2024

Harris
Southern California

Business Directory and Buyers Guide

MERGENT
Exclusive Provider of
Dun & Bradstreet Library Solutions

dun&bradstreet

HOOVERS™

First Research

HARRIS INFOSOURCE™

Published February 2024 next update February 2025

Publisher

Mergent Inc.
444 Madison Ave
New York, NY 10022

©Mergent Inc All Rights Reserved
2024 Mergent Business Press
ISSN 1080-2614
ISBN 979-8-89251-063-9

TABLE OF CONTENTS

SUMMARY OF CONTENTS

Number of Companies 20,419

Number of Decision Makers 33,576

Minimum Number of Employees (Services) 80

Minimum Number of Employees (Manufacturers) 17

EXPLANATORY NOTES

How to Cross-Reference in This Directory

Sequential Entry Numbers. Each establishment in the Geographic Section is numbered sequentially (G-0000). The number assigned to each establishment is referred to as its "entry number." To make cross-referencing easier, each listing in the Geographic, SIC, Alphabetic and Product Sections includes the establishment's entry number. To facilitate locating an entry in the Geographic Section, the entry numbers for the first listing on the left page and the last listing on the right page are printed at the top of the page next to the city name.

Source Suggestions Welcome

Although all known sources were used to compile this directory, it is possible that companies were inadvertently omitted. Your assistance in calling attention to such omissions would be greatly appreciated. A special form on the facing page will help you in the reporting process.

Analysis

Every effort has been made to contact all firms to verify their information. The one exception to this rule is the annual sales figure, which is considered by many companies to be confidential information. Therefore, estimated sales have been calculated by multiplying the nationwide average sales per employee for the firm's major SIC/NAICS code by the firm's number of employees. Nationwide averages for sales per employee by SIC/NAICS codes are provided by the U.S. Department of Commerce and are updated annually. All sales—sales (est)—have been estimated by this method. The exceptions are parent companies (PA), division headquarters (DH) and headquarter locations (HQ) which may include an actual corporate sales figure—sales (corporate-wide) if available.

Types of Companies

Descriptive and statistical data are included for companies in the entire state. These comprise manufacturers, machine shops, fabricators, assemblers and printers. Also identified are corporate offices in the state.

Employment Data

The employment figure shown in the Products & Services Section includes male and female employees and embraces all levels of the company. This directory includes manufacturing companies with 17 or more employees and service companies with 80 or more employees. This figure is for the facility listed and does not include other plants or offices. It should be recognized that these figures represent an approximate year-round average. These employment figures are broken into codes A through F and used in the Alphabetic and Geographic Sections to further help you in qualifying a company. Be sure to check the footnotes at the bottom of the page for the code breakdowns.

Standard Industrial Classification (SIC)

The Standard Industrial Classification (SIC) system used in this directory was developed by the federal government for use in classifying establishments by the type of activity they are engaged in. The SIC classifications used in this directory are from the 1987 edition published by the U.S. Government's Office of Management and Budget. The SIC system separates all activities into broad industrial divisions (e.g., manufacturing, mining, retail trade). It further subdivides each division. The range of manufacturing industry classes extends from two-digit codes (major industry group) to four-digit codes (product).

For example:

Industry Breakdown	Code	Industry, Product, etc.
*Major industry group	20	Food and kindred products
Industry group	203	Canned and frozen foods
*Industry	2033	Fruits and vegetables, etc.

*Classifications used in this directory

Only two-digit and four-digit codes are used in this directory.

Arrangement

1. The **Geographic Section** contains complete in-depth corporate data. This section is sorted by cities listed in alphabetical order and companies listed alphabetically within each city. A County/City Index for referencing cities within counties precedes this section.

IMPORTANT NOTICE: It is a violation of both federal and state law to transmit an unsolicited advertisement to a facsimile machine. Any user of this product that violates such laws may be subject to civil and criminal penalties, which may exceed $500 for each transmission of an unsolicited facsimile. Mergent Inc. provides fax numbers for lawful purposes only and expressly forbids the use of these numbers in any unlawful manner.

2. The **Standard Industrial Classification (SIC) Section** lists companies under approximately 500 four-digit SIC codes. An alphabetical and a numerical index precedes this section. A company can be listed under several codes. The codes are in numerical order with companies listed alphabetically under each code.

3. The **Alphabetic Section** lists all companies with their full physical or mailing addresses and telephone number.

4. The **Product & Services Section** lists companies under unique Harris categories. An index preceding this section lists all product categories in alphabetical order. Companies can be listed under several categories.

USER'S GUIDE TO LISTINGS

PRODUCT & SERVICES SECTION

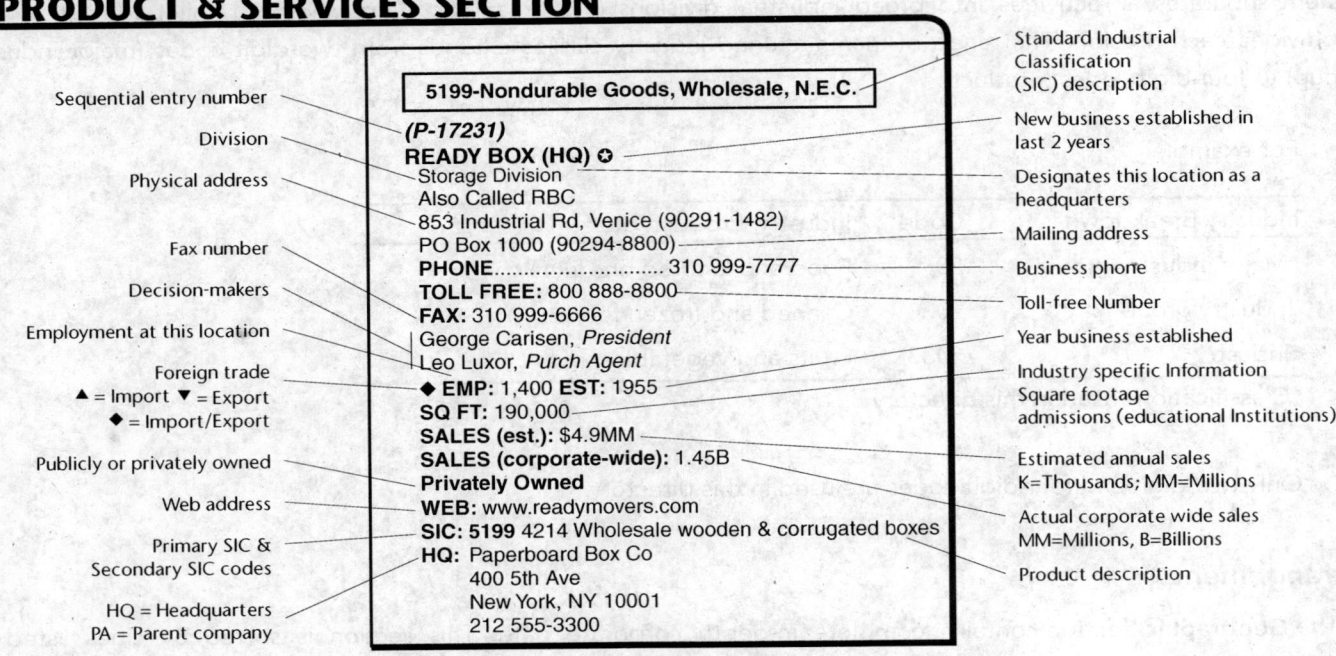

Sequential entry number

Division

Physical address

Fax number

Decision-makers

Employment at this location

Foreign trade
▲ = Import ▼ = Export
◆ = Import/Export

Publicly or privately owned

Web address

Primary SIC &
Secondary SIC codes

HQ = Headquarters
PA = Parent company

Standard Industrial
Classification
(SIC) description

New business established in
last 2 years

Designates this location as a
headquarters

Mailing address

Business phone

Toll-free Number

Year business established

Industry specific Information
Square footage
admissions (educational Institutions)

Estimated annual sales
K=Thousands; MM=Millions

Actual corporate wide sales
MM=Millions, B=Billions

Product description

5199-Nondurable Goods, Wholesale, N.E.C.

(P-17231)
READY BOX (HQ) ✪
Storage Division
Also Called RBC
853 Industrial Rd, Venice (90291-1482)
PO Box 1000 (90294-8800)
PHONE............................ 310 999-7777
TOLL FREE: 800 888-8800
FAX: 310 999-6666
George Carisen, *President*
Leo Luxor, *Purch Agent*
◆ **EMP:** 1,400 **EST:** 1955
SQ FT: 190,000
SALES (est.): $4.9MM
SALES (corporate-wide): 1.45B
Privately Owned
WEB: www.readymovers.com
SIC: 5199 4214 Wholesale wooden & corrugated boxes
HQ: Paperboard Box Co
400 5th Ave
New York, NY 10001
212 555-3300

ALPHABETIC SECTION

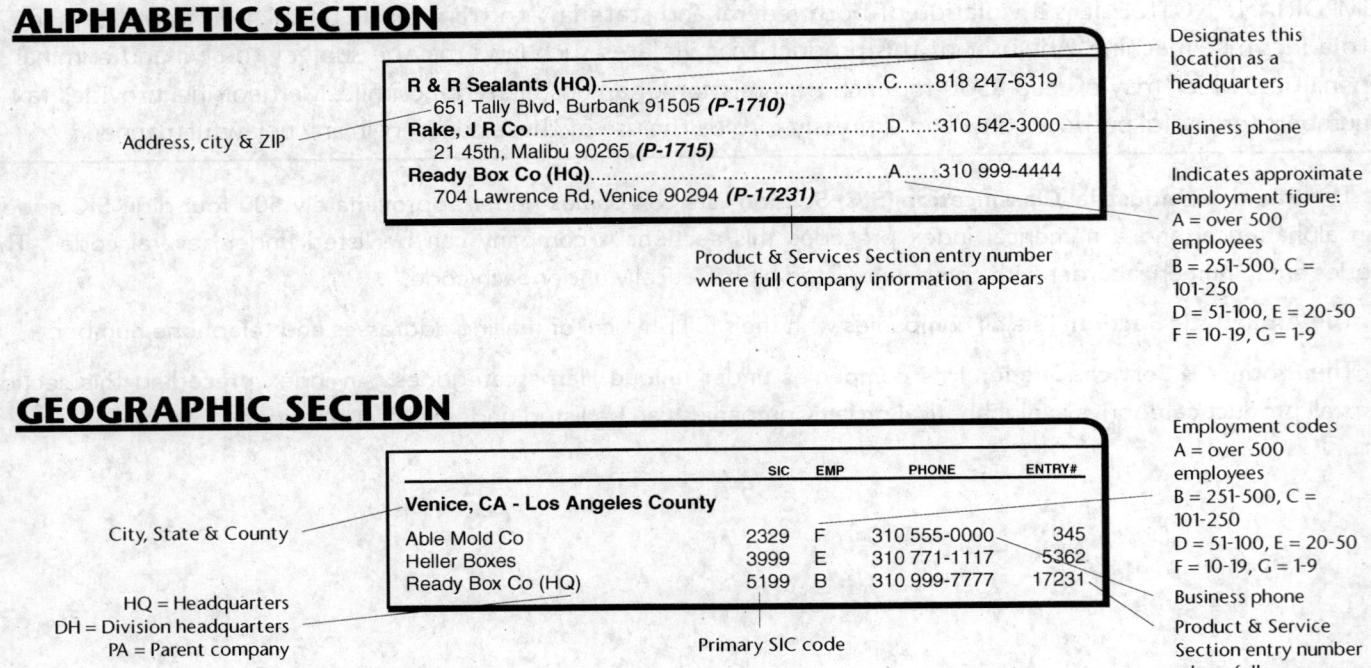

Address, city & ZIP

R & R Sealants (HQ).............................C......818 247-6319
651 Tally Blvd, Burbank 91505 *(P-1710)*
Rake, J R Co...D.....:310 542-3000
21 45th, Malibu 90265 *(P-1715)*
Ready Box Co (HQ)....................................A.......310 999-4444
704 Lawrence Rd, Venice 90294 *(P-17231)*

Designates this
location as a
headquarters

Business phone

Indicates approximate
employment figure:
A = over 500
employees
B = 251-500, C =
101-250
D = 51-100, E = 20-50
F = 10-19, G = 1-9

Product & Services Section entry number
where full company information appears

GEOGRAPHIC SECTION

City, State & County

HQ = Headquarters
DH = Division headquarters
PA = Parent company

	SIC	EMP	PHONE	ENTRY#
Venice, CA - Los Angeles County				
Able Mold Co	2329	F	310 555-0000	345
Heller Boxes	3999	E	310 771-1117	5362
Ready Box Co (HQ)	5199	B	310 999-7777	17231

Primary SIC code

Employment codes
A = over 500
employees
B = 251-500, C =
101-250
D = 51-100, E = 20-50
F = 10-19, G = 1-9

Business phone

Product & Service
Section entry number
where full company
information appears

6

NUMERICAL INDEX of SIC DESCRIPTIONS
ALPHABETICAL INDEX of SIC DESCRIPTIONS

PRODUCTS & SERVICES SECTION

Companies listed alphabetically under their primary SIC
In-depth company data listed

ALPHABETIC SECTION

Company listings in alphabetical order

GEOGRAPHIC INDEX

Companies sorted by city in alphabetical order

SIC

PRDTS & SVCS

ALPHABETIC

GEOGRAPHIC

SIC INDEX

Standard Industrial Classification Numerical Index

SIC NO	PRODUCT

01 agricultural production - crops

0131 Cotton
0134 Irish potatoes
0139 Field crops, except cash grain
0161 Vegetables and melons
0171 Berry crops
0172 Grapes
0173 Tree nuts
0174 Citrus fruits
0175 Deciduous tree fruits
0179 Fruits and tree nuts, nec
0181 Ornamental nursery products
0182 Food crops grown under cover
0191 General farms, primarily crop

02 agricultural production - livestock and animal specialties

0241 Dairy farms
0252 Chicken eggs
0279 Animal specialties, nec
0291 General farms, primarily animals

07 agricultural services

0711 Soil preparation services
0722 Crop harvesting
0723 Crop preparation services for market
0742 Veterinary services, specialties
0751 Livestock services, except veterinary
0752 Animal specialty services
0762 Farm management services
0781 Landscape counseling and planning
0782 Lawn and garden services
0783 Ornamental shrub and tree services

08 forestry

0811 Timber tracts
0851 Forestry services

10 metal mining

1021 Copper ores
1041 Gold ores
1081 Metal mining services
1099 Metal ores, nec

12 coal mining

1221 Bituminous coal and lignite-surface mining
1231 Anthracite mining
1241 Coal mining services

13 oil and gas extraction

1311 Crude petroleum and natural gas
1321 Natural gas liquids
1381 Drilling oil and gas wells
1382 Oil and gas exploration services
1389 Oil and gas field services, nec

14 mining and quarrying of nonmetallic minerals, except fuels

1411 Dimension stone
1422 Crushed and broken limestone
1423 Crushed and broken granite
1429 Crushed and broken stone, nec
1442 Construction sand and gravel
1446 Industrial sand
1455 Kaolin and ball clay
1474 Potash, soda, and borate minerals
1481 Nonmetallic mineral services
1499 Miscellaneous nonmetallic mining

15 construction - general contractors & operative builders

1521 Single-family housing construction
1522 Residential construction, nec
1531 Operative builders
1541 Industrial buildings and warehouses

1542 Nonresidential construction, nec

16 heamy construction, except building construction, contractor

1611 Highway and street construction
1622 Bridge, tunnel, and elevated highway
1623 Water, sewer, and utility lines
1629 Heavy construction, nec

17 construction - special trade contractors

1711 Plumbing, heating, air-conditioning
1721 Painting and paper hanging
1731 Electrical work
1741 Masonry and other stonework
1742 Plastering, drywall, and insulation
1743 Terrazzo, tile, marble, mosaic work
1751 Carpentry work
1752 Floor laying and floor work, nec
1761 Roofing, siding, and sheetmetal work
1771 Concrete work
1781 Water well drilling
1791 Structural steel erection
1793 Glass and glazing work
1794 Excavation work
1795 Wrecking and demolition work
1796 Installing building equipment
1799 Special trade contractors, nec

20 food and kindred products

2011 Meat packing plants
2013 Sausages and other prepared meats
2015 Poultry slaughtering and processing
2021 Creamery butter
2022 Cheese; natural and processed
2023 Dry, condensed, evaporated products
2024 Ice cream and frozen deserts
2026 Fluid milk
2032 Canned specialties
2033 Canned fruits and specialties
2034 Dehydrated fruits, vegetables, soups
2035 Pickles, sauces, and salad dressings
2037 Frozen fruits and vegetables
2038 Frozen specialties, nec
2041 Flour and other grain mill products
2043 Cereal breakfast foods
2045 Prepared flour mixes and doughs
2047 Dog and cat food
2048 Prepared feeds, nec
2051 Bread, cake, and related products
2052 Cookies and crackers
2053 Frozen bakery products, except bread
2061 Raw cane sugar
2063 Beet sugar
2064 Candy and other confectionery products
2066 Chocolate and cocoa products
2068 Salted and roasted nuts and seeds
2076 Vegetable oil mills, nec
2077 Animal and marine fats and oils
2079 Edible fats and oils
2082 Malt beverages
2083 Malt
2084 Wines, brandy, and brandy spirits
2085 Distilled and blended liquors
2086 Bottled and canned soft drinks
2087 Flavoring extracts and syrups, nec
2091 Canned and cured fish and seafoods
2092 Fresh or frozen packaged fish
2095 Roasted coffee
2096 Potato chips and similar snacks
2097 Manufactured ice
2098 Macaroni and spaghetti
2099 Food preparations, nec

21 tobacco products

2111 Cigarettes

2131 Chewing and smoking tobacco

22 textile mill products

2211 Broadwoven fabric mills, cotton
2221 Broadwoven fabric mills, manmade
2231 Broadwoven fabric mills, wool
2241 Narrow fabric mills
2252 Hosiery, nec
2253 Knit outerwear mills
2257 Weft knit fabric mills
2258 Lace and warp knit fabric mills
2259 Knitting mills, nec
2261 Finishing plants, cotton
2262 Finishing plants, manmade
2269 Finishing plants, nec
2273 Carpets and rugs
2281 Yarn spinning mills
2284 Thread mills
2295 Coated fabrics, not rubberized
2297 Nonwoven fabrics
2298 Cordage and twine
2299 Textile goods, nec

23 apparel, finished products from fabrics & similar materials

2311 Men's and boy's suits and coats
2321 Men's and boy's furnishings
2323 Men's and boy's neckwear
2325 Men's and boy's trousers and slacks
2326 Men's and boy's work clothing
2329 Men's and boy's clothing, nec
2331 Women's and misses' blouses and shirts
2335 Women's, junior's, and misses' dresses
2337 Women's and misses' suits and coats
2339 Women's and misses' outerwear, nec
2341 Women's and children's underwear
2342 Bras, girdles, and allied garments
2353 Hats, caps, and millinery
2361 Girl's and children's dresses, blouses
2369 Girl's and children's outerwear, nec
2381 Fabric dress and work gloves
2384 Robes and dressing gowns
2386 Leather and sheep-lined clothing
2387 Apparel belts
2389 Apparel and accessories, nec
2391 Curtains and draperies
2392 Household furnishings, nec
2393 Textile bags
2394 Canvas and related products
2395 Pleating and stitching
2396 Automotive and apparel trimmings
2399 Fabricated textile products, nec

24 lumber and wood products, except furniture

2411 Logging
2421 Sawmills and planing mills, general
2426 Hardwood dimension and flooring mills
2431 Millwork
2434 Wood kitchen cabinets
2435 Hardwood veneer and plywood
2439 Structural wood members, nec
2441 Nailed wood boxes and shook
2448 Wood pallets and skids
2449 Wood containers, nec
2451 Mobile homes
2452 Prefabricated wood buildings
2491 Wood preserving
2493 Reconstituted wood products
2499 Wood products, nec

25 furniture and fixtures

2511 Wood household furniture
2512 Upholstered household furniture
2514 Metal household furniture
2515 Mattresses and bedsprings

SIC NO	PRODUCT	SIC NO	PRODUCT	SIC NO	PRODUCT

2517 Wood television and radio cabinets
2519 Household furniture, nec
2521 Wood office furniture
2522 Office furniture, except wood
2531 Public building and related furniture
2541 Wood partitions and fixtures
2542 Partitions and fixtures, except wood
2591 Drapery hardware and blinds and shades
2599 Furniture and fixtures, nec

26 paper and allied products

2611 Pulp mills
2621 Paper mills
2631 Paperboard mills
2652 Setup paperboard boxes
2653 Corrugated and solid fiber boxes
2655 Fiber cans, drums, and similar products
2656 Sanitary food containers
2657 Folding paperboard boxes
2671 Paper; coated and laminated packaging
2672 Paper; coated and laminated, nec
2673 Bags: plastic, laminated, and coated
2674 Bags: uncoated paper and multiwall
2675 Die-cut paper and board
2676 Sanitary paper products
2677 Envelopes
2678 Stationery products
2679 Converted paper products, nec

27 printing, publishing and allied industries

2711 Newspapers
2721 Periodicals
2731 Book publishing
2741 Miscellaneous publishing
2752 Commercial printing, lithographic
2754 Commercial printing, gravure
2759 Commercial printing, nec
2761 Manifold business forms
2782 Blankbooks and looseleaf binders
2789 Bookbinding and related work
2791 Typesetting
2796 Platemaking services

28 chemicals and allied products

2812 Alkalies and chlorine
2813 Industrial gases
2816 Inorganic pigments
2819 Industrial inorganic chemicals, nec
2821 Plastics materials and resins
2822 Synthetic rubber
2824 Organic fibers, noncellulosic
2833 Medicinals and botanicals
2834 Pharmaceutical preparations
2835 Diagnostic substances
2836 Biological products, except diagnostic
2841 Soap and other detergents
2842 Polishes and sanitation goods
2843 Surface active agents
2844 Toilet preparations
2851 Paints and allied products
2865 Cyclic crudes and intermediates
2869 Industrial organic chemicals, nec
2873 Nitrogenous fertilizers
2875 Fertilizers, mixing only
2879 Agricultural chemicals, nec
2891 Adhesives and sealants
2892 Explosives
2893 Printing ink
2895 Carbon black
2899 Chemical preparations, nec

29 petroleum refining and related industries

2911 Petroleum refining
2951 Asphalt paving mixtures and blocks
2952 Asphalt felts and coatings
2992 Lubricating oils and greases
2999 Petroleum and coal products, nec

30 rubber and miscellaneous plastic products

3011 Tires and inner tubes
3021 Rubber and plastics footwear
3052 Rubber and plastics hose and beltings

3053 Gaskets; packing and sealing devices
3061 Mechanical rubber goods
3069 Fabricated rubber products, nec
3081 Unsupported plastics film and sheet
3082 Unsupported plastics profile shapes
3083 Laminated plastics plate and sheet
3084 Plastics pipe
3085 Plastics bottles
3086 Plastics foam products
3088 Plastics plumbing fixtures
3089 Plastics products, nec

31 leather and leather products

3111 Leather tanning and finishing
3131 Footwear cut stock
3142 House slippers
3143 Men's footwear, except athletic
3144 Women's footwear, except athletic
3149 Footwear, except rubber, nec
3161 Luggage
3171 Women's handbags and purses
3172 Personal leather goods, nec
3199 Leather goods, nec

32 stone, clay, glass, and concrete products

3211 Flat glass
3221 Glass containers
3229 Pressed and blown glass, nec
3231 Products of purchased glass
3241 Cement, hydraulic
3251 Brick and structural clay tile
3253 Ceramic wall and floor tile
3259 Structural clay products, nec
3261 Vitreous plumbing fixtures
3262 Vitreous china table and kitchenware
3263 Semivitreous table and kitchenware
3264 Porcelain electrical supplies
3269 Pottery products, nec
3271 Concrete block and brick
3272 Concrete products, nec
3273 Ready-mixed concrete
3275 Gypsum products
3281 Cut stone and stone products
3291 Abrasive products
3295 Minerals, ground or treated
3296 Mineral wool
3297 Nonclay refractories
3299 Nonmetallic mineral products,

33 primary metal industries

3312 Blast furnaces and steel mills
3313 Electrometallurgical products
3315 Steel wire and related products
3316 Cold finishing of steel shapes
3317 Steel pipe and tubes
3321 Gray and ductile iron foundries
3322 Malleable iron foundries
3324 Steel investment foundries
3325 Steel foundries, nec
3331 Primary copper
3334 Primary aluminum
3339 Primary nonferrous metals, nec
3341 Secondary nonferrous metals
3353 Aluminum sheet, plate, and foil
3354 Aluminum extruded products
3355 Aluminum rolling and drawing, nec
3356 Nonferrous rolling and drawing, nec
3357 Nonferrous wiredrawing and insulating
3363 Aluminum die-castings
3364 Nonferrous die-castings except aluminum
3365 Aluminum foundries
3366 Copper foundries
3369 Nonferrous foundries, nec
3398 Metal heat treating
3399 Primary metal products

34 fabricated metal products

3411 Metal cans
3412 Metal barrels, drums, and pails
3421 Cutlery
3423 Hand and edge tools, nec
3425 Saw blades and handsaws

3429 Hardware, nec
3431 Metal sanitary ware
3432 Plumbing fixture fittings and trim
3433 Heating equipment, except electric
3441 Fabricated structural metal
3442 Metal doors, sash, and trim
3443 Fabricated plate work (boiler shop)
3444 Sheet metalwork
3446 Architectural metalwork
3448 Prefabricated metal buildings
3449 Miscellaneous metalwork
3451 Screw machine products
3452 Bolts, nuts, rivets, and washers
3462 Iron and steel forgings
3463 Nonferrous forgings
3465 Automotive stampings
3469 Metal stampings, nec
3471 Plating and polishing
3479 Metal coating and allied services
3483 Ammunition, except for small arms, nec
3484 Small arms
3489 Ordnance and accessories, nec
3491 Industrial valves
3492 Fluid power valves and hose fittings
3493 Steel springs, except wire
3494 Valves and pipe fittings, nec
3495 Wire springs
3496 Miscellaneous fabricated wire products
3498 Fabricated pipe and fittings
3499 Fabricated metal products, nec

35 industrial and commercial machinery and computer equipment

3511 Turbines and turbine generator sets
3519 Internal combustion engines, nec
3523 Farm machinery and equipment
3524 Lawn and garden equipment
3531 Construction machinery
3532 Mining machinery
3533 Oil and gas field machinery
3534 Elevators and moving stairways
3535 Conveyors and conveying equipment
3536 Hoists, cranes, and monorails
3537 Industrial trucks and tractors
3541 Machine tools, metal cutting type
3542 Machine tools, metal forming type
3543 Industrial patterns
3544 Special dies, tools, jigs, and fixtures
3545 Machine tool accessories
3546 Power-driven handtools
3547 Rolling mill machinery
3548 Welding apparatus
3549 Metalworking machinery, nec
3552 Textile machinery
3554 Paper industries machinery
3555 Printing trades machinery
3556 Food products machinery
3559 Special industry machinery, nec
3561 Pumps and pumping equipment
3562 Ball and roller bearings
3563 Air and gas compressors
3564 Blowers and fans
3565 Packaging machinery
3566 Speed changers, drives, and gears
3567 Industrial furnaces and ovens
3568 Power transmission equipment, nec
3569 General industrial machinery,
3571 Electronic computers
3572 Computer storage devices
3575 Computer terminals
3577 Computer peripheral equipment, nec
3578 Calculating and accounting equipment
3579 Office machines, nec
3581 Automatic vending machines
3582 Commercial laundry equipment
3585 Refrigeration and heating equipment
3589 Service industry machinery, nec
3592 Carburetors, pistons, rings, valves
3593 Fluid power cylinders and actuators
3594 Fluid power pumps and motors
3596 Scales and balances, except laboratory
3599 Industrial machinery, nec

SIC NO	PRODUCT

36 electronic & other electrical equipment & components

3612 Transformers, except electric
3613 Switchgear and switchboard apparatus
3621 Motors and generators
3624 Carbon and graphite products
3625 Relays and industrial controls
3629 Electrical industrial apparatus
3631 Household cooking equipment
3632 Household refrigerators and freezers
3634 Electric housewares and fans
3639 Household appliances, nec
3641 Electric lamps
3643 Current-carrying wiring devices
3644 Noncurrent-carrying wiring devices
3645 Residential lighting fixtures
3646 Commercial lighting fixtures
3647 Vehicular lighting equipment
3648 Lighting equipment, nec
3651 Household audio and video equipment
3652 Prerecorded records and tapes
3661 Telephone and telegraph apparatus
3663 Radio and t.v. communications equipment
3669 Communications equipment, nec
3671 Electron tubes
3672 Printed circuit boards
3674 Semiconductors and related devices
3675 Electronic capacitors
3676 Electronic resistors
3677 Electronic coils and transformers
3678 Electronic connectors
3679 Electronic components, nec
3691 Storage batteries
3692 Primary batteries, dry and wet
3694 Engine electrical equipment
3695 Magnetic and optical recording media
3699 Electrical equipment and supplies, nec

37 transportation equipment

3711 Motor vehicles and car bodies
3713 Truck and bus bodies
3714 Motor vehicle parts and accessories
3715 Truck trailers
3716 Motor homes
3721 Aircraft
3724 Aircraft engines and engine parts
3728 Aircraft parts and equipment, nec
3731 Shipbuilding and repairing
3732 Boatbuilding and repairing
3743 Railroad equipment
3751 Motorcycles, bicycles, and parts
3761 Guided missiles and space vehicles
3764 Space propulsion units and parts
3769 Space vehicle equipment, nec
3792 Travel trailers and campers
3795 Tanks and tank components
3799 Transportation equipment, nec

38 measuring, photographic, medical, & optical goods, & clocks

3812 Search and navigation equipment
3821 Laboratory apparatus and furniture
3822 Environmental controls
3823 Process control instruments
3824 Fluid meters and counting devices
3825 Instruments to measure electricity
3826 Analytical instruments
3827 Optical instruments and lenses
3829 Measuring and controlling devices, nec
3841 Surgical and medical instruments
3842 Surgical appliances and supplies
3843 Dental equipment and supplies
3844 X-ray apparatus and tubes
3845 Electromedical equipment
3851 Ophthalmic goods
3861 Photographic equipment and supplies
3873 Watches, clocks, watchcases, and parts

39 miscellaneous manufacturing industries

3911 Jewelry, precious metal
3914 Silverware and plated ware
3915 Jewelers' materials and lapidary work
3931 Musical instruments

3942 Dolls and stuffed toys
3944 Games, toys, and children's vehicles
3949 Sporting and athletic goods, nec
3951 Pens and mechanical pencils
3952 Lead pencils and art goods
3953 Marking devices
3955 Carbon paper and inked ribbons
3961 Costume jewelry
3965 Fasteners, buttons, needles, and pins
3991 Brooms and brushes
3993 Signs and advertising specialties
3996 Hard surface floor coverings, nec
3999 Manufacturing industries, nec

40 railroad transportation

4011 Railroads, line-haul operating

41 local & suburban transit & interurban highway transportation

4111 Local and suburban transit
4119 Local passenger transportation, nec
4121 Taxicabs
4131 Intercity and rural bus transportation
4141 Local bus charter service
4142 Bus charter service, except local
4151 School buses
4173 Bus terminal and service facilities

42 motor freight transportation

4212 Local trucking, without storage
4213 Trucking, except local
4214 Local trucking with storage
4215 Courier services, except by air
4221 Farm product warehousing and storage
4222 Refrigerated warehousing and storage
4225 General warehousing and storage
4226 Special warehousing and storage, nec

44 water transportation

4424 Deep sea domestic transportation of freight
4481 Deep sea passenger transportation, except ferry
4489 Water passenger transportation
4491 Marine cargo handling
4492 Towing and tugboat service
4493 Marinas
4499 Water transportation services, nec

45 transportation by air

4512 Air transportation, scheduled
4513 Air courier services
4522 Air transportation, nonscheduled
4581 Airports, flying fields, and services

46 pipelines, except natural gas

4613 Refined petroleum pipelines

47 transportation services

4724 Travel agencies
4725 Tour operators
4729 Passenger transportation arrangement
4731 Freight transportation arrangement
4783 Packing and crating
4785 Inspection and fixed facilities
4789 Transportation services, nec

48 communications

4812 Radiotelephone communication
4813 Telephone communication, except radio
4822 Telegraph and other communications
4832 Radio broadcasting stations
4833 Television broadcasting stations
4841 Cable and other pay television services
4899 Communication services, nec

49 electric, gas and sanitary services

4911 Electric services
4922 Natural gas transmission
4924 Natural gas distribution
4931 Electric and other services combined
4932 Gas and other services combined
4939 Combination utilities, nec
4941 Water supply

4952 Sewerage systems
4953 Refuse systems
4959 Sanitary services, nec
4971 Irrigation systems

50 wholesale trade - durable goods

5012 Automobiles and other motor vehicles
5013 Motor vehicle supplies and new parts
5014 Tires and tubes
5021 Furniture
5023 Homefurnishings
5031 Lumber, plywood, and millwork
5032 Brick, stone, and related material
5033 Roofing, siding, and insulation
5039 Construction materials, nec
5043 Photographic equipment and supplies
5044 Office equipment
5045 Computers, peripherals, and software
5046 Commercial equipment, nec
5047 Medical and hospital equipment
5048 Ophthalmic goods
5049 Professional equipment, nec
5051 Metals service centers and offices
5063 Electrical apparatus and equipment
5064 Electrical appliances, television and radio
5065 Electronic parts and equipment, nec
5072 Hardware
5074 Plumbing and hydronic heating supplies
5075 Warm air heating and air conditioning
5078 Refrigeration equipment and supplies
5082 Construction and mining machinery
5083 Farm and garden machinery
5084 Industrial machinery and equipment
5085 Industrial supplies
5087 Service establishment equipment
5088 Transportation equipment and supplies
5091 Sporting and recreation goods
5092 Toys and hobby goods and supplies
5093 Scrap and waste materials
5094 Jewelry and precious stones
5099 Durable goods, nec

51 wholesale trade - nondurable goods

5111 Printing and writing paper
5112 Stationery and office supplies
5113 Industrial and personal service paper
5122 Drugs, proprietaries, and sundries
5131 Piece goods and notions
5136 Men's and boy's clothing
5137 Women's and children's clothing
5139 Footwear
5141 Groceries, general line
5142 Packaged frozen goods
5143 Dairy products, except dried or canned
5144 Poultry and poultry products
5145 Confectionery
5146 Fish and seafoods
5147 Meats and meat products
5148 Fresh fruits and vegetables
5149 Groceries and related products, nec
5153 Grain and field beans
5159 Farm-product raw materials, nec
5162 Plastics materials and basic shapes
5169 Chemicals and allied products, nec
5171 Petroleum bulk stations and terminals
5172 Petroleum products, nec
5181 Beer and ale
5182 Wine and distilled beverages
5191 Farm supplies
5192 Books, periodicals, and newspapers
5193 Flowers and florists supplies
5194 Tobacco and tobacco products
5198 Paints, varnishes, and supplies
5199 Nondurable goods, nec

52 building materials, hardware, garden supplies & mobile homes

5211 Lumber and other building materials
5231 Paint, glass, and wallpaper stores
5251 Hardware stores
5261 Retail nurseries and garden stores

SIC NO	PRODUCT

53 general merchandise stores

5311 Department stores
5331 Variety stores
5399 Miscellaneous general merchandise

54 food stores

5411 Grocery stores
5431 Fruit and vegetable markets
5461 Retail bakeries
5499 Miscellaneous food stores

55 automotive dealers and gasoline service stations

5511 New and used car dealers
5521 Used car dealers
5531 Auto and home supply stores
5541 Gasoline service stations
5551 Boat dealers
5561 Recreational vehicle dealers
5571 Motorcycle dealers
5599 Automotive dealers, nec

56 apparel and accessory stores

5611 Men's and boys' clothing stores
5621 Women's clothing stores
5632 Women's accessory and specialty stores
5651 Family clothing stores
5661 Shoe stores
5699 Miscellaneous apparel and accessories

57 home furniture, furnishings and equipment stores

5712 Furniture stores
5713 Floor covering stores
5714 Drapery and upholstery stores
5719 Miscellaneous homefurnishings
5722 Household appliance stores
5734 Computer and software stores
5736 Musical instrument stores

58 eating and drinking places

5812 Eating places
5813 Drinking places

59 miscellaneous retail

5912 Drug stores and proprietary stores
5921 Liquor stores
5932 Used merchandise stores
5941 Sporting goods and bicycle shops
5942 Book stores
5943 Stationery stores
5944 Jewelry stores
5945 Hobby, toy, and game shops
5946 Camera and photographic supply stores
5947 Gift, novelty, and souvenir shop
5949 Sewing, needlework, and piece goods
5961 Catalog and mail-order houses
5963 Direct selling establishments
5992 Florists
5993 Tobacco stores and stands
5994 News dealers and newsstands
5995 Optical goods stores
5999 Miscellaneous retail stores, nec

60 depository institutions

6011 Federal reserve banks
6021 National commercial banks
6022 State commercial banks
6029 Commercial banks, nec
6035 Federal savings institutions
6036 Savings institutions, except federal
6061 Federal credit unions
6062 State credit unions
6091 Nondeposit trust facilities
6099 Functions related to depository banking

61 nondepository credit institutions

6111 Federal and federally sponsored credit
6141 Personal credit institutions
6153 Short-term business credit
6159 Miscellaneous business credit
6162 Mortgage bankers and correspondents
6163 Loan brokers

62 security & commodity brokers, dealers, exchanges & services

6211 Security brokers and dealers
6221 Commodity contracts brokers, dealers
6282 Investment advice
6289 Security and commodity service

63 insurance carriers

6311 Life insurance
6321 Accident and health insurance
6324 Hospital and medical service plans
6331 Fire, marine, and casualty insurance
6351 Surety insurance
6361 Title insurance
6371 Pension, health, and welfare funds

64 insurance agents, brokers and service

6411 Insurance agents, brokers, and service

65 real estate

6512 Nonresidential building operators
6513 Apartment building operators
6514 Dwelling operators, except apartments
6515 Mobile home site operators
6519 Real property lessors, nec
6531 Real estate agents and managers
6541 Title abstract offices
6552 Subdividers and developers, nec
6553 Cemetery subdividers and developers

67 holding and other investment offices

6712 Bank holding companies
6719 Holding companies, nec
6722 Management investment, open-ended
6726 Investment offices, nec
6732 Trusts: educational, religious, etc.
6733 Trusts, nec
6794 Patent owners and lessors
6798 Real estate investment trusts
6799 Investors, nec

70 hotels, rooming houses, camps, and other lodging places

7011 Hotels and motels
7021 Rooming and boarding houses
7032 Sporting and recreational camps
7033 Trailer parks and campsites
7041 Membership-basis organization hotels

72 personal services

7211 Power laundries, family and commercial
7213 Linen supply
7215 Coin-operated laundries and cleaning
7216 Drycleaning plants, except rugs
7217 Carpet and upholstery cleaning
7218 Industrial launderers
7219 Laundry and garment services, nec
7221 Photographic studios, portrait
7231 Beauty shops
7261 Funeral service and crematories
7291 Tax return preparation services
7299 Miscellaneous personal services

73 business services

7311 Advertising agencies
7312 Outdoor advertising services
7313 Radio, television, publisher representatives
7319 Advertising, nec
7322 Adjustment and collection services
7323 Credit reporting services
7331 Direct mail advertising services
7334 Photocopying and duplicating services
7335 Commercial photography
7336 Commercial art and graphic design
7338 Secretarial and court reporting
7342 Disinfecting and pest control services
7349 Building maintenance services, nec
7352 Medical equipment rental
7353 Heavy construction equipment rental
7359 Equipment rental and leasing, nec
7361 Employment agencies
7363 Help supply services

7371 Custom computer programming services
7372 Prepackaged software
7373 Computer integrated systems design
7374 Data processing and preparation
7375 Information retrieval services
7376 Computer facilities management
7378 Computer maintenance and repair
7379 Computer related services, nec
7381 Detective and armored car services
7382 Security systems services
7383 News syndicates
7384 Photofinish laboratories
7389 Business services, nec

75 automotive repair, services and parking

7513 Truck rental and leasing, without drivers
7514 Passenger car rental
7515 Passenger car leasing
7519 Utility trailer rental
7521 Automobile parking
7532 Top and body repair and paint shops
7534 Tire retreading and repair shops
7537 Automotive transmission repair shops
7538 General automotive repair shops
7539 Automotive repair shops, nec
7542 Carwashes
7549 Automotive services, nec

76 miscellaneous repair services

7622 Radio and television repair
7623 Refrigeration service and repair
7629 Electrical repair shops
7641 Reupholstery and furniture repair
7692 Welding repair
7694 Armature rewinding shops
7699 Repair services, nec

78 motion pictures

7812 Motion picture and video production
7819 Services allied to motion pictures
7822 Motion picture and tape distribution
7829 Motion picture distribution services
7832 Motion picture theaters, except drive-in
7833 Drive-in motion picture theaters
7841 Video tape rental

79 amusement and recreation services

7911 Dance studios, schools, and halls
7922 Theatrical producers and services
7929 Entertainers and entertainment groups
7933 Bowling centers
7941 Sports clubs, managers, and promoters
7948 Racing, including track operation
7991 Physical fitness facilities
7992 Public golf courses
7993 Coin-operated amusement devices
7996 Amusement parks
7997 Membership sports and recreation clubs
7999 Amusement and recreation, nec

80 health services

8011 Offices and clinics of medical doctors
8021 Offices and clinics of dentists
8031 Offices and clinics of osteopathic physicians
8041 Offices and clinics of chiropractors
8042 Offices and clinics of optometrists
8049 Offices of health practitioner
8051 Skilled nursing care facilities
8052 Intermediate care facilities
8059 Nursing and personal care, nec
8062 General medical and surgical hospitals
8063 Psychiatric hospitals
8069 Specialty hospitals, except psychiatric
8071 Medical laboratories
8072 Dental laboratories
8082 Home health care services
8092 Kidney dialysis centers
8093 Specialty outpatient clinics, nec
8099 Health and allied services, nec

81 legal services

8111 Legal services

SIC NO	PRODUCT	SIC NO	PRODUCT	SIC NO	PRODUCT

82 educational services

8211 Elementary and secondary schools
8221 Colleges and universities
8222 Junior colleges
8231 Libraries
8243 Data processing schools
8249 Vocational schools, nec
8299 Schools and educational services

83 social services

8322 Individual and family services
8331 Job training and related services
8351 Child day care services
8361 Residential care
8399 Social services, nec

84 museums, art galleries and botanical and zoological gardens

8412 Museums and art galleries
8422 Botanical and zoological gardens

86 membership organizations

8611 Business associations
8621 Professional organizations
8631 Labor organizations
8641 Civic and social associations
8661 Religious organizations
8699 Membership organizations, nec

87 engineering, accounting, research, and management services

8711 Engineering services
8712 Architectural services
8713 Surveying services
8721 Accounting, auditing, and bookkeeping
8731 Commercial physical research
8732 Commercial nonphysical research
8733 Noncommercial research organizations
8734 Testing laboratories
8741 Management services
8742 Management consulting services
8743 Public relations services
8744 Facilities support services
8748 Business consulting, nec

89 services, not elsewhere classified

8999 Services, nec

91 executive, legislative & general government, except finance

9111 Executive offices
9131 Executive and legislative combined
9199 General government, nec

92 justice, public order and safety

9221 Police protection
9222 Legal counsel and prosecution

94 administration of human resource programs

9431 Administration of public health programs
9441 Administration of social and manpower programs

96 administration of economic programs

9621 Regulation, administration of transportation
9641 Regulation of agricultural marketing

S I C

SIC INDEX

Standard Industrial Classification Alphabetical Index

SIC NO	PRODUCT

A

3291 Abrasive products
6321 Accident and health insurance
8721 Accounting, auditing, and bookkeeping
2891 Adhesives and sealants
7322 Adjustment and collection services
9431 Administration of public health programs
9441 Administration of social and manpower programs
7311 Advertising agencies
7319 Advertising, nec
2879 Agricultural chemicals, nec
3563 Air and gas compressors
4513 Air courier services
4522 Air transportation, nonscheduled
4512 Air transportation, scheduled
3721 Aircraft
3724 Aircraft engines and engine parts
3728 Aircraft parts and equipment, nec
4581 Airports, flying fields, and services
2812 Alkalies and chlorine
3363 Aluminum die-castings
3354 Aluminum extruded products
3365 Aluminum foundries
3355 Aluminum rolling and drawing, nec
3353 Aluminum sheet, plate, and foil
3483 Ammunition, except for small arms, nec
7999 Amusement and recreation, nec
7996 Amusement parks
3826 Analytical instruments
2077 Animal and marine fats and oils
0279 Animal specialties, nec
0752 Animal specialty services
1231 Anthracite mining
6513 Apartment building operators
2389 Apparel and accessories, nec
2387 Apparel belts
3446 Architectural metalwork
8712 Architectural services
7694 Armature rewinding shops
2952 Asphalt felts and coatings
2951 Asphalt paving mixtures and blocks
5531 Auto and home supply stores
3581 Automatic vending machines
7521 Automobile parking
5012 Automobiles and other motor vehicles
2396 Automotive and apparel trimmings
5599 Automotive dealers, nec
7539 Automotive repair shops, nec
7549 Automotive services, nec
3465 Automotive stampings
7537 Automotive transmission repair shops

B

2673 Bags: plastic, laminated, and coated
2674 Bags: uncoated paper and multiwall
3562 Ball and roller bearings
6712 Bank holding companies
7231 Beauty shops
5181 Beer and ale
2063 Beet sugar
0171 Berry crops
2836 Biological products, except diagnostic
1221 Bituminous coal and lignite-surface mining
2782 Blankbooks and looseleaf binders
3312 Blast furnaces and steel mills
3564 Blowers and fans
5551 Boat dealers
3732 Boatbuilding and repairing
3452 Bolts, nuts, rivets, and washers
2731 Book publishing
5942 Book stores
2789 Bookbinding and related work
5192 Books, periodicals, and newspapers
8422 Botanical and zoological gardens
2086 Bottled and canned soft drinks
7933 Bowling centers

2342 Bras, girdles, and allied garments
2051 Bread, cake, and related products
3251 Brick and structural clay tile
5032 Brick, stone, and related material
1622 Bridge, tunnel, and elevated highway
2211 Broadwoven fabric mills, cotton
2221 Broadwoven fabric mills, manmade
2231 Broadwoven fabric mills, wool
3991 Brooms and brushes
7349 Building maintenance services, nec
4142 Bus charter service, except local
4173 Bus terminal and service facilities
8611 Business associations
8748 Business consulting, nec
7389 Business services, nec

C

4841 Cable and other pay television services
3578 Calculating and accounting equipment
5946 Camera and photographic supply stores
2064 Candy and other confectionery products
2091 Canned and cured fish and seafoods
2033 Canned fruits and specialties
2032 Canned specialties
2394 Canvas and related products
3624 Carbon and graphite products
2895 Carbon black
3955 Carbon paper and inked ribbons
3592 Carburetors, pistons, rings, valves
1751 Carpentry work
7217 Carpet and upholstery cleaning
2273 Carpets and rugs
7542 Carwashes
5961 Catalog and mail-order houses
3241 Cement, hydraulic
6553 Cemetery subdividers and developers
3253 Ceramic wall and floor tile
2043 Cereal breakfast foods
2022 Cheese; natural and processed
2899 Chemical preparations, nec
5169 Chemicals and allied products, nec
2131 Chewing and smoking tobacco
0252 Chicken eggs
8351 Child day care services
2066 Chocolate and cocoa products
2111 Cigarettes
0174 Citrus fruits
8641 Civic and social associations
1241 Coal mining services
2295 Coated fabrics, not rubberized
7993 Coin-operated amusement devices
7215 Coin-operated laundries and cleaning
3316 Cold finishing of steel shapes
8221 Colleges and universities
4939 Combination utilities, nec
7336 Commercial art and graphic design
6029 Commercial banks, nec
5046 Commercial equipment, nec
3582 Commercial laundry equipment
3646 Commercial lighting fixtures
8732 Commercial nonphysical research
7335 Commercial photography
8731 Commercial physical research
2754 Commercial printing, gravure
2752 Commercial printing, lithographic
2759 Commercial printing, nec
6221 Commodity contracts brokers, dealers
4899 Communication services, nec
3669 Communications equipment, nec
5734 Computer and software stores
7376 Computer facilities management
7373 Computer integrated systems design
7378 Computer maintenance and repair
3577 Computer peripheral equipment, nec
7379 Computer related services, nec
3572 Computer storage devices

3575 Computer terminals
5045 Computers, peripherals, and software
3271 Concrete block and brick
3272 Concrete products, nec
1771 Concrete work
5145 Confectionery
5082 Construction and mining machinery
3531 Construction machinery
5039 Construction materials, nec
1442 Construction sand and gravel
2679 Converted paper products, nec
3535 Conveyors and conveying equipment
2052 Cookies and crackers
3366 Copper foundries
1021 Copper ores
2298 Cordage and twine
2653 Corrugated and solid fiber boxes
3961 Costume jewelry
0131 Cotton
4215 Courier services, except by air
2021 Creamery butter
7323 Credit reporting services
0722 Crop harvesting
0723 Crop preparation services for market
1311 Crude petroleum and natural gas
1423 Crushed and broken granite
1422 Crushed and broken limestone
1429 Crushed and broken stone, nec
3643 Current-carrying wiring devices
2391 Curtains and draperies
7371 Custom computer programming services
3281 Cut stone and stone products
3421 Cutlery
2865 Cyclic crudes and intermediates

D

0241 Dairy farms
5143 Dairy products, except dried or canned
7911 Dance studios, schools, and halls
7374 Data processing and preparation
8243 Data processing schools
0175 Deciduous tree fruits
4424 Deep sea domestic transportation of freight
4481 Deep sea passenger transportation, except ferry
2034 Dehydrated fruits, vegetables, soups
3843 Dental equipment and supplies
8072 Dental laboratories
5311 Department stores
7381 Detective and armored car services
2835 Diagnostic substances
2675 Die-cut paper and board
1411 Dimension stone
7331 Direct mail advertising services
5963 Direct selling establishments
7342 Disinfecting and pest control services
2085 Distilled and blended liquors
2047 Dog and cat food
3942 Dolls and stuffed toys
5714 Drapery and upholstery stores
2591 Drapery hardware and blinds and shades
1381 Drilling oil and gas wells
5813 Drinking places
7833 Drive-in motion picture theaters
5912 Drug stores and proprietary stores
5122 Drugs, proprietaries, and sundries
2023 Dry, condensed, evaporated products
7216 Drycleaning plants, except rugs
5099 Durable goods, nec
6514 Dwelling operators, except apartments

E

5812 Eating places
2079 Edible fats and oils
4931 Electric and other services combined
3634 Electric housewares and fans
3641 Electric lamps

SIC NO	PRODUCT	SIC NO	PRODUCT	SIC NO	PRODUCT

4911 Electric services
5063 Electrical apparatus and equipment
5064 Electrical appliances, television and radio
3699 Electrical equipment and supplies, nec
3629 Electrical industrial apparatus
7629 Electrical repair shops
1731 Electrical work
3845 Electromedical equipment
3313 Electrometallurgical products
3671 Electron tubes
3675 Electronic capacitors
3677 Electronic coils and transformers
3679 Electronic components, nec
3571 Electronic computers
3678 Electronic connectors
5065 Electronic parts and equipment, nec
3676 Electronic resistors
8211 Elementary and secondary schools
3534 Elevators and moving stairways
7361 Employment agencies
3694 Engine electrical equipment
8711 Engineering services
7929 Entertainers and entertainment groups
2677 Envelopes
3822 Environmental controls
7359 Equipment rental and leasing, nec
1794 Excavation work
9131 Executive and legislative combined
9111 Executive offices
2892 Explosives

F

2381 Fabric dress and work gloves
3499 Fabricated metal products, nec
3498 Fabricated pipe and fittings
3443 Fabricated plate work (boiler shop)
3069 Fabricated rubber products, nec
3441 Fabricated structural metal
2399 Fabricated textile products, nec
8744 Facilities support services
5651 Family clothing stores
5083 Farm and garden machinery
3523 Farm machinery and equipment
0762 Farm management services
4221 Farm product warehousing and storage
5191 Farm supplies
5159 Farm-product raw materials, nec
3965 Fasteners, buttons, needles, and pins
6111 Federal and federally sponsored credit
6061 Federal credit unions
6011 Federal reserve banks
6035 Federal savings institutions
2875 Fertilizers, mixing only
2655 Fiber cans, drums, and similar products
0139 Field crops, except cash grain
2261 Finishing plants, cotton
2262 Finishing plants, manmade
2269 Finishing plants, nec
6331 Fire, marine, and casualty insurance
5146 Fish and seafoods
3211 Flat glass
2087 Flavoring extracts and syrups, nec
5713 Floor covering stores
1752 Floor laying and floor work, nec
5992 Florists
2041 Flour and other grain mill products
5193 Flowers and florists supplies
3824 Fluid meters and counting devices
2026 Fluid milk
3593 Fluid power cylinders and actuators
3594 Fluid power pumps and motors
3492 Fluid power valves and hose fittings
2657 Folding paperboard boxes
0182 Food crops grown under cover
2099 Food preparations, nec
3556 Food products machinery
5139 Footwear
3131 Footwear cut stock
3149 Footwear, except rubber, nec
0851 Forestry services
4731 Freight transportation arrangement
5148 Fresh fruits and vegetables

2092 Fresh or frozen packaged fish
2053 Frozen bakery products, except bread
2037 Frozen fruits and vegetables
2038 Frozen specialties, nec
5431 Fruit and vegetable markets
0179 Fruits and tree nuts, nec
6099 Functions related to depository banking
7261 Funeral service and crematories
5021 Furniture
2599 Furniture and fixtures, nec
5712 Furniture stores

G

3944 Games, toys, and children's vehicles
4932 Gas and other services combined
3053 Gaskets; packing and sealing devices
5541 Gasoline service stations
7538 General automotive repair shops
0291 General farms, primarily animals
0191 General farms, primarily crop
9199 General government, nec
3569 General industrial machinery,
8062 General medical and surgical hospitals
4225 General warehousing and storage
5947 Gift, novelty, and souvenir shop
2361 Girl's and children's dresses, blouses
2369 Girl's and children's outerwear, nec
1793 Glass and glazing work
3221 Glass containers
1041 Gold ores
5153 Grain and field beans
0172 Grapes
3321 Gray and ductile iron foundries
5149 Groceries and related products, nec
5141 Groceries, general line
5411 Grocery stores
3761 Guided missiles and space vehicles
3275 Gypsum products

H

3423 Hand and edge tools, nec
3996 Hard surface floor coverings, nec
5072 Hardware
5251 Hardware stores
3429 Hardware, nec
2426 Hardwood dimension and flooring mills
2435 Hardwood veneer and plywood
2353 Hats, caps, and millinery
8099 Health and allied services, nec
3433 Heating equipment, except electric
7353 Heavy construction equipment rental
1629 Heavy construction, nec
7363 Help supply services
1611 Highway and street construction
5945 Hobby, toy, and game shops
3536 Hoists, cranes, and monorails
6719 Holding companies, nec
8082 Home health care services
5023 Homefurnishings
2252 Hosiery, nec
6324 Hospital and medical service plans
7011 Hotels and motels
3142 House slippers
5722 Household appliance stores
3639 Household appliances, nec
3651 Household audio and video equipment
3631 Household cooking equipment
2392 Household furnishings, nec
2519 Household furniture, nec
3632 Household refrigerators and freezers

I

2024 Ice cream and frozen deserts
8322 Individual and family services
5113 Industrial and personal service paper
1541 Industrial buildings and warehouses
3567 Industrial furnaces and ovens
2813 Industrial gases
2819 Industrial inorganic chemicals, nec
7218 Industrial launderers
5084 Industrial machinery and equipment
3599 Industrial machinery, nec

2869 Industrial organic chemicals, nec
3543 Industrial patterns
1446 Industrial sand
5085 Industrial supplies
3537 Industrial trucks and tractors
3491 Industrial valves
7375 Information retrieval services
2816 Inorganic pigments
4785 Inspection and fixed facilities
1796 Installing building equipment
3825 Instruments to measure electricity
6411 Insurance agents, brokers, and service
4131 Intercity and rural bus transportation
8052 Intermediate care facilities
3519 Internal combustion engines, nec
6282 Investment advice
6726 Investment offices, nec
6799 Investors, nec
0134 Irish potatoes
3462 Iron and steel forgings
4971 Irrigation systems

J

3915 Jewelers' materials and lapidary work
5094 Jewelry and precious stones
5944 Jewelry stores
3911 Jewelry, precious metal
8331 Job training and related services
8222 Junior colleges

K

1455 Kaolin and ball clay
8092 Kidney dialysis centers
2253 Knit outerwear mills
2259 Knitting mills, nec

L

8631 Labor organizations
3821 Laboratory apparatus and furniture
2258 Lace and warp knit fabric mills
3083 Laminated plastics plate and sheet
0781 Landscape counseling and planning
7219 Laundry and garment services, nec
3524 Lawn and garden equipment
0782 Lawn and garden services
3952 Lead pencils and art goods
2386 Leather and sheep-lined clothing
3199 Leather goods, nec
3111 Leather tanning and finishing
9222 Legal counsel and prosecution
8111 Legal services
8231 Libraries
6311 Life insurance
3648 Lighting equipment, nec
7213 Linen supply
5921 Liquor stores
0751 Livestock services, except veterinary
6163 Loan brokers
4111 Local and suburban transit
4141 Local bus charter service
4119 Local passenger transportation, nec
4214 Local trucking with storage
4212 Local trucking, without storage
2411 Logging
2992 Lubricating oils and greases
3161 Luggage
5211 Lumber and other building materials
5031 Lumber, plywood, and millwork

M

2098 Macaroni and spaghetti
3545 Machine tool accessories
3541 Machine tools, metal cutting type
3542 Machine tools, metal forming type
3695 Magnetic and optical recording media
3322 Malleable iron foundries
2083 Malt
2082 Malt beverages
8742 Management consulting services
6722 Management investment, open-ended
8741 Management services
2761 Manifold business forms

SIC NO	PRODUCT
2097	Manufactured ice
3999	Manufacturing industries, nec
4493	Marinas
4491	Marine cargo handling
3953	Marking devices
1741	Masonry and other stonework
2515	Mattresses and bedsprings
3829	Measuring and controlling devices, nec
2011	Meat packing plants
5147	Meats and meat products
3061	Mechanical rubber goods
5047	Medical and hospital equipment
7352	Medical equipment rental
8071	Medical laboratories
2833	Medicinals and botanicals
8699	Membership organizations, nec
7997	Membership sports and recreation clubs
7041	Membership-basis organization hotels
5136	Men's and boy's clothing
2329	Men's and boy's clothing, nec
2321	Men's and boy's furnishings
2323	Men's and boy's neckwear
2311	Men's and boy's suits and coats
2325	Men's and boy's trousers and slacks
2326	Men's and boy's work clothing
5611	Men's and boys' clothing stores
3143	Men's footwear, except athletic
3412	Metal barrels, drums, and pails
3411	Metal cans
3479	Metal coating and allied services
3442	Metal doors, sash, and trim
3398	Metal heat treating
2514	Metal household furniture
1081	Metal mining services
1099	Metal ores, nec
3431	Metal sanitary ware
3469	Metal stampings, nec
5051	Metals service centers and offices
3549	Metalworking machinery, nec
2431	Millwork
3296	Mineral wool
3295	Minerals, ground or treated
3532	Mining machinery
5699	Miscellaneous apparel and accessories
6159	Miscellaneous business credit
3496	Miscellaneous fabricated wire products
5499	Miscellaneous food stores
5399	Miscellaneous general merchandise
5719	Miscellaneous homefurnishings
3449	Miscellaneous metalwork
1499	Miscellaneous nonmetallic mining
7299	Miscellaneous personal services
2741	Miscellaneous publishing
5999	Miscellaneous retail stores, nec
6515	Mobile home site operators
2451	Mobile homes
6162	Mortgage bankers and correspondents
7822	Motion picture and tape distribution
7812	Motion picture and video production
7829	Motion picture distribution services
7832	Motion picture theaters, except drive-in
3716	Motor homes
3714	Motor vehicle parts and accessories
5013	Motor vehicle supplies and new parts
3711	Motor vehicles and car bodies
5571	Motorcycle dealers
3751	Motorcycles, bicycles, and parts
3621	Motors and generators
8412	Museums and art galleries
5736	Musical instrument stores
3931	Musical instruments

N

SIC NO	PRODUCT
2441	Nailed wood boxes and shook
2241	Narrow fabric mills
6021	National commercial banks
4924	Natural gas distribution
1321	Natural gas liquids
4922	Natural gas transmission
5511	New and used car dealers
5994	News dealers and newsstands
7383	News syndicates
2711	Newspapers
2873	Nitrogenous fertilizers
3297	Nonclay refractories
8733	Noncommercial research organizations
3644	Noncurrent-carrying wiring devices
6091	Nondeposit trust facilities
5199	Nondurable goods, nec
3364	Nonferrous die-castings except aluminum
3463	Nonferrous forgings
3369	Nonferrous foundries, nec
3356	Nonferrous rolling and drawing, nec
3357	Nonferrous wiredrawing and insulating
3299	Nonmetallic mineral products,
1481	Nonmetallic mineral services
6512	Nonresidential building operators
1542	Nonresidential construction, nec
2297	Nonwoven fabrics
8059	Nursing and personal care, nec

O

SIC NO	PRODUCT
5044	Office equipment
2522	Office furniture, except wood
3579	Office machines, nec
8041	Offices and clinics of chiropractors
8021	Offices and clinics of dentists
8011	Offices and clinics of medical doctors
8042	Offices and clinics of optometrists
8031	Offices and clinics of osteopathic physicians
8049	Offices of health practitioner
1382	Oil and gas exploration services
3533	Oil and gas field machinery
1389	Oil and gas field services, nec
1531	Operative builders
3851	Ophthalmic goods
5048	Ophthalmic goods
5995	Optical goods stores
3827	Optical instruments and lenses
3489	Ordnance and accessories, nec
2824	Organic fibers, noncellulosic
0181	Ornamental nursery products
0783	Ornamental shrub and tree services
7312	Outdoor advertising services

P

SIC NO	PRODUCT
5142	Packaged frozen goods
3565	Packaging machinery
4783	Packing and crating
5231	Paint, glass, and wallpaper stores
1721	Painting and paper hanging
2851	Paints and allied products
5198	Paints, varnishes, and supplies
3554	Paper industries machinery
2621	Paper mills
2671	Paper; coated and laminated packaging
2672	Paper; coated and laminated, nec
2631	Paperboard mills
2542	Partitions and fixtures, except wood
7515	Passenger car leasing
7514	Passenger car rental
4729	Passenger transportation arrangement
6794	Patent owners and lessors
3951	Pens and mechanical pencils
6371	Pension, health, and welfare funds
2721	Periodicals
6141	Personal credit institutions
3172	Personal leather goods, nec
2999	Petroleum and coal products, nec
5171	Petroleum bulk stations and terminals
5172	Petroleum products, nec
2911	Petroleum refining
2834	Pharmaceutical preparations
7334	Photocopying and duplicating services
7384	Photofinish laboratories
3861	Photographic equipment and supplies
5043	Photographic equipment and supplies
7221	Photographic studios, portrait
7991	Physical fitness facilities
2035	Pickles, sauces, and salad dressings
5131	Piece goods and notions
1742	Plastering, drywall, and insulation
3085	Plastics bottles
3086	Plastics foam products
5162	Plastics materials and basic shapes
2821	Plastics materials and resins
3084	Plastics pipe
3088	Plastics plumbing fixtures
3089	Plastics products, nec
2796	Platemaking services
3471	Plating and polishing
2395	Pleating and stitching
5074	Plumbing and hydronic heating supplies
3432	Plumbing fixture fittings and trim
1711	Plumbing, heating, air-conditioning
9221	Police protection
2842	Polishes and sanitation goods
3264	Porcelain electrical supplies
1474	Potash, soda, and borate minerals
2096	Potato chips and similar snacks
3269	Pottery products, nec
5144	Poultry and poultry products
2015	Poultry slaughtering and processing
7211	Power laundries, family and commercial
3568	Power transmission equipment, nec
3546	Power-driven handtools
3448	Prefabricated metal buildings
2452	Prefabricated wood buildings
7372	Prepackaged software
2048	Prepared feeds, nec
2045	Prepared flour mixes and doughs
3652	Prerecorded records and tapes
3229	Pressed and blown glass, nec
3334	Primary aluminum
3692	Primary batteries, dry and wet
3331	Primary copper
3399	Primary metal products
3339	Primary nonferrous metals, nec
3672	Printed circuit boards
5111	Printing and writing paper
2893	Printing ink
3555	Printing trades machinery
3823	Process control instruments
3231	Products of purchased glass
5049	Professional equipment, nec
8621	Professional organizations
8063	Psychiatric hospitals
2531	Public building and related furniture
7992	Public golf courses
8743	Public relations services
2611	Pulp mills
3561	Pumps and pumping equipment

R

SIC NO	PRODUCT
7948	Racing, including track operation
3663	Radio and t.v. communications equipment
7622	Radio and television repair
4832	Radio broadcasting stations
7313	Radio, television, publisher representatives
4812	Radiotelephone communication
3743	Railroad equipment
4011	Railroads, line-haul operating
2061	Raw cane sugar
3273	Ready-mixed concrete
6531	Real estate agents and managers
6798	Real estate investment trusts
6519	Real property lessors, nec
2493	Reconstituted wood products
5561	Recreational vehicle dealers
4613	Refined petroleum pipelines
4222	Refrigerated warehousing and storage
3585	Refrigeration and heating equipment
5078	Refrigeration equipment and supplies
7623	Refrigeration service and repair
4953	Refuse systems
9641	Regulation of agricultural marketing
9621	Regulation, administration of transportation
3625	Relays and industrial controls
8661	Religious organizations
7699	Repair services, nec
8361	Residential care
1522	Residential construction, nec
3645	Residential lighting fixtures
5461	Retail bakeries
5261	Retail nurseries and garden stores
7641	Reupholstery and furniture repair

S I C

SIC NO	PRODUCT

2095 Roasted coffee
2384 Robes and dressing gowns
3547 Rolling mill machinery
5033 Roofing, siding, and insulation
1761 Roofing, siding, and sheetmetal work
7021 Rooming and boarding houses
3021 Rubber and plastics footwear
3052 Rubber and plastics hose and beltings

S

2068 Salted and roasted nuts and seeds
2656 Sanitary food containers
2676 Sanitary paper products
4959 Sanitary services, nec
2013 Sausages and other prepared meats
6036 Savings institutions, except federal
3425 Saw blades and handsaws
2421 Sawmills and planing mills, general
3596 Scales and balances, except laboratory
4151 School buses
8299 Schools and educational services
5093 Scrap and waste materials
3451 Screw machine products
3812 Search and navigation equipment
3341 Secondary nonferrous metals
7338 Secretarial and court reporting
6289 Security and commodity service
6211 Security brokers and dealers
7382 Security systems services
3674 Semiconductors and related devices
3263 Semivitreous table and kitchenware
5087 Service establishment equipment
3589 Service industry machinery, nec
7819 Services allied to motion pictures
8999 Services, nec
2652 Setup paperboard boxes
4952 Sewerage systems
5949 Sewing, needlework, and piece goods
3444 Sheet metalwork
3731 Shipbuilding and repairing
5661 Shoe stores
6153 Short-term business credit
3993 Signs and advertising specialties
3914 Silverware and plated ware
1521 Single-family housing construction
8051 Skilled nursing care facilities
3484 Small arms
2841 Soap and other detergents
8399 Social services, nec
0711 Soil preparation services
3764 Space propulsion units and parts
3769 Space vehicle equipment, nec
3544 Special dies, tools, jigs, and fixtures
3559 Special industry machinery, nec
1799 Special trade contractors, nec
4226 Special warehousing and storage, nec
8069 Specialty hospitals, except psychiatric
8093 Specialty outpatient clinics, nec
3566 Speed changers, drives, and gears
3949 Sporting and athletic goods, nec
5091 Sporting and recreation goods
7032 Sporting and recreational camps
5941 Sporting goods and bicycle shops
7941 Sports clubs, managers, and promoters

6022 State commercial banks
6062 State credit unions
5112 Stationery and office supplies
2678 Stationery products
5943 Stationery stores
3325 Steel foundries, nec
3324 Steel investment foundries
3317 Steel pipe and tubes
3493 Steel springs, except wire
3315 Steel wire and related products
3691 Storage batteries
3259 Structural clay products, nec
1791 Structural steel erection
2439 Structural wood members, nec
6552 Subdividers and developers, nec
6351 Surety insurance
2843 Surface active agents
3841 Surgical and medical instruments
3842 Surgical appliances and supplies
8713 Surveying services
3613 Switchgear and switchboard apparatus
2822 Synthetic rubber

T

3795 Tanks and tank components
7291 Tax return preparation services
4121 Taxicabs
4822 Telegraph and other communications
3661 Telephone and telegraph apparatus
4813 Telephone communication, except radio
4833 Television broadcasting stations
1743 Terrazzo, tile, marble, mosaic work
8734 Testing laboratories
2393 Textile bags
2299 Textile goods, nec
3552 Textile machinery
7922 Theatrical producers and services
2284 Thread mills
0811 Timber tracts
7534 Tire retreading and repair shops
3011 Tires and inner tubes
5014 Tires and tubes
6541 Title abstract offices
6361 Title insurance
5194 Tobacco and tobacco products
5993 Tobacco stores and stands
2844 Toilet preparations
7532 Top and body repair and paint shops
4725 Tour operators
4492 Towing and tugboat service
5092 Toys and hobby goods and supplies
7033 Trailer parks and campsites
3612 Transformers, except electric
5088 Transportation equipment and supplies
3799 Transportation equipment, nec
4789 Transportation services, nec
4724 Travel agencies
3792 Travel trailers and campers
0173 Tree nuts
3713 Truck and bus bodies
7513 Truck rental and leasing, without drivers
3715 Truck trailers
4213 Trucking, except local
6733 Trusts, nec

6732 Trusts: educational, religious, etc.
3511 Turbines and turbine generator sets
2791 Typesetting

U

3081 Unsupported plastics film and sheet
3082 Unsupported plastics profile shapes
2512 Upholstered household furniture
5521 Used car dealers
5932 Used merchandise stores
7519 Utility trailer rental

V

3494 Valves and pipe fittings, nec
5331 Variety stores
2076 Vegetable oil mills, nec
0161 Vegetables and melons
3647 Vehicular lighting equipment
0742 Veterinary services, specialties
7841 Video tape rental
3262 Vitreous china table and kitchenware
3261 Vitreous plumbing fixtures
8249 Vocational schools, nec

W

5075 Warm air heating and air conditioning
3873 Watches, clocks, watchcases, and parts
4489 Water passenger transportation
4941 Water supply
4499 Water transportation services, nec
1781 Water well drilling
1623 Water, sewer, and utility lines
2257 Weft knit fabric mills
3548 Welding apparatus
7692 Welding repair
5182 Wine and distilled beverages
2084 Wines, brandy, and brandy spirits
3495 Wire springs
5632 Women's accessory and specialty stores
5137 Women's and children's clothing
2341 Women's and children's underwear
2331 Women's and misses' blouses and shirts
2339 Women's and misses' outerwear, nec
2337 Women's and misses' suits and coats
5621 Women's clothing stores
3144 Women's footwear, except athletic
3171 Women's handbags and purses
2335 Women's, junior's, and misses' dresses
2449 Wood containers, nec
2511 Wood household furniture
2434 Wood kitchen cabinets
2521 Wood office furniture
2448 Wood pallets and skids
2541 Wood partitions and fixtures
2491 Wood preserving
2499 Wood products, nec
2517 Wood television and radio cabinets
1795 Wrecking and demolition work

X

3844 X-ray apparatus and tubes

Y

2281 Yarn spinning mills

PRODUCTS & SERVICES SECTION

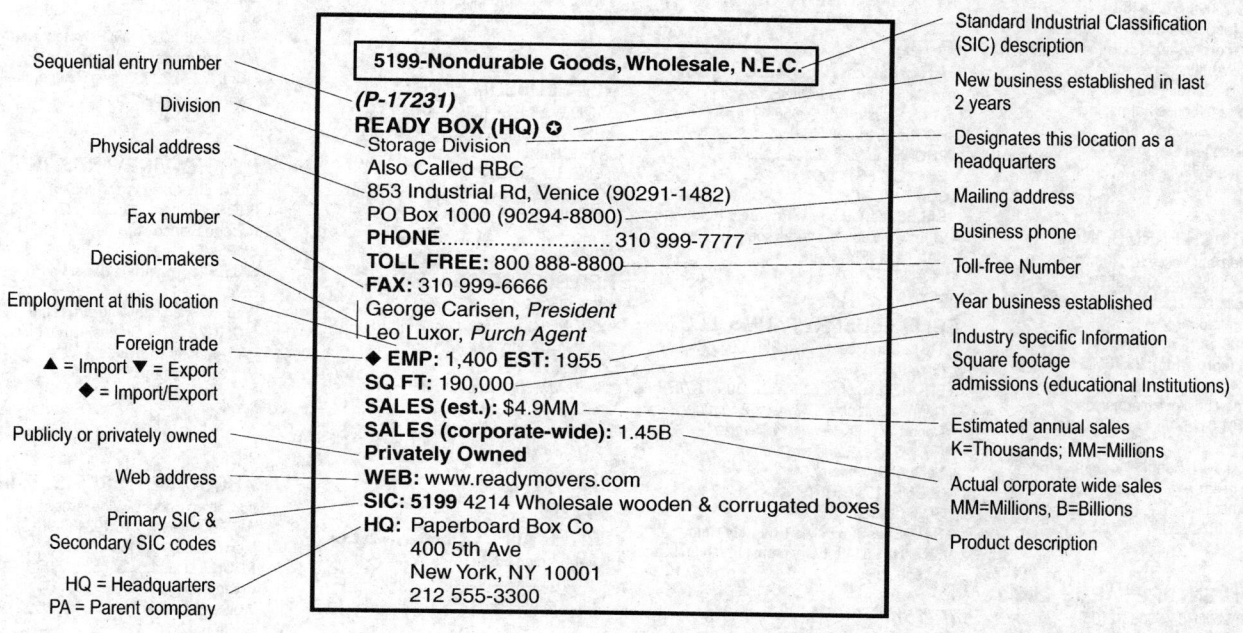

Sequential entry number — Division — Physical address — Fax number — Decision-makers — Employment at this location — Foreign trade ▲ = Import ▼ = Export ◆ = Import/Export — Publicly or privately owned — Web address — Primary SIC & Secondary SIC codes — HQ = Headquarters PA = Parent company

5199-Nondurable Goods, Wholesale, N.E.C.

(P-17231)
READY BOX (HQ) ✪
Storage Division
Also Called RBC
853 Industrial Rd, Venice (90291-1482)
PO Box 1000 (90294-8800)
PHONE............................. 310 999-7777
TOLL FREE: 800 888-8800
FAX: 310 999-6666
George Carisen, *President*
Leo Luxor, *Purch Agent*
◆ **EMP:** 1,400 **EST:** 1955
SQ FT: 190,000
SALES (est.): $4.9MM
SALES (corporate-wide): 1.45B
Privately Owned
WEB: www.readymovers.com
SIC: 5199 4214 Wholesale wooden & corrugated boxes
HQ: Paperboard Box Co
400 5th Ave
New York, NY 10001
212 555-3300

Standard Industrial Classification (SIC) description — New business established in last 2 years — Designates this location as a headquarters — Mailing address — Business phone — Toll-free Number — Year business established — Industry specific Information Square footage admissions (educational Institutions) — Estimated annual sales K=Thousands; MM=Millions — Actual corporate wide sales MM=Millions, B=Billions — Product description

- Companies in this section are listed numerically under their primary SIC Companies are in alphabetical order under each code.
- A numerical and alphabetical index precedes this section.
- **Sequential Entry Numbers.** Each establishment in this section is numbered sequentially. The number assigned to each establishment's Entry Number. To make cross-referencing easier, each listing in the Product's & Services, Alphabetic and Geographical Section includes the establishment's entry number. To facilitate locating an entry in this section, the entry numbers for the first listing on the left page and the last listing on the right page are printed at the top of the page next to the Standard Industrial Classification (SIC) description.
- Further information can be found in the Explanatory Notes starting on page 5.
- See the footnotes for symbols and abbreviations.

IMPORTANT NOTICE: It is a violation of both federal and state law to transmit an unsolicited advertisement to a facsimile machine. Any user of this product that violates such laws may be subject to civil and criminal penalties which may exceed $500 for each transmission of an unsolicited facsimile. Mergent Inc. provides fax numbers for lawful purposes only and expressly forbids the use of these numbers in any unlawful manner.

PRODUCTS & SVCS

0131 Cotton

(P-1)
J G BOSWELL COMPANY
21101 Bear Mountain Blvd (93311-9412)
P.O. Box 9759 (93389-9759)
PHONE............................661 327-7721
Dave Cosyns, *Mgr*
EMP: 397
SALES (corp-wide): 370.2MM **Privately Held**
Web: www.eastlakeco.com
SIC: 0131 0111 0724 Cotton; Wheat; Cotton ginning
PA: J. G. Boswell Company
101 W Walnut St
Pasadena CA
626 583-3000

(P-2)
VIGNOLO FARMS INC
33342 Dresser Ave (93308-9634)
P.O. Box 1270 (93263-1270)
PHONE............................661 746-2148
Robert J Vignolo, *Pr*
EMP: 150 **EST:** 1938
SQ FT: 2,500
SALES (est): 4.86MM **Privately Held**
Web: www.topbrassmarketing.com
SIC: 0131 0172 0134 Cotton; Grapes; Irish potatoes

0134 Irish Potatoes

(P-3)
TASTEFUL SELECTIONS LLC
13003 Di Giorgio Rd (93203-9529)
PHONE............................661 854-3998
EMP: 160 **EST:** 2010
SALES (est): 37.91MM **Privately Held**
Web: www.tastefulselections.com
SIC: 0134 5148 0723 Irish potatoes; Potatoes, fresh; Crop preparation services for market

0139 Field Crops, Except Cash Grain

(P-4)
GARLIC COMPANY
18602 Zerker Rd (93263-9101)
PHONE............................661 393-4212
John Layous, *Mng Pt*
Joe Lane, *
◆ **EMP:** 125 **EST:** 1980
SQ FT: 150,000
SALES (est): 36.52MM **Privately Held**
Web: www.thegarliccompany.com
SIC: 0139 2099 0191 Herb or spice farm; Food preparations, nec; General farms, primarily crop

(P-5)
MEDTERRA CBD LLC
18500 Von Karman Ave (92612-0518)
PHONE............................800 971-1288
John Hartenbach, *CEO*

John Preston Larsen, *
EMP: 89 **EST:** 2017
SALES (est): 12.09MM **Privately Held**
Web: www.medterracbd.com
SIC: 0139 Herb or spice farm

0161 Vegetables And Melons

(P-6)
AMAZING COACHELLA INC
Also Called: Peter Rabbit Farms
85810 Peter Rabbit Ln (92236-1897)
PHONE............................760 398-0151
EMP: 100 **EST:** 1950
SALES (est): 16.04MM **Privately Held**
Web: www.peterrabbitfarms.com
SIC: 0161 Vegetables and melons

(P-7)
BOLTHOUSE FARMS
3200 E Brundage Ln (93304)
PHONE............................661 366-7205

William Bolthouse, *Owner*
◆ **EMP:** 2300 **EST:** 1915
SALES (est): 39.11MM
SALES (corp-wide): 1.33B **Privately Held**
Web: www.bolthouse.com
SIC: 0161 Carrot farm
HQ: Wm. Bolthouse Farms, Inc.
7200 E Brundage Ln
Bakersfield CA
661 366-7209

(P-8)
BOSKOVICH FARMS INC
4224 Pleasant Valley Rd (93012-8533)
P.O. Box 1352 (93032-1352)
PHONE..........................805 987-1443
Ken Mumford, *Mgr*
EMP: 105
SALES (corp-wide): 93.16MM **Privately Held**
Web: www.boskovichfarms.com
SIC: 0161 0115 Vegetables and melons; Corn
PA: Boskovich Farms, Inc.
711 Diaz Ave
Oxnard CA
805 487-2299

(P-9)
FRESH VENTURE FARMS LLC
1181 S Wolff Rd (93033-2105)
PHONE..........................805 754-4449
EMP: 80 **EST:** 2012
SQ FT: 4,000
SALES (est): 2.15MM **Privately Held**
SIC: 0161 0191 Vegetables and melons; General farms, primarily crop

(P-10)
GENERIS HOLDINGS LP (PA)
7200 E Brundage Ln (93307-3016)
PHONE..........................661 366-7209
Jeffrey Dunn, *CEO*
EMP: 241 **EST:** 2019
SALES (est): 1.33B
SALES (corp-wide): 1.33B **Privately Held**
Web: www.bolthouse.com
SIC: 0161 2037 2033 2099 Carrot farm; Fruit juices; Vegetable juices: packaged in cans, jars, etc.; Sauce, gravy, dressing, and dip mixes

(P-11)
SAN MIGUEL PRODUCE INC
Also Called: Cut N Clean Greens
600 E Hueneme Rd (93033-8298)
PHONE..........................805 488-0981
Roy I Nishimori, *CEO*
Jan Berk, *
▲ **EMP:** 500 **EST:** 1979
SALES (est): 34.38MM **Privately Held**
Web: www.sanmiguelproduce.com
SIC: 0161 0723 4212 Vegetables and melons; Vegetable packing services; Farm to market haulage, local

(P-12)
SANTA BARBARA FARMS LLC
1105 Union Sugar Ave (93436-9737)
PHONE..........................805 736-5608
EMP: 190
SALES (corp-wide): 30.6MM **Privately Held**
SIC: 0161 0181 Vegetables and melons; Florists' greens and flowers
PA: Santa Barbara Farms, Llc
1200 Union Sugar Ave
Lompoc CA
805 736-9776

0171 Berry Crops

(P-13)
DARENSBERRIES LLC
Also Called: D B Specialty Farms
714 S Blosser Rd (93458-4914)
P.O. Box 549 (93456-0549)
PHONE..........................805 937-8000
EMP: 250 **EST:** 1994
SQ FT: 1,500
SALES (est): 9.63MM **Privately Held**
Web: www.darensberries.com
SIC: 0171 Strawberry farm

(P-14)
ECLIPSE BERRY FARMS LLC
11812 San Vicente Blvd Ste 250 (90049-6632)
PHONE..........................310 207-7879
Norman Gilfenbain, *Managing Member*
Robert Wiviott, *Managing Member**
Rudy Garza, *Managing Member**
Ventura Strawberry, *
▼ **EMP:** 100 **EST:** 1999
SQ FT: 2,500
SALES (est): 8.84MM **Privately Held**
SIC: 0171 5148 Berry crops; Fresh fruits and vegetables

(P-15)
ETCHANDY FARMS LLC
4324 E Vineyard Ave (93036-1056)
P.O. Box 5770 (93031-5770)
PHONE..........................805 983-4700
EMP: 99 **EST:** 2014
SQ FT: 400
SALES (est): 2.39MM **Privately Held**
SIC: 0171 Strawberry farm

(P-16)
FRESHWAY FARMS LLC
2165 W Main St (93458-9739)
P.O. Box 5369 (93456-5369)
PHONE..........................805 349-7170
Paul M Allen, *Managing Member*
EMP: 150 **EST:** 2014
SALES (est): 8.85MM **Privately Held**
Web: www.mainstreetproduce.com
SIC: 0171 0161 Strawberry farm; Broccoli farm

(P-17)
J&G BERRY FARMS LLC
720 Rosemary Rd (93454-8007)
PHONE..........................831 750-9408
Jose Luis Rocha, *Managing Member*
Guadalupe Rocha, *
EMP: 220 **EST:** 2016
SALES (est): 2.89MM **Privately Held**
SIC: 0171 7389 Strawberry farm; Business Activities at Non-Commercial Site

(P-18)
LAS POSAS BERRY FARMS LLC
730 S A St (93030-7138)
PHONE..........................805 483-1000
Manuel Magdaleno, *CEO*
EMP: 100 **EST:** 2013
SALES (est): 1.87MM **Privately Held**
SIC: 0171 Berry crops

(P-19)
ORANGE COUNTY PRODUCE LLC
210 W Walnut Ave (92832-2347)
PHONE..........................949 451-0880
Matthew K Kawamura, *Managing Member*
EMP: 100 **EST:** 1998

SALES (est): 9.85MM **Privately Held**
Web: www.ocproduce.com
SIC: 0171 Strawberry farm

(P-20)
RED BLOSSOM FARMS INC
1389 W Main St (93458-4903)
PHONE..........................805 686-4747
David Lawrence, *Pr*
EMP: 99 **EST:** 2021
SALES (est): 544.07K **Privately Held**
SIC: 0171 Berry crops

(P-21)
RED BLOSSOM SALES INC
865 Black Rd (93458-9701)
PHONE..........................805 349-9404
Ruben Trevino, *Mgr*
EMP: 572
Web: www.redblossom.com
SIC: 0171 Strawberry farm
PA: Red Blossom Sales, Inc.
400 W Ventura Blvd # 140
Camarillo CA

(P-22)
REITER AFFL COMPANIES LLC
124 Carmen Ln Ste A (93458-7768)
PHONE..........................805 925-8577
Mario Pena, *Mgr*
EMP: 108
SALES (corp-wide): 43.32MM **Privately Held**
Web: www.berry.net
SIC: 0171 Berry crops
PA: Reiter Affiliated Companies, Llc
730 S A St
Oxnard CA
805 483-1000

(P-23)
RINCON PACIFIC LLC
1312 Del Norte Rd (93010-8502)
PHONE..........................805 986-8806
EMP: 100 **EST:** 2001
SALES (est): 4.44MM **Privately Held**
SIC: 0171 Strawberry farm

(P-24)
SANTA ROSA BERRY FARMS LLC
3500 Camino Ave Ste 250 (93030-7999)
PHONE..........................805 981-3060
EMP: 300 **EST:** 2010
SQ FT: 3,500
SALES (est): 8.84MM **Privately Held**
Web: www.srbfarms.com
SIC: 0171 Berry crops

(P-25)
SUPERIOR FRUIT LLC
4324 E Vineyard Ave (93036-1056)
PHONE..........................805 485-2519
Richard Jones, *
EMP: 200 **EST:** 2017
SQ FT: 6,000
SALES (est): 3.21MM **Privately Held**
SIC: 0171 Strawberry farm

0172 Grapes

(P-26)
7TH STANDARD RANCH COMPANY
Also Called: Sun Pacific Farming
33374 Lerdo Hwy (93308-9782)
PHONE..........................661 399-0416
Berne Evans, *Pt*

Robert Reniers, *Pt*
EMP: 500 **EST:** 1986
SQ FT: 140,000
SALES (est): 20.8MM **Privately Held**
Web: www.sunpacific.com
SIC: 0172 4222 Grapes; Refrigerated warehousing and storage

(P-27)
ANTHONY VINEYARDS INC
52301 Enterprise Way (92236)
PHONE..........................760 391-5488
Roberto Bianco, *Mgr*
EMP: 100
SALES (corp-wide): 12.58MM **Privately Held**
Web: www.anthonyvineyards.com
SIC: 0172 0174 Grapes; Grapefruit grove
PA: Anthony Vineyards, Inc.
5512 Valpredo Ave
Bakersfield CA
661 858-6211

(P-28)
BABCOCK ENTERPRISES INC
Also Called: Babcock Vineyards
5175 E Highway 246 (93436-9613)
P.O. Box 637 (93438-0637)
PHONE..........................805 736-1455
Bryan Babcock, *Pr*
Walter Babcock, *
Bryan Babcock, *VP*
Mona Babcock, *
EMP: 25 **EST:** 1979
SALES (est): 2.42MM **Privately Held**
Web: www.babcockwinery.com
SIC: 0172 2084 8734 Grapes; Wines; Food testing service

(P-29)
BECKMEN VINEYARDS
2670 Ontiveros Rd (93441)
P.O. Box 542 (93441-0542)
PHONE..........................805 688-8664
Thomas Beckmen, *Owner*
▲ **EMP:** 23 **EST:** 1985
SQ FT: 3,000
SALES (est): 5.59MM **Privately Held**
Web: www.beckmenvineyards.com
SIC: 0172 2084 Grapes; Wine cellars, bonded: engaged in blending wines

(P-30)
GIUMARRA VINEYARDS CORPORATION
Giumarra Winery
11220 Edison Hwy (93307-8431)
P.O. Box 1969 (93303-1969)
PHONE..........................661 395-7071
Barry Douglas, *Mgr*
EMP: 184
SALES (corp-wide): 134.67MM **Privately Held**
Web: www.giumarravineyards.com
SIC: 0172 Grapes
PA: Giumarra Vineyards Corporation
11220 Edison Hwy
Edison CA
661 395-7000

(P-31)
GIUMARRA VINEYARDS CORPORATION (PA)
11220 Edison Hwy (93220)
P.O. Box 1969 (93303-1969)
PHONE..........................661 395-7000
Wayne Childress, *CEO*
Mimi Corsaro-dorsey, *Sec*
Jeffrey Giumarra, *
◆ **EMP:** 500 **EST:** 1946

▲ = Import ▼ = Export
◆ = Import/Export

SQ FT: 10,000
SALES (est): 134.67MM
SALES (corp-wide): 134.67MM Privately Held
Web: www.giumarravineyards.com
SIC: 0172 2084 2086 Grapes; Wines; Fruit drinks (less than 100% juice): packaged in cans, etc.

(P-32)
J & L VINEYARDS
1850 Ramada Dr Ste 3 (93446-3932)
PHONE..................559 268-1627
Donald Laub, *Pt*
Raymond Jacobson, *Pt*
EMP: 100 EST: 1980
SALES (est): 2.46MM Privately Held
SIC: 0172 Grapes

(P-33)
JAKOV DULCICH AND SONS LLC
31956 Peterson Rd (93250-9606)
PHONE..................661 792-6360
Jakov Dulcich, *Prin*
▲ EMP: 250 EST: 1963
SALES (est): 14.69MM Privately Held
Web: www.dulcich.com
SIC: 0172 Grapes

(P-34)
M CARATAN DISC INC
Also Called: Caliente Farms
33787 Cecil Ave (93215-9597)
PHONE..................661 725-2566
Martin Caratin, *CEO*
▼ EMP: 150 EST: 1946
SQ FT: 6,000
SALES (est): 13.53MM Privately Held
Web: www.mcaratan.com
SIC: 0172 0174 0723 Grapes; Orange grove; Almond hulling and shelling services

(P-35)
RENZONI VINEYARDS INC
Also Called: Robert Rnzoni Vineyards Winery
37350 De Portola Rd (92592-9024)
PHONE..................951 302-8466
Robert Renzoni, *Pr*
Fred Renzoni, *
▲ EMP: 37 EST: 2007
SALES (est): 2.03MM Privately Held
Web: www.robertrenzonivineyards.com
SIC: 0172 2084 Grapes; Wines

(P-36)
TREASURY WINE ESTATES AMERICAS
Also Called: Meridian Vineyards
7000 E Highway 46 (93446-7390)
P.O. Box 3289 (93447-3289)
PHONE..................805 237-6000
Jim Schaefer, *Mgr*
EMP: 22
Web: www.tweglobal.com
SIC: 0172 2084 Grapes; Wines, brandy, and brandy spirits
HQ: Treasury Wine Estates Americas Company
555 Gateway Dr
Napa CA
707 259-4500

0173 Tree Nuts

(P-37)
J G BOSWELL COMPANY
36889 Hwy 58 (93206-9616)

PHONE..................661 764-9000
EMP: 328
SALES (corp-wide): 370.2MM Privately Held
Web: www.eastlakeco.com
SIC: 0173 0161 0131 Pistachio grove; Tomato farm; Cotton
PA: J. G. Boswell Company
101 W Walnut St
Pasadena CA
626 583-3000

(P-38)
SUPREME ALMONDS CALIFORNIA INC
16897 Highway 43 (93280-9611)
PHONE..................661 746-6475
Randy Loemhof, *Pr*
◆ EMP: 100 EST: 2008
SALES (est): 4.46MM Privately Held
Web: www.supremealmonds.com
SIC: 0173 Almond grove

(P-39)
WONDERFUL ORCHARDS LLC
Also Called: Wonderfulpistachiosandalmonds
13646 Highway 33 (93249-9719)
P.O. Box 400 (93249-0400)
PHONE..................661 797-6400
Dennis Elam, *Brnch Mgr*
EMP: 262
SALES (corp-wide): 2.04B Privately Held
Web: www.wonderfulorchards.com
SIC: 0173 0191 Almond grove; General farms, primarily crop
HQ: Wonderful Orchards Llc
6801 E Lerdo Hwy
Shafter CA
661 399-4456

(P-40)
WONDERFUL ORCHARDS LLC
21707 Lerdo Hwy (93251-9758)
PHONE..................661 797-2509
Robert Baker, *Mgr*
EMP: 98
SALES (corp-wide): 2.04B Privately Held
Web: www.wonderfulorchards.com
SIC: 0173 0191 Almond grove; General farms, primarily crop
HQ: Wonderful Orchards Llc
6801 E Lerdo Hwy
Shafter CA
661 399-4456

(P-41)
WONDERFUL ORCHARDS LLC (HQ)
6801 E Lerdo Hwy (93263-9610)
PHONE..................661 399-4456
◆ EMP: 150 EST: 1998
SQ FT: 10,000
SALES (est): 157.67MM
SALES (corp-wide): 2.04B Privately Held
Web: www.wonderfulorchards.com
SIC: 0173 0179 Almond grove; Olive grove
PA: The Wonderful Company Llc
11444 W Olympic Blvd # 210
Los Angeles CA
310 966-5700

0174 Citrus Fruits

(P-42)
EXETER PACKERS INC
Also Called: Sun Pacific Shippers
1095 E Green St (91106-2503)
PHONE..................626 993-6245
Bob Reniers, *Genl Mgr*

EMP: 119
SALES (corp-wide): 41.55MM Privately Held
Web: www.sunpacific.com
SIC: 0174 0172 0161 0723 Orange grove; Grapes; Tomato farm; Fruit (fresh) packing services
PA: Exeter Packers, Inc.
1250 E Myer Ave
Exeter CA
559 592-5168

(P-43)
HRONIS INC A CALIFORNIA CORP (PA)
10443 Hronis Rd (93215-9556)
PHONE..................661 725-2503
Kosta Hronis, *Pr*
Pete Hronis, *
▼ EMP: 145 EST: 1945
SQ FT: 150,000
SALES (est): 30.34MM
SALES (corp-wide): 30.34MM Privately Held
Web: www.hronis.net
SIC: 0174 0172 Citrus fruits; Grapes

(P-44)
SATICOY LEMON ASSOCIATION
Also Called: Saticoy Fruit Exchange
7560 Bristol Rd (93003-7027)
P.O. Box 46 (93061-0046)
PHONE..................805 654-6500
John Elliott, *Brnch Mgr*
EMP: 99
SALES (corp-wide): 26.61MM Privately Held
Web: www.saticoylemon.com
SIC: 0174 Lemon grove
PA: Saticoy Lemon Association
103 N Peck Rd
Santa Paula CA
805 654-6500

(P-45)
WONDERFUL COMPANY LLC
Also Called: Paramount Citrus
1901 S Lexington St (93215-9207)
PHONE..................661 720-2400
Freddie Hernandez, *Mgr*
EMP: 273
SALES (corp-wide): 2.04B Privately Held
Web: www.wonderful.com
SIC: 0174 3911 Citrus fruits; Jewelry, precious metal
PA: The Wonderful Company Llc
11444 W Olympic Blvd # 210
Los Angeles CA
310 966-5700

0175 Deciduous Tree Fruits

(P-46)
NISSHO OF CALIFORNIA INC
89055 64th Ave (92274-9607)
PHONE..................760 727-9719
Abel Bustamante, *Mgr*
EMP: 309
SALES (corp-wide): 23.11MM Privately Held
Web: www.nisshoca.com
SIC: 0175 Deciduous tree fruits
PA: Nissho Of California, Inc.
1902 S Santa Fe Ave
Vista CA
760 727-9719

0179 Fruits And Tree Nuts, Nec

(P-47)
C C GRABER CO
Also Called: Graber Olive House
315 E 4th St (91764-2709)
PHONE..................909 983-1761
Clifford C Graber Ii, *Pr*
Mary E Graber, *VP*
Robert D Graber, *Ch Bd*
EMP: 18 EST: 1894
SQ FT: 10,000
SALES (est): 1.1MM Privately Held
Web: www.graberolives.com
SIC: 0179 5947 2033 2032 Olive grove; Artcraft and carvings; Canned fruits and specialties; Canned specialties

(P-48)
DOLE HOLDING COMPANY LLC
1 Dole Dr (91362-7300)
PHONE..................818 879-6600
David H Murdock, *Ch Bd*
EMP: 74999 EST: 2004
SALES (est): 424.16K Privately Held
SIC: 0179 0174 0175 0161 Pineapple farm; Citrus fruits; Deciduous tree fruits; Lettuce farm
PA: Dhm Holding Company, Inc.
1 Dole Dr
Westlake Village CA

(P-49)
MUNGER BROS LLC
Also Called: Munger Farm
786 Road 188 (93215-9508)
PHONE..................661 721-0390
Kewel K Munger, *
▲ EMP: 600 EST: 1998
SQ FT: 50,000
SALES (est): 24.34MM Privately Held
SIC: 0179 2033 Avocado orchard; Canned fruits and specialties

0181 Ornamental Nursery Products

(P-50)
COLOR SPOT HOLDINGS INC (PA)
Also Called: Color Spot Nurseries
3742 Blue Bird Canyon Rd (92084-7432)
PHONE..................760 695-1430
Rodney Omps, *Sec*
Jerry Halamuda, *CEO*
Oscar Truyol, *COO*
Chip Mello, *COO*
EMP: 1498 EST: 2007
SALES (est): 229.55MM
SALES (corp-wide): 229.55MM Privately Held
SIC: 0181 Bedding plants, growing of

(P-51)
DEVIL MOUNTAIN WHL NURS LLC
Also Called: Devil Mountain Wholesale Nursery, LLC
29001 Ortega Hwy (92675)
PHONE..................949 496-9356
EMP: 93
Web: www.devilmountainnursery.com
SIC: 0181 Nursery stock, growing of
PA: Devil Mountain Wholesale Nursery, Llc
9885 Alcosta Blvd
San Ramon CA

PRODUCTS & SVCS

(P-52)
DRAMM AND ECHTER INC
Also Called: D&E Propagators
1150 Quail Gardens Dr (92024-2365)
PHONE..............................760 436-0188
◆ EMP: 85 EST: 1972
SALES (est): 4.52MM Privately Held
Web: www.drammechter.com
SIC: 0181 5193 Flowers: grown under cover
(e.g., greenhouse production); Flowers and
nursery stock

(P-53)
**EUROAMERICAN
PROPAGATORS LLC**
32149 Aquaduct Rd (92003-4807)
PHONE..............................760 731-6029
▲ EMP: 375
Web: www.euroamericanpropagators.com
SIC: 0181 Ornamental nursery products

(P-54)
**FLORAL GIFT HM DECOR INTL
INC**
3200 Golf Course Dr Ste B (93003-7615)
P.O. Box 2673 (93011-2673)
PHONE..............................818 849-8832
Dolly Ives, CEO
Edwin M Ives, *
▲ EMP: 25 EST: 1973
SALES (est): 2.02MM Privately Held
SIC: 0181 3999 Florists' greens, cultivated:
growing of; Foliage, artificial and preserved

(P-55)
GLAD-A-WAY GARDENS INC
2669 E Clark Ave (93455-5815)
P.O. Box 2550 (93457-2550)
PHONE..............................805 938-0569
Brian Caird, Pr
Erin Caird, *
Lance Runels, *
▲ EMP: 172 EST: 1964
SQ FT: 15,000
SALES (est): 9.93MM Privately Held
Web: www.gladaway.com
SIC: 0181 Flowers: grown under cover (e.g.,
greenhouse production)

(P-56)
HINES GROWERS INC
Also Called: Cshg Holdings
27368 Via Industria Ste 201 (92590-4855)
PHONE..............................800 554-4065
▲ EMP: 942 EST: 2012
SALES (est): 434.05K
SALES (corp-wide): 229.55MM Privately
Held
SIC: 0181 5261 Ornamental nursery products
; Retail nurseries and garden stores
HQ: Csn Winddown, Inc.
27368 Via Industria # 20
Temecula CA

(P-57)
HINES HORTICULTURE INC (PA)
Also Called: Hines Nurseries
12621 Jeffery Rd (92620)
PHONE..............................949 559-4444
▲ EMP: 500 EST: 1920
SALES (est): 446.34MM Privately Held
SIC: 0181 5261 Ornamental nursery products
; Retail nurseries and garden stores

(P-58)
JIMENEZ NURSERY INC
Also Called: Jimenez Nursery and
Landscapes
3800 Via Real (93013-3051)

P.O. Box 2460 (93120-2460)
PHONE..............................805 684-7955
Manuel Jimenez, CEO
Alicia Jimenez, Sec
EMP: 100 EST: 1996
SALES (est): 6.8MM Privately Held
Web: www.jimeneznursery.com
SIC: 0181 Nursery stock, growing of

(P-59)
MARATHON LAND INC
2599 E Hueneme Rd (93033-8112)
P.O. Box 579 (93044-0579)
PHONE..............................805 488-3585
TOLL FREE: 800
Jurgen Gramckow, Pr
EMP: 130 EST: 1977
SQ FT: 3,000
SALES (est): 3.45MM Privately Held
Web: www.sod.com
SIC: 0181 Sod farms

(P-60)
**MONROVIA NURSERY
COMPANY (PA)**
Also Called: Monrovia Growes
817 E Monrovia Pl (91702-6297)
P.O. Box 1385 (91702-1385)
PHONE..............................626 334-9321
Miles R Rosedale, CEO
Richard Van Landinghan, Pr
William B Usrey, Pr
Dennis Conner, General Vice President
▲ EMP: 567 EST: 1926
SQ FT: 50,000
SALES (est): 436.68MM
SALES (corp-wide): 436.68MM Privately
Held
Web: www.monrovia.com
SIC: 0181 5193 5261 Nursery stock, growing
of; Flowers and florists supplies; Retail
nurseries and garden stores

(P-61)
MULROSES USA INC
741 S San Pedro St (90014-2417)
PHONE..............................213 489-1761
Patricio Nasser, Mgr
EMP: 100 EST: 2010
SALES (est): 1.55MM Privately Held
SIC: 0181 Roses, growing of

(P-62)
NORMANS NURSERY INC
Also Called: Norman's Nursery
5770 Casitas Pass Rd (93013-3061)
PHONE..............................805 684-1411
Martin Manzo, Mgr
EMP: 142
SALES (corp-wide): 95.85MM Privately
Held
Web: www.nngrower.com
SIC: 0181 Nursery stock, growing of
PA: Norman's Nursery, Inc.
8665 Duarte Rd
San Gabriel CA
626 285-9795

(P-63)
OLIVE HILL GREENHOUSES INC
3508 Olive Hill Rd (92028-8296)
P.O. Box 1510 (92088-1510)
PHONE..............................760 728-4596
George A Godfrey, Owner
▲ EMP: 100 EST: 1974
SQ FT: 2,000
SALES (est): 5.41MM Privately Held
Web: www.olivehill.net
SIC: 0181 Nursery stock, growing of

(P-64)
**PACIFIC ERTH RSRCES LTD A
CAL**
Also Called: Pacific Sod
315 Hueneme Rd (93012-8522)
P.O. Box 240 (93011-0240)
PHONE..............................209 892-3000
Raymond Freitas, Mgr
EMP: 90
SALES (corp-wide): 8.63MM Privately
Held
SIC: 0181 Sod farms
PA: Pacific Earth Resources, Ltd., A
California Limited Partnership
305 Hueneme Rd
Camarillo CA
805 986-8277

(P-65)
**PACIFIC ERTH RSRCES LTD A
CAL (PA)**
Also Called: Pacific Sd/Pcfic Arbor Nrsries
305 Hueneme Rd (93012-8522)
P.O. Box 240 (93011-0240)
PHONE..............................805 986-8277
Richard Rogers, Mng Pt
Elizabeth Rogers, Pt
EMP: 80 EST: 1958
SQ FT: 8,000
SALES (est): 8.63MM
SALES (corp-wide): 8.63MM Privately
Held
SIC: 0181 Sod farms

(P-66)
PLANTEL NURSERIES INC
3990 Foxen Canyon Rd (93454-9666)
PHONE..............................805 934-4300
Gerald Tonascia, Mgr
EMP: 270
SALES (corp-wide): 19.39MM Privately
Held
Web: www.plantelnurseries.com
SIC: 0181 5193 Seeds, vegetable: growing of
; Nursery stock
PA: Plantel Nurseries, Inc.
2775 E Clark Ave
Santa Maria CA
805 349-8952

(P-67)
PLANTEL NURSERIES INC (PA)
Also Called: Plantel Tranplanting Services
2775 E Clark Ave (93455-5813)
PHONE..............................805 349-8952
Scott Nicholson, Pr
Les Graulich, Sec
Craig Reade, VP
EMP: 20 EST: 1985
SQ FT: 1,300,000
SALES (est): 19.39MM
SALES (corp-wide): 19.39MM Privately
Held
Web: www.plantelnurseries.com
SIC: 0181 5193 3523 Seeds, vegetable:
growing of; Nursery stock; Transplanters

(P-68)
PLUG CONNECTION INC
2627 Ramona Dr (92084-1634)
PHONE..............................760 631-0992
Tim Wada, Pr
Bradley Rhoads, *
▲ EMP: 80 EST: 1987
SQ FT: 350,000
SALES (est): 17.28MM Privately Held
Web: www.plugconnection.com
SIC: 0181 Nursery stock, growing of

(P-69)
RICHARD WILSON WELLINGTON
Also Called: Colorama Wholesale Nursery
1025 N Todd Ave (91702-1602)
P.O. Box 1328 (91740-1328)
PHONE..............................626 812-7881
Richard Wilson, Owner
▲ EMP: 100 EST: 1984
SQ FT: 70,000
SALES (est): 3.09MM Privately Held
Web: www.coloramanursery.com
SIC: 0181 5193 Nursery stock, growing of;
Nursery stock

(P-70)
RIVER RIDGE FARMS INC
3135 Los Angeles Ave (93036-1010)
PHONE..............................805 647-6880
Rieuwert Jan Vis, Pr
▲ EMP: 95 EST: 1992
SQ FT: 440
SALES (est): 2.42MM Privately Held
Web: www.riverridgefarms.net
SIC: 0181 5193 Flowers, grown in field
nurseries; Plants, potted

(P-71)
SUPERIOR SOD I LP
17821 17th St Ste 165 (92780-2172)
P.O. Box 1911 (93581-5911)
PHONE..............................909 923-5068
Michael Considine, Pt
Richard H Considine, Pt
Peter Moore, Pt
Trudy Considine, Pt
EMP: 125 EST: 1988
SQ FT: 1,400
SALES (est): 4.5MM Privately Held
Web: www.superiorsod.com
SIC: 0181 0782 Sod farms; Lawn and
garden services

(P-72)
TWIN OAKS GROWERS INTL INC
Also Called: Twin Oaks Growers Intl
1969 Marilyn Ln (92069-9769)
PHONE..............................760 744-5581
Bas Denbraver, Pr
Mady Denbraver, VP
EMP: 20 EST: 1978
SQ FT: 120,000
SALES (est): 2.06MM Privately Held
Web: www.twinoaksgrowers.com
SIC: 0181 3999 Nursery stock, growing of;
Plants, artificial and preserved

(P-73)
WESTERLAY ORCHIDS LP
Also Called: Westerlay Orchids
3504 Via Real (93013-3048)
PHONE..............................805 684-5411
Antoine Overgaag, Pr
▲ EMP: 117 EST: 2003
SALES (est): 9.94MM Privately Held
Web: www.westerlay.com
SIC: 0181 Flowers: grown under cover (e.g.,
greenhouse production)

0182 Food Crops Grown Under Cover

(P-74)
HOKTO KINOKO COMPANY
130 S Myers St (90033-3212)
PHONE..............................323 526-1155
EMP: 94
Web: www.hokto-kinoko.com

SIC: 0182 Mushrooms, grown under cover
HQ: Hokto Kinoko Company
2033 Marilyn Ln
San Marcos CA

(P-75)
HOUWELINGS CAMARILLO INC
645 Laguna Rd (93012-8523)
PHONE...................805 250-1600
Cornelius Houweling, *CEO*
EMP: 338 EST: 2021
SQ FT: 3,000,000
SALES (est): 520MM **Privately Held**
Web: www.houwelings.com
SIC: 0182 Food crops grown under cover

0191 General Farms, Primarily Crop

(P-76)
BLACKJACK FRMS DE LA CSTA CNTL
Also Called: Black Jack Farms
2385 A St (93455-1073)
PHONE...................805 347-1333
Jose Garcia, *CEO*
EMP: 140 EST: 2017
SALES (est): 2.31MM **Privately Held**
SIC: 0191 General farms, primarily crop

(P-77)
BRAGA FRESH FAMILY FARMS INC
Also Called: Braga Fresh Imperial
817 W Hackleman Rd (92243-9508)
PHONE...................760 353-1155
Asa Braga, *Owner*
EMP: 180
SALES (corp-wide): 150MM **Privately Held**
Web: www.bragafresh.com
SIC: 0191 General farms, primarily crop
PA: Braga Fresh Family Farms, Inc.
33750 Moranda Rd
Soledad CA
831 675-2154

(P-78)
CENTRAL COAST AGRICULTURE INC (PA)
8701 Santa Rosa Rd (93427-8406)
PHONE...................805 694-8594
EMP: 25 EST: 2015
SALES (est): 21.85MM **Privately Held**
Web: www.ccagriculture.com
SIC: 0191 2099 General farms, primarily crop ; Food preparations, nec

(P-79)
CRYSTAL ORGANIC FARMS LLC
10000 Stockdale Hwy Ste 200
(93311-3601)
PHONE...................661 845-5200
Jeff Meger, *Pr*
EMP: 809 EST: 2003
SALES (est): 1.67MM
SALES (corp-wide): 1.86B **Privately Held**
SIC: 0191 General farms, primarily crop
PA: Grimmway Enterprises, Inc.
14141 Di Giorgio Rd
Arvin CA
800 301-3101

(P-80)
DV CUSTOM FARMING LLC
2101 Mettler Frontage Rd E (93307-9649)
PHONE...................661 858-2888
EMP: 80 EST: 2004

SALES (est): 2.49MM **Privately Held**
SIC: 0191 General farms, primarily crop

(P-81)
EARTHRISE NUTRITIONALS LLC (HQ)
2151 Michelson Dr Ste 262 (92612-1374)
PHONE...................949 623-0980
Ichi Kato, *
▲ EMP: 25 EST: 1981
SALES (est): 21.94MM **Privately Held**
Web: www.earthrise.com
SIC: 0191 2099 2834 General farms, primarily crop; Food preparations, nec; Pharmaceutical preparations
PA: Dic Corporation
3-7-20, Nihombashi
Chuo-Ku TKY

(P-82)
GREENHEART FARMS INC
Also Called: Greenheart
902 Zenon Way (93420-5807)
PHONE...................805 481-2234
Hoy Buell, *CEO*
Henry Katzenstein, *
Leo Wolf, *
▲ EMP: 350 EST: 1979
SQ FT: 225,000
SALES (est): 18.19MM **Privately Held**
Web: www.greenheartfarms.com
SIC: 0191 General farms, primarily crop

(P-83)
JOE HEGER FARMS LLC
1625 Drew Rd (92243-9584)
PHONE...................760 353-5111
EMP: 150 EST: 1999
SALES (est): 4.85MM **Privately Held**
SIC: 0191 General farms, primarily crop

(P-84)
MURANAKA FARM
11018 W Los Angeles Ave (93021-9744)
P.O. Box 189 (93020-0189)
PHONE...................805 529-0201
EMP: 237
SALES (corp-wide): 23.08MM **Privately Held**
Web: www.muranakafarm.com
SIC: 0191 General farms, primarily crop
PA: Muranaka Farm
11018 E Los Angeles Ave
Moorpark CA
805 529-0201

(P-85)
RANCHO LAGUNA FARMS LLC
2410 W Main St (93458-9712)
P.O. Box 6617 (93456-6617)
PHONE...................805 925-7805
Larry Ferini, *Managing Member*
Tracy Ferini, *
EMP: 100 EST: 1996
SALES (est): 9.82MM **Privately Held**
Web: www.lagunaproduce.com
SIC: 0191 General farms, primarily crop

(P-86)
SAN DIEGO FARMS LLC
Also Called: Fresh Origins
570 Quarry Rd (92069-9744)
PHONE...................760 736-4072
Norma St Amant, *CEO*
Carlos Pancardo, *
EMP: 177 EST: 1996
SALES (est): 17.43MM **Privately Held**
Web: www.freshorigins.com

SIC: 0191 General farms, primarily crop

(P-87)
SCARBOROUGH FARMS INC
731 Pacific Ave (93030-7322)
P.O. Box 1267 (93032-1267)
PHONE...................805 483-9113
Ann Stein, *Pr*
Wayne G Jansen, *
Ann Stein, *VP*
EMP: 150 EST: 1986
SALES (est): 9.21MM **Privately Held**
Web: www.scarboroughfarms.com
SIC: 0191 General farms, primarily crop

(P-88)
TREESAP FARMS LLC
Also Called: Everde Growers
2500 Rainbow Valley Blvd (92028-9778)
PHONE...................760 990-7770
Jonathan Saperstein, *Brnch Mgr*
EMP: 166
SALES (corp-wide): 121.71MM **Privately Held**
Web: www.everde.com
SIC: 0191 General farms, primarily crop
PA: Treesap Farms, Llc
5151 Mitchelldale St B2
Houston TX
713 613-5600

0241 Dairy Farms

(P-89)
ALTA-DENA CERTIFIED DAIRY LLC (DH)
17637 E Valley Blvd (91744-5731)
PHONE...................626 964-6401
Jack Tewers, *
Steve Schaffer, *
Bob Pettigrew, *
EMP: 370 EST: 1945
SQ FT: 100,000
SALES (est): 49.72MM **Privately Held**
SIC: 0241 Dairy farms
HQ: Dean West Ii, Llc
2515 Mckinney Ave # 1100
Dallas TX

(P-90)
HOLLANDIA DAIRY INC (PA)
622 E Mission Rd (92069-1999)
PHONE...................760 744-3222
TOLL FREE: 800
Peter De Jong, *CEO*
Patrick Schallberger, *
Arie H Dejong, *
EMP: 185 EST: 1950
SQ FT: 20,000
SALES (est): 44.68MM
SALES (corp-wide): 44.68MM **Privately Held**
Web: www.hollandiadairy.com
SIC: 0241 Milk production

0252 Chicken Eggs

(P-91)
DEMLER BROTHERS LLC
25818 Highway 78 (92065-6309)
PHONE...................760 789-2457
EMP: 99 EST: 2016
SALES (est): 2.56MM **Privately Held**
SIC: 0252 Chicken eggs

0279 Animal Specialties, Nec

(P-92)
HONEY ISABELLS INC
Also Called: Isabell's Honey Farm
539 N Glenoaks Blvd Ste 207b
(91502-3201)
PHONE...................800 708-8485
Oganes Kabakchuzyan, *CEO*
EMP: 46 EST: 2019
SALES (est): 2.16MM **Privately Held**
Web: www.isabellshoneyfarm.com
SIC: 0279 2099 Apiary (bee and honey farm) ; Honey, strained and bottled

0291 General Farms, Primarily Animals

(P-93)
BAJA FRESH SUPERMARKET
Also Called: Monrovia Ranch Market
14827 Seventh St (92395-4023)
P.O. Box 661912 (91066-1912)
PHONE...................760 843-7730
EMP: 330
SIC: 0291 General farms, primarily animals
PA: E & T Foods, Inc.
328 W Huntington Dr
Monrovia CA

(P-94)
R RANCH MARKET
1112 Walnut Ave (92780-5607)
PHONE...................714 573-1182
Jubira Martinez, *Owner*
EMP: 142 EST: 2011
SALES (corp-wide): 56.64MM **Privately Held**
Web: www.rranchmarkets.com
SIC: 0291 General farms, primarily animals
PA: R-Ranch Market, Incorporated
13985 Live Oak Ave
Irwindale CA
626 814-2900

0711 Soil Preparation Services

(P-95)
AC IRRIGATION HOLDCO LLC
10000 Stockdale Hwy Ste 100
(93311-3602)
PHONE...................661 368-3550
Derek Yurosek, *Managing Member*
Jonathan Thomas, *CEO*
EMP: 163 EST: 2018
SALES (est): 2.95MM **Privately Held**
SIC: 0711 Soil preparation services

0722 Crop Harvesting

(P-96)
BOSWELL PROPERTIES INC
101 W Walnut St (91103-3636)
PHONE...................626 583-3000
Curt Rowe, *Pr*
Melvin L Eltiste, *
Joseph A Morris, *
Sherm Railsback, *
EMP: 427 EST: 1982
SALES (est): 478.81K
SALES (corp-wide): 370.2MM **Privately Held**
Web: www.tulago.com

PRODUCTS & SVCS

SIC: 0722 6552 Cotton, machine harvesting services; Subdividers and developers, nec
PA: J. G. Boswell Company
101 W Walnut St
Pasadena CA
626 583-3000

(P-97)
NOBLESSE OBLIGE INC
Also Called: Eight Star Equipment
2015 Silsbee Rd (92243-9671)
PHONE....................760 353-3336
Alex Abatti Junior, *Pr*
David Wells, *
Sid Swarthout, *
EMP: 250 **EST:** 1985
SALES (est): 1.79MM **Privately Held**
Web: www.abatti.com
SIC: 0722 Combining services

0723 Crop Preparation Services For Market

(P-98)
APEEL TECHNOLOGY INC (PA)
Also Called: Apeel Sciences
71 S Los Carneros Rd (93117-5506)
PHONE....................805 203-0146
James Rogers, *CEO*
William Strong, *CFO*
EMP: 283 **EST:** 2012
SALES (est): 48.97MM
SALES (corp-wide): 48.97MM **Privately Held**
Web: www.apeel.com
SIC: 0723 2099 Crop preparation services for market; Almond pastes

(P-99)
BOSKOVICH FARMS INC (PA)
711 Diaz Ave (93030-7247)
P.O. Box 1352 (93032-1352)
PHONE....................805 487-2299
George S Boskovich Junior, *CEO*
Philip J Boskovich Junior, *Pr*
▲ **EMP:** 205 **EST:** 1915
SQ FT: 7,000
SALES (est): 93.16MM
SALES (corp-wide): 93.16MM **Privately Held**
Web: www.boskovichfarms.com
SIC: 0723 5812 0161 Crop preparation services for market; Eating places; Rooted vegetable farms

(P-100)
CAL TREEHOUSE ALMONDS LLC
2115 Road 144 (93215-9524)
P.O. Box 286 (93216-0286)
PHONE....................661 725-6334
Robert Houston, *Pr*
EMP: 122
SQ FT: 68,803
SALES (corp-wide): 18.64MM **Privately Held**
Web: www.treehousealmonds.com
SIC: 0723 Crop preparation services for market
PA: Treehouse California Almonds Llc
6914 Road 160
Earlimart CA
559 757-5020

(P-101)
CORONA - CLLEGE HTS ORNGE LMON
8000 Lincoln Ave (92504-4343)

PHONE....................951 359-6451
John Demshki, *Pr*
▼ **EMP:** 300 **EST:** 1905
SQ FT: 180,000
SALES (est): 20.93MM **Privately Held**
Web: www.cchcitrus.com
SIC: 0723 Fruit (fresh) packing services

(P-102)
FISHER RANCH LLC
10610 Ice Plant Rd (92225-2757)
PHONE....................760 922-4151
EMP: 99 **EST:** 1998
SALES (est): 4.32MM **Privately Held**
Web: www.fisherranch.com
SIC: 0723 Field crops, except cash grains, market preparation services

(P-103)
GRIMMWAY ENTERPRISES INC
6101 Zerker Rd (93263-9611)
P.O. Box 81498 (93380-1498)
PHONE....................661 393-3320
Bob Grimm, *Prin*
EMP: 355
SALES (corp-wide): 1.86B **Privately Held**
Web: www.grimmway.com
SIC: 0723 Vegetable packing services
PA: Grimmway Enterprises, Inc.
14141 Di Giorgio Rd
Arvin CA
800 301-3101

(P-104)
GRIMMWAY ENTERPRISES INC
Also Called: Grimmway Frozen Foods
830 Sycamore Rd (93203-2132)
P.O. Box 81498 (93380-1498)
PHONE....................661 854-6250
Brandon Grimm, *Mgr*
EMP: 372
SALES (corp-wide): 1.86B **Privately Held**
Web: www.grimmway.com
SIC: 0723 Vegetable packing services
PA: Grimmway Enterprises, Inc.
14141 Di Giorgio Rd
Arvin CA
800 301-3101

(P-105)
GRIMMWAY ENTERPRISES INC
Also Called: Grimmway Farms
11412 Malaga Rd (93203-9641)
P.O. Box 81498 (93380-1498)
PHONE....................661 854-6200
EMP: 968
SALES (corp-wide): 1.86B **Privately Held**
Web: www.grimmway.com
SIC: 0723 4783 Vegetable packing services; Containerization of goods for shipping
PA: Grimmway Enterprises, Inc.
14141 Di Giorgio Rd
Arvin CA
800 301-3101

(P-106)
GRIMMWAY ENTERPRISES INC
Also Called: Grimmway Farms
6900 Mountain View Rd (93307-9627)
P.O. Box 81498 (93380-1498)
PHONE....................661 845-5200
EMP: 200
SALES (corp-wide): 1.86B **Privately Held**
Web: www.grimmway.com
SIC: 0723 Vegetable packing services
PA: Grimmway Enterprises, Inc.
14141 Di Giorgio Rd
Arvin CA
800 301-3101

(P-107)
KERN RIDGE GROWERS LLC
25429 Barbara St (93203-9748)
P.O. Box 455 (93203-0455)
PHONE....................661 854-3141
▼ **EMP:** 500 **EST:** 1973
SQ FT: 53,000
SALES (est): 48.27MM **Privately Held**
Web: www.kernridge.com
SIC: 0723 5148 Vegetable packing services; Vegetables, fresh

(P-108)
MISSION PRODUCE INC (PA)
Also Called: MISSION
2710 Camino Del Sol (93030-7967)
P.O. Box 5267 (93031-5267)
PHONE....................805 981-3650
◆ **EMP:** 244 **EST:** 1983
SALES (est): 1.05B
SALES (corp-wide): 1.05B **Publicly Held**
Web: www.missionproduce.com
SIC: 0723 0179 5431 Fruit (fresh) packing services; Avocado orchard; Fruit stands or markets

(P-109)
MONARCH NUT COMPANY LLC
Also Called: Munger Farms
786 Road 188 (93215-9508)
PHONE....................661 725-6458
Kamie Munger, *Managing Member*
David Munger, *
◆ **EMP:** 250 **EST:** 1986
SQ FT: 20,000
SALES (est): 19.2MM **Privately Held**
SIC: 0723 7389 Tree nuts (general) hulling and shelling services; Packaging and labeling services

(P-110)
RAMCO ENTERPRISES LP
Also Called: Ramco Employment Services
520 E 3rd St Ste B (93030-0182)
PHONE....................805 486-9328
EMP: 372
SALES (corp-wide): 125.53MM **Privately Held**
Web: www.ramcoenterpriseslp.com
SIC: 0723 Crop preparation services for market
PA: Ramco Enterprises, L.P.
710 La Guardia St
Salinas CA
831 758-5272

(P-111)
SATICOY LEMON ASSOCIATION (PA)
Also Called: Saticoy Fruit Exchange
103 N Peck Rd (93060-3013)
P.O. Box 46 (93061-0046)
PHONE....................805 654-6500
Glenn A Miller, *Pr*
Jerry Pogorzelski, *
Jima Garrett, *
▲ **EMP:** 100 **EST:** 1933
SALES (est): 26.61MM
SALES (corp-wide): 26.61MM **Privately Held**
Web: www.saticoylemon.com
SIC: 0723 Fruit (fresh) packing services

(P-112)
SUN WORLD INC
5544 California Ave Ste 280 (93309-1616)
PHONE....................805 833-6460
Howard P Margulea, *Ch Bd*
David O Marguleas, *VP Mktg*
John P Brincko, *Pr*

Paul W Knupp, *Sec*
◆ **EMP:** 1500 **EST:** 1977
SQ FT: 17,441
SALES (est): 10.67MM **Privately Held**
Web: www.sun-world.com
SIC: 0723 Crop preparation services for market

(P-113)
SUN WORLD INTERNATIONAL INC (PA)
16351 Driver Rd (93308-9733)
P.O. Box 80298 (93380-0298)
PHONE....................661 392-5000
◆ **EMP:** 1500 **EST:** 1976
SQ FT: 160,000
SALES (est): 44.92MM **Privately Held**
Web: www.sun-world.com
SIC: 0723 0172 0174 0175 Vegetable crops market preparation services; Grapes; Citrus fruits; Deciduous tree fruits

(P-114)
TALLEY FARMS
2900 Lopez Dr (93420-4999)
P.O. Box 360 (93421-0360)
PHONE....................805 489-2508
Brian Talley, *Pr*
Rayn Talley, *
Todd Talley, *
Rosemary Talley, *
EMP: 175 **EST:** 1954
SQ FT: 2,000
SALES (est): 21.28MM **Privately Held**
Web: www.talleyfarmsfreshharvest.com
SIC: 0723 0161 Vegetable packing services; Vegetables and melons

(P-115)
TANIMURA ANTLE FRESH FOODS INC
Also Called: Salad Time Farms
4401 Foxdale St (91706-2161)
P.O. Box 4070 (93912-4070)
PHONE....................831 424-6100
Randy Sipled, *Mgr*
EMP: 150
SALES (corp-wide): 321.47MM **Privately Held**
Web: www.taproduce.com
SIC: 0723 Vegetable packing services
PA: Tanimura & Antle Fresh Foods, Inc.
1 Harris Rd
Salinas CA
831 455-2950

(P-116)
THE WONDERFUL COMPANY LLC (PA)
Also Called: Teleflora
11444 W Olympic Blvd Ste 210 (90064-1507)
P.O. Box 30119 (90030-0119)
PHONE....................310 966-5700
◆ **EMP:** 250 **EST:** 2010
SALES (est): 2.04B
SALES (corp-wide): 2.04B **Privately Held**
Web: www.wonderful.com
SIC: 0723 2084 Fruit crops market preparation services; Wines

(P-117)
WEST PAK AVOCADO INC (PA)
Also Called: Avocado Packer & Shipper
38655 Sky Canyon Dr (92563-2536)
PHONE....................951 296-5757
▲ **EMP:** 110 **EST:** 1982
SALES (est): 86.69MM
SALES (corp-wide): 86.69MM **Privately Held**

Web: www.westpakavocado.com
SIC: 0723 Crop preparation services for
market

(P-118)
**WONDERFUL CITRUS PACKING
LLC (HQ)**
Also Called: Paramount Citrus Packing Co
1901 S Lexington St (93215-9207)
PHONE..............................661 720-2400
Craig B Cooper, *Managing Member*
◆ EMP: 273 EST: 1950
SQ FT: 400,000
SALES (est): 280.36MM
SALES (corp-wide): 2.04B Privately Held
Web: www.wonderfulcitrus.com
SIC: 0723 0174 2033 Fruit (fresh) packing
services; Orange grove; Fruit juices: fresh
PA: The Wonderful Company Llc
11444 W Olympic Blvd # 210
Los Angeles CA
310 966-5700

(P-119)
WONDERFUL COMPANY LLC
5001 California Ave (93309-1671)
PHONE..............................559 781-7438
EMP: 960
SALES (corp-wide): 2.04B Privately Held
Web: www.wonderful.com
SIC: 0723 Fruit crops market preparation
services
PA: The Wonderful Company Llc
11444 W Olympic Blvd # 210
Los Angeles CA
310 966-5700

(P-120)
WONDERFUL COMPANY LLC
6801 E Lerdo Hwy (93263-9610)
PHONE..............................661 399-4456
EMP: 1727
SALES (corp-wide): 2.04B Privately Held
Web: www.wonderful.com
SIC: 0723 Fruit crops market preparation
services
PA: The Wonderful Company Llc
11444 W Olympic Blvd # 210
Los Angeles CA
310 966-5700

(P-121)
WONDERFUL COMPANY LLC
11444 W Olympic Blvd Ste 210
(90064-1559)
PHONE..............................661 720-2609
Craig B Cooper, *Mgr*
EMP: 336
SALES (corp-wide): 2.04B Privately Held
Web: www.wonderful.com
SIC: 0723 Fruit (fresh) packing services
PA: The Wonderful Company Llc
11444 W Olympic Blvd # 210
Los Angeles CA
310 966-5700

0742 Veterinary Services, Specialties

(P-122)
**ADVANCED CRTCAL CARE
EMRGNCY S**
9599 Jefferson Blvd (90232-2917)
PHONE..............................310 558-6111
Richard Mills, *CEO*
Amy Grant, *Pr*
EMP: 126 EST: 2004
SALES (est): 9.48MM Privately Held

Web: www.accessanimalhospitals.com
SIC: 0742 Animal hospital services, pets and
other animal specialties

(P-123)
MERCY FOR ANIMALS INC
8033 W Sunset Blvd Ste 864 (90046-2401)
PHONE..............................347 839-6464
Nathan Runkle, *CEO*
EMP: 117 EST: 2015
SALES (est): 18.22MM Privately Held
Web: www.mercyforanimals.org
SIC: 0742 Veterinary services, specialties

(P-124)
PEOPLE PETS AND VETS LLC
Also Called: Prestige Animal Hospital South
10986 Sierra Ave Ste 400 (92337-7673)
PHONE..............................909 453-4213
Sudeep Wahla, *Brnch Mgr*
EMP: 223
SALES (corp-wide): 75.43MM Privately
Held
Web: www.prestigeanimalhospital.com
SIC: 0742 Animal hospital services, pets and
other animal specialties
HQ: People, Pets And Vets, Llc
6541 Sexton Dr Nw Ste G
Olympia WA
360 866-7331

(P-125)
PEOPLE PETS AND VETS LLC
Also Called: Prestige Animal Hospital North
16055 Sierra Lakes Pkwy Ste 100 (92336)
PHONE..............................909 329-2860
Sudeep S Wahla, *Brnch Mgr*
EMP: 240
SALES (corp-wide): 75.43MM Privately
Held
Web: www.prestigeanimalhospital.com
SIC: 0742 Animal hospital services, pets and
other animal specialties
HQ: People, Pets And Vets, Llc
6541 Sexton Dr Nw Ste G
Olympia WA
360 866-7331

(P-126)
**V C A CENTRAL ANIMAL
HOSPITAL**
281 N Central Ave (91786-4215)
PHONE..............................909 981-2855
Doctor Ronald L Beeley, *Pr*
Leanne Palm, *
Richard T Johnson, *
Theresa Dieringer, *
Marjorie Fong, *
EMP: 84 EST: 1973
SALES (est): 4.86MM
SALES (corp-wide): 42.84B Privately Held
Web: www.vcahospitals.com
SIC: 0742 Animal hospital services, pets and
other animal specialties
HQ: Vca Inc.
12401 W Olympic Blvd
Los Angeles CA
310 571-6500

(P-127)
**VALLEY ANIMAL MEDICAL
CENTER**
46920 Jefferson St (92201-7920)
PHONE..............................760 342-4711
Gary Homec, *Pr*
EMP: 801 EST: 1979
SQ FT: 12,000
SALES (est): 2.3MM Privately Held
Web: www.animalmedicalvets.com

SIC: 0742 Animal hospital services, pets and
other animal specialties
PA: Pet Drx Veterinary Group, Inc.
560 S Winchester Blvd
San Jose CA

(P-128)
VCA ANIMAL HOSPITALS INC
Also Called: VCA West Los Angles Anmal
Hosp
1900 S Sepulveda Blvd (90025-5620)
PHONE..............................310 473-2951
David Bruyette, *Brnch Mgr*
EMP: 88
SALES (corp-wide): 42.84B Privately Held
Web: www.petschoice.com
SIC: 0742 Animal hospital services, pets and
other animal specialties
HQ: Vca Animal Hospitals, Inc.
12401 W Olympic Blvd
Los Angeles CA

(P-129)
**VETERINARY PRACTICE ASSOC
INC**
Also Called: Veterinary Specialty Hospital
10435 Sorrento Valley Rd (92121-1607)
PHONE..............................949 833-9020
Keith P Richter, *CEO*
EMP: 150 EST: 2004
SQ FT: 26,280
SALES (est): 21.06MM Privately Held
Web: www.ethosvet.com
SIC: 0742 Animal hospital services, pets and
other animal specialties

(P-130)
VETERINARY SPECIALTY HOSP
Also Called: Veterinary Specialty Hospital
10435 Sorrento Valley Rd (92121-1607)
PHONE..............................858 875-7500
James Robert Dennis, *Pt*
EMP: 149 EST: 2007
SALES (est): 12.66MM Privately Held
Web: vshsd.ethosvet.com
SIC: 0742 Animal hospital services, pets and
other animal specialties

(P-131)
VICAR OPERATING INC (DH)
Also Called: Veterinary Centers America VCA
12401 W Olympic Blvd (90064-1022)
PHONE..............................310 571-6500
Robert Antin, *Pr*
EMP: 91 EST: 1985
SALES (est): 97.06MM
SALES (corp-wide): 42.84B Privately Held
Web: www.vcahospitals.com
SIC: 0742 Animal hospital services, pets and
other animal specialties
HQ: Vca Inc.
12401 W Olympic Blvd
Los Angeles CA
310 571-6500

0751 Livestock Services, Except Veterinary

(P-132)
AMERICAN BEEF PACKERS INC
13677 Yorba Ave (91710-5059)
PHONE..............................909 628-4888
Lawrence Miller, *Pr*
EMP: 250 EST: 2008
SALES (est): 20.7MM Privately Held
SIC: 0751 2011 5147 Slaughtering: custom
livestock services; Beef products, from beef
slaughtered on site; Meats and meat
products

0752 Animal Specialty Services

(P-133)
**CAMP BOW WOW
FRANCHISING INC**
Also Called: Camp Bow Wow
12401 W Olympic Blvd (90064-1022)
PHONE..............................310 571-6500
Robert Antin, *Pr*
EMP: 171 EST: 2014
SALES (est): 1.98MM
SALES (corp-wide): 42.84B Privately Held
Web: www.campbowwow.com
SIC: 0752 Grooming services, pet and
animal specialties
HQ: Vicar Operating, Inc.
12401 W Olympic Blvd
Los Angeles CA
310 571-6500

0762 Farm Management Services

(P-134)
**AG-WISE ENTERPRISES INC
(PA)**
5100 California Ave Ste 209 (93309-0716)
P.O. Box 9729 (93389-9729)
PHONE..............................661 325-1567
Bruce Berreta, *Pr*
Ed Ray, *
EMP: 150 EST: 1983
SQ FT: 4,400
SALES (est): 17.05MM Privately Held
Web: www.ag-wiseinc.com
SIC: 0762 Farm management services

(P-135)
ESPARZA ENTERPRISES INC
251 W Main St Ste G&F (92227-2201)
PHONE..............................760 344-2031
Luis Esparza, *Brnch Mgr*
EMP: 792
SALES (corp-wide): 135MM Privately
Held
Web: www.esparzainc.com
SIC: 0762 Farm management services
PA: Esparza Enterprises, Inc.
3851 Fruitvale Ave
Bakersfield CA
661 831-0002

(P-136)
ILLUME AGRICULTURE LLC
9100 Ming Ave Ste 200 (93311-1382)
P.O. Box 22020 (93390-2020)
PHONE..............................661 587-5198
Jeffrey Fabbri, *Managing Member*
Dan Fabbri, *
EMP: 120 EST: 1939
SALES (est): 15.14MM Privately Held
Web: www.illumeag.com
SIC: 0762 5963 Farm management services;
Food services, direct sales

(P-137)
LARRY JACINTO FARMING INC
9555 N Wabash Ave (92374-2714)
P.O. Box 275 (92359-0275)
PHONE..............................909 794-2276
EMP: 100 EST: 1992
SQ FT: 3,000
SALES (est): 2.05MM Privately Held
Web: www.jacintofarms.com
SIC: 0762 Farm management services

PRODUCTS & SVCS

(P-138)
SUN PACIFIC FARMING COOP INC
Also Called: Sun Pacific Farms
33374 Lerdo Hwy (93308-9782)
PHONE..............................661 399-0376
Ernie Larson, *Mgr*
EMP: 96
SALES (corp-wide): 49.23MM **Privately Held**
Web: www.sunpacific.com
SIC: 0762 5148 0174 Citrus grove management and maintenance services; Fresh fruits and vegetables; Citrus fruits
PA: Sun Pacific Farming Cooperative, Inc.
   1250 E Myer Ave
   Exeter CA
   559 592-7121

0781 Landscape Counseling And Planning

(P-139)
AMERICAN LANDSCAPE INC
Also Called: American Golf Construction
7013 Owensmouth Ave (91303-2006)
PHONE..............................818 999-2041
Gary Peterson, *Pr*
Jamie Tsui, *
▲ **EMP:** 250 **EST:** 1973
SQ FT: 14,000
SALES (est): 28.48MM **Privately Held**
Web: www.americanlandscape.com
SIC: 0781 Landscape services

(P-140)
AMERICAN LANDSCAPE MGT INC (PA)
Also Called: Custom Lawn Services
7013 Owensmouth Ave (91303-2006)
PHONE..............................818 999-2041
Mickey Strauss, *Pr*
Gary Peterson, *
EMP: 125 **EST:** 1975
SQ FT: 14,000
SALES (est): 21.82MM **Privately Held**
Web: www.americanlandscape.com
SIC: 0781 Landscape services

(P-141)
AZTECA LANDSCAPE
4073 Mennes Ave (92509-6722)
PHONE..............................951 369-9210
EMP: 85
SIC: 0781 Landscape services
PA: Azteca Landscape
   1180 Olympic Dr Ste 207
   Corona CA

(P-142)
BENCHMARK LANDSCAPE SVCS INC
12575 Stowe Dr (92064-6805)
PHONE..............................858 513-7190
John A Mohns, *Pr*
Sharon R Mohns, *
EMP: 220 **EST:** 1984
SQ FT: 18,000
SALES (est): 20.23MM **Privately Held**
Web: www.benchmarklandscape.com
SIC: 0781 Landscape services

(P-143)
BENNETT ENTPS A CAL LDSCP CNTG
Also Called: Bennett Landscape
25889 Belle Porte Ave (90710-3393)
PHONE..............................310 534-3543
Sean Bennett, *Pr*
EMP: 90 **EST:** 1977
SQ FT: 10,500
SALES (est): 9.48MM **Privately Held**
Web: www.bennett-landscape.com
SIC: 0781 Landscape services

(P-144)
BILL & DAVES LDSCP MAINT INC
1401 E Edinger Ave (92705-4814)
PHONE..............................714 850-0213
EMP: 101
SALES (corp-wide): 2.13MM **Privately Held**
Web: www.billanddaves.com
SIC: 0781 Landscape services
PA: Bill & Dave's Landscape Maintenance, Inc.
   32750 Keller Rd
   Winchester CA
   951 943-6455

(P-145)
BRIGHTVIEW GOLF MAINT INC
405 Glen Annie Rd (93117-1427)
PHONE..............................805 968-6400
Richard Hasah, *Mgr*
EMP: 99
SALES (corp-wide): 2.82B **Publicly Held**
SIC: 0781 Landscape services
HQ: Brightview Golf Maintenance, Inc.
   980 Jolly Rd
   Blue Bell PA
   818 223-8500

(P-146)
BRIGHTVIEW LANDSCAPE DEV INC
8450 Miramar Pl (92121-2528)
PHONE..............................858 458-9900
Vince Germann, *Mgr*
EMP: 300
SQ FT: 16,050
SALES (corp-wide): 2.82B **Publicly Held**
Web: www.brightview.com
SIC: 0781 Landscape services
HQ: Brightview Landscape Development, Inc.
   27001 Agoura Rd Ste 350
   Calabasas CA
   818 223-8500

(P-147)
BRIGHTVIEW LANDSCAPE SVCS INC
8500 Miramar Pl (92121-2530)
PHONE..............................858 458-1900
Patrick Ceatter, *Mgr*
EMP: 114
SALES (corp-wide): 2.82B **Publicly Held**
Web: www.brightview.com
SIC: 0781 Landscape services
HQ: Brightview Landscape Services, Inc.
   27001 Agoura Rd Ste 350
   Agoura Hills CA
   818 223-8500

(P-148)
BRIGHTVIEW LANDSCAPE SVCS INC
415 W 30th St (91950-7207)
PHONE..............................619 474-4478
Curtis Brook, *Pr*
EMP: 87
SALES (corp-wide): 2.82B **Publicly Held**
Web: www.brightview.com
SIC: 0781 Landscape services
HQ: Brightview Landscape Services, Inc.
   27001 Agoura Rd Ste 350
   Agoura Hills CA
   818 223-8500

(P-149)
BRIGHTVIEW LANDSCAPE SVCS INC
8726 Calabash Ave (92335-3040)
PHONE..............................909 946-3196
Leon Vitort, *Brnch Mgr*
EMP: 114
SALES (corp-wide): 2.82B **Publicly Held**
Web: www.brightview.com
SIC: 0781 Landscape services
HQ: Brightview Landscape Services, Inc.
   27001 Agoura Rd Ste 350
   Agoura Hills CA
   818 223-8500

(P-150)
BRIGHTVIEW LANDSCAPE SVCS INC
2064 Eastman Ave Ste 104 (93003-7787)
PHONE..............................805 642-9300
Frank Annino, *Mgr*
EMP: 130
SALES (corp-wide): 2.82B **Publicly Held**
Web: www.brightview.com
SIC: 0781 Landscape services
HQ: Brightview Landscape Services, Inc.
   27001 Agoura Rd Ste 350
   Agoura Hills CA
   818 223-8500

(P-151)
BRIGHTVIEW LANDSCAPE SVCS INC
32202 Paseo Adelanto (92675-3601)
PHONE..............................714 546-7843
EMP: 101
SALES (corp-wide): 2.82B **Publicly Held**
Web: www.brightview.com
SIC: 0781 Landscape services
HQ: Brightview Landscape Services, Inc.
   27001 Agoura Rd Ste 350
   Agoura Hills CA
   818 223-8500

(P-152)
BRIGHTVIEW LANDSCAPE SVCS INC
1960 S Yale St (92704-3929)
PHONE..............................714 546-7843
Dave Hanson, *Mgr*
EMP: 274
SALES (corp-wide): 2.82B **Publicly Held**
Web: www.brightview.com
SIC: 0781 0782 Landscape services; Lawn and garden services
HQ: Brightview Landscape Services, Inc.
   27001 Agoura Rd Ste 350
   Agoura Hills CA
   818 223-8500

(P-153)
BRIGHTVIEW LANDSCAPE SVCS INC
17813 S Main St Ste 105 (90248-3542)
PHONE..............................310 327-8700
Andrea Musick, *Mgr*
EMP: 245
SQ FT: 1,530
SALES (corp-wide): 2.82B **Publicly Held**
Web: www.brightview.com
SIC: 0781 0782 Landscape services; Landscape contractors
HQ: Brightview Landscape Services, Inc.
   27001 Agoura Rd Ste 350
   Agoura Hills CA
   818 223-8500

(P-154)
BRIGHTVIEW TREE CARE SVCS INC
715 W La Cadena Dr (92501-1338)
PHONE..............................951 684-2730
Todd Huffman, *Pr*
Steven Guarneri, *
EMP: 99 **EST:** 2005
SALES (est): 7.33MM
SALES (corp-wide): 2.82B **Publicly Held**
SIC: 0781 Landscape services
PA: Brightview Holdings, Inc.
   980 Jolly Rd Ste 300
   Blue Bell PA
   484 567-7204

(P-155)
BRIGHTVIEW TREE COMPANY
P.O. Box 1611 (92307-0031)
PHONE..............................760 955-2560
EMP: 86
Web: www.devilmountainnursery.com
SIC: 0781 Landscape services
HQ: Brightview Tree Company
   24151 Ventura Blvd # 100
   Calabasas CA
   818 223-8500

(P-156)
CALIFORNIA SKATEPARKS
285 N Benson Ave (91786-5614)
PHONE..............................909 949-1601
Joseph M Ciaglia Junior, *CEO*
Joseph M Ciaglia Junior, *Pr*
EMP: 150 **EST:** 1977
SALES (est): 12.75MM **Privately Held**
Web: www.californiaskateparks.com
SIC: 0781 Landscape services

(P-157)
CENTRESCAPES INC
165 Gentry St (91767-2184)
PHONE..............................909 392-3303
Mark Marcus, *Pr*
Grace Loya, *
EMP: 88 **EST:** 1992
SQ FT: 7,000
SALES (est): 2.26MM **Privately Held**
Web: www.centrescapes.com
SIC: 0781 Landscape services

(P-158)
CRESTVIEW LANDSCAPE INC
13915 Saticoy St (91402-6521)
PHONE..............................818 962-7771
Harold Young, *CEO*
Augustine Bucio, *
EMP: 100 **EST:** 2020
SALES (est): 2.53MM **Privately Held**
Web: www.crestviewlandscape.com
SIC: 0781 Landscape services

(P-159)
DL LONG LANDSCAPING INC
5475 G St (91710-5233)
PHONE..............................909 628-5531
David L Long, *Pr*
EMP: 100 **EST:** 1974
SQ FT: 1,550
SALES (est): 4.61MM **Privately Held**
SIC: 0781 Landscape architects

(P-160)
EXECUTIVE LANDSCAPE INC
2131 Huffstatler (92028-8861)
P.O. Box 1075 (92088-1075)
PHONE..............................760 731-9036
Edwin Earle, *CEO*
Kathleen D Earle, *

Walter Earle, *
EMP: 230 **EST:** 1993
SQ FT: 1,800
SALES (est): 9.54MM **Privately Held**
Web: www.executivelandscapeinc.com
SIC: 0781 Landscape services

(P-161)
FINLEYS TREE & LANDCARE INC
1209 W 228th St (90502-2325)
PHONE..............................310 326-9818
Steve Finley, *Prin*
EMP: 150 **EST:** 2006
SALES (est): 2.78MM **Privately Held**
Web:
www.treelandscapeconcretesouthbay.com
SIC: 0781 Landscape services

(P-162)
GOTHIC LANDSCAPING INC
Also Called: Gothic Grounds Mgmt
27413 Tourney Rd Ste 200 (91355-5606)
PHONE..............................661 257-5085
Ron Georgio, *Pr*
EMP: 107
SALES (corp-wide): 119.26MM **Privately Held**
Web: www.gothiclandscape.com
SIC: 0781 0782 Landscape services; Lawn and garden services
PA: Gothic Landscaping, Inc.
27413 Tourney Rd
Santa Clarita CA
661 678-1400

(P-163)
GREENSCREEN
Also Called: Atmospheric-Greenscreen
725 S Figueroa St Ste 1825 (90017-2827)
PHONE..............................310 837-0526
EMP: 25 **EST:** 1995
SQ FT: 1,200
SALES (est): 2.45MM **Privately Held**
Web: www.greenscreen.com
SIC: 0781 7363 3446 Landscape planning services; Help supply services; Architectural metalwork

(P-164)
HARVEST LANDSCAPE ENTPS INC (PA)
Also Called: Harvest Landscape Maintenance
8030 E Crystal Dr (92807-2524)
P.O. Box 3877 (92857-0877)
PHONE..............................714 693-8100
Stephen G Schinhofen, *CEO*
Robert Gavela, *CPO**
EMP: 156 **EST:** 2003
SALES (est): 28.03MM
SALES (corp-wide): 28.03MM **Privately Held**
Web: www.hlei.us
SIC: 0781 Landscape services

(P-165)
I PWLC INC
408 Olive Ave (92083-3438)
P.O. Box 3557 (92085-3557)
PHONE..............................760 630-0231
Richard Ruiz, *CEO*
EMP: 90 **EST:** 2004
SQ FT: 1,000
SALES (est): 2.37MM **Privately Held**
Web: www.pacwestlandcare.com
SIC: 0781 Landscape services

(P-166)
MARINA MAINTENANCE GROUP INC
Also Called: Marina Landscape Maint Inc
1900 S Lewis St (92805-6718)
PHONE..............................714 939-6600
Robert B Cowan, *CEO*
EMP: 450 **EST:** 2014
SALES (est): 21.31MM
SALES (corp-wide): 2.82B **Publicly Held**
Web: www.marinaco.com
SIC: 0781 Landscape services
HQ: Brightview Landscapes, Llc
980 Jolly Rd Ste 300
Blue Bell PA
484 567-7204

(P-167)
MERCHANTS LANDSCAPE SERVICES
8748 Industrial Ln # 1 (91730-4526)
PHONE..............................909 981-1022
Freddy Martinez, *Mgr*
EMP: 96
SALES (corp-wide): 90.51MM **Privately Held**
Web: www.merchantslandscape.com
SIC: 0781 Landscape planning services
HQ: Merchants Landscape Services, Inc
1639 E Edinger Ave Ste C
Santa Ana CA
714 972-8200

(P-168)
MISSION LDSCP COMPANIES INC
536 E Dyer Rd (92707-3737)
P.O. Box 16069 (92623-6069)
PHONE..............................714 545-9962
David Dubois, *CEO*
Beth Du Boise, *
Cindy Clark, *
EMP: 200 **EST:** 1973
SQ FT: 11,000
SALES (est): 20.31MM **Privately Held**
Web: www.missionlandscape.com
SIC: 0781 Landscape services

(P-169)
MISSION LDSCP COMPANIES INC
16672 Millikan Ave (92606-5008)
P.O. Box 16069 (92623-6069)
PHONE..............................800 545-9963
David Dubois, *CEO*
EMP: 90 **EST:** 1977
SALES (est): 33.29MM **Privately Held**
Web: www.missionlandscape.com
SIC: 0781 Landscape counseling services

(P-170)
NATURES IMAGE INC
20361 Hermana Cir (92630-8701)
PHONE..............................949 680-4400
EMP: 95 **EST:** 1996
SQ FT: 13,800
SALES (est): 9.8MM **Privately Held**
Web: www.naturesimage.net
SIC: 0781 0782 Landscape services; Landscape contractors

(P-171)
NIEVES LANDSCAPE INC
1629 E Edinger Ave (92705-5001)
PHONE..............................714 835-7332
Gregorio Nieves, *Pr*
Patricia White, *
EMP: 150 **EST:** 1985
SALES (est): 8.38MM **Privately Held**

Web: www.nieveslandscape.com
SIC: 0781 Landscape services

(P-172)
NISSHO OF CALIFORNIA INC (PA)
1902 S Santa Fe Ave (92083-7721)
PHONE..............................760 727-9719
Nobu J Kato, *CEO*
Ed Trotter, *
EMP: 111 **EST:** 1989
SQ FT: 10,000
SALES (est): 23.11MM
SALES (corp-wide): 23.11MM **Privately Held**
Web: www.nisshoca.com
SIC: 0781 0782 Landscape services; Turf installation services, except artificial

(P-173)
NN JAESCHKE INC
9610 Waples St (92121-2955)
PHONE..............................858 550-7900
Ned Heiskell, *Pr*
Kelley Brewster, *Ex VP*
EMP: 48 **EST:** 2004
SALES (est): 1.89MM **Privately Held**
Web: www.nnj.com
SIC: 0781 7349 1389 Landscape services; Janitorial service, contract basis; Construction, repair, and dismantling services

(P-174)
PAC WEST LAND CARE INC
Also Called: Pacific West Tree Service
408 Olive Ave (92083-3438)
P.O. Box 99 (92085-0099)
PHONE..............................760 630-0231
Barry Blue, *Pr*
EMP: 130 **EST:** 1979
SQ FT: 3,000
SALES (est): 1.86MM **Privately Held**
Web: www.pacwestlandcare.com
SIC: 0781 Landscape services

(P-175)
PACIFIC GREEN LANDSCAPE INC (PA)
8834 Winter Gardens Blvd (92040-5419)
PHONE..............................619 390-1546
Michael C Regan, *Pr*
EMP: 109 **EST:** 1979
SQ FT: 1,450
SALES (est): 10.85MM
SALES (corp-wide): 10.85MM **Privately Held**
Web: www.pacificgreenlandscape.com
SIC: 0781 Landscape services

(P-176)
PIERRE LANDSCAPE INC
5455 2nd St (91706-2072)
PHONE..............................626 587-2121
Harold Young, *CEO*
Joseph Lowden, *
Monty Khouri, *
EMP: 200 **EST:** 1980
SQ FT: 9,425
SALES (est): 48.36MM **Privately Held**
Web: www.pierrelandscape.com
SIC: 0781 Landscape architects

(P-177)
PLATINUM LANDSCAPE INC
42575 Melanie Pl Ste C (92211-5162)
PHONE..............................760 200-3673
Christopher Johnson, *Pr*
Cherie Johnson, *

EMP: 150 **EST:** 2002
SQ FT: 3,000
SALES (est): 7.61MM **Privately Held**
Web: www.platinumlandscapeinc.com
SIC: 0781 Landscape services

(P-178)
SAN VAL CORP (PA)
Also Called: San Val Alarm System
72203 Adelaid St (92276-2321)
P.O. Box 12860 (92255-2860)
PHONE..............................760 346-3999
Robert L Sandifer, *Pr*
Sharon L Sandifer, *
EMP: 425 **EST:** 1975
SALES (est): 17.31MM
SALES (corp-wide): 17.31MM **Privately Held**
Web: www.sunshinelandscapecv.com
SIC: 0781 7381 Landscape services; Burglary protection service

(P-179)
SOUTHWEST LANDSCAPE INC
2205 S Standard Ave (92707-3036)
P.O. Box 15611 (92735-0611)
PHONE..............................714 545-1084
Dan Hansen, *Pr*
Robert Hansen, *
EMP: 80 **EST:** 1982
SQ FT: 7,800
SALES (est): 2.39MM **Privately Held**
Web: www.southwestlandscape.org
SIC: 0781 Landscape services

(P-180)
SPERBER LDSCP COMPANIES LLC (PA)
30700 Russell Ranch Rd Ste 120 (91362-9503)
PHONE..............................818 437-1029
Richard A Sperber, *CEO*
EMP: 240 **EST:** 2018
SALES (est): 103.65MM
SALES (corp-wide): 103.65MM **Privately Held**
SIC: 0781 Landscape services

(P-181)
TERRA PACIFIC LANDSCAPE (HQ)
12891 Nelson St (92840-5018)
PHONE..............................714 567-0177
Rich Wingard, *Pr*
EMP: 89 **EST:** 1988
SALES (est): 17.78MM
SALES (corp-wide): 119.26MM **Privately Held**
Web: www.terrapac.com
SIC: 0781 Landscape services
PA: Gothic Landscaping, Inc.
27413 Tourney Rd
Santa Clarita CA
661 678-1400

(P-182)
TREEBEARD LANDSCAPE INC
9917 Campo Rd (91977-1609)
P.O. Box 2777 (91979-2777)
PHONE..............................619 697-8302
Tim Hillman, *Pr*
Craig Des Lauriers, *
EMP: 100 **EST:** 1974
SQ FT: 2,500
SALES (est): 4.66MM **Privately Held**
Web: www.treebeardlandscape.com
SIC: 0781 Landscape services

0782 Lawn And Garden Services

(P-183)
AZTEC LANDSCAPING INC (PA)
7980 Lemon Grove Way (91945-1820)
PHONE.............................619 464-3303
Genaro Garcia, *Pr*
Ramon Aguilar, *
Rafael Aguilar, *
EMP: 180 **EST:** 1981
SQ FT: 30,000
SALES (est): 23.16MM
SALES (corp-wide): 23.16MM **Privately Held**
Web: www.azteclandscaping.com
SIC: 0782 0783 7349 Landscape contractors; Ornamental shrub and tree services; Janitorial service, contract basis

(P-184)
BRIGHTVIEW COMPANIES LLC
11555 Coley River Cir (92708-4224)
PHONE.............................714 437-1586
EMP: 220
Web: www.brightview.com
SIC: 0782 Landscape contractors
PA: Brightview Companies, Llc
2275 Research Blvd
Rockville MD

(P-185)
CAL-WEST NURSERIES INC
138 North Dr (92860-1637)
PHONE.............................951 270-0667
Michael Whiting, *Pr*
EMP: 150 **EST:** 1968
SQ FT: 1,700
SALES (est): 4.55MM **Privately Held**
Web: www.calwestlandscape.com
SIC: 0782 0181 Landscape contractors; Nursery stock, growing of

(P-186)
CALIFORNIA LDSCP & DESIGN INC
Also Called: CA Landscape and Design
273 N Benson Ave (91786-5614)
PHONE.............................909 949-1601
Joseph Ciaglia Junior, *CEO*
Margaret Mingura, *
EMP: 120 **EST:** 1988
SQ FT: 1,500
SALES (est): 9.95MM **Privately Held**
Web: www.calandscape.com
SIC: 0782 Landscape contractors

(P-187)
DESERT HAVEN ENTERPRISES
43437 Copeland Cir (93535-4672)
P.O. Box 2110 (93539-2110)
PHONE.............................661 948-8402
Jenni C Moran, *CEO*
Roberta Terry, *
EMP: 543 **EST:** 1954
SQ FT: 15,000
SALES (est): 10.94MM **Privately Held**
Web: www.deserthaven.org
SIC: 0782 8331 Lawn and garden services; Work experience center

(P-188)
DIVERSCAPE INC
Also Called: Diversified Landscape Co
21730 Bundy Canyon Rd (92595-8780)
PHONE.............................951 245-1686
Vicki Moralez, *Pr*
Paul Moralez, *
EMP: 90 **EST:** 1989
SQ FT: 4,000
SALES (est): 10.03MM **Privately Held**
Web: www.diversifiedlandscape.com
SIC: 0782 1611 Garden maintenance services; General contractor, highway and street construction

(P-189)
DOOSE LANDSCAPE INCORPORATED
785 E Mission Rd (92069-1903)
PHONE.............................760 591-4500
Robert J Doose, *Pr*
Tom Doose, *
Susan Daugherty, *
Shelley Nolet, *
EMP: 85 **EST:** 1967
SQ FT: 11,300
SALES (est): 4.71MM **Privately Held**
Web: www.doose.com
SIC: 0782 Landscape contractors

(P-190)
EXCEL LANDSCAPE INC
710 Rimpau Ave Ste 108 (92879-5724)
P.O. Box 77995 (92877-0133)
PHONE.............................951 735-9650
Jose Alfaro, *Pr*
▲ **EMP:** 120 **EST:** 1975
SQ FT: 1,200
SALES (est): 5.9MM **Privately Held**
Web: www.excellandscape.com
SIC: 0782 Lawn care services

(P-191)
FENDERSCAPE INCORPORATED
Also Called: Proscape Landscape
1446 E Hill St (90755-3527)
PHONE.............................562 988-2228
David Fender, *Pr*
Linda Fender, *
EMP: 127 **EST:** 1984
SQ FT: 1,893
SALES (est): 4.48MM **Privately Held**
Web: www.proscapelandscaping.com
SIC: 0782 Landscape contractors

(P-192)
GOTHIC LANDSCAPING INC (PA)
Also Called: Gothic Ground Management
27413 Tourney Rd (91355-5602)
PHONE.............................661 678-1400
Jon S Georgio, *Pr*
Mike Georgio, *Prin*
Roger Zino, *Vice Chairman*
Ronald Georgio, *VP*
EMP: 200 **EST:** 1984
SQ FT: 5,000
SALES (est): 119.26MM
SALES (corp-wide): 119.26MM **Privately Held**
Web: www.gothiclandscape.com
SIC: 0782 Landscape contractors

(P-193)
GS BROTHERS INC (PA)
20331 Main St (90745-1033)
PHONE.............................310 833-1369
Alan M Gaudenti, *Pr*
Robert M Gaudenti, *
EMP: 190 **EST:** 1963
SALES (est): 7.17MM **Privately Held**
Web: www.gsbrothers.com
SIC: 0782 Landscape contractors

(P-194)
HEAVILAND ENTERPRISES INC
8710 Miramar Pl (92121-2551)
PHONE.............................858 412-1576
EMP: 115
SALES (corp-wide): 12.13MM **Privately Held**
Web: www.brightview.com
SIC: 0782 Landscape contractors
PA: Heaviland Enterprises, Inc.
2180 La Mirada Dr
Vista CA
760 598-7065

(P-195)
IRRISCAPE CONSTRUCTION INC
20182 Carancho Rd (92590-4348)
PHONE.............................951 694-6936
Robert Smith, *Pr*
EMP: 100 **EST:** 1983
SQ FT: 1,500
SALES (est): 5.03MM **Privately Held**
Web: www.irriscapeconstruction.com
SIC: 0782 Landscape contractors

(P-196)
JAMES H COWAN & ASSOCIATES INC
5126 Clareton Dr Ste 200 (91301-4529)
PHONE.............................310 457-2574
Clark J Cowan, *Pr*
Kendall Whitney, *
EMP: 95 **EST:** 1952
SQ FT: 3,500
SALES (est): 4.26MM **Privately Held**
SIC: 0782 Landscape contractors

(P-197)
KITSON LANDSCAPE MGT INC
5787 Thornwood Dr (93117-3801)
PHONE.............................805 681-9460
Sarah Kitson, *Pr*
Brent Kitson, *
Sally Kitson, *
David Fudurich, *
EMP: 80 **EST:** 1969
SQ FT: 52,272
SALES (est): 5.46MM **Privately Held**
Web: www.kitsonlandscape.com
SIC: 0782 Landscape contractors

(P-198)
LANDCARE USA LLC
Also Called: Trugreen
5248 Governor Dr (92122-2800)
PHONE.............................858 453-1755
Craig Gerber, *Mgr*
EMP: 183
SALES (corp-wide): 124.7MM **Privately Held**
Web: www.trugreen.com
SIC: 0782 Lawn care services
PA: Landcare Usa L.L.C.
5295 Westview Dr Ste 100
Frederick MD
301 874-3300

(P-199)
LANDCARE USA LLC
Also Called: Trugreen
216 N Clara St (92703-3518)
PHONE.............................949 559-7771
Kenny Stites, *Brnch Mgr*
EMP: 91
SALES (corp-wide): 124.7MM **Privately Held**
Web: www.trugreen.com

SIC: 0782 Lawn care services
PA: Landcare Usa L.L.C.
5295 Westview Dr Ste 100
Frederick MD
301 874-3300

(P-200)
LANDSCAPE DEVELOPMENT INC (PA)
28447 Witherspoon Pkwy (91355-4174)
PHONE.............................661 295-1970
Mark J Crutcher, *CEO*
Gary Horton, *
Casper Correll, *
Tim Myers, *
Jenny Lunde, *
▲ **EMP:** 350 **EST:** 1983
SALES (est): 89.85MM
SALES (corp-wide): 89.85MM **Privately Held**
Web: www.landscapedevelopment.com
SIC: 0782 5039 Landscape contractors; Soil erosion control fabrics

(P-201)
LANDSCAPE DEVELOPMENT INC
1290 Carbide Dr (92881-7268)
PHONE.............................951 371-9370
Tom Mcdaniel, *Pr*
EMP: 148
SALES (corp-wide): 89.85MM **Privately Held**
Web: www.landscapedevelopment.com
SIC: 0782 Landscape contractors
PA: Landscape Development, Inc.
28447 Witherspoon Pkwy
Valencia CA
661 295-1970

(P-202)
LIBERTY LANDSCAPING INC (PA)
5212 El Rivino Rd (92509-1807)
PHONE.............................951 683-2999
Alejandro Casillas, *Pr*
EMP: 200 **EST:** 1997
SQ FT: 43,560
SALES (est): 11.55MM
SALES (corp-wide): 11.55MM **Privately Held**
Web: www.libertylandscaping.com
SIC: 0782 0783 Landscape contractors; Tree trimming services for public utility lines

(P-203)
MARINA LANDSCAPE INC
Also Called: Marina
3707 W Garden Grove Blvd (92868-4803)
PHONE.............................714 939-6600
EMP: 430 **EST:** 1982
SALES (est): 52.81MM **Privately Held**
Web: www.marinaco.com
SIC: 0782 Landscape contractors

(P-204)
MARIPOSA LANDSCAPES INC (PA)
Also Called: Mariposa Horticultural Entps
6232 Santos Diaz St (91702-3267)
PHONE.............................626 960-0196
Terry Noriega, *Pr*
Antonio Valenzuela, *
EMP: 98 **EST:** 1977
SQ FT: 2,000
SALES (est): 26.18MM
SALES (corp-wide): 26.18MM **Privately Held**
Web: www.mariposa-ca.com

▲ = Import ▼ = Export
◆ = Import/Export

SIC: 0782 Garden maintenance services

(P-205)
MERCHANTS LANDSCAPE SERVICES
2865 Main St Ste A (91911-4848)
PHONE.................................619 778-6239
Eric Anderson, *Mgr*
EMP: 97
SALES (corp-wide): 90.51MM **Privately Held**
Web: www.merchantslandscape.com
SIC: 0782 Landscape contractors
HQ: Merchants Landscape Services, Inc
1639 E Edinger Ave Ste C
Santa Ana CA
714 972-8200

(P-206)
MPL ENTERPRISES INC
Also Called: Mike Parker Landscape
2302 S Susan St (92704-4421)
PHONE.................................714 545-1717
Michael Parker, *Pr*
EMP: 90 **EST:** 1976
SQ FT: 2,000
SALES (est): 2.11MM **Privately Held**
Web: www.mikeparkerlandscape.com
SIC: 0782 Landscape contractors

(P-207)
NAMVARS INC
11815 Sorrento Valley Rd Ste A
(92121-1046)
P.O. Box 400 (92003-0400)
PHONE.................................858 792-5461
Ali A Namvar, *Prin*
EMP: 80 **EST:** 1988
SALES (est): 852.77K **Privately Held**
Web: www.roya.com
SIC: 0782 Landscape contractors

(P-208)
NEW WAY LANDSCAPE & TREE SVCS
7485 Ronson Rd (92111-1507)
PHONE.................................858 505-8300
Randy Newhard, *CEO*
Kathryn Dejong, *
Dan Suhovecky, *
Debra Newhard, *
EMP: 175 **EST:** 1980
SQ FT: 6,400
SALES (est): 20.37MM **Privately Held**
Web: www.newwaypro.com
SIC: 0782 Landscape contractors

(P-209)
OCONNELL LANDSCAPE MAINT INC
Also Called: O'Connell Landscape Maint
860 E Watson Center Rd (90745-4120)
PHONE.................................800 339-1106
EMP: 557
SALES (corp-wide): 50.47MM **Privately Held**
Web: www.oclm.com
SIC: 0782 Landscape contractors
PA: O'connell Landscape Maintenance Inc.
23091 Arroyo Vis
Rcho Sta Marg CA
949 589-2007

(P-210)
PARK WEST LANDSCAPE INC
13105 Crenshaw Blvd (90250-5513)
PHONE.................................310 363-4100
Rose Vargas, *Brnch Mgr*
EMP: 95

SALES (corp-wide): 99.29MM **Privately Held**
Web: www.parkwestinc.com
SIC: 0782 Landscape contractors
HQ: Park West Landscape, Inc.
22421 Gilberto Ste A
Rcho Sta Marg CA

(P-211)
PARK WEST LANDSCAPE MAINT INC (PA)
Also Called: Park Landscape Maint 1-2-3-4
22421 Gilberto Ste A (92688-2104)
PHONE.................................949 546-8300
Robert Morrison, *Pr*
Mike Tracy, *
Tom Tracy, *Stockholder*
Tom England, *
EMP: 300 **EST:** 1986
SQ FT: 10,000
SALES (est): 4.3MM
SALES (corp-wide): 4.3MM **Privately Held**
SIC: 0782 Lawn care services

(P-212)
PARKWOOD LANDSCAPE MAINT INC
16443 Hart St (91406-4608)
PHONE.................................818 988-9677
David Melito, *Pr*
EMP: 95 **EST:** 1988
SQ FT: 1,500
SALES (est): 4.97MM **Privately Held**
Web: www.parkwoodlandscape.com
SIC: 0782 Landscape contractors

(P-213)
PENNEY LAWN SERVICE INC
Also Called: Penny Lawn Service
4000 Allen Rd (93314-9091)
PHONE.................................661 587-4788
Dan Penny, *Owner*
Sandy Penny, *
EMP: 100 **EST:** 1989
SQ FT: 1,275
SALES (est): 4.53MM **Privately Held**
Web: www.penneylawnservice.com
SIC: 0782 Landscape contractors

(P-214)
RESIDENT GROUP SERVICES INC (PA)
Also Called: Rgs Services
1156 N Grove St (92806-2109)
PHONE.................................714 630-5300
TOLL FREE: 800
James M Gilly, *Pr*
Michael K Hayde, *
EMP: 149 **EST:** 1983
SQ FT: 15,000
SALES (est): 19.85MM
SALES (corp-wide): 19.85MM **Privately Held**
Web: www.rgsls.com
SIC: 0782 Landscape contractors

(P-215)
RICHMOND ENGINEERING CO INC
Also Called: Lewis Lifetime Tools
15472 Markar Rd (92064-2313)
PHONE.................................800 589-7058
Daniel Wright, *Pr*
✿ **EMP:** 120 **EST:** 1954
SQ FT: 120,000
SALES (est): 8.88MM **Privately Held**
Web: www.yardbutler.com
SIC: 0782 Lawn and garden services

(P-216)
SUNSET LANDSCAPE MAINTENANCE
27201 Burbank (92610-2500)
P.O. Box 1333 (91702-1333)
PHONE.................................949 455-4636
James Roughan, *Pr*
Claudia Roughan, *
EMP: 100 **EST:** 1976
SQ FT: 6,300
SALES (est): 4.53MM **Privately Held**
Web: www.andrelandscape.com
SIC: 0782 Landscape contractors

(P-217)
TROPICAL PLAZA NURSERY INC
9642 Santiago Blvd (92867-2521)
PHONE.................................714 998-4100
Leslie T Fields, *Pr*
Mike Feilds, *
EMP: 100 **EST:** 1950
SQ FT: 5,000
SALES (est): 4.49MM **Privately Held**
Web: www.tropicalplaza.com
SIC: 0782 Landscape contractors

(P-218)
ULTIMATE LANDSCAPING MGT
700 E Sycamore St (92805-2831)
PHONE.................................714 502-9711
James Berne, *Pr*
EMP: 80 **EST:** 1984
SALES (est): 2.38MM **Privately Held**
SIC: 0782 Landscape contractors

(P-219)
VENCO WESTERN INC
2400 Eastman Ave (93030-5187)
PHONE.................................805 981-2400
TOLL FREE: 800
Linda Del Nagro Burr, *Pr*
William Burr Stcklder, *Prin*
EMP: 200 **EST:** 1977
SQ FT: 15,000
SALES (est): 12.51MM **Privately Held**
Web: www.vencowestern.com
SIC: 0782 Landscape contractors

(P-220)
VINTAGE ASSOCIATES INC
Also Called: Vintage Nursery
78755 Darby Rd (92203-9621)
P.O. Box 5250 (92248-5250)
PHONE.................................760 772-3673
Gregory Gritters, *Pr*
EMP: 160 **EST:** 1989
SQ FT: 1,000
SALES (est): 12.83MM **Privately Held**
Web: www.thevintageco.com
SIC: 0782 5193 5261 Landscape contractors
; Nursery stock; Retail nurseries

(P-221)
WEST COAST ARBORISTS INC (PA)
2200 E Via Burton (92806-1221)
PHONE.................................714 991-1900
EMP: 100 **EST:** 1972
SALES (est): 53.7MM
SALES (corp-wide): 53.7MM **Privately Held**
Web: www.wcainc.com
SIC: 0782 Landscape contractors

0783 Ornamental Shrub And Tree Services

(P-222)
CLS LANDSCAPE MANAGEMENT INC
Also Called: Cls Landscape Management
4329 State St Ste B (91763-6082)
PHONE.................................909 628-3005
Kevin L Davis, *Pr*
Kimberly Davis, *
EMP: 325 **EST:** 1983
SQ FT: 2,500
SALES (est): 21.09MM **Privately Held**
Web: www.clslandscape.com
SIC: 0783 0782 Ornamental shrub and tree services; Lawn and garden services

(P-223)
ORIGINAL MOWBRAYS TREE SVC INC (PA)
686 E Mill St (92408-1610)
PHONE.................................909 383-7009
Dwight Anderson, *Prin*
EMP: 105 **EST:** 1972
SQ FT: 1,000
SALES (est): 53.16MM **Privately Held**
Web: www.mowbrays.com
SIC: 0783 Tree trimming services for public utility lines

(P-224)
PACIFIC COAST TREE EXPERTS
21525 Strathern St (91304-4137)
PHONE.................................805 506-1211
Nicolas Pinedo, *Prin*
Armando Valdez, *
Antonio Ramirez Bonilla, *
Nicolas Pinedo, *Pr*
EMP: 150 **EST:** 2010
SALES (est): 8.34MM **Privately Held**
Web: www.pacificcoasttreeexperts.com
SIC: 0783 Planting, pruning, and trimming services

(P-225)
WEST COAST ARBORISTS INC
21718 Walnut Ave (92313-4437)
PHONE.................................909 783-6544
Patrick Mahoney, *Pr*
EMP: 117
SALES (corp-wide): 53.7MM **Privately Held**
Web: www.westcoastarborists.com
SIC: 0783 Planting, pruning, and trimming services
PA: West Coast Arborists, Inc.
2200 E Via Burton
Anaheim CA
714 991-1900

(P-226)
WEST COAST ARBORISTS INC
11405 Nardo St (93004-3201)
PHONE.................................805 671-5092
Lorenzo Perez, *Owner*
EMP: 116
SALES (corp-wide): 53.7MM **Privately Held**
Web: www.westcoastarborists.com
SIC: 0783 Planting, pruning, and trimming services
PA: West Coast Arborists, Inc.
2200 E Via Burton
Anaheim CA
714 991-1900

P R O D U C T S & S V C S

0811 Timber Tracts

(P-227)
BRIGHTVIEW TREE COMPANY
Also Called: Environmental Industries
3200 W Telegraph Rd (93015-9623)
PHONE......................714 546-7975
Susan Flores, *Brnch Mgr*
EMP: 86
Web: www.brightview.com
SIC: 0811 0782 Tree farm; Lawn services
HQ: Brightview Tree Company
24151 Ventura Blvd # 100
Calabasas CA
818 223-8500

(P-228)
BRIGHTVIEW TREE COMPANY
Also Called: Specimen Contracting
9500 Foothill Blvd (91040-1857)
PHONE......................818 951-5500
Tadd Russikoff, *Mgr*
EMP: 86
Web: www.brightview.com
SIC: 0811 Tree farm
HQ: Brightview Tree Company
24151 Ventura Blvd # 100
Calabasas CA
818 223-8500

(P-229)
HOLIDAY TREE FARMS INC
329 Van Norman Rd (90640-5314)
P.O. Box 1688 (91793-1688)
PHONE......................323 276-1900
Greg Rondeau, *Prin*
EMP: 126
SALES (corp-wide): 40.29MM **Privately Held**
Web: www.holidaytreefarm.com
SIC: 0811 Tree farm
PA: Holiday Tree Farms, Inc.
800 Nw Cornell Ave
Corvallis OR
541 753-3236

0851 Forestry Services

(P-230)
BRADCO INDUSTRIAL CORPORATION
Also Called: Bradco Environmental
1671 Sessums Dr (92374-1906)
P.O. Box 390 (92325-0390)
PHONE......................888 272-3261
Brad Bauder, *Pr*
Tracey Bauder, *Sec*
EMP: 17 EST: 2002
SQ FT: 900
SALES (est): 458.14K **Privately Held**
Web: www.bradcoenvironmental.com
SIC: 0851 2411 Forestry services; Wood chips, produced in the field

1021 Copper Ores

(P-231)
LUSTROS INC
9025 Carlton Hills Blvd Ste A (92071-7905)
PHONE......................619 449-4800
William Farley, *Ch Bd*
EMP: 44 EST: 2012
SQ FT: 1,530
SALES (est): 2.02MM **Privately Held**
Web: www.perfectdomain.com
SIC: 1021 Copper ore mining and preparation

1041 Gold Ores

(P-232)
DV NATURAL RESOURCES LLC
Also Called: Briggs Mine The
8 Miles S Ballarat Wingate Rd (93562)
EMP: 19
SALES (corp-wide): 2.1MM **Privately Held**
SIC: 1041 Gold ores mining
PA: Dv Natural Resources, Llc
7908 Us Highway 169 B
Bovey MN
540 458-3776

(P-233)
GOLDEN QUEEN MINING CO LLC
2818 Silver Queen Rd (93501-7021)
P.O. Box 1030 (93502-1030)
PHONE......................661 824-4300
Thomas Clay, *Ch Bd*
Robert Walish, *
Andree St-germain, *CFO*
EMP: 180 EST: 2014
SQ FT: 2,500
SALES (est): 92.48MM
SALES (corp-wide): 57.04MM **Privately Held**
SIC: 1041 Gold ores mining
PA: Golden Queen Mining Co. Ltd
580 Hornby St Suite 880
Vancouver BC
604 417-7952

(P-234)
LOST DUTCHMANS MININGS ASSN (DH)
43445 Bus Pk Dr Ste 113 (92590-3671)
P.O. Box 891509 (92589-1509)
PHONE......................951 699-4749
▲ EMP: 30 EST: 1995
SQ FT: 3,200
SALES (est): 11.1MM
SALES (corp-wide): 144.91MM **Privately Held**
Web: www.goldprospectors.org
SIC: 1041 Gold ores
HQ: Outdoor Channel Holdings, Inc.
1000 Chopper Cir
Denver CO

(P-235)
STAVATTI INDUSTRIES LTD
3670 El Camino Dr (92404-2025)
P.O. Box 211258 (55121-2658)
PHONE......................651 238-5369
Christopher R Beskar, *Brnch Mgr*
EMP: 42
SALES (corp-wide): 4.22MM **Privately Held**
Web: www.stavatti.com
SIC: 1041 1081 3511 3533 Gold ores mining; Metal mining exploration and development services; Turbines and turbine generator set units, complete; Oil and gas field machinery
PA: Stavatti Industries Ltd
1061 Tiffany Dr
Eagan MN
651 238-5369

1081 Metal Mining Services

(P-236)
NATIONAL EWP INC
Also Called: National Explrtion Wells Pumps
5566 Arrow Hwy (91763-1606)
PHONE......................909 931-4014
Tom Moreland, *Brnch Mgr*
EMP: 19
SALES (corp-wide): 29.93MM **Privately Held**
Web: www.nationalewp.com
SIC: 1081 Metal mining exploration and development services
PA: National Ewp, Inc.
3707 Manzanita Ln
Elko NV
775 753-7355

(P-237)
PERERA CNSTR & DESIGN INC
2890 Inland Empire Blvd Ste 102 (91764-4649)
PHONE......................909 484-6350
Henry Perera Junior, *CEO*
Henry Perera, *CFO*
EMP: 35 EST: 1989
SQ FT: 20,000
SALES (est): 35.16MM **Privately Held**
Web: www.pererainc.com
SIC: 1081 Metal mining exploration and development services

(P-238)
UNICO INCORPORATED
8880 Rio San Diego Dr Fl 8 (92108-1634)
PHONE......................619 209-6124
Mark A Lopez, *Pr*
Charles M Madsen, *Ex VP*
Kenneth Wiedrich, *CFO*
C Wayne Hartle, *Sec*
EMP: 17 EST: 1966
SALES (est): 257.99K **Privately Held**
Web: www.unicosystem.com
SIC: 1081 Metal mining exploration and development services

1099 Metal Ores, Nec

(P-239)
MP MATERIALS CORP
67750 Bailey Rd (92366)
PHONE......................702 844-6111
EMP: 35
SALES (corp-wide): 527.51MM **Publicly Held**
Web: www.mpmaterials.com
SIC: 1099 Rare-earth ores mining
PA: Mp Materials Corp.
1700 S Pavilion Center Dr # 800
Las Vegas NV
702 844-6111

1221 Bituminous Coal And Lignite-surface Mining

(P-240)
CHEVRON MINING INC
Moly
67750 Bailey Rd (92366)
PHONE......................760 856-7625
EMP: 245
SALES (corp-wide): 162.47B **Publicly Held**
SIC: 1221 Surface mining, bituminous, nec
HQ: Chevron Mining Inc.
116 Invrneco Dr E Ste 207
Englewood CO
303 930-3600

1231 Anthracite Mining

(P-241)
MIDSTREAM ENERGY PARTNERS USA
9224 Tupman Rd (93276)
PHONE......................661 765-4087
EMP: 32 EST: 2012
SALES (est): 26.3MM **Privately Held**
Web: www.midstreamenergy.us
SIC: 1231 1382 1311 1321 Anthracite mining; Oil and gas exploration services; Crude petroleum and natural gas; Natural gas liquids

1241 Coal Mining Services

(P-242)
RIO TINTO MINERALS INC
Also Called: Reno Tenco
14486 Borax Rd (93516-2017)
PHONE......................760 762-7121
Xiaoling Liu, *CEO*
Hugo Bague, *
Preston Chiaro, *
◆ EMP: 150 EST: 2006
SALES (est): 100.81MM
SALES (corp-wide): 55.55B **Privately Held**
Web: www.borax.com
SIC: 1241 Coal mining services
HQ: U.S. Borax Inc.
200 E Randolph St # 7100
Chicago IL
773 270-6500

(P-243)
TAFT PRODUCTION COMPANY
950 Petroleum Club Rd (93268-9748)
P.O. Box 1277 (93268-1277)
PHONE......................661 765-7194
Daniel S Jaffee, *Pr*
EMP: 95 EST: 2002
SALES (est): 28.51MM
SALES (corp-wide): 413.02MM **Publicly Held**
Web: www.oildri.com
SIC: 1241 1081 Coal mining services; Metal mining services
PA: Oil-Dri Corporation Of America
410 N Michigan Ave # 400
Chicago IL
312 321-1515

1311 Crude Petroleum And Natural Gas

(P-244)
AERA ENERGY LLC
Also Called: Kernridge Division
19590 7th Standard Rd (93251-9709)
PHONE......................661 334-3100
Marie Crosby, *Prin*
EMP: 96
SALES (corp-wide): 381.31B **Privately Held**
Web: www.aeraenergy.com
SIC: 1311 Natural gas production
HQ: Aera Energy Services Company
10000 Ming Ave
Bakersfield CA
661 665-5000

(P-245)
AERA ENERGY LLC
10000 Ming Ave (93311-1301)
P.O. Box 11164 (93389-1164)
PHONE......................661 665-5000

Erik Bartsch, *Pr*
Ted Witt, *COO*
Sergio De Castro, *CFO*
Lynne Carrithers, *Legal*
Sara Oneill-bouton Senior, *External Affairs Vice President*
EMP: 918 **EST:** 1994
SALES (est): 33.94MM **Privately Held**
SIC: 1311 Crude petroleum production

(P-246)
BENTLEY-SIMONSON INC
1746f S Victoria Ave Ste 382 (93003-6190)
PHONE................805 650-2794
James Bentley, *Ch Bd*
Theodore Bentley, *Ch Bd*
Clifton O Simonson, *Pr*
Petter Romming, *VP*
EMP: 30 **EST:** 1987
SQ FT: 1,000
SALES (est): 2.94MM **Privately Held**
SIC: 1311 Crude petroleum production

(P-247)
BERRY PETROLEUM COMPANY LLC (HQ)
11117 River Run Blvd (93311-8957)
PHONE................661 616-3900
Trem Smith, *Pr*
EMP: 24 **EST:** 1985
SALES (est): 130.26MM
SALES (corp-wide): 918.34MM **Publicly Held**
Web: www.bry.com
SIC: 1311 Crude petroleum production
PA: Berry Corporation (Bry)
16000 Dallas Pkwy Ste 500
Dallas TX
661 616-3900

(P-248)
BERRY PETROLEUM COMPANY LLC
25121 Sierra Hwy (91321-2007)
PHONE................661 255-6066
Eddie Azevedo, *Mgr*
EMP: 51
SALES (corp-wide): 918.34MM **Publicly Held**
Web: www.bry.com
SIC: 1311 Crude petroleum production
HQ: Berry Petroleum Company, Llc
11117 River Run Blvd
Bakersfield CA
661 616-3900

(P-249)
BERRY PETROLEUM COMPANY LLC
28700 Hovey Hills Rd (93268)
P.O. Box 925 (93268-0925)
PHONE................661 769-8820
Tom Cruise, *Mgr*
EMP: 51
SALES (corp-wide): 918.34MM **Publicly Held**
Web: www.bry.com
SIC: 1311 Crude petroleum production
HQ: Berry Petroleum Company, Llc
11117 River Run Blvd
Bakersfield CA
661 616-3900

(P-250)
BETA OPERATING COMPANY LLC
Also Called: Beta Offshore
111 W Ocean Blvd (90802-4633)
PHONE................562 628-1526

EMP: 54
SALES (corp-wide): 458.46MM **Publicly Held**
Web: www.betaoffshore.com
SIC: 1311 Crude petroleum production
HQ: Beta Operating Company, Llc
500 Dallas St Ste 1600
Houston TX

(P-251)
BREA CANON OIL CO INC
23903 Normandie Ave (90710-1400)
PHONE................310 326-4002
Andrew Barkler, *Pr*
Rod Benny, *Mgr*
Ray Javier, *VP*
Andrew Barkler, *Pr*
EMP: 17 **EST:** 2004
SALES (est): 2.45MM **Privately Held**
SIC: 1311 Crude petroleum production

(P-252)
BREITBURN ENERGY PARTNERS LP
707 Wilshire Blvd Ste 4600 (90017-3612)
PHONE................213 225-5900
EMP: 671
SIC: 1311 Crude petroleum production

(P-253)
BREITBURN GP LLC
707 Wilshire Blvd # 4600 (90017-3501)
PHONE................213 225-5900
Halbert S Washburn, *CEO*
EMP: 26 **EST:** 2006
SALES (est): 1.07MM **Privately Held**
SIC: 1311 Crude petroleum and natural gas

(P-254)
CALIFORNIA RESOURCES CORP (PA)
Also Called: CRC
1 World Trade Ctr Ste 1500 (90831-0002)
PHONE................888 848-4754
Francisco J Leon, *Pr*
Tiffany Thom Cepak, *
Manuela Molina, *Ex VP*
Shawn M Kerns, *Ex VP*
Michael L Preston, *Chief Strategy Officer*
EMP: 65 **EST:** 2014
SALES (est): 2.71B
SALES (corp-wide): 2.71B **Publicly Held**
Web: www.crc.com
SIC: 1311 Crude petroleum and natural gas

(P-255)
CALIFORNIA RESOURCES PROD CORP (HQ)
Also Called: Vintage Production California
27200 Tourney Rd Ste 200 (91355-4910)
PHONE................661 869-8000
EMP: 125 **EST:** 2005
SALES (est): 101.88MM
SALES (corp-wide): 2.71B **Publicly Held**
SIC: 1311 1382 Crude petroleum production; Oil and gas exploration services
PA: California Resources Corporation
1 World Trade Ctr Ste 150
Long Beach CA
888 848-4754

(P-256)
CALIFORNIA RESOURCES PROD CORP
4900 W Lokern Rd (93251-9764)
PHONE................661 869-8000
EMP: 25
SALES (corp-wide): 2.71B **Publicly Held**

SIC: 1311 1382 Crude petroleum production; Oil and gas exploration services
HQ: California Resources Production Corporation
27200 Tourney Rd Ste 200
Santa Clarita CA

(P-257)
CALNRG OPERATING LLC (PA)
1536 Eastman Ave (93003-7773)
PHONE................805 477-9805
Clif Simonson, *COO*
EMP: 22
SALES (est): 11.69MM
SALES (corp-wide): 11.69MM **Privately Held**
SIC: 1311 Natural gas production

(P-258)
CARBON CALIFORNIA COMPANY LLC
270 Quail Ct Ste 201 (93060-9206)
PHONE................805 933-1901
Patrick R Mcdonald, *CEO*
Mark D Pierce, *Pr*
Kevin D Struzeski, *CFO*
EMP: 33 **EST:** 2016
SALES (est): 5.03MM
SALES (corp-wide): 116.63MM **Privately Held**
SIC: 1311 Crude petroleum and natural gas
PA: Carbon Energy Corporation
1700 S Broadway Ste 1170
Denver CO
720 407-7043

(P-259)
COOPER & BRAIN INC
Also Called: Cooper
655 E D St (90744-6003)
P.O. Box 1177 (90748-1177)
PHONE................310 834-4411
Robert E Brain, *Pr*
Joel A Cooper, *Sec*
EMP: 26 **EST:** 1948
SQ FT: 4,000
SALES (est): 2.49MM **Privately Held**
SIC: 1311 Crude petroleum production

(P-260)
GREGG HAMMORK ENTERPRISES INC
Also Called: Gregg's Mission Viejo Mobile
23002 Alicia Pkwy (92692-1636)
PHONE................949 586-7902
Gregg Hammork, *Pr*
EMP: 25 **EST:** 1990
SQ FT: 3,000
SALES (est): 4.18MM **Privately Held**
SIC: 1311 Crude petroleum and natural gas production

(P-261)
HATHAWAY LLC
4205 Atlas Ct (93308-4510)
P.O. Box 81385 (93380-1385)
PHONE................661 393-2004
Charles Hathaway, *
EMP: 38 **EST:** 2000
SQ FT: 4,500
SALES (est): 15.29MM **Privately Held**
Web: www.hathawayllc.com
SIC: 1311 Crude petroleum production

(P-262)
HELLMAN PROPERTIES LLC
711 First St (90740)
P.O. Box 2398 (90740-1398)
PHONE................562 431-6022

EMP: 20 **EST:** 1920
SQ FT: 200
SALES (est): 3MM **Privately Held**
SIC: 1311 Crude petroleum production

(P-263)
NAFTEX WESTSIDE PARTNERS LIMIT
1900 Avenue Of The Stars (90067-4301)
PHONE................310 277-9004
Hormoz Ameri, *Genl Pt*
EMP: 38 **EST:** 1988
SQ FT: 1,200
SALES (est): 1.74MM **Privately Held**
SIC: 1311 Crude petroleum production

(P-264)
OCCIDENTAL PETROLEUM CORPORATION OF CALIFORNIA
Also Called: OXY
10889 Wilshire Blvd Fl 10 (90024-4213)
EMP: 3600
SIC: 1311 Crude petroleum production

(P-265)
SEQUOIA EXPLORATION INC
5913 Sundale Ave (93309-2829)
PHONE................661 303-0564
EMP: 22 **EST:** 1991
SALES (est): 5.48MM **Privately Held**
SIC: 1311 Crude petroleum production

(P-266)
THE STRAND ENERGY COMPANY
515 S Flower St Ste 4800 (90071-2241)
PHONE................213 225-5900
EMP: 380
SIC: 1311 Crude petroleum and natural gas production

(P-267)
THUMS LONG BEACH COMPANY
111 W Ocean Blvd Ste 800 (90802-7930)
PHONE................562 624-3400
EMP: 205
SIC: 1311 Crude petroleum production

(P-268)
TIDELANDS OIL PRODUCTION INC
Also Called: Partnrship Prmnt Ptro Chnse En
301 E Ocean Blvd St 300 (90802-4830)
PHONE................562 436-9918
EMP: 30
SIC: 1311 8748 4925 Crude petroleum production; Business consulting, nec; Gas production and/or distribution

(P-269)
TRI-VALLEY CORPORATION
4927 Calloway Dr Ste 101 (93312-9719)
PHONE................661 864-0500
EMP: 25
Web: www.tri-valleycorp.com
SIC: 1311 1382 1041 Crude petroleum and natural gas; Oil and gas exploration services ; Gold ores

(P-270)
UNIFIED FIELD SERVICES CORP
6906 Downing Ave (93308-5812)
PHONE................661 325-8962
Wesley R Furrh Junior, *Pr*
EMP: 28 **EST:** 2015
SALES (est): 67.76MM **Privately Held**
Web: www.unifiedfsc.com

PRODUCTS & SVCS

SIC: 1311 Crude petroleum and natural gas

(P-271)
VAQUERO ENERGY INCORPORATED
15545 Hermosa Rd (93307-9477)
PHONE..................661 363-7240
Ken Hunter, *Pr*
EMP: 50 **EST:** 2007
SALES (est): 10.34MM **Privately Held**
Web: www.vaqueroenergy.com
SIC: 1311 Crude petroleum production

(P-272)
WEST NEWPORT OIL COMPANY
5800 W Coast Hwy (92663-2002)
P.O. Box 1487 (92659-0487)
PHONE..................949 631-1100
Robert A Armstrong, *Pr*
Jay Stair, *VP*
Margaret Armstrong, *Sec*
EMP: 24 **EST:** 1975
SALES (est): 4.91MM
SALES (corp-wide): 4.91MM **Privately Held**
SIC: 1311 Crude petroleum production
PA: Armstrong Petroleum Corporation
5800 W Coast Hwy
Newport Beach CA
949 650-4000

(P-273)
WORLD OIL CORP
9302 Garfield Ave (90280-3896)
P.O. Box 1 (90280-0001)
PHONE..................562 928-0100
EMP: 140 **EST:** 1973
SALES (est): 134.75MM **Privately Held**
Web: www.worldoilcorp.com
SIC: 1311 Crude petroleum and natural gas

1321 Natural Gas Liquids

(P-274)
HEXAGON AGILITY INC
3335 Susan St Ste 100 (92626-1647)
PHONE..................949 236-5520
Hans Peter Havdal, *CEO*
Seung Baik, *Pr*
EMP: 99 **EST:** 2016
SALES (est): 63.23MM **Privately Held**
Web: www.hexagonagility.com
SIC: 1321 Natural gas liquids production
PA: Hexagon Composites Asa
Korsegata 4b
Alesund

1381 Drilling Oil And Gas Wells

(P-275)
AERA ENERGY SERVICES COMPANY
Also Called: Security Front Desk
59231 Main Camp Rd (93251-9740)
PHONE..................661 665-4400
Mike Brown, *Prin*
EMP: 128
SALES (corp-wide): 381.31B **Privately Held**
Web: www.aeraenergy.com
SIC: 1381 Directional drilling oil and gas wells
HQ: Aera Energy Services Company
10000 Ming Ave
Bakersfield CA
661 665-5000

(P-276)
AERA ENERGY SERVICES COMPANY
Also Called: Aera Energy South Midway
29235 Highway 33 (93252-9793)
PHONE..................661 665-3200
Andy Anderson, *Mgr*
EMP: 128
SALES (corp-wide): 381.31B **Privately Held**
Web: www.aeraenergy.com
SIC: 1381 Directional drilling oil and gas wells
HQ: Aera Energy Services Company
10000 Ming Ave
Bakersfield CA
661 665-5000

(P-277)
AERA ENERGY SERVICES COMPANY (HQ)
10000 Ming Ave (93311-1301)
P.O. Box 11164 (93389-1164)
PHONE..................661 665-5000
Erik Bartsch, *Pr*
EMP: 800 **EST:** 1994
SALES (est): 1.73B
SALES (corp-wide): 381.31B **Privately Held**
Web: www.aeraenergy.com
SIC: 1381 Directional drilling oil and gas wells
PA: Shell Plc
Shell Centre
London
800 731-8888

(P-278)
BLE INC
Also Called: Beryl Lockhart Enterprises
11360 Goss St (91352-3205)
PHONE..................818 504-9577
Beryl P Lockhart, *CEO*
EMP: 37 **EST:** 1965
SQ FT: 2,200
SALES (est): 1.92MM **Privately Held**
SIC: 1381 Drilling oil and gas wells

(P-279)
DICK HOWELLS HOLE DRLG SVC INC
Also Called: Howell Drilling
2579 E 67th St (90805-1701)
PHONE..................562 633-9898
Richard Howell Junior, *Pr*
Paul Howell, *VP*
Patty Howell, *Sec*
EMP: 18 **EST:** 1971
SALES (est): 2.49MM **Privately Held**
Web: www.howelldrilling.com
SIC: 1381 1629 1741 Drilling oil and gas wells; Blasting contractor, except building demolition; Foundation building

(P-280)
ELYSIUM JENNINGS LLC
1600 Norris Rd (93308-2234)
PHONE..................661 679-1700
EMP: 145 **EST:** 2003
SALES (est): 4.12MM **Privately Held**
SIC: 1381 Drilling oil and gas wells
PA: E & B Natural Resources Management Corporation
1608 Norris Rd
Bakersfield CA

(P-281)
EXCALIBUR WELL SERVICES CORP
12625 Jomani Dr Ste 104 (93312-3454)

22034 Rosedale Hwy (93314-9704)
PHONE..................661 589-5338
Stephen Layton, *Pr*
Stephen Layton, *CEO*
Frachsco Galesi, *
Gordon Isbel, *
EMP: 120 **EST:** 2006
SALES (est): 20.11MM **Privately Held**
Web: www.excaliburwellservices.com
SIC: 1381 1389 Drilling oil and gas wells; Fishing for tools, oil and gas field

(P-282)
GEO GUIDANCE DRILLING SVCS INC (PA)
200 Old Yard Dr (93307-4268)
P.O. Box 42647 (93384-2647)
PHONE..................661 833-9999
EMP: 25 **EST:** 2011
SQ FT: 3,000
SALES (est): 13.89MM **Privately Held**
Web: www.geoguidancedrilling.com
SIC: 1381 Drilling oil and gas wells

(P-283)
GOLDEN STATE DRILLING INC
3500 Fruitvale Ave (93308-5106)
PHONE..................661 589-0730
Philip F Phelps, *Pr*
Velma Phelps, *
James Phelps, *
EMP: 75 **EST:** 1977
SALES (est): 11.47MM **Privately Held**
Web: www.gsdrilling.com
SIC: 1381 Directional drilling oil and gas wells

(P-284)
KUSTER CO OIL WELL SERVICES
Also Called: Kuster Company
2900 E 29th St (90806-2398)
PHONE..................562 595-0661
John Davidson, *CEO*
▲ **EMP:** 23 **EST:** 1996
SALES (est): 4.82MM **Privately Held**
Web: www.probe1.com
SIC: 1381 Drilling oil and gas wells
PA: Probe Holdings, Inc.
1132 Everman Pkwy Ste 100
Fort Worth TX

(P-285)
LEGEND PUMP & WELL SERVICE INC
1324 W Rialto Ave (92410-1611)
PHONE..................909 384-1000
Keith Collier, *Pr*
EMP: 20 **EST:** 2010
SALES (est): 2.55MM **Privately Held**
Web: www.legendpump.net
SIC: 1381 1781 Service well drilling; Servicing, water wells

(P-286)
LEON KROUS DRILLING INC
9300 Borden Ave (91352-2006)
PHONE..................818 833-4654
Leon Krus, *Pr*
EMP: 25 **EST:** 1981
SQ FT: 1,000
SALES (est): 7.64MM **Privately Held**
Web: leonkrousdrilling.thebluebook.com
SIC: 1381 Directional drilling oil and gas wells

(P-287)
PETRO-LUD INC
12625 Jomani Dr Ste 104 (93312-3454)

PHONE..................661 747-4779
Clayton Ludington, *Prin*
EMP: 23 **EST:** 2012
SALES (est): 1.97MM **Privately Held**
Web: www.petro-lud.com
SIC: 1381 Drilling oil and gas wells

(P-288)
SCIENTIFIC DRILLING INTL INC
31101 Coberly Rd (93263-9702)
PHONE..................661 831-0636
Joe Williams, *Mgr*
EMP: 28
SALES (corp-wide): 400.64MM **Privately Held**
Web: www.scientificdrilling.com
SIC: 1381 Drilling oil and gas wells
PA: Scientific Drilling International, Inc.
16071 Grnspint Pk Dr Ste
Houston TX
281 443-3300

(P-289)
WEST AMERICAN ENERGY CORP
4949 Buckley Way Ste 207 (93309-4882)
P.O. Box 22016 (93390-2016)
PHONE..................661 747-7732
Howard Caywood, *Pr*
EMP: 17 **EST:** 2000
SQ FT: 640
SALES (est): 934.61K **Privately Held**
SIC: 1381 Drilling oil and gas wells

1382 Oil And Gas Exploration Services

(P-290)
ARGUELLO INC
17100 Calle Mariposa Reina (93117-9737)
PHONE..................805 567-1632
James C Flores, *Pr*
John F Wombwell, *
Doss Dourgeois, *
Winston Taldert, *
EMP: 40 **EST:** 1999
SALES (est): 8.87MM
SALES (corp-wide): 22.78B **Publicly Held**
SIC: 1382 Oil and gas exploration services
HQ: Freeport-Mcmoran Oil & Gas Llc
700 Milam St Ste 3100
Houston TX
713 579-6000

(P-291)
BNK PETROLEUM (US) INC
925 Broadbeck Dr Ste 220 (91320-1272)
PHONE..................805 484-3613
Wolf E Regener, *Pr*
Gary W Johnson, *
Ray W Payne, *OF US Operations*
Steven M Warshauer, *Exploration Vice President*
EMP: 25 **EST:** 2006
SALES (est): 8.38MM **Privately Held**
Web: www.kolibrienergy.com
SIC: 1382 Oil and gas exploration services

(P-292)
BREITBURN ENERGY HOLDINGS LLC
707 Wilshire Blvd Ste 4600 (90017-3501)
PHONE..................213 225-5900
EMP: 17 **EST:** 2009
SALES (est): 1.2MM **Privately Held**
Web: www.mavresources.com
SIC: 1382 Oil and gas exploration services

(P-293)
CALIFORNIA RESOURCES CORP
5000 Stockdale Hwy (93309-2650)
PHONE..............................661 395-8000
EMP: 44
SALES (corp-wide): 2.71B Publicly Held
Web: www.crc.com
SIC: 1382 Oil and gas exploration services
PA: California Resources Corporation
1 World Trade Ctr Ste 150
Long Beach CA
888 848-4754

(P-294)
CALIFRNIA RSRCES ELK HILLS LLC
27200 Tourney Rd Ste 200 (91355-4910)
PHONE..............................661 412-0000
Michael L Preston, *
Marshall D Smith, *
EMP: 400 EST: 1997
SALES (est): 84.49MM
SALES (corp-wide): 2.71B Publicly Held
SIC: 1382 Oil and gas exploration services
PA: California Resources Corporation
1 World Trade Ctr Ste 150
Long Beach CA
888 848-4754

(P-295)
CALIFRNIA RSURCES LONG BCH INC
27200 Tourney Rd Ste 200 (91355-4910)
PHONE..............................888 848-4754
EMP: 98 EST: 1989
SALES (est): 8.28MM
SALES (corp-wide): 2.71B Publicly Held
SIC: 1382 Oil and gas exploration services
PA: California Resources Corporation
1 World Trade Ctr Ste 150
Long Beach CA
888 848-4754

(P-296)
CRC SERVICES LLC
27200 Tourney Rd Ste 200 (91355-4910)
PHONE..............................888 848-4754
EMP: 18 EST: 2014
SALES (est): 6.47MM
SALES (corp-wide): 2.71B Publicly Held
SIC: 1382 Oil and gas exploration services
PA: California Resources Corporation
1 World Trade Ctr Ste 150
Long Beach CA
888 848-4754

(P-297)
DCOR LLC (PA)
Also Called: Dcor
1000 Town Center Dr Fl 6 (93036-1132)
P.O. Box 3401 (93006-3401)
PHONE..............................805 535-2000
Andrew Prestridge, *
Alan C Templeton, *
Jeff Warren, *
Bob Garcia, *
EMP: 193 EST: 2001
SALES (est): 89.01MM
SALES (corp-wide): 89.01MM Privately Held
Web: www.dcorllc.com
SIC: 1382 Oil and gas exploration services

(P-298)
DEMENNO KERDOON
2000 N Alameda St (90222-2799)
PHONE..............................310 537-7100
Shane Bamelin, Prin
Jim Tice, *

Shane Bamelin, Ch
Jim Ennis, *
EMP: 20 EST: 2007
SQ FT: 11,614
SALES (est): 5.75MM Privately Held
SIC: 1382 Oil and gas exploration services

(P-299)
DRILLMEC INC
8140 Rosecrans Ave (90723-2754)
PHONE..............................281 885-0777
Paulo Brando Ballerini, Pr
Massimo Tartagni, *
◆ EMP: 74 EST: 1998
SALES (est): 24.66MM
SALES (corp-wide): 578.09MM Privately Held
SIC: 1382 Oil and gas exploration services
HQ: Soilmec Spa
Via Dismano 5819
Cesena FC
054 731-8548

(P-300)
E & B NTRAL RESOURCES MGT CORP (PA)
1608 Norris Rd (93308-2234)
PHONE..............................661 679-1714
Steve Layton, Pr
Jeff Blesener, *
Jeff Jones, *
Steven K Porter, *
Frank J Ronkese, *
EMP: 65 EST: 1972
SALES (est): 169.42MM Privately Held
Web: www.ebresources.com
SIC: 1382 Oil and gas exploration services

(P-301)
E & B NTRAL RESOURCES MGT CORP
1848 Perkins Rd (93254)
P.O. Box 179 (93254-0179)
PHONE..............................661 766-2501
Edward Fetterman, Brnch Mgr
EMP: 21
Web: www.ebresources.com
SIC: 1382 Oil and gas exploration services
PA: E & B Natural Resources Management
Corporation
1608 Norris Rd
Bakersfield CA

(P-302)
EAGLE DOMINION ENERGY CORP
Also Called: Eagle Dominion Trust
200 N Hayes Ave (93030-5420)
P.O. Box 7004 (93031-7004)
PHONE..............................805 272-9557
Roger H Shears, Admn
Roger H Shears, Pr
Nancy Davis, *
Mary Pickford, Prin
EMP: 35 EST: 1997
SQ FT: 1,500
SALES (est): 2.04MM Privately Held
SIC: 1382 Oil and gas exploration services

(P-303)
ELK HILLS POWER LLC
101 Ash St (92101-3017)
PHONE..............................661 763-2730
EMP: 42 EST: 1987
SALES (est): 3.48MM
SALES (corp-wide): 2.71B Publicly Held
SIC: 1382 Oil and gas exploration services
PA: California Resources Corporation
1 World Trade Ctr Ste 150

Long Beach CA
888 848-4754

(P-304)
FREEPORT-MCMORAN OIL & GAS LLC
760 W Hueneme Rd (93033-9013)
PHONE..............................805 567-1601
Eric Vang, Brnch Mgr
EMP: 17
SALES (corp-wide): 22.78B Publicly Held
SIC: 1382 Oil and gas exploration services
HQ: Freeport-Mcmoran Oil & Gas Llc
700 Milam St Ste 3100
Houston TX
713 579-6000

(P-305)
FREEPORT-MCMORAN OIL & GAS LLC
5640 S Fairfax Ave (90056-1266)
PHONE..............................323 298-2200
Charlotte Hargett, Dir
EMP: 27
SALES (corp-wide): 22.78B Publicly Held
Web: www.fcx.com
SIC: 1382 Oil and gas exploration services
HQ: Freeport-Mcmoran Oil & Gas Llc
700 Milam St Ste 3100
Houston TX
713 579-6000

(P-306)
FREEPORT-MCMORAN OIL & GAS LLC
1200 Discovery Dr Ste 500 (93309-7038)
PHONE..............................661 322-7600
Kiran Leal, Mgr
EMP: 30
SALES (corp-wide): 22.78B Publicly Held
SIC: 1382 Oil and gas exploration services
HQ: Freeport-Mcmoran Oil & Gas Llc
700 Milam St Ste 3100
Houston TX
713 579-6000

(P-307)
GREKA INTEGRATED INC (PA)
Also Called: Greka
1700 Sinton Rd (93458-9708)
P.O. Box 5489 (93456-5489)
PHONE..............................805 347-8700
Randeep S Grewal, CEO
Susan Whalen, VP
Ken Miller, CFO
▲ EMP: 121 EST: 2000
SALES (est): 23.58MM
SALES (corp-wide): 23.58MM Privately Held
Web: www.greka.com
SIC: 1382 Oil and gas exploration services

(P-308)
HESS CONTRACTING INC
1024 Pine Dr (92020-7247)
PHONE..............................619 442-6333
John Hess, CEO
EMP: 24 EST: 2005
SALES (est): 1.86MM Privately Held
SIC: 1382 Oil and gas exploration services

(P-309)
LINN ENERGY LLC
Also Called: Linn Western Operating
2000 Tonner Canyon Rd (92821-2659)
PHONE..............................714 257-1600
EMP: 20
SALES (corp-wide): 917.71MM Privately Held

SIC: 1382 Oil and gas exploration services
PA: Linn Energy, Inc.
600 Travis St Ste 5100
Houston TX
281 840-4000

(P-310)
LINNCO LLC
5201 Truxtun Ave (93309-0421)
PHONE..............................661 616-3900
EMP: 888
SALES (corp-wide): 127.72MM Privately Held
SIC: 1382 Oil and gas exploration services
PA: Linnco, Llc
600 Travis St Ste 5100
Houston TX
281 840-4000

(P-311)
MACPHERSON OIL COMPANY LLC
24118 Round Mountain Rd (93308-9115)
P.O. Box 5368 (93388-5368)
PHONE..............................661 556-6096
Wes Duncan, Mgr
EMP: 22
SALES (corp-wide): 918.34MM Publicly Held
Web: www.macphersonenergy.com
SIC: 1382 1311 Oil and gas exploration services; Crude petroleum and natural gas production
HQ: Macpherson Oil Company Llc
11117 River Run Blvd
Bakersfield CA
310 452-3880

(P-312)
MAGNETRON POWER INVENTIONS INC
2226 W 232nd St (90501-5720)
PHONE..............................310 462-6970
Ninan N Johnson, CEO
EMP: 22 EST: 1999
SQ FT: 2,500
SALES (est): 1.98MM Privately Held
Web: www.magnetronusa.com
SIC: 1382 Oil and gas exploration services

(P-313)
NEWPORT ENERGY
19200 Von Karman Ave Ste 400 (92612-1541)
PHONE..............................408 230-7545
Nyle Khan, CEO
Gordon Burk, COO
EMP: 25 EST: 1984
SQ FT: 5,000
SALES (est): 1.64MM Privately Held
SIC: 1382 Oil and gas exploration services

(P-314)
OCCIDENTAL PETROLEUM INVESTMENT CO INC
10889 Wilshire Blvd Fl 10 (90024-4213)
PHONE..............................310 208-8800
EMP: 4000
SIC: 1382 8744 Oil and gas exploration services; Facilities support services

(P-315)
PHOENIX CPITL GROUP HLDNGS LLC
18575 Jamboree Rd Ste 830 (92612-2557)
PHONE..............................303 749-0074
Lindsey Wilson, Mgr
EMP: 50 EST: 2019
SALES (est): 10.18MM Privately Held

Web: www.phxcapitalgroup.com
SIC: 1382 Oil and gas exploration services

(P-316)
QRE OPERATING LLC
707 Wilshire Blvd Ste 4600 (90017-3501)
PHONE..................213 225-5900
EMP: 82 EST: 2010
SALES (est): 921.8K Privately Held
SIC: 1382 Oil and gas exploration services
PA: Qr Energy, Lp
707 Wilshire Blvd # 4600
Los Angeles CA

(P-317)
SAMEDAN OIL CORPORATION
Also Called: Noble Energy
1360 Landing Ave (90740-6525)
PHONE..................661 319-5038
EMP: 446
SALES (corp-wide): 80.5MM Privately Held
SIC: 1382 Oil and gas exploration services
PA: Samedan Oil Corporation
1001 Noble Energy Way
Houston TX
580 223-4110

(P-318)
SANTA MARIA ENRGY HOLDINGS LLC
2811 Airpark Dr (93455-1417)
P.O. Box 7202 (93456-7202)
PHONE..................805 938-3320
EMP: 20 EST: 2008
SALES (est): 1.27MM Privately Held
Web: www.santamaria.com
SIC: 1382 Oil and gas exploration services

(P-319)
SENTINEL PEAK RSOURCES CAL LLC
5640 S Fairfax Ave (90056-1266)
PHONE..................323 298-2200
EMP: 79
SALES (corp-wide): 89.69MM Privately Held
Web: www.sentinelpeakresources.com
SIC: 1382 Oil and gas exploration services
HQ: Sentinel Peak Resources California Llc
6501 E Belleview Ave # 400
Englewood CO
720 749-1105

(P-320)
SENTINEL PEAK RSOURCES CAL LLC
1200 Discovery Dr Ste 100 (93309-7033)
PHONE..................661 395-5214
EMP: 79
SALES (corp-wide): 89.69MM Privately Held
Web: www.sentinelpeakresources.com
SIC: 1382 Oil and gas exploration services
HQ: Sentinel Peak Resources California Llc
6501 E Belleview Ave # 400
Englewood CO
720 749-1105

(P-321)
SIGNAL HILL PETROLEUM INC
2633 Cherry Ave (90755-2008)
PHONE..................562 595-6440
Jerrel Barto, Ch Bd
Craig C Barto, *
EMP: 49 EST: 1984
SALES (est): 27.4MM Privately Held
Web: www.shpi.net

SIC: 1382 Geological exploration, oil and gas field

(P-322)
TERMO COMPANY
3275 Cherry Ave (90807-5213)
P.O. Box 2767 (90801-2767)
PHONE..................562 595-7401
David E Combs, Pr
Donna Sheaffer, Sec
Francis Roth, VP
Norbert Buss, VP
EMP: 21 EST: 1933
SQ FT: 18,034
SALES (est): 14.68MM Privately Held
Web: www.termoco.com
SIC: 1382 Oil and gas exploration services

(P-323)
UNIVERSAL DYNAMICS INC
5313 3rd St (91706-2085)
PHONE..................626 480-0035
Issa Alasker, Pr
EMP: 18 EST: 2004
SQ FT: 15,000
SALES (est): 2.53MM Privately Held
Web: www.udinc.net
SIC: 1382 7382 Oil and gas exploration services; Security systems services

(P-324)
WARREN E&P INC
Also Called: Warren E & P
400 Oceangate Ste 200 (90802-4306)
PHONE..................214 393-9688
James A Watt, CEO
Romy Massey, Contact Person*
EMP: 67 EST: 1973
SQ FT: 7,000
SALES (est): 18.42K Privately Held
SIC: 1382 Oil and gas exploration services
PA: Warren Resources, Inc.
14131 Midway Rd Ste 500
Addison TX

1389 Oil And Gas Field Services, Nec

(P-325)
ALL RISK SHIELD INC
1244 Pine St Ste 211 (93446-7241)
P.O. Box 300 (93465-0300)
PHONE..................866 991-7190
Joe Torres, CEO
EMP: 20 EST: 2017
SALES (est): 1.74MM Privately Held
Web: www.allriskshield.com
SIC: 1389 7389 0851 Construction, repair, and dismantling services; Fire protection service other than forestry or public; Fire prevention services, forest

(P-326)
ALLY ENTERPRISES
5001 E Commercecenter Dr Ste 260 (93309-1659)
P.O. Box 20580 (93390-0580)
PHONE..................661 412-9933
Rick Noland, Pr
EMP: 20 EST: 2016
SALES (est): 1.47MM Privately Held
SIC: 1389 Oil field services, nec

(P-327)
ANATESCO INC
128 Bedford Way (93308-1702)
P.O. Box 5694 (93388-5694)
PHONE..................661 399-6990

Douglas Paul Denesha, Pr
Jean Denesha, VP
EMP: 18 EST: 1978
SQ FT: 3,000
SALES (est): 4.64MM Privately Held
Web: www.anatesco.com
SIC: 1389 Oil field services, nec

(P-328)
B & B PIPE AND TOOL CO (PA)
3035 Walnut Ave (90807-5221)
PHONE..................562 424-0704
Craig Braly, Pr
Stephanie Braly, *
▲ EMP: 23 EST: 1951
SQ FT: 2,000
SALES (est): 11.4MM
SALES (corp-wide): 11.4MM Privately Held
Web: www.bbpipe.com
SIC: 1389 Oil field services, nec

(P-329)
BASIC ENERGY SERVICES INC
6710 Stewart Way (93308)
PHONE..................661 588-3800
EMP: 34
SALES (corp-wide): 411.38MM Privately Held
Web: www.basicenergyservices.com
SIC: 1389 Oil field services, nec
PA: Basic Energy Services, Inc.
801 Cherry St Ste 2100
Fort Worth TX
817 334-4100

(P-330)
BLACK GOLD PUMP & SUPPLY INC
2459 Lewis Ave (90755-3427)
PHONE..................323 298-0077
Michael L Bair, CEO
Michael L Bair, VP
Thomas E Casec, Sec
James L Hurd, Pr
▲ EMP: 17 EST: 1982
SALES (est): 4.94MM Privately Held
Web: www.blackgoldpump.com
SIC: 1389 Oil field services, nec

(P-331)
C & H TESTING SERVICE INC (PA)
6224 Price Way (93308-5117)
P.O. Box 9907 (93389-1907)
PHONE..................661 589-4030
Donald T Hoover, Pr
Karen K Hoover, *
EMP: 20 EST: 1981
SQ FT: 1,500
SALES (est): 4.54MM
SALES (corp-wide): 4.54MM Privately Held
SIC: 1389 Oil field services, nec

(P-332)
C&J WELL SERVICES LLC
3752 Allen Rd (93314-9242)
PHONE..................661 589-5220
Joana Lerma, Managing Member
Danielle Hunter, *
EMP: 900 EST: 2021
SALES (est): 45.15MM Privately Held
Web: www.cjwellservices.com
SIC: 1389 Servicing oil and gas wells

(P-333)
CAL COAST ACIDIZING CO
Also Called: Cal Coast Acidizing Service

6226 Dominion Rd (93454-9177)
P.O. Box 2050 (93457-2050)
PHONE..................805 934-2411
Bruce Edward Conway, CEO
EMP: 45 EST: 1966
SQ FT: 2,000
SALES (est): 4.37MM Privately Held
Web: www.ccacidizing.com
SIC: 1389 Oil field services, nec

(P-334)
CALPI INC
7141 Downing Ave (93308-5815)
P.O. Box 81795 (93380-1795)
PHONE..................661 589-5648
Robert Larkie Barnett, Pr
Jeff Barnett, VP
EMP: 23 EST: 1981
SQ FT: 5,032
SALES (est): 914.83K Privately Held
Web: www.calpiinc.com
SIC: 1389 4959 Cleaning wells; Toxic or hazardous waste cleanup

(P-335)
CAPSULE MANUFACTURING INC
Also Called: Capsule Mfg
1399 N Miller St (92806-1412)
PHONE..................949 245-4151
Chad Bowker, Pr
EMP: 68 EST: 2015
SALES (est): 4.3MM Privately Held
Web: www.capsulemfg.com
SIC: 1389 Construction, repair, and dismantling services

(P-336)
CASING SPECIALTIES INC
12454 Snow Rd (93314-8015)
PHONE..................661 399-5522
Russell C Davis, Owner
EMP: 25 EST: 2010
SALES (est): 5.03MM Privately Held
Web: www.casingspecialties.com
SIC: 1389 Cementing oil and gas well casings

(P-337)
CENTRAL CALIFORNIA CNSTR INC
7221 Downing Ave (93308-5817)
PHONE..................661 978-8230
Dereke Gerecke, Prin
Tammie K Rankin-gerecke, Prin
EMP: 24 EST: 2005
SALES (est): 2.27MM Privately Held
SIC: 1389 Construction, repair, and dismantling services

(P-338)
CJ BERRY WELL SERVICES MGT LLC
3752 Allen Rd (93314-9242)
PHONE..................661 589-5220
Joana Lerma, Prin
Danielle Hunter, *
Stacy Urbina, *
EMP: 900 EST: 2021
SALES (est): 34.51MM Privately Held
SIC: 1389 Servicing oil and gas wells

(P-339)
CJD CONSTRUCTION SVCS INC
503 E Route 66 (91740-3506)
PHONE..................626 335-1116
Diego A Debenedetto, Pr
Diego Dibenedetto, *
EMP: 40 EST: 2004
SALES (est): 2.2MM Privately Held

▲ = Import ▼ = Export
◆ = Import/Export

Web: www.canyonair.com
SIC: **1389** Construction, repair, and dismantling services

(P-340)
CL KNOX INC
Also Called: Advanced Industrial Services
34933 Imperial Ave (93308-9579)
PHONE.................................661 837-0477
Leslie Knox, *Pr*
Chris Knox, *
EMP: 80 **EST:** 1992
SALES (est): 10MM **Privately Held**
Web: www.aisleaders.com
SIC: **1389** 8742 Oil field services, nec; Industrial consultant

(P-341)
CUMMINGS VACUUM SERVICE INC
Also Called: Cummings Transportation
19605 Broken Ct (93263-9583)
PHONE.................................661 746-1786
Pam Cummings, *Pr*
Ted Cummings, *
EMP: 60 **EST:** 1980
SQ FT: 3,000
SALES (est): 8.4MM **Privately Held**
Web: www.cummings2.com
SIC: **1389** Oil field services, nec

(P-342)
DE VRIES INTERNATIONAL INC (PA)
17671 Armstrong Ave (92614-5727)
PHONE.................................949 252-1212
Don Devries, *Pr*
◆ **EMP:** 27 **EST:** 1984
SALES (est): 9.46MM
SALES (corp-wide): 9.46MM **Privately Held**
Web: www.devriesintl.com
SIC: **1389** Lease tanks, oil field: erecting, cleaning, and repairing

(P-343)
DWAYNES ENGINEERING & CNSTR
3559 Addie Ave (93224-9634)
PHONE.................................661 762-7261
EMP: 23 **EST:** 1979
SALES (est): 2.15MM **Privately Held**
SIC: **1389** Construction, repair, and dismantling services

(P-344)
ENGEL & GRAY INC
745 W Betteravia Rd Ste A (93455-1298)
P.O. Box 5020 (93456-5020)
PHONE.................................805 925-2771
Carl W Engel Junior, *Pr*
Robert Engel, *
EMP: 35 **EST:** 1946
SQ FT: 3,000
SALES (est): 4.9MM **Privately Held**
Web: www.engelandgray.com
SIC: **1389** 1623 7389 2875 Construction, repair, and dismantling services; Pipeline construction, nsk; Crane and aerial lift service; Compost

(P-345)
ENGINEERED WELL SVC INTL INC
3120 Standard St (93308-6241)
PHONE.................................866 913-6283
Paul Sturgeon, *CEO*
John E Powell Junior, *Prin*
EMP: 19 **EST:** 2009

SALES (est): 4.08MM **Privately Held**
SIC: **1389** Oil field services, nec

(P-346)
ETHOSENERGY FIELD SERVICES LLC (DH)
10455 Slusher Dr # 12 (90670-3750)
PHONE.................................310 639-3523
Mark Jones, *Pr*
Patricia Lelito, *CFO*
Mike Fieldhouse, *VP Opers*
EMP: 45 **EST:** 1970
SALES (est): 38.2MM
SALES (corp-wide): 5.43B **Privately Held**
Web: www.ethosenergyfs.com
SIC: **1389** 8711 3462 Oil consultants; Industrial engineers; Pump, compressor, and turbine forgings
HQ: Ethosenergy Gts Holdings (Us), Llc
3100 S Sam Houston Pkwy E
Houston TX

(P-347)
FIRST ENERGY SERVICES INC
1031 Carrier Parkway Ave (93308-9670)
P.O. Box 80844 (93380-0844)
PHONE.................................661 387-1972
Richard Chase, *Pr*
Jack Chase, *VP*
Charlotte Maddon, *Treas*
EMP: 20 **EST:** 1996
SQ FT: 7,000
SALES (est): 2.22MM **Privately Held**
SIC: **1389** Oil field services, nec

(P-348)
GRAYSON SERVICE INC
1845 Greeley Rd (93314-9547)
PHONE.................................661 589-5444
Carol A Grayson, *Pr*
Cheryl Grayson, *
EMP: 18 **EST:** 1969
SALES (est): 859.15K **Privately Held**
SIC: **1389** Servicing oil and gas wells

(P-349)
GROUP H ENGINEERING
2030 Vista Ave (91024-1554)
PHONE.................................818 999-0999
Michael Karaiban, *Pt*
Anke Hamalian, *Pt*
EMP: 30 **EST:** 2001
SALES (est): 892.32K **Privately Held**
SIC: **1389** Construction, repair, and dismantling services

(P-350)
HALLIBURTON COMPANY
34722 7th Standard Rd (93314-9435)
PHONE.................................661 393-8111
Dennis Lovett, *Brnch Mgr*
EMP: 51
Web: www.halliburton.com
SIC: **1389** Oil field services, nec
PA: Halliburton Company
3000 N Sam Houston Pkwy E
Houston TX

(P-351)
HAMO CONSTRUCTION
3650 Altura Ave (91214-2463)
PHONE.................................818 415-3334
Hamlet Karamyan, *Owner*
EMP: 47 **EST:** 2013
SALES (est): 525K **Privately Held**
SIC: **1389** Construction, repair, and dismantling services

(P-352)
HILLS WLDG & ENGRG CONTR INC
Also Called: Hwe Mechanical
22038 Stockdale Hwy (93314-8889)
PHONE.................................661 746-5400
Debora M Hill, *VP*
Robert Hill, *Stockholder*
EMP: 92 **EST:** 1999
SALES (est): 9.58MM **Privately Held**
Web: www.hillswelding.com
SIC: **1389** Testing, measuring, surveying, and analysis services

(P-353)
HIRSH INC
Also Called: Better Mens Clothes
860 S Los Angeles St # 900 (90014-3311)
PHONE.................................213 622-9441
EMP: 50
SALES (est): 1.09MM **Privately Held**
SIC: **1389** Lease tanks, oil field: erecting, cleaning, and repairing

(P-354)
HORIZON WELL LOGGING INC
711 Saint Andrews Way (93436-1326)
PHONE.................................805 733-0972
Doug Milham, *Pr*
William Gilmore, *Dir*
James Eastes, *Dir*
▲ **EMP:** 22 **EST:** 1992
SALES (est): 11.08MM **Privately Held**
Web: www.horizon-well-logging.com
SIC: **1389** Oil field services, nec

(P-355)
INSTRUMENT CONTROL SERVICES
Also Called: I C S
6085 King Dr Unit 100 (93003-7679)
PHONE.................................805 642-1999
Michael Leblanc, *Pr*
Joseph Edward Locklear, *
EMP: 45 **EST:** 1994
SQ FT: 6,100
SALES (est): 11.33MM **Privately Held**
Web: www.instrumentcontrol.com
SIC: **1389** 7699 7373 7299 Construction, repair, and dismantling services; Industrial equipment services; Systems integration services; Banquet hall facilities

(P-356)
JERRY MELTON & SONS CNSTR INC
Also Called: Jerry Melton & Sons Cnstr
100 Jamison Ln (93268-4329)
PHONE.................................661 765-5546
Jerry W Melton, *Pr*
Judy Melton, *
Steven Melton, *
Karen Melton, *
EMP: 85 **EST:** 1971
SALES (est): 9.3MM **Privately Held**
SIC: **1389** Oil and gas wells: building, repairing and dismantling

(P-357)
JOHN M PHILLIPS LLC
Also Called: John M Phillips Oil Field Eqp
2800 Gibson St (93308-6106)
PHONE.................................661 327-3118
Melody Shamaker, *Off Mgr*
EMP: 35
SALES (corp-wide): 8.38MM **Privately Held**
Web: www.johnmphillips.com

SIC: **1389** Oil field services, nec
PA: John M. Phillips, Llc
2755 Dawson Ave
Signal Hill CA
562 595-7363

(P-358)
K C RESTORATION CO INC
1514 W 130th St (90249-2104)
PHONE.................................310 280-0597
Carolyn Lehne Macleod, *Pr*
Steve Lehne, *
Katherine Cecilia Lehne, *
EMP: 35 **EST:** 1991
SALES (est): 4.57MM **Privately Held**
Web: www.kcrestorationinc.com
SIC: **1389** 2431 1752 1741 Construction, repair, and dismantling services; Windows and window parts and trim, wood; Wood floor installation and refinishing; Masonry and other stonework

(P-359)
M-I LLC
Also Called: M-I Swaco
4400 Fanucchi Way (93263-9552)
PHONE.................................661 321-5400
EMP: 31
Web: www.slb.com
SIC: **1389** Mud service, oil field drilling
HQ: M-I L.L.C.
5950 N Course Dr
Houston TX
281 561-1300

(P-360)
MARK SHEFFIELD CNSTR INC
Also Called: Sheffield Construction
9105 Langley Rd (93312-2156)
PHONE.................................661 589-8520
Mark Sheffield, *Pr*
Steven Sheffield, *VP*
Linda Sheffield, *Treas*
EMP: 18 **EST:** 1977
SALES (est): 1.98MM **Privately Held**
SIC: **1389** 7389 Oil field services, nec; Crane and aerial lift service

(P-361)
MDM SOLUTIONS LLC
575 Anton Blvd Ste 300 (92626-7169)
PHONE.................................800 669-6361
Michael Flower, *Managing Member*
Michael Bryant, *
Cynthia Williams, *
Doug Sipe, *
EMP: 310 **EST:** 2015
SALES (est): 16.56MM **Privately Held**
Web: www.mdmcorp.com
SIC: **1389** Oil and gas wells: building, repairing and dismantling

(P-362)
MEC-CCC S ALL N ONE
13800 Parkcenter Ln Apt 304 (92782)
PHONE.................................909 529-0013
Emma Jones, *Pr*
EMP: 50 **EST:** 2016
SALES (est): 800.52K **Privately Held**
SIC: **1389** 1799 Construction, repair, and dismantling services; Welding on site

(P-363)
MMI SERVICES INC
4042 Patton Way (93308-5030)
PHONE.................................661 589-9366
Steve Mcgowan, *CEO*
Steve Mcgowan, *Pr*
Mel Mcgowan, *CEO*
Eric Olson, *

EMP: 250 **EST:** 1985
SQ FT: 4,500
SALES (est): 39.65MM **Privately Held**
Web: www.mmi-services.com
SIC: 1389 Oil field services, nec

(P-364)
MTS SOLUTIONS LLC
7131 Charity Ave (93308-5870)
PHONE.................................661 589-5804
EMP: 36
SALES (est): 1.15MM **Privately Held**
SIC: 1389 Oil and gas field services, nec

(P-365)
NABORS WELL SERVICES CO
19431 S Santa Fe Ave (90221-5912)
PHONE.................................310 639-7074
EMP: 73
Web: www.nabors.com
SIC: 1389 Oil field services, nec
HQ: Nabors Well Services Co.
515 W Greens Rd Ste 1000
Houston TX
281 874-0035

(P-366)
NABORS WELL SERVICES CO
2567 N Ventura Ave # C (93001-1201)
PHONE.................................805 648-2731
Paul Smith, *Mgr*
EMP: 94
Web: www.nabors.com
SIC: 1389 Oil field services, nec
HQ: Nabors Well Services Co.
515 W Greens Rd Ste 1000
Houston TX
281 874-0035

(P-367)
NABORS WELL SERVICES CO
1025 Earthmover Ct (93314-9529)
PHONE.................................661 588-6140
Tom Jaquez, *Mgr*
EMP: 152
Web: www.nabors.com
SIC: 1389 Oil field services, nec
HQ: Nabors Well Services Co.
515 W Greens Rd Ste 1000
Houston TX
281 874-0035

(P-368)
NABORS WELL SERVICES CO
7515 Rosedale Hwy (93308-5727)
PHONE.................................661 589-3970
Alan Pounds, *Mgr*
EMP: 247
Web: www.nabors.com
SIC: 1389 1382 Servicing oil and gas wells;
Oil and gas exploration services
HQ: Nabors Well Services Co.
515 W Greens Rd Ste 1000
Houston TX
281 874-0035

(P-369)
NABORS WELL SERVICES CO
1954 James Rd (93308-9749)
PHONE.................................661 392-7668
EMP: 210
Web: www.nabors.com
SIC: 1389 Oil field services, nec
HQ: Nabors Well Services Co.
515 W Greens Rd Ste 1000
Houston TX
281 874-0035

(P-370)
OIL WELL SERVICE COMPANY
Also Called: Oil Well Service
1015 Mission Rock Rd (93060-9730)
PHONE.................................805 525-2103
Harvey Himinell, *Mgr*
EMP: 60
SALES (corp-wide): 35.06MM **Privately Held**
Web: www.ows1.com
SIC: 1389 Oil field services, nec
PA: Oil Well Service Company
1241 E Burnett St
Signal Hill CA
562 612-0600

(P-371)
OIL WELL SERVICE COMPANY
10255 Enos Ln (93263-9572)
PHONE.................................661 746-4809
Rick Hobbs, *Off Mgr*
EMP: 60
SALES (corp-wide): 35.06MM **Privately Held**
Web: www.ows1.com
SIC: 1389 Swabbing wells
PA: Oil Well Service Company
1241 E Burnett St
Signal Hill CA
562 612-0600

(P-372)
OIL WELL SERVICE COMPANY (PA)
1241 E Burnett St (90755-3594)
PHONE.................................562 612-0600
Jack Frost, *Pr*
Matt Hensley, *
Connie Laws, *
Richard Laws, *
EMP: 105 **EST:** 1940
SALES (est): 35.06MM
SALES (corp-wide): 35.06MM **Privately Held**
Web: www.ows1.com
SIC: 1389 Oil field services, nec

(P-373)
ONE STRUCTURAL INC
19326 Ventura Blvd Ste 200 (91356-3016)
PHONE.................................626 252-0778
David Tashroudian, *Pr*
EMP: 35 **EST:** 2015
SALES (est): 2.13MM **Privately Held**
SIC: 1389 Construction, repair, and
dismantling services

(P-374)
PACIFIC PERFORATING INC
25090 Highway 33 (93224-9777)
PHONE.................................661 768-9224
Troy Ducharme, *Pr*
Perry Parker, *
▼ **EMP:** 26 **EST:** 1969
SQ FT: 4,000
SALES (est): 4.91MM **Privately Held**
Web: www.variperm.com
SIC: 1389 Oil field services, nec

(P-375)
PACIFIC PETROLEUM CALIFORNIA INC
Also Called: Oil Field Services
1615 E Betteravia Rd Ste A (93454-9000)
P.O. Box 2646 (93457-2646)
PHONE.................................805 925-1947
EMP: 285 **EST:** 2005
SALES (est): 46.86MM **Privately Held**
Web: www.pacpetrol.com

SIC: 1389 7353 Lease tanks, oil field:
erecting, cleaning, and repairing; Oil field
equipment, rental or leasing

(P-376)
PACIFIC PROCESS SYSTEMS INC (PA)
7401 Rosedale Hwy (93308-5736)
PHONE.................................661 321-9681
▼ **EMP:** 90 **EST:** 1995
SQ FT: 7,000
SALES (est): 35.14MM **Privately Held**
Web: www.pps-equipment.com
SIC: 1389 7353 5082 Testing, measuring,
surveying, and analysis services; Oil field
equipment, rental or leasing; Oil field
equipment

(P-377)
PALMER TANK & CONSTRUCTION INC
2464 S Union Ave (93307-5007)
PHONE.................................661 834-1110
Jerry Palmer, *Pr*
EMP: 32 **EST:** 1971
SQ FT: 1,200
SALES (est): 4.58MM **Privately Held**
Web: www.palmertanks.com
SIC: 1389 5731 Oil and gas wells: building,
repairing and dismantling; Antennas

(P-378)
PC MECHANICAL INC
2803 Industrial Pkwy (93455-1811)
PHONE.................................805 925-2888
Lew Parker, *Pr*
Mitch Caron, *
Mary Parker, *
Brandon Burginger, *
EMP: 50 **EST:** 1991
SQ FT: 67,000
SALES (est): 10.07MM **Privately Held**
Web: www.pcmechanical.com
SIC: 1389 Oil field services, nec

(P-379)
PRODUCTION DATA INC
1210 33rd St (93301-2124)
P.O. Box 3266 (93385-3266)
PHONE.................................661 327-4776
Gerald Tonnelli, *Pr*
EMP: 25 **EST:** 1972
SQ FT: 1,800
SALES (est): 10.25MM **Privately Held**
Web: www.productiondatainc.com
SIC: 1389 Oil field services, nec

(P-380)
PROS INCORPORATED
3400 Patton Way (93308-5722)
P.O. Box 20996 (93390-0996)
PHONE.................................661 589-5400
Robert Lewis, *Pr*
EMP: 58 **EST:** 2007
SALES (est): 23.43MM **Privately Held**
Web: www.proswelltesting.com
SIC: 1389 Oil field services, nec

(P-381)
PSC INDUSTRIAL OUTSOURCING LP
Also Called: Hydrochempsc
200 Old Yard Dr (93307-4268)
PHONE.................................661 833-9991
EMP: 61
SALES (corp-wide): 5.17B **Publicly Held**
Web: www.hpc-industrial.com
SIC: 1389 Oil field services, nec
HQ: Psc Industrial Outsourcing, Lp
900 Georgia Ave

Deer Park TX
713 393-5600

(P-382)
ROBERT HEELY CONSTRUCTION LP (PA)
Also Called: Robert Heely Construction
5401 Woodmere Dr (93313-2777)
PHONE.................................661 617-1400
Robert Heely, *Ch*
Craig Bonna, *Pr*
EMP: 20 **EST:** 1974
SQ FT: 7,000
SALES (est): 53.09MM
SALES (corp-wide): 53.09MM **Privately Held**
Web: www.rhcteam.com
SIC: 1389 Oil field services, nec

(P-383)
RPC INC
1100 N Magnolia Ave Ste H (92020-1953)
PHONE.................................619 334-6244
Roger Ramos, *Prin*
EMP: 18 **EST:** 2008
SALES (est): 3.79MM **Privately Held**
Web: www.usrpc.com
SIC: 1389 Oil field services, nec

(P-384)
SCHLUMBERGER TECHNOLOGY CORP
Also Called: Dowell Schlumberger
6120 Snow Rd (93308-9531)
P.O. Box 81437 (93380-1437)
PHONE.................................661 864-4721
FAX: 661 393-6525
EMP: 100
SIC: 1389 1382 Oil field services, nec; Oil
and gas exploration services
HQ: Schlumberger Technology Corp
100 Gillingham Ln
Sugar Land TX
281 285-8500

(P-385)
THETA OILFIELD SERVICES INC
5201 California Ave Ste 370 (93309-1674)
PHONE.................................661 633-2792
Dan A Newman, *Pr*
EMP: 44 **EST:** 2007
SALES (est): 6.93MM
SALES (corp-wide): 3.81B **Publicly Held**
Web: www.thetaportal.com
SIC: 1389 Oil field services, nec
PA: Championx Corporation
2445 Tech Frest Blvd Bldg
The Woodlands TX
281 403-5772

(P-386)
TIGER CASED HOLE SERVICES INC
Also Called: Tiger Case Hole Services
2828 Junipero Ave (90755-2112)
PHONE.................................562 426-4044
Minnie P Baxter, *Sec*
Joseph S Baxter, *Treas*
▲ **EMP:** 43 **EST:** 1994
SQ FT: 6,000
SALES (est): 6.44MM
SALES (corp-wide): 2.65B **Publicly Held**
SIC: 1389 Oil field services, nec
HQ: Nextier Oilfield Solutions Llc
3990 Rogerdale Rd
Houston TX
713 325-6000

▲ = Import ▼ = Export
◆ = Import/Export

(P-387)
TITAN OILFIELD SERVICES INC
Also Called: Titan Oilfield Services
21535 Kratzmeyer Rd (93314-9482)
PHONE..............................661 861-1630
Terry Hibbitts, *CEO*
Terry Hibbitts, *Pr*
Tim Barman, *
Tony Palacpac, *
EMP: 68 **EST:** 2011
SALES (est): 9.95MM **Privately Held**
Web: www.vinemarketing.com
SIC: 1389 Oil field services, nec

(P-388)
TOTAL-WESTERN INC (HQ)
8049 Somerset Blvd (90723-4396)
PHONE..............................562 220-1450
Paul F Conrad, *CEO*
Earl Grebing, *
Mary A Pool, *
Jerry Balos, *
Payman Farrokhyar, *
EMP: 49 **EST:** 1972
SQ FT: 13,000
SALES (est): 78.84MM
SALES (corp-wide): 489.53MM **Privately Held**
Web: www.total-western.com
SIC: 1389 Oil field services, nec
PA: Bragg Investment Company, Inc.
6251 N Paramount Blvd
Long Beach CA
562 984-2400

(P-389)
TRUITT OILFIELD MAINT CORP
1051 James Rd (93308-9753)
P.O. Box 5066 (93388-5066)
PHONE..............................661 871-4099
Kimberly Sue New, *Pr*
Steve New, *
EMP: 300 **EST:** 1978
SQ FT: 3,000
SALES (est): 23.72MM **Privately Held**
Web: www.truittcorp.com
SIC: 1389 Oil field services, nec

(P-390)
TRYAD SERVICE CORPORATION
5900 E Lerdo Hwy (93263-4023)
PHONE..............................661 391-1524
James Varner, *Pr*
Danny Seely, *
▲ **EMP:** 90 **EST:** 1933
SALES (est): 9.18MM **Privately Held**
Web: www.jdrush.com
SIC: 1389 Oil and gas wells: building,
repairing and dismantling

(P-391)
TUBOSCOPE PIPELINE SVCS INC
Also Called: Tuboscope
3003 Fairhaven Dr Ste B (93308-6114)
PHONE..............................661 328-5500
Scott Sprague, *Mgr*
EMP: 19
SALES (corp-wide): 7.24B **Publicly Held**
SIC: 1389 Pipe testing, oil field service
HQ: Tuboscope Pipeline Services Inc.
2835 Holmes Rd
Houston TX

(P-392)
U S WEATHERFORD L P
2815 Fruitvale Ave (93308-5907)
PHONE..............................661 589-9483
Rick Benton, *Brnch Mgr*
EMP: 226

Web: www.weatherford.com
SIC: 1389 Oil field services, nec
HQ: U S Weatherford L P
179 Weatherford Dr
Schriever LA
985 493-6100

(P-393)
VANDERRA RESOURCES LLC
1801 Century Park E Ste 2400
(90067-2326)
PHONE..............................817 439-2220
EMP: 500
SIC: 1389 Oil field services, nec

(P-394)
VAQUERO ENERGY INC
4700 Stockdale Hwy Ste 120 (93309-2654)
P.O. Box 13550 (93389-3550)
PHONE..............................661 616-0600
Kenneth H Hunter, *CEO*
Seth Hunter, *VP*
Cary Nikkel, *Sec*
EMP: 21 **EST:** 2000
SALES (est): 10.33MM **Privately Held**
Web: www.vaqueroenergy.com
SIC: 1389 Testing, measuring, surveying,
and analysis services

(P-395)
WEATHERFORD INTERNATIONAL LLC
201 Hallock Dr (93060-9647)
P.O. Box 31 (93061-0031)
PHONE..............................805 933-0242
Larry Brixey, *Mgr*
EMP: 18
Web: www.weatherford.com
SIC: 1389 Oil field services, nec
HQ: Weatherford International, Llc
2000 Saint James Pl
Houston TX
713 693-4000

(P-396)
WELBILT INC ✪
3835 E Thousand Oaks Blvd Unit 315
(91362)
PHONE..............................310 339-1555
Ben Hunter, *CEO*
EMP: 25 **EST:** 2022
SALES (est): 502.86K **Privately Held**
Web: www.welbiltinc.us
SIC: 1389 Construction, repair, and
dismantling services

1411 Dimension Stone

(P-397)
CHANDLER AGGREGATES INC (PA)
24867 Maitri Rd (92883-5136)
P.O. Box 78450 (92877-0148)
PHONE..............................951 277-1341
Larry Werner, *Pr*
EMP: 20 **EST:** 1994
SALES (est): 8.61MM **Privately Held**
Web: www.wernercorp.net
SIC: 1411 1422 Dimension stone; Crushed
and broken limestone

1422 Crushed And Broken Limestone

(P-398)
AZUSA ROCK LLC
3605 Dehesa Rd (92019-2903)

PHONE..............................619 440-2363
Tom Nelson, *Mgr*
EMP: 44
SIC: 1422 Crushed and broken limestone
HQ: Azusa Rock, Llc
3901 Fish Canyon Rd
Azusa CA
858 530-9444

(P-399)
CALMAT CO
16101 Hwy 156 (93252)
P.O. Box 22800 (93390-2800)
PHONE..............................661 858-2673
Angela Bailey, *Mgr*
EMP: 152
Web: www.vulcanmaterials.com
SIC: 1422 Crushed and broken limestone
HQ: Calmat Co.
500 N Brand Blvd Ste 500 # 500
Glendale CA
818 553-8821

1423 Crushed And Broken Granite

(P-400)
JUNIPER ROCK CORPORATION
Also Called: ARB
26000 Commercentre Dr (92630-8816)
PHONE..............................949 500-1797
Eric Amlee, *Genl Mgr*
EMP: 18 **EST:** 2009
SALES (est): 4.75MM **Publicly Held**
SIC: 1423 Crushed and broken granite
PA: Primoris Services Corporation
2300 N Field St Ste 1900
Dallas TX

1429 Crushed And Broken Stone, Nec

(P-401)
NORBERG CRUSHING INC
592 Tyrone St (92020-2233)
PHONE..............................619 390-4200
Stephen Norberg, *Pr*
Dana Farrell, *VP*
Heidi Spicer, *CFO*
EMP: 18 **EST:** 2001
SQ FT: 3,500
SALES (est): 1.44MM **Privately Held**
SIC: 1429 Igneus rock, crushed and broken-
quarrying

(P-402)
PAUL HUBBS CONSTRUCTION CO INC (PA)
542 W C St (92324-2140)
PHONE..............................951 360-3990
Jay P Hubbs, *Pr*
John L Hubbs, *
Lucile M Hubbs, *
Pat Hubbs, *
EMP: 18 **EST:** 1961
SQ FT: 4,000
SALES (est): 2.36MM
SALES (corp-wide): 2.36MM **Privately Held**
SIC: 1429 Riprap quarrying

(P-403)
TRIANGLE ROCK PRODUCTS LLC
500 N Brand Blvd Ste 500 (91203-3319)
PHONE..............................818 553-8820
Stanley G Bass, *Pr*

EMP: 272 **EST:** 1978
SQ FT: 20,000
SALES (est): 4.63MM **Publicly Held**
SIC: 1429 1442 2951 3273 Igneus rock,
crushed and broken-quarrying;
Construction sand and gravel; Asphalt
paving mixtures and blocks; Ready-mixed
concrete
HQ: Calmat Co.
500 N Brand Blvd Ste 500 # 500
Glendale CA
818 553-8821

1442 Construction Sand And Gravel

(P-404)
ALAMEDA CONSTRUCTION SVCS INC
2528 E 125th St (90222-1502)
PHONE..............................310 635-3277
Kevin Ramsey, *CEO*
Tracey Watson, *VP*
EMP: 20 **EST:** 1992
SQ FT: 8,000
SALES (est): 6.09MM **Privately Held**
Web: www.alamedaconstruction.com
SIC: 1442 Construction sand and gravel

(P-405)
ENNISS INC
12535 Vigilante Rd (92040-1167)
P.O. Box 1769 (92040-0917)
PHONE..............................619 561-1101
David Von Bhren, *Pr*
D Lois Miller, *
EMP: 40 **EST:** 2002
SQ FT: 4,700
SALES (est): 9.43MM **Privately Held**
Web: www.ennissinc.com
SIC: 1442 4212 3271 4953 Sand mining;
Local trucking, without storage;
Architectural concrete: block, split, fluted,
screen, etc.; Recycling, waste materials

(P-406)
GAIL MATERIALS INC
10060 Dawson Canyon Rd (92883-2112)
PHONE..............................951 667-6106
Nick Leinen, *CEO*
Mitch Leinen, *
▲ **EMP:** 26 **EST:** 1987
SQ FT: 5,000
SALES (est): 8.43MM **Privately Held**
Web: www.gailmaterials.net
SIC: 1442 Construction sand and gravel

(P-407)
NORTH COUNTY SAND AND GRAV INC
26227 Sherman Rd (92585-9223)
PHONE..............................951 928-2881
M J La Paglia Iii, *Pr*
Michael J La Paglia Iii, *Pr*
Tracy Paglia, *CFO*
EMP: 18 **EST:** 1985
SALES (est): 2.49MM **Privately Held**
Web:
www.northcountysandandgravel.com
SIC: 1442 5032 Construction sand and
gravel; Sand, construction

(P-408)
PTI SAND & GRAVEL INC
14925 River Rd (92880-8935)
P.O. Box 6019 (92860-8034)
PHONE..............................951 272-0140
Michael Ellena, *Pr*

Mark Horner, *
EMP: 28 **EST:** 1948
SALES (est): 4.15MM **Privately Held**
Web: www.ptisag.com
SIC: 1442 Construction sand and gravel

1446 Industrial Sand

(P-409)
PIONEER SANDS LLC
31302 Ortega Hwy (92675)
PHONE................................949 728-0171
Mike Miclette, *Brnch Mgr*
EMP: 31
SALES (corp-wide): 24.29B **Publicly Held**
SIC: 1446 Silica sand mining
HQ: Pioneer Sands Llc
     777 Hidden Rdg
     Irving TX
     972 444-9001

(P-410)
PIONEER SANDS LLC
9952 Enos Lane (93314)
PHONE................................661 746-5789
Donna Bartlett, *Brnch Mgr*
EMP: 28
SALES (corp-wide): 24.29B **Publicly Held**
Web: www.pwgillibrand.com
SIC: 1446 Silica mining
HQ: Pioneer Sands Llc
     777 Hidden Rdg
     Irving TX
     972 444-9001

(P-411)
PW GILLIBRAND CO INC (PA)
4537 Ish Dr (93063-7667)
P.O. Box 1019 (93062-1019)
PHONE................................805 526-2195
Celine Gillibrand, *CEO*
Richard Valencia, *
Jim Costello, *
EMP: 48 **EST:** 1957
SQ FT: 11,000
SALES (est): 25.29MM
SALES (corp-wide): 25.29MM **Privately Held**
Web: www.pwgillibrand.com
SIC: 1446 Grinding sand mining

1455 Kaolin And Ball Clay

(P-412)
CP KELCO US INC
Also Called: CP Kelco
2025 Harbor Dr (92113-2214)
PHONE................................619 595-5000
Andrew Currie, *Brnch Mgr*
EMP: 20
SALES (corp-wide): 1.24B **Privately Held**
Web: www.cpkelco.com
SIC: 1455 Kaolin mining
HQ: Cp Kelco U.S., Inc.
     3100 Cumberland Blvd Se # 600
     Atlanta GA
     678 247-7300

1474 Potash, Soda, And Borate Minerals

(P-413)
5E BORON AMERICAS LLC
27555 Hector Rd (92365-8905)
PHONE................................442 292-2120
Michael Schlumpberger, *CEO*
EMP: 38

Web: www.5eadvancedmaterials.com
SIC: 1474 Borate compounds (natural) mining
HQ: 5e Boron Americas, Llc
     9329 Mariposa Rd Ste 210
     Hesperia CA
     419 371-3331

1481 Nonmetallic Mineral Services

(P-414)
MP MINE OPERATIONS LLC
67750 Bailey Rd (92366)
PHONE................................702 277-0848
James H Litinsky, *CEO*
Michael Rosethal, *
EMP: 108 **EST:** 2017
SALES (est): 47.09MM
SALES (corp-wide): 527.51MM **Publicly Held**
SIC: 1481 1099 Mine exploration, nonmetallic minerals; Rare-earth ores mining
PA: Mp Materials Corp.
     1700 S Pavilion Center Dr # 800
     Las Vegas NV
     702 844-6111

1499 Miscellaneous Nonmetallic Mining

(P-415)
ATLAS LITHIUM CORPORATION
433 N Camden Dr Ste 810 (90210-4412)
PHONE................................213 590-2500
Marc Fogassa, *Ch Bd*
Gustavo Pereira De Aguiar, *CAO*
Brian W Bernier, *IR*
Joel De Paiva Monteiro, *Operations*
Volodymyr Myadzel Senior, *Geology Vice President*
EMP: 33 **EST:** 2012
SALES (est): 6.76K **Privately Held**
SIC: 1499 Diamond mining, industrial

(P-416)
DICAPERL CORPORATION (DH)
Also Called: Grefco Dicaperl
23705 Crenshaw Blvd # 10 (90505-5236)
PHONE................................610 667-6640
Ray Perelman, *CEO*
Glenn Jones, *
Mike Cull, *
Barry Katz, *
▼ **EMP:** 90 **EST:** 1992
SQ FT: 5,000
SALES (est): 20.49MM **Privately Held**
Web: www.dicalite.com
SIC: 1499 3677 Perlite mining; Filtration devices, electronic
HQ: Grefco Minerals Inc.
     1 Bala Ave Ste 310
     Bala Cynwyd PA
     610 660-8820

(P-417)
IMERYS MINERALS CALIFORNIA INC (HQ)
2500 San Miguelito Rd (93436-9743)
P.O. Box 519 (93438-0519)
PHONE................................805 736-1221
Douglas A Smith, *Pr*
John Oskam, *
John Leichty, *
◆ **EMP:** 67 **EST:** 1991
SQ FT: 11,600
SALES (est): 276.98MM

SALES (corp-wide): 276.98MM **Privately Held**
Web: www.imerys.com
SIC: 1499 3295 Diatomaceous earth mining; Minerals, ground or treated
PA: Imerys Filtration Minerals, Inc.
     2500 San Miguelito Rd
     Lompoc CA
     805 736-1221

1521 Single-family Housing Construction

(P-418)
1ST CENTURY BUILDERS INC
5737 Kanan Rd (91301-1601)
PHONE................................818 254-7183
Colin Pratt, *CEO*
EMP: 18 **EST:** 2017
SALES (est): 2.37MM **Privately Held**
SIC: 1521 1389 New construction, single-family houses; Construction, repair, and dismantling services

(P-419)
A CLARK/MCCARTHY JOINT VENTURE
18201 Von Karman Ave # 800 (92612-1000)
PHONE................................714 429-9779
EMP: 1125
SIC: 1521 Single-family housing construction

(P-420)
APTIM FEDERAL SERVICES LLC
1230 Columbia St Ste 1200 (92101-8517)
PHONE................................619 239-1690
Eric Malcolm, *Brnch Mgr*
EMP: 538
SALES (corp-wide): 2.39B **Privately Held**
Web: www.aptim.com
SIC: 1521 Single-family housing construction
HQ: Aptim Federal Services, Llc
     1200 Brickyard Ln Ste 202
     Baton Rouge LA
     225 932-2500

(P-421)
AZ CONSTRUCTION INC (PA)
Also Called: Ace Fence Company
727 Glendora Ave (91744-4014)
PHONE................................626 333-0727
Amy Tsui, *Pr*
America Tang, *VP*
EMP: 114 **EST:** 2013
SALES (est): 11.65MM
SALES (corp-wide): 11.65MM **Privately Held**
Web: www.acefencecompany.com
SIC: 1521 Single-family housing construction

(P-422)
BROOKFELD STHLAND HOLDINGS LLC
Also Called: Brookfield Residential
3200 Park Center Dr Ste 1000 (92626-7163)
PHONE................................714 427-6868
EMP: 160 **EST:** 1996
SALES (est): 43.89MM
SALES (corp-wide): 69.06B **Privately Held**
SIC: 1521 Single-family housing construction
HQ: Brookfield Homes (Us) Llc
     3201 Jermantown Rd
     Fairfax VA
     703 270-1400

(P-423)
BROWNCO CONSTRUCTION CO INC
Also Called: Brownco Construction
1000 E Katella Ave (92805-6617)
PHONE................................714 935-9600
Scot Alan Brown, *Pr*
Jeff Radtke, *
EMP: 87 **EST:** 1999
SQ FT: 15,000
SALES (est): 24.04MM **Privately Held**
Web: www.browncoinc.com
SIC: 1521 Single-family housing construction

(P-424)
CALVILLO CONSTRUCTION CORP
Also Called: Tiling and Stone Counter Tops
1133 Brooks St Ste C (91762-3662)
PHONE................................310 985-3911
Luciano Calvillo, *Owner*
Luciano Calvillo, *Pr*
EMP: 26 **EST:** 2011
SALES (est): 1.56MM **Privately Held**
SIC: 1521 1522 1411 1743 Single-family housing construction; Hotel/motel and multi-family home construction; Limestone and marble dimension stone; Tile installation, ceramic

(P-425)
CHAMPION HOME BUILDERS INC
299 N Smith Ave (92878-3241)
PHONE................................951 256-4617
EMP: 79
SALES (corp-wide): 2.61B **Publicly Held**
Web: www.championhomes.com
SIC: 1521 2451 New construction, single-family houses; Mobile homes, except recreational
HQ: Champion Home Builders, Inc.
     755 W Big Beavr Rd # 1000
     Troy MI
     248 614-8200

(P-426)
COASTLINE CNSTR & AWNG CO INC
5742 Research Dr (92649-1617)
PHONE................................714 891-9798
John W Almquist, *Pr*
EMP: 100 **EST:** 1980
SQ FT: 1,600
SALES (est): 4.88MM **Privately Held**
Web: www.coastlineconawn.com
SIC: 1521 Mobile home repair, on site

(P-427)
COUNTY OF RIVERSIDE
Facilities Mgmt
3450 14th St (92501-3812)
PHONE................................951 955-4800
Michael Sylvester, *Dir*
EMP: 100
SALES (corp-wide): 4.58B **Privately Held**
Web: www.countyofriverside.us
SIC: 1521 9532 7349 Single-family housing construction; Urban and community development; Building maintenance services, nec
PA: County Of Riverside
     4080 Lemon St Fl 11
     Riverside CA
     951 955-1110

▲ = Import ▼ = Export
◆ = Import/Export

(P-428)

DENNIS ALLEN ASSOCIATES (PA)
Also Called: Allen Associates
201 N Milpas St (93103-3201)
PHONE..............................805 884-8777
Dennis W Allen, *Pr*
Ian Cronshaw, *
Jennifer Cushnie, *
EMP: 95 EST: 1983
SALES (est): 40.76MM **Privately Held**
Web: www.buildallen.com
SIC: 1521 1542 General remodeling, single-family houses; Commercial and office buildings, renovation and repair

(P-429)

DISASTER RSTRTION PRFSSNALS IN
Also Called: Service Master By ARS
1517 W 130th St (90249-2103)
PHONE..............................310 301-8030
Ahmad Elzarou, *CEO*
EMP: 80 EST: 2003
SALES (est): 8.91MM **Privately Held**
SIC: 1521 7299 1542 Repairing fire damage, single-family houses; Home improvement and renovation contractor agency; Commercial and office building contractors

(P-430)

EBC INC (PA)
Also Called: Ellis Building Contractors
219 Manhattan Beach Blvd Ste 3 (90266-5324)
PHONE..............................310 753-6407
Brad Ellis, *Pr*
Patricia Ellis, *
EMP: 95 EST: 1980
SALES (est): 4.89MM
SALES (corp-wide): 4.89MM **Privately Held**
SIC: 1521 1542 New construction, single-family houses; Commercial and office building, new construction

(P-431)

ELEVEN WESTERN BUILDERS INC (PA)
2862 Executive Pl (92029-1524)
PHONE..............................760 796-6346
Rick W Backus, *CEO*
Richard Huey, *
EMP: 82 EST: 1983
SQ FT: 20,000
SALES (est): 49.34MM
SALES (corp-wide): 49.34MM **Privately Held**
Web: www.ewbinc.com
SIC: 1521 New construction, single-family houses

(P-432)

EXCEL CONTRACTORS INC
Also Called: Progression Drywall
348 E Avenue K8 Ste B (93535-4514)
PHONE..............................661 942-6944
John Rockey, *Pr*
Rose Rockey, *
EMP: 100 EST: 1987
SALES (est): 18.65MM **Privately Held**
SIC: 1521 1742 1542 Single-family home remodeling, additions, and repairs; Drywall; Commercial and office building, new construction

(P-433)

GENERATION CONSTRUCTION INC

15650 El Prado Rd (91710-9108)
P.O. Box 991 (91708-0991)
PHONE..............................909 923-2077
Antwan De Paul, *Pr*
EMP: 150 EST: 1986
SALES (est): 24.43MM **Privately Held**
Web: www.gconstruction.com
SIC: 1521 Single-family housing construction

(P-434)

GRAY CONSTRUCTION INC
421 E Cerritos Ave (92805-6320)
PHONE..............................714 491-1315
Bob Moore, *Brnch Mgr*
EMP: 182
SALES (corp-wide): 623.17MM **Privately Held**
Web: www.gray.com
SIC: 1521 Single-family housing construction
HQ: Gray Construction, Inc.
10 Quality St
Lexington KY
859 281-5000

(P-435)

INNOVATIVE COMMUNITIES INC (PA)
1282 Pacific Oaks Pl (92029-2917)
PHONE..............................760 690-5225
Thomas P Dobron, *Pr*
EMP: 93 EST: 1990
SQ FT: 4,698
SALES (est): 14.06MM
SALES (corp-wide): 14.06MM **Privately Held**
Web: www.innovative-resort.com
SIC: 1521 Single-family housing construction

(P-436)

JAMES ALLISON ESTATES & HOMES
1902 Wright Pl (92008-6583)
PHONE..............................866 463-5780
EMP: 175 EST: 2008
SALES (est): 8.27MM **Privately Held**
SIC: 1521 New construction, single-family houses

(P-437)

JF SHEA CONSTRUCTION INC (HQ)
Also Called: Shea Homes For Active Adults
655 Brea Canyon Rd (91789-3078)
P.O. Box 489 (91788-0489)
PHONE..............................909 594-9500
▲ EMP: 200 EST: 1958
SALES (est): 516.43MM
SALES (corp-wide): 2.1B **Privately Held**
Web: www.jfshea.com
SIC: 1521 1622 6512 New construction, single-family houses; Tunnel construction; Commercial and industrial building operation
PA: J. F. Shea Co., Inc.
655 Brea Canyon Rd
Walnut CA
909 594-9500

(P-438)

JMH ENGINEERING AND CNSTR
2457 Brayton Ave (90755-3508)
PHONE..............................562 317-1700
EMP: 80
SALES (corp-wide): 9.86MM **Privately Held**
Web: www.jmheandc.com
SIC: 1521 Single-family housing construction
PA: Jmh Engineering And Construction
3291 Wendy Way

Los Alamitos CA
562 547-8270

(P-439)

KATERRA
1950 W Corporate Way (92801-5373)
PHONE..............................720 449-3909
EMP: 92 EST: 2019
SALES (est): 1.21MM **Privately Held**
SIC: 1521 Single-family housing construction

(P-440)

KATERRA CONSTRUCTION LLC
1950 W Corporate Way (92801-5373)
PHONE..............................720 449-3909
EMP: 728
SALES (corp-wide): 1.13B **Privately Held**
Web: www.katerra.com
SIC: 1521 Single-family housing construction
HQ: Katerra Construction Llc
2494 Sand Hill Rd Ste 100
Menlo Park CA
650 422-3572

(P-441)

KB HOME GRATER LOS ANGELES INC (HQ)
10990 Wilshire Blvd Ste 700 (90024-3913)
PHONE..............................310 231-4000
Jeffrey Mezge, *Pr*
EMP: 90 EST: 1957
SQ FT: 40,000
SALES (est): 64.08MM
SALES (corp-wide): 6.9B **Publicly Held**
Web: www.kbhome.com
SIC: 1521 1522 Single-family home remodeling, additions, and repairs; Multi-family dwelling construction, nec
PA: Kb Home
10990 Wilshire Blvd Fl 7
Los Angeles CA
310 231-4000

(P-442)

KB HOME GRATER LOS ANGELES INC
36310 Inland Valley Dr (92595-7595)
PHONE..............................951 691-5300
George Brenner, *Mgr*
EMP: 164
SALES (corp-wide): 6.9B **Publicly Held**
Web: www.kbhome.com
SIC: 1521 1522 Single-family home remodeling, additions, and repairs; Multi-family dwelling construction, nec
HQ: Kb Home Greater Los Angeles Inc.
10990 Wilshire Blvd # 700
Los Angeles CA
310 231-4000

(P-443)

KOTA CONSTRUCTION LLC
1200 Lawrence Dr Ste 180 (91320-1316)
PHONE..............................855 800-5682
EMP: 98 EST: 2020
SALES (est): 1.25MM **Privately Held**
SIC: 1521 Single-family housing construction

(P-444)

LARGO CONCRETE INC
591 Camino De La Reina Ste 620 (92108)
PHONE..............................619 356-2142
EMP: 219
Web: www.largoconcrete.com
SIC: 1521 Single-family housing construction
PA: Largo Concrete, Inc.
2741 Walnut Ave Ste 110
Tustin CA

(P-445)

MARTIN BROWN CONSTRUCTION INC
10777 Eureka Rd (91978-1109)
PHONE..............................619 660-0988
Martin Brown, *Pr*
EMP: 17 EST: 1956
SALES (est): 819.38K **Privately Held**
SIC: 1521 1741 2511 Single-family housing construction; Masonry and other stonework; Wood household furniture

(P-446)

MC&A USA LLC
19700 Mariner Ave (90503-1648)
PHONE..............................504 267-8145
EMP: 99 EST: 2019
SALES (est): 2.62MM **Privately Held**
SIC: 1521 Single-family housing construction

(P-447)

MGB CONSTRUCTION INC
91 Commercial Ave (92507-1111)
PHONE..............................951 342-0303
Emily Beach, *Pr*
Emilly Beach, *
EMP: 150 EST: 2001
SALES (est): 18.96MM **Privately Held**
Web: www.mgbconstruction.net
SIC: 1521 Single-family housing construction

(P-448)

NHS WESTERN DIVISION INC
Also Called: Fixd Construction Co.
115 S Palm Ave (91762-3847)
PHONE..............................909 947-9931
Damien Melle, *CEO*
Mia Melle, *
EMP: 89 EST: 2012
SALES (est): 4.91MM **Privately Held**
SIC: 1521 Single-family housing construction

(P-449)

PACIFIC CAST CNSTR WTRPROOFING
390 Oak Ave Ste A (92008-2966)
PHONE..............................760 298-3170
James Schilling, *Pr*
EMP: 23 EST: 2012
SALES (est): 2.33MM **Privately Held**
Web: www.pacificcoastcorporate.com
SIC: 1521 1389 Single-family housing construction; Construction, repair, and dismantling services

(P-450)

PGC CONSTRUCTION INC
Also Called: Architectural Shtmtl Contr
41731 Corporate Center Ct (92562-7084)
PHONE..............................760 549-4121
Philip G Chapman, *CEO*
EMP: 25 EST: 2008
SALES (est): 4MM **Privately Held**
SIC: 1521 3444 1761 Single-family housing construction; Skylights, sheet metal; Architectural sheet metal work

(P-451)

ROMERO GENERAL CNSTR CORP
8320 Nelson Way (92026-5211)
PHONE..............................760 715-0154
Jerusha Finster, *Brnch Mgr*
EMP: 102
Web: www.romerogc.com
SIC: 1521 Single-family housing construction
PA: Romero General Construction Corp.
2150 N Cntre Cy Pkwy Ste

P R O D U C T S & S V C S

Escondido CA

(P-452)
SCENARIO COCKRAM USA INC
16340 Roscoe Blvd (91406-1204)
PHONE..................................407 613-2949
EMP: 207
Web: www.cockramscenario.com
SIC: 1521 Single-family housing construction
HQ: Scenario Cockram Usa Inc.
7600 Kingspointe Pkwy # 101
Orlando FL
818 650-0999

(P-453)
SEARS HOME IMPRV PDTS INC
Also Called: Sears
730 S Orange Ave (91790-2613)
PHONE..................................626 671-1892
EMP: 119
SALES (corp-wide): 4.18B Privately Held
Web: www.searshomeservices.com
SIC: 1521 General remodeling, single-family houses
HQ: Sears Home Improvement Products, Inc.
1024 Florida Central Pkwy
Longwood FL
407 767-0990

(P-454)
SEARS HOME IMPRV PDTS INC
Also Called: Sears
2900 N Bellflower Blvd (90815-1149)
PHONE..................................562 485-4904
EMP: 119
SALES (corp-wide): 4.18B Privately Held
Web: www.searshomeservices.com
SIC: 1521 General remodeling, single-family houses
HQ: Sears Home Improvement Products, Inc.
1024 Florida Central Pkwy
Longwood FL
407 767-0990

(P-455)
SEARS HOME IMPRV PDTS INC
Also Called: Sears
5665 Rosemead Blvd (91780-1804)
PHONE..................................626 988-9134
EMP: 119
SALES (corp-wide): 4.18B Privately Held
Web: www.searshomeservices.com
SIC: 1521 General remodeling, single-family houses
HQ: Sears Home Improvement Products, Inc.
1024 Florida Central Pkwy
Longwood FL
407 767-0990

(P-456)
SEATTLE TNNEL PRTNERS A JINT V
555 Anton Blvd Ste 1000 (92626-7019)
PHONE..................................206 971-8701
▲ EMP: 300 EST: 2010
SALES (est): 15.47MM Privately Held
SIC: 1521 Single-family home remodeling, additions, and repairs

(P-457)
SHEA HOMES AT MONTAGE LLC
655 Brea Canyon Rd (91789-3078)
PHONE..................................909 594-9500
John C Morrissey, Prin
EMP: 143 EST: 2013

SALES (est): 1.67MM
SALES (corp-wide): 2.1B Privately Held
SIC: 1521 Single-family housing construction
HQ: Shea Homes Limited Partnership, A California Limited Partnership
655 Brea Canyon Rd
Walnut CA

(P-458)
SHIMMICK CONSTRUCTION CO INC
16481 Scientific Bldg 2 (92618-4394)
PHONE..................................510 777-5000
Trina Clay, Prin
EMP: 161
SALES (corp-wide): 14.38B Publicly Held
Web: www.shimmick.com
SIC: 1521 Single-family housing construction
HQ: Shimmick Construction Company Incorporated
530 Technology Dr Ste 300
Irvine CA

(P-459)
SILVERADO FRAMING & CNSTR
Also Called: Residential Framer
3091 E La Cadena Dr (92507-2630)
P.O. Box 2941 (92516-2941)
PHONE..................................951 352-1100
Ed Solis, Pr
EMP: 100 EST: 2011
SQ FT: 2,500
SALES (est): 9.68MM Privately Held
Web: www.silveradoframing.com
SIC: 1521 Single-family housing construction

(P-460)
SUPERIOR CONSTRUCTION INC
265 N Joy St (92879-0600)
P.O. Box 1148 (92878-1148)
PHONE..................................951 808-8780
Kenneth Day, Pr
EMP: 100 EST: 1976
SQ FT: 3,000
SALES (est): 9.05MM Privately Held
Web: www.superiorconstruction.com
SIC: 1521 1542 New construction, single-family houses; Commercial and office building, new construction

(P-461)
TRICON AMERICAN HOMES LLC
15771 Red Hill Ave (92780-7333)
P.O. Box 15086 (92735-0086)
PHONE..................................844 874-2661
Kevin Baldridge, Managing Member
EMP: 155 EST: 2012
SALES (est): 35.69MM
SALES (corp-wide): 645.59MM Privately Held
Web: www.triconresidential.com
SIC: 1521 Single-family home remodeling, additions, and repairs
PA: Tricon Residential Inc
7 St Thomas St Suite 801
Toronto ON
416 925-7228

(P-462)
ULTIMATE BUILDERS INC
Also Called: ULTIMATE BUILDERS INC
23679 Calabasas Rd (91302-1502)
PHONE..................................818 481-2627
EMP: 85
SALES (corp-wide): 8.59MM Privately Held
Web: www.repipe1.com
SIC: 1521 New construction, single-family houses
PA: Ultimate Builders, Inc.
19326 Ventura Blvd # 201

Tarzana CA
818 342-2568

(P-463)
ULTIMATE REMOVAL INC
Also Called: Ultimate Demo
2168 Pomona Blvd (91768-3332)
P.O. Box 1220 (91769-1220)
PHONE..................................909 524-0800
EMP: 124 EST: 1995
SQ FT: 9,900
SALES (est): 9.8MM Privately Held
Web: www.ultimateremoval.com
SIC: 1521 Single-family housing construction

(P-464)
US BEST REPAIR SERVICE INC
Also Called: US Best Repairs
1652 Edinger Ave Ste E (92780-6530)
PHONE..................................888 750-2378
EMP: 101 EST: 2008
SALES (est): 20.15MM Privately Held
Web: www.usbestrepairs.com
SIC: 1521 1522 1542 Single-family home remodeling, additions, and repairs; Remodeling, multi-family dwellings; Commercial and office buildings, renovation and repair

(P-465)
WARMINGTON RESIDENTIAL CAL INC
3090 Pullman St (92626-5901)
PHONE..................................714 557-5511
James Warmington Junior, Pr
Matt Tingler, *
Mike Riddlesberger, *
EMP: 150 EST: 2003
SALES (est): 22.87MM Privately Held
Web: www.homesbywarmington.com
SIC: 1521 New construction, single-family houses

(P-466)
WEST COAST ARBORISTS INC
8163 Commercial St (91942-2928)
PHONE..................................858 566-4204
EMP: 116
SALES (corp-wide): 53.7MM Privately Held
Web: www.westcoastarborists.com
SIC: 1521 0783 Single-family home remodeling, additions, and repairs; Ornamental shrub and tree services
PA: West Coast Arborists, Inc.
2200 E Via Burton
Anaheim CA
714 991-1900

1522 Residential Construction, Nec

(P-467)
BERNARDS BUILDERS INC
555 1st St (91340-3051)
PHONE..................................818 898-1521
Doug Bernards, Ch
Jeffrey G Bernards, *
Greg Simons, *
Ken Menager, *
John Kramer, *
EMP: 330 EST: 2013
SALES (est): 64.61MM
SALES (corp-wide): 98.91MM Privately Held
SIC: 1522 Residential construction, nec
PA: Bernards Bros. Inc.
555 1st St
San Fernando CA
818 898-1521

(P-468)
BLH CONSTRUCTION COMPANY
20750 Ventura Blvd Ste 155 (91364-2338)
PHONE..................................818 905-3837
Charles Brumbaugh, CEO
Brian Holland, *
EMP: 150 EST: 2001
SALES (est): 45.91MM Privately Held
SIC: 1522 Apartment building construction

(P-469)
CONDON-JOHNSON & ASSOC INC
3434 Grove St (91945-1812)
PHONE..................................858 530-9165
George Burr, Genl Mgr
EMP: 100
SALES (corp-wide): 103.7MM Privately Held
Web: www.condon-johnson.com
SIC: 1522 Residential construction, nec
PA: Condon-Johnson & Associates, Inc.
480 Roland Way Ste 200
Oakland CA
510 636-2100

(P-470)
FAIRFIELD DEVELOPMENT INC (PA)
Also Called: Ffd II
5355 Mira Sorrento Pl Ste 100 (92121-3812)
PHONE..................................858 457-2123
Christopher E Hashioka, Prin
James L Bosler, *
Ted Bradford, *
Jay Walker, *
Alan G Bear, *
▲ EMP: 225 EST: 1985
SALES (est): 332.75MM
SALES (corp-wide): 332.75MM Privately Held
SIC: 1522 Multi-family dwelling construction, nec

(P-471)
KENNARD DEVELOPMENT GROUP
Also Called: Kdg Construction Consulting
1025 N Brand Blvd Ste 300 (91202-3633)
PHONE..................................818 241-0800
Lydia Kennard, CEO
Jeffrey Lilly, *
EMP: 98 EST: 1980
SQ FT: 2,500
SALES (est): 15.65MM Privately Held
Web: www.kdgaviation.com
SIC: 1522 1541 1623 1611 Residential construction, nec; Industrial buildings and warehouses; Water, sewer, and utility lines; Highway and street construction

(P-472)
REBCO COMMUNITIES INC
Also Called: Warmington Homes California
3090 Pullman St (92626-5901)
P.O. Box 2946 (92628-2946)
PHONE..................................714 557-5511
EMP: 310
SIC: 1522 Residential construction, nec

(P-473)
REGIS CONTRACTORS LP
18825 Bardeen Ave (92612-1520)
PHONE..................................949 253-0455
EMP: 297 EST: 1995
SQ FT: 18,000
SALES (est): 1.97MM
SALES (corp-wide): 95.9MM Privately Held

SIC: **1522** Apartment building construction
PA: Sares Regis Group Operating, Inc.
18802 Bardeen Ave
Irvine CA
949 756-5959

(P-474)
SBHIS
740 Bay Blvd (91910-5254)
PHONE.............................619 427-2689
EMP: 87 EST: 2014
SALES (est): 2.27MM **Privately Held**
Web: www.sbhis.net
SIC: 1522 Residential construction, nec

(P-475)
SHEA HOMES VANTIS LLC
Also Called: Shea Homes
655 Brea Canyon Rd (91789-3078)
PHONE.............................909 594-9500
EMP: 95 EST: 2011
SALES (est): 1.39MM
SALES (corp-wide): 2.1B **Privately Held**
Web: www.jfshea.com
SIC: 1522 Apartment building construction
HQ: Shea Homes Limited Partnership, A
California Limited Partnership
655 Brea Canyon Rd
Walnut CA

(P-476)
TRI POINTE HOMES INC (HQ)
Also Called: Tri Pointe
3161 Michelson Dr Ste 1500 (92612-4400)
P.O. Box 57088 (92619-7088)
PHONE.............................949 438-1400
Douglas Bauer, *CEO*
Barry S Sternlicht, *
Douglas F Bauer, *
Thomas J Mitchell, *Pr*
Michael D Grubbs, *CFO*
EMP: 100 EST: 2009
SALES (est): 1.38B
SALES (corp-wide): 4.35B **Publicly Held**
Web: www.tripointehomes.com
SIC: 1522 Residential construction, nec
PA: Tri Pointe Homes, Inc.
940 Suthwood Blvd Ste 200
Incline Village NV
775 413-1030

(P-477)
TRI POINTE HOMES INC
57 Furlong (92602-1812)
PHONE.............................714 389-5933
Paul Faubion, *Brnch Mgr*
EMP: 135
SALES (corp-wide): 4.35B **Publicly Held**
Web: www.tripointehomes.com
SIC: 1522 Residential construction, nec
HQ: Tri Pointe Homes, Inc.
3161 Michelson Dr # 1500
Irvine CA

(P-478)
WALTON CONSTRUCTION INC
Also Called: Walton Construction Services
358 E Foothill Blvd Ste 100 (91773-1204)
PHONE.............................909 267-7777
Blake Jackson, *Pr*
E Lee Jackson, *
Rick Walker, *
David Jackson, *
EMP: 80 EST: 2004
SQ FT: 8,000
SALES (est): 23.54MM **Privately Held**
Web: www.waltonci.com
SIC: 1522 1542 Apartment building
construction; Commercial and office
building contractors

(P-479)
WERMERS MULTI-FAMILY CORP
Also Called: Wermers
5120 Shoreham Pl Ste 150 (92122-5936)
PHONE.............................858 535-1475
Thomas W Wermers, *Pr*
Jeff Bunker, *
Barry Weber, *
Richard Wood, *
Tom Wermers, *
EMP: 130 EST: 1997
SQ FT: 7,000
SALES (est): 37.93MM **Privately Held**
Web: www.wermerscompanies.com
SIC: 1522 Hotel/motel and multi-family home
construction

(P-480)
WESTERN NATIONAL PRPTS LLC (PA)
Also Called: Arkebauer Properties
8 Executive Cir (92614-6746)
P.O. Box 19528 (92623-9528)
PHONE.............................949 862-6200
David Stone, *Ch Bd*
Michael K Hayde, *
Rex Delong, *
Debra Meute, *
Jeffrey R Scott, *
▲ **EMP: 129 EST:** 1981
SQ FT: 37,000
SALES (est): 60.61MM
SALES (corp-wide): 60.61MM **Privately Held**
Web: www.wng.com
SIC: 1522 6513 6512 6531 Apartment
building construction; Apartment building
operators; Nonresidential building operators
; Real estate agents and managers

(P-481)
ZASTROW CONSTRUCTION INC
Also Called: Reliance Company
3267 Verdugo Rd (90065-2035)
PHONE.............................323 478-1956
Mark Zastrow, *Pr*
Kai Wilson, *
Patti Eldridge, *
EMP: 88 EST: 1976
SQ FT: 2,000
SALES (est): 7.12MM **Privately Held**
Web: www.leisdstudent.ws
SIC: 1522 Multi-family dwelling construction,
nec

1531 Operative Builders

(P-482)
BEAZER MORTGAGE CORPORATION
Also Called: Beazer
1800 E Imperial Hwy Ste 200 (92821-6062)
PHONE.............................714 480-1635
John Short, *Mgr*
EMP: 100
SALES (corp-wide): 2.21B **Publicly Held**
Web: www.beazer.com
SIC: 1531 Speculative builder, single-family
houses
HQ: Beazer Mortgage Corporation
2002 Summit Blvd
Brookhaven GA

(P-483)
FIELDSTONE COMMUNITIES INC (PA)
16 Technology Dr Ste 125 (92618-2325)
PHONE.............................949 790-5400
William H Mcfarland, *CEO*

Frank Foster, *
Peter Ochs, *
David Langlois, *
Alan Arthur, *
EMP: 130 EST: 1986
SQ FT: 15,000
SALES (est): 22.74MM **Privately Held**
SIC: 1531 Speculative builder, single-family
houses

(P-484)
KB HOME (PA)
10990 Wilshire Blvd Fl 7 (90024-3907)
PHONE.............................310 231-4000
Jeffrey T Mezger, *Ch Bd*
Matthew W Mandino, *Ex VP*
Jeff J Kaminski, *Ex VP*
Brian J Woram, *Ex VP*
Albert Z Praw, *Executive Real Estate Vice
President*
EMP: 100 EST: 1957
SALES (est): 6.9B
SALES (corp-wide): 6.9B **Publicly Held**
Web: www.kbhome.com
SIC: 1531 Operative builders

(P-485)
LENNAR CORPORATION
15131 Alton Pkwy Ste 190 (92618-2384)
PHONE.............................949 349-8000
Jonathan Jaffe, *COO*
EMP: 100
SALES (corp-wide): 33.67B **Publicly Held**
Web: www.lennar.com
SIC: 1531 Speculative builder, single-family
houses
PA: Lennar Corporation
5505 Blue Lagoon Dr
Miami FL
305 559-4000

(P-486)
LEWIS COMPANIES (PA)
1156 N Mountain Ave (91786-3633)
PHONE.............................909 985-0971
Richard A Lewis, *Pr*
Goldy S Lewis, *
Robert E Lewis, *
Roger G Lewis, *
Randall W Lewis, *
EMP: 200 EST: 1973
SALES (est): 40.14MM
SALES (corp-wide): 40.14MM **Privately Held**
Web: www.lewisgroupofcompanies.com
SIC: 1531 Operative builders

(P-487)
THE RYLAND GROUP INC
3011 Townsgate Rd Ste 200 (91361-5878)
PHONE.............................805 367-3800
▼ **EMP: 1502**
SIC: 1531 1521 6162 Operative builders;
Single-family housing construction;
Mortgage bankers and loan correspondents

(P-488)
TRI POINTE HOMES INC
5 Peters Canyon Rd Ste 100 (92606-1791)
PHONE.............................949 478-8600
Sarah Shahin, *Off Mgr*
EMP: 135
SALES (corp-wide): 4.35B **Publicly Held**
Web: www.tripointehomes.com
SIC: 1531 Speculative builder, single-family
houses
HQ: Tri Pointe Homes, Inc.
3161 Michelson Dr # 1500
Irvine CA

(P-489)
VAN DAELE DEVELOPMENT CORP
Also Called: Van Daele Homes
2900 Adams St Ste C25 (92504-4334)
PHONE.............................951 354-6800
Michael B Van Daele, *CEO*
Jeff Hack, *
Michael Van Daele, *Prin*
EMP: 110 EST: 1987
SQ FT: 6,000
SALES (est): 40.23MM **Privately Held**
Web: www.vandaele.com
SIC: 1531 Speculative builder, single-family
houses

(P-490)
WARMINGTON HOMES (PA)
3090 Pullman St (92626-7936)
PHONE.............................714 434-4435
Timothy P Hogan, *Pr*
James P Warmington, *Ch Bd*
Michael Riddlesperger, *CFO*
▲ **EMP: 120 EST:** 1972
SQ FT: 40,000
SALES (est): 49.31MM
SALES (corp-wide): 49.31MM **Privately Held**
Web: www.homesbywarmington.com
SIC: 1531 Speculative builder, single-family
houses

(P-491)
WARMINGTON HOMES
15615 Alton Pkwy Ste 150 (92618-7302)
PHONE.............................949 679-3100
EMP: 127
SALES (corp-wide): 49.31MM **Privately Held**
Web: www.homesbywarmington.com
SIC: 1531 Speculative builder, single-family
houses
PA: Warmington Homes
3090 Pullman St
Costa Mesa CA
714 434-4435

1541 Industrial Buildings And Warehouses

(P-492)
AMAYA CURIEL CORPORATION
Also Called: Amaya Curiel Y CIA S.A.
9775 Marconi Dr Ste G (92154-7267)
PHONE.............................619 661-1230
Roberto Curiel, *Prin*
EMP: 900 EST: 1972
SALES (est): 30.26MM **Privately Held**
SIC: 1541 Warehouse construction

(P-493)
AMERICAN DE ROSA LAMPARTS LLC
Also Called: Luminance
10650 4th St (91730-5918)
PHONE.............................800 777-4440
EMP: 95
SALES (corp-wide): 31.1MM **Privately Held**
Web: www.luminancebrands.com
SIC: 1541 Industrial buildings and
warehouses
HQ: American De Rosa Lamparts, Llc
370 Falls Commerce Pkwy
Cuyahoga Falls OH

PRODUCTS & SVCS

(P-494)
BAKELL LLC
Also Called: Jdi Distribution
24723 Redlands Blvd Ste F (92354-4021)
PHONE.............................800 292-2137
Private Information, *Managing Member*
Justin Jordan, *
Deborah Blevins, *
EMP: 65 EST: 2015
SALES (est): 11.86MM Privately Held
Web: www.bakell.com
SIC: 1541 5149 2051 3299 Food products
manufacturing or packing plant construction
; Baking supplies; Bakery: wholesale or
wholesale/retail combined; Mica products

(P-495)
BETHLEHEM CONSTRUCTION INC
425 J St (93280-2335)
PHONE.............................661 758-1001
Michael J Addleman, *Brnch Mgr*
EMP: 86
SALES (corp-wide): 48.14MM Privately
Held
Web: www.bethlehemconstruction.com
SIC: 1541 1542 Warehouse construction;
Commercial and office building, new
construction
PA: Bethlehem Construction Incorporated
5505 Titchenal Way
Cashmere WA
509 782-1001

(P-496)
BIOTIX INC
Also Called: BIOTIX, INC.
6995 Calle De Linea Ste 106 (92154-8015)
PHONE.............................858 875-5479
EMP: 40
Web: www.biotix.com
SIC: 1541 2869 Industrial buildings and
warehouses; Laboratory chemicals, organic
HQ: Biotix
10636 Scripps Summit Ct # 130
San Diego CA
858 875-7696

(P-497)
CALIFORNIA SHTMTL WORKS INC
Also Called: California Sheet Metal
1020 N Marshall Ave (92020-1829)
PHONE.............................619 562-7010
Robin Hoffos, *Pr*
Joe Isom, *
▲ EMP: 90 EST: 1913
SQ FT: 15,000
SALES (est): 45.23MM Privately Held
Web: www.califsheetmetal.com
SIC: 1541 3444 Renovation, remodeling and
repairs: industrial buildings; Sheet
metalwork

(P-498)
CLARK CNSTR GROUP - CAL INC
18201 Von Karman Ave Ste 800
(92612-1092)
PHONE.............................714 754-0764
Richard M Heim, *Pr*
EMP: 450 EST: 2012
SALES (est): 143.48MM
SALES (corp-wide): 1.66B Privately Held
SIC: 1541 1542 Industrial buildings and
warehouses; Nonresidential construction,
nec
HQ: Clark Construction Group, Llc
7500 Old Georgetown Rd # 600

Bethesda MD
301 272-8100

(P-499)
CMC REBAR WEST
10840 Norwalk Blvd (90670-3826)
PHONE.............................714 692-7082
Lee Albright, *Brnch Mgr*
EMP: 88
SIC: 1541 Industrial buildings and
warehouses
HQ: Cmc Rebar West
3880 Murphy Canyon Rd # 100
San Diego CA

(P-500)
CMC REBAR WEST
7326 Mission Gorge Rd (92120-1224)
PHONE.............................858 737-7700
EMP: 126
SIC: 1541 Steel building construction
HQ: Cmc Rebar West
3880 Murphy Canyon Rd # 100
San Diego CA

(P-501)
EDNA H PAGEL INC
Also Called: Sweetener Products
2050 E 38th St (90058-1615)
P.O. Box 58426 (90058-0426)
PHONE.............................323 234-2200
EMP: 96
SIC: 1541 5153 4213 Food products
manufacturing or packing plant construction
; Soybeans; Trucking, except local

(P-502)
FRIZE CORPORATION
16605 Gale Ave (91745-1802)
PHONE.............................800 834-2127
James N Frize, *Pr*
EMP: 80 EST: 1981
SQ FT: 25,000
SALES (est): 36.61MM Privately Held
Web: www.frizecorp.com
SIC: 1541 1542 Industrial buildings and
warehouses; Commercial and office
building contractors

(P-503)
FULLMER CONSTRUCTION
1725 S Grove Ave (91761-4530)
PHONE.............................909 947-9467
Robert A Fullmer, *Pr*
Gary Fullmer, *
Brad Anderson, *
James Fullmer, *
Gered Yetter, *
◆ EMP: 120 EST: 1946
SQ FT: 20,000
SALES (est): 63.17MM Privately Held
Web: www.fullmerco.com
SIC: 1541 Industrial buildings, new
construction, nec

(P-504)
GRAY WEST CONSTRUCTION INC
Also Called: Gray Wc
421 E Cerritos Ave (92805-6320)
PHONE.............................714 491-1317
Brian Silver, *CEO*
EMP: 175 EST: 1999
SALES (est): 11.03MM Privately Held
SIC: 1541 Renovation, remodeling and
repairs: industrial buildings

(P-505)
GRIMMWAY ENTERPRISES INC
Grimmway Farm
12020 Malaga Rd (93203-9527)
PHONE.............................661 854-6240
EMP: 180
SALES (corp-wide): 1.86B Privately Held
Web: www.grimmway.com
SIC: 1541 1542 Industrial buildings and
warehouses; Nonresidential construction,
nec
PA: Grimmway Enterprises, Inc.
14141 Di Giorgio Rd
Arvin CA
800 301-3101

(P-506)
HAL HAYS CONSTRUCTION INC (PA)
4181 Latham St (92501-1729)
PHONE.............................951 788-0703
Hal Hays, *Ex Dir*
EMP: 113 EST: 1990
SQ FT: 28,400
SALES (est): 56.37MM Privately Held
Web: www.halhays.com
SIC: 1541 1542 1623 1629 Industrial
buildings and warehouses; Commercial and
office buildings, renovation and repair;
Water, sewer, and utility lines; Dams,
waterways, docks, and other marine
construction

(P-507)
ISEC INCORPORATED
10105 Carroll Canyon Rd (92131-1109)
PHONE.............................858 279-9085
Louis L Anderson, *Pr*
EMP: 129
SALES (corp-wide): 317.22MM Privately
Held
Web: www.isecinc.com
SIC: 1541 Industrial buildings, new
construction, nec
PA: Isec, Incorporated
6000 Greenwood Plaza Blvd # 200
Greenwood Village CO
303 790-1444

(P-508)
KEVCON INC
10679 Westview Pkwy (92126-2961)
PHONE.............................760 432-0307
Kevin Kutina, *Pr*
EMP: 84 EST: 1988
SQ FT: 600
SALES (est): 5.26MM Privately Held
Web: www.kevcon.us
SIC: 1541 1542 8741 Industrial buildings
and warehouses; Commercial and office
building contractors; Management services

(P-509)
KUSTOM KANOPIES INC
210 Senior Cir (93436-1491)
PHONE.............................801 399-3400
TOLL FREE: 800
Wesley R Robison, *Pr*
Ronald E Schwartz, *
Sharee Robison, *
EMP: 30 EST: 1987
SQ FT: 56,000
SALES (est): 4.02MM Privately Held
SIC: 1541 5999 3444 Industrial buildings
and warehouses; Awnings; Sheet metalwork

(P-510)
LEDCOR CMI INC
6405 Mira Mesa Blvd Ste 100 (92121-4147)
PHONE.............................602 595-3017

David W Lede, *Ch*
Cliff Lede, *Vice Chairman*
EMP: 82 EST: 2003
SALES (est): 12.29MM Privately Held
Web: www.ledcor.com
SIC: 1541 1611 1629 1623 Industrial
buildings and warehouses; Highway and
street construction; Mine loading and
discharging station construction; Pipeline
construction, nsk

(P-511)
MINSHEW BROTHERS STL CNSTR INC
12578 Vigilante Rd (92040-1112)
P.O. Box 1000 (92040-0902)
EMP: 105 EST: 1992
SQ FT: 22,000
SALES (est): 34.93MM Privately Held
SIC: 1541 1791 Steel building construction;
Structural steel erection

(P-512)
MORLEY BUILDERS INC (PA)
Also Called: Benchmark Contractors
3330 Ocean Park Blvd (90405-3202)
PHONE.............................310 399-1600
EMP: 140 EST: 1984
SALES (est): 92.7MM
SALES (corp-wide): 92.7MM Privately
Held
Web: www.morleybuilders.com
SIC: 1541 1522 1542 1771 Industrial
buildings and warehouses; Multi-family
dwelling construction, nec; Commercial and
office building contractors; Concrete work

(P-513)
OLTMANS CONSTRUCTION CO
270 Conejo Ridge Ave Ste 210
(91361-4957)
PHONE.............................805 495-9553
Robert Larson, *Mgr*
EMP: 438
SQ FT: 2,600
SALES (corp-wide): 153.33K Privately
Held
Web: www.oltmans.com
SIC: 1541 1542 Industrial buildings and
warehouses; Nonresidential construction,
nec
PA: The Oltmans Construction Co
10005 Mission Mill Rd
Whittier CA
562 948-4242

(P-514)
OLTMANS CONSTRUCTION CO (PA)
10005 Mission Mill Rd (90601-1739)
P.O. Box 985 (90608-0985)
PHONE.............................562 948-4242
Joseph O Oltmans Ii, *Ch Bd*
John Gormly, *
Charles Roy, *SERV*
Jim Woodside, *
Gerald Singh, *
▼ EMP: 85 EST: 1932
SQ FT: 33,000
SALES (est): 153.33K
SALES (corp-wide): 153.33K Privately
Held
Web: www.oltmans.com
SIC: 1541 1542 Industrial buildings, new
construction, nec; Commercial and office
building, new construction

(P-515)
RQ CONSTRUCTION LLC
1620 Faraday Ave (92008-7313)
PHONE.................................760 631-7707
EMP: 170 EST: 1996
SALES (est): 218.46MM Privately Held
Web: www.rqconstruction.com
SIC: 1541 Industrial buildings, new construction, nec

(P-516)
SHIMS BARGAIN INC
Also Called: JC Sales
7030 E Slauson Ave (90040-3621)
PHONE.................................323 726-8800
Andy Kim, Mgr
EMP: 115
Web: www.jcsalesweb.com
SIC: 1541 Industrial buildings and warehouses
PA: Shims Bargain, Inc.
2600 S Soto St
Vernon CA

(P-517)
SMITH MCHNCL-LCTRICAL-PLUMBING
Also Called: Smith Electric Service
1340 W Betteravia Rd (93455-1030)
PHONE.................................805 621-5000
Michael Brannon, Pr
Larry Brannon, *
EMP: 150 EST: 1980
SQ FT: 10,000
SALES (est): 56.64MM Privately Held
Web: www.smith-electric.com
SIC: 1541 1711 1731 1542 Industrial buildings, new construction, nec; Plumbing, heating, air-conditioning; Fire detection and burglar alarm systems specialization; Nonresidential construction, nec

(P-518)
SPECTRUM CNSTR GROUP INC
514 Via De La Valle Ste 210 (92075-2459)
PHONE.................................949 299-1400
Bisher Aljazzar, CEO
EMP: 99 EST: 2016
SALES (est): 23.55MM Privately Held
Web: www.spectrumcgi.com
SIC: 1541 1622 1542 1611 Steel building construction; Bridge, tunnel, and elevated highway construction; Commercial and office building, new construction; Highway and street construction

(P-519)
SQUARE H BRANDS INC
3615 E Vernon Ave (90058-1815)
PHONE.................................323 267-4600
Bobby Codilla, Prin
EMP: 100
SALES (corp-wide): 24.17MM Privately Held
Web: www.hoffybrand.com
SIC: 1541 Food products manufacturing or packing plant construction
PA: Square H Brands, Inc.
2731 S Soto St
Vernon CA
323 267-4600

(P-520)
STANTRU RESOURCES INC
Also Called: Stantru Reinforcing Steel
11175 Redwood Ave (92337-7137)
P.O. Box 310189 (92331-0189)
PHONE.................................909 587-1441
Ida Ichen, Pr
William M Klorman, *

EMP: 83 EST: 1991
SALES (est): 8.31MM Privately Held
Web: www.stantru.com
SIC: 1541 1542 Industrial buildings, new construction, nec; Commercial and office building, new construction

(P-521)
SYNEAR FOODS USA LLC
Also Called: Synear Foods
9601 Canoga Ave (91311-4115)
PHONE.................................818 341-3588
EMP: 31 EST: 2015
SALES (est): 17.33MM Privately Held
SIC: 1541 2038 Food products manufacturing or packing plant construction; Breakfasts, frozen and packaged
PA: Zhengzhou Synear Food Co., Ltd.
No. 13 Yingcai Street, Huiji District
Zhengzhou HA

(P-522)
T B PENICK & SONS INC
15435 Innovation Dr Ste 200 (92128-3443)
PHONE.................................858 558-1800
Marc E Penick, CEO
Timothy Penick, Pr
John T Boyd, CFO
Keely Prochaska Ctrl, Prin
EMP: 150 EST: 1905
SQ FT: 30,000
SALES (est): 115.43MM Privately Held
Web: www.tbpenick.com
SIC: 1541 1542 Industrial buildings and warehouses; Nonresidential construction, nec

(P-523)
TAISEI CONSTRUCTION CORPORATION
970 W 190th St Ste 920 (90502-1063)
PHONE.................................714 886-1530
▲ EMP: 120
SIC: 1541 1542 Industrial buildings and warehouses; Nonresidential construction, nec

(P-524)
TAWA SUPERMARKET INC
6363 Regio Ave (90620-1025)
PHONE.................................714 521-8899
EMP: 86
SALES (corp-wide): 490.41MM Privately Held
Web: www.168markets.com
SIC: 1541 Industrial buildings and warehouses
PA: Tawa Supermarket, Inc.
6281 Regio Ave
Buena Park CA
714 521-8899

(P-525)
UNIVERSAL DUST CLLCTR MFG SUP (PA)
Also Called: UDC
1041 N Kraemer Pl (92806-2611)
PHONE.................................714 630-8588
Theresa A Shaffer, CEO
Curt Schendel, *
George G Shaffer, *
Deborah Huerta, *
EMP: 89 EST: 1984
SQ FT: 30,000
SALES (est): 36.57MM
SALES (corp-wide): 36.57MM Privately Held
Web: www.udccorporation.com
SIC: 1541 Industrial buildings, new construction, nec

(P-526)
WEST COAST DISTRIBUTION INC
4440 E 26th St (90058-4318)
PHONE.................................323 588-6508
EMP: 82
SALES (corp-wide): 9.4MM Privately Held
Web: www.montagefulfillment.com
SIC: 1541 4789 Industrial buildings and warehouses; Pipeline terminal facilities, independently operated
PA: West Coast Distribution, Inc.
2602 E 37th St
Vernon CA
323 588-6508

1542 Nonresidential Construction, Nec

(P-527)
ABHE & SVOBODA INC
880 Tavern Rd (91901-3810)
PHONE.................................619 659-1320
David Grant, Mgr
EMP: 81
SALES (corp-wide): 1.96MM Privately Held
Web: www.abheonline.com
SIC: 1542 Commercial and office building, new construction
PA: Abhe & Svoboda, Inc.
18100 Dairy Ln
Jordan MN
952 447-6025

(P-528)
AIS CONSTRUCTION COMPANY
7015 Vista Del Rincon Dr (93001)
P.O. Box 4209 (93403-4209)
PHONE.................................805 928-9467
Andy Sheaffer, Pr
EMP: 85 EST: 1996
SQ FT: 4,000
SALES (est): 12.4MM Privately Held
Web: www.aisconstruction.com
SIC: 1542 Commercial and office building contractors

(P-529)
ANDERSON BURTON CNSTR INC (PA)
121 Nevada St (93420-2609)
PHONE.................................805 481-5096
Joann Anderson, Pr
EMP: 99 EST: 1999
SQ FT: 5,000
SALES (est): 47.58MM Privately Held
Web: www.andersonburton.com
SIC: 1542 1522 Commercial and office building, new construction; Residential construction, nec

(P-530)
ANDREW L YOUNGQUIST CNSTR INC
3187 Red Hill Ave Ste 200 (92626-3454)
PHONE.................................949 862-5611
EMP: 90 EST: 1996
SQ FT: 10,319
SALES (est): 13.25MM Privately Held
SIC: 1542 1522 8741 Commercial and office building contractors; Residential construction, nec; Construction management

(P-531)
AUSTIN COMMERCIAL LP
402 W Broadway Ste 400 (92101-3554)
PHONE.................................619 446-5637
James Cole, Off Mgr
EMP: 122
SALES (corp-wide): 2.22B Privately Held
Web: www.austin-ind.com
SIC: 1542 Commercial and office building, new construction
HQ: Austin Commercial, Lp
3535 Travis St Ste 300
Dallas TX
214 443-5500

(P-532)
AUSTIN COMMERCIAL LP
5901 W Century Blvd Ste 600 (90045-5442)
PHONE.................................310 421-0269
Clive Buchan, Brnch Mgr
EMP: 152
SALES (corp-wide): 2.22B Privately Held
Web: www.austin-ind.com
SIC: 1542 Commercial and office building, new construction
HQ: Austin Commercial, Lp
3535 Travis St Ste 300
Dallas TX
214 443-5500

(P-533)
BALFOUR BEATTY CNSTR LLC
13520 Evening Creek Dr N Ste 270 (92128-8105)
PHONE.................................858 635-7400
EMP: 100
SALES (corp-wide): 9.19B Privately Held
Web: www.balfourbeattyus.com
SIC: 1542 Commercial and office building, new construction
HQ: Balfour Beatty Construction, Llc
3100 Mckinnon St Fl 3
Dallas TX
214 451-1000

(P-534)
BARNHART INC
10620 Treena St Ste 300 (92131-1141)
P.O. Box 270399 (92198-2399)
PHONE.................................858 635-7400
◆ EMP: 291
SIC: 1542 8741 Commercial and office building, new construction; Construction management

(P-535)
BERGMAN KPRS LLC (PA)
2850 Saturn St Ste 100 (92821-1701)
PHONE.................................714 924-7000
Mark C Bergman, Prin
Joel H Stensby, *
Lev Rabinovich, *
Paul Kristedja, *
EMP: 125 EST: 1982
SQ FT: 7,500
SALES (est): 50.79MM
SALES (corp-wide): 50.79MM Privately Held
Web: www.bergmankprs.com
SIC: 1542 Restaurant construction

(P-536)
BOMEL CONSTRUCTION CO INC
939 E Francis St (91761-5631)
PHONE.................................909 923-3319
Richard Laughlin, Mgr
EMP: 91
SALES (corp-wide): 102.23MM Privately Held

PRODUCTS & SVCS

Web: www.bomelconstruction.com
SIC: 1542 Commercial and office building, new construction
PA: Bomel Construction Co., Inc.
96 Corporate Park Ste 100
Irvine CA
714 921-1660

(P-537)
BR BUILDING RESOURCES CO
2247 Lindsay Way (91740-5398)
P.O. Box 2090 (91740-2090)
PHONE....................................626 963-4880
Gary Pellant, *Pr*
Juan Banos, *
Jose Banos, *
Vanessa Banos, *
Ramon Banos, *
EMP: 120 **EST:** 2009
SQ FT: 9,000
SALES (est): 28MM **Privately Held**
Web: www.brco.com
SIC: 1542 Commercial and office buildings, renovation and repair

(P-538)
BYCOR GENERAL CONTRACTORS INC
Also Called: Bycor General Contractors
6490 Marindustry Dr (92121-5297)
PHONE....................................858 587-1901
Scott Kaats, *CEO*
Richard A Byer, *
EMP: 90 **EST:** 1975
SQ FT: 10,041
SALES (est): 118.05MM **Privately Held**
Web: www.bycor.com
SIC: 1542 Commercial and office building, new construction

(P-539)
C W DRIVER INCORPORATED
Also Called: C. W. DRIVER, INCORPORATED
7588 Metropolitan Dr (92108-4401)
PHONE....................................619 696-5100
Joe Grosshart, *Dir*
EMP: 113
SALES (corp-wide): 186.96MM **Privately Held**
Web: www.cwdriver.com
SIC: 1542 Commercial and office building, new construction
PA: C. W. Driver, Llc
468 N Rosemead Blvd
Pasadena CA
626 351-8800

(P-540)
CALIFORNIA STRL CONCEPTS INC
28358 Constellation Rd Ste 660 (91355-5010)
PHONE....................................661 257-6903
Jeffrey Horne, *CEO*
Penny Horne, *
EMP: 85 **EST:** 2006
SALES (est): 9.4MM **Privately Held**
Web: www.cscbuilding.net
SIC: 1542 Commercial and office building, new construction

(P-541)
CASTLE & COOKE INVESTMENTS INC
1 Dole Dr (91362-7300)
PHONE....................................310 208-3636
EMP: 200 **EST:** 2008
SALES (est): 32.02MM **Privately Held**

SIC: 1542 7011 7359 1522 Commercial and office building, new construction; Resort hotel; Equipment rental and leasing, nec; Hotel/motel, new construction

(P-542)
CLARK CNSTR GROUP - CAL LP
18201 Von Karman Ave Ste 800 (92612-1092)
PHONE....................................714 429-9779
Richard M Heim, *CEO*
EMP: 393 **EST:** 2004
SQ FT: 5,000
SALES (est): 144.65MM
SALES (corp-wide): 1.66B **Privately Held**
SIC: 1542 Commercial and office building, new construction
HQ: Clark Construction Group, Llc
7500 Old Georgetown Rd # 600
Bethesda MD
301 272-8100

(P-543)
CLAY CORONA COMPANY (PA)
22079 Knabe Rd (92883-7111)
PHONE....................................951 277-2667
Gerald K Deleo, *Pr*
Craig Deleo, *
Joyce Deleo, *
EMP: 23 **EST:** 1947
SALES (est): 9.48MM
SALES (corp-wide): 9.48MM **Privately Held**
Web: www.coronaclayco.com
SIC: 1542 3295 8711 1794 Commercial and office building contractors; Minerals, ground or treated; Construction and civil engineering; Excavation work

(P-544)
CREW BUILDERS INC
8130 Commercial St (91942-2926)
P.O. Box 6205 (92166-0205)
PHONE....................................619 587-2033
Jeff D Salewsky, *CEO*
Jon Archer, *
EMP: 120 **EST:** 2006
SALES (est): 27.16MM **Privately Held**
Web: www.crewbuilders.com
SIC: 1542 Commercial and office building, new construction

(P-545)
DAVID L MANWARREN CORP
9146 9th St (91730-4405)
PHONE....................................909 989-5883
David L Manwarren, *Pr*
Jean Manwarren, *
▼ **EMP:** 22 **EST:** 1981
SQ FT: 44,000
SALES (est): 2.23MM **Privately Held**
Web: www.dlmanwarren.com
SIC: 1542 3999 Design and erection, combined: non-residential; Foliage, artificial and preserved

(P-546)
DPR CONSTRUCTION A GEN PARTNR
5010 Shoreham Pl Ste 100 (92122-6900)
PHONE....................................858 646-0757
Peter Salvati, *Dir*
EMP: 248
Web: www.dpr.com
SIC: 1542 Commercial and office building, new construction
HQ: Dpr Construction, A General Partnership
1450 Veterans Blvd
Redwood City CA

(P-547)
DPR CONSTRUCTION A GEN PARTNR
88 W Colorado Blvd Ste 301 (91105)
PHONE....................................626 463-1265
Dal Swain, *Brnch Mgr*
EMP: 98
Web: www.dpr.com
SIC: 1542 Commercial and office building, new construction
HQ: Dpr Construction, A General Partnership
1450 Veterans Blvd
Redwood City CA

(P-548)
ENGEL HOLDINGS INC
Also Called: Cabrillo Hoist
14754 Ceres Ave (92335-4205)
P.O. Box 3179 (91729-3179)
PHONE....................................866 950-9862
Conal Molloy, *Pr*
▲ **EMP:** 103 **EST:** 1977
SQ FT: 2,000
SALES (est): 36.31MM
SALES (corp-wide): 2.16B **Privately Held**
Web: www.safwayatlantic.com
SIC: 1542 Commercial and office building contractors
HQ: Safway Atlantic, Llc
700 Commercial Ave
Carlstadt NJ
201 636-5500

(P-549)
ENVIRONMENTAL CONSTRUCTION INC
21550 Oxnard St Ste 1060 (91367-7123)
PHONE....................................818 449-8920
Farid Soroudi, *CEO*
Zia Abhari, *
EMP: 90 **EST:** 2004
SQ FT: 2,500
SALES (est): 26.52MM **Privately Held**
Web: www.environmentalconstructioninc.com
SIC: 1542 Commercial and office building contractors

(P-550)
ERICKSON-HALL CONSTRUCTION CO (PA)
500 Corporate Dr (92029-1517)
PHONE....................................760 796-7700
Dave Erickson, *CEO*
Mike Hall, *
Mike Conroy, *
Mat Gates, *
EMP: 86 **EST:** 1998
SALES (est): 52.91MM
SALES (corp-wide): 52.91MM **Privately Held**
Web: www.ericksonhall.com
SIC: 1542 Commercial and office building, new construction

(P-551)
FJ WILLERT CONTRACTING CO
1869 Nirvana Ave (91911-6117)
PHONE....................................619 421-1980
Fred M Willert, *Pr*
EMP: 110 **EST:** 1972
SQ FT: 11,748
SALES (est): 49.84MM **Privately Held**
Web: www.fjwillert.com
SIC: 1542 Commercial and office building, new construction

(P-552)
GALKOS CONSTRUCTION INC
15262 Pipeline Ln (92649-1136)
PHONE....................................714 373-8545
Lonnie Gialketsis, *VP*
EMP: 95
SALES (corp-wide): 18.05MM **Privately Held**
Web: www.galkos.com
SIC: 1542 Nonresidential construction, nec
PA: Galkos Construction, Inc.
15262 Pipeline Ln
Huntington Beach CA
714 373-8545

(P-553)
GGG DEMOLITION INC (PA)
1130 W Trenton Ave (92867-3536)
PHONE....................................714 699-9350
Gregg Miller, *Sec*
EMP: 97 **EST:** 2012
SALES (est): 16.47MM
SALES (corp-wide): 16.47MM **Privately Held**
Web: www.gggdemo.com
SIC: 1542 Specialized public building contractors

(P-554)
GRANI INSTALLATION INC (PA)
5411 Commercial Dr (92649-1231)
PHONE....................................714 898-0441
Gregory A Grani, *CEO*
EMP: 100 **EST:** 1973
SQ FT: 6,000
SALES (est): 23.05MM
SALES (corp-wide): 23.05MM **Privately Held**
Web: www.grani.biz
SIC: 1542 1742 Commercial and office buildings, renovation and repair; Acoustical and ceiling work

(P-555)
HAR-BRO LLC (HQ)
2750 Signal Pkwy (90755-2207)
PHONE....................................562 528-8000
EMP: 80 **EST:** 1956
SALES (est): 49.46MM
SALES (corp-wide): 161.86MM **Privately Held**
Web: www.goblusky.com
SIC: 1542 1521 1522 Commercial and office building, new construction; New construction, single-family houses; Apartment building construction
PA: Blusky Restoration Contractors, Llc
9110 E Nichols Ave # 180
Centennial CO
303 789-4258

(P-556)
HARVEY INC
Also Called: Harvey General Contracting
9455 Ridgehaven Ct Ste 200 (92123-1632)
PHONE....................................858 769-4000
EMP: 125 **EST:** 2005
SALES (est): 31.33MM **Privately Held**
Web: www.harveyusa.com
SIC: 1542 Commercial and office building, new construction

(P-557)
HITT CONTRACTING INC
3733 Motor Ave Ste 200 (90034-6403)
PHONE....................................424 326-1042
EMP: 320
SALES (corp-wide): 1.22B **Privately Held**
Web: www.hitt.com

▲ = Import ▼ = Export
◆ = Import/Export

SIC: 1542 1531 Nonresidential construction, nec; Operative builders
PA: Hitt Contracting, Inc.
2900 Fairview Park Dr
Falls Church VA
703 846-9000

(P-558)
HOUALLA ENTERPRISES LTD
Also Called: Metro Bldrs & Engineers Group
2610 Avon St (92663-4706)
PHONE..................................949 515-4350
Fouad Houalla, *Pr*
▲ **EMP:** 85 **EST:** 1987
SQ FT: 1,200
SALES (est): 22.44MM **Privately Held**
Web: www.metrobuilders.com
SIC: 1542 Commercial and office building, new construction

(P-559)
INTERIOR LGIC GROUP HLDNGS IV (PA)
10 Bunsen (92618-4210)
PHONE..................................800 959-8333
Alan K Davenport, *Pr*
Jason Peel, *CFO*
Bob Hess, *CAO*
Anne Liu, *CAO*
Chris Filandro, *CIO*
EMP: 87 **EST:** 2018
SALES (est): 97.93MM
SALES (corp-wide): 97.93MM **Privately Held**
Web: www.interiorlogicgroup.com
SIC: 1542 Commercial and office building contractors

(P-560)
JOHN M FRANK CONSTRUCTION INC
Also Called: John M Frank Service Group
913 E 4th St (92701-4748)
PHONE..................................714 210-3600
John M Frank, *CEO*
Laurie Dawson, *
EMP: 80 **EST:** 1984
SALES (est): 31.92MM **Privately Held**
Web: www.johnmfrankconstruction.com
SIC: 1542 5411 5812 Commercial and office building, new construction; Supermarkets; Family restaurants

(P-561)
JONES BROTHERS CNSTR CORP (PA)
Also Called: Peck Jones Construction
1601 Cloverfield Blvd (90404-4082)
PHONE..................................310 470-1885
J Gregory Jones, *Pr*
EMP: 98 **EST:** 1923
SALES (est): 9.35MM
SALES (corp-wide): 9.35MM **Privately Held**
SIC: 1542 Commercial and office building contractors

(P-562)
KIEWIT CORPORATION
Also Called: Measure of Excellence Cabinets
12700 Stowe Dr Ste 180 (92064-8883)
PHONE..................................858 208-4285
EMP: 80
SALES (corp-wide): 17.08B **Privately Held**
SIC: 1542 Commercial and office building contractors
HQ: Kiewit Corporation
3555 Farnam St Ste 1000
Omaha NE
402 342-2052

(P-563)
KOLL CONSTRUCTION LP
4343 Von Karman Ave Ste 150 (92660-1200)
PHONE..................................949 833-3030
Donald M Koll, *Managing Member*
EMP: 100 **EST:** 1996
SALES (est): 19.8MM **Privately Held**
SIC: 1542 Nonresidential construction, nec

(P-564)
KPRS CONSTRUCTION SERVICES INC (PA)
Also Called: Kprs
2850 Saturn St Ste 110 (92821-1701)
PHONE..................................714 672-0800
Joel H Stensby, *Pr*
Paul Kristedja, *
Lev Rabinovich, *
EMP: 91 **EST:** 1995
SQ FT: 31,000
SALES (est): 80.12MM
SALES (corp-wide): 80.12MM **Privately Held**
Web: www.kprsinc.com
SIC: 1542 8711 Commercial and office building, new construction; Building construction consultant

(P-565)
LMC HOLLYWOOD HIGHLAND
Also Called: Lennar Multi Family Community
95 Enterprise Ste 200 (92656-2611)
PHONE..................................949 448-1600
Todd Farrell, *CEO*
EMP: 500 **EST:** 2013
SALES (est): 43.15MM **Privately Held**
SIC: 1542 Commercial and office building contractors

(P-566)
MCCARTHY BLDG COMPANIES INC
20401 Sw Birch St Ste 200 (92660-1796)
PHONE..................................949 851-8383
EMP: 347
SALES (corp-wide): 5.39B **Privately Held**
Web: www.mccarthy.com
SIC: 1542 1541 Institutional building construction; Industrial buildings, new construction, nec
HQ: Mccarthy Building Companies, Inc.
12851 Manchester Rd
Saint Louis MO
314 968-3300

(P-567)
MCCARTHY BLDG COMPANIES INC
1113 Bush (92868-4222)
PHONE..................................949 851-8383
Pat Peterson, *Brnch Mgr*
EMP: 92
SALES (corp-wide): 5.39B **Privately Held**
Web: www.mccarthy.com
SIC: 1542 Commercial and office building, new construction
HQ: Mccarthy Building Companies, Inc.
12851 Manchester Rd
Saint Louis MO
314 968-3300

(P-568)
MERUELO ENTERPRISES INC (PA)
9550 Firestone Blvd Ste 105 (90241-5560)
PHONE..................................562 745-2300
Alex Meruelo, *CEO*
Al Stoller, *
Joe Marchica, *
EMP: 501 **EST:** 1986
SALES (est): 528.99MM
SALES (corp-wide): 528.99MM **Privately Held**
Web: www.merueloenterprises.com
SIC: 1542 Nonresidential construction, nec

(P-569)
NEVELL GROUP INC (PA)
Also Called: N G I
3001 Enterprise St Ste 200 (92821-6210)
PHONE..................................714 579-7501
Michael J Nevell, *Pr*
Bruce Pasqua, *
Bryan Bodine, *
Chris Taylor, *
EMP: 125 **EST:** 2002
SQ FT: 35,000
SALES (est): 99.42MM
SALES (corp-wide): 99.42MM **Privately Held**
Web: www.nevellgroup.com
SIC: 1542 Commercial and office building, new construction

(P-570)
NEVELL GROUP INC
Also Called: Nevell Group Inc San Diego
3284 Grey Hawk Ct (92010-6651)
PHONE..................................760 598-3501
Greg Thomas, *Brnch Mgr*
EMP: 388
SALES (corp-wide): 120.36MM **Privately Held**
Web: www.nevellgroup.com
SIC: 1542 Commercial and office building, new construction
PA: The Nevell Group Inc
3001 Enterprise St # 200
Brea CA
714 579-7501

(P-571)
PACIFIC BUILDING GROUP (PA)
9752 Aspen Creek Ct Ste 100 (92126-1082)
PHONE..................................858 552-0600
Gregory A Rogers, *CEO*
Jim Roherty, *
Ron Maize, *
Lisa Hitt, *
William Hansen, *
▲ **EMP:** 96 **EST:** 1984
SQ FT: 17,880
SALES (est): 59.16MM
SALES (corp-wide): 59.16MM **Privately Held**
Web: www.pacificbuildinggroup.com
SIC: 1542 Commercial and office building, new construction

(P-572)
PARKCO BUILDING COMPANY
24795 State Highway 74 (92570-8759)
PHONE..................................714 444-1441
W Adrian Hoyle, *Pr*
EMP: 99 **EST:** 2013
SALES (est): 8.3MM **Privately Held**
Web: www.parkcobuilding.com
SIC: 1542 1771 1799 Commercial and office building, new construction; Foundation and footing contractor; Erection and dismantling of forms for poured concrete

(P-573)
PCL CONSTRUCTION SERVICES INC
4690 Executive Dr Ste 100 (92121-3073)
PHONE..................................858 657-3400
EMP: 121
SALES (corp-wide): 5.99B **Privately Held**
SIC: 1542 Commercial and office building, new construction
HQ: Pcl Construction Services, Inc.
2000 S Colo Blvd Ste 2-50
Denver CO
303 365-6500

(P-574)
PCL CONSTRUCTION SERVICES INC
655 N Central Ave Ste 1600 (91203-1438)
PHONE..................................818 246-3481
Dale Kain, *Mgr*
EMP: 191
SQ FT: 17,619
SALES (corp-wide): 5.99B **Privately Held**
SIC: 1542 Commercial and office building, new construction
HQ: Pcl Construction Services, Inc.
2000 S Colo Blvd Ste 2-50
Denver CO
303 365-6500

(P-575)
PCL CONSTRUCTION SERVICES INC
100 Universal City Plz (91608-1002)
PHONE..................................818 509-7816
EMP: 99
SALES (corp-wide): 5.99B **Privately Held**
SIC: 1542 Commercial and office building, new construction
HQ: Pcl Construction Services, Inc.
2000 S Colo Blvd Ste 2-50
Denver CO
303 365-6500

(P-576)
PCL INDUSTRIAL SERVICES INC
1500 S Union Ave (93307-4144)
PHONE..................................661 832-3995
Joe W Carrieri, *CEO*
Gary L Basher, *
EMP: 300 **EST:** 2002
SALES (est): 128.25MM **Privately Held**
SIC: 1542 Commercial and office building, new construction

(P-577)
PENWAL INDUSTRIES INC
10611 Acacia St (91730-5410)
PHONE..................................909 466-1555
Chris A Pennington, *Prin*
▲ **EMP:** 100 **EST:** 1981
SQ FT: 65,000
SALES (est): 26.16MM **Privately Held**
Web: www.penwal.com
SIC: 1542 3999 8742 3993 Shopping center construction; Advertising display products; Management consulting services; Signs and advertising specialties

(P-578)
PERRY COAST CONSTRUCTION INC
Also Called: West Coast Construction
3811 Wacker Dr (91752-1142)
PHONE..................................951 774-0677
Robert Perry, *Pr*
Erin Perry, *
Britney Perry, *
EMP: 105 **EST:** 2012
SALES (est): 21.35MM **Privately Held**
Web: www.wcconcrete.com
SIC: 1542 Restaurant construction

(P-579)
PHILMONT MANAGEMENT INC
3450 Wilshire Blvd Ste 850 (90010-2211)
PHONE....................................213 380-0159
Monica Nam, *Pr*
EMP: 99 **EST:** 1997
SQ FT: 6,000
SALES (est): 10.77MM **Privately Held**
Web: www.philmontinc.com
SIC: 1542 Commercial and office building,
new construction

(P-580)
PLATINUM CONSTRUCTION INC
865 S East St (92805-5356)
PHONE....................................714 527-0700
Darrin W Streilein, *Pr*
EMP: 100 **EST:** 2005
SALES (est): 20.62MM **Privately Held**
SIC: 1542 1541 1742 Commercial and office
building contractors; Steel building
construction; Plastering, drywall, and
insulation

(P-581)
R J LANTHIER COMPANY INC
485 Corporate Dr (92029-1507)
PHONE....................................760 738-9798
EMP: 80
SIC: 1542 1711 Nonresidential construction,
nec; Warm air heating and air conditioning
contractor

(P-582)
R Q CONSTRUCTION INC
1620 Faraday Ave (92008-7313)
PHONE....................................760 631-7707
EMP: 140 **EST:** 1996
SALES (est): 37.99MM **Privately Held**
Web: www.rqconstruction.com
SIC: 1542 Commercial and office building,
new construction

(P-583)
RBA BUILDERS INC
16490 Harbor Blvd Ste A (92708-1392)
PHONE....................................714 895-9000
Robert Anderson, *CEO*
EMP: 82 **EST:** 2007
SALES (est): 49.78MM **Privately Held**
Web: www.rbabuildersinc.com
SIC: 1542 Commercial and office building,
new construction

(P-584)
RD OLSON CONSTRUCTION INC
400 Spectrum Center Dr Ste 1200
(92618-5022)
PHONE....................................949 474-2001
EMP: 125 **EST:** 1979
SALES (est): 41.12MM
SALES (corp-wide): 41.12MM **Privately
Held**
Web: www.rdolson.com
SIC: 1542 1522 Commercial and office
buildings, renovation and repair; Hotel/
motel and multi-family home construction
PA: The Robert D Olson Corporation
400 Spectrum Center Dr # 12
Irvine CA
949 474-2001

(P-585)
**ROBERT CLAPPER CNSTR
SVCS INC**
Also Called: RC Construction Services
700 New York St (92374-2921)
PHONE....................................909 829-3688
Robert W Clapper, *Prin*

Rebecca Clapper, *
EMP: 100 **EST:** 1994
SALES (est): 25.57MM **Privately Held**
Web: www.rcconstruction.com
SIC: 1542 1771 Commercial and office
building, new construction; Concrete work

(P-586)
RUDOLPH AND SLETTEN INC
2855 Michelle Ste 350 (92606-1013)
PHONE....................................949 252-1919
EMP: 109
SALES (corp-wide): 3.79B **Publicly Held**
Web: www.rsconstruction.com
SIC: 1542 1541 Commercial and office
building, new construction; Industrial
buildings and warehouses
HQ: Rudolph And Sletten, Inc.
120 Constitution Dr
Menlo Park CA
650 216-3600

(P-587)
**SAN-MAR CONSTRUCTION CO
INC**
4875 E La Palma Ave Ste 602
(92807-1955)
PHONE....................................714 693-5400
Sandra Drew, *CEO*
EMP: 200 **EST:** 1993
SQ FT: 3,000
SALES (est): 32.3MM **Privately Held**
Web: www.san-mar.com
SIC: 1542 Commercial and office building,
new construction

(P-588)
SANDER LANGSTON LP
Also Called: Snyder Langston
17962 Cowan (92614-6026)
PHONE....................................949 863-9200
TOLL FREE: 800
Stephen Jones Senior, *Ch*
John Rochford, *
Jason Rich, *
Gary Campanaro, *
EMP: 175 **EST:** 1986
SQ FT: 16,000
SALES (est): 413MM **Privately Held**
Web: www.snyderlangston.com
SIC: 1542 8742 1522 Commercial and office
building, new construction; Real estate
consultant; Residential construction, nec

(P-589)
**SHAWMUT WOODWORKING &
SUP INC**
Also Called: Shawmut Design and Cnstr
11390 W Olympic Blvd Fl 2 (90064-1607)
PHONE....................................323 602-1000
Leonard Porzio, *Prin*
EMP: 145
SALES (corp-wide): 278.72MM **Privately
Held**
Web: www.shawmut.com
SIC: 1542 Commercial and office building,
new construction
PA: Shawmut Woodworking & Supply, Inc.
560 Harrison Ave Ste 200
Boston MA
617 622-7000

(P-590)
SIERRA PACIFIC CONSTRS INC
Also Called: Sierra Pacific Constructors
22212 Ventura Blvd Ste 300 (91364-1517)
PHONE....................................747 888-5000
Cary Gerhardt, *Prin*
Cary Gerhardt, *CEO*
Ken Laspada, *

EMP: 99 **EST:** 1983
SQ FT: 13,500
SALES (est): 46.03MM **Privately Held**
Web: www.spcinc.com
SIC: 1542 Commercial and office buildings,
renovation and repair

(P-591)
**SILVER CREEK INDUSTRIES
LLC**
2830 Barrett Ave (92571-3258)
PHONE....................................951 943-5393
Brett D Bashaw, *CEO*
Micheal Rhodes, *
EMP: 175 **EST:** 2005
SQ FT: 25,000
SALES (est): 91.07MM **Privately Held**
Web: www.silvercreekmodular.com
SIC: 1542 2452 Commercial and office
building contractors; Prefabricated wood
buildings

(P-592)
SOLPAC INC
Also Called: Soltek Pacific
2424 Congress St (92110-2819)
PHONE....................................619 296-6247
Stephen W Thompson, *CEO*
Dave Carlin, *
John Myers, *
Kevin Cammall, *
EMP: 245 **EST:** 1994
SQ FT: 7,386
SALES (est): 50.12MM **Privately Held**
Web: www.soltekpacific.com
SIC: 1542 Commercial and office building,
new construction

(P-593)
STREAMLINE FINISHES INC
26429 Rancho Pkwy S Ste 140
(92630-8330)
PHONE....................................949 600-8964
William Seidel, *Pr*
EMP: 80 **EST:** 2004
SQ FT: 6,000
SALES (est): 25.18MM **Privately Held**
Web: www.streamlinefinishes.com
SIC: 1542 Commercial and office building
contractors

(P-594)
SUMMER SYSTEMS INC
28942 Hancock Pkwy (91355-1069)
PHONE....................................661 257-4419
Don London, *Pr*
Connie London, *
EMP: 80 **EST:** 1988
SQ FT: 20,000
SALES (est): 25.94MM **Privately Held**
Web: www.summersystems.net
SIC: 1542 Nonresidential construction, nec

(P-595)
TECHNO COATINGS INC (PA)
Also Called: Techno West
1391 S Allec St (92805-6304)
PHONE....................................714 635-1130
EMP: 200 **EST:** 1974
SALES (est): 41.05MM
SALES (corp-wide): 41.05MM **Privately
Held**
Web: www.technocoatings.com
SIC: 1542 1629 1721 1799 Commercial and
office buildings, renovation and repair;
Blasting contractor, except building
demolition; Painting and paper hanging;
Coating of concrete structures with plastic

(P-596)
**TRITON STRUCTURAL
CONCRETE INC**
15435 Innovation Dr Ste 225 (92128-3442)
PHONE....................................858 866-2450
Tim Penick, *CEO*
John Boyd, *
EMP: 250 **EST:** 2007
SALES (est): 35.13MM **Privately Held**
Web: www.tritonstructural.com
SIC: 1542 Commercial and office building,
new construction

(P-597)
**TURNER CONSTRUCTION
COMPANY**
1900 S State College Blvd Ste 200
(92806-6197)
PHONE....................................714 940-9000
Bernie Morrissey, *VP*
EMP: 300
Web: www.turnerconstruction.com
SIC: 1542 Commercial and office building,
new construction
HQ: Turner Construction Company Inc
66 Hudson Blvd E Fl 36
New York NY
212 229-6000

(P-598)
**TUTOR PERINI CORPORATION
(PA)**
Also Called: TUTOR PERINI
15901 Olden St (91342-1051)
PHONE....................................818 362-8391
Ronald N Tutor, *Ch Bd*
Michael R Klein, *
Gary G Smalley, *Ex VP*
Ghassan M Ariqat, *Ex VP*
Michael F Smithson, *Ex VP*
▲ **EMP:** 160 **EST:** 1894
SALES (est): 3.79B
SALES (corp-wide): 3.79B **Publicly Held**
Web: www.tutorperini.com
SIC: 1542 8741 1611 1791 Commercial and
office building contractors; Construction
management; Concrete construction:
roads, highways, sidewalks, etc.; Structural
steel erection

(P-599)
**TUTOR-SALIBA CORPORATION
(HQ)**
15901 Olden St (91342-1051)
PHONE....................................818 362-8391
Ronald N Tutor, *CEO*
David L Randall, *
William B Sparks, *
Jack Frost, *
John D Barrett, *
▲ **EMP:** 100 **EST:** 2003
SQ FT: 20,000
SALES (est): 242.56MM
SALES (corp-wide): 3.79B **Publicly Held**
Web: www.tutorperini.com
SIC: 1542 1629 7353 1799 Commercial and
office building, new construction; Subway
construction; Cranes and aerial lift
equipment, rental or leasing; Rigging and
scaffolding
PA: Tutor Perini Corporation
15901 Olden St
Rancho Cascades CA
818 362-8391

(P-600)
TUTOR-SALIBA PERINI
15901 Olden St (91342-1051)
PHONE....................................818 362-8391

EMP: 7733
SIC: 1542 1611 1622 Specialized public building contractors; Highway and street construction; Bridge, tunnel, and elevated highway construction

(P-601)
USS CAL BUILDERS INC
8031 Main St (90680-2452)
PHONE....................714 828-4882
Allen Othman, *CEO*
Jennifer Hotrum, *
Eric Othman, *
EMP: 135 **EST:** 1992
SALES (est): 49.41MM **Privately Held**
Web: www.usscalbuilders.com
SIC: 1542 Specialized public building contractors

(P-602)
WE ONEIL CONSTRUCTION CO CAL
Also Called: W E O'Neil Construction
9485 Haven Ave Ste 101 (91730-5877)
PHONE..............................909 466-5300
John Finn, *Brnch Mgr*
EMP: 161
SALES (corp-wide): 233.95MM **Privately Held**
Web: www.weoneil.com
SIC: 1542 1541 1522 1521 Commercial and office building, new construction; Industrial buildings and warehouses; Residential construction, nec; New construction, single-family houses
HQ: W.E. O'neil Construction Co Of California
909 N Pcf Cast Hwy Ste 40
El Segundo CA
310 643-7900

(P-603)
WEBCOR CONSTRUCTION LP
Also Called: Webcor Builders
2150 W Washington St Ste 308 (92110-2044)
PHONE..............................619 798-3891
Matt Rosie, *CEO*
EMP: 131
Web: www.webcor.com
SIC: 1542 Nonresidential construction, nec
HQ: Webcor Construction L.P.
207 King St Ste 300
San Francisco CA

(P-604)
WEBCOR CONSTRUCTION LP
Also Called: Webcor Builders
333 S Grand Ave Ste 4400 (90071-1548)
PHONE..............................213 239-2800
Leo Bandini, *Mgr*
EMP: 131
Web: www.webcor.com
SIC: 1542 Commercial and office building, new construction
HQ: Webcor Construction L.P.
207 King St Ste 300
San Francisco CA

(P-605)
WEST PACIFIC SERVICES INC
4445 Eastgate Mall Ste 200 (92121)
PHONE..............................888 401-0188
Joshua L Prado, *CEO*
EMP: 138 **EST:** 2009
SALES (est): 11.84MM **Privately Held**
SIC: 1542 Nonresidential construction, nec

(P-606)
WHITING-TURNER CONTRACTING CO
250 Commerce Ste 150 (92602-1345)
PHONE..............................949 863-0800
Len Cannatelli Junior, *Ex VP*
EMP: 388
SALES (corp-wide): 8.62B **Privately Held**
Web: www.whiting-turner.com
SIC: 1542 1541 Commercial and office building, new construction; Industrial buildings and warehouses
PA: The Whiting-Turner Contracting Company
300 E Joppa Rd Ste 800
Baltimore MD
410 821-1100

1611 Highway And Street Construction

(P-607)
ADOPT-A-HIGHWAY MAINTENANCE
Also Called: Adopt-A-Beach
3158 Red Hill Ave Ste 200 (92626-3416)
PHONE..............................800 200-0003
Peter Morin, *CEO*
Patricia Nelson, *
Dennis Day, *
Dan Day, *
EMP: 104 **EST:** 1990
SQ FT: 6,000
SALES (est): 29.52MM **Privately Held**
Web: www.adoptahighway.com
SIC: 1611 4959 Highway and street maintenance; Sanitary services, nec

(P-608)
ALL AMERICAN ASPHALT
All American Service and Sup
1776 All American Way (92879-2070)
P.O. Box 2229 (92878-2229)
PHONE..............................951 736-7617
Kim Mcguire Managing, *Brnch Mgr*
EMP: 179
SALES (corp-wide): 142.17MM **Privately Held**
Web: www.allamericanasphalt.com
SIC: 1611 Highway and street paving contractor
PA: All American Asphalt
400 E 6th St
Corona CA
951 736-7600

(P-609)
ATKINSON CONSTRUCTION INC
18201 Von Karman Ave Ste 800 (92612-1092)
PHONE..............................303 410-2540
John O'keefe, *Pr*
EMP: 450 **EST:** 2004
SALES (est): 122.5MM
SALES (corp-wide): 1.66B **Privately Held**
Web: www.clarkconstruction.com
SIC: 1611 1622 Highway and street construction; Bridge, tunnel, and elevated highway construction
HQ: Clark Construction Group, Llc
7500 Old Georgetown Rd # 600
Bethesda MD
301 272-8100

(P-610)
BEADOR CONSTRUCTION CO INC
2900 Bristol St (92626-5941)

PHONE..............................951 674-7352
EMP: 80 **EST:** 1996
SALES (est): 23.45MM **Privately Held**
SIC: 1611 General contractor, highway and street construction

(P-611)
BENS ASPHALT & MAINT CO INC
Also Called: Medina Construction
2537 Rubidoux Blvd (92509-2142)
PHONE..............................951 248-1103
EMP: 90
Web: www.bensasphalt.com
SIC: 1611 Surfacing and paving
PA: Ben's Asphalt & Maintenance Company, Inc.
2200 S Yale St Ste A
Santa Ana CA

(P-612)
BRUTOCO ENGINEERING & CONSTRUCTION INC
Also Called: Brutoco Engineering
1272 Center Court Dr Ste 101 (91724-3667)
EMP: 200 **EST:** 1967
SALES (est): 20.21MM **Privately Held**
Web: www.brutoco.net
SIC: 1611 1629 1622 General contractor, highway and street construction; Dams, waterways, docks, and other marine construction; Bridge construction

(P-613)
CITY OF PASO ROBLES
747 Spring St Ste B (93446-2898)
PHONE..............................805 237-3999
EMP: 80 **EST:** 1989
SALES (est): 5.54MM **Privately Held**
Web: www.prcity.com
SIC: 1611 Highway and street construction

(P-614)
CITY OF SAN DIEGO
2781 Caminito Chollas (92105-5039)
PHONE..............................619 527-7482
EMP: 187
SALES (corp-wide): 2.67B **Privately Held**
Web: www.sandiego.gov
SIC: 1611 9199 Highway and street maintenance; General government administration
PA: City Of San Diego
202 C St
San Diego CA
619 236-6330

(P-615)
DRAGADOS USA INC
3200 Park Center Dr Ste 600 (92626-7163)
PHONE..............................657 229-7800
John Edward Mcgrath, *Brnch Mgr*
EMP: 93
Web: www.dragados-usa.com
SIC: 1611 General contractor, highway and street construction
HQ: Dragados Usa, Inc.
810 7th Ave Fl 9
New York NY

(P-616)
EBS GENERAL ENGINEERING INC
1345 Quarry St Ste 101 (92879-1734)
PHONE..............................951 279-6869
Joseph Nanci, *Pr*
EMP: 90 **EST:** 1994
SQ FT: 4,000
SALES (est): 11.67MM **Privately Held**

Web: www.ebs-inc.us
SIC: 1611 Highway and street construction

(P-617)
EMERALD ACQUISITION LLC
Also Called: Emerald Paving Company
6381 Industry Way (92683-3693)
PHONE..............................714 891-8752
Derek M Davis, *CEO*
Derek M Davis, *Pr*
Mike Clarke, *Ex VP*
Erinn Steingold, *CFO*
EMP: 132 **EST:** 2006
SQ FT: 20,000
SALES (est): 12.7MM **Privately Held**
Web: www.empave.com
SIC: 1611 Surfacing and paving
PA: M A C Contracting Corp.
6301 W Sunrise Blvd
Plantation FL

(P-618)
GRANITE CONSTRUCTION COMPANY
Also Called: Southern California Regional
38000 Monroe St (92203-9500)
PHONE..............................760 775-7500
Jay Mcquillen, *Mgr*
EMP: 393
Web: www.graniteconstruction.com
SIC: 1611 1771 General contractor, highway and street construction; Concrete work
HQ: Granite Construction Company
585 W Beach St
Watsonville CA
831 724-1011

(P-619)
GRANITE CONSTRUCTION COMPANY
5335 Debbie Rd (93111-2001)
P.O. Box 6744 (93160-6744)
PHONE..............................805 964-9951
Bruce Mcgowan, *Mgr*
EMP: 169
SQ FT: 65,396
Web: www.graniteconstruction.com
SIC: 1611 General contractor, highway and street construction
HQ: Granite Construction Company
585 W Beach St
Watsonville CA
831 724-1011

(P-620)
GRANITE CONSTRUCTION INC
213 Columbia Way (93535-5335)
PHONE..............................805 667-8210
EMP: 95
Web: www.graniteconstruction.com
SIC: 1611 General contractor, highway and street construction
PA: Granite Construction Incorporated
585 W Beach St
Watsonville CA

(P-621)
GRIFFITH COMPANY
1128 Carrier Parkway Ave (93308-9666)
P.O. Box 70157 (93387-0157)
PHONE..............................661 392-6640
Rus Grigg, *Mgr*
EMP: 341
SALES (corp-wide): 350MM **Privately Held**
Web: www.griffithcompany.net
SIC: 1611 General contractor, highway and street construction
PA: Griffith Company
3050 E Birch St

P R O D U C T S & S V C S

Brea CA
714 984-5500

(P-622)
GRIFFITH COMPANY (PA)
Also Called: Tahoe Stag
3050 E Birch St (92821-6248)
PHONE..............................714 984-5500
Jamie Angus, *Pr*
Jim Waltze, *
Thomas L Foss, *
Ryan Aukerman, *
Steve Ruelas, *
EMP: 187 **EST:** 1922
SQ FT: 100,000
SALES (est): 350MM
SALES (corp-wide): 350MM **Privately Held**
Web: www.griffithcompany.net
SIC: 1611 General contractor, highway and street construction

(P-623)
HARDY & HARPER INC
32 Rancho Cir (92630-8325)
PHONE..............................714 444-1851
Daniel Thomas Maas, *CEO*
Fred T Maas Senior, *Dir*
EMP: 50 **EST:** 1946
SALES (est): 14.04MM **Privately Held**
Web: www.hardyandharper.com
SIC: 1611 2951 Surfacing and paving; Asphalt paving mixtures and blocks

(P-624)
HARPER FEDERAL CNSTR LLC
14130 Biscayne Pl (92064-6640)
PHONE..............................619 543-1296
Jeffrey A Harper, *Managing Member*
Ronald D Harper, *
EMP: 80 **EST:** 2007
SALES (est): 8.42MM **Privately Held**
SIC: 1611 1711 1751 1742 Grading; Plumbing, heating, air-conditioning; Carpentry work; Plastering, drywall, and insulation

(P-625)
IES COMMERCIAL INC
Also Called: Ies
6885 Flanders Dr Ste A (92121-2933)
PHONE..............................858 210-4900
Brad Sandman, *Prin*
EMP: 146
Web: www.ielectric.com
SIC: 1611 1812 1623 7382 General contractor, highway and street construction; Audio-visual program production; Cable laying construction; Security systems services
HQ: Ies Commercial, Inc.
2801 S Fair Ln Ste 101
Tempe AZ
480 379-6200

(P-626)
INTERNATIONAL PAVING SVCS INC
Also Called: I P S
1199 Opal Ave (92359-1284)
P.O. Box 10458 (92423-0458)
PHONE..............................909 794-2101
Brent Rieger, *Pr*
EMP: 80 **EST:** 2007
SALES (est): 18.92MM **Privately Held**
Web: www.ipspaving.com
SIC: 1611 Surfacing and paving

(P-627)
KEC ENGINEERING
26320 Lester Cir (92883-6399)
P.O. Box 909 (92878-0909)
PHONE..............................951 734-3010
James Elfring, *Pr*
Les Card, *
Scott Pfeiffer, *Ex VP*
EMP: 110 **EST:** 1953
SALES (est): 21.7MM **Privately Held**
Web: www.kecengineering.com
SIC: 1611 General contractor, highway and street construction

(P-628)
KIEWIT INFRASTRUCTURE WEST CO
10704 Shoemaker Ave (90670-4040)
PHONE..............................562 946-1816
Ken Riley, *Mgr*
EMP: 125
SQ FT: 12,514
SALES (corp-wide): 10.41B **Privately Held**
Web: www.kiewit.com
SIC: 1611 1542 1541 General contractor, highway and street construction; Nonresidential construction, nec; Industrial buildings and warehouses
HQ: Kiewit Infrastructure West Co.
2200 Columbia House Blvd
Vancouver WA
402 342-2052

(P-629)
LARRY JACINTO CONSTRUCTION INC
9555 N Wabash Ave (92374-2714)
P.O. Box 615 (92359-0615)
PHONE..............................909 794-2151
Larry Frankland Jacinto, *CEO*
EMP: 80 **EST:** 1971
SQ FT: 8,500
SALES (est): 22.22MM **Privately Held**
Web: www.larryjacintoconstruction.com
SIC: 1611 Grading

(P-630)
LB3 ENTERPRISES INC
12485 Highway 67 # 3 (92040)
P.O. Box 130 (92022-0130)
PHONE..............................619 579-6161
Lawrence Lee Brown, *Pr*
Debra Brown, *
EMP: 90 **EST:** 2004
SALES (est): 25.37MM **Privately Held**
Web: www.lb3enterprises.com
SIC: 1611 1623 7389 Grading; Water, sewer, and utility lines; Business services, nec

(P-631)
MACRO-Z-TECHNOLOGY COMPANY (PA)
Also Called: M Z T
841 E Washington Ave (92701-3878)
PHONE..............................714 564-1130
Bryan J Zatica, *CEO*
EMP: 97 **EST:** 1989
SQ FT: 3,000
SALES (est): 30.96MM **Privately Held**
Web: www.mztco.com
SIC: 1611 1542 8711 Concrete construction: roads, highways, sidewalks, etc.; Commercial and office building contractors; Engineering services

(P-632)
MAMCO INC (PA)
Also Called: Alabbasi
764 Ramona Expy Ste C (92571-9716)

PHONE..............................951 776-9300
EMP: 116 **EST:** 2002
SQ FT: 2,200
SALES (est): 33.61MM **Privately Held**
Web: www.alabbasi.biz
SIC: 1611 General contractor, highway and street construction

(P-633)
MARATHON GENERAL INC
1728 Mission Rd (92029-1111)
PHONE..............................760 738-9714
Mark Miller, *Pr*
Steven Gallant, *
Donald Tolen, *
EMP: 80 **EST:** 1988
SQ FT: 3,000
SALES (est): 32.51MM **Privately Held**
Web: www.mgipaving.com
SIC: 1611 General contractor, highway and street construction

(P-634)
MATICH CORPORATION (PA)
1596 E Harry Shepard Blvd (92408-0197)
P.O. Box 10 (92346-1010)
PHONE..............................909 382-7400
Stephen A Matich, *CEO*
Martin A Matich, *
Randall Valadez, *
Robert M Matich, *
Patrick A Matich, *
EMP: 60 **EST:** 1918
SQ FT: 10,000
SALES (est): 47.71MM
SALES (corp-wide): 47.71MM **Privately Held**
Web: www.matichcorp.com
SIC: 1611 2951 General contractor, highway and street construction; Asphalt paving mixtures and blocks

(P-635)
MESA CONTRACTING CORPORATION
22845 Savi Ranch Pkwy Ste D (92887-4628)
EMP: 120 **EST:** 1978
SALES (est): 10.46MM **Privately Held**
Web: www.mesacontracting.com
SIC: 1611 Grading

(P-636)
MYERS & SONS CONSTRUCTION LP
5777 W Century Blvd Ste 600 (90045-5636)
PHONE..............................424 227-3285
EMP: 141
Web: www.myers-sons.com
SIC: 1611 Highway and street construction
HQ: Myers & Sons Construction, L.P.
45 Morrison Ave
Sacramento CA

(P-637)
OTAY RIVER CONSTRUCTORS LLC
860 Harold Pl (91914-3550)
P.O. Box 600 (92346-0600)
PHONE..............................619 397-7500
Rich Linford, *Pr*
▲ **EMP:** 130 **EST:** 2002
SQ FT: 17,000
SALES (est): 21.73MM **Privately Held**
SIC: 1611 Highway and street construction

(P-638)
PALP INC
Also Called: Excel Paving Co
2230 Lemon Ave (90806-5124)
P.O. Box 16405 (90806-0995)
PHONE..............................562 599-5841
Curtis P Brown, *CEO*
George Mcrae, *Sr VP*
Bruce Flatt, *
Michelle Drakulich, *
EMP: 225 **EST:** 1976
SQ FT: 11,000
SALES (est): 49.18MM **Privately Held**
Web: www.excelpavingcompany.com
SIC: 1611 8711 Highway and street paving contractor; Engineering services

(P-639)
PAVER DECOR MASONRY INC
Also Called: Alpha & Omega Pavers
987 Calimesa Blvd (92320-1138)
P.O. Box 727 (92320-0727)
PHONE..............................909 795-8474
Adam Cuevas, *Pr*
Mary Cuevas, *
EMP: 25 **EST:** 1995
SQ FT: 2,500
SALES (est): 5.03MM **Privately Held**
Web: www.paverdecor.com
SIC: 1611 3531 Highway and street paving contractor; Pavers

(P-640)
RICK HAMM CONSTRUCTION INC
201 W Carleton Ave (92867-3607)
PHONE..............................714 532-0815
Rick Hamm, *Pr*
Llana Hamm, *
EMP: 90 **EST:** 1977
SQ FT: 25,000
SALES (est): 19.49MM **Privately Held**
Web: www.rickhamm.com
SIC: 1611 1771 1791 1741 General contractor, highway and street construction; Patio construction, concrete; Precast concrete structural framing or panels, placing of; Masonry and other stonework

(P-641)
RIVERSIDE CONSTRUCTION COMPANY INC
4225 Garner Rd (92501-1057)
P.O. Box 1146 (92502-1146)
PHONE..............................951 682-8308
EMP: 150 **EST:** 1966
SALES (est): 22.61MM **Privately Held**
Web: www.rivconstruct.com
SIC: 1611 General contractor, highway and street construction

(P-642)
RJ NOBLE COMPANY (PA)
15505 E Lincoln Ave (92865-1015)
P.O. Box 620 (92856-9020)
PHONE..............................714 637-1550
Michael J Carver, *Pr*
Craig Porter, *
James N Ducote, *
EMP: 144 **EST:** 1950
SQ FT: 5,500
SALES (est): 60.76MM
SALES (corp-wide): 60.76MM **Privately Held**
Web: www.rjnoblecompany.com
SIC: 1611 Highway and street paving contractor

(P-643)
RSVC COMPANY
Also Called: Reliable Service Company
3051 Myers St Ste B (92503-5525)
P.O. Box 7189 (92513-7189)
PHONE.................................951 684-6578
Mark David Aldaco, *Pr*
Mark David Aldaco, *CEO*
Keith Gruber, *
EMP: 188 **EST:** 2004
SALES (est): 48.53MM **Privately Held**
Web: www.rsvc.com
SIC: 1611 8741 8712 General contractor, highway and street construction; Management services; Architectural services

(P-644)
S & S PAVING INC
23875 Ventura Blvd Ste 202 (91302-1464)
PHONE.................................818 591-0668
Jose Hurtado, *Pr*
Virginia Martinez, *
Jan Pick, *
EMP: 50 **EST:** 1971
SQ FT: 1,600
SALES (est): 1.89MM **Privately Held**
Web: www.sspavinginc.com
SIC: 1611 2951 1629 Grading; Asphalt paving mixtures and blocks; Land leveling

(P-645)
SECURITY PAVING COMPANY INC (PA)
Also Called: Valley Base Materials
3075 Towngate Rd Ste 210 # 200 (91361-3027)
PHONE.................................818 362-9200
Mike Mattivi, *CEO*
Mike Mattivi, *Prin*
Albert Mattivi, *
Thomas J Mattivi, *
EMP: 99 **EST:** 1947
SALES (est): 74.25MM
SALES (corp-wide): 74.25MM **Privately Held**
Web: www.securitypaving.com
SIC: 1611 Highway and street paving contractor

(P-646)
SEMA CONSTRUCTION INC
320 Goddard Ste 150 (92618-4630)
PHONE.................................949 470-0500
Steve Mills, *Mgr*
EMP: 100
Web: www.sema.inc
SIC: 1611 1771 Highway and street construction; Concrete work
PA: Sema Construction, Inc.
7353 S Eagle St
Centennial CO

(P-647)
SKANSKA USA CVIL W CAL DST INC (DH)
1995 Agua Mansa Rd (92509-2405)
PHONE.................................951 684-5360
Richard Cavallero, *CEO*
Michael Aparicio, *
Todd Sutton, *
Joseph Nogues, *
Michael Cobelli, *
EMP: 700 **EST:** 1919
SQ FT: 15,000
SALES (est): 475.28MM
SALES (corp-wide): 15.55B **Privately Held**
Web: usa.skanska.com

SIC: 1611 1622 1629 8711 General contractor, highway and street construction; Bridge construction; Dam construction; Engineering services
HQ: Skanska Usa Civil Inc.
7520 Astoria Blvd Ste 200
East Elmhurst NY
718 340-0777

(P-648)
SULLY-MILLER HOLDING CORP
135 S State College Blvd Ste 400 (92821-5819)
PHONE.................................714 578-9600
George W Sully, *Pr*
EMP: 125
SALES (est): 2.04MM
SALES (corp-wide): 114.31MM **Privately Held**
Web: www.sully-miller.com
SIC: 1611 Highway and street paving contractor
HQ: Colas Inc.
73 Hedqrters Plz N Towe 1
Morristown NJ

(P-649)
SUPERIOR PAVING COMPANY INC
Also Called: United Paving Company
1880 N Delilah St (92879-1892)
PHONE.................................951 739-9200
Sabas Trujillo, *CEO*
EMP: 85 **EST:** 2008
SQ FT: 3,000
SALES (est): 25.33MM **Privately Held**
Web: www.united-paving.com
SIC: 1611 Highway and street paving contractor

(P-650)
SYSTEM PAVERS LLC
Also Called: System Pavers
1570 Brookhollow Dr (92705-5438)
PHONE.................................949 243-2072
Larry Green, *Mgr*
EMP: 249 **EST:** 2021
SALES (est): 9.97MM **Privately Held**
Web: www.systempavers.com
SIC: 1611 Surfacing and paving

(P-651)
UNITED ROCK PRODUCTS CORP
Also Called: Sully Miller Contracting
135 S State College Blvd Ste 400 (92821-5819)
PHONE.................................714 578-9600
John Harrington, *Pr*
▲ **EMP:** 103 **EST:** 1988
SQ FT: 2,000
SALES (est): 10.43MM
SALES (corp-wide): 114.31MM **Privately Held**
Web: www.sully-miller.com
SIC: 1611 Highway and street paving contractor
HQ: Sully-Miller Contracting Company Inc
135 S State College Blvd # 400
Brea CA
714 578-9600

1622 Bridge, Tunnel, And Elevated Highway

(P-652)
FLATIRON WEST INC
16341 Chino Corona Rd (91708-9233)

PHONE.................................909 597-8413
Thomas J Rademacher, *CEO*
EMP: 160
Web: www.flatironi-15.com
SIC: 1622 1611 Bridge construction; Highway and street construction
HQ: Flatiron West, Inc.
12121 Scripps Summit Dr # 400
San Diego CA

(P-653)
FLUOR DANIEL CONSTRUCTION CO (DH)
Also Called: Fluor Daniel Construction
3 Polaris Way (92656-5338)
PHONE.................................949 349-2000
Paul Buckham, *Pr*
EMP: 500 **EST:** 1953
SALES (est): 102.17MM
SALES (corp-wide): 13.74B **Publicly Held**
SIC: 1622 Bridge, tunnel, and elevated highway construction
HQ: Fluor Enterprises, Inc.
6700 Las Colinas Blvd
Irving TX
469 398-7000

(P-654)
HAZARD CONSTRUCTION COMPANY
Also Called: Hazard Construction
10529 Vine St Ste 1 (92040-2447)
P.O. Box 229000 (92192-9000)
PHONE.................................858 587-3600
Jason Mordhorst, *Pr*
Klaus Guttau, *VP*
EMP: 100 **EST:** 1926
SALES (est): 99.35MM **Privately Held**
Web: www.hazardconstruction.com
SIC: 1622 1611 Bridge construction; Highway and street construction

(P-655)
STEVE P RADOS INC
1638 Pioneer Way (92020-1636)
PHONE.................................619 328-1360
Steve Rados, *Mgr*
EMP: 110
SALES (corp-wide): 68.32MM **Privately Held**
Web: www.rados.com
SIC: 1622 Highway construction, elevated
HQ: Steve P Rados Inc
2002 E Mcfadden Ave # 200
Santa Ana CA
714 835-4612

1623 Water, Sewer, And Utility Lines

(P-656)
A & H COMMUNICATIONS INC
15 Chrysler (92618-2009)
PHONE.................................949 250-4555
Brian Elliott, *Pr*
Brett Howard, *
EMP: 250 **EST:** 2000
SALES (est): 24.09MM **Privately Held**
Web: www.aandh.com
SIC: 1623 Cable laying construction

(P-657)
AIRX UTILITY SURVEYORS INC (PA)
785 E Mission Rd # 100 (92069-1903)
PHONE.................................760 480-2347
Gail Mcmorran, *Pr*
EMP: 55 **EST:** 1999

SALES (est): 9.17MM
SALES (corp-wide): 9.17MM **Privately Held**
Web: www.airxus.com
SIC: 1623 1389 3272 1611 Underground utilities contractor; Testing, measuring, surveying, and analysis services; Monuments, concrete; Highway and street construction

(P-658)
ARB INC (HQ)
Also Called: California Arb, Inc.
26000 Commercentre Dr (92630-8816)
PHONE.................................949 598-9242
Tom Mccormick, *CEO*
Scott Summers, *
Timothy Healy, *
John P Schauerman, *
John M Perisich, *Corporate Secretary*
▲ **EMP:** 140 **EST:** 1960
SALES (est): 459.34MM **Publicly Held**
Web: www.prim.com
SIC: 1623 1629 Oil and gas line and compressor station construction; Industrial plant construction
PA: Primoris Services Corporation
2300 N Field St Ste 1900
Dallas TX

(P-659)
ARIZONA PIPELINE COMPANY
1745 Sampson Ave (92879-1864)
PHONE.................................951 270-3100
John Guzlow, *Div Mgr*
EMP: 200
SALES (corp-wide): 214.75MM **Privately Held**
Web: www.arizonapipeline.com
SIC: 1623 8711 Underground utilities contractor; Engineering services
PA: Arizona Pipeline Company
17372 Lilac St
Hesperia CA
760 244-8212

(P-660)
ARIZONA PIPELINE COMPANY (PA)
17372 Lilac St (92345-5162)
P.O. Box 401865 (92340-1865)
PHONE.................................760 244-8212
Lowell Duane Moyers, *Ch*
Nina Moyers, *CEO*
Phyliss Moyers, *Dir*
Tom Seals, *Sec*
EMP: 400 **EST:** 1979
SQ FT: 5,000
SALES (est): 214.75MM
SALES (corp-wide): 214.75MM **Privately Held**
Web: www.arizonapipeline.com
SIC: 1623 Pipeline construction, nsk

(P-661)
BALI CONSTRUCTION INC
9852 Joe Vargas Way (91733-3108)
PHONE.................................626 442-8003
Ted Polich Iii, *Pr*
Michael E Brooks, *
EMP: 100 **EST:** 1987
SQ FT: 7,000
SALES (est): 58.08MM **Privately Held**
Web: www.baliconstruction.com
SIC: 1623 Underground utilities contractor

(P-662)
BLOIS CONSTRUCTION INC
3201 Sturgis Rd (93030-8931)
P.O. Box 672 (93032-0672)

PHONE.............................805 485-0011
James B Blois, *Pr*
Steve Woodworth, *
Dan Schultz, *
EMP: 150 **EST:** 1965
SQ FT: 10,000
SALES (est): 44.91MM **Privately Held**
Web: www.bloisconstruction.com
SIC: 1623 Underground utilities contractor

(P-663)
BOUDREAU PIPELINE CORPORATION
Also Called: A & B Equipment
463 N Smith Ave (92878-4305)
PHONE.............................951 493-6780
EMP: 300 **EST:** 2000
SQ FT: 14,000
SALES (est): 66.84MM **Privately Held**
Web: www.boudreaupipeline.com
SIC: 1623 Pipeline construction, nsk

(P-664)
CA STATION MANAGEMENT INC
3200 E Guasti Rd Ste 100 (91761-8661)
PHONE.............................909 245-6251
Taqi Chaudry, *CEO*
EMP: 250 **EST:** 2016
SALES (est): 23.62MM **Privately Held**
SIC: 1623 7389 8082 Underground utilities contractor; Telephone answering service; Home health care services

(P-665)
CAMERON INTRSTATE PIPELINE LLC
488 8th Ave (92101-7123)
PHONE.............................619 696-3110
Ryan O'neal, *VP*
EMP: 200 **EST:** 2005
SALES (est): 28.44MM **Privately Held**
Web: www.sempra.com
SIC: 1623 Oil and gas pipeline construction

(P-666)
CASS CONSTRUCTION INC (PA)
Also Called: Cass
1100 Wagner Dr. (92020-3047)
P.O. Box 309 (92022-0309)
PHONE.............................619 590-0929
Jimmie Nelson, *Ch Bd*
Kyle P Nelson, *
Laura Nelson, *
EMP: 345 **EST:** 1974
SQ FT: 5,700
SALES (est): 43.87MM
SALES (corp-wide): 43.87MM **Privately Held**
Web: www.cassarrieta.com
SIC: 1623 1611 Underground utilities contractor; Grading

(P-667)
CONSTRUCTION SPECIALTY SVC INC
Also Called: C S S
4550 Buck Owens Blvd (93308-4948)
P.O. Box 9429 (93389-9429)
PHONE.............................661 864-7573
Daniel I George, *Pr*
Denise George, *
EMP: 53 **EST:** 2008
SQ FT: 1,000
SALES (est): 14.22MM **Privately Held**
Web: www.cssincorp.biz
SIC: 1623 3271 Pipeline construction, nsk; Concrete block and brick

(P-668)
DIVERSIFIED UTILITY SVCS INC
3105 Unicorn Rd (93308-6858)
P.O. Box 80417 (93380-0417)
PHONE.............................661 325-3212
Leigh Ann Anderson, *CEO*
Steven S Anderson, *
William Mitchell, *Stockholder*
Cody Anderson, *Stockholder*
EMP: 272 **EST:** 1997
SALES (est): 48.45MM **Privately Held**
Web: www.diversifiedutilityservices.com
SIC: 1623 Underground utilities contractor

(P-669)
DOTY BROS EQUIPMENT CO (HQ)
11232 Firestone Blvd (90650-2201)
PHONE.............................562 864-6566
EMP: 100 **EST:** 1931
SALES (est): 55.5MM
SALES (corp-wide): 528.99MM **Privately Held**
Web: www.dotybros.com
SIC: 1623 Pipeline construction, nsk
PA: Meruelo Enterprises, Inc.
9550 Firestone Blvd # 105
Downey CA
562 745-2300

(P-670)
GENERAL PRODUCTION SVC CAL INC
Also Called: G P S
1333 Kern St (93268-9700)
P.O. Box 344 (93268-0344)
PHONE.............................661 765-5330
Charles Beard, *CEO*
Oreste Risi, *
EMP: 180 **EST:** 1967
SALES (est): 49.99MM **Privately Held**
Web: www.genprod.com
SIC: 1623 Oil and gas pipeline construction

(P-671)
HCI LLC (HQ)
Also Called: H C I
6830 Airport Dr (92504-1904)
P.O. Box 5389 (92860-8097)
PHONE.............................951 520-4200
Steven G Silagi, *Pr*
◆ **EMP:** 300 **EST:** 1981
SALES (est): 105.09MM
SALES (corp-wide): 118.73MM **Privately Held**
Web: www.hci-inc.com
SIC: 1623 Telephone and communication line construction
PA: Lombardy Holdings, Inc.
151 Kalmus Dr Ste F6
Costa Mesa CA
951 808-4550

(P-672)
HENKELS & MCCOY INC
2840 Ficus St (91766-6501)
PHONE.............................909 517-3011
Michael Giarratano, *Sr VP*
EMP: 300
SALES (corp-wide): 9.78B **Publicly Held**
Web: www.henkels.com
SIC: 1623 Electric power line construction
HQ: Henkels & Mccoy, Inc
985 Jolly Rd
Blue Bell PA
215 283-7600

(P-673)
HERMAN WEISSKER INC (HQ)
1645 Brown Ave (92509-1859)
PHONE.............................951 826-8800
Luis Alberto Armona, *CEO*
Ron Politte, *
Marty Mayeda, *
EMP: 176 **EST:** 1959
SQ FT: 12,000
SALES (est): 107.21MM
SALES (corp-wide): 528.99MM **Privately Held**
Web: www.hermanweissker.com
SIC: 1623 1731 Underground utilities contractor; Electrical work
PA: Meruelo Enterprises, Inc.
9550 Firestone Blvd # 105
Downey CA
562 745-2300

(P-674)
HP COMMUNICATIONS INC (PA)
13341 Temescal Canyon Rd (92883-4980)
PHONE.............................951 572-1200
Nicholas Goldman, *Pr*
Ahmad Olomi, *Ex VP*
Chris Price, *VP*
EMP: 82 **EST:** 1998
SQ FT: 130,680
SALES (est): 101.53MM
SALES (corp-wide): 101.53MM **Privately Held**
Web: www.hpcomminc.com
SIC: 1623 Communication line and transmission tower construction

(P-675)
IRISH COMMUNICATION COMPANY (DH)
2649 Stingle Ave (91770-3326)
P.O. Box 457 (91770-0457)
PHONE.............................626 288-6170
Gregory C Warde, *CEO*
Dan Mitchell, *
Pat D Furnare, *
Larry Manke Rcdd, *VP*
Dennis Brackney, *
EMP: 100 **EST:** 1985
SQ FT: 9,000
SALES (est): 48.45MM
SALES (corp-wide): 64.03MM **Privately Held**
Web: www.irishteam.com
SIC: 1623 8748 1731 Telephone and communication line construction; Telecommunications consultant; Communications specialization
HQ: Irish Construction
2641 River Ave
Rosemead CA
626 288-8530

(P-676)
IRISH CONSTRUCTION (HQ)
2641 River Ave (91770-3392)
P.O. Box 579 (91770-0579)
PHONE.............................626 288-8530
Gregory C Warde, *Ch Bd*
William E Wilbanks, *
Randall W Dale, *
Jerry L Olmscheid, *
Ken West, *
EMP: 150 **EST:** 1947
SQ FT: 15,000
SALES (est): 64.03MM
SALES (corp-wide): 64.03MM **Privately Held**
Web: www.irishteam.com
SIC: 1623 Telephone and communication line construction

PA: Manhattan Capital Corporation
2641 River Ave
Rosemead CA
626 288-8530

(P-677)
JR FILANC CNSTR CO INC (PA)
740 N Andreasen Dr (92029-1414)
PHONE.............................760 941-7130
Mark E Filanc, *CEO*
Vincent L Diaz, *
Linda Stangel, *
EMP: 100 **EST:** 1952
SQ FT: 13,200
SALES (est): 89.94MM
SALES (corp-wide): 89.94MM **Privately Held**
Web: www.filanc.com
SIC: 1623 1629 Pumping station construction; Waste water and sewage treatment plant construction

(P-678)
K S FABRICATION & MACHINE INC
Also Called: KS Fabrication & Machine
6205 District Blvd (93313-2141)
P.O. Box 41630 (93384-1630)
PHONE.............................661 617-1700
Kevin S Small, *CEO*
Becky Scott, *
EMP: 150 **EST:** 1999
SALES (est): 24.06MM **Privately Held**
Web: www.ksilp.com
SIC: 1623 Water, sewer, and utility lines

(P-679)
KANA PIPELINE INC
12620 Magnolia Ave (92503-4636)
PHONE.............................714 986-1400
Dan Locke, *Pr*
EMP: 100 **EST:** 1984
SQ FT: 55,000
SALES (est): 31.69MM **Privately Held**
Web: www.kanapipeline.com
SIC: 1623 1629 Water main construction; Drainage system construction

(P-680)
KS INDUSTRIES LP (PA)
Also Called: K S I
6205 District Blvd (93313-2141)
P.O. Box 41630 (93384-1630)
PHONE.............................661 617-1700
Kevin Small, *Pt*
EMP: 2000 **EST:** 1979
SQ FT: 20,000
SALES (est): 490.64MM
SALES (corp-wide): 490.64MM **Privately Held**
Web: www.ksilp.com
SIC: 1623 Water, sewer, and utility lines

(P-681)
LOMBARDY HOLDINGS INC (PA)
151 Kalmus Dr Ste F6 (92626-5965)
P.O. Box 6019 (92860-8034)
PHONE.............................951 808-4550
Marc Laulhere, *CEO*
Pam Laulhere, *
EMP: 200 **EST:** 1940
SQ FT: 80,000
SALES (est): 118.73MM
SALES (corp-wide): 118.73MM **Privately Held**
SIC: 1623 5211 Telephone and communication line construction; Electrical construction materials

(P-682)

MURRIETA DEVELOPMENT COMPANY INC

42540 Rio Nedo (92590-3727)
PHONE..............................951 719-1680
EMP: 126 **EST:** 1981
SALES (est): 24.35MM **Privately Held**
Web: www.murrietadevelopment.com
SIC: 1623 Water, sewer, and utility lines

(P-683)

NTS INC

Also Called: Newberry Technical Services
8200 Stockdale Hwy Ste M10306
(93311-1029)
PHONE..............................661 588-8514
EMP: 425
Web: www.ntsinc.com
SIC: 1623 1541 1771 Pipeline construction, nsk; Industrial buildings, new construction, nec; Concrete work

(P-684)

ORION CONSTRUCTION CORPORATION

2185 La Mirada Dr (92081-8830)
PHONE..............................760 597-9660
Richard Dowsing, *CEO*
Mark Dowsing, *
EMP: 80 **EST:** 1987
SQ FT: 7,000
SALES (est): 29.24MM **Privately Held**
Web: www.orionconstruction.com
SIC: 1623 1629 1542 Water, sewer, and utility lines; Industrial plant construction; Nonresidential construction, nec

(P-685)

PRECISION PIPELINE LLC

10400 Trademark St (91730-5826)
PHONE..............................909 229-6858
EMP: 441
SALES (corp-wide): 9.78B **Publicly Held**
Web: www.precisionpipelinellc.com
SIC: 1623 Pipeline construction, nsk
HQ: Precision Pipeline Llc
  3314 56th St
  Eau Claire WI
  715 874-4510

(P-686)

PRIMORIS SERVICES CORPORATION

26000 Commercentre Dr (92630-8816)
PHONE..............................949 598-9242
Peter J Moerbeek, *Prin*
EMP: 123
Web: www.prim.com
SIC: 1623 Pipeline construction, nsk
PA: Primoris Services Corporation
  2300 N Field St Ste 1900
  Dallas TX

(P-687)

S E PIPE LINE CONSTRUCTION CO

11832 Bloomfield Ave (90670-4610)
PHONE..............................562 868-9771
Charles Rikel, *Pr*
James Doulames, *VP*
Thomas Tustin, *Sec*
EMP: 100 **EST:** 1946
SQ FT: 5,000
SALES (est): 23.83MM **Privately Held**
Web: www.sepipeline.com
SIC: 1623 Gas main construction

(P-688)

SCHILLING PARADISE CORP

697 Greenfield Dr (92021-2983)
PHONE..............................619 449-4141
EMP: 175 **EST:** 2009
SALES (est): 28.19MM **Privately Held**
Web: www.schillingcorp.com
SIC: 1623 1731 Underground utilities contractor; General electrical contractor

(P-689)

SCW CONTRACTING CORPORATION

2525 Old Highway 395 (92028-8794)
PHONE..............................760 728-1308
Jeffrey Dean Scrape, *CEO*
Susanne Scrape, *
EMP: 70 **EST:** 1980
SQ FT: 3,000
SALES (est): 15.39MM **Privately Held**
Web: www.scwcompanies.com
SIC: 1623 1791 3449 Underground utilities contractor; Structural steel erection; Miscellaneous metalwork

(P-690)

SEMPRA LNG INTERNATIONAL LLC

488 8th Ave (92101-7123)
PHONE..............................661 399-2077
Lisa Glatch, *Pr*
EMP: 82 **EST:** 2015
SALES (est): 4.49MM **Privately Held**
Web: www.sempra.com
SIC: 1623 4922 Natural gas compressor station construction; Pipelines, natural gas

(P-691)

SHOFFEITT PIPELINE INC

15801 Rockfield Blvd Ste L (92618-2869)
PHONE..............................949 581-1600
Kathy Shoffeitt, *Pr*
John Shoffeitt, *
John Shoffeitt Junior, *Sec*
EMP: 80 **EST:** 2013
SQ FT: 3,200
SALES (est): 9.58MM **Privately Held**
Web: www.shoffeittpipeline.com
SIC: 1623 Underground utilities contractor

(P-692)

SOLEX CONTRACTING INC

42146 Remington Ave (92590-2547)
PHONE..............................951 308-1706
Jerry Allen, *Pr*
EMP: 110 **EST:** 2004
SQ FT: 12,000
SALES (est): 40.3MM **Privately Held**
Web: www.solexcontracting.com
SIC: 1623 1542 1541 Communication line and transmission tower construction; Commercial and office building, new construction; Renovation, remodeling and repairs: industrial buildings

(P-693)

SOUTHWEST CONTRACTORS (PA)

Also Called: Bowman Pipeline Contractors
136 Allen Rd # 100 (93314-3710)
PHONE..............................661 588-0484
Floyd E Bowman Junior, *CEO*
Kathy Bowman, *
EMP: 25 **EST:** 1981
SALES (est): 23.28MM
SALES (corp-wide): 23.28MM **Privately Held**
Web: www.southwestcontractors.net

SIC: 1623 3443 Oil and gas pipeline construction; Industrial vessels, tanks, and containers

(P-694)

SPINIELLO COMPANIES

2650 Pomona Blvd (91768-3220)
PHONE..............................909 629-1000
Priscilla Moyer, *Mgr*
EMP: 152
SALES (corp-wide): 92.17MM **Privately Held**
Web: www.spiniello.com
SIC: 1623 Underground utilities contractor
PA: Spiniello Companies
  354 Eisenhower Pkwy # 1200
  Livingston NJ
  973 808-8383

(P-695)

SUKUT CONSTRUCTION LLC

4010 W Chandler Ave (92704-5202)
PHONE..............................714 540-5351
Michael Crawford, *Prin*
Paul Kuliev, *
EMP: 99 **EST:** 2014
SALES (est): 20.61MM **Privately Held**
Web: www.sukut.com
SIC: 1623 1629 1611 Water, sewer, and utility lines; Earthmoving contractor; Grading

(P-696)

T C CONSTRUCTION COMPANY INC

Also Called: Tc Construction Company
10540 Prospect Ave (92071-4529)
PHONE..............................619 448-4560
Terry W Cameron, *CEO*
Austin Cameron, *
Derek Franken, *
Jack Gieffels, *
Darren Tharp, *
EMP: 230 **EST:** 1976
SQ FT: 16,000
SALES (est): 62.22MM **Privately Held**
Web: www.tcincsd.com
SIC: 1623 1611 Underground utilities contractor; Highway and street paving contractor

(P-697)

THE ORTIZ CORPORATION

2000 Mckinley Ave (91950-5427)
PHONE..............................619 434-7925
EMP: 88 **EST:** 2021
SALES (est): 13.24MM **Privately Held**
Web: www.ortizcorporation.com
SIC: 1623 Underground utilities contractor

(P-698)

THERMAL ENERGY SOLUTIONS INC

100 Quantico Ave (93307-2839)
PHONE..............................661 489-4100
Nelson Ivan Ayala, *CEO*
Gabriela Lopez De Ayala, *
Nelson Ayala, *
EMP: 27 **EST:** 2008
SALES (est): 2.74MM **Privately Held**
Web: www.thermalenergyinc.com
SIC: 1623 1711 3494 7699 Oil and gas line and compressor station construction; Process piping contractor; Line strainers, for use in piping systems; Tank and boiler cleaning service

(P-699)

TURN AROUND COMMUNICATIONS INC

100 N Barranca St Ste 260 (91791-1637)
P.O. Box 6121 (91734-2121)
PHONE..............................626 443-2400
Sayeid Kouhkan, *Pr*
EMP: 170 **EST:** 2002
SALES (est): 25.77MM **Privately Held**
Web: www.turnaroundcommunications.net
SIC: 1623 Telephone and communication line construction

(P-700)

VADNAIS TRENCHLESS SVCS INC

11858 Bernardo Plaza Ct Ste 100 (92128-2440)
PHONE..............................858 550-1460
Paul Vadnais, *CEO*
Jeff Anderson, *
Jesse Mangan, *
▲ **EMP:** 100 **EST:** 1964
SALES (est): 9.26MM **Privately Held**
Web: www.vadnaiscorp.com
SIC: 1623 Sewer line construction

(P-701)

VALVERDE CONSTRUCTION INC

10936 Shoemaker Ave (90670-4533)
P.O. Box 3223 (90670-0223)
PHONE..............................562 906-1826
Joe A Valverde, *Pr*
Joe A Valverde, *Pr*
Edward Valverde, *
Rose Valverde, *
Christopher Valverde, *
EMP: 135 **EST:** 1972
SQ FT: 9,000
SALES (est): 25.68MM **Privately Held**
Web: valverde.webflow.io
SIC: 1623 Water main construction

(P-702)

VCI CONSTRUCTION LLC (HQ)

1921 W 11th St Ste A (91786-3508)
PHONE..............................909 946-0905
John Xanthos, *Pr*
Logan Teal, *
Vic Marovish, *
EMP: 100 **EST:** 1998
SQ FT: 29,500
SALES (est): 95.76MM
SALES (corp-wide): 3.81B **Publicly Held**
Web: www.vcicom.com
SIC: 1623 Underground utilities contractor
PA: Dycom Industries, Inc.
  11780 Us Highway 1 # 600
  Palm Beach Gardens FL
  561 627-7171

(P-703)

W A RASIC CNSTR CO INC (PA)

4150 Long Beach Blvd (90807-2650)
PHONE..............................562 928-6111
Peter L Rasic, *CEO*
EMP: 147 **EST:** 1978
SQ FT: 8,500
SALES (est): 121.56MM
SALES (corp-wide): 121.56MM **Privately Held**
Web: www.warasic.com
SIC: 1623 Sewer line construction

(P-704)

W M LYLES CO

42142 Roick Dr (92590-3695)
PHONE..............................951 296-2354
EMP: 113
SALES (corp-wide): 17.85MM **Privately Held**
Web: www.wmlylesco.com

PRODUCTS & SVCS

SIC: 1623 Water, sewer, and utility lines
HQ: W. M. Lyles Co.
525 W Alluvial Ave
Fresno CA
559 441-1900

1629 Heavy Construction, Nec

(P-705)
ANAERGIA SERVICES LLC
705 Palomar Airport Rd Ste 200
(92011-1029)
PHONE...............................760 436-8870
Andrew Benedek, *CEO*
Arun Sharma, *Pr*
Hani Kaissi, *CFO*
EMP: 22 EST: 2011
SALES (est): 15.55MM
SALES (corp-wide): 121.24MM **Privately
Held**
Web: www.anaergia.com
SIC: 1629 4911 7699 4953 Waste water and
sewage treatment plant construction;
Distribution, electric power; Waste cleaning
services; Recycling, waste materials
PA: Anaergia Inc
4210 South Service Rd
Burlington ON
905 766-3333

(P-706)
BEMUS LANDSCAPE INC
951 Calle Negocio Ste D (92673-6202)
P.O. Box 74268 (92673-0143)
PHONE...............................714 557-7910
William Howard Bemus, *Pr*
Jonathon Parry, *
Martine Bemus, *
EMP: 300 EST: 1973
SQ FT: 7,000
SALES (est): 47.49MM **Privately Held**
Web: www.bemus.com
SIC: 1629 0782 Drainage system
construction; Landscape contractors

(P-707)
CURTIN MARITIME CORP
725 Pier T Ave (90802-6234)
P.O. Box 2531 (90801-2531)
PHONE...............................562 983-7257
Martin Jeremiah Curtin Junior, *CEO*
Kelly Curtin, *
EMP: 326 EST: 1997
SQ FT: 65,340
SALES (est): 104.65MM **Privately Held**
Web: www.curtinmaritime.com
SIC: 1629 4492 Marine construction;
Tugboat service

(P-708)
**ENVIROGENICS SYSTEMS
COMPANY**
9255 Telstar Ave (91731-2845)
PHONE...............................818 573-9220
Doctor Fadi Abbash, *Pr*
R Kadaj, *
EMP: 100 EST: 1967
SQ FT: 91,000
SALES (est): 6.48MM **Privately Held**
SIC: 1629 Industrial plant construction

(P-709)
FOUNDATION PILE INC
8375 Almeria Ave (92335-3283)
P.O. Box 97 (94561-0097)
PHONE...............................909 350-1584
Derek Halecky, *CEO*
Peter Brandl, *
Dermot Fallon, *

Earl Robbins, *
Nikki Sjoblom, *
EMP: 97 EST: 1978
SALES (est): 15.7MM
SALES (corp-wide): 49.44MM **Privately
Held**
Web: www.foundationpiledriving.com
SIC: 1629 1794 Pile driving contractor;
Excavation and grading, building
construction
PA: Foundation Constructors, Inc.
81 Big Break Rd
Oakley CA
925 754-6633

(P-710)
HELLAS CONSTRUCTION INC
5135 Avenida Encinas Ste A (92008-4341)
PHONE...............................760 891-8090
James Towsley, *Owner*
EMP: 387
Web: www.hellasconstruction.com
SIC: 1629 Athletic and recreation facilities
construction
HQ: Hellas Construction, Inc.
12000 W Parmer Ln
Cedar Park TX
800 233-5714

(P-711)
HERZOG CONTRACTING CORP
3760 Kilroy Airport Way Ste 120
(90806-2455)
P.O. Box 1089 (64502-1089)
PHONE...............................562 595-7414
EMP: 88
SALES (corp-wide): 479.93MM **Privately
Held**
Web: www.herzog.com
SIC: 1629 1611 4953 Railroad and railway
roadbed construction; Highway and street
paving contractor; Sanitary landfill operation
HQ: Herzog Contracting Corp.
600 S Riverside Rd
Saint Joseph MO
816 233-9001

(P-712)
IRWIN INDUSTRIES INC
2301 Rosecrans Ave Ste 3185
(90245-4918)
P.O. Box 8678 (25303-0678)
PHONE...............................704 457-5117
EMP: 710
SIC: 1629 1731 1796 7353 Power plant
construction; Electric power systems
contractors; Power generating equipment
installation; Heavy construction equipment
rental

(P-713)
J CLOUD INCORPORATED
2094 Willow Glen Dr (92019-3903)
PHONE...............................619 593-9020
Jon E Cloud, *CEO*
Jon Cloud, *Pr*
James Cloud, *VP*
EMP: 25 EST: 1993
SALES (est): 2.3MM **Privately Held**
SIC: 1629 1771 5032 1423 Earthmoving
contractor; Concrete work; Aggregate;
Crushed and broken granite

(P-714)
RAIN BIRD DISTRIBUTION CORP
1000 W Sierra Madre Ave (91702-1700)
P.O. Box 37 (91702-0037)
PHONE...............................626 963-9311
Anthony Lafetra, *CEO*
Anthony W Lafetra, *

Arthur Ludwick, *
EMP: 27 EST: 1946
SQ FT: 20,000
SALES (est): 6.64MM **Privately Held**
Web: www.rainbird.com
SIC: 1629 3523 Irrigation system
construction; Fertilizing, spraying, dusting,
and irrigation machinery

(P-715)
**SHIMMICK CONSTRUCTION CO
INC (HQ)**
Also Called: Transprtion Oprtons MGT Slton
530 Technology Dr Ste 300 (92618-1350)
PHONE...............................949 591-5922
Steve Richards, *Pr*
Greg Dukellis, *
Andrew Sloane, *
John White, *
Devin Nordhagen, *
EMP: 119 EST: 1990
SQ FT: 30,000
SALES (est): 575.38MM
SALES (corp-wide): 14.38B **Publicly Held**
Web: www.shimmick.com
SIC: 1629 1623 Earthmoving contractor;
Sewer line construction
PA: Aecom
13355 Noel Rd Ste 400
Dallas TX
972 788-1000

(P-716)
SHIMMICK CORPORATION
530 Technology Dr Ste 300 (92618-1350)
PHONE...............................510 777-5000
Steven E Richards, *CEO*
Mitchell B Goldsteen, *Ofcr*
Devin J Nordhagen, *Ex VP*
EMP: 1500 EST: 1990
SQ FT: 6,000
SALES (est): 664.16MM **Privately Held**
SIC: 1629 Irrigation system construction

(P-717)
SLATER INC
11045 Rose Ave (92337-7051)
P.O. Box 759 (92334-0759)
PHONE...............................909 822-6800
Phillip S Slater, *CEO*
Steve David, *VP*
Edward Johnson, *CFO*
EMP: 97 EST: 1981
SQ FT: 6,000
SALES (est): 20.59MM **Privately Held**
Web: www.slaterinc.com
SIC: 1629 8711 Drainage system
construction; Engineering services

(P-718)
TIMEC COMPANIES INC
Also Called: Timec
2997 E Maria St (90221-5801)
PHONE...............................310 885-4710
Craig Crowder, *CEO*
EMP: 238
Web: www.timec.com
SIC: 1629 Industrial plant construction
HQ: Timec Companies Inc
473 E Channel Rd
Benicia CA
707 642-2222

(P-719)
US JOINER LLC
Also Called: Marine Interiors
2800 Harbor Dr (92113)
P.O. Box 13117 (92170-3117)
PHONE...............................619 233-3993
Andy How, *Brnch Mgr*

EMP: 42
SALES (corp-wide): 513.66MM **Privately
Held**
Web: www.tridentllc.com
SIC: 1629 5551 5091 3731 Marine
construction; Boat dealers; Sporting and
recreation goods; Shipbuilding and repairing
HQ: Us Joiner Llc
5690 Three Notch D Rd # 200
Crozet VA
434 220-8500

(P-720)
VISTA STEEL CO INC
Also Called: VISTA STEEL CO INC
331 W Lewis St (93001-1394)
PHONE...............................805 653-1189
John Swaffar, *Brnch Mgr*
EMP: 24
SALES (corp-wide): 4.72MM **Privately
Held**
Web: www.vistasteelcompany.com
SIC: 1629 3449 Dams, waterways, docks,
and other marine construction;
Miscellaneous metalwork
PA: Vista Steel Company
6100 Francis Botello Rd
Goleta CA
805 964-4732

(P-721)
**WARREN COLLINS AND ASSOC
INC (PA)**
Also Called: Collins Company
5470 Daniels St (91710-9012)
PHONE...............................909 548-6708
Larry W Collins, *Pr*
Nancy Collins, *
▲ **EMP: 23 EST:** 1975
SQ FT: 8,000
SALES (est): 6.46MM
SALES (corp-wide): 6.46MM **Privately
Held**
Web: www.collinscompany.com
SIC: 1629 3949 1799 3446 Athletic and
recreation facilities construction; Sporting
and athletic goods, nec; Scaffolding;
Scaffolds, mobile or stationary: metal

1711 Plumbing, Heating, Air-
conditioning

(P-722)
**20/20 PLUMBING & HEATING
INC (PA)**
Also Called: Honeywell Authorized Dealer
7343 Orangewood Dr Ste B (92504-1027)
PHONE...............................951 396-2020
Thomas Lew Baker, *CEO*
EMP: 97 EST: 2014
SALES (est): 46.55MM
SALES (corp-wide): 46.55MM **Privately
Held**
Web: www.2020ph.com
SIC: 1711 Plumbing contractors

(P-723)
**20/20 PLUMBING & HEATING
INC**
674 Rancheros Dr (92069-3005)
PHONE...............................760 535-3101
EMP: 103
SALES (corp-wide): 46.55MM **Privately
Held**
Web: www.2020ph.com
SIC: 1711 Plumbing contractors
PA: 20/20 Plumbing & Heating, Inc.
7343 Orangewood Dr Ste B
Riverside CA
951 396-2020

(P-724)
A & D FIRE PROTECTION INC
7130 Convoy Ct (92111-1019)
PHONE...............................619 258-7697
Andrew R Otero, *Pr*
EMP: 80 **EST:** 1988
SQ FT: 10,000
SALES (est): 11.2MM **Privately Held**
Web: www.adfiresprinklers.com
SIC: 1711 1542 Fire sprinkler system
installation; Nonresidential construction, nec

(P-725)
A O REED & CO LLC
4777 Ruffner St (92111-1578)
P.O. Box 85226 (92186-5226)
PHONE...............................858 565-4131
Steve Andrade, *Ch Bd*
David Clarkin, *
Craig Koehler, *
EMP: 500 **EST:** 1914
SQ FT: 55,000
SALES (est): 148.26MM **Privately Held**
Web: www.aoreed.com
SIC: 1711 Mechanical contractor

(P-726)
**ACCO ENGINEERED SYSTEMS
INC (PA)**
Also Called: Acco
888 E Walnut St (91101-1895)
PHONE...............................818 244-6571
EMP: 900 **EST:** 1934
SALES (est): 1.51B
SALES (corp-wide): 1.51B **Privately Held**
Web: www.accoes.com
SIC: 1711 7623 3448 Process piping
contractor; Air conditioning repair;
Buildings, portable: prefabricated metal

(P-727)
**ACH MECHANICAL
CONTRACTORS INC**
411 Business Center Ct (92373-8084)
PHONE...............................909 307-2850
Hector Vargas, *
EMP: 80 **EST:** 2000
SQ FT: 14,450
SALES (est): 20.46MM **Privately Held**
Web: www.achmechanical.com
SIC: 1711 Mechanical contractor

(P-728)
AIRE-RITE AC & RFRGN LLC
Also Called: Imperial Rfrgn & Ice Mchs
15122 Bolsa Chica St (92649-1025)
P.O. Box 3419 (92605-3419)
PHONE...............................714 895-2338
Donald Langston, *CEO*
David Langston, *
Carol Langston, *
EMP: 97 **EST:** 1972
SQ FT: 22,000
SALES (est): 21.5MM
SALES (corp-wide): 627.87MM **Privately
Held**
Web: www.airerite.com
SIC: 1711 Plumbing, heating, air-conditioning
PA: Ares Holdings, Llc
1045 S John Rodes Blvd
Melbourne FL
321 727-2865

(P-729)
ALPHA MECHANICAL INC
4990 Greencraig Ln Ste A (92123-1673)
PHONE...............................858 278-3500
Boris Barshak, *Brnch Mgr*
EMP: 115

Web: www.alphamechanical.com
SIC: 1711 Fire sprinkler system installation
PA: Alpha Mechanical, Inc.
1866 Friendship Dr
El Cajon CA

(P-730)
**ALPHA MECHANICAL HEATING
& AIR CONDITIONING INC**
4885 Greencraig Ln (92123-1664)
PHONE...............................858 279-1300
EMP: 250
SIC: 1711 Sprinkler contractors

(P-731)
**AMPAM PARKS MECHANICAL
INC**
17036 Avalon Blvd (90746-1206)
PHONE...............................310 835-1532
Charles E Parks Iii, *CEO*
John D Parks, *
James C Wright, *
Chris Kennedy, *
▲ **EMP:** 800 **EST:** 1997
SQ FT: 16,000
SALES (est): 156.98MM **Privately Held**
Web: www.ampam.com
SIC: 1711 Plumbing contractors

(P-732)
**AMS AMERICAN MECH SVCS
MD INC**
2116 E Walnut Ave (92831-4845)
PHONE...............................714 888-6820
Charles S Knight, *Genl Mgr*
EMP: 170
SALES (corp-wide): 1.52B **Privately Held**
Web: www.amsofusa.com
SIC: 1711 Mechanical contractor
HQ: Ams American Mechanical Services Of
Maryland, Inc.
13300 Mid Atlantic Blvd
Laurel MD
301 206-5070

(P-733)
**ANDERSEN COMMERCIAL
PLBG INC**
1608 Yeager Ave (91750-5853)
PHONE...............................909 599-5950
Paul Andersen, *CEO*
Duane Kerr, *
EMP: 101 **EST:** 1993
SQ FT: 2,000
SALES (est): 11.64MM **Privately Held**
Web: www.andersenplumbing.com
SIC: 1711 Plumbing contractors

(P-734)
**ARROWHEAD BRASS &
PLUMBING LLC**
5147 Alhambra Ave (90032-3413)
PHONE...............................800 332-4267
Fred Schneider, *CEO*
▲ **EMP:** 80 **EST:** 1936
SQ FT: 35,000
SALES (est): 9.87MM **Privately Held**
Web: www.arrowheadbrass.com
SIC: 1711 Plumbing contractors

(P-735)
ASI HASTINGS INC
Also Called: Asi Heating, Air and Solar
4870 Viewridge Ave Ste 200 (92123)
PHONE...............................619 590-9300
TOLL FREE: 800
Philip Justo, *Pr*
Kenneth Justo, *

EMP: 120 **EST:** 1952
SQ FT: 2,000
SALES (est): 23.86MM
SALES (corp-wide): 91.05MM **Privately
Held**
Web: www.asiheatingandair.com
SIC: 1711 Heating systems repair and
maintenance
PA: Service Champions, Llc
3150 E Birch St
Brea CA
714 777-7777

(P-736)
ASSOCIATE MECH CONTRS INC
622 S Vinewood St (92029-1925)
PHONE...............................760 294-3517
Richard Reinholz, *Pr*
Laura Reinholz, *Corporate Secretary*
Christina Payne, *
EMP: 150 **EST:** 2011
SALES (est): 47.38MM **Privately Held**
Web: www.amechinc.com
SIC: 1711 Mechanical contractor

(P-737)
**ASTRO MECHANICAL
CONTRACTORS INC**
603 S Marshall Ave (92020-4214)
PHONE...............................619 442-9686
EMP: 85 **EST:** 1960
SALES (est): 15.88MM **Privately Held**
Web: www.astro-mech.com
SIC: 1711 1542 Plumbing contractors;
Nonresidential construction, nec

(P-738)
ATLAS MECHANICAL INC (PA)
Also Called: Honeywell Authorized Dealer
8260 Camino Santa Fe Ste B (92121)
PHONE...............................858 554-0700
EMP: 74 **EST:** 1991
SALES (est): 57.7MM **Privately Held**
Web: www.atlasmechanical.com
SIC: 1711 3531 Ventilation and duct work
contractor; Construction machinery

(P-739)
AWHAP ACQUISITION CORP
28358 Constellation Rd Ste 698
(91355-5010)
PHONE...............................888 611-4328
Alex Stuckey, *CEO*
EMP: 152 **EST:** 2020
SALES (est): 7.79MM **Privately Held**
SIC: 1711 Plumbing, heating, air-conditioning

(P-740)
BARR ENGINEERING INC
19 Castano (92688-1662)
PHONE...............................562 944-1722
Peter Buongiorno, *Pr*
Pamela Price-recchia, *Sec*
Mike Buongiorno, *
EMP: 82 **EST:** 1958
SALES (est): 21.69MM **Privately Held**
Web: www.barrengineering.com
SIC: 1711 Warm air heating and air
conditioning contractor

(P-741)
**BAYWA RE OPERATION SVCS
LLC**
Also Called: Baywa R.E.
18575 Jamboree Rd Ste 850 (92612-2558)
PHONE...............................949 398-3915
Jam Attari, *CEO*
EMP: 21 **EST:** 2019
SALES (est): 2.52MM **Privately Held**

Web: us.baywa-re.com
SIC: 1711 8711 3621 Solar energy contractor
; Energy conservation engineering;
Windmills, electric generating

(P-742)
BCM CUSTOMER SERVICE
12155 Kirkham Rd (92064-6870)
PHONE...............................858 679-5757
Brian R Cox, *CEO*
EMP: 90 **EST:** 1996
SQ FT: 30,000
SALES (est): 4.66MM **Privately Held**
SIC: 1711 1796 Plumbing, heating, air-
conditioning; Installing building equipment

(P-743)
BERNEL INC
Also Called: Vfs Fire Protection Services
501 W Southern Ave (92865-3217)
PHONE...............................714 778-6070
Randy Roland Nelson, *CEO*
Kevin Berthoud, *
Mario Lopez, *
EMP: 140 **EST:** 1994
SQ FT: 7,800
SALES (est): 29.35MM **Privately Held**
Web: www.vfsfire.com
SIC: 1711 7382 Fire sprinkler system
installation; Security systems services

(P-744)
BILL HOWE PLUMBING INC
Also Called: Am-PM Sewer & Drain Cleaning
9210 Sky Park Ct (92123-4478)
PHONE...............................800 245-5469
William Howe, *Pr*
Tina Howe, *
EMP: 85 **EST:** 1982
SALES (est): 24.09MM **Privately Held**
Web: www.billhowe.com
SIC: 1711 Plumbing contractors

(P-745)
BONESO BROTHERS CNSTR INC
2758 Concrete Ct (93446-5936)
PHONE...............................805 227-4450
Steve Boneso, *Pr*
Rob Boneso, *
EMP: 80 **EST:** 1999
SQ FT: 4,000
SALES (est): 40MM **Privately Held**
Web:
www.bonesobrothersconstruction.com
SIC: 1711 1542 Mechanical contractor;
Nonresidential construction, nec

(P-746)
BREEZE AIR CONDITIONING LLC
75145 Saint Charles Pl Ste A (92211-9048)
PHONE...............................760 346-0855
Joe Coker, *Managing Member*
EMP: 59 **EST:** 1980
SQ FT: 33,000
SALES (est): 8.59MM **Privately Held**
Web: www.breezeac.com
SIC: 1711 3444 5075 3433 Warm air heating
and air conditioning contractor; Sheet
metalwork; Warm air heating and air
conditioning; Logs, gas fireplace

(P-747)
**BRIGHTVIEW LANDSCAPE DEV
INC**
8 Hughes Ste 125 (92618-2079)
PHONE...............................714 546-7975
Gins Garmann, *Mgr*
EMP: 166
SALES (corp-wide): 2.82B **Publicly Held**
Web: www.brightview.com

P
R
O
D
U
C
T
S
&
S
V
C
S

SIC: **1711** 0781 Irrigation sprinkler system installation; Landscape services
HQ: Brightview Landscape Development, Inc.
27001 Agoura Rd Ste 350
Calabasas CA
818 223-8500

(P-748)
BROMIC HEATING PTY LIMITED
7595 Irvine Center Dr Ste 100 (92618-2958)
PHONE..................855 552-7432
EMP: 100 EST: 2017
SALES (est): 4.49MM **Privately Held**
Web: www.bromic.com
SIC: **1711** Mechanical contractor

(P-749)
C & L REFRIGERATION CORP
Also Called: HONEYWELL AUTHORIZED DEALER
4111 N Palm St (92835-1025)
P.O. Box 2319 (92822-2319)
PHONE..................800 901-4822
Ronald J Cassell, *CEO*
Ronald J Cassell Junior, *CEO*
Denise Lowe, *CFO*
Larry Jaslove, *
EMP: 150 EST: 1978
SQ FT: 18,000
SALES (est): 50.97MM **Privately Held**
Web: www.clrefrigeration.com
SIC: **1711** Refrigeration contractor

(P-750)
CASCADE THERMAL SOLUTIONS LLC (PA)
1890 Cordell Ct Ste 102 (92020-0913)
PHONE..................619 562-8852
Romulo Lambert Smith, *CEO*
Romulo Lambert Smith, *Pr*
Kay Smith, *
EMP: 49 EST: 1989
SQ FT: 55,000
SALES (est): 19.03MM **Privately Held**
Web: www.fullspectrumlabservices.com
SIC: **1711** 3821 7699 Refrigeration contractor; Laboratory apparatus and furniture; Scientific equipment repair service

(P-751)
CFP FIRE PROTECTION INC
153 Technology Dr Ste 200 (92618-2461)
PHONE..................949 727-3277
EMP: 100 EST: 2002
SQ FT: 21,960
SALES (est): 13.22MM **Privately Held**
Web: www.cfpfire.com
SIC: **1711** Fire sprinkler system installation
PA: Mx Holdings Us, Inc.
153 Technology Dr Ste 200
Irvine CA

(P-752)
CHRISTIAN BROTHERS MECHANICAL SERVICES INC
Also Called: CB Controls
11140 Thurston Ln (91752-1426)
PHONE..................951 361-2247
EMP: 110 EST: 1985
SALES (est): 18.35MM **Privately Held**
Web: www.cbhvac.com
SIC: **1711** Warm air heating and air conditioning contractor

(P-753)
CIRCULATING AIR INC (PA)
Also Called: Honeywell Authorized Dealer

7337 Varna Ave (91605-4009)
PHONE..................818 764-0530
TOLL FREE: 800
Joseph Gallagher, *Ex VP*
Susan Gallagher, *
Marcy Ahlstrom, *
EMP: 100 EST: 1965
SQ FT: 13,000
SALES (est): 24.86MM
SALES (corp-wide): 24.86MM **Privately Held**
Web: www.circulatingair.com
SIC: **1711** Mechanical contractor

(P-754)
CLAY DUNN ENTERPRISES INC
Also Called: Air-TEC
1606 E Carson St (90745-2504)
P.O. Box 5444 (90749-5444)
PHONE..................310 549-1698
Clayton N Dunn, *Pr*
Hayley Amberg, *
EMP: 138 EST: 1969
SQ FT: 18,000
SALES (est): 45.04MM **Privately Held**
Web: www.airtecperforms.com
SIC: **1711** Warm air heating and air conditioning contractor

(P-755)
CONTROL AIR CONDITIONING CORPORATION
Also Called: Honeywell Authorized Dealer
5200 E La Palma Ave (92807-2019)
PHONE..................714 777-8600
EMP: 360
SIC: **1711** 3444 Warm air heating and air conditioning contractor; Ducts, sheet metal

(P-756)
COOLSYS COML INDUS SLTIONS INC (DH)
145 S State College Blvd Ste 200 (92821-5818)
PHONE..................714 510-9609
EMP: 155 EST: 1995
SALES (est): 480.58MM
SALES (corp-wide): 3.06B **Publicly Held**
Web: www.sourcerefrigeration.com
SIC: **1711** Refrigeration contractor
HQ: Coolsys, Inc.
145 S State College Blvd
Brea CA
714 510-9577

(P-757)
COUNTYWIDE MECH SYSTEMS LLC
1400 N Johnson Ave Ste 114 (92020-1651)
PHONE..................619 449-9900
Paul Duke, *Pr*
David Cimpl, *
EMP: 230 EST: 2011
SQ FT: 5,000
SALES (est): 93.71MM
SALES (corp-wide): 281.74MM **Privately Held**
Web: www.countywidems.com
SIC: **1711** Mechanical contractor
PA: Modigent, Llc
3930 E Watkins St Ste 300
Phoenix AZ
888 293-5334

(P-758)
COUTS HEATING & COOLING INC
1693 Rimpau Ave (92881-3202)
PHONE..................951 278-5560

EMP: 160 EST: 1978
SALES (est): 27.77MM **Privately Held**
Web: www.couts.com
SIC: **1711** Warm air heating and air conditioning contractor

(P-759)
CRITCHFELD MECH INC STHERN CAL
15391 Springdale St (92649-1100)
PHONE..................949 390-2900
Mike Pearlman, *CEO*
EMP: 100 EST: 2004
SALES (est): 4.17MM **Privately Held**
Web: www.cmihvac.com
SIC: **1711** Warm air heating and air conditioning contractor

(P-760)
DAC HEATING AND AC
Also Called: Dac Heating and Air
190 Sierra Ct Ste B3 (93550-7608)
PHONE..................661 441-2787
Alex Beltran, *CEO*
EMP: 18 EST: 2017
SALES (est): 2.02MM **Privately Held**
Web: www.dachvac.com
SIC: **1711** 8711 3634 3564 Plumbing, heating, air-conditioning; Heating and ventilation engineering; Heating units, electric (radiant heat): baseboard or wall; Filters, air: furnaces, air conditioning equipment, etc.

(P-761)
DAVE WILLIAMS PLBG & ELEC INC
75140 Saint Charles Pl Ste C (92211-9044)
PHONE..................760 296-1397
Daniel Williams, *Pr*
Dave Williams, *
EMP: 110 EST: 2008
SALES (est): 4.83MM **Privately Held**
Web: www.dwpeinc.com
SIC: **1711** Plumbing contractors

(P-762)
DAVIDSONS AC & HTG INC
Also Called: Davidsons AC Htg & Sh
495 S Sierra Way (92408-1444)
PHONE..................909 885-2703
Richard S Davidson, *Pr*
EMP: 20 EST: 1985
SQ FT: 2,500
SALES (est): 869.89K **Privately Held**
Web: www.davidsonsairandheat.com
SIC: **1711** 3444 Warm air heating and air conditioning contractor; Sheet metal specialties, not stamped

(P-763)
DESERT MECHANICAL INC
Also Called: Dmi
15870 Olden St (91342-1241)
PHONE..................702 873-7333
Casey M Condron, *Pr*
Alex L Hodson, *
Andre Burnthon, *
Joseph Guglielmo, *
Dan Naylor, *
EMP: 1100 EST: 1977
SQ FT: 25,000
SALES (est): 97.67MM
SALES (corp-wide): 3.79B **Publicly Held**
Web: www.lvdmi.com
SIC: **1711** Plumbing contractors
PA: Tutor Perini Corporation
15901 Olden St
Rancho Cascades CA
818 362-8391

(P-764)
DYNAMIC PLUMBING SYSTEMS INC
5920 Winterhaven Ave (92504-1048)
PHONE..................951 343-1200
EMP: 306
SIC: **1711** Plumbing contractors

(P-765)
ECB CORP (PA)
Also Called: Omniduct
6400 Artesia Blvd (90620-1006)
PHONE..................714 385-8900
Robert Brumleu, *Pr*
▲ EMP: 100 EST: 1980
SQ FT: 56,000
SALES (est): 57.91MM
SALES (corp-wide): 57.91MM **Privately Held**
Web: www.omniduct.com
SIC: **1711** 3444 Ventilation and duct work contractor; Ducts, sheet metal

(P-766)
ENERGY ENTERPRISES USA INC (PA)
Also Called: Canopy Energy
6842 Van Nuys Blvd Ste 800 (91405-4650)
PHONE..................424 339-0005
Lior Agam, *CEO*
EMP: 100 EST: 2011
SQ FT: 11,000
SALES (est): 16.07MM
SALES (corp-wide): 16.07MM **Privately Held**
Web: www.canopyenergy.com
SIC: **1711** Solar energy contractor

(P-767)
ENVISE (HQ)
Also Called: Envise
12131 Western Ave (92841-2914)
PHONE..................800 613-6240
Chris Lofaso, *CEO*
EMP: 113 EST: 2015
SALES (est): 88.86MM
SALES (corp-wide): 2.03B **Privately Held**
Web: www.southlandind.com
SIC: **1711** Plumbing, heating, air-conditioning
PA: Southland Industries
12131 Western Ave
Garden Grove CA
800 613-6240

(P-768)
ESS LLC
Also Called: Evergreen Solar Services
5227 Dantes View Dr (91301-2313)
PHONE..................888 303-6424
Jacob Stephens, *Pr*
Eliahu Arbib, *Prin*
Shaul Arbiv, *Prin*
EMP: 100 EST: 2011
SALES (est): 3.04MM **Privately Held**
SIC: **1711** Solar energy contractor

(P-769)
FREEDOM FOREVER LLC
3322 Garfield Ave (90040-3102)
PHONE..................714 955-8735
EMP: 1904
SALES (corp-wide): 227.62MM **Privately Held**
Web: www.freedomforever.com
SIC: **1711** Solar energy contractor
PA: Freedom Forever Llc
43445 Bus Pk Dr Ste 104
Temecula CA
888 557-6431

(P-770)
FREEDOM FOREVER LLC (PA)
43445 Business Park Dr Ste 104 (92590-3670)
PHONE..................888 557-6431
EMP: 89 **EST:** 2016
SALES (est): 227.62MM
SALES (corp-wide): 227.62MM **Privately Held**
Web: www.freedomforever.com
SIC: 1711 Solar energy contractor

(P-771)
FREEDOM SOLAR SERVICES
Also Called: Freedom Forever
43445 Business Park Dr Ste 110 (92590-3671)
PHONE..................888 557-6431
Brett Leon Bouchy, *CEO*
EMP: 150 **EST:** 2012
SALES (est): 13.15MM **Privately Held**
Web: www.freedomforever.com
SIC: 1711 Solar energy contractor

(P-772)
FRONTIER MECHANICAL INC
Also Called: Frontier Plumbing
6309 Seven Seas Ave (93308-5133)
PHONE..................661 589-6203
Rick Palmer, *Pr*
Brenda Palmer, *Stockholder**
EMP: 93 **EST:** 1987
SQ FT: 120,000
SALES (est): 9.12MM **Privately Held**
Web: www.frontier-plumbing.com
SIC: 1711 1521 Plumbing contractors; New construction, single-family houses

(P-773)
GENERAL UNDERGROUND
701 W Grove Ave (92865-3213)
P.O. Box 29830 (92809-0194)
PHONE..................714 632-8646
Robert Anderson, *CEO*
Terry Householder, *
Karla Distrola, *
EMP: 110 **EST:** 1985
SQ FT: 8,000
SALES (est): 23.69MM **Privately Held**
Web: www.gufpinc.com
SIC: 1711 Fire sprinkler system installation

(P-774)
GREATER SAN DIEGO AC CO INC
Also Called: Honeywell Authorized Dealer
3883 Ruffin Rd Ste C (92123-4813)
PHONE..................619 469-7818
Randy Baillargeon, *Pr*
Ryan Baillargeon, *
EMP: 115 **EST:** 1993
SQ FT: 8,500
SALES (est): 21.8MM **Privately Held**
Web: www.gsdac.com
SIC: 1711 Warm air heating and air conditioning contractor

(P-775)
H L MOE CO INC (PA)
Also Called: Keefe Plumbing Services
526 Commercial St (91203-1510)
PHONE..................818 572-2100
Martha Tennyson, *CEO*
Michael C Davis, *
Bernice Davis, *
Richard Herrera, *
Robert Francis, *
EMP: 130 **EST:** 1927
SALES (est): 21.94MM
SALES (corp-wide): 21.94MM **Privately Held**

Web: www.moeplumbing.com
SIC: 1711 Plumbing contractors

(P-776)
HELIX MECHANICAL INC
1100 N Magnolia Ave Ste L (92020-1953)
PHONE..................619 440-1518
Stephen Baker, *CEO*
Michael Hurley, *
Patrick Harrelson, *
EMP: 109 **EST:** 2003
SALES (est): 15.84MM **Privately Held**
Web: www.helixmechanical.com
SIC: 1711 1751 Mechanical contractor; Carpentry work

(P-777)
HPS MECHANICAL INC (PA)
3100 E Belle Ter (93307-6830)
PHONE..................661 397-2121
Les Denherder, *Pr*
Scott Denherder, *
EMP: 127 **EST:** 1959
SALES (est): 47.31MM
SALES (corp-wide): 47.31MM **Privately Held**
Web: www.hpsmechanical.com
SIC: 1711 Plumbing contractors

(P-778)
INDUSTRIAL COML SYSTEMS INC
Also Called: San Marcos Mechanical
1165 Joshua Way (92081-7840)
PHONE..................760 300-4094
Robin Sides, *Pr*
Matt Harbin, *
Cindy Sides, *
EMP: 160 **EST:** 1982
SQ FT: 15,000
SALES (est): 35.44MM **Privately Held**
Web: www.1ics.net
SIC: 1711 Ventilation and duct work contractor

(P-779)
INFINITY PLUMBING DESIGNS INC
9182 Stellar Ct (92883-4923)
PHONE..................951 737-4436
Andrew D Carlson, *Pr*
EMP: 300 **EST:** 2006
SQ FT: 5,925
SALES (est): 27.1MM **Privately Held**
Web: www.infinityplumbingdesigns.com
SIC: 1711 Plumbing contractors

(P-780)
INTEGRATED ENERGY GROUP LLC ✪
3929 E Guasti Rd Ste F (91761-1546)
PHONE..................605 381-7859
Shane Scaletti, *
EMP: 155 **EST:** 2023
SALES (est): 60MM **Privately Held**
SIC: 1711 Solar energy contractor

(P-781)
JACKSON & BLANC
7929 Arjons Dr (92126-4301)
PHONE..................858 831-7900
Kirk Jackson, *CEO*
John Fusca, *
▲ **EMP:** 110 **EST:** 1931
SQ FT: 36,000
SALES (est): 65.48MM **Privately Held**
Web: www.jacksonandblanc.com
SIC: 1711 Mechanical contractor

(P-782)
K & S AIR CONDITIONING INC
Also Called: K&S
143 E Meats Ave (92865-3309)
PHONE..................714 685-0077
Steven Patz, *Pr*
Renee Patz, *
EMP: 140 **EST:** 1952
SQ FT: 18,000
SALES (est): 26.8MM **Privately Held**
Web: www.kandsair.com
SIC: 1711 Warm air heating and air conditioning contractor

(P-783)
KEN STARR INC
Also Called: Home Comfort USA
1120 N Tustin Ave (92807-1712)
PHONE..................714 632-8789
Ken Starr, *Pr*
Paul Buono, *
EMP: 80 **EST:** 2011
SQ FT: 9,000
SALES (est): 19.68MM **Privately Held**
Web: www.homecomfortusa.com
SIC: 1711 Warm air heating and air conditioning contractor

(P-784)
LA SOLAR GROUP INC
Also Called: LA SOLAR GROUP
560 Library St (91340-2524)
PHONE..................818 373-0077
Ara Petrosyan, *CEO*
EMP: 91 **EST:** 2012
SALES (est): 55.41MM **Privately Held**
Web: www.la-solargroup.com
SIC: 1711 Solar energy contractor

(P-785)
LDI MECHANICAL INC (PA)
Also Called: Honeywell Authorized Dealer
1587 E Bentley Dr (92879-1740)
PHONE..................951 340-9685
Lloyd Smith, *Pr*
Mike Smith, *
Robert Smith, *
Steve Buren, *
Jeff Minarik, *
EMP: 155 **EST:** 1985
SQ FT: 38,000
SALES (est): 94.22MM
SALES (corp-wide): 94.22MM **Privately Held**
Web: www.ldimechanical.com
SIC: 1711 Mechanical contractor

(P-786)
LITE SOLAR CORP
Also Called: Lite Solar
3553 Atlantic Ave (90807-4515)
PHONE..................562 256-1249
EMP: 150
Web: www.litesolar.com
SIC: 1711 Solar energy contractor

(P-787)
LOZANO PLUMBING SERVICES INC
Also Called: Plumbing Master
3615 Presley Ave (92507-4448)
P.O. Box 53137 (92517-4137)
PHONE..................951 683-4840
Andrew Lozano, *Pr*
Felipe Lozano, *
Andrew Lozano, *Sec*
EMP: 130 **EST:** 2004
SALES (est): 13.56MM **Privately Held**
Web: www.plumbingmaster.com

SIC: 1711 Plumbing contractors

(P-788)
LPSH HOLDINGS INC
Also Called: Horizon Solar Power
3570 W Florida Ave Ste 168 (92545-3518)
PHONE..................951 926-1176
Zachary Allman, *Acctg Mgr*
EMP: 429
SALES (corp-wide): 50.62MM **Privately Held**
SIC: 1711 Solar energy contractor
PA: Lpsh Holdings, Inc.
7100 W Florida Ave
Hemet CA
855 647-5061

(P-789)
LPSH HOLDINGS INC (PA)
Also Called: Horizon Solar Power
7100 W Florida Ave (92545-3410)
PHONE..................855 647-5061
Frank Kneller, *CEO*
Leroy Polvoorde, *
Gail Polvoorde, *
EMP: 96 **EST:** 2013
SALES (est): 50.62MM
SALES (corp-wide): 50.62MM **Privately Held**
SIC: 1711 Solar energy contractor

(P-790)
M & M PLUMBING INC
6782 Columbus St (92504-1118)
PHONE..................951 354-5388
Robert Malcom, *Pr*
Glenn Malcolm, *
EMP: 80 **EST:** 2002
SALES (est): 4.7MM **Privately Held**
Web: www.mmplumbing.net
SIC: 1711 Plumbing contractors

(P-791)
MAINSTREAM ENERGY CORPORATION
Also Called: Rec Solar
775 Fiero Ln Ste 200 (93401-7904)
PHONE..................805 528-9705
EMP: 493
Web: www.mainstreamenergy.com
SIC: 1711 5049 Solar energy contractor; Scientific and engineering equipment and supplies

(P-792)
MDDR INC
Also Called: Econo Air
1921 Petra Ln (92870-6749)
PHONE..................714 792-1993
Michael Richards, *Pr*
Rhonda Richards, *
EMP: 110 **EST:** 1991
SALES (est): 23.89MM **Privately Held**
Web: www.myeconoair.com
SIC: 1711 1731 Warm air heating and air conditioning contractor; Electrical work

(P-793)
MEMEGED TEVUOT SHEMESH (PA)
Also Called: Titan Solar
5550 Topanga Canyon Blvd Ste 280 (91367-6478)
PHONE..................866 575-1211
Ofir Haimoff, *Pr*
EMP: 152 **EST:** 2011
SQ FT: 20,000
SALES (est): 7.72MM
SALES (corp-wide): 7.72MM **Privately Held**

PRODUCTS & SVCS

SIC: **1711** 5074 Solar energy contractor; Heating equipment and panels, solar

(P-794)
MESA ENERGY SYSTEMS INC (HQ)
Also Called: Emcor Services Mesa Energy
2 Cromwell (92618-1816)
PHONE...........................949 460-0460
Robert A Lake, *Pr*
Charles G Fletcher Junior, *VP*
Michael Ecshner, *
Kip Bagley, *
Steve Hunt, *
EMP: 210 EST: 1984
SQ FT: 55,000
SALES (est): 114.02MM
SALES (corp-wide): 11.08B Publicly Held
Web: www.mesaenergy.com
SIC: **1711** 7623 Warm air heating and air conditioning contractor; Refrigeration service and repair
PA: Emcor Group, Inc.
301 Merritt 7 Fl 6
Norwalk CT
203 849-7800

(P-795)
MUIR-CHASE PLUMBING CO INC
Also Called: M C
4530 Brazil St Ste 1 (90039-1002)
PHONE...........................818 500-1940
Don Chase, *Pr*
Jay Chase, *
James M Muir, *
Grant Muir, *
Gail Comstock, *
EMP: 90 EST: 1975
SQ FT: 5,000
SALES (est): 23.76MM Privately Held
Web: www.muirchase.com
SIC: **1711** 7699 Plumbing contractors; Sewer cleaning and rodding

(P-796)
MURRAY PLUMBING AND HTG CORP (PA)
Also Called: Murray Company
18414 S Santa Fe Ave (90221-5612)
PHONE...........................310 637-1500
Kevan Steffey, *Ch*
James De Flavio, *
EMP: 326 EST: 1913
SQ FT: 26,000
SALES (est): 354.84MM
SALES (corp-wide): 354.84MM Privately Held
Web: www.murraycompany.com
SIC: **1711** Plumbing contractors

(P-797)
NATIONAL AIR INC
Also Called: National Air and Energy
2053 Kurtz St (92110-2014)
PHONE...........................619 299-2500
Jared M Wells, *CEO*
EMP: 110 EST: 1995
SQ FT: 10,500
SALES (est): 24.49MM Privately Held
Web: www.natlair.com
SIC: **1711** Mechanical contractor

(P-798)
NEW POWER INC
887 Marlborough Ave (92507-2133)
PHONE...........................800 980-9825
Thomas Shaffer, *Pr*
Matt Collins, *

EMP: 83 EST: 2009
SALES (est): 7.73MM Privately Held
Web: www.newpower.company
SIC: **1711** Solar energy contractor

(P-799)
NEXGEN AC & HTG LLC
Also Called: Nexgen Air Conditioning & Plbg
700 N Valley St Ste K (92801-3824)
PHONE...........................760 616-5870
Ismael Valdez, *CEO*
Yanela Valdez, *
EMP: 84 EST: 2015
SALES (est): 11.92MM
SALES (corp-wide): 215.03MM Privately Held
SIC: **1711** Warm air heating and air conditioning contractor
PA: Wrench Group Llc
1787 Williams Dr
Marietta GA
678 784-2260

(P-800)
NEXGEN AIR LOS ANGELES
Also Called: Nexgen Air Heating and Plbg
19205 Parthenia St (91324-3643)
PHONE...........................818 900-2525
EMP: 110
SALES (corp-wide): 8.63MM Privately Held
Web: www.nexgenairandplumbing.com
SIC: **1711** Warm air heating and air conditioning contractor
PA: Nexgen Air Los Angeles
5472 E La Palma Ave
Anaheim CA
714 331-9633

(P-801)
NP MECHANICAL INC
9129 Stellar Ct (92883-4924)
P.O. Box 309 (92878-0309)
PHONE...........................951 667-4220
Cecil J Hallinan, *CEO*
Richard Hallinan, *
EMP: 400 EST: 2005
SALES (est): 60.32MM Privately Held
Web: www.npmechanicalinc.net
SIC: **1711** Mechanical contractor

(P-802)
ONE CALL PLUMBER SANTA BARBARA
1016 Cliff Dr Apt 309 (93109-1784)
PHONE...........................805 364-6337
EMP: 100 EST: 2017
SALES (est): 2.49MM Privately Held
SIC: **1711** Plumbing contractors

(P-803)
ORANGE COUNTY SERVICES INC
Also Called: George Brazil Plbg Htg & AC
3022 N Hesperian St (92706-1151)
PHONE...........................714 541-9753
Mike Jones, *Genl Mgr*
EMP: 94
SIC: **1711** 1731 Plumbing contractors; Electrical work
PA: Orange County Services, Inc.
3801 Lenawee Ave
Culver City CA

(P-804)
PACIFIC RIM MECH CONTRS INC
1701 E Edinger Ave Ste F2 (92705-5028)
PHONE...........................714 285-2600
John Heusner, *Mgr*

EMP: 250
SALES (corp-wide): 227.5MM Privately Held
Web: www.prmech.com
SIC: **1711** Mechanical contractor
PA: Pacific Rim Mechanical Contractors, Inc.
9125 Rehco Rd
San Diego CA
858 974-6500

(P-805)
PACIFIC RIM MECH CONTRS INC (PA)
Also Called: Honeywell Authorized Dealer
9125 Rehco Rd (92121-2270)
PHONE...........................858 974-6500
Joseph Mucher, *CEO*
Eric Bader, *
Theodore J Keenan, *
Brian Turner, *
Colin Cook, *
EMP: 400 EST: 2002
SQ FT: 50,000
SALES (est): 227.5MM
SALES (corp-wide): 227.5MM Privately Held
Web: www.prmech.com
SIC: **1711** Mechanical contractor

(P-806)
PAN-PACIFIC MECHANICAL LLC
Also Called: Pan-Pacific Plumbing & Mech
11622 El Camino Real Ste 100 (92130-2049)
PHONE...........................858 764-2464
EMP: 425
SALES (corp-wide): 405.33MM Privately Held
Web: www.ppmechanical.com
SIC: **1711** Mechanical contractor
PA: Pan-Pacific Mechanical Llc
18250 Euclid St
Fountain Valley CA
949 474-9170

(P-807)
PAN-PACIFIC MECHANICAL LLC (PA)
Also Called: Pan-Pacific Mechanical
18250 Euclid St (92708-6112)
PHONE...........................949 474-9170
Reed Mcmackin, *CEO*
Cindy Lanette Mcmackin, *Pr*
Rex Mcmackin, *VP*
Joe Koh, *
Jon Houchin, *
▲ **EMP: 150 EST: 1947**
SQ FT: 60,000
SALES (est): 405.33MM
SALES (corp-wide): 405.33MM Privately Held
Web: www.ppmechanical.com
SIC: **1711** Plumbing contractors

(P-808)
PLUMBING PIPING & CNSTR INC
5950 Lakeshore Dr (90630-3371)
PHONE...........................714 821-0490
Bruce Cook Junior, *Pr*
EMP: 100 EST: 1960
SQ FT: 12,600
SALES (est): 27.37MM Privately Held
Web: www.1ppc.com
SIC: **1711** Plumbing, heating, air-conditioning

(P-809)
PPC ENTERPRISES INC
Also Called: Premier Plumbing Company
5920 Rickenbacker Ave (92504-1042)

PHONE...........................951 354-5402
Jeffrey Geiger, *Pr*
Dawn Geiger, *
EMP: 125 EST: 1982
SQ FT: 10,000
SALES (est): 12.16MM Privately Held
Web: www.premierplumbingcompany.com
SIC: **1711** Plumbing contractors

(P-810)
PRECISE AIR SYSTEMS INC
Also Called: Hvac Installation and Repair
5467 W San Fernando Rd (90039-1014)
P.O. Box 39609 (90039-0609)
PHONE...........................818 646-9757
TOLL FREE: 877
Fred Khachekian, *Pr*
EMP: 91 EST: 1975
SQ FT: 3,200
SALES (est): 18.5MM Privately Held
Web: www.preciseairsystems.com
SIC: **1711** Warm air heating and air conditioning contractor

(P-811)
PRO TRAFFIC SERVICES INC
321 Hunter St (92065-3005)
PHONE...........................760 906-6961
Janet Andrews, *Pr*
Neil Treffers, *
Greg Wakeman, *
EMP: 99 EST: 2018
SALES (est): 3.56MM Privately Held
Web: www.ptats.com
SIC: **1711** Plumbing, heating, air-conditioning

(P-812)
PRO-CRAFT CONSTRUCTION INC
500 Iowa St Ste 100 (92373-8068)
PHONE...........................909 790-5222
Timothy Mcfayden, *Pr*
Susan Mc Fayden, *
EMP: 142 EST: 2006
SALES (est): 27.03MM Privately Held
Web: www.procraftci.com
SIC: **1711** Plumbing contractors

(P-813)
R & R MECHANICAL CONTRACTORS INC
1400 N Johnson Ave # 114 (92020-1616)
PHONE...........................619 449-9900
EMP: 100 EST: 1998
SALES (est): 8.97MM Privately Held
SIC: **1711** Mechanical contractor

(P-814)
RAM PLUMBING
14745 Addison St (91403-1635)
PHONE...........................800 487-5812
EMP: 88
SALES (corp-wide): 835.47K Privately Held
Web: www.ramplumbing.com
SIC: **1711** Plumbing contractors
PA: Ram Plumbing
14431 Ventura Blvd
Sherman Oaks CA
818 907-5812

(P-815)
RC MAINTENANCE HOLDINGS INC
569 Bateman Cir (92878-4012)
PHONE...........................951 903-6303
Richard Collins Junior, *Pr*
Christine Meva, *Acctg Mgr*

EMP: 130 EST: 2020
SALES (est): 22.14MM **Privately Held**
Web: www.rcstoremaintenance.com
SIC: 1711 Plumbing, heating, air-conditioning

(P-816)
REC SOLAR COMMERCIAL CORP
Also Called: Rec Solar
3450 Broad St Ste 105 (93401-7214)
PHONE..............................844 732-7652
Matt Walz, *CEO*
Gary Morris, *
EMP: 200 EST: 2013
SQ FT: 15,000
SALES (est): 87.92MM
SALES (corp-wide): 28.77B **Publicly Held**
Web: www.northern-pine.com
SIC: 1711 Solar energy contractor
PA: Duke Energy Corporation
526 S Church St
Charlotte NC
704 382-3853

(P-817)
RELIABLE ENERGY MANAGEMENT INC
Also Called: Honeywell Authorized Dealer
6829 Walthall Way (90723-2028)
PHONE..............................562 984-5511
EMP: 80 EST: 1995
SALES (est): 18.92MM **Privately Held**
Web: www.relenergy.com
SIC: 1711 Warm air heating and air conditioning contractor

(P-818)
RIGHT ANGLE SOLUTIONS INC
6315 Pedley Rd (92509-6007)
P.O. Box 965 (91752-0965)
PHONE..............................951 934-3081
Duane Eric Cook, *CEO*
EMP: 25 EST: 2009
SALES (est): 6.31MM **Privately Held**
Web: www.rightanglesolutionsinc.com
SIC: 1711 3569 4959 8744 Plumbing contractors; Filters and strainers, pipeline; Environmental cleanup services; Facilities support services

(P-819)
S S W MECHANICAL CNSTR INC
Also Called: Ssw
670 S Oleander Rd (92264-1502)
P.O. Box 3160 (92263-3160)
PHONE..............................760 327-1481
Sean Wood, *Pr*
W T Hayes, *
EMP: 140 EST: 1996
SQ FT: 7,000
SALES (est): 23.51MM **Privately Held**
Web: www.sswmechanical.com
SIC: 1711 Plumbing contractors

(P-820)
SDG ENTERPRISES
Also Called: Century West Plumbing
822 Hampshire Rd Ste H (91361-2850)
PHONE..............................805 777-7978
Nick Simili, *Pr*
Robert Garcia, *
Vincent Simili, *
Vincent Dipinto, *
EMP: 100 EST: 1999
SQ FT: 3,000
SALES (est): 5MM **Privately Held**
SIC: 1711 Plumbing contractors

(P-821)
SERVICE GENIUS LOS ANGELES INC
8925 Fullbright Ave (91311-6124)
PHONE..............................818 200-3379
William Monk, *Pr*
EMP: 100 EST: 2018
SALES (est): 10MM **Privately Held**
Web: www.servicegenius.com
SIC: 1711 Warm air heating and air conditioning contractor

(P-822)
SHELDON MECHANICAL CORPORATION
26015 Avenue Hall (91355-1241)
PHONE..............................661 286-1361
Dan Boute, *Pr*
Stanley Nisenson, *
Beverly Nisenson, *
Chrystal Bout'e, *
EMP: 80 EST: 1984
SQ FT: 45,000
SALES (est): 24.01MM **Privately Held**
Web: www.sheldonmech.com
SIC: 1711 Mechanical contractor

(P-823)
SHERWOOD MECHANICAL INC
6630 Top Gun St (92121-4112)
PHONE..............................858 679-3000
Mitch Roberts, *Pr*
James Robert, *
Bill Smyth, *
EMP: 100 EST: 2003
SALES (est): 22.29MM **Privately Held**
Web: www.sherwoodmechanical.com
SIC: 1711 Mechanical contractor

(P-824)
SKYPOWER HOLDINGS LLC
4700 Wilshire Blvd (90010-3831)
PHONE..............................323 860-4900
Kerry Adler, *CEO*
Avi Shemesh, *Pr*
EMP: 101 EST: 2010
SALES (est): 8.55MM **Privately Held**
Web: www.cimgroup.com
SIC: 1711 Solar energy contractor

(P-825)
SMART ENERGY SOLAR INC
Also Called: Smart Energy USA
1641 Comm St (92880)
PHONE..............................800 405-1978
Leo Joaquin Bautista, *Prin*
EMP: 120 EST: 2013
SALES (est): 20.03MM **Privately Held**
Web: www.smartenergyusa.com
SIC: 1711 Solar energy contractor

(P-826)
SOLAR SPECTRUM LLC
Also Called: Sungevity
27368 Via Industria Ste 101 (92590-4855)
PHONE..............................844 777-6527
Patrick Mcgivern, *CEO*
William Nettles, *
David White, *
EMP: 266 EST: 2017
SALES (est): 51.19MM **Privately Held**
SIC: 1711 8713 Solar energy contractor; Surveying services

(P-827)
SOLCIUS LLC
Also Called: SOLCIUS LLC
12155 Magnolia Ave Ste 12b/C (92503-4967)

PHONE..............................951 772-0030
Bryan Jackson, *Brnch Mgr*
EMP: 227
SALES (corp-wide): 69.13MM **Privately Held**
Web: www.solcius.com
SIC: 1711 Solar energy contractor
PA: Solcius, Llc
1555 N Freedom Blvd
Provo UT
800 960-4150

(P-828)
SOUTH CHINA SHEET METAL INC
Also Called: General Restaurant Equipment
1740 Albion St (90031-2520)
PHONE..............................323 225-1522
Kam C Law, *CEO*
T K Yeung, *
◆ EMP: 28 EST: 1982
SQ FT: 24,000
SALES (est): 862.96K **Privately Held**
SIC: 1711 3589 3444 Ventilation and duct work contractor; Commercial cooking and foodwarming equipment; Sheet metalwork

(P-829)
STERLING PLUMBING INC
3111 W Central Ave (92704-5302)
PHONE..............................714 641-5480
Rodney Robbins, *Pr*
Leslie Schaefer, *
EMP: 100 EST: 2003
SALES (est): 13.16MM **Privately Held**
Web: www.sterlingplumbinginc.com
SIC: 1711 Plumbing contractors

(P-830)
TRILOGY PLUMBING INC
1525 S Sinclair St (92806-5934)
PHONE..............................714 441-2952
Dennis Burk, *Pr*
Linda Burk, *
EMP: 250 EST: 2003
SQ FT: 18,000
SALES (est): 35.79MM **Privately Held**
Web: www.trilogyplumbing.com
SIC: 1711 Septic system construction

(P-831)
TRUE AIR MECHANICAL INC
Also Called: True Home Heating and AC
1801 California Ave (92881-7251)
PHONE..............................888 316-0642
Scott Flora, *CEO*
EMP: 180 EST: 2010
SALES (est): 41.02MM **Privately Held**
Web: www.truehomehvac.com
SIC: 1711 Warm air heating and air conditioning contractor

(P-832)
UNIVERSITY MARELICH MECH INC
1000 N Kraemer Pl (92806-2610)
PHONE..............................714 632-2600
Scott Baker, *Sr VP*
Walter S Baker, *
John R Wycoff, *
John Ellis, *
EMP: 87 EST: 2005
SQ FT: 24,384
SALES (est): 5.2MM
SALES (corp-wide): 11.08B **Publicly Held**
SIC: 1711 Mechanical contractor
PA: Emcor Group, Inc.
301 Merritt 7 Fl 6
Norwalk CT
203 849-7800

(P-833)
WALTER ANDERSON PLUMBING INC
Also Called: Anderson Plbg Htg A Condition
1830 John Towers Ave (92020-1134)
PHONE..............................619 449-7646
Mary Jean Anderson, *CEO*
Kyle Anderson, *
EMP: 125 EST: 1978
SQ FT: 10,000
SALES (est): 26.15MM
SALES (corp-wide): 559.73MM **Privately Held**
Web: www.andersonplumbingheatingandair.com
SIC: 1711 Plumbing contractors
PA: Essential Services Intermediate Holding Corporation
3416 Robards Ct
Louisville KY
502 657-1903

(P-834)
WEST COAST AC CO INC
1155 Pioneer Way Ste 101 (92020-1964)
PHONE..............................619 561-8000
David Dudley, *CEO*
Colin Fisher, *
James Clower, *
EMP: 150 EST: 1960
SQ FT: 24,000
SALES (est): 24.58MM **Privately Held**
Web: www.wcac.com
SIC: 1711 Warm air heating and air conditioning contractor

(P-835)
WESTERN ALLIED CORPORATION
Also Called: Honeywell Authorized Dealer
12046 Florence Ave (90670-4406)
P.O. Box 3628 (90670-1628)
PHONE..............................562 944-6341
Howell L Poe, *CEO*
EMP: 45 EST: 1960
SQ FT: 15,000
SALES (est): 30.27MM **Privately Held**
Web: www.wasocal.com
SIC: 1711 3433 3432 Warm air heating and air conditioning contractor; Heating equipment, except electric; Plumbing fixture fittings and trim

(P-836)
WESTERN FIRE PROTECTION INC (PA)
13630 Danielson St (92064-6830)
PHONE..............................858 513-4949
EMP: 91 EST: 1989
SALES (est): 19.88MM **Privately Held**
Web: www.westernfireprotection.com
SIC: 1711 Fire sprinkler system installation

(P-837)
WILLIAMS EAST HEATING A & PLBG
Also Called: Fortune Energy USA
2290 Agate Ct Ste A (93065-1935)
PHONE..............................818 678-9699
Hailian He, *Pr*
▲ EMP: 84 EST: 2009
SQ FT: 10,000
SALES (est): 13.17MM **Privately Held**
Web: www.fortuneenergy.net
SIC: 1711 Solar energy contractor

(P-838)
XCEL MECHANICAL SYSTEMS INC

1710 W 130th St (90249-2004)
PHONE.................310 660-0090
Kevin Michel, *Pr*
EMP: 175 **EST:** 1996
SQ FT: 10,000
SALES (est): 74.62MM **Privately Held**
Web: www.xcelmech.com
SIC: 1711 Mechanical contractor

(P-839)
ZERO ENERGY CONTRACTING INC
13850 Cerritos Corporate Dr Ste D
(90703-2467)
PHONE.................626 701-3180
Michael Murphy, *Ch Bd*
Paul Hanson, *
Jerry Suk, *
Joseph Power Cbd, *Prin*
EMP: 125 **EST:** 2010
SQ FT: 8,000
SALES (est): 6.73MM **Privately Held**
SIC: 1711 Solar energy contractor

(P-840)
ZERO ENERGY CONTRACTING LLC
13850 Cerritos Corporate Dr Ste D
(90703-2467)
PHONE.................626 701-3180
EMP: 93 **EST:** 2009
SALES (est): 9.9MM **Privately Held**
SIC: 1711 Solar energy contractor

1721 Painting And Paper Hanging

(P-841)
ADVANCED INDUSTRIAL SVCS INC
Also Called: Advanced Industrial Svcs Cal
7831 Alondra Blvd (90723-5005)
PHONE.................562 940-8305
Rex Johnston Junior, *Pr*
EMP: 85 **EST:** 2007
SALES (est): 9.85MM **Privately Held**
Web: www.adinservices.com
SIC: 1721 Industrial painting

(P-842)
ARENA PAINTING CONTRACTORS INC
525 E Alondra Blvd (90248-2903)
PHONE.................310 316-2446
Wilson Grant, *CEO*
Guy Grant Ii, *Pr*
EMP: 100 **EST:** 1982
SQ FT: 10,000
SALES (est): 11.5MM **Privately Held**
Web: www.arenapainting.biz
SIC: 1721 Commercial painting

(P-843)
BORBON INCORPORATED
2560 W Woodland Dr (92801-2636)
PHONE.................714 994-0170
David Morales, *Pr*
EMP: 120 **EST:** 1974
SALES (est): 11.43MM **Privately Held**
Web: www.borbon.net
SIC: 1721 Exterior residential painting
contractor

(P-844)
EMPCC INC
Also Called: Empire Community Painting
1682 Langley Ave Fl 2 (92614-5620)

PHONE.................888 278-8200
Jason Reid, *Pr*
Jeff Gunhus, *
Matt Stewart, *
Spencer Pepe, *
Tracy Meneses, *
EMP: 284 **EST:** 2003
SQ FT: 1,000
SALES (est): 1.1MM **Privately Held**
SIC: 1721 Painting and paper hanging
PA: Mjp Empire, Inc.
1682 Langley Ave Fl 2
Irvine CA

(P-845)
GENERAL COATINGS CORPORATION
600 W Freedom Ave (92865-2537)
PHONE.................858 587-1277
Craig Kinsman, *Brnch Mgr*
EMP: 83
SQ FT: 7,047
SALES (corp-wide): 35.9MM **Privately Held**
Web: www.gencoat.com
SIC: 1721 Painting and paper hanging
PA: General Coatings Corporation
6711 Nancy Ridge Dr
San Diego CA
858 587-1277

(P-846)
GENERAL COATINGS CORPORATION (PA)
6711 Nancy Ridge Dr (92121-2231)
PHONE.................858 587-1277
Craig A Kinsman, *CEO*
Andrew Fluken, *
EMP: 250 **EST:** 1987
SQ FT: 14,000
SALES (est): 35.9MM
SALES (corp-wide): 35.9MM **Privately Held**
Web: www.gencoat.com
SIC: 1721 1799 Painting and paper hanging;
Waterproofing

(P-847)
GENERAL COATINGS CORPORATION
9349 Feron Blvd (91730-4516)
PHONE.................909 204-4150
Craig Kinsman, *Owner*
EMP: 84
SALES (corp-wide): 35.9MM **Privately Held**
Web: www.gencoat.com
SIC: 1721 Painting and paper hanging
PA: General Coatings Corporation
6711 Nancy Ridge Dr
San Diego CA
858 587-1277

(P-848)
GPS PAINTING WALLCOVERING INC
1307 E Saint Gertrude Pl Ste C
(92705-5228)
PHONE.................714 730-8904
Eliot Schneider, *Pr*
EMP: 110 **EST:** 2001
SALES (est): 18.85MM **Privately Held**
Web:
www.gpspaintingandwallcovering.com
SIC: 1721 Painting and paper hanging

(P-849)
J M V B INC
Also Called: Spc Building Services

12118 Severn Way (92503-4804)
P.O. Box 614 (92856-6614)
PHONE.................714 288-9797
Benjamin J Rodriguez, *Pr*
EMP: 80 **EST:** 1993
SALES (est): 2.77MM **Privately Held**
Web: www.spcbs.com
SIC: 1721 Painting and paper hanging

(P-850)
LA WEB INC
Also Called: Chinese La Daily News
9645 Telstar Ave (91731-3012)
PHONE.................626 453-8800
Walter Chang, *Pr*
▲ **EMP:** 18 **EST:** 1989
SALES (est): 2.11MM **Privately Held**
SIC: 1721 2711 Painting and paper hanging;
Newspapers, publishing and printing

(P-851)
LEADING EDGE AVIATION SVCS INC
5251 California Ave # 170 (92617-3077)
PHONE.................714 556-0576
EMP: 800
SIC: 1721 4581 3721 Aircraft painting;
Aircraft maintenance and repair services;
Motorized aircraft

(P-852)
PBC PAVERS INC
Also Called: Peterson Bros Construction
2929 E White Star Ave (92806-2628)
PHONE.................714 278-0488
Robert Peterson, *Pr*
Eldin Peterson, *
▲ **EMP:** 80 **EST:** 1995
SALES (est): 10.06MM **Privately Held**
Web: www.pbccompanies.com
SIC: 1721 Pavement marking contractor

(P-853)
PRIMECO
220 Oceanside Blvd (92054-4903)
PHONE.................760 967-8278
EMP: 90 **EST:** 1992
SQ FT: 2,100
SALES (est): 12.62MM **Privately Held**
Web: www.primeco.com
SIC: 1721 1542 Residential painting;
Commercial and office building contractors

(P-854)
RC WENDT PAINTING INC
21612 Surveyor Cir (92646-7068)
PHONE.................714 960-2700
Robert C Wendt, *Pr*
Scott Wendt, *
Jeri Wendt, *
EMP: 110 **EST:** 1980
SALES (est): 4.02MM **Privately Held**
Web: www.oasisdecksmiami.com
SIC: 1721 Residential painting

(P-855)
RTE ENTERPRISES INC
Also Called: Color Concepts
21530 Roscoe Blvd (91304-4144)
PHONE.................818 999-5300
EMP: 100 **EST:** 1987
SQ FT: 2,000
SALES (est): 4.95MM **Privately Held**
Web: www.ceocolorcon1.com
SIC: 1721 1742 Painting and paper hanging;
Plastering, drywall, and insulation

(P-856)
SANDERS & WOHRMAN CORPORATION
709 N Poplar St (92868-1013)
PHONE.................714 919-0446
John Thomas Wohrman, *Prin*
Todd Wohrman, *
EMP: 150 **EST:** 1979
SQ FT: 12,000
SALES (est): 23.36MM **Privately Held**
Web: www.swcoatings.com
SIC: 1721 Residential painting

(P-857)
WEST COAST INTERIORS INC
Also Called: West Coast Painting
1610 W Linden St (92507-6810)
PHONE.................951 778-3592
Mark Herbert, *CEO*
Dan Slavin, *Marketing**
Santos Garcia, *
Colleen Butler, *
Keith Caneva, *Corporate Controller**
EMP: 600 **EST:** 1968
SQ FT: 8,000
SALES (est): 44.28MM **Privately Held**
Web: www.wcdp.com
SIC: 1721 Wallcovering contractors

1731 Electrical Work

(P-858)
4LIBERTY INC
7675 Dagget St Ste 200 (92111-2256)
PHONE.................619 400-1000
EMP: 85 **EST:** 2010
SALES (est): 5.33MM **Privately Held**
Web: www.4liberty.com
SIC: 1731 Telephone and telephone
equipment installation

(P-859)
A M ORTEGA CONSTRUCTION INC (PA)
Also Called: Western Rim Pipeline
10125 Channel Rd (92040-1703)
PHONE.................619 390-1988
Archie Maurice Ortega, *Pr*
Linda Ortega, *
EMP: 110 **EST:** 1974
SQ FT: 10,000
SALES (est): 55.54MM
SALES (corp-wide): 55.54MM **Privately Held**
Web: www.amortega.com
SIC: 1731 Electrical work

(P-860)
AAA ELCTRCAL CMMUNICATIONS INC (PA)
Also Called: AAA Facility Services
25007 Anza Dr (91355-3414)
PHONE.................800 892-4784
Joann Katinos, *CEO*
Brian Higgins, *Pr*
EMP: 133 **EST:** 1995
SQ FT: 6,000
SALES (est): 34.13MM **Privately Held**
Web: www.aaafacilityservices.com
SIC: 1731 1711 7349 1721 General
electrical contractor; Plumbing, heating, air-
conditioning; Building maintenance
services, nec; Commercial painting

(P-861)
ACS COMMUNICATIONS INC
Also Called: Fiber Optic Technologies
680 Knox St Ste 150 (90502-1325)

PHONE..................310 767-2145
Robby Sawyer, *Pr*
EMP: 94
SIC: 1731 Communications specialization
HQ: Acs Communications, Inc.
2535 Brockton Dr Ste 400
Austin TX
512 837-4400

(P-862)
AJ KIRKWOOD & ASSOCIATES INC
4300 N Harbor Blvd (92835-1091)
PHONE..................714 505-1977
EMP: 500 **EST:** 1996
SALES (est): 144.08MM **Privately Held**
Web: www.ajk-a.com
SIC: 1731 8748 7389 General electrical contractor; Communications consulting; Design services

(P-863)
ALBD ELECTRIC AND CABLE
Also Called: A Lighting By Design
1031 S Leslie St (90631-6843)
PHONE..................949 440-1216
Chad Lambert, *CEO*
James Black, *
EMP: 100 **EST:** 2002
SALES (est): 22.67MM **Privately Held**
Web: www.albdinc.com
SIC: 1731 3651 General electrical contractor; Household audio and video equipment

(P-864)
ALLIED UNIVERSAL
9320 Hazard Way Ste A1 (92123-1227)
PHONE..................619 444-0219
Amy Davis, *Prin*
EMP: 131 **EST:** 2018
SALES (est): 4.98MM **Privately Held**
Web: www.aus.com
SIC: 1731 Safety and security specialization

(P-865)
ALLTECH INDUSTRIES INC
301 E Pomona Blvd (91755-7300)
PHONE..................323 450-2168
Hilda Perez, *Pr*
EMP: 30 **EST:** 2010
SQ FT: 2,000
SALES (est): 2.41MM **Privately Held**
Web: alltechindustriesinc.wordpress.com
SIC: 1731 7381 3669 7382 Fire detection and burglar alarm systems specialization; Security guard service; Burglar alarm apparatus, electric; Fire alarm maintenance and monitoring

(P-866)
AMERICAN SOLAR DIRECT INC
11766 Wilshire Blvd Ste 500 (90025-6551)
PHONE..................424 214-6700
EMP: 107
SIC: 1731 Electrical work

(P-867)
ANDERSON & HOWARD ELECTRIC INC
Also Called: Anderson Howard
15 Chrysler (92618-2009)
PHONE..................949 250-4555
Greg Elliott, *Pr*
Brian E Elliott, *
Tom Howard, *
Charles B Howard, *
EMP: 210 **EST:** 1967
SALES (est): 53.32MM **Privately Held**

Web: www.aandh.com
SIC: 1731 General electrical contractor

(P-868)
BAKER ELECTRIC & RENEWABLES LLC
1298 Pacific Oaks Pl (92029-2900)
PHONE..................760 745-2001
EMP: 586 **EST:** 1938
SALES (est): 127.8MM **Privately Held**
Web: www.baker-electric.com
SIC: 1731 8711 General electrical contractor; Engineering services

(P-869)
BERGELECTRIC CORP (PA)
3182 Lionshead Ave (92010-4701)
PHONE..................760 638-2374
Edward Billig, *Pr*
Ron Wood, *
Steve Buhr, *
William Wingerning, *
Alan Mashburn, *
▲ **EMP:** 100 **EST:** 1946
SALES (est): 705.05MM
SALES (corp-wide): 705.05MM **Privately Held**
Web: www.bergelectric.com
SIC: 1731 General electrical contractor

(P-870)
BERGELECTRIC CORP
3182 Lionshead Ave (92010-4701)
PHONE..................760 746-1003
Tom Anderson, *Brnch Mgr*
EMP: 760
SALES (corp-wide): 705.05MM **Privately Held**
Web: www.bergelectric.com
SIC: 1731 General electrical contractor
PA: Bergelectric Corp.
3182 Lionshead Ave
Carlsbad CA
760 638-2374

(P-871)
BERGELECTRIC CORP
955 Borra Pl (92029-2011)
PHONE..................760 291-8100
Thomas R Anderson, *Ch Bd*
EMP: 94
SALES (corp-wide): 705.05MM **Privately Held**
Web: www.bergelectric.com
SIC: 1731 General electrical contractor
PA: Bergelectric Corp.
3182 Lionshead Ave
Carlsbad CA
760 638-2374

(P-872)
BERGELECTRIC CORP
15776 Gateway Cir (92780-6469)
PHONE..................949 250-7005
Mark Bauer, *Mgr*
EMP: 105
SALES (corp-wide): 705.05MM **Privately Held**
Web: www.bergelectric.com
SIC: 1731 General electrical contractor
PA: Bergelectric Corp.
3182 Lionshead Ave
Carlsbad CA
760 638-2374

(P-873)
BRIGGS ELECTRIC INC (PA)
14381 Franklin Ave (92780-7010)
PHONE..................714 544-2500
Jeff Perry, *

Thomas J Perry, *
Todd Perry, *
▲ **EMP:** 100 **EST:** 1946
SQ FT: 5,500
SALES (est): 51.07MM
SALES (corp-wide): 51.07MM **Privately Held**
Web: www.briggselectric.com
SIC: 1731 General electrical contractor

(P-874)
BUILDING ELCTRONIC CONTRLS INC (PA)
2246 Lindsay Way (91740-5398)
PHONE..................909 305-1600
EMP: 48 **EST:** 1996
SQ FT: 13,000
SALES (est): 17.23MM **Privately Held**
Web: www.becinc.net
SIC: 1731 3699 General electrical contractor; Security control equipment and systems

(P-875)
C G SYSTEMS INC
Also Called: California Gate Entry Systems
1470 N Hundley St (92806-1322)
PHONE..................714 632-8882
Kevin Squire, *CEO*
EMP: 27 **EST:** 1982
SALES (est): 4.98MM **Privately Held**
Web: www.californiagate.com
SIC: 1731 3699 3315 5731 Fire detection and burglar alarm systems specialization; Security devices; Fence gates, posts, and fittings: steel; Video cameras, recorders, and accessories

(P-876)
C T AND F INC
7228 Scout Ave (90201-4902)
PHONE..................562 927-2339
EMP: 80
Web: www.ctandf.net
SIC: 1731 General electrical contractor

(P-877)
CALENERGY LLC
7030 Gentry Rd (92233-9720)
PHONE..................402 231-1527
Bill Fehrman, *Pr*
EMP: 350 **EST:** 2013
SALES (est): 23.9MM **Privately Held**
SIC: 1731 Electric power systems contractors

(P-878)
CAROL ELECTRIC COMPANY INC
3822 Cerritos Ave (90720-2420)
PHONE..................562 431-1870
John R Fuqua, *Ch Bd*
Allen Moffitt, *
Brian Moffitt, *
EMP: 90 **EST:** 1979
SQ FT: 10,000
SALES (est): 17.4MM **Privately Held**
Web: www.carolelectric.com
SIC: 1731 General electrical contractor

(P-879)
CBR ELECTRIC INC
22 Rancho Cir (92630-8325)
PHONE..................949 455-0331
Cary Raffety, *Pr*
EMP: 150 **EST:** 1989
SQ FT: 4,000
SALES (est): 9.76MM **Privately Held**
Web: www.cbrelectric.com
SIC: 1731 General electrical contractor

(P-880)
CITY-WIDE ELECTRONIC SYSTEMS INC
440 Highland Ave (92020-5209)
P.O. Box 2069 (92021-0069)
PHONE..................619 444-0219
EMP: 100
SIC: 1731 General electrical contractor

(P-881)
CLEANTEK ELECTRIC INC
403 W 21st St (90731-5509)
PHONE..................424 400-3315
Carl Pancutt, *CEO*
Carl James Mark Pancutt, *CEO*
EMP: 20 **EST:** 2019
SALES (est): 2.5MM **Privately Held**
Web: www.cleantek.co
SIC: 1731 3621 3694 General electrical contractor; Generators for gas-electric or oil-electric vehicles; Battery charging generators, automobile and aircraft

(P-882)
COMET ELECTRIC INC
21625 Prairie St (91311-5833)
PHONE..................818 340-0965
Adam Saitman, *CEO*
Steve Goad, *VP*
Keith Berson, *Ex VP*
Jason Pennington, *CFO*
EMP: 150 **EST:** 1993
SQ FT: 12,000
SALES (est): 43.92MM
SALES (corp-wide): 101.09MM **Privately Held**
Web: www.cometelectric.com
SIC: 1731 General electrical contractor
PA: Valley Electric Co. Of Mt. Vernon, Inc.,
1100 Merrill Creek Pkwy
Everett WA
425 407-0832

(P-883)
COMMUNCTION WIRG SPCALISTS INC
Also Called: C W S
8909 Complex Dr Ste F (92123-1418)
PHONE..................858 278-4545
Eric Templin, *Pr*
Richard Templin, *
Donna Templin, *Stockholder**
EMP: 80 **EST:** 1991
SQ FT: 5,500
SALES (est): 8.93MM **Privately Held**
Web: www.cwssandiego.com
SIC: 1731 Telephone and telephone equipment installation

(P-884)
COMMUNICATION TECH SVCS LLC
1590 S Milliken Ave Ste H (91761-2326)
PHONE..................508 382-2700
Chris Ungson, *Brnch Mgr*
EMP: 266
Web: www.cts1.com
SIC: 1731 8748 Voice, data, and video wiring contractor; Communications consulting
PA: Communication Technology Services, Llc
33 Locke Dr Ste 201
Marlborough MA

(P-885)
CONTRA COSTA ELECTRIC INC
3208 Landco Dr (93308-6156)
PHONE..................661 322-4036

EMP: 104
SALES (corp-wide): 11.08B **Publicly Held**
Web: www.ccelectric.com
SIC: 1731 General electrical contractor
HQ: Contra Costa Electric, Inc.
825 Howe Rd
Martinez CA
925 229-4250

(P-886)
COOPER LIGHTING LLC
285 Rood Rd Ste 101 (92231-9535)
PHONE..................760 357-4760
EMP: 113
Web: www.cooperlighting.com
SIC: 1731 Lighting contractor
HQ: Cooper Lighting, Llc
1121 Highway 74 S
Peachtree City GA
770 486-4800

(P-887)
CROSSTOWN ELEC & DATA INC
5454 Diaz St (91706-2026)
PHONE..................626 813-6693
Dave Heermance, *CEO*
EMP: 100 **EST:** 1998
SQ FT: 2,500
SALES (est): 28.7MM **Privately Held**
Web: www.crosstowndata.com
SIC: 1731 General electrical contractor

(P-888)
**CSI ELECTRICAL
CONTRACTORS INC**
41769 11th St W Ste B (93551-1418)
PHONE..................661 723-0869
Roland Tamayo, *Brnch Mgr*
EMP: 448
SALES (corp-wide): 3.01B **Publicly Held**
Web: www.csielectric.com
SIC: 1731 General electrical contractor
HQ: Csi Electrical Contractors, Inc.
10623 Fulton Wells Ave
Santa Fe Springs CA

(P-889)
**CSI ELECTRICAL
CONTRACTORS INC**
310 Via Vera Cruz Ste 106 (92078-2631)
PHONE..................760 227-0577
Steve Watts, *Brnch Mgr*
EMP: 449
SALES (corp-wide): 3.01B **Publicly Held**
Web: www.csielectric.com
SIC: 1731 General electrical contractor
HQ: Csi Electrical Contractors, Inc.
10623 Fulton Wells Ave
Santa Fe Springs CA

(P-890)
**CSI ELECTRICAL
CONTRACTORS INC (HQ)**
Also Called: C S I
10623 Fulton Wells Ave (90670-3741)
P.O. Box 2887 (90670-0887)
PHONE..................562 946-0700
Steven M Watts, *Pr*
Paul Pica, *
Rick Yauney, *
William T Macnider, *
Andrew Soffa, *
EMP: 150 **EST:** 1990
SQ FT: 49,044
SALES (est): 146.31MM
SALES (corp-wide): 3.01B **Publicly Held**
Web: www.csielectric.com
SIC: 1731 General electrical contractor
PA: Myr Group Inc.
12150 E 112th Ave

Henderson CO
303 286-8000

(P-891)
DONCO & SONS INC
Also Called: Donco Associates & Sons
2871 E Blue Star St (92806-2508)
PHONE..................714 779-0099
Donavon W Fink, *Pr*
Mark Fink, *
Dave Fink, *
Diane Fink, *
EMP: 38 **EST:** 1980
SALES (est): 9.96MM **Privately Held**
Web: www.donco.com
SIC: 1731 3993 Electrical work; Electric signs

(P-892)
DYNALECTRIC COMPANY
1111 Pioneer Way (92020-1964)
PHONE..................619 328-4007
Daivd Rispolrch, *Mgr*
EMP: 300
SALES (corp-wide): 11.08B **Publicly Held**
Web: www.dynalectric-dc.com
SIC: 1731 General electrical contractor
HQ: Dynalectric Company
22930 Shaw Rd Ste 100
Dulles VA
703 288-2866

(P-893)
**ELECTRICAL &
INSTRUMENTATION UNLIMITED
OF CALIFORNIA INC**
Also Called: Eiu of California
6950 District Blvd (93313-2072)
P.O. Box 40878 (93384-0878)
EMP: 200
SIC: 1731 General electrical contractor

(P-894)
**ELECTRONIC CONTROL
SYSTEMS LLC**
Also Called: Albireo Energy
12575 Kirkham Ct Ste 1 (92064-8844)
PHONE..................858 513-1911
EMP: 145 **EST:** 1996
SQ FT: 17,000
SALES (est): 49.73MM
SALES (corp-wide): 141.55MM **Privately Held**
SIC: 1731 7382 Energy management controls; Security systems services
PA: Albireo Energy, Llc
3 Ethel Rd Ste 300
Edison NJ
732 512-9100

(P-895)
ELITE ELECTRIC
9415 Bellegrave Ave (92509-2741)
PHONE..................951 681-5811
Carl Eric Dawson, *Pr*
EMP: 80 **EST:** 1978
SQ FT: 1,720
SALES (est): 10.05MM **Privately Held**
Web: www.elite-electricinc.com
SIC: 1731 General electrical contractor

(P-896)
ENERGY WATCH
3555 Landco Dr (93308-6169)
PHONE..................661 324-0930
Stefanie Doubert, *Mgr*
EMP: 90 **EST:** 2005
SALES (est): 1.69MM **Privately Held**
Web: www.kernenergywatch.com

SIC: 1731 General electrical contractor

(P-897)
ENERPATH SERVICES INC
1758 Orange Tree Ln (92374-2856)
PHONE..................909 335-1699
Stephen Guthrie, *Pr*
Janina Guthrie, *Treas*
Jonathan Baty, *Sec*
EMP: 86 **EST:** 1989
SQ FT: 4,500
SALES (est): 3.24MM **Privately Held**
SIC: 1731 8748 Lighting contractor; Lighting consultant

(P-898)
ENSIGN US DRLG CAL INC
3701 Fruitvale Ave (93308-5109)
PHONE..................661 387-8400
Brian Watts, *Prin*
EMP: 247
SALES (corp-wide): 1.17B **Privately Held**
Web: www.ensignusd.com
SIC: 1731 Energy management controls
HQ: Ensign United States Drilling (California) Inc.
7001 Charity Ave
Bakersfield CA

(P-899)
FAITH ELECTRIC LLC
1980 Orange Tree Ln Ste 106 (92374-2803)
PHONE..................909 767-2682
Elijah Adams, *Managing Member*
EMP: 200 **EST:** 2014
SQ FT: 5,000
SALES (est): 80MM **Privately Held**
Web: www.faithelectricllc.com
SIC: 1731 General electrical contractor

(P-900)
FIRST FIRE SYSTEMS INC (PA)
Also Called: Fire Systems
5947 Burchard Ave (90034-1701)
PHONE..................310 559-0900
Juda Roshanzamir, *Pr*
Robbie Kashani, *
EMP: 99 **EST:** 1980
SQ FT: 9,400
SALES (est): 11.88MM
SALES (corp-wide): 11.88MM **Privately Held**
Web: www.ffstech.com
SIC: 1731 Fire detection and burglar alarm systems specialization

(P-901)
FISHEL COMPANY
5878 Autoport Mall (92121-2514)
PHONE..................858 658-0830
Sal Padula, *Brnch Mgr*
EMP: 109
SALES (corp-wide): 758.31MM **Privately Held**
Web: www.teamfishel.com
SIC: 1731 1623 Telephone and telephone equipment installation; Water main construction
PA: The Fishel Company
1366 Dublin Rd
Columbus OH
614 274-8100

(P-902)
FISK ELECTRIC COMPANY
15870 Olden St (91342-1241)
PHONE..................818 884-1166
Orvil Anthony, *Sr VP*
EMP: 165

SALES (corp-wide): 3.79B **Publicly Held**
Web: www.fiskcorp.com
SIC: 1731 General electrical contractor
HQ: Fisk Electric Company
10855 Westview Dr
Houston TX
713 868-6111

(P-903)
FOSHAY ELECTRIC CO INC
950 Industrial Blvd (91911-1608)
PHONE..................858 277-7676
Theresa M Faucher, *Pr*
Mark Faucher, *
Michael Beringhaus, *
EMP: 100 **EST:** 1947
SALES (est): 9.92MM **Privately Held**
Web: www.foshayelectric.com
SIC: 1731 General electrical contractor

(P-904)
GOULD ELECTRIC INC
12975 Brookprinter Pl Ste 280 (92064-8895)
P.O. Box 504377 (92150-4377)
PHONE..................858 486-1727
EMP: 125
Web: www.gouldelect.com
SIC: 1731 General electrical contractor

(P-905)
GREGG ELECTRIC INC
608 W Emporia St (91762-3709)
PHONE..................909 983-1794
Randall F Fehlman, *Pr*
James Fehlman, *
Victoria Mensen, *
EMP: 150 **EST:** 1961
SQ FT: 15,000
SALES (est): 23.43MM **Privately Held**
Web: www.greggelectric.com
SIC: 1731 General electrical contractor

(P-906)
HELIX ELECTRIC INC
13100 Alondra Blvd Ste 108 (90703-2262)
P.O. Box 85298 (92186-5298)
PHONE..................562 941-7200
Acey Long, *VP*
EMP: 890
SALES (corp-wide): 408.8MM **Privately Held**
Web: www.helixelectric.com
SIC: 1731 General electrical contractor
PA: Helix Electric, Inc.
6795 Flanders Dr
San Diego CA
858 535-0505

(P-907)
HELIX ELECTRIC INC (PA)
Also Called: Helix Renewables
6795 Flanders Dr (92121-2903)
P.O. Box 85298 (92186-5298)
PHONE..................858 535-0505
EMP: 220 **EST:** 1985
SALES (est): 408.8MM
SALES (corp-wide): 408.8MM **Privately Held**
Web: www.helixelectric.com
SIC: 1731 General electrical contractor

(P-908)
HMT ELECTRIC INC
2340 Meyers Ave (92029-1008)
PHONE..................858 458-9771
Brian Hudak, *CEO*
EMP: 85 **EST:** 2007
SQ FT: 2,000
SALES (est): 24.33MM **Privately Held**

▲ = Import ▼ = Export
◆ = Import/Export

Web: www.hmtelectric.com
SIC: **1731** General electrical contractor

(P-909)
IPITEK INC
Also Called: Ipitek
2461 Impala Dr (92010-7227)
P.O. Box 130878 (92013-0878)
PHONE..............................760 438-1010
Michael M Salour, *Ch Bd*
EMP: 170 EST: 1982
SQ FT: 40,000
SALES (est): 21.12MM **Privately Held**
SIC: **1731** Fiber optic cable installation

(P-910)
KDC INC (HQ)
Also Called: Kdc Systems
4462 Corporate Center Dr (90720-2539)
PHONE..............................714 828-7000
Earnest Lee Brown, *Pr*
Ben Martin, *
Dusty Lord, *
EMP: 207 EST: 1976
SQ FT: 57,000
SALES (est): 99.86MM
SALES (corp-wide): 11.08B **Publicly Held**
Web: www.kdc-systems.com
SIC: **1731** 1611 3823 General electrical
contractor; General contractor, highway and
street construction; Process control
instruments
PA: Emcor Group, Inc.
301 Merritt 7 Fl 6
Norwalk CT
203 849-7800

(P-911)
KITE ELECTRIC INCORPORATED
Also Called: K E
2 Thomas (92618-2512)
PHONE..............................949 380-7471
Tracy Adams, *Pr*
EMP: 120 EST: 2000
SALES (est): 9.35MM **Privately Held**
Web: www.kiteelectric.com
SIC: **1731** Electrical work

(P-912)
LASER ELECTRIC INC
650 Opper St (92029-1020)
PHONE..............................760 658-6626
Denise Hartnett, *CEO*
Kevin Hartnett, *
EMP: 120 EST: 1987
SQ FT: 11,000
SALES (est): 36.15MM **Privately Held**
Web: www.laserelectric.com
SIC: **1731** General electrical contractor

(P-913)
LEED ELECTRIC INC
13138 Arctic Cir (90670-5508)
PHONE..............................562 270-9500
Seth Jamali Dinan, *Pr*
EMP: 135 EST: 1979
SQ FT: 8,480
SALES (est): 21.38MM **Privately Held**
Web: www.leedelectric.com
SIC: **1731** General electrical contractor

(P-914)
LITTLEJOHN-REULAND CORPORATION
4575 Pacific Blvd (90058-2207)
P.O. Box 58487 (90058-0487)
PHONE..............................323 587-5255
Richard Pena, *Pr*
Dolores Robinson, *
Barry Mileski, *
EMP: 45 EST: 1926
SQ FT: 50,000
SALES (est): 13.82MM **Privately Held**
Web: www.littlejohn-reuland.com
SIC: **1731** 7694 5063 5511 General
electrical contractor; Armature rewinding
shops; Electrical supplies, nec; New and
used car dealers

(P-915)
MARK LAND ELECTRIC INC
7876 Deering Ave (91304-5005)
PHONE..............................818 883-5110
Lloyd Saitman, *CEO*
Stewart Franklin, *
John Bennet, *
EMP: 141 EST: 1981
SQ FT: 10,000
SALES (est): 26.38MM **Privately Held**
Web: www.lmela.com
SIC: **1731** General electrical contractor

(P-916)
MB HERZOG ELECTRIC INC
15709 Illinois Ave (90723-4112)
PHONE..............................562 531-2002
Ryan M Herzog, *CEO*
Kevin Ryan, *
EMP: 200 EST: 1974
SQ FT: 6,200
SALES (est): 35.18MM **Privately Held**
Web: www.herzogelectric.com
SIC: **1731** General electrical contractor

(P-917)
MEDLEY COMMUNICATIONS INC (PA)
43015 Black Deer Loop Ste 203
(92590-3567)
PHONE..............................951 245-5200
Darrin Medley, *Pr*
EMP: 175 EST: 1985
SALES (est): 9.23MM **Privately Held**
Web: www.medleycom.net
SIC: **1731** 8748 Cable television installation;
Communications consulting

(P-918)
MOBIZ IT INC
Also Called: Mobiz
1175 Idaho St Ste 103 (92374-4591)
PHONE..............................909 453-6700
Hamad Riaz, *CEO*
EMP: 100 EST: 2017
SALES (est): 30MM **Privately Held**
SIC: **1731** 8742 7373 7371 Electrical work;
Management consulting services; Systems
integration services; Computer software
systems analysis and design, custom

(P-919)
MORROW-MEADOWS CORPORATION
13000 Kirkham Way Ste 101 (92064-7148)
PHONE..............................858 974-3650
Gary Dadmon, *Mgr*
EMP: 381
SALES (corp-wide): 302.64MM **Privately Held**
Web: www.morrow-meadows.com
SIC: **1731** General electrical contractor
PA: Morrow-Meadows Corporation
231 Benton Ct
City Of Industry CA
858 974-3650

(P-920)
MORROW-MEADOWS CORPORATION (PA)
Also Called: Cherry City Electric
231 Benton Ct (91789-5213)
PHONE..............................858 974-3650
Robert E Meadows, *VP*
EMP: 850 EST: 1964
SQ FT: 55,000
SALES (est): 302.64MM
SALES (corp-wide): 302.64MM **Privately Held**
Web: www.morrow-meadows.com
SIC: **1731** General electrical contractor

(P-921)
OBRYANT ELECTRIC INC (PA)
9314 Eton Ave (91311-5809)
PHONE..............................818 407-1986
Cathy O'bryant, *Pr*
Steve O'bryant, *Sec*
EMP: 120 EST: 1978
SQ FT: 25,000
SALES (est): 46.42MM
SALES (corp-wide): 46.42MM **Privately Held**
Web: www.obryantelectric.com
SIC: **1731** General electrical contractor

(P-922)
PACIFIC COAST CABLING INC (PA)
Also Called: PCC Network Solutions
20717 Prairie St (91311-6011)
PHONE..............................818 407-1911
EMP: 47 EST: 1985
SALES (est): 16.49MM
SALES (corp-wide): 16.49MM **Privately Held**
Web: www.pccinc.com
SIC: **1731** 3613 Computer installation;
Control panels, electric

(P-923)
PARADISE ELECTRIC INC
697 Greenfield Dr (92021-2983)
PHONE..............................619 449-4141
Mike Manos, *Pr*
Jeff Platt, *
EMP: 389 EST: 1988
SQ FT: 7,000
SALES (est): 2.82MM
SALES (corp-wide): 81.49MM **Privately Held**
Web: www.schillingcorp.com
SIC: **1731** General electrical contractor
HQ: Builders Tradesource Corp
697 Greenfield Dr
El Cajon CA

(P-924)
PATRIC COMMUNICATIONS INC (PA)
Also Called: Advanced Electronic Solutions
15215 Alton Pkwy Ste 200 (92618-2613)
PHONE..............................619 579-2898
Sean P Mcdermott, *Pr*
Richard P Apgar, *
Kathy Alford, *
EMP: 70 EST: 1981
SALES (est): 10MM **Privately Held**
SIC: **1731** 1751 3699 Fire detection and
burglar alarm systems specialization;
Carpentry work; Security devices

(P-925)
PAVLETICH ELC CMMNICATIONS INC (PA)
Also Called: Pavletich Electric
6308 Seven Seas Ave (93308-5132)
PHONE..............................661 589-9473
EMP: 89 EST: 1994

SQ FT: 15,000
SALES (est): 15.14MM **Privately Held**
Web: www.pavelectric.com
SIC: **1731** General electrical contractor

(P-926)
PINNACLE NETWORKING SVCS INC
Also Called: PINNACLE COMMUNICATION SERVICE
730 Fairmont Ave (91203-1078)
PHONE..............................818 241-6009
Avo Amirian, *CEO*
Joe Licursi, *
EMP: 130 EST: 1994
SQ FT: 10,000
SALES (est): 19.9MM **Privately Held**
Web: www.pinnacleinc.com
SIC: **1731** 8748 Communications
specialization; Telecommunications
consultant

(P-927)
PIVOT INTERIORS INC
Pivot Interiors-Receiving Only
3200 Park Center Dr Ste 100 (92626-7104)
PHONE..............................949 988-5400
Ken Baugh, *CEO*
EMP: 93
SALES (corp-wide): 91.38MM **Privately Held**
Web: www.pivotinteriors.com
SIC: **1731** Electrical work
PA: Pivot Interiors, Inc.
3355 Scott Blvd Ste 110
Santa Clara CA
408 432-5600

(P-928)
PORTERMATT ELECTRIC INC
5431 Production Dr (92649-1524)
PHONE..............................714 596-8788
Tim Matthews, *Pr*
John F Porter Iii, *VP*
EMP: 90 EST: 1998
SQ FT: 5,300
SALES (est): 19.31MM **Privately Held**
Web: www.portermatt.com
SIC: **1731** 1799 General electrical contractor
; Athletic and recreation facilities
construction

(P-929)
PROFESSNAL ELEC CNSTR SVCS INC
Also Called: Pecs
9112 Santa Anita Ave (91730-6143)
PHONE..............................909 373-4100
EMP: 102 EST: 2007
SQ FT: 15,000
SALES (est): 21.52MM **Privately Held**
Web: www.pecs.biz
SIC: **1731** 8711 1542 General electrical
contractor; Engineering services;
Nonresidential construction, nec

(P-930)
PYRO-COMM SYSTEMS INC (PA)
Also Called: Pyro
15215 Alton Pkwy (92618-2359)
PHONE..............................714 902-8000
Michael Donahue, *Pr*
Nanci Donahue, *
EMP: 150 EST: 1980
SALES (est): 38.45MM
SALES (corp-wide): 38.45MM **Privately Held**
Web: www.pyrocomm.com

SIC: **1731** 5063 Fire detection and burglar alarm systems specialization; Fire alarm systems

(P-931)
ROSENDIN ELECTRIC INC
1730 S Anaheim Way (92805-6537)
PHONE................................714 739-1334
Cliff Thompson, *Brnch Mgr*
EMP: 668
SALES (corp-wide): 2.06B **Privately Held**
Web: www.rosendin.com
SIC: 1731 General electrical contractor
PA: Rosendin Electric, Inc.
    880 Mabury Rd
    San Jose CA
    408 286-2800

(P-932)
SBE ELECTRICAL CONTRACTING INC
2817 Mcgaw Ave (92614-5835)
PHONE................................714 544-5066
Jeffery S Wilson, *CEO*
EMP: 105 **EST:** 2016
SALES (est): 9.4MM **Privately Held**
Web: www.sbeoc.com
SIC: 1731 General electrical contractor

(P-933)
SEAL ELECTRIC INC
1162 Greenfield Dr (92021-3314)
PHONE................................619 449-7323
EMP: 145 **EST:** 1996
SQ FT: 5,000
SALES (est): 23.53MM **Privately Held**
Web: www.sealelectric.com
SIC: 1731 General electrical contractor

(P-934)
SFADIA INC
Also Called: Green Energy Innovations
8485 Artesia Blvd Ste A (90621-4194)
PHONE................................323 622-1930
Pilje Park, *Pr*
Pil Soon Um, *
▲ **EMP:** 86 **EST:** 2010
SALES (est): 8.8MM **Privately Held**
Web: www.geinnovationsinc.com
SIC: 1731 Energy management controls

(P-935)
SOL NOVA ELECTRIC LLC
330 Rancheros Dr Ste 116 (92069-2939)
PHONE................................833 765-6682
EMP: 110 **EST:** 2017
SALES (est): 28.52MM **Privately Held**
Web: www.gosolnova.com
SIC: 1731 Electrical work

(P-936)
SOUND RIVER CORPORATION
Also Called: Atk Audiotek
28238 Avenue Crocker (91355-1248)
PHONE................................661 705-3700
Michael M Macdonald, *Pr*
James Harmala, *
John M Stewart, *
EMP: 85 **EST:** 1983
SQ FT: 25,000
SALES (est): 24.1MM **Privately Held**
Web: www.atkaudiotek.com
SIC: 1731 7359 Voice, data, and video wiring contractor; Sound and lighting equipment rental

(P-937)
SOUTHERN CONTRACTING COMPANY

559 N Twin Oaks Valley Rd (92069-1710)
P.O. Box 445 (92079-0445)
PHONE................................760 744-0760
Timothy R Mcbride, *CEO*
Richard W Mc Bride, *
Tim Mc Bride, *
▲ **EMP:** 125 **EST:** 1963
SQ FT: 8,400
SALES (est): 36.56MM **Privately Held**
Web: www.southerncontracting.com
SIC: 1731 General electrical contractor

(P-938)
SPECIALTY CONSTRUCTION INC
645 Clarion Ct (93401-8177)
PHONE................................805 543-1706
Rudolph Bachmann, *Pr*
Jeffrey Martin, *
Chris Teaford, *
Doug Clay, *
Steve Haymaker, *
EMP: 80 **EST:** 1992
SQ FT: 8,000
SALES (est): 27.35MM **Privately Held**
Web: www.specialtyconstruction.com
SIC: 1731 Telephone and telephone equipment installation

(P-939)
SRBRAY LLC
Also Called: Power Plus
229 N Sherman Ave (92882-1844)
PHONE................................951 898-3850
EMP: 83
Web: www.powerplus.com
SIC: 1731 7359 Standby or emergency power specialization; Equipment rental and leasing, nec
PA: S.R.Bray Llc
    5500 E La Palma Ave
    Anaheim CA

(P-940)
STEINY AND COMPANY INC
221 N Ardmore Ave (90004-4503)
PHONE................................213 382-2331
EMP: 300
Web: www.steinyco.com
SIC: 1731 General electrical contractor

(P-941)
SUN ELECTRIC LP
2101 S Yale St Ste B (92704-4424)
PHONE................................714 210-3744
Jeffery J Ber Bernardino, *Ltd Pt*
EMP: 100 **EST:** 2003
SALES (est): 7.33MM **Privately Held**
SIC: 1731 General electrical contractor

(P-942)
SUNSHINE COMMUNICATIONS SE INC
350 Cypress Ln Ste D (92020-1664)
P.O. Box 3509 (33572-1005)
PHONE................................619 448-7600
Robert Straub, *CEO*
EMP: 235 **EST:** 1998
SALES (est): 22.95MM **Privately Held**
Web: www.sunshinecom.com
SIC: 1731 Cable television installation

(P-943)
SUNWEST ELECTRIC INC
3064 E Mariloma (92806-1810)
PHONE................................714 630-8700
Brien Pariseau, *Pr*
Doug Lyvers, *
EMP: 175 **EST:** 1985

SQ FT: 20,000
SALES (est): 23.79MM **Privately Held**
Web: www.sunwestelectric.net
SIC: 1731 Electrical work

(P-944)
SUPERIOR ELEC MECH & PLBG INC
8613 Helms Ave (91730-4521)
PHONE................................909 357-9400
David A Stone Junior, *CEO*
Walt Schobel, *
Pam Metzer, *
EMP: 291 **EST:** 2001
SQ FT: 50,000
SALES (est): 40.09MM **Privately Held**
Web: www.superioremp.com
SIC: 1731 1711 General electrical contractor ; Mechanical contractor

(P-945)
T MCGEE ELECTRIC INC
2390 S Reservoir St (91766-6410)
P.O. Box 1111 (91708-1111)
PHONE................................909 591-6461
Trent L Mc Gee, *Pr*
EMP: 100 **EST:** 1986
SALES (est): 7.71MM **Privately Held**
Web: www.tmcgeeelectric.com
SIC: 1731 General electrical contractor

(P-946)
TAFT ELECTRIC COMPANY (PA)
1694 Eastman Ave (93003-5782)
P.O. Box 3416 (93006-3416)
PHONE................................805 642-0121
James Marsh, *Pr*
Carol A Smith, *
Jeff Wofford, *
EMP: 209 **EST:** 1942
SQ FT: 40,000
SALES (est): 99.9MM
SALES (corp-wide): 99.9MM **Privately Held**
Web: www.taftelectric.com
SIC: 1731 1629 General electrical contractor ; Waste water and sewage treatment plant construction

(P-947)
TRI-SIGNAL INTEGRATION INC (PA)
Also Called: Honeywell Authorized Dealer
28110 Avenue Stanford Unit D (91355-1119)
PHONE................................818 566-8558
Robert Mckibben, *Pr*
Rett Hicks, *
Michael Swisher, *
Dennis Furden, *
EMP: 100 **EST:** 1998
SQ FT: 16,000
SALES (est): 44.75MM
SALES (corp-wide): 44.75MM **Privately Held**
Web: www.tri-signal.com
SIC: 1731 Fire detection and burglar alarm systems specialization

(P-948)
TRL SYSTEMS INCORPORATED
Also Called: T R L
9531 Milliken Ave (91730-6006)
PHONE................................909 390-8392
Lynn Purdy, *Ch*
Mark L Purdy, *
EMP: 100 **EST:** 1980
SQ FT: 14,000
SALES (est): 50.75MM **Privately Held**
Web: www.trlsystems.com

SIC: 1731 General electrical contractor

(P-949)
TWIN POWER USA LLC
Also Called: Twin Power Indus Solutions
40424 Jacob Way (92563-4916)
PHONE................................714 609-6014
Michael Darwish, *CEO*
David Darwich, *Mgr*
David Darwish, *VP*
EMP: 20 **EST:** 2014
SALES (est): 2.16MM **Privately Held**
Web: www.twinpowerusa.com
SIC: 1731 8748 8711 8742 General electrical contractor; Systems analysis and engineering consulting services; Consulting engineer; Management engineering

(P-950)
VECTOR RESOURCES INC (PA)
Also Called: Vectorusa
20917 Higgins Ct (90501-1723)
PHONE................................310 436-1000
TOLL FREE: 800
David Zukerman, *Pr*
Robert Messinger, *
John Schuman, *Dist Vice President**
Jeffrey Zukerman, *
EMP: 169 **EST:** 1988
SALES (est): 89.14MM
SALES (corp-wide): 89.14MM **Privately Held**
Web: www.vectorusa.com
SIC: 1731 3651 7373 Communications specialization; Clock radio and telephone combinations; Systems engineering, computer related

(P-951)
WEST COAST LTG & ENRGY INC
18550 Minthorn St (92530-2784)
PHONE................................951 296-0680
Johnny Odell Leach, *Pr*
Johnny Odell Leach, *Pr*
Tammy Leach, *
EMP: 90 **EST:** 1994
SQ FT: 2,646
SALES (est): 13.39MM **Privately Held**
Web: www.wcleinc.com
SIC: 1731 General electrical contractor

(P-952)
WORLD WIND ELECTRICAL SVCS INC
Also Called: World Wind & Solar
228 W Tehachapi Blvd (93561-1634)
PHONE................................661 822-4877
Edward Cummings, *Pr*
EMP: 396 **EST:** 2009
SALES (est): 3.76MM
SALES (corp-wide): 581.19MM **Privately Held**
SIC: 1731 3621 8742 Electrical work; Windmills, electric generating; Maintenance management consultant
HQ: Pearce Services, Llc
    1222 Vine St Ste 301
    Paso Robles CA
    805 467-2528

(P-953)
WORLDWIND SERVICES LLC
Also Called: World Wind & Solar
1222 Vine St Ste 301 (93446-2333)
PHONE................................661 822-4877
Mark Mclanahan, *CEO*
Kristin Osborn, *
Matthew Gillette, *
EMP: 700 **EST:** 2007
SALES (est): 85.19MM

SALES (corp-wide): 581.19MM **Privately Held**
Web: www.worldwindsolar.com
SIC: 1731 1389 8742 Electrical work; Construction, repair, and dismantling services; Maintenance management consultant
HQ: Pearce Services, Llc
　1222 Vine St Ste 301
　Paso Robles CA
　805 467-2528

(P-954)
X3 MANAGEMENT SERVICES INC
700 La Terraza Blvd Ste 110 (92025)
P.O. Box 460669 (92046-0669)
PHONE...............................760 597-9336
David G Cranford, *CEO*
Arlette Zuniga, *
EMP: 85 **EST:** 2005
SALES (est): 22.84MM **Privately Held**
Web: www.x3corp.net
SIC: 1731 1531 1541 1711 Electrical work; Operative builders; Industrial buildings and warehouses; Solar energy contractor

1741 Masonry And Other Stonework

(P-955)
B&B INDUSTRIAL SERVICES INC (PA)
14549 Manzanita Dr (92335-5378)
PHONE...............................909 428-3167
Lyndon Brewer, *Pr*
Ted Brewer, *
Tim Brewer, *
EMP: 261 **EST:** 1993
SQ FT: 12,000
SALES (est): 22.11MM **Privately Held**
Web: www.midphase.com
SIC: 1741 Refractory or acid brick masonry

(P-956)
FRANK S SMITH MASONRY INC
2830 Pomona Blvd (91768-3224)
PHONE...............................909 468-0525
Frank E Smith, *Pr*
Brian E Smith, *
Kevin J Smith, *
EMP: 100 **EST:** 1938
SQ FT: 54,000
SALES (est): 9.63MM **Privately Held**
Web: www.franksmithmasonry.com
SIC: 1741 Bricklaying

(P-957)
GBC CONCRETE MASNRY CNSTR INC
561 Birch St (92530-2732)
PHONE...............................951 245-2355
Tom Daniel, *Pr*
EMP: 170 **EST:** 1985
SQ FT: 8,000
SALES (est): 23.25MM **Privately Held**
Web: www.gbcconstruction.com
SIC: 1741 1771 Foundation building; Concrete work

(P-958)
HBA INCORPORATED
512 E Vermont Ave (92805-5603)
P.O. Box 25861 (92825-5861)
PHONE...............................714 635-8602
EMP: 100 **EST:** 2006
SALES (est): 6.68MM **Privately Held**
Web: www.hbabuild.com

SIC: 1741 Masonry and other stonework

(P-959)
J GINGER MASONRY LP (PA)
8188 Lincoln Ave Ste 100 (92504-4329)
PHONE...............................951 688-5050
John L Ginger, *Ltd Pt*
EMP: 265 **EST:** 1978
SALES (est): 48.92MM **Privately Held**
Web: www.jgingermasonry.com
SIC: 1741 Masonry and other stonework

(P-960)
MASONRY CONCEPTS INC
15408 Cornet St (90670-5534)
PHONE...............................562 802-3700
Dana Kemp, *Pr*
Ronald O Udall, *
Peter Sturdivant, *
Russell Knight, *
EMP: 100 **EST:** 1983
SQ FT: 10,000
SALES (est): 17.18MM **Privately Held**
Web: www.masonry-concepts.com
SIC: 1741 Masonry and other stonework

(P-961)
MASONRY GROUP NEVADA INC
8188 Lincoln Ave Ste 99 (92504-4329)
PHONE...............................951 509-5300
EMP: 99
SALES (est): 1.15MM **Privately Held**
SIC: 1741 Masonry and other stonework

(P-962)
SPECTRA COMPANY
2510 Supply St (91767-2113)
PHONE...............................909 599-0760
Ray Adamyk, *CEO*
Ann Dresselhaus, *
▲ **EMP:** 125 **EST:** 1985
SQ FT: 7,000
SALES (est): 16.09MM **Privately Held**
Web: www.spectracompany.com
SIC: 1741 1771 1743 1721 Masonry and other stonework; Concrete work; Terrazzo, tile, marble and mosaic work; Painting and paper hanging

(P-963)
VINCENT CONTRACTORS INC
Also Called: Vincent Scaffolding
4501 E La Palma Ave Ste 200 (92807-1904)
PHONE...............................714 660-0165
Justin Erdtsieck, *Pr*
Kenny Vo, *
EMP: 430 **EST:** 2016
SQ FT: 5,538
SALES (est): 23.86MM **Privately Held**
SIC: 1741 1742 Masonry and other stonework; Plastering, drywall, and insulation

(P-964)
WIRTZ QUALITY INSTALLATIONS
7932 Armour St (92111-3718)
PHONE...............................858 569-3816
Victor Fox, *Pr*
Ida Wirtz, *
John Wirtz, *
Ryan Wilson, *
EMP: 85 **EST:** 2009
SALES (est): 3.6MM **Privately Held**
Web: www.wirtzquality.com
SIC: 1741 1752 1743 1799 Masonry and other stonework; Floor laying and floor work, nec; Terrazzo, tile, marble and mosaic work; Cleaning building exteriors, nec

1742 Plastering, Drywall, And Insulation

(P-965)
A A GONZALEZ INC
13264 Ralston Ave (91342-7607)
P.O. Box 408 (91341-0408)
PHONE...............................818 367-2242
EMP: 100 **EST:** 1992
SALES (est): 4.87MM **Privately Held**
Web: www.aagonz.com
SIC: 1742 Plastering, drywall, and insulation

(P-966)
ALL WALL INC
46150 Commerce St Ste 102 (92201-3418)
PHONE...............................760 600-5108
Saul M Gonzalez, *Pr*
Yvette Ambriz, *
Saul Miranda, *
EMP: 89 **EST:** 2012
SALES (est): 4.38MM **Privately Held**
Web: www.allwalldi.com
SIC: 1742 1721 7389 Drywall; Exterior residential painting contractor; Business Activities at Non-Commercial Site

(P-967)
ANCCA CORPORATION
Also Called: N-U Enterprise
7 Goddard (92618-4600)
PHONE...............................949 553-0084
Nicole Hunt, *Sec*
EMP: 99 **EST:** 2008
SALES (est): 3.99MM **Privately Held**
SIC: 1742 Plastering, drywall, and insulation

(P-968)
BERGER BROS INC
154 N Aspan Ave (91702-4224)
PHONE...............................626 334-2699
EMP: 350
Web: www.bergerbro.com
SIC: 1742 Plastering, plain or ornamental

(P-969)
BEST INTERIORS INC (PA)
2100 E Via Burton (92806-1219)
PHONE...............................714 490-7999
Dennis Ayres, *Pr*
Michael Herrig, *
EMP: 150 **EST:** 1986
SQ FT: 20,000
SALES (est): 39.63MM
SALES (corp-wide): 39.63MM **Privately Held**
Web: www.bestinteriors.net
SIC: 1742 Drywall

(P-970)
BEST INTERIORS INC
4395 Murphy Canyon Rd (92123-4337)
PHONE...............................858 715-3760
EMP: 80
SALES (corp-wide): 39.63MM **Privately Held**
Web: www.bestinteriors.net
SIC: 1742 Drywall
PA: Best Interiors, Inc.
　2100 E Via Burton
　Anaheim CA
　714 490-7999

(P-971)
BRADY COMPANY/SAN DIEGO INC
8100 Center St (91942-2925)
P.O. Box 968 (91944-0968)

PHONE...............................619 462-2600
Scott Brady, *CEO*
EMP: 300 **EST:** 1946
SQ FT: 4,000
SALES (est): 23.48MM **Privately Held**
Web: www.brady.com
SIC: 1742 1542 Plastering, plain or ornamental; Commercial and office buildings, renovation and repair

(P-972)
BRADY SOCAL INCORPORATED
8100 Center St (91942-2925)
PHONE...............................619 462-2600
Ricky Marshall, *Pr*
Scott Brady, *
EMP: 99 **EST:** 2009
SALES (est): 18.81MM **Privately Held**
Web: www.brady.com
SIC: 1742 1751 Drywall; Window and door installation and erection

(P-973)
CALDERON DRYWALL CONTRS INC
1931 E Meats Ave Trlr 127 (92865-4002)
PHONE...............................714 696-2977
EMP: 84
SALES (corp-wide): 4.59MM **Privately Held**
SIC: 1742 Drywall
PA: Calderon Drywall Contractors Inc.
　2085 N Nordic St
　Orange CA
　714 900-1863

(P-974)
CAPITAL DRYWALL LP
333 S Grand Ave Ste 4070 (90071-1544)
PHONE...............................909 599-6818
Frank Scardino, *Pr*
Art Toscano, *
Angela Gates, *
EMP: 249 **EST:** 1980
SQ FT: 8,000
SALES (est): 2.45MM **Privately Held**
SIC: 1742 Drywall
PA: U.S. Builder Services, Llc
　272 E Deerpath Ste 308
　Lake Forest IL

(P-975)
CASTON INC
354 S Allen St (92408-1508)
PHONE...............................909 381-1619
James I Malachowski Junior, *Pr*
EMP: 100 **EST:** 2010
SALES (est): 18.13MM **Privately Held**
Web: www.castoninc.com
SIC: 1742 Drywall

(P-976)
CHURCH & LARSEN INC
16103 Avenida Padilla (91702-3223)
PHONE...............................626 303-8741
Raymond W Larsen, *Pr*
Kenneth R Larsen, *
Kenneth P Larsen, *
EMP: 250 **EST:** 1980
SQ FT: 10,800
SALES (est): 9.54MM **Privately Held**
Web: www.churchandlarsen.com
SIC: 1742 Drywall

(P-977)
FARWEST INSULATION CONTRACTING
Also Called: Pacific Insulation
2741 Yates Ave (90040-2623)

PRODUCTS & SVCS

PHONE..................310 634-2800
Linda Chadarria, *Mgr*
EMP: 88
SALES (corp-wide): 26.97MM **Privately Held**
Web: www.farwestinsulation.com
SIC: 1742 Insulation, buildings
PA: Farwest Insulation Contracting, Inc
1220 S Sherman St
Anaheim CA
714 520-5600

(P-978)
FIVE STAR PLASTERING INC
23022 La Cadena Dr Ste 200 (92653-1362)
PHONE..................949 683-5091
EMP: 100 **EST:** 2010
SALES (est): 3.86MM **Privately Held**
Web: www.fivestarplastering.com
SIC: 1742 Drywall

(P-979)
HI-TEMP INSULATION INC
4700 Calle Alto (93012-8537)
PHONE..................805 484-2774
Sieg Borck, *CEO*
Fecialita Allen, *
▲ **EMP:** 410 **EST:** 1964
SQ FT: 100,000
SALES (est): 48.41MM **Privately Held**
Web: www.hi-tempinsulation.com
SIC: 1742 Insulation, buildings

(P-980)
INTERIOR EXPERTS GEN BLDRS INC
4534 Carter Ct (91710-5060)
PHONE..................909 203-4922
Adam Lopez, *Pr*
EMP: 80 **EST:** 1992
SQ FT: 9,000
SALES (est): 11.08MM **Privately Held**
Web: www.interiorexpertsgc.com
SIC: 1742 Drywall

(P-981)
JOHN JORY CORPORATION (PA)
2180 N Glassell St (92865-3308)
P.O. Box 6050 (92863-6050)
PHONE..................714 279-7901
Kenneth Johnson, *CEO*
Jack Jory, *
EMP: 385 **EST:** 1965
SALES (est): 28.26MM
SALES (corp-wide): 28.26MM **Privately Held**
Web: www.johnjorycorp.com
SIC: 1742 Drywall

(P-982)
MARTIN BROS/MARCOWALL INC (PA)
17104 S Figueroa St (90248-3021)
P.O. Box 2089 (90247-0089)
PHONE..................310 532-5335
Mohammad Chahine, *CEO*
EMP: 110 **EST:** 1966
SQ FT: 6,000
SALES (est): 45.05MM
SALES (corp-wide): 45.05MM **Privately Held**
Web: www.martinbros.net
SIC: 1742 Drywall

(P-983)
MARTIN INTEGRATED SYSTEMS
Also Called: Martin Integrated
1525 W Orange Grove Ave Ste D
(92868-1109)

PHONE..................714 998-9100
Cory Hovivian, *Pr*
Marshall Hovivian, *
Anne Reizer, *
EMP: 30 **EST:** 1989
SALES (est): 4.23MM **Privately Held**
Web: www.martinintegrated.com
SIC: 1742 3446 3296 Acoustical and ceiling work; Acoustical suspension systems, metal ; Acoustical board and tile, mineral wool

(P-984)
MOWERY THOMASON INC
1225 N Red Gum St (92806-1821)
PHONE..................714 666-1717
Robert J Heimerl, *Pr*
Todd Heimerl, *
Toni Heimerl, *
EMP: 175 **EST:** 1957
SQ FT: 8,000
SALES (est): 20.21MM **Privately Held**
Web: www.mowerythomason.com
SIC: 1742 Drywall

(P-985)
OJ INSULATION LP (PA)
Also Called: Abco Insulation
600 S Vincent Ave (91702-5145)
PHONE..................800 707-9278
Pamela A Henson, *Pt*
EMP: 148 **EST:** 2006
SQ FT: 12,000
SALES (est): 22.6MM
SALES (corp-wide): 22.6MM **Privately Held**
Web: www.ojinc.com
SIC: 1742 1751 1741 Insulation, buildings; Carpentry work; Masonry and other stonework

(P-986)
ORANGE COUNTY PLST CO INC
3191 Airport Loop Dr Ste B1 (92626)
PHONE..................714 957-1971
EMP: 128 **EST:** 1995
SALES (est): 7.92MM **Privately Held**
SIC: 1742 Plastering, plain or ornamental

(P-987)
ORANGE COUNTY THERMAL INDS INC
1350 N Hundley St (92806-1301)
PHONE..................714 279-9416
Eduardo Olivares, *Pr*
EMP: 51 **EST:** 2010
SQ FT: 10,000
SALES (est): 9.51MM **Privately Held**
Web: www.teamocti.com
SIC: 1742 3296 Insulation, buildings; Acoustical board and tile, mineral wool

(P-988)
PACIFIC BUILDING GROUP
13541 Stoney Creek Rd (92129-2050)
PHONE..................858 552-0600
Jim Roherty, *Brnch Mgr*
EMP: 94
SALES (corp-wide): 59.16MM **Privately Held**
Web: www.pacificbuildinggroup.com
SIC: 1742 Acoustical and ceiling work
PA: Pacific Building Group
9752 Aspen Creek Ct # 100
San Diego CA
858 552-0600

(P-989)
PACIFIC SYSTEMS INTERIORS INC

190 E Arrow Hwy Ste D (91773-3314)
PHONE..................310 436-6820
Michelle Orr Mcneal, *Dir*
EMP: 150 **EST:** 1987
SQ FT: 30,000
SALES (est): 39.51MM **Privately Held**
Web: www.psi.builders
SIC: 1742 1542 Drywall; Nonresidential construction, nec

(P-990)
PADILLA CONSTRUCTION COMPANY
Also Called: Garris Plastering
1620 N Brian St (92867-3422)
PHONE..................714 685-8500
Ralph Padilla, *Prin*
EMP: 250 **EST:** 1963
SALES (est): 23.42MM **Privately Held**
Web: www.padillaconstruction.com
SIC: 1742 Plastering, drywall, and insulation

(P-991)
PETROCHEM INSULATION INC
Also Called: Petrochem
3117 E South St (90805-3742)
PHONE..................310 638-6663
Erich Freudenthaler, *Mgr*
EMP: 115
SALES (corp-wide): 2.72B **Privately Held**
Web: www.petrocheminc.com
SIC: 1742 3531 Insulation, buildings; Construction machinery
HQ: Petrochem Insulation, Inc.
1501 W Ftnhead Pkwy # 550
Tempe AZ
707 644-7455

(P-992)
PROWALL LATH AND PLASTER
360 S Spruce St (92025-4052)
P.O. Box 3058 (92033-3058)
PHONE..................760 480-9001
Mary Kathawa, *Pr*
EMP: 99 **EST:** 2009
SALES (est): 2.68MM **Privately Held**
Web: www.prowalllathandplaster.net
SIC: 1742 Plastering, plain or ornamental

(P-993)
QUALITY PRODUCTION SVCS INC
18711 S Broadwick St (90220-6427)
PHONE..................310 406-3350
Arshak George Kotoyantz, *Pr*
EMP: 100 **EST:** 1995
SALES (est): 11.61MM **Privately Held**
Web: www.qpscompany.com
SIC: 1742 Drywall

(P-994)
ROYAL WEST DRYWALL INC
2008 2nd St (92860-2804)
PHONE..................951 271-4600
Paul Diguiseppe, *CEO*
EMP: 100 **EST:** 1988
SQ FT: 20,473
SALES (est): 9.3MM **Privately Held**
Web: www.royalwestdrywall.com
SIC: 1742 Drywall

(P-995)
RUTHERFORD CO INC (PA)
2107 Crystal St (90039-2901)
PHONE..................323 666-5284
Paul Rutherford, *Pr*
Sheila Rutherford, *
Brad Rutherford, *
James Rutherford, *

EMP: 100 **EST:** 1970
SQ FT: 15,000
SALES (est): 9.17MM
SALES (corp-wide): 9.17MM **Privately Held**
Web: www.rutherfordco.net
SIC: 1742 Plastering, plain or ornamental

(P-996)
SIERRA LATHING COMPANY INC
1189 Leiske Dr (92376-8633)
PHONE..................909 421-0211
Gary K Waldron, *CEO*
Connie Waldron, *
EMP: 200 **EST:** 1958
SQ FT: 10,000
SALES (est): 8.55MM **Privately Held**
SIC: 1742 1751 Drywall; Framing contractor

(P-997)
SPECIALTY TEAM PLASTERING INC
4652 Vintage Ranch Ln (93110-2079)
PHONE..................805 966-3858
Jaime Melgosa, *Pr*
Robin Melgosa, *
EMP: 130 **EST:** 1993
SQ FT: 1,000
SALES (est): 9.28MM **Privately Held**
Web: www.specialtyteamplastering.com
SIC: 1742 Plastering, plain or ornamental

(P-998)
STANDARD DRYWALL INC (HQ)
Also Called: S D I
9831 Channel Rd (92040-3173)
PHONE..................619 443-7034
Robert E Caya, *CEO*
Blaine Caya, *
EMP: 300 **EST:** 1956
SALES (est): 118.19MM **Privately Held**
Web: www.standarddrywall.com
SIC: 1742 Drywall
PA: E M P Interiors Inc
9831 Channel Rd
Lakeside CA

(P-999)
SUNSHINE METAL CLAD INC
7201 Edison Hwy (93307-9011)
PHONE..................661 366-0575
James R Eudy, *Pr*
Linda Payne, *
▲ **EMP:** 100 **EST:** 1979
SQ FT: 50,000
SALES (est): 9.89MM **Privately Held**
Web: www.smcinsulation.com
SIC: 1742 Insulation, buildings

(P-1000)
SUPERIOR WALL SYSTEMS INC
Also Called: Sws
1232 E Orangethorpe Ave (92831-5224)
PHONE..................714 278-0000
Ronald Lee Hudson, *CEO*
Greg Smith, *
EMP: 500 **EST:** 1979
SQ FT: 40,000
SALES (est): 48MM **Privately Held**
Web: www.superiorwallsystems.com
SIC: 1742 Drywall

(P-1001)
THERMO POWER INDUSTRIES
Also Called: Thermo Power Industries
10570 Humbolt St (90720-2439)
PHONE..................562 799-0087
Edward Lydic, *CEO*
John G Carroll, *
EMP: 50 **EST:** 1986

SQ FT: 5,500
SALES (est): 9.38MM **Privately Held**
Web: www.thermopowerindustries.com
SIC: 1742 1721 3479 Insulation, buildings;
Commercial painting; Coating, rust
preventive

(P-1002)
WEST COAST DRYWALL & CO INC
Also Called: West Coast Drywall & Paint
1610 W Linden St (92507-6810)
PHONE...............................951 778-3592
Mark Herbert, *CEO*
Dan Slavin, *
Santos Garcia, *
Colleen Butler, *
Keith Caneva, *Corporate Controller*
EMP: 400 **EST:** 2002
SQ FT: 18,962
SALES (est): 36.86MM **Privately Held**
Web: www.wcdp.com
SIC: 1742 Drywall

1743 Terrazzo, Tile, Marble, Mosaic Work

(P-1003)
ALEXS TILE WORKS INC
5920 Matthews St (93117-3922)
P.O. Box 810 (93102-0810)
PHONE...............................805 967-5308
Vitali Drohomyrecky, *Pr*
Ruthe Drohomyrecky, *
Leonid Bondarenko, *
EMP: 25 **EST:** 1989
SALES (est): 2.48MM **Privately Held**
Web: www.alexstile.com
SIC: 1743 3272 Tile installation, ceramic;
Floor slabs and tiles, precast concrete

(P-1004)
COASTAL TILE INC
Also Called: Coastal The
13226 Moorpark St Apt 104 (91423-5177)
PHONE...............................818 988-6134
Ronig Yemini, *Pr*
Eyal Reguev, *
▲ **EMP:** 100 **EST:** 1993
SALES (est): 3.91MM **Privately Held**
SIC: 1743 Tile installation, ceramic

(P-1005)
KIRBY INDUSTRIES INC
2109 S Lyon St (92705-5303)
PHONE...............................714 437-0789
Scott Kirby, *Pr*
Thomas Jackson, *VP*
Jerald Kirby, *CFO*
EMP: 18 **EST:** 1988
SALES (est): 827.03K **Privately Held**
Web: kirby-industries.hub.biz
SIC: 1743 3281 Tile installation, ceramic;
Marble, building: cut and shaped

(P-1006)
PARAGON INDUSTRIES INC
Also Called: Bedrosian's Tile
16450 Foothill Blvd Ste 100 (91342)
PHONE...............................818 833-0550
Josie Cox, *Brnch Mgr*
EMP: 23
SQ FT: 108,362
SALES (corp-wide): 251.57MM **Privately Held**
Web: www.bedrosians.com

SIC: 1743 3253 5032 5211 Tile installation,
ceramic; Ceramic wall and floor tile;
Ceramic wall and floor tile, nec; Tile,
ceramic
PA: Paragon Industries, Inc.
4285 N Golden State Blvd
Fresno CA
559 275-5000

(P-1007)
TILE & MARBLE DESIGN CO INC
Also Called: Marbleworks
7421 Vincent Cir (92648-1246)
PHONE...............................714 847-6472
David Blataric, *CEO*
EMP: 32 **EST:** 2005
SALES (est): 3.2MM **Privately Held**
SIC: 1743 3281 Tile installation, ceramic;
Marble, building: cut and shaped

1751 Carpentry Work

(P-1008)
CLOSET WORLD INC
14438 Don Julian Rd (91746-3101)
PHONE...............................626 855-0846
EMP: 90
Web: www.closetworld.com
SIC: 1751 5211 Cabinet building and
installation; Closets, interiors and
accessories
PA: Closet World, Inc.
3860 Capitol Ave
City Of Industry CA

(P-1009)
COMMERCIAL WOOD PRODUCTS COMPANY
Also Called: Cwp
10019 Yucca Rd (92301-2242)
PHONE...............................760 246-4530
EMP: 115
Web: www.commercialwood.com
SIC: 1751 Cabinet building and installation

(P-1010)
CRAFTSMAN LATH AND PLASTER INC
8325 63rd St (92509-6004)
PHONE...............................951 685-9922
Kevin Tunstill, *Pr*
EMP: 350 **EST:** 2015
SALES (est): 9.68MM **Privately Held**
Web: www.craftsmanlp.com
SIC: 1751 Carpentry work

(P-1011)
CWP CABINETS INC
15447 Anacapa Rd Ste 102 (92392-2481)
PHONE...............................760 246-4530
Michael Rodriguez, *CEO*
EMP: 115 **EST:** 2011
SALES (est): 9.81MM **Privately Held**
SIC: 1751 2434 2541 5712 Cabinet building
and installation; Wood kitchen cabinets;
Wood partitions and fixtures; Cabinet work,
custom

(P-1012)
GRANT CONSTRUCTION INC
7702 Meany Ave Ste 103 (93308-5199)
PHONE...............................661 588-4586
Grant Fraysier, *Pr*
EMP: 93 **EST:** 1994
SQ FT: 1,000
SALES (est): 23.84MM **Privately Held**
Web: www.grant-construction.com

SIC: 1751 1771 Framing contractor;
Concrete work

(P-1013)
GRESEAN INDUSTRIES INC
6320 Caballero Blvd (90620-1126)
P.O. Box 928 (92075-0928)
EMP: 25 **EST:** 1986
SALES (est): 2.73MM **Privately Held**
Web: www.cabinetsystems.com
SIC: 1751 2421 Cabinet and finish carpentry
; Flooring (dressed lumber), softwood

(P-1014)
HAKES SASH & DOOR INC
31945 Corydon St (92530-8524)
PHONE...............................951 674-2414
Allen J Hakes, *Pr*
EMP: 190 **EST:** 2005
SQ FT: 2,000
SALES (est): 24.49MM **Privately Held**
Web: www.hakesdoor.net
SIC: 1751 3442 5211 Window and door
installation and erection; Window and door
frames; Sash, wood or metal

(P-1015)
HOME ORGANIZERS INC
Also Called: Closet World, The
3860 Capitol Ave (90601-1733)
PHONE...............................562 699-9945
Frank Melkonian, *Pr*
EMP: 660 **EST:** 2001
SALES (est): 41.37MM **Privately Held**
Web: www.closetworld.com
SIC: 1751 2541 Cabinet building and
installation; Cabinets, lockers, and shelving

(P-1016)
ISEC INCORPORATED
Also Called: Intermountain Specialty Eqp
20 Centerpointe Dr Ste 140 (90623-2563)
PHONE...............................714 761-5151
Greg Timmerman, *VP*
EMP: 130
SQ FT: 5,000
SALES (corp-wide): 317.22MM **Privately Held**
Web: www.isecinc.com
SIC: 1751 Cabinet and finish carpentry
PA: Isec, Incorporated
6000 Greenwood Plaza Blvd # 200
Greenwood Village CO
303 790-1444

(P-1017)
JT WINDOWS INC
9261 Independence Ave (91311-5905)
P.O. Box 4317 (91359-1317)
PHONE...............................818 709-7950
Tom Burns, *Pr*
Janet Burns, *
EMP: 40 **EST:** 1978
SQ FT: 34,000
SALES (est): 2.72MM **Privately Held**
Web: www.jtwindows.com
SIC: 1751 2431 Window and door
installation and erection; Millwork

(P-1018)
LAURENCE-HOVENIER INC
179 N Maple St (92878-3260)
PHONE...............................951 736-2990
Ronald Laurence, *Pr*
Fred Hovenier, *
EMP: 190 **EST:** 1979
SQ FT: 6,000
SALES (est): 24.69MM **Privately Held**
SIC: 1751 Framing contractor

(P-1019)
LOZANO CASEWORKS INC
242 W Hanna St (92324-2772)
PHONE...............................909 783-7530
EMP: 70
SIC: 1751 2522 Cabinet building and
installation; Cabinets, office: except wood

(P-1020)
NORCAL INC
Also Called: Seeley Brothers
1400 Moonstone (92821-2801)
PHONE...............................714 224-3949
Michael Seeley, *Pt*
Phil Norys, *
Joe Calvillo, *
EMP: 175 **EST:** 1987
SQ FT: 62,000
SALES (est): 48.78MM **Privately Held**
Web: www.seeleybros.com
SIC: 1751 Finish and trim carpentry

(P-1021)
PARS INDUSTRIES INC
Also Called: Wood Craft Company, The
8594 Siempre Viva Rd # C (92154-6270)
PHONE...............................619 671-9663
Mehdi R Govari, *Prin*
Mehdi Govari, *
EMP: 24 **EST:** 1983
SQ FT: 15,000
SALES (est): 458.95K **Privately Held**
SIC: 1751 2531 Finish and trim carpentry;
Public building and related furniture

(P-1022)
PRIME TECH CABINETS INC
2215 S Standard Ave (92707-3036)
PHONE...............................949 757-4900
Hassan Farjamrad, *Pr*
Zora Farjamrad, *
EMP: 110 **EST:** 1988
SALES (est): 9.36MM **Privately Held**
Web: www.ptcabinets.com
SIC: 1751 Cabinet building and installation

(P-1023)
SURECRAFT SUPPLY INC
2875 Executive Pl (92029-1524)
EMP: 131
Web: www.surecraft.com
SIC: 1751 Carpentry work

(P-1024)
TRIMCO FINISH INC
3130 W Harvard St (92704-3937)
PHONE...............................714 708-0300
EMP: 160
Web: www.trimcofinish.com
SIC: 1751 Finish and trim carpentry

(P-1025)
TWR ENTERPRISES INC
1661 Railroad St (92878-5003)
PHONE...............................951 279-2000
Thomas W Rhodes, *Pr*
EMP: 200 **EST:** 1985
SQ FT: 20,000
SALES (est): 19.94MM **Privately Held**
Web: www.twrframing.com
SIC: 1751 Framing contractor

(P-1026)
UNITED MARKETING GROUP INC
Also Called: Elite Gates
5957 S St Andrews Pl (90047-1308)
PHONE...............................323 778-4283
EMP: 95

SALES (corp-wide): 2.16MM **Privately Held**
SIC: **1751** Garage door, installation or erection
PA: United Marketing Group, Inc.
3226 Escollera Ave
Santa Rosa Valley CA
310 842-7453

(P-1027)
VORTEX INDUSTRIES INC (PA)
Also Called: Vortex Doors
20 Odyssey (92618-3144)
PHONE.................714 434-8000
Elizabeth Turner Everett, *CEO*
▲ **EMP:** 25 **EST:** 1937
SQ FT: 10,000
SALES (est): 127.18MM
SALES (corp-wide): 127.18MM **Privately Held**
Web: www.vortexdoors.com
SIC: **1751** 3441 7699 Garage door, installation or erection; Fabricated structural metal; Door and window repair

(P-1028)
WESLAR INC
28310 Constellation Rd (91355-5078)
PHONE.................661 702-1362
Larry Kern, *Pr*
Wes Toy, *
EMP: 100 **EST:** 1981
SQ FT: 5,500
SALES (est): 4.11MM **Privately Held**
SIC: **1751** Framing contractor

(P-1029)
WIN-DOR INC (PA)
450 Delta Ave (92821-2935)
PHONE.................714 576-2030
TOLL FREE: 800
Gary Templin, *CEO*
Wolfgang Wirthgen, *
EMP: 170 **EST:** 1994
SQ FT: 73,000
SALES (est): 46.75MM **Privately Held**
Web: www.windorsystems.com
SIC: **1751** 3446 Window and door (prefabricated) installation; Guards, made from pipe

1752 Floor Laying And Floor Work, Nec

(P-1030)
HOME CARPET INVESTMENT INC (PA)
Also Called: Americas Finest Carpet Company
730 Design Ct Ste 401 (91911-6160)
PHONE.................619 262-8040
Carlos Ledesma, *CEO*
EMP: 81 **EST:** 1998
SQ FT: 2,500
SALES (est): 22.39MM **Privately Held**
Web: www.americasfinestcarpet.com
SIC: **1752** 7217 Carpet laying; Carpet and upholstery cleaning

(P-1031)
HY-TECH TILE INC
1130 Palmyrita Ave Ste 350 (92507-1706)
P.O. Box 5577 (92517-5577)
PHONE.................951 788-0550
Brian Lyman, *Pr*
Tom Shoemaker, *
Cristina Olteanu, *
Narcis Postolache, *
EMP: 110 **EST:** 1994

SQ FT: 12,000
SALES (est): 16.37MM **Privately Held**
Web: www.hytechtile.com
SIC: **1752** 1743 Ceramic floor tile installation ; Terrazzo, tile, marble and mosaic work

(P-1032)
INTERIOR SPECIALISTS INC
Also Called: Interior Logic Group HM Rmdlg
18565 Jamboree Rd Ste 125 (92612-2543)
PHONE.................800 959-8333
EMP: 273
SALES (corp-wide): 499.75MM **Privately Held**
Web: www.interiorlogicgroup.com
SIC: **1752** Carpet laying
HQ: Interior Specialists, Inc.
1630 Faraday Ave
Carlsbad CA
760 929-6700

(P-1033)
J W FLOOR COVERING INC (PA)
Also Called: J. W. Floor Covering
9881 Carroll Centre Rd (92126-4554)
PHONE.................858 536-8565
John Wallace, *Owner*
John S Wallace, *
Gary Grado, *
EMP: 140 **EST:** 1983
SQ FT: 20,500
SALES (est): 48.9MM
SALES (corp-wide): 48.9MM **Privately Held**
Web: www.jwfloors.com
SIC: **1752** Floor laying and floor work, nec

(P-1034)
PRO INSTALLATIONS INC (HQ)
Also Called: Prospectra Contract Flooring
13250 Gregg St Ste F (92064-7164)
▲ **EMP:** 20 **EST:** 1997
SALES (est): 6.04MM
SALES (corp-wide): 557.41MM **Privately Held**
SIC: **1752** 2273 Carpet laying; Carpets and rugs
PA: Diverzify+ Llc
865 W Irving Park Rd
Itasca IL
847 250-4600

(P-1035)
WEST COAST SURFACES INC
27620 Commerce Center Dr Ste 107 (92590-2539)
PHONE.................951 699-0600
Thomas Lahood, *Pr*
Kristi Lewis, *Off Mgr*
EMP: 20 **EST:** 2011
SQ FT: 2,400
SALES (est): 1.48MM **Privately Held**
SIC: **1752** 1743 3281 3253 Ceramic floor tile installation; Terrazzo, tile, marble and mosaic work; Granite, cut and shaped; Ceramic wall and floor tile

1761 Roofing, Siding, And Sheetmetal Work

(P-1036)
A CLASS PRECISION INC
13395 Estelle St (92879-1881)
PHONE.................951 549-9706
Scott Broadbent, *Managing Member*
Kim Vasile, *Managing Member*
Rene Acero, *Managing Member*
EMP: 18 **EST:** 2006
SQ FT: 9,000

SALES (est): 2.4MM **Privately Held**
Web: www.classaprecision.com
SIC: **1761** 3599 Sheet metal work, nec; Machine and other job shop work

(P-1037)
BEST CONTRACTING SERVICES INC (PA)
Also Called: Construction
19027 S Hamilton Ave (90248-4408)
PHONE.................310 328-9176
Sean Tabazadeh, *CEO*
Modjtaba Tabazadeh, *
Fatemeh Tabazadeh, *
▲ **EMP:** 400 **EST:** 1982
SQ FT: 57,000
SALES (est): 120.29MM
SALES (corp-wide): 120.29MM **Privately Held**
Web: www.bestcontracting.com
SIC: **1761** Roofing contractor

(P-1038)
CHALLENGER SHEET METAL INC
9353 Abraham Way Ste A (92071-5641)
PHONE.................619 596-8040
Joel Quinonez, *CEO*
Robert Basso, *
▲ **EMP:** 80 **EST:** 1987
SQ FT: 18,000
SALES (est): 18.62MM **Privately Held**
Web: www.challengersm.com
SIC: **1761** Sheet metal work, nec

(P-1039)
CMF INC
Also Called: Custom Metal Fabricators
1317 W Grove Ave (92865-4137)
PHONE.................714 637-2409
David Duclett, *CEO*
Mark Allen, *
Darren Sagert, *
EMP: 100 **EST:** 1956
SQ FT: 11,000
SALES (est): 31.58MM **Privately Held**
Web: www.cmfinc.com
SIC: **1761** Sheet metal work, nec

(P-1040)
DANNY LETNER INC
Also Called: Letner Roofing Company
1490 N Glassell St (92867-3612)
PHONE.................714 633-0030
EMP: 230 **EST:** 1957
SALES (est): 62.43MM **Privately Held**
Web: www.letner.com
SIC: **1761** Roofing contractor

(P-1041)
DRI COMMERCIAL CORPORATION
Also Called: D R I
2081 Business Center Dr Ste 195 (92612)
PHONE.................949 266-1900
EMP: 159
Web: www.dricommercial.com
SIC: **1761** Roofing contractor

(P-1042)
DRI COMPANIES
2081 Business Center Dr Ste 195 (92612)
PHONE.................949 266-1900
EMP: 264
Web: www.dricompanies.com
SIC: **1761** Roofing contractor

(P-1043)
DUKE PACIFIC INC
13950 Monte Vista Ave (91710-5535)
P.O. Box 1800 (91708-1800)
PHONE.................909 591-0191
Gregory C Severson, *Pr*
Judith E Braaten, *
EMP: 100 **EST:** 1958
SQ FT: 10,000
SALES (est): 16.33MM **Privately Held**
Web: www.dukepacific.com
SIC: **1761** Roofing contractor

(P-1044)
EBERHARD
15220 Raymer St (91405-1016)
PHONE.................818 782-4604
Brian Lee Mowatt, *CEO*
Dave Stefko, *Sr VP*
EMP: 150 **EST:** 1976
SALES (est): 23.61MM **Privately Held**
Web: www.eberhardco.com
SIC: **1761** 1799 Roofing contractor; Waterproofing

(P-1045)
EDJE-ENTERPRISES
18500 Pasadena St Ste B (92530-2775)
PHONE.................951 245-7070
Edward Joseph Jennen, *CEO*
Maryjane Jennen, *
EMP: 82 **EST:** 2006
SALES (est): 7.9MM **Privately Held**
Web: www.edje-enterprises.com
SIC: **1761** Architectural sheet metal work

(P-1046)
EHMCKE SHEET METAL CORP
840 W 19th St (91950-5406)
P.O. Box 13010 (92170-3010)
PHONE.................619 477-6484
John F Cornell, *CEO*
Dennis Isaacs, *
Dennis Stainbrook, *
Richard Parra, *
▲ **EMP:** 55 **EST:** 1927
SQ FT: 25,000
SALES (est): 13.33MM **Privately Held**
Web: www.ehmckesheetmetal.com
SIC: **1761** 8712 3446 Sheet metal work, nec; Architectural services; Architectural metalwork

(P-1047)
KAISER AIR CONDITIONING AND SHEET METAL INC
Also Called: Kaiser Air Conditioning
600 Pacific Ave (93030-7318)
PHONE.................805 988-1800
EMP: 25 **EST:** 1981
SALES (est): 2.71MM **Privately Held**
Web: www.kaiserac.com
SIC: **1761** 1711 3444 Architectural sheet metal work; Warm air heating and air conditioning contractor; Sheet metalwork

(P-1048)
LEONARD ROOFING INC
43280 Business Park Dr Ste 107 (92590-3676)
PHONE.................951 506-3811
Bruce S Leonard, *Pr*
▲ **EMP:** 98 **EST:** 2004
SALES (est): 15.82MM **Privately Held**
SIC: **1761** Roofing contractor

(P-1049)
PACIFIC STRUCFRAME LLC
1600 Chicago Ave Ste R11 (92507-2040)

PHONE..................951 405-8536
John B Hanna, *Pr*
EMP: 91 **EST:** 2017
SQ FT: 2,000
SALES (est): 4.73MM **Privately Held**
Web: www.pacificstrucframe.com
SIC: 1761 Roofing, siding, and sheetmetal work

(P-1050)
PERFORMANCE SHEETS LLC
440 Baldwin Park Blvd (91746-1407)
PHONE..................626 333-0195
Mike Crosson, *Pr*
Michael Feterik, *Managing Member**
Greg Hall, *Managing Member**
Forest Felvey, *
▲ **EMP:** 125 **EST:** 2006
SALES (est): 24.56MM **Privately Held**
Web: www.performancesheets.net
SIC: 1761 Sheet metal work, nec
HQ: Smurfit Kappa North America Llc
125 E John Carpenter Fwy
Irving TX
800 306-8326

(P-1051)
PLATINUM ROOFING INC
11500 W Olympic Blvd Ste 530 (90064-1509)
PHONE..................408 280-5028
Bill Shevlin, *CEO*
Sean Marzola, *
EMP: 80 **EST:** 2000
SALES (est): 13.56MM **Privately Held**
Web: www.platinumroofinginc.com
SIC: 1761 Roofing contractor

(P-1052)
RED POINTE ROOFING LP (PA)
1814 N Neville St (92865-4216)
PHONE..................714 685-0010
Aaron Martin, *Pt*
John Patterson, *Pt*
Sean Brophy, *Pt*
EMP: 83 **EST:** 2013
SALES (est): 24.96MM
SALES (corp-wide): 24.96MM **Privately Held**
Web: www.redpointeroofing.com
SIC: 1761 Roofing contractor

(P-1053)
ROYAL WESTLAKE ROOFING LLC
Also Called: Boral Industries
3093 Industry St Ste A (92054-4895)
PHONE..................760 967-0827
Jose Davila, *Mgr*
EMP: 122
SIC: 1761 Roofing contractor
HQ: Royal Westlake Roofing Llc
2700 Post Oak Blvd # 1900
Houston TX
949 756-1605

(P-1054)
SBB ROOFING INC (PA)
Also Called: Bilt-Well Roofing & Mtl Co
3310 Verdugo Rd (90065-2845)
P.O. Box 65827 (90065-0827)
PHONE..................323 254-2888
Bruce Radenbaugh, *Pr*
Steven Radenbaugh, *
EMP: 180 **EST:** 1984
SQ FT: 5,000
SALES (est): 8.87MM
SALES (corp-wide): 8.87MM **Privately Held**
Web: www.biltwellroofing.com

SIC: 1761 Roofing contractor

(P-1055)
TINCO SHEET METAL INC
958 N Eastern Ave (90063-1308)
PHONE..................323 263-0511
Brian Powell, *Pr*
Michael Nevarez, *
Laura Nevarez, *
Jim Stock, *
▲ **EMP:** 250 **EST:** 2003
SQ FT: 18,000
SALES (est): 38MM **Privately Held**
Web: www.tincosheetmetal.com
SIC: 1761 Roofing contractor

(P-1056)
WEISS SHEET METAL COMPANY
Also Called: Metcoe Skylight Specialites
1715 W 135th St (90249-2507)
PHONE..................310 354-2700
Andre Sarai, *Pr*
Steve Linder, *
Morris Saraie, *
▼ **EMP:** 45 **EST:** 1937
SQ FT: 33,000
SALES (est): 8.82MM **Privately Held**
Web: www.metcoe.com
SIC: 1761 3211 Skylight installation; Skylight glass

(P-1057)
WESTERN PACIFIC ROOFING CORP
3462 E La Campana Way (92262-5416)
PHONE..................661 273-1336
EMP: 110
SALES (corp-wide): 11.21MM **Privately Held**
Web: www.westpacroof.com
SIC: 1761 1799 Roofing contractor; Waterproofing
PA: Western Pacific Roofing Corp.
2229 E Avenue Q
Palmdale CA
661 273-1336

1771 Concrete Work

(P-1058)
ARCIERO BROTHERS INC
5614 E La Palma Ave (92807-2110)
PHONE..................714 238-6600
EMP: 130
SIC: 1771 Concrete repair

(P-1059)
BAYMARR CONSTRUCTORS INC
6950 Mcdivitt Dr (93313-2046)
P.O. Box 22074 (93390-2074)
PHONE..................661 395-1676
Eric Recktenwald, *CEO*
Jack Whitney, *
Pat Howes, *
EMP: 111 **EST:** 1988
SQ FT: 10,000
SALES (est): 18.24MM **Privately Held**
Web: www.baymarr.com
SIC: 1771 Concrete work

(P-1060)
BEACH PAVING INC
749 N Poplar St (92868-1013)
P.O. Box 10442 (92627-0162)
PHONE..................714 978-2414
Curtis Rummel, *Pr*
EMP: 24 **EST:** 1979

SQ FT: 1,000
SALES (est): 1.65MM **Privately Held**
Web: www.beachpavinginc.com
SIC: 1771 2951 Blacktop (asphalt) work; Asphalt paving mixtures and blocks

(P-1061)
BEN F SMITH INC
Also Called: Concrete Construction
8655 Miramar Pl Ste B (92121-2567)
PHONE..................858 271-4320
Stuart Shelton, *Mgr*
EMP: 180
SALES (corp-wide): 8.67MM **Privately Held**
Web: www.benfsmithinc.com
SIC: 1771 Concrete work
PA: Ben F. Smith, Inc.
4420 Baldwin Ave
El Monte CA
626 444-2543

(P-1062)
CASPER COMPANY
3825 Bancroft Dr (91977-2122)
PHONE..................619 589-6001
Roger Casper, *CEO*
William R Haithcock, *
Ken S Ringer, *
Greg T Casper, *
Steven Casper, *
EMP: 143 **EST:** 1984
SQ FT: 6,000
SALES (est): 48.02MM **Privately Held**
Web: www.caspercompany.com
SIC: 1771 Concrete work

(P-1063)
CELL-CRETE CORPORATION (PA)
Also Called: Cell-Crete
135 Railroad Ave (91016-4652)
PHONE..................626 357-3500
EMP: 80 **EST:** 1965
SALES (est): 92.86MM
SALES (corp-wide): 92.86MM **Privately Held**
Web: www.cell-crete.com
SIC: 1771 Flooring contractor

(P-1064)
CEMENT CUTTING INC
3610 Hancock St Frnt (92110-4335)
PHONE..................619 296-9592
Harold O Grafton, *CEO*
John Gregory Becker, *
Steven Morgan, *
Steve Quinn, *
EMP: 80 **EST:** 1977
SQ FT: 7,000
SALES (est): 15.85MM **Privately Held**
Web: www.cementcutting.com
SIC: 1771 Concrete work

(P-1065)
CENTURY WEST CONCRETE INC
9782 Indiana Ave (92503-5563)
PHONE..................951 712-4065
Esteban Damian C Diaz, *CEO*
EMP: 310 **EST:** 2014
SALES (est): 7.85MM **Privately Held**
Web: www.centurywestconcrete.com
SIC: 1771 Concrete work

(P-1066)
COFFMAN SPECIALTIES INC (PA)
9685 Via Excelencia Ste 200 (92126-7500)

PHONE..................858 536-3100
Colleen Coffman, *Pr*
Kevin Coffman, *
EMP: 247 **EST:** 1990
SQ FT: 6,000
SALES (est): 125.39MM **Privately Held**
Web: www.coffmanspecialties.com
SIC: 1771 Concrete work

(P-1067)
CORNERSTONE CONCRETE INC
255 Benjamin Dr (92879-6509)
PHONE..................951 279-2221
Matthew R Valente, *Prin*
EMP: 87 **EST:** 2011
SALES (est): 2.63MM **Privately Held**
Web: www.contractorsincollaboration.com
SIC: 1771 Concrete work

(P-1068)
CRAWFORD ASSOCIATES
2635 E Chanslor Way (92225-9805)
P.O. Box 807 (92226-0807)
PHONE..................760 922-6804
Bill Crawford, *Pt*
Tommy Crawford, *Pt*
Cody Crawford, *Pt*
EMP: 27 **EST:** 1975
SQ FT: 1,500
SALES (est): 9.5MM **Privately Held**
Web: www.crawfordconcrete.com
SIC: 1771 3273 Concrete work; Ready-mixed concrete

(P-1069)
DIVERSIFIED COATINGS LININGS
4810 Cheyenne Way (91710-5509)
P.O. Box 741 (91788-0741)
PHONE..................909 591-6366
Charlotte Smullen, *Pr*
EMP: 20 **EST:** 1984
SQ FT: 7,000
SALES (est): 404.72K **Privately Held**
SIC: 1771 2851 Flooring contractor; Epoxy coatings

(P-1070)
EKEDAL CONCRETE INC
19600 Fairchild Ste 123 (92612-2509)
PHONE..................949 729-8082
Dave Ekedal, *Pr*
Ryan Ekedal, *
EMP: 100 **EST:** 1974
SALES (est): 8.28MM **Privately Held**
Web: www.ekedalconcrete.com
SIC: 1771 Concrete work

(P-1071)
GENERAL PAVEMENT MANAGEMENT INC
Also Called: GPM
850 Lawrence Dr Ste 100 (91320-1508)
PHONE..................805 933-0909
EMP: 85 **EST:** 1957
SALES (est): 23.13MM **Privately Held**
Web: www.gpmpavement.com
SIC: 1771 1721 1611 Blacktop (asphalt) work ; Pavement marking contractor; Surfacing and paving

(P-1072)
GONSALVES & SANTUCCI INC
Also Called: Conco Cement Co
13052 Dahlia St (92337-6926)
PHONE..................909 350-0474
Steve Gonzales, *Pr*
EMP: 475

SALES (corp-wide): 164.76MM **Privately Held**
Web: www.conconow.com
SIC: **1771** Concrete pumping
PA: Gonsalves & Santucci, Inc.
5141 Commercial Cir
Concord CA
925 685-6799

(P-1073)
GUY YOCOM CONSTRUCTION INC (PA)
3299 Horseless Carriage Rd Ste H (92860-3604)
PHONE.....................951 284-3456
Guy W Yocom, *Prin*
Richard Majestic, *
Dave Kent, *
Greg Wilson, *
Shirley Kowalke, *
EMP: 212 EST: 1978
SQ FT: 41,000
SALES (est): 128.83MM
SALES (corp-wide): 128.83MM **Privately Held**
Web: www.yocominc.com
SIC: **1771** Concrete work

(P-1074)
HB PARKCO CONSTRUCTION INC (PA)
24795 State Highway 74 (92570-8759)
PHONE.....................714 567-4752
Brett D Behrns, *VP*
W Adrian Hoyle, *
Micheal Barry, *
EMP: 394 EST: 2002
SALES (est): 2.56K
SALES (corp-wide): 2.56K **Privately Held**
Web: www.hbparkco.com
SIC: **1771** Parking lot construction

(P-1075)
INLAND CC INC
Also Called: ICC
7010 Wyndham Hill Dr (92506-7506)
PHONE.....................909 355-1318
Marvin Hawkins, *CEO*
Karen Hawkins, *
EMP: 150 EST: 1995
SALES (est): 22.78MM **Privately Held**
Web: www.inlandconcrete.net
SIC: **1771** Foundation and footing contractor

(P-1076)
JEZOWSKI & MARKEL CONTRS INC
749 N Poplar St (92868-1013)
PHONE.....................714 978-2222
Leonard Michael Barth, *Prin*
Joseph Dean, *
Dorothy Destefano, *
EMP: 145 EST: 1953
SQ FT: 4,500
SALES (est): 24.5MM **Privately Held**
Web: www.jmcontractors.com
SIC: **1771** Foundation and footing contractor

(P-1077)
JT WIMSATT CONTG CO INC (PA)
28064 Avenue Stanford Unit B (91355-1159)
PHONE.....................661 775-8090
John Ewing Wimsatt, *CEO*
John E Wimsatt Iii, *Pr*
Tricia Wimsatt, *
EMP: 270 EST: 1992
SALES (est): 63.72MM **Privately Held**
Web: www.jtwimsatt.com

SIC: **1771** Concrete work

(P-1078)
LARGO CONCRETE INC
1690 W Foothill Blvd Ste B (91786-8433)
PHONE.....................909 981-7844
Paul Burkel, *Prin*
EMP: 220
Web: www.largoconcrete.com
SIC: **1771** Concrete work
PA: Largo Concrete, Inc.
2741 Walnut Ave Ste 110
Tustin CA

(P-1079)
MORLEY CONSTRUCTION COMPANY (HQ)
3330 Ocean Park Blvd (90405-3202)
PHONE.....................310 399-1600
Mark Benjamin, *Pr*
Mark Benjamin, *Ch Bd*
Bert Lewitt, *
Reginald Jackson, *
Tod Paris, *
▲ EMP: 80 EST: 1947
SQ FT: 20,000
SALES (est): 30.27MM
SALES (corp-wide): 92.7MM **Privately Held**
Web: www.morleyconcrete.com
SIC: **1771 1522 1542** Concrete work; Condominium construction; Commercial and office building, new construction
PA: Morley Builders, Inc.
3330 Ocean Park Blvd
Santa Monica CA
310 399-1600

(P-1080)
PACIFIC PAVINGSTONE INC
Also Called: Pacific Outdoor Living
8309 Tujunga Ave Unit 201 (91352-3215)
PHONE.....................818 244-4000
Terry Morrill, *Pr*
Trent Morrill, *
Chad Morrill, *
EMP: 115 EST: 1999
SALES (est): 13.09MM **Privately Held**
Web: www.pacificpavingstone.com
SIC: **1771** Driveway contractor

(P-1081)
PACIFIC STHWEST STRUCTURES INC
7845 Lemon Grove Way Ste A (91945-1880)
PHONE.....................619 469-2323
Daniel Fitzgerald, *Pr*
EMP: 150 EST: 1995
SQ FT: 7,500
SALES (est): 14.6MM **Privately Held**
Web: www.pssiconcrete.com
SIC: **1771** Concrete work

(P-1082)
PACIFIC STRUCTURES SC INC (PA)
Also Called: Pacific Structures
1212 Abbot Kinney Blvd Apt A (90291-3366)
PHONE.....................415 970-5434
Ross Edwards, *Ch Bd*
David E Williams, *Pr*
Ron Marano, *CFO*
Eric Horn, *Treas*
Scott Brauninger, *Dir*
EMP: 249 EST: 2008
SALES (est): 50.65MM
SALES (corp-wide): 50.65MM **Privately Held**

Web: www.pacific-structures.com
SIC: **1771** Concrete work

(P-1083)
PENHALL HOLDING COMPANY
1801 W Penhall Way (92801-6700)
PHONE.....................714 772-6450
Kathy Wall, *Sec*
EMP: 109 EST: 2010
SALES (est): 10.42MM **Privately Held**
Web: www.penhall.com
SIC: **1771** Concrete work

(P-1084)
PETERSON BROTHERS CNSTR INC
Also Called: Pbc Companies
2929 E White Star Ave (92806-2628)
PHONE.....................714 278-0488
Elden Peterson, *CEO*
Robert K Peterson, *
Patrick Burns, *
Mike Hoefnagels, *
Jack Saldate, *
▲ EMP: 600 EST: 1983
SALES (est): 66.72MM **Privately Held**
Web: www.pbccompanies.com
SIC: **1771 3531 1741** Concrete work; Pavers ; Concrete block masonry laying

(P-1085)
SANTA ANA CREEK DEVELOPMENT COMPANY
Also Called: Mark Company
2288 N Batavia St (92865-3106)
PHONE.....................714 685-3462
EMP: 100 EST: 1964
SALES (est): 16.91MM **Privately Held**
Web: www.themarkco.com
SIC: **1771 1611 1623** Concrete work; Grading; Pipeline construction, nsk

(P-1086)
SERVICON SYSTEMS INC
3329 Jack Northrop Ave (90250-4426)
PHONE.....................310 970-0700
Julio E Ramirez, *Brnch Mgr*
EMP: 1472
SALES (corp-wide): 83.82MM **Privately Held**
Web: www.servicon.com
SIC: **1771** Flooring contractor
PA: Servicon Systems, Inc.
3965 Landmark St
Culver City CA
310 204-5040

(P-1087)
SOUTHLAND PAVING INC
361 N Hale Ave (92029-1716)
PHONE.....................760 747-6895
Richard Fleck, *CEO*
Daniel Devlin, *
Robert Kennedy, *
Anne Fleck, *
EMP: 75 EST: 1983
SQ FT: 35,000
SALES (est): 25.3MM **Privately Held**
Web: www.southlandpaving.com
SIC: **1771 2951** Blacktop (asphalt) work; Asphalt paving mixtures and blocks

(P-1088)
STRUCTRAL PRSRVTION SYSTEMS LL
11800 Monarch St (92841-2113)
PHONE.....................714 891-9080
Mike Szoke, *Mgr*
EMP: 314

Web: www.structural.net
SIC: **1771** Concrete repair
HQ: Structural Preservation Systems, Llc
10150 Old Columbia Rd
Columbia MD

(P-1089)
SUPERIOR GUNITE (HQ)
12306 Van Nuys Blvd (91342-6049)
PHONE.....................818 896-9199
Anthony L Federico, *Pr*
David Bowers, *
Steve Crawford, *
EMP: 145 EST: 1964
SQ FT: 5,000
SALES (est): 46.72MM
SALES (corp-wide): 3.79B **Publicly Held**
Web: www.shotcrete.com
SIC: **1771** Gunite contractor
PA: Tutor Perini Corporation
15901 Olden St
Rancho Cascades CA
818 362-8391

(P-1090)
TEAM FINISH INC
155 Arovista Cir Ste A (92821-3842)
PHONE.....................714 671-9190
Thomas M Stangl, *Pr*
Mary Stangl, *
EMP: 80 EST: 1996
SQ FT: 1,200
SALES (est): 4.99MM **Privately Held**
SIC: **1771** Concrete work

(P-1091)
UNITED BROTHERS CONCRETE INC
41905 Boardwalk Ste K (92211-9091)
PHONE.....................760 346-1013
Lauro Barcenas, *Pr*
Luis Barcenas, *
Oscar Barcenas, *
EMP: 150 EST: 1999
SQ FT: 2,000
SALES (est): 24.2MM **Privately Held**
SIC: **1771** Concrete work

(P-1092)
Z-BEST CONCRETE INC
2575 Main St (92501-2238)
PHONE.....................951 774-1870
Roger Crott, *Pr*
Jerry Faust, *
EMP: 80 EST: 1989
SQ FT: 2,400
SALES (est): 12.41MM **Privately Held**
SIC: **1771 1741** Concrete work; Masonry and other stonework

1781 Water Well Drilling

(P-1093)
BRAX COMPANY INC
31248 Valley Center Rd (92082-6757)
PHONE.....................760 749-2209
Steven Tweed, *Pr*
EMP: 37 EST: 1985
SQ FT: 3,000
SALES (est): 9.37MM **Privately Held**
Web: www.braxcompany.com
SIC: **1781 5084 3563** Water well drilling; Water pumps (industrial); Air and gas compressors

(P-1094)
GREGG DRILLING LLC
2726 Walnut Ave (90755-1832)
PHONE.....................562 427-6899

John Gregg, *Pr*
Patrick Keating, *
Chris Christensen, *
Sonja De Keyser-meurs, *Sec*
EMP: 160 **EST:** 2018
SQ FT: 17,000
SALES (est): 8MM **Privately Held**
Web: www.greggdrilling.com
SIC: **1781** Water well drilling

(P-1095)
KENAI DRILLING LIMITED
2651 Patton Way (93308-5745)
PHONE..................661 587-0117
Gene Kramer, *Brnch Mgr*
EMP: 131
Web: www.kenaidrilling.com
SIC: **1781** Servicing, water wells
PA: Kenai Drilling Limited
6430 Cat Canyon Rd
Santa Maria CA

(P-1096)
YELLOW JACKET DRLG SVCS LLC
9460 Lucas Ranch Rd (91730-5743)
PHONE..................909 989-8563
EMP: 126
SALES (corp-wide): 21.45MM **Privately Held**
Web: www.yellowjacketdrilling.com
SIC: **1781** Water well drilling
PA: Yellow Jacket Drilling Services, Llc
3922 E University Dr # 1
Phoenix AZ
602 453-3252

(P-1097)
ZIM INDUSTRIES INC
Bakersfield Well & Pump Co
7212 Fruitvale Ave (93308-9529)
PHONE..................661 393-9661
John Zimmerer, *Mgr*
EMP: 140
SALES (corp-wide): 40.49MM **Privately Held**
Web: www.zimindustries.com
SIC: **1781 7699** Servicing, water wells; Pumps and pumping equipment repair
PA: Zim Industries, Inc.
4532 E Jefferson Ave
Fresno CA
559 834-1551

1791 Structural Steel Erection

(P-1098)
ALLIED STEEL CO INC
1027 Palmyrita Ave (92507-1701)
PHONE..................951 241-7000
Brian P Chapman, *Pr*
Perry K Chapman, *
Nicky Chapman, *
Jeanette Chapman, *
EMP: 60 **EST:** 1944
SQ FT: 48,000
SALES (est): 11.13MM **Privately Held**
Web: www.alliedsteelco.com
SIC: **1791 3441** Structural steel erection; Fabricated structural metal

(P-1099)
ANVIL STEEL CORPORATION
Also Called: Anvil Iron
134 W 168th St (90248-2729)
PHONE..................310 329-5811
Gerry Bustrum, *CEO*
Paul Schifino, *
Mike Norton, *

▲ **EMP:** 90 **EST:** 1973
SQ FT: 4,000
SALES (est): 24.92MM **Privately Held**
Web: www.anvilsteel.com
SIC: **1791** Iron work, structural

(P-1100)
ARTIMEX IRON INC
315 Cypress Ln (92020-1695)
PHONE..................619 444-3155
EMP: 116 **EST:** 1973
SALES (est): 9.4MM **Privately Held**
Web: www.artimexiron.com
SIC: **1791** Iron work, structural

(P-1101)
BAPKO METAL INC
721 S Parker St Ste 300 (92868-4732)
PHONE..................714 639-9380
Fred Bagatourian, *Pr*
Heather Wiliams, *
Clint Rieber, *
EMP: 80 **EST:** 1978
SALES (est): 25.64MM **Privately Held**
Web: www.bapko.com
SIC: **1791 3441** Structural steel erection; Fabricated structural metal

(P-1102)
CAL-STATE STEEL CORPORATION
1397 Lynnmere Dr (91360-1946)
PHONE..................310 632-2772
Salvador Valenzuelam, *CEO*
Les Furdek, *
David Olson, *
▲ **EMP:** 150 **EST:** 1963
SQ FT: 10,000
SALES (est): 4.68MM **Privately Held**
Web: www.calstatesteel.com
SIC: **1791** Iron work, structural

(P-1103)
COAST IRON & STEEL CO
12300 Lakeland Rd (90670-3869)
P.O. Box 2846 (90670-0846)
PHONE..................562 946-4421
Greg White, *Pr*
Cyndi White Cramer, *Stockholder**
Carrie White, *Stockholder**
Jared White, *Stockholder**
Duane Westrup, *
▲ **EMP:** 50 **EST:** 1953
SQ FT: 360,000
SALES (est): 13.67MM **Privately Held**
Web: www.rsac.com
SIC: **1791 3441** Structural steel erection; Fabricated structural metal

(P-1104)
HEAVY METAL STEEL COMPANY INC
12130 Lomica Dr (92128-2716)
PHONE..................858 433-4800
Linda Rosenberg, *Pr*
Linda D Rosenberg, *
Arnold Rosenberg, *
EMP: 25 **EST:** 2014
SALES (est): 2MM **Privately Held**
Web: www.heavymetalsteel.com
SIC: **1791 3449** Structural steel erection; Fabricated bar joists and concrete reinforcing bars

(P-1105)
INTEGRITY REBAR PLACERS
1345 Nandina Ave (92571-9402)
PHONE..................951 696-6843
Kenneth Negrete, *Pr*

Richard Rabay, *
Mario Duran, *Prin*
▲ **EMP:** 200 **EST:** 2005
SALES (est): 21.23MM **Privately Held**
Web: www.integrityrebarplacers.com
SIC: **1791** Structural steel erection

(P-1106)
KCB TOWERS INC
27260 Meines St (92346-4223)
P.O. Box 100 (92346-0100)
PHONE..................909 862-0322
S Lynn Bogh, *CEO*
Miles Bogh, *
Sharon Bogh, *
EMP: 100 **EST:** 1982
SQ FT: 12,000
SALES (est): 18.1MM **Privately Held**
Web: www.kcbtowers.com
SIC: **1791 3441** Concrete reinforcement, placing of; Fabricated structural metal

(P-1107)
LEGACY REINFORCING STEEL LLC
1057 Tierra Del Rey Ste F (91910-7882)
PHONE..................619 646-0205
Brian Briggs, *Pr*
EMP: 75 **EST:** 2019
SALES (est): 2.65MM **Privately Held**
SIC: **1791 3449** Structural steel erection; Bars, concrete reinforcing: fabricated steel

(P-1108)
M BAR C CONSTRUCTION INC
1770 La Costa Meadows Dr (92078-5106)
PHONE..................760 744-4131
Michael Jason Ianni, *CEO*
EMP: 85 **EST:** 2005
SALES (est): 41.41MM **Privately Held**
Web: www.mbarconline.com
SIC: **1791 1623** Structural steel erection; Electric power line construction

(P-1109)
MARTINEZ STEEL CORPORATION
1500 S Haven Ave Ste 150 (91761-2971)
PHONE..................909 946-0686
Harry Williams, *CEO*
Debbie Martinez, *
Joe Martinez, *
EMP: 200 **EST:** 1994
SALES (est): 22.13MM **Privately Held**
Web: www.martinezsteel.com
SIC: **1791** Structural steel erection

(P-1110)
MILLENNIUM REINFORCING INC
1046 Calle Recodo (92673-6261)
P.O. Box 73698 (92673-0124)
PHONE..................949 361-9730
Matthew Taylor, *CEO*
EMP: 265 **EST:** 2009
SALES (est): 8.58MM **Privately Held**
Web: www.millenniumreinforcing.com
SIC: **1791** Structural steel erection

(P-1111)
QUALITY REINFORCING INC
13275 Gregg St (92064-7120)
PHONE..................858 748-8400
Bryan Miller, *Pr*
▲ **EMP:** 85 **EST:** 1987
SQ FT: 5,000
SALES (est): 9.85MM **Privately Held**
Web: www.qualityreinforcing.com
SIC: **1791** Concrete reinforcement, placing of

(P-1112)
R & B REINFORCING STEEL CORP
13581 5th St (91710-5166)
PHONE..................909 591-1726
David Mcdaniel, *CEO*
Robert Bessette, *
Nancy Bessette, *
EMP: 80 **EST:** 1983
SQ FT: 30,000
SALES (est): 9.24MM **Privately Held**
Web: www.rbsteel.net
SIC: **1791** Iron work, structural

(P-1113)
REBAR ENGINEERING INC
10706 Painter Ave (90670-4581)
P.O. Box 3986 (90670-1986)
PHONE..................562 946-2461
Charles L Krebs, *Pr*
Jack Garroutte, *
EMP: 250 **EST:** 1963
SQ FT: 6,500
SALES (est): 34.55MM **Privately Held**
Web: www.rebarengineering.com
SIC: **1791** Concrete reinforcement, placing of

(P-1114)
RICHWELL STEEL CO INC
134 W 168th St (90248-2729)
PHONE..................310 324-4455
Stephen William Pronchow, *Pr*
Chris Prochnow, *
Nick Prochnow, *
EMP: 42 **EST:** 1947
SALES (est): 2.07MM **Privately Held**
Web: www.i-am-not-government-property.com
SIC: **1791 3441** Iron work, structural; Fabricated structural metal

(P-1115)
RIKA CORPORATION
Also Called: Diversified Metal Works
332 W Brenna Ln (92867-5637)
PHONE..................949 830-9050
John E Ferguson, *CEO*
Justin Ferguson, *
▲ **EMP:** 100 **EST:** 1977
SQ FT: 8,000
SALES (est): 5.64MM **Privately Held**
Web: www.dmwk.com
SIC: **1791** Structural steel erection

(P-1116)
RIVERTON STEEL CONSTRUCTION
10130 Adella Ave (90280-5314)
P.O. Box 4063 (90280-8463)
PHONE..................323 564-1881
Claude Ritchot, *CEO*
James Hanson, *
EMP: 17 **EST:** 1984
SQ FT: 100,000
SALES (est): 507.81K **Privately Held**
SIC: **1791 3449 3441** Structural steel erection; Miscellaneous metalwork; Fabricated structural metal

(P-1117)
WHITES STEEL INC (PA)
45524 Towne St (92201-4446)
P.O. Box 846 (92274-0846)
PHONE..................760 347-3401
Edwin Neumeyer, *CEO*
EMP: 17 **EST:** 1995
SALES (est): 10.06MM
SALES (corp-wide): 10.06MM **Privately Held**

P R O D U C T S & S V C S

Web: www.whitessteel.com
SIC: **1791** 3446 3599 Structural steel erection; Architectural metalwork; Machine shop, jobbing and repair

1793 Glass And Glazing Work

(P-1118)
GIROUX GLASS INC (PA)
Also Called: Giroux
850 W Washington Blvd Ste 200 (90015-3359)
PHONE.................213 747-7406
Nataline Lomedico, *CEO*
Anne-merelie Murrell, *Ch Bd*
Stephanie Lamb, *
Robert Bob Burkhammer, *Ex VP*
Bob Linford, *
▲ **EMP:** 120 **EST:** 1946
SALES (est): 49.64MM
SALES (corp-wide): 49.64MM **Privately Held**
Web: www.girouxglass.com
SIC: **1793** Glass and glazing work

(P-1119)
RYNOCLAD TECHNOLOGIES INC
780 E Francis St Ste M (91761-5553)
PHONE.................951 264-3441
EMP: 200 **EST:** 2011
SALES (est): 25MM **Privately Held**
Web: www.rynoclad.com
SIC: **1793** Glass and glazing work

(P-1120)
TOWER GLASS INC
9570 Pathway St Ste A (92071-4100)
PHONE.................619 596-6199
Evelyn Dee Swaim, *CEO*
Barry Swaim, *
EMP: 100 **EST:** 1989
SQ FT: 15,000
SALES (est): 22.44MM **Privately Held**
Web: www.towerglass.com
SIC: **1793** Glass and glazing work

(P-1121)
WOODBRIDGE GLASS INC
14321 Myford Rd (92780-7022)
PHONE.................714 838-4444
Virginia Siciliani, *Pr*
John Siciliani, *
Jim Siciliani, *
▲ **EMP:** 205 **EST:** 1981
SQ FT: 8,500
SALES (est): 47.51MM **Privately Held**
Web: www.woodbridgeglass.com
SIC: **1793** 5231 Glass and glazing work; Glass, leaded or stained

1794 Excavation Work

(P-1122)
ARNETT CONSTRUCTION INC
Also Called: A A Construction
626 W 1st St (92376-5715)
P.O. Box 488 (92377-0488)
PHONE.................909 421-7960
Albert Arnett, *Pr*
Shirley Arnett, *VP*
Lea Ann Hibbetts, *Sec*
Wayne Arnett, *Treas*
EMP: 20 **EST:** 1983
SQ FT: 1,200
SALES (est): 2.03MM **Privately Held**

SIC: **1794** 1611 1542 3531 Excavation and grading, building construction; Concrete construction: roads, highways, sidewalks, etc.; Nonresidential construction, nec; Plows: construction, excavating, and grading

(P-1123)
LOVCO CONSTRUCTION INC
Also Called: Lovco Construction
1300 E Burnett St (90755-3512)
P.O. Box 90335 (90809-0335)
PHONE.................562 595-1601
Terry C Lovingier, *Pr*
Steve Barnett, *
Katie Lovingier, *
Matt Lovinger, *
Mike Mcgougan, *VP*
EMP: 125 **EST:** 1988
SQ FT: 2,500
SALES (est): 22.19MM **Privately Held**
Web: www.lovcoconstruction.com
SIC: **1794** 1771 1611 Excavation and grading, building construction; Concrete work; Highway and street construction

(P-1124)
MGE UNDERGROUND INC
2501 Golden Hill Rd (93446-6391)
P.O. Box 4189 (93447-4189)
PHONE.................805 238-3510
Michael Joe Goldstein, *Pr*
Summer Golstein, *
EMP: 372 **EST:** 1997
SALES (est): 110.99MM **Privately Held**
Web: www.mgeunderground.com
SIC: **1794** Excavation work

(P-1125)
REED THOMAS COMPANY INC
1025 Santiago St (92701-3800)
PHONE.................714 558-7691
Harvey T Biegle, *Pr*
EMP: 90 **EST:** 1981
SQ FT: 8,800
SALES (est): 11.05MM **Privately Held**
Web: www.reedthomas.com
SIC: **1794** Excavation and grading, building construction

(P-1126)
STURGEON SON GRADING & PAV INC (PA)
3511 Gilmore Ave (93308-6205)
P.O. Box 2840 (93303-2840)
PHONE.................661 322-4408
John E Powell, *CEO*
Oliver Sturgeon, *
Paul Sturgeon, *
EMP: 180 **EST:** 1927
SQ FT: 3,500
SALES (est): 47.93MM
SALES (corp-wide): 47.93MM **Privately Held**
SIC: **1794** 8711 Excavation work; Engineering services

(P-1127)
SUKUT CONSTRUCTION INC
4010 W Chandler Ave (92704-5202)
PHONE.................714 540-5351
Michael Crawford, *Pr*
Myron Sukut, *
Paul Kuliev, *
▲ **EMP:** 200 **EST:** 1968
SQ FT: 12,000
SALES (est): 137.75MM **Privately Held**
Web: www.sukut.com

SIC: **1794** 1611 1623 1629 Excavation and grading, building construction; General contractor, highway and street construction; Water and sewer line construction; Dams, waterways, docks, and other marine construction

(P-1128)
TIDWELL EXCAV ACQUISITION INC
Also Called: Tidwell Excavating
1691 Los Angeles Ave (93004-3213)
PHONE.................805 647-4707
Alex Miruello, *Pr*
Timothy Wayne Goodwin, *
Louis Armona, *
EMP: 90 **EST:** 1956
SALES (est): 9.78MM
SALES (corp-wide): 528.99MM **Privately Held**
Web: www.tidwell-inc.com
SIC: **1794** Excavation and grading, building construction
PA: Meruelo Enterprises, Inc.
9550 Firestone Blvd # 105
Downey CA
562 745-2300

1795 Wrecking And Demolition Work

(P-1129)
AMERICAN WRECKING INC
2459 Lee Ave (91733-1407)
PHONE.................626 350-8303
EMP: 100 **EST:** 1989
SQ FT: 1,000
SALES (est): 35.43MM **Privately Held**
Web: www.americanwreckinginc.com
SIC: **1795** Demolition, buildings and other structures

(P-1130)
CLAUSS CONSTRUCTION
9911 Maine Ave (92040-3107)
PHONE.................619 390-4940
Joshua Clauss, *CEO*
Patrick Michael Clauss, *
EMP: 80 **EST:** 1991
SALES (est): 17.18MM **Privately Held**
Web: www.claussconstruction.com
SIC: **1795** 1629 4959 Wrecking and demolition work; Earthmoving contractor; Toxic or hazardous waste cleanup

(P-1131)
DANNY RYAN PRECISION CONTG INC
Also Called: Precision Contracting
16782 Millikan Ave (92606-5010)
PHONE.................949 642-6664
Danny Ryan, *Pr*
EMP: 90 **EST:** 1991
SALES (est): 13.04MM **Privately Held**
Web: www.adepprecision.com
SIC: **1795** 1799 Demolition, buildings and other structures; Asbestos removal and encapsulation

(P-1132)
EMPIRE DEMOLITION INC
137 N Joy St (92879-1321)
PHONE.................909 393-8300
Kris Huff, *CEO*
Collin Cumbee, *
EMP: 100 **EST:** 1997
SALES (est): 11.13MM **Privately Held**
Web: www.empiredemolition.com

SIC: **1795** Demolition, buildings and other structures

(P-1133)
GD HEIL INC
1031 Segovia Cir (92870-7137)
PHONE.................714 687-9100
James A Langford, *CEO*
James A Langford, *CEO*
Gary Heil, *
Steve Mc Clain, *
Laura Heil, *
EMP: 160 **EST:** 1992
SQ FT: 20,770
SALES (est): 23.24MM **Privately Held**
Web: www.gdheil.com
SIC: **1795** Demolition, buildings and other structures

(P-1134)
INTERIOR RMOVAL SPECIALIST INC
8990 Atlantic Ave (90280-3505)
PHONE.................323 357-6900
Carlos Herrera, *CEO*
Isabel Herrera, *
EMP: 150 **EST:** 1994
SALES (est): 225 **Privately Held**
Web: www.irsdemo.com
SIC: **1795** Demolition, buildings and other structures

(P-1135)
MILLER ENVIRONMENTAL INC
1130 W Trenton Ave (92867-3536)
PHONE.................714 385-0099
Gregg Miller, *Pr*
Rob Schaefer, *
Mindy Peek, *General* *
EMP: 150 **EST:** 1999
SQ FT: 3,000
SALES (est): 32.31MM **Privately Held**
Web: www.miller-env.com
SIC: **1795** 4953 Demolition, buildings and other structures; Hazardous waste collection and disposal

(P-1136)
NORTHSTAR DEM & REMEDIATION LP (DH)
404 N Berry St (92821-3104)
PHONE.................714 672-3500
Jose Alonso, *VP*
Gregory G Dicarlo, *
Jeffrey P Adix, *
Gary Thibodeaux, *
Kamal Sookram, *
EMP: 174 **EST:** 2007
SQ FT: 19,000
SALES (est): 92.89MM
SALES (corp-wide): 776.44MM **Privately Held**
SIC: **1795** 1799 8744 Demolition, buildings and other structures; Decontamination services; Environmental remediation
HQ: Northstar Group Services, Inc.
370 7th Ave Ste 1803
New York NY
212 951-3660

1796 Installing Building Equipment

(P-1137)
MAINTECH RESOURCES INC
5042 Northwestern Way (92683-2729)
PHONE.................562 804-0664
John Ellen, *Pr*

EMP: 36 **EST:** 1984
SALES (est): 4.48MM **Privately Held**
Web: www.maintech-hq.com
SIC: 1796 1731 8711 3498 Installing building equipment; General electrical contractor; Structural engineering; Coils, pipe; fabricated from purchased pipe

(P-1138)
PERFORMANCE CONTRACTING INC
4955 E Landon Dr (92807-1972)
PHONE...............................913 310-7120
William Massey, *Mgr*
EMP: 99
SALES (corp-wide): 1.11B **Privately Held**
Web: www.performancecontracting.com
SIC: 1796 Installing building equipment
HQ: Performance Contracting, Inc.
16220 Rdmond Wdnvlle Rd N
Woodinville WA
913 888-8600

(P-1139)
UNITED RIGGERS & ERECTORS INC (PA)
4188 Valley Blvd (91789-1446)
P.O. Box 728 (91788-0728)
PHONE...............................909 978-0400
Brian D Kelley, *CEO*
Thomas J Kruss, *
EMP: 100 **EST:** 1966
SQ FT: 58,000
SALES (est): 20.54MM
SALES (corp-wide): 20.54MM **Privately Held**
Web: www.ure-inc.com
SIC: 1796 Machinery installation

(P-1140)
WEST COAST IRON INC
Also Called: Westcoast Iron
9302 Jamacha Rd (91977-4203)
PHONE...............................619 464-8456
EMP: 75 **EST:** 1988
SALES (est): 18.68MM **Privately Held**
Web: www.westcoastiron.com
SIC: 1796 1541 3441 Installing building equipment; Steel building construction; Building components, structural steel

---

1799 Special Trade Contractors, Nec

(P-1141)
A-1 ENTERPRISES INC
Also Called: A-1 Fence
2831 E La Cresta Ave (92806-1817)
PHONE...............................714 630-3390
TOLL FREE: 800
Norman Shepherd, *Pr*
James Sypitkowski, *
EMP: 45 **EST:** 1953
SQ FT: 39,000
SALES (est): 9.56MM **Privately Held**
Web: www.a1fence.com
SIC: 1799 3446 Fence construction; Acoustical suspension systems, metal

(P-1142)
ANTIS ROOFG WATERPROOFING LLC
Also Called: Antis Roofing
2649 Campus Dr (92612-1601)
PHONE...............................949 461-9222
EMP: 85 **EST:** 1988
SALES (est): 18.8MM **Privately Held**
Web: www.antisroofing.com

SIC: 1799 1761 Waterproofing; Roofing contractor

(P-1143)
ATI RESTORATION LLC (PA)
Also Called: ATI
3360 E La Palma Ave (92806-2814)
PHONE...............................714 283-9990
Gary Moore, *CEO*
Ryan Moore, *
Jeff Moore, *
Scott Moore, *OF OPRS & ENVIRONMENTAL HEALTH SERVICES*
Yun Kim, *
▲ **EMP:** 128 **EST:** 1989
SQ FT: 57,000
SALES (est): 287.11MM **Privately Held**
Web: www.atirestoration.com
SIC: 1799 1541 1742 1731 Antenna installation; Industrial buildings and warehouses; Plastering, drywall, and insulation; Electrical work

(P-1144)
BIG BEAR BOWLING BARN INC
Also Called: Fun Flex
40625 Big Bear Blvd (92315)
P.O. Box 1152 (92315-1152)
PHONE...............................909 878-2695
William D Ross, *Pr*
William Douglas Ross, *Pr*
EMP: 20 **EST:** 2010
SALES (est): 1.94MM **Privately Held**
Web: www.bowlingbarn.com
SIC: 1799 3949 Bowling alley installation; Bowling alleys and accessories

(P-1145)
BRAVO SIGN & DESIGN INC
520 S Central Park Ave E (92802-1472)
PHONE...............................714 284-0500
Frank Fiore, *Pr*
EMP: 18 **EST:** 1990
SQ FT: 12,000
SALES (est): 1.98MM **Privately Held**
Web: www.bravosign.com
SIC: 1799 3993 Sign installation and maintenance; Signs and advertising specialties

(P-1146)
CALIFORNIA CLOSET COMPANY INC
Also Called: California Closet Co
5921 Skylab Rd (92647-2062)
PHONE...............................714 899-4905
Mike Cassidy, *Genl Mgr*
EMP: 115
SALES (corp-wide): 3.75B **Privately Held**
Web: www.californiaclosets.com
SIC: 1799 Closet organizers, installation and design
HQ: California Closet Company, Inc.
2001 W Phelps Rd Ste 1
Phoenix AZ
510 763-2033

(P-1147)
CLEAR SIGN & DESIGN INC
170 Navajo St (92078-2506)
PHONE...............................760 736-8111
Steve Weddell, *Pr*
Gabe Griffin, *Genl Mgr*
EMP: 19 **EST:** 1981
SQ FT: 18,000
SALES (est): 6.99MM **Privately Held**
Web: www.clearsigns.com
SIC: 1799 3993 Sign installation and maintenance; Signs and advertising specialties

(P-1148)
CLOSET FACTORY INC (PA)
12800 S Bdwy (90061-1116)
PHONE...............................310 516-7000
John La Barbera, *CEO*
Greg Stein, *
Kathryn La Barbera, *
EMP: 107 **EST:** 1983
SQ FT: 40,000
SALES (est): 61.86MM
SALES (corp-wide): 61.86MM **Privately Held**
Web: www.closetfactory.com
SIC: 1799 Closet organizers, installation and design

(P-1149)
COURTNEY INC (PA)
16781 Millikan Ave (92606-5009)
PHONE...............................949 222-2050
George Courtney, *CEO*
Mildred Courtney, *
EMP: 80 **EST:** 1994
SALES (est): 34.89MM **Privately Held**
Web: www.courtneyinc.com
SIC: 1799 Waterproofing

(P-1150)
CROWN FENCE CO
12070 Telegraph Rd Ste 340 (90670)
PHONE...............................562 864-5177
TOLL FREE: 800
Eric Fiedler, *Prin*
Chris E Nickelatti, *Prin*
Lief Nicolaisen, *Prin*
Eric W Fiedler, *
Doug Eustace, *Prin*
▲ **EMP:** 96 **EST:** 1923
SALES (est): 20.38MM **Privately Held**
Web: www.crownfence.com
SIC: 1799 5039 Fence construction; Wire fence, gates, and accessories

(P-1151)
D&A ENDEAVORS INC
Also Called: SERVPRO of Beverly Hills
8484 Wilshire Blvd Ste 605 (90211-3227)
PHONE...............................310 390-7540
Arezo Jeffries, *CEO*
Daniel Jeffries, *
EMP: 80 **EST:** 2014
SALES (est): 5.31MM **Privately Held**
Web: www.servprobeverlyhillswestwood.com
SIC: 1799 8744 7349 1741 Construction site cleanup; Environmental remediation; Building maintenance services, nec; Tuckpointing or restoration

(P-1152)
DAVIDSON ENTERPRISES INC
3223 Brittan St (93308-4902)
PHONE...............................661 325-2145
Robert Davidson, *Ch Bd*
Philip R Davidson, *
Donna Davidson, *Sec*
Margaret Davidson, *Treas*
▲ **EMP:** 20 **EST:** 1959
SALES (est): 4.23MM **Privately Held**
Web: www.davidsontank.com
SIC: 1799 3531 7699 Petroleum storage tanks, pumping and draining; Trucks, off-highway; Industrial equipment services

(P-1153)
DEHART INC
Also Called: California Closet Co
7550 Miramar Rd Ste 300 (92126-4217)
PHONE...............................858 695-0882
Mike Cayheart, *Pr*

EMP: 21 **EST:** 1983
SQ FT: 5,700
SALES (est): 912.2K **Privately Held**
Web: www.californiaclosets.com
SIC: 1799 2541 2521 1751 Closet organizers, installation and design; Wood partitions and fixtures; Wood office furniture ; Carpentry work

(P-1154)
DEMOR ENTERPRISES INC
Also Called: 911 Restoration of San Diego
4174 Sorrento Valley Blvd Ste H (92121-1424)
PHONE...............................858 625-0003
Roni Dahar, *CEO*
EMP: 20 **EST:** 2009
SALES (est): 2.39MM **Privately Held**
Web: www.911restorationofsandiego.com
SIC: 1799 1389 8322 1742 Fireproofing buildings; Construction, repair, and dismantling services; Disaster service; Insulation, buildings

(P-1155)
EXCEL MDULAR SCAFFOLD LSG CORP
2555 Birch St (92081-8433)
PHONE...............................760 598-0050
Benjamin Bartlett, *Brnch Mgr*
EMP: 1197
Web: www.excelscaffold.com
SIC: 1799 Rigging and scaffolding
PA: Excel Modular Scaffold And Leasing Corporation
720 Washington St Unit 5
Hanover MA

(P-1156)
FENCECORP INC
3045 Industry St (92054-4834)
PHONE...............................760 721-2101
Gary Hansen, *Prin*
EMP: 85
SALES (corp-wide): 49.18MM **Privately Held**
Web: www.fencecorp.us
SIC: 1799 Fence construction
HQ: Fencecorp, Inc.
18440 Van Buren Blvd
Riverside CA

(P-1157)
FENCECORP INC (HQ)
18440 Van Buren Blvd (92508-9258)
PHONE...............................951 686-3170
T Perrry Massie, *CEO*
Dale Marriott, *
Floyd Nixon, *
Gary Hansen, *
EMP: 170 **EST:** 2006
SQ FT: 5,000
SALES (est): 23.93MM
SALES (corp-wide): 49.18MM **Privately Held**
Web: www.fencecorp.us
SIC: 1799 Fence construction
PA: Fenceworks, Inc.
870 Main St
Riverside CA
951 788-5620

(P-1158)
FENCEWORKS INC (PA)
Also Called: Golden State Fence Co.
870 Main St (92501-1016)
PHONE...............................951 788-5620
Jason Ostrander, *CEO*
Mel Kay, *

PRODUCTS & SVCS

▲ **EMP:** 250 **EST:** 1998
SQ FT: 20,000
SALES (est): 49.18MM
SALES (corp-wide): 49.18MM **Privately Held**
Web: www.fenceworks.us
SIC: 1799 Fence construction

(P-1159)
G W SURFACES (PA)
Also Called: Showershapes
2432 Palma Dr (93003-5732)
PHONE...............................805 642-5004
James A Garver, *Pr*
Georgann Garver, *
Tidus Gutierrez, *
EMP: 100 **EST:** 1976
SQ FT: 30,000
SALES (est): 18.65MM
SALES (corp-wide): 18.65MM **Privately Held**
Web: www.gwsurfaces.com
SIC: 1799 Counter top installation

(P-1160)
HARTMARK CAB DESIGN & MFG INC
Also Called: Hartmark Cabinet Design
3575 Grapevine St (91752-3505)
P.O. Box 54204 (92619-4204)
PHONE...............................909 591-9153
Gary Allen Hartmark, *Pr*
Gary Allen Hartmark, *Pr*
Marnell Hartmark, *
EMP: 45 **EST:** 1986
SQ FT: 44,000
SALES (est): 11.97MM **Privately Held**
Web: www.hartmark.com
SIC: 1799 2434 1751 Kitchen cabinet installation; Wood kitchen cabinets; Cabinet and finish carpentry

(P-1161)
HERZOG CONTRACTING CORP
2155 Hancock St (92110-2012)
PHONE...............................619 849-6990
EMP: 87
SALES (corp-wide): 479.93MM **Privately Held**
Web: www.herzog.com
SIC: 1799 Antenna installation
HQ: Herzog Contracting Corp.
600 S Riverside Rd
Saint Joseph MO
816 233-9001

(P-1162)
IN-LINE FENCE & RAILING CO INC
Also Called: In-Line Construction
1307 Walnut St (92065-1840)
P.O. Box 2637 (92065-0945)
PHONE...............................760 789-0282
David Ortiz, *Pr*
EMP: 28 **EST:** 1998
SALES (est): 3.61MM **Privately Held**
Web: www.inlinerail.com
SIC: 1799 1611 3441 1542 Fence construction; General contractor, highway and street construction; Building components, structural steel; Commercial and office building, new construction

(P-1163)
J&M KEYSTONE INC
2709 Via Orange Way Ste A (91978-1745)
PHONE...............................619 466-9876
David Carpenter, *CEO*
Kevin Casenhiser, *
Gary Moore, *

Ryan Moore, *
Jeffrey Moore, *
EMP: 117 **EST:** 1991
SQ FT: 9,100
SALES (est): 17.4MM **Privately Held**
Web: www.jmkeystone.com
SIC: 1799 1542 8744 7349 Steam cleaning of building exteriors; Commercial and office buildings, renovation and repair; Environmental remediation; Air duct cleaning
PA: Ati Restoration, Llc
3360 E La Palma Ave
Anaheim CA

(P-1164)
JEFFRIES GLOBAL INC
Also Called: SERVPRO Jeffries Global
8484 Wilshire Blvd Ste 605 (90211-3227)
PHONE...............................888 255-3488
Daniel Jeffries, *Prin*
EMP: 85 **EST:** 2020
SALES (est): 5.69MM **Privately Held**
SIC: 1799 Asbestos removal and encapsulation

(P-1165)
KELLER NORTH AMERICA INC
1780 E Lemonwood Dr (93060-9510)
PHONE...............................805 933-1331
Alan Ringen, *Brnch Mgr*
EMP: 95
Web: www.keller-na.com
SIC: 1799 Building site preparation
HQ: Keller North America, Inc.
7550 Teague Rd Ste 300
Hanover MD
410 551-8200

(P-1166)
KITCHEN EXPO
7458 La Jolla Blvd (92037-5029)
EMP: 18 **EST:** 1984
SALES (est): 1.34MM **Privately Held**
Web: www.kitchenexpo.com
SIC: 1799 5211 2434 1752 Kitchen and bathroom remodeling; Lumber and other building materials; Wood kitchen cabinets; Floor laying and floor work, nec

(P-1167)
LAYFIELD USA CORPORATION (DH)
10038 Marathon Pkwy (92040-2771)
PHONE...............................619 562-1200
Thomas Rose, *CEO*
Rob Rempel, *
Steve Palubiski, *
▲ **EMP:** 100 **EST:** 2004
SALES (est): 48.68MM
SALES (corp-wide): 3.77MM **Privately Held**
Web: www.layfieldgroup.com
SIC: 1799 Building board-up contractor
HQ: Layfield Group Limited
11120 Silversmith Pl
Richmond BC
604 275-5588

(P-1168)
M GAW INC
Also Called: Jet Sets
6910 Farmdale Ave (91605-6210)
PHONE...............................818 503-7997
Michael Gaw, *Pr*
EMP: 90 **EST:** 1991
SQ FT: 15,000
SALES (est): 9.24MM **Privately Held**
Web: www.jetsets.com

SIC: 1799 Prop, set or scenery construction, theatrical

(P-1169)
MISSION POOLS OF ESCONDIDO
Also Called: Mission Pools of Lake Forest
22600 Lambert St Ste 1104 (92630-1627)
PHONE...............................949 588-0100
Don Ogden, *Mgr*
EMP: 105
SALES (corp-wide): 24.07MM **Privately Held**
Web: www.missionpools.com
SIC: 1799 Swimming pool construction
PA: Mission Pools Of Escondido
755 W Grand Ave
Escondido CA
760 743-2605

(P-1170)
MP AERO LLC
7701 Woodley Ave (91406-1721)
PHONE...............................818 901-9828
EMP: 85 **EST:** 2013
SQ FT: 165,000
SALES (est): 10.62MM **Privately Held**
Web: www.mpaero.com
SIC: 1799 3721 Renovation of aircraft interiors; Research and development on aircraft by the manufacturer

(P-1171)
NAVAL COATING INC
2080 Cambridge Ave (92007-1708)
PHONE...............................619 234-8366
Alan Lerchbacker, *Pr*
EMP: 149 **EST:** 1969
SALES (est): 24.79MM **Privately Held**
Web: www.navalcoating.us
SIC: 1799 1721 2851 Sandblasting of building exteriors; Industrial painting; Paints and allied products

(P-1172)
NITE-LITE SIGNS INC
25583 Avenue Stanford (91355-1101)
PHONE...............................818 341-0987
John Due, *CEO*
Warren Due, *VP*
EMP: 21 **EST:** 1975
SQ FT: 4,500
SALES (est): 678.08K **Privately Held**
Web: www.nlsign.com
SIC: 1799 3993 Sign installation and maintenance; Signs and advertising specialties

(P-1173)
PARKING NETWORK INC
1625 W Olympic Blvd (90015-3853)
PHONE...............................213 613-1500
Frank Zelaya, *CEO*
Rose Zelaya, *
EMP: 120 **EST:** 2001
SALES (est): 9.84MM **Privately Held**
SIC: 1799 8748 Parking lot maintenance; Business consulting, nec

(P-1174)
PSG FENCING CORPORATION
330 Main St (92501-1028)
PHONE...............................951 275-9252
EMP: 83
Web: www.psgfencinginc.com
SIC: 1799 Fence construction
PA: P.S.G. Fencing Corporation
1218 D St
Los Banos CA

(P-1175)
REPUBLIC FENCE CO INC (PA)
11309 Danube Ave (91344-4323)
PHONE...............................818 341-5323
David Woolf, *Pr*
Bonnie Woolf, *
EMP: 26 **EST:** 1973
SQ FT: 11,000
SALES (est): 2.33MM
SALES (corp-wide): 2.33MM **Privately Held**
Web: www.republicfenceco.com
SIC: 1799 3312 5085 Fence construction; Structural shapes and pilings, steel; Fasteners and fastening equipment

(P-1176)
REY-CREST ROOFG WATERPROOFING
Also Called: Rey-Crest Roofg Waterproofing
3065 Verdugo Rd (90065-2014)
PHONE...............................323 257-9329
George Reyes, *Pr*
Georgia Reyes, *
EMP: 80 **EST:** 1969
SQ FT: 10,000
SALES (est): 8.84MM **Privately Held**
Web: www.rey-crestroofing.com
SIC: 1799 1761 Waterproofing; Roofing contractor

(P-1177)
SCENIC EXPRESS INC
9380 San Fernando Rd (91352-1419)
PHONE...............................323 254-4351
Kevin Gadd, *Pr*
EMP: 20 **EST:** 1978
SQ FT: 25,000
SALES (est): 2.18MM **Privately Held**
Web: cmflores72.wixsite.com
SIC: 1799 2541 Prop, set or scenery construction, theatrical; Wood partitions and fixtures

(P-1178)
TEAM WEST CONTRACTING CORP
2733 S Vista Ave (92316-3269)
PHONE...............................951 340-3426
Dawn Lilly, *Prin*
Jerry R Pacheco, *
Stephen Knehans, *
EMP: 92 **EST:** 2009
SQ FT: 7,200
SALES (est): 8.54MM **Privately Held**
Web: www.twc-corp.com
SIC: 1799 Fence construction

(P-1179)
TESERRA (PA)
Also Called: California Pools
86100 Avenue 54 (92236-3813)
P.O. Box 1280 (92236-1280)
PHONE...............................760 340-9000
Bob Smith, *Pr*
James Harebottle, *
EMP: 399 **EST:** 1985
SQ FT: 10,000
SALES (est): 42.96MM
SALES (corp-wide): 42.96MM **Privately Held**
Web: www.teserraoutdoors.com
SIC: 1799 Swimming pool construction

(P-1180)
TURN KEY SCAFFOLD LLC
410 W 30th St (91950-7269)
P.O. Box 120340 (91912-3440)
PHONE...............................619 642-0880

Alvin Ruis Iii, *Pr*
EMP: 106 **EST:** 2017
SALES (est): 7.36MM **Privately Held**
Web: www.tksscaffold.com
SIC: 1799 Scaffolding

(P-1181)
WASHINGTON ORNA IR WORKS INC (PA)
Also Called: Washington Iron Works
17926 S Broadway (90248-3540)
P.O. Box 460 (90247-0846)
PHONE...............................310 327-8660
Daniel Welsh, *CEO*
Tom Pederson, *
Luke Welsh, *
Chris Powell, *
EMP: 117 **EST:** 1966
SQ FT: 141,240
SALES (est): 25.62MM
SALES (corp-wide): 25.62MM **Privately Held**
SIC: 1799 3446 Ornamental metal work; Architectural metalwork

(P-1182)
WAYNE PERRY INC (PA)
8281 Commonwealth Ave (90621-2537)
PHONE...............................714 826-0352
Wayne Perry, *Pr*
Adam Leiter, *
Ron Perry, *
Greg Nicholson, *
Daniel Mcgill, *VP*
EMP: 185 **EST:** 1969
SQ FT: 4,000
SALES (est): 33.36MM
SALES (corp-wide): 33.36MM **Privately Held**
Web: www.wpinc.com
SIC: 1799 8711 Decontamination services; Engineering services

(P-1183)
WEST COAST COUNTERTOPS INC
1200 Marlborough Ave Ste B (92507-2158)
PHONE...............................951 719-3670
▲ **EMP:** 90 **EST:** 1990
SALES (est): 9.04MM **Privately Held**
SIC: 1799 5211 Counter top installation; Counter tops

(P-1184)
WEST COAST FIRESTOPPING INC
1130 W Trenton Ave (92867-3536)
PHONE...............................714 935-1104
Karl Stoll, *Pr*
EMP: 80 **EST:** 2007
SALES (est): 9.79MM **Privately Held**
Web: www.westcoastfirestop.com
SIC: 1799 Fireproofing buildings

(P-1185)
WESTAR MANUFACTURING INC
Also Called: Quik-Shor
13217 Laureldale Ave (90242-5140)
PHONE...............................562 633-0581
Bill Fick, *VP Fin*
EMP: 25 **EST:** 1985
SALES (est): 1.94MM **Privately Held**
SIC: 1799 3531 Shoring and underpinning work; Construction machinery

(P-1186)
WOODS MAINTENANCE SERVICES INC
Also Called: Hydro-Pressure Systems

7250 Coldwater Canyon Ave (91605-4203)
PHONE...............................818 764-2515
Barry Woods, *Pr*
Barry Woods, *Pr*
Diane Woods, *
Jeff Woods, *
Josh Woods, *
EMP: 135 **EST:** 1975
SALES (est): 9.36MM **Privately Held**
Web: www.graffiticontrol.com
SIC: 1799 Cleaning building exteriors, nec

(P-1187)
YYK ENTERPRISES OPERATIONS LLC (PA)
3475 E St (92102-3335)
PHONE...............................619 474-6229
Ted Kines, *CEO*
Steve Johnstone, *
EMP: 190 **EST:** 1981
SQ FT: 4,000
SALES (est): 24.02MM
SALES (corp-wide): 24.02MM **Privately Held**
Web: www.yykenterprises.com
SIC: 1799 1721 3731 Sandblasting of building exteriors; Ship painting; Shipbuilding and repairing

2011 Meat Packing Plants

(P-1188)
ASIA FOOD INC
566 Monterey Pass Rd (91754-2417)
PHONE...............................626 284-1328
Bingham Lee, *CEO*
Chui Lee, *Pr*
▲ **EMP:** 46 **EST:** 1993
SQ FT: 15,000
SALES (est): 1.03MM **Privately Held**
SIC: 2011 2032 2092 2037 Meat packing plants; Chinese foods, nec: packaged in cans, jars, etc.; Fresh or frozen packaged fish; Frozen fruits and vegetables

(P-1189)
BLOOMFIELD FOOD INC
Also Called: Manufacturing
4740 E Hunter Ave (92807-1939)
PHONE...............................714 779-7273
Matthew Kang, *Pr*
EMP: 20 **EST:** 2011
SALES (est): 2.23MM **Privately Held**
Web: www.bloomfieldfood.com
SIC: 2011 Meat packing plants

(P-1190)
BURNETT & SON MEAT CO INC
Also Called: Burnett Fine Foods
1420 S Myrtle Ave (91016-4153)
PHONE...............................626 357-2165
Donald L Burnett, *Pr*
▲ **EMP:** 80 **EST:** 1978
SQ FT: 20,000
SALES (est): 23.89MM **Privately Held**
Web: www.burnettandson.com
SIC: 2011 Meat by-products, from meat slaughtered on site

(P-1191)
CARGILL MEAT SOLUTIONS CORP
13034 Excelsior Dr (90650-6867)
PHONE...............................562 345-5240
EMP: 38
SALES (corp-wide): 176.74B **Privately Held**
Web: www.cargill.com

SIC: 2011 Meat packing plants
HQ: Cargill Meat Solutions Corp
825 E Douglas Ave
Wichita KS
316 291-2500

(P-1192)
CARGILL MEAT SOLUTIONS CORP
Cargill Food Distribution
10602 N Trademark Pkwy Ste 500 (91730-5937)
PHONE...............................909 476-3120
Guy Milam, *Genl Mgr*
EMP: 51
SALES (corp-wide): 176.74B **Privately Held**
Web: www.cargill.com
SIC: 2011 Meat by-products, from meat slaughtered on site
HQ: Cargill Meat Solutions Corp
825 E Douglas Ave
Wichita KS
316 291-2500

(P-1193)
CLOUGHERTY PACKING LLC (DH)
Also Called: Smithfield Foods
3049 E Vernon Ave (90058-1800)
P.O. Box 58870 (90058-0870)
PHONE...............................323 583-4621
Kenneth J Baptist, *Pr*
EMP: 300 **EST:** 1937
SQ FT: 1,000,000
SALES (est): 217.93MM **Privately Held**
Web: farmerjohn.sfdbrands.com
SIC: 2011 2013 Meat packing plants; Sausages and other prepared meats
HQ: Smithfield Foods, Inc.
200 Commerce St
Smithfield VA
757 365-3000

(P-1194)
FIRSTCLASS FOODS - TROJAN INC
Also Called: First Class Foods
12500 Inglewood Ave (90250-4217)
P.O. Box 2397 (90251-2397)
PHONE...............................310 676-2500
Salomon Benzimra, *Pr*
Felix Benzimra, *VP Sls*
Albert Benzimra, *Sec*
Lucy Benzimra, *CFO*
EMP: 135 **EST:** 1963
SQ FT: 45,000
SALES (est): 20.89MM **Publicly Held**
SIC: 2011 5147 Meat packing plants; Meats and meat products
HQ: Us Foods, Inc.
9399 W Higgins Rd # 100
Rosemont IL

(P-1195)
GAYLORDS HRI MEATS
Also Called: Gaylord's Meat Co
1100 E Ash Ave Ste C (92831-5004)
PHONE...............................714 526-2278
Michael Smith, *Ch Bd*
Vance Dixon, *Pr*
EMP: 18 **EST:** 1975
SQ FT: 10,000
SALES (est): 1.93MM **Privately Held**
SIC: 2011 5147 5144 Meat packing plants; Meats and meat products; Poultry and poultry products

(P-1196)
GOLDEN WEST FOOD GROUP INC (PA)
4401 S Downey Rd (90058-2518)
PHONE...............................888 807-3663
Erik Litmanovich, *CEO*
EMP: 50 **EST:** 2011
SALES (est): 452.76MM
SALES (corp-wide): 452.76MM **Privately Held**
Web: www.gwfg.com
SIC: 2011 2013 2015 Meat packing plants; Sausages and other prepared meats; Poultry, slaughtered and dressed

(P-1197)
HEATHERFIELD FOODS INC
Also Called: Villa Roma Sausage Co
1150 Brooks St (91762-3606)
PHONE...............................877 460-3060
EMP: 25 **EST:** 1987
SALES (est): 4.92MM **Privately Held**
Web: www.villaromasausage.com
SIC: 2011 Sausages, from meat slaughtered on site

(P-1198)
JOBBERS MEAT PACKING CO LLC
Also Called: Wilmar
3336 Fruitland Ave (90058-3714)
P.O. Box 58368 (90058-0368)
PHONE...............................323 585-6328
Martin Evanson, *CEO*
EMP: 234 **EST:** 1978
SQ FT: 19,000
SALES (est): 22.62MM **Privately Held**
SIC: 2011 Beef products, from beef slaughtered on site

(P-1199)
K & M PACKING CO INC
Also Called: K & M Meat Co
2443 E 27th St (90058-1219)
PHONE...............................323 585-5318
Felix Goldberg, *Pr*
EMP: 37 **EST:** 1977
SQ FT: 30,000
SALES (est): 1.8MM **Privately Held**
Web: www.kmfoodservice.com
SIC: 2011 Meat packing plants

(P-1200)
NAGLES VEAL INC
1411 E Base Line St (92410-4113)
PHONE...............................909 383-7075
Michael Lemler, *Pr*
▲ **EMP:** 50 **EST:** 1983
SQ FT: 12,500
SALES (est): 8.26MM **Privately Held**
Web: www.nagleveal.com
SIC: 2011 Veal, from meat slaughtered on site

(P-1201)
OLLI SALUMERIA AMERICANA LLC
1301 Rocky Point Dr (92056-5864)
▲ **EMP:** 65 **EST:** 2010
SALES (est): 18.24MM **Privately Held**
Web: www.olli.com
SIC: 2011 Meat packing plants

(P-1202)
OWB PACKERS LLC
57 Shank Rd (92227-9616)
PHONE...............................760 351-2700
Eric W Brandt, *Managing Member*

P R O D U C T S & S V C S

EMP: 41 EST: 2016
SALES (est): 10.35MM **Privately Held**
Web: www.owbpackers.com
SIC: **2011** Meat packing plants

(P-1203)
R B R MEAT COMPANY INC
Also Called: Rightway
5151 Alcoa Ave (90058-3715)
P.O. Box 58225 (90058-0225)
PHONE.............................323 973-4868
Irwin Miller, *Pr*
Larry Vanden Bos, *
James Craig, *
EMP: 72 EST: 1951
SQ FT: 65,000
SALES (est): 2.28MM **Privately Held**
SIC: **2011** Meat packing plants

(P-1204)
SERV-RITE MEAT COMPANY INC
Also Called: Packers Bar M
2515 N San Fernando Rd (90065-1325)
P.O. Box 65026 (90065-0026)
PHONE.............................323 227-1911
Gary Marks, *CEO*
Norman Marks, *
Norma Marks, *
EMP: 55 EST: 1976
SQ FT: 55,000
SALES (est): 10.34MM **Privately Held**
Web: www.bar-m.com
SIC: **2011** Meat packing plants

(P-1205)
SSRE HOLDINGS LLC
Also Called: Signature Fresh
18901 Railroad St (91748-1322)
PHONE.............................800 314-2098
Stanley J Wetch, *Managing Member*
Stanley Joseph Wetch, *Managing Member*
EMP: 100 EST: 2014
SALES (est): 10.78MM **Privately Held**
SIC: **2011** Meat by-products, from meat
slaughtered on site

(P-1206)
V J PROVISION INC
Also Called: Jacobellis
410 S Varney St (91502-2124)
PHONE.............................818 843-3945
Sam Jacobellis, *Pr*
Vito Jacobellis, *VP*
George Jacobellis, *Treas*
Tony Jacobellis, *Sec*
EMP: 18 EST: 1974
SQ FT: 11,300
SALES (est): 240.25K **Privately Held**
SIC: **2011** Meat packing plants

(P-1207)
VENUS FOODS INC
770 S Stimson Ave (91745-1638)
PHONE.............................626 369-5188
Gin Shen Wu, *Ch Bd*
Robert Y Tsai, *Pr*
T K Chow, *VP*
Shih-ai Meng, *Treas*
▲ EMP: 20 EST: 1980
SQ FT: 20,000
SALES (est): 2.16MM **Privately Held**
Web: www.venusfoods.com
SIC: **2011** 2099 Meat packing plants; Food
preparations, nec

(P-1208)
VIZ CATTLE CORPORATION
Also Called: Sukarne
17890 Castleton St Ste 350 (91748-5793)
PHONE.............................310 884-5260

▲ EMP: 39 EST: 1992
SALES (est): 11.29MM **Privately Held**
SIC: **2011** 5154 Meat packing plants; Cattle
HQ: Grupo Viz, S.A.P.I. De C.V.
Av. Diana Tang No. 59 - A
Culiacan SIN

(P-1209)
WEST LAKE FOOD CORPORATION (PA)
Also Called: Tay Ho
301 N Sullivan St (92703-3417)
PHONE.............................714 973-2286
Jayce Yenson, *CEO*
Chieu Nguyen, *
Chuong Nguyen, *
Jayce Yenson, *Sec*
◆ EMP: 39 EST: 1986
SALES (est): 7.89MM
SALES (corp-wide): 7.89MM **Privately
Held**
SIC: **2011** Beef products, from beef
slaughtered on site

2013 Sausages And Other Prepared Meats

(P-1210)
ALPENA SAUSAGE INC
5329 Craner Ave (91601-3313)
PHONE.............................818 505-9482
Frederick Thaller, *Pr*
EMP: 22 EST: 1969
SQ FT: 6,000
SALES (est): 208.67K **Privately Held**
SIC: **2013** Sausages, from purchased meat

(P-1211)
ARIES BEEF LLC
17 W Magnolia Blvd (91502-1719)
PHONE.............................818 526-4855
Steven Zoll, *Managing Member*
EMP: 36 EST: 2021
SALES (est): 4.35MM **Privately Held**
SIC: **2013** Sausages and other prepared
meats

(P-1212)
BAR-S FOODS CO
Also Called: Bar-S Foods Co. Los Angeles
4919 Alcoa Ave (90058-3022)
PHONE.............................323 589-3600
EMP: 59
Web: www.bar-s.com
SIC: **2013** Sausages and other prepared
meats
HQ: Bar-S Foods Co.
5090 N 40th St Ste 300
Phoenix AZ
602 264-7272

(P-1213)
BEYOND MEAT INC
888 N Douglas St Ste 100 (90245-2569)
PHONE.............................866 756-4112
Ethan Brown, *CEO*
EMP: 250
SALES (corp-wide): 418.93MM **Publicly
Held**
Web: www.beyondmeat.com
SIC: **2013** 2038 Frozen meats, from
purchased meat; Frozen specialties, nec
PA: Beyond Meat, Inc.
119 Standard St
El Segundo CA
866 756-4112

(P-1214)
BOYD SPECIALTIES LLC
1016 E Cooley Dr Ste N (92324-3962)
PHONE.............................909 219-5120
▲ EMP: 52 EST: 2008
SQ FT: 10,000
SALES (est): 6MM **Privately Held**
Web: www.boydspecialtiesjerky.com
SIC: **2013** Snack sticks, including jerky: from
purchased meat

(P-1215)
CATTANEO BROS INC
Also Called: Cattaneo Bros
769 Caudill St (93401-5729)
PHONE.............................805 543-7188
Mike Kaney, *Pr*
Jayne Kaney, *Sec*
EMP: 20 EST: 1946
SQ FT: 5,500
SALES (est): 2.55MM **Privately Held**
Web: www.cattaneobros.com
SIC: **2013** 5961 Beef, dried: from purchased
meat; Food, mail order

(P-1216)
CTI FOODS AZUSA LLC
Also Called: S & S Foods LLC
1120 W Foothill Blvd (91702-2818)
PHONE.............................626 633-1609
Robert Horowitz, *CEO*
Horst Sieben, *CFO*
Pam Cardinale, *Dir Fin*
▲ EMP: 220 EST: 1998
SQ FT: 115,000
SALES (est): 48.23MM
SALES (corp-wide): 972MM **Privately
Held**
SIC: **2013** Cooked meats, from purchased
meat
HQ: Cti Foods Holding Co., Llc
2106 E State Highway 114 # 400
Southlake TX

(P-1217)
DEREK AND CONSTANCE LEE CORP (PA)
Also Called: Great River Food
19355 San Jose Ave (91748-1420)
PHONE.............................909 595-8831
Derek E Lee, *Pr*
▲ EMP: 95 EST: 1985
SQ FT: 50,000
SALES (est): 8.72MM
SALES (corp-wide): 8.72MM **Privately
Held**
Web: www.greatriverfood.com
SIC: **2013** 1541 Sausages and other
prepared meats; Food products
manufacturing or packing plant construction

(P-1218)
FORMOSA MEAT COMPANY INC
Also Called: Universal Meat Company
10646 Fulton Ct (91730-4848)
PHONE.............................909 987-0470
▲ EMP: 40 EST: 1995
SQ FT: 23,000
SALES (est): 6.61MM **Privately Held**
Web: www.formosa.com
SIC: **2013** Snack sticks, including jerky: from
purchased meat

(P-1219)
GAYTAN FOODS LLC
15430 Proctor Ave (91745-1024)
P.O. Box 3385 (91744-0385)
PHONE.............................626 330-4553
EMP: 100
Web: www.thelabelshoppe.com

SIC: **2013** 2099 2022 2011 Sausages and
other prepared meats; Food preparations,
nec; Cheese; natural and processed; Meat
packing plants

(P-1220)
HAWA CORPORATION (PA)
Also Called: Beef Jerky Factory
125 E Laurel St (92324-2462)
PHONE.............................909 825-8882
Waleed Saab, *VP*
EMP: 18 EST: 2009
SQ FT: 34,500
SALES (est): 4.9MM
SALES (corp-wide): 4.9MM **Privately Held**
Web: www.enjoybeefjerky.com
SIC: **2013** Beef, dried: from purchased meat

(P-1221)
HORMEL FOODS CORP SVCS LLC
Also Called: Hormel
2 Venture Ste 250 (92618-7408)
PHONE.............................949 753-5350
Randy Kemmipz, *Mgr*
EMP: 21
SALES (corp-wide): 12.11B **Publicly Held**
Web: www.hormelfoods.com
SIC: **2013** Canned meats (except baby
food), from purchased meat
HQ: Hormel Foods Corporate Services, Llc
1 Hormel Pl
Austin MN

(P-1222)
KITCHEN CUTS LLC
6045 District Blvd (90270-3560)
PHONE.............................323 560-7415
Raul Tapia Senior, *CEO*
EMP: 100 EST: 2011
SALES (est): 2.74MM
SALES (corp-wide): 86.67MM **Privately
Held**
Web: www.kitchen-cuts.com
SIC: **2013** Beef stew, from purchased meat
PA: Tapia Enterprises, Inc.
6067 District Blvd
Maywood CA
323 560-7415

(P-1223)
KMB FOODS INC (PA)
1010 S Sierra Way (92408-2124)
PHONE.............................626 447-0545
Scott Biedermann, *Pr*
Sam Mangiaterra, *COO*
▲ EMP: 20 EST: 1998
SQ FT: 6,000
SALES (est): 4.31MM
SALES (corp-wide): 4.31MM **Privately
Held**
Web: www.kmbfoods.com
SIC: **2013** 2099 Prepared beef products,
from purchased beef; Food preparations,
nec

(P-1224)
KRUSE AND SON INC
235 Kruse Ave (91016-4899)
P.O. Box 945 (91017-0945)
PHONE.............................626 358-4536
David R Kruse, *CEO*
EMP: 25 EST: 1949
SQ FT: 20,000
SALES (est): 8.39MM **Privately Held**
Web: www.kruseandson.com
SIC: **2013** Ham, smoked: from purchased
meat

(P-1225)
LA ESPANOLA MEATS INC
25020 Doble Ave (90710-3155)
PHONE.....................310 539-0455
Alex Motamedi, *CEO*
Juana Faraone, *
Frank Faraone, *
◆ EMP: 25 EST: 1975
SQ FT: 8,800
SALES (est): 3.82MM **Privately Held**
Web: www.laespanolameats.com
SIC: 2013 5421 Sausages and related
products, from purchased meat; Meat
markets, including freezer provisioners

(P-1226)
MONDELEZ GLOBAL LLC
Also Called: Kraft Foods
6201 Knott Ave (90620-1010)
PHONE.....................714 690-7428
Jeferey Orchard, *Brnch Mgr*
EMP: 18
Web: www.mondelezinternational.com
SIC: 2013 Sausages and other prepared
meats
HQ: Mondelez Global Llc
905 W Fulton Market # 200
Chicago IL
847 943-4000

(P-1227)
OLD BBH INC
280 10th Ave (92101-7406)
P.O. Box 85362 (92186-5362)
PHONE.....................858 715-4000
◆ EMP: 550
SIC: 2013 2032 2033 Beef stew, from
purchased meat; Chili, with or without meat:
packaged in cans, jars, etc.; Vegetables
and vegetable products, in cans, jars, etc.

(P-1228)
PAMPANGA FOOD COMPANY INC
1835 N Orangethorpe Park Ste A
(92801-1143)
PHONE.....................714 773-0537
Ray Reyes, *Pr*
Coni Reyes, *VP*
EMP: 49 EST: 1984
SQ FT: 11,000
SALES (est): 9.12MM **Privately Held**
Web: www.pampangafood.com
SIC: 2013 5812 8742 2011 Sausages and
other prepared meats; Eating places; Food
and beverage consultant; Sausages, from
meat slaughtered on site

(P-1229)
PAPA CANTELLAS INCORPORATED
Also Called: Papa Cantella's Sausage Plant
3341 E 50th St (90058-3003)
PHONE.....................323 584-7272
Thomas P Cantella, *CEO*
Chris Stafford, *
EMP: 60 EST: 1981
SQ FT: 13,000
SALES (est): 13.3MM **Privately Held**
Web: www.papacantella.com
SIC: 2013 Sausages, from purchased meat

(P-1230)
POCINO FOODS COMPANY
14250 Lomitas Ave (91746-3014)
P.O. Box 2219 (91746-0219)
PHONE.....................626 968-8000
Frank J Pocino, *Pr*
Frank G Pocino, *

Ravi Sheshadri, *
▲ EMP: 100 EST: 1933
SQ FT: 70,000
SALES (est): 30.62MM **Privately Held**
Web: www.pocinofoods.com
SIC: 2013 Sausages, from purchased meat

(P-1231)
PROVENA FOODS INC (HQ)
5010 Eucalyptus Ave (91710-9216)
PHONE.....................909 627-1082
Theodore L Arena, *Pr*
Santo Zito, *
Ronald A Provera, *
Thomas J Mulroney, *CAO*
▲ EMP: 60 EST: 1960
SALES (est): 26.01MM
SALES (corp-wide): 12.11B **Publicly Held**
SIC: 2013 2032 2098 Sausages and other
prepared meats; Canned specialties;
Macaroni and spaghetti
PA: Hormel Foods Corporation
1 Hormel Pl
Austin MN
507 437-5611

(P-1232)
RAEMICA INC
Also Called: Far West Meats
7759 Victoria Ave (92346-5637)
P.O. Box 248 (92346-0248)
PHONE.....................909 864-1990
Thomas R Serrato, *CEO*
Wade Snyder, *
Michael Serrato, *
EMP: 41 EST: 1978
SQ FT: 35,000
SALES (est): 4.48MM **Privately Held**
Web: www.farwestmeat.com
SIC: 2013 5421 Cured meats, from
purchased meat; Meat markets, including
freezer provisioners

(P-1233)
RICE FIELD CORPORATION
14500 Valley Blvd (91746-2918)
PHONE.....................626 968-6917
Derek Lee, *Pr*
▲ EMP: 120 EST: 1997
SQ FT: 100,000
SALES (est): 18.91MM **Privately Held**
Web: www.ricefieldcorporation.com
SIC: 2013 Sausages and other prepared
meats

(P-1234)
SAAB ENTERPRISES INC
Also Called: Enjoy Food
1433 Miller Dr (92324-2456)
PHONE.....................909 823-2228
Waleed Saab, *Pr*
Walleb Saab, *
Saadi Kabab, *
EMP: 24 EST: 2001
SQ FT: 38,000
SALES (est): 1.11MM **Privately Held**
SIC: 2013 Beef, dried: from purchased meat

(P-1235)
SETTLERS JERKY INC
307 Paseo Sonrisa (91789-2721)
PHONE.....................909 444-3999
Cherron L Hart, *CEO*
Aaron J Anderson, *
EMP: 27 EST: 2011
SQ FT: 20,000
SALES (est): 4.58MM **Privately Held**
Web: www.settlersjerky.com
SIC: 2013 Snack sticks, including jerky: from
purchased meat

(P-1236)
STAR FOOD SNACKS INTL INC
Also Called: Star Food Snacks
125 E Laurel St (92324-2462)
PHONE.....................909 825-8882
Aida Hawa, *CEO*
Waleed Saab, *
Asber Hawa, *
EMP: 80 EST: 2010
SALES (est): 8.25MM **Privately Held**
Web: www.enjoybeefjerky.com
SIC: 2013 Beef, dried: from purchased meat

(P-1237)
SWIFT BEEF COMPANY
Also Called: Jbs Case Ready
15555 Meridian Pkwy (92518-3046)
PHONE.....................951 571-2237
Andre Nogueira, *CEO*
EMP: 200 EST: 2015
SALES (est): 51.47MM **Publicly Held**
SIC: 2013 Beef, dried: from purchased meat
HQ: Jbs Usa Food Company
1770 Promontory Cir
Greeley CO
970 506-8000

(P-1238)
T&J SAUSAGE KITCHEN INC
Also Called: T & J Sausage Kitchen
2831 E Miraloma Ave (92806-1804)
PHONE.....................714 632-8350
Tom Drozdowski, *CEO*
David Armendariz, *
EMP: 45 EST: 1984
SQ FT: 20,000
SALES (est): 9.22MM **Privately Held**
Web: www.tandjsausage.com
SIC: 2013 Sausages and other prepared
meats

(P-1239)
TFI OF CALIFORNIA INC
9955 6th St (91730-5752)
PHONE.....................844 362-3222
EMP: 107
SALES (corp-wide): 53.28B **Publicly Held**
SIC: 2013 Snack sticks, including jerky: from
purchased meat
HQ: Tfi Of California, Inc.
10646 Fulton Ct
Rancho Cucamonga CA
844 362-3222

(P-1240)
TFI OF CALIFORNIA INC (DH)
Also Called: Golden Island Jerky Co Inc
10646 Fulton Ct (91730-4848)
PHONE.....................844 362-3222
Cheng Shih, *Pr*
▲ EMP: 20 EST: 2012
SALES (est): 3.95MM
SALES (corp-wide): 53.28B **Publicly Held**
SIC: 2013 Snack sticks, including jerky: from
purchased meat
HQ: The Hillshire Brands Company
400 S Jefferson St Ste 1n
Chicago IL
312 614-6000

(P-1241)
YONEKYU USA INC
611 N 20th St (90640-3135)
PHONE.....................323 581-4194
▼ EMP: 52 EST: 1992
SALES (est): 21.31MM **Privately Held**
Web: www.yqusa.com
SIC: 2013 Sausages, from purchased meat
HQ: Yonekyu Corp. Inc.
1259, Terabayashi, Okanomiya

Numazu SZO

2015 Poultry Slaughtering And Processing

(P-1242)
COMMODITY SALES CO
517 S Clarence St (90033-4225)
PHONE.....................323 980-5463
William T Zant, *Pr*
EMP: 120 EST: 1967
SQ FT: 14,522
SALES (est): 5.21MM **Privately Held**
SIC: 2015 5144 5142 Poultry slaughtering
and processing; Poultry and poultry
products; Packaged frozen goods

(P-1243)
FOSTER POULTRY FARMS
Also Called: FOSTER POULTRY FARMS
1805 N Santa Fe Ave (90221-1009)
PHONE.....................310 223-1499
Ronald Altman, *Brnch Mgr*
EMP: 727
SALES (corp-wide): 1.25B **Privately Held**
Web: www.fosterfarms.com
SIC: 2015 Poultry slaughtering and
processing
PA: Foster Poultry Farms, Llc
1000 Davis St
Livingston CA
209 394-7901

(P-1244)
GLENOAKS FOOD INC
11030 Randall St (91352-2621)
PHONE.....................818 768-9091
John J Fallon Iii, *CEO*
Marvin Caeser, *Stockholder*
Katty Majailovic, *Stockholder*
John J Fallon Iii, *Pr*
EMP: 40 EST: 1996
SQ FT: 30,000
SALES (est): 5.06MM **Privately Held**
Web: www.jcrivers.com
SIC: 2015 2013 3999 2091 Poultry
slaughtering and processing; Beef, dried:
from purchased meat; Pet supplies; Fish,
dried

(P-1245)
INGENUE INC
Also Called: Q C Poultry
1111 W Olympic Blvd (90640-5123)
P.O. Box 17238 (92817-7238)
PHONE.....................323 726-8084
Nick Macis, *Pr*
Michelle Macis, *
EMP: 100 EST: 1998
SQ FT: 10,000
SALES (est): 8.51MM **Privately Held**
Web: www.qcpoultry.com
SIC: 2015 Poultry slaughtering and
processing

(P-1246)
KIFUKI USA CO INC (HQ)
15547 1st St (91706-6201)
PHONE.....................626 334-8090
Kuniaki Ishikaiwa, *Pr*
▲ EMP: 90 EST: 1989
SQ FT: 52,000
SALES (est): 52.69MM **Privately Held**
Web: kifukiusa.openfos.com
SIC: 2015 2013 2035 Eggs, processed:
dehydrated; Beef, dried: from purchased
meat; Seasonings and sauces, except
tomato and dry
PA: Kewpie Corporation
1-4-13, Shibuya

P
R
O
D
U
C
T
S
&
S
V
C
S

Shibuya-Ku TKY

(P-1247)
LOS ANGELES POULTRY CO INC
4816 Long Beach Ave (90058-1915)
P.O. Box 58328 (90058-0328)
PHONE.....................323 232-1619
David Dahan, *Pr*
Dror Dahan, *
EMP: 88 **EST:** 1988
SQ FT: 32,000
SALES (est): 8.35MM **Privately Held**
Web: www.lapoultry.com
SIC: 2015 Poultry slaughtering and processing

(P-1248)
RICH CHICKS LLC
13771 Gramercy Pl (90249-2470)
PHONE.....................209 879-4104
Charlie Brust, *VP Opers*
EMP: 20
Web: www.richchicks.com
SIC: 2015 Chicken, processed: frozen
PA: Rich Chicks, Llc
4276 N Tracy Blvd
Tracy CA

(P-1249)
WESTERN SUPREME INC
Also Called: California Poultry
846 Produce Ct (90021-1832)
P.O. Box 21441 (90021-0441)
PHONE.....................213 627-3861
Frank Fogarty, *Pr*
Marlene Fogarty, *
EMP: 125 **EST:** 1991
SQ FT: 10,000
SALES (est): 9.81MM **Privately Held**
SIC: 2015 Chicken slaughtering and processing

2021 Creamery Butter

(P-1250)
VENTURA FOODS LLC
Also Called: Saffola Quality Foods
2900 Jurupa St (91761-2915)
PHONE.....................323 262-9157
EMP: 42
Web: www.venturafoods.com
SIC: 2021 2035 5199 2079 Creamery butter; Dressings, salad: raw and cooked (except dry mixes); Oils, animal or vegetable; Edible fats and oils
PA: Ventura Foods, Llc
40 Pointe Dr
Brea CA

2022 Cheese; Natural And Processed

(P-1251)
ARIZA CHEESE CO INC
7602 Jackson St (90723-4912)
PHONE.....................562 630-4144
Fatima Cristina Ariza, *CEO*
Ausencio Ariza, *
EMP: 40 **EST:** 1970
SQ FT: 8,000
SALES (est): 4.74MM **Privately Held**
Web: www.arizacheeseco.com
SIC: 2022 Natural cheese

(P-1252)
ARIZA GLOBAL FOODS INC
7602 Jackson St (90723-4912)
PHONE.....................562 630-4144
Pablo Gonzalez, *CEO*
EMP: 23 **EST:** 2015
SALES (est): 2.11MM **Privately Held**
SIC: 2022 Cheese; natural and processed

(P-1253)
EINSTEIN NOAH REST GROUP INC
Also Called: Noah's New York Bagels
16304 Beach Blvd (92683-7857)
PHONE.....................714 847-4609
Fransico Valdez, *Mgr*
EMP: 172
Web: www.bagelbrands.com
SIC: 2022 5812 Spreads, cheese; Cafe
PA: Einstein Noah Restaurant Group, Inc.
555 Zang St Ste 300
Lakewood CO

(P-1254)
EXCELPRO INC (PA)
1630 Amapola Ave (90501-3101)
PHONE.....................323 415-8544
Peter Ernster, *Pr*
Gregg Rowland, *CFO*
John H Ernster Junior, *Sec*
EMP: 19 **EST:** 1973
SQ FT: 36,000
SALES (est): 2.06MM
SALES (corp-wide): 2.06MM **Privately Held**
SIC: 2022 2023 Processed cheese; Dietary supplements, dairy and non-dairy based

(P-1255)
KAROUN DAIRIES INC (PA)
Also Called: Karoun Cheese
13023 Arroyo St (91340-1540)
PHONE.....................818 767-7000
Anto Baghdassarian, *Pr*
Ohan Baghdassarian, *
Rostom Baghdassarian, *
Seta Baghdassarian, *
Tsolak Khatcherian, *
▲ **EMP:** 40 **EST:** 1991
SQ FT: 70,000
SALES (est): 53.58MM **Privately Held**
Web: www.karouncheese.com
SIC: 2022 5143 Natural cheese; Cheese

(P-1256)
LIFE IS LIFE LLC
Also Called: Parmela Creamery
2611 Cottonwood Ave (92553-8089)
PHONE.....................310 584-7541
Ryan Hayes Salomone, *Managing Member*
EMP: 28 **EST:** 2012
SALES (est): 2.83MM **Privately Held**
SIC: 2022 Imitation cheese

(P-1257)
SAPUTO CHEESE USA INC
5611 Imperial Hwy (90280-7419)
PHONE.....................562 862-7686
Rick Mckenney, *Brnch Mgr*
EMP: 545
SALES (corp-wide): 3.79B **Privately Held**
Web: www.saputo.com
SIC: 2022 5143 Natural cheese; Cheese
HQ: Saputo Cheese Usa Inc.
10700 W Res Dr Ste 400
Milwaukee WI

(P-1258)
SIERRA CHEESE MANUFACTURING COMPANY INC
Also Called: Sierra
916 S Santa Fe Ave (90221-4333)
PHONE.....................310 635-1216
EMP: 39 **EST:** 1959
SALES (est): 4.77MM **Privately Held**
Web: www.sierracheese.com
SIC: 2022 Natural cheese

2023 Dry, Condensed, Evaporated Products

(P-1259)
ARMOR DERMALOGICS LLC
9151 Atlanta Ave # 5864 (92615-2639)
PHONE.....................714 202-6424
EMP: 50 **EST:** 2018
SALES (est): 1.17MM **Privately Held**
SIC: 2023 Dietary supplements, dairy and non-dairy based

(P-1260)
BETTER BAR MANUFACTURING LLC
6975 Arlington Ave (92503-1537)
PHONE.....................951 525-3111
EMP: 20 **EST:** 2015
SALES (est): 1.39MM **Privately Held**
SIC: 2023 Dietary supplements, dairy and non-dairy based

(P-1261)
BETTER NUTRITIONALS LLC
3380 Horseless Carriage Rd (92860-3635)
PHONE.....................310 356-9019
Roger Tyre, *Brnch Mgr*
EMP: 100
SALES (corp-wide): 96.69MM **Privately Held**
SIC: 2023 Dietary supplements, dairy and non-dairy based
PA: Better Nutritionals, Llc
3390 Hrseless Carriage Dr
Norco CA

(P-1262)
BETTER NUTRITIONALS LLC
3350 Horseless Carriage Rd (92860-3635)
PHONE.....................310 356-9019
Roger Tyre, *Brnch Mgr*
EMP: 100
SALES (corp-wide): 96.69MM **Privately Held**
SIC: 2023 Dietary supplements, dairy and non-dairy based
PA: Better Nutritionals, Llc
3390 Hrseless Carriage Dr
Norco CA

(P-1263)
BETTER NUTRITIONALS LLC
17120 S Figueroa St Ste B (90248-3024)
PHONE.....................310 356-9019
Sharon Hoffman, *Brnch Mgr*
EMP: 50
SALES (corp-wide): 96.69MM **Privately Held**
Web: www.betternutritionals.com
SIC: 2023 Dietary supplements, dairy and non-dairy based
PA: Better Nutritionals, Llc
3390 Hrseless Carriage Dr
Norco CA

(P-1264)
BIO-NUTRITIONAL RES GROUP INC
Also Called: Bnrg
6 Morgan Ste 100 (92618-1920)
P.O. Box 3669 (90510-3669)
PHONE.....................714 427-6990
Kevin Lawrence, *CEO*
Karen L Stensby, *
Curtis Steinhaus, *
EMP: 185 **EST:** 1991
SQ FT: 3,000
SALES (est): 49.64MM **Privately Held**
Web: www.powercrunch.com
SIC: 2023 Dietary supplements, dairy and non-dairy based

(P-1265)
CAMPER PACKAGING LLC
Also Called: Phoenix Custom Packaging
13208 Arctic Cir (90670-5510)
PHONE.....................562 239-6167
EMP: 19 **EST:** 2019
SALES (est): 1.52MM **Privately Held**
SIC: 2023 Dry, condensed and evaporated dairy products

(P-1266)
CAPTEK HOLDINGS LLC
16218 Arthur St (90703-2131)
PHONE.....................562 921-9511
EMP: 18 **EST:** 2011
SALES (est): 491K **Privately Held**
Web: www.capteksoftgel.com
SIC: 2023 Dietary supplements, dairy and non-dairy based

(P-1267)
EL INDIO SHOPS INCORPORATED
Also Called: El Indio Mexican Restaurant
3695 India St (92103-4799)
PHONE.....................619 299-0333
Ralph R Pesqueira Junior, *Pr*
Eva Sanchez, *
EMP: 55 **EST:** 1940
SQ FT: 10,000
SALES (est): 5.8MM **Privately Held**
Web: www.elindiosandiego.net
SIC: 2023 5812 Evaporated buttermilk; Mexican restaurant

(P-1268)
ESPERER WEBSTORES LLC
Also Called: Diatomaceous Earth.com
3820 State St Ste B (93105-3182)
PHONE.....................805 880-1900
David Stephen Sorensen, *Managing Member*
EMP: 19 **EST:** 2016
SALES (est): 2.32MM **Privately Held**
SIC: 2023 5499 Dietary supplements, dairy and non-dairy based; Vitamin food stores

(P-1269)
FEIHE INTERNATIONAL INC (PA)
2275 Huntington Dr Ste 278 (91108-2640)
PHONE.....................626 757-8885
You-bin Leng, *Pr*
Hua Liu, *
EMP: 1932 **EST:** 1985
SALES (est): 362.97MM **Privately Held**
SIC: 2023 Dry, condensed and evaporated dairy products

(P-1270)
FENCHEM INC (HQ)
Also Called: Fenchem
15308 El Prado Rd Bldg 8 (91710-7659)

PHONE....................909 597-8880
Shufeng Fan, *CEO*
▲ **EMP:** 22 **EST:** 2007
SALES (est): 9.4MM **Privately Held**
Web: www.fenchem.com
SIC: 2023 Dietary supplements, dairy and
non-dairy based
PA: Fenchem Biotek Ltd.
Room 1917, No. 359, Hongwu Road,
Qinhuai District
Nanjing JS

(P-1271)
FOREVER RICH
INTERNATIONAL LLC
14622 Ventura Blvd (91403-3600)
PHONE....................310 867-4723
Leon Katz, *Pr*
EMP: 25 **EST:** 2013
SALES (est): 1.75MM **Privately Held**
SIC: 2023 Dietary supplements, dairy and
non-dairy based

(P-1272)
GERLAIT GROUP INC
9255 Towne Centre Dr (92121-3033)
PHONE....................858 587-0400
Pamela Jeffery, *Brnch Mgr*
EMP: 22
SALES (corp-wide): 220.41K **Privately
Held**
Web: www.gerlait.com
SIC: 2023 Condensed, concentrated, and
evaporated milk products
PA: Gerlait Group Inc.
4225 Executive Sq Ste 950
La Jolla CA
858 587-0400

(P-1273)
HERITAGE DISTRIBUTING
COMPANY
Also Called: Ninth Avenue Foods
425 S 9th Ave (91746-3314)
PHONE....................626 333-9526
Ted De Groot, *Brnch Mgr*
EMP: 22
SIC: 2023 2026 Dry, condensed and
evaporated dairy products; Fluid milk
PA: Heritage Distributing Company
5743 Smithway St Ste 105
Commerce CA

(P-1274)
KERRY INC
64405 Lincoln St (92254-6501)
P.O. Box 398 (92254-0398)
PHONE....................760 396-2116
Darren Worden, *Pr*
EMP: 63
Web: www.kerry.com
SIC: 2023 Dry, condensed and evaporated
dairy products
HQ: Kerry Inc.
3400 Millington Rd
Beloit WI
608 363-1200

(P-1275)
LIEF ORGANICS LLC (PA)
Also Called: Lief Labs
28903 Avenue Paine (91355-4169)
PHONE....................661 775-2500
Adel Villalobos, *CEO*
Steve Chopp, *
Victor Leyson, *
Nathan Cox, *Development*
EMP: 25 **EST:** 2008
SALES (est): 57.27MM
SALES (corp-wide): 57.27MM **Privately
Held**

Web: www.lieflabs.com
SIC: 2023 Dietary supplements, dairy and
non-dairy based

(P-1276)
LONIX PHARMACEUTICAL INC
5001 Earle Ave (91770-1169)
PHONE....................626 287-4700
Chak Yeung Chan, *Pr*
Chak Yeung Chan, *Pr*
Wendy Cheung, *Off Mgr*
EMP: 18 **EST:** 2013
SQ FT: 5,000
SALES (est): 1.26MM **Privately Held**
SIC: 2023 Dietary supplements, dairy and
non-dairy based

(P-1277)
MEGANUTRA INC
17332 Irvine Blvd Ste 232 (92780-3022)
PHONE....................949 331-2503
Hai Ou, *Brnch Mgr*
EMP: 22
SALES (corp-wide): 470.78K **Privately
Held**
Web: www.naturesnutra.com
SIC: 2023 Dietary supplements, dairy and
non-dairy based
PA: Meganutra, Inc.
128 Carnegie Row Ste 107
Norwood MA
781 762-9600

(P-1278)
NATURALIFE ECO VITE LABS
Also Called: Paragon Laboratories
20433 Earl St (90503-2414)
PHONE....................310 370-1563
Jay Kaufman, *CEO*
Richard Kaufman, *
Claire Kaufman, *
Steven Billis, *
▲ **EMP:** 100 **EST:** 1971
SQ FT: 25,000
SALES (est): 22.91MM **Privately Held**
Web: www.paragonlabsusa.com
SIC: 2023 2844 2834 5122 Dietary
supplements, dairy and non-dairy based;
Toilet preparations; Suppositories; Vitamins
and minerals

(P-1279)
NESTLE USA INC
3285 De Forest Cir (91752-3239)
PHONE....................877 463-7853
EMP: 73
Web: www.nestleusa.com
SIC: 2023 Evaporated milk
HQ: Nestle Usa, Inc.
1812 N Moore St
Arlington VA
703 682-4600

(P-1280)
NESTLE USA INC
800 N Brand Blvd (91203-1245)
PHONE....................818 549-6000
EMP: 143
Web: www.nestle.com
SIC: 2023 Evaporated milk
HQ: Nestle Usa, Inc.
1812 N Moore St
Arlington VA
703 682-4600

(P-1281)
NESTLE USA INC
7301 District Blvd (93313-2042)
PHONE....................661 398-3536
EMP: 254

Web: www.nestleusa.com
SIC: 2023 Evaporated milk
HQ: Nestle Usa, Inc.
1812 N Moore St
Arlington VA
703 682-4600

(P-1282)
PHARMACHEM
LABORATORIES LLC
Also Called: PHARMACHEM
LABORATORIES, LLC
2929 E White Star Ave (92806-2628)
PHONE....................714 630-6000
George Joseph, *VP*
EMP: 41
SALES (corp-wide): 2.19B **Publicly Held**
SIC: 2023 Dietary supplements, dairy and
non-dairy based
HQ: Pharmachem Laboratories Llc
265 Harrison Tpke
Kearny NJ
201 246-1000

(P-1283)
PROLACTA BIOSCIENCE INC
1800 Highland Ave (91010-2837)
PHONE....................626 599-9260
Scott A Elster, *CEO*
EMP: 304
SALES (corp-wide): 130.35MM **Privately
Held**
Web: www.prolacta.com
SIC: 2023 Dried and powdered milk and milk
products
PA: Prolacta Bioscience, Inc.
757 Baldwin Park Blvd
City Of Industry CA
626 599-9260

(P-1284)
SOURCE OF HEALTH INC
1055 Bay Blvd Ste A (91911-1628)
PHONE....................619 409-9500
Oskar Thorvaldsson, *Pr*
▲ **EMP:** 20 **EST:** 2000
SALES (est): 969.66K **Privately Held**
SIC: 2023 Dietary supplements, dairy and
non-dairy based

(P-1285)
TEAM BEACHBODY CANADA
LLC
400 Continental Blvd Ste 400 (90245-5089)
PHONE....................310 883-9000
Carl Deikler, *Pr*
EMP: 26 **EST:** 2016
SALES (est): 1.22MM **Privately Held**
SIC: 2023 Dietary supplements, dairy and
non-dairy based

(P-1286)
TRIPLE FIVE NUTRITION LLC
17120 S Figueroa St (90248-3016)
PHONE....................310 502-2277
Sharon Hoffman, *Managing Member*
EMP: 20
SALES (est): 612.52K **Privately Held**
SIC: 2023 Dietary supplements, dairy and
non-dairy based

(P-1287)
TROPICAL FUNCTIONAL LABS
LLC
Also Called: Tahiti Trading Company
7111 Arlington Ave Ste F (92503-1522)
PHONE....................951 688-2619
▲ **EMP:** 22 **EST:** 1999
SALES (est): 1.42MM **Privately Held**

SIC: 2023 Dietary supplements, dairy and
non-dairy based

(P-1288)
UQORA INC
4250 Executive Sq (92037-1482)
PHONE....................888 313-1372
Vivian Rhoads, *Pr*
Jenna Ryan, *
Spencer Gordon, *
EMP: 43 **EST:** 2017
SALES (est): 25.33MM **Privately Held**
Web: www.uqora.com
SIC: 2023 Dietary supplements, dairy and
non-dairy based
HQ: Pharmavite Llc
8531 Fallbrook Ave
West Hills CA
818 221-6200

(P-1289)
VITAWEST NUTRACEUTICALS
INC
Also Called: Chocolates and Health
1502 Arrow Hwy (91750-5318)
PHONE....................888 557-8012
Iraiz Gomez, *CEO*
EMP: 25 **EST:** 1974
SALES (est): 2.48MM **Privately Held**
Web: www.vitawestnutra.com
SIC: 2023 Dietary supplements, dairy and
non-dairy based

(P-1290)
WELLINGTON FOODS INC
1930 California Ave (92881-6491)
PHONE....................951 547-7000
Anthony E Harnack Senior, *Ch*
Tony Mauer, *
▲ **EMP:** 148 **EST:** 1974
SQ FT: 50,000
SALES (est): 26.42MM **Privately Held**
Web: www.wellingtonfoods.com
SIC: 2023 Dietary supplements, dairy and
non-dairy based

(P-1291)
YBCC INC
17800 Castleton St Ste 386 (91748-1791)
PHONE....................626 213-3945
Xiuhua Song, *Pr*
EMP: 38 **EST:** 1986
SALES (est): 2.25MM **Privately Held**
SIC: 2023 Dietary supplements, dairy and
non-dairy based

2024 Ice Cream And Frozen Deserts

(P-1292)
BAKED BEAR LLC
587 S Coast Highway 101 (92024-3532)
PHONE....................760 704-8140
Nick Calderon, *Genl Mgr*
EMP: 19 **EST:** 2013
SALES (est): 1.12MM **Privately Held**
Web: www.thebakedbear.com
SIC: 2024 Dairy based frozen desserts

(P-1293)
BERENICE 2 AM CORP
Also Called: Bobboi Natural Gelato
8008 Girard Ave Ste 150 (92037-4159)
PHONE....................858 255-8693
Andrea Racca, *CEO*
Andrea Racca, *Ofcr*
EMP: 20 **EST:** 2014
SQ FT: 900

SALES (est): 1.82MM **Privately Held**
Web: www.bobboi.com
SIC: 2024 Ice cream and frozen deserts

(P-1294)
BIG TRAIN INC
Also Called: Big T Industries
25392 Commercentre Dr (92630-8823)
PHONE...............................949 340-8800
◆ **EMP:** 150
Web: www.kerryfoodservice.com
SIC: 2024 2086 Ice cream and frozen deserts
; Fruit drinks (less than 100% juice):
packaged in cans, etc.

(P-1295)
**BROTHERS INTL DESSERTS
(PA)**
Also Called: Brothers Desserts
3400 W Segerstrom Ave (92704-6405)
PHONE...............................949 655-0080
Gary M Winkler, *CEO*
▲ **EMP:** 84 **EST:** 1974
SALES (est): 61.12MM
SALES (corp-wide): 61.12MM **Privately Held**
Web: www.brothersdesserts.com
SIC: 2024 Ice cream, bulk

(P-1296)
DANONE US LLC
3500 Barranca Pkwy Ste 240 (92606-8226)
PHONE...............................949 474-9670
John Mastrotaolo, *Dir*
EMP: 42
SALES (corp-wide): 718.68MM **Privately Held**
Web: www.danonenorthamerica.com
SIC: 2024 Ice cream and frozen deserts
HQ: Danone Us, Llc
1 Maple Ave
White Plains NY
914 872-8400

(P-1297)
FARCHITECTURE BB LLC
Also Called: Coolhaus
8588 Washington Blvd (90232-7463)
PHONE...............................917 701-2777
Natasha Case, *Managing Member*
Daniel Fishman, *Pr*
EMP: 30 **EST:** 2009
SALES (est): 4.94MM **Privately Held**
SIC: 2024 Ice cream, packaged: molded, on
sticks, etc.

(P-1298)
**HIGH ROAD CRAFT ICE CREAM
INC (PA)**
12243 Branford St (91352-1010)
PHONE...............................678 701-7623
EMP: 25 **EST:** 2010
SALES (est): 20.81MM **Privately Held**
Web: www.highroadcraft.com
SIC: 2024 Ice cream and frozen deserts

(P-1299)
**MACKIE INTERNATIONAL INC
(PA)**
Also Called: Sun Ice USA
4193 Flat Rock Dr Ste 200 (92505-7113)
PHONE...............................951 346-0530
Ernesto U Dacay Junior, *Pr*
◆ **EMP:** 40 **EST:** 1983
SALES (est): 9.74MM
SALES (corp-wide): 9.74MM **Privately Held**
Web: www.mackieinternational.net

SIC: 2024 2086 5199 Ices, flavored (frozen
dessert); Fruit drinks (less than 100%
juice): packaged in cans, etc.; Baskets

(P-1300)
THRIFTY PAYLESS INC
Thrifty Ice Cream
9200 Telstar Ave (91731-2814)
PHONE...............................626 571-0122
EMP: 16149
SALES (corp-wide): 24.09B **Publicly Held**
SIC: 2024 Ice cream and frozen deserts
HQ: Thrifty Payless, Inc.
1200 Intrepid Ave Ste 2
Philadelphia PA

(P-1301)
TROPICALE FOODS LLC (PA)
1237 W State St (91762-4015)
P.O. Box 2224 (91708-2224)
PHONE...............................909 635-1000
Steven C Schiller, *CEO*
▲ **EMP:** 54 **EST:** 1999
SALES (est): 113.67MM
SALES (corp-wide): 113.67MM **Privately Held**
Web: www.tropicalefoods.com
SIC: 2024 Ice milk, packaged: molded, on
sticks, etc.

(P-1302)
WE THE PIE PEOPLE LLC
Also Called: Jc's Pie Pops
9909 Topanga Canyon Blvd # 159
(91311-3602)
PHONE...............................818 349-1880
Jennifer Constantine, *Managing Member*
Thomas Spler, *
▲ **EMP:** 50 **EST:** 2012
SALES (est): 2.25MM **Privately Held**
Web: www.piepops.com
SIC: 2024 Nondairy based frozen desserts

(P-1303)
ZIEGENFELDER COMPANY
12262 Colony Ave (91710-2095)
PHONE...............................909 509-0493
Donovan Arriaga, *Dir*
EMP: 65
Web: www.twinpops.com
SIC: 2024 Fruit pops, frozen
HQ: The Ziegenfelder Company
87 18th St
Wheeling WV
304 232-6360

(P-1304)
ZIEGENFELDER COMPANY
12290 Colony Ave (91710-2095)
PHONE...............................909 590-0493
EMP: 65
Web: www.twinpops.com
SIC: 2024 Ice cream, packaged: molded, on
sticks, etc.
HQ: The Ziegenfelder Company
87 18th St
Wheeling WV
304 232-6360

2026 Fluid Milk

(P-1305)
AYO FOODS LLC
Also Called: Ayo Food
927 Main St (93215-1729)
P.O. Box 1987 (93216-1987)
PHONE...............................661 345-5457
Matt Billings, *Managing Member*
EMP: 50 **EST:** 2018

SALES (est): 100K **Privately Held**
Web: www.ayoyogurt.com
SIC: 2026 Yogurt

(P-1306)
BERKELEY FARMS LLC
Also Called: Buds Ice Cream San Francisco
17637 E Valley Blvd (91744-5731)
P.O. Box 4616 (94540-4616)
PHONE...............................510 265-8600
▲ **EMP:** 400
SIC: 2026 0241 5143 Fluid milk; Dairy farms;
Butter

(P-1307)
CALIFORNIA DAIRIES INC
11709 Artesia Blvd (90701-3803)
PHONE...............................562 809-2595
Joe Heffington, *Brnch Mgr*
EMP: 65
SALES (corp-wide): 33.2B **Privately Held**
Web: www.californiadairies.com
SIC: 2026 Milk processing (pasteurizing,
homogenizing, bottling)
PA: California Dairies, Inc.
2000 N Plaza Dr
Visalia CA
559 625-2200

(P-1308)
DAIRY FARMERS AMERICA INC
4375 N Ventura Ave (93001-1124)
PHONE...............................805 653-0042
Kevin Clark, *Mgr*
EMP: 52
SALES (corp-wide): 24.52B **Privately Held**
Web: www.dfamilk.com
SIC: 2026 2022 2021 2023 Milk processing
(pasteurizing, homogenizing, bottling);
Natural cheese; Creamery butter;
Condensed milk
PA: Dairy Farmers Of America, Inc.
1405 N 98th St
Kansas City KS
816 801-6455

(P-1309)
DEAN SOCAL LLC
Also Called: Swiss Dairy
17637 E Valley Blvd (91744-5731)
PHONE...............................951 734-3950
EMP: 140
SIC: 2026 Fluid milk

(P-1310)
FARMDALE CREAMERY INC
Also Called: Farmdale
1049 W Base Line St (92411-2310)
PHONE...............................909 888-4938
Norman R Shotts Ii, *CEO*
Nicholas J Sibilio, *
Norman R Shotts Iii, *Genl Mgr*
Michael Shotts, *General Vice President*
Florence Shotts, *
▲ **EMP:** 100 **EST:** 1978
SQ FT: 110,000
SALES (est): 21.82MM **Privately Held**
Web: www.farmdale.net
SIC: 2026 2022 Buttermilk, cultured; Natural
cheese

(P-1311)
GENERAL MILLS INC
Also Called: General Mills
1055 Sandhill Ave (90746-1312)
P.O. Box 4589 (90749-4589)
PHONE...............................310 605-6108
Jeff Crandle, *Mgr*
EMP: 51
SQ FT: 62,497

SALES (corp-wide): 20.09B **Publicly Held**
Web: www.generalmills.com
SIC: 2026 2041 Yogurt; Flour mixes
PA: General Mills, Inc.
1 General Mills Blvd
Minneapolis MN
763 764-7600

(P-1312)
GOOD CULTURE LLC
22 Corporate Park (92606-3117)
PHONE...............................949 545-9945
Jesse Merrill, *Managing Member*
Anders Eisner, *Managing Member*
EMP: 25 **EST:** 2014
SALES (est): 2MM **Privately Held**
Web: www.goodculture.com
SIC: 2026 2023 Fluid milk; Dry, condensed
and evaporated dairy products

(P-1313)
**HERITAGE DISTRIBUTING
COMPANY (PA)**
Also Called: Rex Creamery
5743 Smithway St Ste 105 (90040-1548)
P.O. Box 668 (90241-0668)
PHONE...............................323 838-1225
Ted S Degroot, *Pr*
EMP: 24 **EST:** 1998
SALES (est): 49.67MM **Privately Held**
SIC: 2026 Milk processing (pasteurizing,
homogenizing, bottling)

(P-1314)
PAC FILL INC
Also Called: Sun Dairy Co
5471 W San Fernando Rd (90039-1014)
PHONE...............................818 409-0117
Vahik Sarkissian, *CEO*
Edward Sarkissian, *
Jerry Nicoghosian, *
EMP: 25 **EST:** 1977
SQ FT: 22,000
SALES (est): 4.9MM **Privately Held**
Web: www.sundairy.com
SIC: 2026 2086 Yogurt; Carbonated soft
drinks, bottled and canned

(P-1315)
PARAMOUNT DAIRY INC
15255 Texaco Ave (90723-3917)
PHONE...............................562 361-1800
Phillip C Chang, *Brnch Mgr*
EMP: 135
SALES (corp-wide): 3.07MM **Privately Held**
Web: www.paramount-dairy.com
SIC: 2026 Yogurt
PA: Paramount Dairy, Inc.
17801 Cartwright Rd
Irvine CA
949 265-8077

(P-1316)
**STREMICKS HERITAGE FOODS
LLC (HQ)**
Also Called: Heritage Foods
4002 Westminster Ave (92703-1310)
PHONE...............................714 775-5000
Louis J Stremick, *Managing Member*
Michael W Malone, *
Jack P Noenickx, *Managing Member*
▼ **EMP:** 300 **EST:** 1916
SALES (est): 448.96MM
SALES (corp-wide): 24.52B **Privately Held**
Web: www.heritage-foods.com
SIC: 2026 Cream, sour
PA: Dairy Farmers Of America, Inc.
1405 N 98th St
Kansas City KS
816 801-6455

▲ = Import ▼ = Export
◆ = Import/Export

(P-1317)
WIN SOON INC
Also Called: Epoca Yocool
4569 Firestone Blvd (90280-3343)
PHONE................................323 564-5070
Jun Sang Lee, *Pr*
▲ **EMP:** 25 **EST:** 1993
SQ FT: 7,000
SALES (est): 6.59MM **Privately Held**
Web: www.winsoonepoca.com
SIC: 2026 5149 Yogurt; Soft drinks

(P-1318)
WWF OPERATING COMPANY LLC
Also Called: White Wave Foods
18275 Arenth Ave Bldg 1 (91748-1225)
PHONE................................626 810-1775
EMP: 72
SALES (corp-wide): 718.68MM **Privately Held**
Web: www.danonenorthamerica.com
SIC: 2026 Milk processing (pasteurizing, homogenizing, bottling)
HQ: Wwf Operating Company, Llc
   12002 Airport Way
   Broomfield CO

2032 Canned Specialties

(P-1319)
ADESA INTERNATIONAL LLC (PA)
1440 S Vineyard Ave (91761-8042)
PHONE................................909 321-8240
EMP: 24 **EST:** 2013
SQ FT: 1,500
SALES (est): 3.23MM
SALES (corp-wide): 3.23MM **Privately Held**
Web: www.adesa.com
SIC: 2032 Mexican foods, nec: packaged in cans, jars, etc.

(P-1320)
CAER INC
Also Called: Yumi
8070 Melrose Ave (90046-7015)
PHONE................................415 879-9864
Angela Sutherland, *CEO*
Evelyn Rusli, *
▲ **EMP:** 27 **EST:** 2015
SALES (est): 3.4MM **Privately Held**
Web: www.helloyumi.com
SIC: 2032 7389 Baby foods, including meats: packaged in cans, jars, etc.; Business Activities at Non-Commercial Site

(P-1321)
CALI FOOD COMPANY INC
Cali Noodles
8258 Saigon Pl (92844-1087)
PHONE................................714 821-8630
EMP: 37
SALES (corp-wide): 179.71K **Privately Held**
Web: www.califoodco.com
SIC: 2032 Italian foods, nec: packaged in cans, jars, etc.
PA: Cali Food Company, Inc.
   45401 Research Ave
   Fremont CA
   408 515-3178

(P-1322)
CORN MAIDEN FOODS INC
24201 Frampton Ave (90710-2105)
PHONE................................310 784-0400

EMP: 65 **EST:** 1995
SQ FT: 40,000
SALES (est): 8.15MM **Privately Held**
Web: www.cornmaidenfoods.com
SIC: 2032 Canned specialties

(P-1323)
DOLORES CANNING CO INC
1020 N Eastern Ave (90063-3214)
P.O. Box 63187 (90063-0187)
PHONE................................323 263-9155
David Munoz, *Pr*
Steve A Munoz, *
Frank T Munoz, *
EMP: 25 **EST:** 1956
SQ FT: 5,000
SALES (est): 4.91MM **Privately Held**
Web: www.dolorescanning.com
SIC: 2032 2011 Mexican foods, nec: packaged in cans, jars, etc.; Meat packing plants

(P-1324)
EXPRO MANUFACTURING CORPORATION
2800 Ayers Ave (90058-4302)
PHONE................................323 415-8544
▲ **EMP:** 20
SIC: 2032 Canned specialties

(P-1325)
FRESH PACKING CORPORATION
4333 S Maywood Ave (90058-2521)
P.O. Box 3009 (91803-0009)
PHONE................................213 612-0136
Monica Zambada Lopez, *CEO*
EMP: 20 **EST:** 2009
SALES (est): 4.86MM **Privately Held**
Web: www.freshpacking.net
SIC: 2032 Chili, with or without meat: packaged in cans, jars, etc.

(P-1326)
JIMENEZ MEXICAN FOODS INC
20343 Harvill Ave (92570-7237)
PHONE................................951 351-0102
Veronica Jimenez, *Admn*
Roberto Jimenez, *CEO*
EMP: 20 **EST:** 2001
SALES (est): 2.17MM **Privately Held**
Web: www.casajimenezmexicanrestaurant.com
SIC: 2032 Mexican foods, nec: packaged in cans, jars, etc.

(P-1327)
JUANITAS FOODS
Also Called: Pico Pica Foods
645 N. Eubank Ave (90744)
P.O. Box 847 (90748-0847)
PHONE................................310 834-5339
Aaron De La Torre, *CEO*
Mark De La Torre, *
James Steveson, *
EMP: 125 **EST:** 1946
SQ FT: 85,000
SALES (est): 50.24MM **Privately Held**
Web: www.juanitas.com
SIC: 2032 Mexican foods, nec: packaged in cans, jars, etc.

(P-1328)
KRAFT HEINZ FOODS COMPANY
Heinz
2450 White Rd (92614-6250)
PHONE................................949 250-4080
Dan Foss, *Brnch Mgr*
EMP: 34

SALES (corp-wide): 26.48B **Publicly Held**
Web: www.kraftfoodsgroup.com
SIC: 2032 2035 Soups, except seafood: packaged in cans, jars, etc.; Seasonings and sauces, except tomato and dry
HQ: Kraft Heinz Foods Company
   1 Ppg Pl Ste 3400
   Pittsburgh PA
   412 456-5700

(P-1329)
MASONGATE INC
2800 Ayers Ave (90058-4302)
PHONE................................323 415-8544
EMP: 20
SIC: 2032 6552 Canned specialties; Subdividers and developers, nec

(P-1330)
SALICO FARMS INC
4231 Us Highway 86 Ste 4 (92227-9648)
P.O. Box 1531 (92227-0229)
PHONE................................760 344-5375
Niaz Mohamed Junior, *Pr*
Sara Ann Mohamed, *
Martin Mohamed, *
EMP: 120 **EST:** 1981
SQ FT: 2,400
SALES (est): 9.61MM **Privately Held**
SIC: 2032 Beans and bean sprouts, canned, jarred, etc.

(P-1331)
SHINE FOOD INC (PA)
19216 Normandie Ave (90502-1011)
PHONE................................310 329-3829
Stephen Y S Lee, *CEO*
Tracy Lee, *
▲ **EMP:** 50 **EST:** 1986
SQ FT: 30,000
SALES (est): 13.37MM
SALES (corp-wide): 13.37MM **Privately Held**
Web: www.shinefoods.com
SIC: 2032 Canned specialties

(P-1332)
SUPERIOR QUALITY FOODS INC
Also Called: Superior Touch
2355 E Francis St (91761-7727)
P.O. Box 908 (30162-0908)
PHONE................................909 923-4733
▲ **EMP:** 63
SIC: 2032 2034 Canned specialties; Dried and dehydrated soup mixes

(P-1333)
T & T FOODS INC
Also Called: Colonel Lee's Enterprises
3080 E 50th St (90058-2918)
PHONE................................323 588-2158
Michelle Ma, *CEO*
David Ma, *VP*
EMP: 50 **EST:** 1967
SQ FT: 19,000
SALES (est): 9.27MM **Privately Held**
Web: www.tandtfoods.net
SIC: 2032 2099 Ethnic foods, canned jarred, etc.; Food preparations, nec

(P-1334)
WING HING FOODS LLC
Also Called: Wing Hing
1659 E 23rd St (90011-1803)
PHONE................................323 232-8899
▲ **EMP:** 90
Web: www.passportglobalfoods.com
SIC: 2032 Ethnic foods, canned, jarred, etc.

2033 Canned Fruits And Specialties

(P-1335)
ASEPTIC TECHNOLOGY LLC
Also Called: Aseptic Technology
24855 Corbit Pl (92887-5543)
PHONE................................714 694-0168
Julie Hodson, *
Noel Calma, *
Clay White, *
Lan Pham, *
EMP: 117 **EST:** 2013
SQ FT: 59,300
SALES (est): 13.77MM **Privately Held**
Web: www.asepticllc.com
SIC: 2033 Canned fruits and specialties

(P-1336)
BEAUMONT JUICE INC
Also Called: Perricone Juices
550 B St (92223-2672)
PHONE................................951 769-7171
Robert Paul Rovzar, *CEO*
Thomas M Carmody, *
Joe Perricone, *
Paul Golub, *
▲ **EMP:** 98 **EST:** 1994
SQ FT: 30,000
SALES (est): 24.59MM
SALES (corp-wide): 24.59MM **Privately Held**
Web: www.perriconefarms.com
SIC: 2033 Fruit juices: fresh
PA: G B & P Citrus Co Inc
   1601 E Olympic Blvd Ste 1
   Los Angeles CA
   213 312-1380

(P-1337)
HUY FONG FOODS INC
4800 Azusa Canyon Rd (91706-1938)
PHONE................................626 286-8328
David Tran, *Pr*
Ada Tran, *VP*
Donna Lam, *Sec*
◆ **EMP:** 20 **EST:** 1980
SQ FT: 68,000
SALES (est): 8.61MM **Privately Held**
Web: www.huyfong.com
SIC: 2033 Chili sauce, tomato: packaged in cans, jars, etc.

(P-1338)
J M SMUCKER COMPANY
800 Commercial Ave (93030-7234)
P.O. Box 5161 (93031-5161)
PHONE................................805 487-5483
Al Yamamoto, *Mgr*
EMP: 66
SQ FT: 20,000
SALES (corp-wide): 8.53B **Publicly Held**
Web: www.jmsmucker.com
SIC: 2033 Canned fruits and specialties
PA: The J M Smucker Company
   1 Strawberry Ln
   Orrville OH
   330 682-3000

(P-1339)
JACKSON MANUFACTURING LLC
Also Called: Bear State Kitchen
3515 W Washington Blvd (90018-1122)
PHONE................................213 399-9300
EMP: 18 **EST:** 2020
SALES (est): 1.17MM **Privately Held**
SIC: 2033 Canned fruits and specialties

P
R
O
D
U
C
T
S
&
S
V
C
S

(P-1340)
KRAFT HEINZ FOODS COMPANY
Also Called: Kraft Foods
1500 E Walnut Ave (92831-4731)
PHONE.................................714 870-8235
Robert Pech, *Brnch Mgr*
EMP: 54
SQ FT: 2,878
SALES (corp-wide): 26.48B **Publicly Held**
Web: www.kraftfoodsgroup.com
SIC: 2033 Canned fruits and specialties
HQ: Kraft Heinz Foods Company
   1 Ppg Pl Ste 3400
   Pittsburgh PA
   412 456-5700

(P-1341)
LUDFORDS INC
3038 Pleasant St (92507-5554)
PHONE.................................909 948-0797
EMP: 40 EST: 1926
SALES (est): 35.84MM **Privately Held**
Web: www.ludfordsinc.com
SIC: 2033 Fruit juices: packaged in cans, jars, etc.

(P-1342)
NASCO GOURMET FOODS INC
Also Called: Platinum Distribution
22720 Savi Ranch Pkwy (92887-4608)
PHONE.................................714 279-2100
Burhan Nasser, *Pr*
Jerry Pascoe, *
Mary Beth Nasser, *
EMP: 90 EST: 1990
SQ FT: 42,000
SALES (est): 2.11MM
SALES (corp-wide): 44.16MM **Privately Held**
Web: www.nasserco.com
SIC: 2033 Seasonings, tomato: packaged in cans, jars, etc.
PA: Nasser Company, Inc.
   22720 Savi Ranch Pkwy
   Yorba Linda CA
   714 279-2100

(P-1343)
REFRESCO BEVERAGES US INC
Also Called: Crosby Fruit Products
11751 Pacific Ave (92337-6961)
PHONE.................................951 685-0481
EMP: 150
SQ FT: 99,500
Web: www.refresco-na.com
SIC: 2033 Fruit juices: packaged in cans, jars, etc.
HQ: Refresco Beverages Us Inc.
   8112 Woodland Center Blvd
   Tampa FL

(P-1344)
SATICOY FOODS CORPORATION
554 Todd Rd (93060-9725)
P.O. Box 4547 (93007-0547)
PHONE.................................805 647-5266
EMP: 40 EST: 1967
SALES (est): 13.77MM
SALES (corp-wide): 63.59MM **Privately Held**
SIC: 2033 Vegetables: packaged in cans, jars, etc.
PA: Moody Dunbar, Inc.
   2000 Waters Edge Dr # 21
   Johnson City TN
   423 952-0100

(P-1345)
SUNDOWN FOODS USA INC
Also Called: Sundown Foods

10891 Business Dr (92337-8235)
PHONE.................................909 606-6797
Jeff Wartell, *Pr*
▲ EMP: 30 EST: 1998
SALES (est): 4.14MM **Privately Held**
Web: www.sundownfoods.com
SIC: 2033 Vegetables and vegetable products, in cans, jars, etc.

(P-1346)
SUNNYGEM LLC (PA)
Also Called: Sunnygem
500 N F St (93280-1435)
PHONE.................................661 758-0491
John Vidovich, *Managing Member*
Ajit Sidhu, *
◆ EMP: 300 EST: 2005
SQ FT: 270,000
SALES (est): 60.45MM **Privately Held**
Web: www.sunnygem.com
SIC: 2033 3556 Fruit juices: fresh; Juice extractors, fruit and vegetable: commercial type

(P-1347)
TROPICAL PRESERVING CO INC
5 Lewiston Ct (92694-0532)
PHONE.................................213 748-5108
Ronald Randall, *Pr*
EMP: 23 EST: 1928
SALES (est): 4.08MM **Privately Held**
Web: www.tropicalpreserving.com
SIC: 2033 Jams, jellies, and preserves, packaged in cans, jars, etc.

(P-1348)
TROPICANA PRODUCTS INC
Also Called: Tropicana
240 N Orange Ave (91744-3433)
PHONE.................................626 968-1299
Kevin Frebert, *Manager*
EMP: 21
SQ FT: 1,512
SALES (corp-wide): 1.11B **Privately Held**
Web: www.tropicana.com
SIC: 2033 Fruit juices: fresh
PA: Tropicana Products, Inc.
   1001 13th Ave E
   Bradenton FL
   941 747-4461

(P-1349)
VITA JUICE CORPORATION
10725 Sutter Ave (91331-2553)
PHONE.................................818 899-1195
EMP: 100
SIC: 2033 Fruit juices: concentrated, hot pack

(P-1350)
VITA-PAKT CITRUS PRODUCTS CO (PA)
10000 Stockdale Hwy Ste 390 (93311-3601)
P.O. Box 309 (91723-0309)
PHONE.................................626 332-1101
James R Boyles, *CEO*
Lloyd Shimizu, *
◆ EMP: 50 EST: 1957
SALES (est): 47.18MM
SALES (corp-wide): 47.18MM **Privately Held**
Web: www.vita-pakt.com
SIC: 2033 2037 Apple sauce: packaged in cans, jars, etc.; Fruit juices, frozen

(P-1351)
VIVE ORGANIC INC
2554 Lincoln Blvd Ste 772 (90291-5043)
PHONE.................................877 774-9291

EMP: 35 EST: 2015
SALES (est): 5.27MM
SALES (corp-wide): 52.72MM **Privately Held**
Web: www.viveorganic.com
SIC: 2033 Fruit juices: packaged in cans, jars, etc.
PA: Suja Life, Llc
   3831 Ocean Ranch Blvd
   Oceanside CA
   855 879-7852

(P-1352)
WALKER FOODS INC
Also Called: La Flora Del Sur
237 N Mission Rd (90033-2103)
PHONE.................................323 268-5191
Robert L Walker Junior, *Pr*
Denise Walker, *
EMP: 65 EST: 1914
SQ FT: 150,000
SALES (est): 15.06MM **Privately Held**
Web: www.walkerfoods.net
SIC: 2033 2032 2099 Canned fruits and specialties; Canned specialties; Ready-to-eat meals, salads, and sandwiches

(P-1353)
WONDERFUL CITRUS PACKING LLC
1701 S Lexington St (93215-9200)
PHONE.................................661 720-2400
EMP: 18
SALES (corp-wide): 2.04B **Privately Held**
Web: www.wonderfulcitrus.com
SIC: 2033 Fruit juices: fresh
HQ: Wonderful Citrus Packing Llc
   1901 S Lexington St
   Delano CA

2034 Dehydrated Fruits, Vegetables, Soups

(P-1354)
AMERICAN FOOD INGREDIENTS INC
4021 Avenida De La Plata Ste 501 (92056)
PHONE.................................760 967-6287
Karen Koppenhaver, *CEO*
▲ EMP: 30 EST: 1993
SQ FT: 2,000
SALES (est): 9.07MM **Privately Held**
Web: www.americanfoodingredients.com
SIC: 2034 Dried and dehydrated vegetables

(P-1355)
INLAND EMPIRE FOODS INC (PA)
5425 Wilson St (92509-2434)
PHONE.................................951 682-8222
Mark H Sterner, *Pr*
Paul Stiritz, *
▼ EMP: 35 EST: 1985
SQ FT: 85,000
SALES (est): 10.88MM
SALES (corp-wide): 10.88MM **Privately Held**
Web: www.inlandempirefoods.com
SIC: 2034 Vegetables, dried or dehydrated (except freeze-dried)

(P-1356)
LAUMIERE GOURMET FRUITS CO LLC
3331 Pegasus Dr Ste 101 (93308-6870)
PHONE.................................661 218-9768
EMP: 18 EST: 2019
SALES (est): 2.16MM **Privately Held**

Web: www.laumieregourmet.com
SIC: 2034 Dried and dehydrated fruits, vegetables and soup mixes

(P-1357)
NAMAR FOODS
Also Called: Namar Company
6830 Walthall Way (90723-2028)
PHONE.................................562 531-2744
EMP: 38 EST: 1962
SALES (est): 5.11MM **Privately Held**
Web: www.namar.com
SIC: 2034 Dried and dehydrated fruits, vegetables and soup mixes

(P-1358)
STUTZ PACKING LLC
Also Called: Stutz Packing Company
82689 Avenue 45 (92201-2386)
PHONE.................................760 342-1666
Jack Stutz, *Prin*
EMP: 35 EST: 2021
SALES (est): 2.33MM **Privately Held**
Web: www.stutzpacking.com
SIC: 2034 Dried and dehydrated fruits, vegetables and soup mixes

2035 Pickles, Sauces, And Salad Dressings

(P-1359)
GEDNEY FOODS COMPANY
12243 Branford St (91352-1010)
P.O. Box 8 (55318-0008)
PHONE.................................952 448-2612
Charles Weil, *CEO*
Barry Stecter, *
Carl Tuttle, *
James R Cook, *Technology Vice President*
▲ EMP: 125 EST: 1881
SALES (est): 19.3MM **Privately Held**
Web: www.gedneyfoods.com
SIC: 2035 Pickles, vinegar

(P-1360)
GFF INC
Also Called: Girard Food Service
145 Willow Ave (91746-2047)
PHONE.................................323 232-6255
Emanuel Marti, *CEO*
Bill Perry, *Pr*
William Perry, *Pr*
▲ EMP: 89 EST: 1981
SQ FT: 92,000
SALES (est): 34.72MM **Privately Held**
Web: www.girardsdressings.com
SIC: 2035 Pickles, sauces, and salad dressings
PA: Haco Holding Ag
   Worbstrasse 262
   GÜmligen BE

(P-1361)
LEE KUM KEE (USA) FOODS INC (PA)
14455 Don Julian Rd (91746-3102)
PHONE.................................626 709-1888
Simon Wu, *Pr*
Dickson Chan, *
EMP: 99 EST: 1996
SQ FT: 54,000
SALES (est): 17.13MM
SALES (corp-wide): 17.13MM **Privately Held**
Web: usa.lkk.com
SIC: 2035 Seasonings and sauces, except tomato and dry

80   2024 Southern California
Business Directory and Buyers Guide   ▲ = Import ▼ = Export
◆ = Import/Export

(P-1362)
MOREHOUSE FOODS INC
760 Epperson Dr (91748-1336)
PHONE..................................626 854-1655
David L Latter Senior, *Ch*
David L Latter Junior, *Pr*
◆ **EMP:** 50 **EST:** 1898
SQ FT: 65,000
SALES (est): 12.78MM **Privately Held**
Web: www.morehousefoods.com
SIC: 2035 5149 Mustard, prepared (wet);
Seasonings, sauces, and extracts

(P-1363)
PACIFICA FOODS LLC
Also Called: Stir Foods
1851 N Delilah St (92879-1800)
PHONE..................................951 371-3123
Ming Milton Liu, *
EMP: 140 **EST:** 2000
SALES (est): 60MM
SALES (corp-wide): 240.72MM **Privately
Held**
Web: www.stirfoods.com
SIC: 2035 5149 2033 Seasonings and
sauces, except tomato and dry; Sauces;
Tomato products, packaged in cans, jars,
etc.
PA: Corona-Orange Foods Intermediate
Holdings Llc
1581 N Main St
Orange CA
714 637-6050

(P-1364)
Q & B FOODS INC (DH)
15547 1st St (91706-6201)
PHONE..................................626 334-8090
Kuniaki Ishikaiwa, *Pr*
Jerry Shepherd, *Ex VP*
Akio Okumura, *CEO*
◆ **EMP:** 69 **EST:** 1982
SQ FT: 52,000
SALES (est): 52.69MM **Privately Held**
Web: www.qbfoods.com
SIC: 2035 Dressings, salad: raw and cooked
(except dry mixes)
HQ: Kifuki U.S.A. Co., Inc.
15547 1st St
Irwindale CA

(P-1365)
**VANLAW FOOD PRODUCTS INC
(HQ)**
Also Called: Coron-Rnge Fods Intrmdate Hldn
2325 Moore Ave (92833-2510)
P.O. Box 2388 (92837-0388)
PHONE..................................714 870-9091
EMP: 72 **EST:** 1945
SALES (est): 54.82MM
SALES (corp-wide): 240.72MM **Privately
Held**
SIC: 2035 2087 Pickles, sauces, and salad
dressings; Syrups, drink
PA: Corona-Orange Foods Intermediate
Holdings Llc
1581 N Main St
Orange CA
714 637-6050

2037 Frozen Fruits And Vegetables

(P-1366)
CANADAS FINEST FOODS INC
Also Called: Reliant Foodservice
26090 Ynez Rd (92591-6000)
PHONE..................................951 296-1040
David Canada, *Pr*

▲ **EMP:** 70 **EST:** 1996
SQ FT: 102,000
SALES (est): 16.81MM **Privately Held**
Web: www.reliantfoods.com
SIC: 2037 2024 Fruit juices; Dairy based
frozen desserts

(P-1367)
CLEUGHS FROZEN FOODS INC
6571 Altura Blvd Ste 200 (90620-1020)
EMP: 20 **EST:** 1933
SALES (est): 2.09MM **Privately Held**
SIC: 2037 Frozen fruits and vegetables

(P-1368)
CROWN CITRUS COMPANY INC
551 W Main St (92227-2262)
PHONE..................................760 344-1930
Mark Mcbroom, *Pr*
EMP: 21 **EST:** 2007
SALES (est): 746.55K **Privately Held**
Web: www.fivecrowns.com
SIC: 2037 Citrus pulp, dried

(P-1369)
**DOLE PACKAGED FOODS LLC
(HQ)**
Also Called: Glacier Foods Division
3059 Townsgate Rd Ste 400 (91361-2936)
P.O. Box 5132 (91359-5132)
PHONE..................................805 601-5500
David A Delorenzo, *Managing Member*
Gregory Costley, *Managing Member**
Ann Wiese, *
Jim Johnston, *
Tim Nelson, *
◆ **EMP:** 550 **EST:** 1967
SQ FT: 81,000
SALES (est): 256.93MM **Privately Held**
Web: www.dolesunshine.com
SIC: 2037 Fruits, quick frozen and cold pack
(frozen)
PA: Itochu Corporation
2-5-1, Kitaaoyama
Minato-Ku TKY

(P-1370)
HUSKS UNLIMITED (PA)
9925 Airway Rd # C (92154-7932)
PHONE..................................619 476-8301
Luis Duenas, *CEO*
Eric Brenk, *Pr*
EMP: 22 **EST:** 2012
SALES (est): 7.1MM
SALES (corp-wide): 7.1MM **Privately Held**
Web: www.husksunlimitedinc.com
SIC: 2037 Frozen fruits and vegetables

(P-1371)
IMPERIAL VALLEY FOODS INC
1961 Buchanan Ave (92231-4306)
P.O. Box 233 Paulin Ave (92231)
PHONE..................................760 203-1896
Gustavo Cabellero, *CEO*
Gustavo Cabellero Junior, *Pr*
Fernando Cabellero, *
Edna Cabellero, *
▲ **EMP:** 300 **EST:** 2006
SALES (est): 21.48MM **Privately Held**
SIC: 2037 Frozen fruits and vegetables

(P-1372)
**J HELLMAN FROZEN FOODS
INC (PA)**
1601 E Olympic Blvd Ste 200 (90021-1941)
P.O. Box 86267 (90086-0267)
PHONE..................................213 243-9105
Tracy Hellman, *CEO*
Bryce Hellman, *

EMP: 50 **EST:** 1990
SQ FT: 21,000
SALES (est): 4.65MM
SALES (corp-wide): 4.65MM **Privately
Held**
Web: www.jhellmanfrozenfoods.com
SIC: 2037 Frozen fruits and vegetables

(P-1373)
KOR SHOTS INC
29160 Heathercliff Rd Unit 4273
(90264-1083)
PHONE..................................805 351-0700
Jordan Retamar, *CEO*
EMP: 20 **EST:** 2017
SALES (est): 2.03MM **Privately Held**
Web: www.korshots.com
SIC: 2037 2033 Fruit juices; Fruit juices:
fresh

(P-1374)
LA ALOE LLC
2301 E 7th St Ste A152 (90023-1044)
PHONE..................................888 968-2563
▲ **EMP:** 21 **EST:** 2011
SQ FT: 47,000
SALES (est): 1.99MM **Privately Held**
Web: www.lalibations.com
SIC: 2037 Fruit juices

(P-1375)
LANGERS JUICE COMPANY INC
129 Stephen St (91744)
PHONE..................................626 336-3100
EMP: 300 **EST:** 2016
SALES (est): 11.5MM **Privately Held**
Web: www.langers.com
SIC: 2037 Fruit juices

(P-1376)
LIVE FRESH CORPORATION
1055 E Cooley Ave (92408-2819)
PHONE..................................909 478-0895
▲ **EMP:** 180 **EST:** 1993
SALES (est): 8.89MM **Privately Held**
SIC: 2037 Fruit juices

(P-1377)
OXNARD LEMON COMPANY
2001 Sunkist Cir (93033-3902)
P.O. Box 2240 (93034-2240)
PHONE..................................805 483-1173
Sam Mayhew, *Genl Mgr*
Nancy Low, *Off Mgr*
Tom Mayhew, *Superintnt*
EMP: 26 **EST:** 1996
SALES (est): 2.43MM **Privately Held**
Web: www.oxnardlemon.com
SIC: 2037 0723 5148 Frozen fruits and
vegetables; Crop preparation services for
market; Fresh fruits and vegetables

(P-1378)
QUALITY PRODUCED LLC
Also Called: Pulp Story
987 N Enterprise St (92867-5448)
PHONE..................................310 592-8834
EMP: 26
SALES (corp-wide): 765.36K **Privately
Held**
Web: www.sweetlyproduced.work
SIC: 2037 Fruit juices
PA: Quality Produced Llc
11693 San Vicente Blvd
Los Angeles CA
310 592-8834

(P-1379)
SUNSATION INC
100 S Cambridge Ave (91711-4842)
PHONE..................................909 542-0280
Perry Eichor, *CEO*
Perry Eichor, *Pr*
David Bryant, *
Saul Kusnier, *Prin*
EMP: 48 **EST:** 2003
SQ FT: 30,000
SALES (est): 6.26MM **Privately Held**
SIC: 2037 Fruit juices

(P-1380)
VENTURA COASTAL LLC (PA)
2325 Vista Del Mar Dr (93001-3751)
P.O. Box 69 (93002-0069)
PHONE..................................805 653-7000
Donald Dames, *
Bill Borgers, *Managing Member**
Rolph Scherer, *
Don Uhlrich, *
◆ **EMP:** 51 **EST:** 1951
SQ FT: 25,000
SALES (est): 31.97K
SALES (corp-wide): 31.97K **Privately Held**
Web: www.venturacoastal.com
SIC: 2037 Fruit juice concentrates, frozen

(P-1381)
**WM BOLTHOUSE FARMS INC
(HQ)**
Also Called: Bolthouse Farms
7200 E Brundage Ln (93307-3016)
PHONE..................................661 366-7209
Jeffrey Dunn, *CEO*
Mike Rosenthal, *
◆ **EMP:** 1000 **EST:** 1970
SQ FT: 700,000
SALES (est): 618.7MM
SALES (corp-wide): 1.33B **Privately Held**
Web: www.bolthouse.com
SIC: 2037 0161 2033 2099 Fruit juices;
Carrot farm; Vegetable juices: packaged in
cans, jars, etc.; Sauce, gravy, dressing, and
dip mixes
PA: Generis Holdings, Lp
7200 E Brundage Ln
Bakersfield CA
661 366-7209

2038 Frozen Specialties, Nec

(P-1382)
**AJINOMOTO FOODS NORTH
AMER INC**
Also Called: Windsor Foods
4200 Concours Ste 100 (91764-4982)
PHONE..................................909 477-4700
Steve Charles, *Mgr*
EMP: 244
Web: www.ajinomotofoods.com
SIC: 2038 5142 Frozen specialties, nec;
Packaged frozen goods
HQ: Ajinomoto Foods North America, Inc.
4200 Concours Ste 100
Ontario CA

(P-1383)
**AJINOMOTO FOODS NORTH
AMER INC (DH)**
4200 Concours Ste 100 (91764-4982)
PHONE..................................909 477-4700
Hiroshi Kaho, *CEO*
Sumio Maeda, *
Taro Komura, *
James Caltabiano, *
Daniel O'brien, *CIO*
▲ **EMP:** 100 **EST:** 2015

SQ FT: 56,000
SALES (est): 844.87MM **Privately Held**
Web: www.ajinomotofoods.com
SIC: 2038 2037 Frozen specialties, nec;
Frozen fruits and vegetables
HQ: Ajinomoto North America Holdings, Inc.
7124 N Marine Dr
Portland OR
503 505-5783

(P-1384)
ASTROCHEF LLC
Also Called: Pegasus Foods
1111 Mateo St (90021-1717)
P.O. Box 86404 (90086-0404)
PHONE.....................213 627-9860
Jim Zaferis, *CEO*
Evangelos Ambatielos, *
Steve Koufoudakis, *
EMP: 55 **EST:** 1998
SQ FT: 60,000
SALES (est): 15.47MM **Privately Held**
Web: www.astrochef.com
SIC: 2038 Frozen specialties, nec

(P-1385)
BEYOND MEAT INC (PA)
119 Standard St (90245-3833)
PHONE.....................866 756-4112
Ethan Brown, *Pr*
Seth Goldman, *Ch Bd*
Lubi Kutua, *CFO*
Dariush Ajami, *CIO*
Teri L Witteman, *CLO*
▲ **EMP:** 20 **EST:** 2009
SALES (est): 418.93MM
SALES (corp-wide): 418.93MM **Publicly Held**
Web: www.beyondmeat.com
SIC: 2038 2013 Frozen specialties, nec;
Frozen meats, from purchased meat

(P-1386)
CARDENAS MARKETS LLC
1621 E Francis St (91761-8324)
PHONE.....................909 923-7426
Javier Ramirez, *COO*
EMP: 297
SALES (corp-wide): 10.5MM **Privately Held**
Web: www.cardenasmarkets.com
SIC: 2038 5411 Frozen specialties, nec;
Grocery stores
HQ: Cardenas Markets Llc
2501 E Guasti Rd
Ontario CA
909 923-7426

(P-1387)
CULINARY BRANDS INC (PA)
3280 E 44th St (90058-2426)
PHONE.....................626 289-3000
Frank Calma, *Pr*
Mohsen Ganeian, *Prin*
EMP: 41 **EST:** 2011
SQ FT: 2,000
SALES (est): 10.14MM
SALES (corp-wide): 10.14MM **Privately Held**
Web: www.culinaryinternational.com
SIC: 2038 Frozen specialties, nec

(P-1388)
DEL REAL LLC (PA)
Also Called: Del Real Foods
11041 Inland Ave (91752-1155)
PHONE.....................951 681-0395
Michael Axelrod, *CEO*
Jesus Cardenas, *Managing Member*
Viviano Del Villar Junior, *COO*

Manuel Martinez, *CFO*
EMP: 72 **EST:** 2003
SQ FT: 175,000
SALES (est): 68.65MM
SALES (corp-wide): 68.65MM **Privately Held**
Web: www.delrealfoods.com
SIC: 2038 Ethnic foods, nec, frozen

(P-1389)
DON MIGUEL MEXICAN FOODS INC (HQ)
Also Called: Don Miguel Foods
333 S Anita Dr Ste 1000 (92868-3318)
PHONE.....................714 385-4500
Jeff Frank, *CEO*
Saralyn Brown, *
Mike Elliott, *
Terry Girch, *
Michael Chaignot, *
▲ **EMP:** 45 **EST:** 1908
SQ FT: 80,000
SALES (est): 113.34MM **Privately Held**
Web: www.donmiguel.com
SIC: 2038 Frozen specialties, nec
PA: Megamex Foods, Llc
333 S Anita Dr Ste 1000
Orange CA

(P-1390)
EXCELLINE FOOD PRODUCTS LLC
833 N Hollywood Way (91505-2814)
PHONE.....................818 701-7710
EMP: 27 **EST:** 1979
SQ FT: 23,000
SALES (est): 1.93MM **Privately Held**
Web: www.excellinefoods.com
SIC: 2038 Ethnic foods, nec, frozen

(P-1391)
GOLDEN STATE FOODS CORP
640 S 6th Ave (91746-3086)
PHONE.....................626 465-7500
Chad Buechel, *Brnch Mgr*
EMP: 350
SALES (corp-wide): 1.36B **Privately Held**
Web: www.goldenstatefoods.com
SIC: 2038 2087 2026 2051 Frozen
specialties, nec; Flavoring extracts and
syrups, nec; Fluid milk; Bread, cake, and
related products
PA: Golden State Foods Corp.
18301 Von Karman Ave # 1
Irvine CA
949 247-8000

(P-1392)
HARVEST FARMS INC
45000 Yucca Ave (93534-2526)
PHONE.....................661 945-3636
Craig Shugert, *CEO*
Eric Shiring, *
▲ **EMP:** 100 **EST:** 1947
SQ FT: 18,000
SALES (est): 24.09MM
SALES (corp-wide): 519.54MM **Privately Held**
Web: www.harvestfarms.com
SIC: 2038 5144 Lunches, frozen and
packaged; Poultry and poultry products
HQ: Good Source Solutions, Inc.
3115 Melrose Dr Ste 160
Carlsbad CA
858 455-4800

(P-1393)
LA MEXICANA LLC
6535 Caballero Blvd A (90620-8106)
PHONE.....................323 277-3660

Angelo Fraggos, *CEO*
EMP: 40 **EST:** 2006
SALES (est): 5.77MM
SALES (corp-wide): 469.89MM **Privately Held**
SIC: 2038 Ethnic foods, nec, frozen
PA: Blue Point Capital Partners Llc
127 Public Sq Ste 5100
Cleveland OH
216 535-4700

(P-1394)
LA MOUSSE DESSERTS INC
Also Called: La Mousse
18211 S Broadway (90248-3535)
PHONE.....................310 478-6051
Leah Noble, *Pr*
EMP: 24 **EST:** 2017
SQ FT: 11,000
SALES (est): 2.42MM **Privately Held**
Web: www.lamoussedesserts.com
SIC: 2038 Frozen specialties, nec

(P-1395)
LANGLOIS FANCY FROZEN FOODS INC
2975 Laguna Canyon Rd (92651-1148)
PHONE.....................949 497-1741
EMP: 49 **EST:** 1951
SALES (est): 4.49MM **Privately Held**
Web: www.langloisfoods.com
SIC: 2038 Dinners, frozen and packaged

(P-1396)
NESTLE USA INC
Also Called: Nestle Dist Ctr & Logistics
3450 Dulles Dr (91752-3242)
PHONE.....................951 360-7200
EMP: 481
Web: www.nestleusa.com
SIC: 2038 Frozen specialties, nec
HQ: Nestle Usa, Inc.
1812 N Moore St
Arlington VA
703 682-4600

(P-1397)
PASCO CORPORATION OF AMERICA
19191 S Vermont Ave Ste 420 (90502-1051)
PHONE.....................503 289-6500
Hiroyuki Horie, *CEO*
◆ **EMP:** 38 **EST:** 1979
SALES (est): 1.11MM **Privately Held**
Web: www.pascoamerica.com
SIC: 2038 Ethnic foods, nec, frozen
PA: Pasco Shikishima Corporation
5-3, Shirakabe, Higashi-Ku
Nagoya AIC

(P-1398)
PICTSWEET COMPANY
732 Hanson Way (93458-9710)
P.O. Box 5878 (93456-5878)
PHONE.....................805 928-4414
Thomas Kerulas, *Brnch Mgr*
EMP: 300
SALES (corp-wide): 403.32MM **Privately Held**
Web: www.pictsweetfarms.com
SIC: 2038 2099 Frozen specialties, nec;
Food preparations, nec
PA: The Pictsweet Company
10 Pictsweet Dr
Bells TN
731 663-7600

(P-1399)
REAL VISION FOODS LLC
Also Called: Real Vision Foods
72 Knollglen (92614-7485)
PHONE.....................253 228-5050
Joseph H Ertman, *Pr*
Joseph Ertman, *
EMP: 50 **EST:** 2019
SALES (est): 4.07MM **Privately Held**
Web: www.realvisionfoods.com
SIC: 2038 Snacks, incl. onion rings, cheese
sticks, etc.

(P-1400)
SHINE FOOD INC
Jesse Lord
21100 S Western Ave (90501-1700)
PHONE.....................310 533-6010
John Freschi, *Mgr*
EMP: 90
SALES (corp-wide): 13.37MM **Privately Held**
Web: www.shinefoods.com
SIC: 2038 2053 2052 2051 Frozen
specialties, nec; Frozen bakery products,
except bread; Cookies and crackers;
Bread, cake, and related products
PA: Shine Food, Inc.
19216 Normandie Ave
Torrance CA
310 329-3829

(P-1401)
SPECIALTY BRANDS INCORPORATED
4200 Concours Ste 100 (91764-4982)
P.O. Box 51467 (91761-1057)
PHONE.....................909 477-4851
EMP: 1900
SIC: 2038 5142 Frozen specialties, nec;
Packaged frozen goods

(P-1402)
STAR FOOD 316 INC
2370 E 48th St (90058-2026)
PHONE.....................213 858-2512
EMP: 49
SALES (corp-wide): 254.58K **Privately Held**
SIC: 2038 Dinners, frozen and packaged
PA: Star Food 316, Inc.
1206 E 6th St
Los Angeles CA
323 896-2103

(P-1403)
STIR FOODS LLC
1851 N Delilah St (92879-1800)
PHONE.....................714 871-9231
Phil Decarion, *CEO*
EMP: 44
SALES (corp-wide): 240.72MM **Privately Held**
Web: www.stirfoods.com
SIC: 2038 2099 Frozen specialties, nec;
Food preparations, nec
HQ: Stir Foods, Llc
1581 N Main St
Orange CA

(P-1404)
TAWA SUPERMARKET INC (PA)
Also Called: 99 Ranch Market
6281 Regio Ave (90620-1023)
PHONE.....................714 521-8899
Chang Hua K Chen, *CEO*
▲ **EMP:** 87 **EST:** 1985
SQ FT: 117,000
SALES (est): 490.41MM
SALES (corp-wide): 490.41MM **Privately Held**

▲ = Import ▼ = Export
◆ = Import/Export

Web: www.168markets.com
SIC: 2038 5411 Breakfasts, frozen and packaged; Supermarkets, chain

(P-1405)
WINDSOR QUALITY FOOD COMPANY LTD
Also Called: Windsor Foods
4200 Concours Ste 100 (91764-4982)
PHONE..............................713 843-5200
EMP: 3300
SIC: 2038 Frozen specialties, nec

2041 Flour And Other Grain Mill Products

(P-1406)
ANDREW LLC
Also Called: Sanluisina
17058 Lagos Dr (91709-3998)
PHONE..............................909 270-9356
Miriam Navarro, *Managing Member*
EMP: 18 EST: 2012
SALES (est): 1.5MM **Privately Held**
SIC: 2041 Corn meal

(P-1407)
ARDENT MILLS LLC
2020 E Steel Rd (92324-4008)
PHONE..............................951 201-1170
Brad Beckwith, *Brnch Mgr*
EMP: 24
SALES (corp-wide): 571.31MM **Privately Held**
Web: www.ardentmills.com
SIC: 2041 Flour and other grain mill products
PA: Ardent Mills, Llc
    1875 Lawrence St Ste 1400
    Denver CO
    800 851-9618

(P-1408)
ARDENT MILLS LLC
Also Called: Cargill Flour Milling Division
19684 Cajon Blvd (92407-1813)
PHONE..............................909 887-3407
Nelson Selmer, *Brnch Mgr*
EMP: 21
SQ FT: 26,180
SALES (corp-wide): 571.31MM **Privately Held**
Web: www.ardentmills.com
SIC: 2041 Flour mills, cereal (except rice)
PA: Ardent Mills, Llc
    1875 Lawrence St Ste 1400
    Denver CO
    800 851-9618

(P-1409)
GENERAL MILLS INC
Also Called: General Mills
4309 Fruitland Ave (90058-3176)
PHONE..............................323 584-3433
Jeff Shapiro, *Brnch Mgr*
EMP: 26
SQ FT: 81,186
SALES (corp-wide): 20.09B **Publicly Held**
Web: www.generalmills.com
SIC: 2041 Flour mills, cereal (except rice)
PA: General Mills, Inc.
    1 General Mills Blvd
    Minneapolis MN
    763 764-7600

(P-1410)
GK FOODS INC
Also Called: San Marcos Trading Company
133 Mata Way Ste 101 (92069-2946)

PHONE..............................760 752-5230
Laurence Hickerson, *CEO*
Laurence James Hickerson, *CEO*
John Bartelt, *Sec*
EMP: 20 EST: 2002
SQ FT: 15,000
SALES (est): 4.81MM **Privately Held**
Web: www.globalkaizen.com
SIC: 2041 7389 5149 Flour and other grain mill products; Packaging and labeling services; Organic and diet food

(P-1411)
GRAIN CRAFT INC
Also Called: California Milling Co
1861 E 55th St (90058-3836)
PHONE..............................323 585-0131
Kurt Gallehugh, *Brnch Mgr*
EMP: 61
Web: www.graincraft.com
SIC: 2041 Flour mills, cereal (except rice)
PA: Grain Craft, Inc.
    201 W Main St Ste 203
    Chattanooga TN

(P-1412)
HONEYVILLE GRAIN INC
9175 Milliken Ave (91730-5509)
PHONE..............................909 243-1050
Ed Hemphill, *Prin*
EMP: 29 EST: 1951
SALES (est): 1.48MM **Privately Held**
Web: www.honeyville.com
SIC: 2041 Flour and other grain mill products

(P-1413)
LT FOODS AMERICAS INC (HQ)
11130 Warland Dr (90630-5032)
PHONE..............................562 340-4040
Abhinav Arora, *CEO*
Mukesh Agrawal, *
◆ EMP: 17 EST: 1992
SQ FT: 30,000
SALES (est): 26.46MM **Privately Held**
Web: www.ltfoodsglobal.com
SIC: 2041 5149 Flour and other grain mill products; Pasta and rice
PA: Lt Foods Limited
    4th Floor, Mvl-I Park, Sector 15
    Gurugram HR

(P-1414)
ORGANIC GEMINI LLC
Also Called: Gemini Superfoods
325 N Maple Dr Ste 5088 (90210-3428)
PHONE..............................347 662-2900
EMP: 23
SALES (corp-wide): 705.73K **Privately Held**
Web: www.organicgemini.com
SIC: 2041 Flour mixes
PA: Organic Gemini, Llc
    68 33rd St Unit 4
    Brooklyn NY
    347 662-2900

(P-1415)
PILLSBURY COMPANY LLC
Also Called: Pillsbury
220 S Kenwood St Ste 202 (91205-1671)
PHONE..............................818 522-3952
Linda Goodman, *Brnch Mgr*
EMP: 31
SALES (corp-wide): 20.09B **Publicly Held**
Web: www.lgpillsbury.com
SIC: 2041 Doughs and batters
HQ: The Pillsbury Company Llc
    1 General Mills Blvd
    Minneapolis MN

(P-1416)
SING KUNG CORP
12061 Clark St (91006-5829)
PHONE..............................626 358-5838
Louis Choy, *Pr*
◆ EMP: 25 EST: 1997
SQ FT: 7,000
SALES (est): 2.1MM **Privately Held**
Web: www.singkung.com
SIC: 2041 Flour and other grain mill products

(P-1417)
SUNOPTA GRAINS AND FOODS INC
12128 Center St (90280-8046)
PHONE..............................323 774-6000
EMP: 62
SALES (corp-wide): 934.66MM **Publicly Held**
Web: www.sunopta.com
SIC: 2041 5153 Flour and other grain mill products; Grains
HQ: Sunopta Grains And Foods Inc.
    7078 Shady Oak Rd
    Eden Prairie MN

(P-1418)
THE SWEET LIFE ENTERPRISES INC
Also Called: Aryzta Sweet Life
2350 Pullman St (92705-5507)
PHONE..............................949 261-7400
EMP: 115
Web: www.sweetlifeinc.com
SIC: 2041 5149 Doughs and batters; Crackers, cookies, and bakery products

2043 Cereal Breakfast Foods

(P-1419)
CALIFRNIA NUTRITIONAL PDTS INC ✪
64405 Lincoln St (92254-6501)
PHONE..............................760 485-3000
Minh Nguyen, *CEO*
EMP: 65 EST: 2022
SALES (est): 5.5MM **Privately Held**
SIC: 2043 Cereal breakfast foods

(P-1420)
EAST WEST TEA COMPANY LLC
Also Called: Golden Temple
1616 Preuss Rd (90035-4212)
PHONE..............................310 275-9891
EMP: 226
SALES (corp-wide): 97.82MM **Privately Held**
Web: www.yogiproducts.com
SIC: 2043 2099 2064 8721 Cereal breakfast foods; Tea blending; Candy and other confectionery products; Billing and bookkeeping service
PA: East West Tea Company, Llc
    1325 Westec Dr
    Eugene OR
    541 461-2160

(P-1421)
INTELLIGENT BLENDS LP
5330 Eastgate Mall (92121-2804)
PHONE..............................858 888-7937
Michael Ishayik, *Pr*
▲ EMP: 38 EST: 2013
SALES (est): 15.05MM **Privately Held**
Web: www.intelligentblends.com
SIC: 2043 Cereal breakfast foods

(P-1422)
JULIANS FOODS LLC
3021 Industry St (92054-4834)
PHONE..............................760 583-9358
EMP: 21
SALES (est): 1.13MM **Privately Held**
SIC: 2043 Granola and muesli, except bars and clusters

(P-1423)
ORGANIC MILLING INC (PA)
505 W Allen Ave (91773-1487)
PHONE..............................800 638-8686
Wolfgang Buehler, *CEO*
Lupe Martinez, *
EMP: 89 EST: 2009
SALES (est): 8.5MM **Privately Held**
Web: www.organicmilling.com
SIC: 2043 Cereal breakfast foods

2045 Prepared Flour Mixes And Doughs

(P-1424)
LANGLOIS COMPANY
Also Called: Langlois Flour Company
10810 San Sevaine Way (91752-1116)
PHONE..............................951 360-3900
Richard W Langlois, *Pr*
Sally Langlois, *
Lynn Langlois Nye, *
▼ EMP: 50 EST: 1950
SQ FT: 48,000
SALES (est): 8.85MM **Privately Held**
Web: www.langloiscompany.com
SIC: 2045 2035 2079 2099 Blended flour: from purchased flour; Mayonnaise; Vegetable refined oils (except corn oil); Gelatin dessert preparations

(P-1425)
POPLA INTERNATIONAL INC
1740 S Sacramento Ave (91761-7744)
PHONE..............................909 923-6899
Mike Shinozaki, *Pr*
Ashley Shinozaki, *
◆ EMP: 41 EST: 1986
SQ FT: 8,000
SALES (est): 4.17MM **Privately Held**
Web: www.popla.com
SIC: 2045 Prepared flour mixes and doughs

2047 Dog And Cat Food

(P-1426)
ARIES PREPARED BEEF COMPANY
11850 Sheldon St (91352-1507)
PHONE..............................818 771-0181
EMP: 18
SALES (corp-wide): 10.06MM **Privately Held**
Web: www.registrar-transfers.com
SIC: 2047 Dog food
PA: Aries Prepared Beef Company
    17 W Magnolia Blvd
    Burbank CA
    818 526-4855

(P-1427)
ARTHUR DOGSWELL LLC (PA)
Also Called: Dogswell
11301 W Olympic Blvd Ste 520 (90064-1603)
PHONE..............................888 559-8833
Brad Casper, *Managing Member*
Gianmarco Giannini, *Managing Member*

PRODUCTS & SVCS

Berenice Officer, *
▲ **EMP:** 33 **EST:** 2003
SQ FT: 2,000
SALES (est): 21.2MM
SALES (corp-wide): 21.2MM **Privately Held**
Web: www.dogswell.com
SIC: 2047 5149 Dog food; Pet foods

(P-1428)
CANINE CAVIAR PET FOODS DE INC
4131 Tigris Way (92503-4844)
PHONE................714 223-1800
Jeff A Baker, *Prin*
EMP: 18 **EST:** 2019
SALES (est): 1.62MM **Privately Held**
Web: www.caninecaviar.com
SIC: 2047 Dog and cat food

(P-1429)
HONEST KITCHEN INC
350 Camino De La Reina Ste 140 (92108)
PHONE................619 544-0018
Michael Greenwell, *CEO*
Jacob Fuller, *
Nathan Kredich, *
Mike Steck, *
EMP: 73 **EST:** 2002
SALES (est): 20.68MM **Privately Held**
Web: www.thehonestkitchen.com
SIC: 2047 Dog and cat food

(P-1430)
J&R TAYLOR BROTHERS ASSOC INC
Also Called: Premium Pet Foods
16321 Arrow Hwy (91706-2018)
PHONE................626 334-9301
Rick Taylor, *Pr*
◆ **EMP:** 58 **EST:** 1967
SALES (est): 23.83MM
SALES (corp-wide): 3.31B **Publicly Held**
SIC: 2047 2048 Dog food; Prepared feeds, nec
PA: Central Garden & Pet Company
1340 Treat Blvd Ste 600
Walnut Creek CA
925 948-4000

(P-1431)
JE RICH COMPANY
Also Called: Sittin Pretty Natural Dog Bky
7225 Edison Ave (91762-7507)
PHONE................909 464-1872
EMP: 21
SALES (corp-wide): 273.93K **Privately Held**
Web: www.adlvet.com
SIC: 2047 Dog and cat food
PA: J.E. Rich Company
7225 Edison Ave
Ontario CA
714 368-1895

(P-1432)
JUSTFOODFORDOGS LLC (PA)
17851 Sky Park Cir Ste A (92614-6113)
PHONE................866 726-9509
Richard Shawn Buckley, *Managing Member*
EMP: 18 **EST:** 2006
SALES (est): 30.8MM
SALES (corp-wide): 30.8MM **Privately Held**
Web: www.justfoodfordogs.com
SIC: 2047 5149 Dog food; Dog food

(P-1433)
MARS PETCARE US INC
2765 Lexington Way (92407-1842)
PHONE................909 887-8131
Ed Skokan, *Mgr*
EMP: 50
SQ FT: 76,000
SALES (corp-wide): 42.84B **Privately Held**
Web: www.marspetcare.com
SIC: 2047 2048 Dog food; Prepared feeds, nec
HQ: Mars Petcare Us, Inc.
2013 Ovation Pkwy
Franklin TN
615 807-4626

(P-1434)
MARS PETCARE US INC
13243 Nutro Way (92395-7789)
PHONE................760 261-7900
EMP: 63
SALES (corp-wide): 42.84B **Privately Held**
Web: www.marspetcare.com
SIC: 2047 Cat food
HQ: Mars Petcare Us, Inc.
2013 Ovation Pkwy
Franklin TN
615 807-4626

(P-1435)
NESTLE PURINA PETCARE COMPANY
800 N Brand Blvd Fl 5 (91203-4281)
PHONE................314 982-1000
EMP: 46
Web: www.purina.com
SIC: 2047 Dog and cat food
HQ: Nestle Purina Petcare Company
800 Chouteau Ave
Saint Louis MO
314 982-1000

(P-1436)
NESTLE PURINA PETCARE COMPANY
Also Called: Nestle Purina Factory
1710 Golden Cat Rd (93252)
PHONE................661 769-8261
Mike Ashmore, *Mgr*
EMP: 125
Web: www.purina.com
SIC: 2047 Dog and cat food
HQ: Nestle Purina Petcare Company
800 Chouteau Ave
Saint Louis MO
314 982-1000

2048 Prepared Feeds, Nec

(P-1437)
A SHOC BEVERAGE LLC
844 Production Pl (92663-2810)
PHONE................949 490-1612
Lance Collins, *Managing Member*
Kyle Ostrowsky, *
EMP: 50 **EST:** 2018
SALES (est): 5.86MM **Privately Held**
Web: www.ashoc.com
SIC: 2048 Mineral feed supplements

(P-1438)
CANINE CAVIAR PET FOODS INC
4131 Tigris Way (92503-4844)
P.O. Box 5872 (92860-8029)
PHONE................714 223-1800
Jeff Baker, *Pr*
Gary Ward, *

◆ **EMP:** 30 **EST:** 1996
SQ FT: 6,000
SALES (est): 5.08MM **Privately Held**
Web: www.caninecaviar.com
SIC: 2048 Canned pet food (except dog and cat)

(P-1439)
DEXT COMPANY OF MARYLAND (DH)
Also Called: Reconserve of Maryland
2811 Wilshire Blvd Ste 410 (90403-4803)
P.O. Box 2211 (90407-2211)
PHONE................310 458-1574
Meyer Luskin, *Ch Bd*
Robert Mcmullen, *Pr*
Rida Hamed, *VP Fin*
Gerald Truelove, *General Vice President*
EMP: 20 **EST:** 1985
SQ FT: 4,000
SALES (est): 8.59MM
SALES (corp-wide): 203.79MM **Privately Held**
SIC: 2048 Prepared feeds, nec
HQ: Reconserve, Inc.
2811 Wilshire Blvd # 410
Santa Monica CA
310 458-1574

(P-1440)
GARMON CORPORATION (PA)
Also Called: Naturvet
27461 Via Industria (92590-3752)
PHONE................888 628-8783
Scott Garmon, *CEO*
Debra O'brien, *CFO*
Jodi Hoefler, *Sec*
▲ **EMP:** 60 **EST:** 1979
SQ FT: 18,500
SALES (est): 24.1MM
SALES (corp-wide): 24.1MM **Privately Held**
Web: www.naturvet.com
SIC: 2048 Feed supplements

(P-1441)
HARBOR GREEN GRAIN LP
13181 Crossroads Pkwy N Ste 200 (91746)
PHONE................310 991-8089
Shing Lo, *Pr*
Zach Xu, *CEO*
Kevin Yoon, *COO*
◆ **EMP:** 45 **EST:** 2014
SALES (est): 4.96MM **Privately Held**
SIC: 2048 Alfalfa, cubed

(P-1442)
HRK PET FOOD PRODUCTS INC
12924 Pierce St (91331-2526)
PHONE................818 897-2521
Joey Herrick, *Pr*
Lynnda Herrick, *VP*
▲ **EMP:** 19 **EST:** 1999
SQ FT: 30,000
SALES (est): 628.71K **Privately Held**
SIC: 2048 Canned pet food (except dog and cat)

(P-1443)
INTERNATIONAL PROCESSING CORP (DH)
233 Wilshire Blvd Ste 310 (90401-1206)
P.O. Box 2211 (90407-2211)
PHONE................310 458-1574
Bob Mcmullen, *Pr*
EMP: 25 **EST:** 1953
SALES (est): 41.3MM
SALES (corp-wide): 203.79MM **Privately Held**

SIC: 2048 Prepared feeds, nec
HQ: Reconserve, Inc.
2811 Wilshire Blvd # 410
Santa Monica CA
310 458-1574

(P-1444)
LEGACY EPOCH LLC
21011 Warner Center Ln Ste A (91367-6509)
PHONE................844 673-7305
Shawn Lipman, *CEO*
Gary Puterman, *
Robert Roizen, *
Brian Roizen, *Chief Architect**
Igor Roizen, *Chief Scientist**
EMP: 83 **EST:** 2015
SALES (est): 12.47MM
SALES (corp-wide): 279.07MM **Publicly Held**
Web: www.feedonomics.com
SIC: 2048 Chicken feeds, prepared
PA: Bigcommerce Holdings, Inc.
11305 Four Points Dr I
Austin TX
512 865-4500

(P-1445)
MANCHESTER FEEDS INC (PA)
Also Called: Manchester Feeds San Marcos
1520 E Barham Dr (92078-4505)
P.O. Box 1987 (92572-1987)
PHONE................714 637-7062
William Richard Cramer, *Pr*
Bertrum Bonner, *Treas*
EMP: 19 **EST:** 1962
SQ FT: 7,542
SALES (est): 2.62MM
SALES (corp-wide): 2.62MM **Privately Held**
Web: www.manchesterfeeds.com
SIC: 2048 Chicken feeds, prepared

(P-1446)
NATURAL BALANCE PET FOODS LLC (PA)
2358 University Ave Ste 2280 (92104-2720)
P.O. Box 397 (91785-0397)
PHONE................800 829-4493
Brian Connolly, *CEO*
▲ **EMP:** 64 **EST:** 1989
SQ FT: 55,000
SALES (est): 29.94MM **Privately Held**
SIC: 2048 5199 Prepared feeds, nec; Pet supplies

(P-1447)
NATURAL BALANCE PET FOODS INC
Also Called: NATURAL BALANCE PET FOODS, INC.
1224 Montague Unit 1 (91331)
PHONE................800 829-4493
EMP: 68
SIC: 2048 Prepared feeds, nec
PA: Natural Balance Pet Foods, Llc
2358 University Ave # 2280
San Diego CA

(P-1448)
RECONSERVE INC (HQ)
Also Called: Dext Company
2811 Wilshire Blvd Ste 410 (90403-4803)
P.O. Box 2211 (90407-2211)
PHONE................310 458-1574
Meyer Luskin, *CEO*
David Luskin, *
EMP: 25 **EST:** 1966
SQ FT: 5,000

SALES (est): 160.91MM
SALES (corp-wide): 203.79MM **Privately Held**
Web: www.reconserve.com
SIC: **2048** Livestock feeds
PA: Scope Industries
2811 Wilshire Blvd # 410
Santa Monica CA
310 458-1574

(P-1449)
STAR MILLING CO
23901 Water St (92570-9094)
P.O. Box 1987 (92572-1987)
PHONE..................................951 657-3143
William R Cramer Junior, *Pr*
Paul R Cramer, *
Greg W Carls, *
◆ EMP: 118 EST: 1952
SALES (est): 41.06MM **Privately Held**
Web: www.starmilling.com
SIC: **2048** Poultry feeds

(P-1450)
SUN-GRO COMMODITIES INC (PA)
34575 Famoso Rd (93308-9769)
PHONE..................................661 393-2612
Donald G Smith, *CEO*
Scott Smith, *
Lori Melendez, *
Wendy Smith, *
EMP: 25 EST: 1974
SQ FT: 1,400
SALES (est): 3.88MM
SALES (corp-wide): 3.88MM **Privately Held**
Web: www.sun-gro.com
SIC: **2048 4212** Livestock feeds; Local trucking, without storage

---

2051 Bread, Cake, And Related Products

(P-1451)
BAKE R US INC
Also Called: Dave's Baking Goods
2632 Wilshire Blvd Ste 463 (90403-4623)
PHONE..................................310 630-5873
EMP: 178
SALES (corp-wide): 2.37MM **Privately Held**
SIC: **2051** Doughnuts, except frozen
PA: Bake R Us, Inc.
13400 S Western Ave
Gardena CA
310 630-5873

(P-1452)
BAKED IN THE SUN
Also Called: S & S Bakery
2560 Progress St (92081-8465)
PHONE..................................760 591-9045
EMP: 250
Web: www.bakedinthesun.com
SIC: **2051** Bagels, fresh or frozen

(P-1453)
BAKERS KNEADED LLC
148 W 132nd St Ste D (90061-1649)
PHONE..................................310 819-8700
Carlos Enriquez, *CEO*
Carlos Enriquez, *Managing Member*
Paul Cox, *
EMP: 28 EST: 2017
SALES (est): 2.24MM **Privately Held**
SIC: **2051** Bread, all types (white, wheat, rye, etc); fresh or frozen

(P-1454)
BESTWAY SANDWICHES INC (PA)
28209 Avenue Stanford (91355-3984)
PHONE..................................818 361-1800
EMP: 46 EST: 2008
SALES (est): 9.71MM **Privately Held**
SIC: **2051** Bread, all types (white, wheat, rye, etc); fresh or frozen

(P-1455)
BIMBO BAKERIES USA INC
Also Called: Bimbo Bakeries USA, Inc
480 S Vail Ave (90640-4947)
PHONE..................................323 720-6099
Edgar Jaramillo, *Brnch Mgr*
EMP: 18
Web: www.bimbobakeriesusa.com
SIC: **2051** Bakery: wholesale or wholesale/retail combined
HQ: Bimbo Bakeries Usa, Inc.
255 Business Center Dr # 200
Horsham PA
215 347-5500

(P-1456)
BRILL INC
2111 W Valley Blvd (92324-1814)
PHONE..................................909 825-7343
EMP: 184
Web: www.risebakingcompany.com
SIC: **2051 2053** Bread, cake, and related products; Pies, bakery; frozen
HQ: Brill, Inc.
1912 Montreal Rd
Tucker GA

(P-1457)
BUBBLES BAKING COMPANY
15215 Keswick St (91405-1014)
P.O. Box 2a (93287-0002)
PHONE..................................818 786-1700
FAX: 818 786-3617
EMP: 50
SQ FT: 23,000
SALES (est): 13.38MM **Privately Held**
SIC: **2051** Cakes, bakery: except frozen

(P-1458)
CALIFORNIA CHURROS CORPORATION
751 Via Lata (92324-3930)
PHONE..................................909 370-4777
Jorge D Martinez, *CEO*
Jorge D Martinez Senior, *Pr*
Eva A Martinez, *
Frank Ruvalcaba, *
EMP: 251 EST: 1980
SQ FT: 54,800
SALES (est): 2.93MM
SALES (corp-wide): 1.56B **Publicly Held**
Web: www.churros.com
SIC: **2051** Pastries, e.g. danish: except frozen
HQ: J & J Snack Foods Corp. Of California
5353 S Downey Rd
Vernon CA
323 581-0171

(P-1459)
CORBIN-HILL INC
Also Called: Corbin Foods
2961 W Macarthur Blvd Ste 117 (92704-6913)
P.O. Box 28139 (92799-8139)
PHONE..................................714 966-6695
Jl Corbin, *Ch Bd*
A Moreno, *
R W Carlyle, *

Karen Kelley, *
EMP: 23 EST: 1982
SQ FT: 20,000
SALES (est): 864.7K **Privately Held**
SIC: **2051** Bread, cake, and related products

(P-1460)
DANISH BAKING CO INC
Also Called: Bubbles Baking Company
15215 Keswick St (91405-1014)
PHONE..................................818 786-1700
EMP: 70
SIC: **2051** Bread, cake, and related products

(P-1461)
DAWN FOOD PRODUCTS INC
15601 Mosher Ave Ste 230 (92780-6426)
PHONE..................................714 258-1223
Joe Barsoppi, *Genl Mgr*
EMP: 150
SALES (corp-wide): 1.73B **Privately Held**
Web: www.dawnfoods.com
SIC: **2051** Pastries, e.g. danish: except frozen
HQ: Dawn Food Products, Inc.
3333 Sargent Rd
Jackson MI

(P-1462)
DISTINCT INDULGENCE INC
Also Called: Mrs Appletree's Bakery
5018 Lante St (91706-1839)
PHONE..................................818 546-1700
Robert W Gray, *Pr*
Suzanne Gray, *
▲ EMP: 38 EST: 1985
SQ FT: 10,000
SALES (est): 7.8MM **Privately Held**
Web: www.mrsappletree.com
SIC: **2051 5499** Bakery: wholesale or wholesale/retail combined; Health and dietetic food stores

(P-1463)
EL METATE INC
Also Called: El Metate Market
817 W 19th St (92627-3518)
PHONE..................................949 646-9362
Brian Murrieta, *Brnch Mgr*
EMP: 190
SALES (corp-wide): 24.5MM **Privately Held**
Web: www.elmetate.com
SIC: **2051 2052 2099 5812** Breads, rolls, and buns; Cookies; Tortillas, fresh or refrigerated; Mexican restaurant
PA: El Metate, Inc.
838 E 1st St
Santa Ana CA
714 542-3913

(P-1464)
EL SEGUNDO BREAD BAR LLC
Also Called: Bread Bar
701 E El Segundo Blvd (90245-4108)
PHONE..................................310 615-9898
Myrna Al-midani, *Managing Member*
▲ EMP: 32 EST: 2004
SQ FT: 8,000
SALES (est): 2.43MM **Privately Held**
Web: www.breadbar.la
SIC: **2051 5149** Bread, all types (white, wheat, rye, etc); fresh or frozen; Bakery products

(P-1465)
FEEMSTER CO INC
Also Called: Some Crust Bakery
119 Yale Ave (91711-4723)
PHONE..................................909 621-9772

Larry Feemster, *Pr*
Sandra Feemster, *
EMP: 17 EST: 1997
SQ FT: 3,000
SALES (est): 865.49K **Privately Held**
Web: www.somecrust.com
SIC: **2051 5461** Bread, cake, and related products; Retail bakeries

(P-1466)
FIESTA MEXICAN FOODS INC
979 G St (92227-2615)
PHONE..................................760 344-3580
Raymond Armenta, *Pr*
EMP: 30 EST: 1956
SQ FT: 4,000
SALES (est): 2.5MM **Privately Held**
SIC: **2051 2099** Pastries, e.g. danish: except frozen; Tortillas, fresh or refrigerated

(P-1467)
FLOWERS BKG CO HENDERSON LLC
21540 Blythe St (91304-4910)
PHONE..................................818 884-8970
EMP: 63
SALES (corp-wide): 4.81B **Publicly Held**
Web: www.flowersfoods.com
SIC: **2051** Breads, rolls, and buns
HQ: Flowers Baking Co. Of Henderson, Llc
501 Conestoga Way
Henderson NV
702 567-6401

(P-1468)
FLOWERS BKG CO HENDERSON LLC
3800 W Century Blvd (90303-1011)
PHONE..................................310 695-9846
EMP: 63
SALES (corp-wide): 4.81B **Publicly Held**
Web: www.flowersfoods.com
SIC: **2051** Breads, rolls, and buns
HQ: Flowers Baking Co. Of Henderson, Llc
501 Conestoga Way
Henderson NV
702 567-6401

(P-1469)
FOOD FOR LIFE BAKING CO INC (PA)
Also Called: Natural Food Mill
2991 Doherty St (92879-5811)
P.O. Box 1434 (92878-1434)
PHONE..................................951 273-3031
R James Torres, *Pr*
Charles Torres, *
▲ EMP: 100 EST: 1970
SQ FT: 170,000
SALES (est): 24.55MM
SALES (corp-wide): 24.55MM **Privately Held**
Web: www.foodforlife.com
SIC: **2051** Bakery: wholesale or wholesale/retail combined

(P-1470)
FRESH START BAKERIES INC
Also Called: Fresh Start Bakeries N Amer
145 S State College Blvd Ste 200 (92821)
PHONE..................................714 256-8900
▲ EMP: 600
SIC: **2051** Bread, cake, and related products

(P-1471)
FRISCO BAKING COMPANY INC
Also Called: Frisco Baking Company
621 W Avenue 26 (90065-1095)
PHONE..................................323 225-6111

PRODUCTS & SVCS

Aldo Pricco Junior, *CEO*
James Pricco, *
Ronald Perata, *
John Pricco, *
Mary Anne Fetter, *
EMP: 115 **EST:** 1938
SQ FT: 18,000
SALES (est): 9.11MM **Privately Held**
Web: www.friscobakingcompany.com
SIC: 2051 Bread, all types (white, wheat, rye, etc); fresh or frozen

(P-1472)
FUSION FOOD FACTORY
Also Called: La Jolla Baking Co
8980 Crestmar Pt (92121-3222)
PHONE......................858 578-8001
Steve Kwon, *Pr*
EMP: 19 **EST:** 1998
SALES (est): 909.78K **Privately Held**
SIC: 2051 Bread, cake, and related products

(P-1473)
GIULIANO-PAGANO CORPORATION
Also Called: Giuliano's Bakery
1264 E Walnut St (90746-1319)
PHONE......................310 537-7700
Nancy Ritmire Giuliano, *Ch Bd*
Gregory Ritmire, *
EMP: 100 **EST:** 1952
SQ FT: 40,000
SALES (est): 24.25MM **Privately Held**
SIC: 2051 Bakery: wholesale or wholesale/retail combined

(P-1474)
GLOBAL IMPACT INV PARTNERS LLC
1410 Westwood Blvd Apt 260 (90024-4974)
PHONE......................310 592-2000
EMP: 25 **EST:** 2014
SQ FT: 16,400
SALES (est): 977.37K **Privately Held**
SIC: 2051 Cakes, bakery: except frozen

(P-1475)
GOLD COAST BAKING COMPANY LLC (PA)
Also Called: Kanan Baking Company
21250 Califa St Ste 104 (91367-5040)
PHONE......................818 575-7280
Edward H Rogers Iii, *CEO*
EMP: 57 **EST:** 2003
SQ FT: 60,000
SALES (est): 45.39MM **Privately Held**
Web: www.goldcoastbakery.com
SIC: 2051 Bakery: wholesale or wholesale/retail combined

(P-1476)
GOLD COAST BAKING COMPANY INC
Also Called: Gold Coast Baking Company, Inc.
1590 E Saint Gertrude Pl (92705-5310)
PHONE......................714 545-2253
EMP: 26
Web: www.goldcoastbakery.com
SIC: 2051 Bread, cake, and related products
PA: Gold Coast Baking Company, Llc
21250 Califa St Ste 104
Woodland Hills CA

(P-1477)
HANNAHMAX BAKING INC
14601 S Main St (90248-1916)
PHONE......................310 380-6778
Joanne Adirim, *CEO*

Stuart Scwartz, *
EMP: 145 **EST:** 1993
SQ FT: 15,000
SALES (est): 8.65MM **Privately Held**
Web: www.hannahmax.com
SIC: 2051 Bakery: wholesale or wholesale/retail combined

(P-1478)
JEANNINES BKG CO SANTA BARBARA (PA)
Also Called: Jeannine's Bakery
3607 State St (93105-2521)
P.O. Box 8929 (93118-8929)
PHONE......................805 687-8701
EMP: 19 **EST:** 1991
SQ FT: 1,800
SALES (est): 4.52MM **Privately Held**
Web: www.jeannines.com
SIC: 2051 5812 Bread, cake, and related products; American restaurant

(P-1479)
LAURAS ORGNAL BSTON BRWNIES IN
Also Called: Bhu Food
2735 Cactus Rd Ste 101 (92154-8024)
PHONE......................619 855-3258
Laura Katleman, *CEO*
EMP: 18 **EST:** 2013
SQ FT: 4,000
SALES (est): 2.84MM **Privately Held**
Web: www.bhufoods.com
SIC: 2051 2052 Bread, cake, and related products; Cookies and crackers

(P-1480)
LAVASH CORPORATION OF AMERICA
Also Called: Toneonel Lavash
2835 Newell St (90039-3817)
PHONE......................323 663-5249
Edmond Hartounin, *Pr*
EMP: 25 **EST:** 1980
SQ FT: 10,000
SALES (est): 2.44MM **Privately Held**
Web: www.organicflatbread.net
SIC: 2051 Bakery: wholesale or wholesale/retail combined

(P-1481)
LITTLE BROTHERS BAKERY LLC
Also Called: Little Brothers Bakery
320 W Alondra Blvd (90248-2423)
PHONE......................310 225-3790
Paul C Giuliano, *Managing Member*
Anthony S Giuliano, *
Joann Giuliano, *
▲ **EMP:** 65 **EST:** 1999
SQ FT: 15,000
SALES (est): 9.86MM **Privately Held**
Web: www.littlebrothersbakery.com
SIC: 2051 5149 Bakery: wholesale or wholesale/retail combined; Bakery products

(P-1482)
LUPITAS BAKERY INC (PA)
1848 W Florence Ave (90047-2123)
PHONE......................323 752-2391
Able Diaz, *Pr*
Martha Diaz, *Sec*
EMP: 18 **EST:** 1985
SQ FT: 8,000
SALES (est): 1.78MM
SALES (corp-wide): 1.78MM **Privately Held**
Web: www.mylupitasbakery.com

SIC: 2051 5461 Bread, all types (white, wheat, rye, etc); fresh or frozen; Bread

(P-1483)
MOCHI ICE CREAM COMPANY LLC (PA)
Also Called: Mikawaya
5563 Alcoa Ave (90058-3730)
PHONE......................323 587-5504
Jerry Bucan, *CEO*
Joel Friedman, *Ofcr*
◆ **EMP:** 30 **EST:** 1910
SQ FT: 10,000
SALES (est): 19.62MM
SALES (corp-wide): 19.62MM **Privately Held**
Web: www.mymochi.com
SIC: 2051 2024 5451 Cakes, pies, and pastries; Ice cream and frozen deserts; Ice cream (packaged)

(P-1484)
MRS REDDS PIE CO INC
150 S La Cadena Dr (92324-3416)
P.O. Box 555 (92324-0555)
PHONE......................909 825-4800
Tom P Telliard, *Pr*
Nick Telliard, *VP*
EMP: 20 **EST:** 1956
SQ FT: 76,030
SALES (est): 2.51MM **Privately Held**
SIC: 2051 Cakes, bakery: except frozen

(P-1485)
NE-MOS
416 N Hale Ave (92029-1420)
PHONE......................800 325-2692
Ed Smith, *Prin*
EMP: 17 **EST:** 2010
SALES (est): 5.21MM **Privately Held**
SIC: 2051 Bakery: wholesale or wholesale/retail combined

(P-1486)
NOUSHIG INC
Also Called: Amoretti
451 Lombard St (93030-5143)
PHONE......................805 983-2903
Jack Barsoumian, *CEO*
Hayop L Barsoumian, *Pr*
Maral Barsoumian, *Sec*
◆ **EMP:** 50 **EST:** 1998
SQ FT: 10,000
SALES (est): 10.86MM **Privately Held**
Web: www.amoretti.com
SIC: 2051 5149 Bread, cake, and related products; Soft drinks

(P-1487)
OAKHURST INDUSTRIES INC (PA)
Also Called: Freund Baking
2050 S Tubeway Ave (90040-1624)
P.O. Box 911457 (90091-1238)
PHONE......................323 724-3000
James Freund, *Pr*
Ronald Martin, *
Jonathan Freund, *
Linda F Freund, *
EMP: 140 **EST:** 1981
SQ FT: 81,000
SALES (est): 51.88MM **Privately Held**
Web: www.oakhurstmetals.com
SIC: 2051 5149 Buns, bread type: fresh or frozen; Groceries and related products, nec

(P-1488)
ORANGE BAKERY INC (HQ)
17751 Cowan (92614-6064)

PHONE......................949 863-1377
Yukinobu Saito, *CEO*
Yokinobu Saito, *
Mikio Kobayashi, *
Yoshiaki Okazaki, *
Kota Ueki, *
▲ **EMP:** 19 **EST:** 1978
SQ FT: 45,000
SALES (est): 49.04MM **Privately Held**
Web: www.orangebakery.com
SIC: 2051 Bread, cake, and related products
PA: Rheon Automatic Machinery Co.,Ltd.
2-3, Nozawamachi
Utsunomiya TCG

(P-1489)
PASCAL PATISSERIE
21040 Victory Blvd (91367-2601)
PHONE......................818 712-9375
Bruno Marcy, *Pr*
EMP: 18 **EST:** 2015
SALES (est): 1.5MM **Privately Held**
SIC: 2051 Bakery: wholesale or wholesale/retail combined

(P-1490)
PYRENEES FRENCH BAKERY INC
717 E 21st St (93305-5240)
P.O. Box 3626 (93385-3626)
PHONE......................661 322-7159
Marianne Laxague, *Pr*
Juanita Laxague, *
EMP: 20 **EST:** 1945
SQ FT: 33,750
SALES (est): 879.98K **Privately Held**
Web: www.pyreneesfrenchbakery.com
SIC: 2051 5461 Bakery: wholesale or wholesale/retail combined; Retail bakeries

(P-1491)
ROSSMOOR PASTRIES MGT INC
2325 Redondo Ave (90755-4019)
PHONE......................562 498-2253
Charles Feder, *CEO*
Janice Ahlgren, *
EMP: 80 **EST:** 2000
SALES (est): 9.32MM **Privately Held**
Web: www.rossmoorpastries.com
SIC: 2051 Bread, cake, and related products

(P-1492)
SGB BETTER BAKING CO LLC
14528 Blythe St (91402-6006)
PHONE......................818 787-9992
Chris Botticella, *CEO*
Ash Aghasi, *
EMP: 57 **EST:** 2019
SALES (est): 6.14MM
SALES (corp-wide): 22.62MM **Privately Held**
SIC: 2051 5149 Bakery: wholesale or wholesale/retail combined; Bakery products
PA: Surge Global Bakeries Holdings Llc
13336 Paxton St
Pacoima CA
818 896-0525

(P-1493)
SGB BUBBLES BAKING CO LLC
15215 Keswick St (91405-1014)
PHONE......................818 786-1700
Lewis Sharp, *
EMP: 100 **EST:** 2019
SQ FT: 50,000
SALES (est): 10.21MM **Privately Held**
SIC: 2051 5461 Bread, cake, and related products; Retail bakeries

(P-1494)
SUGAR FOODS LLC
6190 E Slauson Ave (90040-3010)
PHONE.................................323 727-8290
EMP: 100
SALES (corp-wide): 286.33MM **Privately Held**
Web: www.sugarfoods.com
SIC: 2051 2052 2099 Bread, cake, and related products; Cookies and crackers; Food preparations, nec
PA: Sugar Foods Llc
3059 Townsgate Rd Ste 101
Westlake Village CA
805 396-5000

(P-1495)
TALLGRASS PICTURES LLC
Also Called: Izola
710 13th St Ste 300 (92101-7351)
PHONE.................................619 227-2701
Jeffrey Lamont Brown, *Managing Member*
EMP: 29 **EST:** 2004
SALES (est): 2.5MM **Privately Held**
Web: www.izolabakery.com
SIC: 2051 Bakery: wholesale or wholesale/retail combined

(P-1496)
UNITED STATES BAKERY
Also Called: Franz Family Bakeries
457 E Martin Luther King Jr Blvd
(90011-5650)
PHONE.................................323 232-6124
EMP: 29
SALES (corp-wide): 497.81MM **Privately Held**
Web: www.franzbakery.com
SIC: 2051 Bread, cake, and related products
PA: United States Bakery
315 Ne 10th Ave
Portland OR
503 232-2191

(P-1497)
VBC HOLDINGS INC
134 Main St (90245-3801)
PHONE.................................310 322-7357
James N Desisto, *CEO*
Larry De Sisto, *
EMP: 40 **EST:** 1959
SQ FT: 35,000
SALES (est): 4.87MM **Privately Held**
Web: www.venicebakery.com
SIC: 2051 5149 Bread, all types (white, wheat, rye, etc); fresh or frozen; Baking supplies

(P-1498)
VURGER CO (USA) CORP ✪
1800 Century Park E Ste 600 (90067-1501)
PHONE.................................929 318-9546
Rachel Hugh, *CEO*
EMP: 50 **EST:** 2022
SALES (est): 1.44MM **Privately Held**
SIC: 2051 Bakery: wholesale or wholesale/retail combined

(P-1499)
WESTERN BAGEL BAKING CORP
21749 Ventura Blvd (91364-1835)
PHONE.................................818 887-5451
Tim Brennen, *Prin*
EMP: 26
SALES (corp-wide): 60.98MM **Privately Held**
Web: www.westernbagel.com

SIC: 2051 5461 Bagels, fresh or frozen; Bagels
PA: Western Bagel Baking Corp
7814 Sepulveda Blvd
Van Nuys CA
818 786-5847

(P-1500)
WESTERN BAGEL BAKING CORP (PA)
7814 Sepulveda Blvd (91405-1020)
PHONE.................................818 786-5847
Steven Ustin, *Pr*
▼ **EMP:** 225 **EST:** 1946
SQ FT: 23,500
SALES (est): 60.98MM
SALES (corp-wide): 60.98MM **Privately Held**
Web: www.westernbagel.com
SIC: 2051 5461 Bagels, fresh or frozen; Bagels

2052 Cookies And Crackers

(P-1501)
ADRIENNES GOURMET FOODS
849 Ward Dr (93111-2920)
PHONE.................................805 964-6848
▲ **EMP:** 60
SIC: 2052 2099 2098 Cookies and crackers; Food preparations, nec; Macaroni and spaghetti

(P-1502)
AMAYS BAKERY & NOODLE CO INC (PA)
837 E Commercial St (90012-3413)
PHONE.................................213 626-2713
Kee Hom, *CEO*
▲ **EMP:** 63 **EST:** 1968
SQ FT: 20,000
SALES (est): 9.6MM
SALES (corp-wide): 9.6MM **Privately Held**
Web: www.amaysbakery.com
SIC: 2052 2098 Cookies; Noodles (e.g. egg, plain, and water), dry

(P-1503)
ASPIRE BAKERIES HOLDCO LLC (HQ)
6701 Center Dr W Ste 850 (90045-1695)
PHONE.................................844 992-7747
Tyson Yu, *Pr*
Didier Vinamont, *
Chris Woo, *
EMP: 86 **EST:** 2021
SALES (est): 1.61B
SALES (corp-wide): 1.77B **Privately Held**
SIC: 2052 2053 2051 Cookies; Frozen bakery products, except bread; Cakes, pies, and pastries
PA: Goldberg Lindsay & Co. Llc
630 5th Ave Fl 30
New York NY
212 651-1100

(P-1504)
ASPIRE BAKERIES HOLDINGS LLC (DH)
6701 Center Dr W Ste 850 (90045-1695)
PHONE.................................844 992-7747
Tyson Yu, *Pr*
Didier Vinamont, *CFO*
Chris Woo, *Sec*
EMP: 19 **EST:** 2021
SALES (est): 1.61B
SALES (corp-wide): 1.77B **Privately Held**

SIC: 2052 2053 2051 Cookies; Frozen bakery products, except bread; Cakes, pies, and pastries
HQ: Aspire Bakeries Midco Llc
6701 Center Dr W Ste 850
Los Angeles CA
844 992-7747

(P-1505)
ASPIRE BAKERIES LLC (DH)
6701 Center Dr W Ste 850 (90045-1695)
PHONE.................................844 992-7747
Tyson Yu, *CEO*
◆ **EMP:** 235 **EST:** 1977
SQ FT: 90,000
SALES (est): 1.6B
SALES (corp-wide): 1.77B **Privately Held**
Web: www.aspirebakeries.com
SIC: 2052 2053 2051 Cookies; Frozen bakery products, except bread; Cakes, pies, and pastries
HQ: Aspire Bakeries Holdings Llc
6701 Center Dr W Ste 850
Los Angeles CA
844 992-7747

(P-1506)
ASPIRE BAKERIES LLC
15963 Strathern St (91406-1313)
PHONE.................................818 904-8230
Marcus Garcia, *Brnch Mgr*
EMP: 233
SALES (corp-wide): 1.77B **Privately Held**
Web: www.aspirebakeries.com
SIC: 2052 Cookies
HQ: Aspire Bakeries Llc
6701 Center Dr W Ste 850
Los Angeles CA
844 992-7747

(P-1507)
ASPIRE BAKERIES LLC
357 W Santa Ana Ave (92316-2901)
PHONE.................................714 478-4656
Armando Villalpando, *Mgr*
EMP: 111
SALES (corp-wide): 1.77B **Privately Held**
Web: www.aspirebakeries.com
SIC: 2052 Cookies
HQ: Aspire Bakeries Llc
6701 Center Dr W Ste 850
Los Angeles CA
844 992-7747

(P-1508)
ASPIRE BAKERIES MIDCO LLC (DH)
6701 Center Dr W Ste 850 (90045-1695)
PHONE.................................844 992-7747
Tyson Yu, *Pr*
Didier Vinamont, *
Chris Woo, *
EMP: 17 **EST:** 2021
SALES (est): 1.61B
SALES (corp-wide): 1.77B **Privately Held**
SIC: 2052 2053 2051 Cookies; Frozen bakery products, except bread; Cakes, pies, and pastries
HQ: Aspire Bakeries Holdco Llc
6701 Center Dr W Ste 850
Los Angeles CA
844 992-7747

(P-1509)
BETTER BAKERY LLC
Also Called: Better Bakery Co
444 E Santa Clara St (93001-2749)
PHONE.................................661 294-9882
EMP: 212

SIC: 2052 Bakery products, dry

(P-1510)
BISCOMERICA CORP
565 West Slover Ave (92377)
P.O. Box 1070 (92377-1070)
PHONE.................................909 877-5997
Nadi Soltan, *Ch Bd*
Ayad Fargo, *
◆ **EMP:** 252 **EST:** 1979
SQ FT: 250,000
SALES (est): 71.62MM **Privately Held**
Web: www.biscomericacorp.com
SIC: 2052 2064 Cookies; Candy and other confectionery products

(P-1511)
BLOOMFIELD BAKERS
Also Called: Bloomfield Bakers
10711 Bloomfield St (90720-2503)
PHONE.................................626 610-2253
William R Ross, *Genl Pt*
Gary Marx, *Brnch Mgr*
▼ **EMP:** 600 **EST:** 1992
SQ FT: 75,000
SALES (est): 104.92MM
SALES (corp-wide): 3.45B **Publicly Held**
Web: www.bloomfieldbakers.com
SIC: 2052 2064 Cookies; Candy and other confectionery products
HQ: Treehouse Private Brands, Inc.
2021 Spring Rd Ste 600
Oak Brook IL

(P-1512)
CHARLIES SPECIALTIES INC
501 Airpark Dr (92833-2501)
PHONE.................................724 346-2350
Jay Thier, *Pr*
Edward G Byrnes Junior, *Ch*
Thomas C Byrnes, *
EMP: 108 **EST:** 1967
SALES (est): 981.63K
SALES (corp-wide): 38.32MM **Privately Held**
SIC: 2052 5149 5142 2045 Cookies; Groceries and related products, nec; Packaged frozen goods; Prepared flour mixes and doughs
PA: Byrnes And Kiefer Company
131 Kline Ave
Callery PA
724 538-5200

(P-1513)
CRUMBL COOKIES
23702 El Toro Rd Ste B (92630-8905)
PHONE.................................949 519-0791
Spencer Hanks, *Owner*
EMP: 70 **EST:** 2021
SALES (est): 1.7MM **Privately Held**
Web: www.crumblcookies.com
SIC: 2052 Cookies

(P-1514)
D F STAUFFER BISCUIT CO INC
Laguna Cookie Company
4041 W Garry Ave (92704-6315)
PHONE.................................714 546-6855
Albert Ovalle, *Mgr*
EMP: 50
Web: www.meijiamerica.com
SIC: 2052 Cookies
HQ: D F Stauffer Biscuit Co Inc
360 S Belmont St
York PA
717 815-4600

P
R
O
D
U
C
T
S

&

S
V
C
S

(P-1515)
DIBELLA BAKING COMPANY INC
Also Called: Dibella
3524 Seagate Way Ste 110 (92056-2673)
PHONE...................................951 797-4144
EMP: 65
Web: www.dibellafamiglia.com
SIC: 2052 Cookies

(P-1516)
ELEMENTS FOOD GROUP INC
5560 Brooks St (91763-4522)
P.O. Box 4020 (92661-4020)
PHONE...................................909 983-2011
Wayne Sorensen, *Pr*
EMP: 60 **EST:** 2004
SQ FT: 23,000
SALES (est): 7.21MM **Privately Held**
Web: www.elementsfoods.com
SIC: 2052 2038 Bakery products, dry;
Breakfasts, frozen and packaged

(P-1517)
FANTASY COOKIE CORPORATION (PA)
Also Called: Fantasy Cookie Company
12322 Gladstone Ave (91342-5318)
PHONE...................................818 361-6901
▲ **EMP:** 34 **EST:** 1979
SALES (est): 11.44MM
SALES (corp-wide): 11.44MM **Privately Held**
Web: www.fantasycookie.com
SIC: 2052 Cookies and crackers

(P-1518)
GRANDVILLE LLC
Also Called: Jihwaja Rice Bakery
1670 Cordova St (90007-1112)
PHONE...................................213 382-3878
EMP: 26
SALES (corp-wide): 373.44K **Privately Held**
SIC: 2052 Rice cakes
PA: Grandville, Llc.
1001 S Vermont Ave # 110
Los Angeles CA
213 382-3878

(P-1519)
INTERNTNAL DESSERTS DELICACIES (PA)
Also Called: Cookie Lovers
4700 District Blvd (90058-2714)
PHONE...................................818 549-0056
Robbie Jacobs, *Pr*
Bonnie Jacobs, *VP*
Jeffrey Jacobs, *Sec*
EMP: 18 **EST:** 1983
SQ FT: 4,000
SALES (est): 4.64MM
SALES (corp-wide): 4.64MM **Privately Held**
Web:
www.uncleeddiesvegancookies.com
SIC: 2052 Cookies

(P-1520)
J & J SNACK FOODS CORP CAL (HQ)
5353 S Downey Rd (90058-3725)
PHONE...................................323 581-0171
Dennis Moore, *VP*
▲ **EMP:** 112 **EST:** 1978
SQ FT: 132,000
SALES (est): 103.41MM
SALES (corp-wide): 1.56B **Publicly Held**
Web: www.jjsnack.com

SIC: 2052 5149 Pretzels; Cookies
PA: J & J Snack Foods Corp.
350 Fellowship Rd
Mount Laurel NJ
856 665-9533

(P-1521)
LAGUNA COOKIE COMPANY INC
4041 W Garry Ave (92704-6315)
PHONE...................................714 546-6855
Takeshi Izumi, *CEO*
EMP: 100 **EST:** 1981
SQ FT: 55,000
SALES (est): 28.39MM **Privately Held**
SIC: 2052 Cookies
HQ: D F Stauffer Biscuit Co Inc
360 S Belmont St
York PA
717 815-4600

(P-1522)
PAK GROUP LLC
Also Called: Dellarise
236 N Chester Ave Ste 200 (91106-5166)
PHONE...................................626 316-6555
Walter Postelwait, *Managing Member*
▲ **EMP:** 24 **EST:** 2012
SQ FT: 6,200
SALES (est): 2.5MM
SALES (corp-wide): 2.5MM **Privately Held**
Web: www.bellarise.com
SIC: 2052 2099 5149 Bakery products, dry;
Food preparations, nec; Yeast
PA: Tech Us Corp
236 N Chester Ave Ste 200
Pasadena CA
626 316-6555

(P-1523)
PHENIX GOURMET LLC
Also Called: Monaco Baking Company
4225 N Palm St (92835-1045)
PHONE...................................562 404-5028
▲ **EMP:** 135
SIC: 2052 Cookies

(P-1524)
SOUTH COAST BAKING LLC (PA)
Also Called: South Coast Baking Co.
1711 Kettering (92614-5615)
PHONE...................................949 851-9654
Kent Hayden, *CEO*
Rick Ptak, *
◆ **EMP:** 55 **EST:** 2011
SALES (est): 88.26MM **Privately Held**
SIC: 2052 5149 Cookies; Cookies

(P-1525)
UTBBB INC
10711 Bloomfield St (90720-2503)
PHONE...................................562 594-4411
Gary Marks, *CEO*
William R Ross, *
Gene Kester, *
◆ **EMP:** 92 **EST:** 1985
SQ FT: 1,000
SALES (est): 3.94MM
SALES (corp-wide): 3.45B **Publicly Held**
SIC: 2052 5141 Cookies and crackers; Food brokers
HQ: Treehouse Private Brands, Inc.
2021 Spring Rd Ste 600
Oak Brook IL

2053 Frozen Bakery Products, Except Bread

(P-1526)
BONERTS INCORPORATED
Also Called: Bonert's Slice of Pie
3144 W Adams St (92704-5808)
PHONE...................................714 540-3535
Tim Rooney, *Mgr*
EMP: 50
Web: www.bonertspies.com
SIC: 2053 2051 Frozen bakery products,
except bread; Bread, cake, and related products
PA: Bonert's Incorporated
273 S Canon Dr
Beverly Hills CA

(P-1527)
NEMOS BAKERY INC (HQ)
416 N Hale Ave (92029-1420)
PHONE...................................760 741-5725
Phillip S Estes, *CEO*
Bob Yurick, *VP*
Sam Delucca Junior, *Sr VP*
▲ **EMP:** 70 **EST:** 1975
SALES (est): 16.86MM **Privately Held**
Web: www.nemosbakery.com
SIC: 2053 Cakes, bakery: frozen
PA: Horizon Holdings, Llc
1 Bush St Ste 650
San Francisco CA

(P-1528)
OPERA PATISSERIE
Also Called: Opera Patisserie
8480 Redwood Creek Ln (92126-1067)
PHONE...................................858 536-5800
Diane Anderson, *Prin*
Vincent Garcia, *
EMP: 61 **EST:** 2002
SQ FT: 9,000
SALES (est): 4.71MM **Privately Held**
Web: www.operapatisserie.com
SIC: 2053 5812 Pastries, e.g. danish: frozen;
Cafe

(P-1529)
RICH PRODUCTS CORPORATION
3401 W Segerstrom Ave (92704-6404)
PHONE...................................714 338-1145
EMP: 21
SALES (corp-wide): 4.81B **Privately Held**
Web: www.richs.com
SIC: 2053 Frozen bakery products, except bread
PA: Rich Products Corporation
1 Robert Rich Way
Buffalo NY
716 878-8000

2061 Raw Cane Sugar

(P-1530)
AZUMEX CORP
2365 Michael Faraday Dr (92154-7257)
PHONE...................................619 710-8855
Fabian Gomez-ibarra, *CEO*
EMP: 28 **EST:** 2011
SALES (est): 2.34MM **Privately Held**
Web: www.azumexsugar.com
SIC: 2061 Granulated cane sugar

2063 Beet Sugar

(P-1531)
SPRECKELS SUGAR COMPANY INC
395 W Keystone Rd (92227-9739)
P.O. Box 581 (92227-0581)
PHONE...................................760 344-3110
John Richmond, *Pr*
John Richmond, *CEO*
Neil Rudeen, *
Jeff Plathe, *
▲ **EMP:** 260 **EST:** 1905
SALES (est): 47.8MM
SALES (corp-wide): 376.83MM **Privately Held**
SIC: 2063 Beet sugar, from beet sugar refinery
PA: Southern Minnesota Beet Sugar Cooperative
83550 County Road 21
Renville MN
320 329-8305

2064 Candy And Other Confectionery Products

(P-1532)
180 SNACKS INC
Also Called: Mareblu Naturals
1173 N Armando St (92806-2609)
PHONE...................................714 238-1192
Michael Kim, *Pr*
Katherine Kim, *VP*
▲ **EMP:** 47 **EST:** 2004
SALES (est): 9.16MM **Privately Held**
Web: www.180snacks.com
SIC: 2064 2034 2068 Granola and muesli,
bars and clusters; Dried and dehydrated
fruits; Salted and roasted nuts and seeds

(P-1533)
ADAMS AND BROOKS INC
4345 Hallmark Pkwy (92407-1829)
P.O. Box 9940 (92427-0940)
PHONE...................................909 880-2305
▲ **EMP:** 160 **EST:** 1932
SALES (est): 23MM **Privately Held**
Web: www.adams-brooks.com
SIC: 2064 Nuts, candy covered

(P-1534)
CALIFORNIA SNACK FOODS INC
Also Called: California Candy
2131 Tyler Ave (91733-2754)
PHONE...................................626 444-4508
Murl W Nelson, *CEO*
Steve Nelson, *
Paul Mullen, *
Mary Nelson, *
EMP: 45 **EST:** 1961
SQ FT: 30,000
SALES (est): 4.64MM **Privately Held**
Web: www.californiasnackfoods.com
SIC: 2064 2024 2099 2051 Fruits candied,
crystallized, or glazed; Juice pops, frozen;
Popcorn, packaged: except already popped
; Cakes, pies, and pastries

(P-1535)
CHOCOLATES A LA CARTE INC
24836 Avenue Rockefeller (91355-3467)
PHONE...................................661 257-3700
▲ **EMP:** 165
Web: www.candymaker.com

SIC: **2064** 2066 Chocolate candy, except solid chocolate; Chocolate and cocoa products

(P-1536)
COUNTRY HOUSE
Also Called: Seloah Gourmet Food
2852 Walnut Ave Ste C1 (92780-7033)
PHONE..............................714 505-8988
Monica Ching, *Owner*
▲ **EMP: 18 EST:** 1994
SQ FT: 9,400
SALES (est): 1.12MM **Privately Held**
Web: www.countryhousenatural.com
SIC: **2064** Candy and other confectionery products

(P-1537)
EL SUPER LEON PNCHIN SNCKS INC
2545 Britannia Blvd Ste A (92154-7427)
PHONE..............................619 426-2968
Alfonso Guerrero, *Pr*
EMP: 21
Web: www.elsuperleoninc.com
SIC: **2064** Candy and other confectionery products
PA: El Super Leon Ponchin Snacks, Inc.
2545 Britannia Blvd
San Diego CA

(P-1538)
EZAKI GLICO USA CORPORATION
Also Called: Ezaki Glico
18022 Cowan Ste 110 (92614-6805)
PHONE..............................949 251-0144
Akitoshi Oku, *Pr*
▲ **EMP:** 19 **EST:** 1996
SALES (est): 10.47MM **Privately Held**
Web: www.glicousa.com
SIC: **2064** 8111 Candy and other confectionery products; General practice attorney, lawyer
PA: Ezaki Glico Co.,Ltd.
4-6-5, Utajima, Nishiyodogawa-Ku
Osaka OSK

(P-1539)
FOOD TECHNOLOGY AND DESIGN LLC (PA)
Also Called: Food Pharma
10012 Painter Ave (90670-3016)
PHONE..............................562 944-7821
Glen Marinelli, *Managing Member*
Remmell Gopez, *Managing Member*
EMP: 27 **EST:** 2001
SQ FT: 20,000
SALES (est): 10.76MM
SALES (corp-wide): 10.76MM **Privately Held**
Web: www.foodpharma.com
SIC: **2064** Candy and other confectionery products

(P-1540)
GENESIS FOODS CORPORATION
Also Called: Garvey Nut & Candy
8825 Mercury Ln (90660-6707)
PHONE..............................323 890-5890
TOLL FREE: 800
▲ **EMP:** 60
Web: www.garveycandy.com
SIC: **2064** 5149 Candy and other confectionery products; Cookies

(P-1541)
HGC HOLDINGS INC
3303 Martin Luther King Jr Blvd
(90262-1905)

PHONE..............................323 567-2226
Robert I Hadgraft, *CEO*
David Worth, *
Robert Worth, *
▲ **EMP:** 23 **EST:** 1944
SQ FT: 90,000
SALES (est): 1.07MM **Privately Held**
SIC: **2064** 5441 Chocolate candy, except solid chocolate; Candy

(P-1542)
HIRA PARIS INC
Also Called: Andy Anand Chocolates
3811 Schaefer Ave Ste B (91710-5400)
PHONE..............................909 634-3900
Thaminder Singh Anand, *Pr*
Sing Datu, *VP*
EMP: 200 **EST:** 2020
SALES (est): 10.57MM **Privately Held**
SIC: **2064** 5149 Candy bars, including chocolate covered bars; Chocolate

(P-1543)
HOTLIX (PA)
Also Called: Hotlix Candy
966 Griffin St (93433-3019)
P.O. Box 447 (93483-0447)
PHONE..............................805 473-0596
Larry Peterman, *Pr*
▼ **EMP:** 25 **EST:** 1983
SQ FT: 1,500
SALES (est): 4.92MM
SALES (corp-wide): 4.92MM **Privately Held**
Web: www.hotlix.com
SIC: **2064** Lollipops and other hard candy

(P-1544)
ISLAND SNACKS INC
Also Called: Island Products
7650 Stage Rd (90621-1226)
PHONE..............................714 994-1228
Alin Barak, *Pr*
◆ **EMP:** 20 **EST:** 1980
SQ FT: 6,600
SALES (est): 5.73MM **Privately Held**
Web: www.islandsnacksinc.com
SIC: **2064** Candy and other confectionery products

(P-1545)
MAVE ENTERPRISES INC
Also Called: It's Delish
11555 Cantara St Ste B-E (91605-1652)
P.O. Box 480620 (90048-1620)
PHONE..............................818 767-4533
Amy Grawitzky, *CEO*
Moshe Grawitzky, *
Rochell Legarreta, *
▲ **EMP:** 35 **EST:** 1992
SQ FT: 35,000
SALES (est): 4.51MM **Privately Held**
SIC: **2064** 2099 2033 2068 Candy and other confectionery products; Seasonings and spices; Canned fruits and specialties; Salted and roasted nuts and seeds

(P-1546)
MCKEEVER DANLEE CONFECTIONARY
760 N Mckeever Ave (91702-2349)
PHONE..............................626 334-8964
EMP: 91 **EST:** 1994
SQ FT: 10,000
SALES (est): 1.68MM
SALES (corp-wide): 179.18MM **Privately Held**
SIC: **2064** Candy and other confectionery products
HQ: Morris National, Inc.
760 N Mckeever Ave

Azusa CA
626 385-2000

(P-1547)
NELLSON NUTRACEUTICAL INC
5115 E La Palma Ave (92807-2018)
PHONE..............................844 635-5766
Scott Greenwood, *CEO*
Ben Muhlenkamp, *
Jeff Moran, *
Paul Hanson, *
Manuel Martinez, *CFO*
▲ **EMP:** 297 **EST:** 1961
SQ FT: 100,000
SALES (est): 21.63MM **Privately Held**
Web: www.nellsonllc.com
SIC: **2064** Candy bars, including chocolate covered bars

(P-1548)
SANDERS CANDY FACTORY INC
5051 Calmview Ave (91706-1802)
PHONE..............................626 814-2038
Timothy Sanders, *CEO*
Mark Sanders, *VP*
Steven L Peralez, *Sec*
EMP: 20 **EST:** 1989
SQ FT: 40,000
SALES (est): 10.47MM **Privately Held**
SIC: **2064** Candy and other confectionery products

(P-1549)
SUGARFINA INC
779 Americana Way (91210-1507)
PHONE..............................818 302-0765
EMP: 21
SALES (corp-wide): 13.43MM **Privately Held**
Web: www.sugarfina.com
SIC: **2064** Candy and other confectionery products
PA: Sugarfina, Inc.
5275 W Diablo Dr 1
Las Vegas NV
424 256-9489

(P-1550)
SUGARFINA INC
4353 La Jolla Village Dr (92122-1242)
PHONE..............................949 301-9482
EMP: 21
SALES (corp-wide): 13.43MM **Privately Held**
Web: www.sugarfina.com
SIC: **2064** Candy and other confectionery products
PA: Sugarfina, Inc.
5275 W Diablo Dr 1
Las Vegas NV
424 256-9489

(P-1551)
SUGARFINA INC
840 S Pacific Coast Hwy (90245-4834)
PHONE..............................424 290-0777
EMP: 21
SALES (corp-wide): 13.43MM **Privately Held**
Web: www.sugarfina.com
SIC: **2064** Candy and other confectionery products
PA: Sugarfina, Inc.
5275 W Diablo Dr 1
Las Vegas NV
424 256-9489

(P-1552)
SUGARFINA INC
20 Hugus Aly (91103-3644)

PHONE..............................424 284-8518
EMP: 21
SALES (corp-wide): 13.43MM **Privately Held**
Web: www.sugarfina.com
SIC: **2064** Candy and other confectionery products
PA: Sugarfina, Inc.
5275 W Diablo Dr 1
Las Vegas NV
424 256-9489

(P-1553)
SUGARFINA INC
9495 Santa Monica Blvd (90210-4620)
PHONE..............................855 784-2734
Josh Resnick, *Brnch Mgr*
EMP: 21
SALES (corp-wide): 13.43MM **Privately Held**
Web: www.sugarfina.com
SIC: **2064** 5441 Candy and other confectionery products; Candy
PA: Sugarfina, Inc.
5275 W Diablo Dr 1
Las Vegas NV
424 256-9489

2066 Chocolate And Cocoa Products

(P-1554)
CFP CHOCOLATE HOLDINGS LLC
1100a John Reed Ct (91745-1813)
PHONE..............................661 257-3700
EMP: 140
SIC: **2066** Chocolate and cocoa products

(P-1555)
VERY SPECIAL CHOCOLATS INC
760 N Mckeever Ave (91702-2349)
PHONE..............................626 334-7838
Gerry Morris Zubatoff, *CEO*
Gerald Morris, *
Bram Morris, *
David Pistole, *
▲ **EMP:** 183 **EST:** 1986
SQ FT: 40,000
SALES (est): 2.26MM
SALES (corp-wide): 179.18MM **Privately Held**
SIC: **2066** Chocolate and cocoa products
HQ: Morris National, Inc.
760 N Mckeever Ave
Azusa CA
626 385-2000

2068 Salted And Roasted Nuts And Seeds

(P-1556)
MELLACE FAMILY BRANDS INC
6195 El Camino Real (92009-1602)
P.O. Box 22831 (92192-2831)
PHONE..............................760 448-1940
Michael Mellace, *Pr*
▲ **EMP:** 50 **EST:** 2001
SQ FT: 45,000
SALES (est): 934.66K **Privately Held**
SIC: **2068** Nuts: dried, dehydrated, salted or roasted

(P-1557)
MELLACE FAMILY BRANDS CAL INC

6195 El Camino Real (92009-1602)
P.O. Box 22831 (92192-2831)
PHONE..................760 448-1940
EMP: 50 **EST:** 2011
SQ FT: 50,000
SALES (est): 4.71MM
SALES (corp-wide): 394.19MM **Privately Held**
SIC: 2068 Salted and roasted nuts and seeds
PA: Johnvince Foods
555 Steeprock Dr
North York ON
416 663-6146

(P-1558)
MFB LIQUIDATION INC
Also Called: Mama Mellaces Old World Treats
6195 El Camino Real (92009-1602)
PHONE..................760 448-1940
▲ **EMP:** 50 **EST:** 1962
SALES (est): 6.27MM **Privately Held**
SIC: 2068 Salted and roasted nuts and seeds

(P-1559)
MIXED NUTS INC
7909 Crossway Dr (90660-4449)
PHONE..................323 587-6887
Vanik Hartounian, *Pr*
◆ **EMP:** 25 **EST:** 1986
SALES (est): 7.68MM **Privately Held**
Web: www.mixednutsinc.com
SIC: 2068 5145 Nuts: dried, dehydrated, salted or roasted; Nuts, salted or roasted

(P-1560)
NEW CENTURY SNACKS LLC
5560 E Slauson Ave (90040-2921)
PHONE..................323 278-9578
▲ **EMP:** 25
SIC: 2068 2099 Salted and roasted nuts and seeds; Food preparations, nec

(P-1561)
PRIMEX FARMS LLC (PA)
16070 Wildwood Rd (93280-9210)
PHONE..................661 758-7790
Ali Amin, *CEO*
Ignasius Handoko, *
EMP: 30 **EST:** 2002
SQ FT: 136,837
SALES (est): 264.21MM
SALES (corp-wide): 264.21MM **Privately Held**
Web: www.primex.us
SIC: 2068 Nuts: dried, dehydrated, salted or roasted

(P-1562)
SNAK CLUB LLC
Also Called: New Century Snacks
5560 E Slauson Ave (90040-2921)
PHONE..................323 278-9578
Farhad Morshed, *Pr*
EMP: 98
SALES (corp-wide): 177.61MM **Privately Held**
Web: www.snakclub.com
SIC: 2068 2099 Salted and roasted nuts and seeds; Food preparations, nec
HQ: Snak Club, Llc
607 N Nash St
El Segundo CA
310 322-4400

(P-1563)
WONDERFUL PSTCHIOS ALMONDS LLC (HQ)
Also Called: Paramount Farms
11444 W Olympic Blvd Ste 310 (90064-1549)

P.O. Box 200937 (75320-0937)
PHONE..................310 966-4650
Stewart Resnick, *Pr*
Michael Hohmann, *
Craig B Cooper, *Senior Vice President Managing*
Bill Phillimore, *
◆ **EMP:** 25 **EST:** 1989
SQ FT: 15,000
SALES (est): 915.31MM
SALES (corp-wide): 2.04B **Privately Held**
Web: www.wonderful.com
SIC: 2068 Salted and roasted nuts and seeds
PA: The Wonderful Company Llc
11444 W Olympic Blvd # 210
Los Angeles CA
310 966-5700

2076 Vegetable Oil Mills, Nec

(P-1564)
GLOBAL AGRI-TRADE (PA)
Also Called: Gatc Ghq
15500 S Avalon Blvd (90220-3205)
PHONE..................562 320-8550
Haresh Kumar Bhatt, *CEO*
Jignesh Bhatt, *VP*
Lynn Willis, *Contrlr*
▲ **EMP:** 21 **EST:** 2006
SQ FT: 2,500
SALES (est): 9.8MM
SALES (corp-wide): 9.8MM **Privately Held**
Web: www.globalagritrade.com
SIC: 2076 5199 Palm kernel oil; Oils, animal or vegetable

(P-1565)
SMART FOODS LLC
3398 Leonis Blvd (90058-3014)
PHONE..................800 284-2250
◆ **EMP:** 25 **EST:** 2015
SALES (est): 3.26MM **Privately Held**
Web: www.avocadooilusa.com
SIC: 2076 2046 Vegetable oil mills, nec; Corn oil, refined

2077 Animal And Marine Fats And Oils

(P-1566)
BAKER COMMODITIES INC (PA)
Also Called: Corenco
4020 Bandini Blvd (90058-4274)
PHONE..................323 268-2801
TOLL FREE: 800
James M Andreoli, *Pr*
Mitchell Ebright, *
Denis Luckey, *
◆ **EMP:** 150 **EST:** 1948
SQ FT: 12,000
SALES (est): 153.63MM
SALES (corp-wide): 153.63MM **Privately Held**
Web: www.bakercommodities.com
SIC: 2077 2048 Tallow rendering, inedible; Poultry feeds

(P-1567)
D & D SERVICES INC
Also Called: D & D Cremations Service
4105 Bandini Blvd (90058-4208)
P.O. Box 55338 (91385-0338)
PHONE..................323 261-4176
William M Gorman, *Pr*
Vincent Gorman, *
Roseanne Gorman, *
EMP: 41 **EST:** 1967
SQ FT: 100,000

SALES (est): 4.67MM **Privately Held**
SIC: 2077 Animal and marine fats and oils

(P-1568)
DARLING INGREDIENTS INC
2626 E 25th St (90058-1212)
P.O. Box 58725 (90058-0725)
PHONE..................323 583-6311
Thomas Nunley, *Genl Mgr*
EMP: 44
SALES (corp-wide): 6.53B **Publicly Held**
Web: www.darlingii.com
SIC: 2077 2048 Animal and marine fats and oils; Prepared feeds, nec
PA: Darling Ingredients Inc.
5601 N Macarthur Blvd
Irving TX
972 717-0300

(P-1569)
PARK WEST ENTERPRISES INC
Also Called: Co-West Commodities
2586 Shenandoah Way (92407-1845)
PHONE..................909 383-8341
Sergio Perez, *CEO*
Freddie Peterson, *
EMP: 18 **EST:** 1996
SALES (est): 2.43MM **Privately Held**
Web: www.co-west.com
SIC: 2077 Animal and marine fats and oils

2079 Edible Fats And Oils

(P-1570)
COAST PACKING COMPANY
3275 E Vernon Ave (90058-1820)
P.O. Box 58918 (90058-0918)
PHONE..................323 277-7700
EMP: 60 **EST:** 1922
SALES (est): 22.23MM **Privately Held**
Web: www.coastpacking.com
SIC: 2079 Edible fats and oils

(P-1571)
GEMSA ENTERPRISES LLC
Also Called: Gemsa Oils
14370 Gannet St (90638-5221)
P.O. Box 1447 (90637-1447)
PHONE..................714 521-1736
▲ **EMP:** 20 **EST:** 1996
SQ FT: 60,000
SALES (est): 10.13MM **Privately Held**
Web: www.gemsaoils.com
SIC: 2079 Olive oil

(P-1572)
LIBERTY VEGETABLE OIL COMPANY
15306 Carmenita Rd (90670-5606)
P.O. Box 4207 (90703-4207)
PHONE..................562 921-3567
Irwin Field, *Pr*
Ronald Field, *
◆ **EMP:** 40 **EST:** 1948
SQ FT: 30,000
SALES (est): 5.3MM **Privately Held**
Web: www.libertyvegetableoil.com
SIC: 2079 Olive oil

(P-1573)
VENTURA FOODS LLC
2900 Jurupa St (91761-2915)
PHONE..................714 257-3700
Wayne Kess, *Mgr*
EMP: 68
Web: www.venturafoods.com

SIC: 2079 2035 Vegetable shortenings (except corn oil); Pickles, sauces, and salad dressings
PA: Ventura Foods, Llc
40 Pointe Dr
Brea CA

(P-1574)
VENTURA FOODS LLC (PA)
Also Called: Lou Ana Foods
40 Pointe Dr (92821-3652)
PHONE..................714 257-3700
◆ **EMP:** 200 **EST:** 1996
SALES (est): 2.05B **Privately Held**
Web: www.venturafoods.com
SIC: 2079 2035 Vegetable shortenings (except corn oil); Pickles, sauces, and salad dressings

(P-1575)
WILSEY FOODS INC
40 Pointe Dr (92821-3652)
PHONE..................714 257-3700
Takashi Fukunaga, *CEO*
Steve Takagi, *Pr*
Hiro Matsumura, *VP*
◆ **EMP:** 1000 **EST:** 1919
SQ FT: 103,378
SALES (est): 52.94MM **Privately Held**
Web: www.venturafoods.com
SIC: 2079 5149 Cooking oils, except corn: vegetable refined; Shortening, vegetable
HQ: Mbk Usa Holdings, Inc.
200 Park Ave Fl 36
New York NY
212 878-6773

2082 Malt Beverages

(P-1576)
ANGEL CITY PUBLIC HSE & BREWRY
216 S Alameda St (90012-4201)
PHONE..................562 983-6880
Vincent Barrios, *Prin*
▲ **EMP:** 26 **EST:** 2013
SALES (est): 964.35K **Privately Held**
Web: www.angelcitybrewery.com
SIC: 2082 Beer (alcoholic beverage)

(P-1577)
ANHEUSER-BUSCH LLC
Also Called: Anheuser-Busch
2800 S Reservoir St (91766-6525)
PHONE..................951 782-3935
TOLL FREE: 800
Yo Sanchez, *Mgr*
EMP: 115
SALES (corp-wide): 1.31B **Privately Held**
Web: www.budweisertours.com
SIC: 2082 Beer (alcoholic beverage)
HQ: Anheuser-Busch, Llc
1 Busch Pl
Saint Louis MO
800 342-5283

(P-1578)
ANHEUSER-BUSCH LLC
Also Called: Anheuser-Busch
12065 Pike St (90670-2964)
P.O. Box 3988 (90670-1988)
PHONE..................562 699-3424
EMP: 21
SALES (corp-wide): 1.31B **Privately Held**
Web: www.ab-inbev.com
SIC: 2082 5181 Malt beverage products; Beer and ale
HQ: Anheuser-Busch, Llc
1 Busch Pl

Saint Louis MO
800 342-5283

(P-1579)
ANHEUSER-BUSCH LLC
Also Called: Anheuser-Busch
20499 S Reeves Ave (90810-1011)
PHONE..............................310 761-4600
Damian Bonnenfant, *Mgr*
EMP: 43
SALES (corp-wide): 1.31B **Privately Held**
Web: www.budweisertours.com
SIC: 2082 Beer (alcoholic beverage)
HQ: Anheuser-Busch, Llc
    1 Busch Pl
    Saint Louis MO
    800 342-5283

(P-1580)
ANHEUSER-BUSCH LLC
Also Called: Anheuser-Busch
5959 Santa Fe St (92109-1623)
P.O. Box 80758 (92138-0758)
PHONE..............................858 581-7000
Denise Cooper, *Genl Mgr*
EMP: 56
SALES (corp-wide): 1.31B **Privately Held**
Web: www.ab-inbev.com
SIC: 2082 Beer (alcoholic beverage)
HQ: Anheuser-Busch, Llc
    1 Busch Pl
    Saint Louis MO
    800 342-5283

(P-1581)
**ASSOCIATED
MICROBREWERIES INC**
9675 Scranton Rd (92121-1761)
PHONE..............................858 587-2739
Bryan King, *Brnch Mgr*
EMP: 70
SALES (corp-wide): 45.99MM **Privately
Held**
Web: www.karlstrauss.com
SIC: 2082 Beer (alcoholic beverage)
PA: Associated Microbreweries, Inc.
    5985 Santa Fe St
    San Diego CA
    858 273-2739

(P-1582)
**ASSOCIATED
MICROBREWERIES INC**
Also Called: Karl Strauss Brewery & Rest
1157 Columbia St (92101-3511)
PHONE..............................619 234-2739
EMP: 70
SALES (corp-wide): 45.99MM **Privately
Held**
Web: www.karlstrauss.com
SIC: 2082 5812 Beer (alcoholic beverage);
    Eating places
PA: Associated Microbreweries, Inc.
    5985 Santa Fe St
    San Diego CA
    858 273-2739

(P-1583)
**ASSOCIATED
MICROBREWERIES INC (PA)**
Also Called: Karl Strauss Brewery Garden
5985 Santa Fe St (92109-1623)
PHONE..............................858 273-2739
Christopher W Cramer, *Pr*
Matthew H Rattner, *
EMP: 50 **EST:** 1988
SQ FT: 2,000
SALES (est): 45.99MM
SALES (corp-wide): 45.99MM **Privately
Held**

Web: www.karlstrauss.com
SIC: 2082 5812 Beer (alcoholic beverage);
    Eating places

(P-1584)
**ASSOCIATED
MICROBREWERIES INC**
901 S Coast Dr Ste A (92626-7790)
PHONE..............................714 546-2739
David Sadeler, *Mgr*
EMP: 70
SALES (corp-wide): 45.99MM **Privately
Held**
Web: www.karlstrauss.com
SIC: 2082 Beer (alcoholic beverage)
PA: Associated Microbreweries, Inc.
    5985 Santa Fe St
    San Diego CA
    858 273-2739

(P-1585)
**ASSOCTED MCRBRWRIES LTD
A CAL**
Also Called: Karl Strauss Brewing Company
5985 Santa Fe St (92109-1623)
PHONE..............................858 273-2739
Christopher W Cramer, *Prin*
EMP: 18 **EST:** 1988
SALES (est): 1.55MM **Privately Held**
Web: www.karlstrauss.com
SIC: 2082 Beer (alcoholic beverage)

(P-1586)
DUDES BREWING COMPANY
1840 W 208th St (93066)
P.O. Box 276 (93066-0276)
PHONE..............................424 271-2915
Toby Humes, *Owner*
EMP: 20 **EST:** 2013
SALES (est): 880.6K **Privately Held**
Web: www.thedudesbrew.com
SIC: 2082 5921 Beer (alcoholic beverage);
    Beer (packaged)

(P-1587)
FERMENTED SCIENCES INC
3200 Golf Course Dr (93003-7696)
PHONE..............................818 427-8442
William Moses, *CEO*
William Castagna, *Sec*
Chelsea Brewders, *CFO*
David Whatley, *Dir*
Robert Adams, *Dir*
EMP: 44 **EST:** 2016
SALES (est): 2.48MM **Privately Held**
SIC: 2082 Beer (alcoholic beverage)

(P-1588)
FIRESTONE WALKER INC
1332 Vendels Cir (93446-3802)
PHONE..............................805 226-8514
Adam Firestone, *Brnch Mgr*
EMP: 86
SALES (corp-wide): 155.51MM **Privately
Held**
Web: www.firestonebeer.com
SIC: 2082 Beer (alcoholic beverage)
PA: Firestone Walker, Inc.
    1400 Ramada Dr
    Paso Robles CA
    805 225-5911

(P-1589)
FIRESTONE WALKER INC (PA)
Also Called: Firestone Walker Brewing Co
1400 Ramada Dr (93446-3993)
PHONE..............................805 225-5911
David Walker, *CEO*
Adam Firestone, *

◆ **EMP:** 156 **EST:** 1997
SALES: 155.51MM
SALES (est): 155.51MM **Privately
Held**
Web: www.firestonebeer.com
SIC: 2082 Beer (alcoholic beverage)

(P-1590)
FIRESTONE WALKER INC
Also Called: Firestone Walker Brewing Co
620 Mcmurray Rd (93427-2511)
PHONE..............................805 254-4205
Patrick Mcalary, *Genl Mgr*
EMP: 86
SALES (corp-wide): 155.51MM **Privately
Held**
Web: www.firestonebeer.com
SIC: 2082 Beer (alcoholic beverage)
PA: Firestone Walker, Inc.
    1400 Ramada Dr
    Paso Robles CA
    805 225-5911

(P-1591)
HOME BREW MART INC
9045 Carroll Way (92121-2405)
PHONE..............................858 790-6900
Jim Buechler, *CEO*
Jack White, *
Yuseff Cherney, *
Rick Morgan, *
Julie Buechler, *
▲ **EMP:** 425 **EST:** 1992
SQ FT: 107,000
SALES (est): 47.43MM
SALES (corp-wide): 9.45B **Publicly Held**
Web: www.ballastpoint.com
SIC: 2082 5999 Ale (alcoholic beverage);
    Alcoholic beverage making equipment and
    supplies
PA: Constellation Brands, Inc.
    207 High Point Dr # 100
    Victor NY
    585 678-7100

(P-1592)
J&L EPPIG BREWING LLC
Also Called: Eppig Brewing
1347 Keystone Way Ste C (92081-8311)
PHONE..............................760 295-2009
Todd Warshaw, *Mgr*
Clayton Leblanc, *Mgr*
Stephanie Eppig, *Mgr*
EMP: 18 **EST:** 2015
SALES (est): 938.37K **Privately Held**
Web: www.eppigbrewing.com
SIC: 2082 Malt beverages

(P-1593)
JDZ INC
Also Called: Alesmith Brewing Company
9990 Alesmith Ct (92126-4200)
P.O. Box 993 (92038-0993)
PHONE..............................858 549-9888
Peter Zien, *CEO*
EMP: 54 **EST:** 2014
SALES (est): 4.79MM **Privately Held**
SIC: 2082 Beer (alcoholic beverage)

(P-1594)
K A MCNAIR BREWING CO LLC
Also Called: North Park Beer Co.
3038 University Ave (92104-3002)
PHONE..............................858 254-3238
EMP: 20 **EST:** 2013
SALES (est): 2.4MM **Privately Held**
Web: www.northparkbeer.com
SIC: 2082 Malt beverages

(P-1595)
**KARL STRAUSS BREWING
COMPANY (PA)**
5985 Santa Fe St (92109-1623)
P.O. Box 5965 (92165-5965)
PHONE..............................858 273-2739
Chris Cramer, *CEO*
Matt Rattner, *Prin*
EMP: 50 **EST:** 1989
SALES (est): 15.92MM **Privately Held**
Web: www.karlstrauss.com
SIC: 2082 Beer (alcoholic beverage)

(P-1596)
KINGS & CONVICTS BP LLC
2215 India St (92101-1725)
PHONE..............................619 255-7213
EMP: 112
SALES (corp-wide): 99.31MM **Privately
Held**
Web: www.ballastpoint.com
SIC: 2082 Malt beverages
HQ: Kings & Convicts Bp, Llc
    9045 Carroll Way
    San Diego CA
    858 790-6900

(P-1597)
KINGS & CONVICTS BP LLC
5401 Linda Vista Rd Ste 406 (92110-2402)
PHONE..............................619 295-2337
Jim Johnson, *Brnch Mgr*
EMP: 50
SALES (corp-wide): 99.31MM **Privately
Held**
Web: www.ballastpoint.com
SIC: 2082 Malt beverages
HQ: Kings & Convicts Bp, Llc
    9045 Carroll Way
    San Diego CA
    858 790-6900

(P-1598)
**LA QUINTA BREWING
COMPANY LLC**
74714 Technology Dr (92211-5803)
PHONE..............................760 200-2597
Scott Stokes, *Managing Member*
Scott Stoaks, *
EMP: 55 **EST:** 2013
SALES (est): 3.54MM **Privately Held**
Web: www.laquintabrewing.com
SIC: 2082 5813 Beer (alcoholic beverage);
    Beer garden (drinking places)

(P-1599)
**MIKKELLER BREWING SAN
DIEGO**
9368 Cabot Dr (92126-4311)
PHONE..............................858 381-3500
Stella Polly, *Prin*
EMP: 23 **EST:** 2016
SALES (est): 1.6MM **Privately Held**
Web: www.mikkellersd.com
SIC: 2082 Beer (alcoholic beverage)

(P-1600)
MILLER BREWING CO
15801 1st St (91706-2069)
PHONE..............................626 353-1604
EMP: 23 **EST:** 2016
SALES (est): 4.65MM **Privately Held**
Web: www.molsoncoors.com
SIC: 2082 Beer (alcoholic beverage)

(P-1601)
OTAY LAKES BREWERY LLC
Also Called: Novo Brasil Brewing Co.

PRODUCTS & SVCS

901 Lane Ave Ste 100 (91914-3536)
PHONE..................619 768-0172
EMP: 20 **EST:** 2014
SALES (est): 5.29MM **Privately Held**
Web: www.novobrew.com
SIC: 2082 Ale (alcoholic beverage)

(P-1602)
POWER BRANDS CONSULTING LLC
Also Called: Bevpack
5805 Sepulveda Blvd Ste 501 (91411-2551)
PHONE..................818 989-9646
EMP: 40 **EST:** 2006
SQ FT: 5,000
SALES (est): 8.53MM **Privately Held**
Web: www.powerbrands.us
SIC: 2082 8742 Malt beverage products; Food and beverage consultant

(P-1603)
PROST LLC
8179 Center St (91942-2907)
PHONE..................619 954-4189
EMP: 25 **EST:** 2013
SALES (est): 1.76MM **Privately Held**
SIC: 2082 Malt beverages

(P-1604)
PURE PROJECT LLC
1305 Hot Springs Way (92081-7876)
PHONE..................760 552-7873
Mat Robar, *Managing Member*
EMP: 67 **EST:** 2015
SALES (est): 6MM **Privately Held**
Web: www.purebrewing.org
SIC: 2082 Beer (alcoholic beverage)

(P-1605)
TAPROOM BEER CO
2000 El Cajon Blvd (92104-1007)
PHONE..................619 539-7738
Kevin Conover, *Pt*
EMP: 30 **EST:** 2020
SALES (est): 1.15MM **Privately Held**
Web: www.taproombeerco.com
SIC: 2082 Beer (alcoholic beverage)

(P-1606)
TEMBLOR BREWING LLC
3200 Buck Owens Blvd (93308-6318)
PHONE..................661 489-4855
Donald Bynum, *CEO*
EMP: 49 **EST:** 2014
SQ FT: 19,000
SALES (est): 4.15MM **Privately Held**
Web: www.temblorbrewing.com
SIC: 2082 5813 Ale (alcoholic beverage); Bars and lounges

(P-1607)
TOWNE PARK BREW INC
1566 W Lincoln Ave (92801-5850)
PHONE..................714 844-2492
Brett Lawrence, *Pr*
EMP: 25 **EST:** 2014
SQ FT: 20,000
SALES (est): 1.95MM **Privately Held**
SIC: 2082 5149 Beer (alcoholic beverage); Beverages, except coffee and tea

(P-1608)
TSB2 LLC
Also Called: Thorn Street Brewing Company
1745 National Ave (92113-1010)
PHONE..................619 255-9679
EMP: 83
SALES (corp-wide): 3.65MM **Privately Held**

Web: www.thorn.beer
SIC: 2082 Malt beverages
PA: Tsb2, Llc.
3176 Thorn St
San Diego CA
619 501-2739

2083 Malt

(P-1609)
GREAT WESTERN MALTING CO
995 Joshua Way Ste B (92081-7856)
PHONE..................360 991-0888
Mike O'toole, *Pr*
EMP: 99
Web: www.greatwesternmalting.com
SIC: 2083 Malt
HQ: Great Western Malting Co.
1705 Nw Harborside Dr
Vancouver WA
360 693-3661

2084 Wines, Brandy, And Brandy Spirits

(P-1610)
AGUA DULCE VINEYARDS LLC
9640 Sierra Hwy (91390-4622)
PHONE..................661 268-7402
EMP: 20 **EST:** 2001
SALES (est): 1.79MM **Privately Held**
Web: www.aguadulcewinery.com
SIC: 2084 5921 Wines; Wine

(P-1611)
ARC VINEYARDS LLC
5391 Presquile Dr (93455-5811)
PHONE..................805 937-3901
EMP: 30
SALES (corp-wide): 1.09MM **Privately Held**
Web: www.presquilewine.com
SIC: 2084 Wines
PA: Arc Vineyards, Llc
2529b Professional Pkwy
Santa Maria CA
805 310-9322

(P-1612)
BLENDING LAB INC
25327 Avenue Stanford Ste 105 (91355)
PHONE..................323 424-4051
Magdalena Wojcik, *Mgr*
EMP: 23
SALES (corp-wide): 485.13K **Privately Held**
SIC: 2084 Wines
PA: The Blending Lab Inc
7948 W 3rd St
Los Angeles CA
323 424-4051

(P-1613)
BOTTAIA WINES LP
35601 Rancho California Rd (92591-4024)
PHONE..................951 252-1799
EMP: 20 **EST:** 2016
SALES (est): 5.09MM **Privately Held**
Web: www.bottaiawinery.com
SIC: 2084 Wines, brandy, and brandy spirits

(P-1614)
CALLAWAY VINEYARD & WINERY
32720 Rancho California Rd (92591-4925)
P.O. Box 9014 (92589-9014)
PHONE..................951 676-4001

Mike Jellison, *Pr*
▲ **EMP:** 70 **EST:** 1969
SALES (est): 5.13MM **Privately Held**
Web: www.callawaywinery.com
SIC: 2084 Wine cellars, bonded: engaged in blending wines

(P-1615)
CASA BARRANCA INC
208 E Ojai Ave (93023-2737)
PHONE..................805 640-1255
William Moses, *CEO*
EMP: 20 **EST:** 2008
SALES (est): 755.28K **Privately Held**
Web: www.casabarranca.com
SIC: 2084 Wines

(P-1616)
CENTRAL COAST WINE WAREHOUSE (PA)
Also Called: Central Coast Wine Services
2717 Aviation Way Ste 101 (93455-1506)
PHONE..................805 928-9210
Jim Lunt, *Ltd Pt*
Jeff Maiken, *Ltd Pt*
▲ **EMP:** 17 **EST:** 1988
SQ FT: 35,000
SALES (est): 4.81MM **Privately Held**
SIC: 2084 5182 7389 Wines; Bottling wines and liquors; Field warehousing

(P-1617)
CORBETT VINEYARDS LLC
Also Called: Kitchen and Rail
2195 Corbett Canyon Rd (93420-4974)
PHONE..................805 782-9463
William Swanson, *Managing Member*
Bill Swanson, *
Rob Rossi, *
▲ **EMP:** 25 **EST:** 2008
SALES (est): 2.47MM **Privately Held**
Web: www.coewine.com
SIC: 2084 Wines

(P-1618)
COURTSIDE CELLARS LLC
2425 Mission St (93451-9556)
PHONE..................805 467-2882
David Mchenry, *Genl Mgr*
EMP: 17
SALES (corp-wide): 10.27MM **Privately Held**
Web: www.tolosawinery.com
SIC: 2084 Wine cellars, bonded: engaged in blending wines
PA: Courtside Cellars, Llc
4910 Edna Rd
San Luis Obispo CA
805 782-0500

(P-1619)
COURTSIDE CELLARS LLC (PA)
Also Called: Tolosa Winery
4910 Edna Rd (93401-7938)
PHONE..................805 782-0500
James Efird, *
Robin Baggett, *
▲ **EMP:** 30 **EST:** 1998
SQ FT: 70,000
SALES (est): 10.27MM
SALES (corp-wide): 10.27MM **Privately Held**
Web: www.tolosawinery.com
SIC: 2084 Wines

(P-1620)
CYDEA INC
Also Called: Beveragefactory.com
8510 Miralani Dr (92126-4351)
PHONE..................800 710-9939

Craig Costanzo, *CEO*
Michael Costanzo, *
Barbara Costanzo, *
◆ **EMP:** 49 **EST:** 1997
SQ FT: 12,000
SALES (est): 8.42MM **Privately Held**
Web: www.beveragefactory.com
SIC: 2084 2082 5046 5078 Wines, brandy, and brandy spirits; Beer (alcoholic beverage); Coffee brewing equipment and supplies; Refrigeration equipment and supplies

(P-1621)
DANZA DEL SOL WINERY INC
39050 De Portola Rd (92592-8833)
P.O. Box 892889 (92589-2889)
PHONE..................951 302-6363
Robert Olson, *Pr*
EMP: 25 **EST:** 2015
SALES (est): 1.95MM **Privately Held**
Web: www.danzadelsolwinery.com
SIC: 2084 Wines

(P-1622)
DAOU FAMILY ESTATES LLC
2777 Hidden Mountain Rd (93446-8712)
PHONE..................805 226-5460
Georges Daou, *Managing Member*
EMP: 64 **EST:** 2017
SALES (est): 2.93MM **Privately Held**
Web: www.daouvineyards.com
SIC: 2084 Wines

(P-1623)
DIERBERG STARLANE VINEYARD
1280 Drum Canyon Rd (93436-9418)
PHONE..................805 736-0757
Kurt Ammann, *Ofcr*
EMP: 18 **EST:** 2013
SALES (est): 832.51K **Privately Held**
Web: www.dierbergvineyard.com
SIC: 2084 Wines

(P-1624)
EOS ESTATE WINERY
Also Called: Eos
2300 Airport Rd (93446-8549)
P.O. Box 1287 (93447-1287)
PHONE..................805 239-2562
TOLL FREE: 800
Frank Arciero, *Pt*
Phil Arciero, *Pt*
Fern Underwood, *Pt*
▲ **EMP:** 47 **EST:** 1986
SALES (est): 4.83MM **Privately Held**
Web: www.eosvintage.com
SIC: 2084 0172 3172 Wines; Grapes; Personal leather goods, nec

(P-1625)
EUROBIZUSA INC
Also Called: Terravino
572 E Green St Ste 301 (91101-2080)
PHONE..................626 793-0032
Valerio Chiarotti, *CEO*
EMP: 18 **EST:** 2006
SALES (est): 1.79MM **Privately Held**
SIC: 2084 Wines, brandy, and brandy spirits

(P-1626)
FALKNER WINERY INC
40620 Calle Contento (92591-5041)
PHONE..................951 676-6741
EMP: 65 **EST:** 1993
SALES (est): 9.11MM **Privately Held**
Web: www.falknerwinery.com

▲ = Import ▼ = Export
◆ = Import/Export

SIC: 2084 7299 Wines; Banquet hall facilities

(P-1627)
FERTILE SOIL LLC
79 Dunmore (92620-3693)
PHONE.....................949 981-9026
Xunbin Jiang, *Mgr*
EMP: 18
SALES (corp-wide): 91.15K **Privately Held**
Web: www.thefertilesoil.com
SIC: 2084 Wines
PA: Fertile Soil, Llc
43085 Bus Pk Dr Ste B
Temecula CA
949 981-9026

(P-1628)
FIRESTONE VINEYARD LP
Also Called: Curtis Winery
5000 Zaca Station Rd (93441-4566)
P.O. Box 244 (93441-0244)
PHONE.....................805 688-3940
Michael L Gravelle, *Pt*
Adam Firestone, *Pt*
▲ EMP: 85 EST: 1976
SQ FT: 45,000
SALES (est): 8.65MM
SALES (corp-wide): 69.09MM **Privately Held**
Web: www.firestonewine.com
SIC: 2084 0172 Wines; Grapes
HQ: Foley Family Wines, Inc.
200 Concourse Blvd
Santa Rosa CA

(P-1629)
FLOOD RANCH COMPANY
Also Called: Rancho Sisquoc Winery
6600 Foxen Canyon Rd (93454-9656)
PHONE.....................805 937-3616
Ed A Holt, *Mgr*
EMP: 33
SALES (corp-wide): 5.04MM **Privately Held**
Web: www.ranchosisquoc.com
SIC: 2084 Wines
PA: Flood Ranch Company
870 Market St Ste 1100
San Francisco CA
415 982-5645

(P-1630)
FOLEY FMLY WINES HOLDINGS INC
90 Easy St (93427-9566)
PHONE.....................805 450-7225
EMP: 93
SALES (corp-wide): 69.09MM **Privately Held**
Web: www.foleyfoodandwinesociety.com
SIC: 2084 Wines
PA: Foley Family Wines Holdings, Inc.
200 Concourse Blvd
Santa Rosa CA
707 708-7600

(P-1631)
FOXEN VINEYARD INC
Also Called: Foxen Canyon Winery & Vineyard
7600 Foxen Canyon Rd (93454-9170)
PHONE.....................805 937-4251
Richard Dore, *Pr*
William Wathen, *
EMP: 35 EST: 1987
SQ FT: 4,000
SALES (est): 4.39MM **Privately Held**
Web: www.foxenvineyard.com
SIC: 2084 Wines

(P-1632)
GAINEY VINEYARD
3950 E Highway 246 (93460)
P.O. Box 910 (93460-0910)
PHONE.....................805 688-0558
Daniel H Gainey, *Pr*
▲ EMP: 23 EST: 1983
SQ FT: 20,000
SALES (est): 7.36MM **Privately Held**
Web: www.gaineyvineyard.com
SIC: 2084 Wines

(P-1633)
GIUMARRA VINEYARDS CORPORATION
11220 Edison Hwy (93307-8431)
P.O. Box 1968 (93303-1968)
PHONE.....................661 395-7000
EMP: 93
SALES (corp-wide): 134.67MM **Privately Held**
Web: www.giumarravineyards.com
SIC: 2084 Wines, brandy, and brandy spirits
PA: Giumarra Vineyards Corporation
11220 Edison Hwy
Edison CA
661 395-7000

(P-1634)
HALTER PROPERTIES LLC
Also Called: Halter Ranch Vineyard
8910 Adelaida Rd (93446-8798)
PHONE.....................805 226-9455
Hanjorg Wyss, *Prin*
▲ EMP: 25 EST: 2000
SALES (est): 4.99MM **Privately Held**
Web: www.halterranch.com
SIC: 2084 Wines

(P-1635)
HALTER WINERY LLC (PA)
Also Called: Chaparral Blend
8910 Adelaida Rd (93446-8798)
PHONE.....................805 226-9455
EMP: 22 EST: 2002
SALES (est): 16.4MM **Privately Held**
Web: www.halterranch.com
SIC: 2084 Wines

(P-1636)
HEARST RANCH WINERY
7300 N River Rd (93446-7101)
PHONE.....................805 467-2241
Bill Grant, *Prin*
EMP: 17 EST: 2012
SALES (est): 1.76MM **Privately Held**
Web: www.hearstranchwinery.com
SIC: 2084 Wines

(P-1637)
HILLIARD BRUCE VINEYARDS LLC (PA)
2097 Vineyard View Ln (93436-2628)
PHONE.....................805 736-5366
John C Hilliard, *Managing Member*
EMP: 19 EST: 2006
SALES (est): 1.12MM **Privately Held**
Web: www.hellinthearmory.com
SIC: 2084 Wines

(P-1638)
J LOHR WINERY CORPORATION
6169 Airport Rd (93446-9547)
PHONE.....................805 239-8900
J Lohr, *Owner*
EMP: 31
SALES (corp-wide): 49.49MM **Privately Held**
Web: www.jlohr.com

SIC: 2084 Wines
PA: J. Lohr Winery Corporation
1000 Lenzen Ave
San Jose CA
408 288-5057

(P-1639)
JACKSON FAMILY WINES INC
Also Called: Cambria Winery
5475 Chardonnay Ln (93454-9600)
PHONE.....................805 938-7300
Bill Hammond, *Brnch Mgr*
EMP: 30
Web: www.cambriawines.com
SIC: 2084 Wines
PA: Jackson Family Wines, Inc.
425 Aviation Blvd
Santa Rosa CA

(P-1640)
JAMES TOBIN CELLARS INC
8950 Union Rd (93446-9356)
PHONE.....................805 239-2204
Tobin J Shumrick, *Pr*
Claire Silver, *Stockholder**
EMP: 25 EST: 1987
SQ FT: 10,000
SALES (est): 5.53MM **Privately Held**
Web: www.tobinjames.com
SIC: 2084 Wines

(P-1641)
KUGLER WINES LLC
300 N 12th St Ste 4b (93436-9444)
PHONE.....................630 306-4634
EMP: 20
SALES (corp-wide): 532.53K **Privately Held**
SIC: 2084 Wines
PA: Kugler Wines Llc
3506 Newridge Dr
Rancho Palos Verdes CA
310 345-2934

(P-1642)
LAETITIA VINEYARD & WINERY INC
Also Called: Laetitia Winery
453 Laetitia Vineyard Dr (93420-9701)
PHONE.....................805 481-1772
Selim K Zilkha, *Pr*
▲ EMP: 65 EST: 1994
SALES (est): 9.05MM **Privately Held**
Web: www.laetitiawine.com
SIC: 2084 Wines

(P-1643)
LEONESSE CELLARS LLC
38311 De Portola Rd (92592-8923)
P.O. Box 1371 (92593-1371)
PHONE.....................951 302-7601
Gary Winder, *Managing Member*
Michael Rennie, *
▲ EMP: 25 EST: 2003
SQ FT: 6,000
SALES (est): 4.51MM **Privately Held**
Web: www.leonessecellars.com
SIC: 2084 Wines

(P-1644)
LEVECKE LLC
Also Called: Chaco Flaco Drinks
10810 Inland Ave (91752-3235)
PHONE.....................951 681-8600
Tim Levecke, *Managing Member*
Reed Levecke, *Managing Member**
Neil Levecke, *Managing Member**
▲ EMP: 23 EST: 1949
SQ FT: 150,000
SALES (est): 971.07K **Privately Held**

Web: www.levecke.com
SIC: 2084 Wines, brandy, and brandy spirits

(P-1645)
LORIMAR WINERY
42031 Main St Ste C (92590-2792)
PHONE.....................951 240-5177
Lawrie Lipton, *Prin*
EMP: 25 EST: 2012
SALES (est): 820.18K **Privately Held**
Web: www.lorimarwinery.com
SIC: 2084 Wines

(P-1646)
LOUIDAR LLC
Also Called: Mount Palomar Winery
33820 Rancho California Rd (92591-4930)
P.O. Box 891510 (92589-1510)
PHONE.....................951 676-5047
Peter Poole, *Prin*
Louis Darwish, *Managing Member*
EMP: 30 EST: 1997
SQ FT: 4,000
SALES (est): 4.33MM **Privately Held**
Web: www.mountpalomarwinery.com
SIC: 2084 Wines

(P-1647)
MAURICE CARRIE WINERY
34225 Rancho California Rd (92591-5054)
PHONE.....................951 676-1711
Buddy Linn, *Pr*
Cheri Linn, *
EMP: 17 EST: 1958
SQ FT: 14,000
SALES (est): 839.55K **Privately Held**
Web: www.ultimatevineyards.com
SIC: 2084 5921 0172 Wines; Wine; Grapes

(P-1648)
NINER WINE ESTATES LLC
2400 W Highway 46 (93446-8602)
PHONE.....................805 239-2233
▲ EMP: 32 EST: 2004
SALES (est): 5.14MM **Privately Held**
Web: www.ninerwine.com
SIC: 2084 Wines

(P-1649)
ONEILL BEVERAGES CO LLC
2975 Mitchell Ranch Way (93446)
PHONE.....................805 239-1616
Jeffrey O'neill, *Pr*
EMP: 22
SALES (corp-wide): 113.24MM **Privately Held**
Web: www.oneillwine.com
SIC: 2084 Wines
PA: O'neill Beverages Co. Llc
101 Larkspur Landing Cir
Larkspur CA
559 638-3544

(P-1650)
OPOLO VINEYARDS INC
2801 Townsgate Rd Ste 123 (91361-3033)
P.O. Box 277 (93447-0277)
PHONE.....................805 238-9593
EMP: 57
SALES (est): 11.22MM **Privately Held**
Web: www.opolo.com
SIC: 2084 Wines
PA: Opolo Vineyards, Inc.
7110 Vineyard Dr
Paso Robles CA
805 238-9593

P
R
O
D
U
C
T
S
&
S
V
C
S

(P-1651)
ORFILA VINEYARDS INC (PA)
Also Called: Orfila Vineyards & Winery
13455 San Pasqual Rd (92025-7833)
PHONE....................760 738-6500
Alejandro Orfila, Pr
Helga Orfila, *
Justin Mund, *
Danica Gvozden, *
▲ EMP: 19 EST: 1989
SQ FT: 12,000
SALES (est): 3.37MM Privately Held
Web: www.orfila.com
SIC: 2084 0172 7299 Wines; Grapes;
　Wedding chapel, privately operated

(P-1652)
PONTE WINERY
35053 Rancho California Rd (92591-4008)
PHONE....................951 694-8855
EMP: 32 EST: 2016
SALES (est): 4.99MM Privately Held
Web: www.pontewinery.com
SIC: 2084 Wines

(P-1653)
POURING WITH HEART LLC
515 W 7th St (90014-2500)
PHONE....................213 817-5321
EMP: 64 EST: 2019
SALES (est): 1.54MM Privately Held
Web: www.pouringwithheart.com
SIC: 2084 Wines

(P-1654)
PROMISE WINE LLC
14909 La Cumbre Dr (90272-4457)
PHONE....................707 260-9094
EMP: 55
SALES (corp-wide): 958.19K Privately
Held
Web: www.promisewine.com
SIC: 2084 Wines
PA: Promise Wine, Llc
　3524 Silverado Trl N
　Saint Helena CA
　707 963-6053

(P-1655)
RBZ VINEYARDS LLC
Also Called: Sextant Wines
2324 W Highway 46 (93446-8602)
P.O. Box 391 (93447-0391)
PHONE....................805 542-0133
Craig Stoller, Prin
EMP: 30 EST: 2006
SALES (est): 4.46MM Privately Held
Web: www.sextantwines.com
SIC: 2084 Wines

(P-1656)
RIVERBENCH LLC
137 Anacapa St (93101-1848)
PHONE....................805 324-4100
Laura Booras, Brnch Mgr
EMP: 50
Web: www.riverbench.com
SIC: 2084 0172 Wines; Grapes
PA: Riverbench Llc
　6020 Foxen Canyon Rd
　Santa Maria CA

(P-1657)
ROLLING HILLS VINEYARD INC
4213 Pascal Pl (90274-3943)
PHONE....................310 541-5098
EMP: 23
SALES (corp-wide): 211.41K Privately
Held

SIC: 2084 Wines, brandy, and brandy spirits
PA: Rolling Hills Vineyard, Inc.
　6200 E Canyon Rim Rd # 201
　Anaheim CA

(P-1658)
ROYAL WINE CORPORATION
Also Called: Herzog Wine Cellars
3201 Camino Del Sol (93030-8915)
PHONE....................805 983-1560
Joseph Herzog, Brnch Mgr
EMP: 21
SALES (corp-wide): 87.37MM Privately
Held
Web: www.herzogwine.com
SIC: 2084 5182 Wines; Wine
PA: Royal Wine Corporation
　63 Lefante Dr
　Bayonne NJ
　718 384-2400

(P-1659)
SAN ANTONIO WINERY INC (PA)
Also Called: San Antonio Gift Shop
737 Lamar St (90031-2514)
PHONE....................323 223-1401
Santo Riboli, CEO
Maddelena Riboli, *
Cathey Riboli, *
◆ EMP: 101 EST: 1917
SQ FT: 310,000
SALES (est): 50.72MM
SALES (corp-wide): 50.72MM Privately
Held
Web: www.sanantoniowinery.com
SIC: 2084 5182 5812 Wines; Wine; Eating
places

(P-1660)
SOUTH COAST WINERY INC
Also Called: South Coast Winery Resort Spa
34843 Rancho California Rd (92591-4006)
PHONE....................951 587-9463
James A Carter, Pr
▲ EMP: 32 EST: 2001
SALES (est): 10.48MM
SALES (corp-wide): 22.31MM Privately
Held
Web: www.southcoastwinery.com
SIC: 2084 7011 7991 Wines; Resort hotel;
Spas
PA: Spruce Grove, Inc.
　3719 S Plaza Dr
　Santa Ana CA
　714 546-4255

(P-1661)
TABLAS CREEK VINEYARD LLC
9339 Adelaida Rd (93446-9785)
PHONE....................805 237-1231
Bob Haas Mg, Pt
▲ EMP: 18 EST: 1990
SQ FT: 40,000
SALES (est): 3.67MM Privately Held
Web: www.tablascreek.com
SIC: 2084 Wines

(P-1662)
TEMECULA VALLEY WINERY MGT LLC
Also Called: Leonesse Cellars
27495 Diaz Rd (92590-3414)
PHONE....................951 699-8896
EMP: 56 EST: 2008
SQ FT: 40,000
SALES (est): 11.86MM Privately Held
Web: www.tvwinerymanagement.com
SIC: 2084 Wines

(P-1663)
TERRAVANT WINE COMPANY LLC
Also Called: Summerland Wine Brands
35 Industrial Way (93427-9565)
PHONE....................805 686-9400
Lew Eisaguirre, Pr
EMP: 66
Web: www.summerlandwinebrands.com
SIC: 2084 Wines
PA: Terravant Wine Company, Llc
　70 Industrial Way
　Buellton CA

(P-1664)
TERRAVANT WINE COMPANY LLC (PA)
Also Called: Terravant Wine
70 Industrial Way (93427-9567)
PHONE....................805 688-4245
Lew Eisaguirre, Pr
Diane Turner, *
Fred Kayne, Managing Member*
Eric J Guerra, *
▲ EMP: 44 EST: 2006
SQ FT: 25,000
SALES (est): 23.54MM Privately Held
Web: www.summerlandwinebrands.com
SIC: 2084 Wines

(P-1665)
THORNTON WINERY
Also Called: Cafe Champagne
32575 Rancho California Rd (92591-4935)
P.O. Box 9008 (92589-9008)
PHONE....................951 699-0099
John M Thornton, Ch Bd
Steve Thornton, *
EMP: 98 EST: 1975
SQ FT: 41,000
SALES (est): 7.74MM Privately Held
Web: www.thorntonwine.com
SIC: 2084 5812 5947 Wine cellars, bonded:
engaged in blending wines; Eating places;
Gift shop

(P-1666)
TREANA WINERY LLC
Also Called: Liberty School
4280 Second Wind Way (93446-6309)
P.O. Box 3260 (93447-3260)
PHONE....................805 237-2932
Charles Wagner, *
▲ EMP: 30 EST: 1996
SALES (est): 4.46MM Privately Held
Web: www.hopefamilywines.com
SIC: 2084 Wines

(P-1667)
WG BEST WEINKELLEREI INC
Also Called: Montesquieu Winery
888 W E St (92101-5915)
PHONE....................858 627-1747
Fonda Hopkins, CEO
Fonda Hopkins, Pr
Frank Kryger, Sec
▲ EMP: 18 EST: 1985
SALES (est): 3.41MM Privately Held
SIC: 2084 5182 5921 Wine cellars, bonded:
engaged in blending wines; Wine; Wine

(P-1668)
WIENS CELLARS LLC
35055 Via Del Ponte (92592-8022)
PHONE....................951 694-9892
EMP: 40 EST: 2001
SALES (est): 8.99MM Privately Held
Web: www.wienscellars.com
SIC: 2084 Wines

(P-1669)
WILSON CREEK WNERY VNYARDS INC
Also Called: Wilson Creek Winery
35960 Rancho California Rd (92591-5088)
PHONE....................951 699-9463
William J Wilson, CEO
Michael Wilson, *
Craig Johns, *
EMP: 110 EST: 2000
SQ FT: 6,000
SALES (est): 24.19MM Privately Held
Web: www.wilsoncreekwinery.com
SIC: 2084 8999 Wines; Personal services

(P-1670)
WINC INC
927 S Santa Fe Ave (90021-1726)
PHONE....................855 282-5829
Alexander Oxman, CEO
EMP: 146 EST: 2007
SALES (est): 23.11MM Privately Held
SIC: 2084 Wines

2085 Distilled And Blended Liquors

(P-1671)
BAR NONE INC
1302 Santa Fe Dr (92780-6434)
PHONE....................714 259-8450
John Underwood, Pr
Elizabeth Underwood, Sec
EMP: 18 EST: 1963
SQ FT: 20,000
SALES (est): 4.8MM
SALES (corp-wide): 810.02MM Publicly
Held
Web: www.barnoneinc.com
SIC: 2085 2087 3565 Cocktails, alcoholic;
Beverage bases, concentrates, syrups,
powders and mixes; Bottling machinery:
filling, capping, labeling
PA: First Advantage Corporation
　1 Concrse Pkwy Ne Ste 200
　Atlanta GA
　888 314-9761

(P-1672)
BOOCHERY INC
Also Called: Boochcraft
684 Anita St Ste F (91911-7170)
PHONE....................619 207-0530
Michael Kent, CEO
Adam Hiner, *
Andrew Clark, *
Michael Kent, Sec
EMP: 65 EST: 2015
SQ FT: 5,000
SALES (est): 9.63MM Privately Held
Web: www.boochcraft.com
SIC: 2085 Distilled and blended liquors

(P-1673)
HAMMOND INC WHICH WILL DO BUS
404 S Coast Hwy (92054-4007)
PHONE....................925 381-5392
Nicholas Hammond, Pr
EMP: 25 EST: 2018
SALES (est): 2.51MM Privately Held
Web: www.paccoastspirits.com
SIC: 2085 Ethyl alcohol for beverage
purposes

(P-1674)
ROKIT DRINKS LLC
17383 W Sunset Blvd Ste 300
(90272-4181)

PHONE..............................323 654-2740
Jonathan Kendrick, *CEO*
Graham Higgins, *COO*
EMP: 21 **EST:** 2014
SALES (est): 1.59MM
SALES (corp-wide): 17.12MM **Privately Held**
SIC: 2085 Rum (alcoholic beverage)
PA: Rokit Stars Limited
    Rok House
    Wolverhampton W MIDLANDS
    190 237-4896

(P-1675)
SAZERAC COMPANY INC
Barton Brands of California
2202 E Del Amo Blvd (90749)
P.O. Box 6263 (90749-6263)
PHONE..............................310 604-8717
Michael Dominick, *Mgr*
EMP: 51
SALES (corp-wide): 1.28B **Privately Held**
Web: www.sazerac.com
SIC: 2085 Distilled and blended liquors
PA: Sazerac Company, Inc.
    101 Magazine St Fl 5
    New Orleans LA
    866 729-3722

(P-1676)
STILLHOUSE LLC
8201 Beverly Blvd Ste 300 (90048-4542)
PHONE..............................323 498-1111
EMP: 32 **EST:** 2009
SALES (est): 4.76MM **Privately Held**
Web: www.stillhouse.com
SIC: 2085 Corn whiskey
PA: Bacardi Limited
    C/O Conyers Corporate Services
    (Bermuda) Limited
    Hamilton

2086 Bottled And Canned Soft Drinks

(P-1677)
AMERICAN BOTTLING COMPANY
1166 Arroyo St (91340-1824)
PHONE..............................818 898-1471
Ed Nemecek, *Brnch Mgr*
EMP: 76
Web: www.keurigdrpepper.com
SIC: 2086 5149 Soft drinks: packaged in cans, bottles, etc.; Soft drinks
HQ: The American Bottling Company
    6425 Hall Of Fame Ln
    Frisco TX

(P-1678)
AMERICAN BOTTLING COMPANY
Also Called: Dr Pepper Snapple Group
1188 Mt Vernon Ave (92507-1829)
PHONE..............................951 341-7500
Vince Spurgeon, *Mgr*
EMP: 76
Web: www.drpepper.com
SIC: 2086 5149 Soft drinks: packaged in cans, bottles, etc.; Soft drinks
HQ: The American Bottling Company
    6425 Hall Of Fame Ln
    Frisco TX

(P-1679)
AMERICAN BOTTLING COMPANY
Also Called: 7 Up / R C Bottling Co

3220 E 26th St (90058-8008)
PHONE..............................323 268-7779
Russ Wolfe, *Contlr*
EMP: 113
Web: www.keurigdrpepper.com
SIC: 2086 5149 Soft drinks: packaged in cans, bottles, etc.; Groceries and related products, nec
HQ: The American Bottling Company
    6425 Hall Of Fame Ln
    Frisco TX

(P-1680)
AMERICAN BOTTLING COMPANY
1166 Arroyo St (92865)
PHONE..............................714 974-8560
Mark Jones, *Mgr*
EMP: 185
Web: www.keurigdrpepper.com
SIC: 2086 5149 Soft drinks: packaged in cans, bottles, etc.; Soft drinks
HQ: The American Bottling Company
    6425 Hall Of Fame Ln
    Frisco TX

(P-1681)
AMERICAN BOTTLING COMPANY
230 E 18th St (93305-5609)
PHONE..............................661 323-7921
Brian Sutton, *Mgr*
EMP: 76
Web: www.keurigdrpepper.com
SIC: 2086 5149 Soft drinks: packaged in cans, bottles, etc.; Soft drinks
HQ: The American Bottling Company
    6425 Hall Of Fame Ln
    Frisco TX

(P-1682)
AMERICAN BOTTLING COMPANY
618 Hanson Way (93458-9734)
PHONE..............................805 928-1001
Richard Roese, *Brnch Mgr*
EMP: 53
Web: www.keurigdrpepper.com
SIC: 2086 Soft drinks: packaged in cans, bottles, etc.
HQ: The American Bottling Company
    6425 Hall Of Fame Ln
    Frisco TX

(P-1683)
AMERIPEC INC
6965 Aragon Cir (90620-1118)
PHONE..............................714 690-9191
Ping C Wu, *CEO*
Ed Muratori, *
EMP: 150 **EST:** 1988
SQ FT: 215,000
SALES (est): 22.52MM **Privately Held**
Web: www.ameripec.com
SIC: 2086 Carbonated soft drinks, bottled and canned
HQ: President Global Corporation
    6965 Aragon Cir
    Buena Park CA

(P-1684)
AQUAHYDRATE INC
5870 W Jefferson Blvd Ste D (90016-3159)
P.O. Box 69798 (90069-0798)
PHONE..............................310 559-5058
◆ **EMP:** 49 **EST:** 2003
SALES (est): 9.97MM **Privately Held**
Web: www.aquahydrate.com

SIC: 2086 Mineral water, carbonated: packaged in cans, bottles, etc.

(P-1685)
BEVERAGES & MORE INC
Also Called: Bevmo
28011 Greenfield Dr (92677-4428)
PHONE..............................949 643-3020
Christoph Killin, *Brnch Mgr*
EMP: 135
SALES (corp-wide): 1.61B **Privately Held**
Web: www.bevmo.com
SIC: 2086 5149 5921 Bottled and canned soft drinks; Beverages, except coffee and tea; Beer (packaged)
HQ: Beverages & More, Inc.
    1401 Willow Pass Rd # 90
    Concord CA

(P-1686)
BLK INTERNATIONAL LLC (PA)
26565 Agoura Rd Ste 205 (91302-3595)
PHONE..............................424 282-3443
Sara Bergstein, *CEO*
Jacqueline Wilkie, *Mgr*
Louise Wilkie, *Mgr*
John Kim, *COO*
EMP: 21 **EST:** 2016
SQ FT: 5,500
SALES (est): 5.33MM
SALES (corp-wide): 5.33MM **Privately Held**
Web: www.getblk.com
SIC: 2086 Water, natural: packaged in cans, bottles, etc.

(P-1687)
BLUECAN COMPANY LLC ✪
956 Griswold Ave (91340-1454)
PHONE..............................818 450-3290
Denis Brunk, *CEO*
EMP: 20 **EST:** 2022
SALES (est): 1.12MM **Privately Held**
SIC: 2086 Water, natural: packaged in cans, bottles, etc.

(P-1688)
BOTTLING GROUP LLC
Also Called: Pepsico
6659 Sycamore Canyon Blvd (92507-0733)
PHONE..............................951 697-3200
EMP: 37 **EST:** 2011
SALES (est): 19.61MM **Privately Held**
Web: www.pepsico.com
SIC: 2086 Carbonated soft drinks, bottled and canned

(P-1689)
CALIFORNIA SPIRITS COMPANY LLC
2946 Norman Strasse Rd (92069-5933)
PHONE..............................619 677-7066
Sam Alexander, *Managing Member*
Kyle Clarke, *Managing Member**
Casey Miles, *Managing Member**
Justin Wilkinson, *Managing Member**
EMP: 30 **EST:** 2016
SALES (est): 4.28MM **Privately Held**
Web: www.calspirits.com
SIC: 2086 Carbonated soft drinks, bottled and canned

(P-1690)
CHAMELEON BEVERAGE COMPANY INC (PA)
6444 E 26th St (90040-3214)
PHONE..............................323 724-8223
◆ **EMP:** 68 **EST:** 1995
SQ FT: 100,000

SALES (est): 12.42MM **Privately Held**
Web: www.chameleonbeverage.com
SIC: 2086 5149 Water, natural: packaged in cans, bottles, etc.; Soft drinks

(P-1691)
COCA-COLA COMPANY
Also Called: Coca-Cola
1650 S Vintage Ave (91761-3656)
PHONE..............................909 975-5200
Melvin Robinson, *Mgr*
EMP: 63
SALES (corp-wide): 43B **Publicly Held**
Web: www.coca-colacompany.com
SIC: 2086 Bottled and canned soft drinks
PA: The Coca-Cola Company
    1 Coca Cola Plz Nw
    Atlanta GA
    404 676-2121

(P-1692)
CRYSTAL GEYSER WATER COMPANY
1233 E California Ave (93307-1205)
PHONE..............................661 323-6296
Gerhard Gaugel, *Brnch Mgr*
EMP: 68
Web: www.crystalgeyser.com
SIC: 2086 5141 2099 2033 Mineral water, carbonated: packaged in cans, bottles, etc.; Groceries, general line; Food preparations, nec; Canned fruits and specialties
HQ: Crystal Geyser Water Company
    501 Washington St
    Calistoga CA
    707 265-3900

(P-1693)
CRYSTAL GEYSER WATER COMPANY
2351 E Brundage Ln Ste A (93307-3063)
PHONE..............................661 321-0896
Robert Hofferd, *Mgr*
EMP: 34
Web: www.crystalgeyser.com
SIC: 2086 Mineral water, carbonated: packaged in cans, bottles, etc.
HQ: Crystal Geyser Water Company
    501 Washington St
    Calistoga CA
    707 265-3900

(P-1694)
GENIUS PRODUCTS NT INC
556 N Diamond Bar Blvd Ste 101 (91765-1000)
PHONE..............................510 671-0219
Chris Clifford, *CEO*
EMP: 110 **EST:** 2019
SALES (est): 7.4MM **Privately Held**
SIC: 2086 Carbonated beverages, nonalcoholic: pkged. in cans, bottles

(P-1695)
GREEN SPOT PACKAGING INC
Also Called: Green Spot USA
100 S Cambridge Ave (91711-4842)
PHONE..............................909 625-8771
Greg Saust, *CEO*
EMP: 20 **EST:** 1934
SQ FT: 100,000
SALES (est): 8.44MM **Privately Held**
Web: www.greenspotusa.com
SIC: 2086 Fruit drinks (less than 100% juice): packaged in cans, etc.
PA: Green Spot International
    C/O Grand Pavilion Main Entrance
    West Bay GR CAYMAN

PRODUCTS & SVCS

(P-1696)
GTS LIVING FOODS LLC
4646 Hampton St (90058-2116)
PHONE..............................323 581-7787
Gt Dave, *Mgr*
EMP: 20
SIC: 2086 Bottled and canned soft drinks
PA: Gt's Living Foods, Llc
  4415 Bandini Blvd
  Vernon CA

(P-1697)
GTS LIVING FOODS LLC (PA)
Also Called: Synergy Beverages
4415 Bandini Blvd (90058-4309)
P.O. Box 2352 (90213-2352)
PHONE..............................323 581-7787
EMP: 700 **EST:** 1994
SALES (est): 172.15MM **Privately Held**
Web: www.gtslivingfoods.com
SIC: 2086 Bottled and canned soft drinks

(P-1698)
**J & R BOTTLING AND
DISTRIBUTING INC**
1130 S Vail Ave (90640-6021)
PHONE..............................323 724-4076
EMP: 20
SIC: 2086 Soft drinks: packaged in cans,
  bottles, etc.

(P-1699)
KERNS BEVERAGES LLC (DH)
4002 Westminster Ave (92703-1310)
PHONE..............................888 655-3767
Louis J Stremick Mng, *Mgr*
▲ **EMP:** 34 **EST:** 2004
SQ FT: 2,700
SALES (est): 807.9K
SALES (corp-wide): 24.52B **Privately Held**
SIC: 2086 Carbonated beverages,
  nonalcoholic: pkged. in cans, bottles
HQ: Stremicks Heritage Foods, Llc
  4002 Westminster Ave
  Santa Ana CA
  714 775-5000

(P-1700)
KEURIG GREEN MOUNTAIN INC
26875 Pioneer Ave (92374-2026)
PHONE..............................909 557-6513
Jeffery Jenkins, *Brnch Mgr*
EMP: 20
Web: www.keurigdrpepper.com
SIC: 2086 Soft drinks: packaged in cans,
  bottles, etc.
HQ: Keurig Green Mountain, Inc.
  1 Rotarian Pl
  Waterbury VT
  877 879-2326

(P-1701)
KEVITA INC (HQ)
Also Called: Kevita
2220 Celsius Ave Ste A (93030-5181)
PHONE..............................805 200-2250
Chakra Earthsong, *CEO*
Cynthia Nastanski, *
Ada Cheng, *
EMP: 58 **EST:** 2009
SQ FT: 17,000
SALES (est): 21.55MM
SALES (corp-wide): 86.39B **Publicly Held**
Web: www.kevita.com
SIC: 2086 Bottled and canned soft drinks
PA: Pepsico, Inc.
  700 Anderson Hill Rd
  Purchase NY
  914 253-2000

(P-1702)
LA BOTTLEWORKS INC
1605 Beach St (90640-5432)
PHONE..............................323 724-4076
Ryan Marsh, *CEO*
Matthew Marsh, *VP*
EMP: 20 **EST:** 2013
SALES (est): 323.31K
SALES (corp-wide): 1.29MM **Privately
Held**
Web: www.labottleworks.com
SIC: 2086 Bottled and canned soft drinks
PA: Entertainment Arts Research, Inc.
  19109 W Catwba Ave # 200
  Cornelius NC
  980 999-0270

(P-1703)
**LIQUID DEATH MOUNTAIN
WATER** ☯
1447 2nd St Ste 200 (90401-3404)
PHONE..............................818 521-5500
EMP: 23 **EST:** 2022
SALES (est): 4.44MM **Privately Held**
Web: www.liquiddeath.com
SIC: 2086 Water, natural: packaged in cans,
  bottles, etc.

(P-1704)
**MONSTER BEVERAGE 1990
CORPORATION**
1 Monster Way (92879-7101)
PHONE..............................951 739-6200
◆ **EMP:** 2001
SIC: 2086 Soft drinks: packaged in cans,
  bottles, etc.

(P-1705)
**MONSTER BEVERAGE
COMPANY**
1990 Pomona Rd (92878-4355)
PHONE..............................866 322-4466
EMP: 36 **EST:** 2010
SALES (est): 8.17MM
SALES (corp-wide): 6.31B **Publicly Held**
Web: www.monsterbevcorp.com
SIC: 2086 Soft drinks: packaged in cans,
  bottles, etc.
PA: Monster Beverage Corporation
  1 Monster Way
  Corona CA
  951 739-6200

(P-1706)
**MONSTER BEVERAGE
CORPORATION (PA)**
1 Monster Way (92879-7101)
PHONE..............................951 739-6200
Rodney C Sacks, *Ch Bd*
Hilton H Schlosberg, *
Thomas J Kelly, *CFO*
EMP: 1923 **EST:** 1985
SQ FT: 141,000
SALES (est): 6.31B
SALES (corp-wide): 6.31B **Publicly Held**
Web: www.monsterbevcorp.com
SIC: 2086 Carbonated beverages,
  nonalcoholic: pkged. in cans, bottles

(P-1707)
ORANGE BANG INC
13115 Telfair Ave (91342-3574)
PHONE..............................818 833-1000
David Fox, *Pr*
EMP: 40 **EST:** 1971
SQ FT: 33,000
SALES (est): 2.3MM **Privately Held**
Web: www.orangebang.com

SIC: 2086 Soft drinks: packaged in cans,
  bottles, etc.

(P-1708)
PEPSI-COLA BOTTLING GROUP
Also Called: Pepsico
215 E 21st St (93305-5186)
PHONE..............................661 635-1100
Steve Longfield, *Brnch Mgr*
EMP: 62
SALES (corp-wide): 86.39B **Publicly Held**
Web: www.pepsico.com
SIC: 2086 Carbonated soft drinks, bottled
  and canned
HQ: Pepsi-Cola Bottling Group
  700 Anderson Hill Rd
  Purchase NY

(P-1709)
**PEPSI-COLA BTLG CO
BAKERSFIELD**
Also Called: Pepsi-Cola
215 E 21st St (93305-5186)
PHONE..............................661 327-9992
James B Lindsey Junior, *Pr*
Marjorie Lindsey, *
Fay W Penney, *
EMP: 22 **EST:** 1953
SQ FT: 30,000
SALES (est): 764.02K **Privately Held**
Web: www.pepsico.com
SIC: 2086 Soft drinks: packaged in cans,
  bottles, etc.

(P-1710)
**PEPSI-COLA METRO BTLG CO
INC**
Also Called: Pepsi-Cola
2471 Nadeau St (93501-1507)
PHONE..............................661 824-2051
Blaine Sherritt, *Mgr*
EMP: 38
SALES (corp-wide): 86.39B **Publicly Held**
Web: www.pepsico.com
SIC: 2086 5149 Bottled and canned soft
  drinks; Soft drinks
HQ: Pepsi-Cola Metropolitan Bottling
  Company, Inc.
  700 Anderson Hill Rd
  Purchase NY
  914 767-6000

(P-1711)
**PEPSI-COLA METRO BTLG CO
INC**
Also Called: Pepsi-Cola
1200 Arroyo St (91340-1545)
PHONE..............................818 898-3829
Bob Simpson, *Brnch Mgr*
EMP: 74
SALES (corp-wide): 86.39B **Publicly Held**
Web: www.pepsico.com
SIC: 2086 Carbonated soft drinks, bottled
  and canned
HQ: Pepsi-Cola Metropolitan Bottling
  Company, Inc.
  700 Anderson Hill Rd
  Purchase NY
  914 767-6000

(P-1712)
**PEPSI-COLA METRO BTLG CO
INC**
Also Called: Pepsico
2345 Thompson Way (93455-1050)
PHONE..............................805 739-2160
Joe Pearson, *Brnch Mgr*
EMP: 36
SALES (corp-wide): 86.39B **Publicly Held**

Web: www.pepsico.com
SIC: 2086 Carbonated soft drinks, bottled
  and canned
HQ: Pepsi-Cola Metropolitan Bottling
  Company, Inc.
  700 Anderson Hill Rd
  Purchase NY
  914 767-6000

(P-1713)
**PEPSI-COLA METRO BTLG CO
INC**
Also Called: Pepsico
10057 Marathon Pkwy (92040-2771)
PHONE..............................858 560-6735
Art Brennan, *Brnch Mgr*
EMP: 158
SALES (corp-wide): 86.39B **Publicly Held**
Web: www.pepsico.com
SIC: 2086 Carbonated soft drinks, bottled
  and canned
HQ: Pepsi-Cola Metropolitan Bottling
  Company, Inc.
  700 Anderson Hill Rd
  Purchase NY
  914 767-6000

(P-1714)
**PEPSI-COLA METRO BTLG CO
INC**
Also Called: Pepsi-Cola
19700 Figueroa St (90745-1098)
PHONE..............................310 327-4222
Stefan Freeman, *Mgr*
EMP: 228
SALES (corp-wide): 86.39B **Publicly Held**
Web: www.pepsico.com
SIC: 2086 5149 Carbonated soft drinks,
  bottled and canned; Soft drinks
HQ: Pepsi-Cola Metropolitan Bottling
  Company, Inc.
  700 Anderson Hill Rd
  Purchase NY
  914 767-6000

(P-1715)
**PEPSI-COLA METRO BTLG CO
INC**
Also Called: Pepsico
27717 Aliso Creek Rd (92656-3804)
PHONE..............................949 643-5700
EMP: 92
SALES (corp-wide): 86.39B **Publicly Held**
Web: www.pepsico.com
SIC: 2086 Carbonated soft drinks, bottled
  and canned
HQ: Pepsi-Cola Metropolitan Bottling
  Company, Inc.
  700 Anderson Hill Rd
  Purchase NY
  914 767-6000

(P-1716)
**PEPSI-COLA METRO BTLG CO
INC**
Also Called: Pepsi-Cola
6261 Caballero Blvd (90620-1191)
PHONE..............................714 522-9635
Margaret Gramann, *Mgr*
EMP: 247
SALES (corp-wide): 86.39B **Publicly Held**
Web: www.pepsico.com
SIC: 2086 5149 Carbonated soft drinks,
  bottled and canned; Soft drinks
HQ: Pepsi-Cola Metropolitan Bottling
  Company, Inc.
  700 Anderson Hill Rd
  Purchase NY
  914 767-6000

(P-1717)
PEPSICO
Also Called: Pepsico
1650 E Central Ave (92408-2611)
PHONE.................................562 818-9429
EMP: 45 **EST:** 2015
SALES (est): 2.58MM **Privately Held**
Web: www.pepsico.com
SIC: 2086 Carbonated soft drinks, bottled and canned

(P-1718)
PEPSICO INC
Also Called: Pepsico
8530 Wilshire Blvd Ste 300 (90211-3122)
PHONE.................................323 785-2820
Taylor Liptak, *Mktg Mgr*
EMP: 18
SALES (corp-wide): 86.39B **Publicly Held**
Web: www.pepsico.com
SIC: 2086 Carbonated soft drinks, bottled and canned
PA: Pepsico, Inc.
700 Anderson Hill Rd
Purchase NY
914 253-2000

(P-1719)
PEPSICO INC
Also Called: Pepsico
4416 Azusa Canyon Rd (91706-2740)
PHONE.................................626 338-5531
Kip Zaughan, *Mgr*
EMP: 23
SALES (corp-wide): 86.39B **Publicly Held**
Web: www.pepsico.com
SIC: 2086 Carbonated soft drinks, bottled and canned
PA: Pepsico, Inc.
700 Anderson Hill Rd
Purchase NY
914 253-2000

(P-1720)
PEPSICO INC
Also Called: Pepsico
20445 Business Pkwy (91789-2939)
PHONE.................................909 718-8229
EMP: 24 **EST:** 2015
SALES (est): 317.57K **Privately Held**
Web: www.pepsico.com
SIC: 2086 Carbonated soft drinks, bottled and canned

(P-1721)
PURE-FLO WATER CO (PA)
Also Called: Pure Flo Water
2169 Orange Ave (92029-4302)
P.O. Box 660579 (75266-0579)
PHONE.................................619 596-4130
Braian Grant, *CEO*
Marian Grant, *
EMP: 75 **EST:** 1969
SALES (est): 8.78MM
SALES (corp-wide): 8.78MM **Privately Held**
Web: www.pureflo.com
SIC: 2086 Water, natural: packaged in cans, bottles, etc.

(P-1722)
RED BULL MEDIA HSE N AMER INC
1630 Stewart St Ste A (90404-4020)
PHONE.................................310 393-4647
Jennifer Barney, *Brnch Mgr*
EMP: 54
SALES (corp-wide): 10.06B **Privately Held**
SIC: 2086 Carbonated beverages, nonalcoholic: pkged. in cans, bottles
HQ: Red Bull Media House North America, Inc.
1740 Stewart St
Santa Monica CA
310 393-4647

(P-1723)
REFRESCO BEVERAGES US INC
631 S Waterman Ave (92408-2329)
PHONE.................................909 915-1400
Armando Martinez, *Brnch Mgr*
EMP: 20
Web: www.refresco-na.com
SIC: 2086 Carbonated beverages, nonalcoholic: pkged. in cans, bottles
HQ: Refresco Beverages Us Inc.
8112 Woodland Center Blvd
Tampa FL

(P-1724)
REFRESCO BEVERAGES US INC
Also Called: San Bernardino Canning Co.
499 E Mill St (92408-1523)
PHONE.................................909 915-1430
Ed Williams, *Mgr*
EMP: 34
SQ FT: 76,180
Web: www.refresco-na.com
SIC: 2086 5149 Carbonated beverages, nonalcoholic: pkged. in cans, bottles; Soft drinks
HQ: Refresco Beverages Us Inc.
8112 Woodland Center Blvd
Tampa FL

(P-1725)
REYES COCA-COLA BOTTLING LLC
Also Called: Coca-Cola
15346 Anacapa Rd (92392-2448)
PHONE.................................760 241-2653
Rose Wols, *Mgr*
EMP: 33
SALES (corp-wide): 850.14MM **Privately Held**
Web: www.reyescocacola.com
SIC: 2086 Bottled and canned soft drinks
PA: Reyes Coca-Cola Bottling, L.L.C.
3 Park Plz Ste 600
Irvine CA
213 744-8616

(P-1726)
REYES COCA-COLA BOTTLING LLC
Also Called: Coca-Cola
5335 Walker St (93003-7406)
PHONE.................................805 644-2211
Jim Donelson, *Mgr*
EMP: 40
SALES (corp-wide): 850.14MM **Privately Held**
Web: www.reyescocacola.com
SIC: 2086 5149 Bottled and canned soft drinks; Groceries and related products, nec
PA: Reyes Coca-Cola Bottling, L.L.C.
3 Park Plz Ste 600
Irvine CA
213 744-8616

(P-1727)
REYES COCA-COLA BOTTLING LLC
Also Called: Coca-Cola
120 E Jones St (93454-5101)
PHONE.................................805 925-2629
Dan Suchecki, *Mgr*

EMP: 20
SQ FT: 50
SALES (corp-wide): 850.14MM **Privately Held**
Web: www.reyescocacola.com
SIC: 2086 Bottled and canned soft drinks
PA: Reyes Coca-Cola Bottling, L.L.C.
3 Park Plz Ste 600
Irvine CA
213 744-8616

(P-1728)
REYES COCA-COLA BOTTLING LLC
Also Called: Coca-Cola
1000 Fairway Dr (93455-1512)
PHONE.................................805 614-3702
Dan Suchecki, *Mgr*
EMP: 26
SALES (corp-wide): 850.14MM **Privately Held**
Web: www.reyescocacola.com
SIC: 2086 Bottled and canned soft drinks
PA: Reyes Coca-Cola Bottling, L.L.C.
3 Park Plz Ste 600
Irvine CA
213 744-8616

(P-1729)
REYES COCA-COLA BOTTLING LLC
Also Called: Coca-Cola
126 S 3rd St (92243-2542)
PHONE.................................760 352-1561
EMP: 20
SALES (corp-wide): 850.14MM **Privately Held**
Web: www.reyescocacola.com
SIC: 2086 Bottled and canned soft drinks
PA: Reyes Coca-Cola Bottling, L.L.C.
3 Park Plz Ste 600
Irvine CA
213 744-8616

(P-1730)
REYES COCA-COLA BOTTLING LLC
4320 Ride St (93313-4831)
PHONE.................................661 324-6531
Ed Shell, *Mgr*
EMP: 59
SALES (corp-wide): 850.14MM **Privately Held**
Web: www.reyescocacola.com
SIC: 2086 Bottled and canned soft drinks
PA: Reyes Coca-Cola Bottling, L.L.C.
3 Park Plz Ste 600
Irvine CA
213 744-8616

(P-1731)
REYES COCA-COLA BOTTLING LLC
Also Called: Coca-Cola
10670 6th St (91730-5912)
PHONE.................................909 980-3121
Sid Campa, *Mgr*
EMP: 310
SALES (corp-wide): 850.14MM **Privately Held**
Web: www.reyescocacola.com
SIC: 2086 5149 Bottled and canned soft drinks; Groceries and related products, nec
PA: Reyes Coca-Cola Bottling, L.L.C.
3 Park Plz Ste 600
Irvine CA
213 744-8616

(P-1732)
REYES COCA-COLA BOTTLING LLC
Also Called: Coca-Cola
5255 Federal Blvd (92105-5710)
PHONE.................................619 266-6300
Randy Cleveland, *Mgr*
EMP: 354
SALES (corp-wide): 850.14MM **Privately Held**
Web: www.reyescocacola.com
SIC: 2086 5149 Bottled and canned soft drinks; Groceries and related products, nec
PA: Reyes Coca-Cola Bottling, L.L.C.
3 Park Plz Ste 600
Irvine CA
213 744-8616

(P-1733)
REYES COCA-COLA BOTTLING LLC
666 Union St (90640-6624)
PHONE.................................323 278-2600
Gary Drees, *Mgr*
EMP: 236
SQ FT: 127,556
SALES (corp-wide): 850.14MM **Privately Held**
Web: www.reyescocacola.com
SIC: 2086 Bottled and canned soft drinks
PA: Reyes Coca-Cola Bottling, L.L.C.
3 Park Plz Ste 600
Irvine CA
213 744-8616

(P-1734)
REYES COCA-COLA BOTTLING LLC
Also Called: Coca-Cola
1338 E 14th St (90021-2344)
PHONE.................................213 744-8659
Perry Fitch, *Genl Mgr*
EMP: 26
SALES (corp-wide): 850.14MM **Privately Held**
Web: www.reyescocacola.com
SIC: 2086 Bottled and canned soft drinks
PA: Reyes Coca-Cola Bottling, L.L.C.
3 Park Plz Ste 600
Irvine CA
213 744-8616

(P-1735)
REYES COCA-COLA BOTTLING LLC
Also Called: Coca-Cola
700 W Grove Ave (92865-3214)
PHONE.................................714 974-1901
Thomas Murphy, *Brnch Mgr*
EMP: 75
SQ FT: 7,043
SALES (corp-wide): 850.14MM **Privately Held**
Web: www.reyescocacola.com
SIC: 2086 Bottled and canned soft drinks
PA: Reyes Coca-Cola Bottling, L.L.C.
3 Park Plz Ste 600
Irvine CA
213 744-8616

(P-1736)
REYES COCA-COLA BOTTLING LLC (PA)
Also Called: Coca-Cola
3 Park Plz Ste 600 (92614-2575)
PHONE.................................213 744-8616
James Quincy, *CEO*
Nehal Desai, *
◆ **EMP:** 300 **EST:** 1902

PRODUCTS & SVCS

SQ FT: 80,000
SALES (est): 850.14MM
SALES (corp-wide): 850.14MM **Privately Held**
Web: www.reyescocacola.com
SIC: 2086 Bottled and canned soft drinks

(P-1737)
REYES COCA-COLA BOTTLING LLC
Also Called: Coca-Cola
86375 Industrial Way (92236-2729)
PHONE..........................760 396-4500
Andrell Gritley, *Genl Mgr*
EMP: 66
SALES (corp-wide): 850.14MM **Privately Held**
Web: www.reyescocacola.com
SIC: 2086 Bottled and canned soft drinks
PA: Reyes Coca-Cola Bottling, L.L.C.
3 Park Plz Ste 600
Irvine CA
213 744-8616

(P-1738)
REYES COCA-COLA BOTTLING LLC
Also Called: Coca-Cola
8729 Cleta St (90241-5202)
PHONE..........................562 803-8100
Kim Curtis, *Mgr*
EMP: 90
SQ FT: 76,395
SALES (corp-wide): 850.14MM **Privately Held**
Web: www.coca-cola.com
SIC: 2086 5149 Bottled and canned soft drinks; Groceries and related products, nec
PA: Reyes Coca-Cola Bottling, L.L.C.
3 Park Plz Ste 600
Irvine CA
213 744-8616

(P-1739)
SBM DAIRIES INC
Also Called: Heartland Farms
17851 Railroad St (91748-1118)
PHONE..........................626 923-3000
▼ **EMP:** 300
Web: www.gcd.com
SIC: 2086 2026 2033 Fruit drinks (less than 100% juice): packaged in cans, etc.; Fluid milk; Canned fruits and specialties

(P-1740)
SHASTA BEVERAGES INC
14405 Artesia Blvd (90638-5886)
PHONE..........................714 523-2280
Bruce Mcdowell, *Mgr*
EMP: 63
SALES (corp-wide): 1.17B **Publicly Held**
Web: www.shastapop.com
SIC: 2086 5149 Soft drinks: packaged in cans, bottles, etc.; Soft drinks
HQ: Shasta Beverages, Inc.
26901 Indl Blvd
Hayward CA
954 581-0922

(P-1741)
STRATUS GROUP DUO LLC
4401 S Downey Rd (90058-2518)
PHONE..........................323 581-3663
Dara Killilea, *Managing Member*
EMP: 30 **EST:** 2018
SALES (est): 30K **Privately Held**
SIC: 2086 Bottled and canned soft drinks

(P-1742)
TOGNAZZINI BEVERAGE SERVICE
Also Called: Coca-Cola
241 Roemer Way (93454-1129)
PHONE..........................805 928-1144
TOLL FREE: 800
Jim Tognazzini, *Owner*
EMP: 20 **EST:** 1965
SQ FT: 18,000
SALES (est): 1.67MM **Privately Held**
Web: www.togbev.com
SIC: 2086 7699 Bottled and canned soft drinks; Fountain repair

(P-1743)
UNIX PACKAGING LLC (PA)
Also Called: Mammoth Water
9 Minson Way (90640-6744)
PHONE..........................213 627-5050
Bobby Melamed, *CEO*
Shawn Arianpour, *
Kourosh Melamed, *
▲ **EMP:** 110 **EST:** 2010
SQ FT: 125,000
SALES (est): 93.6MM
SALES (corp-wide): 93.6MM **Privately Held**
Web: www.unixpackaging.com
SIC: 2086 Pasteurized and mineral waters, bottled and canned

(P-1744)
WISER FOODS INC
5405 E Village Rd Unit 8219 (90808-7030)
P.O. Box 8219 (90808-0219)
PHONE..........................310 895-0888
Jeri Powers, *CEO*
Jeri Diane Powers, *
EMP: 100 **EST:** 2017
SALES (est): 6.94MM **Privately Held**
Web: www.wiserfoods.global
SIC: 2086 5169 1541 8742 Bottled and canned soft drinks; Alcohols; Food products manufacturing or packing plant construction; Administrative services consultant

(P-1745)
ZEVIA LLC
15821 Ventura Blvd Ste 145 (91436-5201)
PHONE..........................310 202-7000
Padraic Spence, *Managing Member*
EMP: 75 **EST:** 2007
SALES (est): 110.03MM
SALES (corp-wide): 163.18MM **Publicly Held**
Web: www.zevia.com
SIC: 2086 Bottled and canned soft drinks
PA: Zevia Pbc
15821 Ventura Blvd # 145
Encino CA
855 469-3842

(P-1746)
ZEVIA PBC (PA)
15821 Ventura Blvd Ste 145 (91436-2915)
PHONE..........................855 469-3842
Padraic Spence, *Ch Bd*
Amy Taylor, *Pr*
Harry Margolis, *COO*
Denise Beckles, *CFO*
Lorna R Simms, *Corporate Secretary*
EMP: 23 **EST:** 2007
SALES (est): 163.18MM
SALES (corp-wide): 163.18MM **Publicly Held**
SIC: 2086 Bottled and canned soft drinks

(P-1747)
ZICO BEVERAGES LLC (HQ)
Also Called: Zico
2101 E El Segundo Blvd Ste 403 (90245-4503)
P.O. Box 1734 (30301-1734)
PHONE..........................866 729-9426
Ronald J Lewis, *Managing Member*
Marie D Quintero-johnson, *Managing Member*
▲ **EMP:** 20 **EST:** 2009
SQ FT: 10,000
SALES (est): 17.18MM
SALES (corp-wide): 43B **Publicly Held**
Web: www.zico.com
SIC: 2086 Bottled and canned soft drinks
PA: The Coca-Cola Company
1 Coca Cola Plz Nw
Atlanta GA
404 676-2121

2087 Flavoring Extracts And Syrups, Nec

(P-1748)
AMERICAN FRUITS & FLAVORS LLC
1527 Knowles Ave (90063-1606)
PHONE..........................818 899-9574
Daron Canales, *Mgr*
EMP: 25
SALES (corp-wide): 6.31B **Publicly Held**
Web: www.americanfruits-flavors.com
SIC: 2087 Concentrates, drink
HQ: American Fruits And Flavors, Llc
10725 Sutter Ave
Pacoima CA
818 899-9574

(P-1749)
AMERICAN FRUITS & FLAVORS LLC
1565 Knowles Ave (90063-1606)
PHONE..........................818 899-9574
Daron Canales, *Mgr*
EMP: 25
SALES (corp-wide): 6.31B **Publicly Held**
Web: www.americanfruits-flavors.com
SIC: 2087 Concentrates, drink
HQ: American Fruits And Flavors, Llc
10725 Sutter Ave
Pacoima CA
818 899-9574

(P-1750)
AMERICAN FRUITS & FLAVORS LLC
400 S Central Ave (90013-1712)
PHONE..........................213 624-1831
Terry Miller, *Mgr*
EMP: 64
SALES (corp-wide): 6.31B **Publicly Held**
Web: www.americanfruits-flavors.com
SIC: 2087 Concentrates, drink
HQ: American Fruits And Flavors, Llc
10725 Sutter Ave
Pacoima CA
818 899-9574

(P-1751)
AMERICAN FRUITS & FLAVORS LLC
Also Called: Ability
22560 Lucerne St (90745-4303)
PHONE..........................310 522-1844
Ricardo Velasquez, *Mgr*
EMP: 55
SALES (corp-wide): 6.31B **Publicly Held**

Web: www.americanfruits-flavors.com
SIC: 2087 Concentrates, drink
HQ: American Fruits And Flavors, Llc
10725 Sutter Ave
Pacoima CA
818 899-9574

(P-1752)
AMERICAN FRUITS & FLAVORS LLC
Also Called: Lineage
3001 Sierra Pine Ave (90058-4120)
PHONE..........................323 881-8321
Julio Tovar, *Mgr*
EMP: 47
SALES (corp-wide): 6.31B **Publicly Held**
Web: www.americanfruits-flavors.com
SIC: 2087 Concentrates, drink
HQ: American Fruits And Flavors, Llc
10725 Sutter Ave
Pacoima CA
818 899-9574

(P-1753)
AMERICAN FRUITS & FLAVORS LLC
13530 Rosecrans Ave (90670-5023)
PHONE..........................562 320-2802
Michael Mallette, *Mgr*
EMP: 34
SALES (corp-wide): 6.31B **Publicly Held**
Web: www.americanfruits-flavors.com
SIC: 2087 Concentrates, drink
HQ: American Fruits And Flavors, Llc
10725 Sutter Ave
Pacoima CA
818 899-9574

(P-1754)
AMERICAN FRUITS & FLAVORS LLC (HQ)
Also Called: Juice Division
10725 Sutter Ave (91331-2553)
P.O. Box 331060 (91333-1060)
PHONE..........................818 899-9574
Jack Haddad, *
◆ **EMP:** 125 **EST:** 1975
SQ FT: 10,000
SALES (est): 82.8MM
SALES (corp-wide): 6.31B **Publicly Held**
Web: www.americanfruits-flavors.com
SIC: 2087 Concentrates, drink
PA: Monster Beverage Corporation
1 Monster Way
Corona CA
951 739-6200

(P-1755)
AMERICAN FRUITS & FLAVORS LLC
Also Called: Weber
9345 Santa Anita Ave (91730-6126)
PHONE..........................909 291-2620
Brian Maton, *Mgr*
EMP: 48
SALES (corp-wide): 6.31B **Publicly Held**
Web: www.americanfruits-flavors.com
SIC: 2087 Concentrates, drink
HQ: American Fruits And Flavors, Llc
10725 Sutter Ave
Pacoima CA
818 899-9574

(P-1756)
BERRI PRO INC
840 Apollo St Ste 100 (90245-4641)
PHONE..........................781 929-8288
Jerome Joseph Tse, *CEO*
EMP: 19 **EST:** 2015

SALES (est): 2.25MM **Privately Held**
Web: www.berriorganics.com
SIC: 2087 Concentrates, drink

(P-1757)
BETTER BEVERAGES INC (PA)
Also Called: Chem-Mark of Orange County
10624 Midway Ave (90703-1581)
P.O. Box 1399 (90707-1399)
PHONE..................................562 924-8321
H Ronald Harris, *CEO*
Tricia Harris, *
William Kendig, *General Vice President*
Patrick Dickson, *
▲ **EMP: 40 EST:** 1946
SQ FT: 15,000
SALES (est): 8.26MM
SALES (corp-wide): 8.26MM **Privately Held**
Web: www.betbev.com
SIC: 2087 7359 5169 Beverage bases;
Equipment rental and leasing, nec;
Industrial gases

(P-1758)
BI NUTRACEUTICALS INC
2384 E Pacifica Pl (90220-6214)
PHONE..................................310 669-2100
◆ **EMP:** 120
SIC: 2087 2833 5122 5149 Flavoring
extracts and syrups, nec; Medicinals and
botanicals; Vitamins and minerals;
Seasonings, sauces, and extracts

(P-1759)
BLUE PACIFIC FLAVORS INC (PA)
1354 Marion Ct (91745-2418)
PHONE..................................626 934-0099
Donald F Wilkes, *Pr*
▲ **EMP: 28 EST:** 1993
SQ FT: 40,000
SALES (est): 9.05MM **Privately Held**
Web: www.bluepacificflavors.com
SIC: 2087 2869 Extracts, flavoring;
Perfumes, flavorings, and food additives

(P-1760)
BYRNES & KIEFER CO
501 Airpark Dr (92833-2501)
PHONE..................................714 554-4000
EMP: 55 EST: 2012
SALES (est): 3.86MM **Privately Held**
Web: www.bkcompany.com
SIC: 2087 Colorings, confectioners'

(P-1761)
CALIFRNIA CSTM FRITS FLVORS IN (PA)
Also Called: California Cstm Frt & Flavors
15800 Tapia St (91706-2178)
PHONE..................................626 736-4130
Mike Mulhausen, *Pr*
◆ **EMP: 35 EST:** 1984
SALES (est): 33.86MM
SALES (corp-wide): 33.86MM **Privately Held**
Web: www.ccff.com
SIC: 2087 2033 2099 5083 Extracts, flavoring
; Fruits: packaged in cans, jars, etc.; Food
preparations, nec; Dairy machinery and
equipment

(P-1762)
CARMI FLVR & FRAGRANCE CO INC (PA)
Also Called: Carmi Flavors
6030 Scott Way (90040-3516)
PHONE..................................323 888-9240

Eliot Carmi, *Pr*
▲ **EMP: 40 EST:** 1980
SQ FT: 35,000
SALES (est): 19.68MM
SALES (corp-wide): 19.68MM **Privately Held**
Web: www.carmiflavors.com
SIC: 2087 2844 Extracts, flavoring;
Perfumes, cosmetics and other toilet
preparations

(P-1763)
COMMON COLLABS LLC (PA)
Also Called: Hangar 1
1820 E Walnut Ave (92831-4844)
PHONE..................................714 519-3245
Freddy Lopez, *Managing Member*
EMP: 34 EST: 2019
SALES (est): 4.6MM
SALES (corp-wide): 4.6MM **Privately Held**
Web: www.commoncollabs.com
SIC: 2087 Beverage bases

(P-1764)
CUSTOM INGREDIENTS INC (PA)
Also Called: Custom Flavors
160 Calle Iglesia (92672-7551)
PHONE..................................949 276-7995
Michael L Wendling, *CEO*
Steven Bishop, *CFO*
Alexander Wendling, *Pr*
EMP: 24 EST: 2000
SALES (est): 13.35MM **Privately Held**
Web: www.customflavors.com
SIC: 2087 Beverage bases, concentrates,
syrups, powders and mixes

(P-1765)
DELANO GROWERS GRAPE PRODUCTS
32351 Bassett Ave (93215-9699)
PHONE..................................661 725-3255
Jim Cesare, *Pr*
▲ **EMP: 55 EST:** 1940
SQ FT: 40,000
SALES (est): 11.85MM **Privately Held**
Web:
www.delanogrowersgrapeproducts.com
SIC: 2087 Concentrates, drink

(P-1766)
DR SMOOTHIE BRANDS INC
1730 Raymer Ave (92833-2530)
PHONE..................................714 449-9787
Sam Lteif, *CEO*
▼ **EMP: 25 EST:** 2006
SQ FT: 30,000
SALES (est): 6.41MM
SALES (corp-wide): 26.2MM **Privately Held**
Web: www.drsmoothie.com
SIC: 2087 Beverage bases, concentrates,
syrups, powders and mixes
PA: Juice Tyme, Inc.
4401 S Oakley Ave
Chicago IL
773 579-1291

(P-1767)
DR SMOOTHIE ENTERPRISES
1730 Raymer Ave (92833-2530)
PHONE..................................714 449-9787
Bill Haugh, *Pr*
William P Haugh, *Prin*
▼ **EMP: 21 EST:** 1998
SQ FT: 30,000
SALES (est): 4.27MM **Privately Held**
Web: www.drsmoothie.com
SIC: 2087 Beverage bases, concentrates,
syrups, powders and mixes

(P-1768)
FELBRO FOOD PRODUCTS INC
Also Called: Felbro
5700 W Adams Blvd (90016-2402)
PHONE..................................323 936-5266
TOLL FREE: 800
Michael Feldmar, *CEO*
Barton J Feldmar, *
Barton Feldmar, *
EMP: 49 EST: 1946
SQ FT: 35,000
SALES (est): 10.32MM **Privately Held**
Web: www.felbro.com
SIC: 2087 Syrups, drink

(P-1769)
FLAVOR HOUSE INC
16378 Koala Rd (92301-3916)
PHONE..................................760 246-9131
Richard Staley, *Pr*
▲ **EMP: 45 EST:** 1977
SQ FT: 23,600
SALES (est): 3.99MM **Privately Held**
Web: www.flavorhouseinc.com
SIC: 2087 Flavoring extracts and syrups, nec

(P-1770)
FLAVOR INFUSION LLC
Also Called: Fisa
332 Forest Ave Ste 19 (92651-2100)
PHONE..................................949 715-4369
◆ **EMP:** 40
SIC: 2087 Syrups, drink

(P-1771)
FLAVOR PRODUCERS LLC (PA)
Also Called: Flavor Producers
8521 Fallbrook Ave Ste 380 (91304)
PHONE..................................661 257-3400
EMP: 47 EST: 1981
SALES (est): 40.88MM
SALES (corp-wide): 40.88MM **Privately Held**
Web: www.flavorproducers.com
SIC: 2087 Concentrates, flavoring (except
drink)

(P-1772)
FPG OC INC
24855 Corbit Pl Ste B (92887-5543)
PHONE..................................714 692-2950
Joshua Cua, *CEO*
Priscilla Latter, *
Julie Hodson, *
◆ **EMP: 21 EST:** 2003
SQ FT: 74,300
SALES (est): 905.37K **Privately Held**
SIC: 2087 Extracts, flavoring

(P-1773)
FROZEN BEAN INC
9238 Bally Ct (91730-5313)
PHONE..................................855 837-6936
John Bae, *CEO*
▼ **EMP: 30 EST:** 2011
SALES (est): 4.39MM **Privately Held**
Web: www.thefrozenbean.com
SIC: 2087 Beverage bases, concentrates,
syrups, powders and mixes

(P-1774)
FRUTAROM
790 E Harrison St (92879-1348)
PHONE..................................951 734-6620
Imtiaz Syed, *Brnch Mgr*
EMP: 34
SALES (corp-wide): 8.77MM **Privately Held**
Web: www.frutarom.com

SIC: 2087 Extracts, flavoring
HQ: Frutarom Industries Ltd
2 Hamanofim, Entrance
Herzliya

(P-1775)
GOLDEN STATE FOODS CORP (PA)
Also Called: Golden State Foods
18301 Von Karman Ave Ste 1100
(92612-1009)
PHONE..................................949 247-8000
Brian Dick, *Pr*
Mark Wetterau, *
John E Page, *
Ed Rodriguez, *Chief Human Resources Officer*
William Sanderson, *
◆ **EMP: 35 EST:** 1969
SALES (est): 1.36B
SALES (corp-wide): 1.36B **Privately Held**
Web: www.goldenstatefoods.com
SIC: 2087 5142 5148 5149 Syrups, drink;
Packaged frozen goods; Vegetables;
Condiments

(P-1776)
HERBALIFE MANUFACTURING LLC (DH)
800 W Olympic Blvd Ste 406 (90015-1360)
PHONE..................................866 866-4744
Richard Caloca, *
◆ **EMP: 36 EST:** 2008
SQ FT: 145,000
SALES (est): 78.31MM **Privately Held**
Web: www.herbalife.com
SIC: 2087 2023 Beverage bases,
concentrates, syrups, powders and mixes;
Dietary supplements, dairy and non-dairy
based
HQ: Herbalife International, Inc.
800 W Olympic Blvd # 406
Los Angeles CA
310 410-9600

(P-1777)
J & J PROCESSING INC
Also Called: Custom Foods
14715 Anson Ave (90670-5305)
PHONE..................................562 926-2333
James B Nelson, *CEO*
Paul Nelson, *
▲ **EMP: 50 EST:** 1972
SQ FT: 44,000
SALES (est): 8.65MM **Privately Held**
Web: www.custom-foods.com
SIC: 2087 2041 2099 Beverage bases; Flour
and other grain mill products; Seasonings:
dry mixes

(P-1778)
JAVO BEVERAGE COMPANY INC
1311 Specialty Dr (92081-8521)
PHONE..................................760 560-5286
▲ **EMP: 100 EST:** 2001
SQ FT: 39,000
SALES (est): 39.27MM **Privately Held**
Web: www.javobeverage.com
SIC: 2087 Extracts, flavoring

(P-1779)
KEY ESSENTIALS INC
Also Called: Agilex Flavors & Fragrances
1916 S Tubeway Ave (90040-1612)
▲ **EMP:** 60
SIC: 2087 Flavoring extracts and syrups, nec

(P-1780)
LA PAZ PRODUCTS INC
345 Oak Pl (92821-4122)
P.O. Box 459 (92822-0459)
PHONE.....................714 990-0982
Suanne Casey, *CEO*
▼ **EMP:** 18 **EST:** 1968
SQ FT: 18,000
SALES (est): 3.4MM **Privately Held**
Web: www.lapazproducts.com
SIC: 2087 Cocktail mixes, nonalcoholic

(P-1781)
NEWPORT FLAVORS & FRAGRANCES
Also Called: Nature's Flavors
833 N Elm St (92867-7909)
PHONE.....................714 771-2200
William R Sabo, *CEO*
Jeanne A Rossman, *
▲ **EMP:** 30 **EST:** 1984
SALES (est): 4.9MM **Privately Held**
Web: www.newportflavours.com
SIC: 2087 Extracts, flavoring

(P-1782)
SCISOREK & SON FLAVORS INC
Also Called: S&S Flavours
2951 Enterprise St (92821-6212)
PHONE.....................714 524-0550
Mark Tuerffs, *Pr*
Dan Hart, *
EMP: 50 **EST:** 1928
SQ FT: 33,000
SALES (est): 6.69MM **Privately Held**
Web: www.ssflavors.com
SIC: 2087 Extracts, flavoring

(P-1783)
SOVEREIGN FLAVORS INC
4030 W Chandler Ave (92704-5202)
PHONE.....................760 455-0446
EMP: 25 **EST:** 2015
SALES (est): 1.13MM **Privately Held**
Web: www.sovereignflavors.com
SIC: 2087 Extracts, flavoring

(P-1784)
SUNOPTA FRUIT GROUP INC
12128 Center St (90280-8046)
P.O. Box 2218 (90280-9218)
PHONE.....................323 774-6000
◆ **EMP:** 62
SIC: 2087 Flavoring extracts and syrups, nec

(P-1785)
T HASEGAWA USA INC
25882 Wright (92610-3503)
PHONE.....................949 461-3344
EMP: 20
Web: www.thasegawa.com
SIC: 2087 Flavoring extracts and syrups, nec
HQ: T. Hasegawa U.S.A. Inc.
14017 183rd St
Cerritos CA
714 522-1900

(P-1786)
T HASEGAWA USA INC (HQ)
14017 183rd St (90703-7000)
PHONE.....................714 522-1900
Tom Damiano, *CEO*
Tokujiro Hasegawa, *
▲ **EMP:** 50 **EST:** 1978
SQ FT: 56,000
SALES (est): 61.26MM **Privately Held**
Web: www.thasegawa.com
SIC: 2087 Extracts, flavoring
PA: T.Hasegawa Co., Ltd.
4-4-14, Nihombashihoncho

Chuo-Ku TKY

(P-1787)
T HASEGAWA USA INC
8720 Rochester Ave (91730-4907)
PHONE.....................714 522-1900
Tom Damiano, *Prin*
EMP: 20
Web: www.thasegawa.com
SIC: 2087 Flavoring extracts and syrups, nec
HQ: T. Hasegawa U.S.A. Inc.
14017 183rd St
Cerritos CA
714 522-1900

(P-1788)
UNITED BRANDS COMPANY INC
5930 Cornerstone Ct W Ste 170 (92121-3772)
PHONE.....................619 461-5220
Michael Michail, *Pr*
Philip W Oneil, *CRO*
EMP: 43 **EST:** 2001
SQ FT: 1,800
SALES (est): 4.53MM **Privately Held**
Web: www.unitedbrandsco.com
SIC: 2087 2082 Beverage bases; Ale (alcoholic beverage)

(P-1789)
WEIDER HEALTH AND FITNESS
21100 Erwin St (91367-3772)
PHONE.....................818 884-6800
Eric Weider, *Pr*
George Lengvari, *
Bernard J Cartoon, *
Lian Katz, *
Tonja Fuller, *
EMP: 466 **EST:** 1940
SQ FT: 6,000
SALES (est): 24.35MM **Privately Held**
SIC: 2087 7991 7999 Beverage bases, concentrates, syrups, powders and mixes; Physical fitness facilities; Physical fitness instruction

(P-1790)
WEST COAST NATURALS LLC
4591 Firestone Blvd (90280-3343)
PHONE.....................310 467-3007
EMP: 20 **EST:** 2017
SALES (est): 1.16MM **Privately Held**
Web: www.wcnfoods.com
SIC: 2087 Bitters (flavoring concentrates)

2091 Canned And Cured Fish And Seafoods

(P-1791)
AQUAMAR INC
10888 7th St (91730-5421)
PHONE.....................909 481-4700
Hugo Yamakawa, *Pr*
Taka Iwasaki, *
◆ **EMP:** 150 **EST:** 1987
SQ FT: 42,000
SALES (est): 27.96MM **Privately Held**
Web: www.aquamarseafood.com
SIC: 2091 2092 Shellfish, canned and cured; Fresh or frozen packaged fish
PA: Lm Foods, Llc
100 Raskulinecz Rd
Carteret NJ

(P-1792)
BUMBLE BEE FOODS LLC (HQ)
280 10th Ave (92101-7406)
PHONE.....................800 800-8572

Jerry Chou, *CEO*
EMP: 17 **EST:** 2019
SALES (est): 366.7MM **Privately Held**
Web: www.thebumblebeecompany.com
SIC: 2091 Tuna fish: packaged in cans, jars, etc.
PA: Fcf Co., Ltd.
28f, No. 8, Minquan 2nd Rd.
Kaohsiung City

(P-1793)
BUMBLE BEE FOODS LLC
13100 Arctic Cir (90670-5508)
PHONE.....................562 483-7474
Jan Tharp, *Brnch Mgr*
EMP: 72
Web: www.bumblebee.com
SIC: 2091 Canned and cured fish and seafoods
HQ: Bumble Bee Foods, Llc
280 10th Ave
San Diego CA
800 800-8572

(P-1794)
BUMBLE BEE SEAFOODS LP
280 10th Ave (92101-7406)
P.O. Box 85362 (92186-5362)
PHONE.....................858 715-4000
Christopher Lischewsky, *Pt*
◆ **EMP:** 150 **EST:** 1997
SALES (est): 23.39MM **Privately Held**
Web: www.bumblebee.com
SIC: 2091 2047 Tuna fish: packaged in cans, jars, etc.; Dog and cat food

(P-1795)
PACIFIC AMERICAN FISH CO INC (PA)
Also Called: Pafco
5525 S Santa Fe Ave (90058-3523)
PHONE.....................323 319-1551
Peter Huh, *CEO*
Paul Huh, *
◆ **EMP:** 150 **EST:** 1977
SQ FT: 100,000
SALES (est): 44.99MM
SALES (corp-wide): 44.99MM **Privately Held**
Web: www.pafco.net
SIC: 2091 5146 Fish, filleted (boneless); Fish, fresh

(P-1796)
SOUTHWIND FOODS LLC (PA)
Also Called: Great Amercn Seafood Import Co
20644 S Fordyce Ave (90810-1018)
P.O. Box 86021 (90086-0021)
PHONE.....................323 262-8222
Sebastiano Buddy Galletti, *CEO*
Jim Lee, *
Paul Galletti, *
Sam Galletti, *
Salvatori Perri, *
▲ **EMP:** 125 **EST:** 1999
SQ FT: 80,000
SALES (est): 99.06MM
SALES (corp-wide): 99.06MM **Privately Held**
Web: www.southwindfoods.com
SIC: 2091 Seafood products: packaged in cans, jars, etc.

(P-1797)
YAMASA ENTERPRISES
Also Called: Yamasa Fish Cake
515 Stanford Ave (90013-2189)
PHONE.....................213 626-2211
Frank Kawana, *CEO*
Yuji Kawana, *

Sachie Kawana, *
▲ **EMP:** 27 **EST:** 1939
SQ FT: 20,000
SALES (est): 4.77MM **Privately Held**
Web: www.yamasafishcake.com
SIC: 2091 Fish and seafood cakes: packaged in cans, jars, etc.

2092 Fresh Or Frozen Packaged Fish

(P-1798)
ADVANCED FRESH CNCPTS FRNCHISE
Also Called: Afcfc
19700 Mariner Ave (90503-1648)
PHONE.....................310 604-3200
Jeffery Seiler, *CEO*
▲ **EMP:** 38 **EST:** 2002
SALES (est): 14.16MM
SALES (corp-wide): 48.2MM **Privately Held**
Web: www.afcsushi.com
SIC: 2092 6794 Fresh or frozen packaged fish; Franchises, selling or licensing
PA: Advanced Fresh Concepts Corp.
19205 S Laurel Park Rd
Rancho Dominguez CA
310 604-3630

(P-1799)
ATLANTIS SEAFOOD LLC
Also Called: Seacatch Seafoods
10501 Valley Blvd Ste 1820 (91731-3623)
PHONE.....................626 626-4900
EMP: 85
SIC: 2092 Seafoods, frozen: prepared

(P-1800)
BLUE NALU INC
Also Called: Bluenalu
6060 Nancy Ridge Dr Ste 100 (92121)
PHONE.....................858 703-8703
Henry Louis Cooperhouse, *CEO*
Chris Somogyi, *
Deja Westerson, *
EMP: 42 **EST:** 2017
SALES (est): 6.11MM **Privately Held**
Web: www.bluenalu.com
SIC: 2092 Fresh or frozen packaged fish

(P-1801)
CFWF INC
842 Flint Ave (90744-3739)
PHONE.....................310 221-6280
▲ **EMP:** 102
SIC: 2092 5146 Fresh or frozen packaged fish; Fish and seafoods

(P-1802)
CUSA PROPERTIES INC
4643 Hackett Ave (90713-2632)
PHONE.....................562 432-7300
Tony Delucia, *Pr*
Star Delucia, *
EMP: 24 **EST:** 1921
SQ FT: 50,000
SALES (est): 819.78K **Privately Held**
SIC: 2092 5146 Fresh or frozen packaged fish; Fish and seafoods

(P-1803)
ETHOS SEAFOOD GROUP LLC
18531 S Broadwick St (90220-6440)
PHONE.....................312 858-3474
EMP: 77 **EST:** 2012
SALES (est): 1.04MM
SALES (corp-wide): 105.89MM **Privately Held**

▲ = Import ▼ = Export
◆ = Import/Export

Web: www.smseafoodcr.com
SIC: 2092 5146 Fresh or frozen packaged fish; Fish and seafoods
PA: Santa Monica Seafood Company
18531 S Broadwick St
Rancho Dominguez CA
310 886-7900

(P-1804)
FIG313 INC
313 N El Camino Real (92672-4716)
PHONE...............................949 218-4406
Ghassan Dahabreh, *CEO*
Malgorzata Napiorkowska, *Prin*
EMP: 20 **EST:** 2014
SALES (est): 1.29MM **Privately Held**
Web: www.fig313.com
SIC: 2092 Fresh or frozen packaged fish

(P-1805)
FISH HOUSE FOODS INC
1263 Linda Vista Dr (92078-3827)
PHONE...............................760 597-1270
Ron Butler, *Pr*
Ronald J Butler, *
Rex Butler, *
Karen Butler, *
EMP: 274 **EST:** 1985
SQ FT: 52,000
SALES (est): 4.28MM
SALES (corp-wide): 18.65MM **Privately Held**
Web: www.fishhousefoods.com
SIC: 2092 5149 Seafoods, fresh: prepared; Groceries and related products, nec
PA: The Fish House Vera Cruz Inc
3585 Main St Ste 212
Riverside CA
760 744-8000

(P-1806)
FISHERMANS PRIDE PRCESSORS INC
Also Called: Neptune Foods
4510 S Alameda St (90058-2011)
PHONE...............................323 232-1980
Howard Choi, *CEO*
Hector Poon, *
◆ **EMP:** 300 **EST:** 1954
SQ FT: 125,000
SALES (est): 46.31MM **Privately Held**
SIC: 2092 Fresh or frozen packaged fish

(P-1807)
INLAND COLD STORAGE
2356 Fleetwood Dr (92509-2409)
PHONE...............................951 369-0230
William Hendricksen, *CEO*
EMP: 38 **EST:** 2013
SALES (est): 259.82K **Privately Held**
Web: www.inlandcold.com
SIC: 2092 Fresh or frozen packaged fish

(P-1808)
J DELUCA FISH COMPANY INC
Also Called: Nautilus Seafood
505 E Harry Bridges Blvd (90744-6607)
PHONE...............................310 221-6500
Wayne Berman, *Brnch Mgr*
EMP: 38
SALES (corp-wide): 24.4MM **Privately Held**
Web: www.nautilussfd.com
SIC: 2092 Fresh or frozen packaged fish
PA: J Deluca Fish Company, Inc.
2194 Signal Pl
San Pedro CA
310 684-5180

(P-1809)
NIKKO ENTERPRISE CORPORATION
Also Called: Hanna Fuji Sushi
13168 Sandoval St (90670-6600)
PHONE...............................562 941-6080
Tlang T Mawii, *CEO*
Robby Sharma, *VP*
Sein Myint, *Stockholder*
EMP: 23 **EST:** 1995
SQ FT: 5,000
SALES (est): 2.35MM **Privately Held**
Web: www.necsushi.com
SIC: 2092 Fresh or frozen fish or seafood chowders, soups, and stews

(P-1810)
OCEAN DIRECT LLC (HQ)
Also Called: Boardwalk Solutions
13771 Gramercy Pl (90249-2470)
PHONE...............................424 266-9300
▼ **EMP:** 184 **EST:** 2003
SQ FT: 20,000
SALES (est): 54.9MM
SALES (corp-wide): 94.06MM **Privately Held**
Web: www.oceandirect.com
SIC: 2092 2022 2037 2033 Fresh or frozen fish or seafood chowders, soups, and stews ; Natural cheese; Frozen fruits and vegetables; Vegetables and vegetable products, in cans, jars, etc.
PA: Richmond Wholesale Meat, Llc
2920 Regatta Blvd
Richmond CA
510 233-5111

(P-1811)
SANTA MONICA SEAFOOD COMPANY (PA)
Also Called: Santa Monica Seafood
18531 S Broadwick St (90220-6440)
PHONE...............................310 886-7900
TOLL FREE: 888
Roger O'brien, *CEO*
Michael Cigliano Ii, *VP*
▲ **EMP:** 100 **EST:** 1939
SQ FT: 65,000
SALES (est): 105.89MM
SALES (corp-wide): 105.89MM **Privately Held**
Web: www.santamonicaseafood.com
SIC: 2092 5146 Seafoods, frozen: prepared; Seafoods

(P-1812)
SIMPLY FRESH LLC
Also Called: Rojo's
11215 Knott Ave Ste A (90630-5495)
PHONE...............................714 562-5000
Dale Jabour, *CEO*
▼ **EMP:** 160 **EST:** 1987
SQ FT: 20,000
SALES (est): 44.28MM
SALES (corp-wide): 113.55MM **Privately Held**
Web: www.simplyff.com
SIC: 2092 Fresh or frozen packaged fish
PA: Lakeview Farms, Llc
1600 Gressel Dr
Delphos OH
419 695-9925

(P-1813)
STATE FISH CO INC
624 W 9th St Ste 100 (90731-7288)
PHONE...............................310 547-9530
◆ **EMP:** 230
Web: www.statefish.com

SIC: 2092 5146 Fresh or frozen packaged fish; Fish, frozen, unpackaged

2095 Roasted Coffee

(P-1814)
APFFELS COFFEE INC
Also Called: Apffels Coffee
12115 Pacific St (90670-2989)
P.O. Box 2506 (90670-0506)
PHONE...............................562 309-0400
Darryl Blunk, *CEO*
Alvin Apffel, *
Edward Apffel, *
Mike Rogers, *
◆ **EMP:** 67 **EST:** 1914
SQ FT: 100,000
SALES (est): 9.82MM **Privately Held**
Web: www.apffels.com
SIC: 2095 5149 Coffee roasting (except by wholesale grocers); Coffee, green or roasted

(P-1815)
BLACK DROP COFFEE INC
225 W Fairview Ave (91776-2942)
PHONE...............................323 742-5666
Mark Stiles, *CEO*
EMP: 17 **EST:** 2015
SALES (est): 824.97K **Privately Held**
SIC: 2095 Coffee roasting (except by wholesale grocers)

(P-1816)
CAFFE DAMORE INC
1916 S Tubeway Ave (90040-1612)
▲ **EMP:** 105
Web: www.kerryfoodservice.com
SIC: 2095 5046 Instant coffee; Coffee brewing equipment and supplies

(P-1817)
EBERINE ENTERPRISES INC
Also Called: Euro Coffee
3360 Fruitland Ave (90058-3714)
PHONE...............................323 587-1111
▲ **EMP:** 29 **EST:** 1983
SALES (est): 2.33MM **Privately Held**
Web: www.eurocoffee.com
SIC: 2095 Roasted coffee

(P-1818)
EQUAL EXCHANGE INC
2920 Norman Strasse Rd (92069-5935)
PHONE...............................619 335-6259
Nanelle Newbom, *Mgr*
EMP: 79
SALES (corp-wide): 6.36MM **Privately Held**
Web: shop.equalexchange.coop
SIC: 2095 Coffee roasting (except by wholesale grocers)
PA: Equal Exchange, Inc.
3460 Nw Industrial St
Portland OR
503 847-2000

(P-1819)
F GAVINA & SONS INC
Also Called: Gavia
2700 Fruitland Ave (90058-2893)
PHONE...............................323 582-0671
Pedro Gavina, *Pr*
Francisco M Gavina, *
Leonora Gavina, *
Jose Gavina, *
▲ **EMP:** 295 **EST:** 1870
SQ FT: 239,000
SALES (est): 77.47MM **Privately Held**

Web: www.gavina.com
SIC: 2095 Coffee roasting (except by wholesale grocers)

(P-1820)
GOURMET COFFEE WAREHOUSE INC (PA)
Also Called: Groundwork Coffee Company
920 N Formosa Ave (90046-6702)
PHONE...............................323 871-8930
EMP: 20 **EST:** 1991
SQ FT: 10,000
SALES (est): 6.1MM **Privately Held**
SIC: 2095 5149 5499 Coffee roasting (except by wholesale grocers); Coffee and tea; Coffee

(P-1821)
GROUNDWORK COFFEE ROASTERS LLC
Also Called: Groundwork Coffee
5457 Cleon Ave (91601-2834)
PHONE...............................818 506-6020
EMP: 160 **EST:** 2011
SQ FT: 4,650
SALES (est): 16.69MM **Privately Held**
Web: www.groundworkcoffee.com
SIC: 2095 5812 5149 Roasted coffee; Contract food services; Coffee, green or roasted

(P-1822)
SON OF A BARISTA USA LLC (PA) ✪
5401 S Soto St (90058-3618)
PHONE...............................323 780-8250
Don Waldman, *COO*
Oana Cioaca Taylor Vpo, *Prin*
EMP: 50 **EST:** 2023
SALES (est): 1.51MM
SALES (corp-wide): 1.51MM **Privately Held**
SIC: 2095 Roasted coffee

2096 Potato Chips And Similar Snacks

(P-1823)
ANITAS MEXICAN FOODS CORP
3392 N Mike Daley Dr (92407-1892)
PHONE...............................909 884-8706
EMP: 23
SALES (corp-wide): 50MM **Privately Held**
SIC: 2096 Potato chips and similar snacks
PA: Anita's Mexican Foods Corp.
3454 N Mike Daley Dr
San Bernardino CA
909 884-8706

(P-1824)
ANITAS MEXICAN FOODS CORP (PA)
3454 N Mike Daley Dr (92407-1890)
PHONE...............................909 884-8706
Ricardo Alvarez, *Pr*
Ricardo Robles, *
Rene Robles, *
Jacqueline Robles, *
▲ **EMP:** 57 **EST:** 1936
SQ FT: 330,000
SALES (est): 50MM
SALES (corp-wide): 50MM **Privately Held**
Web: www.anitasmfc.com
SIC: 2096 Potato chips and similar snacks

(P-1825)
FRITO-LAY NORTH AMERICA INC
Also Called: Frito-Lay
635 W Valley Blvd (92316-2200)
PHONE..............................909 877-0902
Fred Schmidt, *Brnch Mgr*
EMP: 23
SQ FT: 18,220
SALES (corp-wide): 86.39B **Publicly Held**
Web: www.fritolay.com
SIC: **2096** 5145 5149 4226 Potato chips and similar snacks; Confectionery; Groceries and related products, nec; Special warehousing and storage, nec
HQ: Frito-Lay North America, Inc.
7701 Legacy Dr
Plano TX

(P-1826)
GRUMA CORPORATION
Also Called: Mission Foods
11559 Jersey Blvd Ste A (91730-4924)
PHONE..............................909 980-3566
Victor Cervantes, *Manager*
EMP: 102
Web: www.missionfoods.com
SIC: **2096** Tortilla chips
HQ: Gruma Corporation
5601 Executive Dr Ste 800
Irving TX
972 232-5000

(P-1827)
GRUMA CORPORATION
Also Called: Mission Foods
5505 E Olympic Blvd (90022-5129)
PHONE..............................323 803-1400
Bob Solano, *Brnch Mgr*
EMP: 500
Web: www.missionfoods.com
SIC: **2096** Tortilla chips
HQ: Gruma Corporation
5601 Executive Dr Ste 800
Irving TX
972 232-5000

(P-1828)
KING HENRYS INC
Also Called: Manufacturing
29124 Hancock Pkwy 1 (91355-1066)
PHONE..............................818 536-3692
Trina Davidian, *CEO*
◆ **EMP:** 45 **EST:** 1989
SQ FT: 44,000
SALES (est): 10.14MM **Privately Held**
Web: www.kinghenrys.com
SIC: **2096** 2064 Cheese curls and puffs; Breakfast bars

(P-1829)
MARQUEZ MARQUEZ INC
Also Called: Marquez & Marquez Food PR
11821 Industrial Ave (90280-7914)
PHONE..............................562 408-0960
Elias Marquez, *Pr*
EMP: 29 **EST:** 1993
SALES (est): 2.33MM **Privately Held**
Web: www.marquezmarquez.com
SIC: **2096** 2041 Corn chips and other corn-based snacks; Flour

(P-1830)
POPSALOT LLC
Also Called: Popsalot Gourmet Popcorn
7723 Somerset Blvd (90723-4104)
P.O. Box 7040 (90212-7040)
PHONE..............................213 761-0156
Victoria Ho, *Prin*
▼ **EMP:** 20 **EST:** 2005

SQ FT: 8,400
SALES (est): 3.22MM **Privately Held**
Web: www.popsalot.com
SIC: **2096** Popcorn, already popped (except candy covered)

(P-1831)
SNACK IT FORWARD LLC
Also Called: World Peas Brand
6080 Center Dr Ste 600 (90045-1574)
PHONE..............................310 242-5517
Nick Desai, *CEO*
Bryan Cameron, *COO*
EMP: 23 **EST:** 2011
SQ FT: 500
SALES (est): 5.16MM **Privately Held**
Web: www.peatos.com
SIC: **2096** Cheese curls and puffs

(P-1832)
SNAK-KING LLC (PA)
16150 Stephens St (91745-1718)
PHONE..............................626 336-7711
◆ **EMP:** 500 **EST:** 1978
SALES (est): 174.35MM
SALES (corp-wide): 174.35MM **Privately Held**
Web: www.snakking.com
SIC: **2096** Potato chips and similar snacks

(P-1833)
TACO WORKS INC
3424 Sacramento Dr (93401-7128)
PHONE..............................805 541-1556
Roy D Bayly, *Pr*
Theresa Bayly, *Sec*
EMP: 20 **EST:** 1976
SQ FT: 9,900
SALES (est): 2.28MM **Privately Held**
Web: www.tacoworks.net
SIC: **2096** 5145 Tortilla chips; Snack foods

(P-1834)
TACUPETO CHIPS & SALSA INC
1330 Distribution Way Ste A (92081-8837)
PHONE..............................760 597-9400
Gilberto Pablo Fajardo, *Pr*
Gilberto Ramon Fajardo, *VP*
EMP: 18 **EST:** 2009
SALES (est): 1.65MM **Privately Held**
Web: www.tacupetochipsandsalsa.com
SIC: **2096** Corn chips and other corn-based snacks

2097 Manufactured Ice

(P-1835)
ARCTIC GLACIER USA INC
17011 Central Ave (90746-1303)
PHONE..............................310 638-0321
Sharon Cooper, *Mgr*
EMP: 200
SALES (corp-wide): 576.1MM **Privately Held**
Web: www.arcticglacier.com
SIC: **2097** Manufactured ice
HQ: Arctic Glacier U.S.A., Inc.
1654 Marthaler Ln
Saint Paul MN
204 784-5873

(P-1836)
FRESH INNOVATIONS LLC
Also Called: Terminal Freezers
908 E 3rd St (93030-6119)
P.O. Box 472 (93032-0472)
PHONE..............................805 483-2265
John Brashear, *Mgr*
EMP: 41

SALES (corp-wide): 4.69MM **Privately Held**
Web: www.petersonfarmsinc.com
SIC: **2097** 4222 Manufactured ice; Refrigerated warehousing and storage
PA: Fresh Innovations, Llc
1135 Mountain View Ave
Oxnard CA
805 201-2331

(P-1837)
KAR ICE SERVICE INC (PA)
2521 Solar Way (92311-3616)
P.O. Box 1197 (92312-1197)
PHONE..............................760 256-2648
Tom Lewis, *Pr*
Carol Lewis, *Sec*
Micheal Lewis, *CFO*
EMP: 18 **EST:** 1980
SQ FT: 14,400
SALES (est): 1.2MM
SALES (corp-wide): 1.2MM **Privately Held**
SIC: **2097** Ice cubes

(P-1838)
MOUNTAIN WATER ICE COMPANY INC (PA)
17011 Central Ave (90746-1303)
PHONE..............................310 638-0321
EMP: 54 **EST:** 1925
SALES (est): 4.83MM
SALES (corp-wide): 4.83MM **Privately Held**
SIC: **2097** Manufactured ice

2098 Macaroni And Spaghetti

(P-1839)
FUNGS VILLAGE INC
5339 E Washington Blvd (90040-2111)
PHONE..............................323 881-1600
Albert Lee, *Pr*
▲ **EMP:** 20 **EST:** 1984
SQ FT: 18,000
SALES (est): 2.15MM **Privately Held**
Web: www.fungsvillage.com
SIC: **2098** Noodles (e.g. egg, plain, and water), dry

(P-1840)
MARUCHAN INC
1902 Deere Ave (92606-4819)
PHONE..............................949 789-2300
EMP: 242
Web: www.maruchan.com
SIC: **2098** 5146 Noodles (e.g. egg, plain, and water), dry; Fish, cured
HQ: Maruchan, Inc.
15800 Laguna Canyon Rd
Irvine CA
949 789-2300

(P-1841)
MONZU HOLDINGS LLC
780 Hollister St (92154-1333)
PHONE..............................619 255-5032
EMP: 72
SALES (corp-wide): 220.04K **Privately Held**
SIC: **2098** Macaroni and spaghetti
PA: Monzu Holdings Llc
455 10th Ave
San Diego CA
619 255-5032

(P-1842)
NISSIN FOODS USA COMPANY INC (DH)

2001 W Rosecrans Ave (90249-2994)
PHONE..............................310 327-8478
Hiroyuki Yoshida, *CEO*
Takahiro Enomoto, *VP*
Michael J Price, *Pr*
◆ **EMP:** 200 **EST:** 1970
SQ FT: 200,000
SALES (est): 123.55MM **Privately Held**
Web: www.nissinfoods.com
SIC: **2098** 2038 Noodles (e.g. egg, plain, and water), dry; Ethnic foods, nec, frozen
HQ: Nissin Food Products Co., Ltd.
6-28-1, Shinjuku
Shinjuku-Ku TKY

(P-1843)
PEKING NOODLE CO INC
1514 N San Fernando Rd (90065-1282)
PHONE..............................323 223-0897
Frank Tong, *Pr*
Stephen Tong, *
Donna Tong, *
▲ **EMP:** 40 **EST:** 1928
SQ FT: 40,000
SALES (est): 4.79MM **Privately Held**
Web: www.pekingnoodle.com
SIC: **2098** 2052 Noodles (e.g. egg, plain, and water), dry; Cookies and crackers

(P-1844)
SANYO FOODS CORP AMERICA (DH)
Also Called: Yorba Linda Country Club
11955 Monarch St (92841-2111)
PHONE..............................714 891-3671
Junichiro Ida, *CEO*
Hiroaki Obuchi, *Sec*
◆ **EMP:** 30 **EST:** 1978
SQ FT: 130,000
SALES (est): 20MM **Privately Held**
Web: www.sanyofoodsamerica.com
SIC: **2098** 7997 Noodles (e.g. egg, plain, and water), dry; Golf club, membership
HQ: Sanyo Foods Co., Ltd.
1-1-1, Higashihama
Ichikawa CHI

2099 Food Preparations, Nec

(P-1845)
AB MAURI FOOD INC
Also Called: Fleis Chmanns Vinegar
12604 Hiddencreek Way Ste A
(90703-2137)
PHONE..............................562 483-4619
Dave Billings, *Pr*
EMP: 23
SALES (corp-wide): 24.92B **Privately Held**
Web: www.abmna.com
SIC: **2099** 2087 Vinegar; Flavoring extracts and syrups, nec
HQ: Ab Mauri Food Inc.
4240 Duncan Ave Ste 150
Saint Louis MO
314 392-0800

(P-1846)
ADELANTO ELEMENTARY SCHOOL DST
Also Called: Desert Trils Prpratory Academy
14350 Bellflower St (92301-4246)
P.O. Box 400880 (92340-0880)
PHONE..............................760 530-7680
Mandy Plantz, *Prin*
EMP: 50
SALES (corp-wide): 149.42MM **Privately Held**
Web: www.dtpacademy.com

SIC: 2099 Food preparations, nec
PA: Adelanto Elementary School District
11824 Air Expy
Adelanto CA
760 246-8691

(P-1847)
ALBANY FARMS INC (PA)
10680 W Pico Blvd Ste 230 (90064-7203)
PHONE...............................877 832-8269
William Saller, *CEO*
EMP: 22 **EST:** 2014
SQ FT: 50,000
SALES (est): 1.5MM
SALES (corp-wide): 1.5MM **Privately Held**
Web: www.albanyfarms.com
SIC: 2099 Noodles, uncooked: packaged with other ingredients

(P-1848)
ALBANY FARMS INC
625 Fair Oaks Ave Ste 125 (91030-2688)
PHONE...............................213 330-6573
William Saller, *CEO*
EMP: 39
SALES (corp-wide): 1.5MM **Privately Held**
Web: www.albanyfarms.com
SIC: 2099 Food preparations, nec
PA: Albany Farms Inc.
10680 W Pico Blvd Ste 230
Los Angeles CA
877 832-8269

(P-1849)
ALFRED LOUIE INCORPORATED
4501 Shepard St (93313-2310)
PHONE...............................661 831-2520
Victor Louie, *Pr*
Gordon Louie, *Sec*
Samuel Louie, *Stockholder*
Maryann Louie, *Stockholder*
EMP: 17 **EST:** 1979
SQ FT: 28,000
SALES (est): 1.82MM **Privately Held**
SIC: 2099 0182 Noodles, fried (Chinese); Bean sprouts, grown under cover

(P-1850)
AMERICAN NATURALS COMPANY LLC
3737 Longridge Ave (91423-4919)
PHONE...............................323 201-6891
Carlo Brandon, *CEO*
EMP: 22 **EST:** 2014
SALES (est): 963.41K **Privately Held**
SIC: 2099 Bouillon cubes

(P-1851)
AMERICAN YEAST CORPORATION
5455 District Blvd (93313-2123)
PHONE...............................661 834-1050
Lloyd Fry, *Mgr*
EMP: 28
SALES (corp-wide): 300K **Privately Held**
SIC: 2099 Food preparations, nec
HQ: American Yeast Corporation
8215 Beachwood Rd
Baltimore MD
410 477-3700

(P-1852)
AREVALO TORTILLERIA INC
3033 Supply Ave (90040-2709)
P.O. Box 788 (90078-0788)
PHONE...............................323 888-1711
Edward Arello, *Mgr*
EMP: 30
SALES (corp-wide): 18.86MM **Privately Held**

Web: www.arevalos.com
SIC: 2099 Tortillas, fresh or refrigerated
PA: Arevalo Tortilleria, Inc.
1537 W Mines Ave
Montebello CA
323 888-1711

(P-1853)
AREVALO TORTILLERIA INC (PA)
1537 W Mines Ave (90640-5414)
P.O. Box 788 (90640-0788)
PHONE...............................323 888-1711
Jose Luis Arevalo, *CEO*
Emilia Arevalo, *
▲ **EMP:** 82 **EST:** 1985
SQ FT: 20,000
SALES (est): 18.86MM
SALES (corp-wide): 18.86MM **Privately Held**
Web: www.arevalos.com
SIC: 2099 Food preparations, nec

(P-1854)
ASIANA CUISINE ENTERPRISES INC
Also Called: Ace Sushi
22771 S Western Ave Ste 100 (90501)
PHONE...............................310 327-2223
Harlan Chin, *Pr*
Gary Chin, *
▲ **EMP:** 560 **EST:** 1990
SQ FT: 6,000
SALES (est): 25.43MM **Privately Held**
Web: www.acesushi.com
SIC: 2099 5812 8741 Ready-to-eat meals, salads, and sandwiches; Fast food restaurants and stands; Management services

(P-1855)
BCD FOOD INC
13507 S Normandie Ave (90249-2605)
PHONE...............................310 323-1200
Tae Ro Lee, *Pr*
▲ **EMP:** 18 **EST:** 2006
SALES (est): 1.31MM **Privately Held**
SIC: 2099 Box lunches, for sale off premises

(P-1856)
BENEVOLENCE FOOD PRODUCTS LLC
2761 Saturn St Ste D (92821-6707)
PHONE...............................888 832-3738
EMP: 24 **EST:** 2010
SALES (est): 982.03K **Privately Held**
SIC: 2099 Food preparations, nec

(P-1857)
BEST FORMULATIONS LLC (HQ)
Also Called: Best Formulations
17758 Rowland St (91748-1148)
PHONE...............................626 912-9998
Jeffrey Goh, *CEO*
Eugene Ung, *Executive Manager*
Kelly Ung, *
◆ **EMP:** 39 **EST:** 1984
SQ FT: 50,000
SALES (est): 86.35MM **Privately Held**
Web: www.bestformulations.com
SIC: 2099 8748 5149 2834 Food preparations, nec; Business consulting, nec; Health foods; Pharmaceutical preparations
PA: Sirio Pharma Co., Ltd.
No.83, Taishan Rd., Longhu District
Shantou GD

(P-1858)
BITCHIN INC (PA)
Also Called: Bitchin Sauce
6211 Yarrow Dr Ste C (92011-1538)
PHONE...............................760 224-7447
Starr Edwards, *CEO*
Harrison Edwards, *CMO*
EMP: 30 **EST:** 2012
SALES (est): 10.35MM
SALES (corp-wide): 10.35MM **Privately Held**
Web: www.bitchinsauce.com
SIC: 2099 Sauce, gravy, dressing, and dip mixes

(P-1859)
BITCHIN SAUCE LLC
Also Called: Bitchin' Sauce
6211 Yarrow Dr Ste C (92011-1539)
PHONE...............................737 248-2446
Starr Edwards, *Ch Bd*
EMP: 75 **EST:** 2020
SALES (est): 9.72MM
SALES (corp-wide): 10.35MM **Privately Held**
Web: www.bitchinsauce.com
SIC: 2099 Sauce, gravy, dressing, and dip mixes
PA: Bitchin' Inc.
6211 Yarrow Dr Ste C
Carlsbad CA
760 224-7447

(P-1860)
BRISTOL FARMS (HQ)
915 E 230th St (90745-5005)
PHONE...............................310 233-4700
Adam Caldecott, *CEO*
EMP: 100 **EST:** 1982
SQ FT: 73,667
SALES (est): 94.53MM **Privately Held**
Web: www.bristolfarms.com
SIC: 2099 5411 Ready-to-eat meals, salads, and sandwiches; Grocery stores, chain
PA: The Endeavour Capital Fund Limited Partnership
920 Sw 6th Ave Ste 1400
Portland OR

(P-1861)
C & F FOODS INC
12400 Wilshire Blvd Ste 1180 (90025-1058)
PHONE...............................626 723-1000
◆ **EMP:** 400
Web: www.cnf-foods.com
SIC: 2099 Food preparations, nec

(P-1862)
CADENCE GOURMET LLC (PA)
Also Called: Cadence Gourmet Involve Foods
155 Klug Cir (92878-5424)
PHONE...............................951 444-9269
Brian J Wynn, *CEO*
David Wells, *
▲ **EMP:** 18 **EST:** 2004
SQ FT: 12,000
SALES (est): 4.63MM
SALES (corp-wide): 4.63MM **Privately Held**
SIC: 2099 Food preparations, nec

(P-1863)
CALAVO GROWERS INC (PA)
Also Called: Calavo
1141 Cummings Rd Ste A (93060-9118)
PHONE...............................805 525-1245
Lecil Cole, *Pr*
Steven Hollister, *
Shawn Munsell, *CFO*
Mark Lodge, *COO*

Ronald A Araiza, *FOODS & RFG SLS*
EMP: 91 **EST:** 1924
SALES (est): 1.19B
SALES (corp-wide): 1.19B **Publicly Held**
Web: www.calavo.com
SIC: 2099 5148 Salads, fresh or refrigerated; Fruits

(P-1864)
CALI-NAT PRODUCTS INC
Also Called: J Spices
534 S 6th Ave (91746-3023)
PHONE...............................626 581-5555
Kun Yuan, *CEO*
EMP: 30
SALES (corp-wide): 87.04K **Privately Held**
SIC: 2099 Seasonings and spices
PA: Cali-Nat Products, Inc
538 S 6th Ave
City Of Industry CA
626 581-5555

(P-1865)
CAMINO REAL FOODS INC (PA)
Also Called: Camino Real Kitchens
2638 E Vernon Ave (90058-1825)
P.O. Box 30729 (90030-0729)
PHONE...............................323 585-6599
Rob Cross, *Pr*
Richard Lunsford, *
EMP: 150 **EST:** 1980
SALES (est): 55.44MM
SALES (corp-wide): 55.44MM **Privately Held**
Web: www.caminorealkitchens.com
SIC: 2099 Food preparations, nec

(P-1866)
CANTARE FOODS INC
900 Glenneyre St (92651-2707)
▲ **EMP:** 42 **EST:** 1992
SALES (est): 1.86MM **Privately Held**
Web: www.cantarefoods.com
SIC: 2099 2022 Food preparations, nec; Cheese; natural and processed

(P-1867)
CARGILL MEAT SOLUTIONS CORP
3501 E Vernon Ave (90058-1813)
PHONE...............................515 735-9800
Hans Kabat, *Pr*
EMP: 191
SALES (corp-wide): 176.74B **Privately Held**
Web: www.cargill.com
SIC: 2099 Food preparations, nec
HQ: Cargill Meat Solutions Corp
825 E Douglas Ave
Wichita KS
316 291-2500

(P-1868)
CEDARLANE NATURAL FOODS INC (PA)
717 E Artesia Blvd Ste A (90746-1202)
PHONE...............................310 886-7720
Robert Atallah, *CEO*
Neil Holmes, *
▲ **EMP:** 100 **EST:** 1981
SALES (est): 81.29MM
SALES (corp-wide): 81.29MM **Privately Held**
Web: www.cedarlanefoods.com
SIC: 2099 Food preparations, nec

(P-1869)
CHEF MERITO LLC (PA)
Also Called: Merito.com

7915 Sepulveda Blvd (91405-1032)
PHONE............................818 787-0100
Margaret Crow, *CEO*
Jose J Corugedo, *
Natt Hasson, *
▲ **EMP:** 42 **EST:** 1985
SQ FT: 30,000
SALES (est): 30.65MM
SALES (corp-wide): 30.65MM **Privately Held**
Web: www.chefmerito.com
SIC: 2099 2033 2032 2044 Spices, including grinding; Jellies, edible, including imitation: in cans, jars, etc.; Soups, except seafood: packaged in cans, jars, etc.; Enriched rice (vitamin and mineral fortified)

(P-1870)
CHEFMASTER
501 Airpark Dr (92833-2501)
PHONE................................714 554-4000
Aaron G Byrnes, *Pr*
▲ **EMP:** 35 **EST:** 1939
SALES (est): 7.13MM **Privately Held**
Web: www.chefmaster.com
SIC: 2099 Sugar powdered, from purchased ingredients

(P-1871)
CJ FOODS INC (HQ)
Also Called: CJ America
4 Centerpointe Dr Ste 100 (90623-1074)
PHONE................................714 367-7200
Pious Jung, *CEO*
EMP: 78 **EST:** 1995
SALES (est): 54.82MM **Privately Held**
Web: www.cjfoods.com
SIC: 2099 Food preparations, nec
PA: Cj Cheiljedang Corporation
330 Dongho-Ro, Jung-Gu
Seoul

(P-1872)
CLW FOODS LLC
3425 E Vernon Ave (90058-1811)
PHONE................................323 432-4600
EMP: 17
SALES (corp-wide): 5.53MM **Privately Held**
Web: www.clwfoods.com
SIC: 2099 Dessert mixes and fillings
PA: Clw Foods, Llc
8765 E 3rd St
Hanford CA
559 639-6661

(P-1873)
COSMOS FOOD CO INC
16015 Phoenix Dr (91745-1624)
PHONE................................323 221-9142
David Kim, *Pr*
EMP: 45 **EST:** 1971
SQ FT: 85,000
SALES (est): 5.41MM **Privately Held**
Web: www.cosmosfood.com
SIC: 2099 5149 Tortillas, fresh or refrigerated; Groceries and related products, nec

(P-1874)
CRAVE FOODS INC
Also Called: Crave Foods
2043 Imperial St (90021-3203)
PHONE................................562 900-7272
Shaheda Sayed, *Pr*
Riaz A Surti, *
▲ **EMP:** 40 **EST:** 1992
SQ FT: 20,000
SALES (est): 3.54MM **Privately Held**
Web: www.hearthyfoods.com

SIC: 2099 Food preparations, nec

(P-1875)
CREATIVE FIRE KILN AND KIT LLC
13612 Van Nuys Blvd (91331-3657)
PHONE................................818 486-3899
EMP: 25
SALES (corp-wide): 69.95K **Privately Held**
Web: www.creativefirekilnandkitchen.com
SIC: 2099 Sauce, gravy, dressing, and dip mixes
PA: Creative Fire Kiln And Kitchen Llc
11061 Swinton Ave
Granada Hills CA
818 486-3899

(P-1876)
CREATIVE FOODS LLC
12622 Poway Rd # A (92064-4451)
PHONE................................858 748-0070
Frank Interlandi, *Managing Member*
EMP: 25 **EST:** 2007
SALES (est): 1.29MM **Privately Held**
SIC: 2099 5812 Food preparations, nec; Eating places

(P-1877)
CULINARY INTERNATIONAL LLC (PA)
3280 E 44th St (90058-2426)
PHONE................................626 289-3000
EMP: 249 **EST:** 2017
SALES (est): 22.47MM
SALES (corp-wide): 22.47MM **Privately Held**
Web: www.culinaryinternational.com
SIC: 2099 2038 5149 Food preparations, nec; Ethnic foods, nec, frozen; Natural and organic foods

(P-1878)
CULINARY SPECIALTIES INC
Also Called: Culinary Specialties
1231 Linda Vista Dr (92078-3809)
PHONE................................760 744-8220
Chris Schragner, *Pr*
Patrick O Farrell, *
EMP: 53 **EST:** 1997
SQ FT: 6,400
SALES (est): 7.94MM **Privately Held**
Web: www.culinaryspecialties.net
SIC: 2099 2038 Emulsifiers, food; Frozen specialties, nec

(P-1879)
CURATION FOODS INC (HQ)
2811 Airpark Dr (93455-1417)
P.O. Box 727 (93434-0727)
PHONE................................800 454-1355
James G Hall, *Pr*
◆ **EMP:** 80 **EST:** 1979
SQ FT: 200,000
SALES (est): 161.79MM
SALES (corp-wide): 185.79MM **Publicly Held**
Web: www.apioinc.com
SIC: 2099 0723 Food preparations, nec; Vegetable packing services
PA: Lifecore Biomedical, Inc.
3515 Lyman Blvd
Chaska MN
952 368-4300

(P-1880)
DAD INVESTMENTS
2929 Halladay St (92705-5622)
PHONE................................714 751-8500

EMP: 22
SALES (est): 959.12K **Privately Held**
SIC: 2099 5812 Food preparations, nec; Caterers

(P-1881)
DEAN DISTRIBUTORS INC
5015 Hallmark Pkwy (92407-1871)
PHONE................................323 587-8147
John D Garinger, *Brnch Mgr*
EMP: 21
SALES (corp-wide): 5.35MM **Privately Held**
Web: www.deandistributors.com
SIC: 2099 2087 2834 Sauces: dry mixes; Syrups, flavoring (except drink); Pharmaceutical preparations
PA: Dean Distributors, Inc.
899 Northgate Dr Ste 405
San Rafael CA
800 792-0816

(P-1882)
DELORI-NUTIFOOD PRODUCTS INC
Also Called: Delori Foods
17043 Green Dr (91745-1812)
P.O. Box 92668 (91715-2668)
PHONE................................626 965-3006
Jaime Brown, *CEO*
Blanca Brown, *
▲ **EMP:** 32 **EST:** 1991
SALES (est): 4.7MM **Privately Held**
Web: www.deloriproducts.com
SIC: 2099 Jelly, corncob (gelatin)

(P-1883)
DIANAS MEXICAN FOOD PDTS INC
2905 Durfee Ave (91732-3517)
PHONE................................626 444-0555
Samuel Magana, *Owner*
EMP: 59
SQ FT: 13,530
SALES (corp-wide): 26.49MM **Privately Held**
Web: www.dianas.net
SIC: 2099 5812 Tortillas, fresh or refrigerated; Mexican restaurant
PA: Diana's Mexican Food Products, Inc.
16330 Pioneer Blvd
Norwalk CA
562 926-5802

(P-1884)
DIANAS MEXICAN FOOD PDTS INC (PA)
Also Called: La Bonita
16330 Pioneer Blvd (90650-7042)
P.O. Box 369 (90651-0369)
PHONE................................562 926-5802
Samuel Magana, *CEO*
Hortensia Magana, *
EMP: 50 **EST:** 1975
SQ FT: 4,068
SALES (est): 26.49MM
SALES (corp-wide): 26.49MM **Privately Held**
Web: www.dianas.net
SIC: 2099 5812 Tortillas, fresh or refrigerated; Ethnic food restaurants

(P-1885)
DIVINE PASTA COMPANY
140 W Providencia Ave (91502-2121)
P.O. Box 15425 (90209-1425)
PHONE................................818 559-7440
EMP: 42

SIC: 2099 Pasta, rice, and potato, packaged combination products

(P-1886)
EARTHRISE NUTRITIONALS LLC
113 E Hoober Rd (92233-9703)
P.O. Box 270 (92233-0270)
PHONE................................760 348-5027
Jose Perez, *Mgr*
EMP: 29
Web: www.earthrise.com
SIC: 2099 Chicory root, dried
HQ: Earthrise Nutritionals Llc
2151 Michelson Dr Ste 262
Irvine CA
949 623-0980

(P-1887)
EL GALLITO MARKET INC
12242 Valley Blvd (91732-3108)
PHONE................................626 442-1190
Sandra Veisaga, *Pr*
Mario Rodriguez, *
EMP: 35 **EST:** 1974
SQ FT: 1,200
SALES (est): 2.36MM **Privately Held**
Web: www.elgallitonicamexcocina.com
SIC: 2099 5421 5411 Tortillas, fresh or refrigerated; Meat and fish markets; Grocery stores

(P-1888)
ESPERANZAS TORTILLERIA
750 Rock Springs Rd (92025-1625)
PHONE................................760 743-5908
Victor Martinez, *Pr*
Teresa Martinez, *
Hugo Martinez, *
Leonor Batista, *
EMP: 46 **EST:** 1980
SALES (est): 2.64MM **Privately Held**
Web: www.esperanzastortilleria.com
SIC: 2099 Tortillas, fresh or refrigerated

(P-1889)
EVERSON SPICE COMPANY INC
2667 Gundry Ave (90755-1808)
PHONE................................562 595-4785
Kim Everson, *CEO*
Ken Hopkins, *
Thomas L Everson, *Prin*
▲ **EMP:** 35 **EST:** 1987
SQ FT: 35,000
SALES (est): 5.6MM **Privately Held**
Web: www.eversonspice.com
SIC: 2099 Spices, including grinding

(P-1890)
EVERYTABLE PBC
Also Called: Everytable
3650 W Martin Luther King Jr Blvd (90008-1700)
PHONE................................323 296-0311
EMP: 38
SALES (corp-wide): 61.38MM **Privately Held**
Web: www.everytable.com
SIC: 2099 Box lunches, for sale off premises
PA: Everytable, Pbc
3305 E Vernon Ave
Vernon CA
917 319-6156

(P-1891)
F I O IMPORTS INC
Also Called: Contessa Premium Foods
5980 Alcoa Ave (90058-3925)
PHONE................................323 263-5100
Dirk Leuenberger, *Pr*
Bob Nielsen, *CFO*

EMP: 180 EST: 2002
SALES (est): 24.07MM Privately Held
SIC: 2099 Food preparations, nec
HQ: Aqua Star (Usa), Corp.
2025 1st Ave Ste 200
Seattle WA
800 232-6280

(P-1892)
FAMILY LOOMPYA CORPORATION
2626 Southport Way Ste F (91950-8753)
PHONE...............................619 477-2125
Alen Enriquez, *Pr*
▲ EMP: 25 EST: 1973
SQ FT: 10,000
SALES (est): 2.43MM Privately Held
Web: www.loompya.com
SIC: 2099 5149 Food preparations, nec;
Specialty food items

(P-1893)
FIVE STAR GOURMET FOODS INC (PA)
3880 Ebony St (91761-1500)
PHONE...............................909 390-0032
Tal Shoshan, *CEO*
Michelle Eoff, *Ex VP*
Masha Simonian, *CFO*
Michael Solomon, *Pr*
EMP: 199 EST: 1999
SQ FT: 130,000
SALES (est): 114.45MM
SALES (corp-wide): 114.45MM Privately Held
Web: www.fivestargourmetfoods.com
SIC: 2099 Ready-to-eat meals, salads, and sandwiches

(P-1894)
FLEISCHMANNS VINEGAR COMPANY INC (DH)
12604 Hiddencreek Way Ste A (90703-2137)
PHONE...............................562 483-4619
EMP: 20 EST: 1920
SALES (est): 55.82MM Privately Held
Web: www.fleischmannsvinegar.com
SIC: 2099 2087 Vinegar; Flavoring extracts and syrups, nec
HQ: Kerry Inc.
3400 Millington Rd
Beloit WI
608 363-1200

(P-1895)
FOODOLOGY LLC
Also Called: Sproutime
8920 Norris Ave (91352-2740)
PHONE...............................818 252-1888
EMP: 75 EST: 1980
SQ FT: 20,000
SALES (est): 7.77MM Privately Held
SIC: 2099 Ready-to-eat meals, salads, and sandwiches

(P-1896)
FOODS ON FLY LLC
7004 Carroll Rd (92121-2213)
PHONE...............................858 404-0642
Peter Didomizio, *Managing Member*
Budy Kubursi, *
EMP: 38 EST: 2019
SALES (est): 2.54MM Privately Held
SIC: 2099 Sandwiches, assembled and packaged: for wholesale market

(P-1897)
FOUR SEASONS HUMMUS INC
11030 Randall St (91352-2621)
PHONE...............................305 409-0449
Claudia Mejia, *Pr*
Francisco Mejia, *Dir*
EMP: 17 EST: 2019
SALES (est): 1.16MM Privately Held
SIC: 2099 1541 Sauce, gravy, dressing, and dip mixes; Food products manufacturing or packing plant construction

(P-1898)
FRESH & READY FOODS LLC (PA)
1145 Arroyo St Ste B (91340-1842)
PHONE...............................818 837-7600
Art Sezgin, *Pr*
John Saladino, *
EMP: 99 EST: 2015
SALES (est): 23.22MM
SALES (corp-wide): 23.22MM Privately Held
SIC: 2099 Salads, fresh or refrigerated

(P-1899)
FRESHREALM INC (PA)
1330 Calle Avanzado (92673-6351)
P.O. Box 2770 (93002-2770)
PHONE...............................800 264-1297
Michael R Lippold, *CEO*
Sophie Cecchini, *VP*
EMP: 125 EST: 2013
SQ FT: 5,000
SALES (est): 212.4MM
SALES (corp-wide): 212.4MM Privately Held
Web: www.freshrealm.com
SIC: 2099 Food preparations, nec

(P-1900)
FUJI FOOD PRODUCTS INC (PA)
14420 Bloomfield Ave (90670-5410)
PHONE...............................562 404-2590
Farrell Hirsch, *CEO*
Javier Aceves, *
▲ EMP: 100 EST: 2010
SQ FT: 90,000
SALES (est): 93.01MM
SALES (corp-wide): 93.01MM Privately Held
Web: www.fujisansushi.com
SIC: 2099 Food preparations, nec

(P-1901)
FUJI FOOD PRODUCTS INC
8660 Miramar Rd Ste N (92126-4362)
PHONE...............................619 268-3118
Kenny Sung, *Brnch Mgr*
EMP: 150
SALES (corp-wide): 93.01MM Privately Held
Web: www.fujifood.com
SIC: 2099 Food preparations, nec
PA: Fuji Food Products, Inc.
14420 Bloomfield Ave
Santa Fe Springs CA
562 404-2590

(P-1902)
FUJI NATURAL FOODS INC (HQ)
13500 S Hamner Ave (91761-2605)
P.O. Box 3728 (91761-0973)
PHONE...............................909 947-1008
Katsuhiro Nakagawa, *CEO*
Ikuzo Sugiyama, *
◆ EMP: 72 EST: 1979
SQ FT: 65,000
SALES (est): 13.81MM Privately Held
Web: www.fujinf.com

(P-1903)
GLUTEN FREE FOODS MFG LLC (PA)
5010 Eucalyptus Ave (91710-9216)
PHONE...............................909 823-8230
Luis Faura, *Managing Member*
EMP: 20 EST: 2015
SALES (est): 864.98K
SALES (corp-wide): 864.98K Privately Held
Web: www.glutenfreefoodsmfg.com
SIC: 2099 Pasta, uncooked: packaged with other ingredients

(P-1904)
GOLD COAST INGREDIENTS INC
2429 Yates Ave (90040-1917)
PHONE...............................323 724-8935
Clarence H Brasher, *CEO*
James A Sgro, *
Laurie Goddard, *
◆ EMP: 53 EST: 1985
SQ FT: 50,000
SALES (est): 24.91MM Privately Held
Web: www.goldcoastinc.com
SIC: 2099 Almond pastes

(P-1905)
GOLD STAR FOODS INC (HQ)
3781 E Airport Dr (91761-1558)
P.O. Box 4328 (91761-8828)
PHONE...............................909 843-9600
Sean Leer, *Pr*
C Scott Salmon, *Strategy Vice President*
Joe Villarreal, *
Greg Johnson, *
Les Wong, *
▲ EMP: 64 EST: 2007
SQ FT: 38,000
SALES (est): 329.25MM
SALES (corp-wide): 519.54MM Privately Held
Web: www.goldstarfoods.com
SIC: 2099 Ready-to-eat meals, salads, and sandwiches
PA: Highview Capital, Llc
11755 Wilshire Blvd # 14
Los Angeles CA
310 806-9780

(P-1906)
GOLDEN SPECIALTY FOODS LLC
14605 Best Ave (90650-5258)
PHONE...............................562 802-2537
Philip Pisciotta, *CEO*
Philip Pisciotta, *Managing Member*
Jeff Chan, *
Deryk Howard, *
◆ EMP: 25 EST: 1979
SQ FT: 31,000
SALES (est): 5.19MM Privately Held
Web: www.goldenspecialtyfoods.com
SIC: 2099 2032 Food preparations, nec; Canned specialties

(P-1907)
GOODMAN FOOD PRODUCTS INC (PA)
Also Called: Don Lee Farms
200 E Beach Ave Fl 1 (90302-3404)
PHONE...............................310 674-3180
Donald Goodman, *CEO*
▲ EMP: 250 EST: 1982

SQ FT: 55,000
SALES (est): 98.93MM
SALES (corp-wide): 98.93MM Privately Held
Web: www.donleefarms.com
SIC: 2099 Food preparations, nec

(P-1908)
GPDE SLVA SPCES INCRPORATION (PA)
Also Called: Peterson's Spices
8531 Loch Lomond Dr (90660-2509)
PHONE...............................562 407-2643
Ravi De Silva, *Pr*
Rupa De Silva, *
Binuka De Silva, *
Nalin Kulasooriya, *
◆ EMP: 80 EST: 2008
SQ FT: 60,000
SALES (est): 13.27MM Privately Held
Web: www.cinnamononline.com
SIC: 2099 5149 Chili pepper or powder; Spices and seasonings

(P-1909)
HALIBURTON INTERNATIONAL FOODS INC
3855 Jurupa St (91761-1404)
PHONE...............................909 428-8520
▲ EMP: 278 EST: 1992
SALES (est): 60.37MM Privately Held
Web: www.haliburton.net
SIC: 2099 Food preparations, nec

(P-1910)
HESPERIA UNIFIED SCHOOL DST
Also Called: Hesperia Usd Food Service
11176 G Ave (92345-8315)
PHONE...............................760 948-1051
EMP: 63
SALES (corp-wide): 116.14MM Privately Held
Web: www.hesperiausd.org
SIC: 2099 8322 8299 Box lunches, for sale off premises; Geriatric social service; Arts and crafts schools
PA: Hesperia Unified School District
15576 Main St
Hesperia CA
760 244-4411

(P-1911)
HONEY
333 E Haley St (93101-1712)
PHONE...............................805 963-8300
EMP: 17 EST: 2019
SALES (est): 83.31K Privately Held
Web: www.joinhoney.com
SIC: 2099 Honey, strained and bottled

(P-1912)
HONEY BENNETTS FARM
3176 Honey Ln (93015-2026)
PHONE...............................805 521-1375
Gilebert Vannoy, *Pr*
Ann Lindsay Bennett, *
EMP: 25 EST: 1978
SQ FT: 20,000
SALES (est): 2.66MM Privately Held
Web: www.bennetthoney.com
SIC: 2099 5191 0279 Honey, strained and bottled; Farm supplies; Apiary (bee and honey farm)

(P-1913)
HOUSE FOODS AMERICA CORP (HQ)
Also Called: Hinoichi Tofu

PRODUCTS & SVCS

7351 Orangewood Ave (92841-1411)
PHONE....................714 901-4350
Tsuyoshi Kido, *Pr*
Tadashi Okamoto, *
▲ EMP: 41 EST: 1947
SQ FT: 30,000
SALES (est): 74.4MM Privately Held
Web: www.house-foods.com
SIC: 2099 Food preparations, nec
PA: House Foods Group Inc.
　1-5-7, Mikuriyasakaemachi
　Higashi-Osaka OSK

(P-1914)
IMPERFECT FOODS INC (HQ)
Also Called: Imperfect Produce
351 Cheryl Ln (91789-3003)
PHONE....................510 595-6683
Abhi Ramesh, *CEO*
EMP: 75 EST: 2017
SALES (corp-wide): 25MM Privately Held
Web: www.imperfectfoods.com
SIC: 2099 Vegetables, peeled for the trade
PA: Misfits Market, Inc.
　7481 Coca Cola Dr Ste 100
　Hanover MD
　678 559-7970

(P-1915)
INGREDIENTS BY NATURE LLC
5555 Brooks St (91763-4547)
PHONE....................909 230-6200
Matt Outz, *Pr*
EMP: 24 EST: 2010
SALES (est): 10.77MM Privately Held
Web: www.ingredientsbynature.com
SIC: 2099 Molasses, mixed or blended: from purchased ingredients

(P-1916)
INTERNTIONAL TEA IMPORTERS INC (PA)
Also Called: India Tea Importers
2140 Davie Ave (90040-1706)
PHONE....................562 801-9600
◆ EMP: 32 EST: 1992
SQ FT: 21,500
SALES (est): 9.68MM Privately Held
Web: www.teavendor.com
SIC: 2099 5149 Tea blending; Coffee and tea

(P-1917)
JAYONE FOODS INC
7212 Alondra Blvd (90723-3902)
PHONE....................562 633-7400
Seung Hoon Lee, *Pr*
Chil Park, *
◆ EMP: 50 EST: 1999
SQ FT: 28,000
SALES (est): 50MM Privately Held
Web: www.jayonefoods.com
SIC: 2099 Food preparations, nec

(P-1918)
JIMENES FOOD INC
7046 Jackson St (90723-4835)
PHONE....................562 602-2505
Reyna Jimenez, *Pr*
Juan Jimenez, *
EMP: 30 EST: 1998
SQ FT: 11,000
SALES (est): 4.4MM Privately Held
Web: www.juanjs.com
SIC: 2099 Tortillas, fresh or refrigerated

(P-1919)
JSL FOODS INC (PA)
3550 Pasadena Ave (90031-1946)
PHONE....................323 223-2484

Teiji Kawana, *Pr*
Koji Kawana, *
◆ EMP: 71 EST: 1990
SALES (est): 91.01MM Privately Held
Web: www.jslfoods.com
SIC: 2099 5142 2052 Pasta, uncooked: packaged with other ingredients; Packaged frozen goods; Cookies

(P-1920)
JUNESHINE INC
10051 Old Grove Rd Ste A (92131-1654)
PHONE....................619 501-8311
Greg Serrao, *CEO*
EMP: 131 EST: 2017
SALES (est): 6.15MM Privately Held
Web: www.juneshine.com
SIC: 2099 Tea blending

(P-1921)
KATE FARMS INC
101 Innovation Pl (93108-2268)
P.O. Box 50840 (93150-0840)
PHONE....................805 845-2446
Richard Laver, *Pr*
Richard Laver, *Prin*
Michelle Laver, *
Tom Beecher, *Executive Corporate Development Vice President*
EMP: 123 EST: 2015
SALES (est): 40.72MM Privately Held
Web: www.katefarms.com
SIC: 2099 Ready-to-eat meals, salads, and sandwiches

(P-1922)
KHYBER FOODS INCORPORATED
Also Called: Sun Glo Foods
500 S Acacia Ave (92831-5102)
P.O. Box 4324 (92834-4324)
PHONE....................714 879-0900
A R Ray Ghafoori, *Pr*
Larry Ballard, *
▲ EMP: 19 EST: 1964
SQ FT: 55,000
SALES (est): 583.93K Privately Held
SIC: 2099 Food preparations, nec

(P-1923)
KTS KITCHENS INC
1065 E Walnut St Ste C (90746-1384)
PHONE....................310 764-0850
Kathleen D Taggares, *CEO*
Joan Paris, *
EMP: 250 EST: 1987
SALES (est): 37.33MM Privately Held
Web: www.ktskitchens.com
SIC: 2099 2035 Pizza, refrigerated: except frozen; Dressings, salad: raw and cooked (except dry mixes)

(P-1924)
LA BARCA TORTILLERIA INC
3047 Whittier Blvd (90023-1651)
P.O. Box 23548 (90023-0548)
PHONE....................323 268-1744
Jose Luis Arevalo, *CEO*
Antonio Arevalo, *
Alexander Arevalo, *
EMP: 50 EST: 1988
SQ FT: 6,000
SALES (est): 4.6MM Privately Held
SIC: 2099 Tortillas, fresh or refrigerated

(P-1925)
LA CHAPALITA INC (PA)
1724 Chico Ave (91733-2942)
PHONE....................626 443-8556
Luis E Moya Senior, *Pr*

Luis E Moya Junior, *Genl Mgr*
EMP: 20 EST: 1981
SQ FT: 15,000
SALES (est): 2.05MM
SALES (corp-wide): 2.05MM Privately Held
Web: www.lachapalita.com
SIC: 2099 Tortillas, fresh or refrigerated

(P-1926)
LA COLONIAL TORTILLA PDTS INC
Also Called: La Colonial Mexican Foods
543 Monterey Pass Rd (91754-2416)
PHONE....................626 289-3647
Daniel Robles, *Pr*
EMP: 185 EST: 1950
SQ FT: 27,000
SALES (est): 15.6MM Privately Held
Web: www.lacolonial-la.com
SIC: 2099 Tortillas, fresh or refrigerated

(P-1927)
LA COPA DE ORO
Also Called: Productos Oropeza
3321 W 1st St (92703-3423)
PHONE....................714 554-9925
Jose Oropeza, *Owner*
EMP: 20 EST: 1975
SQ FT: 2,400
SALES (est): 850.37K Privately Held
SIC: 2099 Tortillas, fresh or refrigerated

(P-1928)
LA FORTALEZA INC
525 N Ford Blvd (90022-1104)
PHONE....................323 261-1211
Hermila Josefina Ortiz, *CEO*
David Ortiz, *
Ramiro Ortiz Junior, *VP*
EMP: 98 EST: 1990
SQ FT: 40,000
SALES (est): 9.63MM Privately Held
Web: www.lafortalezaproducts.net
SIC: 2099 2096 Tortillas, fresh or refrigerated ; Potato chips and similar snacks

(P-1929)
LA GLORIA FOODS CORP
Also Called: La Gloria Flour Tortillas
3285 E Cesar E Chavez Ave (90063-2853)
PHONE....................323 263-6755
Daniel Torrez, *Mgr*
EMP: 20
SALES (corp-wide): 7MM Privately Held
Web: www.lagloriafoods.com
SIC: 2099 5461 Tortillas, fresh or refrigerated ; Retail bakeries
PA: La Gloria Foods Corp.
　3455 E 1st St
　Los Angeles CA
　323 262-0410

(P-1930)
LA GLORIA FOODS CORP (PA)
Also Called: La Gloria Tortilleria
3455 E 1st St (90063-2945)
PHONE....................323 262-0410
Maria De La Luz Vera, *CEO*
▼ EMP: 80 EST: 1954
SQ FT: 8,000
SALES (est): 7MM
SALES (corp-wide): 7MM Privately Held
Web: www.lagloriafoods.com
SIC: 2099 5461 5812 Tortillas, fresh or refrigerated; Bread; Mexican restaurant

(P-1931)
LA PRINCESITA TORTILLERIA INC (PA)
Also Called: Abalquiga
3432 E Cesar E Chavez Ave (90063-4146)
PHONE....................323 267-0673
Francisco Ramirez, *Pr*
EMP: 19 EST: 1974
SQ FT: 2,195
SALES (est): 2.69MM
SALES (corp-wide): 2.69MM Privately Held
Web: www.la-princesita.com
SIC: 2099 Tortillas, fresh or refrigerated

(P-1932)
LABRUCHERIE PRODUCE LLC
1407 S La Brucherie Rd (92243-9677)
PHONE....................760 352-2170
Jean Labrucherie, *Managing Member*
Tim Labrucherie, *Prin*
EMP: 42 EST: 2011
SALES (est): 3.87MM
SALES (corp-wide): 6.02MM Privately Held
Web: www.lbproduce.com
SIC: 2099 0191 Vegetables, peeled for the trade; General farms, primarily crop
PA: Tjl Capital, Inc.
　1407 S La Brucherie Rd
　El Centro CA
　760 352-2170

(P-1933)
LEHMAN FOODS INC
Also Called: Fresh & Ready
1145 Arroyo St Ste B (91340-1842)
PHONE....................818 837-7600
EMP: 25 EST: 1990
SQ FT: 15,000
SALES (est): 4.98MM Privately Held
SIC: 2099 Salads, fresh or refrigerated

(P-1934)
LETS DO LUNCH
Also Called: Integrated Food Service
310 W Alondra Blvd (90248-2423)
PHONE....................310 523-3664
Paul G Giuliano, *CEO*
Paul G Giuliano, *Pr*
Jon Sugimoto, *
David Watzke, *
▲ EMP: 300 EST: 1991
SQ FT: 57,000
SALES (est): 59.66MM Privately Held
Web: www.integratedfoodservice.com
SIC: 2099 Sandwiches, assembled and packaged: for wholesale market

(P-1935)
LEY GRAND FOODS CORPORATION
287 S 6th Ave (91746-2916)
PHONE....................626 336-2244
Frank Chen, *Pr*
J J Chen, *Sec*
Chien Chen, *VP*
▲ EMP: 23 EST: 1989
SQ FT: 4,000
SALES (est): 2.01MM Privately Held
Web: www.leygrandfoods.com
SIC: 2099 Food preparations, nec

(P-1936)
LIVING WELLNESS PARTNERS LLC
Also Called: Buddha Teas
3305 Tyler St (92008-3056)
PHONE....................800 642-3754

Nicholas Narier, *
EMP: 30 EST: 2013
SQ FT: 10,000
SALES (est): 4.53MM Privately Held
Web: www.buddhateas.com
SIC: 2099 Tea blending

(P-1937)
LOS PERICOS FOOD PRODUCTS LLC
2301 Valley Blvd (91768-1105)
PHONE..........................909 623-5625
Marcelino Ortega, Pt
Luis Ortega, Pt
Guadalupe Ortega, Pt
EMP: 46 EST: 1962
SQ FT: 20,000
SALES (est): 4.21MM Privately Held
Web: www.lospericosfood.com
SIC: 2099 Tortillas, fresh or refrigerated

(P-1938)
MARS FOOD US LLC (HQ)
Also Called: Mars Food North America
2001 E Cashdan St Ste 201 (90220-6438)
PHONE..........................310 933-0670
Vincent Howell, Managing Member
◆ EMP: 500 EST: 1936
SALES (est): 221.15MM
SALES (corp-wide): 42.84B Privately Held
SIC: 2099 Food preparations, nec
PA: Mars, Incorporated
6885 Elm St Ste 1
Mc Lean VA
703 821-4900

(P-1939)
MARUCHAN INC (HQ)
15800 Laguna Canyon Rd (92618-3103)
PHONE..........................949 789-2300
Noritaka Sumimoto, CEO
Mutsuhiko Oda, *
◆ EMP: 450 EST: 1972
SQ FT: 300,000
SALES (est): 243.06MM Privately Held
Web: www.maruchan.com
SIC: 2099 Food preparations, nec
PA: Toyo Suisan Kaisha, Ltd.
2-13-40, Konan
Minato-Ku TKY

(P-1940)
MARUKAN VINEGAR U S A INC (HQ)
Also Called: Marukan Vinegar
16203 Vermont Ave (90723-5042)
PHONE..........................562 630-6060
Yasuo Sasada, Ch Bd
Denzaemon Sasada, *
Toshio Takeuchi, *
Shugi Yamada, General Vice President*
Junichi Oyama, *
◆ EMP: 20 EST: 1649
SQ FT: 20,000
SALES (est): 9.02MM Privately Held
Web: www.marukan-usa.com
PA: Marukan Vinegar Co.,Ltd.
5-6, Koyochonishi, Higashinada-Ku
Kobe HYO

(P-1941)
MARUKAN VINEGAR U S A INC
7755 Monroe St (90723-5020)
PHONE..........................562 630-6060
Yasuo Sasada, Ch Bd
EMP: 42
Web: www.marukan-usa.com
SIC: 2099 Vinegar
HQ: Marukan Vinegar (U. S. A.) Inc.
16203 Vermont Ave

Paramount CA
562 630-6060

(P-1942)
MARUKOME USA INC
17132 Pullman St (92614-5524)
PHONE..........................949 863-0110
Takeshi Azuma, CEO
Toshio Abe, Sec
Kazuhiko Fushimi, S&M/Dir
Shigeru Kiuchi, Ofcr
▲ EMP: 17 EST: 2004
SQ FT: 134,172
SALES (est): 7.58MM Privately Held
Web: www.marukomeusa.com
SIC: 2099 Seasonings and spices
PA: Marukome Co.,Ltd.
883, Amori
Nagano NAG

(P-1943)
MCI FOODS INC
Also Called: Los Cabos Mexican Foods
13013 Molette St (90670-5521)
PHONE..........................562 977-4000
Daniel Southard, Pr
Alberta Southard, *
John M Southard, *
EMP: 140 EST: 1970
SQ FT: 15,000
SALES (est): 22.81MM Privately Held
Web: www.mcifoods.com
SIC: 2099 Food preparations, nec

(P-1944)
MCK ENTERPRISES INC
Also Called: Valley Spuds
910 Commercial Ave (93030-7232)
PHONE..........................805 483-5292
Evelyn Gardiner, Pr
Al Melino, *
Travis Dergan, *
Evelyn Gardner, *
EMP: 87 EST: 2004
SQ FT: 60,000
SALES (est): 4.53MM Privately Held
Web: www.valleyspuds.com
SIC: 2099 Food preparations, nec

(P-1945)
MILLERS AMERICAN HONEY INC
Also Called: Superior Honey Company
1455 Riverview Dr (92408-2931)
P.O. Box 500 (92324-0500)
PHONE..........................909 825-1722
George T Murdock, CEO
Steve Smith, General Vice President*
◆ EMP: 18 EST: 1894
SQ FT: 33,000
SALES (est): 702.88K Privately Held
Web: www.millershoney.com
SIC: 2099 Honey, strained and bottled

(P-1946)
MINSLEY INC
989 S Monterey Ave (91761-3463)
PHONE..........................909 458-1100
Song Tae Jin, CEO
▲ EMP: 40 EST: 2002
SQ FT: 42,000
SALES (est): 5.14MM Privately Held
Web: www.minsley.com
SIC: 2099 Pasta, rice, and potato, packaged combination products

(P-1947)
MIZKAN AMERICA INC
Also Called: Indian Summer
10037 8th St (91730-5210)

PHONE..........................909 484-8743
Pete Marsing, Brnch Mgr
EMP: 133
SQ FT: 58,500
Web: www.mizkan.com
SIC: 2099 Vinegar
HQ: Mizkan America, Inc.
1661 Feehanville Dr 100a
Mount Prospect IL
847 590-0059

(P-1948)
MOJAVE FOODS CORPORATION (HQ)
6200 E Slauson Ave (90040-3012)
PHONE..........................323 890-8900
Richard D Lipka, CEO
Craig M Berger, *
◆ EMP: 200 EST: 1953
SQ FT: 110,000
SALES (est): 47.55MM
SALES (corp-wide): 6.35B Publicly Held
SIC: 2099 Butter, renovated and processed
PA: Mccormick & Company Incorporated
24 Schilling Rd Ste 1
Hunt Valley MD
410 771-7301

(P-1949)
MOORE FARMS INC
916 S Derby St (93203-2312)
P.O. Box 698 (93203-0698)
PHONE..........................661 854-5588
John Moore, Pr
EMP: 22 EST: 1955
SQ FT: 2,000
SALES (est): 840.14K Privately Held
Web: www.moorefarmsca.com
SIC: 2099 0134 Potatoes, peeled for the trade; Irish potatoes

(P-1950)
MORINAGA NUTRITIONAL FOODS INC (HQ)
3838 Del Amo Blvd Ste 201 (90503-7709)
P.O. Box 7969 (90504-9369)
PHONE..........................310 787-0200
Hiroyuki Imanishi, Pr
Tetsuhisa Tato, *
▼ EMP: 19 EST: 1985
SQ FT: 2,782
SALES (est): 53.33MM Privately Held
Web: www.morinaga-usa.com
SIC: 2099 Food preparations, nec
PA: Morinaga Milk Industry Co.,Ltd.
5-33-1, Shiba
Minato-Ku TKY

(P-1951)
MR TORTILLA INC
1112 Arroyo St (91340-1850)
PHONE..........................818 233-8932
Anthony Alcazar, CEO
Ronald Alcazar, *
EMP: 50 EST: 2012
SALES (est): 6.3MM Privately Held
Web: www.mrtortilla.com
SIC: 2099 Tortillas, fresh or refrigerated

(P-1952)
MRS FOODS INCORPORATED (PA)
Also Called: La Rancherita Tortilleria Deli
4406 W 5th St (92703-3224)
PHONE..........................714 554-2791
Laura Perez, Pr
Shirley Serna, *
Roxana Perez, *
▲ EMP: 40 EST: 1981

SQ FT: 4,000
SALES (est): 4.82MM
SALES (corp-wide): 4.82MM Privately Held
SIC: 2099 5812 Tortillas, fresh or refrigerated ; Fast-food restaurant, independent

(P-1953)
NATREN INC
3105 Willow Ln (91361-4919)
PHONE..........................805 371-4737
Yordan Trenev, CEO
Natasha Trenev, *
Odessa Braza, *
EMP: 60 EST: 1983
SQ FT: 22,000
SALES (est): 11.65MM Privately Held
Web: www.natren.com
SIC: 2099 8011 Food preparations, nec; Offices and clinics of medical doctors

(P-1954)
NATURES FLAVORS
833 N Elm St (92867-7909)
PHONE..........................714 744-3700
Bill Sabo, Prin
▲ EMP: 25 EST: 1998
SALES (est): 3.11MM Privately Held
Web: www.naturesflavors.com
SIC: 2099 Food preparations, nec

(P-1955)
NINA MIA INC
Also Called: Pasta Mia
826 Enterprise Way (92831-5015)
PHONE..........................714 773-5588
Diego Mazza, Pr
▲ EMP: 80 EST: 1984
SQ FT: 32,000
SALES (est): 14.99MM Privately Held
Web: www.pastamia.com
SIC: 2099 Pasta, uncooked: packaged with other ingredients

(P-1956)
NINAS MEXICAN FOODS INC
20631 Valley Blvd Ste A (91789-2751)
PHONE..........................909 468-5888
Ruben Vasquez, Pr
▲ EMP: 40 EST: 1989
SQ FT: 14,000
SALES (est): 4.34MM Privately Held
SIC: 2099 Tortillas, fresh or refrigerated

(P-1957)
OASIS DATE GARDEN INC
59111 Grapefruit Blvd (92274-8813)
P.O. Box 757 (92274-0757)
PHONE..........................760 399-5665
James Freimuth, Pr
Chris Nelsen, *
▲ EMP: 20 EST: 1918
SQ FT: 14,000
SALES (est): 2.34MM Privately Held
Web: www.oasisdate.com
SIC: 2099 5431 5148 0179 Food preparations, nec; Fruit stands or markets; Fruits; Date orchard

(P-1958)
ORGANIC MILLING CORPORATION
305 S Acacia St Ste A (91773-2928)
PHONE..........................909 305-0185
Lupe Martinez, Brnch Mgr
EMP: 32
SALES (corp-wide): 25.19MM Privately Held
Web: www.organicmilling.com

P
R
O
D
U
C
T
S

&
S
V
C
S

SIC: **2099** Food preparations, nec
PA: Organic Milling Corporation
505 W Allen Ave
San Dimas CA
909 599-0961

(P-1959)

ORGANIC MILLING CORPORATION (PA)
505 W Allen Ave (91773-1487)
PHONE..................................909 599-0961
Bruce Olsen, *Pr*
Nick Bishop, *Dir*
John Duenas, *Prin*
◆ **EMP: 108 EST:** 2001
SQ FT: 43,000
SALES (est): 25.19MM
SALES (corp-wide): 25.19MM **Privately Held**
Web: www.organicmilling.com
SIC: **2099** Food preparations, nec

(P-1960)

OSI INDUSTRIES LLC
1155 Mt Vernon Ave (92507-1830)
PHONE..................................951 684-4500
Sheldon Lavin, *CEO*
▲ **EMP: 431**
Web: www.osigroup.com
SIC: **2099** Ready-to-eat meals, salads, and sandwiches
HQ: Osi Industries, Llc
1225 Corp Blvd Ste 105
Aurora IL
630 851-6600

(P-1961)

OTAFUKU FOODS INC
13117 Molette St (90670-5523)
PHONE..................................562 404-4700
Naoyoshi Saki, *Ch*
Takamitsu Ozawa, *Pr*
▲ **EMP: 22 EST:** 1998
SQ FT: 2,000
SALES (est): 7.84MM **Privately Held**
Web: www.otafukufoods.com
SIC: **2099** Food preparations, nec
PA: Otafuku Holdings Co., Ltd.
7-4-27, Shoko-Center, Nishi-Ku
Hiroshima HIR

(P-1962)

OUT OF SHELL LLC
Also Called: Ling's
9658 Remer St (91733-3033)
PHONE..................................626 401-1923
Bing Yang, *
EMP: 200 EST: 1999
SALES (est): 21.26MM **Privately Held**
SIC: **2099** Food preparations, nec

(P-1963)

OVERHILL FARMS INC (DH)
Also Called: Chicago Brothers
2727 E Vernon Ave (90058-1822)
P.O. Box 58806 (90058-0806)
PHONE..................................323 582-9977
James Rudis, *Pr*
Robert C Bruning, *
Robert A Olivarez, *
Rick Alvarez, *
EMP: 101 EST: 1995
SQ FT: 170,000
SALES (est): 23.07MM **Privately Held**
Web: www.overhillfarms.com
SIC: **2099** Food preparations, nec
HQ: Bellisio Foods, Inc
701 Washington Ave N # 400
Minneapolis MN

(P-1964)

PACIFIC CULINARY GROUP INC
566 Monterey Pass Rd (91754-2417)
PHONE..................................626 284-1328
Bingham Lee, *CEO*
Lin Ma, *Pr*
EMP: 20 EST: 2013
SALES (est): 1.06MM **Privately Held**
SIC: **2099** Food preparations, nec

(P-1965)

PACIFIC SPICE COMPANY INC
Also Called: Pacific Natural Spices
6430 E Slauson Ave (90040-3108)
PHONE..................................323 726-9190
Gershon Schlussel, *CEO*
Gershon D Schlussel, *
Akiba E Schlussel, *
Sharon Schlussel, *
◆ **EMP: 130 EST:** 1966
SQ FT: 150,000
SALES (est): 25.25MM **Privately Held**
Web: www.pacificspice.com
SIC: **2099** 5149 Spices, including grinding; Spices and seasonings

(P-1966)

PALERMO FAMILY LP
Also Called: Divine Pasta Company
140 W Providencia Ave (91502-2121)
PHONE..................................213 542-3300
Alexander Palermo, *Prin*
EMP: 49 EST: 1991
SQ FT: 30,000
SALES (est): 8.77MM **Privately Held**
Web: www.divinepasta.com
SIC: **2099** Pasta, rice, and potato, packaged combination products

(P-1967)

PASSPORT FOOD GROUP LLC
Also Called: Wing Hing Noodle Company
2539 E Philadelphia St (91761-7774)
PHONE..................................909 627-7312
▲ **EMP: 150**
SIC: **2099** Pasta, rice, and potato, packaged combination products

(P-1968)

PASSPORT FOODS (SVC) LLC
2539 E Philadelphia St (91761-7774)
PHONE..................................909 627-7312
Mark Thomson, *CEO*
EMP: 150 EST: 2019
SALES (est): 9.4MM **Privately Held**
SIC: **2099** Pasta, rice, and potato, packaged combination products

(P-1969)

PENGUIN NATURAL FOODS INC
5659 Mansfield Way (90201-6300)
PHONE..................................323 488-6000
EMP: 28
Web: www.penguinfoods.com
SIC: **2099** Food preparations, nec
PA: Penguin Natural Foods, Inc.
4400 Alcoa Ave
Vernon CA

(P-1970)

PENGUIN NATURAL FOODS INC (PA)
4400 Alcoa Ave (90058-2412)
PHONE..................................323 727-7980
▲ **EMP: 45 EST:** 1993
SALES (est): 10.11MM **Privately Held**
Web: www.penguinfoods.com
SIC: **2099** Pasta, rice, and potato, packaged combination products

(P-1971)

PLANT RANCH LLC
242 N Avenue 25 Ste 114 (90031-1881)
PHONE..................................818 384-9727
Gary Robert Huerta, *Managing Member*
EMP: 17 EST: 2016
SALES (est): 875.34K **Privately Held**
Web: www.plantranchfoods.com
SIC: **2099** Food preparations, nec

(P-1972)

QUOC VIET FOODS
Also Called: Cafvina Coffee & Tea
12221 Monarch St (92841-2906)
PHONE..................................714 283-3663
Tuan Nguyen, *Pr*
Theresa Nguyen, *Ex VP*
Kim Vu, *Stockholder*
Khanh Nguyen, *Stockholder*
Alan Khoa Nguyen, *Stockholder*
▲ **EMP: 80 EST:** 2002
SQ FT: 2,000
SALES (est): 18.03MM **Privately Held**
Web: www.quocviet.com
SIC: **2099** 2095 5149 2034 Seasonings and spices; Coffee roasting (except by wholesale grocers); Coffee and tea; Soup mixes

(P-1973)

RAMA FOOD MANUFACTURE CORP (PA)
1486 E Cedar St (91761-8300)
P.O. Box 4045 (91761-1002)
PHONE..................................909 923-5305
Karen Trang Ving, *CEO*
▲ **EMP: 19 EST:** 1984
SQ FT: 25,000
SALES (est): 5.17MM
SALES (corp-wide): 5.17MM **Privately Held**
Web: www.ramafood.com
SIC: **2099** Noodles, fried (Chinese)

(P-1974)

RANCHO LOMITA FOOD INDS INC
912 Cardiff St (92114-5018)
PHONE..................................619 464-2800
Nasser Beydoun, *Pr*
EMP: 25 EST: 1991
SQ FT: 10,000
SALES (est): 1.45MM **Privately Held**
SIC: **2099** 2096 Tortillas, fresh or refrigerated ; Tortilla chips

(P-1975)

READY PAC FOODS INC (HQ)
4401 Foxdale St (91706-2161)
PHONE..................................626 856-8686
Mary Thompson, *CEO*
Tim Clark, *Chief*
Jay Ellis, *SO*
Dan Redfern, *CFO*
Scott Mcguire, *SCO*
◆ **EMP: 2000 EST:** 2000
SQ FT: 135,000
SALES (est): 973.11MM
SALES (corp-wide): 2.67MM **Privately Held**
Web: www.readypac.com
SIC: **2099** 5148 Salads, fresh or refrigerated; Vegetables, fresh
PA: Bonduelle
Rue De La Woestyne
Renescure
328426060

(P-1976)

REYNALDOS MEXICAN FOOD CO LLC (PA)
3301 E Vernon Ave (90058-1809)
PHONE..................................562 803-3188
Douglas Reed, *CFO*
Marisol Scrugham, *
Al Soto, *Managing Member**
EMP: 160 EST: 2006
SALES (est): 24.77MM **Privately Held**
Web: www.sabrosurafoods.com
SIC: **2099** Food preparations, nec

(P-1977)

RICH PRODUCTS CORPORATION
12805 Busch Pl (90670-3023)
PHONE..................................562 946-6396
Mike Ball, *Mgr*
EMP: 63
SALES (corp-wide): 4.81B **Privately Held**
Web: www.richs.com
SIC: **2099** 2051 Desserts, ready-to-mix; Bread, cake, and related products
PA: Rich Products Corporation
1 Robert Rich Way
Buffalo NY
716 878-8000

(P-1978)

RISVOLDS INC
1234 W El Segundo Blvd (90247-1522)
PHONE..................................323 770-2674
Tim Brandon, *CEO*
Ed Scoullar, *
EMP: 65 EST: 1937
SQ FT: 30,000
SALES (est): 9.1MM **Privately Held**
Web: www.risvolds.com
SIC: **2099** Salads, fresh or refrigerated

(P-1979)

ROMEROS FOOD PRODUCTS INC (PA)
15155 Valley View Ave (90670-5323)
PHONE..................................562 802-1858
Richard Scandalito, *CEO*
Leon Romero Senior, *Pr*
Raul Romero Senior, *VP*
Leon S Romero, *
EMP: 100 EST: 1971
SQ FT: 20,000
SALES (est): 21.87MM
SALES (corp-wide): 21.87MM **Privately Held**
Web: www.romerosfood.com
SIC: **2099** 2096 5461 Tortillas, fresh or refrigerated; Tortilla chips; Retail bakeries

(P-1980)

RUIZ MEXICAN FOODS INC (PA)
Also Called: Ruiz Flour Tortillas
1200 Marlborough Ave Ste A (92507-2158)
PHONE..................................909 947-7811
Dolores C Ruiz, *CEO*
▼ **EMP: 120 EST:** 1976
SQ FT: 38,000
SALES (est): 9.89MM
SALES (corp-wide): 9.89MM **Privately Held**
Web: www.ruizflourtortillas.com
SIC: **2099** 3556 Tortillas, fresh or refrigerated ; Food products machinery

(P-1981)

SABATER USA INC (PA)
Also Called: Npms Natural Products Mil Svcs
14824 S Main St (90248-1919)
PHONE..................................310 518-2227

Jose Sabater Sanchez, *CEO*
David Solomon, *Prin*
▲ **EMP:** 33 **EST:** 1999
SQ FT: 80,000
SALES (est): 12.77MM
SALES (corp-wide): 12.77MM **Privately Held**
Web: www.bdsnatural.com
SIC: 2099 5149 Seasonings and spices; Natural and organic foods

(P-1982)
SALADISH INC
12 W Colorado Blvd (91105-1923)
PHONE..................626 304-3100
Seung Hee Lee, *Prin*
EMP: 67
SALES (corp-wide): 454.96K **Privately Held**
SIC: 2099 Ready-to-eat meals, salads, and sandwiches
PA: Saladish, Inc.
28901 S Wstn Ave Ste 123
Rancho Palos Verdes CA
310 521-0300

(P-1983)
SAUER BRANDS INC
Also Called: Sauer Brands, Inc
184 Suburban Rd (93401-7502)
PHONE..................805 597-8900
William W Lovette, *CEO*
EMP: 65
SALES (corp-wide): 111.61MM **Privately Held**
Web: www.sauers.com
SIC: 2099 Seasonings and spices
PA: Sauer Brands, Inc.
2000 W Broad St
Richmond VA
804 359-5786

(P-1984)
SHORE FRONT LLC
Also Called: Subway
3973 Trolley Ct (92823-1054)
PHONE..................714 612-3751
Anil Kumar, *
Ajay Maini, *CEO*
EMP: 40 **EST:** 2009
SALES (est): 4.29MM **Privately Held**
Web: order.subway.com
SIC: 2099 5812 Ready-to-eat meals, salads, and sandwiches; Eating places

(P-1985)
SILAO TORTILLERIA INC
Also Called: Silao Tortilleria
18316 Senteno St (91748-4433)
PHONE..................626 961-0761
Leandro Espinosa Senior, *Pr*
Leandro Espinosa Junior, *VP*
EMP: 44 **EST:** 1955
SALES (est): 4.21MM **Privately Held**
SIC: 2099 Tortillas, fresh or refrigerated

(P-1986)
SINCERE ORIENT COMMERCIAL CORP
Also Called: Sincere Orient Food Company
15222 Valley Blvd (91746-3323)
PHONE..................626 333-8882
Andy Khun, *Pr*
▲ **EMP:** 70 **EST:** 1984
SQ FT: 12,000
SALES (est): 4.9MM **Privately Held**
Web: www.sincereorient.com
SIC: 2099 Pasta, rice, and potato, packaged combination products

(P-1987)
SONORA MILLS FOODS INC (PA)
Also Called: Pop Chips
3064 E Maria St (90221-5804)
PHONE..................310 639-5333
Patrick Turpin, *CEO*
Martin Basch, *
▲ **EMP:** 191 **EST:** 1991
SQ FT: 80,000
SALES (est): 22.58MM
SALES (corp-wide): 22.58MM **Privately Held**
SIC: 2099 Food preparations, nec

(P-1988)
SOUP BASES LOADED INC
2355 E Francis St (91761-7727)
PHONE..................909 230-6890
Alan Portney, *Pr*
EMP: 45 **EST:** 1997
SQ FT: 27,000
SALES (est): 9.95MM **Privately Held**
Web: www.soupbasesloaded.com
SIC: 2099 2034 Seasonings: dry mixes; Dried and dehydrated soup mixes

(P-1989)
SOUTHWEST PRODUCTS LLC
8411 Siempre Viva Rd (92154-6299)
PHONE..................619 263-8000
▲ **EMP:** 250
Web: www.circlefoods.com
SIC: 2099 Tortillas, fresh or refrigerated

(P-1990)
SOYFOODS OF AMERICA
1091 Hamilton Rd (91010-2743)
PHONE..................626 358-3836
Ka Nin Lee, *Pr*
EMP: 27 **EST:** 1981
SQ FT: 15,000
SALES (est): 2.49MM **Privately Held**
Web: www.soyfoodsusa.com
SIC: 2099 Food preparations, nec

(P-1991)
STANESS JONEKOS ENTPS INC
Also Called: Eat Like A Woman
4000 W Magnolia Blvd D (91505-2827)
PHONE..................818 606-2710
Staness Jonekos, *Owner*
EMP: 27 **EST:** 1988
SALES (est): 1.32MM **Privately Held**
Web: www.eatlikeawoman.com
SIC: 2099 Food preparations, nec

(P-1992)
SUN RICH FOODS INTL CORP
1240 N Barsten Way (92806-1822)
PHONE..................714 632-7577
Walid A Barakat, *Pr*
Shirley Barakat, *CFO*
Alex Barakat, *VP*
EMP: 19 **EST:** 1981
SQ FT: 6,500
SALES (est): 861.42K **Privately Held**
Web: www.sunrichfoods.com
SIC: 2099 Food preparations, nec

(P-1993)
SUNRISE GROWERS INC
Also Called: Oxnard 2 Warehouse
2640 Sturgis Rd (93030-7931)
PHONE..................612 619-9545
Jill Barnett, *Pr*
EMP: 576 **EST:** 2011
SALES (est): 3.02MM **Privately Held**

SIC: 2099 Food preparations, nec
PA: Sunopta Foods Inc.
7078 Shady Oak Rd
Eden Prairie MN

(P-1994)
T HASEGAWA USA INC
2026 Cecilia Cir (92881-3389)
PHONE..................951 264-1121
EMP: 20
Web: www.thasegawa.com
SIC: 2099 Food preparations, nec
HQ: T. Hasegawa U.S.A. Inc.
14017 183rd St
Cerritos CA
714 522-1900

(P-1995)
TAMPICO SPICE CO INCORPORATED
Also Called: Tampico Spice Company
5901 S Central Ave # 5941 (90001-1128)
P.O. Box 1229 (90001-0229)
PHONE..................323 235-3154
George Martinez, *CEO*
Delia Navarro, *Sec*
▲ **EMP:** 40 **EST:** 1946
SQ FT: 150,000
SALES (est): 8.45MM **Privately Held**
Web: www.tampicospice.com
SIC: 2099 Spices, including grinding

(P-1996)
TEVA FOODS INC
4401 S Downey Rd (90058-2518)
P.O. Box 58128 (90058-0128)
PHONE..................323 267-8110
Erik Litmanovich, *Pr*
EMP: 21 **EST:** 2008
SALES (est): 747.02K **Privately Held**
Web: www.gwfg.com
SIC: 2099 Salads, fresh or refrigerated

(P-1997)
THE HUNTER SPICE INC
184 Suburban Rd (93401-7502)
P.O. Box 8110 (93403-8110)
PHONE..................805 597-8900
▲ **EMP:** 65
SIC: 2099 Seasonings and spices

(P-1998)
THG BRANDS INC
Also Called: Hummus Guy, The
1810 Abalone Ave (90501-3703)
P.O. Box 1039 (90278-0039)
PHONE..................844 694-8327
Noel D Bonn, *CEO*
John Molino, *CFO*
Mohamed Cherif, *COO*
EMP: 20 **EST:** 2014
SQ FT: 4,000
SALES (est): 2.49MM **Privately Held**
SIC: 2099 Food preparations, nec

(P-1999)
TRIPLE H FOOD PROCESSORS LLC
5821 Wilderness Ave (92504-1004)
PHONE..................951 352-5700
Richard J Harris, *
▲ **EMP:** 60 **EST:** 1976
SQ FT: 120,000
SALES (est): 17.18MM **Privately Held**
Web: www.triplehfoods.com
SIC: 2099 2035 2033 Food preparations, nec; Pickles, sauces, and salad dressings; Jams, jellies, and preserves, packaged in cans, jars, etc.

(P-2000)
TU MADRE ROMANA INC
13633 S Western Ave (90249-2503)
P.O. Box 1275 (90249-0275)
PHONE..................323 321-6041
EMP: 215
Web: www.ramonas.com
SIC: 2099 5812 Tortillas, fresh or refrigerated; Delicatessen (eating places)

(P-2001)
UCE HOLDINGS INC
411 Center St (90012-3435)
PHONE..................213 217-4235
Gary Kawaguchi, *CEO*
Edward Shelley, *
◆ **EMP:** 87 **EST:** 2006
SQ FT: 45,000
SALES (est): 164.91K **Privately Held**
Web: www.uppercrustent.com
SIC: 2099 Bread crumbs, except made in bakeries

(P-2002)
VALUE WHOLESALER INC
1830 Flower Ave (91010-2931)
PHONE..................626 263-5933
Jintian Ye, *CEO*
Xiuxia Ye, *CFO*
EMP: 18 **EST:** 2011
SALES (est): 944.68K **Privately Held**
Web: www.valuewindowsdoors.com
SIC: 2099 Sandwiches, assembled and packaged: for wholesale market

(P-2003)
VILLAGE GREEN FOODS INC
1732 Kaiser Ave (92614-5706)
PHONE..................949 261-0111
EMP: 25 **EST:** 1970
SALES (est): 3.19MM **Privately Held**
Web: www.villagegreenfoods.com
SIC: 2099 Food preparations, nec

(P-2004)
WORLDWIDE SPECIALTIES INC
Also Called: California Specialty Farms
2420 Modoc St (90021-2916)
PHONE..................323 587-2200
EMP: 120
Web: www.newcsf.com
SIC: 2099 Almond pastes
PA: Worldwide Specialties, Inc.
2421 E 16th St 1
Los Angeles CA

2111 Cigarettes

(P-2005)
HOOK IT UP
1513 S Grand Ave (92705-4410)
PHONE..................714 600-0100
Zack Zakari, *CEO*
EMP: 23 **EST:** 2014
SQ FT: 5,000
SALES (est): 461.15K **Privately Held**
SIC: 2111 Cigarettes

(P-2006)
R J REYNOLDS TOBACCO COMPANY
8380 Miramar Mall Ste 117 (92121-2548)
PHONE..................858 625-8453
Ken Stevens, *Prin*
EMP: 86
Web: www.rjrt.com
SIC: 2111 Cigarettes
HQ: R. J. Reynolds Tobacco Company
401 N Main St

PRODUCTS & SVCS

Winston Salem NC
336 741-5000

(P-2007)
USA SALES INC
Also Called: Statewide Distributors
1560 S Archibald Ave (91761-7629)
PHONE..............................909 390-9606
Kabiruddin Ali, *CEO*
EMP: 20 **EST:** 2005
SALES (est): 4.41MM **Privately Held**
Web: www.usasalesinc.net
SIC: 2111 2121 Cigarettes; Cigars

2131 Chewing And Smoking Tobacco

(P-2008)
FANTASIA DISTRIBUTION INC
Also Called: Fantasia Hookah Tobacco
1566 W Embassy St (92802-1016)
PHONE..............................714 817-8300
Randy Jacob Bahbah, *CEO*
Issa Bahbah, *
◆ **EMP:** 17 **EST:** 2007
SALES (est): 2.53MM **Privately Held**
SIC: 2131 Smoking tobacco

2211 Broadwoven Fabric Mills, Cotton

(P-2009)
ALSTYLE APPAREL LLC
1501 E Cerritos Ave (92805-6400)
PHONE..............................714 765-0400
EMP: 2079 **EST:** 2014
SALES (est): 583.08K
SALES (corp-wide): 3.24B **Privately Held**
SIC: 2211 Apparel and outerwear fabrics, cotton
HQ: Alstyle Apparel & Activewear
Management Co.
1501 E Cerritos Ave
Anaheim CA
714 765-0400

(P-2010)
ARTCRAFT BEDSPREADS MFG INC
Also Called: Artcraft Bedding and Draperies
6466 Fleet St (90040-1710)
▲ **EMP:** 22 **EST:** 1992
SQ FT: 16,000
SALES (est): 658.72K **Privately Held**
SIC: 2211 2392 5719 Broadwoven fabric mills, cotton; Household furnishings, nec; Bedding (sheets, blankets, spreads, and pillows)

(P-2011)
AVITEX INC (PA)
Also Called: Veratex
20362 Plummer St (91311-5371)
PHONE..............................818 994-6487
Avi Cohen, *CEO*
▲ **EMP:** 250 **EST:** 1992
SQ FT: 15,000
SALES (est): 18.88MM **Privately Held**
Web: www.veratex.com
SIC: 2211 5131 Sheets, bedding and table cloths: cotton; Linen piece goods, woven

(P-2012)
BELAGIO ENTERPRISES INC
3737 Ross St (90058-1635)
PHONE..............................323 731-6934
Ruben Melamed, *CEO*

▲ **EMP:** 20 **EST:** 2002
SALES (est): 1.74MM **Privately Held**
Web: www.belagioenterprises.com
SIC: 2211 2269 Decorative trim and specialty fabrics, including twist weave; Decorative finishing of narrow fabrics

(P-2013)
BONDED FIBERLOFT INC
2748 Tanager Ave (90040-2721)
PHONE..............................323 726-7820
EMP: 299 **EST:** 1998
SQ FT: 96,000
SALES (est): 806.93K **Privately Held**
SIC: 2211 2823 2299 Broadwoven fabric mills, cotton; Cellulosic manmade fibers; Batts and batting: cotton mill waste and related material
PA: Western Synthetic Fiber Inc
2 Atlantic Ave Fl 4
Boston MA

(P-2014)
BTS TRADING INC
Also Called: Manufacture
3449 S Main St (90007-4413)
PHONE..............................213 800-6755
Euisoo Kim, *Pr*
EMP: 35 **EST:** 2020
SALES (est): 553.95K **Privately Held**
SIC: 2211 Apparel and outerwear fabrics, cotton

(P-2015)
CALA ACTION INC
2440 Troy Ave (91733-1432)
PHONE..............................213 272-9759
Hongfang Li, *CEO*
EMP: 25 **EST:** 2017
SALES (est): 1.21MM **Privately Held**
SIC: 2211 Apparel and outerwear fabrics, cotton

(P-2016)
COLORMAX INDUSTRIES INC (PA)
1627 Paloma St (90021-3013)
PHONE..............................213 748-6600
Gholamreza Amighi, *Pr*
Goodarz Haydarzadeh, *
EMP: 25 **EST:** 1988
SQ FT: 64,000
SALES (est): 3.65MM
SALES (corp-wide): 3.65MM **Privately Held**
SIC: 2211 2269 2261 2254 Broadwoven fabric mills, cotton; Finishing plants, nec; Finishing plants, cotton; Dyeing and finishing knit underwear

(P-2017)
CREATIVE COSTUMING DESIGNS INC
Also Called: Creative Costuming & Designs
15402 Electronic Ln (92649-1334)
PHONE..............................714 895-0982
Noreen Roberts, *Pr*
Noreen Roberts, *CEO*
Kevin Roberts, *
EMP: 35 **EST:** 2009
SQ FT: 5,300
SALES (est): 2.75MM **Privately Held**
Web: www.creative-costuming.com
SIC: 2211 Apparel and outerwear fabrics, cotton

(P-2018)
DEAR JOHN DENIM INC
Also Called: Dear John American Classic

12318 Lower Azusa Rd (91006-5872)
PHONE..............................626 350-5100
Chiu Yeung, *CEO*
▲ **EMP:** 19 **EST:** 2013
SALES (est): 1.99MM **Privately Held**
Web: www.dearjohndenim.com
SIC: 2211 Denims

(P-2019)
EAST SHORE GARMENT COMPANY LLC
3250 E Olympic Blvd (90023-3709)
PHONE..............................323 923-4454
EMP: 20 **EST:** 2017
SALES (est): 2.28MM
SALES (corp-wide): 50.48MM **Privately Held**
Web: www.eastshoregarment.com
SIC: 2211 Broadwoven fabric mills, cotton
PA: Lakeshirts Llc
750 Randolph Rd
Detroit Lakes MN
800 627-2780

(P-2020)
FACTORY ONE STUDIO INC
6700 Avalon Blvd Ste 101 (90003-1920)
PHONE..............................323 752-1670
Steve C Rhee, *CEO*
EMP: 52 **EST:** 2017
SALES (est): 10MM **Privately Held**
Web: www.factoryonestudio.com
SIC: 2211 Denims

(P-2021)
FIRST FINISH INC
11126 Wright Rd (90262-3122)
PHONE..............................310 631-6717
Keyomars Fard, *Pr*
▲ **EMP:** 25 **EST:** 2003
SQ FT: 10,000
SALES (est): 2.66MM **Privately Held**
SIC: 2211 Jean fabrics

(P-2022)
G KAGAN AND SONS INC (PA)
Also Called: Kagan Trim Center
3957 S Hill St (90037-1313)
PHONE..............................323 583-1400
Jed Kagan, *Pr*
Rod Kagan, *
◆ **EMP:** 25 **EST:** 1946
SQ FT: 50,000
SALES (est): 4.58MM
SALES (corp-wide): 4.58MM **Privately Held**
Web: www.kagantrim.com
SIC: 2211 Apparel and outerwear fabrics, cotton

(P-2023)
GDA INC
13563 Alondra Blvd (90670-5602)
PHONE..............................702 260-1949
Michael H Chung, *Pr*
Garon Donofrio, *CFO*
EMP: 18 **EST:** 2017
SALES (est): 763.3K **Privately Held**
Web: www.getdownart.com
SIC: 2211 Shirting fabrics, cotton

(P-2024)
HIDDEN JEANS INC
Also Called: Cello Jeans
7210 Dominion Cir (90040-3647)
PHONE..............................213 746-4223
Kenny Park, *CEO*
Adam Lee, *
◆ **EMP:** 30 **EST:** 2007
SQ FT: 4,000

SALES (est): 4.92MM **Privately Held**
Web: www.hiddenjean.com
SIC: 2211 2339 Denims; Jeans: women's, misses', and juniors'

(P-2025)
JML TEXTILE INC
Also Called: W & M Textile
5801 S 2nd St (90058-3403)
PHONE..............................323 584-2323
Seung Choon Lim, *CEO*
Seung Hoon Lim, *
▲ **EMP:** 18 **EST:** 2005
SQ FT: 350,000
SALES (est): 914.37K **Privately Held**
SIC: 2211 Apparel and outerwear fabrics, cotton

(P-2026)
KNIT GENERATION GROUP INC
3818 S Broadway (90037-1412)
PHONE..............................213 221-5081
Joseph Dania, *CEO*
EMP: 25 **EST:** 2013
SALES (est): 2.38MM **Privately Held**
Web: www.knitgeneration.net
SIC: 2211 Broadwoven fabric mills, cotton

(P-2027)
LINKSOUL LLC
530 S Coast Hwy (92054-4009)
PHONE..............................760 231-7069
Dave Seymour Cfo, *COO*
EMP: 29 **EST:** 2013
SALES (est): 2.95MM **Privately Held**
Web: www.linksoul.com
SIC: 2211 Apparel and outerwear fabrics, cotton

(P-2028)
MASTERPIECE ARTIST CANVAS LLC
Also Called: Canvas Concepts
1401 Air Wing Rd (92154-7705)
PHONE..............................619 710-2500
John M Sooklaris, *Pr*
◆ **EMP:** 50 **EST:** 1965
SQ FT: 1,000
SALES (est): 5.7MM **Privately Held**
Web: masterpiecearts.shptron.com
SIC: 2211 Canvas

(P-2029)
MSP GROUP INC
206 W 140th St (90061-1006)
PHONE..............................310 660-0022
Jong H Lim, *Pr*
▲ **EMP:** 27 **EST:** 1996
SQ FT: 1,000
SALES (est): 1.67MM **Privately Held**
Web: www.mspsteel.com
SIC: 2211 Apparel and outerwear fabrics, cotton

(P-2030)
PJY LLC
Also Called: Intimo Industry
3251 Leonis Blvd (90058-3018)
PHONE..............................323 583-7737
Ryan Fisher, *CEO*
▲ **EMP:** 40 **EST:** 2001
SALES (est): 5.05MM **Privately Held**
Web: www.intimoindustry.com
SIC: 2211 Long cloth, cotton

(P-2031)
SOCAL GARMENT WORKS LLC
4700 S Boyle Ave Ste C (90058-3032)
PHONE..............................323 300-5717

Michael Burns, *Managing Member*
Joseph Burns, *Managing Member*
Sho Kato, *Managing Member*
EMP: 43 **EST:** 2020
SALES (est): 3.08MM **Privately Held**
SIC: 2211 2221 Apparel and outerwear fabrics, cotton; Apparel and outerwear fabric, manmade fiber or silk

(P-2032)
STANZINO INC (PA)
Also Called: Apparel House USA
16325 S Avalon Blvd (90248-2909)
PHONE..............................213 746-8822
David Ghods, *CEO*
EMP: 25 **EST:** 2011
SALES (est): 20.91MM
SALES (corp-wide): 20.91MM **Privately Held**
SIC: 2211 Apparel and outerwear fabrics, cotton

(P-2033)
STANZINO INC
17937 Santa Rita St (91316-3602)
PHONE..............................818 602-5171
David Ghods, *Brnch Mgr*
EMP: 120
SALES (corp-wide): 20.91MM **Privately Held**
SIC: 2211 Apparel and outerwear fabrics, cotton
PA: Stanzino, Inc.
16325 S Avalon Blvd
Gardena CA
213 746-8822

(P-2034)
TWIN DRAGON MARKETING INC (PA)
Also Called: Tdmi
14600 S Broadway (90248-1812)
PHONE..............................310 715-7070
Dominic Poon, *CEO*
Joseph Tse, *Treas*
◆ **EMP:** 49 **EST:** 1980
SQ FT: 39,000
SALES (est): 21.88MM
SALES (corp-wide): 21.88MM **Privately Held**
Web: www.tdmi-us.com
SIC: 2211 Denims

(P-2035)
XCVI LLC (PA)
15236 Burbank Blvd (91411-3504)
PHONE..............................213 749-2661
Alon Zeltzer, *CEO*
Mordechia Zelter, *
Gita Zeltzer, *
▲ **EMP:** 60 **EST:** 1996
SALES (est): 20.86MM
SALES (corp-wide): 20.86MM **Privately Held**
Web: www.xcvi.com
SIC: 2211 Apparel and outerwear fabrics, cotton

2221 Broadwoven Fabric Mills, Manmade

(P-2036)
DAE SHIN USA INC
610 N Gilbert St (92833-2555)
PHONE..............................714 578-8900
Jae Weon Lee, *CEO*
▲ **EMP:** 100 **EST:** 1999
SQ FT: 10,000
SALES (est): 14.04MM **Privately Held**

SIC: 2221 Textile mills, broadwoven: silk and manmade, also glass
PA: Daeshin Textile Co.,Ltd.
16 Haean-Ro 397beon-Gil, Danwon-Gu
Ansan

(P-2037)
DOOL FNA INC
Also Called: Grand Textile
16624 Edwards Rd (90703-2438)
PHONE..............................562 483-4100
Jae Weon Lee, *CEO*
▲ **EMP:** 120 **EST:** 1999
SALES (est): 9.72MM **Privately Held**
SIC: 2221 Textile mills, broadwoven: silk and manmade, also glass

(P-2038)
FABRICMATE SYSTEMS INC
Also Called: Fabricmate
2781 Golf Course Dr Unit A (93003-7941)
PHONE..............................805 642-7470
Craig Lanuza, *Pr*
Manoj Pradhan, *
▲ **EMP:** 30 **EST:** 1995
SQ FT: 16,116
SALES (est): 4.92MM **Privately Held**
Web: www.fabricmate.com
SIC: 2221 Upholstery, tapestry, and wall covering fabrics

(P-2039)
FABTEX INC
Also Called: Ft Textiles
615 S State College Blvd (92831-5115)
PHONE..............................714 538-0877
William P Friese, *Brnch Mgr*
▲ **EMP:** 105
SALES (corp-wide): 54.75MM **Privately Held**
Web: www.fabtex.com
SIC: 2221 2515 2392 2391 Draperies and drapery fabrics, manmade fiber and silk; Mattresses and bedsprings; Household furnishings, nec; Curtains and draperies
PA: Fabtex, Inc.
111 Woodbine Ln
Danville PA
800 778-2791

(P-2040)
GROUND CONTROL BUSINESS MGT (DH)
Also Called: Savitsky Stin Bcon Bcci A Cal
2049 Century Park E Ste 1400 (90067-3101)
PHONE..............................310 315-6200
Chris Bucci, *CEO*
EMP: 18 **EST:** 1997
SALES (est): 20.94MM
SALES (corp-wide): 1.8B **Privately Held**
Web: www.gcbm.com
SIC: 2221 Satins
HQ: Nfp Corp.
200 Park Ave Rm 3202
New York NY
212 301-4000

(P-2041)
JUICY COUTURE INC
1580 Jesse St (90021-1317)
PHONE..............................888 824-8826
Pamela Levy, *CEO*
Edgar O Huber, *Pr*
Lisa Rodericks, *
Ellen Rodriguez, *
▲ **EMP:** 160 **EST:** 1990
SALES (est): 48.81K **Publicly Held**
Web: www.juicycouture.com

SIC: 2221 Broadwoven fabric mills, manmade
HQ: Kate Spade Holdings Llc
5822 Haverford Ave Ste 2
Philadelphia PA
212 354-4900

(P-2042)
NEXT AUTO TECH CENTER
6821 Crenshaw Blvd (90043-4666)
PHONE..............................323 483-6767
Admiral Jay Park, *Prin*
EMP: 25 **EST:** 2018
SALES (est): 1.02MM **Privately Held**
Web: next-auto-tech-center.business.site
SIC: 2221 Automotive fabrics, manmade fiber

(P-2043)
S&B DEVELOPMENT GROUP LLC
1901 Avenue Of The Stars 235 (90067-6064)
PHONE..............................213 446-2818
Nathalio Ortez, *CEO*
EMP: 48 **EST:** 2008
SQ FT: 50,000
SALES (est): 4.16MM **Privately Held**
SIC: 2221 5023 Broadwoven fabric mills, manmade; Sheets, textile

(P-2044)
SPD MANUFACTURING INC
1101 E Truslow Ave (92831-4625)
PHONE..............................985 302-,902
Debra Macaluso, *CEO*
EMP: 19 **EST:** 2018
SALES (est): 1.24MM **Privately Held**
SIC: 2221 Apparel and outerwear fabric, manmade fiber or silk

---

2231 Broadwoven Fabric Mills, Wool

(P-2045)
AMERICAN AP DYG & FINSHG INC
Also Called: American Apparel
747 Warehouse St (90021-1106)
P.O. Box 5129 (39047-5129)
PHONE..............................310 644-4001
Sang H Lim, *Pr*
Sang Ho Lim, *Pr*
▲ **EMP:** 46 **EST:** 2004
SALES (est): 3.22MM
SALES (corp-wide): 3.24B **Privately Held**
SIC: 2231 Dyeing and finishing: wool or similar fibers
HQ: App Winddown, Llc
747 Warehouse St
Los Angeles CA

(P-2046)
CALIFORNIA INDUSTRIAL FABRICS
2325 Marconi Ct (92154-7241)
PHONE..............................619 661-7166
TOLL FREE: 800
Michael Kent Lindsey, *Pr*
Patrick Dickey, *
Erin Mcnamara, *CFO*
◆ **EMP:** 30 **EST:** 1978
SQ FT: 24,000
SALES (est): 3.99MM **Privately Held**
Web: www.cifabrics.com
SIC: 2231 Broadwoven fabric mills, wool

(P-2047)
CMK MANUFACTURING LLC
Also Called: Green Dragon
10375 Wilshire Blvd Apt 2h (90024-4728)
▲ **EMP:** 31 **EST:** 2003
SALES (est): 2.51MM **Privately Held**
Web: www.freesocietyclothing.com
SIC: 2231 5632 Cloth, wool: mending; Apparel accessories

(P-2048)
COMFORT INDUSTRIES INC
301 W Las Tunas Dr (91776-1201)
PHONE..............................562 692-8288
Kevin D.o.s., *CEO*
Ken Quach, *
Mike D.o.s., *Treas*
Kevin Deal, *
◆ **EMP:** 35 **EST:** 1998
SALES (est): 4.54MM **Privately Held**
SIC: 2231 Upholstery fabrics, wool

(P-2049)
FAM LLC (PA)
Also Called: Fam Brands
5553 Bandini Blvd B (90201)
PHONE..............................323 888-7755
Frank Zarabi, *Pr*
Rich Campanelli, *
Rich Lyons, *
Nazy Salamat, *
Carrie Henley, *
▲ **EMP:** 64 **EST:** 1985
SQ FT: 75,000
SALES (est): 100.37MM **Privately Held**
Web: www.fambrands.com
SIC: 2231 2221 Apparel and outerwear broadwoven fabrics; Apparel and outerwear fabric, manmade fiber or silk

(P-2050)
LEKOS DYE & FINISHING INC (PA)
3131 E Harcourt St (90221-5505)
PHONE..............................310 763-0900
Ilgun Lee, *Pr*
▲ **EMP:** 65 **EST:** 2003
SQ FT: 72,000
SALES (est): 6.57MM
SALES (corp-wide): 6.57MM **Privately Held**
SIC: 2231 Dyeing and finishing: wool or similar fibers

(P-2051)
ROSHAN TRADING INC
Also Called: Envirofabrics
3631 Union Pacific Ave (90023-3255)
PHONE..............................213 622-9904
David Roshan, *CEO*
◆ **EMP:** 40 **EST:** 1986
SALES (est): 5.53MM **Privately Held**
Web: www.lagunafabrics.com
SIC: 2231 5131 Broadwoven fabric mills, wool; Textiles, woven, nec

(P-2052)
TRI-STAR DYEING & FINSHG INC
15125 Marquardt Ave (90670-5705)
PHONE..............................562 483-0123
Jang You, *Prin*
▲ **EMP:** 63 **EST:** 2006
SQ FT: 60,000
SALES (est): 8.14MM **Privately Held**
Web: www.tristar-df.com
SIC: 2231 Dyeing and finishing: wool or similar fibers

2241 Narrow Fabric Mills

(P-2053)
AX II INC
Also Called: Gin'l Fabrics
13921 S Figueroa St (90061-1027)
PHONE..............................310 292-6523
Anthony Xepolis, *Pr*
Ginny Xepolis, *VP*
EMP: 22 **EST:** 1981
SALES (est): 400.61K **Privately Held**
SIC: 2241 2396 Narrow fabric mills;
   Automotive and apparel trimmings

(P-2054)
CHUA & SONS CO INC
Also Called: Reliable Tape Products
3300 E 50th St (90058-3004)
P.O. Box 58261 (90058-0261)
PHONE..............................323 588-8044
Shirley Chua, *Pr*
▲ **EMP:** 23 **EST:** 1984
SQ FT: 67,000
SALES (est): 2.19MM **Privately Held**
SIC: 2241 Fabric tapes

(P-2055)
HOLLYWOOD RIBBON INDUSTRIES INC
9000 Rochester Ave (91730-5522)
P.O. Box 428 (18603-0428)
PHONE..............................323 266-0670
◆ **EMP:** 400
Web: www.hollywoodribbon.com
SIC: 2241 Ribbons, nec

(P-2056)
UNIVERSAL ELASTIC & GARMENT SUPPLY INC
2200 S Alameda St (90058-1308)
PHONE..............................213 748-2995
▲ **EMP:** 23 **EST:** 1991
SALES (est): 2.41MM **Privately Held**
Web: www.universalelastic.com
SIC: 2241 5131 Narrow fabric mills; Piece
   goods and notions

(P-2057)
WEST COAST TRIMMING CORP
7100 Wilson Ave (90001-2249)
PHONE..............................323 587-0701
Arnold F Pretz Junior, *Pr*
James R Mcbride, *VP*
Robert D Clarke, *Sec*
▲ **EMP:** 21 **EST:** 1922
SQ FT: 12,000
SALES (est): 1.3MM **Privately Held**
Web: www.westcoasttrimming.com
SIC: 2241 5131 Trimmings, textile; Drapery
   material, woven

2252 Hosiery, Nec

(P-2058)
GILDAN USA INC
Also Called: GILDAN USA INC.
28200 Highway 189 (92352-9700)
PHONE..............................909 485-1475
EMP: 18
SALES (corp-wide): 3.24B **Privately Held**
Web: www.gildancorp.com
SIC: 2252 Hosiery, nec
HQ: Gildan Usa Llc
   1980 Clements Ferry Rd
   Charleston SC

(P-2059)
K B SOCKS INC (DH)
Also Called: K Bell
550 N Oak St (90302-2942)
PHONE..............................310 670-3235
▲ **EMP:** 51 **EST:** 1985
SALES (est): 11.78MM
SALES (corp-wide): 3.26B **Privately Held**
Web: www.kbellsocks.com
SIC: 2252 Socks
HQ: Renfro Llc
   661 Linville Rd
   Mount Airy NC
   336 719-8000

(P-2060)
SAY IT WITH A SOCK LLC
11111 Santa Monica Blvd Ste 1100
(90025-3333)
PHONE..............................800 208-0879
EMP: 19
SALES (corp-wide): 456.37K **Privately Held**
Web: www.sayitwithasock.com
SIC: 2252 Socks
PA: Say It With A Sock Llc
   10200 Venice Blvd Ste 108
   Culver City CA
   424 284-8416

(P-2061)
SOXNET INC
235 S 6th Ave (91746-2916)
PHONE..............................626 934-9400
Miri Ryu, *CEO*
▲ **EMP:** 17 **EST:** 2002
SQ FT: 30,434
SALES (est): 1.57MM **Privately Held**
Web: www.soxnetinc.com
SIC: 2252 Men's, boys', and girls' hosiery

(P-2062)
UNIVERSAL HOSIERY INC
28337 Constellation Rd (91355-5048)
PHONE..............................661 702-8444
Johnathan Ekizian, *Pr*
▲ **EMP:** 75 **EST:** 1994
SQ FT: 44,000
SALES (est): 4.93MM **Privately Held**
Web: www.universalhosiery.com
SIC: 2252 Socks

2253 Knit Outerwear Mills

(P-2063)
BALBOA MANUFACTURING CO LLC (PA)
Also Called: Bobster Eyewear
4909 Murphy Canyon Rd Ste 310
(92123-4301)
PHONE..............................858 715-0060
▲ **EMP:** 26 **EST:** 1996
SQ FT: 40,000
SALES (est): 5.65MM **Privately Held**
Web: www.zanheadgear.com
SIC: 2253 2211 Hats and headwear, knit;
   Apparel and outerwear fabrics, cotton

(P-2064)
BYER CALIFORNIA
Alfred Paquette Division
1201 Rio Vista Ave (90023-2609)
PHONE..............................323 780-7615
Jan Shostak, *Mgr*
EMP: 114
SQ FT: 10,000
SALES (corp-wide): 127.6MM **Privately Held**
Web: www.byerca.com

SIC: 2253 2339 2335 Dresses, knit;
   Women's and misses' outerwear, nec;
   Women's, junior's, and misses' dresses
PA: Byer California
   66 Potrero Ave
   San Francisco CA
   415 626-7844

(P-2065)
CREW KNITWEAR LLC
2155 E 7th St Ste 125 (90023-1031)
PHONE..............................323 526-3888
Fredrick Ken, *Mgr*
EMP: 66
Web: www.crewknitwear.com
SIC: 2253 Dresses, knit
PA: Crew Knitwear, Llc
   660 S Myers St
   Los Angeles CA

(P-2066)
DELTA PACIFIC ACTIVEWEAR INC
331 S Hale Ave (92831-4805)
PHONE..............................714 871-9281
Imran Parekh, *Pr*
▲ **EMP:** 80 **EST:** 1998
SALES (est): 4.96MM **Privately Held**
Web: www.delpacific.com
SIC: 2253 2331 2321 T-shirts and tops, knit;
   Women's and misses' blouses and shirts;
   Men's and boy's furnishings

(P-2067)
DESIGN KNIT INC
Also Called: DK
1636 Staunton Ave (90021-3132)
PHONE..............................213 742-1234
▲ **EMP:** 21 **EST:** 1985
SALES (est): 2.15MM **Privately Held**
Web: www.designknit.com
SIC: 2253 Knit outerwear mills

(P-2068)
FANTASY ACTIVEWEAR INC (PA)
Also Called: Fantasy Manufacturing
5383 Alcoa Ave (90058-3734)
PHONE..............................213 705-4111
Anwar Gajiani, *CEO*
Yassmin Gajiani, *
▲ **EMP:** 38 **EST:** 1991
SQ FT: 20,000
SALES (est): 9.85MM **Privately Held**
SIC: 2253 2331 2321 T-shirts and tops, knit;
   Women's and misses' blouses and shirts;
   Men's and boy's furnishings

(P-2069)
FANTASY DYEING & FINISHING INC
5383 Alcoa Ave (90058-3734)
PHONE..............................323 983-9988
Anwar M Gajiani, *CEO*
EMP: 36 **EST:** 2003
SALES (est): 4.14MM **Privately Held**
SIC: 2253 Dyeing and finishing knit
   outerwear, excl. hosiery and glove

(P-2070)
FORTUNE SWIMWEAR LLC (HQ)
Also Called: Palisades Beach Club
2340 E Olympic Blvd Ste A (90021-2544)
PHONE..............................310 733-2130
Stephen Soller, *Managing Member*
Craig Soller, *
Gary Bub, *
Ann Kennedy, *
◆ **EMP:** 30 **EST:** 2002

SQ FT: 10,000
SALES (est): 34.7MM **Privately Held**
Web: www.fortuneswimwear.com
SIC: 2253 2335 Bathing suits and swimwear,
   knit; Women's, junior's, and misses' dresses
PA: Coast Style Group, Llc
   860 S Los Angeles St # 540
   Los Angeles CA

(P-2071)
INSTA-LETTERING MACHINE CO (PA)
Also Called: Insta Graphic Systems
13925 166th St (90703-2431)
P.O. Box 7900 (90702-7900)
PHONE..............................562 404-3000
◆ **EMP:** 90 **EST:** 1959
SALES (est): 8.72MM
SALES (corp-wide): 8.72MM **Privately Held**
Web: www.instagraph.com
SIC: 2253 2752 2396 T-shirts and tops, knit;
   Transfers, decalcomania or dry;
   lithographed; Screen printing on fabric
   articles

(P-2072)
ISIQALO LLC
Also Called: Spectra USA
5610 Daniels St (91710-9024)
PHONE..............................714 683-2820
Nick Agakanian, *
▼ **EMP:** 350 **EST:** 2012
SALES (est): 22.72MM **Privately Held**
Web: www.spectrausa.net
SIC: 2253 5136 5137 2321 T-shirts and tops,
   knit; Men's and boy's clothing; Women's
   and children's clothing; Sport shirts, men's
   and boys': from purchased materials

(P-2073)
LATIGO INC
4371 E 49th St (90058-3122)
PHONE..............................323 583-8000
EMP: 30 **EST:** 2011
SQ FT: 18,000
SALES (est): 2.56MM **Privately Held**
Web: www.latigousa.com
SIC: 2253 Knit outerwear mills

(P-2074)
MAD ENGINE GLOBAL LLC (HQ)
Also Called: Mad Engine
6740 Cobra Way Ste 100 (92121-4109)
PHONE..............................858 558-5270
Danish Gajiani, *CEO*
Faizan Bakali, *
Erik Johnson, *
◆ **EMP:** 54 **EST:** 1987
SQ FT: 50,000
SALES (est): 638.25MM
SALES (corp-wide): 638.25MM **Privately Held**
Web: www.madengine.com
SIC: 2253 2261 T-shirts and tops, knit;
   Screen printing of cotton broadwoven
   fabrics
PA: Mad Acquisition Corporation
   360 N Crescent Dr
   Beverly Hills CA
   858 558-5270

(P-2075)
PATTERN KNITTING MILLS INC
7963 Paramount Blvd (90660-4809)
PHONE..............................310 801-1126
Amir Henry Asgarynejad, *Pr*
EMP: 25 **EST:** 1988
SQ FT: 60,000
SALES (est): 1.5MM **Privately Held**

SIC: **2253** Knit outerwear mills

(P-2076)
STUDIO9D8 INC
9743 Alesia St (91733-3008)
PHONE..............................626 350-0832
Ann Lem, *CEO*
EMP: 30 **EST:** 2011
SALES (est): 2.5MM **Privately Held**
Web: www.studio9d8.com
SIC: **2253** 2515 T-shirts and tops, knit;
   Studio couches

(P-2077)
SUNSETS INC
Also Called: Sunsets Separates
24511 Frampton Ave (90710-2108)
PHONE..............................310 784-3600
▲ **EMP:** 35 **EST:** 1984
SALES (est): 3.59MM **Privately Held**
Web: www.sunsetsinc.com
SIC: **2253** Bathing suits and swimwear, knit

(P-2078)
THIENES APPAREL INC
1811 Floradale Ave (91733-3605)
PHONE..............................626 575-2818
Chao Wen Chang, *Prin*
▲ **EMP:** 20 **EST:** 1997
SQ FT: 17,500
SALES (est): 795.65K **Privately Held**
Web: www.thienes.com
SIC: **2253** Blouses, knit

2257 Weft Knit Fabric Mills

(P-2079)
SHARA-TEX INC
3338 E Slauson Ave (90058-3915)
PHONE..............................323 587-7200
Shahram Fahimian, *Ch Bd*
S Tony Souferian, *
▲ **EMP:** 45 **EST:** 1989
SQ FT: 55,000
SALES (est): 8.64MM **Privately Held**
Web: www.shara-tex.com
SIC: **2257** Weft knit fabric mills

(P-2080)
TENENBLATT CORPORATION
Also Called: Antex Knitting Mills
3750 Broadway Pl (90007-4400)
PHONE..............................323 232-2061
William Tenenblatt, *Pr*
Anna Tenenblatt, *
◆ **EMP:** 109 **EST:** 1973
SQ FT: 60,000
SALES (est): 1.41MM
SALES (corp-wide): 66.31MM **Privately
Held**
SIC: **2257** Dyeing and finishing circular knit
   fabrics
PA: Matchmaster Dyeing & Finishing, Inc.
   3750 S Broadway
   Los Angeles CA
   323 232-2061

2258 Lace And Warp Knit Fabric Mills

(P-2081)
COSMO TEXTILES INC
13984 Orange Ave (90723-2029)
PHONE..............................562 220-1177
EMP: 60 **EST:** 1995
SQ FT: 45,000
SALES (est): 4.84MM **Privately Held**

SIC: **2258** 2257 Cloth, warp knit; Weft knit
fabric mills

(P-2082)
**JIF-PAK MANUFACTURING INC
(PA)**
1451 Engineer St Ste A (92081-8841)
PHONE..............................760 597-2665
▲ **EMP:** 96 **EST:** 1989
SALES (est): 18.63MM **Privately Held**
Web: jifpak.kallegroup.com
SIC: **2258** Netting, knit

2259 Knitting Mills, Nec

(P-2083)
AZITEX TRADING CORP
Also Called: Azitex Knitting Mills
1850 E 15th St (90021-2820)
PHONE..............................213 745-7072
Michael Azizi, *Pr*
Mozie Azizi, *
Andrew Azizi, *
▲ **EMP:** 60 **EST:** 1986
SQ FT: 50,000
SALES (est): 9.41MM **Privately Held**
Web:
azitex-trading-co-knitting-mills.business.site
SIC: **2259** 2253 Convertors, knit goods; Knit
   outerwear mills

(P-2084)
MIDTHRUST IMPORTS INC
Also Called: Midthrust
830 E 14th Pl (90021-2120)
PHONE..............................213 749-6651
Kamran Noman, *CEO*
▲ **EMP:** 20 **EST:** 1983
SALES (est): 2.8MM **Privately Held**
Web: kiosk.midthrust.com
SIC: **2259** Convertors, knit goods

(P-2085)
PIERCAN USA INC
160 Bosstick Blvd (92069-5930)
PHONE..............................760 599-4543
▲ **EMP:** 62 **EST:** 1995
SALES (est): 10.05MM **Privately Held**
Web: www.piercanusa.com
SIC: **2259** 3842 3089 2673 Work gloves, knit
   ; Gloves, safety; Gloves or mittens, plastics;
   Plastic and pliofilm bags

(P-2086)
SAS TEXTILES INC
3100 E 44th St (90058-2406)
PHONE..............................323 277-5555
Sohrab Sassounian, *Pr*
Soheil Sassounian, *
Albert Sassounian, *
▲ **EMP:** 70 **EST:** 1991
SQ FT: 40,000
SALES (est): 9.5MM **Privately Held**
Web: www.sastextile.com
SIC: **2259** 2257 7389 Convertors, knit goods
   ; Weft knit fabric mills; Textile and apparel
   services

2261 Finishing Plants, Cotton

(P-2087)
**CAITAC GARMENT
PROCESSING INC**
14725 S Broadway (90248-1813)
PHONE..............................310 217-9888
Muneyuki Ishii, *CEO*
Azusa Sahara, *
▲ **EMP:** 270 **EST:** 1991

SQ FT: 200,000
SALES (est): 40.78MM **Privately Held**
Web: www.caitacgarment.com
SIC: **2261** 2339 2325 5651 Screen printing
   of cotton broadwoven fabrics; Women's
   and misses' outerwear, nec; Men's and
   boy's trousers and slacks; Jeans stores
PA: Caitac Holdings Corp.
   3-12, Showacho, Kita-Ku
   Okayama OKA

(P-2088)
CUSTOM LOGOS INC
7889 Clairemont Mesa Blvd (92111-1618)
PHONE..............................858 277-1886
▲ **EMP:** 44 **EST:** 1982
SALES (est): 5.57MM **Privately Held**
Web: www.customlogos.com
SIC: **2261** Screen printing of cotton
   broadwoven fabrics

(P-2089)
HARRYS DYE AND WASH INC
Also Called: Harry's Dye & Wash
1015 E Orangethorpe Ave (92801-1135)
PHONE..............................714 446-0300
Harry Choung, *Pr*
Kang Ho Lee, *
EMP: 30 **EST:** 1994
SQ FT: 20,000
SALES (est): 2.02MM **Privately Held**
SIC: **2261** 2269 Finishing plants, cotton;
   Finishing plants, nec

(P-2090)
**LORBER INDUSTRIES
CALIFORNIA**
Also Called: Lorber Industries of Claif
823 N Roxbury Dr (90210-3017)
PHONE..............................310 275-1568
Tom Lorber, *Pr*
Greg Lorber, *
Michael Painter, *
Michael Gruener, *OF MIS*
John Robertson, *
EMP: 19 **EST:** 1969
SALES (est): 464.62K **Privately Held**
SIC: **2261** 2262 2253 2257 Screen printing
   of cotton broadwoven fabrics; Screen
   printing: manmade fiber and silk
   broadwoven fabrics; Knit outerwear mills;
   Weft knit fabric mills

(P-2091)
SILK SCREEN SHIRTS INC
Also Called: SSS
6185 El Camino Real (92009-1602)
PHONE..............................760 233-3900
Stephen H Taylor, *Pr*
Laura D Wile, *
William Regan, *
▲ **EMP:** 30 **EST:** 1969
SQ FT: 20,000
SALES (est): 4.96MM **Privately Held**
Web: www.silkscreenshirtsinc.com
SIC: **2261** 2396 Screen printing of cotton
   broadwoven fabrics; Automotive and
   apparel trimmings

(P-2092)
SUPER DYEING LLC
Also Called: Super Dyeing and Finishing
8825 Millergrove Dr (90670-2003)
PHONE..............................562 692-9500
▲ **EMP:** 75 **EST:** 1995
SALES (est): 4.84MM **Privately Held**
Web: www.superdyeing.com
SIC: **2261** Dyeing cotton broadwoven fabrics

(P-2093)
TOMORROWS LOOK INC
Also Called: Dimensions In Screen Printing
17462 Von Karman Ave (92614-6206)
PHONE..............................949 596-8400
Steven E Mellgren, *CEO*
Torrey Mellgren, *
EMP: 70 **EST:** 1986
SQ FT: 36,000
SALES (est): 4.3MM **Privately Held**
SIC: **2261** Screen printing of cotton
   broadwoven fabrics

(P-2094)
**WASHINGTON GRMENT DYG
FNSHG IN**
1332 E 18th St (90021-3027)
PHONE..............................213 747-1111
Pradip Shah, *Mgr*
EMP: 35
SALES (corp-wide): 3.86MM **Privately
Held**
Web: www.washingtongarment.com
SIC: **2261** 2262 Finishing plants, cotton;
   Finishing plants, manmade
PA: Washington Garment Dyeing &
   Finishing, Inc.
   1341 E Washington Blvd
   Los Angeles CA
   213 747-1111

2262 Finishing Plants, Manmade

(P-2095)
FINAL FINISH INC
10910 Norwalk Blvd (90670-3828)
PHONE..............................562 777-7774
Luis Ibarria, *Pr*
EMP: 17 **EST:** 1987
SQ FT: 20,000
SALES (est): 1MM **Privately Held**
SIC: **2262** Preshrinking: manmade fiber and
   silk broadwoven fabrics

(P-2096)
INX PRINTS INC
1802 Kettering (92614-5618)
PHONE..............................949 660-9190
Harold A Haase Junior, *CEO*
David Van Steenhuyse, *
▼ **EMP:** 100 **EST:** 2004
SQ FT: 26,000
SALES (est): 9.63MM **Privately Held**
Web: inx-prints-inc.hub.biz
SIC: **2262** Screen printing: manmade fiber
   and silk broadwoven fabrics

(P-2097)
**PRINT PLUS MANUFACTURING
INC**
Also Called: Print Plus
1939 S Susan St (92704-3901)
▲ **EMP:** 24 **EST:** 2004
SALES (est): 841.44K **Privately Held**
SIC: **2262** Screen printing: manmade fiber
   and silk broadwoven fabrics

(P-2098)
SPREADCO INC
803 Us Highway 78 (92227-9514)
P.O. Box 1400 (92227-1320)
PHONE..............................760 351-0747
EMP: 20 **EST:** 2007
SALES (est): 1.92MM **Privately Held**
Web: www.spreadco.net

**P
R
O
D
U
C
T
S

&

S
V
C
S**

SIC: 2262 Chemical coating or treating of manmade broadwoven fabrics

(P-2099)
WASHINGTON GARMENT DYEING (PA)
1341 E Washington Blvd (90021-3037)
PHONE....................213 747-1111
Vijay Shah, *Pr*
Pradip Shah, *
EMP: 25 **EST:** 1988
SQ FT: 20,000
SALES (est): 3.86MM
SALES (corp-wide): 3.86MM **Privately Held**
Web: www.washingtongarment.com
SIC: 2262 2261 2269 Dyeing: manmade fiber and silk broadwoven fabrics; Dyeing cotton broadwoven fabrics; Finishing plants, nec

2269 Finishing Plants, Nec

(P-2100)
EXPO DYEING & FINISHING INC
1365 N Knollwood Cir (92801-1312)
PHONE....................714 220-9583
Eduardo J Kim, *Pr*
▲ **EMP:** 170 **EST:** 1987
SQ FT: 86,000
SALES (est): 21.46MM **Privately Held**
Web: www.expodye.com
SIC: 2269 Dyeing: raw stock, yarn, and narrow fabrics

(P-2101)
GEARMENT INC (PA)
Also Called: GEARMENT
14801 Able Ln Ste 102 (92647-2059)
PHONE....................866 236-5476
Ton Le, *Pr*
Tom Le, *Pr*
Sang D.o.s., *CMO*
EMP: 195 **EST:** 2016
SALES (est): 33.6MM
SALES (corp-wide): 33.6MM **Privately Held**
Web: www.gearment.com
SIC: 2269 Printing of narrow fabrics

(P-2102)
J MICHELLE OF CALIFORNIA
Also Called: Edie Lee
6409 Gayhart St (90040-2505)
PHONE....................323 585-8500
Paul Bogner, *Pr*
EMP: 19 **EST:** 1985
SALES (est): 906.62K **Privately Held**
SIC: 2269 Finishing plants, nec

(P-2103)
MATCHMASTER DYG & FINSHG INC (PA)
Also Called: Antex Knitting Mills
3750 S Broadway (90007-4436)
PHONE....................323 232-2061
William Tenenblatt, *Pr*
◆ **EMP:** 250 **EST:** 1977
SQ FT: 66,000
SALES (est): 66.31MM
SALES (corp-wide): 66.31MM **Privately Held**
Web: www.antex.com
SIC: 2269 Dyeing: raw stock, yarn, and narrow fabrics

(P-2104)
PACIFIC COAST BACH LABEL INC
3015 S Grand Ave (90007-3814)
PHONE....................213 612-0314
Dan Finnegan, *Pr*
▲ **EMP:** 23 **EST:** 1989
SALES (est): 2.12MM **Privately Held**
Web: www.pcblabel.com
SIC: 2269 2679 Labels, cotton: printed; Labels, paper: made from purchased material

(P-2105)
PACIFIC CONTNTL TEXTILES INC
Also Called: Pct
2880 E Ana St (90221-5602)
P.O. Box 1330 (90801-1330)
PHONE....................310 639-1500
Edmund Kim, *CEO*
◆ **EMP:** 98 **EST:** 1983
SALES (est): 22.14MM
SALES (corp-wide): 23.19MM **Privately Held**
SIC: 2269 2329 Finishing plants, nec; Men's and boys' sportswear and athletic clothing
PA: Edmund Kim International, Inc.
2880 E Ana St
Compton CA
310 604-1100

(P-2106)
REZEX CORPORATION
Also Called: Geltman Industries
1930 E 51st St (90058-2804)
PHONE....................213 622-2015
Shari Rezai, *Pr*
Amir R Rezai, *
EMP: 25 **EST:** 1981
SALES (est): 4.16MM **Privately Held**
Web: www.geltman.com
SIC: 2269 Finishing plants, nec

(P-2107)
TAG-IT PACIFIC INC
21900 Burbank Blvd Ste 270 (91367-7461)
PHONE....................818 444-4100
Colin Dyne, *CEO*
Steven Forte, *
◆ **EMP:** 34 **EST:** 1991
SALES (est): 2.14MM **Privately Held**
Web: www.taloninternational.com
SIC: 2269 Labels, cotton: printed
PA: Talon International, Inc.
21900 Burbank Blvd # 101
Woodland Hills CA

2273 Carpets And Rugs

(P-2108)
AMERICAN COVER DESIGN 26 INC
2131 E 52nd St (90058-3498)
PHONE....................323 582-8666
Daniel Mahgerefteh, *CEO*
EMP: 26 **EST:** 2001
SALES (est): 2.29MM **Privately Held**
Web: www.americancoverdesign.com
SIC: 2273 Rugs, machine woven

(P-2109)
ATLAS CARPET MILLS INC
3201 S Susan St (92704-6838)
P.O. Box 11467 (36671-0467)
PHONE....................323 724-7930
James Horwich, *Pr*
Ada Horwich, *

Stan Dunford, *
Mark Hesther, *
Markos Varpas, *
▲ **EMP:** 229 **EST:** 1969
SALES (est): 47.71MM
SALES (corp-wide): 303.57MM **Publicly Held**
Web: www.atlascarpetmills.com
SIC: 2273 Rugs, tufted
HQ: Tdg Operations, Llc
716 Bill Myles Dr
Saraland AL
251 679-3512

(P-2110)
BENTLEY MILLS INC (PA)
Also Called: Bentley Mills
14641 Don Julian Rd (91746-3106)
PHONE....................626 333-4585
Jay Brown, *Pr*
Nancy Agger-nielsen, *CFO*
◆ **EMP:** 250 **EST:** 1980
SQ FT: 390,000
SALES (est): 127.73MM
SALES (corp-wide): 127.73MM **Privately Held**
Web: www.bentleymills.com
SIC: 2273 2299 Carpets, textile fiber; Batting, wadding, padding and fillings

(P-2111)
CATALINA CARPET MILLS INC (PA)
Also Called: Catalina Home
14418 Best Ave (90670-5133)
PHONE....................562 926-5811
Duane Jensen, *Pr*
Jack Heinrich, *
▲ **EMP:** 38 **EST:** 1975
SQ FT: 60,000
SALES (est): 8.11MM
SALES (corp-wide): 8.11MM **Privately Held**
Web: www.catalinahome.com
SIC: 2273 5023 Finishers of tufted carpets and rugs; Floor coverings

(P-2112)
CREATIVE ACCENTS
6294 Curtis Pl (93505-6006)
P.O. Box 2510 (93581-2510)
PHONE....................760 373-1222
Mike Hensler, *Pr*
▲ **EMP:** 20 **EST:** 1967
SQ FT: 22,000
SALES (est): 1.85MM **Privately Held**
Web: www.creativeaccents.com
SIC: 2273 Carpets and rugs

(P-2113)
DURKAN PATTERNED CARPETS INC
3633 Lenawee Ave # 120 (90016-4319)
PHONE....................310 838-2898
Kathy Stein, *Mgr*
EMP: 248
SIC: 2273 Carpets, hand and machine made
HQ: Durkan Patterned Carpets, Inc.
121 Goodwill Dr
Dalton GA
706 278-7037

(P-2114)
FABRICA INTERNATIONAL INC
Also Called: Fabrica Fine Carpet
3201 S Susan St (92704-6838)
P.O. Box 2007 (30722-2007)
PHONE....................949 261-7181
Greg Uttecht, *Pr*
Jon A Faulkner, *

▲ **EMP:** 167 **EST:** 1974
SQ FT: 107,000
SALES (est): 36.33MM
SALES (corp-wide): 303.57MM **Publicly Held**
SIC: 2273 Carpets, hand and machine made
PA: The Dixie Group Inc
475 Reed Rd Ste 100
Dalton GA
706 876-5800

(P-2115)
INTERFACEFLOR LLC
1111 S Grand Ave Ste 103 (90015-2164)
PHONE....................213 741-2139
EMP: 61
SALES (corp-wide): 1.3B **Publicly Held**
Web: www.interface.com
SIC: 2273 Finishers of tufted carpets and rugs
HQ: Interfaceflor, Llc
1503 Orchard Hill Rd
Lagrange GA

(P-2116)
MARSPRING CORPORATION (PA)
Also Called: Marflex
4920 S Boyle Ave (90058-3017)
P.O. Box 58643 (90058-0643)
PHONE....................323 589-5637
Ronald J Greitzer, *Pr*
Stan Greitzer, *
▲ **EMP:** 34 **EST:** 1950
SQ FT: 54,008
SALES (est): 6.62MM
SALES (corp-wide): 6.62MM **Privately Held**
Web: www.reliancecarpetcushion.com
SIC: 2273 Carpets, textile fiber

(P-2117)
MAT CACTUS MFG CO
930 W 10th St (91702-1936)
PHONE....................626 969-0444
Debra Hartranft-dering, *Pr*
Cailey Dering, *Treas*
▲ **EMP:** 20 **EST:** 1934
SQ FT: 35,000
SALES (est): 4.21MM **Privately Held**
Web: www.cactusmat.com
SIC: 2273 5023 3069 Carpets and rugs; Floor coverings; Mats or matting, rubber, nec

(P-2118)
MOHAWK INDUSTRIES INC
9687 Transportation Way (92335-2604)
PHONE....................909 357-1064
Lisa Gomez, *Brnch Mgr*
EMP: 26
Web: www.mohawkind.com
SIC: 2273 3253 Finishers of tufted carpets and rugs; Ceramic wall and floor tile
PA: Mohawk Industries, Inc.
160 S Industrial Blvd
Calhoun GA

(P-2119)
ROYALTY CARPET MILLS INC
Also Called: Royalty
17111 Red Hill Ave (92614-5607)
PHONE....................949 474-4000
▲ **EMP:** 800
SIC: 2273 Carpets, hand and machine made

(P-2120)
SHAW INDUSTRIES GROUP INC
Also Called: Carriage Carpet Mills
11411 Valley View St (90630-5368)

PHONE..................562 430-4445
EMP: 28
SALES (corp-wide): 302.09B **Publicly Held**
Web: www.shawinc.com
SIC: 2273 5713 5023 Finishers of tufted carpets and rugs; Floor covering stores; Homefurnishings
HQ: Shaw Industries Group, Inc.
616 E Walnut Ave
Dalton GA
706 278-3812

(P-2121)
STANTON CARPET CORP
Also Called: Hibernia Woolen Mills
2209 Pine Ave (90266-2832)
PHONE..................562 945-8711
Debbie Dearo, *Mgr*
EMP: 50
SALES (corp-wide): 48.41MM **Privately Held**
Web: www.stantoncarpet.com
SIC: 2273 Carpets and rugs
PA: Stanton Carpet Corp.
100 Sunnyside Blvd # 100
Woodbury NY
516 822-5878

2281 Yarn Spinning Mills

(P-2122)
KUK RIM USA INC
Also Called: Encore Tex Inc
7507 Roseberry Ave (90255)
PHONE..................323 277-9256
Sang Yoon Lee, *Pr*
EMP: 200 **EST:** 1990
SALES (est): 9MM **Privately Held**
SIC: 2281 Yarn spinning mills

2284 Thread Mills

(P-2123)
AMERICAN & EFIRD LLC
6098 Rickenbacker Rd (90040-3030)
PHONE..................323 724-6884
Juan Anbric, *Mgr*
EMP: 18
SALES (corp-wide): 1.98B **Privately Held**
Web: www.amefird.com
SIC: 2284 Thread mills
HQ: American & Efird Llc
22 American St
Mount Holly NC
704 827-4311

2295 Coated Fabrics, Not Rubberized

(P-2124)
AOC LLC
Also Called: AOC California Plant
19991 Seaton Ave (92570-8724)
PHONE..................951 657-5161
EMP: 100
Web: www.aocresins.com
SIC: 2295 2821 5169 Resin or plastic coated fabrics; Plastics materials and resins; Synthetic resins, rubber, and plastic materials
HQ: Aoc, Llc
955 Highway 57
Piperton TN

(P-2125)
CALIFORNIA COMBINING CORP
5607 S Santa Fe Ave (90058-3525)
P.O. Box 509 (90280-0509)
PHONE..................323 589-5727
Charlette Heller, *CEO*
Vincent Rosato, *
Kathy Diaz, *
▲ **EMP:** 37 **EST:** 1947
SQ FT: 68,000
SALES (est): 2.38MM **Privately Held**
Web: www.flamelaminatingcorp.com
SIC: 2295 Coated fabrics, not rubberized

(P-2126)
J MILLER CANVAS LLC
2429 S Birch St (92707-3406)
PHONE..................714 641-0052
EMP: 26 **EST:** 2018
SALES (est): 2.35MM **Privately Held**
Web: www.jmillercanvas.com
SIC: 2295 Waterproofing fabrics, except rubberizing

(P-2127)
SHERWIN-WILLIAMS COMPANY
Also Called: Sherwin-Williams
5501 E Slauson Ave (90040-2920)
PHONE..................323 726-7272
EMP: 45
SALES (corp-wide): 22.15B **Publicly Held**
Web: www.sherwin-williams.com
SIC: 2295 Resin or plastic coated fabrics
PA: The Sherwin-Williams Company
101 W Prospect Ave # 1020
Cleveland OH
216 566-2000

(P-2128)
SOLECTA INC (PA)
4113 Avenida De La Plata (92056-6002)
PHONE..................760 630-9643
Jim Ford, *CEO*
Michael Ahearn, *
▲ **EMP:** 24 **EST:** 2014
SALES (est): 9.62MM
SALES (corp-wide): 9.62MM **Privately Held**
Web: www.solecta.com
SIC: 2295 Chemically coated and treated fabrics

2297 Nonwoven Fabrics

(P-2129)
TEXOLLINI INC
2575 E El Presidio St (90810-1114)
PHONE..................310 537-3400
Daniel Kadisha, *Pr*
◆ **EMP:** 250 **EST:** 1989
SQ FT: 200,000
SALES (est): 38.98MM **Privately Held**
Web: www.texollini.com
SIC: 2297 2262 2269 2221 Nonwoven fabrics ; Dyeing: manmade fiber and silk broadwoven fabrics; Finishing plants, nec; Broadwoven fabric mills, manmade

2298 Cordage And Twine

(P-2130)
CABLECO
13100 Firestone Blvd (90670-5517)
PHONE..................562 942-8076
Greg Bailey, *Prin*
▲ **EMP:** 22 **EST:** 2002
SALES (est): 1.19MM **Privately Held**
Web: www.carpenterrigging.com

SIC: 2298 Cable, fiber

(P-2131)
DYNAMEX CORPORATION
155 E Albertoni St (90746-1405)
PHONE..................310 329-0399
Ben Bravin, *Pr*
◆ **EMP:** 52 **EST:** 1975
SALES (est): 1.02MM **Privately Held**
SIC: 2298 Cable, fiber

(P-2132)
LIFT-IT MANUFACTURING CO INC
Also Called: Lift It
1603 W 2nd St (91766-1252)
PHONE..................909 469-2251
▲ **EMP:** 46 **EST:** 1979
SALES (est): 9.71MM **Privately Held**
Web: www.lift-it.com
SIC: 2298 Slings, rope

2299 Textile Goods, Nec

(P-2133)
ALANIC INTERNATIONAL CORP
Also Called: Dioz Group, The
8730 Wilshire Blvd Ph (90211-2709)
PHONE..................855 525-2642
Farhan Beig, *Pr*
Johnny Beig, *CEO*
Tony Beig, *Sr VP*
▲ **EMP:** 38 **EST:** 2013
SALES (est): 3.34MM **Privately Held**
Web: www.alanic.com
SIC: 2299 Broadwoven fabrics: linen, jute, hemp, and ramie

(P-2134)
AMERICAN DAWN INC (PA)
Also Called: ADI
401 W Artesia Blvd (90220-5518)
PHONE..................800 821-2221
Adnan Rawjee, *Pr*
Mahmud G Rawjee, *
◆ **EMP:** 60 **EST:** 1980
SQ FT: 212,000
SALES (est): 25.02MM
SALES (corp-wide): 25.02MM **Privately Held**
Web: www.americandawn.com
SIC: 2299 5023 5131 2393 Linen fabrics; Linens and towels; Textiles, woven, nec; Cushions, except spring and carpet: purchased materials

(P-2135)
AMERICAN FOAM FIBER & SUPS INC (PA)
Also Called: Foam Depot
255 S 7th Ave Ste A (91746-3256)
PHONE..................626 969-7268
▲ **EMP:** 26 **EST:** 2006
SALES (est): 3.82MM **Privately Held**
Web: www.affsinc.com
SIC: 2299 Hair, curled: for upholstery, pillow, and quilt filling

(P-2136)
AMPM MAINTENANCE CORPORATION
1010 E 14th St (90021-2212)
PHONE..................424 230-1300
Mohammad Saderi, *Pr*
EMP: 48 **EST:** 2020
SALES (est): 1.55MM **Privately Held**
SIC: 2299 Textile goods, nec

(P-2137)
AMRAPUR OVERSEAS INCORPORATED (PA)
Also Called: Colonial Home Textiles
1560 E 6th St Ste 101 (92879-1712)
PHONE..................714 893-8808
Chandru H Wadhwani, *CEO*
Laxmi Wadhwani, *
◆ **EMP:** 25 **EST:** 1983
SQ FT: 130,000
SALES (est): 9.2MM
SALES (corp-wide): 9.2MM **Privately Held**
Web: www.amrapur.com
SIC: 2299 2269 5023 Linen fabrics; Linen fabrics: dyeing, finishing, and printing; Linens and towels

(P-2138)
CORNERSTONE APPAREL INC
Also Called: Cornerstore Apparel
101 W Avenida Vista Hermosa (92672)
PHONE..................949 498-2664
EMP: 42
SALES (corp-wide): 67.6MM **Privately Held**
Web: www.papayaclothing.com
SIC: 2299 Jute and flax textile products
PA: Cornerstone Apparel, Inc.
1001 S Melrose St
Placentia CA
323 724-3600

(P-2139)
DECCOFELT CORPORATION
555 S Vermont Ave (91741-6206)
P.O. Box 156 (91740-0156)
PHONE..................626 963-8511
Gerald L Heinrich, *CEO*
▲ **EMP:** 24 **EST:** 1951
SQ FT: 33,000
SALES (est): 4.69MM **Privately Held**
Web: www.deccofelt.com
SIC: 2299 Felts and felt products

(P-2140)
ETRADE 24 INC
16600 Calneva Dr (91436-4130)
PHONE..................818 712-0574
EMP: 25 **EST:** 2018
SALES (est): 2.06MM **Privately Held**
Web: us.etrade.com
SIC: 2299 2326 7389 Batting, wadding, padding and fillings; Medical and hospital uniforms, men's; Brokers' services

(P-2141)
J H TEXTILES INC
2301 E 55th St (90058-3435)
PHONE..................323 585-4124
Jong Soon Hur, *CEO*
▲ **EMP:** 25 **EST:** 2003
SQ FT: 80,000
SALES (est): 2.38MM **Privately Held**
Web: www.jhtextilesinc.com
SIC: 2299 Textile mill waste and remnant processing

(P-2142)
NEW HAVEN COMPANIES INC
13571 Vaughn St Unit E (91340-3006)
PHONE..................818 686-7020
Alex Franco, *Mgr*
EMP: 55
Web: www.newhaven-usa.com
SIC: 2299 3537 2298 2273 Batting, wadding, padding and fillings; Industrial trucks and tractors; Cordage and twine; Carpets and rugs
PA: The New Haven Companies Inc
4820 Suthpoint Dr Ste 102

Fredericksburg VA

(P-2143)
NEXTRADE INC (PA)
Also Called: Nextex International
12411 Industrial Ave (90280-8221)
PHONE.................................562 944-9950
Jang R Cho, *CEO*
◆ **EMP:** 20 **EST:** 1998
SQ FT: 40,000
SALES (est): 2.31MM
SALES (corp-wide): 2.31MM **Privately Held**
SIC: 2299 Batting, wadding, padding and fillings

(P-2144)
OTT TEXTILE INC
Also Called: Ott Textile, Inc.
21708 Lasso Ln (91789-1457)
PHONE.........................626 217-5132
Allen Ge Jun Wang, *Brnch Mgr*
EMP: 40
SALES (corp-wide): 215.37K **Privately Held**
SIC: 2299 Fabrics: linen, jute, hemp, ramie
PA: Ott Textile Inc.
　10507 Valley Blvd Ste 858
　El Monte CA
　626 566-5858

(P-2145)
PACESETTER FABRICS LLC (HQ)
11450 Sheldon St (91352-1121)
PHONE.........................213 741-9999
◆ **EMP:** 17 **EST:** 1997
SQ FT: 36,000
SALES (est): 7.74MM **Privately Held**
SIC: 2299 Tops and top processing, manmade or other fiber
PA: Unitex Industries, Inc.
　1401 Griffith Ave
　Los Angeles CA

(P-2146)
REDWOOD WELLNESS LLC
1950 W Corporate Way (92801-5373)
PHONE.........................323 843-2676
Robert Rosenheck, *CEO*
EMP: 38 **EST:** 2017
SALES (est): 1.99MM **Privately Held**
SIC: 2299 Hemp yarn, thread, roving, and textiles

(P-2147)
STONE HARBOR INC
5015 District Blvd (90058-2719)
PHONE.........................323 277-2777
▲ **EMP:** 18 **EST:** 2003
SALES (est): 1.98MM **Privately Held**
SIC: 2299 Textile mill waste and remnant processing

2311 Men's And Boy's Suits And Coats

(P-2148)
AMWEAR USA INC
Also Called: Tactsquad
250 Benjamin Dr (92879-6508)
PHONE.........................800 858-6755
Hong Li Hawkins, *CEO*
Hang Guo, *Prin*
EMP: 34 **EST:** 2017
SALES (est): 4.82MM **Privately Held**
Web: www.tactsquad.com
SIC: 2311 5699 Men's and boys' uniforms; Uniforms

(P-2149)
BARCO UNIFORMS INC
350 W Rosecrans Ave (90248-1728)
PHONE.........................310 323-7315
Ron Wagensiel, *CEO*
Danny Robertson, *
David Ayers, *
Kathy Peterson, *
David Aquino, *
◆ **EMP:** 372 **EST:** 1929
SQ FT: 74,000
SALES (est): 56.82MM **Privately Held**
Web: www.barcomade.com
SIC: 2311 2326 2337 Men's and boys' uniforms; Men's and boy's work clothing; Uniforms, except athletic: women's, misses', and juniors'

(P-2150)
BLUE SPHERE INC
Also Called: Lucky-13 Apparel
10869 Portal Dr (90720-2508)
PHONE.........................714 953-7555
▲ **EMP:** 55 **EST:** 1989
SALES (est): 1.97MM **Privately Held**
Web: www.bluespheremfg.com
SIC: 2311 2331 2369 Men's and boy's suits and coats; Women's and misses' blouses and shirts; Girl's and children's outerwear, nec

(P-2151)
CROSSPORT MOCEAN
Also Called: Mocean
1611 Babcock St (92663-2805)
PHONE.........................949 646-1701
Bill Levitt, *Pr*
Tim Hindman, *Sec*
Pamela Green, *Treas*
▲ **EMP:** 18 **EST:** 1991
SQ FT: 3,000
SALES (est): 1.62MM **Privately Held**
Web: www.mocean.net
SIC: 2311 Policemen's uniforms: made from purchased materials

(P-2152)
NEW CHEF FASHION INC
3223 E 46th St (90058-2407)
PHONE.........................323 581-0300
Guy Lucien Salama, *Pr*
Chantal Salama, *
▲ **EMP:** 70 **EST:** 1989
SALES (est): 11.21MM **Privately Held**
Web: www.newchef.com
SIC: 2311 2339 2326 5137 Men's and boys' uniforms; Women's and misses' outerwear, nec; Men's and boy's work clothing; Uniforms, women's and children's

(P-2153)
NO SECOND THOUGHTS INC
Also Called: Nst
1333 30th St Ste D (92154-3487)
PHONE.........................619 428-5992
Audrey Swirsky, *Pr*
Onnie Ramos, *
EMP: 52 **EST:** 1999
SALES (est): 4.44MM **Privately Held**
Web: www.nst2.com
SIC: 2311 2329 2326 Men's and boys' uniforms; Men's and boys' sportswear and athletic clothing; Medical and hospital uniforms, men's

(P-2154)
STRINGKING INC (PA)
19100 S Vermont Ave (90248-4413)
PHONE.........................310 503-8901
Jake Mccampbell, *CEO*

EMP: 23 **EST:** 2020
SALES (est): 50MM
SALES (corp-wide): 50MM **Privately Held**
Web: www.stringking.com
SIC: 2311 Men's and boys' uniforms

(P-2155)
TYLER TRAFFICANTE INC (PA)
Also Called: Richard Tyler
700 S Palm Ave (91803-1528)
PHONE.........................323 869-9299
Lisa Trafficante, *Pr*
Richard Tyler, *
EMP: 24 **EST:** 1986
SQ FT: 30,000
SALES (est): 3.83MM
SALES (corp-wide): 3.83MM **Privately Held**
Web: www.hbpta.org
SIC: 2311 2335 5611 5621 Tailored suits and formal jackets; Gowns, formal; Suits, men's ; Dress shops

2321 Men's And Boy's Furnishings

(P-2156)
COTTON LINKS LLC
1360 Ritchey St (92705-4727)
PHONE.........................714 444-4700
Robby Khalek, *Managing Member*
EMP: 25 **EST:** 2011
SALES (est): 7MM **Privately Held**
Web: www.cottonlinks.net
SIC: 2321 Men's and boy's furnishings

(P-2157)
CREATIVE DESIGN INDUSTRIES
2587 Otay Center Dr (92154-7612)
PHONE.........................619 710-2525
▲ **EMP:** 125 **EST:** 1982
SALES (est): 10.57MM **Privately Held**
SIC: 2321 5137 Men's and boy's furnishings; Sportswear, women's and children's

(P-2158)
GINO CORPORATION
Also Called: Shaka Wear
555 E Jefferson Blvd (90011-2430)
PHONE.........................323 234-7979
Sung Uk Park, *CEO*
Eugene Park, *Ex VP*
◆ **EMP:** 25 **EST:** 2004
SALES (est): 4.12MM **Privately Held**
Web: www.shakawear.com
SIC: 2321 5136 Men's and boys' dress shirts ; Shirts, men's and boys'

(P-2159)
JL DESIGN ENTERPRISES INC
Also Called: Jl Racing.com
1451 Edinger Ave Ste C (92780-6250)
PHONE.........................714 479-0240
Jolene Sparza, *Pr*
Kenneth Mills, *
▲ **EMP:** 63 **EST:** 1983
SALES (est): 5.57MM **Privately Held**
SIC: 2321 Sport shirts, men's and boys': from purchased materials

(P-2160)
JUST FOR FUN INC
Also Called: Jff Uniforms
557 Van Ness Ave (90501-1424)
P.O. Box 9012 (90508-9012)
PHONE.........................310 320-1327
Corinne Stolz, *Pr*
Gary Stolz, *

▲ **EMP:** 24 **EST:** 1975
SQ FT: 11,000
SALES (est): 1.92MM **Privately Held**
Web: www.jffuniforms.com
SIC: 2321 2337 2339 2326 Uniform shirts: made from purchased materials; Uniforms, except athletic: women's, misses', and juniors'; Women's and misses' outerwear, nec; Men's and boy's work clothing

(P-2161)
LISA FACTORY INC
144 N Swall Dr (90211-1943)
PHONE.........................213 536-5326
Abrar Ahmed, *CEO*
EMP: 52 **EST:** 2020
SALES (est): 48.66MM **Privately Held**
SIC: 2321 5199 Men's and boys' dress shirts ; General merchandise, non-durable

(P-2162)
STARLION INC
Also Called: Star Lion
706 E 32nd St (90011-2406)
PHONE.........................323 233-8823
Mike Lim, *Pr*
Moon Lim, *Prin*
EMP: 26 **EST:** 1984
SQ FT: 11,000
SALES (est): 979.25K **Privately Held**
Web: www.fashionface.com
SIC: 2321 2331 Men's and boys' dress shirts ; Women's and misses' blouses and shirts

(P-2163)
TEXTILE UNLIMITED CORPORATION (PA)
20917 Higgins Ct (90501-1723)
PHONE.........................310 263-7400
James Y Park, *CEO*
Sam Lee, *Pr*
Stanley Kim, *Pr*
Yumi Park, *Sec*
◆ **EMP:** 61 **EST:** 1994
SALES (est): 33.91MM **Privately Held**
Web: www.tuc.net
SIC: 2321 2339 2329 2331 Men's and boy's furnishings; Women's and misses' athletic clothing and sportswear; Men's and boys' athletic uniforms; Women's and misses' blouses and shirts

(P-2164)
TOP HEAVY CLOTHING COMPANY INC (PA)
28381 Vincent Moraga Dr (92590-3653)
PHONE.........................951 442-8839
▲ **EMP:** 65 **EST:** 1995
SQ FT: 40,000
SALES (est): 9.85MM **Privately Held**
Web: www.topheavyclothing.com
SIC: 2321 Men's and boys' dress shirts

(P-2165)
TRUE CLASSIC TEES LLC
26635 Agoura Rd Ste 105 (91302-3807)
PHONE.........................323 419-1092
Ryan Bartlett, *Managing Member*
EMP: 22 **EST:** 2018
SALES (est): 5.2MM **Privately Held**
Web: www.trueclassictees.com
SIC: 2321 Men's and boys' dress shirts

2323 Men's And Boy's Neckwear

(P-2166)
FASHIONGO

2250 Maple Ave (90011-1190)
PHONE..................213 745-2667
EMP: 19
SALES (est): 546.54K Privately Held
Web: www.fashiongo.net
SIC: 2323 Men's and boy's neckwear

2325 Men's And Boy's Trousers And Slacks

(P-2167)
AG ADRIANO GOLDSCHMIED INC (PA)
Also Called: AG Jeans
2741 Seminole Ave (90280-5550)
PHONE..................323 357-1111
U Yul Ku, CEO
Adriano Suarez, *
▲ EMP: 50 EST: 2000
SQ FT: 150,000
SALES (est): 28.18MM
SALES (corp-wide): 28.18MM Privately Held
Web: www.agjeans.com
SIC: 2325 2339 5136 5137 Men's and boy's trousers and slacks; Women's and misses' outerwear, nec; Men's and boy's clothing; Women's and children's clothing

(P-2168)
J&C APPAREL
757 Towne Ave Unit B (90021-1419)
PHONE..................323 490-8260
Cipriano Serrano, Pr
EMP: 40 EST: 2017
SALES (est): 1.37MM Privately Held
SIC: 2325 Men's and boy's trousers and slacks

(P-2169)
KI-P C USA JEANS INC
6738 Los Verdes Dr Apt 2 (90275-7603)
PHONE..................310 234-8185
EMP: 80 EST: 1996
SALES (est): 4.07MM Privately Held
SIC: 2325 2339 Jeans: men's, youths', and boys'; Jeans: women's, misses', and juniors'

(P-2170)
LEE
111 Pacifica Ste 310 (92618-7428)
PHONE..................213 200-1000
Christopher L Bonney, Prin
EMP: 24 EST: 2010
SALES (est): 614.06K Privately Held
Web: www.lee-associates.com
SIC: 2325 Jeans: men's, youths', and boys'

(P-2171)
ROB INC
Also Called: Robin's Jeans
6760 Foster Bridge Blvd (90201-2030)
PHONE..................562 806-5589
Robert Chretien, CEO
Gilberto Jimenez, *
◆ EMP: 90 EST: 2005
SQ FT: 26,000
SALES (est): 20.15MM Privately Held
Web: www.robinsjean.com
SIC: 2325 2339 2369 Jeans: men's, youths', and boys'; Women's and misses' culottes, knickers and shorts; Shorts (outerwear): girls' and children's

(P-2172)
TRUE RELIGION APPAREL INC (HQ)
Also Called: True Religion Brand Jeans

500 W 190th St Ste 300 (90248-4269)
PHONE..................323 266-3072
Michael Buckley, CEO
Lynne Koplin, Pr
Peter F Collins, CFO
Kelly Gvildys, VP Opers
David Chiovetti, Sr VP
▲ EMP: 300 EST: 2005
SALES (est): 270.02MM
SALES (corp-wide): 350MM Privately Held
Web: www.truereligion.com
SIC: 2325 2339 2369 Men's and boy's trousers and slacks; Women's and misses' outerwear, nec; Jeans: girls', children's, and infants'
PA: Trlg Corporate Holdings, Llc
1888 Rosecrans Ave
Manhattan Beach CA
323 266-3072

2326 Men's And Boy's Work Clothing

(P-2173)
FIGS INC
2834 Colorado Ave Ste 100 (90404-3644)
PHONE..................424 300-8330
Catherine Spear, CEO
Heather Hasson, *
Daniella Turenshine, CFO
▲ EMP: 313 EST: 2013
SALES (est): 505.83MM Privately Held
Web: www.wearfigs.com
SIC: 2326 5699 Work apparel, except uniforms; Work clothing

(P-2174)
IMAGE APPAREL FOR BUSINESS INC
1618 E Edinger Ave (92705-5019)
PHONE..................714 541-5247
Keith Knerr, CEO
Robert Duffield, *
EMP: 25 EST: 2009
SALES (est): 2.87MM Privately Held
Web: www.ia4b.com
SIC: 2326 2339 2353 7213 Men's and boy's work clothing; Uniforms, athletic: women's, misses', and juniors'; Uniform hats and caps ; Linen supply

(P-2175)
IMAGE SOLUTIONS APPAREL INC
Also Called: Image Solutions
19571 Magellan Dr (90502-1136)
PHONE..................310 464-8991
Christopher Kelley, Pr
Christopher Kelley, Pr
Paula Fox, *
▲ EMP: 111 EST: 1997
SQ FT: 4,500
SALES (est): 24.41MM Privately Held
Web: www.imageinc.com
SIC: 2326 2337 Work uniforms; Uniforms, except athletic: women's, misses', and juniors'

(P-2176)
INDIE SOURCE
940 Venice Blvd (90291-4978)
PHONE..................424 200-2027
Jesse Dombrowiak, Pr
EMP: 20 EST: 2014
SALES (est): 2.24MM Privately Held
Web: www.indiesource.com

SIC: 2326 7336 Men's and boy's work clothing; Graphic arts and related design

(P-2177)
KNK APPAREL INC
223 W Rosecrans Ave (90248-1831)
PHONE..................310 768-3333
John Kang, Pr
EMP: 18 EST: 1993
SQ FT: 90,000
SALES (est): 373.98K Privately Held
SIC: 2326 2339 Men's and boy's work clothing; Women's and misses' outerwear, nec

(P-2178)
LA TRIUMPH INC
Also Called: Medgear
13336 Alondra Blvd (90703-2205)
PHONE..................562 404-7657
Hasina Lakhani, CEO
Amin Lakhani, *
▲ EMP: 24 EST: 2003
SQ FT: 40,000
SALES (est): 2.46MM Privately Held
Web: www.pacuniforms.com
SIC: 2326 Medical and hospital uniforms, men's

(P-2179)
MARSHA VICKI ORIGINALS INC
Also Called: Vicki Marsha Uniforms
5292 Production Dr (92649-1521)
PHONE..................714 895-6371
Diane Cologne, Pr
Timothy Cologne, VP
EMP: 17 EST: 1947
SQ FT: 14,500
SALES (est): 452.87K Privately Held
Web: www.vickimarsha.com
SIC: 2326 Aprons, work, except rubberized and plastic: men's

(P-2180)
MED COUTURE INC
Also Called: Peaches
9800 De Soto Ave (91311-4411)
PHONE..................214 231-2500
Barry Rothschild, Pr
Mark Wilcoxson, *
◆ EMP: 87 EST: 1987
SALES (est): 22.53MM Privately Held
Web: www.medcouture.com
SIC: 2326 Work uniforms

(P-2181)
MEXAPPAREL INC (PA)
2344 E 38th St (90058-1627)
PHONE..................323 364-8600
Maria Maniatis, Pr
Hubert Guez, *
Fred Kalmar, *
Nomaan Yousef, *
EMP: 21 EST: 1991
SQ FT: 277,000
SALES (est): 4.37MM Privately Held
SIC: 2326 Service apparel (baker, barber, lab, etc.), washable: men's

(P-2182)
OFFLINE INC (PA)
2931 S Alameda St (90058-1326)
PHONE..................213 742-9001
Charles Park, Pr
Karen Park, CFO
▲ EMP: 45 EST: 2002
SALES (est): 5.83MM
SALES (corp-wide): 5.83MM Privately Held
Web: www.offlineinc.com

SIC: 2326 2342 Industrial garments, men's and boys'; Foundation garments, women's

(P-2183)
PPD HOLDING LLC (PA)
10119 Jefferson Blvd (90232-3519)
PHONE..................310 733-2100
Paige Adams-geller, Chief Design Officer
EMP: 63 EST: 2012
SALES (est): 49.17MM
SALES (corp-wide): 49.17MM Privately Held
SIC: 2326 2331 6719 Men's and boy's work clothing; Women's and misses' blouses and shirts; Investment holding companies, except banks

(P-2184)
PROVIDENCE INDUSTRIES LLC
Also Called: Mydyer.com
18191 Von Karman Ave Ste 100 (92612-7103)
PHONE..................562 420-9091
Daniel S Kang, Pr
Dan Kang, *
Jennifer Gim, *
Krystal Park, *
James Lee, *
◆ EMP: 60 EST: 1997
SALES (est): 9.04MM Privately Held
Web: www.mydyer.com
SIC: 2326 2331 Men's and boy's work clothing; Blouses, women's and juniors': made from purchased material

(P-2185)
ROF LLC
Also Called: Ring of Fire
7800 Airport Business Pkwy (91406)
PHONE..................818 933-4000
Eran Bitton, *
▲ EMP: 45 EST: 2007
SQ FT: 60,000
SALES (est): 5.18MM Privately Held
Web: www.ringoffireclothing.com
SIC: 2326 5651 5136 Men's and boy's work clothing; Jeans stores; Men's and boys' outerwear

(P-2186)
STRATEGIC DISTRIBUTION L P
Also Called: Cherokee Uniforms
9800 De Soto Ave (91311-4411)
PHONE..................818 671-2100
▲ EMP: 240 EST: 2003
SALES (est): 51.44MM Privately Held
Web: www.careismatic.com
SIC: 2326 2337 3143 3144 Work uniforms; Uniforms, except athletic: women's, misses', and juniors'; Men's footwear, except athletic; Women's footwear, except athletic
PA: Careismatic Brands, Llc
1119 Colorado Ave
Santa Monica CA

(P-2187)
WAY OUT WEST INC
1440 W 135th St (90249-2218)
PHONE..................310 769-6937
Michael C Goldberg, Pr
Mark J Goldberg, *
Michael Goldberg, *
▲ EMP: 22 EST: 1979
SALES (est): 1.89MM Privately Held
Web: www.wayoutwestinc.com
SIC: 2326 2385 Industrial garments, men's and boys'; Waterproof outerwear

2329 Men's And Boy's Clothing, Nec

(P-2188)
3 POINT DISTRIBUTION LLC
Also Called: Ezekiel
2139 Placentia Ave (92627-3301)
P.O. Box 2568 (92659-1668)
PHONE..............................949 266-2700
◆ **EMP:** 20 **EST:** 2000
SQ FT: 42,000
SALES (est): 4.93MM **Privately Held**
Web: www.3pointdistribution.com
SIC: 2329 Men's and boys' sportswear and athletic clothing

(P-2189)
4 WHAT ITS WORTH INC (PA)
Also Called: Tyte Jeans
5815 Smithway St (90040-1605)
PHONE..............................323 728-4503
Alden J Halpern, *Dir*
Kyle Soladay, *CFO*
◆ **EMP:** 51 **EST:** 1993
SQ FT: 38,000
SALES (est): 9.76MM **Privately Held**
Web: www.rewash.com
SIC: 2329 5961 5651 5699 Knickers, dress (separate): men's and boys'; Electronic shopping; Jeans stores; Designers, apparel

(P-2190)
A AND G INC (HQ)
Also Called: Alstyle Apparel
11296 Harrel St (91752-3715)
PHONE..............................714 765-0400
Keith S Walters, *Pr*
Keith S Walters, *Prin*
Michael D Magill Same, *Sec*
◆ **EMP:** 627 **EST:** 1978
SALES (est): 94.5MM
SALES (corp-wide): 3.24B **Privately Held**
Web: www.alstyle.com
SIC: 2329 2253 Athletic clothing, except uniforms: men's, youths' and boys'; T-shirts and tops, knit
PA: Les Vetements De Sport Gildan Inc
  600 Boul De Maisonneuve O 33eme Etage
  Montreal QC
  514 735-2023

(P-2191)
ACTIVEAPPAREL INC (PA)
11076 Venture Dr (91752-3234)
PHONE..............................951 361-0060
▲ **EMP:** 19 **EST:** 1993
SQ FT: 30,000
SALES (est): 9.7MM **Privately Held**
Web: www.3dcartstores.com
SIC: 2329 2339 7389 Men's and boys' sportswear and athletic clothing; Women's and misses' athletic clothing and sportswear ; Sewing contractor

(P-2192)
ANDARI FASHION INC
Also Called: Andari
9626 Telstar Ave (91731-3004)
PHONE..............................626 575-2759
Wei Chen Wang, *Pr*
Lillian Wang, *
Charles Chang, *
◆ **EMP:** 120 **EST:** 1991
SQ FT: 50,000
SALES (est): 12.54MM **Privately Held**
Web: www.andari.com

SIC: 2329 2339 2253 5199 Sweaters and sweater jackets, men's and boys'; Women's and misses' accessories; Sweaters and sweater coats, knit; Art goods and supplies

(P-2193)
ANTAEUS FASHIONS GROUP INC
2400 Chico Ave (91733-1613)
PHONE..............................626 452-0797
Yungchieh Lin, *CEO*
Shangwen Lin, *
Peter Lin, *
▲ **EMP:** 19 **EST:** 1991
SQ FT: 10,000
SALES (est): 518.97K **Privately Held**
Web: www.atfusa.com
SIC: 2329 2339 Men's and boys' sportswear and athletic clothing; Women's and misses' athletic clothing and sportswear

(P-2194)
ARIES 33 LLC
3400 S Main St (90007-4412)
PHONE..............................310 355-8330
Daniel Guez, *CEO*
Robin Saeks, *CFO*
EMP: 20 **EST:** 2017
SQ FT: 28,000
SALES (est): 2.46MM **Privately Held**
SIC: 2329 7389 2339 Men's and boys' sportswear and athletic clothing; Apparel designers, commercial; Women's and misses' outerwear, nec

(P-2195)
ASHWORTH INC
Also Called: Ashworth Studio
2765 Loker Ave W (92010-6601)
PHONE..............................760 438-6610
◆ **EMP:** 598
Web: us.ashworthgolf.com
SIC: 2329 2339 2353 Men's and boys' sportswear and athletic clothing; Athletic clothing: women's, misses', and juniors'; Hats, caps, and millinery

(P-2196)
BIRDWELL ENTERPRISES INC
Also Called: Birdwell Beach Britches
8801 Research Dr (92618-4236)
PHONE..............................714 557-7040
Vivian Richardson, *Pr*
William Robert Mann, *
EMP: 25 **EST:** 1962
SALES (est): 2.85MM **Privately Held**
Web: www.birdwell.com
SIC: 2329 2339 2326 Bathing suits and swimwear: men's and boys'; Women's and misses' outerwear, nec; Men's and boy's work clothing

(P-2197)
BOA INC
580 W Lambert Rd Ste L (92821-3913)
PHONE..............................714 256-8960
David Fleming, *Pr*
Pamela Fleming, *
▲ **EMP:** 34 **EST:** 1992
SQ FT: 6,000
SALES (est): 3.18MM **Privately Held**
Web: www.boausa.com
SIC: 2329 2337 2339 Men's and boys' sportswear and athletic clothing; Women's and misses' suits and coats; Women's and misses' outerwear, nec

---

(P-2198)
BOARDRIDERS INC (HQ)
Also Called: Billabong
5600 Argosy Ave Ste 100 (92649-1063)
PHONE..............................714 889-5404
Arne Arens, *CEO*
Greg Healy, *Pr*
Thomas Chambolle, *INTERIM PRESIDENT EMEA*
Stephen Coulombe, *CRO*
Carol Scherman, *Ex VP*
▼ **EMP:** 599 **EST:** 1986
SALES (est): 494.99MM **Privately Held**
Web: www.boardriders.com
SIC: 2329 2339 3949 5136 Men's and boys' sportswear and athletic clothing; Women's and misses' athletic clothing and sportswear ; Sporting and athletic goods, nec; Sportswear, men's and boys'
PA: Authentic Brands Group Llc
  1411 Broadway Fl 4
  New York NY

(P-2199)
BODY GLOVE INTERNATIONAL LLC
Also Called: Body Glove
6255 W Sunset Blvd Ste 650 (90028-7403)
PHONE..............................310 374-3441
Cory M Baker, *COO*
Warren Clamen, *CFO*
◆ **EMP:** 31 **EST:** 1997
SALES (est): 592.3K **Privately Held**
Web: www.bodyglove.com
SIC: 2329 2339 2369 3069 Bathing suits and swimwear: men's and boys'; Bathing suits: women's, misses', and juniors'; Bathing suits and swimwear: girls', children's, and infants'; Wet suits, rubber

(P-2200)
DC SHOES INC (DH)
Also Called: DC
5600 Argosy Ave Ste 100 (92649-1063)
PHONE..............................714 889-4206
Arne Arens, *CEO*
Francis Roy, *CFO*
Maryn Miller, *Sec*
◆ **EMP:** 27 **EST:** 1993
SQ FT: 100,000
SALES (est): 30.3MM **Privately Held**
Web: www.dcshoes.com
SIC: 2329 5136 5137 5139 Men's and boys' sportswear and athletic clothing; Men's and boy's clothing; Women's and children's clothing; Footwear
HQ: Boardriders, Inc.
  5600 Argosy Ave Ste 100
  Huntington Beach CA
  714 889-5404

(P-2201)
DOH QUEST LLC
8939 S Sepulveda Blvd (90045-3631)
PHONE..............................213 651-3441
EMP: 20
SALES (est): 1.29MM **Privately Held**
SIC: 2329 Riding clothes: men's, youths', and boys'

(P-2202)
EDMUND KIM INTERNATIONAL INC (PA)
2880 E Ana St (90221-5602)
P.O. Box 1330 (90801-1330)
PHONE..............................310 604-1100
Edmund K Kim, *Pr*
Reza Farmehr, *Sec*
◆ **EMP:** 20 **EST:** 1997
SALES (est): 23.19MM

SALES (corp-wide): 23.19MM **Privately Held**
Web: www.ekii.com
SIC: 2329 2261 7218 2253 Athletic clothing, except uniforms: men's, youths' and boys'; Dyeing cotton broadwoven fabrics; Industrial launderers; Dresses and skirts

(P-2203)
FEAR OF GOD LLC
558 S Alameda St (90013-1726)
PHONE..............................310 466-9751
EMP: 45
Web: www.fearofgod.com
SIC: 2329 Sweaters and sweater jackets, men's and boys'
PA: Fear Of God, Llc
  3940 Lrl Cyn Blvd Ste 42
  Studio City CA

(P-2204)
FETISH GROUP INC (PA)
Also Called: Tag Rag
1013 S Los Angeles St Ste 700 (90015-1782)
PHONE..............................323 587-7873
Raphael Sabbah, *CEO*
Orly Dahan, *
▲ **EMP:** 39 **EST:** 1986
SQ FT: 28,000
SALES (est): 4.81MM
SALES (corp-wide): 4.81MM **Privately Held**
SIC: 2329 2339 2369 Men's and boys' sportswear and athletic clothing; Women's and misses' athletic clothing and sportswear ; Girl's and children's outerwear, nec

(P-2205)
FUNNY-BUNNY INC (PA)
Also Called: Cachcach
1513b E Saint Gertrude Pl (92705-5309)
PHONE..............................714 957-1114
Paul Kohne, *Pr*
▲ **EMP:** 95 **EST:** 1983
SQ FT: 25,000
SALES (est): 8.04MM
SALES (corp-wide): 8.04MM **Privately Held**
SIC: 2329 2369 Men's and boys' sportswear and athletic clothing; Slacks: girls' and children's

(P-2206)
GLOBAL CASUALS INC
18505 S Broadway (90248-4632)
PHONE..............................310 817-2828
Jack Tsao, *Genl Mgr*
▲ **EMP:** 70 **EST:** 1995
SQ FT: 2,000
SALES (est): 423.63K
SALES (corp-wide): 54.44MM **Privately Held**
SIC: 2329 Men's and boys' sportswear and athletic clothing
PA: Seattle Pacific Industries, Inc.
  1633 W Lake Ave N Ste 300
  Seattle WA
  253 872-8822

(P-2207)
HURLEY INTERNATIONAL LLC (PA)
Also Called: Hurley
3080 Bristol St (92626-3093)
PHONE..............................949 548-9375
Adrian L Bell, *
Ann M Miller, *
◆ **EMP:** 200 **EST:** 2001
SALES (est): 99.67MM

SALES (corp-wide): 99.67MM **Privately Held**
Web: www.hurley.com
SIC: **2329** 5137 Knickers, dress (separate): men's and boys'; Women's and children's clothing

(P-2208)
JH DESIGN GROUP
940 W Washington Blvd (90015-3312)
PHONE..............................213 747-5700
▲ **EMP:** 60 **EST:** 1987
SALES (est): 9.91MM **Privately Held**
Web: www.jhdesigngroup.com
SIC: **2329** 2337 Jackets (suede, leatherette, etc.), sport: men's and boys'; Women's and misses' capes and jackets

(P-2209)
JOE WELLS ENTERPRISES INC
Also Called: Max Muscle
1500 S Sunkist St Ste D (92806-5815)
P.O. Box 825 (92781-0825)
◆ **EMP:** 26
Web: www.maxmuscle.com
SIC: **2329** 2023 2339 6794 Men's and boys' sportswear and athletic clothing; Dietary supplements, dairy and non-dairy based; Sportswear, women's; Franchises, selling or licensing

(P-2210)
JS APPAREL INC
1751 E Del Amo Blvd (90746-2938)
PHONE..............................310 631-6333
Ki S Kim, *CEO*
▲ **EMP:** 99 **EST:** 2004
SALES (est): 10.29MM **Privately Held**
Web: www.jsapparel.net
SIC: **2329** 2339 Men's and boys' sportswear and athletic clothing; Women's and misses' outerwear, nec

(P-2211)
KORAL LLC
Also Called: Koral Activewear
1334 3rd Street Promenade Ste 200 (90401-1313)
PHONE..............................323 391-1060
Marcelo Kugel, *Managing Member*
Peter Koral, *
Liz Hampshire, *
Ilana Kugel, *
EMP: 36 **EST:** 2002
SALES (est): 2.2MM **Privately Held**
Web: www.koral.com
SIC: **2329** 2339 Men's and boys' sportswear and athletic clothing; Women's and misses' athletic clothing and sportswear

(P-2212)
L A CSTM AP & PROMOTIONS INC (PA)
2680 Temple Ave (90806-2209)
PHONE..............................562 595-1770
Chris Roybal, *Pr*
EMP: 33 **EST:** 1984
SQ FT: 10,000
SALES (est): 5.24MM **Privately Held**
SIC: **2329** 5136 Athletic clothing, except uniforms: men's, youths' and boys'; Men's and boy's clothing

(P-2213)
LEEMARC INDUSTRIES LLC
Also Called: Canari
340 Rancheros Dr Ste 172 (92069-2980)
PHONE..............................760 598-0505
Christopher Robinson, *Managing Member*
▲ **EMP:** 55 **EST:** 2000

SALES (est): 5.32MM **Privately Held**
Web: www.canari.com
SIC: **2329** 2339 Athletic clothing, except uniforms: men's, youths' and boys'; Women's and misses' outerwear, nec

(P-2214)
LIQUID GRAPHICS INC
2701 S Harbor Blvd Unit A (92704-5803)
PHONE..............................949 486-3588
Josh Merrell, *Pr*
Mark Hyman, *
◆ **EMP:** 130 **EST:** 1997
SQ FT: 100,000
SALES (est): 22.01MM **Privately Held**
Web: www.liquidgraphicsmfg.com
SIC: **2329** Men's and boys' sportswear and athletic clothing

(P-2215)
LOST INTERNATIONAL LLC
170 Technology Dr (92618-2401)
PHONE..............................949 600-6950
Mike Reola, *Managing Member*
▲ **EMP:** 61 **EST:** 1999
SALES (est): 840.16K **Privately Held**
SIC: **2329** Athletic clothing, except uniforms: men's, youths' and boys'

(P-2216)
MORTEX CORPORATION
Also Called: Mortex Apparel
40 E Verdugo Ave (91502-1931)
P.O. Box 127 (27591-0127)
EMP: 225
SIC: **2329** 2339 5699 Men's and boys' sportswear and athletic clothing; Sportswear, women's; Sports apparel

(P-2217)
PATAGONIA INC (HQ)
Also Called: Great Pacific Patagonia
259 W Santa Clara St (93001-2545)
P.O. Box 150 (93002-0150)
PHONE..............................805 643-8616
◆ **EMP:** 500 **EST:** 1979
SALES (est): 342.14MM
SALES (corp-wide): 415.44MM **Privately Held**
Web: www.patagoniaprovisions.com
SIC: **2329** 2339 Athletic clothing, except uniforms: men's, youths' and boys'; Athletic clothing: women's, misses', and juniors'
PA: Patagonia Works
259 W Santa Clara St
Ventura CA
805 643-8616

(P-2218)
SAUVAGE INC (PA)
7717 Formula Pl (92121-2419)
PHONE..............................858 408-0100
Elizabeth Southwood, *Pr*
Simon Southwood, *Sec*
EMP: 17 **EST:** 1981
SQ FT: 10,000
SALES (est): 2.41MM
SALES (corp-wide): 2.41MM **Privately Held**
Web: www.sauvagewear.com
SIC: **2329** 2339 Men's and boys' sportswear and athletic clothing; Bathing suits: women's, misses', and juniors'

(P-2219)
SPEEDO USA INC
Also Called: Speedo USA
6251 Katella Ave (90630-5234)
PHONE..............................657 465-3800
Jim Gerson, *Pr*

◆ **EMP:** 400 **EST:** 1990
SQ FT: 10,000
SALES (est): 122.99MM
SALES (corp-wide): 436.88K **Privately Held**
Web: us.speedo.com
SIC: **2329** 2339 2321 3949 Athletic clothing, except uniforms: men's, youths' and boys'; Bathing suits: women's, misses', and juniors'; Men's and boys' sports and polo shirts; Water sports equipment
HQ: Pentland Capital Limited
8 Manchester Square
London
207 535-3820

(P-2220)
SPORTSROBE INC
8654 Hayden Pl (90232-2902)
PHONE..............................310 559-3999
Allen Ruegsegger, *Pr*
Mary Ann Ruegsegger, *
EMP: 49 **EST:** 1979
SQ FT: 14,000
SALES (est): 3.85MM **Privately Held**
SIC: **2329** Baseball uniforms: men's, youths', and boys'

(P-2221)
STEADY CLOTHING INC
2851 E White Star Ave Ste A (92806-2550)
PHONE..............................714 444-2058
Eric Anthony, *Pr*
Joshua Brownfield, *VP*
▲ **EMP:** 17 **EST:** 1994
SALES (est): 2.45MM **Privately Held**
Web: www.steadyclothing.com
SIC: **2329** 2339 Men's and boys' sportswear and athletic clothing; Sportswear, women's

(P-2222)
STRAIGHT DOWN ENTERPRISES (PA)
Also Called: Straight Down Clothing Company
625 Clarion Ct (93401-8177)
PHONE..............................805 543-3086
Michael Rowley, *CEO*
▲ **EMP:** 20 **EST:** 1989
SQ FT: 21,000
SALES (est): 4.89MM
SALES (corp-wide): 4.89MM **Privately Held**
Web: www.straightdown.com
SIC: **2329** 2339 Men's and boys' sportswear and athletic clothing; Women's and misses' outerwear, nec

(P-2223)
STREAMLINE DSIGN SLKSCREEN INC (PA)
Also Called: Old Guys Rule
1299 S Wells Rd (93004-1901)
PHONE..............................805 884-1025
Thom Hill, *CEO*
▲ **EMP:** 60 **EST:** 1995
SQ FT: 33,000
SALES (est): 9.86MM **Privately Held**
Web: www.oldguysrule.com
SIC: **2329** 5136 5611 Men's and boys' sportswear and athletic clothing; Men's and boy's clothing; Men's and boys' clothing stores

(P-2224)
TARTAN FASHION INC
4357 Rowland Ave (91731-1119)
PHONE..............................626 575-2828
Joann Sun, *Pr*
◆ **EMP:** 20 **EST:** 2002
SQ FT: 20,363

SALES (est): 1.8MM **Privately Held**
SIC: **2329** Men's and boys' sportswear and athletic clothing

(P-2225)
THIRTY THREE THREADS INC (PA)
Also Called: Toesox
1330 Park Center Dr (92081-8300)
PHONE..............................877 486-3769
Barry Buchholtz, *CEO*
Joseph Patterson, *Dir*
Deedee Wilson, *Dir*
▲ **EMP:** 34 **EST:** 2004
SALES (est): 10.8MM
SALES (corp-wide): 10.8MM **Privately Held**
Web: www.thirtythreethreads.com
SIC: **2329** 2252 Athletic clothing, except uniforms: men's, youths' and boys'; Socks

(P-2226)
TRAVISMATHEW LLC (HQ)
15202 Graham St (92649-1109)
PHONE..............................562 799-6900
Ryan Ellis, *CEO*
Chris Rossassen, *
John Kruger, *
Nick Beranek, *
▲ **EMP:** 38 **EST:** 2007
SALES (est): 64.95MM
SALES (corp-wide): 4B **Publicly Held**
Web: www.travismathew.com
SIC: **2329** 5699 5651 5661 Athletic clothing, except uniforms: men's, youths' and boys'; Sports apparel; Unisex clothing stores; Men's shoes
PA: Topgolf Callaway Brands Corp.
2180 Rutherford Rd
Carlsbad CA
760 931-1771

(P-2227)
WATERFRONT DESIGN GROUP LLC
122 E Washington Blvd (90015-3601)
PHONE..............................213 746-5800
EMP: 23 **EST:** 2001
SALES (est): 1.66MM **Privately Held**
SIC: **2329** Men's and boys' sportswear and athletic clothing

(P-2228)
ZK ENTERPRISES INC
Also Called: Unique Sales
4368 District Blvd (90058-3124)
PHONE..............................213 622-7012
Ron Kelfer, *Pr*
Kathy Kelfer, *
EMP: 40 **EST:** 1985
SQ FT: 13,000
SALES (est): 3.7MM **Privately Held**
Web: www.uniquesalesco.com
SIC: **2329** 2339 Athletic clothing, except uniforms: men's, youths' and boys'; Jogging and warmup suits: women's, misses', and juniors'

2331 Women's And Misses' Blouses And Shirts

(P-2229)
ALLIANCE APPAREL INC
Also Called: Blu Heaven
3422 Garfield Ave (90040-3104)
PHONE..............................323 888-8900
Tae Hoo Shin, *Pr*
Michael Park, *

P
R
O
D
U
C
T
S

&

S
V
C
S

▲ **EMP:** 40 **EST:** 1999
SQ FT: 17,500
SALES (est): 3.32MM **Privately Held**
Web: www.imagenationapparel.com
SIC: 2331 Blouses, women's and juniors':
made from purchased material

(P-2230)
ALPINESTARS USA
Also Called: Alpinestars USA
2780 W 237th St (90505-5270)
PHONE...................................310 891-0222
Giovanni Mazzarolo, *CEO*
▲ **EMP:** 82 **EST:** 1986
SQ FT: 28,380
SALES (est): 23.52MM
SALES (corp-wide): 319.08MM **Privately
Held**
Web: www.alpinestar.com
SIC: 2331 2326 3751 5571 Women's and
misses' blouses and shirts; Men's and boy's
work clothing; Motorcycle accessories;
Motorcycle parts and accessories
HQ: Alpinestars Spa
Viale Enrico Fermi 5
Asolo TV
042 352-9571

(P-2231)
BLTEE LLC
7101 Telegraph Rd (90640-6511)
P.O. Box 2762 (90670-0762)
PHONE...................................213 802-1736
Elano Miguel Elias, *Managing Member*
EMP: 45 **EST:** 2013
SQ FT: 4,900
SALES (est): 3.48MM **Privately Held**
SIC: 2331 5136 Women's and misses'
blouses and shirts; Shirts, men's and boys'

(P-2232)
BLUPRINT CLOTHING CORP
6013 Randolph St (90040-3417)
PHONE...................................323 780-4347
Ju Hyun Kim, *CEO*
Liz Lee, *
▲ **EMP:** 75 **EST:** 2005
SALES (est): 30MM **Privately Held**
Web: www.bluprintcorp.com
SIC: 2331 Women's and misses' blouses
and shirts

(P-2233)
BOULEVARD STYLE INC
Also Called: Blvd
1680 E 40th Pl (90011-2223)
PHONE...................................213 749-1551
Joseph Huh, *Prin*
EMP: 44
Web: www.blvdstyle.com
SIC: 2331 Women's and misses' blouses
and shirts
PA: Boulevard Style, Inc.
1015 Crocker St Ste 27
Los Angeles CA

(P-2234)
C-QUEST INC
Also Called: Ava James
1439 S Herbert Ave (90023-4047)
PHONE...................................323 980-1400
Nam H Paik, *CEO*
◆ **EMP:** 22 **EST:** 2003
SQ FT: 100,000
SALES (est): 4.68MM **Privately Held**
SIC: 2331 Women's and misses' blouses
and shirts

(P-2235)
**COLON MANUFACTURING INC
(PA)**
Also Called: Coc Inc
1100 S San Pedro St Ste 0-08
(90015-2328)
PHONE...................................213 749-6149
Thomas T Byun, *Pr*
Julia Anna Byun, *Sec*
EMP: 19 **EST:** 1991
SALES (est): 2.9MM **Privately Held**
SIC: 2331 2335 2337 Women's and misses'
blouses and shirts; Women's, junior's, and
misses' dresses; Women's and misses'
suits and coats

(P-2236)
CRESTONE LLC
Also Called: Hazel Clothes
2511 S Alameda St (90058-1309)
PHONE...................................323 588-8857
Robert Cho, *CEO*
▲ **EMP:** 20 **EST:** 2005
SQ FT: 10,000
SALES (est): 2.41MM **Privately Held**
SIC: 2331 2361 Women's and misses'
blouses and shirts; Girl's and children's
dresses, blouses

(P-2237)
EASTWEST CLOTHING INC (PA)
Also Called: Language Los Angeles
40 E Verdugo Ave (91502-1931)
PHONE...................................323 980-1177
Michael Schreier, *CEO*
Arvril Ozen, *COO*
▲ **EMP:** 19 **EST:** 1995
SQ FT: 10,000
SALES (est): 3.68MM **Privately Held**
Web: www.languagelosangeles.com
SIC: 2331 Women's and misses' blouses
and shirts

(P-2238)
ETRO USA INCORPORATED
9501 Wilshire Blvd (90212-2404)
PHONE...................................310 248-2855
Janine Masaki, *Mgr*
▲ **EMP:** 18 **EST:** 2007
SALES (est): 490.95K **Privately Held**
Web: www.etro.com
SIC: 2331 2339 2341 5137 Women's and
misses' blouses and shirts; Women's and
misses' outerwear, nec; Women's and
children's underwear; Women's and
children's clothing

(P-2239)
FINAL TOUCH APPAREL INC
Also Called: Final Touch Apparel
4801 Pacific Blvd (90058-2211)
PHONE...................................323 484-9621
Mark Min Hyuk Kim, *CEO*
June Lim, *
EMP: 19 **EST:** 2017
SQ FT: 16,000
SALES (est): 1.67MM **Privately Held**
Web: www.finaltouchapparel.com
SIC: 2331 5632 5137 Women's and misses'
blouses and shirts; Apparel accessories;
Women's and children's clothing

(P-2240)
FORTUNE CASUALS LLC (PA)
Also Called: Judy Ann
10119 Jefferson Blvd (90232-3519)
PHONE...................................310 733-2100
Fred Kayne, *Managing Member*
◆ **EMP:** 100 **EST:** 1999
SQ FT: 40,000

SALES (est): 9.52MM
SALES (corp-wide): 9.52MM **Privately
Held**
SIC: 2331 2339 2321 T-shirts and tops,
women's: made from purchased materials;
Slacks: women's, misses', and juniors';
Men's and boy's furnishings

(P-2241)
GLORIA LANCE INC (PA)
Also Called: Electric Designs
15616 S Broadway (90248-2211)
P.O. Box 3941 (90247-7519)
PHONE...................................310 767-4400
Robert Hempling, *Pr*
Zvia Hempling, *
Miguel Lopez, *
Gloria Lopez, *
◆ **EMP:** 90 **EST:** 1983
SQ FT: 25,000
SALES (est): 14.83MM
SALES (corp-wide): 14.83MM **Privately
Held**
SIC: 2331 2339 2335 Blouses, women's and
juniors': made from purchased material;
Sportswear, women's; Bridal and formal
gowns

(P-2242)
GURU KNITS INC
Also Called: Antex Knitting Mills
225 W 38th St (90037-1405)
PHONE...................................323 235-9424
Kevin Port, *CEO*
William Tenenblatt, *
◆ **EMP:** 60 **EST:** 2007
SALES (est): 6.59MM **Privately Held**
Web: www.aceross.com
SIC: 2331 2361 Women's and misses'
blouses and shirts; Blouses: girls,
children's, and infants'

(P-2243)
HARARI INC (PA)
9646 Brighton Way (90016)
PHONE...................................323 734-5302
EMP: 45 **EST:** 1979
SALES (est): 3.48MM
SALES (corp-wide): 3.48MM **Privately
Held**
Web: www.harariinc.com
SIC: 2331 5621 Women's and misses'
blouses and shirts; Women's clothing stores

(P-2244)
**HARKHAM INDUSTRIES INC
(PA)**
Also Called: Jonathan Martin
857 S San Pedro St Ste 300 (90014-2432)
PHONE...................................323 586-4600
Uri Harkham, *Pr*
◆ **EMP:** 50 **EST:** 1974
SQ FT: 140,000
SALES (est): 5.58MM
SALES (corp-wide): 5.58MM **Privately
Held**
Web: www.jonathanmartin.com
SIC: 2331 2335 2337 2339 Blouses,
women's and juniors': made from
purchased material; Women's, junior's, and
misses' dresses; Skirts, separate: women's,
misses', and juniors'; Women's and misses'
outerwear, nec

(P-2245)
J HEYRI INC
Also Called: Everleigh
219 E 32nd St (90011-1917)
PHONE...................................323 588-1234
Tiffany Lin, *Pr*

Sunny Choi, *VP*
Alexis Kwak, *VP*
◆ **EMP:** 20 **EST:** 2010
SALES (est): 2.39MM **Privately Held**
SIC: 2331 Women's and misses' blouses
and shirts

(P-2246)
JUDY ANN OF CALIFORNIA INC
Also Called: Landing Gear
1936 Mateo St (90021-2833)
PHONE...................................213 623-9233
Michael Geller, *Pr*
EMP: 150 **EST:** 1985
SALES (est): 9.19MM **Privately Held**
SIC: 2331 2339 T-shirts and tops, women's:
made from purchased materials; Slacks:
women's, misses', and juniors'

(P-2247)
JUNTEE OF CALIFORNIA INC
1031 S Broadway Rm 327 (90015-4006)
PHONE...................................213 742-0246
Jamshid Younesi, *Pr*
Azam Shirzeh, *
EMP: 35 **EST:** 1987
SQ FT: 3,000
SALES (est): 2.8MM **Privately Held**
SIC: 2331 Women's and misses' blouses
and shirts

(P-2248)
K TOO
Also Called: K-Too
800 E 12th St Ste 117 (90021-2199)
PHONE...................................213 747-7766
Jae Hee Kim, *CEO*
Kelley Kim, *
◆ **EMP:** 41 **EST:** 2007
SALES (est): 2.68MM **Privately Held**
Web: www.ktoousa.com
SIC: 2331 Women's and misses' blouses
and shirts

(P-2249)
**KANDY KISS OF CALIFORNIA
INC**
14761 Califa St (91411-3107)
▲ **EMP:** 60
Web: www.perfectdomain.com
SIC: 2331 2335 2361 Women's and misses'
blouses and shirts; Women's, junior's, and
misses' dresses; Shirts: girls', children's,
and infants'

(P-2250)
KSM GARMENT INC
Also Called: Alex and Jane
5613 Maywood Ave (90270-2503)
PHONE...................................323 585-8811
EMP: 42
SIC: 2331 Women's and misses' blouses
and shirts

(P-2251)
LA MAMBA LLC
150 N Myers St (90033-2109)
PHONE...................................323 526-3526
Fabian Oberfeld, *Managing Member*
Denni Kopelan, *
Stephen Brown, *
▲ **EMP:** 31 **EST:** 2008
SALES (est): 3.36MM **Privately Held**
SIC: 2331 Blouses, women's and juniors':
made from purchased material

(P-2252)
LEEBE APPAREL INC
Also Called: Leebe

▲ = Import ▼ = Export
◆ = Import/Export

3499 S Main St (90007-4413)
PHONE.................................323 897-5585
Won Joo Lee, *Pr*
▲ **EMP:** 25 **EST:** 2007
SQ FT: 8,000
SALES (est): 2.52MM **Privately Held**
SIC: 2331 Women's and misses' blouses
and shirts

(P-2253)
LF SPORTSWEAR INC (PA)
Also Called: Furst
13336 Beach Ave (90292-5622)
PHONE.................................310 437-4100
Phillip L Furst, *CEO*
Marsha Furst, *
Steve Katz, *
◆ **EMP:** 30 **EST:** 1980
SALES (est): 9.4MM
SALES (corp-wide): 9.4MM **Privately Held**
Web: www.lfstores.com
SIC: 2331 5137 2211 Women's and misses'
blouses and shirts; Women's and children's
dresses, suits, skirts, and blouses; Denims

(P-2254)
LOVEMARKS INC
2050 E 51st St (90058-2819)
PHONE.................................213 514-5888
EMP: 88
SALES (corp-wide): 1.99MM **Privately
Held**
SIC: 2331 Women's and misses' blouses
and shirts
PA: Lovemarks, Inc.
3251 E 26th St
Vernon CA
213 514-5888

(P-2255)
LSPACE AMERICA LLC
Also Called: L Space
14420 Myford Rd (92606-1017)
PHONE.................................949 750-2292
◆ **EMP:** 62 **EST:** 2008
SALES (est): 8.45MM **Privately Held**
Web: www.lspace.com
SIC: 2331 2253 Women's and misses'
blouses and shirts; Bathing suits and
swimwear, knit

(P-2256)
MF INC
Also Called: Welovefine
2010 E 15th St (90021-2823)
PHONE.................................213 627-2498
Danish Gajiani, *CEO*
Faizan Bakali, *Pr*
Bill Bussiere, *CFO*
Dean Allen, *CMO*
◆ **EMP:** 120 **EST:** 1999
SQ FT: 700,000
SALES (est): 30.56MM
SALES (corp-wide): 638.25MM **Privately
Held**
SIC: 2331 2253 T-shirts and tops, women's:
made from purchased materials; T-shirts
and tops, knit
HQ: Mad Engine Global, Llc
6740 Cobra Way Ste 100
San Diego CA
858 558-5270

(P-2257)
MONROW INC
Also Called: Monrow
1404 S Main St Ste C (90015-2566)
PHONE.................................213 741-6007
Megan George, *Pr*
EMP: 29 **EST:** 2007

SALES (est): 4.04MM **Privately Held**
Web: www.monrow.com
SIC: 2331 T-shirts and tops, women's: made
from purchased materials

(P-2258)
MXF DESIGNS INC
Also Called: Nally & Millie
5327 Valley Blvd (90032-3930)
PHONE.................................323 266-1451
James Park, *Pr*
Nally Park, *Stockholder*
▼ **EMP:** 95 **EST:** 1994
SALES (est): 6.11MM **Privately Held**
Web: www.nallyandmillie.com
SIC: 2331 Blouses, women's and juniors':
made from purchased material

(P-2259)
MYMICHELLE COMPANY LLC (HQ)
Also Called: My Michelle
13077 Temple Ave (91746-1418)
PHONE.................................626 934-4166
Arthur Gordon, *Pr*
Arthur Gordon, *Pr*
Roger D Joseph, *
◆ **EMP:** 300 **EST:** 1948
SQ FT: 600,000
SALES (est): 23.87MM
SALES (corp-wide): 618.9MM **Privately
Held**
SIC: 2331 2337 2335 2361 Blouses,
women's and juniors': made from
purchased material; Skirts, separate:
women's, misses', and juniors';
Dresses,paper, cut and sewn; Blouses:
girls', children's, and infants'
PA: Kellwood Company, Llc
13071 Temple Ave
City Of Industry CA
626 934-4122

(P-2260)
NOTHING TO WEAR INC
Also Called: Subtle Luxury
630 Maple Ave (90503-5001)
PHONE.................................310 328-0408
EMP: 19
Web: www.subtletones.com
SIC: 2331 Women's and misses' blouses
and shirts
PA: Nothing To Wear, Inc.
630 Maple Ave
Torrance CA

(P-2261)
NOTHING TO WEAR INC (PA)
Also Called: Figure 8
630 Maple Ave (90503-5001)
PHONE.................................310 328-0408
Cindy Nunes Freeman, *Pr*
Darrin Freeman, *
◆ **EMP:** 35 **EST:** 1991
SQ FT: 18,000
SALES (est): 4.67MM **Privately Held**
Web: www.subtletones.com
SIC: 2331 2335 2339 Women's and misses'
blouses and shirts; Women's, junior's, and
misses' dresses; Women's and misses'
accessories

(P-2262)
PAIGE LLC (HQ)
Also Called: Paige Premium Denim
10119 Jefferson Blvd (90232-3519)
PHONE.................................310 733-2100
Paige Adams-geller, *Chief Design Officer*
Walter Lacher, *
Michael Henschel, *

Caroline Blanchard, *
◆ **EMP:** 150 **EST:** 2004
SQ FT: 40,000
SALES (est): 49.17MM
SALES (corp-wide): 49.17MM **Privately
Held**
Web: www.paige.com
SIC: 2331 2326 Women's and misses'
blouses and shirts; Men's and boy's work
clothing
PA: Ppd Holding, Llc
10119 Jefferson Blvd
Culver City CA
310 733-2100

(P-2263)
PROJECT SOCIAL T LLC
615 S Clarence St (90023-1107)
PHONE.................................323 266-4500
EMP: 30 **EST:** 2011
SALES (est): 2.96MM **Privately Held**
Web: www.projectsocialt.com
SIC: 2331 5137 5621 Women's and misses'
blouses and shirts; Women's and children's
clothing; Women's clothing stores

(P-2264)
STONY APPAREL CORP (PA)
Also Called: Eyeshadow
1201 S Grand Ave (90015-2105)
PHONE.................................323 981-9080
▲ **EMP:** 175 **EST:** 1996
SALES (est): 44.25MM **Privately Held**
Web: www.stonyapparel.com
SIC: 2331 2335 7389 Women's and misses'
blouses and shirts; Women's, junior's, and
misses' dresses; Apparel designers,
commercial

(P-2265)
T2C INC
1348 S Flower St (90015-2908)
PHONE.................................213 741-5232
Shawn Janet, *Pr*
EMP: 18 **EST:** 2002
SQ FT: 3,500
SALES (est): 1.94MM **Privately Held**
SIC: 2331 Women's and misses' blouses
and shirts

(P-2266)
TIANELLO INC
Also Called: Tianello By Steve Barraza
138 W 38th St (90037-1404)
PHONE.................................323 231-0599
Steven Barraza, *Pr*
▲ **EMP:** 185 **EST:** 1992
SQ FT: 25,000
SALES (est): 9.75MM **Privately Held**
Web: www.tianello.com
SIC: 2331 5621 2339 Women's and misses'
blouses and shirts; Women's clothing stores
; Women's and misses' outerwear, nec

(P-2267)
UMGEE USA INC
1565 E 23rd St (90011-1801)
PHONE.................................323 526-9138
Boyng Ki Gi, *Pr*
◆ **EMP:** 18 **EST:** 2001
SALES (est): 2.43MM **Privately Held**
Web: www.umgeeusa.com
SIC: 2331 2335 Women's and misses'
blouses and shirts; Women's, junior's, and
misses' dresses

(P-2268)
UNGER FABRIK LLC (PA)
18525 Railroad St (91748-1316)
PHONE.................................626 469-8080

Yongbin Luo, *CEO*
◆ **EMP:** 110 **EST:** 1998
SQ FT: 300,000
SALES (est): 10.2MM
SALES (corp-wide): 10.2MM **Privately
Held**
Web: www.oneworldapparel.com
SIC: 2331 Women's and misses' blouses
and shirts

(P-2269)
VEEZEE INC
Also Called: Honulua Surf Co
121 Waterworks Way (92618-7719)
PHONE.................................949 265-0800
Paul Naude, *Pr*
▲ **EMP:** 20 **EST:** 2001
SALES (est): 9.2MM
SALES (corp-wide): 2.67MM **Privately
Held**
SIC: 2331 5099 Women's and misses'
blouses and shirts; Sunglasses
HQ: Billabong International Pty Ltd
5 Billabong Place
Burleigh Waters QLD

(P-2270)
W5 CONCEPTS INC
2049 E 38th St (90058-1614)
PHONE.................................323 231-2415
Kyung Eun Kim, *CEO*
EMP: 20 **EST:** 2014
SQ FT: 3,800
SALES (est): 2.59MM **Privately Held**
Web: www.w5concepts.com
SIC: 2331 Women's and misses' blouses
and shirts

(P-2271)
YS GARMENTS LLC (HQ)
Also Called: Next Level Apparel
588 Crenshaw Blvd (90503-1705)
PHONE.................................310 631-4955
▲ **EMP:** 36 **EST:** 2003
SALES (est): 36.05MM
SALES (corp-wide): 36.05MM **Privately
Held**
Web: www.nextlevelapparel.com
SIC: 2331 2326 5136 5137 Women's and
misses' blouses and shirts; Men's and boy's
work clothing; Men's and boy's clothing;
Blouses
PA: Next Level Holdings Company Llc
588 Crenshaw Blvd
Torrance CA
310 631-4955

2335 Women's, Junior's, And Misses' Dresses

(P-2272)
AGS USA LLC
Also Called: American Garment Sewing
1210 Rexford Ave (91107-1713)
PHONE.................................323 588-2200
▲ **EMP:** 150
Web: www.agsusallc.com
SIC: 2335 2326 2331 2339 Women's,
junior's, and misses' dresses; Men's and
boy's work clothing; Women's and misses'
blouses and shirts; Jeans: women's,
misses', and juniors'

(P-2273)
ALL ACCESS APPAREL INC (PA)
Also Called: Self Esteem
1515 Gage Rd (90640-6613)
PHONE.................................323 889-4300
◆ **EMP:** 130 **EST:** 1997

SQ FT: 122,000
SALES (est): 23.68MM **Privately Held**
Web: www.selfesteemclothing.com
SIC: **2335** 2331 2361 Women's, junior's, and misses' dresses; Women's and misses' blouses and shirts; Girl's and children's dresses, blouses

(P-2274)
ALMACK LINERS INC
9541 Cozycroft Ave (91311-5102)
PHONE..............................818 718-5878
Susana Almack, *Pr*
EMP: 25 EST: 1985
SQ FT: 3,000
SALES (est): 3.48MM **Privately Held**
Web: www.almackliners.com
SIC: **2335** 2329 Women's, junior's, and misses' dresses; Men's and boys' sportswear and athletic clothing

(P-2275)
AQUARIUS RAGS LLC (PA)
Also Called: ABS By Allen Schwartz
15821 Ventura Blvd Ste 270 (91436-4775)
PHONE..............................213 895-4400
Allen Schwartz, *Managing Member*
▲ EMP: 75 EST: 2003
SALES (est): 13.11MM
SALES (corp-wide): 13.11MM **Privately Held**
SIC: **2335** Women's, junior's, and misses' dresses

(P-2276)
AVALON APPAREL LLC (PA)
Also Called: Disorderly Kids
2520 W 6th St (90057-3174)
PHONE..............................323 581-3511
Elliot Schutzer, *Managing Member*
Jason Schutzer, *
Jill Grossman, *
Terri Cohen, *
EMP: 165 EST: 2004
SQ FT: 5,000
SALES (est): 25.02MM **Privately Held**
Web: www.avalonapparel.com
SIC: **2335** Ensemble dresses: women's, misses', and juniors'

(P-2277)
AWAKE INC
Also Called: JEM SPORTSWEAR
10700 Valley View St (90630-4835)
PHONE..............................818 365-9361
Jeffrey A Marine, *CEO*
Orna Stark, *
▲ EMP: 40 EST: 2001
SALES (est): 356.56K **Privately Held**
SIC: **2335** Women's, junior's, and misses' dresses

(P-2278)
CALIFORNIA BLUE APPAREL INC
Also Called: Ever Blue
245 W 28th St (90007-3312)
PHONE..............................213 745-5400
▲ EMP: 30
Web: www.californiablue.com
SIC: **2335** 2339 2331 Women's, junior's, and misses' dresses; Women's and misses' outerwear, nec; Women's and misses' blouses and shirts

(P-2279)
CAROL ANDERSON INC (PA)
Also Called: Carol Anderson By Invitation
18700 S Laurel Park Rd (90220-6003)
PHONE..............................310 638-3333

Jan Janura, *Pr*
Carol M Anderson, *
Jan A Janura, *
◆ EMP: 25 EST: 1977
SQ FT: 50,000
SALES (est): 8.74MM
SALES (corp-wide): 8.74MM **Privately Held**
Web: www.cabionline.com
SIC: **2335** 2339 Women's, junior's, and misses' dresses; Shorts (outerwear): women's, misses', and juniors'

(P-2280)
CHOON INC (PA)
Also Called: Pezeme
1443 E 4th St (90033-4214)
PHONE..............................213 225-2500
Choon S Nakamura, *Pr*
Daniel Nakamura, *
◆ EMP: 31 EST: 1972
SALES (est): 3.92MM
SALES (corp-wide): 3.92MM **Privately Held**
Web: www.choon.com
SIC: **2335** Women's, junior's, and misses' dresses

(P-2281)
COMPLETE CLOTHING COMPANY (PA)
Also Called: Willow
4950 E 49th St (90058-2736)
PHONE..............................323 277-1470
▲ EMP: 43 EST: 1995
SQ FT: 30,000
SALES (est): 8.72MM **Privately Held**
Web: www.shopwillow.com
SIC: **2335** 2339 2337 2331 Women's, junior's, and misses' dresses; Sportswear, women's; Women's and misses' suits and coats; Women's and misses' blouses and shirts

(P-2282)
J C TRIMMING COMPANY INC
Also Called: JC Industries
3800 S Hill St (90037-1416)
PHONE..............................323 235-4458
Eric Shin, *CEO*
◆ EMP: 65 EST: 1993
SALES (est): 10.14MM **Privately Held**
SIC: **2335** 2326 Women's, junior's, and misses' dresses; Men's and boy's work clothing

(P-2283)
JODI KRISTOPHER LLC (PA)
Also Called: City Triangles
1950 Naomi Ave (90011-1342)
PHONE..............................323 890-8000
Adir Haroni, *CEO*
Juduth Naka, *
▲ EMP: 83 EST: 1990
SALES (est): 22.74MM **Privately Held**
Web: www.hottempered.com
SIC: **2335** Women's, junior's, and misses' dresses

(P-2284)
JWC STUDIO INC (PA)
Also Called: Johnny Was Showroom
2423 E 23rd St (90058-1201)
PHONE..............................323 231-8222
Eli Levite, *Pr*
▼ EMP: 26 EST: 1994
SQ FT: 30,000
SALES (est): 4.81MM
SALES (corp-wide): 4.81MM **Privately Held**

SIC: **2335** Women's, junior's, and misses' dresses

(P-2285)
LOTUS ORIENT CORP (PA)
Also Called: Venus Bridal Gowns
411 S California St (91776-2527)
P.O. Box 280 (91778-0280)
PHONE..............................626 285-5796
Eugene Wu, *Pr*
▲ EMP: 18 EST: 1985
SQ FT: 6,400
SALES (est): 2.44MM
SALES (corp-wide): 2.44MM **Privately Held**
Web: www.lotusorient.com
SIC: **2335** 5621 Wedding gowns and dresses ; Bridal shops

(P-2286)
OLA NATION LLC
Also Called: Go Sales.us
915 W Barbara Ave (91790-4135)
PHONE..............................310 256-0638
Oscar Linares, *Pr*
EMP: 20 EST: 2007
SALES (est): 1.05MM **Privately Held**
SIC: **2335** Bridal and formal gowns

(P-2287)
PRIVATE BRAND MDSG CORP
Also Called: Jody of California
214 W Olympic Blvd (90015-1605)
P.O. Box 260923 (91426-0923)
PHONE..............................213 749-0191
William Berman, *Pr*
Rochelle Berman, *Sec*
John Berman, *VP Sls*
EMP: 23 EST: 1954
SQ FT: 6,000
SALES (est): 2.27MM **Privately Held**
Web: privatebm.openfos.com
SIC: **2335** 2339 Women's, junior's, and misses' dresses; Sportswear, women's

(P-2288)
PROMISES PROMISES INC
3121 S Grand Ave (90007-3816)
PHONE..............................213 749-7725
Eugene M Hardy, *Pr*
▲ EMP: 29 EST: 1978
SALES (est): 3.82MM **Privately Held**
SIC: **2335** Women's, junior's, and misses' dresses

(P-2289)
SUBLITEX INC
Also Called: Sublitex Sublimation Tech
1515 E 15th St (90021-2711)
PHONE..............................323 582-9596
EMP: 35 EST: 2008
SALES (est): 3.4MM **Privately Held**
SIC: **2335** 7389 Women's, junior's, and misses' dresses; Printing broker

(P-2290)
TLMF INC
Also Called: Big Strike
1515 E 15th St (90021-2711)
PHONE..............................212 764-2334
▲ EMP: 100
Web: www.heartsoul.org
SIC: **2335** 2337 Women's, junior's, and misses' dresses; Women's and misses' suits and coats

(P-2291)
TRINITY SPORTS INC
2067 E 55th St (90058-3441)

PHONE..............................323 277-9288
▲ EMP: 300
Web: www.trinitysportsinc.com
SIC: **2335** 2339 2325 Women's, junior's, and misses' dresses; Women's and misses' outerwear, nec; Men's and boy's trousers and slacks

(P-2292)
TRIXXI CLOTHING COMPANY INC (PA)
6817 E Acco St (90040-1901)
PHONE..............................323 585-4200
Annette Soufrine, *CEO*
Leslie Flores, *
▲ EMP: 49 EST: 2001
SQ FT: 35,000
SALES (est): 10.09MM
SALES (corp-wide): 10.09MM **Privately Held**
Web: www.trixxi.com
SIC: **2335** 2331 Women's, junior's, and misses' dresses; Blouses, women's and juniors': made from purchased material

2337 Women's And Misses' Suits And Coats

(P-2293)
KELLER CLASSICS INC (PA)
Also Called: Nannette Keller
102 S Robinson St (93561-1723)
PHONE..............................805 524-1322
Nannette Keller, *Pr*
Roger Keller, *CFO*
Richard Scott, *Sec*
Doctor Landon, *Prin*
EMP: 35 EST: 1993
SQ FT: 12,000
SALES (est): 2.94MM **Privately Held**
Web: www.nannettekeller.com
SIC: **2337** 5621 Women's and misses' suits and skirts; Women's clothing stores

(P-2294)
KOMAROV ENTERPRISES INC
Also Called: Kisca
10939 Venice Blvd (90034-7015)
PHONE..............................213 244-7000
Dimitri Komarov, *Pr*
Dimitri Leiberman, *
Shelley Komvarov, *
▲ EMP: 75 EST: 1997
SALES (est): 9.52MM **Privately Held**
Web: www.komarov.com
SIC: **2337** 2331 Women's and misses' suits and coats; Women's and misses' blouses and shirts

(P-2295)
R B III ASSOCIATES INC
Also Called: Teamwork Athletic Apparel
2386 Faraday Ave Ste 125 (92008-7263)
PHONE..............................760 471-5370
Matthew Lehrer, *CEO*
Dave Caserta, *
Andy Lehrer, *
▲ EMP: 150 EST: 1976
SALES (est): 24.58MM **Privately Held**
SIC: **2337** 2329 Uniforms, except athletic: women's, misses', and juniors'; Men's and boys' athletic uniforms

(P-2296)
TOPSON DOWNS CALIFORNIA INC
3545 Motor Ave (90034-4806)
PHONE..............................310 558-0300

▲ = Import ▼ = Export
◆ = Import/Export

Kris Scott, *Brnch Mgr*
EMP: 131
SALES (corp-wide): 62.4MM **Privately Held**
Web: www.topsondowns.com
SIC: 2337 5621 Women's and misses' suits and coats; Ready-to-wear apparel, women's
PA: Topson Downs Of California, Inc.
3840 Watseka Ave
Culver City CA
310 558-0300

2339 Women's And Misses' Outerwear, Nec

(P-2297)
AARON CORPORATION
Also Called: J P Sportswear
2645 Industry Way (90262-4007)
PHONE................................323 235-5959
Paul Shechet, *Pr*
Francisco Balleste, *
▲ **EMP:** 170 **EST:** 1955
SALES (est): 17.82MM **Privately Held**
Web: www.jpsportswear.us
SIC: 2339 Women's and misses' athletic clothing and sportswear

(P-2298)
AB&R INC
Also Called: Billy Blues
5849 Smithway St (90040-1605)
PHONE................................323 727-0007
Rene Allison Thomas, *Pr*
William Scott Curtis, *VP*
▲ **EMP:** 21 **EST:** 1997
SQ FT: 10,500
SALES (est): 578.32K **Privately Held**
Web: www.mybillyblues.com
SIC: 2339 Women's and misses' outerwear, nec

(P-2299)
ABS BY ALLEN SCHWARTZ LLC (HQ)
15821 Ventura Blvd Ste 270 (91436-4775)
PHONE................................213 895-4400
Allen Schwartz, *Managing Member*
Kirk Foster, *
▲ **EMP:** 22 **EST:** 2004
SALES (est): 8.91MM
SALES (corp-wide): 13.11MM **Privately Held**
Web: www.allenschwartz.com
SIC: 2339 5621 Women's and misses' outerwear, nec; Women's clothing stores
PA: Aquarius Rags, Llc
15821 Ventura Blvd # 270
Encino CA
213 895-4400

(P-2300)
AMBIANCE USA INC
Also Called: Wax Jean By Ambiance
930 Towne Ave (90021-2022)
PHONE................................213 765-9600
EMP: 34
SALES (corp-wide): 18.45MM **Privately Held**
Web: www.waxjean.com
SIC: 2339 Jeans: women's, misses', and juniors'
PA: Ambiance U.S.A., Inc.
2415 E 15th St
Los Angeles CA
323 587-0007

(P-2301)
AMBIANCE USA INC
2465 E 23rd St (90058-1201)
PHONE................................323 587-0007
EMP: 33
SALES (corp-wide): 18.45MM **Privately Held**
Web: www.waxjean.com
SIC: 2339 Women's and misses' outerwear, nec
PA: Ambiance U.S.A., Inc.
2415 E 15th St
Los Angeles CA
323 587-0007

(P-2302)
AMBIANCE USA INC (PA)
Also Called: Ambiance Apparel
2415 E 15th St (90021-2936)
PHONE................................323 587-0007
Sang Noh, *CEO*
In Y Noh, *
✦ **EMP:** 100 **EST:** 1999
SALES (est): 18.45MM
SALES (corp-wide): 18.45MM **Privately Held**
Web: www.ambianceapparel.com
SIC: 2339 5137 Women's and misses' outerwear, nec; Women's and children's clothing

(P-2303)
APPAREL PROD SVCS GLOBL LLC
Also Called: APS Global
8954 Lurline Ave (91311-6103)
P.O. Box 5011 (91365-5011)
PHONE................................818 700-3700
✦ **EMP:** 42 **EST:** 2013
SQ FT: 15,000
SALES (est): 8.42MM **Privately Held**
SIC: 2339 2329 Women's and misses' athletic clothing and sportswear; Men's and boys' sportswear and athletic clothing

(P-2304)
BARE NOTHINGS INC (PA)
17705 Sampson Ln (92647-6790)
PHONE................................714 848-8532
Ann Mase, *Pr*
Ronald Mase, *VP*
EMP: 22 **EST:** 1977
SALES (est): 1.82MM
SALES (corp-wide): 1.82MM **Privately Held**
Web: www.barenothings.com
SIC: 2339 Bathing suits: women's, misses', and juniors'

(P-2305)
BB CO INC
Also Called: Wild Lizard
1753 E 21st St (90058-1006)
PHONE................................213 550-1158
Kyoung K Frazier, *Pr*
Kyoung K Frazier, *Pr*
Cecy Mendoza, *
▲ **EMP:** 30 **EST:** 1998
SQ FT: 22,000
SALES (est): 7.5MM **Privately Held**
SIC: 2339 Women's and misses' athletic clothing and sportswear

(P-2306)
BE BOP CLOTHING
Also Called: Rebel Jeans
5833 Avalon Blvd (90003-1307)
PHONE................................323 846-0121
Guillermo Granados, *Pr*
Marcus Sphatt, *

Michael Harb, *
EMP: 350 **EST:** 1987
SQ FT: 100,000
SALES (est): 19.8MM **Privately Held**
SIC: 2339 Sportswear, women's

(P-2307)
BOARDRIDERS WHOLESALE LLC
Dakine
6201 Oak Cyn Ste 100 (92618-5232)
PHONE................................949 916-3060
EMP: 62
Web: www.quiksilver.com
SIC: 2339 2331 Women's and misses' outerwear, nec; Women's and misses' blouses and shirts
HQ: Boardriders Wholesale, Llc
5600 Argosy Ave Ste 100
Huntington Beach CA
714 889-2200

(P-2308)
BURNING TORCH INC
1738 Cordova St (90007-1129)
PHONE................................323 733-7700
Karyn Craven, *Pr*
▲ **EMP:** 20 **EST:** 1999
SQ FT: 5,000
SALES (est): 2.62MM **Privately Held**
Web: www.burningtorchinc.com
SIC: 2339 Sportswear, women's

(P-2309)
C M G INC (PA)
Also Called: Tarrant Apparel Group
801 S Figueroa St (90017-5504)
PHONE................................323 780-8250
Charles Ghailian, *Pr*
Julie Ghailian, *
EMP: 25 **EST:** 1988
SALES (est): 2.7MM
SALES (corp-wide): 2.7MM **Privately Held**
SIC: 2339 Women's and misses' athletic clothing and sportswear

(P-2310)
CAMP SMIDGEMORE INC (DH)
Also Called: Renee Claire Inc
3641 10th Ave (90018-4114)
PHONE................................323 634-0333
Wendy Luttrel, *CEO*
Renee Bertrand, *Pr*
▲ **EMP:** 22 **EST:** 2001
SQ FT: 13,000
SALES (est): 7.74MM
SALES (corp-wide): 359.75MM **Privately Held**
SIC: 2339 2341 Women's and misses' outerwear, nec; Pajamas and bedjackets: women's and children's
HQ: Komar Intimates, Llc
90 Hudson St
Jersey City NJ
212 725-1500

(P-2311)
CARBON 38 INC
10000 Washington Blvd Ste 100 (90232-2728)
PHONE................................888 723-5838
Katherine Johnson, *CEO*
EMP: 90 **EST:** 2012
SALES (est): 11.76MM **Privately Held**
Web: www.carbon38.com
SIC: 2339 Sportswear, women's

(P-2312)
CAROL WIOR INC
Also Called: Slimsuit
7533 Garfield Ave (90201-4817)
PHONE................................562 927-0052
Carol Wior, *Pr*
Niki Wior, *
Lucy Weddell, *
Troy Berg, *
Julie Wilson, *
▲ **EMP:** 30 **EST:** 1991
SQ FT: 77,000
SALES (est): 1.1MM **Privately Held**
Web: www.carolwiorinc.com
SIC: 2339 5699 Bathing suits: women's, misses', and juniors'; Bathing suits

(P-2313)
CITIZENS OF HUMANITY LLC (PA)
Also Called: Goldsign
5715 Bickett St (90255-2624)
PHONE................................323 923-1240
Jerome Dahan, *CEO*
Amy Williams, *Pr*
✦ **EMP:** 158 **EST:** 2005
SQ FT: 70,000
SALES (est): 54.81MM
SALES (corp-wide): 54.81MM **Privately Held**
Web: www.citizensofhumanity.com
SIC: 2339 Jeans: women's, misses', and juniors'

(P-2314)
CLOTHING ILLUSTRATED INC (PA)
Also Called: Love Stitch
836 Traction Ave (90013-1816)
PHONE................................213 403-9950
Danny Hanasab Foruzesh, *CEO*
Cyrous Forouzesh, *CFO*
▲ **EMP:** 35 **EST:** 2002
SALES (est): 8.95MM **Privately Held**
Web: www.shoplovestitch.com
SIC: 2339 Women's and misses' accessories

(P-2315)
CREW KNITWEAR LLC (PA)
Also Called: Hiatus
660 S Myers St (90023-1015)
PHONE................................323 526-3888
Tricia Franklin, *CEO*
Chris Y Jung, *Pr*
Peter Jung, *CFO*
▲ **EMP:** 58 **EST:** 2001
SQ FT: 39,000
SALES (est): 13.6MM **Privately Held**
Web: www.crewknitwear.com
SIC: 2339 Women's and misses' outerwear, nec

(P-2316)
DAVID GRMENT CTNG FSING SVC IN
Also Called: Clothng/Pparel/Uniform/ppe Mfg
5008 S Boyle Ave (90058-3904)
PHONE................................323 216-1574
Mario Alvarado, *CEO*
David Alvarado, *
Mario Alvarado, *VP*
▲ **EMP:** 45 **EST:** 1987
SQ FT: 15,000
SALES (est): 4.97MM **Privately Held**
SIC: 2339 2326 2329 Women's and misses' athletic clothing and sportswear; Men's and boy's work clothing; Men's and boys' sportswear and athletic clothing

---

(P-2317)
DDA HOLDINGS INC
Also Called: A Commom Thread
834 S Broadway Ste 600 (90014-3217)
PHONE....................213 624-5200
Anthony Graham, *CEO*
Sandra Balestier, *
▲ **EMP:** 25 **EST:** 2007
SQ FT: 15,000
SALES (est): 5.29MM **Privately Held**
Web: www.ddaholdings.com
SIC: 2339 Women's and misses' athletic
clothing and sportswear

(P-2318)
DESIGN TODAYS INC (PA)
11707 Cetona Way (91326-4604)
PHONE....................213 745-3091
Sung Ok Hong, *Pr*
EMP: 26 **EST:** 1987
SALES (est): 2.35MM **Privately Held**
SIC: 2339 Women's and misses' outerwear,
nec

(P-2319)
DHM INTERNATIONAL CORP
Also Called: Sunshine Enterprises
901 Monterey Pass Rd (91754-3610)
PHONE....................323 263-3888
Scott Yuen, *Pr*
Joe Yuen, *VP*
Ross Yuen, *VP*
▲ **EMP:** 18 **EST:** 2003
SQ FT: 28,000
SALES (est): 528.34K **Privately Held**
SIC: 2339 2326 Women's and misses'
outerwear, nec; Men's and boy's work
clothing

(P-2320)
DMBM LLC
2445 E 12th St Ste C (90021-2954)
PHONE....................714 321-6032
David Chong, *Owner*
EMP: 23
SIC: 2339 2369 Women's and misses'
outerwear, nec; Girl's and children's
outerwear, nec
PA: Dmbm, Llc
2701 S Santa Fe Ave
Vernon CA

(P-2321)
DNAM APPAREL INDUSTRIES LLC
Also Called: Ed Hardy
4938 Triggs St (90022-4832)
PHONE....................323 859-0114
Michael Cohen, *
▲ **EMP:** 32 **EST:** 2004
SALES (est): 2.71MM **Privately Held**
SIC: 2339 5137 Service apparel, washable:
women's; Women's and children's clothing

(P-2322)
EV R INC
Also Called: Skinny Minnie
3400 Slauson Ave (90270-2525)
PHONE....................323 312-5400
▲ **EMP:** 50
SIC: 2339 Athletic clothing: women's,
misses', and juniors'

(P-2323)
FINESSE APPAREL INC
Also Called: Finesse
815 Fairview Ave Unit 101 (91030-2490)
PHONE....................213 747-7077
▲ **EMP:** 45

Web: www.finesseusa.com
SIC: 2339 Women's and misses' athletic
clothing and sportswear

(P-2324)
GAZE USA INC
2011 E 25th St (90058-1127)
PHONE....................213 622-0022
Ji S Hong, *CEO*
Stephen S Whang, *
EMP: 25 **EST:** 2010
SALES (est): 2.31MM **Privately Held**
SIC: 2339 5651 3999 Women's and misses'
athletic clothing and sportswear; Unisex
clothing stores; Bristles, dressing of

(P-2325)
GOOD AMERICAN LLC (PA)
3125 S La Cienega Blvd (90016-3110)
P.O. Box 888 (90232-0888)
PHONE....................213 357-5100
Emma Grede, *CEO*
Khloe Kardashian, *
EMP: 42 **EST:** 2016
SALES (est): 19.95MM
SALES (corp-wide): 19.95MM **Privately
Held**
Web: www.goodamerican.com
SIC: 2339 5137 5621 Jeans: women's,
misses', and juniors'; Women's and
children's clothing; Women's clothing stores

(P-2326)
GYPSY 05 INC
3200 Union Pacific Ave (90023-4203)
PHONE....................323 265-2700
Dotan Shoham, *Pr*
▲ **EMP:** 27 **EST:** 2005
SALES (est): 2.28MM **Privately Held**
Web: www.gypsy05.com
SIC: 2339 Women's and misses' athletic
clothing and sportswear

(P-2327)
HEARTS DELIGHT
4035 N Ventura Ave (93001-1163)
PHONE....................805 648-7123
Deborah Mesker, *Owner*
EMP: 27 **EST:** 1986
SQ FT: 2,000
SALES (est): 1.77MM **Privately Held**
Web: shop.heartsdelightclothiers.com
SIC: 2339 5621 Women's and misses'
outerwear, nec; Boutiques

(P-2328)
HEATHER BY BORDEAUX INC
Also Called: Bordeaux
5983 Malburg Way (90058-3945)
PHONE....................213 622-0555
Afshin Raminfar, *CEO*
▲ **EMP:** 39 **EST:** 2003
SALES (est): 3.74MM **Privately Held**
Web: www.heatherfashion.com
SIC: 2339 Service apparel, washable:
women's

(P-2329)
HYLETE INC
Also Called: Hylete
11622 El Camino Real Ste 100 (92130)
PHONE....................858 225-8998
Adam Colton, *CEO*
Ron L Wilson Ii, *Interim Chief Financial
Officer*
Matthew Paulson, *VP*
EMP: 20 **EST:** 2012
SQ FT: 4,300
SALES (est): 11.69MM **Privately Held**
Web: www.hylete.com

SIC: 2339 5091 2329 Women's and misses'
athletic clothing and sportswear; Athletic
goods; Athletic clothing, except uniforms:
men's, youths' and boys'

(P-2330)
IT JEANS INC
Also Called: It Campus
2425 E 38th St (90058-1708)
PHONE....................323 588-2156
▲ **EMP:** 23
Web: www.itjeans.com
SIC: 2339 2369 Jeans: women's, misses',
and juniors'; Girl's and children's outerwear,
nec

(P-2331)
J & F DESIGN INC
Also Called: Next Generation
2042 Garfield Ave (90040-1804)
PHONE....................323 526-4444
Jack Farshi, *Pr*
◆ **EMP:** 67 **EST:** 1991
SQ FT: 100,000
SALES (est): 23MM **Privately Held**
Web: www.bobbyjackbrand.com
SIC: 2339 Sportswear, women's

(P-2332)
JANIN
10031 Hunt Ave (90280-6310)
PHONE....................323 564-0995
Jose Estevez, *Owner*
EMP: 210 **EST:** 1987
SQ FT: 10,000
SALES (est): 5.47MM **Privately Held**
SIC: 2339 Neckwear and ties: women's,
misses', and juniors'

(P-2333)
JAYA APPAREL GROUP LLC (PA)
5175 S Soto St (90058-3620)
PHONE....................323 584-3500
Jane Siskin, *Managing Member*
Don Lewis, *
Jalal Elbasri, *
◆ **EMP:** 67 **EST:** 2005
SALES (est): 24.28MM
SALES (corp-wide): 24.28MM **Privately
Held**
Web: www.jayaapparelgroup.com
SIC: 2339 2337 Women's and misses'
jackets and coats, except sportswear;
Women's and misses' suits and skirts

(P-2334)
JD/CMC INC
Also Called: Color ME Cotton
2834 E 11th St (90023-3406)
PHONE....................818 767-2260
Mari Tatevosian, *Pr*
Anait Grigorian, *
◆ **EMP:** 35 **EST:** 1991
SQ FT: 12,000
SALES (est): 3.21MM **Privately Held**
Web: www.cmcclick.com
SIC: 2339 Women's and misses' outerwear,
nec

(P-2335)
JNJ APPAREL INC
18788 Fairfield Rd (91326-3922)
PHONE....................323 584-9700
Chan Hyoung Park, *Pr*
▲ **EMP:** 30 **EST:** 2001
SALES (est): 2.76MM **Privately Held**
SIC: 2339 Women's and misses' athletic
clothing and sportswear

(P-2336)
JOLYN CLOTHING COMPANY LLC
16390 Pacific Coast Hwy Ste 201 (92649)
PHONE....................714 794-2149
Warren Lief Pedersen, *Pr*
Ann Dawson, *
Brandon Molina, *
EMP: 30 **EST:** 2007
SALES (est): 3.03MM **Privately Held**
Web: www.jolyn.com
SIC: 2339 5621 Women's and misses'
athletic clothing and sportswear; Women's
sportswear

(P-2337)
JOWETT GARMENTS FACTORY INC
Also Called: Jowett Group
10359 Rush St (91733-3341)
PHONE....................626 350-0515
◆ **EMP:** 40
Web: www.jowett.com
SIC: 2339 Athletic clothing: women's,
misses', and juniors'

(P-2338)
JT DESIGN STUDIO INC (PA)
Also Called: 860, Shameless, Hot Wire
860 S Los Angeles St Ste 912
(90014-3302)
PHONE....................213 891-1500
Ted Cooper, *Pr*
Robert Grossman, *
▲ **EMP:** 24 **EST:** 1998
SALES (est): 2.28MM
SALES (corp-wide): 2.28MM **Privately
Held**
Web: www.jtdesignstudio.com
SIC: 2339 Women's and misses' athletic
clothing and sportswear

(P-2339)
JUST FOR WRAPS INC (PA)
Also Called: A-List
4871 S Santa Fe Ave (90058-2103)
PHONE....................213 239-0503
Vrajesh Lal, *CEO*
Rakesh Lal, *
▲ **EMP:** 130 **EST:** 1980
SALES (est): 24.11MM
SALES (corp-wide): 24.11MM **Privately
Held**
Web: www.wrapper.com
SIC: 2339 2335 2337 Sportswear, women's;
Women's, junior's, and misses' dresses;
Women's and misses' suits and coats

(P-2340)
KAYO OF CALIFORNIA (PA)
Also Called: Kayo Clothing Company
11854 Alameda St (90262-4019)
PHONE....................323 233-6107
Jack Ostrovsky, *Ch Bd*
Jeffrey Michaels, *
Jonathan Kaye, *
Annabelle Wall, *
▲ **EMP:** 45 **EST:** 1968
SALES (est): 7.93MM
SALES (corp-wide): 7.93MM **Privately
Held**
Web: www.kayo.com
SIC: 2339 2337 Sportswear, women's;
Skirts, separate: women's, misses', and
juniors'

(P-2341)
KIM & CAMI PRODUCTIONS INC
2950 Leonis Blvd (90058-2916)

▲ = Import ▼ = Export
◆ = Import/Export

PHONE..................323 584-1300
Kimberly A Hiatt, *Pr*
Cami Gasmer, *
▲ EMP: 40 EST: 1999
SQ FT: 1,000
SALES (est): 5.29MM Privately Held
SIC: 2339 Sportswear, women's

(P-2342)
KLK FORTE INDUSTRY INC (PA)
Also Called: Honey Punch
1535 Rio Vista Ave (90023-2619)
PHONE..................323 415-9181
Katherine Kim, *CEO*
◆ EMP: 45 EST: 2012
SQ FT: 30,000
SALES (est): 3.1MM
SALES (corp-wide): 3.1MM Privately Held
SIC: 2339 Women's and misses' outerwear, nec

(P-2343)
KORAL INDUSTRIES LLC (PA)
Also Called: Koral Los Angeles
1334 3rd Street Promenade Ste 200 (90401-1310)
PHONE..................323 585-5343
Peter Koral, *
▲ EMP: 31 EST: 2012
SALES (est): 8.71MM
SALES (corp-wide): 8.71MM Privately Held
Web: www.koral.com
SIC: 2339 Service apparel, washable: women's

(P-2344)
L Y A GROUP INC
1317 S Grand Ave (90015-3008)
PHONE..................213 683-1123
Claudia L Blanco, *CEO*
Augustin Ramirez, *Pr*
▲ EMP: 25 EST: 2003
SALES (est): 607.1K Privately Held
SIC: 2339 Jeans: women's, misses', and juniors'

(P-2345)
L&L MANUFACTURING CO INC
Also Called: L & L Distributors
12400 Wilshire Blvd Ste 360 (90025-1059)
EMP: 270
SIC: 2339 2329 2369 8741 Sportswear, women's; Men's and boys' sportswear and athletic clothing; Girl's and children's outerwear, nec; Management services

(P-2346)
LAT LLC
Also Called: G Girl Clothing
2618 Fruitland Ave (90058-2220)
PHONE..................323 233-3017
▲ EMP: 40 EST: 1999
SALES (est): 4.68MM Privately Held
Web: www.latapparel.com
SIC: 2339 Women's and misses' outerwear, nec

(P-2347)
LEE THOMAS INC (PA)
13800 S Figueroa St (90061-1026)
PHONE..................310 532-7560
Lee Opolinsky, *Pr*
Thomas Mahoney, *
EMP: 30 EST: 1981
SQ FT: 45,000
SALES (est): 4.22MM
SALES (corp-wide): 4.22MM Privately Held

SIC: 2339 Women's and misses' athletic clothing and sportswear

(P-2348)
LEFTY PRODUCTION CO LLC
318 W 9th St Ste 1010 (90015-1546)
PHONE..................323 515-9266
Marta Abrams, *Managing Member*
EMP: 39 EST: 2012
SALES (est): 4.61MM Privately Held
Web: www.leftyproductionco.com
SIC: 2339 Athletic clothing: women's, misses', and juniors'

(P-2349)
MARCEA INC
1742 Crenshaw Blvd (90501-3311)
P.O. Box 48317 (90048-0317)
PHONE..................213 746-5191
Marcia D Lane, *Pr*
EMP: 19 EST: 1988
SQ FT: 2,500
SALES (est): 703.46K Privately Held
Web: www.marcea.com
SIC: 2339 Sportswear, women's

(P-2350)
MARIKA LLC
5553 Bandini Blvd B (90201)
PHONE..................323 888-7755
▲ EMP: 100 EST: 1982
SQ FT: 160,000
SALES (est): 10.02MM Privately Held
Web: www.marika.com
SIC: 2339 5137 Athletic clothing: women's, misses', and juniors'; Women's and children's outerwear

(P-2351)
MAX LEON INC (PA)
Also Called: Max Studio.com
3100 New York Dr Ste 100 (91107-1554)
P.O. Box 70879 (91117-7879)
PHONE..................626 797-6886
Leon Max, *CEO*
Ernest E Hoffer, *
Kerri Specker, *
▲ EMP: 100 EST: 1979
SQ FT: 65,000
SALES (est): 53.28MM
SALES (corp-wide): 53.28MM Privately Held
Web: www.maxstudio.com
SIC: 2339 5632 Sportswear, women's; Apparel accessories

(P-2352)
MGT INDUSTRIES INC (PA)
Also Called: California Dynasty
13889 S Figueroa St (90061-1025)
PHONE..................310 516-5900
Jeffrey P Mirvis, *CEO*
Alessandra Strahl, *
Mike Brooks, *
Phil Nathanson, *
▲ EMP: 68 EST: 1983
SQ FT: 82,000
SALES (est): 4.18K
SALES (corp-wide): 4.18K Privately Held
Web: www.mgtind.com
SIC: 2339 Women's and misses' outerwear, nec

(P-2353)
MONTEREY CANYON LLC (PA)
1515 E 15th St (90021-2711)
PHONE..................213 741-0209
Richard Sneider, *
▲ EMP: 70 EST: 1977
SALES (est): 7.13MM

SALES (corp-wide): 7.13MM Privately Held
SIC: 2339 Sportswear, women's

(P-2354)
NEW FASHION PRODUCTS INC
3600 E Olympic Blvd (90023-3121)
PHONE..................310 354-0090
▲ EMP: 170 EST: 1975
SALES (est): 22.58MM Privately Held
SIC: 2339 2325 Slacks: women's, misses', and juniors'; Men's and boy's trousers and slacks

(P-2355)
NEXXEN APPAREL INC (PA)
Also Called: Check It Out
1555 Los Palos St (90023-3218)
PHONE..................323 267-9900
Jai Sim, *Pr*
Carol Chang, *VP*
Billy Sim, *VP*
EMP: 18 EST: 1998
SQ FT: 10,000
SALES (est): 2.38MM
SALES (corp-wide): 2.38MM Privately Held
SIC: 2339 Women's and misses' outerwear, nec

(P-2356)
PACIFIC ATHLETIC WEAR INC
7340 Lampson Ave (92841-2902)
PHONE..................714 751-8006
John Hillenbrand, *Pr*
Gabriela Hillenbrand, *
▲ EMP: 70 EST: 1994
SALES (est): 6.47MM Privately Held
Web: www.pacificathleticwear.com
SIC: 2339 Uniforms, athletic: women's, misses', and juniors'

(P-2357)
PATTERSON KINCAID LLC
5175 S Soto St (90058-3620)
PHONE..................323 584-3559
◆ EMP: 45 EST: 2010
SQ FT: 35,000
SALES (est): 1.13MM
SALES (corp-wide): 24.28MM Privately Held
SIC: 2339 Women's and misses' outerwear, nec
PA: Jaya Apparel Group Llc
5175 S Soto St
Vernon CA
323 584-3500

(P-2358)
PIERRE MITRI (PA)
Also Called: Watch L.A.
1138 Wall St (90015-2320)
PHONE..................213 747-1838
Pierre D Mitri, *Owner*
▲ EMP: 17 EST: 1989
SQ FT: 6,000
SALES (est): 1.91MM Privately Held
Web: www.lashowroom.com
SIC: 2339 Jeans: women's, misses', and juniors'

(P-2359)
PIET RETIEF INC
Also Called: Peter Cohen Companies
1914 6th Ave (90018-1124)
PHONE..................323 732-8312
Peter Cohen, *Pr*
Lee Stuart Cox, *
Anna Cohen, *
EMP: 34 EST: 1983

SQ FT: 4,800
SALES (est): 2.21MM Privately Held
SIC: 2339 Sportswear, women's

(P-2360)
POINT CONCEPTION INC
Also Called: Kechika
23121 Arroyo Vis Ste A (92688-2633)
PHONE..................949 589-6890
Jeff Jung, *CEO*
Jamie Jung, *
Victoria Jung, *
◆ EMP: 35 EST: 1979
SQ FT: 20,000
SALES (est): 2.23MM Privately Held
Web: www.kechika.com
SIC: 2339 Bathing suits: women's, misses', and juniors'

(P-2361)
POLYMOND DK INC
777 E 10th St Ste 110 (90021-2083)
PHONE..................213 327-0771
EMP: 26
SALES (corp-wide): 300.63K Privately Held
Web: polymond-dk-ca.hub.biz
SIC: 2339 5136 Women's and misses' athletic clothing and sportswear; Men's and boy's clothing
PA: Polymond Dk, Inc.
655 S Santa Fe Ave # 25
Los Angeles CA
213 327-0771

(P-2362)
PUTNAM ACCESSORY GROUP INC
4455 Fruitland Ave (90058-3222)
PHONE..................323 306-1330
John Putnam, *Pr*
John Putnam Pers, *Prin*
▲ EMP: 20 EST: 2012
SALES (est): 1.85MM Privately Held
Web: www.putnamaccessorygroup.com
SIC: 2339 2389 Women's and misses' accessories; Men's miscellaneous accessories

(P-2363)
Q&A7 LLC
Also Called: Q&A Clothing
2155 E 7th St Ste 150 (90023-1032)
PHONE..................323 364-4250
◆ EMP: 19 EST: 2016
SQ FT: 10,000
SALES (est): 1.79MM Privately Held
SIC: 2339 5137 Women's and misses' athletic clothing and sportswear; Women's and children's clothing

(P-2364)
RAJ MANUFACTURING LLC
Also Called: Rajswim
2712 Dow Ave (92780-7210)
PHONE..................714 838-3110
Barinder Bhathal, *Pr*
Jennifer Renish, *Contrlr*
EMP: 25 EST: 2006
SALES (est): 4.38MM Privately Held
Web: www.rajswim.com
SIC: 2339 Bathing suits: women's, misses', and juniors'

(P-2365)
RAJ MANUFACTURING INC (PA)
Also Called: Athena Pick Your Fit
2712 Dow Ave (92780-7210)
PHONE..................714 838-3110
◆ EMP: 17 EST: 1963

P R O D U C T S & S V C S

SALES (est): 4.91MM
SALES (corp-wide): 4.91MM **Privately Held**
Web: www.rajswim.com
SIC: 2339 Athletic clothing: women's, misses', and juniors'

(P-2366)
RHAPSODY CLOTHING INC
Also Called: Epilogue and Arrested
810 E Pico Blvd Ste 24 (90021-2375)
PHONE..........................213 614-8887
▲ **EMP:** 65 **EST:** 1994
SALES (est): 5.28MM **Privately Held**
Web: www.rhapsodyclothing.com
SIC: 2339 Shorts (outerwear): women's, misses', and juniors'

(P-2367)
ROTAX INCORPORATED
Also Called: Gamma
2940 Leonis Blvd (90058-2916)
P.O. Box 58071 (90058-0071)
PHONE..........................323 589-5999
Arthur Torssien, *Pr*
Ripsick Kepenekian, *
▲ **EMP:** 40 **EST:** 1993
SALES (est): 2.5MM **Privately Held**
Web: www.rotax1.com
SIC: 2339 2329 Women's and misses' outerwear, nec; Men's and boys' sportswear and athletic clothing

(P-2368)
ROYAL APPAREL INC
4331 Baldwin Ave (91731-1103)
PHONE..........................626 579-5168
Kung-shih Steward Yang, *Pr*
Michael Hsu, *
Sheena Yang, *
▲ **EMP:** 29 **EST:** 1987
SQ FT: 24,000
SALES (est): 1.97MM **Privately Held**
Web: www.royalapparel.net
SIC: 2339 Leotards: women's, misses', and juniors'

(P-2369)
SECOND GENERATION INC
Also Called: Fish Bowl
21650 Oxnard St Ste 500 (91367-4911)
▲ **EMP:** 68 **EST:** 1996
SQ FT: 11,000
SALES (est): 9.88MM **Privately Held**
Web: www.bebopclothing.com
SIC: 2339 5621 Women's and misses' athletic clothing and sportswear; Women's clothing stores

(P-2370)
SOLOW
2907 Glenview Ave (90039-2823)
PHONE..........................323 664-7772
▲ **EMP:** 30 **EST:** 1999
SQ FT: 20,000
SALES (est): 3.39MM **Privately Held**
SIC: 2339 Sportswear, women's

(P-2371)
SPIRIT CLOTHING COMPANY
Also Called: Spirit Active Wear
2211 E 37th St (90058-1427)
PHONE..........................213 784-0251
TOLL FREE: 800
Jake Pitaszink, *Pr*
▼ **EMP:** 172 **EST:** 1983
SQ FT: 19,000
SALES (est): 19.44MM **Privately Held**
Web: www.spiritjersey.com

SIC: 2339 2329 Athletic clothing: women's, misses', and juniors'; Men's and boys' sportswear and athletic clothing

(P-2372)
SSC APPAREL INC
Also Called: Soprano
2025 Long Beach Ave (90058-1021)
P.O. Box 1358 (90717-5358)
PHONE..........................213 748-5511
Julie Kim, *CEO*
Alexis Kim, *Pr*
▲ **EMP:** 17 **EST:** 2000
SQ FT: 20,000
SALES (est): 373.3K **Privately Held**
SIC: 2339 Women's and misses' athletic clothing and sportswear

(P-2373)
ST JOHN KNITS INC (DH)
Also Called: St John Knits
17522 Armstrong Ave (92614-5876)
PHONE..........................949 863-1171
Eran Cohen, *CEO*
EMP: 243 **EST:** 1962
SALES (est): 107.75MM
SALES (corp-wide): 462.29MM **Privately Held**
Web: www.stjohncafe.com
SIC: 2339 2253 2389 Women's and misses' accessories; Knit outerwear mills; Men's miscellaneous accessories
HQ: St. John Knits International, Incorporated
17522 Armstrong Ave
Irvine CA
949 863-1171

(P-2374)
ST JOHN KNITS INTL INC (HQ)
Also Called: St John Knits
17522 Armstrong Ave (92614-5726)
PHONE..........................949 863-1171
Geoffroy Van Raemdonck, *CEO*
Glenn Mcmahon, *CEO*
Bernd Beetz, *
Tammy Storino, *
Bruce Fetter, *
◆ **EMP:** 150 **EST:** 1962
SQ FT: 71,100
SALES (est): 462.29MM
SALES (corp-wide): 462.29MM **Privately Held**
SIC: 2339 Sportswear, women's
PA: Gray Vestar Investors Llc
17622 Armstrong Ave
Irvine CA
949 863-1171

(P-2375)
TCJ MANUFACTURING LLC
Also Called: Velvet Heart
2744 E 11th St (90023-3404)
PHONE..........................213 488-8400
▲ **EMP:** 43 **EST:** 2008
SALES (est): 5.23MM **Privately Held**
SIC: 2339 Athletic clothing: women's, misses', and juniors'

(P-2376)
TCW TRENDS INC
2886 Columbia St (90503-3808)
PHONE..........................310 533-5177
Charanjiv Mansingh, *CEO*
▲ **EMP:** 28 **EST:** 2001
SQ FT: 10,000
SALES (est): 5.2MM **Privately Held**
Web: www.tcwusa.com

SIC: 2339 2326 5137 Aprons, except rubber or plastic: women's, misses', juniors'; Men's and boy's work clothing; Coordinate sets: women's, children's, and infants'

(P-2377)
TEMPTED APPAREL CORP
4516 Loma Vista Ave (90058-2602)
PHONE..........................323 859-2480
▲ **EMP:** 58 **EST:** 1996
SALES (est): 4.39MM **Privately Held**
Web: www.temptedapparel.com
SIC: 2339 Women's and misses' outerwear, nec

(P-2378)
THE ORIGINAL CULT INC
Also Called: Lip Service
40 E Verdugo Ave (91502-1931)
PHONE..........................323 260-7308
▲ **EMP:** 71
SIC: 2339 2311 2399 Women's and misses' outerwear, nec; Men's and boy's suits and coats; Emblems, badges, and insignia

(P-2379)
TOAD & CO INTERNATIONAL INC (PA)
Also Called: Toad & Co
2020 Alameda Padre Serra Ste 125 (93103-1756)
P.O. Box 21508 (93121-1508)
PHONE..........................800 865-8623
Gordon Seabury, *Pr*
▲ **EMP:** 35 **EST:** 1991
SQ FT: 7,000
SALES (est): 17.72MM **Privately Held**
Web: www.toadandco.com
SIC: 2339 2329 Women's and misses' athletic clothing and sportswear; Men's and boys' sportswear and athletic clothing

(P-2380)
TREIVUSH INDUSTRIES INC
Also Called: B B Blu
940 W Washington Blvd (90015-3312)
PHONE..........................213 745-7774
Menachem Treivush, *Pr*
EMP: 100 **EST:** 1983
SQ FT: 125,000
SALES (est): 9.15MM **Privately Held**
Web: www.treivush.com
SIC: 2339 5137 Sportswear, women's; Sportswear, women's and children's

(P-2381)
VICTORY PROFESSIONAL PDTS INC
Also Called: Victory Koredrry
5601 Engineer Dr (92649-1123)
PHONE..........................714 887-0621
Marc Spitaleri, *Pr*
▲ **EMP:** 28 **EST:** 1979
SQ FT: 8,500
SALES (est): 3MM **Privately Held**
Web: www.victorybuiltusa.com
SIC: 2339 2329 2393 Women's and misses' athletic clothing and sportswear; Men's and boys' sportswear and athletic clothing; Textile bags

(P-2382)
VXB & ORFWID INC
Also Called: Lost & Wander
5041 S Santa Fe Ave Unit B (90058-2123)
PHONE..........................213 222-0030
Jillian J Yoo, *CEO*
EMP: 20 **EST:** 2014
SALES (est): 1.89MM **Privately Held**

Web: www.lostandwander.com
SIC: 2339 Sportswear, women's

(P-2383)
W & W CONCEPT INC
Also Called: Perseption
4890 S Alameda St (90058-2806)
PHONE..........................323 803-3090
▲ **EMP:** 55 **EST:** 1996
SQ FT: 45,000
SALES (est): 8.3MM **Privately Held**
Web: www.perseption.com
SIC: 2339 5137 Sportswear, women's; Women's and children's outerwear

(P-2384)
YMI JEANSWEAR INC
1015 Wall St Ste 115 (90015-2392)
PHONE..........................213 746-6681
Ronan Vered, *Brnch Mgr*
EMP: 54
SALES (corp-wide): 16.4MM **Privately Held**
Web: www.ymijeans.com
SIC: 2339 2325 Jeans: women's, misses', and juniors'; Men's and boys' jeans and dungarees
PA: Y.M.I Jeanswear, Inc.
1155 S Boyle Ave
Los Angeles CA
323 581-7700

(P-2385)
ZOOEY APPAREL INC
1526 Cloverfield Blvd C (90404-3772)
PHONE..........................310 315-2880
Alice Heller, *Pr*
Viet D.o.s., *COO*
EMP: 24 **EST:** 2003
SQ FT: 5,000
SALES (est): 2.47MM **Privately Held**
SIC: 2339 Women's and misses' outerwear, nec

2341 Women's And Children's Underwear

(P-2386)
AFR APPAREL INTERNATIONAL INC
Also Called: Parisa Lingerie & Swim Wear
25365 Prado De La Felicidad (91302-3652)
PHONE..........................818 773-5000
Amir Moghadam, *Pr*
Brenda J Moghadam, *
▲ **EMP:** 60 **EST:** 1992
SALES (est): 25MM **Privately Held**
Web: www.parisausa.com
SIC: 2341 2342 2369 5137 Women's and children's nightwear; Bras, girdles, and allied garments; Bathing suits and swimwear: girls', children's, and infants'; Lingerie

(P-2387)
CHARLES KOMAR & SONS INC
Also Called: Komar Distribution Services
11850 Riverside Dr (91752-1001)
PHONE..........................951 934-1377
EMP: 307
SALES (corp-wide): 359.75MM **Privately Held**
Web: www.komarbrands.com
SIC: 2341 Women's and children's underwear
PA: Charles Komar & Sons, Inc.
90 Hudson St Fl 9
Jersey City NJ
212 725-1500

(P-2388)
DELTA GALIL USA INC
777 S Alameda St Fl 3 (90021-1657)
PHONE....................................213 488-4859
EMP: 303
Web: www.deltagalil.com
SIC: 2341 Women's and children's
undergarments
HQ: Delta Galil Usa Inc.
1 Harmon Plz Fl 5
Secaucus NJ
201 902-0055

(P-2389)
GUESS INC (PA)
Also Called: GUESS?
1444 S Alameda St (90021-2433)
PHONE....................................213 765-3100
Carlos Alberini, *CEO*
Alex Yemenidjian, *Non-Executive Chairman of the Board**
Paul Marciano, *CCO**
Markus Neubrand, *CFO*
Dennis Secor, *Ex VP*
◆ **EMP: 700 EST:** 1981
SQ FT: 341,700
SALES (est): 2.69B
SALES (corp-wide): 2.69B **Publicly Held**
Web: www.guess.com
SIC: 2341 2325 2369 6794 Women's and children's underwear; Men's and boy's trousers and slacks; Girl's and children's outerwear, nec; Copyright buying and licensing

(P-2390)
HARPER WILDE INC
10866 Wilshire Blvd Ste 1650 (90024-4321)
PHONE....................................213 510-1608
Jane Fisher, *CEO*
EMP: 23 **EST:** 2016
SALES (est): 2.91MM **Privately Held**
Web: www.harperwilde.com
SIC: 2341 Women's and children's underwear

(P-2391)
HONEST COMPANY INC (PA)
Also Called: Honest
12130 Millennium Ste 500 (90094-2946)
PHONE....................................310 917-9199
▲ **EMP: 171 EST:** 2011
SQ FT: 46,518
SALES (est): 313.65MM **Publicly Held**
Web: www.honest.com
SIC: 2341 2833 5961 Panties: women's, misses', children's, and infants'; Vitamins, natural or synthetic: bulk, uncompounded; Catalog and mail-order houses

(P-2392)
NATIONAL CORSET SUPPLY HOUSE (PA)
Also Called: Louden Madelon
3240 E 26th St (90058-8008)
PHONE....................................323 261-0265
Roy Schlobohm, *CEO*
◆ **EMP: 65 EST:** 1948
SQ FT: 25,000
SALES (est): 9.74MM
SALES (corp-wide): 9.74MM **Privately Held**
Web: www.shirleyofhollywood.com
SIC: 2341 5137 Women's and children's undergarments; Corsets

(P-2393)
SELECTRA INDUSTRIES CORP
5166 Alcoa Ave (90058-3716)
PHONE....................................323 581-8500

John Neman, *Pr*
Mark Neman, *
Malek Neman, *
▲ **EMP: 85 EST:** 2000
SQ FT: 30,000
SALES (est): 12.46MM **Privately Held**
Web: www.selectraindustries.com
SIC: 2341 2339 Women's and children's underwear; Sportswear, women's

2342 Bras, Girdles, And Allied Garments

(P-2394)
BRAGEL INTERNATIONAL INC
Also Called: Brava
3383 Pomona Blvd (91768-3297)
PHONE....................................909 598-8808
Clotilde Chen, *CEO*
Alice Chen, *
Kenny Chen, *Stockholder**
▲ **EMP: 45 EST:** 1989
SQ FT: 30,000
SALES (est): 7.35MM **Privately Held**
Web: www.bragel.com
SIC: 2342 Brassieres

(P-2395)
FOH GROUP INC (PA)
Also Called: Fredericks.com
6255 W Sunset Blvd Ste 2212 (90028-7403)
◆ **EMP: 38 EST:** 1935
SQ FT: 23,000
SALES (est): 86.6MM
SALES (corp-wide): 86.6MM **Privately Held**
SIC: 2342 2339 5621 5632 Bras, girdles, and allied garments; Women's and misses' outerwear, nec; Women's clothing stores; Women's accessory and specialty stores

(P-2396)
METRIC PRODUCTS INC (PA)
4630 Leahy St (90232-3515)
PHONE....................................310 815-9000
Shirley Magidson, *Pr*
Debra Magidson, *Sec*
Rita Haft, *VP*
▲ **EMP: 20 EST:** 1948
SQ FT: 25,000
SALES (est): 7.94MM
SALES (corp-wide): 7.94MM **Privately Held**
Web: www.metric-products.com
SIC: 2342 3496 Brassieres; Fabrics, woven wire

2353 Hats, Caps, And Millinery

(P-2397)
AGRON INC (PA)
2440 S Sepulveda Blvd Ste 201 (90064-1748)
PHONE....................................310 473-7223
Wade Siegel, *Pr*
Anton Schiff, *
◆ **EMP: 60 EST:** 1989
SQ FT: 10,000
SALES (est): 18.63MM **Privately Held**
Web: sales.agron.com
SIC: 2353 2393 3949 3171 Hats, caps, and millinery; Canvas bags; Sporting and athletic goods, nec; Women's handbags and purses

(P-2398)
AUGUST HAT COMPANY INC (PA)
Also Called: August Accessories
2021 Calle Yucca (91360-2257)
PHONE....................................805 983-4651
Roque Valladares, *Pr*
Ann Valladares, *Sec*
▲ **EMP: 23 EST:** 1990
SALES (est): 3.35MM **Privately Held**
SIC: 2353 2381 2339 Hats, caps, and millinery; Fabric dress and work gloves; Scarves, hoods, headbands, etc.: women's

(P-2399)
CALI-FAME LOS ANGELES INC
Also Called: Kennedy Athletics
20934 S Santa Fe Ave (90810-1131)
PHONE....................................310 747-5263
Michael G Kennedy, *CEO*
Brian Kennedy, *
Timothy Kennedy, *
Linelle Kennedy, *
▲ **EMP: 92 EST:** 1925
SQ FT: 30,000
SALES (est): 11.74MM **Privately Held**
Web: www.califame.com
SIC: 2353 Uniform hats and caps

(P-2400)
LEGENDARY HOLDINGS INC
Also Called: Legendary Headwear
2295 Paseo De Las Americas Ste 19 (92154-7909)
PHONE....................................619 872-6100
◆ **EMP:** 38
Web: www.legendaryholdings.com
SIC: 2353 Hats, caps, and millinery

(P-2401)
MAGIC APPAREL GROUP INC
Also Called: Magic Apparel & Magic Headwear
1100 W Walnut St (90220-5114)
P.O. Box 2308 (90274-8308)
PHONE....................................310 223-4000
◆ **EMP:** 30
SIC: 2353 Baseball caps

(P-2402)
NIKE INC
Nike
20001 Ellipse (92610-3001)
PHONE....................................949 616-4042
Matt Ross, *Mgr*
EMP: 17
SALES (corp-wide): 51.22B **Publicly Held**
Web: www.nike.com
SIC: 2353 5137 5136 Baseball caps; Women's and children's clothing; Men's and boy's clothing
PA: Nike, Inc.
1 Sw Bowerman Dr
Beaverton OR
503 671-6453

(P-2403)
PETER GRIMM LTD
Also Called: Gold Coast Sunwear
550 Rancheros Dr (92069-2911)
PHONE....................................800 664-4287
Peter Niedermeyer, *Pr*
Glen Walker, *VP*
Peter Grimm, *Prin*
◆ **EMP: 20 EST:** 1989
SQ FT: 6,000
SALES (est): 4.35MM **Privately Held**
Web: www.petergrimm.com

SIC: 2353 5136 Hats, caps, and millinery; Hats, men's and boys'

2361 Girl's And Children's Dresses, Blouses

(P-2404)
A THANKS MILLION INC
8195 Mercury Ct Ste 140 (92111-1231)
PHONE....................................858 432-7744
Lowell J Cohen, *CEO*
Peter Mouostaos, *Pr*
Ian Barrow, *CFO*
◆ **EMP: 19 EST:** 2003
SALES (est): 1.68MM **Privately Held**
Web: www.justaddakid.com
SIC: 2361 2329 T-shirts and tops: girls', children's, and infants'; Shirt and slack suits: men's, youths', and boys'

(P-2405)
AST SPORTSWEAR INC (PA)
2701 E Imperial Hwy (92821-6713)
P.O. Box 17219 (92817-7219)
PHONE....................................714 223-2030
▲ **EMP: 85 EST:** 1995
SQ FT: 42,000
SALES (est): 49.1MM **Privately Held**
Web: www.astsportswear.com
SIC: 2361 2331 5699 T-shirts and tops: girls', children's, and infants'; T-shirts and tops, women's: made from purchased materials; Sports apparel

(P-2406)
COTTON GENERATION INC
Also Called: Trouble At The Mill
6051 Maywood Ave (90255-3211)
PHONE....................................323 581-8555
Mohamad Toluee, *Pr*
Masoud Parvinjah, *VP*
EMP: 19 **EST:** 1994
SQ FT: 45,000
SALES (est): 791.96K **Privately Held**
Web: www.cottongeneration.com
SIC: 2361 2339 7389 T-shirts and tops: girls', children's, and infants'; Sportswear, women's; Textile and apparel services

(P-2407)
EVY OF CALIFORNIA INC
2042 Garfield Av (90040-1804)
P.O. Box 812030 (90081-0018)
PHONE....................................213 746-4647
▲ **EMP:** 140
Web: www.evy.com
SIC: 2361 2369 Dresses: girls', children's, and infants'; Warm-up, jogging, and sweat suits: girls' and children's

(P-2408)
KWDZ MANUFACTURING LLC (PA)
337 S Anderson St (90033-3742)
PHONE....................................323 526-3526
Gene Bonilla, *
◆ **EMP: 75 EST:** 1999
SQ FT: 45,000
SALES (est): 5.16MM
SALES (corp-wide): 5.16MM **Privately Held**
Web: www.calfashion.org
SIC: 2361 T-shirts and tops: girls', children's, and infants'

(P-2409)
L A S A M INC
Also Called: Natural Elements

3844 S Santa Fe Ave (90058-1713)
PHONE.....................323 586-8717
Sandy Maroney, *Pr*
Dennis Maroney, *Sec*
EMP: 18 **EST:** 1981
SQ FT: 5,000
SALES (est): 494.17K **Privately Held**
SIC: 2361 Girl's and children's dresses, blouses

(P-2410)
LEIGH JERRY CALIFORNIA INC (PA)
Also Called: Jerry Leigh Entertainment AP
7860 Nelson Rd (91402-6044)
PHONE.....................818 909-6200
Andrew Leigh, *CEO*
Barbara Leigh, *
◆ **EMP:** 251 **EST:** 1962
SQ FT: 40,000
SALES (est): 95.93MM
SALES (corp-wide): 95.93MM **Privately Held**
Web: www.jerryleigh.com
SIC: 2361 5137 Girl's and children's dresses, blouses; Sportswear, women's and children's

(P-2411)
MISYD CORP (PA)
Also Called: Ruby Rox
30 Fremont Pl (90005-3858)
PHONE.....................213 742-1800
Robert Borman, *Pr*
Joseph Hanasab, *
▲ **EMP:** 79 **EST:** 1993
SQ FT: 35,000
SALES (est): 7.83MM **Privately Held**
Web: www.misyd.com
SIC: 2361 Shirts: girls', children's, and infants'

(P-2412)
WINSTAR TEXTILE INC
16815 E Johnson Dr (91745-2417)
PHONE.....................626 357-1133
Der Yeu Lu, *CEO*
Davis Lu, *Pr*
Huimin Dou, *Prin*
▲ **EMP:** 17 **EST:** 1999
SQ FT: 3,400
SALES (est): 845.45K **Privately Held**
SIC: 2361 2325 Blouses: girls', children's, and infants'; Men's and boy's trousers and slacks

2369 Girl's And Children's Outerwear, Nec

(P-2413)
BABY GUESS INC
Also Called: Guess
1444 S Alameda St (90021-2433)
PHONE.....................213 765-3100
Maurice Marciano, *Ch Bd*
EMP: 20 **EST:** 1999
SALES (est): 835.22K
SALES (corp-wide): 2.69B **Publicly Held**
Web: www.guess.com
SIC: 2369 Jackets: girls', children's, and infants'
PA: Guess , Inc.
1444 S Alameda St
Los Angeles CA
213 765-3100

(P-2414)
BODYWAVES INC (PA)
Also Called: Aks, Amy K Su
12362 Knott St (92841-2802)
PHONE.....................714 898-9900
EMP: 47 **EST:** 1986
SALES (est): 4.71MM
SALES (corp-wide): 4.71MM **Privately Held**
Web: www.elleven.com
SIC: 2369 2335 2331 2325 Girl's and children's outerwear, nec; Dresses,paper, cut and sewn; Women's and misses' blouses and shirts; Men's and boy's trousers and slacks

(P-2415)
FRANKIES BIKINIS LLC
Also Called: Frankies Bikinis
4030 Del Rey Ave (90292-5602)
PHONE.....................323 354-4133
Francheska Aiello, *CEO*
Miriam Aiello, *
Frank Messmann, *
EMP: 36 **EST:** 2013
SALES (est): 4.39MM **Privately Held**
Web: www.frankiesbikinis.com
SIC: 2369 Bathing suits and swimwear: girls', children's, and infants'

(P-2416)
GRACING BRAND MANAGEMENT INC
Also Called: Gbm
1108 W Valley Blvb Ste 660 (91803)
PHONE.....................626 297-2472
Sabrina Yam, *CEO*
Vico Yam, *
EMP: 492 **EST:** 2017
SALES (est): 20.17MM **Privately Held**
SIC: 2369 5137 5131 2211 Bathing suits and swimwear: girls', children's, and infants'; Swimsuits: women's, children's, and infants' ; Trimmings, apparel; Apparel and outerwear fabrics, cotton

(P-2417)
MANHATTAN BEACHWEAR LLC (PA)
10855 Business Center Dr Ste C (90630)
PHONE.....................657 384-2110
EMP: 65 **EST:** 2020
SALES (est): 24.1MM
SALES (corp-wide): 24.1MM **Privately Held**
Web: www.mbwswim.com
SIC: 2369 2329 Bathing suits and swimwear: girls', children's, and infants'; Bathing and swimwear: men's and boys'

(P-2418)
THE LUNADA BAY CORPORATION (PA)
Also Called: Becca
2000 E Winston Rd (92806-5546)
PHONE.....................714 490-1313
▲ **EMP:** 54 **EST:** 1980
SALES (est): 24.3MM
SALES (corp-wide): 24.3MM **Privately Held**
Web: www.lunadabayswim.com
SIC: 2369 Bathing suits and swimwear: girls', children's, and infants'

(P-2419)
TRLG CORPORATE HOLDINGS LLC (PA)
1888 Rosecrans Ave (90266-3701)
PHONE.....................323 266-3072

Dalli Snyder, *CFO*
Alan Weiss, *VP*
Eugene Davis, *Dir*
Steve Perrella, *Dir*
◆ **EMP:** 84 **EST:** 2017
SQ FT: 119,000
SALES (est): 350MM
SALES (corp-wide): 350MM **Privately Held**
SIC: 2369 2325 2339 Girl's and children's outerwear, nec; Men's and boy's trousers and slacks; Women's and misses' outerwear, nec

(P-2420)
UN DEUX TROIS INC (PA)
2301 E 7th St (90023-1043)
PHONE.....................323 588-1067
Colin Shorkend, *Pr*
Cydney Shorkend, *
Beverly Shorkend, *
Erin Shorkend, *
▲ **EMP:** 24 **EST:** 1988
SALES (est): 4.97MM **Privately Held**
Web: www.udtfashion.com
SIC: 2369 5137 Girl's and children's outerwear, nec; Fur clothing, women's and children's

(P-2421)
VESTURE GROUP INCORPORATED
Also Called: Pinky Los Angeles
3405 W Pacific Ave (91505-1555)
PHONE.....................818 842-0200
Robert Galishoff, *CEO*
Gayle Lupacchini, *
▲ **EMP:** 72 **EST:** 2007
SQ FT: 3,500
SALES (est): 9.41MM **Privately Held**
Web: www.vesturegroupinc.com
SIC: 2369 2335 Skirts: girls', children's, and infants'; Women's, junior's, and misses' dresses

2381 Fabric Dress And Work Gloves

(P-2422)
MECHANIX WEAR LLC (PA)
Also Called: Mechanix Wear
27335 Tourney Rd (91355-2200)
PHONE.....................800 222-4296
Jesse Spungin, *CEO*
Bari Waalk, *
Kevin Reynolds, *CFO*
Sherrie Hale, *
Michael Hale, *Vice Chairman*
▲ **EMP:** 38 **EST:** 1984
SQ FT: 24,000
SALES (est): 47.26MM
SALES (corp-wide): 47.26MM **Privately Held**
Web: www.mechanix.com
SIC: 2381 Fabric dress and work gloves

(P-2423)
SVO ENTERPRISE LLC
9854 Baldwin Pl (91731-2202)
PHONE.....................626 406-4770
Scott Streitfld C.p.a., *Admn*
EMP: 25 **EST:** 2013
SALES (est): 1.26MM **Privately Held**
Web: www.svoenterprises.com
SIC: 2381 Fabric dress and work gloves

2384 Robes And Dressing Gowns

(P-2424)
TERRY TOWN CORPORATION
8851 Kerns St Ste 100 (92154-6298)
PHONE.....................619 421-5354
Saip Ereren, *CEO*
◆ **EMP:** 100 **EST:** 1988
SALES (est): 33.19MM **Privately Held**
Web: www.terrytown.com
SIC: 2384 5023 5719 Bathrobes, men's and women's: made from purchased materials; Linens and towels; Bedding (sheets, blankets, spreads, and pillows)

2386 Leather And Sheep-lined Clothing

(P-2425)
AJG INC
Also Called: Astrologie California
7220 E Slauson Ave (90040-3625)
PHONE.....................323 346-0171
Angelo Ghailian, *CEO*
▲ **EMP:** 20 **EST:** 2003
SALES (est): 4.72MM **Privately Held**
Web: www.astrologieca.com
SIC: 2386 5131 5199 Leather and sheep-lined clothing; Knit fabrics; Fabrics, yarns, and knit goods

(P-2426)
CHROME HEARTS LLC (PA)
915 N Mansfield Ave (90038-2311)
PHONE.....................323 957-7544
Richard Stark, *Managing Member*
Robert Bowman, *
Mario D Lejtman, *
▲ **EMP:** 50 **EST:** 2005
SQ FT: 50,000
SALES (est): 25.76MM
SALES (corp-wide): 25.76MM **Privately Held**
Web: www.chromehearts.com
SIC: 2386 3911 2511 2371 Leather and sheep-lined clothing; Jewelry, precious metal; Wood household furniture; Fur goods

(P-2427)
DISTINCTIVE INDS TEXAS INC
9419 Ann St (90670-2613)
PHONE.....................323 889-5766
Dwight Forrester, *Brnch Mgr*
EMP: 25
SIC: 2386 Coats and jackets, leather and sheep-lined
PA: Distinctive Industries Of Texas, Inc.
4516 Seton Center Pkwy # 13
Austin TX

(P-2428)
DISTINCTIVE INDS TEXAS INC
Also Called: Roadwire Distinctive Inds
10618 Shoemaker Ave (90670-4038)
PHONE.....................512 491-3500
Dwight Forrester, *Prin*
EMP: 25
SIC: 2386 Leather and sheep-lined clothing
PA: Distinctive Industries Of Texas, Inc.
4516 Seton Center Pkwy # 13
Austin TX

(P-2429)
EURO BELLO USA
10660 Wilshire Blvd Apt 601 (90024-4522)
PHONE.....................213 446-2818

Bijan Israel, *Pr*
Natalio Oscar, *
EMP: 46 EST: 2014
SQ FT: 20,000
SALES (est): 4.63MM **Privately Held**
SIC: 2386 2211 Garments, leather; Apparel and outerwear fabrics, cotton

(P-2430)
FLIGHT SUITS
Also Called: Gibson & Barnes
1900 Weld Blvd Ste 140 (92020-0503)
PHONE...............................619 440-2700
▲ **EMP:** 100 **EST:** 1977
SALES (est): 15.33MM **Privately Held**
Web: www.gibson-barnes.com
SIC: 2386 Coats and jackets, leather and sheep-lined

(P-2431)
KRASNES INC
Also Called: Cop Shopper
2222 Commercial St (92113-1111)
PHONE...............................619 232-2066
Jerry Krasne, *Pr*
Gail Wilson, *
Kurt Krasne, *
▲ **EMP:** 90 **EST:** 1947
SQ FT: 28,000
SALES (est): 5.3MM **Privately Held**
Web: www.triplek.com
SIC: 2386 3484 Leather and sheep-lined clothing; Small arms

(P-2432)
OHECK LLC
5830 Bickett St (90255-2627)
PHONE...............................323 923-2700
Eric Jweon, *Managing Member*
EMP: 19 **EST:** 2012
SQ FT: 52,000
SALES (est): 1.53MM **Privately Held**
SIC: 2386 Garments, leather

(P-2433)
SCULLY SPORTSWEAR INC (PA)
Also Called: Scully Leather Wear
1701 Pacific Ave (93033-1879)
PHONE...............................805 483-6339
Daniel Scully Iii, *CEO*
Robert Swink, *
▲ **EMP:** 60 **EST:** 1906
SQ FT: 80,000
SALES (est): 13.2MM
SALES (corp-wide): 13.2MM **Privately Held**
Web: www.scullyleather.com
SIC: 2386 5099 Coats and jackets, leather and sheep-lined; Luggage

---

2387 Apparel Belts

(P-2434)
LEJON OF CALIFORNIA INC
Also Called: Lejon Tulliani
1229 Railroad St (92882-1838)
PHONE...............................951 736-1229
John W Shirinian, *Pr*
Jack Shirinian, *
▲ **EMP:** 40 **EST:** 1968
SQ FT: 33,000
SALES (est): 4.58MM **Privately Held**
Web: www.lejon.com
SIC: 2387 3172 Apparel belts; Personal leather goods, nec

(P-2435)
STREETS AHEAD INC
Also Called: Hyde

5510 S Soto St Unit B (90058-3623)
PHONE...............................323 277-0860
David Sack, *CEO*
Michael Fructuoso, *Contrlr*
▲ **EMP:** 20 **EST:** 1982
SQ FT: 28,000
SALES (est): 2.17MM **Privately Held**
Web: www.streetsaheadinc.com
SIC: 2387 Apparel belts

(P-2436)
WESTSIDE ACCESSORIES INC (PA)
8920 Vernon Ave Ste 128 (91763-1663)
PHONE...............................626 858-5452
Carol Cantagallo, *Pr*
▲ **EMP:** 17 **EST:** 1991
SALES (est): 1.16MM **Privately Held**
Web: www.belts-etc.com
SIC: 2387 Apparel belts

2389 Apparel And Accessories, Nec

(P-2437)
ACADEMIC CH CHOIR GWNS MFG INC
Also Called: ACADEMIC CAP & GOWN
8944 Mason Ave (91311-6107)
PHONE...............................818 886-8697
TOLL FREE: 800
Michael Cronan, *Pr*
Mike Cronan, *
Evelyn Cronan, *
Mark Cronan, *
◆ **EMP:** 30 **EST:** 1947
SQ FT: 13,000
SALES (est): 1.34MM **Privately Held**
Web: www.academicapparel.com
SIC: 2389 2353 Clergymen's vestments; Hats, caps, and millinery

(P-2438)
AHS TRINITY GROUP INC (PA)
11041 Vanowen St (91605-6314)
PHONE...............................818 508-2105
Eddie Marks, *Pr*
Bill Haber, *CFO*
EMP: 25 **EST:** 1989
SALES (est): 8.87MM **Privately Held**
Web: www.westerncostume.com
SIC: 2389 7299 6512 Costumes; Costume rental; Commercial and industrial building operation

(P-2439)
AMERICAN APPAREL (USA) LLC
Also Called: American Apparel
747 Warehouse St (90021-1106)
P.O. Box 5129 (39047-5129)
PHONE...............................213 488-0226
▲ **EMP:** 22 **EST:** 2007
SALES (est): 1.18MM **Privately Held**
SIC: 2389 5961 Men's miscellaneous accessories; Women's apparel, mail order

(P-2440)
ANAYA BROTHERS CUTTING LLC
3130 Leonis Blvd (90058-3012)
PHONE...............................323 582-5758
Martin Anaya Junior, *Owner*
EMP: 90
SALES (est): 4.82MM **Privately Held**
SIC: 2389 Apparel and accessories, nec

(P-2441)
APP WINDDOWN LLC (HQ)
Also Called: American Apparel
747 Warehouse St (90021-1106)
P.O. Box 5129 (39047-5129)
◆ **EMP:** 141 **EST:** 2005
SALES (est): 84.39MM
SALES (corp-wide): 3.24B **Privately Held**
SIC: 2389 2311 2331 Men's miscellaneous accessories; Men's and boy's suits and coats; Women's and misses' blouses and shirts
PA: Les Vetements De Sport Gildan Inc
600 Boul De Maisonneuve O 33eme Etage
Montreal QC
514 735-2023

(P-2442)
BLUE AND BUTTER LLC
6828 Ripple Ct (91752-2749)
PHONE...............................951 763-8808
Courtney Oaks, *CEO*
EMP: 17 **EST:** 2020
SALES (est): 758.3K **Privately Held**
Web: www.blueandbutter.com
SIC: 2389 Men's miscellaneous accessories

(P-2443)
CALIFRNIA CSTUME CLLCTIONS INC (PA)
Also Called: California Costume Int'l
210 S Anderson St (90033-3205)
PHONE...............................323 262-8383
Tak Kwan Woo, *CEO*
Peter Woo, *Pr*
Charles C K Woo, *Sec*
◆ **EMP:** 280 **EST:** 1992
SQ FT: 300,000
SALES (est): 24.56MM **Privately Held**
Web: www.californiacostumes.com
SIC: 2389 5699 Costumes; Costumes, masquerade or theatrical

(P-2444)
CHARADES LLC (PA)
20579 Valley Blvd (91789-2730)
PHONE...............................626 435-0077
▲ **EMP:** 238 **EST:** 2000
SALES (est): 9.73MM
SALES (corp-wide): 9.73MM **Privately Held**
Web: www.rubies.com
SIC: 2389 Costumes

(P-2445)
CONQUER NATION INC
6100 Wilmington Ave (90001-1826)
PHONE...............................310 651-5555
Jerry Saeedian, *CEO*
EMP: 142 **EST:** 2014
SALES (est): 15MM **Privately Held**
Web: www.conquernation.com
SIC: 2389 Hospital gowns

(P-2446)
CUSTOM CHARACTERS INC
621 Thompson Ave (91201-2032)
PHONE...............................818 507-5940
Ryan Rhodes, *Pr*
Drew Herron, *VP*
EMP: 18 **EST:** 1985
SQ FT: 5,200
SALES (est): 1.88MM **Privately Held**
Web: www.customcharacters.com
SIC: 2389 3999 Costumes; Stage hardware and equipment, except lighting

(P-2447)
DECKERS OUTDOOR CORPORATION (PA)
Also Called: DECKERS BRANDS
250 Coromar Dr (93117-3697)
PHONE...............................805 967-7611
David Powers, *Pr*
Michael F Devine Iii, *Ch Bd*
Steven J Fasching, *CFO*
Thomas Garcia, *Chief*
Angela Ogbechie, *Chief Supply Chain Officer*
▲ **EMP:** 2657 **EST:** 1975
SQ FT: 185,094
SALES (est): 3.63B
SALES (corp-wide): 3.63B **Publicly Held**
Web: www.deckers.com
SIC: 2389 2339 3021 Men's miscellaneous accessories; Women's and misses' accessories; Sandals, rubber

(P-2448)
DIAMOND COLLECTION LLC
Also Called: Charades
20579 Valley Blvd (91789-2730)
PHONE...............................626 435-0077
EMP: 30 **EST:** 2016
SALES (est): 1.5MM **Privately Held**
SIC: 2389 5137 Costumes; Dresses

(P-2449)
DIANA DID-IT DESIGNS INC
Also Called: Princess Paradise
20579 Valley Blvd (91789-2730)
PHONE...............................970 226-5062
Diana Clements, *Pr*
Brad Clements, *
◆ **EMP:** 26 **EST:** 1980
SALES (est): 2.07MM **Privately Held**
Web: www.rubies.com
SIC: 2389 7299 Costumes; Costume rental

(P-2450)
DISGUISE INC (HQ)
12120 Kear Pl (92064-7132)
PHONE...............................858 391-3600
Stephen Berman, *CEO*
Benoit Pousset, *Pr*
◆ **EMP:** 45 **EST:** 1987
SQ FT: 206,000
SALES (est): 22.88MM **Publicly Held**
Web: www.disguise.com
SIC: 2389 7299 Costumes; Costume rental
PA: Jakks Pacific, Inc.
2951 28th St
Santa Monica CA

(P-2451)
GILLI INC
1100 S San Pedro St Ste C07 (90015-2385)
PHONE...............................213 744-9808
Hae Yun Suh, *Brnch Mgr*
EMP: 18
SALES (corp-wide): 9.49MM **Privately Held**
Web: www.gilliclothing.com
SIC: 2389 5137 Uniforms and vestments; Women's and children's clothing
PA: Gilli, Inc.
2939 Bandini Blvd
Vernon CA
323 235-3722

(P-2452)
HAVUNI LLC
11321 Iowa Ave (90025-3178)
PHONE...............................917 428-1183
EMP: 22
SALES (est): 922.3K **Privately Held**

SIC: 2389 Apparel and accessories, nec

(P-2453)
LETS GO APPAREL INC (PA)
Also Called: Uptown
1729 E Washington Blvd (90021-3124)
PHONE..............................213 863-1767
Chang Wha Yoon, *Pr*
▼ **EMP:** 22 **EST:** 2013
SQ FT: 30,000
SALES (est): 4.17MM
SALES (corp-wide): 4.17MM **Privately Held**
SIC: 2389 5661 5632 Academic vestments (caps and gowns); Shoes, custom; Apparel accessories

(P-2454)
LOS ANGELES APPAREL INC (PA)
Also Called: La Apparel
1020 E 59th St (90001-1010)
PHONE..............................213 275-3120
Dov Charney, *CEO*
Morris Charney, *
David Nisenbaum, *
EMP: 450 **EST:** 2016
SALES (est): 80.47MM
SALES (corp-wide): 80.47MM **Privately Held**
Web: www.losangelesapparel.net
SIC: 2389 Uniforms and vestments

(P-2455)
MDC INTERIOR SOLUTIONS LLC
Also Called: Komar Apparel Supply
6900 E Washington Blvd (90040-1908)
PHONE..............................800 621-4006
Gary Rothschild, *Mgr*
EMP: 23
SALES (corp-wide): 75.23MM **Privately Held**
Web: www.mdcwall.com
SIC: 2389 Men's miscellaneous accessories
PA: Mdc Interior Solutions, Llc
   400 High Grove Blvd
   Glendale Heights IL
   847 437-4000

(P-2456)
ML KISHIGO MFG CO LLC
11250 Slater Ave (92708-5421)
PHONE..............................949 852-1963
Loren H Wall, *CEO*
Karen Wall, *
▲ **EMP:** 86 **EST:** 1971
SALES (est): 14.09MM
SALES (corp-wide): 14.5B **Privately Held**
Web: www.kishigo.com
SIC: 2389 5099 Men's miscellaneous accessories; Safety equipment and supplies
PA: Bunzl Public Limited Company
   York House
   London
   207 725-5000

(P-2457)
OUTER REBEL INC
760 W 16th St Ste A2 (92627-4319)
PHONE..............................949 548-3630
Michael A Carlson, *CEO*
EMP: 17 **EST:** 2008
SALES (est): 628.32K **Privately Held**
SIC: 2389 5651 Apparel for handicapped; Unisex clothing stores

(P-2458)
R & R INDUSTRIES INC
204 Avenida Fabricante (92672-7538)
PHONE..............................800 234-5611

Robert Pare, *Pr*
Roger Poulin, *
▲ **EMP:** 30 **EST:** 1978
SQ FT: 8,150
SALES (est): 3.61MM **Privately Held**
Web: www.rrind.com
SIC: 2389 2759 Uniforms and vestments; Promotional printing

(P-2459)
RG COSTUMES & ACCESSORIES INC
726 Arrow Grand Cir (91722-2147)
PHONE..............................626 858-9559
Roger Lee, *Pr*
Michael Lee, *
◆ **EMP:** 30 **EST:** 1982
SQ FT: 21,000
SALES (est): 1.87MM **Privately Held**
Web: www.rgcostume.com
SIC: 2389 7299 Costumes; Costume rental

(P-2460)
TRUE WARRIOR LLC
21226 Lone Star Way (91390-4226)
PHONE..............................661 237-6588
EMP: 20 **EST:** 2017
SALES (est): 508.62K **Privately Held**
SIC: 2389 3069 Apparel and accessories, nec; Boot or shoe products, rubber

(P-2461)
WALT DSNEY IMGNRING RES DEV IN
Also Called: Disney
1200 N Miller St Unit D (92806-1954)
PHONE..............................714 781-3152
Mark Hollingworth, *Brnch Mgr*
EMP: 28
SALES (corp-wide): 88.9B **Publicly Held**
Web: www.disneyimaginations.com
SIC: 2389 Masquerade costumes
HQ: Walt Disney Imagineering Research & Development, Inc.
   1401 Flower St
   Glendale CA
   818 544-6500

2391 Curtains And Draperies

(P-2462)
AMTEX CALIFORNIA INC
Also Called: Ameritex International
113 S Utah St (90033-3213)
PHONE..............................323 859-2200
Saq Hafeez, *Pr*
Alia Hafeez, *
◆ **EMP:** 45 **EST:** 1991
SQ FT: 40,000
SALES (est): 4.18MM **Privately Held**
Web: ameritexinternational.americommerce.com
SIC: 2391 2392 5023 Draperies, plastic and textile: from purchased materials; Bedspreads and bed sets: made from purchased materials; Curtains

(P-2463)
SEW WHAT INC
Also Called: Rent What
1978 E Gladwick St (90220-6201)
PHONE..............................310 639-6000
Megan Duckett, *Pr*
Adam Duckett, *
◆ **EMP:** 35 **EST:** 1997
SQ FT: 15,000
SALES (est): 5.41MM **Privately Held**
Web: www.sewwhatinc.com

SIC: 2391 5049 Curtains and draperies; Theatrical equipment and supplies

(P-2464)
SUPERIOR WINDOW COVERINGS INC
7683 N San Fernando Rd (91505-1073)
PHONE..............................818 762-6685
Marco Bonilla, *Pr*
▲ **EMP:** 35 **EST:** 1979
SQ FT: 4,000
SALES (est): 2.4MM **Privately Held**
Web: www.superiorshades.com
SIC: 2391 2591 Draperies, plastic and textile: from purchased materials; Blinds vertical

---

2392 Household Furnishings, Nec

(P-2465)
ANATOMIC GLOBAL INC
1241 Old Temescal Rd # 103 (92881-7266)
PHONE..............................800 874-7237
▲ **EMP:** 115 **EST:** 1991
SALES (est): 12.14MM **Privately Held**
SIC: 2392 Bedspreads and bed sets: made from purchased materials

(P-2466)
BIG LEAGUE PILLOWS LLC
1600 Vine St Apt 1034 (90028-8845)
PHONE..............................949 422-8443
EMP: 18
SALES (corp-wide): 85.83K **Privately Held**
Web: www.bigleaguepillows.com
SIC: 2392 Cushions and pillows
PA: Big League Pillows Llc
   100 N Fairway Dr Ste 116
   Vernon Hills IL
   917 662-8860

(P-2467)
BOJER INC
177 S Peckham Rd (91702-3237)
PHONE..............................626 334-1711
Doris Gabai, *Pr*
Joey Gabai, *VP*
EMP: 20 **EST:** 1991
SQ FT: 12,974
SALES (est): 2.35MM **Privately Held**
Web: www.bojeroutdoor.com
SIC: 2392 Cushions and pillows

(P-2468)
BRENTWOOD ORIGINALS INC (PA)
Also Called: Brentwood Originals
3780 Kilroy Airport Way Ste 540 (90806-2451)
PHONE..............................310 637-6804
Joy Stewart, *CEO*
Loren Sweet, *
Bill Bronstein, *
Craig Torrey, *
Tom Rose, *
◆ **EMP:** 215 **EST:** 1958
SALES (est): 103.82MM
SALES (corp-wide): 103.82MM **Privately Held**
Web: www.brentwoodoriginals.com
SIC: 2392 Cushions and pillows

(P-2469)
CLASSIC SLIP COVERS INC
4300 District Blvd (90058-3110)
PHONE..............................323 583-0804
David Illulian, *CEO*

Chris Wroolie, *Pr*
▲ **EMP:** 18 **EST:** 1993
SQ FT: 15,000
SALES (est): 979.93K **Privately Held**
Web: www.theslipcovercompany.com
SIC: 2392 5714 Slip covers: made of fabric, plastic, etc.; Slip covers

(P-2470)
COOP HOME GOODS LLC
Also Called: Coop
7860 Paramount Blvd (90660-4311)
PHONE..............................888 316-1886
Zachary Kramer, *Managing Member*
EMP: 50 **EST:** 2021
SALES (est): 3.48MM **Privately Held**
Web: www.coopsleepgoods.com
SIC: 2392 Pillows, bed: made from purchased materials

(P-2471)
CUSTOM QUILTING INC
2832 Walnut Ave Ste D (92780-7002)
PHONE..............................714 731-7271
Alfredo Zermeno, *Owner*
Elda Zermeno, *
EMP: 28 **EST:** 1983
SALES (est): 1.66MM **Privately Held**
Web: www.customquiltinginc.com
SIC: 2392 5719 Bedspreads and bed sets: made from purchased materials; Bedding (sheets, blankets, spreads, and pillows)

(P-2472)
INSTANT TUCK INC
9663 Santa Monica Blvd (90210-4303)
PHONE..............................310 955-8824
Adrian Gluck, *CEO*
EMP: 30 **EST:** 2019
SALES (est): 1.12MM **Privately Held**
SIC: 2392 Mattress pads

(P-2473)
JOMAR TABLE LINENS INC
Also Called: Linen Lovers
4000 E Airport Dr Ste A (91761-1566)
PHONE..............................909 390-1444
EMP: 80 **EST:** 1982
SALES (est): 4.14MM **Privately Held**
SIC: 2392 7336 Tablecloths: made from purchased materials; Silk screen design

(P-2474)
KIDS LINE LLC
10541 Humbolt St (90720-5401)
P.O. Box 16712 (92623-6712)
PHONE..............................310 660-0110
◆ **EMP:** 140
SIC: 2392 Blankets, comforters and beddings

(P-2475)
LAMBS & IVY INC
Also Called: Bed Time Originals
2042 E Maple Ave (90245-5008)
PHONE..............................310 322-3800
Barbara Laiken, *Pr*
Cathy Ravdin, *
◆ **EMP:** 39 **EST:** 1979
SQ FT: 30,000
SALES (est): 5.16MM **Privately Held**
Web: www.lambsivy.com
SIC: 2392 Blankets, comforters and beddings

(P-2476)
LOFTA
9225 Brown Deer Rd (92121-2268)
PHONE..............................858 299-8000
Jay B Levitt, *CEO*
EMP: 35 **EST:** 2016

▲ = Import ▼ = Export
◆ = Import/Export

SALES (est): 4.72MM **Publicly Held**
Web: www.lofta.com
SIC: 2392 Mattress pads
HQ: Apria, Inc.
7353 Company Dr
Indianapolis IN
800 990-9799

(P-2477)
MATTEO LLC
1000 E Cesar E Chavez Ave (90033-1204)
PHONE............................213 617-2813
▲ EMP: 50 EST: 1996
SQ FT: 25,000
SALES (est): 8.21MM **Privately Held**
Web: www.matteola.com
SIC: 2392 Blankets, comforters and beddings

(P-2478)
MICRONOVA MANUFACTURING INC
3431 Lomita Blvd (90505-5010)
PHONE............................310 784-6990
Audrey J Reynolds Lowman, *CEO*
▲ EMP: 30 EST: 1984
SQ FT: 28,310
SALES (est): 7.36MM **Privately Held**
Web: www.micronova-mfg.com
SIC: 2392 Mops, floor and dust

(P-2479)
NORTHWESTERN CONVERTING CO
Also Called: Premier Mop & Broom
2395 Railroad St (92878-5411)
P.O. Box 78328 (92877-0144)
PHONE............................800 959-3402
Tom Buckles, *Pr*
Thomas M Buckles, *
▲ EMP: 100 EST: 1935
SALES (est): 16.35MM **Privately Held**
Web: northwesternc.openfos.com
SIC: 2392 Household furnishings, nec

(P-2480)
OMNIA LEATHER MOTION INC
Also Called: Cathy Ireland Home
4950 Edison Ave (91710-5713)
PHONE............................909 393-4400
Peter Zolferino, *Pr*
Luie Nastri, *
▲ EMP: 200 EST: 1989
SALES (est): 8.9MM **Privately Held**
Web: www.omnialeather.com
SIC: 2392 Household furnishings, nec

(P-2481)
PACIFIC CAST FTHER CUSHION LLC (HQ)
Also Called: Pacific Coast Feather Cushion
7600 Industry Ave (90660-4302)
PHONE............................562 801-9995
◆ EMP: 110 EST: 1986
SQ FT: 100,000
SALES (est): 12.84MM
SALES (corp-wide): 99.44MM **Privately Held**
Web: www.pcfcushion.com
SIC: 2392 Cushions and pillows
PA: Pacific Coast Feather, Llc
901 W Yamato Rd Ste 250
Boca Raton FL
206 624-1057

(P-2482)
PACIFIC COAST HOME FURN INC (PA)
Also Called: Sherry Kline
2424 Saybrook Ave (90040-2510)

PHONE............................323 838-7808
Parviz Banafshe, *Pr*
Shahrokh Samani, *VP*
▲ EMP: 19 EST: 1988
SQ FT: 35,000
SALES (est): 5.35MM
SALES (corp-wide): 5.35MM **Privately Held**
Web:
www.pacificcoasthomefurnishings.com
SIC: 2392 3261 Cushions and pillows;
Bathroom accessories/fittings, vitreous
china or earthenware

(P-2483)
PACIFIC URETHANES LLC
Also Called: Pacific Urethanes
1671 Champagne Ave Ste A (91761-3660)
PHONE............................909 390-8400
▲ EMP: 200 EST: 2010
SQ FT: 250,000
SALES (est): 44.62MM
SALES (corp-wide): 5.15B **Publicly Held**
SIC: 2392 5021 Blankets, comforters and
beddings; Beds and bedding
PA: Leggett & Platt, Incorporated
1 Leggett Rd
Carthage MO
417 358-8131

(P-2484)
PARACHUTE HOME INC
3525 Eastham Dr (90232-2440)
PHONE............................310 903-0353
Ariel Kaye, *CEO*
EMP: 227 EST: 2013
SQ FT: 13,000
SALES (est): 10.05MM **Privately Held**
Web: www.parachutehome.com
SIC: 2392 5719 Sheets, fabric: made from
purchased materials; Bedding (sheets,
blankets, spreads, and pillows)

(P-2485)
PRO-MART INDUSTRIES INC
Also Called: Promart Dazz
17421 Von Karman Ave (92614-6205)
PHONE............................949 428-7700
Azad Sabounjian, *CEO*
▲ EMP: 40 EST: 1970
SQ FT: 120,000
SALES (est): 8.94MM **Privately Held**
Web: www.shopsmartdesign.com
SIC: 2392 1799 5085 Bags, laundry: made
from purchased materials; Closet
organizers, installation and design; Bins
and containers, storage

(P-2486)
RELIANCE UPHOLSTERY SUP CO INC
Also Called: Reliance Carpet Cushion
4920 S Boyle Ave (90255)
P.O. Box 58584 (90058-0584)
PHONE............................323 321-2300
Ronald J Greitzer, *CEO*
Stanley Grietzer, *
Sheldon P Wallach, *
EMP: 95 EST: 1931
SQ FT: 360,000
SALES (est): 5.23MM **Privately Held**
Web: www.reliancecarpetcushion.com
SIC: 2392 Linings, carpet: textile, except felt

(P-2487)
ROYAL BLUE INC
9025 Wilshire Blvd Ste 301 (90211-1831)
PHONE............................310 888-0156
Diana Moinian, *Pr*
▲ EMP: 21 EST: 2005

SALES (est): 1.76MM **Privately Held**
Web: www.royalblueintl.com
SIC: 2392 2299 Household furnishings, nec;
Towels and towelings, linen and linen-and-
cotton mixtures

(P-2488)
SIBYL SHEPARD INC
Also Called: Sarris Interiors
8225 Alondra Blvd (90723-4401)
PHONE............................562 531-8612
C Nicholas Sarris, *Pr*
Chris Andrew Sarris, *VP*
Byron Sarris, *Dir*
EMP: 23 EST: 1957
SQ FT: 15,000
SALES (est): 630.82K **Privately Held**
Web: www.sarrisinteriors.com
SIC: 2392 Bedspreads and bed sets: made
from purchased materials

(P-2489)
UNIVERSAL CUSHION COMPANY INC (PA)
Also Called: Cloud Nine Comforts
1610 Mandeville Canyon Rd (90049-2524)
PHONE............................323 887-8000
Sharyl G Bloom, *Pr*
Sharyl Bloom, *
▲ EMP: 34 EST: 1989
SALES (est): 4.04MM **Privately Held**
Web: www.cloudninecomforts.com
SIC: 2392 2221 2211 Cushions and pillows;
Comforters and quilts, manmade fiber and
silk; Sheets and sheetings, cotton

(P-2490)
VFT INC
Also Called: Vertical Fiber Technologies
1040 S Vail Ave (90640-6020)
PHONE............................323 728-2280
John Chang, *Pr*
▲ EMP: 40 EST: 1998
SQ FT: 70,000
SALES (est): 3.34MM **Privately Held**
SIC: 2392 Household furnishings, nec

2393 Textile Bags

(P-2491)
ACTION BAG & COVER INC
18401 Mount Langley St (92708-6904)
PHONE............................714 965-7777
Byung Ki Lee, *Pr*
▲ EMP: 80 EST: 1978
SQ FT: 15,000
SALES (est): 4.32MM **Privately Held**
Web: www.actionbaginc.com
SIC: 2393 Canvas bags

(P-2492)
CONTINENTAL MARKETING SVC INC
Also Called: Continental Marketing
15381 Proctor Ave (91745-1022)
PHONE............................626 626-8888
Dawn Du, *Pr*
EMP: 17 EST: 1986
SALES (est): 2.48MM **Privately Held**
SIC: 2393 Bags and containers, except
sleeping bags: textile

(P-2493)
CTA MANUFACTURING INC
Also Called: Bagmasters
1160 California Ave (92881-3324)
PHONE............................951 280-2400
Richard Whittier, *Pr*

Gayne Whittier, *
▲ EMP: 40 EST: 1922
SQ FT: 23,000
SALES (est): 8.42MM **Privately Held**
Web: www.bagmasters.com
SIC: 2393 Textile bags

(P-2494)
GMI INC ✿
Also Called: Gary Manufacturing
2626 Southport Way Ste E (91950-8754)
PHONE............................619 429-4479
Kathryn Smith, *CEO*
Andrea Beagle, *
EMP: 36 EST: 2022
SALES (est): 1.79MM **Privately Held**
SIC: 2393 2392 2394 2385 Textile bags;
Tablecloths: made from purchased materials
; Liners and covers, fabric: made from
purchased materials; Diaper covers,
waterproof: made from purchased materials

(P-2495)
GOLD CREST INDUSTRIES INC
1018 E Acacia St (91761-4553)
P.O. Box 939 (91769-0939)
PHONE............................909 930-9069
Jose Garcia, *Pr*
EMP: 40 EST: 1963
SQ FT: 14,000
SALES (est): 2.59MM **Privately Held**
Web: www.goldcrestind.com
SIC: 2393 3999 2392 Cushions, except
spring and carpet: purchased materials;
Umbrellas, garden or wagon; Household
furnishings, nec

(P-2496)
OUTDOOR RCRTION GROUP HLDNGS L (PA)
Also Called: Outdoor Products
3450 Mount Vernon Dr (90008-4936)
PHONE............................323 226-0830
Andrew Altshule, *CEO*
Joel Altshule, *
George Aba, *
◆ EMP: 37 EST: 1946
SQ FT: 90,000
SALES (est): 14MM
SALES (corp-wide): 14MM **Privately Held**
Web: www.outdoorproducts.com
SIC: 2393 3949 Textile bags; Camping
equipment and supplies

2394 Canvas And Related Products

(P-2497)
A&R TARPAULINS INC
Also Called: AR Tech Aerospace
16246 Valley Blvd (92335-7831)
P.O. Box 1400 (92334-1400)
PHONE............................909 829-4444
Carmen Weisbart, *Pr*
Bud Weisbart, *
Charles Rosselet, *
EMP: 34 EST: 1977
SQ FT: 15,000
SALES (est): 5.36MM **Privately Held**
Web: www.artarpaulins.com
SIC: 2394 Awnings, fabric: made from
purchased materials

(P-2498)
A-AZTEC RENTS & SELLS INC (PA)
Also Called: Aztec Tents
2665 Columbia St (90503-3801)

PHONE..................................310 347-3010
TOLL FREE: 800
Chuck Miller, *CEO*
Alex Kouzmanoff, *
◆ **EMP:** 125 **EST:** 1967
SQ FT: 70,000
SALES (est): 18.63MM
SALES (corp-wide): 18.63MM **Privately Held**
Web: www.aztectent.com
SIC: 2394 Canvas and related products

(P-2499)
BRIDPORT-AIR CARRIER INC (HQ)
Also Called: Amsafe Bridport
6900 Orangethorpe Ave Ste B
(90620-1390)
PHONE..................................253 872-7205
Michael Lisman, *Pr*
Liza Sabol, *Dir*
Halle Martin, *Dir*
▲ **EMP:** 53 **EST:** 1958
SQ FT: 18,000
SALES (est): 2.27MM
SALES (corp-wide): 6.58B **Publicly Held**
SIC: 2394 2296 2399 2298 Canvas and related products; Tire cord and fabrics; Seat belts, automobile and aircraft; Cordage and twine
PA: Transdigm Group Incorporated
1301 E 9th St Ste 3000
Cleveland OH
216 706-2960

(P-2500)
CANVAS CONCEPTS INC
649 Anita St Ste A2 (91911-4658)
PHONE..................................619 424-3428
EMP: 41 **EST:** 2000
SQ FT: 9,600
SALES (est): 885.25K **Privately Held**
Web: www.canvasstore.com
SIC: 2394 Awnings, fabric: made from purchased materials

(P-2501)
CANVAS SPECIALTY INC
1309 S Eastern Ave (90040-5610)
▲ **EMP:** 25 **EST:** 1942
SQ FT: 84,000
SALES (est): 1.69MM **Privately Held**
Web: www.can-spec.com
SIC: 2394 5199 Tarpaulins, fabric: made from purchased materials; Canvas products

(P-2502)
CARAVAN CANOPY INTL INC
Also Called: Caravan Canopy
17510-17512 Studebaker Rd (90703)
PHONE..................................714 367-3000
Lindy Jung Park, *CEO*
David Hudrlik, *
◆ **EMP:** 70 **EST:** 1999
SQ FT: 50,000
SALES (est): 14.66MM **Privately Held**
Web: www.caravancanopy.com
SIC: 2394 3444 2392 Canvas and related products; Awnings and canopies; Chair covers and pads: made from purchased materials

(P-2503)
EIDE INDUSTRIES INC
16215 Piuma Ave (90703-1528)
PHONE..................................562 402-8335
Don Araiza, *Pr*
Jesus Borrego, *
Dan Neill, *
Joe Belli, *

◆ **EMP:** 80 **EST:** 1938
SQ FT: 41,000
SALES (est): 20.64MM **Privately Held**
Web: www.eideindustries.com
SIC: 2394 Tents: made from purchased materials

(P-2504)
FRAMETENT INC
Also Called: Central Tent
26480 Summit Cir (91350-2991)
PHONE..................................661 290-3375
◆ **EMP:** 30 **EST:** 1994
SALES (est): 1.94MM **Privately Held**
SIC: 2394 5999 Tents: made from purchased materials; Tents

(P-2505)
GMA COVER CORP
1170 Somera Rd (90077-2628)
▲ **EMP:** 179
SIC: 2394 3812 Canvas and related products; Defense systems and equipment

(P-2506)
INTERNATIONAL E-Z UP INC (PA)
1900 2nd St (92860-2803)
PHONE..................................800 457-4233
Leonardo Pais, *CEO*
Katie Melzer, *
◆ **EMP:** 89 **EST:** 1983
SQ FT: 115,000
SALES (est): 24.62MM
SALES (corp-wide): 24.62MM **Privately Held**
Web: www.ezup.com
SIC: 2394 5999 Shades, canvas: made from purchased materials; Tents

(P-2507)
PARADISE MANUFACTURING CO INC
Also Called: Arden/Paradise Manufacturing
13364 Aerospace Dr # 100 (92394-7902)
PHONE..................................909 477-3460
Robert Sachs, *Pr*
Michael Sachs, *
EMP: 20 **EST:** 1934
SALES (est): 418.27K **Privately Held**
SIC: 2394 Air cushions and mattresses, canvas

(P-2508)
ROLL-RITE LLC
Also Called: Pulltarps Manufacturing
1404 N Marshall Ave (92020-1521)
PHONE..................................619 449-8860
EMP: 48
SALES (corp-wide): 392.02MM **Privately Held**
Web: www.pulltarps.com
SIC: 2394 3479 Tarpaulins, fabric: made from purchased materials; Bonderizing of metal or metal products
HQ: Roll-Rite Llc
650 Industrial Dr
Gladwin MI

(P-2509)
STARK MFG CO
Also Called: Stark Awning & Canvas
76 Broadway (91910-1422)
PHONE..................................619 425-5880
Turner Stark, *Ch*
EMP: 29 **EST:** 1953
SQ FT: 3,500
SALES (est): 2.37MM **Privately Held**
Web: www.starkmfgco.com

SIC: 2394 3444 Awnings, fabric: made from purchased materials; Sheet metalwork

(P-2510)
SUPERIOR AWNING INC
14555 Titus St (91402-4920)
PHONE..................................818 780-7200
Brian Hotchkiss, *Pr*
Julie Hotchkiss, *
EMP: 40 **EST:** 1984
SQ FT: 11,776
SALES (est): 4.74MM **Privately Held**
Web: www.superiorawning.com
SIC: 2394 5999 3444 Awnings, fabric: made from purchased materials; Awnings; Sheet metalwork

(P-2511)
TRANSPORTATION EQUIPMENT INC
Also Called: Pulltarps Manufacturing
1404 N Marshall Ave (92020-1521)
PHONE..................................619 449-8860
TOLL FREE: 800
▲ **EMP:** 48
Web: www.pulltarps.com
SIC: 2394 3479 Tarpaulins, fabric: made from purchased materials; Bonderizing of metal or metal products

(P-2512)
VAE INDUSTRIES CORPORATION
Also Called: Vitabri Canopies
5402 Research Dr (92649-1542)
PHONE..................................714 842-7500
Damien Vieille, *CEO*
Mathieu Hayaud, *VP*
◆ **EMP:** 22 **EST:** 2010
SQ FT: 7,500
SALES (est): 3.18MM **Privately Held**
Web: www.instent.com
SIC: 2394 5999 Canopies, fabric: made from purchased materials; Banners

---

2395 Pleating And Stitching

(P-2513)
AMERICAN QUILTING COMPANY INC
Also Called: Antaky Quilting Company
1540 Calzona St (90023-3254)
PHONE..................................323 233-2500
Derek Antaky, *CEO*
Elias Antaky Junior, *VP*
▲ **EMP:** 30 **EST:** 1917
SALES (est): 1.99MM **Privately Held**
Web: www.antakyquilting.com
SIC: 2395 Quilting: for the trade

(P-2514)
BEST- IN- WEST
Also Called: Best-In-West Emblem Co
2279 Eagle Glen Pkwy Ste 112
(92883-0785)
PHONE..................................909 947-6507
Eric Roberts, *Pr*
Heriberto Perez, *
Beatriz Roberts, *
EMP: 23 **EST:** 1980
SQ FT: 15,000
SALES (est): 403.17K **Privately Held**
SIC: 2395 Embroidery products, except Schiffli machine; Commercial printing, nec

(P-2515)
J & M RICHMAN CORPORATION
1501 Beach St (90640-5431)
PHONE..................................800 422-9646
James D Richman, *Pr*
Tom Shapiro, *
Maury Rice, *
EMP: 25 **EST:** 1992
SALES (est): 5.3MM **Privately Held**
Web: www.cabanasbyacademy.com
SIC: 2395 5999 3448 Quilted fabrics or cloth; Awnings; Buildings, portable: prefabricated metal

(P-2516)
LA PALM FURNITURES & ACC INC (PA)
Also Called: Royal Plasticware
1650 W Artesia Blvd (90248-3217)
PHONE..................................310 217-2700
Dorra Ngan, *CEO*
Donna Sada, *VP*
Gino Lam, *Dir*
John Lee, *Dir*
Shawn Morse, *Sls Dir*
▲ **EMP:** 27 **EST:** 1996
SQ FT: 30,000
SALES (est): 11.23MM
SALES (corp-wide): 11.23MM **Privately Held**
SIC: 2395 Embroidery products, except Schiffli machine

(P-2517)
LAKESHIRTS LLC
Also Called: Yesterdays Sportswear
1400 Railroad St Ste 104 (93446-1771)
PHONE..................................805 239-1290
Mark Fritz, *Brnch Mgr*
EMP: 45
SALES (corp-wide): 50.48MM **Privately Held**
Web: www.yessport.com
SIC: 2395 Embroidery and art needlework
PA: Lakeshirts Llc
750 Randolph Rd
Detroit Lakes MN
800 627-2780

(P-2518)
MANHATTAN STITCHING CO INC
Also Called: Manhattan Stitching Co
8362 Artesia Blvd Ste E (90621-4179)
PHONE..................................714 521-9479
Maxine Jossel, *Pr*
Lynne Miller, *
Cory Miller, *
EMP: 37 **EST:** 2005
SQ FT: 750
SALES (est): 1.85MM **Privately Held**
Web: www.manhattanstitching.com
SIC: 2395 2759 7389 Embroidery products, except Schiffli machine; Promotional printing; Advertising, promotional, and trade show services

(P-2519)
MELMARC PRODUCTS INC
752 S Campus Ave (91761-1728)
PHONE..................................714 549-2170
Brian Hirth, *Pr*
Leila Drager, *
Harish Naran, *
▲ **EMP:** 160 **EST:** 1987
SQ FT: 85,000
SALES (est): 24.5MM **Privately Held**
Web: www.melmarc.com
SIC: 2395 2396 Pleating and stitching; Screen printing on fabric articles

(P-2520)
MODERN EMBROIDERY INC
3701 W Moore Ave (92704-6836)
PHONE.............................714 436-9960
EMP: 42 EST: 1996
SALES (est): 3.59MM **Privately Held**
Web: www.modernembroidery.com
SIC: 2395 Embroidery and art needlework

(P-2521)
N STITCHES PRINTS INC
16009 S Broadway (90248-2417)
PHONE.............................310 366-7537
Ali Amir, *Pr*
EMP: 21 EST: 1999
SQ FT: 3,800
SALES (est): 485.53K **Privately Held**
Web: www.snpink.com
SIC: 2395 Embroidery products, except
Schiffli machine

(P-2522)
NATIONAL EMBLEM INC (PA)
3925 E Vernon St (90815-1727)
P.O. Box 15680 (90815-0680)
PHONE.............................310 515-5055
TOLL FREE: 800
Milton H Lubin Senior, *Pr*
Milton H Lubin Junior, *VP*
▲ EMP: 250 EST: 1972
SQ FT: 60,000
SALES (est): 23.6MM
SALES (corp-wide): 23.6MM **Privately Held**
Web: www.nationalemblem.com
SIC: 2395 2396 Emblems, embroidered;
Automotive and apparel trimmings

(P-2523)
OUTLOOK RESOURCES INC
Also Called: Leftbank Art
14930 Alondra Blvd (90638-5752)
PHONE.............................562 623-9328
Chris Hyun, *Pr*
◆ EMP: 100 EST: 2008
SALES (est): 9.48MM **Privately Held**
Web: www.leftbankart.com
SIC: 2395 5999 Pleating and stitching; Art
dealers

(P-2524)
REBECCA INTERNATIONAL INC
4587 E 48th St (90058-3201)
PHONE.............................323 973-2602
Eli Kahen, *Owner*
EMP: 25 EST: 2015
SQ FT: 1,500
SALES (est): 1.33MM **Privately Held**
Web: www.rebeccainternational.com
SIC: 2395 2759 7299 Embroidery products,
except Schiffli machine; Screen printing;
Stitching services

2396 Automotive And Apparel Trimmings

(P-2525)
ABSOLUTE SCREENPRINT INC
333 Cliffwood Park St (92821-4104)
P.O. Box 9069 (92822-9069)
PHONE.............................714 529-2120
Steven Restivo, *CEO*
Andrea Restivo, *
▲ EMP: 250 EST: 1991
SQ FT: 65,000
SALES (est): 24.87MM **Privately Held**
Web: www.absolutescreenprint.com

SIC: 2396 3993 2759 Screen printing on
fabric articles; Signs and advertising
specialties; Screen printing

(P-2526)
AMOSEASTERN APPAREL INC
2684 Lacy St Apt 307 (90031-1977)
PHONE.............................323 909-1010
EMP: 39
Web: www.amoseastern.com
SIC: 2396 Apparel and other linings, except
millinery
PA: Amoseastern Apparel Inc.
251 W 39th St Fl 12
New York NY

(P-2527)
ATELIER LUXURY GROUP LLC
Also Called: Amiri
1330 Channing St (90021-2411)
PHONE.............................310 751-2444
Michael Amiri, *Managing Member*
EMP: 45 EST: 2019
SQ FT: 30,000
SALES (est): 5.22MM **Privately Held**
SIC: 2396 2311 2321 2331 Apparel and
other linings, except millinery; Men's and
boy's suits and coats; Men's and boy's
furnishings; Women's and misses' blouses
and shirts

(P-2528)
D AND J MARKETING INC
Also Called: DJM Suspension
580 W 184th St (90248-4202)
PHONE.............................310 538-1583
Jeffery J Ullmann, *Pr*
Mark Dunham, *
▲ EMP: 32 EST: 1985
SQ FT: 18,000
SALES (est): 3.42MM **Privately Held**
Web: www.djmsuspension.com
SIC: 2396 2531 3714 Automotive trimmings,
fabric; Public building and related furniture;
Motor vehicle parts and accessories

(P-2529)
DISTINCTIVE INDUSTRIES
Also Called: Specialty Division
10618 Shoemaker Ave (90670-4038)
PHONE.............................800 421-9777
Dwight Forrister, *CEO*
Aaron Forrister, *
▲ EMP: 410 EST: 1969
SQ FT: 110,000
SALES (est): 48.69MM **Privately Held**
Web: www.distinctiveindustries.com
SIC: 2396 3086 Automotive trimmings, fabric
; Plastics foam products
PA: Distinctive Industries Of Texas, Inc.
4516 Seton Center Pkwy # 13
Austin TX

(P-2530)
**FOUR SEASONS DESIGN INC
(PA)**
2451 Britannia Blvd (92154-7405)
PHONE.............................619 761-5151
John Borsini, *Pr*
▲ EMP: 25 EST: 2000
SALES (est): 24.18MM
SALES (corp-wide): 24.18MM **Privately Held**
Web: www.fourseasonsdesign.com
SIC: 2396 Screen printing on fabric articles

(P-2531)
GRAPHIC PRINTS INC
Also Called: Pipeline
904 Silver Spur Rd Ste 415 (90274-3800)

P.O. Box 459 (90248-0459)
PHONE.............................310 870-1239
Alan Greenberg, *CEO*
Tamotsu Inouye, *
Richard Greenberg, *
EMP: 45 EST: 1971
SQ FT: 22,000
SALES (est): 2.31MM **Privately Held**
Web: www.pipelinegear.com
SIC: 2396 2339 2329 Screen printing on
fabric articles; Women's and misses'
athletic clothing and sportswear; Men's and
boys' sportswear and athletic clothing

(P-2532)
I D BRAND LLC
3185 Airway Ave Ste A (92626-4601)
PHONE.............................949 422-7057
▲ EMP: 36 EST: 1995
SQ FT: 6,400
SALES (est): 4.62MM **Privately Held**
Web: www.brandid.com
SIC: 2396 Apparel findings and trimmings

(P-2533)
J & H PRODUCTION
4481 S Santa Fe Ave (90058-2101)
PHONE.............................323 261-6600
Joseph Hendifar, *Pt*
Sassan Kohan, *Pt*
EMP: 20 EST: 1988
SQ FT: 8,000
SALES (est): 1.09MM **Privately Held**
SIC: 2396 Pads, shoulder: for coats, suits,
etc.

(P-2534)
KAMM INDUSTRIES INC
Also Called: Prp Seats
43352 Business Park Dr (92590-3665)
PHONE.............................800 317-6253
▲ EMP: 43 EST: 2009
SALES (est): 5.49MM **Privately Held**
Web: www.prpseats.com
SIC: 2396 Automotive trimmings, fabric

(P-2535)
KAPAN - KENT COMPANY INC
3540 Seagate Way Ste 100 (92056-2672)
PHONE.............................760 631-1716
Arnold Kapen Senior, *Pr*
▲ EMP: 35 EST: 1958
SALES (est): 2.13MM **Privately Held**
Web: www.kapankent.com
SIC: 2396 3231 Screen printing on fabric
articles; Decorated glassware: chipped,
engraved, etched, etc.

(P-2536)
**NORTH AMERICAN TEXTILE CO
LLC (PA)**
Also Called: N A T C O
346 W Cerritos Ave (91204-2704)
PHONE.............................818 409-0019
◆ EMP: 49 EST: 1991
SQ FT: 18,000
SALES (est): 9.77MM **Privately Held**
Web: www.natcoglobal.com
SIC: 2396 7389 Apparel findings and
trimmings; Textile and apparel services

(P-2537)
ORBO MANUFACTURING INC
12740 Lakeland Rd (90670-4633)
PHONE.............................562 222-4535
Roberto Galvez, *CEO*
EMP: 25 EST: 2021
SALES (est): 1.42MM **Privately Held**

SIC: 2396 Furniture trimmings, fabric

(P-2538)
**SECURITY TEXTILE
CORPORATION**
1457 E Washington Blvd (90021-3039)
PHONE.............................213 747-2673
Doug Weitman, *CEO*
Brian Weitman, *
▲ EMP: 20 EST: 1972
SQ FT: 85,000
SALES (est): 638.81K **Privately Held**
Web: www.stc-qst.com
SIC: 2396 5131 Automotive and apparel
trimmings; Sewing supplies and notions

(P-2539)
SIMSO TEX SUBLIMATION (PA)
Also Called: Simso Tex
3028 E Las Hermanas St (90221-5511)
PHONE.............................310 885-9717
Joe Simsoly, *CEO*
Eli Simsollo, *
Kaden Simsollo, *
▲ EMP: 36 EST: 2001
SQ FT: 38,000
SALES (est): 6.31MM
SALES (corp-wide): 6.31MM **Privately
Held**
SIC: 2396 Fabric printing and stamping

(P-2540)
**SJ&L BIAS BINDING & TEX CO
INC**
Also Called: Superior Bias Trims
1950 E 20th St (90058-1005)
PHONE.............................213 747-5271
Lynn Menichiwi, *CEO*
Joseph Menichini, *
▲ EMP: 45 EST: 1950
SQ FT: 11,000
SALES (est): 982.07K **Privately Held**
SIC: 2396 Pads, shoulder: for coats, suits,
etc.

(P-2541)
SMOOTHREADS INC
Also Called: 2.95 Guys
13750 Stowe Dr Ste A (92064-8828)
PHONE.............................800 536-5959
Lance Beesley, *Pr*
▲ EMP: 28 EST: 1987
SQ FT: 12,000
SALES (est): 2.3MM **Privately Held**
Web: www.295guys.com
SIC: 2396 2395 Screen printing on fabric
articles; Embroidery products, except
Schiffli machine

(P-2542)
**WESTIN AUTOMOTIVE
PRODUCTS INC (PA)**
Also Called: Westin
320 W Covina Blvd (91773-2907)
PHONE.............................626 960-6762
Robert West, *Pr*
▲ EMP: 35 EST: 1994
SQ FT: 10,000
SALES (est): 15.59MM **Privately Held**
Web: www.westinautomotive.com
SIC: 2396 Automotive and apparel trimmings

2399 Fabricated Textile Products, Nec

(P-2543)
A LOT TO SAY INC
1541 S Vineyard Ave (91761-7717)

PRODUCTS & SVCS

PHONE..................877 366-8448
Jennifer Spannich Danmiller, *CEO*
Alisson Spannich Powers, *COO*
EMP: 20 **EST:** 2008
SALES (est): 1.23MM **Privately Held**
SIC: 2399 Banners, made from fabric

(P-2544)
ACTION EMBROIDERY CORP (PA)
Also Called: Action
1315 W Brooks St (91762-3612)
PHONE..................909 983-1359
Ira Newman, *Pr*
Steven Mendelow, *
Ozzie Silna Stkhlr, *Prin*
▲ **EMP:** 120 **EST:** 1986
SQ FT: 12,000
SALES (est): 9.7MM
SALES (corp-wide): 9.7MM **Privately Held**
Web: www.actionembroiderycorp.com
SIC: 2399 2395 Emblems, badges, and insignia: from purchased materials; Pleating and stitching

(P-2545)
AIRBORNE SYSTEMS N AMER CA INC
3100 W Segerstrom Ave (92704-5812)
PHONE..................714 662-1400
Bryce Wiedeman, *Pr*
Sean P Maroney, *
Halle F Terrion, *
Terrance M Paradie, *
▼ **EMP:** 200 **EST:** 1919
SQ FT: 160,000
SALES (est): 55.29MM
SALES (corp-wide): 6.58B **Publicly Held**
Web: www.airborne-sys.com
SIC: 2399 Parachutes
HQ: Airborne Systems North America Inc.
　5800 Magnolia Ave
　Pennsauken NJ
　856 663-1275

(P-2546)
AUTOLIV ASP INC
Also Called: Autoliv Akr Fcilty -Casa Whse
9355 Airway Rd (92154-7931)
PHONE..................619 662-8018
EMP: 27
SALES (corp-wide): 8.84B **Publicly Held**
SIC: 2399 Seat belts, automobile and aircraft
HQ: Autoliv Asp, Inc.
　3350 Airport Rd
　Ogden UT

(P-2547)
AUTOLIV SAFETY TECHNOLOGY INC
2475 Paseo De Las Americas Ste A (92154-7255)
PHONE..................619 662-8000
Bradley J Murray, *Pr*
Anthony J Nellis, *Sec*
Raymond B Pekar, *Treas*
EMP: 1003 **EST:** 1989
SALES (est): 43.65MM **Privately Held**
Web: www.autoliv.com
SIC: 2399 Seat belts, automobile and aircraft

(P-2548)
DISPLAY FABRICATION GROUP INC
1231 N Miller St Ste 100 (92806-1950)
PHONE..................714 373-2100
Luis Ocampo, *Pr*
Luis Ocampo, *Pr*
◆ **EMP:** 50 **EST:** 2002

SQ FT: 100,000
SALES (est): 5.05MM **Privately Held**
Web: www.displayfg.com
SIC: 2399 Belting, fabric: made from purchased materials

(P-2549)
DSY EDUCATIONAL CORPORATION
Also Called: Main Street Banner
525 Maple St (93013-2070)
P.O. Box 41829 (93140-1829)
PHONE..................805 684-8111
David Yothers, *Pr*
Sharon Yothers, *Sec*
EMP: 21 **EST:** 1960
SQ FT: 15,000
SALES (est): 397K **Privately Held**
SIC: 2399 7336 Banners, made from fabric; Commercial art and graphic design

(P-2550)
EEVELLE LLC
5928 Balfour Ct (92008-7304)
PHONE..................760 434-2231
Charles Mckee, *Managing Member*
▲ **EMP:** 24 **EST:** 1994
SALES (est): 2.38MM **Privately Held**
Web: www.eevelle.com
SIC: 2399 Automotive covers, except seat and tire covers

(P-2551)
EXXEL OUTDOORS INC
343 Baldwin Park Blvd (91746-1406)
PHONE..................626 369-7278
EMP: 158
SALES (corp-wide): 123.41MM **Privately Held**
Web: www.exxel.com
SIC: 2399 Sleeping bags
PA: Exxel Outdoors, Inc.
　300 American Blvd
　Haleyville AL
　205 486-5258

(P-2552)
FLEXSYSTEMS USA INC
1308 N Magnolia Ave Ste J (92020-1646)
PHONE..................619 401-1858
Diane Chapman, *Pr*
▲ **EMP:** 19 **EST:** 1994
SALES (est): 2.42MM **Privately Held**
Web: www.flexsystems.com
SIC: 2399 2396 Emblems, badges, and insignia; Apparel findings and trimmings

(P-2553)
FXC CORPORATION
Guardian Parachute Division
3050 Red Hill Ave (92626-4524)
PHONE..................714 557-8032
Frank X Chevrier, *Mgr*
EMP: 64
SALES (corp-wide): 9.82MM **Privately Held**
Web: www.fxcguardian.com
SIC: 2399 3429 Parachutes; Parachute hardware
PA: Fxc Corporation
　3050 Red Hill Ave
　Costa Mesa CA
　714 556-7400

(P-2554)
HITEX DYEING & FINISHING INC
355 Vineland Ave (91746-2321)
PHONE..................626 363-0160
Young C Kim, *Pr*
▲ **EMP:** 25 **EST:** 2010

SALES (est): 466.71K **Privately Held**
Web: www.hitexdye.com
SIC: 2399 2257 Nets, launderers and dyers; Dyeing and finishing circular knit fabrics

(P-2555)
PRESTIGE FLAG & BANNER CO INC
Also Called: Prestige Flag
591 Camino De La Reina Ste 917 (92108)
PHONE..................619 497-2220
▼ **EMP:** 100 **EST:** 1991
SALES (est): 9.81MM **Privately Held**
Web: www.prestigeflag.com
SIC: 2399 Flags, fabric

(P-2556)
REFLEX CORPORATION
1825 Aston Ave Ste A (92008-7341)
PHONE..................760 931-9009
John C Levy Junior, *Pr*
▲ **EMP:** 20 **EST:** 1976
SQ FT: 20,000
SALES (est): 1.07MM **Privately Held**
Web: www.premiumtuflock.com
SIC: 2399 Horse and pet accessories, textile

(P-2557)
SCOTTEX INC
12828 S Broadway (90061-1116)
PHONE..................310 516-1411
▲ **EMP:** 25 **EST:** 1995
SQ FT: 19,000
SALES (est): 551.75K **Privately Held**
Web: it.scottex.com
SIC: 2399 Hand woven and crocheted products

(P-2558)
SEABORN CANVAS
435 N Harbor Blvd Ste B1 (90731-2271)
PHONE..................310 519-1208
Juanita Wade, *Owner*
▼ **EMP:** 25 **EST:** 1987
SQ FT: 5,000
SALES (est): 888.33K **Privately Held**
SIC: 2399 2394 Banners, pennants, and flags; Canvas and related products

(P-2559)
VANGUARD INDUSTRIES EAST INC
2440 Impala Dr (92010-7226)
PHONE..................800 433-1334
William M Gershen, *Brnch Mgr*
EMP: 30
SALES (corp-wide): 12.95MM **Privately Held**
Web: www.vanguardmil.com
SIC: 2399 Military insignia, textile
PA: Vanguard Industries East, Inc.
　1172 Azalea Garden Rd
　Norfolk VA
　757 665-8405

(P-2560)
VANGUARD INDUSTRIES WEST INC (PA)
2440 Impala Dr (92010-7226)
PHONE..................760 438-4437
William M Gershen, *Pr*
Michael Harrison, *
Bill Gershen, *
▲ **EMP:** 107 **EST:** 1980
SQ FT: 36,000
SALES (est): 14.9MM
SALES (corp-wide): 14.9MM **Privately Held**
Web: www.vanguardmil.com

SIC: 2399 2395 Military insignia, textile; Pleating and stitching

(P-2561)
WESSCO INTL LTD A CAL LTD PRTN (PA)
Also Called: Wessco International
11400 W Olympic Blvd Ste 450 (90064-1550)
PHONE..................310 477-4272
Robert Bregman, *Pr*
Tyler Shepodd, *CFO*
Nick Bregman, *COO*
◆ **EMP:** 54 **EST:** 1979
SQ FT: 7,000
SALES (est): 9.17MM
SALES (corp-wide): 9.17MM **Privately Held**
Web: www.wessco.net
SIC: 2399 2393 3161 2273 Sleeping bags; Textile bags; Traveling bags; Bathmats and sets, textile

---

2411 Logging

(P-2562)
WASHBURN GROVE MANAGEMENT INC
27781 Fairview Ave (92544-8521)
PHONE..................909 322-4690
Dennis Washburn, *Pr*
David Washburn, *VP*
EMP: 20 **EST:** 1991
SALES (est): 915.7K **Privately Held**
SIC: 2411 0783 Logging; Ornamental shrub and tree services

(P-2563)
WELL ANALYSIS CORPORATION INC (PA)
Also Called: Welaco
5500 Woodmere Dr (93313-2776)
P.O. Box 20008 (93390-0008)
PHONE..................661 283-9510
Judy L Bebout, *CEO*
Brenda Muniozguren, *
Robert Muniozguren, *
Dan Bebout, *
▲ **EMP:** 26 **EST:** 1989
SQ FT: 1,400
SALES (est): 9.28MM **Privately Held**
Web: www.welacogroup.com
SIC: 2411 1389 Logging; Oil field services, nec

2421 Sawmills And Planing Mills, General

(P-2564)
ARTESIA SAWDUST PRODUCTS INC
13434 S Ontario Ave (91761-7956)
PHONE..................909 947-5983
TOLL FREE: 800
Brigitte De Laura-espinoza, *Pr*
Anthony Espinoza, *
EMP: 35 **EST:** 1960
SQ FT: 2,700
SALES (est): 5.41MM **Privately Held**
Web: www.artesiasawdust.com
SIC: 2421 Sawdust and shavings

(P-2565)
CABINETS GLORE ORANGE CNTY INC
Also Called: Cabinets Galore Oc
9279 Cabot Dr Ste D (92126-4364)

▲ = Import ▼ = Export
◆ = Import/Export

PHONE..................858 586-0555
Barry Jacobs, *Pr*
Adi Jacobs, *VP*
Luke Breandt, *Prin*
EMP: 20 **EST:** 1986
SQ FT: 10,000
SALES (est): 3MM **Privately Held**
Web: www.cabinetsgalore.net
SIC: 2421 1751 Furniture dimension stock, softwood; Cabinet and finish carpentry

(P-2566)
HMR BUILDING SYSTEMS LLC
620 Newport Center Dr Fl 12 (92660-6420)
PHONE..................951 749-4700
▲ **EMP:** 79 **EST:** 2008
SQ FT: 90,000
SALES (est): 688.35K **Privately Held**
SIC: 2421 Building and structural materials, wood
PA: Rsi Holding Llc
620 Nwport Ctr Fl 12 Flr 12
Newport Beach CA

(P-2567)
STRATA FOREST PRODUCTS INC (PA)
Also Called: Profile Planing Mill
2600 S Susan St (92704-5816)
PHONE..................714 751-0800
TOLL FREE: 800
Richard W Hormuth, *Pr*
John Hormuth, *
▲ **EMP:** 50 **EST:** 1991
SQ FT: 38,000
SALES (est): 9.95MM
SALES (corp-wide): 9.95MM **Privately Held**
Web: www.strataforest.com
SIC: 2421 Planing mills, nec

2426 Hardwood Dimension And Flooring Mills

(P-2568)
BAXSTRA INC
Also Called: Martin Erattrud Co
1224 W 132nd St (90247-1506)
PHONE..................323 770-4171
Patrick Baxter, *VP*
Allan Stratford, *
EMP: 23 **EST:** 1997
SALES (est): 543.73K **Privately Held**
Web: www.martinbrattrud.com
SIC: 2426 Frames for upholstered furniture, wood

(P-2569)
BMW OF PALM SPRINGS
3737 E Palm Canyon Dr (92264-5205)
PHONE..................760 324-7071
Frank Hickinbotham, *Prin*
EMP: 23 **EST:** 2015
SALES (est): 4.4MM **Privately Held**
Web: www.bmwpalmsprings.com
SIC: 2426 3545 Vehicle stock, hardwood; Thread cutting dies

(P-2570)
FURNITURE TECHNOLOGIES INC
17227 Columbus St (92301)
P.O. Box 1076 (92301-1076)
PHONE..................760 246-9180
Kenneth Drum, *CEO*
EMP: 24 **EST:** 1998
SQ FT: 31,000
SALES (est): 2.36MM **Privately Held**

Web: www.ftical.com
SIC: 2426 Furniture stock and parts, hardwood

(P-2571)
HALLMARK HOME INTERIORS INC (PA)
Also Called: Hallmark Floors
2360 S Archibald Ave (91761-8520)
PHONE..................909 947-7736
Zheng Qing Pan, *Pr*
EMP: 17 **EST:** 2020
SALES (est): 1.67MM
SALES (corp-wide): 1.67MM **Privately Held**
SIC: 2426 Flooring, hardwood

(P-2572)
HARDWOOD FLRG LIQUIDATORS INC (PA)
Also Called: Republic Flooring
7227 Telegraph Rd (90640-6512)
PHONE..................323 201-4200
Rotem Eylor, *CEO*
▲ **EMP:** 100 **EST:** 2008
SALES (est): 52.37MM
SALES (corp-wide): 52.37MM **Privately Held**
Web: www.republicfloor.com
SIC: 2426 Flooring, hardwood

(P-2573)
HOGUE BROS INC
Also Called: Hogue Grips
550 Linne Rd (93446-8454)
P.O. Box 1138 (93447-1138)
PHONE..................805 239-1440
▲ **EMP:** 36
Web: www.hogueinc.com
SIC: 2426 3489 Hardwood dimension and flooring mills; Guns, howitzers, mortars, and related equipment

(P-2574)
LA HARDWOOD FLOORING INC (PA)
Also Called: Eternity Floors
9880 San Fernando Rd (91331-2603)
PHONE..................818 361-0099
Doron Gal, *CEO*
Eliyahu Shuat, *Prin*
▲ **EMP:** 17 **EST:** 2005
SQ FT: 12,000
SALES (est): 9.37MM
SALES (corp-wide): 9.37MM **Privately Held**
Web: www.eternityflooring.com
SIC: 2426 5211 Flooring, hardwood; Flooring, wood

(P-2575)
LEXAR INCORPORATED
Also Called: Diamondcore Tools
380 Vernon Way Ste J (92020-1931)
PHONE..................619 252-8265
Nancy Oakes, *Managing Member*
Robert Oaks, *Owner*
EMP: 18 **EST:** 2010
SALES (est): 4.25MM **Privately Held**
Web: www.diamondcoretools.com
SIC: 2426 5961 5251 5945 Carvings, furniture: wood; Tools and hardware, mail order; Tools, hand; Arts and crafts supplies

(P-2576)
MCMURTRIE & MCMURTRIE INC
Also Called: Tru-Wood Products
915 W 5th St (91702-3311)
P.O. Box 1940 (91017-5940)

PHONE..................626 815-0177
Richard Mcmurtrie, *CEO*
Bill Cherry, *
▲ **EMP:** 36 **EST:** 1990
SQ FT: 97,000
SALES (est): 760.83K **Privately Held**
SIC: 2426 2431 5031 Frames for upholstered furniture, wood; Trim, wood; Lumber, plywood, and millwork

(P-2577)
MONTCLAIR WOOD CORPORATION
545 N Mountain Ave Ste 104 (91786-5073)
PHONE..................909 985-0302
John Slavek Grey, *Pr*
John Slavek Grey, *Pr*
Louis Jimenez, *
EMP: 23 **EST:** 1990
SQ FT: 70,000
SALES (est): 678.86K **Privately Held**
SIC: 2426 5031 Furniture stock and parts, hardwood; Lumber: rough, dressed, and finished

(P-2578)
PARQUET BY DIAN
16601 S Main St (90248-2722)
PHONE..................310 527-3779
Anatoli Efros, *CEO*
Dima Efros, *Pr*
EMP: 92 **EST:** 1993
SALES (est): 4.57MM **Privately Held**
Web: www.parquet.com
SIC: 2426 Parquet flooring, hardwood

(P-2579)
RTMEX INC
Also Called: Best Redwood
1202 Piper Ranch Rd (92154-7714)
P.O. Box 8662 (91912-8662)
PHONE..................619 391-9913
Jorje Sampietro, *Pr*
EMP: 108 **EST:** 2010
SQ FT: 15,000
SALES (est): 6.8MM **Privately Held**
SIC: 2426 Carvings, furniture: wood

(P-2580)
WEST COAST FURN FRAMERS INC
17402 Eucalyptus St (92345-5118)
PHONE..................760 669-5275
Katelynn Galiana-baca, *Pr*
Katelynn Baca, *
Javier Galiana, *
EMP: 27 **EST:** 2017
SALES (est): 2.52MM **Privately Held**
SIC: 2426 Frames for upholstered furniture, wood

2431 Millwork

(P-2581)
ABC CUSTOM WOOD SHUTTERS INC
Also Called: Golden West Shutters
20561 Pascal Way (92630-8119)
PHONE..................949 595-0300
David Harris, *VP*
John Stahman, *
EMP: 35 **EST:** 1991
SALES (est): 2.25MM **Privately Held**
Web: www.gwshutters.com
SIC: 2431 Door shutters, wood

(P-2582)
AMERICAN CABINET WORKS INC
13518 S Normandie Ave (90249-2606)
PHONE..................310 715-6815
Alex Medrano, *Owner*
EMP: 22 **EST:** 1999
SQ FT: 5,000
SALES (est): 2.47MM **Privately Held**
Web: www.americancabinetworks.com
SIC: 2431 Millwork

(P-2583)
ANDERCO INC
540 Airpark Dr (92833-2503)
PHONE..................714 446-9508
Peter Johnson, *Pr*
Ralph Johnson, *
▲ **EMP:** 50 **EST:** 1983
SQ FT: 70,000
SALES (est): 4.73MM **Privately Held**
SIC: 2431 5031 Door frames, wood; Doors and windows

(P-2584)
ARCHITCTRAL MLLWK SNTA BARBARA
Also Called: Manufacturers of Wood Products
8 N Nopal St (93103-3317)
P.O. Box 4699 (93140-4699)
PHONE..................805 965-7011
Thomas G Mathews, *Pr*
Glenice Mathews, *
Joseph J Mathews, *
Ronald Mathews, *Stockholder*
EMP: 40 **EST:** 1968
SQ FT: 10,000
SALES (est): 4.87MM **Privately Held**
Web: www.archmill.com
SIC: 2431 Millwork

(P-2585)
ART GLASS ETC INC
Also Called: AG Millworks
3111 Golf Course Dr (93003-7604)
PHONE..................805 644-4494
Rachid El Etel, *Pr*
Aida El Etel, *
▲ **EMP:** 50 **EST:** 1986
SALES (est): 7.45MM **Privately Held**
Web: www.agmillworks.com
SIC: 2431 Doors and door parts and trim, wood

(P-2586)
AVALON SHUTTERS INC
3407 N Perris Blvd (92571-3100)
PHONE..................909 937-4900
Douglas Noel Serbin, *CEO*
▲ **EMP:** 215 **EST:** 1986
SQ FT: 85,000
SALES (est): 49.69MM **Privately Held**
Web: www.avalonshutters.com
SIC: 2431 Window shutters, wood

(P-2587)
CALIFORNIA MILLWORKS CORP
Also Called: California Classics
27772 Avenue Scott (91355-3417)
PHONE..................661 294-2345
Steven Gadol, *Pr*
Lay Cho, *Pr*
Edmond Cho, *VP*
Steven Godol, *Pr*
EMP: 22 **EST:** 1981
SQ FT: 149,000
SALES (est): 3.52MM
SALES (corp-wide): 4.35MM **Privately Held**

Web: www.california-classics.com
SIC: 2431 Doors, wood
PA: Old English Milling & Woodworks, Inc.
27772 Avenue Scott
Santa Clarita CA
661 294-9171

(P-2588)
CALIFRNIA DLUXE WNDOWS INDS IN (PA)
20735 Superior St (91311-4416)
PHONE............................818 349-5566
Aaron Adirim, *Pr*
EMP: 46 EST: 1999
SQ FT: 60,000
SALES (est): 12.36MM
SALES (corp-wide): 12.36MM **Privately Held**
Web: www.cdwindows.com
SIC: 2431 2824 Windows and window parts and trim, wood; Vinyl fibers

(P-2589)
CANYON GRAPHICS INC
3738 Ruffin Rd (92123-1812)
PHONE............................858 646-0444
Scott Moncrieff, *CEO*
EMP: 60 EST: 1981
SALES (est): 10.03MM **Privately Held**
Web: www.canyongraphics.com
SIC: 2431 2754 Moldings and baseboards, ornamental and trim; Labels: gravure printing

(P-2590)
CONTRACTORS WARDROBE INC (PA)
Also Called: Contractors Wardrobe
26121 Avenue Hall (91355-3490)
P.O. Box 800790 (91380-0790)
PHONE............................661 257-1177
▲ EMP: 200 EST: 1972
SALES (est): 136.14MM
SALES (corp-wide): 136.14MM **Privately Held**
Web: www.cwdoors.com
SIC: 2431 3088 Doors, wood; Shower stalls, fiberglass and plastics

(P-2591)
CUSTOM WIN & DOOR DESIGN INC
3242 Production Ave (92058-1308)
PHONE............................760 439-6213
Mark Alvey, *Pr*
Andrew Alvey, *Sec*
EMP: 22 EST: 1982
SQ FT: 30,000
SALES (est): 496.19K **Privately Held**
SIC: 2431 Doors, wood

(P-2592)
DANMER INC
Also Called: Danmer Custom Shutters
8000 Woodley Ave (91406-1226)
PHONE............................516 670-5125
▲ EMP: 250
Web: www.danmer.com
SIC: 2431 5023 Window shutters, wood; Window covering parts and accessories

(P-2593)
DAY STAR INDUSTRIES
13727 Excelsior Dr (90670-5104)
PHONE............................562 926-8800
Dan R Prigmore, *Pr*
Anne Prigmore, *Treas*
EMP: 19 EST: 1985
SALES (est): 3.15MM **Privately Held**

Web: www.daystarindustries.com
SIC: 2431 Millwork

(P-2594)
DECORE-ATIVE SPC NC LLC (PA)
2772 Peck Rd (91016-5005)
PHONE............................626 254-9191
Jack Lansford Senior, *CEO*
Jack Lansford Junior, *Pr*
Eric Lansford, *
Billie Lansford, *
▲ EMP: 650 EST: 1969
SALES (est): 202.63MM
SALES (corp-wide): 202.63MM **Privately Held**
Web: www.decore.com
SIC: 2431 Millwork

(P-2595)
DECORE-ATIVE SPC NC LLC
4414 Azusa Canyon Rd (91706-2740)
PHONE............................626 960-7731
David Thompson, *Brnch Mgr*
EMP: 111
SALES (corp-wide): 202.63MM **Privately Held**
Web: www.decore.com
SIC: 2431 Millwork
PA: Decore-Ative Specialties Nc Llc
2772 Peck Rd
Monrovia CA
626 254-9191

(P-2596)
DESIGN SYNTHESIS INC
9855 Black Mountain Rd (92126-4512)
PHONE............................858 271-8480
EMP: 20 EST: 1976
SALES (est): 4.97MM **Privately Held**
Web: www.designsynthesis.net
SIC: 2431 2434 Doors, wood; Wood kitchen cabinets

(P-2597)
DREES WOOD PRODUCTS INC
14020 Orange Ave (90723-2018)
PHONE............................562 633-7337
Ed Drees, *Mgr*
EMP: 50
SALES (corp-wide): 10.61MM **Privately Held**
Web: www.dreeswoodproducts.com
SIC: 2431 Doors, wood
PA: Drees Wood Products, Inc.
14003 Orange Ave
Paramount CA
562 633-7337

(P-2598)
ECMD INC
10863 Jersey Blvd 100 (91730-5151)
PHONE............................909 980-1775
EMP: 62
SALES (corp-wide): 186.49MM **Privately Held**
Web: www.ecmd.com
SIC: 2431 Moldings, wood: unfinished and prefinished
PA: Ecmd, Inc.
2 Grandview St
North Wilkesboro NC
336 667-5976

(P-2599)
EL & EL WOOD PRODUCTS CORP (DH)
6011 Schaefer Ave (91710-7043)
P.O. Box 5105 (91708-5105)

PHONE............................909 591-0339
Cathy Vidas, *Pr*
◆ EMP: 53 EST: 1963
SQ FT: 72,000
SALES (est): 27.7MM
SALES (corp-wide): 183.49MM **Privately Held**
Web: www.elandelwoodproducts.com
SIC: 2431 Millwork
HQ: Metrie Canada Ltd
1055 Dunsmuir St Suite 3500
Vancouver BC
604 691-9100

(P-2600)
FINELINE WOODWORKING INC
Also Called: Fineline Architectural Mllwk
1139 Baker St (92626-4114)
PHONE............................714 540-5468
Marc Butman, *CEO*
Jon Muller, *
Tom Crone, *
Julie Butman, *OF EVENTS & SOCIAL MEDIA*
EMP: 60 EST: 2006
SQ FT: 20,000
SALES (est): 6.44MM **Privately Held**
Web: www.finelinewood.com
SIC: 2431 Millwork

(P-2601)
GL WOODWORKING INC
Also Called: Millers Woodworking
14341 Franklin Ave (92780-7010)
PHONE............................949 515-2192
Grant Miller, *Owner*
EMP: 63 EST: 2004
SALES (est): 7.02MM **Privately Held**
SIC: 2431 Millwork

(P-2602)
GMS MOLDS
732 Avenue C (90277-4841)
PHONE............................310 403-9870
Bradley Gardner, *Brnch Mgr*
EMP: 23
Web: www.gmsmolds.com
SIC: 2431 Moldings and baseboards, ornamental and trim
PA: Gms Molds
729 E 223rd St
Carson CA

(P-2603)
HALEY BROS INC
1575 Riverview Dr (92408-2922)
PHONE............................800 854-5951
EMP: 110
SALES (corp-wide): 98.98MM **Privately Held**
Web: www.haleybros.com
SIC: 2431 Doors, wood
HQ: Haley Bros., Inc.
6291 Orangethorpe Ave
Buena Park CA

(P-2604)
HALEY BROS INC (HQ)
6291 Orangethorpe Ave (90620-1339)
PHONE............................714 670-2112
Thomas J Cobb, *CEO*
Thomas Cobb, *Sec*
▲ EMP: 90 EST: 1987
SQ FT: 24,000
SALES (est): 33.94MM
SALES (corp-wide): 98.98MM **Privately Held**
Web: www.haleybros.com
SIC: 2431 Doors, wood
PA: T. M. Cobb Company
500 Palmyrita Ave

Riverside CA
951 248-2400

(P-2605)
HIGHLAND LUMBER SALES INC
300 E Santa Ana St (92805-3953)
PHONE............................714 778-2293
Richard Phillips, *Pr*
Daniel Lobue, *
▲ EMP: 31 EST: 1991
SQ FT: 2,000
SALES (est): 4.76MM **Privately Held**
Web: www.highlandlumber.com
SIC: 2431 5031 2493 5211 Millwork; Lumber: rough, dressed, and finished; Reconstituted wood products; Lumber products

(P-2606)
HIS LIFE WOODWORKS
22651 Gaycrest Ave (90505-3327)
PHONE............................310 756-0170
John Johnson Junior, *Pr*
Garrett Brim, *
EMP: 40 EST: 1978
SALES (est): 4.18MM **Privately Held**
Web: www.hislifewoodworks.com
SIC: 2431 Millwork

(P-2607)
HOSPITALITY WOOD PRODUCTS INC
7206 E Gage Ave (90040-3813)
PHONE............................562 806-5564
Michael Romero, *Pr*
Victor Garcia, *VP*
Carlos Escalante, *Treas*
EMP: 17 EST: 2001
SALES (est): 2.46MM **Privately Held**
SIC: 2431 Interior and ornamental woodwork and trim

(P-2608)
JELD-WEN INC
Also Called: International Wood Products
3760 Convoy St Ste 111 (92111-3743)
PHONE............................800 468-3667
Hugo Hernadez, *Off Mgr*
EMP: 140
Web: www.jeld-wen.com
SIC: 2431 Doors, wood
HQ: Jeld-Wen, Inc.
2645 Silver Crescent Dr
Charlotte NC
800 535-3936

(P-2609)
KASTLE STAIR INC (PA)
7422 Mountjoy Dr (92648-1231)
PHONE............................714 596-2600
Rose Phillips, *Pr*
EMP: 20 EST: 1983
SALES (est): 5.77MM
SALES (corp-wide): 5.77MM **Privately Held**
SIC: 2431 Staircases and stairs, wood

(P-2610)
KL DECORATOR SALES
Also Called: K & L Shutters
10120 Artesia Pl (90706-6729)
PHONE............................562 920-0268
FAX: 562 920-3865
EMP: 20
SIC: 2431 Window shutters, wood
PA: Kl Decorator Sales
3848 N Mckinley St 11o
Corona CA

(P-2611)
KLS DOORS LLC
Chaparral A Division Kls Door
501 Kettering Dr (91761-8150)
PHONE..............................909 605-6468
EMP: 85
SALES (corp-wide): 503.27K **Privately Held**
SIC: 2431 Doors and door parts and trim, wood
PA: Kls Doors Llc
501 Kettering Dr
Ontario CA
909 605-6468

(P-2612)
L & L CUSTOM SHUTTERS INC
3133 Yukon Ave (92626-2921)
PHONE..............................714 996-9539
Larry Allen, *Pr*
Lillian Allen, *
Ralph Gerardo, *
EMP: 17 EST: 1980
SQ FT: 9,000
SALES (est): 588.66K **Privately Held**
Web: www.llshutters.com
SIC: 2431 Window shutters, wood

(P-2613)
LEEPERS WOOD TURNING CO INC (PA)
Also Called: Leeper's Stair Products
341 Bonnie Cir Ste 104 (92878-5182)
P.O. Box 17098 (90807-7098)
PHONE..............................562 422-6525
Michael Skinner, *Pr*
Barbara Skinner, *
Molly Rubio, *
◆ EMP: 38 EST: 1946
SQ FT: 29,000
SALES (est): 5.31MM
SALES (corp-wide): 5.31MM **Privately Held**
Web: www.ljsmith.com
SIC: 2431 Staircases and stairs, wood

(P-2614)
MASONITE ENTRY DOOR CORP
25100 Globe St (92551-9528)
PHONE..............................951 243-2261
Lawrence Repar, *Pr*
▲ EMP: 18 EST: 2006
SALES (est): 352.99K **Privately Held**
SIC: 2431 Doors, wood

(P-2615)
MILLCRAFT INC
2850 E White Star Ave (92806-2517)
PHONE..............................714 632-9621
Lars Eppick, *Pr*
Ray Pfeifer, *
Philip De Marco, *
Reginald Skipcott, *
EMP: 70 EST: 1983
SQ FT: 34,000
SALES (est): 5.19MM **Privately Held**
Web: www.millcraft.com
SIC: 2431 2434 Doors, wood; Wood kitchen cabinets

(P-2616)
MILLER WOODWORKING INC
1429 259th St (90710-3326)
PHONE..............................310 257-6806
Steve Miller, *Pr*
EMP: 20 EST: 1986
SQ FT: 17,000
SALES (est): 4.73MM **Privately Held**
Web: www.millerwoodworking.com
SIC: 2431 Millwork

(P-2617)
MILLWORKS BY DESIGN INC
4525 Runway St (93063-3479)
PHONE..............................818 597-1326
Daniel S Parish, *CEO*
Zachary D Eglit, *Pr*
▲ EMP: 44 EST: 2007
SALES (est): 5.27MM **Privately Held**
Web: www.millworksbydesign.com
SIC: 2431 Millwork

(P-2618)
MOLDINGS PLUS INC
1856 S Grove Ave (91761-5613)
PHONE..............................909 947-3310
Robert Bryant, *Pr*
Steve Totri, *VP*
▲ EMP: 20 EST: 1972
SQ FT: 13,500
SALES (est): 2.43MM **Privately Held**
Web: www.moldingsplus.com
SIC: 2431 Moldings, wood: unfinished and prefinished

(P-2619)
MTD KITCHEN INC
13213 Sherman Way (91605-4649)
PHONE..............................818 764-2254
Gil Alkoby, *CEO*
EMP: 85 EST: 2012
SALES (est): 7.24MM **Privately Held**
Web: www.mtdkitchen.com
SIC: 2431 2441 1799 2434 Millwork; Cases, wood; Kitchen cabinet installation; Vanities, bathroom: wood

(P-2620)
NEWMAN BROS CALIFORNIA INC (PA)
Also Called: A-1 Grit Co
1901 Massachusetts Ave (92507-2618)
P.O. Box 5675 (92517-5675)
PHONE..............................951 782-0102
Harold Newman, *CEO*
EMP: 19 EST: 1973
SALES (est): 2.39MM **Privately Held**
Web: www.a1grit.com
SIC: 2431 3291 5199 8711 Millwork; Grit, steel; Architects' supplies (non-durable); Consulting engineer

(P-2621)
NORTHWESTERN INC
10153 1/2 Riverside Dr # 250 (91602-2561)
PHONE..............................818 786-1581
▲ EMP: 40
SIC: 2431 Woodwork, interior and ornamental, nec

(P-2622)
NOVO MANUFACTURING LLC
25956 Commercentre Dr (92630-8815)
PHONE..............................949 609-0544
Danny Umemoto, *Mgr*
EMP: 20
SALES (corp-wide): 805.03MM **Privately Held**
Web: www.ljsmith.com
SIC: 2431 Millwork
HQ: Novo Manufacturing, Llc
35280 Scio Bowerston Rd
Bowerston OH
740 269-9515

(P-2623)
OHLINE CORPORATION
1930 W 139th St (90249-2408)
PHONE..............................310 327-4630
EMP: 33

SIC: 2431 Door shutters, wood

(P-2624)
OLD ENGLISH MIL WOODWORKS INC (PA)
Also Called: Old English Mil & Woodworks
27772 Avenue Scott (91355-3417)
PHONE..............................661 294-9171
Lay Cho, *Pr*
Edmond Cho, *
EMP: 30 EST: 1977
SQ FT: 30,000
SALES (est): 4.35MM
SALES (corp-wide): 4.35MM **Privately Held**
Web: www.oldenglishmilling.com
SIC: 2431 2439 1751 Staircases and stairs, wood; Structural wood members, nec; Carpentry work

(P-2625)
ORANGE WOODWORKS INC
1215 N Parker St (92867-4613)
PHONE..............................714 997-2600
Jeff Mcmillian, *Pr*
EMP: 45 EST: 1984
SQ FT: 120,000
SALES (est): 5.25MM **Privately Held**
Web: www.orangewoodworks.com
SIC: 2431 Millwork

(P-2626)
PACIFIC ARCHTECTURAL MLLWK INC
101 E Commwl Ave Ste A (92832)
PHONE..............................714 525-2059
EMP: 62
Web: www.pacmillwork.com
SIC: 2431 Window shutters, wood
PA: Pacific Architectural Millwork, Inc.
101 E Commwl Ave Ste A
Fullerton CA

(P-2627)
PACIFIC ARCHTECTURAL MLLWK INC
1435 Pioneer St (92821-3721)
PHONE..............................562 905-9282
EMP: 38
SALES (est): 1.4MM **Privately Held**
Web: www.pacmillwork.com
SIC: 2431 Millwork

(P-2628)
PACIFIC ARCHTECTURAL MLLWK INC
Also Called: Reveal Windows & Doors
1031 S Leslie St (90631-6843)
PHONE..............................562 905-3200
John Higman, *CEO*
Roy Gustin, *
Alice Vanberpool, *
◆ EMP: 100 EST: 2007
SALES (est): 13.34MM **Privately Held**
Web: www.pacmillwork.com
SIC: 2431 Planing mill, millwork

(P-2629)
PARAMOUNT WINDOWS & DOORS
Also Called: Paramount Window & Doors
723 W Mill St (92410-3347)
PHONE..............................909 888-4688
Don Mc Farland, *CEO*
EMP: 17 EST: 1999
SQ FT: 10,000
SALES (est): 1.79MM **Privately Held**

SIC: 2431 5211 Windows and window parts and trim, wood; Door and window products

(P-2630)
QUALITY SHUTTERS INC
3359 Chicago Ave Ste A (92507-6820)
PHONE..............................951 683-4939
Agustin Flores, *Owner*
EMP: 49 EST: 2002
SALES (est): 3.44MM **Privately Held**
SIC: 2431 Window frames, wood

(P-2631)
RENAISSNCE FRNCH DORS SASH INC (PA)
Also Called: Renaissance Doors & Windows
38 Segada (92688-2744)
PHONE..............................714 578-0090
Michael Jenkins, *Pr*
Thomas Jenkins, *
James Jenkins, *
EMP: 129 EST: 1982
SQ FT: 75,000
SALES (est): 9.26MM
SALES (corp-wide): 9.26MM **Privately Held**
SIC: 2431 Doors, wood

(P-2632)
SEMIHANDMADE LLC
3017 W Burbank Blvd (91505-2312)
PHONE..............................818 561-4350
John Mcdonald, *Prin*
EMP: 47 EST: 2014
SALES (est): 83.2K **Privately Held**
Web: www.semihandmade.com
SIC: 2431 Millwork

(P-2633)
SOUTH COAST STAIRS INC
30251 Tomas (92688-2123)
PHONE..............................949 858-1685
Chris Galloway, *Pr*
Mary Galloway, *
Tamera Selchau, *
EMP: 40 EST: 1980
SQ FT: 2,000
SALES (est): 2.78MM **Privately Held**
Web: www.scstairs.com
SIC: 2431 2439 5211 Staircases and stairs, wood; Structural wood members, nec; Millwork and lumber

(P-2634)
T M COBB COMPANY (PA)
Also Called: Haley Bros
500 Palmyrita Ave (92507-1801)
PHONE..............................951 248-2400
Jeffrey Cobb, *Pr*
Thomas J Cobb, *VP*
▲ EMP: 23 EST: 1947
SALES (est): 98.98MM
SALES (corp-wide): 98.98MM **Privately Held**
Web: www.tmcobb.com
SIC: 2431 3442 Door frames, wood; Window and door frames

(P-2635)
TABER COMPANY INC
121 Waterworks Way Ste 100 (92618-7719)
PHONE..............................714 543-7100
Brian Taber, *Pr*
EMP: 65 EST: 2002
SALES (est): 22.63MM **Privately Held**
Web: www.taberco.net
SIC: 2431 Millwork

(P-2636)

TALBERT ARCHTCTRAL PANL DOOR I
711 S Stimson Ave (91745-1627)
PHONE..............................714 671-9700
Jeff Tustin, *Pr*
Nick Parrino, *
Angie Talbert, *Corporate Secretary**
Heidi Gordon Ctrl, *Prin*
EMP: 65 EST: 2005
SALES (est): 18MM **Privately Held**
Web: www.talbertusa.com
SIC: 2431 Millwork

(P-2637)

THE ENKEBOLL CO
Also Called: Enkeboll Design
16506 Avalon Blvd (90746-1007)
PHONE..............................310 532-1400
EMP: 27 EST: 1955
SALES (est): 3.25MM **Privately Held**
Web: www.enkebolldesigns.com
SIC: 2431 Ornamental woodwork: cornices, mantels, etc.

(P-2638)

TRAVIS-AMERICAN GROUP LLC
Also Called: Travis Industries
11450 Sheldon St (91352-1121)
PHONE..............................714 258-1200
Thomas D Bell, *Pr*
Stephen Saponaro, *
Lyle Zastrow, *
Robert Kincaid, *
Robert Levine, *
EMP: 21 EST: 1978
SQ FT: 5,300
SALES (est): 747.84K **Privately Held**
SIC: 2431 2499 2426 2591 Moldings, wood: unfinished and prefinished; Veneer work, inlaid; Furniture stock and parts, hardwood; Venetian blinds

(P-2639)

TRINITY WOODWORKS INC
2620 Temple Heights Dr (92056-3512)
PHONE..............................760 639-5351
Jeffrey D Hollenbeck, *CEO*
EMP: 23 EST: 2011
SALES (est): 4.21MM **Privately Held**
Web: www.trinitywoodworksinc.com
SIC: 2431 Millwork

(P-2640)

W B POWELL INC
630 Parkridge Ave (92860-3124)
PHONE..............................951 270-0095
Charles G Mayhew, *CEO*
Chuck Mayhew, *
Doug Westra, *
EMP: 57 EST: 1993
SALES (est): 12.79MM
SALES (corp-wide): 86.81MM **Privately Held**
Web: www.wbpowell.com
SIC: 2431 2439 Millwork; Structural wood members, nec
PA: Plymold, Inc.
    615 Centennial Dr
    Kenyon MN
    507 789-5111

(P-2641)

WESTERN INTEGRATED MTLS INC (PA)
3310 E 59th St (90805-4504)
PHONE..............................562 634-2823
Larry Farrah, *Pr*
Edward G Farrah, *

Jim Halbrook, *
Alex Rojas, *
Debra Price, *
▲ EMP: 30 EST: 1975
SQ FT: 20,000
SALES (est): 5.36MM
SALES (corp-wide): 5.36MM **Privately Held**
Web: www.aluminumdoorframes.com
SIC: 2431 3442 Millwork; Window and door frames

(P-2642)

WOODWORK PIONEERS CORP
1757 S Claudina Way (92805-6544)
PHONE..............................714 991-1017
Karina Avalos, *Pr*
EMP: 50 EST: 2016
SALES (est): 2.45MM **Privately Held**
Web: www.woodworkpioneers.com
SIC: 2431 Millwork

(P-2643)

WW WOODWORKS
9771 Cedar St (92344-0563)
PHONE..............................760 887-4708
Timothy Wilson, *Prin*
EMP: 32 EST: 2010
SALES (est): 167.48K **Privately Held**
SIC: 2431 Millwork

2434 Wood Kitchen Cabinets

(P-2644)

ACCURATE LAMINATED PDTS INC
1826 Dawns Way (92831-5323)
PHONE..............................714 632-2773
Daniel Dunn, *Pr*
Patricia Dunn, *
EMP: 30 EST: 1989
SQ FT: 5,000
SALES (est): 4.04MM **Privately Held**
Web: www.accuratelaminated.com
SIC: 2434 Wood kitchen cabinets

(P-2645)

AMERICAN WOODMARK CORPORATION
Also Called: RSI Home Products
400 E Orangethorpe Ave (92801-1046)
PHONE..............................714 449-2200
EMP: 334
SALES (corp-wide): 2.07B **Publicly Held**
Web: www.americanwoodmark.com
SIC: 2434 Vanities, bathroom: wood
PA: American Woodmark Corporation
    561 Shady Elm Rd
    Winchester VA
    540 665-9100

(P-2646)

ARCADIA CABINETRY LLC
5467 Brooks St (91763-4563)
PHONE..............................909 550-0074
Kathy Massey, *Prin*
EMP: 17 EST: 2018
SALES (est): 951.24K **Privately Held**
SIC: 2434 Wood kitchen cabinets

(P-2647)

ARTCRAFTERS CABINETS
5446 Cleon Ave (91601-2897)
PHONE..............................818 752-8960
Jack R Walter, *Pr*
Sharon E Walter, *
EMP: 50 EST: 1949
SQ FT: 20,000

SALES (est): 3.35MM **Privately Held**
Web: www.artcrafter.com
SIC: 2434 2521 2431 Wood kitchen cabinets ; Wood office furniture; Millwork

(P-2648)

B YOUNG ENTERPRISES INC
Also Called: Mission Vly Cab / Counter Tech
12254 Iavelli Way (92064-6818)
PHONE..............................858 748-0935
EMP: 75
SIC: 2434 2521 5031 5211 Wood kitchen cabinets; Cabinets, office: wood; Kitchen cabinets; Cabinets, kitchen

(P-2649)

BROMACK COMPANY
3005 Humboldt St (90031-1830)
PHONE..............................323 227-5000
Kurt Webster, *Managing Member*
Kurt Webster, *Prin*
Brown Mcpherson Iii, *Prin*
EMP: 24 EST: 2010
SALES (est): 1.02MM **Privately Held**
SIC: 2434 Wood kitchen cabinets

(P-2650)

CABINETS 2000 LLC
11100 Firestone Blvd (90650-2269)
PHONE..............................562 868-0909
Frank Hamadani, *Ch*
Nematollah Abdollahi, *
Sherwood Prusso, *
Azam Abdollahi, *
Sue Abdollahi, *
EMP: 180 EST: 1988
SQ FT: 103,000
SALES (est): 27.21MM
SALES (corp-wide): 2.54B **Privately Held**
Web: www.cabinets2000.com
SIC: 2434 1751 Wood kitchen cabinets; Cabinet and finish carpentry
PA: Cabinetworks Group, Inc.
    20000 Victor Pkwy Ste 100
    Livonia MI
    734 205-4600

(P-2651)

CABINETS BY PRCISION WORKS INC
81101 Indio Blvd Ste D22 (92201-1922)
PHONE..............................760 342-1133
EMP: 50 EST: 1993
SQ FT: 16,000
SALES (est): 4.8MM **Privately Held**
Web: www.cabinetsbyprecision.com
SIC: 2434 2431 Wood kitchen cabinets; Millwork

(P-2652)

CABINETS R US
1240 N Fee Ana St (92807-1817)
PHONE..............................562 483-6886
◆ EMP: 20 EST: 2013
SALES (est): 1.56MM **Privately Held**
Web: www.cabinetsrus.us
SIC: 2434 Wood kitchen cabinets

(P-2653)

CALIFORNIA WOODWORKING INC
1726 Ives Ave (93033-4072)
PHONE..............................805 982-9090
Edward Vickery, *Pr*
Lucas Vickery, *
Susan Vickery, *
EMP: 30 EST: 1990
SQ FT: 8,000
SALES (est): 3.86MM **Privately Held**

Web: www.calwoodinc.com
SIC: 2434 Wood kitchen cabinets

(P-2654)

CALIFRNIA DSGNERS CHICE CSTM C
547 Constitution Ave Ste F (93012-8572)
PHONE..............................805 987-5820
Mark Mulchay, *Pr*
Russell Leavitt, *
EMP: 38 EST: 1989
SALES (est): 5MM **Privately Held**
Web: www.cdcc-inc.com
SIC: 2434 Wood kitchen cabinets

(P-2655)

CORONA MILLWORKS COMPANY (PA)
5572 Edison Ave (91710-6936)
PHONE..............................909 606-3288
Jose Corona, *CEO*
▲ EMP: 63 EST: 1995
SQ FT: 8,700
SALES (est): 22.88MM
SALES (corp-wide): 22.88MM **Privately Held**
Web: www.coronamillworks.com
SIC: 2434 Wood kitchen cabinets

(P-2656)

DREES WOOD PRODUCTS INC (PA)
14003 Orange Ave (90723-2017)
PHONE..............................562 633-7337
Ed Drees, *CEO*
EMP: 50 EST: 1982
SALES (est): 10.61MM
SALES (corp-wide): 10.61MM **Privately Held**
Web: www.dreeswoodproducts.com
SIC: 2434 Wood kitchen cabinets

(P-2657)

ELITE STONE & CABINET INC
1655 E Mission Blvd (91766-2321)
PHONE..............................909 629-6988
Yiyong Huang, *CEO*
EMP: 30 EST: 2015
SALES (est): 2.44MM **Privately Held**
Web: www.elitestonegroup.com
SIC: 2434 5032 1741 Wood kitchen cabinets ; Building stone; Stone masonry

(P-2658)

EXCEL CABINETS INC
225 Jason Ct (92879-6199)
PHONE..............................951 279-4545
Charles W Ketzel, *CEO*
Kevin Ketzel, *
Sandra Ketzel, *
▲ EMP: 35 EST: 1990
SALES (est): 5.54MM **Privately Held**
Web: www.excelcabinetsinc.com
SIC: 2434 Wood kitchen cabinets

(P-2659)

FINISHING TOUCH MOULDING INC
6190 Corte Del Cedro (92011-1515)
PHONE..............................760 444-1019
Roland Chaney, *Pr*
EMP: 55 EST: 2013
SALES (est): 4.82MM **Privately Held**
Web: www.ftmillwork.com
SIC: 2434 1751 Wood kitchen cabinets; Carpentry work

(P-2660)

HOLLANDS CUSTOM CABINETS INC

14511 Olde Highway 80 (92021-2877)
PHONE................................619 443-6081
Robert Holland, *Managing Member*
Robert Holland, *Pr*
Jed Richard, *
EMP: 38 **EST:** 1977
SQ FT: 10,000
SALES (est): 4.87MM **Privately Held**
Web: www.hollandscustomcabinets.com
SIC: 2434 Wood kitchen cabinets

(P-2661)

I AND E CABINETS INC

14660 Raymer St (91405-1217)
PHONE................................818 933-6480
Israel Chlomovitz, *CEO*
Ettie Chlomovitz, *
EMP: 34 **EST:** 1981
SQ FT: 9,000
SALES (est): 2.4MM **Privately Held**
Web: www.iecabinets.com
SIC: 2434 Wood kitchen cabinets

(P-2662)

K & Z CABINET CO INC

1450 S Grove Ave (91761-4523)
PHONE................................909 947-3567
Dennis Chan, *Pr*
EMP: 60 **EST:** 1975
SQ FT: 59,000
SALES (est): 10.13MM **Privately Held**
Web: www.kzcabt.com
SIC: 2434 2431 Wood kitchen cabinets;
Millwork

(P-2663)

KITCHEN PRO CABINETRY INC

8910 Quartz Ave (91324-3339)
PHONE................................877 210-6361
Yaron Goren, *Pr*
Ben Guttman, *VP*
▼ **EMP:** 20 **EST:** 2006
SALES (est): 1.8MM **Privately Held**
Web: www.kpmoderncabinetry.com
SIC: 2434 Wood kitchen cabinets

(P-2664)

KOBIS WINDOWS & DOORS MFG INC

7326 Laurel Canyon Blvd (91605-3710)
PHONE................................818 764-6400
Kobi Louria, *CEO*
▲ **EMP:** 25 **EST:** 1999
SALES (est): 2.62MM **Privately Held**
Web: www.kobiwindows.net
SIC: 2434 2431 1522 Vanities, bathroom:
wood; Millwork; Residential construction,
nec

(P-2665)

LA BATH VANITY INC (PA)

1071 W 9th St (91786-5702)
PHONE................................909 303-3323
EMP: 18 **EST:** 2018
SALES (est): 1.72MM **Privately Held**
SIC: 2434 Vanities, bathroom: wood

(P-2666)

MASTERBRAND CABINETS LLC

3700 S Riverside Ave (92324-3329)
PHONE................................951 682-1535
Michael Mejia, *Mgr*
EMP: 46
SALES (corp-wide): 3.28B **Publicly Held**
Web: www.masterbrand.com

SIC: 2434 Wood kitchen cabinets
HQ: Masterbrand Cabinets Llc
1 Masterbrand Cabinets Dr
Jasper IN
812 482-2527

(P-2667)

MCCONNELL CABINETS INC

Also Called: Coastal Wood Products
13110 Louden Ln (91746-1507)
PHONE................................626 937-2200
▲ **EMP:** 740
Web: www.mcconnellinc.com
SIC: 2434 Wood kitchen cabinets

(P-2668)

MIKADA CABINETS LLC

Also Called: Mikada Cabinets
11777 San Vicente Blvd (90049-5067)
PHONE................................713 681-6116
Tom Moodie, *CEO*
Kevin Horton, *
Monette Stephens, *
Debbie Thompson, *
EMP: 60 **EST:** 1965
SALES (est): 9.23MM **Privately Held**
Web: www.mikadacabinets.com
SIC: 2434 Wood kitchen cabinets

(P-2669)

MULTITASKR

2576 Catamaran Way (91914-4533)
PHONE................................619 391-3371
EMP: 42 **EST:** 2020
SALES (est): 2.84MM **Privately Held**
Web: www.gomultitaskr.com
SIC: 2434 1799 1522 1521 Wood kitchen
cabinets; Special trade contractors, nec;
Residential construction, nec; Single-family
housing construction

(P-2670)

N K CABINETS INC

Also Called: Universal Custom Cabinets
11015 Glenoaks Blvd Ste 22 (91331-1646)
PHONE................................818 897-7909
Norik Kagramanyan, *CEO*
Norik Kayramanyon, *
EMP: 26 **EST:** 1998
SALES (est): 2.18MM **Privately Held**
Web: www.nkcabinets.com
SIC: 2434 Wood kitchen cabinets

(P-2671)

PRECISION WOODWORKS

10 Hammond Ste 300 (92618-1626)
PHONE................................949 215-1185
EMP: 17 **EST:** 2018
SALES (est): 195.92K **Privately Held**
Web: www.precisionwoodworksoc.com
SIC: 2434 Wood kitchen cabinets

(P-2672)

PROFESSIONAL CABINET SOLUTIONS

2111 Eastridge Ave (92507-0778)
PHONE................................909 614-2900
EMP: 139
SALES (corp-wide): 2.07B **Publicly Held**
Web: www.pcscabinetry.com
SIC: 2434 Wood kitchen cabinets
HQ: Professional Cabinet Solutions
2111 Eastridge Ave
Riverside CA

(P-2673)

PROFESSIONAL CABINET SOLUTIONS (DH)

2111 Eastridge Ave (92507-0778)

PHONE................................909 614-2900
EMP: 111 **EST:** 1996
SALES (est): 39.63MM
SALES (corp-wide): 2.07B **Publicly Held**
Web: www.pcscabinetry.com
SIC: 2434 Wood kitchen cabinets
HQ: Rsi Home Products Llc
400 E Orangethorpe Ave
Anaheim CA
714 449-2200

(P-2674)

QUALITY CABINET AND FIXTURE CO (HQ)

7955 Saint Andrews Ave (92154-8224)
PHONE................................619 266-1011
Michael J Floyd, *CEO*
Donald Paradise, *
Tim Paradise, *
Andrew Meek, *
Nicholas P Willems, *
▲ **EMP:** 23 **EST:** 1966
SQ FT: 55,000
SALES (est): 5.16MM
SALES (corp-wide): 30.54MM **Privately Held**
SIC: 2434 Wood kitchen cabinets
PA: Glenn Rieder, Llc
6520 W Becher Pl
Milwaukee WI
414 449-2888

(P-2675)

REBORN CABINETS LLC (PA)

Also Called: Reborn Bath Solutions
5515 E La Palma Ave Ste 250
(92807-2131)
PHONE................................714 630-2220
TOLL FREE: 800
Vincent Nardolillo, *Managing Member*
Anthony Nardolillo, *
EMP: 484 **EST:** 1983
SALES (est): 119.18MM
SALES (corp-wide): 119.18MM **Privately Held**
Web: www.reborncabinets.com
SIC: 2434 2431 Wood kitchen cabinets;
Millwork

(P-2676)

ROYAL CABINETS INC

Also Called: Royal Cabinets
1299 E Phillips Blvd (91766-5429)
PHONE................................909 629-8565
Clay Smith, *Pr*
Bill Roan, *
▲ **EMP:** 600 **EST:** 1984
SQ FT: 70,000
SALES (est): 49.46MM **Privately Held**
Web: www.royalcabinets.com
SIC: 2434 2511 Wood kitchen cabinets;
Wood household furniture

(P-2677)

ROYAL INDUSTRIES INC

Also Called: Royal Cabinets
1299 E Phillips Blvd (91766-5429)
PHONE................................909 629-8565
Clay R Smith, *CEO*
Dan Mcginn, *Pr*
Kathy Goodrow, *
Gus Danjoi, *
EMP: 130 **EST:** 1985
SALES (est): 19.17MM **Privately Held**
Web: www.royalcabinets.com
SIC: 2434 Vanities, bathroom: wood

(P-2678)

SANTA MONICA MILLWORKS

2568 Channel Dr (93003-4563)

PHONE................................805 643-0010
William Lunche, *Pr*
EMP: 20 **EST:** 1996
SALES (est): 1.23MM **Privately Held**
SIC: 2434 Wood kitchen cabinets

(P-2679)

SOUTHCOAST CABINET INC (PA)

755 Pinefalls Ave (91789-3027)
PHONE................................909 594-3089
Dante M Senese, *CEO*
John Lopez, *
EMP: 42 **EST:** 1983
SQ FT: 108,000
SALES (est): 8.56MM
SALES (corp-wide): 8.56MM **Privately Held**
Web: www.southcoastcabinet.com
SIC: 2434 Wood kitchen cabinets

(P-2680)

TESSA MIA CORP

9565 Vassar Ave (91311-4141)
PHONE................................877 740-5757
Zack Karni, *CEO*
Yom Tov Yohanan, *
EMP: 27 **EST:** 2019
SALES (est): 5.5MM **Privately Held**
SIC: 2434 Wood kitchen cabinets

(P-2681)

ULTRA BUILT KITCHENS INC

1814 E 43rd St (90058-1517)
PHONE................................323 232-3362
Iris Yanes, *Pr*
Eduardo Yanes, *
Daisy Blanco, *
EMP: 28 **EST:** 1993
SQ FT: 18,000
SALES (est): 2.35MM **Privately Held**
Web: www.ultrabuiltkitchens.net
SIC: 2434 Vanities, bathroom: wood

(P-2682)

UNITED CABINET COMPANY INC

1510 S Mountain View Ave (92408-3134)
PHONE................................909 796-3015
Dennis Rice, *Pr*
Jeffery Westrom, *VP*
Doris Rice, *Sec*
Gayle L Rice, *Stockholder*
EMP: 20 **EST:** 1963
SQ FT: 10,000
SALES (est): 2.36MM **Privately Held**
SIC: 2434 Wood kitchen cabinets

(P-2683)

VCSD INC

Also Called: Valley Cabinet
585 Vernon Way (92020-1934)
PHONE................................619 579-6886
Larry Doyle, *Pr*
Susan Raymond, *
EMP: 49 **EST:** 2011
SALES (est): 4.72MM **Privately Held**
Web: www.vcsdinc.com
SIC: 2434 Wood kitchen cabinets

(P-2684)

W L RUBOTTOM CO

320 W Lewis St (93001-1335)
PHONE................................805 648-6943
Gary Mccoy, *Pr*
Lawrence Rubottom, *
EMP: 55 **EST:** 1946
SQ FT: 40,000
SALES (est): 4.35MM **Privately Held**

P
R
O
D
U
C
T
S
&
S
V
C
S

Web: www.wlrubottom.com
SIC: **2434** Wood kitchen cabinets

(P-2685)
WOODPECKER CABINETS INC
21512 Nordhoff St (91311-5822)
PHONE..............................310 404-4805
Izaac Sananes, *CEO*
River Cook, *Mgr*
EMP: 20 **EST:** 2005
SALES (est): 1.76MM **Privately Held**
SIC: **2434** 1799 Wood kitchen cabinets;
  Kitchen cabinet installation

(P-2686)
WYNDHAM COLLECTION LLC
1175 Aviation Pl (91340-1460)
PHONE..............................888 522-8476
Martin Symes, *Managing Member*
EMP: 26 **EST:** 2011
SQ FT: 100,000
SALES (est): 2.46MM **Privately Held**
Web: www.wyndhamcollection.com
SIC: **2434** Vanities, bathroom: wood

2435 Hardwood Veneer And Plywood

(P-2687)
G - L VENEER CO INC (PA)
2224 E Slauson Ave (90255-2728)
PHONE..............................323 582-5203
▲ **EMP:** 96 **EST:** 1977
SALES (est): 17.99MM
SALES (corp-wide): 17.99MM **Privately Held**
Web: www.glveneer.com
SIC: **2435** Hardwood veneer and plywood

(P-2688)
GENERAL VENEER MFG CO
8652 Otis St (90280-3220)
P.O. Box 1607 (90280-1607)
PHONE..............................323 564-2661
William Dewitt, *Pr*
Ed Bewitt, *
Douglas Bradley, *
EMP: 50 **EST:** 1942
SQ FT: 200,000
SALES (est): 8.74MM **Privately Held**
Web: www.generalveneer.com
SIC: **2435** 3365 Hardwood veneer and plywood; Aerospace castings, aluminum

(P-2689)
JC HANSCOM INC
Also Called: Panel Works
10472 Caribou Way (92782-1470)
PHONE..............................562 789-9955
John C Hanscom, *Pr*
Marsha Hanscom, *VP*
EMP: 18 **EST:** 1999
SALES (est): 444.5K **Privately Held**
SIC: **2435** Panels, hardwood plywood

(P-2690)
PLYCRAFT INDUSTRIES INC
Also Called: Concepts & Wood
2100 E Slauson Ave (90255-2727)
PHONE..............................323 587-8101
Ashley Joffe, *Pr*
Nathan Joffe, *
Donald R Greenberg, *
▲ **EMP:** 180 **EST:** 1979
SQ FT: 71,187
SALES (est): 7.93MM **Privately Held**
Web: www.plycraft.com

SIC: **2435** Plywood, hardwood or hardwood faced

(P-2691)
SONORA FACE CO
5233 Randolph St (90270-3448)
PHONE..............................323 560-8188
Ossiel Calvillo, *Pr*
▲ **EMP:** 25 **EST:** 1984
SQ FT: 20,000
SALES (est): 2.48MM **Privately Held**
Web: sonora-face-co.hub.biz
SIC: **2435** Veneer stock, hardwood

(P-2692)
SWANER HARDWOOD CO INC (PA)
5 W Magnolia Blvd (91502-1719)
PHONE..............................818 953-5350
Gary Swaner, *Pr*
Keith M Swaner, *
Beverly Swaner, *
Stephen Haag, *
▲ **EMP:** 70 **EST:** 1967
SQ FT: 4,500
SALES (est): 36.61MM
SALES (corp-wide): 36.61MM **Privately Held**
Web: www.swanerhardwood.com
SIC: **2435** 5031 Hardwood veneer and plywood; Lumber: rough, dressed, and finished

2439 Structural Wood Members, Nec

(P-2693)
BROWN HNYCUTT TRUSS SYSTEMS IN
16775 Smoke Tree St (92345-6165)
P.O. Box 401804 (92340-1804)
PHONE..............................760 244-8887
Michael Hough, *Pr*
Pedro Sanchez, *Stockholder*
EMP: 18 **EST:** 1968
SQ FT: 1,800
SALES (est): 939.29K **Privately Held**
SIC: **2439** Trusses, wooden roof

(P-2694)
CALIFORNIA TRUSFRAME LLC (HQ)
Also Called: Ctf
23665 Cajalco Rd (92570-8181)
PHONE..............................951 350-4880
EMP: 90 **EST:** 2011
SALES (est): 324.09MM
SALES (corp-wide): 22.73B **Publicly Held**
Web: www.bldr.com
SIC: **2439** Trusses, wooden roof
PA: Builders Firstsource, Inc.
  6031 Connection Dr # 400
  Irving TX
  214 880-3500

(P-2695)
CALIFORNIA TRUSFRAME LLC
23447 Cajalco Rd (92570-8435)
PHONE..............................951 657-7491
EMP: 206
SALES (corp-wide): 22.73B **Publicly Held**
Web: www.bldr.com
SIC: **2439** Trusses, wooden roof
HQ: California Trusframe, Llc
  23665 Cajalco Rd
  Perris CA

(P-2696)
CALIFORNIA TRUSS COMPANY (PA)
23665 Cajalco Rd (92570-8181)
PHONE..............................951 657-7491
Kenneth M Cloyd, *Pr*
Mike Ruede, *VP*
Jim Butler, *CFO*
EMP: 87 **EST:** 1970
SQ FT: 5,000
SALES (est): 19.37MM
SALES (corp-wide): 19.37MM **Privately Held**
Web: www.caltruss.com
SIC: **2439** Trusses, wooden roof

(P-2697)
ESCONDIDO ROOF TRUSS CO INC
430 Via Vera Cruz (92078-1134)
P.O. Box 1625 (92079-1625)
PHONE..............................760 744-4040
TOLL FREE: 800
Howard M Brubeck, *Pr*
Howard E Brubeck, *Pr*
Robert Reynolds, *VP*
Wesley Carter, *Sec*
EMP: 18 **EST:** 1973
SQ FT: 130,000
SALES (est): 496.52K **Privately Held**
Web: www.escondidotruss.com
SIC: **2439** Trusses, wooden roof

(P-2698)
GOLDENWOOD TRUSS CORPORATION
11032 Nardo St (93004-3210)
PHONE..............................805 659-2520
Kevin Tollefson, *Pr*
Darin Ranson, *
Myron Hodgson, *
EMP: 80 **EST:** 1998
SALES (est): 9.74MM **Privately Held**
Web: www.goldenwoodtruss.com
SIC: **2439** Trusses, wooden roof

(P-2699)
HANSON TRUSS INC
13950 Yorba Ave (91710-5520)
PHONE..............................909 591-9256
Donald R Hanson, *Pr*
Tom Hanson, *
EMP: 300 **EST:** 1985
SQ FT: 4,000
SALES (est): 24.73MM **Privately Held**
SIC: **2439** Trusses, wooden roof

(P-2700)
HESPERIA HOLDING INC
9780 E Ave (92345-6174)
PHONE..............................760 244-8787
William Nalls, *Pr*
Mark Presgraves, *
Don Shimp, *
EMP: 74 **EST:** 2000
SALES (est): 5.69MM **Privately Held**
Web: www.hesperia.com
SIC: **2439** Structural wood members, nec

(P-2701)
INLAND TRUSS INC (PA)
275 W Rider St (92571-3225)
PHONE..............................951 300-1758
Dan Irwin, *Pr*
Ernie Castro, *
EMP: 66 **EST:** 1991
SQ FT: 1,200
SALES (est): 7MM **Privately Held**
Web: www.inlandempiretruss.com

SIC: **2439** Trusses, wooden roof

(P-2702)
SIMPSON STRONG-TIE COMPANY INC
12246 Holly St (92509-2314)
PHONE..............................714 871-8373
Dave Bastian, *Brnch Mgr*
EMP: 250
SQ FT: 40,845
SALES (corp-wide): 2.12B **Publicly Held**
Web: www.strongtie.com
SIC: **2439** 3429 Structural wood members, nec; Hardware, nec
HQ: Simpson Strong-Tie Company Inc.
  5956 W Las Positas Blvd
  Pleasanton CA
  925 560-9000

(P-2703)
SPATES FABRICATORS INC
Also Called: Spates Fabricators
85435 Middleton St (92274-9619)
PHONE..............................760 397-4122
Tom Spates, *Pr*
David Spates, *
Frankie Spates, *
EMP: 51 **EST:** 1976
SQ FT: 40,000
SALES (est): 9.52MM **Privately Held**
Web: www.spates.com
SIC: **2439** Trusses, except roof: laminated lumber

(P-2704)
T L TIMMERMAN CNSTR INC
Also Called: Timco
9845 Santa Fe Ave E (92345-6216)
P.O. Box 402563 (92340-2563)
PHONE..............................760 244-2532
Timothy L Timmerman, *Pr*
Anita Timmerman, *
EMP: 30 **EST:** 1976
SQ FT: 7,700
SALES (est): 2.15MM **Privately Held**
SIC: **2439** Trusses, wooden roof

(P-2705)
TRI STATE TRUSS CORPORATION
600 River Rd (92363)
P.O. Box 628 (92363-0628)
PHONE..............................760 326-3868
Richard C Huebner, *CEO*
Mike Terry, *Pr*
EMP: 31 **EST:** 1978
SQ FT: 1,500
SALES (est): 941.1K **Privately Held**
SIC: **2439** Trusses, wooden roof

(P-2706)
TRI-CO BUILDING SUPPLY INC
Also Called: Truspro
695 Obispo St (93434-1631)
P.O. Box 850 (93434-0850)
PHONE..............................805 343-2555
TOLL FREE: 800
Patrick A Herring Senior, *Pr*
Steve Herring, *
Memory Herring, *
EMP: 25 **EST:** 1975
SQ FT: 2,500
SALES (est): 2.04MM **Privately Held**
Web: www.truspro.com
SIC: **2439** Trusses, wooden roof

2441 Nailed Wood Boxes And Shook

(P-2707)
A & J INDUSTRIES INC
Also Called: A & J Manufacturing
1430 240th St (90710-1307)
P.O. Box 90596 (90009-0596)
PHONE..............................310 216-2170
TOLL FREE: 800
Patrick Doucette, CEO
Keith Bell, Sec
◆ EMP: 18 EST: 1945
SQ FT: 40,000
SALES (est): 2.61MM Privately Held
Web: www.ajcases.com
SIC: 2441 Chests and trunks, wood

(P-2708)
ARMORED GROUP INC
Also Called: Innerspace Cases
11555 Cantara St (91605-1652)
PHONE..............................818 767-3030
Louis Kaye, Pr
Loretta Kaye, Sec
EMP: 23 EST: 1986
SQ FT: 15,000
SALES (est): 1.76MM Privately Held
Web: www.innerspacecases.com
SIC: 2441 Cases, wood

(P-2709)
BASAW MANUFACTURING INC
Also Called: Basaw
13340 Raymer (91605-4101)
PHONE..............................818 765-6650
EMP: 22
SALES (corp-wide): 9.51MM Privately Held
Web: www.basaw.com
PA: Basaw Manufacturing, Inc.
11323 Hartland St
North Hollywood CA
818 765-6650
SIC: 2441 Shipping cases, wood: nailed or lock corner

(P-2710)
BASAW MANUFACTURING INC (PA)
Also Called: Basaw Manufacturing
11323 Hartland St (91605-6310)
PHONE..............................818 765-6650
Robert Allen, Pr
Hugh Mullen, *
Eleazar Padilla, *
Jorge Cea, *
Martha Rivera, *
▲ EMP: 32 EST: 1990
SALES (est): 9.51MM
SALES (corp-wide): 9.51MM Privately Held
Web: www.basaw.com
SIC: 2441 7389 Shipping cases, wood: nailed or lock corner; Packaging and labeling services

(P-2711)
CAL-COAST PKG & CRATING INC
2040 E 220th St (90810-1603)
PHONE..............................310 518-7215
Dale Loughry, Pr
▲ EMP: 35 EST: 1957
SQ FT: 58,000
SALES (est): 2.6MM Privately Held
Web: www.calcoastpacking.com

SIC: 2441 2449 Shipping cases, wood: nailed or lock corner; Wood containers, nec

(P-2712)
NELSON CASE CORPORATION
Also Called: Nelson Case
650 S Jefferson St Ste A (92870-6640)
PHONE..............................714 528-2215
Edward Bobadilla, CEO
John Bovadilla Junior, CEO
Virginia Sandburg, CFO
EMP: 20 EST: 1995
SALES (est): 2.43MM Privately Held
Web: www.nelsoncasecorp.com
SIC: 2441 5199 5099 2449 Packing cases, wood: nailed or lock corner; Bags, baskets, and cases; Carrying cases; Shipping cases, wood: wirebound

2448 Wood Pallets And Skids

(P-2713)
AAA PALLET RECYCLING & MFG INC
Also Called: AAA Pallet
23120 Oleander Ave (92570-5662)
PHONE..............................951 681-7748
EMP: 22 EST: 1994
SQ FT: 152,460
SALES (est): 5MM Privately Held
SIC: 2448 Pallets, wood

(P-2714)
ARNIES SUPPLY SERVICE LTD (PA)
1541 N Ditman Ave (90063-2501)
P.O. Box 26 (91754-0026)
PHONE..............................323 263-1696
Arnold Espino, Pr
Madeline Espino, *
Maria Espino, *
EMP: 25 EST: 1975
SALES (est): 4.4MM
SALES (corp-wide): 4.4MM Privately Held
Web: www.arniessupply.com
SIC: 2448 Pallets, wood

(P-2715)
COMMERCIAL LBR & PALLET CO INC (PA)
135 Long Ln (91746-2633)
PHONE..............................626 968-0631
Raymond Gutierrez, Pr
EMP: 150 EST: 1941
SQ FT: 10,000
SALES (est): 30.43MM
SALES (corp-wide): 30.43MM Privately Held
Web: www.clcpallets.com
SIC: 2448 5031 Pallets, wood; Lumber: rough, dressed, and finished

(P-2716)
CORTEZ PALLETS SERVICE INC (PA)
14739 Proctor Ave (91746-3203)
P.O. Box 2552 (91746-0552)
PHONE..............................626 961-9891
Salvadore Cortez, Pr
Julia Cortez, VP
Salvadore Cortez Junior, Sec
EMP: 18 EST: 1976
SQ FT: 2,000
SALES (est): 2.16MM
SALES (corp-wide): 2.16MM Privately Held
Web: www.industrypallets.com
SIC: 2448 Pallets, wood

(P-2717)
E VASQUEZ DISTRIBUTORS INC
Also Called: Oxnard Pallet Company
4524 E Pleasant Valley Rd (93033-2309)
P.O. Box 1748 (93032-1748)
PHONE..............................805 487-8458
EMP: 30 EST: 1989
SQ FT: 480
SALES (est): 4.59MM Privately Held
Web: www.oxnardpalletco.com
SIC: 2448 4214 Pallets, wood; Local trucking with storage

(P-2718)
G C PALLETS INC
5490 26th St (92509-2212)
PHONE..............................909 357-8515
Mayra Gaona, CEO
Sebastian Gaona, *
EMP: 30 EST: 2001
SALES (est): 2.45MM Privately Held
Web: www.gcpalletsusa.com
SIC: 2448 Pallets, wood

(P-2719)
HARDING CONTAINERS INTL INC
4000 Santa Fe Ave (90810-1832)
PHONE..............................310 549-7272
Victor Hsing, Pr
Keith R Mayer, VP
▲ EMP: 26 EST: 1992
SQ FT: 1,000
SALES (est): 971.63K Privately Held
SIC: 2448 Cargo containers, wood and wood with metal

(P-2720)
IFCO SYSTEMS US LLC
8950 Rochester Ave Ste 150 (91730-5541)
PHONE..............................909 484-4332
Mike Ellis, Prin
EMP: 56
Web: www.ifco.com
SIC: 2448 Pallets, wood
PA: Ifco Systems Us, Llc
3030 N Rocky Point Dr W # 300
Tampa FL

(P-2721)
PALLET MASTERS INC
655 E Florence Ave (90001-2319)
PHONE..............................323 758-1713
Stephen H Anderson, Pr
EMP: 55 EST: 1991
SQ FT: 105,000
SALES (est): 9.01MM Privately Held
Web: www.palletmasters.com
SIC: 2448 2441 2439 Pallets, wood; Boxes, wood; Structural wood members, nec

(P-2722)
PRIORITY PALLET INC
1060 E Third St (92223-3020)
PHONE..............................951 769-9399
Raymond Guiterrez, Pr
EMP: 19 EST: 1999
SALES (est): 1.45MM Privately Held
Web: www.clcpallets.com
SIC: 2448 Pallets, wood

(P-2723)
RAMIREZ PALLETS INC
8431 Sultana Ave (92335-3298)
PHONE..............................909 822-2066
Cresencio Ramirez, Pr
EMP: 35 EST: 1977
SALES (est): 2.65MM Privately Held
Web: www.ramirezpallets.com
SIC: 2448 Pallets, wood

(P-2724)
ROGER R CARUSO ENTERPRISES INC
Also Called: Century Pallets
2911 Norton Ave (90262-1810)
PHONE..............................714 778-6006
Roger R Caruso, Pr
Rose Caruso, Sec
▲ EMP: 20 EST: 1973
SQ FT: 92,000
SALES (est): 2.29MM Privately Held
Web: www.centurypallets.com
SIC: 2448 Pallets, wood

(P-2725)
ROYAL PALLETS INC
849 E 29th St (90011-2015)
PHONE..............................323 580-4364
EMP: 17
SALES (corp-wide): 259.08K Privately Held
SIC: 2448 Pallets, wood
PA: Royal Pallets, Inc.
2637 E El Segundo Blvd
Compton CA

(P-2726)
SATCO INC (PA)
Also Called: Satco
1601 E El Segundo Blvd (90245-4334)
PHONE..............................310 322-4719
Mike Proctor, CEO
Micheal Proctor, *
Vincent Voong, *
Richard Weis, *
▲ EMP: 125 EST: 1968
SQ FT: 27,000
SALES (est): 71.22MM
SALES (corp-wide): 71.22MM Privately Held
Web: www.satco-inc.com
SIC: 2448 3537 Pallets, wood and metal combination; Containers (metal), air cargo

(P-2727)
STANDARD LUMBER COMPANY INC (HQ)
Also Called: United Wholesale Lumber Co
27770 Entertainment Dr (91355-1092)
PHONE..............................559 651-2037
Thomas J Thayer, CEO
EMP: 35 EST: 1950
SQ FT: 10,000
SALES (est): 5.52MM
SALES (corp-wide): 222.6MM Privately Held
SIC: 2448 2441 Pallets, wood; Nailed wood boxes and shook
PA: Fruit Growers Supply Company Inc
27770 N Entrmt Dr Fl 3 Flr 3
Valencia CA
888 997-4855

(P-2728)
VOTAW WOOD PRODUCTS INC
Also Called: Pomona Box Co
301 W Imperial Hwy (90631-7263)
P.O. Box 536 (90633-0536)
PHONE..............................714 871-0932
EMP: 30 EST: 1929
SALES (est): 2.23MM Privately Held
Web: www.pomonabox.com
SIC: 2448 2441 5085 Pallets, wood; Boxes, wood; Boxes, crates, etc., other than paper

PRODUCTS & SVCS

2449 Wood Containers, Nec

(P-2729)
A & S CASE COMPANY INC
5260 Vineland Ave (91601-3221)
PHONE...............................800 394-6181
TOLL FREE: 800
FAX: 818 509-1397
EMP: 22
SQ FT: 21,000
SALES (est): 1.5MM **Privately Held**
Web: www.ascase.com
SIC: **2449** 3089 Shipping cases and drums,
wood: wirebound and plywood; Cases,
plastics

(P-2730)
APEX DRUM COMPANY INC
Also Called: Apex Container Services
6226 Ferguson Dr (90022-5399)
PHONE...............................323 721-8994
Abe Michlin, *CEO*
Sybil Flom, *Sec*
EMP: 19 EST: 1946
SQ FT: 40,000
SALES (est): 4.07MM **Privately Held**
Web: www.apexdrum.com
SIC: **2449** 5085 Containers, plywood and
veneer wood; Cooperage stock

(P-2731)
**FRANK KAMS & ASSOCIATES
INC**
Also Called: California Redwood Products
242 W Hanna St (92324-2772)
PHONE...............................909 382-0047
Frank L Kams, *CEO*
Eleanor Kams, *
▲ EMP: 25 EST: 1976
SQ FT: 44,700
SALES (est): 519.96K **Privately Held**
SIC: **2449** 5083 Rectangular boxes and
crates, wood; Lawn and garden machinery
and equipment

(P-2732)
GREIF INC
6001 S Eastern Ave (90040-3413)
PHONE...............................323 724-7500
EMP: 28
SALES (corp-wide): 6.35B **Publicly Held**
Web: www.greif.com
SIC: **2449** 2655 Shipping cases and drums,
wood: wirebound and plywood; Fiber cans,
drums, and similar products
PA: Greif, Inc.
425 Winter Rd
Delaware OH
740 549-6000

(P-2733)
PICNIC AT ASCOT INC
3237 W 131st St (90250-5514)
PHONE...............................310 674-3098
Paul Whitlock, *Pr*
Jill Brown, *
◆ EMP: 30 EST: 1992
SQ FT: 20,000
SALES (est): 2.75MM **Privately Held**
Web: www.picnicatascot.com
SIC: **2449** 5947 Baskets: fruit and vegetable,
round stave, till, etc.; Gift, novelty, and
souvenir shop

2451 Mobile Homes

(P-2734)
CAVCO INDUSTRIES INC
Also Called: Fleetwood Homes
7007 Jurupa Ave (92504-1015)
P.O. Box 49991 (92514-1991)
PHONE...............................951 688-5353
Mike Hayes, *Brnch Mgr*
EMP: 46
SALES (corp-wide): 2.14B **Publicly Held**
Web: www.cavcoindustries.com
SIC: **2451** 2452 Mobile homes;
Prefabricated buildings, wood
PA: Cavco Industries, Inc.
3636 N Central Ave # 1200
Phoenix AZ
602 256-6263

(P-2735)
**CHAMPION HOME BUILDERS
INC**
Also Called: Champion
7825 Fay Ave Ste 200 (92037-4270)
PHONE...............................858 456-3507
EMP: 56
SALES (corp-wide): 2.61B **Publicly Held**
Web: www.championhomes.com
SIC: **2451** Mobile homes, except recreational
HQ: Champion Home Builders, Inc.
755 W Big Beavr Rd # 1000
Troy MI
248 614-8200

(P-2736)
D-MAC INC
1105 E Discovery Ln (92801-1121)
PHONE...............................714 808-3918
David A Wade, *Prin*
EMP: 26 EST: 1998
SALES (est): 4.42MM **Privately Held**
Web: www.d-macinc.com
SIC: **2451** 5039 5032 Mobile home frames;
Structural assemblies, prefabricated: non-
wood; Paving materials

(P-2737)
DVELE INC
25525 Redlands Blvd (92354-2009)
P.O. Box 1710 (92354-0150)
PHONE...............................909 796-2561
EMP: 45
SALES (corp-wide): 4.52MM **Privately
Held**
Web: www.dvele.com
SIC: **2451** 2452 Mobile homes, except
recreational; Prefabricated buildings, wood
PA: Dvele, Inc.
5521 La Jolla Blvd
La Jolla CA

(P-2738)
DVELE OMEGA CORPORATION
Also Called: Hallmark Southwest
25525 Redlands Blvd (92354-2009)
P.O. Box 1710 (92354-0150)
PHONE...............................909 796-2561
Luca Brammer, *Pr*
EMP: 100 EST: 2018
SQ FT: 5,000
SALES (est): 9.73MM **Privately Held**
Web: www.dvele.com
SIC: **2451** 2452 Mobile homes, personal or
private use; Prefabricated wood buildings

(P-2739)
**FLEETWOOD HOMES
CALIFORNIA INC (DH)**
Also Called: Fleetwood Homes
7007 Jurupa Ave (92504-1015)
P.O. Box 7638 (92513-7638)
PHONE...............................951 351-2494
Elvin Smith, *Pr*
Boyd R Plowman, *Ex VP*
Forrest D Theobald, *Sr VP*
Lyle N Larkin, *VP*
Roger L Howsmon, *Sr VP*
▲ EMP: 176 EST: 1963
SQ FT: 262,900
SALES (est): 53.85MM **Privately Held**
SIC: **2451** Mobile homes
HQ: Fleetwood Enterprises, Inc.
1351 Pomona Rd Ste 230
Corona CA
951 354-3000

(P-2740)
**FLEETWOOD HOMES OF
FLORIDA (DH)**
Also Called: Fleetwood Homes
3125 Myers St (92503-5527)
P.O. Box 7638 (92513-7638)
PHONE...............................909 261-4274
Edward B Caudill, *Pr*
Boyd R Plowman, *Ex VP*
Forrest D Theobald, *Sr VP*
Lyle N Larkin, *VP*
▲ EMP: 242 EST: 1970
SQ FT: 262,900
SALES (est): 9.76MM **Privately Held**
SIC: **2451** Mobile homes, except recreational
HQ: Fleetwood Enterprises, Inc.
1351 Pomona Rd Ste 230
Corona CA
951 354-3000

(P-2741)
**FLEETWOOD HOMES OF
KENTUCKY (DH)**
Also Called: Fleetwood Homes
1351 Pomona Rd Ste 230 (92882-7165)
PHONE...............................800 688-1745
Elden L Smith, *Prin*
Edward B Caudill, *Prin*
Boyd R Plowman, *Ex VP*
Forrest D Theobald, *Sr VP*
Lyle N Larkin, *VP*
EMP: 22 EST: 1998
SALES (est): 1.93MM **Privately Held**
SIC: **2451** Mobile homes
HQ: Fleetwood Enterprises, Inc.
1351 Pomona Rd Ste 230
Corona CA
951 354-3000

(P-2742)
SKYLINE HOMES INC
499 W Esplanade Ave (92583-5001)
P.O. Box 670 (92581-0670)
PHONE...............................951 654-9321
Jim Claverie, *Genl Mgr*
EMP: 115
SALES (corp-wide): 2.61B **Publicly Held**
Web: www.skylinehomes.com
SIC: **2451** Mobile homes
HQ: Skyline Homes, Inc.
2520 Bypass Rd
Elkhart IN
574 294-6521

2452 Prefabricated Wood Buildings

(P-2743)
**APPLIED POLYTECH SYSTEMS
INC**
Also Called: A P S
26000 Springbrook Ave Ste 102
(91350-2590)
PHONE...............................818 504-9261
Christine Wagner, *Pr*
EMP: 30 EST: 1988
SQ FT: 6,000
SALES (est): 2.43MM **Privately Held**
Web: www.apsincprecast.com
SIC: **2452** Prefabricated wood buildings

(P-2744)
PLH PRODUCTS INC
10541 Calle Lee Ste 119 (90720-6782)
PHONE...............................714 739-6622
Seung Woo Lee, *Ch Bd*
Kyung Min Park, *
Won Yong Lee, *
◆ EMP: 405 EST: 1992
SALES (est): 24.43MM **Privately Held**
Web: www.plhproducts.com
SIC: **2452** 2449 5999 Sauna rooms,
prefabricated, wood; Hot tubs, wood;
Sauna equipment and supplies

(P-2745)
WALDEN STRUCTURES INC
1000 Bristol St N # 126 (92660-8916)
PHONE...............................909 389-9100
EMP: 400 EST: 1996
SQ FT: 150,000
SALES (est): 48.47MM **Privately Held**
Web: www.silvercreekmodular.com
SIC: **2452** Modular homes, prefabricated,
wood

2491 Wood Preserving

(P-2746)
**HOOVER TREATED WOOD PDTS
INC**
Also Called: Hoover Treated Wood Pdts Plant
5601 District Blvd (93313-2129)
PHONE...............................661 833-0429
EMP: 23
SALES (corp-wide): 3.92B **Publicly Held**
Web: www.frtw.com
SIC: **2491** Structural lumber and timber,
treated wood
HQ: Hoover Treated Wood Products, Inc.
154 Wire Rd
Thomson GA
706 595-5058

(P-2747)
SC BLUWOOD INC
2604b El Camino Real Ste 356 (92008)
PHONE...............................909 519-5470
Stephen Conboy, *Pr*
EMP: 18 EST: 2006
SALES (est): 424.57K **Privately Held**
SIC: **2491** Structural lumber and timber,
treated wood

(P-2748)
**WEST COAST WOOD
PRESERVING LLC**
5601 District Blvd (93313-2129)
PHONE...............................661 833-0429
▲ EMP: 125

▲ = Import ▼ = Export
◆ = Import/Export

SIC: **2491** Preserving (creosoting) of wood

2493 Reconstituted Wood Products

(P-2749)
REGARDS ENTERPRISES INC
Also Called: Quality Marble & Granite
731 S Taylor Ave (91761-1847)
PHONE..............................909 983-0655
Evan Cohen, *CEO*
▲ **EMP:** 19 **EST:** 2013
SQ FT: 95,000
SALES (est): 2.58MM **Privately Held**
SIC: 2493 3281 Marbleboard (stone face hard board); Granite, cut and shaped

2499 Wood Products, Nec

(P-2750)
ALACO LADDER COMPANY
5167 G St (91710-5143)
PHONE..............................909 591-7561
Gil Jacobs, *Pr*
Mario Garcia, *
▼ **EMP:** 25 **EST:** 1946
SQ FT: 26,000
SALES (est): 4.44MM
SALES (corp-wide): 5.71MM **Privately Held**
Web: www.alacoladder.com
SIC: 2499 3354 3499 Ladders, wood; Aluminum extruded products; Metal ladders
PA: B, E & P Enterprises, Llc
5167 G St
Chino CA
909 591-7561

(P-2751)
B E & P ENTERPRISES LLC (PA)
Also Called: Alaco Ladder Company
5167 G St (91710-5143)
PHONE..............................909 591-7561
Fred Evans, *
Gil Jacobs, *
Stephen Bernstein, *
EMP: 24 **EST:** 1946
SALES (est): 5.71MM
SALES (corp-wide): 5.71MM **Privately Held**
Web: www.alacoladder.com
SIC: 2499 3499 3354 Ladders, wood; Ladders, portable: metal; Aluminum extruded products

(P-2752)
BRENT-WOOD PRODUCTS INC
17071 Hercules St (92345-7621)
P.O. Box 17037 (90807-7037)
PHONE..............................800 400-7335
Lawrence D Hobbs, *CEO*
Birgitta Olin, *
Anna Pinili, *
▼ **EMP:** 30 **EST:** 1963
SQ FT: 26,000
SALES (est): 5.58MM **Privately Held**
Web: www.brent-wood.com
SIC: 2499 Reels, plywood

(P-2753)
CRI 2000 LP (PA)
Also Called: Lso
2245 San Diego Ave Ste 125 (92110-2942)
PHONE..............................619 542-1975
Mitchell G Lynn, *Pt*
◆ **EMP:** 50 **EST:** 2002
SQ FT: 10,000
SALES (est): 10.42MM **Privately Held**

Web: www.cri-global.com
SIC: 2499 5112 5049 5092 Picture frame molding, finished; Office supplies, nec; School supplies; Arts and crafts equipment and supplies

(P-2754)
LARSON-JUHL US LLC
Also Called: Larson Picture Frames
12206 Bell Ranch Dr (90670-3361)
PHONE..............................562 946-6873
Anthony Eikenberry, *Mgr*
EMP: 31
SALES (corp-wide): 302.09B **Publicly Held**
Web: www.larsonjuhl.com
SIC: 2499 Picture frame molding, finished
HQ: Larson-Juhl Us Llc
990 Pchtree Indus Blvd Un
Suwanee GA
770 279-5200

(P-2755)
MAGIC-FLIGHT GENERAL MFG INC
3417 Hancock St (92110-4307)
P.O. Box 3758 (92067-3758)
PHONE..............................619 288-4638
Forrest Landry, *CEO*
Tamara Ward, *
EMP: 21 **EST:** 2009
SQ FT: 17,000
SALES (est): 372.5K **Privately Held**
Web: www.magic-flight.com
SIC: 2499 Woodenware, kitchen and household

(P-2756)
MODERN WOODWORKS INC
Also Called: Modern Woodworks
7949 Deering Ave (91304-5009)
PHONE..............................800 575-3475
George Mekhtarian, *CEO*
Allen Mekhtarian, *
▲ **EMP:** 35 **EST:** 1996
SQ FT: 10,000
SALES (est): 4.04MM **Privately Held**
Web: www.californialightworks.com
SIC: 2499 3648 Carved and turned wood; Lighting equipment, nec

(P-2757)
OUTDOOR DIMENSIONS LLC
5325 E Hunter Ave (92807-2054)
PHONE..............................714 578-9555
Brian Pickler, *Pr*
Donald Pickler, *
Brian Pickler, *VP*
EMP: 160 **EST:** 1974
SQ FT: 80,000
SALES (est): 39.28MM **Privately Held**
Web: www.outdoordimensions.com
SIC: 2499 3993 3281 Signboards, wood; Signs and advertising specialties; Cut stone and stone products

(P-2758)
PACIFIC PANEL PRODUCTS CORP
Also Called: Pacific Panel Products
15601 Arrow Hwy (91706-2004)
P.O. Box 2204 (91706-1126)
PHONE..............................626 851-0444
Jon R Dickey, *CEO*
▲ **EMP:** 39 **EST:** 1994
SQ FT: 79,800
SALES (est): 4.8MM **Privately Held**
Web: www.pacificpanel.com
SIC: 2499 Decorative wood and woodwork

(P-2759)
PRO TOUR MEMORABILIA LLC
Also Called: Ptm Images
700 N San Vicente Blvd Ste G696 (90069-5073)
P.O. Box 15084 (90209-1084)
PHONE..............................424 303-7200
◆ **EMP:** 25 **EST:** 1995
SQ FT: 8,000
SALES (est): 2.69MM **Privately Held**
Web: www.protourmemorabilia.com
SIC: 2499 Picture and mirror frames, wood

(P-2760)
QUALITY FIRST WOODWORKS INC
1264 N Lakeview Ave (92807-1831)
PHONE..............................714 632-0480
Mark Nappy, *Pr*
Chad Nappy, *
EMP: 115 **EST:** 1989
SQ FT: 30,000
SALES (est): 9.11MM **Privately Held**
Web: www.qfwinc.com
SIC: 2499 1751 Decorative wood and woodwork; Cabinet building and installation

(P-2761)
RAPHAELS INC
4460 Braeburn Rd (92116-2126)
▲ **EMP:** 17 **EST:** 1976
SALES (est): 1.25MM **Privately Held**
Web: www.raphaelsap.com
SIC: 2499 Picture and mirror frames, wood

(P-2762)
ROMA MOULDING INC
6230 N Irwindale Ave (91702-3208)
PHONE..............................626 334-2539
Jon Mathews, *Opers Mgr*
EMP: 27
SALES (corp-wide): 28.86MM **Privately Held**
Web: www.romamoulding.com
SIC: 2499 5023 Picture frame molding, finished; Frames and framing, picture and mirror
PA: Roma Moulding Inc
360 Hanlan Rd
Woodbridge ON
905 850-1500

(P-2763)
SURVEY STAKE AND MARKER INC
Also Called: Nichols Lumber
13470 Dalewood St (91706-5834)
PHONE..............................626 960-4802
Judith A Nichols, *Pr*
Evelyn M Rumsey, *VP*
Charles F Nichols, *Sec*
EMP: 29 **EST:** 1956
SQ FT: 3,000
SALES (est): 847.15K **Privately Held**
Web: www.nicholslumber.com
SIC: 2499 Surveyors' stakes, wood

(P-2764)
TIMMONS WOOD PRODUCTS INC
4675 Wade Ave (92571-7494)
PHONE..............................951 940-4700
Eddie Timmons, *Pr*
EMP: 26 **EST:** 1948
SQ FT: 45,000
SALES (est): 769.6K **Privately Held**
SIC: 2499 Handles, poles, dowels and stakes: wood

(P-2765)
UNIVERSITY FRAMES INC
Also Called: Campus Images
3060 E Miraloma Ave (92806-1810)
PHONE..............................714 575-5100
John G Winn, *CEO*
Diane Winn, *
▲ **EMP:** 50 **EST:** 1996
SQ FT: 20,000
SALES (est): 9.24MM **Privately Held**
Web: www.universityframes.com
SIC: 2499 5999 Picture frame molding, finished; Picture frames, ready made

(P-2766)
WALTON COMPANY INC
17900 Sampson Ln (92647-7149)
PHONE..............................714 847-8800
Don Walton, *CEO*
◆ **EMP:** 17 **EST:** 1960
SQ FT: 12,000
SALES (est): 942.77K **Privately Held**
Web: www.thewaltoncompany.com
SIC: 2499 Cork and cork products

2511 Wood Household Furniture

(P-2767)
BAU FURNITURE MFG INC
21 Kelly Ln (92694-1463)
PHONE..............................949 643-2729
Thomas Bau, *Pr*
Linda Bau, *
EMP: 52 **EST:** 1978
SALES (est): 4.42MM **Privately Held**
SIC: 2511 2512 2521 Tables, household: wood; Upholstered household furniture; Tables, office: wood

(P-2768)
BIG TREE FURNITURE & INDS INC (PA)
760 S Vail Ave (90640-4954)
PHONE..............................310 894-7500
Joe Ho, *CEO*
◆ **EMP:** 47 **EST:** 1985
SALES (est): 8.58MM **Privately Held**
SIC: 2511 Wood household furniture

(P-2769)
BROWNWOOD FURNITURE INC
9805 6th St Ste 104 (91730-5751)
PHONE..............................909 945-5613
Rick Vartanian, *Pr*
Pat Eberly, *
Jose Navarro, *
◆ **EMP:** 150 **EST:** 1979
SQ FT: 107,000
SALES (est): 5.36MM **Privately Held**
Web: www.brownwoodfurniture.com
SIC: 2511 Wood bedroom furniture

(P-2770)
DEDON INC
8687 Melrose Ave Ste B188 (90069-5708)
PHONE..............................310 388-4721
EMP: 34
SALES (corp-wide): 355.83K **Privately Held**
Web: www.dedon.de
SIC: 2511 Lawn furniture: wood
HQ: Dedon, Inc.
657 Brigham Rd Ste C
Greensboro NC

PRODUCTS & SVCS

(P-2771)
DOREL HOME FURNISHINGS INC
5400 Shea Center Dr (91761-7892)
PHONE..............................909 390-5705
EMP: 67
SALES (corp-wide): 1.57B Privately Held
Web: www.ameriwoodhome.com
SIC: 2511 Console tables: wood
HQ: Dorel Home Furnishings, Inc.
  410 E 1st St S
  Wright City MO
  636 745-3351

(P-2772)
DOUG MOCKETT & COMPANY INC
1915 Abalone Ave (90501-3706)
P.O. Box 3333 (90266-1333)
PHONE..............................310 318-2491
Tyra Cunningham, *Pr*
Susan Darby Gordon, *
Sonia Marie H Mockett, *
◆ EMP: 65 EST: 1984
SALES (est): 11.53MM Privately Held
Web: www.mockett.com
SIC: 2511 5072 Unassembled or unfinished
  furniture, household: wood; Furniture
  hardware, nec

(P-2773)
FREMARC INDUSTRIES INC (PA)
Also Called: Fremarc Designs
18810 San Jose Ave (91748-1325)
P.O. Box 1086 (91788-1086)
PHONE..............................626 965-0802
Maurice M Donenfeld, *Pr*
Harriette Donenfeld, *
▲ EMP: 78 EST: 1971
SQ FT: 45,000
SALES (est): 5.31MM
SALES (corp-wide): 5.31MM Privately Held
Web: www.fremarc.com
SIC: 2511 Wood household furniture

(P-2774)
FURNITURE TECHNICS INC
Also Called: Furniture Techniques
2900 Supply Ave (90040-2708)
PHONE..............................562 802-0261
Cesar Rousseau, *Pr*
Ricardo Flores, *
EMP: 25 EST: 1988
SALES (est): 1.89MM Privately Held
SIC: 2511 2426 Wood household furniture;
  Furniture stock and parts, hardwood

(P-2775)
HOLLYWOOD CHAIRS
Also Called: Totally Bamboo
1880 Diamond St (92078-5100)
PHONE..............................760 471-6600
Joanne Sullivan, *CEO*
Thomas Sullivan, *
◆ EMP: 39 EST: 1998
SQ FT: 10,000
SALES (est): 6.86MM Privately Held
Web: www.totallybamboo.com
SIC: 2511 Wood household furniture

(P-2776)
JP PRODUCTS LLC
2054 Davie Ave (90040-1705)
PHONE..............................310 237-6237
Patrick Mooney, *Managing Member*
Jacqueline Mooney, *Managing Member**
EMP: 46 EST: 2010
SQ FT: 35,000

SALES (est): 3.57MM Privately Held
SIC: 2511 Wood household furniture

(P-2777)
LANPAR INC
Also Called: Oakwood Interiors
1333 S Bon View Ave (91761-4404)
PHONE..............................541 484-1962
Nick Lanphier, *Ch Bd*
▲ EMP: 21 EST: 1982
SQ FT: 180,000
SALES (est): 373.44K Privately Held
Web: www.fineoak.com
SIC: 2511 Wood bedroom furniture

(P-2778)
LAUREN ANTHONY & CO INC
11425 Woodside Ave Ste B (92071-4726)
PHONE..............................619 590-1141
Randy T Passanisi, *Pr*
EMP: 23 EST: 2004
SALES (est): 2MM Privately Held
Web: www.anthonylauren.com
SIC: 2511 Wood household furniture

(P-2779)
LEGACY COMMERCIAL HOLDINGS INC
Also Called: Armen Living
28939 Avenue Williams (91355-4183)
PHONE..............................818 767-6626
Kevin Kevonian, *Pr*
Kevon Kevonian, *
Honigsfeld Lee, *
▲ EMP: 35 EST: 2007
SALES (est): 34.18MM Privately Held
Web: www.armenliving.com
SIC: 2511 2514 2531 2521 Kitchen and
  dining room furniture; Metal lawn and
  garden furniture; Public building and related
  furniture; Wood office furniture

(P-2780)
MIKHAIL DARAFEEV INC (PA)
5075 Edison Ave (91710-5716)
PHONE..............................909 613-1818
Antonina Darafeev, *Pr*
Paul Darafeev, *
George Darafeev, *
▲ EMP: 50 EST: 1957
SALES (est): 9.95MM
SALES (corp-wide): 9.95MM Privately Held
Web: www.darafeev.com
SIC: 2511 Stools, household: wood

(P-2781)
MORETTIS DESIGN COLLECTION INC
16926 Keegan Ave Ste C (90746-1322)
PHONE..............................310 638-5555
Mori Afshar, *Pr*
▲ EMP: 30 EST: 1992
SALES (est): 1.91MM Privately Held
Web: www.morettisdesign.com
SIC: 2511 Wood household furniture

(P-2782)
NELSON ADAMS NACO CORPORATION
420 S E St (92401-2013)
PHONE..............................909 256-8938
Rafael Rangel, *Pr*
EMP: 20 EST: 2008
SALES (est): 4.81MM Privately Held
Web: www.nelsonadamsnaco.com
SIC: 2511 Coffee tables: wood

(P-2783)
NEWCO INTERNATIONAL INC
Also Called: Harmony Kids
13600 Vaughn St (91340-3017)
PHONE..............................818 834-7100
Howard Napolske, *Pr*
Ernest Johnston, *
▲ EMP: 29 EST: 2004
SQ FT: 20,000
SALES (est): 1.33MM Privately Held
Web:
www.therockabyeglidercompany.com
SIC: 2511 Children's wood furniture

(P-2784)
NOVA LIFESTYLE INC (PA)
6565 E Washington Blvd (90040-1821)
PHONE..............................323 888-9999
Thanh H Lam, *Ch Bd*
Min Su, *Corporate Secretary**
Jeffery Chuang, *CFO*
Mark Chapman, *VP Mktg*
Steven Qiang Liu, *VP*
EMP: 24 EST: 2011
SALES (est): 12.74MM
SALES (corp-wide): 12.74MM Publicly Held
Web: www.novalifestyle.com
SIC: 2511 2512 Wood household furniture;
  Upholstered household furniture

(P-2785)
OAK TREE FURNITURE INC
13681 Newport Ave Ste 8 (92780-7815)
PHONE..............................562 944-0754
Tim Sopp, *Pr*
Elaine Sopp, *
▲ EMP: 17 EST: 1977
SALES (est): 640.06K Privately Held
SIC: 2511 Wood household furniture

(P-2786)
RADFORD CABINETS INC
216 E Avenue K8 (93535-4527)
PHONE..............................661 729-8931
Steven Radford, *Pr*
Robert Mendoza, *
Sharon Radford, *
EMP: 70 EST: 1992
SQ FT: 20,000
SALES (est): 9.26MM Privately Held
Web: www.radfordcabinetsinc.com
SIC: 2511 2434 2521 Kitchen and dining
  room furniture; Wood kitchen cabinets;
  Cabinets, office: wood

(P-2787)
RUSS BASSETT CORP
Also Called: Group Five
8189 Byron Rd (90606-2615)
PHONE..............................562 945-2445
Mike Dressendorfer, *CEO*
Peter Fink, *
▲ EMP: 115 EST: 1959
SQ FT: 112,000
SALES (est): 21.9MM Privately Held
Web: www.russbassett.com
SIC: 2511 Wood household furniture

(P-2788)
SAN DIEGO ARCFT INTERIORS INC
2381 Boswell Rd (91914-3509)
PHONE..............................619 474-1997
Juan Carlos Vasquez, *Pr*
▲ EMP: 23 EST: 2009
SALES (est): 2.65MM Privately Held
Web: www.sdaircraftinteriors.com
SIC: 2511 Chairs, household, except
  upholstered: wood

(P-2789)
SANDBERG FURNITURE MFG CO INC (PA)
Also Called: Sandberg Furniture
5705 Alcoa Ave (90058-3794)
P.O. Box 58291 (90058-0291)
PHONE..............................323 582-0711
John Sandberg, *CEO*
Mark Nixon, *Sr VP*
▲ EMP: 225 EST: 1918
SALES (est): 32.99MM
SALES (corp-wide): 32.99MM Privately Held
Web: www.sandbergfurniture.com
SIC: 2511 Wood bedroom furniture

(P-2790)
TEXTURED DESIGN FURNITURE INC
Also Called: Texture Design
1303 S Claudina St (92805-6235)
PHONE..............................714 502-9121
J Luis Gonzales, *Pr*
▲ EMP: 29 EST: 1985
SQ FT: 34,000
SALES (est): 807.64K Privately Held
SIC: 2511 Wood household furniture

(P-2791)
TREND MANOR FURN MFG CO INC
17047 Gale Ave (91745-1808)
PHONE..............................626 964-6493
Theodore Vecchione, *Pr*
▲ EMP: 42 EST: 1946
SQ FT: 63,000
SALES (est): 5.22MM Privately Held
Web: www.trendmanor.com
SIC: 2511 Wood household furniture

(P-2792)
WHALEN LLC (DH)
Also Called: Whalen Furniture Manufacturing
1578 Air Wing Rd (92154-7706)
PHONE..............................619 423-9948
Jose Luis Laparte, *Pr*
David Levinson, *
◆ EMP: 26 EST: 1991
SQ FT: 100,000
SALES (est): 49.33MM Privately Held
Web: www.whalenfurniture.com
SIC: 2511 Wood household furniture
HQ: Li & Fung Development (China) Limited
  11/F Lifung Twr
  Cheung Sha Wan KLN

2512 Upholstered Household Furniture

(P-2793)
A RUDIN INC (PA)
Also Called: A Rudin Designs
6062 Alcoa Ave (90058-3902)
PHONE..............................323 589-5547
Arnold Rudin, *Pr*
Ralph Rudin, *
◆ EMP: 92 EST: 1918
SQ FT: 117,000
SALES (est): 8.06MM
SALES (corp-wide): 8.06MM Privately Held
Web: www.arudin.com
SIC: 2512 5021 Upholstered household
  furniture; Household furniture

(P-2794)
AMERASIA FURN CMPNNTS MFG IMPR
2772 Norton Ave (90262-1835)
PHONE..............................310 638-0570
Khue Van Cao, *CEO*
Alfred Varela Junior, *Pr*
▲ EMP: 24 EST: 2006
SQ FT: 55,000
SALES (est): 631.56K Privately Held
SIC: 2512 Upholstered household furniture

(P-2795)
ARDMORE HOME DESIGN INC (PA)
Also Called: Pigeon and Poodle
918 S Stimson Ave (91745-1640)
PHONE..............................626 803-7769
Chris Dewitt, *CEO*
Oscar Yague, *
◆ EMP: 49 EST: 2012
SALES (est): 22.93MM
SALES (corp-wide): 22.93MM Privately Held
Web: www.madegoods.com
SIC: 2512 Upholstered household furniture

(P-2796)
BURTON JAMES INC
428 Turnbull Canyon Rd (91745-1011)
PHONE..............................626 961-7221
Raymond Zoref, *CEO*
Raymond Zoref, *Pr*
Ralph Hipsman, *Prin*
Harry Robbins, *
EMP: 80 EST: 1983
SQ FT: 28,000
SALES (est): 9.71MM Privately Held
Web: www.burtonjames.com
SIC: 2512 Upholstered household furniture

(P-2797)
CISCO BROS CORP (PA)
Also Called: Cisco & Brothers Designs
474 S Arroyo Pkwy (91105-2530)
PHONE..............................323 778-8612
Francisco Pinedo, *CEO*
Alba E Pinedo, *
◆ EMP: 145 EST: 1993
SALES (est): 25.36MM Privately Held
Web: www.ciscohome.net
SIC: 2512 Upholstered household furniture

(P-2798)
COMMERCIAL INTR RESOURCES INC
Also Called: Contract Resources
6077 Rickenbacker Rd (90040-3031)
PHONE..............................562 926-5885
Roberta Tuchman, *CEO*
Stanley Rice, *
Barbara Rice, *
Stephanie Lesko, *
EMP: 65 EST: 1982
SQ FT: 28,000
SALES (est): 9.51MM Privately Held
Web: www.villahallmark.com
SIC: 2512 Upholstered household furniture

(P-2799)
DELLAROBBIA INC (PA)
119 Waterworks Way (92618-3110)
PHONE..............................949 251-9532
David Soonlan, *Pr*
Sunee Soonlan, *
▲ EMP: 48 EST: 1979
SQ FT: 27,000
SALES (est): 1.95MM
SALES (corp-wide): 1.95MM Privately Held

Web: www.dellarobbia.com
SIC: 2512 Upholstered household furniture

(P-2800)
E J LAUREN LLC
Also Called: Ejl
2690 Pellissier Pl (90601-1507)
PHONE..............................562 803-1113
Antonio Ocampo, *Managing Member*
◆ EMP: 50 EST: 2009
SALES (est): 4.98MM Privately Held
Web: www.ejlauren.com
SIC: 2512 Upholstered household furniture

(P-2801)
ELITE LEATHER LLC
1620 5th Ave Ste 400 (92101-2738)
PHONE..............................909 548-8600
▲ EMP: 100
Web: www.oneforvictory.com
SIC: 2512 Living room furniture: upholstered on wood frames

(P-2802)
GENESIS TC INC
Also Called: Genesis 2000
524 Hofgaarden St (91744-5529)
PHONE..............................626 968-4455
Anthony Moreno, *Pr*
EMP: 22 EST: 2003
SALES (est): 483.89K Privately Held
SIC: 2512 Wood upholstered chairs and couches

(P-2803)
GOMEN FURNITURE MFG INC
11612 Wright Rd (90262-3945)
PHONE..............................310 635-4894
Leonardo Gonzalez, *Pr*
▲ EMP: 30 EST: 1990
SALES (est): 1.84MM Privately Held
SIC: 2512 7641 Upholstered household furniture; Upholstery work

(P-2804)
HAMMER COLLECTION INC
14427 S Main St (90248-1913)
P.O. Box 2458 (90267-2458)
PHONE..............................310 515-0276
Frank Hammer, *Pr*
Eva Hammer, *
▲ EMP: 19 EST: 1989
SQ FT: 30,000
SALES (est): 615.86K Privately Held
Web: www.hammerfinefurniture.com
SIC: 2512 2511 Upholstered household furniture; Wood household furniture

(P-2805)
HARBOR FURNITURE MFG INC (PA)
Also Called: Harbor House
15817 Whitepost Ln (90638-3126)
PHONE..............................323 636-1201
Malcolm Tuttleton Junior, *Pr*
Brent Tuttleton, *
▲ EMP: 25 EST: 1929
SALES (est): 2.56MM
SALES (corp-wide): 2.56MM Privately Held
SIC: 2512 2511 6514 2521 Upholstered household furniture; Wood household furniture; Dwelling operators, except apartments; Wood office furniture

(P-2806)
HUNTINGTON INDUSTRIES INC
12520 Chadron Ave (90250-4808)
PHONE..............................323 772-5575

▲ EMP: 150
SIC: 2512 Upholstered household furniture

(P-2807)
M&J DESIGN INC
Also Called: M&J Design Furniture
1303 S Claudina St (92805-6235)
PHONE..............................714 687-9918
Jorge Mojica, *CEO*
EMP: 23 EST: 2018
SALES (est): 2.49MM Privately Held
Web: www.mjdesignus.com
SIC: 2512 2541 5712 Upholstered household furniture; Wood partitions and fixtures; Custom made furniture, except cabinets

(P-2808)
MARGE CARSON INC (PA)
555 W 5th St (90013-2670)
P.O. Box 1283 (91769-1283)
PHONE..............................626 571-1111
James Labarge, *CEO*
Dominic Ching, *
▲ EMP: 82 EST: 1951
SALES (est): 9.82MM
SALES (corp-wide): 9.82MM Privately Held
Web: www.margecarson.com
SIC: 2512 2511 Living room furniture: upholstered on wood frames; Wood household furniture

(P-2809)
MARLIN DESIGNS LLC
13845 Alton Pkwy Ste C (92618-1643)
PHONE..............................949 637-7257
Ronald Whitlock, *Managing Member*
EMP: 150 EST: 1995
SALES (est): 13MM Privately Held
Web: www.marlin-designs.com
SIC: 2512 Upholstered household furniture

(P-2810)
MARTIN/BRATTRUD INC
1231 W 134th St (90247-1902)
PHONE..............................323 770-4171
Allan G Stratford, *Pr*
Patrick Baxter, *
EMP: 95 EST: 1946
SQ FT: 38,000
SALES (est): 14.35MM Privately Held
Web: www.martinbrattrud.com
SIC: 2512 2511 Upholstered household furniture; Tables, household: wood

(P-2811)
MINSON CORPORATION
Also Called: Mallin Casual Furniture
11701 Wilshire Blvd Ste 15a (90025-1599)
PHONE..............................323 513-1041
▲ EMP: 300
Web: www.minson.com
SIC: 2512 2514 Wood upholstered chairs and couches; Lawn furniture: metal

(P-2812)
MPB FURNITURE CORPORATION
Also Called: Ashley Furniture
414 W Ridgecrest Blvd (93555-4015)
PHONE..............................760 375-4800
Mike Mcgee, *Pr*
Bill Farris, *Genl Mgr*
EMP: 30 EST: 2005
SQ FT: 18,000
SALES (est): 1.15MM Privately Held
Web: www.ashleyfurniture.com
SIC: 2512 Upholstered household furniture

(P-2813)
R C FURNITURE INC
1111 Jellick Ave (91748-1212)
PHONE..............................626 964-4100
Rene Cazares, *Pr*
▲ EMP: 81 EST: 1986
SQ FT: 25,000
SALES (est): 17.02MM Privately Held
Web: www.renecazares.com
SIC: 2512 5021 Upholstered household furniture; Furniture

(P-2814)
REPUBLIC FURNITURE MFG INC
2241 E 49th St (90058-2822)
PHONE..............................323 235-2144
Karen Rosen-hirsch, *Pr*
Judy Rosen, *
EMP: 18 EST: 1963
SQ FT: 38,000
SALES (est): 977.77K Privately Held
Web: www.republic-furniture.com
SIC: 2512 2515 Living room furniture: upholstered on wood frames; Mattresses and bedsprings

(P-2815)
ROBERT MICHAEL LTD
10035 Geary Ave (90670-3237)
P.O. Box 2397 (90670-0397)
PHONE..............................562 758-6789
◆ EMP: 263
Web: www.robertmichaellimited.com
SIC: 2512 Upholstered household furniture

(P-2816)
ROYAL CUSTOM DESIGNS LLC
13951 Monte Vista Ave (91710-5536)
PHONE..............................909 591-8990
Jeff Sladick, *Pr*
▲ EMP: 133 EST: 1970
SQ FT: 35,000
SALES (est): 17.44MM
SALES (corp-wide): 27.84MM Privately Held
Web: www.royalcustomdesigns.com
SIC: 2512 Upholstered household furniture
PA: Makers & Craftsmen Llc
396 E Jefferson Ave
Pomona CA
909 525-5181

(P-2817)
RTMH INC (PA)
Also Called: Rose Tarlow-Melrose House
425 N Robertson Blvd (90048-1735)
PHONE..............................323 651-2202
Rose Tarlow, *CEO*
▲ EMP: 17 EST: 1981
SALES (est): 9.15MM
SALES (corp-wide): 9.15MM Privately Held
Web: www.rosetarlow.com
SIC: 2512 2511 Upholstered household furniture; Wood household furniture

(P-2818)
SOFA U LOVE LLC (PA)
Also Called: Factory Showroom Exchange
1207 N Western Ave (90029-1018)
PHONE..............................323 464-3397
Varougan Karapetian, *Pr*
EMP: 22 EST: 1976
SQ FT: 22,000
SALES (est): 3.75MM
SALES (corp-wide): 3.75MM Privately Held
Web: www.sofaulove.com
SIC: 2512 5712 Upholstered household furniture; Furniture stores

P
R
O
D
U
C
T
S

&

S
V
C
S

(P-2819)
SOLE DESIGNS INC
11685 Mcbean Dr (91732-1104)
PHONE.............................626 452-8642
Linda Le, *CEO*
Lam Tran, *Pr*
▲ EMP: 17 EST: 1996
SQ FT: 8,000
SALES (est): 3.46MM Privately Held
Web: www.soledesigns.com
SIC: 2512 Upholstered household furniture

(P-2820)
STITCH INDUSTRIES INC
Also Called: Joybird
767 S Alameda St Ste 360 (90021-1633)
PHONE.............................888 282-0842
Kurt L Darrow, *CEO*
EMP: 50 EST: 2013
SALES (est): 23.26MM
SALES (corp-wide): 2.35B Publicly Held
Web: www.joybird.com
SIC: 2512 5961 5712 Upholstered
household furniture; Catalog and mail-order
houses; Furniture stores
PA: La-Z-Boy Incorporated
1 Lazboy Dr
Monroe MI
734 242-1444

(P-2821)
SUPERB CHAIR CORPORATION
Also Called: Patricia Edwards
6861 Watcher St (90040-3715)
PHONE.............................562 776-1771
Audrey Smith, *Pr*
Julie Smith, *
James E Smith, *
EMP: 26 EST: 1971
SQ FT: 36,000
SALES (est): 557.31K Privately Held
Web: www.patriciaedwards.com
SIC: 2512 Living room furniture: upholstered
on wood frames

(P-2822)
TERRA FURNITURE INC
1950 Salto Dr (91745-4209)
▲ EMP: 41 EST: 1964
SALES (est): 2.41MM Privately Held
Web: www.terrafurniture.com
SIC: 2512 2514 2522 2511 Upholstered
household furniture; Metal household
furniture; Office furniture, except wood;
Wood lawn and garden furniture

(P-2823)
YEN-NHAI INC
Also Called: Nathan Anthony Furniture
4940 District Blvd (90058-2718)
PHONE.............................323 584-1315
Khai Mai, *Pr*
EMP: 40 EST: 1995
SALES (est): 3.65MM Privately Held
Web: www.nafurniture.com
SIC: 2512 Upholstered household furniture

2514 Metal Household Furniture

(P-2824)
A A CATER TRUCK MFG CO INC
Also Called: Hizco Truck Body
750 E Slauson Ave (90011-5236)
PHONE.............................323 233-2343
Vahe Karapetian, *Pr*
EMP: 24 EST: 1971
SQ FT: 60,000

SALES (est): 1.99MM Privately Held
Web: www.aacatertruck.com
SIC: 2514 7538 Metal household furniture;
General truck repair

(P-2825)
**ATLANTIC REPRESENTATIONS
INC**
Also Called: Snowsound USA
10018 Santa Fe Springs Rd (90670-2922)
P.O. Box 2399 (90670-0399)
PHONE.............................562 903-9550
Shahriar Dardashti, *Pr*
Farnaz Dardashti, *
Leo Dardashti, *
▲ EMP: 30 EST: 1984
SQ FT: 150,000
SALES (est): 8.62MM Privately Held
Web: www.atlantic-inc.com
SIC: 2514 2511 Metal household furniture;
Wood household furniture

(P-2826)
**ATLAS SURVIVAL SHELTERS
LLC**
7407 Telegraph Rd (90640-6515)
PHONE.............................323 727-7084
Ronal D Hubbard, *Managing Member*
EMP: 25 EST: 2011
SQ FT: 30,000
SALES (est): 2.34MM Privately Held
Web: www.atlassurvivalshelters.com
SIC: 2514 Beds, including folding and
cabinet, household: metal

(P-2827)
CASUALWAY USA LLC
Also Called: Casualway Home & Garden
1623 Lola Way (93030-5080)
PHONE.............................805 660-7408
Guoxiang Wu, *Pr*
Ralph Ybarra, *VP*
EMP: 99
SALES (est): 1.92MM Privately Held
SIC: 2514 Garden furniture, metal

(P-2828)
**DOUGLAS FURNITURE OF
CALIFORNIA LLC**
809 Tyburn Rd (90274-2843)
PHONE.............................310 749-0003
▲ EMP: 2400
SIC: 2514 2512 Dinette sets: metal;
Recliners: upholstered on wood frames

(P-2829)
EARTHLITE LLC (DH)
Also Called: Earthlite
990 Joshua Way (92081-7855)
P.O. Box 51245 (90051-5545)
PHONE.............................760 599-1112
James Chenevey, *CEO*
Philippe Barret, *
Tara Grodjesk, *WELLNESS*
◆ EMP: 95 EST: 1987
SQ FT: 68,000
SALES (est): 42.65MM
SALES (corp-wide): 98.64MM Privately
Held
Web: www.earthlite.com
SIC: 2514 5091 2531 Tables, household:
metal; Spa equipment and supplies; Chairs,
portable folding
HQ: Earthlite Holdings, Llc
150 E 58th St Fl 37
New York NY
212 317-2004

(P-2830)
ELLIOTTS DESIGNS INC
2473 E Rancho Del Amo Pl (90220-6311)
PHONE.............................310 631-4931
Elliott Jones, *Pr*
Julie Jones, *
EMP: 30 EST: 1974
SQ FT: 127,000
SALES (est): 2.27MM Privately Held
SIC: 2514 5021 Beds, including folding and
cabinet, household: metal; Furniture

(P-2831)
**GRACO CHILDRENS
PRODUCTS INC**
17182 Nevada St (92394-7806)
PHONE.............................770 418-7200
EMP: 293
SALES (corp-wide): 9.46B Publicly Held
SIC: 2514 Juvenile furniture, household:
metal
HQ: Graco Children's Products Inc.
6655 Pachtree Dunwoody Rd
Atlanta GA
770 418-7200

(P-2832)
JBI LLC
Also Called: Buchbinder, Jay Industries
18521 S Santa Fe Ave (90221-5624)
PHONE.............................310 537-2910
Claudio Luna, *Mgr*
EMP: 48
SALES (corp-wide): 63.16MM Privately
Held
Web: www.jbi-interiors.com
SIC: 2514 2221 2511 Tables, household:
metal; Fiberglass fabrics; Wood household
furniture
PA: Jbi, Llc
2650 E El Presidio St
Long Beach CA
310 886-8034

(P-2833)
M724 INC
949 N Cataract Ave Ste E (91773-1464)
PHONE.............................951 314-1333
EMP: 17
SALES (est): 1.05MM Privately Held
SIC: 2514 Metal household furniture

(P-2834)
**MURRAYS IRON WORKS INC
(PA)**
7355 E Slauson Ave (90040-3626)
PHONE.............................323 521-1100
▲ EMP: 165 EST: 1966
SALES (est): 9.07MM
SALES (corp-wide): 9.07MM Privately
Held
Web: www.murraysiw.com
SIC: 2514 3446 5021 5961 Metal household
furniture; Fences or posts, ornamental iron
or steel; Furniture; Furniture and
furnishings, mail order

(P-2835)
RSI HOME PRODUCTS INC
RSI HOME PRODUCTS, INC.
620 Newport Center Dr Ste 1030 (92660)
PHONE.............................949 720-1116
EMP: 83
SALES (corp-wide): 2.07B Publicly Held
Web: www.americanwoodmark.com
SIC: 2514 2541 1751 Metal household
furniture; Wood partitions and fixtures;
Cabinet and finish carpentry
HQ: Rsi Home Products Llc
400 E Orangethorpe Ave

Anaheim CA
714 449-2200

(P-2836)
RSI HOME PRODUCTS LLC (HQ)
Also Called: RSI
400 E Orangethorpe Ave (92801-1046)
PHONE.............................714 449-2200
Alex Calabrese, *CEO*
Jeff Hoeft, *
David Lowrie, *
▲ EMP: 700 EST: 1994
SQ FT: 675,000
SALES (est): 1.03B
SALES (corp-wide): 2.07B Publicly Held
Web: www.americanwoodmark.com
SIC: 2514 2541 3281 2434 Kitchen cabinets:
metal; Counter and sink tops; Cut stone
and stone products; Wood kitchen cabinets
PA: American Woodmark Corporation
561 Shady Elm Rd
Winchester VA
540 665-9100

(P-2837)
SANDUSKY LEE LLC
16125 Widmere Rd (93203-9307)
P.O. Box 517 (93203-0517)
PHONE.............................661 854-5551
Jim Coontz, *Brnch Mgr*
EMP: 26
SALES (corp-wide): 24.67MM Privately
Held
Web: www.sanduskycabinets.com
SIC: 2514 2522 Metal household furniture;
Office furniture, except wood
PA: Sandusky Lee Llc
80 Keystone St
Littlestown PA
717 359-4111

(P-2838)
SURROUNDING ELEMENTS LLC
33051 Calle Aviador Ste A (92675-4780)
PHONE.............................949 582-9000
Moss Shacter, *Managing Member*
EMP: 20 EST: 2001
SQ FT: 15,000
SALES (est): 2.48MM Privately Held
Web: www.surroundingelements.com
SIC: 2514 Lawn furniture: metal

(P-2839)
**TROPITONE FURNITURE CO
INC (DH)**
5 Marconi (92618-2594)
PHONE.............................949 595-2010
Randy Danielson, *Ex VP*
◆ EMP: 300 EST: 1954
SQ FT: 100,000
SALES (est): 100MM
SALES (corp-wide): 342.49MM Privately
Held
Web: www.tropitone.com
SIC: 2514 2522 Garden furniture, metal;
Office furniture, except wood
HQ: Jordan Brown Inc
475 W Town Pl Ste 200
Saint Augustine FL

(P-2840)
WESLEY ALLEN INC
Also Called: Iron Beds of America
1001 E 60th St (90001-1018)
PHONE.............................323 231-4275
Victor Sawan, *CEO*
▲ EMP: 150 EST: 1976
SQ FT: 100,000
SALES (est): 19.05MM Privately Held
Web: www.wesleyallen.com

SIC: 2514 Metal household furniture

2515 Mattresses And Bedsprings

(P-2841)
ADVANCED INNVTIVE RCVERY TECH
3401 Space Center Ct Ste 811b (91752-1128)
PHONE..............................949 273-8100
Brad Bannister, *Mgr*
EMP: 30
SALES (corp-wide): 9.08MM **Privately Held**
Web: www.airtechinnovation.com
SIC: 2515 Mattresses, containing felt, foam rubber, urethane, etc.
PA: Advanced Innovative Recovery Technologies, Inc.
1715 E Wilshire Ave # 72
Santa Ana CA
949 273-8100

(P-2842)
AMERICAN NATIONAL MFG INC
252 Mariah Cir (92879-1751)
PHONE..............................951 273-7888
Eve Miller, *Pr*
Craig Miller, *VP*
◆ EMP: 65 EST: 1993
SQ FT: 75,000
SALES (est): 10.11MM **Privately Held**
Web: www.americannationalmfg.com
SIC: 2515 5712 Mattresses and bedsprings; Furniture stores

(P-2843)
AMF SUPPORT SURFACES INC (DH)
1691 N Delilah St (92879-1885)
PHONE..............................951 549-6800
Fredrick Kohnke, *CEO*
Curt Wyatt, *
Charles C Wyatt, *
Carole A Wyatt, *
▲ EMP: 162 EST: 1932
SQ FT: 40,000
SALES (est): 27.03MM
SALES (corp-wide): 15.11B **Publicly Held**
SIC: 2515 Mattresses, containing felt, foam rubber, urethane, etc.
HQ: Anodyne Medical Device, Inc.
1069 State Road 46 E
Batesville IN

(P-2844)
BANNER MATTRESS INC
1501 E Cooley Dr Ste B (92324-3991)
PHONE..............................909 835-4200
▲ EMP: 57
Web: www.bannermattressonline.com
SIC: 2515 5021 Bedsprings, assembled; Mattresses

(P-2845)
BRENTWOOD HOME LLC (PA)
Also Called: Silverrest
701 Burning Tree Rd Ste A (92833-1447)
PHONE..............................562 949-3759
Vy Nguyen, *CEO*
EMP: 128 EST: 2015
SQ FT: 80,000
SALES (est): 24.13MM
SALES (corp-wide): 24.13MM **Privately Held**
Web: www.brentwoodhome.com

SIC: 2515 5021 5712 Mattresses, containing felt, foam rubber, urethane, etc.; Mattresses ; Mattresses

(P-2846)
CRISTAL MATERIALS INC
6825 Mckinley Ave (90001-1525)
PHONE..............................323 855-1688
Luis Ponce, *CEO*
EMP: 30 EST: 2013
SALES (est): 2.22MM **Privately Held**
SIC: 2515 5999 3086 Mattresses, containing felt, foam rubber, urethane, etc.; Foam and foam products; Plastics foam products

(P-2847)
DELLA ROBBIA INC
Also Called: Focus One Home
796 E Harrison St (92879-1348)
PHONE..............................951 372-9199
David Soonlan, *Pr*
▲ EMP: 20 EST: 1980
SQ FT: 72,000
SALES (est): 5MM **Privately Held**
Web: www.dellarobbia.com
SIC: 2515 Sofa beds (convertible sofas)

(P-2848)
ES KLUFT & COMPANY INC (DH)
11096 Jersey Blvd Ste 101 (91730-5158)
PHONE..............................909 373-4211
David Binke, *CEO*
Brad Goodshaw, *CFO*
Ron Bruneau, *COO*
◆ EMP: 174 EST: 2004
SALES (est): 110.87MM **Privately Held**
Web: www.aireloom.com
SIC: 2515 Mattresses, innerspring or box spring
HQ: Vi - Spring Limited
Ernesettle Lane
Plymouth
175 236-6311

(P-2849)
G & M MATTRESS AND FOAM CORPORATION
Also Called: Fun Furnishings
1943 N White Ave (91750-5663)
P.O. Box 7220 (91750-7220)
PHONE..............................909 593-1000
EMP: 80 EST: 1987
SALES (est): 13MM **Privately Held**
SIC: 2515 Mattresses, containing felt, foam rubber, urethane, etc.

(P-2850)
GATEWAY MATTRESS CO INC
624 S Vail Ave (90640-4952)
PHONE..............................323 725-1923
EMP: 65 EST: 1961
SALES (est): 4.57MM **Privately Held**
Web: www.gatewaymattress.com
SIC: 2515 Mattresses, innerspring or box spring

(P-2851)
GOLDEN MATTRESS CO INC
11680 Wright Rd (90262-3945)
PHONE..............................323 887-1888
San Dang, *CEO*
Phuc Nguyen, *
◆ EMP: 52 EST: 1980
SALES (est): 4.58MM **Privately Held**
Web: www.goldenmattressus.com
SIC: 2515 5021 Mattresses and foundations; Mattresses

(P-2852)
IDEAL MATTRESS COMPANY INC
1901 Main St (92113-2129)
PHONE..............................619 595-0003
Jesse Hernandez, *Pr*
John Hernandez, *
Patrick Goularte, *
Estella Goularte, *
EMP: 25 EST: 1929
SQ FT: 10,000
SALES (est): 2.5MM **Privately Held**
SIC: 2515 Mattresses, containing felt, foam rubber, urethane, etc.

(P-2853)
KINGDOM MATTRESS CO INC
Also Called: Kingdom Matress Company
2425 S Malt Ave (90040-3201)
PHONE..............................562 630-5531
Jose Flores, *Pr*
EMP: 29 EST: 1999
SALES (est): 1.34MM **Privately Held**
Web: www.kingdommattress.com
SIC: 2515 Mattresses and bedsprings

(P-2854)
LEGGETT & PLATT INCORPORATED
Also Called: Lpcc 6008
1050 S Dupont Ave (91761-1578)
PHONE..............................909 937-1010
Barry Kubasak, *Mgr*
EMP: 96
SALES (corp-wide): 5.15B **Publicly Held**
Web: www.leggett.com
SIC: 2515 Mattresses, innerspring or box spring
PA: Leggett & Platt, Incorporated
1 Leggett Rd
Carthage MO
417 358-8131

(P-2855)
MARSPRING CORPORATION
Also Called: Los Angeles Fiber Co
5190 S Santa Fe Ave (90058-3532)
P.O. Box 58643 (90058-0643)
PHONE..............................310 484-6849
Ronald Greitzer, *Pr*
EMP: 56
SALES (corp-wide): 6.62MM **Privately Held**
Web: www.reliancecarpetcushion.com
SIC: 2515 Spring cushions
PA: Marspring Corporation
4920 S Boyle Ave
Vernon CA
323 589-5637

(P-2856)
MIRACLE BEDDING CORPORATION
3700 Capitol Ave (90601-1731)
PHONE..............................562 908-2370
Cam Hua, *Pr*
Cam Tu Hua, *Pr*
Quyen Lieu, *Treas*
▲ EMP: 23 EST: 1991
SQ FT: 100,000
SALES (est): 458.32K **Privately Held**
SIC: 2515 5719 5712 Mattresses, containing felt, foam rubber, urethane, etc.; Bedding (sheets, blankets, spreads, and pillows); Mattresses

(P-2857)
PURA NATURALS INC
3401 Space Center Ct Ste 811a (91752-1128)

PHONE..............................949 273-8100
Brad Bannister, *Mgr*
EMP: 30
SALES (corp-wide): 9.08MM **Privately Held**
Web: www.puranaturalsproducts.com
SIC: 2515 Mattresses, containing felt, foam rubber, urethane, etc.
HQ: Pura Naturals, Inc.
23615 El Toro Rd Ste X300
Lake Forest CA
949 273-8100

(P-2858)
SERTA SIMMONS BEDDING LLC
23700 Cactus Ave (92553-8900)
PHONE..............................951 807-8467
Stephanie Mckibbon, *Brnch Mgr*
EMP: 50
Web: www.sertasimmons.com
SIC: 2515 Mattresses and bedsprings
PA: Serta Simmons Bedding, Llc
2451 Industry Ave
Doraville GA

(P-2859)
SKY RIDER EQUIPMENT CO INC
1180 N Blue Gum St (92806-2409)
PHONE..............................714 632-6890
Martin Villegas, *CEO*
Carl Gray, *
Dev Donnelley, *
Karl Keranen, *
▲ EMP: 30 EST: 1984
SQ FT: 12,000
SALES (est): 7.23MM **Privately Held**
Web: www.sky-rider.com
SIC: 2515 7349 5719 Foundations and platforms; Window cleaning; Window shades, nec

(P-2860)
SOUTH BAY INTERNATIONAL INC
8570 Hickory Ave (91739-9632)
PHONE..............................909 718-5000
Guohai Tang, *CEO*
Guohai Tang, *
Daniella Serven, *
Weijun She, *
Wendiao Hou, *
▲ EMP: 25 EST: 1993
SALES (est): 50.07MM **Privately Held**
Web: www.southbayinternational.com
SIC: 2515 Mattresses and bedsprings

(P-2861)
STRESS-O-PEDIC MATTRESS CO INC
Also Called: Stress-O-Pedic
2060 S Wineville Ave Ste A (91761-3633)
PHONE..............................909 605-2010
▲ EMP: 58
Web: www.stressopedic.com
SIC: 2515 Mattresses, innerspring or box spring

(P-2862)
TEMPO INDUSTRIES INC
2137 E 55th St (90058-3439)
P.O. Box 1822 (91353-1822)
PHONE..............................415 552-8074
▲ EMP: 134
Web: www.tempofurniture.com
SIC: 2515 Sleep furniture

(P-2863)
VISIONARY SLEEP LLC
2060 S Wineville Ave Ste A (91761-3633)

PHONE..............................909 605-2010
Carter Gronbach, *Mgr*
EMP: 58
SALES (corp-wide): 9.22MM **Privately Held**
SIC: 2515 Mattresses, innerspring or box spring
PA: Visionary Sleep, Llc
1721 Moon Lake Blvd # 205
Hoffman Estates IL
812 945-4155

(P-2864)
WIDLY INC
Also Called: American Furniture Alliance
785 E Harrison St Ste 100 (92879-1350)
PHONE..............................951 279-0900
▲ **EMP:** 130
SIC: 2515 5021 Mattresses and bedsprings; Furniture

2517 Wood Television And Radio Cabinets

(P-2865)
ANA GLOBAL LLC (PA)
2360 Marconi Ct (92154-7241)
PHONE..............................619 482-9990
▲ **EMP:** 90 **EST:** 1953
SALES (est): 44.49MM
SALES (corp-wide): 44.49MM **Privately Held**
Web: www.anaglb.com
SIC: 2517 5999 Television cabinets, wood; Medical apparatus and supplies

(P-2866)
GILBERT MARTIN WDWKG CO INC (PA)
Also Called: Martin Furniture
2345 Britannia Blvd (92154-8313)
PHONE..............................800 268-5669
Gilbert Martin, *Pr*
Mark Mitchell, *
◆ **EMP:** 30 **EST:** 1980
SQ FT: 210,000
SALES (est): 13.58MM
SALES (corp-wide): 13.58MM **Privately Held**
Web: www.martinfurniture.com
SIC: 2517 2511 2521 5021 Home entertainment unit cabinets, wood; Wood household furniture; Wood office furniture; Furniture

---

2519 Household Furniture, Nec

(P-2867)
ACRYLIC DISTRIBUTION CORP
Also Called: Acrylic Distribution
8421 Lankershim Blvd (91352-3125)
PHONE..............................818 767-8448
Shlomi Haziza, *Prin*
Soli Amor, *
Nick Enriques, *
▲ **EMP:** 34 **EST:** 1992
SALES (est): 6.08MM **Privately Held**
SIC: 2519 Furniture, household: glass, fiberglass, and plastic

(P-2868)
ARKTURA LLC (HQ)
966 Sandhill Ave (90746-1217)
PHONE..............................310 532-1050
Chris Kabatsi, *Managing Member*
▲ **EMP:** 30 **EST:** 2008

SALES (est): 10.35MM
SALES (corp-wide): 1.23B **Publicly Held**
Web: www.arktura.com
SIC: 2519 Furniture, household: glass, fiberglass, and plastic
PA: Armstrong World Industries, Inc.
2500 Columbia Ave
Lancaster PA
717 397-0611

(P-2869)
CALIFRNIA FURN COLLECTIONS INC
Also Called: Artifacts International
150 Reed Ct Ste A (91911-5890)
PHONE..............................619 621-2455
Eric Vogt, *Pr*
EMP: 114 **EST:** 1986
SQ FT: 40,000
SALES (est): 9.92MM **Privately Held**
Web: www.artifactsinternational.com
SIC: 2519 2514 2511 2512 Household furniture, except wood or metal: upholstered; Metal household furniture; Wood household furniture; Upholstered household furniture

(P-2870)
DON ALDERSON ASSOCIATES INC
3327 La Cienega Pl (90016-3116)
PHONE..............................310 837-5141
Juan Guardado, *Prin*
EMP: 40 **EST:** 1979
SALES (est): 1.46MM **Privately Held**
SIC: 2519 Household furniture, except wood or metal: upholstered

(P-2871)
MICHAEL NICHOLAS DESIGNS INC
2330 Raymer Ave (92833-2515)
PHONE..............................714 562-8101
Michael A Cimarusti Senior, *CEO*
Michael J Cimarusti II, *
▲ **EMP:** 120 **EST:** 2003
SALES (est): 21.79MM **Privately Held**
Web: www.mndca.com
SIC: 2519 Household furniture, except wood or metal: upholstered

(P-2872)
NEXT DAY FRAME INC
11560 Wright Rd (90262-3944)
PHONE..............................310 886-0851
Nancy Abelar, *CEO*
EMP: 65 **EST:** 2012
SALES (est): 2.56MM **Privately Held**
SIC: 2519 Household furniture, except wood or metal: upholstered

(P-2873)
SEATING COMPONENT MFG INC
3951 E Miraloma Ave (92806-6201)
PHONE..............................714 693-3376
Daryl Fossier, *Pr*
EMP: 24 **EST:** 1991
SQ FT: 12,000
SALES (est): 817.56K **Privately Held**
Web: www.seatingcomponentmfg.com
SIC: 2519 Fiberglass furniture, household: padded or plain

(P-2874)
STANDDESK INC
5042 Wilshire Blvd # 44689 (90036-4305)
PHONE..............................213 634-0665
Steven Yu, *Pr*
▲ **EMP:** 20 **EST:** 2013

SQ FT: 1,300
SALES (est): 1.6MM **Privately Held**
Web: www.standdesk.co
SIC: 2519 2522 Household furniture, except wood or metal: upholstered; Benches, office: except wood

(P-2875)
STONE YARD INC
Also Called: Carlsbad Manufacturing
6056 Corte Del Cedro (92011-1514)
PHONE..............................858 586-1580
Mitchell Brean, *Pr*
◆ **EMP:** 18 **EST:** 1967
SALES (est): 1.77MM **Privately Held**
Web: www.stoneyardinc.com
SIC: 2519 Household furniture, except wood or metal: upholstered

---

2521 Wood Office Furniture

(P-2876)
A M CABINETS INC (PA)
239 E Gardena Blvd (90248-2813)
PHONE..............................310 532-1919
Alex H Mc Kay Junior, *CEO*
Alex H Mc Kay Junior, *Pr*
Nancy Wolfinger, *
EMP: 88 **EST:** 1975
SQ FT: 35,000
SALES (est): 14.89MM
SALES (corp-wide): 14.89MM **Privately Held**
Web: www.amcabinets.com
SIC: 2521 2434 2541 Wood office furniture; Wood kitchen cabinets; Counters or counter display cases, wood

(P-2877)
AMERICON
900 Flynn Rd (93012-8703)
PHONE..............................805 987-0412
Bill Farrah, *Pr*
EMP: 17 **EST:** 1982
SQ FT: 30,000
SALES (est): 2.53MM **Privately Held**
Web: www.americon-usa.com
SIC: 2521 3663 Wood office furniture; Radio and t.v. communications equipment

(P-2878)
BAUSMAN AND COMPANY INC (PA)
1500 Crafton Ave (92359-1329)
PHONE..............................909 947-0139
Craig L Johnson, *CEO*
Craig Johnson, *CEO*
Robert Williams, *VP*
EMP: 249 **EST:** 1971
SALES (est): 22.14MM
SALES (corp-wide): 22.14MM **Privately Held**
Web: www.bausman.net
SIC: 2521 2511 Wood office furniture; Wood household furniture

(P-2879)
CASEWORX INC (PA)
Also Called: Caseworx
1130 Research Dr (92374-4562)
PHONE..............................909 799-8550
Bruce Humphrey, *Pr*
Gregg Schneider, *Sec*
▲ **EMP:** 37 **EST:** 1992
SQ FT: 28,000
SALES (est): 6.19MM **Privately Held**
Web: www.caseworx.com
SIC: 2521 Cabinets, office: wood

(P-2880)
COMMERCIAL FURNITURE
1261 N Lakeview Ave (92807-1834)
PHONE..............................714 350-7045
Bob Gomez, *Pr*
EMP: 19 **EST:** 1993
SQ FT: 8,500
SALES (est): 591.44K **Privately Held**
Web: www.cfi12345.com
SIC: 2521 7641 Wood office furniture; Upholstery work

(P-2881)
CRI SUB 1 (DH)
Also Called: E O C
1715 S Anderson Ave (90220-5005)
PHONE..............................310 537-1657
Ken Bodger, *CEO*
Richard L Sinclair Junior, *Pr*
Charles Hess, *VP*
▲ **EMP:** 27 **EST:** 1969
SQ FT: 120,000
SALES (est): 9.91MM
SALES (corp-wide): 67.75MM **Privately Held**
SIC: 2521 Cabinets, office: wood
HQ: Chromcraft Revington, Inc.
140 Bradford Dr Ste A
West Berlin NJ

(P-2882)
DESKMAKERS INC
6525 Flotilla St (90040-1713)
PHONE..............................323 264-2260
Philip Polishook, *CEO*
John Bornstein, *
◆ **EMP:** 50 **EST:** 1982
SQ FT: 105,000
SALES (est): 9.82MM **Privately Held**
Web: www.deskmakers.com
SIC: 2521 Desks, office: wood

(P-2883)
FORTRESS INC
Also Called: Off Broadway
1721 Wright Ave (91750-5841)
PHONE..............................909 593-8600
Donald I Wolper, *Pr*
▲ **EMP:** 35 **EST:** 1959
SQ FT: 100
SALES (est): 5.32MM **Privately Held**
Web: www.fortresseating.com
SIC: 2521 2522 Chairs, office: padded, upholstered, or plain: wood; Chairs, office: padded or plain: except wood

(P-2884)
FURNITURE SOLUTIONS INC
1347 N Blue Gum St (92806-1750)
P.O. Box 3578 (92834-3578)
PHONE..............................714 666-0424
Karen Valverde, *Ex VP*
Karen Valverde, *VP*
Daniel Nolazco, *Pr*
EMP: 24 **EST:** 1993
SQ FT: 25,000
SALES (est): 579.57K **Privately Held**
Web: www.furnituresolutions.us
SIC: 2521 2511 Wood office furniture; Wood household furniture

(P-2885)
GALTECH COMPUTER CORPORATION
Also Called: Galtech International
501 Flynn Rd (93012-8756)
P.O. Box 305 (91319-0305)
PHONE..............................805 376-1060
Fei Lin Ko, *CEO*
Robert Ko, *Pr*

Jim Lai, *Stockholder*
▲ **EMP**: 20 **EST**: 1991
SQ FT: 32,000
SALES (est): 3.4MM **Privately Held**
Web: www.galtechcorp.com
SIC: 2521 Benches, office: wood

(P-2886)
INTERIOR WOOD OF SAN DIEGO
1215 W Nutmeg St (92101-1230)
PHONE..............................619 295-6469
Alan Marshall, *Pr*
EMP: 18 **EST**: 1975
SQ FT: 10,000
SALES (est): 1.74MM **Privately Held**
Web: www.interiorwood.com
SIC: 2521 Cabinets, office: wood

(P-2887)
KUSHWOOD CHAIR INC
1290 E Elm St (91761-4025)
PHONE..............................909 930-2100
Daniel Kusvhinikov, *Pr*
Roger Douglas, *
EMP: 20 **EST**: 1979
SQ FT: 450,000
SALES (est): 451.1K **Privately Held**
SIC: 2521 2511 Wood office furniture;
Unassembled or unfinished furniture,
household: wood

(P-2888)
MONTBLEAU & ASSOCIATES
INC (PA)
555 Raven St (92102-4523)
PHONE..............................619 263-5550
Ron P Montbleau, *Pr*
Marti Montbleau, *
David Zammit, *
Barton Ward, *
EMP: 87 **EST**: 1980
SQ FT: 32,000
SALES (est): 18.62MM
SALES (corp-wide): 18.62MM **Privately
Held**
Web: www.montbleau.com
SIC: 2521 1751 2434 Wood office furniture;
Cabinet building and installation; Wood
kitchen cabinets

(P-2889)
NAKAMURA-BEEMAN INC
8520 Wellsford Pl (90670-2226)
PHONE..............................562 696-1400
Mike Beeman, *Pr*
EMP: 40 **EST**: 1978
SQ FT: 20,000
SALES (est): 4.91MM **Privately Held**
Web: www.nbifixtures.com
SIC: 2521 3429 2541 Wood office furniture;
Cabinet hardware; Display fixtures, wood

(P-2890)
NEW MAVERICK DESK INC
Also Called: Maverick Desk
15100 S Figueroa St (90248-1724)
PHONE..............................310 217-1554
John Long, *CEO*
Ted Jaroszewicz, *
Rich Mealey, *
▲ **EMP**: 150 **EST**: 1997
SQ FT: 1,000
SALES (est): 25.86MM **Privately Held**
Web: www.maverickdesk.com
SIC: 2521 Wood office furniture
HQ: Workstream Inc.
   3158 Production Dr
   Fairfield OH

(P-2891)
NORSTAR OFFICE PRODUCTS
INC (PA)
Also Called: Boss
5353 Jillson St (90040-2115)
PHONE..............................323 262-1919
William W Huang, *Pr*
◆ **EMP**: 40 **EST**: 1991
SQ FT: 150,000
SALES (est): 97.07MM **Privately Held**
Web: www.boss-chair.com
SIC: 2521 2522 Chairs, office: padded,
upholstered, or plain: wood; Chairs, office:
padded or plain: except wood

(P-2892)
OAK DESIGN CORPORATION
13272 6th St (91710-4108)
PHONE..............................909 628-9597
Ismaell Castellanos, *Pr*
Julio Salas, *Pr*
Ismael Castellanos, *Prin*
EMP: 18 **EST**: 1991
SALES (est): 4.82MM **Privately Held**
Web: www.odcproducts.com
SIC: 2521 2434 2511 Wood office furniture;
Wood kitchen cabinets; Wood bedroom
furniture

(P-2893)
OFFICE CHAIRS INC
Also Called: Oci
14815 Radburn Ave (90670-5319)
PHONE..............................562 802-0464
Sharon Klapper, *Pr*
Donald J Simek, *
Joseph J Klapper Junior, *Sec*
▲ **EMP**: 60 **EST**: 1974
SQ FT: 60,000
SALES (est): 9.32MM **Privately Held**
Web: www.ocisitwell.com
SIC: 2521 2512 Wood office furniture;
Chairs: upholstered on wood frames

(P-2894)
OFS BRANDS HOLDINGS INC
5559 Mcfadden Ave (92649-1317)
P.O. Box 100 (47542-0100)
PHONE..............................714 903-2257
Craig Baker, *Pr*
EMP: 660 **EST**: 2018
SALES (est): 2.38MM
SALES (corp-wide): 228.87MM **Privately
Held**
SIC: 2521 Wood office furniture
PA: Ofs Brands Holdings Inc.
   1204 E 6th St
   Huntingburg IN
   800 521-5381

(P-2895)
PARKINSON ENTERPRISES INC
Also Called: Salman
135 S State College Blvd Ste 625
(92821-5811)
PHONE..............................714 626-0275
Michael Parkinson, *CEO*
Carolyn Parkinson, *
EMP: 70 **EST**: 1993
SQ FT: 75,000
SALES (est): 3.98MM **Privately Held**
SIC: 2521 Wood office furniture

(P-2896)
RBF GROUP INTERNATIONAL
Also Called: Rbf Lifestyle Holdings
1441 W 2nd St (91766-1202)
PHONE..............................626 333-5700
Robert Brown, *CEO*
▲ **EMP**: 19 **EST**: 2007

SALES (est): 932.17K **Privately Held**
SIC: 2521 Chairs, office: padded,
upholstered, or plain: wood

(P-2897)
RBF LIFESTYLE HOLDINGS LLC
Also Called: Beverly Furniture
1441 W 2nd St (91766-1202)
PHONE..............................626 333-5700
▲ **EMP**: 45
SIC: 2521 2511 Chairs, office: padded,
upholstered, or plain: wood; Dining room
furniture: wood

(P-2898)
S & H CABINETS AND MFG INC
10860 Mulberry Ave (92337-7027)
PHONE..............................909 357-0551
Michael Hansen, *CEO*
EMP: 40 **EST**: 1954
SQ FT: 22,000
SALES (est): 6.21MM **Privately Held**
Web: www.shcabinets.com
SIC: 2521 2541 2431 Cabinets, office: wood;
Table or counter tops, plastic laminated;
Millwork

(P-2899)
SPACESTOR INC
16411 Carmenita Rd (90703-2216)
PHONE..............................310 410-0220
▲ **EMP**: 21 **EST**: 1974
SALES (est): 24.74MM **Privately Held**
Web: www.spacestor.com
SIC: 2521 2522 5712 Wood office furniture;
Office furniture, except wood; Office
furniture

(P-2900)
STOLO CABINETS INC (PA)
Also Called: Stolo Custom Cabinets
860 Challenger St (92821-2946)
PHONE..............................714 529-7303
Gary Stolo, *VP*
Justin Stolo, *
Robert F Stolo, *
EMP: 45 **EST**: 1953
SQ FT: 15,000
SALES (est): 9.55MM
SALES (corp-wide): 9.55MM **Privately
Held**
Web: www.stolocabinets.com
SIC: 2521 Cabinets, office: wood

(P-2901)
VALLEY OAKS INDUSTRIES
Also Called: Valley Oak Cabinets
3550 E Highway 246 Ste Ae (93460-9480)
P.O. Box 1097 (93460-1097)
PHONE..............................805 688-2754
Tom Carlson, *Pr*
Kim Carlson, *VP*
EMP: 17 **EST**: 1982
SALES (est): 2.39MM **Privately Held**
Web: www.valleyoakindustries.com
SIC: 2521 2511 Wood office furniture; Wood
household furniture

2522 Office Furniture, Except
Wood

(P-2902)
AMERICAN FURNITURE
SYSTEMS INC
Also Called: Advantage Custom Fixtures
14105 Avalon Blvd (90061-2637)
P.O. Box 1235 (91778-1235)
PHONE..............................626 457-9900

Allen Sterris, *Pr*
EMP: 23 **EST**: 1930
SQ FT: 50,000
SALES (est): 1.07MM **Privately Held**
Web: www.americanfurnituresys.com
SIC: 2522 5411 Office furniture, except wood
; Convenience stores

(P-2903)
ANGELL & GIROUX INC
2727 Alcazar St (90033-1106)
P.O. Box 33156 (90033-0156)
PHONE..............................323 269-8596
Richard M Hart, *CEO*
Carol A Hart, *
Kenneth Hart, *
EMP: 52 **EST**: 1956
SQ FT: 13,000
SALES (est): 8.92MM **Privately Held**
Web: www.angellandgiroux.com
SIC: 2522 3479 Cabinets, office: except
wood; Painting, coating, and hot dipping

(P-2904)
ARTE DE MEXICO INC (PA)
1000 Chestnut St (91506-1623)
PHONE..............................818 753-4559
Gerald J Stoffers, *CEO*
▲ **EMP**: 90 **EST**: 1982
SQ FT: 103,000
SALES (est): 9.36MM
SALES (corp-wide): 9.36MM **Privately
Held**
Web: www.artedemexico.com
SIC: 2522 3645 Office furniture, except wood
; Residential lighting fixtures

(P-2905)
AUTONOMOUS INC
21800 Opportunity Way (92518-3100)
PHONE..............................844 949-3879
Geoffrey Handley, *Pr*
EMP: 30 **EST**: 2013
SALES (est): 3.77MM **Privately Held**
Web: www.autonomous.ai
SIC: 2522 Office furniture, except wood

(P-2906)
CARTERS METAL
FABRICATORS INC
935 W 5th St (91702-3311)
PHONE..............................626 815-4225
EMP: 30
Web: www.cartersmetal.com
SIC: 2522 Office furniture, except wood

(P-2907)
CRAFTWOOD INDUSTRIES INC
222 Shelbourne (92620-2176)
P.O. Box 2068 (49422-2068)
PHONE..............................616 796-1209
Terry W Beckering, *Pr*
Roger Steensma, *
Kathy Prominski, *Corporate Secretary*
EMP: 35 **EST**: 1995
SALES (est): 2.65MM **Privately Held**
Web: www.craftwoodindustries.com
SIC: 2522 2531 2426 2511 Office furniture,
except wood; Public building and related
furniture; Hardwood dimension and flooring
mills; Wood household furniture

(P-2908)
ELITE MFG CORP
Also Called: Elite Modern
12143 Altamar Pl (90670-2501)
PHONE..............................888 354-8356
Peter Luong, *CEO*
Robinson Ho, *
▲ **EMP**: 102 **EST**: 1988

P
R
O
D
U
C
T
S

&

S
V
C
S

SQ FT: 62,000
SALES (est): 16.12MM **Privately Held**
Web: www.elitemodern.com
SIC: 2522 2514 Office furniture, except wood
; Metal household furniture

(P-2909)
**ERGOCRAFT CONTRACT
SOLUTIONS**
Also Called: Ergocraft Office Furniture
6055 E Washington Blvd Ste 500
(90040-2426)
▲ **EMP:** 25 **EST:** 2001
SALES (est): 3.11MM **Privately Held**
Web: www.ecs-designs.com
SIC: 2522 Office furniture, except wood

(P-2910)
**ERGONONMIC COMFORT
DESIGN INC**
9140 Stellar Ct Ste B (92883-4902)
P.O. Box 79018 (92877-0167)
PHONE..........................951 277-1558
▲ **EMP:** 18 **EST:** 1994
SQ FT: 22,000
SALES (est): 2.24MM **Privately Held**
Web: www.ecdergo.com
SIC: 2522 Office chairs, benches, and
stools, except wood

(P-2911)
EXEMPLIS LLC
Also Called: Sit On It
6280 Artesia Blvd (90620-1004)
PHONE..........................714 995-4800
Paul Devries, *Mgr*
EMP: 21
Web: www.exemplis.com
SIC: 2522 2521 2512 Chairs, office: padded
or plain: except wood; Wood office furniture
; Upholstered household furniture
PA: Exemplis Llc
6415 Katella Ave Ste 100
Cypress CA

(P-2912)
EXEMPLIS LLC (PA)
Also Called: Sitonit
6415 Katella Ave (90630-5245)
PHONE..........................714 995-4800
◆ **EMP:** 40 **EST:** 1996
SQ FT: 20,000
SALES (est): 157.5MM **Privately Held**
Web: www.exemplis.com
SIC: 2522 Chairs, office: padded or plain:
except wood

(P-2913)
**HIGHMARK SMART RELIABLE
SEATING INC**
Also Called: Highmark
5559 Mcfadden Ave (92649-1317)
PHONE..........................714 903-2257
◆ **EMP:** 200
SIC: 2522 Chairs, office: padded or plain:
except wood

(P-2914)
KORDEN INC
601 S Milliken Ave (91761-8103)
PHONE..........................909 988-8979
Barjona S Meek, *Prin*
Thomas Mc Cormick, *Pr*
Jim Ethridge, *Ex VP*
EMP: 48 **EST:** 1949
SALES (est): 6.96MM **Privately Held**
Web: www.modernspace.com
SIC: 2522 Stools, office: except wood

(P-2915)
**MCDOWELL CRAIG OFF
SYSTEMS INC**
Also Called: McDowell-Craig Office Furn
13146 Firestone Blvd (90650)
P.O. Box 349 (90651-0349)
PHONE..........................562 921-4441
Brent G Mcdowell, *Pr*
Jeffrey C Mcdowell, *Sec*
EMP: 70 **EST:** 1995
SQ FT: 117,000
SALES (est): 8.06MM **Privately Held**
Web: www.mcdowellcraig.com
SIC: 2522 Office furniture, except wood

(P-2916)
**MODULAR OFFICE SOLUTIONS
INC**
11701 6th St (91730-6030)
PHONE..........................909 476-4200
Daniel G Coelho, *CEO*
Jorge E Robles, *
▲ **EMP:** 40 **EST:** 1999
SQ FT: 173,000
SALES (est): 725.26K **Privately Held**
Web: www.chicagoofficefurniture.com
SIC: 2522 2521 Office furniture, except wood
; Wood office furniture

(P-2917)
**SUPER STRUCT BLDG
SYSTEMS INC**
1251 Montalvo Way Ste F (92263)
P.O. Box 1014 (92247-1014)
PHONE..........................760 322-2522
John G Kalogeris, *Pr*
Chris Kalogeris, *
EMP: 40 **EST:** 1960
SQ FT: 10,000
SALES (est): 3.01MM **Privately Held**
SIC: 2522 2439 Panel systems and
partitions, office: except wood; Trusses,
wooden roof

(P-2918)
VERSA PRODUCTS INC (PA)
Also Called: Versatables.com
14105 Avalon Blvd (90061-2637)
PHONE..........................310 353-7100
Christopher Laudadio, *CEO*
▲ **EMP:** 108 **EST:** 2000
SQ FT: 35,000
SALES (est): 21.68MM
SALES (corp-wide): 21.68MM **Privately
Held**
Web: www.versatables.com
SIC: 2522 Office desks and tables, except
wood

(P-2919)
X-CHAIR LLC
6415 Katella Ave (90630-5245)
PHONE..........................844 492-4247
Anthony Mazlish, *Managing Member*
EMP: 39 **EST:** 2015
SALES (est): 5.53MM **Privately Held**
Web: www.xchair.com
SIC: 2522 Office furniture, except wood
PA: Exemplis Llc
6415 Katella Ave Ste 100
Cypress CA

2531 Public Building And Related Furniture

(P-2920)
AEROFOAM INDUSTRIES INC
Also Called: Quality Foam Packaging

31855 Corydon St (92530-8501)
PHONE..........................951 245-4429
Noel Castellon, *Pr*
Noel Castellon Junior, *VP*
Jim Barrett, *
Ruth Castellon, *
Darlene Garay, *
▲ **EMP:** 80 **EST:** 2010
SQ FT: 150,000
SALES (est): 9.82MM **Privately Held**
Web: www.aerofoams.com
SIC: 2531 Seats, aircraft

(P-2921)
AIRO INDUSTRIES COMPANY
429 Jessie St (91340-2541)
PHONE..........................818 838-1008
Bahram Salem, *Pr*
Mike Salem, *
▲ **EMP:** 25 **EST:** 1989
SQ FT: 20,000
SALES (est): 4.2MM **Privately Held**
Web: www.airoindustries.com
SIC: 2531 4581 Seats, aircraft; Aircraft
upholstery repair

(P-2922)
CLARIOS LLC
Also Called: Johnson Controls
4100 Guardian St (93063-6717)
PHONE..........................805 522-5555
Dimitri Dorfan, *Mgr*
EMP: 36
SALES (corp-wide): 1.54B **Privately Held**
Web: www.clarios.com
SIC: 2531 Seats, automobile
HQ: Clarios, Llc
5757 N Green Bay Ave
Milwaukee WI

(P-2923)
CLARIOS LLC
Also Called: Johnson Controls
39312 Leopard St Ste A (92211-1129)
PHONE..........................760 200-5225
EMP: 38
SALES (corp-wide): 1.54B **Privately Held**
Web: www.clarios.com
SIC: 2531 Seats, automobile
HQ: Clarios, Llc
5757 N Green Bay Ave
Milwaukee WI

(P-2924)
COD USA INC
Also Called: Creative Outdoor Distrs USA
25954 Commercentre Dr (92630-8815)
PHONE..........................949 381-7367
Heather Smulson, *Pr*
Brian Horowitz, *CEO*
Barbara Tolbert, *COO*
◆ **EMP:** 23 **EST:** 2016
SQ FT: 34,000
SALES (est): 2.74MM **Privately Held**
SIC: 2531 Chairs, portable folding

(P-2925)
ECR4KIDS LP
Also Called: Early Childhood Resources
5630 Kearny Mesa Rd Ste B (92111-1323)
PHONE..........................619 323-2005
Lee Siegel, *Pt*
◆ **EMP:** 25 **EST:** 2003
SALES (est): 9.33MM **Privately Held**
Web: www.ecr4kids.com
SIC: 2531 3944 2511 5021 Chairs, table and
arm; Craft and hobby kits and sets;
Children's wood furniture; Chairs
PA: Cri 2000, L.P.
2245 San Diego Ave # 125

San Diego CA

(P-2926)
**EUROTEC SEATING
INCORPORATED**
1000 S Euclid St (90631-6806)
PHONE..........................562 806-6171
◆ **EMP:** 50
SIC: 2531 Seats, automobile

(P-2927)
HOLGUIN & HOLGUIN INC
Also Called: Seating Resource
968 W Foothill Blvd (91702-2842)
PHONE..........................626 815-0168
Gilda Vega, *Pr*
John H Holguin, *
EMP: 45 **EST:** 1994
SQ FT: 25,000
SALES (est): 4.76MM **Privately Held**
Web: www.seatingresource.com
SIC: 2531 Public building and related
furniture

(P-2928)
J L FURNISHINGS LLC
Also Called: J L F/Lone Meadow
1620 5th Ave Ste 400 (92101-2738)
PHONE..........................310 605-6600
◆ **EMP:** 300
Web: www.thestandardbyrcd.com
SIC: 2531 2521 Chairs, table and arm;
Wood office chairs, benches and stools

(P-2929)
JOHNSON CONTROLS INC
Also Called: Johnson Controls
12393 Slauson Ave (90606-2824)
PHONE..........................562 698-8301
Stephen Roell, *Brnch Mgr*
EMP: 22
Web: www.johnsoncontrols.com
SIC: 2531 1711 Seats, automobile; Warm air
heating and air conditioning contractor
HQ: Johnson Controls, Inc.
5757 N Green Bay Ave
Milwaukee WI
920 245-6409

(P-2930)
JOHNSON CONTROLS INC
Also Called: Johnson Controls
5770 Warland Dr Ste A (90630-5047)
PHONE..........................562 594-3200
Dough Beebe, *Mgr*
EMP: 150
Web: www.johnsoncontrols.com
SIC: 2531 1711 5075 5065 Seats, automobile
; Heating systems repair and maintenance;
Warm air heating and air conditioning;
Electronic parts and equipment, nec
HQ: Johnson Controls, Inc.
5757 N Green Bay Ave
Milwaukee WI
920 245-6409

(P-2931)
KRUEGER INTERNATIONAL INC
16510 Bake Pkwy Ste 100 (92618-4663)
PHONE..........................949 748-7000
EMP: 23
SALES (corp-wide): 682.99MM **Privately
Held**
Web: www.ki.com
SIC: 2531 School furniture
PA: Krueger International, Inc.
1330 Bellevue St
Green Bay WI
920 468-8100

▲ = Import ▼ = Export
◆ = Import/Export

(P-2932)
LOUIS SARDO UPHOLSTERY INC (PA)
Also Called: Sardo Bus & Coach Upholstery
512 W Rosecrans Ave (90248-1515)
PHONE..............................310 327-0532
Louis Sardo, *Pr*
Jeanie Sardo, *
EMP: 55 EST: 1916
SQ FT: 10,000
SALES (est): 5.06MM
SALES (corp-wide): 5.06MM **Privately Held**
Web: www.sardobus.com
SIC: 2531 3713 7641 Seats, automobile; Truck and bus bodies; Reupholstery and furniture repair

(P-2933)
MORTECH MANUFACTURING
411 N Aerojet Dr (91702-3253)
PHONE..............................626 334-1471
Gino Joseph, *Pr*
Gino Joseph, *CEO*
Paul Joseph, *
Christy Haines, *
◆ **EMP: 82 EST:** 1986
SQ FT: 43,000
SALES (est): 11.64MM **Privately Held**
Web: www.mortechmfg.com
SIC: 2531 5087 Altars and pulpits; Funeral director's equipment and supplies

(P-2934)
ORBO CORPORATION (PA)
Also Called: Eurotec Seating
1000 S Euclid St (90631-6806)
PHONE..............................562 806-6171
Oscar Galvez, *Pr*
EMP: 63 EST: 2001
SALES (est): 9.1MM
SALES (corp-wide): 9.1MM **Privately Held**
Web: www.4seating.com
SIC: 2531 Seats, automobile

(P-2935)
PACIFIC HOSPITALITY DESIGN INC
Also Called: PH Design
2620 S Malt Ave (90040-3206)
PHONE..............................323 278-7998
Gilberto Martinez, *CEO*
Ana Martinez, *
EMP: 25 EST: 1979
SQ FT: 14,000
SALES (est): 2.31MM **Privately Held**
Web: www.phdesign.com
SIC: 2531 Public building and related furniture

(P-2936)
SAN DIEGO UNIFIED SCHOOL DST
3426 School St (92116-3423)
PHONE..............................619 600-5321
EMP: 20
SALES (corp-wide): 1.97B **Privately Held**
Web: www.sandiegounified.org
SIC: 2531 Public building and related furniture
PA: San Diego Unified School District
4100 Normal St
San Diego CA
619 725-8000

(P-2937)
SEATING CONCEPTS LLC
4229 Ponderosa Ave Ste B (92123-1519)
PHONE..............................619 491-3159

Juan Carlos Letayf, *Managing Member*
Bill Overton, *
Jose Letayf, *
◆ **EMP: 30 EST:** 1982
SALES (est): 5.65MM **Privately Held**
Web: www.barstoolmanufacturers.com
SIC: 2531 5021 Theater furniture; Chairs

(P-2938)
TALIMAR SYSTEMS INC
3105 W Alpine St (92704-6911)
PHONE..............................714 557-4884
David G Wesdell, *Pr*
▲ **EMP: 37 EST:** 1988
SQ FT: 11,000
SALES (est): 5.1MM **Privately Held**
Web: www.talimarsystems.com
SIC: 2531 5712 7389 5932 Public building and related furniture; Furniture stores; Merchandise liquidators; Office furniture, secondhand

(P-2939)
VILLA FURNITURE MFG CO
Also Called: Villa International
13760 Midway St (90703-2331)
PHONE..............................714 535-7272
Andrew M Greenthal, *Pr*
▲ **EMP: 125 EST:** 1949
SQ FT: 75,000
SALES (est): 9.24MM **Privately Held**
Web: www.villainternational.com
SIC: 2531 2522 Vehicle furniture; Office furniture, except wood

(P-2940)
VIRCO MFG CORPORATION (PA)
2027 Harpers Way (90501-1524)
PHONE..............................310 533-0474
Robert A Virtue, *Ch Bd*
Douglas A Virtue, *
J Scott Bell, *Sr VP*
Robert E Dose, *Sr VP*
Patricia Quinones, *Sr VP*
◆ **EMP: 88 EST:** 1950
SQ FT: 560,000
SALES (est): 231.06MM
SALES (corp-wide): 231.06MM **Publicly Held**
Web: www.virco.com
SIC: 2531 2522 2511 School furniture; Office furniture, except wood; Wood household furniture

---

2541 Wood Partitions And Fixtures

(P-2941)
ALL AMERICAN CABINETRY INC
Also Called: All American Sterile Coat
13901 Saticoy St (91402-6521)
PHONE..............................818 376-0500
Chris Zepatos, *Pr*
EMP: 18 EST: 1996
SALES (est): 920.67K **Privately Held**
Web: www.allamericancabinets.us
SIC: 2541 Cabinets, lockers, and shelving

(P-2942)
AMTREND CORPORATION
1458 Manhattan Ave (92831-5222)
PHONE..............................714 630-2070
Hamid A Malik, *Pr*
Javeeda Malik, *
EMP: 85 EST: 1980
SQ FT: 45,000
SALES (est): 16.52MM **Privately Held**
Web: www.amtrend.com

SIC: 2541 2521 7641 2512 Wood partitions and fixtures; Wood office furniture; Upholstery work; Upholstered household furniture

(P-2943)
ARCHITECTURAL WOODWORKING CO
582 Monterey Pass Rd (91754-2417)
PHONE..............................626 570-4125
John K Jack Heydorff, *Pr*
John F Heydorff, *Stockholder*
Richard A Schaub, *
Edward Illig, *
Thomas C Heydorff, *
EMP: 100 EST: 1963
SQ FT: 60,000
SALES (est): 9.58MM **Privately Held**
Web: www.awcla.com
SIC: 2541 1751 Office fixtures, wood; Carpentry work

(P-2944)
BLOCK TOPS INC (PA)
Also Called: Top Source, The
1321 S Sunkist St (92806-5614)
PHONE..............................714 978-5080
Vanessa Bates, *CEO*
Nate Kolenski, *
▲ **EMP: 34 EST:** 1977
SQ FT: 10,000
SALES (est): 4.8MM
SALES (corp-wide): 4.8MM **Privately Held**
Web: www.blocktops.com
SIC: 2541 2519 3281 2821 Table or counter tops, plastic laminated; Furniture, household: glass, fiberglass, and plastic; Cut stone and stone products; Plastics materials and resins

(P-2945)
BRISTOL OMEGA INC
9441 Opal Ave Ste 2 (92359-9900)
PHONE..............................909 794-6862
Ralf G Zacky, *CEO*
EMP: 27 EST: 1993
SALES (est): 2.03MM **Privately Held**
Web: www.bristolomega.com
SIC: 2541 1611 Wood partitions and fixtures; General contractor, highway and street construction

(P-2946)
CCM ENTERPRISES (PA)
10848 Wheatlands Ave (92071-2855)
PHONE..............................619 562-2605
Cody L Nosko, *CEO*
Duane Nosco, *
Virginia Jaggi, *
EMP: 60 EST: 1995
SQ FT: 67,543
SALES (est): 5MM **Privately Held**
Web: www.ccmmfg.com
SIC: 2541 1799 Counter and sink tops; Kitchen and bathroom remodeling

(P-2947)
CK MANUFACTURING & TRADING INC
Also Called: Kosakura Associates
3 Holland (92618-2506)
P.O. Box 1190 (75483-1190)
PHONE..............................949 529-3400
▲ **EMP:** 35
SIC: 2541 Display fixtures, wood

(P-2948)
CLOSETS BY DESIGN INC
Also Called: Closets By Design

3860 Capitol Ave (90601-1733)
PHONE..............................562 699-9945
Frank Melkonian, *Pr*
EMP: 28 EST: 1982
SALES (est): 1.45MM **Privately Held**
Web: www.closetsbydesign.com
SIC: 2541 2521 Lockers, except refrigerated: wood; Wood office filing cabinets and bookcases

(P-2949)
COLUMBIA SHOWCASE & CAB CO INC
11034 Sherman Way Ste A (91352-4927)
PHONE..............................818 765-9710
Samuel M Patterson Junior, *CEO*
▲ **EMP: 125 EST:** 1950
SQ FT: 170,000
SALES (est): 14.56MM **Privately Held**
SIC: 2541 1542 Cabinets, except refrigerated: show, display, etc.: wood; Commercial and office building contractors

(P-2950)
COMPATICO INC
1901 S Archibald Ave (91761-8548)
PHONE..............................616 940-1772
John Rea, *Pr*
Richard Posthumus, *
William Boer, *
Cheryl Daniels, *
Carrie Boer, *
◆ **EMP: 45 EST:** 1989
SALES (est): 4.55MM **Privately Held**
Web: www.compatico.com
SIC: 2541 Wood partitions and fixtures

(P-2951)
CUSTOM DISPLAYS INC
411 W 157th St (90248-2118)
PHONE..............................323 770-8074
Thomas Otani, *Pr*
Ben Hasuike, *
EMP: 21 EST: 1970
SQ FT: 16,000
SALES (est): 637.68K **Privately Held**
SIC: 2541 3827 3993 Display fixtures, wood; Triplet magnifying instruments, optical; Signs and advertising specialties

(P-2952)
EUROPEAN WHOLESALE COUNTER
10051 Prospect Ave (92071-4321)
PHONE..............................619 562-0565
Pete Sciarrino, *CEO*
EMP: 150 EST: 2008
SQ FT: 40,000
SALES (est): 14.66MM **Privately Held**
Web: www.europeancompany.com
SIC: 2541 1799 Counter and sink tops; Counter top installation

(P-2953)
F-J-E INC
Also Called: Jf Fixtures & Design
546 W Esther St (90813-1529)
PHONE......:.......................562 437-7466
Frank Ernandes, *Pr*
Barbara Ernandes, *
EMP: 25 EST: 1983
SQ FT: 26,000
SALES (est): 4.7MM **Privately Held**
Web: www.jffixtures.com
SIC: 2541 2542 Store fixtures, wood; Fixtures, store: except wood

P R O D U C T S & S V C S

(P-2954)
HERITAGE CABINET CO INC
21740 Marilla St (91311-4125)
PHONE...............818 786-4900
Robert Geyer, *Pr*
Kathy Geyer, *Sec*
EMP: 17 **EST:** 1982
SQ FT: 12,000
SALES (est): 713.35K **Privately Held**
SIC: 2541 5211 2521 2517 Cabinets, except refrigerated: show, display, etc.: wood; Lumber and other building materials; Wood office furniture; Wood television and radio cabinets

(P-2955)
IDEAL PRODUCTS INC
4025 Garner Rd (92501-1043)
P.O. Box 4090 (91761-1006)
PHONE...............951 727-8600
Robert L Martin Junior, *CEO*
Virginia Martin, *
EMP: 35 **EST:** 1976
SALES (est): 5.14MM **Privately Held**
Web: www.idealockers.com
SIC: 2541 Lockers, except refrigerated: wood

(P-2956)
IVARS DISPLAY (PA)
Also Called: Ivar's Displays
2314 E Locust Ct (91761-7613)
PHONE...............909 923-2761
Ivan Gundersen, *CFO*
Karl Gundersen, *
Linda Pulice, *
Jason Gundersen, *
▲ **EMP:** 87 **EST:** 1966
SQ FT: 95,000
SALES (est): 18.21MM
SALES (corp-wide): 18.21MM **Privately Held**
Web: www.ivarsdisplay.com
SIC: 2541 2542 Store fixtures, wood; Shelving, office and store, except wood

(P-2957)
JUDITH VON HOPF INC
1525 W 13th St Ste H (91786-7528)
PHONE...............909 481-1884
▲ **EMP:** 25 **EST:** 1976
SALES (est): 4.06MM **Privately Held**
Web: www.judithvonhopf.com
SIC: 2541 Display fixtures, wood

(P-2958)
KILLION INDUSTRIES INC (PA)
1380 Poinsettia Ave (92081-8504)
PHONE...............760 727-5102
Richard W Killion, *Pr*
Larry Edward, *
◆ **EMP:** 80 **EST:** 1981
SQ FT: 185,000
SALES (est): 28.58MM
SALES (corp-wide): 28.58MM **Privately Held**
Web: www.killionindustries.com
SIC: 2541 Store and office display cases and fixtures

(P-2959)
LA CABINET & MILLWORK INC
Also Called: Bromack
3005 Humboldt St (90031-1830)
PHONE...............323 227-5000
EMP: 25 **EST:** 2005
SQ FT: 17,000
SALES (est): 3.71MM **Privately Held**

(P-2960)
LEONARDS CARPET SERVICE INC (PA)
Also Called: Xgrass Turf Direct
1121 N Red Gum St (92806-2582)
PHONE...............714 630-1930
Leonard Nagel, *Pr*
Joel Nagel, *
▲ **EMP:** 75 **EST:** 1970
SQ FT: 52,000
SALES (est): 23.06MM
SALES (corp-wide): 23.06MM **Privately Held**
Web: www.leonardscarpetservice.com
SIC: 2541 1771 1799 Table or counter tops, plastic laminated; Flooring contractor; Artificial turf installation

(P-2961)
NICO NAT MFG CORP
Also Called: Niconat Manufacturing
2624 Yates Ave (90040-2622)
PHONE...............323 721-1900
Jose Valdez, *CEO*
Francisco Valdez, *Stockholder**
EMP: 45 **EST:** 2008
SALES (est): 9.97MM **Privately Held**
Web: www.niconatmfg.com
SIC: 2541 Store and office display cases and fixtures

(P-2962)
OAK-IT INC
845 Sandhill Ave (90746-1210)
P.O. Box 4733 (90241-1733)
PHONE...............310 719-3999
Lori Barrett, *Pr*
Sean Kittiko, *
◆ **EMP:** 22 **EST:** 1983
SQ FT: 8,000
SALES (est): 4.57MM **Privately Held**
Web: www.oakitinc.com
SIC: 2541 2431 5046 Store fixtures, wood; Millwork; Store fixtures

(P-2963)
OMNI ENCLOSURES INC
Also Called: Omni Pacific
505 Raleigh Ave (92020-3139)
PHONE...............619 579-6664
Thomas P Burke, *Pr*
▲ **EMP:** 27 **EST:** 1981
SQ FT: 20,000
SALES (est): 5.52MM **Privately Held**
Web: www.omnilabsolutions.com
SIC: 2541 Office fixtures, wood

(P-2964)
PACIFIC WESTLINE INC
1536 W Embassy St (92802-1016)
PHONE...............714 956-2442
Daniel G Mcleith, *CEO*
EMP: 90 **EST:** 1975
SQ FT: 62,000
SALES (est): 7.82MM **Privately Held**
Web: www.pacificwestline.com
SIC: 2541 2431 Cabinets, except refrigerated: show, display, etc.: wood; Millwork

(P-2965)
SPALINGER ENTERPRISES INC
Also Called: Skyline Cabinet & Millworks
800 S Mount Vernon Ave (93307-2889)
PHONE...............661 834-4550
David Spalinger, *Pr*
J W Spalinger, *VP*
Melody Spalinger, *Sec*
▲ **EMP:** 30 **EST:** 1948
SQ FT: 8,500
SALES (est): 2.69MM **Privately Held**
Web: www.skylinecabinets.com
SIC: 2541 Cabinets, except refrigerated: show, display, etc.: wood

(P-2966)
SPOONERS WOODWORKS INC
Also Called: Spooners Woodworks
12460 Kirkham Ct (92064-6819)
PHONE...............858 679-9086
Tom Spooner, *Admn*
Thomas Spooner, *
Stephen Spooner, *
Valerie Spooner, *
Rosemary Spooner, *
EMP: 120 **EST:** 1979
SQ FT: 22,000
SALES (est): 23.76MM **Privately Held**
Web: www.spoonerwoodworks.com
SIC: 2541 Store fixtures, wood

(P-2967)
SW FIXTURES INC
3940 Valley Blvd Ste C (91789-1541)
PHONE...............909 595-2506
Daniel Zachary, *Pr*
EMP: 18 **EST:** 1985
SQ FT: 22,500
SALES (est): 2.48MM **Privately Held**
Web: www.swfixtures.com
SIC: 2541 2431 Display fixtures, wood; Planing mill, millwork

(P-2968)
TEMEKA ADVERTISING INC
Also Called: Temeka Group
9073 Pulsar Ct (92883-7346)
PHONE...............951 277-2525
Michael D Wilson, *CEO*
Paul Mieboer, *Stockholder**
Marlene Kelly, *
▲ **EMP:** 55 **EST:** 1991
SQ FT: 24,000
SALES (est): 9.92MM **Privately Held**
Web: www.temekagroup.com
SIC: 2541 Store and office display cases and fixtures

(P-2969)
V TWEST INC
16222 Phoebe Ave (90638-5610)
PHONE...............714 521-2167
EMP: 17
SALES (corp-wide): 434.93MM **Privately Held**
Web: www.vtindustries.com
SIC: 2541 Counter and sink tops
HQ: V T.West Inc.
1000 Industrial Park
Holstein IA

(P-2970)
YOSHIMASA DISPLAY CASE INC
Also Called: Yoshimasa
108 Pico St (91766-2137)
PHONE...............213 637-9999
Toro Hayashi, *Pr*
Michael Y Yoo, *
Alma Kim Oprtn, *Mgr*
▲ **EMP:** 35 **EST:** 2011
SQ FT: 15,000
SALES (est): 3.1MM **Privately Held**
Web: www.yoshimasausa.com

SIC: 2541 3564 Store and office display cases and fixtures; Aircurtains (blower)

2542 Partitions And Fixtures, Except Wood

(P-2971)
ABTECH INCORPORATED
3420 W Fordham Ave (92704-4422)
PHONE...............714 550-9961
James Herr, *CEO*
Cheryl Herr, *
▲ **EMP:** 33 **EST:** 1992
SQ FT: 11,000
SALES (est): 4.84MM **Privately Held**
Web: www.abtech.net
SIC: 2542 3448 Partitions and fixtures, except wood; Prefabricated metal buildings and components

(P-2972)
ADVANCED EQUIPMENT CORPORATION (PA)
2401 W Commonwealth Ave (92833-2999)
PHONE...............714 635-5350
Wesley B Dickson, *Ch*
W Scott Dickson, *Senior President**
W Dickson, *
Bryan Dickson, *
Frank Manning, *
◆ **EMP:** 50 **EST:** 1957
SQ FT: 51,000
SALES (est): 10.17MM
SALES (corp-wide): 10.17MM **Privately Held**
Web: www.advancedequipment.com
SIC: 2542 2541 Partitions for floor attachment, prefabricated: except wood; Wood partitions and fixtures

(P-2973)
BOBRICK WASHROOM EQUIPMENT INC (HQ)
Also Called: Gamco
6901 Tujunga Ave (91605-5882)
PHONE...............818 764-1000
◆ **EMP:** 100 **EST:** 1906
SALES (est): 129.48MM
SALES (corp-wide): 132.97MM **Privately Held**
Web: www.bobrick.com
SIC: 2542 Partitions for floor attachment, prefabricated: except wood
PA: The Bobrick Corporation
6901 Tujunga Ave
North Hollywood CA
818 764-1000

(P-2974)
BRITCAN INC
Also Called: Rich Limited
3809 Ocean Ranch Blvd Ste 110 (92056-8606)
PHONE...............760 722-2300
James B Hollen, *CEO*
◆ **EMP:** 20 **EST:** 1992
SQ FT: 23,000
SALES (est): 4.83MM **Privately Held**
Web: www.richltd.com
SIC: 2542 3089 Racks, merchandise display or storage: except wood; Air mattresses, plastics

(P-2975)
CAL PARTITIONS INC
23814 President Ave (90710-1390)
PHONE...............310 539-1911
Alan Anderson, *Pr*

Sarah Anderson, *Sec*
EMP: 23 **EST:** 1959
SQ FT: 13,000
SALES (est): 570.47K **Privately Held**
Web: www.calpartitionsinc.com
SIC: 2542 5046 3231 2631 Partitions for floor attachment, prefabricated: except wood; Partitions; Products of purchased glass; Paperboard mills

(P-2976)
CALIFORNIA COUNTERTOP INC (PA)
7811 Alvarado Rd (91942-0665)
PHONE..............................619 460-0205
Wayne J Krumenacker, *Pr*
EMP: 19 **EST:** 1984
SQ FT: 8,300
SALES (est): 2.51MM
SALES (corp-wide): 2.51MM **Privately Held**
Web: www.californiacountertop.com
SIC: 2542 1799 2541 5211 Counters or counter display cases, except wood; Counter top installation; Wood partitions and fixtures; Cabinets, kitchen

(P-2977)
CTA FIXTURES INC
5721 Santa Ana St Ste B (91761-8617)
PHONE..............................909 390-6744
Carlos Gutierrez, *CEO*
▲ **EMP:** 62 **EST:** 1994
SQ FT: 90,000
SALES (est): 8.72MM **Privately Held**
Web: www.ctafixtures.com
SIC: 2542 Partitions and fixtures, except wood

(P-2978)
CUTTING EDGE CREATIVE LLC
9944 Flower St (90706-5411)
PHONE..............................562 907-7007
▲ **EMP:** 75 **EST:** 1996
SALES (est): 9.45MM **Privately Held**
SIC: 2542 3496 7319 Racks, merchandise display or storage: except wood; Miscellaneous fabricated wire products; Display advertising service

(P-2979)
FELBRO INC
3666 E Olympic Blvd (90023-3147)
PHONE..............................323 263-8686
Howard Feldner, *Ch Bd*
Norman Feldner, *
Jeffrey Feldner, *
▲ **EMP:** 180 **EST:** 1945
SQ FT: 75,000
SALES (est): 20.02MM **Privately Held**
Web: www.felbrodisplays.com
SIC: 2542 Racks, merchandise display or storage: except wood

(P-2980)
FIELD MANUFACTURING CORP (PA)
1751 Torrance Blvd Ste N (90501-1726)
PHONE..............................310 781-9292
Patrick Field, *Pr*
▲ **EMP:** 36 **EST:** 1955
SQ FT: 20,000
SALES (est): 8.23MM
SALES (corp-wide): 8.23MM **Privately Held**
Web: www.field-manufacturing.com
SIC: 2542 3089 Partitions and fixtures, except wood; Injection molding of plastics

(P-2981)
IDX LOS ANGELES LLC
Also Called: West Coast Mfg & Whsng
5005 E Philadelphia St (91761-2816)
PHONE..............................909 212-8333
Graham Fownes, *Genl Mgr*
◆ **EMP:** 109 **EST:** 2012
SALES (est): 26.18MM
SALES (corp-wide): 9.63B **Publicly Held**
Web: www.idxcorporation.com
SIC: 2542 Partitions and fixtures, except wood
PA: Ufp Industries, Inc.
2801 E Beltline Ave Ne
Grand Rapids MI
616 364-6161

(P-2982)
JCM INDUSTRIES INC (PA)
Also Called: Advance Storage Products
15302 Pipeline Ln (92649-1138)
PHONE..............................714 902-9000
John Vr Krummell, *Pr*
Ken Blankenhorn, *Pr*
John Warren, *CFO*
▼ **EMP:** 21 **EST:** 1970
SQ FT: 10,000
SALES (est): 44.06MM
SALES (corp-wide): 44.06MM **Privately Held**
Web: www.advancestorageproducts.com
SIC: 2542 Racks, merchandise display or storage: except wood

(P-2983)
K-JACK ENGINEERING CO INC
5672 Buckingham Dr (92649-1160)
P.O. Box 2320 (90247-0320)
PHONE..............................310 327-8389
▲ **EMP:** 60 **EST:** 1963
SALES (est): 4.9MM **Privately Held**
Web: www.kjack.com
SIC: 2542 Racks, merchandise display or storage: except wood

(P-2984)
LLC WALKER WEST
Also Called: Impac International
5500 Jurupa St (91761-3668)
PHONE..............................800 767-9378
Kory Levoy, *Brnch Mgr*
EMP: 53
Web: www.premierenclosuresystems.com
SIC: 2542 3444 Cabinets: show, display, or storage: except wood; Sheet metalwork
PA: Walker West, Llc
1555 S Vintage Ave
Ontario CA

(P-2985)
PACIFIC MANUFACTURING MGT INC
Also Called: Greneker Solutions
3110 E 12th St (90023-3616)
PHONE..............................323 263-9000
Erik Johnson, *Pr*
Steven Beckman, *
▲ **EMP:** 60 **EST:** 2003
SQ FT: 60,000
SALES (est): 9.65MM **Privately Held**
Web: www.greneker.com
SIC: 2542 2541 Fixtures: display, office, or store: except wood; Display fixtures, wood

(P-2986)
RACK INSTALLATION SERVICES INC
1256 Brooks St Ste E (91762-3663)
PHONE..............................909 261-2243

Gabriel Caliana, *CEO*
EMP: 20 **EST:** 2018
SALES (est): 1.02MM **Privately Held**
SIC: 2542 1796 Partitions and fixtures, except wood; Installing building equipment

(P-2987)
RAP SECURITY INC
4630 Cecilia St (90201-5814)
PHONE..............................323 560-3493
Angelo Palmer, *Pr*
Bob Palmer, *
◆ **EMP:** 55 **EST:** 1984
SQ FT: 40,000
SALES (est): 4.98MM **Privately Held**
SIC: 2542 Fixtures, store: except wood

(P-2988)
RAPID RACK HOLDINGS INC✶
1370 Valley Vista Dr Ste 100 (91765-3950)
EMP: 618
SIC: 2542 Postal lock boxes, mail racks, and related products

(P-2989)
RAPID RACK INDUSTRIES INC
1370 Valley Vista Dr # 100 (91765-3911)
▲ **EMP:** 75
SIC: 2542 Partitions and fixtures, except wood

(P-2990)
REEVE STORE EQUIPMENT COMPANY (PA)
9131 Bermudez St (90660-4507)
PHONE..............................562 949-2535
TOLL FREE: 800
John Frackelton, *Pr*
Robert Frackelton, *
Mary Ann Crysler, *
▲ **EMP:** 100 **EST:** 1932
SQ FT: 170,000
SALES (est): 16.22MM
SALES (corp-wide): 16.22MM **Privately Held**
Web: www.reeveco.com
SIC: 2542 3471 Counters or counter display cases, except wood; Electroplating of metals or formed products

(P-2991)
SALSBURY INDUSTRIES INC (PA)
Also Called: Salsbury Industries
18300 Central Ave (90746-4008)
PHONE..............................800 624-5269
TOLL FREE: 800
Dennis Fraher, *Pr*
Brian Fraher, *VP*
John Fraher, *Ch*
Michael N Lobasso, *CFO*
◆ **EMP:** 344 **EST:** 1936
SQ FT: 600,000
SALES (est): 94.73MM **Privately Held**
Web: www.mailboxes.com
SIC: 2542 Locker boxes, postal service: except wood

(P-2992)
SAMSON PRODUCTS INC
Also Called: J L Industries
6285 Randolph St (90040-3514)
PHONE..............................323 726-9070
John Reissner, *Pr*
Robert Dunn, *
EMP: 34 **EST:** 1955
SQ FT: 20,000
SALES (est): 8.34MM
SALES (corp-wide): 142.69MM **Privately Held**

Web: usa.samsongroup.com
SIC: 2542 Cabinets: show, display, or storage: except wood
PA: Activar, Inc.
9700 Newton Ave S
Bloomington MN
952 392-8445

(P-2993)
SPECTRUM INTL HOLDINGS
14421 Bonelli St (91746-3021)
PHONE..............................626 333-7225
Matthew Harrison, *Ch Bd*
Robert A Davies, *VP Fin*
EMP: 620 **EST:** 1997
SALES (est): 30.74MM **Privately Held**
SIC: 2542 Postal lock boxes, mail racks, and related products

(P-2994)
STEVES PLATING CORPORATION
3111 N San Fernando Blvd (91504-2527)
PHONE..............................818 842-2184
Terry Knezevich, *CEO*
Roger C Knezevich, *
EMP: 140 **EST:** 1956
SQ FT: 80,000
SALES (est): 15.18MM **Privately Held**
Web: www.stevesplating.com
SIC: 2542 3446 3471 7692 Fixtures, store: except wood; Ladders, for permanent installation: metal; Plating of metals or formed products; Welding repair

(P-2995)
TEICHMAN ENTERPRISES INC
Also Called: T & H Store Fixtures
6100 Bandini Blvd (90040-3112)
PHONE..............................323 278-9000
Ruth Teichman, *Pr*
Steve Teichman, *
Bernard Teichman, *
Sidney Teichman, *
Alan Teichman, *
▲ **EMP:** 50 **EST:** 1956
SALES (est): 5.14MM **Privately Held**
Web: www.teichman.net
SIC: 2542 Fixtures: display, office, or store: except wood

(P-2996)
THE BOBRICK CORPORATION (PA)
6901 Tujunga Ave (91605-6213)
PHONE..............................818 764-1000
◆ **EMP:** 100 **EST:** 1906
SALES (est): 132.97MM
SALES (corp-wide): 132.97MM **Privately Held**
Web: www.bobrick.com
SIC: 2542 Partitions for floor attachment, prefabricated: except wood

(P-2997)
TURTLE STORAGE LTD
Also Called: American Bicycle Security Co
401 S Beckwith Rd (93060-3047)
P.O. Box 7359 (93006-7359)
PHONE..............................805 933-3688
Thomas Volk, *CEO*
Thomas M Volk, *CEO*
Thomas Volk, *Pr*
EMP: 20 **EST:** 1986
SQ FT: 16,000
SALES (est): 4.97MM **Privately Held**
Web: www.ameribike.com
SIC: 2542 1799 Lockers (not refrigerated): except wood; Fiberglass work

PRODUCTS & SVCS

(P-2998)
UNIWEB INC (PA)
Also Called: Uniweb
222 S Promenade Ave (92879-1743)
PHONE..............................951 279-7999
Karl F Weber, *CEO*
▲ EMP: 90 EST: 1979
SQ FT: 170,000
SALES (est): 14.27MM
SALES (corp-wide): 14.27MM **Privately Held**
Web: www.uniwebinc.com
SIC: 2542 Fixtures: display, office, or store: except wood

(P-2999)
WESTERN PCF STOR SOLUTIONS INC (PA)
300 E Arrow Hwy (91773-3339)
PHONE..............................909 451-0303
Tom Rogers, *Pr*
Peter G Dunn, *
Angie Bosley, *
Soheir Hakim, *
Paul Bautista, *
EMP: 100 EST: 1985
SQ FT: 165,000
SALES (est): 33.85MM
SALES (corp-wide): 33.85MM **Privately Held**
Web: www.wpss.com
SIC: 2542 Shelving, office and store, except wood

2591 Drapery Hardware And Blinds And Shades

(P-3000)
ALL STRONG INDUSTRY (USA) INC (PA)
326 Paseo Tesoro (91789-2725)
PHONE..............................909 598-6494
Pei-hsiang Hsu, *Ch Bd*
Frank Hsu, *
◆ EMP: 30 EST: 1992
SQ FT: 52,000
SALES (est): 4.86MM **Privately Held**
SIC: 2591 Mini blinds

(P-3001)
BONDED WINDOW COVERINGS INC
7831 Ostrow St (92111-3602)
P.O. Box 710130 (92171-0130)
PHONE..............................858 576-8400
EMP: 21 EST: 1976
SALES (est): 459.64K **Privately Held**
Web: www.bondedwindowcoverings.com
SIC: 2591 Drapery hardware and window blinds and shades

(P-3002)
C & M WOOD INDUSTRIES
17229 Lemon St Ste D (92345-5125)
PHONE..............................760 949-3292
Calvin Lam, *Pr*
Roger Mccarvel, *VP*
▲ EMP: 41 EST: 1987
SQ FT: 55,000
SALES (est): 1.1MM **Privately Held**
Web: www.cmwood.com
SIC: 2591 Venetian blinds

(P-3003)
CENTURY BLINDS INC
300 S Promenade Ave (92879-1754)
P.O. Box 77940 (92877-0131)
PHONE..............................951 734-3762

Mitch Shapiro, *CEO*
▲ EMP: 100 EST: 1992
SALES (est): 23.71MM **Privately Held**
Web: www.altawindowfashions.com
SIC: 2591 3429 5719 5023 Blinds vertical; Hardware, nec; Vertical blinds; Vertical blinds
HQ: Hunter Douglas Scandinavia Ab
    Kristineholmsvagen 14a
    AlingsAs
    32277500

(P-3004)
CUSTOM BRANDS GROUP
9255 Customhouse Plz Ste A (92154-7636)
PHONE..............................213 749-6333
EMP: 30 EST: 2016
SALES (est): 2.25MM **Privately Held**
SIC: 2591 Window blinds
HQ: Hunter Douglas N.V.
    Dokweg 19
    Willemstad

(P-3005)
ELWIN INC
6910 8th St (90620-1036)
PHONE..............................714 752-6962
Josh W Kim, *CEO*
EMP: 20 EST: 2015
SALES (est): 1.75MM **Privately Held**
SIC: 2591 5719 Window blinds; Window shades, nec

(P-3006)
HD WINDOW FASHIONS INC (DH)
Also Called: M & B Window Fashions
1818 Oak St (90015-3302)
PHONE..............................213 749-6333
Wayne Gourlay, *Pr*
Dominique Au Yeung, *
▲ EMP: 500 EST: 1975
SQ FT: 200,000
SALES (est): 71.9MM **Privately Held**
SIC: 2591 Mini blinds
HQ: Hunter Douglas Inc.
    1 Blue Hill Plz Ste 1569
    Pearl River NY
    845 664-7000

(P-3007)
HUNTER DOUGLAS INC
Hunter Douglas Contract
9900 Gidley St (91731-1112)
PHONE..............................858 679-7500
Rich Ries, *Brnch Mgr*
EMP: 261
Web: www.hunterdouglas.com
SIC: 2591 3446 Drapery hardware and window blinds and shades; Architectural metalwork
HQ: Hunter Douglas Inc.
    1 Blue Hill Plz Ste 1569
    Pearl River NY
    845 664-7000

(P-3008)
JC WINDOW FASHIONS INC
Also Called: JC Window Fashions
2438 Peck Rd (90601-1604)
PHONE..............................909 364-8888
Jennifer Chiao, *CEO*
▲ EMP: 28 EST: 2011
SALES (est): 4.79MM **Privately Held**
Web: www.jcwindowfashions.com
SIC: 2591 Drapery hardware and window blinds and shades

(P-3009)
KITTRICH CORPORATION (PA)
1585 W Mission Blvd (91766-1233)
PHONE..............................714 736-1000
Robert Friedland, *CEO*
◆ EMP: 130 EST: 1978
SQ FT: 237,000
SALES (est): 125.59MM
SALES (corp-wide): 125.59MM **Privately Held**
Web: www.kittrich.com
SIC: 2591 2392 2381 Blinds vertical; Household furnishings, nec; Fabric dress and work gloves

(P-3010)
L C PRINGLE SALES INC (PA)
Also Called: Pringle's Draperies
12020 Western Ave (92841-2913)
PHONE..............................714 892-1524
Larry C Pringle, *Pr*
Carolyn Pringle, *
Curtis L Pringle, *
Susan Pringle Kusinsky, *
Pamela Pringle Skinner, *
EMP: 30 EST: 1968
SQ FT: 11,000
SALES (est): 2.89MM
SALES (corp-wide): 2.89MM **Privately Held**
Web: www.pringlesdraperies.com
SIC: 2591 7216 2391 7211 Blinds vertical; Drapery, curtain drycleaning; Draperies, plastic and textile: from purchased materials; Power laundries, family and commercial

(P-3011)
PHASE II PRODUCTS INC (PA)
Also Called: Phase II
501 W Broadway Ste 2090 (92101-8563)
PHONE..............................619 236-9699
Charles Hunt, *CEO*
Gordon Peiper, *
John Bowie, *
▲ EMP: 18 EST: 1999
SQ FT: 4,800
SALES (est): 9.63MM
SALES (corp-wide): 9.63MM **Privately Held**
Web: www.phaseii.com
SIC: 2591 Drapery hardware and window blinds and shades

(P-3012)
ROBERSON CONSTRUCTION
Also Called: Architectural Window Shades
22 Central Ct (91105-2060)
P.O. Box 3286 (91731)
PHONE..............................626 578-1936
▲ EMP: 35
Web: www.openinfo.com
SIC: 2591 Window shades

(P-3013)
ROLL-A-SHADE INC (PA)
12101 Madera Way (92503-4849)
PHONE..............................951 245-5077
◆ EMP: 22 EST: 1996
SQ FT: 10,000
SALES (est): 9.46MM **Privately Held**
Web: www.rollashade.com
SIC: 2591 1799 Window shades; Window treatment installation

(P-3014)
SHEWARD & SON & SONS (PA)
Also Called: Solar Shading Systems
3000 Airway Ave Frnt (92626-6023)
PHONE..............................866 432-8400
▲ EMP: 39 EST: 1939

SALES (est): 7.81MM
SALES (corp-wide): 7.81MM **Privately Held**
Web: www.shewards.com
SIC: 2591 1799 2221 1752 Curtain and drapery rods, poles, and fixtures; Window treatment installation; Draperies and drapery fabrics, manmade fiber and silk; Carpet laying

(P-3015)
SHOWDOGS INC
Also Called: Wholesale Shade
168 S Pacific St (92078-2527)
PHONE..............................760 603-3269
Patrick Howe, *Pr*
EMP: 30 EST: 2013
SQ FT: 10,000
SALES (est): 2.32MM **Privately Held**
Web: www.wholesaleshade.com
SIC: 2591 Blinds vertical

(P-3016)
SPEED-O-PIN INTERNATIONAL
1401 Freeman Ave (90804-2518)
PHONE..............................562 433-4911
Jeffrey Jacobson, *Pr*
EMP: 17 EST: 1952
SQ FT: 20,000
SALES (est): 354.19K **Privately Held**
SIC: 2591 2672 Drapery hardware and window blinds and shades; Paper; coated and laminated, nec

(P-3017)
VERTICAL DOORS INC
Also Called: Vdi Motor Sports
542 3rd St (92530-2729)
PHONE..............................951 273-1069
Rob Baum, *Pr*
EMP: 17 EST: 2003
SALES (est): 734.97K **Privately Held**
Web: www.verticaldoors.com
SIC: 2591 Blinds vertical

2599 Furniture And Fixtures, Nec

(P-3018)
1PERFECTCHOICE
21908 Valley Blvd (91789-0938)
PHONE..............................909 594-8855
Chi Ching Lin, *CEO*
Brian Lin, *CFO*
EMP: 18 EST: 2014
SQ FT: 5,000
SALES (est): 2.15MM **Privately Held**
Web: www.1perfectchoice.com
SIC: 2599 5021 5712 Hospital furniture, except beds; Furniture; Furniture stores

(P-3019)
6TH STREET PARTNERS LLC
3950 W 6th St 201 (90020-4251)
PHONE..............................213 377-5277
EMP: 17 EST: 2015
SALES (est): 1.03MM **Privately Held**
SIC: 2599 Bar, restaurant and cafeteria furniture

(P-3020)
ALEGACY FDSRVICE PDTS GROUP IN
Also Called: Alegacy
12683 Corral Pl (90670-4748)
PHONE..............................562 320-3100
Jesse Gross, *Prin*
Brett Gross, *

Eric Gross, *
◆ **EMP:** 60 **EST:** 2000
SQ FT: 130,000
SALES (est): 9.72MM **Privately Held**
Web: www.alegacy.com
SIC: 2599 3263 Carts, restaurant equipment;
Cookware, fine earthenware

(P-3021)
**COMMERCIAL CSTM STING
UPHL INC**
12601 Western Ave (92841-4014)
PHONE................................714 850-0520
Robert Francis, *CEO*
Lynn D.o.s., *Sec*
▲ **EMP:** 90 **EST:** 1988
SQ FT: 50,000
SALES (est): 21.05MM **Privately Held**
Web: www.ccs-ind.com
SIC: 2599 Restaurant furniture, wood or
metal

(P-3022)
DAVID HAID
Also Called: HAID, DAVID
8619 Crocker St (90003-3516)
PHONE................................323 752-8096
EMP: 20
SIC: 2599 5199 Factory furniture and fixtures
; Advertising specialties
PA: David Haid
3931 Topanga Canyon Blvd
Malibu CA

(P-3023)
ERGONOM CORPORATION
Also Called: Erg International
390 Lombard St (93030-7209)
PHONE................................805 981-9978
Roy Zaki, *Pr*
EMP: 70
SALES (corp-wide): 22.15MM **Privately
Held**
SIC: 2599 2531 Hospital furniture, except
beds; School furniture
PA: Ergonom Corporation
361 Bernoulli Cir
Oxnard CA
805 981-9978

(P-3024)
ERGONOM CORPORATION (PA)
Also Called: E R G International
361 Bernoulli Cir (93030-5164)
PHONE................................805 981-9978
George Zaki, *CEO*
Roy Zaki, *
▲ **EMP:** 90 **EST:** 1981
SALES (est): 22.15MM
SALES (corp-wide): 22.15MM **Privately
Held**
SIC: 2599 2531 Hospital furniture, except
beds; School furniture

(P-3025)
FORBES INDUSTRIES DIV
1933 E Locust St (91761-7608)
PHONE................................909 923-4559
Tim Sweetland, *Pr*
Peter Sweetland, *
▼ **EMP:** 210 **EST:** 1919
SQ FT: 110,000
SALES (est): 25.84MM
SALES (corp-wide): 47.64MM **Privately
Held**
Web: www.forbesindustries.com
SIC: 2599 Carts, restaurant equipment
PA: The Winsford Corporation
1933 E Locust St
Ontario CA
909 923-4559

(P-3026)
HIRE ELEGANCE
8333 Arjons Dr Ste E (92126-6320)
PHONE................................858 740-7862
Stuart Simble, *Prin*
EMP: 17 **EST:** 2010
SALES (est): 1.66MM **Privately Held**
Web: www.hire-elegance.com
SIC: 2599 Furniture and fixtures, nec

(P-3027)
JBI LLC (PA)
Also Called: Jbi Interiors
2650 E El Presidio St (90810-1115)
PHONE................................310 886-8034
Pete Jensen, *Music Manager*
Bonnie Holt, *
Michael Buchbinder, *
Gregg Buchbinder, *
◆ **EMP:** 200 **EST:** 1968
SQ FT: 270,000
SALES (est): 63.16MM
SALES (corp-wide): 63.16MM **Privately
Held**
Web: www.jbi-interiors.com
SIC: 2599 5046 Restaurant furniture, wood
or metal; Restaurant equipment and
supplies, nec

(P-3028)
MASHINDUSTRIES INC
7150 Village Dr (90621-2261)
PHONE................................714 736-9600
Bernard Brucha, *CEO*
Michelle Blemel, *Corporate Secretary**
Lisa Boardman, *
Jennifer Olsen Ctrl, *Prin*
EMP: 47 **EST:** 2013
SALES (est): 4.36MM **Privately Held**
Web: www.mashindustries.com
SIC: 2599 Factory furniture and fixtures

(P-3029)
**NLP FURNITURE INDUSTRIES
INC**
1425 Corporate Center Dr Ste 200
(92154-6629)
P.O. Box 530659 (92153-0659)
PHONE................................619 661-5170
Joseph B Cabrera, *Pr*
Louis J Rodriguez, *
▲ **EMP:** 25 **EST:** 1985
SQ FT: 9,000
SALES (est): 1.51MM **Privately Held**
Web: www.nlpfurniture.com
SIC: 2599 Hospital furniture, except beds

(P-3030)
R & J FABRICATORS INC
1121 Railroad St Ste 102 (92882-8219)
PHONE................................951 817-0300
James Ciarletta, *CEO*
Jay Warren Ciarletta, *VP*
EMP: 20 **EST:** 1982
SQ FT: 20,000
SALES (est): 2.35MM **Privately Held**
SIC: 2599 Restaurant furniture, wood or
metal

(P-3031)
STAINLESS FIXTURES INC
1250 E Franklin Ave (91766-5449)
PHONE................................909 622-1615
Randy Rodriguez, *Pr*
EMP: 35 **EST:** 1989
SQ FT: 36,000
SALES (est): 8.4MM **Privately Held**
SIC: 2599 Restaurant furniture, wood or
metal

(P-3032)
TAHITI CABINETS INC
5419 E La Palma Ave (92807-2022)
PHONE................................714 693-0618
Mark Ramsey, *Pr*
Doreen Ramsey, *
EMP: 58 **EST:** 1975
SQ FT: 32,000
SALES (est): 9.79MM **Privately Held**
Web: www.tahiticabinets.com
SIC: 2599 2431 2434 Cabinets, factory;
Millwork; Wood kitchen cabinets

(P-3033)
TRESTON IAC LLC
8175 E Brookdale Ln (92807-2526)
PHONE................................714 990-8997
EMP: 34
Web: www.iacindustries.com
SIC: 2599 Bar furniture
HQ: Treston Iac Llc
3831 S Bullard Ave
Goodyear AZ
714 989-5363

(P-3034)
WEST COAST INDUSTRIES INC
707 E 7th St (90021-1403)
PHONE................................213 627-1113
Andy Ozolos, *Genl Mgr*
▲ **EMP:** 34
SALES (corp-wide): 9.29MM **Privately
Held**
Web: www.westcoastindustries.com
SIC: 2599 Restaurant furniture, wood or
metal
PA: West Coast Industries, Inc.
361 Bernoulli Cir
Oxnard CA
415 621-6656

(P-3035)
**WEST COAST INDUSTRIES INC
(PA)**
Also Called: W C I
361 Bernoulli Cir (93030-5164)
PHONE................................415 621-6656
◆ **EMP:** 23 **EST:** 1941
SALES (est): 9.29MM
SALES (corp-wide): 9.29MM **Privately
Held**
Web: www.westcoastindustries.com
SIC: 2599 Bar, restaurant and cafeteria
furniture

(P-3036)
**WESTERN MILL FABRICATORS
INC**
670 S Jefferson St Ste B (92870-6638)
PHONE................................714 993-3667
Kimball Boyack, *CEO*
EMP: 30 **EST:** 1987
SALES (est): 2.23MM **Privately Held**
Web: www.wmfinc.com
SIC: 2599 Bar, restaurant and cafeteria
furniture

2611 Pulp Mills

(P-3037)
NEW GREEN DAY LLC
1710 E 111th St (90059-1910)
P.O. Box 72147 (90002-0147)
PHONE................................323 566-7603
Brian Kelly, *CEO*
David Holt, *
Kirk Sanford, *Managing Member**
Daniel Montoya, *

Randi Yamamoto, *
EMP: 25 **EST:** 2004
SQ FT: 25,000
SALES (est): 5MM **Privately Held**
Web: www.ngdla.com
SIC: 2611 Pulp manufactured from waste or
recycled paper

(P-3038)
**WESTERN PACIFIC PULP AND
PAPER (HQ)**
9400 Hall Rd (90241-5365)
PHONE................................562 803-4401
Ralph Ho, *Ch Bd*
Kevin Duncombe, *
Jim Forkey, *
▼ **EMP:** 51 **EST:** 1983
SALES (est): 23.7MM
SALES (corp-wide): 26.98MM **Privately
Held**
Web: www.wppp.com
SIC: 2611 5093 Pulp manufactured from
waste or recycled paper; Waste paper
PA: Y. F. International
180 Park Rd
Burlingame CA
650 342-6560

2621 Paper Mills

(P-3039)
ACME UNITED CORPORATION
630 Young St (92705-5633)
PHONE................................714 557-2001
EMP: 22
SALES (corp-wide): 193.96MM **Publicly
Held**
Web: www.acmeunited.com
SIC: 2621 Absorbent paper
PA: Acme United Corporation
1 Waterview Dr Ste 200
Shelton CT
203 254-6060

(P-3040)
ALLIED WEST PAPER CORP
11101 Etiwanda Ave Unit 100 (92337-6984)
PHONE................................909 349-0710
Ray Ovanessian, *CEO*
Mike Ovanessian, *
Eric Ovanessian, *
◆ **EMP:** 95 **EST:** 1989
SQ FT: 300,000
SALES (est): 31.21MM **Privately Held**
Web: www.alliedwestpaper.com
SIC: 2621 Paper mills

(P-3041)
**AMERICAN GRAPHIC BOARD
INC**
5880 E Slauson Ave (90040-3018)
PHONE................................323 721-0585
Don Zeccola, *Pr*
Michael Carmody, *
Peter Kang, *
▲ **EMP:** 84 **EST:** 2003
SQ FT: 135,000
SALES (est): 3.39MM **Privately Held**
SIC: 2621 Paper mills

(P-3042)
BOISE CASCADE COMPANY
3221 Hutchison Ave (90034-3246)
PHONE................................310 815-2200
Paul Hurty, *Brnch Mgr*
EMP: 19
SALES (corp-wide): 8.39B **Publicly Held**
Web: www.bc.com
SIC: 2621 Paper mills

**P
R
O
D
U
C
T
S

&

S
V
C
S**

PA: Boise Cascade Company
1111 W Jefferson St # 100
Boise ID
208 384-6161

(P-3043)
CROWN PAPER CONVERTING INC
Also Called: Crown Paper Converting
1380 S Bon View Ave (91761-4403)
P.O. Box 3277 (91761-0928)
PHONE.................................909 923-5226
Bruce Hale, *Prin*
Lisa Hale, *
EMP: 40 **EST:** 1983
SQ FT: 34,000
SALES (est): 9.74MM **Privately Held**
Web: www.crownpaperconverting.com
SIC: 2621 Paper mills

(P-3044)
DYNAMIC RESOURCES INC
7894 Dagget St Ste 202e (92111-2323)
PHONE.................................619 268-3070
Kwang Kim, *CFO*
Cheong Won Bae, *CEO*
EMP: 60 **EST:** 2010
SQ FT: 9,000
SALES (est): 5.27MM **Privately Held**
Web: www.dynamicresources.biz
SIC: 2621 2672 Lithograph paper; Adhesive
papers, labels, or tapes; from purchased
material

(P-3045)
ENVELOPMENTS INC
13091 Sandhurst Pl (92705-2135)
PHONE.................................714 569-3300
▲ **EMP:** 39 **EST:** 1993
SALES (est): 5.14MM **Privately Held**
Web: www.envelopments.com
SIC: 2621 5112 Stationary, envelope and
tablet papers; Stationery

(P-3046)
GLOBAL PAPER SOLUTIONS INC
100 S Anaheim Blvd Ste 250 (92805-3872)
PHONE.................................714 687-6102
Chi Mi Chung, *Pr*
▲ **EMP:** 42 **EST:** 2004
SALES (est): 1.34MM **Privately Held**
Web: www.globalpapersolutions.com
SIC: 2621 Paper mills

(P-3047)
HARVARD LABEL LLC
Also Called: Harvard Card Systems
111 Baldwin Park Blvd (91746-1402)
PHONE.................................626 333-8881
Michael Tang, *CEO*
David Banducci, *
▲ **EMP:** 115 **EST:** 1996
SQ FT: 125,000
SALES (est): 38.13MM **Privately Held**
SIC: 2621 2675 2752 Greeting card paper;
Stencil cards, die-cut: made from
purchased materials; Cards, lithographed
PA: Plasticard - Locktech International, Llc
1220 Trade Dr
North Las Vegas NV

(P-3048)
INTERNATIONAL PAPER COMPANY
International Paper
601 E Ball Rd (92805-5910)
PHONE.................................714 776-6060
Terry Tockey, *Brnch Mgr*

EMP: 65
SALES (corp-wide): 21.16B **Publicly Held**
Web: www.internationalpaper.com
SIC: 2621 Paper mills
PA: International Paper Company
6400 Poplar Ave
Memphis TN
901 419-7000

(P-3049)
INTERNATIONAL PAPER COMPANY
Also Called: International Paper
9211 Norwalk Blvd (90670-2923)
PHONE.................................562 692-9465
Lee Bekiarian, *Brnch Mgr*
EMP: 50
SALES (corp-wide): 21.16B **Publicly Held**
Web: www.internationalpaper.com
SIC: 2621 Paper mills
PA: International Paper Company
6400 Poplar Ave
Memphis TN
901 419-7000

(P-3050)
INTERNATIONAL PAPER COMPANY
Also Called: International Paper
1350 E 223rd St (90745-4381)
PHONE.................................310 549-5525
Melanie Kastner, *Brnch Mgr*
EMP: 50
SALES (corp-wide): 21.16B **Publicly Held**
Web: www.internationalpaper.com
SIC: 2621 Paper mills
PA: International Paper Company
6400 Poplar Ave
Memphis TN
901 419-7000

(P-3051)
INTERNATIONAL PAPER COMPANY
Also Called: International Paper
19615 S Susana Rd (90221-5717)
PHONE.................................310 639-2310
Joseph Winters, *Genl Mgr*
EMP: 35
SALES (corp-wide): 21.16B **Publicly Held**
Web: www.internationalpaper.com
SIC: 2621 Paper mills
PA: International Paper Company
6400 Poplar Ave
Memphis TN
901 419-7000

(P-3052)
J R C INDUSTRIES INC
11804 Wakeman St (90670-2129)
PHONE.................................562 698-0171
Leonard Fishelberg, *CEO*
EMP: 20 **EST:** 1976
SQ FT: 32,000
SALES (est): 1.11MM **Privately Held**
Web: www.jrcenvelopes.com
SIC: 2621 Paper mills

(P-3053)
KUI CO INC
266 Calle Pintoresco (92672-7504)
PHONE.................................949 369-7949
EMP: 40 **EST:** 1996
SQ FT: 14,800
SALES (est): 4.49MM **Privately Held**
Web: www.kuicoinc.com
SIC: 2621 3089 Molded pulp products;
Plastics processing

(P-3054)
LD PRODUCTS INC
Also Called: 4inkjets
3700 Cover St (90808-1782)
PHONE.................................888 321-2552
Aaron Leon, *CEO*
Patrick Devane, *Sr VP*
◆ **EMP:** 193 **EST:** 1999
SQ FT: 25,000
SALES (est): 51.65MM **Privately Held**
Web: www.ldproducts.com
SIC: 2621 5045 Stationary, envelope and
tablet papers; Printers, computer

(P-3055)
NEW-INDY CONTAINERBOARD LLC (DH)
Also Called: International Paper
3500 Porsche Way Ste 150 (91764-4909)
P.O. Box 519 (93044-0519)
PHONE.................................909 296-3400
Richard Hartman, *CEO*
Mike Conkey, *
▲ **EMP:** 95 **EST:** 2012
SALES (est): 304.23MM
SALES (corp-wide): 679.24MM **Privately
Held**
Web: www.newindycontainerboard.com
SIC: 2621 Paper mills
HQ: New-Indy Containerboard Hold Co Llc
1 Patriot Pl
Foxborough MA

(P-3056)
NEW-INDY ONTARIO LLC
Also Called: New-Indy Containerboard
5100 Jurupa St (91761-3618)
PHONE.................................909 390-1055
Richard Hartman, *CEO*
Mike Conkey, *
EMP: 110 **EST:** 2012
SALES (est): 67.55MM
SALES (corp-wide): 679.24MM **Privately
Held**
Web: www.newindycontainerboard.com
SIC: 2621 Paper mills
HQ: New-Indy Containerboard Llc
3500 Porsche Way Ste 150
Ontario CA
909 296-3400

(P-3057)
NEW-INDY OXNARD LLC
Also Called: New-Indy Containerboard
5936 Perkins Rd (93033-9044)
P.O. Box 519 (93044-0519)
PHONE.................................805 986-3881
Richard Hartman, *CEO*
Mike Conkey, *VP*
▲ **EMP:** 224 **EST:** 2012
SALES (est): 52.2MM
SALES (corp-wide): 679.24MM **Privately
Held**
Web: www.newindycontainerboard.com
SIC: 2621 Paper mills
HQ: New-Indy Containerboard Llc
3500 Porsche Way Ste 150
Ontario CA
909 296-3400

(P-3058)
OEM MATERIALS & SUPPLIES INC
Also Called: OEM Materials
1500 Ritchey St (92705-4731)
PHONE.................................714 564-9600
Wendy King, *CEO*
Randall K Johnson, *Pr*
Michael Cavazos, *Acctg Mgr*
Gloria Montoya, *Acctnt*

EMP: 20 **EST:** 2008
SALES (est): 9.6MM **Privately Held**
Web: www.oemmaterials.com
SIC: 2621 2631 5084 2671 Wrapping and
packaging papers; Container, packaging,
and boxboard; Processing and packaging
equipment; Paper; coated and laminated
packaging

(P-3059)
PACON INC
4249 Puente Ave (91706-3420)
PHONE.................................626 814-4654
Robert M Austin, *CEO*
Michael Austin, *
◆ **EMP:** 103 **EST:** 1977
SQ FT: 44,000
SALES (est): 20.6MM **Privately Held**
Web: www.paconinc.com
SIC: 2621 Paper mills

(P-3060)
PAPER SURCE CONVERTING MFG INC
Also Called: Soft-Touch Tissue
2015 E 48th St (90058-2021)
PHONE.................................323 583-3800
Jacob Khobian, *CEO*
▲ **EMP:** 50 **EST:** 1996
SQ FT: 55,000
SALES (est): 21.41MM **Privately Held**
Web: www.papersourcemfg.com
SIC: 2621 Tissue paper

(P-3061)
SAN DIEGO DAILY TRANSCRIPT
Also Called: Daily Transcript
34 Emerald Gln (92677-9379)
P.O. Box 85469 (92186-5469)
PHONE.................................619 232-4381
Ed Frederickson, *Pr*
EMP: 63 **EST:** 1886
SQ FT: 30,000
SALES (est): 10.95MM
SALES (corp-wide): 13.77MM **Privately
Held**
SIC: 2621 4813 Printing paper; Online
service providers
PA: Calcomco, Inc.
5544 S Red Pine Cir
Kalamazoo MI
313 885-9228

(P-3062)
SAPPI NORTH AMERICA INC
21700 Copley Dr Ste 165 (91765-4434)
PHONE.................................714 456-0600
EMP: 44
Web: www.sappi.com
SIC: 2621 Paper mills
HQ: Sappi North America, Inc.
255 State St Fl 4
Boston MA
617 423-7300

(P-3063)
SPECIALTY PAPER MILLS INC
8844 Millergrove Dr (90670-2004)
P.O. Box 3188 (90670-0188)
PHONE.................................562 692-8737
Ronald Gabriel, *Pr*
Aldo De Soto, *
Agnes Gabriel, *
EMP: 200 **EST:** 1959
SQ FT: 45,000
SALES (est): 32.16MM
SALES (corp-wide): 32.16MM **Privately
Held**
SIC: 2621 2631 Paper mills; Paperboard
mills

PA: Gabriel Container
8844 Millergrove Dr
Santa Fe Springs CA
562 699-1051

(P-3064)
SPILL MAGIC INC
630 Young St (92705-5633)
PHONE................714 557-2001
Susan Wampler, *Pr*
David Wampler, *VP*
▲ **EMP:** 22 **EST:** 1995
SQ FT: 30,000
SALES (est): 5.42MM
SALES (corp-wide): 193.96MM **Publicly Held**
Web: www.firstaidonly.com
SIC: 2621 Absorbent paper
PA: Acme United Corporation
1 Waterview Dr Ste 200
Shelton CT
203 254-6060

2631 Paperboard Mills

(P-3065)
CALIFRNIA TRADE CONVERTERS INC
9816 Variel Ave (91311-4316)
PHONE................818 899-1455
Carlos Martinez, *Pr*
EMP: 25 **EST:** 1997
SALES (est): 3.9MM **Privately Held**
SIC: 2631 2675 Paperboard mills; Paper die-cutting

(P-3066)
CARAUSTAR INDUSTRIES INC
4502 E Airport Dr (91761-7820)
PHONE................951 685-5544
D Wever Paul Potter, *Mgr*
EMP: 21
SALES (corp-wide): 6.35B **Publicly Held**
Web: www.greif.com
SIC: 2631 Paperboard mills
HQ: Caraustar Industries, Inc.
5000 Astell Pwdr Sprng Rd
Austell GA
770 948-3101

(P-3067)
EASTWEST CONTAINER GROUP INC
5521 Schaefer Ave (91710-9070)
PHONE................626 523-1523
Nongwang Lai, *CEO*
Jialin Wu, *CFO*
EMP: 20 **EST:** 2019
SALES (est): 2.01MM **Privately Held**
Web: www.2eastwest.com
SIC: 2631 Container, packaging, and boxboard

(P-3068)
FIRST CLASS PACKAGING INC
280 Cypress Ln Ste D (92020-1662)
PHONE................619 579-7166
Sandra L Brock, *Pr*
EMP: 22 **EST:** 1987
SQ FT: 18,500
SALES (est): 4.51MM
SALES (corp-wide): 7.37MM **Privately Held**
Web: www.larsonpkg.com
SIC: 2631 2449 3086 5085 Packaging board ; Rectangular boxes and crates, wood; Plastics foam products; Bins and containers, storage
PA: Larson Packaging Holdings, Inc.
280 Cypress Ln

El Cajon CA
408 946-4971

(P-3069)
ONE UP MANUFACTURING LLC
550 E Airline Way (90248-2502)
PHONE................310 749-8347
Nielson Ballon, *Managing Member*
Kavish Mehta, *
Nathan Miller, *
EMP: 25 **EST:** 2017
SALES (est): 3.46MM **Privately Held**
SIC: 2631 Container, packaging, and boxboard

(P-3070)
PREFERRED PRINTING & PACKAGING INC
1493 E Philadelphia St (91761-5729)
PHONE................909 923-2053
EMP: 30 **EST:** 1991
SALES (est): 6.8MM **Privately Held**
Web: www.preferredpnp.com
SIC: 2631 Folding boxboard

(P-3071)
SONOCO PRODUCTS COMPANY
Also Called: Sonoco Industrial Products Div
166 Baldwin Park Blvd (91746-1498)
PHONE................626 369-6611
Dhamo Srinivasan, *Mgr*
EMP: 116
SALES (corp-wide): 7.25B **Publicly Held**
Web: www.sonoco.com
SIC: 2631 2611 Paperboard mills; Pulp mills
PA: Sonoco Products Company
1 N 2nd St
Hartsville SC
843 383-7000

(P-3072)
SONOCO PRODUCTS COMPANY
12851 Leyva St (90650-6853)
PHONE................562 921-0881
Jeff Blaine, *Mgr*
EMP: 63
SQ FT: 164,934
SALES (corp-wide): 7.25B **Publicly Held**
Web: www.sonoco.com
SIC: 2631 2655 Paperboard mills; Fiber cans, drums, and similar products
PA: Sonoco Products Company
1 N 2nd St
Hartsville SC
843 383-7000

(P-3073)
UNION CARBIDE CORPORATION
19206 Hawthorne Blvd (90503-1590)
PHONE................310 214-5300
Patrick E Gottschalk, *Prin*
EMP: 36
SQ FT: 15,269
SALES (corp-wide): 56.9B **Publicly Held**
Web: www.unioncarbide.com
SIC: 2631 Latex board
HQ: Union Carbide Corporation
7501 State Hwy 185 N
Seadrift TX
361 553-2997

(P-3074)
WATERBOX LLC
2500 E Imperial Hwy Ste 201 (92821-6122)
PHONE................323 743-8070
EMP: 20 **EST:** 2017
SALES (est): 2.38MM **Privately Held**
Web: www.waterboxllc.com

SIC: 2631 Container, packaging, and boxboard

(P-3075)
ZAPP PACKAGING INC
1921 S Business Pkwy (91761-8539)
PHONE................909 930-1500
Vincent Randazzo, *CEO*
William L Finn, *
Bruce Altshuler, *
▲ **EMP:** 60 **EST:** 1931
SQ FT: 80,000
SALES (est): 12.71MM **Privately Held**
Web: www.autajon.com
SIC: 2631 Folding boxboard

2652 Setup Paperboard Boxes

(P-3076)
MOZAIK LLC
245 W Carl Karcher Way (92801-2499)
PHONE................562 207-1900
Sharon Carton Ctrl, *Prin*
▲ **EMP:** 24 **EST:** 2006
SQ FT: 27,000
SALES (est): 5.5MM **Privately Held**
Web: www.mozaik.net
SIC: 2652 Filing boxes, paperboard: made from purchased materials

2653 Corrugated And Solid Fiber Boxes

(P-3077)
ABEX DISPLAY SYSTEMS INC (PA)
Also Called: Abex Exhibit Systems
355 Parkside Dr (91340-3036)
PHONE................800 537-0231
Robbie Blumenfeld, *Pr*
Max Canditotty, *
◆ **EMP:** 105 **EST:** 1982
SQ FT: 85,000
SALES (est): 9.05MM
SALES (corp-wide): 9.05MM **Privately Held**
Web: www.abex.com
SIC: 2653 2541 Display items, solid fiber: made from purchased materials; Store and office display cases and fixtures

(P-3078)
ADVANCE PAPER BOX COMPANY
Also Called: Packaging Spectrum
6100 S Gramercy Pl (90047-1397)
PHONE................323 750-2550
Martin Gardner, *CEO*
Martin Gardner, *Pr*
Nick Silk, *
Carlo Mendoza, *
Devan Gardner, *
▲ **EMP:** 250 **EST:** 1924
SQ FT: 500,000
SALES (est): 43.34MM **Privately Held**
Web: www.advancepaperbox.com
SIC: 2653 3082 2657 Boxes, corrugated: made from purchased materials; Unsupported plastics profile shapes; Folding paperboard boxes

(P-3079)
ANDROP PACKAGING INC
Also Called: Ontario Foam Products
4400 E Francis St (91761-2327)
PHONE................909 605-8842

Cesar Flores, *Pr*
▲ **EMP:** 23 **EST:** 1974
SQ FT: 52,000
SALES (est): 4.25MM **Privately Held**
Web: www.androppkg.com
SIC: 2653 3086 Boxes, corrugated: made from purchased materials; Plastics foam products

(P-3080)
AWARD PACKAGING SPC CORP
12855 Midway Pl (90703-2141)
PHONE................323 727-1200
Alfred Espinoza, *CEO*
Virginia S Espinoza, *
EMP: 20 **EST:** 1978
SQ FT: 800
SALES (est): 747.46K **Privately Held**
SIC: 2653 Boxes, corrugated: made from purchased materials

(P-3081)
BAY CITIES CONTAINER CORP
9206 Santa Fe Springs Rd (90670-2618)
PHONE................562 302-2552
EMP: 18
SALES (corp-wide): 150.82MM **Privately Held**
Web: www.bay-cities.com
SIC: 2653 Boxes, corrugated: made from purchased materials
PA: Bay Cities Container Corp
5138 Industry Ave Frnt
Pico Rivera CA
562 948-3751

(P-3082)
BAY CITIES CONTAINER CORP (PA)
Also Called: Bay Cities Logistics
5138 Industry Ave (90660-2503)
PHONE................562 948-3751
Greg A Tucker, *CEO*
Patrick Donohoe, *
Michael Musgrave, *
▲ **EMP:** 94 **EST:** 1956
SALES (est): 150.82MM
SALES (corp-wide): 150.82MM **Privately Held**
Web: www.bay-cities.com
SIC: 2653 3993 5113 Boxes, corrugated: made from purchased materials; Signs and advertising specialties; Corrugated and solid fiber boxes

(P-3083)
BLOWER-DEMPSAY CORPORATION
Also Called: Pacific Western Container
4044 W Garry Ave (92704-6300)
PHONE................714 547-9266
Ken Ito, *Mgr*
EMP: 20
SQ FT: 30,000
SALES (corp-wide): 99.99MM **Privately Held**
Web: pacificwestern.blowerdempsay.com
SIC: 2653 5199 5113 Boxes, corrugated: made from purchased materials; Packaging materials; Corrugated and solid fiber boxes
PA: Blower-Dempsay Corporation
4042 W Garry Ave
Santa Ana CA
714 481-3800

(P-3084)
BLOWER-DEMPSAY CORPORATION (PA)
Also Called: Pak West Paper & Packaging

4042 W Garry Ave (92704-6300)
PHONE..................714 481-3800
James Blower, *Pr*
Linda Dempsay, *
Serge Poirier, *
▲ **EMP:** 217 **EST:** 1973
SQ FT: 190,000
SALES (est): 99.99MM
SALES (corp-wide): 99.99MM **Privately Held**
Web: pakwest.blowerdempsay.com
SIC: 2653 Boxes, corrugated: made from purchased materials

(P-3085)
BLUE RIBBON CONT & DISPLAY INC
5450 Dobbs Ave (90621)
PHONE..................562 944-1217
Kenneth G Overfield, *Pr*
EMP: 22 **EST:** 1991
SQ FT: 32,000
SALES (est): 2.3MM **Privately Held**
Web: www.brcbox.com
SIC: 2653 5199 5113 2621 Boxes, corrugated: made from purchased materials; Packaging materials; Boxes and containers; Paper mills

(P-3086)
BOXES R US INC
Also Called: Ultimate Paper Box Company
15051 Don Julian Rd (91746-3302)
PHONE..................626 820-5410
Janak P Patel, *Pr*
Dipak Patel, *
▲ **EMP:** 70 **EST:** 1996
SQ FT: 38,000
SALES (est): 18.71MM **Privately Held**
SIC: 2653 Boxes, corrugated: made from purchased materials

(P-3087)
C B SHEETS INC
13901 Carmenita Rd (90670-4916)
PHONE..................562 921-1223
John Widera, *CEO*
Mackey Davis, *Pr*
EMP: 21 **EST:** 2001
SALES (est): 9.07MM
SALES (corp-wide): 33.56MM **Privately Held**
Web: www.calbox.com
SIC: 2653 Boxes, corrugated: made from purchased materials
PA: California Box Company
13901 Carmenita Rd
Santa Fe Springs CA
562 921-1223

(P-3088)
CALIFORNIA BOX COMPANY (PA)
13901 Carmenita Rd (90670-4916)
PHONE..................562 921-1223
▲ **EMP:** 29 **EST:** 1990
SALES (est): 33.56MM
SALES (corp-wide): 33.56MM **Privately Held**
Web: www.calbox.com
SIC: 2653 Corrugated and solid fiber boxes

(P-3089)
CD CONTAINER INC
Also Called: Carton Design
7343 Paramount Blvd (90660-3713)
PHONE..................562 948-1910
Juan De La Cruz, *Pr*
Juan De La Cruz, *Pr*
Jose De La Cruz, *

▲ **EMP:** 70 **EST:** 1987
SQ FT: 46,000
SALES (est): 9.46MM **Privately Held**
Web: www.cdcontainerinc.com
SIC: 2653 Boxes, corrugated: made from purchased materials

(P-3090)
CFLUTE CORP
Also Called: Montebello Container
13220 Molette St (90670-5526)
P.O. Box 788 (90637-0788)
PHONE..................562 404-6221
▲ **EMP:** 170
SIC: 2653 Boxes, corrugated: made from purchased materials

(P-3091)
COASTAL CONTAINER INC
8455 Loch Lomond Dr (90660-2508)
PHONE..................562 801-4595
Richard Rudell, *Pr*
Roberta Noble, *VP*
EMP: 21 **EST:** 1993
SQ FT: 3,000
SALES (est): 2.13MM **Privately Held**
SIC: 2653 5113 Boxes, corrugated: made from purchased materials; Corrugated and solid fiber boxes

(P-3092)
COMMANDER PACKAGING WEST INC
602 S Rockefeller Ave Ste D (91761-8191)
PHONE..................714 921-9350
Joseph F Kindlon, *Ch Bd*
Brian R Webber, *
EMP: 37 **EST:** 1987
SQ FT: 48,000
SALES (est): 5.02MM **Privately Held**
SIC: 2653 7389 5113 Boxes, corrugated: made from purchased materials; Packaging and labeling services; Corrugated and solid fiber boxes
PA: Cano Container Corporation
3920 Enterprise Ct Ste A
Aurora IL

(P-3093)
CORRU-KRAFT IV
1911 E Rosslynn Ave (92831-5141)
PHONE..................714 773-0124
Bob Dunford, *Prin*
EMP: 19 **EST:** 2008
SALES (est): 3.69MM **Privately Held**
Web: www.ororapackagingsolutions.com
SIC: 2653 Boxes, corrugated: made from purchased materials

(P-3094)
CORRUGADOS DE BAJA CALIFORNIA
2475 Paseo De Las A (92154)
PHONE..................619 662-8672
Smurfit Kappa, *Owner*
EMP: 900 **EST:** 2008
SALES (est): 52.32MM **Privately Held**
SIC: 2653 Corrugated and solid fiber boxes

(P-3095)
CROCKETT GRAPHICS INC (PA)
Also Called: Folding Cartons
980 Avenida Acaso (93012-8759)
PHONE..................805 987-8577
Edward Randall Crockett, *Pr*
Edward Randall Crockett, *Pr*
Rod K Rieth, *
▲ **EMP:** 60 **EST:** 1994
SALES (est): 17.11MM

SALES (corp-wide): 17.11MM **Privately Held**
Web: www.garedgraphics.com
SIC: 2653 Corrugated boxes, partitions, display items, sheets, and pad

(P-3096)
CROWN CARTON COMPANY INC
1820 E 48th Pl (90058-1946)
PHONE..................323 582-3053
Jeffrey P Marks, *Pr*
EMP: 20 **EST:** 1953
SQ FT: 28,000
SALES (est): 2.41MM **Privately Held**
Web: www.crowncarton.com
SIC: 2653 Boxes, corrugated: made from purchased materials

(P-3097)
ECKO PRODUCTS GROUP LLC
Also Called: Ecko Print & Packaging
740 S Milliken Ave Ste C (91761-7842)
PHONE..................909 628-5678
Eric Rogers, *CFO*
Christopher Hively, *Pr*
◆ **EMP:** 23 **EST:** 2002
SQ FT: 17,000
SALES (est): 7.41MM **Privately Held**
Web: www.eckopg.com
SIC: 2653 5085 2759 Boxes, corrugated: made from purchased materials; Abrasives and adhesives; Commercial printing, nec

(P-3098)
EMPIRE CONTAINER CORPORATION
1161 E Walnut St (90746-1382)
PHONE..................310 537-8190
Donald Simmons, *Pr*
Gregory V Hall, *
Patrick Fox, *Stockholder*
▲ **EMP:** 66 **EST:** 1970
SQ FT: 61,000
SALES (est): 7.48MM **Privately Held**
Web: www.empirecontainercorp.com
SIC: 2653 3578 Boxes, corrugated: made from purchased materials; Point-of-sale devices

(P-3099)
EXPRESS CONTAINER INC
5450 Dodds Ave (90621-1209)
P.O. Box 230 (92373-0064)
PHONE..................909 798-3857
Gilles Roy, *Pr*
EMP: 22 **EST:** 1984
SALES (est): 2.42MM **Privately Held**
Web: www.expresscontainerline.com
SIC: 2653 Boxes, corrugated: made from purchased materials

(P-3100)
FLEETWOOD FIBRE LLC
Also Called: Fleetwood Fibre Pkg & Graphics
15250 Don Julian Rd (91745-1001)
PHONE..................626 968-8503
EMP: 225 **EST:** 1952
SALES (est): 37.11MM
SALES (corp-wide): 317.12MM **Privately Held**
SIC: 2653 Boxes, corrugated: made from purchased materials
PA: Golden West Packaging Group Llc
15400 Don Julian Rd
City Of Industry CA
888 501-5893

(P-3101)
FRUIT GROWERS SUPPLY COMPANY (PA)
27770 Entertainment Dr Ste 120 (91355)
PHONE..................888 997-4855
Jim Phillips, *CEO*
Charles Boyce, *
William O Knox, *
◆ **EMP:** 50 **EST:** 1907
SQ FT: 10,000
SALES (est): 222.6MM
SALES (corp-wide): 222.6MM **Privately Held**
Web: www.fruitgrowerssupply.com
SIC: 2653 0811 5191 2448 Boxes, corrugated: made from purchased materials; Timber tracts; Farm supplies; Pallets, wood

(P-3102)
GABRIEL CONTAINER (PA)
Also Called: Recycled Paper Products
8844 Millergrove Dr (90670-2004)
P.O. Box 3188 (90670-0188)
PHONE..................562 699-1051
Ronald H Gabriel, *Pr*
Agnes Gabriel, *
▲ **EMP:** 199 **EST:** 1935
SQ FT: 72,000
SALES (est): 32.16MM
SALES (corp-wide): 32.16MM **Privately Held**
Web: www.gabrielcontainer.com
SIC: 2653 2621 Boxes, corrugated: made from purchased materials; Paper mills

(P-3103)
GENERAL CONTAINER
235 Radio Rd (92879-1725)
PHONE..................714 562-8700
Tim G Black, *CEO*
Scott Black, *
EMP: 72 **EST:** 1976
SALES (est): 19.64MM
SALES (corp-wide): 46.83MM **Privately Held**
Web: www.gcbox.com
SIC: 2653 Boxes, corrugated: made from purchased materials
PA: U.S. Display Group, Inc.
810 S Washington St
Tullahoma TN
931 455-9585

(P-3104)
GLOBAL PACKAGING SOLUTIONS INC
6259 Progressive Dr Ste 200 (92154-6644)
PHONE..................619 710-2661
Jawed Ghias, *CEO*
Anila Parikh, *
Rajnikanth Parikh, *
Tariq Butt, *
Henry Romo, *Stockholder*
▲ **EMP:** 280 **EST:** 2006
SALES (est): 8.19MM **Privately Held**
Web: www.globsoln.com
SIC: 2653 3089 Corrugated and solid fiber boxes; Injection molding of plastics
PA: Global Packaging Solutions, S.A. De C.V.
Calle 7 Norte No.108
Tijuana BCN

(P-3105)
GOLDEN WEST PACKG GROUP LLC (PA)
15400 Don Julian Rd (91745-1004)
PHONE..................888 501-5893

Brad Jordan, *Pr*
EMP: 381 **EST:** 2017
SALES (est): 317.12MM
SALES (corp-wide): 317.12MM **Privately Held**
Web: www.goldenwestpackaging.com
SIC: 2653 Boxes, corrugated: made from purchased materials

(P-3106)
GOLDENCORR SHEETS LLC
13890 Nelson Ave (91746-2050)
P.O. Box 90968 (91715-0968)
PHONE..............................626 369-6446
Tom Anderson, *Managing Member*
John Webb, *Managing Member**
Glen Tucker, *Managing Member**
Jeffrey Erseluis, *Managing Member**
John Perullo, *
▲ **EMP:** 150 **EST:** 1999
SALES (est): 23.62MM **Privately Held**
Web: www.goldencorr.net
SIC: 2653 Corrugated boxes, partitions, display items, sheets, and pad

(P-3107)
HERITAGE CONTAINER INC
4777 Felspar St (92509-3040)
P.O. Box 605 (91752-0605)
PHONE..............................951 360-1900
Richard Gabriel, *CEO*
Thomas Gabriel, *
Nancy Zuniga, *
EMP: 100 **EST:** 1988
SQ FT: 95,000
SALES (est): 16.5MM **Privately Held**
Web: www.heritagecontainer.com
SIC: 2653 5199 Boxes, corrugated: made from purchased materials; Packaging materials

(P-3108)
HERITAGE PAPER CO (HQ)
2400 S Grand Ave (92705-5211)
PHONE..............................714 540-9737
Ron Scagliotti, *CEO*
Lenet Derksen, *
▲ **EMP:** 75 **EST:** 1976
SQ FT: 150,000
SALES (est): 28.99MM
SALES (corp-wide): 50.82MM **Privately Held**
Web: www.heritagepaper.net
SIC: 2653 5199 Boxes, corrugated: made from purchased materials; Packaging materials
PA: Pioneer Packing, Inc.
2430 S Grand Ave
Santa Ana CA
714 540-9751

(P-3109)
HOOVER CONTAINERS INC
19570 San Jose Ave (91748-1404)
P.O. Box 10366 (92838-6366)
PHONE..............................909 444-9454
▲ **EMP:** 60
SIC: 2653 5113 Boxes, corrugated: made from purchased materials; Corrugated and solid fiber boxes

(P-3110)
HPI LIQUIDATIONS INC
13100 Danielson St (92064-6840)
PHONE..............................858 391-7302
EMP: 245
SIC: 2653 5199 Boxes, corrugated: made from purchased materials; Packaging materials

(P-3111)
INTERNATIONAL PAPER COMPANY
Also Called: International Paper
11211 Greenstone Ave (90670-4616)
PHONE..............................323 946-6100
Marc Bailey, *Genl Mgr*
EMP: 33
SALES (corp-wide): 21.16B **Publicly Held**
Web: www.internationalpaper.com
SIC: 2653 Boxes, corrugated: made from purchased materials
PA: International Paper Company
6400 Poplar Ave
Memphis TN
901 419-7000

(P-3112)
JELLCO CONTAINER INC
1151 N Tustin Ave (92807-1736)
PHONE..............................714 666-2728
Jeff Erselius, *Pr*
Rick Leininger, *
EMP: 72 **EST:** 1977
SQ FT: 42,000
SALES (est): 20.16MM **Privately Held**
Web: www.jellco.com
SIC: 2653 Boxes, corrugated: made from purchased materials

(P-3113)
JKV INC
Also Called: Atlantic Box & Carton Company
8343 Loch Lomond Dr (90660-2507)
PHONE..............................562 948-3000
Michael Valov, *Pr*
Jack Valov, *
Elena Valov, *
EMP: 40 **EST:** 1971
SQ FT: 30,000
SALES (est): 5.01MM **Privately Held**
Web: www.atlanticboxncarton.com
SIC: 2653 Boxes, corrugated: made from purchased materials

(P-3114)
LIBERTY CONTAINER COMPANY
Also Called: Key Container
4224 Santa Ana St (90280-2557)
PHONE..............................323 564-4211
Robert J Watts, *Pr*
William J Watts, *
▲ **EMP:** 110 **EST:** 1956
SQ FT: 300,000
SALES (est): 20.42MM **Privately Held**
Web: www.keycontainer.com
SIC: 2653 Boxes, corrugated: made from purchased materials

(P-3115)
LIBERTY DIVERSIFIED INTL INC
Also Called: Harbor Packaging
13100 Danielson St (92064-6840)
PHONE..............................858 391-7302
EMP: 245
SALES (corp-wide): 1.02B **Privately Held**
Web: www.libertydiversified.com
SIC: 2653 5199 Boxes, corrugated: made from purchased materials; Packaging materials
PA: Liberty Diversified International, Inc.
5600 Highway 169 N
New Hope MN
763 536-6600

(P-3116)
LIFOAM INDUSTRIES LLC
15671 Industry Ln (92649-1536)
PHONE..............................714 891-5035
EMP: 50

SALES (corp-wide): 1.86B **Privately Held**
Web: www.lifoam.com
SIC: 2653 Corrugated and solid fiber boxes
HQ: Lifoam Industries, Llc
1303 S Batesville Rd
Greer SC
410 889-1023

(P-3117)
MARFRED INDUSTRIES
Also Called: Amatix
12708 Branford St (91353)
▲ **EMP:** 300
SIC: 2653 5113 Boxes, solid fiber: made from purchased materials; Shipping supplies

(P-3118)
MCDONALD PACKAGING INC
Also Called: Rightpaq
2601 S Garnsey St (92707-3338)
EMP: 150
SALES (est): 19.56MM **Privately Held**
SIC: 2653 5199 Boxes, corrugated: made from purchased materials; Packaging materials

(P-3119)
NUMATECH WEST (KMP) LLC
Also Called: Kmp Numatech Pacific
1201 E Lexington Ave (91766-5520)
P.O. Box 357 (92871-0357)
PHONE..............................909 706-3627
John Neate, *Managing Member*
▲ **EMP:** 100 **EST:** 1986
SQ FT: 65,000
SALES (est): 2.36MM
SALES (corp-wide): 19.33MM **Privately Held**
SIC: 2653 Boxes, corrugated: made from purchased materials
PA: Nw Packaging Llc
1201 E Lexington Ave
Pomona CA
909 706-3627

(P-3120)
PACIFIC QUALITY PACKAGING CORP
660 Neptune Ave (92821-2909)
PHONE..............................714 257-1234
Frederick H Chau, *Pr*
▲ **EMP:** 65 **EST:** 1984
SQ FT: 44,000
SALES (est): 8.04MM **Privately Held**
SIC: 2653 3993 Boxes, corrugated: made from purchased materials; Signs and advertising specialties

(P-3121)
PACKAGING CORPORATION AMERICA
Also Called: PCA/South Gate 378
9700 E Frontage Rd Ste 20 (90280-5421)
PHONE..............................562 927-7741
EMP: 114
SALES (corp-wide): 8.48B **Publicly Held**
Web: www.packagingcorp.com
SIC: 2653 Boxes, corrugated: made from purchased materials
PA: Packaging Corporation Of America
1 N Field Ct
Lake Forest IL
847 482-3000

(P-3122)
PACKAGING CORPORATION AMERICA
Also Called: PCA/Los Angeles 349
4240 Bandini Blvd (90058-4207)

PHONE..............................323 263-7581
Mark Beyma, *Brnch Mgr*
EMP: 135
SALES (corp-wide): 8.48B **Publicly Held**
Web: www.packagingcorp.com
SIC: 2653 Boxes, corrugated: made from purchased materials
PA: Packaging Corporation Of America
1 N Field Ct
Lake Forest IL
847 482-3000

(P-3123)
PACKAGING CORPORATION AMERICA
Also Called: City of Industry Sheet Plant
19570 San Jose Ave (91748-1404)
PHONE..............................909 595-0401
EMP: 21
SALES (corp-wide): 8.48B **Publicly Held**
Web: www.packagingcorp.com
SIC: 2653 Boxes, corrugated: made from purchased materials
PA: Packaging Corporation Of America
1 N Field Ct
Lake Forest IL
847 482-3000

(P-3124)
PACKAGING CORPORATION AMERICA
Also Called: San Bernardino Sheet Plant
879 E Rialto Ave (92408-1202)
PHONE..............................909 888-7008
EMP: 31
SALES (corp-wide): 8.48B **Publicly Held**
Web: www.packagingcorp.com
SIC: 2653 Boxes, corrugated: made from purchased materials
PA: Packaging Corporation Of America
1 N Field Ct
Lake Forest IL
847 482-3000

(P-3125)
PNC PROACTIVE NTHRN CONT LLC
Also Called: Proactive Northern Container
602 S Rockefeller Ave A (91761-8190)
PHONE..............................909 390-5624
Gary Hartog, *Managing Member*
▲ **EMP:** 44 **EST:** 2005
SQ FT: 362,000
SALES (est): 1.92MM **Privately Held**
SIC: 2653 Boxes, corrugated: made from purchased materials
PA: Fourth Third Llc
375 Park Ave Ste 3304
New York NY

(P-3126)
RELIABLE CONTAINER CORPORATION
9206 Santa Fe Springs Rd (90670-2618)
PHONE..............................562 861-6226
EMP: 275
SIC: 2653 5113 Boxes, corrugated: made from purchased materials; Corrugated and solid fiber boxes

(P-3127)
SAN DIEGO CRATING & PKG INC
12678 Brookprinter Pl (92064-6809)
PHONE..............................858 748-0100
Jacqueline H Peterson, *Prin*
Jacqueline H Peterson, *CEO*
Lee Peterson, *Pr*
EMP: 17 **EST:** 1975
SQ FT: 12,000

PRODUCTS & SVCS

SALES (est): 2.34MM **Privately Held**
Web: www.sdcrate.com
SIC: 2653 4783 Boxes, corrugated: made from purchased materials; Crating goods for shipping

(P-3128)
SCOPE PACKAGING INC
Also Called: Sp
13400 Nelson Ave (91746-2331)
PHONE...................714 998-4411
TOLL FREE: 800
Mike E Flinn, *CEO*
Cindy Baker, *
▲ **EMP:** 75 **EST:** 1966
SQ FT: 70,000
SALES (est): 1.98MM **Privately Held**
SIC: 2653 7389 Boxes, corrugated: made from purchased materials; Packaging and labeling services

(P-3129)
SILICA GEL DESSICANT PDTS CO
1144 E Hyde Park Blvd (90302-1804)
PHONE...................800 426-1529
EMP: 35
SALES (corp-wide): 187.9K **Privately Held**
Web: www.silicagelco.com
SIC: 2653 Corrugated and solid fiber boxes
PA: Silica Gel Dessicant Products Company
6326 West Blvd
Los Angeles CA
310 258-9121

(P-3130)
SOUTHLAND BOX COMPANY
4201 Fruitland Ave (90058-3118)
P.O. Box 512214 (90051-0214)
PHONE...................323 583-2231
▲ **EMP:** 170 **EST:** 1945
SALES (est): 69.74MM **Privately Held**
Web: www.southlandbox.com
SIC: 2653 5113 Corrugated boxes, partitions, display items, sheets, and pad; Corrugated and solid fiber boxes
PA: Tomoku Co., Ltd.
2-2-2, Marunouchi
Chiyoda-Ku TKY

(P-3131)
SOUTHLAND CONTAINER CORP
Also Called: Concept Packaging Group
1600 Champagne Ave (91761-3612)
PHONE...................909 937-9781
Tom Heinz, *Brnch Mgr*
EMP: 234
SALES (corp-wide): 371.15MM **Privately Held**
Web: www.southlandcontainer.com
SIC: 2653 Boxes, corrugated: made from purchased materials
PA: Southland Container Corporation
60 Fairview Church Rd
Spartanburg SC
864 578-0085

(P-3132)
ST WORTH CONTAINER LLC
727 S Wanamaker Ave (91761-8116)
PHONE...................909 390-4550
EMP: 82 **EST:** 1994
SALES (est): 9.64MM **Privately Held**
Web: www.goldenwestpackaging.com
SIC: 2653 Corrugated boxes, partitions, display items, sheets, and pad

(P-3133)
TRIPLE A CONTAINERS INC
16069 Shoemaker Ave (90703-2234)
P.O. Box 6111 (90702-6111)
PHONE...................562 404-7433
EMP: 88 **EST:** 1957
SALES (est): 10.14MM **Privately Held**
SIC: 2653 3993 Corrugated boxes, partitions, display items, sheets, and pad; Signs and advertising specialties

(P-3134)
US DISPLAY GROUP INC
235 Radio Rd (92879-1725)
PHONE...................951 444-4567
Gabriel Perez, *Dir*
EMP: 50
SALES (corp-wide): 46.83MM **Privately Held**
Web: www.usdisplaygroup.com
SIC: 2653 Boxes, corrugated: made from purchased materials
PA: U.S. Display Group, Inc.
810 S Washington St
Tullahoma TN
931 455-9585

(P-3135)
WESTERN CORRUGATED DESIGN INC
8741 Pioneer Blvd (90670-2021)
PHONE...................562 695-9295
John Brendlinger, *CEO*
▲ **EMP:** 50 **EST:** 2004
SALES (est): 10.4MM **Privately Held**
SIC: 2653 Boxes, corrugated: made from purchased materials

2655 Fiber Cans, Drums, And Similar Products

(P-3136)
GREIF BROS CORP
3042 Inland Empire Blvd (91764-6549)
PHONE...................909 941-4570
▼ **EMP:** 25 **EST:** 2009
SALES (est): 5.84MM
SALES (corp-wide): 6.35B **Publicly Held**
Web: www.greif.com
SIC: 2655 Fiber cans, drums, and similar products
PA: Greif, Inc.
425 Winter Rd
Delaware OH
740 549-6000

(P-3137)
PLASTOPAN INDUSTRIES INC (PA)
Also Called: Plastopan
812 E 59th St (90001-1006)
PHONE...................323 231-2225
Ronald D Miller, *Pr*
Catherine M Bump, *
Sofia G Miller, *
Martin L Miller, *
EMP: 30 **EST:** 1992
SQ FT: 48,000
SALES (est): 5.55MM **Privately Held**
SIC: 2655 Fiber cans, drums, and similar products

(P-3138)
SGL COMPOSITES INC (DH)
1551 W 139th St (90249-2603)
PHONE...................424 329-5250
David Otterson, *CEO*
Jeff Schade, *

▼ **EMP:** 90 **EST:** 1995
SALES: 70.91MM
SALES (corp-wide): 1.18B **Privately Held**
Web: www.sglcarbon.com
SIC: 2655 Fiber cans, drums, and similar products
HQ: Sgl Carbon, Llc
10715 David Taylor Dr # 4
Charlotte NC
704 593-5100

(P-3139)
SPIRAL PPR TUBE & CORE CO INC
5200 Industry Ave (90660-2506)
PHONE...................562 801-9705
George Hibard, *CEO*
Summer Hibard, *
▲ **EMP:** 45 **EST:** 1949
SQ FT: 40,000
SALES (est): 9.91MM **Privately Held**
Web: www.spiralpaper.com
SIC: 2655 Fiber cans, drums, and similar products

(P-3140)
TUBE-TAINER INC
8174 Byron Rd (90606-2616)
PHONE...................562 945-3711
Mike Mundia, *Pr*
▲ **EMP:** 45 **EST:** 1967
SQ FT: 44,000
SALES (est): 9.22MM **Privately Held**
Web: www.tubetainer.com
SIC: 2655 Tubes, fiber or paper: made from purchased material

2656 Sanitary Food Containers

(P-3141)
AMSCAN INC
Ampro
804 W Town & Country Rd (92868-4712)
PHONE...................714 972-2626
EMP: 48
SALES (corp-wide): 2.17B **Publicly Held**
Web: www.amscan.com
SIC: 2656 Cups, paper: made from purchased material
HQ: Amscan Inc.
1 Celebration Sq
Woodcliff Lake NJ
800 444-8887

(P-3142)
FINELINE SETTINGS LLC
2041 S Turner Ave Unit 30 (91761-8510)
PHONE...................845 369-6100
Abraham Feig, *Brnch Mgr*
▲ **EMP:** 42
SALES (corp-wide): 3.48B **Privately Held**
Web: www.finelinesettings.com
SIC: 2656 Sanitary food containers
HQ: Fineline Settings, Llc
135 Crotty Rd Ste 1
Middletown NY
845 369-6100

(P-3143)
HARVEST PACK INC
12336 Lower Azusa Rd (91006-5872)
PHONE...................888 727-7225
Christina Pou, *CEO*
EMP: 17 **EST:** 2013
SALES (est): 2.46MM **Privately Held**
Web: www.harvest-pack.com
SIC: 2656 Plates, paper: made from purchased material

2657 Folding Paperboard Boxes

(P-3144)
88 SPECIAL SWEET INC
2437 Lee Ave (91733-1407)
PHONE...................909 525-7055
EMP: 22
SALES (corp-wide): 231.36K **Privately Held**
SIC: 2657 Food containers, folding: made from purchased material
PA: 88 Special Sweet Inc
4934 Walnut Grove Ave
San Gabriel CA

(P-3145)
ABSOLUTE PACKAGING INC
1201 N Miller St (92806-1933)
PHONE...................714 630-3020
Ramin Kohan, *Pr*
EMP: 35 **EST:** 2020
SALES (est): 2.64MM **Privately Held**
Web: www.absolutepackaginginc.com
SIC: 2657 5199 Folding paperboard boxes; Packaging materials

(P-3146)
T & T BOX COMPANY INC
Also Called: Thomas Container & Packaging
1353 Philadelphia St Ste 101 (91766-5554)
PHONE...................909 465-0848
Thomas Murphy, *CEO*
Andy Murphy, *VP*
EMP: 22 **EST:** 1972
SQ FT: 60,000
SALES (est): 2.02MM **Privately Held**
Web: www.thomascontainer.com
SIC: 2657 2653 Folding paperboard boxes; Corrugated and solid fiber boxes

(P-3147)
YAVAR MANUFACTURING CO INC
Also Called: National Packaging Products
1900 S Tubeway Ave (90040-1612)
PHONE...................323 722-2040
Massoud Afari, *CEO*
Ben Afari, *
▲ **EMP:** 48 **EST:** 1998
SQ FT: 50,000
SALES (est): 14.43MM **Privately Held**
Web: www.nationalpkg.com
SIC: 2657 2631 Folding paperboard boxes; Folding boxboard

2671 Paper; Coated And Laminated Packaging

(P-3148)
AMCOR FLEXIBLES LLC
Also Called: Amcor Flexibles Healthcare
5416 Union Pacific Ave (90022-5117)
PHONE...................323 721-6777
EMP: 1206
SALES (corp-wide): 14.69B **Privately Held**
SIC: 2671 2621 2821 3081 Plastic film, coated or laminated for packaging; Packaging paper; Plastics materials and resins; Packing materials, plastics sheet
HQ: Amcor Flexibles Llc
3 Parkway North Blvd # 300
Deerfield IL
224 313-7000

(P-3149)
AUDIO VIDEO COLOR CORPORATION (PA)
17707 S Santa Fe Ave (90221-5419)
PHONE..............................424 213-7500
Kali J Limath, *CEO*
Guy Marrom, *
Michael Baker, *Prin*
▲ **EMP: 145 EST:** 1990
SQ FT: 78,000
SALES (est): 45.46MM **Privately Held**
SIC: 2671 Paper; coated and laminated packaging

(P-3150)
BAY CITIES CONTAINER CORP
9206 Santa Fe Springs Rd (90670-2618)
PHONE..............................562 551-2946
Greg Tucker, *CEO*
EMP: 32
SALES (corp-wide): 150.82MM **Privately Held**
Web: www.bay-cities.com
SIC: 2671 Paper; coated and laminated packaging
PA: Bay Cities Container Corp
5138 Industry Ave Frnt
Pico Rivera CA
562 948-3751

(P-3151)
FEDERATED DIVERSIFIED SLS INC
Also Called: FDS Manufacturing Company Svcs
2200 S Reservoir St (91766-6408)
P.O. Box 45 (91769-0045)
PHONE..............................909 591-1733
EMP: 89 **EST:** 1957
SALES (est): 5.82MM **Privately Held**
SIC: 2671 2631 2653 3086 Paper; coated and laminated packaging; Container, packaging, and boxboard; Corrugated and solid fiber boxes; Cups and plates, foamed plastics

(P-3152)
GLOBAL LINK SOURCING INC
41690 Corporate Center Ct (92562-7084)
PHONE..............................951 698-1977
Jullie Annet, *Pr*
▲ **EMP:** 70 **EST:** 2006
SQ FT: 80,000
SALES (est): 6.57MM **Privately Held**
Web: www.globallinksourcing.com
SIC: 2671 Paper; coated and laminated packaging

(P-3153)
IRONWOOD PACKAGING LLC
8975 Cottage Ave (91730-5235)
PHONE..............................909 581-0077
Bill O'melveny, *CEO*
William O'melveny, *Managing Member*
▲ **EMP:** 21 **EST:** 1998
SQ FT: 35,000
SALES (est): 4.73MM **Privately Held**
Web: www.ironwoodpackaging.com
SIC: 2671 Plastic film, coated or laminated for packaging

(P-3154)
PAPERCUTTERS INC
6900 Washington Blvd (90640-5424)
PHONE..............................323 888-1330
Susan Feinstein, *Pr*
Beth Feinstein, *VP*
Joyce Feinstein, *Sec*
▲ **EMP:** 21 **EST:** 1983

SALES (est): 4.95MM **Privately Held**
Web: www.papercutters.net
SIC: 2671 5113 Paper; coated and laminated packaging; Paper, wrapping or coarse, and products

(P-3155)
PGAC CORP (PA)
Also Called: Pgi
9630 Ridgehaven Ct Ste B (92123-5605)
PHONE..............................858 560-8213
Mark Grantham, *Pr*
Florentina Shields, *
EMP: 75 **EST:** 1975
SALES (est): 45.04MM **Privately Held**
Web: www.pgisd.com
SIC: 2671 Paper, coated or laminated for packaging

(P-3156)
PRECISION LABEL LLC
659 Benet Rd (92058-1208)
P.O. Box 766 (92075-0766)
PHONE..............................760 757-7533
Robert A Wilcox, *Pr*
EMP: 30 **EST:** 1991
SQ FT: 7,000
SALES (est): 6.33MM
SALES (corp-wide): 4.71B **Privately Held**
Web: www.p-label.com
SIC: 2671 2759 Paper; coated and laminated packaging; Labels and seals: printing, nsk
HQ: Inovar Packaging Group, Llc
9001 Sterling St
Irving TX

(P-3157)
SHERPA CLINICAL PACKAGING LLC
6920 Carroll Rd (92121-2211)
PHONE..............................858 282-0928
Derek Truninger, *Prin*
EMP: 20 **EST:** 2010
SALES (est): 1.47MM **Privately Held**
SIC: 2671 Plastic film, coated or laminated for packaging

(P-3158)
THERMECH CORPORATION
Also Called: Thermech Engineering
1773 W Lincoln Ave Ste I (92801-6713)
PHONE..............................714 533-3183
Jim Shah, *CEO*
Richard Gorman, *
EMP: 23 **EST:** 1949
SQ FT: 24,000
SALES (est): 2.25MM **Privately Held**
Web: www.thermech.com
SIC: 2671 3083 Paper; coated and laminated packaging; Plastics finished products, laminated

(P-3159)
TRANSCONTINENTAL ONTARIO INC
5601 Santa Ana St (91761-8622)
PHONE..............................909 390-8866
Brian Reid, *CEO*
EMP: 48 **EST:** 2003
SALES (est): 8.35MM
SALES (corp-wide): 2.15B **Privately Held**
SIC: 2671 Paper, coated or laminated for packaging
HQ: Transcontinental Us Llc
8700 W Bryn Mawr Ave
Chicago IL
773 877-3300

(P-3160)
TRI-PACK ENTERPRISES INC
Also Called: Custom Blow Molding
946 S Andreasen Dr (92029-1914)
PHONE..............................760 737-7995
◆ **EMP:** 170
SIC: 2671 3085 Plastic film, coated or laminated for packaging; Plastics bottles

(P-3161)
TRIUNE ENTERPRISES INC
Also Called: Triune Enterprises Mfg
13711 S Normandie Ave (90249-2609)
PHONE..............................310 719-1600
◆ **EMP:** 23 **EST:** 1996
SQ FT: 29,000
SALES (est): 2.68MM **Privately Held**
Web: www.triuneent.com
SIC: 2671 5162 Plastic film, coated or laminated for packaging; Plastics materials and basic shapes

(P-3162)
VINYL TECHNOLOGY INC (PA)
200 Railroad Ave (91016-4643)
PHONE..............................626 443-5257
Carlos A Mollura, *Ch Bd*
Daniel Mullora, *
Carlos Mollura Junior, *VP*
Rodney Mollura, *
Haydee Mollura, *
◆ **EMP:** 199 **EST:** 1981
SQ FT: 68,000
SALES (est): 46.38MM
SALES (corp-wide): 46.38MM **Privately Held**
Web: www.vinyltechnology.com
SIC: 2671 7389 Plastic film, coated or laminated for packaging; Sewing contractor

2672 Paper; Coated And Laminated, Nec

(P-3163)
AVERY DENNISON CORPORATION
11195 Eucalyptus St (91730-3836)
PHONE..............................909 987-4631
Marta E Corfaelb, *Mgr*
EMP: 62
SALES (corp-wide): 9.04B **Publicly Held**
Web: www.averydennison.com
SIC: 2672 Tape, pressure sensitive: made from purchased materials
PA: Avery Dennison Corporation
8080 Norton Pkwy
Mentor OH
440 534-6000

(P-3164)
AVERY DENNISON CORPORATION
50 Pointe Dr (92821-3648)
PHONE..............................714 674-8500
Rick Alonzo, *Mgr*
EMP: 400
SALES (corp-wide): 9.04B **Publicly Held**
Web: www.averydennison.com
SIC: 2672 3081 3497 2678 Adhesive papers, labels, or tapes: from purchased material; Unsupported plastics film and sheet; Metal foil and leaf; Stationery products
PA: Avery Dennison Corporation
8080 Norton Pkwy
Mentor OH
440 534-6000

(P-3165)
AVERY DENNISON CORPORATION
2900 Bradley St (91107-1560)
PHONE..............................626 304-2000
Dave Edwards, *VP*
EMP: 120
SQ FT: 67,580
SALES (corp-wide): 9.04B **Publicly Held**
Web: www.averydennison.com
SIC: 2672 2679 Adhesive papers, labels, or tapes: from purchased material; Labels, paper: made from purchased material
PA: Avery Dennison Corporation
8080 Norton Pkwy
Mentor OH
440 534-6000

(P-3166)
AVERY DENNISON FOUNDATION
207 N Goode Ave Ste 500 (91203-1301)
PHONE..............................626 304-2000
Alicia Maddox, *Pr*
EMP: 85 **EST:** 1978
SALES (est): 2.46MM **Privately Held**
SIC: 2672 Paper; coated and laminated, nec

(P-3167)
BECKERS FABRICATION INC
Also Called: B F I Labels
22465 La Palma Ave (92887-3803)
PHONE..............................714 692-1600
Mark Becker, *CEO*
Dan Becker, *
EMP: 24 **EST:** 1981
SQ FT: 6,500
SALES (est): 4.96MM **Privately Held**
Web: www.beckersfab.com
SIC: 2672 2759 Paper; coated and laminated, nec; Screen printing

(P-3168)
CINTON LLC
Also Called: West Coast Labels
620 Richfield Rd (92870-6727)
PHONE..............................714 961-8808
Salvatore Scaffide, *Pr*
Romona Scaffide, *
Cindi Montgomery, *
EMP: 46 **EST:** 1972
SQ FT: 23,000
SALES (est): 10.79MM **Privately Held**
SIC: 2672 2679 Paper; coated and laminated, nec; Labels, paper: made from purchased material
PA: Fortis Solutions Group, Llc
2505 Hawkeye Ct
Virginia Beach VA

(P-3169)
CLARIANT CORPORATION
926 S 8th St (92324-3500)
P.O. Box 610 (92324-0610)
PHONE..............................909 825-1793
Kenneth Golder, *Pr*
EMP: 32
Web: www.clariant.com
SIC: 2672 7389 5199 Paper; coated and laminated, nec; Packaging and labeling services; Packaging materials
HQ: Clariant Corporation
500 E Morehead St Ste 400
Charlotte NC
704 331-7000

(P-3170)
EDWARDS ASSOC CMMNICATIONS INC (PA)
Also Called: Edwards Label

2277 Knoll Dr Ste A (93003-5878)
PHONE....................805 658-2626
Joel Horacio Gomez-avila, *Pr*
John Edwards, *
EMP: 150 **EST:** 1984
SQ FT: 44,000
SALES (est): 42.02MM
SALES (corp-wide): 42.02MM **Privately Held**
Web: www.edwardslabel.com
SIC: 2672 Labels (unprinted), gummed: made from purchased materials

(P-3171)
FELIX SCHOELLER NORTH AMER INC
1260 N Lakeview Ave (92807-1831)
PHONE....................315 298-8425
EMP: 25
SALES (corp-wide): 29.22MM **Privately Held**
Web: www.schoeller.com
SIC: 2672 Paper; coated and laminated, nec
HQ: Felix Schoeller North America Inc.
      179 County Route 2a
      Pulaski NY
      315 298-8425

(P-3172)
HARRIS INDUSTRIES INC (PA)
5181 Argosy Ave (92649-1058)
P.O. Box 3269 (92605-3269)
PHONE....................714 898-8048
William Helzer, *Pr*
Gail Helzer, *
◆ **EMP:** 50 **EST:** 1987
SQ FT: 25,000
SALES (est): 9.97MM
SALES (corp-wide): 9.97MM **Privately Held**
Web: www.harrisind.com
SIC: 2672 Tape, pressure sensitive: made from purchased materials

(P-3173)
PRECISION DYNAMICS CORPORATION (HQ)
Also Called: Pdc-Identicard
25124 Springfield Ct Ste 200 (91355)
PHONE....................818 897-1111
J Michael Nauman, *CEO*
Robin Barber, *
Robert Case, *
John Park, *
◆ **EMP:** 161 **EST:** 1956
SQ FT: 75,000
SALES (est): 74.12MM
SALES (corp-wide): 1.33B **Publicly Held**
Web: www.pdcorp.com
SIC: 2672 2754 5047 3069 Adhesive papers, labels, or tapes: from purchased material; Labels: gravure printing; Instruments, surgical and medical; Tape, pressure sensitive: rubber
PA: Brady Corporation
      6555 W Good Hope Rd
      Milwaukee WI
      414 358-6600

(P-3174)
SC LIQUIDATION COMPANY LLC
566 Vanguard Way (92821-3928)
PHONE....................714 482-1006
EMP: 103
Web: www.spinps.com
SIC: 2672 Labels (unprinted), gummed: made from purchased materials
HQ: Sc Liquidation Company, Llc
      550 Summit Ave
      Troy OH
      937 332-6500

(P-3175)
SEAL METHODS INC (PA)
11915 Shoemaker Ave (90670-4717)
P.O. Box 2604 (90670-0604)
PHONE....................562 944-0291
Eugene Welter, *Prin*
Geri Welter, *
◆ **EMP:** 90 **EST:** 1974
SQ FT: 75,000
SALES (est): 24.2MM
SALES (corp-wide): 24.2MM **Privately Held**
Web: www.sealmethodsinc.com
SIC: 2672 3053 5085 Masking tape: made from purchased materials; Gaskets, all materials; Gaskets

(P-3176)
TAPE AND LABEL CONVERTERS INC
8231 Allport Ave (90670-2105)
P.O. Box 398 (90660-0398)
PHONE....................562 945-3486
TOLL FREE: 888
Robert Varela Senior, *Pr*
Jeanette Verela, *Sec*
EMP: 20 **EST:** 1996
SQ FT: 3,625
SALES (est): 2.31MM **Privately Held**
Web: www.stickybiz.com
SIC: 2672 2782 2752 2671 Labels (unprinted), gummed: made from purchased materials; Blankbooks and looseleaf binders; Commercial printing, lithographic; Paper; coated and laminated packaging

(P-3177)
UPM RAFLATAC INC
1105 Auto Center Dr (91761-2213)
PHONE....................909 390-4657
Alan Punch, *Mgr*
EMP: 17
Web: www.upmraflatac.com
SIC: 2672 2679 Paper; coated and laminated, nec; Labels, paper: made from purchased material
HQ: Upm Raflatac, Inc.
      400 Broadpointe Dr
      Mills River NC
      828 651-4800

2673 Bags: Plastic, Laminated, And Coated

(P-3178)
ASIA PLASTICS INC
9347 Rush St (91733-2544)
PHONE....................626 448-8100
Kent Ung, *CEO*
Hung Tran, *CFO*
Tracy Ung, *Sec*
▲ **EMP:** 20 **EST:** 1982
SQ FT: 11,000
SALES (est): 2.29MM **Privately Held**
SIC: 2673 Plastic bags: made from purchased materials

(P-3179)
CALIFORNIA PLASTIX INC
1319 E 3rd St (91766-2212)
PHONE....................909 629-8288
▼ **EMP:** 25 **EST:** 1994
SQ FT: 44,000
SALES (est): 4MM **Privately Held**
Web: www.californiaplastix.com
SIC: 2673 3089 Garment and wardrobe bags, (plastic film); Extruded finished plastics products, nec

(P-3180)
CF&B MANUFACTURING INC
Also Called: Cleanroom Film & Bags
1700 Barcelona Cir (92870-6630)
P.O. Box 807 (92811-0807)
PHONE....................714 744-8361
Michael Hoffman, *CEO*
Kyle Purcell, *CFO*
EMP: 20 **EST:** 2004
SQ FT: 10,000
SALES (est): 9.02MM **Privately Held**
Web: www.cleanroomfilm.com
SIC: 2673 Plastic bags: made from purchased materials
HQ: C. P. Converters, Inc.
      15 Grumbacher Rd
      York PA
      717 764-1193

(P-3181)
CROWN POLY INC
Also Called: Pull-N-Pac
5700 Bickett St (90255-2625)
PHONE....................323 585-5522
Ebrahim Simhaee, *CEO*
◆ **EMP:** 150 **EST:** 1991
SQ FT: 40,000
SALES (est): 47.65MM **Privately Held**
Web: www.crownpoly.com
SIC: 2673 Plastic bags: made from purchased materials

(P-3182)
DURABAG COMPANY INC
Also Called: Superpak
1432 Santa Fe Dr (92780-6417)
PHONE....................714 259-8811
Frank C S Huang, *VP*
Daniel Huang, *
Feng Jung Huang, *
▲ **EMP:** 70 **EST:** 1985
SQ FT: 150,000
SALES (est): 12.95MM **Privately Held**
Web: www.durabag.net
SIC: 2673 Food storage and frozen food bags, plastic

(P-3183)
GREAT AMERICAN PACKAGING
4361 S Soto St (90058-2311)
PHONE....................323 582-2247
Greg Gurewitz, *Pr*
Marlene Gurewitz, *
Bruce Carter, *
Bob Clarke, *
Fito Perez Outside Sales, *Prin*
EMP: 50 **EST:** 1966
SQ FT: 40,000
SALES (est): 9.19MM **Privately Held**
Web: www.greatampack.com
SIC: 2673 3081 3082 Plastic bags: made from purchased materials; Plastics film and sheet; Unsupported plastics profile shapes

(P-3184)
LIBERTY PACKG & EXTRUDING INC
Also Called: Liberty Film
3015 Supply Ave (90040-2709)
PHONE....................323 722-5124
Derek De Heras, *CEO*
Derek De Heras, *Pr*
Bonnie Hudson, *
Mary Hudson, *
Mary Anne Bove, *
EMP: 40 **EST:** 1986
SQ FT: 25,000
SALES (est): 5.11MM **Privately Held**
Web: www.libertypkg.com

SIC: 2673 7389 Plastic and pliofilm bags; Packaging and labeling services

(P-3185)
LINDAMAR INDUSTRIES INC
1603 Commerce Way (93446-3644)
P.O. Box 2180 (93447-2180)
PHONE....................805 237-1910
EMP: 63
Web: www.lindamarindustries.com
SIC: 2673 Bags: plastic, laminated, and coated

(P-3186)
MERCURY PLASTICS INC (HQ)
14825 Salt Lake Ave (91746-3131)
PHONE....................626 961-0165
Benjamin Deutsch, *CEO*
Stanley Tzenkov, *CFO*
Kamyar Mirdamadi, *
Yathira Munoz, *
▲ **EMP:** 415 **EST:** 1987
SQ FT: 140,000
SALES (est): 85.22MM **Privately Held**
Web: www.mercplastics.com
SIC: 2673 2759 3089 Plastic bags: made from purchased materials; Bags, plastic: printing, nsk; Plastics containers, except foam
PA: Alpha Industries Management, Inc.
      2919 Center Port Cir
      Pompano Beach FL

(P-3187)
MOHAWK WESTERN PLASTICS INC
1496 Arrow Hwy (91750-5219)
P.O. Box 463 (91750-0463)
PHONE....................909 593-7547
John R Mordoff, *CEO*
J Christopher Mordoff, *
EMP: 40 **EST:** 1965
SQ FT: 28,000
SALES (est): 7.43MM **Privately Held**
Web: www.mohawkwestern.com
SIC: 2673 3081 Plastic bags: made from purchased materials; Unsupported plastics film and sheet

(P-3188)
NORMAN PAPER AND FOAM CO INC
Also Called: Norman International
4501 S Santa Fe Ave (90058-2129)
PHONE....................323 582-7132
Norman Levine, *Pr*
Dawnn Winter, *VP*
Christopher Werner, *CFO*
Ellen Levine, *Sec*
▲ **EMP:** 23 **EST:** 1980
SQ FT: 40,000
SALES (est): 4.56MM **Privately Held**
Web: www.normaninternational.com
SIC: 2673 2671 3086 Bags: plastic, laminated, and coated; Paper; coated and laminated packaging; Packaging and shipping materials, foamed plastics

(P-3189)
NOVOLEX HOLDINGS LLC
515 Turnbull Canyon Rd (91745-1118)
PHONE....................626 961-6766
EMP: 73
SALES (corp-wide): 10.97B **Publicly Held**
Web: www.novolex.com
SIC: 2673 Plastic bags: made from purchased materials
HQ: Novolex Holdings, Llc
      101 E Carolina Ave
      Hartsville SC
      800 845-6051

(P-3190)
REPUBLIC BAG INC (PA)
580 E Harrison St (92879-1344)
PHONE.................................951 734-9740
Richard Schroeder, *CEO*
Steven Fritz, *
Mark Teo, *
▲ EMP: 80 EST: 1976
SQ FT: 59,000
SALES (est): 18.95MM
SALES (corp-wide): 18.95MM **Privately Held**
Web: www.republicbag.com
SIC: 2673 Plastic bags: made from purchased materials

(P-3191)
SUN PLASTICS INC
7140 E Slauson Ave (90040-3663)
PHONE.................................323 888-6999
Vahan Bagamian, *Pr*
Movses Shrikian, *
EMP: 50 EST: 1979
SQ FT: 60,000
SALES (est): 8.75MM **Privately Held**
Web: www.sunplastics.com
SIC: 2673 Plastic bags: made from purchased materials

(P-3192)
SUNSHINE FPC INC
Also Called: Sunshine
1600 Gage Rd (90640-6616)
PHONE.................................323 721-8168
▲ EMP: 65 EST: 1981
SALES (est): 8.99MM **Privately Held**
Web: www.sunshinefpc.com
SIC: 2673 Plastic bags: made from purchased materials

(P-3193)
TDI2 CUSTOM PACKAGING INC
17391 Mount Cliffwood Cir (92708-4102)
PHONE.................................714 751-6782
Stephen Deniger, *CEO*
Catharina Deniger, *Sec*
EMP: 17 EST: 1975
SQ FT: 19,000
SALES (est): 2.44MM **Privately Held**
Web: www.tdicustompackaging.com
SIC: 2673 Plastic bags: made from purchased materials

(P-3194)
THE HEAT FACTORY INC
2793 Loker Ave W (92010-6601)
PHONE.................................760 893-8300
Chris Treptow, *CEO*
▲ EMP: 35 EST: 1980
SALES (est): 8.49MM **Privately Held**
Web: www.heatfactory.com
SIC: 2673 2381 Bags: plastic, laminated, and coated; Fabric dress and work gloves

(P-3195)
TRANSCONTINENTAL US LLC
Also Called: Coveris
5601 Santa Ana St (91761-8622)
PHONE.................................909 390-8866
EMP: 20
SALES (corp-wide): 2.15B **Privately Held**
SIC: 2673 Bags: plastic, laminated, and coated
HQ: Transcontinental Us Llc
8700 W Bryn Mawr Ave
Chicago IL
773 877-3300

(P-3196)
WESTERN STATES PACKAGING INC
13276 Paxton St (91331-2356)
PHONE.................................818 686-6045
▲ EMP: 50 EST: 1995
SQ FT: 35,000
SALES (est): 8.18MM **Privately Held**
Web: www.wspusa.com
SIC: 2673 5113 5162 Plastic bags: made from purchased materials; Bags, paper and disposable plastic; Plastics materials, nec

2674 Bags: Uncoated Paper And Multiwall

(P-3197)
BAGCRAFTPAPERCON I LLC
Also Called: Papercon Packaging Division
515 Turnbull Canyon Rd (91745-1118)
PHONE.................................626 961-6766
Hector Lourido, *Mgr*
EMP: 100
SALES (corp-wide): 10.97B **Publicly Held**
Web: www.novolex.com
SIC: 2674 2671 Bags: uncoated paper and multiwall; Paper; coated and laminated packaging
HQ: Bagcraftpapercon I, Llc
3900 W 43rd St
Chicago IL
800 621-8468

(P-3198)
E-Z MIX INC (PA)
11450 Tuxford St (91352-2638)
PHONE.................................818 768-0568
William Frenzel, *CEO*
Sunjiv Parekh, *
EMP: 33 EST: 1992
SQ FT: 50,000
SALES (est): 10.3MM **Privately Held**
Web: www.ezmixinc.com
SIC: 2674 Cement bags: made from purchased materials

(P-3199)
ENDPAK PACKAGING INC
9101 Perkins St (90660-4512)
PHONE.................................562 801-0281
Edgar A Garcia, *CEO*
Carlos Garcia, *
EMP: 90 EST: 1992
SQ FT: 45,600
SALES (est): 16.71MM **Privately Held**
Web: www.endpak.com
SIC: 2674 5199 Paper bags: made from purchased materials; Packaging materials

(P-3200)
PACOBOND INC
9344 Glenoaks Blvd (91352-1533)
PHONE.................................818 768-5002
Arsine Seraydarian, *CEO*
Gerard Seradarian, *
▲ EMP: 50 EST: 1985
SALES (est): 9.65MM **Privately Held**
Web: www.pacobond.com
SIC: 2674 5162 Shopping bags: made from purchased materials; Plastics materials, nec

(P-3201)
SIDAKK DISTRIBUTORS
2109 Newton Ave (92113-2210)
PHONE.................................619 391-0950
EMP: 30 EST: 2017
SALES (est): 1.23MM **Privately Held**
Web: www.sidakk.com

SIC: 2674 Shipping and shopping bags or sacks

2675 Die-cut Paper And Board

(P-3202)
J J FOIL COMPANY INC
1734 W Sequoia Ave (92868-1016)
PHONE.................................714 998-9920
Tiffany Dang, *Pr*
EMP: 29 EST: 1991
SALES (est): 971K **Privately Held**
Web: www.jjfoil.com
SIC: 2675 2759 Paper die-cutting; Embossing on paper

(P-3203)
K & D GRAPHICS
Also Called: K & D Graphics Prtg & Packg
1432 N Main St Ste C (92867-3450)
PHONE.................................714 639-8900
Don Chew, *CEO*
Kim Chew, *
Montri Chew, *
Bebe Chew, *
Gus Chew, *
▲ EMP: 48 EST: 1981
SQ FT: 75,500
SALES (est): 9.07MM **Privately Held**
Web: www.kdgpp.com
SIC: 2675 2752 Die-cut paper and board; Offset printing

(P-3204)
PRESENTATION FOLDER INC
1130 N Main St (92867-3421)
PHONE.................................714 289-7000
Joseph Tardie Junior, *Pr*
Joseph Tardie Senior, *VP*
◆ EMP: 45 EST: 1988
SQ FT: 70,000
SALES (est): 11.04MM **Privately Held**
Web: www.presentationfolder.com
SIC: 2675 2759 2672 Folders, filing, die-cut: made from purchased materials; Embossing on paper; Paper; coated and laminated, nec

2676 Sanitary Paper Products

(P-3205)
GEORGIA PACIFIC HOLDINGS INC
13208 Hadley St Apt 1 (90601-4531)
PHONE.................................626 926-1474
Jorge Arroyo, *CEO*
EMP: 860 EST: 2008
SQ FT: 1,000
SALES (est): 155.07MM
SALES (corp-wide): 36.93B **Privately Held**
SIC: 2676 2656 2435 2821 Sanitary paper products; Sanitary food containers; Hardwood veneer and plywood; Plastics materials and resins
PA: Koch Industries, Inc.
4111 E 37th St N
Wichita KS
316 828-5500

(P-3206)
PRINCESS PAPER INC
4455 Fruitland Ave (90058-3222)
PHONE.................................323 588-4777
Abraham Hakimi, *Pr*
▲ EMP: 45 EST: 1989
SQ FT: 150,000
SALES (est): 8.23MM **Privately Held**
Web: www.princesspaper.com

SIC: 2676 Towels, napkins, and tissue paper products

(P-3207)
PROCTER & GAMBLE PAPER PDTS CO
Also Called: Procter & Gamble
800 N Rice Ave (93030-8910)
PHONE.................................805 485-8871
Shirley Boone, *Mgr*
EMP: 2361
SALES (corp-wide): 82.01B **Publicly Held**
Web: us.pg.com
SIC: 2676 Towels, paper: made from purchased paper
HQ: The Procter & Gamble Paper Products Company
1 Procter And Gamble Plz
Cincinnati OH
513 983-1100

(P-3208)
RAEL INC
6940 Beach Blvd Unit D301 (90621-6827)
PHONE.................................800 573-1516
Aness Han, *CEO*
Yanghee Park, *Pr*
EMP: 20 EST: 2017
SALES (est): 4.86MM **Privately Held**
Web: www.getrael.com
SIC: 2676 Feminine hygiene paper products

(P-3209)
UI MEDICAL LLC
1670 W Park Ave (92373-8048)
PHONE.................................562 453-1515
Joseph Baum Harris, *Ex Dir*
Wade Johnson, *
Nicolas Soichet, *
Christian Bluhm, *
Aaron Johnson, *
EMP: 25 EST: 2016
SALES (est): 3.69MM **Privately Held**
Web: www.quickchange.com
SIC: 2676 Diapers, paper (disposable): made from purchased paper

2677 Envelopes

(P-3210)
ASTRO CONVERTERS INC (PA)
Also Called: Astro Paper & Envelopes
2370 Oak Ridge Way Ste B (92081-8345)
PHONE.................................800 752-5003
EMP: 22 EST: 1970
SALES (est): 4.7MM
SALES (corp-wide): 4.7MM **Privately Held**
Web: www.astropaper.com
SIC: 2677 2621 2678 Envelopes; Paper mills; Stationery products

(P-3211)
INLAND ENVELOPE COMPANY
150 N Park Ave (91768-3835)
PHONE.................................909 622-2016
Bernard Kloenne, *CEO*
Otilia Kloenne, *Corporate Secretary*
EMP: 55 EST: 1966
SQ FT: 45,000
SALES (est): 9.55MM **Privately Held**
Web: www.inlandenvelope.com
SIC: 2677 Envelopes

(P-3212)
LA ENVELOPE INCORPORATED
1053 S Vail Ave (90640-6019)
PHONE.................................323 838-9300
Gary T Earls, *Pr*
Louise Earls, *

EMP: 35 **EST:** 1986
SQ FT: 25,000
SALES (est): 4.76MM **Privately Held**
Web: www.laenvelope.com
SIC: 2677 2752 Envelopes; Offset printing

(P-3213)
SEABOARD ENVELOPE CO INC
15601 Cypress Ave (91706-2120)
P.O. Box 721 (92625-0721)
PHONE...............................626 960-4559
Ronald Neidringhaus, *Pr*
Richard Riggle, *
Valerie Niedringhaus, *Prin*
EMP: 25 **EST:** 1939
SQ FT: 72,000
SALES (est): 2.19MM **Privately Held**
Web: www.seaboardenvelope.com
SIC: 2677 Envelopes

(P-3214)
SOUTHLAND ENVELOPE COMPANY INC
10111 Riverford Rd (92040-2741)
PHONE...............................619 449-3553
Dianne Gonzalez, *CEO*
Frank Soloman Junior, *Pr*
Rita Soloman, *
EMP: 115 **EST:** 1970
SQ FT: 80,000
SALES (est): 24.68MM **Privately Held**
Web: www.southlandenvelope.com
SIC: 2677 Envelopes

(P-3215)
VISION ENVELOPE & PRTG CO INC (PA)
13707 S Figueroa St (90061-1045)
PHONE...............................310 324-7062
Mark Fisher, *Prin*
Michael J Leeny, *
Ericka Fisher, *Prin*
Joe Barretto, *Prin*
Kraig Herrera, *Prin*
EMP: 50 **EST:** 1993
SQ FT: 45,000
SALES (est): 8.37MM **Privately Held**
Web: www.vision-envelope.com
SIC: 2677 2752 Envelopes; Offset printing

2678 Stationery Products

(P-3216)
AVERY DENNISON OFFICE PRODUCTS CO INC
Also Called: Dennison Division
50 Pointe Dr (92821-3652)
▼ **EMP:** 2410
SIC: 2678 3951 2672 2891 Notebooks: made from purchased paper; Markers, soft tip (felt, fabric, plastic, etc.); Labels (unprinted), gummed: made from purchased materials; Adhesives

(P-3217)
AVERY DNNSON RET INFO SVCS LLC (HQ)
207 N Goode Ave Fl 6 (91203-1364)
PHONE...............................626 304-2000
EMP: 51 **EST:** 2008
SALES (est): 23.41MM
SALES (corp-wide): 9.04B **Publicly Held**
SIC: 2678 3497 Notebooks: made from purchased paper; Metal foil and leaf
PA: Avery Dennison Corporation
8080 Norton Pkwy
Mentor OH
440 534-6000

(P-3218)
AVERY PRODUCTS CORPORATION (DH)
Also Called: ID&c
50 Pointe Dr (92821-3648)
PHONE...............................714 674-8500
Mark Cooper, *CEO*
Jeff Lattanzio, *
Bohdan Sirota, *
◆ **EMP:** 127 **EST:** 2012
SALES (est): 325.82MM
SALES (corp-wide): 4.75B **Privately Held**
Web: www.avery.com
SIC: 2678 3951 2672 2891 Notebooks: made from purchased paper; Markers, soft tip (felt, fabric, plastic, etc.); Labels (unprinted), gummed: made from purchased materials; Adhesives
HQ: Ccl Industries Corporation
161 Worcester Rd Ste 403
Framingham MA

(P-3219)
AVERY PRODUCTS CORPORATION
6987 Calle De Linea Ste 101 (92154-8016)
PHONE...............................619 671-1022
Geoff Martin, *Pr*
EMP: 144
SALES (corp-wide): 4.75B **Privately Held**
Web: www.avery.com
SIC: 2678 Stationery products
HQ: Avery Products Corporation
50 Pointe Dr
Brea CA
714 674-8500

(P-3220)
COAST INDEX CO INC
Also Called: Coast Index 965
850 Lawrence Dr (91320-1508)
PHONE...............................805 499-6844
EMP: 75 **EST:** 1982
SALES (est): 7.58MM **Privately Held**
Web: www.coastindex.com
SIC: 2678 2782 Stationery: made from purchased materials; Library binders, looseleaf

(P-3221)
CONTIXO INC
13947 Central Ave (91710-5556)
PHONE...............................909 465-5668
Pujie Sui, *CEO*
EMP: 20 **EST:** 2013
SALES (est): 1.51MM **Privately Held**
Web: www.contixo.com
SIC: 2678 5092 Tablets and pads, book and writing: from purchased materials; Educational toys

(P-3222)
PENCIL GRIP INC (PA)
21200 Superior St Ste A (91311-4324)
P.O. Box 3787 (91313-3787)
PHONE...............................310 315-3545
Alexander Provda, *CEO*
Alexander Provda, *Pr*
Asher Provda, *CEO*
Steve George, *Dir*
Julia Boyle, *VP*
◆ **EMP:** 17 **EST:** 1991
SQ FT: 12,000
SALES (est): 4.97MM **Privately Held**
Web: www.thepencilgrip.com
SIC: 2678 Stationery products

(P-3223)
PIPSTICKS INC
Also Called: Pipsticks
872 Higuera St (93401-3610)
P.O. Box 13260 (93406-3260)
PHONE...............................805 439-1692
Nathan Vazquez, *CEO*
Maureen D Vazquez, *Prin*
EMP: 22 **EST:** 2016
SALES (est): 2.85MM **Privately Held**
Web: www.pipsticks.com
SIC: 2678 Stationery products

(P-3224)
TREE HOUSE PAD & PAPER INC
2341 Pomona Rd Ste 108 (92878-4330)
PHONE...............................800 213-4184
David Moncrief, *Pr*
Darrin Monroe, *
EMP: 55 **EST:** 1998
SQ FT: 50,000
SALES (est): 10.81MM **Privately Held**
Web: www.treehousepaper.com
SIC: 2678 Stationery products

(P-3225)
VIVA HOLDINGS LLC (PA)
Also Called: Viva Concepts
4210 Charter St (90058-2520)
PHONE...............................818 243-1363
EMP: 18 **EST:** 2011
SALES (est): 14.77MM
SALES (corp-wide): 14.77MM **Privately Held**
Web: www.vivaconcepts.com
SIC: 2678 Memorandum books, except printed: purchased materials

(P-3226)
VIVA PRINT LLC (HQ)
1025 N Brand Blvd Ste 300 (91202-3633)
PHONE...............................818 243-1363
EMP: 17 **EST:** 2013
SQ FT: 28,000
SALES (est): 4.77MM
SALES (corp-wide): 14.77MM **Privately Held**
SIC: 2678 Memorandum books, except printed: purchased materials
PA: Viva Holdings, Llc
4210 Charter St
Vernon CA
818 243-1363

2679 Converted Paper Products, Nec

(P-3227)
88 SPECIAL SWEET INC
2437 Lee Ave (91733-1407)
PHONE...............................909 525-7055
Stella Sotoodeh, *CEO*
EMP: 78 **EST:** 2005
SALES (est): 5.61MM **Privately Held**
Web: www.stellateaproducts.com
SIC: 2679 Cups, pressed and molded pulp: made from purchased material

(P-3228)
A PLUS LABEL INC
3215 W Warner Ave (92704-5314)
PHONE...............................714 229-9811
EMP: 50 **EST:** 1995
SQ FT: 6,400
SALES (est): 4.84MM **Privately Held**
Web: www.apluslabel.com
SIC: 2679 Tags and labels, paper

(P-3229)
APPLE PAPER CONVERTING INC
3800 E Miraloma Ave (92806-2108)
P.O. Box 768 (92811-0768)
PHONE...............................714 632-3195
Jorge Daniel Podboj, *Pr*
Louis Salavar, *Pr*
George Podboj, *VP*
EMP: 20 **EST:** 2001
SALES (est): 2.1MM **Privately Held**
Web: www.applepaperconverting.com
SIC: 2679 Paper products, converted, nec

(P-3230)
ARTISSIMO DESIGNS LLC (HQ)
2100 E Grand Ave Ste 400 (90245-5169)
PHONE...............................310 906-3700
Ravi Bhagavatula, *Managing Member*
▲ **EMP:** 50 **EST:** 2015
SQ FT: 13,000
SALES (est): 46.61MM
SALES (corp-wide): 47.03MM **Privately Held**
SIC: 2679 Wallboard, decorated: made from purchased material
PA: Excelsior Capital Partners, Llc
4695 Macarthur Ct Ste 370
Newport Beach CA
949 566-8110

(P-3231)
ARTISTRY IN MOTION INC
19411 Londelius St (91324-3512)
PHONE...............................818 994-7388
Roger Wachtell, *CEO*
Richard Graves, *Pr*
▼ **EMP:** 22 **EST:** 1995
SALES (est): 2.94MM **Privately Held**
Web: www.artistryinmotion.com
SIC: 2679 5947 Confetti: made from purchased material; Gifts and novelties

(P-3232)
CALPACO PAPERS INC (PA)
3155 Universe Dr (91752-3252)
PHONE...............................323 767-2800
Paul Maier, *Pr*
Francis A Maier, *
▲ **EMP:** 136 **EST:** 1968
SQ FT: 606,000
SALES (est): 9.99MM
SALES (corp-wide): 9.99MM **Privately Held**
Web: www.actfulfillment.com
SIC: 2679 5111 Paper products, converted, nec; Printing and writing paper

(P-3233)
CONTINENTAL DATALABEL INC
Also Called: American Single Sheets
211 Business Center Ct (92373-4404)
PHONE...............................909 307-3600
Patrick Flynn, *Brnch Mgr*
EMP: 19
SALES (corp-wide): 24.95MM **Privately Held**
Web: www.datalabel.com
SIC: 2679 2672 Labels, paper: made from purchased material; Paper; coated and laminated, nec
PA: Continental Datalabel, Inc.
1855 Fox Ln
Elgin IL
847 742-1600

(P-3234)
DIETZGEN CORPORATION
1522 E Bentley Dr (92879-1741)
PHONE...............................951 278-3259
Darren A Letang, *Pr*

▲ = Import ▼ = Export
◆ = Import/Export

EMP: 20
SALES (corp-wide): 61.87MM **Privately Held**
Web: www.dietzgen.com
SIC: 2679 Paper products, converted, nec
HQ: Dietzgen Corporation
121 Kelsey Ln Ste G
Tampa FL

(P-3235)
DIGITAL LABEL SOLUTIONS LLC
1177 N Grove St (92806-2110)
PHONE...............................714 982-5000
Joel H Mark, *CEO*
Sandy Petersen, *
Suzie Dobyns, *
EMP: 29 EST: 2006
SALES (est): 9.37MM **Privately Held**
Web: www.digitallabelsolutions.com
SIC: 2679 Tags and labels, paper
PA: Brook & Whittle Limited
20 Carter Dr
Guilford CT

(P-3236)
ENCORR SHEETS LLC
5171 E Francis St (91761-3661)
PHONE...............................626 523-4661
EMP: 40 EST: 2016
SALES (est): 10.73MM **Privately Held**
SIC: 2679 Corrugated paper: made from purchased material

(P-3237)
FDS MANUFACTURING COMPANY (PA)
2200 S Reservoir St (91766-6408)
P.O. Box 3120 (91769-3120)
PHONE...............................909 591-1733
Robert B Stevenson, *CEO*
Samuel B Stevenson, *
Chuck O'connor, *VP*
Kevin Stevenson, *
▲ EMP: 100 EST: 1950
SQ FT: 240,000
SALES (est): 24.16MM
SALES (corp-wide): 24.16MM **Privately Held**
Web: www.fdsmfg.com
SIC: 2679 3089 Corrugated paper: made from purchased material; Plastics containers, except foam

(P-3238)
GOLDEN KRAFT INC
15500 Valley View Ave (90638-5230)
PHONE...............................562 926-8888
Dan August, *Genl Mgr*
▲ EMP: 356 EST: 1982
SQ FT: 63,200
SALES (est): 17.29MM
SALES (corp-wide): 36.93B **Privately Held**
SIC: 2679 2631 Corrugated paper: made from purchased material; Paperboard mills
HQ: Georgia-Pacific Corrugated Iii Llc
5645 W 82nd St
Indianapolis IN

(P-3239)
NCLA INC
1388 W Foothill Blvd (91702-2846)
PHONE...............................562 926-6252
John Mcgee, *Pr*
EMP: 17 EST: 1997
SALES (est): 562.38K **Privately Held**
Web: www.nclainc.com
SIC: 2679 3083 Paper products, converted, nec; Plastics finished products, laminated

(P-3240)
NON-STOP LABEL CORP
16221 Arthur St (90703-2130)
PHONE...............................562 949-2885
▼ EMP: 18 EST: 1988
SALES (est): 1.91MM **Privately Held**
SIC: 2679 Labels, paper: made from purchased material

(P-3241)
P & R PAPER SUPPLY CO INC
1350 Piper Ranch Rd (92154-7708)
PHONE...............................619 671-2400
Bruce Overmeyer, *Mgr*
EMP: 180
SALES (corp-wide): 1.63B **Privately Held**
Web: www.prpaper.com
SIC: 2679 2621 Paper products, converted, nec; Paper mills
HQ: P. & R. Paper Supply Company, Inc.
1898 E Colton Ave
Redlands CA
909 389-1807

(P-3242)
PACIFIC PULP MOLDING INC
11285 Forestview Ln (92131-1359)
PHONE...............................619 977-5617
John Mcneil, *CEO*
Christine Elliot, *Prin*
EMP: 25 EST: 1997
SQ FT: 25,000
SALES (est): 1.46MM **Privately Held**
Web: www.pacificpulp.com
SIC: 2679 Pressed fiber and molded pulp products, except food products

(P-3243)
POSITIVE CONCEPTS INC (PA)
Also Called: Ameri-Fax
2021 N Glassell St (92865-3305)
PHONE...............................714 685-5800
Lambert C Thom, *CEO*
▼ EMP: 22 EST: 1989
SQ FT: 20,000
SALES (est): 8.04MM
SALES (corp-wide): 8.04MM **Privately Held**
Web: www.posconcepts.com
SIC: 2679 5084 Paper products, converted, nec; Machine tools and accessories

(P-3244)
PRIME CONVERTING CORPORATION
9121 Pittsburgh Ave Ste 100 (91730)
P.O. Box 3207 (91729-3207)
PHONE...............................909 476-9500
Robert J Nielsen, *Pr*
▲ EMP: 24 EST: 2003
SALES (est): 13.91MM **Privately Held**
Web: www.primecc.com
SIC: 2679 Paper products, converted, nec

(P-3245)
PROGRESSIVE CONVERTING INC
280 W Bonita Ave (91767-1850)
PHONE...............................909 392-2201
Eric Briones, *Mgr*
EMP: 18
Web: www.pro-con.net
SIC: 2679 Paper products, converted, nec
PA: Progressive Converting, Inc.
2430 E Glendale Ave
Appleton WI

(P-3246)
PROGRESSIVE LABEL INC
2545 Yates Ave (90040-2619)
P.O. Box 911430 (90091-1238)
PHONE...............................323 415-9770
Gus Garcia, *Pr*
Adam Flores, *
Julie Lawrence, *
David Lawrence, *Stockholder*
▲ EMP: 39 EST: 1988
SQ FT: 18,000
SALES (est): 7.26MM **Privately Held**
Web: www.progressivelabel.com
SIC: 2679 2672 2671 2241 Tags and labels, paper; Paper; coated and laminated, nec; Paper; coated and laminated packaging; Narrow fabric mills

(P-3247)
SUMMIT ENTERPRISES INC
Also Called: Summit Erosion Control
2471 Montecito Rd Ste A (92065-1641)
P.O. Box 880335 (92168-0335)
PHONE...............................858 679-2100
Larry Holley, *CEO*
Timothy R Binder, *
EMP: 50 EST: 2005
SALES (est): 9.14MM **Privately Held**
Web: www.summiterosion.com
SIC: 2679 Book covers, paper

(P-3248)
TAGTIME USA INC
4601 District Blvd (90058-2731)
PHONE...............................323 587-1555
Cort Johnson, *Pr*
Darryl Rudnick, *
Mindy Knox, *
David Scott, *
▲ EMP: 480 EST: 2001
SQ FT: 23,000
SALES (est): 40.13MM **Privately Held**
Web: www.tagtimeusa.com
SIC: 2679 Labels, paper: made from purchased material

(P-3249)
TEKNI-PLEX INC
Also Called: Natvar
19555 Arenth Ave (91748-1403)
PHONE...............................909 589-4366
Joleen Kennelley, *Brnch Mgr*
EMP: 97
SALES (corp-wide): 996.3MM **Privately Held**
Web: www.tekni-plex.com
SIC: 2679 3061 Egg cartons, molded pulp: made from purchased material; Medical and surgical rubber tubing (extruded and lathe-cut)
PA: Tekni-Plex, Inc.
460 E Swedesford Rd # 300
Wayne PA
484 690-1520

(P-3250)
THOMPSON PIPE GROUP INC (PA)
3011 N Laurel Ave (92377-3725)
PHONE...............................909 822-0200
Kenneth D Thompson, *CEO*
EMP: 27 EST: 2018
SALES (est): 20.15MM
SALES (corp-wide): 20.15MM **Privately Held**
Web: www.thompsonpipegroup.com
SIC: 2679 Pipes and fittings, fiber: made from purchased material

(P-3251)
TRIPLE D AND DS
Also Called: Baron Paper Company
4040 Calle Platino Ste 105 (92056-5833)
EMP: 23 EST: 2002
SALES (est): 3.46MM **Privately Held**
SIC: 2679 Paper products, converted, nec

(P-3252)
W/S PACKAGING GROUP INC
W/S Packaging Fullerton
531 Airpark Dr (92833-2501)
PHONE...............................714 992-2574
Mathew Edwards, *Genl Mgr*
EMP: 92
SALES (corp-wide): 6.8B **Privately Held**
SIC: 2679 2671 2759 Labels, paper: made from purchased material; Paper; coated and laminated packaging; Labels and seals: printing, nsk
HQ: W/S Packaging Group, Inc.
2571 S Hemlock Rd
Green Bay WI
800 818-5481

2711 Newspapers

(P-3253)
2100 FREEDOM INC (HQ)
625 N Grand Ave (92701-4347)
PHONE...............................714 796-7000
Richard E Mirman, *CEO*
Aaron Kushner, *
EMP: 100 EST: 2012
SALES (est): 1.04B
SALES (corp-wide): 1.04B **Privately Held**
SIC: 2711 2721 7313 2741 Newspapers, publishing and printing; Periodicals; Newspaper advertising representative; Miscellaneous publishing
PA: 2100 Trust, Llc
625 N Grand Ave
Santa Ana CA
877 469-7344

(P-3254)
ACORN NEWSPAPER INC
30423 Canwood St Ste 108 (91301-4313)
PHONE...............................818 706-0266
Jim Rule, *Pr*
EMP: 35 EST: 1974
SQ FT: 3,000
SALES (est): 2.36MM **Privately Held**
Web: www.theacornonline.com
SIC: 2711 Newspapers: publishing only, not printed on site

(P-3255)
ANTELOPE VALLEY NEWSPAPERS INC
Also Called: Antelope Valley Press
44939 10th St W (93534-2313)
PHONE...............................661 940-1000
Tammy Valdes, *Mgr*
EMP: 29
SALES (corp-wide): 11.82MM **Privately Held**
Web: www.avpress.com
SIC: 2711 7313 2741 Newspapers: publishing only, not printed on site; Newspaper advertising representative; Miscellaneous publishing
PA: Antelope Valley Newspapers Inc.
37404 Sierra Hwy
Palmdale CA
661 273-2700

PRODUCTS & SVCS

(P-3256)
ARGONAUT
5355 Mcconnell Ave (90066-7025)
PHONE....................................310 822-1629
David Asper Johnson, Pr
George Drury Smith, *
EMP: 22 EST: 1971
SQ FT: 10,000
SALES (est): 494.68K Privately Held
Web: www.argonautnews.com
SIC: 2711 Newspapers: publishing only, not printed on site

(P-3257)
ASIA-PACIFIC CALIFORNIA INC
Also Called: The China Press
923 E Valley Blvd Ste 203 (91776-3684)
PHONE....................................626 281-8500
Non Hiand, Genl Mgr
EMP: 35
SIC: 2711 Newspapers, publishing and printing
PA: Asia-Pacific California, Inc.
2121 W Mission Rd Ste 207
Alhambra CA

(P-3258)
ASSOCIATED DESERT NEWSPAPER (DH)
Also Called: Imperial Valley Press
205 N 8th St (92243-2301)
P.O. Box 2641 (92244-2641)
PHONE....................................760 337-3400
Mayer Malone, Pr
David Leone, *
Teresa Zimmer, *
Clifford James, *
John Yanni, *
EMP: 40 EST: 1950
SQ FT: 30,000
SALES (est): 22.47MM
SALES (corp-wide): 3.68B Publicly Held
Web: www.ivpressonline.com
SIC: 2711 Newspapers, publishing and printing
HQ: Schurz Communications, Inc.
1301 E Douglas Rd Ste 200
Mishawaka IN
574 247-7237

(P-3259)
ASSOCIATED STUDENTS UCLA
Also Called: Asucla Publications
308 Westwood Plz Ste 118 (90095-8355)
PHONE....................................310 825-2787
Arvli Ward, Mgr
EMP: 148
SALES (corp-wide): 47.49MM Privately Held
Web: asucla.ucla.edu
SIC: 2711 2741 2721 Newspapers: publishing only, not printed on site; Miscellaneous publishing; Periodicals
PA: Associated Students U.C.L.A.
308 Westwood Plz
Los Angeles CA
310 794-8836

(P-3260)
CALIFORNIA COMMUNITY NEWS LLC
Also Called: Burbank Leader
221 N Brand Blvd Fl 2 (91203-2609)
PHONE....................................818 843-8700
Danette Goulet, Mgr
EMP: 56
SIC: 2711 Newspapers: publishing only, not printed on site
HQ: California Community News, Llc
2000 E 8th St

Los Angeles CA

(P-3261)
CALIFORNIA COMMUNITY NEWS LLC (DH)
2000 E 8th St (90021-2474)
PHONE....................................626 388-1017
Eddy Hartenstein, Pr
Judy Kendall, *
Julie Xanders, *
EMP: 349 EST: 1993
SALES (est): 26.12B Privately Held
SIC: 2711 Newspapers, publishing and printing
HQ: Tribune Publishing Company
560 W Grand Ave
Chicago IL
312 222-9100

(P-3262)
CALIFRNIA NWSPAPERS LTD PARTNR (DH)
Also Called: Inland Valley Daily Bulletin
605 E Huntington Dr Ste 100 (91016-3636)
P.O. Box 1259 (91722-0259)
PHONE....................................626 962-8811
Ron Hasse, Pr
Mark Welches, VP
EMP: 450 EST: 1997
SALES (est): 199.57MM
SALES (corp-wide): 1.96B Privately Held
SIC: 2711 Newspapers, publishing and printing
HQ: Medianews Group, Inc.
5990 Washington St
Denver CO

(P-3263)
CALIFRNIA NWSPAPERS LTD PARTNR
Also Called: Inland Valley Daily Bulletin
3200 E Guasti Rd Ste 100 (91761-8661)
PHONE....................................909 987-6397
Bob Balzer, Mgr
EMP: 42
SALES (corp-wide): 1.96B Privately Held
SIC: 2711 Newspapers, publishing and printing
HQ: California Newspapers Limited Partnership
605 E Huntington Dr # 100
Monrovia CA
626 962-8811

(P-3264)
CALIFRNIA NWSPAPERS LTD PARTNR
Also Called: Redlands Daily Facts
19 E Citrus Ave Ste 102 (92373-4763)
PHONE....................................909 793-3221
Peggy Del Torro, Mgr
EMP: 42
SQ FT: 8,301
SALES (corp-wide): 1.96B Privately Held
SIC: 2711 7313 Newspapers, publishing and printing; Newspaper advertising representative
HQ: California Newspapers Limited Partnership
605 E Huntington Dr # 100
Monrovia CA
626 962-8811

(P-3265)
CHURM PUBLISHING INC (PA)
Also Called: O.C. Metro Magazine
1451 Quail St Ste 201 (92660-2741)
PHONE....................................714 796-7000
Steve Churm, Pr

Peter Churm, *
Brian O'neill, CFO
EMP: 47 EST: 1982
SQ FT: 7,000
SALES (est): 4.57MM
SALES (corp-wide): 4.57MM Privately Held
Web: www.ocmetro.com
SIC: 2711 Newspapers, publishing and printing

(P-3266)
COAST NEWS INC
Also Called: Beach News
531 Encinitas Blvd Ste 204 (92024-3773)
P.O. Box 232550 (92023-2550)
PHONE....................................760 436-9737
James Kydd, CEO
EMP: 39 EST: 1987
SALES (est): 4MM Privately Held
Web: www.thecoastnews.com
SIC: 2711 2741 Newspapers, publishing and printing; Miscellaneous publishing

(P-3267)
COMMUNITY MEDIA CORPORATION (PA)
Also Called: San Dego Nghborhood Newspapers
5119 Ball Rd (90630-3645)
PHONE....................................714 220-0292
Kathy Verdugo, Pr
EMP: 37 EST: 1993
SQ FT: 4,000
SALES (est): 4.65MM Privately Held
Web: www.communitymediaus.com
SIC: 2711 Newspapers, publishing and printing

(P-3268)
CYCLE NEWS INC (PA)
Also Called: CN Publishing Group
17771 Mitchell N (92614-6028)
PHONE....................................949 863-7082
Sharon Clayton, Pr
EMP: 32 EST: 1965
SQ FT: 10,000
SALES (est): 4.75MM
SALES (corp-wide): 4.75MM Privately Held
Web: www.cyclenews.com
SIC: 2711 Newspapers, publishing and printing

(P-3269)
DAILY BREEZE
5215 Torrance Blvd (90503-4077)
PHONE....................................310 540-5622
EMP: 34
SALES (corp-wide): 517.17K Privately Held
Web: www.dailybreeze.com
SIC: 2711 Newspapers, publishing and printing
PA: Daily Breeze
21250 Hawthorne Blvd # 170
Torrance CA
310 540-5511

(P-3270)
DAILY JOURNAL CORPORATION (PA)
915 E 1st St (90012-4042)
PHONE....................................213 229-5300
Steven Myhill-jones, Interim Chief Executive Officer
Tu To, CFO
EMP: 66 EST: 1888
SQ FT: 34,000
SALES (est): 54.01MM

SALES (corp-wide): 54.01MM Publicly Held
Web: www.dailyjournal.com
SIC: 2711 2721 7313 7372 Newspapers, publishing and printing; Magazines: publishing and printing; Newspaper advertising representative; Prepackaged software

(P-3271)
DAILY NEXUS
P.O. Box 13402 (93107-3402)
PHONE....................................805 893-4006
Mingchen Shen, Dir
EMP: 53 EST: 2008
SALES (est): 290.09K Privately Held
Web: www.dailynexus.com
SIC: 2711 Newspapers, publishing and printing

(P-3272)
DAILYMEDIA INC (PA)
8 E Figueroa St Ste 220 (93101-2716)
PHONE....................................541 821-5207
Scott Blum, Pr
EMP: 19 EST: 2005
SQ FT: 5,000
SALES (est): 1.18MM Privately Held
SIC: 2711 Newspapers, publishing and printing

(P-3273)
DESERT SUN PUBLISHING CO (DH)
Also Called: Desert Sun The
750 N Gene Autry Trl (92262-5463)
P.O. Box 2734 (92263-2734)
PHONE....................................760 322-8889
EMP: 200 EST: 1974
SQ FT: 30,621
SALES (est): 63.87MM
SALES (corp-wide): 2.95B Publicly Held
Web: www.desertsun.com
SIC: 2711 Newspapers, publishing and printing
HQ: Gannett Media Corp.
7950 Jones Branch Dr Fl 8
Mc Lean VA
703 854-6000

(P-3274)
E Z BUY & E Z SELL RECYCL CORP (DH)
Also Called: Recycler Classified
4954 Van Nuys Blvd Ste 201 (91403-1719)
PHONE....................................310 886-7808
Niki Ruoksuo, Pr
Jim Fullmer, *
EMP: 200 EST: 1973
SQ FT: 13,000
SALES (est): 57.49MM
SALES (corp-wide): 5.21MM Publicly Held
SIC: 2711 2741 Newspapers: publishing only, not printed on site; Miscellaneous publishing
HQ: Tribune Media Company
515 N State St Ste 2400
Chicago IL
312 222-3394

(P-3275)
EASY READER INC
832 Hermosa Ave (90254-4116)
P.O. Box 427 (90254-0427)
PHONE....................................310 372-4611
Kevin Cody, Pr
EMP: 25 EST: 1970
SQ FT: 3,400
SALES (est): 4.17MM Privately Held

Web: www.easyreadernews.com
SIC: 2711 Newspapers: publishing only, not printed on site

(P-3276)
EL CLASIFICADO (PA)
11205 Imperial Hwy (90650-2229)
PHONE...............................323 837-4095
Martha C Dela Torre, *Pr*
Gil Garcia, *
Joseph Badame, *
EMP: 42 EST: 1988
SALES (est): 24.96MM **Privately Held**
Web: www.elclasificado.com
SIC: 2711 Newspapers, publishing and printing

(P-3277)
FREEDOM COMMUNICATIONS INC
Also Called: Freedom Newspapers
625 N Grand Ave (92701-4347)
P.O. Box 11450 (92711-1450)
PHONE...............................714 796-7000
▲ EMP: 7542
SIC: 2711 2721 7313 2741 Newspapers, publishing and printing; Periodicals; Newspaper advertising representative; Miscellaneous publishing

(P-3278)
GARDENA VALLEY NEWS INC
Also Called: Valley News Gardens
15005 S Vermont Ave (90247-3004)
P.O. Box 219 (90248-0219)
PHONE...............................310 329-6351
George D Algie, *Pr*
Ruriko Yatabe, *
EMP: 40 EST: 1904
SQ FT: 8,200
SALES (est): 2.02MM **Privately Held**
Web: www.gardenavalleynews.org
SIC: 2711 Commercial printing and newspaper publishing combined

(P-3279)
GRACE COMMUNICATIONS INC (PA)
Also Called: Metropolitan News Company
210 S Spring St (90012-3710)
P.O. Box 86308 (90086-0308)
PHONE...............................213 628-4384
Joann W Grace, *Pr*
Roger M Grace, *
EMP: 43 EST: 1901
SQ FT: 21,000
SALES (est): 8.87MM
SALES (corp-wide): 8.87MM **Privately Held**
Web: www.mnc.net
SIC: 2711 Newspapers, publishing and printing

(P-3280)
HARRELL HOLDINGS (PA)
1707 Eye St Ste 102 (93301-5208)
P.O. Box 440 (93302-0440)
PHONE...............................661 322-5627
Richard Beene, *Pr*
Virginia Fritts Moorhouse, *
Gizel Bermudez, *
Michelle Hirst, *
Logan Molen, *
EMP: 188 EST: 1897
SALES (est): 29.74MM
SALES (corp-wide): 29.74MM **Privately Held**
Web: www.bakersfield.com
SIC: 2711 Commercial printing and newspaper publishing combined

(P-3281)
HI-DESERT PUBLISHING COMPANY
Also Called: Yuciapa & Calimesa News Mirror
35154 Yucaipa Blvd (92399-4339)
P.O. Box 760 (92399-0760)
PHONE...............................909 795-8145
Jerry Bean, *Mgr*
EMP: 27
SALES (corp-wide): 151.22MM **Privately Held**
Web: www.newsmirror.net
SIC: 2711 Newspapers, publishing and printing
HQ: Hi-Desert Publishing Company
56445 29 Palms Hwy
Yucca Valley CA

(P-3282)
HI-DESERT PUBLISHING COMPANY
Also Called: Mountain News & Shopper
28200 Highway 189 Bldg O-1 (92352-9700)
P.O. Box 2410 (92352-2410)
PHONE...............................909 336-3555
Harry Bradley, *Mgr*
EMP: 41
SALES (corp-wide): 151.51MM **Privately Held**
SIC: 2711 Commercial printing and newspaper publishing combined
HQ: Hi-Desert Publishing Company
56445 29 Palms Hwy
Yucca Valley CA

(P-3283)
HI-DESERT PUBLISHING COMPANY (HQ)
56445 29 Palms Hwy (92284-2861)
PHONE...............................760 365-3315
Cindy Melland, *Publisher*
Stacy Moore, *
EMP: 70 EST: 1990
SALES (est): 10.35MM
SALES (corp-wide): 151.22MM **Privately Held**
SIC: 2711 Newspapers, publishing and printing
PA: Brehm Communications, Inc.
16644 W Bernardo Dr # 300
San Diego CA
858 451-6200

(P-3284)
HIGHLANDER NEWSPAPER
4158 Chestnut St (92501-3539)
PHONE...............................951 827-3457
Erin Mahoney, *Prin*
EMP: 21 EST: 2016
SALES (est): 93.79K **Privately Held**
Web: www.highlandernews.org
SIC: 2711 Newspapers, publishing and printing

(P-3285)
HOLLYWOOD REPORTER
6715 W Sunset Blvd (90028-7107)
PHONE...............................323 525-2000
Janice Min, *Prin*
EMP: 207 EST: 2010
SALES (est): 1.97MM **Privately Held**
Web: www.hollywoodreporter.com
SIC: 2711 Newspapers, publishing and printing

(P-3286)
HOLLYWOOD REPORTER
100 N Crescent Dr Ste Gl-1 (90210-5408)
PHONE...............................323 525-2150

Janice Min, *Pr*
EMP: 33 EST: 2015
SALES (est): 903.81K **Privately Held**
Web: www.hollywoodreporter.com
SIC: 2711 Newspapers, publishing and printing

(P-3287)
HOLLYWOOD REPORTER LLC
100 N Crescent Dr Ste Gl-1 (90210-5408)
PHONE...............................323 525-2000
EMP: 24 EST: 2010
SALES (est): 1.54MM **Privately Held**
Web: www.hollywoodreporter.com
SIC: 2711 Newspapers, publishing and printing

(P-3288)
INTERNATIONAL DAILY NEWS INC (PA)
870 Monterey Pass Rd (91754-3688)
PHONE...............................323 265-1317
Jessica G Elnitiarta, *Pr*
▲ EMP: 20 EST: 1981
SQ FT: 10,000
SALES (est): 2.03MM
SALES (corp-wide): 2.03MM **Privately Held**
Web: www.chinesetoday.com
SIC: 2711 Newspapers, publishing and printing

(P-3289)
INVESTORS BUSINESS DAILY INC (HQ)
5900 Wilshire Blvd Ste 2950 (90036-5013)
PHONE...............................800 831-2525
William O'neil, *Pr*
Kathy Sherman, *
Edward Skolarus, *CDO*
▲ EMP: 200 EST: 1984
SQ FT: 180,000
SALES (est): 70.76MM
SALES (corp-wide): 335.64MM **Privately Held**
Web: www.investors.com
SIC: 2711 Newspapers, publishing and printing
PA: Data Analysis Inc.
12655 Beatrice St
Los Angeles CA
310 448-6800

(P-3290)
JOONG-ANG DAILY NEWS CAL INC
Also Called: Joong-Ang Daily News California, Inc.
7750 Dagget St Ste 208 (92111-2236)
PHONE...............................858 573-1111
Kwong Luk Chang, *Brnch Mgr*
▲ EMP: 60
Web: www.koreadaily.com
SIC: 2711 Newspapers, publishing and printing
HQ: Joongangilbo Usa, Inc.
690 Wilshire Pl
Los Angeles CA
213 368-2512

(P-3291)
JOONGANGILBO USA INC (DH)
Also Called: Joong-Ang Daily News Cal Inc
690 Wilshire Pl (90005-3930)
PHONE...............................213 368-2512
Kae Hong Ko, *CEO*
In Taek Park, *
◆ EMP: 200 EST: 1974
SQ FT: 70,000

SALES (est): 92.11MM **Privately Held**
Web: www.koreadaily.com
SIC: 2711 Commercial printing and newspaper publishing combined
HQ: Joongang Ilbo Co.,Ltd.
48-6 Sangamsan-Ro, Mapo-Gu
Seoul

(P-3292)
KAAR DRECT MAIL FLFILLMENT LLC
1225 Exposition Way Ste 160 (92154)
PHONE...............................619 382-3670
EMP: 25 EST: 2013
SALES (est): 3.05MM **Privately Held**
Web: www.kaardm.com
SIC: 2711 5963 2752 8742 Commercial printing and newspaper publishing combined; Direct sales, telemarketing; Publication printing, lithographic; Marketing consulting services

(P-3293)
LA OPINION LP
210 E Washington Blvd (90015-3603)
PHONE...............................213 896-2222
Carlos Marina, *Mgr*
EMP: 359
SALES (corp-wide): 94.23MM **Privately Held**
Web: www.laopinion.com
SIC: 2711 Newspapers, publishing and printing
HQ: La Opinion, L.P.
915 Wilshire Blvd Ste 915 # 915
Los Angeles CA
213 891-9191

(P-3294)
LA OPINION LP (HQ)
Also Called: Lozano Enterprises
915 Wilshire Blvd Ste 915 (90017-3474)
P.O. Box 71847 (90071-0847)
PHONE...............................213 891-9191
Monica C Lozano, *CEO*
EMP: 54 EST: 1926
SALES (est): 49.49MM
SALES (corp-wide): 94.23MM **Privately Held**
Web: www.laopinion.com
SIC: 2711 Newspapers, publishing and printing
PA: Impremedia, Llc
41 Flatbush Ave Ste 1
Brooklyn NY
212 807-4600

(P-3295)
LA TIMES
202 W 1st St Ste 500 (90012-4401)
PHONE...............................213 237-2279
Raymond Jansen, *CEO*
EMP: 42 EST: 2008
SALES (est): 1.52MM **Privately Held**
Web: www.latimes.com
SIC: 2711 Newspapers, publishing and printing

(P-3296)
LATINA & ASSOCIATES INC (PA)
Also Called: El Latino Newspaper
1105 Broadway (91911-2767)
P.O. Box 120550 (92112-0550)
PHONE...............................619 426-1491
Fanny Miller, *CEO*
EMP: 25 EST: 1985
SQ FT: 2,500
SALES (est): 1.94MM
SALES (corp-wide): 1.94MM **Privately Held**

Web: www.ellatinoonline.com
SIC: 2711 Newspapers: publishing only, not
printed on site

(P-3297)
LOS ANGELES DAILY NEWS
PUBG CO
21860 Burbank Blvd Ste 200 (91367-6477)
PHONE.................................818 713-3883
EMP: 39 EST: 1999
SALES (est): 1.47MM
SALES (corp-wide): 1.96B Privately Held
SIC: 2711 Newspapers, publishing and
printing
HQ: Medianews Group, Inc.
5990 Washington St
Denver CO

(P-3298)
LOS ANGELES SENTINEL INC
Also Called: La Sentinel Newspaper
3800 Crenshaw Blvd (90008-1813)
PHONE.................................323 299-3800
Jennifer Thomas, Pr
Brik Booker, *
EMP: 51 EST: 1933
SALES (est): 5.25MM Privately Held
Web: www.lasentinel.net
SIC: 2711 Newspapers, publishing and
printing

(P-3299)
LOS ANGLES TMES
CMMNCTIONS LLC (PA)
Also Called: Los Angeles Times
2300 E Imperial Hwy (90245-2813)
PHONE.................................213 237-5000
Ross Levinsohn, CEO
Scott Mckibben, Pr
Don Reis S, VP
▲ EMP: 3518 EST: 1884
SQ FT: 162,000
SALES (est): 930.82MM
SALES (corp-wide): 930.82MM Privately
Held
Web: www.latimes.com
SIC: 2711 Newspapers, publishing and
printing

(P-3300)
LOUDLABS NEWS LLC
11932 Heritage Cir (90241-4326)
PHONE.................................310 877-8374
Scott Pacheco, Brnch Mgr
EMP: 18
SALES (corp-wide): 138.4K Privately Held
SIC: 2711 Newspapers, publishing and
printing
PA: Loudlabs News Llc
13337 South St
Cerritos CA

(P-3301)
MALIBU TIMES INC
3864 Las Flores Canyon Rd (90265-5239)
P.O. Box 1127 (90265-1127)
PHONE.................................310 456-5507
Arnold York, Pr
Karen York, VP
EMP: 19 EST: 1946
SQ FT: 2,000
SALES (est): 664.19K Privately Held
Web: www.malibutimes.com
SIC: 2711 Newspapers: publishing only, not
printed on site

(P-3302)
MAMMOTH MEDIA INC
1447 2nd St (90401-3404)

PHONE.................................832 315-0833
Benoit Vatere, CEO
Mike Jones, *
EMP: 64 EST: 2016
SALES (est): 7.65MM Privately Held
Web: www.mammoth.la
SIC: 2711 Newspapers

(P-3303)
MEDIANEWS GROUP INC
Long Beach Press-Telegram
300 Oceangate Ste 150 (90802-6801)
PHONE.................................562 435-1161
Barbie Brodeur, Brnch Mgr
EMP: 25
SALES (corp-wide): 1.96B Privately Held
Web: www.medianewsgroup.com
SIC: 2711 Newspapers, publishing and
printing
HQ: Medianews Group, Inc.
5990 Washington St
Denver CO

(P-3304)
MEDIANEWS GROUP INC
Also Called: Daily News
605 E Huntington Dr Ste 100 (91016-6352)
P.O. Box 4200 (91365-4200)
PHONE.................................818 713-3000
Douglas Hanes, Publisher
EMP: 175
SALES (corp-wide): 1.96B Privately Held
Web: www.dailynews.com
SIC: 2711 Newspapers, publishing and
printing
HQ: Medianews Group, Inc.
5990 Washington St
Denver CO

(P-3305)
MEDIANEWS GROUP INC
Also Called: Daily Breeze
5215 Torrance Blvd (90503-4009)
PHONE.................................310 540-5511
EMP: 22
SALES (corp-wide): 1.96B Privately Held
Web: www.medianewsgroup.com
SIC: 2711 Newspapers, publishing and
printing
HQ: Medianews Group, Inc.
5990 Washington St
Denver CO

(P-3306)
MET NEWS
210 S Spring St (90012-3710)
PHONE.................................310 346-0033
Joann Grace, Prin
▲ EMP: 23 EST: 2003
SALES (est): 432.44K Privately Held
SIC: 2711 Newspapers, publishing and
printing

(P-3307)
METROPOLITAN NEWS
COMPANY
Also Called: Riverside Blltin Jrupa This We
3540 12th St (92501-3802)
P.O. Box 60859 (90060-0859)
PHONE.................................951 369-5890
Roger Gray, Pr
EMP: 29 EST: 1998
SALES (est): 1.33MM Privately Held
SIC: 2711 Newspapers, publishing and
printing

(P-3308)
NATIONAL MEDIA INC (HQ)
Also Called: Beach Reporter
609 Deep Valley Dr Ste 200 (90274-3629)

P.O. Box 2609 (90274-8609)
PHONE.................................310 377-6877
Stephen C Laxineta, Pr
Simon M Tam, *
William Dean Singleton, *
EMP: 30 EST: 1983
SQ FT: 12,000
SALES (est): 16.16MM
SALES (corp-wide): 1.96B Privately Held
Web: www.dailybreeze.com
SIC: 2711 Newspapers: publishing only, not
printed on site
PA: Digital First Media, Llc
101 W Colfax Ave Fl 11
Denver CO
303 954-6360

(P-3309)
NGUOI VIET VTNAMESE
PEOPLE INC (PA)
Also Called: Nguoi Viet Newspaper
14771 Moran St (92683-5553)
PHONE.................................714 892-9414
Dat Pham, Ch
Hoang Tong, *
Dieu Le, *
▲ EMP: 30 EST: 1978
SQ FT: 10,000
SALES (est): 5.31MM
SALES (corp-wide): 5.31MM Privately
Held
Web: www.nguoi-viet.com
SIC: 2711 5994 2741 Newspapers:
publishing only, not printed on site; News
dealers and newsstands; Miscellaneous
publishing

(P-3310)
NOOZHAWK
1327a State St (93101-2609)
PHONE.................................805 456-7267
EMP: 19 EST: 2017
SALES (est): 223.56K Privately Held
Web: www.noozhawk.com
SIC: 2711 Newspapers, publishing and
printing

(P-3311)
NORTH COUNTY TIMES (DH)
Also Called: Californian, The
350 Camino De La Reina (92108-3007)
PHONE.................................800 533-8830
▲ EMP: 250 EST: 1962
SQ FT: 45,000
SALES (est): 49.32MM
SALES (corp-wide): 691.14MM Publicly
Held
Web: www.caseybrownco.com
SIC: 2711 Newspapers, publishing and
printing
HQ: Lee Publications, Inc.
4600 E 53rd St
Davenport IA
563 383-2100

(P-3312)
NORTH COUNTY TIMES
28441 Rancho California Rd Ste 103
(92590-3618)
PHONE.................................951 676-4315
EMP: 45
SALES (corp-wide): 691.14MM Publicly
Held
Web: www.caseybrownco.com
SIC: 2711 Newspapers, publishing and
printing
HQ: North County Times
350 Camino De La Reina
San Diego CA
800 533-8830

(P-3313)
NORTHEAST NEWSPAPERS INC
621 W Beverly Blvd (90640-3623)
PHONE.................................213 727-1117
Art Aguilar, Pr
Tom Morrison, *
EMP: 32 EST: 1905
SALES (est): 2.58MM Privately Held
SIC: 2711 Newspapers, publishing and
printing

(P-3314)
PACIFIC COAST BUS TIMES INC
14 E Carrillo St Ste A (93101-2769)
PHONE.................................805 560-6950
Henry Dubroff, Pr
EMP: 23 EST: 1999
SQ FT: 2,200
SALES (est): 2.28MM Privately Held
Web: www.pacbiztimes.com
SIC: 2711 Newspapers, publishing and
printing

(P-3315)
PASADENA NEWSPAPERS INC
(PA)
Also Called: Pasadena Star-News
605 E Huntington Dr Ste 100 (91016-6352)
PHONE.................................626 578-6300
Dean Singleton, Pr
▲ EMP: 190 EST: 1884
SALES (est): 10.49MM Privately Held
Web: www.pasadenastarnews.com
SIC: 2711 7313 Commercial printing and
newspaper publishing combined;
Newspaper advertising representative

(P-3316)
PRESS-ENTERPRISE COMPANY
(PA)
3450 14th St (92501-3862)
P.O. Box 792 (92502-0792)
PHONE.................................951 684-1200
Ronald Redfern, Pr
Kathy Weiermiller, VP
Sue Barry, VP
Ed Lasak, CFO
▲ EMP: 700 EST: 2011
SQ FT: 190,000
SALES (est): 149.78MM
SALES (corp-wide): 149.78MM Privately
Held
Web: www.pressenterprise.com
SIC: 2711 Commercial printing and
newspaper publishing combined

(P-3317)
RAFU SHIMPO
Also Called: L A Japanese Daily News
701 E 3rd St Ste 130 (90013-1789)
PHONE.................................213 629-2231
Michael M Komai, Pr
EMP: 22 EST: 1903
SQ FT: 20,000
SALES (est): 866.29K Privately Held
Web: www.rafunews.com
SIC: 2711 Newspapers, publishing and
printing

(P-3318)
RUNWAY BEAUTY INC ✪
Also Called: Runway
6075 Rodgerton Dr (90068-1961)
PHONE.................................844 240-2250
Vincent Mazzotta, CEO
EMP: 18 EST: 2022
SALES (est): 1.28MM Privately Held
SIC: 2711 Newspapers, publishing and
printing

▲ = Import ▼ = Export
◆ = Import/Export

(P-3319)

SAN DIEGO UNION-TRIBUNE LLC
San Diego Union Tribune
600 B St (92101-4501)
P.O. Box 120191 (92112-0191)
PHONE..............................619 299-3131
Roy E Gene Bell, *CEO*
EMP: 39
SQ FT: 400,000
Web: www.sandiegouniontribune.com
SIC: 2711 7313 Newspapers: publishing only, not printed on site; Newspaper advertising representative
PA: The San Diego Union-Tribune Llc
600 B St Ste 1201
San Diego CA

(P-3320)

SAN DIEGO UNION-TRIBUNE LLC (PA)
Also Called: San Diego Union Tribune, The
600 B St Ste 1201 (92101-4505)
P.O. Box 120191 (92112-0191)
PHONE..............................619 299-3131
Jeff Light, *Pr*
EMP: 600 **EST:** 2009
SALES (est): 136.6MM **Privately Held**
Web: www.sandiegouniontribune.com
SIC: 2711 7313 7383 Newspapers: publishing only, not printed on site; Newspaper advertising representative; News reporting services for newspapers and periodicals

(P-3321)

SAN LUIS OBSPO COCMMNTY CLGDST
2800 Buena Vista Dr (93446-8556)
PHONE..............................805 591-6200
EMP: 17 **EST:** 2015
SALES (est): 555.76K **Privately Held**
Web: www.cuesta.edu
SIC: 2711 Newspapers, publishing and printing

(P-3322)

SANTA BARBARA INDEPENDENT INC
Also Called: Independent
1715 State St (93101-2521)
PHONE..............................805 965-5205
M Partridge Poette, *Pr*
Marianne Partridge Poette, *
Brandi Rivera, *
EMP: 40 **EST:** 1984
SALES (est): 7.7MM **Privately Held**
Web: www.independent.com
SIC: 2711 Newspapers, publishing and printing

(P-3323)

SIGNAL
Also Called: Newhall Signal
26330 Diamond Pl Ste 100 (91350-5819)
P.O. Box 801870 (91380-1870)
PHONE..............................661 259-1234
Charles Morris, *Pr*
EMP: 76 **EST:** 1919
SQ FT: 32,000
SALES (est): 2.02MM
SALES (corp-wide): 285.74MM **Privately Held**
Web: www.signalscv.com
SIC: 2711 Newspapers, publishing and printing
PA: Morris Multimedia, Inc.
27 Abercorn St
Savannah GA
912 233-1281

(P-3324)

SING TAO NEWSPAPERS LTD
Also Called: Sing Tao Nwspapers Los Angeles
17059 Green Dr (91745-1812)
PHONE..............................626 956-8200
Sau K Cheung, *Mgr*
EMP: 52
Web: std.stheadline.com
SIC: 2711 Newspapers, publishing and printing
HQ: Sing Tao Limited
Sing Tao News Corporation Bldg
Tseung Kwan O NT

(P-3325)

SLO NEW TIMES INC
Also Called: New Times Media Group
1010 Marsh St (93401-3630)
PHONE..............................805 546-8208
Bob Rucker, *CEO*
EMP: 26 **EST:** 1987
SALES (est): 4.35MM **Privately Held**
Web: www.newtimesslo.com
SIC: 2711 Newspapers, publishing and printing

(P-3326)

SUN CMPANY OF SAN BRNRDINO CAL (HQ)
Also Called: San Bernardino County Sun, The
4030 Georgia Blvd (92407-1847)
PHONE..............................909 889-9666
Bob Balzer, *Pr*
Douglass H Mccorkindale, *Prin*
EMP: 400 **EST:** 1964
SQ FT: 110,000
SALES (est): 63.65MM
SALES (corp-wide): 2.95B **Publicly Held**
Web: www.sbsun.com
SIC: 2711 Newspapers, publishing and printing
PA: Gannett Co., Inc.
7950 Jones Branch Dr Fl 8
Mc Lean VA
703 854-6000

(P-3327)

TAKE A BREAK PAPER
263 W Olive Ave # 307 (91502-1825)
PHONE..............................323 333-7773
Albert Moran, *Pt*
EMP: 30 **EST:** 2013
SALES (est): 961.7K **Privately Held**
Web: elpiojito.godaddysites.com
SIC: 2711 Newspapers, publishing and printing

(P-3328)

TERIS - SAN DIEGO LLC
600 W Broadway Ste 340 (92101-3352)
PHONE..............................619 231-3282
Stefan Wikstrom, *CEO*
Kip Hauser, *CCO*
EMP: 21 **EST:** 1997
SALES (est): 138.48K **Privately Held**
SIC: 2711 Newspapers, publishing and printing

(P-3329)

THE KOREA TIMES LOS ANGELES INC (PA)
Also Called: Korea Times
3731 Wilshire Blvd Ste 1000 (90010-2819)
PHONE..............................323 692-2000
▲ **EMP:** 200 **EST:** 1969
SALES (est): 23.89MM
SALES (corp-wide): 23.89MM **Privately Held**

Web: www.koreatimes.com
SIC: 2711 Newspapers, publishing and printing

(P-3330)

THEWRAP
2260 S Centinela Ave Ste 150 (90064-1007)
PHONE..............................424 273-4787
EMP: 59 **EST:** 2016
SALES (est): 1.17MM **Privately Held**
Web: www.thewrap.com
SIC: 2711 Newspapers

(P-3331)

TIDINGS
Also Called: VIDA NUEVA
3424 Wilshire Blvd (90010-2263)
PHONE..............................213 637-7360
Roger Mahoney, *Pr*
EMP: 23 **EST:** 1895
SALES (est): 2.09MM **Privately Held**
Web: www.angelusnews.com
SIC: 2711 Newspapers: publishing only, not printed on site

(P-3332)

TRIBE MDIA CORP A CAL NNPRFIT
Also Called: Jewish Journal, The
3250 Wilshire Blvd (90010-1577)
PHONE..............................213 368-1661
Rob Eshman, *Publisher*
EMP: 27 **EST:** 1985
SQ FT: 4,500
SALES (est): 4.93MM **Privately Held**
Web: www.jewishjournal.com
SIC: 2711 Newspapers, publishing and printing

(P-3333)

U-T DIRECT
350 Camino De La Reina (92108-3007)
PHONE..............................619 293-1484
Laura Tarabini, *Prin*
EMP: 19 **EST:** 2010
SALES (est): 421.84K **Privately Held**
SIC: 2711 Newspapers, publishing and printing

(P-3334)

VILLAGE NEWS INC
Also Called: Fallbrook Bonsall Village News
41740 Enterprise Cir S (92590-4881)
PHONE..............................760 451-3488
Julie Reeder, *Pr*
Michelle Howard, *Advt Dir*
EMP: 39 **EST:** 1997
SQ FT: 1,500
SALES (est): 4.96MM **Privately Held**
Web: www.villagenews.com
SIC: 2711 Newspapers, publishing and printing

(P-3335)

VOICE OF SAN DIEGO
110 W A St Ste 650 (92101-3708)
PHONE..............................619 325-0525
Scott Lewis, *CEO*
Julianne Markow, *COO*
EMP: 24 **EST:** 2004
SALES (est): 2.34MM **Privately Held**
Web: www.voiceofsandiego.org
SIC: 2711 Newspapers: publishing only, not printed on site

(P-3336)

WAVE COMMUNITY NEWSPAPERS INC (PA)

Also Called: The Wave
1007 N Sepulveda Blvd (90266-5964)
PHONE..............................323 290-3000
Pluria Marshall, *Pr*
Andy Wiedlin, *Chief Business Officer**
▲ **EMP:** 30 **EST:** 1970
SALES (est): 4.92MM
SALES (corp-wide): 4.92MM **Privately Held**
SIC: 2711 Commercial printing and newspaper publishing combined

(P-3337)

WESTERN OUTDOORS PUBLICATIONS (PA)
Also Called: Western Outdoor News
901 Calle Amanecer Ste 115 (92673-4216)
P.O. Box 73370 (92673-0113)
PHONE..............................949 366-0030
Robert Twilegar, *Pr*
Lori Twilegar, *
EMP: 28 **EST:** 1953
SALES (est): 2.43MM
SALES (corp-wide): 2.43MM **Privately Held**
Web: www.wonews.com
SIC: 2711 2721 Newspapers: publishing only, not printed on site; Periodicals

(P-3338)

WICK COMMUNICATIONS CO
Also Called: Kern Valley Sun
6404 Lake Isabella Blvd (93240-9475)
P.O. Box 3074 (93240-3074)
PHONE..............................760 379-3667
Cliff Urfeth, *Mgr*
EMP: 31
SALES (corp-wide): 87.63MM **Privately Held**
Web: www.kernvalleysun.com
SIC: 2711 Newspapers, publishing and printing
HQ: Wick Communications Co.
333 W Wilcox Dr Ste 302
Sierra Vista AZ
520 458-0200

(P-3339)

WORLD JOURNAL LA LLC (HQ)
1588 Corporate Center Dr (91754-7624)
PHONE..............................323 268-4982
James Guon, *CEO*
▲ **EMP:** 170 **EST:** 1981
SQ FT: 45,000
SALES (est): 20.7MM **Privately Held**
SIC: 2711 Newspapers, publishing and printing
PA: United Daily News Co., Ltd.
No. 369, Datong Rd., Sec. 1
New Taipei City TAP

2721 Periodicals

(P-3340)

ADAMS TRADE PRESS LP (PA)
Also Called: Adams Business Media
420 S Palm Canyon Dr (92262-7304)
PHONE..............................760 318-7000
Mark Adams, *Pt*
EMP: 30 **EST:** 1994
SQ FT: 2,000
SALES (est): 4.03MM **Privately Held**
SIC: 2721 Magazines: publishing only, not printed on site

(P-3341)

ADVANSTAR COMMUNICATIONS INC
2525 Main St Ste 300 (92614-6680)

PHONE..............714 513-8400
FAX: 714 513-8403
EMP: 80
SALES (corp-wide): 1.06B **Privately Held**
SIC: 2721 7389 Magazines: publishing only, not printed on site; Trade show arrangement
HQ: Advanstar Communications Inc.
2501 Colorado Ave Ste 280
Santa Monica CA
310 857-7500

(P-3342)
AEROTECH NEWS AND REVIEW INC (PA)
Also Called: Astro News
220 E Avenue K4 Ste 4 (93535-4687)
P.O. Box 1332 (93584-1332)
PHONE..............661 945-5634
Paul Kinison, *Pr*
EMP: 42 EST: 1986
SALES (est): 4.44MM
SALES (corp-wide): 4.44MM **Privately Held**
Web: www.aerotechnews.com
SIC: 2721 2741 2752 Trade journals: publishing only, not printed on site; Miscellaneous publishing; Commercial printing, lithographic

(P-3343)
AFFLUENT TARGET MARKETING INC
Also Called: Affluent Living Publication
3855 E La Palma Ave Ste 250 (92807-1765)
P.O. Box 18507 (92817-8507)
PHONE..............714 446-6280
Wally Hicks, *Pr*
EMP: 21 EST: 1980
SQ FT: 3,500
SALES (est): 2.16MM **Privately Held**
Web: www.businessvideoconsulting.com
SIC: 2721 Magazines: publishing only, not printed on site

(P-3344)
ALTERNATIVE PRESS MAGAZINE INC
4321 W Magnolia Blvd (91505-2728)
PHONE..............216 631-1510
Michael P Shea, *Pr*
EMP: 25 EST: 1985
SALES (est): 987.19K **Privately Held**
Web: www.altpress.com
SIC: 2721 Magazines: publishing only, not printed on site

(P-3345)
BBM FAIRWAY INC (PA)
3520 Challenger St (90503-1640)
P.O. Box 2703 (90509-2703)
EMP: 120 EST: 1961
SALES (est): 10.07MM
SALES (corp-wide): 10.07MM **Privately Held**
Web: www.bobit.com
SIC: 2721 7319 8742 Magazines: publishing only, not printed on site; Media buying service; Marketing consulting services

(P-3346)
BOBIT BUSINESS MEDIA INC
3520 Challenger St (90503-1640)
PHONE..............310 533-2400
Richard Rivera, *CEO*
EMP: 273 EST: 2018
SALES (est): 7.21MM
SALES (corp-wide): 957.36MM **Privately Held**

Web: www.bobit.com
SIC: 2721 Magazines: publishing only, not printed on site
PA: Gemspring Capital, Llc
54 Wilton Rd
Westport CT
203 842-8886

(P-3347)
CBJ LP
Also Called: San Fernando Valley Bus Jurnl
11150 Santa Monica Blvd Ste 350 (90025-3314)
PHONE..............818 676-1750
Pegi Matsuda, *Mgr*
EMP: 76
SALES (corp-wide): 23.64MM **Privately Held**
Web: www.sfvbj.com
SIC: 2721 Magazines: publishing only, not printed on site
PA: Cbj, L.P.
7101 College Blvd # 1100
Shawnee Mission KS
913 451-9000

(P-3348)
CBJ LP
Also Called: Los Angeles Business Journal
11150 Santa Monica Blvd (90025-3314)
PHONE..............323 549-5225
Matt Toledo, *Brnch Mgr*
EMP: 40
SALES (corp-wide): 23.64MM **Privately Held**
Web: www.labusinessjournal.com
SIC: 2721 2711 8742 Periodicals, publishing only; Newspapers; General management consultant
PA: Cbj, L.P.
7101 College Blvd # 1100
Shawnee Mission KS
913 451-9000

(P-3349)
CBJ LP
Also Called: Orange County Business Journal
18500 Von Karman Ave Ste 150 (92612-0504)
PHONE..............949 833-8373
Janet Cox, *Mgr*
EMP: 40
SALES (corp-wide): 23.64MM **Privately Held**
Web: www.ocbj.com
SIC: 2721 2711 7313 Trade journals: publishing only, not printed on site; Newspapers; Newspaper advertising representative
PA: Cbj, L.P.
7101 College Blvd # 1100
Shawnee Mission KS
913 451-9000

(P-3350)
CBJ LP
Also Called: San Diego Business Journal
4909 Murphy Canyon Rd Ste 200 (92123-4349)
PHONE..............858 277-6359
Armon Mills, *Prin*
EMP: 25
SQ FT: 10,000
SALES (corp-wide): 23.64MM **Privately Held**
Web: www.sdbj.com
SIC: 2721 2741 2711 Trade journals: publishing and printing; Miscellaneous publishing; Newspapers
PA: Cbj, L.P.
7101 College Blvd # 1100

Shawnee Mission KS
913 451-9000

(P-3351)
CLIQUE BRANDS INC (PA)
Also Called: Who What Wear
750 N San Vicente Blvd Ste 800 (90069-5788)
PHONE..............310 623-6916
Katherine Power, *CEO*
Hilary Kerr, *Pr*
Mika Onishi, *COO*
David Thomas, *Dir*
EMP: 25 EST: 2007
SQ FT: 2,200
SALES (est): 8.15MM
SALES (corp-wide): 8.15MM **Privately Held**
SIC: 2721 5621 Magazines: publishing only, not printed on site; Women's specialty clothing stores

(P-3352)
CREATIVE AGE PUBLICATIONS INC
Also Called: Nailpro
15975 High Knoll Rd (91436-3426)
PHONE..............818 782-7328
Deborah Carver, *Pr*
Mindy Rosiejka, *
EMP: 50 EST: 1972
SALES (est): 4.13MM **Privately Held**
Web: www.creativeage.co.uk
SIC: 2721 2731 Magazines: publishing only, not printed on site; Book publishing

(P-3353)
CURTCO ROBB MEDIA LLC (PA)
29160 Heathercliff Rd Ste 200 (90265-6310)
PHONE..............310 589-7700
Stephen Colvin, *CEO*
William J Curtis, *
Christopher Fabian, *
David Arnold, *
EMP: 30 EST: 2001
SALES (est): 9.03MM
SALES (corp-wide): 9.03MM **Privately Held**
Web: www.curtco.com
SIC: 2721 Magazines: publishing and printing

(P-3354)
DAISY PUBLISHING COMPANY INC
Also Called: Hi-Torque Publications
25233 Anza Dr (91355-1289)
P.O. Box 957 (91380-9057)
PHONE..............661 295-1910
Roland Hinz, *Pr*
Lila Hinz, *
EMP: 55 EST: 1969
SQ FT: 16,000
SALES (est): 4.12MM **Privately Held**
Web: www.hi-torque.com
SIC: 2721 Magazines: publishing and printing

(P-3355)
DESERT PUBLICATIONS INC (PA)
Also Called: Desert Grafics
303 N Indian Canyon Dr (92262-6015)
P.O. Box 2724 (92263-2724)
PHONE..............760 325-2333
Franklin Jones, *VP*
EMP: 47 EST: 1965
SQ FT: 25,000
SALES (est): 9.61MM
SALES (corp-wide): 9.61MM **Privately Held**

Web: www.palmspringslife.com
SIC: 2721 7311 Magazines: publishing only, not printed on site; Advertising agencies

(P-3356)
DISNEY PUBLISHING WORLDWIDE (DH)
Also Called: Disney Editions
500 S Buena Vista St (91521-0001)
PHONE..............212 633-4400
R Russell Hampton Junior, *Ch*
▲ EMP: 100 EST: 1992
SALES (est): 89.09MM
SALES (corp-wide): 88.9B **Publicly Held**
Web: www.thewaltdisneycompany.com
SIC: 2721 Magazines: publishing only, not printed on site
HQ: Disney Enterprises, Inc.
500 S Buena Vista St
Burbank CA
818 560-1000

(P-3357)
DUNCAN MCINTOSH COMPANY INC (PA)
Also Called: Sea Magazine
18475 Bandilier Cir (92708-7012)
P.O. Box 1337 (92659-0337)
PHONE..............949 660-6150
Duncan R Mcintosh, *CEO*
Teresa Mcintosh, *Sec*
EMP: 35 EST: 1967
SQ FT: 15,728
SALES (est): 7.73MM
SALES (corp-wide): 7.73MM **Privately Held**
Web: www.duncanmcintoshco.com
SIC: 2721 7389 Magazines: publishing and printing; Trade show arrangement

(P-3358)
ENTREPRENEUR MEDIA INC (PA)
Also Called: Entrepeneur Magazine
18061 Fitch (92614-6018)
P.O. Box 19787 (92623-9787)
PHONE..............949 261-2325
Ryan Shea, *CEO*
Neil Perlman, *
Joe Goodman, *
Ronald Young, *
▲ EMP: 80 EST: 1986
SQ FT: 30,000
SALES (est): 20.42MM **Privately Held**
Web: www.entrepreneur.com
SIC: 2721 Magazines: publishing only, not printed on site

(P-3359)
FLAUNT MAGAZINE
1418 N Highland Ave (90028-7611)
PHONE..............323 836-1044
Luis A Barajas Junior, *Pr*
▲ EMP: 18 EST: 1998
SALES (est): 3.16MM **Privately Held**
Web: www.flaunt.com
SIC: 2721 Magazines: publishing only, not printed on site

(P-3360)
GOLD PROSPECTORS ASSN AMER LLC
Also Called: Gold Prospectors Assn Amer
25819 Jefferson Ave Ste 110 (92562-6964)
P.O. Box 891509 (92589-1509)
PHONE..............951 699-4749
Thomas Massie, *Managing Member*
Richard Dixon, *Managing Member*
EMP: 28 EST: 1966

SALES (est): 9.51MM **Privately Held**
Web: www.goldprospectors.org
SIC: **2721** 4833 Magazines: publishing only, not printed on site; Television broadcasting stations

(P-3361)

HAYMARKET WORLDWIDE INC

17030 Red Hill Ave (92614-5626)
PHONE..............................949 417-6700
Peter Foubister, *CEO*
▲ **EMP:** 24 **EST:** 1992
SQ FT: 4,000
SALES (est): 2.08MM
SALES (corp-wide): 208.52MM **Privately Held**
SIC: **2721** Magazines: publishing only, not printed on site
HQ: Haymarket Media, Inc.
275 7th Ave Fl 10
New York NY
646 638-6000

(P-3362)

INLAND EMPIRE MEDIA GROUP INC

Also Called: Inland Empire Magazine
36095 Monte De Oro Rd (92592-8123)
PHONE..............................951 682-3026
Don Lorenzi, *Pr*
Don Lorenzi, *Pr*
Richard Lorenzi, *Sec*
EMP: 31 **EST:** 1972
SALES (est): 4.37MM **Privately Held**
Web: www.inlandempiremagazine.com
SIC: **2721** Magazines: publishing and printing

(P-3363)

KELLEY BLUE BOOK CO INC (DH)

195 Technology Dr (92618-2402)
P.O. Box 19691 (92623-9691)
PHONE..............................949 770-7704
Jared Rowe, *CEO*
John Morrison, *
EMP: 92 **EST:** 1926
SALES (est): 113.99MM
SALES (corp-wide): 16.61B **Privately Held**
Web: www.kbb.com
SIC: **2721** Trade journals: publishing only, not printed on site
HQ: Autotrader.Com, Inc.
3003 Summit Blvd Fl 200
Brookhaven GA
404 568-8000

(P-3364)

L F P INC (PA)

Also Called: Flynt, Larry Publishing
8484 Wilshire Blvd Ste 900 (90211-3211)
PHONE..............................323 651-3525
Larry Flynt, *Ch Bd*
Michael H Klein, *
▲ **EMP:** 100 **EST:** 1976
SQ FT: 10,000
SALES (est): 33.18MM
SALES (corp-wide): 33.18MM **Privately Held**
Web: www.lfp.com
SIC: **2721** Magazines: publishing only, not printed on site

(P-3365)

LANDSCAPE COMMUNICATIONS INC

Also Called: Landscape Contract National
14771 Plaza Dr Ste A (92780-2779)
P.O. Box 1126 (92781-1126)
PHONE..............................714 979-5276

George Schmok, *Pr*
EMP: 25 **EST:** 1991
SQ FT: 1,618
SALES (est): 3.11MM **Privately Held**
Web: www.landscapearchitect.com
SIC: **2721** Trade journals: publishing only, not printed on site

(P-3366)

LOCALE LIFESTYLE MAGAZINE LLC

Also Called: Locale Magazine
2755 Bristol St Ste 295 (92626-5968)
P.O. Box 2971 (92659-0459)
PHONE..............................949 436-8910
Erik Hale, *CEO*
EMP: 35 **EST:** 2010
SQ FT: 2,000
SALES (est): 2MM **Privately Held**
Web: www.localemagazine.com
SIC: **2721** Magazines: publishing only, not printed on site

(P-3367)

LOS ANGELES BUS JURNL ASSOC

11150 Santa Monica Blvd Ste 350 (90025-3314)
PHONE..............................323 549-5225
Matt Toledo, *Pr*
EMP: 37 **EST:** 1975
SALES (est): 570.23K **Privately Held**
Web: www.labusinessjournal.com
SIC: **2721** Magazines: publishing only, not printed on site

(P-3368)

LUNDBERG SURVEY INCORPORATED

911 Via Alondra (93012-8048)
PHONE..............................805 383-2400
Trilby Lundberg, *Pr*
EMP: 21 **EST:** 1949
SALES (est): 2.68MM **Privately Held**
Web: www.lundbergsurvey.com
SIC: **2721** 8748 2741 Statistical reports (periodicals): publishing only; Business consulting, nec; Miscellaneous publishing

(P-3369)

MAXWELL PETERSEN ASSOCIATES

Also Called: Dynamic Chiropractic
412 Olive Ave Ste 208 (92648-5142)
PHONE..............................714 230-3150
Donald M Petersen, *Pr*
EMP: 34 **EST:** 1977
SQ FT: 2,000
SALES (est): 4.41MM **Privately Held**
Web: www.mpamedia.com
SIC: **2721** Magazines: publishing only, not printed on site

(P-3370)

MCKINNON ENTERPRISES

Also Called: San Dego HM Grdn Lfestyles Mag
4577 Viewridge Ave (92123-1623)
P.O. Box 719001 (92171-9001)
PHONE..............................858 571-1818
Michael Dean Mckinnon, *Pt*
EMP: 18 **EST:** 1978
SALES (est): 240.82K **Privately Held**
Web: www.sandiegohomegarden.com
SIC: **2721** Magazines: publishing only, not printed on site

(P-3371)

MINORITY SUCCESS PUBG GROUP

Also Called: Minorities & Success
23505 Crenshaw Blvd (90505-5223)
PHONE..............................310 736-2462
Farimah Farahpour, *Pr*
Ali F Chegini, *VP*
EMP: 20 **EST:** 1990
SALES (est): 2.41MM **Privately Held**
Web: www.minoritysuccess.us
SIC: **2721** Magazines: publishing only, not printed on site

(P-3372)

MNM CORPORATION (PA)

Also Called: Apparel Newsgroup, The
110 E 9th St Ste A777 (90079-1300)
PHONE..............................213 627-3737
Martin Wernicke, *CEO*
▲ **EMP:** 25 **EST:** 1985
SQ FT: 11,000
SALES (est): 9.6MM
SALES (corp-wide): 9.6MM **Privately Held**
Web: www.apparelnews.net
SIC: **2721** 8721 Magazines: publishing only, not printed on site; Accounting, auditing, and bookkeeping

(P-3373)

OMICS GROUP INC

5716 Corsa Ave Ste 110 (91362-7354)
PHONE..............................650 268-9744
Srinu B Gedela, *Brnch Mgr*
EMP: 460
SALES (corp-wide): 109.68MM **Privately Held**
Web: www.omicsonline.org
SIC: **2721** Trade journals: publishing and printing
PA: Omics Group Inc
2360 Corp Cir Ste 400
Henderson NV
888 843-8169

(P-3374)

ORANGE COAST MAGAZINE LLC

Also Called: Orange Coast Magazine
5900 Wilshire Blvd # 10 (90036-5013)
PHONE..............................949 862-1133
Gary Thoe, *Pr*
EMP: 146 **EST:** 1975
SALES (est): 4.83MM
SALES (corp-wide): 39.71MM **Privately Held**
Web: www.orangecoast.com
SIC: **2721** 5812 Magazines: publishing only, not printed on site; Eating places
HQ: Emmis Publishing, L.P.
40 Monument Cir Ste 100
Indianapolis IN

(P-3375)

PAISANO PUBLICATIONS LLC (PA)

Also Called: V Twin Magazine
28210 Dorothy Dr (91301-2693)
PHONE..............................818 889-8740
John Lagana, *CEO*
John Lagana, *Publisher*
Joseph Teresi, *
Robert Davis, *
EMP: 60 **EST:** 1971
SQ FT: 40,000
SALES (est): 9.4MM
SALES (corp-wide): 9.4MM **Privately Held**
Web: www.tattoomag.com

SIC: **2721** Magazines: publishing only, not printed on site

(P-3376)

PAISANO PUBLICATIONS INC

Also Called: V/ Twins
28210 Dorothy Dr (91301-2693)
P.O. Box 3000 (91376-3000)
PHONE..............................818 889-8740
Bill Prather, *Pr*
Allen Ribakoff, *
Joseph Teresi, *
Robert Davis, *
EMP: 52 **EST:** 1993
SALES (est): 941.32K
SALES (corp-wide): 9.4MM **Privately Held**
SIC: **2721** 7812 Magazines: publishing and printing; Commercials, television: tape or film
PA: Paisano Publications, Llc
28210 Dorothy Dr
Agoura Hills CA
818 889-8740

(P-3377)

PALM SPRINGS LIFE

303 N Indian Canyon Dr (92262-6015)
P.O. Box 2724 (92263-2724)
PHONE..............................760 325-2333
Joan Braunstein, *Mgr*
EMP: 58 **EST:** 2016
SALES (est): 1.56MM **Privately Held**
Web: www.palmspringslife.com
SIC: **2721** Magazines: publishing only, not printed on site

(P-3378)

PARTNER CONCEPTS INC

811 Camino Viejo (93108-2313)
PHONE..............................805 745-7199
William J Kasch, *Pr*
William L Coulson, *
EMP: 75 **EST:** 1983
SALES (est): 18.57MM **Privately Held**
SIC: **2721** Magazines: publishing only, not printed on site

(P-3379)

PENSKE BUSINESS MEDIA LLC

11175 Santa Monica Blvd (90025-3368)
PHONE..............................310 321-5000
EMP: 22 **EST:** 2016
SALES (est): 2.81MM
SALES (corp-wide): 29.15MM **Privately Held**
Web: www.pmc.com
SIC: **2721** Periodicals
PA: Penske Media Corporation
11175 Santa Monica Blvd # 9
Los Angeles CA
310 321-5000

(P-3380)

PLAYBOY ENTERPRISES INC

10960 Wilshire Blvd Fl 22 (90024-3808)
PHONE..............................310 424-1800
John Luther, *Mgr*
EMP: 79
SALES (corp-wide): 266.93MM **Publicly Held**
Web: www.plbygroup.com
SIC: **2721** Magazines: publishing and printing
HQ: Playboy Enterprises, Inc.
10960 Wilshire Blvd Fl 22
Los Angeles CA
310 424-1800

(P-3381)

PLAYBOY JAPAN INC

9346 Civic Center Dr # 200 (90210-3604)

PHONE..................310 424-1800
EMP: 23 **EST:** 2010
SALES (est): 2.28MM
SALES (corp-wide): 266.93MM **Publicly Held**
SIC: 2721 Magazines: publishing and printing
HQ: Playboy Enterprises, Inc.
   10960 Wilshire Blvd Fl 22
   Los Angeles CA
   310 424-1800

(P-3382)
PUBLISHERS DEVELOPMENT CORP
Also Called: American Handgunner and Guns
225 W Valley Pkwy Ste 100 (92025-2613)
PHONE..................858 605-0200
Thomas Von Rosen, *CEO*
Thomas M Hollander,   *
EMP: 40 **EST:** 1941
SALES (est): 2.36MM **Privately Held**
Web: www.americanhandgunner.com
SIC: 2721 Magazines: publishing only, not printed on site

(P-3383)
QG PRINTING CORP
6688 Box Springs Blvd (92507-0726)
PHONE..................951 571-2500
EMP: 49
SALES (corp-wide): 3.22B **Publicly Held**
SIC: 2721 2752 Periodicals; Commercial printing, lithographic
HQ: Qg Printing Corp.
   N61w23044 Harrys Way
   Sussex WI

(P-3384)
R T C GROUP
Also Called: Cots Journal Magazine
905 Calle Amanecer Ste 250 (92673-6226)
PHONE..................949 226-2000
John Reardon, *Owner*
EMP: 18 **EST:** 1985
SALES (est): 1.91MM **Privately Held**
Web: www.rtcgroup.com
SIC: 2721 Magazines: publishing only, not printed on site

(P-3385)
RANGEFINDER PUBLISHING CO INC
Also Called: After Capture
11835 W Olympic Blvd Ste 550e (90064-5001)
PHONE..................310 846-4770
Stephen Sheanin, *Pr*
EMP: 22 **EST:** 1971
SQ FT: 12,000
SALES (est): 2.05MM
SALES (corp-wide): 325.9MM **Publicly Held**
SIC: 2721 Magazines: publishing only, printed on site
HQ: Emerald X, Llc
   31910 Del Obispo St # 20
   San Juan Capistrano CA

(P-3386)
ROBB CURTCO MEDIA LLC
22741 Pacific Coast Hwy Ste 401 (90265)
PHONE..................310 589-7700
EMP: 33
SALES (corp-wide): 9.03MM **Privately Held**
Web: www.curtco.com
SIC: 2721 Magazines: publishing and printing
PA: Curtco Robb Media Llc
   29160 Heathercliff Rd # 1
   Malibu CA
   310 589-7700

(P-3387)
ROBB REPORT COLLECTION
29160 Heathercliff Rd Ste 200 (90265-6306)
PHONE..................310 589-7700
John S Geer, *Prin*
EMP: 21 **EST:** 2008
SALES (est): 643.17K **Privately Held**
Web: www.robbreport.com
SIC: 2721 Magazines: publishing and printing

(P-3388)
SABOT PUBLISHING INC (PA)
Also Called: A Media
300 Continental Blvd Ste 650 (90245-5042)
PHONE..................310 356-4100
Gibb Zimbalist, *Pr*
William Berry, *CFO*
EMP: 20 **EST:** 1999
SQ FT: 4,400
SALES (est): 7.56MM
SALES (corp-wide): 7.56MM **Privately Held**
SIC: 2721 2731 Magazines: publishing and printing; Book publishing

(P-3389)
SAN DIEGO FAMILY MAGAZINE LLC
Also Called: San Diego Family
1475 6th Ave Ste 500 (92101-3200)
P.O. Box 23960 (92193-3960)
PHONE..................619 685-6970
EMP: 24 **EST:** 1982
SQ FT: 4,000
SALES (est): 3.75MM **Privately Held**
Web: www.sandiegofamily.com
SIC: 2721 Magazines: publishing and printing

(P-3390)
SAN DIEGO MAGAZINE PUBG CO
Also Called: San Diego Magazine
1230 Columbia St Ste 800 (92101-3571)
PHONE..................619 230-9292
James Fitzpatrick, *CEO*
Claire Johnson,   *
EMP: 30 **EST:** 1948
SALES (est): 5.52MM
SALES (corp-wide): 7.64MM **Privately Held**
Web: www.sandiegomagazine.com
SIC: 2721 Magazines: publishing only, not printed on site
PA: Curtco, Publishing
   29160 Heathercliff Rd # 1
   Malibu CA
   310 589-7700

(P-3391)
TL ENTERPRISES LLC
Also Called: Highways Magazine
2750 Park View Ct Ste 240 (93036-5458)
PHONE..................805 981-8393
EMP: 200
Web: rv.campingworld.com
SIC: 2721 Magazines: publishing only, not printed on site

(P-3392)
TWELVE SIGNS INC
Also Called: Starscroll
3369 S Robertson Blvd (90034-3309)
PHONE..................310 553-8000
Richard W Housman, *Pr*
H Kim,   *
EMP: 18 **EST:** 1967
SQ FT: 25,000
SALES (est): 416.17K **Privately Held**

SIC: 2721 Magazines: publishing only, not printed on site

(P-3393)
UBM CANON LLC (DH)
2901 28th St Ste 100 (90405-2975)
PHONE..................310 445-4200
Sally Shankland, *CEO*
Scott Schulman,   *
Sally Shankland, *Pr*
Stephen Corrick,   *
Fred Gysi,   *
EMP: 31 **EST:** 1996
SQ FT: 50,000
SALES (est): 24.29MM
SALES (corp-wide): 2.72B **Privately Held**
Web: www.informamarkets.com
SIC: 2721 7389 Magazines: publishing only, not printed on site; Trade show arrangement
HQ: Informa Tech Holdings Llc
   1983 Marcus Ave Ste 250
   New Hyde Park NY
   516 562-7800

(P-3394)
WEST WORLD PRODUCTIONS INC
420 N Camden Dr (90210-4507)
PHONE..................310 276-9500
Yuri Spiro, *Pr*
EMP: 21 **EST:** 1980
SQ FT: 9,000
SALES (est): 862.67K **Privately Held**
SIC: 2721 Trade journals: publishing only, not printed on site

(P-3395)
XBIZ
Also Called: Adnet Media
4929 Wilshire Blvd Ste 960 (90010-3808)
PHONE..................310 820-0228
Alec Helmy, *Prin*
EMP: 19 **EST:** 2013
SALES (est): 821.49K **Privately Held**
Web: www.xbiz.com
SIC: 2721 Magazines: publishing only, not printed on site

(P-3396)
XPLAIN CORPORATION
Also Called: Mactech Magazine
705 Lakefield Rd Ste I (91361-5903)
P.O. Box 5200 (91359-5200)
PHONE..................805 494-9797
Neil Ticktin, *Pr*
Andrea Sniderman, *CFO*
EMP: 25 **EST:** 1992
SALES (est): 3.24MM **Privately Held**
Web: www.xplain.com
SIC: 2721 5994 Magazines: publishing only, not printed on site; Magazine stand

---

2731 Book Publishing

(P-3397)
ABC - CLIO INC (HQ)
Also Called: ABC-Clio
147 Castilian Dr (93117-3025)
P.O. Box 1911 (93116-1911)
PHONE..................805 968-1911
Ronald Boehm, *CEO*
EMP: 115 **EST:** 1955
SALES (est): 30.93MM
SALES (corp-wide): 325.4MM **Privately Held**
Web: www.abc-clio.com
SIC: 2731 Books, publishing only
PA: Bloomsbury Publishing Plc
   50 Bedford Square

   London
   207 631-5600

(P-3398)
AVN MEDIA NETWORK INC
Also Called: Adult Video News
9400 Penfield Ave (91311-6549)
PHONE..................818 718-5788
Tony Rios, *CEO*
EMP: 30 **EST:** 1982
SQ FT: 15,000
SALES (est): 5.11MM **Privately Held**
Web: www.avn.com
SIC: 2731 2721 Book publishing; Periodicals

(P-3399)
BERTELSMANN INC
Also Called: Arvato Services
29011 Commerce Center Dr (91355-4195)
PHONE..................661 702-2700
Janet Adams, *Mgr*
EMP: 9648
SALES (corp-wide): 54.57MM **Privately Held**
Web: www.bertelsmann.com
SIC: 2731 Books, publishing only
HQ: Bertelsmann, Inc.
   1745 Broadway
   New York NY
   212 782-1000

(P-3400)
BRIDGE PUBLICATIONS INC (PA)
Also Called: Bpi Records
5600 E Olympic Blvd (90022-5128)
PHONE..................323 888-6200
Blake Silber, *CEO*
Lis Astrupgaard,   *
Marilyn Pisani,   *
Suzanne Riley,   *
▲ **EMP:** 40 **EST:** 1981
SQ FT: 15,000
SALES (est): 20.95MM
SALES (corp-wide): 20.95MM **Privately Held**
Web: www.bridgepub.com
SIC: 2731 3652 Books, publishing only; Prerecorded records and tapes

(P-3401)
CHICK PUBLICATIONS INC
8780 Archibald Ave (91730-4697)
P.O. Box 3500 (91761-1019)
PHONE..................909 987-0771
Jack T Chick, *Pr*
George A Collins,   *
Ronald Rockney,   *
◆ **EMP:** 21 **EST:** 1961
SQ FT: 10,000
SALES (est): 1.79MM **Privately Held**
Web: www.chick.com
SIC: 2731 5961 Books, publishing only; Mail order house, nec

(P-3402)
COGNELLA INC
Also Called: University Readers
3970 Sorrento Valley Blvd Ste 500 (92121-1416)
PHONE..................858 552-1120
Bassin Hamadeh, *CEO*
EMP: 65 **EST:** 1997
SQ FT: 8,000
SALES (est): 14.79MM **Privately Held**
Web: www.cognella.com
SIC: 2731 Textbooks: publishing only, not printed on site

(P-3403)
CPP/BELWIN INC
16320 Roscoe Blvd Ste 100 (91406-1216)
P.O. Box 10003 (91410-0003)
PHONE..............................818 891-5999
Steven Manus, *Pr*
▲ **EMP:** 282 **EST:** 1988
SQ FT: 142,000
SALES (est): 481.55K **Privately Held**
SIC: 2731 Book music: publishing only, not
printed on site
PA: Alfred Music Group Inc.
16320 Roscoe Blvd Ste 100
Van Nuys CA

(P-3404)
CREATIVE TEACHING PRESS INC (PA)
6262 Katella Ave (90630-5204)
PHONE..............................714 799-2100
James M Connelly, *CEO*
Luella Connelly, *
Susan Connelly, *
Patrick Connelly, *
◆ **EMP:** 95 **EST:** 1965
SQ FT: 85,000
SALES (est): 12.61MM
SALES (corp-wide): 12.61MM **Privately Held**
Web: www.creativeteaching.com
SIC: 2731 Books, publishing only

(P-3405)
DAWN SIGN PRESS INC
6130 Nancy Ridge Dr (92121-3223)
PHONE..............................858 625-0600
Joe Dannis, *CEO*
Thomas Schlegel, *
Tina Jo Breindel, *
◆ **EMP:** 28 **EST:** 1977
SQ FT: 16,500
SALES (est): 2.5MM **Privately Held**
Web: www.dawnsign.com
SIC: 2731 Books, publishing only

(P-3406)
DISNEY BOOK GROUP LLC (DH)
Also Called: Hyperion Books For Children
500 S Buena Vista St (91521-0001)
PHONE..............................818 560-1000
EMP: 24 **EST:** 1999
SALES (est): 2.45MM
SALES (corp-wide): 88.9B **Publicly Held**
Web: www.thewaltdisneycompany.com
SIC: 2731 Book publishing
HQ: Twdc Enterprises 18 Corp.
500 S Buena Vista St
Burbank CA

(P-3407)
HOUGHTON MIFFLIN HARCOURT PUBG
Also Called: Harcourt Trade Publishers
525 B St Ste 1900 (92101-4495)
PHONE..............................617 351-5000
Barbara Fisch, *Brnch Mgr*
EMP: 20
SALES (corp-wide): 1.05B **Privately Held**
Web: www.hmhco.com
SIC: 2731 Textbooks: publishing only, not
printed on site
HQ: Houghton Mifflin Harcourt Publishing
Company
125 High St Ste 900
Boston MA
617 351-5000

(P-3408)
JUDY O PRODUCTIONS INC
4858 W Pico Blvd Ste 331 (90019-4225)
PHONE..............................323 938-8513
Judy Ostarch, *Pr*
▲ **EMP:** 28 **EST:** 1999
SALES (est): 1.52MM **Privately Held**
SIC: 2731 Book publishing

(P-3409)
MANSON WESTERN LLC
Also Called: Western Psychological Services
625 Alaska Ave (90503-5124)
PHONE..............................424 201-8800
EMP: 117 **EST:** 1996
SALES (est): 16.01MM **Privately Held**
Web: www.wpspublish.com
SIC: 2731 Book publishing

(P-3410)
MICROFILM COMPANY OF CAL INC
Also Called: Library Reproduction Service
14214 S Figueroa St (90061-1034)
PHONE..............................310 354-2610
Joan Miller, *Pr*
Peter Jones, *General Vice President*
EMP: 18 **EST:** 1946
SQ FT: 7,000
SALES (est): 689.71K **Privately Held**
SIC: 2731 7389 Books, publishing and
printing; Microfilm recording and developing
service

(P-3411)
NARCOTICS ANNYMOUS WRLD SVCS I (PA)
Also Called: WORLD SERVICE OFFICE
19737 Nordhoff Pl (91311-6606)
P.O. Box 9999 (91409-9099)
PHONE..............................818 773-9999
Anthony Edmondson, *CEO*
▲ **EMP:** 45 **EST:** 1953
SQ FT: 35,000
SALES (est): 8.17MM
SALES (corp-wide): 8.17MM **Privately Held**
Web: www.na.org
SIC: 2731 Books, publishing only

(P-3412)
PLURAL PUBLISHING INC
9177 Aero Dr (92123-2400)
PHONE..............................858 492-1555
Sadanand Singh, *Pr*
▲ **EMP:** 27 **EST:** 2004
SALES (est): 4.97MM **Privately Held**
Web: www.pluralpublishing.com
SIC: 2731 Textbooks: publishing only, not
printed on site

(P-3413)
SADDLEBACK EDUCATIONAL INC
Also Called: Saddleback Educational Pubg
151 Kalmus Dr Ste J1 (92626-5919)
P.O. Box 3239 (92659-1239)
PHONE..............................714 640-5200
Arianne M Mchugh, *Pr*
Tim Mchugh, *VP Sls*
▲ **EMP:** 19 **EST:** 1982
SQ FT: 5,000
SALES (est): 4.83MM **Privately Held**
Web: www.sdlback.com
SIC: 2731 5192 Books, publishing only;
Books

(P-3414)
SAGE PUBLICATIONS INC (PA)
Also Called: Cq Press Fairfax Co
2455 Teller Rd (91320-2234)
PHONE..............................805 499-0721
▲ **EMP:** 201 **EST:** 1965
SALES (est): 106.19MM
SALES (corp-wide): 106.19MM **Privately Held**
Web: us.sagepub.com
SIC: 2731 Book publishing

(P-3415)
STONEYBROOK PUBLISHING INC
10815 Rancho Bernardo Rd Ste 300 (92127)
PHONE..............................858 674-4600
Aaron Combs, *Pr*
Dave Stone, *CEO*
EMP: 21 **EST:** 1984
SALES (est): 859.53K **Privately Held**
Web: www.stoneybrookpublishing.com
SIC: 2731 2741 7331 Pamphlets: publishing
only, not printed on site; Newsletter
publishing; Direct mail advertising services

(P-3416)
TEACHER CREATED RESOURCES INC
12621 Western Ave (92841-4014)
PHONE..............................714 230-7060
Mary Smith, *CEO*
Sarah Fournier, *
Darin Smith, *
◆ **EMP:** 103 **EST:** 2004
SALES (est): 28.85MM **Privately Held**
Web: www.teachercreated.com
SIC: 2731 Books, publishing and printing

(P-3417)
THE FULL VOID 2 INC
Also Called: Alfred Music Publishing
16320 Roscoe Blvd Ste 100 (91406-1216)
P.O. Box 10003 (91410-0003)
PHONE..............................818 891-5999
◆ **EMP:** 275
SIC: 2731 Book publishing

(P-3418)
TOKYOPOP INC (PA)
4136 Del Rey Ave (90292-5604)
PHONE..............................323 920-5967
Stuart J Levy, *Pr*
John Parker, *
Victor Chin, *
◆ **EMP:** 90 **EST:** 1997
SALES (est): 7.69MM
SALES (corp-wide): 7.69MM **Privately Held**
Web: www.tokyopop.com
SIC: 2731 3652 7812 7371 Books,
publishing only; Compact laser discs,
prerecorded; Video tape production;
Custom computer programming services

(P-3419)
WALTER FOSTER PUBLISHING INC
6 Orchard Ste 100 (92630-8351)
PHONE..............................949 380-7510
▲ **EMP:** 26
Web: www.walterfoster.com
SIC: 2731 Books, publishing only

(P-3420)
WEST PUBLISHING CORPORATION
Also Called: The Rutter Group
5161 Lankershim Blvd (91601-4962)
PHONE..............................800 747-3161
William Rutter, *Brnch Mgr*
EMP: 382
SALES (corp-wide): 10.66B **Publicly Held**
Web: home.westacademic.com
SIC: 2731 8111 Book publishing; General
practice attorney, lawyer
HQ: West Publishing Corporation
610 Opperman Dr
Eagan MN
651 687-7000

2741 Miscellaneous Publishing

(P-3421)
418 MEDIA LLC
Also Called: 418 Media
1875 Century Park E Ste 370 (90067-2253)
PHONE..............................614 350-3960
EMP: 20 **EST:** 2010
SALES (est): 633.67K **Privately Held**
Web: www.lewishowes.com
SIC: 2741 Internet publishing and
broadcasting

(P-3422)
ACCEPTEDCOM LLC
2229 S Canfield Ave (90034-1114)
PHONE..............................310 815-9553
Linda Abraham, *Pr*
EMP: 27 **EST:** 2002
SALES (est): 3.81MM **Privately Held**
Web: www.accepted.com
SIC: 2741 Miscellaneous publishing

(P-3423)
ACTIVISION
9465 Wilshire Blvd Ste 400 (90212-2612)
PHONE..............................424 320-9000
EMP: 25 **EST:** 2019
SALES (est): 867.63K **Privately Held**
Web: www.activision.com
SIC: 2741 Miscellaneous publishing

(P-3424)
ADVANCED PUBLISHING TECH INC
1105 N Hollywood Way (91505-2528)
PHONE..............................818 557-3035
D Kraai, *Owner*
EMP: 18
Web: www.advpubtech.com
SIC: 2741 Miscellaneous publishing
PA: Advanced Publishing Technology, Inc.
140 S Buena Vista St M
Burbank CA

(P-3425)
AIO ACQUISITION INC (HQ)
Also Called: Personnel Concepts
3200 E Guasti Rd Ste 300 (91761-8661)
P.O. Box 3353 9003 (91761)
PHONE..............................800 333-3795
▲ **EMP:** 92 **EST:** 1989
SALES (est): 28.25MM
SALES (corp-wide): 1.33B **Publicly Held**
Web: www.personnelconcepts.com
SIC: 2741 7319 Posters: publishing and
printing; Circular and handbill distribution
PA: Brady Corporation
6555 W Good Hope Rd
Milwaukee WI
414 358-6600

(P-3426)
ALG INC
120 Broadway Ste 200 (90401-2385)
P.O. Box 61207 (93160-1207)
PHONE...............................424 258-8026
James Nguyen, *Pr*
Michael Guthrie, *
Jeff Swart, *
Scott Watkinson, *
Bernard Brenner, *
EMP: 333 **EST:** 1972
SALES (est): 2.14MM **Publicly Held**
Web: www.automotiveleaseguide.com
SIC: 2741 Guides: publishing only, not printed on site
PA: Truecar, Inc.
120 Broadway Ste 200
Santa Monica CA

(P-3427)
AMERICAN SOC CMPSERS ATHORS PB
Also Called: Ascap
7920 W Sunset Blvd Ste 300 (90046-3300)
PHONE...............................323 883-1000
Daniel Gonzales, *Genl Mgr*
EMP: 79
SALES (corp-wide): 101.46MM **Privately Held**
Web: www.ascap.com
SIC: 2741 Miscellaneous publishing
PA: American Society Of Composers, Authors And Publishers
250 W 57th St Ste 1300
New York NY
212 621-6000

(P-3428)
ASSOCIATED DESERT SHOPPERS INC (DH)
Also Called: The White Sheet
73400 Highway 111 (92260-3908)
PHONE...............................760 346-1729
Harold Paradis, *Pr*
Esperanza Barrett, *
Rey Verdugo Senior, *Dir Opers*
EMP: 75 **EST:** 1987
SQ FT: 4,000
SALES (est): 11.47MM
SALES (corp-wide): 3.68B **Publicly Held**
SIC: 2741 7313 Shopping news: publishing and printing; Newspaper-advertising representative
HQ: Schurz Communications, Inc.
1301 E Douglas Rd Ste 200
Mishawaka IN
574 247-7237

(P-3429)
AUDIENCE INC
5670 Wilshire Blvd Ste 100 (90036-5686)
PHONE...............................323 413-2370
EMP: 27 **EST:** 2011
SALES (est): 2.86MM **Privately Held**
Web: www.theaudience.com
SIC: 2741 Miscellaneous publishing
PA: Al Ahli Holding Group
Dubai Al-Ain Road Route 66 Blue Glasses Building, Dubai Outlet C
Dubai

(P-3430)
BINGO PUBLISHERS INCORPORATED
24881 Alicia Pkwy Ste E (92653-4617)
PHONE...............................949 581-5410
Charles Sloan, *Pr*
EMP: 22 **EST:** 1990
SQ FT: 3,000
SALES (est): 477.05K **Privately Held**
Web: www.localbingohalls.com
SIC: 2741 Miscellaneous publishing

(P-3431)
BLAVITY INC
600 Wilshire Blvd Ste 1650 (90017-3228)
PHONE...............................818 669-9162
Morgan Rose Debaun, *CEO*
Mike Hadgis, *CRO*
EMP: 161 **EST:** 2018
SALES (est): 4.32MM **Privately Held**
Web: www.blavityinc.com
SIC: 2741 Internet publishing and broadcasting

(P-3432)
BREMIK INTERNATIONAL INC
Also Called: Bremik Press
14403 S Main St (90248-1913)
PHONE...............................310 715-6622
Alan Saloner, *Pr*
EMP: 55 **EST:** 1992
SQ FT: 17,500
SALES (est): 4.35MM **Privately Held**
SIC: 2741 Posters: publishing and printing

(P-3433)
BROWNTROUT PUBLISHERS INC (PA)
Also Called: Browntrout
201 Continental Blvd Ste 200 (90245-4514)
PHONE...............................424 290-6122
William Michael Brown, *CEO*
Gray Peterson, *
▲ **EMP:** 40 **EST:** 1993
SQ FT: 11,000
SALES (est): 13.98MM **Privately Held**
Web: www.browntrout.com
SIC: 2741 Miscellaneous publishing

(P-3434)
BRUD INC
837 N Spring St Ste 101 (90012-2594)
PHONE...............................310 806-2283
Trevor Mcfedries, *Pr*
EMP: 17 **EST:** 2017
SALES (est): 1.15MM **Privately Held**
Web: www.dapperlabs.com
SIC: 2741 Internet publishing and broadcasting

(P-3435)
C PUBLISHING LLC
Also Called: C Magazine
1543 7th St Ste 202 (90401-2645)
PHONE...............................310 393-3800
Jennifer Smith Hale, *Managing Member*
Jennifer Smith Hale, *Mgr*
Jenny Murray, *IN*
Lesley Canpoy, *Publisher*
EMP: 25 **EST:** 2005
SALES (est): 4.44MM **Privately Held**
Web: www.magazinec.com
SIC: 2741 Miscellaneous publishing

(P-3436)
CHINESE OVERSEAS MKTG SVC CORP (PA)
Also Called: Chinese Consumer Yellow Pages
3940 Rosemead Blvd (91770-1952)
PHONE...............................626 280-8588
Alan Kao, *Pr*
Gorden Kao, *Dir*
▲ **EMP:** 60 **EST:** 1982
SQ FT: 9,298
SALES (est): 8.06MM
SALES (corp-wide): 8.06MM **Privately Held**
Web: www.ccyp.com
SIC: 2741 7389 8742 Directories, telephone: publishing only, not printed on site; Trade show arrangement; Marketing consulting services

(P-3437)
COLBI TECHNOLOGIES INC
13891 Newport Ave Ste 150 (92780-7897)
PHONE...............................714 505-9544
Charles Olsen, *Prin*
Larry Goshorn, *
Francisco Javier Oseguera, *
Jamin Boggs, *
Lettie Cowie, *
EMP: 43 **EST:** 2008
SALES (est): 4.14MM **Privately Held**
Web: www.colbitech.com
SIC: 2741 Miscellaneous publishing

(P-3438)
COYNE COMPANIES LLC
2351 S 4th St (92243-6004)
PHONE...............................760 353-1016
EMP: 17 **EST:** 2012
SALES (est): 1.3MM **Privately Held**
SIC: 2741 Miscellaneous publishing

(P-3439)
DANIELS INC (PA)
Also Called: Big Nickel
74745 Leslie Ave (92260-2030)
PHONE...............................801 621-3355
Daniel Murphy, *Pr*
Dennis Porter, *Sec*
EMP: 23 **EST:** 1968
SQ FT: 10,000
SALES (est): 2.1MM
SALES (corp-wide): 2.1MM **Privately Held**
Web: www.danielsdki.com
SIC: 2741 Shopping news: publishing and printing

(P-3440)
DEN EDITORIAL LLC
2332 S Centinela Ave (90064-1071)
PHONE...............................949 292-6475
EMP: 33 **EST:** 2019
SALES (est): 442.59K **Privately Held**
Web: www.thedeneditorial.com
SIC: 2741 Miscellaneous publishing

(P-3441)
DIVERSIFIED PRINTERS INC
12834 Maxwell Dr (92782-0914)
PHONE...............................714 994-3400
Kenneth Bittner, *Pr*
Jerry Tominaga, *
Paul R Nassar, *
EMP: 51 **EST:** 1986
SQ FT: 105,000
SALES (est): 3.38MM **Privately Held**
SIC: 2741 2759 2789 Directories, nec: publishing and printing; Commercial printing, nec; Bookbinding and related work

(P-3442)
ECT NEWS NETWORK INC
16133 Ventura Blvd Ste 700 (91436-2403)
P.O. Box 18500 (91416-8500)
PHONE...............................818 461-9700
Richard Kern, *Prin*
EMP: 23 **EST:** 2004
SALES (est): 1.12MM **Privately Held**
Web: www.ectnews.com
SIC: 2741 Internet publishing and broadcasting

(P-3443)
EDUCATIONAL IDEAS INCORPORATED
Also Called: Ballard & Tighe Publishers
471 Atlas St (92821-3118)
P.O. Box 219 (92822-0219)
PHONE...............................714 990-4332
Dorothy Roberts, *Ch Bd*
Mark Espinola, *
Kent Roberts, *
◆ **EMP:** 48 **EST:** 1976
SQ FT: 12,000
SALES (est): 4.71MM **Privately Held**
Web: www.ballard-tighe.com
SIC: 2741 Miscellaneous publishing

(P-3444)
ELECTRIC SOLIDUS LLC
26565 Agoura Rd Ste 200 (91302-1990)
PHONE...............................917 692-7764
EMP: 25 **EST:** 2019
SALES (est): 1.09MM **Privately Held**
SIC: 2741 Internet publishing and broadcasting

(P-3445)
ELSEVIER INC
Also Called: Elsevier
10620 Treena St (92131-1140)
PHONE...............................619 231-6616
Kristen Chrisman, *Brnch Mgr*
EMP: 67
SALES (corp-wide): 10.3B **Privately Held**
Web: www.elsevier.com
SIC: 2741 Miscellaneous publishing
HQ: Elsevier Inc.
230 Park Ave Fl 7
New York NY
212 309-8100

(P-3446)
ELSEVIER INC
Also Called: Elsevier Academic Press
525 B St (92101-4420)
PHONE...............................619 231-6616
EMP: 30
SALES (corp-wide): 10.3B **Privately Held**
Web: www.elsevier.com
SIC: 2741 Technical manuals: publishing only, not printed on site
HQ: Elsevier Inc.
230 Park Ave Fl 7
New York NY
212 309-8100

(P-3447)
EQUITY FORD RESEARCH
11722 Sorrento Valley Rd Ste I
(92121-1021)
PHONE...............................858 755-1327
Timothy R Alward, *Pr*
Jonathan Worrall, *Ch*
EMP: 22 **EST:** 1970
SQ FT: 5,500
SALES (est): 480.14K **Privately Held**
Web: www.lseg.com
SIC: 2741 6282 Miscellaneous publishing; Investment advice

(P-3448)
G R LEONARD & CO INC
Also Called: Leonard's Guide
181 N Vermont Ave (91741-3321)
PHONE...............................847 797-8101
David Ercolani, *CEO*
Ahmed Hawari, *
Elizabeth Stern, *
▲ **EMP:** 26 **EST:** 1912
SALES (est): 2.19MM **Privately Held**
Web: www.leonardsguide.com

▲ = Import ▼ = Export
◆ = Import/Export

SIC: **2741** Directories, nec: publishing only, not printed on site

(P-3449)
GLOBAL COMPLIANCE INC
Also Called: Compliance Poster
438 W Chestnut Ave Ste A (91016-1129)
P.O. Box 607 (91017-0607)
PHONE..................................626 303-6855
Patricia A Blum, *Pr*
EMP: 25 EST: 1990
SALES (est): 4.39MM **Privately Held**
Web: www.accupostdocs.com
SIC: **2741** Posters: publishing and printing

(P-3450)
GLS US FREIGHT INC
3561 Philadelphia St (91710-2089)
PHONE..................................909 627-2538
Erin Craig, *Mgr*
EMP: 21
SALES (corp-wide): 89.98MM **Privately Held**
Web: freight.gls-us.com
SIC: **2741** Miscellaneous publishing
PA: Gls Us Freight, Inc.
6750 Longe St Ste 100
Stockton CA
209 823-2168

(P-3451)
GOLDEN STATE COMPANY LLC
200 N Pacific Coast Hwy Ste 110 (90245-5606)
PHONE..................................310 376-7800
EMP: 21 EST: 2017
SALES (est): 2.45MM **Privately Held**
Web: www.goldenstate.is
SIC: **2741** Miscellaneous publishing

(P-3452)
GOOD WORLDWIDE LLC
6380 Wilshire Blvd # 15 (90048-5003)
PHONE..................................323 206-6495
EMP: 44 EST: 2010
SALES (est): 3.6MM **Privately Held**
Web: www.good.is
SIC: **2741** Miscellaneous publishing

(P-3453)
GRAPHIQ LLC
101a Innovation Pl (93108-2268)
P.O. Box 1259 (93067-1259)
PHONE..................................805 335-2433
Kevin Oconnor, *Pr*
Scott Leonard, *
EMP: 120 EST: 2009
SALES (est): 18.63MM **Publicly Held**
Web: www.graphiq.com
SIC: **2741** 4813 Internet publishing and broadcasting; Web search portals
PA: Amazon.Com, Inc.
410 Terry Ave N
Seattle WA

(P-3454)
GREAT EASTERN ENTERTAINMENT CO (PA)
610 W Carob St (90220-5210)
PHONE..................................310 638-5058
▲ EMP: 23 EST: 1995
SQ FT: 6,000
SALES (est): 2.22MM **Privately Held**
Web: www.geanimation.com
SIC: **2741** Posters: publishing and printing

(P-3455)
HANLEY WOOD MEDIA INC (HQ)
Also Called: Zonda Media

4000 Macarthur Blvd Ste 400 (92660-2543)
PHONE..................................202 736-3300
Peter Goldstone, *CEO*
Matthew Flynn, *CFO*
EMP: 17 EST: 2013
SALES (est): 97.02MM
SALES (corp-wide): 179.03MM **Privately Held**
Web: www.jlconline.com
SIC: **2741** Business service newsletters: publishing and printing
PA: Hw Holdco, Llc
1 Thomas Cir Nw Ste 600
Washington DC
202 452-0800

(P-3456)
HI TORQUE PUBLICATIO
25233 Anza Dr (91355-1289)
PHONE..................................661 367-2134
EMP: 23 EST: 2019
SALES (est): 1.08MM **Privately Held**
Web: www.hi-torque.com
SIC: **2741** Miscellaneous publishing

(P-3457)
INFORMA BUSINESS MEDIA INC
Sourceesb
16815 Von Karman Ave # 150 (92606-2406)
PHONE..................................949 252-1146
EMP: 30
SALES (corp-wide): 3.12B **Privately Held**
SIC: **2741** Directories, nec: publishing only, not printed on site
HQ: Informa Business Media, Inc.
605 3rd Ave
New York NY
212 204-4200

(P-3458)
JUMPER MEDIA LLC
Also Called: Jumper Media
1719 Alta La Jolla Dr (92037-7103)
PHONE..................................831 333-6202
Colton Bollinger, *CEO*
EMP: 99 EST: 2016
SALES (est): 4.27MM **Privately Held**
Web: www.jumpermedia.co
SIC: **2741** Internet publishing and broadcasting

(P-3459)
JUNGOTV LLC
4605 Lankershim Blvd Ste 180 (91602-1818)
PHONE..................................650 207-6227
George Chung, *CEO*
EMP: 60 EST: 2015
SALES (est): 1.27MM **Privately Held**
Web: www.jungotv.com
SIC: **2741** Internet publishing and broadcasting

(P-3460)
JUNIPER PUBLISHERS
1890 W Hillcrest Dr (91320-2390)
PHONE..................................909 563-8215
EMP: 24 EST: 2016
SALES (est): 41.35K **Privately Held**
Web: www.juniperpublishers.com
SIC: **2741** Miscellaneous publishing

(P-3461)
LA XPRESS AIR & HEATING SVCS
6400 E Washington Blvd Ste 121 (90040-1820)
PHONE..................................310 856-9678
Jesus A Chavez, *CEO*

EMP: 67 EST: 2013
SALES (est): 2.38MM **Privately Held**
SIC: **2741** Miscellaneous publishing

(P-3462)
LEADMMATIC LLC
5154 Don Pio Dr (91364-1730)
PHONE..................................310 857-4511
Aaron Beck, *Brnch Mgr*
EMP: 29
SALES (corp-wide): 487.67K **Privately Held**
Web: www.leadmmatic.com
SIC: **2741** Internet publishing and broadcasting
PA: Leadmmatic, Llc
74998 Country Club Dr # 22
Palm Desert CA

(P-3463)
MARCOA MEDIA LLC (PA)
9955 Black Mountain Rd (92126-4514)
P.O. Box 509100 (92150-9100)
PHONE..................................858 635-9627
Michael Martella, *Managing Member*
Matt Benedict, *
EMP: 40 EST: 1967
SQ FT: 40,000
SALES (est): 16.01MM
SALES (corp-wide): 16.01MM **Privately Held**
Web: www.mybaseguide.com
SIC: **2741** Atlas, map, and guide publishing

(P-3464)
MARCOA QUALITY PUBLISHING LLC
9955 Black Mountain Rd (92126-4514)
P.O. Box 509100 (92150-9100)
PHONE..................................858 695-9600
EMP: 17 EST: 2010
SALES (est): 1.09MM **Privately Held**
SIC: **2741** Miscellaneous publishing

(P-3465)
MITCHELL REPAIR INFO CO LLC (HQ)
Also Called: Mitchell1
16067 Babcock St (92127-3690)
PHONE..................................858 391-5000
EMP: 20 EST: 1996
SALES (est): 87.41MM
SALES (corp-wide): 4.49B **Publicly Held**
Web: www.mitchell.com
SIC: **2741** 2731 5251 Technical manuals: publishing only, not printed on site; Book publishing; Hardware stores
PA: Snap-On Incorporated
2801 80th St
Kenosha WI
262 656-5200

(P-3466)
MRC MEDIA LLC (PA)
100 N Crescent Dr Ste 100 (90210-5447)
PHONE..................................212 493-4100
▲ EMP: 17 EST: 2009
SALES (est): 819.97K **Privately Held**
SIC: **2741** Miscellaneous publishing

(P-3467)
NATIONAL APPRAISAL GUIDES INC
Also Called: Nada Appraisal Guide
3186 Airway Ave Ste K (92626-4650)
PHONE..................................714 556-8511
Donald D Christy Junior, *Pr*
Jody Christy, *
Robin Lewis, *

EMP: 33 EST: 1968
SQ FT: 20,000
SALES (est): 4.41MM **Privately Held**
Web: www.jdpower.com
SIC: **2741** Guides: publishing and printing

(P-3468)
NEIL A KJOS MUSIC COMPANY (PA)
Also Called: Kjos Music
4382 Jutland Dr (92117-3642)
P.O. Box 178270 (92177-8270)
PHONE..................................858 270-9800
Neil A Kjos Junior, *Ch Bd*
Ryan Nowlin, *
Barbara G Kjos, *
▲ EMP: 40 EST: 1985
SQ FT: 72,000
SALES (est): 11.47MM
SALES (corp-wide): 11.47MM **Privately Held**
Web: www.kjos.com
SIC: **2741** Music, book: publishing and printing

(P-3469)
NETMARBLE US INC
600 Wilshire Blvd Ste 1100 (90005-3983)
PHONE..................................213 222-7712
Chul Min Sim, *CEO*
EMP: 66 EST: 2012
SQ FT: 2,500
SALES (est): 7.82MM **Privately Held**
SIC: **2741** 5734 Miscellaneous publishing; Software, computer games
PA: Netmarble Corporation
G-Tower
Seoul

(P-3470)
PARROT COMMUNICATIONS INTL INC
Also Called: Parrot Media Network
25461 Rye Canyon Rd (91355-1206)
PHONE..................................818 567-4700
Robert W Mertz, *CEO*
▲ EMP: 50 EST: 1989
SALES (est): 4.99MM **Privately Held**
Web: www.parrotmedia.com
SIC: **2741** 7331 4822 7375 Directories, nec: publishing only, not printed on site; Direct mail advertising services; Facsimile transmission services; Information retrieval services

(P-3471)
PASSION PLANNER LLC
1608 Grayson Ct (91913-1501)
PHONE..................................619 777-3451
Angelia Trinidad, *Brnch Mgr*
EMP: 31
SALES (corp-wide): 2.87MM **Privately Held**
Web: www.passionplanner.com
SIC: **2741** Miscellaneous publishing
PA: Passion Planner Llc
101 E 30th St Ste E
National City CA
619 693-7606

(P-3472)
PENINSULA PUBLISHING INC
1602 Monrovia Ave (92663-2808)
PHONE..................................949 631-1307
Nick Slevin, *Pr*
EMP: 17 EST: 1998
SALES (est): 1.88MM **Privately Held**
Web: www.penpubinc.com
SIC: **2741** Miscellaneous publishing

PRODUCTS & SVCS

(P-3473)
PENNYSAVER USA PUBLISHING LLC
Also Called: Original Pennysaver, The
2830 Orbiter St (92821-6224)
P.O. Box 8900 (92822-8900)
PHONE..................................866 640-3900
EMP: 1000
Web: www.pennysaverusa.com
SIC: 2741 Shopping news: publishing only, not printed on site

(P-3474)
PLANETIZEN INC
Also Called: Planetizen
3530 Wilshire Blvd Ste 1285 (90010-2328)
PHONE..................................877 260-7526
Chris Steins, Pr
EMP: 22 EST: 2011
SALES (est): 484.76K Privately Held
Web: www.planetizen.com
SIC: 2741 Internet publishing and broadcasting

(P-3475)
PLAYBOY ENTERPRISES INTL INC
Also Called: Peei
10960 Wilshire Blvd Ste 2200 (90024-3808)
PHONE..................................310 424-1800
Christopher Pachler, Ex VP
Christopher Pachler, CAO
Hugh Heffner, Chief Creative Officer
EMP: 100 EST: 1964
SALES (est): 21.05MM
SALES (corp-wide): 266.93MM Publicly Held
Web: www.playboy.com
HQ: Playboy Enterprises, Inc.
    10960 Wilshire Blvd Fl 22
    Los Angeles CA
    310 424-1800

(P-3476)
POLLSTAR LLC
Also Called: Pollstar.com
1100 Glendon Ave Ste 2100 (90024-3592)
PHONE..................................559 271-7900
Gary Bongiovanni, Pr
Gary Smith, *
EMP: 58 EST: 1981
SALES (est): 9.39MM Privately Held
Web: store.pollstar.com
SIC: 2741 Miscellaneous publishing

(P-3477)
PRISON RIDE SHARE NETWORK
Also Called: Prison Rideshare Network
25310 Stephvon Way (92544-2021)
PHONE..................................314 703-5245
Keisha Joseph-beard, Owner
EMP: 20 EST: 2016
SALES (est): 741.74K Privately Held
SIC: 2741 8742 4729 Telephone and other directory publishing; Transportation consultant; Carpool/vanpool arrangement

(P-3478)
PROTOTYPE INDUSTRIES INC (PA)
26035 Acero Ste 100 (92691-7951)
PHONE..................................949 680-4890
Irene Grigoriadis, CEO
EMP: 28 EST: 1991
SQ FT: 4,000
SALES (est): 2.48MM Privately Held
Web: www.prototypeindustries.com

(P-3479)
QUADRIGA AMERICAS LLC
17800 S Main St Ste 113 (90248-3511)
PHONE..................................424 634-4900
EMP: 21
SALES (corp-wide): 1.66MM Privately Held
SIC: 2741 Internet publishing and broadcasting
PA: Quadriga Americas, Llc
    480 Olde Worthington Rd
    Westerville OH
    614 890-6090

(P-3480)
RASPADOXPRESS
8610 Van Nuys Blvd (91402-7205)
PHONE..................................818 892-6969
Oscar Limon, Brnch Mgr
EMP: 56
SALES (corp-wide): 1.42MM Privately Held
Web: www.raspadoxpress.com
SIC: 2741 Miscellaneous publishing
PA: Raspadoxpress
    9765 Laurel Canyon Blvd
    Pacoima CA
    818 890-4111

(P-3481)
REAL MARKETING
8470 Redwood Creek Ln Ste 200 (92126-1000)
PHONE..................................858 847-0335
David Collins, Pr
▼ EMP: 28 EST: 2007
SALES (est): 5.44MM Privately Held
Web: www.realmarketing4you.com
SIC: 2741 2759 2721 Newsletter publishing; Promotional printing; Magazines: publishing and printing

(P-3482)
RIYE GROUP LLC
2110 W 103rd St (90047-4113)
PHONE..................................820 203-9215
Lanon Johnson, Pr
EMP: 49 EST: 2021
SALES (est): 711.77K Privately Held
SIC: 2741 8742 8741 7514 Internet publishing and broadcasting; Marketing consulting services; Administrative management; Passenger car rental

(P-3483)
SCHUBERT MUSIC PUBLISHING INC
18233 Rayen St (91325-2741)
PHONE..................................310 409-7326
EMP: 25 EST: 2013
SALES (est): 204.43K Privately Held
Web: www.schubertmusic.com
SIC: 2741 Miscellaneous publishing

(P-3484)
SIEMENS ENERGY INC
6 Journey Ste 200 (92656-5321)
PHONE..................................949 448-0600
Ralph Sonnseld, Brnch Mgr
EMP: 29
SALES (corp-wide): 33.81B Privately Held
Web: www.siemens.com
SIC: 2741 Miscellaneous publishing
HQ: Siemens Energy, Inc.
    4400 N Alafaya Trl
    Orlando FL
    407 736-2000

(P-3485)
SPIDELL PUBLISHING INC
1134 N Gilbert St (92801-1401)
P.O. Box 61044 (92803-6144)
PHONE..................................714 776-7850
Lynn Freer, Pr
EMP: 27 EST: 1975
SQ FT: 2,500
SALES (est): 5.21MM
SALES (corp-wide): 9.46MM Privately Held
Web: www.caltax.com
SIC: 2741 Guides: publishing only, not printed on site
PA: Cerifi, Llc
    3625 Brookside Pkwy # 450
    Alpharetta GA
    877 850-9291

(P-3486)
STORIES INTERNATIONAL INC
400 Corporate Pointe (90230-7615)
PHONE..................................310 242-8409
Tomoya Suzuki, CEO
EMP: 20 EST: 2013
SALES (est): 1.76MM Privately Held
Web: www.stories-llc.com
SIC: 2741 Miscellaneous publishing

(P-3487)
STUDIO SYSTEMS INC (PA)
5700 Wilshire Blvd Ste 600 (90036-3659)
PHONE..................................323 634-3400
Gary Hiller, Pr
EMP: 20 EST: 1999
SQ FT: 13,000
SALES (est): 4.42MM
SALES (corp-wide): 4.42MM Privately Held
Web: www.studiosystem.com
SIC: 2741 Miscellaneous publishing

(P-3488)
SUPERBAM INC
214 Main St (90245-3803)
PHONE..................................310 845-5784
Rian Bosak, CEO
EMP: 27 EST: 2018
SALES (est): 1.98MM Privately Held
Web: www.superbam.com
SIC: 2741 Internet publishing and broadcasting

(P-3489)
SUPERMEDIA LLC
Also Called: Verizon
3131 Katella Ave (90720-2335)
P.O. Box 3770 (90720-0377)
PHONE..................................562 594-5101
Del Humenik, Mgr
EMP: 79
SQ FT: 150,078
SALES (corp-wide): 1.2B Publicly Held
SIC: 2741 7372 2791 Directories, telephone: publishing only, not printed on site; Prepackaged software; Typesetting
HQ: Supermedia Llc
    2200 W Airfield Dr
    Dfw Airport TX
    972 453-7000

(P-3490)
TABOR COMMUNICATIONS INC
Also Called: Hpcwire
8445 Camino Santa Fe Ste 101 (92121)
PHONE..................................858 625-0070
Debra Goldfarb, Pr
Thomas Taber, Ch Bd
Lara Kisielewska, CMO
EMP: 42 EST: 2002

SQ FT: 15,000
SALES (est): 6.36MM Privately Held
Web: www.taborcommunications.com
SIC: 2741 Miscellaneous publishing

(P-3491)
TEACHER CREATED MATERIALS INC
5301 Oceanus Dr (92649-1030)
P.O. Box 1040 (92647-1040)
PHONE..................................714 891-2273
Rachelle Cracchiolo, CEO
Corinne Burton, *
Deanne Mendoza, *
Rich Levitt, *
◆ EMP: 110 EST: 1979
SQ FT: 10,000
SALES (est): 40.44MM Privately Held
Web: www.teachercreatedmaterials.com
SIC: 2741 Miscellaneous publishing

(P-3492)
TECHTURE INC
1010 Wilshire Blvd Apt 1206 (90017-5662)
PHONE..................................323 347-6209
Muhammad Zubair Khan, Pr
Chris M Joseph, *
EMP: 35 EST: 2021
SALES (est): 1.4MM Privately Held
SIC: 2741 Internet publishing and broadcasting

(P-3493)
THOMSON REUTERS CORPORATION
3280 Motor Ave Ste 200 (90034-3700)
PHONE..................................310 287-2360
Ayanna Chambliss, Brnch Mgr
EMP: 25
SQ FT: 900
SALES (corp-wide): 10.66B Publicly Held
Web: www.thomsonreuters.com
SIC: 2741 Miscellaneous publishing
HQ: Thomson Reuters Corporation
    333 Bay St
    Toronto ON
    416 687-7500

(P-3494)
THOMSON REUTERS CORPORATION
163 Albert Pl (92627-1744)
PHONE..................................949 400-7782
EMP: 19
SALES (corp-wide): 10.66B Publicly Held
Web: www.thomsonreuters.com
SIC: 2741 Miscellaneous publishing
HQ: Thomson Reuters Corporation
    333 Bay St
    Toronto ON
    416 687-7500

(P-3495)
TLM PUBLISHING INC
110 E 9th St Ste A777 (90079-1300)
PHONE..................................213 627-3737
EMP: 20 EST: 2019
SALES (est): 969.7K Privately Held
Web: www.apparelnews.net
SIC: 2741 Miscellaneous publishing

(P-3496)
TRANSWESTERN PUBLISHING COMPANY LLC
Also Called: Transwestern Publishing
8344 Clairemont Mesa Blvd (92111-1307)
PHONE..................................858 467-2800
EMP: 1869

SIC: 2741 Directories, telephone: publishing and printing

(P-3497)
UNIVERSAL MUS GROUP DIST CORP (DH)
Also Called: Umgd
2220 Colorado Ave (90404-3506)
PHONE............................310 235-4700
Jim Urie, *Pr*
Kevin Lipson, *VP*
EMP: 76 **EST:** 1989
SALES (est): 211.94MM **Privately Held**
Web: www.universalmusic.com
SIC: 2741 Miscellaneous publishing
HQ: Vivendi Holding I Llc
1755 Broadway Frnt 2
New York NY
212 445-3800

(P-3498)
UNIVERSAL MUSIC PUBLISHING INC
Also Called: Universal Christian Music Pubg
1601 Cloverfield Blvd (90404-4082)
PHONE............................310 235-4700
Jody Gerson, *CEO*
EMP: 149 **EST:** 1999
SALES (est): 16.43MM **Privately Held**
SIC: 2741 Miscellaneous publishing
HQ: Universal Music Group, Inc.
2220 Colorado Ave
Santa Monica CA
310 865-0770

(P-3499)
UPPER DECK COMPANY (PA)
5830 El Camino Real (92008-8816)
PHONE............................800 873-7332
Jason Masherah, *Pr*
Don Utic, *Treas*
EMP: 30 **EST:** 2003
SQ FT: 33,424
SALES (est): 25.3MM **Privately Held**
Web: www.upperdeck.com
SIC: 2741 Music, book: publishing and printing

(P-3500)
WARNER/CHAPPELL MUSIC INC (DH)
Also Called: Warner Geometric Music
777 S Santa Fe Ave (90021-1750)
PHONE............................310 441-8600
Cameron Strang, *CEO*
Ira Pianko, *
Jay Morgenstern, *
Brian Roberts, *
Scott Francis, *
EMP: 110 **EST:** 1984
SALES (est): 113.45MM **Publicly Held**
Web: www.warnerchappellpm.com
SIC: 2741 Music book and sheet music publishing
HQ: Warner Music Inc.
1633 Broadway
New York NY

(P-3501)
WB MUSIC CORP (DH)
10585 Santa Monica Blvd Ste 200 (90025-4950)
PHONE............................310 441-8600
Leslie Bider, *CEO*
EMP: 125 **EST:** 1994
SALES (est): 23.53MM **Publicly Held**
SIC: 2741 Music, sheet: publishing only, not printed on site
HQ: Warner Music Inc.
1633 Broadway

New York NY

(P-3502)
WEDDINGCHANNELCOM INC
5757 Wilshire Blvd Ste 504 (90036-5810)
PHONE............................213 599-4100
Adam Berger, *Pr*
Donald Drapkin, *
Greg Franchina, *CIO*
Lee Essmer, *
EMP: 247 **EST:** 1996
SQ FT: 18,000
SALES (est): 4.98MM **Privately Held**
SIC: 2741 5621 Miscellaneous publishing; Women's clothing stores
HQ: Xo Group Inc.
2 Wisconsin Cir Ste 300
Chevy Chase MD

(P-3503)
WEST PUBLISHING CORPORATION
2801 Camino Del Rio S (92108-3800)
PHONE............................619 296-7862
Wes Askins, *Brnch Mgr*
EMP: 286
SALES (corp-wide): 10.66B **Publicly Held**
Web: home.westacademic.com
SIC: 2741 Miscellaneous publishing
HQ: West Publishing Corporation
610 Opperman Dr
Eagan MN
651 687-7000

(P-3504)
YAMAGATA AMERICA INC
3760 Convoy St Ste 219 (92111-3744)
PHONE............................858 751-1010
EMP: 102 **EST:** 2009
SQ FT: 4,630
SALES (est): 1.95MM **Privately Held**
Web: www.yamagatadsa.com
SIC: 2741 Technical manuals: publishing and printing
HQ: Yamagata Holdings America, Inc.
3760 Convoy St Ste 219
San Diego CA

2752 Commercial Printing, Lithographic

(P-3505)
ACE COMMERCIAL INC
Also Called: Press Colorcom
10310 Pioneer Blvd Ste 1 (90670-3737)
PHONE............................562 946-6664
EMP: 40 **EST:** 1988
SQ FT: 22,000
SALES (est): 5.78MM **Privately Held**
Web: www.acecommercial.com
SIC: 2752 7331 2791 2789 Offset printing; Direct mail advertising services; Typesetting ; Bookbinding and related work

(P-3506)
ADVANCED COLOR GRAPHICS
Also Called: Acg Ecopack
1921 S Business Pkwy (91761-8539)
PHONE............................909 930-1500
Steve Thompson, *Pr*
Mike Mullens, *
EMP: 60 **EST:** 1992
SQ FT: 70,000
SALES (est): 8.53MM **Privately Held**
SIC: 2752 Offset printing

(P-3507)
ADVANCED VSUAL IMAGE DSIGN LLC
Also Called: Avid Ink
229 N Sherman Ave (92614)
PHONE............................951 279-2138
Jennie Enholm, *
▲ **EMP:** 44 **EST:** 1997
SQ FT: 20,000
SALES (est): 3.73MM **Privately Held**
SIC: 2752 Offset printing

(P-3508)
ALPHA PRINTING & GRAPHICS INC
12758 Schabarum Ave (91706-6801)
PHONE............................626 851-9800
Stacey Chen, *Pr*
Kelly Ngo, *CEO*
▲ **EMP:** 20 **EST:** 1990
SQ FT: 5,000
SALES (est): 2.39MM **Privately Held**
Web: www.alphaprinting.com
SIC: 2752 Offset printing

(P-3509)
AMERICAN PCF PRTRS COLLEGE INC
Also Called: Kenny The Printer
675 N Main St (92868-1103)
PHONE............................949 250-3212
TOLL FREE: 800
David Smith, *CEO*
Cal Laird, *
EMP: 36 **EST:** 1981
SALES (est): 3.99MM **Privately Held**
Web: www.westprint.com
SIC: 2752 Offset printing

(P-3510)
AMERICHIP INC (PA)
Also Called: Americhip
19032 S Vermont Ave (90248-4412)
PHONE............................310 323-3697
Timothy Clegg, *CEO*
Kevin Clegg, *Pr*
John Clegg, *VP*
Primoz Samardzija, *Ex VP*
Francis Logan, *Corporate Counsel*
▲ **EMP:** 45 **EST:** 1995
SQ FT: 30,000
SALES (est): 18.59MM
SALES (corp-wide): 18.59MM **Privately Held**
Web: www.americhip.com
SIC: 2752 Promotional printing, lithographic

(P-3511)
ANCHORED PRINTS
1199 N Grove St (92806-2110)
PHONE............................714 929-9317
Samuel I Schinhofen, *CEO*
Samuel Schinhofen, *CEO*
EMP: 23 **EST:** 2018
SALES (est): 2.34MM **Privately Held**
Web: www.anchoredprints.com
SIC: 2752 Commercial printing, lithographic

(P-3512)
ANDERSON LA INC
Also Called: Anderson Printing
3550 Tyburn St (90065-1427)
PHONE............................323 460-4115
▲ **EMP:** 95
SIC: 2752 2759 Commercial printing, lithographic; Letterpress printing

(P-3513)
APPLE GRAPHICS INC
3550 Tyburn St (90065-1427)
PHONE............................626 301-4287
EMP: 50
SIC: 2752 2791 2789 Lithographing on metal ; Typesetting; Bookbinding and related work

(P-3514)
AVION GRAPHICS INC
27192 Burbank (92610-2503)
PHONE............................949 472-0438
Craig Greiner, *Pr*
Michele Morris, *
Mary Kay Swanson, *Stockholder*
EMP: 33 **EST:** 1984
SQ FT: 6,800
SALES (est): 6.12MM **Privately Held**
Web: www.aviongraphics.com
SIC: 2752 7336 3993 5999 Decals, lithographed; Commercial art and graphic design; Signs and advertising specialties; Decals

(P-3515)
AXIOMPRINT INC
Also Called: Axiom Designs & Printing
4544 San Fernando Rd Ste 210 (91204-5014)
PHONE............................747 888-7777
Garnik Bayatyan, *CEO*
▼ **EMP:** 17 **EST:** 2009
SALES (est): 2.39MM **Privately Held**
Web: www.axiomprint.com
SIC: 2752 5999 2741 7312 Offset printing; Banners, flags, decals, and posters; Posters: publishing and printing; Poster advertising, outdoor

(P-3516)
B AND Z PRINTING INC
1300 E Wakeham Ave # B (92705-4145)
PHONE............................714 892-2000
Frank Buono, *Pr*
James Zimmer, *
EMP: 45 **EST:** 1984
SQ FT: 40,000
SALES (est): 2.68MM **Privately Held**
Web: www.bandzprinting.com
SIC: 2752 2789 Offset printing; Bookbinding and related work

(P-3517)
BARRYS PRINTING INC
Also Called: All About Printing
9005 Eton Ave Ste D (91304-1617)
PHONE............................818 998-8600
Barry Shapiro, *CEO*
EMP: 30 **EST:** 1996
SALES (est): 2.09MM **Privately Held**
Web: barrysprinting.mfgpages.com
SIC: 2752 7334 Offset printing; Photocopying and duplicating services

(P-3518)
BERT-CO INDUSTRIES INC
Also Called: Bert-Co
2150 S Parco Ave (91761-5768)
P.O. Box 4150 (91761-1068)
PHONE............................323 669-5700
▲ **EMP:** 154
SIC: 2752 Commercial printing, lithographic

(P-3519)
BIG HORN WEALTH MANAGEMENT INC
2577 Research Dr (92882-7607)
PHONE............................951 273-7900
▲ **EMP:** 64

SIC: 2752 Offset printing

(P-3520)
BOONE PRINTING & GRAPHICS INC
70 S Kellogg Ave Ste 8 (93117-6408)
PHONE..............................805 683-2349
EMP: 52 EST: 1988
SQ FT: 15,000
SALES (est): 11.63MM Privately Held
Web: www.boonegraphics.net
SIC: 2752 Offset printing

(P-3521)
BOSS LITHO INC
1544 Hauser Blvd (90019-3940)
PHONE..............................626 912-7088
Jean Paul Nataf, Pr
EMP: 48 EST: 2010
SALES (est): 8.02MM Privately Held
Web: www.bosslitho.com
SIC: 2752 Offset printing

(P-3522)
BREHM COMMUNICATIONS INC (PA)
Also Called: B C I
16644 W Bernardo Dr Ste 300 (92127-1901)
P.O. Box 28429 (92198-0429)
PHONE..............................858 451-6200
Bill Brehm Junior, Pr
Tom Taylor, *
Mona Brehm, *
W J Brehm, *
EMP: 29 EST: 1919
SQ FT: 6,000
SALES (est): 151.22MM
SALES (corp-wide): 151.22MM Privately Held
Web: www.brehmcommunications.com
SIC: 2752 2711 Offset printing; Commercial printing and newspaper publishing combined

(P-3523)
C & L GRAPHICS INC
6825 Valjean Ave (91406-4713)
PHONE..............................818 785-8310
Charles Ball, Pr
Laurie Ball, Sec
EMP: 18 EST: 1985
SQ FT: 10,500
SALES (est): 2.45MM Privately Held
Web: www.clgraphicsinc.com
SIC: 2752 Offset printing

(P-3524)
CAL SOUTHERN GRAPHICS CORP (HQ)
Also Called: California Graphics
9655 De Soto Ave (91311-5013)
PHONE..............................310 559-3600
Timothy Toomey, CEO
▲ EMP: 91 EST: 1959
SALES (est): 20.03MM
SALES (corp-wide): 23.29MM Privately Held
Web: www.socalgraph.com
SIC: 2752 2759 2754 Lithographing on metal ; Commercial printing, nec; Commercial printing, gravure
PA: Gpa Printing Ca Llc
9655 De Soto Ave
Chatsworth CA
818 237-9771

(P-3525)
CALIFORNIA OFFSET PRINTERS INC (PA)
Also Called: Cop Communications
5075 Brooks St (91763-4804)
PHONE..............................818 291-1100
TOLL FREE: 800
John Hedlund, Ch Bd
William R Rittwage, Pr
EMP: 100 EST: 1962
SQ FT: 55,000
SALES (est): 11.82MM
SALES (corp-wide): 11.82MM Privately Held
Web: www.copprints.com
SIC: 2752 2741 2721 Offset printing; Miscellaneous publishing; Periodicals

(P-3526)
CALIFORNIA PRTG SOLUTIONS INC
Also Called: Printing Solutions
1950 W Park Ave (92373-3133)
P.O. Box 11451 (92423-1451)
PHONE..............................909 307-2032
Mark Smith, Pr
▲ EMP: 18 EST: 1996
SQ FT: 20,000
SALES (est): 717.9K Privately Held
Web: www.printingsolutions.tv
SIC: 2752 Offset printing

(P-3527)
CDR GRAPHICS INC (PA)
1207 E Washington Blvd (90021-3035)
P.O. Box 15311 (90015-0311)
PHONE..............................310 474-7600
Homan Hadawi, Pr
EMP: 23 EST: 2010
SALES (est): 2.33MM
SALES (corp-wide): 2.33MM Privately Held
Web: www.cdrgraphics.com
SIC: 2752 Offset printing

(P-3528)
CHALLENGE GRAPHICS INC
7661 Densmore Ave Ste 3 (91406-2016)
PHONE..............................818 892-0123
Robert F Ritter, Pr
Sally A Ritter, *
Kathy Burtoft, *
Tara Curtis, *
EMP: 17 EST: 1975
SALES (est): 377.61K Privately Held
Web: www.challenge-graphics.com
SIC: 2752 Offset printing

(P-3529)
CHROMATIC INC LITHOGRAPHERS
127 Concord St (91203-2456)
PHONE..............................818 242-5785
Keith Sevigny, Pr
Michael Sevigny, *
Mary Gene Sevigny, *
Marlene Lunn, *
▲ EMP: 32 EST: 1969
SALES (est): 4.97MM Privately Held
Web: www.chromaticinc.com
SIC: 2752 Offset printing

(P-3530)
CLASSIC LITHO & DESIGN INC
340 Maple Ave (90503-2600)
PHONE..............................310 224-5200
Masoud Nikravan, CEO
Firouzeh Nikravan, *
EMP: 30 EST: 1976

SQ FT: 12,500
SALES (est): 6.05MM Privately Held
Web: www.classiclitho.com
SIC: 2752 Offset printing

(P-3531)
CLEAR IMAGE PRINTING INC
12744 San Fernando Rd (91342-3853)
PHONE..............................818 547-4684
Anthony Toven, Pr
EMP: 28 EST: 2007
SQ FT: 18,000
SALES (est): 4.8MM Privately Held
Web: www.clearimageprinting.com
SIC: 2752 Offset printing

(P-3532)
COLOR INC
1600 Flower St (91201-2319)
PHONE..............................818 240-1350
Barry D Hamm, Pr
James E Hamm, *
EMP: 35 EST: 1968
SQ FT: 16,000
SALES (est): 2.48MM Privately Held
Web: www.colorincorporated.com
SIC: 2752 2796 Color lithography; Platemaking services

(P-3533)
COLOR WEST INC
Also Called: Color West Printing & Packg
2228 N Hollywood Way (91505-1112)
P.O. Box 10879 (91510-0879)
PHONE..............................818 840-8881
EMP: 170
Web: www.colorwestprinting.com
SIC: 2752 Commercial printing, lithographic

(P-3534)
COLORCOM INC
2437 S Eastern Ave (90040-1414)
PHONE..............................323 246-4640
John Youn, Pr
Young Kim, Stockholder
EMP: 34 EST: 1992
SALES (est): 3.63MM Privately Held
Web: www.colorcom.net
SIC: 2752 Offset printing

(P-3535)
COLORFAST DYE & PRINT HSE INC
5075 Pacific Blvd (90058-2215)
PHONE..............................323 581-1656
Enrique Ruiz, Pr
Jose Ramos, *
EMP: 20 EST: 1999
SQ FT: 30,000
SALES (est): 467.53K Privately Held
SIC: 2752 2396 2269 Commercial printing, lithographic; Screen printing on fabric articles; Dyeing: raw stock, yarn, and narrow fabrics

(P-3536)
COLORFX INC
11050 Randall St (91352-2621)
P.O. Box 12357 (91224-5357)
PHONE..............................818 767-7671
EMP: 50 EST: 1996
SQ FT: 28,000
SALES (est): 9.55MM Privately Held
Web: www.colorfxweb.com
SIC: 2752 Offset printing

(P-3537)
COLOUR CONCEPTS INC
Also Called: Partner Printing

1225 Los Angeles St (91204-2403)
EMP: 150 EST: 1989
SQ FT: 36,000
SALES (est): 22.86MM Privately Held
Web: www.partnerprinting.com
SIC: 2752 7371 Offset printing; Computer software development

(P-3538)
COMPREHENSIVE PRINT GROUP LLC
Also Called: Westprint
675 N Main St (92868-1103)
PHONE..............................949 255-4067
Stanley K Spencer, Managing Member
EMP: 25 EST: 2020
SALES (est): 705.45K Privately Held
SIC: 2752 Commercial printing, lithographic

(P-3539)
CONTINENTAL GRAPHICS CORP
Also Called: Continental Data Graphics
9302 Pittsburgh Ave Ste 100 (91730)
PHONE..............................909 758-9800
Steve Meade, Brnch Mgr
EMP: 27
SALES (corp-wide): 66.61B Publicly Held
Web: services.boeing.com
SIC: 2752 7336 Promotional printing, lithographic; Graphic arts and related design
HQ: Continental Graphics Corporation
4060 N Lakewood Blvd # 8
Long Beach CA
714 503-4200

(P-3540)
CONTINENTAL GRAPHICS CORP
Also Called: Continental Engineering Svcs
6910 Carroll Rd (92121-2211)
PHONE..............................858 552-6520
Manuel Defaria, Brnch Mgr
EMP: 27
SALES (corp-wide): 66.61B Publicly Held
Web: services.boeing.com
SIC: 2752 7336 Promotional printing, lithographic; Graphic arts and related design
HQ: Continental Graphics Corporation
4060 N Lakewood Blvd # 8
Long Beach CA
714 503-4200

(P-3541)
CONTINENTAL GRAPHICS CORP
Also Called: Continental Data Graphics
4060 N Lakewood Blvd Bldg 801 (90808-1700)
PHONE..............................714 827-1752
Warren Smith, Mgr
EMP: 28
SALES (corp-wide): 66.61B Publicly Held
Web: services.boeing.com
SIC: 2752 7336 Promotional printing, lithographic; Graphic arts and related design
HQ: Continental Graphics Corporation
4060 N Lakewood Blvd # 8
Long Beach CA
714 503-4200

(P-3542)
CONTINENTAL GRAPHICS CORP
Also Called: Continental Data Graphics
4000 N Lakewood Blvd (90808-1700)
PHONE..............................714 503-4200
Steve Meade, Mgr
EMP: 28
SALES (corp-wide): 66.61B Publicly Held
Web: services.boeing.com
SIC: 2752 Promotional printing, lithographic
HQ: Continental Graphics Corporation
4060 N Lakewood Blvd # 8

Long Beach CA
714 503-4200

(P-3543)
CONTINENTAL GRAPHICS CORP
Also Called: Continental Data Graphics
222 N Pacific Coast Hwy Ste 300
(90245-5648)
PHONE..............................310 662-2307
Mike Parvin, *Mgr*
EMP: 27
SALES (corp-wide): 66.61B **Publicly Held**
Web: services.boeing.com
SIC: 2752 7336 Promotional printing,
lithographic; Graphic arts and related design
HQ: Continental Graphics Corporation
4060 N Lakewood Blvd # 8
Long Beach CA
714 503-4200

(P-3544)
CONTINENTAL LITHO INC
1360 Park Center Dr (92081-8300)
PHONE..............................760 598-0291
Stephen Tomacelli, *Pr*
Stephen Tomacelli, *Pr*
EMP: 21 **EST:** 1988
SQ FT: 37,000
SALES (est): 447.77K **Privately Held**
Web: www.continental-litho.com
SIC: 2752 Offset printing

(P-3545)
COPY SOLUTIONS INC
919 S Fremont Ave Ste 398 (91803-4701)
PHONE..............................323 307-0900
Roger Zhao, *Pr*
EMP: 20 **EST:** 1995
SQ FT: 5,000
SALES (est): 2.42MM **Privately Held**
Web: www.copysolution.com
SIC: 2752 Offset printing

(P-3546)
**CORPORATE GRAPHICS &
PRINTING**
335 Science Dr (93021-2092)
PHONE..............................805 529-5333
Harry A Stidham, *Pr*
Harry Stidham, *Pr*
EMP: 17 **EST:** 2002
SQ FT: 20,000
SALES (est): 3MM **Privately Held**
Web: www.corgfx.com
SIC: 2752 Offset printing

(P-3547)
**CORPORATE GRAPHICS INTL
INC**
Also Called: Corporate Graphics West
4909 Alcoa Ave (90058-3022)
PHONE..............................323 826-3440
Robert Gonynor, *Genl Mgr*
EMP: 65
SALES (corp-wide): 3.81B **Privately Held**
Web: www.taylor.com
SIC: 2752 2759 Offset printing; Embossing
on paper
HQ: Corporate Graphics International, Inc.
1750 Tower Blvd
North Mankato MN

(P-3548)
**COYLE REPRODUCTIONS INC
(PA)**
2850 Orbiter St (92821-6224)
PHONE..............................866 269-5373
Frank T Cutrone Junior, *CEO*
Frank T Cutrone, *Ch Bd*

EMP: 112 **EST:** 1963
SQ FT: 85,000
SALES (est): 23.45MM
SALES (corp-wide): 23.45MM **Privately
Held**
Web: www.coylerepro.com
SIC: 2752 2759 Offset printing; Screen
printing

(P-3549)
CREATIVE PRESS LLC (PA)
Also Called: Creative Press
1350 S Caldwell Cir (92805-6408)
PHONE..............................714 774-5060
EMP: 29 **EST:** 2007
SQ FT: 31,000
SALES (est): 9.26MM **Privately Held**
Web: www.creativepressinc.net
SIC: 2752 2791 2789 Offset printing;
Typesetting; Bookbinding and related work

(P-3550)
CREATIVE PRESS LLC
1600 E Ball Rd (92805-5990)
PHONE..............................714 774-5060
EMP: 36
Web: www.creativepressinc.net
SIC: 2752 2791 2789 Offset printing;
Typesetting; Bookbinding and related work
PA: Creative Press, L.L.C.
1350 S Caldwell Cir
Anaheim CA

(P-3551)
CRESCENT INC
Also Called: Print Printing
670 S Jefferson St (92870-6638)
PHONE..............................714 992-6030
Reza Mohkami, *Pr*
Ira Heshmati, *
Tahereh Mohkami, *
EMP: 25 **EST:** 1980
SALES (est): 2.04MM **Privately Held**
Web: www.csitx.com
SIC: 2752 7549 Offset printing; Do-it-
yourself garages

(P-3552)
CRESTEC USA INC
Also Called: Crestec Los Angeles
2410 Mira Mar Ave (90815-1756)
PHONE..............................310 327-9000
Takeomi Kurisawa, *CEO*
Mike Burk, *
▲ **EMP:** 50 **EST:** 1967
SALES (est): 10.26MM **Privately Held**
Web: www.crestecusa.com
SIC: 2752 Offset printing
PA: Crestec Inc.
69, Higashimikatacho, Kita-Ku
Hamamatsu SZO

(P-3553)
CRT COLOR PRINTING INC
Also Called: C R T
13201 Barton Cir (90670)
PHONE..............................562 906-1517
Yo Yo, *CEO*
Rosanna Tung, *Pr*
Roger Tung, *VP*
EMP: 17 **EST:** 1996
SQ FT: 14,000
SALES (est): 537.48K **Privately Held**
SIC: 2752 Offset printing

(P-3554)
CYU LITHOGRAPHICS INC
Also Called: Choice Lithographics
6951 Oran Cir (90621-3305)
PHONE..............................888 878-9898

Michael Wang, *Pr*
▲ **EMP:** 25 **EST:** 1983
SQ FT: 13,000
SALES (est): 3.3MM **Privately Held**
SIC: 2752 2721 Color lithography;
Magazines: publishing only, not printed on
site

(P-3555)
D & J PRINTING INC
Also Called: Bang Printing
600 W Technology Dr (93551-3748)
PHONE..............................661 265-1995
EMP: 59
SALES (corp-wide): 654.01MM **Privately
Held**
Web: www.sheridan.com
SIC: 2752 Offset printing
HQ: D. & J. Printing, Inc.
3323 Oak St
Brainerd MN
218 829-2877

(P-3556)
DAVID B ANDERSON
Also Called: Central Coast Printing
174 Suburban Rd Ste 100 (93401-7522)
PHONE..............................805 489-0661
David B Anderson, *Owner*
EMP: 26 **EST:** 1978
SALES (est): 2MM **Privately Held**
SIC: 2752 Offset printing

(P-3557)
**DELTA PRINTING SOLUTIONS
INC**
28210 Avenue Stanford (91355-3983)
PHONE..............................661 257-0584
Tony Richardson, *Pr*
EMP: 130 **EST:** 2003
SQ FT: 100,000
SALES (est): 9.1MM **Privately Held**
Web: www.deltaprintingsolutions.com
SIC: 2752 Offset printing

(P-3558)
**DENNIS BOLTON ENTERPRISES
INC**
7285 Coldwater Canyon Ave (91605-4204)
PHONE..............................818 982-1800
Dennis Bolton, *Pr*
Max Guerrero, *VP*
Carlo Bernal, *Sec*
Osvaldo Acosta, *Treas*
EMP: 17 **EST:** 1971
SQ FT: 14,780
SALES (est): 655.33K **Privately Held**
Web: www.printingbydbe.com
SIC: 2752 7334 7311 Offset printing;
Photocopying and duplicating services;
Advertising consultant

(P-3559)
DIEGO & SON PRINTING INC
2277 National Ave (92113-3614)
P.O. Box 13100 (92170-3100)
PHONE..............................619 233-5373
Nicholas Aguilera, *Pr*
Rebecca Aguilera, *VP*
Isabelle Aguilera, *Sec*
EMP: 22 **EST:** 1972
SALES (est): 2.14MM **Privately Held**
Web: www.diegoandson.com
SIC: 2752 2759 Offset printing; Commercial
printing, nec

(P-3560)
DIGITAL ONE COLOR
13367 Kirkham Way Ste 110 (92064-7118)

PHONE..............................858 576-3600
Kathreen Moebius, *CEO*
Michael Uriell, *Prin*
Paul Moebius, *Pr*
EMP: 17 **EST:** 2005
SALES (est): 925.28K **Privately Held**
Web: www.dpidirect.com
SIC: 2752 Offset printing

(P-3561)
**DIGITAL PRINTING SYSTEMS
INC (PA)**
2350 Panorama Ter (90039-2536)
PHONE..............................626 815-1888
Donald J Nores, *Ch*
Donald J Nores, *Ch Bd*
Peter Young, *
Jim Nores, *
Joyce Nores, *
◆ **EMP:** 68 **EST:** 1971
SALES (est): 8.36MM
SALES (corp-wide): 8.36MM **Privately
Held**
Web: www.digifab.com
SIC: 2752 Offset printing

(P-3562)
DIGITAL SUPERCOLOR INC
Also Called: Supercolor
PHONE..............................949 622-0010
▲ **EMP:** 55
Web: www.supercolor.com
SIC: 2752 7336 2759 Commercial printing,
lithographic; Commercial art and graphic
design; Commercial printing, nec

(P-3563)
DIGITALPRO INC
Also Called: Dpi Direct
13257 Kirkham Way (92064-7116)
PHONE..............................858 874-7750
Sam Mousavi, *Pr*
Mohammed Khaki, *
Paul Moebius, *Development**
EMP: 65 **EST:** 2001
SQ FT: 38,000
SALES (est): 12.6MM **Privately Held**
Web: www.dpidirect.com
SIC: 2752 Offset printing

(P-3564)
DOCUMOTION RESEARCH INC
Also Called: Stickypos
2020 S Eastwood Ave (92705-5208)
PHONE..............................714 662-3800
EMP: 17 **EST:** 2010
SQ FT: 10,000
SALES (est): 3.23MM **Privately Held**
Web: www.documotionresearch.com
SIC: 2752 Commercial printing, lithographic

(P-3565)
DOT CORP
1801 S Standard Ave (92707-2465)
PHONE..............................714 708-5960
EMP: 39
SALES (corp-wide): 3.01MM **Privately
Held**
Web: www.thedotcorp.com
SIC: 2752 Offset printing
PA: The Dot Corp
2525 Pullman St
Santa Ana CA
714 708-5800

(P-3566)
DOT PRINTER INC (PA)
2424 Mcgaw Ave (92614-5834)
PHONE..............................949 474-1100
Bruce M Carson, *Pr*

P
R
O
D
U
C
T
S

&

S
V
C
S

Jim Voss, *
Stan Lowe, *
▲ **EMP:** 95 **EST:** 1980
SQ FT: 40,000
SALES (est): 39.35MM
SALES (corp-wide): 39.35MM **Privately Held**
Web: www.thedotcorp.com
SIC: 2752 2732 3555 Offset printing; Book printing; Printing trades machinery

(P-3567)
EARTH PRINT INC
Also Called: Cr Print
31115 Via Colinas Ste 301 (91362-4507)
PHONE.........................818 879-6050
Jim Friedl, *Pr*
Edward Corridori, *Sec*
EMP: 19 **EST:** 1994
SQ FT: 7,500
SALES (est): 2.42MM **Privately Held**
Web: www.crprint.com
SIC: 2752 7334 Offset printing; Photocopying and duplicating services

(P-3568)
ECLIPSE PRTG & GRAPHICS LLC
Also Called: James Litho
4462 E Airport Dr (91761-7804)
PHONE.........................909 390-2452
Jeff James, *Mgr*
Jeff James, *Managing Member*
EMP: 23 **EST:** 1999
SQ FT: 25,000
SALES (est): 3.49MM **Privately Held**
Web: www.jameslitho.com
SIC: 2752 Offset printing

(P-3569)
ELITE 4 PRINT INC
851 E Walnut St (90746-1214)
PHONE.........................310 366-1344
▲ **EMP:** 20 **EST:** 2008
SALES (est): 2.25MM **Privately Held**
Web: www.elite4print.com
SIC: 2752 Offset printing

(P-3570)
ELUM DESIGNS INC
Also Called: Elum
8969 Kenamar Dr Ste 113 (92121-2441)
PHONE.........................858 650-3586
Bradley Foster, *CEO*
Melissa Foster, *
▲ **EMP:** 27 **EST:** 2001
SALES (est): 4.69MM **Privately Held**
Web: www.elumdesigns.com
SIC: 2752 Offset printing

(P-3571)
FB PRODUCTIONS INC
12722 Riverside Dr Ste 204 (91607)
PHONE.........................818 773-9337
Frank Barbarino, *Pr*
Jerry Cheney, *
David Wohl, *
EMP: 28 **EST:** 1989
SQ FT: 60,000
SALES (est): 1.02MM **Privately Held**
SIC: 2752 2675 Offset printing; Die-cut paper and board

(P-3572)
FGS-WI LLC
5401 Jurupa St (91761-3621)
PHONE.........................909 467-8300
Ron Roger, *Mgr*
EMP: 21
SALES (corp-wide): 101.33MM **Privately Held**

Web: www.fgs.com
SIC: 2752 Offset printing
HQ: Fgs-Wi, Llc
1101 S Janesville St
Milton WI
608 373-6500

(P-3573)
FIREBRAND MEDIA LLC
Also Called: Laguna Beach Magazine
900 Glenneyre St (92651-2707)
PHONE.........................949 715-4100
Vincent Zepezauer, *Managing Member*
Steve Zepezauer, *CEO*
Carrie Robles, *Dir*
Cindy Mendaros, *Off Mgr*
EMP: 17 **EST:** 2015
SALES (est): 2.77MM **Privately Held**
Web: www.firebrandmediainc.com
SIC: 2752 Commercial printing, lithographic

(P-3574)
FISHER PRINTING INC (PA)
2257 N Pacific St (92865-2615)
PHONE.........................714 998-9200
Thomas Fischer, *Ch*
Will Fischer, *
Tom Scarpati, *
EMP: 150 **EST:** 1933
SQ FT: 60,000
SALES (est): 60.13MM
SALES (corp-wide): 60.13MM **Privately Held**
Web: www.gofisher.net
SIC: 2752 Offset printing

(P-3575)
FOSTER PRINTING COMPANY INC
700 E Alton Ave (92705-5610)
PHONE.........................714 731-2000
Dennis M Blackburn, *CEO*
EMP: 47 **EST:** 1988
SQ FT: 35,000
SALES (est): 6.73MM **Privately Held**
Web: www.fosterprint.com
SIC: 2752 Offset printing

(P-3576)
FRANCHISE SERVICES INC (PA)
26722 Plaza (92691-8051)
PHONE.........................949 348-5400
Don F Lowe, *Ch Bd*
Daniel J Conger, *CFO*
EMP: 20 **EST:** 1968
SQ FT: 44,000
SALES (est): 19.99MM
SALES (corp-wide): 19.99MM **Privately Held**
Web: www.franserv.com
SIC: 2752 6159 Commercial printing, lithographic; Machinery and equipment finance leasing

(P-3577)
G PRINTING INC
1815 Ayers Way (91501-1106)
PHONE.........................818 246-1156
George Ouzounian, *Pr*
John Melkonian, *VP*
EMP: 18 **EST:** 1974
SALES (est): 636.07K **Privately Held**
SIC: 2752 Offset printing

(P-3578)
GEORGE CORIATY
Also Called: Sir Speedy
7240 Greenleaf Ave (90602-1312)
PHONE.........................562 698-7513
George Coriaty, *Owner*

EMP: 32 **EST:** 1979
SQ FT: 12,000
SALES (est): 4.28MM **Privately Held**
Web: www.sirspeedy.com
SIC: 2752 7334 Commercial printing, lithographic; Photocopying and duplicating services

(P-3579)
GOLDEN COLOR PRINTING INC
9353 Rush St (91733-2544)
PHONE.........................626 455-0850
EMP: 19 **EST:** 1996
SQ FT: 11,000
SALES (est): 478.26K **Privately Held**
Web: www.goldencolorprinting.com
SIC: 2752 Color lithography

(P-3580)
GRAPHIC COLOR SYSTEMS INC
Also Called: Continental Colorcraft
1166 W Garvey Ave (91754-2511)
PHONE.........................323 283-3000
Andy Scheidegger, *Pr*
Linda Clarke, *
Maria Donhauser, *
EMP: 52 **EST:** 1968
SQ FT: 28,000
SALES (est): 7.93MM **Privately Held**
Web: www.continentalcolorcraft.com
SIC: 2752 2796 2791 2759 Offset printing; Color separations, for printing; Typesetting; Commercial printing, nec

(P-3581)
GRAPHIC VISIONS INC
7119 Fair Ave (91605-6304)
PHONE.........................818 845-8393
Randall Avazian, *CEO*
Kenneth Langer, *
▲ **EMP:** 23 **EST:** 1940
SALES (est): 4.36MM **Privately Held**
Web: www.graphicvisionsla.com
SIC: 2752 Offset printing

(P-3582)
GSG PRINTING INC (PA)
Also Called: Golden State Graphics
2304 Faraday Ave (92008-7216)
PHONE.........................760 752-9500
David Hyman, *
▲ **EMP:** 20 **EST:** 2000
SALES (est): 2.28MM
SALES (corp-wide): 2.28MM **Privately Held**
Web: www.goldenstategraphics.com
SIC: 2752 Offset printing

(P-3583)
GW REED PRINTING INC
4071 Greystone Dr (91761-3100)
PHONE.........................909 947-0599
EMP: 40
SIC: 2752 7336 Offset printing; Commercial art and graphic design

(P-3584)
HANDBILL PRINTERS LP
Also Called: Handbill Printers
820 E Parkridge Ave (92879-6611)
PHONE.........................951 547-5910
Don J Messick, *Pr*
Kenneth Messick, *Pt*
Michael Messick, *Pt*
Mark Messick, *Pt*
Dane Messick, *Pt*
EMP: 45 **EST:** 1984
SQ FT: 62,500
SALES (est): 8.94MM **Privately Held**
Web: www.handbillprinters.com

SIC: 2752 7336 Offset printing; Graphic arts and related design

(P-3585)
HARMAN PRESS INC
Also Called: Harman Envelopes
6840 Vineland Ave (91605-6409)
PHONE.........................818 432-0570
Jay Goldner, *Pr*
Phillip Goldner, *
Deborah Goldner-watson, *Sec*
EMP: 38 **EST:** 1963
SQ FT: 10,000
SALES (est): 6.37MM **Privately Held**
Web: www.harmanpress.com
SIC: 2752 Offset printing

(P-3586)
HIGH FIVE INC
Also Called: Printech
625 Fee Ana St (92870-6704)
PHONE.........................714 847-2200
Steve Kramer, *Pr*
Katherine Kramer, *
▼ **EMP:** 20 **EST:** 1987
SALES (est): 2.25MM **Privately Held**
Web: www.printechusa.com
SIC: 2752 Offset printing

(P-3587)
HOUSE OF PRINTING INC
3336 E Colorado Blvd (91107-3885)
PHONE.........................626 793-7034
Eugene F Pittroff Senior, *Pr*
Walter E Pittroff, *VP*
Edna Pittroff, *Sec*
Marguerite Pittroff, *Treas*
EMP: 22 **EST:** 1942
SQ FT: 6,500
SALES (est): 2.32MM **Privately Held**
Web: www.thehouseofprinting.com
SIC: 2752 2791 2789 Offset printing; Typesetting; Bookbinding and related work

(P-3588)
IDEAL PRINTING COMPANY
17855 Maclaren St (91744-5799)
PHONE.........................626 964-2019
Richard Mancino, *Pr*
Yolanda Mancino, *VP*
EMP: 20 **EST:** 1961
SQ FT: 30,000
SALES (est): 1.9MM **Privately Held**
Web: www.idealprintingcompany.com
SIC: 2752 Offset printing

(P-3589)
IKONICK LLC
705 W 9th St Apt 1404 (90015-1696)
PHONE.........................516 680-7765
Mark Mastrandrea, *Pr*
EMP: 35 **EST:** 2017
SALES (est): 2.4MM **Privately Held**
Web: www.ikonick.com
SIC: 2752 7336 Commercial printing, lithographic; Commercial art and graphic design

(P-3590)
IMAGEMOVER INC
13031 Bradley Ave (91342-3832)
PHONE.........................818 485-8840
EMP: 17 **EST:** 2009
SALES (est): 3.24MM **Privately Held**
Web: www.imagemoverinc.com
SIC: 2752 Commercial printing, lithographic

▲ = Import ▼ = Export
◆ = Import/Export

(P-3591)
IMAGIC
2810 N Lima St (91504-2510)
PHONE......................818 333-1670
EMP: 59
SIC: 2752 Commercial printing, lithographic

(P-3592)
IMPACT PRINTING & GRAPHICS
15150 Sierra Bonita Ln (91710-8903)
PHONE......................909 614-1678
Bill Mcginley, *Pr*
EMP: 25 EST: 1995
SQ FT: 14,000
SALES (est): 2.37MM **Privately Held**
Web: www.impactpkgco.com
SIC: 2752 Offset printing

(P-3593)
IMPERIAL PRINTERS (PA)
Also Called: Imperial Printers Rocket Copy
430 W Main St (92243-3019)
PHONE......................760 352-4374
Rudy Rodgruegos, *Pr*
Marvin Wieben Junior, *VP*
Rodolfo Rodriguez, *VP*
EMP: 18 EST: 1977
SQ FT: 8,725
SALES (est): 2.37MM
SALES (corp-wide): 2.37MM **Privately Held**
Web: www.imperialprinters.com
SIC: 2752 2796 Offset printing; Letterpress plates, preparation of

(P-3594)
IMPRESS COMMUNICATIONS INC
9320 Lurline Ave (91311-6041)
PHONE......................818 701-8800
Paul Marino, *CEO*
▲ EMP: 92 EST: 1974
SQ FT: 50,000
SALES (est): 16.5MM **Privately Held**
Web: www.impress1.com
SIC: 2752 7336 7319 Offset printing; Commercial art and graphic design; Display advertising service

(P-3595)
INK & COLOR INC
Also Called: Acuprint
5920 Bowcroft St (90016-4302)
PHONE......................310 280-6060
Saman Sowlaty, *CEO*
Mojgan Sowalty, *
▲ EMP: 30 EST: 1985
SQ FT: 17,000
SALES (est): 4.63MM **Privately Held**
Web: www.acuprint.net
SIC: 2752 Offset printing

(P-3596)
INK SPOT INC
9737 Bell Ranch Dr (90670-2951)
PHONE......................626 338-4500
Somsak Reuanglith, *CEO*
EMP: 26 EST: 2004
SALES (est): 4.66MM **Privately Held**
Web: www.inkspotinc.com
SIC: 2752 Offset printing

(P-3597)
INKOVATION INC
13659 Excelsior Dr (90670-5103)
PHONE......................800 465-4174
Janak Savaliya, *Pr*
EMP: 17 EST: 2010
SALES (est): 864.3K **Privately Held**
Web: www.inkovation.net
SIC: 2752 Offset printing

(P-3598)
INKWRIGHT LLC
5822 Research Dr (92649-1348)
PHONE......................714 892-3300
EMP: 30 EST: 2010
SALES (est): 2.3MM **Privately Held**
Web: www.inkwright.com
SIC: 2752 Offset and photolithographic printing

(P-3599)
INLAND LITHO LLC
Also Called: Inland Group
4305 E La Palma Ave (92807-1843)
PHONE......................714 993-6000
Kathy Urbanovitch, *
EMP: 60 EST: 1984
SQ FT: 40,000
SALES (est): 9.15MM **Privately Held**
Web: www.inlandgroupllc.com
SIC: 2752 Offset printing

(P-3600)
INSTANT IMPRINTS FRANCHISING
7310 Miramar Rd (92126-4225)
PHONE......................858 642-4848
Leo Kats, *Pr*
Lev Kats, *CEO*
EMP: 18 EST: 2001
SALES (est): 466.75K **Privately Held**
Web: www.instantimprints.com
SIC: 2752 Commercial printing, lithographic

(P-3601)
INSTANT WEB LLC
Also Called: Iwco Direct - Downey
7300 Flores St (90242-4010)
PHONE......................562 658-2020
Jake Hertel, *Brnch Mgr*
EMP: 112
SALES (corp-wide): 6.55B **Privately Held**
Web: www.iwco.com
SIC: 2752 Commercial printing, lithographic
HQ: Instant Web, Llc
7951 Powers Blvd
Chanhassen MN
952 474-0961

(P-3602)
INSUA GRAPHICS INCORPORATED
9121 Glenoaks Blvd (91352-2612)
PHONE......................818 767-7007
Jose Miguel Insua, *CEO*
Eric Insua, *
Albert Insua, *
◆ EMP: 35 EST: 1996
SQ FT: 28,000
SALES (est): 5.08MM **Privately Held**
Web: www.insua.com
SIC: 2752 Offset printing

(P-3603)
INTEGRATED COMMUNICATIONS INC
208 N Broadway (92701-4863)
PHONE......................310 851-8066
Peter Levshin, *CEO*
David Humphrey, *
▲ EMP: 24 EST: 1986
SALES (est): 2.34MM **Privately Held**
Web: www.icla.com
SIC: 2752 Commercial printing, lithographic

(P-3604)
INTERLINK INC
Also Called: Precision Plastics Packaging
3845 E Coronado St (92807-1606)
PHONE......................714 905-7700
Bob Bhagat, *Pr*
Hathin Bhagat, *
▲ EMP: 85 EST: 1963
SQ FT: 50,000
SALES (est): 18MM **Privately Held**
Web: www.pppc.com
SIC: 2752 Commercial printing, lithographic

(P-3605)
JA FERRARI PRINT IMAGING LLC
Also Called: Allegra Print & Imaging
7515 Metropolitan Dr Ste 405 (92108)
PHONE......................619 295-8307
EMP: 19 EST: 2006
SALES (est): 1.65MM **Privately Held**
Web: www.allegramarketingprint.com
SIC: 2752 Offset printing

(P-3606)
JD BUSINESS SOLUTIONS INC
Also Called: Printing Impressions
1351 Holiday Hill Rd (93117-1815)
P.O. Box 1729 (93116-1729)
PHONE......................805 962-8193
James Denion, *Pr*
Michael Gregory, *Prin*
Jeannine Denion, *Sec*
EMP: 25 EST: 1982
SQ FT: 9,000
SALES (est): 759.85K **Privately Held**
SIC: 2752 Offset printing

(P-3607)
JEFF LANE
Also Called: Pj Printers
1530 Lakeview Loop (92807)
PHONE......................714 779-8484
EMP: 45 EST: 1983
SALES (est): 6.69MM **Privately Held**
Web: www.pjprinters.com
SIC: 2752 Commercial printing, lithographic

(P-3608)
K-1 PACKAGING GROUP
Also Called: K-1 Packaging Group
2001 W Mission Blvd (91766-1020)
PHONE......................626 964-9384
EMP: 134
Web: www.k1packaging.com
SIC: 2752 Offset and photolithographic printing
PA: K-1 Packaging Group Llc
17989 Arenth Ave
City Of Industry CA

(P-3609)
K-1 PACKAGING GROUP LLC (PA)
17989 Arenth Ave (91748-1126)
PHONE......................626 964-9384
Mike Tsai, *Pr*
◆ EMP: 77 EST: 1992
SALES (est): 22.96MM **Privately Held**
Web: www.k1packaging.com
SIC: 2752 Offset and photolithographic printing

(P-3610)
K2 LABEL & PRINTING INC
633 Great Bend Dr (91765-2034)
PHONE......................626 922-8108
Jack Dam, *Brnch Mgr*
EMP: 21

SALES (corp-wide): 236K **Privately Held**
SIC: 2752 Commercial printing, lithographic
PA: K2 Label & Printing, Inc.
23535 Palomino Dr
Diamond Bar CA

(P-3611)
KELMSCOTT COMMUNICATIONS LLC
Also Called: Orange County Printing
2485 Da Vinci (92614-5844)
PHONE......................949 475-1900
Paz Calaci, *Brnch Mgr*
EMP: 320
SALES (corp-wide): 15B **Privately Held**
Web: www.rrd.com
SIC: 2752 Offset printing
HQ: Kelmscott Communications Llc
5858 Westheimer Rd # 410
Houston TX
713 787-0977

(P-3612)
KINDRED LITHO INCORPORATED
10833 Bell Ct (91730-4835)
PHONE......................909 944-4015
Kurt Kindred, *Pr*
Cherie Kindred, *Sec*
EMP: 26 EST: 1971
SQ FT: 8,000
SALES (est): 2.09MM **Privately Held**
Web: www.kindredcorp.com
SIC: 2752 Offset printing

(P-3613)
KM PRINTING PRODUCTION INC
218 Longden Ave (91706-1328)
PHONE......................626 821-0008
Chim Moon Ming, *Pr*
Kerwin Ngo, *VP*
Wendy Lui, *Acctg Mgr*
EMP: 18 EST: 1994
SQ FT: 600
SALES (est): 2.32MM **Privately Held**
Web: www.kmppi.com
SIC: 2752 Offset printing

(P-3614)
KOVIN CORPORATION INC
Also Called: Neb Cal Printing
9240 Mira Este Ct (92126-6336)
PHONE......................858 558-0100
Mervin Kodesh, *Pr*
Sandra Kodesh, *
Debbie Dykstra, *
EMP: 30 EST: 1984
SQ FT: 10,000
SALES (est): 2.08MM **Privately Held**
SIC: 2752 2789 Offset printing; Bookbinding and related work

(P-3615)
L & L PRINTERS CARLSBAD LLC
Also Called: Specialist Media Group
6200 Yarrow Dr (92011-1537)
PHONE......................760 477-0321
William Anderson, *Pr*
EMP: 50 EST: 2006
SALES (est): 9.34MM **Privately Held**
Web: www.llprinters.com
SIC: 2752 Offset printing

(P-3616)
L T LITHO & PRINTING CO
16811 Noyes Ave (92606-5122)
PHONE......................949 466-8584
Craig Thomas, *Pr*

Mark Thomas, *CEO*
EMP: 22 **EST:** 1970
SQ FT: 16,000
SALES (est): 598.7K **Privately Held**
Web: www.expiredwixdomain.com
SIC: 2752 2759 Offset printing; Commercial
printing, nec

(P-3617)
LA PRINTING & GRAPHICS INC
Also Called: L A Press
13951 S Main St (90061-2140)
PHONE...................................310 527-4526
Kevin Sheu Chhim Kaing, *CEO*
Sheu C Kevin Kaing, *
Lor Yik, *Corporate Secretary*
EMP: 26 **EST:** 1989
SQ FT: 32,000
SALES (est): 2.22MM **Privately Held**
SIC: 2752 Offset printing

(P-3618)
LABORLAWCENTER LLC
Also Called: Laborlawcenter.com
1651 E Saint Andrew Pl (92705-4932)
PHONE...................................800 745-9970
Duyen La, *Pr*
EMP: 25 **EST:** 2004
SALES (est): 3.05MM **Privately Held**
Web: www.laborlawcenter.com
SIC: 2752 Commercial printing, lithographic

(P-3619)
LAVA PRODUCTS INC
Also Called: Lava Products
2358 E Walnut Ave (92831-4937)
PHONE...................................949 951-7191
Michael Freitas, *CEO*
▲ **EMP:** 22 **EST:** 1997
SALES (est): 4.73MM **Privately Held**
Web: www.lavapartners.com
SIC: 2752 Offset printing

(P-3620)
LAYTON PRINTING & MAILING
Also Called: Layton Printing
1538 Arrow Hwy (91750-5318)
PHONE...................................909 592-4419
Michael Layton, *Pr*
Mary Ellen Layton, *Sec*
EMP: 18 **EST:** 1996
SQ FT: 20,000
SALES (est): 2.47MM **Privately Held**
Web: www.laytonprinting.com
SIC: 2752 Offset printing

(P-3621)
LEGAL VISION GROUP LLC
2030 Paddock Ln (92860-2663)
PHONE...................................310 945-5550
EMP: 30 **EST:** 2018
SALES (est): 1.26MM **Privately Held**
SIC: 2752 7389 7374 7335 Commercial
printing, lithographic; Mailing and
messenger services; Data processing and
preparation; Commercial photography

(P-3622)
LESTER LITHOGRAPH INC
1128 N Gilbert St (92801-1401)
PHONE...................................714 491-3981
Robert Miller, *CEO*
Georgiana Lester, *
Larry Lester, *
Larita Miller, *
James Jim Witt, *VP*
EMP: 50 **EST:** 1980
SQ FT: 25,000
SALES (est): 5.38MM **Privately Held**
Web: www.lesterlitho.com

SIC: 2752 Offset printing

(P-3623)
LICHER DIRECT MAIL INC
980 Seco St (91103-2816)
PHONE...................................626 795-3333
Wayne Licher Senior, *Pr*
Wayne Licher Junior, *VP*
Besse Licher, *Sec*
EMP: 33 **EST:** 1946
SQ FT: 17,000
SALES (est): 4.84MM **Privately Held**
Web: www.licherdm.com
SIC: 2752 7331 Offset printing; Direct mail
advertising services

(P-3624)
LITHOGRAPHIX INC (PA)
12250 Crenshaw Blvd (90250-3332)
PHONE...................................323 770-1000
Herbert Zebrack, *Pr*
Jeffrey Zebrack, *
Victor Wolfe, *
▲ **EMP:** 305 **EST:** 1949
SQ FT: 250,000
SALES (est): 50.19MM
SALES (corp-wide): 50.19MM **Privately
Held**
Web: www.lithographix.com
SIC: 2752 2759 Offset printing; Commercial
printing, nec

(P-3625)
LIVING WAY INDUSTRIES INC
Also Called: Creative Graphic Services
20734 Centre Pointe Pkwy (91350-2966)
PHONE...................................661 298-3200
Ronald Niner, *Pr*
Charlene E Niner, *Sec*
EMP: 18 **EST:** 1970
SQ FT: 22,500
SALES (est): 2.44MM **Privately Held**
Web: www.creativegraphicservices.com
SIC: 2752 Commercial printing, lithographic

(P-3626)
LOMBARD ENTERPRISES INC
Also Called: Lombard Graphics
3619 San Gabriel River Pkwy (90660-1403)
PHONE...................................562 692-7070
EMP: 20 **EST:** 1993
SQ FT: 10,000
SALES (est): 2.46MM **Privately Held**
Web: www.lombardgraphics.com
SIC: 2752 Offset printing

(P-3627)
MADISN/GRHAM CLOR GRAPHICS INC
Also Called: Colorgraphics
150 N Myers St (90033-2109)
PHONE...................................323 261-7171
Cappy Childs, *CEO*
Arthur Bell, *
Chris Madison, *
Terry Bell, *
▲ **EMP:** 380 **EST:** 1953
SQ FT: 96,000
SALES (est): 21.39MM **Privately Held**
Web: www.colorgraphics.com
SIC: 2752 7336 2796 Offset printing;
Graphic arts and related design;
Platemaking services

(P-3628)
MAIL HANDLING GROUP INC
Also Called: Mail Handling Services
2840 Madonna Dr (92835-1830)
PHONE...................................952 975-5000
Brian Ostenso, *President COOC*

Michael Murphy, *
EMP: 120 **EST:** 1977
SALES (est): 9.98MM **Privately Held**
SIC: 2752 7331 7374 Offset printing; Mailing
service; Data processing service

(P-3629)
MAN-GROVE INDUSTRIES INC
Also Called: Lithocraft Co
1201 N Miller St (92806-1933)
PHONE...................................714 630-3020
EMP: 64
Web: www.lithocraft-files.com
SIC: 2752 Offset printing

(P-3630)
MARINA GRAPHIC CENTER INC
Also Called: Brotherwise Games
12901 Cerise Ave (90250-5520)
PHONE...................................310 970-1777
EMP: 115 **EST:** 1964
SALES (est): 17.53MM **Privately Held**
Web: www.marinagraphics.com
SIC: 2752 Offset printing

(P-3631)
MARRS PRINTING INC
Also Called: Mars Printing and Packaging
860 Tucker Ln (91789-2914)
PHONE...................................909 594-9459
Walter H Marrs, *CEO*
Scott Marrs, *
Teresa Grisby, *
Jackie Marrs, *
EMP: 82 **EST:** 1971
SQ FT: 27,000
SALES (est): 9.96MM **Privately Held**
Web: www.marrs.com
SIC: 2752 Offset printing

(P-3632)
MATSUDA HOUSE PRINTING INC
Also Called: B & G House of Printing
1825 W 169th St Ste A (90247-5270)
PHONE...................................310 532-1533
Benjamin Matsuda, *CEO*
Darren Matsuda, *
Patsy Matsuda, *
▲ **EMP:** 31 **EST:** 1975
SALES (est): 2.39MM **Privately Held**
Web: www.bgprinting.com
SIC: 2752 Lithographing on metal

(P-3633)
MEKONG PRINTING INC
Also Called: Mk Printing
2421 W 1st St (92703-3509)
PHONE...................................714 558-9595
Hoan Truong, *CEO*
Hoan Truong, *Pr*
Nancy Luu, *VP*
EMP: 22 **EST:** 1986
SQ FT: 20,000
SALES (est): 2.16MM **Privately Held**
SIC: 2752 Offset printing

(P-3634)
MERIDIAN GRAPHICS INC
2652 Dow Ave (92780-7208)
PHONE...................................949 833-3500
David R Melin, *Pr*
Paul Valencia, *
David Melin, *
Craig Miller, *
▲ **EMP:** 65 **EST:** 2000
SQ FT: 40,000
SALES (est): 9.69MM **Privately Held**
Web: www.mglitho.com

SIC: 2752 2759 Offset printing; Letterpress
printing

(P-3635)
METRO DIGITAL PRINTING INC
Also Called: Metro Digital
3311 W Macarthur Blvd (92704-6803)
PHONE...................................714 545-8400
Mike Jafari, *Pr*
Sherri Taheri, *
EMP: 22 **EST:** 1986
SQ FT: 15,000
SALES (est): 862.2K **Privately Held**
Web: store.metrodigitalinc.com
SIC: 2752 Offset printing

(P-3636)
MICROSCALE INDUSTRIES INC
18435 Bandilier Cir (92708-7012)
PHONE...................................714 593-1422
David Williams, *Pr*
EMP: 19 **EST:** 1933
SQ FT: 10,626
SALES (est): 960.87K **Privately Held**
Web: www.microscale.com
SIC: 2752 5945 Decals, lithographed;
Hobby, toy, and game shops

(P-3637)
MIDNIGHT OIL AGENCY LLC
Also Called: Midnight Oil Agency, Inc.
3800 W Vanowen St Ste 101 (91505-1173)
PHONE...................................818 295-6100
EMP: 285 **EST:** 1989
SALES (est): 39.54MM
SALES (corp-wide): 430.34MM **Privately
Held**
Web: www.moagency.com
SIC: 2752 8742 Commercial printing,
lithographic; Marketing consulting services
PA: The Imagine Group Llc
1000 Valley Park Dr
Shakopee MN
800 942-7088

(P-3638)
MITTERA GROUP INC
Also Called: Mittera-CA
3791 Catalina St (90720-2402)
PHONE...................................562 598-2446
EMP: 47 **EST:** 2020
SALES (est): 1.73MM **Privately Held**
Web: www.mittera.com
SIC: 2752 Offset printing

(P-3639)
MODERN PRINTING & MAILING INC
3535 Enterprise St (92110-3211)
PHONE...................................619 222-0535
Steve Hire, *Pr*
Alice Hire, *
EMP: 28 **EST:** 1962
SQ FT: 12,000
SALES (est): 2.04MM **Privately Held**
Web: www.modernsd.com
SIC: 2752 7331 2759 Offset printing; Mailing
service; Commercial printing, nec

(P-3640)
MOLINO COMPANY
Also Called: Melcast
13712 Alondra Blvd (90703-2316)
PHONE...................................323 726-1000
Melchor Castano, *Pr*
EMP: 85 **EST:** 1976
SQ FT: 200,000
SALES (est): 8.89MM **Privately Held**
SIC: 2752 Offset printing

▲ = Import ▼ = Export
◆ = Import/Export

(P-3641)
MONARCH LITHO INC (PA)
1501 Date St (90640-6324)
PHONE..............................323 727-0300
Robert Lopez, *Pr*
George Lopez, *VP*
Victor Neri, *Sec*
Eddie Audelo, *Contrlr*
EMP: 50 **EST:** 1974
SQ FT: 153,000
SALES (est): 45.69MM
SALES (corp-wide): 45.69MM **Privately Held**
Web: www.monarchlitho.com
SIC: 2752 Offset printing

(P-3642)
NATIONAL GRAPHICS LLC
Also Called: Jano Graphics
200 N Elevar St (93030-7969)
PHONE..............................805 644-9212
Mike Scher, *Pr*
EMP: 40 **EST:** 1960
SALES (est): 10.11MM **Privately Held**
Web: www.janoprint.com
SIC: 2752 Offset printing

(P-3643)
NEYENESCH PRINTERS INC
2750 Kettner Blvd (92101-1295)
P.O. Box 81184 (92138-1184)
PHONE..............................619 297-2281
Carl A Bentley, *CEO*
Clifford Neyenesch, *
Dave Pauley, *
Kandy Neyenesch, *
EMP: 70 **EST:** 1899
SQ FT: 30,000
SALES (est): 18.65MM **Privately Held**
Web: www.neyenesch.com
SIC: 2752 Offset printing

(P-3644)
NIKNEJAD INC
Also Called: Colornet Press
6855 Hayvenhurst Ave (91406-4718)
PHONE..............................310 477-0407
Kamran Niknejad, *Pr*
Rashid Yassamy, *
Sima Fouladi, *
EMP: 40 **EST:** 1981
SQ FT: 5,000
SALES (est): 5.5MM **Privately Held**
Web: www.colornetpress.com
SIC: 2752 7336 2791 Offset printing; Graphic arts and related design; Typesetting

(P-3645)
NO BOUNDARIES INC
Also Called: Greenbox Art and Culture
789 Gateway Center Way (92102-4539)
PHONE..............................619 266-2349
Thomas Capp, *CEO*
Karen Capp, *
▲ **EMP:** 50 **EST:** 2002
SQ FT: 3,500
SALES (est): 9.76MM **Privately Held**
Web: www.shopgreenboxart.com
SIC: 2752 Offset printing

(P-3646)
OCPC INC
Also Called: The Orange County Printing Co
2485 Da Vinci (92614-5844)
PHONE..............................949 475-1900
Miguel Jacobowitz, *Prin*
EMP: 60 **EST:** 1986
SQ FT: 18,000
SALES (est): 9.92MM **Privately Held**
Web: www.rrd.com

SIC: 2752 Offset printing

(P-3647)
ODCOMBE PRESS (NASHVILLE)
Also Called: Haynes Publications
2801 Townsgate Rd (91361-3010)
PHONE..............................615 793-5414
John H Haynes, *Ch Bd*
▲ **EMP:** 22 **EST:** 1993
SALES (est): 2.07MM **Privately Held**
SIC: 2752 Offset printing
HQ: Haynes Group Limited
Sparkford
Yeovil
196 344-0635

(P-3648)
ORANGE COAST REPROGRAPHICS INC
Also Called: Mouse Graphics
659 W 19th St (92627-2715)
PHONE..............................949 548-5571
Constance Mary Lane, *CEO*
EMP: 22 **EST:** 1947
SQ FT: 9,000
SALES (est): 4.92MM **Privately Held**
Web: www.sendmouse.com
SIC: 2752 7336 2789 2759 Commercial printing, lithographic; Commercial art and graphic design; Bookbinding and related work; Commercial printing, nec

(P-3649)
PACER PRINT
9207 Eton Ave (91311-5808)
PHONE..............................888 305-3144
Peter Varady, *CEO*
Naomi Gonzalez, *
EMP: 35 **EST:** 2016
SALES (est): 3.91MM **Privately Held**
Web: www.pacerprint.com
SIC: 2752 Offset printing

(P-3650)
PACIFIC WEST LITHO INC
Also Called: Pacific West
3291 E Miraloma Ave (92806-1910)
PHONE..............................714 579-0868
Chang Che Chou, *CEO*
EMP: 70 **EST:** 1984
SQ FT: 24,000
SALES (est): 9.2MM **Privately Held**
Web: www.pacificwestlitho.com
SIC: 2752 Lithographing on metal

(P-3651)
PACKAGING MANUFACTURING INC
2285 Michael Faraday Dr Ste 12 (92154-7926)
PHONE..............................619 498-9199
Salvatore Anza, *CEO*
Jim Belcher, *
Gayle Cronin, *
EMP: 240 **EST:** 2009
SALES (est): 30MM **Privately Held**
Web: pm.domeprinting.com
SIC: 2752 Commercial printing, lithographic

(P-3652)
PARADISE PRINTING INC
13474 Pumice St (90650-5247)
PHONE..............................714 228-9628
Paul B Pistone, *CEO*
EMP: 24 **EST:** 1980
SQ FT: 48,000
SALES (est): 2.2MM **Privately Held**
Web: www.paradiseprinting.com
SIC: 2752 Offset printing

(P-3653)
PARS PUBLISHING CORP
Also Called: Grapheex
6029 Fairview Pl (91301-1851)
PHONE..............................818 280-0540
Mehran Kiankarimi, *Pr*
Mike Kian, *
Mahnaz Shidfar, *
Vincent Fisher, *
Allan Yegani, *
EMP: 28 **EST:** 1996
SALES (est): 398.76K **Privately Held**
SIC: 2752 Offset printing

(P-3654)
PDF PRINT COMMUNICATIONS INC (PA)
2630 E 28th St (90755-2202)
PHONE..............................562 426-6978
Robert Albert Mullaney, *CEO*
Kevin J Mullaney, *
Shirley Mullaney, *
EMP: 52 **EST:** 1973
SQ FT: 23,000
SALES (est): 16.91MM
SALES (corp-wide): 16.91MM **Privately Held**
Web: www.pdfpc.com
SIC: 2752 2761 Offset printing; Manifold business forms

(P-3655)
PEGASUS INTERPRINT INC
7111 Hayvenhurst Ave (91406-3807)
PHONE..............................800 926-9873
▲ **EMP:** 24
SIC: 2752 Offset printing

(P-3656)
PGI PACIFIC GRAPHICS INTL
Also Called: Pgi
14938 Nelson Ave (91744-4330)
PHONE..............................626 336-7707
Yvonne Castillo Wasson, *CEO*
Ricardo Wasson, *
EMP: 25 **EST:** 1989
SQ FT: 17,000
SALES (est): 4.78MM **Privately Held**
Web: www.pacgraphics.com
SIC: 2752 2759 8742 7331 Offset printing; Commercial printing, nec; Marketing consulting services; Mailing service

(P-3657)
PHOENIX MARKETING SERVICES INC
651 Wharton Dr (91711-4819)
PHONE..............................909 399-4000
▲ **EMP:** 95
Web: www.phoenixmarketing.net
SIC: 2752 5199 Offset printing; Advertising specialties

(P-3658)
PINE GROVE INDUSTRIES INC
Also Called: Custom Printing
2001 Cabot Pl (93030-2666)
PHONE..............................805 485-3700
Charles Utts, *Pr*
Becky Utts, *
EMP: 26 **EST:** 1975
SQ FT: 10,000
SALES (est): 1.7MM **Privately Held**
Web: www.customprintinginc.com
SIC: 2752 Offset printing

(P-3659)
PM CORPORATE GROUP INC (PA)
Also Called: PM Packaging
2285 Michael Faraday Dr Ste 12 (92154-7924)
PHONE..............................619 498-9199
Salvatore Anza, *CEO*
Jim Belcher, *Pr*
Gayle Cronin, *COO*
EMP: 47 **EST:** 2007
SALES (est): 59.63MM
SALES (corp-wide): 59.63MM **Privately Held**
Web: pm.domeprinting.com
SIC: 2752 Offset printing

(P-3660)
POSTAL INSTANT PRESS INC (HQ)
Also Called: PIP Printing
26722 Plaza (92691-8051)
P.O. Box 9077 (92690-9077)
PHONE..............................949 348-5000
Dan Lowe, *Ch Bd*
Richard Low, *
Dan Conger, *
EMP: 40 **EST:** 1996
SQ FT: 25,000
SALES (est): 2.61MM
SALES (corp-wide): 19.99MM **Privately Held**
Web: www.pip.com
SIC: 2752 6159 Offset printing; Machinery and equipment finance leasing
PA: Franchise Services, Inc.
26722 Plaza
Mission Viejo CA
949 348-5400

(P-3661)
PRECISION LITHO INC
Also Called: Rrd Pckaging Solutions - Vista
1185 Joshua Way (92081-7840)
PHONE..............................760 727-9400
Daniel Knotts, *Pr*
Elif Sagsen-ercel, *Ex VP*
EMP: 35 **EST:** 1981
SQ FT: 40,000
SALES (est): 4.61MM
SALES (corp-wide): 15B **Privately Held**
Web: www.rrd.com
SIC: 2752 Offset printing
HQ: Consolidated Graphics, Inc.
5858 Westheimer Rd # 200
Houston TX

(P-3662)
PRECISION OFFSET INC
Also Called: Precision Services Group
15201 Woodlawn Ave (92780-6418)
PHONE..............................949 752-1714
Lawrence Smith, *CEO*
EMP: 75 **EST:** 1979
SQ FT: 15,000
SALES (est): 20.83MM **Privately Held**
SIC: 2752 Offset printing

(P-3663)
PRIMARY COLOR SYSTEMS CORP
3500 W Burbank Blvd (91505-2268)
PHONE..............................818 643-5944
EMP: 53
SALES (corp-wide): 122.08MM **Privately Held**
Web: www.primarycolor.com
SIC: 2752 Offset printing
PA: Primary Color Systems Corporation
11130 Holder St Ste 210
Cypress CA
949 660-7080

(P-3664)
PRINTING MANAGEMENT ASSOCIATES
17128 Edwards Rd (90703-2424)
P.O. Box 5037 (90703-5037)
PHONE...................................562 407-9977
Jeffrey Brady, *CEO*
Michael Lane, *Pr*
Rich Russell, *VP*
Clif Mcdougall, *Ex VP*
▲ **EMP:** 19 **EST:** 1991
SQ FT: 12,600
SALES (est): 4.4MM **Privately Held**
Web: www.printmgt.com
SIC: 2752 5111 Offset printing; Printing paper

(P-3665)
PRINTING PALACE INC (PA)
2300 Lincoln Blvd (90405-2530)
PHONE...................................310 451-5151
Eli Albek, *Pr*
EMP: 19 **EST:** 1982
SQ FT: 8,000
SALES (est): 2.35MM
SALES (corp-wide): 2.35MM **Privately Held**
Web: www.printingpalace.com
SIC: 2752 Offset printing

(P-3666)
PRINTIVITY LLC
Also Called: Printivity
8840 Kenamar Dr Ste 405 (92121-2450)
PHONE...................................877 649-5463
Lawrence Chou, *CEO*
EMP: 30 **EST:** 2010
SALES (est): 7.13MM **Privately Held**
Web: www.printivity.com
SIC: 2752 2711 2721 Offset printing; Commercial printing and newspaper publishing combined; Magazines: publishing and printing

(P-3667)
PRINTRUNNER LLC
Also Called: U-Nited Printing and Copy Ctr
8000 Haskell Ave (91406-1321)
PHONE...................................888 296-5760
Dean Rabbani, *Managing Member*
Mike Zaya, *
Adam Berger, *
Kamie Davison, *
EMP: 27 **EST:** 1999
SQ FT: 50,000
SALES (est): 1.23MM **Privately Held**
Web: www.printrunner.com
SIC: 2752 Offset printing

(P-3668)
PRINTS 4 LIFE
43145 Business Ctr Pkwy (93535-4564)
PHONE...................................661 942-2233
EMP: 27
Web: www.learn4life.org
SIC: 2752 Commercial printing, lithographic

(P-3669)
PRO DOCUMENT SOLUTIONS INC (PA)
Also Called: Pro Vote Solutions
1760 Commerce Way (93446-3620)
PHONE...................................805 238-6680
George Phillips, *CEO*
Brad Stier, *
Noal Phillips, *
Molly Comin, *
Diana Phillips, *
▲ **EMP:** 50 **EST:** 1979
SQ FT: 35,000

SALES (est): 9.7MM
SALES (corp-wide): 9.7MM **Privately Held**
Web: www.prodocumentsolutions.com
SIC: 2752 Forms, business: lithographed

(P-3670)
PROCESSORS MAILING INC
Also Called: Processors The
761 N Dodsworth Ave (91724-2408)
PHONE...................................626 358-5600
Anthony N Perone, *Pr*
EMP: 21 **EST:** 1974
SQ FT: 8,000
SALES (est): 754.93K **Privately Held**
Web: www.theprocessors.com
SIC: 2752 7331 2791 Offset printing; Mailing service; Typesetting

(P-3671)
PROGRAPHICS INC
9200 Lower Azusa Rd (91770-1593)
PHONE...................................626 287-0417
Christina Stevens, *CEO*
Timothy Stevens, *
Jaime Colacio, *
EMP: 38 **EST:** 1967
SQ FT: 23,000
SALES (est): 6.7MM **Privately Held**
Web: www.prographicsllc.com
SIC: 2752 Offset printing

(P-3672)
PRPCO
Also Called: Poor Richard's Press
2226 Beebee St (93401-5505)
PHONE...................................805 543-6844
Todd P Ventura, *Pr*
Richard C Blake, *
Mary Monroe, *
EMP: 35 **EST:** 2000
SALES (est): 4.07MM **Privately Held**
Web: www.prpco.com
SIC: 2752 Offset printing

(P-3673)
Q TEAM
Also Called: Ryan Press
6400 Dale St (90621-3115)
PHONE...................................714 228-4465
Mike Quibodeaux, *CEO*
Donna Quibodeaux, *
Mike Quibodeaux, *VP*
James Quibodeaux, *
EMP: 45 **EST:** 1980
SQ FT: 13,000
SALES (est): 4.84MM **Privately Held**
Web: www.ryanpress.com
SIC: 2752 Offset printing

(P-3674)
QG PRINTING IL LLC
Also Called: Quad Graphics
6688 Box Springs Blvd (92507-0726)
PHONE...................................951 571-2500
Georg Decker, *Brnch Mgr*
EMP: 136
SALES (corp-wide): 3.22B **Publicly Held**
SIC: 2752 Offset printing
HQ: Qg Printing Ii Llc
N61w23044 Harrys Way
Sussex WI

(P-3675)
QUAD/GRAPHICS INC
Also Called: QUAD/GRAPHICS INC.
6688 Box Springs Blvd (92507-0726)
PHONE...................................951 689-1122
Uli Oels, *Genl Mgr*
EMP: 45
SALES (corp-wide): 3.22B **Publicly Held**

Web: www.quad.com
SIC: 2752 7336 Offset printing; Commercial art and graphic design
PA: Quad/Graphics, Inc.
N61w23044 Harrys Way
Sussex WI
414 566-6000

(P-3676)
QUEEN BEACH PRINTERS INC
937 Pine Ave (90813-4375)
P.O. Box 540 (90801-0540)
PHONE...................................562 436-8201
Nicholas W Edwards, *CEO*
William L Edwards Senior, *Pr*
William L Edwards Junior, *VP*
Virginia Noyes, *
EMP: 30 **EST:** 1944
SQ FT: 25,000
SALES (est): 3.74MM **Privately Held**
Web: www.qbprinters.com
SIC: 2752 7336 Offset printing; Commercial art and graphic design

(P-3677)
RANROY COMPANY
Also Called: Ranroy Printing Company
9265 Activity Rd Ste 112 (92126-4444)
PHONE...................................858 571-8800
Randall S Roy, *Pr*
EMP: 23 **EST:** 1982
SQ FT: 20,000
SALES (est): 954.44K **Privately Held**
Web: www.ranroy.com
SIC: 2752 5112 Offset printing; Envelopes

(P-3678)
RED BRICK CORPORATION
Also Called: Design Printing
5364 Venice Blvd (90019-5240)
PHONE...................................323 549-9444
Parviz Bina, *CEO*
Bijan Bina, *VP*
EMP: 18 **EST:** 1984
SQ FT: 8,000
SALES (est): 4.88MM **Privately Held**
Web: www.dprintla.com
SIC: 2752 Offset printing

(P-3679)
RESOURCE LABEL GROUP LLC
Also Called: Best Label Company
13260 Moore St (90703-2228)
PHONE...................................562 926-1432
EMP: 17
Web: www.resourcelabel.com
SIC: 2752 Commercial printing, lithographic
PA: Resource Label Group, Llc
2550 Meridian Blvd # 370
Franklin TN

(P-3680)
ROBO 3D INC
Also Called: Robo 3d Printer
5070 Santa Fe St Ste C (92109-1610)
PHONE...................................844 476-2233
Braydon Moreno, *CEO*
Randall Waynick, *
▲ **EMP:** 25 **EST:** 2013
SALES (est): 2.37MM **Privately Held**
Web: www.robo3d.com
SIC: 2752 Commercial printing, lithographic

(P-3681)
RUSH PRESS INC
Also Called: Arts & Crafts Press
955 Gateway Center Way (92102-4542)
PHONE...................................619 296-7874
EMP: 48
Web: www.rushpress.com

SIC: 2752 Offset printing

(P-3682)
SAN DIEGO PRINTING GROUP INC
Also Called: Mesa Reprographics
5560 Ruffin Rd Ste 2 (92123-1332)
PHONE...................................858 541-1500
Karen Moreno, *Pr*
EMP: 17 **EST:** 2014
SALES (est): 494.94K **Privately Held**
SIC: 2752 Offset printing

(P-3683)
SAN DIEGUITO PUBLISHERS INC
Also Called: San Dieguito Printers
1880 Diamond St (92078-5100)
P.O. Box 885 (92075-0885)
PHONE...................................760 593-5139
▲ **EMP:** 59 **EST:** 1964
SALES (est): 5.19MM **Privately Held**
Web: www.sd-print.com
SIC: 2752 Offset printing

(P-3684)
SCHOLASTIC SPORTS INC
4878 Ronson Ct Ste Kl (92111-1806)
PHONE...................................858 496-9221
EMP: 90
SQ FT: 5,500
SALES (est): 867.63K **Privately Held**
SIC: 2752 Commercial printing, lithographic

(P-3685)
SELECT GRAPHICS
11931 Euclid St (92840-2200)
PHONE...................................714 537-5250
Yung Phan, *Prin*
EMP: 20 **EST:** 1988
SQ FT: 2,703
SALES (est): 871.5K **Privately Held**
Web: www.selectgp.com
SIC: 2752 2759 Offset printing; Commercial printing, nec

(P-3686)
SIR SPEEDY INC (HQ)
Also Called: Sir Speedy
26722 Plaza (92691-6390)
P.O. Box 9077 (92690-9077)
PHONE...................................949 348-5000
Don Lowe, *CEO*
Richard Lowe, *
Dan Conger, *
EMP: 43 **EST:** 1968
SQ FT: 44,000
SALES (est): 7.99MM
SALES (corp-wide): 19.99MM **Privately Held**
Web: www.sirspeedy.com
SIC: 2752 Commercial printing, lithographic
PA: Franchise Services, Inc.
26722 Plaza
Mission Viejo CA
949 348-5400

(P-3687)
SOUTHWEST OFFSET PRTG CO INC (PA)
13650 Gramercy Pl (90249-2453)
PHONE...................................310 965-9154
Greg Mcdonald, *CEO*
Jennifer Mcdonald, *VP*
Art Spear, *
▲ **EMP:** 275 **EST:** 1986
SQ FT: 45,000
SALES (est): 42.54MM
SALES (corp-wide): 42.54MM **Privately Held**

Web: www.southwestoffset.com
SIC: 2752 Offset printing

(P-3688)
SPORT CARD CO LLC
5830 El Camino Real (92008-8816)
PHONE..............................800 873-7332
Richard Mc William, *CEO*
Jason Masherah, *
Roz Nowicki, *
◆ **EMP: 400 EST:** 1988
SQ FT: 247,000
SALES (est): 99.18MM **Privately Held**
Web: www.upperdeck.com
SIC: 2752 5947 Souvenir cards, lithographed
; Gift, novelty, and souvenir shop

(P-3689)
STOUGHTON PRINTING CO
130 N Sunset Ave (91744-3595)
PHONE..............................626 961-3678
Jack Stoughton Junior, *Pr*
Clay Stoughton, *
EMP: 28 EST: 1952
SQ FT: 21,000
SALES (est): 5.22MM **Privately Held**
Web: www.stoughtonprinting.com
SIC: 2752 Offset printing

(P-3690)
SUPERIOR LITHOGRAPHICS INC
3055 Bandini Blvd (90058-4109)
PHONE..............................323 263-8400
Douglas Rawson, *CEO*
Carol Rawson, *
▲ **EMP: 90 EST:** 1982
SQ FT: 60,000
SALES (est): 19.68MM **Privately Held**
Web: www.superiorlithographics.com
SIC: 2752 Offset printing

(P-3691)
SUPREME GRAPHICS INC
1201 N Miller St (92806-1933)
PHONE..............................310 531-8300
Ramin Kohanteb, *Pr*
EMP: 18 EST: 2005
SALES (est): 2.25MM **Privately Held**
Web: www.supremegraphicsinc.com
SIC: 2752 Offset printing

(P-3692)
TAILGATE PRINTING INC
2930 S Fairview St (92704-6503)
PHONE..............................714 966-3035
Maria C Vega, *CEO*
EMP: 90 EST: 2008
SQ FT: 80,000
SALES (est): 9.42MM **Privately Held**
Web: www.tailgateprinting.com
SIC: 2752 Offset printing

(P-3693)
TAJEN GRAPHICS INC
Also Called: Apollo Printing & Graphics
2100 W Lincoln Ave Ste B (92801-5642)
PHONE..............................714 527-3122
Dhansukhlal Ratanjee, *Pr*
Ken Ratanjee, *
EMP: 30 EST: 1977
SQ FT: 1,800
SALES (est): 4.88MM **Privately Held**
Web: www.apganaheim.com
SIC: 2752 2791 Offset printing; Typesetting,
computer controlled

(P-3694)
TAM PRINTING INC
2961 E White Star Ave (92806-2630)
PHONE..............................714 224-4488
Tam Bui, *Pr*
EMP: 19 EST: 1986
SQ FT: 10,000
SALES (est): 2.41MM **Privately Held**
Web: www.tamprinting.com
SIC: 2752 Offset printing

(P-3695)
TECHNOLOGY TRAINING CORP
Also Called: Avalon Communications
3238 W 131st St (90250-5517)
PHONE..............................310 644-7777
Richard D Lytle, *Pr*
EMP: 54
SALES (corp-wide): 4.84MM **Privately Held**
Web: www.ttcus.com
SIC: 2752 7331 3577 Offset printing; Direct
mail advertising services; Computer
peripheral equipment, nec
PA: Technology Training Corp
369 Van Ness Way Ste 735
Torrance CA
310 320-8110

(P-3696)
TEEFOR2 INC
5460 Vine St (91710-5247)
PHONE..............................909 613-0055
EMP: 18 EST: 2015
SALES (est): 971.87K **Privately Held**
Web: www.teefor2.net
SIC: 2752 Commercial printing, lithographic

(P-3697)
THE LIGATURE INC (HQ)
Also Called: Echelon Fine Printing
4909 Alcoa Ave (90058-3022)
PHONE..............................323 585-6000
Linda H Pennell, *
Denyse Owens, *
Dave Meyer, *
Tom Clifford, *
EMP: 50 EST: 1920
SQ FT: 47,415
SALES (est): 12.43MM
SALES (corp-wide): 3.81B **Privately Held**
Web: www.echelonprint.com
SIC: 2752 2759 Offset printing; Invitation
and stationery printing and engraving
PA: Taylor Corporation
1725 Roe Crest Dr
North Mankato MN
507 625-2828

(P-3698)
TREND OFFSET PRINTING SERVICES INC (HQ)
Also Called: Trend Offset Printing
3701 Catalina St (90720-2402)
P.O. Box 3008 (90720-1308)
PHONE..............................562 598-2446
◆ **EMP: 41 EST:** 1986
SALES (est): 86.66MM
SALES (corp-wide): 487.58MM **Privately Held**
Web: www.mittera.com
SIC: 2752 Offset printing
PA: Mittera Group, Inc.
1312 Locust St Ste 202
Des Moines IA
515 343-5353

(P-3699)
TREND OFFSET PRINTING SVCS INC
Also Called: TREND OFFSET PRINTING
SERVICES INCORPORATED
3791 Catalina St (90720-2402)
PHONE..............................562 598-2446
Paul Rhilindger, *Mgr*
EMP: 425
SALES (corp-wide): 487.58MM **Privately Held**
Web: www.mittera.com
SIC: 2752 2732 Offset printing; Books,
printing and binding
HQ: Trend Offset Printing Services, Inc.
3701 Catalina St
Los Alamitos CA
562 598-2446

(P-3700)
TYPECRAFT INC
Also Called: Typecraft Wood & Jones
2040 E Walnut St (91107-5804)
PHONE..............................626 795-8093
D Harry Montgomery, *Pr*
Jeffrey J Gish, *
EMP: 38 EST: 1947
SQ FT: 19,000
SALES (est): 6.35MM **Privately Held**
Web: www.typecraft.com
SIC: 2752 Offset printing

(P-3701)
ULTIMATE PRINT SOURCE INC
Also Called: Printing 4him
2070 S Hellman Ave (91761-8018)
PHONE..............................909 947-5292
Jeffrey J Ferrazzano, *CEO*
Desiree Ferrazzano, *
Edith Le Leux, *
Jon Le Leux, *
EMP: 30 EST: 1987
SQ FT: 20,000
SALES (est): 4.74MM **Privately Held**
Web: www.ultimateprintsource.com
SIC: 2752 Offset printing

(P-3702)
UNI-SPORT INC
16933 Gramercy Pl (90247-5207)
PHONE..............................310 217-4587
Thomas Hebert, *Pr*
◆ **EMP: 25 EST:** 2006
SQ FT: 10,000
SALES (est): 2.25MM **Privately Held**
Web: www.uni-sport.com
SIC: 2752 Commercial printing, lithographic

(P-3703)
V3 PRINTING CORPORATION
Also Called: V 3
200 N Elevar St (93030-7969)
PHONE..............................805 981-2600
David Wilson, *Pr*
Michael Szanger, *
EMP: 80 EST: 1959
SQ FT: 4,000
SALES (est): 18.07MM **Privately Held**
Web: www.printv3.com
SIC: 2752 Lithographing on metal

(P-3704)
VALLEY BUSINESS PRINTERS INC
Also Called: Valley Printers
6355 Topanga Canyon Blvd Ste 225
(91367-2118)
PHONE..............................818 362-7771
Michael Flannery, *CEO*

Bruce Bolkin, *
Karen S Flannery, *
▲ **EMP: 92 EST:** 1965
SALES (est): 9.28MM **Privately Held**
Web: www.valleyprinters.net
SIC: 2752 2759 Offset printing; Commercial
printing, nec

(P-3705)
VENTURA PRINTING INC (PA)
Also Called: V3
200 N Elevar St (93030-7969)
PHONE..............................805 981-2600
David Wilson, *Pr*
▲ **EMP: 99 EST:** 1946
SALES (est): 4.26MM
SALES (corp-wide): 4.26MM **Privately Held**
Web: www.venturaprint.com
SIC: 2752 Offset printing

(P-3706)
VOMELA SPECIALTY COMPANY
Also Called: Vomela
9810 Bell Ranch Dr (90670-2952)
PHONE..............................562 944-3853
Loren Maxwell, *Brnch Mgr*
EMP: 123
SALES (corp-wide): 258.06MM **Privately Held**
Web: www.vomela.com
SIC: 2752 7336 Poster and decal printing,
lithographic; Commercial art and graphic
design
PA: Vomela Specialty Company
845 Minnehaha Ave E
Saint Paul MN
651 228-2200

(P-3707)
WE DO GRAPHICS INC
1150 N Main St (92867-3421)
PHONE..............................714 997-7390
Douglas K Le Mieux, *Pr*
Steven I Lehrer, *
Heidi G Le Mieux, *
▲ **EMP: 27 EST:** 1980
SQ FT: 23,000
SALES (est): 1.6MM **Privately Held**
Web: www.wedographics.com
SIC: 2752 Offset printing

(P-3708)
WEBER PRINTING COMPANY INC
1124 E Del Amo Blvd (90807-1010)
PHONE..............................310 639-5064
Richard M Weber, *Pr*
Steven Weber, *
Lynda Slack, *
EMP: 35 EST: 1946
SQ FT: 30,000
SALES (est): 4.77MM **Privately Held**
Web: www.weberprint.com
SIC: 2752 Offset printing

(P-3709)
WESTAMERICA GRAPHICS CORPORATION
26012 Atlantic Ocean Dr (92630-8843)
PHONE..............................949 462-3600
EMP: 57
Web: www.wagraphics.com
SIC: 2752 Offset printing

(P-3710)
WESTERN PRTG & GRAPHICS LLC (PA)
Also Called: Western Printing and Label

675 N Main St (92868-1103)
PHONE..................714 532-3946
EMP: 22 **EST:** 1981
SALES (est): 2.67MM
SALES (corp-wide): 2.67MM **Privately Held**
Web: www.westprint.com
SIC: 2752 2791 2759 2741 Offset printing; Typesetting; Commercial printing, nec; Miscellaneous publishing

(P-3711)
WESTMINSTER PRESS INC
4906 W 1st St (92703-3110)
PHONE..................714 210-2881
Gary Tang, *CEO*
Thoai Tang, *VP*
Tri Tang, *VP*
▲ **EMP:** 50 **EST:** 1986
SQ FT: 10,000
SALES (est): 7.67MM **Privately Held**
SIC: 2752 Color lithography

(P-3712)
WESTROCK CP LLC
MPS Corona
2577 Research Dr (92882-7607)
PHONE..................951 273-7900
Steven Voorhees, *CEO*
EMP: 64
SALES (corp-wide): 20.31B **Publicly Held**
Web: www.westrock.com
SIC: 2752 Offset printing
HQ: Westrock Cp, Llc
1000 Abernathy Rd Ste 125
Atlanta GA

(P-3713)
WIRZ & CO
444 Colton Ave (92324-3019)
PHONE..................909 825-6970
Charles Fred Wirz, *Owner*
EMP: 18 **EST:** 1985
SQ FT: 8,000
SALES (est): 1.81MM **Privately Held**
Web: www.wirzco.com
SIC: 2752 Offset printing

(P-3714)
WOODRIDGE PRESS INC
2485 Da Vinci (92614-5844)
PHONE..................949 475-1900
EMP: 50
Web: www.woodridgepress.com
SIC: 2752 2796 Offset printing; Platemaking services

(P-3715)
WS PACKAGING-BLAKE PRINTERY
Also Called: Poor Richards Press
2224 Beebee St (93401-5505)
PHONE..................805 543-6844
Bruce Dickinson, *Brnch Mgr*
EMP: 34
SQ FT: 3,500
SALES (corp-wide): 5.44B **Privately Held**
SIC: 2752 2621 2791 Offset printing; Wrapping paper; Typesetting, computer controlled
HQ: Ws Packaging-Blake Printery
2222 Beebee St
San Luis Obispo CA
805 543-6843

(P-3716)
WTPC INC
Also Called: World Trade Printing Company
12082 Western Ave (92841-2913)
PHONE..................714 903-2500

Joe Ratanjee, *CEO*
▲ **EMP:** 30 **EST:** 1991
SQ FT: 25,000
SALES (est): 10.86MM **Privately Held**
Web: www.wtpcenter.com
SIC: 2752 Offset printing

(P-3717)
ZOO PRINTING INC (PA)
Also Called: Zoo Printing Trade Printer
1225 Los Angeles St (91204-2403)
PHONE..................310 253-7751
Dan Doron, *Pr*
Maria Camins, *
▲ **EMP:** 43 **EST:** 2001
SALES (est): 18.91MM
SALES (corp-wide): 18.91MM **Privately Held**
Web: www.zooprinting.com
SIC: 2752 Offset printing

(P-3718)
ZUZA LLC
2304 Faraday Ave (92008-7216)
PHONE..................760 494-9000
Philip M Lurie, *CEO*
Philip M Lurie, *Pr*
Martin Solarish, *
EMP: 72 **EST:** 1992
SQ FT: 23,000
SALES (est): 15.49MM **Privately Held**
Web: www.zuzaprint.com
SIC: 2752 Offset printing

2754 Commercial Printing, Gravure

(P-3719)
KMR LABEL LLC
Also Called: Axiom Label Group
1360 W Walnut Pkwy (90220-5029)
PHONE..................310 603-8910
EMP: 50
SIC: 2754 2752 Labels: gravure printing; Commercial printing, lithographic

(P-3720)
MC ALLISTER INDUSTRIES INC (PA)
731 S Highway 101 Ste 2 (92075-2629)
PHONE..................858 755-0683
Robert Mc Allister, *Pr*
▲ **EMP:** 20 **EST:** 1998
SQ FT: 2,500
SALES (est): 2.41MM **Privately Held**
Web: www.mcallisterindustries.com
SIC: 2754 Cards, except greeting: gravure printing

(P-3721)
ONEIL CAPITAL MANAGEMENT INC
12655 Beatrice St (90066-7003)
PHONE..................310 448-6400
William O Neil, *CEO*
▲ **EMP:** 152 **EST:** 1973
SQ FT: 70,000
SALES (est): 51.03MM
SALES (corp-wide): 335.64MM **Privately Held**
Web: www.oneildigitalsolutions.com
SIC: 2754 2732 2741 2711 Catalogs: gravure printing, not published on site; Book printing; Miscellaneous publishing; Newspapers
PA: Data Analysis Inc.
12655 Beatrice St
Los Angeles CA
310 448-6800

(P-3722)
QPE INC
Also Called: Quality Packaging and Engrg
1372 Mcgaw Ave (92614-5539)
PHONE..................949 263-0381
Kirk Wei, *Pr*
Joseph S Chiang, *Sec*
▲ **EMP:** 18 **EST:** 1986
SQ FT: 10,000
SALES (est): 2.22MM **Privately Held**
Web: www.qpeinc.com
SIC: 2754 7389 Labels: gravure printing; Packaging and labeling services

(P-3723)
RESOURCE LABEL GROUP LLC
Also Called: Axiom Label & Packaging
1360 W Walnut Pkwy (90220-5029)
PHONE..................310 603-8910
Kieron Delahunt, *Brnch Mgr*
EMP: 50
Web: www.resourcelabel.com
SIC: 2754 2752 Labels: gravure printing; Commercial printing, lithographic
PA: Resource Label Group, Llc
2550 Meridian Blvd # 370
Franklin TN

(P-3724)
STUART F COOPER CO
1565 E 23rd St (90011-1801)
P.O. Box 11306 (90011-0306)
PHONE..................213 747-7141
EMP: 150
SIC: 2754 Announcements: gravure printing

2759 Commercial Printing, Nec

(P-3725)
4 OVER LLC (HQ)
Also Called: 4 Over
1225 Los Angeles St (91204-2403)
PHONE..................818 246-1170
Zarik Megerdichian, *CEO*
Tina Hartounian, *
▲ **EMP:** 49 **EST:** 2000
SALES (est): 172.36MM
SALES (corp-wide): 172.36MM **Privately Held**
Web: www.4over.com
SIC: 2759 7336 Commercial printing, nec; Commercial art and graphic design
PA: Four Cents Holdings, Inc.
16111 Nw 13th Ave
North Miami Beach FL

(P-3726)
ABC IMAGING OF WASHINGTON
17240 Red Hill Ave (92614-5628)
PHONE..................949 419-3728
EMP: 19
SALES (corp-wide): 96.92MM **Privately Held**
Web: www.abcimaging.com
SIC: 2759 Commercial printing, nec
PA: Abc Imaging Of Washington, Inc
5290 Shawnee Rd Ste 300
Alexandria VA
202 429-8870

(P-3727)
ABC IMAGING OF WASHINGTON
Also Called: ABC Imaging
13573 Larwin Cir (90670-5032)
PHONE..................562 375-7280
EMP: 17
SALES (corp-wide): 96.92MM **Privately Held**

Web: www.abcimaging.com
SIC: 2759 Advertising literature: printing, nsk
PA: Abc Imaging Of Washington, Inc
5290 Shawnee Rd Ste 300
Alexandria VA
202 429-8870

(P-3728)
ABF PRINTS INC
102 N Riverside Ave (92376-5922)
PHONE..................909 875-7163
Kevin M Danko, *CEO*
EMP: 18 **EST:** 2005
SQ FT: 10,000
SALES (est): 924.84K **Privately Held**
Web: www.abfprints.com
SIC: 2759 7323 Commercial printing, nec; Credit reporting services

(P-3729)
ADCRAFT PRODUCTS CO INC
Also Called: Adcraft Labels
1230 S Sherman St (92805-6455)
PHONE..................714 776-1230
Randy C Mottram, *Pr*
Keith A Mottram, *
EMP: 27 **EST:** 1977
SALES (est): 4.86MM **Privately Held**
Web: www.adcraftlabels.com
SIC: 2759 Labels and seals: printing, nsk

(P-3730)
ADVANCED WEB OFFSET INC
Also Called: Awo
2260 Oak Ridge Way (92081-8341)
PHONE..................760 727-1700
Stephen F Shoemaker, *Pr*
David Altomare, *
EMP: 75 **EST:** 1989
SQ FT: 65,000
SALES (est): 11.96MM **Privately Held**
Web: www.awoink.com
SIC: 2759 2752 Newspapers: printing, nsk; Offset and photolithographic printing

(P-3731)
ALL-STAR LETTERING INC
9419 Ann St (90670-2613)
PHONE..................562 404-5995
Paul Possemato, *Pr*
Susan Possemato, *
Palma Possemato, *
EMP: 20 **EST:** 1969
SALES (est): 4.78MM **Privately Held**
Web: www.allstarlettering.com
SIC: 2759 3555 2396 Screen printing; Printing trades machinery; Automotive and apparel trimmings

(P-3732)
AMERICAN FOOTHILL PUBG CO INC
10009 Commerce Ave (91042-2303)
PHONE..................818 352-7878
Doris Horwith, *Pr*
Douglas Horwith, *
EMP: 40 **EST:** 1920
SQ FT: 13,000
SALES (est): 2.25MM **Privately Held**
Web: www.americanfoothillpublishing.com
SIC: 2759 Newspapers: printing, nsk

(P-3733)
AMERICAN ZABIN INTL INC
3933 S Hill St (90037-1313)
PHONE..................213 746-3770
◆ **EMP:** 32 **EST:** 1993
SQ FT: 18,000
SALES (est): 2.27MM **Privately Held**

Web: www.zabin.com
SIC: 2759 Tags: printing, nsk

(P-3734)
ARACA MERCHANDISE LP
Araca Ink
459 Park Ave (91340-2525)
PHONE..............................818 743-5400
Judy Courney, *Mgr*
EMP: 97
Web: www.araca.com
SIC: 2759 Screen printing
HQ: Araca Merchandise L.P.
545 W 45th St Fl 10
New York NY

(P-3735)
ARTISAN NAMEPLATE AWARDS CORP
Also Called: Weber Precision Graphics
2730 S Shannon St (92704-5232)
PHONE..............................714 556-6222
Henry G Weber, *Pr*
Margaret Weber, *
EMP: 33 EST: 1972
SQ FT: 12,160
SALES (est): 5.09MM Privately Held
Web: www.weberpg.com
SIC: 2759 3479 Labels and seals: printing, nsk; Coating of metals with plastic or resins

(P-3736)
ARTISAN SCREEN PRINTING INC
1055 W 5th St (91702-3313)
PHONE..............................626 815-2700
Vasant N Doabria, *Pr*
Praful Bajaria, *
C P Kheni, *
▲ EMP: 120 EST: 2004
SQ FT: 90,000
SALES (est): 6.51MM Privately Held
Web: www.artisanscreen.com
SIC: 2759 Screen printing

(P-3737)
BLACKBURN ALTON INVSTMENTS LLC
Also Called: Foster Print
700 E Alton Ave (92705-5610)
PHONE..............................714 731-2000
EMP: 34 EST: 2011
SALES (est): 1.64MM Privately Held
SIC: 2759 Commercial printing, nec

(P-3738)
BLC WC INC (PA)
Also Called: Imperial Marking Systems
13260 Moore St (90703-2228)
PHONE..............................562 926-1452
TOLL FREE: 800
Ernest Wong, *Pr*
Donald Ingle, *
Timothy Koontz, *
EMP: 120 EST: 1989
SQ FT: 60,000
SALES (est): 21.29MM
SALES (corp-wide): 21.29MM Privately Held
Web: www.resourcelabel.com
SIC: 2759 Labels and seals: printing, nsk

(P-3739)
BRETKERI CORPORATION
Also Called: So Cal Graphics
8316 Clairemont Mesa Blvd Ste 105 (92111-1316)
PHONE..............................858 292-4919
Bret Catcott, *Pr*

Keri Catcott, *Sec*
EMP: 19 EST: 1982
SQ FT: 4,500
SALES (est): 5.07MM Privately Held
Web: www.socalgraphics.com
SIC: 2759 7336 Commercial printing, nec; Graphic arts and related design

(P-3740)
BRIXEN & SONS INC
2100 S Fairview St (92704-4516)
PHONE..............................714 566-1444
Martin Corey Brixen, *Pr*
Son Nguyen, *
▲ EMP: 27 EST: 1992
SQ FT: 32,000
SALES (est): 4.71MM Privately Held
Web: www.brixen.com
SIC: 2759 3993 Screen printing; Signs and advertising specialties

(P-3741)
BROOK & WHITTLE LIMITED
Also Called: Label Impressions
1177 N Grove St (92806-2110)
PHONE..............................714 634-3466
Remy Zada, *Brnch Mgr*
EMP: 42
Web: www.brookandwhittle.com
SIC: 2759 Labels and seals: printing, nsk
PA: Brook & Whittle Limited
20 Carter Dr
Guilford CT

(P-3742)
C T L PRINTING INDS INC
Also Called: Cal Tape & Label
1741 W Lincoln Ave Ste A (92801-6716)
PHONE..............................714 635-2980
James Edward Hudson, *CEO*
J J Hudson, *
Dave Adams, *
EMP: 25 EST: 1960
SQ FT: 8,950
SALES (est): 4.74MM Privately Held
Web: ctlprintingindustries.openfos.com
SIC: 2759 Labels and seals: printing, nsk

(P-3743)
CCL LABEL INC
Pharmaceutical Label Systems
576 College Commerce Way (91786-4377)
PHONE..............................909 608-2655
Kieorn Delahunt, *Brnch Mgr*
EMP: 92
SQ FT: 43,000
SALES (corp-wide): 4.75B Privately Held
Web: www.cclind.com
SIC: 2759 Labels and seals: printing, nsk
HQ: Ccl Label, Inc.
161 Worcester Rd Ste 403
Framingham MA
508 872-4511

(P-3744)
CCL LABEL (DELAWARE) INC
576 College Commerce Way (91786-4377)
PHONE..............................909 608-2260
Kieron Delahunt, *Mgr*
EMP: 238
SALES (corp-wide): 4.75B Privately Held
SIC: 2759 Labels and seals: printing, nsk
HQ: Ccl Label (Delaware), Inc.
15 Controls Dr
Shelton CT
203 926-1253

(P-3745)
COASTAL TAG & LABEL INC
13233 Barton Cir (90605-3255)

P.O. Box 3303 (90670-1303)
PHONE..............................562 946-4318
Fred Elhami, *Pr*
Ruth Elhami, *
EMP: 94 EST: 1982
SALES (est): 9.5MM Privately Held
SIC: 2759 2672 2671 Labels and seals: printing, nsk; Paper; coated and laminated, nec; Paper; coated and laminated packaging
PA: A F E Industries, Inc.
13233 Barton Cir
Whittier CA

(P-3746)
COASTWIDE TAG & LABEL CO INC
7647 Industry Ave (90660-4301)
PHONE..............................323 721-1501
Jay Sullivan, *Pr*
Jerry Sullivan, *
EMP: 26 EST: 1946
SQ FT: 6,000
SALES (est): 576.04K Privately Held
Web: www.coastwidetag.com
SIC: 2759 Labels and seals: printing, nsk

(P-3747)
COLMOL INC
Also Called: King Graphics
8517 Production Ave (92121-2204)
PHONE..............................858 693-7575
Sean P Mundy, *CEO*
▲ EMP: 45 EST: 1991
SQ FT: 14,000
SALES (est): 4.77MM Privately Held
Web: www.kinggraph.com
SIC: 2759 Screen printing

(P-3748)
CONSOLIDATED GRAPHICS INC
Anderson La
3550 Tyburn St (90065-1427)
PHONE..............................323 460-4115
Luke Westlake, *Grp VP*
EMP: 62
SALES (corp-wide): 15B Privately Held
Web: www.consolidatedgraphicsinc.com
SIC: 2759 2752 Commercial printing, nec; Offset printing
HQ: Consolidated Graphics, Inc.
5858 Westheimer Rd # 200
Houston TX

(P-3749)
CORPORATE IMPRESSIONS LA INC
Also Called: Dorado Pkg
10742 Burbank Blvd (91601-2516)
PHONE..............................818 761-9295
Jennifer L Freund, *Pr*
EMP: 27 EST: 1982
SQ FT: 10,000
SALES (est): 2.39MM Privately Held
Web: www.impressionsla.com
SIC: 2759 7389 Screen printing; Packaging and labeling services

(P-3750)
COSMO FIBER CORPORATION (PA)
1802 Santo Domingo Ave (91010-2933)
PHONE..............................626 256-6098
Sidney Ru, *Pr*
Sissy Ru, *Sec*
◆ EMP: 19 EST: 1990
SQ FT: 4,000
SALES (est): 4.55MM Privately Held
Web: www.cosmopromos.com

SIC: 2759 7389 Promotional printing; Advertising, promotional, and trade show services

(P-3751)
CR & A CUSTOM APPAREL INC
Also Called: Cr & A Custom
312 W Pico Blvd (90015-2437)
PHONE..............................213 749-4440
Masoud Rad, *COO*
Carmen Rad, *Pr*
Dino Maquiddang, *
◆ EMP: 30 EST: 1993
SQ FT: 26,500
SALES (est): 5.7MM Privately Held
Web: www.cracustom.com
SIC: 2759 Posters, including billboards: printing, nsk

(P-3752)
DEAN HESKETH COMPANY INC
Also Called: Mpressions
2551 W La Palma Ave (92801-2622)
PHONE..............................714 236-2138
Matthew Hesketh, *Pr*
▲ EMP: 35 EST: 1956
SQ FT: 6,000
SALES (est): 3.59MM Privately Held
Web: www.mpressions.graphics
SIC: 2759 Commercial printing, nec

(P-3753)
DIGITAL ROOM HOLDINGS INC (HQ)
Also Called: New Printing
8000 Haskell Ave (91406-1321)
PHONE..............................310 575-4440
Michael Turner, *CEO*
Brett Zane, *CFO*
▲ EMP: 63 EST: 2016
SALES (est): 188.44MM Publicly Held
Web: www.digitalroominc.com
SIC: 2759 7336 Commercial printing, nec; Graphic arts and related design
PA: Sycamore Partners Management, L.P.
9 W 57th St Ste 3100
New York NY

(P-3754)
DIVERSIFIED IMAGES INC
1230 N Jefferson St Ste J (92807-1631)
PHONE..............................661 702-0003
Robert W Waycott, *Pr*
Barbara Waycott, *VP*
EMP: 18 EST: 1966
SALES (est): 452.28K Privately Held
Web: www.diversifiedimages.com
SIC: 2759 2752 3479 Screen printing; Decals, lithographed; Etching and engraving

(P-3755)
DM LUXURY LLC
875 Prospect St Ste 300 (92037-4264)
PHONE..............................858 366-9721
EMP: 107
SALES (corp-wide): 79.5MM Privately Held
Web: www.modernluxurymedia.com
SIC: 2759 Advertising literature: printing, nsk
PA: Dm Luxury, Llc
3414 Peachtree Rd Ne # 48
Atlanta GA
404 443-1180

(P-3756)
ECLECTIC PRINTING & DESIGN LLC
1030 Ortega Way Ste A (92870-7161)
P.O. Box 6667 (92834-6667)

PHONE...............714 528-8040
Jeffrey Abraham, *Pr*
Jeff Abraham, *Owner*
EMP: 18 **EST:** 2007
SALES (est): 1.44MM **Privately Held**
Web: www.eclecticprinting.com
SIC: 2759 Screen printing

(P-3757)
ELECTRONIC PRTG SOLUTIONS LLC
4879 Ronson Ct Ste C (92111-1811)
PHONE...............858 576-3000
Grant Freeman, *Managing Member*
EMP: 20 **EST:** 1997
SQ FT: 7,600
SALES (est): 3.37MM **Privately Held**
Web: www.epsolution.com
SIC: 2759 2732 Magazines: printing, nsk; Book printing

(P-3758)
EXPRESS BUSINESS SYSTEMS INC
Also Called: Express
9155 Trade Pl (92126-4377)
P.O. Box 537 (92038-0537)
PHONE...............858 549-9828
Briggs Keiffer, *Pr*
Maureen O'malley, *Sec*
EMP: 37 **EST:** 1987
SQ FT: 7,000
SALES (est): 5.06MM **Privately Held**
Web: www.expresscorp.com
SIC: 2759 3993 2672 2671 Labels and seals: printing, nsk; Signs and advertising specialties; Paper; coated and laminated, nec; Paper; coated and laminated packaging

(P-3759)
FABFAD LLC
1901 E 7th Pl (90021-1601)
PHONE...............213 488-0456
Lolita Mejia, *VP Opers*
EMP: 19 **EST:** 2017
SALES (est): 1.48MM **Privately Held**
Web: www.fabfad.com
SIC: 2759 Screen printing

(P-3760)
G-2 GRAPHIC SERVICE INC
5510 Cleon Ave (91601-2835)
PHONE...............818 623-3100
John C Beard, *CEO*
Joe Cotrupe, *
Pamela Beard-cotrupe, *VP*
Scott Dewinkeleer, *
◆ **EMP:** 52 **EST:** 1969
SQ FT: 35,000
SALES (est): 9.55MM **Privately Held**
Web: www.g2online.com
SIC: 2759 7331 Commercial printing, nec; Direct mail advertising services

(P-3761)
GACHUPIN ENTERPRISES LLC
Also Called: Speedwear.com
5671 Engineer Dr (92649-1123)
PHONE...............714 375-4111
Kai Gachupin, *Owner*
David Thomas, *Mgr*
▲ **EMP:** 18 **EST:** 2010
SQ FT: 11,000
SALES (est): 2.04MM **Privately Held**
SIC: 2759 7389 3949 Screen printing; Embroidery advertising; Sporting and athletic goods, nec

(P-3762)
GOLDEN APPLEXX CO INC
19805 Harrison Ave (91789-2849)
PHONE...............909 594-9788
Peter Lee, *Pr*
Shio-ru Lee, *VP*
◆ **EMP:** 20 **EST:** 1986
SALES (est): 963.87K **Privately Held**
Web: www.goldenapplexx.com
SIC: 2759 2396 Promotional printing; Automotive and apparel trimmings

(P-3763)
GRAPHIC TRENDS INCORPORATED
7301 Adams St (90723-4007)
PHONE...............562 531-2339
Kieu V Tran, *Prin*
EMP: 40 **EST:** 1983
SQ FT: 20,984
SALES (est): 5.34MM **Privately Held**
Web: www.graphictrends.net
SIC: 2759 7336 Screen printing; Graphic arts and related design

(P-3764)
GRAPHICS 2000 LLC
1600 E Valencia Dr (92831-4735)
PHONE...............714 879-1188
EMP: 54
SIC: 2759 2396 Letterpress and screen printing; Automotive and apparel trimmings

(P-3765)
GREAT WESTERN PACKAGING LLC
8230 Haskell Ave 8240 (91406)
PHONE...............818 464-3800
Michael C Warner, *Managing Member*
Victoria Warner Kaplan, *
EMP: 68 **EST:** 1970
SALES (est): 3.55MM **Privately Held**
Web: www.greatwesternpackaging.com
SIC: 2759 Commercial printing, nec

(P-3766)
HB PRODUCTS LLC
Also Called: Lean Merch
5671 Engineer Dr (92649-1123)
PHONE...............714 799-6967
EMP: 20 **EST:** 2000
SALES (est): 2.13MM **Privately Held**
SIC: 2759 Screen printing

(P-3767)
HEARTLAND LABEL PRINTERS LLC
9817 7th St Ste 703 (91730-7802)
PHONE...............909 243-7151
John Wojcik, *Prin*
EMP: 575
Web: www.hrtlp.com
SIC: 2759 Labels and seals: printing, nsk
HQ: Heartland Label Printers, Llc
1700 Stephen St
Little Chute WI
920 687-4145

(P-3768)
HUDSON PRINTING INC
Also Called: Hudson Printing
2780 Loker Ave W (92010-6611)
PHONE...............760 602-1260
James Fairweather, *Pr*
Tom Fairweather, *VP*
Anne Fairweather, *Treas*
EMP: 23 **EST:** 2004
SQ FT: 6,000

SALES (est): 7.43MM **Privately Held**
Web: www.hudsonsd.com
SIC: 2759 2752 Screen printing; Offset printing

(P-3769)
ID SUPPLY
3183 Red Hill Ave (92626-3401)
PHONE...............714 728-6478
Brandon Ruddach, *CEO*
Brandon Rudach, *
EMP: 34 **EST:** 2017
SALES (est): 2.51MM **Privately Held**
Web: www.idsupplyco.com
SIC: 2759 Screen printing

(P-3770)
INK FX CORPORATION
513 S La Serena Dr (91723-3202)
PHONE...............909 673-1950
Joe Metz, *Pr*
Mike Machrone, *
EMP: 25 **EST:** 1993
SALES (est): 2.35MM **Privately Held**
Web: www.inkfx.com
SIC: 2759 Screen printing

(P-3771)
INTERNTIONAL COLOR POSTERS INC
Also Called: ICP West
8081 Orangethorpe Ave (90621-3801)
PHONE...............949 768-1005
Eric Guerineau, *Pr*
▲ **EMP:** 38 **EST:** 1985
SQ FT: 26,000
SALES (est): 1.81MM **Privately Held**
SIC: 2759 Screen printing

(P-3772)
INVESTMENT ENTERPRISES INC (PA)
Also Called: A2z Color Graphics
8230 Haskell Ave Ste 8240 (91406-1322)
PHONE...............818 464-3800
Michael Warner, *Pr*
Denise Scanlon, *
Jack Wickson, *
EMP: 43 **EST:** 1970
SALES (est): 4.03MM
SALES (corp-wide): 4.03MM **Privately Held**
SIC: 2759 Magazines: printing, nsk

(P-3773)
IRIS GROUP INC
Also Called: Modern Postcard
1675 Faraday Ave (92008-7314)
PHONE...............760 431-1103
Steve Hoffman, *CEO*
EMP: 250 **EST:** 1977
SQ FT: 75,000
SALES (est): 45.45MM **Privately Held**
Web: www.modernpostcard.com
SIC: 2759 5961 Commercial printing, nec; Mail order house, nec

(P-3774)
KIERAN LABEL CORP
2321 Siempre Viva Ct Ste 101 (92154-6301)
PHONE...............619 449-4457
Denis Vanier, *CEO*
William Walker, *
Bill Walker, *
▲ **EMP:** 44 **EST:** 1979
SALES (est): 10.43MM **Privately Held**
Web: www.kieranlabel.com

SIC: 2759 Commercial printing, nec
PA: I.D. Images Llc
1120 W 130th St
Brunswick OH

(P-3775)
L A SUPPLY CO
Also Called: Label House
4241 E Brickell St (91761-1512)
PHONE...............949 470-9900
Randolph William Austin, *CEO*
▲ **EMP:** 31 **EST:** 1947
SALES (est): 4.32MM **Privately Held**
SIC: 2759 2752 2672 2396 Labels and seals: printing, nsk; Commercial printing, lithographic; Paper; coated and laminated, nec; Automotive and apparel trimmings

(P-3776)
LABEL IMPRESSIONS INC
1831 W Sequoia Ave (92868-1017)
PHONE...............714 634-3466
EMP: 42
SIC: 2759 Labels and seals: printing, nsk

(P-3777)
LABEL SPECIALTIES INC
704 Dunn Way (92870-6805)
PHONE...............714 961-8074
Michael A Gyure, *Pr*
Tom Wetterhus, *VP*
EMP: 26 **EST:** 1981
SQ FT: 11,000
SALES (est): 1.25MM **Privately Held**
Web: www.labelspec.com
SIC: 2759 Labels and seals: printing, nsk

(P-3778)
LABELING HURST SYSTEMS LLC
Also Called: Hurst International
20747 Dearborn St (91311-5914)
P.O. Box 5169 (91313-5169)
PHONE...............818 701-0710
Aron Lichtenberg, *Pr*
▲ **EMP:** 18 **EST:** 1995
SQ FT: 12,875
SALES (est): 2.41MM **Privately Held**
Web: www.hurst-international.com
SIC: 2759 Labels and seals: printing, nsk

(P-3779)
LABELTRONIX LLC (HQ)
Also Called: Rethink Label Systems
2419 E Winston Rd (92806-5544)
PHONE...............800 429-4321
▲ **EMP:** 73 **EST:** 1993
SQ FT: 48,000
SALES (est): 15.75MM
SALES (corp-wide): 28.01MM **Privately Held**
Web: www.awtlabelpack.com
SIC: 2759 Labels and seals: printing, nsk
PA: Advanced Web Technologies, Inc.
600 Hoover St Ne Ste 500
Minneapolis MN
612 706-3700

(P-3780)
LAWEB OFFSET PRINTING INC
Also Called: Chinese-La Daily News
9645 Telstar Ave (91731-3012)
PHONE...............626 454-2469
Walter Chang, *Pr*
Chi-kwang Chiang, *VP*
Ya-tang Fu, *Stockholder*
▲ **EMP:** 19 **EST:** 1990
SALES (est): 676.29K **Privately Held**
Web: www.lawebprint.com

SIC: 2759 2752 Newspapers: printing, nsk; Offset printing

(P-3781)
LCA PROMOTIONS INC
3073 Cicero Ct (93063-1606)
PHONE..............................818 773-9170
Terrence R Aleck, *Pr*
EMP: 20 EST: 1992
SALES (est): 2.03MM **Privately Held**
Web: www.lcapromotions.com
SIC: 2759 Screen printing

(P-3782)
LEGION CREATIVE GROUP
500 N Brand Blvd Ste 1800 (91203-3305)
PHONE..............................323 498-1100
Kathleen Fliiler, *Owner*
EMP: 25 EST: 2015
SALES (est): 3.09MM **Privately Held**
Web: www.legioncreative.us
SIC: 2759 Advertising literature: printing, nsk

(P-3783)
LPS AGENCY SALES & POSTING INC
3210 El Camino Real Ste 200 (92602)
PHONE..............................714 247-7500
EMP: 79
SALES (corp-wide): 658.5K **Privately Held**
SIC: 2759 Publication printing
PA: Lps Agency Sales And Posting, Inc.
3210 El Cmino Real Ste 20
Irvine CA
714 247-7503

(P-3784)
MARCO FINE ARTS GALLERIES INC
4860 W 147th St (90250-6706)
PHONE..............................310 615-1818
Al Marco, *Pr*
Kristoff Honeymany, *
▲ EMP: 24 EST: 1986
SQ FT: 10,000
SALES (est): 4.48MM **Privately Held**
Web: www.marcofinearts.com
SIC: 2759 5199 5023 Commercial printing, nec; Art goods; Frames and framing, picture and mirror

(P-3785)
MARTIN E-Z STICK LABELS
12921 Sunnyside Pl (90670-4645)
PHONE..............................562 906-1577
Francisco Martinez, *Pr*
Moncia Martinez, *Sec*
Sylvia Martinez, *Treas*
EMP: 18 EST: 1979
SQ FT: 14,800
SALES (est): 2.44MM **Privately Held**
Web: www.martinezsticklabels.com
SIC: 2759 Labels and seals: printing, nsk

(P-3786)
MATRIX DOCUMENT IMAGING INC
527 E Rowland St Ste 214 (91723-3267)
PHONE..............................626 966-9959
Thomas Smith, *Pr*
Mercedes Uribe, *
EMP: 19 EST: 2006
SALES (est): 809.53K **Privately Held**
Web: www.legal-records.us
SIC: 2759 8111 Laser printing; Legal services

(P-3787)
MILLION CORPORATION
Also Called: Able Card Corporation
1300 W Optical Dr Ste 600 (91702-3285)
PHONE..............................626 969-1888
Herman Ho, *CEO*
Hector Dominguez, *
Donny Yu, *
EMP: 70 EST: 1989
SQ FT: 45,000
SALES (est): 7.93MM **Privately Held**
SIC: 2759 Commercial printing, nec
PA: First Nations Capital Partners, Llc
7676 Hazard Center Dr # 5
San Diego CA

(P-3788)
MORELAND MANUFACTURING INC
Also Called: Coast Label Company
17406 Mount Cliffwood Cir (92708-4101)
PHONE..............................714 426-1411
EMP: 20 EST: 1970
SALES (est): 4.43MM **Privately Held**
Web: www.coastlabel.com
SIC: 2759 Labels and seals: printing, nsk

(P-3789)
NEFT VODKA USA INC
144 Penn St (90245-3907)
PHONE..............................415 846-0359
Christopher Holtzer, *Prin*
EMP: 27 EST: 2017
SALES (est): 1.17MM **Privately Held**
Web: www.neftvodkaus.com
SIC: 2759 Screen printing

(P-3790)
NOWDOCS INTERNATIONAL INC
Also Called: Nowdocs
3230 E Imperial Hwy # 302 (92821-6721)
PHONE..............................714 986-1559
EMP: 24
SIC: 2759 Commercial printing, nec

(P-3791)
ONE STOP LABEL CORPORATION
1641 S Baker Ave (91761-8025)
PHONE..............................909 230-9380
Maria Navarro, *Pr*
Jorge Navarro, *VP*
EMP: 22 EST: 1996
SQ FT: 12,000
SALES (est): 905.38K **Privately Held**
Web: www.onestoplabel.com
SIC: 2759 Labels and seals: printing, nsk

(P-3792)
OPTEC LASER SYSTEMS LLC
11622 El Camino Real Ste 100 (92130-2049)
PHONE..............................858 220-1070
EMP: 25 EST: 2017
SALES (est): 1.24MM **Privately Held**
Web: www.optec-laser-systems.com
SIC: 2759 Laser printing

(P-3793)
ORANGE CIRCLE STUDIO CORP (PA)
Also Called: Studio OH
2 Technology Dr (92618-5317)
PHONE..............................949 727-0800
Daniel H Whang, *CEO*
Scott Whang, *Ch*
◆ EMP: 40 EST: 2009
SALES (est): 10.68MM

SALES (corp-wide): 10.68MM **Privately Held**
Web: www.studiooh.com
SIC: 2759 Calendars: printing, nsk

(P-3794)
ORORA VISUAL LLC
1600 E Valencia Dr (92831-4735)
PHONE..............................714 879-2400
James R Hamel, *Pr*
▲ EMP: 100 EST: 1987
SALES (est): 9.07MM **Privately Held**
Web: www.ororagroup.com
SIC: 2759 Screen printing

(P-3795)
PAX TAG & LABEL INC
9528 Rush St Ste C (91733-1551)
PHONE..............................626 579-2000
Michael Brown, *Pr*
EMP: 20 EST: 1994
SQ FT: 10,000
SALES (est): 2.38MM **Privately Held**
Web: www.paxtag.com
SIC: 2759 2679 Tags: printing, nsk; Tags, paper (unprinted): made from purchased paper

(P-3796)
POLYCRAFT INC
42075 Avenida Alvarado (92590-3486)
PHONE..............................951 296-0860
William D Verstegen, *Pr*
Patricia Verstegen, *Prin*
Bryan Nealy, *Prin*
EMP: 20 EST: 1974
SQ FT: 21,000
SALES (est): 3.69MM **Privately Held**
Web: www.polycraftinc.com
SIC: 2759 2671 Screen printing; Paper; coated and laminated packaging

(P-3797)
PRESIDENT ENTERPRISE LLC
Also Called: Lotus Labels
655 Tamarack Ave (92821-3213)
PHONE..............................714 671-9577
George Wu, *Pr*
Shu-feng T Wu, *VP*
▲ EMP: 20 EST: 1992
SALES (est): 4.77MM **Privately Held**
Web: www.lotuslabels.net
SIC: 2759 Labels and seals: printing, nsk

(P-3798)
PRIMARY COLOR SYSTEMS CORP (PA)
11130 Holder St Ste 210 (90630-5162)
PHONE..............................949 660-7080
Daniel Hirt, *CEO*
Michael Hirt, *
▲ EMP: 305 EST: 1984
SQ FT: 40,000
SALES (est): 122.08MM
SALES (corp-wide): 122.08MM **Privately Held**
Web: www.primarycolor.com
SIC: 2759 2752 Commercial printing, nec; Offset printing

(P-3799)
PRIMARY COLOR SYSTEMS CORP
401 Coral Cir (90245-4622)
PHONE..............................310 841-0250
Ed Philipps, *Brnch Mgr*
EMP: 53
SALES (corp-wide): 122.08MM **Privately Held**

Web: www.primarycolor.com
SIC: 2759 2752 Commercial printing, nec; Commercial printing, lithographic
PA: Primary Color Systems Corporation
11130 Holder St Ste 210
Cypress CA
949 660-7080

(P-3800)
PROFESSNAL RPRGRAPHIC SVCS INC
Also Called: Pro Group
17622 Armstrong Ave (92614-5728)
PHONE..............................949 748-5400
Cindy Kennedy, *Pr*
Thomas Brian Kennedy, *
EMP: 25 EST: 2008
SALES (est): 7.48MM **Privately Held**
Web: professionalreprographic.mfgpages.com
SIC: 2759 Commercial printing, nec

(P-3801)
PROGRAPHICS SCREENPRINTING INC
1975 Diamond St (92078-5122)
PHONE..............................760 744-4555
Bruce Heid, *Pr*
Barbara Heid, *
EMP: 41 EST: 1989
SQ FT: 18,000
SALES (est): 6.21MM **Privately Held**
Web: www.prografx.com
SIC: 2759 3993 2396 5112 Screen printing; Signs and advertising specialties; Automotive and apparel trimmings; Pens and/or pencils

(P-3802)
PROGRSSIVE INTGRATED SOLUTIONS
Also Called: Progressive Manufacturing
377 S Acacia Ave (92831-4748)
PHONE..............................714 237-0980
Rodney Dean Boehme, *Pr*
EMP: 76 EST: 1988
SALES (est): 4.01MM **Privately Held**
Web: www.progressiveusa.com
SIC: 2759 2752 Envelopes: printing, nsk; Offset printing

(P-3803)
R R DONNELLEY & SONS COMPANY
Los Angeles Manufacturing Div
19681 Pacific Gateway Dr (90502-1116)
PHONE..............................310 516-3100
Barbara Dowell, *Dir*
EMP: 54
SQ FT: 80,000
SALES (corp-wide): 15B **Privately Held**
Web: www.rrd.com
SIC: 2759 2752 Publication printing; Commercial printing, lithographic
HQ: R. R. Donnelley & Sons Company
35 W Wacker Dr
Chicago IL
800 782-4892

(P-3804)
R R DONNELLEY & SONS COMPANY
Also Called: R R Donnelley
955 Gateway Center Way (92102-4542)
PHONE..............................619 527-4600
Boyd Richardson, *Brnch Mgr*
EMP: 56
SALES (corp-wide): 15B **Privately Held**
Web: www.rrd.com

P R O D U C T S & S V C S

SIC: 2759 Commercial printing, nec
HQ: R. R. Donnelley & Sons Company
　　35 W Wacker Dr
　　Chicago IL
　　800 782-4892

(P-3805)
RESOURCE LABEL GROUP LLC
1511 E Edinger Ave (92705-4907)
PHONE..............................714 619-7100
Robert Simko, *Mgr*
EMP: 80
Web: www.resourcelabel.com
SIC: 2759 2752 Commercial printing, nec;
　　Commercial printing, lithographic
PA: Resource Label Group, Llc
　　2550 Meridian Blvd # 370
　　Franklin TN

(P-3806)
RESPONSE ENVELOPE INC (PA)
1340 S Baker Ave (91761-7742)
PHONE..............................909 923-5855
Jonas Ulrich, *CEO*
Philip Ulrich, *
▲ EMP: 104 EST: 1986
SQ FT: 85,000
SALES (est): 9.5MM
SALES (corp-wide): 9.5MM **Privately Held**
Web: www.response-envelope.com
SIC: 2759 2677 Envelopes: printing, nsk;
　　Envelopes

(P-3807)
RETAIL PRINT MEDIA INC
2355 Crenshaw Blvd Ste 135 (90501-3329)
PHONE..............................424 488-6950
Raymond Young, *CEO*
Karli Sikich, *
EMP: 35 EST: 2015
SALES (est): 4.64MM **Privately Held**
Web: www.retailprintmedia.com
SIC: 2759 7371 Advertising literature:
　　printing, nsk; Computer software writing
　　services

(P-3808)
RJ ACQUISITION CORP (PA)
Also Called: Ad Art Company
3260 E 26th St (90058-8008)
PHONE..............................323 318-1107
Joe M Demarco, *Pr*
Roger Keech, *
Eddie Leon, *Prin*
Jose Puentes Plant, *Prin*
▲ EMP: 215 EST: 1944
SQ FT: 200,000
SALES (est): 39.34MM
SALES (corp-wide): 39.34MM **Privately
Held**
Web: www.adartco.com
SIC: 2759 Screen printing

(P-3809)
ROBINSON PRINTING INC
Also Called: Robinson Printing
42685 Rio Nedo (92590-3711)
PHONE..............................951 296-0300
David Robinson, *CEO*
Mike Robinson, *
▲ EMP: 46 EST: 1981
SQ FT: 24,000
SALES (est): 5.2MM **Privately Held**
Web: www.robinsonprinting.com
SIC: 2759 2621 Screen printing; Packaging
　　paper

(P-3810)
**SAN BRNRDINO CMNTY
COLLEGE DST**

Also Called: Print Shop
701 S Mount Vernon Ave (92410-2705)
PHONE..............................909 888-6511
Louie Chavira, *Supervisor*
EMP: 56
SALES (corp-wide): 46.53MM **Privately
Held**
Web: www.sbccd.edu
SIC: 2759 Commercial printing, nec
PA: San Bernardino Community College
　　District
　　550 E Hospitality Ln # 200
　　San Bernardino CA
　　909 382-4000

(P-3811)
SHORETT PRINTING INC (PA)
Also Called: Crown Printers
250 W Rialto Ave (92408-1017)
PHONE..............................714 545-4689
Charles D Shorett Junior, *CEO*
John Shorett, *
EMP: 30 EST: 1970
SALES (est): 6.4MM
SALES (corp-wide): 6.4MM **Privately Held**
Web: www.crownconnect.com
SIC: 2759 2752 Commercial printing, nec;
　　Offset printing

(P-3812)
**SPECIALIZED SCREEN PRTG
INC**
18435 Bandilier Cir (92708-7012)
PHONE..............................714 964-1230
David Williams, *CEO*
Jim Keisker, *
EMP: 17 EST: 1998
SQ FT: 20,000
SALES (est): 675.68K **Privately Held**
Web:
www.specializedscreenprinting.com
SIC: 2759 2752 2396 Screen printing;
　　Commercial printing, lithographic;
　　Automotive and apparel trimmings

(P-3813)
SUPACOLOR USA INC
16198 Gramercy Pl Ste B (90247)
PHONE..............................844 973-2862
Ramneek Walia, *CEO*
EMP: 91 EST: 2019
SALES (est): 5.2MM **Privately Held**
Web: www.supacolor.com
SIC: 2759 Letterpress and screen printing

(P-3814)
**SUPER COLOR DIGITAL LLC
(PA)**
Also Called: Super Color Digital
16761 Hale Ave (92606-5006)
PHONE..............................949 622-0010
Peyman Rashtchi, *Managing Member*
▲ EMP: 25 EST: 2006
SQ FT: 48,043
SALES (est): 58.79MM **Privately Held**
Web: www.supercolor.com
SIC: 2759 Commercial printing, nec

(P-3815)
SUPERIOR PRINTING INC
Also Called: Superior Press
9440 Norwalk Blvd (90670-2928)
PHONE..............................888 590-7998
Robert Traut, *Pr*
Kevin Traut, *
Jason Traut, *
EMP: 95 EST: 1953
SQ FT: 32,000
SALES (est): 20.15MM **Privately Held**
Web: www.superiorpress.com

SIC: 2759 5112 Commercial printing, nec;
　　Business forms

(P-3816)
**TARGET MDIA PRTNERS
INTRCTIVE (HQ)**
Also Called: Target Mdia Prtners Intractive
5200 Lankershim Blvd Ste 350
(91601-3109)
PHONE..............................323 930-3123
Dave Duckwitz, *CEO*
EMP: 35 EST: 1998
SALES (est): 15.06MM
SALES (corp-wide): 24.59MM **Privately
Held**
Web: www.targetmediapartners.com
SIC: 2759 7331 Commercial printing, nec;
　　Direct mail advertising services
PA: Responselogix, Inc.
　　6991 E Camelback Rd B30
　　Scottsdale AZ
　　888 713-8958

(P-3817)
TAYLOR GRAPHICS INC
1582 Browning (92606-4807)
PHONE..............................949 752-5200
Dean S Taylor, *CEO*
Carla Spicer, *
EMP: 23 EST: 1950
SQ FT: 7,500
SALES (est): 4.22MM **Privately Held**
SIC: 2759 Screen printing

(P-3818)
**TAYLOR TECHNOLOGY
SERVICES INC**
Nowdocs
3230 E Imperial Hwy Ste 302 (92821-6721)
PHONE..............................714 986-1559
EMP: 70
SALES (corp-wide): 3.81B **Privately Held**
Web: www.taylor.com
SIC: 2759 Commercial printing, nec
HQ: Taylor Technology Services, Inc.
　　1725 Roe Crest Dr
　　North Mankato MN

(P-3819)
TEC COLOR CRAFT (PA)
Also Called: TEC Color Craft Products
1860 Wright Ave (91750-5824)
PHONE..............................909 392-9000
Edgar A Frenkiel, *CEO*
▲ EMP: 40 EST: 1960
SQ FT: 8,000
SALES (est): 4.82MM
SALES (corp-wide): 4.82MM **Privately
Held**
Web: www.teccolorcraft.com
SIC: 2759 Screen printing

(P-3820)
TEE STYLED INC
5383 Alcoa Ave (90058-3734)
PHONE..............................323 983-9988
Anwar Gajiani, *Pr*
EMP: 41 EST: 2019
SALES (est): 4.64MM **Privately Held**
SIC: 2759 Screen printing
PA: Fantasy Activewear, Inc.
　　5383 Alcoa Ave
　　Vernon CA

(P-3821)
THREE MAN CORPORATION
Also Called: San Diego Printers
10025 Huennekens St (92121-2967)
PHONE..............................858 684-5200

John Barros, *Pr*
Wayne Ihms, *VP*
EMP: 20 EST: 1999
SQ FT: 14,000
SALES (est): 3.72MM **Privately Held**
Web: www.sdprinters.com
SIC: 2759 2752 Commercial printing, nec;
　　Commercial printing, lithographic

(P-3822)
**VITACHROME GRAPHICS
GROUP INC**
Also Called: Vitachrome Graphics
3710 Park Pl (91020-1623)
P.O. Box 2924 (90670-0924)
PHONE..............................818 957-0900
Gary Durbin, *Pr*
Tony Won, *
EMP: 45 EST: 1971
SQ FT: 43,000
SALES (est): 4.82MM **Privately Held**
Web: www.adahotelsigns.com
SIC: 2759 Decals: printing, nsk

(P-3823)
VOMAR PRODUCTS INC
Also Called: Vomar
7800 Deering Ave (91304-5005)
PHONE..............................818 610-5115
Paul Van Ostrand, *CEO*
Herbert Paul Van Ostrand, *
Jason Van Ostrand, *
EMP: 38 EST: 1961
SQ FT: 29,000
SALES (est): 6.14MM **Privately Held**
Web: www.vomarproducts.com
SIC: 2759 3993 Commercial printing, nec;
　　Name plates: except engraved, etched,
　　etc.: metal

(P-3824)
WES GO INC
Also Called: GP Color Imaging Group
8211 Lankershim Blvd (91605-1614)
PHONE..............................818 504-1200
Wesley Adams, *CEO*
Thomas Wilhelm, *
▲ EMP: 24 EST: 2001
SALES (est): 5.25MM **Privately Held**
Web: www.gpcolor.com
SIC: 2759 Posters, including billboards:
　　printing, nsk

(P-3825)
**WESTERN CONVERTING SPC
INC**
Also Called: Consolidated Design West
2886 Metropolitan Pl (91767-1854)
PHONE..............................909 392-4578
Chad Junkin, *Pr*
EMP: 20 EST: 1980
SQ FT: 8,000
SALES (est): 1.96MM **Privately Held**
Web: www.westernconverting.com
SIC: 2759 Commercial printing, nec

(P-3826)
**WESTERN STATES ENVELOPE
CORP**
2301 Raymer Ave (92833-2514)
P.O. Box 2607 (92837-0607)
PHONE..............................714 449-0909
Lisa Hoehle, *Pr*
EMP: 60 EST: 1968
SQ FT: 24,000
SALES (est): 4.44MM **Privately Held**
Web: www.wseca.com
SIC: 2759 Commercial printing, nec

(P-3827)
WILSONS ART STUDIO INC
Also Called: Solutions Unlimited
501 S Acacia Ave (92831-5101)
PHONE...............................714 870-7030
William L Goetsch, *Pr*
N Jim Goetsch, *
Roberta C Goetsch, *
EMP: 63 **EST:** 1958
SQ FT: 50,000
SALES (est): 5MM **Privately Held**
Web: www.solutions-unlimited.net
SIC: 2759 2396 Screen printing; Automotive and apparel trimmings

2761 Manifold Business Forms

(P-3828)
APPERSON INC (PA)
17315 Studebaker Rd Ste 211
(90703-2563)
P.O. Box 480309 (28269-5338)
PHONE...............................562 356-3333
Kelly Doherty, *CEO*
Brian Apperson, *
William Apperson, *
▲ **EMP:** 70 **EST:** 1955
SQ FT: 80,080
SALES (est): 20.25MM
SALES (corp-wide): 20.25MM **Privately Held**
Web: www.apperson.com
SIC: 2761 Continuous forms, office and business

(P-3829)
BESTFORMS INC
1135 Avenida Acaso (93012-8740)
PHONE...............................805 388-0503
Joe Valdez, *Pr*
Patrick Valdez, *
EMP: 48 **EST:** 1985
SQ FT: 31,000
SALES (est): 8.36MM **Privately Held**
Web: www.bestforms.com
SIC: 2761 Manifold business forms

(P-3830)
COMPLYRIGHT DIST SVCS INC
3451 Jupiter Ct (93030-8957)
PHONE...............................805 981-0992
Richard Roddis, *CEO*
EMP: 44 **EST:** 2006
SALES (est): 9.18MM
SALES (corp-wide): 3.81B **Privately Held**
Web: www.complyrightdealer.com
SIC: 2761 Manifold business forms
PA: Taylor Corporation
1725 Roe Crest Dr
North Mankato MN
507 625-2828

(P-3831)
NBS SYSTEMS INC (PA)
2477 E Orangethorpe Ave (92831-5303)
PHONE...............................217 999-3472
Bill Gascon, *Pr*
EMP: 35 **EST:** 1963
SALES (est): 2.1MM
SALES (corp-wide): 2.1MM **Privately Held**
Web: www.nbschecks.com
SIC: 2761 2759 Continuous forms, office and business; Commercial printing, nec

(P-3832)
PRINTEGRA CORP
23281 La Palma Ave (92887-4768)
PHONE...............................714 692-2221
Terri Reynolds, *Mgr*
EMP: 65
SQ FT: 38,000
SALES (corp-wide): 431.84MM **Publicly Held**
Web: www.printegra.com
SIC: 2761 2782 Continuous forms, office and business; Blankbooks and looseleaf binders
HQ: Printegra Corp
1560 Westfork Dr
Lithia Springs GA
770 487-5151

(P-3833)
TST/IMPRESO INC
10589 Business Dr (92337-8223)
PHONE...............................909 357-7190
▲ **EMP:** 42
SALES (corp-wide): 117.52MM **Privately Held**
Web: www.tstimpreso.com
SIC: 2761 Manifold business forms
HQ: Tst/Impreso, Inc.
652 Southwestern Blvd
Coppell TX
972 462-0100

(P-3834)
WRIGHT BUSINESS GRAPHICS LLC
Also Called: Wright Business Graphics Calif
13602 12th St Ste A (91710-5200)
P.O. Box 20489 (97294-0489)
PHONE...............................909 614-6700
Gene Snitker, *Prin*
EMP: 29
SALES (corp-wide): 431.84MM **Publicly Held**
Web: www.wrightbg.com
SIC: 2761 Manifold business forms
HQ: Wright Business Graphics Llc
18440 Ne San Rafael St
Portland OR
800 547-8397

2782 Blankbooks And Looseleaf Binders

(P-3835)
CHECKWORKS INC
315 Cloverleaf Dr Ste J (91706-6510)
P.O. Box 60065 (91716-0065)
PHONE...............................626 333-1444
EMP: 55 **EST:** 1995
SQ FT: 15,000
SALES (est): 4.52MM **Privately Held**
Web: www.checkworks.com
SIC: 2782 Checkbooks

(P-3836)
CONTINENTAL BDR SPECIALTY CORP (PA)
407 W Compton Blvd (90248-1703)
PHONE...............................310 324-8227
Andrew Lisardi, *CEO*
Jack Gray, *
▼ **EMP:** 120 **EST:** 1978
SQ FT: 31,000
SALES (est): 8.03MM
SALES (corp-wide): 8.03MM **Privately Held**
Web: www.continentalbinder.com
SIC: 2782 2759 2675 2396 Looseleaf binders and devices; Commercial printing, nec; Die-cut paper and board; Automotive and apparel trimmings

(P-3837)
DOCUPAK INC
1702 Edinger Ave (92780-6511)
PHONE...............................714 670-7944
William Lyons, *Pr*
Pat Lyons, *VP*
John Flores, *CFO*
EMP: 17 **EST:** 1993
SALES (est): 1.95MM **Privately Held**
Web: www.docupakinc.com
SIC: 2782 Looseleaf binders and devices

(P-3838)
HANOVER ACCESSORIES CORP
6049 E Slauson Ave (90040-3007)
▲ **EMP:** 120
SIC: 2782 Library binders, looseleaf

(P-3839)
PIONEER PHOTO ALBUMS INC (PA)
9801 Deering Ave (91311-4398)
P.O. Box 2497 (91313-2497)
PHONE...............................818 882-2161
Shell Plutsky, *CEO*
Jason Reubens, *
Rick Collies, *
◆ **EMP:** 150 **EST:** 1972
SQ FT: 100,000
SALES (est): 16.64MM
SALES (corp-wide): 16.64MM **Privately Held**
Web: www.pioneerphotoalbums.com
SIC: 2782 Albums

(P-3840)
SHARON HAVRILUK
Also Called: American Mailing & Prtg Svc
1164 N Kraemer Pl (92806-1922)
PHONE...............................714 630-1313
Sharon Havriluk, *Owner*
EMP: 20 **EST:** 1966
SQ FT: 10,000
SALES (est): 1.68MM **Privately Held**
Web: www.ampls.com
SIC: 2782 7331 Account books; Mailing list compilers

(P-3841)
ULTRA PRO ACQUISITION LLC
6049 E Slauson Ave (90040-3007)
PHONE...............................323 725-1975
▲ **EMP:** 24 **EST:** 2007
SALES (est): 2.49MM **Privately Held**
SIC: 2782 Library binders, looseleaf
PA: Marlin Equity Partners, Llc
1301 Manhattan Ave
Hermosa Beach CA

(P-3842)
VAGRANT RECORDS INC
6351 Wilshire Blvd Ste 101 (90048-5021)
PHONE...............................323 302-0100
Richard A Egan, *Pr*
Jon Cohen, *VP*
EMP: 18 **EST:** 1993
SALES (est): 801.84K **Privately Held**
Web: www.vagrant.com
SIC: 2782 5735 Record albums; Records

(P-3843)
VAPOR DELUX INC
2148 Glendale Galleria (91210-2101)
PHONE...............................818 370-8308
EMP: 22
SALES (corp-wide): 565.75K **Privately Held**
Web: www.vapordelux.com
SIC: 2782 Checkbooks

PA: Vapor Delux Inc
11152 Fleetwood St Ste 1
Sun Valley CA
818 856-3750

2789 Bookbinding And Related Work

(P-3844)
B J BINDERY INC
833 S Grand Ave (92705-4117)
PHONE...............................714 835-7342
Naresh Arya, *CEO*
Renu Arya, *
▲ **EMP:** 80 **EST:** 1970
SQ FT: 29,000
SALES (est): 4.07MM **Privately Held**
Web: www.bjbindery.com
SIC: 2789 Binding only: books, pamphlets, magazines, etc.

(P-3845)
GENERAL REWINDING INC
Also Called: General Newsprint
888 W Crowther Ave (92870-6348)
PHONE...............................714 776-5561
▲ **EMP:** 20 **EST:** 1980
SALES (est): 1.3MM **Privately Held**
SIC: 2789 Paper cutting

(P-3846)
GOLDEN RULE BINDERY INC
Also Called: Golden Rule Packaging
1315 Hot Springs Way Ste 102
(92081-7878)
PHONE...............................760 471-2013
Jerry Kiley, *Pr*
Fred Antor, *Treas*
EMP: 22 **EST:** 1957
SQ FT: 6,400
SALES (est): 1.41MM **Privately Held**
Web: www.goldenrulebindery.com
SIC: 2789 Bookbinding and related work

(P-3847)
KATER-CRAFTS INCORPORATED
Also Called: Book Binders
4860 Gregg Rd (90660-2107)
PHONE...............................562 692-0665
Bruce Kavin, *Pr*
Richard Kavin, *
EMP: 40 **EST:** 1948
SQ FT: 20,000
SALES (est): 4.85MM **Privately Held**
Web: www.katercrafts.com
SIC: 2789 Binding only: books, pamphlets, magazines, etc.

(P-3848)
ROSS BINDERY INC
15310 Spring Ave (90670-5644)
PHONE...............................562 623-4565
George Jackson, *CEO*
▲ **EMP:** 120 **EST:** 1969
SQ FT: 65,000
SALES (est): 9.27MM **Privately Held**
Web: www.rossbindery.com
SIC: 2789 Pamphlets, binding

(P-3849)
S & S BINDERY INC
2366 1st St (91750-5545)
PHONE...............................909 596-2213
Steve Thompson, *Pr*
Scott Fehrensen, *VP*
▼ **EMP:** 20 **EST:** 1998
SQ FT: 13,750

P R O D U C T S & S V C S

SALES (est): 2.37MM **Privately Held**
SIC: 2789 Binding only: books, pamphlets, magazines, etc.

2791 Typesetting

(P-3850)
AUTOMATION PRINTING CO (PA)
1230 Long Beach Ave (90021-2320)
PHONE.........................213 488-1230
David Tobman, *Pr*
Ann Tobman, *
EMP: 37 EST: 1949
SQ FT: 30,000
SALES (est): 3.4MM
SALES (corp-wide): 3.4MM **Privately Held**
Web: www.automation-123.com
SIC: 2791 2796 2759 2732 Typesetting; Platemaking services; Commercial printing, nec; Book printing

(P-3851)
GRANT DAHLSTROM INC
Also Called: Castle Press
1222 N Fair Oaks Ave (91103-2514)
PHONE.........................626 798-0858
EMP: 19 EST: 1931
SALES (est): 825.86K **Privately Held**
SIC: 2791 2752 7336 2789 Typesetting; Offset printing; Commercial art and graphic design; Bookbinding and related work

2796 Platemaking Services

(P-3852)
EFFECTIVE GRAPHICS NC INC
40 E Verdugo Ave (91502-1931)
PHONE.........................310 323-2223
Roger Sanders, *CEO*
David Curtis, *
Michael Vascellaro, *
EMP: 23 EST: 1977
SQ FT: 47,970
SALES (est): 810.74K **Privately Held**
SIC: 2796 2752 Color separations, for printing; Commercial printing, lithographic

(P-3853)
FLEXLINE INCORPORATED
3727 S Meyler St (90731-6431)
PHONE.........................562 921-4141
John Bateman, *Pr*
William Hall, *
EMP: 28 EST: 1991
SALES (est): 2.38MM **Privately Held**
SIC: 2796 2759 3555 Platemaking services; Commercial printing, nec; Printing plates

(P-3854)
GEMINI GEL LLC
8365 Melrose Ave (90069-5419)
PHONE.........................323 651-0513
Sidney B Felsen, *Pr*
Stanley Grinstein, *VP*
EMP: 20 EST: 1966
SQ FT: 6,000
SALES (est): 1.23MM **Privately Held**
Web: www.geminigel.com
SIC: 2796 2752 Etching on copper, steel, wood, or rubber: printing plates; Commercial printing, lithographic

2812 Alkalies And Chlorine

(P-3855)
ARKEMA INC
Also Called: Arkema Coating Resins
19206 Hawthorne Blvd (90503-1505)
PHONE.........................310 214-5327
EMP: 66
SALES (corp-wide): 129.02MM **Privately Held**
Web: www.arkema.com
SIC: 2812 2819 2869 2899 Chlorine, compressed or liquefied; Industrial inorganic chemicals, nec; Industrial organic chemicals, nec; Metal treating compounds
HQ: Arkema Inc.
900 1st Ave
King Of Prussia PA
610 205-7000

(P-3856)
HASA INC (PA)
23119 Drayton St (91350-2547)
P.O. Box 761 (90213-0761)
PHONE.........................661 259-5848
EMP: 95 EST: 1964
SALES (est): 149.04MM
SALES (corp-wide): 149.04MM **Privately Held**
Web: www.hasa.com
SIC: 2812 Chlorine, compressed or liquefied

(P-3857)
HILL BROTHERS CHEMICAL COMPANY
Also Called: Desert Brand
15017 Clark Ave (91745-1409)
PHONE.........................626 333-2251
TOLL FREE: 800
Ron Hill, *Pr*
EMP: 18
SQ FT: 17,203
SALES (corp-wide): 125.44MM **Privately Held**
Web: www.hillbrothers.com
SIC: 2812 2851 2819 Chlorine, compressed or liquefied; Paints and allied products; Industrial inorganic chemicals, nec
PA: Hill Brothers Chemical Company
3000 E Birch St Ste 108
Brea CA
714 998-8800

(P-3858)
JCI JONES CHEMICALS INC
Also Called: Jones Chemicals
1401 Del Amo Blvd (90501-1630)
PHONE.........................310 523-1629
Mike Reddinton, *Mgr*
EMP: 19
SALES (corp-wide): 196.9MM **Privately Held**
Web: www.jcichem.com
SIC: 2812 2899 Alkalies; Chemical preparations, nec
PA: Jci Jones Chemicals, Inc.
1765 Ringling Blvd
Sarasota FL
941 330-1537

(P-3859)
OLIN CHLOR ALKALI LOGISTICS
Also Called: Chlor Alkali Products & Vinyls
11600 Pike St (90670-2938)
PHONE.........................562 692-0510
John Bilac, *Brnch Mgr*
EMP: 127
SALES (corp-wide): 9.38B **Publicly Held**
Web: www.olinchloralkali.com

SIC: 2812 Alkalies and chlorine
HQ: Olin Chlor Alkali Logistics Inc
490 Stuart Rd Ne
Cleveland TN
423 336-4850

2813 Industrial Gases

(P-3860)
AIR LIQUIDE ELECTRONICS US LP
1502 W Anaheim St (90744-2303)
PHONE.........................310 549-7079
EMP: 4366
SALES (corp-wide): 109.44MM **Privately Held**
Web: www.airliquide.com
SIC: 2813 3564 8631 2819 Industrial gases; Blowers and fans; Labor organizations; Industrial inorganic chemicals, nec
HQ: Air Liquide Electronics U.S. Lp
9101 Lyndon B Johnson Fwy # 800
Dallas TX
972 301-5200

(P-3861)
AIR PRODUCTS AND CHEMICALS INC
Air Products
1969 Palomar Oaks Way (92011-1307)
PHONE.........................760 931-9555
EMP: 371
SALES (corp-wide): 12.7B **Publicly Held**
Web: www.airproducts.com
SIC: 2813 3625 2899 2865 Industrial gases; Relays and industrial controls; Chemical preparations, nec; Cyclic crudes and intermediates
PA: Air Products And Chemicals, Inc.
1940 Air Products Blvd
Allentown PA
610 481-4911

(P-3862)
AIR SOURCE INDUSTRIES INC
3976 Cherry Ave (90807-3727)
PHONE.........................562 426-4017
EMP: 19 EST: 1938
SALES (est): 3.97MM **Privately Held**
Web: www.air-source.com
SIC: 2813 5999 Industrial gases; Convalescent equipment and supplies

(P-3863)
AIRGAS INC
Also Called: Airgas
3737 Worsham Ave (90808-1774)
P.O. Box 93500 (90809-3500)
PHONE.........................510 429-4216
EMP: 43
SALES (corp-wide): 109.44MM **Privately Held**
Web: www.airgas.com
SIC: 2813 Industrial gases
HQ: Airgas, Inc.
259 N Radnor Chester Rd # 100
Radnor PA
610 687-5253

(P-3864)
AIRGAS USA LLC
8832 Dice Rd (90670-2516)
PHONE.........................562 945-1383
Rafael Motta, *Brnch Mgr*
EMP: 59
SQ FT: 29,887
SALES (corp-wide): 109.44MM **Privately Held**
Web: www.airgas.com

SIC: 2813 5084 Industrial gases; Industrial machinery and equipment
HQ: Airgas Usa, Llc
259 N Radnor Chester Rd
Radnor PA
216 642-6600

(P-3865)
AIRGAS USA LLC
9756 Santa Fe Springs Rd (90670-2920)
PHONE.........................562 906-8700
Cynthia Aragundi, *Mgr*
EMP: 23
SALES (corp-wide): 109.44MM **Privately Held**
Web: www.airgas.com
SIC: 2813 5169 Industrial gases; Oxygen
HQ: Airgas Usa, Llc
259 N Radnor Chester Rd
Radnor PA
216 642-6600

(P-3866)
H2U TECHNOLOGIES INC
20360 Plummer St (91311-5371)
PHONE.........................626 344-0505
Mark Mcgough, *Pr*
EMP: 21 EST: 2021
SALES (est): 9.62MM **Privately Held**
Web: www.h2utechnologies.com
SIC: 2813 Hydrogen

(P-3867)
LINDE INC
Praxair
5705 E Airport Dr (91761-8611)
PHONE.........................909 390-0283
M M Stenberg, *Brnch Mgr*
EMP: 35
Web: www.lindeus.com
SIC: 2813 Industrial gases
HQ: Linde Inc.
10 Riverview Dr
Danbury CT
203 837-2000

(P-3868)
MATHESON TRI-GAS INC
16125 Ornelas St (91706-2037)
PHONE.........................626 334-2905
Fermin Reyes, *Mgr*
EMP: 22
SQ FT: 19,472
Web: www.mathesongas.com
SIC: 2813 5169 Industrial gases; Industrial gases
HQ: Matheson Tri-Gas, Inc.
3 Mountainview Rd Ste 3 # 3
Warren NJ
908 991-9200

(P-3869)
MESSER LLC
Also Called: Cryostar USA
13117 Meyer Rd (90605-3555)
PHONE.........................562 903-1290
Mark Sutton, *Brnch Mgr*
EMP: 52
SALES (corp-wide): 1.63B **Privately Held**
Web: www.messeramericas.com
SIC: 2813 3561 Oxygen, compressed or liquefied; Pumps and pumping equipment
HQ: Messer Llc
200 Smrst Corp Blvd # 7000
Bridgewater NJ
800 755-9277

(P-3870)
MESSER LLC
2535 Del Amo Blvd (90503-1706)

PHONE.............................310 533-8394
Jason Lacasella, *Brnch Mgr*
EMP: 85
SALES (corp-wide): 1.63B Privately Held
Web: www.messeramericas.com
SIC: 2813 Carbon dioxide
HQ: Messer Llc
200 Smrst Corp Blvd # 7000
Bridgewater NJ
800 755-9277

(P-3871)
NEON ROSE INC
5158 Bristol Rd (92116-2130)
PHONE.............................619 218-6103
Erin Cutler, *Prin*
EMP: 25 EST: 2018
SALES (est): 4.4MM Privately Held
Web: www.neonroseagency.com
SIC: 2813 Neon

(P-3872)
PLZ CORP
840 Tourmaline Dr (91320-1205)
PHONE.............................805 498-4531
James Seastrom, *Brnch Mgr*
EMP: 43
SALES (corp-wide): 766.3MM Privately Held
Web: www.plzcorp.com
SIC: 2813 Aerosols
PA: Plz Corp.
2651 Wrrnvlle Rd Stre 300 300 Stre
Downers Grove IL
630 628-3000

(P-3873)
PRAXAIR DISTRIBUTION INC
Also Called: Praxair
1555 E Edinger Ave (92705-4907)
PHONE.............................714 564-7311
Vince Biagiotti, *Pr*
EMP: 26 EST: 1997
SALES (est): 1.24MM Privately Held
SIC: 2813 Oxygen, compressed or liquefied

2816 Inorganic Pigments

(P-3874)
DAY-GLO COLOR CORP
Also Called: Day-Glo
4615 Ardine St (90201-5801)
PHONE.............................323 560-2000
Joe Cummings, *Mgr*
EMP: 19
SQ FT: 100,000
SALES (corp-wide): 7.26B Publicly Held
Web: www.dayglo.com
SIC: 2816 5169 2865 2851 Inorganic
pigments; Synthetic resins, rubber, and
plastic materials; Color pigments, organic;
Paints and allied products
HQ: Day-Glo Color Corp.
4515 Saint Clair Ave
Cleveland OH
216 391-7070

(P-3875)
OXERRA AMERICAS LLC
Davis Colors
3700 E Olympic Blvd (90023-3123)
P.O. Box 23100 (90023-0100)
PHONE.............................323 269-7311
Nick Paris, *VP*
EMP: 70
SQ FT: 540,000
Web: www.daviscolors.com
SIC: 2816 2865 Inorganic pigments; Cyclic
crudes and intermediates

HQ: Oxerra Americas, Llc
10001 Woodloch Forest Dr
The Woodlands TX
281 465-6700

(P-3876)
RYVEC INC
251 E Palais Rd (92805-6239)
PHONE.............................714 520-5592
Michael Ryan, *CEO*
Aristeo Figueroa, *CFO*
◆ EMP: 23 EST: 1982
SQ FT: 43,000
SALES (est): 9.78MM Privately Held
Web: www.ryvec.com
SIC: 2816 2865 2821 Color pigments; Dyes
and pigments; Polyurethane resins

(P-3877)
SOLOMON COLORS INC
1371 Laurel Ave (92376-3011)
PHONE.............................909 873-9444
Jeff Bowers, *Brnch Mgr*
EMP: 31
SQ FT: 80,000
SALES (corp-wide): 100.37MM Privately
Held
Web: www.solomoncolors.com
SIC: 2816 Inorganic pigments
PA: Solomon Colors, Inc.
4050 Color Plant Rd
Springfield IL
217 522-3112

(P-3878)
SPECTRA COLOR INC
9116 Stellar Ct (92883-4923)
P.O. Box 79527 (92877-0184)
PHONE.............................951 277-0200
Robert Shedd, *Pr*
John Shedd, *
▲ EMP: 42 EST: 1976
SQ FT: 40,000
SALES (est): 8.05MM Privately Held
Web: www.spectracolor.com
SIC: 2816 3089 2821 Color pigments;
Coloring and finishing of plastics products;
Plastics materials and resins

2819 Industrial Inorganic Chemicals, Nec

(P-3879)
ADVANCED CHEMICAL TECHNOLOGY
Also Called: Advanced Chemical Technology
3540 E 26th St (90058-4103)
PHONE.............................800 527-9607
Daniel Anthony Earley, *CEO*
EMP: 40 EST: 1996
SALES (est): 9.97MM Privately Held
Web: www.actglobal.net
SIC: 2819 2899 5169 Industrial inorganic
chemicals, nec; Antiscaling compounds,
boiler; Anti-corrosion products

(P-3880)
AMBER CHEMICAL INC
5201 Boylan St (93308-4567)
PHONE.............................661 325-2072
▲ EMP: 24 EST: 1983
SALES (est): 8.99MM Privately Held
Web: www.amberchem.com
SIC: 2819 5169 Industrial inorganic
chemicals, nec; Industrial chemicals

(P-3881)
CAL-PAC CHEMICAL CO INC
6231 Maywood Ave (90255-4530)
PHONE.............................323 585-2178
Charles F Duane, *Pr*
EMP: 17 EST: 1955
SQ FT: 37,000
SALES (est): 2.57MM Privately Held
Web: www.calpacchem.com
SIC: 2819 Industrial inorganic chemicals, nec

(P-3882)
CALIFORNIA CARBON COMPANY INC
615 W 17th St (90813-1515)
PHONE.............................562 436-1962
Franklin Liu, *Pr*
Richard Liu, *VP*
Rita L Wu, *Sec*
▲ EMP: 21 EST: 1962
SALES (est): 2.18MM Privately Held
Web: www.californiacarbon.com
SIC: 2819 Carbides

(P-3883)
CALIFORNIA SILICA PRODUCTS LLC
12808 Rancho Rd (92301-2719)
PHONE.............................909 947-0028
EMP: 84
SALES (corp-wide): 813.38K Privately
Held
Web: www.calsilica.net
SIC: 2819 Silica compounds
PA: California Silica Products, Llc
1420 S Bon View Ave
Ontario CA
760 885-5358

(P-3884)
CALIFORNIA SULPHUR COMPANY
2250 E Pacific Coast Hwy (90744-2917)
P.O. Box 176 (90748-0176)
PHONE.............................562 437-0768
John Babbitt, *Prin*
▼ EMP: 28 EST: 1958
SQ FT: 900
SALES (est): 4.6MM Privately Held
Web:
www.california-sulphur-company.com
SIC: 2819 Industrial inorganic chemicals, nec

(P-3885)
CAR SOUND EXHAUST SYSTEM INC
Environmental Catalyst Tech
1901 Corporate Centre Dr (92056-5831)
PHONE.............................949 888-1625
EMP: 94
SALES (corp-wide): 122.75MM Privately
Held
Web: www.magnaflow.com
SIC: 2819 Catalysts, chemical
PA: Car Sound Exhaust System, Inc.
1901 Corporate Ctr
Oceanside CA
949 858-5900

(P-3886)
CARBOMER INC
6324 Ferris Sq Ste B (92121-3238)
P.O. Box 261026 (92196-1026)
PHONE.............................858 552-0992
EMP: 85 EST: 1995
SALES (est): 9.79MM Privately Held
Web: www.carbomer.com
SIC: 2819 Industrial inorganic chemicals, nec

(P-3887)
CARBON ACTIVATED CORPORATION (PA)
2250 S Central Ave (90220-5311)
PHONE.............................310 885-4555
◆ EMP: 50 EST: 1993
SALES (est): 20.93MM Privately Held
Web: www.activatedcarbon.com
SIC: 2819 5074 Charcoal (carbon), activated
; Water purification equipment

(P-3888)
CDTI ADVANCED MATERIALS INC (PA)
Also Called: Cdti
1641 Fiske Pl (93033-1862)
PHONE.............................805 639-9458
EMP: 47 EST: 1994
SALES (est): 26.59MM Privately Held
Web: www.cdti.com
SIC: 2819 3823 Catalysts, chemical;
Process control instruments

(P-3889)
CHAMPIONX LLC
Also Called: Nalco Champion
6321 District Blvd (93313-2143)
PHONE.............................661 834-0454
Tom Pappas, *Mgr*
EMP: 30
SQ FT: 5,000
SALES (corp-wide): 3.81B Publicly Held
Web: www.championx.com
SIC: 2819 7349 Industrial inorganic
chemicals, nec; Chemical cleaning services
HQ: Championx Llc
2445 Tech Frest Blvd Bldg
The Woodlands TX
281 632-6500

(P-3890)
CYTEC SOLVAY GROUP
1440 N Kraemer Blvd (92806-1404)
PHONE.............................714 630-9400
EMP: 22 EST: 2020
SALES (est): 2.18MM Privately Held
SIC: 2819 Industrial inorganic chemicals, nec

(P-3891)
ECO SERVICES OPERATIONS CORP
20720 S Wilmington Ave (90810-1034)
PHONE.............................310 885-6719
Stephen Caro, *Brnch Mgr*
EMP: 51
SALES (corp-wide): 745MM Privately
Held
Web: www.pqcorp.com
SIC: 2819 Sulfuric acid, oleum
HQ: Eco Services Operations Corp.
300 Lindenwood Dr
Malvern PA
610 251-9118

(P-3892)
ELEMENTIS SPECIALTIES INC
31763 Mountain View Rd (92365-9763)
PHONE.............................760 257-9112
Mike Mcgath, *Mgr*
EMP: 68
SALES (corp-wide): 736.4MM Privately
Held
Web: www.elementis.com
SIC: 2819 Industrial inorganic chemicals, nec
HQ: Elementis Specialties, Inc.
469 Old Trenton Rd
East Windsor NJ

PRODUCTS & SVCS

(P-3893)
ENVIRNMENTAL CATALYST TECH LLC
3937 Ocean Ranch Blvd (92056-2670)
PHONE..............................949 459-3870
Gennaro Paolone, *Pr*
▲ EMP: 20 EST: 2000
SALES (est): 5.09MM
SALES (corp-wide): 122.75MM **Privately Held**
Web: www.ect-catalyst.com
SIC: 2819 Catalysts, chemical
PA: Car Sound Exhaust System, Inc.
1901 Corporate Ctr
Oceanside CA
949 858-5900

(P-3894)
ENVIRONMENTAL CATALYST TECH ✪
22961 Arroyo Vis (92688-2601)
PHONE..............................949 888-1625
Jerry Poloni, *Prin*
EMP: 20 EST: 2022
SALES (est): 1.88MM **Privately Held**
SIC: 2819 Catalysts, chemical

(P-3895)
JM HUBER MICROPOWDERS INC
Also Called: Nutri Granulations
16024 Phoebe Ave (90638-5606)
PHONE..............................714 994-7855
Mike Marberry, *Pr*
EMP: 35
SQ FT: 45,000
SALES (corp-wide): 1.24B **Privately Held**
Web: www.nutrigranulations.com
SIC: 2819 Industrial inorganic chemicals, nec
HQ: J.M. Huber Micropowders Inc.
3100 Cumberland Blvd Se # 600
Atlanta GA
732 549-8600

(P-3896)
KEMIRA WATER SOLUTIONS INC
14000 San Bernardino Ave (92335-5258)
PHONE..............................909 350-5678
Keith Heasley, *Mgr*
EMP: 29
SALES (corp-wide): 3.71B **Privately Held**
Web: www.californiasteel.com
SIC: 2819 Industrial inorganic chemicals, nec
HQ: Kemira Water Solutions, Inc.
1000 Parkwood Cir Se # 500
Atlanta GA

(P-3897)
MARCHEM TECHNOLOGIES LLC
20851 S Santa Fe Ave (90810-1130)
PHONE..............................310 638-9352
◆ EMP: 30
Web: www.marchemtechnologies.com
SIC: 2819 2899 Industrial inorganic chemicals, nec; Chemical preparations, nec

(P-3898)
MATERIA INC (DH)
60 N San Gabriel Blvd (91107-3748)
PHONE..............................626 584-8400
Karen Mckee, *Pr*
◆ EMP: 120 EST: 1998
SQ FT: 30,000
SALES (est): 49.65MM
SALES (corp-wide): 413.68B **Publicly Held**
Web: www.materia-inc.com

SIC: 2819 Catalysts, chemical
HQ: Exxonmobil Chemical Company
22777 Sprngwoods Vlg Pkwy
Spring TX
800 243-9966

(P-3899)
MERELEX CORPORATION
Also Called: American Elements
10884 Weyburn Ave (90024-2917)
PHONE..............................310 208-0551
Michael Silver, *Pr*
▲ EMP: 22 EST: 1996
SALES (est): 5.04MM **Privately Held**
Web: www.americanbiochemistry.com
SIC: 2819 Chemicals, high purity: refined from technical grade

(P-3900)
MORAVEK BIOCHEMICALS INC (PA)
Also Called: Moravek
577 Mercury Ln (92821-4831)
P.O. Box 1716 (92822-1716)
PHONE..............................714 990-2018
Paul Moravek, *Pr*
Joseph Moravek, *
Helen Moravek, *
▲ EMP: 25 EST: 1976
SQ FT: 6,000
SALES (est): 10.06MM
SALES (corp-wide): 10.06MM **Privately Held**
Web: www.moravek.com
SIC: 2819 Industrial inorganic chemicals, nec

(P-3901)
OMYA CALIFORNIA INC
Also Called: O M Y A
7299 Crystal Creek Rd (92356-8646)
PHONE..............................760 248-7306
▲ EMP: 100
SIC: 2819 8741 3281 Calcium compounds and salts, inorganic, nec; Management services; Cut stone and stone products

(P-3902)
OMYA INC
7299 Crystal Creek Rd (92356-8646)
PHONE..............................760 248-5200
Rainer Seidler, *CEO*
EMP: 100
Web: www.omya.com
SIC: 2819 8741 3281 Calcium compounds and salts, inorganic, nec; Management services; Cut stone and stone products
HQ: Omya Inc.
9987 Carver Rd Ste 300
Blue Ash OH
513 387-4600

(P-3903)
PCT-GW CARBIDE TOOLS USA INC
13701 Excelsior Dr (90670-5104)
PHONE..............................562 921-7898
Shamir Seth, *Pr*
▲ EMP: 17 EST: 2005
SALES (est): 598.06K **Privately Held**
SIC: 2819 Carbides

(P-3904)
PERIMETER SOLUTIONS LP
Wildfire Control Division
10667 Jersey Blvd (91730-5110)
PHONE..............................909 983-0772
Vinayak Sharma, *Mgr*
EMP: 20
Web: www.perimeter-solutions.com

SIC: 2819 Industrial inorganic chemicals, nec
HQ: Perimeter Solutions Lp
8000 Maryland Ave Ste 350
Saint Louis MO
314 983-7500

(P-3905)
PHIBRO-TECH INC
8851 Dice Rd (90670-2515)
PHONE..............................562 698-8036
Mark Alling, *Mgr*
EMP: 50
SALES (corp-wide): 977.89MM **Publicly Held**
Web: www.pahc.com
SIC: 2819 2899 Inorganic metal compounds or salts, nec; Chemical preparations, nec
HQ: Phibro-Tech, Inc.
300 Frank W Burr Blvd
Teaneck NJ

(P-3906)
PQ LLC
8401 Quartz Ave (90280-2536)
PHONE..............................323 326-1100
Jim Olivier, *Mgr*
EMP: 135
SALES (corp-wide): 745MM **Privately Held**
Web: www.pqcorp.com
SIC: 2819 Industrial inorganic chemicals, nec
PA: Pq Llc
300 Lindenwood Dr
Malvern PA
610 651-4200

(P-3907)
QUALITY CAR CARE PRODUCTS INC
2734 Huntington Dr (91010-2301)
PHONE..............................626 359-9174
Edward R Justice Junior, *Pr*
EMP: 38 EST: 1947
SQ FT: 25,000
SALES (est): 4.73MM **Privately Held**
SIC: 2819 Industrial inorganic chemicals, nec

(P-3908)
REAGENT CHEMICAL & RES INC
Also Called: White Fire Tagets
1454 S Sunnyside Ave (92408-2810)
PHONE..............................909 796-4059
Dan Sumnter, *Brnch Mgr*
EMP: 63
SQ FT: 99,400
SALES (corp-wide): 517MM **Privately Held**
Web: www.whiteflyer.com
SIC: 2819 3949 Sulfur, recovered or refined, incl. from sour natural gas; Targets, archery and rifle shooting
PA: Reagent Chemical & Research, Inc.
115 Rte 202
Ringoes NJ
908 284-2800

(P-3909)
SINGOD INVESTORS VI LLC
Also Called: Element Anheim Rsort Cnvntion
1600 S Clementine St (92802-2901)
PHONE..............................714 326-7800
Padmesh Patel, *Prin*
EMP: 55 EST: 2016
SALES (est): 6.9MM **Privately Held**
SIC: 2819 Elements

(P-3910)
SOLVAY AMERICA INC
Also Called: SOLVAY AMERICA, INC.
1440 N Kraemer Blvd (92806-1404)

PHONE..............................714 688-4403
Michele Jenkins, *Brnch Mgr*
EMP: 116
SALES (corp-wide): 146.05MM **Privately Held**
SIC: 2819 Industrial inorganic chemicals, nec
HQ: Solvay America Llc
3737 Buffalo Spdwy Ste 80
Houston TX
713 525-4000

(P-3911)
SOLVAY AMERICA INC
Also Called: SOLVAY AMERICA, INC.
645 N Cypress St (92867-6603)
PHONE..............................225 361-3376
EMP: 52
SALES (corp-wide): 146.05MM **Privately Held**
SIC: 2819 Industrial inorganic chemicals, nec
HQ: Solvay America Llc
3737 Buffalo Spdwy Ste 80
Houston TX
713 525-4000

(P-3912)
SOLVAY AMERICA INC
Also Called: SOLVAY AMERICA, INC.
12801 Ann St (90670-3025)
PHONE..............................562 906-3300
EMP: 114
SALES (corp-wide): 146.05MM **Privately Held**
SIC: 2819 Industrial inorganic chemicals, nec
HQ: Solvay America Llc
3737 Buffalo Spdwy Ste 80
Houston TX
713 525-4000

(P-3913)
SOLVAY CHEMICALS INC
645 N Cypress St (92867-6603)
PHONE..............................714 744-5610
EMP: 25
SALES (corp-wide): 146.05MM **Privately Held**
Web: www.solvay.com
SIC: 2819 Industrial inorganic chemicals, nec
HQ: Solvay Chemicals, Inc.
1201 Fannin St Ste 262
Houston TX
713 525-6800

(P-3914)
SOLVAY USA INC
Also Called: Marchem Solvay Group
20851 S Santa Fe Ave (90810-1130)
PHONE..............................310 669-5300
Maria Johnson, *Mgr*
EMP: 424
SALES (corp-wide): 146.05MM **Privately Held**
Web: www.solvay
SIC: 2819 Industrial inorganic chemicals, nec
HQ: Solvay Usa Llc
504 Carnegie Ctr
Princeton NJ
609 860-4000

(P-3915)
SPECIALTY MINERALS INC
Minerals Technology
6565 Meridian Rd (92356-8602)
P.O. Box 558 (92356-0558)
PHONE..............................760 248-5300
Doug Mayger, *Brnch Mgr*
EMP: 150
Web: www.mineralstech.com
SIC: 2819 Industrial inorganic chemicals, nec
HQ: Specialty Minerals Inc.
622 3rd Ave Fl 38

New York NY

(P-3916)
TONBO BIOTECHNOLOGIES CORP
Also Called: Tonbo Biosciences
10840 Thornmint Rd (92127-2404)
PHONE..............................858 888-7300
Todd Robert Nelson, *CEO*
Chrisopher Coarke, *CIO*
EMP: 20 **EST:** 2011
SALES (est): 4.47MM **Privately Held**
Web: www.cytekbio.com
SIC: 2819 Inorganic metal compounds or salts, nec

(P-3917)
US BORAX INC
14486 Borax Rd (93516-2017)
PHONE..............................760 762-7000
Joe A Carrabba, *Brnch Mgr*
EMP: 900
SALES (corp-wide): 55.55B **Privately Held**
Web: www.borax.com
SIC: 2819 Industrial inorganic chemicals, nec
HQ: U.S. Borax Inc.
   200 E Randolph St # 7100
   Chicago IL
   773 270-6500

(P-3918)
VENUS LABORATORIES INC
Earth Friendly Products
11150 Hope St (90630-5236)
PHONE..............................714 891-3100
Firas Jamal, *Mgr*
EMP: 70
SALES (corp-wide): 76.72MM **Privately Held**
Web: www.ecos.com
SIC: 2819 2844 2842 2841 Industrial inorganic chemicals, nec; Perfumes, cosmetics and other toilet preparations; Polishes and sanitation goods; Soap and other detergents
PA: Venus Laboratories, Inc.
   111 S Rohlwing Rd
   Addison IL
   630 595-1900

(P-3919)
W R GRACE & CO
Also Called: W R Grace Construction Pdts
7237 E Gage Ave (90040-3812)
PHONE..............................562 927-8513
Suzanne Parsons, *Mgr*
EMP: 19
SQ FT: 18,595
SALES (corp-wide): 6.27B **Privately Held**
Web: www.grace.com
SIC: 2819 Industrial inorganic chemicals, nec
HQ: W. R. Grace & Co.
   7500 Grace Dr
   Columbia MD
   410 531-4000

2821 Plastics Materials And Resins

(P-3920)
ACP NOXTAT INC
1112 E Washington Ave (92701-4221)
PHONE..............................714 547-5477
Anthony Floyd Richard, *Pr*
EMP: 19 **EST:** 2004
SALES (est): 1.93MM **Privately Held**
Web: www.noxtat.com
SIC: 2821 Plastics materials and resins

(P-3921)
ALPHA CORPORATION OF TENNESSEE
Also Called: Alpha-Owens Corning
19991 Seaton Ave (92570-8724)
PHONE..............................951 657-5161
John Mulrine, *Mgr*
EMP: 136
Web: www.aocresins.com
SIC: 2821 Polyethylene resins
HQ: The Alpha Corporation Of Tennessee
   955 Highway 57
   Piperton TN
   901 854-2800

(P-3922)
AMERICAN PACIFIC PLASTIC FABRICATORS INC
Also Called: Sterling Sleep Systems
7130 Fenwick Ln (92683-5248)
PHONE..............................714 891-3191
▲ **EMP:** 25 **EST:** 1987
SALES (est): 11.04MM **Privately Held**
Web: www.appf.com
SIC: 2821 3089 5021 2515 Polyvinyl chloride resins, PVC; Air mattresses, plastics; Mattresses; Mattresses and bedsprings

(P-3923)
AMERICAS STYRENICS LLC
305 Crenshaw Blvd (90503-1701)
PHONE..............................424 488-3757
Brad Crocker, *Brnch Mgr*
EMP: 83
SALES (corp-wide): 6.85B **Privately Held**
Web: www.amsty.com
SIC: 2821 Plastics materials and resins
HQ: Americas Styrenics Llc
   24 Waterway Ave Ste 1200
   The Woodlands TX

(P-3924)
APTCO LLC (PA)
31381 Pond Rd Bldg 2 (93250-9795)
PHONE..............................661 792-2107
◆ **EMP:** 99 **EST:** 1996
SALES (est): 16.07MM **Privately Held**
Web: www.aptcollc.com
SIC: 2821 Thermoplastic materials

(P-3925)
AQSEPTENCE GROUP INC
Also Called: AQSEPTENCE GROUP, INC.
1901 E Brundage Ln Ste A (93307-2761)
PHONE..............................661 323-1506
EMP: 131
SALES (corp-wide): 355.83K **Privately Held**
Web: www.aqseptence.com
SIC: 2821 Polyvinyl chloride resins, PVC
HQ: Johnson Screens, Inc.
   1950 Old Highway 8 Nw
   New Brighton MN
   651 636-3900

(P-3926)
AVIENT CORPORATION
2104 E 223rd St (90810-1611)
P.O. Box 9077 (90810-0077)
PHONE..............................310 513-7100
Rod Myers, *Brnch Mgr*
EMP: 23
Web: www.avient.com
SIC: 2821 Polyvinyl chloride resins, PVC
PA: Avient Corporation
   33587 Walker Rd
   Avon Lake OH

(P-3927)
B & B PLASTICS INC
1892 W Casmalia St (92377-4112)
PHONE..............................909 829-3606
Baltazar Mejia, *CEO*
EMP: 21 **EST:** 2014
SALES (est): 5.26MM **Privately Held**
Web: www.bbplasticsinc.com
SIC: 2821 Thermoplastic materials

(P-3928)
BDC EPOXY SYSTEMS INC
12903 Sunshine Ave (90670-4732)
P.O. Box 2445 (90670-0445)
PHONE..............................562 944-6177
Fred Benson, *CEO*
Matt Benson, *
Laura Benson, *
▲ **EMP:** 27 **EST:** 1976
SQ FT: 15,000
SALES (est): 4.68MM **Privately Held**
Web: www.bdcepoxysystems.com
SIC: 2821 Epoxy resins

(P-3929)
BJB ENTERPRISES INC
14791 Franklin Ave (92780-7215)
PHONE..............................714 734-8450
Brian Stransky, *Pr*
EMP: 27 **EST:** 1970
SQ FT: 38,000
SALES (est): 7.16MM **Privately Held**
Web: www.bjbenterprises.com
SIC: 2821 3087 5162 Polyurethane resins; Custom compound purchased resins; Plastics materials and basic shapes

(P-3930)
CGPC AMERICA CORPORATION
Also Called: Enduratex
4 Latitude Way Unit 108 (92881-4918)
PHONE..............................951 332-4100
Quentin Wu, *Ch Bd*
Doctor Dean Lee, *VP*
Amy Pan, *CFO*
▲ **EMP:** 22 **EST:** 1985
SALES (est): 9.01MM **Privately Held**
Web: www.enduratex.com
SIC: 2821 Plastics materials and resins
PA: China General Plastics Corporation
   12th Floor , No.37 , Ji-Hu Rd.
   Taipei City TAP

(P-3931)
COASTAL ENTERPRISES
Also Called: Coastal Enterprises Company
1925 W Collins Ave (92867-5426)
P.O. Box 4875 (92863-4875)
PHONE..............................714 771-4969
Chuck Miller, *Owner*
▲ **EMP:** 20 **EST:** 1970
SQ FT: 25,000
SALES (est): 3.54MM **Privately Held**
Web: www.precisionboard.com
SIC: 2821 Plastics materials and resins

(P-3932)
COMPOSITES HORIZONS LLC (DH)
1629 W Industrial Park St (91722-3418)
PHONE..............................626 331-0861
Renee Fahmy, *
▲ **EMP:** 140 **EST:** 1974
SQ FT: 25,000
SALES (est): 33.9MM
SALES (corp-wide): 302.09B **Publicly Held**
Web: www.pccstructurals.com
SIC: 2821 3844 3728 Plastics materials and resins; X-ray apparatus and tubes; Aircraft parts and equipment, nec
HQ: Precision Castparts Corp.
   5885 Meadows Rd Ste 620
   Lake Oswego OR
   503 946-4800

(P-3933)
COSMIC PLASTICS INC (PA)
28410 Industry Dr (91355-4108)
PHONE..............................661 257-3274
George Luh, *CEO*
Edwin Luh, *
◆ **EMP:** 30 **EST:** 1960
SQ FT: 846,000
SALES (est): 5MM
SALES (corp-wide): 5MM **Privately Held**
Web: www.cosmicplastics.com
SIC: 2821 Plastics materials and resins

(P-3934)
CROSSFIELD PRODUCTS CORP (PA)
Also Called: Dex-O-Tex Division
3000 E Harcourt St (90221-5589)
PHONE..............................310 886-9100
Richard Watt, *Ch Bd*
W Brad Watt, *
Ronald Borum, *
◆ **EMP:** 47 **EST:** 1938
SQ FT: 23,000
SALES (est): 23.79MM
SALES (corp-wide): 23.79MM **Privately Held**
Web: www.crossfieldproducts.com
SIC: 2821 Plastics materials and resins

(P-3935)
CYTEC ENGINEERED MATERIALS INC
Also Called: Cytec
1191 N Hawk Cir (92807-1723)
PHONE..............................714 632-8444
George Slayton, *Brnch Mgr*
EMP: 20
SALES (corp-wide): 146.05MM **Privately Held**
SIC: 2821 2822 Plastics materials and resins ; Synthetic rubber
HQ: Cytec Engineered Materials Inc.
   2085 E Tech Cir Ste 102
   Tempe AZ

(P-3936)
DOW COMPANY FOUNDATION
Dow Chemical
11266 Jersey Blvd (91730-5114)
P.O. Box 748 (91729-0748)
PHONE..............................909 476-4127
Steve Rynders, *Prin*
EMP: 159
SALES (corp-wide): 56.9B **Publicly Held**
Web: corporate.dow.com
SIC: 2821 Thermoplastic materials
HQ: Dow Company Foundation
   2030 Dow Ctr
   Midland MI
   989 636-1000

(P-3937)
ECOWISE INC
13538 Excelsior Dr Unit B (90670-5616)
PHONE..............................626 759-3997
Sheng Xu, *Pr*
EMP: 30 **EST:** 2019
SALES (est): 2.82MM **Privately Held**
Web: www.ecowisepcr.com
SIC: 2821 Polyethylene resins

PRODUCTS & SVCS

(P-3938)
ELASCO INC
Also Called: E Sales
11377 Markon Dr (92841-1402)
PHONE..............................714 373-4767
Henry Larrucea, *Pr*
Janet Lurrucea, *
Gary Stull, *
David Schindler, *
▲ EMP: 100 EST: 1979
SQ FT: 28,000
SALES (est): 11.6MM **Privately Held**
Web: www.elascourethane.com
SIC: 2821 2891 2822 Polyurethane resins;
   Adhesives and sealants; Synthetic rubber

(P-3939)
ELASCO URETHANE INC
11377 Markon Dr (92841-1402)
PHONE..............................714 895-7031
John Frasco, *CEO*
EMP: 34 EST: 2014
SALES (est): 3.84MM **Privately Held**
Web: www.elascourethane.com
SIC: 2821 2891 2822 Polyurethane resins;
   Adhesives and sealants; Synthetic rubber

(P-3940)
FERCO COLOR INC (PA)
Also Called: Ferco Plastic Products
5498 Vine St (91710-5247)
PHONE..............................909 930-0773
Jennifer Thaw, *Pr*
EMP: 48 EST: 1989
SQ FT: 20,000
SALES (est): 1.2MM **Privately Held**
Web: www.fercocolor.com
SIC: 2821 2865 Polyethylene resins; Color
   pigments, organic

(P-3941)
HENNIS ENTERPRISES INC
2646 Palma Dr Ste 430 (93003-7798)
PHONE..............................805 477-0257
Rodney Hennis, *Pr*
Christopher Hennis, *VP*
EMP: 21 EST: 1975
SQ FT: 10,000
SALES (est): 930.79K **Privately Held**
Web: www.hennisenterprises.com
SIC: 2821 Polyurethane resins

(P-3942)
**HOFFMAN PLASTIC
COMPOUNDS INC**
16616 Garfield Ave (90723-5305)
PHONE..............................323 636-3346
Ronald P Hoffman, *Pr*
Susan Hoffman, *
▲ EMP: 66 EST: 1976
SQ FT: 46,000
SALES (est): 10.46MM **Privately Held**
Web: www.hoffmanplastic.com
SIC: 2821 3087 Polyvinyl chloride resins,
   PVC; Custom compound purchased resins

(P-3943)
**HUNTSMAN ADVANCED
MATERIALS AM**
Also Called: Huntsman
5121 W San Fernando Rd (90039-1011)
PHONE..............................818 265-7221
Glenn Bauernschmidt, *Mgr*
EMP: 120
SALES (corp-wide): 8.02B **Publicly Held**
Web: www.huntsman.com
SIC: 2821 Plastics materials and resins

HQ: Huntsman Advanced Materials
   Americas Llc
   10003 Woodloch Forest Dr # 260
   The Woodlands TX
   281 719-6000

(P-3944)
**INDORAMA VNTRES SSTNBLE
SLTION**
11591 Etiwanda Ave (92337-6927)
PHONE..............................951 727-8318
John Wang, *CEO*
EMP: 54 EST: 2018
SALES (est): 9.43MM **Privately Held**
SIC: 2821 Plastics materials and resins
HQ: Indorama Ventures Public Company
   Limited
   75/102 Soi Sukhumvit 19 (Vadhana),
   Asok Road
   Vadhana

(P-3945)
INDUSPAC CALIFORNIA INC
Also Called: Pacific Foam
1550 Champagne Ave (91761-3600)
PHONE..............................909 390-4422
Keith Tatum, *Genl Mgr*
EMP: 30
Web: www.protecpac.com
SIC: 2821 Polyethylene resins
HQ: Induspac California, Inc.
   38505 Cherry St Ste H
   Newark CA

(P-3946)
INEOS COMPOSITES US LLC
6608 E 26th St (90040-3216)
P.O. Box 22118 (90022-0118)
PHONE..............................323 767-1300
Reid Mork, *Brnch Mgr*
EMP: 60
SQ FT: 45,845
SALES (corp-wide): 1.03MM **Privately
Held**
Web: www.ineos.com
SIC: 2821 Plastics materials and resins
HQ: Ineos Composites Us, Llc
   5220 Blazer Pkwy
   Dublin OH
   614 790-9299

(P-3947)
INEOS POLYPROPYLENE LLC
Also Called: Ineos
2384 E 223rd St (90810-1615)
PHONE..............................310 847-8523
Jim Ratcliffe, *Ch*
▲ EMP: 46 EST: 1998
SALES (est): 23.63MM
SALES (corp-wide): 1.03MM **Privately
Held**
Web: www.ineos.com
SIC: 2821 Plastics materials and resins
HQ: Ineos Usa Llc
   2600 S Shore Blvd Ste 500
   League City TX

(P-3948)
IP CORPORATION
Also Called: Silmar Division
12335 S Van Ness Ave (90250-3320)
PHONE..............................323 757-1801
Doug Johnson, *Brnch Mgr*
EMP: 40
SQ FT: 56,425
SALES (corp-wide): 497.64MM **Privately
Held**
Web: www.nacomposites.com

SIC: 2821 5169 Plastics materials and resins
   ; Synthetic resins, rubber, and plastic
   materials
PA: Ip Corporation
   1225 Willow Lake Blvd
   Saint Paul MN
   651 481-6860

(P-3949)
**J-M MANUFACTURING
COMPANY INC**
10990 Hemlock Ave (92337-7250)
PHONE..............................909 822-3009
Stephen Yang, *Mgr*
EMP: 92
SQ FT: 72,000
SALES (corp-wide): 998.24MM **Privately
Held**
Web: www.jmeagle.com
SIC: 2821 3084 5051 3085 Polyvinyl
   chloride resins, PVC; Plastics pipe; Pipe
   and tubing, steel; Plastics bottles
PA: J-M Manufacturing Company, Inc.
   5200 W Century Blvd
   Los Angeles CA
   310 693-8200

(P-3950)
**J-M MANUFACTURING
COMPANY INC**
Also Called: JM Eagle
23711 Rider St (92570-7114)
PHONE..............................951 657-7400
Robert Johnson, *Mgr*
EMP: 24
SALES (corp-wide): 998.24MM **Privately
Held**
Web: www.jmeagle.com
SIC: 2821 Polyvinyl chloride resins, PVC
PA: J-M Manufacturing Company, Inc.
   5200 W Century Blvd
   Los Angeles CA
   310 693-8200

(P-3951)
JOES PLASTICS INC
Also Called: Joes Plastics
5725 District Blvd (90058-5519)
PHONE..............................323 771-8433
Joe La Fountain Junior, *CEO*
▼ EMP: 40 EST: 1974
SQ FT: 130,000
SALES (est): 4.94MM **Privately Held**
SIC: 2821 Plastics materials and resins

(P-3952)
LAMKIN CORPORATION (PA)
6530 Gateway Park Dr (92154-7599)
PHONE..............................619 661-7090
▲ EMP: 21 EST: 1925
SALES (est): 4.83MM
SALES (corp-wide): 4.83MM **Privately
Held**
Web: www.lamkingrips.com
SIC: 2821 3069 Thermoplastic materials;
   Grips or handles, rubber

(P-3953)
MAPEI CORPORATION
5415 Industrial Pkwy (92407-1803)
PHONE..............................909 475-4100
Jose Granillo, *Mgr*
EMP: 44
SALES (corp-wide): 4.13B **Privately Held**
Web: www.mapei.com
SIC: 2821 Acrylic resins
HQ: Mapei Corporation
   1144 E Newport Center Dr
   Deerfield Beach FL
   954 246-8888

(P-3954)
MER-KOTE PRODUCTS INC
4125 E La Palma Ave Ste 250
(92807-1860)
P.O. Box 17866 (92817-7866)
PHONE..............................714 778-2266
EMP: 30
SIC: 2821 Thermoplastic materials

(P-3955)
MULTI-PLASTICS INC
Also Called: Multi Plastics
11625 Los Nietos Rd (90670-2009)
PHONE..............................562 692-1202
Rafael Enriquez, *Brnch Mgr*
EMP: 34
SALES (corp-wide): 98.55MM **Privately
Held**
Web: www.multi-plastics.com
SIC: 2821 Plastics materials and resins
PA: Multi-Plastics, Inc.
   7770 N Central Dr
   Lewis Center OH
   740 548-4894

(P-3956)
MUM INDUSTRIES INC
2320 Meyers Ave (92029-1006)
PHONE..............................800 729-1314
EMP: 61
SALES (corp-wide): 24.44MM **Privately
Held**
Web: www.mumindustries.com
SIC: 2821 Plasticizer/additive based plastic
   materials
PA: Mum Industries Inc.
   8989 Tyler Blvd
   Mentor OH
   440 269-4966

(P-3957)
**NATURAL ENVMTL
PROTECTION CO**
Also Called: Nepco
750 S Reservoir St (91766-3815)
PHONE..............................909 620-8028
Young Su Shin, *Pr*
▲ EMP: 31 EST: 2006
SQ FT: 3,600
SALES (est): 10.1MM **Privately Held**
SIC: 2821 Polystyrene resins
PA: Kumsung Industrial Co.Ltd
   57-6 Gubong-Gil, Donghwa-Myeon
   Jangseong

(P-3958)
**NEW TECHNOLOGY PLASTICS
INC**
7110 Fenwick Ln (92683-5248)
PHONE..............................562 941-6034
EMP: 35 EST: 1996
SALES (est): 4.48MM **Privately Held**
Web: www.newtechnologyplastics.com
SIC: 2821 5162 Molding compounds, plastics
   ; Plastics materials and basic shapes

(P-3959)
**NORTH AMERICAN
COMPOSITES CO**
Also Called: Interplastic
4990 Vanderbilt St (91761-2202)
PHONE..............................909 605-8977
Mark Prost, *VP*
David Englesgard, *VP Fin*
▲ EMP: 19 EST: 2000
SALES (est): 2.37MM **Privately Held**
Web: www.nacomposites.com
SIC: 2821 Plastics materials and resins

(P-3960)

ORION PLASTICS CORPORATION

700 W Carob St (90220-5225)
PHONE..................310 223-0370
Patricia Conkling, *Prin*
▲ **EMP:** 75 **EST:** 2000
SQ FT: 60,000
SALES (est): 18.4MM **Privately Held**
Web: www.orionplastics.net
SIC: 2821 Plastics materials and resins

(P-3961)

PERFORMANCE MATERIALS CORP (HQ)

Also Called: Tencate Performance Composite
1150 Calle Suerte (93012-8051)
PHONE..................805 482-1722
Thomas W Smith, *Pr*
◆ **EMP:** 100 **EST:** 1986
SQ FT: 50,000
SALES (est): 36.21MM **Privately Held**
Web: www.toraytac.com
SIC: 2821 Plastics materials and resins
PA: Toray Industries, Inc.
2-1-1, Nihombashimuromachi
Chuo-Ku TKY

(P-3962)

PEXCO AEROSPACE INC

5451 Argosy Ave (92649-1038)
PHONE..................714 894-9922
Julio Cuevas, *Manager*
EMP: 40
SALES (corp-wide): 6.58B **Publicly Held**
Web: www.pexcoaerospace.com
SIC: 2821 Plastics materials and resins
HQ: Pexco Aerospace, Inc.
2405 S 3rd Ave
Union Gap WA

(P-3963)

PLASKOLITE WEST LLC

Also Called: Continental Acrylics
2225 E Del Amo Blvd (90220-6303)
PHONE..................310 637-2103
Rick Larkin, *CFO*
▲ **EMP:** 30 **EST:** 2000
SALES (est): 7.41MM
SALES (corp-wide): 443.48MM **Privately Held**
SIC: 2821 Acrylic resins
PA: Plaskolite, Llc
400 W Nationwide Blvd # 400
Columbus OH
614 294-3281

(P-3964)

PROFESSIONAL PLASTICS INC (PA)

1810 E Valencia Dr (92831-4847)
PHONE..................714 446-6500
TOLL FREE: 800
EMP: 50 **EST:** 1984
SALES (est): 110.43MM
SALES (corp-wide): 110.43MM **Privately Held**
Web: www.professionalplastics.com
SIC: 2821 5162 3083 3081 Plastics materials and resins; Plastics materials and basic shapes; Laminated plastics plate and sheet; Plastics film and sheet

(P-3965)

QYCELL CORPORATION

600 Etiwanda Ave (91761-8635)
PHONE..................909 390-6644
Grant Kesler, *CEO*
▲ **EMP:** 25 **EST:** 1990
SQ FT: 45,000
SALES (est): 14MM **Privately Held**
Web: www.qycellfoam.com
SIC: 2821 Plastics materials and resins

(P-3966)

R K FABRICATION INC

1283 N Grove St (92806-2114)
PHONE..................714 630-9654
Roger King, *CEO*
Sarah King, *Treas*
EMP: 18 **EST:** 1989
SQ FT: 10,000
SALES (est): 4.83MM **Privately Held**
Web: www.rkfabrication.com
SIC: 2821 3714 1799 Plastics materials and resins; Exhaust systems and parts, motor vehicle; Fiberglass work

(P-3967)

ROCK WEST COMPOSITES INC (PA)

7625 Panasonic Way (92154-8204)
PHONE..................858 537-6260
James P Gormican, *CEO*
EMP: 54 **EST:** 2006
SALES (est): 51.31MM **Privately Held**
Web: www.rockwestcomposites.com
SIC: 2821 Plastics materials and resins

(P-3968)

SAINT-GOBAIN PRFMCE PLAS CORP

7301 Orangewood Ave (92841-1411)
PHONE..................714 893-0470
Greg Maki, *Brnch Mgr*
EMP: 190
SALES (corp-wide): 397.78MM **Privately Held**
Web: www.saint-gobain.com
SIC: 2821 Plastics materials and resins
HQ: Saint-Gobain Performance Plastics Corporation
20 Moores Rd
Malvern PA
440 836-6900

(P-3969)

SAINT-GOBAIN PRFMCE PLAS CORP

Also Called: High Performance Seals
7301 Orangewood Ave (92841-1411)
PHONE..................714 630-5818
Thomas Kinisky, *CEO*
EMP: 91
SALES (corp-wide): 397.78MM **Privately Held**
Web: www.saint-gobain.com
SIC: 2821 Plastics materials and resins
HQ: Saint-Gobain Performance Plastics Corporation
20 Moores Rd
Malvern PA
440 836-6900

(P-3970)

SK CHEMICALS AMERICA INC

3 Park Plz Ste 430 (92614-2579)
PHONE..................949 336-8088
Michael Tae, *Pr*
▲ **EMP:** 24 **EST:** 2002
SALES (est): 2.21MM **Privately Held**
SIC: 2821 Plastics materials and resins

(P-3971)

SOUTHERN CALIFORNIA PLAS INC

3122 Maple St (92707-4408)
PHONE..................714 751-7084

▲ **EMP:** 54 **EST:** 1995
SQ FT: 240,000
SALES (est): 7.9MM **Privately Held**
SIC: 2821 Plastics materials and resins

(P-3972)

SOUTHLAND POLYMERS INC

14030 Gannet St (90670-5314)
PHONE..................562 921-0444
Henry Hsi, *Pr*
◆ **EMP:** 22 **EST:** 1979
SQ FT: 64,000
SALES (est): 9.19MM **Privately Held**
Web: www.southlandpolymers.com
SIC: 2821 5162 Plastics materials and resins; Plastics resins

(P-3973)

SPHERE ALLIANCE INC

Also Called: Advanced Aircraft Seal
3087 12th St (92507-4904)
PHONE..................951 352-2400
EMP: 37 **EST:** 2011
SALES (est): 3.85MM **Privately Held**
SIC: 2821 Plastics materials and resins

(P-3974)

ST CLAIR PLASTICS INC

10031 Freeman Ave (90670-3405)
PHONE..................562 946-3115
EMP: 20 **EST:** 1988
SALES (est): 3.51MM **Privately Held**
SIC: 2821 Plastics materials and resins

(P-3975)

STEPAN COMPANY

Also Called: Anaheim Plant
1208 N Patt St (92801-2549)
PHONE..................714 776-9870
Tom Szczeblowski, *Mgr*
EMP: 423
SQ FT: 10,412
SALES (corp-wide): 2.77B **Publicly Held**
Web: www.stepan.com
SIC: 2821 2843 Plastics materials and resins; Surface active agents
PA: Stepan Company
1101 Skokie Blvd Ste 500
Northbrook IL
847 446-7500

(P-3976)

TA AEROSPACE CO

Also Called: Ta Division
28065 Franklin Pkwy (91355-4117)
PHONE..................661 702-0448
Jim Sweeney, *Pr*
EMP: 180
SQ FT: 78,124
SALES (corp-wide): 6.58B **Publicly Held**
Web: www.taaerospace.com
SIC: 2821 3429 Elastomers, nonvulcanizable (plastics); Clamps, metal
HQ: Ta Aerospace Co.
28065 Franklin Pkwy
Valencia CA
661 775-1100

(P-3977)

TAMMY TAYLOR NAILS INC

2001 E Deere Ave (92705-5724)
PHONE..................949 250-9287
Tammy Taylor, *Pr*
▼ **EMP:** 45 **EST:** 1982
SQ FT: 11,500
SALES (est): 8.68MM **Privately Held**
Web: www.tammytaylornails.com
SIC: 2821 7231 5087 Acrylic resins; Beauty shops; Beauty parlor equipment and supplies

(P-3978)

TECHMER PM INC

18420 S Laurel Park Rd (90220-6015)
PHONE..................310 632-9211
John R Manuck, *Pr*
◆ **EMP:** 500 **EST:** 1982
SQ FT: 40,000
SALES (est): 61.8MM **Privately Held**
Web: www.techmerpm.com
SIC: 2821 Plastics materials and resins

(P-3979)

TEKNOR APEX COMPANY

Maclin Company
420 S 6th Ave (91746-3128)
P.O. Box 2307 (91746-0307)
PHONE..................626 968-4656
Tony Patrizio, *Mgr*
EMP: 104
SALES (corp-wide): 1.03B **Privately Held**
Web: www.teknorapex.com
SIC: 2821 3081 3089 Vinyl resins, nec; Unsupported plastics film and sheet; Plastics processing
PA: Teknor Apex Company
505 Central Ave
Pawtucket RI
401 725-8000

(P-3980)

TEKNOR COLOR COMPANY

Also Called: Teknor Apex
420 S 6th Ave (91746-3128)
P.O. Box 2307 (91746-0307)
PHONE..................626 336-7709
Tony Patrizio, *Genl Mgr*
EMP: 29
SALES (corp-wide): 1.03B **Privately Held**
Web: www.teknorapex.com
SIC: 2821 3089 Plastics materials and resins; Plastics processing
HQ: Teknor Color Company Llc
505 Central Ave
Pawtucket RI

(P-3981)

UREMET CORPORATION

7012 Belgrave Ave (92841-2808)
PHONE..................657 257-4027
Steve Zamollo, *CEO*
Mark Moore, *
John Cockriel, *
▲ **EMP:** 26 **EST:** 1989
SQ FT: 9,500
SALES (est): 9.81MM **Privately Held**
Web: www.uremet.com
SIC: 2821 Polyurethane resins

(P-3982)

US BLANKS LLC (PA)

14700 S San Pedro St (90248-2001)
P.O. Box 486 (90248-0486)
PHONE..................310 225-6774
Kimberly Thress, *
▲ **EMP:** 48 **EST:** 2006
SALES (est): 7.84MM
SALES (corp-wide): 7.84MM **Privately Held**
Web: www.usblanks.com
SIC: 2821 Plastics materials and resins

(P-3983)

XERXES CORPORATION

1210 N Tustin Ave (92807-1617)
PHONE..................714 630-0012
Rudy Tapia, *Mgr*
EMP: 119
SALES (corp-wide): 934.5MM **Privately Held**
Web: www.xerxes.com

SIC: 2821 5999 3444 Polystyrene resins; Fiberglass materials, except insulation; Sheet metalwork
HQ: Xerxes Corporation
7901 Xerxes Ave S Ste 201
Minneapolis MN
952 887-1890

2822 Synthetic Rubber

(P-3984)
ARNCO
5141 Firestone Pl (90280-3535)
PHONE..............................323 249-7500
◆ **EMP:** 50 **EST:** 1971
SALES (est): 5.76MM **Privately Held**
SIC: 2822 2821 3089 5084 Synthetic rubber; Plastics materials and resins; Casting of plastics; Paint spray equipment, industrial

(P-3985)
CRITICALPOINT CAPITAL LLC
Arlon Materials For Elec Div
9433 Hyssop Dr (91730-6107)
PHONE..............................909 987-9533
Roy Baulmer, *Brnch Mgr*
EMP: 100
SALES (corp-wide): 38.96MM **Privately Held**
Web: www.criticalpointpartners.com
SIC: 2822 3672 2821 Silicone rubbers; Printed circuit boards; Plastics materials and resins
PA: Criticalpoint Capital, Llc
2101 Rosecrans Ave # 4255
El Segundo CA
310 321-4400

2824 Organic Fibers, Noncellulosic

(P-3986)
MATCHES INC
1700 E Araby St Ste 64 (92264)
PHONE..............................760 899-1919
Jinle Chen, *Ch Bd*
Zhimeng Zhao, *CAO*
Xiqing Zhang, *COO*
EMP: 359 **EST:** 2009
SALES (est): 10.49MM **Privately Held**
SIC: 2824 Polyester fibers

(P-3987)
ST PAUL BRANDS INC
11842 Monarch St (92841-2113)
PHONE..............................714 903-1000
Jimmy Ngo, *Pr*
Henry Smith, *
Fred Evans, *
▲ **EMP:** 25 **EST:** 2004
SALES (est): 2.48MM **Privately Held**
Web: probactive.en.ec21.com
SIC: 2824 Protein fibers

(P-3988)
TURNER FIBERFILL INC
1600 Date St (90640-6371)
P.O. Box 460 (90640-0460)
PHONE..............................323 724-7957
Paul Turner, *Pr*
▲ **EMP:** 35 **EST:** 2003
SALES (est): 4.17MM **Privately Held**
SIC: 2824 Polyester fibers

2833 Medicinals And Botanicals

(P-3989)
ALLERMED LABORATORIES INC
7203 Convoy Ct (92111-1020)
PHONE..............................858 292-1060
H S Nielsen, *Pr*
EMP: 30 **EST:** 1972
SQ FT: 20,000
SALES (est): 4.5MM **Privately Held**
Web: www.stallergenesgreer.com
SIC: 2833 2836 Medicinals and botanicals; Biological products, except diagnostic

(P-3990)
AMASS BRANDS INC
860 E Stowell Rd (93454-7006)
PHONE..............................619 204-2560
Mark Thomas Lynn, *CEO*
EMP: 24 **EST:** 2019
SALES (est): 8.56MM **Privately Held**
Web: www.amass.com
SIC: 2833 Alkaloids and other botanical based products

(P-3991)
B & C NUTRITIONAL PRODUCTS INC
Also Called: Merical
2995 E Miraloma Ave (92806-1805)
PHONE..............................714 238-7225
EMP: 77
SIC: 2833 2048 2834 Medicinals and botanicals; Prepared feeds, nec; Vitamin preparations

(P-3992)
BEACON MANUFACTURING INC
Also Called: North West Pharmanaturals
1000 Beacon St (92821-2938)
PHONE..............................714 529-0980
Jack L Brown, *CEO*
Patrick D K Brown, *CFO*
EMP: 20 **EST:** 2015
SQ FT: 25,000
SALES (est): 3.19MM **Privately Held**
Web: www.northwestpn.com
SIC: 2833 Vitamins, natural or synthetic: bulk, uncompounded

(P-3993)
BIO-RAD LABORATORIES INC
Bio-RAD E.C S
9500 Jeronimo Rd (92618-2017)
PHONE..............................949 598-1200
Kelly Knapps, *Brnch Mgr*
EMP: 86
SALES (corp-wide): 2.8B **Publicly Held**
Web: www.bio-rad.com
SIC: 2833 2835 Medicinals and botanicals; Diagnostic substances
PA: Bio-Rad Laboratories, Inc.
1000 Alfred Nobel Dr
Hercules CA
510 724-7000

(P-3994)
CARGILL INCORPORATED
Also Called: Cargill
600 N Gilbert St (92833-2555)
PHONE..............................714 449-6708
Steve Hoemoller, *Mgr*
EMP: 52
SALES (corp-wide): 176.74B **Privately Held**
Web: www.cargill.com

SIC: 2833 2079 5199 Vegetable oils, medicinal grade: refined or concentrated; Edible fats and oils; Oils, animal or vegetable
PA: Cargill, Incorporated
15407 Mcginty Rd W
Wayzata MN
800 227-4455

(P-3995)
CHROMADEX CORPORATION (PA)
Also Called: Chromadex
10900 Wilshire Blvd Ste 600 (90024-6535)
PHONE..............................310 388-6706
Robert Fried, *CEO*
Frank Jaksch Junior, *Ex Ch Bd*
Kevin Farr, *CFO*
Lisa Hatton Harrington, *Corporate Secretary*
EMP: 31 **EST:** 2000
SQ FT: 15,000
SALES (est): 72.05MM
SALES (corp-wide): 72.05MM **Publicly Held**
Web: www.chromadex.com
SIC: 2833 Medicinals and botanicals

(P-3996)
CREATONS GRDN NTRAL FD MKTS IN
Also Called: Cgnfm
24849 Anza Dr (91355-1259)
PHONE..............................661 877-4280
Dino Guglielmelli, *CEO*
EMP: 21 **EST:** 1999
SALES (est): 436.52K **Privately Held**
SIC: 2833 Medicinals and botanicals

(P-3997)
DOCTORS SIGNATURE SALES (PA)
Also Called: Life Force International
495 Raleigh Ave (92020-3137)
PHONE..............................800 531-4877
Ron Hillman, *Pr*
Kathleen Meadows, *VP*
Marjorie Lynn, *Sec*
Geraldine L Hillman, *Ch Bd*
▲ **EMP:** 23 **EST:** 1992
SQ FT: 24,000
SALES (est): 7.66MM **Privately Held**
SIC: 2833 2048 Drugs and herbs: grading, grinding, and milling; Prepared feeds, nec

(P-3998)
ERBAVIVA INC
Also Called: Erba Organics
19831 Nordhoff Pl Ste 116 (91311-6608)
PHONE..............................818 998-7112
Robin Brown, *CEO*
Robin Brown, *Prin*
Anna C Brown, *VP*
▲ **EMP:** 20 **EST:** 2010
SQ FT: 10,000
SALES (est): 5.16MM **Privately Held**
Web: www.erbaviva.com
SIC: 2833 Organic medicinal chemicals: bulk, uncompounded

(P-3999)
ESMOND NATURAL INC
Also Called: Hopkins Labratory Co
5316 Irwindale Ave Ste B (91706-2034)
PHONE..............................626 337-1588
▲ **EMP:** 25 **EST:** 1994
SALES (est): 4.69MM **Privately Held**
Web: www.esmondnatural.com
SIC: 2833 Vitamins, natural or synthetic: bulk, uncompounded

(P-4000)
EVOLIFE SCIENTIFIC LLC
3150 Long Beach Blvd (90807-5061)
PHONE..............................888 750-0310
EMP: 23 **EST:** 2019
SALES (est): 1.42MM **Privately Held**
Web: www.evolifescientific.com
SIC: 2833 Medicinals and botanicals

(P-4001)
EXCELSIOR NUTRITION INC
Also Called: 4excelsior
1206 N Miller St Unit D (92806-1960)
PHONE..............................657 999-5188
Yisheng Lin, *Pr*
Jian Wu, *
EMP: 61 **EST:** 2014
SQ FT: 78,000
SALES (est): 10.36MM **Privately Held**
Web: www.4excelsior.com
SIC: 2833 Medicinals and botanicals

(P-4002)
J & D LABORATORIES INC
2710 Progress St (92081-8449)
PHONE..............................760 734-6800
David Wood, *CEO*
Fon Wong, *CFO*
▲ **EMP:** 300 **EST:** 1988
SQ FT: 32,000
SALES (est): 62.65MM
SALES (corp-wide): 203.23MM **Privately Held**
Web: www.capteksoftgel.com
SIC: 2833 Vitamins, natural or synthetic: bulk, uncompounded; Pharmaceutical preparations
HQ: Captek Softgel International, Inc.
16218 Arthur St
Cerritos CA

(P-4003)
MIDNIGHT MANUFACTURING LLC
2535 Conejo Spectrum St Bldg 4 (91320-1453)
PHONE..............................714 833-6130
Kevin A Shaw, *Pr*
EMP: 25 **EST:** 2019
SALES (est): 4.57MM **Privately Held**
Web: www.midnightmanufacturing.com
SIC: 2833 Medicinals and botanicals

(P-4004)
MRO MARYRUTH LLC
1171 S Robertson Blvd Ste 148 (90035-1403)
PHONE..............................424 343-6650
Colleen Boehmer, *Managing Member*
Dave Hsu, *CFO*
EMP: 105 **EST:** 2021
SALES (est): 11.21MM **Privately Held**
SIC: 2833 Drugs and herbs: grading, grinding, and milling

(P-4005)
NATURAL ALTERNATIVES INTL INC (PA)
Also Called: Nai
1535 Faraday Ave (92008-7319)
PHONE..............................760 736-7700
Mark A Ledoux, *Ch Bd*
Kenneth E Wolf, *Pr*
Michael E Fortin, *CFO*
▲ **EMP:** 178 **EST:** 1980
SQ FT: 20,981
SALES (est): 154.01MM
SALES (corp-wide): 154.01MM **Publicly Held**

▲ = Import ▼ = Export
◆ = Import/Export

Web: www.nai-online.com
SIC: 2833 2834 Medicinals and botanicals;
Pharmaceutical preparations

(P-4006)
NORTH WEST
PHARMANATURALS INC
Also Called: Vitamins Unlimited
1000 Beacon St (92821-2938)
PHONE...............................714 529-0980
▲ **EMP:** 20
SIC: 2833 Vitamins, natural or synthetic:
bulk, uncompounded

(P-4007)
NU-HEALTH PRODUCTS CO
Also Called: Nu Health Products
20875 Currier Rd (91789-3081)
PHONE...............................909 869-0666
▲ **EMP:** 25 **EST:** 1991
SQ FT: 12,000
SALES (est): 2.39MM **Privately Held**
Web: www.nu-health.com
SIC: 2833 2048 5149 Vitamins, natural or
synthetic: bulk, uncompounded; Prepared
feeds, nec; Organic and diet food

(P-4008)
ORGAIN LLC
16851 Hale Ave (92606-5020)
P.O. Box 4918 (92616-4918)
PHONE...............................888 881-4246
Andrew Abraham, *CEO*
EMP: 47 **EST:** 2019
SALES (est): 19.84MM **Privately Held**
Web: www.orgain.com
SIC: 2833 5499 Medicinals and botanicals;
Health and dietetic food stores

(P-4009)
ORGANIC BY NATURE INC (PA)
Also Called: Organic
2610 Homestead Pl (90220-5610)
PHONE...............................562 901-0177
Amy L Venner Hamdi, *CEO*
David Sandoval, *
▲ **EMP:** 36 **EST:** 1993
SQ FT: 30,000
SALES (est): 10.32MM **Privately Held**
Web: www.organicbynatureinc.com
SIC: 2833 Adrenal derivatives

(P-4010)
PALETTE LIFE SCIENCES INC
27 E Cota St Ste 402 (93101-7632)
PHONE...............................805 869-7020
Per Lango, *CEO*
Hank Courson, *
EMP: 87 **EST:** 2018
SALES (est): 9.02MM **Privately Held**
Web: www.palettelifesciences.com
SIC: 2833 Medicinal chemicals

(P-4011)
PHARMAVITE LLC (DH)
8531 Fallbrook Ave (91304-3232)
PHONE...............................818 221-6200
Jeff Boutelle, *CEO*
Brian Beams, *
Christine Burdick-bell J.d., *VP*
Rhonda Hoffman, *CMO**
▲ **EMP:** 300 **EST:** 1971
SQ FT: 45,000
SALES (est): 555.17MM **Privately Held**
Web: www.pharmavite.com
SIC: 2833 2834 Vitamins, natural or
synthetic: bulk, uncompounded;
Pharmaceutical preparations
HQ: Otsuka America, Inc.
1 Embarcadero Ctr # 2020

San Francisco CA

(P-4012)
PHILIP B INC
Also Called: Philip B
9053 Nemo St (90069-5511)
PHONE...............................888 376-8236
Philip Bloom, *CEO*
EMP: 20 **EST:** 2005
SALES (est): 2.4MM **Privately Held**
Web: www.philipb.com
SIC: 2833 Medicinals and botanicals

(P-4013)
PROMEGA BIOSCIENCES LLC
277 Granada Dr (93401-7396)
PHONE...............................805 544-8524
EMP: 55 **EST:** 1999
SQ FT: 40,000
SALES (est): 21.39MM
SALES (corp-wide): 743.96MM **Privately
Held**
Web: www.promega.com
SIC: 2833 2835 Medicinal chemicals;
Diagnostic substances
PA: Promega Corporation
2800 Woods Hollow Rd
Fitchburg WI
608 274-4330

(P-4014)
RON TEEGUARDEN
ENTERPRISES INC (PA)
Also Called: Dragon Herbs
10940 Wilshire Blvd (90024-3915)
PHONE...............................323 556-8188
Ron Teagarden, *Pr*
Yanlin Teeguarden, *
◆ **EMP:** 23 **EST:** 1994
SALES (est): 4.9MM
SALES (corp-wide): 4.9MM **Privately Held**
Web: www.dragonherbs.com
SIC: 2833 5122 Drugs and herbs: grading,
grinding, and milling; Medicinals and
botanicals

(P-4015)
S&B PHARMA INC
Also Called: Norac Pharma
405 S Motor Ave (91702-3232)
PHONE...............................626 334-2908
Doctor Daniel Levin, *Pr*
▲ **EMP:** 66 **EST:** 2012
SALES (est): 10.36MM **Privately Held**
Web: www.noracpharma.com
SIC: 2833 8731 2834 Medicinals and
botanicals; Commercial physical research;
Pharmaceutical preparations
PA: Alkem Laboratories Limited
Devashish Building, Alkem House,
Mumbai MH

(P-4016)
SABRE SCIENCES INC
2233 Faraday Ave Ste K (92008-7214)
PHONE...............................760 448-2750
Victor Salerno, *Pr*
Anna Salerno, *Treas*
Michael Borkin, *Prin*
EMP: 18 **EST:** 1999
SQ FT: 8,000
SALES (est): 4.05MM **Privately Held**
Web: www.sabresciences.com
SIC: 2833 8731 Hormones or derivatives;
Commercial physical research

(P-4017)
SAPPHIRE ENERGY INC
10996 Torreyana Rd Ste 280 (92121-1159)
PHONE...............................858 768-4700

James Levine, *CEO*
Thomas Willardson, *CFO*
EMP: 55 **EST:** 2007
SALES (est): 9.74MM **Privately Held**
Web: www.sapphireenergy.com
SIC: 2833 Medicinals and botanicals

(P-4018)
STAUBER CALIFORNIA INC
Also Called: Stauber USA
4120 N Palm St (92835-1026)
PHONE...............................714 441-3900
▲ **EMP:** 95
SIC: 2833 Medicinals and botanicals

(P-4019)
STAUBER PRFMCE
INGREDIENTS INC (HQ)
Also Called: Stauber
4120 N Palm St (92835-1026)
PHONE...............................714 441-3900
Patrick Hawkins, *CEO*
Dan Stauber, *Chief Brand Officer*
EMP: 66 **EST:** 1969
SALES (est): 46.9MM
SALES (corp-wide): 935.1MM **Publicly
Held**
Web: www.stauberusa.com
SIC: 2833 Medicinals and botanicals
PA: Hawkins, Inc.
2381 Rosegate
Roseville MN
612 331-6910

(P-4020)
TIKUN OLAM ADELANTO LLC
541 S Spring St Unit 213 (90013-1657)
PHONE...............................833 468-4586
David Librush, *Brnch Mgr*
EMP: 35
SALES (corp-wide): 1.96MM **Privately
Held**
Web: www.tikunolam.com
SIC: 2833 Medicinals and botanicals
PA: Tikun Olam Adelanto Llc
16605 Koala Rd
Adelanto CA
833 468-4586

(P-4021)
UNI-CAPS LLC
540 Lambert Rd (92821)
PHONE...............................714 529-8400
Sang H Kim, *Managing Member*
▲ **EMP:** 22 **EST:** 2006
SALES (est): 9.31MM **Privately Held**
Web: www.unicapsllc.com
SIC: 2833 Vitamins, natural or synthetic:
bulk, uncompounded

(P-4022)
VITAJOY USA INC
14165 Ramona Ave (91710-5753)
PHONE...............................626 965-8830
Dan Gu, *CEO*
Charles Kuo, *CFO*
▲ **EMP:** 22 **EST:** 2012
SALES (est): 4.75MM **Privately Held**
Web: www.vitajoyusa.com
SIC: 2833 Vitamins, natural or synthetic:
bulk, uncompounded

(P-4023)
VYTALOGY WELLNESS LLC
15233 Ventura Blvd (91403-2201)
PHONE...............................818 867-4440
Nina Barton, *Managing Member*
EMP: 130 **EST:** 2021
SALES (est): 14.75MM **Privately Held**
Web: www.vytalogy.com

SIC: 2833 Vitamins, natural or synthetic:
bulk, uncompounded

(P-4024)
WESTAR NUTRITION CORP (PA)
350 Paularino Ave (92626-4616)
PHONE...............................949 645-6100
David Fan, *Pr*
Lucy Fan, *VP*
▼ **EMP:** 20 **EST:** 1973
SQ FT: 55,000
SALES (est): 22.12MM
SALES (corp-wide): 22.12MM **Privately
Held**
Web: www.westarnutrition.com
SIC: 2833 2834 2844 7389 Vitamins, natural
or synthetic: bulk, uncompounded;
Pharmaceutical preparations; Cosmetic
preparations; Packaging and labeling
services

2834 Pharmaceutical Preparations

(P-4025)
1859 INC
11425 Sorrento Valley Rd Ste 2
(92121-1351)
PHONE...............................858 648-2470
Devon M Cayer, *CEO*
EMP: 63 **EST:** 2019
SALES (est): 8.28MM **Privately Held**
SIC: 2834 Proprietary drug products

(P-4026)
A Q PHARMACEUTICALS INC
11555 Monarch St Ste C (92841-1814)
PHONE...............................714 903-1000
Tracy Nguyen, *Pr*
Henry Smith, *
▲ **EMP:** 30 **EST:** 2001
SQ FT: 3,000
SALES (est): 3.97MM **Privately Held**
Web: www.aqpharmaceuticals.com
SIC: 2834 Pharmaceutical preparations

(P-4027)
AADI BIOSCIENCE INC (PA)
Also Called: Aadi
17383 W Sunset Blvd Ste A250
(90272-4181)
PHONE...............................424 744-8055
Dave Lennon, *Pr*
Scott Giacobello, *CFO*
Neil Desai, *Ex Ch Bd*
Caley Castelein, *Ch Bd*
Loretta M Itri, *CMO*
EMP: 49 **EST:** 2007
SQ FT: 2,760
SALES (est): 15.22MM
SALES (corp-wide): 15.22MM **Publicly
Held**
Web: www.aerpio.com
SIC: 2834 Pharmaceutical preparations

(P-4028)
ABBOTT LABORATORIES
15900 Valley View Ct (91342-3577)
PHONE...............................818 493-2388
Dee Vetter, *Prin*
EMP: 27
SALES (corp-wide): 43.65B **Publicly Held**
Web: www.abbott.com
SIC: 2834 Pharmaceutical preparations
PA: Abbott Laboratories
100 Abbott Park Rd
Abbott Park IL
224 667-6100

P R O D U C T S & S V C S

(P-4029)
ABBOTT VASCULAR INC
26531 Ynez Rd (92591-4630)
PHONE....................951 941-2400
Ronald Dollens, *Brnch Mgr*
EMP: 500
SALES (corp-wide): 43.65B **Publicly Held**
Web: www.cardiovascular.abbott
SIC: 2834 Pharmaceutical preparations
HQ: Abbott Vascular Inc.
3200 Lakeside Dr
Santa Clara CA
408 845-3000

(P-4030)
ABRAXIS BIOSCIENCE LLC (DH)
11755 Wilshire Blvd Fl 20 (90025-1543)
PHONE....................800 564-0216
EMP: 232 **EST:** 2007
SALES (est): 99.9MM
SALES (corp-wide): 46.16B **Publicly Held**
SIC: 2834 Pharmaceutical preparations
HQ: Abraxis Bioscience, Inc.
86 Morris Ave
Summit NJ

(P-4031)
ACADIA PHARMACEUTICALS INC (PA)
Also Called: Acadia
12830 El Camino Real Ste 400 (92130)
PHONE....................858 558-2871
▲ **EMP:** 570 **EST:** 1993
SQ FT: 98,000
SALES (est): 517.24MM **Publicly Held**
Web: www.acadia.com
SIC: 2834 Pharmaceutical preparations

(P-4032)
ACCOLADE PHARMA USA
13260 Temple Ave (91746-1511)
PHONE....................626 279-9699
Spencer Liu, *CEO*
EMP: 20 **EST:** 2018
SALES (est): 2.49MM **Privately Held**
Web: www.accoladepharma.us
SIC: 2834 Pharmaceutical preparations

(P-4033)
ACTAVIS LLC
132 Business Center Dr (92878-3224)
PHONE....................951 493-5582
EMP: 30
Web: www.actavis.com
SIC: 2834 Pharmaceutical preparations
HQ: Actavis Llc
1150 S Northpoint Blvd
Waukegan IL
862 261-7000

(P-4034)
ACTAVIS LLC
311 Bonnie Cir (92878-5182)
P.O. Box 1149 (92878-1149)
PHONE....................909 270-1400
Allen Chao, *Brnch Mgr*
EMP: 79
Web: www.actavis.com
SIC: 2834 Pharmaceutical preparations
HQ: Actavis Llc
1150 S Northpoint Blvd
Waukegan IL
862 261-7000

(P-4035)
ADAM NUTRITION INC
11010 Hopkins St Ste B (91752-3279)
PHONE....................951 361-1120
◆ **EMP:** 130

Web: www.adamnutrition.com
SIC: 2834 Vitamin, nutrient, and hematinic preparations for human use

(P-4036)
AEGIS LIFE INC
Also Called: Aegis Biodefense
3033 Science Park Rd Ste 270
(92121-1167)
PHONE....................650 666-5287
Hong Jiang, *COO*
John Lewis, *CEO*
EMP: 30 **EST:** 2020
SALES (est): 2.52MM **Privately Held**
Web: www.aegis.life
SIC: 2834 Pharmaceutical preparations

(P-4037)
AGOURON PHARMACEUTICALS INC (HQ)
10777 Science Center Dr (92121-1111)
PHONE....................858 622-3000
Catherine Mackey Ph.D., *Sr VP*
EMP: 50 **EST:** 1984
SALES (est): 147.08MM
SALES (corp-wide): 100.33B **Publicly Held**
Web: www.agi.org
SIC: 2834 5122 8731 Pharmaceutical preparations; Pharmaceuticals; Commercial physical research
PA: Pfizer Inc.
66 Hudson Blvd E Fl 20
New York NY
212 733-2323

(P-4038)
AKCEA THERAPEUTICS INC (HQ)
Also Called: Akcea Therapeutics
2850 Gazelle Ct (92010)
PHONE....................617 207-0202
Brett Monia, *Pr*
Elizabeth Hougen, *Treas*
Melissa Yoon, *Sec*
Michael Pollock, *Chief Commercial Officer*
Tracy Berns, *Chief Compliance Officer*
EMP: 76 **EST:** 2017
SALES (est): 488.54MM
SALES (corp-wide): 587.37MM **Publicly Held**
Web: www.ionispharma.com
SIC: 2834 8731 Pharmaceutical preparations; Biological research
PA: Ionis Pharmaceuticals, Inc.
2855 Gazelle Ct
Carlsbad CA
760 931-9200

(P-4039)
ALLERGAN SALES LLC (DH)
2525 Dupont Dr (92612-1599)
P.O. Box 19534 (92623-9534)
PHONE....................862 261-7000
Brenton L Saunders, *Ch*
William Meury, *CCO**
Matthew M Walsh, *
A Robert D Bailey, *CLO**
Karen L Ling, *Chief Human Resource Officer**
▲ **EMP:** 600 **EST:** 1986
SQ FT: 10,000
SALES (est): 1.32B
SALES (corp-wide): 58.05B **Publicly Held**
Web: www.abbvie.com
SIC: 2834 Pharmaceutical preparations
HQ: Allergan, Inc.
1 N Waukegan Rd
North Chicago IL
862 261-7000

(P-4040)
ALLERGAN SPCLTY THRPEUTICS INC
Also Called: Allergan
2525 Dupont Dr (92612-1599)
PHONE....................714 246-4500
David Pyott, *Pr*
EMP: 1500 **EST:** 1997
SALES (est): 472.74MM
SALES (corp-wide): 58.05B **Publicly Held**
SIC: 2834 Pharmaceutical preparations
HQ: Allergan, Inc.
1 N Waukegan Rd
North Chicago IL
862 261-7000

(P-4041)
ALLERGAN USA INC
Also Called: Pacific Communications
18581 Teller Ave (92612-1627)
P.O. Box 19534 (92623-9534)
PHONE....................714 427-1900
David E I Pyott, *CEO*
Craig Sullivan, *Pr*
Jeffrey L Edwards, *VP*
Douglas S Ingram, *Sec*
James M Hindman, *Treas*
EMP: 2000 **EST:** 2007
SALES (est): 228.87MM
SALES (corp-wide): 58.05B **Publicly Held**
Web: www.pacificcommunications.com
SIC: 2834 Druggists' preparations (pharmaceuticals)
HQ: Allergan, Inc.
1 N Waukegan Rd
North Chicago IL
862 261-7000

(P-4042)
AMBIT BIOSCIENCES CORPORATION
10201 Wateridge Cir Ste 200 (92121)
PHONE....................858 334-2100
Michael A Martino, *Pr*
Faheem Hasnain, *Ch Bd*
Alan Fuhrman, *CFO*
Annette North, *Sr VP*
Mario Orlando, *Sr VP*
EMP: 53 **EST:** 2000
SQ FT: 20,000
SALES (est): 21.35MM **Privately Held**
Web: www.ambitbio.com
SIC: 2834 Pharmaceutical preparations
PA: Daiichi Sankyo Company, Limited
3-5-1, Nihombashihoncho
Chuo-Ku TKY

(P-4043)
AMBRX INC (PA)
10975 N Torrey Pines Rd Ste 100
(92037-1051)
PHONE....................858 875-2400
Tiecheng Qiao, *CEO*
John D Diekman, *
John W Wallen Iii, *VP*
Ho Cho, *
Simon Allen, *Chief Business Officer**
EMP: 56 **EST:** 2003
SALES (est): 25MM
SALES (corp-wide): 25MM **Privately Held**
Web: www.ambrx.com
SIC: 2834 Druggists' preparations (pharmaceuticals)

(P-4044)
AMERIPHARMA SPECIALTY PHRM DIV
132 S Anita Dr (92868-3317)
PHONE....................877 778-3773

EMP: 17 **EST:** 2017
SALES (est): 2.16MM **Privately Held**
Web: www.ameripharma.com
SIC: 2834 Pharmaceutical preparations

(P-4045)
AMGEN INC
1840 De Havilland Dr (91320-1789)
PHONE....................805 447-1000
EMP: 178
SALES (corp-wide): 26.32B **Publicly Held**
Web: www.amgen.com
SIC: 2834 Pharmaceutical preparations
PA: Amgen Inc.
1 Amgen Center Dr
Thousand Oaks CA
805 447-1000

(P-4046)
AMGEN USA INC (HQ)
1 Amgen Center Dr (91320-1799)
PHONE....................805 447-1000
EMP: 96 **EST:** 2010
SALES (est): 27.37MM
SALES (corp-wide): 26.32B **Publicly Held**
Web: www.amgen.com
SIC: 2834 Pharmaceutical preparations
PA: Amgen Inc.
1 Amgen Center Dr
Thousand Oaks CA
805 447-1000

(P-4047)
AMPHASTAR PHARMACEUTICALS INC (PA)
Also Called: Amphastar
11570 6th St (91730-6025)
PHONE....................909 980-9484
Jack Yongfeng Zhang, *CSO*
Jack Yongfeng Zhang, *CSO*
Mary Ziping Luo, *Chief Scientist**
William J Peters, *
▲ **EMP:** 102 **EST:** 1996
SQ FT: 267,674
SALES (est): 498.99MM
SALES (corp-wide): 498.99MM **Publicly Held**
Web: www.amphastar.com
SIC: 2834 Pharmaceutical preparations

(P-4048)
AMPHASTAR PHARMACEUTICALS INC
Also Called: Amphastar Pharmaceuticals
13760 Magnolia Ave (91710-7018)
PHONE....................909 590-1828
Jack Zhang, *Mgr*
EMP: 28
SQ FT: 11,432
SALES (corp-wide): 498.99MM **Publicly Held**
Web: www.amphastar.com
SIC: 2834 Pharmaceutical preparations
PA: Amphastar Pharmaceuticals Inc
11570 6th St
Rancho Cucamonga CA
909 980-9484

(P-4049)
AMYLIN OHIO LLC
9360 Towne Centre Dr (92121-3057)
PHONE....................858 552-2200
EMP: 1300
SIC: 2834 Pharmaceutical preparations

(P-4050)
ANABOLIC INCORPORATED
Also Called: Vitamer Laboratories
17802 Gillette Ave (92614-6502)

▲ = Import ▼ = Export
◆ = Import/Export

P.O. Box 19516 (92623-9516)
PHONE..............................949 863-0340
Steven R Brown, *Pr*
Jane Drinkwalter, *
▲ **EMP:** 25 **EST:** 1959
SALES (est): 956.3K **Privately Held**
SIC: 2834 Vitamin preparations

(P-4051)
ANAPTYSBIO INC (PA)
Also Called: Anaptysbio
10770 Wateridge Cir Ste 210 (92121)
PHONE..............................858 362-6295
Hamza Suria, *Pr*
John Orwin, *Ch Bd*
Eric Loumeau, *COO*
Dennis Mulroy, *CFO*
Paul F Lizzul, *CMO*
EMP: 94 **EST:** 2005
SQ FT: 45,000
SALES (est): 10.29MM **Publicly Held**
Web: www.anaptysbio.com
SIC: 2834 Pharmaceutical preparations

(P-4052)
ANCHEN PHARMACEUTICALS INC
5 Goodyear (92618-2000)
PHONE..............................949 639-8100
Phillip Brancazio, *Brnch Mgr*
EMP: 236
Web: www.parpharm.com
SIC: 2834 Druggists' preparations
(pharmaceuticals)
HQ: Anchen Pharmaceuticals, Inc.
300 Tice Blvd Ste 230
Woodcliff Lake NJ
949 639-8100

(P-4053)
AOE INTERNATIONAL INC
20611 Belshaw Ave (90746-3507)
▲ **EMP:** 35 **EST:** 1998
SQ FT: 12,500
SALES (est): 3.48MM **Privately Held**
SIC: 2834 Vitamin, nutrient, and hematinic
preparations for human use

(P-4054)
APPLIED MLECULAR EVOLUTION INC (HQ)
10300 Campus Point Dr Ste 200
(92121-1504)
PHONE..............................858 597-4990
Thomas Bumol, *Pr*
EMP: 50 **EST:** 1990
SQ FT: 43,000
SALES (est): 29.64MM
SALES (corp-wide): 28.54B **Publicly Held**
SIC: 2834 Pharmaceutical preparations
PA: Eli Lilly And Company
Lilly Corporate Ctr
Indianapolis IN
317 276-2000

(P-4055)
ARCTURUS THRPTICS HOLDINGS INC (PA)
Also Called: Arcturus
10628 Science Center Dr Ste 250
(92121-1116)
PHONE..............................858 900-2660
Joseph E Payne, *Pr*
Peter Farrell, *Ch Bd*
Andy Sassine, *CFO*
Padmanabh Chivukula, *CSO*
Steven Hughes, *CDO*
EMP: 114 **EST:** 2013
SQ FT: 24,700

SALES (est): 206MM
SALES (corp-wide): 206MM **Publicly Held**
Web: www.arcturusrx.com
SIC: 2834 Pharmaceutical preparations

(P-4056)
ARCUTIS BIOTHERAPEUTICS INC (PA)
Also Called: ARCUTIS BIOTHERAPEUTICS
3027 Townsgate Rd Ste 300 (91361-5873)
PHONE..............................805 418-5006
Todd Franklin Watanabe, *Pr*
Todd Franklin Watanabe, *Pr*
Patrick J Heron, *Ch Bd*
John W Smither, *CFO*
EMP: 50 **EST:** 2016
SQ FT: 4,741
SALES (est): 3.69MM
SALES (corp-wide): 3.69MM **Publicly
Held**
Web: www.arcutis.com
SIC: 2834 Pharmaceutical preparations

(P-4057)
ARIZEKE PHARMACUETICALS INC
6828 Nncy Rdge Dr Ste 400 (92121)
PHONE..............................858 455-6907
Daniel Henderson, *Pr*
Seth Goldman, *
Dave Sodolsky, *
EMP: 44 **EST:** 1996
SQ FT: 17,707
SALES (est): 2.83MM **Privately Held**
SIC: 2834 Pharmaceutical preparations

(P-4058)
ARROWHEAD PHARMACEUTICALS INC
10102 Hoyt Park Dr (92131-3000)
PHONE..............................626 304-3400
EMP: 34
Web: www.arrowheadpharma.com
SIC: 2834 Pharmaceutical preparations
PA: Arrowhead Pharmaceuticals, Inc.
177 E Colo Blvd Ste 700
Pasadena CA

(P-4059)
ATXCO INC
3030 Bunker Hill St Ste 325 (92109-5754)
PHONE..............................650 334-2079
Robert Williamson, *CEO*
EMP: 21 **EST:** 2019
SALES (est): 1.01MM **Privately Held**
SIC: 2834 Pharmaceutical preparations

(P-4060)
AUSPEX PHARMACEUTICALS INC
3333 N Torrey Pines Ct Ste 400
(92037-1022)
P.O. Box 49272 (90049-0272)
PHONE..............................858 558-2400
Larry Downey, *Pr*
Deborah A Griffin, *
Austin D Kim, *
EMP: 30 **EST:** 2001
SALES (est): 9.48MM **Privately Held**
Web: www.tevapharm.com
SIC: 2834 Pharmaceutical preparations
PA: Teva Pharmaceutical Industries Limited
5 Bazel
Petah Tikva

(P-4061)
AVANIR PHARMACEUTICALS INC (DH)

30 Enterprise Ste 200 (92656-7112)
PHONE..............................949 389-6700
Rohan Palekar, *Pr*
Gregory J Flesher, *Sr VP*
Joao Siffert, *Sr VP*
Christine G Ocampo, *VP*
EMP: 67 **EST:** 1988
SALES (est): 98.77MM **Privately Held**
Web: www.otsuka-us.com
SIC: 2834 Pharmaceutical preparations
HQ: Otsuka Pharmaceutical Co., Ltd.
2-16-4, Konan
Minato-Ku TKY

(P-4062)
AVID BIOSERVICES INC (PA)
Also Called: Avid Bioservices
14191 Myford Rd (92780-7020)
PHONE..............................714 508-6100
Nicholas S Green, *Pr*
Joseph Carleone, *Non-Executive Chairman
of the Board**
Daniel R Hart, *CFO*
Matthew Kwietniak, *CCO*
Mark R Ziebell, *Corporate Secretary*
EMP: 120 **EST:** 1981
SALES (est): 149.27MM
SALES (corp-wide): 149.27MM **Publicly
Held**
Web: www.avidbio.com
SIC: 2834 Pharmaceutical preparations

(P-4063)
AVID BIOSERVICES INC
14272 Franklin Ave Ste 115 (92780-7064)
PHONE..............................714 508-6000
Steven W King, *Pr*
EMP: 145
SALES (corp-wide): 149.27MM **Publicly
Held**
Web: www.avidbio.com
SIC: 2834 Pharmaceutical preparations
PA: Avid Bioservices, Inc.
14191 Myford Rd
Tustin CA
714 508-6100

(P-4064)
AVIDITY BIOSCIENCES INC
Also Called: Avidity Biosciences
10578 Science Center Dr Ste 125
(92121-1145)
PHONE..............................858 401-7900
Sarah Boyce, *Pr*
Troy Wilson, *
Joseph Baroldi, *COO*
Michael F Maclean, *CFO*
Arthur A Levin, *CSO*
EMP: 38 **EST:** 2012
SQ FT: 8,561
SALES (est): 9.22MM **Privately Held**
Web: www.aviditybiosciences.com
SIC: 2834 Pharmaceutical preparations

(P-4065)
BACHEM AMERICAS INC
Also Called: Bachem Vista BSD
1271 Avenida Chelsea (92081-8315)
PHONE..............................888 422-2436
Brian Gregg, *Pr*
EMP: 58
Web: www.bachem.com
SIC: 2834 Pharmaceutical preparations
HQ: Bachem Americas, Inc.
3132 Kashiwa St
Torrance CA
310 784-4440

(P-4066)
BAXALTA US INC
4501 Colorado Blvd (90039-1103)
PHONE..............................818 240-5600
Raul Navarro, *Brnch Mgr*
EMP: 686
SIC: 2834 Pharmaceutical preparations
HQ: Baxalta Us Inc.
1200 Lakeside Dr
Bannockburn IL
224 948-2000

(P-4067)
BAXCO PHARMACEUTICAL INC
2393 Bateman Ave (91010-3313)
PHONE..............................626 610-7088
Dennis Wong, *Pr*
Joseph Meuse, *COO*
Koki Luu, *CFO*
Rose Ibarra, *Genl Mgr*
▲ **EMP:** 17 **EST:** 2000
SALES (est): 4.64MM **Privately Held**
Web: www.baxcoinc.com
SIC: 2834 Pharmaceutical preparations

(P-4068)
BEAUTY & HEALTH INTERNATIONAL
7541 Anthony Ave (92841-4005)
P.O. Box 890 (92684-0890)
PHONE..............................714 903-9730
▲ **EMP:** 50 **EST:** 1993
SQ FT: 12,000
SALES (est): 6.49MM **Privately Held**
SIC: 2834 2844 5122 5149. Vitamin
preparations; Cosmetic preparations;
Vitamins and minerals; Health foods

(P-4069)
BEST FORMULATIONS INC
Also Called: BEST FORMULATIONS INC.
17775 Rowland St (91748-1138)
PHONE..............................626 912-9998
EMP: 166
Web: www.bestformulations.com
SIC: 2834 Pharmaceutical preparations
HQ: Best Formulations Llc
17758 Rowland St
City Of Industry CA
626 912-9998

(P-4070)
BF SUMA PHARMACEUTICALS INC
5077 Walnut Grove Ave (91776-2023)
PHONE..............................626 285-8366
▲ **EMP:** 37 **EST:** 2006
SQ FT: 10,000
SALES (est): 3.43MM **Privately Held**
SIC: 2834 Pharmaceutical preparations

(P-4071)
BIMEDA INC
5539 Ayon Ave (91706-2057)
PHONE..............................626 815-1680
Tim Tynan, *Brnch Mgr*
EMP: 187
SALES (corp-wide): 3.12B **Privately Held**
Web: www.bimedaus.com
SIC: 2834 3841 Veterinary pharmaceutical
preparations; Surgical and medical
instruments
HQ: Bimeda Inc.
1 Tower Ln Ste 2250
Oakbrook Terrace IL
630 928-0361

(P-4072)
BIO-NUTRACEUTICALS INC (PA)
Also Called: Bni
21820 Marilla St (91311-4127)
PHONE..................818 727-0246
EMP: 17 **EST:** 2004
SALES (est): 10.1MM
SALES (corp-wide): 10.1MM **Privately Held**
Web: bionutraceutical.elementor.cloud
SIC: 2834 Tablets, pharmaceutical

(P-4073)
BIOMED CALIFORNIA INC
Also Called: Soleo Health
721 S Glasgow Ave Ste C (90301-3016)
PHONE..................310 665-1121
John Ginzler, *CFO*
Drew Walk, *CEO*
EMP: 22 **EST:** 2007
SALES (est): 2.27MM **Privately Held**
SIC: 2834 5912 Druggists' preparations (pharmaceuticals); Drug stores and proprietary stores
HQ: Biomed Healthcare, Inc.
950 Calcon Hook Rd Ste 19
Sharon Hill PA
888 244-2340

(P-4074)
BIORX PHARMACEUTICALS INC
Also Called: Biorx Laboratories
6320 Chalet Dr (90040-3706)
PHONE..................323 725-3100
Amin Jack, *Pr*
EMP: 32 **EST:** 2010
SALES (est): 2.4MM **Privately Held**
Web: www.biorxlabs.com
SIC: 2834 2844 Pharmaceutical preparations; Perfumes, cosmetics and other toilet preparations

(P-4075)
BIOVAIL TECHNOLOGIES LTD
1 Enterprise (92656-2606)
PHONE..................703 995-2400
David Tierney, *Pr*
EMP: 61 **EST:** 1988
SQ FT: 55,000
SALES (est): 3.74MM
SALES (corp-wide): 8.05B **Privately Held**
SIC: 2834 8731 3841 2087 Pharmaceutical preparations; Commercial physical research; Surgical and medical instruments; Flavoring extracts and syrups, nec
PA: Bausch Health Companies Inc.
2150 Boul Saint-Elzear O
Laval QC
514 744-6792

(P-4076)
BMS FINANCE INC
3705 El Cajon Blvd (92105-1004)
PHONE..................619 284-9801
EMP: 23 **EST:** 1998
SALES (est): 182.92K **Privately Held**
SIC: 2834 Pharmaceutical preparations

(P-4077)
BMS INVESTMENTS LLC
Also Called: Jiffy Lube
12626 Hackberry Ln (92553-4796)
PHONE..................714 376-2535
Byron Marroquin, *Pr*
Byron Marroquin, *Managing Member*
David Orlando Marroquin, *Managing Member*
EMP: 23 **EST:** 2015
SALES (est): 1.54MM **Privately Held**
Web: www.jiffylube.com

SIC: 2834 Pharmaceutical preparations

(P-4078)
CALPORTA THERAPEUTICS INC
11099 N Torrey Pines Rd Ste 290 (92037-1029)
PHONE..................858 750-4700
Sanford J Madigan, *CEO*
EMP: 26 **EST:** 2015
SALES (est): 3.03MM
SALES (corp-wide): 59.28B **Publicly Held**
Web: www.avalonbioventures.com
SIC: 2834 Pharmaceutical preparations
PA: Merck & Co., Inc.
126 E Lincoln Ave
Rahway NJ
908 740-4000

(P-4079)
CAPRICOR THERAPEUTICS INC (PA)
Also Called: Capricor Therapeutics
10865 Road To The Cure Ste 150 (92121-1154)
PHONE..................310 358-3200
Linda Marban, *Pr*
Frank Litvack, *Ex Ch Bd*
Anthony Bergmann, *Corporate Treasurer*
Karen G Krasney, *Ex VP*
EMP: 19 **EST:** 2005
SALES (est): 2.55MM
SALES (corp-wide): 2.55MM **Publicly Held**
Web: www.capricor.com
SIC: 2834 Pharmaceutical preparations

(P-4080)
CAPTEK MIDCO INC
2710 Progress St (92081-8449)
PHONE..................760 734-6800
EMP: 66
SALES (corp-wide): 203.23MM **Privately Held**
Web: www.capteksoftgel.com
SIC: 2834 Pharmaceutical preparations
HQ: Captek Midco, Inc.
16218 Arthur St
Cerritos CA
562 921-9511

(P-4081)
CAPTEK SOFTGEL INTL INC (DH)
16218 Arthur St (90703-2131)
PHONE..................562 921-9511
▲ **EMP:** 300 **EST:** 1995
SQ FT: 90,000
SALES (est): 203.23MM
SALES (corp-wide): 203.23MM **Privately Held**
Web: www.capteksoftgel.com
SIC: 2834 Vitamin, nutrient, and hematinic preparations for human use
HQ: Captek Midco, Inc.
16218 Arthur St
Cerritos CA
562 921-9511

(P-4082)
CAPTEK SOFTGEL INTL INC
Also Called: Captek Pharma
14535 Industry Cir (90638-5814)
PHONE..................657 325-0412
Paul Hwang, *Genl Mgr*
EMP: 50
SALES (corp-wide): 203.23MM **Privately Held**
Web: www.capteksoftgel.com
SIC: 2834 Pharmaceutical preparations
HQ: Captek Softgel International, Inc.
16218 Arthur St

Cerritos CA

(P-4083)
CARDINAL HEALTH 414 LLC
640 S Jefferson St (92870-6600)
PHONE..................714 572-9900
Shanam Biglari, *Mgr*
EMP: 20
SALES (corp-wide): 205.01B **Publicly Held**
SIC: 2834 5912 Pharmaceutical preparations; Drug stores and proprietary stores
HQ: Cardinal Health 414, Llc
7000 Cardinal Pl
Dublin OH
614 757-5000

(P-4084)
CARLSBAD TECHNOLOGY INC
Also Called: Carlsbad Tech
5923 Balfour Ct (92008-7304)
PHONE..................760 431-8284
EMP: 70
Web: www.carlsbadtech.com
SIC: 2834 Druggists' preparations (pharmaceuticals)
HQ: Carlsbad Technology Inc.
5922 Farnsworth Ct # 102
Carlsbad CA

(P-4085)
CARLSBAD TECHNOLOGY INC (DH)
Also Called: Carlsbad Tech
5922 Farnsworth Ct Ste 102 (92008-7398)
PHONE..................760 431-8284
Robert Wan, *CEO*
Andy Cheng, *
▲ **EMP:** 30 **EST:** 1990
SQ FT: 27,000
SALES (est): 23.67MM **Privately Held**
Web: www.carlsbadtech.com
SIC: 2834 Druggists' preparations (pharmaceuticals)
HQ: Yung Shin Pharm. Ind. Co., Ltd.
No. 1191, Zhongshan Rd., Sec. 1,
Taichung City

(P-4086)
CATALENT PHARMA SOLUTIONS INC
Also Called: Pharmatek
7330 Carroll Rd Ste 200 (92121-2364)
PHONE..................858 805-6383
EMP: 200
Web: www.catalent.com
SIC: 2834 Pharmaceutical preparations
HQ: Catalent Pharma Solutions, Inc.
14 Schoolhouse Rd
Somerset NJ

(P-4087)
CATALENT PHARMA SOLUTIONS INC
8926 Ware Ct (92121-2222)
PHONE..................877 587-1835
EMP: 31
Web: www.catalent.com
SIC: 2834 Pharmaceutical preparations
HQ: Catalent Pharma Solutions, Inc.
14 Schoolhouse Rd
Somerset NJ

(P-4088)
CELGENE CORPORATION
Also Called: Celgene Signal Research
10300 Campus Point Dr Ste 100 (92121-1504)
PHONE..................858 795-4961

Alan Lewis, *Brnch Mgr*
EMP: 45
SALES (corp-wide): 46.16B **Publicly Held**
Web: www.bms.com
SIC: 2834 Pharmaceutical preparations
HQ: Celgene Corporation
86 Morris Ave
Summit NJ
908 673-9000

(P-4089)
CG ONCOLOGY INC
400 Spectrum Center Dr Ste 2040 (92618-4934)
PHONE..................949 409-3700
Arthur Kuan, *CEO*
EMP: 33 **EST:** 2010
SALES (est): 2.98MM **Privately Held**
Web: www.cgoncology.com
SIC: 2834 8733 Pharmaceutical preparations; Biotechnical research, noncommercial

(P-4090)
CH LABORATORIES INC (PA)
1243 W 130th St (90247-1501)
PHONE..................310 516-8273
Brid Nolan, *Pr*
EMP: 24 **EST:** 2001
SQ FT: 30,000
SALES (est): 4.4MM
SALES (corp-wide): 4.4MM **Privately Held**
Web: www.chlabs.com
SIC: 2834 Vitamin preparations

(P-4091)
COMPRHNSIVE CRDVSCLAR SPCLSTS (PA)
220 S 1st St Ste 101 (91801-3705)
PHONE..................626 281-8663
Peter Fung Md, *Pr*
EMP: 17 **EST:** 2002
SALES (est): 4.93MM
SALES (corp-wide): 4.93MM **Privately Held**
Web: www.ccsheartcare.com
SIC: 2834 8111 Drugs acting on the cardiovascular system, except diagnostic; Legal services

(P-4092)
CONTINENTAL VITAMIN CO INC
Also Called: Cvc Specialties
4510 S Boyle Ave (90058-2418)
PHONE..................323 581-0176
Ron Beckenfeld, *Pr*
Lillian Beckenfeld, *
EMP: 60 **EST:** 1969
SQ FT: 80,000
SALES (est): 9.54MM **Privately Held**
Web: www.cvc4health.com
SIC: 2834 5122 Vitamin preparations; Vitamins and minerals

(P-4093)
COSMEDX SCIENCE INC
3550 Vine St Ste 210 (92507-4175)
P.O. Box 1925 (92878-1925)
PHONE..................951 371-0509
▲ **EMP:** 50
Web: www.cosmedxscience.com
SIC: 2834 Dermatologicals

(P-4094)
COUGAR BIOTECHNOLOGY INC
10990 Wilshire Blvd Ste 1200 (90024-3919)
PHONE..................310 943-8040
Alan H Auerbach, *Pr*
Charles Eyler, *VP Fin*
Gloria Lee Md, *Clinical Vice President*
Arie S Belldegrun Md, *Ch Bd*

▲ = Import ▼ = Export
◆ = Import/Export

EMP: 58 EST: 2003
SQ FT: 7,300
SALES (est): 16.24MM
SALES (corp-wide): 94.94B **Publicly Held**
SIC: 2834 Drugs affecting neoplasms and endrocrine systems
PA: Johnson & Johnson
1 Johnson And Johnson Plz
New Brunswick NJ
732 524-0400

(P-4095)
CRINETICS PHARMACEUTICALS INC (PA)
Also Called: CRINETICS
10222 Barnes Canyon Rd Ste 200 (92121-2711)
PHONE..............................858 450-6464
R Scott Struthers, *Pr*
Wendell Wierenga, *Ch Bd*
Jeff Knight, *COO*
Marc Wilson, *CFO*
Alan Krasner, *CMO*
EMP: 92 EST: 2008
SQ FT: 29,499
SALES (est): 4.74MM **Publicly Held**
Web: www.crinetics.com
SIC: 2834 Pharmaceutical preparations

(P-4096)
CV SCIENCES INC (PA)
9530 Padgett St Ste 107 (92126-4449)
PHONE..............................866 290-2157
Joseph Dowling, *CEO*
Michael Mona Iii, *Pr*
Joerg Grasser, *CFO*
EMP: 38 EST: 2013
SALES (est): 16.2MM
SALES (corp-wide): 16.2MM **Privately Held**
Web: www.cvsciences.com
SIC: 2834 Pharmaceutical preparations

(P-4097)
CYMBIOTIKA LLC (PA)
5825 Oberlin Dr Ste 5 (92121-3777)
PHONE..............................770 910-4945
Shahab Elmi, *CEO*
EMP: 32 EST: 2018
SALES (est): 26.4MM
SALES (corp-wide): 26.4MM **Privately Held**
Web: www.cymbiotika.com
SIC: 2834 Pharmaceutical preparations

(P-4098)
CYMBIOTIKA LLC
8885 Rehco Rd (92121-3261)
PHONE..............................949 652-8177
Anya Bytnar, *Mgr*
EMP: 58
SALES (corp-wide): 26.4MM **Privately Held**
Web: www.cymbiotika.com
SIC: 2834 Pharmaceutical preparations
PA: Cymbiotika Llc
5825 Oberlin Dr Ste 5
San Diego CA
770 910-4945

(P-4099)
DEFENDER SD MANUFACTURING LLC
3443 Tripp Ct (92121-1032)
PHONE..............................314 697-1330
Barry Feinberg, *Pr*
Barry Feinberg, *Managing Member*
David Helton, *
EMP: 28 EST: 2020
SALES (est): 3.53MM **Privately Held**

SIC: 2834 Pharmaceutical preparations

(P-4100)
DENDREON PHARMACEUTICALS LLC (HQ)
1700 Saturn Way (90740-5618)
PHONE..............................562 252-7500
Jason Oneill, *CEO*
Matthew Kemp, *CCO**
Christina Yi, *
Chris Carr, *
EMP: 50 EST: 2015
SALES (est): 115.38MM **Privately Held**
Web: www.dendreon.com
SIC: 2834 Pharmaceutical preparations
PA: Nanjing Xinjiekou Department Store Co., Ltd.
No.1, Zhongshan South Road, Qinhuai District
Nanjing JS

(P-4101)
DESIGN THERAPEUTICS INC
Also Called: DESIGN THERAPEUTICS
6005 Hidden Valley Rd Ste 110 (92011-4222)
PHONE..............................858 293-4900
Joao Siffert, *Pr*
Pratik Shah, *Ex Ch Bd*
Sean Jeffries, *COO*
Jae Kim, *CMO*
EMP: 22 EST: 2017
Web: www.designtx.com
SIC: 2834 Pharmaceutical preparations

(P-4102)
DNIB UNWIND INC
333 S Grand Ave Ste 4070 (90071-1544)
PHONE..............................213 617-2717
EMP: 114
SIC: 2834 Pharmaceutical preparations

(P-4103)
EDWARDS LIFESCIENCES LLC (HQ)
1 Edwards Way (92614-5688)
PHONE..............................949 250-2500
Michael A Mussallem, *CEO*
John H Kehl Junior, *VP*
▲ EMP: 1700 EST: 1958
SALES (est): 529.14MM
SALES (corp-wide): 5.38B **Publicly Held**
Web: www.edwards.com
SIC: 2834 Pharmaceutical preparations
PA: Edwards Lifesciences Corp
1 Edwards Way
Irvine CA
949 250-2500

(P-4104)
ELITRA PHARMACEUTICALS
3510 Dunhill St Ste A (92121-1201)
PHONE..............................858 410-3030
Paul R Hamelin, *CEO*
Harry Hixson Junior, *Ch Bd*
J Gordon Foulkes, *Senior Vice President Research & Development*
EMP: 65 EST: 1997
SQ FT: 35,735
SALES (est): 4.81MM **Privately Held**
Web: www.elitra.net
SIC: 2834 8731 Pharmaceutical preparations ; Commercial physical research

(P-4105)
ENDO PHARMACEUTICALS INC
9601 Jeronimo Rd (92618-2025)
PHONE..............................949 767-9420
EMP: 30

Web: www.endo.com
SIC: 2834 Pharmaceutical preparations
HQ: Endo Pharmaceuticals, Inc.
1400 Atwater Dr
Malvern PA
484 216-0000

(P-4106)
ENTOS PHARMACEUTICALS INC
3040 Science Park Rd (92121-1102)
PHONE..............................800 727-0884
John D Lewis, *CEO*
Jason Ding, *Chief Business Officer*
EMP: 18 EST: 2021
SALES (est): 2.56MM **Privately Held**
SIC: 2834 Pharmaceutical preparations

(P-4107)
EQUILLIUM INC (PA)
2223 Avenida De La Playa Ste 105 (92037)
PHONE..............................858 412-5302
Bruce D Steel, *Pr*
Daniel M Bradbury, *Ex Ch Bd*
Jason A Keyes, *CFO*
Stephen Connelly, *CSO*
Joel Rothman, *Chief Development Officer*
EMP: 18 EST: 2017
SQ FT: 1,750
SALES (est): 15.76MM
SALES (corp-wide): 15.76MM **Publicly Held**
Web: www.equilliumbio.com
SIC: 2834 2836 Pharmaceutical preparations ; Biological products, except diagnostic

(P-4108)
ERASCA INC
10835 Road To The Cure Ste 140 (92121-1130)
PHONE..............................858 465-6511
Jonathan E Lim, *Ch Bd*
David M Chacko, *Chief Business Officer*
Nik Chetwyn, *COO*
Ebun S Garner, *Corporate Secretary*
Shannon R Morris, *Chief Medical Officer*
EMP: 102 EST: 2018
SQ FT: 16,153
Web: www.erasca.com
SIC: 2834 Pharmaceutical preparations

(P-4109)
ESSENTIAL PHARMACEUTICAL CORP
1906 W Holt Ave (91768-3351)
PHONE..............................909 623-4565
Bruce Lin, *CEO*
Po Chia Lin, *Sec*
▲ EMP: 20 EST: 1986
SQ FT: 7,642
SALES (est): 4.21MM **Privately Held**
Web: www.essentialpharmaceutical.com
SIC: 2834 Vitamin preparations

(P-4110)
EVOFEM BIOSCIENCES INC (PA)
Also Called: Evofem
12400 High Bluff Dr Ste 600 (92130-3077)
PHONE..............................858 550-1900
Saundra Pelletier, *CEO*
William Hall, *Ch Bd*
Albert Altro, *Interim Chief Financial Officer*
Kelly Culwell, *CMO*
Russell Barrans, *CCO*
EMP: 42 EST: 2009
SQ FT: 33,290
SALES (est): 16.84MM **Publicly Held**
Web: www.evofem.com
SIC: 2834 Pharmaceutical preparations

(P-4111)
EVOLUS INC (PA)
Also Called: EVOLUS
520 Newport Center Dr Ste 1200 (92660)
PHONE..............................949 284-4555
David Moatazedi, *Pr*
Vikram Malik, *Non-Executive Chairman of the Board*
Lauren Silvernail, *Executive Corporate Development Vice President*
Rui Avelar, *Chief Medical Officer*
EMP: 98 EST: 2012
SQ FT: 17,758
SALES (est): 148.62MM **Publicly Held**
Web: www.evolus.com
SIC: 2834 Pharmaceutical preparations

(P-4112)
FORMEX LLC
9601 Jeronimo Rd (92618-2025)
PHONE..............................858 529-6600
Cyrus K Mirsaidi, *Pr*
Ian Wisenberg, *
J Blair West, *CSO**
EMP: 32 EST: 2013
SALES (est): 6.9MM **Privately Held**
Web: www.formexllc.com
SIC: 2834 8731 8071 Tablets, pharmaceutical; Biological research; Testing laboratories
PA: Bioduro Llc
11011 Torreyana Rd
San Diego CA

(P-4113)
FP NUTRACEUTICALS LLC
3851 Schaufele Ave (90808-1703)
PHONE..............................562 944-7821
John Bornstein, *Mgr*
EMP: 66
SALES (corp-wide): 1.05MM **Privately Held**
SIC: 2834 Pharmaceutical preparations
PA: Fp Nutraceuticals, Llc
10012 Painter Ave
Santa Fe Springs CA
562 944-7821

(P-4114)
GENENTECH INC
1 Antibody Way (92056-5701)
PHONE..............................760 231-2440
Amr Elkhayat, *Dir*
EMP: 5045
Web: www.gene.com
SIC: 2834 Pharmaceutical preparations
HQ: Genentech, Inc.
1 Dna Way
South San Francisco CA
650 225-1000

(P-4115)
GENETRONICS INC
10480 Wateridge Cir (92121-5773)
PHONE..............................858 410-3112
EMP: 24 EST: 2019
SALES (est): 776.95K **Publicly Held**
SIC: 2834 Pharmaceutical preparations
PA: Inovio Pharmaceuticals, Inc.
660 W Germantown Pike # 1
Plymouth Meeting PA

(P-4116)
GENVIVO INCORPORATED
Also Called: Genvivo Incorporated
1981 E Locust St (91761-7608)
PHONE..............................626 441-6695
Chris Bergman, *Brnch Mgr*
EMP: 59
SALES (corp-wide): 2.02MM **Privately Held**

Web: www.genvivoinc.com
SIC: 2834 Pharmaceutical preparations
PA: Genvivo, Inc.
435 Huntington Dr
San Marino CA
626 441-6695

(P-4117)
GENZYME CORPORATION
Also Called: Genzyme Genetics
655 E Huntington Dr (91016-3636)
PHONE...............................626 471-9922
Jane Willis, *Brnch Mgr*
EMP: 77
Web: www.sanofi.com
SIC: 2834 Pharmaceutical preparations
HQ: Genzyme Corporation
450 Water St
Cambridge MA
617 252-7500

(P-4118)
GILEAD PALO ALTO INC
Also Called: Gilead Scientist
550 Cliffside Dr (91773-2978)
PHONE...............................909 394-4000
Chris Beley, *CEO*
EMP: 125
SALES (corp-wide): 27.28B Publicly Held
Web: www.gilead.com
SIC: 2834 Drugs acting on the
cardiovascular system, except diagnostic
HQ: Alto Gilead Palo Inc
333 Lakeside Dr
Foster City CA

(P-4119)
GILEAD PALO ALTO INC
4049 Avenida De La Plata (92056-5802)
PHONE...............................760 945-7701
EMP: 125
SALES (corp-wide): 27.28B Publicly Held
Web: www.gilead.com
SIC: 2834 Drugs acting on the
cardiovascular system, except diagnostic
HQ: Alto Gilead Palo Inc
333 Lakeside Dr
Foster City CA

(P-4120)
GILEAD SCIENCES INC
Also Called: Nexstar Pharmaceutical
650 Cliffside Dr (91773-2957)
PHONE...............................909 394-4000
EMP: 33
SALES (corp-wide): 27.28B Publicly Held
Web: www.gilead.com
SIC: 2834 Drugs affecting parasitic and
infective diseases
PA: Gilead Sciences, Inc.
333 Lakeside Dr
Foster City CA
650 574-3000

(P-4121)
GILEAD SCIENCES INC
1800 Wheeler St (91750-5801)
PHONE...............................650 522-2771
Michael Lee, *Prin*
EMP: 99 EST: 1987
SALES (est): 12.69MM Privately Held
Web: www.gilead.com
SIC: 2834 Pharmaceutical preparations

(P-4122)
GMP LABORATORIES AMERICA INC (PA)
Also Called: Gmp Labratories of America
2931 E La Jolla St (92806-1306)
PHONE...............................714 630-2467

Mohammad Ishaq, *CEO*
Suhail Ishaq, *
▲ EMP: 92 EST: 1994
SQ FT: 90,000
SALES (est): 23MM Privately Held
Web: www.gmplabs.com
SIC: 2834 Pharmaceutical preparations

(P-4123)
GOSSAMER BIO INC (PA)
3013 Science Park Rd Ste 200
(92121-1101)
PHONE...............................858 684-1300
Sheila Gujrathi, *Pr*
Faheem Hasnain, *Ex Ch Bd*
Bryan Giraudo, *CFO*
Jakob Dupont, *CMO*
Christian Waage, *Ex VP*
EMP: 26 EST: 2015
SQ FT: 63,667
Web: www.gossamerbio.com
SIC: 2834 Pharmaceutical preparations

(P-4124)
GREENWICH BIOSCIENCES LLC (DH)
Also Called: Greenwich Biosciences, Inc.
5750 Fleet St Ste 200 (92008-4700)
PHONE...............................760 795-2200
Julian Gangolli, *Pr*
Justin Gover, *
Scott Giacobello, *
EMP: 23 EST: 2013
SQ FT: 4,911
SALES (est): 19.22MM Privately Held
Web: www.jazzpharma.com
SIC: 2834 Pharmaceutical preparations
HQ: Gw Pharmaceuticals Limited
Sovereign House
Cambridge CAMBS
122 326-6800

(P-4125)
GSMS INC (PA)
5187 Camino Ruiz (93012-8601)
PHONE...............................805 477-9866
Michael Bornitz, *Pr*
EMP: 22 EST: 2012
SALES (est): 47.53MM
SALES (corp-wide): 47.53MM Privately
Held
Web: www.gsms.us
SIC: 2834 Pharmaceutical preparations

(P-4126)
GUCKENHEIMER ENTERPRISES INC
4010 Ocean Ranch Blvd (92056-5700)
PHONE...............................760 414-3659
EMP: 74
SALES (corp-wide): 127.53MM Privately
Held
Web: www.gilead.com
SIC: 2834 Pharmaceutical preparations
PA: Guckenheimer Enterprises, Inc.
1850 Gateway Dr Ste 500
San Mateo CA
650 592-3800

(P-4127)
GYRE THERAPEUTICS INC (PA)
12730 High Bluff Dr Ste 250 (92130-2075)
PHONE...............................650 266-8674
Charles Wu, *CEO*
Ying Luo, *
Songjiang Ma, *Pr*
Ruoyu Chen, *Interim Chief Financial Officer*
Weiguo Ye, *COO*
EMP: 81 EST: 2002
SALES (est): 794K Publicly Held

Web: www.catalystbiosciences.com
SIC: 2834 Pharmaceutical preparations

(P-4128)
H J HARKINS COMPANY INC
Also Called: Pharma Pac
1400 W Grand Ave Ste F (93433-4221)
PHONE...............................805 929-1333
Norma Jean Erenius, *CEO*
Charles Smith, *
EMP: 50 EST: 1984
SQ FT: 10,000
SALES (est): 5.05MM Privately Held
Web: www.pharmapac.com
SIC: 2834 Pharmaceutical preparations

(P-4129)
HARPERS PHARMACY INC
Also Called: Ameripharma
132 S Anita Dr Ste 210 (92868-3317)
PHONE...............................877 778-3773
Andrew A Harper, *CEO*
Gor Mnatsakanyan, *
EMP: 187 EST: 2016
SALES (est): 27.44MM Privately Held
Web: www.ameripharma.com
SIC: 2834 Pharmaceutical preparations

(P-4130)
HERON THERAPEUTICS INC (PA)
4242 Campus Point Ct Ste 200
(92121-1570)
PHONE...............................858 251-4400
Craig Collard, *CEO*
Adam Morgan, *
John Poyhonen, *CCO*
David Szekeres, *Ex VP*
Lisa Peraza, *CAO*
EMP: 199 EST: 1983
SQ FT: 52,148
SALES (est): 107.67MM
SALES (corp-wide): 107.67MM Publicly
Held
Web: www.herontx.com
SIC: 2834 Pharmaceutical preparations

(P-4131)
HIKMA PHARMACEUTICALS USA INC
2325 Camino Vida Roble Ste B (92011)
PHONE...............................760 683-0901
Sigurdur Olafsson, *Brnch Mgr*
EMP: 45
SALES (corp-wide): 2.52B Privately Held
Web: www.hikma.com
SIC: 2834 Pharmaceutical preparations
HQ: Hikma Pharmaceuticals Usa Inc.
200 Connell Dr Ste 4100
Berkeley Heights NJ
908 673-1030

(P-4132)
HYLANDS CONSUMER HEALTH INC (PA)
Also Called: Hyland's Homeopathic
13301 S Main St (90061-1611)
P.O. Box 61067 (90061-0067)
PHONE...............................310 768-0700
Daniel M Krombach, *Pr*
Will Righeimer, *
Dan Krombach, *
Stephen Schnack, *
▲ EMP: 300 EST: 1903
SQ FT: 150
SALES (est): 77.48MM
SALES (corp-wide): 77.48MM Privately
Held
Web: www.hylands.com

SIC: 2834 5912 Pharmaceutical preparations
; Drug stores *

(P-4133)
IMCD US LLC
16050 Canary Ave (90638-5507)
PHONE...............................714 562-7660
EMP: 93
Web: www.imcdus.com
SIC: 2834 Pharmaceutical preparations
HQ: Imcd Us, Llc
2 Equity Way Ste 210
Westlake OH
216 228-8900

(P-4134)
IMPRIMISRX LLC
1000 Aviara Dr Ste 220 (92011-4218)
PHONE...............................844 446-6979
EMP: 68 EST: 2019
SALES (est): 23.73MM Publicly Held
Web: www.imprimisrx.com
SIC: 2834 Pharmaceutical preparations
PA: Harrow, Inc.
102 Woodmont Blvd Ste 610
Nashville TN

(P-4135)
INOVA DIAGNOSTICS INC
9889 Willow Creek Rd (92131-1119)
PHONE...............................858 586-9900
EMP: 143
Web: www.werfen.com
SIC: 2834 Pharmaceutical preparations
HQ: Inova Diagnostics, Inc.
9900 Old Grove Rd
San Diego CA
858 586-9900

(P-4136)
INSTACURE HEALING PRODUCTS
235 N Moorpark Rd Unit 2022
(91358-7001)
PHONE...............................818 222-9600
David Traub, *Owner*
EMP: 33 EST: 2015
SQ FT: 6,000
SALES (est): 2.9MM Privately Held
Web: www.instacure.net
SIC: 2834 Lip balms

(P-4137)
INTERNATIONAL VITAMIN CORP
Also Called: Adam Nutrition, A Division Ivc
1 Park Plz Ste 800 (92614-5998)
PHONE...............................951 361-1120
Iliu Elisara, *Brnch Mgr*
EMP: 125
Web: www.ivcinc.com
SIC: 2834 Vitamin, nutrient, and hematinic
preparations for human use
PA: International Vitamin Corporation
1050 Woodruff Rd
Greenville SC

(P-4138)
INTERNTNAL MDCTION SYSTEMS LTD
Also Called: IMS
1886 Santa Anita Ave (91733-3414)
PHONE...............................626 442-6757
Jack Zhang, *Pr*
Mary Luo Zhang, *
▲ EMP: 720 EST: 1963
SALES (est): 228.87MM
SALES (corp-wide): 498.99MM Publicly
Held
Web: www.amphastar.com

SIC: **2834** 2833 3841 Drugs acting on the central nervous system & sense organs; Anesthetics, in bulk form; Surgical and medical instruments
PA: Amphastar Pharmaceuticals Inc
11570 6th St
Rancho Cucamonga CA
909 980-9484

(P-4139)
IONIS PHARMACEUTICALS INC
2282 Faraday Ave (92008-7208)
PHONE.............................760 603-3567
Stanley Crooke, *Brnch Mgr*
EMP: 29
SALES (corp-wide): 587.37MM **Publicly Held**
Web: www.ionispharma.com
SIC: **2834** Pharmaceutical preparations
PA: Ionis Pharmaceuticals, Inc.
2855 Gazelle Ct
Carlsbad CA
760 931-9200

(P-4140)
IONIS PHARMACEUTICALS INC
1896 Rutherford Rd (92008-7326)
PHONE.............................760 931-9200
Alfred Chappell, *Brnch Mgr*
EMP: 100
SALES (corp-wide): 587.37MM **Publicly Held**
Web: www.ionispharma.com
SIC: **2834** Pharmaceutical preparations
PA: Ionis Pharmaceuticals, Inc.
2855 Gazelle Ct
Carlsbad CA
760 931-9200

(P-4141)
IONIS PHARMACEUTICALS INC (PA)
Also Called: Ionis
2855 Gazelle Ct (92010-6670)
PHONE.............................760 931-9200
Brett P Monia, *CEO*
Joseph Loscalzo, *
Elizabeth L Hougen, *Ex VP*
Joseph T Baroldi, *Chief Business Officer*
C Frank Bennett, *CSO*
▲ EMP: 340 EST: 1989
SALES (est): 587.37MM
SALES (corp-wide): 587.37MM **Publicly Held**
Web: www.ionispharma.com
SIC: **2834** 8731 3845 Pharmaceutical preparations; Medical research, commercial ; Electromedical equipment

(P-4142)
ISTA PHARMACEUTICALS INC
50 Technology Dr (92618-2301)
P.O. Box 25169 (18002-5169)
PHONE.............................949 788-6000
EMP: 330
SIC: **2834** Pharmaceutical preparations

(P-4143)
JANSSEN RESEARCH & DEV LLC
3210 Merryfield Row (92121-1126)
PHONE.............................858 450-2000
Steve Schuetzle, *Mgr*
EMP: 228
SALES (corp-wide): 94.94MM **Publicly Held**
Web: www.janssenlabs.com
SIC: **2834** Pharmaceutical preparations
HQ: Janssen Research & Development, Llc
920 Us Highway 202
Raritan NJ
908 704-4000

(P-4144)
JANUX THERAPEUTICS INC
10955 Vista Sorrento Pkwy Ste 300 (92130-8699)
PHONE.............................858 751-4493
David Campbell, *Pr*
Jay Lichter, *Ch Bd*
Wayne Godfrey, *CMO*
Andy Meyer, *Chief Business Officer*
EMP: 20 EST: 2017
SALES (est): 8.61MM **Privately Held**
Web: www.januxrx.com
SIC: **2834** Pharmaceutical preparations

(P-4145)
JARROW INDUSTRIES LLC (PA)
12246 Hawkins St (90670-3365)
PHONE.............................562 906-1919
Jarrow Rogovin, *Ch Bd*
Mohammed Khalid, *
Ben Khowong, *
David Chen, *
▲ EMP: 74 EST: 2000
SQ FT: 125,000
SALES (est): 50.38MM
SALES (corp-wide): 50.38MM **Privately Held**
Web: www.jarrowindustries.com
SIC: **2834** Vitamin preparations

(P-4146)
JARROW INDUSTRIES LLC
12342 Hawkins St (90670-3367)
PHONE.............................562 631-9330
Jackie Kelley, *Mgr*
EMP: 22
SALES (corp-wide): 50.38MM **Privately Held**
Web: www.jarrowindustries.com
SIC: **2834** Vitamin preparations
PA: Jarrow Industries, L.L.C.
12246 Hawkins St
Santa Fe Springs CA
562 906-1919

(P-4147)
JARROW INDUSTRIES LLC
10226 Palm Dr (90670-3368)
PHONE.............................562 631-9330
Jackie Kelley, *Mgr*
EMP: 22
SALES (corp-wide): 50.38MM **Privately Held**
Web: www.jarrowindustries.com
SIC: **2834** Vitamin preparations
PA: Jarrow Industries, L.L.C.
12246 Hawkins St
Santa Fe Springs CA
562 906-1919

(P-4148)
JARROW INDUSTRIES LLC
12328 Hawkins St (90670-3367)
PHONE.............................562 631-9330
Jackie Kelley, *Mgr*
EMP: 22
SALES (corp-wide): 50.38MM **Privately Held**
Web: www.jarrowindustries.com
SIC: **2834** Vitamin preparations
PA: Jarrow Industries, L.L.C.
12246 Hawkins St
Santa Fe Springs CA
562 906-1919

(P-4149)
K-MAX HEALTH PRODUCTS CORP
1468 E Mission Blvd (91766-2229)
PHONE.............................909 455-0158

Lei Ye, *CEO*
EMP: 17 EST: 1999
SALES (est): 921.34K **Privately Held**
SIC: **2834** Vitamin, nutrient, and hematinic preparations for human use

(P-4150)
KATE SOMERVILLE SKINCARE LLC (HQ)
Also Called: Kate Smrvlle Skin Hlth Experts
144 S Beverly Dr Ste 500 (90212-3023)
PHONE.............................323 655-7546
Kate Somerville, *Managing Member*
Michelle Taylor, *
Laura Shaff, *
Jeff Hansen, *
▲ EMP: 51 EST: 2005
SALES (est): 25.75MM
SALES (corp-wide): 62.39B **Privately Held**
Web: www.katesomerville.com
SIC: **2834** 5122 Pharmaceutical preparations ; Toiletries
PA: Unilever Plc
Unilever House
London
207 572-1202

(P-4151)
KC PHARMACEUTICALS INC (PA)
3201 Producer Way (91768-3916)
PHONE.............................909 598-9499
Lieutenant Khouw, *Ch Bd*
Doctor Pramuditya Oen, *CEO*
Joseph Sutedjo, *
▲ EMP: 62 EST: 1987
SQ FT: 20,000
SALES (est): 22.86MM
SALES (corp-wide): 22.86MM **Privately Held**
Web: www.kc-ph.com
SIC: **2834** Solutions, pharmaceutical

(P-4152)
KINDEVA DRUG DELIVERY LP
19901 Nordhoff St (91324-3213)
P.O. Box 1001 (91328-1001)
PHONE.............................818 341-1300
Carol Beesley, *Brnch Mgr*
EMP: 400
Web: www.kindevadd.com
SIC: **2834** Pharmaceutical preparations
PA: Kindeva Drug Delivery L.P.
42 Water St W Bldg 75
Saint Paul MN

(P-4153)
KURA ONCOLOGY INC (PA)
12730 High Bluff Dr Ste 400 (92130-2079)
PHONE.............................858 500-8800
EMP: 36 EST: 2007
SQ FT: 13,420
Web: www.kuraoncology.com
SIC: **2834** Pharmaceutical preparations

(P-4154)
KYOWA KIRIN PHRM RES INC (DH)
9420 Athena Cir (92037-1387)
PHONE.............................858 952-7000
Kinya Ohgami, *Pr*
Hiroshi Makino, *
▲ EMP: 31 EST: 1988
SQ FT: 3,000
SALES (est): 23.51MM **Privately Held**
Web: www.kyowakirin.com
SIC: **2834** Pharmaceutical preparations
HQ: Kyowa Kirin Co., Ltd.
1-9-2, Otemachi

Chiyoda-Ku TKY

(P-4155)
KYTHERA BIOPHARMACEUTICALS INC
30930 Russell Ranch Rd Fl 3 (91362-7378)
PHONE.............................818 587-4500
A Robert D Bailey, *Pr*
John W Smither, *CFO*
Elisabeth A Sandoval, *CCO*
Frederick Beddingfield Iii, *CMO*
EMP: 106 EST: 2005
SQ FT: 33,198
SALES (est): 25.08MM
SALES (corp-wide): 58.05B **Publicly Held**
Web: www.mykybella.com
SIC: **2834** Dermatologicals
HQ: Allergan Unlimited Company
Clonshaugh Business & Technology Park
Coolock

(P-4156)
LEINER HEALTH PRODUCTS INC (DH)
Also Called: Leiner Health Products
901 E 233rd St (90745-6204)
PHONE.............................631 200-2000
Jeffrey A Nagel, *CEO*
Michael Collins, *
Harvey Kamil, *
◆ EMP: 200 EST: 1952
SQ FT: 488,000
SALES (est): 208.09MM **Privately Held**
Web: www.leiner.com
SIC: **2834** 5122 Vitamin, nutrient, and hematinic preparations for human use; Vitamins and minerals
HQ: Nhs U.S., Llc
121 River St Ste 9
Hoboken NJ
631 200-2000

(P-4157)
LEINER HEALTH PRODUCTS INC
Also Called: Leiner Health Products
7366 Orangewood Ave (92841-1412)
PHONE.............................714 898-9936
James Smith, *Mgr*
EMP: 45
Web: www.leiner.com
SIC: **2834** 2844 2833 5122 Vitamin, nutrient, and hematinic preparations for human use; Perfumes, cosmetics and other toilet preparations; Medicinals and botanicals; Vitamins and minerals
HQ: Leiner Health Products, Inc.
901 E 233rd St
Carson CA
631 200-2000

(P-4158)
LEVENA BIOPHARMA US INC
11760 Sorrento Valley Rd Ste N (92121-1018)
PHONE.............................858 720-1439
Hui Li, *Pr*
EMP: 36 EST: 2016
SALES (est): 1.12MM
SALES (corp-wide): 62.84MM **Publicly Held**
Web: www.levenabiopharma.com
SIC: **2834** Pharmaceutical preparations
PA: Sorrento Therapeutics, Inc.
4955 Directors Pl Ste 100
San Diego CA
858 203-4100

(P-4159)
LIFEBLOOM CORPORATION
Also Called: B&A Health Products Co
970 Challenger St (92821-2930)
PHONE..................562 944-6800
Cathy Ann, *CEO*
Chong Ann, *CFO*
◆ **EMP:** 20 **EST:** 2002
SALES (est): 4.55MM **Privately Held**
Web: www.lifebloomcorp.com
SIC: 2834 Vitamin preparations

(P-4160)
LONGBOARD PHARMACEUTICALS INC
4275 Executive Sq Ste 950 (92037-9208)
PHONE..................619 592-9775
Kevin Lind, *CEO*
Kevin R Lind, *
Paul J Sekhri, *
Brandi L Roberts, *CFO*
Philip Perera, *CMO*
EMP: 28 **EST:** 2020
Web: www.longboardpharma.com
SIC: 2834 Pharmaceutical preparations

(P-4161)
LOREM CYTORI USA INC
8659 Production Ave (92121-2206)
PHONE..................858 746-8696
Jonathan Soneff, *CEO*
EMP: 40 **EST:** 2019
SALES (est): 1.88MM **Privately Held**
Web: www.cytori.com
SIC: 2834 Pharmaceutical preparations

(P-4162)
MANNA HEALTH LLC
Also Called: Manna
216 Nautilus St (92037-5918)
PHONE..................877 576-2662
EMP: 20 **EST:** 2020
SALES (est): 1.35MM **Privately Held**
SIC: 2834 Vitamin preparations

(P-4163)
MARAVAI LFSCENCES HOLDINGS INC (PA)
Also Called: Maravai Lifesciences
10770 Wateridge Cir Ste 200 (92121)
PHONE..................858 546-0004
William Martin Iii, *CEO*
Eric Tardif, *Pr*
Kevin Herde, *CFO*
Brian Neel Coo Nucleic Acid Pr oduction, *Prin*
Christine Dolan Coo Biologics Safety Testing, *Prin*
EMP: 27 **EST:** 2014
SQ FT: 119,000
SALES (est): 883MM
SALES (corp-wide): 883MM **Publicly Held**
Web: www.maravai.com
SIC: 2834 Pharmaceutical preparations

(P-4164)
MCGUFF OTSURCING SOLUTIONS INC ♻
2921 W Macarthur Blvd # 1 (92704-6909)
PHONE..................800 603-4795
Ron Mcguff, *CEO*
EMP: 20 **EST:** 2022
SALES (est): 1.39MM **Privately Held**
SIC: 2834 Pharmaceutical preparations

(P-4165)
MCKENNA LABS INC (PA)
1601 E Orangethorpe Ave (92831-5230)
PHONE..................714 687-6888

Dennis Alexander Owen, *Pr*
◆ **EMP:** 38 **EST:** 1998
SQ FT: 62,000
SALES (est): 11.6MM
SALES (corp-wide): 11.6MM **Privately Held**
Web: www.mckennalabs.com
SIC: 2834 2844 Pharmaceutical preparations ; Perfumes, cosmetics and other toilet preparations

(P-4166)
MED-PHARMEX INC
2727 Thompson Creek Rd (91767-1861)
PHONE..................909 593-7875
Paul Hays, *CEO*
▲ **EMP:** 117 **EST:** 1982
SQ FT: 18,000
SALES (est): 37.61MM **Privately Held**
Web: www.medpharmex.com
SIC: 2834 Pharmaceutical preparations
PA: Dechra Pharmaceuticals Plc
24 Cheshire Avenue
Northwich

(P-4167)
MEI PHARMA INC
Also Called: MEI Pharma
11455 El Camino Real Ste 250 (92130)
PHONE..................858 369-7100
David M Urso, *Pr*
Charles V Baltic Iii, *Ch Bd*
Richard G Ghalie, *CMO*
Justin J File, *CFO*
EMP: 46 **EST:** 2002
SQ FT: 45,100
SALES (est): 48.82MM **Privately Held**
Web: www.meipharma.com
SIC: 2834 Pharmaceutical preparations

(P-4168)
METABASIS THERAPEUTICS INC
11085 N Torrey Pines Rd Ste 300 (92037-1015)
PHONE..................858 550-7500
John L Higgins, *Pr*
EMP: 22 **EST:** 1997
SQ FT: 82,000
SALES (est): 2.54MM
SALES (corp-wide): 196.25MM **Publicly Held**
Web: www.metabasistherapeutics.com
SIC: 2834 Pharmaceutical preparations
PA: Ligand Pharmaceuticals Incorporated
5980 Horton St Ste 405
Emeryville CA
858 550-7500

(P-4169)
METACRINE INC
Also Called: Metacrine
3985 Sorrento Valley Blvd Ste C (92121-1497)
PHONE..................858 369-7800
Preston Klassen, *Pr*
Richard Heyman, *
Patricia Millican, *CFO*
Hubert Chen, *CMO*
EMP: 32 **EST:** 2014
SQ FT: 20,475
Web: www.metacrine.com
SIC: 2834 Pharmaceutical preparations

(P-4170)
MIRATI THERAPEUTICS INC (PA)
Also Called: Mirati
3545 Cray Ct (92121-1169)
PHONE..................858 332-3410
Charles M Baum, *Interim Chief Executive Officer*

Faheem Hasnain, *Ch Bd*
Alan Sandler, *CMO*
Laurie Stelzer, *CFO*
James Christensen, *CSO*
EMP: 574 **EST:** 1995
SQ FT: 118,000
SALES (est): 12.44MM
SALES (corp-wide): 12.44MM **Publicly Held**
Web: www.mirati.com
SIC: 2834 8731 Pharmaceutical preparations ; Biotechnical research, commercial

(P-4171)
MURAD LLC
Also Called: Murad
8207 W 3rd St (90048-4302)
PHONE..................310 906-3100
EMP: 97
SALES (corp-wide): 62.39B **Privately Held**
Web: www.murad.com
SIC: 2834 Pharmaceutical preparations
HQ: Murad, Llc
2121 Park Pl Fl 1
El Segundo CA

(P-4172)
MURAD LLC (HQ)
2121 Park Pl Fl 1 (90245-4843)
PHONE..................310 726-0600
Elizabeth Ashmun, *
▲ **EMP:** 160 **EST:** 1990
SQ FT: 8,000
SALES (est): 94.06MM
SALES (corp-wide): 62.39B **Privately Held**
Web: www.murad.com
SIC: 2834 5122 Vitamin, nutrient, and hematinic preparations for human use; Pharmaceuticals
PA: Unilever Plc
Unilever House
London
207 572-1202

(P-4173)
MYOGENIX INCORPORATED
Also Called: Alchemi
4725 Allene Way (93401-8734)
PHONE..................800 950-0348
Adam G Nielson, *Pr*
▲ **EMP:** 17 **EST:** 2002
SALES (est): 2.14MM **Privately Held**
Web: www.myogenix.com
SIC: 2834 Pharmaceutical preparations

(P-4174)
NANOCELLECT BIOMEDICAL INC
6865 Flanders Dr (92121-2949)
PHONE..................877 745-7678
Jose Morachis, *Pr*
EMP: 22 **EST:** 2011
SALES (est): 918.42K **Privately Held**
Web: www.nanocellect.com
SIC: 2834 Druggists' preparations (pharmaceuticals)

(P-4175)
NATALS INC
Also Called: Ritual
3576 Eastham Dr (90232-2409)
PHONE..................323 475-6033
Katerina Schneider, *CEO*
Elizabeth Reifsnyder, *
EMP: 110 **EST:** 2015
SALES (est): 16.32MM **Privately Held**
Web: www.ritual.com
SIC: 2834 Vitamin preparations

(P-4176)
NATIONAL RESILIENCE INC (PA)
Also Called: Resilience
3115 Merryfield Row Ste 200 (92121)
PHONE..................888 737-2460
Rahul Singhvi, *CEO*
Sandy Mahatme, *Pr*
Elliot Menschik, *Chief Digital Officer*
Georgeta Puscalau, *Chief Quality Officer*
EMP: 23 **EST:** 2020
SALES (est): 174.83MM
SALES (corp-wide): 174.83MM **Privately Held**
Web: www.resilience.com
SIC: 2834 Pharmaceutical preparations

(P-4177)
NATROL INC
21411 Prairie St (91311-5829)
PHONE..................818 739-6000
◆ **EMP:** 230
SIC: 2834 2833 Vitamin, nutrient, and hematinic preparations for human use; Medicinals and botanicals

(P-4178)
NATROL LLC (PA)
21411 Prairie St (91311-5829)
PHONE..................818 739-6000
Nina Barton, *CEO*
◆ **EMP:** 130 **EST:** 2014
SALES (est): 121.68MM
SALES (corp-wide): 121.68MM **Privately Held**
Web: www.natrolkids.com
SIC: 2834 Pharmaceutical preparations

(P-4179)
NATURELAB NORTH AMERICA INC (HQ)
8149 Santa Monica Blvd Ste 361 (90046-4912)
PHONE..................424 901-0707
Keigo Hishiya, *Pr*
EMP: 109 **EST:** 2017
SALES (est): 51.79MM **Privately Held**
Web: www.naturelab.com
SIC: 2834 5912 Vitamin preparations; Proprietary (non-prescription medicine) stores
PA: Naturelab. Co., Ltd.
1-1-39, Hiroo
Shibuya-Ku TKY

(P-4180)
NBTY MANUFACTURING LLC
Also Called: Omni-Pak Industries
5115 E La Palma Ave (92807-2018)
PHONE..................714 765-8323
Steve Cahillane, *CEO*
Harvey Kamil, *Managing Member*
Scott Rudolph, *
Hans Lindgren, *
▼ **EMP:** 224 **EST:** 1978
SALES (est): 50.11MM **Privately Held**
SIC: 2834 Vitamin preparations
HQ: Nhs U.S., Llc
121 River St Ste 9
Hoboken NJ
631 200-2000

(P-4181)
NEURELIS INC (PA)
3430 Carmel Mountain Rd Ste 300 (92121-1071)
PHONE..................858 251-2111
Craig Chambliss, *CEO*
George Stuart, *CFO*
Charles Dewildt, *Chief Commercial Officer*
Brittany Bradrick, *CFO*

Adrian L Rabinowicz, *CMO*
EMP: 30 **EST:** 2008
SQ FT: 100
SALES (est): 12.17MM
SALES (corp-wide): 12.17MM **Privately Held**
Web: www.neurelis.com
SIC: 2834 Druggists' preparations (pharmaceuticals)

(P-4182)
NEW GENERATION WELLNESS INC (PA)
Also Called: Nexgen Pharma
46 Corporate Park Ste 200 (92606-3120)
P.O. Box 19516 (92623-9516)
PHONE..............................949 863-0340
Kyle Brown, *Pr*
Mark Nishi, *
Chris Limer, *OF DIETARY SUPPLEMENT*
EMP: 190 **EST:** 1935
SQ FT: 50,000
SALES (est): 52.38MM
SALES (corp-wide): 52.38MM **Privately Held**
Web: www.nexgenpharma.com
SIC: 2834 Pharmaceutical preparations

(P-4183)
NHK LABORATORIES INC (PA)
12230 Florence Ave (90670-3806)
PHONE..............................562 903-5835
Karim Amirul, *CEO*
Nasima A Karim, *
Mohammad H Haque, *
Shafiel Ahmed, *
▲ **EMP:** 35 **EST:** 1987
SQ FT: 90,000
SALES (est): 21.21MM **Privately Held**
Web: www.nhklabs.com
SIC: 2834 5122 Vitamin preparations; Vitamins and minerals

(P-4184)
NHK LABORATORIES INC
10603 Norwalk Blvd (90670-3821)
PHONE..............................562 204-5002
Shafiel Ahmed, *CEO*
EMP: 55
Web: www.nhklabs.com
SIC: 2834 5122 Vitamin preparations; Vitamins and minerals
PA: Nhk Laboratories, Inc.
　12230 Florence Ave
　Santa Fe Springs CA

(P-4185)
NITTO
10614 Science Center Dr (92121-1150)
PHONE..............................858 750-2012
EMP: 22 **EST:** 2019
SALES (est): 77.29K **Privately Held**
Web: www.nittobiopharma.com
SIC: 2834 Pharmaceutical preparations

(P-4186)
NITTO AVECIA PHARMA SVCS INC (DH)
10 Vanderbilt (92618-2010)
PHONE..............................949 951-4425
Raymond Kaczmarek, *Pr*
EMP: 18 **EST:** 2016
SQ FT: 62,000
SALES (est): 25.49MM **Privately Held**
Web: www.aveciapharma.com
SIC: 2834 Pharmaceutical preparations
HQ: Nitto Denko Avecia Inc.
　125 Fortune Blvd
　Milford MA

(P-4187)
NURA USA LLC
2652 White Rd (92614-6248)
PHONE..............................949 946-5700
Lily Ruan, *Pr*
EMP: 30 **EST:** 2018
SALES (est): 5.67MM **Privately Held**
Web: www.nurausa.com
SIC: 2834 Vitamin preparations

(P-4188)
NUTRAWISE HEALTH & BEAUTY CORP
Also Called: Nutrawise
9600 Toledo Way (92618-1808)
PHONE..............................949 900-2400
Darren Rude, *CEO*
Patty Terzo-rude, *Pr*
Theresa Rude, *
EMP: 95 **EST:** 2009
SQ FT: 130,000
SALES (est): 26.01MM **Privately Held**
Web: www.youtheory.com
SIC: 2834 Vitamin, nutrient, and hematinic preparations for human use

(P-4189)
ONYX PHARMACEUTICALS INC
1 Amgen Center Dr (91320-1730)
PHONE..............................650 266-0000
Pablo Cagnoni, *Pr*
Bob Goeltz, *Ex Dir*
Matthew K Fust, *Ex VP*
Suzanne M Shema, *Ex VP*
Helen Torley, *Ex VP*
EMP: 741 **EST:** 2013
SQ FT: 297,111
SALES (est): 106.32MM
SALES (corp-wide): 26.32B **Publicly Held**
SIC: 2834 8049 Drugs affecting parasitic and infective diseases; Occupational therapist
PA: Amgen Inc.
　1 Amgen Center Dr
　Thousand Oaks CA
　805 447-1000

(P-4190)
OREXIGEN THERAPEUTICS INC
Also Called: Orexigen
3344 N Torrey Pines Ct Ste 200 (92037-1024)
PHONE..............................858 875-8600
Thomas P Lynch, *Pr*
Thomas P Lynch, *Pr*
Lota S Zoth, *
EMP: 100 **EST:** 2003
SQ FT: 29,935
SALES (est): 27.18MM
SALES (corp-wide): 52.98MM **Privately Held**
Web: www.curraxpharma.com
SIC: 2834 Pharmaceutical preparations
HQ: Nalpropion Pharmaceuticals, Llc
　155 Franklin Rd Ste 450
　Brentwood TN
　800 793-2145

(P-4191)
OTONOMY INC
Also Called: OTONOMY
4796 Executive Dr (92121-3090)
PHONE..............................619 323-2200
David A Weber, *Pr*
Jay Lichter, *
Paul E Cayer, *Chief Business Officer*
EMP: 56 **EST:** 2008
SQ FT: 62,000
SALES (est): 125K **Privately Held**
Web: www.otonomy.com

SIC: 2834 Pharmaceutical preparations

(P-4192)
P & L DEVELOPMENT LLC
Also Called: Pl Development
11865 Alameda St (90262-4022)
PHONE..............................323 567-2482
Jim Smith, *Genl Mgr*
EMP: 152
Web: www.pldevelopments.com
SIC: 2834 2841 2844 Pharmaceutical preparations; Soap and other detergents; Perfumes, cosmetics and other toilet preparations
PA: P & L Development, Llc
　200 Hicks St
　Westbury NY

(P-4193)
PACIFIC PHARMA INC
18600 Von Karman Ave (92612-1513)
PHONE..............................714 246-4600
Roger Maffia, *Dir*
EMP: 2000 **EST:** 1997
SALES (est): 105.06MM
SALES (corp-wide): 58.05B **Publicly Held**
SIC: 2834 Pharmaceutical preparations
HQ: Allergan, Inc.
　1 N Waukegan Rd
　Madison NJ
　862 261-7000

(P-4194)
PACIFIC SHORE HOLDINGS INC
Also Called: Nature-Cide
8236 Remmet Ave (91304-4156)
PHONE..............................818 998-0996
Matthew Mills, *Pr*
Jennifer Mills, *
Ronald J Tchorzewski, *
David E Toomey, *
▲ **EMP:** 24 **EST:** 1981
SQ FT: 13,000
SALES (est): 4.7MM
SALES (corp-wide): 4.7MM **Privately Held**
Web: www.pac-sh.com
SIC: 2834 2879 Pharmaceutical preparations ; Pesticides, agricultural or household
HQ: X Med Inc
　8236 Remmet Ave
　Canoga Park CA
　818 349-2870

(P-4195)
PACIRA PHARMACEUTICALS INC (HQ) ✪
10410 Science Center Dr (92121-1119)
PHONE..............................858 625-2424
Chuck Laranjeira, *Pr*
EMP: 49 **EST:** 2022
SALES (est): 46.2MM **Publicly Held**
Web: www.pacira.com
SIC: 2834 Pharmaceutical preparations
PA: Pacira Biosciences, Inc.
　5401 W Knnedy Blvd Lincoln
　Tampa FL

(P-4196)
PACIRA PHARMACEUTICALS INC ✪
10578 Science Center Dr (92121-1149)
PHONE..............................858 625-2424
Chuck Laranjeira, *Pr*
EMP: 73 **EST:** 2022
SALES (est): 7.63MM **Publicly Held**
Web: www.pacira.com
SIC: 2834 Pharmaceutical preparations
PA: Pacira Biosciences, Inc.
　5401 W Knnedy Blvd Lincoln
　Tampa FL

(P-4197)
PEARL MANAGEMENT GROUP INC
14950 Delano St (91411-2122)
PHONE..............................818 217-0218
Michael Ben Perlman, *Brnch Mgr*
EMP: 47
SALES (corp-wide): 914.12K **Privately Held**
SIC: 2834 Pharmaceutical preparations
PA: Pearl Management Group Inc.
　2150 Bluebell Dr
　Santa Rosa CA
　818 383-0095

(P-4198)
PELICAN BIOPHARMA LLC
23215 Early Ave (90505-4002)
PHONE..............................310 326-4700
EMP: 19 **EST:** 2013
SALES (est): 1.08MM **Privately Held**
Web: www.pelican.com
SIC: 2834 Pharmaceutical preparations

(P-4199)
PFENEX INC
Also Called: Pfenex
10790 Roselle St (92121-1508)
PHONE..............................858 352-4400
Evert B Schimmelpennink, *
Evert B Schimmelpennink, *
Jason Grenfell-gardner, *Ch Bd*
Shawn A Scranton, *Sr VP*
Patrick K Lucy, *Chief Business Officer*
EMP: 81 **EST:** 2009
SQ FT: 46,959
SALES (est): 19.58MM
SALES (corp-wide): 196.25MM **Publicly Held**
Web: www.pelicanexpression.com
SIC: 2834 Pharmaceutical preparations
PA: Ligand Pharmaceuticals Incorporated
　5980 Horton St Ste 405
　Emeryville CA
　858 550-7500

(P-4200)
PFIZER INC
Also Called: Pfizer
10777 Science Center Dr (92121-1111)
PHONE..............................858 622-3000
Karen Katen, *Brnch Mgr*
EMP: 63
SALES (corp-wide): 100.33B **Publicly Held**
Web: www.pfizer.com
SIC: 2834 Pharmaceutical preparations
PA: Pfizer Inc.
　66 Hudson Blvd E Fl 20
　New York NY
　212 733-2323

(P-4201)
PFIZER INC
Also Called: Pfizer
10646 Science Center Dr (92121-1150)
PHONE..............................858 622-3001
Mary Mateja, *Mgr*
EMP: 43
SALES (corp-wide): 100.33B **Publicly Held**
Web: www.pfizer.com
SIC: 2834 Pharmaceutical preparations
PA: Pfizer Inc.
　66 Hudson Blvd E Fl 20
　New York NY
　212 733-2323

(P-4202)
PHARMACEUTIC LITHO LABEL INC
3990 Royal Ave (93063-3380)
PHONE..................805 285-5162
Timothy Laurence, *Pr*
Tom Moore, *Pr*
Rick Machale, *VP*
▲ **EMP**: 85 **EST**: 1964
SQ FT: 32,000
SALES (est): 21.15MM **Privately Held**
Web: www.pharmaceuticlitho.com
SIC: 2834 Pharmaceutical preparations

(P-4203)
PHARMION CORPORATION
12481 High Bluff Dr Ste 200 (92130-3585)
PHONE..................858 335-5744
Jeffry Howbert, *Brnch Mgr*
EMP: 20
SALES (corp-wide): 46.16B **Publicly Held**
Web: www.bms.com
SIC: 2834 Pharmaceutical preparations
HQ: Pharmion Corporation
86 Morris Ave
Summit NJ
908 673-9000

(P-4204)
POLARIS PHARMACEUTICALS INC (PA)
10675 Sorrento Valley Rd Ste 200
(92121-1617)
PHONE..................858 452-6688
Bor Wen Wu, *CEO*
John Bomalaski, *VP*
Robert E Hoffman, *Mgr*
EMP: 28 **EST**: 2006
SALES (est): 6.02MM
SALES (corp-wide): 6.02MM **Privately Held**
Web: www.polarispharma.com
SIC: 2834 Pharmaceutical preparations

(P-4205)
POLYPEPTIDE LABS SAN DIEGO LLC
9395 Cabot Dr (92126-4310)
PHONE..................858 408-0808
EMP: 72 **EST**: 1986
SQ FT: 43,000
SALES (est): 42.06MM **Privately Held**
Web: www.polypeptide.com
SIC: 2834 2833 8731 Pharmaceutical
preparations; Medicinals and botanicals;
Biotechnical research, commercial
HQ: Polypeptide Laboratories Inc.
365 Maple Ave
Torrance CA

(P-4206)
PRESCIENT HOLDINGS GROUP LLC
10181 Scripps Gateway Ct (92131-5152)
PHONE..................858 790-7004
Christine Nguyen, *Pr*
Debra Minich, *Dir*
Ethan Dargie, *VP*
Mike Schneider, *VP*
Vasu Bobba, *VP*
EMP: 30 **EST**: 2021
SALES (est): 122.32K **Privately Held**
Web: www.prescientholdingsgroup.com
SIC: 2834 Pharmaceutical preparations

(P-4207)
PRIMAPHARMA INC
3443 Tripp Ct (92121-1032)
PHONE..................858 259-0969

Mark Livingston, *Pr*
Tony Dziabo, *
Larry Braga, *
Nayaz Ahmed, *
Arshad Chaudry, *
EMP: 35 **EST**: 2015
SQ FT: 24,000
SALES (est): 5.2MM **Privately Held**
Web: www.primapharma.net
SIC: 2834 Pharmaceutical preparations

(P-4208)
PROMETHEUS BIOSCIENCES INC
3050 Science Park Rd (92121-1102)
PHONE..................858 422-4300
Mark C Mckenna, *Ch Bd*
Keith W Marshall, *CFO*
Mark Stenhouse, *COO*
EMP: 72 **EST**: 2016
SALES (est): 6.81MM **Privately Held**
Web: www.prometheusbiosciences.com
SIC: 2834 Pharmaceutical preparations

(P-4209)
PROMETHEUS LABORATORIES INC
5739 Pacific Center Blvd (92121-4203)
PHONE..................858 583-0131
EMP: 23 **EST**: 2019
SALES (est): 833.11K **Privately Held**
Web: www.prometheuslabs.com
SIC: 2834 Pharmaceutical preparations

(P-4210)
PROMETHEUS LABORATORIES INC
9410 Carroll Park Dr (92121-5201)
PHONE..................858 824-0895
EMP: 405 **EST**: 1996
SQ FT: 99,000
SALES (est): 105.96MM **Privately Held**
Web: www.prometheuslabs.com
SIC: 2834 8011 Pharmaceutical preparations
; Offices and clinics of medical doctors

(P-4211)
PROMETHEUS RXDX INC
9410 Carroll Park Dr (92121-5201)
PHONE..................858 824-0895
EMP: 23 **EST**: 2010
SALES (est): 225.43K **Privately Held**
Web: www.prometheuslabs.com
SIC: 2834 Pharmaceutical preparations

(P-4212)
PROMETHEUS THERAPEUTICS &DIAGN
9410 Carroll Park Dr (92121-5201)
PHONE..................858 824-0895
EMP: 19 **EST**: 2014
SALES (est): 804.03K **Privately Held**
Web: www.prometheuslabs.com
SIC: 2834 Pharmaceutical preparations

(P-4213)
PROTAB LABORATORIES
25902 Towne Centre Dr (92610-3436)
PHONE..................949 635-1930
Min W Chen, *CEO*
Randy L Pollan, *VP*
Shafiqul Islam, *VP*
Joanne Hsu, *Dir Opers*
▲ **EMP**: 150 **EST**: 2004
SQ FT: 100,000
SALES (est): 23.49MM **Privately Held**
Web: www.protablabs.com

SIC: 2834 2023 Vitamin preparations;
Dietary supplements, dairy and non-dairy
based

(P-4214)
PUMA BIOTECHNOLOGY INC (PA)
10880 Wilshire Blvd Ste 2150 (90024-4106)
P.O. Box 64945 (55164-0945)
PHONE..................424 248-6500
Alan H Auerbach, *Ch Bd*
Charles R Eyler, *VP Fin*
Richard P Bryce, *CMO CSO*
Steven Lo, *CCO*
Douglas Hunt, *Senior Vice President Regulatory Affairs*
EMP: 318 **EST**: 2007
SQ FT: 25,700
SALES (est): 228.03MM
SALES (corp-wide): 228.03MM **Publicly Held**
Web: www.pumabiotechnology.com
SIC: 2834 Pharmaceutical preparations

(P-4215)
PURETEK CORPORATION (PA)
1145 Arroyo St Ste D (91340-1820)
PHONE..................818 361-3316
Barry Pressman, *CEO*
◆ **EMP**: 50 **EST**: 1991
SQ FT: 114,000
SALES (est): 55.92MM **Privately Held**
Web: www.puretekcorp.com
SIC: 2834 Pharmaceutical preparations

(P-4216)
PURETEK CORPORATION
7900 Nelson Rd Unit A (91402-6828)
PHONE..................818 361-3949
Jeff Pressman, *Brnch Mgr*
EMP: 130
Web: www.puretekcorp.com
SIC: 2834 2844 Pharmaceutical preparations
; Cosmetic preparations
PA: Puretek Corporation
1145 Arroyo St Ste D
San Fernando CA

(P-4217)
QUANTICEL PHARMACUETICALS INC
9393 Towne Centre Dr Ste 110
(92121-3070)
PHONE..................858 956-3747
Steve Kaldor, *Brnch Mgr*
EMP: 20
SIC: 2834 Pharmaceutical preparations
PA: Quanticel Pharmacueticals, Inc.
1500 Owens St Ste 500
San Francisco CA

(P-4218)
QUOREX PHARM INC (PA)
2232 Rutherford Rd (92008-8814)
PHONE..................760 602-1910
Robert Robb, *Pr*
Robert Robb, *Pr*
Jeffrey Stein, *Chief Scientist**
Krzysztof Appelt, *Technology**
Gary J G Atkinson, *CFO*
EMP: 42 **EST**: 1999
SQ FT: 23,500
SALES (est): 5.65MM
SALES (corp-wide): 5.65MM **Privately Held**
SIC: 2834 Pharmaceutical preparations

(P-4219)
RAYZEBIO INC
5505 Morehouse Dr Ste 300 (92121-1720)
PHONE..................619 937-2754
Ken Song, *Pr*
Richard Heyman, *Non-Executive Chairman of the Board**
Arvind Kush, *CFO*
Susan Moran, *CMO*
EMP: 88 **EST**: 2020
SQ FT: 28,000
Web: www.rayzebio.com
SIC: 2834 8731 Pharmaceutical preparations
; Medical research, commercial

(P-4220)
RECEPTOS INC
3033 Science Park Rd Ste 300
(92121-1168)
PHONE..................858 652-5700
Faheem Hasnain, *Pr*
Marcus F Boehm, *
Graham Cooper, *
Shiela Gujrathi, *CMO**
Robert J Peach, *CSO**
EMP: 32 **EST**: 2009
SALES (est): 7.27MM
SALES (corp-wide): 46.16B **Publicly Held**
Web: www.celgene.com
SIC: 2834 Pharmaceutical preparations
HQ: Celgene Corporation
86 Morris Ave
Summit NJ
908 673-9000

(P-4221)
REDWOOD SCIENTIFIC TECH INC
245 E Main St Ste 115 (91801-7507)
PHONE..................310 693-5401
Jason E Cardiff, *Pr*
Eunjung Cardiff, *
Jacques Poujade, *
Rhonda Pearlman, *
M Salah Zaki, *CMO**
EMP: 24 **EST**: 2014
SALES (est): 2.98MM **Privately Held**
SIC: 2834 Druggists' preparations
(pharmaceuticals)

(P-4222)
REMPEX PHARMACEUTICALS INC
3013 Science Park Rd 1st Fl (92121-1101)
PHONE..................858 875-2840
EMP: 40 **EST**: 2013
SQ FT: 60
SALES (est): 1.31MM
SALES (corp-wide): 6.14MM **Privately Held**
SIC: 2834 Pharmaceutical preparations
PA: The Medicines Company
8 Sylvan Way
Parsippany NJ
973 290-6000

(P-4223)
RESILIENCE US INC (HQ)
3115 Merryfield Row Ste 200 (92121)
PHONE..................984 202-0854
Rahul Singhvi, *CEO*
Sandy Mahatme, *Pr*
EMP: 23 **EST**: 2020
SALES (est): 133.37MM
SALES (corp-wide): 174.83MM **Privately Held**
SIC: 2834 3559 Pharmaceutical preparations
; Pharmaceutical machinery
PA: National Resilience, Inc.
3115 Mrryfield Row Ste 200

San Diego CA
888 737-2460

(P-4224)
ROBINSON PHARMA INC
3701 W Warner Ave (92704-5218)
PHONE....................................714 241-0235
Tam H Nguyen, *CEO*
EMP: 121
Web: www.robinsonpharma.com
SIC: 2834 7389 Pharmaceutical preparations
; Packaging and labeling services
PA: Robinson Pharma, Inc.
3330 S Harbor Blvd
Santa Ana CA

(P-4225)
ROBINSON PHARMA INC (PA)
3330 S Harbor Blvd (92704-6831)
PHONE....................................714 241-0235
Tuong Nguyen, *CEO*
Tam Nguyen, *
Elaine Phan, *
◆ EMP: 310 EST: 1989
SQ FT: 124,000
SALES (est): 207.9MM **Privately Held**
Web: www.robinsonpharma.com
SIC: 2834 Medicines, capsuled or ampuled

(P-4226)
ROBINSON PHARMA INC
3300 W Segerstrom Ave (92704-6403)
PHONE....................................714 241-0235
Gulfam Sheikh, *Mgr*
EMP: 120
Web: www.robinsonpharma.com
SIC: 2834 Medicines, capsuled or ampuled
PA: Robinson Pharma, Inc.
3330 S Harbor Blvd
Santa Ana CA

(P-4227)
S K LABORATORIES INC
Also Called: S K Labs
5420 E La Palma Ave (92807-2023)
PHONE....................................714 695-9800
Bansi Patel, *Pr*
Ramila B Patel, *
▲ EMP: 100 EST: 1992
SQ FT: 60,000
SALES (est): 25MM **Privately Held**
Web: www.sklabs.com
SIC: 2834 Pharmaceutical preparations

(P-4228)
SAMSON PHARMACEUTICALS INC
5635 Smithway St (90040-1545)
PHONE....................................323 722-3066
Jay Kassir, *Pr*
▲ EMP: 40 EST: 2001
SALES (est): 9.3MM **Privately Held**
Web: www.samsonpharmaceutical.com
SIC: 2834 Pharmaceutical preparations

(P-4229)
SANTARUS INC
3611 Valley Centre Dr Ste 400 (92130)
PHONE....................................858 314-5700
Blake Boland, *Prin*
EMP: 21 EST: 2014
SALES (est): 834.38K **Privately Held**
SIC: 2834 5122 Pharmaceutical preparations
; Pharmaceuticals

(P-4230)
SENJU USA INC
21515 Hawthorne Blvd (90503-6570)
PHONE....................................818 719-7190

Ag Katayama, *Pr*
EMP: 23 EST: 2007
SALES (est): 4.75MM **Privately Held**
Web: www.senju-usa.com
SIC: 2834 Druggists' preparations
(pharmaceuticals)
PA: Senju Pharmaceutical Co., Ltd.
3-1-9, Kawaramachi, Chuo-Ku
Osaka OSK

(P-4231)
SENTYNL THERAPEUTICS INC
420 Stevens Ave Ste 200 (92075-2076)
PHONE....................................888 227-8725
Matt Heck, *CEO*
Daniel Stokely, *
Michael Hercz, *General*
Darren Pincus, *
Shawn Scranton, *
EMP: 30 EST: 2011
SALES (est): 6.4MM **Privately Held**
Web: www.sentynl.com
SIC: 2834 Pharmaceutical preparations
HQ: Zydus Lifesciences Limited
Zydus Corporate Park Scheme No. 63,
Survey No. 536
Ahmedabad GJ

(P-4232)
SHIRE
1445 Lawrence Dr (91320-1311)
PHONE....................................805 372-3000
John Sandstrom, *Prin*
EMP: 64 EST: 2018
SALES (est): 796.31K **Privately Held**
SIC: 2834 Pharmaceutical preparations

(P-4233)
SHIRE RGENERATIVE MEDICINE INC
Also Called: Advanced Biohealing.com
11095 Torreyana Rd (92121-1104)
PHONE....................................858 754-5396
EMP: 50
SIC: 2834 Pharmaceutical preparations
HQ: Shire Regenerative Medicine, Inc.
36 Church Ln
Westport CT
877 422-4463

(P-4234)
SICOR INC (HQ)
19 Hughes (92618-1902)
PHONE....................................949 455-4700
Carlo Salvi, *Vice Chairman*
▲ EMP: 800 EST: 1986
SQ FT: 170,000
SALES (est): 139.6MM **Privately Held**
Web: www.tevausa.com
SIC: 2834 8731 Drugs acting on the
cardiovascular system, except diagnostic;
Medical research, commercial
PA: Teva Pharmaceutical Industries Limited
5 Bazel
Petah Tikva

(P-4235)
SIGNAL PHARMACEUTICALS LLC
10300 Campus Point Dr Ste 100
(92121-1504)
PHONE....................................858 795-4700
Alan J Lewis Ph.D., *Pr*
Shripad Bhagwat, *Drug Discovery Vice President*
David R Webb, *Research Vice President*
EMP: 134 EST: 1992
SQ FT: 78,202
SALES (est): 26.97MM
SALES (corp-wide): 46.16B **Publicly Held**

SIC: 2834 Pharmaceutical preparations
HQ: Celgene Corporation
86 Morris Ave
Summit NJ
908 673-9000

(P-4236)
SIMPSON INDUSTRIES INC
Also Called: Simpsonsimpson Industries
1093 E Bedmar St (90746-3601)
PHONE....................................310 605-1224
Rick Simpson, *CEO*
Robert Simpson, *
EMP: 50 EST: 2011
SALES (est): 8.32MM **Privately Held**
Web: www.simpsonindustries.com
SIC: 2834 Proprietary drug products

(P-4237)
SKINMEDICA INC
18655 Teller Ave (92612-1610)
P.O. Box 19534 (92623-9534)
PHONE....................................760 929-2600
▲ EMP: 275
Web: www.skinmedica.com
SIC: 2834 2844 Dermatologicals; Perfumes,
cosmetics and other toilet preparations

(P-4238)
SOCIETAL CDMO SAN DIEGO LLC
6828 Nancy Ridge Dr Ste 100 (92121)
PHONE....................................858 623-1520
J David Enloe Junior, *Pr*
Ryan Lake, *
Scott Rizzo, *
EMP: 55 EST: 2015
SQ FT: 24,100
SALES (est): 10.09MM **Publicly Held**
SIC: 2834 Druggists' preparations
(pharmaceuticals)
PA: Societal Cdmo, Inc.
490 Lapp Rd
Malvern PA

(P-4239)
SOFT GEL TECHNOLOGIES INC (HQ)
6982 Bandini Blvd (90040-3326)
PHONE....................................323 726-0700
Steve Holtby, *CEO*
Ronald Udell, *
Hiroshi Kishimoto, *
▲ EMP: 21 EST: 1994
SQ FT: 21,000
SALES (est): 27.28MM **Privately Held**
Web: www.soft-gel.com
SIC: 2834 Medicines, capsuled or ampuled
PA: Kenko Corporation
3-1-2, Iwamotocho
Chiyoda-Ku TKY

(P-4240)
ST JUDE MEDICAL LLC
Also Called: Sjm Facility
2375 Morse Ave (92614-6233)
PHONE....................................949 769-5000
EMP: 30
SALES (corp-wide): 43.65B **Publicly Held**
Web: www.cardiovascular.abbott
SIC: 2834 Pharmaceutical preparations
HQ: St. Jude Medical, Llc
1 Saint Jude Medical Dr
Saint Paul MN
651 756-2000

(P-4241)
STA PHARMACEUTICAL US LLC
6114 Nancy Ridge Dr (92121-3223) *

PHONE....................................609 606-6499
Chen Hui, *CFO*
EMP: 40 EST: 2016
SALES (est): 5.49MM **Privately Held**
Web: www.stapharma.com
SIC: 2834 Pharmaceutical preparations

(P-4242)
STERISYN INC
Also Called: Sterisyn Scientific
11969 Challenger Ct (93021-7119)
PHONE....................................805 991-9694
Julie Anne, *Admn*
Timothy Henry, *CEO*
EMP: 30 EST: 2015
SALES (est): 2.37MM **Privately Held**
Web: www.sterisyn.com
SIC: 2834 Pharmaceutical preparations

(P-4243)
SUHEUNG-AMERICA CORPORATION
540 W Lambert Rd (92821-3914)
PHONE....................................714 671-9095
Joo Hwan Yang, *Brnch Mgr*
EMP: 44
Web: www.embocaps.com
SIC: 2834 Medicines, capsuled or ampuled
HQ: Suheung-America Corporation
428 Saturn St
Brea CA
714 854-9882

(P-4244)
SYNTHORX INC
Also Called: Synthorx
11099 N Torrey Pines Rd Ste 190
(92037-1029)
PHONE....................................858 352-5100
John Reed, *Pr*
Marie Debans, *
EMP: 38 EST: 2014
SQ FT: 8,636
Web: www.sanofi.com
SIC: 2834 8731 Pharmaceutical preparations
; Biotechnical research, commercial
HQ: Aventis Inc.
55 Corporate Dr
Bridgewater NJ

(P-4245)
TBP INDOOR FACILITIES INC
3905 State St (93105-3138)
PHONE....................................877 778-9587
Adrian Sedlin, *CEO*
EMP: 95 EST: 2016
SALES (est): 2.5MM **Privately Held**
Web: www.canndescent.com
SIC: 2834 Pharmaceutical preparations

(P-4246)
TEVA PARENTERAL MEDICINES INC
19 Hughes (92618-1902)
P.O. Box 57049 (92619-7049)
PHONE....................................949 455-4700
Phillip Frost, *Ch Bd*
Amir Elstein, *
Karin Shanahan, *
Nir Baron, *
Iris Beck-codner, *VP*
▲ EMP: 830 EST: 1990
SQ FT: 148,000
SALES (est): 110.36MM **Privately Held**
SIC: 2834 Pills, pharmaceutical
HQ: Teva Pharmaceuticals Usa, Inc.
400 Interpace Pkwy Ste A1
Parsippany NJ
215 591-3000

**P
R
O
D
U
C
T
S

&

S
V
C
S**

(P-4247)
TRAVERE THERAPEUTICS INC (PA)
Also Called: TRAVERE
3611 Valley Centre Dr Ste 300 (92130)
PHONE..............................888 969-7879
EMP: 248 **EST:** 2008
SQ FT: 149,123
SALES (est): 212.02MM **Publicly Held**
Web: www.travere.com
SIC: 2834 8731 Pharmaceutical preparations ; Biotechnical research, commercial

(P-4248)
TRIUS THERAPEUTICS LLC
4747 Executive Dr Ste 1100 (92121-3095)
PHONE..............................858 452-0370
Jeffrey Stein, *Pr*
John P Schmid, *
Michael Morneau, *CAO*
Kenneth Bartizal, *Chief Development Officer*
John Finn, *
EMP: 139 **EST:** 2007
SQ FT: 39,000
SALES (est): 27.53MM
SALES (corp-wide): 59.28B **Publicly Held**
Web: www.triusrx.com
SIC: 2834 Antibiotics, packaged
HQ: Cubist Pharmaceuticals Llc
2000 Galloping Hill Rd
Kenilworth NJ

(P-4249)
UNIVERSAL PRTEIN SPPLMNTS CORP
3441 Gato Ct (92507-6800)
PHONE..............................732 545-3130
Michael Rockoff, *Pr*
EMP: 18
SALES (corp-wide): 44.52MM **Privately Held**
Web: www.universalusa.com
SIC: 2834 2032 Vitamin, nutrient, and hematinic preparations for human use; Canned specialties
PA: Universal Protein Supplements Corporation
3 Terminal Rd
New Brunswick NJ
732 545-3130

(P-4250)
UROVANT SCIENCES INC
5281 California Ave Ste 100 (92617-3218)
PHONE..............................949 226-6029
James Robinson, *CEO*
Ajay Bansal, *CFO*
Ryan Card, *Ex VP*
Betzy Estrada, *Ex VP*
Laura Genatossio, *Sr VP*
EMP: 50 **EST:** 2016
SQ FT: 8,000
SALES (est): 8.92MM **Privately Held**
Web: www.urovant.com
SIC: 2834 Pharmaceutical preparations

(P-4251)
VERTEX PHRMCTCALS SAN DEGO LLC (HQ)
3215 Merryfield Row (92121-1126)
PHONE..............................858 404-6600
▲ **EMP:** 235 **EST:** 2001
SQ FT: 81,000
SALES (est): 55.79MM **Publicly Held**
Web: www.vrtx.com
SIC: 2834 Pharmaceutical preparations
PA: Vertex Pharmaceuticals Incorporated
50 Northern Ave

Boston MA

(P-4252)
VIKING THERAPEUTICS INC (PA)
12340 El Camino Real Ste 250 (92130)
PHONE..............................858 704-4660
Brian Lian, *Pr*
Lawson Macartney, *Ch Bd*
Marianne Mancini, *COO*
Greg Zante, *CFO*
EMP: 20 **EST:** 2012
SQ FT: 7,149
Web: www.vikingtherapeutics.com
SIC: 2834 Pharmaceutical preparations

(P-4253)
VITATECH NUTRITIONAL SCIENCES INC
2802 Dow Ave (92780-7212)
PHONE..............................714 832-9700
▲ **EMP:** 285
SIC: 2834 Vitamin preparations

(P-4254)
WACKER BIOTECH US INC
10390 Pacific Center Ct (92121-4340)
PHONE..............................858 875-4700
Doctor Philippe Cronet, *CEO*
Keith Hall, *
EMP: 24 **EST:** 2018
SQ FT: 68,400
SALES (est): 11.01MM
SALES (corp-wide): 8.53B **Privately Held**
Web: www.genopis.com
SIC: 2834 Pharmaceutical preparations
HQ: Wacker Chemical Corporation
4950 S State Rd
Ann Arbor MI
517 264-8500

(P-4255)
WAKUNAGA OF AMERICA CO LTD (HQ)
Also Called: Kyolic
23501 Madero (92691-2744)
PHONE..............................949 855-2776
Kazuhiko Nomura, *Pr*
Hiyoshi Sakai, *
◆ **EMP:** 64 **EST:** 1972
SQ FT: 36,000
SALES (est): 31.05MM **Privately Held**
Web: www.kyolic.com
SIC: 2834 Pharmaceutical preparations
PA: Wakunaga Pharmaceutical Co., Ltd.
13-4, Arakicho
Shinjuku-Ku TKY

(P-4256)
WEST COAST LABORATORIES INC
156 E 162nd St (90248-2802)
PHONE..............................310 527-6163
Maurice Ovadia, *Mgr*
EMP: 35
SQ FT: 4,000
SALES (corp-wide): 6.35MM **Privately Held**
Web: www.westcoastlabsinc.com
SIC: 2834 Vitamin preparations
PA: West Coast Laboratories, Inc.
116 E Alondra Blvd
Gardena CA
323 321-4774

(P-4257)
XENCOR INC
Also Called: Xencor
465 N Halstead St Ste 200 (91107-3291)

PHONE..............................626 305-5900
Bassil I Dahiyat, *Pr*
Paul Foster, *CMO*
John R Desjarlais, *Senior Vice President Research*
John J Kuch, *VP Fin*
Celia Eckert, *VP*
EMP: 114 **EST:** 1997
SQ FT: 129,543
SALES (est): 164.58MM **Privately Held**
Web: www.xencor.com
SIC: 2834 Pharmaceutical preparations

(P-4258)
YOUCARE PHARMA (USA) INC
132 Business Center Dr (92878-3224)
P.O. Box 668 (92878-0668)
PHONE..............................951 258-3114
Weishi Yu, *CEO*
EMP: 60 **EST:** 2015
SQ FT: 160,000
SALES (est): 20.9MM **Privately Held**
SIC: 2834 Pharmaceutical preparations
PA: Youcare Pharmaceutical Group Co., Ltd
No. 6, Hongda Middle Road, Economic And Technological Area
Beijing BJ

(P-4259)
ZOETIS INC
16420 Via Esprillo (92127-1702)
PHONE..............................858 312-7082
EMP: 18 **EST:** 2018
SALES (est): 1.83MM **Privately Held**
Web: www.zoetis.com
SIC: 2834 Pharmaceutical preparations

(P-4260)
ZP OPCO INC
Also Called: Zosano
355 S Grand Ave Ste 1450 (90071-3152)
PHONE..............................510 745-1200
Konstantinos Alataris, *CEO*
Konstantinos Alataris, *Pr*
Winnie W Tso, *CFO*
EMP: 32 **EST:** 2006
SALES (est): 448.57K
SALES (corp-wide): 785K **Privately Held**
SIC: 2834 Pharmaceutical preparations
PA: Zosano Pharma Corporation
34790 Ardentech Ct
Fremont CA
510 745-1200

2835 Diagnostic Substances

(P-4261)
ACON LABORATORIES INC (PA)
10125 Mesa Rim Rd (92121-2915)
PHONE..............................858 875-8000
Jinn-nan Lin, *Pr*
▲ **EMP:** 47 **EST:** 1999
SQ FT: 36,000
SALES (est): 19.24MM **Privately Held**
Web: www.aconlabs.com
SIC: 2835 Diagnostic substances

(P-4262)
ALERE INC
9975 Summers Ridge Rd (92121-2997)
PHONE..............................858 805-2000
Sabina Roaldset, *Brnch Mgr*
EMP: 61
SALES (corp-wide): 43.65B **Publicly Held**
Web: www.globalpointofcare.abbott
SIC: 2835 Diagnostic substances
HQ: Alere Inc.
51 Sawyer Rd Ste 200

Waltham MA
781 647-3900

(P-4263)
ALERE INC
Also Called: Alere of San Diego
5995 Pacific Center Blvd Ste 108 (92121)
PHONE..............................858 805-3810
EMP: 17
SALES (corp-wide): 43.65B **Publicly Held**
Web: www.globalpointofcare.abbott
SIC: 2835 Diagnostic substances
HQ: Alere Inc.
51 Sawyer Rd Ste 200
Waltham MA
781 647-3900

(P-4264)
ALERE SAN DIEGO INC (DH)
9975 Summers Ridge Rd (92121-2997)
PHONE..............................858 455-4808
Christopher Scoggins, *CEO*
Karen Peterson, *
▲ **EMP:** 106 **EST:** 1988
SQ FT: 350,000
SALES (est): 228.87MM
SALES (corp-wide): 43.65B **Publicly Held**
Web: www.globalpointofcare.abbott
SIC: 2835 Diagnostic substances
HQ: Alere Inc.
51 Sawyer Rd Ste 200
Waltham MA
781 647-3900

(P-4265)
ALERE SAN DIEGO INC
Also Called: Immunalysis
829 Towne Center Dr (91767-5901)
PHONE..............................909 482-0840
Bob Funck, *Brnch Mgr*
EMP: 897
SALES (corp-wide): 43.65B **Publicly Held**
Web: www.globalpointofcare.abbott
SIC: 2835 3841 Diagnostic substances; Diagnostic apparatus, medical
HQ: Alere San Diego, Inc.
9975 Summers Ridge Rd
San Diego CA
858 455-4808

(P-4266)
ALFA SCIENTIFIC DESIGNS INC
13200 Gregg St (92064-7121)
PHONE..............................858 513-3888
Chai Bunyagidj, *CEO*
Chai Bunyagidj, *Pr*
Naishu Wang, *
Angela Shen, *
Claudia Shen, *
▲ **EMP:** 94 **EST:** 1996
SQ FT: 39,000
SALES (est): 18.89MM **Privately Held**
Web: www.alfascientific.com
SIC: 2835 Diagnostic substances

(P-4267)
BIOCELL LABORATORIES INC
2001 E University Dr (90220-6411)
PHONE..............................310 537-3300
▲ **EMP:** 35 **EST:** 1972
SALES (est): 2.86MM **Privately Held**
Web: www.biocell.com
SIC: 2835 2836 Diagnostic substances; Biological products, except diagnostic

(P-4268)
BIOMERICA INC (PA)
Also Called: BIOMERICA
17571 Von Karman Ave (92614-6207)
PHONE..............................949 645-2111

Zackary Irani, *Ch Bd*
Allen Barbieri, *Executive Vice Chairman of the Board*
Gary Lu, *CAO*
▲ **EMP:** 18 **EST:** 1971
SQ FT: 22,000
SALES (est): 5.34MM
SALES (corp-wide): 5.34MM **Publicly Held**
Web: www.biomerica.com
SIC: 2835 Diagnostic substances

(P-4269)
BIOSERV CORPORATION
Also Called: Bioserve
5340 Eastgate Mall (92121-2804)
PHONE................917 817-1326
Henry Ji Ph.d., *Pr*
Kevin Herde, *
EMP: 27 **EST:** 1988
SALES (est): 838.22K
SALES (corp-wide): 62.84MM **Publicly Held**
Web: www.bioservamerica.com
SIC: 2835 2834 Diagnostic substances; Pharmaceutical preparations
PA: Sorrento Therapeutics, Inc.
    4955 Directors Pl Ste 100
    San Diego CA
    858 203-4100

(P-4270)
BIOSOURCE INTERNATIONAL INC
5791 Van Allen Way (92008-7321)
PHONE................805 659-5759
Terrance J Bieker, *Pr*
Alan Edrick, *Ex VP*
Kevin J Reagan Ph.d., *Executive Technical Vice President*
Jean-pierre L Conte, *Ch Bd*
Jozef Vangenechten, *Executive Commercial Vice President*
EMP: 30 **EST:** 1989
SQ FT: 51,821
SALES (est): 1.39MM **Privately Held**
SIC: 2835 Diagnostic substances

(P-4271)
DERMTECH INC (PA)
12340 El Camino Real (92130-3078)
PHONE................866 450-4223
Bret Christensen, *Pr*
Matthew Posard, *Non-Executive Chairman of the Board*
Kevin Sun, *CFO*
Claudia Ibarra, *COO*
Todd Wood, *Chief Commercial Officer*
EMP: 35 **EST:** 1995
SQ FT: 28,655
SALES (est): 14.52MM
SALES (corp-wide): 14.52MM **Publicly Held**
Web: www.dermtech.com
SIC: 2835 8071 Diagnostic substances; Testing laboratories

(P-4272)
DIASORIN MOLECULAR LLC
11331 Valley View St (90630-5300)
PHONE................562 240-6500
Carlo Rosa, *CEO*
EMP: 200 **EST:** 2016
SALES (est): 90MM **Privately Held**
Web: int.diasorin.com
SIC: 2835 5047 In vitro diagnostics; Diagnostic equipment, medical
HQ: Diasorin Inc.
    1951 Northwestern Ave S
    Stillwater MN
    651 439-9710

(P-4273)
EPICUREN DISCOVERY
31 Journey Ste 100 (92656-3334)
PHONE................949 588-5807
Colleen Lohrman, *Pr*
▲ **EMP:** 65 **EST:** 1999
SALES (est): 8.7MM **Privately Held**
Web: www.epicuren.com
SIC: 2835 Enzyme and isoenzyme diagnostic agents

(P-4274)
GATEWAY GENOMICS LLC
11436 Sorrento Valley Rd (92121-1350)
P.O. Box 99129 (92169-1129)
PHONE................858 886-7250
Christopher Jacob, *CEO*
EMP: 53 **EST:** 2018
SALES (est): 11.26MM **Publicly Held**
Web: www.gatewaygenomics.org
SIC: 2835 Microbiology and virology diagnostic products
PA: Myriad Genetics, Inc.
    322 N 2200 W
    Salt Lake City UT

(P-4275)
GEN-PROBE INCORPORATED
10210 Genetic Center Dr (92121-4394)
PHONE................858 410-8000
EMP: 74
SALES (corp-wide): 3.91B **Publicly Held**
Web: www.gen-probe.com
SIC: 2835 In vitro diagnostics
HQ: Gen-Probe Incorporated
    250 Campus Dr
    Marlborough MA
    508 263-8937

(P-4276)
HELICA BIOSYSTEMS INC
3310 W Macarthur Blvd (92704-6804)
PHONE................714 578-7830
Wondu Wolde Mariam, *Pr*
EMP: 17 **EST:** 1999
SQ FT: 7,500
SALES (est): 1.98MM **Privately Held**
Web: www.helica.com
SIC: 2835 2836 In vitro diagnostics; Biological products, except diagnostic

(P-4277)
INNOVACON INC
9975 Summers Ridge Rd (92121-2997)
PHONE................858 805-8900
▲ **EMP:** 82 **EST:** 2006
SALES (est): 14.41MM
SALES (corp-wide): 43.65B **Publicly Held**
SIC: 2835 Diagnostic substances
HQ: Alere Inc.
    51 Sawyer Rd Ste 200
    Waltham MA
    781 647-3900

(P-4278)
INOVA DIAGNOSTICS INC
9675 Businesspark Ave (92131-1644)
PHONE................858 586-9900
Roger Ingles, *Brnch Mgr*
EMP: 143
Web: www.werfen.com
SIC: 2835 Diagnostic substances
HQ: Inova Diagnostics, Inc.
    9900 Old Grove Rd
    San Diego CA
    858 586-9900

(P-4279)
LEHMAN MILLET INCORPORATED
Also Called: Leham Millet West
3 Macarthur Pl Ste 700 (92707-6078)
PHONE................714 850-7900
Bruce Lehman, *CEO*
EMP: 49
SALES (corp-wide): 51.21MM **Privately Held**
Web: www.precisioneffect.com
SIC: 2835 Diagnostic substances
HQ: Lehman Millet Incorporated
    101 Tremont St Ste 205
    Boston MA
    617 722-0019

(P-4280)
LIFE TECHNOLOGIES CORPORATION (HQ)
5781 Van Allen Way (92008-7321)
P.O. Box 1039 (92018-1039)
PHONE................760 603-7200
Seth Hoogasian, *CEO*
Mark P Stevenson, *
John A Cottingham, *
◆ **EMP:** 140 **EST:** 1997
SALES (est): 888.72MM
SALES (corp-wide): 44.91B **Publicly Held**
Web: www.thermofisher.com
SIC: 2835 2836 Diagnostic substances; Biological products, except diagnostic
PA: Thermo Fisher Scientific Inc.
    168 3rd Ave
    Waltham MA
    781 622-1000

(P-4281)
LIFEOME BIOLABS INC
10054 Mesa Ridge Ct (92121-2945)
PHONE................619 302-0129
Zheng Chaojun, *Pr*
EMP: 20
SALES (corp-wide): 4.49MM **Privately Held**
Web: www.lifeome.com
SIC: 2835 8731 Microbiology and virology diagnostic products; Biological research
PA: Lifeome Biolabs Inc.
    1895 Avenida Del Oro # 6554
    Oceanside CA
    619 302-0129

(P-4282)
MOLECULAR PROBES INC
5781 Van Allen Way (92008-7321)
PHONE................760 603-7200
EMP: 99
SALES (corp-wide): 44.91B **Publicly Held**
SIC: 2835 Diagnostic substances
HQ: Molecular Probes, Inc.
    29851 Willow Creek Rd
    Eugene OR
    760 603-7200

(P-4283)
MONOCENT INC
Also Called: Monocent
8920 Quartz Ave (91324-3339)
PHONE................424 310-0777
Shervin Taheri, *CEO*
EMP: 18 **EST:** 2019
SALES (est): 4.63MM **Privately Held**
Web: www.monocent.com
SIC: 2835 In vitro diagnostics

(P-4284)
ONCOCYTE CORPORATION (PA)
15 Cushing (92618-4220)

PHONE................949 409-7600
EMP: 17 **EST:** 2009
SALES (est): 958K **Publicly Held**
Web: www.oncocyte.com
SIC: 2835 Diagnostic substances

(P-4285)
ORTHO-CLINICAL DIAGNOSTICS INC
612 W Katella, Ste-B (92867-4608)
PHONE................714 639-2323
Robert Black, *Brnch Mgr*
EMP: 27
SQ FT: 2,200
SALES (corp-wide): 3.27B **Publicly Held**
Web: go.orthoclinicaldiagnostics.com
SIC: 2835 Blood derivative diagnostic agents
HQ: Ortho-Clinical Diagnostics, Inc.
    1001 Route 202
    Raritan NJ
    908 218-8000

(P-4286)
PACIFIC BIOTECH INC
10165 Mckellar Ct (92121-4201)
PHONE................858 552-1100
Wayne Kay, *Pr*
EMP: 45 **EST:** 1981
SQ FT: 70,000
SALES (est): 8.61MM
SALES (corp-wide): 3.27B **Publicly Held**
SIC: 2835 Pregnancy test kits
HQ: Quidel Corporation
    9975 Summers Ridge Rd
    San Diego CA
    858 552-1100

(P-4287)
QUANTIMETRIX
2005 Manhattan Beach Blvd (90278-1205)
PHONE................310 536-0006
Monty Ban, *Pr*
Edward Cleek, *
Abdee Akhavan, *
EMP: 70 **EST:** 1974
SQ FT: 86,400
SALES (est): 17.51MM **Privately Held**
Web: www.quantimetrix.com
SIC: 2835 Diagnostic substances

(P-4288)
QUIDEL CORPORATION
10165 Mckellar Ct (92121-4299)
PHONE................858 552-1100
EMP: 70
SALES (corp-wide): 3.27B **Publicly Held**
Web: www.quidelortho.com
SIC: 2835 Diagnostic substances
HQ: Quidel Corporation
    9975 Summers Ridge Rd
    San Diego CA
    858 552-1100

(P-4289)
QUIDEL CORPORATION (HQ)
9975 Summers Ridge Rd (92121-2997)
PHONE................858 552-1100
Douglas C Bryant, *Pr*
Randall J Steward, *CFO*
Robert J Bujarski, *Senior Vice President Business Development*
Werner Kroll, *Senior Vice President Research & Development*
EMP: 99 **EST:** 1977
SQ FT: 30,000
SALES (est): 1.7B
SALES (corp-wide): 3.27B **Publicly Held**
Web: www.quidelortho.com
SIC: 2835 Pregnancy test kits
PA: Quidelortho Corporation
    9975 Summers Ridge Rd

P R O D U C T S & S V C S

San Diego CA
858 552-1100

(P-4290)
QUIDELORTHO CORPORATION (PA)
9975 Summers Ridge Rd (92121-2997)
PHONE................................858 552-1100
Douglas C Bryant, *Pr*
Kenneth F Buechler, *Non-Executive Chairman of the Board*
Robert J Bujarski, *Ex VP*
Joseph M Busky, *CFO*
Michael S Iskra, *CCO*
EMP: 27 **EST:** 2021
SALES (est): 3.27B
SALES (corp-wide): 3.27B **Publicly Held**
Web: ir.quidelortho.com
SIC: 2835 Pregnancy test kits

(P-4291)
RESPONSE GENETICS INC
1640 Marengo St Ste 7 (90033-1057)
PHONE................................323 224-3900
EMP: 113
Web: www.responsegenetics.com
SIC: 2835 Diagnostic substances

(P-4292)
SEKISUI AMERICA CORPORATION
Genzyme Diagnostics
6659 Top Gun St (92121-4113)
PHONE................................858 452-3198
Brian Danieli, *Brnch Mgr*
EMP: 80
Web: www.sekisui-corp.com
SIC: 2835 Diagnostic substances
HQ: Sekisui America Corporation
300 Lighting Way Ste 320
Secaucus NJ
201 423-7960

(P-4293)
SYNBIOTICS LLC
16420 Via Esprillo (92127-1702)
PHONE................................858 451-3771
Keith A Butler, *Brnch Mgr*
EMP: 22
SALES (corp-wide): 8.08B **Publicly Held**
SIC: 2835 Veterinary diagnostic substances
HQ: Synbiotics Llc
12200 N Ambassador Dr # 202
Kansas City MO
816 464-3500

(P-4294)
SYNTRON BIORESEARCH INC
2774 Loker Ave W (92010-6610)
PHONE................................760 930-2200
Charles Yu, *Pr*
▲ **EMP:** 278 **EST:** 1986
SALES (est): 32.73MM **Privately Held**
Web: www.syntron.net
SIC: 2835 5122 Diagnostic substances;
Biologicals and allied products

(P-4295)
TECO DIAGNOSTICS
1268 N Lakeview Ave (92807-1831)
PHONE................................714 693-7788
K C Chen, *Pr*
◆ **EMP:** 70 **EST:** 1985
SQ FT: 40,000
SALES (est): 17.09MM **Privately Held**
Web: www.tecodiagnostics.com
SIC: 2835 5049 Diagnostic substances;
Laboratory equipment, except medical or dental

(P-4296)
TYRA BIOSCIENCES INC
2656 State St (92008-1626)
PHONE................................619 728-4760
Todd Harris, *Pr*
Robert More, *
Daniel Bensen, *COO*
Esther Van Den Boom, *CFO*
EMP: 25 **EST:** 2018
SQ FT: 4,734
Web: www.tyra.bio
SIC: 2835 Microbiology and virology diagnostic products

2836 Biological Products, Except Diagnostic

(P-4297)
AMERICAN PEPTIDE COMPANY INC
1271 Avenida Chelsea (92081-8315)
PHONE................................408 733-7604
▲ **EMP:** 86
SIC: 2836 5169 Biological products, except diagnostic; Chemicals and allied products, nec

(P-4298)
AMGEN INC (PA)
1 Amgen Center Dr (91320-1799)
PHONE................................805 447-1000
Robert A Bradway, *Ch Bd*
Peter H Griffith, *Ex VP*
Jonathan P Graham, *Ex VP*
Nancy A Grygiel, *CCO*
Linda H Louie, *CAO*
◆ **EMP:** 2577 **EST:** 1980
SALES (est): 26.32B
SALES (corp-wide): 26.32B **Publicly Held**
Web: www.amgen.com
SIC: 2836 Biological products, except diagnostic

(P-4299)
ARK ANIMAL HEALTH INC
4955 Directors Pl (92121-3836)
PHONE................................858 203-4100
EMP: 30 **EST:** 2017
SALES (est): 931.35K
SALES (corp-wide): 62.84MM **Publicly Held**
Web: www.arkanimalhealth.com
SIC: 2836 Biological products, except diagnostic
PA: Sorrento Therapeutics, Inc.
4955 Directors Pl Ste 100
San Diego CA
858 203-4100

(P-4300)
ARMATA PHARMACEUTICALS INC (PA)
Also Called: Armata Pharmaceuticals
4503 Glencoe Ave (90292-6372)
PHONE................................310 665-2928
Todd R Patrick, *CEO*
Brian Varnum, *CDO*
Steve R Martin, *CFO*
Duane Morris, *VP*
EMP: 24 **EST:** 1989
SQ FT: 35,500
SALES (est): 5.51MM **Publicly Held**
Web: www.armatapharma.com
SIC: 2836 Biological products, except diagnostic

(P-4301)
ATARA BIOTHERAPEUTICS INC (PA)
Also Called: Atara Bio
2380 Conejo Spectrum St Ste 200 (91320-1444)
PHONE................................650 278-8930
Pascal Touchon, *Pr*
Ronald C Renaud, *
Jakob Dupont, *Ex VP*
Utpal Koppikar, *Sr VP*
Amar Murugan, *Sr VP*
EMP: 568 **EST:** 2012
SQ FT: 13,670
SALES (est): 63.57MM
SALES (corp-wide): 63.57MM **Publicly Held**
Web: www.atarabio.com
SIC: 2836 8731 Biological products, except diagnostic; Biotechnical research, commercial

(P-4302)
ATYR PHARMA INC (PA)
Also Called: Atyr Pharma
10240 Sorrento Valley Rd Ste 300 (92121-1605)
PHONE................................858 731-8389
Sanjay S Shukla, *Pr*
John K Clarke, *Ch Bd*
Jill M Broadfoot, *CFO*
Nancy E Denyes, *Corporate Secretary*
EMP: 42 **EST:** 2005
SQ FT: 23,696
SALES (est): 10.39MM **Publicly Held**
Web: www.atyrpharma.com
SIC: 2836 2834 Biological products, except diagnostic; Pharmaceutical preparations

(P-4303)
BACHEM AMERICAS INC (DH)
Also Called: Bachem California
3132 Kashiwa St (90505-4011)
PHONE................................310 784-4440
Brian Gregg, *CEO*
Michael Brenk, *
Najib Masloub, *
▲ **EMP:** 32 **EST:** 1971
SQ FT: 70,000
SALES (est): 112.08MM **Privately Held**
Web: www.bachem.com
SIC: 2836 2834 Biological products, except diagnostic; Pharmaceutical preparations
HQ: Bachem Holding Ag
Hauptstrasse 144
Bubendorf BL

(P-4304)
BACHEM AMERICAS INC
3152 Kashiwa St (90505-4011)
PHONE................................310 784-4440
EMP: 58
Web: www.bachem.com
SIC: 2836 2834 Biological products, except diagnostic; Pharmaceutical preparations
HQ: Bachem Americas, Inc.
3132 Kashiwa St
Torrance CA
310 784-4440

(P-4305)
BACHEM BIOSCIENCE INC
Also Called: Bachem
3132 Kashiwa St (90505-4087)
PHONE................................310 784-7322
Peter Grogg, *Ch Bd*
Peter Grogg, *Ch*
Rolf Nyfeler, *
Michael Pennington, *
David Floyd, *

▲ **EMP:** 45 **EST:** 1987
SALES (est): 13.42MM **Privately Held**
Web: www.bachem.com
SIC: 2836 2899 Biological products, except diagnostic; Chemical preparations, nec
HQ: Bachem Holding Ag
Hauptstrasse 144
Bubendorf BL

(P-4306)
BIOATLA INC
Also Called: BIOATLA
11085 Torreyana Rd (92121-1104)
PHONE................................858 558-0708
Jay M Short, *Ch Bd*
Scott Smith, *
Eric Sievers, *CMO*
Richard A Waldron, *Sr VP*
Christian Vasquez, *Corporate Controller*
EMP: 36 **EST:** 2007
SQ FT: 43,377
Web: www.bioatla.com
SIC: 2836 Biological products, except diagnostic

(P-4307)
CAMBRIDGE EQUITIES LP
9922 Jefferson Blvd (90232-3506)
PHONE................................858 350-2300
EMP: 46 **EST:** 2011
SALES (est): 4.95MM **Privately Held**
SIC: 2836 Biological products, except diagnostic

(P-4308)
CAPSIDA BIOTHERAPEUTICS INC (PA)
3075 Townsgate Rd (91361-3076)
PHONE................................805 410-2673
Robert Cuddihy, *CEO*
Pamela Wapnick, *CFO*
EMP: 53 **EST:** 2019
SALES (est): 10.2MM
SALES (corp-wide): 10.2MM **Privately Held**
Web: www.capsida.com
SIC: 2836 Biological products, except diagnostic

(P-4309)
CIDARA THERAPEUTICS INC (PA)
Also Called: Cidara
6310 Nancy Ridge Dr Ste 101 (92121)
PHONE................................858 752-6170
Jeffrey L Stein, *Pr*
Daniel D Burgess, *Ch Bd*
Preetam Shah, *Chief Business Officer*
Paul Daruwala, *COO*
Taylor Sandison, *CMO*
EMP: 71 **EST:** 2012
SQ FT: 29,638
SALES (est): 64.29MM
SALES (corp-wide): 64.29MM **Publicly Held**
Web: www.cidara.com
SIC: 2836 8731 Biological products, except diagnostic; Biotechnical research, commercial

(P-4310)
CLINIQA CORPORATION
258 La Moree Rd (92078-4381)
PHONE................................760 744-1900
Charles G Haugh, *CEO*
EMP: 58
SALES (corp-wide): 1.14B **Publicly Held**
Web: www.cliniqa.com
SIC: 2836 Biological products, except diagnostic

HQ: Cliniqa Corporation
495 Enterprise St
San Marcos CA
760 744-1900

(P-4311)
CLINIQA CORPORATION (HQ)
Also Called: Cliniqa
495 Enterprise St (92078-4364)
PHONE..............................760 744-1900
Kevin Gould, Pr
C Granger Haugh, *
Dean Harriman, *
Shing Kwan, *
Larry Beaty, *
▼ EMP: 29 EST: 1976
SQ FT: 25,000
SALES (est): 20.7MM
SALES (corp-wide): 1.14B Publicly Held
Web: www.cliniqa.com
SIC: 2836 Biological products, except
diagnostic
PA: Bio-Techne Corporation
614 Mckinley Pl Ne
Minneapolis MN
612 379-8854

(P-4312)
DNATRIX INC
2659 State St # 100 (92008-1627)
PHONE..............................832 930-2401
Jeffrey Knapp, CEO
Imran Alibhai, Sr VP
Reenie Mccarthy, Prin
Frank Tufaro Ph.d., Prin
EMP: 20 EST: 2005
SALES (est): 2.38MM Privately Held
Web: www.dnatrix.com
SIC: 2836 Biological products, except
diagnostic

(P-4313)
EMD MILLIPORE CORPORATION
Also Called: Bioscience Research Reagents
28820 Single Oak Dr (92590-3607)
PHONE..............................951 676-8080
John Ambroziak, Mgr
EMP: 69
SALES (corp-wide): 23.09B Privately Held
Web: www.millipore.com
SIC: 2836 2835 3826 Biological products,
except diagnostic; Diagnostic substances;
Liquid testing apparatus
HQ: Emd Millipore Corporation
400 Summit Dr
Burlington MA
800 645-5476

(P-4314)
EXCELLOS INCORPORATED
1155 Island Ave (92101-7230)
PHONE..............................619 400-8235
David Wellis, CEO
EMP: 20 EST: 2020
SALES (est): 3.6MM Privately Held
Web: www.excellos.com
SIC: 2836 Vaccines and other immunizing
products

(P-4315)
FUJIFILM DSYNTH BTCHNLGIES CAL
2430 Conejo Spectrum St (91320-1445)
PHONE..............................914 789-8100
Martin Meeson, Pr
Gerry Farrell, COO
Hideru Sato, Treas
Steve Lee, Sec
EMP: 22
SALES (est): 8.19MM Privately Held

SIC: 2836 Biological products, except
diagnostic
HQ: Fujifilm Diosynth Biotechnologies Uk
Limited
New Billingham House
Billingham

(P-4316)
FUJIFILM DSYNTH BTCHNLGIES USA
2430 Conejo Spectrum St (91320-1445)
PHONE..............................805 699-5579
Takatoshi Ishikawa, Brnch Mgr
EMP: 134
Web: www.atarabio.com
SIC: 2836 Biological products, except
diagnostic
HQ: Fujifilm Diosynth Biotechnologies
U.S.A., Inc.
101 J Morris Comns Ln
Morrisville NC

(P-4317)
FUJIFILM IRVINE SCIENTIFIC INC (DH)
Also Called: Irvine Scientific
1830 E Warner Ave (92705-5505)
PHONE..............................949 261-7800
Yutaka Yamaguchi, CEO
Judy Malillo, Sec
Ryo Iguchi, CFO
▲ EMP: 44 EST: 1970
SQ FT: 20,000
SALES (est): 124.93MM Privately Held
Web: www.irvinesci.com
SIC: 2836 5047 Blood derivatives; Medical
laboratory equipment
HQ: Fujifilm Holdings America Corporation
200 Summit Lake Dr Fl 2
Valhalla NY

(P-4318)
GB007 INC
3013 Science Park Rd (92121-1101)
PHONE..............................858 684-1300
Sheila Gujrathi, CEO
EMP: 26 EST: 2004
SALES (est): 927.08K Publicly Held
SIC: 2836 Biological products, except
diagnostic
PA: Gossamer Bio, Inc.
3013 Science Park Rd # 200
San Diego CA
858 684-1300

(P-4319)
GRIFOLS BIOLOGICALS LLC (DH)
5555 Valley Blvd (90032-3520)
PHONE..............................323 225-2221
David Bell, *
Max Debrouwer, *
Willie Zuniga, *
▲ EMP: 67 EST: 2003
SALES (est): 185.52MM Privately Held
Web: www.grifols.com
SIC: 2836 2834 Plasmas; Pharmaceutical
preparations
HQ: Grifols Shared Services North
America, Inc.
2410 Lillyvale Ave
Los Angeles CA
323 225-2221

(P-4320)
GRIFOLS USA LLC
Also Called: Access Biologicals
995 Park Center Dr (92081-8312)
PHONE..............................760 931-8444

EMP: 71
Web: www.grifols.com
SIC: 2836 Biological products, except
diagnostic
HQ: Grifols Usa, Llc
2410 Grifols Way
Los Angeles CA
323 225-2221

(P-4321)
HALOZYME THERAPEUTICS INC (PA)
Also Called: Halozyme
12390 El Camino Real (92130-3190)
PHONE..............................858 794-8889
Helen I Torley, Pr
Connie L Matsui, Ch Bd
Nicole Labrosse, Sr VP
Mark Snyder, CCO
Michael J Labarre, Sr VP
EMP: 62 EST: 1998
SQ FT: 50,000
SALES (est): 660.12MM
SALES (corp-wide): 660.12MM Publicly
Held
Web: www.halozyme.com
SIC: 2836 2834 Biological products, except
diagnostic; Pharmaceutical preparations

(P-4322)
IMMUNITYBIO INC (PA)
3530 John Hopkins Ct (92121-1121)
PHONE..............................844 696-5235
EMP: 56 EST: 2002
SQ FT: 44,681
SALES (est): 240K Publicly Held
Web: www.immunitybio.com
SIC: 2836 Biological products, except
diagnostic

(P-4323)
INHIBRX INC (PA)
Also Called: Inhibrx
11025 N Torrey Pines Rd Ste 200
(92037-1030)
PHONE..............................858 795-4220
Mark P Lappe, Ch Bd
Kelly Deck, CFO
Klaus W Wagner, CMO
Brendan P Eckelman, CSO
David Matly, CCO
EMP: 37 EST: 2010
SQ FT: 34,000
SALES (est): 2.19MM
SALES (corp-wide): 2.19MM Publicly
Held
Web: inhibrxv1stag.wpengine.com
SIC: 2836 Biological products, except
diagnostic

(P-4324)
LINEAGE CELL THERAPEUTICS INC (PA)
Also Called: LINEAGE
2173 Salk Ave Ste 200 (92008-7354)
PHONE..............................510 521-3390
Brian M Culley, CEO
Alfred D Kingsley, Ch Bd
Kevin L Cook, CFO
Gary S Hogge, Sr VP
George A Samuel Iii, Corporate Secretary
EMP: 20 EST: 1990
SQ FT: 8,841
SALES (est): 14.7MM Publicly Held
Web: www.biotimeinc.com
SIC: 2836 8731 Biological products, except
diagnostic; Biotechnical research,
commercial

(P-4325)
NEUROCRINE BIOSCIENCES INC (PA)
Also Called: Neurocrine
12780 El Camino Real Ste 100
(92130-2042)
PHONE..............................858 617-7600
Kevin C Gorman, Pr
William H Rastetter, *
Matthew C Abernethy, CFO
Julie S Cooke, Chief Human Resources
Officer
Darin M Lippoldt, CLO
EMP: 1178 EST: 1992
SQ FT: 141,000
SALES (est): 1.49B Publicly Held
Web: www.neurocrine.com
SIC: 2836 Biological products, except
diagnostic

(P-4326)
NEUROCRINE CONTINENTAL INC
12790 El Camino Real (92130-2008)
PHONE..............................858 617-7941
Kevin Gorman, CEO
EMP: 20 EST: 2017
SALES (est): 6.1MM Publicly Held
Web: www.neurocrine.com
SIC: 2836 Biological products, except
diagnostic
PA: Neurocrine Biosciences, Inc.
12780 El Camino Real
San Diego CA

(P-4327)
POSEIDA THERAPEUTICS INC (PA)
Also Called: Poseida
9390 Towne Centre Dr Ste 200 (92121)
PHONE..............................858 779-3100
Mark J Gergen, Ch Bd
Harry J Leonhardt, CCO
Johanna M Mylet, CFO
Brent Warner, Pr
Kristin Yarema, Pr
EMP: 313 EST: 2014
SQ FT: 87,000
SALES (est): 130.49MM
SALES (corp-wide): 130.49MM Publicly
Held
Web: www.poseida.com
SIC: 2836 2834 Biological products, except
diagnostic; Pharmaceutical preparations

(P-4328)
PROLACTA BIOSCIENCE INC (PA)
757 Baldwin Park Blvd (91746-1504)
PHONE..............................626 599-9260
Scott A Elster, CEO
Scott A Elster, CEO
Joseph Fournell, VP
Alan Kofsky, VP
Tami D Ciranna, CFO
▼ EMP: 132 EST: 1999
SQ FT: 65,000
SALES (est): 130.35MM
SALES (corp-wide): 130.35MM Privately
Held
Web: www.prolacta.com
SIC: 2836 Biological products, except
diagnostic

(P-4329)
REPLIGEN CORPORATION
Also Called: Artesyn Offices and Mfg Fcilty
2685 Park Center Dr Ste C (93065-6211)
PHONE..............................775 235-5200

PRODUCTS & SVCS

EMP: 17
SALES (corp-wide): 801.54MM **Publicly Held**
SIC: 2836 Biological products, except diagnostic
PA: Repligen Corporation
　41 Seyon St Ste 100
　Waltham MA
　781 250-0111

(P-4330)
SCRIPPS LABORATORIES
6838 Flanders Dr (92121-2904)
PHONE.................858 546-5800
Simon C Khoury, *Pr*
James Scoffin, *Treas*
EMP: 20 **EST:** 1984
SQ FT: 32,000
SALES (est): 5.44MM
SALES (corp-wide): 4.06B **Privately Held**
Web: www.scrippslabs.com
SIC: 2836 2835 Biological products, except diagnostic; Diagnostic substances
PA: Scripps Health
　10140 Campus Point Dr # 415
　San Diego CA
　800 727-4777

(P-4331)
SORRENTO THERAPEUTICS INC (PA)
4955 Directors Pl (92121-3837)
PHONE.................858 203-4100
Henry Ji, *Ch Bd*
EMP: 65 **EST:** 2006
SQ FT: 30,000
SALES (est): 62.84MM
SALES (corp-wide): 62.84MM **Publicly Held**
Web: www.sorrentotherapeutics.com
SIC: 2836 Biological products, except diagnostic

2841 Soap And Other Detergents

(P-4332)
ALL ONE GOD FAITH INC (PA)
Also Called: Dr. Bronners Magic Soaps
1335 Park Center Dr (92081-8357)
P.O. Box 1958 (92085-1958)
PHONE.................844 937-2551
David Bronner, *CEO*
Michael Bronner, *
Trudy Bronner, *
◆ **EMP:** 170 **EST:** 1973
SQ FT: 126,000
SALES (est): 56.18MM **Privately Held**
Web: www.drbronner.com
SIC: 2841 2834 2844 Soap: granulated, liquid, cake, flaked, or chip; Lip balms; Lotions, shaving

(P-4333)
ALL ONE GOD FAITH INC
Also Called: Dr. Bronners Magic Soaps
1225 Park Center Dr Ste D (92081-8353)
PHONE.................760 599-4010
David Bronner, *CEO*
EMP: 70
Web: www.drbronner.com
SIC: 2841 Soap: granulated, liquid, cake, flaked, or chip
PA: All One God Faith, Inc.
　1335 Park Center Dr
　Vista CA

(P-4334)
BRADFORD SOAP MEXICO INC
1778 Zinetta Rd Ste G (92231-9510)
PHONE.................760 768-4539
John Howland, *CEO*
EMP: 493
SALES (corp-wide): 227.55MM **Privately Held**
Web: www.bradfordsoap.com
SIC: 2841 Soap: granulated, liquid, cake, flaked, or chip
HQ: Bradford Soap Mexico, Inc.
　200 Providence St
　West Warwick RI
　401 821-2141

(P-4335)
CHURCH & DWIGHT CO INC
17486 Nisqualli Rd (92395-7740)
PHONE.................609 613-1551
EMP: 28
SALES (corp-wide): 5.38B **Publicly Held**
Web: www.churchdwight.com
SIC: 2841 Soap and other detergents
PA: Church & Dwight Co., Inc.
　500 Charles Ewing Blvd
　Ewing NJ
　609 806-1200

(P-4336)
ECOLAB
5640 S Fairfax Ave (90056-1266)
PHONE.................323 292-7752
EMP: 79 **EST:** 2016
SALES (est): 249.98K **Privately Held**
Web: www.ecolab.com
SIC: 2841 Soap and other detergents

(P-4337)
GOODWIN AMMONIA COMPANY LLC
Also Called: The Goodwin Company
12361 Monarch St (92841-2908)
PHONE.................714 894-0531
Tom Goodwin, *Pr*
EMP: 68
SALES (corp-wide): 35.27MM **Privately Held**
Web: www.goodwininc.com
SIC: 2841 Soap and other detergents
PA: The Goodwin Ammonia Company Llc
　12361 Monarch St
　Garden Grove CA
　714 894-0531

(P-4338)
KINGMAN INDUSTRIES INC
26370 Beckman Ct Ste A (92562-1005)
PHONE.................951 698-1812
Barbara Mandel, *CEO*
Paul Mandel Junior, *Pr*
Mitch Mayer, *Pr*
▲ **EMP:** 20 **EST:** 1974
SQ FT: 23,000
SALES (est): 4MM **Privately Held**
Web: www.kingmanlabs.com
SIC: 2841 2869 5169 5122 Soap and other detergents; Industrial organic chemicals, nec; Detergents and soaps, except specialty cleaning; Cosmetics

(P-4339)
MISSION KLEENSWEEP PROD INC
Also Called: Mission Laboratories
13644 Live Oak Ln (91706-1317)
PHONE.................323 223-1405
TOLL FREE: 888
Helen Rosenbaum, *Pr*

EMP: 53 **EST:** 1936
SQ FT: 75,000
SALES (est): 4.8MM **Privately Held**
SIC: 2841 2842 Soap and other detergents; Polishes and sanitation goods

(P-4340)
PANROSA ENTERPRISES INC
550 Monica Cir (92878-5496)
PHONE.................951 339-5888
Peter Chengjian Pan, *Pr*
Jingwen Zhao, *
Chenyang Sun, *
▲ **EMP:** 60 **EST:** 2003
SALES (est): 8.75MM **Privately Held**
Web: www.panrosa.com
SIC: 2841 Soap and other detergents

2842 Polishes And Sanitation Goods

(P-4341)
3D/INTERNATIONAL INC
20724 Centre Pointe Pkwy Unit 1 (91350)
PHONE.................661 250-2020
Tony Goren, *Mgr*
EMP: 142
SALES (corp-wide): 4.2B **Publicly Held**
SIC: 2842 Automobile polish
HQ: 3d/International, Inc.
　2200 West Loop S Ste 200
　Houston TX
　713 871-7000

(P-4342)
AMREP INC
1555 S Cucamonga Ave (91761-4512)
PHONE.................770 422-2071
William Redmond, *Pr*
EMP: 353
Web: www.amrepproducts.com
SIC: 2842 Specialty cleaning
HQ: Amrep, Inc.
　600 Galleria Pkwy Se # 1500
　Atlanta GA
　877 428-9937

(P-4343)
AWESOME PRODUCTS INC (PA)
Also Called: La's Totally Awesome
6370 Altura Blvd (90620-1001)
PHONE.................714 562-8873
Loksarang D Hardas, *CEO*
◆ **EMP:** 125 **EST:** 1983
SQ FT: 250,000
SALES (est): 45.34MM
SALES (corp-wide): 45.34MM **Privately Held**
Web: www.lastotallyawesome.com
SIC: 2842 Cleaning or polishing preparations, nec

(P-4344)
B&D INVESTMENT PARTNERS INC (PA)
20950 Centre Pointe Pkwy (91350-2975)
PHONE.................661 255-0955
Darrell Mahler, *CEO*
Glenn Mahler, *
George D Stroesenreuther, *
◆ **EMP:** 48 **EST:** 1960
SQ FT: 100,000
SALES (est): 18.11MM
SALES (corp-wide): 18.11MM **Privately Held**
Web: www.bc-labs.com
SIC: 2842 2844 Cleaning or polishing preparations, nec; Perfumes, cosmetics and other toilet preparations

(P-4345)
BURNS ENVIRONMENTAL SVCS INC
19360 Rinaldi St Ste 381 (91326-1607)
PHONE.................800 577-4009
EMP: 23 **EST:** 2005
SALES (est): 620.59K **Privately Held**
Web: www.burns-enviro.com
SIC: 2842 Polishes and sanitation goods

(P-4346)
CALIFORNIA SCENTS LLC
18850 Von Karman Ave Ste 200 (92612-1586)
◆ **EMP:** 50 **EST:** 1993
SQ FT: 13,000
SALES (est): 9.15MM
SALES (corp-wide): 2.96B **Publicly Held**
Web: www.californiascents.com
SIC: 2842 2844 Polishes and sanitation goods; Perfumes, cosmetics and other toilet preparations
PA: Energizer Holdings, Inc.
　533 Maryville Univ Dr
　Saint Louis MO
　314 985-2000

(P-4347)
CILAJET LLC
16425 Ishida Ave (90248-2924)
PHONE.................310 320-8000
Jaci Warren, *Pr*
EMP: 25 **EST:** 2006
SALES (est): 4.05MM **Privately Held**
Web: www.cilajet.com
SIC: 2842 7542 Automobile polish; Washing and polishing, automotive

(P-4348)
CLOROX MANUFACTURING COMPANY
Also Called: Clorox
2300 W San Bernardino Ave (92374-5000)
PHONE.................909 307-2756
EMP: 56
SALES (corp-wide): 7.39B **Publicly Held**
Web: www.thecloroxcompany.com
SIC: 2842 Polishes and sanitation goods
HQ: Clorox Manufacturing Company
　1221 Broadway
　Oakland CA

(P-4349)
FLO-KEM INC
19402 S Susana Rd (90221-5712)
PHONE.................310 632-7124
EMP: 48
SIC: 2842 Cleaning or polishing preparations, nec

(P-4350)
GENLABS (PA)
5568 Schaefer Ave (91710-9041)
P.O. Box 1697 (91708-1697)
PHONE.................909 591-8451
EMP: 135 **EST:** 1968
SALES (est): 33.66MM
SALES (corp-wide): 33.66MM **Privately Held**
Web: www.genlabscorp.com
SIC: 2842 2841 5169 7389 Polishes and sanitation goods; Soap and other detergents; Chemicals and allied products, nec; Packaging and labeling services

(P-4351)
GPS ASSOCIATES INC
1803 Carnegie Ave (92705-5502)
PHONE.................949 408-3162

Joe Parisi, *CEO*
Renee Gaudreau, *
EMP: 49 **EST:** 1993
SALES (est): 7.54MM
SALES (corp-wide): 7.54MM **Publicly Held**
Web: www.guardrxhandsanitizer.com
SIC: 2842 Sanitation preparations, disinfectants and deodorants
PA: Mountain High Acquisitions Corp.
4350 Executive Dr Ste 200
San Diego CA
760 402-5105

(P-4352)
GRANITE GOLD INC
12780 Danielson Ct Ste A (92064-8857)
PHONE...................858 499-8933
Lenny Sciarrino, *CEO*
Scott Martin, *COO*
Leonard Pellegrino, *VP*
EMP: 91 **EST:** 2002
SALES (est): 5.14MM **Privately Held**
Web: www.granitegold.com
SIC: 2842 Cleaning or polishing preparations, nec

(P-4353)
GRANITIZE PRODUCTS INC
11022 Vulcan St (90280-7621)
P.O. Box 2306 (90280-9306)
PHONE...................562 923-5438
Tony Raymondo, *CEO*
Betty Raymondo, *
◆ **EMP:** 75 **EST:** 1930
SQ FT: 30,000
SALES (est): 19.81MM **Privately Held**
Web: www.granitize.com
SIC: 2842 Automobile polish

(P-4354)
JASON MARKK INC (PA)
15325 Blackburn Ave (90650-6842)
PHONE...................213 687-7060
Jason M Angsuvarn, *CEO*
▲ **EMP:** 32 **EST:** 2007
SALES (est): 4.76MM
SALES (corp-wide): 4.76MM **Privately Held**
Web: www.jasonmarkk.com
SIC: 2842 Shoe polish or cleaner

(P-4355)
KIK-SOCAL INC
Also Called: Kik
9028 Dice Rd (90670-2520)
PHONE...................562 946-6427
Jeffrey M Nodland, *CEO*
Stratis Katsiris, *
William Smith, *
Ben W Kaak, *
EMP: 3000 **EST:** 1995
SQ FT: 3,000,000
SALES (est): 259.9MM
SALES (corp-wide): 2.37B **Privately Held**
SIC: 2842 Bleaches, household: dry or liquid
HQ: Kik International Llc
1725 N Brown Rd
Lawrenceville GA

(P-4356)
LAB CLEAN INC
3627 Briggeman Dr (90720-2475)
PHONE...................714 689-0063
Mark Cunningham, *CEO*
Mark Cunningham, *Managing Member*
Matthew Bays, *
EMP: 25 **EST:** 2005
SQ FT: 40,000
SALES (est): 2.29MM **Privately Held**

Web: www.bayescleaners.com
SIC: 2842 Cleaning or polishing preparations, nec

(P-4357)
LMC ENTERPRISES (PA)
Also Called: Chemco Products Company
6401 Alondra Blvd (90723-3758)
PHONE...................562 602-2116
Elaine S Cooper, *CEO*
Janis Utz, *
John D Grimes, *
EMP: 70 **EST:** 1962
SQ FT: 15,000
SALES (est): 41.67MM
SALES (corp-wide): 41.67MM **Privately Held**
Web: www.chemcoprod.com
SIC: 2842 Cleaning or polishing preparations, nec

(P-4358)
LMC ENTERPRISES
Also Called: Flo-Kem
19402 S Susana Rd (90221-5712)
PHONE...................310 632-7124
Elaine Cooper, *CEO*
EMP: 50
SQ FT: 20,000
SALES (corp-wide): 41.67MM **Privately Held**
Web: www.chemcoprod.com
SIC: 2842 Cleaning or polishing preparations, nec
PA: Lmc Enterprises
6401 Alondra Blvd
Paramount CA
562 602-2116

(P-4359)
MAINTEX INC (PA)
13300 Nelson Ave (91746-1516)
P.O. Box 7110 (91744-7110)
PHONE...................800 446-1888
TOLL FREE: 800
▲ **EMP:** 140 **EST:** 1960
SALES (est): 35.04MM
SALES (corp-wide): 35.04MM **Privately Held**
Web: www.maintex.com
SIC: 2842 5087 Cleaning or polishing preparations, nec; Janitors' supplies

(P-4360)
MEGUIARS INC (HQ)
Also Called: Brilliant Solutions
213 Technology Dr (92618-2400)
PHONE...................949 752-8000
Barry J Meguiar, *Pr*
Michael W Meguiar, *
Catherine E Bayless, *
◆ **EMP:** 50 **EST:** 1901
SALES (est): 50.87MM
SALES (corp-wide): 34.23B **Publicly Held**
Web: www.meguiars.com
SIC: 2842 Cleaning or polishing preparations, nec
PA: 3m Company
3m Center
Saint Paul MN
651 733-1110

(P-4361)
MORGAN GALLACHER INC
Also Called: Custom Chemical Formulators
8707 Millergrove Dr (90670-2001)
PHONE...................562 695-1232
Harriet Von Luft, *Ch Bd*
David M Smith, *
Tam Sarmiento, *

▼ **EMP:** 46 **EST:** 1964
SQ FT: 100,000
SALES (est): 5.28MM **Privately Held**
Web: www.morgan-gallacher.com
SIC: 2842 5169 Cleaning or polishing preparations, nec; Industrial chemicals

(P-4362)
MPM BUILDING SERVICES INC
Also Called: Mpm & Associates
7011 Hayvenhurst Ave Ste F (91406-3822)
PHONE...................818 708-9676
EMP: 33 **EST:** 1975
SQ FT: 35,000
SALES (est): 890.5K **Privately Held**
Web: www.mpmco.com
SIC: 2842 Polishes and sanitation goods

(P-4363)
MYSMILE ORAL CARE INC ✪
8238 Mayten Ave (91730-3922)
PHONE...................909 908-4615
Hong Chen, *CEO*
EMP: 20 **EST:** 2022
SALES (est): 835.08K **Privately Held**
SIC: 2842 Polishes and sanitation goods

(P-4364)
NO PRSSURE PRSSURE WSHG SVCS L
Also Called: No Pressure Landscape Services
41880 Kalmia St Ste 165 (92562-8838)
PHONE...................951 477-1988
Lennix Gibson, *Managing Member*
EMP: 20 **EST:** 2015
SALES (est): 2.3MM **Privately Held**
SIC: 2842 0782 8744 4971 Polishes and sanitation goods; Lawn and garden services ; Facilities support services; Irrigation systems

(P-4365)
OIL-DRI CORPORATION AMERICA
950 Petroleum Club Rd (93268-9748)
P.O. Box 1277 (93268-1277)
PHONE...................661 765-7194
EMP: 64
SALES (corp-wide): 413.02MM **Publicly Held**
Web: www.oildri.com
SIC: 2842 Sweeping compounds, oil or water absorbent, clay or sawdust
PA: Oil-Dri Corporation Of America
410 N Michigan Ave # 400
Chicago IL
312 321-1515

(P-4366)
OLYMPUS WATER HOLDINGS IV LP
360 N Crescent Dr Bldg S (90210-2529)
PHONE...................310 739-6325
Mary Ann Sigler, *Pr*
EMP: 9000 **EST:** 2020
SALES (est): 66.03MM **Privately Held**
SIC: 2842 Polishes and sanitation goods

(P-4367)
PEERLESS MATERIALS COMPANY
4442 E 26th St (90058-4318)
P.O. Box 33228 (90033-0228)
PHONE...................323 266-0313
Louis J Buty, *Pr*
Peter H Pritchard, *
▲ **EMP:** 40 **EST:** 1967
SQ FT: 35,000
SALES (est): 4.37MM **Privately Held**

Web: www.americantex.com
SIC: 2842 Sweeping compounds, oil or water absorbent, clay or sawdust

(P-4368)
SOAPTRONIC LLC
20562 Crescent Bay Dr (92630-8845)
PHONE...................949 465-8955
Horst Binderbauer, *Managing Member*
◆ **EMP:** 25 **EST:** 1998
SALES (est): 4.91MM **Privately Held**
Web: www.germstar.com
SIC: 2842 2841 Sanitation preparations, disinfectants and deodorants; Soap and other detergents

(P-4369)
SUNSHINE MAKERS INC (PA)
Also Called: Simple Green
15922 Pacific Coast Hwy (92649-1894)
PHONE...................562 795-6000
Bruce P Fabrizio, *
Bruce P Fabrizio, *
Rose Concilia, *
Jeffrey Hyder, *
Patrick Sheehan, *
▼ **EMP:** 51 **EST:** 1981
SQ FT: 25,000
SALES (est): 23MM
SALES (corp-wide): 23MM **Privately Held**
Web: www.simplegreen.com
SIC: 2842 Cleaning or polishing preparations, nec

(P-4370)
SYNSUS PRVATE LBEL PRTNERS LLC
980 Rancheros Dr (92069)
PHONE...................713 714-0225
Greg Crawford, *Brnch Mgr*
EMP: 118
SALES (corp-wide): 11.37MM **Privately Held**
Web: www.synsus.com
SIC: 2842 Polishes and sanitation goods
PA: Synsus Private Label Partners, Llc
18211 Katy Fwy Ste 325
Houston TX
713 714-0225

(P-4371)
US CONTINENTAL MARKETING INC (PA)
Also Called: U.S. Continental
310 Reed Cir (92879-1349)
PHONE...................951 808-8888
David Lee Williams, *Pr*
◆ **EMP:** 81 **EST:** 1988
SQ FT: 40,000
SALES (est): 25.33MM **Privately Held**
Web: www.uscontinental.com
SIC: 2842 Leather dressings and finishes

2843 Surface Active Agents

(P-4372)
CHEMEOR INC (PA)
727 Arrow Grand Cir (91722-2148)
PHONE...................626 966-3808
Yongchun Tang, *Ch Bd*
Pat Mills, *
Patrick Shuler, *
Carl Aften, *
▲ **EMP:** 29 **EST:** 2005
SQ FT: 16,000
SALES (est): 9.29MM **Privately Held**
Web: www.chemeor.com

SIC: 2843 1389 2911 Surface active agents; Chemically treating wells; Aromatic chemical products

(P-4373)
HENKEL US OPERATIONS CORP
21551 Prairie St (91311-5831)
PHONE....................818 435-0889
EMP: 41
SALES (corp-wide): 23.26B **Privately Held**
Web: www.henkel-northamerica.com
SIC: 2843 Surface active agents
HQ: Henkel Us Operations Corporation
1 Henkel Way
Rocky Hill CT
860 571-5100

(P-4374)
HENKEL US OPERATIONS CORP
20021 S Susana Rd (90221-5721)
PHONE....................562 297-6840
EMP: 175
SALES (corp-wide): 23.26B **Privately Held**
Web: www.henkel.com
SIC: 2843 Surface active agents
HQ: Henkel Us Operations Corporation
1 Henkel Way
Rocky Hill CT
860 571-5100

(P-4375)
JUSTICE BROS DIST CO INC
Also Called: Justice Bros-J B Car Care Pdts
2734 Huntington Dr (91010-2301)
PHONE....................626 359-9174
Edward R Justice Senior, *Ch Bd*
Edward R Justice Junior, *Pr*
▲ **EMP:** 25 **EST:** 1947
SQ FT: 33,000
SALES (est): 2.16MM **Privately Held**
Web: www.justicebrothers.com
SIC: 2843 2899 Surface active agents; Chemical preparations, nec

---

2844 Toilet Preparations

(P-4376)
ADONIS INC
475 N Sheridan St (92878-4021)
PHONE....................951 432-3960
Helga Arminak, *CEO*
EMP: 50 **EST:** 2020
SQ FT: 73,200
SALES (est): 7MM **Privately Held**
Web:
www.adoniscontractmanufacturer.com
SIC: 2844 Perfumes, cosmetics and other toilet preparations

(P-4377)
ALASTIN SKINCARE INC
3129 Tiger Run Ct Ste 109 (92010-6511)
PHONE....................844 858-7546
Amber Edwards, *CEO*
Alan Widgerow, *CMO**
John Garruto, *
Tom Christenson, *
Cam Garner, *Ch Bd*
EMP: 150 **EST:** 2015
SALES (est): 32.27MM **Privately Held**
Web: www.alastin.com
SIC: 2844 Perfumes, cosmetics and other toilet preparations

(P-4378)
AMERICAN INTL INDS INC
Also Called: Aii Beauty
2220 Gaspar Ave (90040-1516)
PHONE....................323 728-2999

David Eisenstein, *CEO*
◆ **EMP:** 1100 **EST:** 1998
SQ FT: 224,000
SALES (est): 39.49MM **Privately Held**
Web: www.aiibeauty.com
SIC: 2844 Perfumes, cosmetics and other toilet preparations

(P-4379)
ARCHIPELAGO INC
Also Called: Archipelago Botanicals
1548 18th St (90404-3404)
PHONE....................213 743-9200
David Klass, *CEO*
Gregory Corzine, *
◆ **EMP:** 110 **EST:** 1994
SALES (est): 21.75MM **Privately Held**
Web: www.shoparchipelago.com
SIC: 2844 3999 Perfumes, cosmetics and other toilet preparations; Candles

(P-4380)
AWARE PRODUCTS INC
9250 Mason Ave (91311-6005)
PHONE....................818 206-6700
Joe Pender, *Pr*
EMP: 19 **EST:** 1971
SALES (est): 565.29K **Privately Held**
SIC: 2844 Perfumes, cosmetics and other toilet preparations

(P-4381)
AWARE PRODUCTS LLC
Also Called: Voyant Beauty
9250 Mason Ave (91311-6005)
PHONE....................818 206-6700
Richard Mcevoy, *CEO*
Bill Saracco, *
▲ **EMP:** 150 **EST:** 1973
SQ FT: 60,000
SALES (est): 44.89MM
SALES (corp-wide): 2.37B **Privately Held**
SIC: 2844 Hair preparations, including shampoos
PA: Voyant Beauty Holdings, Inc.
6710 River Rd
Hodgkins IL
708 482-8881

(P-4382)
BBEAUTIFUL LLC
Also Called: Chrislie Formulations
1361 Mountain View Cir (91702-1649)
PHONE....................626 610-2332
◆ **EMP:** 40
SIC: 2844 5999 Cosmetic preparations; Cosmetics

(P-4383)
BLUE CROSS BEAUTY PRODUCTS INC
557 Jessie St (91340-2542)
PHONE....................818 896-8681
Ray J Friedman, *Ch Bd*
Mark Friedman, *
Lorraine Friedman, *
▲ **EMP:** 27 **EST:** 1942
SQ FT: 12,000
SALES (est): 835.94K **Privately Held**
SIC: 2844 Manicure preparations

(P-4384)
BLUEFIELD ASSOCIATES INC
14900 Hilton Dr (92336-4026)
PHONE....................909 476-6027
Iheatu N Obioha, *CEO*
Chimere K Obioha, *
Tembi Sukuta, *
◆ **EMP:** 30 **EST:** 1986
SQ FT: 30,000

SALES (est): 2.5MM **Privately Held**
Web: www.bluefieldinc.com
SIC: 2844 5122 Cosmetic preparations; Cosmetics, perfumes, and hair products

(P-4385)
BOTANX LLC
3357 E Miraloma Ave Ste 156 (92806-1937)
PHONE....................714 854-1601
James Mcgee, *Managing Member*
▲ **EMP:** 50 **EST:** 2005
SALES (est): 5.04MM **Privately Held**
Web: www.botanx.com
SIC: 2844 Cosmetic preparations

(P-4386)
BUDS COTTON INC
1240 N Fee Ana St (92807-1817)
P.O. Box 18073 (92817-8073)
PHONE....................714 223-7800
Dewitt Paul, *Ch Bd*
Barry Williams, *Pr*
▲ **EMP:** 26 **EST:** 1991
SQ FT: 30,000
SALES (est): 504.59K **Privately Held**
Web: www.cottonbuds.com
SIC: 2844 Perfumes, cosmetics and other toilet preparations

(P-4387)
CALI CHEM INC
Also Called: Be Beauty
14271 Corporate Dr Ste B (92843-5000)
PHONE....................714 265-3740
Tung Doan, *CEO*
Duc Doan, *
Amy Doan, *
▲ **EMP:** 25 **EST:** 2005
SQ FT: 50,000
SALES (est): 3.86MM **Privately Held**
Web: www.bebeautyproducts.com
SIC: 2844 Face creams or lotions

(P-4388)
CLASSIC COSMETICS INC (PA)
9530 De Soto Ave (91311-5010)
PHONE....................818 773-9042
Ida Csiszar, *CEO*
Steve Csiszar, *
Frank Csiszar, *
▲ **EMP:** 125 **EST:** 1988
SQ FT: 70,000
SALES (est): 20.86MM **Privately Held**
Web: www.classiccosmetics.com
SIC: 2844 Cosmetic preparations

(P-4389)
CLM GROUP INC
20730 Dearborn St (91311-5912)
PHONE....................818 349-2549
Joseph Caputo, *CEO*
EMP: 25 **EST:** 2018
SALES (est): 1.02MM **Privately Held**
SIC: 2844 Cosmetic preparations

(P-4390)
COBE CHEMICAL CO INC
Also Called: Cobe Laboratories
1016 S Vail Ave (90640-6020)
PHONE....................877 691-3590
▲ **EMP:** 75
Web: www.cobechem.com
SIC: 2844 5999 5122 Perfumes, cosmetics and other toilet preparations; Cosmetics; Cosmetics, perfumes, and hair products

(P-4391)
COLONIAL ENTERPRISES INC
690 Knox St Ste 200 (90502-1323)
PHONE....................909 822-8700
Louis Navarro, *COO*
EMP: 40 **EST:** 1977
SALES (est): 4.92MM **Privately Held**
SIC: 2844 2087 Shampoos, rinses, conditioners: hair; Powders, drink

(P-4392)
COOLA LLC
Also Called: Coola Suncare
6134 Innovation Way (92009-1728)
PHONE....................760 940-2125
EMP: 56 **EST:** 2004
SALES (est): 11.37MM **Privately Held**
Web: www.coola.com
SIC: 2844 5722 Suntan lotions and oils; Suntanning equipment and supplies

(P-4393)
COSMETIC ENTERPRISES LTD
12848 Pierce St (91331-2524)
PHONE....................818 896-5355
Richard Saute, *Pr*
Arda Saute, *Treas*
▲ **EMP:** 19 **EST:** 1980
SQ FT: 65,000
SALES (est): 5.27MM **Privately Held**
Web: www.cosmeticent.com
SIC: 2844 Hair preparations, including shampoos

(P-4394)
COSMETIC GROUP USA INC
12708 Branford St (91331-4203)
PHONE....................818 767-2889
Andrea Chuchvara, *CEO*
Judy Zegarelli, *
▼ **EMP:** 180 **EST:** 1984
SQ FT: 80,000
SALES (est): 47.46MM **Privately Held**
Web: www.cosmeticgroupusa.com
SIC: 2844 Cosmetic preparations

(P-4395)
COSMETIC TECHNOLOGIES LLC
2585 Azurite Cir (91320-1202)
PHONE....................805 376-9960
▲ **EMP:** 60
Web: www.cosmetictechnologies.com
SIC: 2844 Cosmetic preparations

(P-4396)
COSMO INTERNATIONAL CORP
Also Called: Cosmo International Fragrances
9200 W Sunset Blvd Ste 401 (90069-3502)
PHONE....................310 271-1100
Axel Van Liempt, *Brnch Mgr*
EMP: 63
SALES (corp-wide): 47.19MM **Privately Held**
Web: www.cosmo-fragrances.com
SIC: 2844 Perfumes, natural or synthetic
PA: Cosmo International Corp
1341 W Newport Center Dr
Deerfield Beach FL
954 798-4500

(P-4397)
COSRICH GROUP INC
12243 Branford St (91352-1010)
PHONE....................818 686-2500
EMP: 35
SALES (corp-wide): 1.71B **Privately Held**
Web: www.ouchiesonline.com
SIC: 2844 Perfumes, cosmetics and other toilet preparations

▲ = Import ▼ = Export
◆ = Import/Export

HQ: Cosrich Group, Inc.
51 La France Ave 55
Bloomfield NJ
866 771-7473

(P-4398)

COSWAY COMPANY INC (PA)
20633 S Fordyce Ave (90810-1019)
PHONE................................310 900-4100
Richard L Hough, *CEO*
▲ **EMP:** 20 **EST:** 1963
SALES (est): 67.33MM
SALES (corp-wide): 67.33MM **Privately Held**
Web: www.cosway.com
SIC: 2844 Face creams or lotions

(P-4399)

DAVIDS NATURAL TOOTHPASTE INC
33360 Zeiders Rd Ste 106 (92584-1408)
PHONE................................949 933-1185
Eric Buss, *CEO*
Eric Buss, *Pr*
EMP: 20 **EST:** 2015
SALES (est): 1.38MM **Privately Held**
Web: www.davids-usa.com
SIC: 2844 Toothpastes or powders, dentifrices

(P-4400)

DEN-MAT CORPORATION (DH)
236 S Bdwy (93455-4605)
PHONE................................805 922-8491
Robert L Ibsen, *CEO*
Noreen Freitas, *
▲ **EMP:** 500 **EST:** 1972
SQ FT: 2,500
SALES (est): 95.51MM
SALES (corp-wide): 167.38MM **Privately Held**
Web: www.denmat.com
SIC: 2844 3843 Toothpastes or powders, dentifrices; Dental materials
HQ: Den-Mat Holdings, Llc
1017 W Central Ave
Lompoc CA

(P-4401)

DEN-MAT CORPORATION
21515 Vanowen St Ste 200 (91303-2715)
PHONE................................800 445-0345
Robert Brennis, *Mgr*
EMP: 179
SALES (corp-wide): 167.38MM **Privately Held**
Web: www.denmat.com
SIC: 2844 Toothpastes or powders, dentifrices
HQ: Den-Mat Corporation
236 S Broadway St
Orcutt CA
805 922-8491

(P-4402)

DERMALOGICA LLC (HQ)
Also Called: Dermal Group, The
1535 Beachey Pl (90746-4005)
PHONE................................310 900-4000
Aurelian Lis, *Pr*
Jane Wurwand, *
◆ **EMP:** 150 **EST:** 1983
SQ FT: 52,000
SALES (est): 125.33MM
SALES (corp-wide): 62.39B **Privately Held**
Web: www.dermalogica.com
SIC: 2844 Cosmetic preparations
PA: Unilever Plc
Unilever House
London
207 572-1202

(P-4403)

DIAMOND WIPES INTL INC
320 Clary Ave (91776-1306)
PHONE................................626 309-0033
EMP: 62
SALES (corp-wide): 51.1MM **Privately Held**
Web: www.diamondwipes.com
SIC: 2844 Towelettes, premoistened
PA: Diamond Wipes International, Inc.
4651 Schaefer Ave
Chino CA
909 230-9888

(P-4404)

DIAMOND WIPES INTL INC
4200 E Mission Blvd (91761-2952)
PHONE................................909 230-9888
EMP: 62
SALES (corp-wide): 51.1MM **Privately Held**
Web: www.diamondwipes.com
SIC: 2844 Towelettes, premoistened
PA: Diamond Wipes International, Inc.
4651 Schaefer Ave
Chino CA
909 230-9888

(P-4405)

DIAMOND WIPES INTL INC
13775 Ramona Ave (91710-5405)
PHONE................................909 230-9888
EMP: 31
SALES (corp-wide): 51.1MM **Privately Held**
Web: www.diamondwipes.com
SIC: 2844 Towelettes, premoistened
PA: Diamond Wipes International, Inc.
4651 Schaefer Ave
Chino CA
909 230-9888

(P-4406)

DIAMOND WIPES INTL INC (PA)
Also Called: Diamond Wipes
4651 Schaefer Ave (91710-5542)
PHONE................................909 230-9888
Steve Gallo, *CEO*
Jessica Lum, *Pr*
Vivian Kul, *VP*
Neville Kadimi, *CFO*
▲ **EMP:** 95 **EST:** 1994
SALES (est): 51.1MM
SALES (corp-wide): 51.1MM **Privately Held**
Web: www.diamondwipes.com
SIC: 2844 Towelettes, premoistened

(P-4407)

DR SQUATCH LLC
4065 Glencoe Ave Apt 300b (90292-6079)
PHONE................................631 229-7068
Josh Friedman, *Pr*
Daniel Larson, *CFO*
EMP: 250 **EST:** 2013
SALES (est): 72.08MM **Privately Held**
Web: www.drsquatch.com
SIC: 2844 7389 Perfumes, cosmetics and other toilet preparations; Business services, nec

(P-4408)

EDEN BEAUTY CONCEPTS INC
Also Called: Eufora
5876 Owens Ave Ste 200 (92008-5519)
PHONE................................760 330-9941
Donald Bewley, *CEO*
Don Bewley, *CEO*
▲ **EMP:** 20 **EST:** 1994
SALES (est): 8.47MM **Privately Held**

Web: www.eufora.net
SIC: 2844 5087 Shampoos, rinses, conditioners: hair; Beauty salon and barber shop equipment and supplies

(P-4409)

EVERBRANDS INC
401 N Oak St (90302-3314)
PHONE................................855 595-2999
Michael Florman, *CEO*
Joshua Wallace, *
EMP: 45 **EST:** 2013
SQ FT: 6,000
SALES (est): 5.99MM **Privately Held**
Web: www.eversmilewhite.com
SIC: 2844 Oral preparations

(P-4410)

FNC MEDICAL CORPORATION
Also Called: Show Off Time
6000 Leland St (93003-7605)
PHONE................................805 644-7576
Samuel S Pattillo, *Pr*
Samuel Pattillo, *
Synora Pattillo, *VP*
EMP: 20 **EST:** 1992
SQ FT: 36,000
SALES (est): 2.41MM **Privately Held**
Web: www.3dcartstores.com
SIC: 2844 Cosmetic preparations

(P-4411)

FORMOLOGY LAB INC
9174 Deering Ave (91311-5801)
PHONE................................424 452-0377
Oren Ezra, *CEO*
EMP: 20 **EST:** 2017
SALES (est): 1.01MM **Privately Held**
Web: www.formologylab.com
SIC: 2844 Perfumes, cosmetics and other toilet preparations

(P-4412)

GAR LABORATORIES INC
1844 Massachusetts Ave (92507)
PHONE................................951 788-0700
▲ **EMP:** 110 **EST:** 1978
SALES (est): 22.48MM **Privately Held**
Web: www.garlabs.com
SIC: 2844 Perfumes, cosmetics and other toilet preparations

(P-4413)

GIOVANNI COSMETICS INC
Also Called: Giovanni Hair Care & Cosmetics
2064 E University Dr (90220-6419)
P.O. Box 6990 (90212-6990)
PHONE................................310 952-9960
Giovanni J Guidotti, *CEO*
Arthur Guidotti, *
◆ **EMP:** 56 **EST:** 1979
SALES (est): 11.54MM **Privately Held**
Web: www.giovannicosmetics.com
SIC: 2844 5122 5999 Cosmetic preparations ; Cosmetics, perfumes, and hair products; Cosmetics

(P-4414)

GLAM AND GLITS NAIL DESIGN INC
Also Called: Kiara Sky Professional Nails
8700 Swigert Ct Unit 209 (93311-9696)
PHONE................................661 393-4800
Khoa Duong, *CEO*
▲ **EMP:** 65 **EST:** 2013
SALES (est): 7.35MM **Privately Held**
Web: www.glamandglits.com
SIC: 2844 Manicure preparations

(P-4415)

GLOBAL SALES INC
Also Called: Aniise Skin Care
1732 Westwood Blvd (90024-5608)
PHONE................................310 474-7700
Sheida Kimiabakhsh, *CEO*
Sharareh Kimiabakhsh, *VP*
▲ **EMP:** 25 **EST:** 2011
SALES (est): 1.4MM **Privately Held**
Web: www.aniise.com
SIC: 2844 5999 Hair preparations, including shampoos; Toiletries, cosmetics, and perfumes

(P-4416)

GRAHAM WEBB INTERNATIONAL INC (HQ)
6109 De Soto Ave (91367-3709)
PHONE................................760 918-3600
Rick Kornbluth, *Pr*
Thomas P Baumann, *VP*
EMP: 70 **EST:** 1989
SQ FT: 30,000
SALES (est): 44.43MM **Publicly Held**
SIC: 2844 Hair preparations, including shampoos
PA: Coty Inc.
350 5th Ave Ste 2700
New York NY

(P-4417)

GSCM VENTURES INC
Also Called: Pacific Naturals
12924 Pierce St (91331-2526)
PHONE................................818 303-2600
Gary Mcnelley, *Pr*
Gary Neeley, *
David Rivero, *
▼ **EMP:** 25 **EST:** 2002
SQ FT: 5,000
SALES (est): 684.75K **Privately Held**
SIC: 2844 Toilet preparations

(P-4418)

HAIN CELESTIAL GROUP INC
Also Called: Jason's Natural
5630 Rickenbacker Rd (90201-6412)
PHONE................................323 859-0553
David Vazquez, *Brnch Mgr*
EMP: 150
Web: www.hain.com
SIC: 2844 Perfumes, cosmetics and other toilet preparations
PA: The Hain Celestial Group Inc
221 River St Ste 12
Hoboken NJ

(P-4419)

HENKEL US OPERATIONS CORP
Joico Laboratories Division
5800 Bristol Pkwy (90230-6696)
PHONE................................626 321-4100
Annie Hu, *Brnch Mgr*
EMP: 29
SALES (corp-wide): 23.26B **Privately Held**
Web: www.henkel.com
SIC: 2844 Hair preparations, including shampoos
HQ: Henkel Us Operations Corporation
1 Henkel Way
Rocky Hill CT
860 571-5100

(P-4420)

HENKEL US OPERATIONS CORP
12155 Paine Pl (92064-7154)
PHONE................................203 655-8911
Tracy Henslin, *Brnch Mgr*
EMP: 46
SALES (corp-wide): 23.26B **Privately Held**

Web: www.henkel.com
SIC: **2844** Hair preparations, including
  shampoos
HQ: Henkel Us Operations Corporation
  1 Henkel Way
  Rocky Hill CT
  860 571-5100

(P-4421)
IBG HOLDINGS INC
24841 Avenue Tibbitts (91355-3405)
PHONE...............................661 702-8680
Richard Mayne, *Pr*
Marissa Pomerantz, *VP*
▲ **EMP:** 20 **EST:** 2002
SQ FT: 5,000
SALES (est): 1.77MM **Privately Held**
Web: www.colorevolution.com
SIC: **2844** Cosmetic preparations

(P-4422)
**INNOVATIVE BIOSCIENCES
CORP**
Also Called: Innovative Body Science
1849 Diamond St (92078-5127)
PHONE...............................760 603-0772
Michelle Barton, *Pr*
▲ **EMP:** 20 **EST:** 1987
SQ FT: 16,000
SALES (est): 4.92MM **Privately Held**
Web: www.innovativebodyscience.com
SIC: **2844** Perfumes, cosmetics and
  other toilet preparations; Management
  consulting services

(P-4423)
INSPARATION INC
Also Called: Brian Guy Electric Ltg Svcs Co
11950 Hertz Ave (93021-7145)
PHONE...............................805 553-0820
Lori Guy, *CEO*
EMP: 38 **EST:** 1987
SALES (est): 4.55MM **Privately Held**
Web: www.insparation.com
SIC: **2844** Cosmetic preparations

(P-4424)
**JOHNSON & JOHNSON
CONSUMER INC**
Also Called: Neutrogena
5760 W 96th St (90045-5544)
PHONE...............................310 642-1150
EMP: 72
SALES (corp-wide): 94.94B **Publicly Held**
Web: www.kenvue.com
SIC: **2844** Perfumes, cosmetics and other
  toilet preparations
HQ: Johnson & Johnson Consumer Inc.
  199 Grandview Rd
  Skillman NJ
  908 874-1000

(P-4425)
JOICO LABORATORIES INC
5800 Bristol Pkwy (90230-6696)
PHONE...............................626 321-4100
Sara Jones, *Pr*
Akira Mochizuki, *
Takahiro Iwabuchi, *
▲ **EMP:** 149 **EST:** 1976
SALES (est): 1.35MM **Privately Held**
Web: www.joico.com
SIC: **2844** Hair preparations, including
  shampoos

(P-4426)
KAMSUT INCORPORATED
Also Called: Kama Sutra
5260 Kazuko Ct (93021-1789)

PHONE...............................805 495-7479
Joseph Bolstad, *Pr*
▲ **EMP:** 20 **EST:** 1968
SALES (est): 2.43MM **Privately Held**
Web: www.kamasutra.com
SIC: **2844** Cosmetic preparations

(P-4427)
**KDC/ONE CHATSWORTH INC
(DH)**
20245 Sunburst St (91311-6219)
PHONE...............................818 709-1345
Nicholas Whitley, *CEO*
EMP: 121 **EST:** 2020
SALES (est): 107.49MM
SALES (corp-wide): 1.7B **Privately Held**
Web: www.kdc-one.com
SIC: **2844** Shampoos, rinses, conditioners:
  hair
HQ: Kdc Us Holdings, Inc.
  4400 S Hamilton Rd
  Groveport OH

(P-4428)
KDC/ONE CHATSWORTH INC
Also Called: Cosmetic Laboratories-America
20320 Prairie St (91311-6026)
PHONE...............................818 709-1345
Nicholas Whitley, *CEO*
EMP: 199
SALES (corp-wide): 1.7B **Privately Held**
Web: www.kdc-one.com
SIC: **2844** Cosmetic preparations
HQ: Kdc/One Chatsworth, Inc.
  20245 Sunburst St
  Chatsworth CA
  818 709-1345

(P-4429)
KIM LAUBE & COMPANY INC
Also Called: Kelco
2221 Statham Blvd (93033-3913)
PHONE...............................805 240-1300
Kim E Laube, *Pr*
▲ **EMP:** 40 **EST:** 1982
SALES (est): 4.2MM **Privately Held**
Web: www.laubeshop.com
SIC: **2844** **3999** Hair preparations, including
  shampoos; Hair clippers for human use,
  hand and electric

(P-4430)
KUM KANG TRADING USA INC
Also Called: Black N Gold
6433 Alondra Blvd (90723-3758)
PHONE...............................562 531-6111
Yoon Oh, *Pr*
◆ **EMP:** 25 **EST:** 1987
SQ FT: 20,000
SALES (est): 2.11MM **Privately Held**
SIC: **2844** Hair preparations, including
  shampoos

(P-4431)
**LANZA RESEARCH
INTERNATIONAL**
429 Santa Monica Blvd Ste 510
(90401-3401)
PHONE...............................310 393-5227
Robert De Lanza, *Pr*
Dana Story, *
Jo-ann Stamp, *Sec*
EMP: 25 **EST:** 1983
SQ FT: 40,000
SALES (est): 1.21MM **Privately Held**
Web: www.lanza.com
SIC: **2844** **5122** Shampoos, rinses,
  conditioners: hair; Cosmetics

(P-4432)
LEE PHARMACEUTICALS
1434 Santa Anita Ave (91733-3312)
PHONE...............................626 442-3141
Ronald G Lee, *CEO*
Mike Agresti, *
▲ **EMP:** 82 **EST:** 1971
SALES (est): 9.9MM **Privately Held**
Web: www.leepharmaceuticals.com
SIC: **2844** **2834** **3843** Manicure preparations
  ; Pharmaceutical preparations; Enamels,
  dentists'

(P-4433)
MASTEY DE PARIS INC
24841 Avenue Tibbitts (91355-1269)
PHONE...............................661 257-4814
Stephen Mastey, *Pr*
Lesley Mastey, *
Henri Mastey, *
EMP: 50 **EST:** 1976
SALES (est): 4.51MM **Privately Held**
Web: www.mastey.com
SIC: **2844** Hair preparations, including
  shampoos

(P-4434)
MELISSA TRINIDAD
Also Called: Paisleyriversoapco
3589 Vine St (93446-1014)
PHONE...............................805 536-0954
Melissa Trinidad, *Owner*
EMP: 21 **EST:** 2021
SALES (est): 882.06K **Privately Held**
SIC: **2844** Bath salts

(P-4435)
**MERLE NORMAN COSMETICS
INC (PA)**
Also Called: Merle Norman Cosmetics
9130 Bellanca Ave (90045-4772)
PHONE...............................310 641-3000
Jack B Nethercutt, *Ch Bd*
Amy Hackbart, *
Michael Cassidy, *
Helen Nethercutt, *
Rick Rosa, *
▲ **EMP:** 345 **EST:** 1974
SQ FT: 354,000
SALES (est): 64MM
SALES (corp-wide): 64MM **Privately Held**
Web: www.merlenorman.com
SIC: **2844** **5999** Cosmetic preparations;
  Cosmetics

(P-4436)
**NATURAL THOUGHTS
INCORPORATED**
Also Called: Biotone Professional Products
4757 Old Cliffs Rd (92120-1134)
PHONE...............................619 582-0027
▲ **EMP:** 38 **EST:** 1978
SALES (est): 7.21MM **Privately Held**
Web: www.biotone.com
SIC: **2844** **5122** Cosmetic preparations;
  Drugs, proprietaries, and sundries

(P-4437)
NEUTRADERM INC
20660 Nordhoff St (91311-6114)
PHONE...............................818 534-3190
Samuel D Raoof, *CEO*
Toora J Raoof, *
▲ **EMP:** 25 **EST:** 2003
SALES (est): 9.83MM **Privately Held**
Web: www.neutraderm.com
SIC: **2844** Cosmetic preparations

(P-4438)
NYX LOS ANGELES INC
Also Called: Nyx Cosmetics
588 Crenshaw Blvd (90503-1705)
PHONE...............................323 869-9420
◆ **EMP:** 140
SIC: **2844** **5122** Perfumes, cosmetics and
  other toilet preparations; Cosmetics

(P-4439)
O P I PRODUCTS INC (HQ)
13034 Saticoy St (91605-3510)
PHONE...............................818 759-8688
Jules Kaufman, *CEO*
John Heffner, *
Susan Weiss-fischmann, *Ex VP*
Eric Schwartz, *
William Halfacre, *Executive Sales &
Marketing Vice President*
◆ **EMP:** 500 **EST:** 1981
SQ FT: 250,000
SALES (est): 93.34MM **Publicly Held**
Web: www.opi.com
SIC: **2844** Perfumes, cosmetics and other
  toilet preparations
PA: Coty Inc.
  350 5th Ave Ste 2700
  New York NY

(P-4440)
ORLY INTERNATIONAL INC (PA)
Also Called: Sparitual
7710 Haskell Ave (91406-1905)
PHONE...............................818 994-1001
Jeff Pink, *Pr*
◆ **EMP:** 99 **EST:** 1977
SQ FT: 65,000
SALES (est): 24.77MM
SALES (corp-wide): 24.77MM **Privately
Held**
Web: www.orlybeauty.com
SIC: **2844** Cosmetic preparations

(P-4441)
OYEWAN INC
20501 Earlgate St (91789-2909)
PHONE...............................909 869-6200
Nick Whitley, *CEO*
▲ **EMP:** 20 **EST:** 2007
SALES (est): 6.95MM
SALES (corp-wide): 1.7B **Privately Held**
Web: www.vmlcosmetics.com
SIC: **2844** Cosmetic preparations
PA: Corporation Developpement Knowlton
  Inc.
  375 Boul Roland-Therrien Suite 210
  Longueuil QC
  450 243-2000

(P-4442)
**PACIFIC WORLD CORPORATION
(PA)**
100 Technology Dr Ste 200 (92618-2466)
PHONE...............................949 598-2400
William George, *CEO*
Stuart Noyes, *
Bart Dibie, *
Justin Martini, *
Bob Nabholz, *
◆ **EMP:** 99 **EST:** 1947
SALES (est): 21.42MM
SALES (corp-wide): 21.42MM **Privately
Held**
Web: www.pacificworldcorp.com
SIC: **2844** **3421** **3999** **5199** Cosmetic
  preparations; Clippers, fingernail and toenail
  ; Fingernails, artificial; General
  merchandise, non-durable

(P-4443)
PERSON & COVEY INC
616 Allen Ave (91201-2014)
P.O. Box 25018 (91221-5018)
PHONE................................818 937-5000
Lorne Person Junior, *CEO*
Lorne Person Senior, *Ch Bd*
Sue Person, *
EMP: 45 **EST:** 1941
SQ FT: 36,000
SALES (est): 9.42MM **Privately Held**
Web: www.personandcovey.com
SIC: 2844 2834 Cosmetic preparations;
Dermatologicals

(P-4444)
**PHYSICIANS FORMULA INC
(DH)**
22067 Ferrero (91789-5214)
PHONE................................626 334-3395
Ingrid Jackel, *CEO*
Jeff Rogers, *
Rick Kirchhoff, *
Joseph J Jaeger, *
Richard John Almeida External Reporting,
Mgr
▲ **EMP:** 57 **EST:** 1980
SQ FT: 82,800
SALES (est): 22.27MM
SALES (corp-wide): 270.93MM **Privately
Held**
Web: www.physiciansformula.com
SIC: 2844 Cosmetic preparations
HQ: Physicians Formula Holdings, Inc.
22067 Ferrero
Walnut CA

(P-4445)
**PHYSICIANS FORMULA COSMT
INC**
22067 Ferrero (91789-5214)
PHONE................................626 334-3395
Jeffrey P Rogers, *Pr*
Joseph J Jaeger, *CFO*
EMP: 70 **EST:** 1937
SALES (est): 2.47MM
SALES (corp-wide): 270.93MM **Privately
Held**
Web: www.physiciansformula.com
SIC: 2844 Cosmetic preparations
HQ: Physicians Formula, Inc.
22067 Ferrero
City Of Industry CA
626 334-3395

(P-4446)
PLZ CORP
2321 3rd St (92507-3306)
PHONE................................951 683-2912
Ian Sishman, *Mgr*
EMP: 69
SALES (corp-wide): 766.3MM **Privately
Held**
Web: www.plzcorp.com
SIC: 2844 5122 5087 Cosmetic preparations
; Cosmetics, perfumes, and hair products;
Beauty parlor equipment and supplies
PA: Plz Corp.
2651 Wrrnvlle Rd Stre 300 300 Stre
Downers Grove IL
630 628-3000

(P-4447)
PLZ CORP
2375 3rd St (92507-3306)
PHONE................................951 683-2912
Marcelo Jimenez, *Brnch Mgr*
EMP: 126
SALES (corp-wide): 766.3MM **Privately
Held**

Web: www.plzcorp.com
SIC: 2844 Cosmetic preparations
PA: Plz Corp.
2651 Wrrnvlle Rd Stre 300 300 Stre
Downers Grove IL
630 628-3000

(P-4448)
PLZ CORP
14425 Yorba Ave (91710-5733)
PHONE................................909 393-9475
Mikel Pruett, *Brnch Mgr*
EMP: 64
SALES (corp-wide): 766.3MM **Privately
Held**
Web: www.plzcorp.com
SIC: 2844 Cosmetic preparations
PA: Plz Corp.
2651 Wrrnvlle Rd Stre 300 300 Stre
Downers Grove IL
630 628-3000

(P-4449)
PROLABS FACTORY INC
15001 Oxnard St (91411-2613)
P.O. Box 492419 (90049-8419)
PHONE................................818 646-3677
EMP: 26 **EST:** 2020
SALES (est): 1.1MM **Privately Held**
SIC: 2844 Cosmetic preparations

(P-4450)
**RADIANCE BEAUTY &
WELLNESS INC**
9016 Fullbright Ave (91311-6125)
PHONE................................818 812-9740
Debra Q Saavedra, *CFO*
Hugo Saavedra, *CEO*
EMP: 22 **EST:** 2021
SALES (est): 2.08MM **Privately Held**
SIC: 2844 Perfumes, cosmetics and other
toilet preparations

(P-4451)
REVLON INC
Creative Nail Design
1125 Joshua Way Ste 12 (92081-7840)
PHONE................................619 372-1379
Jim Northstrum, *Brnch Mgr*
EMP: 74
Web: www.revloncorp.com
SIC: 2844 Cosmetic preparations
HQ: Revlon, Inc.
55 Water St Fl 43
New York NY

(P-4452)
SAMUEL RAOOF
Also Called: Brandmd Skin Care
20660 Nordhoff St (91311-6114)
PHONE................................818 534-3180
Samuel Raoof, *Owner*
EMP: 32 **EST:** 2014
SALES (est): 334.98K **Privately Held**
Web: www.brandmd.com
SIC: 2844 Deodorants, personal

(P-4453)
SEPHORA CO LLC (PA)
6103 Obispo Ave (90805-3799)
PHONE................................760 798-7654
Oscar Sadegi, *Managing Member*
◆ **EMP:** 20 **EST:** 2003
SQ FT: 20,000
SALES (est): 3.08MM
SALES (corp-wide): 3.08MM **Privately
Held**
SIC: 2844 Cosmetic preparations

(P-4454)
SHADOW HOLDINGS LLC
Also Called: Bocchi Laboratories
26421 Ruether Ave (91350-2621)
PHONE................................661 252-3807
Robert J Bocchi, *Managing Member*
EMP: 205
SQ FT: 86,200
SALES (corp-wide): 249.82MM **Privately
Held**
Web: www.brightinnovationlabs.com
SIC: 2844 Perfumes, cosmetics and other
toilet preparations
HQ: Shadow Holdings, Llc
26455 Ruether Ave
Santa Clarita CA
661 252-3807

(P-4455)
SHADOW HOLDINGS LLC (HQ)
Also Called: Bocchi Laboratories
26455 Ruether Ave (91350-2621)
PHONE................................661 252-3807
Ed Gotch, *Managing Member*
Wayne Byrne, *Managing Member*
EMP: 295 **EST:** 2007
SQ FT: 88,500
SALES (est): 105.71MM
SALES (corp-wide): 249.82MM **Privately
Held**
Web: www.brightinnovationlabs.com
SIC: 2844 Perfumes, cosmetics and other
toilet preparations
PA: Bright Holdco, Llc
9002 Smiths Mill Rd
New Albany OH
614 741-7458

(P-4456)
SHANI DARDEN SKINCARE INC
1800 Century Park E Ste 400 (90067-1501)
PHONE................................310 745-3150
Jessica Goldin, *CEO*
EMP: 21 **EST:** 2016
SALES (est): 2.37MM **Privately Held**
Web: www.shanidarden.com
SIC: 2844 5122 5961 Perfumes, cosmetics
and other toilet preparations; Cosmetics,
perfumes, and hair products; Cosmetics
and perfumes, mail order

(P-4457)
SPATZ CORPORATION
Also Called: Spatz Laboratories
1600 Westar Dr (93033-2423)
PHONE................................805 487-2122
Joel Lynn Nelson, *CEO*
Laura Nelson, *
George Jefferson, *
John Nelson, *
▲ **EMP:** 145 **EST:** 1954
SQ FT: 62,000
SALES (est): 44.34MM **Privately Held**
Web: www.spatzlabs.com
SIC: 2844 3089 Cosmetic preparations;
Plastics containers, except foam

(P-4458)
STEARNS CORPORATION
Also Called: Derma E
2280 Ward Ave Ste 100 (93065-2075)
PHONE................................805 582-2710
Brenda Wu, *Pr*
Linda Miles, *
Barbara Roll, *
▲ **EMP:** 25 **EST:** 1981
SALES (est): 4.69MM **Privately Held**
Web: www.dermae.com
SIC: 2844 Face creams or lotions
PA: Topix Pharmaceuticals Inc.
174 Route 109 Ste 2

West Babylon NY

(P-4459)
SUMMER FRIDAYS LLC
9180 Wilshire Blvd (90212-3414)
PHONE................................612 804-0868
EMP: 21 **EST:** 2017
SALES (est): 378.48K **Privately Held**
Web: www.summerfridays.com
SIC: 2844 Face creams or lotions

(P-4460)
SUNEVA MEDICAL INC (PA)
5870 Pacific Center Blvd (92121-4204)
PHONE................................858 550-9999
Patricia Altavilla, *CEO*
Joseph A Newcomb, *
Stewart M Brown, *
Nicola Selley, *
Brian Pilcher, *CSO*
EMP: 42 **EST:** 2009
SALES (est): 15.41MM
SALES (corp-wide): 15.41MM **Privately
Held**
Web: www.sunevamedical.com
SIC: 2844 3842 Cosmetic preparations;
Cosmetic restorations

(P-4461)
TRADEMARK COSMETICS INC
545 Columbia Ave (92507-2183)
PHONE................................951 683-2631
David Ryngler, *CEO*
Eko Handoko, *
Joy Boiani, *
▲ **EMP:** 38 **EST:** 1994
SQ FT: 38,000
SALES (est): 8.13MM **Privately Held**
Web: www.trademarkcosmetics.com
SIC: 2844 7231 5999 5122 Hair
preparations, including shampoos; Beauty
shops; Cosmetics; Cosmetics

(P-4462)
TU-K INDUSTRIES INC
5702 Firestone Pl (90280-3714)
PHONE................................562 927-3365
Arman Cornell, *Prin*
Alpin K Kaler, *
Eleanor Kaler, *
▲ **EMP:** 50 **EST:** 1970
SQ FT: 40,000
SALES (est): 5.45MM **Privately Held**
Web: www.tukindusries.com
SIC: 2844 Cosmetic preparations

(P-4463)
**TWILA TRUE
COLLABORATIONS LLC**
Also Called: Trueclass
27156 Burbank (92610-2503)
PHONE................................949 258-9720
EMP: 20 **EST:** 2018
SALES (est): 1.51MM **Privately Held**
Web: www.twilatruecollaborations.com
SIC: 2844 2389 Perfumes, cosmetics and
other toilet preparations; Men's
miscellaneous accessories

(P-4464)
**UNIVERSAL PACKG SYSTEMS
INC (PA)**
Also Called: Paklab
14570 Monte Vista Ave (91710-5743)
PHONE................................909 517-2442
Jeffery Morlando, *CEO*
Alan Kristel, *COO*
William Wachtel, *Sec*
◆ **EMP:** 750 **EST:** 1987

SALES (est): 379.38MM
SALES (corp-wide): 379.38MM **Privately Held**
Web: www.paklab.com
SIC: 2844 7389 3565 2671 Cosmetic preparations; Packaging and labeling services; Bottling machinery: filling, capping, labeling; Plastic film, coated or laminated for packaging

(P-4465)
USP INC
Also Called: Enjoy Haircare
1818 Ord Way (92056-1502)
PHONE....................760 842-7700
Patrick Dockry, *Prin*
Gordon Fletcher, *
▲ **EMP:** 60 **EST:** 1995
SQ FT: 60,000
SALES (est): 18.03MM **Privately Held**
Web: www.enjoyhaircare.com
SIC: 2844 Hair preparations, including shampoos

(P-4466)
VEGE - KURL INC
Also Called: Vege-Tech Company
412 W Cypress St (91204-2402)
PHONE....................818 956-5582
Eric W Huffman, *Pr*
Helen Huffman, *
EMP: 60 **EST:** 1959
SALES (est): 9.8MM **Privately Held**
Web: www.vegelabs.com
SIC: 2844 2833 5122 Shampoos, rinses, conditioners: hair; Medicinals and botanicals ; Cosmetics, perfumes, and hair products

(P-4467)
WELLA CORPORATION (HQ)
4500 Park Granada # 100 (91302-1665)
PHONE....................800 422-2336
◆ **EMP:** 250 **EST:** 1935
SALES (est): 1.44B **Publicly Held**
Web: us.wella.professionalstore.com
SIC: 2844 Toilet preparations
PA: Kkr & Co. Inc.
30 Hudson Yards
New York NY

(P-4468)
WESTRIDGE LABORATORIES INC
1671 E Saint Andrew Pl (92705-4932)
PHONE....................714 259-9400
Gregg Richard Haskell, *CEO*
John Speelman, *
▲ **EMP:** 28 **EST:** 1993
SALES (est): 5.18MM **Privately Held**
Web: www.idlube.com
SIC: 2844 Cosmetic preparations

(P-4469)
WESTWOOD LABORATORIES LLC (PA)
710 S Ayon Ave (91702-5123)
PHONE....................626 969-3305
Paul Schirmer, *CEO*
Brian Surpia Ctrl, *Prin*
▲ **EMP:** 47 **EST:** 2004
SALES (est): 9.58MM **Privately Held**
Web: www.westwoodlabs.com
SIC: 2844 Perfumes, cosmetics and other toilet preparations

(P-4470)
YG LABORATORIES INC
Also Called: Youthglow
11520 Warner Ave (92708-2512)
PHONE....................714 474-2800
EMP: 28 **EST:** 1977
SALES (est): 4.05MM **Privately Held**
Web: www.yglabs.com
SIC: 2844 Cosmetic preparations

(P-4471)
YOUTH TO PEOPLE INC
888 N Douglas St (90245-2839)
PHONE....................309 648-5500
Joseph Cloyes, *CEO*
Greg Gonzalez, *
EMP: 95 **EST:** 2018
SALES (est): 7.29MM
SALES (corp-wide): 5.95B **Privately Held**
Web: www.youthtothepeople.com
SIC: 2844 Lotions, shaving
PA: L'oreal
Mugler Beaute
Paris
140206000

(P-4472)
ZO SKIN HEALTH INC (DH)
9685 Research Dr (92618-4657)
PHONE....................949 988-7524
Mark Williams, *CEO*
Kevin Cornett, *
▲ **EMP:** 80 **EST:** 2006
SQ FT: 12,000
SALES (est): 38.31MM
SALES (corp-wide): 8.52B **Publicly Held**
Web: www.zoskinhealth.com
SIC: 2844 Face creams or lotions
HQ: Blackstone Tactical Opportunities Advisors L.L.C.
345 Park Ave
New York NY
212 583-5000

(P-4473)
ZO SKIN HEALTH INC
15375 Barranca Pkwy (92618-2217)
PHONE....................949 988-3153
EMP: 17
SALES (corp-wide): 8.52B **Publicly Held**
Web: www.zoskinhealth.com
SIC: 2844 Face creams or lotions
HQ: Zo Skin Health, Inc.
9685 Research Dr
Irvine CA

2851 Paints And Allied Products

(P-4474)
AMERICA WOOD FINISHES INC
728 E 59th St (90001-1004)
PHONE....................323 232-8256
Manuel Padilla, *Pr*
Elvira Padilla, *Sec*
▲ **EMP:** 20 **EST:** 2002
SALES (est): 904.32K **Privately Held**
SIC: 2851 Paints, waterproof

(P-4475)
BEHR HOLDINGS CORPORATION (HQ)
3400 W Segerstrom Ave (92704-6405)
PHONE....................714 545-7101
EMP: 23 **EST:** 1997
SALES (est): 1.5B
SALES (corp-wide): 8.68B **Publicly Held**
Web: www.behr.com
SIC: 2851 Paints and paint additives
PA: Masco Corporation
17450 College Pkwy
Livonia MI
313 274-7400

(P-4476)
BEHR PROCESS CORPORATION (DH)
Also Called: Behr Paint Company
1801 E Saint Andrew Pl (92705-5044)
PHONE....................714 545-7101
▼ **EMP:** 700 **EST:** 1947
SQ FT: 220,000
SALES (est): 1.5B
SALES (corp-wide): 8.68B **Publicly Held**
Web: www.behr.com
SIC: 2851 Paints and paint additives
HQ: Behr Holdings Corporation
3400 W Segerstrom Ave
Santa Ana CA

(P-4477)
BEHR PROCESS CORPORATION
1603 W Alton Ave (92704-7258)
PHONE....................714 545-7101
Jeffrey D Filley, *Brnch Mgr*
EMP: 18
SQ FT: 54,819
SALES (corp-wide): 8.68B **Publicly Held**
Web: www.behr.com
SIC: 2851 Paints and paint additives
HQ: Behr Process Corporation
1801 E Saint Andrew Pl
Santa Ana CA

(P-4478)
BEHR PROCESS CORPORATION
3400 W Garry Ave (92704-6421)
PHONE....................714 545-7101
EMP: 17
SALES (corp-wide): 8.68B **Publicly Held**
Web: www.behr.com
SIC: 2851 Paints and paint additives
HQ: Behr Process Corporation
1801 E Saint Andrew Pl
Santa Ana CA

(P-4479)
BEHR PROCESS CORPORATION
3130 S Harbor Blvd Ste 520 (92704-6820)
PHONE....................714 545-7101
EMP: 20
SALES (corp-wide): 8.68B **Publicly Held**
Web: www.behr.com
SIC: 2851 Paints and paint additives
HQ: Behr Process Corporation
1801 E Saint Andrew Pl
Santa Ana CA

(P-4480)
BEHR PROCESS CORPORATION
3500 W Segerstrom Ave (92704-6406)
PHONE....................714 545-7101
EMP: 18
SALES (corp-wide): 8.68B **Publicly Held**
Web: www.behr.com
SIC: 2851 Paints and paint additives
HQ: Behr Process Corporation
1801 E Saint Andrew Pl
Santa Ana CA

(P-4481)
BEHR SALES INC (HQ)
Also Called: Behr Paint Corp.
3400 W Segerstrom Ave (92704-6405)
PHONE....................714 545-7101
Jeffrey D Filley, *CEO*
Jonathan M Sullivan, *
Anthony Demiro, *
EMP: 169 **EST:** 1948
SQ FT: 54,000
SALES (est): 531.5MM
SALES (corp-wide): 8.68B **Publicly Held**
Web: www.behr.com

SIC: 2851 Paints and paint additives
PA: Masco Corporation
17450 College Pkwy
Livonia MI
313 274-7400

(P-4482)
CARDINAL INDUSTRIAL FINISHES (PA)
1329 Potrero Ave Ca (91733-3088)
P.O. Box 9296 (91733-0965)
PHONE....................626 444-9274
Lawrence C Felix, *CEO*
◆ **EMP:** 100 **EST:** 1952
SQ FT: 50,000
SALES (est): 24.84MM
SALES (corp-wide): 24.84MM **Privately Held**
Web: www.cardinalpaint.com
SIC: 2851 Lacquers, varnishes, enamels, and other coatings

(P-4483)
CARDINAL PAINT AND POWDER INC
1329 Potrero Ave (91733-3012)
PHONE....................626 444-9274
EMP: 59 **EST:** 2016
SALES (est): 5.99MM **Privately Held**
Web: www.cardinalpaint.com
SIC: 2851 Paints and allied products

(P-4484)
CARDINAL PAINT AND POWDER INC
15010 Don Julian Rd (91746-3301)
PHONE....................626 937-6767
Stanley W Ekstrom, *Brnch Mgr*
EMP: 143
SALES (corp-wide): 99.3MM **Privately Held**
Web: www.cardinalpaint.com
SIC: 2851 Paints and allied products
PA: Cardinal Paint And Powder, Inc.
1900 Aerojet Way
North Las Vegas NV
702 852-2333

(P-4485)
CONSOLIDATED COLOR CORPORATION
12316 Carson St (90716-1604)
PHONE....................562 420-7714
Michael J Muldown, *Pr*
Deborah Muldown, *
EMP: 25 **EST:** 1993
SQ FT: 30,000
SALES (est): 2.68MM **Privately Held**
Web: www.consolidatedcolorcorp.com
SIC: 2851 2865 Paints and paint additives; Cyclic crudes and intermediates

(P-4486)
DURA TECHNOLOGIES INC
2720 S Willow Ave Ste A (92316-3259)
P.O. Box 333 (92316-0333)
PHONE....................909 877-8477
Douglas L Dennis, *Pr*
Gina L Dennis, *
▲ **EMP:** 150 **EST:** 1977
SQ FT: 14,000
SALES (est): 8.35MM **Privately Held**
SIC: 2851 Paints and allied products

(P-4487)
ENGINEERED COATING TECH INC
2838 E 54th St (90058-3632)

PHONE.....................323 588-0260
Gloria Navarro, *Pr*
EMP: 26 **EST:** 1984
SQ FT: 17,000
SALES (est): 1.12MM **Privately Held**
SIC: 2851 Paints and allied products

(P-4488)
ENNIS TRAFFIC SAFETY SOLUTIONS
Also Called: Colorama Paints
6624 Stanford Ave (90001-1538)
P.O. Box 1496 (90001-0496)
PHONE.....................323 758-1147
EMP: 48
SIC: 2851 Paints and allied products

(P-4489)
EPMAR CORPORATION
9930 Painter Ave (90605-2759)
PHONE.....................562 946-8781
Peter Weissman, *Pr*
Joe Matrange, *
◆ **EMP:** 38 **EST:** 1980
SQ FT: 26,000
SALES (est): 13.69MM
SALES (corp-wide): 1.94B **Publicly Held**
Web: www.epmar.com
SIC: 2851 2891 2821 3087 Epoxy coatings;
Adhesives and sealants; Plastics materials
and resins; Custom compound purchased
resins
PA: Quaker Chemical Corporation
901 E Hector St
Conshohocken PA
610 832-4000

(P-4490)
FRAZEE INDUSTRIES INC
Also Called: Frazee Paint & Wallcovering
6625 Miramar Rd (92121-2508)
PHONE.....................858 626-3600
EMP: 900
Web: www.sherwin-williams.com
SIC: 2851 5198 5231 Paints, waterproof;
Paints; Paint

(P-4491)
FSI COATING TECHNOLOGIES INC
45 Parker Ste 100 (92618-1658)
PHONE.....................949 540-1140
Antonios Grigoriou, *Pr*
Richard Chang, *CFO*
EMP: 24 **EST:** 1986
SALES (est): 2.46MM **Privately Held**
Web: www.fsicti.com
SIC: 2851 Lacquers, varnishes, enamels,
and other coatings
HQ: Sdc Technologies, Inc.
45 Parker Ste 100
Irvine CA
714 939-8300

(P-4492)
LAIRD COATINGS CORPORATION
Also Called: Coatings Resource
15541 Commerce Ln (92649-1601)
PHONE.....................714 894-5252
Jeff Laird, *CEO*
▲ **EMP:** 51 **EST:** 1976
SQ FT: 17,500
SALES (est): 10.61MM **Privately Held**
Web: www.coatingsresource.com
SIC: 2851 2865 Paints and paint additives;
Dyes, synthetic organic

(P-4493)
MAST TECHNOLOGIES LLC
8380 Camino Santa Fe Ste 200 (92121)
PHONE.....................858 452-1700
Andrew Sundsmo, *Pr*
Mike Vanderby, *Treas*
Steve Burningham, *Sec*
Steven Chevillotte, *VP*
EMP: 18 **EST:** 2020
SQ FT: 4,995
SALES (est): 5.39MM
SALES (corp-wide): 137.12MM **Privately Held**
Web: www.masttechnologies.com
SIC: 2851 2891 Paints and allied products;
Adhesives and sealants
PA: Sanders Industries Holdings, Inc.
3701 E Conant St
Long Beach CA
562 354-2920

(P-4494)
MASTER POWDER COATING INC
13721 Bora Dr (90670-5007)
PHONE.....................562 863-4135
Judith Flores, *CEO*
Juan Renteria, *
EMP: 21 **EST:** 2006
SALES (est): 2.45MM **Privately Held**
Web: www.masterpowdercoating.com
SIC: 2851 Paints and allied products

(P-4495)
MICROBLEND INC
Also Called: Microblend Technologies
543 Country Club Dr (93065-0637)
PHONE.....................330 998-4602
John E Tyson, *CEO*
Melvin J Sauder, *
Dan Trevino, *
John Bond, *
Jennifer Haslip, *
◆ **EMP:** 46 **EST:** 2014
SALES (est): 7.39MM **Privately Held**
Web: www.microblend.com
SIC: 2851 Paints and paint additives

(P-4496)
OLIVE REFINISH
9990 Glenoaks Blvd (91352-1048)
PHONE.....................805 273-5072
Albert Banoun, *Owner*
EMP: 25 **EST:** 2004
SALES (est): 1.53MM **Privately Held**
Web: www.oliverefinish.com
SIC: 2851 Paints and allied products

(P-4497)
POLY-FIBER INC (PA)
Also Called: Consolidated Aircraft Coatings
4343 Fort Dr (92509-6784)
P.O. Box 3129 (92519-3129)
PHONE.....................951 684-4280
Jon Goldenbaum, *Pr*
Greg Albarin, *Genl Mgr*
EMP: 17 **EST:** 1992
SQ FT: 75,000
SALES (est): 4.71MM **Privately Held**
Web: www.conaircraft.com
SIC: 2851 Undercoatings, paint

(P-4498)
PPG INDUSTRIES INC
Also Called: Industrial Coatings Division
15541 Commerce Ln (92649-1601)
PHONE.....................714 894-5252
Jeff Laird, *Mgr*
EMP: 21
SALES (corp-wide): 17.65B **Publicly Held**

Web: www.ppg.com
SIC: 2851 Paints and allied products
PA: Ppg Industries, Inc.
1 Ppg Pl
Pittsburgh PA
412 434-3131

(P-4499)
PPG INDUSTRIES INC
10060 Mission Mill Rd (90601-1738)
PHONE.....................562 692-4010
Gerald Roberts, *Mgr*
EMP: 17
SALES (corp-wide): 17.65B **Publicly Held**
Web: www.ppg.com
SIC: 2851 Paints and allied products
PA: Ppg Industries, Inc.
1 Ppg Pl
Pittsburgh PA
412 434-3131

(P-4500)
PPG INDUSTRIES INC
11601 United St (93501-7048)
PHONE.....................661 824-4532
Michelle Brown, *Mgr*
EMP: 24
SALES (corp-wide): 17.65B **Publicly Held**
Web: www.ppg.com
SIC: 2851 Paints and allied products
PA: Ppg Industries, Inc.
1 Ppg Pl
Pittsburgh PA
412 434-3131

(P-4501)
PPG PAINTS
12780 San Fernando Rd (91342-3728)
PHONE.....................818 362-6711
James Romano, *Mgr*
EMP: 19 **EST:** 1990
SALES (est): 1.66MM **Privately Held**
Web: www.ppg.com
SIC: 2851 Paints and allied products

(P-4502)
PRO-LINE PAINT COMPANY
2646 Main St (92113-3613)
PHONE.....................619 232-8968
Anthony A Mitchell, *CEO*
▼ **EMP:** 18 **EST:** 1961
SALES (est): 883.4K **Privately Held**
SIC: 2851 5198 5231 Paints and allied
products; Paints; Paint

(P-4503)
R & S MANUFACTURING & SUP INC
16616 Garfield Ave (90723-5305)
PHONE.....................909 622-5881
Ronald Hoffman, *Prin*
Susan Hoffman, *Sec*
EMP: 18 **EST:** 1976
SQ FT: 20,000
SALES (est): 3.82MM **Privately Held**
Web: www.rsmfgsupply.com
SIC: 2851 Colors in oil, except artists'

(P-4504)
RHINO LININGS CORPORATION (PA)
9747 Businesspark Ave (92131-1661)
PHONE.....................858 450-0441
Pierre M Gagnon, *CEO*
Russel Lewis, *
Sandra S Roberts, *
◆ **EMP:** 65 **EST:** 1988
SQ FT: 20,000
SALES (est): 86.26MM

SALES (corp-wide): 86.26MM **Privately Held**
Web: www.rhinolinings.com
SIC: 2851 Coating, air curing

(P-4505)
SIERRACIN CORPORATION (HQ)
12780 San Fernando Rd (91342-3796)
PHONE.....................818 741-1656
Barry N Gillespie, *CEO*
David B Navikas, *
Michael H Mcgarry, *Ex VP*
Frank S Sklarsky, *
Viktoras R Sekmakas, *
▲ **EMP:** 550 **EST:** 1952
SQ FT: 287,000
SALES (est): 178.27MM
SALES (corp-wide): 17.65B **Publicly Held**
Web: www.ppgaerospace.com
SIC: 2851 Paints and allied products
PA: Ppg Industries, Inc.
1 Ppg Pl
Pittsburgh PA
412 434-3131

(P-4506)
SPECIALIZED MILLING CORP
Also Called: Specialty Finishes
10330 Elm Ave (92337-7319)
PHONE.....................909 357-7890
Jack Neems, *Pr*
Seymour S Neems, *Ch Bd*
Adele Neems, *Treas*
EMP: 53 **EST:** 1968
SQ FT: 11,000
SALES (est): 2.48MM **Privately Held**
SIC: 2851 Paints and allied products

(P-4507)
SPECIALTY COATINGS & CHEM INC
Also Called: Special-T
7360 Varna Ave (91605-4008)
P.O. Box 32459 (90032-0459)
PHONE.....................818 983-0055
Alaistair Macdonald, *Pr*
W Daniel Ernt, *
Larry Wick, *
▲ **EMP:** 24 **EST:** 1964
SQ FT: 15,000
SALES (est): 861.59K **Privately Held**
Web: www.special-tcoatings.com
SIC: 2851 Plastics base paints and varnishes

(P-4508)
VINYLVISIONS COMPANY LLC
Also Called: Trim Quick
1233 Enterprise Ct (92882-7126)
PHONE.....................800 321-8746
John P Halle, *Managing Member*
Helen Halle, *Managing Member*
EMP: 20 **EST:** 2001
SQ FT: 40,000
SALES (est): 5.26MM
SALES (corp-wide): 19.56MM **Privately Held**
Web: www.vinylvisions.com
SIC: 2851 Vinyl coatings, strippable
PA: Halle-Hopper, Llc
5380 E Larry Caldwell Dr
Prescott AZ
951 284-7373

2865 Cyclic Crudes And Intermediates

(P-4509)
COLOR SCIENCE INC
Also Called: C S I

P
R
O
D
U
C
T
S
&
S
V
C
S

1230 E Glenwood Pl (92707-3000)
PHONE.................714 434-1033
Jocelyn Eubank, *CEO*
Mark Hoffenberg, *
EMP: 45 **EST:** 1989
SQ FT: 9,000
SALES (est): 22.22MM
SALES (corp-wide): 24.9MM **Privately Held**
Web: www.modifiedplastics.com
SIC: 2865 Color pigments, organic
PA: Modified Plastics, Inc.
1240 E Glenwood Pl
Santa Ana CA
714 546-4667

2869 Industrial Organic Chemicals, Nec

(P-4510)
AEROJET ROCKETDYNE DE INC (DH)
Also Called: Aerojet Rocketdyne
8900 De Soto Ave (91304-1967)
P.O. Box 7922 (91309-7922)
PHONE.................818 586-1000
Eileen P Drake, *CEO*
Pete Gleszer, *
Jerry Tucker, *
▲ **EMP:** 248 **EST:** 2005
SALES (est): 652.03MM
SALES (corp-wide): 17.06B **Publicly Held**
Web: www.l3harris.com
SIC: 2869 3724 Rocket engine fuel, organic; Aircraft engines and engine parts
HQ: Aerojet Rocketdyne Holdings, Inc.
222 N Pcf Cast Hwy Ste 50
El Segundo CA
310 252-8100

(P-4511)
AEROJET ROCKETDYNE DE INC
8495 Carla Ln (91304-3201)
PHONE.................818 586-9629
EMP: 281
SALES (corp-wide): 17.06B **Publicly Held**
Web: www.l3harris.com
SIC: 2869 3724 Rocket engine fuel, organic; Aircraft engines and engine parts
HQ: Inc Aerojet Rocketdyne Of De
8900 De Soto Ave
Canoga Park CA
818 586-1000

(P-4512)
AEROJET ROCKETDYNE DE INC
9001 Lurline Ave (91311-6122)
P.O. Box 7922 (91309-7922)
PHONE.................818 586-1000
Helen Lubin, *Brnch Mgr*
EMP: 115
SALES (corp-wide): 17.06B **Publicly Held**
Web: www.l3harris.com
SIC: 2869 3724 Rocket engine fuel, organic; Aircraft engines and engine parts
HQ: Inc Aerojet Rocketdyne Of De
8900 De Soto Ave
Canoga Park CA
818 586-1000

(P-4513)
AVIENT COLORANTS USA LLC
14355 Ramona Ave (91710-5740)
PHONE.................909 606-1325
Mike Urbano, *Brnch Mgr*
EMP: 44
Web: www.avient.com
SIC: 2869 Industrial organic chemicals, nec
HQ: Avient Colorants Usa Llc
85 Industrial Dr

Holden MA
508 829-6321

(P-4514)
BASF CORPORATION
138 E Meats Ave (92865-3310)
PHONE.................714 921-1430
John Zomer, *Mgr*
EMP: 127
SQ FT: 10,000
SALES (corp-wide): 90.7B **Privately Held**
Web: www.basf.com
SIC: 2869 2821 Industrial organic chemicals, nec; Plastics materials and resins
HQ: Basf Corporation
100 Park Ave
Florham Park NJ
800 962-7831

(P-4515)
BASF CORPORATION
6700 8th St (90620-1097)
PHONE.................714 521-6085
Tim Stmarseille, *Mgr*
EMP: 27
SALES (corp-wide): 90.7B **Privately Held**
Web: www.basf.com
SIC: 2869 Industrial organic chemicals, nec
HQ: Basf Corporation
100 Park Ave
Florham Park NJ
800 962-7831

(P-4516)
BASF ENZYMES LLC (DH)
3550 John Hopkins Ct (92121-1121)
PHONE.................858 431-8520
◆ **EMP:** 51 **EST:** 1992
SALES (est): 25.59MM
SALES (corp-wide): 90.7B **Privately Held**
Web: www.basf.com
SIC: 2869 Industrial organic chemicals, nec
HQ: Basf Corporation
100 Park Ave
Florham Park NJ
800 962-7831

(P-4517)
CAL-INDIA FOODS INTERNATIONAL
Also Called: Specilty Enzymes Btechnologies
13591 Yorba Ave (91710-5071)
PHONE.................909 613-1660
Vic Rathi, *Pr*
▲ **EMP:** 20 **EST:** 1982
SQ FT: 12,000
SALES (est): 6.25MM **Privately Held**
Web: www.specialtyenzymes.com
SIC: 2869 Enzymes

(P-4518)
CHEMLOGICS GROUP LLC
Also Called: Envirochem Technologies
7305 Morro Rd Ste 200 (93422-4445)
PHONE.................805 591-3314
EMP: 35
SIC: 2869 Industrial organic chemicals, nec

(P-4519)
CLARIANT CORPORATION
3355 Olive Ave (90755-4619)
PHONE.................562 322-6647
Devon Bench, *Mgr*
EMP: 18
Web: www.clariant.com
SIC: 2869 Industrial organic chemicals, nec
HQ: Clariant Corporation
500 E Morehead St Ste 400
Charlotte NC
704 331-7000

(P-4520)
FIRMENICH
424 S Atchison St (92805-4045)
PHONE.................714 535-2871
EMP: 89
SALES (est): 38.34MM **Privately Held**
Web: www.firmenich.com
SIC: 2869 Industrial organic chemicals, nec

(P-4521)
FIRMENICH INCORPORATED
Also Called: Firmenich Inc
424 S Atchison St (92805-4045)
PHONE.................714 535-2871
EMP: 74
Web: www.firmenich.com
SIC: 2869 Industrial organic chemicals, nec
HQ: Firmenich Incorporated
250 Plainsboro Rd
Plainsboro NJ
609 452-1000

(P-4522)
INNOVATIVE ORGANICS INC
4905 E Hunter Ave (92807-2058)
PHONE.................714 701-3900
Robert E Futrell Junior, *Pr*
EMP: 18 **EST:** 1990
SQ FT: 30,000
SALES (est): 3.58MM **Privately Held**
Web: ceramicsrefractories.saint-gobain.com
SIC: 2869 2899 Industrial organic chemicals, nec; Chemical preparations, nec

(P-4523)
INTERNATIONAL ACADEMY OF FIN (PA)
Also Called: Cordova Industries
13177 Foothill Blvd (91342-4830)
P.O. Box 922079 (91392-2079)
PHONE.................818 361-7724
Sam Cordova, *Pr*
Steven M Cordova, *
Rodrick Cordova, *
Sam Scott Cordova, *
Steven Schector, *
EMP: 24 **EST:** 1963
SQ FT: 6,000
SALES (est): 14.32MM **Privately Held**
SIC: 2869 3944 2879 Alcohols, industrial: denatured (non-beverage); Video game machines, except coin-operated; Insecticides, agricultural or household

(P-4524)
LAMB FUELS INC
725 Main St Ste B (91911-6168)
PHONE.................619 777-9135
Gregory Scott Lamb, *Pr*
Gregory Scott Lamb, *CEO*
Rochelle Lamb, *Sec*
▼ **EMP:** 21 **EST:** 1985
SALES (est): 5.63MM **Privately Held**
Web: www.lambfuels.com
SIC: 2869 Fuels

(P-4525)
MERCFUEL LLC
2780 Skypark Dr Ste 300 (90505-7518)
PHONE.................310 827-5778
Eric Beelar, *Pr*
EMP: 17
SALES (corp-wide): 243.17MM **Privately Held**
Web: www.mercuryaviation.org
SIC: 2869 Fuels
HQ: Mercfuel, Llc
500 Jefferson St Ste 1990
Houston TX

(P-4526)
PROVIVI INC (PA)
1701 Colorado Ave (90404-3436)
PHONE.................310 828-2307
Pedro S L Coelho, *CEO*
Peter Meinhold, *
Eduardo Sein, *
Teri Quinn Gray, *
EMP: 48 **EST:** 2012
SALES (est): 28.82MM
SALES (corp-wide): 28.82MM **Privately Held**
SIC: 2869 Laboratory chemicals, organic

(P-4527)
S FUEL LLC
4860 Llano Dr (91364-3040)
PHONE.................818 914-4849
EMP: 26
SALES (corp-wide): 442.8K **Privately Held**
SIC: 2869 Fuels
PA: S. Fuel, Llc
800 W 6th St Ste 320
Los Angeles CA

(P-4528)
SAINT-GOBAIN CERAMICS PLAS INC
Innovative Organics Division
4905 E Hunter Ave (92807-2058)
PHONE.................714 701-3900
Robert E Futrell Junior, *Brnch Mgr*
EMP: 257
SALES (corp-wide): 397.78MM **Privately Held**
Web: www.saint-gobain.com
SIC: 2869 2899 Industrial organic chemicals, nec; Chemical preparations, nec
HQ: Saint-Gobain Ceramics & Plastics, Inc.
20 Moores Rd
Malvern PA

(P-4529)
SOLVAY USA INC
7305 Morro Rd Ste 200 (93422-4445)
PHONE.................805 591-3314
EMP: 21
SALES (corp-wide): 11.45MM **Privately Held**
SIC: 2869 Industrial organic chemicals, nec
HQ: Solvay Usa Inc.
504 Carnegie Ctr
Princeton NJ
609 860-4000

(P-4530)
SPECILTY ENZYMES BTECHNOLOGIES
Also Called: Seb
13591 Yorba Ave (91710-5071)
PHONE.................909 613-1660
EMP: 18 **EST:** 2011
SALES (est): 9.38MM **Privately Held**
Web: www.specialtyenzymes.com
SIC: 2869 Enzymes

(P-4531)
STRATOS RENEWABLES CORPORATION
Also Called: A Development Stage Company
9440 Santa Monica Blvd Ste 401 (90210-4653)
PHONE.................310 402-5901
Thomas Snyder, *Pr*
Julio Cesar Alonso, *
Valerie Broadbent, *
Jorge Eduardo Aza, *
Sanjay Pai, *Chief Strategy Officer*
EMP: 28 **EST:** 2004

SALES (est): 4.01MM **Privately Held**
Web: www.stratosrenewables.com
SIC: 2869 0133 Ethyl alcohol, ethanol;
Sugarcane and sugar beets

(P-4532)
SUGAR FOODS LLC (PA)
Also Called: Sugar Foods
3059 Townsgate Rd Ste 101 (91361-2936)
PHONE..............................805 396-5000
Marty Wilson, *Pr*
Donald G Tober, *
Stephen Odell, *
Jack Vivinetto, *
◆ **EMP:** 34 **EST:** 1961
SQ FT: 10,000
SALES (est): 286.33MM
SALES (corp-wide): 286.33MM **Privately
Held**
Web: www.sugarfoods.com
SIC: 2869 2023 2099 2068 Sweeteners,
synthetic; Cream substitutes; Sugar; Salted
and roasted nuts and seeds

(P-4533)
TASTEPOINT INC
Also Called: Tastepoint By Iff
790 E Harrison St (92879-1348)
PHONE..............................951 734-6620
EMP: 188
SALES (corp-wide): 12.44B **Publicly Held**
Web: www.tastepoint.com
SIC: 2869 Flavors or flavoring materials,
synthetic
HQ: Tastepoint Inc.
7800 Holstein Ave
Philadelphia PA
215 365-7800

(P-4534)
USL PARALLEL PRODUCTS CAL
12281 Arrow Rte (91739-9601)
PHONE..............................909 980-1200
Gene Kiesel, *CEO*
Ken Reese, *
Jim Russell, *
Bob Pasma, *
Tim Cusson, *
▲ **EMP:** 35 **EST:** 1981
SQ FT: 6,000
SALES (est): 10.63MM
SALES (corp-wide): 87.06MM **Privately
Held**
Web: www.parallelproducts.com
SIC: 2869 Alcohols, industrial: denatured
(non-beverage)
PA: Parallel Environmental Services
Corporation
401 Industry Rd
Louisville KY
502 471-2444

(P-4535)
UTAK LABORATORIES INC
25020 Avenue Tibbitts (91355-3447)
PHONE..............................661 294-3935
James D Plutchak, *CEO*
EMP: 26 **EST:** 1974
SQ FT: 12,000
SALES (est): 9.82MM **Privately Held**
Web: www.utak.com
SIC: 2869 Industrial organic chemicals, nec

(P-4536)
VERENIUM CORPORATION
3550 John Hopkins Ct (92121-1121)
P.O. Box 685 (07932-0685)
PHONE..............................858 431-8500
▲ **EMP:** 111

SIC: 2869 Industrial organic chemicals, nec

(P-4537)
**WACKER CHEMICAL
CORPORATION**
Also Called: Precision Silicones
13910 Oaks Ave (91710-7010)
PHONE..............................909 590-8822
Sudipta Das, *Brnch Mgr*
EMP: 96
SALES (corp-wide): 8.53B **Privately Held**
Web: www.wacker.com
SIC: 2869 5169 Silicones; Industrial
chemicals
HQ: Wacker Chemical Corporation
4950 S State Rd
Ann Arbor MI
517 264-8500

2873 Nitrogenous Fertilizers

(P-4538)
CVR NITROGEN LP (HQ)
10877 Wilshire Blvd Fl 10 (90024-4251)
PHONE..............................310 571-9800
Keith B Forman, *CEO*
John H Diesch, *Pr*
Jeffrey R Spain, *CFO*
EMP: 39 **EST:** 2015
SALES (est): 340.73MM **Publicly Held**
SIC: 2873 Ammonium nitrate, ammonium
sulfate
PA: Cvr Partners, Lp
2277 Plaza Dr Ste 500
Sugar Land TX

(P-4539)
GRO-POWER INC
15065 Telephone Ave (91710-9614)
PHONE..............................909 393-3744
Brent Holden, *Pr*
▼ **EMP:** 25 **EST:** 1966
SALES (est): 4.12MM **Privately Held**
Web: www.gropower.com
SIC: 2873 0782 0721 Fertilizers: natural
(organic), except compost; Lawn and
garden services; Crop planting and
protection

(P-4540)
HYPONEX CORPORATION
Also Called: Scotts- Hyponex
12273 Brown Ave (92509-1828)
PHONE..............................909 597-2811
Roclund White, *Brnch Mgr*
EMP: 264
SALES (corp-wide): 3.55B **Publicly Held**
Web: www.scots.com
SIC: 2873 Fertilizers: natural (organic),
except compost
HQ: Hyponex Corporation
14111 Scottslawn Rd
Marysville OH
937 644-0011

(P-4541)
**RENTECH NTRGN PASADENA
SPA LLC**
10877 Wilshire Blvd Ste 710 (90024-4341)
PHONE..............................310 571-9805
EMP: 36 **EST:** 1987
SALES (est): 853.96K **Publicly Held**
SIC: 2873 Nitrogenous fertilizers
HQ: Cvr Nitrogen, Lp
10877 Wilshire Blvd Fl 10
Los Angeles CA
310 571-9800

(P-4542)
SCOTTS COMPANY LLC
742 Industrial Way (93263-4018)
PHONE..............................661 387-9555
Aaron Leach, *Brnch Mgr*
EMP: 23
SALES (corp-wide): 3.55B **Publicly Held**
Web: www.scotts.com
SIC: 2873 Fertilizers: natural (organic),
except compost
HQ: The Scotts Company Llc
14111 Scottslawn Rd
Marysville OH
937 644-0011

(P-4543)
**WHITTIER FERTILIZER
COMPANY**
9441 Kruse Rd (90660-1492)
PHONE..............................562 699-3461
Robert Osborn, *CEO*
Janet Osborn, *
▲ **EMP:** 51 **EST:** 1930
SQ FT: 20,000
SALES (est): 9.92MM **Privately Held**
Web: www.whittierfertilizer.com
SIC: 2873 5261 2875 Fertilizers: natural
(organic), except compost; Garden supplies
and tools, nec; Fertilizers, mixing only

2875 Fertilizers, Mixing Only

(P-4544)
JH BIOTECH INC (PA)
Also Called: Jh Biotech
4951 Olivas Park Dr (93003-7667)
P.O. Box 3538 (93006-3538)
PHONE..............................805 650-8933
Hsinhung John Hsu, *Pr*
◆ **EMP:** 23 **EST:** 1986
SQ FT: 3,000
SALES (est): 15.43MM
SALES (corp-wide): 15.43MM **Privately
Held**
Web: www.jhbiotech.com
SIC: 2875 Fertilizers, mixing only

2879 Agricultural Chemicals, Nec

(P-4545)
**AMERICAN VANGUARD
CORPORATION (PA)**
Also Called: Avd
4695 Macarthur Ct (92660-1882)
PHONE..............................949 260-1200
Eric G Wintemute, *Ch Bd*
Ulrich G Trogele, *Ex VP*
David T Johnson, *VP*
Timothy J Donnelly, *Chief*
◆ **EMP:** 67 **EST:** 1969
SQ FT: 19,953
SALES (est): 609.62MM
SALES (corp-wide): 609.62MM **Publicly
Held**
Web: www.american-vanguard.com
SIC: 2879 Pesticides, agricultural or
household

(P-4546)
**AMVAC CHEMICAL
CORPORATION (HQ)**
4695 Macarthur Ct Ste 1200 (92660-8859)
PHONE..............................323 264-3910
Eric G Wintemute, *Ch*
Bob Trogele, *
David T Johnson, *

Glen Johnson, *
Cindy Baker Smith, *
◆ **EMP:** 36 **EST:** 1945
SQ FT: 152,000
SALES (est): 212.13MM
SALES (corp-wide): 609.62MM **Publicly
Held**
Web: www.amvac.com
SIC: 2879 Pesticides, agricultural or
household
PA: American Vanguard Corporation
4695 Macarthur Ct
Newport Beach CA
949 260-1200

(P-4547)
CERTIS USA LLC
Also Called: Thermo Trilogy
720 5th St (93280-1420)
PHONE..............................661 758-8471
Michael Hillberry, *Prin*
EMP: 40
Web: www.certisbio.com
SIC: 2879 5191 Pesticides, agricultural or
household; Insecticides
HQ: Certis U.S.A. L.L.C.
9145 Guilford Rd Ste 175
Columbia MD

(P-4548)
CIBUS INC
6455 Nancy Ridge Dr (92121-2249)
PHONE..............................858 450-0008
Rory Riggs, *Ch Bd*
Peter Beetham, *Pr*
Wade King, *CFO*
Greg Gocal, *CSO*
EMP: 237 **EST:** 2010
SQ FT: 53,423
SALES (est): 157K **Privately Held**
Web: www.calyxt.com
SIC: 2879 8731 0721 Agricultural chemicals,
nec; Agricultural research; Crop planting
and protection

(P-4549)
**DECCO US POST-HARVEST INC
(HQ)**
1713 S California Ave (91016-4623)
P.O. Box 120 (91017-0120)
PHONE..............................800 221-0925
Francois Girin, *Pr*
◆ **EMP:** 18 **EST:** 2009
SALES (est): 19.08MM **Privately Held**
Web: www.deccous.com
SIC: 2879 Agricultural chemicals, nec
PA: Upl Limited
Upl House, 610 B/2, Bandra Village,
Mumbai MH

(P-4550)
**ECOSMART TECHNOLOGIES
INC**
1585 W Mission Blvd (91766-1233)
PHONE..............................770 667-0006
EMP: 25
SIC: 2879 Insecticides and pesticides

(P-4551)
GROW MORE INC
15600 New Century Dr (90248-2129)
PHONE..............................310 515-1700
◆ **EMP:** 62 **EST:** 1918
SQ FT: 43,560
SALES (est): 11.18MM **Privately Held**
Web: www.growmore.com
SIC: 2879 2899 2873 2869 Agricultural
chemicals, nec; Chemical preparations, nec
; Nitrogenous fertilizers; Industrial organic
chemicals, nec

(P-4552)
MONSANTO COMPANY
Also Called: Monsanto
2700 Camino Del Sol (93030-7967)
PHONE..................................805 827-2341
EMP: 23
SALES (corp-wide): 52.7B **Privately Held**
Web: www.monsanto.com
SIC: 2879 Agricultural chemicals, nec
HQ: Bayer Northern Production Co., Llc
800 N Lindbergh Blvd
Saint Louis MO
314 694-1000

(P-4553)
TRICAL INC
1029 Railroad St (92882-2416)
PHONE..................................951 737-6960
Joanne Vargas, *Mgr*
EMP: 22
SALES (corp-wide): 68.13MM **Privately Held**
Web: www.trical.com
SIC: 2879 Agricultural chemicals, nec
PA: Trical, Inc.
8100 Arroyo Cir
Gilroy CA
831 637-0195

(P-4554)
TRICAL INC
1667 Purdy Rd (93501-7403)
PHONE..................................661 824-2494
EMP: 22
SALES (corp-wide): 68.13MM **Privately Held**
Web: www.trical.com
SIC: 2879 Agricultural chemicals, nec
PA: Trical, Inc.
8100 Arroyo Cir
Gilroy CA
831 637-0195

2891 Adhesives And Sealants

(P-4555)
AC PRODUCTS INC
Also Called: Quaker
9930 Painter Ave (90605-2759)
PHONE..................................714 630-7311
Peter Weissman, *Pr*
Joseph Matrange, *
Hugh H Muller, *
Sheldon I Weinstein, *
◆ **EMP:** 35 **EST:** 1972
SQ FT: 28,000
SALES (est): 10.4MM
SALES (corp-wide): 1.94B **Publicly Held**
Web: www.acpmaskants.com
SIC: 2891 2952 8731 Adhesives and
sealants; Coating compounds, tar;
Chemical laboratory, except testing
PA: Quaker Chemical Corporation
901 E Hector St
Conshohocken PA
610 832-4000

(P-4556)
ADVANCED CHEMISTRY & TECHNOLOGY INC
Also Called: AC Tech
7341 Anaconda Ave (92841-2921)
PHONE..................................714 373-8118
▲ **EMP:** 70
Web: www.actechaero.com
SIC: 2891 Sealants

(P-4557)
ADVANTAGE ADHESIVES INC
8345 White Oak Ave (91730-3896)
PHONE..................................909 204-4990
Greg Lane, *Pr*
▲ **EMP:** 26 **EST:** 1998
SQ FT: 25,620
SALES (est): 4.57MM **Privately Held**
Web: www.advantageadhesives.com
SIC: 2891 Adhesives

(P-4558)
AXIOM MATERIALS INC
2320 Pullman St (92705-5507)
PHONE..................................949 623-4400
Murat Oguz Arca, *CEO*
Olcay Demirkesen, *
▲ **EMP:** 35 **EST:** 2009
SQ FT: 15,000
SALES (est): 18.58MM **Privately Held**
Web: www.axiommaterials.com
SIC: 2891 2295 Epoxy adhesives; Resin or
plastic coated fabrics
HQ: Kordsa, Inc.
4501 N Access Rd
Chattanooga TN
423 643-8300

(P-4559)
BOSTIK INC
27460 Bostik Ct (92590-3698)
PHONE..................................951 296-6425
Ed Lui, *Brnch Mgr*
EMP: 50
SALES (corp-wide): 129.02MM **Privately Held**
Web: www.bostik.com
SIC: 2891 2899 Adhesives; Chemical
preparations, nec
HQ: Bostik, Inc.
11320 W Watertwn Plnk Rd
Wauwatosa WI
414 774-2250

(P-4560)
CTS CEMENT MANUFACTURING CORP
Also Called: CTS Cement Manufacturing Co
2077 Linda Flora Dr (90077-1406)
PHONE..................................310 472-4004
EMP: 23
SALES (corp-wide): 48.4MM **Privately Held**
Web: www.ctscement.com
SIC: 2891 Cement, except linoleum and tile
PA: Cts Cement Manufacturing Corporation
12442 Knott St
Garden Grove CA
714 379-8260

(P-4561)
CUSTOM BUILDING PRODUCTS LLC (DH)
Also Called: Custom Building Products
7711 Center Ave Ste 500 (92647-3076)
PHONE..................................800 272-8786
Don Devine, *CEO*
Thomas Peck Junior, *Pr*
Marc Powell, *
◆ **EMP:** 65 **EST:** 2005
SQ FT: 15,000
SALES (est): 543.07MM **Privately Held**
Web: www.custombuildingproducts.com
SIC: 2891 Adhesives and sealants
HQ: The Quikrete Companies Llc
5 Concourse Pkwy Ste 1900
Atlanta GA
404 634-9100

(P-4562)
CUSTOM BUILDING PRODUCTS LLC
6511 Salt Lake Ave (90201-2126)
PHONE..................................323 582-0846
Tom Milan, *Manager*
EMP: 141
Web: www.custombuildingproducts.com
SIC: 2891 3273 2899 5032 Adhesives and
sealants; Ready-mixed concrete; Chemical
preparations, nec; Ceramic wall and floor
tile, nec
HQ: Custom Building Products Llc
7711 Center Ave Ste 500
Huntington Beach CA
800 272-8786

(P-4563)
DESMOND VENTURES INC
17451 Von Karman Ave (92614-6205)
P.O. Box 19507 (92623-9507)
PHONE..................................949 474-0400
▲ **EMP:** 135
SIC: 2891 2851 Adhesives and sealants;
Lacquers, varnishes, enamels, and other
coatings

(P-4564)
ESSENTRA INTERNATIONAL LLC
Also Called: Duraco Express
21303 Ferrero (91789-5231)
PHONE..................................708 315-7498
EMP: 1091
SALES (corp-wide): 406.82MM **Privately Held**
Web: www.essentra.com
SIC: 2891 Adhesives and sealants
HQ: Essentra International Llc
2 Westbrook Corp Ctr
Westchester IL
866 800-0775

(P-4565)
FLAMEMASTER CORPORATION
Also Called: Chemseal
13576 Desmond St (91331-2315)
P.O. Box 4510 (91333-4500)
PHONE..................................818 890-1401
Joshua Mazin, *Pr*
▲ **EMP:** 28 **EST:** 1942
SALES (est): 5.72MM **Privately Held**
Web: www.flamemaster.com
SIC: 2891 Sealants

(P-4566)
GENERAL SEALANTS
300 Turnbull Canyon Rd (91745-1009)
P.O. Box 3855 (91744-0855)
PHONE..................................626 961-0211
Bradley Boyle, *Pr*
Patricia Boyle, *
Patrick Boyle, *
◆ **EMP:** 120 **EST:** 1964
SQ FT: 96,000
SALES (est): 16.17MM **Privately Held**
Web: www.generalsealants.com
SIC: 2891 Adhesives

(P-4567)
HENKEL CHEMICAL MANAGEMENT LLC
Also Called: Henkel Electronic Mtls LLC
14000 Jamboree Rd (92606-1730)
PHONE..................................888 943-6535
Benoit Pouliquen, *VP*
Alan P Syzdek, *
Paul R Berry, *
EMP: 170 **EST:** 2010
SQ FT: 75,000

SALES (est): 77.5MM
SALES (corp-wide): 23.26B **Privately Held**
Web: www.henkel.com
SIC: 2891 Adhesives
PA: Henkel Ag & Co. Kgaa
Henkelstr. 67
Dusseldorf NW
2117970

(P-4568)
HENKEL CORPORATION
14000 Jamboree Rd (92606-1730)
PHONE..................................714 368-8000
EMP: 165
SALES (corp-wide): 23.26B **Privately Held**
Web: www.henkel.com
SIC: 2891 Adhesives and sealants
HQ: Henkel Corporation
1 Henkel Way
Rocky Hill CT
860 571-5100

(P-4569)
HENKEL US OPERATIONS CORP
Dexter Electronics Mtls Div
15051 Don Julian Rd (91746-3302)
P.O. Box 1282 (91749-1282)
PHONE..................................626 968-6511
Jim Dehart, *Mgr*
EMP: 60
SALES (corp-wide): 23.26B **Privately Held**
Web: www.henkel.com
SIC: 2891 Adhesives
HQ: Henkel Us Operations Corporation
1 Henkel Way
Rocky Hill CT
860 571-5100

(P-4570)
INTERNATIONAL COATINGS CO INC (PA)
Also Called: International Coatings
13929 166th St (90703-2431)
PHONE..................................562 926-1010
Stephen W Kahane, *CEO*
Herbert A Wells, *
Janet Wells, *
◆ **EMP:** 40 **EST:** 1957
SQ FT: 50,000
SALES (est): 9.92MM
SALES (corp-wide): 9.92MM **Privately Held**
Web: www.iccink.com
SIC: 2891 2899 3555 2893 Adhesives; Ink or
writing fluids; Printing trades machinery;
Printing ink

(P-4571)
IPS CORPORATION (HQ)
Also Called: Weld-On Adhesives
455 W Victoria St (90220-6064)
PHONE..................................310 898-3300
Tracy Bilbrough, *CEO*
Will Barton, *
Gary Rosenfield, *
◆ **EMP:** 180 **EST:** 1953
SQ FT: 22,000
SALES (est): 497.43MM **Privately Held**
Web: www.ipscorp.com
SIC: 2891 Adhesives, plastic
PA: Centerbridge Partners, L.P.
375 Park Ave Fl 12c
New York NY

(P-4572)
MASK-OFF COMPANY INC
345 W Maple Ave (91016-3331)
PHONE..................................626 359-3261
Steven B Sites, *Pr*
Dimitrianne Wood, *Sec*

Jim Sites, *Dir*
▲ **EMP:** 18 **EST:** 1950
SQ FT: 28,160
SALES (est): 4.45MM **Privately Held**
Web: www.mask-off.com
SIC: 2891 Adhesives

(P-4573)
MITSUBISHI CHEMICAL CRBN FBR
Also Called: Mitsubishi Chemical Carbon
Fiber and Composites, Inc.
1822 Reynolds Ave (92614-5714)
PHONE................................800 929-5471
Takashi Sasaki, *VP*
EMP: 110
Web: www.mccfc.com
SIC: 2891 5169 Adhesives; Chemical
additives
HQ: Mitsubishi Chemical Carbon Fiber And
Composites, Inc
5900 88th St
Sacramento CA

(P-4574)
PACER TECHNOLOGY (HQ)
Also Called: Super Glue
3281 E Guasti Rd Ste 260 (91761-7621)
PHONE................................909 987-0550
E T Gravette, *CEO*
Ronald T Gravette, *Pr*
Kristine Wright, *CFO*
James Gallagher, *VP*
Marsha Gravette, *VP Mktg*
◆ **EMP:** 107 **EST:** 1975
SQ FT: 47,700
SALES (est): 24.1MM
SALES (corp-wide): 24.1MM **Privately
Held**
Web: www.supergluecorp.com
SIC: 2891 3089 3085 Adhesives and
sealants; Plastics containers, except foam;
Plastics bottles
PA: Cyan Holding Corporation
9420 Santa Anita Ave
Rancho Cucamonga CA
909 987-0550

(P-4575)
PACKAGING SYSTEMS INC
26435 Summit Cir (91350-2991)
PHONE................................661 253-5700
Raymond J Gray, *CEO*
Steve Gray, *
Patricia Gray, *
▼ **EMP:** 42 **EST:** 1976
SQ FT: 25,700
SALES (est): 17.02MM **Privately Held**
Web: www.pkgsys.net
SIC: 2891 Adhesives and sealants

(P-4576)
PRC - DESOTO INTERNATIONAL INC
Also Called: PPG Aerospace
11601 United St (93501-7048)
PHONE................................661 824-4532
Dave Richardson, *Brnch Mgr*
EMP: 130
SALES (corp-wide): 17.65B **Publicly Held**
Web: guide13227.guidechem.com
SIC: 2891 Sealing compounds, synthetic
rubber or plastic
HQ: Prc - Desoto International, Inc.
24811 Ave Rockefeller
Valencia CA
661 678-4209

(P-4577)
PRC - DESOTO INTERNATIONAL INC (HQ)
Also Called: PPG Aerospace
24811 Avenue Rockefeller (91355-3468)
PHONE................................661 678-4209
Michael H Mcgarry, *Pr*
Barry Gillespie, *
David P Morris, *
John Machin, *
Donna Lee Walker, *Tax Administration Vice
President*
▲ **EMP:** 320 **EST:** 1945
SQ FT: 200,000
SALES (est): 138.57MM
SALES (corp-wide): 17.65B **Publicly Held**
Web: www.ppgaerospace.com
SIC: 2891 3089 Sealing compounds,
synthetic rubber or plastic; Plastics
containers, except foam
PA: Ppg Industries, Inc.
1 Ppg Pl
Pittsburgh PA
412 434-3131

(P-4578)
QSPAC INDUSTRIES INC (PA)
Also Called: Quality Service Pac Industry
15020 Marquardt Ave (90670-5704)
PHONE................................562 407-3868
Jow-lin Tang, *Pr*
Wu-hsiung Chung, *CFO*
Vic Lee, *
◆ **EMP:** 52 **EST:** 2009
SQ FT: 96,000
SALES (est): 16.9MM **Privately Held**
Web: www.qspac.com
SIC: 2891 Adhesives

(P-4579)
RELIABLE PACKAGING SYSTEMS INC
Also Called: Astro Packaging
1300 N Jefferson St (92807-1614)
PHONE................................714 572-1094
Debra Lynn Dillon, *Pr*
Debra Dillon, *Pr*
EMP: 17 **EST:** 1994
SQ FT: 5,500
SALES (est): 4.56MM **Privately Held**
Web: www.astropackaging.com
SIC: 2891 3565 5084 5169 Adhesives and
sealants; Packaging machinery; Packaging
machinery and equipment; Adhesives and
sealants

(P-4580)
SEAL FOR LIFE INDUSTRIES LLC (PA)
2290 Enrico Fermi Dr Ste 22 (92154-7206)
PHONE................................619 671-0932
Jeffrey Oravitz, *CEO*
Dirk Totte, *Pr*
Mauricio Perini, *CFO*
▲ **EMP:** 26 **EST:** 2012
SQ FT: 260,831
SALES (est): 47.28MM
SALES (corp-wide): 47.28MM **Privately
Held**
Web: www.sealforlife.com
SIC: 2891 2952 Sealing compounds,
synthetic rubber or plastic; Coating
compounds, tar

(P-4581)
SIGNATURE FLEXIBLE PACKG LLC (PA)
Also Called: Dazpak Flexible Packaging
19310 San Jose Ave (91748-1419)

PHONE................................909 598-7844
Adrian Backer, *Pr*
Jeff Sewel, *VP*
Kelly Redding, *Sec*
▲ **EMP:** 28 **EST:** 1954
SALES (est): 29.26MM
SALES (corp-wide): 29.26MM **Privately
Held**
Web: www.dazpak.com
SIC: 2891 2673 Adhesives and sealants;
Bags: plastic, laminated, and coated

(P-4582)
STIC-ADHESIVE PRODUCTS CO INC
3950 Medford St (90063-1675)
PHONE................................323 268-2956
Junho Suh, *Pr*
EMP: 150 **EST:** 1975
SQ FT: 75,000
SALES (est): 9.5MM **Privately Held**
Web: www.sticadhesive.com
SIC: 2891 2851 Adhesives; Paints and allied
products

(P-4583)
TECHNICOTE INC
1587 E Bentley Dr (92879-1788)
PHONE................................951 372-0627
George Parker, *Mgr*
EMP: 40
SALES (corp-wide): 69.44MM **Privately
Held**
Web: www.technicote.com
SIC: 2891 2675 Adhesives; Die-cut paper
and board
PA: Technicote, Inc.
222 Mound Ave
Miamisburg OH
800 358-4448

2892 Explosives

(P-4584)
TELEDYNE REYNOLDS INC
1001 Knox St (90502-1030)
PHONE................................310 823-5491
EMP: 250
SIC: 2892 3489 3678 3643 Explosives;
Ordnance and accessories, nec; Electronic
connectors; Current-carrying wiring services

(P-4585)
TELEDYNE RISI INC (HQ)
19735 Dearborn St (91311-6510)
P.O. Box 359 (95378-0359)
PHONE................................818 718-6640
Al Pichelli, *CEO*
EMP: 21 **EST:** 1984
SQ FT: 5,000
SALES (est): 22MM
SALES (corp-wide): 5.46B **Publicly held**
Web:
www.teledynedefenseelectronics.com
SIC: 2892 Explosives
PA: Teledyne Technologies Inc
1049 Camino Dos Rios
Thousand Oaks CA
805 373-4545

2893 Printing Ink

(P-4586)
BOMARK INC
601 S 6th Ave (91746-3026)
PHONE................................626 968-1666
Herman R Schowe Junior, *Ch Bd*
H Mark Schowe, *

Kathie Virgil, *
EMP: 43 **EST:** 1961
SQ FT: 21,000
SALES (est): 1.18MM **Privately Held**
SIC: 2893 Printing ink

(P-4587)
DIVERSFIED NANO SOLUTIONS CORP
12140 Community Rd (92064-6871)
PHONE................................858 924-1013
EMP: 21
SALES (corp-wide): 9.76MM **Privately
Held**
Web: www.diversifiednano.com
SIC: 2893 Printing ink
PA: Diversified Nano Solutions Corporation
2900 S Highland Dr Ste 17
Las Vegas NV
858 924-1005

(P-4588)
GANS INK AND SUPPLY CO INC (PA)
1441 Boyd St (90033-3790)
P.O. Box 33806 (90033-0806)
PHONE................................323 264-2200
Jeffrey Koppelman, *Pr*
◆ **EMP:** 50 **EST:** 1950
SQ FT: 28,000
SALES (est): 20.46MM
SALES (corp-wide): 20.46MM **Privately
Held**
Web: www.gansink.com
SIC: 2893 Printing ink

(P-4589)
HADDADS FINE ARTS INC
Also Called: Curated Image, The
3855 E Miraloma Ave (92806-2124)
PHONE................................714 996-2100
Paula Haddad, *Pr*
EMP: 24 **EST:** 1958
SQ FT: 17,000
SALES (est): 897K **Privately Held**
Web: giclee.haddadsfinearts.com
SIC: 2893 Lithographic ink

(P-4590)
INK SYSTEMS INC (PA)
2311 S Eastern Ave (90040-1430)
PHONE................................323 720-4000
▲ **EMP:** 55 **EST:** 1985
SALES (est): 24.96MM
SALES (corp-wide): 24.96MM **Privately
Held**
Web: www.inksystems.com
SIC: 2893 Printing ink

(P-4591)
SUN CHEMICAL CORPORATION
General Printing Ink Division
12963 Park St (90670-4083)
PHONE................................562 946-2327
Paul Stack, *Mgr*
EMP: 28
Web: www.sunchemical.com
SIC: 2893 5084 Printing ink; Printing trades
machinery, equipment, and supplies
HQ: Sun Chemical Corporation
35 Waterview Blvd Ste 104
Parsippany NJ
973 404-6000

2895 Carbon Black

(P-4592)
ALDILA MATERIALS TECH CORP (DH)
13450 Stowe Dr (92064-6860)
PHONE..............................858 486-6970
Pete Matthewson, *Pr*
▼ **EMP:** 33 **EST:** 1997
SALES (est): 43.98MM **Privately Held**
Web: www.aldila.com
SIC: 2895 Carbon black
HQ: Aldila, Inc.
  1945 Kellogg Ave
  Carlsbad CA
  858 513-1801

2899 Chemical Preparations, Nec

(P-4593)
ACORN ENGINEERING COMPANY (PA)
Also Called: Morris Group International
15125 Proctor Ave (91746-3327)
P.O. Box 3527 (91744-0527)
PHONE..............................800 488-8999
Donald E Morris, *CEO*
William D Morris, *
Kristin E Kahle, *
Randal Morris, *
Barrett Morris, *
◆ **EMP:** 702 **EST:** 1955
SQ FT: 120,000
SALES (est): 99.15MM
SALES (corp-wide): 99.15MM **Privately Held**
Web: www.acorneng.com
SIC: 2899 3431 Distilled water; Drinking fountains, metal

(P-4594)
ALL AMERICAN PRODUCTS GROUP INC
Also Called: All American Drill Bushing
1135 Aviation Pl (91340-1460)
P.O. Box 190 (91341-0190)
PHONE..............................818 361-0059
EMP: 22 **EST:** 1941
SALES (est): 1.74MM **Privately Held**
SIC: 2899 3599 3429 3398 Metal treating compounds; Machine shop, jobbing and repair; Hardware, nec; Metal heat treating

(P-4595)
AMERICAN CONSUMER PRODUCTS LLC
120 E 8th St Ste 908 (90014-3332)
PHONE..............................323 289-6610
David Molayem, *Pr*
David Molayem, *
Kam Jahanbigloo, *
Daryoosh Molayem, *
◆ **EMP:** 73 **EST:** 1999
SALES (est): 2.39MM
SALES (corp-wide): 50.24MM **Privately Held**
Web:
www.american-consumer-products.com
SIC: 2899 2844 2834 Chemical preparations, nec; Cosmetic preparations; Pharmaceutical preparations
PA: Tabletops Unlimited, Inc.
  23000 Avalon Blvd
  Carson CA
  310 549-6000

(P-4596)
AT APOLLO TECHNOLOGIES LLC
31441 Santa Margarita Pkwy Ste A219 (92688-1836)
PHONE..............................949 888-0573
Austin Browning, *Managing Member*
EMP: 23 **EST:** 1980
SALES (est): 3.42MM **Privately Held**
Web: www.apolloh2o.com
SIC: 2899 Water treating compounds

(P-4597)
AVISTA TECHNOLOGIES INC
140 Bosstick Blvd (92069-5930)
PHONE..............................760 744-0536
Dave Walker, *Pr*
Greg Leiser, *Ex VP*
Takefumi Shimoda, *Ex VP*
▼ **EMP:** 19 **EST:** 1999
SQ FT: 15,500
SALES (est): 5.34MM **Privately Held**
Web:
www.avistamembranesolutions.com
SIC: 2899 Chemical supplies for foundries
PA: Kurita Water Industries Ltd.
  4-10-1, Nakano
  Nakano-Ku TKY

(P-4598)
CALIFORNIA RESPIRATORY CARE
16055 Ventura Blvd # 715 (91436-2601)
PHONE..............................818 379-9999
EMP: 55
SALES (est): 4.18MM **Privately Held**
SIC: 2899 5047 5169 Chemical preparations, nec; Medical and hospital equipment; Oxygen

(P-4599)
CHEMDIV INC
Also Called: Chemical Diversity Labs
12730 High Bluff Dr (92130-2076)
PHONE..............................858 794-4860
Nikolay P Savchuk, *CEO*
A Ivachtchenko, *Ch*
EMP: 45 **EST:** 1995
SALES (est): 9.74MM **Privately Held**
Web: www.chemdiv.com
SIC: 2899 Chemical preparations, nec

(P-4600)
CHEMTREAT INC
Also Called: Trident Technologies
8885 Rehco Rd (92121-3261)
PHONE..............................804 935-2000
EMP: 129
SALES (corp-wide): 31.47B **Publicly Held**
Web: www.chemtreat.com
SIC: 2899 Water treating compounds
HQ: Chemtreat, Inc.
  5640 Cox Rd Ste 300
  Glen Allen VA
  804 935-2000

(P-4601)
COATINC UNITED STATES INC
325 W Washington St Ste 2340 (92103-1930)
PHONE..............................619 638-7261
Paul Mcsweeney, *CEO*
EMP: 21 **EST:** 2014
SALES (est): 166.04K **Privately Held**
Web: www.coatinc.com
SIC: 2899 Fluxes: brazing, soldering, galvanizing, and welding

(P-4602)
CP KELCO US INC
2031 E Belt St (92113)
PHONE..............................619 652-5326
EMP: 20
SALES (corp-wide): 1.24B **Privately Held**
Web: www.cpkelco.com
HQ: Cp Kelco U.S., Inc.
  3100 Cumberland Blvd Se # 600
  Atlanta GA
  678 247-7300

(P-4603)
CYTEC ENGINEERED MATERIALS INC
645 N Cypress St (92867-6603)
PHONE..............................714 630-9400
Ron Martin, *Brnch Mgr*
EMP: 130
SQ FT: 300,000
SALES (corp-wide): 146.05MM **Privately Held**
SIC: 2899 Chemical preparations, nec
HQ: Cytec Engineered Materials Inc.
  2085 E Tech Cir Ste 102
  Tempe AZ

(P-4604)
EVERSPRING CHEMICAL INC
Also Called: Everspring
11577 W Olympic Blvd (90064-1522)
PHONE..............................310 707-1600
Marvin Lai, *CEO*
▲ **EMP:** 21 **EST:** 2005
SQ FT: 2,000
SALES (est): 1.64MM **Privately Held**
Web: www.everspringchem.com
SIC: 2899 Chemical preparations, nec

(P-4605)
EVONIK CORPORATION
Also Called: Air Products
3305 E 26th St (90058-4101)
PHONE..............................323 264-0311
William Ayacha, *Brnch Mgr*
EMP: 110
SALES (corp-wide): 2.27B **Privately Held**
Web: corporate.evonik.com
SIC: 2899 2891 2821 Chemical preparations, nec; Adhesives and sealants; Plastics materials and resins
HQ: Evonik Corporation
  2 Turner Pl
  Piscataway NJ
  973 929-8000

(P-4606)
FIRMENICH INCORPORATED
10636 Scripps Summit Ct (92131-3965)
PHONE..............................858 646-8323
Kym Coleman, *Brnch Mgr*
EMP: 22
Web: www.firmenich.com
SIC: 2899 Essential oils
HQ: Firmenich Incorporated
  250 Plainsboro Rd
  Plainsboro NJ
  609 452-1000

(P-4607)
GGTW LLC
Also Called: South Bay Salt Works
1470 Bay Blvd (91911-3942)
PHONE..............................619 423-3388
Glenn Warner, *Owner*
Tracy Strahl, *Prin*
▼ **EMP:** 28 **EST:** 1930
SALES (est): 2.46MM **Privately Held**
SIC: 2899 Salt

(P-4608)
HEMOSURE INC
5358 Irwindale Ave (91706-2086)
PHONE..............................888 436-6787
Doctor John Wan, *Pr*
Sherry Wang, *
EMP: 40 **EST:** 2003
SALES (est): 9.57MM **Privately Held**
Web: www.hemosure.com
SIC: 2899 3841 Chemical preparations, nec; Surgical and medical instruments
PA: W.H.P.M. Inc.
  5358 Irwindale Ave
  Irwindale CA

(P-4609)
HOME & BODY COMPANY (PA)
Also Called: Direct Chemicals
5800 Skylab Rd (92647-2054)
PHONE..............................714 842-8000
Hazem H Haddad, *Pr*
Nadene Haddad, *
▲ **EMP:** 349 **EST:** 1997
SALES (est): 51.12MM
SALES (corp-wide): 51.12MM **Privately Held**
Web: www.homeandbodyco.com
SIC: 2899 5999 2842 2844 Essential oils; Toiletries, cosmetics, and perfumes; Bleaches, household: dry or liquid; Face creams or lotions

(P-4610)
HYDRANAUTICS (DH)
401 Jones Rd (92058-1216)
PHONE..............................760 901-2500
Masaaki Ando, *Pr*
Michael Concannon, *
Randolph Truby, *
Marek Wilf, *
Norio Ikeyama, *
◆ **EMP:** 400 **EST:** 1987
SQ FT: 150,000
SALES (est): 88.4MM **Privately Held**
Web: www.membranes.com
SIC: 2899 3589 Chemical preparations, nec; Water treatment equipment, industrial
HQ: Nitto Americas, Inc.
  400 Frank W Burr Blvd
  Teaneck NJ
  510 445-5400

(P-4611)
INDIO PRODUCTS INC
Cultural Heritage Candle Co
5331 E Slauson Ave (90040-2916)
PHONE..............................323 720-9117
Marty Mayer, *Owner*
EMP: 33
SALES (corp-wide): 25.3MM **Privately Held**
Web: www.indioproducts.com
SIC: 2899 3999 5199 5049 Incense; Candles ; Candles; Religious supplies
PA: Indio Products, Inc.
  12910 Mulberry Dr Unit A
  Whittier CA
  323 720-1188

(P-4612)
INSULTECH LLC (PA)
Also Called: Insultech
3530 W Garry Ave (92704-6423)
PHONE..............................714 384-0506
Ryan Barto, *Managing Member*
◆ **EMP:** 45 **EST:** 1994
SQ FT: 30,000
SALES (est): 15.61MM **Privately Held**
Web: www.insultech.com

▲ = Import ▼ = Export
◆ = Import/Export

SIC: 2899 Insulating compounds

(P-4613)

KEMIRA WATER SOLUTIONS INC

Also Called: Kemiron Pacific
14000 San Bernardino Ave (92335-5258)
PHONE..................909 350-5678
EMP: 24
SALES (corp-wide): 3.71B **Privately Held**
Web: www.kemira.com
SIC: 2899 Water treating compounds
HQ: Kemira Water Solutions, Inc.
1000 Parkwood Cir Se # 500
Atlanta GA

(P-4614)

KIK POOL ADDITIVES INC

5160 E Airport Dr (91761-7824)
PHONE..................909 390-9912
John A Christensen, *Pr*
David M Christensen, *VP*
Debra Schonk, *VP*
Brian Patterson, *CFO*
Chet Yoakum, *VP*
▲ EMP: 140 EST: 1958
SALES (est): 16.87MM **Privately Held**
Web: www.kem-tek.com
SIC: 2899 3089 7389 5169 Chemical
preparations, nec; Plastics hardware and
building products; Packaging and labeling
services; Swimming pool and spa chemicals

(P-4615)

L M SCOFIELD COMPANY (DH)

12767 Imperial Hwy (90670-4711)
PHONE..................323 720-3000
Phillip J Arnold, *Pr*
◆ EMP: 50 EST: 1915
SQ FT: 36,000
SALES (est): 27.84MM **Privately Held**
Web: usa.sika.com
SIC: 2899 Concrete curing and hardening
compounds
HQ: Sika Corporation
201 Polito Ave
Lyndhurst NJ
201 933-8800

(P-4616)

LG NANOH2O LLC

Also Called: Lg Nanoh2o, Inc.
21250 Hawthorne Blvd Ste 330
(90503-5506)
PHONE..................424 218-4000
Jeff Green, *CEO*
Michael Demartino, *VP*
John Markovich, *CFO*
Doug Barnes, *COO*
Cj Kurth, *VP*
▲ EMP: 35 EST: 2005
SQ FT: 2,000
SALES (est): 7.3MM **Privately Held**
SIC: 2899 Distilled water
PA: Lg Chem, Ltd.
128 Yeoui-Daero, Yeongdeungpo-Gu
Seoul

(P-4617)

LUBRIZOL GLOBAL MANAGEMENT INC

3115 Propeller Dr (93446-8524)
PHONE..................805 239-1550
Daniel Mccornack, *Prin*
EMP: 35
SALES (corp-wide): 302.09B **Publicly Held**
Web: www.lubrizol.com
SIC: 2899 Chemical preparations, nec
HQ: Lubrizol Global Management, Inc.
9911 Brecksville Rd

Cleveland OH
216 447-5000

(P-4618)

MASTER BUILDERS LLC

Degussa Construction
9060 Haven Ave (91730-5405)
PHONE..................909 987-1758
Dave Lougheed, *Mgr*
EMP: 911
Web: master-builders-solutions.basf.us
SIC: 2899 Chemical preparations, nec
HQ: Master Builders, Llc
23700 Chagrin Blvd
Beachwood OH
800 228-3318

(P-4619)

MATSUI INTERNATIONAL CO INC (HQ)

Also Called: Unimark
1501 W 178th St (90248-3203)
PHONE..................310 767-7812
Masa Matsui, *Pr*
Yoshi Haga, *
◆ EMP: 180 EST: 1987
SQ FT: 30,000
SALES (est): 26.09MM **Privately Held**
Web: www.matsui-color.com
SIC: 2899 Ink or writing fluids
PA: Matsui Shikiso Chemical Co., Ltd.
64, Sakuradani, Kamikazan,
Yamashina-Ku
Kyoto KYO

(P-4620)

MC PRODUCTS INC

23331 Antonio Pkwy (92688-2664)
PHONE..................949 888-7100
Dave Maietta, *Pr*
EMP: 26 EST: 2003
SQ FT: 36,000
SALES (est): 1.13MM **Privately Held**
SIC: 2899 Waterproofing compounds

(P-4621)

MEDICAL CHEMICAL CORPORATION

Also Called: M C C
19250 Van Ness Ave (90501-1102)
P.O. Box 6217 (90504-0217)
PHONE..................310 787-6800
Emmanuel Didier, *Pr*
Patrick Braden, *
Andy Rocha, *
Kris Kontis, *
◆ EMP: 45 EST: 1954
SALES (est): 9.47MM **Privately Held**
Web: www.med-chem.com
SIC: 2899 2841 Chemical preparations, nec;
Soap and other detergents

(P-4622)

MOC PRODUCTS COMPANY INC (PA)

Also Called: Auto Edge Solutions
12306 Montague St (91331-2279)
PHONE..................818 794-3500
Mark Waco, *CEO*
Dave Waco, *
◆ EMP: 75 EST: 1954
SQ FT: 100,000
SALES (est): 73.97MM
SALES (corp-wide): 73.97MM **Privately Held**
Web: www.mocproducts.com
SIC: 2899 7549 5169 Corrosion preventive
lubricant; Automotive maintenance services
; Chemicals and allied products, nec

(P-4623)

MORTON SALT INC

1050 Pier F Ave (90802-6215)
P.O. Box 2289 (90801-2289)
PHONE..................562 437-0071
Ken Dobson, *Brnch Mgr*
EMP: 135
SALES (corp-wide): 1.22B **Privately Held**
Web: www.mortonsalt.com
SIC: 2899 Salt
HQ: Morton Salt, Inc.
444 W Lake St Ste 3000
Chicago IL

(P-4624)

OLDE THOMPSON LLC (DH)

3250 Camino Del Sol (93030-8998)
PHONE..................805 983-0388
David Sugarman, *CEO*
Jeffrey M Shumway, *Ch*
◆ EMP: 21 EST: 1917
SQ FT: 88,000
SALES (est): 114.1MM
SALES (corp-wide): 476.62MM **Privately Held**
Web: www.oldethompson.com
SIC: 2899 2099 5149 Salt; Seasonings and
spices; Spices and seasonings
HQ: Olam Food Ingredients Vietnam Pte.
Ltd.
7 Straits View
Singapore

(P-4625)

PACIFIC WTRPRFING RSTRTION INC

2845 Pomona Blvd (91768-3242)
PHONE..................909 444-3052
Ronald Bithell, *CEO*
EMP: 18 EST: 2005
SALES (est): 727.96K **Privately Held**
Web: www.pacificwaterproofing.com
SIC: 2899 7641 Waterproofing compounds;
Antique furniture repair and restoration

(P-4626)

PHIBRO ANIMAL HEALTH CORP

Phibro-Tech
8851 Dice Rd (90670-2515)
PHONE..................562 698-8036
Mark Alling, *Mgr*
EMP: 55
SALES (corp-wide): 977.89MM **Publicly Held**
Web: www.pahc.com
SIC: 2899 2819 Chemical preparations, nec;
Industrial inorganic chemicals, nec
HQ: Phibro Animal Health Corporation
300 Frank W Burr Blvd
Teaneck NJ
201 329-7300

(P-4627)

PRESTONE PRODUCTS CORPORATION

Also Called: Kik Custom Products
19500 Mariner Ave (90503-1644)
PHONE..................424 271-4836
Raymond Yu, *Manager*
EMP: 30
SALES (corp-wide): 118.94MM **Privately Held**
Web: www.prestone.com
SIC: 2899 5531 5169 Antifreeze compounds
; Automotive parts; Anti-freeze compounds
HQ: Prestone Products Corporation
6250 N River Rd Ste 6000
Rosemont IL

(P-4628)

RELTON CORPORATION

317 Rolyn Pl (91007-2838)
P.O. Box 60019 (91066-6019)
PHONE..................800 423-1505
William Kinard, *Ch*
Wm Craig Kinard, *
Craig Kinard, *
Kevin Kinard, *
Chris Kinard, *
◆ EMP: 65 EST: 1946
SQ FT: 20,000
SALES (est): 9.03MM **Privately Held**
Web: www.relton.com
SIC: 2899 3423 3546 2992 Chemical
preparations, nec; Masons' hand tools;
Power-driven handtools; Lubricating oils
and greases

(P-4629)

ROYAL ADHESIVES & SEALANTS LLC

800 E Anaheim St (90744-3637)
PHONE..................310 830-9904
Theodore M Clark, *Managing Member*
▲ EMP: 20 EST: 2006
SALES (est): 5.17MM
SALES (corp-wide): 3.75B **Publicly Held**
Web: www.hbfuller.com
SIC: 2899 3479 Waterproofing compounds;
Painting, coating, and hot dipping
PA: H.B. Fuller Company
1200 Willow Lake Blvd
Saint Paul MN
651 236-5900

(P-4630)

SIGMA-ALDRICH CORPORATION

Also Called: Safc Pharma
6211 El Camino Real (92009-1604)
PHONE..................760 710-6213
Tim Quinn, *Mgr*
EMP: 50
SALES (corp-wide): 23.09B **Privately Held**
Web: www.sigmaaldrich.com
SIC: 2899 Chemical preparations, nec
HQ: Sigma-Aldrich Corporation
3050 Spruce St
Saint Louis MO
314 771-5765

(P-4631)

SIKA CORPORATION

12767 Imperial Hwy (90670-4711)
PHONE..................562 941-0231
Jerry Monarch, *Brnch Mgr*
EMP: 17
SQ FT: 26,186
Web: usa.sika.com
SIC: 2899 Concrete curing and hardening
compounds
HQ: Sika Corporation
201 Polito Ave
Lyndhurst NJ
201 933-8800

(P-4632)

SNF HOLDING COMPANY

Also Called: Polypure
4690 Worth St (90063-1630)
PHONE..................323 266-4435
EMP: 18
SQ FT: 15,044
Web: www.snf.com
SIC: 2899 Water treating compounds
HQ: Snf Holding Company
1 Chemical Plant Rd
Riceboro GA

(PA)=Parent Co (HQ)=Headquarters
✿ = New Business established in last 2 years

(P-4633)
THE LUBRIZOL CORPORATION
30211 Avenida De Las Bandera (92688)
PHONE..................949 212-1863
EMP: 19
SALES (corp-wide): 302.09B **Publicly Held**
Web: www.lubrizol.com
SIC: 2899 Chemical preparations, nec
HQ: The Lubrizol Corporation
4400 Eston Cmmons Way Ste
Columbus OH
440 943-4200

(P-4634)
TORAY MEMBRANE USA INC (DH)
13435 Danielson St (92064-6825)
PHONE..................858 218-2360
Steve Cappos, *CEO*
Tak Wakisaka, *
Gabriel Juarez, *
◆ EMP: 85 EST: 2006
SQ FT: 90,000
SALES (est): 13.93MM **Privately Held**
Web: www.water.toray
SIC: 2899 Water treating compounds
HQ: Toray Holding (U.S.A), Inc.
461 5th Ave Fl 9
New York NY
212 697-8150

(P-4635)
UNITED PHARMA LLC
2317 Moore Ave (92833-2510)
PHONE..................714 738-8999
Bill Wang, *Pr*
▲ EMP: 130 EST: 2006
SQ FT: 53,000
SALES (est): 23.8MM **Privately Held**
Web: www.unitedpharmallc.com
SIC: 2899 Gelatin: edible, technical, photographic, or pharmaceutical

(P-4636)
USC HSC PURCHASING SVC
3560 Watt Way Mc0656 (90089-0084)
PHONE..................213 740-8165
Kim Henige, *Prin*
EMP: 18 EST: 2009
SALES (est): 879.12K **Privately Held**
SIC: 2899 Chemical preparations, nec

(P-4637)
VEOLIA WTS USA INC
Also Called: GE Water & Process Tech
8.5 Miles Nw Avila Beach (93424)
PHONE..................805 545-3743
EMP: 90
Web: www.watertechnologies.com
SIC: 2899 Water treating compounds
HQ: Veolia Wts Usa, Inc.
3600 Horizon Blvd
Trevose PA
866 439-2837

2911 Petroleum Refining

(P-4638)
ACCU-BLEND CORPORATION
364 Malbert St (92570-8336)
PHONE..................626 334-7744
Xia Wang, *CEO*
Kenny Wang, *Pr*
▲ EMP: 17 EST: 2005
SALES (est): 3.56MM **Privately Held**
Web: www.accu-blend.com
SIC: 2911 Paraffin wax

(P-4639)
CASTAIC TRUCK STOP INC
31611 Castaic Rd (91384-3939)
PHONE..................661 295-1374
Sarkis Khrimian, *Pr*
Refe Dimmuck, *
EMP: 26 EST: 1994
SQ FT: 2,000
SALES (est): 3.92MM **Privately Held**
Web: www.castaictruckstop.com
SIC: 2911 7389 5812 Diesel fuels; Flea market; American restaurant

(P-4640)
DE MENNO-KERDOON TRADING CO (HQ)
2000 N Alameda St (90222-2702)
PHONE..................310 537-7100
Jim Ennis, *COO*
Jay Demel, *
EMP: 149 EST: 1990
SQ FT: 60,000
SALES (est): 38.18MM
SALES (corp-wide): 128.17MM **Privately Held**
SIC: 2911 Oils, fuel
PA: World Oil Marketing Company
9302 Garfield Ave
South Gate CA
562 928-0100

(P-4641)
GOLDEN WEST REFINING COMPANY
13116 Imperial Hwy (90670-4817)
P.O. Box 2128 (90670-0138)
PHONE..................562 921-3581
Ted Orden, *Pr*
Moshe Sassover, *Sr VP*
EMP: 20 EST: 1978
SALES (est): 4.17MM
SALES (corp-wide): 9.39MM **Privately Held**
SIC: 2911 Gas, refinery
PA: Thrifty Oil Co.
13116 Imperial Hwy
Santa Fe Springs CA
562 921-3581

(P-4642)
KERN OIL & REFINING CO (HQ)
Also Called: Kern Energy
7724 E Panama Ln (93307-9210)
PHONE..................661 845-0761
EMP: 125 EST: 1971
SALES (est): 51.82MM
SALES (corp-wide): 101.77MM **Privately Held**
Web: www.kernoil.com
SIC: 2911 Petroleum refining
PA: Casey Company
180 E Ocean Blvd Ste 1010
Long Beach CA
562 436-9685

(P-4643)
LION TANK LINE INC
5801 Randolph St (90040-3415)
PHONE..................323 726-1966
Levon Termandjyan, *Pr*
EMP: 19 EST: 1992
SQ FT: 6,000
SALES (est): 999.92K **Privately Held**
SIC: 2911 4213 Diesel fuels; Liquid petroleum transport, non-local

(P-4644)
M ARGESO & CO INC
Also Called: Argeso
2628 River Ave (91770-3302)
PHONE..................626 573-3000
EMP: 22 EST: 2001
SALES (est): 2.48MM **Privately Held**
Web: www.paramelt.com
SIC: 2911 Paraffin wax

(P-4645)
MOLECULUM
3128 Red Hill Ave (92626-4525)
PHONE..................714 619-5139
EMP: 18 EST: 2015
SALES (est): 1.36MM **Privately Held**
Web: www.moleculum.com
SIC: 2911 Aromatic chemical products

(P-4646)
NEW LEAF BIOFUEL LLC
2285 Newton Ave (92113-3619)
PHONE..................619 236-8500
Jennifer Case, *Pt*
Nicole Kennard, *Managing Member*
▲ EMP: 35 EST: 2006
SALES (est): 6.14MM **Privately Held**
Web: www.newleafbiofuel.com
SIC: 2911 8742 Diesel fuels; Restaurant and food services consultants

(P-4647)
PARAMOUNT PETROLEUM CORP (DH)
Also Called: Paramount Asphalt
14700 Downey Ave (90723-4526)
PHONE..................562 531-2060
W S Lovejoy, *CEO*
◆ EMP: 155 EST: 1980
SQ FT: 6,000
SALES (est): 55.34MM
SALES (corp-wide): 20.25B **Publicly Held**
Web: www.alon.com
SIC: 2911 Petroleum refining
HQ: Alon Usa Energy, Inc.
310 Seven Springs Way # 500
Brentwood TN

(P-4648)
PBF ENERGY WESTERN REGION LLC (DH)
3760 Kilroy Airport Way Ste 640 (90806-2490)
PHONE..................973 455-7500
Thomas J Nimbley, *CEO*
EMP: 24 EST: 2015
SALES (est): 414.75MM
SALES (corp-wide): 46.83B **Publicly Held**
Web: www.pbfenergy.com
SIC: 2911 2992 Petroleum refining; Lubricating oils
HQ: Pbf Holding Company Llc
1 Sylvan Way Ste 2
Parsippany NJ

(P-4649)
SACAHN JV
15916 Bernardo Center Dr (92127-1828)
PHONE..................858 924-1110
EMP: 99 EST: 2014
SQ FT: 3,000
SALES (est): 4.22MM **Privately Held**
SIC: 2911 Oils, fuel

(P-4650)
SAN JOAQUIN REFINING CO INC
3500 Shell St (93308-5215)

P.O. Box 5576 (93388-5576)
PHONE..................661 327-4257
Kenneth E Fait, *Ch Bd*
Majid Mojibi, *
Dorothy A Gribben, *
EMP: 130 EST: 1979
SQ FT: 15,000
SALES (est): 47.17MM **Privately Held**
Web: www.sjr.com
SIC: 2911 Oils, fuel

(P-4651)
TESORO REFINING & MKTG CO LLC
5905 N Paramount Blvd (90805-3709)
PHONE..................562 728-2215
EMP: 79
SIC: 2911 5541 Petroleum refining; Gasoline service stations
HQ: Tesoro Refining & Marketing Company Llc
19100 Ridgewood Pkwy
San Antonio TX
210 626-6000

(P-4652)
TORRANCE REFINING COMPANY LLC
3700 W 190th St (90504-5733)
PHONE..................310 212-2800
Thomas J Nimbley, *CEO*
EMP: 600 EST: 2015
SALES (est): 90.51MM
SALES (corp-wide): 46.83B **Publicly Held**
Web: www.pbfenergy.com
SIC: 2911 2992 Petroleum refining; Lubricating oils
HQ: Pbf Energy Western Region Llc
3760 Kilroy Arprt Way # 640
Long Beach CA
973 455-7500

(P-4653)
TRICOR REFINING LLC
1134 Manor St (93308-3553)
P.O. Box 5877 (93388-5877)
PHONE..................661 393-7110
Majid Mojibi, *Managing Member*
Don Brookes, *Managing Member*
Kenneth E Fait, *Managing Member*
EMP: 28 EST: 2001
SALES (est): 9.96MM **Privately Held**
Web: www.tricorrefining.com
SIC: 2911 Oils, fuel

(P-4654)
ULTRAMAR INC
Also Called: Village Center Ultramar
9508 E Palmdale Blvd (93591-2202)
PHONE..................661 944-2496
Ken Berglund, *Mgr*
EMP: 35
SALES (corp-wide): 176.38B **Publicly Held**
Web: www.valero.com
SIC: 2911 Petroleum refining
HQ: Ultramar Inc.
1 Valero Way
San Antonio TX
210 345-2000

(P-4655)
VALERO REF COMPANY-CALIFORNIA
Also Called: Valero
2401 E Anaheim St (90744-4009)
PHONE..................562 491-6754
Mark Thair, *Mgr*
EMP: 828

SALES (corp-wide): 176.38B **Publicly Held**
Web: www.valero.com
SIC: 2911 Petroleum refining
HQ: Valero Refining Company-California
1 Valero Way
San Antonio TX
210 345-2000

(P-4656)
WD-40 COMPANY
Also Called: Hdp Holdings
9715 Businesspark Ave (92131-1642)
PHONE...............................619 275-1400
Garry Ridge, *Pr*
EMP: 233
SALES (corp-wide): 537.25MM **Publicly Held**
Web: www.wd40.com
SIC: 2911 Oils, lubricating
PA: Wd-40 Company
9715 Businesspark Ave
San Diego CA
619 275-1400

2951 Asphalt Paving Mixtures And Blocks

(P-4657)
CALMAT CO (DH)
Also Called: Vulcan Materials
500 N Brand Blvd Ste 500 (91203-1904)
PHONE...............................818 553-8821
Tom Hill, *CEO*
James W Smack, *
Daniel F Sansone, *
Danny R Shepherd, *
EMP: 150 EST: 1891
SQ FT: 40,000
SALES (est): 976.92MM **Publicly Held**
Web: www.vulcanmaterials.com
SIC: 2951 1442 1429 3273 Asphalt and asphaltic paving mixtures (not from refineries); Construction sand and gravel; Igneus rock, crushed and broken-quarrying; Ready-mixed concrete
HQ: Legacy Vulcan, Llc
1200 Urban Center Dr
Vestavia AL
205 298-3000

(P-4658)
DELTA TRADING LP
Also Called: Crimson Resource Management
17731 Millux Rd (93311-9714)
PHONE...............................661 834-5560
Mike Purdy, *Pt*
Rob Mcelroy, *Genl Mgr*
EMP: 20 EST: 2004
SALES (est): 4.47MM **Privately Held**
Web: www.deltatradinglp.com
SIC: 2951 Asphalt paving mixtures and blocks

(P-4659)
DESERT BLOCK CO INC
11374 Tuxford St (91352-2636)
PHONE...............................661 824-2624
Bill Fenzel, *Pr*
William Gapastione, *VP*
EMP: 22 EST: 1991
SALES (est): 843.66K **Privately Held**
SIC: 2951 3272 Concrete, asphaltic (not from refineries); Concrete products, precast, nec

(P-4660)
GOLDSTAR ASPHALT PRODUCTS INC

1354 Jet Way (92571-7466)
PHONE...............................951 940-1610
Jeff S Nelson, *Pr*
EMP: 32 EST: 1997
SALES (est): 2.89MM **Privately Held**
Web: www.goldstarasphalt.com
SIC: 2951 Asphalt paving mixtures and blocks

(P-4661)
LEWIS BARRICADE INC
4000 Westerly Pl Ste 100 (92660-2347)
PHONE...............................661 363-0912
John R Lewis, *Pr*
Teresa Lewis, *
EMP: 50 EST: 1998
SQ FT: 20,000
SALES (est): 1.88MM **Privately Held**
SIC: 2951 7353 Concrete, asphaltic (not from refineries); Heavy construction equipment rental

(P-4662)
NPG INC (PA)
Also Called: Goldstar Asphalt Products
1354 Jet Way (92571-7466)
P.O. Box 1515 (92572-1515)
PHONE...............................951 940-0200
Jeff Nelson, *Pr*
Sharon Nelson, *
EMP: 54 EST: 1962
SQ FT: 6,900
SALES (est): 22.79MM **Privately Held**
Web: www.goldstarasphalt.com
SIC: 2951 1799 1771 Asphalt and asphaltic paving mixtures (not from refineries); Parking lot maintenance; Driveway, parking lot, and blacktop contractors

(P-4663)
PAVEMENT RECYCLING SYSTEMS INC
Also Called: West Coast Milling
48028 90th St W (93536-9366)
PHONE...............................661 948-5599
Steve Ward, *Mgr*
EMP: 60
Web: www.pavementrecycling.com
SIC: 2951 1611 Asphalt paving mixtures and blocks; Surfacing and paving
PA: Pavement Recycling Systems, Inc.
10240 San Sevaine Way
Jurupa Valley CA

(P-4664)
PETROCHEM MANUFACTURING INC
Also Called: PMI
6168 Innovation Way (92009-1728)
PHONE...............................760 603-0961
EMP: 54 EST: 2002
SALES (est): 2.25MM **Privately Held**
Web: www.pmitechnology.com
SIC: 2951 1522 Asphalt paving mixtures and blocks; Residential construction, nec

(P-4665)
RECYCLED AGGREGATE MTLS CO INC (HQ)
Also Called: Ramco
2655 1st St Ste 210 (93065-1578)
PHONE...............................805 522-1646
Dennis L Newman, *Pr*
EMP: 18 EST: 2006
SALES (est): 6.21MM
SALES (corp-wide): 2.24B **Publicly Held**
Web: ramco.us.com
SIC: 2951 Concrete, asphaltic (not from refineries)

PA: Arcosa, Inc.
500 N Akard St Ste 400
Dallas TX
972 942-6500

(P-4666)
SURFACE-TECH LLC
888 Prospect St Ste 200 (92037-4261)
PHONE...............................619 880-0265
EMP: 18 EST: 2013
SALES (est): 2.28MM **Privately Held**
Web: www.surface-tech.com
SIC: 2951 Asphalt paving mixtures and blocks

2952 Asphalt Felts And Coatings

(P-4667)
ASPHALT DR INC
7440 Downing Ave (93308-5006)
P.O. Box 9914 (93389-1914)
PHONE...............................661 437-5995
Jeffrey Marvin White, *Pr*
EMP: 20 EST: 2014
SALES (est): 2.84MM **Privately Held**
Web: www.asphaltdoctr.com
SIC: 2952 Asphalt felts and coatings

(P-4668)
FONTANA PAPER MILLS INC
13733 Valley Blvd (92335-5291)
P.O. Box 339 (92334-0339)
PHONE...............................909 823-4100
George Thagard Iii, *Pr*
Jeff Thagard, *
Ray G Thagard Junior, *Sec*
EMP: 56 EST: 1967
SQ FT: 28,000
SALES (est): 9.41MM **Privately Held**
Web: www.fontanaroof.com
SIC: 2952 2621 Roofing materials; Felts, building

(P-4669)
HCO HOLDING II CORPORATION
999 N Pacific Coast Hwy Ste 800 (90245-2714)
PHONE...............................310 955-9200
Brian C Strauss, *Pr*
EMP: 560 EST: 2005
SALES (est): 98.92MM
SALES (corp-wide): 254.17MM **Privately Held**
SIC: 2952 2821 2891 Roof cement: asphalt, fibrous, or plastic; Polyurethane resins; Sealants
HQ: Hco Holding I Corporation
999 N Pacific Coast Hwy # 80
El Segundo CA
323 583-5000

(P-4670)
HENRY COMPANY LLC (HQ)
Also Called: Henry Building Products
999 N Pacific Coast Hwy Ste 800 (90245)
PHONE...............................310 955-9200
Frank Ready, *Pr*
Jason Peel, *
◆ EMP: 100 EST: 1981
SALES (est): 212.61MM
SALES (corp-wide): 6.59B **Publicly Held**
Web: www.henry.com
SIC: 2952 2821 2891 Roof cement: asphalt, fibrous, or plastic; Polyurethane resins; Sealants
PA: Carlisle Companies Incorporated
16430 N Scottsdale Rd
Scottsdale AZ
480 781-5000

(P-4671)
HNC PARENT INC (PA)
999 N Pacific Coast Hwy Ste 800 (90245-2714)
PHONE...............................310 955-9200
Rob Newbold, *Prin*
EMP: 100 EST: 2012
SALES (est): 254.17MM
SALES (corp-wide): 254.17MM **Privately Held**
SIC: 2952 2821 2891 Roof cement: asphalt, fibrous, or plastic; Polyurethane resins; Sealants

(P-4672)
JAMES HARDIE TRADING CO INC
26300 La Alameda Ste 400 (92691-8372)
PHONE...............................949 582-2378
Bryon G Borgardt, *Pr*
EMP: 160 EST: 1995
SALES (est): 30.07MM **Privately Held**
Web: www.jameshardie.com
SIC: 2952 Siding materials
HQ: James Hardie Transition Co., Inc.
26300 La Alameda Ste 400
Mission Viejo CA
949 348-1800

(P-4673)
LUNDAY-THAGARD COMPANY
9301 Garfield Ave (90280-3804)
P.O. Box 1519 (90280-1519)
PHONE...............................562 928-6990
John Todorovich, *VP Opers*
EMP: 369
SALES (corp-wide): 128.17MM **Privately Held**
SIC: 2952 2951 Roofing materials; Asphalt paving mixtures and blocks
HQ: Lunday-Thagard Company
9302 Garfield Ave
South Gate CA
562 928-7000

(P-4674)
NATIONAL COATINGS CORPORATION
1201 Calle Suerte (93012-8087)
PHONE...............................805 388-7112
▲ EMP: 20 EST: 1981
SALES (est): 10.66MM
SALES (corp-wide): 6.59B **Publicly Held**
Web: www.nationalcoatings.com
SIC: 2952 Roofing felts, cements, or coatings, nec
HQ: Henry Company Llc
999 N Pcf Cast Hwy Ste 80
El Segundo CA
310 955-9200

(P-4675)
OWENS CORNING SALES LLC
Also Called: Owens Corning
1501 N Tamarind Ave (90222-4130)
P.O. Box 5665 (90224-5665)
PHONE...............................310 631-1062
David Randalph, *Brnch Mgr*
EMP: 162
Web: www.owenscorning.com
SIC: 2952 2951 1761 Roofing felts, cements, or coatings, nec; Asphalt paving mixtures and blocks; Roofing, siding, and sheetmetal work
HQ: Owens Corning Sales, Llc
1 Owens Corning Pkwy
Toledo OH
419 248-8000

PRODUCTS & SVCS

(P-4676)
REP-KOTE PRODUCTS INC
10938 Beech Ave (92337-7260)
PHONE..............................909 355-1288
Robert Wang, *Pr*
EMP: 18 EST: 1981
SQ FT: 20,000
SALES (est): 219.34K Privately Held
SIC: 2952 5084 Asphalt felts and coatings;
Water pumps (industrial)

2992 Lubricating Oils And Greases

(P-4677)
AOCLSC INC
Also Called: Aocusa
8015 Paramount Blvd (90660-4811)
PHONE..............................813 248-1988
Harry Barkett, *Brnch Mgr*
EMP: 150
SALES (corp-wide): 110.41MM Privately
Held
SIC: 2992 Lubricating oils
HQ: Aoclsc, Inc.
1601 Mcclosky Blvd
Tampa FL
813 248-1988

(P-4678)
AOCLSC INC
Also Called: Aocusa
3365 E Slauson Ave (90058-3914)
PHONE..............................562 776-4000
Stephen Milam, *CEO*
EMP: 30
SALES (corp-wide): 110.41MM Privately
Held
SIC: 2992 Lubricating oils and greases
HQ: Aoclsc, Inc.
1601 Mcclosky Blvd
Tampa FL
813 248-1988

(P-4679)
CHEM ARROW CORP
13643 Live Oak Ln (91706-1317)
P.O. Box 2366 (91706-1198)
PHONE..............................626 358-2255
Alphonse Spalding, *Ch Bd*
Hemith Mitchello, *
▼ EMP: 25 EST: 1977
SQ FT: 36,000
SALES (est): 5.53MM Privately Held
Web: www.chemarrow.com
SIC: 2992 2899 Lubricating oils; Fuel tank or
engine cleaning chemicals

(P-4680)
CHEMTOOL INCORPORATED
1300 Goodrick Dr (93561-1508)
PHONE..............................661 823-7190
Bill Hart, *Mgr*
EMP: 125
SALES (corp-wide): 302.09B Publicly
Held
Web: www.lubrizol.com
SIC: 2992 2899 5172 Oils and greases,
blending and compounding; Chemical
preparations, nec; Lubricating oils and
greases
HQ: Chemtool Incorporated
801 W Rockton Rd
Rockton IL
815 957-4140

(P-4681)
DEMENNO/KERDOON HOLDINGS (DH)
Also Called: Demenno-Kerdoon
9302 Garfield Ave (90280-3805)
PHONE..............................562 231-1550
Robert Roth, *Ch Bd*
Bruce Demenno, *
Steve Kerdoon, *
Mark Snell, *Prin*
EMP: 67 EST: 1971
SQ FT: 21,000
SALES (est): 37.15MM
SALES (corp-wide): 128.17MM Privately
Held
Web: www.worldoilcorp.com
SIC: 2992 2911 Oils and greases, blending
and compounding; Petroleum refining
HQ: De Menno-Kerdoon Trading Company
2000 N Alameda St
Compton CA

(P-4682)
DEMENNO/KERDOON HOLDINGS
Also Called: D K Environmental
3650 E 26th St (90058-4104)
PHONE..............................323 268-3387
Rodney Ananda, *Mgr*
EMP: 27
SALES (corp-wide): 128.17MM Privately
Held
Web: www.worldoilcorp.com
SIC: 2992 4953 Oils and greases, blending
and compounding; Refuse systems
HQ: Demenno/Kerdoon Holdings
9302 Garfield Ave
South Gate CA
562 231-1550

(P-4683)
EVERGREEN HOLDINGS INC (PA)
18952 Macarthur Blvd Ste 410
(92612-1402)
PHONE..............................949 757-7770
Jacob Voogd, *Ch Bd*
Gary Colbert, *Pr*
Jesus Romero, *CFO*
Atam Gossain, *Sec*
▲ EMP: 20 EST: 1981
SQ FT: 6,200
SALES (est): 10.57MM
SALES (corp-wide): 10.57MM Privately
Held
SIC: 2992 4953 Re-refining lubricating oils
and greases, nec; Liquid waste, collection
and disposal

(P-4684)
EVERGREEN OIL INC (HQ)
Also Called: Evergreen Environmental Svcs
18025 S Broadway (90248-3539)
PHONE..............................949 757-7770
Jake Voogd, *CEO*
George Lamont, *Ex VP*
Obert Gwaltney, *VP Opers*
Jesus Romero, *VP*
EMP: 23 EST: 1983
SALES (est): 49.7MM
SALES (corp-wide): 5.17B Publicly Held
SIC: 2992 2911 4953 Lubricating oils and
greases; Petroleum refining; Refuse
systems
PA: Clean Harbors, Inc.
42 Longwater Dr
Norwell MA
781 792-5000

(P-4685)
EZ LUBE LLC
532 W Florida Ave (92543-4007)
PHONE..............................951 766-1996
Richie Berling, *Mgr*
EMP: 75
SALES (corp-wide): 21.83MM Privately
Held
Web: www.ezlube.com
SIC: 2992 Lubricating oils
PA: Ez Lube, Llc
3540 Howard Way Ste 200
Costa Mesa CA

(P-4686)
LUBECO INC
6859 Downey Ave (90805-1967)
PHONE..............................562 602-1791
Steven Rossi, *Pr*
EMP: 45 EST: 1958
SQ FT: 20,000
SALES (est): 6.4MM Privately Held
Web: www.lubecoinc.com
SIC: 2992 2851 Lubricating oils and greases
; Paints and allied products

(P-4687)
LUBRICATING SPECIALTIES COMPANY
Also Called: AOC USA
8015 Paramount Blvd (90660-4811)
PHONE..............................562 776-4000
◆ EMP: 170
SIC: 2992 Lubricating oils

(P-4688)
SOUTH WEST LUBRICANTS INC
Also Called: Maxima Racing Oils
9266 Abraham Way (92071-5611)
PHONE..............................619 449-5000
Daniel J Massie, *CEO*
◆ EMP: 54 EST: 1979
SQ FT: 50,000
SALES (est): 9.78MM Privately Held
Web: www.maximausa.com
SIC: 2992 5172 Lubricating oils and greases
; Lubricating oils and greases

(P-4689)
WD-40 COMPANY (PA)
9715 Businesspark Ave (92131-1642)
PHONE..............................619 275-1400
Steven A Brass, *Pr*
Gregory A Sandfort, *
Sara K Hyzer, *VP Fin*
Phenix Q Kiamilev, *Corporate Secretary*
Jeffrey G Lindeman, *Chief Human
Resources Officer*
EMP: 133 EST: 1953
SALES (est): 537.25MM
SALES (corp-wide): 537.25MM Publicly
Held
Web: www.wd40.com
SIC: 2992 2851 Lubricating oils; Removers
and cleaners

2999 Petroleum And Coal Products, Nec

(P-4690)
LUNDAY-THAGARD COMPANY (HQ)
Also Called: Ltr
9302 Garfield Ave (90280-3805)
P.O. Box 1519 (90280-1519)
PHONE..............................562 928-7000
Bernard B Roth, *Ch Bd*
Robert Roth, *

Steve Roth, *
Bert Wootan, *
Peter Stockhausen, *
EMP: 106 EST: 1937
SQ FT: 16,000
SALES (est): 47.41MM
SALES (corp-wide): 128.17MM Privately
Held
SIC: 2999 2951 2911 Coke; Paving blocks;
Gases and liquefied petroleum gases
PA: World Oil Marketing Company
9302 Garfield Ave
South Gate CA
562 928-0100

(P-4691)
RENTECH INC (PA)
10880 Wilshire Blvd Ste 1101 (90024-4101)
PHONE..............................310 571-9800
Keith Forman, *Pr*
Halbert S Washburn, *
Keith B Forman, *
Paul M Summers, *
Colin M Morris, *
EMP: 51 EST: 1981
SQ FT: 600
SALES (est): 144.69MM
SALES (corp-wide): 144.69MM Privately
Held
Web: www.rentechinc.com
SIC: 2999 2873 6794 Waxes, petroleum: not
produced in petroleum refineries;
Nitrogenous fertilizers; Patent buying,
licensing, leasing

3011 Tires And Inner Tubes

(P-4692)
AMERICAN GENERAL TOOL GROUP
929 Poinsettia Ave Ste 101 (92081-8459)
PHONE..............................760 745-7993
Nasreen Godil, *Pr*
EMP: 40 EST: 2014
SALES (est): 5.11MM Privately Held
Web: www.americangeneraltools.com
SIC: 3011 3492 3535 3822 Pneumatic tires,
all types; Control valves, aircraft: hydraulic
and pneumatic; Pneumatic tube conveyor
systems; Switches, pneumatic positioning
remote

(P-4693)
BIG BRAND TIRE & SERVICE
Also Called: Big Brand Tire & Svc - Menifee
26920 Newport Rd (92584-9076)
PHONE..............................951 679-6266
EMP: 99 EST: 2020
SALES (est): 2.65MM Privately Held
SIC: 3011 Automobile tires, pneumatic

(P-4694)
BRIDGESTONE AMERICAS INC
Also Called: Firestone Cmplete Auto Care 79
3690 Murphy Canyon Rd (92123-4455)
PHONE..............................858 874-3109
EMP: 47
Web: www.bridgestonetire.com
SIC: 3011 Tires and inner tubes
HQ: Bridgestone Americas, Inc.
200 4th Ave S Ste 100
Nashville TN
615 937-1000

(P-4695)
DESSER TIRE & RUBBER CO LLC (DH)
Also Called: Desser Tire & Rubber Co
6900 W Acco St (90640-5435)

P.O. Box 1028 (90640-1028)
PHONE..............................323 721-4900
◆ EMP: 35 EST: 1995
SALES (est): 22.97MM
SALES (corp-wide): 949.76MM **Publicly Held**
Web: www.desser.com
SIC: 3011 Airplane tires, pneumatic
HQ: Desser Holding Company, Llc
    6900 W Acco St
    Montebello CA
    323 721-4900

(P-4696)
EUHOMY LLC
1230 Santa Anita Ave (91733-3861)
PHONE..............................213 265-5081
EMP: 20
SALES (est): 1.4MM **Privately Held**
SIC: 3011 Tires and inner tubes

(P-4697)
HSB HOLDINGS INC
14050 Day St (92553-9106)
PHONE..............................951 214-6590
Ohannes Beudjekian, *Ch Bd*
Sarkis Beudjeaian, *
▲ EMP: 40 EST: 1989
SQ FT: 80,000
SALES (est): 5.25MM **Privately Held**
Web: www.basrecycling.com
SIC: 3011 Tires, cushion or solid rubber

(P-4698)
ITW GLOBAL TIRE REPAIR INC
Also Called: Access Marketing
125 Venture Dr Ste 210 (93401-9105)
PHONE..............................805 489-0490
E Scott Santi, *Ch Bd*
◆ EMP: 71 EST: 1993
SQ FT: 20,000
SALES (est): 16.45MM
SALES (corp-wide): 15.93B **Publicly Held**
Web: www.slime.com
SIC: 3011 Tire and inner tube materials and
    related products
PA: Illinois Tool Works Inc.
    155 Harlem Ave
    Glenview IL
    847 724-7500

(P-4699)
SKAT-TRAK
654 Avenue K (92320-1115)
P.O. Box 518 (92320-0518)
PHONE..............................909 795-2505
Ken Stuart, *Pr*
Diane Stuart, *
EMP: 24 EST: 1952
SQ FT: 3,000
SALES (est): 4.37MM **Privately Held**
Web: www.skat-trak.com
SIC: 3011 3599 3366 Tires and inner tubes;
    Propellers, ship and boat: machined;
    Copper foundries

(P-4700)
**TOYO TIRE HLDINGS
AMERICAS INC (HQ)**
3565 Harbor Blvd (92626-1405)
PHONE..............................714 229-6100
Tomoshige Mizutani, *CEO*
▲ EMP: 20 EST: 1988
SALES (est): 1.03B **Privately Held**
Web: www.toyotires.com
SIC: 3011 Automobile inner tubes
PA: Toyo Tire Corporation
    2-2-13, Fujinoki
    Itami HYO

(P-4701)
**YOKOHAMA CORP NORTH
AMERICA (HQ)**
Also Called: Yokohama Tire
1 Macarthur Pl (92707-5927)
PHONE..............................540 389-5426
Yasuo Tominaga, *CEO*
Takaharu Fushimi, *
◆ EMP: 250 EST: 1917
SALES (est): 792.7MM **Privately Held**
Web: www.yokohamatire.com
SIC: 3011 5014 Tires and inner tubes; Tires
    and tubes
PA: Yokohama Rubber Company, Limited,
    The
    2-1, Oiwake
    Hiratsuka KNG

3021 Rubber And Plastics Footwear

(P-4702)
FOUR STAR DISTRIBUTION
206 Calle Conchita (92672-5404)
PHONE..............................949 369-4420
Markus Bohi, *CEO*
Raul Ries, *
▲ EMP: 20 EST: 1991
SALES (est): 1.28MM **Privately Held**
SIC: 3021 Shoes, plastic soles molded to
    fabric uppers

(P-4703)
K-SWISS INC (DH)
Also Called: K-Swiss
523 W 6th St Ste 534 (90014-1225)
PHONE..............................323 675-2700
Philip Jeong, *Ch Bd*
Barney Waters, *CMO*
◆ EMP: 31 EST: 1990
SALES (est): 85.79MM **Privately Held**
Web: www.kswiss.com
SIC: 3021 Rubber and plastics footwear
HQ: Xtep International Holdings Limited
    Rm A 27/F Billion Ctr Twr A
    Kowloon Bay KLN

(P-4704)
K-SWISS SALES CORP
523 W 6th St Ste 534 (90014-1225)
PHONE..............................323 675-2700
Cheryl Kuchinka, *Pr*
EMP: 206 EST: 1999
SALES (est): 2.5MM **Privately Held**
Web: www.kswiss.com
SIC: 3021 Rubber and plastics footwear
HQ: K-Swiss Inc.
    523 W 6th St Ste 534
    Los Angeles CA
    323 675-2700

(P-4705)
**PLS DIABETIC SHOE COMPANY
INC**
21500 Osborne St (91304-1522)
PHONE..............................818 734-7080
Ambartsum Kumuryan, *Pr*
Konstandin Kumuryan, *
▲ EMP: 32 EST: 2004
SQ FT: 24,031
SALES (est): 4.55MM **Privately Held**
Web: www.pedorthiclab.com
SIC: 3021 Shoes, rubber or plastic molded
    to fabric

(P-4706)
PRINCIPLE PLASTICS
1136 W 135th St (90247-1919)

P.O. Box 2408 (90247-0408)
PHONE..............................310 532-3411
David Hoyt, *Pr*
Robert Hoyt, *
▲ EMP: 27 EST: 1948
SQ FT: 28,000
SALES (est): 7.54MM **Privately Held**
Web: www.sloggers.com
SIC: 3021 3949 2519 Galoshes, plastic; Golf
    equipment; Lawn and garden furniture,
    except wood and metal

(P-4707)
SKECHERS COLLECTION LLC
Also Called: SKECHERS
228 Manhattan Beach Blvd (90266-5347)
PHONE..............................310 318-3100
Robert Greenberg, *Managing Member*
◆ EMP: 20 EST: 1999
SALES (est): 260.86K **Publicly Held**
Web: www.skechers.com
SIC: 3021 5661 Shoes, rubber or plastic
    molded to fabric; Shoe stores
PA: Skechers U.S.A., Inc.
    228 Manhattan Beach Blvd # 200
    Manhattan Beach CA

(P-4708)
VANS INC (DH)
Also Called: Vans Shoes
1588 S Coast Dr (92626-1549)
PHONE..............................714 755-4000
Arthur I Carver, *Senior Vice President
Global Operations*
Robert L Nagel, *
Craig E Gosselin, *
Scott J Blechman, *
Marissa Pardini, *PRODUCT Merchandising*
▲ EMP: 279 EST: 1987
SQ FT: 185,000
SALES (est): 606.78MM
SALES (corp-wide): 11.61B **Publicly Held**
Web: www.vans.com
SIC: 3021 2321 2329 2325 Canvas shoes,
    rubber soled; Men's and boys' sports and
    polo shirts; Men's and boys' sportswear and
    athletic clothing; Slacks: men's,
    youths', and boys'
HQ: Vf Outdoor, Llc
    1551 Wewatta St
    Denver CO
    855 500-8639

3052 Rubber And Plastics Hose And Beltings

(P-4709)
**AMFLEX PLASTICS
INCORPORATED**
Also Called: Nationwide and International
4039 Calle Platino Ste G (92056-5827)
PHONE..............................760 643-1756
EMP: 21 EST: 1996
SQ FT: 18,000
SALES (est): 4.15MM **Privately Held**
Web: www.amflex.com
SIC: 3052 3089 Rubber and plastics hose
    and beltings; Extruded finished plastics
    products, nec

(P-4710)
**NORTH AMERICAN FIRE HOSE
CORP**
Also Called: Nafhc
910 Noble Way (93454-1506)
P.O. Box 1968 (93456-1968)
PHONE..............................805 922-7076
Michael S Aubuchon, *CEO*
Virginia Aubuchon, *

▲ EMP: 55 EST: 1980
SQ FT: 43,000
SALES (est): 6.4MM **Privately Held**
Web: www.nafhc.com
SIC: 3052 Fire hose, rubber

(P-4711)
**PARKER-HANNIFIN
CORPORATION**
Also Called: Parker Service Center
8460 Kass Dr (90621-3808)
PHONE..............................714 522-8840
Chris Wright, *Brnch Mgr*
EMP: 87
SALES (corp-wide): 19.07B **Publicly Held**
Web: www.parker.com
SIC: 3052 3429 Rubber and plastics hose
    and beltings; Hardware, nec
PA: Parker-Hannifin Corporation
    6035 Parkland Blvd
    Cleveland OH
    216 896-3000

(P-4712)
SANI-TECH WEST INC (HQ)
Also Called: Sanisure
1020 Flynn Rd (93012-8705)
PHONE..............................805 389-0400
Richard J Shor, *Pr*
Sherry Maxson, *VP Opers*
EMP: 61 EST: 1991
SQ FT: 27,000
SALES (est): 49.21MM
SALES (corp-wide): 5.69B **Privately Held**
Web: www.sani-techwest.com
SIC: 3052 3053 Rubber hose; Gasket
    materials
PA: 3i Group Plc
    16 Palace Street
    London
    207 928-3131

(P-4713)
STEWARD PLASTICS INC
Also Called: Smooth-Bor Plastics
23322 Del Lago Dr (92653-1310)
PHONE..............................949 581-9530
▼ EMP: 75 EST: 1971
SALES (est): 9.42MM **Privately Held**
Web: www.smoothborplastics.com
SIC: 3052 Plastic hose

(P-4714)
TECHNICAL HEATERS INC
Also Called: Thermolab
10959 Tuxford St (91352-2626)
PHONE..............................818 361-7185
Bruce W Jones, *Pr*
EMP: 18 EST: 1969
SQ FT: 35,000
SALES (est): 3.02MM **Privately Held**
Web: www.techheat.com
SIC: 3052 Plastic hose

(P-4715)
TK PAX INC
Also Called: P A X Industries
1545 Macarthur Blvd (92626-1407)
PHONE..............................714 850-1330
Tom Kawaguchi, *Pr*
Randy Tamura, *
▲ EMP: 30 EST: 1985
SALES (est): 4.62MM **Privately Held**
Web: www.paxindustries.com
SIC: 3052 3053 Rubber hose; Gaskets, all
    materials

P R O D U C T S & S V C S

(P-4716)
TTI FLOOR CARE NORTH AMER INC
13055 Valley Blvd (92335-2603)
PHONE................................440 996-2802
Ross Verrocchi, *Mgr*
EMP: 100
Web: www.ttifloorcare.com
SIC: 3052 5722 Vacuum cleaner hose, plastic; Vacuum cleaners
HQ: Tti Floor Care North America, Inc.
8405 Ibm Dr
Charlotte NC

(P-4717)
WESTFLEX INC (PA)
Also Called: Western Hose & Gasket
325 W 30th St (91950-7205)
PHONE................................619 474-7400
Dixon G Legros, *Pr*
Paula Legros, *
◆ **EMP:** 24 **EST:** 1981
SQ FT: 56,000
SALES (est): 5.94MM
SALES (corp-wide): 5.94MM **Privately Held**
Web: www.westflex.com
SIC: 3052 3053 5085 Rubber and plastics hose and beltings; Gaskets; packing and sealing devices; Hose, belting, and packing

---

3053 Gaskets; Packing And Sealing Devices

(P-4718)
ABLE INDUSTRIAL PRODUCTS INC (PA)
2006 S Baker Ave (91761-7709)
PHONE................................909 930-1585
Gilbert J Martinez, *CEO*
Debbie Viramontes, *
Gloria Martinez, *CTRL*
▲ **EMP:** 30 **EST:** 1974
SQ FT: 21,120
SALES (est): 11.08MM
SALES (corp-wide): 11.08MM **Privately Held**
Web: www.able123.com
SIC: 3053 3069 5085 Gaskets, all materials; Weather strip, sponge rubber; Industrial supplies

(P-4719)
BRYANT RUBBER CORP (PA)
1580 W Carson St (90810-1455)
PHONE................................310 530-2530
Steven Bryant, *Prin*
Steven Bryant, *Prin*
Robert Tracewell, *Prin*
Brogan Bryant, *Prin*
Tracy Hunter, *
EMP: 37 **EST:** 1971
SALES (est): 24.17MM
SALES (corp-wide): 24.17MM **Privately Held**
Web: www.bryantrubber.com
SIC: 3053 Gaskets; packing and sealing devices

(P-4720)
BRYANT RUBBER CORP
Also Called: Ingla Rubber Products
1083 W 251st St. (90706)
PHONE................................310 530-2530
EMP: 113
SALES (corp-wide): 24.17MM **Privately Held**
Web: www.bryantrubber.com

SIC: 3053 3061 Gaskets; packing and sealing devices; Mechanical rubber goods
PA: Bryant Rubber Corp.
1580 W Carson St
Long Beach CA
310 530-2530

(P-4721)
CANNON GASKET INC
7784 Edison Ave (92336-3635)
PHONE................................909 355-1547
Billy Cannon, *Pr*
Billy Jr P Cannon, *
Candy Houle, *
▲ **EMP:** 27 **EST:** 1971
SQ FT: 10,000
SALES (est): 4.35MM **Privately Held**
Web: www.cannongasket.com
SIC: 3053 Gaskets, all materials

(P-4722)
CHAVERS GASKET CORPORATION
23325 Del Lago Dr (92653-1309)
PHONE................................949 472-8118
Riley Cole, *CEO*
Christopher Cole, *
EMP: 25 **EST:** 1986
SQ FT: 13,000
SALES (est): 2.5MM **Privately Held**
Web: www.chaversgasket.com
SIC: 3053 Gaskets, all materials

(P-4723)
CIASONS INDUSTRIAL INC
1615 Boyd St (92705-5103)
PHONE................................714 259-0838
Paul Hsieh, *Pr*
Grace S P Hsieh, *
Samuel Hsieh, *
▲ **EMP:** 30 **EST:** 1985
SQ FT: 25,000
SALES (est): 2MM **Privately Held**
Web: www.ciasons.com
SIC: 3053 3563 Packing: steam engines, pipe joints, air compressors, etc.; Air and gas compressors

(P-4724)
D W MACK CO INC
900 W 8th St (91702-2216)
P.O. Box 1247 (91017-1247)
PHONE................................626 969-1817
Danny J Mack, *Pr*
Joseph Demarco, *
Dennis S Mack, *
▲ **EMP:** 40 **EST:** 1979
SALES (est): 4.71MM **Privately Held**
Web: www.dwmack.com
SIC: 3053 Gaskets, all materials

(P-4725)
DAN-LOC GROUP LLC
Also Called: Dan-Loc Bolt & Gasket
20444 Tillman Ave (90746-3516)
PHONE................................310 538-2822
Rudy Estrada, *Brnch Mgr*
EMP: 66
SALES (corp-wide): 23.23MM **Privately Held**
Web: www.danlocgroup.com
SIC: 3053 3452 Gaskets and sealing devices ; Bolts, nuts, rivets, and washers
PA: Dan-Loc Group, Llc
725 N Drennan St
Houston TX
713 356-3500

(P-4726)
DAR-KEN INC
Also Called: K & S Enterprises
10515 Rancho Rd (92301-3414)
PHONE................................760 246-4010
Ken Mc Gilp, *Pt*
Darla Mc Gilp, *
EMP: 32 **EST:** 1965
SQ FT: 10,000
SALES (est): 2.33MM **Privately Held**
Web: www.ksentusa.com
SIC: 3053 3728 Gaskets; packing and sealing devices; Aircraft parts and equipment, nec

(P-4727)
ERIKS NORTH AMERICA INC
15500 Blackburn Ave (90650-6845)
PHONE................................562 802-7782
EMP: 74
SALES (corp-wide): 484.16MM **Privately Held**
Web: www.eriksna.com
SIC: 3053 3965 3052 2992 Gaskets, all materials; Fasteners; Heater hose, rubber; Lubricating oils
PA: Eriks North America, Inc.
650 Washington Rd Ste 500
Pittsburgh PA
412 787-2400

(P-4728)
FREUDENBERG-NOK GENERAL PARTNR
Also Called: International Seal Company
2041 E Wilshire Ave (92705-4726)
PHONE................................714 834-0602
John Hudspeth, *Mgr*
EMP: 150
SQ FT: 28,928
SALES (corp-wide): 12.23B **Privately Held**
Web: www.fst.com
SIC: 3053 Gaskets and sealing devices
HQ: Freudenberg-Nok General Partnership
47774 W Anchor Ct
Plymouth MI
734 451-0020

(P-4729)
G F COLE CORPORATION (PA)
21735 S Western Ave (90501-3718)
PHONE................................310 320-0601
Fritz Cole, *Pr*
Cathy Cole, *
▼ **EMP:** 18 **EST:** 1982
SQ FT: 26,000
SALES (est): 4.45MM
SALES (corp-wide): 4.45MM **Privately Held**
Web: www.gfcole.com
SIC: 3053 3069 Gaskets, all materials; Hard rubber and molded rubber products

(P-4730)
GASKET ASSOCIATES LP (PA)
10816 Kurt St (91342-6844)
PHONE................................310 217-5630
Dewain R Butler, *Pt*
Edward R Hare, *Pt*
David L Price, *Pt*
Mureen Lador, *Owner*
EMP: 17 **EST:** 1991
SALES (est): 5.69MM **Privately Held**
SIC: 3053 Gaskets, all materials

(P-4731)
GASKET MANUFACTURING CO
8427 Secura Way (90670-2215)
PHONE................................310 217-5600
TOLL FREE: 800

Maureen E Labor, *CEO*
Dewain R Butler, *
Maureen E Labor, *Pr*
Vince Labor, *
EMP: 33 **EST:** 1937
SALES (est): 5.69MM **Privately Held**
Web: www.gasketmfg.com
SIC: 3053 Gaskets, all materials
PA: Gasket Associates Lp
10816 Kurt St
Sylmar CA

(P-4732)
HDZ BROTHERS INC
1924 E Mcfadden Ave (92705-4705)
PHONE................................714 953-4010
Zeferino Hernandez, *Pr*
EMP: 23 **EST:** 2007
SALES (est): 1.37MM **Privately Held**
SIC: 3053 Gaskets; packing and sealing devices

(P-4733)
HUTCHINSON SEAL CORPORATION (DH)
Also Called: National O Rings
11634 Patton Rd (90241-5212)
PHONE................................248 375-4190
▲ **EMP:** 120 **EST:** 1996
SQ FT: 125,000
SALES (est): 44.95MM
SALES (corp-wide): 788.22K **Publicly Held**
Web: www.hutchinson-seal.com
SIC: 3053 Gaskets and sealing devices
HQ: Hutchinson Corporation
460 Fuller Ave Ne
Grand Rapids MI
616 459-4541

(P-4734)
INDUSTRIAL GASKET AND SUP CO
Also Called: Gasketfab Division
23018 Normandie Ave (90502-2691)
P.O. Box 4138 (90510-4138)
PHONE................................310 530-1771
William P Hynes, *Pr*
Kevin P Treacy, *VP*
Theresa Holmes, *Sec*
EMP: 23 **EST:** 1970
SQ FT: 11,000
SALES (est): 2.41MM **Privately Held**
SIC: 3053 5085 Gaskets, all materials; Gaskets

(P-4735)
INERTECH SUPPLY INC
Also Called: Inertech
641 Monterey Pass Rd (91754-2418)
PHONE................................626 282-2000
James Huang, *Pr*
Charlie C Miskell, *
Bruce Wang, *
Walter Lee, *
▲ **EMP:** 75 **EST:** 1991
SQ FT: 14,000
SALES (est): 4.62MM **Privately Held**
Web: www.inertech.com
SIC: 3053 5085 2891 Gasket materials; Gaskets; Adhesives and sealants

(P-4736)
J MILLER CO INC
Also Called: Miller Gasket Co
11537 Bradley Ave (91340-2519)
PHONE................................818 837-0181
TOLL FREE: 800
Dennis D Miller, *Pr*
Elaine Miller, *

▲ **EMP:** 35 **EST:** 1961
SQ FT: 20,000
SALES (est): 2.32MM **Privately Held**
Web: www.millergasket.com
SIC: 3053 Gaskets, all materials

(P-4737)
KIRKHILL INC
Also Called: Haskon, Div of
300 E Cypress St (92821-4007)
PHONE......................714 529-4901
Michael Harden, *Brnch Mgr*
EMP: 700
SALES (corp-wide): 6.58B **Publicly Held**
Web: www.kirkhill.com
SIC: 3053 3728 2822 Gaskets; packing and
   sealing devices; Aircraft parts and
   equipment, nec; Synthetic rubber
HQ: Kirkhill Inc.
   300 E Cypress St
   Brea CA
   714 529-4901

(P-4738)
**MORGAN POLYMER SEALS
LLC (PA)**
2475a Paseo De Las Americas Ste 3303
(92154-7255)
PHONE......................619 498-9221
Kevin Morgan, *Pr*
Ed Ditz, *Contrlr*
▲ **EMP:** 314 **EST:** 1997
SQ FT: 33,500
SALES (est): 23.5MM
SALES (corp-wide): 23.5MM **Privately
Held**
Web: www.morganpolymerseals.com
SIC: 3053 Gaskets, all materials

(P-4739)
PARCO LLC (DH)
1801 S Archibald Ave (91761-7677)
PHONE......................909 947-2200
Adam Morrison Burgener, *CEO*
Angie Garcia, *VP*
▲ **EMP:** 113 **EST:** 1989
SALES (est): 50.97MM **Privately Held**
Web: www.parcoinc.com
SIC: 3053 Gaskets; packing and sealing
   devices
HQ: Datwyler Schweiz Ag
   Militarstrasse 7
   Schattdorf UR

(P-4740)
REAL SEAL CO INC
Also Called: Real Seal
1971 Don Lee Pl (92029-1141)
PHONE......................760 743-7263
Patrick Thomas Tobin, *CEO*
Rose Ann Tobin, *
◆ **EMP:** 25 **EST:** 1970
SQ FT: 22,000
SALES (est): 2.59MM **Privately Held**
Web: www.real-seal.com
SIC: 3053 5085 Oil seals, rubber; Industrial
   supplies

(P-4741)
ROETTELE INDUSTRIES
15485 Dupont Ave (91710-7605)
PHONE......................909 606-8252
Mark Roettele, *Pr*
Maurice Roettele, *Ch Bd*
Lon Roettele, *VP*
Randal Roettele, *Treas*
▲ **EMP:** 19 **EST:** 1979
SQ FT: 15,000
SALES (est): 2.33MM **Privately Held**
Web: www.roetteleindustries.com

SIC: 3053 5085 Gaskets, all materials;
   Industrial supplies

(P-4742)
RPM PRODUCTS INC (PA)
Also Called: Rubber Plastic & Metal Pdts
23201 Antonio Pkwy (92688-2653)
PHONE......................949 888-8543
Mark Paolella, *Pr*
Suzanne Paolella, *
▲ **EMP:** 35 **EST:** 1994
SALES (est): 9.32MM **Privately Held**
Web: www.rpmproducts.com
SIC: 3053 3089 5085 Gaskets and sealing
   devices; Injection molding of plastics;
   Gaskets and seals

(P-4743)
SEAL SCIENCE INC (HQ)
Also Called: S S I
3701 E Conant St (90808-1783)
PHONE......................949 253-3130
Frederick E Tuliper, *CEO*
Patricia Tuliper, *
▲ **EMP:** 68 **EST:** 1985
SALES (est): 16.33MM
SALES (corp-wide): 137.12MM **Privately
Held**
Web: www.sealscience.com
SIC: 3053 3089 3061 Gaskets, all materials;
   Injection molding of plastics; Mechanical
   rubber goods
PA: Sanders Industries Holdings, Inc.
   3701 E Conant St
   Long Beach CA
   562 354-2920

(P-4744)
SEALING CORPORATION
7353 Greenbush Ave # B (91605-4004)
PHONE......................818 765-7327
John Patterson, *Pr*
Adrian Patterson, *Sec*
▲ **EMP:** 22 **EST:** 1973
SQ FT: 2,600
SALES (est): 419.35K **Privately Held**
Web: www.selcoseal.com
SIC: 3053 Gaskets, all materials

(P-4745)
SEWING COLLECTION INC
3113 E 26th St (90058-8006)
PHONE......................323 264-2223
Touraj Tour, *Pr*
Houshang Tour, *VP*
◆ **EMP:** 100 **EST:** 1991
SQ FT: 135,000
SALES (est): 24.36MM **Privately Held**
Web: www.sewingcollection.com
SIC: 3053 5199 4953 Packing materials;
   Packaging materials; Recycling, waste
   materials

(P-4746)
SPIRA MANUFACTURING CORP
650 Jessie St (91340-2233)
PHONE......................818 764-8222
George M Kunkel, *Pr*
Bonnie Paul, *
Michael Kunkel, *
Wendy Kunkel, *
EMP: 30 **EST:** 1972
SQ FT: 15,000
SALES (est): 4.33MM **Privately Held**
Web: www.spira-emi.com
SIC: 3053 Gaskets, all materials

(P-4747)
SWABPLUS INC
9669 Hermosa Ave (91730-5813)

PHONE......................909 987-7898
Tom Y Lee, *CEO*
Garry Tsaur, *
Eddy C Wan, *
▲ **EMP:** 41 **EST:** 1998
SALES (est): 4.82MM **Privately Held**
SIC: 3053 Packing materials

(P-4748)
WEST COAST GASKET CO
300 Ranger Ave (92821-6217)
PHONE......................714 869-0123
Louis Russell, *Prin*
Jean Grey, *
EMP: 75 **EST:** 1979
SQ FT: 50,000
SALES (est): 16.07MM **Privately Held**
Web: www.westcoastgasket.com
SIC: 3053 3061 3469 5085 Gaskets, all
   materials; Mechanical rubber goods; Metal
   stampings, nec; Industrial supplies

3061 Mechanical Rubber Goods

(P-4749)
CRM CO LLC (PA)
Also Called: C R M
1301 Dove St Ste 940 (92660-2483)
PHONE......................949 263-9100
H Barry Takallou, *CEO*
▲ **EMP:** 19 **EST:** 1998
SALES (est): 8.55MM
SALES (corp-wide): 8.55MM **Privately
Held**
Web: www.crmrubber.com
SIC: 3061 Mechanical rubber goods

(P-4750)
MIKRON PRODUCTS INC
3701 E Conant St (90808-1783)
PHONE......................909 545-8600
Nicholas Carone, *Pr*
Palma Carone, *
EMP: 37 **EST:** 1974
SALES (est): 1.11MM **Privately Held**
SIC: 3061 Mechanical rubber goods

(P-4751)
OMNI SEALS INC
11031 Jersey Blvd Ste A (91730-5150)
PHONE......................909 946-0181
EMP: 68
SIC: 3061 Mechanical rubber goods

(P-4752)
**R D RUBBER TECHNOLOGY
CORP**
12870 Florence Ave (90670-4540)
PHONE......................562 941-4800
Walter V Hopkins Junior, *Pr*
Rosanne Dukowitz, *
EMP: 27 **EST:** 1986
SQ FT: 15,600
SALES (est): 3.7MM **Privately Held**
Web: www.rdrubber.com
SIC: 3061 Mechanical rubber goods

(P-4753)
**RUBBERCRAFT CORP CAL LTD
(HQ)**
Also Called: Rubber Teck Division
3701 E Conant St (90808-1783)
PHONE......................562 354-2800
Marc Sanders, *CEO*
Eric Sanders, *
EMP: 238 **EST:** 1984
SQ FT: 40,000

SALES (est): 48.96MM
SALES (corp-wide): 137.12MM **Privately
Held**
Web: www.rubbercraft.com
SIC: 3061 Appliance rubber goods
   (mechanical)
PA: Sanders Industries Holdings, Inc.
   3701 E Conant St
   Long Beach CA
   562 354-2920

3069 Fabricated Rubber Products, Nec

(P-4754)
3M COMPANY
Also Called: 3M
1601 S Shamrock Ave (91016-4248)
PHONE......................626 358-0136
Bob Palmer, *Mgr*
EMP: 29
SALES (corp-wide): 34.23B **Publicly Held**
Web: www.3m.com
SIC: 3069 Rubber coated fabrics and clothing
PA: 3m Company
   3m Center
   Saint Paul MN
   651 733-1110

(P-4755)
ABBA ROLLER LLC (DH)
1351 E Philadelphia St (91761-5719)
PHONE......................909 947-1244
▲ **EMP:** 19 **EST:** 2010
SQ FT: 4,000
SALES (est): 5.62MM **Privately Held**
Web: www.abbaroller.com
SIC: 3069 Roll coverings, rubber
HQ: Electro-Coatings, Inc.
   216 Baywood St
   Houston TX
   713 923-5935

(P-4756)
AMES RUBBER MFG CO INC
Also Called: Ames Industrial
4516 Brazil St (90039-1002)
PHONE......................818 240-9313
TOLL FREE: 800
Timothy L Brown, *CEO*
Pat Brown, *
▲ **EMP:** 30 **EST:** 1954
SQ FT: 20,000
SALES (est): 4.59MM **Privately Held**
Web: www.amesrubberonline.com
SIC: 3069 3061 Medical and laboratory
   rubber sundries and related products;
   Mechanical rubber goods

(P-4757)
**APON MEDICAL MOLDING AND
ASSEMBLY INC**
10005 Marconi Dr Ste B (92154-5207)
PHONE......................619 793-4887
EMP: 99 **EST:** 2005
SALES (est): 4.09MM **Privately Held**
SIC: 3069 Molded rubber products

(P-4758)
**CALIFORNIA GASKET AND RBR
CORP (PA)**
533 W Collins Ave (92867-5509)
PHONE......................310 323-4250
Scott H Franklin, *VP*
Armando Rodriguez, *
EMP: 36 **EST:** 1942
SQ FT: 51,000
SALES (est): 5.34MM

P
R
O
D
U
C
T
S

&

S
V
C
S

SALES (corp-wide): 5.34MM **Privately Held**
Web: www.californiagasket.com
SIC: **3069** 3053 3469 3061 Molded rubber products; Gaskets; packing and sealing devices; Metal stampings, nec; Appliance rubber goods (mechanical)

(P-4759)
COI RUBBER PRODUCTS INC
19255 San Jose Ave Unit D-1 (91748-1418)
PHONE............................626 965-9966
David Chao, *CEO*
EMP: 450 EST: 2013
SQ FT: 2,500
SALES (est): 22.53MM **Privately Held**
Web: www.coirubber.com
SIC: **3069** Medical and laboratory rubber sundries and related products

(P-4760)
DURO-FLEX RUBBER PRODUCTS INC
13215 Lakeland Rd (90670-4522)
PHONE............................562 946-5533
John A Lozano, *Pr*
EMP: 21 EST: 1967
SQ FT: 6,000
SALES (est): 484.79K **Privately Held**
Web: www.duroflexrubber.com
SIC: **3069** Molded rubber products

(P-4761)
EXROX INC
535 Ceres Ave (90013-1716)
PHONE............................213 536-5290
Alex Echeverry, *Brnch Mgr*
EMP: 21
SALES (corp-wide): 32MM **Privately Held**
SIC: **3069** Rubber coated fabrics and clothing
PA: Exrox Inc.
323 S Clarence St
Los Angeles CA
213 536-5290

(P-4762)
FALCON WATERFREE TECH LLC (HQ)
2255 Barry Ave (90064-1401)
PHONE............................310 209-7250
◆ EMP: 20 EST: 2000
SALES (est): 10.76MM
SALES (corp-wide): 20.04MM **Privately Held**
Web: www.falconwatertech.com
SIC: **3069** Pump sleeves, rubber
PA: Management Kingsley Llc Mapleton
9952 Santa Monica Blvd
Beverly Hills CA
310 282-0780

(P-4763)
FLEX COMPANY (PA)
318 Lincoln Blvd Ste 204 (90291-2828)
PHONE............................424 209-2711
Lauren Schulte, *CEO*
Brian Wang, *Sec*
EMP: 25 EST: 2015
SQ FT: 4,500
SALES (est): 5.61MM
SALES (corp-wide): 5.61MM **Privately Held**
Web: www.flexfits.com
SIC: **3069** 5999 5122 Birth control devices, rubber; Toiletries, cosmetics, and perfumes; Drugs, proprietaries, and sundries

(P-4764)
GOOD-WEST RUBBER CORP (PA)
Also Called: Goodyear Rbr Co Southern Cal
9615 Feron Blvd (91730-4503)
PHONE............................909 987-1774
Christian Groche, *Pr*
Harold W Sears, *
Patrick Sears, *
Fred Ledesma, *
▲ EMP: 145 EST: 1961
SQ FT: 56,000
SALES (est): 19.69MM
SALES (corp-wide): 19.69MM **Privately Held**
Web: www.goodyearrubber.com
SIC: **3069** 3061 5531 Molded rubber products; Mechanical rubber goods; Automotive tires

(P-4765)
GOODWEST RUBBER LININGS INC
Also Called: Goodwest Linings & Coatings
8814 Industrial Ln (91730-4528)
PHONE............................888 499-0085
Ryan Sears, *Pr*
Larry Sears, *Sec*
Patrick Sears, *VP*
Fred Ledesma, *VP*
EMP: 20 EST: 1995
SQ FT: 300,000
SALES (est): 4.83MM **Privately Held**
Web: www.goodwestlining.com
SIC: **3069** Linings, vulcanizable rubber

(P-4766)
HITT COMPANIES
Also Called: Hitt Marking Devices I D Tech
3231 W Macarthur Blvd (92704-6801)
PHONE............................714 979-1405
Harold G Hitt, *Pr*
Ken Hitt, *
Heidi Hitt, *
▲ EMP: 24 EST: 1987
SQ FT: 10,000
SALES (est): 4.4MM **Privately Held**
Web: www.hittcompanies.com
SIC: **3069** 3993 5199 Stationer's rubber sundries; Signs and advertising specialties; Badges

(P-4767)
HUTCHINSON AROSPC & INDUST INC
Also Called: Barry Controls Aerospace
4510 W Vanowen St (91505-1135)
P.O. Box 7710 (91510-7710)
PHONE............................818 843-1000
Grant Hintze, *CEO*
EMP: 156
SALES (corp-wide): 788.22K **Publicly Held**
Web: www.hutchinsonai.com
SIC: **3069** Molded rubber products
HQ: Hutchinson Aerospace & Industry, Inc.
82 South St
Hopkinton MA
508 417-7000

(P-4768)
INNOCOR WEST LLC
300 S Tippecanoe Ave 310 (92408)
PHONE............................909 307-3737
Carol S Eicher, *CEO*
Doug Vaughan, *CFO*
▲ EMP: 361 EST: 2003
SQ FT: 150,000
SALES (est): 2.08MM **Privately Held**

SIC: **3069** 5021 Pillows, sponge rubber; Mattresses
HQ: Innocor, Inc.
200 Schulz Dr Ste 2
Red Bank NJ

(P-4769)
INTERNATIONAL RUBBER PDTS INC (HQ)
Also Called: Irp
1035 Calle Amanecer (92673-6260)
PHONE............................909 947-1244
Rich Mcmanus, *CEO*
▲ EMP: 58 EST: 2003
SQ FT: 45,000
SALES (est): 23.55MM
SALES (corp-wide): 137.12MM **Privately Held**
Web: www.irpi.com
SIC: **3069** Medical and laboratory rubber sundries and related products
PA: Sanders Industries Holdings, Inc.
3701 E Conant St
Long Beach CA
562 354-2920

(P-4770)
JJ ACQUISITIONS LLC
8501 Fllbrook Ave Ste 370 (91304)
PHONE............................818 772-0100
Matthew Matsudaira, *Managing Member*
EMP: 41 EST: 2014
SALES (est): 7MM **Privately Held**
SIC: **3069** Toys, rubber

(P-4771)
KIRKHILL INC
1451 S Carlos Ave (91761-7676)
P.O. Box 7012 (90242-7012)
PHONE............................562 803-1117
Robert L Harold, *Ch*
Bruce Mekjian, *
Arlene Hite, *
Gary Riopelle, *
EMP: 95 EST: 1941
SALES (est): 9.29MM **Privately Held**
Web: www.kirkhill.com
SIC: **3069** Acid bottles, rubber

(P-4772)
KIRKHILL RUBBER COMPANY
2500 E Thompson St (90805-1836)
PHONE............................562 803-1117
David Schlothauer, *Pr*
Edward Reker, *
EMP: 99 EST: 2018
SALES (est): 19.97MM
SALES (corp-wide): 231.22K **Privately Held**
Web: www.kirkhill.com
SIC: **3069** Medical and laboratory rubber sundries and related products
HQ: Hexpol Holding Inc.
14330 Kinsman Rd
Burton OH
440 834-4644

(P-4773)
KMC ACQUISITION LLC (PA)
Also Called: Kirkhill Manufacturing Company
1451 S Carlos Ave (91761-7676)
PHONE............................562 396-0121
▲ EMP: 51 EST: 1996
SALES (est): 24.5MM **Privately Held**
Web: www.rubbersales.com
SIC: **3069** Molded rubber products

(P-4774)
LEONARDS MOLDED PRODUCTS INC
25031 Anza Dr (91355-3414)
PHONE............................661 253-2227
Randy Smith, *Pr*
Randy Smith, *Pr*
Frank Smith, *
EMP: 25 EST: 1984
SQ FT: 5,000
SALES (est): 2.79MM **Privately Held**
SIC: **3069** Molded rubber products

(P-4775)
LINE ONE LABORATORIES INC USA
Also Called: Line One Laboratories
9600 Lurline Ave (91311-5107)
PHONE............................818 886-2288
▲ EMP: 17 EST: 1990
SQ FT: 22,000
SALES (est): 1.82MM **Privately Held**
Web: www.lineonelabsusa.com
SIC: **3069** 5122 Medical and laboratory rubber sundries and related products; Medical rubber goods

(P-4776)
MATZ RUBBER COMPANY INC
1209 Chestnut St (91506-1626)
PHONE............................323 849-5170
Carmela B San Diego, *CEO*
Jan Jensen, *Sec*
EMP: 20 EST: 1954
SQ FT: 12,000
SALES (est): 2.42MM **Privately Held**
Web: www.matzabrasive.com
SIC: **3069** 3541 3291 Rubber covered motor mounting rings (rubber bonded); Machine tools, metal cutting type; Abrasive products

(P-4777)
MITCHELL PROCESSING LLC
2778 Pomona Blvd (91768-3222)
PHONE............................909 519-5759
EMP: 20 EST: 2012
SQ FT: 100,000
SALES (est): 1.6MM **Privately Held**
Web: www.mitchellkidcover.com
SIC: **3069** Custom compounding of rubber materials

(P-4778)
MITCHELL RUBBER PRODUCTS LLC (PA)
1880 Iowa Ave Ste 400 (92507-2405)
PHONE............................951 681-5655
Theodore Ballou, *CEO*
Mark Mitchell, *Corporate Secretary*
◆ EMP: 120 EST: 1967
SALES (est): 26.42MM
SALES (corp-wide): 26.42MM **Privately Held**
Web: www.mitchellrubber.com
SIC: **3069** 2891 2822 Mats or matting, rubber, nec; Adhesives and sealants; Synthetic rubber

(P-4779)
MODUS ADVANCED INC
2772 Loker Ave W (92010-6610)
PHONE............................925 960-8700
Richard Mackirdy Junior, *CEO*
Don E Ulery, *
Natalia Spruiell, *
▲ EMP: 53 EST: 1976
SALES (est): 14.66MM **Privately Held**
Web: www.modusadvanced.com

SIC: 3069 3599 3053 Molded rubber products; Machine and other job shop work; Gaskets; packing and sealing devices

(P-4780)
NEWBY RUBBER INC
320 Industrial St (93307-2706)
PHONE..............................661 327-5137
TOLL FREE: 800
Kelly Newby, *Pr*
Lori Newby, *
▼ EMP: 25 EST: 1958
SQ FT: 80,000
SALES (est): 4.39MM **Privately Held**
Web: www.newbyrubber.com
SIC: 3069 Molded rubber products

(P-4781)
NUSIL TECHNOLOGY LLC (DH)
Also Called: Nusil
1050 Cindy Ln (93013-2906)
PHONE..............................805 684-8780
◆ EMP: 400 EST: 1980
SALES (est): 131.69MM
SALES (corp-wide): 7.51B **Publicly Held**
Web: nusil.avantorsciences.com
SIC: 3069 Medical and laboratory rubber sundries and related products
HQ: Avantor Performance Materials, Llc
100 W Matsonford Rd Ste 1
Radnor PA
610 573-2600

(P-4782)
OXYSTRAP INTERNATIONAL INC
8705 Complex Dr (92123-1401)
PHONE..............................800 699-6901
Bruce L Gertsch, *CEO*
EMP: 28 EST: 2015
SALES (est): 588.5K **Privately Held**
Web: www.oxystrap.com
SIC: 3069 2326 3949 Medical and laboratory rubber sundries and related products; Medical and hospital uniforms, men's; Team sports equipment

(P-4783)
PACIFICTECH MOLDED PDTS INC
22695 Old Canal Rd (92887-4601)
PHONE..............................714 279-9928
Jane Xu, *Pr*
▲ EMP: 18 EST: 2006
SALES (est): 2.21MM **Privately Held**
Web: www.pacifictechmold.com
SIC: 3069 Rubber automotive products

(P-4784)
PLAYMAX SURFACING INC
Also Called: Califrnia Rcrtion Instllations
1950 Compton Ave Ste 111 (92881-6471)
P.O. Box 77372 (92877-0112)
PHONE..............................951 250-6039
Chris Wolf, *Pr*
EMP: 19 EST: 2014
SQ FT: 3,500
SALES (est): 2.14MM **Privately Held**
Web: www.playmaxsurfacing.com
SIC: 3069 5091 1752 1771 Flooring, rubber: tile or sheet; Sporting and recreation goods; Floor laying and floor work, nec; Flooring contractor

(P-4785)
PMR PRECISION MFG & RBR CO INC
1330 Etiwanda Ave (91761-8605)
PHONE..............................909 605-7525

Samuel Surh, *Pr*
George Surh, *
EMP: 30 EST: 1996
SQ FT: 36,800
SALES (est): 2.67MM **Privately Held**
Web: www.pmrubbertech.com
SIC: 3069 2295 Rubberized fabrics; Coated fabrics, not rubbered

(P-4786)
PROMOTONAL DESIGN CONCEPTS INC
Also Called: Creative Inflatables
9872 Rush St (91733-2635)
PHONE..............................626 579-4454
Adam Melendez, *CEO*
◆ EMP: 71 EST: 1984
SALES (est): 7.87MM **Privately Held**
Web: www.promotionaldesigngroup.com
SIC: 3069 7389 5092 2394 Balloons, advertising and toy: rubber; Balloons, novelty and toy; Toy novelties and amusements; Canvas and related products

(P-4787)
PURUS INTERNATIONAL INC
82860 Avenue 45 (92201-2396)
PHONE..............................760 775-4500
Dennis Baldwin, *Pr*
Jessica Baldwin, *CFO*
◆ EMP: 19 EST: 2002
SQ FT: 3,000
SALES (est): 3.4MM **Privately Held**
Web: www.purusint.com
SIC: 3069 2381 Mats or matting, rubber, nec ; Glove linings, except fur

(P-4788)
R & R RUBBER MOLDING INC
2444 Loma Ave (91733-1416)
P.O. Box 3533 (91733-0533)
PHONE..............................626 575-8105
Richard P Norman, *Pr*
EMP: 35 EST: 1977
SQ FT: 6,100
SALES (est): 3.26MM **Privately Held**
Web: www.rrrubber.com
SIC: 3069 Molded rubber products

(P-4789)
R & R SERVICES CORPORATION
Also Called: Geolabs Westlake Village
3595 Old Conejo Rd (91320-2122)
PHONE..............................818 889-2562
Ronald Z Shmerling, *Pr*
EMP: 25 EST: 1983
SALES (est): 2.14MM **Privately Held**
SIC: 3069 8999 8711 Laboratory sundries: cases, covers, funnels, cups, etc.; Geological consultant; Engineering services

(P-4790)
R & S PROCESSING CO INC
15712 Illinois Ave (90723-4113)
P.O. Box 2037 (90723-8037)
PHONE..............................562 531-0738
Karen A Kelly, *Pr*
Linda M Inga, *
Anthony J Inga, *
EMP: 73 EST: 1959
SQ FT: 53,000
SALES (est): 8.16MM **Privately Held**
Web: www.rsprocessing.com
SIC: 3069 Reclaimed rubber (reworked by manufacturing processes)

(P-4791)
ROGERS CORPORATION
Also Called: Diversified Silicone
13937 Rosecrans Ave (90670-5209)

PHONE..............................562 404-8942
Brian Lindey, *Genl Mgr*
EMP: 60
SALES (corp-wide): 971.17MM **Publicly Held**
Web: www.rogerscorp.com
SIC: 3069 Bags, rubber or rubberized fabric
PA: Rogers Corporation
2225 W Chandler Blvd
Chandler AZ
480 917-6000

(P-4792)
RUBBER-TRIM PRODUCTS INC
Also Called: Trim-Lok
6855 Hermosa Cir (90620-1151)
P.O. Box 6180 (90622-6180)
PHONE..............................714 562-0500
EMP: 26 EST: 1983
SALES (est): 982.64K **Privately Held**
Web: www.trimlok.com
SIC: 3069 3061 Molded rubber products; Mechanical rubber goods

(P-4793)
S & H RUBBER CO
1141 E Elm Ave (92831-5023)
PHONE..............................714 525-0277
Stephen Haney, *Pr*
Mike Haney, *Mgr*
EMP: 28 EST: 1967
SQ FT: 5,406
SALES (est): 2.89MM **Privately Held**
Web: www.shrubber.com
SIC: 3069 Washers, rubber

(P-4794)
SANTA FE RUBBER PRODUCTS INC
12306 Washington Blvd (90606-2597)
PHONE..............................562 693-2776
William Krames, *Pr*
Mike Peterman, *
EMP: 50 EST: 1966
SQ FT: 30,000
SALES (est): 5.06MM **Privately Held**
Web: www.santaferubber.com
SIC: 3069 Molded rubber products

(P-4795)
SHERCON LLC
Also Called: Shercon, Inc.
18704 S Ferris Pl (90220-6400)
▲ EMP: 60 EST: 1966
SQ FT: 50,000
SALES (est): 12.03MM
SALES (corp-wide): 2.13B **Privately Held**
Web: www.caplugs.com
SIC: 3069 3089 2672 Tape, pressure sensitive: rubber; Injection molded finished plastics products, nec; Paper; coated and laminated, nec
HQ: Caplugs, Inc.
2150 Elmwood Ave
Buffalo NY
716 876-9855

(P-4796)
SPANGLER INDUSTRIES INC
Also Called: A S I American
1711 N Delilah St (92879-1865)
P.O. Box 1445 (92878-1445)
PHONE..............................951 735-5000
Bernard D Spangler, *Pr*
Greg Spangler, *
EMP: 165 EST: 1970
SQ FT: 37,897
SALES (est): 8.53MM **Privately Held**
SIC: 3069 Rubber bands

(P-4797)
TA AEROSPACE CO (DH)
28065 Franklin Pkwy (91355-4117)
PHONE..............................661 775-1100
Carol Marinello, *Pr*
▲ EMP: 250 EST: 1919
SQ FT: 100,000
SALES (est): 193.2MM
SALES (corp-wide): 6.58B **Publicly Held**
Web: www.taaerospace.com
SIC: 3069 Reclaimed rubber and specialty rubber compounds
HQ: Esterline Technologies Corp
1301 E 9th St Ste 3000
Cleveland OH
216 706-2960

(P-4798)
TIMEMED LABELING SYSTEMS INC (DH)
27770 Entertainment Dr Ste 200 (91355)
PHONE..............................818 897-1111
Cecil Kost, *CEO*
Mark Segal, *
Tracey Carpentier, *
EMP: 100 EST: 1953
SQ FT: 75,000
SALES (est): 37.7MM
SALES (corp-wide): 1.33B **Publicly Held**
SIC: 3069 Tape, pressure sensitive: rubber
HQ: Precision Dynamics Corporation
25124 Sprngfeld Ct Ste 20
Valencia CA
818 897-1111

(P-4799)
US RUBBER RECYCLING INC
1231 Lincoln St (92324-3533)
PHONE..............................909 825-1200
Rick Snyder, *Pr*
▲ EMP: 22 EST: 1996
SQ FT: 30,000
SALES (est): 7.48MM **Privately Held**
Web: www.usrubber.com
SIC: 3069 Acid bottles, rubber

(P-4800)
US RUBBER ROLLER COMPANY INC
1516 7th St (92507-4421)
PHONE..............................951 682-2221
Jose Uribe, *Pr*
Lebizia Uribe, *VP*
Ramie Uribe, *Sec*
EMP: 18 EST: 1994
SQ FT: 10,000
SALES (est): 2.37MM **Privately Held**
Web: www.usrubberroller.com
SIC: 3069 Medical and laboratory rubber sundries and related products

(P-4801)
VIKING RUBBER PRODUCTS INC
2600 Homestead Pl (90220-5610)
PHONE..............................310 868-5200
Rod Trujillo, *CEO*
Leigh Munsell, *Pr*
Ricardo Ordonez, *CFO*
EMP: 19 EST: 1981
SALES (est): 3.37MM
SALES (corp-wide): 137.12MM **Privately Held**
Web: www.irpi.com
SIC: 3069 3061 Custom compounding of rubber materials; Mechanical rubber goods
HQ: International Rubber Products, Inc.
1035 Calle Amanecer
San Clemente CA

(P-4802)
VIP RUBBER COMPANY INC (PA)
540 S Cypress St (90631-6127)
PHONE.....................562 905-3456
Bernardyne Louise Campana, Pr
Howard Vipperman, *
Deena Campana, *
Kathy Leclair, *
Thomas Leclair, *
▲ EMP: 107 EST: 1970
SQ FT: 58,000
SALES (est): 23.69MM
SALES (corp-wide): 23.69MM Privately Held
Web: www.viprubber.com
SIC: 3069 3089 3061 Rubber hardware; Plastics hardware and building products; Mechanical rubber goods

(P-4803)
WEST AMERICAN RUBBER CO LLC
Also Called: Warco
750 N Main St (92868-1106)
P.O. Box 6146 (92863-6146)
PHONE.....................714 532-3355
Renan Mendez, Com Operations Vice President
EMP: 165
SALES (corp-wide): 48.04MM Privately Held
Web: www.warco.com
SIC: 3069 Sheets, hard rubber
PA: West American Rubber Company Llc
1337 W Braden Ct
Orange CA
714 532-3355

(P-4804)
WEST AMERICAN RUBBER CO LLC (PA)
Also Called: Warco
1337 W Braden Ct (92868-1123)
P.O. Box 6146 (92863-6146)
PHONE.....................714 532-3355
Tim Hemstreet, Managing Member
▲ EMP: 124 EST: 1910
SQ FT: 12,500
SALES (est): 48.04MM
SALES (corp-wide): 48.04MM Privately Held
Web: www.warco.com
SIC: 3069 3061 3053 Sheets, hard rubber; Mechanical rubber goods; Gaskets, all materials

3081 Unsupported Plastics Film And Sheet

(P-4805)
ARLON GRAPHICS LLC (HQ)
200 Boysenberry Ln (92870-6413)
PHONE.....................714 985-6300
◆ EMP: 150 EST: 2011
SALES (est): 56.17MM
SALES (corp-wide): 314.36MM Privately Held
Web: www.arlon.com
SIC: 3081 Vinyl film and sheet
PA: Flexcon Company, Inc.
1 Flexcon Industrial Park
Spencer MA
508 885-8200

(P-4806)
ARVINYL LAMINATES LP
233 N Sherman Ave (92882-1844)
PHONE.....................951 371-7800

Andy Peters, Pt
EMP: 36 EST: 2011
SALES (est): 30.52MM Privately Held
Web: www.arvinyl.com
SIC: 3081 Vinyl film and sheet

(P-4807)
BERRY GLOBAL FILMS LLC
14000 Monte Vista Ave (91710-5537)
PHONE.....................909 517-2872
J Brendan Barba, Pr
EMP: 237
SQ FT: 63,480
Web: www.berryglobal.com
SIC: 3081 2673 Polyethylene film; Bags: plastic, laminated, and coated
HQ: Berry Global Films, Llc
95 Chestnut Ridge Rd
Montvale NJ
201 641-6600

(P-4808)
CREATIVE IMPRESSIONS INC
7697 9th St (90621-2898)
PHONE.....................714 521-4441
Marc D Abbott, Pr
▲ EMP: 17 EST: 1991
SQ FT: 8,000
SALES (est): 1.22MM Privately Held
Web: www.emenucovers.com
SIC: 3081 Plastics film and sheet

(P-4809)
DELSTAR HOLDING CORP
9225 Isaac St (92071-5615)
PHONE.....................619 258-1503
Scott Anglin, Brnch Mgr
▲ EMP: 26
Web: www.swmintl.com
SIC: 3081 Polypropylene film and sheet
HQ: Delstar Holding Corp.
100 N Point Ctr E Ste 600
Alpharetta GA
800 514-0186

(P-4810)
DELSTAR TECHNOLOGIES INC
Also Called: Swm
1306 Fayette St (92020-1513)
PHONE.....................619 258-1503
Mark Laughlin, Mgr
EMP: 50
Web: www.swmintl.com
SIC: 3081 Polypropylene film and sheet
HQ: Delstar Technologies, Inc.
601 Industrial Dr
Middletown DE
302 378-8888

(P-4811)
FLEXCON COMPANY INC
12840 Reservoir St (91710-2944)
PHONE.....................909 465-0408
David R Trujillo, Mgr
EMP: 143
SALES (corp-wide): 314.36MM Privately Held
Web: www.flexcon.com
SIC: 3081 2679 Plastics film and sheet; Labels, paper: made from purchased material
PA: Flexcon Company, Inc.
1 Flexcon Industrial Park
Spencer MA
508 885-8200

(P-4812)
GRAFFITI SHIELD INC
2940 E La Palma Ave Ste D (92806)
PHONE.....................714 575-1100

Jeffrey Green, CEO
EMP: 22 EST: 2013
SALES (est): 6.11MM Privately Held
Web: www.graffiti-shield.com
SIC: 3081 Floor or wall covering, unsupported plastics

(P-4813)
LAIRD PLASTICS INC
Also Called: Eplastics
5535 Ruffin Rd (92123-1314)
PHONE.....................858 560-1551
Jason Askew, Brnch Mgr
EMP: 58
Web: www.lairdplastics.com
SIC: 3081 3082 5162 2541 Unsupported plastics film and sheet; Unsupported plastics profile shapes; Plastics materials and basic shapes; Wood partitions and fixtures
HQ: Laird Plastics, Inc.
5800 Campus Circle Dr E # 1
Irving TX
469 299-7000

(P-4814)
MERCURY PLASTICS INC
Poly Pak Packaging Division
2939 E Washington Blvd (90023-4218)
PHONE.....................323 264-2400
Benjamin Deutsch, Brnch Mgr
EMP: 95
Web: www.polypak.com
SIC: 3081 2677 Polyethylene film; Envelopes
HQ: Mercury Plastics, Inc.
14825 Salt Lake Ave
City Of Industry CA
626 961-0165

(P-4815)
MONTEBELLO PLASTICS LLC
601 W Olympic Blvd (90640-5229)
P.O. Box 789 (90640-0789)
PHONE.....................323 728-6814
EMP: 50 EST: 1982
SQ FT: 25,000
SALES (est): 8.71MM Privately Held
Web: www.montebelloplastics.com
SIC: 3081 2673 3089 Packing materials, plastics sheet; Trash bags (plastic film): made from purchased materials; Extruded finished plastics products, nec

(P-4816)
OCEANIA INC
14209 Gannet St (90638-5220)
PHONE.....................562 926-8886
Tai Leong, CEO
Angela Leung, *
▲ EMP: 30 EST: 2014
SALES (est): 4.84MM Privately Held
SIC: 3081 Plastics film and sheet

(P-4817)
POLY PAK AMERICA INC
2939 E Washington Blvd (90023-4277)
PHONE.....................323 264-2400
TOLL FREE: 800
EMP: 95
Web: www.polypak.com
SIC: 3081 2677 Polyethylene film; Envelopes

(P-4818)
PROVIDIEN THERMOFORMING INC
6740 Nancy Ridge Dr (92121-2230)
PHONE.....................858 850-1591
Jeffrey S Goble, CEO
Jenny Ames, *
Frank Ames Junior, Sec

Paul Jazwin, *
▲ EMP: 48 EST: 1982
SQ FT: 25,500
SALES (est): 27.92MM Privately Held
Web: www.providienmedical.com
SIC: 3081 Unsupported plastics film and sheet
PA: Providien, Llc
6740 Nancy Ridge Dr
San Diego CA

(P-4819)
RIDOUT PLASTICS COMPANY (PA)
Also Called: Eplastics
5535 Ruffin Rd (92123-1314)
PHONE.....................858 560-1551
TOLL FREE: 800
Elliot Rabin, Pr
◆ EMP: 58 EST: 1915
SQ FT: 32,000
SALES (est): 15.59MM
SALES (corp-wide): 15.59MM Privately Held
Web: www.eplastics.com
SIC: 3081 3082 5162 2541 Unsupported plastics film and sheet; Unsupported plastics profile shapes; Plastics materials and basic shapes; Wood partitions and fixtures

(P-4820)
SAINT-GOBAIN SOLAR GARD LLC (DH)
Also Called: Saint-Gobain Performance Plas
4540 Viewridge Ave (92123-1637)
P.O. Box 2864 (52733-2864)
PHONE.....................866 300-2674
M Shawn Puccio, *
◆ EMP: 88 EST: 2001
SQ FT: 65,000
SALES (est): 82.56MM
SALES (corp-wide): 397.78MM Privately Held
Web: www.solargard.com
SIC: 3081 5162 3479 Plastics film and sheet; Plastics film; Coating of metals and formed products
HQ: Saint-Gobain Performance Plastics Corporation
20 Moores Rd
Malvern PA
440 836-6900

(P-4821)
SIGMA EXTRUDING CORP
Also Called: Sigma Stretch Film
1565 Eastwood Ct (92507-2411)
PHONE.....................951 781-8807
EMP: 28
Web: www.sigmastretchtools.com
SIC: 3081 Unsupported plastics film and sheet
HQ: Sigma Extruding Corp.
808 Page Ave Bldg 8
Lyndhurst NJ
201 933-5353

(P-4822)
SOLVAY DRAKA INC (DH)
6900 Elm St (90040-2625)
PHONE.....................323 725-7010
▲ EMP: 120 EST: 1986
SALES (est): 79.02MM
SALES (corp-wide): 2.67MM Privately Held
Web: www.renolit.com
SIC: 3081 3087 Vinyl film and sheet; Custom compound purchased resins
HQ: Renolit Se
Horchheimer Str. 50

Worms RP
62413030

(P-4823)

TRAFFIC WORKS INC
5720 Soto St (90255-2631)
PHONE..............................323 582-0616
Steve Josephson, *Owner*
▲ **EMP:** 20 **EST:** 1983
SQ FT: 20,000
SALES (est): 2.55MM **Privately Held**
Web: www.trafficworksinc.com
SIC: 3081 2678 Packing materials, plastics
sheet; Stationery: made from purchased
materials

(P-4824)

TRM MANUFACTURING INC
375 Trm Cir (92879-1758)
P.O. Box 77520 (92877-0117)
PHONE..............................951 256-8550
Ted Moore, *Pr*
Anaisa Moore, *
▲ **EMP:** 200 **EST:** 1978
SQ FT: 200,000
SALES (est): 2.2MM **Privately Held**
Web: www.trmmfg.com
SIC: 3081 Polyethylene film

(P-4825)

W PLASTICS INC
Also Called: Western Plastics Temecula
41573 Dendy Pkwy Ste 2543 (92590-3757)
PHONE..............................800 442-9727
Michael T F Cunningham, *Pr*
Patrick Cunningham, *VP*
Thomas C Cunningham, *Treas*
◆ **EMP:** 35 **EST:** 1991
SQ FT: 65,000
SALES (est): 4.3MM **Privately Held**
Web: www.wplastics.com
SIC: 3081 1799 Plastics film and sheet;
Food service equipment installation

(P-4826)

WESTERN SUMMIT MFG CORP
Also Called: Southern International Packg
30200 Cartier Dr (90275-5722)
PHONE..............................626 333-3333
Donald K Clark, *Pr*
EMP: 20 **EST:** 1978
SQ FT: 55,000
SALES (est): 482.32K **Privately Held**
SIC: 3081 2759 2673 Unsupported plastics
film and sheet; Commercial printing, nec;
Bags: plastic, laminated, and coated

3082 Unsupported Plastics Profile Shapes

(P-4827)

ALL WEST PLASTICS INC
5451 Argosy Ave (92649-1038)
PHONE..............................714 894-9922
L Scott Leishman, *Pr*
EMP: 20 **EST:** 1978
SQ FT: 35,000
SALES (est): 901.78K **Privately Held**
SIC: 3082 Unsupported plastics profile
shapes

(P-4828)

BIRD B GONE LLC
1921 E Edinger Ave (92705-4720)
PHONE..............................949 472-3122
◆ **EMP:** 86 **EST:** 1992
SQ FT: 7,100
SALES (est): 28.24MM **Privately Held**

Web: www.birdbgone.com
SIC: 3082 Unsupported plastics profile
shapes
HQ: Pelsis Limited
Sterling House
Knaresborough
800 988-5359

(P-4829)

C&M MANUFACTURING COMPANY INC (PA)
Also Called: C & M Manufacturing
9640b Mission Gorge Rd Ste 165
(92071-3854)
PHONE..............................619 449-7200
Curt Moore, *Pr*
Lori Moore, *VP*
EMP: 29 **EST:** 1986
SALES (est): 5.03MM **Privately Held**
Web: www.centralizers.com
SIC: 3082 Unsupported plastics profile
shapes

(P-4830)

JSN PACKAGING PRODUCTS INC
9700 Jeronimo Rd (92618-2019)
PHONE..............................949 458-0050
Jim Nagel, *Pr*
Sandra Nagel, *
James H Nagel Junior, *CEO*
EMP: 65 **EST:** 1985
SALES (est): 9.16MM **Privately Held**
Web: www.jsn.com
SIC: 3082 3089 Tubes, unsupported plastics
; Caps, plastics

3083 Laminated Plastics Plate And Sheet

(P-4831)

ALCHEM PLASTICS INC
Also Called: Spartech Plastics
14263 Gannet St (90638-5220)
PHONE..............................714 523-2260
▲ **EMP:** 130
SIC: 3083 Thermoplastics laminates: rods,
tubes, plates, and sheet

(P-4832)

CUSTOM LAMINATORS INC
1350 S Claudina St (92805-6234)
P.O. Box 2744 (92859-0744)
PHONE..............................714 778-0895
Stephen C Navelski, *Pr*
EMP: 22 **EST:** 1977
SQ FT: 12,000
SALES (est): 533.31K **Privately Held**
Web: www.aglinc.com
SIC: 3083 Laminated plastics sheets

(P-4833)

INNOVATIVE PLASTICS INC
5502 Buckingham Dr (92649-5701)
PHONE..............................714 891-8800
Gary Elmer, *Pr*
EMP: 20 **EST:** 1989
SQ FT: 10,500
SALES (est): 873.46K **Privately Held**
Web: www.plasticfab.com
SIC: 3083 5947 3089 Plastics finished
products, laminated; Gift, novelty, and
souvenir shop; Plastics processing

(P-4834)

JOHNSON LAMINATING COATING INC
20631 Annalee Ave (90746-3502)

PHONE..............................310 635-4929
Scott Davidson, *Pr*
▲ **EMP:** 75 **EST:** 1960
SQ FT: 50,000
SALES (est): 22.67MM **Privately Held**
Web: www.johnsonlaminating.com
SIC: 3083 3081 2891 1541 Laminated
plastics sheets; Unsupported plastics film
and sheet; Adhesives and sealants; Food
products manufacturing or packing plant
construction

(P-4835)

LINDSEY DOORS INC
Also Called: Lindsey Mfg
81101 Indio Blvd Ste D16 (92201-1920)
PHONE..............................760 775-1959
Pierre Letellier, *Pr*
Katherine Letellier, *Sec*
EMP: 22 **EST:** 1996
SALES (est): 4.05MM **Privately Held**
Web: www.lindseydoors.com
SIC: 3083 1521 Thermoplastics laminates:
rods, tubes, plates, and sheet; Single-family
housing construction

(P-4836)

LITE EXTRUSIONS MFG INC
Also Called: Lite Extrusions
15025 S Main St (90248-1922)
PHONE..............................323 770-4298
Paul Puga, *Pr*
William Puga, *
Barbara Puga, *
EMP: 30 **EST:** 1973
SQ FT: 23,500
SALES (est): 2.62MM **Privately Held**
Web: www.liteextrusions.com
SIC: 3083 Thermoplastics laminates: rods,
tubes, plates, and sheet

(P-4837)

NELCO PRODUCTS INC
1100 E Kimberly Ave (92801-1101)
PHONE..............................714 879-4293
▲ **EMP:** 135
Web: www.nelcoproducts.com
SIC: 3083 Laminated plastics plate and sheet

(P-4838)

PLASTICS RESEARCH CORPORATION
Also Called: PRC
1400 S Campus Ave (91761-4330)
PHONE..............................909 391-9050
Gene Gregory, *CEO*
Robert Black, *
Michael Maedel, *
▲ **EMP:** 100 **EST:** 1972
SQ FT: 105,000
SALES (est): 15.35MM **Privately Held**
Web: www.prccal.com
SIC: 3083 Laminated plastics plate and sheet

(P-4839)

PLASTIFAB INC
Also Called: Plastifab/Leed Plastics
1425 Palomares St (91750-5294)
PHONE..............................909 596-1927
Rick Donnelly, *Pr*
EMP: 30 **EST:** 1977
SQ FT: 15,000
SALES (est): 4.62MM **Privately Held**
Web: www.plastifabonline.com
SIC: 3083 5162 3089 Laminated plastics
sheets; Plastics sheets and rods; Plastics
processing

(P-4840)

PLASTIFAB SAN DIEGO
12145 Paine St (92064-7124)
PHONE..............................858 679-6600
EMP: 18 **EST:** 1986
SQ FT: 15,000
SALES (est): 3.11MM **Privately Held**
Web: www.plastifabsd.com
SIC: 3083 5162 3089 Laminated plastics
sheets; Plastics sheets and rods; Plastics
processing

(P-4841)

PTM & W INDUSTRIES INC
10640 Painter Ave (90670-4092)
PHONE..............................562 946-4511
Charles E Owen, *CEO*
William Ryan, *
▲ **EMP:** 25 **EST:** 1959
SQ FT: 25,000
SALES (est): 4.76MM **Privately Held**
Web: www.ptm-w.com
SIC: 3083 2992 2891 2851 Plastics finished
products, laminated; Lubricating oils and
greases; Adhesives and sealants; Paints
and allied products

(P-4842)

REPET INC
14207 Monte Vista Ave (91710-5724)
PHONE..............................909 594-5333
Shubin Zhao, *Pr*
▲ **EMP:** 145 **EST:** 2009
SALES (est): 22.26MM **Privately Held**
Web: www.repetinc.com
SIC: 3083 Plastics finished products,
laminated

(P-4843)

SIMMONS FAMILY CORPORATION
Also Called: Teklam
350 W Rincon St (92880-2004)
PHONE..............................951 278-4563
▲ **EMP:** 80
SIC: 3083 Laminated plastics plate and sheet

(P-4844)

VANDERVEER INDUSTRIAL PLAS LLC
Also Called: Vanderveer Industrial Plastics
515 S Melrose St (92870-6337)
PHONE..............................714 579-7700
Greg Geiss, *Managing Member*
EMP: 46 **EST:** 2012
SQ FT: 29,000
SALES (est): 11.67MM
SALES (corp-wide): 89.99MM **Privately
Held**
Web: www.vanderveerplastics.com
SIC: 3083 Laminated plastics plate and sheet
PA: The Gund Company Inc
9333 Dielman Indus Dr
Saint Louis MO
314 423-5200

(P-4845)

VCLAD LAMINATES INC
2103 Seaman Ave (91733-2628)
PHONE..............................626 442-2100
David Thomson, *Pr*
▲ **EMP:** 20 **EST:** 2002
SALES (est): 2.47MM **Privately Held**
Web: www.vclad.com
SIC: 3083 2434 Laminated plastics sheets;
Wood kitchen cabinets

(P-4846)
VILLANUEVA PLASTIC COMPANY INC
372 W Tullock St (92376-7702)
PHONE..............................909 581-3870
Jose C Villanueva, *Pr*
EMP: 20 **EST:** 2008
SALES (est): 2.13MM **Privately Held**
SIC: 3083 Plastics finished products, laminated

3084 Plastics Pipe

(P-4847)
EXCALIBUR EXTRUSION INC
110 E Crowther Ave (92870-5637)
PHONE..............................714 528-8834
EMP: 50
Web: www.viprubber.com
SIC: 3084 3089 Plastics pipe; Fittings for pipe, plastics

(P-4848)
GEORG FISCHER HARVEL LLC
7001 Schirra Ct (93313-2165)
PHONE..............................661 396-0653
EMP: 30
SIC: 3084 Plastics pipe
HQ: Georg Fischer Harvel Llc
300 Kuebler Rd
Easton PA
610 252-7355

(P-4849)
HANCOR INC
140 Vineland Rd (93307-9515)
PHONE..............................661 366-1520
James Tingle, *Mgr*
EMP: 45
SALES (corp-wide): 3.07B **Publicly Held**
Web: www.adspipe.com
SIC: 3084 5051 Plastics pipe; Pipe and tubing, steel
HQ: Hancor, Inc.
4640 Trueman Blvd
Hilliard OH
614 658-0050

(P-4850)
J-M MANUFACTURING COMPANY INC (PA)
Also Called: JM Eagle
5200 W Century Blvd (90045-5928)
PHONE..............................310 693-8200
Walter Wang, *Ch*
Shirley Wang, *
◆ **EMP:** 150 **EST:** 1982
SQ FT: 24,000
SALES (est): 998.24MM
SALES (corp-wide): 998.24MM **Privately Held**
Web: www.jmeagle.com
SIC: 3084 2821 3082 Plastics pipe; Polyvinyl chloride resins, PVC; Unsupported plastics profile shapes

(P-4851)
KAKUICHI AMERICA INC
23540 Telo Ave (90505-4013)
PHONE..............................310 539-1590
Yasuo Ogami, *CEO*
Kenichi Tanaka, *
▲ **EMP:** 100 **EST:** 1973
SQ FT: 110,000
SALES (est): 25MM **Privately Held**
Web: www.pacificecho.com
SIC: 3084 Plastics pipe
HQ: Kakuichi Co., Ltd.
1415, Midoricho, Tsuruga

Nagano NAG

(P-4852)
PACIFIC PLASTICS INC
111 S Berry St (92821-4827)
PHONE..............................714 990-9050
Anayat Raminfar, *Pr*
Farhad Bahremand, *
Rahim Arian, *
John Ramin, *
Ata Ramin, *
▲ **EMP:** 71 **EST:** 1980
SQ FT: 32,000
SALES (est): 23.86MM **Privately Held**
Web: www.pacificplastics.us
SIC: 3084 Plastics pipe

(P-4853)
PW EAGLE INC
Also Called: JM Eagle
5200 W Century Blvd (90045-5928)
PHONE..............................800 621-4404
▼ **EMP:** 1087
SIC: 3084 Plastics pipe

(P-4854)
SPEARS MANUFACTURING CO
15860 Olden St (91342-1241)
PHONE..............................818 364-1611
EMP: 51
SALES (corp-wide): 1.37B **Privately Held**
Web: www.spearsmfg.net
SIC: 3084 Plastics pipe
PA: Spears Manufacturing Co.
15853 Olden St
Rancho Cascades CA
818 364-1611

(P-4855)
VALENCIA PIPE COMPANY
Also Called: Home-Flex
28305 Livingston Ave (91355-4164)
PHONE..............................661 257-3923
Andrew Dervin, *CEO*
Curt Meyer, *
Peter Dervin, *
Uriel Sandoval, *
▲ **EMP:** 28 **EST:** 2007
SALES (est): 14.11MM **Privately Held**
Web: www.valenciapipe.com
SIC: 3084 5074 3479 3312 Plastics pipe; Pipes and fittings, plastic; Coating or wrapping steel pipe; Galvanized pipes, plates, sheets, etc.: iron and steel

3085 Plastics Bottles

(P-4856)
ALTIUM PACKAGING LLC
Mayfair Plastics
1500 E 223rd St (90745-4316)
PHONE..............................310 952-8736
Larry Lindsey, *Mgr*
EMP: 55
SALES (corp-wide): 14.04B **Publicly Held**
Web: www.altiumpkg.com
SIC: 3085 2656 Plastics bottles; Sanitary food containers
HQ: Altium Packaging Llc
2500 Windy Ridge Pkwy Se # 1400
Atlanta GA
678 742-4600

(P-4857)
CLASSIC CONTAINERS INC
1700 S Hellman Ave (91761-7638)
PHONE..............................909 930-3610
Manny G Hernandez Senior, *CEO*
Ernie Hernandez, *

Maria Hernandez, *
Manny Hernandez Junior, *Treas*
EMP: 280 **EST:** 1988
SQ FT: 60,000
SALES (est): 25.66MM **Privately Held**
Web: www.classiccontainers.com
SIC: 3085 3089 5085 Plastics bottles; Plastics containers, except foam; Industrial supplies

(P-4858)
LIQUI-BOX CORPORATION
Liqui-Box Division
5772 Jurupa St Ste C (91761-3643)
PHONE..............................909 390-4646
Lou Pershin, *Prin*
EMP: 26
SALES (corp-wide): 5.64B **Publicly Held**
Web: www.liquibox.com
SIC: 3085 3089 2656 Plastics bottles; Plastics processing; Sanitary food containers
HQ: Liqui-Box Corporation
901 E Byrd St Ste 1105
Richmond VA
804 325-1400

(P-4859)
MUNCHKIN INC
27334 San Bernardino Ave (92374-5051)
PHONE..............................818 893-5000
Steven Dunn, *Brnch Mgr*
EMP: 31
Web: www.munchkin.com
SIC: 3085 Plastics bottles
PA: Munchkin, Inc.
7835 Gloria Ave
Van Nuys CA

(P-4860)
MUNCHKIN INC (PA)
7835 Gloria Ave (91406-1822)
PHONE..............................800 344-2229
Steven Dunn, *CEO*
Andrew Keimach, *
David Dunn, *
Gary Rolfes, *
Jeff Hale, *
◆ **EMP:** 123 **EST:** 1991
SQ FT: 63,000
SALES (est): 71.01MM **Privately Held**
Web: www.munchkin.com
SIC: 3085 3069 5999 Plastics bottles; Teething rings, rubber; Infant furnishings and equipment

(P-4861)
NARAYAN CORPORATION
Also Called: Plastic Processing Co
13432 Estrella Ave (90248-1513)
PHONE..............................310 719-7330
Harshad Desai, *Pr*
▲ **EMP:** 37 **EST:** 2002
SALES (est): 2.87MM **Privately Held**
Web: www.plasticprocessing.net
SIC: 3085 3089 Plastics bottles; Bottle caps, molded plastics

(P-4862)
PLASCOR INC
972 Columbia Ave (92507-2140)
PHONE..............................951 328-1010
David Harrigan, *Pr*
▼ **EMP:** 135 **EST:** 1993
SQ FT: 50,000
SALES (est): 20.52MM **Privately Held**
Web: www.plascorinc.net
SIC: 3085 Plastics bottles

(P-4863)
PLAXICON HOLDING CORPORATION
Also Called: Plaxicon Co
10660 Acacia St (91730-5409)
PHONE..............................909 944-6868
EMP: 1846 **EST:** 1983
SQ FT: 150,000
SALES (est): 3.55MM **Privately Held**
SIC: 3085 3089 Plastics bottles; Plastics containers, except foam
PA: Graham Packaging Company Europe Llc
700 Indian Springs Dr # 100
Lancaster PA

(P-4864)
POLY-TAINER INC (PA)
Also Called: Custom Molded Devices
450 W Los Angeles Ave (93065-1646)
PHONE..............................805 526-3424
TOLL FREE: 800
Julie Williams, *CEO*
Paul Strong, *Pr*
Stephanie Strong, *VP*
Tim Williams, *CFO*
▲ **EMP:** 120 **EST:** 1970
SQ FT: 95,000
SALES (est): 47.83MM
SALES (corp-wide): 47.83MM **Privately Held**
Web: www.polytainer.com
SIC: 3085 Plastics bottles

(P-4865)
POLYCYCLE SOLUTIONS LLC
4516 Azusa Canyon Rd (91706-2742)
PHONE..............................626 856-2100
▲ **EMP:** 60
SIC: 3085 Plastics bottles

(P-4866)
RING CONTAINER TECH LLC
8275 Almeria Ave (92335-3280)
PHONE..............................909 350-8416
Fred Miller, *Brnch Mgr*
EMP: 53
SQ FT: 60,800
SALES (corp-wide): 1.37B **Privately Held**
Web: www.ringcontainer.com
SIC: 3085 3411 3089 Plastics bottles; Food containers, metal; Blow molded finished plastics products, nec
HQ: Ring Container Technologies, Llc.
1 Industrial Park
Oakland TN
800 280-7464

(P-4867)
TRIPLE DOT CORP
3302 S Susan St (92704-6841)
PHONE..............................714 241-0888
Tony T Tsai, *Pr*
Jason Tsai, *
Elaine Chang, *
◆ **EMP:** 36 **EST:** 1990
SQ FT: 35,000
SALES (est): 4.13MM **Privately Held**
Web: www.triple-dot.com
SIC: 3085 5085 3089 Plastics bottles; Glass bottles; Plastics containers, except foam

3086 Plastics Foam Products

(P-4868)
ABAD FOAM INC
6560 Caballero Blvd (90620-1130)
PHONE..............................714 994-2223
Cesar Chavez, *CEO*

▲ **EMP:** 50 **EST:** 1974
SALES (est): 15.33MM **Privately Held**
SIC: 3086 Plastics foam products

(P-4869)
ADVANCED FOAM INC
1745 W 134th St (90249-2015)
PHONE................................310 515-0728
James Conley, *Pr*
Susan L Conley, *
EMP: 18 **EST:** 1983
SQ FT: 17,500
SALES (est): 3.38MM **Privately Held**
Web: www.advancedfoam.com
SIC: 3086 3299 Packaging and shipping
materials, foamed plastics; Ornamental and
architectural plaster work

(P-4870)
AGRI-CEL INC
401 Road 192 (93215-9598)
P.O. Box 100 (93216-0100)
PHONE................................661 792-2107
Louis Pandol, *Pr*
Jack Pandol, *
Steve Pandol, *
▲ **EMP:** 25 **EST:** 1980
SQ FT: 30,000
SALES (est): 794.39K **Privately Held**
Web: www.agri-cel.com
SIC: 3086 Packaging and shipping
materials, foamed plastics

(P-4871)
ALTIUM PACKAGING LP
Also Called: A Division Continental Can Co
1217 E Saint Gertrude Pl (92707-3029)
PHONE................................714 241-6640
Cesare Calabrese, *Brnch Mgr*
EMP: 57
SALES (corp-wide): 14.04B **Publicly Held**
Web: www.altiumpkg.com
SIC: 3086 3085 Plastics foam products;
Plastics bottles
HQ: Altium Packaging Lp
3101 Towercreek Pkwy Se
Atlanta GA
678 742-4600

(P-4872)
AMFOAM INC (PA)
Also Called: American Foam & Packaging
15110 S Broadway (90248-1822)
PHONE................................310 327-4003
Brian Leecing, *Pr*
Alex Gelbard, *
▲ **EMP:** 45 **EST:** 1993
SQ FT: 42,000
SALES (est): 15.58MM **Privately Held**
Web: www.amfoaminc.com
SIC: 3086 5199 Packaging and shipping
materials, foamed plastics; Foam rubber

(P-4873)
ARTISTIC COVERINGS INC
Also Called: Sports Venue Padding
14135 Artesia Blvd (90703-7025)
PHONE................................562 404-9343
Troy Robinson, *Pr*
Michelle Robinson, *
▲ **EMP:** 30 **EST:** 2000
SQ FT: 24,000
SALES (est): 4.76MM **Privately Held**
Web: www.sportsvenuepadding.com
SIC: 3086 3949 2759 Padding, foamed
plastics; Track and field athletic equipment;
Commercial printing, nec

(P-4874)
ATLAS FOAM PRODUCTS
12836 Arroyo St (91342-5304)
PHONE................................818 837-3626
Sal Damji, *Pr*
Jeff Naples, *Pr*
Sandra Naples, *Sec*
EMP: 18 **EST:** 1957
SQ FT: 28,000
SALES (est): 4.93MM **Privately Held**
Web: www.atlasfoam.com
SIC: 3086 Plastics foam products

(P-4875)
ATLAS ROOFING CORPORATION
2335 Roll Dr Ste 4121 (92154-7298)
PHONE................................626 334-5358
Edith Villegas, *Mgr*
EMP: 28
Web: www.atlasmoldedproducts.com
SIC: 3086 Insulation or cushioning material,
foamed plastics
HQ: Atlas Roofing Corporation
802 Highway 19 N Ste 190
Meridian MS
601 484-8900

(P-4876)
BACK SUPPORT SYSTEMS INC
1064 N E St (92410-3506)
P.O. Box 961 (92240-0907)
PHONE................................760 329-1472
Jeffrey A Kalatsky, *Pr*
▲ **EMP:** 17 **EST:** 1989
SQ FT: 9,800
SALES (est): 2.54MM **Privately Held**
Web: www.backsupportsystems.com
SIC: 3086 5047 Plastics foam products;
Therapy equipment

(P-4877)
CARPENTER CO
Also Called: Carpenter E R Co
7809 Lincoln Ave (92504-4442)
P.O. Box 7788 (92513-7788)
PHONE................................951 354-7550
Jim Nanfeldt, *Mgr*
EMP: 55
SALES (corp-wide): 1.85B **Privately Held**
Web: www.carpenter.com
SIC: 3086 2821 7389 5033 Insulation or
cushioning material, foamed plastics;
Plastics materials and resins; Furniture
finishing; Insulation materials
PA: Carpenter Co.
5016 Monument Ave
Richmond VA
804 359-0800

(P-4878)
CLEAN CUT TECHNOLOGIES LLC
1145 N Ocean Cir (92806-1939)
PHONE................................714 864-3500
EMP: 100
Web: www.oliverhcp.com
SIC: 3086 Packaging and shipping
materials, foamed plastics

(P-4879)
DART CONTAINER CORP CALIFORNIA (PA)
Also Called: Dtx
150 S Maple Center (92880)
PHONE................................951 735-8115
Robert C Dart, *CEO*
Kevin Fox, *
▲ **EMP:** 300 **EST:** 1937
SQ FT: 50,000

SALES (est): 77.17MM
SALES (corp-wide): 77.17MM **Privately Held**
SIC: 3086 Cups and plates, foamed plastics

(P-4880)
EPE INDUSTRIES USA INC (HQ)
Also Called: Epe USA
17835 Newhope St Ste G (92708-5428)
PHONE................................800 315-0336
EMP: 18 **EST:** 2010
SALES (est): 62.27MM **Privately Held**
Web: www.epeusa.com
SIC: 3086 Ice chests or coolers (portable),
foamed plastics
PA: Epe Corporation
2-57-5, Nishinippori
Arakawa-Ku TKY

(P-4881)
FIVE STAR FOOD CONTAINERS INC
250 Eastgate Rd (92311-3224)
PHONE................................626 437-6219
Larry Luc, *Pr*
▲ **EMP:** 60 **EST:** 2016
SALES (est): 4.73MM **Privately Held**
SIC: 3086 Plastics foam products

(P-4882)
FOAM CONCEPTS INC
4729 E Wesley Dr (92807-1941)
PHONE................................714 693-1037
Stephen C Ross, *Owner*
▲ **EMP:** 20 **EST:** 1995
SQ FT: 9,000
SALES (est): 2.31MM **Privately Held**
Web: www.foamconcepts.net
SIC: 3086 Packaging and shipping
materials, foamed plastics

(P-4883)
FOAM FACTORY INC
17515 S Santa Fe Ave (90221-5400)
PHONE................................310 603-9808
Felipe Alcazar, *Pr*
▼ **EMP:** 45 **EST:** 1989
SQ FT: 40,000
SALES (est): 4.78MM **Privately Held**
SIC: 3086 3069 5199 5087 Insulation or
cushioning material, foamed plastics; Foam
rubber; Foams and rubber; Upholsterers'
equipment and supplies

(P-4884)
FOAM MOLDERS AND SPECIALTIES
20004 State Rd (90703-6495)
PHONE................................562 924-7757
EMP: 50
SALES (corp-wide): 15.38MM **Privately Held**
Web: www.foammolders.com
SIC: 3086 Packaging and shipping
materials, foamed plastics
PA: Foam Molders And Specialties
11110 Business Cir
Cerritos CA
562 924-7757

(P-4885)
FOAM MOLDERS AND SPECIALTIES (PA)
Also Called: Foam Specialties
11110 Business Cir (90703-5523)
PHONE................................562 924-7757
Daniel M Doke, *Pr*
Dan Doke, *
Rory Strammer, *

Roberta J Doke, *
Norman Himel, *
▲ **EMP:** 50 **EST:** 1973
SQ FT: 35,600
SALES (est): 15.38MM
SALES (corp-wide): 15.38MM **Privately Held**
Web: www.foammolders.com
SIC: 3086 3089 Plastics foam products;
Thermoformed finished plastics products,
nec

(P-4886)
FOAM-CRAFT INC
2441 Cypress Way (92831-5103)
PHONE................................714 459-9971
Bruce Schneider, *Pr*
Michael Blatt, *
▲ **EMP:** 165 **EST:** 1965
SQ FT: 110,000
SALES (est): 22.07MM
SALES (corp-wide): 495.02MM **Privately Held**
SIC: 3086 Plastics foam products
PA: Future Foam, Inc.
1610 Avenue N
Council Bluffs IA
712 323-9122

(P-4887)
FOAMEX LP
Also Called: Foamex
1400 E Victoria Ave (92408-2924)
PHONE................................909 824-8981
Ron Paez, *Mgr*
EMP: 24
Web: www.fxi.com
SIC: 3086 Carpet and rug cushions, foamed
plastics
PA: Foamex L.P.
100 W Matsonford Rd # 5
Wayne PA

(P-4888)
FUTURE FOAM INC
Also Called: Future Foam
2441 Cypress Way (92831-5103)
PHONE................................714 459-9971
EMP: 165
SALES (corp-wide): 495.02MM **Privately Held**
Web: www.futurefoam.com
SIC: 3086 Plastics foam products
PA: Future Foam, Inc.
1610 Avenue N
Council Bluffs IA
712 323-9122

(P-4889)
FUTURE FOAM INC
2451 Cypress Way (92831-5103)
PHONE................................714 871-2344
Randall Lake, *Mgr*
EMP: 30
SALES (corp-wide): 495.02MM **Privately Held**
Web: www.futurefoam.com
SIC: 3086 Insulation or cushioning material,
foamed plastics
PA: Future Foam, Inc.
1610 Avenue N
Council Bluffs IA
712 323-9122

(P-4890)
HUHTAMAKI INC
4209 Noakes St (90023-4024)
PHONE................................323 269-0151
Mark Pettigrew, *Brnch Mgr*
EMP: 119

SALES (corp-wide): 4.65B **Privately Held**
Web: www.huhtamaki.com
SIC: 3086 3089 2657 2656 Cups and plates,
foamed plastics; Plastics containers, except
foam; Folding paperboard boxes; Sanitary
food containers
HQ: Huhtamaki, Inc.
9201 Packaging Dr
De Soto KS
913 583-3025

(P-4891)
INTER-PACKING INC
Also Called: Flexy Foam
12315 Colony Ave (91710-2092)
PHONE..............................909 465-5555
Alfonso Cardenas, *Pr*
EMP: 18 EST: 1985
SQ FT: 10,000
SALES (est): 2.36MM **Privately Held**
SIC: 3086 2653 Padding, foamed plastics;
Corrugated boxes, partitions, display items,
sheets, and pad

(P-4892)
KB FOAM INC
2525 Camino Del Rio S Ste 145 (92108)
PHONE..............................619 661-1870
Kenji Kasahara, *Ch Bd*
Yo Kojima, *
Masahiro Ieyoshi, *
▲ EMP: 17 EST: 1989
SALES (est): 2.04MM **Privately Held**
Web: www.kbfoam.com
SIC: 3086 Packaging and shipping
materials, foamed plastics

(P-4893)
**MARKO FOAM PRODUCTS INC
(PA)**
Also Called: Marko Foam Products
7441 Vincent Cir (92648-1246)
PHONE..............................949 417-3307
Donald J Peterson, *Ch Bd*
Tyson Peterson, *
▲ EMP: 30 EST: 1962
SQ FT: 114,000
SALES (est): 22.66MM
SALES (corp-wide): 22.66MM **Privately
Held**
Web: www.markofoam.com
SIC: 3086 5999 Packaging and shipping
materials, foamed plastics; Packaging
materials: boxes, padding, etc.

(P-4894)
**MULTI-LINK INTERNATIONAL
CORP**
933 Montecito Dr (91776-2336)
PHONE..............................562 941-5380
Sai Hung Chan, *Pr*
◆ EMP: 20 EST: 1993
SALES (est): 2.36MM **Privately Held**
Web: www.multilinkintl.com
SIC: 3086 Plastics foam products

(P-4895)
**NORTH AMRCN FOAM PPR
CNVERTERS**
11835 Wicks St (91352-1906)
PHONE..............................818 255-3383
Bijan Toobian, *CEO*
Haydeh Toobian, *
▲ EMP: 25 EST: 1998
SQ FT: 30,000
SALES (est): 4.87MM **Privately Held**
SIC: 3086 2672 5087 Plastics foam products
; Paper; coated and laminated, nec;
Laundry equipment and supplies

(P-4896)
**PLASTIC SERVICES AND
PRODUCTS**
Also Called: General Plastics
12243 Branford St (91352-1010)
P.O. Box 1367 (91353-1367)
PHONE..............................818 896-1101
◆ EMP: 3000
SIC: 3086 3674 2865 2816 Plastics foam
products; Semiconductors and related
devices; Food dyes or colors, synthetic;
Color pigments

(P-4897)
PMC GLOBAL INC (PA)
12243 Branford St (91352-1010)
PHONE..............................818 896-1101
Philip Kamins, *CEO*
Gary Kamins, *
Thian Cheong, *
Steven Cohen, *
◆ EMP: 75 EST: 1996
SALES (est): 1.71B
SALES (corp-wide): 1.71B **Privately Held**
Web: www.pmcglobalinc.com
SIC: 3086 3674 2865 2816 Plastics foam
products; Semiconductors and related
devices; Food dyes or colors, synthetic;
Color pigments

(P-4898)
**PMC LEADERS IN CHEMICALS
INC (HQ)**
12243 Branford St (91352-1010)
PHONE..............................818 896-1101
Gary Kamins, *Pr*
EMP: 200 EST: 1992
SQ FT: 180,000
SALES (est): 224.15MM
SALES (corp-wide): 1.71B **Privately Held**
Web: www.pmcglobalinc.com
SIC: 3086 5169 Plastics foam products;
Chemicals and allied products, nec
PA: Pmc Global, Inc.
12243 Branford St
Sun Valley CA
818 896-1101

(P-4899)
POMONA QUALITY FOAM LLC
1279 Philadelphia St (91766-5536)
PHONE..............................909 628-7844
EMP: 67 EST: 2015
SQ FT: 70,000
SALES (est): 5.04MM **Privately Held**
Web: www.pomonaqualityfoam.com
SIC: 3086 Plastics foam products

(P-4900)
PREMIER PACKAGING LLC
10700 Business Dr Ste 100 (92337-8201)
PHONE..............................909 749-5123
EMP: 38
Web: www.prempack.com
SIC: 3086 5085 5113 Packaging and
shipping materials, foamed plastics;
Packing, industrial; Corrugated and solid
fiber boxes
PA: Premier Packaging, Llc
3900 Produce Rd
Louisville KY

(P-4901)
**QUALITY FOAM PACKAGING
INC**
31855 Corydon St (92530-8501)
PHONE..............................951 245-4429
Noel A Castellon, *Pr*
Ruth Castellon, *Sec*

James Barrett, *VP*
▲ EMP: 25 EST: 1973
SQ FT: 56,000
SALES (est): 16.08MM **Privately Held**
Web: www.qualityfoam.com
SIC: 3086 Packaging and shipping
materials, foamed plastics

(P-4902)
**SABRED INTERNATIONAL
PACKG INC**
3740 Prospect Ave (92886-1742)
P.O. Box 566 (92885-0566)
PHONE..............................714 996-2800
Sabrina Sierra, *Pr*
Edward A Sierra, *VP*
EMP: 20 EST: 1991
SQ FT: 15,000
SALES (est): 576.48K **Privately Held**
SIC: 3086 5199 5113 5087 Packaging and
shipping materials, foamed plastics;
Packaging materials; Corrugated and solid
fiber boxes; Janitors' supplies

(P-4903)
SEALED AIR CORPORATION
Also Called: Special Products Group
2311 Boswell Rd Ste 8 (91914-3512)
PHONE..............................619 421-9003
David Rader, *Mgr*
EMP: 50
SALES (corp-wide): 5.64B **Publicly Held**
Web: www.sealedair.com
SIC: 3086 Packaging and shipping
materials, foamed plastics
PA: Sealed Air Corporation
2415 Cascade Pointe Blvd
Charlotte NC
980 221-3235

(P-4904)
SEALED AIR CORPORATION
Packaging Products Div
19440 Arenth Ave (91748-1424)
PHONE..............................909 594-1791
EMP: 126
SALES (corp-wide): 5.64B **Publicly Held**
Web: www.sealedair.com
SIC: 3086 Packaging and shipping
materials, foamed plastics
PA: Sealed Air Corporation
2415 Cascade Pointe Blvd
Charlotte NC
980 221-3235

(P-4905)
SLEEPCOMP WEST LLC
Also Called: Latexco West
10006 Santa Fe Springs Rd (90670-2922)
PHONE..............................562 946-3222
Roger Coffey, *Pr*
▲ EMP: 40 EST: 2002
SQ FT: 53,000
SALES (est): 4.42MM **Privately Held**
Web: www.latexco.com
SIC: 3086 Plastics foam products

(P-4906)
SPECIALTY ENTERPRISES CO
Also Called: Seco Industries
6858 E Acco St (90040-1902)
PHONE..............................323 726-9721
Charles De Heras, *Pr*
▲ EMP: 100 EST: 1983
SQ FT: 60,000
SALES (est): 23.69MM **Privately Held**
SIC: 3086 3565 Plastics foam products;
Packaging machinery
HQ: Cnh Industrial America Llc
6900 Veterans Blvd

Burr Ridge IL
630 887-2233

(P-4907)
STYROTEK INC
345 Road 176 (93215-9471)
P.O. Box 2870 (93303-2870)
PHONE..............................661 725-4957
Martin Caratan, *Pr*
Dale Arthur, *
▲ EMP: 110 EST: 1973
SQ FT: 18,500
SALES (est): 8.7MM **Privately Held**
Web: www.styrotek.com
SIC: 3086 Packaging and shipping
materials, foamed plastics

(P-4908)
UFP TECHNOLOGIES INC
20211 S Susana Rd (90221-5725)
PHONE..............................714 662-0277
Richard Tunila, *Brnch Mgr*
EMP: 50
SALES (corp-wide): 353.79MM **Publicly
Held**
Web: www.ufpt.com
SIC: 3086 Packaging and shipping
materials, foamed plastics
PA: Ufp Technologies, Inc.
100 Hale St
Newburyport MA
978 352-2200

(P-4909)
VEFO INC
3202 Factory Dr (91768-3903)
PHONE..............................909 598-3856
Roger Voss, *Pr*
Pat Voss, *Sec*
EMP: 20 EST: 1970
SQ FT: 11,000
SALES (est): 2.46MM **Privately Held**
Web: www.vefofoamshapes.com
SIC: 3086 Plastics foam products

(P-4910)
WALTER N COFFMAN INC
5180 Naranja St (92114-3515)
PHONE..............................619 266-2642
Walter N Coffman, *CEO*
EMP: 70 EST: 2000
SALES (est): 9.29MM **Privately Held**
Web: www.wncfoam.com
SIC: 3086 Cups and plates, foamed plastics

3088 Plastics Plumbing
Fixtures

(P-4911)
AQUATIC CO
1700 N Delilah St (92879-1893)
PHONE..............................714 993-1220
Gary Anderson, *Pr*
EMP: 278
SALES (corp-wide): 535.81MM **Privately
Held**
Web: www.aquaticbath.com
SIC: 3088 Plastics plumbing fixtures
HQ: Aquatic Co.
665 Industrial Rd
Savannah TN

(P-4912)
AQUATIC CO
Lasco Bathware
8101 E Kaiser Blvd Ste 200 (92808-2287)
PHONE..............................714 993-1220
Scott Hartman, *Mgr*

EMP: 110
SQ FT: 5,000
SALES (corp-wide): 535.81MM **Privately Held**
Web: www.aquaticbath.com
SIC: 3088 1711 5211 Shower stalls, fiberglass and plastics; Plumbing, heating, air-conditioning; Bathroom fixtures, equipment and supplies
HQ: Aquatic Co.
665 Industrial Rd
Savannah TN

(P-4913)
AQUATIC INDUSTRIES INC
8101 E Kaiser Blvd Ste 200 (92808-2287)
PHONE.........................800 877-2005
Anthony Reading, *CEO*
Margaret Voskamp, *
EMP: 33 **EST:** 1999
SQ FT: 78,004
SALES (est): 6.7MM **Privately Held**
Web: www.aquaticbath.com
SIC: 3088 5999 3949 Plastics plumbing fixtures; Hot tub and spa chemicals, equipment, and supplies; Sporting and athletic goods, nec

(P-4914)
EUROTECH SHOWERS INC
Also Called: Eurotech Luxury Shower Doors
23552 Commerce Center Dr Ste B (92653-1514)
PHONE.........................949 716-4099
James Simmons, *Pr*
EMP: 25 **EST:** 2006
SQ FT: 2,800
SALES (est): 2.52MM **Privately Held**
Web: www.eurotechshowers.com
SIC: 3088 Shower stalls, fiberglass and plastics

(P-4915)
FIBER CARE BATHS INC
9832 Yucca Rd Ste A (92301-2471)
PHONE.........................760 246-0019
EMP: 275 **EST:** 1996
SQ FT: 6,000
SALES (est): 48.99MM **Privately Held**
Web: www.fibercarebaths.com
SIC: 3088 Shower stalls, fiberglass and plastics

(P-4916)
JACUZZI PRODUCTS CO (DH)
13925 City Center Dr Ste 200 (91709-5438)
PHONE.........................909 606-1416
Thomas D Koos, *CEO*
Philip Weeks, *
▲ **EMP:** 120 **EST:** 1959
SALES (est): 105.28MM
SALES (corp-wide): 423.13K **Privately Held**
Web: www.jacuzzi.com
SIC: 3088 Tubs (bath, shower, and laundry), plastics
HQ: Jacuzzi Inc.
17872 Gillette Ave # 300
Irvine CA
909 606-7733

(P-4917)
JACUZZI PRODUCTS CO
14525 Monte Vista Ave (91710-5721)
PHONE.........................909 548-7732
Jim Barry, *Mgr*
EMP: 340
SALES (corp-wide): 423.13K **Privately Held**
Web: www.jacuzzi.com

SIC: 3088 5091 Tubs (bath, shower, and laundry), plastics; Fitness equipment and supplies
HQ: Jacuzzi Products Co.
13925 City Center Dr # 200
Chino Hills CA
909 606-1416

(P-4918)
KING BROS ENTERPRISES LLC
29101 The Old Rd (91355-1014)
P.O. Box 9203 (91392-9203)
PHONE.........................661 257-3262
▲ **EMP:** 125
SIC: 3088 5169 Plastics plumbing fixtures; Synthetic resins, rubber, and plastic materials

(P-4919)
LE ELEGANT BATH INC
Also Called: American Bath Factory
13405 Estelle St (92879-1877)
P.O. Box 127 (92878-0127)
PHONE.........................951 734-0238
Richard Wheeler, *Pr*
Debbie Wheeler, *
◆ **EMP:** 120 **EST:** 1984
SQ FT: 18,000
SALES (est): 22.04MM **Privately Held**
Web: www.americanbathfactory.com
SIC: 3088 Tubs (bath, shower, and laundry), plastics

(P-4920)
PAINTED RHINO INC (PA)
14310 Veterans Way (92553-9058)
PHONE.........................951 656-5524
Ryan Franklin, *Pr*
▲ **EMP:** 35 **EST:** 2007
SQ FT: 25,000
SALES (est): 3.75MM
SALES (corp-wide): 3.75MM **Privately Held**
Web: www.paintedrhino.com
SIC: 3088 Shower stalls, fiberglass and plastics

(P-4921)
VANTAGE ASSOCIATES INC
Glassform
12333 Los Nietos Rd (90670-2911)
PHONE.........................800 995-8322
Paul Roy, *CEO*
EMP: 25
SALES (corp-wide): 21.95MM **Privately Held**
Web: www.vantageassoc.com
SIC: 3088 2519 Plastics plumbing fixtures; Fiberglass and plastic furniture
PA: Vantage Associates Inc.
12333 Los Nietos Rd
Santa Fe Springs CA
619 477-6940

(P-4922)
WATKINS MANUFACTURING CORP
1325 Hot Springs Way (92081-8360)
PHONE.........................760 598-6464
EMP: 289
SALES (corp-wide): 8.68B **Publicly Held**
Web: masco.wd1.myworkdayjobs.com
SIC: 3088 Hot tubs, plastics or fiberglass
HQ: Watkins Manufacturing Corporation
1280 Park Center Dr
Vista CA
760 598-6464

3089 Plastics Products, Nec

(P-4923)
10 DAY PARTS INC
Also Called: Westfall Technik
20109 Paseo Del Prado (91789-2665)
PHONE.........................951 279-4810
Brian Laibach, *Dir Opers*
EMP: 35 **EST:** 2018
SALES (est): 9.93MM
SALES (corp-wide): 568.49MM **Privately Held**
Web: www.westfalltechnik.com
SIC: 3089 Injection molding of plastics
PA: Westfall Technik, Inc.
3883 Howard Hughes Pkwy # 590
Las Vegas NV
702 659-9898

(P-4924)
3D CAM INC
Also Called: 3 D CAM
9801 Variel Ave (91311-4317)
PHONE.........................818 407-0220
EMP: 21
Web: www.3d-cam.com
SIC: 3089 8711 3369 3544 Injection molded finished plastics products, nec; Machine tool design; Nonferrous foundries, nec; Special dies, tools, jigs, and fixtures

(P-4925)
A & S MOLD AND DIE CORP
9705 Eton Ave (91311-4306)
PHONE.........................818 341-5393
Arno Adlhoch, *CEO*
Karen Adlhoch, *
▲ **EMP:** 90 **EST:** 1969
SQ FT: 35,000
SALES (est): 8.75MM **Privately Held**
Web: www.aandsmold.com
SIC: 3089 3544 Injection molding of plastics; Special dies, tools, jigs, and fixtures

(P-4926)
A&A GLOBAL IMPORTS LLC (PA)
Also Called: A&A Fulfillment Center
1801 E 41st St (90058-1533)
PHONE.........................888 315-2453
David Aryan, *Pr*
Brian Anowns, *
James Bunting, *
Adam Wolf, *
▲ **EMP:** 59 **EST:** 2011
SALES (est): 21.48MM
SALES (corp-wide): 21.48MM **Privately Held**
Web: www.aaglobalimports.com
SIC: 3089 3999 Injection molded finished plastics products, nec

(P-4927)
ACORN-GENCON PLASTICS LLC
13818 Oaks Ave (91710-7008)
PHONE.........................909 591-8461
Donald E Morris, *Managing Member*
▲ **EMP:** 68 **EST:** 2001
SQ FT: 94,000
SALES (est): 12.27MM
SALES (corp-wide): 99.15MM **Privately Held**
Web: www.acorn-gencon.com
SIC: 3089 3088 3821 3082 Injection molded finished plastics products, nec; Plastics plumbing fixtures; Laboratory apparatus and furniture; Unsupported plastics profile shapes

HQ: Acorn Plastics, Inc.
13818 Oaks Ave
Chino CA
909 591-8461

(P-4928)
ADVANCED CMPSITE PDTS TECH INC
Also Called: Acpt
15602 Chemical Ln (92649-1507)
PHONE.........................714 895-5544
James C Leslie Ii, *Pr*
EMP: 45 **EST:** 1984
SQ FT: 25,300
SALES (est): 8.77MM **Privately Held**
Web: www.acpt.com
SIC: 3089 8748 Hardware, plastics; Business consulting, nec

(P-4929)
ADVANCED ENGRG MLDING TECH INC
6510 Box Springs Blvd Ste B (92507-0740)
P.O. Box 5620 (92517-5620)
PHONE.........................888 264-0392
Donald Furness, *Pr*
Helen Furness, *VP*
▲ **EMP:** 20 **EST:** 1968
SQ FT: 12,000
SALES (est): 3.49MM **Privately Held**
Web: www.aemt.com
SIC: 3089 Molding primary plastics

(P-4930)
ADVANCED MATERIALS INC (HQ)
20211 S Susana Rd (90221-5725)
PHONE.........................310 537-5444
Steve Scott, *Pr*
◆ **EMP:** 29 **EST:** 1959
SQ FT: 56,000
SALES (est): 4.92MM
SALES (corp-wide): 353.79MM **Publicly Held**
SIC: 3089 Injection molding of plastics
PA: Ufp Technologies, Inc.
100 Hale St
Newburyport MA
978 352-2200

(P-4931)
ADVANCED THRMLFORMING ENTP INC
Also Called: A T E
3750 Oceanic Way (92056-2650)
PHONE.........................760 722-4400
Hai Parson, *Pr*
David Cox, *VP Opers*
Anh Doan, *Stockholder*
EMP: 21 **EST:** 1998
SALES (est): 429.77K **Privately Held**
SIC: 3089 Thermoformed finished plastics products, nec

(P-4932)
AKRA PLASTIC PRODUCTS INC
1504 E Cedar St (91761-5761)
PHONE.........................909 930-1999
Alexander Semeczko, *CEO*
R Wayne Callaway, *
Bentley Callaway, *
Alex Semeczko, *
EMP: 37 **EST:** 1972
SQ FT: 36,000
SALES (est): 4.43MM **Privately Held**
Web: www.akraplastics.com

P R O D U C T S & S V C S

SIC: **3089** 2821 2542 5063 Plastics processing; Plastics materials and resins; Office and store showcases and display fixtures; Lighting fixtures, commercial and industrial

(P-4933)
ALLEN MOLD INC
1100 W Katella Ave Ste N (92867-3515)
PHONE................................714 538-6517
Clayton Allen, *Pr*
EMP: 18 **EST:** 1997
SQ FT: 5,800
SALES (est): 2.46MM **Privately Held**
Web: www.allenmold.com
SIC: **3089** Injection molding of plastics

(P-4934)
ALLTEC INTEGRATED MFG INC
Also Called: New Age Enclosures
2240 S Thornburg St (93455-1248)
PHONE................................805 595-3500
Randall Dennis, *CEO*
◆ **EMP:** 40 **EST:** 2002
SQ FT: 13,500
SALES (est): 9.38MM **Privately Held**
Web: www.newageenclosures.com
SIC: **3089** 2821 Injection molding of plastics; Plastics materials and resins

(P-4935)
ALTIUM HOLDINGS LLC
Also Called: California Plastics
12165 Madera Way (92503-4849)
PHONE................................951 340-9390
Steve Thompson, *Mgr*
EMP: 886
SALES (corp-wide): 483.23MM **Privately Held**
Web: www.altiumpkg.com
SIC: **3089** Plastics containers, except foam
PA: Altium Holdings Llc
    2500 Windy Ridge Pkwy Se # 1400
    Atlanta GA
    678 742-4600

(P-4936)
ALTIUM PACKAGING
Also Called: ALTIUM PACKAGING
4516 Azusa Canyon Rd (91706-2742)
PHONE................................626 856-2100
EMP: 60
SALES (corp-wide): 14.04B **Publicly Held**
Web: www.altiumpkg.com
SIC: **3089** Plastics containers, except foam
HQ: Altium Packaging Llc
    2500 Windy Ridge Pkwy Se # 1400
    Atlanta GA
    678 742-4600

(P-4937)
ALTIUM PACKAGING LLC
Also Called: Reid Plastics Customer Svcs
1070 Samuelson St (91748-1219)
PHONE................................888 425-7343
Fred Braham, *Prin*
EMP: 57
SALES (corp-wide): 14.04B **Publicly Held**
Web: www.altiumpkg.com
SIC: **3089** 3085 Plastics containers, except foam; Plastics bottles
HQ: Altium Packaging Llc
    2500 Windy Ridge Pkwy Se # 1400
    Atlanta GA
    678 742-4600

(P-4938)
ALTIUM PACKAGING LP
Envision Plastics
14312 Central Ave (91710-5752)

PHONE................................909 590-7334
EMP: 50
SALES (corp-wide): 14.04B **Publicly Held**
Web: www.altiumpkg.com
SIC: **3089** Plastics containers, except foam
HQ: Altium Packaging Lp
    3101 Towercreek Pkwy Se
    Atlanta GA
    678 742-4600

(P-4939)
AMERICAN INTEGRITY CORP
13510 Central Rd (92308-6561)
P.O. Box 999 (92307-0017)
PHONE................................760 247-1082
EMP: 50
Web: www.americanintegrity.com
SIC: **3089** 5211 Window frames and sash, plastics; Lumber and other building materials

(P-4940)
AMS PLASTICS INC (HQ)
20109 Paseo Del Prado (91789-2665)
PHONE................................619 713-2000
Thomas G Plein, *CEO*
Diane L Plein, *Sec*
▲ **EMP:** 96 **EST:** 1983
SALES (est): 33.44MM
SALES (corp-wide): 568.49MM **Privately Held**
Web: www.westfalltechnik.com
SIC: **3089** Injection molding of plastics
PA: Westfall Technik, Inc.
    3883 Howard Hughes Pkwy # 590
    Las Vegas NV
    702 659-9898

(P-4941)
ANAHEIM CUSTOM EXTRUDERS INC
Also Called: Ace
1360 N Mccan St (92806-1316)
PHONE................................714 693-8508
TOLL FREE: 800
William A Czapar, *Ch Bd*
Chrintina Smith, *
EMP: 48 **EST:** 1977
SALES (est): 7.46MM **Privately Held**
Web: www.acextrusions.com
SIC: **3089** 3082 Extruded finished plastics products, nec; Unsupported plastics profile shapes

(P-4942)
ANURA PLASTIC ENGINEERIGN
5050 Rivergrade Rd (91706-1405)
PHONE................................626 814-9684
Wolfgang Buehler, *CEO*
Anura Welikala, *
EMP: 20 **EST:** 1997
SQ FT: 35,000
SALES (est): 487.12K **Privately Held**
SIC: **3089** Injection molding of plastics

(P-4943)
API KIRK CONTAINERS
2131 Garfield Ave (90040-1805)
PHONE................................323 278-5400
Arthur Marounian, *VP*
▼ **EMP:** 31 **EST:** 2005
SALES (est): 11.19MM **Privately Held**
Web: www.apikirkcontainers.com
SIC: **3089** Plastics containers, except foam

(P-4944)
APON INDUSTRIES CORP
10005 Marconi Dr Ste 2 (92154-5208)
▲ **EMP:** 200 **EST:** 1998
SALES (est): 24.94MM **Privately Held**

Web: www.aponindustries.com
SIC: **3089** Injection molding of plastics

(P-4945)
ARC PLASTICS INC
14010 Shoemaker Ave (90650-4536)
PHONE................................562 802-3299
Richard Renaudo, *Pr*
Olga Peralta, *VP*
EMP: 20 **EST:** 2002
SQ FT: 1,600
SALES (est): 2.47MM **Privately Held**
Web: arcplastics.tripod.com
SIC: **3089** Injection molded finished plastics products, nec

(P-4946)
ARGEE MFG CO SAN DIEGO INC
Also Called: Argee
9550 Pathway St (92071-4169)
PHONE................................619 449-5050
Robert Goldman, *Pr*
Ruth Goldman, *
▲ **EMP:** 75 **EST:** 1961
SQ FT: 65,000
SALES (est): 9.71MM **Privately Held**
Web: www.argeecorp.com
SIC: **3089** Plastics hardware and building products

(P-4947)
ARLON LLC
Arlon Adhesives-Films Division
2811 S Harbor Blvd (92704-5805)
P.O. Box 5260 (92704-0260)
PHONE................................714 540-2811
Elmer Pruim, *Pr*
EMP: 150
SQ FT: 124,478
SALES (corp-wide): 971.17MM **Publicly Held**
Web: www.arlonecp.com
SIC: **3089** 3081 2672 Plastics hardware and building products; Unsupported plastics film and sheet; Paper; coated and laminated, nec
HQ: Arlon Llc
    1100 Governor Lea Rd
    Bear DE

(P-4948)
ARMORCAST PRODUCTS COMPANY INC
500 S Dupont Ave (91761-1508)
PHONE................................909 390-1365
Paul Boghossian, *Brnch Mgr*
EMP: 40
SALES (corp-wide): 4.95B **Publicly Held**
Web: www.armorcastprod.com
SIC: **3089** 5092 Plastics processing; Toys, nec
HQ: Armorcast Products Company, Inc.
    9140 Lurline Ave
    Chatsworth CA
    818 982-3600

(P-4949)
ARTHURMADE PLASTICS INC
Also Called: Kirk Containers
2131 Garfield Ave (90040-1805)
PHONE................................323 721-7325
Kirk Marounian, *Pr*
Silva Marounian, *
Arthur Marounian, *
EMP: 75 **EST:** 1984
SQ FT: 20,000
SALES (est): 10.32MM **Privately Held**
SIC: **3089** Injection molding of plastics

(P-4950)
AXIUM PACKAGING LLC
5701 Clark St (91761-3640)
PHONE................................909 969-0766
Kulwinder Singh, *Mgr*
EMP: 579
Web: www.axiumplastics.com
SIC: **3089** Plastics containers, except foam
PA: Axium Packaging Llc
    9005 Smiths Mill Rd
    New Albany OH

(P-4951)
B & S PLASTICS INC
Also Called: Waterway Plastics
2200 Sturgis Rd (93030-8978)
PHONE................................805 981-0262
Bill Spears, *CEO*
Sandy Spears, *
◆ **EMP:** 105 **EST:** 1973
SQ FT: 240,000
SALES (est): 43.56MM **Privately Held**
Web: www.waterwayplastics.com
SIC: **3089** Injection molding of plastics

(P-4952)
B AND P PLASTICS INC
Also Called: Advance Plastics
225 W 30th St (91950-7203)
PHONE................................619 477-1893
Bruce Browne, *Pr*
Patricia Browne, *
▲ **EMP:** 35 **EST:** 1974
SQ FT: 10,000
SALES (est): 6.54MM **Privately Held**
Web: www.advanceplastics.com
SIC: **3089** 3061 Molding primary plastics; Mechanical rubber goods

(P-4953)
BACE MANUFACTURING INC (HQ)
Also Called: Spm
3125 E Coronado St (92806-1915)
PHONE................................714 630-6002
Richard R Harris, *Pr*
Shannon White, *
EMP: 700 **EST:** 1989
SQ FT: 200,000
SALES (est): 137.76MM
SALES (corp-wide): 137.76MM **Privately Held**
SIC: **3089** Injection molding of plastics
PA: Medplast Group, Inc.
    7865 Northcourt Rd # 100
    Houston TX
    480 553-6400

(P-4954)
BALDA C BREWER INC (DH)
Also Called: C Brewer Company
4501 E Wall St (91761-8143)
PHONE................................714 630-6810
Christoph Klaus, *CEO*
Steve Holland, *Pr*
Harold Hee, *VP*
▲ **EMP:** 66 **EST:** 1968
SQ FT: 60,000
SALES (est): 42.58MM
SALES (corp-wide): 2.67MM **Privately Held**
SIC: **3089** 3544 Molding primary plastics; Special dies, tools, jigs, and fixtures
HQ: Clere Ag
    Schluterstr. 45
    Berlin BE
    302 130-0430

(P-4955)
BANDLOCK CORPORATION
1734 S Vineyard Ave (91761-7746)
PHONE..............................909 947-7500
EMP: 68
SIC: 3089 3492 3082 Extruded finished
plastics products, nec; Hose and tube
couplings, hydraulic/pneumatic;
Unsupported plastics profile shapes

(P-4956)
**BARBER-WEBB COMPANY INC
(PA)**
12912 Lakeland Rd (90670-4517)
PHONE..............................541 488-4821
TOLL FREE: 800
Donald B Barber Junior, *Pr*
Brian Barber, *
James Barber, *
Wr Greenbecker, *
▼ EMP: 30 EST: 1945
SALES (est): 8.9MM
SALES (corp-wide): 8.9MM **Privately Held**
Web: www.barber-webb.com
SIC: 3089 Plastics processing

(P-4957)
BARNES PLASTICS INC
Also Called: Barnes Plastics
18903 Anelo Ave (90248-4598)
PHONE..............................310 329-6301
Charles Walker, *CEO*
Scott Piepmeyer, *
▲ EMP: 30 EST: 1930
SQ FT: 30,000
SALES (est): 4.46MM **Privately Held**
Web: www.barnesplastics.com
SIC: 3089 Injection molding of plastics

(P-4958)
BEEMAK PLASTICS LLC
Also Called: Beemak-Idl Display Products
1515 S Harris Ct (92806-5932)
PHONE..............................800 421-4393
John Davis, *Managing Member*
Fred Garcy, *
Winfred Ross, *
▲ EMP: 100 EST: 1951
SALES (est): 25MM
SALES (corp-wide): 475.79MM **Privately
Held**
Web: www.beemak.com
SIC: 3089 Injection molding of plastics
HQ: Deflecto, Llc
7035 E 86th St
Indianapolis IN
317 849-9555

(P-4959)
BENT MANUFACTURING CO INC
Also Called: Bent Manufacturing Company
17311 Nichols Ln (92647-5721)
PHONE..............................714 842-0600
EMP: 85
Web: www.bentmfg.com
SIC: 3089 3069 Blow molded finished
plastics products, nec; Hard rubber and
molded rubber products

(P-4960)
BERICAP LLC
Also Called: Bericap
1671 Champagne Ave Ste B (91761-3650)
PHONE..............................905 634-2248
Steve Buckley, *Pr*
Steve Buckley, *Managing Member*
David Andison, *
▲ EMP: 67 EST: 2001
SALES (est): 28.9MM
SALES (corp-wide): 2.67MM **Privately
Held**

Web: www.bericap.com
SIC: 3089 Injection molding of plastics
HQ: Bericap Holding Gmbh
Kirchstr. 5
Budenheim RP
613929020

(P-4961)
BERRY GLOBAL INC
14000 Monte Vista Ave (91710-5537)
PHONE..............................909 465-9055
Salama Elsayed, *Brnch Mgr*
EMP: 200
Web: www.berryglobal.com
SIC: 3089 3081 Bottle caps, molded plastics;
Unsupported plastics film and sheet
HQ: Berry Global, Inc.
101 Oakley St
Evansville IN

(P-4962)
BERRY GLOBAL INC
4875 E Hunter Ave (92807-2005)
PHONE..............................714 777-5200
Don Parodi, *Mgr*
EMP: 56
Web: www.berryglobal.com
SIC: 3089 3081 Bottle caps, molded plastics;
Unsupported plastics film and sheet
HQ: Berry Global, Inc.
101 Oakley St
Evansville IN

(P-4963)
BH-TECH INC
6174 Lemonglaze Ct (92130-5034)
PHONE..............................858 694-0900
Seung Hoon Han, *CEO*
Woo Hyuk Choi, *CFO*
EMP: 700 EST: 2018
SALES (est): 50MM **Privately Held**
SIC: 3089 Injection molding of plastics

(P-4964)
BLOW MOLDED PRODUCTS INC
Also Called: Bmp
4720 Felspar St (92509-3068)
PHONE..............................951 360-6055
EMP: 40
Web: www.blowmoldedproducts.com
SIC: 3089 Injection molding of plastics

(P-4965)
BM EXTRUSION INC
1575 Omaha Ct (92507-2444)
PHONE..............................951 782-9020
Bacilio Mejia, *Pr*
EMP: 24 EST: 2006
SALES (est): 1.75MM **Privately Held**
SIC: 3089 Plastics containers, except foam

(P-4966)
BOLERO INDS INC A CAL CORP
Also Called: Bolero Plastics
11850 Burke St (90670-2536)
PHONE..............................562 693-3000
Daniel Imasdounian, *CEO*
Daniel Imasdounian, *Pr*
Annie Imasdounian, *TRAE*
Vasken Imasdounian, *VP*
EMP: 20 EST: 1975
SQ FT: 19,500
SALES (est): 2.59MM **Privately Held**
Web: www.boleroplastics.com
SIC: 3089 Injection molding of plastics

(P-4967)
BOMATIC INC (DH)
Also Called: Bmi

43225 Business Park Dr (92590-3648)
PHONE..............................909 947-3900
Kjeld R Hestehave, *Pr*
Borge Hestehave, *
Mary Ann, *
Kirk Franks, *
Kresten Hestehave, *
▲ EMP: 40 EST: 1969
SQ FT: 35,000
SALES (est): 21.72MM **Privately Held**
Web: www.bomatic.com
SIC: 3089 Plastics containers, except foam
HQ: Universal Packaging West, Inc.
43225 Business Park Dr
Temecula CA
603 889-8311

(P-4968)
BOMATIC INC
2181 E Francis St (91761-7723)
PHONE..............................909 947-3900
Back Melon, *Mgr*
EMP: 60
Web: www.bomatic.com
SIC: 3089 Plastics containers, except foam
HQ: Bomatic, Inc.
43225 Business Park Dr
Temecula CA
909 947-3900

(P-4969)
BOTTLEMATE INC (PA)
2095 Leo Ave (90040-1626)
PHONE..............................323 887-9009
Kai-win Chuang, *CEO*
Anderson Chuang, *
Mei-li Chang, *Sec*
▲ EMP: 23 EST: 1982
SQ FT: 25,000
SALES (est): 2.53MM **Privately Held**
Web: www.bottlemate.com
SIC: 3089 5162 Blow molded finished
plastics products, nec; Plastics products,
nec

(P-4970)
**BRADLEY MANUFACTURING CO
INC**
Also Called: Bradley's Plastic Bag Co
9368 Stewart And Gray Rd (90241-5316)
PHONE..............................562 923-5556
Keith Smith, *Pr*
Richard Lane, *
EMP: 28 EST: 1933
SALES (est): 2.36MM **Privately Held**
Web: www.bradleypackaging.com
SIC: 3089 3069 3083 2673 Plastics
processing; Tubing, rubber; Laminated
plastics plate and sheet; Bags: plastic,
laminated, and coated

(P-4971)
C & G PLASTICS
Also Called: C & G Mercury Plastics
12729 Foothill Blvd (91342-5314)
PHONE..............................818 837-3773
Greg Leighton, *Pr*
▲ EMP: 25 EST: 1963
SQ FT: 6,000
SALES (est): 4.91MM **Privately Held**
Web: www.cgplastics.net
SIC: 3089 Injection molding of plastics

(P-4972)
C & R MOLDS INC
2737 Palma Dr (93003-7651)
P.O. Box 5644 (93005-0644)
PHONE..............................805 658-7098
Randall Ohnemus, *Pr*
Marla Ohnemus, *

▲ EMP: 24 EST: 1984
SQ FT: 12,000
SALES (est): 4.96MM **Privately Held**
Web: www.crmolds.com
SIC: 3089 3544 Injection molding of plastics;
Special dies, tools, jigs, and fixtures

(P-4973)
C G MOTOR SPORTS INC
Also Called: Anzo USA
5150 Eucalyptus Ave Ste A (91710-9218)
PHONE..............................909 628-1440
Debbie Law, *Pr*
▲ EMP: 18 EST: 2006
SALES (est): 1.42MM **Privately Held**
SIC: 3089 Automotive parts, plastic

(P-4974)
C-PAK INDUSTRIES INC
4925 Hallmark Pkwy (92407-1870)
PHONE..............................909 880-6017
Arch Young, *Pr*
EMP: 28 EST: 1999
SQ FT: 25,000
SALES (est): 3.52MM **Privately Held**
Web: www.c-pak.net
SIC: 3089 Injection molding of plastics

(P-4975)
**CAL-MIL PLASTIC PRODUCTS
INC (PA)**
Also Called: Cal-Mil
4079 Calle Platino (92056-5805)
PHONE..............................800 321-9069
Johnny Callahan, *CEO*
Barney Callahan, *
◆ EMP: 20 EST: 1965
SQ FT: 60,000
SALES (est): 9.23MM
SALES (corp-wide): 9.23MM **Privately
Held**
Web: www.calmil.com
SIC: 3089 Plastics containers, except foam

(P-4976)
CALIFORNIA QUALITY PLAS INC
Also Called: Bel-Air Cases
2104 S Cucamonga Ave (91761-5609)
PHONE..............................909 930-5667
Erik Calcott, *Brnch Mgr*
EMP: 20
SALES (corp-wide): 12.63MM **Privately
Held**
Web: www.calplastics.com
SIC: 3089 Plastics containers, except foam
PA: California Quality Plastics, Inc.
2226 S Castle Harbour Pl
Ontario CA
909 930-5535

(P-4977)
**CAMBRO MANUFACTURING
COMPANY**
Also Called: Cambro Manufacturing
5801 Skylab Rd (92647-2051)
PHONE..............................714 848-1555
Argyle Campbell, *Pr*
EMP: 69
SALES (corp-wide): 307.89MM **Privately
Held**
Web: www.cambro.com
SIC: 3089 Trays, plastics
PA: Cambro Manufacturing Company Inc
5801 Skylab Rd
Huntington Beach CA
714 848-1555

(P-4978)
CAMBRO MANUFACTURING COMPANY (PA)
Also Called: Cambro
5801 Skylab Rd (92647-2051)
P.O. Box 2000 (92647-2000)
PHONE..............................714 848-1555
Argyle Campbell, *CEO*
◆ **EMP:** 500 **EST:** 1951
SQ FT: 300,000
SALES (est): 307.89MM
SALES (corp-wide): 307.89MM **Privately Held**
Web: www.cambro.com
SIC: 3089 Trays, plastics

(P-4979)
CAMBRO MANUFACTURING COMPANY
7601 Clay Ave (92648-2219)
PHONE..............................714 848-1555
David Capestro, *Mgr*
EMP: 242
SALES (corp-wide): 307.89MM **Privately Held**
Web: www.cambro.com
SIC: 3089 Plastics containers, except foam
PA: Cambro Manufacturing Company Inc
5801 Skylab Rd
Huntington Beach CA
714 848-1555

(P-4980)
CANYON PLASTICS LLC
28455 Livingston Ave (91355-4173)
PHONE..............................800 350-6325
TOLL FREE: 800
Karshan A Gajera, *CEO*
▲ **EMP:** 78 **EST:** 1982
SQ FT: 110,950
SALES (est): 17.37MM **Privately Held**
Web: www.canyonplastics.com
SIC: 3089 3544 Plastics containers, except foam; Forms (molds), for foundry and plastics working machinery

(P-4981)
CAPCO/PSA
Also Called: California Art Products Co
11125 Vanowen St (91605-6316)
PHONE..............................818 762-4276
TOLL FREE: 800
Zaven P Berberian, *Pr*
EMP: 19 **EST:** 1967
SQ FT: 18,000
SALES (est): 498.15K **Privately Held**
Web: www.californiaartproducts.com
SIC: 3089 2821 Planters, plastics; Plastics materials and resins

(P-4982)
CAPLUGS INC
Also Called: Caplugs
18704 S Ferris Pl (90220-6400)
PHONE..............................310 537-2300
Fred Karam, *Brnch Mgr*
EMP: 60
SALES (corp-wide): 2.13B **Privately Held**
Web: www.caplugs.com
SIC: 3089 Injection molding of plastics
HQ: Caplugs, Inc.
2150 Elmwood Ave
Buffalo NY
716 876-9855

(P-4983)
CAPLUGS INC
Also Called: Caplugs
18704 S Ferris Pl (90745)

PHONE..............................310 900-8323
EMP: 23
SALES (corp-wide): 2.13B **Privately Held**
Web: www.caplugs.com
SIC: 3089 3822 Molding primary plastics; Temperature controls, automatic
HQ: Caplugs, Inc.
2150 Elmwood Ave
Buffalo NY
716 876-9855

(P-4984)
CARR MANAGEMENT INC
22324 Temescal Canyon Rd (92883-4622)
PHONE..............................951 277-4800
Nick Rende, *Brnch Mgr*
EMP: 70
Web: www.altiumpkg.com
SIC: 3089 Plastics containers, except foam
PA: Carr Management, Inc.
1 Tara Blvd Ste 303
Nashua NH

(P-4985)
CARSON INDUSTRIES LLC
Also Called: Oldcastle Prcast Enclsure Slto
2434 Rubidoux Blvd (92509-2144)
P.O. Box 99697 (60696-7497)
PHONE..............................951 788-9720
◆ **EMP:** 3000
SIC: 3089 Boxes, plastics

(P-4986)
CCI INDUSTRIES INC (PA)
Also Called: Cool Curtain CCI
350 Fischer Ave Ste A (92626-4508)
PHONE..............................714 662-3879
Michael Robinson, *Pr*
▲ **EMP:** 27 **EST:** 1976
SQ FT: 15,000
SALES (est): 2.75MM
SALES (corp-wide): 2.75MM **Privately Held**
Web: www.coolcurtain.com
SIC: 3089 3564 3496 Doors, folding: plastics or plastics coated fabric; Aircurtains (blower); Grilles and grillework, woven wire

(P-4987)
CCL TUBE INC (HQ)
2250 E 220th St (90810-1638)
PHONE..............................310 635-4444
Andreas Iseli, *CEO*
▲ **EMP:** 108 **EST:** 1984
SQ FT: 300,000
SALES (est): 44.41MM
SALES (corp-wide): 4.75B **Privately Held**
Web: www.ccltube.com
SIC: 3089 Injection molded finished plastics products, nec
PA: Ccl Industries Inc.
111 Gordon Baker Rd Suite 801
Toronto ON
416 756-8500

(P-4988)
CERTIFIED THERMOPLASTICS INC
Also Called: Certified Thermoplastics LLC
26381 Ferry Ct (91350-2998)
PHONE..............................661 222-3006
Robert Duncan, *Pr*
▲ **EMP:** 35 **EST:** 1978
SQ FT: 30,000
SALES (est): 10.43MM
SALES (corp-wide): 712.54MM **Publicly Held**
Web: www.ctplastics.com
SIC: 3089 Injection molding of plastics
HQ: Ducommun Labarge Technologies, Inc.
1601 E Broadway Rd

Phoenix AZ
480 998-0733

(P-4989)
CHARMAINE PLASTICS INC
Also Called: Crafttech
2941 E La Jolla St (92806-1306)
PHONE..............................714 630-8117
John Butler, *Pr*
Alfredo Bonetto, *
John Ayers, *
Douglas Barker, *Product Vice President*
Steven Lawson, *
▲ **EMP:** 88 **EST:** 1979
SQ FT: 35,000
SALES (est): 20.54MM
SALES (corp-wide): 43.66MM **Privately Held**
Web: www.craftechcorp.com
SIC: 3089 3559 Injection molding of plastics; Plastics working machinery
PA: Sage Park Acq. Ct Llc
725 Cool Springs Blvd # 2
Franklin TN
615 637-8030

(P-4990)
CHUBBY GORILLA INC (PA)
4320 N Harbor Blvd (92835-1091)
PHONE..............................844 365-5218
Ibraheim Hamsa Aboabdo, *CEO*
Eyad Aboabdo, *
EMP: 27 **EST:** 2015
SALES (est): 5.54MM
SALES (corp-wide): 5.54MM **Privately Held**
Web: www.chubbygorilla.com
SIC: 3089 Closures, plastics

(P-4991)
CLACK CORPORATION
8728 Dice Rd (90670-2514)
PHONE..............................562 789-1702
EMP: 62
SALES (corp-wide): 96.84MM **Privately Held**
Web: www.clackcorp.com
SIC: 3089 Injection molding of plastics
PA: Clack Corporation
4462 Duraform Ln
Windsor WI
608 846-3010

(P-4992)
CLEAR-AD INC
Also Called: Brochure Holders 4u
2410 W 3rd St (92703-3519)
PHONE..............................866 627-9718
Juan Diaz, *CEO*
John Diaz, *Prin*
Bruce Kelly, *
EMP: 30 **EST:** 1972
SQ FT: 17,006
SALES (est): 4.71MM **Privately Held**
Web: www.clearadplastics.com
SIC: 3089 3544 3993 3061 Injection molded finished plastics products, nec; Forms (molds), for foundry and plastics working machinery; Displays and cutouts, window and lobby; Medical and surgical rubber tubing (extruded and lathe-cut)

(P-4993)
CODAN US CORPORATION
Also Called: Codan US
3501 W Sunflower Ave (92704-6923)
PHONE..............................714 545-2111
Peter Schwark, *
Bernd J Larsen, *
Deon Miller, *

▲ **EMP:** 145 **EST:** 1971
SALES (est): 28.94MM
SALES (corp-wide): 64.2K **Privately Held**
Web: www.codanusa.com
SIC: 3089 Molding primary plastics
PA: Codan Holding Gmbh & Co. Kg
Stig Husted-Andersen Str. 11
Lensahn SH
43635111

(P-4994)
CONTAINER OPTIONS
1493 E San Bernardino Ave (92408-2927)
PHONE..............................909 478-0045
EMP: 18 **EST:** 1995
SQ FT: 43,000
SALES (est): 2.6MM **Privately Held**
SIC: 3089 Plastics containers, except foam

(P-4995)
COOL-PAK LLC
Also Called: Bunzl Agrclture Group Chstrfel
401 N Rice Ave (93030-7936)
PHONE..............................805 981-2434
Nick Weber, *
Jim Borchard, *
Derek Goodin, *
Patrick Larmon, *
▲ **EMP:** 85 **EST:** 2001
SQ FT: 124,000
SALES (est): 22.08MM
SALES (corp-wide): 14.5B **Privately Held**
Web: www.cool-pak.com
SIC: 3089 Plastics containers, except foam
HQ: Bunzl Distribution Usa, Llc
1 Cityplace Dr Ste 200
Saint Louis MO

(P-4996)
CORNUCOPIA TOOL & PLASTICS INC
448 Sherwood Rd (93446-3554)
P.O. Box 1915 (93447-1915)
PHONE..............................805 238-7660
Larry Horn, *Pr*
Art Horn, *
EMP: 47 **EST:** 1969
SQ FT: 20,000
SALES (est): 10.09MM **Privately Held**
Web: www.cornucopiaplastics.com
SIC: 3089 3544 Injection molding of plastics; Industrial molds

(P-4997)
CPD INDUSTRIES
Also Called: Custom Packaging Design
4665 State St (91763-6130)
PHONE..............................909 465-5596
Carlos Hurtado, *Pr*
Sergio Briceno, *
EMP: 29 **EST:** 1985
SQ FT: 22,000
SALES (est): 4.49MM **Privately Held**
Web: www.cpdindustries.com
SIC: 3089 Plastics containers, except foam

(P-4998)
CREU LLC
12750 Baltic Ct (91739-8957)
PHONE..............................909 483-4888
Anthony Quezada, *CEO*
EMP: 25 **EST:** 2014
SALES (est): 2.1MM **Privately Held**
SIC: 3089 5063 Automotive parts, plastic; Lighting fixtures

(P-4999)
CUSTOM ENGINEERING PLASTICS LP

Also Called: Custom Engineering Plastics
8558 Miramar Pl (92121-2530)
PHONE..............................858 452-0961
Sylvia Hammond, *Mng Pt*
Jack Hammond, *Pt*
▲ **EMP:** 18 **EST:** 1987
SQ FT: 11,400
SALES (est): 2.43MM **Privately Held**
Web: www.cepi.com
SIC: 3089 3544 Injection molding of plastics;
Forms (molds), for foundry and plastics
working machinery

(P-5000)
DACHA ENTERPRISES INC (HQ)
Also Called: Accent Plastics
13948 Mountain Ave (91710-9018)
PHONE..............................951 273-7777
Thomas A Pridonoff, *CEO*
Bonnie Pridonoff, *
Denise Parks, *
◆ **EMP:** 21 **EST:** 1965
SALES (est): 16.72MM
SALES (corp-wide): 18.38MM **Privately
Held**
Web: www.accentplastics.com
SIC: 3089 Injection molding of plastics
PA: Syntech Development And
Manufacturing, Inc.
13948 Mountain Ave
Chino CA
909 465-5554

(P-5001)
DACHA ENTERPRISES INC
1915 Elise Cir (92879-1882)
PHONE..............................951 273-7777
EMP: 77
SALES (corp-wide): 18.38MM **Privately
Held**
Web: www.accentplastics.com
SIC: 3089 Injection molding of plastics
HQ: Dacha Enterprises, Inc.
13948 Mountain Ave
Chino CA
951 273-7777

(P-5002)
DAMAR PLASTICS INC
1035 Pioneer Way Ste 160 (92020-1978)
PHONE..............................619 283-2300
EMP: 45 **EST:** 1970
SALES (est): 5.01MM **Privately Held**
Web: www.damarplastics.com
SIC: 3089 Plastics processing

(P-5003)
DELAMO MANUFACTURING INC
7171 Telegraph Rd (90640-6511)
PHONE..............................323 936-3566
Fred Morad, *CEO*
EMP: 80 **EST:** 2008
SQ FT: 120,000
SALES (est): 7.88MM **Privately Held**
Web: www.delamo-mfg.com
SIC: 3089 Plastics kitchenware, tableware,
and houseware

(P-5004)
DELFIN DESIGN & MFG INC
15672 Producer Ln (92649-1310)
PHONE..............................949 888-4644
John M Rief, *Pr*
Paul Iverson, *
Rita Williams, *
▲ **EMP:** 28 **EST:** 1991
SALES (est): 8.62MM
SALES (corp-wide): 463.17K **Privately
Held**
Web: www.delfinfs.com

SIC: 3089 3083 Thermoformed finished
plastics products, nec; Plastics finished
products, laminated
HQ: Steelite International U.S.A. Inc.
154 Keystone Dr
New Castle PA

(P-5005)
DEMOLDCO PLASTICS INC
3931 E Miraloma Ave (92806-6201)
PHONE..............................714 577-9391
Nick Trees, *Pr*
EMP: 42 **EST:** 1994
SQ FT: 6,600
SALES (est): 2.18MM **Privately Held**
SIC: 3089 Injection molding of plastics

(P-5006)
DESIGN WEST TECHNOLOGIES INC
2701 Dow Ave (92780-7209)
PHONE..............................714 731-0201
Ryan Hur, *Pr*
▲ **EMP:** 65 **EST:** 1994
SQ FT: 60,000
SALES (est): 16.26MM **Privately Held**
Web: www.dwtusa.com
SIC: 3089 8711 Injection molded finished
plastics products, nec; Electrical or
electronic engineering

(P-5007)
DESIGNER SASH AND DOOR SYS INC
Also Called: Designer Fashion Door
45899 Via Tornado (92590-3359)
PHONE..............................951 657-4179
Ross Eberhart, *Pr*
Kenneth Mcbride, *Sec*
EMP: 24 **EST:** 1988
SQ FT: 20,000
SALES (est): 1.47MM **Privately Held**
SIC: 3089 2431 5211 Windows, plastics;
Doors, wood; Door and window products

(P-5008)
DIAL INDUSTRIES INC
Also Called: All-Power Plastcs Div Dial
3616 Noakes St (90023-3200)
PHONE..............................323 263-6878
Richard Oxford, *Pr*
EMP: 100
SALES (corp-wide): 9.77MM **Privately
Held**
Web: www.dialind.com
SIC: 3089 3354 Plastics kitchenware,
tableware, and houseware; Aluminum
extruded products
PA: Dial Industries, Inc.
3628 Noakes St
Los Angeles CA
323 263-6878

(P-5009)
DIAL INDUSTRIES INC (PA)
3628 Noakes St (90023-3222)
PHONE..............................323 263-6878
▲ **EMP:** 80 **EST:** 1968
SALES (est): 9.77MM
SALES (corp-wide): 9.77MM **Privately
Held**
Web: www.dialind.com
SIC: 3089 Plastics kitchenware, tableware,
and houseware

(P-5010)
DISPENSING DYNAMICS INTL INC (PA)
Also Called: Perrin Craft

1940 Diamond St (92078-5120)
PHONE..............................626 961-3691
Dean Debuhr, *Ch*
Larry Maccormack, *
Scott Strachan, *
Michael Severyn, *
Rocky Wilske, *
◆ **EMP:** 99 **EST:** 1932
SALES (est): 45.23MM
SALES (corp-wide): 45.23MM **Privately
Held**
Web: www.dispensingdynamics.com
SIC: 3089 3993 Injection molding of plastics;
Signs and advertising specialties

(P-5011)
DISTINCTIVE PLASTICS INC
1385 Decision St (92081-8523)
PHONE..............................760 599-9100
Timothy Curnutt, *Pr*
Violeta Curnutt, *
▲ **EMP:** 62 **EST:** 1982
SQ FT: 44,500
SALES (est): 11.29MM **Privately Held**
Web: www.dpi-tech.com
SIC: 3089 3312 Injection molding of plastics;
Tool and die steel

(P-5012)
DIVERSE OPTICS INC
10339 Dorset St (91730-3067)
PHONE..............................909 593-9330
Erik Fleming, *Pr*
EMP: 20 **EST:** 1987
SALES (est): 2.78MM **Privately Held**
Web: www.diverseoptics.com
SIC: 3089 3827 Injection molding of plastics;
Lenses, optical: all types except ophthalmic

(P-5013)
DIVERSIFIED PLASTICS INC
Also Called: Pacific Plas Injection Molding
1333 Keystone Way (92081-8311)
PHONE..............................760 598-5333
Rob Gilman, *Genl Mgr*
EMP: 30
SALES (corp-wide): 11.23MM **Privately
Held**
Web: www.divplast.com
SIC: 3089 3544 Injection molding of plastics;
Industrial molds
PA: Diversified Plastics, Inc.
8617 Xylon Ct
Minneapolis MN
763 424-2525

(P-5014)
DOMINO PLASTICS MFG INC
601 Gateway Ct (93307-6827)
PHONE..............................661 396-3744
W Thomas Bathe Iii, *CEO*
Neil Conway, *Pr*
EMP: 21 **EST:** 1971
SQ FT: 16,000
SALES (est): 3.12MM **Privately Held**
Web: www.dominoplastics.com
SIC: 3089 Billfold inserts, plastics

(P-5015)
DOREL JUVENILE GROUP INC
9950 Calabash Ave (92335-5210)
PHONE..............................909 428-0295
Carrisa John, *Prin*
EMP: 120
SALES (corp-wide): 1.57B **Privately Held**
Web: na.doreljuvenile.com
SIC: 3089 Plastics kitchenware, tableware,
and houseware
HQ: Dorel Juvenile Group, Inc.
2525 State St

Columbus IN
800 457-5276

(P-5016)
DOREL JUVENILE GROUP INC
Also Called: Cosco Home & Office Products
5400 Shea Center Dr (91761-7892)
PHONE..............................909 390-5705
Rick Mc Cook, *Mgr*
EMP: 159
SALES (corp-wide): 1.57B **Privately Held**
Web: www.doreljuvenile.com
SIC: 3089 Plastics kitchenware, tableware,
and houseware
HQ: Dorel Juvenile Group, Inc.
2525 State St
Columbus IN
800 457-5276

(P-5017)
DPP 2020 INC (DH)
533 E Third St (92223-2715)
P.O. Box 2097 (92223-0997)
PHONE..............................951 845-3161
Kevin Rost, *CEO*
Monica Rost, *
◆ **EMP:** 31 **EST:** 1974
SQ FT: 150,000
SALES (est): 39.84MM **Privately Held**
Web: www.duraplastics.com
SIC: 3089 Fittings for pipe, plastics
HQ: Tigre S/A Participacoes
Rua Xavantes 54
Joinvile SC

(P-5018)
EAGLE MOLD TECHNOLOGIES INC
12330 Crosthwaite Cir (92064-6823)
PHONE..............................858 530-0888
Ulrich Bark, *Pr*
Gregory Bark, *VP*
David Bark, *VP*
Ronald Bark, *VP*
Rosemary Bark, *Treas*
EMP: 20 **EST:** 1969
SQ FT: 10,500
SALES (est): 3.85MM **Privately Held**
SIC: 3089 3544 Injection molded finished
plastics products, nec; Special dies, tools,
jigs, and fixtures

(P-5019)
EDCO PLASTICS INC
2110 E Winston Rd (92806-6534)
PHONE..............................714 772-1986
Edward A Contreras, *Pr*
Maria Contreras, *
▲ **EMP:** 49 **EST:** 1984
SQ FT: 25,000
SALES (est): 9MM **Privately Held**
Web: www.edcoplastics.com
SIC: 3089 Molding primary plastics

(P-5020)
EDGE PLASTICS INC (PA)
Also Called: O D I
3016 Kansas Ave Bldg 3 (92507-3442)
PHONE..............................951 786-4750
◆ **EMP:** 28 **EST:** 1990
SQ FT: 23,000
SALES (est): 5.97MM
SALES (corp-wide): 5.97MM **Privately
Held**
Web: www.edgeplastics.com
SIC: 3089 5199 5091 Injection molding of
plastics; Advertising specialties; Bicycle
parts and accessories

P
R
O
D
U
C
T
S
&
S
V
C
S

(P-5021)
EDRIS PLASTICS MFG INC
4560 Pacific Blvd (90058-2208)
PHONE...............................323 581-7000
Hovanes Hovik Issagholian, *CEO*
▲ **EMP:** 26 **EST:** 1991
SQ FT: 27,000
SALES (est): 4.82MM **Privately Held**
Web:
edrisplastics-com.3dcartstores.com
SIC: 3089 Injection molding of plastics

(P-5022)
ELASTPRO SILICONE
SHEETING LLC
13937 Rosecrans Ave (90670-5209)
PHONE...............................562 348-2348
EMP: 19 **EST:** 2019
SALES (est): 2.43MM **Privately Held**
Web: www.elastapro.com
SIC: 3089 Injection molding of plastics

(P-5023)
EMBER TECHNOLOGIES INC
880 Hampshire Rd (91361-2811)
PHONE...............................520 400-9337
Clayton Alexander, *CEO*
John Stone, *Marketing Officer*
Phil Poel, *
EMP: 50 **EST:** 2017
SALES (est): 4.95MM **Privately Held**
Web: www.ember.com
SIC: 3089 5999 Cups, plastics, except foam;
Electronic parts and equipment

(P-5024)
ENGINEERING MODEL ASSOC
INC (PA)
Also Called: Ema
1020 Wallace Way (91748-1027)
PHONE...............................626 912-7011
John Jay Wanderman, *Pr*
John Jay Wanderman, *Pr*
Leon Katz, *
EMP: 25 **EST:** 1955
SQ FT: 28,000
SALES (est): 9.43MM
SALES (corp-wide): 9.43MM **Privately**
Held
SIC: 3089 5162 Plastics processing; Plastics
products, nec

(P-5025)
ENVISION PLASTICS
INDUSTRIES LLC
Also Called: Envision Plastics
14312 Central Ave (91710-5752)
PHONE...............................909 590-7334
EMP: 50
SIC: 3089 Lamp bases and shades, plastics

(P-5026)
EXPANDED RUBBER &
PLASTICS CORP
Also Called: Erp
19200 S Laurel Park Rd (90220-6008)
PHONE...............................310 324-6692
EMP: 37 **EST:** 1957
SALES (est): 5.91MM **Privately Held**
Web: www.expandedrubber.com
SIC: 3089 3086 5088 Molding primary
plastics; Plastics foam products; Aircraft
and space vehicle supplies and parts

(P-5027)
EXTRUMED INC (DH)
Also Called: Vesta
547 Trm Cir (92879-1768)

PHONE...............................951 547-7400
Phil Estes, *Pr*
Chris Guglielmi, *
Eric R Schnur, *
EMP: 28 **EST:** 1990
SQ FT: 53,000
SALES (est): 28.86MM
SALES (corp-wide): 302.09B **Publicly**
Held
SIC: 3089 Injection molding of plastics
HQ: Vesta Intermediate Funding, Inc.
9900 S 57th St
Franklin WI
414 423-0550

(P-5028)
FISCHER MOLD INCORPORATED
393 Meyer Cir (92879-1078)
PHONE...............................951 279-1140
Robert Fischer, *Pr*
Eleanor Fischer, *
▲ **EMP:** 60 **EST:** 1969
SQ FT: 32,000
SALES (est): 10.48MM **Privately Held**
Web: www.fischermold.com
SIC: 3089 3544 Injection molding of plastics;
Special dies, tools, jigs, and fixtures

(P-5029)
FIT-LINE INC
Also Called: Fit-Line Global
2901 S Tech Center Dr (92705-5657)
PHONE...............................714 549-9091
▼ **EMP:** 50 **EST:** 1993
SQ FT: 4,500
SALES (est): 5.53MM **Privately Held**
Web: www.fit-lineglobal.com
SIC: 3089 Fittings for pipe, plastics

(P-5030)
FLUIDMASTER INC (PA)
30800 Rancho Viejo Rd (92675-1564)
PHONE...............................949 728-2000
Robert Andersonschoepe, *CEO*
Michael Draves, *
Robert Connell, *
Terry Bland, *
◆ **EMP:** 127 **EST:** 1957
SALES (est): 135.53MM
SALES (corp-wide): 135.53MM **Privately**
Held
Web: www.fluidmaster.com
SIC: 3089 3432 1711 Injection molding of
plastics; Plumbing fixture fittings and trim;
Plumbing contractors

(P-5031)
FORMULA PLASTICS INC
451 Tecate Rd Ste 2b (91980)
PHONE...............................866 307-1362
Alexander Mora, *CEO*
Elias Mora, *
Joe Mora, *
Monica Mora, *
▲ **EMP:** 500 **EST:** 1984
SQ FT: 20,000
SALES (est): 93.42MM **Privately Held**
Web: www.formulaplastics.com
SIC: 3089 Injection molding of plastics

(P-5032)
FRUTH CUSTOM PLASTICS INC
Also Called: Cal-AZ Sales & Marketing
701 Richfield Rd (92870-6729)
P.O. Box 807 (92811-0807)
PHONE...............................714 993-9955
EMP: 80 **EST:** 1980
SALES (est): 14.13MM **Privately Held**
Web: www.fruth.com

SIC: 3089 3081 2673 Plastics containers,
except foam; Plastics film and sheet;
Plastic bags: made from purchased
materials
HQ: C. P. Converters, Inc.
15 Grumbacher Rd
York PA
717 764-1193

(P-5033)
G B REMANUFACTURING INC
2040 E Cherry Industrial Cir (90805-4410)
PHONE...............................562 272-7333
Michael J Kitching, *CEO*
Michael J Kitching, *Pr*
F William Kitching, *
Patricia Kitching, *
▲ **EMP:** 70 **EST:** 1986
SQ FT: 26,400
SALES (est): 13.74MM **Privately Held**
Web: www.gbreman.com
SIC: 3089 Injection molded finished plastics
products, nec

(P-5034)
GARY MANUFACTURING INC
2626 Southport Way Ste E (91950-8754)
PHONE...............................619 429-4479
Brian Smith, *Pr*
Helen Smith, *
▲ **EMP:** 35 **EST:** 1958
SQ FT: 10,000
SALES (est): 4.89MM **Privately Held**
Web: www.garymanufacturing.com
SIC: 3089 2392 5162 2673 Plastics
containers, except foam; Napkins, fabric
and nonwoven: made from purchased
materials; Plastics materials and basic
shapes; Bags: plastic, laminated, and
coated

(P-5035)
GEIGER PLASTICS INC
16150 S Maple Ave # A (90248-2837)
PHONE...............................310 327-9926
Charlotte May, *Pr*
Vangie Ramirez, *Sec*
EMP: 20 **EST:** 1964
SQ FT: 10,000
SALES (est): 2.2MM **Privately Held**
Web: www.geigerplastics.com
SIC: 3089 3559 Injection molding of plastics;
Plastics working machinery

(P-5036)
GEMINI FILM & BAG INC (PA)
Also Called: Gemini Plastics
3574 Fruitland Ave (90270-2008)
P.O. Box 806 (92811-0806)
PHONE...............................323 582-0901
James Fruth, *Pr*
Brian Kunisch, *
EMP: 25 **EST:** 1966
SQ FT: 12,000
SALES (est): 2.31MM
SALES (corp-wide): 2.31MM **Privately**
Held
SIC: 3089 8742 Extruded finished plastics
products, nec; Manufacturing management
consultant

(P-5037)
GEO PLASTICS
2200 E 52nd St (90058-3446)
PHONE...............................323 277-8106
Michael Abraham Morris, *CEO*
Justin Hunt, *
▲ **EMP:** 27 **EST:** 1992
SALES (est): 5.03MM **Privately Held**
Web: www.geoplastics.com

SIC: 3089 Extruded finished plastics
products, nec

(P-5038)
GETPART LA INC
13705 Cimarron Ave (90249-2463)
PHONE...............................424 331-9599
Ilya S Shchelokov, *CEO*
EMP: 23 **EST:** 2016
SALES (est): 3.53MM **Privately Held**
Web: www.fitparts.com
SIC: 3089 Automotive parts, plastic

(P-5039)
GIBRALTAR PLASTIC PDTS
CORP
12885 Foothill Blvd (91342-5317)
PHONE...............................818 365-9318
Harvey J Jacobs, *Pr*
EMP: 25 **EST:** 1964
SQ FT: 30,000
SALES (est): 4.8MM **Privately Held**
Web: www.gibraltarplastic.com
SIC: 3089 Injection molded finished plastics
products, nec

(P-5040)
GILL CORPORATION (PA)
4056 Easy St (91731-1054)
PHONE...............................626 443-6094
Stephen E Gill, *Ch*
William Heinze, *
Irv Freund, *Business Development*
Don Clark, *
◆ **EMP:** 236 **EST:** 1945
SQ FT: 390,000
SALES (est): 225.82MM
SALES (corp-wide): 225.82MM **Privately**
Held
Web: www.thegillcorp.com
SIC: 3089 3469 3272 2448 Laminating of
plastics; Honeycombed metal; Panels and
sections, prefabricated concrete; Cargo
containers, wood and metal combination

(P-5041)
GKN ARSPACE TRNSPRNCY
SYSTEMS
12122 Western Ave (92841-2915)
PHONE...............................714 893-7531
John Danley, *CEO*
Mike Mccann Ceo Aeostructures N
America, *Prin*
Joakim Anderson, *Chief Executive Officer*
Engine Systems
Gavin Wesson, *
Russ Dunn, *Technology*
▲ **EMP:** 360 **EST:** 1946
SQ FT: 324,000
SALES (est): 116.69MM
SALES (corp-wide): 1.51MM **Privately**
Held
Web: www.gkn.com
SIC: 3089 3231 3827 3728 Windows, plastics
; Mirrors, truck and automobile: made from
purchased glass; Optical instruments and
lenses; Aircraft parts and equipment, nec
HQ: Gkn America Corp.
1180 Peachtree St Ne # 2450
Atlanta GA
630 972-9300

(P-5042)
GRAND FUSION HOUSEWARES
INC
Also Called: GRAND FUSION
HOUSEWARES, INC
9375 Customhouse Plz (92154-7653)
PHONE...............................909 292-5776

▲ = Import ▼ = Export
◆ = Import/Export

Hilton Blieden, *Pr*
EMP: 48
SALES (corp-wide): 7.08MM **Privately Held**
Web: www.grandfusionhousewares.com
SIC: 3089 Kitchenware, plastics
PA: Grand Fusion Housewares, Llc
12 Partridge
Irvine CA
888 614-7263

(P-5043)
GRIFF INDUSTRIES INC
4515 Runway Dr (93536-8530)
PHONE.................................661 728-0111
Michael Griffin, *Pr*
◆ **EMP:** 19 **EST:** 1999
SQ FT: 8,400
SALES (est): 2.75MM **Privately Held**
Web: www.griffindustries.com
SIC: 3089 Injection molding of plastics

(P-5044)
GT STYLING CORP
2830 E Via Martens (92806-1751)
PHONE.................................714 644-9214
EMP: 27 **EST:** 2001
SALES (est): 1.68MM **Privately Held**
SIC: 3089 Molding primary plastics

(P-5045)
**HEE ENVIRONMENTAL
ENGINEERING LLC**
16605 Koala Rd (92301-3925)
PHONE.................................760 530-1409
EMP: 38
SIC: 3089 Plastics and fiberglass tanks

(P-5046)
**HI-REL PLASTICS & MOLDING
CORP**
7575 Jurupa Ave (92504-1012)
PHONE.................................951 354-0258
Rakesh Bajaria, *CEO*
Rick Bajria, *
Harry Thummer, *
Dennis Sovalia, *
▲ **EMP:** 50 **EST:** 1984
SQ FT: 15,000
SALES (est): 8.01MM **Privately Held**
Web: www.hirelplastics.com
SIC: 3089 3549 3599 Injection molded
finished plastics products, nec; Assembly
machines, including robotic; Machine shop,
jobbing and repair

(P-5047)
HIGGINS HARDWOOD INC
Also Called: Pacific Coast Laminating
450 B St Ste 1900 (92101-8005)
PHONE.................................775 856-1653
John Parr, *Genl Mgr*
EMP: 18 **EST:** 2003
SALES (est): 503.47K **Privately Held**
SIC: 3089 Panels, building: plastics, nec

(P-5048)
HIGHLAND PLASTICS INC
Also Called: Hi-Plas
3650 Dulles Dr (91752-3260)
PHONE.................................951 360-9587
James L Nelson, *Prin*
William B Warren, *
◆ **EMP:** 130 **EST:** 1974
SQ FT: 150,000
SALES (est): 19.76MM **Privately Held**
SIC: 3089 Injection molding of plastics

(P-5049)
HILLCOR DISTRIBUTION INC
5100 Commerce Dr (91706-1450)
PHONE.................................626 960-8789
Harry O Hill Iii, *Pr*
▲ **EMP:** 18 **EST:** 1962
SQ FT: 18,000
SALES (est): 1.85MM **Privately Held**
Web: www.hillcorplastics.com
SIC: 3089 Injection molding of plastics

(P-5050)
**HOME CONCEPTS PRODUCTS
INC**
4199 Bandini Blvd (90058-4208)
PHONE.................................866 981-0500
Michael Moghavem, *Pr*
Ata Moghavem, *VP*
Perry Rahban, *VP*
Charles Rahban, *Sec*
▲ **EMP:** 23 **EST:** 2004
SALES (est): 444.45K **Privately Held**
SIC: 3089 5023 Kitchenware, plastics;
Kitchenware

(P-5051)
HOOD MANUFACTURING INC
Also Called: Thermobile
2621 S Birch St (92707-3410)
PHONE.................................714 979-7681
Michael Hood, *Pr*
Patrica Hood, *
Michele Rauschenbach, *CIO*
EMP: 60 **EST:** 1948
SQ FT: 24,000
SALES (est): 7.28MM **Privately Held**
Web: www.hoodmfg.com
SIC: 3089 3585 Injection molded finished
plastics products, nec; Refrigeration and
heating equipment

(P-5052)
HOOSIER INC
1152 California Ave (92881-3324)
P.O. Box 78926 (92877-0164)
PHONE.................................951 272-3070
Robert G Simms, *CEO*
EMP: 80 **EST:** 1979
SQ FT: 45,000
SALES (est): 22.05MM **Privately Held**
Web: www.hoosierinc.com
SIC: 3089 Injection molding of plastics

(P-5053)
HOPE PLASTICS CO INC
5353 Strohm Ave (91601-3526)
PHONE.................................818 769-5560
Steven Borden, *Pr*
Bill Borden, *VP*
Hope Borden, *Sec*
▲ **EMP:** 20 **EST:** 1964
SQ FT: 17,000
SALES (est): 2.22MM **Privately Held**
Web: www.hopeplastics.com
SIC: 3089 Injection molding of plastics

(P-5054)
**HOUSEWARES
INTERNATIONAL INC**
Also Called: American Household Company
1933 S Broadway Ste 867 (90007-4523)
PHONE.................................323 581-3000
Kamyar Solouki, *CEO*
Sean Solouki, *
◆ **EMP:** 35 **EST:** 1988
SALES (est): 5.33MM **Privately Held**
Web: www.housewaresintl.com
SIC: 3089 5023 Kitchenware, plastics;
Kitchenware

(P-5055)
**HUSKY INJCTION MLDING
SYSTEMS**
5245 Maureen Ln (93021-7125)
PHONE.................................805 523-9593
EMP: 67
Web: www.husky.co
SIC: 3089 Injection molding of plastics
HQ: Husky Injection Molding Systems, Inc.
288 Nrd
Milton VT
802 859-8000

(P-5056)
**HUSKY INJCTION MLDING
SYSTEMS**
3505 Cadillac Ave Ste N4 (92626-1433)
PHONE.................................714 545-8200
Michael Smith, *Mgr*
EMP: 67
SQ FT: 6,501
Web: www.husky.co
SIC: 3089 Injection molding of plastics
HQ: Husky Injection Molding Systems, Inc.
288 Nrd
Milton VT
802 859-8000

(P-5057)
IDEMIA AMERICA CORP
3150 E Ana St (90221-5607)
PHONE.................................310 884-7900
Eric Daniele, *Dir*
EMP: 161
SALES (corp-wide): 2.44B **Privately Held**
Web: www.idemia.com
SIC: 3089 3083 Identification cards, plastics;
Plastics finished products, laminated
HQ: Idemia America Corp.
11951 Freedom Dr Ste 1800
Reston VA
703 775-7800

(P-5058)
IKEGAMI MOLD CORP AMERICA
4025 Camino Del Rio S # 301 (92108)
PHONE.................................619 858-6855
Masatomo Ikegami, *Pr*
Yoshiyuki Koga, *VP*
▲ **EMP:** 17 **EST:** 1988
SALES (est): 4.79MM **Privately Held**
Web: www.ikegami-mold.com
SIC: 3089 Injection molding of plastics
PA: Ikegami Mold Engineering Co.,Ltd.
2-664-8, Toyonodai
Kazo STM

(P-5059)
**INCA PLASTICS MOLDING CO
INC**
17129 Koala Rd (92301-2248)
PHONE.................................760 246-8087
Howard Haigh, *CEO*
EMP: 18 **EST:** 2016
SALES (est): 1.04MM **Privately Held**
SIC: 3089 Injection molding of plastics

(P-5060)
**INCA PLASTICS MOLDING CO
INC**
948 E Belmont St (91761-4549)
PHONE.................................909 923-3235
Howard L Haigh, *Pr*
▲ **EMP:** 17 **EST:** 1960
SQ FT: 33,000
SALES (est): 4.47MM **Privately Held**
Web: www.incaplastics.com

SIC: 3089 3714 3544 3443 Injection molding
of plastics; Motor vehicle parts and
accessories; Special dies, tools, jigs, and
fixtures; Fabricated plate work (boiler shop)

(P-5061)
INLINE PLASTICS INC
1950 S Baker Ave (91761-7755)
PHONE.................................909 923-1033
Kelly Orr, *CEO*
Alfredo Perez, *
EMP: 25 **EST:** 1996
SQ FT: 21,000
SALES (est): 4.02MM **Privately Held**
Web: www.inlineplasticsinc.com
SIC: 3089 Injection molding of plastics

(P-5062)
INTERTRADE INDUSTRIES LTD
14600 Hoover St (92683-5346)
PHONE.................................714 894-5566
EMP: 56 **EST:** 1975
SALES (est): 14.73MM **Privately Held**
SIC: 3089 Plastics boats and other marine
equipment
PA: American Innotek, Inc.
2655 Vista Pacific Dr
Oceanside CA

(P-5063)
IPS INDUSTRIES INC
Also Called: Spectrum Bags
12641 166th St (90703-2101)
PHONE.................................562 623-2555
Frank Su, *CEO*
Peter Hii, *
David Silva, *
Ben Tran, *
Betty Green, *
◆ **EMP:** 80 **EST:** 1990
SQ FT: 150,000
SALES (est): 21.08MM **Privately Held**
Web: www.ipspi.com
SIC: 3089 3629 Battery cases, plastics or
plastics combination; Battery chargers,
rectifying or nonrotating

(P-5064)
**J & L CSTM PLSTIC EXTRSONS
INC**
850 Lawson St (91748-1103)
PHONE.................................626 442-0711
Edwin Woo, *CEO*
Louis Salmon, *
Jaime Lizarraga, *
EMP: 30 **EST:** 1974
SALES (est): 2.35MM **Privately Held**
Web: www.jlplastic.com
SIC: 3089 Plastics hardware and building
products

(P-5065)
J A ENGLISH II INC
Also Called: Pacific Plstcs-Njction Molding
1333 Keystone Way (92081-8311)
PHONE.................................760 598-5333
▲ **EMP:** 25
SIC: 3089 3544 Injection molding of plastics;
Industrial molds

(P-5066)
JACOBSON PLASTICS INC
1401 Freeman Ave (90804-2518)
PHONE.................................562 433-4911
Jeff Jacobson, *Pr*
▲ **EMP:** 75 **EST:** 1962
SQ FT: 25,000
SALES (est): 8.55MM **Privately Held**
Web: www.jacobsonplastics.com

**P
R
O
D
U
C
T
S
&
S
V
C
S**

SIC: **3089** 3544 Injection molding of plastics;
Special dies, tools, jigs, and fixtures

(P-5067)
JASON TOOL AND ENGINEERING INC
7101 Honold Cir (92841-1424)
PHONE..............................714 895-5067
Jack Winterswyk, *Pr*
Curtis H Thompson, *
▲ **EMP:** 30 **EST:** 1979
SQ FT: 30,000
SALES (est): 4.47MM **Privately Held**
Web: www.jasontool.com
SIC: 3089 3544 Injection molding of plastics;
Dies, plastics forming

(P-5068)
JB BRANANNE INC
6 Orchard (92630-8335)
PHONE..............................949 215-7704
Jay Kim, *CEO*
EMP: 20 **EST:** 1993
SALES (est): 50MM **Privately Held**
Web: www.jbbrananne.com
SIC: 3089 Automotive parts, plastic

(P-5069)
JB PLASTICS INC
1921 E Edinger Ave (92705-4720)
PHONE..............................714 541-8500
Joseph N Chiodo, *Pr*
Bruce Donoho, *
EMP: 45 **EST:** 2000
SQ FT: 30,000
SALES (est): 7.95MM **Privately Held**
Web: www.jb-plastics.com
SIC: 3089 Injection molding of plastics

(P-5070)
JDR ENGINEERING CONS INC (PA)
3122 Maple St (92707-4408)
PHONE..............................714 751-7084
Dionisio Rodriguez, *Pr*
Janet Rodriguez, *VP*
▲ **EMP:** 68 **EST:** 1969
SQ FT: 25,000
SALES (est): 10.13MM
SALES (corp-wide): 10.13MM **Privately Held**
SIC: 3089 Injection molding of plastics

(P-5071)
JEM-HD CO INC
10030 Via De La Amistad Ste F (92154-7275)
PHONE..............................619 710-1443
Jae Man Lee, *CEO*
EMP: 22 **EST:** 2005
SALES (est): 444.8K **Privately Held**
SIC: 3089 Injection molding of plastics

(P-5072)
JET PLASTICS (PA)
941 N Eastern Ave (90063-1307)
PHONE..............................323 268-6706
TOLL FREE: 800
Lee R Johnson, *Pr*
Lee Johnson, *
Lon Johnson, *
Lowel Johnson, *
◆ **EMP:** 50 **EST:** 1948
SQ FT: 30,000
SALES (est): 14.63MM
SALES (corp-wide): 14.63MM **Privately Held**
Web: www.jetplastics.com

(P-5073)
JG PLASTICS GROUP LLC
335 Fischer Ave (92626-4522)
PHONE..............................714 751-4266
◆ **EMP:** 50 **EST:** 1975
SQ FT: 32,000
SALES (est): 13.93MM **Privately Held**
Web: www.jgplastics.com
SIC: 3089 3544 Injection molding of plastics;
Special dies, tools, jigs, and fixtures

(P-5074)
JSN INDUSTRIES INC
9700 Jeronimo Rd (92618-2019)
PHONE..............................949 458-0050
James H Nagel Junior, *CEO*
Sandra Nagel, *
EMP: 70 **EST:** 1984
SQ FT: 65,000
SALES (est): 9.83MM **Privately Held**
Web: www.jsn.com
SIC: 3089 Injection molding of plastics

(P-5075)
KARAT PACKAGING INC (PA)
Also Called: Karat
6185 Kimball Ave (91708-9126)
PHONE..............................626 965-8882
Alan Yu, *Ch Bd*
Joanne Wang, *COO*
Ann T Sabahat, *CFO*
Marvin Cheng, *VP Mfg*
EMP: 28 **EST:** 2001
SALES (est): 364.24MM
SALES (corp-wide): 364.24MM **Publicly Held**
Web: www.karatpackaging.com
SIC: 3089 5113 Plastics containers, except
foam; Disposable plates, cups, napkins,
and eating utensils

(P-5076)
KAS ENGINEERING INC (PA)
1714 14th St (90404-4341)
PHONE..............................310 450-8925
EMP: 24 **EST:** 1958
SALES (est): 4.83MM
SALES (corp-wide): 4.83MM **Privately Held**
Web: www.kasengineering.com
SIC: 3089 3541 Injection molding of plastics;
Machine tools, metal cutting type

(P-5077)
KELCOURT PLASTICS INC (DH)
Also Called: Kelpac Medical
1000 Calle Recodo (92673-6225)
PHONE..............................949 361-0774
John Wolf, *CEO*
Rob Bonatakis, *
▲ **EMP:** 80 **EST:** 1982
SQ FT: 20,000
SALES (est): 20MM
SALES (corp-wide): 13.02B **Publicly Held**
Web: www.spectrumplastics.com
SIC: 3089 Injection molding of plastics
HQ: Ppc Industries Inc.
10101 78th Ave
Pleasant Prairie WI
262 947-0900

(P-5078)
KEPNER PLAS FABRICATORS INC
3131 Lomita Blvd (90505-5158)
PHONE..............................310 325-3162
Frank Meyers, *CEO*
Meryl Bayley, *

▲ **EMP:** 26 **EST:** 1960
SQ FT: 50,000
SALES (est): 2.43MM **Privately Held**
Web: www.kepnerplastics.com
SIC: 3089 Injection molding of plastics

(P-5079)
KING BROS INDUSTRIES
29101 The Old Rd (91355-1014)
◆ **EMP:** 170
Web: www.kbico.com
SIC: 3089 Plastics hardware and building
products

(P-5080)
KING PLASTICS INC
840 N Elm St (92867-7908)
P.O. Box 6229 (92863-6229)
PHONE..............................714 997-7540
Larry E Lathrum, *CEO*
◆ **EMP:** 96 **EST:** 1962
SQ FT: 100,000
SALES (est): 15.01MM **Privately Held**
Web: www.kingplastics.com
SIC: 3089 Plastics kitchenware, tableware,
and houseware

(P-5081)
L & H MOLD & ENGINEERING INC (PA)
Also Called: L & H Molds
140 Atlantic St (91768-3285)
PHONE..............................909 930-1547
Stan Hillary, *CEO*
Steve Hillary, *Pr*
Brenda Bishop, *Sec*
EMP: 23 **EST:** 1974
SQ FT: 6,000
SALES (est): 3.41MM
SALES (corp-wide): 3.41MM **Privately Held**
SIC: 3089 Injection molding of plastics

(P-5082)
LAMSCO WEST INC
29101 The Old Rd (91355-1014)
PHONE..............................661 295-8620
Steve Griffith, *Pr*
Scott Wilkinson, *
Rick Casillas, *
EMP: 99 **EST:** 1993
SQ FT: 31,280
SALES (est): 20.87MM
SALES (corp-wide): 123.82MM **Privately Held**
Web: www.lamscowest.com
SIC: 3089 Injection molding of plastics
HQ: Avantus Aerospace, Inc.
29101 The Old Rd
Valencia CA
661 295-8620

(P-5083)
LEADING INDUSTRY INC
Also Called: Pinnacle Plastic Containers
1151 Pacific Ave (93033-2472)
PHONE..............................805 385-4100
◆ **EMP:** 100
Web: www.ldind.com
SIC: 3089 Plastics processing

(P-5084)
LEHRER BRLLNPRFKTION WERKS INC
Also Called: Lbi - USA
20801 Nordhoff St (91311-5925)
P.O. Box 3519 (91313-3519)
PHONE..............................818 407-1890
Keith Lehrer, *Pr*

Chett Lehrer, *
▲ **EMP:** 65 **EST:** 1949
SQ FT: 38,000
SALES (est): 5.5MM **Privately Held**
SIC: 3089 Cases, plastics

(P-5085)
LINER TECHNOLOGIES INC
Also Called: Flexi-Liner
4821 Chino Ave (91710-5132)
PHONE..............................909 594-6610
Tait Eyre, *Pr*
Angela Eyre, *Sec*
▼ **EMP:** 20 **EST:** 1953
SQ FT: 20,000
SALES (est): 4.11MM **Privately Held**
Web: www.flexi-liner.com
SIC: 3089 Plastics containers, except foam

(P-5086)
LLC WALKER WEST
1555 S Vintage Ave (91761-3655)
PHONE..............................909 390-4300
Frank San Roman, *CEO*
Frank San Roman, *Managing Member*
EMP: 175 **EST:** 1954
SALES (est): 11.89MM **Privately Held**
SIC: 3089 Automotive parts, plastic

(P-5087)
LORITZ & ASSOCIATES INC
Also Called: L & A Plastics
24895 La Palma Ave (92887-5531)
PHONE..............................714 694-0200
Edward F Loritz, *CEO*
Ken Loritz, *
Anita Court, *
◆ **EMP:** 46 **EST:** 1982
SQ FT: 6,000
SALES (est): 11.82MM **Privately Held**
Web: www.lacontainer.com
SIC: 3089 Plastics processing

(P-5088)
M & A PLASTICS INC
11735 Sheldon St (91352-1580)
PHONE..............................818 768-0479
Guillermo S Morales, *Pr*
Nancy M Morales, *
EMP: 18 **EST:** 1979
SQ FT: 20,000
SALES (est): 992.8K **Privately Held**
Web: www.maplastics.com
SIC: 3089 Injection molding of plastics

(P-5089)
MAGIC PLASTICS INC (PA)
25215 Avenue Stanford (91355-3923)
PHONE..............................800 369-0303
John Sarno, *CEO*
Patrick Madormo, *
Tony Madormo, *
Nan Sarno, *
▲ **EMP:** 22 **EST:** 1985
SQ FT: 75,000
SALES (est): 13.47MM
SALES (corp-wide): 13.47MM **Privately Held**
Web: www.magicplastics.com
SIC: 3089 Injection molding of plastics

(P-5090)
MAKABI 26 INC
Also Called: Best Buy Imports
2850 E 44th St (90058-2402)
PHONE..............................323 588-7666
Benham Makabi, *CEO*
EMP: 19 **EST:** 1998
SQ FT: 12,000
SALES (est): 629.36K **Privately Held**

▲ = Import ▼ = Export
◆ = Import/Export

SIC: 3089 Plastics kitchenware, tableware, and houseware

(P-5091)
MARTIN CHANCEY CORPORATION
Also Called: Taral Plastics
525 Malloy Ct (92878-4045)
PHONE..............................510 972-6300
Chancey Price Martin, CEO
Emily Martin, Sec
▲ EMP: 25 EST: 2003
SALES (est): 4.48MM Privately Held
Web: www.taralplastics.com
SIC: 3089 5085 Jars, plastics; Plastic bottles

(P-5092)
MEDEGEN LLC (DH)
4501 E Wall St (91761-8143)
P.O. Box 515111 (90051-5111)
PHONE..............................909 390-9080
Michael E Stanley, *
W Mark Dorris, *
Paul M Ellis, *
Jeffrey S Goble, *
▲ EMP: 50 EST: 2001
SQ FT: 3,000
SALES (est): 135.67MM
SALES (corp-wide): 19.37B Publicly Held
Web: www.medegenmed.com
SIC: 3089 Injection molded finished plastics products, nec
HQ: Carefusion Corporation
3750 Torrey View Ct
San Diego CA

(P-5093)
MEDEGEN INC
930 S Wanamaker Ave (91761-8151)
PHONE..............................909 390-9080
▲ EMP: 180
SIC: 3089 3544 Injection molded finished plastics products, nec; Special dies, tools, jigs, and fixtures

(P-5094)
MEDICAL EXTRUSION TECH INC (PA)
Also Called: M E T
26608 Pierce Cir Ste A (92562-1008)
PHONE..............................951 698-4346
Tom E Bauer, CEO
I Rikki Bauer, VP
EMP: 20 EST: 1990
SQ FT: 16,645
SALES (est): 9.21MM Privately Held
Web: www.medicalextrusion.com
SIC: 3089 Injection molding of plastics

(P-5095)
MEDWAY PLASTICS CORPORATION
2250 E Cherry Industrial Cir (90805-4414)
PHONE..............................562 630-1175
Thomas Hutchinson Junior, CEO
Mary Hutchinson, *
Gerry Hutchinson, *
Rick Hutchinson, *
Sheryl Mcdaniel, VP
◆ EMP: 141 EST: 1974
SALES (est): 29.79MM Privately Held
Web: www.medwayplastics.com
SIC: 3089 Injection molding of plastics

(P-5096)
MERGER SUB GOTHAM 2 LLC
6261 Katella Ave Ste 250 (90630-5200)
PHONE..............................714 462-4603
Nicholas Kovacevich, CEO

EMP: 109 EST: 2021
SALES (est): 11.2MM
SALES (corp-wide): 137.09MM Publicly Held
SIC: 3089 5085 Plastics containers, except foam; Industrial supplies
PA: Greenlane Holdings, Inc.
1095 Broken Sound Pkwy Nw # 100
Boca Raton FL
877 292-7660

(P-5097)
MERRICK ENGINEERING INC (PA)
1275 Quarry St (92879-1707)
PHONE..............................951 737-6040
Abraham M Abdi, Pr
Katina Brown, *
Mina Abdi, *
◆ EMP: 250 EST: 1971
SQ FT: 150,000
SALES (est): 95.41MM
SALES (corp-wide): 95.41MM Privately Held
Web: www.merrickengineering.com
SIC: 3089 Injection molding of plastics

(P-5098)
MI TECHNOLOGIES INC
Also Called: Lutema
2215 Paseo De Las Americas Ste 30 (92154-7908)
PHONE..............................619 710-2637
Amir Tafreshi, CEO
Ali Irani-tehrani, Prin
John Celms, *
▲ EMP: 700 EST: 2004
SQ FT: 8,000
SALES (est): 71.57MM Privately Held
Web: www.discount-merchant.com
SIC: 3089 3672 5731 3999 Injection molding of plastics; Printed circuit boards; Consumer electronic equipment, nec; Barber and beauty shop equipment

(P-5099)
MICRODYNE PLASTICS INC
1901 E Cooley Dr (92324-6322)
PHONE..............................909 503-4010
Judy Lopez, CEO
▲ EMP: 100 EST: 1977
SQ FT: 33,000
SALES (est): 23.33MM Privately Held
Web: www.microdyneplastics.com
SIC: 3089 Blow molded finished plastics products, nec

(P-5100)
MILGARD MANUFACTURING LLC
Also Called: Milgard Windows
26879 Diaz Rd (92590-3470)
PHONE..............................480 763-6000
Cory Hall, Brnch Mgr
EMP: 317
SALES (corp-wide): 822.1MM Privately Held
Web: www.milgard.com
SIC: 3089 3442 5211 3231 Windows, plastics ; Sash, door or window: metal; Door and window products; Products of purchased glass
HQ: Milgard Manufacturing Llc
1010 54th Ave E
Tacoma WA
253 922-4343

(P-5101)
MISSION CUSTOM EXTRUSION INC
10904 Beech Ave (92337-7260)
P.O. Box 310302 (92331-0302)
PHONE..............................909 822-1581
Moses Tersaud, Pr
EMP: 20 EST: 2005
SQ FT: 23,400
SALES (est): 943.96K Privately Held
Web: www.missioncustomextrusions.com
SIC: 3089 Awnings, fiberglass and plastics combination

(P-5102)
MISSION PLASTICS INC
1930 S Parco Ave (91761-8312)
PHONE..............................909 947-7287
Patrick Dauphinee, CEO
Charles Montes, *
▲ EMP: 120 EST: 1982
SQ FT: 20,000
SALES (est): 1.41MM Privately Held
Web: www.missionplastics.com
SIC: 3089 Injection molding of plastics

(P-5103)
MODERN CONCEPTS INC
3121 E Ana St (90221-5606)
PHONE..............................310 637-0013
Richard J Warpack, Pr
◆ EMP: 60 EST: 1983
SQ FT: 42,000
SALES (est): 7.25MM Privately Held
SIC: 3089 3087 Coloring and finishing of plastics products; Custom compound purchased resins

(P-5104)
MODIFIED PLASTICS INC (PA)
1240 E Glenwood Pl (92707-3000)
PHONE..............................714 546-4667
Robert Estep, CEO
Jocelyn Eubank, *
▲ EMP: 27 EST: 1976
SQ FT: 18,000
SALES (est): 24.9MM
SALES (corp-wide): 24.9MM Privately Held
Web: www.modifiedplastics.com
SIC: 3089 Injection molding of plastics

(P-5105)
MOLDED FIBER GL COMPANIES - W
Also Called: M F G West
9400 Holly Rd (92301-3900)
P.O. Box 675 (44005-0675)
PHONE..............................760 246-4042
Richard Morrison, CEO
Dave Denny, *
Jim Sommer, *
▲ EMP: 100 EST: 1958
SQ FT: 66,000
SALES (est): 23.33MM
SALES (corp-wide): 360.86MM Privately Held
Web: www.moldedfiberglass.com
SIC: 3089 Air mattresses, plastics
PA: Molded Fiber Glass Companies
2925 Mfg Pl
Ashtabula OH
440 997-5851

(P-5106)
MOLDING CORPORATION AMERICA
10349 Norris Ave (91331-2220)

PHONE..............................818 890-7877
Mark Hurley, CEO
Sandra Rinder, VP
▲ EMP: 50 EST: 1967
SQ FT: 59,000
SALES (est): 6.34MM Privately Held
Web: www.pepincplastics.com
SIC: 3089 Injection molding of plastics

(P-5107)
MOLDING INTL & ENGRG INC
Also Called: M I E
42136 Avenida Alvarado (92590-3400)
PHONE..............................951 296-5010
Bradway B Adams, CEO
EMP: 22 EST: 1985
SQ FT: 27,000
SALES (est): 808.57K Privately Held
SIC: 3089 3544 2821 Injection molded finished plastics products, nec; Industrial molds; Plastics materials and resins

(P-5108)
MONCO PRODUCTS INC
7562 Acacia Ave (92841-4057)
PHONE..............................714 891-2788
Tom Monson, Pr
Jerry Monson, *
▲ EMP: 34 EST: 1979
SQ FT: 15,000
SALES (est): 2.09MM Privately Held
Web: www.moncoproducts.com
SIC: 3089 Injection molding of plastics

(P-5109)
MORRIS ENTERPRISES INC
16799 Schoenborn St (91343-6107)
PHONE..............................818 894-9103
Morris Weinberg, Pr
Benjamin Weinberg, VP
EMP: 17 EST: 1959
SQ FT: 5,000
SALES (est): 184.11K Privately Held
SIC: 3089 3676 3674 3577 Blow molded finished plastics products, nec; Electronic resistors; Semiconductors and related devices; Computer peripheral equipment, nec

(P-5110)
NATIONAL DIVERSIFIED SALES INC (HQ)
Also Called: Nds
21300 Victory Blvd Ste 215 (91367-7721)
P.O. Box 339 (93247-0339)
PHONE..............................559 562-9888
Michael Gummeson, Pr
Randall Stott, *
Josie Malonado, *
◆ EMP: 200 EST: 1978
SQ FT: 5,000
SALES (est): 210.51MM Privately Held
Web: www.ndspro.com
SIC: 3089 Plastics hardware and building products
PA: Norma Group Se
Edisonstr. 4
Maintal HE

(P-5111)
NATIONAL MEDICAL PRODUCTS INC
57 Parker (92618-1605)
PHONE..............................949 768-1147
Dahyabhai Patel, Pr
Kaushik Patel, CFO
Jack Kay, R&D Mgr
EMP: 22 EST: 1989
SQ FT: 28,630
SALES (est): 1.72MM Privately Held

PRODUCTS & SVCS

Web: www.jtip.com
SIC: **3089** Injection molded finished plastics products, nec

(P-5112)
NEOPACIFIC HOLDINGS INC
Also Called: Pro-Action Products
14940 Calvert St (91411-2603)
PHONE......................818 786-2900
Steve Chan, *Pr*
▲ **EMP: 48 EST:** 1981
SQ FT: 24,000
SALES (est): 8.04MM **Privately Held**
Web: www.proactionproducts.com
SIC: **3089** Injection molding of plastics

(P-5113)
NEW WEST PRODUCTS INC
Also Called: ITW Space Bag
7520 Airway Rd Ste 1 (92154-8304)
PHONE......................619 671-9022
◆ **EMP:** 46
Web: www.ziploc.com
SIC: **3089** 2673 Plastics containers, except foam; Bags: plastic, laminated, and coated

(P-5114)
NEWELL BRANDS INC
17182 Nevada St (92394-7806)
PHONE......................760 246-2700
EMP: 21
SALES (corp-wide): 9.46B **Publicly Held**
Web: www.newellbrands.com
SIC: **3089** Plastics kitchenware, tableware, and houseware
PA: Newell Brands Inc.
6655 Pachtree Dunwoody Rd
Atlanta GA
770 418-7000

(P-5115)
NEWLIGHT TECHNOLOGIES INC
Also Called: Aircarbon
14382 Astronautics Ln (92647-2081)
PHONE......................714 556-4500
Mark Herrema, *CEO*
Kenton Kimmel, *
Evan Creelman, *
EMP: 29 **EST:** 2007
SALES (est): 11.62MM **Privately Held**
Web: www.newlight.com
SIC: **3089** Plastics processing

(P-5116)
NEWPORT LAMINATES INC
3121 W Central Ave (92704-5302)
PHONE......................714 545-8335
Brad A Bollman, *Pr*
Wendy Bollman, *
EMP: 40 **EST:** 1974
SQ FT: 24,000
SALES (est): 4.26MM **Privately Held**
Web: www.newportlaminates.com
SIC: **3089** Fiber, vulcanized

(P-5117)
NISHIBA INDUSTRIES CORPORATION
2360 Marconi Ct (92154-7241)
PHONE......................619 661-8866
Yoshiaki Nishiba, *Pr*
▲ **EMP:** 72 **EST:** 1987
SQ FT: 2,500
SALES (est): 9.23MM **Privately Held**
Web: www.anaglb.com
SIC: **3089** 3544 5162 Plastics hardware and building products; Special dies, tools, jigs, and fixtures; Plastics materials and basic shapes
PA: Nishiba Industry Co., Ltd.
5-1350, Hirosawacho

Kiryu GNM

(P-5118)
NORCO INJECTION MOLDING INC
Also Called: Norco Plastics
14325 Monte Vista Ave (91710-5726)
P.O. Box 2528 (91708-2528)
PHONE......................909 393-4000
Jack Williams, *Pr*
John Williams, *CFO*
▲ **EMP:** 100 **EST:** 1974
SQ FT: 45,000
SALES (est): 7.26MM **Privately Held**
Web: www.niminc.com
SIC: **3089** 3544 Injection molding of plastics; Special dies, tools, jigs, and fixtures

(P-5119)
NORCO PLASTICS INC
14325 Monte Vista Ave (91710-5726)
P.O. Box 2528 (91708-2528)
PHONE......................909 393-4000
John Williams, *CEO*
▲ **EMP:** 90 **EST:** 2010
SALES (est): 9.33MM **Privately Held**
Web: www.norcoplastics.com
SIC: **3089** Plastics containers, except foam

(P-5120)
NORTON PACKAGING INC
5800 S Boyle Ave (90058-3927)
PHONE......................323 588-6167
Joe Schrick, *Brnch Mgr*
EMP: 25
SALES (corp-wide): 55.58MM **Privately Held**
Web: www.nortonpackaging.com
SIC: **3089** 5162 Plastics containers, except foam; Resins
PA: Norton Packaging, Inc.
20670 Corsair Blvd
Hayward CA
510 786-1922

(P-5121)
NSA HOLDINGS INC
Also Called: Amerex Company
888 Marlborough Ave (92507-2117)
PHONE......................951 686-1400
Donald H Circosta, *Pr*
EMP: 22 **EST:** 1972
SQ FT: 15,500
SALES (est): 385.69K **Privately Held**
SIC: **3089** Injection molding of plastics

(P-5122)
NUBS PLASTICS INC
991 Park Center Dr (92081-8312)
PHONE......................760 598-2525
Niyogi Ramolia, *Pr*
▼ **EMP:** 30 **EST:** 1993
SQ FT: 13,000
SALES (est): 5.61MM **Privately Held**
Web: www.nubsplasticsinc.com
SIC: **3089** Injection molding of plastics

(P-5123)
NUCLEUS ENTERPRISES LLC
888 Prospect St Ste 200 (92037-4261)
PHONE......................619 517-8747
Ernesto Mendiola Otero, *Managing Member*
Manuel Mendiola Rios, *Managing Member*
Luis Escobedo, *
Luis Antonio Rodriguez, *
◆ **EMP:** 51 **EST:** 2015
SQ FT: 1,200
SALES (est): 1MM **Privately Held**

SIC: **3089** Injection molding of plastics

(P-5124)
NUCONIC PACKAGING LLC
4889 Loma Vista Ave (90058-3216)
PHONE......................323 588-9033
Alan Franz, *CEO*
Christopher Winkler, *
Skip Farber, *
Jason Farber, *
▲ **EMP:** 31 **EST:** 2008
SQ FT: 30,000
SALES (est): 4.6MM **Privately Held**
Web: www.easypak.com
SIC: **3089** 4783 Plastics containers, except foam; Packing and crating

(P-5125)
NYPRO INC
Also Called: Nypro Healthcare Baja
505 Main St Rm 107 (91911-6059)
PHONE......................619 498-9250
Gregg Lambert, *Genl Mgr*
EMP: 75
SALES (corp-wide): 34.7B **Publicly Held**
Web: www.jabil.com
SIC: **3089** 3559 Injection molding of plastics; Robots, molding and forming plastics
HQ: Nypro Inc.
101 Union St
Clinton MA
978 365-9721

(P-5126)
NYPRO SAN DIEGO INC
505 Main St (91911-6075)
PHONE......................619 482-7033
Gordon Lankton, *Sec*
Ernie Rice, *
▼ **EMP:** 80 **EST:** 1988
SQ FT: 66,000
SALES (est): 18.55MM
SALES (corp-wide): 34.7B **Publicly Held**
SIC: **3089** Injection molding of plastics
HQ: Nypro Inc.
101 Union St
Clinton MA
978 365-9721

(P-5127)
OMNI RESOURCE RECOVERY INC
1495 N 8th St Ste 150 (92324-1451)
PHONE......................909 327-2900
EMP: 250
Web: www.omnirecovery.com
SIC: **3089** Extruded finished plastics products, nec

(P-5128)
PACTIV LLC
2024 Norris Rd (93308-2238)
PHONE......................661 392-4000
Steve Stewart, *Mgr*
EMP: 103
Web: www.pactiv.com
SIC: **3089** 3086 Kitchenware, plastics; Plastics foam products
HQ: Pactiv Llc
1900 W Field Ct
Lake Forest IL
847 482-2000

(P-5129)
PARADIGM PACKAGING EAST LLC
Also Called: Paradigm Packaging West
9595 Utica Ave (91730-5921)
P.O. Box 10 (91785-0010)

PHONE......................909 985-2750
Steve Costecki, *Mgr*
EMP: 27
SALES (corp-wide): 112.7MM **Privately Held**
SIC: **3089** Plastics containers, except foam
HQ: Paradigm Packaging East Llc
141 5th St
Saddle Brook NJ
201 909-3400

(P-5130)
PARAMOUNT PANELS INC (PA)
Also Called: California Plasteck
1531 E Cedar St (91761-5762)
PHONE......................909 947-8008
Arthur G Thorne, *Pr*
John G Thorne, *
EMP: 32 **EST:** 1962
SQ FT: 12,000
SALES (est): 5.56MM
SALES (corp-wide): 5.56MM **Privately Held**
Web: www.paramountpanels.com
SIC: **3089** 3812 3728 Plastics processing; Search and navigation equipment; Aircraft parts and equipment, nec

(P-5131)
PARAMUNT PLSTIC FBRICATORS INC
Also Called: Paramount Fabricators
11251 Jersey Blvd (91730-5147)
PHONE......................909 987-4757
Peter M Smits, *Pr*
Rose I Smits, *VP*
EMP: 17 **EST:** 1958
SQ FT: 60,000
SALES (est): 494.93K **Privately Held**
Web: www.paramountfabricators.com
SIC: **3089** Injection molding of plastics

(P-5132)
PC VAUGHAN MFG CORP
Also Called: Rostar Filters
1278 Mercantile St (93030-7522)
PHONE......................805 278-2555
Jeff Starin, *CEO*
Jeff Starin, *Pr*
EMP: 65 **EST:** 1979
SQ FT: 40,000
SALES (est): 7.67MM **Privately Held**
Web: www.rostarfilters.com
SIC: **3089** 3569 3714 5085 Automotive parts, plastic; Filters; Filters: oil, fuel, and air, motor vehicle; Filters, industrial

(P-5133)
PEERLESS INJECTION MOLDING LLC
Also Called: Proplas Technologies
14321 Corp Dr (92843)
PHONE......................714 689-1920
Scott Taylor, *Pr*
▲ **EMP:** 50 **EST:** 1977
SQ FT: 51,112
SALES (est): 11.64MM
SALES (corp-wide): 74.47MM **Privately Held**
SIC: **3089** Injection molding of plastics
PA: Comar, Inc.
201 Laurel Rd Fl 2
Voorhees NJ
856 692-6100

(P-5134)
PERFORMNCE ENGINEERED PDTS INC
Also Called: Honor Plastics

▲ = Import ▼ = Export
◆ = Import/Export

3270 Pomona Blvd (91768-3282)
PHONE..............................909 594-7487
Dinesh Savalia, *CEO*
EMP: 48 **EST:** 2016
SQ FT: 42,000
SALES (est): 9MM **Privately Held**
Web: www.honorplastics.com
SIC: 3089 Injection molding of plastics

(P-5135)
PIERCO INCORPORATED
Also Called: Pierco
3900 Hamner Ave (91752-1017)
PHONE..............................951 361-6400
Erik Fleming, *Pr*
Edward T Fleming, *
EMP: 58 **EST:** 1966
SQ FT: 170,000
SALES (est): 1.14MM **Privately Held**
SIC: 3089 Injection molding of plastics

(P-5136)
PINNPACK CAPITAL HOLDINGS LLC
1151 Pacific Ave (93033-2472)
PHONE..............................805 385-4100
Ira Maroofian, *CEO*
Sriram Kailasam, *CFO*
EMP: 205 **EST:** 2021
SALES (est): 16MM **Privately Held**
Web: www.pinnpack.com
SIC: 3089 Plastics containers, except foam

(P-5137)
PITBULL GYM INCORPORATED
Also Called: Art Plates
10782 Edison Ct (91730-4845)
PHONE..............................909 980-7960
Gary John Vandenlangenberg, *Pr*
◆ **EMP:** 20 **EST:** 1988
SQ FT: 10,120
SALES (est): 3.03MM **Privately Held**
Web: www.switchplates.com
SIC: 3089 5072 Bottle caps, molded plastics; Hardware

(P-5138)
PLAINFIELD MOLDING INC
Also Called: Plainfield Companies
135 S State College Blvd # 200 (92821-5823)
PHONE..............................815 436-7806
EMP: 69
SIC: 3089 Molding primary plastics

(P-5139)
PLAINFIELD TOOL AND ENGINEERING INC
Also Called: Plainfield Stamping-Illinois
135 S College Blvd St (92821)
PHONE..............................815 436-5671
▲ **EMP:** 305
SIC: 3089 3469 Injection molding of plastics; Metal stampings, nec

(P-5140)
PLASIDYNE ENGINEERING & MFG
3230 E 59th St (90805-4502)
P.O. Box 5578 (90805-0578)
PHONE..............................562 531-0510
Dean C Sutherland, *Pr*
EMP: 22 **EST:** 1969
SQ FT: 15,000
SALES (est): 3.32MM **Privately Held**
Web: www.plasidyne.com
SIC: 3089 Injection molding of plastics

(P-5141)
PLASTHEC MOLDING INC
1945 S Grove Ave (91761-5616)
PHONE..............................909 947-4267
Hector Carrion, *Pr*
James Downey, *
EMP: 21 **EST:** 1978
SQ FT: 34,000
SALES (est): 949.29K **Privately Held**
SIC: 3089 Injection molding of plastics

(P-5142)
PLASTIC AND METAL CENTER INC
23162 La Cadena Dr (92653-1405)
PHONE..............................949 770-0610
Faramarz Khaladj, *Pr*
Fred Carr, *
Denise Khaladj, *
EMP: 25 **EST:** 1993
SQ FT: 20,000
SALES (est): 4.42MM **Privately Held**
Web: www.plastic-metal.com
SIC: 3089 Injection molding of plastics

(P-5143)
PLASTIC DRESS-UP COMPANY
11077 Rush St (91733-3546)
PHONE..............................626 442-7711
Myron H Funk, *Pr*
◆ **EMP:** 68 **EST:** 1952
SQ FT: 130,000
SALES (est): 919.42K **Privately Held**
SIC: 3089 Novelties, plastics

(P-5144)
PLASTIC FABRICATION TECH LLC
2320 E Cherry Indus Cir (90805-4417)
PHONE..............................773 509-1700
Mary Hutchinson, *
EMP: 17 **EST:** 1997
SQ FT: 20,000
SALES (est): 347.91K **Privately Held**
SIC: 3089 Injection molding of plastics

(P-5145)
PLASTIC MOLDED COMPONENTS INC
Also Called: P M C
5920 Lakeshore Dr (90630-3371)
PHONE..............................714 229-0133
EMP: 40 **EST:** 1979
SALES (est): 4.3MM **Privately Held**
Web: www.moldedplasticcomponents.com
SIC: 3089 Molding primary plastics

(P-5146)
PLASTIC SPECIALTIES & TECH INC
Action Technology
19555 Arenth Ave (91748-1403)
PHONE..............................909 869-8069
Roy Anderson, *Brnch Mgr*
EMP: 130
SALES (corp-wide): 996.3MM **Privately Held**
SIC: 3089 Plastics containers, except foam
HQ: Plastic Specialties And Technologies Inc.
101 Railroad Ave
Ridgefield NJ
201 941-2900

(P-5147)
PLASTIC TECHNOLOGIES INC
Also Called: Blow Molded Products

4720 Felspar St (92509-3068)
PHONE..............................951 360-6055
Meir Ben-david, *Pr*
Diane Ben-david, *VP*
EMP: 50 **EST:** 2018
SALES (est): 5.02MM **Privately Held**
Web: www.blowmoldedproducts.com
SIC: 3089 Injection molding of plastics

(P-5148)
PLASTICS DEVELOPMENT CORP
960 Calle Negocio (92673-6201)
PHONE..............................949 492-0217
Inder Jain, *Pr*
Sanie Jain, *VP*
Vijay Jain, *Sec*
▲ **EMP:** 23 **EST:** 1969
SQ FT: 7,000
SALES (est): 3.59MM **Privately Held**
Web: www.plasticsdev.com
SIC: 3089 Injection molding of plastics

(P-5149)
PLASTICS PLUS TECHNOLOGY INC
1495 Research Dr (92374-4584)
PHONE..............................909 747-0555
Kathy Bodor, *CEO*
EMP: 33 **EST:** 1980
SQ FT: 35,000
SALES (est): 7.94MM **Privately Held**
Web: www.plasticsplus.com
SIC: 3089 3544 Injection molding of plastics; Forms (molds), for foundry and plastics working machinery

(P-5150)
PLASTIQUE UNIQUE INC
3383 Livonia Ave (90034-3127)
PHONE..............................310 839-3968
Christine Galonska, *Pr*
Lionel Funes, *
Silvia Totado, *
EMP: 17 **EST:** 1970
SQ FT: 5,000
SALES (est): 900.06K **Privately Held**
Web: www.plastiquequniqueinc.com
SIC: 3089 Injection molding of plastics

(P-5151)
PLASTO TECH INTERNATIONAL INC
4 Autry (92618-2708)
PHONE..............................949 458-1880
Ben Khalaj, *Pr*
Jacqueline Khalaj, *CEO*
▲ **EMP:** 25 **EST:** 1985
SQ FT: 16,530
SALES (est): 2.32MM **Privately Held**
Web: www.plastotech.com
SIC: 3089 5084 8711 7389 Injection molding of plastics; Industrial machinery and * equipment; Consulting engineer; Design, commercial and industrial

(P-5152)
PLASTPRO 2000 INC (PA)
Also Called: Plastpro Doors
5200 W Century Blvd (90045-5928)
PHONE..............................310 693-8600
◆ **EMP:** 126 **EST:** 1994
SALES (est): 31.01MM **Privately Held**
Web: www.plastproinc.com
SIC: 3089 Fiberglass doors

(P-5153)
POLYMER LOGISTICS INC
1725 Sierra Ridge Dr (92507-7133)

PHONE..............................951 567-2900
Albert Terrazas, *Brnch Mgr*
EMP: 60
SALES (corp-wide): 217.91MM **Privately Held**
Web: www.toscaltd.com
SIC: 3089 5085 5162 Pallets, plastics; Boxes, crates, etc., other than paper; Plastics materials and basic shapes
HQ: Polymer Logistics, Inc.
1175 Peachtree St Ne # 1900
Atlanta GA

(P-5154)
PPP LLC
601 W Olympic Blvd (90640-5229)
P.O. Box 789 (90640-0789)
PHONE..............................323 832-9627
Evelyn Garcia, *Managing Member*
EMP: 17 **EST:** 2001
SALES (est): 965.2K **Privately Held**
SIC: 3089 Injection molding of plastics

(P-5155)
PRC COMPOSITES LLC (PA)
1400 S Campus Ave (91761-4330)
PHONE..............................909 391-2006
John Upsher, *Managing Member*
Gene Gregory, *
EMP: 79 **EST:** 2014
SALES (est): 18.14MM
SALES (corp-wide): 18.14MM **Privately Held**
Web: www.prccal.com
SIC: 3089 Plastics containers, except foam

(P-5156)
PRC COMPOSITES LLC
Also Called: Globe Plastics
13477 12th St (91710-5206)
PHONE..............................909 464-1520
John Upsher, *Brnch Mgr*
EMP: 20
SALES (corp-wide): 18.14MM **Privately Held**
Web: www.globecomposites.com
SIC: 3089 3544 Injection molding of plastics; Special dies, tools, jigs, and fixtures
PA: Prc Composites, Llc
1400 S Campus Ave
Ontario CA
909 391-2006

(P-5157)
PRECISE AEROSPACE MFG INC
Also Called: Precise Plastic Products
22951 La Palma Ave (92887-6701)
PHONE..............................951 898-0500
Ronnie E Harwood, *CEO*
Roxanne Abdi, *
▲ **EMP:** 42 **EST:** 1965
SQ FT: 39,000
SALES (est): 9.32MM **Privately Held**
Web: www.precisemfg.com
SIC: 3089 3544 Molding primary plastics; Industrial molds

(P-5158)
PRECISION MOLDED PRODUCTS INC
12660 Magnolia Ave (92503-4636)
PHONE..............................951 354-0779
Chris Kozloski, *Pr*
Sabrina Kozloski, *CFO*
▲ **EMP:** 37 **EST:** 1967
SQ FT: 15,000
SALES (est): 1.76MM **Privately Held**
Web: www.precisionmoldpro.com

SIC: **3089** 3083 Injection molded finished plastics products, nec; Laminated plastics plate and sheet

(P-5159)
PREMIUM PLASTICS MACHINE INC
15956 Downey Ave (90723-5190)
PHONE..................................562 633-7723
David Pennington, *Pr*
Suzanne Pennington, *VP*
Michael Robert Pennington, *Ex VP*
▲ **EMP:** 19 **EST:** 1976
SQ FT: 6,241
SALES (est): 982.47K **Privately Held**
Web: www.premiumplasticsmachine.com
SIC: 3089 Injection molding of plastics

(P-5160)
PREPRODUCTION PLASTICS INC
Also Called: P P I
210 Teller St (92879-1886)
PHONE..................................951 340-9680
Koby Loosen, *Pr*
Ron Loosen, *
Barbara Loosen, *
▲ **EMP:** 50 **EST:** 1978
SQ FT: 45,000
SALES (est): 8.44MM **Privately Held**
Web: www.ppiplastics.com
SIC: 3089 3544 Molding primary plastics; Forms (molds), for foundry and plastics working machinery

(P-5161)
PRES-TEK PLASTICS INC (PA)
10700 7th St (91730-5404)
PHONE..................................909 360-1600
Donna C Pursell, *CEO*
EMP: 22 **EST:** 2005
SALES (est): 23.72MM
SALES (corp-wide): 23.72MM **Privately Held**
Web: www.prestekplastics.com
SIC: 3089 Injection molding of plastics

(P-5162)
PRETIUM PACKAGING LLC
Also Called: Pretium Packaging
13980 Mountain Ave (91710-9018)
PHONE..................................714 777-9580
Lisa Engert, *Mgr*
EMP: 150
SALES (corp-wide): 868.81MM **Privately Held**
Web: www.pretiumpkg.com
SIC: 3089 3544 3085 5113 Blow molded finished plastics products, nec; Industrial molds; Plastics bottles; Bags, paper and disposable plastic
PA: Pretium Packaging, L.L.C.
1555 Page Industrial Blvd
Saint Louis MO
314 727-8200

(P-5163)
PRIME PLASTIC PRODUCTS INC
1351 Distribution Way Ste 8 (92081)
PHONE..................................760 734-3900
EMP: 18 **EST:** 1993
SALES (est): 4.87MM **Privately Held**
Web: www.primeplastic.com
SIC: 3089 Plastics processing

(P-5164)
PRINCE LIONHEART INC (PA)
2421 Westgate Rd (93455-1075)
PHONE..................................805 922-2250
Kelly Griffiths, *CEO*
Debbie Di Nardi, *
▲ **EMP:** 40 **EST:** 1973
SQ FT: 80,000
SALES (est): 9.65MM
SALES (corp-wide): 9.65MM **Privately Held**
Web: www.princelionheart.com
SIC: 3089 Injection molding of plastics

(P-5165)
PRINCETON CASE-WEST INC
1444 W Mccoy Ln (93455-1005)
PHONE..................................805 928-8840
Douglas Laggrenm, *
EMP: 20 **EST:** 1964
SQ FT: 22,000
SALES (est): 1.8MM **Privately Held**
Web: www.princetoncasewest.com
SIC: 3089 3161 Cases, plastics; Luggage

(P-5166)
PRO DESIGN GROUP INC
438 E Alondra Blvd (90248-2902)
PHONE..................................310 767-1032
Chris Raab, *Pr*
Christopher Allen Raab, *
Maria Chanlder, *
▲ **EMP:** 35 **EST:** 1990
SQ FT: 50,000
SALES (est): 5.74MM **Privately Held**
Web: www.theprodesigngroup.com
SIC: 3089 Plastics kitchenware, tableware, and houseware

(P-5167)
PRODUCTIVITY CALIFORNIA INC
Also Called: Pro Cal
10533 Sessler St (90280-7251)
PHONE..................................562 923-3100
Gary Vollers, *Pr*
Don Uchiyama, *
EMP: 80 **EST:** 1983
SQ FT: 100,000
SALES (est): 7.17MM
SALES (corp-wide): 899.55MM **Publicly Held**
Web: www.myersindustries.com
SIC: 3089 Injection molding of plastics
PA: Myers Industries, Inc.
1293 S Main St
Akron OH
330 253-5592

(P-5168)
PROULX MANUFACTURING INC
Also Called: Universal Products
11433 6th St (91730-6024)
PHONE..................................909 980-0662
Richard Proulx, *Pr*
Lorraine Proulx, *
Raymond E Proulx, *
◆ **EMP:** 45 **EST:** 1970
SALES (est): 6.5MM **Privately Held**
Web: www.proulxmfg.com
SIC: 3089 Plastics hardware and building products

(P-5169)
PROVIDIEN INJCTION MOLDING INC
Also Called: Pedi
6740 Nancy Ridge Dr (92121-2230)
PHONE..................................760 931-1844
Jeffrey S Goble, *CEO*
Richard D Witchey Junior, *Pr*
Louise Witchey, *
Paul Jazwin, *
◆ **EMP:** 74 **EST:** 1985

SALES (est): 25.79MM **Privately Held**
Web: www.providienmedical.com
SIC: 3089 Injection molded finished plastics products, nec
HQ: Witco Industries, Inc.
2731 Loker Ave W
Carlsbad CA

(P-5170)
R V BEST INC
Also Called: Shademaster Products
9335 Stevens Rd (92071-2809)
PHONE..................................619 448-7300
Steven Smoot, *Pr*
Mike Scheller, *
Dan Smoot, *
EMP: 45 **EST:** 1983
SQ FT: 15,000
SALES (est): 6.1MM **Privately Held**
SIC: 3089 5999 Awnings, fiberglass and plastics combination; Awnings

(P-5171)
RAKAR INCORPORATED
1680 Universe Cir (93033-2441)
PHONE..................................805 487-2721
Theresa Padilla, *CEO*
EMP: 48 **EST:** 1951
SALES (est): 9.05MM **Privately Held**
Web: www.rakarinc.com
SIC: 3089 3544 Injection molding of plastics; Forms (molds), for foundry and plastics working machinery

(P-5172)
RAMKO INJECTION INC
3551 Tanya Ave (92545-9447)
PHONE..................................951 929-0360
EMP: 100 **EST:** 2007
SALES (est): 20.25MM **Privately Held**
Web: www.ramko-inj.com
SIC: 3089 3364 Blow molded finished plastics products, nec; Nonferrous die-castings except aluminum

(P-5173)
RAMTEC ASSOCIATES INC
Also Called: Con-Tech Plastics
3200 E Birch St Ste B (92821-6287)
PHONE..................................714 996-7477
Ralph Riehl, *Pr*
Vernon Meurer, *
▲ **EMP:** 28 **EST:** 1984
SQ FT: 35,000
SALES (est): 4.85MM **Privately Held**
SIC: 3089 Molding primary plastics

(P-5174)
RAY PRODUCTS COMPANY INC
1700 Chablis Ave (91761-3610)
PHONE..................................888 776-9014
EMP: 50 **EST:** 1949
SALES (est): 8.17MM **Privately Held**
Web: www.rayplastics.com
SIC: 3089 Thermoformed finished plastics products, nec

(P-5175)
REEVES EXTRUDED PRODUCTS INC
1032 Stockton Ave (93203-2330)
PHONE..................................661 854-5970
Matthew Cobbs, *CEO*
Steve Reeves, *
Beverly Palmer, *
Sandy Shelton, *
EMP: 75 **EST:** 1967
SQ FT: 45,000
SALES (est): 9.87MM **Privately Held**
Web: www.reevesextruded.com

SIC: **3089** Injection molding of plastics

(P-5176)
REHAU CONSTRUCTION LLC
1250 Corona Pointe Ct Ste 301 (92879-2099)
PHONE..................................951 549-9017
Joe Lepire, *Mgr*
EMP: 64
Web: www.rehau.com
SIC: 3089 Plastics processing
HQ: Rehau Construction Llc
1501 Edwards Ferry Rd Ne
Leesburg VA

(P-5177)
REHRIG PACIFIC COMPANY (HQ)
4010 E 26th St (90058-4401)
PHONE..................................323 262-5145
William J Rehrig, *Pr*
Michael J Doka, *
James L Drew, *
Rajesh Luhar, *
◆ **EMP:** 150 **EST:** 1997
SQ FT: 200,000
SALES (est): 447.31MM **Privately Held**
Web: www.rehrigpacific.com
SIC: 3089 2821 Cases, plastics; Plasticizer/additive based plastic materials
PA: Rehrig Pacific Holdings, Inc.
4010 E 26th St
Vernon CA

(P-5178)
REHRIG PACIFIC HOLDINGS INC (PA)
4010 E 26th St (90058-4477)
PHONE..................................323 262-5145
EMP: 98 **EST:** 1998
SALES (est): 499.72MM **Privately Held**
Web: www.rehrigpacific.com
SIC: 3089 2821 Cases, plastics; Plasticizer/additive based plastic materials

(P-5179)
REINHOLD INDUSTRIES INC (DH)
12827 Imperial Hwy (90670-4761)
PHONE..................................562 944-3281
Clarence Hightower, *CEO*
Carl Walker, *CFO*
▲ **EMP:** 145 **EST:** 1984
SQ FT: 130,000
SALES (est): 24.64MM **Publicly Held**
Web: www.reinhold-ind.com
SIC: 3089 3764 2531 Molding primary plastics; Space propulsion units and parts; Seats, aircraft
HQ: Reinhold Holdings, Inc.
12827 Imperial Hwy
Santa Fe Springs CA

(P-5180)
RENY & CO INC
Also Called: Renymed
4505 Littlejohn St (91706-2239)
PHONE..................................626 962-3078
EMP: 18 **EST:** 1985
SALES (est): 4.81MM **Privately Held**
Web: www.renymed.com
SIC: 3089 Plastics hardware and building products

(P-5181)
RESINART CORPORATION
Also Called: Resinart Plastics
1621 Placentia Ave (92627-4311)
PHONE..................................949 642-3665
Gary Uecker, *Pr*

Gene Chandler, *
Frank Uecker, *
EMP: 40 **EST:** 1969
SQ FT: 15,000
SALES (est): 3.45MM **Privately Held**
Web: www.resinart.com
SIC: 3089 Molding primary plastics

(P-5182)
REYRICH PLASTICS INC
1704 S Vineyard Ave (91761-7746)
PHONE..............................909 484-8444
Tina Richter, *Pr*
Sandy Reyes, *Pr*
Tina Richter, *CFO*
EMP: 21 **EST:** 2012
SALES (est): 2.34MM **Privately Held**
Web: www.reyrichplastics.com
SIC: 3089 Injection molding of plastics

(P-5183)
ROLENN MANUFACTURING INC (PA)
2065 Roberta St (92507-2644)
PHONE..............................951 682-1185
Thomas J Accatino, *Pr*
Christie Accatino, *Sec*
EMP: 20 **EST:** 1965
SQ FT: 9,000
SALES (est): 10.09MM
SALES (corp-wide): 10.09MM **Privately Held**
Web: www.rolenn.com
SIC: 3089 3599 Injection molding of plastics; Machine and other job shop work

(P-5184)
RONCO PLASTICS INC
Also Called: Ronco Plastics
15022 Parkway Loop Ste B (92780-6518)
PHONE..............................714 259-1385
Raul L Barajas, *Pr*
Ronald L Pearson, *
EMP: 28 **EST:** 1976
SQ FT: 28,000
SALES (est): 4.84MM **Privately Held**
Web: www.ronco-plastics.com
SIC: 3089 Plastics products, except foam

(P-5185)
RONFORD PRODUCTS INC
1116 E 2nd St (91766-2114)
PHONE..............................909 622-7446
Carl Higgins, *Mgr*
EMP: 28
SALES (corp-wide): 4.03MM **Privately Held**
SIC: 3089 5093 Injection molding of plastics; Plastics scrap
PA: Ronford Products, Inc.
16616 Garfield Ave
Paramount CA
562 408-1081

(P-5186)
ROTATIONAL MOLDING INC
Also Called: R M I
17038 S Figueroa St (90248-3089)
PHONE..............................310 327-5401
EMP: 80 **EST:** 2010
SALES (est): 13.13MM **Privately Held**
Web: www.rotationalmoldinginc.com
SIC: 3089 Plastics containers, except foam
PA: Tank Holding Corp.
6940 O St Ste 100
Lincoln NE

(P-5187)
ROTO DYNAMICS INC
1925 N Lime St (92865-4123)
PHONE..............................714 685-0183
Yogindra Saran, *CEO*
Rishi Saran, *
EMP: 24 **EST:** 2005
SALES (est): 1.77MM **Privately Held**
Web: www.rotodynamics.com
SIC: 3089 Plastics containers, except foam

(P-5188)
ROTO LITE INC
84701 Avenue 48 (92236-1201)
PHONE..............................909 923-4353
Sandy Canzone, *Pr*
John Hammond, *
Dan Hammond, *
EMP: 27 **EST:** 2003
SALES (est): 3.25MM **Privately Held**
Web: www.rotoliteinc.com
SIC: 3089 0781 Plastics containers, except foam; Landscape services

(P-5189)
ROYAL INTERPACK NORTH AMER INC
475 Palmyrita Ave (92507-1812)
PHONE..............................951 787-6925
▲ **EMP:** 45 **EST:** 2011
SALES (est): 10.32MM **Privately Held**
Web: www.royalinterpackmidwest.com
SIC: 3089 Thermoformed finished plastics products, nec

(P-5190)
RPLANET ERTH LOS ANGLES HLDNGS
5300 S Boyle Ave (90058-3921)
PHONE..............................833 775-2638
EMP: 51 **EST:** 2015
SALES (est): 13.33MM **Privately Held**
Web: www.rplanetearth.com
SIC: 3089 Injection molding of plastics

(P-5191)
RPM PLASTIC MOLDING INC
2821 E Miraloma Ave (92806-1804)
PHONE..............................714 630-9300
Michael Ferik, *CEO*
Phil Hothan, *
▲ **EMP:** 25 **EST:** 1995
SALES (est): 4.66MM **Privately Held**
Web: www.rpmselect.com
SIC: 3089 Injection molding of plastics

(P-5192)
RSK TOOL INCORPORATED
410 W Carob St (90220-5213)
PHONE..............................310 537-3302
Ronald Kohagura, *Pr*
Virginia Kohagura, *
Mark Kohagura, *
EMP: 35 **EST:** 1974
SQ FT: 27,000
SALES (est): 2.66MM **Privately Held**
Web: www.rsktool.com
SIC: 3089 Injection molding of plastics

(P-5193)
RUSSELL-STANLEY
Also Called: Russell-Stanley West
9449 Santa Anita Ave (91730-6118)
PHONE..............................909 980-7114
Robert Singleton, *Pr*
Daniel Miller, *
▼ **EMP:** 24 **EST:** 1984
SQ FT: 75,000
SALES (est): 2.43MM **Privately Held**

SIC: 3089 Plastics containers, except foam
HQ: Mauser Usa, Llc
2 Tower Center Blvd
East Brunswick NJ

(P-5194)
S&B INDUSTRY INC
Also Called: Fxp Technologies
105 S Puente St (92821-3844)
PHONE..............................909 569-4155
Paul H Shiung, *Pr*
EMP: 39
SIC: 3089 Injection molded finished plastics products, nec
HQ: S&B Industry, Inc.
13301 Park Vista Blvd # 100
Fort Worth TX

(P-5195)
SAN DIEGO ACE INC
5363 Sweetwater Trl (92130-5040)
P.O. Box 486 (91980-0486)
PHONE..............................619 206-7339
Kyung Min Kim, *CEO*
▲ **EMP:** 200 **EST:** 1992
SALES (est): 16.51MM **Privately Held**
Web: www.sandiegoace.com
SIC: 3089 Molding primary plastics

(P-5196)
SANDEE PLASTIC EXTRUSIONS
14932 Gwenchris Ct (90723-3423)
PHONE..............................323 979-4020
Thomas Kunkel, *Pr*
EMP: 22 **EST:** 1982
SQ FT: 14,000
SALES (est): 5.21MM
SALES (corp-wide): 15.46MM **Privately Held**
Web: www.sandeeplastics.com
SIC: 3089 Injection molding of plastics
PA: Sandee Manufacturing Co.
10520 Waveland Ave
Franklin Park IL
847 671-1335

(P-5197)
SANDIA PLASTICS INC
Also Called: Ultimate Solutions
15571 Container Ln (92649-1530)
PHONE..............................714 901-8400
▲ **EMP:** 31 **EST:** 1996
SQ FT: 2,500
SALES (est): 4.66MM **Privately Held**
Web: www.sandiaplastics.com
SIC: 3089 Injection molded finished plastics products, nec

(P-5198)
SANTA CLRITA PLSTIC MLDING COR
24735 Avenue Rockefeller (91355-3466)
PHONE..............................661 294-2257
Walter Schrey, *Pr*
Thomas Schrey, *Prin*
EMP: 29 **EST:** 1998
SALES (est): 561.68K **Privately Held**
Web: www.valenciaplastics.com
SIC: 3089 Injection molding of plastics

(P-5199)
SANTA FE EXTRUDERS INC
15315 Marquardt Ave (90670-5709)
P.O. Box 524 (62450-0524)
PHONE..............................562 921-8991
Brick Pinckney, *Pr*
Jeanne Pinckney, *
EMP: 20 **EST:** 1981
SQ FT: 30,000
SALES (est): 792.19K **Privately Held**

Web: www.sfext.com
SIC: 3089 3083 3081 2673 Extruded finished plastics products, nec; Laminated plastics plate and sheet; Unsupported plastics film and sheet; Bags: plastic, laminated, and coated

(P-5200)
SCHAFFER MARINE SERVICES INC
Also Called: SCHAFFER MARINE SERVICES INC
3154 Petaluma Ave (90808-4238)
PHONE..............................562 480-8085
Gary K Schaffer, *Brnch Mgr*
EMP: 17
SIC: 3089 Plastics boats and other marine equipment
PA: Schaffer Marine Services, Inc.
6444 E Spring St Ste 248
Long Beach CA

(P-5201)
SCR MOLDING INC
2340 Pomona Rd (92878-4329)
PHONE..............................951 736-5490
Carl E Thompson, *Pr*
Richard H Mccray, *VP*
Karen Thompson, *Sec*
EMP: 17 **EST:** 1984
SQ FT: 21,000
SALES (est): 1.79MM **Privately Held**
Web: www.scrmolding.com
SIC: 3089 Injection molding of plastics

(P-5202)
SERCO MOLD INC (PA)
Also Called: Serpac Electronic Enclosures
2009 Wright Ave (91750-5812)
PHONE..............................626 331-0517
Patricia Ann Serio, *CEO*
Don Serio Junior, *VP*
▲ **EMP:** 29 **EST:** 1978
SQ FT: 85,000
SALES (est): 8.81MM
SALES (corp-wide): 8.81MM **Privately Held**
Web: www.serpac.com
SIC: 3089 3544 5999 Injection molding of plastics; Industrial molds; Electronic parts and equipment

(P-5203)
SETCO LLC
4875 E Hunter Ave (92807-2005)
PHONE..............................812 424-2904
Patty Harper, *Brnch Mgr*
EMP: 150
Web: www.setco.com
SIC: 3089 Plastics containers, except foam
HQ: Setco, Llc
101 Oakley St
Evansville IN
812 424-2904

(P-5204)
SIERRACIN/SYLMAR CORPORATION
Also Called: PPG Aerospace
12780 San Fernando Rd (91342-3728)
PHONE..............................818 362-6711
Barry Gillespie, *CEO*
◆ **EMP:** 600 **EST:** 1952
SQ FT: 300,000
SALES (est): 106.76MM
SALES (corp-wide): 17.65B **Publicly Held**
Web: www.ppgaerospace.com

SIC: 3089 3812 3621 3231 Windshields, plastics; Search and navigation equipment; Motors and generators; Products of purchased glass
PA: Ppg Industries, Inc.
1 Ppg Pl
Pittsburgh PA
412 434-3131

(P-5205)
SILGAN WHITE CAP CORPORATION
21600 Oxnard St Ste 1600 (91367-5082)
PHONE..................................818 710-3700
EMP: 25 **EST:** 2003
SALES (est): 181.59K **Publicly Held**
SIC: 3089 3221 5085 Plastics containers, except foam; Food containers, glass; Cans for fruits and vegetables
PA: Silgan Holdings Inc.
4 Landmark Sq Ste 400
Stamford CT

(P-5206)
SKB CORPORATION (PA)
434 W Levers Pl (92867-3605)
PHONE..................................714 637-1252
Steven A Kottman, *CEO*
David Sanderson, *
Don Weber, *
◆ **EMP:** 350 **EST:** 1975
SALES (est): 46.72MM
SALES (corp-wide): 46.72MM **Privately Held**
Web: www.skbcases.com
SIC: 3089 3161 Cases, plastics; Luggage

(P-5207)
SMART LLC
Also Called: Smart Wax
3501 Sepulveda Blvd (90505-2537)
PHONE..................................866 822-3670
David Knotek, *CEO*
Paul Schneider, *
▼ **EMP:** 40 **EST:** 2003
SALES (est): 11.68MM
SALES (corp-wide): 11.68MM **Privately Held**
Web: www.chemicalguys.com
SIC: 3089 5013 Automotive parts, plastic; Automotive supplies and parts
PA: Advanced Auto Detailing, Llc
3501 Sepulveda Blvd
Torrance CA
310 674-8135

(P-5208)
SNAPWARE CORPORATION
Also Called: Corningware Corelle & More
2325 Cottonwood Ave (92508-2309)
PHONE..................................951 361-3100
Kris Malkoski, *CEO*
Ken Tran, *
Grant Hartman, *
◆ **EMP:** 180 **EST:** 1991
SALES (est): 55.17MM
SALES (corp-wide): 995.97MM **Privately Held**
Web: www.snapware.com
SIC: 3089 Plastics kitchenware, tableware, and houseware
HQ: Instant Brands Llc
3025 Highland Pkwy # 700
Downers Grove IL
847 233-8600

(P-5209)
SOL-PAK THERMOFORMING INC
3388 Fruitland Ave (90058-3714)

PHONE..................................323 582-3333
Moussa Soleimani-kashi, *Pr*
Joseph Soleimani, *VP*
Joubin Soleimani-kashi, *CFO*
▲ **EMP:** 23 **EST:** 2004
SALES (est): 4.62MM **Privately Held**
Web: www.solpak.com
SIC: 3089 Plastics containers, except foam

(P-5210)
SONFARREL
3000 E La Jolla St (92806-1310)
PHONE..................................714 630-7280
EMP: 23 **EST:** 1955
SALES (est): 6.07MM **Privately Held**
Web: www.son-aero.com
SIC: 3089 Injection molding of plastics

(P-5211)
SOUTH BAY CSTM PLSTIC EXTRDERS
2554 Commercial St (92113-1132)
P.O. Box 131195 (92170-1195)
PHONE..................................619 544-0808
Abraham Rafiee, *Pr*
Hassan Rafiee, *VP*
EMP: 21 **EST:** 1982
SQ FT: 14,000
SALES (est): 998.84K **Privately Held**
SIC: 3089 Plastics containers, except foam

(P-5212)
SP CRAFTECH I LLC
Also Called: Craftech
2941 E La Jolla St (92806-1306)
PHONE..................................714 630-8117
Thomas Stenglein, *Prin*
Allen Webb, *Prin*
Robert Joubran, *Prin*
EMP: 44 **EST:** 2021
SALES (est): 10.48MM **Privately Held**
Web: www.craftechcorp.com
SIC: 3089 Injection molding of plastics

(P-5213)
SPIN PRODUCTS INC
13878 Yorba Ave (91710-5518)
PHONE..................................909 590-7000
Paul Burlingham, *Pr*
William Burlingham, *
▲ **EMP:** 24 **EST:** 1996
SQ FT: 96,000
SALES (est): 4.29MM **Privately Held**
Web: www.spinproducts.com
SIC: 3089 Plastics containers, except foam

(P-5214)
SR PLASTICS COMPANY LLC
692 Parkridge Ave (92860-3124)
PHONE..................................951 479-5394
EMP: 55
SALES (corp-wide): 4.02MM **Privately Held**
Web: www.srplasticsmolding.com
SIC: 3089 Injection molding of plastics
PA: Sr Plastics Company, Llc
640 Parkridge Ave
Norco CA
951 520-9486

(P-5215)
STAR PLASTIC DESIGN
25914 President Ave (90710-3333)
PHONE..................................310 530-7119
Dana Maltun, *Pr*
▲ **EMP:** 60 **EST:** 1980
SQ FT: 25,000
SALES (est): 4.82MM **Privately Held**
Web: www.starplastic.com

SIC: 3089 Injection molding of plastics

(P-5216)
STAR SHIELD SOLUTIONS LLC
4315 Santa Ana St (91761-7872)
PHONE..................................866 662-4477
Gil Stanfill, *Managing Member*
EMP: 60 **EST:** 2007
SALES (est): 5.88MM **Privately Held**
Web: www.starshieldsolutions.com
SIC: 3089 7389 Automotive parts, plastic; Financial services

(P-5217)
STONE CANYON INDUSTRIES LLC
1875 Century Park E Ste 320 (90067-2337)
PHONE..................................310 570-4869
James H Fordyce, *CEO*
Adam Cohn, *
Michael Neumann, *
Sascha Kaeser, *
Shawn Malleck, *
EMP: 2708 **EST:** 2014
SALES (est): 151.5MM **Privately Held**
Web: www.mauserpackaging.com
SIC: 3089 3411 Plastics containers, except foam; Metal cans

(P-5218)
STRAND ART COMPANY INC
4700 E Hunter Ave (92807-1919)
PHONE..................................714 777-0444
Kevin Strand, *Pr*
Vicky Strand, *
▲ **EMP:** 50 **EST:** 1974
SQ FT: 10,480
SALES (est): 4.81MM **Privately Held**
Web: www.strandart.com
SIC: 3089 Injection molded finished plastics products, nec

(P-5219)
SUPERIOR MOLD CO
1927 E Francis St (91761-7719)
PHONE..................................909 947-7028
Anthony Codet, *CEO*
EMP: 21 **EST:** 1972
SALES (est): 2.39MM **Privately Held**
Web: www.unitindustriesgroup.com
SIC: 3089 Injection molding of plastics

(P-5220)
SYNTECH DEVELOPMENT & MFG INC (PA)
Also Called: S D M
13948 Mountain Ave (91710-9018)
PHONE..................................909 465-5554
Harry N Herbert, *CEO*
Bob Hobbs, *
Eddie Montelongo, *
EMP: 25 **EST:** 1998
SQ FT: 11,000
SALES (est): 18.38MM
SALES (corp-wide): 18.38MM **Privately Held**
Web: www.sdmplastics.com
SIC: 3089 Injection molding of plastics

(P-5221)
TALCO PLASTICS INC
3270 E 70th St (90805-1821)
PHONE..................................562 630-1224
EMP: 64
SALES (corp-wide): 22.23MM **Privately Held**
Web: www.talcoplastics.com

SIC: 3089 4953 Extruded finished plastics products, nec; Recycling, waste materials
PA: Talco Plastics, Inc.
1000 W Rincon St
Corona CA
951 531-2000

(P-5222)
TAMSHELL CORP
Also Called: Tamshell
237 Glider Cir (92878-5034)
PHONE..................................951 272-9395
John Hernandez, *Pr*
Art Pierce, *
EMP: 95 **EST:** 1979
SQ FT: 20,000
SALES (est): 20.25MM **Privately Held**
Web: www.tamshell.com
SIC: 3089 Caps, plastics

(P-5223)
TANK HOLDING CORP
13878 Yorba Ave (91710-5518)
PHONE..................................952 446-1945
EMP: 320
Web: www.tankholding.com
SIC: 3089 Plastics containers, except foam
PA: Tank Holding Corp.
6940 O St Ste 100
Lincoln NE

(P-5224)
TEKSUN INC
1549 N Poinsettia Pl Apt 1 (90046-3662)
PHONE..................................310 479-0794
EMP: 50
SALES (corp-wide): 3.26MM **Privately Held**
Web: www.teksuninc.com
SIC: 3089 Injection molding of plastics
PA: Teksun Inc
1607 S Main St
Milpitas CA
415 851-7851

(P-5225)
TENMA AMERICA CORPORATION
333 H St Ste 5000 (91910-5561)
PHONE..................................619 754-2250
▲ **EMP:** 168 **EST:** 1996
SALES (est): 27.45MM **Privately Held**
Web: www.nket.net
SIC: 3089 Molding primary plastics
PA: Tenma Corporation
1-63-6, Akabane
Kita-Ku TKY

(P-5226)
THERMODYNE INTERNATIONAL LTD
1841 S Business Pkwy (91761-8537)
PHONE..................................909 923-9945
Gary S Ackerman, *Ch Bd*
Scott Ackerman, *
◆ **EMP:** 110 **EST:** 1967
SQ FT: 57,500
SALES (est): 10.32MM **Privately Held**
Web: www.thermodyne.com
SIC: 3089 3694 Plastics containers, except foam; Engine electrical equipment

(P-5227)
THREE-D PLASTICS INC (PA)
Also Called: Three-D Traffics Works
430 N Varney St (91502-1732)
PHONE..................................323 849-1316
Frank J Dvoracek, *CEO*
Joseph Dvoracek, *

Kathleen D Trumbo, *
EMP: 35 **EST:** 1968
SQ FT: 40,000
SALES (est): 4.69MM
SALES (corp-wide): 4.69MM **Privately Held**
Web: www.3dplastics.com
SIC: 3089 Injection molding of plastics

(P-5228)
TNT PLASTIC MOLDING INC (PA)
725 E Harrison St (92879-1350)
PHONE.....................951 808-9700
Diane Mixson, *Pr*
John Chadwick, *
Lynn Chadwick, *
Doug Chadwick, *
Dennis Chadwick, *
▲ **EMP:** 80 **EST:** 1979
SQ FT: 30,000
SALES (est): 24.69MM
SALES (corp-wide): 24.69MM **Privately Held**
Web: www.tntplasticmolding.com
SIC: 3089 Injection molding of plastics

(P-5229)
TOM YORK ENTERPRISES INC
Also Called: Kal Plastics
2050 E 48th St (90058-2022)
PHONE.....................323 581-6194
Tom York, *CEO*
EMP: 35 **EST:** 1958
SQ FT: 45,000
SALES (est): 1.72MM **Privately Held**
Web: www.kal-plastics.com
SIC: 3089 3993 Boxes, plastics; Signs and advertising specialties

(P-5230)
TOTALLY RADICAL ASSOCIATES INC
Also Called: Tra Medical
1025 Ortega Way Ste A (92870-7174)
PHONE.....................714 630-0653
EMP: 25 **EST:** 1994
SQ FT: 8,300
SALES (est): 1.74MM **Privately Held**
SIC: 3089 Injection molding of plastics

(P-5231)
TOTEX MANUFACTURING INC
3050 Lomita Blvd (90505-5103)
PHONE.....................310 326-2028
▲ **EMP:** 70 **EST:** 1998
SALES (est): 11.17MM **Privately Held**
Web: www.totexmfg.com
SIC: 3089 5063 Battery cases, plastics or plastics combination; Batteries, dry cell

(P-5232)
TRELLBORG SLING SLTIONS US INC
3077 Rollie Gates Dr (93446-9500)
PHONE.....................805 239-4284
EMP: 34
SALES (corp-wide): 4.26B **Privately Held**
SIC: 3089 Plastics processing
HQ: Trelleborg Sealing Solutions Us, Inc.
2531 Bremer Rd
Fort Wayne IN
260 749-9631

(P-5233)
TRIM-LOK INC (PA)
6855 Hermosa Cir (90620-1151)
P.O. Box 6180 (90622-6180)
PHONE.....................714 562-0500

Gary Whitener, *Pr*
◆ **EMP:** 178 **EST:** 1971
SQ FT: 57,000
SALES (est): 53.67MM
SALES (corp-wide): 53.67MM **Privately Held**
Web: www.trimlok.com
SIC: 3089 Molding primary plastics

(P-5234)
TRINITY INTERNATIONAL INDS LLC
930 E 233rd St (90745-6203)
PHONE.....................800 985-5506
Cze Chao Tam, *CEO*
▲ **EMP:** 33 **EST:** 2007
SQ FT: 35,000
SALES (est): 5.42MM **Privately Held**
Web: www.trinityii.com
SIC: 3089 2511 2542 Organizers for closets, drawers, etc.: plastics; Storage chests, household: wood; Racks, merchandise display or storage: except wood

(P-5235)
TRU-FORM PLASTICS INC
14600 Hoover St (92683-5346)
PHONE.....................310 327-9444
Douglas W Sahm Senior, *CEO*
John D Evans, *
Anita Lorber, *
Clauve Hurwicz, *
▲ **EMP:** 35 **EST:** 1956
SQ FT: 1,000
SALES (est): 7.24MM **Privately Held**
Web: www.tru-formplastics.com
SIC: 3089 Pallets, plastics

(P-5236)
TST MOLDING LLC
Also Called: All Amrcan Injction Mlding Svc
42322 Avenida Alvarado (92590-3445)
PHONE.....................951 296-6200
EMP: 27 **EST:** 2009
SALES (est): 4.54MM **Privately Held**
Web: www.tstmolding.com
SIC: 3089 Injection molding of plastics

(P-5237)
UFO INC
2110 Belgrave Ave (90255-2713)
P.O. Box 58192 (90058-0192)
PHONE.....................323 588-5450
Efi Youavian, *Pr*
Efraim Youavian, *
▲ **EMP:** 50 **EST:** 1982
SQ FT: 65,000
SALES (est): 9.19MM **Privately Held**
Web: www.ufobrand.com
SIC: 3089 2842 5199 Sponges, plastics; Polishes and sanitation goods; Foams and rubber

(P-5238)
UNIVERSAL PACKAGING WEST INC (HQ)
43225 Business Park Dr (92590-3648)
PHONE.....................603 889-8311
EMP: 28 **EST:** 2018
SALES (est): 21.72MM **Privately Held**
SIC: 3089 Injection molding of plastics
PA: Envases Universales De Mexico, S.A.P.I. De C.V.
Calz. Guadalupe No. 504
Mexico MEX

(P-5239)
URBAN ARMOR GEAR LLC (HQ)
1601 Alton Pkwy (92606-4842)

PHONE.....................949 329-0500
Scott W Hardy, *CEO*
▲ **EMP:** 20 **EST:** 2011
SALES (est): 9.57MM
SALES (corp-wide): 14.95MM **Privately Held**
Web: www.urbanarmorgear.com
SIC: 3089 Cases, plastics
PA: Urban Armor Gear Holdings, Inc.
28202 Cabot Rd Ste 300
Laguna Niguel CA
949 329-0500

(P-5240)
US POLYMERS INC (PA)
Also Called: Duramax Building Products
1057 S Vail Ave (90640-6019)
PHONE.....................323 728-3023
Viken Ohanesian, *CEO*
Jacques Ohanesian, *
Vram Ohanesian, *
Haigan Ohanesian, *
◆ **EMP:** 100 **EST:** 1983
SQ FT: 70,000
SALES (est): 36.29MM
SALES (corp-wide): 36.29MM **Privately Held**
Web: www.uspolymersinc.com
SIC: 3089 3084 Shutters, plastics; Plastics pipe

(P-5241)
V-T INDUSTRIES INC
9818 Firestone Blvd (90241-5595)
PHONE.....................714 521-2008
EMP: 49
SALES (corp-wide): 434.93MM **Privately Held**
Web: www.vtindustries.com
SIC: 3089 3083 4213 2435 Plastics hardware and building products; Plastics finished products, laminated; Trucking, except local; Hardwood veneer and plywood
PA: V-T Industries Inc.
1000 Industrial Park
Holstein IA
712 368-4381

(P-5242)
VANTAGE ASSOCIATES INC
12333 Los Nietos Rd (90670-2911)
PHONE.....................562 968-1400
Paul Roy, *CEO*
EMP: 65
SQ FT: 20,000
SALES (corp-wide): 21.95MM **Privately Held**
Web: www.vantageassoc.com
SIC: 3089 2499 5085 3621 Plastics processing; Spools, reels, and pulleys: wood; Industrial supplies; Motors and generators
PA: Vantage Associates Inc.
12333 Los Nietos Rd
Santa Fe Springs CA
619 477-6940

(P-5243)
VOLEX INC
Also Called: Volex De Mexico
511 E San Ysidro Blvd 509 (92173-3150)
PHONE.....................619 205-4900
EMP: 28
SALES (corp-wide): 722.8MM **Privately Held**
Web: www.volex.com
SIC: 3089 Injection molded finished plastics products, nec
HQ: Volex Inc.
511 E San Ysidro Blvd
San Ysidro CA
669 444-1740

(P-5244)
VOLEX INC (HQ)
Also Called: Powercords
511 E San Ysidro Blvd Ste 509 (92173-3150)
PHONE.....................669 444-1740
Christoph Eisenhardt, *CEO*
James Stuart, *
Nick Parker, *
▲ **EMP:** 30 **EST:** 1979
SQ FT: 10,000
SALES (est): 349.9MM
SALES (corp-wide): 722.8MM **Privately Held**
Web: www.volex.com
SIC: 3089 Injection molded finished plastics products, nec
PA: Volex Plc
Unit C1
Basingstoke HANTS
203 370-8830

(P-5245)
VPET USA LLC
12925b Marlay Ave (92337-6939)
PHONE.....................909 605-1668
Jeff Kellar, *CEO*
Steven Saull, *
EMP: 96 **EST:** 2019
SALES (est): 12.24MM **Privately Held**
Web: www.vpetusa.com
SIC: 3089 Plastics containers, except foam

(P-5246)
WADDINGTON NORTH AMERICA INC
Also Called: Wna City of Industry
1135 Samuelson St (91748-1222)
PHONE.....................626 913-4022
EMP: 112
SALES (corp-wide): 10.97B **Publicly Held**
Web: www.novolex.com
SIC: 3089 Plastics kitchenware, tableware, and houseware
HQ: Waddington North America, Inc.
50 E Rver Ctr Blvd Ste 65
Covington KY

(P-5247)
WCP INC
Also Called: West Coast Vinyl Windows
17730 Crusader Ave (90703-2629)
PHONE.....................562 653-9797
Charles Neubauer, *Pr*
▲ **EMP:** 95 **EST:** 1988
SQ FT: 50,000
SALES (est): 20.41MM **Privately Held**
Web: www.westcoastglass.com
SIC: 3089 3211 Windows, plastics; Insulating glass, sealed units

(P-5248)
WEST-BAG INC
1161 Monterey Pass Rd (91754-3614)
PHONE.....................323 264-0750
Luis Michel, *Pr*
Sixto Michel, *
EMP: 30 **EST:** 1977
SQ FT: 12,000
SALES (est): 2.47MM **Privately Held**
Web: www.west-bag.com
SIC: 3089 5149 Food casings, plastics; Sausage casings

(P-5249)
WESTERN CASE INCORPORATED
231 E Alessandro Blvd (92508-5084)
PHONE.....................951 214-6380

(PA)=Parent Co (HQ)=Headquarters
✪ = New Business established in last 2 years

2024 Southern California
Business Directory and Buyers Guide

255

PRODUCTS & SVCS

TOLL FREE: 877
Paul F Queyrel, *CEO*
Mario Robles, *Prin*
▲ **EMP:** 60 **EST:** 1981
SALES (est): 13.47MM **Privately Held**
Web: www.westerncase.com
SIC: 3089 3544 3444 Cases, plastics;
  Special dies, tools, jigs, and fixtures; Sheet
  metalwork

(P-5250)
WESTFALL TECHNIK INC
1100 Citrus St (92507-1731)
PHONE....................951 734-5600
EMP: 393
SALES (corp-wide): 568.49MM **Privately Held**
Web: www.westfalltechnik.com
SIC: 3089 Molding primary plastics
PA: Westfall Technik, Inc.
  3883 Howard Hughes Pkwy # 590
  Las Vegas NV
  702 659-9898

(P-5251)
WESTLAKE ENGRG ROTO FORM
Also Called: Rotoform Plastics
1041 E Santa Barbara St (93060-2820)
P.O. Box 3504 (91359-0504)
PHONE....................805 525-8800
Wade Zimmerman, *Pr*
Pat Zimmerman, *Sec*
▲ **EMP:** 24 **EST:** 1969
SQ FT: 75,000
SALES (est): 703.94K **Privately Held**
Web: www.jazproducts.com
SIC: 3089 Injection molding of plastics

(P-5252)
WHITE BOTTLE INC
10579 Dale Ave (90680-2641)
PHONE....................949 788-1998
Arash Anvaripour, *Prin*
Robert W Thompson, *Prin*
▲ **EMP:** 20 **EST:** 2009
SALES (est): 2.62MM **Privately Held**
Web: www.whitebottle.com
SIC: 3089 Plastics containers, except foam

(P-5253)
WNA COMET WEST INC
Also Called: Wna City of Industry
927 S Azusa Ave (91748-1015)
PHONE....................626 913-0724
Mike Evans, *Pr*
Rodney Harano, *
Gabriella Flores, *
Janet Parga, *
▲ **EMP:** 230 **EST:** 1982
SALES (est): 23.22MM **Privately Held**
SIC: 3089 Plastics kitchenware, tableware,
  and houseware

3111 Leather Tanning And Finishing

(P-5254)
ANDREW ALEXANDER INC
Also Called: Falltech
1306 S Alameda St (90221-4803)
PHONE....................323 752-0066
◆ **EMP:** 100 **EST:** 1992
SQ FT: 100,000
SALES (est): 27.37MM **Privately Held**
Web: www.falltech.com
SIC: 3111 Harness leather

(P-5255)
BELLA K
724 E 10th St Ste A (90021-2166)
PHONE....................213 559-7916
EMP: 37
SALES (corp-wide): 97.47K **Privately Held**
SIC: 3111 Handbag leather
PA: Bella K
  777 E 10th St
  Los Angeles CA
  213 559-7916

(P-5256)
CUSTOMFAB INC
7345 Orangewood Ave (92841-1411)
PHONE....................714 891-9119
Donald Alhanati, *Pr*
▲ **EMP:** 250 **EST:** 1991
SQ FT: 47,000
SALES (est): 22.78MM **Privately Held**
Web: www.customfabusa.com
SIC: 3111 3842 Accessory products, leather;
  Surgical appliances and supplies

(P-5257)
HERITAGE LEATHER COMPANY INC
4011 E 52nd St (90270-2205)
PHONE....................323 983-0420
Jose C Munoz, *CEO*
Gustavo Gonzalez, *
▲ **EMP:** 30 **EST:** 2000
SQ FT: 5,000
SALES (est): 2.42MM **Privately Held**
Web: www.heritageleather.com
SIC: 3111 Belting leather

(P-5258)
LA LA LAND PRODUCTION & DESIGN
1701 S Santa Fe Ave (90021-2904)
PHONE....................323 406-9223
Alexander M Zar, *CEO*
EMP: 45 **EST:** 2006
SQ FT: 30,000
SALES (est): 4.7MM **Privately Held**
Web: www.lalaland-design.com
SIC: 3111 Accessory products, leather

(P-5259)
LINEA PELLE INC (PA)
Also Called: Linea Pelle
7107 Valjean Ave (91406-3917)
PHONE....................310 231-9950
Meira Katz, *CEO*
Wynn Katz, *Prin*
▲ **EMP:** 17 **EST:** 1986
SQ FT: 5,000
SALES (est): 2.67MM
SALES (corp-wide): 2.67MM **Privately Held**
Web: www.lineapelle.com
SIC: 3111 5621 Accessory products, leather;
  Dress shops

3131 Footwear Cut Stock

(P-5260)
CYDWOQ INC
2102 Kenmere Ave (91504-3413)
PHONE....................818 848-8307
Rafi Balouzian, *Pr*
Richard Delamarter, *Stockholder*
◆ **EMP:** 28 **EST:** 1996
SQ FT: 15,000
SALES (est): 1.82MM **Privately Held**
Web: www.cydwoq.com

SIC: 3131 3199 Laces, shoe and boot;
  leather; Leather belting and strapping

(P-5261)
SOLE SOCIETY GROUP INC
11248 Playa Ct # B (90230-6127)
P.O. Box 5206 (90231)
PHONE....................310 220-0808
Andy Solomon, *Managing Member*
Talitha Peters, *
▲ **EMP:** 200 **EST:** 2011
SALES (est): 32.34MM
SALES (corp-wide): 3.32B **Publicly Held**
SIC: 3131 5661 5621 Boot and shoe
  accessories; Men's boots; Ready-to-wear
  apparel, women's
HQ: Vcs Group Llc
  1407 Broadway Frnt 3
  New York NY
  646 898-1050

(P-5262)
SUNSPORTS LP
7 Holland (92618-2506)
PHONE....................949 273-6202
Jamey Draper, *Pt*
▲ **EMP:** 40 **EST:** 1991
SQ FT: 85,000
SALES (est): 561.43K **Privately Held**
Web: www.sunsportsapparel.com
SIC: 3131 2395 Footwear cut stock;
  Embroidery products, except Schiffli
  machine

3142 House Slippers

(P-5263)
NINE EIGHT NINE LLC
1624 240th St (90710-1311)
PHONE....................310 469-1013
Julie Kim, *Brnch Mgr*
EMP: 25
SIC: 3142 House slippers
PA: Nine Eight Nine Llc
  2938 Briarwood Dr
  Torrance CA

3143 Men's Footwear, Except Athletic

(P-5264)
ALLBIRDS INC
1125 Newport Center Dr (92660-6950)
PHONE....................949 942-1233
EMP: 19
SALES (corp-wide): 297.77MM **Publicly Held**
Web: www.allbirds.com
SIC: 3143 Men's footwear, except athletic
PA: Allbirds, Inc.
  730 Montgomery St
  San Francisco CA
  628 225-4848

(P-5265)
ALLBIRDS INC
860 S Pacific Coast Hwy (90245-4838)
PHONE....................424 502-2383
EMP: 19
SALES (corp-wide): 297.77MM **Publicly Held**
Web: www.allbirds.com
SIC: 3143 Men's footwear, except athletic
PA: Allbirds, Inc.
  730 Montgomery St
  San Francisco CA
  628 225-4848

(P-5266)
ALLBIRDS INC
77 West Colorado Blvd (91105-1927)
PHONE....................626 344-2622
EMP: 19
SALES (corp-wide): 297.77MM **Publicly Held**
Web: www.allbirds.com
SIC: 3143 Men's footwear, except athletic
PA: Allbirds, Inc.
  730 Montgomery St
  San Francisco CA
  628 225-4848

(P-5267)
ALLBIRDS INC
10250 Santa Monica Blvd Ste 1985
(90067-6404)
PHONE....................213 374-2354
EMP: 19
SALES (corp-wide): 297.77MM **Publicly Held**
Web: www.allbirds.com
SIC: 3143 Men's footwear, except athletic
PA: Allbirds, Inc.
  730 Montgomery St
  San Francisco CA
  628 225-4848

(P-5268)
ALLBIRDS INC
12833 Ventura Blvd (91604-2368)
PHONE....................213 374-3533
EMP: 19
SALES (corp-wide): 297.77MM **Publicly Held**
Web: www.allbirds.com
SIC: 3143 Men's footwear, except athletic
PA: Allbirds, Inc.
  730 Montgomery St
  San Francisco CA
  628 225-4848

(P-5269)
ALLBIRDS INC
1335 Abbot Kinney Blvd (90291-3739)
PHONE....................424 295-9968
EMP: 19
SALES (corp-wide): 297.77MM **Publicly Held**
Web: www.allbirds.com
SIC: 3143 Men's footwear, except athletic
PA: Allbirds, Inc.
  730 Montgomery St
  San Francisco CA
  628 225-4848

(P-5270)
ALLBIRDS INC
1923 Calle Barcelona Bldg 3 (92009-8456)
PHONE....................442 273-5519
EMP: 19
SALES (corp-wide): 297.77MM **Publicly Held**
Web: www.allbirds.com
SIC: 3143 Men's footwear, except athletic
PA: Allbirds, Inc.
  730 Montgomery St
  San Francisco CA
  628 225-4848

(P-5271)
ALLBIRDS INC
4301 La Jolla Village Dr Ste 2010
(92122-1298)
PHONE....................858 987-9533
EMP: 19
SALES (corp-wide): 297.77MM **Publicly Held**
Web: www.allbirds.com

SIC: 3143 Men's footwear, except athletic
PA: Allbirds, Inc.
730 Montgomery St
San Francisco CA
628 225-4848

(P-5272)
CAREISMATIC BRANDS LLC (PA)
Also Called: Cherokee Uniform
1119 Colorado Ave (90401-3009)
PHONE.....................818 671-2100
◆ EMP: 203 EST: 1995
SQ FT: 140,000
SALES (est): 189.35MM Privately Held
Web: www.careismatic.com
SIC: 3143 3144 5139 2339 Men's footwear, except athletic; Women's footwear, except athletic; Shoes; Women's and misses' outerwear, nec

(P-5273)
PHOENIX FOOTWEAR GROUP INC (PA)
2236 Rutherford Rd Ste 113 (92008-8836)
PHONE.....................760 602-9688
James R Riedman, Pr
Dennis Nelson, CFO
◆ EMP: 17 EST: 2002
SQ FT: 21,700
SALES (est): 11.89MM
SALES (corp-wide): 11.89MM Publicly Held
Web: www.phoenixfootwear.com
SIC: 3143 3144 2329 2339 Men's footwear, except athletic; Women's footwear, except athletic; Men's and boys' sportswear and athletic clothing; Sportswear, women's

---

3144 Women's Footwear, Except Athletic

(P-5274)
ALPARGATAS USA INC
Also Called: Havaianas
513 Boccaccio Ave (90291-4806)
PHONE.....................646 277-7171
Marcio Moura, CEO
Afonso Fugiyama, *
◆ EMP: 30 EST: 2006
SALES (est): 12.02MM Privately Held
SIC: 3144 Women's footwear, except athletic
PA: Alpargatas S/A
Av. Das Nacoes Unidas 14261
Sao Paulo SP

(P-5275)
EVOLUTION DESIGN LAB INC
Also Called: Jellypop
144 W Colorado Blvd (91105-1953)
PHONE.....................626 960-8388
Jennet Chow, CEO
▲ EMP: 25 EST: 2009
SALES (est): 2.13MM Privately Held
Web: www.jellypop-shoes.com
SIC: 3144 5139 Women's footwear, except athletic; Shoes

(P-5276)
IMPO INTERNATIONAL LLC
Also Called: Chili's
3510 Black Rd (93455-5927)
P.O. Box 639 (93456-0639)
PHONE.....................805 922-7753
Laura Ann Hopkins, Managing Member
◆ EMP: 24 EST: 1968
SQ FT: 30,000
SALES (est): 4.78MM Privately Held

Web: www.impo.com
SIC: 3144 Boots, canvas or leather: women's

(P-5277)
MECO-NAG CORPORATION
Also Called: Dezario Shoe Company
7306 Laurel Canyon Blvd (91605-3710)
P.O. Box 16565 (91615-6565)
PHONE.....................818 764-2020
Krikor Astourian, Pr
Vicki Astourian, *
Cruz Martinez, *
◆ EMP: 18 EST: 1986
SQ FT: 10,000
SALES (est): 427.74K Privately Held
SIC: 3144 Women's footwear, except athletic

(P-5278)
MILLENNIAL BRANDS LLC
126 W 9th St (90015-1500)
PHONE.....................925 230-0617
Catalin Gaitanaru, Prin
EMP: 27
SIC: 3144 Women's footwear, except athletic
PA: Millennial Brands Llc
2002 Diablo Rd
Danville CA

(P-5279)
SURGEON WORLDWIDE INC
3855 S Hill St (90037-1415)
PHONE.....................707 501-7962
Mariko Chambrone, VP
EMP: 27 EST: 2018
SALES (est): 1.83MM Privately Held
SIC: 3144 3143 Women's footwear, except athletic; Men's footwear, except athletic

---

3149 Footwear, Except Rubber, Nec

(P-5280)
NELSON SPORTS INC
12810 Florence Ave (90670-4540)
PHONE.....................562 944-8081
Young Chu, Pr
Sook Hee Chu, *
▲ EMP: 45 EST: 1986
SALES (est): 4.52MM Privately Held
Web: nelsonsportsf.openfos.com
SIC: 3149 3021 Athletic shoes, except rubber or plastic; Rubber and plastics footwear

(P-5281)
SKECHERS USA INC (PA)
Also Called: SKECHERS
228 Manhattan Beach Blvd Ste 200 (90266-5356)
PHONE.....................310 318-3100
Robert Greenberg, Ch Bd
Michael Greenberg, Pr
John Vandemore, CFO
David Weinberg, *
Philip Paccione, Corporate Secretary
▲ EMP: 80 EST: 1992
SQ FT: 213,000
SALES (est): 7.44B Publicly Held
Web: www.skechers.com
SIC: 3149 3021 Athletic shoes, except rubber or plastic; Shoes, rubber or plastic molded to fabric

(P-5282)
SOLE TECHNOLOGY INC (PA)
Also Called: Etnies
26921 Fuerte Dr (92630-8149)
PHONE.....................949 460-2020

Pierre Senizergues, Pr
Paul Migaki, *
◆ EMP: 124 EST: 1996
SALES (est): 57.31MM Privately Held
Web: www.soletechnology.com
SIC: 3149 5139 Athletic shoes, except rubber or plastic; Footwear

---

3161 Luggage

(P-5283)
AMERICAN TRAVELER INC
9509 Feron Blvd (91730-4541)
PHONE.....................909 466-4000
Scott Oh, CEO
June Yi, *
EMP: 25 EST: 2009
SALES (est): 4.3MM Privately Held
Web: www.americantravelerinc.com
SIC: 3161 Luggage

(P-5284)
ANVIL CASES INC
1242 E Edna Pl Unit B (91724-2540)
PHONE.....................626 968-4100
Joseph Calzone, Pr
Vincent Calzone, *
▲ EMP: 125 EST: 1952
SALES (est): 20.3MM
SALES (corp-wide): 20.3MM Privately Held
Web: www.calzoneandanvil.com
SIC: 3161 Musical instrument cases
PA: Calzone, Ltd.
225 Black Rock Ave
Bridgeport CT
203 367-5766

(P-5285)
BLOOM DESIGNS CORP
3347 Michelson Dr Ste 100 (92612-0661)
PHONE.....................949 250-4929
EMP: 18
SALES (corp-wide): 59.98MM Privately Held
Web: www.incase.com
SIC: 3161 Luggage
HQ: Bloom Designs Corp.
6001 Oak Cyn
Irvine CA

(P-5286)
ENCORE CASES INC
5260 Vineland Ave (91601-3221)
PHONE.....................818 768-8803
Gary A Peterson, Pr
▲ EMP: 27 EST: 1988
SALES (est): 2.35MM Privately Held
Web: www.encorecases.com
SIC: 3161 Cases, carrying, nec

(P-5287)
G & G QUALITY CASE CO INC
2025 E 25th St (90058-1127)
P.O. Box 58541 (90058-0541)
PHONE.....................323 233-2482
Efren Guzman, Pr
Ben Germain, *
Maria Germain, *
▲ EMP: 70 EST: 1978
SQ FT: 13,500
SALES (est): 4.22MM Privately Held
Web: www.ggqualitycase.com
SIC: 3161 Musical instrument cases

(P-5288)
HAMMITT INC
2101 Pacific Coast Hwy (90254-2745)
PHONE.....................310 292-5200

Anthony Drockton, Ch
Andrew Forbes, *
▲ EMP: 51 EST: 2008
SQ FT: 3,600
SALES (est): 26.5MM Privately Held
Web: www.hammitt.com
SIC: 3161 3171 Traveling bags; Women's handbags and purses

(P-5289)
HSIAO & MONTANO INC
Also Called: Odyssey Innovative Designs
809 W Santa Anita Ave (91776-1016)
PHONE.....................626 588-2528
▲ EMP: 50 EST: 1995
SALES (est): 9.83MM Privately Held
SIC: 3161 3648 5084 1751 Musical instrument cases; Lighting equipment, nec; Woodworking machinery; Cabinet and finish carpentry

(P-5290)
JAN-AL INNERPRIZES INC
Also Called: Jan-Al Cases
3339 Union Pacific Ave (90023-3812)
P.O. Box 23337 (90023-0337)
PHONE.....................323 260-7212
Miriam Alejandro, Pr
Jan Michael Alejandro, *
EMP: 30 EST: 1983
SQ FT: 16,000
SALES (est): 4.42MM Privately Held
Web: www.janalcase.com
SIC: 3161 Luggage

(P-5291)
NATUS INC
4522 Katella Ave Ste 200 (90720-2624)
PHONE.....................626 355-3746
Jimmy Chen, Pr
◆ EMP: 90 EST: 2009
SALES (est): 3.51MM Privately Held
SIC: 3161 Suitcases

(P-5292)
OGIO INTERNATIONAL INC (HQ)
Also Called: Ogio
2180 Rutherford Rd (92008-7328)
PHONE.....................801 619-4100
Anthony Palma, CEO
Michael Pratt, *
▲ EMP: 24 EST: 1989
SQ FT: 70,000
SALES (est): 28.34MM
SALES (corp-wide): 4B Publicly Held
Web: www.ogio.com
SIC: 3161 2393 Traveling bags; Textile bags
PA: Topgolf Callaway Brands Corp.
2180 Rutherford Rd
Carlsbad CA
760 931-1771

(P-5293)
OGIO INTERNATIONAL INC
Also Called: Ogio Powersports
508 Constitution Ave (93012-8510)
PHONE.....................800 326-6325
EMP: 76
SALES (corp-wide): 4B Publicly Held
Web: www.ogio.com
SIC: 3161 Luggage
HQ: Ogio International, Inc.
2180 Rutherford Rd
Carlsbad CA
801 619-4100

(P-5294)
RJ SINGER INTERNATIONAL INC
Also Called: Ruben and Sharam
3737 Ross St (90058-1635)

PHONE..............................323 735-1717
Reouben Melamed, *Pr*
Farshad Melamed, *
▲ **EMP:** 19 **EST:** 1947
SALES (est): 612.38K **Privately Held**
Web: www.rjsinger.com
SIC: 3161 2393 2335 2331 Cases, carrying, nec; Textile bags; Women's, junior's, and misses' dresses; T-shirts and tops, women's: made from purchased materials

(P-5295)
SANDPIPER OF CALIFORNIA INC
687 Anita St Ste A (91911-4693)
P.O. Box 489 (91908-0489)
PHONE..............................619 424-2222
EMP: 54
SIC: 3161 Luggage

(P-5296)
TARGUS US LLC
1211 N Miller St (92806-1933)
PHONE..............................714 765-5555
Mikel Williams, *CEO*
Victor Streufert, *CFO*
EMP: 50 **EST:** 2015
SQ FT: 200,656
SALES (est): 11.98MM **Publicly Held**
Web: us.targus.com
SIC: 3161 Cases, carrying, nec
HQ: B. Riley Principal Investments, Llc
11100 Santa Monica Blvd
Los Angeles CA
310 966-1444

(P-5297)
TRAVELERS CHOICE TRAVELWARE
Also Called: Golden Pacific
2805 S Reservoir St (91766-6526)
PHONE..............................909 529-7688
Roger Yang, *CEO*
Annie Yang, *CFO*
▲ **EMP:** 55 **EST:** 1993
SQ FT: 12,000
SALES (est): 8.37MM **Privately Held**
Web: www.travelerchoice.com
SIC: 3161 5948 Luggage; Luggage and leather goods stores

3171 Women's Handbags And Purses

(P-5298)
ISABELLE HANDBAG INC
3155 Bandini Blvd Unit A (90058-4134)
PHONE..............................323 277-9888
Roye Xu, *Pr*
James Li, *VP*
▲ **EMP:** 35 **EST:** 2011
SQ FT: 2,000
SALES (est): 3.07MM **Privately Held**
Web: www.isabellehandbags.com
SIC: 3171 5632 Handbags, women's; Handbags

(P-5299)
SBNW LLC (PA)
5600 W Adams Blvd (90016-2563)
PHONE..............................213 234-5122
Jason Rimokh, *
EMP: 110 **EST:** 2018
SALES (est): 14.87MM
SALES (corp-wide): 14.87MM **Privately Held**
SIC: 3171 Handbags, women's

(P-5300)
URBAN EXPRESSIONS INC
5500 Union Pacific Ave (90022-5139)
PHONE..............................310 593-4574
Farbod Shakouri, *CEO*
Arash Vojdani, *Pr*
▲ **EMP:** 20 **EST:** 2005
SALES (est): 3.91MM **Privately Held**
Web: www.urbanexpressions.net
SIC: 3171 5137 Handbags, women's; Handbags

3172 Personal Leather Goods, Nec

(P-5301)
KOLTOV INC (PA)
300 S Lewis Rd Ste A (93012-6620)
P.O. Box 2922 (93011-2922)
PHONE..............................805 764-0280
Joe Covrigaru, *CEO*
Brett Stone, *Pr*
Phillip Shieh, *Prin*
▲ **EMP:** 20 **EST:** 1983
SALES (est): 1.59MM
SALES (corp-wide): 1.59MM **Privately Held**
SIC: 3172 5199 Personal leather goods, nec; Leather, leather goods, and furs

(P-5302)
LEATHER PRO INC
Also Called: Turtleback Case
12900 Bradley Ave (91342-3829)
PHONE..............................818 833-8822
Brian Eremita, *Pr*
Al Eremita, *
▲ **EMP:** 24 **EST:** 2001
SQ FT: 13,000
SALES (est): 2.47MM **Privately Held**
Web: www.turtlebackcase.com
SIC: 3172 Personal leather goods, nec

(P-5303)
MALIBU LEATHER INC
510 W 6th St Ste 1002 (90014-1311)
PHONE..............................310 985-0707
Allen Cinoglu, *Pr*
EMP: 125 **EST:** 2009
SQ FT: 12,000
SALES (est): 6.8MM **Privately Held**
SIC: 3172 5199 5948 Personal leather goods, nec; Leather, leather goods, and furs; Luggage and leather goods stores

(P-5304)
RIDGE WALLET LLC
Also Called: Ridge Wallet, The
2448 Main St (90405-3516)
PHONE..............................818 636-2832
Daniel Kane, *Managing Member*
EMP: 19 **EST:** 2016
SALES (est): 10.74MM **Privately Held**
Web: www.ridge.com
SIC: 3172 Wallets

3199 Leather Goods, Nec

(P-5305)
AKER INTERNATIONAL INC
Also Called: Aker Leather Products
2248 Main St Ste 4 (91911-3932)
PHONE..............................619 423-5182
Kamuran Aker, *CEO*
Laurie Aker, *
Levent Aker, *
▲ **EMP:** 30 **EST:** 1981
SQ FT: 10,000

SALES (est): 4.03MM **Privately Held**
Web: www.akerleather.com
SIC: 3199 Holsters, leather

(P-5306)
CUSTOM LEATHERCRAFT MFG LLC (DH)
Also Called: CLC Work Gear
10240 Alameda St (90280-5551)
PHONE..............................323 752-2221
Ron Pickens, *CEO*
Craig Anderson, *CFO*
◆ **EMP:** 50 **EST:** 1983
SQ FT: 150,000
SALES (est): 26.05MM
SALES (corp-wide): 2.16B **Privately Held**
Web: www.goclc.com
SIC: 3199 2394 3111 Leather belting and strapping; Canvas and related products; Glove leather
HQ: Hultafors Group Ab
J A Wettergrens Gata 7, Inga
VAstra FrOlunda
337237400

(P-5307)
EL JINETE LEATHER & WESTERN
2001 S Garey Ave (91766-5727)
PHONE..............................951 264-8396
Herminia Gaeta, *Owner*
EMP: 17 **EST:** 2002
SALES (est): 241.83K **Privately Held**
SIC: 3199 Leather goods, nec

(P-5308)
ELEANOR RIGBY LEATHER CO
Also Called: Coda Mexico
4660 La Jolla Village Dr Ste 500 Pmb 50054 (92122-4604)
PHONE..............................619 356-5590
Peter Robinson, *CEO*
▲ **EMP:** 70 **EST:** 2011
SQ FT: 2,000
SALES (est): 5.09MM **Privately Held**
Web: www.eleanorrigbyhome.com
SIC: 3199 Leather garments

(P-5309)
MASCORRO LEATHER INC
1303 S Gerhart Ave (90022-4256)
PHONE..............................323 724-6759
Yolanda Mascorro, *Pr*
Antonio Mascorro, *Pr*
Yolanda Mascorro, *Sec*
▲ **EMP:** 21 **EST:** 1977
SQ FT: 20,000
SALES (est): 1.19MM **Privately Held**
Web: www.mascorroleather.com
SIC: 3199 Equestrian related leather articles

(P-5310)
US DUTY GEAR INC
1946 S Grove Ave (91761-5615)
PHONE..............................909 391-8800
Jose Flores, *CEO*
Jose Flores, *Pr*
Estela Flores, *VP*
EMP: 17 **EST:** 2015
SALES (est): 1.24MM **Privately Held**
Web: www.usdutygear.com
SIC: 3199 Aprons: welders', blacksmiths', etc.: leather

3211 Flat Glass

(P-5311)
BUDGET ENTERPRISES LLC
Also Called: Solar Art
23042 Mill Creek Dr (92653-1214)
PHONE..............................949 697-9544
Matthew Darienzo, *CEO*
EMP: 25 **EST:** 2014
SALES (est): 2.48MM **Privately Held**
Web: www.solarart.com
SIC: 3211 Construction glass

(P-5312)
CARDINAL GLASS INDUSTRIES INC
Also Called: Cardinal C G
24100 Cardinal Ave (92551-9545)
PHONE..............................951 485-9007
Scott Paisley, *Brnch Mgr*
EMP: 150
SALES (corp-wide): 1B **Privately Held**
Web: www.cardinalcorp.com
SIC: 3211 5039 3229 Flat glass; Glass construction materials; Pressed and blown glass, nec
PA: Cardinal Glass Industries Inc
775 Pririe Ctr Dr Ste 200
Eden Prairie MN
952 229-2600

(P-5313)
CEVIANS LLC (PA)
3128 Red Hill Ave (92626-4525)
PHONE..............................714 619-5135
Eric Lemay, *Pr*
EMP: 95 **EST:** 2014
SALES (est): 15.21MM
SALES (corp-wide): 15.21MM **Privately Held**
Web: www.cevians.com
SIC: 3211 Flat glass

(P-5314)
CL SOLUTIONS LLC
1900 S Susan St (92704-3924)
PHONE..............................714 597-6499
EMP: 57 **EST:** 2011
SALES (est): 5.31MM **Privately Held**
Web: www.transparentarmorsolutions.com
SIC: 3211 Flat glass

(P-5315)
GWLA ACQUISITION CORP (PA)
8600 Rheem Ave (90280-3333)
PHONE..............................323 789-7800
▲ **EMP:** 17 **EST:** 2002
SALES (est): 84.2MM **Privately Held**
Web: www.glasswerks.com
SIC: 3211 3231 6719 Tempered glass; Mirrored glass; Investment holding companies, except banks

(P-5316)
INTERNATIONAL SKYLIGHTS
Also Called: Acralight International
1831 Ritchey St (92705-5138)
PHONE..............................800 325-4355
EMP: 110
Web: www.acralightsolar.com
SIC: 3211 Skylight glass

(P-5317)
MEDILAND CORPORATION
Also Called: Premium Windows
15 Longitude Way (92881-4911)
PHONE..............................562 630-9696

Carlos Landazuri, *CEO*
Jose Medina, *Corporate Secretary**
▲ **EMP:** 79 **EST:** 2005
SALES (est): 8.46MM **Privately Held**
Web: www.premiumwindows.com
SIC: 3211 3645 Window glass, clear and colored; Garden, patio, walkway and yard lighting fixtures: electric

(P-5318)
SUNDOWN LIQUIDATING CORP (PA)
Also Called: Bristolite
401 Goetz Ave (92707-3709)
PHONE..............................714 540-8950
Randolph Heartfield, *CEO*
Rick Beets, *
◆ **EMP:** 92 **EST:** 1970
SQ FT: 100,000
SALES (est): 9.29MM
SALES (corp-wide): 9.29MM **Privately Held**
SIC: 3211 Skylight glass

(P-5319)
US HORIZON MANUFACTURING INC
Also Called: U.S. Horizon Mfg
28539 Industry Dr (91355-5424)
PHONE..............................661 775-1675
Donald E Friest, *CEO*
Garrett A Russell, *
▲ **EMP:** 39 **EST:** 1998
SQ FT: 44,000
SALES (est): 7.69MM
SALES (corp-wide): 32.72B **Privately Held**
Web: www.ushorizon.com
SIC: 3211 3429 Plate and sheet glass; Hardware, nec
HQ: C. R. Laurence Co., Inc.
2503 E Vernon Ave
Vernon CA
323 588-1281

3221 Glass Containers

(P-5320)
ACME VIAL & GLASS CO
Also Called: Acme Vial
1601 Commerce Way (93446-3626)
PHONE..............................805 239-2666
Debra C Knowles, *Pr*
Kay Anderson, *
▲ **EMP:** 25 **EST:** 1942
SALES (est): 4.75MM **Privately Held**
Web: acmevialglassa.openfos.com
SIC: 3221 3231 5113 Vials, glass; Products of purchased glass; Industrial and personal service paper

(P-5321)
PACIFIC VIAL MFG INC
2738 Supply Ave (90040-2704)
PHONE..............................323 721-7004
Steven Oh, *Prin*
▲ **EMP:** 40 **EST:** 2001
SQ FT: 30,000
SALES (est): 6.52MM **Privately Held**
Web: www.pacificvial.com
SIC: 3221 Vials, glass

3229 Pressed And Blown Glass, Nec

(P-5322)
APUTURE IMAGING INDUSTRIES
1715 N Gower St (90028-5405)

PHONE..............................626 295-6133
Bob Meesterman, *Sls Dir*
EMP: 32 **EST:** 2015
SALES (est): 1.57MM **Privately Held**
Web: www.aputure.com
SIC: 3229 Glass lighting equipment parts

(P-5323)
CARLEY (PA)
1502 W 228th St (90501-5105)
PHONE..............................310 325-8474
James A Carley, *Pr*
▲ **EMP:** 225 **EST:** 1974
SQ FT: 14,000
SALES (est): 24.68MM
SALES (corp-wide): 24.68MM **Privately Held**
Web: www.carleylamps.com
SIC: 3229 3646 3641 Lamp parts and shades, glass; Commercial lighting fixtures; Electric lamps

(P-5324)
DONOCO INDUSTRIES INC
Also Called: Encore Plastics
5642 Research Dr Ste B (92649-1634)
P.O. Box 3208 (92605-3208)
PHONE..............................714 893-7889
Richard Harvey, *CEO*
Donald Okada, *
George West, *
EMP: 25 **EST:** 1993
SQ FT: 12,000
SALES (est): 1.91MM **Privately Held**
Web: www.encoreplastics.com
SIC: 3229 Tableware, glass or glass ceramic

(P-5325)
GLAS WERK INC
29710 Avenida De Las Bandera (92688)
PHONE..............................949 766-1296
Maik Mike Bollhorn, *Pr*
▲ **EMP:** 26 **EST:** 1987
SQ FT: 6,000
SALES (est): 2.46MM **Privately Held**
Web: www.glaswerk.com
SIC: 3229 Scientific glassware

(P-5326)
IFIBER OPTIX INC
14450 Chambers Rd (92780-6914)
PHONE..............................714 665-9796
Sanjeev Jaiswal, *Pr*
▲ **EMP:** 25 **EST:** 2000
SQ FT: 5,731
SALES (est): 4.07MM **Privately Held**
Web: www.ifiberoptix.com
SIC: 3229 Fiber optics strands

(P-5327)
ORBITS LIGHTWAVE INC
41 S Chester Ave (91106-3104)
PHONE..............................626 513-7400
Yaakov Shevy, *CEO*
EMP: 25 **EST:** 1999
SQ FT: 9,700
SALES (est): 1.91MM **Privately Held**
Web: www.orbitslightwave.com
SIC: 3229 Fiber optics strands

(P-5328)
PERFORMANCE COMPOSITES INC
1418 S Alameda St (90221-4802)
PHONE..............................310 328-6661
Francis Hu, *CEO*
EMP: 106 **EST:** 1994
SQ FT: 46,000
SALES (est): 22.36MM **Privately Held**
Web: www.performancecomposites.com

SIC: 3229 3624 3544 Glass fiber products; Carbon and graphite products; Special dies, tools, jigs, and fixtures

(P-5329)
SCI-TECH GLASSBLOWING INC
5555 Tech Cir (93021-1795)
P.O. Box 207 (93020-0207)
PHONE..............................805 523-9790
Glenn Gaydick, *Pr*
Craig Gaydick, *Stockholder*
Glenn Gaydick, *Stockholder*
EMP: 24 **EST:** 1971
SQ FT: 4,600
SALES (est): 468.24K **Privately Held**
SIC: 3229 Pressed and blown glass, nec

(P-5330)
SHAMIR INSIGHT INC
Also Called: Shamir
9938 Via Pasar (92126-4559)
PHONE..............................858 514-8330
Raanan Naftalovich, *CEO*
Richard Dailey, *
Joyce Hornaday, *
▲ **EMP:** 77 **EST:** 1997
SALES (est): 32.1MM
SALES (corp-wide): 2.55MM **Privately Held**
Web: www.shamir.com
SIC: 3229 Optical glass
HQ: Shamir Optical Industry Ltd
Kibbutz
Shamir

(P-5331)
SPOTLITE AMERICA CORPORATION (PA)
9937 Jefferson Blvd Ste 110 (90232-3528)
PHONE..............................310 829-0200
Halston Mikail, *CEO*
▲ **EMP:** 20 **EST:** 2014
SQ FT: 17,000
SALES (est): 4.97MM
SALES (corp-wide): 4.97MM **Privately Held**
Web: www.spotlite-usa.com
SIC: 3229 3699 Bulbs for electric lights; Electrical equipment and supplies, nec

(P-5332)
ZEONS INC
291 S La Cienega Blvd Ste 102 (90211)
PHONE..............................323 302-8299
Naved Jafry, *Pr*
EMP: 312 **EST:** 2014
SQ FT: 3,500
SALES (est): 7.94MM **Privately Held**
SIC: 3229 1629 6211 Insulators, electrical: glass; Power plant construction; Investment certificate sales

3231 Products Of Purchased Glass

(P-5333)
ANTHONY INC
Also Called: Anthony International
12812 Arroyo St (91342-5301)
PHONE..............................818 365-9451
Jeff Clark, *Brnch Mgr*
EMP: 41
SALES (corp-wide): 8.51B **Publicly Held**
Web: www.anthonyintl.com
SIC: 3231 5078 3585 Doors, glass: made from purchased glass; Display cases, refrigerated; Evaporative condensers, heat transfer equipment
HQ: Anthony, Inc.
12391 Montero Ave

Sylmar CA

(P-5334)
AVALON GLASS & MIRROR COMPANY
Also Called: Avalon Glass & Mirror
642 Alondra Blvd (90746-1049)
PHONE..............................323 321-8806
Salvador G Gomez, *Pr*
Randy Seeinberg, *
Ed Rosengrant, *
Ruben Huerta, *
▲ **EMP:** 66 **EST:** 1950
SQ FT: 100,000
SALES (est): 4.37MM **Privately Held**
Web: www.avalonmirrorglass.com
SIC: 3231 5023 5231 3211 Mirrored glass; Glassware; Glass; Flat glass
PA: Gwla Acquisition Corp.
8600 Rheem Ave
South Gate CA

(P-5335)
CARLOS SHOWER DOORS INC
300 Kentucky St (93305-4230)
P.O. Box 6009 (93386-6009)
PHONE..............................661 204-6689
Phillip Calvillo, *Pr*
Loni Amado, *Pr*
Edward Amado, *VP*
Phillip C Calvillo, *Sec*
Steven Amado, *VP*
EMP: 17 **EST:** 1947
SQ FT: 10,000
SALES (est): 552.1K **Privately Held**
Web: www.carlosshowerdoors.com
SIC: 3231 Doors, glass: made from purchased glass

(P-5336)
CHAM-CAL ENGINEERING CO
12722 Western Ave (92841-4017)
PHONE..............................714 898-9721
▲ **EMP:** 85 **EST:** 1970
SALES (est): 9.17MM **Privately Held**
Web: www.chamcal.com
SIC: 3231 8711 Mirrors, truck and automobile: made from purchased glass; Engineering services

(P-5337)
COMMONPATH LLC
Also Called: Ozeri
5963 Olivas Park Dr Ste F (93003-7936)
PHONE..............................858 922-8116
▲ **EMP:** 17 **EST:** 2009
SALES (est): 1.69MM **Privately Held**
Web: www.ozeri.com
SIC: 3231 3365 3596 3829 Decorated glassware: chipped, engraved, etched, etc.; Cooking/kitchen utensils, cast aluminum; Scales and balances, except laboratory; Measuring and controlling devices, nec

(P-5338)
CUSTOM INDUSTRIES INC
1371 N Miller St (92806-1412)
PHONE..............................714 779-9101
Thomas Mcafee, *Pr*
▲ **EMP:** 21 **EST:** 1992
SALES (est): 2.6MM **Privately Held**
Web: www.customglassindustries.com
SIC: 3231 Doors, glass: made from purchased glass

(P-5339)
DENNIS DIGIORGIO
Also Called: Oc Direct Shower Door
333 City Blvd W Ste 1700 (92868-5905)
PHONE..............................714 408-7527

Dennis Digiorgio, *Owner*
EMP: 43 **EST:** 2010
SALES (est): 1MM **Privately Held**
Web: www.ocframeless.com
SIC: 3231 Products of purchased glass

(P-5340)
GAFFOGLIO FMLY MTLCRAFTERS INC (PA)
Also Called: Camera Ready Cars
11161 Slater Ave (92708-4921)
PHONE..............................714 444-2000
George Gaffoglio, *CEO*
Ruben Gaffoglio, *
Mike Alexander, *
EMP: 103 **EST:** 1979
SQ FT: 94,000
SALES (est): 17.2MM
SALES (corp-wide): 17.2MM **Privately Held**
Web: www.metalcrafters.com
SIC: 3231 3711 3365 Mirrors, truck and automobile: made from purchased glass; Automobile assembly, including specialty automobiles; Aerospace castings, aluminum

(P-5341)
GLASSWERKS LA INC (HQ)
Also Called: Glasswerks Group
8600 Rheem Ave (90280-3333)
PHONE..............................888 789-7810
Randy Steinberg, *CEO*
Ruben Huerta, *Sec*
Edwin Rosengrant, *VP Sls*
Michael Torres, *CFO*
▲ **EMP:** 280 **EST:** 1949
SQ FT: 100,000
SALES (est): 72.38MM **Privately Held**
Web: www.glasswerks.com
SIC: 3231 3211 Mirrored glass; Flat glass
PA: Gwla Acquisition Corp.
8600 Rheem Ave
South Gate CA

(P-5342)
GP MERGER SUB INC
Also Called: Glaspro
9401 Ann St (90670-2613)
PHONE..............................562 946-7722
Joseph Green, *Pr*
Jim Martineau, *
Jeff Brown, *
◆ **EMP:** 85 **EST:** 1986
SQ FT: 75,000
SALES (est): 16.85MM **Privately Held**
Web: www.glas-pro.com
SIC: 3231 Laminated glass: made from purchased glass

(P-5343)
INVENIOS LLC
320 N Nopal St (93103-3225)
PHONE..............................805 962-3333
Paul Then, *Pr*
EMP: 83 **EST:** 2017
SALES (est): 9.43MM
SALES (corp-wide): 14.19B **Publicly Held**
Web: www.perfectdomain.com
SIC: 3231 Products of purchased glass
PA: Corning Incorporated
1 Riverfront Plz
Corning NY
607 974-9000

(P-5344)
J & B MANUFACTURING CORP
Also Called: San Diego Mirror and Window
2780 La Mirada Dr Ste C (92081-8404)
PHONE..............................760 846-6316
TOLL FREE: 877

Daniel Jaoudi, *Pr*
EMP: 24 **EST:** 1992
SQ FT: 40,000
SALES (est): 935.39K **Privately Held**
SIC: 3231 5231 5211 Doors, glass: made from purchased glass; Glass; Door and window products

(P-5345)
JUDSON STUDIOS INC
200 S Avenue 66 (90042-3632)
PHONE..............................323 255-0131
David Judson, *Pr*
EMP: 27 **EST:** 1897
SQ FT: 10,000
SALES (est): 6.77MM **Privately Held**
Web: www.judsonstudios.com
SIC: 3231 Stained glass: made from purchased glass

(P-5346)
LARRY MTHVIN INSTALLATIONS INC (HQ)
Also Called: L M I
501 Kettering Dr (91761-8150)
PHONE..............................909 563-1700
Larry Methvin, *CEO*
▲ **EMP:** 200 **EST:** 1975
SQ FT: 28,000
SALES (est): 48.45MM
SALES (corp-wide): 4.88B **Publicly Held**
Web: www.larrymethvin.com
SIC: 3231 3431 1751 Doors, glass: made from purchased glass; Shower stalls, metal; Carpentry work
PA: Patrick Industries, Inc.
107 W Franklin St
Elkhart IN
574 294-7511

(P-5347)
LIPPERT COMPONENTS MFG INC
Hehr Glass Co
1021 Walnut Ave (91766-6528)
PHONE..............................909 628-5557
Pete Adams, *Mgr*
EMP: 50
SALES (corp-wide): 5.21B **Publicly Held**
Web: www.lci1.com
SIC: 3231 5231 Doors, glass: made from purchased glass; Glass
HQ: Lippert Components Manufacturing, Inc.
3501 County Road 6 E
Elkhart IN
574 535-1125

(P-5348)
MILGARD MANUFACTURING LLC
Also Called: Milgard-Simi Valley
355 E Easy St (93065-1801)
PHONE..............................805 581-6325
Wayne Ramay, *Brnch Mgr*
EMP: 110
SALES (corp-wide): 822.1MM **Privately Held**
Web: www.milgard.com
SIC: 3231 Products of purchased glass
HQ: Milgard Manufacturing Llc
1010 54th Ave E
Tacoma WA
253 922-4343

(P-5349)
NEW GLASPRO INC
9401 Ann St (90670-2613)
PHONE..............................800 776-2368

Joseph Green, *Pr*
EMP: 23 **EST:** 2005
SALES (est): 1.19MM **Privately Held**
Web: www.glas-pro.com
SIC: 3231 Products of purchased glass

(P-5350)
NEWPORT INDUSTRIAL GLASS INC
Also Called: Glass Fabrication and Dist
8610 Central Ave (90680-2720)
P.O. Box 127 (90680-0127)
PHONE..............................714 484-7500
Ray Larsen, *Dir*
EMP: 21 **EST:** 1983
SALES (est): 517.33K **Privately Held**
Web: www.newportglass.com
SIC: 3231 3827 3851 5039 Products of purchased glass; Mirrors, optical; Lens grinding, except prescription; ophthalmic; Exterior flat glass: plate or window

(P-5351)
OLDCASTLE BUILDINGENVELOPE INC
5631 Ferguson Dr (90022-5132)
P.O. Box 22243 (90022-0243)
PHONE..............................323 722-2007
Luis Soto, *Prin*
EMP: 51
SQ FT: 200,000
SALES (corp-wide): 1.5B **Privately Held**
Web: www.obe.com
SIC: 3231 5231 Tempered glass: made from purchased glass; Glass
PA: Oldcastle Buildingenvelope, Inc.
5005 Lyndon B Johnson Fwy
Dallas TX
214 273-3400

(P-5352)
PACIFIC ARTGLASS CORPORATION
Also Called: Pacific Glass
125 W 157th St (90248-2225)
PHONE..............................310 516-7828
John Williams, *Pr*
▲ **EMP:** 23 **EST:** 1976
SQ FT: 18,000
SALES (est): 2.37MM **Privately Held**
Web: www.pacificartglass.com
SIC: 3231 5231 Products of purchased glass; Glass, leaded or stained

(P-5353)
PRL GLASS SYSTEMS INC
14760 Don Julian Rd (91746-3107)
PHONE..............................877 775-2586
EMP: 74
Web: www.prlglass.com
SIC: 3231 Products of purchased glass
PA: Prl Glass Systems, Inc.
13644 Nelson Ave
City Of Industry CA

(P-5354)
PRL GLASS SYSTEMS INC (PA)
Also Called: P R L
13644 Nelson Ave (91746-2336)
PHONE..............................626 961-5890
◆ **EMP:** 200 **EST:** 1989
SALES (est): 66.38MM **Privately Held**
Web: www.prlglass.com
SIC: 3231 3354 Products of purchased glass; Aluminum extruded products

(P-5355)
RAYOTEK SCIENTIFIC INC
Also Called: Rayotek Scientific

8845 Rehco Rd (92121-3261)
PHONE..............................858 558-3671
William Raggio, *CEO*
William Raggio, *Pr*
Jessica Yadley, *
EMP: 30 **EST:** 1996
SQ FT: 30,000
SALES (est): 8.35MM **Privately Held**
Web: www.rayotek.com
SIC: 3231 8748 Products of purchased glass; Business consulting, nec

(P-5356)
SREAM INC
12869 Temescal Canyon Rd Ste A (92883-4021)
PHONE..............................951 245-6999
Jarir Farraj, *CEO*
Steve Rodriguez, *
EMP: 34 **EST:** 2013
SALES (est): 2.5MM **Privately Held**
Web: www.liquidsciglass.com
SIC: 3231 5231 Products of purchased glass; Glass

(P-5357)
TOTAL MONT LLC
Also Called: Western States Glass
790 W 12th St (90813-2810)
PHONE..............................562 983-1374
EMP: 44 **EST:** 2020
SALES (est): 4.79MM **Privately Held**
SIC: 3231 3211 Insulating glass: made from purchased glass; Tempered glass

(P-5358)
TRIVIEW GLASS INDUSTRIES LLC
Also Called: Triview
279 Shawnan Ln (90631-8087)
PHONE..............................626 363-7980
Alexander A Kastaniuk, *CEO*
▲ **EMP:** 99 **EST:** 2008
SALES (est): 8.21MM **Privately Held**
Web: trivew-glass.squarespace.com
SIC: 3231 Products of purchased glass

(P-5359)
TWED-DELLS INC
Also Called: California Glass & Mirror Div
1900 S Susan St (92704-3924)
PHONE..............................714 754-6900
Corey M Myer Junior, *Pr*
Gayle Myer, *
▲ **EMP:** 38 **EST:** 1980
SQ FT: 45,000
SALES (est): 4.54MM **Privately Held**
Web: www.tbmglass.com
SIC: 3231 Mirrored glass

(P-5360)
ZADRO INC
14462 Astronautics Ln Ste 101 (92647-2077)
PHONE..............................714 892-9200
Zlatko Zadro, *CEO*
Elizabeth Zadro, *Sec*
Rebecca Zadro, *CFO*
Alexander Zadro, *Dir*
EMP: 20 **EST:** 2007
SALES (est): 1.25MM **Privately Held**
Web: www.zadroinc.com
SIC: 3231 Mirrored glass

(P-5361)
ZADRO PRODUCTS INC
14462 Astronautics Ln Ste 101 (92647-2077)
PHONE..............................714 892-9200
Zlatko Zadro, *Pr*

Becky Zadro, *
◆ **EMP:** 35 **EST:** 1986
SQ FT: 22,000
SALES (est): 4.93MM **Privately Held**
Web: www.zadroinc.com
SIC: 3231 3641 Mirrored glass; Electric lamps

3241 Cement, Hydraulic

(P-5362)
CALPORTLAND COMPANY (DH)
Also Called: Arizona Portland Cement
2025 E Financial Way (91741-4692)
P.O. Box 5025 (91740-0885)
PHONE.....................626 852-6200
Michio Kimura, *Ch Bd*
Allen Hamblen, *
James A Repman, *
James A Wendoll, *
John Renninger, *
▲ **EMP:** 77 **EST:** 1891
SQ FT: 28,000
SALES (est): 864.13MM **Privately Held**
Web: www.calportland.com
SIC: 3241 3273 5032 Portland cement; Ready-mixed concrete; Brick, stone, and related material
HQ: Taiheiyo Cement U.S.A., Inc.
2025 E Fincl Way Ste 200
Glendora CA
626 852-6200

(P-5363)
CALPORTLAND COMPANY
19409 National Trails Hwy (92368-9705)
PHONE.....................760 245-5321
EMP: 40
Web: www.calportland.com
SIC: 3241 3273 5032 Portland cement; Ready-mixed concrete; Brick, stone, and related material
HQ: Calportland Company
2025 E Financial Way
Glendora CA

(P-5364)
CALPORTLAND COMPANY
Also Called: California Portland Cement
9350 Oak Creek Rd (93501-7738)
PHONE.....................661 824-2401
Bruce Shaffer, *Brnch Mgr*
EMP: 130
Web: www.calportland.com
SIC: 3241 5032 5211 Masonry cement; Brick, stone, and related material; Cement
HQ: Calportland Company
2025 E Financial Way
Glendora CA

(P-5365)
CTS CEMENT MANUFACTURING CORP (PA)
12442 Knott St (92841-2832)
PHONE.....................714 379-8260
Walter J Hoyle, *CEO*
▼ **EMP:** 45 **EST:** 1978
SQ FT: 14,000
SALES (est): 48.4MM
SALES (corp-wide): 48.4MM **Privately Held**
Web: www.ctscement.com
SIC: 3241 Cement, hydraulic

(P-5366)
HEADWATERS CONSTRUCTION INC
Also Called: Louis W Osborn Co.
16005 Phoebe Ave (90638-5607)

PHONE.....................714 523-1530
Rudy Valverde, *Genl Mgr*
EMP: 24 **EST:** 1962
SQ FT: 18,000
SALES (est): 446.86K **Privately Held**
SIC: 3241 Cement, hydraulic

(P-5367)
MITSUBISHI CEMENT CORPORATION
1150 Pier F Ave (90802-6252)
PHONE.....................562 495-0600
Marty Marcum, *Mgr*
EMP: 428
Web: www.mitsubishicement.com
SIC: 3241 Cement, hydraulic
HQ: Mitsubishi Cement Corporation
151 Cassia Way
Henderson NV
702 932-3900

(P-5368)
MITSUBISHI CEMENT CORPORATION
5808 State Highway 18 (92356-8179)
PHONE.....................760 248-7373
Jim Russell, *Brnch Mgr*
EMP: 175
Web: www.mitsubishicement.com
SIC: 3241 Portland cement
HQ: Mitsubishi Cement Corporation
151 Cassia Way
Henderson NV
702 932-3900

(P-5369)
NATIONAL CEMENT COMPANY INC (HQ)
15821 Ventura Blvd Ste 475 (91436-2935)
PHONE.....................818 728-5200
James E Rotch, *Ch Bd*
▲ **EMP:** 38 **EST:** 1920
SQ FT: 11,446
SALES (est): 510.16MM
SALES (corp-wide): 564.52MM **Privately Held**
Web: www.nationalcement.com
SIC: 3241 3273 Portland cement; Ready-mixed concrete
PA: Vicat
Les Trois Vallons
L Isle D Abeau
474275900

(P-5370)
RIVERSIDE CEMENT HOLDINGS COMPANY
Also Called: Txi Riverside Cement
1500 Rubidoux Blvd (92509-1840)
P.O. Box 832 (92502-0832)
PHONE.....................951 774-2500
▲ **EMP:** 380
SIC: 3241 3272 Natural cement; Concrete products, nec

3251 Brick And Structural Clay Tile

(P-5371)
ARTO BRICK / CALIFORNIA PAVERS
Also Called: Arto Brick and Cal Pavers
15209 S Broadway (90248-1823)
PHONE.....................310 768-8500
Arto Alajian, *CEO*
EMP: 40 **EST:** 1966
SQ FT: 18,000
SALES (est): 4.74MM **Privately Held**

Web: www.arto.com
SIC: 3251 Brick and structural clay tile

3253 Ceramic Wall And Floor Tile

(P-5372)
ELYSIUM TILES INC
Also Called: Elysium Ceramics
1160 N Anaheim Blvd (92801-2502)
PHONE.....................714 991-7885
Yue Zhou, *CEO*
▲ **EMP:** 17 **EST:** 2009
SALES (est): 2.39MM **Privately Held**
Web: www.elysiumtile.com
SIC: 3253 Mosaic tile, glazed and unglazed: ceramic

(P-5373)
OCEANSIDE GLASSTILE COMPANY (PA)
Also Called: Mandala
5858 Edison Pl (92008-6519)
PHONE.....................760 929-4000
Sean M Gildea, *CEO*
Jim Jensen, *VP*
John Marckx, *Ex VP*
Rick Blacklock, *VP*
Jeff Nibler, *VP*
◆ **EMP:** 375 **EST:** 1992
SQ FT: 48,000
SALES (est): 76.08MM **Privately Held**
Web: www.glasstile.com
SIC: 3253 5032 Mosaic tile, glazed and unglazed: ceramic; Tile, clay or other ceramic, excluding refractory

3259 Structural Clay Products, Nec

(P-5374)
EAGLE ROOFING PRODUCTS FLA LLC
3546 N Riverside Ave (92377-3802)
PHONE.....................909 822-6000
Robert C Burlingame, *Managing Member*
Seamus P Burlingame, *
Kevin C Burlingame, *
EMP: 25 **EST:** 2006
SALES (est): 2.51MM **Privately Held**
Web: www.eagleroofing.com
SIC: 3259 Roofing tile, clay

(P-5375)
MARUHACHI CERAMICS AMERICA INC
1985 Sampson Ave (92879-6006)
PHONE.....................800 736-6221
Yoshihiro Suzuki, *Pr*
▲ **EMP:** 22 **EST:** 1983
SQ FT: 83,250
SALES (est): 5.04MM **Privately Held**
Web: www.mca-tile.com
SIC: 3259 Roofing tile, clay

(P-5376)
UNITED STATES TILE CO
909 Railroad St (92882-1906)
PHONE.....................951 739-4613
◆ **EMP:** 125
SIC: 3259 Roofing tile, clay

3261 Vitreous Plumbing Fixtures

(P-5377)
LOTUS HYGIENE SYSTEMS INC
1621 E Saint Andrew Pl (92705-4932)
PHONE.....................714 259-8805
Xiang Liu, *Pr*
▲ **EMP:** 20 **EST:** 2005
SQ FT: 10,000
SALES (est): 2.03MM **Privately Held**
Web: www.lotusseats.com
SIC: 3261 Vitreous plumbing fixtures

(P-5378)
TUBULAR SPECIALTIES MFG INC
Also Called: T S M
13011 S Spring St (90061-1685)
PHONE.....................310 515-4801
Marcia Lynn Hemphill, *CEO*
L C Huntley, *
Arif Mansuri, *
▲ **EMP:** 62 **EST:** 1966
SQ FT: 38,000
SALES (est): 4.4MM **Privately Held**
Web: www.calltsm.com
SIC: 3261 2656 3446 Bathroom accessories/fittings, vitreous china or earthenware; Sanitary food containers; Railings, prefabricated metal

3262 Vitreous China Table And Kitchenware

(P-5379)
SKY ONE INC
Also Called: Vertex China
1793 W 2nd St (91766-1253)
PHONE.....................909 622-3333
Hoi Shum, *Pr*
Ken Joyce, *VP*
Gary Dallas, *VP*
▲ **EMP:** 19 **EST:** 1976
SQ FT: 14,000
SALES (est): 3.8MM **Privately Held**
Web: www.vertexchina.com
SIC: 3262 Dishes, commercial or household: vitreous china

3263 Semivitreous Table And Kitchenware

(P-5380)
MASTERS IN METAL INC
131 Lombard St (93030-5161)
PHONE.....................805 988-1992
Wayne R Haddox, *Pr*
Dennis Haddox, *
▲ **EMP:** 26 **EST:** 1996
SQ FT: 11,000
SALES (est): 844.32K **Privately Held**
Web: www.mastersinmetal.com
SIC: 3263 3952 Commercial tableware or kitchen articles, fine earthenware; Sizes, gold and bronze; artists'

3264 Porcelain Electrical Supplies

(P-5381)
MAGNET SALES & MFG CO INC (HQ)
Also Called: Integrated Magnetics

11250 Playa Ct (90230-6127)
PHONE..............................310 391-7213
TOLL FREE: 800
Anil Nanji, *Pr*
Anil Nanji, *Pr*
Gary Hooper, *
▲ EMP: 75 EST: 1936
SQ FT: 45,000
SALES (est): 32.15MM
SALES (corp-wide): 46.01MM **Privately Held**
Web: www.intemag.com
SIC: 3264 3621 Porcelain electrical supplies; Servomotors, electric
PA: Integrated Technologies Group, Inc.
11250 Playa Ct
Culver City CA
310 391-7213

3269 Pottery Products, Nec

(P-5382)
ASDAK INTERNATIONAL
Also Called: Oggi Corp
1809 1/2 N Orangethorpe Park (92801-1141)
PHONE..............................714 449-0733
Ajit Das, *Pr*
Barbara Das, *CFO*
◆ EMP: 32 EST: 1992
SQ FT: 29,000
SALES (est): 2.41MM **Privately Held**
SIC: 3269 Pottery cooking and kitchen articles

(P-5383)
BERNEY-KARP INC
3350 E 26th St (90058-4145)
PHONE..............................323 260-7122
Morry Karp, *Pr*
Anna Ramos, *
▲ EMP: 74 EST: 1970
SQ FT: 80,000
SALES (est): 4.8MM **Privately Held**
Web: berneykarp.openfos.com
SIC: 3269 Pottery cooking and kitchen articles

(P-5384)
GAINEY CERAMICS INC
1200 Arrow Hwy (91750-5217)
P.O. Box 1513 (91017-5513)
PHONE..............................909 596-4464
Steve Gainey, *CEO*
▲ EMP: 22 EST: 1952
SQ FT: 75,500
SALES (est): 400.45K **Privately Held**
SIC: 3269 Flower pots, red earthenware

(P-5385)
HAGEN-RENAKER INC (PA)
914 W Cienega Ave (91773-2415)
P.O. Box 41324 (90853-1324)
PHONE..............................909 599-2341
Susan Renaker Nikas, *Pr*
Mary Lou Salas, *
EMP: 80 EST: 1946
SQ FT: 88,964
SALES (est): 5.32MM
SALES (corp-wide): 5.32MM **Privately Held**
Web: www.hagenrenaker.com
SIC: 3269 0181 Figures: pottery, china, earthenware, and stoneware; Nursery stock, growing of

(P-5386)
SANTA BARBARA DESIGN STUDIO (PA)

1600 Pacific Ave (93033-2746)
P.O. Box 6087 (93160-6087)
PHONE..............................805 966-3883
Raymond Markow, *CEO*
◆ EMP: 53 EST: 1972
SQ FT: 2,400
SALES (est): 5.01MM
SALES (corp-wide): 5.01MM **Privately Held**
Web: www.sb-designstudio.com
SIC: 3269 5719 Art and ornamental ware, pottery; Pottery

3271 Concrete Block And Brick

(P-5387)
AIR-VOL BLOCK INC
1 Suburban Rd (93401-7523)
P.O. Box 931 (93406-0931)
PHONE..............................805 543-1314
Robert J Miller, *Pr*
Richard Ayres, *
EMP: 40 EST: 1962
SQ FT: 1,400
SALES (est): 5.46MM **Privately Held**
Web: www.airvolblock.com
SIC: 3271 Blocks, concrete or cinder: standard

(P-5388)
ANGELUS BLOCK CO INC (PA)
11374 Tuxford St (91352-2678)
PHONE..............................714 637-8594
Mario Antonini, *Pr*
Edward Antonini, *
▲ EMP: 50 EST: 1946
SQ FT: 2,000
SALES (est): 46.38MM
SALES (corp-wide): 46.38MM **Privately Held**
Web: www.angelusblock.com
SIC: 3271 Concrete block and brick

(P-5389)
MUTH DEVELOPMENT CO INC
Also Called: Orco Block
11100 Beach Blvd (90680-3219)
PHONE..............................714 527-2239
Richard Muth, *Pr*
Tom Ruggeri, *
Lynn Muth, *
Dwayne Gleason, *
EMP: 21 EST: 1996
SALES (est): 328.37K **Privately Held**
Web: www.orco.com
SIC: 3271 Concrete block and brick

(P-5390)
ORCO BLOCK & HARDSCAPE (PA)
11100 Beach Blvd (90680-3219)
PHONE..............................714 527-2239
Richard J Muth, *CEO*
Mary M Muth, *
EMP: 60 EST: 1946
SQ FT: 5,000
SALES (est): 49.61MM
SALES (corp-wide): 49.61MM **Privately Held**
Web: www.orco.com
SIC: 3271 Architectural concrete: block, split, fluted, screen, etc.

(P-5391)
ORCO BLOCK & HARDSCAPE
4510 Rutile St (92509-2649)
PHONE..............................951 685-1521
Ray Davis, *Off Mgr*

EMP: 17
SALES (corp-wide): 49.61MM **Privately Held**
Web: www.orco.com
SIC: 3271 Concrete block and brick
PA: Orco Block & Hardscape
11100 Beach Blvd
Stanton CA
714 527-2239

(P-5392)
RCP BLOCK & BRICK INC (PA)
8240 Broadway (91945-2004)
P.O. Box 579 (91946-0579)
PHONE..............................619 460-9101
Michael Finch, *CEO*
Charles T Finch, *
Eugene M Chubb, *
EMP: 57 EST: 1947
SQ FT: 4,000
SALES (est): 43.4MM
SALES (corp-wide): 43.4MM **Privately Held**
Web: www.rcpblock.com
SIC: 3271 5211 5032 Blocks, concrete or cinder: standard; Masonry materials and supplies; Concrete building products

(P-5393)
RCP BLOCK & BRICK INC
8755 N Magnolia Ave (92071-4594)
PHONE..............................619 448-2240
Randy Scott, *Brnch Mgr*
EMP: 40
SALES (corp-wide): 43.4MM **Privately Held**
Web: www.rcpblock.com
SIC: 3271 5032 5211 Blocks, concrete or cinder: standard; Concrete and cinder block; Lumber and other building materials
PA: Rcp Block & Brick, Inc.
8240 Broadway
Lemon Grove CA
619 460-9101

(P-5394)
RCP BLOCK & BRICK INC
75 N 4th Ave (91910-1007)
PHONE..............................619 474-1516
Tim Ostrom, *Mgr*
EMP: 41
SALES (corp-wide): 43.4MM **Privately Held**
Web: www.rcpblock.com
SIC: 3271 5032 5211 Blocks, concrete or cinder: standard; Concrete and cinder block; Concrete and cinder block
PA: Rcp Block & Brick, Inc.
8240 Broadway
Lemon Grove CA
619 460-9101

(P-5395)
RCP BLOCK & BRICK INC
577 N Vulcan Ave (92024-2120)
PHONE..............................760 753-1164
Chico Savage, *Mgr*
EMP: 41
SALES (corp-wide): 43.4MM **Privately Held**
Web: www.rcpblock.com
SIC: 3271 5211 Blocks, concrete or cinder: standard; Lumber and other building materials
PA: Rcp Block & Brick, Inc.
8240 Broadway
Lemon Grove CA
619 460-9101

(P-5396)
WESTERN STATES WHOLESALE INC (PA)
Also Called: C-Cure
1420 S Bon View Ave (91761-4405)
P.O. Box 3340 (91761-0934)
PHONE..............................909 947-0028
▲ EMP: 70 EST: 1995
SQ FT: 60,000
SALES (est): 23.04MM **Privately Held**
Web: www.wswcorp.com
SIC: 3271 5072 5032 5211 Concrete block and brick; Bolts; Drywall materials; Lumber products

3272 Concrete Products, Nec

(P-5397)
ACKER STONE INDUSTRIES INC (DH)
13296 Temescal Canyon Rd (92883-5299)
PHONE..............................951 674-0047
Giora Ackerstein, *Ch Bd*
▲ EMP: 50 EST: 1987
SQ FT: 14,000
SALES (est): 25.76MM **Privately Held**
Web: www.ackerstone.com
SIC: 3272 3271 Concrete products, precast, nec; Paving blocks, concrete
HQ: Ackerstein Zvi Ltd.
103 Medinat Hayehudim
Herzliya

(P-5398)
AMERON INTERNATIONAL CORP
Also Called: Ameron Protective Coatings
1020 B St (93015-1024)
PHONE..............................425 258-2616
William Miner, *Brnch Mgr*
EMP: 115
SALES (corp-wide): 7.24B **Publicly Held**
SIC: 3272 Cylinder pipe, prestressed or pretensioned concrete
HQ: Ameron International Corporation
7909 Parkwood Circle Dr
Houston TX
713 375-3700

(P-5399)
AMERON INTERNATIONAL CORP
Ameron Pole Products & Systems
1020 B St (93015-1024)
PHONE..............................805 524-0223
West Allison, *Mgr*
EMP: 100
SALES (corp-wide): 7.24B **Publicly Held**
SIC: 3272 3648 3646 3441 Concrete products, precast, nec; Lighting equipment, nec; Commercial lighting fixtures; Fabricated structural metal
HQ: Ameron International Corporation
7909 Parkwood Circle Dr
Houston TX
713 375-3700

(P-5400)
ASSOCIATED CNSTR & ENGRG INC (PA)
23232 Peralta Dr Ste 206 (92653-1437)
PHONE..............................949 455-2682
Lawrence Gene Wombles, *CEO*
Bryan M Wombles, *Sec*
Shawn P Owens, *Dir*
EMP: 20 EST: 2011
SALES (est): 61.08MM
SALES (corp-wide): 61.08MM **Privately Held**
Web: www.a-c-e-inc.com
SIC: 3272 Tanks, concrete

(P-5401)
AVILAS GARDEN ART (PA)
14608 Merrill Ave (92335-4219)
PHONE.................909 350-4546
Ralph G Avila, *Owner*
EMP: 60 **EST:** 1981
SQ FT: 7,000
SALES (est): 8.64MM
SALES (corp-wide): 8.64MM **Privately Held**
Web: www.avilasgardenart.com
SIC: 3272 5261 5211 5199 Precast terrazzo or concrete products; Lawn ornaments; Masonry materials and supplies; Statuary

(P-5402)
CENTINELA CONSULTING GROUP INC
Also Called: Enderle Vault Co
720 E Florence Ave (90301-1406)
PHONE.................310 674-2115
Walter Birch, *Pr*
EMP: 18 **EST:** 1963
SQ FT: 14,000
SALES (est): 944.57K **Privately Held**
SIC: 3272 Burial vaults, concrete or precast terrazzo

(P-5403)
CLARK - PACIFIC CORPORATION
9367 Holly Rd (92301-3910)
PHONE.................626 962-8755
EMP: 25
SALES (corp-wide): 243.72MM **Privately Held**
Web: www.clarkpacific.com
SIC: 3272 5032 Concrete products, precast, nec; Brick, stone, and related material
PA: Clark - Pacific Corporation
   710 Riverpoint Ct Ste 100
   West Sacramento CA
   916 371-0305

(P-5404)
CLARK - PACIFIC CORPORATION
Also Called: Tecon Pacific
4684 Ontario Mills Pkwy Ste 200 (91764-5151)
PHONE.................909 823-1433
Donald Clark, *Owner*
EMP: 49
SALES (corp-wide): 243.72MM **Privately Held**
Web: www.clarkpacific.com
SIC: 3272 5211 Concrete products, precast, nec; Masonry materials and supplies
PA: Clark - Pacific Corporation
   710 Riverpoint Ct Ste 100
   West Sacramento CA
   916 371-0305

(P-5405)
CLARK - PACIFIC CORPORATION
131 Los Angeles St (91706)
PHONE.................626 962-8751
Ed Wopschall, *Brnch Mgr*
EMP: 24
SALES (corp-wide): 243.72MM **Privately Held**
Web: www.clarkpacific.com
SIC: 3272 Concrete products, precast, nec
PA: Clark - Pacific Corporation
   710 Riverpoint Ct Ste 100
   West Sacramento CA
   916 371-0305

(P-5406)
CORESLAB STRUCTURES LA INC
150 W Placentia Ave (92571-3200)
PHONE.................951 943-9119
Mario Franciosa, *CEO*
Lou Franciosa, *
Robert H Konoske, *General Vice President**
Jorgen Clausen, *
EMP: 200 **EST:** 1955
SQ FT: 25,000
SALES (est): 40.48MM
SALES (corp-wide): 27.34MM **Privately Held**
Web: www.coreslab.com
SIC: 3272 Concrete products, precast, nec
HQ: Coreslab Holdings U S Inc
   332 Jones Rd Suite 1
   Stoney Creek ON
   905 643-0220

(P-5407)
CREATIVE STONE MFG INC (PA)
Also Called: Coronado Stone Products
201 S Cactus Ave (92376-6318)
PHONE.................909 357-8295
Melton Bacon, *Pr*
Scott Ebersole, *
Bob Ratkovic, *
◆ **EMP:** 180 **EST:** 1962
SALES (est): 54.55MM
SALES (corp-wide): 54.55MM **Privately Held**
Web: www.coronado.com
SIC: 3272 Siding, precast stone

(P-5408)
DCC GENERAL ENGRG CONTRS INC
2180 Meyers Ave (92029-1001)
PHONE.................760 480-7400
Frank D'agostini, *Pr*
Scott Woods, *
EMP: 75 **EST:** 1982
SQ FT: 2,100
SALES (est): 9.89MM **Privately Held**
Web: www.dccengineering.com
SIC: 3272 1771 3531 Concrete products, nec ; Curb and sidewalk contractors; Asphalt plant, including gravel-mix type

(P-5409)
EISEL ENTERPRISES INC
714 Fee Ana St (92870-6705)
PHONE.................714 993-1706
Lyle Eisel, *Pr*
Kim Webster, *
Janis Eisel, *
EMP: 24 **EST:** 1970
SQ FT: 4,000
SALES (est): 2.42MM **Privately Held**
Web: www.eiselenterprises.com
SIC: 3272 Meter boxes, concrete

(P-5410)
ELDORADO STONE LLC (DH)
3817 Ocean Ranch Blvd (92056-8607)
P.O. Box 2289 (92079-2289)
PHONE.................800 925-1491
Donald P Newman, *Managing Member*
◆ **EMP:** 50 **EST:** 2000
SALES (est): 302.58MM **Privately Held**
Web: www.eldoradostone.com
SIC: 3272 Concrete products, precast, nec
HQ: Headwaters Incorporated
   10701 S Rver Front Pkwy
   South Jordan UT

(P-5411)
ELK CORPORATION OF TEXAS
Also Called: Elk
6200 Zerker Rd (93263-9612)
PHONE.................661 391-3900
Gus Freshwater, *Brnch Mgr*
EMP: 153
SALES (corp-wide): 6.27B **Privately Held**
SIC: 3272 2952 Precast terrazzo or concrete products; Asphalt felts and coatings
HQ: Elk Corporation Of Texas
   14911 Quorum Dr Ste 600
   Dallas TX

(P-5412)
FARLEY PAVING STONE CO INC
Also Called: Farley Interlocking Pav Stones
39301 Badger St (92211-1162)
P.O. Box 10946 (92255-0946)
PHONE.................760 773-3960
Shon Farley, *VP*
Charissa Farley, *
Hector Gonzalez, *
EMP: 70 **EST:** 1985
SALES (est): 7.53MM **Privately Held**
Web: www.farleypavers.com
SIC: 3272 3531 3281 Paving materials, prefabricated concrete; Pavers; Curbing, paving, and walkway stone

(P-5413)
FIORE STONE INC
1814 Commercenter W Ste E (92408-3332)
PHONE.................909 424-0221
Bruce Raabe, *Pr*
EMP: 45 **EST:** 2009
SALES (est): 5.2MM **Privately Held**
Web: www.fiorestone.com
SIC: 3272 Concrete products, precast, nec

(P-5414)
FORMS AND SURFACES COMPANY LLC
Also Called: Lightform
6395 Cindy Ln (93013-2909)
PHONE.................805 684-8626
EMP: 150 **EST:** 1975
SQ FT: 63,000
SALES (est): 17.73MM **Privately Held**
Web: www.forms-surfaces.com
SIC: 3272 3531 3446 3429 Building materials, except block or brick: concrete; Construction machinery; Architectural metalwork; Hardware, nec

(P-5415)
FORTERRA PIPE & PRECAST LLC
Also Called: South Coast Materials Co
9229 Harris Plant Rd (92145-0001)
P.O. Box 639069 (92163-9069)
PHONE.................858 715-5600
Carol Hartwig, *Brnch Mgr*
EMP: 28
Web: www.rinkerpipe.com
SIC: 3272 Concrete products, nec
HQ: Forterra Pipe & Precast, Llc
   511 E John Carpenter Fwy
   Irving TX
   469 458-7973

(P-5416)
FORTERRA PIPE & PRECAST LLC
26380 Palomar Rd (92585-9811)
PHONE.................951 523-7039
EMP: 41
Web: www.rinkerpipe.com

SIC: 3272 Concrete products, nec
HQ: Forterra Pipe & Precast, Llc
   511 E John Carpenter Fwy
   Irving TX
   469 458-7973

(P-5417)
GOLDEN EMPIRE CON PDTS INC
Also Called: Structurecast
8261 Mccutchen Rd (93311-9407)
PHONE.................661 833-4490
Brent Dezember, *Pr*
Ann Dzember, *
EMP: 65 **EST:** 1997
SQ FT: 10,000
SALES (est): 10.04MM **Privately Held**
Web: www.structurecast.com
SIC: 3272 1791 Precast terrazzo or concrete products; Precast concrete structural framing or panels, placing of

(P-5418)
HANSON ROOF TILE INC
10651 Elm Ave (92337-7324)
P.O. Box 660225 (75266-0225)
PHONE.................888 509-4787
▲ **EMP:** 422
SIC: 3272 Roofing tile and slabs, concrete

(P-5419)
HEADWATERS INCORPORATED
1345 Philadelphia St (91766-5564)
PHONE.................909 627-9066
Jim Johnson, *Mgr*
EMP: 24
Web: www.ecomaterial.com
SIC: 3272 Concrete products, nec
HQ: Headwaters Incorporated
   10701 S River Front Pkwy # 300
   South Jordan UT

(P-5420)
HINTEX
1230 S Glendale Ave (91205-3205)
PHONE.................320 400-0009
EMP: 18 **EST:** 2018
SALES (est): 495.71K **Privately Held**
Web: www.hintex.com
SIC: 3272 3431 Liquid catch basins, tanks, and covers: concrete; Bathtubs: enameled iron, cast iron, or pressed metal

(P-5421)
J & R CONCRETE PRODUCTS INC
440 W Markham St (92571-8138)
PHONE.................951 943-5855
Raul Ramirez, *Pr*
EMP: 42 **EST:** 1981
SQ FT: 40,000
SALES (est): 4.66MM **Privately Held**
Web: www.jrconcreteproducts.com
SIC: 3272 Meter boxes, concrete

(P-5422)
JENSEN ENTERPRISES INC
Also Called: Jensen Precast
14221 San Bernardino Ave (92335-5232)
PHONE.................909 357-7264
TOLL FREE: 800
Carol Kohanle, *Mgr*
EMP: 300
SALES (corp-wide): 237.25MM **Privately Held**
Web: www.jensenprecast.com
SIC: 3272 7699 5211 5039 Concrete products, precast, nec; Waste cleaning services; Masonry materials and supplies; Septic tanks
PA: Jensen Enterprises, Inc.
   9895 Double R Blvd

PRODUCTS & SVCS

Reno NV
775 352-2700

(P-5423)
KTI INCORPORATED
Also Called: Rialto Concrete Products
3011 N Laurel Ave (92377-3725)
PHONE..................................909 434-1888
Kenneth D Thompson, *CEO*
Daniel J Deming, *
Jerry Cowden, *
EMP: 100 **EST:** 1987
SQ FT: 400
SALES (est): 21.49MM **Privately Held**
Web: www.thompsonpipegroup.com
SIC: 3272 Concrete products, precast, nec

(P-5424)
MHK INVESTMENT HOLDINGS INC
Also Called: United Memorial Products, Inc.
4845 Pioneer Blvd (90601-1842)
P.O. Box 721 (90608-0721)
PHONE..................................562 699-3578
Joseph Bartolacci, *Owner*
Mac Sharrock, *Genl Mgr*
▲ **EMP:** 36 **EST:** 1993
SALES (est): 4.45MM
SALES (corp-wide): 1.88B **Publicly Held**
SIC: 3272 3281 Concrete structural support and building material; Cut stone and stone products
PA: Matthews International Corporation
2 N Shore Ctr Ste 200
Pittsburgh PA
412 442-8200

(P-5425)
MID-STATE CONCRETE PDTS INC
1625 E Donovan Rd Ste C (93454-2519)
P.O. Box 219 (93456-0219)
PHONE..................................805 928-2855
TOLL FREE: 800
Ralph Vander Veen, *Pr*
Pat Vander Veen, *VP*
EMP: 23 **EST:** 1975
SQ FT: 2,000
SALES (est): 4.91MM **Privately Held**
Web: www.midstateconcrete.com
SIC: 3272 Concrete products, precast, nec

(P-5426)
MODERN STAIRWAYS INC
3239 Bancroft Dr (91977-2698)
PHONE..................................619 466-1484
Jack Spencer, *Pr*
Deborah Spencer, *VP*
EMP: 26 **EST:** 1962
SQ FT: 1,000
SALES (est): 1.34MM **Privately Held**
SIC: 3272 Burial vaults, concrete or precast terrazzo

(P-5427)
NEWBASIS LLC
2626 Kansas Ave (92507-2600)
PHONE..................................951 787-0600
EMP: 150 **EST:** 2020
SALES (est): 20.59MM
SALES (corp-wide): 20.59MM **Privately Held**
Web: www.newbasis.com
SIC: 3272 Concrete products, nec
PA: Capital Precast Holdings, Llc
250 W Nottingham Dr # 120
San Antonio TX

(P-5428)
NEWBASIS WEST LLC
2626 Kansas Ave (92507-2600)
PHONE..................................951 787-0600
Jennifer Ewing, *
Kim Ruiz, *
◆ **EMP:** 115 **EST:** 1989
SALES (est): 24.81MM
SALES (corp-wide): 24.81MM **Privately Held**
Web: www.newbasis.com
SIC: 3272 Manhole covers or frames, concrete
PA: Echo Rock Ventures, Inc.
370 Hammond Dr
Auburn CA
530 823-9600

(P-5429)
NEWMAN AND SONS INC (PA)
2655 1st St Ste 210 (93065-1578)
PHONE..................................805 522-1646
Dennis L Newman, *Pr*
EMP: 40 **EST:** 1938
SQ FT: 12,500
SALES (est): 2.55MM
SALES (corp-wide): 2.55MM **Privately Held**
Web: ramco.us.com
SIC: 3272 Paving materials, prefabricated concrete

(P-5430)
NUCAST INDUSTRIES INC
Also Called: Robbins Precast
23220 Park Canyon Dr (92883-6006)
PHONE..................................951 277-8888
David Minasian, *Prin*
Anthony Minasian, *Prin*
EMP: 22 **EST:** 1974
SQ FT: 5,000
SALES (est): 785.17K **Privately Held**
Web: www.robbinsprecast.com
SIC: 3272 5211 Concrete products, precast, nec; Masonry materials and supplies

(P-5431)
OLDCAST PRECAST (DH)
Also Called: Riverside Foundary
2434 Rubidoux Blvd (92509-2144)
PHONE..................................951 788-9720
Thomas D Lynch, *Ch Bd*
John R Waren, *
EMP: 35 **EST:** 1966
SQ FT: 7,000
SALES (est): 29.64MM
SALES (corp-wide): 32.72B **Privately Held**
Web: www.inland-concrete.com
SIC: 3272 3271 Concrete products, precast, nec; Concrete block and brick
HQ: Oldcastle Infrastructure, Inc.
7000 Central Pkwy Ste 800
Atlanta GA
770 270-5000

(P-5432)
OLDCASTLE INFRASTRUCTURE INC
Also Called: Utility Vault
10650 Hemlock Ave (92337-7296)
P.O. Box 310039 (92331-0039)
PHONE..................................909 428-3700
Glenn Scheaffer, *Mgr*
EMP: 44
SALES (corp-wide): 32.72B **Privately Held**
Web: www.oldcastleinfrastructure.com
SIC: 3272 Concrete products, precast, nec
HQ: Oldcastle Infrastructure, Inc.
7000 Central Pkwy Ste 800
Atlanta GA
770 270-5000

(P-5433)
OLDCASTLE INFRASTRUCTURE INC
Also Called: Utility Vault
2512 Harmony Grove Rd (92029-2800)
PHONE..................................951 683-8200
EMP: 50
SALES (corp-wide): 29.71B **Privately Held**
SIC: 3272 3446 Concrete products, precast, nec; Open flooring and grating for construction
HQ: Oldcastle Infrastructure, Inc.
7000 Cntl Prkaway Ste 800
Atlanta GA
470 602-2000

(P-5434)
OLDCASTLE INFRASTRUCTURE INC
19940 Hansen Ave (92567-9649)
PHONE..................................951 928-8713
EMP: 30
SALES (corp-wide): 32.72B **Privately Held**
Web: www.oldcastleinfrastructure.com
SIC: 3272 Concrete products, nec
HQ: Oldcastle Infrastructure, Inc.
7000 Central Pkwy Ste 800
Atlanta GA
770 270-5000

(P-5435)
OVER & OVER READY MIX INC
Also Called: Borges Rock Product
8216 Tujunga Ave (91352-3932)
P.O. Box 309 (93020-0309)
PHONE..................................818 983-1588
Ed Borges, *Pr*
EMP: 33 **EST:** 2001
SALES (est): 2.21MM **Privately Held**
SIC: 3272 3273 Concrete products, nec; Ready-mixed concrete

(P-5436)
PACIFIC STONE DESIGN INC
1201 E Wakeham Ave (92705-4145)
PHONE..................................714 836-5757
Scott Sterling, *Pr*
Kathy Sterling, *
EMP: 45 **EST:** 1996
SQ FT: 40,000
SALES (est): 7MM **Privately Held**
Web: www.pacificstone.net
SIC: 3272 Concrete products, precast, nec

(P-5437)
PARAGON BUILDING PRODUCTS INC (PA)
2191 5th St Ste 111 (92860-1966)
P.O. Box 99 (92860-0099)
PHONE..................................951 549-1155
Jeffrey M Goodman, *Pr*
Jack Goodman, *
Richard Goodman, *
▲ **EMP:** 25 **EST:** 1984
SQ FT: 16,500
SALES (est): 22.17MM
SALES (corp-wide): 22.17MM **Privately Held**
Web: www.paragonbp.us
SIC: 3272 3271 5032 Dry mixture concrete; Concrete block and brick; Brick, stone, and related material

(P-5438)
PRE-CON PRODUCTS
240 W Los Angeles Ave (93065-1695)
P.O. Box 940669 (93094-0669)
PHONE..................................805 527-0841
EMP: 70 **EST:** 1964

SALES (est): 9.56MM **Privately Held**
Web: www.preconproducts.com
SIC: 3272 Pipe, concrete or lined with concrete

(P-5439)
PRECAST INNOVATIONS INC
1670 N Main St (92867-3405)
PHONE..................................714 921-4060
Chester Valdovinos, *Pr*
EMP: 28 **EST:** 2011
SQ FT: 20,000
SALES (est): 4.01MM **Privately Held**
Web: www.precastinnovations.com
SIC: 3272 1791 Concrete products, precast, nec; Precast concrete structural framing or panels, placing of

(P-5440)
PRIME FORMING & CNSTR SUPS INC
Also Called: Fitzgerald Formliners
1500a E Chestnut Ave (92701-6321)
PHONE..................................714 547-6710
Edward Fitzgerald, *Pr*
EMP: 46 **EST:** 1988
SQ FT: 30,000
SALES (est): 8.76MM **Privately Held**
SIC: 3272 Concrete products, nec

(P-5441)
PRO-CAST PRODUCTS INC (PA)
27417 3rd St (92346-4258)
P.O. Box 602 (92346-0602)
PHONE..................................909 793-7602
TOLL FREE: 800
EMP: 49 **EST:** 1987
SALES (est): 7.24MM
SALES (corp-wide): 7.24MM **Privately Held**
Web: www.procastproducts.com
SIC: 3272 Concrete products, nec

(P-5442)
QUICK CRETE PRODUCTS CORP
731 Parkridge Ave (92860-3149)
P.O. Box 639 (92860-0639)
PHONE..................................951 737-6240
EMP: 180 **EST:** 1976
SALES (est): 24.38MM **Privately Held**
Web: www.qcp-corp.com
SIC: 3272 Concrete products, precast, nec

(P-5443)
QUIKRETE CALIFORNIA LLC (DH)
Also Called: Quickrete
3940 Temescal Canyon Rd (92883-5618)
PHONE..................................951 277-3155
John O Winshester, *Managing Member*
EMP: 43 **EST:** 2004
SALES (est): 31.36MM **Privately Held**
SIC: 3272 Concrete products, nec
HQ: The Quikrete Companies Llc
5 Concourse Pkwy Ste 1900
Atlanta GA
404 634-9100

(P-5444)
QUIKRETE COMPANIES LLC
Also Called: True Cast Concrete Products
11145 Tuxford St (91352-2632)
PHONE..................................323 875-1367
Greg Gibhel, *Principal B*
EMP: 34
Web: www.quikrete.com
SIC: 3272 3271 5211 Steps, prefabricated concrete; Concrete block and brick; Masonry materials and supplies

HQ: The Quikrete Companies Llc
5 Concourse Pkwy Ste 1900
Atlanta GA
404 634-9100

(P-5445)

RIVER VALLEY PRECAST INC

14796 Washington Dr (92335-6263)
PHONE...............................928 764-3839
Darryl Kerr, *Pr*
EMP: 20 **EST:** 2003
SALES (est): 708.68K **Privately Held**
SIC: 3272 Precast terrazzo or concrete
products

(P-5446)

RMR PRODUCTS INC (PA)

11011 Glenoaks Blvd Ste 1 (91331-1634)
PHONE...............................818 890-0896
David Mckendrick, *CEO*
Jim Mckendrick, *Pr*
EMP: 25 **EST:** 1984
SQ FT: 3,200
SALES (est): 3.29MM
SALES (corp-wide): 3.29MM **Privately
Held**
Web: www.ceormfproducts.com
SIC: 3272 Chimney caps, concrete

(P-5447)

ROYAL WESTLAKE ROOFING LLC

Also Called: Monier Lifetile
3511 N Riverside Ave (92377-3803)
PHONE...............................909 822-4407
Kevin O Neil, *Mgr*
EMP: 19
SIC: 3272 3251 5032 2952 Roofing tile and
slabs, concrete; Brick clay: common face,
glazed, vitrified, or hollow; Cinders; Asphalt
felts and coatings
HQ: Royal Westlake Roofing Llc
2700 Post Oak Blvd # 1900
Houston TX
949 756-1605

(P-5448)

SAN DIEGO PRECAST CONCRETE INC (DH)

Also Called: US Concrete Precast
2735 Cactus Rd (92154-8024)
PHONE...............................619 240-8000
Douglas Mclaughlin, *Pr*
EMP: 27 **EST:** 1999
SQ FT: 1,600
SALES (est): 27.96MM **Publicly Held**
Web: www.sandiego.gov
SIC: 3272 3281 Meter boxes, concrete;
Urns, cut stone
HQ: U.S. Concrete, Inc.
331 N Main St
Euless TX
817 835-4105

(P-5449)

SISSELL BROS

4322 E 3rd St (90022-1501)
PHONE...............................323 261-0106
John F Foote, *Pr*
Dorothy Sissell, *VP*
Joan M Foote, *Sec*
EMP: 23 **EST:** 1930
SQ FT: 7,000
SALES (est): 979.02K **Privately Held**
SIC: 3272 Burial vaults, concrete or precast
terrazzo

(P-5450)

SOUTHER CAST STONE INC

235 Via Del Monte (92058-1223)
P.O. Box 1133 (92595-1133)
PHONE...............................760 754-9697
Phillip Souther, *Pr*
EMP: 38 **EST:** 2002
SQ FT: 7,000
SALES (est): 857K **Privately Held**
SIC: 3272 Concrete products, nec

(P-5451)

SOUTHWEST CONCRETE PRODUCTS

519 S Benson Ave (91762-4002)
PHONE...............................909 983-9789
Bob Dzajkich, *Pr*
Eileen Dzajkich, *
Natalie Dzajkich, *
♣ **EMP:** 160 **EST:** 1966
SQ FT: 25,000
SALES (est): 10.5MM **Privately Held**
SIC: 3272 5032 Manhole covers or frames,
concrete; Brick, stone, and related material
PA: Taiheyo Kenkou Center Co.,Ltd.
164-2, Rokuchome, Yotsukuramachi
Iwaki FSM

(P-5452)

SPEC FORMLINERS INC

1038 E 4th St (92701-4751)
P.O. Box 10277 (92711-0277)
PHONE...............................714 429-9500
Stephen A Deering, *CEO*
Anthony Zaha, *
EMP: 26 **EST:** 1996
SQ FT: 23,000
SALES (est): 8.55MM **Privately Held**
Web: www.specformliners.com
SIC: 3272 Concrete products, nec

(P-5453)

STEPSTONE INC

13238 S Figueroa St (90061-1140)
PHONE...............................310 327-7474
Kelsy Carrington, *Brnch Mgr*
EMP: 25
SALES (corp-wide): 9.34MM **Privately
Held**
Web: www.stepstoneinc.com
SIC: 3272 Concrete products, precast, nec
PA: Stepstone, Inc.
17025 S Main St
Gardena CA
310 327-7474

(P-5454)

STEPSTONE INC (PA)

17025 S Main St (90248-3125)
PHONE...............................310 327-7474
Gordon S Mcwilliams, *CEO*
Paul Mitchell, *
EMP: 50 **EST:** 1963
SQ FT: 15,000
SALES (est): 9.34MM
SALES (corp-wide): 9.34MM **Privately
Held**
Web: www.stepstoneinc.com
SIC: 3272 Concrete products, precast, nec

(P-5455)

VAULT PREP INC

2500 Broadway Ste F125 (90404-3080)
PHONE...............................310 971-9091
EMP: 20 **EST:** 2012
SALES (est): 2.4MM **Privately Held**
Web: www.vault-prep.com

SIC: 3272 8748 Burial vaults, concrete or
precast terrazzo; Testing service,
educational or personnel

(P-5456)

W R MEADOWS INC

Also Called: W. R. Meadows Southern Cal
2300 Valley Blvd (91768-1168)
P.O. Box 667 (91788-0667)
PHONE...............................909 469-2606
Michael Knapp, *Brnch Mgr*
EMP: 27
SALES (corp-wide): 26.89K **Privately Held**
Web: www.wrmeadows.com
SIC: 3272 3444 2899 2891 Concrete
products, nec; Concrete forms, sheet metal;
Chemical preparations, nec; Adhesives and
sealants
PA: W. R. Meadows, Inc.
300 Industrial Dr
Hampshire IL
800 342-5976

3273 Ready-mixed Concrete

(P-5457)

A & A READY MIXED CONCRETE INC (PA)

4621 Teller Ave Ste 130 (92660-2104)
PHONE...............................949 253-2800
Kurt Caillier, *Pr*
Randy Caillier, *Sec*
▲ **EMP:** 45 **EST:** 1956
SQ FT: 8,000
SALES (est): 84.61MM
SALES (corp-wide): 84.61MM **Privately
Held**
Web: www.aareadymix.com
SIC: 3273 Ready-mixed concrete

(P-5458)

ALLIANCE READY MIX INC

310 James Way Ste 210 (93449-2877)
P.O. Box 1163 (93421-1163)
PHONE...............................805 556-3015
Brandt Robertson, *Brnch Mgr*
EMP: 96
SIC: 3273 Ready-mixed concrete
PA: Alliance Ready Mix, Inc.
915 Sheridan Rd
Arroyo Grande CA

(P-5459)

ALPHA MATERIALS INC

6170 20th St (92509-2031)
PHONE...............................951 788-5150
Brian Oaks, *Pr*
EMP: 36 **EST:** 2002
SQ FT: 1,200
SALES (est): 8.64MM **Privately Held**
Web: www.alpha-materials-inc.com
SIC: 3273 Ready-mixed concrete

(P-5460)

ARROW TRANSIT MIX

507 E Avenue L12 (93535-5417)
P.O. Box 6677 (93539-6677)
PHONE...............................661 945-7600
H D Follendore, *Pr*
Christine Follendore, *
EMP: 35 **EST:** 1998
SQ FT: 7,200
SALES (est): 4.95MM **Privately Held**
Web: www.arrowtransitmix.com
SIC: 3273 Ready-mixed concrete

(P-5461)

ASSOCIATED READY MIX CON INC

Also Called: ASSOCIATED READY MIX
CONCRETE, INC.
8946 Bradley Ave (91352-2601)
PHONE...............................818 504-3100
Tim Sullivan, *Mgr*
EMP: 77
Web: www.assocrmc.com
SIC: 3273 Ready-mixed concrete
PA: Associated Ready Mixed Concrete, Inc.
4621 Teller Ave Ste 130
Newport Beach CA

(P-5462)

ASSOCIATED READY MIXED CON INC (PA)

4621 Teller Ave Ste 130 (92660-2165)
PHONE...............................949 253-2800
EMP: 40 **EST:** 1996
SALES (est): 17.83MM **Privately Held**
Web: www.assocrmc.com
SIC: 3273 Ready-mixed concrete

(P-5463)

BEACON CONCRETE INC

Also Called: Lighthouse Trucking
1597 S Bluff Rd (90640-6601)
PHONE...............................323 889-7775
TOLL FREE: 800
Lou Earlabaugh, *Pr*
Suzanne Earlabaugh, *VP*
EMP: 19 **EST:** 1993
SALES (est): 681.52K **Privately Held**
Web: www.beaconconcrete.com
SIC: 3273 Ready-mixed concrete

(P-5464)

BENDER READY MIX INC

Also Called: Bender Ready Mix Concrete
516 S Santa Fe St (92705-4142)
PHONE...............................714 560-0744
Sarah Bender, *CEO*
Greg Bender, *Pr*
EMP: 25 **EST:** 2007
SALES (est): 5.49MM **Privately Held**
Web: www.benderreadymix.com
SIC: 3273 Ready-mixed concrete

(P-5465)

CALIFORNIA COMMERCIAL ASP LLC

4211 Ponderosa Ave Ste C (92123-1665)
PHONE...............................858 513-0611
EMP: 19 **EST:** 2005
SALES (est): 320.24K **Privately Held**
Web: www.heidelbergmaterials.us
SIC: 3273 Ready-mixed concrete

(P-5466)

CALPORTLAND

2025 E Financial Way (91741-4692)
P.O. Box 567 (92276-0567)
PHONE...............................760 343-3403
Terri Stelter, *Pr*
Diane Sarauer, *VP*
Debra Rubenzer, *Sec*
EMP: 28 **EST:** 1973
SQ FT: 480
SALES (est): 981.29K **Privately Held**
Web: www.calportland.com
SIC: 3273 Ready-mixed concrete

(P-5467)

CALPORTLAND COMPANY

Also Called: Califrnia Prtland Cem Dispatch
1862 E 27th St (90058-1120)

PRODUCTS & SVCS

PHONE..............................800 272-1891
Basil Ortiz, *Brnch Mgr*
EMP: 19
Web: www.calportland.com
SIC: 3273 Ready-mixed concrete
HQ: Calportland Company
2025 E Financial Way
Glendora CA

(P-5468)
CAPITAL READY MIX INC
11311 Pendleton St (91352-1530)
PHONE..............................818 771-1122
Tigran Aneian, *CEO*
EMP: 32 **EST:** 2014
SALES (est): 7.59MM **Privately Held**
SIC: 3273 Ready-mixed concrete

(P-5469)
CATALINA PACIFIC CONCRETE
19030 Normandie Ave (90502-1009)
PHONE..............................310 532-4600
Patrick E Greene, *Pr*
EMP: 22 **EST:** 1969
SQ FT: 1,500
SALES (est): 186.46K **Privately Held**
SIC: 3273 Ready-mixed concrete

(P-5470)
CEMEX CEMENT INC
25220 Black Mountain Quarry Rd
(92307-9341)
PHONE..............................760 381-7616
Luis Lopez, *Brnch Mgr*
EMP: 200
SIC: 3273 Ready-mixed concrete
HQ: Cemex Cement, Inc.
10100 Katy Fwy Ste 300
Houston TX
713 650-6200

(P-5471)
CEMEX CNSTR MTLS PCF LLC
Also Called: Readymix -Redlands Rm Dual
8203 Alabama Ave (92346-4255)
PHONE..............................909 335-3105
Erick Garcia, *Brnch Mgr*
EMP: 17
SIC: 3273 Ready-mixed concrete
HQ: Cemex Construction Materials Pacific,
Llc
1501 Belvedere Rd
West Palm Beach FL
561 833-5555

(P-5472)
CEMEX MATERIALS LLC
1205 S Rancho Ave (92324-3343)
PHONE..............................909 825-1500
Lindsey Hank, *Mgr*
EMP: 90
SIC: 3273 Ready-mixed concrete
HQ: Cemex Materials Llc
1720 Centrepark Dr E # 100
West Palm Beach FL
561 833-5555

(P-5473)
**CONCRETE HOLDING CO CAL
INC**
15821 Ventura Blvd Ste 475 (91436-2915)
PHONE..............................818 788-4228
Don Unmacht, *Pr*
Dominique Bidet, *
EMP: 919 **EST:** 1988
SQ FT: 4,000
SALES (est): 9.79MM
SALES (corp-wide): 564.52MM **Privately
Held**

SIC: 3273 Ready-mixed concrete
HQ: National Cement Company, Inc.
15821 Ventura Blvd # 475
Encino CA
818 728-5200

(P-5474)
**CORONET CONCRETE
PRODUCTS INC (PA)**
Also Called: Desert Redi Mix
83801 Avenue 45 (92201-3311)
PHONE..............................760 398-2441
James Richert, *CEO*
EMP: 22 **EST:** 1982
SQ FT: 2,000
SALES (est): 8.32MM
SALES (corp-wide): 8.32MM **Privately
Held**
SIC: 3273 3272 Ready-mixed concrete;
Concrete products, nec

(P-5475)
CPC SERVICES INC
2025 E Financial Way Ste 200 (91741)
PHONE..............................626 852-6200
James Repman, *Pr*
EMP: 21 **EST:** 2002
SALES (est): 694.43K **Privately Held**
SIC: 3273 Ready-mixed concrete

(P-5476)
DIVERSIFIED MINERALS INC
Also Called: Dmi Ready Mix
1100 Mountain View Ave Ste F
(93030-7213)
PHONE..............................805 247-1069
James W Price, *Pr*
Sharron Price, *
▲ **EMP:** 44 **EST:** 1990
SQ FT: 44,482
SALES (est): 9.34MM **Privately Held**
Web: www.dmicement.com
SIC: 3273 4013 3531 3241 Ready-mixed
concrete; Railroad terminals; Bituminous,
cement and concrete related products and
equip.; Pozzolana cement

(P-5477)
GARY BALE REDI-MIX CON INC
16131 Construction Cir W (92606-4410)
PHONE..............................949 786-9441
Kyle Goerlitz, *CEO*
EMP: 80 **EST:** 1968
SALES (est): 9.66MM **Privately Held**
Web: www.garybaleredimix.com
SIC: 3273 Ready-mixed concrete

(P-5478)
GIBBEL BROS INC
Also Called: True Cast Concrete Products
11145 Tuxford St (91352-2632)
PHONE..............................323 875-1367
Gregory Gibbel, *Pr*
EMP: 17 **EST:** 1965
SQ FT: 1,500
SALES (est): 780.41K **Privately Held**
SIC: 3273 3271 Ready-mixed concrete;
Blocks, concrete or cinder: standard

(P-5479)
GIBSON & SCHAEFER INC (PA)
1126 Rock Wood Rd (92249)
P.O. Box 1539 (92249-1539)
PHONE..............................619 352-3535
Don Gibson, *Pr*
P M Schaefer, *
Maria Schaefer, *
Rhoberta Gibson, *
EMP: 50 **EST:** 1989
SQ FT: 1,440

SALES (est): 9.28MM **Privately Held**
Web: www.gibsonandschaeferinc.com
SIC: 3273 5032 Ready-mixed concrete;
Gravel

(P-5480)
**HEIDELBERG MTLS STHWEST
AGG LL**
Also Called: HEIDELBERG MATERIALS
SOUTHWEST AGG LLC
1050 S Prairie Ave (90301-4120)
PHONE..............................310 419-1520
Rick Baedeker, *Brnch Mgr*
EMP: 50
SALES (corp-wide): 21.19B **Privately Held**
Web: www.heidelbergmaterials.us
SIC: 3273 Ready-mixed concrete
HQ: Hanson Aggregates Llc
8505 Freport Pkwy Ste 500
Irving TX
469 417-1200

(P-5481)
HI-GRADE MATERIALS CO
6500 E Avenue T (93543-1722)
P.O. Box 1050 (93543-1050)
PHONE..............................661 533-3100
Rod Elderton, *Mgr*
EMP: 88
SALES (corp-wide): 63.93MM **Privately
Held**
Web: www.robar.com
SIC: 3273 Ready-mixed concrete
HQ: Hi-Grade Materials Co.
17671 Bear Valley Rd
Hesperia CA
760 244-9325

(P-5482)
HOLLIDAY ROCK TRUCKING INC
Also Called: HOLLIDAY ROCK TRUCKING
INC
2300 W Base Line St (92410-1002)
PHONE..............................888 273-2200
Frederick N Holliday, *Brnch Mgr*
EMP: 60
SALES (corp-wide): 5.03MM **Privately
Held**
Web: www.hollidayrock.com
SIC: 3273 Ready-mixed concrete
PA: Holliday Trucking Inc.
1401 N Benson Ave
Upland CA
909 982-1553

(P-5483)
HOLLIDAY TRUCKING INC (PA)
1401 N Benson Ave (91786-2166)
PHONE..............................909 982-1553
Frederick N Holliday, *Pr*
Penny Holliday, *
John Holliday, *
Ronald Chambers, *
EMP: 60 **EST:** 1964
SQ FT: 2,000
SALES (est): 5.03MM
SALES (corp-wide): 5.03MM **Privately
Held**
Web: www.hollidayrock.com
SIC: 3273 4212 Ready-mixed concrete;
Local trucking, without storage

(P-5484)
JP GUNITE INC
9458 New Colt Ct (92021-2323)
PHONE..............................619 938-0228
Juan Padilla, *Pr*
EMP: 20 **EST:** 1990
SALES (est): 1.87MM **Privately Held**
Web: www.jpgunite.com

SIC: 3273 Ready-mixed concrete

(P-5485)
LEBATA INC
Also Called: A & A Ready Mix Concrete
4621 Teller Ave Ste 130 (92660-2165)
PHONE..............................949 253-2800
Kurt Caillier, *Pr*
EMP: 30 **EST:** 1987
SALES (est): 4.98MM **Privately Held**
SIC: 3273 Ready-mixed concrete

(P-5486)
MOUNTAIN MATERIALS INC
1117 Tavern Rd (91901-3817)
PHONE..............................619 445-4150
Daniel Shea, *Pr*
Michele Bracco, *CFO*
Steve Finch, *VP*
EMP: 21 **EST:** 1998
SALES (est): 9.45MM **Privately Held**
Web: www.mountainmaterialsinc.com
SIC: 3273 Ready-mixed concrete

(P-5487)
**NATIONAL CEMENT CO CAL INC
(DH)**
15821 Ventura Blvd Ste 475 (91436-2935)
PHONE..............................818 728-5200
Steven Weiss, *Pr*
Pragati Kapoor, *CFO*
Dominique Bidet, *VP*
▲ **EMP:** 37 **EST:** 1987
SQ FT: 12,000
SALES (est): 270.38MM
SALES (corp-wide): 564.52MM **Privately
Held**
Web: www.nationalcement.com
SIC: 3273 Ready-mixed concrete
HQ: National Cement Company, Inc.
15821 Ventura Blvd # 475
Encino CA
818 728-5200

(P-5488)
**NATIONAL CEMENT COMPANY
INC**
2626 E 26th St (90058-1218)
PHONE..............................323 923-4466
EMP: 17
SALES (corp-wide): 564.52MM **Privately
Held**
Web: www.nationalcement.com
SIC: 3273 Ready-mixed concrete
HQ: National Cement Company, Inc.
15821 Ventura Blvd # 475
Encino CA
818 728-5200

(P-5489)
NATIONAL READY MIX
15821 Ventura Blvd Ste 475 (91436-4778)
PHONE..............................818 728-5200
Edward I Doucette, *Prin*
EMP: 17 **EST:** 2011
SALES (est): 2.41MM **Privately Held**
Web: www.nationalcement.com
SIC: 3273 Ready-mixed concrete

(P-5490)
**NATIONAL READY MIXED CON
CO (DH)**
Also Called: National Cement Ready Mix
15821 Ventura Blvd Ste 475 (91436-4778)
PHONE..............................818 728-5200
Tim Toland, *CEO*
Don Unmacht, *VP*
▲ **EMP:** 20 **EST:** 1946
SQ FT: 40,000

SALES (est): 45.33MM
SALES (corp-wide): 564.52MM **Privately Held**
Web: www.nrmcc.com
SIC: 3273 Ready-mixed concrete
HQ: National Cement Company Of California, Inc.
15821 Ventura Blvd # 475
Encino CA
818 728-5200

(P-5491)
PACIFIC AGGREGATES INC
28251 Lake St (92530-1635)
PHONE..............................951 245-2460
Kai Chin, *CEO*
Dale Kline, *
▲ **EMP:** 75 **EST:** 2002
SQ FT: 1,000
SALES (est): 12.66MM
SALES (corp-wide): 372.87MM **Privately Held**
Web: www.pacificaggregates.com
PA: Castle & Cooke, Inc.
10000 Stockdale Hwy # 300
Bakersfield CA
818 879-6700

(P-5492)
PUENTE READY MIX SERVICES INC (PA)
209 N California Ave (91744-4324)
P.O. Box 3345 (91744-0345)
PHONE..............................626 968-0711
TOLL FREE: 800
Mark Keuning, *Ch Bd*
Ronald A Biang, *
Kevin Keuning, *
Marcia Biang, *
EMP: 22 **EST:** 1949
SQ FT: 5,000
SALES (est): 6.03MM
SALES (corp-wide): 6.03MM **Privately Held**
Web: www.puentereadymix.com
SIC: 3273 Ready-mixed concrete

(P-5493)
RANCHO READY MIX
28251 Lake St (92530-1635)
PHONE..............................951 674-0488
William Summers, *Pr*
Mal Gatherer, *
EMP: 36 **EST:** 1976
SQ FT: 1,000
SALES (est): 3.33MM **Privately Held**
Web: www.ieranchoreadymix.com
SIC: 3273 Ready-mixed concrete

(P-5494)
ROBAR ENTERPRISES INC (PA)
17671 Bear Valley Rd (92345-4902)
PHONE..............................760 244-5456
Jonathan D Hove, *CEO*
Robert E Hove, *
Al Calvanico, *
EMP: 150 **EST:** 1981
SQ FT: 26,000
SALES (est): 63.93MM
SALES (corp-wide): 63.93MM **Privately Held**
Web: www.robar.com
SIC: 3273 5051 3441 Ready-mixed concrete ; Steel; Building components, structural steel

(P-5495)
ROBERTSONS RDYMX LTD A CAL LTD (HQ)

Also Called: Robertson's
200 S Main St Ste 200 (92882-2212)
P.O. Box 3600 (92878-3600)
PHONE..............................951 493-6500
TOLL FREE: 800
Jon Troesh, *Pt*
Greg Edwards, *
▲ **EMP:** 85 **EST:** 1991
SQ FT: 22,008
SALES (est): 511.78MM **Privately Held**
Web: www.rrmca.com
SIC: 3273 3531 5032 2951 Ready-mixed concrete; Bituminous, cement and concrete related products and equip.; Asphalt mixture ; Asphalt paving mixtures and blocks
PA: Mitsubishi Materials Corporation
3-2-3, Marunouchi
Chiyoda-Ku TKY

(P-5496)
ROBERTSONS RDYMX LTD A CAL LTD
27401 3rd St (92346-4242)
PHONE..............................909 425-2930
EMP: 106
Web: www.rrmca.com
SIC: 3273 Ready-mixed concrete
HQ: Robertson's Ready Mix, Ltd., A California Limited Partnership
200 S Main St Ste 200 # 200
Corona CA
951 493-6500

(P-5497)
ROBERTSONS READY MIX LTD
9635 C Ave (92345-6047)
PHONE..............................760 244-7239
EMP: 94
Web: www.rrmca.com
SIC: 3273 Ready-mixed concrete
HQ: Robertson's Ready Mix, Ltd., A California Limited Partnership
200 S Main St Ste 200 # 200
Corona CA
951 493-6500

(P-5498)
ROBERTSONS READY MIX LTD
Also Called: Miramar Plant 33
5692 Eastgate Dr (92121-2816)
PHONE..............................800 834-7557
EMP: 100
Web: www.rrmca.com
SIC: 3273 Ready-mixed concrete
HQ: Robertson's Ready Mix, Ltd., A California Limited Partnership
200 S Main St Ste 200 # 200
Corona CA
951 493-6500

(P-5499)
ROBERTSONS READY MIX LTD
1310 Simpson Way (92029-1377)
PHONE..............................951 685-4600
EMP: 88
Web: www.rrmca.com
SIC: 3273 Ready-mixed concrete
HQ: Robertson's Ready Mix, Ltd., A California Limited Partnership
200 S Main St Ste 200 # 200
Corona CA
951 493-6500

(P-5500)
ROBERTSONS READY MIX LTD
7900 Moss Ave (93505-4311)
PHONE..............................760 373-4815
EMP: 94
Web: www.rrmca.com

SIC: 3273 Ready-mixed concrete
HQ: Robertson's Ready Mix, Ltd., A California Limited Partnership
200 S Main St Ste 200 # 200
Corona CA
951 493-6500

(P-5501)
RWH INC
Also Called: Holiday Transportation
15115 Oxnard St (91411-2615)
PHONE..............................818 782-2350
TOLL FREE: 800
EMP: 30 **EST:** 1964
SALES (est): 4.3MM **Privately Held**
Web: www.bonanzaconcrete.com
SIC: 3273 4212 Ready-mixed concrete; Local trucking, without storage

(P-5502)
SHORT LOAD CONCRETE INC
605 E Commercial St (92801-2511)
PHONE..............................714 524-7013
Ryan Van Derhook, *Pr*
EMP: 20 **EST:** 1996
SALES (est): 3.85MM **Privately Held**
Web: www.shortloadconcrete.com
SIC: 3273 Ready-mixed concrete

(P-5503)
SPRAGUES ROCK AND SAND COMPANY (PA)
Also Called: Spragues Ready Mix
230 Longden Ave (91706-1328)
PHONE..............................626 445-2125
Carole Cotter, *Ch Bd*
Michael Toland, *Pr*
Steven Toland, *VP*
Juli Paez, *Sec*
EMP: 22 **EST:** 1953
SQ FT: 2,100
SALES (est): 8.78MM
SALES (corp-wide): 8.78MM **Privately Held**
Web: www.srmconcrete.com
SIC: 3273 Ready-mixed concrete

(P-5504)
STANDARD CONCRETE PRODUCTS INC (HQ)
Also Called: Associated Ready Mix Concrete
13550 Live Oak Ln (91706-1318)
P.O. Box 15326 (92735-0326)
PHONE..............................310 829-4537
David Hummel, *Pr*
Brian Serra, *VP*
EMP: 20 **EST:** 1986
SQ FT: 2,400
SALES (est): 27.39MM
SALES (corp-wide): 84.61MM **Privately Held**
Web: www.standard-concrete.com
SIC: 3273 Ready-mixed concrete
PA: A & A Ready Mixed Concrete, Inc.
4621 Teller Ave Ste 130
Newport Beach CA
949 253-2800

(P-5505)
STATE READY MIX INC
3127 Los Angeles Ave (93036-1010)
PHONE..............................805 647-2817
Robert Lynch, *Pr*
EMP: 19
SALES (corp-wide): 5.63MM **Privately Held**
Web: www.statereadymix.com
SIC: 3273 Ready-mixed concrete
PA: State Ready Mix, Inc.
1011 Azahar St Ste 1

Ventura CA
805 647-2817

(P-5506)
STATE READY MIX INC (PA)
1011 Azahar St Ste 1 (93004)
PHONE..............................805 647-2817
Russell Cochran, *CEO*
Robert A Lynch, *
EMP: 21 **EST:** 1988
SALES (est): 5.63MM
SALES (corp-wide): 5.63MM **Privately Held**
Web: www.statereadymix.com
SIC: 3273 Ready-mixed concrete

(P-5507)
SUPERIOR READY MIX CONCRETE LP
Also Called: Superior Ready Mix Concrete
24635 Temescal Canyon Rd (92883-5422)
PHONE..............................951 277-3553
Justine Moss, *Brnch Mgr*
EMP: 71
SALES (corp-wide): 205.26MM **Privately Held**
Web: superiorrm.cloudflareaccess.com
SIC: 3273 Ready-mixed concrete
PA: Superior Ready Mix Concrete L.P.
1564 Mission Rd
Escondido CA
760 745-0556

(P-5508)
SUPERIOR READY MIX CONCRETE LP
Also Called: Hemet Ready Mix
1130 N State St (92543-1510)
PHONE..............................951 658-9225
Wayne Heckerman, *Prin*
EMP: 71
SALES (corp-wide): 205.26MM **Privately Held**
Web: superiorrm.cloudflareaccess.com
SIC: 3273 5211 Ready-mixed concrete; Masonry materials and supplies
PA: Superior Ready Mix Concrete L.P.
1564 Mission Rd
Escondido CA
760 745-0556

(P-5509)
SUPERIOR READY MIX CONCRETE LP
Also Called: Superior Ready Mix Concrete
72270 Varner Rd (92276-3341)
PHONE..............................760 343-3418
Mark Higgins, *Mgr*
EMP: 71
SALES (corp-wide): 205.26MM **Privately Held**
Web: superiorrm.cloudflareaccess.com
SIC: 3273 Ready-mixed concrete
PA: Superior Ready Mix Concrete L.P.
1564 Mission Rd
Escondido CA
760 745-0556

(P-5510)
SUPERIOR READY MIX CONCRETE LP (PA)
Also Called: Southland Ready Mix Concrete
1564 Mission Rd (92029-1194)
PHONE..............................760 745-0556
Donald Lee, *Pr*
EMP: 50 **EST:** 1957
SALES (est): 205.26MM
SALES (corp-wide): 205.26MM **Privately Held**

Web: superiorrm.cloudflareaccess.com
SIC: **3273** 1611 5032 Ready-mixed concrete
; Surfacing and paving; Gravel

(P-5511)
SUPERIOR READY MIX CONCRETE LP
Also Called: Srm Contracting & Paving
7192 Mission Gorge Rd (92120-1131)
PHONE.................................619 265-0955
Brent Cooper, *Brnch Mgr*
EMP: 70
SALES (corp-wide): 205.26MM **Privately Held**
Web: superiorrm.cloudflareaccess.com
SIC: **3273** Ready-mixed concrete
PA: Superior Ready Mix Concrete L.P.
1564 Mission Rd
Escondido CA
760 745-0556

(P-5512)
SUPERIOR READY MIX CONCRETE LP
Also Called: Canyon Rock & Asphalt
7500 Mission Gorge Rd (92120-1304)
PHONE.................................619 265-0296
Tracy Mall, *Mgr*
EMP: 70
SALES (corp-wide): 205.26MM **Privately Held**
Web: superiorrm.cloudflareaccess.com
SIC: **3273** Ready-mixed concrete
PA: Superior Ready Mix Concrete L.P.
1564 Mission Rd
Escondido CA
760 745-0556

(P-5513)
SUPERIOR READY MIX CONCRETE LP
Also Called: American Ready Mix
1564 Mission Rd (92029-1194)
PHONE.................................760 728-1128
Greg Sage, *Mgr*
EMP: 71
SALES (corp-wide): 205.26MM **Privately Held**
SIC: **3273** 1442 Ready-mixed concrete;
Construction sand and gravel
PA: Superior Ready Mix Concrete L.P.
1564 Mission Rd
Escondido CA
760 745-0556

(P-5514)
SUPERIOR READY MIX CONCRETE LP
Also Called: TTT Concrete
12494 Highway 67 (92040-1133)
PHONE.................................619 443-7510
Jerry Anderson, *Mgr*
EMP: 71
SQ FT: 3,200
SALES (corp-wide): 205.26MM **Privately Held**
Web: superiorrm.cloudflareaccess.com
SIC: **3273** Ready-mixed concrete
PA: Superior Ready Mix Concrete L.P.
1564 Mission Rd
Escondido CA
760 745-0556

(P-5515)
SUPERIOR READY MIX CONCRETE LP
802 E Main St (92243-9474)
P.O. Box 400 (92244-0400)
PHONE.................................760 352-4341

Donald Lee, *Brnch Mgr*
EMP: 70
SALES (corp-wide): 205.26MM **Privately Held**
Web: superiorrm.cloudflareaccess.com
SIC: **3273** Ready-mixed concrete
PA: Superior Ready Mix Concrete L.P.
1564 Mission Rd
Escondido CA
760 745-0556

(P-5516)
TROESH READYMIX INC
2280 Hutton Rd (93444-9448)
PHONE.................................805 928-3764
Steve Troesh, *Pr*
Renee Troesh, *
EMP: 28 **EST:** 1984
SALES (est): 1.76MM **Privately Held**
Web: www.troeshcoleman.com
SIC: **3273** Ready-mixed concrete

(P-5517)
VULCAN MATERIALS CO
849 W Washington Ave (92025-1634)
PHONE.................................760 737-3486
TOLL FREE: 800
A F Gerstell, *Pr*
EMP: 266 **EST:** 1957
SALES (est): 4.08MM **Publicly Held**
SIC: **3273** Ready-mixed concrete
HQ: Calmat Co.
500 N Brand Blvd Ste 500 # 500
Glendale CA
818 553-8821

(P-5518)
WERNER CORPORATION
Also Called: Foster Sand & Gravel
25050 Maitri Rd (92883-5105)
P.O. Box 77850 (92877-0128)
PHONE.................................951 277-4586
Mark Miller, *Mgr*
EMP: 20
SALES (corp-wide): 16.31MM **Privately Held**
Web: www.wernercorp.net
SIC: **3273** Ready-mixed concrete
PA: Werner Corporation
25555 Maitri Rd
Corona CA
951 277-3900

(P-5519)
WESTWOOD BUILDING MATERIALS CO
15708 Inglewood Ave (90260-2544)
PHONE.................................310 643-9158
Craig St John, *Pr*
Liza Peitzmeier, *
EMP: 36 **EST:** 1941
SQ FT: 23,500
SALES (est): 9.86MM **Privately Held**
Web: www.westwoodbm.com
SIC: **3273** Ready-mixed concrete

3275 Gypsum Products

(P-5520)
PABCO BUILDING PRODUCTS LLC
Also Called: Pabco Paper
4460 Pacific Blvd (90058-2206)
PHONE.................................323 581-6113
Mike Willoughby, *Brnch Mgr*
EMP: 107
SALES (corp-wide): 1.19B **Privately Held**
Web: www.pabcopaper.com

SIC: **3275** Gypsum products
HQ: Pabco Building Products, Llc
10600 White Rock Rd Ste 1
Rancho Cordova CA
510 792-1577

(P-5521)
PROFORM FINISHING PRODUCTS LLC
1850 Pier B St (90813-2604)
P.O. Box 1888 (90801-1888)
PHONE.................................562 435-4465
Tim Fout, *Mgr*
EMP: 39
SALES (corp-wide): 795.88MM **Privately Held**
Web: www.nationalgypsum.com
SIC: **3275** Gypsum products
HQ: Proform Finishing Products, Llc
2001 Rexford Rd
Charlotte NC

(P-5522)
UNITED STATES GYPSUM COMPANY
401 Van Ness Ave (90501-1422)
PHONE.................................908 232-8900
Matt Craig, *Mgr*
EMP: 100
SQ FT: 71,800
SALES (corp-wide): 14.2B **Privately Held**
Web: www.usg.com
SIC: **3275** Gypsum products
HQ: United States Gypsum Company
550 W Adams St Ste 1300
Chicago IL
312 606-4000

(P-5523)
UNITED STATES GYPSUM COMPANY
3810 Evan Hewes Hwy (92251-9529)
P.O. Box 2450 (92244-2450)
PHONE.................................760 358-3200
George Keelan, *Dir Fin*
EMP: 99
SALES (corp-wide): 14.2B **Privately Held**
Web: www.usg.com
SIC: **3275** Gypsum products
HQ: United States Gypsum Company
550 W Adams St Ste 1300
Chicago IL
312 606-4000

3281 Cut Stone And Stone Products

(P-5524)
AMERICAN MARBLE & ONYX CO INC
10321 S La Cienega Blvd (90045-6109)
PHONE.................................323 776-0900
TOLL FREE: 800
Frederick Gherardi, *Pr*
Susan Gibbs, *Treas*
Steve Gherardi, *VP*
▲ **EMP:** 19 **EST:** 1933
SQ FT: 30,000
SALES (est): 774.27K **Privately Held**
Web: www.americanmarble.us
SIC: **3281** 1743 Marble, building: cut and
shaped; Marble installation, interior

(P-5525)
BEST-WAY MARBLE & TILE CO INC
Also Called: Best Way Marble
5037 Telegraph Rd (90022-4922)

PHONE.................................323 266-6794
Shelley Herrera, *Pr*
◆ **EMP:** 28 **EST:** 1981
SQ FT: 16,000
SALES (est): 2.45MM **Privately Held**
Web: www.bestwaymarble.com
SIC: **3281** 1743 Table tops, marble; Marble
installation, interior

(P-5526)
CARNEVALE & LOHR INC
6521 Clara St (90201-5634)
PHONE.................................562 927-8311
Louie Carnevale, *CEO*
Edmund B Lohr Iv, *Prin*
David Carnevale, *
Michael Carnevale, *
▲ **EMP:** 70 **EST:** 1958
SALES (est): 4.01MM **Privately Held**
Web: www.carnevaleandlohr.com
SIC: **3281** 1741 Cut stone and stone
products; Marble masonry, exterior
construction

(P-5527)
COAST FLAGSTONE CO
1810 Colorado Ave (90404-3412)
PHONE.................................310 829-4010
Timothy Wang, *Owner*
EMP: 70 **EST:** 2010
SALES (est): 4.93MM **Privately Held**
Web: www.bourgetbros.com
SIC: **3281** Flagstones

(P-5528)
CORTIMA CO
83778 Avenue 45 (92201-3310)
PHONE.................................760 347-5535
Franz P Jevne Iii, *Pr*
EMP: 17 **EST:** 1976
SQ FT: 23,000
SALES (est): 561.97K **Privately Held**
Web: www.cortima.com
SIC: **3281** Marble, building: cut and shaped

(P-5529)
KAMMERER ENTERPRISES INC
Also Called: American Marble
1280 N Melrose Dr (92083-3469)
PHONE.................................760 560-0550
William S Kammerer, *CEO*
Bill Kammerer, *
Karl Miethke, *
▲ **EMP:** 100 **EST:** 1985
SALES (est): 15.21MM **Privately Held**
SIC: **3281** Curbing, granite or stone

(P-5530)
L&S STONE LLC (DH)
Also Called: L & S Stone and Fireplace Shop
1370 Grand Ave Ste B (92078-2404)
PHONE.................................760 736-3232
◆ **EMP:** 50 **EST:** 1970
SQ FT: 35,000
SALES (est): 15.99MM **Privately Held**
SIC: **3281** Cut stone and stone products
HQ: Eldorado Stone Llc
3817 Ocean Ranch Blvd # 114
Oceanside CA
800 925-1491

(P-5531)
LUX LLC
5206 Phisto Pl (93313-5853)
PHONE.................................661 479-2926
EMP: 28
SALES (corp-wide): 62.17K **Privately Held**
SIC: **3281** Granite, cut and shaped
PA: Lux Llc
3207 W Shields Ave

Fresno CA

(P-5532)

RUGGERI MARBLE AND GRANITE INC
25028 Vermont Ave (90710-3116)
PHONE..............................310 513-2155
Andre Ruggeri, *Pr*
Robert Ruggeri, *
◆ **EMP:** 80 **EST:** 1991
SALES (est): 3.94MM **Privately Held**
Web: www.ruggerimarble.com
SIC: 3281 5032 Marble, building: cut and shaped; Ceramic wall and floor tile, nec

(P-5533)

SAMPLE TILE AND STONE INC
1410 Richardson St (92408-2962)
PHONE..............................951 776-8562
EMP: 45 **EST:** 2011
SQ FT: 13,500
SALES (est): 6.07MM **Privately Held**
Web: www.sampletileandstone.com
SIC: 3281 5032 1411 1743 Cut stone and stone products; Limestone; Limestone and marble dimension stone; Terrazzo, tile, marble and mosaic work

(P-5534)

SIX ELEVEN LIMITED INC
11921 Sherman Way (91605-3726)
PHONE..............................818 764-5810
George Gruber, *Pr*
Mort Braustein, *Prin*
EMP: 18 **EST:** 1986
SALES (est): 219.65K **Privately Held**
SIC: 3281 Bathroom fixtures, cut stone

(P-5535)

STANDRIDGE GRANITE CORPORATION
9437 Santa Fe Springs Rd (90670-2684)
PHONE..............................562 946-6334
Deborah Deleon, *Pr*
EMP: 30 **EST:** 1965
SQ FT: 24,000
SALES (est): 4.83MM **Privately Held**
Web: www.standridgegranite.com
SIC: 3281 1411 Granite, cut and shaped; Dimension stone

(P-5536)

SULLIVANS STONE FACTORY INC
83778 Avenue 45 (92201-3310)
PHONE..............................760 347-5535
Robert J Sullivan, *Pr*
▲ **EMP:** 25 **EST:** 2004
SALES (est): 2.41MM **Privately Held**
Web: www.sullivansstonefactory.com
SIC: 3281 Granite, cut and shaped

(P-5537)

WESTLAKE ROYAL STONE LLC
3817 Ocean Ranch Blvd (92056-8607)
PHONE..............................800 255-1727
Michael Mildenhall, *Managing Member*
EMP: 85 **EST:** 2006
SALES (est): 6.59MM **Publicly Held**
Web: www.elevatewithstone.com
SIC: 3281 Building stone products
HQ: Westlake Pipe & Fittings Corporation
2801 Post Oak Blvd # 600
Houston TX

3291 Abrasive Products

(P-5538)

BUFF AND SHINE MFG INC
2139 E Del Amo Blvd (90220-6301)
PHONE..............................310 886-5111
Richard Umbrell, *Pr*
Elizabeth Umbrell, *
◆ **EMP:** 40 **EST:** 1987
SQ FT: 25,792
SALES (est): 8.71MM **Privately Held**
Web: www.buffandshine.com
SIC: 3291 Buffing or polishing wheels, abrasive or nonabrasive

(P-5539)

COLUMBIA STONE PRODUCTS
663 S Rancho Santa Fe Rd (92078-3973)
PHONE..............................760 737-3215
Faruk Delener, *Prin*
▲ **EMP:** 17 **EST:** 2010
SALES (est): 1.02MM **Privately Held**
Web: www.columbiastone.com
SIC: 3291 Silicon carbide abrasive

(P-5540)

CRATEX MANUFACTURING CO INC
Also Called: Cratex
328 Encinitas Blvd Ste 200 (92024-3723)
PHONE..............................760 942-2877
Allen R Mccasland, *CEO*
Barbara Mccasland, *Sec*
▲ **EMP:** 75 **EST:** 1946
SALES (est): 7.88MM **Privately Held**
Web: www.cratex.com
SIC: 3291 Wheels, grinding: artificial

(P-5541)

FALCON ABRASIVE MFG INC
5490 Brooks St (91763-4520)
P.O. Box 713 (91788-0713)
PHONE..............................909 598-3078
Steve De La Torre, *Pr*
Rosemarie De Latorre, *Sec*
▼ **EMP:** 19 **EST:** 1986
SQ FT: 6,900
SALES (est): 959.14K **Privately Held**
Web: www.falconabrasive.com
SIC: 3291 5085 Wheels, abrasive; Industrial supplies

(P-5542)

JASON INCORPORATED
Jackson Lea Division
13006 Philadelphia St Ste 305 (90601-4210)
PHONE..............................562 921-9821
Ron Locher, *Brnch Mgr*
EMP: 24
SQ FT: 30,000
SALES (corp-wide): 834.99MM **Privately Held**
Web: www.osborn.com
SIC: 3291 2273 3599 Buffing or polishing wheels, abrasive or nonabrasive; Automobile floor coverings, except rubber or plastic; Custom machinery
PA: Jason Incorporated
833 E Michigan St Ste 900
Milwaukee WI

(P-5543)

MAVERICK ABRASIVES CORPORATION
4340 E Miraloma Ave (92807-1886)
PHONE..............................714 854-9531
Rami Aryan, *Pr*

◆ **EMP:** 60 **EST:** 1997
SQ FT: 15,000
SALES (est): 9.83MM **Privately Held**
Web: www.maverickabrasives.com
SIC: 3291 Abrasive products

(P-5544)

SUPREME ABRASIVES
Also Called: Continental Machine Tool Co
1021 Fuller St (92701-4212)
PHONE..............................949 250-8644
William W Taylor, *CEO*
Robert Longman, *VP*
▲ **EMP:** 23 **EST:** 1958
SQ FT: 20,000
SALES (est): 2.45MM **Privately Held**
Web: www.continentalabrasives.com
SIC: 3291 Wheels, abrasive

(P-5545)

TECHNIFEX PRODUCTS LLC
25261 Rye Canyon Rd (91355-1203)
PHONE..............................661 294-3800
Joe Ortiz, *Pr*
▲ **EMP:** 25 **EST:** 1999
SALES (est): 4.87MM **Privately Held**
Web: www.technifex.com
SIC: 3291 Steel wool

(P-5546)

VIBRA FINISH CO (PA)
Also Called: Vibrahone
2220 Shasta Way (93065-1831)
PHONE..............................805 578-0033
Haskel Hall, *Pr*
Jerry Rindal, *VP*
▲ **EMP:** 20 **EST:** 1924
SQ FT: 41,000
SALES (est): 4.63MM
SALES (corp-wide): 4.63MM **Privately Held**
Web: www.vibrafinish.com
SIC: 3291 Abrasive products

(P-5547)

YEAGER ENTERPRISES CORP
Also Called: Pasco
7100 Village Dr (90621-2261)
PHONE..............................714 994-2040
Joseph O'mera, *CEO*
David M Yeager, *
Joan F Yeager, *
▲ **EMP:** 81 **EST:** 1920
SQ FT: 55,000
SALES (est): 8.86MM **Privately Held**
SIC: 3291 Abrasive products

3295 Minerals, Ground Or Treated

(P-5548)

3M COMPANY
Also Called: 3M
18750 Minnesota Rd (92881-4313)
PHONE..............................951 737-3441
Flees Peter, *Brnch Mgr*
EMP: 53
SALES (corp-wide): 34.23B **Publicly Held**
Web: www.3m.com
SIC: 3295 2952 Roofing granules; Asphalt felts and coatings
PA: 3m Company
3m Center
Saint Paul MN
651 733-1110

(P-5549)

DESICCARE INC
3406 Pomona Blvd (91768-3236)
PHONE..............................909 444-8272
Shaneen Aros, *CFO*
EMP: 22
Web: www.desiccare.com
SIC: 3295 Desiccants, clay: activated
PA: Desiccare, Inc.
3930 W Windmill Ln # 100
Las Vegas NV

(P-5550)

JON BROOKS INC (PA)
Also Called: Laguna Clay Company
14400 Lomitas Ave (91746-3018)
PHONE..............................626 330-0631
Jon Brooks, *Pr*
Laurie Brooks, *
◆ **EMP:** 100 **EST:** 1981
SQ FT: 117,000
SALES (est): 20.91MM
SALES (corp-wide): 20.91MM **Privately Held**
Web: www.lagunaclay.com
SIC: 3295 5085 Clay, ground or otherwise treated; Refractory material

(P-5551)

SGL TECHNIC LLC (DH)
Also Called: Inc Polycarbon
28176 Avenue Stanford (91355-1119)
PHONE..............................661 257-0500
Ken Mamon, *Pr*
Brian Green, *VP*
▲ **EMP:** 41 **EST:** 1967
SQ FT: 130,000
SALES (est): 13.74MM
SALES (corp-wide): 1.18B **Privately Held**
Web: www.sglcarbon.com
SIC: 3295 3624 Graphite, natural: ground, pulverized, refined, or blended; Carbon and graphite products
HQ: Sgl Carbon, Llc
10715 David Taylor Dr # 4
Charlotte NC
704 593-5100

3296 Mineral Wool

(P-5552)

C A SCHROEDER INC (PA)
Also Called: Casco Mfg
1318 1st St (91340-2804)
PHONE..............................818 365-9561
Susan A Knudsen, *CEO*
Clifford A Schroeder, *
EMP: 42 **EST:** 1969
SQ FT: 18,500
SALES (est): 7.17MM
SALES (corp-wide): 7.17MM **Privately Held**
Web: www.casco-flex.com
SIC: 3296 3585 3444 3433 Fiberglass insulation; Refrigeration and heating equipment; Sheet metalwork; Heating equipment, except electric

(P-5553)

CONSOLIDATED FIBRGLS PDTS CO
Also Called: Conglas
3801 Standard St (93308-5230)
PHONE..............................661 323-6026
Daron J Thomas, *CEO*
Jack Pfeffer, *
EMP: 60 **EST:** 1972
SQ FT: 20,000
SALES (est): 9.11MM **Privately Held**

SIC: 3296 Fiberglass insulation

(P-5554)
JOHNS MANVILLE CORPORATION
4301 Firestone Blvd (90280-3318)
PHONE..............................323 568-2220
EMP: 54
SALES (corp-wide): 302.09B **Publicly Held**
Web: www.jm.com
SIC: 3296 Mineral wool
HQ: Johns Manville Corporation
717 17th St Ste 800
Denver CO
303 978-2000

(P-5555)
KAINALU BLUE INC
4675 North Ave (92056-3511)
PHONE..............................760 806-6400
Robin Gray, *Pr*
EMP: 30 EST: 1965
SQ FT: 30,000
SALES (est): 5.1MM **Privately Held**
Web: www.lamvin.com
SIC: 3296 3275 Acoustical board and tile, mineral wool; Gypsum products

(P-5556)
LAMART CALIFORNIA INC
7560 Bristow Ct Ste C (92154-7428)
P.O. Box 1648 (07015-1648)
PHONE..............................973 772-6262
Steven Hirsh, *Pr*
Graeme Silbert, *CFO*
EMP: 20 EST: 2016
SALES (est): 3.81MM
SALES (corp-wide): 28.22MM **Privately Held**
Web: www.lamartcorp.com
SIC: 3296 Fiberglass insulation
PA: Lamart Corporation
16 Richmond St
Clifton NJ
973 772-6262

(P-5557)
ROCK STRUCTURES-RIP RAP
11126 Silverton Ct (92881-5626)
PHONE..............................951 371-1112
Antonio Paredes, *Owner*
EMP: 30 EST: 2003
SQ FT: 3,500
SALES (est): 4.47MM **Privately Held**
SIC: 3296 Insulation: rock wool, slag, and silica minerals

(P-5558)
SOUND SEAL INC
Lamvin
4675 North Ave (92056-3511)
PHONE..............................760 806-6400
Robin Gray, *Mgr*
EMP: 25
Web: www.soundseal.com
SIC: 3296 3275 Acoustical board and tile, mineral wool; Gypsum products
HQ: Sound Seal, Inc.
50 Almgren Dr
Agawam MA
413 789-1770

(P-5559)
UNITED STATES MINERAL PDTS CO
Also Called: Isolatek International
4062 Georgia Blvd (92407-1847)
PHONE..............................909 473-3027

Adrienne Bowen, *Brnch Mgr*
EMP: 28
SALES (corp-wide): 74.65MM **Privately Held**
Web: www.isolatek.com
SIC: 3296 Mineral wool insulation products
PA: United States Mineral Products Company Inc
41 Furnace St
Stanhope NJ
973 347-1200

(P-5560)
UPF CORPORATION
3747 Standard St (93308-5228)
PHONE..............................661 323-8227
Jack Pfeffer, *Pr*
▼ EMP: 18 EST: 1988
SALES (est): 919.19K **Privately Held**
Web: www.upfusa.com
SIC: 3296 Fiberglass insulation

3297 Nonclay Refractories

(P-5561)
SIMONS BRICK CORPORATION
4301 Firestone Blvd (90280-3318)
PHONE..............................951 279-1000
John Williams, *Pr*
EMP: 21 EST: 1989
SQ FT: 24,000
SALES (est): 1.67MM
SALES (corp-wide): 1.19B **Privately Held**
SIC: 3297 5211 Brick refractories; Brick
HQ: Basalite Building Products, Llc
2150 Douglas Blvd Ste 260
Roseville CA
707 678-1901

3299 Nonmetallic Mineral Products,

(P-5562)
3M TECHNICAL CERAMICS INC (HQ)
1922 Barranca Pkwy (92606-4826)
PHONE..............................949 862-9600
Joel P Moskowitz, *CEO*
Jerrold J Pellizzon, *Corporate Secretary**
Thomas A Cole, *
Terry M Hart, *
David P Reed, *Assistant Corporate Secretary**
◆ EMP: 78 EST: 1987
SQ FT: 99,000
SALES (est): 284.05MM
SALES (corp-wide): 34.23B **Publicly Held**
Web: www.ceradyne.com
SIC: 3299 3671 Ceramic fiber; Cathode ray tubes, including rebuilt
PA: 3m Company
3m Center
Saint Paul MN
651 733-1110

(P-5563)
3M TECHNICAL CERAMICS INC
17466 Daimler St (92614-5514)
PHONE..............................949 756-0642
Joel Moskowitz, *Brnch Mgr*
EMP: 29
SQ FT: 33,965
SALES (corp-wide): 34.23B **Publicly Held**
Web: www.ceradyne.com
SIC: 3299 3264 Ceramic fiber; Porcelain electrical supplies
HQ: 3m Technical Ceramics, Inc.
1922 Barranca Pkwy

Irvine CA
949 862-9600

(P-5564)
ALS GARDEN ART INC (PA)
311 W Citrus St (92324-1412)
PHONE..............................909 424-0221
Donald Bracci, *Pr*
EMP: 290 EST: 1949
SQ FT: 305,000
SALES (est): 17.07MM
SALES (corp-wide): 17.07MM **Privately Held**
Web: www.alsgardenart.com
SIC: 3299 3272 Statuary: gypsum, clay, papier mache, metal, etc.; Concrete products, nec

(P-5565)
BURLINGAME INDUSTRIES INC
Also Called: Eagle Roofing Products Co
2352 N Locust Ave (92377-5000)
PHONE..............................909 355-7000
Robert Burlingame, *Pr*
EMP: 109
SQ FT: 76,704
SALES (corp-wide): 95.73MM **Privately Held**
Web: www.eagleroofing.com
SIC: 3299 3272 2952 Tile, sand lime; Concrete products, nec; Asphalt felts and coatings
PA: Burlingame Industries, Incorporated
3546 N Riverside Ave
Rialto CA
909 355-7000

(P-5566)
CERADYNE ESK LLC
3169 Red Hill Ave M (92626-3419)
PHONE..............................714 549-0421
Joel P Moskowitz, *CEO*
Jason Smith, *CFO*
EMP: 105 EST: 2004
SALES (est): 10.96MM
SALES (corp-wide): 34.23B **Publicly Held**
SIC: 3299 Ceramic fiber
HQ: 3m Technical Ceramics, Inc.
1922 Barranca Pkwy
Irvine CA
949 862-9600

(P-5567)
FOUNDRY SERVICE & SUPPLIES INC
2029 S Parco Ave (91761-5700)
PHONE..............................909 284-5000
Curt Parnell, *CEO*
Joel Leathers, *
◆ EMP: 24 EST: 1962
SQ FT: 40,000
SALES (est): 4.57MM **Privately Held**
Web: www.foundryservice.com
SIC: 3299 Art goods: plaster of paris, papier mache, and scagliola

(P-5568)
HARRINGTON & SONS INC
Also Called: Storyland Studios
590 Crane St (92530-2737)
PHONE..............................951 674-0998
EMP: 20 EST: 1979
SALES (est): 2.2MM **Privately Held**
SIC: 3299 Ornamental and architectural plaster work

(P-5569)
JP WEAVER & COMPANY
941 Air Way (91201-3001)
PHONE..............................818 500-1740

Lenna Tyler Kast, *Pr*
EMP: 37 EST: 1914
SQ FT: 10,000
SALES (est): 2.16MM **Privately Held**
Web: www.jpweaver.com
SIC: 3299 2431 Moldings, architectural: plaster of paris; Millwork

(P-5570)
MERLEX STUCCO INC
Also Called: Merlex Stucco Mfg
2911 N Orange Olive Rd (92865-1699)
PHONE..............................877 547-8822
Steve Combs, *Pr*
◆ EMP: 20 EST: 1963
SQ FT: 30,000
SALES (est): 1.63MM **Privately Held**
Web: www.merlex.com
SIC: 3299 Stucco

(P-5571)
OMEGA PRODUCTS CORP
282 S Anita Dr 3rd Fl (92868-3308)
P.O. Box 1149 (92856-0149)
PHONE..............................714 935-0900
Todd Martin, *Mgr*
EMP: 39
SALES (corp-wide): 91.19MM **Privately Held**
Web: www.omega-products.com
SIC: 3299 Stucco
HQ: Omega Products Corp.
8111 Fruitridge Rd
Sacramento CA
916 635-3335

(P-5572)
OPAL SERVICE INC (PA)
282 S Anita Dr (92868-3308)
P.O. Box 1149 (92856-0149)
PHONE..............................714 935-0900
Kenneth R Thompson, *CEO*
▲ EMP: 30 EST: 1962
SQ FT: 1,200
SALES (est): 91.19MM
SALES (corp-wide): 91.19MM **Privately Held**
SIC: 3299 5031 5211 Stucco; Doors and windows; Lumber and other building materials

(P-5573)
PAREX USA INC (DH)
2150 Eastridge Ave (92507-0720)
PHONE..............................714 778-2266
Rodrigo Lacerda, *Pr*
◆ EMP: 30 EST: 1926
SALES (est): 118.03MM **Privately Held**
Web: www.parexusa.com
SIC: 3299 5031 Stucco; Building materials, interior
HQ: Sika France
84 Rue Edouard Vaillant
Le Bourget
149928000

(P-5574)
ROLLS-ROYCE HIGH TEMPERATURE COMPOSITES INC
Also Called: Rolls-Royce Htc
5730 Katella Ave (90630-5005)
PHONE..............................714 375-4085
EMP: 50 EST: 1992
SALES (est): 15.85MM
SALES (corp-wide): 16.28B **Privately Held**
SIC: 3299 Mica products

▲ = Import ▼ = Export
◆ = Import/Export

HQ: Rolls-Royce North America (Usa)
Holdings Co.
1900 Reston Metro Plz # 4
Reston VA
703 834-1700

3312 Blast Furnaces And Steel Mills

(P-5575)
2ND SOURCE WIRE & CABLE INC
Also Called: 2nd Source Wire & Cable
20445 E Walnut Dr N (91789-2918)
PHONE..............................714 482-2866
Donna Silvers, *Pr*
Danny Chargualaf, *
Cathy Moorhead, *
Lois Ginn, *
EMP: 65 EST: 1989
SALES (est): 10.18MM
SALES (corp-wide): 1.75B Privately Held
Web: www.2ndsourcewire.com
SIC: 3312 3399 Pipes and tubes; Brads: aluminum, brass, or other nonferrous metal or wire
HQ: Align Precision - Anaheim, Inc.
7100 Belgrave Ave
Garden Grove CA

(P-5576)
AMERICAN PLANT SERVICES INC (PA)
6242 N Paramount Blvd (90805-3714)
P.O. Box 727 (90801-0727)
PHONE..............................562 630-1773
George M Bragg, *Pr*
Mary-ann Pool, *Sec*
EMP: 24 EST: 1981
SALES (est): 4.79MM
SALES (corp-wide): 4.79MM Privately Held
SIC: 3312 Blast furnaces and steel mills

(P-5577)
ARTSONS MANUFACTURING COMPANY
11121 Garfield Ave (90280-7505)
PHONE..............................323 773-3469
Jeffery A Winders, *CEO*
Jeffrey A Winders, *
Steve Winders, *
Art L Winders, *
▲ EMP: 28 EST: 1958
SALES (est): 4.25MM Privately Held
Web: www.artsonswire.com
SIC: 3312 Wire products, steel or iron

(P-5578)
BORRMANN METAL CENTER
12790 Holly St (92509-2364)
PHONE..............................951 367-1510
EMP: 20
SALES (corp-wide): 598.85MM Privately Held
Web: www.borrmannmetals.com
SIC: 3312 Iron and steel products, hot-rolled
HQ: Borrmann Metal Center
110 W Olive Ave
Burbank CA
818 846-7171

(P-5579)
BROWN-PACIFIC INC
Also Called: B P W
13639 Bora Dr (90670-5010)
PHONE..............................562 921-3471
Ron R Nagele, *CEO*

Claudia Nagele, *
Kenneth Brown, *
EMP: 32 EST: 1967
SQ FT: 35,000
SALES (est): 4.56MM Privately Held
Web: www.brownpacific.com
SIC: 3312 3355 3357 3356 Bar, rod, and wire products; Wire, aluminum: made in rolling mills; Nonferrous wiredrawing and insulating; Nonferrous rolling and drawing, nec

(P-5580)
CALABASAS TMS CENTER
Also Called: CALABASAS TMS CENTER
2950 Sycamore Dr (93065-1232)
PHONE..............................805 261-0824
EMP: 51
SALES (corp-wide): 292.82K Privately Held
Web: www.calabasasbehavioralhealth.com
SIC: 3312 Blast furnaces and steel mills
PA: Calabasas Tms Center Inc.
23622 Calabasas Rd # 301
Calabasas CA
818 921-4300

(P-5581)
CALIFORNIA AMFORGE CORPORATION
Also Called: California Amforge
750 N Vernon Ave (91702-2231)
PHONE..............................626 334-4931
William Taylor, *Brnch Mgr*
EMP: 102
SQ FT: 20,000
SALES (corp-wide): 23.78MM Privately Held
Web: www.cal-amforge.com
SIC: 3312 3462 Forgings, iron and steel; Iron and steel forgings
PA: California Amforge Corporation
750 N Vernon Ave
Azusa CA
626 334-4931

(P-5582)
CALIFORNIA STEEL INDS INC
1 California Steel Way (92335)
PHONE..............................909 350-6300
EMP: 415
SALES (corp-wide): 41.51B Publicly Held
Web: www.californiasteel.com
SIC: 3312 3317 Slabs, steel; Pipes, wrought: welded, lock joint, or heavy riveted
HQ: California Steel Industries, Inc.
14000 San Bernardino Ave
Fontana CA
909 350-6300

(P-5583)
CALIFORNIA STEEL INDS INC (HQ)
Also Called: Si
14000 San Bernardino Ave (92335-5259)
P.O. Box 5080 (92334-5080)
PHONE..............................909 350-6300
Marcelo Botelho, *Pr*
Ricardo Bernardes, *Executive Commercial Vice President*
Brett Guge, *Executive Vice President Finance & Administration*
▲ EMP: 266 EST: 1983
SALES (est): 510.44MM
SALES (corp-wide): 41.51B Publicly Held
Web: www.californiasteel.com
SIC: 3312 3317 Slabs, steel; Pipes, wrought: welded, lock joint, or heavy riveted
PA: Nucor Corporation
1915 Rexford Rd Ste 400

Charlotte NC
704 366-7000

(P-5584)
CALPIPE INDUSTRIES LLC
923 Calpipe Rd (93060-9155)
PHONE..............................562 803-4388
Francisco Hernandez, *Prin*
EMP: 38
Web: www.atkore.com
SIC: 3312 Pipes and tubes
HQ: Calpipe Industries, Llc
16100 Lathrop Ave
Harvey IL

(P-5585)
CARTER HOLT HARVEY HOLDINGS
1230 Railroad St (92882-1837)
PHONE..............................951 272-8180
John Miller, *Pr*
EMP: 39 EST: 1994
SQ FT: 60,000
SALES (est): 2MM Privately Held
Web: www.decra.com
SIC: 3312 Blast furnaces and steel mills
HQ: Qeynos New Zealand Limited
173 Captain Springs Road
Auckland AUK

(P-5586)
CHAPALA IRON & MANUFACTURING
1301 Callens Rd (93003-5602)
PHONE..............................805 654-9803
Patrick Davis, *Owner*
EMP: 19 EST: 1973
SQ FT: 3,600
SALES (est): 2.4MM Privately Held
Web: www.chapalairon.com
SIC: 3312 3446 Blast furnaces and steel mills ; Architectural metalwork

(P-5587)
DESIGN SHAPES IN STEEL INC
10315 Rush St (91733-3341)
PHONE..............................626 579-2032
Peter Costruba Ii, *Pr*
EMP: 27 EST: 1979
SQ FT: 10,000
SALES (est): 998.86K Privately Held
Web: design-shapes-in-steel.business.site
SIC: 3312 3446 3444 Primary finished or semifinished shapes; Architectural metalwork; Sheet metalwork

(P-5588)
EASYFLEX INC
Also Called: Easy Flex
2700 N Main St Ste 800 (92705-6672)
PHONE..............................888 577-8999
Sunmin Kim Oh, *Pr*
◆ EMP: 25 EST: 2005
SALES (est): 6.56MM Privately Held
Web: www.easyflexusa.com
SIC: 3312 Stainless steel

(P-5589)
ENGENSE INC
Also Called: Dfndr Armor
2255 Pleasant Valley Rd Ste G (93012-8569)
PHONE..............................805 484-8317
David Fernandez, *Pr*
EMP: 17 EST: 2013
SALES (est): 2.27MM Privately Held
Web: www.engense.com
SIC: 3312 Armor plate

(P-5590)
HARDY FRAMES INC
Also Called: My Tech USA
250 Klug Cir (92878-5409)
PHONE..............................951 245-9525
Clifford Grant, *Brnch Mgr*
EMP: 100
SALES (corp-wide): 11.24MM Privately Held
Web: www.hardyframe.com
SIC: 3312 Stainless steel
PA: Hardy Frames, Inc.
555 S Promenade Ave # 104
Corona CA
805 477-0793

(P-5591)
INTERNATIONAL MFG TECH INC (DH)
Also Called: Nassco
2798 Harbor Dr (92113-3650)
PHONE..............................619 544-7741
Willam J Cuddy, *CEO*
James C Scott, *
▲ EMP: 57 EST: 1990
SALES (est): 47.05MM
SALES (corp-wide): 39.41B Publicly Held
SIC: 3312 3731 Structural and rail mill products; Shipbuilding and repairing
HQ: Nassco Holdings Incorporated
2798 Harbor Dr
San Diego CA

(P-5592)
LEXANI WHEEL CORPORATION
Also Called: Lexani
1121 Olympic Dr (92881-3391)
PHONE..............................951 808-4220
Frank J Hodges, *CEO*
◆ EMP: 33 EST: 1996
SQ FT: 35,000
SALES (est): 9.25MM Privately Held
Web: www.lexani.com
SIC: 3312 Wheels

(P-5593)
MAC PRODUCTS INC
Also Called: Mac Performance Exhaust
43214 Black Deer Loop Ste 113 (92590-3473)
PHONE..............................951 296-3077
Mack Jones Senior, *Pr*
Mack Jones Junior, *Sec*
▲ EMP: 29 EST: 1969
SQ FT: 56,000
SALES (est): 1.02MM Privately Held
SIC: 3312 3751 3714 Tubes, steel and iron; Motorcycles, bicycles and parts; Motor vehicle parts and accessories

(P-5594)
NIPPON STEEL TRDG AMERICAS INC
Also Called: Nsta Foods
3100 Bristol St Ste 525 (92626-3000)
PHONE..............................714 367-3910
EMP: 21
Web: www.nst-us.com
SIC: 3312 Blast furnaces and steel mills
HQ: Nippon Steel Trading Americas, Inc.
200 N Martingale Rd # 801
Schaumburg IL
847 882-6700

(P-5595)
PACIFIC TOLL PROCESSING INC
Also Called: P T P
24724 Wilmington Ave (90745-6127)

PRODUCTS & SVCS

PHONE..................310 952-4992
Anthony Camasta, *CEO*
Anthony J Camasta, *
Mark Proner, *
EMP: 30 **EST:** 1999
SQ FT: 101,000
SALES (est): 5.3MM **Privately Held**
Web: www.pacifictoll.com
SIC: 3312 4785 Structural and rail mill
products; Toll road operation

(P-5596)
PASO ROBLES TANK INC (HQ)
825 26th St (93446-1242)
P.O. Box 3229 (93447-3229)
PHONE..................805 227-1641
Shawn P Owens, *CEO*
Shane P Wombles, *
Eduardo Peralta, *
▲ **EMP:** 63 **EST:** 2000
SALES (est): 46.24MM
SALES (corp-wide): 61.08MM **Privately
Held**
Web: www.pasoroblestank.com
SIC: 3312 3443 Blast furnaces and steel mills
; Tanks, standard or custom fabricated:
metal plate
PA: Associated Construction And
Engineering, Inc.
23232 Peralta Dr Ste 206
Laguna Hills CA
949 455-2682

(P-5597)
PRICE INDUSTRIES INC
Also Called: International Iron Products
10883 Thornmint Rd (92127-2403)
PHONE..................858 673-4451
Kenneth Alan Price, *Pr*
Barbara Price, *
EMP: 75 **EST:** 1968
SQ FT: 4,000
SALES (est): 8.73MM **Privately Held**
Web: www.priceindustries.com
SIC: 3312 3441 1791 5072 Structural and
rail mill products; Fabricated structural metal
; Structural steel erection; Bolts, nuts, and
screws

(P-5598)
RSR STEEL FABRICATION INC
11040 I Ave (92345-5214)
PHONE..................760 244-2210
Hector Grijalva, *Pr*
Ruth Grijalva, *VP*
EMP: 27 **EST:** 1993
SQ FT: 12,000
SALES (est): 2.98MM **Privately Held**
SIC: 3312 Structural shapes and pilings,
steel

(P-5599)
RTM PRODUCTS INC
13120 Arctic Cir (90670-5508)
PHONE..................562 926-2400
Robert M Thierjung, *Prin*
EMP: 23 **EST:** 2007
SALES (est): 4.15MM **Privately Held**
Web: www.rtmproducts.com
SIC: 3312 Tool and die steel and alloys

(P-5600)
SAN DEGO PRCSION
MACHINING INC
9375 Ruffin Ct (92123-5304)
PHONE..................858 499-0379
William Matteson, *CEO*
EMP: 40 **EST:** 1971
SQ FT: 23,000
SALES (est): 5.08MM **Privately Held**

Web: www.sdpm.com
SIC: 3312 3599 Stainless steel; Machine
shop, jobbing and repair

(P-5601)
SEARING INDUSTRIES INC
Also Called: Searing Industries
8901 Arrow Rte (91730-4410)
P.O. Box 3059 (91729-3059)
PHONE..................909 948-3030
Lee Searing, *CEO*
Jim Searing, *Prin*
Mmargaret Cantu, *
◆ **EMP:** 120 **EST:** 1985
SQ FT: 265,000
SALES (est): 25.19MM **Privately Held**
Web: www.searingindustries.com
SIC: 3312 3317 Tubes, steel and iron; Steel
pipe and tubes

(P-5602)
SIMEC USA CORPORATION
Also Called: Pacific Steel
333 H St Ste 5000 (91910-5561)
PHONE..................619 474-7081
Sergio Vigil Gonzalez, *CEO*
Mario Moreno Cortez, *CFO*
Van Haynie, *Sec*
EMP: 20 **EST:** 2009
SALES (est): 12.39MM **Privately Held**
Web: www.gsimec.com.mx
SIC: 3312 Bars, iron: made in steel mills
HQ: Simec International 6, S.A. De C.V.
Av. Lazaro Cardenas No. 601 Edif.
A-3, Piso 4
Guadalajara JAL

(P-5603)
STATE PIPE & SUPPLY INC
Westcoast Pipe Lining Division
2180 N Locust Ave (92377-4166)
PHONE..................909 356-5670
Kenneth Walker, *Mgr*
EMP: 50
Web: www.statepipe.com
SIC: 3312 Blast furnaces and steel mills
HQ: State Pipe & Supply, Inc.
183 S Cedar Ave
Rialto CA
909 877-9999

(P-5604)
TAMCO (HQ)
Also Called: CMC Steel California
5425 Industrial Pkwy (92407-1803)
PHONE..................909 899-0660
Chia Yuan Wang, *CEO*
Harley Scardoelli, *
Vilmar Babot, *
◆ **EMP:** 50 **EST:** 1974
SALES (est): 58.2MM
SALES (corp-wide): 8.8B **Publicly Held**
Web: www.tamcocorp.com
SIC: 3312 Blast furnaces and steel mills
PA: Commercial Metals Company
6565 N Macarthur Blvd # 800
Irving TX
214 689-4300

(P-5605)
TUBE-LINE TECHNOLOGIES
340 Via El Centro (92058-1237)
PHONE..................951 834-3123
Andy Gilmour, *Prin*
Ken Hein, *Prin*
Tuan Le, *Prin*
EMP: 18 **EST:** 2021
SALES (est): 2.1MM **Privately Held**
Web: www.tube-linetechnologies.com

SIC: 3312 Tubes, steel and iron

(P-5606)
WAYNE TOOL & DIE CO
15853 Olden St (91342-1249)
PHONE..................818 364-1611
Kenneth E Ruggles, *Pr*
EMP: 20 **EST:** 1978
SQ FT: 1,200
SALES (est): 275.58K **Privately Held**
SIC: 3312 Tool and die steel

(P-5607)
WEST CAST STL PROC
HLDINGS LLC (PA)
13568 Vintage Pl (91710-5243)
PHONE..................909 393-8405
Erik Gamm, *CEO*
Ron Searcy, *Pr*
EMP: 25 **EST:** 2021
SALES (est): 64.22MM
SALES (corp-wide): 64.22MM **Privately
Held**
Web: www.steelcousa.com
SIC: 3312 6719 3444 5075 Stainless steel;
Investment holding companies, except
banks; Elbows, for air ducts, stovepipes,
etc.: sheet metal; Warm air heating and air
conditioning

(P-5608)
WHEEL AND TIRE CLUB INC
Also Called: Discounted Wheel Warehouse
1301 Burton St (92831-5212)
PHONE..................714 422-3505
Naeem Niamat, *Pr*
◆ **EMP:** 35 **EST:** 2013
SQ FT: 42,000
SALES (est): 5.66MM **Privately Held**
Web:
www.discountedwheelwarehouse.com
SIC: 3312 Locomotive wheels, rolled

3313 Electrometallurgical Products

(P-5609)
R D MATHIS COMPANY
2840 Gundry Ave (90755-1813)
P.O. Box 92916 (90809-2916)
PHONE..................562 426-7049
Robert Lumley, *Pr*
Kirk Bennett, *
Barbara Bennett, *
EMP: 25 **EST:** 1963
SQ FT: 10,000
SALES (est): 3.29MM **Privately Held**
Web: www.rdmathis.com
SIC: 3313 8711 3567 3443 Molybdenum
silicon, not made in blast furnaces;
Engineering services; Industrial furnaces
and ovens; Fabricated plate work (boiler
shop)

3315 Steel Wire And Related Products

(P-5610)
BARRETTE OUTDOOR LIVING
INC
1151 Palmyrita Ave (92507-1703)
PHONE..................800 336-2383
Rick Paulson, *Mgr*
EMP: 18
SALES (corp-wide): 32.72B **Privately Held**
Web: www.barretteoutdoorliving.com

SIC: 3315 Fence gates, posts, and fittings:
steel
HQ: Barrette Outdoor Living, Inc.
7830 Freeway Cir
Middleburg Heights OH
440 891-0790

(P-5611)
CAL STATE SITE SERVICES
4518 Industrial St (93063-3411)
PHONE..................800 499-5757
EMP: 20 **EST:** 2014
SALES (est): 2.28MM **Privately Held**
Web: www.rentfenceandtoilets.com
SIC: 3315 5099 3431 Fencing made in
wiredrawing plants; Toilets, portable;
Bathroom fixtures, including sinks

(P-5612)
DAVIS WIRE CORPORATION
(HQ)
5555 Irwindale Ave (91706-2046)
PHONE..................626 969-7651
Jim Baske, *Pr*
Emily Heisley, *
▲ **EMP:** 150 **EST:** 1927
SQ FT: 265,000
SALES (est): 103.6MM **Privately Held**
Web: www.daviswire.com
SIC: 3315 Wire, ferrous/iron
PA: The Heico Companies, L.L.C.
70 W Madison St Ste 5600
Chicago IL

(P-5613)
DAYTON SUPERIOR
CORPORATION
6001 20th St (92509-2030)
PHONE..................951 782-9517
Jeffrey Bokn, *Brnch Mgr*
EMP: 21
SALES (corp-wide): 69.06B **Privately Held**
Web: www.daytonsuperior.com
SIC: 3315 Steel wire and related products
HQ: Dayton Superior Corporation
1125 Byers Rd
Miamisburg OH
937 866-0711

(P-5614)
EAST WEST ENTERPRISES
Also Called: Service Chemicals
20545 Belshaw Ave (90746-3505)
PHONE..................310 632-9933
Eugene Livshin, *Pt*
Michael Goldenstein, *Prin*
EMP: 26 **EST:** 1990
SQ FT: 30,000
SALES (est): 954.46K **Privately Held**
SIC: 3315 Hangers (garment), wire

(P-5615)
HALSTEEL INC (DH)
4190 Santa Ana St Ste A (91761-1527)
P.O. Box 90100 (92427-1100)
PHONE..................909 937-1001
Rebecca Kalis, *Pr*
Ed Halstead, *VP*
Donald Halstead, *Treas*
EMP: 21 **EST:** 1996
SQ FT: 100,000
SALES (est): 1.99MM
SALES (corp-wide): 251.95MM **Privately
Held**
Web: www.treeisland.com
SIC: 3315 5051 Nails, steel: wire or cut; Nails
HQ: Tree Island Industries Ltd
3933 Boundary Rd
Richmond BC
604 524-3744

(P-5616)
HAMROCK INC
3019 Wilshire Blvd (90403-2301)
PHONE..................................562 944-0255
Stephen R Hamrock, *Prin*
Michael E Hamrock, *Prin*
▲ **EMP:** 250 **EST:** 1976
SALES (est): 23.72MM **Privately Held**
Web: www.hamrock.com
SIC: 3315 2542 3496 3317 Wire and
fabricated wire products; Racks,
merchandise display or storage: except
wood; Miscellaneous fabricated wire
products; Steel pipe and tubes

(P-5617)
HOGAN CO INC
2741 S Lilac Ave (92316-3213)
PHONE..................................909 421-0245
Kraig B Hogan, *Pr*
◆ **EMP:** 20 **EST:** 1939
SQ FT: 9,150
SALES (est): 4.16MM **Privately Held**
Web: www.hoganco.com
SIC: 3315 3531 Spikes, steel: wire or cut;
Bituminous, cement and concrete related
products and equip.

(P-5618)
INWESCO INCORPORATED (PA)
746 N Coney Ave (91702-2239)
PHONE..................................626 334-7115
David L Morris, *CEO*
EMP: 65 **EST:** 1967
SQ FT: 30,000
SALES (est): 24.06MM
SALES (corp-wide): 24.06MM **Privately
Held**
Web: www.inwesco.com
SIC: 3315 Steel wire and related products

(P-5619)
MERCHANTS METALS LLC
Also Called: Merchants Metals
6466 Mission Blvd (92509-4128)
PHONE..................................951 686-1888
Rob Sisco, *Mgr*
EMP: 89
SQ FT: 8,750
SALES (corp-wide): 1.06B **Privately Held**
Web: www.merchantsmetals.com
SIC: 3315 3496 Fence gates, posts, and
fittings: steel; Miscellaneous fabricated wire
products
HQ: Merchants Metals Llc
3 Ravinia Dr Ste 1750
Atlanta GA
770 741-0300

(P-5620)
MK MAGNETICS INC
17030 Muskrat Ave (92301-2258)
PHONE..................................760 246-6373
Magne Stangenes, *Pr*
John Stangenes, *
Jay Runge, *Corporate Secretary**
▲ **EMP:** 53 **EST:** 2003
SQ FT: 45,000
SALES (est): 11.13MM
SALES (corp-wide): 26.47MM **Privately
Held**
Web: www.mkmagnetics.com
SIC: 3315 Steel wire and related products
PA: Stangenes Industries, Inc.
1052 E Meadow Cir
Palo Alto CA
650 855-9926

(P-5621)
NATIONAL WIRE AND CABLE CORPORATION
Àlso Called: National Wire and Cable
136 N San Fernando Rd (90031-1780)
P.O. Box 31307 (90031-0307)
PHONE..................................323 225-5611
EMP: 170 **EST:** 1952
SALES (est): 22.05MM **Privately Held**
Web: www.nationalwire.com
SIC: 3315 5031 Cable, steel: insulated or
armored; Molding, all materials

(P-5622)
PRO DETENTION INC
Also Called: Viking Products
2238 N Glassell St Ste E (92865-2742)
PHONE..................................714 881-3680
Mike Peterson, *CEO*
▲ **EMP:** 70 **EST:** 2012
SALES (est): 9.11MM **Privately Held**
SIC: 3315 Wire and fabricated wire products

(P-5623)
SOUTH BAY WIRE & CABLE CO LLC
54125 Maranatha Dr M-S 67 (92549-0075)
P.O. Box 67 (92549-0067)
PHONE..................................951 659-2183
EMP: 78 **EST:** 2021
SALES (est): 5.71MM **Privately Held**
Web: www.southbaycable.com
SIC: 3315 Wire and fabricated wire products

(P-5624)
TREE ISLAND WIRE (USA) INC
Industrial Alloys
13470 Philadelphia Ave (92337-7700)
PHONE..................................909 594-7511
Rebecca Kalis, *Brnch Mgr*
EMP: 115
SALES (corp-wide): 251.95MM **Privately
Held**
Web: www.treeisland.com
SIC: 3315 Wire, steel: insulated or armored
HQ: Tree Island Wire (Usa), Inc.
3880 Valley Blvd
Walnut CA

(P-5625)
TREE ISLAND WIRE (USA) INC
K-Lath
3880 W Valley Blvd (91769)
PHONE..................................909 595-6617
Ken Stufford, *Mgr*
EMP: 115
SALES (corp-wide): 251.95MM **Privately
Held**
Web: www.treeisland.com
SIC: 3315 Wire, steel: insulated or armored
HQ: Tree Island Wire (Usa), Inc.
3880 Valley Blvd
Walnut CA

(P-5626)
TREE ISLAND WIRE (USA) INC (DH)
Also Called: TI Wire
3880 Valley Blvd (91789-1515)
P.O. Box 90100 (92427-1100)
PHONE..................................909 594-7511
Amar S Doman, *Ch Bd*
Dale R Maclean, *CEO*
Nancy Davies, *CFO*
Stephen Ogden, *VP*
▲ **EMP:** 250 **EST:** 1980
SALES (est): 59.34MM
SALES (corp-wide): 251.95MM **Privately
Held**

Web: www.treeisland.com
SIC: 3315 Steel wire and related products
HQ: Tree Island Industries Ltd
3933 Boundary Rd
Richmond BC
604 524-3744

(P-5627)
US HANGER COMPANY LLC
17501 S Denver Ave (90248-3410)
PHONE..................................310 323-8030
▲ **EMP:** 47 **EST:** 2008
SALES (est): 3.69MM **Privately Held**
SIC: 3315 5199 Hangers (garment), wire;
Clothes hangers

(P-5628)
WIRETECH INC (PA)
6440 Canning St (90040-3122)
PHONE..................................323 722-4933
William Hillpot, *CEO*
Irene Sanchez, *
Garry Goodson, *
Simon Correa, *
▲ **EMP:** 87 **EST:** 2001
SALES (est): 22.2MM
SALES (corp-wide): 22.2MM **Privately
Held**
Web:
wiretechincorporated.wordpress.com
SIC: 3315 Steel wire and related products

3316 Cold Finishing Of Steel Shapes

(P-5629)
KIP STEEL INC
1650 Valley Ln (92833-1718)
PHONE..................................714 461-1051
EMP: 20
SALES (corp-wide): 480.32K **Privately
Held**
Web: www.kipsteel.com
SIC: 3316 Cold finishing of steel shapes
PA: Kip Steel, Inc.
21314 Twisted Willow Ln
Katy TX
714 461-1051

(P-5630)
OMEGA STEEL INC
7140 Bandini Blvd (90040-3325)
PHONE..................................323 726-7669
Thomas B Nelis, *Pr*
Michael Kerby, *VP*
EMP: 25 **EST:** 1988
SQ FT: 40,000
SALES (est): 2.88MM **Privately Held**
Web: www.omegasteel.com
SIC: 3316 3494 3312 Strip, steel, cold-rolled,
nec: from purchased hot-rolled,; Valves and
pipe fittings, nec; Blast furnaces and steel
mills

(P-5631)
REMINGTON ROLL FORMING INC
2445 Chico Ave (91733-1612)
P.O. Box 9325 (91733-0979)
PHONE..................................626 350-5196
Thomas Henry, *Pr*
EMP: 23 **EST:** 1987
SQ FT: 25,000
SALES (est): 848.32K **Privately Held**
SIC: 3316 Cold finishing of steel shapes

3317 Steel Pipe And Tubes

(P-5632)
CHARMAN MANUFACTURING INC
5681 S Downey Rd (90058-3719)
PHONE..................................213 489-7000
Shahab Namvar, *Pr*
Shawn Namvar, *Pr*
Ezra Namvar, *VP*
▲ **EMP:** 19 **EST:** 2006
SALES (est): 6.95MM **Privately Held**
Web: www.charmaninc.com
SIC: 3317 Steel pipe and tubes

(P-5633)
CONTECH ENGNERED SOLUTIONS INC
950 S Coast Dr Ste 145 (92626-7833)
PHONE..................................714 281-7883
EMP: 1250
Web: www.conteches.com
SIC: 3317 Steel pipe and tubes
HQ: Contech Engineered Solutions Inc.
9025 Ctr Pinte Dr Ste 400
West Chester OH
513 645-7000

(P-5634)
IMPERIAL PIPE SERVICES LLC
12375 Brown Ave (92509-1868)
PHONE..................................951 682-3307
EMP: 21 **EST:** 2002
SALES (est): 9.89MM
SALES (corp-wide): 134.62MM **Privately
Held**
Web: www.imperialpipe.com
SIC: 3317 Steel pipe and tubes
PA: Shapco Inc.
1666 20th St Ste 100
Santa Monica CA
310 264-1666

(P-5635)
INTERNATIONAL CONSULTING UNLTD
Also Called: Kns Industrial Supply
10542 Calle Lee (90720-2560)
PHONE..................................657 256-1761
EMP: 157
SALES (corp-wide): 11.23MM **Privately
Held**
Web: www.knsindustrialsupply.com
SIC: 3317 Steel pipe and tubes
PA: International Consulting, Unltd.
1440 N Harbor Blvd # 900
Fullerton CA
714 449-3318

(P-5636)
K-TUBE CORPORATION
Also Called: K Tube Technologies
13400 Kirkham Way Frnt (92064-7167)
PHONE..................................858 513-9229
Greg May, *CEO*
EMP: 100 **EST:** 1982
SQ FT: 75,000
SALES (est): 27.69MM
SALES (corp-wide): 1.61B **Privately Held**
Web: www.k-tube.com
SIC: 3317 Tubing, mechanical or
hypodermic sizes: cold drawn stainless
PA: Cook Group Incorporated
750 N Daniels Way
Bloomington IN
812 339-2235

P R O D U C T S   &   S V C S

(P-5637)
MARUICHI AMERICAN CORPORATION
11529 Greenstone Ave (90670-4622)
PHONE...................562 903-8600
Wataru Morita, *Pr*
Teruo Horikawa, *
Takehiko Katsumata, *
Makoto Ishikawa, *
Takuhiro Ishihara, *
▲ EMP: 96 EST: 1978
SQ FT: 240,000
SALES (est): 21.97MM **Privately Held**
Web: www.macsfs.com
SIC: 3317 Pipes, seamless steel
PA: Maruichi Steel Tube Ltd.
5-1-60, Namba, Chuo-Ku
Osaka OSK

(P-5638)
NORTHWEST PIPE COMPANY
12351 Rancho Rd (92301-2711)
PHONE...................760 246-3191
Charles Koenig, *VP*
EMP: 77
SALES (corp-wide): 457.67MM **Publicly Held**
Web: www.nwpipe.com
SIC: 3317 3321 Pipes, wrought: welded, lock joint, or heavy riveted; Gray and ductile iron foundries
PA: Northwest Pipe Company
201 Ne Park Plaza Dr # 100
Vancouver WA
360 397-6250

(P-5639)
NUCOR WAREHOUSE SYSTEMS INC (HQ)
3851 S Santa Fe Ave (90058-1712)
PHONE...................323 588-4261
TOLL FREE: 800
Dave Olmstead, *Pr*
Steve Rogers, *VP*
Sturgeon Baker, *Contrlr*
Matthew Devries, *Supply Chain Manager*
◆ EMP: 177 EST: 1985
SQ FT: 285,000
SALES (est): 158.73MM
SALES (corp-wide): 41.51B **Publicly Held**
Web: www.nucorwarehousesystems.com
SIC: 3317 Tubes, seamless steel
PA: Nucor Corporation
1915 Rexford Rd Ste 400
Charlotte NC
704 366-7000

(P-5640)
PRIMUS PIPE AND TUBE INC (DH)
5855 Obispo Ave (90805-3715)
PHONE...................562 808-8000
Tommy Grahn, *Pr*
Chris Podsaid, *VP*
Karl Almond, *VP Fin*
Roy Harrison, *VP Opers*
Scott Templeton, *Ex VP*
▲ EMP: 51 EST: 1967
SQ FT: 120,000
SALES (est): 43.43MM **Privately Held**
Web: www.primuspipeandtube.com
SIC: 3317 Steel pipe and tubes
HQ: Ta Chen International, Inc.
5855 Obispo Ave
Long Beach CA
562 808-8000

(P-5641)
ROSCOE MOSS MANUFACTURING CO (PA)
Also Called: Roscoe Moss Company
4360 Worth St (90063-2536)
P.O. Box 31064 (90031-0064)
PHONE...................323 261-4185
Roscoe Moss Junior, *Ch Bd*
George E Moss, *
Robert A Vanvaler, *
Tony Creque, *
Regis Coyle, *Corporate Secretary*
◆ EMP: 90 EST: 1913
SQ FT: 20,000
SALES (est): 28.49MM
SALES (corp-wide): 28.49MM **Privately Held**
Web: www.roscoemoss.com
SIC: 3317 Well casing, wrought: welded, lock joint, or heavy riveted

(P-5642)
VALLEY METALS LLC
Also Called: Leggett & Platt 0768
13125 Gregg St (92064-7122)
P.O. Box 85402 (92186-5402)
PHONE...................858 513-1300
Kirk Nelson, *Managing Member*
EMP: 40 EST: 1946
SQ FT: 47,700
SALES (est): 11.46MM
SALES (corp-wide): 5.15B **Publicly Held**
Web: www.leggettaerospace.com
SIC: 3317 Tubes, wrought: welded or lock joint
HQ: Western Pneumatic Tube Company, Llc
835 6th St S
Kirkland WA
425 822-8271

3321 Gray And Ductile Iron Foundries

(P-5643)
ALHAMBRA FOUNDRY COMPANY LTD
Also Called: Afco
1147 S Meridian Ave (91803-1218)
P.O. Box 469 (91802-0469)
PHONE...................626 289-4294
Arzhang Baghkhanian, *CEO*
James Wright, *
Mike Smalski, *
▲ EMP: 46 EST: 1984
SQ FT: 48,370
SALES (est): 885 **Privately Held**
Web: www.ejco.com
SIC: 3321 3312 5051 Gray iron castings, nec; Structural shapes and pilings, steel; Iron and steel (ferrous) products

(P-5644)
FOX HILLS INDUSTRIES
5831 Research Dr (92649-1385)
PHONE...................714 893-1940
John Burk, *Pr*
Doug Reichard, *
Frank Reilly, *
Raj Mittal, *
▲ EMP: 40 EST: 1947
SQ FT: 20,000
SALES (est): 914.67K **Privately Held**
Web: www.onesourcecc.com
SIC: 3321 3366 3365 3322 Ductile iron castings; Castings (except die), nec, brass; Aluminum foundries; Malleable iron foundries

(P-5645)
GLOBE IRON FOUNDRY INC
5649 Randolph St (90040-3404)
PHONE...................323 723-8983
John M Pratto, *Pr*
Othon Garcia, *
John Pratto Junior, *VP Prd*
Jeff Pratto, *
EMP: 70 EST: 1929
SQ FT: 58,000
SALES (est): 8.59MM **Privately Held**
Web: www.globeiron.com
SIC: 3321 3543 3369 Gray iron castings, nec; Industrial patterns; Nonferrous foundries, nec

(P-5646)
JDH PACIFIC INC (PA)
14821 Artesia Blvd (90638-6006)
PHONE...................818 269-6274
Donald Hu, *CEO*
Donald Hu, *Pr*
▲ EMP: 30 EST: 1989
SQ FT: 103,000
SALES (est): 24.88MM **Privately Held**
Web: www.jdhpacific.com
SIC: 3321 3324 3599 3462 Gray iron castings, nec; Commercial investment castings, ferrous; Crankshafts and camshafts, machining; Iron and steel forgings

(P-5647)
PACIFIC ALLOY CASTING COMPANY INC
5900 Firestone Blvd Fl 1 (90280-3708)
PHONE...................562 928-1387
EMP: 120 EST: 1937
SALES (est): 17.06MM **Privately Held**
Web: www.pacificalloy.com
SIC: 3321 Gray and ductile iron foundries

(P-5648)
PACIFIC SEWER MAINTENANCE CORP
Also Called: PSM
4008 Via Rio Ave (92057-6439)
PHONE...................800 292-9927
Richard Gayman, *Pr*
Brett Gayman, *VP*
Scott Gayman, *VP*
Todd Gayman, *VP*
Mary Gayman, *Sec*
EMP: 19 EST: 1977
SQ FT: 1,400
SALES (est): 2.17MM **Privately Held**
SIC: 3321 1623 Sewer pipe, cast iron; Water and sewer line construction

(P-5649)
THOMPSON GUNDRILLING INC
13840 Saticoy St (91402-6582)
PHONE...................323 873-4045
Michael Thompson, *Pr*
Robert Thompson, *
EMP: 39 EST: 1973
SQ FT: 32,000
SALES (est): 4.84MM **Privately Held**
Web: www.thompsongundrilling.com
SIC: 3321 Gray and ductile iron foundries

3322 Malleable Iron Foundries

(P-5650)
STEVEN HANDELMAN STUDIOS INC (PA)
716 N Milpas St (93103-3029)
PHONE...................805 884-9070
Steven Handelman, *Owner*
EMP: 41 EST: 1973
SALES (est): 4.8MM
SALES (corp-wide): 4.8MM **Privately Held**
Web: www.lightingshs.com
SIC: 3322 Malleable iron foundries

3324 Steel Investment Foundries

(P-5651)
CAST PARTS INC
Also Called: Cpp-City of Industry
16800 Chestnut St (91748-1017)
PHONE...................626 937-3444
David Atwood, *Brnch Mgr*
EMP: 160
SALES (corp-wide): 2.07B **Privately Held**
Web: www.cppcorp.com
SIC: 3324 Aerospace investment castings, ferrous
HQ: Cast Parts, Inc.
4200 Valley Blvd
Walnut CA
909 595-2252

(P-5652)
CAST PARTS INC (HQ)
Also Called: Cpp-Pomona
4200 Valley Blvd (91789-1408)
PHONE...................909 595-2252
Steve Clodfelter, *Pr*
Ali Ghavami, *
EMP: 185 EST: 2000
SQ FT: 300,000
SALES (est): 53.55MM
SALES (corp-wide): 2.07B **Privately Held**
SIC: 3324 3365 Steel investment foundries; Aluminum foundries
PA: Consolidated Precision Products Corp.
1621 Euclid Ave Ste 1850
Cleveland OH
216 453-4800

(P-5653)
CFI HOLDINGS CORP
Also Called: Consolidated Foundries
4200 Valley Blvd (91765)
PHONE...................909 595-2252
Debbie Comstock, *Prin*
EMP: 32 EST: 1979
SALES (est): 536.49K **Privately Held**
SIC: 3324 3365 Steel investment foundries; Aluminum foundries

(P-5654)
HOWMET CORPORATION
900 E Watson Center Rd (90745-4201)
PHONE...................310 847-8152
EMP: 1086
SALES (corp-wide): 5.66B **Publicly Held**
Web: www.howmet.com
SIC: 3324 Commercial investment castings, ferrous
HQ: Howmet Corporation
1 Misco Dr
Whitehall MI
231 894-5686

(P-5655)
HOWMET GLOBL FSTNING SYSTEMS I
Rosan / Eagle Products
800 S State College Blvd (92831-5334)
PHONE...................714 871-1550
Craig Brown, *Mgr*
EMP: 100
SALES (corp-wide): 5.66B **Publicly Held**

SIC: 3324 3365 Aerospace investment castings, ferrous; Aerospace castings, aluminum
HQ: Howmet Global Fastening Systems Inc.
3990a Heritage Oak Ct
Simi Valley CA
805 426-2270

(P-5656)
INITIUM AEROSPACE LLC
4255 Ruffin Rd Ste 100 (92123-1247)
PHONE..................................818 324-3684
Etienne Boisseau, *CEO*
EMP: 17 **EST:** 2018
SQ FT: 2,500
SALES (est): 1.52MM **Privately Held**
SIC: 3324 3369 3365 3812 Aerospace investment castings, ferrous; Aerospace castings, nonferrous: except aluminum; Aerospace castings, aluminum; Aircraft/aerospace flight instruments and guidance systems

(P-5657)
LISI AEROSPACE NORTH AMER INC
2600 Skypark Dr (90505-5314)
PHONE..................................310 326-8110
Christian Darville, *CEO*
◆ **EMP:** 900 **EST:** 2009
SALES (est): 118.86MM
SALES (corp-wide): 2.67MM **Privately Held**
Web: www.lisi-aerospace.com
SIC: 3324 Aerospace investment castings, ferrous
HQ: Lisi Aerospace
42 A 52
Paris
140198200

(P-5658)
MILLER CASTINGS INC (PA)
2503 Pacific Pk Dr (90601-1610)
PHONE..................................562 695-0461
Ralph Miller, *Pr*
Hadi Khandehroo, *
▲ **EMP:** 328 **EST:** 1973
SQ FT: 40,000
SALES (est): 49.35MM
SALES (corp-wide): 49.35MM **Privately Held**
Web: www.millercastings.com
SIC: 3324 Steel investment foundries

(P-5659)
NET SHAPES INC (PA)
1336 E Francis St Ste B (91761-5723)
PHONE..................................909 947-3231
Joseph S Cannone, *Pr*
James Cannone, *VP*
EMP: 63 **EST:** 1986
SQ FT: 43,500
SALES (est): 9.77MM
SALES (corp-wide): 9.77MM **Privately Held**
Web: www.netshapes.com
SIC: 3324 Steel investment foundries

(P-5660)
PAC-RANCHO INC (HQ)
11000 Jersey Blvd (91730-5103)
PHONE..................................909 987-4721
Steve Clodfelter, *Pr*
Ali Ghavami, *
EMP: 180 **EST:** 1984
SQ FT: 55,000
SALES (est): 24.34MM
SALES (corp-wide): 2.07B **Privately Held**

SIC: 3324 3354 3369 Commercial investment castings, ferrous; Aluminum extruded products; Nonferrous foundries, nec
PA: Consolidated Precision Products Corp.
1621 Euclid Ave Ste 1850
Cleveland OH
216 453-4800

3325 Steel Foundries, Nec

(P-5661)
CWI STEEL TECHNOLOGIES CORPORATION
2415 Campus Dr Ste 100 (92612-1502)
PHONE..................................949 476-7600
EMP: 48
SIC: 3325 Steel foundries, nec

(P-5662)
DAMERON ALLOY FOUNDRIES (PA)
6330 Gateway Dr Ste B (90630-4836)
PHONE..................................310 631-5165
John W Dameron, *Pr*
Augustin Huerta, *
▲ **EMP:** 100 **EST:** 1946
SQ FT: 5,000
SALES (est): 23.95MM
SALES (corp-wide): 23.95MM **Privately Held**
Web: www.dameron.net
SIC: 3325 3324 Steel foundries, nec; Commercial investment castings, ferrous

(P-5663)
ENER-TECH METALS INC
7815 Somerset Blvd (90723-4212)
P.O. Box 137 (90723-0137)
PHONE..................................562 529-5034
Franklin Dees, *CEO*
David C Brayton, *Genl Mgr*
Randall Dees, *Prin*
Larry Boren, *Prin*
Paz Gualvez, *Prin*
EMP: 67 **EST:** 1986
SQ FT: 120,000
SALES (est): 6.63MM **Privately Held**
SIC: 3325 Alloy steel castings, except investment

(P-5664)
METAL CAST INC
Also Called: Metalcast
2002 W Chestnut Ave (92703-4341)
P.O. Box 3099 (92703-0099)
PHONE..................................714 285-9792
Rigoberto Urquiza, *Pr*
EMP: 23 **EST:** 1999
SQ FT: 12,000
SALES (est): 652.23K **Privately Held**
Web: www.metalcast.com
SIC: 3325 Alloy steel castings, except investment

(P-5665)
WCS EQUIPMENT HOLDINGS LLC
Also Called: Deluxe Building Products
1350 E Lexington Ave (91766-5521)
PHONE..................................909 993-5700
EMP: 53
SALES (corp-wide): 64.22MM **Privately Held**
Web: www.steelcousa.com
SIC: 3325 Steel foundries, nec
HQ: Wcs Equipment Holdings, Llc
13568 Vintage Pl
Chino CA

(P-5666)
WCS EQUIPMENT HOLDINGS LLC (HQ)
Also Called: Steelco USA
13568 Vintage Pl (91710-5243)
PHONE..................................909 393-8405
Erik Gamm, *CEO*
EMP: 54 **EST:** 2006
SALES (est): 49.58MM
SALES (corp-wide): 64.22MM **Privately Held**
Web: www.steelcousa.com
SIC: 3325 Steel foundries, nec
PA: West Coast Steel & Processing Holdings, Llc
13568 Vintage Pl
Chino CA
909 393-8405

(P-5667)
WEST COAST FOUNDRY LLC (HQ)
2450 E 53rd St (90255)
PHONE..................................323 583-1421
Michael Bargani, *Pr*
John Heine, *CFO*
▲ **EMP:** 20 **EST:** 1972
SQ FT: 18,000
SALES (est): 10.67MM
SALES (corp-wide): 85.77MM **Privately Held**
Web: www.westcoastfoundry.com
SIC: 3325 Alloy steel castings, except investment
PA: Speyside Equity Fund I Lp
430 E 86th St
New York NY
212 994-0308

3331 Primary Copper

(P-5668)
CORRPRO COMPANIES INC
10260 Matern Pl (90670-3248)
PHONE..................................562 944-1636
Randy Galinski, *Prin*
EMP: 23
SALES (corp-wide): 1.27B **Privately Held**
Web: www.aegion.com
SIC: 3331 1799 Cathodes (primary), copper; Corrosion control installation
HQ: Corrpro Companies, Inc.
580 Goddard Ave
Chesterfield MO
636 530-8000

3334 Primary Aluminum

(P-5669)
ALUMINUM PRECISION PDTS INC (PA)
3333 W Warner Ave (92704-5316)
PHONE..................................714 546-8125
Gregory S Keeler, *Pr*
Roark Keeler, *VP*
Simona Manoiu, *CFO*
◆ **EMP:** 550 **EST:** 1965
SALES (est): 80.17MM
SALES (corp-wide): 80.17MM **Privately Held**
Web: www.aluminumprecision.com
SIC: 3334 Primary aluminum

(P-5670)
HOWMET AEROSPACE INC
3016 Lomita Blvd (90505-5103)
PHONE..................................212 836-2674
EMP: 356

SALES (corp-wide): 5.66B **Publicly Held**
Web: www.howmet.com
SIC: 3334 Primary aluminum
PA: Howmet Aerospace Inc.
201 Isabella St Ste 200
Pittsburgh PA
412 553-1950

(P-5671)
INOVATIV INC
1500 W Mckinley St (91702-3218)
PHONE..................................626 969-5300
Patrick Blewett, *CEO*
Tracy Barbosa, *
EMP: 40 **EST:** 2013
SALES (est): 6.22MM **Privately Held**
Web: www.inovativ.com
SIC: 3334 Primary aluminum

(P-5672)
MAURICE & MAURICE ENGRG INC
17579 Mesa St Ste B4 (92345-8308)
P.O. Box 403682 (92340-3682)
PHONE..................................760 949-5151
Jennifer Thomas, *CEO*
Aron Maurice, *
Jennifer Maurice, *
EMP: 27 **EST:** 1973
SQ FT: 22,000
SALES (est): 2.39MM **Privately Held**
SIC: 3334 Primary aluminum

3339 Primary Nonferrous Metals, Nec

(P-5673)
ARGEN CORPORATION (PA)
Also Called: Jelenko
8515 Miralani Dr (92126-4352)
PHONE..................................858 455-7900
Anton Woolf, *CEO*
Jackie Woolf, *
Paul Cascone, *
Neil Wainstein, *
Andrea Ravid, *
▲ **EMP:** 203 **EST:** 1963
SQ FT: 39,609
SALES (est): 75.94MM
SALES (corp-wide): 75.94MM **Privately Held**
Web: www.argen.com
SIC: 3339 3843 Precious metals; Dental equipment and supplies

(P-5674)
COMMODITY RESOURCE ENVMTL INC
Also Called: Commodity Rsource Enviromental
11847 United St (93501-7047)
PHONE..................................661 824-2416
Mike Kelsey, *Mgr*
EMP: 40
SALES (corp-wide): 9.42MM **Privately Held**
Web: www.creweb.com
SIC: 3339 3341 Precious metals; Secondary nonferrous metals
PA: Commodity Resource & Environmental, Inc.
116 E Prospect Ave
Burbank CA
818 843-2811

(P-5675)
PCC ROLLMET INC
1822 Deere Ave (92606-4817)

(PA)=Parent Co (HQ)=Headquarters
✪ = New Business established in last 2 years

2024 Southern California
Business Directory and Buyers Guide

PRODUCTS & SVCS

275

PHONE...............................949 221-5333
EMP: 70 **EST:** 2011
SALES (est): 22.38MM
SALES (corp-wide): 302.09B **Publicly Held**
Web: www.rollmetusa.com
SIC: 3339 Nickel refining (primary)
HQ: Precision Castparts Corp.
5885 Meadows Rd Ste 620
Lake Oswego OR
503 946-4800

(P-5676)
RBC LUBRON BEARING SYSTEMS INC (HQ)
13141 Molette St (90670-5523)
PHONE...............................714 841-3007
Robert James, *Dir*
EMP: 23 **EST:** 2009
SALES (est): 13.34MM
SALES (corp-wide): 1.47B **Publicly Held**
Web: www.rbclubron.com
SIC: 3339 Antifriction bearing metals, lead-base
PA: Rbc Bearings Incorporated
102 Willenbrock Rd Bldg B
Oxford CT
203 267-7001

(P-5677)
WESTERN MESQUITE MINES INC
6502 E Us Highway 78 (92227-9306)
PHONE...............................928 341-4653
Randall Oliphant, *Ch*
Robert Gallagher, *CEO*
Cory Atiyeh, *Pr*
W Hanson P Geo, *VP*
Penny Brian, *Sec*
EMP: 20 **EST:** 1985
SALES (est): 22.91MM
SALES (corp-wide): 952.2MM **Privately Held**
SIC: 3339 Gold refining (primary)
PA: Equinox Gold Corp
1501-700 W Pender St
Vancouver BC
604 558-0560

3341 Secondary Nonferrous Metals

(P-5678)
CERTIFIED ALLOY PRODUCTS INC
3245 Cherry Ave (90807-5213)
P.O. Box 90 (90801-0090)
PHONE...............................562 595-6621
▲ **EMP:** 110 **EST:** 1943
SALES (est): 34.84MM
SALES (corp-wide): 363.11K **Privately Held**
Web: www.doncasters.com
SIC: 3341 3313 3325 3312 Nickel smelting and refining (secondary); Ferroalloys; Steel foundries, nec; Blast furnaces and steel mills
HQ: Doncasters Limited
Repton House
Burton-On-Trent STAFFS
133 286-4900

(P-5679)
DAVID H FELL & CO INC (PA)
6009 Bandini Blvd (90040-2967)
PHONE...............................323 722-9992
TOLL FREE: 800
Larry Fell, *Ch*
Lawrence Fell, *

Sondra Fell, *
▼ **EMP:** 24 **EST:** 1973
SQ FT: 18,000
SALES (est): 7.62MM
SALES (corp-wide): 7.62MM **Privately Held**
Web: www.dhfco.com
SIC: 3341 5094 Secondary precious metals; Bullion, precious metals

(P-5680)
GEMINI INDUSTRIES INC
2311 Pullman St (92705-5506)
PHONE...............................949 250-4011
M Elguindy, *CEO*
Diana Keiffer, *
▲ **EMP:** 75 **EST:** 1973
SALES (est): 16.44MM **Privately Held**
Web: www.gemini-catalyst.com
SIC: 3341 Secondary precious metals

(P-5681)
HERAEUS PRCOUS MTLS N AMER LLC (DH)
15524 Carmenita Rd (90670-5610)
PHONE...............................562 921-7464
Andre Christl, *Managing Member*
Uve Kupka, *
◆ **EMP:** 200 **EST:** 1970
SQ FT: 71,000
SALES (est): 93.93MM
SALES (corp-wide): 2.67MM **Privately Held**
SIC: 3341 2899 Gold smelting and refining (secondary); Chemical preparations, nec
HQ: Heraeus Holding Gesellschaft Mit Beschrankter Haftung
Heraeusstr. 12-14
Hanau HE
6181350

(P-5682)
JOHNSON MATTHEY INC
Also Called: Noble Metals
12205 World Trade Dr (92128-3766)
P.O. Box Orld Trade (92128)
PHONE...............................858 716-2400
Steve Hill, *Brnch Mgr*
EMP: 198
SALES (corp-wide): 17.95B **Privately Held**
Web: www.matthey.com
SIC: 3341 Secondary nonferrous metals
HQ: Johnson Matthey Inc.
435 Devon Park Dr Ste 600
Wayne PA
610 971-3000

(P-5683)
QUEMETCO WEST LLC
720 S 7th Ave (91746-3124)
PHONE...............................626 330-2294
▲ **EMP:** 20 **EST:** 2000
SALES (est): 11.55MM
SALES (corp-wide): 3.88MM **Privately Held**
Web: www.quemetco.com
SIC: 3341 Lead smelting and refining (secondary)
HQ: Eco-Bat Technologies Limited
Cowley Lodge
Matlock

(P-5684)
TEXAS TST INC
13428 Benson Ave (91710-5258)
PHONE...............................951 685-2155
◆ **EMP:** 50
Web: www.tst-inc.com
SIC: 3341 Aluminum smelting and refining (secondary)

(P-5685)
TST INC (PA)
Also Called: Alpase
13428 Benson Ave (91710-5258)
PHONE...............................951 685-2155
Andrew G Stein, *CEO*
Robert A Stein, *
Greg Levine, *
James Davidson, *
◆ **EMP:** 260 **EST:** 1961
SQ FT: 123,000
SALES (est): 45.96MM
SALES (corp-wide): 45.96MM **Privately Held**
Web: www.tst-inc.com
SIC: 3341 5093 Aluminum smelting and refining (secondary); Metal scrap and waste materials

---

3353 Aluminum Sheet, Plate, And Foil

(P-5686)
ALUM-A-FOLD PACIFIC INC
Also Called: AFP
3730 Capitol Ave (90601-1731)
PHONE...............................562 699-4550
▲ **EMP:** 45
Web: www.perfectdomain.com
SIC: 3353 Aluminum sheet, plate, and foil

(P-5687)
HOWMET AEROSPACE INC
Also Called: Howmet Aerospace Inc
1550 Gage Rd (90640-6614)
PHONE...............................323 728-3901
EMP: 135
SALES (corp-wide): 5.66B **Publicly Held**
Web: www.howmet.com
SIC: 3353 Aluminum sheet and strip
PA: Howmet Aerospace Inc.
201 Isabella St Ste 200
Pittsburgh PA
412 553-1950

(P-5688)
KAISER ALUMINUM FAB PDTS LLC (HQ)
Also Called: Kafp
27422 Portola Pkwy Ste 200 (92610-2831)
PHONE...............................949 614-1740
Jack A Hockema, *Pr*
John M Donnan, *
Joseph P Bellino, *
◆ **EMP:** 2200 **EST:** 2006
SALES (est): 456.62MM
SALES (corp-wide): 3.43B **Publicly Held**
Web: www.kaiseraluminum.com
SIC: 3353 3334 3354 3355 Aluminum sheet, plate, and foil; Primary aluminum; Aluminum rod and bar; Wire, aluminum: made in rolling mills
PA: Kaiser Aluminum Corporation
1550 W Mcewen Dr Ste 500
Franklin TN
629 252-7040

(P-5689)
MATERIAL SCIENCES CORPORATION
Also Called: MSC-La
3730 Capitol Ave (90601-1731)
PHONE...............................562 699-4550
Patrick Murley, *CEO*
EMP: 45
SALES (corp-wide): 120.84MM **Privately Held**
Web: www.materialsciencescorp.com

SIC: 3353 Aluminum sheet, plate, and foil
PA: Material Sciences Corporation
6855 Commerce Blvd
Canton MI
734 207-4444

(P-5690)
SOUTHWIRE COMPANY LLC
Southwire Master Service Ctr
9199 Cleveland Ave Ste 100 (91730-8559)
PHONE...............................909 989-2888
David Jordan, *Brnch Mgr*
EMP: 95
SALES (corp-wide): 1.7B **Privately Held**
Web: www.southwire.com
SIC: 3353 Aluminum sheet and strip
PA: Southwire Company, Llc
1 Southwire Dr
Carrollton GA
770 832-4529

(P-5691)
SOUTHWIRE INC
Also Called: Alflex
20250 S Alameda St (90221-6207)
PHONE...............................310 886-8300
Jorge Eulloqui, *Mgr*
EMP: 500
SALES (corp-wide): 1.7B **Privately Held**
Web: www.southwire.com
SIC: 3353 3644 3315 Coils, sheet aluminum; Electric conduits and fittings; Cable, steel: insulated or armored
HQ: Southwire Inc
11695 Pacific Ave
Fontana CA
310 884-8500

(P-5692)
TCI TEXARKANA INC (DH)
5855 Obispo Ave (90805-3715)
PHONE...............................562 808-8000
Johnny Hsieh, *CEO*
James Chang, *VP*
Andrew Chang, *Contrlr*
EMP: 34 **EST:** 2018
SALES (est): 87.93MM **Privately Held**
SIC: 3353 Coils, sheet aluminum
HQ: Ta Chen International, Inc.
5855 Obispo Ave
Long Beach CA
562 808-8000

3354 Aluminum Extruded Products

(P-5693)
ANAHEIM EXTRUSION CO INC
1330 N Kraemer Blvd (92806-1401)
P.O. Box 6380 (92816-0380)
PHONE...............................714 630-3111
EMP: 80 **EST:** 1974
SALES (est): 14.35MM **Privately Held**
Web: www.anaheimextrude.com
SIC: 3354 Aluminum extruded products
HQ: Universal Molding Company
9151 Imperial Hwy
Downey CA
310 886-1750

(P-5694)
CENTURY AMERICAN ALUMINUM INC
1001 S Doubleday Ave (91761-1564)
PHONE...............................909 390-2384
Trang Trong, *Prin*
▲ **EMP:** 17 **EST:** 2009
SALES (est): 467.13K **Privately Held**

SIC: 3354 Aluminum extruded products

(P-5695)
DWA COMPOSITE SPECIALTIES INC
Also Called: Dwa Aluminum Composites
21100 Superior St (91311-4308)
PHONE.............................818 885-8654
EMP: 19
SIC: 3354 Aluminum extruded products

(P-5696)
FRY REGLET CORPORATION (PA)
14013 Marquardt Ave (90670-5018)
P.O. Box 665 (90637-0665)
PHONE.............................800 237-9773
Stephen Reed, *CEO*
Avon M Hall, *
James Tuttle, *
EMP: 75 **EST:** 1945
SQ FT: 20,000
SALES (est): 61.44MM
SALES (corp-wide): 61.44MM **Privately Held**
Web: www.fryreglet.com
SIC: 3354 Aluminum extruded products

(P-5697)
GEMINI ALUMINUM CORPORATION
Also Called: Gemini Aluminum
3255 Pomona Blvd (91768-3291)
P.O. Box 1462 (83864-0866)
PHONE.............................909 595-7403
Alan J Hardy, *Pr*
Healani Hardy, *
EMP: 37 **EST:** 1976
SQ FT: 10,000
SALES (est): 738.7K **Privately Held**
Web: www.geminialuminum.com
SIC: 3354 Aluminum rod and bar

(P-5698)
GLOBAL TRUSS AMERICA LLC
Also Called: Global Truss
4295 Charter St (90058-2520)
PHONE.............................323 415-6225
Charles Davies, *Managing Member*
Kenneth Kahn, *
◆ **EMP:** 55 **EST:** 2004
SQ FT: 60,000
SALES (est): 6.98MM **Privately Held**
Web: www.globaltruss.com
SIC: 3354 Aluminum extruded products

(P-5699)
HYDRO EXTRUSION USA LLC
18111 Railroad St (91748-1216)
PHONE.............................626 964-3411
Matt Zundel, *Sls Dir*
EMP: 300
SIC: 3354 Aluminum extruded products
HQ: Hydro Extrusion Usa, Llc
6250 N River Rd Ste 5000
Rosemont IL

(P-5700)
KAISER ALUMINUM CORPORATION
6250 Bandini Blvd (90040-3168)
PHONE.............................323 726-8011
D F Smith, *Mgr*
EMP: 435
SALES (corp-wide): 3.43B **Publicly Held**
Web: www.kaiseraluminum.com
SIC: 3354 Aluminum extruded products
PA: Kaiser Aluminum Corporation
1550 W Mcewen Dr Ste 500

Franklin TN
629 252-7040

(P-5701)
KAISER ALUMINUM FAB PDTS LLC
6250 E Bandini Blvd (90040-3168)
PHONE.............................323 722-7151
D F Smith, *Brnch Mgr*
EMP: 18
SALES (corp-wide): 3.43B **Publicly Held**
Web: www.kaiseraluminum.com
SIC: 3354 Aluminum extruded products
HQ: Kaiser Aluminum Fabricated Products, Llc
27422 Portola Pkwy # 200
Foothill Ranch CA

(P-5702)
LUXFER INC
1995 3rd St (92507-3483)
PHONE.............................951 684-5110
Brian Mcguire, *Mgr*
EMP: 31
SALES (corp-wide): 423.4MM **Privately Held**
Web: www.luxfercylinders.com
SIC: 3354 3728 Aluminum extruded products ; Aircraft parts and equipment, nec
HQ: Luxfer Inc.
3016 Kansas Ave Bldg 1
Riverside CA
951 684-5110

(P-5703)
MERIT ALUMINUM INC (PA)
2480 Railroad St (92878-5418)
PHONE.............................951 735-1770
Michael Rapport, *CEO*
Evan Rapport, *
▲ **EMP:** 122 **EST:** 1990
SQ FT: 58,000
SALES (est): 39.33MM **Privately Held**
Web: www.meritaluminum.com
SIC: 3354 Aluminum extruded products

(P-5704)
NEAL FEAY COMPANY
Also Called: Troy Metal Products
133 S La Patera Ln (93117-3291)
PHONE.............................805 967-4521
Neal C Rasmussen, *CEO*
N J Rasmussen, *
Alex Rasmussen, *
EMP: 60 **EST:** 1944
SQ FT: 50,000
SALES (est): 9.49MM **Privately Held**
Web: www.nealfeay.com
SIC: 3354 3469 Tube, extruded or drawn, aluminum; Electronic enclosures, stamped or pressed metal

(P-5705)
PENGCHENG ALUMINUM ENTERPRISE INC USA
Also Called: Zhong W Ang Group
19605 E Walnut Dr N (91789-2815)
PHONE.............................909 598-7933
▲ **EMP:** 30
Web: www.pcaus.com
SIC: 3354 Aluminum extruded products

(P-5706)
PRL ALUMINUM INC
14760 Don Julian Rd (91746-3107)
PHONE.............................626 968-7507
Roberto Landeros, *CEO*
EMP: 100 **EST:** 2004
SALES (est): 17.55MM **Privately Held**

Web: www.architecturalglassandmetal.com
SIC: 3354 Aluminum extruded products
PA: Prl Glass Systems, Inc.
13644 Nelson Ave
City Of Industry CA

(P-5707)
SAMUEL SON & CO (USA) INC
Also Called: Sierra Aluminum
2345 Fleetwood Dr (92509-2410)
PHONE.............................951 781-7800
EMP: 24
SALES (corp-wide): 1.54B **Privately Held**
SIC: 3354 Aluminum extruded products
HQ: Samuel, Son & Co. (Usa) Inc.
1401 Davey Rd Ste 300
Woodridge IL
630 783-8900

(P-5708)
SIERRA ALUMINUM COMPANY
2345 Fleetwood Dr (92509-2426)
PHONE.............................951 781-7800
▲ **EMP:** 24
Web: www.samuel.com
SIC: 3354 Aluminum extruded products

(P-5709)
SUN VALLEY PRODUCTS INC (HQ)
4626 Sperry St (90039-1018)
PHONE.............................818 247-8350
Jennifer K Hillman, *Pr*
Rosanne M Kusar, *
Angelica K Clark, *
EMP: 40 **EST:** 1960
SQ FT: 64,980
SALES (est): 8.63MM
SALES (corp-wide): 8.63MM **Privately Held**
Web: www.sunvalleyextrusion.com
SIC: 3354 Aluminum extruded products
PA: Darfield Industries, Inc.
4626 Sperry St
Los Angeles CA
818 247-8350

(P-5710)
SUN VALLEY PRODUCTS INC
Also Called: Sun Valley Extrusion
4640 Sperry St (90039-1018)
PHONE.............................818 247-8350
Kerry Dodge, *Brnch Mgr*
EMP: 20
SALES (corp-wide): 8.63MM **Privately Held**
Web: www.sunvalleyextrusion.com
SIC: 3354 Aluminum extruded products
HQ: Sun Valley Products, Inc.
4626 Sperry St
Los Angeles CA
818 247-8350

(P-5711)
SUPERIOR METAL SHAPES INC
4730 Eucalyptus Ave (91710-9255)
PHONE.............................909 947-3455
David A Stockton, *Pr*
EMP: 40 **EST:** 1983
SQ FT: 64,000
SALES (est): 7.19MM **Privately Held**
Web: www.superiormetalshapes.net
SIC: 3354 Shapes, extruded aluminum, nec

(P-5712)
TRULITE GL ALUM SOLUTIONS LLC
19430 San Jose Ave (91748-1421)

PHONE.............................800 877-8439
Elizabeth Hemsing, *Mgr*
EMP: 72
Web: www.trulite.com
SIC: 3354 Aluminum extruded products
PA: Trulite Glass & Aluminum Solutions, Llc
403 Westpark Ct Ste 201
Peachtree City GA

(P-5713)
UNIVERSAL MLDING EXTRUSION INC (DH)
Also Called: Umex
9151 Imperial Hwy (90242-2808)
PHONE.............................562 401-1015
Dominick L Baione, *CEO*
◆ **EMP:** 43 **EST:** 1988
SALES (est): 63.52MM **Privately Held**
Web: www.umextrude.com
SIC: 3354 Aluminum extruded products
HQ: Universal Molding Company
9151 Imperial Hwy
Downey CA
310 886-1750

(P-5714)
US POLYMERS INC
5910 Bandini Blvd (90040-2963)
PHONE.............................323 727-6888
Vram Ohanesiam, *Mgr*
EMP: 100
SALES (corp-wide): 36.29MM **Privately Held**
Web: www.uspolymersinc.com
SIC: 3354 5719 Aluminum extruded products ; Window furnishings
PA: U.S. Polymers, Inc.
1057 S Vail Ave
Montebello CA
323 728-3023

(P-5715)
VISION SYSTEMS INC
11322 Woodside Ave N (92071-4728)
PHONE.............................619 258-7300
Fred W Witte, *Pr*
James Schlereth, *
▲ **EMP:** 60 **EST:** 1984
SQ FT: 32,000
SALES (est): 17.44MM **Privately Held**
Web: www.visionsystems.com
SIC: 3354 3442 Aluminum extruded products ; Window and door frames

(P-5716)
VISTA METALS CORP (PA)
13425 Whittram Ave (92335-2999)
PHONE.............................909 823-4278
Andrew Primack, *CEO*
Raymond Alpert, *
Steve Chevlin, *
Robert Praefke, *
◆ **EMP:** 235 **EST:** 1968
SQ FT: 17,000
SALES (est): 50.05MM
SALES (corp-wide): 50.05MM **Privately Held**
Web: www.vistametals.com
SIC: 3354 3341 Aluminum extruded products ; Aluminum smelting and refining (secondary)

3355 Aluminum Rolling And Drawing, Nec

(P-5717)
ARCADIA PRODUCTS LLC (HQ)
Also Called: Arcadia Norcal
2301 E Vernon Ave (90058-8052)

PHONE................................323 771-9819
James Schladen, *CEO*
Khan Chow, *CFO*
▲ **EMP:** 250 **EST:** 1985
SQ FT: 50,000
SALES (est): 174.07MM
SALES (corp-wide): 654.09MM **Publicly Held**
Web: www.arcadiainc.com
SIC: 3355 Extrusion ingot, aluminum: made in rolling mills
PA: Dmc Global Inc.
11800 Ridge Pkwy Ste 300
Broomfield CO
303 665-5700

(P-5718)
DIACK 1 INC
19437 Windrose Dr (91748-3994)
PHONE................................626 961-2491
Thomas Gonzalez, *Pr*
Consuelo Diack, *
EMP: 22 **EST:** 1953
SALES (est): 2.49MM **Privately Held**
Web: www.fhc-usa.com
SIC: 3355 Aluminum rolling and drawing, nec

(P-5719)
INTERSTATE STEEL CENTER CO INC
7001 S Alameda St (90001-2204)
PHONE................................323 583-0855
Leon Banks, *Pr*
William Korth, *
EMP: 50 **EST:** 1972
SQ FT: 53,000
SALES (est): 4.88MM **Privately Held**
Web: www.interstateleveling.com
SIC: 3355 3312 Coils, wire aluminum: made in rolling mills; Blast furnaces and steel mills

(P-5720)
METALS USA BUILDING PDTS LP (DH)
Also Called: Metals USA
955 Columbia St (92821-2923)
PHONE................................713 946-9000
Charles Canning, *Pt*
Robert Mcpherson, *Pt*
▲ **EMP:** 700 **EST:** 1960
SQ FT: 60,000
SALES (est): 270.44MM
SALES (corp-wide): 17.02B **Publicly Held**
Web: www.metalsusa.com
SIC: 3355 5031 1542 Structural shapes, rolled, aluminum; Building materials, exterior ; Commercial and office buildings, renovation and repair
HQ: Metals Usa, Inc.
800 W Cypress Creed Rd St
Fort Lauderdale FL
215 673-3595

(P-5721)
METALS USA BUILDING PDTS LP
1951 S Parco Ave Ste C (91761-8315)
PHONE................................800 325-1305
Steve Brang, *Mgr*
EMP: 88
SALES (corp-wide): 17.02B **Publicly Held**
Web: www.metalsusa.com
SIC: 3355 Structural shapes, rolled, aluminum
HQ: Metals Usa Building Products Lp
955 Columbia St
Brea CA
713 946-9000

(P-5722)
WERNER SYSTEMS INC
Also Called: Woodbridge Glass
14321 Myford Rd (92780-7022)
PHONE................................714 838-4444
Virgina Siciliani, *CEO*
Vito Siciliani, *Dir*
▲ **EMP:** 20 **EST:** 1984
SQ FT: 58,000
SALES (est): 4.81MM **Privately Held**
Web: www.woodbridgeglass.com
SIC: 3355 Aluminum rolling and drawing, nec

3356 Nonferrous Rolling And Drawing, Nec

(P-5723)
DYNAMET INCORPORATED
16052 Beach Blvd Ste 221 (92647-3855)
PHONE................................714 375-3150
Tom Proteau, *Mgr*
EMP: 32
SALES (corp-wide): 2.55B **Publicly Held**
Web: ir.carpentertechnology.com
SIC: 3356 Titanium and titanium alloy bars, sheets, strip, etc.
HQ: Dynamet Incorporated
195 Museum Rd
Washington PA
724 228-1000

(P-5724)
INTERSPACE BATTERY INC (PA)
2009 W San Bernardino Rd (91790-1006)
PHONE................................626 813-1234
Paul Godber, *Ch Bd*
Donald W Godber, *Pr*
EMP: 23 **EST:** 1970
SQ FT: 36,000
SALES (est): 3.57MM
SALES (corp-wide): 3.57MM **Privately Held**
Web: www.concordebattery.com
SIC: 3356 3691 Battery metal; Storage batteries

(P-5725)
NEW CNTURY MTALS SOUTHEAST INC
Also Called: Rti Los Angeles
15723 Shoemaker Ave (90650-6863)
PHONE................................562 356-6804
Jeremy S Halford, *CEO*
Marie T Batz, *
EMP: 379 **EST:** 1998
SALES (est): 2.2MM
SALES (corp-wide): 5.66B **Publicly Held**
SIC: 3356 Titanium
HQ: Rmi Titanium Company, Llc
1000 Warren Ave
Niles OH
330 652-9952

(P-5726)
OCEANIA INTERNATIONAL LLC
Also Called: Stanford Advanced Materials
23661 Birtcher Dr (92630-1770)
PHONE................................949 372-8385
Alexander Chen, *Managing Member*
▲ **EMP:** 40 **EST:** 2012
SALES (est): 3.69MM **Privately Held**
Web: www.samaterials.com
SIC: 3356 3313 Titanium and titanium alloy bars, sheets, strip, etc.; Ferromolybdenum

(P-5727)
UMC ACQUISITION CORP (PA)
Also Called: Universal Molding Company

9151 Imperial Hwy (90242-2808)
PHONE................................562 940-0300
Dominick L Baione, *Ch Bd*
Edward L Koch Iii, *Pr*
EMP: 50 **EST:** 1998
SALES (est): 135.02MM **Privately Held**
Web: www.universalmold.com
SIC: 3356 3354 3471 3479 Nonferrous rolling and drawing, nec; Anodizing (plating) of metals or formed products; Aluminum coating of metal products

(P-5728)
UNIVERSAL MOLDING COMPANY (HQ)
9151 Imperial Hwy (90242-2808)
PHONE................................310 886-1750
Dominick L Baione, *Ch Bd*
EMP: 160 **EST:** 1952
SQ FT: 62,000
SALES (est): 130.16MM **Privately Held**
Web: www.universalmold.com
SIC: 3356 3354 3448 3471 Nonferrous rolling and drawing, nec; Aluminum extruded products; Screen enclosures; Anodizing (plating) of metals or formed products
PA: Umc Acquisition Corp.
9151 Imperial Hwy
Downey CA

(P-5729)
VSMPO-TIRUS US INC
Also Called: West Coast Service Center
2850 E Cedar St (91761-8514)
PHONE................................909 230-9020
Dave Richardson, *Mgr*
EMP: 61
Web: www.vsmpo-tirus.com
SIC: 3356 Titanium
HQ: Vsmpo-Tirus, U.S., Inc.
1745 Shea Center Dr # 175
Highlands Ranch CO
720 746-1023

3357 Nonferrous Wiredrawing And Insulating

(P-5730)
BEE WIRE & CABLE INC
2850 E Spruce St (91761-8550)
PHONE................................909 923-5800
Arjan Bera, *Pr*
Kiran Kaneria, *
Nalin Kaneria, *
▲ **EMP:** 26 **EST:** 1979
SQ FT: 34,400
SALES (est): 2.17MM **Privately Held**
SIC: 3357 Building wire and cable, nonferrous

(P-5731)
BELDEN INC
Also Called: Coast Custom Cable
1048 E Burgrove St (90746-3514)
PHONE................................310 639-9473
Michael Dugar, *Brnch Mgr*
EMP: 750
SALES (corp-wide): 2.61B **Publicly Held**
Web: www.alphawire.com
SIC: 3357 3699 Coaxial cable, nonferrous; Electrical equipment and supplies, nec
PA: Belden Inc.
1 N Brentwood Blvd Fl 15
Saint Louis MO
314 854-8000

(P-5732)
BRIDGEWAVE COMMUNICATIONS INC
17034 Camino San Bernardo (92127-5708)
PHONE................................408 567-6900
Amir Makleff, *Pr*
John Keating, *
▲ **EMP:** 25 **EST:** 1998
SALES (est): 4.29MM **Privately Held**
Web: www.bridgewave.com
SIC: 3357 3229 Communication wire; Pressed and blown glass, nec

(P-5733)
BROADATA COMMUNICATIONS INC
2545 W 237th St Ste K (90505-5216)
PHONE................................310 530-1416
Freddie Lin, *Pr*
Patty Shaw, *
◆ **EMP:** 64 **EST:** 2000
SQ FT: 10,000
SALES (est): 13.21MM **Privately Held**
Web: www.broadatacom.com
SIC: 3357 3663 Fiber optic cable (insulated); Television broadcasting and communications equipment

(P-5734)
CABLESYS LLC
2100 E Valencia Dr Ste D (92831-4811)
PHONE................................562 356-3222
Mike Lin, *Managing Member*
▲ **EMP:** 20 **EST:** 1997
SQ FT: 10,000
SALES (est): 1.97MM **Privately Held**
Web: www.cablesys.com
SIC: 3357 Communication wire

(P-5735)
CALIFORNIA FINE WIRE CO (PA)
338 S 4th St (93433-1999)
P.O. Box 446 (93483-0446)
PHONE................................805 489-5144
EMP: 36 **EST:** 1961
SALES (est): 10.36MM
SALES (corp-wide): 10.36MM **Privately Held**
Web: www.calfinewire.com
SIC: 3357 3315 3466 3341 Nonferrous wiredrawing and insulating; Wire, ferrous/iron; Closures, stamped metal; Secondary nonferrous metals

(P-5736)
CALIFORNIA INSULATED WIRE &
3050 N California St (91504-2004)
PHONE................................818 569-4930
Bill Boyd, *Pr*
Micheal Boyd, *
Bruce Boyd, *
Lois Boyd, *
EMP: 60 **EST:** 1978
SQ FT: 26,000
SALES (est): 16.22MM **Privately Held**
Web: www.ciwinc.com
SIC: 3357 Communication wire

(P-5737)
CALMONT ENGRG & ELEC CORP (PA)
Also Called: Calmont Wire & Cable
420 E Alton Ave (92707-4242)
PHONE................................714 549-0336
Barbara Monteleone, *Pr*
Blanche F Chilcote, *
EMP: 36 **EST:** 1970
SQ FT: 24,000
SALES (est): 5.41MM

SALES (corp-wide): 5.41MM **Privately Held**
Web: www.calmont.com
SIC: 3357 3061 Nonferrous wiredrawing and insulating; Medical and surgical rubber tubing (extruded and lathe-cut)

(P-5738)
CENTURUM INFORMATION TECH INC
4250 Pacific Hwy Ste 105 (92110-3219)
PHONE............................619 224-1100
Brad Geiger, *Mgr*
EMP: 26
SALES (corp-wide): 56.12MM **Privately Held**
SIC: 3357 Shipboard cable, nonferrous
HQ: Centurum Information Technology, Inc.
651 Route 73 N Ste 107
Marlton NJ
856 751-1111

(P-5739)
CENTURY WIRE & CABLE INC
7400 E Slauson Ave (90040-3300)
PHONE............................800 999-5566
David Lifschitz, *CEO*
Carl Tom, *
Rowdy Oxford, *
William Suddarth, *
EMP: 100 **EST:** 1982
SALES (est): 25.27MM
SALES (corp-wide): 123.67MM **Privately Held**
Web: www.centurywire.com
SIC: 3357 5063 Nonferrous wiredrawing and insulating; Electrical apparatus and equipment
HQ: Gehr Industries, Inc.
7400 E Slauson Ave
Commerce CA
323 728-5558

(P-5740)
COAST 2 COAST CABLES LLC
3162 E La Palma Ave Ste D (92806-2810)
PHONE............................714 666-1062
Lynn Swearingen, *Managing Member*
EMP: 45 **EST:** 2007
SQ FT: 14,040
SALES (est): 6.79MM
SALES (corp-wide): 28.11MM **Privately Held**
SIC: 3357 Aluminum wire and cable
PA: Nyle, Llc
555 E Lancaster Ave Fl 3
Radnor PA

(P-5741)
FIBEROPTIC SYSTEMS INC
60 Moreland Rd Ste A (93065-1643)
PHONE............................805 579-6600
Sanford S Stark, *Pr*
Kathy Hanau, *
EMP: 29 **EST:** 1982
SQ FT: 14,000
SALES (est): 4.3MM **Privately Held**
Web: www.fiberopticsystems.com
SIC: 3357 3229 Fiber optic cable (insulated); Fiber optics strands

(P-5742)
GEHR INDUSTRIES INC (HQ)
Also Called: Gehr Group
7400 E Slauson Ave (90040-3300)
PHONE............................323 728-5558
David Lifschitz, *CEO*
Carlton Tom, *VP*
Mark Goldman, *COO*
William Suddarth, *VP*

▲ **EMP:** 140 **EST:** 1966
SQ FT: 260,000
SALES (est): 57.64MM
SALES (corp-wide): 123.67MM **Privately Held**
Web: www.gehrindustries.com
SIC: 3357 5063 5072 5085 Nonferrous wiredrawing and insulating; Electrical apparatus and equipment; Hardware; Industrial supplies
PA: The Gehr Group Inc
7400 E Slauson Ave
Commerce CA
323 728-5558

(P-5743)
HELISTRAND INC
707 E Yanonali St (93103-3273)
PHONE............................805 963-4518
EMP: 20 **EST:** 1972
SALES (est): 600K **Privately Held**
Web: www.helistrand.com
SIC: 3357 Aircraft wire and cable, nonferrous

(P-5744)
JEB HOLDINGS CORP
42033 Rio Nedo (92590-3705)
P.O. Box 67 (92549-0067)
PHONE............................951 296-9900
Gordon Brown, *Pr*
EMP: 23
SALES (corp-wide): 23.43MM **Privately Held**
Web: www.southbaycable.com
SIC: 3357 Nonferrous wiredrawing and insulating
PA: Jeb Holdings Corp.
54125 Maranatha Dr
Idyllwild CA
951 659-2183

(P-5745)
OKONITE COMPANY INC
2900 Skyway Dr (93455-1897)
PHONE............................805 922-6682
Rick Flory, *Brnch Mgr*
EMP: 193
SQ FT: 10,000
SALES (corp-wide): 505.89MM **Privately Held**
Web: www.okonite.com
SIC: 3357 Nonferrous wiredrawing and insulating
PA: The Okonite Company Inc
102 Hilltop Rd
Ramsey NJ
201 825-0300

(P-5746)
PHILATRON INTERNATIONAL
15645 Clanton Cir (90670-5613)
PHONE............................562 802-2570
EMP: 20
SALES (corp-wide): 24.17MM **Privately Held**
Web: www.philatron.com
SIC: 3357 Nonferrous wiredrawing and insulating
PA: Philatron International
15315 Cornet St
Santa Fe Springs CA
562 802-0452

(P-5747)
PRECISION FIBER PRODUCTS INC
Also Called: Pfp
642 Palomar St (91911-2626)
PHONE............................408 946-4040
Ray Pierce, *Pr*

◆ **EMP:** 30 **EST:** 2003
SALES (est): 3.47MM **Privately Held**
Web: www.precisionfiberproducts.com
SIC: 3357 Fiber optic cable (insulated)

(P-5748)
PRIME WIRE & CABLE INC
11701 6th St (91730-6030)
PHONE............................323 266-2010
EMP: 104
Web: www.primewirecable.com
SIC: 3357 Nonferrous wiredrawing and insulating
HQ: Prime Wire & Cable, Inc.
1330 Valley Vista Dr
Diamond Bar CA
888 445-9955

(P-5749)
QPC FIBER OPTIC LLC
27612 El Lazo (92677-3913)
PHONE............................949 361-8855
Steven J Wilkes, *Pr*
David Olsen, *
EMP: 30 **EST:** 1999
SQ FT: 1,400
SALES (est): 7.35MM **Privately Held**
Web: www.qpcfiber.com
SIC: 3357 Fiber optic cable (insulated)

(P-5750)
STANDARD WIRE & CABLE CO (PA)
Also Called: American Wire Sales
2050 E Vista Bella Way (90220-6109)
PHONE............................310 609-1811
Russell J Skrable, *Pr*
Dick Hampikian, *Ch Bd*
◆ **EMP:** 22 **EST:** 1947
SQ FT: 45,500
SALES (est): 10.86MM
SALES (corp-wide): 10.86MM **Privately Held**
Web: www.standard-wire.com
SIC: 3357 5063 Coaxial cable, nonferrous; Wire and cable

(P-5751)
SUPERIOR ESSEX INC
5250 Ontario Mills Pkwy Ste 300 (91764-5131)
PHONE............................909 481-4804
EMP: 103
Web: www.superioressex.com
SIC: 3357 Nonferrous wiredrawing and insulating
HQ: Superior Essex Inc.
5770 Powers Ferry Rd
Atlanta GA
770 657-6000

(P-5752)
WAVENET INC (PA)
707 E Sepulveda Blvd (90745-6032)
PHONE............................310 885-4200
Yi Hong Jang, *CEO*
Kevin Chang, *COO*
Keun Hee Chang, *Sec*
▲ **EMP:** 18 **EST:** 1990
SQ FT: 29,000
SALES (est): 3.04MM **Privately Held**
Web: www.wavenetcable.com
SIC: 3357 Fiber optic cable (insulated)

(P-5753)
WINCHSTER INTRCNNECT CM CA INC
Also Called: C B S
1810 Diamond St (92078-5100)

PHONE............................800 848-4257
Lewis Brian Falk, *CEO*
Donald Falk, *
Shannon Baroni, *
▲ **EMP:** 175 **EST:** 1965
SQ FT: 40,000
SALES (est): 46.8MM
SALES (corp-wide): 17.49B **Privately Held**
Web: www.falmat.com
SIC: 3357 5063 Nonferrous wiredrawing and insulating; Wire and cable
HQ: Aptiv Corporation
5820 Innovation Dr
Troy MI

(P-5754)
WIRE TECHNOLOGY CORPORATION
9527 Laurel St (90002-2653)
P.O. Box 1608 (90280-1608)
PHONE............................310 635-6935
Rachel Mendoza, *Pr*
Darlene Delange, *
Robert Mendoza, *
EMP: 25 **EST:** 1970
SQ FT: 4,000
SALES (est): 3.02MM **Privately Held**
Web: www.wiretechnologycorp.com
SIC: 3357 Nonferrous wiredrawing and insulating

3363 Aluminum Die-castings

(P-5755)
AEROTEC ALLOYS INC
10632 Alondra Blvd (90650-5301)
PHONE............................562 809-1378
Robert W Franklin, *CEO*
Mitchell Frahm, *
EMP: 50 **EST:** 1986
SQ FT: 18,000
SALES (est): 7.11MM **Privately Held**
Web: www.aerotecalloys.com
SIC: 3363 3312 3365 3325 Aluminum die-castings; Blast furnaces and steel mills; Aluminum foundries; Steel foundries, nec

(P-5756)
ALLOY DIE CASTING CO
Also Called: ADC Aerospace
6550 Caballero Blvd (90620-1130)
PHONE............................714 521-9800
Rick Simpson, *CEO*
Eric Sanders, *Pr*
Wim Huijs, *VP*
Maeli Garcia, *Dir*
Melissa Duran, *Acctg Mgr*
EMP: 135 **EST:** 1939
SQ FT: 55,000
SALES (est): 23.12MM **Privately Held**
Web: www.adc-aerospace.com
SIC: 3363 Aluminum die-castings

(P-5757)
ALUMINUM DIE CASTING CO INC
10775 San Sevaine Way (91752-1146)
PHONE............................951 681-3900
Steve Bennett, *CEO*
Rudy Bennett, *
James Bennett, *Stockholder**
EMP: 65 **EST:** 1950
SQ FT: 31,000
SALES (est): 8.44MM **Privately Held**
Web: www.adc3900.com
SIC: 3363 3364 Aluminum die-castings; Nonferrous die-castings except aluminum

(PA)=Parent Co (HQ)=Headquarters
✪ = New Business established in last 2 years

2024 Southern California
Business Directory and Buyers Guide

279

P R O D U C T S & S V C S

(P-5758)
EDELBROCK FOUNDRY CORP
1320 S Buena Vista St (92583-4665)
PHONE.................................951 654-6677
Otis Victor Edelbrock, *Pr*
Ronald L Webb, *
Nancy Edelbrock, *
Aristedes Seles, *
Camme Edelbrock, *
EMP: 40 **EST:** 1938
SQ FT: 75,000
SALES (est): 24.95MM **Privately Held**
Web: www.edelbrock.com
SIC: 3363 3365 3325 Aluminum die-castings
; Aluminum foundries; Steel foundries, nec
HQ: Edelbrock, Llc
8649 Hacks Cross Rd
Olive Branch MS
310 781-2222

(P-5759)
HYATT DIE CAST AND
ENGINEERING CORPORATION -
SOUTH (PA)
4656 Lincoln Ave (90630-2650)
P.O. Box 728 (90630-0728)
PHONE.................................714 826-7550
EMP: 80 **EST:** 1956
SALES (est): 25.09MM
SALES (corp-wide): 25.09MM **Privately**
Held
SIC: 3363 Aluminum die-castings

(P-5760)
HYATT DIE CAST ENGRG CORP
- S
12250 Industry St (92841-2816)
PHONE.................................714 622-2131
Mike Senter, *Brnch Mgr*
EMP: 35
SALES (corp-wide): 25.09MM **Privately**
Held
Web: www.hyattdiecast.com
SIC: 3363 Aluminum die-castings
PA: Hyatt Die Cast And Engineering
Corporation - South
4656 Lincoln Ave
Cypress CA
714 826-7550

(P-5761)
KENWALT DIE CASTING CORP
Also Called: Kenwait Die Casting Company
8719 Bradley Ave (91352-2799)
PHONE.................................818 768-5800
TOLL FREE: 800
Ken Zaucha Senior, *Pr*
Rose Zaucha, *Stockholder**
▼ **EMP:** 25 **EST:** 1974
SQ FT: 20,000
SALES (est): 3.55MM **Privately Held**
Web: www.kenwalt.com
SIC: 3363 Aluminum die-castings

(P-5762)
MAGNESIUM ALLOY PDTS CO
INC
2420 N Alameda St (90222-2895)
P.O. Box 4668 (90224-4668)
PHONE.................................310 605-1440
J W Long, *Pr*
M B Long, *
EMP: 46 **EST:** 1945
SQ FT: 90,000
SALES (est): 5.59MM **Privately Held**
Web: www.magnesiumalloy.com
SIC: 3363 Aluminum die-castings

(P-5763)
MAGNESIUM ALLOY
PRODUCTS CO LP
2420 N Alameda St (90222-2895)
PHONE.................................323 636-2276
EMP: 50 **EST:** 1956
SALES (est): 4.5MM **Privately Held**
Web: www.magnesiumalloy.com
SIC: 3363 Aluminum die-castings

(P-5764)
PACIFIC DIE CASTING CORP
6155 S Eastern Ave (90040-3401)
PHONE.................................323 725-1308
Jeff Orlandini, *VP*
Sonny Yun, *Stockholder**
▲ **EMP:** 150 **EST:** 1954
SQ FT: 8,000
SALES (est): 23.12MM **Privately Held**
Web: www.pacdiecast.com
SIC: 3363 Aluminum die-castings

(P-5765)
PERFORMANCE ALUMINUM
PRODUCTS
Also Called: Performance Aluminum
520 S Palmetto Ave (91762-4121)
PHONE.................................909 391-4131
John Reed, *Pr*
▲ **EMP:** 20 **EST:** 1985
SALES (est): 2.17MM **Privately Held**
Web: www.performancealuminum.net
SIC: 3363 Aluminum die-castings

(P-5766)
PIONEER DIECASTERS INC
4209 Chevy Chase Dr (90039-1274)
P.O. Box 406 (91012-0406)
PHONE.................................323 245-6561
Carl H Spahr, *Pr*
Gretchen Perry, *Sec*
EMP: 17 **EST:** 1949
SQ FT: 18,000
SALES (est): 2.19MM **Privately Held**
SIC: 3363 3364 5051 Aluminum die-castings
; Zinc and zinc-base alloy die-castings;
Aluminum bars, rods, ingots, sheets, pipes,
plates, etc.

(P-5767)
RANGERS DIE CASTING CO
10828 Alameda St (90262-1721)
P.O. Box 127 (90262-0127)
PHONE.................................310 764-1800
EMP: 40
Web: www.rangersdiecasting.com
SIC: 3363 3544 3599 Aluminum die-castings
; Special dies, tools, jigs, and fixtures;
Machine and other job shop work

(P-5768)
SEA SHIELD MARINE
PRODUCTS
Also Called: American Zinc Enterprises
20832 Currier Rd (91789-3017)
PHONE.................................909 594-2507
Wendell Walter Godwin, *CEO*
Shelley Lopez, *
Alicia Vongoeben, *
▲ **EMP:** 45 **EST:** 1971
SQ FT: 25,000
SALES (est): 9.94MM **Privately Held**
Web: www.seashieldmarine.com
SIC: 3363 3364 Aluminum die-castings;
Magnesium and magnesium-base alloy die-
castings

(P-5769)
VENUS ALLOYS INC (PA)
1415 S Allec St (92805-6306)
PHONE.................................714 635-8800
E K Venugopal, *Pr*
Kousalya Venugopal, *
EMP: 24 **EST:** 1989
SQ FT: 20,000
SALES (est): 5.41MM **Privately Held**
SIC: 3363 3364 Aluminum die-castings;
Brass and bronze die-castings

3364 Nonferrous Die-castings Except Aluminum

(P-5770)
ALCAST MFG INC
2910 Fisk Ln (90278-5437)
PHONE.................................310 542-3581
EMP: 30
SALES (corp-wide): 9.6MM **Privately Held**
Web: www.alcast-foundry.com
SIC: 3364 3363 Brass and bronze die-
castings; Aluminum die-castings
PA: Alcast Mfg, Inc.
7355 E Slauson Ave
Commerce CA
310 542-3581

(P-5771)
AMERICAN DIE CASTING INC
14576 Fontlee Ln (92335-2599)
PHONE.................................909 356-7768
TOLL FREE: 800
Walter Mueller, *Pr*
Jeffrey Mueller, *
Marjorie Mueller, *
EMP: 50 **EST:** 1992
SQ FT: 20,000
SALES (est): 4.67MM **Privately Held**
Web: www.americandiecasting.com
SIC: 3364 3363 Zinc and zinc-base alloy die-
castings; Aluminum die-castings

(P-5772)
CALIFORNIA DIE CASTING INC
1820 S Grove Ave (91761-5613)
PHONE.................................909 947-9947
EMP: 49 **EST:** 1996
SQ FT: 3,000
SALES (est): 8.52MM **Privately Held**
Web: www.caldiecast.com
SIC: 3364 3363 Nonferrous die-castings
except aluminum; Aluminum die-castings

(P-5773)
DEL MAR INDUSTRIES (PA)
Also Called: Del Mar Die Casting Co
12901 S Western Ave (90249-1917)
P.O. Box 881 (90294-0881)
PHONE.................................323 321-0600
Doctor Taylor, *CEO*
Louis A Cuhrt, *
Judith Taylor, *
Susan Davis, *Stockholder**
EMP: 100 **EST:** 1968
SQ FT: 68,000
SALES (est): 9.9MM
SALES (corp-wide): 9.9MM **Privately Held**
Web: www.delmarindustries.com
SIC: 3364 Zinc and zinc-base alloy die-
castings

(P-5774)
DYNACAST LLC
Also Called: Dynacast, LLC
25952 Commercentre Dr (92630-8815)
PHONE.................................949 707-1211

John Hess, *Brnch Mgr*
EMP: 140
Web: www.dynacast.com
SIC: 3364 Nonferrous die-castings except
aluminum
HQ: Dynacast Us Holdings, Inc.
14045 Balntyn Corp Pl
Charlotte NC
704 927-2790

(P-5775)
FTG AEROSPACE INC (DH)
20740 Marilla St (91311-4407)
PHONE.................................818 407-4024
▼ **EMP:** 42 **EST:** 2011
SQ FT: 13,000
SALES (est): 24.49MM
SALES (corp-wide): 65.73MM **Privately**
Held
Web: www.ftgcorp.com
SIC: 3364 Nonferrous die-castings except
aluminum
HQ: Firan Technology Group (Usa)
Corporation
20750 Marilla St
Chatsworth CA
818 407-4024

(P-5776)
VERTECHS ENTERPRISES INC
(PA)
1071 Industrial Pl (92020-3107)
PHONE.................................858 578-3900
Geosef Straza, *CEO*
George C Straza, *
▲ **EMP:** 46 **EST:** 2007
SALES (est): 9.83MM **Privately Held**
Web: www.vertechsusa.com
SIC: 3364 3724 3544 Copper and copper
alloy die-castings; Aircraft engines and
engine parts; Die sets for metal stamping
(presses)

(P-5777)
WHITEFOX DEFENSE TECH INC
854 Monterey St (93401-3225)
PHONE.................................805 225-4506
Mark Kulam, *Pr*
EMP: 25 **EST:** 2016
SALES (est): 5.62MM **Privately Held**
Web: www.whitefoxdefense.com
SIC: 3364 Nonferrous die-castings except
aluminum

3365 Aluminum Foundries

(P-5778)
ADM WORKS LLC
1343 E Wilshire Ave (92705-4420)
PHONE.................................714 245-0536
Jimmy Garcia, *Managing Member*
EMP: 23 **EST:** 2004
SALES (est): 3.13MM **Privately Held**
Web: www.adm-works.com
SIC: 3365 7389 8711 Aerospace castings,
aluminum; Design services; Engineering
services

(P-5779)
AEROL CO INC
Also Called: Aerol Co
19560 S Rancho Way (90220-6038)
PHONE.................................310 762-2660
▲ **EMP:** 36
Web: www.aerol.com
SIC: 3365 2821 3714 3728 Aluminum
foundries; Plastics materials and resins;
Motor vehicle parts and accessories;
Wheels, aircraft

(P-5780)
ALCAST MFG INC (PA)
7355 E Slauson Ave (90040-3626)
PHONE..............................310 542-3581
Kiwon Ban, *CEO*
Soo Ban, *Treas*
Lily Martinez, *
▲ EMP: 25 EST: 1986
SALES (est): 9.6MM
SALES (corp-wide): 9.6MM **Privately Held**
Web: www.alcast-foundry.com
SIC: 3365 3366 3544 3369 Aluminum and
aluminum-based alloy castings; Brass
foundry, nec; Special dies, tools, jigs, and
fixtures; Nonferrous foundries, nec

(P-5781)
ALUMISTAR INC
Also Called: Pacific Cast Products
520 S Palmetto Ave (91762-4121)
PHONE..............................562 633-6673
Peter Lake, *Pr*
▲ EMP: 26 EST: 1982
SALES (est): 4.8MM **Privately Held**
Web: www.pacificcastproducts.com
SIC: 3365 Aluminum and aluminum-based
alloy castings

(P-5782)
**AMERICAN INTRNTNL-STEEL
CAST D**
Also Called: American International
860 Arroyo St (91340-1832)
PHONE..............................818 365-8000
Ward H White, *Pr*
EMP: 26 EST: 1972
SQ FT: 12,000
SALES (est): 921.92K **Privately Held**
SIC: 3365 Aluminum foundries

(P-5783)
BUDDY BAR CASTING LLC
10801 Sessler St (90280-7222)
PHONE..............................562 861-9664
Edward W Barksdale Senior, *Prin*
Bill Fell, *
Mike Mckeen, *VP*
John Fell, *
▲ EMP: 130 EST: 1953
SQ FT: 25,000
SALES (est): 18.49MM **Privately Held**
Web: www.buddybarcasting.com
SIC: 3365 Aluminum foundries

(P-5784)
CALIDAD INC
1730 S Balboa Ave (91761-7773)
PHONE..............................909 947-3937
Don Cornell, *Pr*
Daniel Garcia, *
EMP: 30 EST: 1986
SQ FT: 10,000
SALES (est): 4.1MM **Privately Held**
Web: www.calidadinc.com
SIC: 3365 3324 Aluminum foundries; Steel
investment foundries

(P-5785)
**CONSOLDTED PRECISION
PDTS CORP**
705 Industrial Way (93041-3505)
PHONE..............................805 488-6451
EMP: 88
SALES (corp-wide): 2.07B **Privately Held**
Web: www.cppcorp.com
SIC: 3365 Aluminum foundries
PA: Consolidated Precision Products Corp.
1621 Euclid Ave Ste 1850
Cleveland OH
216 453-4800

(P-5786)
**CONSOLDTED PRECISION
PDTS CORP**
Also Called: Cpp - Pomona
4200 West Valley Blvd (91769)
PHONE..............................909 595-2252
James Stewart, *CEO*
EMP: 153
SALES (corp-wide): 2.07B **Privately Held**
Web: www.cppcorp.com
SIC: 3365 3324 Aluminum foundries; Steel
investment foundries
PA: Consolidated Precision Products Corp.
1621 Euclid Ave Ste 1850
Cleveland OH
216 453-4800

(P-5787)
**CONSOLIDATED FOUNDRIES
INC**
Also Called: Cpp Cudahy
8333 Wilcox Ave (90201-5919)
P.O. Box 1099 (90201-7099)
PHONE..............................323 773-2363
Steve Gallardo, *Brnch Mgr*
EMP: 130
SALES (corp-wide): 2.07B **Privately Held**
Web: www.cppcorp.com
SIC: 3365 3324 Aluminum foundries; Steel
investment foundries
HQ: Consolidated Foundries, Inc.
1621 Euclid Ave Ste 1850
Cleveland OH

(P-5788)
**CYTEC ENGINEERED
MATERIALS INC**
Also Called: Solvay Composite Materials
1440 N Kraemer Blvd (92806-1404)
PHONE..............................714 632-1174
Ron Martin, *Brnch Mgr*
EMP: 125
SQ FT: 135,055
SALES (corp-wide): 146.05MM **Privately
Held**
SIC: 3365 2891 2851 2823 Aerospace
castings, aluminum; Adhesives and sealants
; Paints and allied products; Cellulosic
manmade fibers
HQ: Cytec Engineered Materials Inc.
2085 E Tech Cir Ste 102
Tempe AZ

(P-5789)
DC PARTNERS INC (PA)
Also Called: Soligen 2006
19329 Bryant St (91324-4114)
PHONE..............................714 558-9444
Yehoram Uziel, *Pr*
Alecia Wagner, *
EMP: 32 EST: 2005
SALES (est): 5.46MM **Privately Held**
Web: www.soligen2006.com
SIC: 3365 3599 Aluminum foundries;
Machine and other job shop work

(P-5790)
**DOWELL ALUMINUM FOUNDRY
INC**
11342 Hartland St (91605-6387)
PHONE..............................323 877-9645
Lynn F Dompe, *Pr*
EMP: 22 EST: 1954
SQ FT: 17,000
SALES (est): 829.8K **Privately Held**
SIC: 3365 3369 Aluminum and aluminum-
based alloy castings; Nonferrous foundries,
nec

(P-5791)
**DWA ALUMINUM COMPOSITES
USA INC**
21100 Superior St (91311-4308)
PHONE..............................818 998-1504
Mark R Van Den Bergh, *CEO*
J J Shah, *CFO*
Gary Wolfe, *COO*
EMP: 20 EST: 2013
SQ FT: 40,000
SALES (est): 4.88MM **Privately Held**
Web: www.dwa-usa.com
SIC: 3365 Aluminum and aluminum-based
alloy castings

(P-5792)
**EMPLOYEE OWNED PCF CAST
PDTS I**
Also Called: Aluminum Casting Company
520 S Palmetto Ave (91762-4121)
PHONE..............................562 633-6673
Alex B Hall, *Pr*
EMP: 24 EST: 2000
SALES (est): 983.13K **Privately Held**
SIC: 3365 Aluminum and aluminum-based
alloy castings

(P-5793)
**FONTANA FOUNDRY
CORPORATION**
8306 Cherry Ave (92335-3026)
PHONE..............................909 822-6128
Jeffrey Ritz, *Pr*
Susan Ritz, *
EMP: 17 EST: 1946
SQ FT: 11,500
SALES (est): 2.16MM **Privately Held**
Web: www.fontanafoundry.com
SIC: 3365 Aluminum and aluminum-based
alloy castings

(P-5794)
GC INTERNATIONAL INC (PA)
Also Called: Alj
4671 Calle Carga (93012-8560)
PHONE..............................805 389-4631
Mark Griffith, *
Richard R Carlson, *Pr*
Mark R Griffith, *VP*
Terry Carlson, *VP*
F Willard Griffith, *CEO*
▼ EMP: 43 EST: 1975
SQ FT: 45,000
SALES (est): 14.34MM
SALES (corp-wide): 14.34MM **Privately
Held**
Web: www.aljcast.com
SIC: 3365 3695 3369 3061 Aluminum and
aluminum-based alloy castings; Magnetic
disks and drums; Lead, zinc, and white
metal; Appliance rubber goods (mechanical)

(P-5795)
GRISWOLD INDUSTRIES (PA)
Also Called: Cla-Val Co
1701 Placentia Ave (92627-4416)
P.O. Box 1325 (92659-0325)
PHONE..............................949 722-4800
◆ EMP: 420 EST: 1936
SALES (est): 75.13MM
SALES (corp-wide): 75.13MM **Privately
Held**
Web: www.cla-val.com
SIC: 3365 3366 3492 3325 Aluminum
foundries; Brass foundry, nec; Control
valves, fluid power: hydraulic and pneumatic
; Steel foundries, nec

(P-5796)
**LYNWOOD PATTERN SERVICE
INC**
603 S Hope Ave (91761-1824)
P.O. Box 536 (90262-0536)
PHONE..............................310 631-2225
Jose Alvarez, *Pr*
Benjamen Alvarez, *VP*
EMP: 20 EST: 1944
SQ FT: 4,000
SALES (est): 964.35K **Privately Held**
Web: www.lynwoodpattern.com
SIC: 3365 3543 Aluminum and aluminum-
based alloy castings; Foundry
patternmaking

(P-5797)
MAGPARTS (HQ)
Also Called: Cpp-Azusa
1545 W Roosevelt St (91702-3281)
P.O. Box 1099 (90201-7099)
PHONE..............................626 334-7897
Richard H Emerson, *Pr*
L Scott Donald Mac, *VP*
Ellen E Skatvold, *
EMP: 140 EST: 1958
SQ FT: 100,000
SALES (est): 24.69MM
SALES (corp-wide): 2.07B **Privately Held**
Web: www.perfectdomain.com
SIC: 3365 3369 Aluminum and aluminum-
based alloy castings; Magnesium and
magnes.-base alloy castings, exc. die-
casting
PA: Consolidated Precision Products Corp.
1621 Euclid Ave Ste 1850
Cleveland OH
216 453-4800

(P-5798)
SONFARREL AEROSPACE LLC
3010 E La Jolla St (92806-1310)
PHONE..............................714 630-7280
Jeffrey Greer, *CEO*
Ken Anderson, *
EMP: 96 EST: 2018
SALES (est): 10.43MM **Privately Held**
Web: www.son-aero.com
SIC: 3365 Aerospace castings, aluminum

(P-5799)
SUPERNAL LLC
15555 Laguna Canyon Rd (92618-7722)
PHONE..............................202 422-3275
Jaiwon Shin, *Brnch Mgr*
EMP: 155
SIC: 3365 Aerospace castings, aluminum
HQ: Supernal, Llc
1101 16th St Nw
Washington DC
202 422-3175

3366 Copper Foundries

(P-5800)
ACME CASTINGS INC
6009 Santa Fe Ave (90255-2723)
PHONE..............................323 583-3129
Lee Lewis, *Pr*
Ruth Lewis, *
EMP: 24 EST: 1963
SQ FT: 25,000
SALES (est): 1.19MM **Privately Held**
Web: www.acme-castings.com
SIC: 3366 3325 3365 3322 Copper foundries
; Alloy steel castings, except investment;
Aluminum foundries; Malleable iron
foundries

PRODUCTS & SVCS

(P-5801)
ART BRONZE INC
11275 San Fernando Rd (91340-3422)
PHONE.............................818 897-2222
Ian G Killips, *CEO*
EMP: 18 **EST:** 1971
SQ FT: 11,400
SALES (est): 2.21MM **Privately Held**
Web: www.artbronze.com
SIC: 3366 3312 Bronze foundry, nec;
Stainless steel

(P-5802)
FLEETWOOD CONTINENTAL INC
19451 S Susana Rd (90221-5713)
PHONE.............................310 609-1477
David J Forster, *Pr*
▲ **EMP:** 75 **EST:** 1965
SQ FT: 5,000
SALES (est): 10.41MM **Privately Held**
Web: www.fleetcon.com
SIC: 3366 3823 3561 3523 Castings (except die), nec, bronze; Turbine flow meters, industrial process type; Pumps and pumping equipment; Farm machinery and equipment

(P-5803)
GALAXY DIE AND ENGINEERING INC
Also Called: Galaxy Bearing Company
24910 Avenue Tibbitts (91355-3426)
PHONE.............................661 775-9301
Jawahar Saini, *Pr*
Hamid Baig, *
Sooltan Ali Bhoy, *
Malkiat Saini, *Stockholder**
EMP: 40 **EST:** 1958
SQ FT: 30,000
SALES (est): 4.76MM **Privately Held**
Web: www.galaxybearing.com
SIC: 3366 3575 Bushings and bearings;
Computer terminals

(P-5804)
MATTHEWS INTERNATIONAL CORP
442 W Esplanade Ave # 105 (92583-5006)
PHONE.............................951 537-6615
Rocky Thornton, *Mgr*
EMP: 17
SALES (corp-wide): 1.88B **Publicly Held**
Web: www.matw.com
SIC: 3366 Copper foundries
PA: Matthews International Corporation
2 N Shore Ctr Ste 200
Pittsburgh PA
412 442-8200

(P-5805)
MONTCLAIR BRONZE INC (PA)
2535 E 57th St (90255-2520)
P.O. Box 2009 (91763-0509)
PHONE.............................909 986-2664
Dan Griffiths, *
Wayne Freeberg, *
Thomas Freeberg, *
EMP: 20 **EST:** 1963
SALES (est): 5.3MM
SALES (corp-wide): 5.3MM **Privately Held**
Web: www.montclairbronze.com
SIC: 3366 3599 Bronze foundry, nec;
Machine shop, jobbing and repair

(P-5806)
PAC FOUNDRIES INC
Also Called: Cpp-Port Hueneme
705 Industrial Way (93041-3505)
PHONE.............................805 986-1308
Steve Clodfelter, *Pr*
EMP: 99 **EST:** 1978
SALES (est): 21.33MM
SALES (corp-wide): 2.07B **Privately Held**
Web: www.cppcorp.com
SIC: 3366 Copper foundries
PA: Consolidated Precision Products Corp.
1621 Euclid Ave Ste 1850
Cleveland OH
216 453-4800

3369 Nonferrous Foundries, Nec

(P-5807)
ALLIEDSIGNAL AROSPC SVC CORP (HQ)
Also Called: Allied Signal Aerospace
2525 W 190th St (90504-6002)
PHONE.............................310 323-9500
Bernd F Kessler, *Pr*
Mary Beth Orson, *
James V Gelly, *
EMP: 53 **EST:** 2003
SALES (est): 101.89MM
SALES (corp-wide): 35.47B **Publicly Held**
SIC: 3369 3822 3812 3769 Nonferrous
foundries, nec; Environmental controls;
Search and navigation equipment; Space
vehicle equipment, nec
PA: Honeywell International Inc.
855 S Mint St
Charlotte NC
704 627-6200

(P-5808)
CAST PARTNER INC
4658 W Washington Blvd (90016-1743)
PHONE.............................323 876-9000
Fridlizius Theo, *Pr*
EMP: 26 **EST:** 2013
SALES (est): 3.17MM **Privately Held**
Web: www.castpartner.com
SIC: 3369 Nonferrous foundries, nec

(P-5809)
CAST-RITE INTERNATIONAL INC (PA)
515 E Airline Way (90248-2501)
PHONE.............................310 532-2080
Donald E Dehaan, *CEO*
Wynn Chapman, *
Howard Watkins, *
◆ **EMP:** 90 **EST:** 1961
SQ FT: 59,330
SALES (est): 24.75MM
SALES (corp-wide): 24.75MM **Privately Held**
Web: www.cast-rite.com
SIC: 3369 Zinc and zinc-base alloy castings, except die-castings

(P-5810)
DECCO CASTINGS INC
1596 Pioneer Way (92020-1638)
PHONE.............................619 444-9437
Carl Decina, *Pr*
EMP: 45 **EST:** 1971
SQ FT: 20,000
SALES (est): 8.32MM **Privately Held**
Web: www.deccocastings.com
SIC: 3369 3365 3325 Nonferrous foundries, nec; Aluminum foundries; Steel foundries, nec

(P-5811)
DELT INDUSTRIES INC
90 W Easy St Ste 2 (93065-6206)
P.O. Box 940067 (93094-0067)
PHONE.............................805 579-0213
EMP: 18 **EST:** 1994
SQ FT: 10,000
SALES (est): 2.46MM **Privately Held**
Web: www.deltindustries.com
SIC: 3369 5088 Nonferrous foundries, nec;
Transportation equipment and supplies

(P-5812)
EXCELITY
Also Called: Solara Engineering
11127 Dora St (91352-3339)
PHONE.............................818 767-1000
Shaun Tan, *Pr*
EMP: 56 **EST:** 2003
SALES (est): 893.13K **Privately Held**
Web: www.ceridian.com
SIC: 3369 3812 Aerospace castings, nonferrous: except aluminum; Acceleration indicators and systems components, aerospace

(P-5813)
FENICO PRECISION CASTINGS INC
7805 Madison St (90723-4220)
PHONE.............................562 634-5000
Don Tomeo, *Pr*
Sherry Tomeo, *
▲ **EMP:** 75 **EST:** 1987
SQ FT: 20,000
SALES (est): 8.68MM **Privately Held**
Web: www.fenicocastings.com
SIC: 3369 3366 3324 3322 Machinery castings, exc. die, nonferrous, exc. alum. copper; Copper foundries; Steel investment foundries; Malleable iron foundries

(P-5814)
FS - PRECISION TECH CO LLC
3025 E Victoria St (90221-5616)
PHONE.............................310 638-0595
Israel M Sanchez, *
▲ **EMP:** 100 **EST:** 2004
SALES (est): 24.83MM **Privately Held**
Web: www.fs-precision.com
SIC: 3369 Titanium castings, except die-casting
PA: Fs-Elliott Company, Inc.
5710 Mellon Rd
Export PA

(P-5815)
INTERNATIONAL DIE CASTING INC
515 E Airline Way (90248-2501)
PHONE.............................310 324-2278
▲ **EMP:** 38 **EST:** 1977
SALES (est): 5.32MM
SALES (corp-wide): 24.75MM **Privately Held**
Web: www.internationaldiecasting.com
SIC: 3369 2842 3364 Zinc and zinc-base alloy castings, except die-castings; Metal polish; Nonferrous die-castings except aluminum
PA: Cast-Rite International, Inc.
515 E Airline Way
Gardena CA
310 532-2080

(P-5816)
ORLANDINI ENTPS PCF DIE CAST
Also Called: Pacific Die Casting

6155 S Eastern Ave (90040-3401)
PHONE.............................323 725-1332
Jeff Orlandini, *Pr*
Vincent Orlandini, *
▲ **EMP:** 125 **EST:** 1955
SQ FT: 45,000
SALES (est): 11.63MM **Privately Held**
Web: www.pacdiecast.com
SIC: 3369 3363 Machinery castings, exc.
die, nonferrous, exc. alum. copper;
Aluminum die-castings

(P-5817)
PANKL AEROSPACE SYSTEMS
16615 Edwards Rd (90703-2437)
PHONE.............................562 207-6300
Horst Rieger, *CEO*
Barry Calvert, *
Wolfgang Plasser, *
Harry Glieder, *
EMP: 75 **EST:** 2000
SQ FT: 63,040
SALES (est): 19.27MM
SALES (corp-wide): 3.39B **Privately Held**
Web: www.pankl.com
SIC: 3369 3724 Aerospace castings, nonferrous: except aluminum; Aircraft engines and engine parts
HQ: Pankl Holdings, Inc.
1902 Mcgaw Ave
Irvine CA

(P-5818)
SYNERTECH PM INC
11711 Monarch St (92841-1830)
PHONE.............................714 898-9151
Charles Barre, *CEO*
Kristen Barre, *Pr*
Victor Samarov, *VP*
◆ **EMP:** 17 **EST:** 2000
SQ FT: 20,000
SALES (est): 2.5MM **Privately Held**
Web: www.synertechpm.com
SIC: 3369 Aerospace castings, nonferrous: except aluminum

(P-5819)
TECHNI-CAST CORP
11220 Garfield Ave (90280-7586)
PHONE.............................562 923-4585
Bryn Jhan Van Hiel Ii, *Pr*
Donald Van Hiel, *
Lynne Van Hiel, *
Elaine M Kay, *
▲ **EMP:** 80 **EST:** 1954
SQ FT: 60,000
SALES (est): 9.67MM **Privately Held**
Web: www.techni-cast.com
SIC: 3369 3599 3364 3325 Lead, zinc, and white metal; Machine shop, jobbing and repair; Nonferrous die-castings except aluminum; Steel foundries, nec

---

3398 Metal Heat Treating

(P-5820)
ABRASIVE FINISHING CO
Also Called: Afco
14920 S Main St (90248-1985)
P.O. Box 2292 (90247-0292)
PHONE.............................310 323-7175
William Swanson, *Pr*
EMP: 17 **EST:** 1957
SQ FT: 2,600
SALES (est): 436.57K **Privately Held**
Web: www.afco.la
SIC: 3398 3471 Shot peening (treating steel to reduce fatigue); Plating and polishing

▲ = Import ▼ = Export
◆ = Import/Export

(P-5821)
ACCURATE STEEL TREATING INC
10008 Miller Way (90280-5496)
PHONE................562 927-6528
Ronald Loyns, *Pr*
Mike Bastin, *
EMP: 38 **EST:** 1962
SQ FT: 10,000
SALES (est): 5.66MM **Privately Held**
Web: www.accuratesteeltreating.com
SIC: 3398 Metal heat treating

(P-5822)
ADB INDUSTRIES
Also Called: Subsidy of Be Aerospace
1400 Manhattan Ave (92831-5222)
PHONE................310 679-9193
Brian Dietz, *Pr*
EMP: 256 **EST:** 1961
SQ FT: 50,000
SALES (est): 4.75MM
SALES (corp-wide): 67.07B **Publicly Held**
SIC: 3398 8711 7692 3444 Brazing
  (hardening) of metal; Engineering services;
  Welding repair; Sheet metalwork
HQ: Tsi Group, Inc.
  94 Tide Mill Rd
  Hampton NH

(P-5823)
AEROCRAFT HEAT TREATING CO INC
15701 Minnesota Ave (90723-4120)
PHONE................562 674-2400
David W Dickson, *CEO*
Robert Lyddon, *
EMP: 57 **EST:** 1957
SQ FT: 18,000
SALES (est): 10.74MM
SALES (corp-wide): 302.09B **Publicly Held**
Web: www.aerocraft-ht.com
SIC: 3398 Metal heat treating
HQ: Precision Castparts Corp.
  5885 Meadows Rd Ste 620
  Lake Oswego OR
  503 946-4800

(P-5824)
AREMAC HEAT TREATING INC
330 S 9th Ave (91746-3311)
P.O. Box 90068 (91715-0068)
PHONE................626 333-3898
B E Kopaskie, *Pr*
Bernard E Kopaskie, *
Doctor Butler, *VP*
Jan Kopaskie, *
EMP: 38 **EST:** 1967
SQ FT: 14,000
SALES (est): 8.82MM **Privately Held**
Web: www.aremac.com
SIC: 3398 Metal heat treating

(P-5825)
ASTRO ALUMINUM TREATING CO
11040 Palmer Ave (90280-7497)
PHONE................562 923-4344
Mark R Dickson, *Pr*
Mike Burns, *
EMP: 90 **EST:** 1977
SQ FT: 4,800
SALES (est): 19.09MM **Privately Held**
Web: www.astroaluminum.com
SIC: 3398 Metal heat treating

(P-5826)
BODYCOTE THERMAL PROC INC
7474 Garden Grove Blvd (92683-2227)
PHONE................714 893-6561
Manuel Granillo, *Brnch Mgr*
EMP: 34
SQ FT: 7,369
SALES (corp-wide): 895.27MM **Privately Held**
Web: www.bodycote.com
SIC: 3398 Metal heat treating
HQ: Bodycote Thermal Processing, Inc.
  12750 Merit Dr Ste 1400
  Dallas TX
  214 904-2420

(P-5827)
BODYCOTE THERMAL PROC INC
9921 Romandel Ave (90670-3441)
PHONE................562 946-1717
Manuel Granillo, *Prin*
EMP: 53
SALES (corp-wide): 895.27MM **Privately Held**
Web: www.bodycote.com
SIC: 3398 Metal heat treating
HQ: Bodycote Thermal Processing, Inc.
  12750 Merit Dr Ste 1400
  Dallas TX
  214 904-2420

(P-5828)
BODYCOTE THERMAL PROC INC
515 W Apra St Ste A (90220-5523)
PHONE................310 604-8000
Jose Catano, *Brnch Mgr*
EMP: 21
SALES (corp-wide): 895.27MM **Privately Held**
Web: www.bodycote.com
SIC: 3398 Metal heat treating
HQ: Bodycote Thermal Processing, Inc.
  12750 Merit Dr Ste 1400
  Dallas TX
  214 904-2420

(P-5829)
BODYCOTE USA INC
2900 S Sunol Dr (90058-4315)
PHONE................323 264-0111
EMP: 2260
SQ FT: 31,717
SALES (corp-wide): 895.27MM **Privately Held**
Web: www.bodycote.com
SIC: 3398 Metal heat treating
HQ: Bodycote Usa, Inc.
  12750 Merit Dr Ste 1400
  Dallas TX
  214 904-2420

(P-5830)
BODYCOTE W CAST ANLYTCAL SVC I
Also Called: Metal Analysis
9840 Alburtis Ave (90670-3208)
PHONE................562 948-2225
Ian Nichol, *Pr*
Mark Batgaz, *
EMP: 24 **EST:** 1967
SQ FT: 13,500
SALES (est): 178.67K **Privately Held**
Web: www.bodycote.com
SIC: 3398 Metal heat treating

(P-5831)
BURBANK STEEL TREATING INC
415 S Varney St (91502-2194)
PHONE................818 842-0975
Mildred Bennett, *Ch Bd*
Larry Bennett, *
Kenneth Bennett, *
EMP: 45 **EST:** 1969
SQ FT: 16,000
SALES (est): 5.05MM **Privately Held**
Web: www.burbanksteel.com
SIC: 3398 Metal heat treating

(P-5832)
CERTIFIED METAL CRAFT INC
877 Vernon Way (92020-1940)
PHONE................619 593-3636
John C Wiederkehr, *Pr*
Mark Wiederkehr, *
EMP: 30 **EST:** 1969
SQ FT: 29,500
SALES (est): 4.59MM **Privately Held**
Web: www.certifiedmetalcraft.com
SIC: 3398 Brazing (hardening) of metal

(P-5833)
CONTINENTAL HEAT TREATING INC
10643 Norwalk Blvd (90670-3821)
PHONE................562 944-8808
James Stull, *Pr*
Shaun Radford, *
Laura Rubio, *
Don Lowman, *
Dennis Hugie, *
EMP: 62 **EST:** 1957
SQ FT: 20,000
SALES (est): 9.92MM **Privately Held**
Web: www.continentalht.com
SIC: 3398 Metal heat treating

(P-5834)
COOK INDUCTION HEATING CO INC
Also Called: Cook Induction Heating Co.
4925 Slauson Ave (90270-3094)
P.O. Box 430 (90270-0430)
PHONE................323 560-1327
Keith Doolittle, *CEO*
Richard Egkan, *VP Sls*
EMP: 21 **EST:** 1945
SQ FT: 24,500
SALES (est): 2.53MM **Privately Held**
Web: www.cookinduction.com
SIC: 3398 3728 Metal heat treating; Aircraft
  assemblies, subassemblies, and parts, nec

(P-5835)
CURTISS-WRIGHT SURFC TECH LLC
2151 S Hathaway St (92705-5247)
PHONE................714 546-4160
EMP: 17
SALES (corp-wide): 2.56B **Publicly Held**
Web: www.cwst.co.uk
SIC: 3398 Metal heat treating
HQ: Curtiss-Wright Surface Technologies
  Llc
  80 E Rte 4 Ste 310
  Paramus NJ
  201 843-7800

(P-5836)
DIVERSFIED MTLLRGICAL SVCS INC
Also Called: Varco Heat Treating
12101 Industry St (92841-2813)
P.O. Box 5500 (92846-0500)
PHONE................714 895-7777
Don A Gay, *Pr*
Winston E Mote, *
EMP: 25 **EST:** 1908
SQ FT: 28,000
SALES (est): 1.37MM **Privately Held**
Web: www.varcoheat.com
SIC: 3398 4924 3479 Metal heat treating;
  Natural gas distribution; Coating of metals
  and formed products

(P-5837)
INDUSTRIAL METAL CLEANING CO
339 Palm Ave (92118-1234)
PHONE................314 621-4209
Dick Pedrotty, *Pr*
Gladys Pedrotty, *Sec*
EMP: 19 **EST:** 1951
SALES (est): 494.24K **Privately Held**
Web: www.indmetcl.com
SIC: 3398 Metal heat treating

(P-5838)
INTERNTONAL METALLURGICAL SVCS
Also Called: Scarrott Metallurgical Co
6371 Arizona Cir (90045-1201)
PHONE................310 645-7300
Dave Scarrott, *Pr*
Ralph Jones, *VP*
EMP: 19 **EST:** 1977
SQ FT: 8,000
SALES (est): 4.79MM **Privately Held**
Web: www.scarrott.com
SIC: 3398 Brazing (hardening) of metal

(P-5839)
KITTYHAWK PRODUCTS CA LLC
11651 Monarch St (92841-1816)
PHONE................714 895-5024
Brandon Creason, *Prin*
Kimberly Dickerson, *Prin*
Daniel Bednar, *Prin*
EMP: 25 **EST:** 2019
SALES (est): 1.06MM **Privately Held**
Web: www.kittyhawkinc.com
SIC: 3398 Metal heat treating

(P-5840)
KPI SERVICES INC
Also Called: Kittyhawk Products
11651 Monarch St (92841-1816)
PHONE................714 895-5024
Charles Barre, *CEO*
Dennis Poor, *
Steve Belloise, *
Dee Dee Poor, *
Lois Barre, *
▲ **EMP:** 35 **EST:** 1995
SQ FT: 12,500
SALES (est): 4.75MM **Privately Held**
Web: www.kittyhawkinc.com
SIC: 3398 Metal heat treating

(P-5841)
METAL IMPROVEMENT COMPANY LLC
Also Called: Para Tech Coating
35 Argonaut Ste A1 (92656-4151)
PHONE................949 855-8010
Bill Gleason, *Mgr*
EMP: 30
SALES (corp-wide): 2.56B **Publicly Held**
Web: www.imrtest.com
SIC: 3398 Shot peening (treating steel to
  reduce fatigue)
HQ: Metal Improvement Company, Llc
  80 E Rte 4 Ste 310
  Paramus NJ
  201 843-7800

(P-5842)
METAL IMPROVEMENT COMPANY LLC
2151 S Hathaway St (92705-5247)
PHONE..............................714 546-4160
Joe Wheaton, *Mgr*
EMP: 21
SALES (corp-wide): 2.56B **Publicly Held**
Web: www.imrtest.com
SIC: 3398 Shot peening (treating steel to reduce fatigue)
HQ: Metal Improvement Company, Llc
80 E Rte 4 Ste 310
Paramus NJ
201 843-7800

(P-5843)
METAL IMPROVEMENT COMPANY LLC
2588 Industry Way Ste A (90262-4015)
PHONE..............................323 585-2168
Amando Yanez, *Mgr*
EMP: 70
SQ FT: 28,260
SALES (corp-wide): 2.56B **Publicly Held**
Web: www.imrtest.com
SIC: 3398 Shot peening (treating steel to reduce fatigue)
HQ: Metal Improvement Company, Llc
80 E Rte 4 Ste 310
Paramus NJ
201 843-7800

(P-5844)
METAL IMPROVEMENT COMPANY LLC
E/M Coatings Solutions
6940 Farmdale Ave (91605-6210)
PHONE..............................818 983-1952
Brent Taylor, *Brnch Mgr*
EMP: 85
SALES (corp-wide): 2.56B **Publicly Held**
Web: www.imrtest.com
SIC: 3398 Shot peening (treating steel to reduce fatigue)
HQ: Metal Improvement Company, Llc
80 E Rte 4 Ste 310
Paramus NJ
201 843-7800

(P-5845)
METAL IMPROVEMENT COMPANY LLC
E/M Coatings Services
20751 Superior St (91311-4416)
PHONE..............................818 407-6280
Brent Taylor, *Brnch Mgr*
EMP: 96
SALES (corp-wide): 2.56B **Publicly Held**
Web: www.imrtest.com
SIC: 3398 Shot peening (treating steel to reduce fatigue)
HQ: Metal Improvement Company, Llc
80 E Rte 4 Ste 310
Paramus NJ
201 843-7800

(P-5846)
NEWTON HEAT TREATING CO INC
19235 E Walnut Dr N (91748-1494)
P.O. Box 8010 (91748-0010)
PHONE..............................626 964-6528
Greg Newton, *Pr*
Linda Malcor, *
EMP: 71 **EST:** 1968
SQ FT: 1,900
SALES (est): 12.13MM **Privately Held**
Web: www.newtonheattreating.com

SIC: 3398 8734 3444 Metal heat treating; X-ray inspection service, industrial; Sheet metalwork

(P-5847)
PRO TECH THERMAL SERVICES
1954 Tandem (92860-3607)
PHONE..............................951 272-5808
Brian Grier, *Pr*
Nathan Smith, *
Carolyn Dearborn, *
EMP: 33 **EST:** 1997
SQ FT: 4,000
SALES (est): 6.97MM **Privately Held**
Web: www.protechthermal.com
SIC: 3398 Metal heat treating

(P-5848)
QUALITY HEAT TREATING INC
3305 Burton Ave (91504-3199)
PHONE..............................818 840-8212
James G Stull, *Pr*
EMP: 34 **EST:** 1945
SQ FT: 20,000
SALES (est): 3.64MM **Privately Held**
Web: www.qualityht.com
SIC: 3398 3471 Metal heat treating; Sand blasting of metal parts

(P-5849)
SOLAR ATMOSPHERES INC
8606 Live Oak Ave (92335-3172)
PHONE..............................909 217-7400
EMP: 24
Web: www.solaratm.com
SIC: 3398 Annealing of metal
PA: Solar Atmospheres, Inc.
1969 Clearview Rd
Souderton PA

(P-5850)
TEAM INC
Also Called: Team Industrial Services
1515 240th St (90710-1308)
PHONE..............................310 514-2312
Bill Pigeon, *Mgr*
EMP: 29
SALES (corp-wide): 840.21MM **Publicly Held**
Web: www.teaminc.com
SIC: 3398 3567 Metal heat treating; Heating units and devices, industrial: electric
HQ: Team, Inc.
5095 Paris St
Denver CO

(P-5851)
THERMAL-VAC TECHNOLOGY INC
Also Called: City Steel Heat Treating
1221 W Struck Ave (92867-3531)
PHONE..............................714 997-2601
Steve Driscol, *CEO*
Aaron Anderson, *
Jennifer Kovatch, *
EMP: 41 **EST:** 1985
SQ FT: 26,800
SALES (est): 8.71MM **Privately Held**
Web: www.thermalvac.com
SIC: 3398 Brazing (hardening) of metal

(P-5852)
TRI-J METAL HEAT TREATING CO (PA)
327 E Commercial St (91767-5505)
PHONE..............................909 622-9999
Debra Cramer, *Sec*
Albert W James Junior, *Pr*
Robert L James, *VP Fin*

Lena James, *Sec*
▲ **EMP:** 19 **EST:** 1976
SQ FT: 17,500
SALES (est): 1.94MM
SALES (corp-wide): 1.94MM **Privately Held**
Web: www.trijonline.com
SIC: 3398 Annealing of metal

(P-5853)
VALLEY METAL TREATING INC
355 Se End Ave (91766-2312)
PHONE..............................909 623-6316
James G Stull, *Pr*
EMP: 38 **EST:** 1986
SQ FT: 8,000
SALES (est): 5.08MM **Privately Held**
Web: www.valleymt.net
SIC: 3398 Metal heat treating

3399 Primary Metal Products

(P-5854)
MELLING TOOL RUSH METALS LLC
Also Called: Melling Sintered Metals
16100 S Figueroa St (90248-2617)
PHONE..............................580 725-3295
Mark Melling, *CEO*
▲ **EMP:** 43 **EST:** 2003
SQ FT: 48,000
SALES (est): 2.13MM
SALES (corp-wide): 206.39MM **Privately Held**
SIC: 3399 Powder, metal
PA: Melling Tool Co.
2620 Saradan Dr
Jackson MI
517 787-8172

(P-5855)
MICRO SURFACE ENGR INC (PA)
Also Called: Ball TEC
1550 E Slauson Ave (90011-5099)
P.O. Box 58611 (90011)
PHONE..............................323 582-7348
TOLL FREE: 800
Eugene A Gleason Junior, *Pr*
Helen Gleason, *
Eugene A Gleason Iii, *Sec*
EMP: 35 **EST:** 1952
SQ FT: 46,000
SALES (est): 9.4MM
SALES (corp-wide): 9.4MM **Privately Held**
Web: www.precisionballs.com
SIC: 3399 Steel balls

(P-5856)
PRECISION PWDRED MET PARTS INC
145 Atlantic St (91768-3286)
PHONE..............................909 595-5656
Maurice Bridgman, *Pr*
David Connelly, *
▲ **EMP:** 48 **EST:** 1978
SQ FT: 25,000
SALES (est): 4.73MM **Privately Held**
Web: www.precisionpm.com
SIC: 3399 Powder, metal

(P-5857)
QUANTUMSPHERE INC
28981 Modjeska Peak Ln (92679-1025)
PHONE..............................714 545-6266
Kevin D Maloney, *Pr*
Stephen Gillings, *CFO*
Stephanie Hargis Administrativ e, *Prin*
EMP: 18 **EST:** 2003

SQ FT: 6,000
SALES (est): 2.4MM **Privately Held**
Web: www.qsinano.com
SIC: 3399 5169 2819 Metal powders, pastes, and flakes; Ammonia; Catalysts, chemical

3411 Metal Cans

(P-5858)
CONTAINER SUPPLY COMPANY INCORPORATED
Also Called: C S C
12571 Western Ave (92841-4012)
P.O. Box 5367 (92846-0367)
PHONE..............................714 892-8321
▲ **EMP:** 105 **EST:** 1947
SALES (est): 21.09MM **Privately Held**
Web: www.containersupplycompany.com
SIC: 3411 2656 Food and beverage containers; Sanitary food containers

(P-5859)
JOSEPH COMPANY INTL INC
1711 Langley Ave (92614-5679)
PHONE..............................949 474-2200
Mitchell J Joseph, *Pr*
▲ **EMP:** 20 **EST:** 2010
SQ FT: 18,000
SALES (est): 3.95MM **Privately Held**
Web: www.chillcan.com
SIC: 3411 Food and beverage containers

(P-5860)
METAL CONTAINER CORPORATION
7155 Central Ave (92504-1400)
PHONE..............................951 354-0444
Bob Parker, *Brnch Mgr*
EMP: 158
SALES (corp-wide): 1.31B **Privately Held**
Web: www.metal-containers.com
SIC: 3411 Can lids and ends, metal
HQ: Metal Container Corporation
3636 S Geyer Rd Ste 100
Saint Louis MO
314 577-2000

(P-5861)
METAL CONTAINER CORPORATION
10980 Inland Ave (91752-1127)
PHONE..............................951 360-4500
Otto Sosapavon, *Prin*
EMP: 158
SALES (corp-wide): 1.31B **Privately Held**
Web: www.metal-containers.com
SIC: 3411 Aluminum cans
HQ: Metal Container Corporation
3636 S Geyer Rd Ste 100
Saint Louis MO
314 577-2000

(P-5862)
SILGAN CAN COMPANY
Also Called: Silgan
21600 Oxnard St Ste 1600 (91367-5082)
PHONE..............................818 348-3700
EMP: 166
SIC: 3411 2032 Metal cans; Canned specialties

(P-5863)
SILGAN CONTAINERS CORPORATION (DH)
Also Called: Silgan
21600 Oxnard St Ste 1600 (91367-3609)
PHONE..............................818 710-3700

Anthony J Allott, *CEO*
Thomas J Snyder, *Ch Bd*
R Phillip Silver, *V Ch Bd*
James D Beam, *Pr*
Joseph Heaney, *VP*
◆ **EMP:** 100 **EST:** 1987
SALES (est): 478.49MM **Publicly Held**
Web: www.silgancontainers.com
SIC: 3411 Food containers, metal
HQ: Silgan Containers Llc
　 21600 Oxnard St Ste 1600
　 Woodland Hills CA
　 818 710-3700

(P-5864)
SILGAN CONTAINERS LLC (HQ)
21600 Oxnard St Ste 1600 (91367-5082)
PHONE..............................818 710-3700
Thomas Snyder, *Pr*
Joseph Heaney, *
Anthony Cost, *
Richard Brewer, *
Michael Beninato, *Supply Chain Management Vice-President**
◆ **EMP:** 100 **EST:** 1997
SALES (est): 1.74B **Publicly Held**
Web: www.silgancontainers.com
SIC: 3411 Food containers, metal
PA: Silgan Holdings Inc.
　 4 Landmark Sq Ste 400
　 Stamford CT

(P-5865)
SILGAN CONTAINERS MFG CORP (DH)
Also Called: Silgan
21600 Oxnard St Ste 1600 (91367-5082)
PHONE..............................818 710-3700
EMP: 128 **EST:** 1997
SALES (est): 481.14MM **Publicly Held**
Web: www.silgancontainers.com
SIC: 3411 Metal cans
HQ: Silgan Containers Llc
　 21600 Oxnard St Ste 1600
　 Woodland Hills CA
　 818 710-3700

(P-5866)
VAN CAN COMPANY
13230 Evening Creek Dr S Ste 212 (92128-4104)
PHONE..............................858 391-8084
▲ **EMP:** 200
Web: www.vancan.com
SIC: 3411 Tin cans

3412 Metal Barrels, Drums, And Pails

(P-5867)
GREIF INC
8250 Almeria Ave (92335-3279)
PHONE..............................909 350-2112
Andy Wade, *Mgr*
EMP: 54
SQ FT: 73,320
SALES (corp-wide): 6.35B **Publicly Held**
Web: www.greif.com
SIC: 3412 2674 2655 2449 Drums, shipping: metal; Bags: uncoated paper and multiwall; Fiber cans, drums, and similar products; Wood containers, nec
PA: Greif, Inc.
　 425 Winter Rd
　 Delaware OH
　 740 549-6000

3421 Cutlery

(P-5868)
KAI USA LTD
6031 Malburg Way (90058-3947)
PHONE..............................323 589-2600
EMP: 30
Web: zt.kaiusa.com
SIC: 3421 Carving sets
HQ: Kai U.S.A., Ltd.
　 18600 Sw Teton Ave
　 Tualatin OR
　 503 682-1966

(P-5869)
NADOLIFE INC
1025 Orange Ave (92118-3405)
PHONE..............................619 522-0077
EMP: 28
SALES (corp-wide): 1.42MM **Privately Held**
SIC: 3421 Table and food cutlery, including butchers'
PA: Nadolife, Inc.
　 2709 Newton Ave
　 San Diego CA
　 619 522-6890

(P-5870)
PACIUGO
122 Main St Ste 122 (92648-5126)
PHONE..............................714 536-5388
EMP: 25 **EST:** 2009
SALES (est): 1.45MM **Privately Held**
SIC: 3421 Table and food cutlery, including butchers'

3423 Hand And Edge Tools, Nec

(P-5871)
ADVANCED CUTTING TOOLS INC
17741 Metzler Ln (92647-6246)
PHONE..............................714 842-9376
Stjepan Herceg, *Pr*
EMP: 30 **EST:** 1987
SQ FT: 10,200
SALES (est): 2.31MM **Privately Held**
Web: www.actincorporated.com
SIC: 3423 3545 5251 Hand and edge tools, nec; Machine tool accessories; Tools

(P-5872)
ALLEGION ACCESS TECH LLC
8380 Camino Santa Fe Ste 100 (92121)
PHONE..............................858 431-5940
Michael Hecker, *Brnch Mgr*
EMP: 32
Web: www.stanleyaccess.com
SIC: 3423 Hand and edge tools, nec
HQ: Allegion Access Technologies Llc
　 65 Scott Swamp Rd
　 Farmington CT

(P-5873)
ALLEGION ACCESS TECH LLC
15750 Jurupa Ave (92337-7329)
PHONE..............................909 628-9272
John Rapisarda, *Mgr*
EMP: 32
Web: www.stanleyaccess.com
SIC: 3423 Hand and edge tools, nec
HQ: Allegion Access Technologies Llc
　 65 Scott Swamp Rd
　 Farmington CT

(P-5874)
AUGERSCOPE INC
Also Called: Marco Products
10375 Wilshire Blvd 1b (90024-4728)
▲ **EMP:** 45 **EST:** 1924
SALES (est): 3.37MM **Privately Held**
SIC: 3423 Plumbers' hand tools

(P-5875)
CALIFORNIA FLEXRAKE CORP
Also Called: Flexrake
9620 Gidley St (91780-4215)
P.O. Box 1289 (91780-1289)
PHONE..............................626 443-4026
John P Mcguire, *Pr*
▲ **EMP:** 25 **EST:** 1946
SALES (est): 2.47MM **Privately Held**
Web: www.flexrake.com
SIC: 3423 Garden and farm tools, including shovels

(P-5876)
CRAFTSMAN CUTTING DIES INC (PA)
Also Called: Ccd
2273 E Via Burton (92806-1222)
PHONE..............................714 776-8995
Thomas Hughes, *Pr*
Ronald Ong, *
Cathy Ong-chan, *Sec*
▲ **EMP:** 21 **EST:** 1986
SQ FT: 11,000
SALES (est): 2.88MM
SALES (corp-wide): 2.88MM **Privately Held**
Web: www.craftsmancuttingdies.com
SIC: 3423 3544 Cutting dies, except metal cutting; Special dies, tools, jigs, and fixtures

(P-5877)
CRAFTSMAN UNITY LLC
2273 E Via Burton (92806-1222)
PHONE..............................714 776-8995
Graham Butler, *Managing Member*
EMP: 175 **EST:** 1986
SALES (est): 9.66MM **Privately Held**
Web: www.craftsmancuttingdies.com
SIC: 3423 Cutting dies, except metal cutting

(P-5878)
DURSTON MANUFACTURING COMPANY
Also Called: Vim Tools
1395 Palomares St (91750-5241)
P.O. Box 340 (91750-0340)
PHONE..............................909 593-1506
Donovan Norton, *CEO*
Mary Dills, *Acctg Mgr*
Donovan Norton, *Sec*
James Maloney, *Treas*
▲ **EMP:** 18 **EST:** 1946
SQ FT: 29,000
SALES (est): 2.24MM **Privately Held**
Web: www.vimtools.com
SIC: 3423 Mechanics' hand tools

(P-5879)
EVEREST GROUP USA INC
2030 S Carlos Ave (91761-8032)
PHONE..............................909 923-1818
Niko Peng, *CEO*
◆ **EMP:** 20 **EST:** 2008
SALES (est): 2.35MM **Privately Held**
Web: www.everestgroupusa.com
SIC: 3423 2298 Jacks: lifting, screw, or ratchet (hand tools); Ropes and fiber cables

(P-5880)
FUN PROPERTIES INC (PA)
Also Called: PEC Tool
2645 Maricopa St (90503-5144)
PHONE..............................310 787-4500
Richard A Luboviski, *CEO*
Sandy Luboviski, *
Bernard Brooks, *
◆ **EMP:** 52 **EST:** 1960
SQ FT: 68,000
SALES (est): 9.46MM
SALES (corp-wide): 9.46MM **Privately Held**
Web: www.pec.tools
SIC: 3423 Hand and edge tools, nec

(P-5881)
GARDEN PALS INC
3632 E Moonlight St Unit 91 (91761)
PHONE..............................909 605-0200
Wei Chun Hsu, *CEO*
Robert Deal, *COO*
◆ **EMP:** 20 **EST:** 1990
SALES (est): 6.17MM **Privately Held**
Web: www.gardenpals.com
SIC: 3423 Garden and farm tools, including shovels
PA: Formosa Tools Co., Ltd.
　 No. 22, Yanhai Rd., Sec. 2
　 Fuxing Township CHA

(P-5882)
HALEX CORPORATION (DH)
4200 Santa Ana St Ste A (91761-1539)
PHONE..............................909 629-6219
Mark Chichak, *Pr*
◆ **EMP:** 43 **EST:** 2002
SALES (est): 48.23MM
SALES (corp-wide): 397.78MM **Privately Held**
Web: www.traxxcorp.com
SIC: 3423 Carpet layers' hand tools
HQ: Gcp Applied Technologies Inc.
　 2325 Lakeview Pkwy # 450
　 Alpharetta GA
　 617 876-1400

(P-5883)
KAL-CAMERON MANUFACTURING CORP (HQ)
Also Called: Pro American Premium Tools
4265 Puente Ave (91706-3420)
PHONE..............................626 338-7308
John Toshima, *Ch Bd*
EMP: 100 **EST:** 1983
SQ FT: 32,000
SALES (est): 8.67MM
SALES (corp-wide): 17.71MM **Privately Held**
SIC: 3423 Mechanics' hand tools
PA: American Kal Enterprises, Inc.
　 4265 Puente Ave
　 Baldwin Park CA
　 626 338-7308

(P-5884)
KEMPER ENTERPRISES INC
13595 12th St (91710-5208)
P.O. Box 696 (91708-0696)
PHONE..............................909 627-6191
Herbert H Stampfl, *Pr*
Librado Cortez, *
▲ **EMP:** 21 **EST:** 1947
SQ FT: 30,000
SALES (est): 1.43MM **Privately Held**
Web: www.kempertools.com
SIC: 3423 Hand and edge tools, nec

(P-5885)
LARIN CORP
5651 Schaefer Ave (91710-9048)
PHONE..............................909 464-0605
Shouyun Zhang, *Pr*
▲ EMP: 20 EST: 1989
SQ FT: 50,000
SALES (est): 2.14MM Privately Held
Web: www.larincorp.com
SIC: 3423 Jacks: lifting, screw, or ratchet (hand tools)

(P-5886)
MONSTER TOOL LLC
2470 Ash St U 2 (92081-8461)
PHONE..............................760 477-1000
Richard Mcintyre, *Pr*
Kevin Zimmerman, *CFO*
EMP: 150 EST: 2021
SALES (est): 27.7MM
SALES (corp-wide): 11.77B Privately Held
Web: www.monstertool.com
SIC: 3423 Hand and edge tools, nec
HQ: Gws Tool Holdings, Llc
   595 County Road 448
   Tavares FL
   352 343-8778

(P-5887)
PACIFIC HANDY CUTTER INC (DH)
Also Called: PHC
170 Technology Dr (92618-2401)
PHONE..............................714 662-1033
Mark Marinovich, *CEO*
▲ EMP: 34 EST: 1960
SALES (est): 9.99MM
SALES (corp-wide): 148.42MM Privately Held
Web: www.phcsafety.com
SIC: 3423 3421 Hand and edge tools, nec; Cutlery
HQ: Phc Sharp Holdings, Inc.
   17819 Gillette Ave
   Irvine CA
   714 662-1033

(P-5888)
PHC MERGER INC
Also Called: PHC
17819 Gillette Ave (92614-6501)
PHONE..............................714 662-1033
▲ EMP: 50
SIC: 3423 3421 Hand and edge tools, nec; Cutlery

(P-5889)
PRODUCTS ENGINEERING CORP
Also Called: PEC
2645 Maricopa St (90503-5144)
PHONE..............................310 787-4500
Hongguang Ren, *Pr*
Jianhua Ren, *
EMP: 49 EST: 1961
SALES (est): 5.68MM Privately Held
Web: www.pec.tools
SIC: 3423 3596 4731 Hand and edge tools, nec; Scales and balances, except laboratory ; Freight transportation arrangement

(P-5890)
TOUGHBUILT INDUSTRIES INC (PA)
Also Called: TOUGHBUILT
8669 Research Dr (92618-4204)
PHONE..............................949 528-3100
Michael Panosian, *Ch Bd*
Martin Galstyan, *CFO*

Joshua Keeler, *CDO*
Zareh Khachatoorian, *COO*
EMP: 255 EST: 2012
SQ FT: 15,500
SALES (est): 95.25MM
SALES (corp-wide): 95.25MM Publicly Held
Web: www.toughbuilt.com
SIC: 3423 3429 3069 Hand and edge tools, nec; Hardware, nec; Kneeling pads, rubber

3425 Saw Blades And Handsaws

(P-5891)
DIAMOND K2
23911 Garnier St Ste C (90505-7523)
P.O. Box 346 (90508-0346)
PHONE..............................310 539-6116
Les Kuzmick, *Ch Bd*
Richard Kirby, *Pr*
EMP: 21 EST: 1993
SQ FT: 7,600
SALES (est): 2.86MM Privately Held
Web: www.k2diamond.com
SIC: 3425 3531 5082 Saw blades and handsaws; Construction machinery; Concrete processing equipment

(P-5892)
HILTI US MANUFACTURING INC
Also Called: Dbi
6601 Darin Way (90630-5130)
P.O. Box 21148 (74121-1148)
PHONE..............................714 230-7410
EMP: 30 EST: 1984
SALES (est): 9.43MM Privately Held
SIC: 3425 Saw blades and handsaws
HQ: Hilti, Inc.
   5400 S 122nd East Ave
   Tulsa OK
   800 879-8000

(P-5893)
WESTERN SAW MANUFACTURERS INC
Also Called: Western Saw
3200 Camino Del Sol (93030-8998)
PHONE..............................805 981-0999
Kevin Baron, *CEO*
Frank Baron, *
Kraig Baron, *
Nancy Pounds, *
◆ EMP: 50 EST: 1930
SQ FT: 70,000
SALES (est): 10.85MM Privately Held
Web: www.westernsaw.com
SIC: 3425 3546 Saw blades and handsaws; Power-driven handtools

3429 Hardware, Nec

(P-5894)
ACCURIDE INTERNATIONAL INC (PA)
12311 Shoemaker Ave (90670-4721)
PHONE..............................562 903-0200
Scott E Jordan, *CEO*
Jeffrey A Dunlap, *
Jerome Barr, *
Kent A Jordan, *
▲ EMP: 47 EST: 1966
SALES (est): 365.22MM
SALES (corp-wide): 365.22MM Privately Held
Web: www.accuride.com
SIC: 3429 Cabinet hardware

(P-5895)
ACTRON MANUFACTURING INC
1841 Railroad St (92878-5012)
PHONE..............................951 371-0885
Frank Rechberg, *CEO*
Dow Rechberg, *
EMP: 93 EST: 1971
SQ FT: 30,000
SALES (est): 16.66MM Privately Held
Web: www.actronmfginc.com
SIC: 3429 Aircraft hardware

(P-5896)
ALARIN AIRCRAFT HINGE INC
Also Called: Commerce
6231 Randolph St (90040-3514)
PHONE..............................323 725-1666
Gregory A Sanders, *Pr*
EMP: 25 EST: 1988
SQ FT: 11,000
SALES (est): 4.73MM Privately Held
Web: www.alarin.com
SIC: 3429 3728 Aircraft hardware; Aircraft parts and equipment, nec

(P-5897)
ASCO SINTERING CO
2750 Garfield Ave (90040-2610)
P.O. Box 911157 (90091-1157)
PHONE..............................323 725-3550
Neil Moore, *CEO*
Robert Lebrun, *VP*
▲ EMP: 33 EST: 1971
SQ FT: 69,000
SALES (est): 6.73MM Privately Held
Web: www.ascosintering.com
SIC: 3429 3714 Hardware, nec; Motor vehicle parts and accessories

(P-5898)
ASSA ABLOY ACC DOOR CNTRLS GRO
Also Called: Markar & Pemko Products
4226 Transport St (93003-5627)
PHONE..............................805 642-2600
EMP: 112
SALES (corp-wide): 11.51B Privately Held
SIC: 3429 3466 Locks or lock sets; Crowns and closures
HQ: Assa Abloy Accessories And Door
   Controls Group, Inc.
   1902 Airport Rd
   Monroe NC
   877 974-2255

(P-5899)
AUTOMOTIVE RACING PRODUCTS INC
Also Called: A R P
1760 E Lemonwood Dr (93060-9510)
PHONE..............................805 525-1497
Michael Holzapsel, *Brnch Mgr*
EMP: 104
SALES (corp-wide): 59.57K Privately Held
Web: www.arp-bolts.com
SIC: 3429 Hardware, nec
PA: Automotive Racing Products, Inc.
   1863 Eastman Ave
   Ventura CA
   805 339-2200

(P-5900)
AUTOMOTIVE RACING PRODUCTS INC (PA)
Also Called: A R P
1863 Eastman Ave (93003-8084)
PHONE..............................805 339-2200
Gary Holzapfel, *CEO*
Mike Holzapfel, *

Robert Flourin, *
Kelly Schau, *
▲ EMP: 65 EST: 1975
SQ FT: 10,000
SALES (est): 59.57K
SALES (corp-wide): 59.57K Privately Held
Web: www.arp-bolts.com
SIC: 3429 3714 3452 Hardware, nec; Motor vehicle parts and accessories; Bolts, nuts, rivets, and washers

(P-5901)
AVANTUS AEROSPACE INC
14957 Gwenchris Ct (90723-3423)
PHONE..............................562 633-6626
Brian Williams, *Brnch Mgr*
EMP: 50
SALES (corp-wide): 123.82MM Privately Held
Web: www.avantusaerospace.com
SIC: 3429 3452 Metal fasteners; Bolts, nuts, rivets, and washers
HQ: Avantus Aerospace, Inc.
   29101 The Old Rd
   Valencia CA
   661 295-8620

(P-5902)
AVIBANK MFG INC
Avk Industrial Products
25323 Rye Canyon Rd (91355-1205)
PHONE..............................661 257-2329
James M Wolpert, *Genl Mgr*
EMP: 85
SQ FT: 23,000
SALES (corp-wide): 302.09B Publicly Held
Web: www.avibank.com
SIC: 3429 3541 3452 Hardware, nec; Machine tools, metal cutting type; Bolts, nuts, rivets, and washers
HQ: Avibank Mfg., Inc.
   11500 Sherman Way
   North Hollywood CA
   818 392-2100

(P-5903)
B & B SPECIALTIES INC (PA)
4321 E La Palma Ave (92807-1887)
PHONE..............................714 985-3000
Bruce Borchardt, *Pr*
▲ EMP: 90 EST: 1971
SQ FT: 40,000
SALES (est): 22.69MM
SALES (corp-wide): 22.69MM Privately Held
Web: www.bbspecialties.com
SIC: 3429 3452 Metal fasteners; Bolts, nuts, rivets, and washers

(P-5904)
BAIER MARINE COMPANY INC
2920 Airway Ave (92626-6008)
PHONE..............................800 455-3917
Mark Smith, *Pr*
Felice Lineberry, *Mgr*
◆ EMP: 20 EST: 2007
SALES (est): 1.95MM Privately Held
Web: www.baiermarine.com
SIC: 3429 Hardware, nec

(P-5905)
BALDWIN HARDWARE CORPORATION (HQ)
Also Called: Baldwin Brass
19701 Da Vinci (92610-2622)
PHONE..............................949 672-4000
David R Lumley, *CEO*
◆ EMP: 816 EST: 1944
SQ FT: 300,000

SALES (est): 104.33MM
SALES (corp-wide): 558.24MM **Privately Held**
Web: www.baldwinhardware.com
SIC: 3429 Builders' hardware
PA: Spectrum Brands, Inc.
3001 Deming Way
Middleton WI
608 275-3340

(P-5906)
BATON LOCK AND HARDWARE CO INC
Also Called: Baton Security
14275 Commerce Dr (92843-4944)
PHONE...............................714 265-3636
Hwei Ying Chen, *Pr*
Fong Peace Shiang Hsu, *Pr*
Sharron Hsu, *VP*
◆ **EMP:** 21 **EST:** 1971
SQ FT: 15,025
SALES (est): 2.03MM **Privately Held**
SIC: 3429 Keys, locks, and related hardware

(P-5907)
BIRMINGHAM FASTENER & SUP INC
Also Called: Pacific Coast Bolt
12748 Florence Ave (90670-3906)
PHONE...............................562 944-9549
Brad Tinney, *Brnch Mgr*
EMP: 38
SALES (corp-wide): 193.68MM **Privately Held**
Web: www.bhamfast.com
SIC: 3429 Hardware, nec
PA: Birmingham Fastener & Supply, Inc.
931 Avenue W
Birmingham AL
205 595-3511

(P-5908)
CAESAR HARDWARE INTL LTD
4985 Hallmark Pkwy (92407-1870)
PHONE...............................800 306-3829
Chao Xu, *CEO*
EMP: 2 **EST:** 2012
SALES (est): 4.21MM **Privately Held**
Web: www.caesarfireplace.com
SIC: 3429 3999 5021 Fireplace equipment, hardware: andirons, grates, screens; Atomizers, toiletry; Outdoor and lawn furniture, nec
PA: Yuyao Super Wing Foreign Trade Co., Ltd
Room 1401, Yangguang International Mansion, No.55, Yuli Road
Yuyao ZJ

(P-5909)
CAL-JUNE INC (PA)
Also Called: Jim-Buoy
5238 Vineland Ave (91601-3221)
P.O. Box 9551 (91609-1551)
PHONE...............................323 877-4164
James H Robertson, *Pr*
Jennifer D Jacobson, *
Melini Robertson, *
Andrea Robertson, *
◆ **EMP:** 30 **EST:** 1966
SQ FT: 3,000
SALES (est): 5.39MM
SALES (corp-wide): 5.39MM **Privately Held**
Web: www.jimbuoy.com
SIC: 3429 Marine hardware

(P-5910)
CALIFORNIA SCREW PRODUCTS CORP
14957 Gwenchris Ct (90723-3423)
P.O. Box 228 (90723-0228)
PHONE...............................562 633-6626
Dan Strangio, *CEO*
Dennis Suedkamp, *
EMP: 75 **EST:** 1966
SQ FT: 20,000
SALES (est): 12.22MM **Privately Held**
Web: www.calscrew.net
SIC: 3429 3452 Metal fasteners; Bolts, nuts, rivets, and washers

(P-5911)
CALMEX FIREPLACE EQP MFG INC
Also Called: Calmex Fireplace Equip Mfg
13629 Talc St (90670-5113)
PHONE...............................716 645-2901
Maria Hirshal, *Pr*
Rosa Franco, *VP*
EMP: 23 **EST:** 1964
SQ FT: 15,000
SALES (est): 736.77K **Privately Held**
SIC: 3429 Fireplace equipment, hardware: andirons, grates, screens

(P-5912)
CONSOLIDATED AEROSPACE MFG LLC
630 E Lambert Rd (92821-4119)
PHONE...............................714 989-2802
EMP: 68 **EST:** 2014
SALES (est): 5.1MM **Privately Held**
Web: www.camaerospace.com
SIC: 3429 Metal fasteners

(P-5913)
CRD MFG INC
615 Fee Ana St (92870-6704)
PHONE...............................714 871-3300
Timothy Carroll, *CEO*
EMP: 27 **EST:** 2011
SALES (est): 3.76MM **Privately Held**
Web: www.crdmfg.com
SIC: 3429 3699 Motor vehicle hardware; Welding machines and equipment, ultrasonic

(P-5914)
CRENSHAW MANUFACTURING INC
7432 Prince Dr (92647-4553)
PHONE...............................949 475-5505
EMP: 20 **EST:** 2013
SALES (est): 306.91K **Privately Held**
SIC: 3429 Hardware, nec

(P-5915)
DARNELL-ROSE INC
1205 Via Roma (92324-3909)
PHONE...............................626 912-1688
Brent Bargar, *Pr*
John Posen, *
Robbie Mccullah, *VP Opers*
EMP: 40 **EST:** 1984
SALES (est): 2.73MM **Privately Held**
Web: www.casters.com
SIC: 3429 Aircraft & marine hardware, inc. pulleys & similar items

(P-5916)
DOVAL INDUSTRIES INC
Also Called: Doval Industries Co
3961 N Mission Rd (90031-2931)
PHONE...............................323 226-0335
Cruz Sandoval, *CEO*
▲ **EMP:** 65 **EST:** 1985
SALES (est): 4.68MM **Privately Held**
Web: www.doval.com
SIC: 3429 5072 2759 Keys, locks, and related hardware; Hardware; Screen printing

(P-5917)
FORESPAR PRODUCTS CORP (PA)
Also Called: Tea Tree Essentials
22322 Gilberto (92688-2110)
PHONE...............................949 858-8820
◆ **EMP:** 23 **EST:** 1964
SALES (est): 9.58MM
SALES (corp-wide): 9.58MM **Privately Held**
Web: www.forespar.com
SIC: 3429 Marine hardware

(P-5918)
FRAMELESS HARDWARE COMPANY LLC
4361 Firestone Blvd (90280-3340)
PHONE...............................888 295-4531
Donald Friese Junior, *Managing Member*
EMP: 37 **EST:** 2020
SALES (est): 14.67MM **Privately Held**
Web: www.fhc-usa.com
SIC: 3429 1793 2591 Builders' hardware; Glass and glazing work; Drapery hardware and window blinds and shades

(P-5919)
FXC CORPORATION (PA)
3050 Red Hill Ave (92626-4524)
PHONE...............................714 556-7400
Irene Chevrier, *CEO*
EMP: 21 **EST:** 1973
SQ FT: 26,000
SALES (est): 9.82MM
SALES (corp-wide): 9.82MM **Privately Held**
Web: www.fxcguardian.com
SIC: 3429 2399 Parachute hardware; Parachutes

(P-5920)
HARTWELL CORPORATION (DH)
Also Called: Hasco
900 Richfield Rd (92870-6732)
PHONE...............................714 993-4200
Dain Miller, *Pr*
▲ **EMP:** 200 **EST:** 1957
SQ FT: 134,000
SALES (est): 173.5MM
SALES (corp-wide): 6.58B **Publicly Held**
Web: www.hartwellcorp.com
SIC: 3429 Aircraft hardware
HQ: Mckechnie Aerospace Investments, Inc.
20 Pacifica Ste 200
Irvine CA

(P-5921)
HODGE PRODUCTS INC
Also Called: Lock People, The
7365 Mission Gorge Rd Ste F (92120-1299)
P.O. Box 1326 (92022-1326)
PHONE...............................800 778-2217
Anthony A Hodge, *CEO*
Allan Hodge, *
▲ **EMP:** 25 **EST:** 1971
SALES (est): 5.34MM **Privately Held**
Web: www.hpionline.com
SIC: 3429 5099 Locks or lock sets; Locks and lock sets

(P-5922)
HOLLYWOOD BED SPRING MFG INC (PA)
Also Called: Hollywood Bed & Spring Mfg
5959 Corvette St (90040-1601)
PHONE...............................323 887-9500
Larry Harrow, *CEO*
Jason Harrow, *
Andrea Harrow, *
◆ **EMP:** 78 **EST:** 1945
SQ FT: 55,000
SALES (est): 17.5MM
SALES (corp-wide): 17.5MM **Privately Held**
Web: www.hollywoodbed.com
SIC: 3429 2515 2511 2514 Hardware, nec; Mattresses and bedsprings; Wood household furniture; Frames for box springs or bedsprings: metal

(P-5923)
INSPIRED FLIGHT TECH INC
Also Called: Inspired Flight
225 Suburban Rd Ste A (93401-7547)
PHONE...............................805 776-3640
Richard Stollmeyer, *CEO*
Marcus Stollmeyer, *
EMP: 34 **EST:** 2017
SALES (est): 3.63MM **Privately Held**
Web: www.inspiredflight.com
SIC: 3429 Aircraft hardware

(P-5924)
J & M PRODUCTS INC
1647 Truman St (91340-3119)
PHONE...............................818 837-0205
EMP: 97 **EST:** 1995
SALES (est): 16.69MM **Privately Held**
Web: www.jmproducts.com
SIC: 3429 3679 Hardware, nec; Harness assemblies, for electronic use: wire or cable

(P-5925)
JONATHAN ENGNRED SLUTIONS CORP (HQ)
250 Commerce Ste 100 (92602-1318)
PHONE...............................714 665-4400
Jack Frickel, *Pr*
Jason Ciancarulo, *
▲ **EMP:** 44 **EST:** 1954
SQ FT: 120,000
SALES (est): 98.46MM
SALES (corp-wide): 397.46MM **Privately Held**
Web: www.jonathanengr.com
SIC: 3429 3562 Hardware, nec; Ball bearings and parts
PA: Jll Partners, Llc
300 Park Ave Fl 18
New York NY
212 286-8600

(P-5926)
KWIKSET CORPORATION
Also Called: Spectrum Brands Hdwr HM Imprv
19701 Da Vinci (92610-2622)
P.O. Box 620992 (53562-0992)
PHONE...............................949 672-4000
▲ **EMP:** 3200
Web: www.kwikset.com
SIC: 3429 Keys, locks, and related hardware

(P-5927)
LIGHT COMPOSITE CORPORATION
Also Called: Forespar
22322 Gilberto (92688-2102)
PHONE...............................949 858-8820

▼ **EMP: 24 EST:** 1991
SALES (est): 2.3MM **Privately Held**
Web: www.forespar.com
SIC: 3429 Marine hardware

(P-5928)
LOCK AMERICA INC
Also Called: Mr Lock
9168 Stellar Ct (92883-4923)
PHONE..............................951 277-5180
Ming Shiao, *Pr*
Frank Minnella, *CEO*
Watson Visuwan, *VP*
◆ **EMP: 19 EST:** 1989
SQ FT: 11,500
SALES (est): 2.42MM **Privately Held**
Web: www.laigroup.com
SIC: 3429 5099 Keys, locks, and related
hardware; Locks and lock sets

(P-5929)
LUCKY LINE PRODUCTS INC
7890 Dunbrook Rd (92126-4369)
PHONE..............................858 549-6699
◆ **EMP: 26 EST:** 1948
SALES (est): 4.98MM **Privately Held**
Web: www.luckyline.com
SIC: 3429 3993 Keys, locks, and related
hardware; Signs and advertising specialties

(P-5930)
M A G ENGINEERING MFG CO
Also Called: M.A.g Engineering & Mfg
17305 Demler St (92614)
▲ **EMP: 40 EST:** 1968
SALES (est): 3.7MM **Privately Held**
SIC: 3429 Locks or lock sets

(P-5931)
MCMAHON STEEL COMPANY INC
1880 Nirvana Ave (91911-6118)
PHONE..............................619 671-9700
Derek J Mcmahon, *Pr*
Kevin Mcmahon, *VP*
EMP: 120 **EST:** 1970
SQ FT: 14,300
SALES (est): 23.18MM **Privately Held**
Web: www.mcmahonsteel.com
SIC: 3429 1791 3441 Hardware, nec;
Structural steel erection; Fabricated
structural metal

(P-5932)
MID-WEST WHOLESALE HARDWARE CO
Also Called: Banner Solutions
1641 S Sunkist St (92806-5813)
PHONE..............................714 630-4751
Terry Olson, *Brnch Mgr*
EMP: 22
SALES (corp-wide): 61.24MM **Privately Held**
Web: www.bannersolutions.com
SIC: 3429 5072 Hardware, nec; Hardware
PA: Mid-West Wholesale Hardware Co Inc
1000 Century Dr
Kansas City MO
816 245-1142

(P-5933)
MOELLER MFG & SUP LLC
630 E Lambert Rd (92821-4119)
PHONE..............................714 999-5551
Stevens Chevillotte, *Pr*
Peter George, *
EMP: 45 **EST:** 1978
SALES (est): 14MM
SALES (corp-wide): 16.95B **Publicly Held**

SIC: 3429 3452 Aircraft hardware; Washers,
metal
HQ: Consolidated Aerospace
Manufacturing, Llc
1425 S Acacia Ave
Fullerton CA
714 989-2797

(P-5934)
MONADNOCK COMPANY
Also Called: Lisi Aerospace
16728 Gale Ave (91745-1803)
PHONE..............................626 964-6581
Christian Darville, *CEO*
Michael Reyes, *
▼ **EMP: 190 EST:** 1987
SQ FT: 90,000
SALES (est): 55.54MM
SALES (corp-wide): 2.67MM **Privately Held**
SIC: 3429 Aircraft hardware
HQ: Lisi Aerospace
42 A 52
Paris
140198200

(P-5935)
MONOGRAM AEROSPACE FAS INC
3423 Garfield Ave (90040-3103)
PHONE..............................323 722-4760
David Adler, *Pr*
John P Schaefer, *
▲ **EMP: 250 EST:** 1990
SQ FT: 97,500
SALES (est): 70.92MM
SALES (corp-wide): 883.83MM **Publicly Held**
Web: www.trsaero.com
SIC: 3429 3452 Hardware, nec; Bolts, metal
PA: Trimas Corporation
38505 Woodward Ave # 200
Bloomfield Hills MI
248 631-5450

(P-5936)
NATIONAL MANUFACTURING CO
Also Called: Stanley National Hardware
19701 Da Vinci (92610-2622)
PHONE..............................800 346-9445
◆ **EMP: 1660 EST:** 1901
SALES (est): 76.57MM
SALES (corp-wide): 16.95B **Publicly Held**
SIC: 3429 Builders' hardware
PA: Stanley Black & Decker, Inc.
1000 Stanley Dr
New Britain CT
860 225-5111

(P-5937)
NUSET INC
2432 Peck Rd (90601-1604)
PHONE..............................626 246-1668
Caron Ng, *CEO*
EMP: 20 **EST:** 2017
SALES (est): 1.35MM **Privately Held**
Web: www.nusetlock.com
SIC: 3429 Keys, locks, and related hardware

(P-5938)
ORION ORNAMENTAL IRON INC
6918 Tujunga Ave (91605-6212)
PHONE..............................818 752-0688
Sunil Patel, *CEO*
Atul Patel, *
▲ **EMP: 40 EST:** 1983
SQ FT: 30,000
SALES (est): 3.37MM **Privately Held**
Web: www.ironartbyorion.com

SIC: 3429 Builders' hardware

(P-5939)
PACIFIC LOCK COMPANY (PA)
25605 Hercules St (91355-5051)
PHONE..............................661 294-3707
Gregory B Waugh, *Pr*
Joshua Fleagane, *
Patty Yang, *
▲ **EMP: 29 EST:** 1998
SQ FT: 18,000
SALES (est): 3.2MM **Privately Held**
Web: www.paclock.com
SIC: 3429 3699 5099 Keys and key blanks;
Security devices; Locks and lock sets

(P-5940)
R C PRODUCTS CORP
22322 Gilberto (92688-2102)
PHONE..............................949 858-8820
Robert R Foresman, *Pr*
Marilyn Holst, *
EMP: 37 **EST:** 1991
SQ FT: 40,000
SALES (est): 701.18K
SALES (corp-wide): 9.58MM **Privately Held**
Web: www.forespar.com
SIC: 3429 Marine hardware
PA: Forespar Products Corp.
22322 Gilberto
Rcho Sta Marg CA
949 858-8820

(P-5941)
RPC LEGACY INC
Also Called: Terry Hinge & Hardware
14600 Arminta St (91402-5902)
PHONE..............................818 787-9000
Authur William, *Brnch Mgr*
EMP: 20
SALES (corp-wide): 9.58MM **Privately Held**
SIC: 3429 Hardware, nec
PA: Rpc Legacy, Inc.
2020 7th St
Rockford IL
815 966-2000

(P-5942)
SATURN FASTENERS INC
425 S Varney St (91502-2193)
PHONE..............................818 973-1807
Raymond David Barker Junior, *C*
Laura Elaine Barker, *
Raymond D Barker Junior, *Pr*
▲ **EMP: 112 EST:** 1989
SQ FT: 38,000
SALES (est): 16.83MM **Privately Held**
Web: www.saturnfasteners.com
SIC: 3429 5085 5072 3452 Metal fasteners;
Industrial supplies; Bolts, nuts, and screws;
Bolts, nuts, rivets, and washers
HQ: Acument Global Technologies, Inc.
6125 18 Mile Rd
Sterling Heights MI
586 254-3900

(P-5943)
SNAPNRACK INC
775 Fiero Ln Ste 200 (93401-7904)
PHONE..............................877 732-2860
Lyn Cowgill, *Off Mgr*
EMP: 23 **EST:** 2014
SALES (est): 3.03MM **Privately Held**
Web: www.snapnrack.com
SIC: 3429 Clamps, couplings, nozzles, and
other metal hose fittings

(P-5944)
SPEP ACQUISITION CORP (PA)
Also Called: Sierra Pacific Engrg & Pdts
4041 Via Oro Ave (90810-1458)
P.O. Box 5246 (90749-5246)
PHONE..............................310 608-0693
Barry Stein, *Pr*
Larry Mirick, *
◆ **EMP: 70 EST:** 1986
SQ FT: 48,300
SALES (est): 20.69MM
SALES (corp-wide): 20.69MM **Privately Held**
Web: www.spep.com
SIC: 3429 8711 5072 Hardware, nec;
Engineering services; Hardware

(P-5945)
STAR DIE CASTING INC
12209 Slauson Ave (90670-2605)
PHONE..............................562 698-0627
Jer Ming Yu, *Pr*
Mei H Yu, *VP*
▲ **EMP: 80 EST:** 1980
SQ FT: 13,290
SALES (est): 5.26MM **Privately Held**
Web: www.stargroupglobal.com
SIC: 3429 3364 3544 Builders' hardware;
Nonferrous die-castings except aluminum;
Special dies and tools

(P-5946)
TOMORROWS HEIRLOOMS INC
Also Called: Stone Manufacturing Company
1636 W 135th St (90249-2506)
P.O. Box 1325 (90249-0325)
PHONE..............................310 323-6720
Amit V Patel, *Pr*
Kumar V Patel, *
Sumi Patel, *
EMP: 20 **EST:** 1957
SQ FT: 22,000
SALES (est): 974.13K **Privately Held**
Web: www.stonemfg.com
SIC: 3429 Fireplace equipment, hardware:
andirons, grates, screens

(P-5947)
TOP LINE MFG INC
7032 Alondra Blvd (90723-3926)
P.O. Box 739 (90723-0739)
PHONE..............................562 633-0605
Anne Graffy, *CEO*
▲ **EMP: 29 EST:** 1982
SQ FT: 20,000
SALES (est): 2.75MM **Privately Held**
Web: www.toplinemfg.com
SIC: 3429 Motor vehicle hardware

(P-5948)
TOWNSTEEL INC
17901 Railroad St (91748-1113)
PHONE..............................626 965-8917
Lydia Meng, *Pr*
Shien Cheng Meng, *VP*
◆ **EMP: 100 EST:** 2001
SQ FT: 10,000
SALES (est): 9.12MM **Privately Held**
Web: www.townsteel.com
SIC: 3429 Door locks, bolts, and checks

(P-5949)
UMPCO INC
7100 Lampson Ave (92841-3914)
P.O. Box 5158 (92846-0158)
PHONE..............................714 897-3531
Dan Miller, *CEO*
EMP: 75 **EST:** 1963
SQ FT: 60,000
SALES (est): 20.67MM **Privately Held**

Web: www.umpco.com
SIC: 3429 Clamps, metal

(P-5950)
VIT PRODUCTS INC
2063 Wineridge Pl (92029-1931)
PHONE...............760 480-6702
Don Pagano, *Pr*
Arthur Arns, *
EMP: 36 **EST:** 1972
SQ FT: 24,000
SALES (est): 5.27MM **Privately Held**
Web: www.strongbox.com
SIC: 3429 2295 Clamps, couplings, nozzles, and other metal hose fittings; Coated fabrics, not rubberized

(P-5951)
W & F MFG INC
10635 Keswick St (91352-4610)
P.O. Box 1219 (91353-1219)
PHONE...............818 394-6060
▲ **EMP:** 50
SIC: 3429 Door opening and closing devices, except electrical

(P-5952)
WEISER LOCK CORPORATION
19701 Da Vinci (92610-2622)
P.O. Box 620992 (53562-0992)
PHONE...............949 672-4000
◆ **EMP:** 18
SIC: 3429 Door locks, bolts, and checks

(P-5953)
WESTERN HARDWARE COMPANY
161 Commerce Way (91789-2719)
PHONE...............909 595-6201
Gayle E Pacheco, *Pr*
▲ **EMP:** 19 **EST:** 1968
SALES (est): 2.19MM **Privately Held**
Web: www.westernhardware.com
SIC: 3429 Hardware, nec

(P-5954)
WINFIELD LOCKS INC
Also Called: Computerized Security Systems
1721 Whittier Ave (92627-4580)
PHONE...............949 722-5400
John Kimes, *Pr*
EMP: 5045 **EST:** 1977
SQ FT: 30,000
SALES (est): 8.11MM
SALES (corp-wide): 8.68B **Publicly Held**
SIC: 3429 Locks or lock sets
HQ: Masco Building Products Corp.
17450 College Pkwy
Livonia MI
313 274-7400

(P-5955)
YOUNG ENGINEERS INC
25841 Commercentre Dr (92630-8812)
P.O. Box 278 (92609-0278)
PHONE...............949 581-9411
Pat Wells, *Pr*
EMP: 64 **EST:** 1963
SQ FT: 26,000
SALES (est): 11.08MM
SALES (corp-wide): 218.18MM **Privately Held**
Web: www.youngengineers.com
SIC: 3429 Aircraft hardware
PA: Novaria Group, L.L.C.
6685 Iron Horse Blvd
North Richland Hills TX
214 707-8980

(P-5956)
YOUNGDALE MANUFACTURING CORP
1216 Liberty Way Ste B (92081-8369)
P.O. Box 3209 (92085-3209)
PHONE...............760 727-0644
Peter Youngdale, *Ch Bd*
Joseph Carrick, *Pr*
Christine Carrick, *VP*
Susan Youngdale, *VP Fin*
▲ **EMP:** 31 **EST:** 1964
SQ FT: 25,000
SALES (est): 1.07MM **Privately Held**
Web: www.youngdale.com
SIC: 3429 Cabinet hardware

3431 Metal Sanitary Ware

(P-5957)
ALTMANS PRODUCTS LLC
Also Called: Altmans
301 N Robertson Blvd (90211-1705)
PHONE...............310 274-5896
Howard Rom, *Brnch Mgr*
EMP: 28
Web: www.altmansproducts.com
SIC: 3431 Sinks: enameled iron, cast iron, or pressed metal
HQ: Altmans Products Llc
7136 Kittyhawk Ave Apt 4
Los Angeles CA
310 559-4093

(P-5958)
HYDRO SYSTEMS INC (PA)
29132 Avenue Paine (91355-5402)
PHONE...............661 775-0686
Scott G Steinhardt, *Pr*
Dave Ortwein, *
Larry Burroughs, *
EMP: 95 **EST:** 1979
SQ FT: 90,000
SALES (est): 18.92MM
SALES (corp-wide): 18.92MM **Privately Held**
Web: www.hydrosystem.com
SIC: 3431 3432 3088 Bathtubs: enameled iron, cast iron, or pressed metal; Plumbing fixture fittings and trim; Plastics plumbing fixtures

(P-5959)
MAG AEROSPACE INDUSTRIES LLC
Also Called: Monogram Systems
1500 Glenn Curtiss St (90746-4012)
P.O. Box 11189 (90749-1189)
PHONE...............801 400-7944
Sebastien Weber, *Pr*
Mark Scott, *VP*
David Conrad, *S&M/VP*
Mike Nieves, *SUPPLY CHAIN*
Tim Birbeck, *VP Engg*
◆ **EMP:** 350 **EST:** 1989
SQ FT: 150,000
SALES (est): 99.67MM
SALES (corp-wide): 650.78MM **Privately Held**
SIC: 3431 3728 Plumbing fixtures: enameled iron, cast iron, or pressed metal; Aircraft parts and equipment, nec
PA: Safran
2 Bd Du General Martial Valin
Paris

(P-5960)
SEACHROME CORPORATION
Also Called: Seachrome
1906 E Dominguez St (90810-1002)

PHONE...............310 427-8010
Sam C Longo Junior, *CEO*
▲ **EMP:** 112 **EST:** 1983
SQ FT: 50,000
SALES (est): 22.1MM **Privately Held**
Web: www.seachrome.com
SIC: 3431 5072 3842 3429 Bathroom fixtures, including sinks; Builders' hardware, nec; Surgical appliances and supplies; Hardware, nec

3432 Plumbing Fixture Fittings And Trim

(P-5961)
ACORNVAC INC
Also Called: Acorn Vac
13818 Oaks Ave (91710-7008)
PHONE...............909 902-1141
Donald E Morris, *CEO*
EMP: 20 **EST:** 2000
SALES (est): 11.25MM
SALES (corp-wide): 99.15MM **Privately Held**
Web: www.acornvac.com
SIC: 3432 Plastic plumbing fixture fittings, assembly
PA: Acorn Engineering Company
15125 Proctor Ave
City Of Industry CA
800 488-8999

(P-5962)
AMERICAN BRASS & ALUM FNDRY CO
2060 Garfield Ave (90040-1804)
P.O. Box 80304 (90040)
PHONE...............800 545-9988
Tony Orapallo Junior, *Pr*
Robert A Orapallo, *VP*
◆ **EMP:** 20 **EST:** 1931
SQ FT: 15,000
SALES (est): 2.38MM **Privately Held**
Web: www.abainc.net
SIC: 3432 Plumbers' brass goods: drain cocks, faucets, spigots, etc.

(P-5963)
BRASSTECH INC (HQ)
Also Called: Newport Brass
2001 Carnegie Ave (92705-5531)
PHONE...............949 417-5207
Jonathan Wood, *CEO*
John G Sznewajs, *
Kenneth G Cole, *
◆ **EMP:** 110 **EST:** 1987
SQ FT: 70,000
SALES (est): 97.64MM
SALES (corp-wide): 8.68B **Publicly Held**
Web: www.brasstech.com
SIC: 3432 Plumbing fixture fittings and trim
PA: Masco Corporation
17450 College Pkwy
Livonia MI
313 274-7400

(P-5964)
BRASSTECH INC
1301 E Wilshire Ave (92705-4420)
PHONE...............714 796-9278
EMP: 230
SALES (corp-wide): 8.68B **Publicly Held**
Web: www.brasstech.com
SIC: 3432 Plumbing fixture fittings and trim
HQ: Brasstech, Inc.
2001 Carnegie Ave
Santa Ana CA
949 417-5207

(P-5965)
CALIFORNIA FAUCETS INC
5231 Argosy Ave (92649-1015)
PHONE...............657 400-1639
Blas Ramierez, *Brnch Mgr*
EMP: 39
Web: www.calfaucets.com
SIC: 3432 Faucets and spigots, metal and plastic
PA: California Faucets, Inc.
5271 Argosy Ave
Huntington Beach CA

(P-5966)
CALIFORNIA FAUCETS INC (PA)
5271 Argosy Ave (92649-1015)
PHONE...............800 822-8855
Jeffrey Howard Silverstein, *CEO*
Sonia Silverstein, *
◆ **EMP:** 36 **EST:** 1988
SALES (est): 23.27MM **Privately Held**
Web: www.calfaucets.com
SIC: 3432 Faucets and spigots, metal and plastic

(P-5967)
CHAMPION-ARROWHEAD LLC
5147 Alhambra Ave (90032-3413)
PHONE...............323 221-9137
Jim Shearer, *Managing Member*
▲ **EMP:** 25 **EST:** 1936
SQ FT: 4,000
SALES (est): 2.47MM **Privately Held**
Web: www.championarrowhead.com
SIC: 3432 Plumbing fixture fittings and trim

(P-5968)
COLLICUTT ENERGY SERVICES INC
12349 Hawkins St (90670-3366)
PHONE...............562 944-4413
TOLL FREE: 866
Tim Rahman, *Brnch Mgr*
EMP: 21
SQ FT: 77,000
SALES (corp-wide): 33.54MM **Privately Held**
Web: www.collicutt.com
SIC: 3432 Plumbing fixture fittings and trim
HQ: Collicutt Energy Services Inc.
940 Riverside Pkwy Ste 80
West Sacramento CA

(P-5969)
COLUMBIA SANITARY PRODUCTS INC
Also Called: Columbia Products Co
1622 Browning (92606-4809)
PHONE...............949 474-0777
Dorothy Lazier, *CEO*
Paul Escalera, *Pr*
▲ **EMP:** 20 **EST:** 1949
SQ FT: 20,000
SALES (est): 2.49MM **Privately Held**
Web: www.columbiasinks.com
SIC: 3432 Plumbing fixture fittings and trim

(P-5970)
G T WATER PRODUCTS INC
5239 N Commerce Ave (93021-1763)
PHONE...............805 529-2900
George Tash, *Pr*
Debra Tash, *VP*
Russell Reasner, *VP*
Steve Schmitt, *VP*
Julie Shipley, *VP*
▲ **EMP:** 17 **EST:** 1971
SQ FT: 20,000
SALES (est): 3.86MM **Privately Held**

PRODUCTS & SVCS

Web: www.gtwaterproducts.com
SIC: **3432** Plumbing fixture fittings and trim

(P-5971)
GMS LANDSCAPES INC
207 Camino Leon (93012-8635)
PHONE..............................805 402-3925
Sarah Corbin, *Pr*
EMP: 85 EST: 2017
SALES (est): 3.75MM **Privately Held**
SIC: **3432** 0781 Plumbing fixture fittings and trim; Landscape services

(P-5972)
PRICE PFISTER INC (HQ)
Also Called: Price Pfister Brass Mfg
19701 Da Vinci (92610-2622)
PHONE..............................949 672-4000
Gregory John Gluchowski, *CEO*
▲ EMP: 800 EST: 1910
SQ FT: 127,612
SALES (est): 128.86MM
SALES (corp-wide): 558.24MM **Privately Held**
Web: www.pfisterfaucets.com
SIC: **3432** Faucets and spigots, metal and plastic
PA: Spectrum Brands, Inc.
3001 Deming Way
Middleton WI
608 275-3340

(P-5973)
RAIN BIRD CORPORATION
Also Called: Rain Bird Golf Division
970 W Sierra Madre Ave (91702-1873)
PHONE..............................626 812-3400
Matt Circle, *Mgr*
EMP: 33
SALES (corp-wide): 433.78MM **Privately Held**
Web: www.rainbird.com
SIC: **3432** 3494 3433 Plumbing fixture fittings and trim; Valves and pipe fittings, nec; Heating equipment, except electric
PA: Rain Bird Corporation
970 W Sierra Madre Ave
Azusa CA
626 812-3400

(P-5974)
SANTEC INC
3501 Challenger St Fl 2 (90503-1697)
PHONE..............................310 542-0063
Nicolas Chen, *CEO*
James S Chen, *
▲ EMP: 50 EST: 1981
SQ FT: 32,000
SALES (est): 8.21MM **Privately Held**
Web: www.santecfaucet.com
SIC: **3432** Faucets and spigots, metal and plastic

(P-5975)
TBS IRRIGATION PRODUCTS INC
Also Called: T.B.S. Irrigation
8787 Olive Ln Bldg 3 (92071-4137)
PHONE..............................619 579-0520
Michael J Folkman, *Pr*
William Butson, *VP*
Neil Faulkman, *Sec*
EMP: 20 EST: 1997
SQ FT: 25,000
SALES (est): 2.32MM **Privately Held**
Web: www.tbsirrigation.com
SIC: **3432** 3523 3088 Lawn hose nozzles and sprinklers; Farm machinery and equipment; Plastics plumbing fixtures

(P-5976)
WATERTITE PRODUCTS INC
455 W Victoria St (90220-6064)
PHONE..............................901 853-5001
Nick Cassella, *CEO*
Zhana Goldblatt, *
▲ EMP: 71 EST: 1972
SQ FT: 70,000
SALES (est): 20.07MM **Privately Held**
Web: www.ipscorp.com
SIC: **3432** Plumbing fixture fittings and trim
HQ: Ips Corporation
455 W Victoria St
Compton CA
310 898-3300

3433 Heating Equipment, Except Electric

(P-5977)
AMERICAN SOLAR LLC
8484 Wilshire Blvd Ste 630 (90211-3227)
PHONE..............................323 250-1307
Meir Yaniv, *CEO*
EMP: 30 EST: 2020
SALES (est): 2.77MM **Privately Held**
SIC: **3433** Solar heaters and collectors

(P-5978)
CAPITAL COOKING EQUIPMENT INC
Also Called: Capital Cooking
1025 E Bedmar St (90746-3601)
PHONE..............................562 903-1168
Roberto Bernal, *
Alejandro Bernal, *
Porfiro Guzman, *
Rafael Romero, *
▲ EMP: 47 EST: 2001
SALES (est): 7.99MM **Privately Held**
Web: www.capital-cooking.com
SIC: **3433** 3631 Stoves, wood and coal burning; Gas ranges, domestic

(P-5979)
EMPIRE PRODUCTS INC
5061 Brooks St (91763-4835)
PHONE..............................909 399-3355
Robert Beck, *Ch Bd*
EMP: 57 EST: 1982
SQ FT: 6,000
SALES (est): 4.79MM **Privately Held**
SIC: **3433** 3429 3631 Logs, gas fireplace; Fireplace equipment, hardware: andirons, grates, screens; Household cooking equipment

(P-5980)
INDEPENDENT ENERGY SOLUTIONS INC
663 S Rancho Santa Fe Rd Ste 682 (92078)
PHONE..............................760 752-9706
▲ EMP: 42
Web: www.indenergysolutions.com
SIC: **3433** Heating equipment, except electric

(P-5981)
INFRARED DYNAMICS INC
3830 Prospect Ave (92886-1742)
PHONE..............................714 572-4050
Robert Cowan, *Pr*
▲ EMP: 21 EST: 1959
SQ FT: 23,500
SALES (est): 2.45MM **Privately Held**
Web: www.infradyne.com

SIC: **3433** 5075 Heating equipment, except electric; Warm air heating equipment and supplies

(P-5982)
OMC-THC LIQUIDATING INC
12131 Community Rd (92064-8893)
PHONE..............................858 486-8846
Frank Polese, *Prin*
EMP: 23 EST: 2005
SALES (est): 962.37K **Privately Held**
Web: www.fralock.com
SIC: **3433** Heating equipment, except electric

(P-5983)
RASMUSSEN IRON WORKS INC
12028 Philadelphia St (90601-3925)
PHONE..............................562 696-8718
Theodore Rasmussen, *Pr*
T E Rasmussen, *
▲ EMP: 62 EST: 1907
SQ FT: 40,000
SALES (est): 6.82MM **Privately Held**
Web: www.radiantpatioheater.com
SIC: **3433** Logs, gas fireplace

(P-5984)
RAYPAK INC (DH)
2151 Eastman Ave (93030-5194)
PHONE..............................805 278-5300
Kevin Mcdonald, *VP*
◆ EMP: 320 EST: 1949
SQ FT: 250,000
SALES (est): 97.79MM **Privately Held**
Web: www.raypak.com
SIC: **3433** Heaters, swimming pool: oil or gas
HQ: Rheem Manufacturing Company Inc
1100 Abernathy Rd # 1700
Atlanta GA
770 351-3000

(P-5985)
SOLARRESERVE LLC (PA)
520 Broadway 6th Fl (90401-2420)
PHONE..............................310 315-2200
Tom Georgis, *CEO*
Kevin Smith, *CEO*
Tim Rosenzweig, *CFO*
Alistair Jessop, *Sr VP*
Stephen Mullennix, *Sr VP*
EMP: 19 EST: 2007
SALES (est): 5.23MM **Privately Held**
Web: www.solarreserve.com
SIC: **3433** 1711 4911 Solar heaters and collectors; Solar energy contractor; Electric services

3441 Fabricated Structural Metal

(P-5986)
A AND M WELDING INC
16935 S Broadway (90248-3111)
PHONE..............................310 329-2700
Tom A Jorgenson, *Pr*
Linda Jorgenson, *VP*
EMP: 23 EST: 1952
SQ FT: 25,000
SALES (est): 2.12MM **Privately Held**
Web: www.ammetalforming.com
SIC: **3441** Fabricated structural metal

(P-5987)
ABLE IRON WORKS
222 Hershey St (91767-5810)
PHONE..............................909 397-5300
Stephen Holmes, *CEO*
EMP: 20 EST: 1993

SQ FT: 12,000
SALES (est): 5.03MM **Privately Held**
Web: www.ableironwork.com
SIC: **3441** Fabricated structural metal

(P-5988)
AEC - ABLE ENGINEERING COMPANY INC
600 Pine Ave (93117-3803)
PHONE..............................805 685-2262
EMP: 120
SIC: **3441** 3769 Fabricated structural metal; Space vehicle equipment, nec

(P-5989)
AEROFAB CORPORATION
4001 E Leaverton Ct (92807-1610)
PHONE..............................714 635-0902
Matthew Owen, *Pr*
George Robinson, *VP*
EMP: 17 EST: 2007
SQ FT: 10,000
SALES (est): 3.89MM **Privately Held**
Web: www.aerofab-corp.com
SIC: **3441** Fabricated structural metal

(P-5990)
AFAKORI INC
Also Called: AAF Steel Structural
18173 Osborne Rd (92394-1600)
P.O. Box 4526 (92690-4526)
PHONE..............................949 859-4277
Amir A Fakori, *Pr*
Luz Marina Agreda, *Sec*
▲ EMP: 20 EST: 2001
SALES (est): 5.69MM **Privately Held**
Web: www.afakori.com
SIC: **3441** Building components, structural steel

(P-5991)
AMAZING STEEL COMPANY
Also Called: Mitchellamazing
4564 Mission Blvd (91763-6106)
PHONE..............................909 590-0393
EMP: 20 EST: 1985
SQ FT: 25,000
SALES (est): 1.84MM **Privately Held**
Web: www.mitchellamazing.com
SIC: **3441** 7692 7699 Fabricated structural metal; Welding repair; Hydraulic equipment repair

(P-5992)
ANDERSON CHRNESKY STRL STL INC
Also Called: Acss
353 Risco Cir (92223-2676)
PHONE..............................951 769-5700
Kevin Charneskey, *Pr*
Kevin Charnesky, *
EMP: 85 EST: 1984
SQ FT: 6,600
SALES (est): 36.73MM **Privately Held**
Web: www.acssteelinc.com
SIC: **3441** Fabricated structural metal

(P-5993)
AZTEC TECHNOLOGY CORPORATION (PA)
Also Called: Aztec Container
2550 S Santa Fe Ave (92084-8005)
PHONE..............................760 727-2300
Brian Hyndman, *CEO*
Catherine Hyndman, *VP*
Michael Hyndman, *Treas*
Steven Hyndman, *Sec*
Teresa Gualtieri, *Contrlr*
EMP: 20 EST: 1969

SQ FT: 3,000
SALES (est): 7.03MM
SALES (corp-wide): 7.03MM Privately Held
Web: www.azteccontainer.com
SIC: 3441 Fabricated structural metal

(P-5994)
BAY CITY MARINE INC (PA)
1625 Cleveland Ave (91950-4212)
PHONE..............................619 477-3991
Paul Ralph, CEO
Michelle Ralph, *
Timothy Dernbach, *
Steve Johnston, *
EMP: 24 EST: 1971
SQ FT: 11,000
SALES (est): 5.87MM
SALES (corp-wide): 5.87MM Privately Held
Web: www.baycmarine.com
SIC: 3441 3731 7699 Fabricated structural metal; Military ships, building and repairing; Boat repair

(P-5995)
BELL BROS STEEL INC
1510 Palmyrita Ave (92507-1629)
PHONE..............................951 784-0903
James Bell, Pr
EMP: 36 EST: 2001
SQ FT: 1,400
SALES (est): 5MM Privately Held
Web: www.bellbrossteel.com
SIC: 3441 Fabricated structural metal

(P-5996)
BELLOWS MFG & RES INC
864 Arroyo St (91340-1832)
PHONE..............................818 838-1333
Arteom Art Bulgadarian, CEO
EMP: 30 EST: 2005
SQ FT: 28,000
SALES (est): 5.56MM Privately Held
Web: www.bellowsmfg.com
SIC: 3441 3724 3764 Fabricated structural metal; Aircraft engines and engine parts; Propulsion units for guided missiles and space vehicles

(P-5997)
BLAZING INDUSTRIAL STEEL INC
9040 Jurupa Rd (92509-3106)
PHONE..............................951 360-8340
Fernando Herrera, Pr
Roberta Calderon, *
Mike Calderon, *
Brad Mcglothlin, Genl Mgr
EMP: 63 EST: 1985
SQ FT: 100,000
SALES (est): 4.03MM Privately Held
Web: www.blazingindustrial.com
SIC: 3441 Fabricated structural metal

(P-5998)
BLUE STAR STEEL INC
12122 Industry Rd (92040-1736)
PHONE..............................619 448-5520
Rodney Walker, Pr
EMP: 45 EST: 1962
SALES (est): 7.11MM Privately Held
Web: www.bluestarsteelinc.com
SIC: 3441 Fabricated structural metal

(P-5999)
BOYD CORPORATION (PA)
Also Called: Boyd Construction
5832 Ohio St (92886-5323)
P.O. Box 6012 (92816-0012)

PHONE..............................714 533-2375
Mitch Aiello, Pr
EMP: 25 EST: 1980
SALES (est): 19.19MM
SALES (corp-wide): 19.19MM Privately Held
Web: www.boydcorp.com
SIC: 3441 2891 Fabricated structural metal; Adhesives

(P-6000)
BRASS UNIQUE INC
9948 Hayward Way (91733-3193)
PHONE..............................626 444-8977
Yi-tai Soong, Pr
EMP: 27 EST: 1991
SQ FT: 15,000
SALES (est): 1.02MM Privately Held
SIC: 3441 Fabricated structural metal for ships

(P-6001)
BRUNTON ENTERPRISES INC
Also Called: Plas-Tal Manufacturing Co
8815 Sorensen Ave (90670-2636)
PHONE..............................562 945-0013
Sean P Brunton, CEO
John W Brunton Junior, Pr
EMP: 125 EST: 1947
SQ FT: 45,000
SALES (est): 22.77MM Privately Held
Web: www.plas-tal.com
SIC: 3441 Fabricated structural metal

(P-6002)
C A BUCHEN CORP
9231 Glenoaks Blvd (91352-2688)
PHONE..............................818 767-5408
John Oster, CEO
Ryan Chapman, *
EMP: 25 EST: 1962
SQ FT: 22,500
SALES (est): 6.64MM Privately Held
Web: www.cabuchen.com
SIC: 3441 1791 3312 Fabricated structural metal; Structural steel erection; Galvanized pipes, plates, sheets, etc.: iron and steel

(P-6003)
CAD WORKS INC
16366 E Valley Blvd (91744-5546)
PHONE..............................626 336-5491
David Paquini, Pr
Avrahan Garcia, VP
Cecilia Chavez, CFO
EMP: 20 EST: 2004
SQ FT: 10,000
SALES (est): 1.6MM Privately Held
Web: www.cadworks.us
SIC: 3441 Fabricated structural metal

(P-6004)
CAMPBELL CERTIFIED INC
1629 Ord Way (92056-3599)
PHONE..............................760 722-9353
EMP: 30 EST: 1991
SQ FT: 45,000
SALES (est): 3.72MM Privately Held
Web: www.campbellcertified.com
SIC: 3441 Fabricated structural metal

(P-6005)
CANYON STEEL FABRICATORS INC
4280 Patterson Ave (92571-9714)
PHONE..............................951 683-2352
Thomas J Baggett, Pr
Ray Magnon, VP
Doug Magnon, Sec
EMP: 22 EST: 2007

SALES (est): 3.23MM Privately Held
Web: www.canyonsteelfab.com
SIC: 3441 Fabricated structural metal

(P-6006)
CAPITOL STEEL FABRICATORS INC
3522 Greenwood Ave (90040-3319)
P.O. Box 640 (91017-0640)
PHONE..............................323 721-5460
James Moreland, Pr
Janice Moreland, *
Eric Jonkey, Stockholder*
EMP: 25 EST: 1984
SALES (est): 7.17MM Privately Held
Web: www.capitolsteel.com
SIC: 3441 Fabricated structural metal

(P-6007)
CARROLL METAL WORKS INC
740 W 16th St (91950-4205)
PHONE..............................619 477-9125
Pat Carroll, Pr
EMP: 95 EST: 1984
SQ FT: 11,500
SALES (est): 8.51MM Privately Held
Web: www.carrollmetalworks.com
SIC: 3441 Fabricated structural metal

(P-6008)
COLUMBIA ALUMINUM PRODUCTS LLC
1150 W Rincon St (92878-9601)
PHONE..............................323 728-7361
Drew D Mumford, Managing Member
Grant Palenske, *
▲ EMP: 70 EST: 1989
SALES (est): 8.61MM Privately Held
Web: www.columbiaaluminumproductsllc.com
SIC: 3441 Fabricated structural metal

(P-6009)
COLUMBIA STEEL INC
2175 N Linden Ave (92377-4445)
PHONE..............................909 874-8840
Gustavo Waldemar Theisen, CEO
William Young, *
Luis Theisen, *
Charmaine Helenihi, *
EMP: 75 EST: 1975
SQ FT: 63,384
SALES (est): 25.8MM Privately Held
Web: www.csirialto.com
SIC: 3441 Building components, structural steel

(P-6010)
COMMERCIAL SHTMTL WORKS INC
Also Called: CSM Metal Fabricating & Engrg
1800 S San Pedro St (90015-3711)
PHONE..............................213 748-7321
Jack L Gardener, CEO
▲ EMP: 27 EST: 1916
SQ FT: 22,000
SALES (est): 4.6MM Privately Held
Web: www.csmworks.com
SIC: 3441 Fabricated structural metal

(P-6011)
COMPLETE METAL FABRICATION INC
596 E Main St (92243-9471)
P.O. Box 1529 (92244-1529)
PHONE..............................760 353-0260
Jesse Ray Riddle, CEO
EMP: 17 EST: 2012
SALES (est): 1.15MM Privately Held

Web: www.cmfab.biz
SIC: 3441 Fabricated structural metal

(P-6012)
CONSTEEL INDUSTRIAL INC
Also Called: Consteel Industrial
15435 Woodcrest Dr (90604-3236)
PHONE..............................562 806-4575
Luis Lagarica, CEO
Russ Lambert, Corporate Secretary*
Maria Torres, *
Robert Geronca, *
Peter Williams, *
EMP: 27 EST: 2012
SALES (est): 1.28MM Privately Held
SIC: 3441 Fabricated structural metal

(P-6013)
CORBELL PRODUCTS INC (PA)
14650 Hawthorne Ave (92335-2509)
PHONE..............................909 574-9139
Frank Stavinski, Pr
Elaine Lucero, Treas
EMP: 18 EST: 1997
SQ FT: 26,000
SALES (est): 2.88MM
SALES (corp-wide): 2.88MM Privately Held
SIC: 3441 Fabricated structural metal

(P-6014)
CRAFTECH METAL FORMING INC
24100 Water Ave Ste B (92570-6738)
PHONE..............................951 940-6444
EMP: 40 EST: 1996
SQ FT: 26,000
SALES (est): 4.94MM Privately Held
Web: www.craftechmetal.com
SIC: 3441 3499 3444 Fabricated structural metal; Fire- or burglary-resistive products; Sheet metalwork

(P-6015)
CROSNO CONSTRUCTION INC
819 Sheridan Rd (93420-5833)
PHONE..............................805 343-7437
Wade Crosno, Pr
Wade Crosno, Pr
Jaime Crosno, *
EMP: 48 EST: 2004
SQ FT: 5,000
SALES (est): 9.17MM Privately Held
Web: www.crosnoconstruction.com
SIC: 3441 Fabricated structural metal

(P-6016)
CUSTOM IRON CORPORATION
26895 Aliso Creek Rd Ste B787 (92656-5301)
PHONE..............................949 939-4379
Michael Knee, Pr
EMP: 27 EST: 2013
SALES (est): 2.37MM Privately Held
Web: www.customironcorp.com
SIC: 3441 Fabricated structural metal

(P-6017)
CUSTOM STEEL FABRICATION INC
Also Called: C & J Industries
11966 Rivera Rd (90670-2232)
PHONE..............................562 907-2777
EMP: 17 EST: 2006
SQ FT: 3,400
SALES (est): 2.87MM Privately Held
Web: www.cnjindustries.com
SIC: 3441 Fabricated structural metal

PRODUCTS & SVCS

(P-6018)
CW INDUSTRIES
1735 Santa Fe Ave (90813-1242)
PHONE....................562 432-5421
Craig Wildvank, *Prin*
EMP: 28 EST: 2006
SALES (est): 729.26K **Privately Held**
Web: www.cwindustries.us
SIC: 3441 3548 5084 Building components, structural steel; Welding apparatus; Oil refining machinery, equipment, and supplies

(P-6019)
D & M STEEL INC
13020 Pierce St (91331-2528)
PHONE....................818 896-2070
Michael Atia, *Pr*
David Dagni, *
EMP: 37 EST: 1980
SQ FT: 16,500
SALES (est): 9.59MM **Privately Held**
Web: www.d-msteel.com
SIC: 3441 Fabricated structural metal

(P-6020)
D D WIRE CO INC (PA)
4335 Temple City Blvd (91780-4229)
PHONE....................626 442-0459
Wes Berry, *Pr*
David Berry, *CFO*
Elizabeth D Berry, *Sec*
James Howe, *COO*
Dorsey Wire, *Prin*
EMP: 22 EST: 1963
SQ FT: 24,000
SALES (est): 4.99MM
SALES (corp-wide): 4.99MM **Privately Held**
Web: www.ddwire.com
SIC: 3441 3469 Fabricated structural metal; Stamping metal for the trade

(P-6021)
DUNCAN BROS INC
21516 Main St (92313-5835)
PHONE....................909 877-1904
EMP: 30
Web: www.duncanbrosinc.com
SIC: 3441 3443 Building components, structural steel; Fabricated plate work (boiler shop)

(P-6022)
EAST CAST REPR FABRICATION LLC
Also Called: West Coast Operations
280 Trousdale Dr Ste E (91910-1079)
PHONE....................619 591-9577
Brett Baker, *Prin*
EMP: 44
SALES (corp-wide): 49.95MM **Privately Held**
Web: www.ecrfab.com
SIC: 3441 Fabricated structural metal
PA: East Coast Repair & Fabrication, L.L.C.
1201 Terminal Ave
Newport News VA
757 455-9600

(P-6023)
EW CORPRTION INDUS FABRICATORS (PA)
1002 E Main St (92243)
P.O. Box 2189 (92244-2189)
PHONE....................760 337-0020
Tiberio R Esparza, *Pr*
◆ EMP: 69 EST: 1973
SQ FT: 100,000
SALES (est): 15.01MM
SALES (corp-wide): 15.01MM **Privately Held**
Web: www.ewcorporation.com
SIC: 3441 Fabricated structural metal

(P-6024)
FABCO STEEL FABRICATION INC
14688 San Bernardino Ave (92335-5319)
P.O. Box 8636 (91701-0636)
PHONE....................909 350-1535
John E Schick, *Pr*
Rich Schick, *
EMP: 35 EST: 1979
SQ FT: 30,000
SALES (est): 5.91MM **Privately Held**
Web: www.fabcosteel.com
SIC: 3441 Fabricated structural metal

(P-6025)
FABRICATION TECH INDS INC
2200 Haffley Ave (91950-6418)
P.O. Box 1447 (91951-1447)
PHONE....................619 477-4141
▲ EMP: 75 EST: 1994
SQ FT: 50,000
SALES (est): 10.04MM **Privately Held**
Web: www.ftisd.com
SIC: 3441 Fabricated structural metal

(P-6026)
FOSS MARITIME COMPANY
Also Called: FOSS MARITIME COMPANY
49 W Pier D St (90802-1020)
PHONE....................562 437-6098
Wendall Koi, *Prin*
EMP: 18
SALES (corp-wide): 2.33B **Privately Held**
Web: www.foss.com
SIC: 3441 Boat and barge sections, prefabricated metal
HQ: Foss Maritime Company, Llc.
450 Alaskan Way S Ste 706
Seattle WA
206 281-3800

(P-6027)
FREEBERG INDUS FBRICATION CORP
Also Called: Freeberg Industrial
2874 Progress Pl (92029-1516)
PHONE....................760 737-7614
Marc Brown, *Pr*
James R St John, *
EMP: 85 EST: 1992
SQ FT: 128,000
SALES (est): 23.39MM **Privately Held**
Web: www.freeberg.com
SIC: 3441 3444 Fabricated structural metal; Sheet metalwork

(P-6028)
GRATING PACIFIC INC (PA)
3651 Sausalito St (90720-2436)
PHONE....................562 598-4314
TOLL FREE: 800
Ronald S Robertson, *Pr*
Jeffrey Robertson, *VP*
▲ EMP: 20 EST: 1971
SQ FT: 40,000
SALES (est): 23.57MM
SALES (corp-wide): 23.57MM **Privately Held**
Web: www.gratingpacific.com
SIC: 3441 3446 Fabricated structural metal; Architectural metalwork

(P-6029)
HITECH METAL FABRICATION CORP
Also Called: H M F
1705 S Claudina Way (92805-6544)
PHONE....................714 635-3505
Ba V Nguyen, *Pr*
Matthew Vu, *
EMP: 60 EST: 1989
SQ FT: 42,850
SALES (est): 10.78MM **Privately Held**
Web: www.hmfcorp.com
SIC: 3441 Fabricated structural metal

(P-6030)
HOMESTEAD SHEET METAL
9031 Memory Ln (91977-2152)
PHONE....................619 469-4373
EMP: 27 EST: 1996
SQ FT: 5,625
SALES (est): 5.81MM **Privately Held**
Web: www.homesteadsheetmetal.com
SIC: 3441 Fabricated structural metal

(P-6031)
IMPERIAL VALLEY STEEL COMPANY
8516 La Jolla Shores Dr (92037-3020)
PHONE....................858 900-2011
Efren Carlos Romero, *Brnch Mgr*
EMP: 41
SALES (corp-wide): 399.88K **Privately Held**
SIC: 3441 Fabricated structural metal
PA: Imperial Valley Steel Company Inc
805 Bowsprit Rd
Chula Vista CA

(P-6032)
INDUSTRIAL MACHINE & MFG CO
Also Called: Immco
2626 Seaman Ave (91733-1930)
PHONE....................626 444-0181
Diane Teresa, *Pr*
Mark Teresa, *VP*
David Teresa, *VP*
Ron Teresa, *Sec*
EMP: 20 EST: 1959
SQ FT: 5,500
SALES (est): 803.32K **Privately Held**
Web: www.immcohandtrucks.com
SIC: 3441 3569 3537 Fabricated structural metal; Assembly machines, non-metalworking; Industrial trucks and tractors

(P-6033)
INTEGRAL ENGRG FABRICATION INC
520 Hofgaarden St (91744-5529)
PHONE....................626 369-0958
John Zheng, *CEO*
Son T Nguyen, *
EMP: 25 EST: 2003
SQ FT: 20,000
SALES (est): 2.5MM **Privately Held**
Web: www.integralfab.com
SIC: 3441 Fabricated structural metal

(P-6034)
J L M C INC
1944 S Bon View Ave (91761-5503)
P.O. Box 3817 (91761-0979)
PHONE....................909 947-2980
EMP: 35 EST: 1984
SALES (est): 4.06MM **Privately Held**
Web: www.jlmc.com
SIC: 3441 Fabricated structural metal

(P-6035)
JCI METAL PRODUCTS (PA)
6540 Federal Blvd (91945-1311)
PHONE....................619 229-8206
Marcel Becker, *CEO*
Mark Withers, *
Rich Bartlett, *
Lorey Topham, *
EMP: 57 EST: 1984
SQ FT: 21,000
SALES (est): 8.68MM **Privately Held**
SIC: 3441 1761 Fabricated structural metal for ships; Architectural sheet metal work

(P-6036)
JOHASEE REBAR INC
Also Called: Johasee Rebar
26365 Earthmover Cir (92883-5270)
PHONE....................661 589-0972
Mike Hill Senior, *CEO*
Tamara L Chapman, *
Michael Hill Junior, *COO*
EMP: 47 EST: 1979
SALES (est): 13.22MM
SALES (corp-wide): 3.49MM **Privately Held**
SIC: 3441 1791 Fabricated structural metal; Concrete reinforcement, placing of
PA: Lms Holdings (Ab) Ltd
7452 132 St
Surrey BC
604 598-9930

(P-6037)
KERN STEEL FABRICATION INC (PA)
627 Williams St (93305-5437)
PHONE....................661 327-9588
Tom Champness, *Pr*
Larkin Mckenzie, *VP*
◆ EMP: 54 EST: 1959
SQ FT: 50,000
SALES (est): 22.92MM
SALES (corp-wide): 22.92MM **Privately Held**
Web: www.kernsteel.com
SIC: 3441 3728 4581 3412 Fabricated structural metal; Aircraft parts and equipment, nec; Aircraft maintenance and repair services; Metal barrels, drums, and pails

(P-6038)
KUMAR INDUSTRIES
4775 Chino Ave (91710-5130)
PHONE....................909 591-0722
EMP: 23 EST: 1980
SALES (est): 5.43MM **Privately Held**
Web: www.kumarindustries.net
SIC: 3441 Building components, structural steel

(P-6039)
LEXINGTON ACQUISITION INC
Also Called: Lexington
11125 Vanowen St (91605-6316)
PHONE....................818 768-5768
EMP: 145
SIC: 3441 Fabricated structural metal

(P-6040)
LIGHTCAP INDUSTRIES INC
Also Called: JC Supply & Manufacturing
1612 S Cucamonga Ave (91761-4513)
PHONE....................909 930-3772
EMP: 50
SIC: 3441 3479 Building components, structural steel; Painting, coating, and hot dipping

(P-6041)
LINDBLADE METALWORKS INC
Also Called: Lindblade Metal Works
14355 Macaw St (90638-5208)
PHONE..................714 670-7172
Vernon Lindblade, *CEO*
Marilyn Lindblade, *VP*
EMP: 20 EST: 1973
SQ FT: 16,250
SALES (est) 2.53MM Privately Held
Web: www.lindblademetalworks.com
SIC: 3441 Fabricated structural metal

(P-6042)
M W REID WELDING INC
Also Called: South Bay Welding
781 Oconner St (92020-1644)
PHONE..................619 401-5880
Bruce A Reid, *Pr*
Timothy Hill, *
Timothy Fair, *
Susan Reid, *
EMP: 78 EST: 1965
SQ FT: 25,000
SALES (est) 16.38MM Privately Held
Web: www.southbaywelding.com
SIC: 3441 Fabricated structural metal

(P-6043)
MADISON INC OF OKLAHOMA
18000 Studebaker Rd (90703-2679)
PHONE..................918 224-6990
John Samuel Frey, *Pr*
Robert E Hansen, *
Barbara Cruncleton, *
EMP: 67 EST: 1946
SALES (est) 22.77MM
SALES (corp-wide): 90.88MM Privately Held
SIC: 3441 1541 3448 3444 Fabricated structural metal; Prefabricated building erection, industrial; Prefabricated metal buildings and components; Sheet metalwork
PA: John S. Frey Enterprises
1900 E 64th St
Los Angeles CA
323 583-4061

(P-6044)
MAXIMUM QUALITY METAL PDTS INC
Also Called: Max Q
1017 E Acacia St (91761-4554)
PHONE..................909 902-5018
John Kim, *Pr*
Paul Kim, *Sec*
John Kim, *Pr*
EMP: 20 EST: 1998
SQ FT: 10,000
SALES (est) 4.9MM Privately Held
Web: www.maxqmetalproducts.com
SIC: 3441 Fabricated structural metal

(P-6045)
MAYA STEEL FABRICATIONS INC
301 E Compton Blvd (90248-2015)
PHONE..................310 532-8830
Meir Amsalam, *CEO*
Yechiel Yogev, *
Sara Haddad, *
EMP: 64 EST: 1982
SQ FT: 65,000
SALES (est) 11.18MM Privately Held
Web: www.mayasteel.com
SIC: 3441 Building components, structural steel

(P-6046)
MCCAIN MANUFACTURING INC
2633 Progress St (92081-8402)
P.O. Box 2307 (92067-2307)
PHONE..................760 295-9290
Jeffrey Lynn Mccain, *CEO*
EMP: 61 EST: 2016
SALES (est) 5.17MM Privately Held
SIC: 3441 Fabricated structural metal

(P-6047)
MCM FABRICATORS INC
Also Called: Global Fabricators
720 Commerce Way (93263-9530)
P.O. Box 80247 (93380-0247)
PHONE..................661 589-2774
Jim L Moses, *Pr*
Gary E Moses, *
Bill Chaney, *
EMP: 140 EST: 1982
SQ FT: 12,000
SALES (est) 17.32MM Privately Held
SIC: 3441 Fabricated structural metal

(P-6048)
MCWHIRTER STEEL INC
42211 7th St E (93535-5400)
PHONE..................661 951-8998
David Mcwhirter, *Pr*
Angela Mcwhirter, *CFO*
Nathan Mcwhirter, *Dir*
EMP: 95 EST: 1992
SQ FT: 21,000
SALES (est) 14.14MM Privately Held
Web: www.mcwhirtersteel.com
SIC: 3441 1791 Fabricated structural metal; Structural steel erection

(P-6049)
MEDSCO FABRICATION & DIST INC
938 N Eastern Ave (90063-1308)
PHONE..................323 263-0511
Michael Nevarez, *Ch Bd*
Brian Powell, *Pr*
Jim Stock, *CFO*
John Millan, *COO*
Laura Nevarez, *Sec*
EMP: 56 EST: 2001
SALES (est) 6.46MM Privately Held
SIC: 3441 Fabricated structural metal

(P-6050)
MERRIMANS INCORPORATED
32195 Dunlap Blvd (92399-1728)
P.O. Box 547 (92320-0547)
PHONE..................909 795-5301
TOLL FREE: 800
Tod Merriman, *Pr*
Janice Merriman, *
Lisa Merriman, *
Elaine Onken, *
EMP: 30 EST: 1965
SQ FT: 5,000
SALES (est) 4.38MM Privately Held
Web: www.merrimansinc.com
SIC: 3441 5271 1521 Building components, structural steel; Mobile home parts and accessories; General remodeling, single-family houses

(P-6051)
METAL SUPPLY LLC
11810 Center St (90280-7832)
PHONE..................562 634-9940
TOLL FREE: 800
Dion Genchi, *Pr*
Bruce E Hubert, *
▼ **EMP: 63 EST:** 1961
SQ FT: 50,000
SALES (est): 9.38MM Privately Held
Web: www.metalsupply.com
SIC: 3441 5051 Fabricated structural metal; Iron and steel (ferrous) products

(P-6052)
METAL TEK COMPANY
3801 S H St (93304-6502)
PHONE..................661 832-6011
EMP: 20 EST: 1979
SALES (est) 1.98MM Privately Held
Web: www.metaltekonline.com
SIC: 3441 Fabricated structural metal

(P-6053)
METALS USA BUILDING PDTS LP
6450 Caballero Blvd Ste A (90620-1007)
PHONE..................714 522-7852
Tom Bush, *Brnch Mgr*
EMP: 103
SALES (corp-wide): 17.02B Publicly Held
Web: www.metalsusa.com
SIC: 3441 3444 Fabricated structural metal; Sheet metalwork
HQ: Metals Usa Building Products Lp
955 Columbia St
Brea CA
713 946-9000

(P-6054)
MIKES METAL WORKS INC
3552 Fowler Canyon Rd (91935-1602)
PHONE..................619 440-8804
Mike Hancock, *Pr*
EMP: 18 EST: 1984
SQ FT: 6,000
SALES (est) 4.54MM Privately Held
Web: www.mikesmetalworks.net
SIC: 3441 Fabricated structural metal

(P-6055)
MILLERS FAB & WELD CORP
6100 Industrial Ave (92504-1120)
PHONE..................951 359-3100
James Miller, *CEO*
EMP: 21 EST: 1964
SQ FT: 2,100
SALES (est) 2.28MM Privately Held
Web: www.millersfab.net
SIC: 3441 Fabricated structural metal

(P-6056)
MITCHELL FABRICATION
Also Called: Amazing Steel
4564 Mission Blvd (91763-6106)
PHONE..................909 590-0393
▲ **EMP: 30 EST:** 1985
SQ FT: 35,000
SALES (est) 3.9MM Privately Held
Web: www.mitchellamazing.com
SIC: 3441 Fabricated structural metal

(P-6057)
MUHLHAUSER ENTERPRISES INC (PA)
Also Called: Muhlhauser Steel
25825 Adams Ave (92562-0601)
P.O. Box 159 (92316-0159)
PHONE..................909 877-2792
William C Muhlhauser, *Pr*
Gisela Muhlhauser, *
EMP: 19 EST: 1961
SALES (est): 8.89MM
SALES (corp-wide): 8.89MM Privately Held
Web: www.msisteel.com
SIC: 3441 1791 Building components, structural steel; Structural steel erection

(P-6058)
MUHLHAUSER STEEL INC
25825 Adams Ave (92562-0601)
P.O. Box 159 (92316-0159)
PHONE..................909 877-2792
William Muhlhauser, *Pr*
Zigfried Muhlhauser, *Sr VP*
EMP: 20 EST: 1988
SALES (est): 7.8MM
SALES (corp-wide): 8.89MM Privately Held
Web: www.msisteel.com
SIC: 3441 1791 Building components, structural steel; Structural steel erection
PA: Muhlhauser Enterprises, Inc.
25825 Adams Ave
Murrieta CA
909 877-2792

(P-6059)
MYWI FABRICATORS INC
2115 Edwards Ave 2119 (91733)
PHONE..................626 279-6994
Henry Yue, *Pr*
Jeanne Yue, *Sec*
EMP: 18 EST: 1993
SQ FT: 5,000
SALES (est) 2.26MM Privately Held
Web: www.mywifabricators.com
SIC: 3441 Fabricated structural metal

(P-6060)
PACIFIC COAST IRONWORKS INC
8831 Miner St (90002-1835)
PHONE..................323 585-1320
Andrew Larkin, *Pr*
Andrew Larkin Junior, *VP*
Mike Larkin, *VP*
Max Gonzalez, *VP*
Ron David, *Sec*
EMP: 20 EST: 1991
SQ FT: 22,000
SALES (est) 2.28MM Privately Held
Web: www.pacificcoastironworks.com
SIC: 3441 Fabricated structural metal

(P-6061)
PACIFIC MARITIME INDS CORP
Also Called: P M I
1790 Dornoch Ct (92154-7206)
PHONE..................619 575-8141
John Atkinson, *CEO*
▲ **EMP: 110 EST:** 1995
SQ FT: 38,000
SALES (est) 20.11MM Privately Held
Web: pacificmaritimeindm.openfos.com
SIC: 3441 Fabricated structural metal

(P-6062)
PARCELL STEEL CORP
Also Called: Parcell Steel
26365 Earthmover Cir (92883-5270)
PHONE..................951 471-3200
EMP: 140
Web: www.parcellsteel.com
SIC: 3441 Fabricated structural metal

(P-6063)
PARK STEEL CO INC
515 E Pine St (90222-2817)
P.O. Box 4787 (90224-4787)
PHONE..................310 638-6101
Gregory M Park, *Pr*
Sally O Park, *Treas*
Randy Park, *Sec*
EMP: 18 EST: 1980
SQ FT: 70,000
SALES (est) 2.9MM Privately Held
Web: www.parksteel.net

P R O D U C T S & S V C S

SIC: **3441** 1791 Bridge sections, prefabricated, highway; Concrete reinforcement, placing of

(P-6064)
PRECISION METAL CRAFTS INC
11965 Rivera Rd (90670-2209)
PHONE.............................562 468-7080
Coleman Conrad Iii, *CEO*
Rosemary Coleman, *Sec*
Coleman Conrad Junior, *CFO*
EMP: 20 **EST:** 2006
SALES (est): 2.14MM **Privately Held**
Web: www.precisionmetalcrafts.com
SIC: **3441** Fabricated structural metal

(P-6065)
PRECISION WELDING INC
241 Enterprise Pkwy (93534-7201)
PHONE.............................661 729-3436
David R Jones, *Pr*
David Jones, *Pr*
EMP: 23 **EST:** 1995
SQ FT: 10,000
SALES (est): 4.26MM **Privately Held**
Web: www.precisionweldingla.com
SIC: **3441** 1799 Fabricated structural metal; Welding on site

(P-6066)
PREMIER STEEL STRUCTURES INC
13345 Estelle St (92879-1881)
PHONE.............................951 356-6655
Armando Rodarte, *Pr*
EMP: 30 **EST:** 2016
SALES (est): 4.9MM **Privately Held**
SIC: **3441** Fabricated structural metal

(P-6067)
R & D STEEL INC
1136 S Santa Fe Ave (90221-4337)
PHONE.............................310 631-6183
Joie A Dunyon, *Pr*
Jim Dunyon, *
▲ **EMP:** 30 **EST:** 1979
SQ FT: 8,000
SALES (est): 2.14MM **Privately Held**
Web: www.rdsteelinc.com
SIC: **3441** Fabricated structural metal

(P-6068)
R & I INDUSTRIES INC
Also Called: R & I
1876 S Taylor Ave (91761-5556)
PHONE.............................909 923-7747
William Franklin Rowan Senior, *CEO*
William Franklin Rowan Junior, *VP*
Ardith Rowan, *
EMP: 40 **EST:** 1978
SQ FT: 12,000
SALES (est): 6.76MM **Privately Held**
Web: www.rimetal.com
SIC: **3441** Building components, structural steel

(P-6069)
RELIABLE BUILDING PRODUCTS INC
Also Called: Reliable Building Products
9314 Gaymont Ave (90240-2669)
PHONE.............................323 566-5000
Jeff Palmer, *Pr*
Nikki Reagan, *VP*
EMP: 24 **EST:** 1989
SALES (est): 993.42K **Privately Held**
Web: www.reliablesteelusa.com
SIC: **3441** Fabricated structural metal

(P-6070)
RICHARDSON STEEL INC
9102 Harness St Ste A (91977-3924)
PHONE.............................619 697-5892
John Richardson, *Pr*
Lance Richardson, *
Natalie N Lautner, *
EMP: 32 **EST:** 1993
SQ FT: 5,000
SALES (est): 5.92MM **Privately Held**
Web: www.richardsonsteelinc.com
SIC: **3441** Fabricated structural metal

(P-6071)
RND CONTRACTORS INC
14796 Jurupa Ave Ste A (92337-7232)
PHONE.............................909 429-8500
Nancy Sauter, *Pr*
EMP: 40 **EST:** 2007
SALES (est): 9.13MM **Privately Held**
Web: www.rndcontractorsinc.com
SIC: **3441** Fabricated structural metal

(P-6072)
S & R ARCHITECTURAL METALS INC
2609 W Woodland Dr (92801-2627)
PHONE.............................714 226-0108
EMP: 45
SIC: **3441** Fabricated structural metal

(P-6073)
SCHROEDER IRON CORPORATION
8417 Beech Ave (92335-1200)
PHONE.............................909 428-6471
Linda Schroeder, *Pr*
EMP: 30 **EST:** 1993
SQ FT: 23,000
SALES (est): 8.61MM **Privately Held**
Web: www.schroederiron.com
SIC: **3441** Building components, structural steel

(P-6074)
SCRAPE CERTIFIED WELDING INC
2525 Old Highway 395 (92028-8794)
PHONE.............................760 728-1308
Jeff D Scrape, *Pr*
EMP: 20 **EST:** 2003
SALES (est): 542.87K **Privately Held**
Web: www.scwcontracting.com
SIC: **3441** Fabricated structural metal

(P-6075)
SO-CAL STRL STL FBRICATION INC
130 S Spruce Ave (92376-9005)
PHONE.............................909 877-1299
EMP: 50 **EST:** 1995
SQ FT: 40,000
SALES (est): 13.25MM **Privately Held**
SIC: **3441** Fabricated structural metal

(P-6076)
SOUTH BAY FOUNDRY INC (HQ)
895 Inland Center Dr (92408-1828)
PHONE.............................909 383-1823
Bill Rogers, *Pr*
Russell Goodsell, *
▲ **EMP:** 35 **EST:** 1990
SQ FT: 12,002
SALES (est): 23.55MM
SALES (corp-wide): 46.84MM **Privately Held**
Web: www.southbayfoundry.com

SIC: **3441** 3322 Fabricated structural metal; Malleable iron foundries
PA: Olympic Foundry Inc.
5200 Airport Way S
Seattle WA
206 764-6200

(P-6077)
SPARTAN INC
3030 M St (93301-2137)
PHONE.............................661 327-1205
John Wood, *Pr*
Louis Stern, *
John D Clemmey, *
Teresa Wood, *
▼ **EMP:** 65 **EST:** 2002
SQ FT: 125,000
SALES (est): 10.96MM **Privately Held**
Web: www.spartaninc.net
SIC: **3441** 8711 Fabricated structural metal; Engineering services

(P-6078)
STEEL-TECH INDUSTRIAL CORP
1268 Sherborn St (92879-2090)
PHONE.............................951 270-0144
Michael R Black, *Pr*
Braebon Black, *
Linda Black, *
Elise Roberts, *
EMP: 47 **EST:** 1984
SQ FT: 15,000
SALES (est): 8.96MM **Privately Held**
Web: www.steeltech.org
SIC: **3441** Fabricated structural metal

(P-6079)
STRUCTURAL STL FABRICATORS INC
10641 Sycamore Ave (90680-2639)
P.O. Box 707 (90680-0707)
PHONE.............................714 761-1695
Rex Shaw, *Pr*
Maureen Shaw, *
EMP: 25 **EST:** 1983
SQ FT: 3,600
SALES (est): 2.74MM **Privately Held**
SIC: **3441** Fabricated structural metal

(P-6080)
TITAN METAL FABRICATORS INC (PA)
Also Called: Titan
352 Balboa Cir (93012-8644)
PHONE.............................805 487-5050
Steve Muscarella, *Pr*
Tom Muscarella, *
▲ **EMP:** 69 **EST:** 1998
SQ FT: 15,000
SALES (est): 20.85MM
SALES (corp-wide): 20.85MM **Privately Held**
Web: www.titanmf.com
SIC: **3441** Fabricated structural metal

(P-6081)
TL FAB LP
2921 E Coronado St (92806-2502)
PHONE.............................562 802-3980
Joseph Schmidt, *Prin*
▲ **EMP:** 117 **EST:** 2012
SALES (est): 20.45MM **Privately Held**
Web: www.tlfab.com
SIC: **3441** Building components, structural steel

(P-6082)
TOBIN STEEL COMPANY INC
817 E Santa Ana Blvd (92701-3909)

P.O. Box 717 (92702-0717)
PHONE.............................714 541-2268
Linda A Robin, *CEO*
Carl Tobin, *
Steve Tobin, *
Jim Tobin, *
EMP: 65 **EST:** 1978
SQ FT: 20,000
SALES (est): 9.44MM **Privately Held**
Web: www.tobinsteel.com
SIC: **3441** Building components, structural steel

(P-6083)
TOLAR MANUFACTURING CO INC
258 Mariah Cir (92879-1751)
PHONE.............................951 808-0081
Gary Tolar, *Pr*
Rhonda Tolar, *
▲ **EMP:** 40 **EST:** 1991
SQ FT: 22,000
SALES (est): 8.58MM **Privately Held**
Web: www.tolarmfg.com
SIC: **3441** 3599 3448 Fabricated structural metal; Machine shop, jobbing and repair; Prefabricated metal buildings and components

(P-6084)
TRIAD BELLOWS DESIGN & MFG INC
Also Called: Triad Bellows
2897 E La Cresta Ave (92806-1817)
PHONE.............................714 204-4444
Michael G Moore, *Pr*
EMP: 26 **EST:** 2010
SALES (est): 4.54MM **Privately Held**
Web: www.triadbellows.com
SIC: **3441** Fabricated structural metal

(P-6085)
TRUSSWORKS INTERNATIONAL INC
1275 E Franklin Ave (91766-5450)
PHONE.............................714 630-2772
Michael Farrell, *Pr*
Ali Shantyaei, *
EMP: 60 **EST:** 2007
SALES (est): 9.21MM **Privately Held**
Web: www.twifab.com
SIC: **3441** 3446 1791 Fabricated structural metal; Architectural metalwork; Building front installation, metal

(P-6086)
ULMER INDUSTRIES INC
15243 Valley Blvd (92335-6358)
P.O. Box 2299 (91740-2299)
PHONE.............................909 823-7111
Herbert Ulmer, *Pr*
Dar Ulmer, *Sec*
EMP: 30 **EST:** 1968
SQ FT: 1,000
SALES (est): 1.46MM **Privately Held**
Web: www.ulmerind.com
SIC: **3441** Fabricated structural metal

(P-6087)
UNIVERSAL STEEL SERVICES INC
5034 Heintz St (91706-1816)
P.O. Box 2428 (91706-1232)
PHONE.............................626 960-1455
Ramon T Lopez, *CEO*
EMP: 54 **EST:** 2001
SALES (est): 4.82MM **Privately Held**
Web: www.universalsteelservices.com

▲ = Import ▼ = Export
◆ = Import/Export

SIC: **3441** Building components, structural steel

(P-6088)

V & F FABRICATION COMPANY INC

13902 Seaboard Cir (92843-3910)
PHONE.............................714 265-0630
Vinh Nguyen, *Pr*
Vinh Van Nguyen, *
Senator Truong, *Sec*
▲ **EMP:** 35 **EST:** 1989
SALES (est): 4.71MM **Privately Held**
SIC: **3441** 3599 3769 3444 Fabricated structural metal; Machine shop, jobbing and repair; Space vehicle equipment, nec; Sheet metalwork

(P-6089)

VALENCE SURFACE TECH LLC

7718 Adams St (90723-4202)
PHONE.............................562 531-7666
Chris Celtruda, *Brnch Mgr*
EMP: 18
SALES (corp-wide): 138.9MM **Privately Held**
Web: www.valencesurfacetech.com
SIC: **3441** Fabricated structural metal
PA: Valence Surface Technologies Llc
300 Continental Blvd # 600
El Segundo CA
888 540-0878

(P-6090)

VISTA STEEL COMPANY (PA)

6100 Francis Botello Rd Ste C (93117-3259)
PHONE.............................805 964-4732
Maria Di Maggio, *Pr*
EMP: 50 **EST:** 1969
SQ FT: 600
SALES (est): 4.72MM
SALES (corp-wide): 4.72MM **Privately Held**
Web: www.vistasteelcompany.com
SIC: **3441** Fabricated structural metal

(P-6091)

WADCO INDUSTRIES INC

Also Called: Wadco Steel Sales
2625 S Willow Ave (92316-3258)
PHONE.............................909 874-7800
David D Scheibel, *CEO*
Salvador Arratia, *
Anthony Salazar, *
Scott Brown, *
EMP: 47 **EST:** 1979
SQ FT: 50,000
SALES (est): 5.02MM **Privately Held**
Web: www.wadcoindustries.com
SIC: **3441** 5051 Building components, structural steel; Steel

(P-6092)

WEISER IRON INC

64 Sundance Dr (91766-4894)
PHONE.............................909 429-4600
David Metoyer, *Pr*
Carmela Metoyer, *
EMP: 18 **EST:** 1985
SALES (est): 1.6MM **Privately Held**
Web: www.weiseriron.com
SIC: **3441** Fabricated structural metal

(P-6093)

WESTCO INDUSTRIES INC

Also Called: Corbell Products
2625 S Willow Ave (92316-3258)
PHONE.............................909 874-8700
David Schibel, *Pr*

▲ **EMP:** 25 **EST:** 2005
SQ FT: 25,000
SALES (est): 1.6MM **Privately Held**
Web: www.westcoind.com
SIC: **3441** Fabricated structural metal

(P-6094)

WESTERN BAY SHEET METAL INC

1410 Hill St (92020-5749)
PHONE.............................619 233-1753
James Lozano, *Pr*
Roy Lozano, *
Helena Lopez, *
▲ **EMP:** 45 **EST:** 1981
SQ FT: 9,800
SALES (est): 8.92MM **Privately Held**
Web: www.westernbay.net
SIC: **3441** 3444 Fabricated structural metal; Sheet metalwork

(P-6095)

ZIA AAMIR

Also Called: Bridge Metals
2043 Imperial St (90021-3203)
PHONE.............................714 337-7861
Aamir Zia, *Owner*
EMP: 25 **EST:** 2017
SALES (est): 1.53MM **Privately Held**
Web: www.bridgemetals.com
SIC: **3441** Fabricated structural metal

3442 Metal Doors, Sash, And Trim

(P-6096)

ACCENT INDUSTRIES INC (PA)

Also Called: Accent Awnings
1600 E Saint Gertrude Pl (92705-5312)
PHONE.............................714 708-1389
TOLL FREE: 800
Karl Desmarais, *CEO*
▲ **EMP:** 17 **EST:** 1993
SQ FT: 26,000
SALES (est): 3.16MM **Privately Held**
Web: www.accentawnings.com
SIC: **3442** 3444 2394 5999 Shutters, door or window: metal; Awnings and canopies; Canvas and related products; Awnings

(P-6097)

ACTIVE WINDOW PRODUCTS

Also Called: Z Industries
5431 W San Fernando Rd (90039-1088)
P.O. Box 39125 (90039-0125)
PHONE.............................323 245-5185
TOLL FREE: 800
Michael Schoenfeld, *Pr*
Rosa Castro, *
▲ **EMP:** 53 **EST:** 1952
SQ FT: 96,000
SALES (est): 7.45MM **Privately Held**
Web: www.activewindowproducts.com
SIC: **3442** Storm doors or windows, metal

(P-6098)

ADVANCE OVERHEAD DOOR INC

15829 Stagg St (91406-1969)
PHONE.............................818 781-5590
Leland S Groshong, *Pr*
Marguerite Groshong, *
Don Henderson, *
EMP: 19 **EST:** 1956
SQ FT: 25,000
SALES (est): 512.08K **Privately Held**

SIC: **3442** 2431 Garage doors, overhead: metal; Garage doors, overhead, wood

(P-6099)

AIR LOUVERS INC

6285 Randolph St (90040-3514)
PHONE.............................800 554-6077
EMP: 50
SALES (corp-wide): 142.69MM **Privately Held**
Web: www.activarcpg.com
SIC: **3442** Metal doors, sash, and trim
HQ: Air Louvers, Inc.
9702 Newton Ave S
Bloomington MN
800 554-6077

(P-6100)

ARCADIA INC

Also Called: Arcadia, Inc.
2323 Firestone Blvd (90280-2684)
PHONE.............................310 665-0490
EMP: 40
SALES (corp-wide): 654.09MM **Publicly Held**
Web: www.arcadiainc.com
SIC: **3442** Window and door frames
HQ: Arcadia Products, Llc
2301 E Vernon Ave
Vernon CA
323 771-9819

(P-6101)

BEST ROLL-UP DOOR INC

13202 Arctic Cir (90670-5510)
PHONE.............................562 802-2233
Edward Choi, *Pr*
▲ **EMP:** 20 **EST:** 1978
SQ FT: 15,000
SALES (est): 2.34MM **Privately Held**
Web: www.bestrollup.com
SIC: **3442** Rolling doors for industrial buildings or warehouses, metal

(P-6102)

COLUMBIA HOLDING CORP

14400 S San Pedro St (90248-2027)
PHONE.............................310 327-4107
Daryl Mccollend, *Ch Bd*
Lawrence Goodman, *
▲ **EMP:** 300 **EST:** 1994
SQ FT: 100,000
SALES (est): 22.73MM **Privately Held**
Web: www.columbiamfg.com
SIC: **3442** 2431 2439 Metal doors, sash, and trim; Millwork; Structural wood members, nec

(P-6103)

DOOR COMPONENTS INC

Also Called: DCI Hollow Metal On Demand
7980 Redwood Ave (92336-1638)
PHONE.............................909 770-5700
Robert Briggs, *Pr*
Ronald Green, *
EMP: 200 **EST:** 1981
SQ FT: 45,000
SALES (est): 41.88MM **Privately Held**
Web: www.dcihollowmetal.com
SIC: **3442** Metal doors

(P-6104)

ELIZABETH SHUTTERS INC

Also Called: Elizabeth Shutters
525 S Rancho Ave (92324-3240)
P.O. Box 1345 (92324-0827)
PHONE.............................909 825-1531
Dean Frost, *CEO*
Maren Frost, *
Maggie Castaneda, *Accounts Payable*

EMP: 45 **EST:** 1996
SQ FT: 51,000
SALES (est): 4.77MM **Privately Held**
Web: www.elizabethshutters.com
SIC: **3442** 5023 5211 2431 Shutters, door or window: metal; Window furnishings; Door and window products; Millwork

(P-6105)

EUROLINE STEEL WINDOWS

Also Called: Euroline Steel Windows & Doors
22600 Savi Ranch Pkwy Ste E (92887-4646)
PHONE.............................877 590-2741
Elyas Balta, *CEO*
▲ **EMP:** 41 **EST:** 2013
SALES (est): 10.51MM **Privately Held**
Web: www.eurolinesteelwindows.com
SIC: **3442** Window and door frames

(P-6106)

FANBOYS WINDOW FACTORY INC (PA)

10750 Saint Louis Dr (91731-2028)
PHONE.............................626 280-8787
Lili Bell, *CEO*
Jeff Bell, *COO*
EMP: 21 **EST:** 2015
SQ FT: 10,000
SALES (est): 2.33MM
SALES (corp-wide): 2.33MM **Privately Held**
SIC: **3442** Window and door frames

(P-6107)

HEHR INTERNATIONAL INC

Also Called: Hehr International Polymers
P.O. Box 39160 (90039-0160)
PHONE.............................323 663-1261
▲ **EMP:** 199
Web: www.hehr-international.com
SIC: **3442** Window and door frames

(P-6108)

J T WALKER INDUSTRIES INC

Also Called: Rite Screen
9322 Hyssop Dr (91730-6103)
PHONE.............................909 481-1909
Dan Harvey, *Pr*
EMP: 2274
SQ FT: 36,929
SALES (corp-wide): 96.16MM **Privately Held**
SIC: **3442** Screen and storm doors and windows
PA: J. T. Walker Industries, Inc.
1310 N Hercules Ave Ste A
Clearwater FL
727 461-0501

(P-6109)

JOANKA INC

Also Called: M & A Custom Doors
25510 Frampton Ave (90710-2907)
PHONE.............................310 326-8940
Manuel A Valenzuela, *Pr*
EMP: 17 **EST:** 1998
SQ FT: 4,640
SALES (est): 245.62K **Privately Held**
SIC: **3442** Window and door frames

(P-6110)

KAWNEER COMPANY INC

925 Marlborough Ave (92507-2138)
PHONE.............................951 410-4779
EMP: 95
SALES (corp-wide): 8.96B **Privately Held**
Web: www.kawneer.us

SIC: **3442** Metal doors, sash, and trim
HQ: Kawneer Company, Inc.
555 Guthridge Ct
Norcross GA
770 449-5555

(P-6111)
LAWRENCE ROLL UP DOORS INC (PA)
4525 Littlejohn St (91706-2239)
PHONE......,....................626 962-4163
TOLL FREE: 800
Paul Weston Freberg, *CEO*
◆ **EMP:** 35 **EST:** 1925
SQ FT: 35,000
SALES (est): 17.42MM
SALES (corp-wide): 17.42MM **Privately Held** ≉
Web: www.lawrencedoors.com
SIC: **3442 3446** Rolling doors for industrial buildings or warehouses, metal; Architectural metalwork

(P-6112)
METAL TITE PRODUCTS (PA)
Also Called: Krieger Speciality Products
4880 Gregg Rd (90660-2107)
PHONE..................................562 695-0645
Robert J Mccluney, *Pr*
A W Mc Cluney, *
William Mc Cluney, *
James Mc Cluney, *Stockholder*
Charles Mc Cluney, *Stockholder*
EMP: 58 **EST:** 1966
SQ FT: 39,000
SALES (est): 10.08MM
SALES (corp-wide): 10.08MM **Privately Held**
Web: www.kriegerproducts.com
SIC: **3442 1751** Metal doors; Window and door (prefabricated) installation

(P-6113)
MILLWORKS ETC INC
Also Called: Steel Works Etc
2230 Statham Blvd Ste 100 (93033-3909)
PHONE..................................805 499-3400
Robin W Shattuck, *CEO*
◆ **EMP:** 25 **EST:** 1985
SALES (est): 4.94MM **Privately Held**
Web: www.millworksetc.com
SIC: **3442** Window and door frames

(P-6114)
MNM MANUFACTURING INC
3019 E Harcourt St (90221-5503)
PHONE..................................310 898-1099
Matt Klein, *Pr*
Elizabeth Klein, *
Marlene Klein, *
EMP: 60 **EST:** 1980
SQ FT: 24,000
SALES (est): 4.53MM **Privately Held**
Web: www.mnmmfg.com
SIC: **3442** Sash, door or window: metal

(P-6115)
PEMKO MANUFACTURING CO
4226 Transport St (93003-5627)
P.O. Box 3780 (93006-3780)
PHONE..................................800 283-9988
◆ **EMP:** 250
SIC: **3442** Weather strip, metal

(P-6116)
PRECISE IRON DOORS INC
12331 Foothill Blvd (91342-6003)
PHONE..................................818 338-6269
Haik Pambuckchyan, *CEO*
EMP: 20 **EST:** 2015

SALES (est): 2.48MM **Privately Held**
Web: www.preciseirondoors.com
SIC: **3442 5031 5999** Metal doors; Metal doors, sash and trim; Miscellaneous retail stores, nec

(P-6117)
QUANEX SCREENS LLC
13611 Santa Ana Ave (92337-8203)
PHONE..................................909 349-0600
Dewayne Williams, *VP*
EMP: 20
Web: www.quanex.com
SIC: **3442** Screen doors, metal
HQ: Quanex Screens Llc
945 Bunker Hill Rd
Houston TX
713 961-4600

(P-6118)
R & S AUTOMATION INC
283 W Bonita Ave (91767-1848)
PHONE..................................800 962-3111
Jerry Bradfield, *Mgr*
EMP: 27
SALES (corp-wide): 4.83MM **Privately Held**
Web: www.rsoperators.com
SIC: **3442 3446 5031 5063** Metal doors; Grillwork, ornamental metal; Doors, nec; Motor controls, starters and relays: electric
PA: R & S Automation, Inc.
2041 W Avenue 140th
San Leandro CA
510 357-4110

(P-6119)
R & S OVRHD DOORS SO-CAL INC
Also Called: Door Doctor
1617 N Orangethorpe Way (92801-1228)
PHONE..................................714 680-0600
TOLL FREE: 800
EMP: 25 **EST:** 1991
SALES (est): 3.22MM **Privately Held**
Web: www.rsdoorsofsocal.com
SIC: **3442 7699 1731 3446** Rolling doors for industrial buildings or warehouses, metal; Door and window repair; Access control systems specialization; Gates, ornamental metal

(P-6120)
S E - G I PRODUCTS INC
20521 Teresita Way (92630-8142)
PHONE..................................949 297-8530
EMP: 180 **EST:** 1976
SALES (est): 19.65MM
SALES (corp-wide): 1.62B **Privately Held**
SIC: **3442** Sash, door or window: metal
HQ: Truck Accessories Group, Llc
28858 Ventura Dr
Elkhart IN
574 522-5337

(P-6121)
SAN JOAQUIN WINDOW INC
Also Called: ATI Windows
1455 Columbia Ave (92507-2013)
PHONE..................................909 946-3697
Stephen Schwartz, *CEO*
Daniel Schwartz, *
EMP: 120 **EST:** 1992
SQ FT: 190,000
SALES (est): 16.14MM **Privately Held**
SIC: **3442 5211** Metal doors, sash, and trim; Door and window products

(P-6122)
SDS INDUSTRIES INC
Also Called: Timely Prefinished Steel
10241 Norris Ave (91331-2292)
PHONE..................................818 492-3500
EMP: 130 **EST:** 1973
SALES (est): 21.7MM **Privately Held**
Web: www.timelyframes.com
SIC: **3442** Window and door frames

(P-6123)
SECURITY METAL PRODUCTS CORP (DH)
5678 Concours (91764-5394)
PHONE..................................310 641-6690
Chris Holloway, *CEO*
EMP: 57 **EST:** 2010
SALES (est): 13.16MM
SALES (corp-wide): 11.51B **Privately Held**
Web: www.assaabloyservicecenters.us
SIC: **3442** Metal doors
HQ: Assa Abloy Inc.
110 Sargent Dr
New Haven CT

(P-6124)
SOLATUBE INTERNATIONAL INC (DH)
Also Called: Solatube
2210 Oak Ridge Way (92081-8341)
PHONE..................................888 765-2882
Robert E Westfall Junior, *CEO*
Francisco Lopez, *
▲ **EMP:** 100 **EST:** 1995
SQ FT: 105,000
SALES (est): 41.55MM **Privately Held**
Web: www.solatube.com
SIC: **3442** Metal doors, sash, and trim
HQ: Kingspan Light & Air Llc
28662 N Ballard Dr
Lake Forest IL
847 816-1060

(P-6125)
STEELWORKS ETC INC
Also Called: Shattuck Group, The
2230 Statham Blvd Ste 100 (93033-3909)
PHONE..................................805 487-3000
Rob Shattuck, *Pr*
EMP: 20 **EST:** 2010
SALES (est): 1.76MM **Privately Held**
Web: www.steelworksetc.com
SIC: **3442** Metal doors, sash, and trim

(P-6126)
TJE COMPANY
Also Called: Onyx Shutters
20805 Currier Rd (91789-3080)
PHONE..................................909 869-7777
Sylvia Lee, *CEO*
Philip Kim, *VP*
◆ **EMP:** 17 **EST:** 2007
SALES (est): 2.17MM **Privately Held**
Web: www.onyxshutters.com
SIC: **3442** Shutters, door or window: metal

(P-6127)
TORRANCE STEEL WINDOW CO INC
1819 Abalone Ave (90501-3704)
PHONE..................................310 328-9181
Dong K Lim, *Pr*
▲ **EMP:** 25 **EST:** 1964
SQ FT: 32,000
SALES (est): 5.3MM **Privately Held**
Web: www.torrancesteelwindow.com
SIC: **3442** Window and door frames

(P-6128)
WINDOW ENTERPRISES INC
Also Called: Torrance Aluminum Window
430 Nevada St (92373-4244)
PHONE..................................951 943-4894
▲ **EMP:** 30 **EST:** 1970
SALES (est): 3.14MM **Privately Held**
SIC: **3442** Storm doors or windows, metal

3443 Fabricated Plate Work (boiler Shop)

(P-6129)
AAR MANUFACTURING INC
Also Called: Telair International
2220 E Cerritos Ave (92806-5709)
PHONE..................................714 634-8807
EMP: 150
SALES (corp-wide): 1.77B **Publicly Held**
SIC: **3443** Containers, shipping (bombs, etc.): metal plate
HQ: Aar Manufacturing, Inc.
1100 N Wood Dale Rd
Wood Dale IL
630 227-2000

(P-6130)
ACD LLC (DH)
Also Called: Nikkiso Acd
2321 Pullman St (92705-5512)
PHONE..................................949 261-7533
◆ **EMP:** 53 **EST:** 1978
SQ FT: 52,000
SALES (est): 43.52MM **Privately Held**
Web: www.nikkisoceig.com
SIC: **3443 3559** Cryogenic tanks, for liquids and gases; Cryogenic machinery, industrial
HQ: Cryogenic Industries, Inc.
27710 Jefferson Ave # 301
Temecula CA
951 677-2081

(P-6131)
AJAX BOILER INC
Also Called: Ace Boiler
2701 S Harbor Blvd (92704-5838)
PHONE..................................714 437-9050
▼ **EMP:** 68
Web: www.aceheaters.com
SIC: **3443** Fabricated plate work (boiler shop)

(P-6132)
ATCO RUBBER PRODUCTS INC
3080 12th St (92507-4903)
PHONE..................................951 788-4345
Bertha Almanza, *Brnch Mgr*
EMP: 18
Web: www.atcoflex.com
SIC: **3443** Fabricated plate work (boiler shop)
HQ: Atco Rubber Products, Inc.
7101 Atco Dr
Fort Worth TX
817 595-2894

(P-6133)
BA HOLDINGS INC (DH)
3016 Kansas Ave Bldg 1 (92507-3445)
PHONE..................................951 684-5110
EMP: 30 **EST:** 1996
SALES (est): 110.24MM
SALES (corp-wide): 423.4MM **Privately Held**
Web: www.mediluxcylinders.com
SIC: **3443 3728** Cylinders, pressure: metal plate; Aircraft parts and equipment, nec
HQ: Luxfer Overseas Holdings Limited
Anchorage Gateway, 5 Anchorage Quay

▲ = Import ▼ = Export
◆ = Import/Export

Salford LANCS

(P-6134)
BASIC INDUSTRIES INTL INC (PA)
Also Called: Pacific Metal Products
10850 Wilshire Blvd (90024-4305)
PHONE..................................951 226-1500
John Wallace, *Pr*
Steven W Burge, *
EMP: 200 **EST:** 2000
SALES (est): 23.88MM
SALES (corp-wide): 23.88MM **Privately Held**
SIC: 3443 3446 Fabricated plate work (boiler shop); Architectural metalwork

(P-6135)
BRYANT FUEL SYSTEMS LLC
1300 32nd St (93301-2144)
PHONE..................................661 334-5462
EMP: 18 **EST:** 2019
SALES (est): 4.93MM **Privately Held**
Web: www.bryantfuelsystems.com
SIC: 3443 Air coolers, metal plate

(P-6136)
CJI PROCESS SYSTEMS INC
Also Called: Lee Ray Sandblasting
12000 Clark St (90670-3709)
PHONE..................................562 777-0614
Archie Cholakian, *Pr*
John Cholakian, *
▼ **EMP:** 70 **EST:** 1982
SQ FT: 35,000
SALES (est): 22.99MM **Privately Held**
Web: www.cjiprocesssystems.com
SIC: 3443 3441 3444 Tanks, lined: metal plate; Fabricated structural metal; Sheet metalwork

(P-6137)
COMMERCIAL METAL FORMING INC
Also Called: Commercial Metal Forming
341 W Collins Ave (92867-5505)
PHONE..................................714 532-6321
William Kowal, *Pr*
Donald E Washdewicz, *
▲ **EMP:** 48 **EST:** 2003
SALES (est): 6.1MM **Privately Held**
SIC: 3443 Fabricated plate work (boiler shop)

(P-6138)
COMPUTRUS INC
250 Klug Cir (92878-5409)
PHONE..................................951 245-9103
William Turnbull, *Pr*
Scott R Carroll, *
EMP: 30 **EST:** 1984
SALES (est): 8.54MM
SALES (corp-wide): 302.09B **Publicly Held**
Web: www.computrusinc.com
SIC: 3443 Truss plates, metal
HQ: Mitek Industries, Inc.
16023 Swinly Rdg
Chesterfield MO
314 434-1200

(P-6139)
CONSOLIDATED FABRICATORS CORP (PA)
Also Called: Confab
14620 Arminta St (91402-5902)
PHONE..................................800 635-8335
Michael J Melideo, *CEO*
Jeff Lombardi, *
▲ **EMP:** 110 **EST:** 1974
SQ FT: 150,000
SALES (est): 39.04MM
SALES (corp-wide): 39.04MM **Privately Held**
Web: www.con-fab.com
SIC: 3443 5051 3444 Dumpsters, garbage; Steel; Studs and joists, sheet metal

(P-6140)
COOK AND COOK INCORPORATED
Also Called: Royal Welding & Fabricating
1000 E Elm Ave (92831-5022)
PHONE..................................714 680-6669
Wallace F Cook, *Pr*
Patricia Cook, *
EMP: 30 **EST:** 1967
SQ FT: 30,000
SALES (est): 5.1MM **Privately Held**
Web: www.royalwelding.com
SIC: 3443 3599 3444 Industrial vessels, tanks, and containers; Amusement park equipment; Sheet metalwork

(P-6141)
DAVIS GREGG ENTERPRISES INC
8525 Roland Acres Dr (92071-4453)
PHONE..................................619 449-4250
Davis Gregg, *Pr*
Mary Gregg, *VP*
▲ **EMP:** 18 **EST:** 1996
SQ FT: 4,800
SALES (est): 1.5MM **Privately Held**
Web: www.davisgreggenterprises.com
SIC: 3443 Tanks, standard or custom fabricated: metal plate

(P-6142)
DESIGN FORM INC
8250 Electric Ave (90680-2640)
PHONE..................................714 952-3700
Glenn Baldwin, *CEO*
EMP: 23 **EST:** 1980
SQ FT: 7,000
SALES (est): 1.87MM **Privately Held**
Web: www.designform.com
SIC: 3443 Tanks, standard or custom fabricated: metal plate

(P-6143)
HAYDEN PRODUCTS LLC
Also Called: Hayden Industrial Products
5199 N Mingo Rd (92408)
PHONE..................................951 736-2600
Harold Lehon, *Managing Member*
James Neitz, *Pr*
▲ **EMP:** 80 **EST:** 1959
SQ FT: 55,000
SALES (est): 13.51MM **Privately Held**
Web: www.haydenindustrial.com
SIC: 3443 Heat exchangers, condensers, and components

(P-6144)
HYUNDAI TRANSLEAD (HQ)
8880 Rio San Diego Dr Ste 600 (92108-1640)
PHONE..................................619 574-1500
Sean Kenney, *CEO*
Glen Harney, *
Jangsoo Choi, *
Hae Sung Park, *
▲ **EMP:** 87 **EST:** 1989
SALES (est): 440.44MM **Privately Held**
Web: www.hyundaitranslead.com
SIC: 3443 3715 3412 Industrial vessels, tanks, and containers; Semitrailers for truck tractors; Metal barrels, drums, and pails
PA: Hyundai Motor Company
12 Heolleung-Ro, Seocho-Gu
Seoul

(P-6145)
MELCO STEEL INC
1100 W Foothill Blvd (91702-2818)
PHONE..................................626 334-7875
Michel Kashou, *Pr*
Mazin Kashou, *
Joann Reese, *
EMP: 30 **EST:** 1971
SQ FT: 25,500
SALES (est): 5.53MM **Privately Held**
Web: www.melcosteel.com
SIC: 3443 Vessels, process or storage (from boiler shops): metal plate

(P-6146)
OMEGA II INC
Also Called: Omega Industrial Marine
3525 Main St (91911-5830)
PHONE..................................619 920-6650
Greg Lewis, *CEO*
Nicholas Ruiz, *MNG*
EMP: 39 **EST:** 1986
SALES (est): 7.01MM **Privately Held**
Web: www.omegaindustrial.net
SIC: 3443 1542 1629 1541 Air coolers, metal plate; Nonresidential construction, nec; Marine construction; Industrial buildings and warehouses

(P-6147)
PACIFIC STEAM EQUIPMENT INC
Also Called: P S E Boilers
11748 Slauson Ave (90670-2227)
PHONE..................................562 906-9292
William S M Shanahan Md, *Pr*
Shin Duk David Kang, *VP*
▲ **EMP:** 25 **EST:** 1954
SQ FT: 22,500
SALES (est): 2.3MM **Privately Held**
Web: www.pacificsteam.com
SIC: 3443 5074 3582 2841 Tanks, standard or custom fabricated: metal plate; Plumbing and hydronic heating supplies; Commercial laundry equipment; Soap and other detergents

(P-6148)
PACIFIC TANK & CNSTR INC
17995 E Highway 46 (93461-9636)
PHONE..................................805 237-2929
Tom Yanaga, *Mgr*
EMP: 30
Web: www.pacifictank.net
SIC: 3443 Fabricated plate work (boiler shop)
PA: Pacific Tank & Construction, Inc.
31551 Avnida Los Cerritos
San Juan Capistrano CA

(P-6149)
PARKER-HANNIFIN CORPORATION
Hydraulic Accumulator Division
14087 Borate St (90670-5336)
PHONE..................................562 404-1938
Mark Gagnon, *Brnch Mgr*
EMP: 44
SALES (corp-wide): 19.07B **Publicly Held**
Web: www.parker.com
SIC: 3443 3052 2822 Fabricated plate work (boiler shop); Rubber and plastics hose and beltings; Synthetic rubber
PA: Parker-Hannifin Corporation
6035 Parkland Blvd
Cleveland OH
216 896-3000

(P-6150)
PLUCKYS DUMP RENTAL LLC
10136 Bowman Ave (90280-6233)
PHONE..................................323 540-3510
EMP: 45 **EST:** 2021
SALES (est): 1.57MM **Privately Held**
SIC: 3443 Dumpsters, garbage

(P-6151)
PROTEC ARISAWA AMERICA INC
2455 Ash St (92081-8424)
PHONE..................................760 599-4800
◆ **EMP:** 50 **EST:** 2005
SALES (est): 9.81MM **Privately Held**
Web: www.protec-arisawa.com
SIC: 3443 Process vessels, industrial: metal plate

(P-6152)
RICHFIELD ENGINEERING INC
Also Called: L W Lefort
1135 Fee Ana St (92870-6761)
PHONE..................................714 524-3741
Don Robinson, *Pr*
EMP: 40 **EST:** 1995
SQ FT: 40,000
SALES (est): 547.43K
SALES (corp-wide): 6.53MM **Privately Held**
SIC: 3443 Metal parts
PA: Robinson Mfg., Inc.
1136 Richfield Rd
Placentia CA
714 524-7395

(P-6153)
RITE ENGINEERING & MANUFACTURING CORPORATION
5832 Garfield Ave (90040-3605)
PHONE..................................562 862-2135
EMP: 25 **EST:** 1952
SALES (est): 4.64MM **Privately Held**
Web: www.riteboiler.com
SIC: 3443 Boilers: industrial, power, or marine

(P-6154)
ROY E HANSON JR MFG (PA)
Also Called: Hanson Tank
1600 E Washington Blvd (90021-3123)
P.O. Box 30507 (90030-0507)
PHONE..................................213 747-7514
Jonathan Goss, *CEO*
Johnathan Goss, *
Cliff Jones, *
Thys Dorenbosch, *
Dorothy Griffen, *
▼ **EMP:** 83 **EST:** 1932
SQ FT: 55,000
SALES (est): 11.72MM
SALES (corp-wide): 11.72MM **Privately Held**
Web: www.hansontank.com
SIC: 3443 Fuel tanks (oil, gas, etc.), metal plate

(P-6155)
S BRAVO SYSTEMS INC
Also Called: Bravo Support
2929 Vail Ave (90040-2615)
PHONE..................................323 888-4133
Paola Bravo Recendez, *CEO*
▲ **EMP:** 26 **EST:** 1986
SQ FT: 40,000
SALES (est): 10MM **Privately Held**
Web: www.sbravo.com

P R O D U C T S & S V C S

SIC: **3443** Containers, shipping (bombs, etc.): metal plate

(P-6156)
SID E PARKER BOILER MFG CO INC
Also Called: Parker Boiler Co
5930 Bandini Blvd (90040-2903)
PHONE.................................323 727-9800
Sid D Danenhauer, *Ch Bd*
Greg G Danenhauer, *
Ed Marchak, *
◆ EMP: 66 EST: 1939
SQ FT: 80,000
SALES (est): 14.65MM **Privately Held**
Web: www.parkerboiler.com
SIC: **3443** 3433 Boilers: industrial, power, or marine; Heating equipment, except electric

(P-6157)
SOUTH GATE ENGINEERING LLC
13477 Yorba Ave (91710-5055)
PHONE.................................909 628-2779
William Paolino, *Managing Member*
EMP: 115 EST: 1947
SALES (est): 22.09MM **Privately Held**
Web: www.southgateengineering.com
SIC: **3443** Vessels, process or storage (from boiler shops): metal plate

(P-6158)
SPX COOLING TECH LLC
Also Called: Recold
550 Mercury Ln (92821-4830)
PHONE.................................714 529-6080
Doug Vickers, *Brnch Mgr*
EMP: 18
SALES (corp-wide): 495.11MM **Privately Held**
Web: www.spxcooling.com
SIC: **3443** Fabricated plate work (boiler shop)
HQ: Spx Cooling Tech, Llc
7401 W 129th St
Overland Park KS
913 664-7400

(P-6159)
SPX FLOW US LLC
Also Called: A P V Crepaco
26561 Rancho Pkwy S (92630-8301)
PHONE.................................949 455-8150
Brian Ahern, *Mgr*
EMP: 28
SALES (corp-wide): 1.53B **Privately Held**
SIC: **3443** Fabricated plate work (boiler shop)
HQ: Spx Flow Us, Llc
135 Mount Read Blvd
Rochester NY
585 436-5550

(P-6160)
STRUCTURAL COMPOSITES INDS LLC (DH)
Also Called: SCI
336 Enterprise Pl (91768-3244)
PHONE.................................909 594-7777
Ken Miller, *Managing Member*
◆ EMP: 49 EST: 2007
SALES (est): 46.78MM
SALES (corp-wide): 423.4MM **Privately Held**
SIC: **3443** Tanks, lined: metal plate
HQ: Luxfer Inc.
3016 Kansas Ave Bldg 1
Riverside CA
951 684-5110

(P-6161)
SUPERIOR TANK CO INC (PA)
Also Called: Stci
9500 Lucas Ranch Rd (91730-5724)
PHONE.................................909 912-0580
Jesus Eric Marquez, *Pr*
George Marquez, *
Lewis A Marquez, *
◆ EMP: 50 EST: 1984
SQ FT: 53,392
SALES (est): 44.83MM
SALES (corp-wide): 44.83MM **Privately Held**
Web: www.superiortank.com
SIC: **3443** 3494 1791 1794 Fuel tanks (oil, gas, etc.), metal plate; Valves and pipe fittings, nec; Structural steel erection; Excavation work

(P-6162)
TAIT & ASSOCIATES INC
2131 S Dupont Dr (92806-6102)
PHONE.................................714 560-8222
Jim Streipz, *Brnch Mgr*
EMP: 51
SALES (corp-wide): 23.79MM **Privately Held**
Web: www.tait.com
SIC: **3443** Fuel tanks (oil, gas, etc.), metal plate
PA: Tait & Associates, Inc.
701 Parkcenter Dr
Santa Ana CA
866 584-0283

(P-6163)
THERMAL EQUIPMENT CORPORATION
Also Called: TEC
2146 E Gladwick St (90220-6203)
PHONE.................................310 328-6600
Nancy Huffman, *Pr*
▼ EMP: 45 EST: 1969
SALES (est): 12.76MM **Privately Held**
Web: www.thermalequipment.com
SIC: **3443** 3821 2842 Autoclaves, industrial; Laboratory apparatus and furniture; Polishes and sanitation goods
PA: Km3 Holdings, Inc.
2030 E University Dr
Rancho Dominguez CA

(P-6164)
THERMLLY ENGNRED MNFCTRED PDTS
Also Called: T E M P
543 W 135th St (90248-1505)
PHONE.................................310 523-9934
▲ EMP: 27 EST: 1994
SQ FT: 50,000
SALES (est): 7.43MM **Privately Held**
Web: www.tempinc.com
SIC: **3443** Heat exchangers, condensers, and components

(P-6165)
THOMPSON TANK INC
8029 Phlox St (90241-4816)
P.O. Box 790 (90714-0790)
PHONE.................................562 869-7711
David B Thompson, *Pr*
Robert I Grue, *Treas*
EMP: 19 EST: 1993
SQ FT: 225,000
SALES (est): 4.57MM **Privately Held**
Web: www.thompsontank.com
SIC: **3443** 7699 3715 3713 Tanks, standard or custom fabricated: metal plate; Tank repair and cleaning services; Truck trailers; Truck and bus bodies

(P-6166)
TODD STREET INC
Also Called: Schweitzers Metal Fabricators
770 N Todd Ave (91702-2227)
P.O. Box 963 (91702-0963)
PHONE.................................626 815-1175
Jerry Childress, *Pr*
Frank Lewis, *Sec*
EMP: 20 EST: 1939
SALES (est): 3.43MM **Privately Held**
Web: www.toddstreetinc.com
SIC: **3443** Tanks, standard or custom fabricated: metal plate

(P-6167)
UNIVERSAL DEFENSE
412 Cucamonga Ave (91711-5019)
P.O. Box 1372 (91711-1372)
PHONE.................................909 626-4178
EMP: 20
SALES (est): 1.72MM **Privately Held**
SIC: **3443** Fabricated plate work (boiler shop)

(P-6168)
WAGNER PLATE WORKS WEST INC (PA)
Also Called: P V T Supply
14015 Garfield Ave (90723-2137)
PHONE.................................562 531-6050
Jack Brian Purtell, *Pr*
EMP: 21 EST: 1994
SQ FT: 60,000
SALES (est): 4.6MM **Privately Held**
SIC: **3443** 5051 Tanks, lined: metal plate; Pipe and tubing, steel

(P-6169)
WATERCREST INC
4850 E Airport Dr (91761-7818)
PHONE.................................909 390-3944
Jeremiah B Robins, *CEO*
Gary F Johnson, *Pr*
▲ EMP: 25 EST: 1996
SQ FT: 29,000
SALES (est): 1.17MM **Privately Held**
Web: www.thermaldynamics.com
SIC: **3443** Heat exchangers, condensers, and components

(P-6170)
WATTS SPACEMAKER INC
Also Called: Spacemaker
1918 W Chestnut Ave (92703-4304)
PHONE.................................714 542-4649
Kristine Uttley, *Treas*
Timothy M Macphee, *
▲ EMP: 31 EST: 1969
SQ FT: 8,500
SALES (est): 9.23MM
SALES (corp-wide): 1.98B **Publicly Held**
SIC: **3443** Metal parts
PA: Watts Water Technologies, Inc.
815 Chestnut St
North Andover MA
978 688-1811

(P-6171)
WELLS STRUTHERS CORPORATION
Also Called: Tei Struthers Wells
10375 Slusher Dr (90670-3748)
PHONE.................................814 726-1000
John C Wallace, *Pr*
John M Carey, *
Burton M Abrams, *
EMP: 30 EST: 1937
SQ FT: 30,000
SALES (est): 2.27MM **Privately Held**

SIC: **3443** Heat exchangers, plate type

(P-6172)
WORTHINGTON CYLINDER CORP
336 Enterprise Pl (91768-3244)
PHONE.................................909 594-7777
EMP: 37
SALES (est): 4.92B **Publicly Held**
Web: www.worthingtonenterprises.com
SIC: **3443** Cylinders, pressure: metal plate
HQ: Worthington Cylinder Corporation
200 W Wilson Bridge Rd
Worthington OH
614 840-3210

3444 Sheet Metalwork

(P-6173)
A & A FEROS NON FEROS MET LLC
640 S Hill St (90014-4000)
PHONE.................................213 622-9995
EMP: 28 EST: 2019
SALES (est): 228.87K **Privately Held**
Web: www.ampreciousmetals.com
SIC: **3444** Sheet metalwork

(P-6174)
A & M SCULPTURED METALS LLC
Also Called: A & M Sculpture Lighting
1781 N Indiana St (90063-2523)
PHONE.................................323 263-2221
EMP: 19 EST: 1986
SQ FT: 10,000
SALES (est): 794.07K **Privately Held**
Web: www.amsculptedmetals.com
SIC: **3444** Sheet metalwork

(P-6175)
A-1 METAL PRODUCTS INC
2707 Supply Ave (90040-2703)
PHONE.................................323 721-3334
Jerry Calsbeek, *Pr*
Patricia Calsbeek, *
EMP: 24 EST: 1952
SQ FT: 40,000
SALES (est): 2.37MM **Privately Held**
Web: www.a1metalproducts.com
SIC: **3444** Sheet metal specialties, not stamped

(P-6176)
ABLE SHEET METAL INC (PA)
614 N Ford Blvd (90022-1195)
PHONE.................................323 269-2181
Dmitri Triphon, *CEO*
Gurgen Tovmasyan, *General Vice President*
◆ EMP: 40 EST: 2001
SQ FT: 25,000
SALES (est): 7.98MM
SALES (corp-wide): 7.98MM **Privately Held**
Web: www.ablemetal.com
SIC: **3444** Sheet metal specialties, not stamped

(P-6177)
ADAMS-CAMPBELL COMPANY LTD (PA)
Also Called: Accent Ceilings
15343 Proctor Ave (91745-1022)
P.O. Box 3867 (91744-0867)
PHONE.................................626 330-3425
EMP: 74 EST: 1909
SALES (est): 12MM

SALES (corp-wide): 12MM **Privately Held**
Web: www.adamscampbell.com
SIC: **3444** 3469 3431 Sheet metalwork;
Metal stampings, nec; Metal sanitary ware

(P-6178)
ADVANCED METAL MFG INC
49 Strathearn Pl (93065-1653)
PHONE..................................805 322-4161
Scott Stewart, *CEO*
Gina Stewart Ctrl, *Prin*
▲ EMP: 30 EST: 2010
SALES (est): 4.13MM **Privately Held**
Web: www.advancedmetalmfg.com
SIC: **3444** Sheet metalwork

(P-6179)
AERO ARC
16634 S Figueroa St (90248-2627)
PHONE..................................310 324-3400
EMP: 38 EST: 1984
SALES (est): 5.07MM **Privately Held**
SIC: **3444** 3498 Sheet metalwork;
Fabricated pipe and fittings

(P-6180)
AERO BENDING COMPANY
560 Auto Center Dr Ste A (93551-4485)
PHONE..................................661 948-2363
Robert Burns, *Pr*
EMP: 80 EST: 1944
SQ FT: 26,000
SALES (est): 10.8MM **Privately Held**
Web: www.aerobendingco.com
SIC: **3444** 5088 Sheet metalwork; Aircraft
engines and engine parts

(P-6181)
AERO PRECISION ENGINEERING
11300 Hindry Ave (90045-6228)
PHONE..................................310 642-9747
Sherry L Martinez, *Pr*
Tom Segotta, *
EMP: 45 EST: 1984
SQ FT: 55,000
SALES (est): 8.89MM **Privately Held**
Web: www.aeroprecisioneng.com
SIC: **3444** 3599 Sheet metal specialties, not
stamped; Machine shop, jobbing and repair

(P-6182)
AIRCRAFT STAMPING COMPANY INC
1285 Paseo Alicia (91773-4407)
PHONE..................................323 283-1239
Michael Nolan, *Pr*
Linda Nolan, *Stockholder*
EMP: 23 EST: 1943
SQ FT: 17,900
SALES (est): 668.42K **Privately Held**
Web: www.aircraftstamping.com
SIC: **3444** 3469 Sheet metal specialties, not
stamped; Metal stampings, nec

(P-6183)
ALL-WAYS METAL INC
401 E Alondra Blvd (90248-2901)
PHONE..................................310 217-1177
Shirley Pickens, *Pr*
Scott Pickens, *
EMP: 30 EST: 1983
SQ FT: 29,000
SALES (est): 5.16MM **Privately Held**
Web: www.allwaysmetal.com
SIC: **3444** Sheet metal specialties, not
stamped

(P-6184)
ALLIANCE METAL PRODUCTS INC
20844 Plummer St (91311-5004)
PHONE..................................818 709-1204
Dan L Rowlett Junior, *CEO*
EMP: 212 EST: 2002
SQ FT: 2,000
SALES (est): 14.73MM **Privately Held**
Web: www.alliancemp.com
SIC: **3444** Sheet metal specialties, not
stamped

(P-6185)
AMD INTERNATIONAL TECH LLC
Also Called: International Rite-Way Pdts
1725 S Campus Ave (91761-4346)
PHONE..................................909 985-8300
EMP: 25 EST: 1994
SQ FT: 17,000
SALES (est): 5.59MM **Privately Held**
Web: www.intlrwp.com
SIC: **3444** 1761 Sheet metal specialties, not
stamped; Sheet metal work, nec

(P-6186)
AMERICAN AIRCRAFT PRODUCTS INC
Also Called: A A P
15411 S Broadway (90248-2207)
PHONE..................................310 532-7434
Gerald R Tupper, *Pr*
EMP: 67 EST: 1975
SQ FT: 54,000
SALES (est): 9.77MM **Privately Held**
Web: www.americanaircraft.com
SIC: **3444** 3599 Sheet metalwork; Machine
shop, jobbing and repair

(P-6187)
AMERICAN RANGE CORPORATION
13592 Desmond St (91331-2315)
PHONE..................................818 897-0808
Shane Demirjian, *Pr*
Mourad Demirjian, *
▲ EMP: 120 EST: 1989
SQ FT: 125,000
SALES (est): 22.74MM **Privately Held**
Web: www.americanrange.com
SIC: **3444** 3631 Hoods, range: sheet metal;
Household cooking equipment

(P-6188)
AMF ANAHEIM LLC
2100 E Orangewood Ave (92806-6108)
PHONE..................................714 363-9206
▲ EMP: 120
SIC: **3444** Sheet metalwork

(P-6189)
ANOROC PRECISION SHTMTL INC
Also Called: Anoroc
19122 S Santa Fe Ave (90221-5910)
PHONE..................................310 515-6015
Roxanne Zavala, *CEO*
Pete Corona, *Lending Vice President*
EMP: 25 EST: 1978
SQ FT: 15,000
SALES (est): 4.1MM **Privately Held**
Web: www.anoroc.com
SIC: **3444** Sheet metal specialties, not
stamped

(P-6190)
AP PRECISION METALS INC
1215 30th St (92154-3477)

PHONE..................................619 628-0003
Lane A Litke, *CEO*
Victor B Miller, *
Susan D Miller, *
EMP: 35 EST: 2000
SALES (est): 5.16MM **Privately Held**
Web: www.apprecision.com
SIC: **3444** Sheet metalwork

(P-6191)
ARMORCAST PRODUCTS COMPANY INC (DH)
9140 Lurline Ave (91311-5923)
PHONE..................................818 982-3600
▲ EMP: 220 EST: 1972
SALES (est): 42.41MM
SALES (corp-wide): 4.95B **Publicly Held**
Web: www.armorcastprod.com
SIC: **3444** 3089 Sheet metalwork; Plastics
processing
HQ: Hubbell Lenoir City, Inc.
3621 Industrial Park Dr
Lenoir City TN
865 986-9726

(P-6192)
ARRK NORTH AMERICA INC
4660 La Jolla Village Dr Ste 100
(92122-4604)
PHONE..................................858 552-1587
Carlos Herrera, *Pr*
Koji Tsujino, *
Takuya Kasai, *
▲ EMP: 145 EST: 1984
SALES (est): 52.42MM **Privately Held**
Web: www.arrk.com
SIC: **3444** Sheet metalwork
HQ: Arrk Corporation
2-2-9, Minamihonmachi, Chuo-Ku
Osaka OSK

(P-6193)
ARTISTIC WELDING
Also Called: Precision Sheet Metal
505 E Gardena Blvd (90248-2915)
PHONE..................................310 515-4922
George R Sandoval, *Pr*
Mary Sandoval, *
EMP: 65 EST: 1974
SQ FT: 85,000
SALES (est): 8.69MM **Privately Held**
Web: www.artistic-welding.com
SIC: **3444** Sheet metalwork

(P-6194)
ASM CONSTRUCTION INC
Also Called: American Sheet Metal
1947 John Towers Ave (92020-1117)
PHONE..................................619 449-1966
Robert Burner, *Pr*
Ron Burner Junior, *CFO*
EMP: 41 EST: 1993
SQ FT: 9,000
SALES (est): 5.03MM **Privately Held**
SIC: **3444** Sheet metalwork

(P-6195)
ATLAS SHEET METAL INC
19 Musick (92618-1638)
PHONE..................................949 600-8787
James M Odlum, *Pr*
EMP: 17 EST: 1998
SQ FT: 5,500
SALES (est): 4.98MM **Privately Held**
Web: www.atlassheetmetal.com
SIC: **3444** Sheet metalwork

(P-6196)
AYMAR ENGINEERING
9434 Abraham Way (92071-5835)
PHONE..................................619 562-1121
Wayne Aymar, *Owner*
EMP: 17 EST: 1979
SQ FT: 13,000
SALES (est): 1.83MM **Privately Held**
Web: www.aymarengineering.com
SIC: **3444** 3469 Sheet metal specialties, not
stamped; Metal stampings, nec

(P-6197)
BARZILLAI MANUFACTURING CO INC
1410 S Cucamonga Ave (91761-4509)
PHONE..................................909 947-4200
Ray Richmond, *Pr*
Garrett Zopf, *Treas*
EMP: 17 EST: 2003
SQ FT: 5,200
SALES (est): 1.99MM **Privately Held**
SIC: **3444** Sheet metalwork

(P-6198)
BASMAT INC (PA)
Also Called: McStarlite
1531 240th St (90710-1308)
PHONE..................................310 325-2063
John W Basso, *CEO*
John Allen Basso, *
Sharon Stelter, *
▲ EMP: 100 EST: 1952
SQ FT: 42,000
SALES (est): 24.23MM
SALES (corp-wide): 24.23MM **Privately Held**
Web: www.mcstarlite.com
SIC: **3444** Sheet metalwork

(P-6199)
BAY CITIES TIN SHOP INC
Also Called: BAY CITIES METAL PRODUCTS
301 E Alondra Blvd (90248-2809)
PHONE..................................310 660-0351
Majid Abai, *CEO*
Henry Kamberg, *
Gary Mugford, *
Debra Childress, *
EMP: 170 EST: 1958
SALES (est): 5.01MM **Privately Held**
Web: www.baycitiesmetalproducts.com
SIC: **3444** Sheet metal specialties, not
stamped

(P-6200)
BAY SHEET METAL INC
9343 Bond Ave Ste C (92021-2839)
PHONE..................................619 401-9270
Michael Hayes, *Pr*
EMP: 22 EST: 2000
SALES (est): 4.77MM **Privately Held**
Web: www.westernbay.net
SIC: **3444** Sheet metalwork

(P-6201)
BEND-TEK INC
2205 S Yale St (92704-4426)
PHONE..................................714 210-8966
Melinda Nguyen, *CEO*
Mac Le, *
Eric Tran, *
EMP: 100 EST: 1999
SQ FT: 7,000
SALES (est): 10.46MM **Privately Held**
Web: www.bendtekinc.com
SIC: **3444** Pipe, sheet metal

PRODUCTS & SVCS

(P-6202)
BLEEKER BROTHERS INC1
10868 Drury Ln (90262-1834)
PHONE..................310 639-4367
Charles Bleeker, *Pr*
EMP: 18 **EST:** 1952
SQ FT: 30,000
SALES (est): 710.29K **Privately Held**
SIC: 3444 3567 3563 Booths, spray:
prefabricated sheet metal; Industrial
furnaces and ovens; Air and gas
compressors

(P-6203)
BOOZAK INC
Also Called: K Squared Metals
508 Chaney St Ste A (92530-2797)
PHONE..................951 245-6045
Kevin Kluzak, *Pr*
Kevin Booth, *
EMP: 45 **EST:** 2004
SALES (est): 5.13MM **Privately Held**
SIC: 3444 Sheet metal specialties, not
stamped

(P-6204)
BROADWAY AC HTG & SHTMTL
Also Called: Broadway Sheet Metal
7855 Burnet Ave (91405-1010)
PHONE..................818 781-1477
Alexander Merzel, *Pr*
Vince Lombardo, *
Anna Merzel, *
EMP: 35 **EST:** 1926
SQ FT: 7,000
SALES (est): 3.06MM **Privately Held**
Web: www.broadwaysm.com
SIC: 3444 Sheet metalwork

(P-6205)
**BRYDENSCOT METAL
PRODUCTS INC**
1299 Riverview Dr (92408-2955)
PHONE..................909 799-0088
EMP: 18 **EST:** 1983
SALES (est): 4.37MM **Privately Held**
Web: www.brydenscot.com
SIC: 3444 Sheet metalwork

(P-6206)
C & J METAL PRODUCTS INC
6323 Alondra Blvd (90723-3750)
PHONE..................562 634-3101
Roy L Chapman, *Pr*
Isabelle Chapman, *
▲ **EMP:** 21 **EST:** 1946
SQ FT: 37,000
SALES (est): 1.9MM **Privately Held**
Web: www.cjmetals.com
SIC: 3444 Ventilators, sheet metal

(P-6207)
**C&O MANUFACTURING
COMPANY INC**
9640 Beverly Rd (90660-2137)
PHONE..................562 692-7525
Cesar Gonzalez, *Pr*
Oscar Valdez, *
EMP: 67 **EST:** 1995
SQ FT: 22,000
SALES (est): 9.99MM **Privately Held**
Web: www.cnomfg.com
SIC: 3444 Sheet metal specialties, not
stamped

(P-6208)
CAL PAC SHEET METAL INC
Also Called: Cal Pac Sheet Metal
2720 S Main St Ste B (92707-3404)

PHONE..................714 979-2733
Marushkah Kurtz, *CEO*
Bob Catalano, *
Carolyn Miller, *
EMP: 40 **EST:** 1977
SQ FT: 5,000
SALES (est): 4.89MM **Privately Held**
Web: www.calpacsheetmetal.com
SIC: 3444 Sheet metal specialties, not
stamped

(P-6209)
CALIFORNIA CHASSIS INC
3356 E La Palma Ave (92806-2814)
PHONE..................714 666-8511
EMP: 110 **EST:** 1947
SALES (est): 15.78MM
SALES (corp-wide): 15.78MM **Privately
Held**
SIC: 3444 2522 Metal housings, enclosures,
casings, and other containers; Office
furniture, except wood
PA: Arroyo Holdings Inc
898 N Fair Oaks Ave
Pasadena CA
626 765-9340

(P-6210)
CARLA SENTER
Also Called: Swift Fab
515 E Alondra Blvd (90248-2903)
PHONE..................310 366-7295
Carla Senter, *Owner*
Robert Senter, *Owner*
EMP: 18 **EST:** 1988
SQ FT: 6,000
SALES (est): 2.48MM **Privately Held**
Web: www.swiftfab.com
SIC: 3444 Sheet metal specialties, not
stamped

(P-6211)
CARTEL INDUSTRIES LLC
Also Called: Cartel Industries
17152 Armstrong Ave (92614-5718)
PHONE..................949 474-3200
Gant Penick, *
▲ **EMP:** 49 **EST:** 1971
SQ FT: 30,000
SALES (est): 9.68MM **Privately Held**
Web: www.cartelind.com
SIC: 3444 Sheet metal specialties, not
stamped

(P-6212)
**CASTLE INDUSTRIES INC OF
CALIFORNIA**
Also Called: M.C. Gill
4056 Easy St (91731-1054)
PHONE..................909 390-0899
EMP: 48
SIC: 3444 Sheet metalwork

(P-6213)
CEMCO LLC (DH)
Also Called: Cemco Steel
13191 Crossroads Pkwy N Ste 325 (91746)
PHONE..................800 775-2362
Tom Porter, *Pr*
Toshihiko Iizuka, *
◆ **EMP:** 68 **EST:** 1973
SQ FT: 40,000
SALES (est): 78.14MM **Privately Held**
Web: www.cemcosteel.com
SIC: 3444 Sheet metalwork
HQ: Shoji Jfe America Holdings Inc
301 E Ocean Blvd Ste 1750
Long Beach CA
562 637-3500

(P-6214)
**CLARKWESTERN DIETRICH
BUILDING**
Also Called: Clarkdietrich Building Systems
6510 General Rd (92509-0103)
PHONE..................951 360-3500
Clark Dietrich, *Owner*
EMP: 20
SALES (corp-wide): 4.92B **Publicly Held**
Web: www.clarkdietrich.com
SIC: 3444 8711 3081 Studs and joists, sheet
metal; Engineering services; Vinyl film and
sheet
HQ: Clarkwestern Dietrich Building
Systems Llc
9050 Cntre Pnte Dr Ste 40
West Chester OH

(P-6215)
COAST SHEET METAL INC
990 W 17th St (92627-4403)
PHONE..................949 645-2224
Wayne Chambers, *Pr*
Marna Chambers, *
EMP: 35 **EST:** 1960
SQ FT: 3,800
SALES (est): 2.65MM **Privately Held**
Web: www.coastsheetmetal.com
SIC: 3444 Sheet metalwork

(P-6216)
**COMPUMERIC ENGINEERING
INC**
Also Called: Bearsaver
1390 S Milliken Ave (91761-1585)
PHONE..................909 605-7666
Jeannie Hankins, *CEO*
EMP: 45 **EST:** 1989
SQ FT: 30,000
SALES (est): 7.32MM **Privately Held**
Web: www.compumeric.com
SIC: 3444 Sheet metalwork

(P-6217)
**COMPUTER METAL PRODUCTS
CORP**
Also Called: Vline Industries
370 E Easy St (93065-1802)
PHONE..................805 520-6966
Jim Visage, *Pr*
Karen Bender, *
EMP: 90 **EST:** 1971
SQ FT: 25,000
SALES (est): 9.19MM **Privately Held**
Web: www.computermetal.com
SIC: 3444 Sheet metalwork

(P-6218)
CONCISE FABRICATORS INC
Also Called: Concise Fabricators
7550 Panasonic Way (92154-8207)
PHONE..................520 746-3226
James Dean Johnson, *Pr*
Bill Maples, *
▼ **EMP:** 50 **EST:** 1981
SQ FT: 120,000
SALES (est): 14.43MM **Privately Held**
SIC: 3444 Sheet metalwork
PA: Blackbird Management Group, Llc
240 E Illinois St # 2004
Chicago IL

(P-6219)
COWELCO
Also Called: Cowelco Steel Contractors
1634 W 14th St (90813-1205)
PHONE..................562 432-5766
EMP: 50 **EST:** 1947
SALES (est): 8.73MM **Privately Held**

Web: www.cowelco.com
SIC: 3444 3441 3443 1791 Sheet metalwork
; Fabricated structural metal; Fabricated
plate work (boiler shop); Structural steel
erection

(P-6220)
COY INDUSTRIES INC
Also Called: E R C Company
2970 E Maria St (90221-5802)
PHONE..................310 603-2970
Michael Coy, *Pr*
James Patrick Coy, *
EMP: 95 **EST:** 1972
SQ FT: 50,000
SALES (est): 16.12MM **Privately Held**
Web: www.ercco.com
SIC: 3444 3469 Sheet metal specialties, not
stamped; Metal stampings, nec

(P-6221)
CPC FABRICATION INC
2904 Oak St (92707-3723)
PHONE..................714 549-2426
Thomas Baker, *CEO*
Lyn Baker, *
EMP: 35 **EST:** 1980
SQ FT: 15,000
SALES (est): 3.42MM **Privately Held**
SIC: 3444 Sheet metal specialties, not
stamped

(P-6222)
CROWN PRODUCTS INC
Also Called: Crown Steel
177 Newport Dr Ste A (92069-1470)
PHONE..................760 471-1188
David J Carr, *Pr*
EMP: 22 **EST:** 1969
SQ FT: 20,000
SALES (est): 2.29MM **Privately Held**
Web: www.crownsteelmfg.net
SIC: 3444 3589 Sheet metalwork;
Commercial cooking and foodwarming
equipment

(P-6223)
DANRICH WELDING CO INC
155 N Eucla Ave (91773-2587)
PHONE..................562 634-4811
Richard Schenk, *Pr*
EMP: 26 **EST:** 1970
SALES (est): 2.3MM **Privately Held**
Web: www.danrichwelding.com
SIC: 3444 7692 Sheet metalwork; Welding
repair

(P-6224)
**DAVE WHIPPLE SHEET METAL
INC**
1077 N Cuyamaca St (92020-1803)
PHONE..................619 562-6962
Dave Whipple Senior, *Pr*
Carol Whipple, *
EMP: 34 **EST:** 1993
SQ FT: 9,000
SALES (est): 4.94MM **Privately Held**
Web: www.whipplesm.com
SIC: 3444 Sheet metalwork

(P-6225)
**DAVIS CALIFORNIA
INDUSTRIES LTD**
Also Called: Davis California Industries
11323 Hartland St (91605-6310)
PHONE..................818 980-6178
EMP: 20
Web: www.dimfg.com

SIC: **3444** 3599 Sheet metal specialties, not stamped; Machine shop, jobbing and repair

(P-6226)
DECRA ROOFING SYSTEMS INC (DH)
Also Called: Decra
1230 Railroad St (92882-1837)
PHONE...................951 272-8180
Willard C Hudson Junior, *Pr*
◆ **EMP:** 70 **EST:** 1998
SQ FT: 60,000
SALES (est): 35.83MM **Privately Held**
Web: www.decra.com
SIC: 3444 Metal roofing and roof drainage equipment
HQ: Fletcher Building Holdings Usa, Inc.
1230 Railroad St
Corona CA
951 272-8180

(P-6227)
DIMIC STEEL TECH INC
145 N 8th Ave (91786-5402)
PHONE...................909 946-6767
Miles Dimic, *Pr*
Anna Dimic, *
▲ **EMP:** 24 **EST:** 1973
SQ FT: 45,000
SALES (est): 4.91MM **Privately Held**
Web: www.dimicsteeltech.com
SIC: 3444 Sheet metal specialties, not stamped

(P-6228)
DUR-RED PRODUCTS
5634 Costa Dr (91709-3996)
PHONE...................323 771-9000
Russell Smith, *Pr*
Linda Harrison, *
EMP: 50 **EST:** 1961
SALES (est): 4.39MM **Privately Held**
Web: www.dur-red.com
SIC: 3444 3446 Sheet metalwork; Architectural metalwork

(P-6229)
DYNAMO AVIATION INC
9601 Mason Ave # A (91311-5207)
P.O. Box 14040 (91409-4040)
PHONE...................818 785-9561
Masoud S Rabadi, *CEO*
Robin C Scott, *
Lary Hockens, *CAO*
Christopher Rabadi, *
Riley Drake, *Finance*
EMP: 86 **EST:** 1986
SQ FT: 27,000
SALES (est): 42.93MM **Privately Held**
Web: www.dynamoaviation.com
SIC: 3444 Sheet metalwork

(P-6230)
EDWARDS SHEET METAL SUPPLY INC
7810 Burnet Ave (91405-1009)
PHONE...................818 785-8600
Edward Der-mesropian, *Pr*
Jacqueline Der-mesropian, *Sec*
EMP: 21 **EST:** 1985
SQ FT: 20,000
SALES (est): 1.87MM **Privately Held**
Web: www.esmsi.com
SIC: 3444 Booths, spray: prefabricated sheet metal

(P-6231)
EMPIRE SHEET METAL INC
1215 S Bon View Ave (91761-4402)

PHONE...................909 923-2927
Martin Layman, *Pr*
EMP: 28 **EST:** 1999
SALES (est): 3.71MM **Privately Held**
Web: www.empiresheetmetal.com
SIC: 3444 Sheet metalwork

(P-6232)
EQUIPMENT DESIGN & MFG INC
119 Explorer St (91768-3278)
PHONE...................909 594-2229
Rick Clewett, *CEO*
Steve Clewett, *
Ryan Clewett, *
EMP: 55 **EST:** 1976
SQ FT: 27,400
SALES (est): 6.53MM **Privately Held**
Web: www.equipmentdesign.net
SIC: 3444 Sheet metalwork

(P-6233)
ESM AEROSPACE INC
1203 W Isabel St (91506-1407)
PHONE...................818 841-3653
Jerome Flament, *Pr*
Rina Flament, *
EMP: 25 **EST:** 2005
SQ FT: 8,900
SALES (est): 2.96MM **Privately Held**
Web: www.esmaerospace.com
SIC: 3444 Casings, sheet metal

(P-6234)
EUGENIOS SHEET METAL INC
2151 Maple Privado (91761-7603)
PHONE...................909 923-2002
Eugenio M Lozano, *Pr*
Maria B Lozano, *Prin*
Reyes B Lozano, *Prin*
EMP: 28 **EST:** 1983
SQ FT: 10,000
SALES (est): 985.42K **Privately Held**
Web: www.eugeniossheetmetal.com
SIC: 3444 Sheet metalwork

(P-6235)
EVANS ALLOYS
15701 Graham St (92649-1612)
PHONE...................714 373-2515
EMP: 25 **EST:** 1963
SALES (est): 2.59MM **Privately Held**
Web: www.evansus.com
SIC: 3444 Sheet metalwork

(P-6236)
EXCEL SHEET METAL INC (PA)
Also Called: Excel Bridge Manufacturing Co.
12001 Shoemaker Ave (90670-4718)
PHONE...................562 944-0701
Craig E Vasquez, *CEO*
Jeffrey Vasquez, *
▼ **EMP:** 53 **EST:** 1952
SQ FT: 16,000
SALES (est): 7.48MM
SALES (corp-wide): 7.48MM **Privately Held**
Web: www.excelsheetmetal.com
SIC: 3444 1622 Sheet metalwork; Bridge construction

(P-6237)
F T B & SON INC
11551 Markon Dr (92841-1808)
PHONE...................714 891-8003
Frank Taylor Brown, *CEO*
Kathy M Ayers, *CFO*
EMP: 44 **EST:** 1972
SQ FT: 37,000
SALES (est): 1.8MM **Privately Held**
Web: www.ftbson.com

SIC: **3444** Ducts, sheet metal

(P-6238)
FABRICATION CONCEPTS CORPORATION
Also Called: Fabcon
1800 E Saint Andrew Pl (92705-5043)
PHONE...................714 881-2000
◆ **EMP:** 180
Web: www.fabcon.com
SIC: 3444 Sheet metalwork

(P-6239)
FABTRONICS INC
5026 Calmview Ave (91706-1899)
PHONE...................626 962-3293
Carlos Duarte, *
David Thompson, *VP*
▼ **EMP:** 20 **EST:** 1976
SQ FT: 26,000
SALES (est): 2.49MM **Privately Held**
Web: www.fabtronics.com
SIC: 3444 3829 Sheet metal specialties, not stamped; Fare registers, for street cars, buses, etc.

(P-6240)
FACILITY MAKERS INC
345 W Freedom Ave (92865-2647)
P.O. Box 60066 (92602-6002)
PHONE...................714 544-1702
Cameron Kazemi, *CEO*
EMP: 20 **EST:** 2009
SALES (est): 3.5MM **Privately Held**
Web: www.facilitymakers.com
SIC: 3444 1542 3446 Sheet metal specialties, not stamped; Commercial and office building, new construction; Architectural metalwork

(P-6241)
FLETCHER BLDG HOLDINGS USA INC (DH)
1230 Railroad St (92882-1837)
PHONE...................951 272-8180
Willard Hudson, *Pr*
John Miller, *
Steve Jones, *
◆ **EMP:** 70 **EST:** 1998
SQ FT: 60,000
SALES (est): 40.43MM **Privately Held**
Web: www.decra.com
SIC: 3444 Metal roofing and roof drainage equipment
HQ: Fletcher Building (Australia) Pty Ltd
Fletcher Building Australia 1051
Nudgee Rd
Banyo QLD

(P-6242)
FOUR SEASONS REST EQP INC
412 Jenks Cir (92878-5006)
PHONE...................951 278-9100
Larry Kaye, *Pr*
EMP: 25 **EST:** 1975
SQ FT: 19,000
SALES (est): 778.02K **Privately Held**
SIC: 3444 Restaurant sheet metalwork

(P-6243)
GAINES MANUFACTURING INC
12200 Kirkham Rd (92064-6806)
PHONE...................858 486-7100
Ted Gaines, *Prin*
EMP: 40 **EST:** 1989
SQ FT: 23,000
SALES (est): 4.67MM **Privately Held**

SIC: **3444** Mail (post office) collection or storage boxes, sheet metal

(P-6244)
GARD INC
Also Called: Reliable Sheet Metal Works
524 E Walnut Ave (92832-2540)
PHONE...................714 738-5891
Arthur Schade, *Pr*
Arthur Schade Junior, *VP*
Dan Schade, *Sec*
EMP: 20 **EST:** 1956
SQ FT: 12,000
SALES (est): 2.48MM **Privately Held**
Web: www.reliablesheetmetal.com
SIC: 3444 Sheet metal specialties, not stamped

(P-6245)
GERARD ROOF PRODUCTS LLC (DH)
Also Called: Gerard Roofing Technologies
721 Monroe Way (92870-6309)
PHONE...................714 529-0407
Donald P Newman, *Managing Member*
EMP: 48 **EST:** 2014
SALES (est): 22.28MM **Privately Held**
SIC: 3444 Sheet metalwork
HQ: Headwaters Incorporated
10701 S Rver Front Pkwy
South Jordan UT

(P-6246)
GKN AEROSPACE CAMARILLO INC
3030 Redhll Ave (92705-5823)
PHONE...................805 383-6684
Richard Oldfield, *CEO*
David Lind, *Pr*
Bernd Hermann, *CFO*
▲ **EMP:** 19 **EST:** 2009
SALES (est): 6.63MM
SALES (corp-wide): 9.07B **Privately Held**
Web: www.gknaerospace.com
SIC: 3444 Sheet metalwork
HQ: Gkn Limited
2nd Floor, One Central Boulevard
Solihull W MIDLANDS
121 210-9800

(P-6247)
GRAYD-A PRCSION MET FBRICATORS
13233 Florence Ave (90670-4509)
PHONE...................562 944-8951
William Gray Junior, *Pr*
William Gray Iii, *VP*
Jo Dell Gray, *Sec*
EMP: 20 **EST:** 1964
SQ FT: 17,500
SALES (est): 2.37MM **Privately Held**
Web: www.grayd-a.com
SIC: 3444 Sheet metal specialties, not stamped

(P-6248)
GREAT PACIFIC ELBOW LLC
Also Called: Great Pacific Elbow Company
13900 Sycamore Way (91710-7016)
PHONE...................909 606-5551
Erik Gamm, *CEO*
Ron Searcy, *Pr*
EMP: 25 **EST:** 2021
SALES (est): 6.39MM
SALES (corp-wide): 64.22MM **Privately Held**
Web: www.greatpacificelbow.com

SIC: **3444** 3827 Elbows, for air ducts, stovepipes, etc.: sheet metal; Telescopes: elbow, panoramic, sighting, fire control, etc.
PA: West Coast Steel & Processing Holdings, Llc
13568 Vintage Pl
Chino CA
909 393-8405

(P-6249)
HAIMETAL DUCT INC
625 Arroyo St (91340-2219)
PHONE.................................818 768-2315
Rouben Hovsepian, *Pr*
EMP: 25 EST: 1980
SQ FT: 10,000
SALES (est): 919.19K **Privately Held**
SIC: **3444** Ducts, sheet metal

(P-6250)
HALLMARK METALS INC
600 W Foothill Blvd (91741-2403)
PHONE.................................626 335-1263
Scott Schoenick, *Pr*
Joseph Allen Zerucha, *
David Peifer, *
Candice Schoenick, *
Marina Carmona, *
EMP: 28 EST: 1959
SQ FT: 23,000
SALES (est): 4.89MM **Privately Held**
Web: www.hallmarkmetals.com
SIC: **3444** 3469 Sheet metalwork; Machine parts, stamped or pressed metal

(P-6251)
HAMILTON METALCRAFT INC
848 N Fair Oaks Ave (91103-3046)
PHONE.................................626 795-4811
Sandra Stahler, *Pr*
EMP: 25 EST: 1966
SQ FT: 10,000
SALES (est): 2.15MM **Privately Held**
Web: www.hmetal.com
SIC: **3444** Casings, sheet metal

(P-6252)
HI-CRAFT METAL PRODUCTS
606 W 184th St (90248-4282)
PHONE.................................310 323-6949
Bill Gerich, *CEO*
Edward P Gerich, *VP*
Liz Gallagher, *Sec*
Ted Gerich, *Stockholder*
Jennifer Gerich, *Stockholder*
EMP: 20 EST: 1948
SQ FT: 11,000
SALES (est): 2.3MM **Privately Held**
Web: www.hicraftmetal.com
SIC: **3444** 3469 Sheet metal specialties, not stamped; Metal stampings, nec

(P-6253)
INLAND METAL TRADING INC
41187 Sandalwood Cir (92562-7003)
PHONE.................................833 396-0740
Kristopher Lanham, *Pr*
EMP: 19 EST: 2018
SALES (est): 1.08MM **Privately Held**
SIC: **3444** 5039 Ducts, sheet metal; Metal buildings

(P-6254)
INTERNATIONAL WEST INC
Also Called: Continental Industries
1025 N Armando St (92806-2606)
PHONE.................................714 632-9190
Jeffery Aaron Hayden, *Pr*
Tami Hayden, *
EMP: 47 EST: 1985

SQ FT: 8,500
SALES (est): 8.65MM **Privately Held**
Web: www.continental-ind.com
SIC: **3444** Sheet metalwork

(P-6255)
JBW PRECISION INC
2650 Lavery Ct (91320-1581)
PHONE.................................805 499-1973
David Ogden, *Pr*
Jack Ogden, *VP*
Dawn Spalding, *Sec*
EMP: 23 EST: 1969
SQ FT: 2,500
SALES (est): 4.18MM **Privately Held**
Web: www.jbwprecision.com
SIC: **3444** Sheet metal specialties, not stamped

(P-6256)
JEFFREY FABRICATION LLC
Also Called: C & J Metal Prducts
6323 Alondra Blvd (90723-3750)
PHONE.................................562 634-3101
Lilly Chang, *Managing Member*
EMP: 50 EST: 2011
SALES (est): 3.12MM **Privately Held**
Web: www.cjmetals.com
SIC: **3444** Sheet metalwork

(P-6257)
JET MANUFACTURING INC
Also Called: Prism Aerospace dba Jet Manufacturing
13445 Estelle St (92879-1877)
PHONE.................................951 736-9316
Eric S Cunningham, *CEO*
▲ EMP: 44 EST: 1997
SQ FT: 45,000
SALES (est): 4.89MM **Privately Held**
Web: www.jetmanufacturing.com
SIC: **3444** 3724 Sheet metalwork; Jet assisted takeoff devices (JATO)

(P-6258)
JORDAHL USA INC
34420 Gateway Dr (92211-0843)
PHONE.................................866 332-6687
Frank Metelmann, *CEO*
EMP: 20 EST: 2019
SALES (est): 2.36MM **Privately Held**
Web: www.jordahlusa.com
SIC: **3444** Sheet metalwork

(P-6259)
KB SHEETMETAL FABRICATION INC
17371 Mount Wynne Cir # B (92708-4107)
PHONE.................................714 979-1780
Cong Nguyen, *Pr*
EMP: 25 EST: 2001
SQ FT: 12,000
SALES (est): 4.81MM **Privately Held**
Web: www.kb-sheetmetal.com
SIC: **3444** 3441 Sheet metalwork; Fabricated structural metal

(P-6260)
KEITH E ARCHAMBEAU SR INC
Also Called: American Precision Sheet Metal
20615 Plummer St (91311-5112)
PHONE.................................818 718-6110
Keith Archambeau Junior, *Pr*
John Wetlsch, *VP*
EMP: 20 EST: 1986
SQ FT: 10,000
SALES (est): 2.38MM **Privately Held**
Web: www.americanprecision.net

SIC: **3444** Sheet metal specialties, not stamped

(P-6261)
L & T PRECISION LLC
12105 Kirkham Rd (92064-6870)
PHONE.................................858 513-7874
Loc Nguyen, *Pr*
Loc Nguyen, *Pr*
Tho Nguyen, *
Tien D Nguyen, *
EMP: 110 EST: 1984
SQ FT: 48,000
SALES (est): 18.78MM **Privately Held**
Web: www.ltprecision.com
SIC: **3444** 3599 Sheet metal specialties, not stamped; Machine and other job shop work

(P-6262)
LLC WALKER WEST
Impac International
11445 Pacific Ave (92337-8227)
PHONE.................................951 685-9660
Kory Lavoy, *Div Mgr*
EMP: 52
Web: www.impac-international.com
SIC: **3444** 3315 Housings for business machines, sheet metal; Steel wire and related products
PA: Walker West, Llc
1555 S Vintage Ave
Ontario CA

(P-6263)
LYNAM INDUSTRIES INC (PA)
11027 Jasmine St (92337-6955)
PHONE.................................951 360-1919
Troy Lindstrom, *Pr*
Greg Traeger Pe, *Dir*
▲ EMP: 85 EST: 1989
SQ FT: 39,000
SALES (est): 14.35MM **Privately Held**
Web: www.lynaminc.com
SIC: **3444** Sheet metal specialties, not stamped

(P-6264)
M-5 STEEL MFG INC (PA)
11778 San Marino St Ste A (91730-6016)
PHONE.................................323 263-9383
Douglas Linkon, *CEO*
▲ EMP: 46 EST: 1970
SALES (est): 5.43MM
SALES (corp-wide): 5.43MM **Privately Held**
Web: www.m5steel.com
SIC: **3444** 3443 Gutters, sheet metal; Fabricated plate work (boiler shop)

(P-6265)
MARATHON FINISHING SYSTEMS INC
Also Called: Manufacturing
42355 Rio Nedo (92590-3701)
PHONE.................................310 791-5601
Christian Rerucha, *Pr*
▲ EMP: 25 EST: 2004
SALES (est): 2.59MM **Privately Held**
Web: www.marathonspraybooths.com
SIC: **3444** Booths, spray: prefabricated sheet metal

(P-6266)
MARINE & REST FABRICATORS INC
3768 Dalbergia St (92113-3815)
PHONE.................................619 232-7267
Carlos Velazquez, *Pr*
EMP: 44 EST: 1986

SQ FT: 7,600
SALES (est): 8.46MM **Privately Held**
Web: www.mrf.bz
SIC: **3444** 3731 Restaurant sheet metalwork ; Military ships, building and repairing

(P-6267)
MASTER ENTERPRISES INC
Also Called: A B C Restaurant Equipment Co
2025 Lee Ave (91733-2505)
PHONE.................................626 442-1821
Brian Kim Lien, *CEO*
Wen Lin, *VP*
Thanh Quach, *Sec*
EMP: 20 EST: 1988
SQ FT: 20,000
SALES (est): 2.48MM **Privately Held**
Web: www.chineserange.com
SIC: **3444** 5087 Restaurant sheet metalwork ; Restaurant supplies

(P-6268)
MAYONI ENTERPRISES
10320 Glenoaks Blvd (91331-1699)
PHONE.................................818 896-0026
Isaac Benyehuda, *CEO*
Isaac Glazer, *
EMP: 60 EST: 1984
SQ FT: 17,000
SALES (est): 7.33MM **Privately Held**
Web: www.mayoni.com
SIC: **3444** 3581 Sheet metal specialties, not stamped; Automatic vending machines

(P-6269)
MEADOWS SHEET METAL AND AC INC
Also Called: Meadows Mechanical
333 Crown Vista Dr (90248-1705)
PHONE.................................310 615-1125
Madonna Rose, *CEO*
Thomas Nolan, *
Dennis Johnson, *
EMP: 50 EST: 1949
SQ FT: 5,000
SALES (est): 11.62MM **Privately Held**
SIC: **3444** 1711 Sheet metalwork; Heating and air conditioning contractors

(P-6270)
METAL ENGINEERING INC
1642 S Sacramento Ave (91761-8052)
PHONE.................................626 334-1819
Arthur A Valenzuela, *Pr*
EMP: 23 EST: 2002
SQ FT: 14,000
SALES (est): 2.46MM **Privately Held**
Web: www.metaleng.com
SIC: **3444** 1761 Awnings and canopies; Sheet metal work, nec

(P-6271)
METAL MASTER INC
4611 Overland Ave (92123-1233)
PHONE.................................858 292-8880
Benito Garrido, *Pr*
Donald Wagner, *
Dianne Yeaman, *
EMP: 41 EST: 1987
SQ FT: 30,000
SALES (est): 9.14MM **Privately Held**
Web: www.metalmasterinc.com
SIC: **3444** 3541 Sheet metalwork; Milling machines

(P-6272)
METAL-FAB SERVICES INDUST INC
2500 E Miraloma Way (92806-1608)

PHONE..............................714 630-7771
Carlos Mondragon, *Pr*
▲ **EMP:** 34 **EST:** 2003
SQ FT: 28,000
SALES (est): 8.47MM **Privately Held**
Web: www.metalfabsi.com
SIC: 3444 Sheet metal specialties, not
stamped

(P-6273)
MMP SHEET METAL INC
501 Commercial Way (90631-6170)
PHONE..............................562 691-1055
Frank Varanelli, *Pr*
EMP: 30 **EST:** 1977
SQ FT: 8,500
SALES (est): 2.94MM **Privately Held**
Web: www.mmp-sheetmetal.com
SIC: 3444 Sheet metal specialties, not
stamped

(P-6274)
**MODERN-AIRE VENTILATING
INC**
Also Called: Modern Aire Ventilating
7319 Lankershim Blvd (91605-3895)
PHONE..............................818 765-9870
Steven Herman, *Pr*
EMP: 23 **EST:** 1956
SQ FT: 20,000
SALES (est): 4.41MM **Privately Held**
Web: www.modernaire.com
SIC: 3444 3645 Hoods, range: sheet metal;
Residential lighting fixtures

(P-6275)
**MODULAR METAL
FABRICATORS INC**
24600 Nandina Ave (92551-9537)
PHONE..............................951 242-3154
E E Gearing, *CEO*
Don Gearing, *
Mike Beam, *
John Wingate, *
Pat Geary, *
▲ **EMP:** 130 **EST:** 1970
SQ FT: 200,000
SALES (est): 21.24MM **Privately Held**
SIC: 3444 Pipe, sheet metal

(P-6276)
MS INDUSTRIAL SHTMTL INC
Also Called: Baghouse and Indus Shtmtl Svcs
1731 Pomona Rd (92878-4363)
PHONE..............................951 272-6610
Nancy Nicola, *CEO*
Warren Lampkin, *
Dan Suffel, *
EMP: 130 **EST:** 1985
SQ FT: 35,000
SALES (est): 28.81MM **Privately Held**
Web: www.1888baghouse.com
SIC: 3444 Sheet metalwork

(P-6277)
OC METALS INC
Also Called: Oc Metals
2720 S Main St Ste B (92707-3404)
PHONE..............................714 668-0783
Marushkah Kurtz, *CEO*
Mari Kurtz, *Pr*
EMP: 20 **EST:** 2000
SQ FT: 23,000
SALES (est): 4.68MM **Privately Held**
Web: www.ocmetals.com
SIC: 3444 Sheet metalwork

(P-6278)
ORECO DUCT SYSTEMS INC
5119 Azusa Canyon Rd (91706-1833)
P.O. Box 1460 (91706-7460)
PHONE..............................626 337-8832
Robert I Havai, *Pr*
EMP: 110 **EST:** 1985
SQ FT: 57,600
SALES (est): 9.54MM **Privately Held**
Web: www.orecoduct.com
SIC: 3444 Sheet metalwork

(P-6279)
ORTRONICS INC
Also Called: Electrorack
1443 S Sunkist St (92806-5626)
PHONE..............................714 776-5420
Mark Panico, *Pr*
Robert Julian, *
James Laperriere, *
Valerie Alsante, *
▲ **EMP:** 120 **EST:** 1955
SQ FT: 50,000
SALES (est): 24.05MM **Privately Held**
Web: www.legrand.us
SIC: 3444 3679 Sheet metalwork; Power
supplies, all types: static
HQ: Legrand Holding, Inc.
60 Woodlawn St
West Hartford CT
860 233-6251

(P-6280)
**OXNARD PRCSION
FABRICATION INC**
Also Called: O P F
2200 Teal Club Rd (93030-8640)
PHONE..............................805 985-0447
David Garza, *Pr*
David Garza, *Pr*
Robert Valles, *
EMP: 30 **EST:** 1987
SQ FT: 107,000
SALES (est): 3.87MM **Privately Held**
Web: www.opfmfg.com
SIC: 3444 3469 3443 Sheet metal
specialties, not stamped; Metal stampings,
nec; Fabricated plate work (boiler shop)

(P-6281)
P A S U INC
1891 Nirvana Ave (91911-6117)
PHONE..............................619 421-1151
Donald R Palumbo, *Pr*
▲ **EMP:** 36 **EST:** 1979
SQ FT: 100,000
SALES (est): 1.94MM **Privately Held**
SIC: 3444 3825 Sheet metalwork; Test
equipment for electronic and electrical
circuits

(P-6282)
P T INDUSTRIES INC
3220 Industry Dr (90755-4014)
PHONE..............................562 961-3431
Kim Nguyen, *Pr*
Thuy Nguyen, *Sec*
EMP: 19 **EST:** 1999
SQ FT: 19,000
SALES (est): 3.05MM **Privately Held**
Web: www.ptindustriesinc.com
SIC: 3444 Sheet metal specialties, not
stamped

(P-6283)
**PACIFIC AWARD METALS INC
(HQ)**
Also Called: Award Metals
1450 Virginia Ave (91706-5819)

PHONE..............................626 814-4410
Brian J Lipke, *CEO*
W Brent Taylor, *
Frank Fulford, *
EMP: 100 **EST:** 2001
SQ FT: 110,000
SALES (est): 85.59MM
SALES (corp-wide): 1.39B **Publicly Held**
Web:
www.gibraltarbuildingproducts.com
SIC: 3444 3312 Sheet metalwork; Blast
furnaces and steel mills
PA: Gibraltar Industries, Inc.
3556 Lake Shore Rd # 100
Buffalo NY
716 826-6500

(P-6284)
PACIFIC AWARD METALS INC
Also Called: Award Metals
10302 Birtcher Dr (91752-1829)
PHONE..............................360 694-9530
EMP: 40
SALES (corp-wide): 1.39B **Publicly Held**
Web:
www.gibraltarbuildingproducts.com
SIC: 3444 3443 Concrete forms, sheet metal
; Fabricated plate work (boiler shop)
HQ: Pacific Award Metals, Inc.
1450 Virginia Ave
Baldwin Park CA
626 814-4410

(P-6285)
PACIFIC DUCT INC
5499 Brooks St (91763-4563)
PHONE..............................909 635-1335
▲ **EMP:** 30 **EST:** 1996
SQ FT: 15,000
SALES (est): 5MM **Privately Held**
Web: www.pacificduct.com
SIC: 3444 5075 5039 Metal ventilating
equipment; Warm air heating and air
conditioning; Air ducts, sheet metal

(P-6286)
**PACIFIC MARINE SHEET METAL
CORPORATION**
Also Called: Southwest Manufacturing Svcs
2650 Jamacha Rd Ste 147 Pmb
(92019-6316)
PHONE..............................858 869-8900
◆ **EMP:** 200
SIC: 3444 Sheet metalwork

(P-6287)
PARIS PRECISION LLC
1650 Ramada Dr (93446-5976)
PHONE..............................805 239-2500
EMP: 150
SIC: 3444 Sheet metalwork

(P-6288)
PCH SHEET METAL & AC INC
118 Calle De Los Molinos (92672-3831)
PHONE..............................949 361-9905
EMP: 18 **EST:** 2002
SQ FT: 6,000
SALES (est): 4.94MM **Privately Held**
Web: www.pchsheetmetal.com
SIC: 3444 Sheet metalwork

(P-6289)
PCI INDUSTRIES INC
6501 Potello St (90040)
PHONE..............................323 728-0004
Greg Skilley, *VP*
EMP: 28
SALES (corp-wide): 46.63MM **Privately
Held**

Web: www.pottorff.com
SIC: 3444 3564 Metal ventilating equipment;
Filters, air: furnaces, air conditioning
equipment, etc.
PA: Pci Industries, Inc.
5101 Blue Mound Rd
Fort Worth TX
817 509-2300

(P-6290)
PCI INDUSTRIES INC
Pottorff
700 S Vail Ave (90640-4954)
PHONE..............................323 889-6770
EMP: 28
SALES (corp-wide): 46.63MM **Privately
Held**
Web: www.pottorff.com
SIC: 3444 Sheet metalwork
PA: Pci Industries, Inc.
5101 Blue Mound Rd
Fort Worth TX
817 509-2300

(P-6291)
PICO METAL PRODUCTS INC
Also Called: Pico Metal Products Since 1919
10640 Springdale Ave (90670-3843)
PHONE..............................562 944-0626
▲ **EMP:** 20
Web: www.picometal.com
SIC: 3444 Sheet metalwork

(P-6292)
**PINNACLE PRECISION SHTMTL
CORP (PA)**
5410 E La Palma Ave (92807-2023)
PHONE..............................714 777-3129
David Oddo, *Pr*
Brian Mclaughlin, *VP*
Paul Oddo, *Stockholder*
EMP: 98 **EST:** 1973
SALES (est): 21.25MM
SALES (corp-wide): 21.25MM **Privately
Held**
Web: www.pinnaclemetal.com
SIC: 3444 Sheet metalwork

(P-6293)
**PINNACLE PRECISION SHTMTL
CORP**
Fabnet
5410 E La Palma Ave (92807-2023)
PHONE..............................714 777-3129
EMP: 51
SALES (corp-wide): 21.25MM **Privately
Held**
Web: www.pinnaclemetal.com
SIC: 3444 3599 Metal housings, enclosures,
casings, and other containers; Machine
shop, jobbing and repair
PA: Pinnacle Precision Sheet Metal
Corporation
5410 E La Palma Ave
Anaheim CA
714 777-3129

(P-6294)
PLENUMS PLUS LLC
67 Brisbane St (91910-1065)
PHONE..............................619 422-5515
EMP: 75 **EST:** 1986
SALES (est): 5.69MM **Privately Held**
Web: www.plenumsplus.com
SIC: 3444 Sheet metalwork

(P-6295)
PNA CONSTRUCTION TECH INC
301 Espee St Ste E (93301-2659)

PHONE..............................661 326-1700
Matt Wilen, *Prin*
EMP: 33
SALES (corp-wide): 5.01MM **Privately Held**
Web: www.pna-inc.com
SIC: 3444 Concrete forms, sheet metal
PA: P.N.A. Construction Technologies, Inc.
1349 W Bryn Mawr Ave
Itasca IL
770 668-9500

(P-6296)
PRECISE INDUSTRIES INC
610 Neptune Ave (92821-2909)
PHONE..............................714 482-2333
Terry D Wells, *Pr*
Robert L Wells, *
▲ **EMP:** 120 **EST:** 2004
SQ FT: 78,000
SALES (est): 16.65MM **Privately Held**
Web: www.preciseind.com
SIC: 3444 3679 3599 Sheet metalwork;
Electronic circuits; Machine and other job
shop work

(P-6297)
PRECISION STEEL PRODUCTS INC
Also Called: Steel Products International
13124 Avalon Blvd (90061-2738)
PHONE..............................310 523-2002
Raul De Latorre, *Pr*
Deborah De Latorre, *Sec*
EMP: 22 **EST:** 1994
SQ FT: 24,000
SALES (est): 3.75MM **Privately Held**
Web: www.steelproducts.biz
SIC: 3444 3441 Sheet metalwork;
Fabricated structural metal

(P-6298)
PRISM AEROSPACE
3087 12th St (92507-4904)
PHONE..............................951 582-2850
Eng Tan, *CEO*
Peng Tan, *
EMP: 50 **EST:** 2014
SQ FT: 100,000
SALES (est): 8.17MM **Privately Held**
Web: biz260.inmotionhosting.com
SIC: 3444 3812 Forming machine work,
sheet metal; Aircraft/aerospace flight
instruments and guidance systems

(P-6299)
QUALITY FABRICATION INC (PA)
9631 Irondale Ave (91311-5009)
PHONE..............................818 407-5015
Pradeep Kumar, *CEO*
▲ **EMP:** 99 **EST:** 1980
SALES (est): 12.3MM
SALES (corp-wide): 12.3MM **Privately Held**
Web: www.quality-fab.com
SIC: 3444 Sheet metal specialties, not
stamped

(P-6300)
R & D METAL FABRICATORS INC
Also Called: R&D Metal
5250 Rancho Rd (92647-2052)
PHONE..............................714 891-4878
EMP: 36 **EST:** 1971
SALES (est): 4.67MM **Privately Held**
SIC: 3444 Sheet metalwork

(P-6301)
R & R DUCTWORK LLC
Also Called: R & R Ductwork
12820 Lakeland Rd (90670-4515)
PHONE..............................562 944-9660
Brian Klebowski, *Managing Member*
EMP: 18 **EST:** 1997
SQ FT: 14,000
SALES (est): 1.5MM **Privately Held**
Web: www.rrductwork.com
SIC: 3444 Ducts, sheet metal

(P-6302)
RAH INDUSTRIES INC (PA)
24800 Avenue Rockefeller (91355-3467)
PHONE..............................661 295-5190
EMP: 185 **EST:** 1971
SALES (est): 21.83MM
SALES (corp-wide): 21.83MM **Privately Held**
Web: www.rah-ind.com
SIC: 3444 3599 Sheet metalwork; Machine
shop, jobbing and repair

(P-6303)
RAMDA METAL SPECIALTIES INC
Also Called: Ramda Metal Specialties
13012 Crenshaw Blvd (90249-1544)
PHONE..............................310 538-2136
Daniel Guevara, *CEO*
EMP: 25 **EST:** 1985
SQ FT: 25,000
SALES (est): 4.12MM **Privately Held**
Web: www.ramda.com
SIC: 3444 Metal housings, enclosures,
casings, and other containers

(P-6304)
RDFABRICATORS INC
11880 Western Ave (90680-3438)
PHONE..............................714 634-2078
Raymond D Foye, *Pr*
EMP: 18 **EST:** 1979
SQ FT: 12,000
SALES (est): 2.3MM **Privately Held**
SIC: 3444 Sheet metal specialties, not
stamped

(P-6305)
RIGOS EQUIPMENT MFG LLC
Also Called: Rigos Sheet Metal
14501 Joanbridge St (91706-1749)
PHONE..............................626 813-6621
EMP: 23 **EST:** 1977
SQ FT: 3,600
SALES (est): 4.91MM **Privately Held**
Web: www.rigosequipment.com
SIC: 3444 Sheet metalwork

(P-6306)
ROBERT F CHAPMAN INC
43100 Exchange Pl (93535-4524)
PHONE..............................661 940-9482
Tim Mitchell, *CEO*
John H Mitchell, *
Paulette Mitchell, *
EMP: 53 **EST:** 1959
SQ FT: 62,000
SALES (est): 4.64MM **Privately Held**
Web: www.robertfchapman.com
SIC: 3444 3549 Sheet metalwork;
Metalworking machinery, nec

(P-6307)
ROMLA CO
Also Called: Romla Ventilator Co
9668 Heinrich Hertz Dr Ste D (92154-7917)
PHONE..............................619 946-1224

Ronald W Haneline, *CEO*
Robert Haneline, *
Bob Haneline, *
▲ **EMP:** 33 **EST:** 1945
SQ FT: 18,000
SALES (est): 8.29MM **Privately Held**
Web: www.romlair.com
SIC: 3444 Metal ventilating equipment

(P-6308)
RUSS INTERNATIONAL INC
1658 W 132nd St (90249-2006)
PHONE..............................310 329-7121
Randy Carter, *CEO*
Edmond Russ, *Ch*
▲ **EMP:** 22 **EST:** 1952
SQ FT: 20,000
SALES (est): 2.17MM **Privately Held**
Web: www.russ-international.com
SIC: 3444 Sheet metal specialties, not
stamped

(P-6309)
SA SERVING LINES INC
Also Called: G A Systems
226 W Carleton Ave (92867-3608)
PHONE..............................714 848-7529
Steve Aderson, *CEO*
Pat Devalle, *CFO*
Virginia Anderson, *Sec*
EMP: 29 **EST:** 2011
SALES (est): 1.66MM **Privately Held**
Web: www.gasystemsmfg.com
SIC: 3444 Metal housings, enclosures,
casings, and other containers

(P-6310)
SANTOURIAN MANUFACTURING INC
2603 Industry St (92054-4808)
PHONE..............................760 754-3811
EMP: 22 **EST:** 1978
SALES (est): 2.42MM **Privately Held**
Web: www.santourian.com
SIC: 3444 7692 Sheet metalwork; Welding
repair

(P-6311)
SCOTT A HUMPHREYS INC (PA)
4600 Industrial St (93063-3413)
PHONE..............................805 581-2971
EMP: 21 **EST:** 1975
SALES (est): 3.11MM
SALES (corp-wide): 3.11MM **Privately Held**
Web: scottahumphreys.mfgpages.com
SIC: 3444 Sheet metalwork

(P-6312)
SHADE STRUCTURES INC
Also Called: Fabritec Structures
115 E 2nd St Ste 101 (92780-3684)
PHONE..............................714 427-6980
Cathy Wanamaker, *Brnch Mgr*
EMP: 71
Web: www.usa-shade.com
SIC: 3444 1799 2394 Sheet metalwork;
Welding on site; Canvas and related
products
HQ: Shade Structures, Inc.
2580 Esters Blvd 100
Dfw Airport TX
214 905-9500

(P-6313)
SHEET METAL ENGINEERING
1780 Voyager Ave (93063-3301)
PHONE..............................805 306-0390
Kenneth Chamberlain, *Pr*
Kenneth Chamberlain, *Pr*

David Reed, *
Kathy Chou, *
▲ **EMP:** 25 **EST:** 1983
SQ FT: 21,000
SALES (est): 4.27MM **Privately Held**
Web: www.sheetmetaleng.com
SIC: 3444 1799 Sheet metal specialties, not
stamped; Welding on site

(P-6314)
SHEET METAL PROTOTYPE INC
19420 Londelius St (91324-3511)
PHONE..............................818 772-2715
Jane E Lamborn, *Pr*
EMP: 21 **EST:** 1983
SQ FT: 7,500
SALES (est): 946.64K **Privately Held**
Web: www.sheetmetalprototypeinc.com
SIC: 3444 Sheet metal specialties, not
stamped

(P-6315)
SHEET METAL SERVICE
2310 E Orangethorpe Ave (92806-1231)
PHONE..............................714 446-0196
EMP: 18 **EST:** 1991
SQ FT: 10,000
SALES (est): 4.19MM **Privately Held**
Web: www.smsfab.com
SIC: 3444 Sheet metalwork

(P-6316)
SHEET METAL SPECIALISTS LLC
11698 Warm Springs Rd (92505-5862)
PHONE..............................951 351-6828
Sandy Sligar, *
EMP: 18 **EST:** 2000
SQ FT: 18,000
SALES (est): 930.61K **Privately Held**
Web: www.sheetmetalspecialists.com
SIC: 3444 Sheet metal specialties, not
stamped

(P-6317)
SHOWERDOORDIRECT LLC
20100 Normandie Ave (90502-1211)
PHONE..............................310 327-8060
▲ **EMP:** 17 **EST:** 2010
SALES (est): 1.91MM
SALES (corp-wide): 14.21MM **Privately Held**
Web: www.showerdoordirect.com
SIC: 3444 Bins, prefabricated sheet metal
PA: Century Shower Door Co., Inc.
20100 Normandie Ave
Torrance CA
310 327-8060

(P-6318)
SMS FABRICATIONS INC
11698 Warm Springs Rd (92505-5862)
PHONE..............................951 351-6828
Michael A Uranga, *CEO*
Sandy Sligar, *
Scott Sligar, *
EMP: 36 **EST:** 2003
SALES (est): 4.96MM **Privately Held**
Web: www.sheetmetalspecialists.com
SIC: 3444 Sheet metalwork

(P-6319)
SPAN-O-MATIC INC
825 Columbia St (92821-2917)
PHONE..............................714 256-4700
Wolfgang Arnold, *Pr*
Lynda Arnold, *
Erik A Arnold, *
Carl Arnold, *
EMP: 40 **EST:** 1972

SQ FT: 50,000
SALES (est): 7.61MM **Privately Held**
Web: www.spanomatic.com
SIC: 3444 Sheet metalwork

(P-6320)
SPEC-BUILT SYSTEMS INC
2150 Michael Faraday Dr (92154-7903)
P.O. Box 531581 (92153-1581)
PHONE..........................619 661-8100
Randy Eifler, *Pr*
EMP: 75 **EST:** 1986
SQ FT: 25,000
SALES (est): 19.94MM **Privately Held**
Web: www.specbuilt.com
SIC: 3444 Sheet metalwork

(P-6321)
SPECIALTY FABRICATIONS INC
2674 Westhills Ct (93065-6234)
PHONE..........................805 579-9730
Mark Zimmerman, *Pr*
Randy Zimmerman, *
EMP: 49 **EST:** 1978
SQ FT: 80,000
SALES (est): 8.06MM **Privately Held**
Web: www.specfabinc.com
SIC: 3444 3599 Sheet metalwork; Machine and other job shop work

(P-6322)
SPRAY ENCLOSURE TECH INC
Also Called: Spray Tech
1427 N Linden Ave (92376-8601)
PHONE..........................909 419-7011
Tyler Rand, *Pr*
▲ **EMP:** 30 **EST:** 1994
SQ FT: 59,000
SALES (est): 7.33MM **Privately Held**
Web: www.spraytech.com
SIC: 3444 Booths, spray: prefabricated sheet metal

(P-6323)
STEELDYNE INDUSTRIES
Also Called: ABC Sheet Metal
2871 E La Cresta Ave (92806-1817)
PHONE..........................714 630-6200
EMP: 40 **EST:** 1995
SQ FT: 20,000
SALES (est): 9.1MM **Privately Held**
Web: www.abcsheetmetal.com
SIC: 3444 Sheet metal specialties, not stamped

(P-6324)
STEIN INDUSTRIES INC (PA)
4005 Artesia Ave (92833-2519)
PHONE..........................714 522-4560
Rudi Steinhilber, *CEO*
Theodore Steinhilber, *
Dave Spivy, *
EMP: 30 **EST:** 1982
SQ FT: 30,800
SALES (est): 6.07MM
SALES (corp-wide): 6.07MM **Privately Held**
SIC: 3444 2599 Sheet metalwork; Work benches, factory

(P-6325)
STOLL METALCRAFT INC
24808 Anza Dr (91355-1258)
PHONE..........................661 295-0401
Gunter Stoll, *Pr*
EMP: 105 **EST:** 1973
SQ FT: 45,000
SALES (est): 24.7MM **Privately Held**
Web: www.stoll-metalcraft.com

SIC: 3444 Sheet metal specialties, not stamped

(P-6326)
STRETCH FORMING CORPORATION
Also Called: Sfc
804 S Redlands Ave (92570-2478)
PHONE..........................951 443-0911
Brian D Geary, *CEO*
▲ **EMP:** 85 **EST:** 2009
SQ FT: 97,000
SALES (est): 14.27MM **Privately Held**
Web: www.stretchformingcorp.com
SIC: 3444 Sheet metalwork

(P-6327)
SUPERIOR DUCT FABRICATION INC
1683 Mount Vernon Ave (91768-3300)
PHONE..........................909 620-8565
Mike Hilgert, *CEO*
Kerry Bootke, *
◆ **EMP:** 107 **EST:** 2002
SQ FT: 3,900
SALES (est): 19.01MM **Privately Held**
Web: www.sdfab.com
SIC: 3444 Ducts, sheet metal

(P-6328)
SUPERIOR METAL FABRICATORS INC
4768 Felspar St (92509-3038)
PHONE..........................951 360-2474
Ron Didonanto, *Pr*
Dave Anderson, *VP*
EMP: 28 **EST:** 1977
SQ FT: 10,000
SALES (est): 1.2MM **Privately Held**
Web: www.superiormetalfabricators.net
SIC: 3444 Sheet metalwork

(P-6329)
SWIFT-COR PRECISION INC
344 W 157th St (90248-2135)
PHONE..........................310 354-1207
Sam Longo Junior, *Pr*
Tony Serge, *
EMP: 42 **EST:** 1981
SQ FT: 100,000
SALES (est): 911.91K **Privately Held**
Web: www.swiftcor.com
SIC: 3444 Sheet metalwork

(P-6330)
T & F SHEET MTLS FAB MCHNING I
15607 New Century Dr (90248-2128)
PHONE..........................310 516-8548
Thomas Medina, *Pr*
Hector Medina, *
EMP: 32 **EST:** 2005
SQ FT: 9,800
SALES (est): 5.48MM **Privately Held**
Web: tandfinc.eazy-ecpt.com
SIC: 3444 Sheet metalwork

(P-6331)
TEE -N -JAY MANUFACTURING INC
9145 Glenoaks Blvd (91352-2612)
PHONE..........................818 504-2961
Jeff Berns, *Pr*
Tamara Berns, *Sec*
EMP: 20 **EST:** 1973
SQ FT: 10,187
SALES (est): 2.39MM **Privately Held**
Web: www.tee-n-jay.com

SIC: 3444 Sheet metalwork

(P-6332)
TFC MANUFACTURING INC
4001 Watson Plaza Dr (90712-4034)
PHONE..........................562 426-9559
Majid Shahbazi, *Pr*
Hamid Sharifat, *
EMP: 81 **EST:** 1999
SQ FT: 28,500
SALES (est): 22.06MM **Privately Held**
Web: www.tfcmfg.com
SIC: 3444 Sheet metalwork

(P-6333)
TN SHEET METAL INC
18385 Bandilier Cir (92708-7001)
PHONE..........................714 593-0100
Thony Quang Nguyen, *CEO*
Christine Lee, *Contrlr*
Thony Quang Nguyen, *Pr*
▲ **EMP:** 19 **EST:** 2001
SQ FT: 12,035
SALES (est): 3.7MM **Privately Held**
Web: www.tnsheetmetal.com
SIC: 3444 Ducts, sheet metal

(P-6334)
TREND TECHNOLOGIES LLC (DH)
Also Called: Trend Technologies
4626 Eucalyptus Ave (91710-9215)
P.O. Box 515001 (00051-5001)
PHONE..........................909 597-7861
Earl Payton, *Managing Member*
▲ **EMP:** 220 **EST:** 2002
SQ FT: 125,000
SALES (est): 145.24MM **Privately Held**
Web: www.trendtechnologies.com
SIC: 3444 3469 3499 3089 Metal housings, enclosures, casings, and other containers; Electronic enclosures, stamped or pressed metal; Aquarium accessories, metal; Injection molding of plastics
HQ: Ttl Holdings, Llc
4626 Eucalyptus Ave
Chino CA
909 597-7861

(P-6335)
TRI PRECISION SHEETMETAL INC
845 N Elm St (92867-7909)
PHONE..........................714 632-8838
Leonardo Cortes, *Pr*
Ross Morrow, *
Rob Morrow, *
EMP: 40 **EST:** 1988
SALES (est): 5.12MM **Privately Held**
Web: www.triprecision.com
SIC: 3444 3542 Sheet metalwork; Sheet metalworking machines

(P-6336)
TRIO METAL STAMPING INC
Also Called: Trio Metal Stamping
15318 Proctor Ave (91745-1023)
PHONE..........................626 336-1228
Damian Rickard, *CEO*
Georgia Boris, *
EMP: 53 **EST:** 1947
SQ FT: 75,000
SALES (est): 5.93MM **Privately Held**
Web: www.triometalstamping.com
SIC: 3444 3469 Sheet metalwork; Stamping metal for the trade

SIC: 3444 Sheet metalwork

(P-6337)
TRU-DUCT INC
2515 Industry St (92054-4807)
PHONE..........................619 660-3858
Drew E Miles, *CEO*
EMP: 45 **EST:** 1991
SALES (est): 9.76MM **Privately Held**
Web: www.tru-duct.com
SIC: 3444 Ducts, sheet metal

(P-6338)
US PRECISION SHEET METAL INC
Also Called: U S Precision Manufacturing
4020 Garner Rd (92501-1006)
PHONE..........................951 276-2611
Amanda Hawkins, *CEO*
Ray Mayo, *
Sal Giulano, *
EMP: 68 **EST:** 1981
SQ FT: 25,000
SALES (est): 7.31MM **Privately Held**
Web: www.usprecision.net
SIC: 3444 Sheet metal specialties, not stamped

(P-6339)
VALLEY PRECISION METAL PRODUCT
Also Called: Valley Engravers
27771 Avenue Hopkins (91355-1223)
P.O. Box 800942 (91380-0942)
PHONE..........................661 607-0100
TOLL FREE: 888
Howard R Vermillion Junior, *Pr*
EMP: 25 **EST:** 1999
SQ FT: 15,000
SALES (est): 599.86K
SALES (corp-wide): 4.69MM **Privately Held**
Web: www.valleyengravers.com
SIC: 3444 3599 Sheet metalwork; Machine shop, jobbing and repair
PA: Valley Precision Metal Products, Inc.
27771 Avenue Hopkins
Valencia CA
661 607-0100

(P-6340)
VERSAFAB CORP (PA)
15919 S Broadway (90248-2489)
PHONE..........................800 421-1822
Edward Penfold Junior, *Ch Bd*
Joe Flynn, *Pr*
EMP: 42 **EST:** 1982
SQ FT: 35,000
SALES (est): 10.24MM
SALES (corp-wide): 10.24MM **Privately Held**
Web: www.versafabcorp.com
SIC: 3444 3465 3496 3469 Sheet metalwork; Moldings or trim, automobile: stamped metal; Miscellaneous fabricated wire products; Metal stampings, nec

(P-6341)
VERSAFORM CORPORATION
1377 Specialty Dr (92081-8521)
PHONE..........................760 599-4477
Ronals S Saks, *Pr*
EMP: 73 **EST:** 1974
SQ FT: 24,000
SALES (est): 11.19MM **Privately Held**
Web: www.lmiaerospace.com
SIC: 3444 3549 3398 Forming machine work, sheet metal; Metalworking machinery, nec; Metal heat treating
HQ: Lmi Aerospace, Inc.
3600 Mueller Rd
Saint Charles MO
636 946-6525

PRODUCTS & SVCS

(P-6342)

VTS SHEETMETAL SPECIALIST CO

1041 N Grove St (92806-2015)
PHONE....................714 237-1420
Thomas Bonnett, *Pr*
Tom Bonnett, *
Sa H Vo, *Sec*
EMP: 31 **EST:** 1986
SQ FT: 21,300
SALES (est): 4.86MM **Privately Held**
Web: www.vtsfab.com
SIC: 3444 Metal housings, enclosures, casings, and other containers

(P-6343)

WCS EQUIPMENT HOLDINGS LLC

Also Called: Steelco USA
13066 14th St (91710-4365)
PHONE....................909 393-8405
Erik Gamm, *Prin*
EMP: 53
SALES (corp-wide): 64.22MM **Privately Held**
Web: www.steelcousa.com
SIC: 3444 Sheet metalwork
HQ: Wcs Equipment Holdings, Llc
13568 Vintage Pl
Chino CA

(P-6344)

WEST COAST CUSTOM SHEET METAL

8125 Lankershim Blvd (91605-1612)
PHONE....................818 252-7500
George Vartan, *Pr*
EMP: 28 **EST:** 2001
SALES (est): 640.9K **Privately Held**
Web: www.westcoastcustomsheetmetal.com
SIC: 3444 Sheet metalwork

(P-6345)

WESTERN SHEET METALS INC

280 E Harrison St (92879-1309)
PHONE....................951 272-3600
Albert Rivera, *Pr*
EMP: 17 **EST:** 1993
SALES (est): 1.11MM **Privately Held**
Web: www.westernsheetmetals.com
SIC: 3444 Sheet metalwork

(P-6346)

WILL-MANN INC

225 E Santa Fe Ave (92832-1917)
P.O. Box 976 (92836-0976)
PHONE....................714 870-0350
Manfred Frischmuth, *Pr*
Lore Frischmuth, *
Sabina Andrassy, *
EMP: 40 **EST:** 1968
SQ FT: 30,000
SALES (est): 4.56MM **Privately Held**
Web: www.will-mann.com
SIC: 3444 7692 3471 Sheet metal specialties, not stamped; Welding repair; Plating and polishing

3446 Architectural Metalwork

(P-6347)

ACCESS PROFESSIONAL INC

Also Called: Access Professional Systems
1955 Cordell Ct Ste 104 (92020-0901)
PHONE....................858 571-4444
Russell Scheppmann, *Pr*
EMP: 18 **EST:** 1994

SALES (est): 3.07MM **Privately Held**
Web: www.accessprofessionals.com
SIC: 3446 7521 1731 Fences, gates, posts, and flagpoles; Automobile parking; Voice, data, and video wiring contractor

(P-6348)

ACE IRON INC

929 Howard St (90292-5518)
PHONE....................510 324-3300
Aejaz Sareshwala, *Pr*
EMP: 28 **EST:** 2000
SQ FT: 60,000
SALES (est): 1.53MM **Privately Held**
SIC: 3446 3441 1791 Fences or posts, ornamental iron or steel; Building components, structural steel; Structural steel erection

(P-6349)

ADF INCORPORATED

Also Called: Able Design and Fabrication
1550 W Mahalo Pl (90220-5422)
PHONE....................310 669-9700
Lou Mannick, *Pr*
EMP: 30 **EST:** 1993
SQ FT: 23,000
SALES (est): 9.46MM
SALES (corp-wide): 99.47MM **Privately Held**
Web: www.adfvisual.com
SIC: 3446 Partitions and supports/studs, including acoustical systems
PA: Peerless Industries, Inc.
2300 White Oak Cir
Aurora IL
630 375-5100

(P-6350)

ALABAMA METAL INDUSTRIES CORP

Also Called: Amico Fontana
11093 Beech Ave (92337-7268)
P.O. Box 310353 (92331-0353)
PHONE....................909 350-9280
Lilly Mc Donalds, *Brnch Mgr*
EMP: 108
SALES (corp-wide): 1.39B **Publicly Held**
Web: www.amicoglobal.com
SIC: 3446 Open flooring and grating for construction
HQ: Alabama Metal Industries Corporation
3245 Fayette Ave
Birmingham AL
205 787-2611

(P-6351)

ARCHITECTURAL ENTERPRISES INC

Also Called: Hi-Tech Iron Works
5821 Randolph St (90040-3415)
PHONE....................323 268-4000
Tom Lee, *Pr*
John S Lee, *
Alma Gutierrez, *
EMP: 40 **EST:** 1984
SQ FT: 20,000
SALES (est): 4.58MM **Privately Held**
SIC: 3446 Fences or posts, ornamental iron or steel

(P-6352)

CANTERBURY DESIGNS INC

Also Called: Canterbury International
6195 Maywood Ave (90255-3213)
PHONE....................323 936-7111
Larry Snyder, *Pr*
Laura Snyder, *VP*
▲ **EMP:** 20 **EST:** 1964
SALES (est): 2.29MM **Privately Held**

Web: www.canterbury-designs.com
SIC: 3446 3873 Architectural metalwork; Clocks, assembly of

(P-6353)

CLARK STEEL FABRICATORS INC

12610 Vigilante Rd (92040-1113)
P.O. Box 1370 (92040-0910)
PHONE....................619 390-1502
Kimberley L Clark, *Pr*
Kevin B Clark, *
EMP: 45 **EST:** 1977
SQ FT: 12,500
SALES (est): 7.68MM **Privately Held**
Web: www.clarksteelfab.com
SIC: 3446 3441 Architectural metalwork; Fabricated structural metal

(P-6354)

COLUMBIA FABRICATING CO INC

5079 Gloria Ave (91436-1553)
PHONE....................818 247-4220
Joseph Goldberg, *CEO*
Dalia Goldberg, *
EMP: 23 **EST:** 1983
SQ FT: 19,000
SALES (est): 835.33K **Privately Held**
SIC: 3446 Architectural metalwork

(P-6355)

CURRAN ENGINEERING COMPANY I

28727 Industry Dr (91355-5414)
P.O. Box 26 (91310-0026)
PHONE....................800 643-6353
Patrick Curran, *CEO*
Douglas M Curran, *CEO*
Patrick Curran, *Pr*
EMP: 20 **EST:** 1947
SQ FT: 20,000
SALES (est): 2.14MM **Privately Held**
Web: www.curranengineering.com
SIC: 3446 Architectural metalwork

(P-6356)

DENNISON INC

Also Called: Maxxon Company
17901 Railroad St (91748-1113)
PHONE....................626 965-8917
◆ **EMP:** 47 **EST:** 1990
SQ FT: 26,000
SALES (est): 4.7MM **Privately Held**
SIC: 3446 Architectural metalwork

(P-6357)

EUROCRAFT ARCHTECTURAL MET INC

5619 Watcher St (90201-1632)
PHONE....................323 771-1323
John Fechter, *Pr*
EMP: 30 **EST:** 1976
SQ FT: 30,000
SALES (est): 4.36MM **Privately Held**
Web: www.eurocraftmetal.com
SIC: 3446 Architectural metalwork

(P-6358)

FORMS AND SURFACES INC

6395 Cindy Ln (93013-2909)
PHONE....................805 684-8626
George Hickmann, *Brnch Mgr*
EMP: 80
SALES (corp-wide): 96.36MM **Privately Held**
Web: www.forms-surfaces.com
SIC: 3446 Architectural metalwork
PA: Forms And Surfaces, Inc.
30 Pine St

Pittsburgh PA
412 781-9003

(P-6359)

J TALLEY CORPORATION (PA)

Also Called: Talley Metal Fabrication
989 W 7th St (92582-3813)
P.O. Box 850 (92581-0850)
PHONE....................951 654-2123
Joe Brown Talley, *CEO*
EMP: 86 **EST:** 1963
SQ FT: 13,400
SALES (est): 18.26MM
SALES (corp-wide): 18.26MM **Privately Held**
Web: www.talleymetalfabrication.com
SIC: 3446 3444 Railings, prefabricated metal ; Sheet metalwork

(P-6360)

JANSEN ORNAMENTAL SUPPLY CO

10926 Schmidt Rd (91733-2708)
PHONE....................626 442-0271
Mike Jansen, *CEO*
Harry Jansen, *
John Jansen, *
▲ **EMP:** 30 **EST:** 1960
SQ FT: 22,000
SALES (est): 4.46MM **Privately Held**
Web: www.jansensupply.com
SIC: 3446 Architectural metalwork

(P-6361)

JMI STEEL INC

8983 San Fernando Rd (91352-1410)
PHONE....................818 768-3955
EMP: 32 **EST:** 1989
SQ FT: 11,000
SALES (est): 957.91K **Privately Held**
SIC: 3446 Fences or posts, ornamental iron or steel

(P-6362)

K & J WIRE PRODUCTS CORP

1220 N Lance Ln (92806-1812)
PHONE....................714 816-0360
Klaus Borutzki, *Pr*
Barbara Borutzki, *
EMP: 25 **EST:** 1989
SQ FT: 21,000
SALES (est): 952.89K **Privately Held**
Web: www.kjwire.com
SIC: 3446 3496 5046 3315 Architectural metalwork; Miscellaneous fabricated wire products; Store fixtures and display equipment; Wire and fabricated wire products

(P-6363)

LAVI INDUSTRIES (PA)

27810 Avenue Hopkins (91355-3409)
PHONE....................877 275-5284
Gavriel Lavi, *Pr*
Susan Lavi, *
◆ **EMP:** 80 **EST:** 1979
SQ FT: 80,000
SALES (est): 26.32MM
SALES (corp-wide): 26.32MM **Privately Held**
Web: www.lavi.com
SIC: 3446 Railings, banisters, guards, etc: made from metal pipe

(P-6364)

LNI CUSTOM MANUFACTURING INC

15542 Broadway Center St (90248-2137)
PHONE....................310 978-2000

Scott Blakely, *CEO*
EMP: 50 **EST:** 1995
SALES (est): 9.48MM **Privately Held**
Web: www.lnisigns.com
SIC: 3446 5046 Architectural metalwork;
Neon signs

(P-6365)
PARAMOUNT METAL & SUPPLY INC
8140 Rosecrans Ave (90723-2754)
PHONE..............................562 634-8180
Vincent Jue, *CEO*
George Jue, *
Helen Jue, *
EMP: 25 **EST:** 1955
SQ FT: 80,000
SALES (est): 4.21MM **Privately Held**
Web: www.paramountmetals.com
SIC: 3446 Architectural metalwork

(P-6366)
RAMI DESIGNS INC
24 Hammond Ste E (92618-1680)
PHONE..............................949 588-8288
Ron Taybi, *Pr*
EMP: 19 **EST:** 1982
SQ FT: 6,000
SALES (est): 2.36MM **Privately Held**
Web: www.ramidesigns.com
SIC: 3446 3299 3229 Architectural metalwork
; Architectural sculptures: gypsum, clay,
papier mache, etc.; Glass furnishings and
accessories

(P-6367)
SANIE MANUFACTURING COMPANY
320 E Alton Ave (92707-4419)
PHONE..............................714 751-7700
Mendi Haidarali, *Pr*
Mohammad Haidari, *VP*
EMP: 18 **EST:** 1981
SALES (est): 5.08MM **Privately Held**
Web: www.saniemfg.com
SIC: 3446 Fences or posts, ornamental iron
or steel

(P-6368)
SAPPHIRE MANUFACTURING INC
505 Porter Way (92870-6454)
PHONE..............................714 401-3117
Hector Garibay, *CEO*
EMP: 20 **EST:** 2015
SQ FT: 25,000
SALES (est): 2.61MM **Privately Held**
Web: www.sapphiremfg.com
SIC: 3446 7371 Fences or posts, ornamental
iron or steel; Computer software
development and applications

(P-6369)
SECURUS INC
Also Called: Holdrite
14284 Danielson St (92064-8885)
◆ **EMP:** 50 **EST:** 1983
SQ FT: 46,000
SALES (est): 19.78MM **Privately Held**
SIC: 3446 3351 3431 5162 Acoustical
suspension systems, metal; Tubing, copper
and copper alloy; Plumbing fixtures:
enameled iron, cast iron,or pressed metal;
Plastics materials and basic shapes

PA: Reliance Worldwide Corporation
Limited
L 26 140 William St
Melbourne VIC

(P-6370)
TAJIMA USA DISSOLVING CORP
Also Called: Tajima /Crl
2503 E Vernon Ave (90058-1826)
PHONE..............................323 588-1281
Bernard P Harris, *Ch Bd*
EMP: 34 **EST:** 1999
SALES (est): 4.33MM
SALES (corp-wide): 32.72B **Privately Held**
SIC: 3446 Architectural metalwork
HQ: C. R. Laurence Co., Inc.
2503 E Vernon Ave
Vernon CA
323 588-1281

(P-6371)
THORNTON STEEL & IR WORKS INC
1323 S State College Pkwy (92806-5242)
PHONE..............................714 491-8800
Ken Thornton, *CEO*
Steven Braseny, *Pr*
Richard Salcedo, *VP*
EMP: 18 **EST:** 1997
SQ FT: 12,200
SALES (est): 5.09MM **Privately Held**
Web: www.thorntonsteelironworks.com
SIC: 3446 Architectural metalwork

(P-6372)
TJS METAL MANUFACTURING INC
10847 Drury Ln (90262-1833)
PHONE..............................310 604-1545
Jose Antonio Gallegos, *CEO*
EMP: 26 **EST:** 1999
SQ FT: 30,000
SALES (est): 5.44MM **Privately Held**
Web: www.tjsmetal.com
SIC: 3446 Architectural metalwork

3448 Prefabricated Metal Buildings

(P-6373)
ALLIED MDULAR BLDG SYSTEMS INC (PA)
642 W Nicolas Ave (92868-1316)
PHONE..............................714 516-1188
Kevin Peithman, *CEO*
Raj Singh, *
Cathy Peithman, *
Richard Navarro, *
EMP: 38 **EST:** 1996
SQ FT: 35,000
SALES (est): 14.08MM **Privately Held**
Web: www.alliedmodular.com
SIC: 3448 Prefabricated metal buildings

(P-6374)
BIG ENTERPRISES
9702 Rush St (91733-1731)
PHONE..............................626 448-1449
EMP: 49 **EST:** 1971
SALES (est): 8.5MM **Privately Held**
Web: www.bigbooth.com
SIC: 3448 Buildings, portable: prefabricated
metal

(P-6375)
CRATE MODULAR INC
3025 E Dominguez St (90810-1437)
PHONE..............................310 405-0829

Rich Rozycki, *CEO*
Natasaha Deski, *
Moises Bada, *
EMP: 99 **EST:** 2018
SALES (est): 17.29MM **Privately Held**
Web: www.cratemodular.com
SIC: 3448 Prefabricated metal buildings and
components

(P-6376)
DURACOLD REFRIGERATION MFG LLC
1551 S Primrose Ave (91016-4542)
PHONE..............................626 358-1710
Harold Monsher, *Genl Pt*
Ben Monsher, *Pt*
EMP: 22 **EST:** 1996
SQ FT: 25,000
SALES (est): 2.18MM **Privately Held**
Web: www.arcticwalkins.com
SIC: 3448 3585 Prefabricated metal
components; Refrigeration and heating
equipment

(P-6377)
FCP INC (PA)
23100 Wildomar Trl (92595-9699)
P.O. Box 1555 (92595-1555)
PHONE..............................951 678-4571
Russell J Greer, *CEO*
Barret Hilzer, *
EMP: 84 **EST:** 1982
SQ FT: 200,000
SALES (est): 12.24MM
SALES (corp-wide): 12.24MM **Privately Held**
Web: www.fcpbarns.com
SIC: 3448 1541 Prefabricated metal
components; Steel building construction

(P-6378)
GCN SUPPLY LLC
9070 Bridgeport Pl (91730-5530)
PHONE..............................909 643-4603
Gustavo Chona Senior, *Managing Member*
EMP: 50 **EST:** 2015
SALES (est): 10MM **Privately Held**
Web: www.gcnsupply.com
SIC: 3448 2671 Prefabricated metal
buildings and components; Plastic film,
coated or laminated for packaging

(P-6379)
H ROBERTS CONSTRUCTION
2165 W Gaylord St (90813-1033)
PHONE..............................562 590-4825
Kathleen F Roberts, *Pr*
EMP: 51 **EST:** 1988
SQ FT: 1,100
SALES (est): 4.42MM **Privately Held**
Web: www.robertsconstructionllc.net
SIC: 3448 Buildings, portable: prefabricated
metal

(P-6380)
JOHN L CONLEY INC
Also Called: Conleys Greenhouse Mfg &
Sales
4344 Mission Blvd (91763-6017)
PHONE..............................909 627-0981
John L Conley, *CEO*
Tom Conley, *
Dean Conley, *
Howard Davis, *
◆ **EMP:** 75 **EST:** 1946
SALES (est): 20.61MM **Privately Held**
Web: www.conleys.com
SIC: 3448 3441 Greenhouses, prefabricated
metal; Fabricated structural metal

(P-6381)
JTS MODULAR INC
7001 Mcdivitt Dr Ste B (93313-2006)
P.O. Box 41765 (93384-1765)
PHONE..............................661 835-9270
Dene Hurlbert, *Pr*
John Hurlbert, *
Lee Hawkins, *
Phillip Engler, *
EMP: 50 **EST:** 2000
SQ FT: 4,000
SALES (est): 8.5MM **Privately Held**
Web: www.jtsmodular.com
SIC: 3448 Prefabricated metal buildings and
components

(P-6382)
MADISON INDUSTRIES (HQ)
2961 W Macarthur Blvd Ste 211
(92704-6913)
PHONE..............................323 583-4061
John Frey Junior, *Pr*
John Samuel Frey, *
Grace Lee, *Corporate Controller*
EMP: 28 **EST:** 1974
SALES (est): 9.64MM
SALES (corp-wide): 90.88MM **Privately
Held**
Web: www.madisonind.com
SIC: 3448 3441 1542 Prefabricated metal
buildings and components; Fabricated
structural metal; Nonresidential
construction, nec
PA: John S. Frey Enterprises
1900 E 64th St
Los Angeles CA
323 583-4061

(P-6383)
MCELROY METAL MILL INC
Also Called: McElroy Metal
17031 Koala Rd (92301-2246)
PHONE..............................760 246-5545
Pete Nadler, *Mgr*
EMP: 42
SQ FT: 37,700
SALES (corp-wide): 362.01MM **Privately
Held**
Web: www.mcelroymetal.com
SIC: 3448 Prefabricated metal components
PA: Mcelroy Metal Mill, Inc.
1500 Hamilton Rd
Bossier City LA
318 747-8000

(P-6384)
MOBILE MINI INC
42207 3rd St E (93535-5314)
P.O. Box 1538 (92377-1538)
PHONE..............................909 356-1690
Craig Nelson, *Genl Mgr*
EMP: 17
SALES (corp-wide): 2.14B **Publicly Held**
Web: www.mobilemini.com
SIC: 3448 Buildings, portable: prefabricated
metal
HQ: Mobile Mini, Inc.
4646 E Van Buren St # 400
Phoenix AZ
480 894-6311

(P-6385)
MOBILE MODULAR MANAGEMENT CORP
Also Called: Trs Rentelco
11450 Mission Blvd (91752-1015)
PHONE..............................800 819-1084
Thomas Sanders, *Mgr*
EMP: 100
SALES (corp-wide): 733.82MM **Publicly
Held**

P R O D U C T S & S V C S

Web: www.mobilemodular.com
SIC: **3448** 7519 Prefabricated metal
buildings and components; Trailer rental
HQ: Mobile Modular Management
    Corporation
    5700 Las Positas Rd
    Livermore CA
    925 443-8052

(P-6386)
MORIN CORPORATION
Also Called: Morin West
10707 Commerce Way (92337-8216)
PHONE................................909 428-3747
Ilhan Eser, *VP*
EMP: 40
Web: group.kingspan.com
SIC: **3448** Prefabricated metal buildings and
components
HQ: Morin Corporation
    685 Middle St Ste 1
    Bristol CT

(P-6387)
NCI GROUP INC
Also Called: Metal Coaters
9123 Center Ave (91730-5312)
PHONE................................909 987-4681
Colin Lally, *Brnch Mgr*
EMP: 25
SALES (corp-wide): 5.58B **Privately Held**
Web:
www.bluescopecoatedproducts.com
SIC: **3448** 3446 Prefabricated metal buildings
; Architectural metalwork
HQ: Nci Group, Inc.
    10943 N Sam Huston Pkwy W
    Houston TX
    281 897-7788

(P-6388)
**ORANGE COUNTY ERECTORS
INC**
517 E La Palma Ave (92801-2536)
PHONE................................714 502-8455
Richard Lewis, *CEO*
Sandra Lewis, *
EMP: 50 EST: 1975
SQ FT: 80,000
SALES (est): 17.63MM **Privately Held**
Web: www.ocerectors.com
SIC: **3448** 3441 1791 Buildings, portable:
prefabricated metal; Fabricated structural
metal; Structural steel erection

(P-6389)
**PROGRESSIVE MARKETING
PDTS INC**
Also Called: Progressive Marketing
4571 Avenida Del Este (92886-3002)
PHONE................................714 888-1700
Leonard Dozier, *CEO*
Scott Hillstrom, *Dir*
Sam Malik, *Ex VP*
Tiffany Dozier, *Ex VP*
◆ EMP: 80 EST: 1977
SALES (est): 19.91MM **Privately Held**
Web: www.premiermounts.com
SIC: **3448** Prefabricated metal buildings and
components

(P-6390)
SHADE STRUCTURES INC
Also Called: Shade Structures
1085 N Main St Ste C (92867-5458)
PHONE................................714 427-6980
Christina Bennett, *Brnch Mgr*
EMP: 37
Web: www.usa-shade.com

SIC: **3448** Prefabricated metal components
HQ: Shade Structures, Inc.
    2580 Esters Blvd 100
    Dfw Airport TX
    214 905-9500

(P-6391)
STELL INDUSTRIES INC
Also Called: C-Thru Sunrooms
1951 S Parco Ave Ste B (91761-8315)
PHONE................................951 369-8777
Gary P Stell Junior, *CEO*
Jason S Albany, *
Mike Leigh, *
EMP: 50 EST: 1947
SALES (est): 8.44MM **Privately Held**
SIC: **3448** Sunrooms, prefabricated metal

(P-6392)
T M P SERVICES INC (PA)
2929 Kansas Ave (92507-2639)
PHONE................................951 213-3900
Prentiss Tarver Junior, *Stockholder*
Shari Taylor, *
EMP: 21 EST: 1993
SQ FT: 32,000
SALES (est): 4.71MM **Privately Held**
Web: www.tmpservices.com
SIC: **3448** Ramps, prefabricated metal

(P-6393)
UNITED CARPORTS LLC
7280 Sycamore Canyon Blvd Ste 1
(92508-2333)
PHONE................................800 757-6742
Ryan Spates, *Pr*
Ryan Spates, *Managing Member*
Garrett Spates, *
EMP: 28 EST: 2011
SQ FT: 5,000
SALES (est): 6.64MM **Privately Held**
Web: www.unitedcarports.com
SIC: **3448** Prefabricated metal buildings and
components

3449 Miscellaneous Metalwork

(P-6394)
AMC MACHINING INC
1540 Commerce Way (93446-3524)
P.O. Box 665 (93447-0665)
PHONE................................805 238-5452
Alex Camp, *Pr*
EMP: 21 EST: 2007
SQ FT: 10,000
SALES (est): 4.41MM **Privately Held**
Web: www.amcmachining.com
SIC: **3449** Miscellaneous metalwork

(P-6395)
CMC STEEL US LLC
Also Called: Gerdau Ameristeel
5425 Industrial Pkwy (92407-1803)
PHONE................................909 646-7827
EMP: 43
SALES (corp-wide): 8.8B **Publicly Held**
Web: www.cmc.com
SIC: **3449** Bars, concrete reinforcing:
fabricated steel
HQ: Cmc Steel Us, Llc
    6565 N Macarthur Blvd # 8
    Irving TX
    214 689-4300

(P-6396)
**DB BUILDING FASTENERS INC
(PA)**

Also Called: Db Building Fasteners
5555 E Gibralter (91764-5121)
P.O. Box 4407 (91729-4407)
PHONE................................909 581-6740
Brent Dooley, *Pr*
John Dooley Iii, *VP*
Andrew Cohn, *Sec*
▲ EMP: 18 EST: 1992
SALES (est): 4.16MM
SALES (corp-wide): 4.16MM **Privately
Held**
Web: www.selfdrillers.com
SIC: **3449** Miscellaneous metalwork

(P-6397)
FAB SERVICES WEST INC
10007 Elm Ave (92335-6318)
PHONE................................909 350-7500
EMP: 77 EST: 2011
SALES (est): 9.8MM **Privately Held**
SIC: **3449** Miscellaneous metalwork
HQ: Fab Holding Llc
    3335 Susan St
    Costa Mesa CA
    949 236-5520

(P-6398)
H WAYNE LEWIS INC
Also Called: Amber Steel Co.
312 S Willow Ave (92376-6313)
P.O. Box 900 (92377-0900)
PHONE................................909 874-2213
H Wayne Lewis, *CEO*
Dan Bergen, *
Janet Lewis, *
Kriss Lewis, *
EMP: 40 EST: 1983
SQ FT: 8,100
SALES (est): 4.72MM **Privately Held**
Web: www.ambersteelco.com
SIC: **3449** Bars, concrete reinforcing:
fabricated steel

(P-6399)
INNOVATIVE METAL INDS INC
Also Called: Southwest Data Products
1330 Riverview Dr (92408-2944)
PHONE................................909 796-6200
Kelly Brodhagan, *CEO*
▲ EMP: 100 EST: 2006
SQ FT: 150,000
SALES (est): 23.61MM **Privately Held**
Web: www.imiac.com
SIC: **3449** Curtain wall, metal

(P-6400)
KING WIRE PARTITIONS INC
Also Called: A A A Partitions
6044 N Figueroa St (90042-4232)
PHONE................................323 256-4848
Max Behshid, *Pr*
Millie Behshid, *
Farid Behshid, *
▲ EMP: 30 EST: 1978
SQ FT: 24,000
SALES (est): 4.91MM **Privately Held**
Web: www.kingwireusa.com
SIC: **3449** 5046 3496 Miscellaneous
metalwork; Partitions; Miscellaneous
fabricated wire products

(P-6401)
**LMS REINFORCING STEEL USA
LP (HQ)**
Also Called: LMS Reinforcing Steel Group
26365 Earthmover Cir (92883-5270)
PHONE................................604 598-9930
Norm Streu, *Pr*
Janice Comeau, *CFO*
Mike Schutz, *VP Fin*

EMP: 49 EST: 2016
SALES (est): 10.63MM
SALES (corp-wide): 3.49MM **Privately
Held**
SIC: **3449** Bars, concrete reinforcing:
fabricated steel
PA: Lms Holdings (Ab) Ltd
    7452 132 St
    Surrey BC
    604 598-9930

(P-6402)
NI INDUSTRIES INC
7300 E Slauson Ave (90040-3627)
PHONE................................309 283-3355
David Adler, *Pr*
Brian Mcguire, *Pr*
Anil Shanehg, *General Vice President*
▲ EMP: 87 EST: 1930
SQ FT: 30,000
SALES (est): 4.5MM
SALES (corp-wide): 883.83MM **Publicly
Held**
SIC: **3449** Miscellaneous metalwork
PA: Trimas Corporation
    38505 Woodward Ave # 200
    Bloomfield Hills MI
    248 631-5450

(P-6403)
NORTH STAR ACQUISITION INC
Also Called: North Star Company
14912 S Broadway (90248-1818)
PHONE................................310 515-2200
EMP: 63 EST: 1950
SALES (est): 4.09MM **Privately Held**
Web: www.northstarcompany.com
SIC: **3449** 3444 3321 3316 Custom roll
formed products; Sheet metalwork; Gray
and ductile iron foundries; Cold finishing of
steel shapes

(P-6404)
PACIFIC STEEL GROUP (PA)
Also Called: Psg
4805 Murphy Canyon Rd (92123-4324)
PHONE................................858 251-1100
Eric Benson, *Prin*
Eric Benson, *CEO*
John Scurlock, *
Monica Kamoss, *
EMP: 114 EST: 2014
SQ FT: 26,000
SALES (est): 119.78MM
SALES (corp-wide): 119.78MM **Privately
Held**
Web: www.pacificsteelgroup.com
SIC: **3449** Bars, concrete reinforcing:
fabricated steel

(P-6405)
**QUALITY STEEL FABRICATORS
INC**
13275 Gregg St (92064-7120)
PHONE................................858 748-8400
Bryan J Miller, *Pr*
Cheryl Wolf, *Contrlr*
EMP: 22 EST: 1997
SALES (est): 1.57MM **Privately Held**
Web: www.qualityreinforcing.com
SIC: **3449** Bars, concrete reinforcing:
fabricated steel

(P-6406)
TAMCO
Also Called: Gerdau Rancho Cucamonga
1000 Quail St Ste 260 (92660-2784)
P.O. Box 13158 (92658-5087)
PHONE................................949 552-9714
EMP: 300

SALES (corp-wide): 8.8B **Publicly Held**
Web: www.tamco.com
SIC: 3449 Bars, concrete reinforcing:
fabricated steel
HQ: Tamco
5425 Industrial Pkwy
San Bernardino CA
909 899-0660

3451 Screw Machine Products

(P-6407)
ABEL AUTOMATICS LLC
Also Called: Abel Reels
165 N Aviador St (93010-8314)
PHONE..................805 388-3721
David Dragoo, *Ch Bd*
◆ **EMP:** 30 **EST:** 1980
SQ FT: 16,000
SALES (est): 2.7MM **Privately Held**
Web: www.abelreels.com
SIC: 3451 3949 Screw machine products;
Reels, fishing

(P-6408)
ALGER PRECISION MACHINING LLC
724 S Bon View Ave (91761-1913)
PHONE..................909 986-4591
Duane Femrite, *Prin*
Jim Hemingway, *Prin*
Danny Hankla, *Prin*
▲ **EMP:** 160 **EST:** 1986
SQ FT: 35,000
SALES (est): 23.2MM **Privately Held**
Web: www.algerprecision.com
SIC: 3451 Screw machine products

(P-6409)
ALPHA OMEGA SWISS INC
23305 La Palma Ave (92887-4773)
PHONE..................714 692-8009
Dale La Rock, *Pr*
Randy L Jones, *
EMP: 20 **EST:** 1980
SQ FT: 15,500
SALES (est): 713.2K **Privately Held**
Web: www.alphaomegaswiss.com
SIC: 3451 3599 Screw machine products;
Machine shop, jobbing and repair

(P-6410)
ANWRIGHT CORPORATION
10225 Glenoaks Blvd (91331-1605)
P.O. Box 330940 (91333-0940)
PHONE..................818 896-2465
Lloyd Anderson, *Pr*
David Richardson, *General Vice President**
EMP: 30 **EST:** 1968
SQ FT: 15,000
SALES (est): 475.58K **Privately Held**
Web: www.anwright.com
SIC: 3451 3599 Screw machine products;
Machine shop, jobbing and repair

(P-6411)
ATHANOR GROUP INC
921 E California St (91761-1918)
PHONE..................909 467-1205
Duane L Femrite, *Pr*
Richard Krause, *VP*
EMP: 22 **EST:** 1958
SQ FT: 35,600
SALES (est): 180.28K **Privately Held**
SIC: 3451 Screw machine products

(P-6412)
BALDA HK PLASTICS INC
Also Called: H K Prcision Turning Machining
3229 Roymar Rd (92058-1311)
PHONE..................760 757-1100
Dan Wannigen, *Mgr*
EMP: 40
SQ FT: 9,808
SALES (corp-wide): 2.67MM **Privately Held**
SIC: 3451 3544 3089 Screw machine
products; Special dies and tools; Injection
molded finished plastics products, nec
HQ: Balda Precision, Inc.
3233 Roymar Rd
Oceanside CA
760 757-1100

(P-6413)
BALDA PRECISION INC (DH)
Also Called: HK Precision Turning Machining
3233 Roymar Rd (92058-1311)
PHONE..................760 757-1100
EMP: 80 **EST:** 1974
SALES (est): 18.8MM
SALES (corp-wide): 2.67MM **Privately Held**
SIC: 3451 3544 3089 Screw machine
products; Special dies and tools; Injection
molded finished plastics products, nec
HQ: Clere Ag
Schluterstr. 45
Berlin BE
302 130-0430

(P-6414)
FASTENER INNOVATION TECH INC
Also Called: F I T
19300 S Susana Rd (90221-5711)
PHONE..................310 538-1111
Larry Valeriano, *Pr*
EMP: 99 **EST:** 1979
SQ FT: 65,000
SALES (est): 15.95MM
SALES (corp-wide): 123.82MM **Privately Held**
Web: www.fitfastener.com
SIC: 3451 3728 3452 3429 Screw machine
products; Aircraft parts and equipment, nec;
Bolts, nuts, rivets, and washers; Hardware,
nec
HQ: Avantus Aerospace, Inc.
29101 The Old Rd
Valencia CA
661 295-8620

(P-6415)
GT PRECISION INC
Also Called: Alard Machine Products
1629 W 132nd St (90249-2005)
PHONE..................310 323-4374
Gregg Thompson, *CEO*
▲ **EMP:** 107 **EST:** 1967
SQ FT: 11,700
SALES (est): 23.08MM **Privately Held**
Web: www.alardmachine.com
SIC: 3451 Screw machine products

(P-6416)
ONYX INDUSTRIES INC (PA)
Also Called: Quad R Tech
1227 254th St (90710-2912)
PHONE..................310 539-8830
Vladimir Reil, *CEO*
▲ **EMP:** 100 **EST:** 1978
SQ FT: 30,000
SALES (est): 24.28MM
SALES (corp-wide): 24.28MM **Privately Held**

Web: www.onyxindustries.com
SIC: 3451 Screw machine products

(P-6417)
ONYX INDUSTRIES INC
521 W Rosecrans Ave (90248-1514)
PHONE..................310 851-6161
Siamak Maghoul, *Brnch Mgr*
EMP: 100
SALES (corp-wide): 24.28MM **Privately Held**
Web: www.studex.com
SIC: 3451 Screw machine products
PA: Onyx Industries Inc.
1227 254th St
Harbor City CA
310 539-8830

(P-6418)
PACIFIC PRECISION INC
1318 Palomares St (91750-5232)
PHONE..................909 392-5610
EMP: 40 **EST:** 1981
SALES (est): 7.22MM **Privately Held**
Web: www.pacificprecisioninc.com
SIC: 3451 Screw machine products

(P-6419)
PRECISION TECHNOLOGY AND MFG
3147 Durahart St (92507-3463)
PHONE..................951 788-0252
Jose Pompa, *Pr*
Juan Pompa, *
Lorraine Pagones, *
EMP: 19 **EST:** 1987
SQ FT: 9,000
SALES (est): 520.18K **Privately Held**
Web: www.p-t-c.com
SIC: 3451 3643 Screw machine products;
Contacts, electrical

(P-6420)
PRICE MANUFACTURING CO INC
372 N Smith Ave (92878-4371)
P.O. Box 1209 (92878-1209)
PHONE..................951 371-5660
Robert P Schiffmacher, *CEO*
Ively Schiffmacher, *
EMP: 32 **EST:** 1979
SQ FT: 15,600
SALES (est): 4.67MM **Privately Held**
Web: www.pricemfg.com
SIC: 3451 Screw machine products

(P-6421)
SORENSON ENGINEERING INC (PA)
32032 Dunlap Blvd (92399-1706)
PHONE..................909 795-2434
David L Sorenson, *Pr*
Paul Sewell, *
◆ **EMP:** 161 **EST:** 1956
SQ FT: 61,000
SALES (est): 63.8MM
SALES (corp-wide): 63.8MM **Privately Held**
Web: www.sorensoneng.com
SIC: 3451 Screw machine products

(P-6422)
SPARTAN MANUFACTURING CO
7081 Patterson Dr (92841-1435)
PHONE..................714 894-1955
R J Horton, *Pr*
Terry Danielson, *
EMP: 26 **EST:** 1957
SQ FT: 16,000
SALES (est): 2.27MM **Privately Held**

Web: www.spartanmfg.com
SIC: 3451 Screw machine products

(P-6423)
SWISS-MICRON INC
22361 Gilberto Ste A (92688-2103)
PHONE..................949 589-0430
Kurt Sollberger, *CEO*
Beverley Sollberger, *
EMP: 53 **EST:** 1984
SQ FT: 16,000
SALES (est): 4.78MM **Privately Held**
Web: www.swissmicron.com
SIC: 3451 Screw machine products

(P-6424)
TL MACHINE INC
14272 Commerce Dr (92843-4942)
PHONE..................714 554-4154
Thanh X Ly, *Pr*
Thanh Ly, *
Tuyen Ly, *
Quang Ly, *
▲ **EMP:** 90 **EST:** 2001
SQ FT: 39,126
SALES (est): 20.85MM **Privately Held**
Web: www.tlmachine.com
SIC: 3451 3561 3593 3728 Screw machine
products; Pumps and pumping equipment;
Fluid power cylinders and actuators;
Aircraft parts and equipment, nec

(P-6425)
TRIUMPH PRECISION PRODUCTS
Also Called: TP Products
13636 Vaughn St Ste A (91340-3052)
PHONE..................818 897-4700
Victor Linares, *Pr*
Javier Cervantes, *VP*
Jesus Cervantes, *Sec*
EMP: 17 **EST:** 1967
SQ FT: 19,500
SALES (est): 474.32K **Privately Held**
SIC: 3451 Screw machine products

(P-6426)
WESTERN SCREW PRODUCTS INC
11770 Slauson Ave (90670-2269)
PHONE..................562 698-5793
Lester P Kovats, *Pr*
Margaret K Doolittle, *
William Doolittle, *
EMP: 50 **EST:** 1940
SQ FT: 30,000
SALES (est): 4.7MM **Privately Held**
Web: www.westernscrew.com
SIC: 3451 Screw machine products

(P-6427)
WYATT PRECISION MACHINE INC
3301 E 59th St (90805-4503)
PHONE..................562 634-0524
Dennis Allison, *Pr*
Paul Layton, *
Allen Harmon, *
EMP: 47 **EST:** 1952
SQ FT: 14,000
SALES (est): 5.29MM **Privately Held**
Web: www.wyattprecisionmachine.com
SIC: 3451 Screw machine products

(P-6428)
ZENITH SCREW PRODUCTS INC
10910 Painter Ave (90670-4552)
P.O. Box 2747 (90670-0747)
PHONE..................562 941-0281

PRODUCTS & SVCS

Kenneth Miller, *Pr*
Donald S Miller, *Ch Bd*
Keith L Miller, *VP*
Connie Miller, *Sec*
EMP: 20 **EST:** 1953
SQ FT: 7,000
SALES (est): 2.22MM **Privately Held**
Web: www.zspinc.com
SIC: 3451 Screw machine products

3452 Bolts, Nuts, Rivets, And Washers

(P-6429)
3-V FASTENER CO INC
630 E Lambert Rd (92821-4119)
PHONE..................................949 888-7700
Peter George, *CEO*
EMP: 56 **EST:** 1982
SQ FT: 18,500
SALES (est): 13.57MM
SALES (corp-wide): 16.95B **Publicly Held**
SIC: 3452 Bolts, metal
HQ: Consolidated Aerospace
　　Manufacturing, Llc
　　1425 S Acacia Ave
　　Fullerton CA
　　714 989-2797

(P-6430)
A J FASTENERS INC
Also Called: Pacific Hardware Sales
2800 E Miraloma Ave (92806-1803)
PHONE..................................714 630-1556
Lawrence Roa, *Pr*
▲ **EMP:** 20 **EST:** 1975
SQ FT: 15,000
SALES (est): 2.49MM **Privately Held**
Web: www.ajfasteners.com
SIC: 3452 5072 3469 Screws, metal; Screws
; Metal stampings, nec

(P-6431)
ANILLO INDUSTRIES INC (PA)
Also Called: Anillo Industries
2090 N Glassell St (92865-3306)
P.O. Box 5586 (92863-5586)
PHONE..................................714 637-7000
Kurt Hilton Koch, *Pr*
Mark Koch, *VP*
EMP: 24 **EST:** 1957
SQ FT: 80,000
SALES (est): 4.59MM
SALES (corp-wide): 4.59MM **Privately Held**
Web: www.anilloinc.com
SIC: 3452 3325 3499 3429 Washers;
　Bushings, cast steel: except investment;
　Shims, metal; Hardware, nec

(P-6432)
AZTEC MANUFACTURING INC (PA)
Also Called: Aztec Washer Company
13821 Danielson St (92064-6891)
PHONE..................................858 513-4350
▲ **EMP:** 25 **EST:** 1970
SALES (est): 24.82MM
SALES (corp-wide): 24.82MM **Privately Held**
Web: www.aztecwasher.com
SIC: 3452 Washers

(P-6433)
BRILES AEROSPACE LLC
1559 W 135th St (90249-2219)
PHONE..................................424 320-3817
Richard Alessi, *Managing Member*
Daniel Yoon, *Dir*

EMP: 44 **EST:** 2012
SQ FT: 22,000
SALES (est): 900K **Privately Held**
Web: www.brilesaerospace.com
SIC: 3452 Bolts, nuts, rivets, and washers

(P-6434)
BRISTOL INDUSTRIES LLC
630 E Lambert Rd (92821-4119)
PHONE..................................714 990-4121
EMP: 152 **EST:** 1973
SALES (est): 47.7MM
SALES (corp-wide): 16.95B **Publicly Held**
Web: www.bristolindustries.com
SIC: 3452 Bolts, nuts, rivets, and washers
HQ: Consolidated Aerospace
　　Manufacturing, Llc
　　1425 S Acacia Ave
　　Fullerton CA
　　714 989-2797

(P-6435)
BUTLER INC
2140 S Dupont Dr (92806-6101)
PHONE..................................310 323-3114
John Hollern, *Pr*
Cynthia Hollern, *VP*
EMP: 19 **EST:** 1974
SALES (est): 515.1K **Privately Held**
Web: www.butlerbolt.com
SIC: 3452 Bolts, metal

(P-6436)
CBS FASTENERS INC
1345 N Brasher St (92807-2046)
PHONE..................................714 779-6368
Vic Luna, *Pr*
Gerald Bozarth, *
EMP: 49 **EST:** 1978
SQ FT: 10,400
SALES (est): 9.12MM **Privately Held**
Web: www.cbsfasteners.com
SIC: 3452 Bolts, metal

(P-6437)
DGL HOLDINGS INC
3850 E Miraloma Ave (92806-2108)
PHONE..................................714 630-7840
George Hennes, *Pr*
David Boehm, *
EMP: 50 **EST:** 1969
SQ FT: 35,500
SALES (est): 9.61MM **Privately Held**
Web: www.mwcomponents.com
SIC: 3452 Bolts, nuts, rivets, and washers

(P-6438)
DOUBLECO INCORPORATED
Also Called: R & D Fasteners
9444 9th St (91730-4509)
P.O. Box 250 (91785-0250)
PHONE..................................909 481-0799
Craig Scheu, *Pr*
EMP: 100 **EST:** 1986
SQ FT: 30,000
SALES (est): 23.62MM **Privately Held**
Web: www.rdfast.com
SIC: 3452 5072 Bolts, metal; Bolts

(P-6439)
DUNCAN BOLT CO
5555 E Gibralter (91764-5121)
PHONE..................................909 581-6740
Brent Dooley, *Mgr*
EMP: 19
SALES (corp-wide): 29.58MM **Privately Held**
Web: www.duncanbolt.com
SIC: 3452 Bolts, nuts, rivets, and washers
PA: Duncan Bolt Co.
　　8535 Dice Rd

Santa Fe Springs CA
562 698-8800

(P-6440)
DUPREE INC
Also Called: Stake Fastener
14395 Ramona Ave (91710-5740)
P.O. Box 1797 (91708-1797)
PHONE..................................909 597-4889
Jim Pon, *Pr*
James D Dupree, *
▲ **EMP:** 31 **EST:** 1958
SQ FT: 60,000
SALES (est): 4.57MM **Privately Held**
Web: www.dupreeinc.com
SIC: 3452 6512 Bolts, metal; Commercial
　and industrial building operation

(P-6441)
FEDERAL MANUFACTURING CORP
9825 De Soto Ave (91311-4412)
PHONE..................................818 341-9825
Helen Rainey, *Pr*
Arthur Rainey, *
Paul Rainey, *
EMP: 42 **EST:** 1951
SQ FT: 36,000
SALES (est): 5.06MM **Privately Held**
Web: www.federalmanufacturing.com
SIC: 3452 3812 3462 3429 Bolts, metal;
　Search and navigation equipment; Iron and
　steel forgings; Hardware, nec

(P-6442)
GALLEHER ACQUISITION CORP
Also Called: Galleher Industries
1384 S Signal Dr (91766-5462)
PHONE..................................909 623-5888
Bradley Bowden, *CEO*
EMP: 50 **EST:** 2021
SALES (est): 4.87MM **Privately Held**
SIC: 3452 Nuts, metal

(P-6443)
GOLDEN BOLT LLC
9361 Canoga Ave (91311-5879)
PHONE..................................818 626-8261
EMP: 74 **EST:** 2016
SALES (est): 4.92MM **Privately Held**
Web: www.goldenboltllc.com
SIC: 3452 Bolts, metal

(P-6444)
HI-SHEAR CORPORATION (DH)
2600 Skypark Dr (90505-5373)
PHONE..................................310 326-8110
Christian Darville, *CEO*
▲ **EMP:** 600 **EST:** 1943
SQ FT: 180,000
SALES (est): 138.97MM
SALES (corp-wide): 2.67MM **Privately Held**
Web: www.hi-shear.com
SIC: 3452 3429 Bolts, nuts, rivets, and
　washers; Aircraft hardware
HQ: Lisi Aerospace
　　42 A 52
　　Paris
　　140198200

(P-6445)
HUCK INTERNATIONAL INC
Also Called: Arconic Fastening Systems
900 E Watson Center Rd (90745-4201)
PHONE..................................310 830-8200
Jim Dawn, *Mgr*
EMP: 203
SALES (corp-wide): 5.66B **Publicly Held**
Web: www.howmet.com

SIC: 3452 Nuts, metal
HQ: Huck International, Inc.
　　3724 E Columbia St
　　Tucson AZ
　　520 519-7400

(P-6446)
INSTRUMENT BEARING FACTORY USA
19360 Rinaldi St (91326-1607)
PHONE..................................818 989-5052
EMP: 50
SQ FT: 30,000
SALES (est): 2.67MM **Privately Held**
SIC: 3452 5085 Bolts, metal; Industrial
　supplies

(P-6447)
JW MANUFACTURING INC
Also Called: Arconic Fstening Systems Rings
12989 Bradley Ave (91342-3830)
PHONE..................................805 498-4594
Jacob Wood, *Pr*
Ali Motamedi D.o.s., *Prin*
▲ **EMP:** 30 **EST:** 1943
SQ FT: 40,000
SALES (est): 525.34K **Privately Held**
SIC: 3452 5072 Nuts, metal; Bolts, nuts, and
　screws

(P-6448)
KING HOLDING CORPORATION
360 N Crescent Dr (90210-4874)
PHONE..................................586 254-3900
EMP: 7970
SIC: 3452 3465 3469 3089 Bolts, nuts,
　rivets, and washers; Automotive stampings;
　Metal stampings, nec; Injection molded
　finished plastics products, nec

(P-6449)
MS AEROSPACE INC
13928 Balboa Blvd (91342-1086)
PHONE..................................818 833-9095
Michel Szostak, *CEO*
Jerome Taieb, *
Jim Cole, *General Vice President**
EMP: 302 **EST:** 1992
SALES (est): 48.8MM **Privately Held**
Web: www.msaerospace.com
SIC: 3452 3728 Bolts, nuts, rivets, and
　washers; Aircraft parts and equipment, nec

(P-6450)
NYLOK LLC
Also Called: Nylok Western Fastener
313 N Euclid Way (92801-6738)
PHONE..................................714 635-3993
Scott Plantiga, *Mgr*
EMP: 45
SALES (corp-wide): 32.23MM **Privately Held**
Web: www.nylok.com
SIC: 3452 Bolts, nuts, rivets, and washers
PA: Nylok, Llc
　　15260 Hallmark Ct
　　Macomb MI
　　586 786-0100

(P-6451)
PAUL R BRILES INC
Also Called: Pb Fasteners
1700 W 132nd St (90249-2008)
PHONE..................................310 323-6222
▲ **EMP:** 1262
SIC: 3452 Bolts, nuts, rivets, and washers

(P-6452)
POWER FASTENERS INC
650 E 60th St (90001-1012)
P.O. Box 512056 (90051-0056)
PHONE...................................323 232-4362
Patrick Harrington, *Pr*
▲ **EMP:** 30 **EST:** 1991
SQ FT: 35,000
SALES (est): 2.36MM **Privately Held**
Web: 041d6c8.netsolhost.com
SIC: 3452 3448 Bolts, nuts, rivets, and
washers; Prefabricated metal components

(P-6453)
RISCO INC
390 Risco Cir (92223-2676)
PHONE...................................951 769-2899
Joseph A Frainee Ii, *CEO*
Cynthia R Frainee, *
▲ **EMP:** 30 **EST:** 1964
SQ FT: 30,000
SALES (est): 4.33MM **Privately Held**
Web: www.risco-fasteners.com
SIC: 3452 Bolts, metal

(P-6454)
SUNLAND AEROSPACE
FASTENERS
12920 Pierce St (91331-2526)
PHONE...................................818 485-8929
Jack Wilson, *CEO*
EMP: 45 **EST:** 2012
SQ FT: 11,000
SALES (est): 4.53MM **Privately Held**
Web: www.sunlandaerospace.com
SIC: 3452 Bolts, nuts, rivets, and washers

(P-6455)
TWIST TITE MFG INC
13344 Cambridge St (90670-4904)
PHONE...................................562 229-0990
Spiro Aykias, *CEO*
Martha Leonard, *
EMP: 32 **EST:** 1994
SQ FT: 18,200
SALES (est): 4.57MM **Privately Held**
Web: www.twisttite.com
SIC: 3452 Bolts, nuts, rivets, and washers

(P-6456)
VALLEY-TODECO INC (DH)
Also Called: Arconic Fastening Systems
135 N Unruh Ave (91744-4427)
PHONE...................................800 992-4444
▲ **EMP:** 57 **EST:** 1995
SALES (est): 25.05MM
SALES (corp-wide): 5.66B **Publicly Held**
SIC: 3452 5085 Bolts, nuts, rivets, and
washers; Fasteners, industrial: nuts, bolts,
screws, etc.
HQ: Howmet Global Fastening Systems Inc.
3990a Heritage Oak Ct
Simi Valley CA
805 426-2270

3462 Iron And Steel Forgings

(P-6457)
ADVANCED STRUCTURAL TECH
INC
Also Called: Asa
950 Richmond Ave (93030-7212)
PHONE...................................805 204-9133
Robert Melsness, *Pr*
Douglas Jones, *
▼ **EMP:** 135 **EST:** 2009
SALES (est): 36.3MM **Privately Held**
Web: www.astforgetech.com

SIC: 3462 Aircraft forgings, ferrous

(P-6458)
AJAX FORGE COMPANY (PA)
1956 E 48th St (90058-2006)
PHONE...................................323 582-6307
TOLL FREE: 800
Fred Goble, *Pr*
Steve Mc Elrath, *Stockholder*
EMP: 19 **EST:** 1939
SQ FT: 10,000
SALES (est): 2.31MM
SALES (corp-wide): 2.31MM **Privately**
Held
Web: www.ajaxforge.com
SIC: 3462 Iron and steel forgings

(P-6459)
FORGED METALS INC
10685 Beech Ave (92337-7212)
PHONE...................................909 350-9260
Torben Kaese, *CEO*
◆ **EMP:** 200 **EST:** 1982
SQ FT: 4,800
SALES (est): 46.8MM
SALES (corp-wide): 5.66B **Publicly Held**
SIC: 3462 Iron and steel forgings
PA: Howmet Aerospace Inc.
201 Isabella St Ste 200
Pittsburgh PA
412 553-1950

(P-6460)
INDEPENDENT FORGE
COMPANY
692 N Batavia St (92868-1221)
PHONE...................................714 997-7337
Rosemary Ruiz, *Pr*
Joe Ramirez, *
Gloria Lopez, *
▲ **EMP:** 40 **EST:** 1975
SQ FT: 11,900
SALES (est): 4.46MM **Privately Held**
Web: www.independentforge.com
SIC: 3462 Iron and steel forgings

(P-6461)
IRONWOOD FABRICATION INC
Also Called: South Coast Iron
761 Monroe Way (92870-6309)
PHONE...................................714 576-7320
Sean Michael, *Pr*
Sean D Michael, *Prin*
EMP: 18 **EST:** 2018
SALES (est): 2.37MM **Privately Held**
Web: www.southcoastiron.com
SIC: 3462 1791 Iron and steel forgings;
Structural steel erection

(P-6462)
JAZ DISTRIBUTION INC
8485 Artesia Blvd Ste B (90621-4195)
PHONE...................................714 521-3888
Tavis Tan, *Pr*
Mark Uchinao, *VP*
▲ **EMP:** 17 **EST:** 1999
SALES (est): 819.39K **Privately Held**
SIC: 3462 5013 Railroad wheels, axles,
frogs, or other equipment: forged;
Automotive supplies and parts

(P-6463)
JMMCA INC (PA)
Also Called: Pmp Forge
850 W Bradley Ave (92020-1218)
PHONE...................................619 448-2711
James Matarese, *CEO*
Betty Matarese, *
▲ **EMP:** 83 **EST:** 1963
SQ FT: 92,000

SALES (est): 18.37MM
SALES (corp-wide): 18.37MM **Privately**
Held
Web: www.pmpforge.com
SIC: 3462 Iron and steel forgings

(P-6464)
KIMS WELDING AND IRON
WORKS
Also Called: Kim's Fence
2331 E Orangethorpe Ave (92831-5330)
PHONE...................................714 680-7700
David S Kim, *Pr*
EMP: 18 **EST:** 1982
SQ FT: 5,000
SALES (est): 474.45K **Privately Held**
Web: www.kimironworks.com
SIC: 3462 1799 Ornamental metal forgings,
ferrous; Welding on site

(P-6465)
MATTCO FORGE INC
7530 Jackson St (90723-4910)
PHONE...................................562 634-8635
Denis B Brady, *CEO*
EMP: 34
SALES (corp-wide): 26.75MM **Privately**
Held
Web: www.mattcoforge.com
SIC: 3462 Iron and steel forgings
HQ: Mattco Forge, Inc.
16443 Minnesota Ave
Paramount CA
562 634-8635

(P-6466)
MATTCO FORGE INC (HQ)
16443 Minnesota Ave (90723-4917)
PHONE...................................562 634-8635
Robert Lewis, *Pr*
Andrew Fite, *
▲ **EMP:** 19 **EST:** 1998
SQ FT: 150,000
SALES (est): 11.17MM
SALES (corp-wide): 26.75MM **Privately**
Held
Web: www.mattcoforge.com
SIC: 3462 Iron and steel forgings
PA: Mattco Forge Holdings, Llc
16443 Minnesota Ave
Paramount CA
562 634-8635

(P-6467)
PACIFIC FORGE INC
10641 Etiwanda Ave (92337-6991)
PHONE...................................909 390-0701
Ronald D Browne, *Pr*
Jacqueline Dyer, *
EMP: 55 **EST:** 1955
SQ FT: 34,816
SALES (est): 12.32MM
SALES (corp-wide): 474.53MM **Privately**
Held
Web: www.pacificforge.com
SIC: 3462 3463 Iron and steel forgings;
Nonferrous forgings
PA: Avis Industrial Corporation
1909 S Main St
Upland IN
765 998-8100

(P-6468)
PARAMOUNT FORGE INC
1721 E Colon St (90744-2210)
P.O. Box 205 (90748-0205)
PHONE...................................323 775-6803
Donald Ferguson, *Pr*
EMP: 20 **EST:** 1962
SALES (est): 1.64MM **Privately Held**

SIC: 3462 Iron and steel forgings

(P-6469)
PERFORMANCE FORGE INC
7401 Telegraph Rd (90640-6500)
PHONE...................................323 722-3460
Wayne Ramay, *Pr*
EMP: 30 **EST:** 2012
SALES (est): 4.66MM **Privately Held**
Web: www.performance-forge.com
SIC: 3462 Iron and steel forgings

(P-6470)
PREMIER GEAR & MACHINING
INC
2360 Pomona Rd (92878-4329)
P.O. Box 2799 (92878-2799)
PHONE...................................951 278-5505
Steve Golden, *Pr*
Huy Nguyen, *
EMP: 25 **EST:** 1986
SQ FT: 21,000
SALES (est): 5.06MM **Privately Held**
Web: www.premiergearinc.com
SIC: 3462 3599 Iron and steel forgings;
Machine shop, jobbing and repair

(P-6471)
PRESS FORGE COMPANY
7700 Jackson St (90723-5029)
P.O. Box 1432 (90723-1432)
PHONE...................................562 531-4962
Jeffrey M Carlton, *CEO*
Michael Buxton, *
Mike Buxton, *
▲ **EMP:** 80 **EST:** 1978
SQ FT: 32,726
SALES (est): 21.04MM
SALES (corp-wide): 302.09B **Publicly**
Held
Web: www.pressforge.com
SIC: 3462 Iron and steel forgings
HQ: Precision Castparts Corp.
5885 Meadows Rd Ste 620
Lake Oswego OR
503 946-4800

(P-6472)
RUBICON GEAR INC
Also Called: Rubicon Gear
225 Citation Cir (92878-5023)
PHONE...................................951 356-3800
Cheryl A Edwards, *Ch Bd*
Ryan B Edwards, *
Frank Salazar, *
EMP: 68 **EST:** 1970
SQ FT: 25,000
SALES (est): 10MM **Privately Held**
Web: www.rubicon-gear.com
SIC: 3462 Gears, forged steel

(P-6473)
TIMKEN GEARS & SERVICES INC
Also Called: Philadelphia Gear
12935 Imperial Hwy (90670-4715)
PHONE...................................310 605-2600
Tony Tartaglio, *Brnch Mgr*
EMP: 20
SALES (corp-wide): 4.5B **Publicly Held**
Web: www.philagear.com
SIC: 3462 Gear and chain forgings
HQ: Timken Gears & Services Inc.
935 1st Ave Ste 200
King Of Prussia PA

(P-6474)
VI-STAR GEAR CO INC
7312 Jefferson St (90723-4094)
PHONE...................................323 774-3750
Thomas R Redfield, *Pr*

Chris Redfield, *
EMP: 30 **EST:** 1960
SQ FT: 12,000
SALES (est): 3.41MM **Privately Held**
Web: www.vistargear.com
SIC: 3462 3728 Iron and steel forgings;
　Gears, aircraft power transmission

3463 Nonferrous Forgings

(P-6475)
ALUM-ALLOY CO INC
603 S Hope Ave (91761-1824)
PHONE....................909 986-0410
David Howell, *CEO*
Marilyn Howell, *
Clark Howell, *
EMP: 40 **EST:** 1961
SQ FT: 20,000
SALES (est): 3.01MM **Privately Held**
Web: www.lynwoodpattern.com
SIC: 3463 3365 Aluminum forgings;
　Aluminum foundries

(P-6476)
CARLTON FORGE WORKS
Also Called: Fw
7743 Adams St (90723-4200)
PHONE....................562 633-1131
◆ **EMP:** 300 **EST:** 1929
SALES (est): 53.95MM
SALES (corp-wide): 302.09B **Publicly
Held**
Web: www.carltonforgeworks.com
SIC: 3463 3462 Nonferrous forgings; Iron
　and steel forgings
HQ: Precision Castparts Corp.
　5885 Meadows Rd Ste 620
　Lake Oswego OR
　503 946-4800

(P-6477)
CONTINENTAL FORGE
COMPANY LLC
412 E El Segundo Blvd (90222-2317)
PHONE....................310 603-1014
Olivier Jarrault, *CEO*
Peter Manos, *
EMP: 90 **EST:** 1968
SQ FT: 27,000
SALES (est): 10.65MM
SALES (corp-wide): 123.83MM **Privately
Held**
Web: www.cforge.com
SIC: 3463 Aluminum forgings
HQ: Forged Solutions Group Limited
　Dale Road North
　Matlock
　114 219-3001

(P-6478)
GEL INDUSTRIES INC
Also Called: Quality Aluminum Forge Div
810 N Lemon St (92867-6616)
PHONE....................714 639-8191
EMP: 150
SIC: 3463 Aluminum forgings

(P-6479)
LINDSEY MANUFACTURING CO
Also Called: Lindsey Systems
760 N Georgia Ave (91702-2249)
P.O. Box 877 (91702-0877)
PHONE....................626 969-3471
Keith E Lindsey, *Pr*
Frederick Findley, *
Lela Lindsey, *
▲ **EMP:** 110 **EST:** 1947
SQ FT: 60,000

SALES (est): 36.9MM **Privately Held**
Web: www.lindsey-usa.com
SIC: 3463 3644 Pole line hardware forgings,
　nonferrous; Noncurrent-carrying wiring
　devices

(P-6480)
LUXFER INC
Superform USA
6825 Jurupa Ave (92504-1039)
PHONE....................951 351-4100
Michael Reynolds, *VP*
EMP: 38
SALES (corp-wide): 423.4MM **Privately
Held**
Web: www.luxfercylinders.com
SIC: 3463 Aluminum forgings
HQ: Luxfer Inc.
　3016 Kansas Ave Bldg 1
　Riverside CA
　951 684-5110

(P-6481)
QUALITY ALUMINUM FORGE
LLC
793 N Cypress St (92867-6605)
PHONE....................714 639-8191
EMP: 230 **EST:** 2011
SALES (est): 44.92MM
SALES (corp-wide): 83.9MM **Publicly
Held**
Web: www.sifco.com
SIC: 3463 Aluminum forgings
PA: Sifco Industries, Inc.
　970 E 64th St
　Cleveland OH
　216 881-8600

(P-6482)
SHULTZ STEEL COMPANY
Also Called: S S
5321 Firestone Blvd (90280-3629)
PHONE....................323 357-3200
◆ **EMP:** 490 **EST:** 1956
SALES (est): 74.94MM
SALES (corp-wide): 302.09B **Publicly
Held**
Web: www.shultzsteel.com
SIC: 3463 3462 Aircraft forgings, nonferrous;
　Aircraft forgings, ferrous
HQ: Precision Castparts Corp.
　5885 Meadows Rd Ste 620
　Lake Oswego OR
　503 946-4800

(P-6483)
STS METALS
Also Called: Sierra Alloys Company
5467 Ayon Ave (91706-2044)
PHONE....................626 969-6711
Craig Culaciati, *CEO*
Ed Brennan, *VP*
Jeff Augustyn, *Ex VP*
▲ **EMP:** 52 **EST:** 1974
SQ FT: 75,000
SALES (est): 17.23MM **Privately Held**
Web: www.tsititanium.com
SIC: 3463 3494 3312 Nonferrous forgings;
　Valves and pipe fittings, nec; Blast furnaces
　and steel mills

(P-6484)
WEBER METALS INC (HQ)
16706 Garfield Ave (90723-5307)
PHONE....................562 602-0260
John R Creed, *CEO*
Paul Dennis, *
◆ **EMP:** 39 **EST:** 1962
SQ FT: 270,000
SALES (est): 148.84MM

SALES (corp-wide): 3.58B **Privately Held**
Web: www.webermetals.com
SIC: 3463 Aluminum forgings
PA: Otto Fuchs Beteiligungen Kg
　Derschlager Str. 26
　Meinerzhagen NW
　2354730

(P-6485)
WEBER METALS INC
233 E Manville St (90220-5602)
PHONE....................562 543-3316
EMP: 461
SALES (corp-wide): 3.58B **Privately Held**
Web: www.webermetals.com
SIC: 3463 Aluminum forgings
HQ: Weber Metals, Inc.
　16706 Garfield Ave
　Paramount CA
　562 602-0260

(P-6486)
WJB BEARINGS INC
535 Brea Canyon Rd (91789-3001)
PHONE....................909 598-6238
John Jun Jiang, *CEO*
▲ **EMP:** 25 **EST:** 1992
SQ FT: 30,000
SALES (est): 4.87MM **Privately Held**
Web: www.wjbgroup.us
SIC: 3463 5085 Bearing and bearing race
　forgings, nonferrous; Bearings

3465 Automotive Stampings

(P-6487)
SALEEN AUTOMOTIVE INC (PA)
2735 Wardlow Rd (92882-2869)
PHONE....................800 888-8945
EMP: 21 **EST:** 2011
SALES (est): 13.71MM **Privately Held**
Web: www.saleen.com
SIC: 3465 3711 Body parts, automobile:
　stamped metal; Automobile assembly,
　including specialty automobiles

(P-6488)
T-REX TRUCK PRODUCTS INC
Also Called: T-Rex Grilles
2365 Railroad St (92878-5411)
PHONE....................800 287-5900
Behrouz Mizban, *Pr*
▼ **EMP:** 55 **EST:** 1995
SQ FT: 45,000
SALES (est): 9.89MM **Privately Held**
Web: www.trexbillet.com
SIC: 3465 Automotive stampings

(P-6489)
TROY SHEET METAL WORKS
INC (PA)
Also Called: Troy Products
1024 S Vail Ave (90640-6020)
PHONE....................323 720-4100
Carl Moses Kahalewai, *CEO*
Paul Alvarado, *Stockholder*
Carol Stewart, *Stockholder*
Marci Norkin, *Stockholder*
Rigo Guadiana, *
EMP: 73 **EST:** 1930
SQ FT: 16,000
SALES (est): 9.82MM
SALES (corp-wide): 9.82MM **Privately
Held**
Web: www.troyproducts.com
SIC: 3465 3444 3714 3564 Automotive
　stampings; Sheet metalwork; Motor vehicle
　parts and accessories; Blowers and fans

3469 Metal Stampings, Nec

(P-6490)
A & J MANUFACTURING
COMPANY
70 Icon (92610-3000)
PHONE....................714 544-9570
Barry Lyerly, *CEO*
Janice Lyerly, *
EMP: 32 **EST:** 1954
SQ FT: 40,000
SALES (est): 7.82MM **Privately Held**
Web: www.aj-racks.com
SIC: 3469 Electronic enclosures, stamped or
　pressed metal

(P-6491)
A-W ENGINEERING COMPANY
INC
8528 Dice Rd (90670-2590)
PHONE....................562 945-1041
Guy Hansen, *Pr*
Anthony Giangrande, *
EMP: 36 **EST:** 1965
SQ FT: 38,000
SALES (est): 8.28MM **Privately Held**
Web: www.aw-eng.com
SIC: 3469 3544 Stamping metal for the trade
　; Special dies and tools

(P-6492)
ACRONTOS MANUFACTURING
INC
Also Called: Al Industries
1641 E Saint Gertrude Pl (92705-5311)
PHONE....................714 850-9133
Ngoc V Hoang, *Pr*
EMP: 30 **EST:** 1991
SQ FT: 22,000
SALES (est): 4.64MM **Privately Held**
SIC: 3469 3599 3441 Stamping metal for the
　trade; Machine and other job shop work;
　Fabricated structural metal

(P-6493)
ACTION STAMPING INC
517 S Glendora Ave (91741-6212)
P.O. Box 778 (91740-0778)
PHONE....................626 914-7466
Henry Reynolds, *CEO*
Terry Reynolds, *
▲ **EMP:** 42 **EST:** 1982
SQ FT: 55,000
SALES (est): 4.54MM **Privately Held**
Web: www.actionstamping.com
SIC: 3469 Stamping metal for the trade

(P-6494)
ALL NEW STAMPING CO
10801 Lower Azusa Rd (91731-1307)
P.O. Box 5948 (91734-1948)
PHONE....................626 443-8813
TOLL FREE: 800
Donald Schuil, *Pr*
Robert Larson, *
EMP: 150 **EST:** 1962
SQ FT: 40,000
SALES (est): 13.09MM **Privately Held**
Web: www.allnewstamping.com
SIC: 3469 3441 3444 Stamping metal for the
　trade; Fabricated structural metal; Sheet
　metal specialties, not stamped

(P-6495)
APT METAL FABRICATORS INC
11164 Bradley Ave (91331-2405)
PHONE....................818 896-7478
Dennis M Vigo, *Pr*

Susan Vigo, *
▼ **EMP:** 26 **EST:** 1975
SQ FT: 18,000
SALES (est): 2.75MM **Privately Held**
Web: www.aptmetal.com
SIC: 3469 Stamping metal for the trade

(P-6496)
ASCENT MANUFACTURING LLC
2545 W Via Palma (92801-2624)
PHONE..............................714 540-6414
Travis Mullen, *CEO*
David Kramer, *
EMP: 34 **EST:** 2001
SQ FT: 17,000
SALES (est): 6.55MM **Privately Held**
Web: www.ascentmfg.com
SIC: 3469 1796 Machine parts, stamped or
pressed metal; Machinery installation

(P-6497)
BANDEL MFG INC
4459 Alger St (90039-1292)
PHONE..............................818 246-7493
Ed Finley, *Pr*
Chester Carlson, *
EMP: 23 **EST:** 1947
SQ FT: 15,000
SALES (est): 4.64MM **Privately Held**
Web: www.bandel.com
SIC: 3469 Stamping metal for the trade

(P-6498)
BERRY-PERUSSI INC
Also Called: Associated Engineering
Company
25131 Arctic Ocean Dr (92630-8852)
P.O. Box 7 (92609-0007)
PHONE..............................949 461-7000
Roberto Perussi, *Pr*
Jerry Berry, *
Ruben Perussi, *
EMP: 40 **EST:** 1972
SQ FT: 4,600
SALES (est): 3.54MM **Privately Held**
SIC: 3469 Machine parts, stamped or
pressed metal

(P-6499)
BINDER METAL PRODUCTS INC
14909 S Broadway (90248-1817)
P.O. Box 2306 (90247-0306)
PHONE..............................800 233-0896
Steve Binder, *Pr*
Adam Binder, *
Ana Weber, *
▲ **EMP:** 75 **EST:** 1925
SQ FT: 35,000
SALES (est): 9.8MM **Privately Held**
Web: www.bindermetal.com
SIC: 3469 Stamping metal for the trade

(P-6500)
BLOOMERS METAL STAMPINGS INC
28615 Braxton Ave (91355-4112)
PHONE..............................661 257-2955
Matt Holland, *CEO*
Perry Bloomer, *
Ella H Bloomer, *
EMP: 30 **EST:** 1976
SQ FT: 25,000
SALES (est): 3.93MM **Privately Held**
Web: www.bloomersmetal.com
SIC: 3469 Stamping metal for the trade

(P-6501)
BRAXTON CARIBBEAN MFG CO INC

2641 Walnut Ave (92780-7005)
P.O. Box 425 (92781-0425)
PHONE..............................714 508-3570
Thomas Ordway, *Pr*
Robert Dionne, *
Joesph Triano, *
EMP: 62 **EST:** 1972
SALES (est): 5MM **Privately Held**
Web: www.braxtonmfg.com
SIC: 3469 Stamping metal for the trade

(P-6502)
C WOLFE INDUSTRIES INC
Also Called: Wolfe Industries
14420 Marquardt Ave (90670-5119)
PHONE..............................626 443-7185
EMP: 21 **EST:** 1991
SALES (est): 5.06MM **Privately Held**
Web: www.wolfeindustries.net
SIC: 3469 Metal stampings, nec

(P-6503)
CABRAC INC
13250 Paxton St (91331-2356)
PHONE..............................818 834-0177
Hans Kaufmann, *Pr*
EMP: 20 **EST:** 1973
SQ FT: 20,000
SALES (est): 2.38MM **Privately Held**
Web: www.cabrac.com
SIC: 3469 Electronic enclosures, stamped or
pressed metal

(P-6504)
CAMISASCA AUTOMOTIVE MFG INC (PA)
20352 Hermana Cir (92630-8701)
PHONE..............................949 452-0195
Henry Camisasca, *CEO*
Georgann Camisasca, *Sec*
▲ **EMP:** 20 **EST:** 1982
SQ FT: 16,000
SALES (est): 7.46MM
SALES (corp-wide): 7.46MM **Privately Held**
Web: www.camincusa.com
SIC: 3469 Automobile license tags, stamped
metal

(P-6505)
CAMISASCA AUTOMOTIVE MFG INC
20341 Hermana Cir (92630-8701)
PHONE..............................949 452-0195
Henry Camisasca, *CEO*
EMP: 20
SALES (corp-wide): 7.46MM **Privately Held**
Web: www.camincusa.com
SIC: 3469 Automobile license tags, stamped
metal
PA: Camisasca Automotive Manufacturing,
Inc.
20352 Hermana Cir
Lake Forest CA
949 452-0195

(P-6506)
CARAN PRECISION ENGINEERING & MANUFACTURING CORP (PA)
2830 Orbiter St (92821-6224)
PHONE..............................714 447-5400
▲ **EMP:** 98 **EST:** 1964
SALES (est): 23.83MM
SALES (corp-wide): 23.83MM **Privately Held**
Web: www.caranprecision.com

SIC: 3469 Metal stampings, nec

(P-6507)
CKD INDUSTRIES INC
501 E Jamie Ave (90631-6842)
PHONE..............................714 871-5600
Rolf Hess, *Pr*
Rose Hess, *VP*
EMP: 19 **EST:** 1986
SQ FT: 15,000
SALES (est): 808.98K **Privately Held**
SIC: 3469 8711 3544 Metal stampings, nec;
Designing: ship, boat, machine, and product
; Special dies and tools

(P-6508)
CYGNET STAMPNG & FABRICTNG INC (PA)
613 Justin Ave (91201-2326)
PHONE..............................818 240-7574
Marko Swan, *Pr*
E Michael Swan, *
John Swan, *
EMP: 29 **EST:** 1976
SQ FT: 28,000
SALES (est): 5.02MM
SALES (corp-wide): 5.02MM **Privately Held**
Web: www.cygnetstamping.com
SIC: 3469 Stamping metal for the trade

(P-6509)
DAVID ENGINEERING & MFG INC
Also Called: David Engineering & Mfg
1230 Quarry St (92879-1708)
P.O. Box 77035 (92877-0101)
PHONE..............................951 735-5200
Mike David, *CEO*
Michael David, *
EMP: 30 **EST:** 2003
SALES (est): 4MM **Privately Held**
Web: www.davidengineering.com
SIC: 3469 3544 Stamping metal for the trade
; Special dies and tools

(P-6510)
DAYTON ROGERS OF CALIFORNIA INC
13630 Saticoy St Van Nuys (91402)
PHONE..............................763 784-7714
EMP: 158
SIC: 3469 Stamping metal for the trade

(P-6511)
DECCO GRAPHICS INC
24411 Frampton Ave (90710-2107)
PHONE..............................310 534-2861
Harry B Line, *Pr*
EMP: 19 **EST:** 1979
SQ FT: 5,000
SALES (est): 2.37MM **Privately Held**
Web: www.deccographics.com
SIC: 3469 2759 Stamping metal for the trade
; Commercial printing, nec

(P-6512)
DIVERSIFIED TOOL & DIE
2585 Birch St (92081-8433)
PHONE..............................760 598-9100
Ernst Wilms, *CEO*
Rosa Wilms, *
EMP: 30 **EST:** 1972
SQ FT: 33,000
SALES (est): 4.64MM **Privately Held**
Web: www.stamping.com
SIC: 3469 3544 Stamping metal for the trade
; Special dies and tools

(P-6513)
EAGLEWARE MANUFACTURING CO INC
12683 Corral Pl (90670-4748)
PHONE..............................562 320-3100
Brett L Gross, *Pr*
Eric Gross, *
▲ **EMP:** 32 **EST:** 1963
SQ FT: 130,000
SALES (est): 2.29MM **Privately Held**
SIC: 3469 3421 Stamping metal for the trade
; Cutlery

(P-6514)
ELIXIR INDUSTRIES
24800 Chrisanta Dr Ste 210 (92691-4833)
PHONE..............................949 860-5000
◆ **EMP:** 64
Web: www.elixirind.com
SIC: 3469 Metal stampings, nec

(P-6515)
ENTERPRISES INDUSTRIES INC
7500 Tyrone Ave (91405-1447)
PHONE..............................818 989-6103
Tony Magnome, *Pr*
Rolando Loera, *
Livino D Ribaya Junior, *VP Mfg*
Frank Ramirez Iii, *VP Engg*
Charles E Shaw, *
EMP: 130 **EST:** 1971
SALES (est): 10.17MM **Privately Held**
SIC: 3469 Stamping metal for the trade

(P-6516)
FALLBROOK INDUSTRIES INC
Also Called: Standish Precision Products
323 Industrial Way Ste 1 (92028-2357)
PHONE..............................760 728-7229
Michael Standish, *Pr*
Dennis Standish, *VP*
▲ **EMP:** 31 **EST:** 1973
SQ FT: 15,000
SALES (est): 3.6MM **Privately Held**
Web: www.standishproducts.com
SIC: 3469 Stamping metal for the trade

(P-6517)
FRED R RIPPY INC
12450 Whittier Blvd (90602-1017)
PHONE..............................562 698-9801
▼ **EMP:** 35 **EST:** 1950
SALES (est): 5.18MM **Privately Held**
Web: www.frrippy.com
SIC: 3469 Metal stampings, nec

(P-6518)
FTR ASSOCIATES INC
11862 Burke St (90670-2536)
PHONE..............................562 945-7504
EMP: 32 **EST:** 1986
SALES (est): 4.75MM **Privately Held**
Web: www.ftrmetalproducts.com
SIC: 3469 Metal stampings, nec

(P-6519)
GLOBAL PCCI (GPC) (PA)
Also Called: Gpc
2465 Campus Dr Ste 100 (92612-1502)
PHONE..............................757 637-9000
Sherri Bovino, *Pt*
EMP: 120 **EST:** 1989
SQ FT: 10,000
SALES (est): 17.65MM **Privately Held**
SIC: 3469 4499 Metal stampings, nec;
Salvaging, distressed vessels and cargoes

(PA)=Parent Co (HQ)=Headquarters
✪ = New Business established in last 2 years

(P-6520)
HANMAR LLC (PA)
Also Called: Metalite Manufacturing
11441 Bradley Ave (91331-2304)
PHONE..................................818 890-2802
John Schachtner, *CEO*
Hannes Michael Schachtner, *
EMP: 52 **EST:** 1969
SQ FT: 25,000
SALES (est): 17MM
SALES (corp-wide): 17MM **Privately Held**
Web: www.metalite.net
SIC: 3469 Spinning metal for the trade

(P-6521)
HI TECH HONEYCOMB INC
9355 Ruffin Ct (92123-5304)
PHONE..................................858 974-1600
Joao J Costa, *CEO*
John J Costa, *
Selma Costa, *
John Costa, *
EMP: 136 **EST:** 1989
SQ FT: 20,000
SALES (est): 20.93MM **Privately Held**
Web: www.hitechhoneycomb.com
SIC: 3469 Honeycombed metal

(P-6522)
HOUSTON BAZZ CO
Also Called: Bazz Houston Co
12700 Western Ave (92841-4017)
PHONE..................................714 898-2666
Javier Castro, *Pr*
Chester O Houston, *
▲ **EMP:** 85 **EST:** 1957
SQ FT: 50,000
SALES (est): 23.33MM **Privately Held**
Web: www.bhisolutions.com
SIC: 3469 3495 3493 Machine parts, stamped or pressed metal; Mechanical springs, precision; Steel springs, except wire

(P-6523)
IMPERIAL CAL PRODUCTS INC
425 Apollo St (92821-3110)
PHONE..................................714 990-9100
Shari Bittel, *Pr*
Kathy Flentye, *
▲ **EMP:** 35 **EST:** 1961
SQ FT: 35,000
SALES (est): 3.8MM **Privately Held**
Web: www.imperialhoods.com
SIC: 3469 Kitchen fixtures and equipment: metal, except cast aluminum

(P-6524)
INNOVATIVE STAMPING INC
Also Called: Innovative Systems
2068 E Gladwick St (90220-6202)
P.O. Box 5327 (90224-5327)
PHONE..................................310 537-6996
Gerald L Czaban, *Pr*
Kim Stevenson, *
▼ **EMP:** 32 **EST:** 1976
SQ FT: 128,000
SALES (est): 4.7MM **Privately Held**
Web: www.innovative-sys.com
SIC: 3469 Stamping metal for the trade

(P-6525)
IPT HOLDING INC (PA)
751 S Kellogg Ave (93117-3806)
PHONE..................................805 683-3414
Stephen Braunheim, *Pr*
Ron Williams, *CFO*
EMP: 18 **EST:** 2002
SALES (est): 21.69MM
SALES (corp-wide): 21.69MM **Privately Held**

SIC: 3469 Stamping metal for the trade

(P-6526)
J-MARK MANUFACTURING INC
Also Called: J-Mark Company
2480 Coral St (92081-8430)
PHONE..................................760 727-6956
Mark Baker, *Pr*
Dale Jackson, *VP*
Debbie Baker, *Treas*
Carol Jackson, *Sec*
EMP: 22 **EST:** 1988
SQ FT: 24,000
SALES (est): 4.98MM **Privately Held**
Web: www.j-markmfg.com
SIC: 3469 3599 Electronic enclosures, stamped or pressed metal; Machine shop, jobbing and repair

(P-6527)
KAGA (USA) INC
2620 S Susan St (92704-5816)
PHONE..................................714 540-2697
Masaaki Nozaki, *Pr*
Takashi Nozaki, *
Nobuharu Nozaki, *
Fumio Shiina, *
▲ **EMP:** 30 **EST:** 1981
SQ FT: 38,400
SALES (est): 7.6MM **Privately Held**
Web: www.kagainc.co.jp
SIC: 3469 Stamping metal for the trade
PA: Kaga,Inc.
    140, Ni, Ota, Tsubatamachi
    Kahoku-Gun ISH

(P-6528)
KB DELTA INC
Also Called: KB Delta Comprsr Valve Parts
3340 Fujita St (90505-4017)
PHONE..................................310 530-1539
Boris Giourof, *CEO*
Katarina Giourof, *
◆ **EMP:** 37 **EST:** 1982
SQ FT: 5,500
SALES (est): 6.47MM **Privately Held**
Web: www.kbdelta.com
SIC: 3469 5085 7699 Machine parts, stamped or pressed metal; Industrial supplies; Compressor repair

(P-6529)
KITCHEN EQUIPMENT MFG CO INC
Also Called: Kemco
2102 Maple Privado (91761-7602)
PHONE..................................909 923-3153
David Rodriguez, *Pr*
EMP: 44 **EST:** 1984
SQ FT: 15,000
SALES (est): 4.04MM **Privately Held**
SIC: 3469 3431 Kitchen fixtures and equipment, porcelain enameled; Metal sanitary ware

(P-6530)
KITCOR CORPORATION
9959 Glenoaks Blvd (91352-1085)
PHONE..................................323 875-2820
Kent Kitchen, *Prin*
Kent Kitchen, *Pr*
Alice Kitchen, *
Jim Kitchen, *
Bob Kitchen, *
EMP: 35 **EST:** 1943
SQ FT: 42,000
SALES (est): 4.73MM **Privately Held**
Web: www.kitcor.com
SIC: 3469 Kitchen fixtures and equipment: metal, except cast aluminum

(P-6531)
KOPYKAKE ENTERPRISES INC (PA)
Also Called: Mayer Baking Co
3699 W 240th St (90505-6002)
PHONE..................................310 373-8906
Gerald G Mayer, *Pr*
Greg Mayer, *VP*
Rick Mayer, *VP*
▲ **EMP:** 19 **EST:** 1970
SQ FT: 22,000
SALES (est): 4.7MM
SALES (corp-wide): 4.7MM **Privately Held**
Web: www.kopykake.com
SIC: 3469 2051 Kitchen fixtures and equipment: metal, except cast aluminum; Bakery: wholesale or wholesale/retail combined

(P-6532)
LARRY SPUN PRODUCTS INC
1533 S Downey Rd (90023-4042)
PHONE..................................323 881-6300
Hilario F Hurtado, *CEO*
EMP: 49 **EST:** 1958
SQ FT: 6,000
SALES (est): 4.95MM **Privately Held**
Web: www.larryspunproducts.com
SIC: 3469 Stamping metal for the trade

(P-6533)
LOCK-RIDGE TOOL COMPANY INC
145 N 8th Ave (91786-5402)
PHONE..................................909 865-8309
Keith Clark, *Pr*
Ashford Clark, *
Penney Clark, *
▲ **EMP:** 52 **EST:** 1962
SALES (est): 8.97MM **Privately Held**
Web: www.lockridgetool.com
SIC: 3469 Stamping metal for the trade

(P-6534)
LUPPEN HOLDINGS INC (PA)
Also Called: Metal Products Engineering
3050 Leonis Blvd (90058-2914)
PHONE..................................323 581-8121
TOLL FREE: 800
Luppe R Luppen, *Ch Bd*
Paula Luppen, *
Ray Woodmansee, *
▲ **EMP:** 23 **EST:** 1940
SQ FT: 40,000
SALES (est): 688.31K
SALES (corp-wide): 688.31K **Privately Held**
Web: www.metalproductseng.com
SIC: 3469 3578 3596 Stamping metal for the trade; Change making machines; Scales and balances, except laboratory

(P-6535)
MC WILLIAM & SON INC
Also Called: California Tool & Die
421 S Irwindale Ave (91702-3217)
PHONE..................................626 969-1821
Dan Mcwilliam, *Pr*
Dana Matejka, *Sec*
EMP: 19 **EST:** 1967
SQ FT: 26,000
SALES (est): 2.42MM **Privately Held**
Web: www.californiatool-die.com
SIC: 3469 3544 Stamping metal for the trade; Special dies, tools, jigs, and fixtures

(P-6536)
METALITE MANUFACTURING COMPANY
Also Called: Metalite Mfg Companys
11441 Bradley Ave (91331-2304)
PHONE..................................818 890-2802
Hanness Schachtner, *CEO*
Jan Schacatner, *
EMP: 38 **EST:** 1923
SQ FT: 58,000
SALES (est): 2.42MM
SALES (corp-wide): 17MM **Privately Held**
Web: www.metalite.net
SIC: 3469 Stamping metal for the trade
PA: Hanmar, Llc
    11441 Bradley Ave
    Pacoima CA
    818 890-2802

(P-6537)
METCO MANUFACTURING INC
Also Called: Metco Fourslide Manufacturing
17540 S Denver Ave (90248-3411)
PHONE..................................310 516-6547
Jack Bishop, *Pr*
Darryl Scholl, *
Shirley Bishop, *
Dana Beisel, *
EMP: 29 **EST:** 1980
SQ FT: 11,200
SALES (est): 4.83MM **Privately Held**
Web: www.metcofourslide.com
SIC: 3469 Stamping metal for the trade

(P-6538)
MICRO MATRIX SYSTEMS (PA)
Also Called: M M S
1899 Salem Ct (91711-2638)
PHONE..................................909 626-8544
Grant P Zarbock, *CEO*
Kerry Zarbock, *
▲ **EMP:** 24 **EST:** 1968
SALES (est): 2.49MM
SALES (corp-wide): 2.49MM **Privately Held**
Web: www.mmsys.biz
SIC: 3469 Stamping metal for the trade

(P-6539)
NANOPRECISION PRODUCTS INC
802 Calle Plano (93012-8557)
PHONE..................................310 597-4991
Michael K Barnoski, *CEO*
EMP: 25 **EST:** 2002
SALES (est): 4.37MM **Privately Held**
Web: www.nanoprecision.com
SIC: 3469 3721 Stamping metal for the trade ; Research and development on aircraft by the manufacturer

(P-6540)
NATIONAL METAL STAMPINGS INC
42110 8th St E (93535-5444)
PHONE..................................661 945-1157
William T Bloomer, *Pr*
Madeleine J Bloomer, *
▲ **EMP:** 70 **EST:** 1979
SQ FT: 20,000
SALES (est): 10.61MM **Privately Held**
Web: www.nationalmetal.com
SIC: 3469 Stamping metal for the trade

(P-6541)
NELLXO LLC
5990 Bald Eagle Dr (92336-4573)
PHONE..................................909 320-8501
EMP: 37 **EST:** 2021
SALES (est): 1.36MM **Privately Held**
SIC: 3469 7389 Household cooking and kitchen utensils, metal; Business services, nec

▲ = Import ▼ = Export
◆ = Import/Export

(P-6542)
NEW GORDON INDUSTRIES LLC
Also Called: New Gordon Industries
13750 Rosecrans Ave (90670-5027)
P.O. Box 599 (90633-0599)
PHONE.................................562 483-7378
EMP: 22
SIC: 3469 Stamping metal for the trade

(P-6543)
ORANGE MTAL SPNNING STMPING IN
2601 Orange Ave (92707-3724)
P.O. Box 80070 (92688-0070)
PHONE.................................714 754-0770
Mario Haber, *Pr*
Enrique Haber, *VP*
Elsa Haber, *Sec*
EMP: 17 **EST:** 1984
SQ FT: 10,000
SALES (est): 917.41K **Privately Held**
Web: www.proformancemfg.com
SIC: 3469 Stamping metal for the trade

(P-6544)
P P MFG CO INC
13130 Arctic Cir (90670-5508)
PHONE.................................562 921-3640
Ronald Burr, *Pr*
Glenn Burr, *VP*
EMP: 17 **EST:** 1948
SQ FT: 10,000
SALES (est): 951.44K **Privately Held**
SIC: 3469 3544 Stamping metal for the trade
; Special dies and tools

(P-6545)
PACIFIC METAL STAMPINGS INC
28415 Witherspoon Pkwy (91355-4174)
PHONE.................................661 257-7656
Brian Schlotfelt, *CEO*
Scott Schlotfelt, *
▲ **EMP:** 30 **EST:** 1954
SQ FT: 21,000
SALES (est): 4.67MM **Privately Held**
Web: www.pacificmetalstampings.com
SIC: 3469 Stamping metal for the trade

(P-6546)
PACIFIC PRECISION METALS INC
Also Called: Tubing Seal Cap Co
1100 E Orangethorpe Ave Ste 253 (92801-1164)
P.O. Box 51481 (91761-0081)
PHONE.................................951 226-1500
Ajay N Thakkar, *Pr*
EMP: 130 **EST:** 1987
SQ FT: 2,063
SALES (est): 23.77MM **Privately Held**
SIC: 3469 3429 2599 8711 Stamping metal for the trade; Door locks, bolts, and checks; Cabinets, factory; Machine tool design
PA: Triyar Sv, Llc
10850 Wilshire Blvd
Los Angeles CA

(P-6547)
PRECISION RESOURCE INC
Also Called: Precision Resource Cal Div
5803 Engineer Dr (92649-1127)
PHONE.................................714 891-4439
Robert Fitzgerald, *Prin*
EMP: 104
SQ FT: 27,000
SALES (corp-wide): 125.54MM **Privately Held**
Web: www.precisionresource.com

SIC: 3469 3544 Stamping metal for the trade
; Special dies, tools, jigs, and fixtures
PA: Precision Resource, Inc.
25 Forest Pkwy
Shelton CT
203 925-0012

(P-6548)
PROFESSNAL FNSHG SYSTEMS SUPS
Also Called: Pfs
12341 Gladstone Ave (91342-5319)
PHONE.................................818 365-8888
Vern Coley, *CEO*
Pat Ramnarine, *VP*
EMP: 17 **EST:** 1980
SQ FT: 14,000
SALES (est): 3.15MM **Privately Held**
Web: www.profinishing.com
SIC: 3469 5084 3471 Machine parts, stamped or pressed metal; Machine tools and metalworking machinery; Plating and polishing

(P-6549)
PROFORMANCE MANUFACTURING INC
1922 Elise Cir (92879-1882)
PHONE.................................951 279-1230
Robert Morales, *Pr*
EMP: 20 **EST:** 1987
SQ FT: 21,000
SALES (est): 2.2MM **Privately Held**
Web: www.proformancemfg.com
SIC: 3469 3599 3451 3312 Machine parts, stamped or pressed metal; Machine and other job shop work; Screw machine products; Blast furnaces and steel mills

(P-6550)
PROTOTYPE & SHORT-RUN SVCS INC
Also Called: Pass
1310 W Collins Ave (92867-5415)
PHONE.................................714 449-9661
Jack Mc Devitt, *Pr*
EMP: 25 **EST:** 1989
SQ FT: 6,700
SALES (est): 6.02MM
SALES (corp-wide): 6.02MM **Privately Held**
Web: www.prototype-shortrun.com
SIC: 3469 Stamping metal for the trade
PA: Apl Manufacturing Inc
1310 W Collins Ave
Orange CA
714 542-1942

(P-6551)
QUICK DRAW AND MACHINING INC
4869 Mcgrath St Ste 130 (93003-7767)
PHONE.................................805 644-7882
EMP: 18 **EST:** 1953
SALES (est): 2.11MM **Privately Held**
Web: www.quickdraw.com
SIC: 3469 Metal stampings, nec

(P-6552)
R ZAMORA INC
Also Called: Tecxel
4645 North Ave Ste 102 (92056-3593)
PHONE.................................760 597-1130
Reggie Zamora, *Pr*
EMP: 21 **EST:** 2001
SQ FT: 10,000
SALES (est): 2.72MM **Privately Held**
Web: www.tecxel.com

SIC: 3469 Machine parts, stamped or pressed metal

(P-6553)
RESEARCH TOOL & DIE WORKS LLC
Also Called: RT&d
17124 Keegan Ave (90746-1379)
PHONE.................................310 639-5722
EMP: 66 **EST:** 1952
SALES (est): 10.16MM
SALES (corp-wide): 653.43MM **Privately Held**
Web: www.fairbanksmorsedefense.com
SIC: 3469 Metal stampings, nec
HQ: Fairbanks Morse, Llc
701 White Ave
Beloit WI
800 356-6955

(P-6554)
SERRA MANUFACTURING CORP (PA)
3039 E Las Hermanas St (90221-5575)
PHONE.................................310 537-4560
Sylvia G Hernandez, *Ch Bd*
John B Hernandez, *
Kris Hernandez, *
EMP: 53 **EST:** 1959
SQ FT: 23,916
SALES (est): 8.52MM
SALES (corp-wide): 8.52MM **Privately Held**
Web: www.serramfg.com
SIC: 3469 Stamping metal for the trade

(P-6555)
SESSA MANUFACTURING & WELDING
2932 Golf Course Dr (93003-7689)
PHONE.................................805 644-2284
Michael J Sessa, *CEO*
Lea Sessa, *Stockholder*
EMP: 39 **EST:** 1980
SQ FT: 15,500
SALES (est): 4.39MM **Privately Held**
Web: www.sessamfg.com
SIC: 3469 Stamping metal for the trade

(P-6556)
SOUTHWEST GREENE INTL INC
Also Called: Greene Group Industries
4055b Calle Platino (92056-5805)
PHONE.................................760 639-4960
Alexis Willingham, *Pr*
▲ **EMP:** 100 **EST:** 1997
SQ FT: 80,000
SALES (est): 18.38MM **Privately Held**
Web: www.greenegroup.com
SIC: 3469 Metal stampings, nec

(P-6557)
SPECIALTY INTERNATIONAL INC
11144 Penrose St Ste 11 (91352-5601)
PHONE.................................818 768-8810
Anthony J Magnone, *Pr*
Jack Mcconnell, *VP*
▲ **EMP:** 46 **EST:** 1978
SALES (est): 1.73MM **Privately Held**
Web: www.specialtyinternational.com
SIC: 3469 Metal stampings, nec

(P-6558)
SPRING R&D & STAMP INC
5757 Chino Ave (91710-5226)
P.O. Box 2875 (91708-2875)
PHONE.................................909 465-5166
EMP: 18 **EST:** 1982

SALES (est): 1.88MM **Privately Held**
Web: www.rdspring.com
SIC: 3469 3493 Metal stampings, nec; Steel springs, except wire

(P-6559)
STEICO INDUSTRIES INC
Also Called: Steico
1814 Ord Way (92056-1502)
PHONE.................................760 438-8015
Troy Steiner, *CEO*
▲ **EMP:** 230 **EST:** 2001
SQ FT: 52,000
SALES (est): 51.17MM
SALES (corp-wide): 1.02B **Privately Held**
Web: www.steicoindustries.com
SIC: 3469 5051 Metal stampings, nec; Metals service centers and offices
HQ: Senior Operations Llc
300 E Devon Ave
Bartlett IL
630 372-3500

(P-6560)
SUNSTONE COMPONENTS GROUP INC (HQ)
Also Called: Sun Stone Sales
42136 Avenida Alvarado (92590-3400)
PHONE.................................951 296-5010
Bradway B Adams, *CEO*
David Bernard, *
EMP: 41 **EST:** 1990
SALES (est): 15.24MM
SALES (corp-wide): 27.84MM **Privately Held**
Web: www.4scg.com
SIC: 3469 Metal stampings, nec
PA: Pancon Corporation
350 Revolutionary Dr
East Taunton MA
781 297-6000

(P-6561)
TEAM MANUFACTURING INC
2625 Homestead Pl (90220-5610)
PHONE.................................310 639-0251
Ed Ellis, *CEO*
James Cheatham, *
▲ **EMP:** 50 **EST:** 1975
SQ FT: 34,000
SALES (est): 7.98MM **Privately Held**
Web: www.teammfg.com
SIC: 3469 3544 Stamping metal for the trade
; Die sets for metal stamping (presses)

(P-6562)
THE MACSMITH CORPORATION
1563 W 130th St (90249-2103)
PHONE.................................323 321-8881
EMP: 20 **EST:** 1961
SALES (est): 2.41MM **Privately Held**
Web: www.macsmithcorp.com
SIC: 3469 3544 Metal stampings, nec; Special dies, tools, jigs, and fixtures

(P-6563)
TOP NOTCH MFG INC
1488 Pioneer Way Ste 17 (92020-1633)
PHONE.................................619 588-2033
Peter Vickonoff, *Pr*
Patricia Santore, *VP*
EMP: 18 **EST:** 2002
SQ FT: 6,000
SALES (est): 2MM **Privately Held**
Web: www.topnotchmanufacturing.com
SIC: 3469 3544 Machine parts, stamped or pressed metal; Sheet metalwork

PRODUCTS & SVCS

(P-6564)
TRU-FORM INDUSTRIES INC (PA)
Also Called: Tru Form Industries
14511 Anson Ave (90670-5393)
PHONE.....................562 802-2041
Vernon M Hildebrandt, *CEO*
▲ EMP: 69 EST: 1974
SQ FT: 50,000
SALES (est): 9.75MM
SALES (corp-wide): 9.75MM Privately Held
Web: www.tru-form.com
SIC: 3469 3496 3429 Metal stampings, nec; Clips and fasteners, made from purchased wire; Hardware, nec

(P-6565)
VANGUARD TOOL & MFG CO INC
Also Called: Vanguard Tool & Manufacturing
8388 Utica Ave (91730-3849)
PHONE.....................909 980-9392
Robert A Scudder, *Pr*
Connie Scudder, *
EMP: 49 EST: 1970
SQ FT: 47,000
SALES (est): 8.86MM Privately Held
Web: www.vanguardtoolmfg.net
SIC: 3469 Stamping metal for the trade

(P-6566)
VERDUGO TOOL & ENGRG CO INC
20600 Superior St (91311-4414)
PHONE.....................818 998-1101
Kevin Gresiak, *Pr*
EMP: 19 EST: 1957
SQ FT: 15,000
SALES (est): 2.37MM Privately Held
Web: www.verdugotool.com
SIC: 3469 3544 Stamping metal for the trade ; Special dies and tools

(P-6567)
VORWERK LLC
Also Called: Thermomix
3255 E Thousand Oaks Blvd Ste B (91362-3452)
PHONE.....................888 867-9375
Louis Ross, *Pr*
EMP: 89 EST: 2016
SALES (est): 19.92MM
SALES (corp-wide): 3.29B Privately Held
Web: www.thermomix.com
SIC: 3469 Kitchen fixtures and equipment: metal, except cast aluminum
PA: Vorwerk Se & Co. Kg
Muhlenweg 17-37
Wuppertal NW
2025640

(P-6568)
WALKER CORPORATION
1555 S Vintage Ave (91761-3655)
P.O. Box 2146 (93303-2146)
PHONE.....................909 390-4300
Randall Walker, *VP*
EMP: 48 EST: 2015
SALES (est): 11.99MM Privately Held
Web: www.walkerstamping.com
SIC: 3469 Stamping metal for the trade

(P-6569)
WALKER SPRING & STAMPING CORP
Also Called: Walker
1555 S Vintage Ave (91761-3655)
PHONE.....................909 390-4300

Lang Walker, *Ch Bd*
Bruce Walker, *Pr*
James D Walker Junior, *VP Mfg*
Randy Walker, *VP Sls*
Carmen Prieto, *Sec*
▲ EMP: 110 EST: 1954
SQ FT: 108,000
SALES (est): 19.83MM Privately Held
SIC: 3469 3495 Stamping metal for the trade ; Precision springs

(P-6570)
WEST COAST MANUFACTURING INC
Also Called: West Coast Manufacturing
11822 Western Ave (90680-3438)
PHONE.....................714 897-4221
Patrick Hundley, *Pr*
Minerva Hundley, *
▲ EMP: 26 EST: 1993
SQ FT: 8,000
SALES (est): 5.95MM Privately Held
Web: www.westcoastmfg.com
SIC: 3469 Machine parts, stamped or pressed metal

(P-6571)
WEST COAST METAL STAMPING INCORPORATED
550 W Crowther Ave (92870-6312)
PHONE.....................714 792-0322
EMP: 32 EST: 1966
SALES (est): 5.2MM Privately Held
Web: www.wcmetalstamping.com
SIC: 3469 Stamping metal for the trade

3471 Plating And Polishing

(P-6572)
A & D PLATING INC
2265 Micro Pl Ste A (92029-1011)
PHONE.....................760 480-4580
Antonio Medina, *Pr*
EMP: 18 EST: 1984
SQ FT: 2,400
SALES (est): 914.44K Privately Held
SIC: 3471 Electroplating of metals or formed products

(P-6573)
AAA PLATING & INSPECTION INC
424 E Dixon St (90222-1420)
PHONE.....................323 979-8930
Gerald Wahlin, *CEO*
Charles Schwan, *
EMP: 95 EST: 1958
SQ FT: 50,000
SALES (est): 11.64MM Privately Held
Web: www.aaaplating.com
SIC: 3471 8734 Anodizing (plating) of metals or formed products; Metallurgical testing laboratory

(P-6574)
ACCURATE PLATING COMPANY
2811 Alcazar St (90033-1108)
P.O. Box 33348 (90033-0348)
PHONE.....................323 268-8567
Dennis Orr, *Pr*
Rigo Rodriguez, *
EMP: 30 EST: 1949
SQ FT: 18,000
SALES (est): 2.47MM Privately Held
Web: www.accurateplatingco.com
SIC: 3471 Electroplating of metals or formed products

(P-6575)
ADVANCE-TECH PLATING INC
1061 N Grove St (92806-2015)
PHONE.....................714 630-7093
Meliton Gomez, *Pr*
EMP: 19 EST: 2001
SQ FT: 9,706
SALES (est): 1.35MM Privately Held
SIC: 3471 Electroplating of metals or formed products

(P-6576)
ALCO PLATING CORP (PA)
Also Called: Modern Plating
1400 Long Beach Ave (90021-2794)
PHONE.....................213 749-7561
E Edward Chuck Manzetti, *Pr*
Emil Edward Chuck Manzetti, *Pr*
David Manzetti, *
▲ EMP: 50 EST: 1929
SQ FT: 65,000
SALES (est): 4.72MM
SALES (corp-wide): 4.72MM Privately Held
Web: www.alconickelchrome.com
SIC: 3471 Electroplating of metals or formed products

(P-6577)
ALERT PLATING COMPANY
Also Called: Alert Plating
9939 Glenoaks Blvd (91352-1023)
PHONE.....................818 771-9304
David La Liberte, *Pr*
Maurice La Liberte, *
Shirley La Liberte, *
Ed Lee, *
EMP: 45 EST: 1968
SQ FT: 22,000
SALES (est): 8.44MM Privately Held
SIC: 3471 Finishing, metals or formed products

(P-6578)
ALL METALS PROCESSING OF SAN DIEGO INC
Also Called: AMC
8401 Standustrial St (90680-2619)
PHONE.....................714 828-8238
EMP: 120
Web: www.allmetalsprocessing.com
SIC: 3471 3479 8734 Electroplating of metals or formed products; Enameling, including porcelain, of metal products; X-ray inspection service, industrial

(P-6579)
ALL MTALS PROC ORANGE CNTY LLC
8401 Standustrial St (90680-2619)
PHONE.....................714 828-8238
Scott Christman, *CFO*
Bob Wolfsberger, *
Rose Blikian, *
Michael Coburn, *
Derek Watson, *
EMP: 125 EST: 2015
SALES (est): 19.36MM Privately Held
Web: www.allmetalsprocessing.com
SIC: 3471 3479 8734 Electroplating of metals or formed products; Enameling, including porcelain, of metal products; X-ray inspection service, industrial

(P-6580)
ALLBLACK CO INC
13090 Park St (90670-4032)
PHONE.....................562 946-2955
Juan F Guerrero, *Pr*

Lorena Guerrero, *
▲ EMP: 39 EST: 1992
SQ FT: 12,000
SALES (est): 4.87MM Privately Held
Web: www.allblackco-inc.com
SIC: 3471 Electroplating of metals or formed products

(P-6581)
ALPHA POLISHING CORPORATION (PA)
Also Called: General Plating
1313 Mirasol St (90023-3108)
PHONE.....................323 263-7593
TOLL FREE: 800
Alan Olick, *Pr*
Alan Olick, *Pr*
Trinidad Gonzales, *
EMP: 60 EST: 1940
SQ FT: 7,500
SALES (est): 3.46MM
SALES (corp-wide): 3.46MM Privately Held
Web: www.generalplatingco.net
SIC: 3471 3911 Plating of metals or formed products; Pins (jewelry), precious metal

(P-6582)
ANADITE CAL RESTORATION TR
Also Called: Metal Finishing Division
10647 Garfield Ave (90280-7391)
P.O. Box 1399 (90280-1399)
PHONE.....................562 861-2205
Margie Gutierrez, *Acctnt*
EMP: 127
SALES (corp-wide): 1.26MM Privately Held
SIC: 3471 Finishing, metals or formed products
PA: Anadite California Restoration Trust
711 W Hurst Blvd
Hurst TX
817 282-9171

(P-6583)
ANAPLEX CORPORATION
15547 Garfield Ave (90723-4033)
PHONE.....................714 522-4481
Carmen Campbell, *CEO*
Bernie Kerper, *
EMP: 48 EST: 1962
SQ FT: 38,000
SALES (est): 6.03MM Privately Held
Web: www.anaplexcorp.com
SIC: 3471 Electroplating of metals or formed products

(P-6584)
ANODIZING INDUSTRIES INC
5222 Alhambra Ave (90032-3403)
P.O. Box 32459 (90032-0459)
PHONE.....................323 227-4916
Eugene J Golling, *Pr*
Amir Afshar, *
▲ EMP: 30 EST: 1980
SQ FT: 8,000
SALES (est): 4.33MM Privately Held
Web: www.anodizingindustries.com
SIC: 3471 3479 2396 Anodizing (plating) of metals or formed products; Painting of metal products; Automotive and apparel trimmings

(P-6585)
ANODYNE INC
2230 S Susan St (92704-4419)
PHONE.....................714 549-3321
Ralph Adams, *Pr*
Patti Kientz, *
EMP: 49 EST: 1960

SQ FT: 30,000
SALES (est): 5.63MM **Privately Held**
Web: www.anodyne.aero
SIC: **3471** 8734 Anodizing (plating) of metals or formed products; Testing laboratories

(P-6586)
ARTISTIC PLTG & MET FINSHG INC
2801 E Miraloma Ave (92806-1804)
PHONE.............................619 661-1691
Kipton Kahler, *Pr*
EMP: 50 EST: 1992
SQ FT: 44,573
SALES (est): 988.12K **Privately Held**
SIC: **3471** Chromium plating of metals or formed products

(P-6587)
ASSOCIATED PLATING COMPANY
9636 Ann St (90670-2902)
PHONE.............................562 946-5525
Michael Evans, *Pr*
Jon Shulkin, *Stockholder*
▲ EMP: 46 EST: 1952
SQ FT: 18,000
SALES (est): 1.92MM **Privately Held**
Web: www.associatedplating.com
SIC: **3471** Finishing, metals or formed products

(P-6588)
AUTOMATION PLATING CORPORATION
927 Thompson Ave (91201-2011)
PHONE.............................323 245-4951
Peter K Wiggins, *
Edward Lee, *
Pat Kinzy, *
Marcia Mitchell, *
EMP: 40 EST: 1941
SQ FT: 65,000
SALES (est): 5.06MM **Privately Held**
Web: www.apczinc.com
SIC: **3471** Plating of metals or formed products

(P-6589)
BARRY AVENUE PLATING CO INC
2210 Barry Ave (90064-1402)
PHONE.............................310 478-0078
Chuck Kearsley, *Pr*
Charles B Kearsley Iv, *Pr*
Kenneth F Kearsley, *
▼ EMP: 88 EST: 1951
SQ FT: 26,000
SALES (est): 16.79MM **Privately Held**
Web: www.barryavenueplating.com
SIC: **3471** Electroplating of metals or formed products

(P-6590)
BHC INDUSTRIES INC
239 E Greenleaf Blvd (90220-4913)
PHONE.............................310 632-2000
Gary Barken, *Pr*
EMP: 25 EST: 2000
SQ FT: 20,000
SALES (est): 2.53MM **Privately Held**
Web: www.barkenshardchrome.com
SIC: **3471** Electroplating of metals or formed products

(P-6591)
BLACK OXIDE INDUSTRIES INC
Also Called: Black Oxide
1745 N Orangethorpe Park Ste A (92801-1139)

PHONE.............................714 870-9610
Pete Mata, *Pr*
Edward Mata, *
Evelyn Mata, *
EMP: 35 EST: 1974
SALES (est): 3.74MM **Privately Held**
Web: www.blackoxideindustries.com
SIC: **3471** 3479 Electroplating of metals or formed products; Coating of metals and formed products

(P-6592)
BLAIRS METAL POLSG PLTG CO INC
Also Called: Blair's Metal Polishing
17760 Crusader Ave (90703-2629)
PHONE.............................562 860-7106
Keith W Blair, *CEO*
Keith Blair, *VP*
EMP: 18 EST: 1950
SQ FT: 10,000
SALES (est): 970.78K **Privately Held**
Web: www.blairsmetalpolishing.net
SIC: **3471** Plating of metals or formed products

(P-6593)
BODYCOTE THERMAL PROC INC
3370 Benedict Way (90255-4517)
PHONE.............................323 583-1231
Chris Hall, *Brnch Mgr*
EMP: 87
SQ FT: 16,694
SALES (corp-wide): 895.27MM **Privately Held**
Web: www.bodycote.com
SIC: **3471** 3398 Plating and polishing; Metal heat treating
HQ: Bodycote Thermal Processing, Inc.
12750 Merit Dr Ste 1400
Dallas TX
214 904-2420

(P-6594)
BOWMAN PLATING CO INC
2631 E 126th St (90222-1599)
P.O. Box 5205 (90224-5205)
PHONE.............................310 639-4343
Mac Esfandi, *Pr*
Rashel Esfandi, *
John Esfandi, *Stockholder*
Cyrus Gipoor, *Stockholder*
EMP: 150 EST: 1952
SALES (est): 18.52MM **Privately Held**
Web: www.bowmanplating.com
SIC: **3471** Electroplating of metals or formed products

(P-6595)
BOWMAN-FIELD INC
Also Called: Chrome Nickel Plating
2800 Martin Luther King Jr Blvd (90262-1829)
PHONE.............................310 638-8519
Hector Flores, *Pr*
Ron Storer, *
▲ EMP: 60 EST: 1946
SQ FT: 20,000
SALES (est): 4.03MM **Privately Held**
SIC: **3471** 3714 Chromium plating of metals or formed products; Motor vehicle parts and accessories

(P-6596)
BRITE PLATING CO INC
1313 Mirasol St (90023-3108)
PHONE.............................323 263-7593
Alan Olick, *CEO*
Kashiam Patel, *
EMP: 25 EST: 1950

SQ FT: 60,000
SALES (est): 869.29K **Privately Held**
SIC: **3471** Electroplating of metals or formed products

(P-6597)
BRONZE-WAY PLATING CORPORATION (PA)
3301 E 14th St (90023-3893)
PHONE.............................323 266-6933
Sarkis Mikhael-fard, *Pr*
Benjamin Mikhael-fard, *VP*
Fiyodor Mikhael-fard, *VP*
Fred Mikhael-fard, *VP*
EMP: 44 EST: 1956
SQ FT: 27,000
SALES (est): 4.64MM
SALES (corp-wide): 4.64MM **Privately Held**
SIC: **3471** Electroplating of metals or formed products

(P-6598)
CAL-AURUM INDUSTRIES
Also Called: Cal-Aurum
15632 Container Ln (92649-1533)
PHONE.............................714 898-0996
Paul A Ginder, *Pr*
Chuck Tygard, *
EMP: 35 EST: 1971
SQ FT: 25,000
SALES (est): 5.05MM **Privately Held**
Web: www.cal-aurum.com
SIC: **3471** Electroplating of metals or formed products

(P-6599)
CAL-TRON PLATING INC
11919 Rivera Rd (90670-2209)
PHONE.............................562 945-1181
Carl Troncale Junior, *CEO*
Carl Troncale Senior, *Ch Bd*
EMP: 45 EST: 1961
SQ FT: 15,000
SALES (est): 4.36MM **Privately Held**
Web: www.cal-tronplating.com
SIC: **3471** Electroplating of metals or formed products

(P-6600)
CEMCOAT INC
4928 W Jefferson Blvd (90016-3923)
PHONE.............................323 733-0125
Farzaneh Aalam, *Pr*
Mike Aalam, *VP*
EMP: 23 EST: 1966
SQ FT: 14,500
SALES (est): 544.32K **Privately Held**
Web: www.cemcoat.com
SIC: **3471** Plating of metals or formed products

(P-6601)
CERTIFIED STEEL TREATING CORP
2454 E 58th St (90058-3592)
PHONE.............................323 583-8711
Janice Davis, *Pr*
Pauline Nicolls, *Stockholder*
Jeff Davis, *
EMP: 42 EST: 1947
SQ FT: 30,000
SALES (est): 7.5MM **Privately Held**
SIC: **3471** 3398 Sand blasting of metal parts; Annealing of metal

(P-6602)
CHROMAL PLATING COMPANY
Also Called: Chromal Plating & Grinding

1748 Workman St (90031-3395)
PHONE.............................323 222-0119
Ethel Bokelman, *Pr*
Ray F Bokelman Junior, *VP*
Diane L Remilinger, *
Robin Bokelman, *
Robin Ospoin, *
EMP: 28 EST: 1946
SQ FT: 20,625
SALES (est): 4.22MM **Privately Held**
Web: www.chromal.com
SIC: **3471** 3999 Electroplating of metals or formed products; Grinding and pulverizing of materials, nec

(P-6603)
CHROME TECH INC
2310 Cape Cod Way (92703-3562)
PHONE.............................714 543-4092
EMP: 107
Web: www.chrometechwheels.com
SIC: **3471** Plating and polishing

(P-6604)
COAST PLATING INC (PA)
Also Called: Valence Los Angeles
128 W 154th St (90248-2202)
PHONE.............................323 770-0240
EMP: 50 EST: 1965
SALES (est): 9.44MM
SALES (corp-wide): 9.44MM **Privately Held**
Web: www.coastplating.com
SIC: **3471** Plating of metals or formed products

(P-6605)
COAST TO COAST MET FINSHG CORP
401 S Raymond Ave (91803-1532)
PHONE.............................626 282-2122
Gildardo Bernal, *Pr*
David Bernal, *
EMP: 25 EST: 1978
SQ FT: 20,000
SALES (est): 3.45MM **Privately Held**
Web: www.ctclightingmfg.com
SIC: **3471** 3646 3645 Finishing, metals or formed products; Commercial lighting fixtures; Residential lighting fixtures

(P-6606)
COASTLINE METAL FINISHING CORP
7061 Patterson Dr (92841-1414)
PHONE.............................714 895-9099
Tracy Glende, *CEO*
Jamie Mitchell, *
Matthew Alty, *
EMP: 83 EST: 1987
SQ FT: 18,600
SALES (est): 11.48MM **Privately Held**
Web: www.valencesurfacetech.com
SIC: **3471** Finishing, metals or formed products

(P-6607)
CONNELL PROCESSING INC
3094 N Avon St (91504-2003)
PHONE.............................818 845-7661
Stephen Lee, *Pr*
David Augustine, *
EMP: 27 EST: 1946
SQ FT: 25,000
SALES (est): 2.22MM **Privately Held**
Web: www.connellprocessing.com
SIC: **3471** Electroplating of metals or formed products

PRODUCTS & SVCS

(P-6608)
CONTINUOUS COATING CORP (PA)
Also Called: Clinch-On Cornerbead Company
500 W Grove Ave (92865-3210)
PHONE..............................714 637-4642
Ralph M Scott, *Pr*
Kenneth N Harel, *
EMP: 72 **EST:** 1956
SALES (est): 14.04MM
SALES (corp-wide): 14.04MM **Privately Held**
Web: www.continuouscoating.com
SIC: 3471 3444 7389 Electroplating of metals or formed products; Sheet metal specialties, not stamped; Metal slitting and shearing

(P-6609)
CP AUTO PRODUCTS INC
3901 Medford St (90063-1608)
P.O. Box 63915 (90063-0915)
PHONE..............................323 266-3850
Tom Longo, *Pr*
▲ **EMP:** 28 **EST:** 1955
SQ FT: 100,000
SALES (est): 934.24K **Privately Held**
Web: www.derale.com
SIC: 3471 3714 3564 Plating of metals or formed products; Motor vehicle parts and accessories; Blowers and fans

(P-6610)
DANCO ANODIZING INC (PA)
Also Called: Danco Metal Surfacing
44 La Porte St (91006-2827)
P.O. Box 660727 (91066-0727)
PHONE..............................626 445-3303
Sherri Vivian Scherer, *Pr*
David Tatge, *
EMP: 40 **EST:** 1971
SQ FT: 10,000
SALES (est): 15.68MM
SALES (corp-wide): 15.68MM **Privately Held**
Web: www.danco.net
SIC: 3471 Electroplating of metals or formed products

(P-6611)
DANCO ANODIZING INC
Also Called: Danco
1750 E Monticello Ct (91761-7740)
PHONE..............................909 923-0562
Joe Galvan, *Mgr*
EMP: 102
SALES (corp-wide): 15.68MM **Privately Held**
Web: www.danco.net
SIC: 3471 Anodizing (plating) of metals or formed products
PA: Danco Anodizing, Inc.
44 La Porte St
Arcadia CA
626 445-3303

(P-6612)
DUNHAM METAL PROCESSING INC
Also Called: Tech Plate
936 N Parker St (92867-5580)
P.O. Box 3736 (92857-0736)
PHONE..............................714 532-5551
Charles H Dunham, *Owner*
EMP: 33 **EST:** 1960
SALES (est): 1.09MM **Privately Held**
Web: www.dunhammetalprocessing.com

SIC: 3471 2396 3341 Anodizing (plating) of metals or formed products; Automotive and apparel trimmings; Secondary nonferrous metals

(P-6613)
E M E INC
Also Called: Electro Machine & Engrg Co
500 E Pine St (90222-2818)
P.O. Box 4998 (90224-4998)
PHONE..............................310 639-1621
Wesley Turnbow, *CEO*
Randy Turnbow, *
Steven Turnbow, *
EMP: 125 **EST:** 1962
SQ FT: 65,000
SALES (est): 10.29MM **Privately Held**
Web: www.emeplating.com
SIC: 3471 2899 Anodizing (plating) of metals or formed products; Chemical preparations, nec

(P-6614)
ELECTRODE TECHNOLOGIES INC
Also Called: Reid Metal Finishing
3110 W Harvard St Ste 14 (92704-3940)
PHONE..............................714 549-3771
Tim A Grandcolas, *Pr*
Ivan Padron, *
▲ **EMP:** 40 **EST:** 1978
SQ FT: 10,000
SALES (est): 5.91MM **Privately Held**
Web: www.rmfusa.com
SIC: 3471 Finishing, metals or formed products

(P-6615)
ELECTROLIZING INC
1947 Hooper Ave (90011-1354)
P.O. Box 11900 (90011-0900)
PHONE..............................213 749-7876
Susan B Grant, *Pr*
Jack Morgan, *
EMP: 26 **EST:** 1947
SQ FT: 10,000
SALES (est): 2.45MM **Privately Held**
Web: www.electrolizingofla.com
SIC: 3471 Electroplating of metals or formed products

(P-6616)
ELECTROLURGY INC
1121 Duryea Ave (92614-5519)
PHONE..............................949 250-4494
Eron G Eklund, *Pr*
June Eklund, *
Sean Eklund, *
Stefni Gritten, *
EMP: 68 **EST:** 1969
SQ FT: 25,000
SALES (est): 8.63MM **Privately Held**
Web: www.electrolurgy.com
SIC: 3471 3429 Electroplating of metals or formed products; Marine hardware

(P-6617)
ELECTRON PLATING III INC
Also Called: Electron Plating
13932 Enterprise Dr (92843-4021)
PHONE..............................714 554-2210
Jose Luis Padilla Senior, *Pr*
EMP: 26 **EST:** 1988
SQ FT: 10,000
SALES (est): 2.84MM **Privately Held**
Web: www.electronplating.com
SIC: 3471 Electroplating of metals or formed products

(P-6618)
ELECTRONIC CHROME GRINDING INC
9128 Dice Rd (90670-2545)
PHONE..............................562 946-6671
Philip Reed, *Pr*
Mike Reed, *VP*
Dale Reed, *VP*
Jeannette Goble, *Sec*
EMP: 22 **EST:** 1956
SQ FT: 55,000
SALES (est): 2.26MM **Privately Held**
Web: www.ecgrinding.com
SIC: 3471 3599 Electroplating of metals or formed products; Machine shop, jobbing and repair

(P-6619)
ELECTRONIC PRECISION SPC INC
545 Mercury Ln (92821-4831)
PHONE..............................714 256-8950
Henry Brown, *
EMP: 34 **EST:** 1980
SQ FT: 4,000
SALES (est): 4.68MM **Privately Held**
Web: www.elecprec.com
SIC: 3471 Electroplating of metals or formed products

(P-6620)
ELITE METAL FINISHING LLC (PA)
Also Called: Metal Finishing Pntg Lab Tstg
540 Spectrum Cir (93030-8988)
PHONE..............................805 983-4320
Joel Clemons, *Pt*
Joe Hansen, *
George Hansen, *
EMP: 109 **EST:** 2001
SQ FT: 55,000
SALES (est): 20.1MM
SALES (corp-wide): 20.1MM **Privately Held**
Web: www.elitemetalfinishing.com
SIC: 3471 8734 Plating of metals or formed products; Testing laboratories

(P-6621)
FLARE GROUP
1571 Macarthur Blvd (92626-1407)
PHONE..............................714 549-0202
EMP: 25
SALES (est): 1.04MM **Privately Held**
SIC: 3471 Plating and polishing

(P-6622)
GENES PLATING WORKS INC (PA)
3498 E 14th St (90023-3819)
PHONE..............................323 269-8748
Harry W Levy, *Pr*
John F Whitney, *VP*
EMP: 30 **EST:** 2002
SQ FT: 13,000
SALES (est): 14.97MM
SALES (corp-wide): 14.97MM **Privately Held**
Web: www.lombardtechnologies.com
SIC: 3471 Plating of metals or formed products

(P-6623)
GLOBAL METAL SOLUTIONS INC
2150 Mcgaw Ave (92614-0912)
PHONE..............................949 872-2995
Mario Robles, *Pr*

Mario Robles, *Pr*
Thomas Linovitz, *
EMP: 35 **EST:** 2016
SALES (est): 2.88MM **Privately Held**
Web: www.gms1.net
SIC: 3471 Polishing, metals or formed products

(P-6624)
GRANATH & GRANATH INC
Also Called: Sonic Plating Company
1930 W Rosecrans Ave (90249-2930)
P.O. Box 5387 (90249-5387)
PHONE..............................310 327-5740
Richard E Granath Junior, *Pr*
Richard E Granath Senior, *VP*
Tina Mc Vey, *Sec*
EMP: 19 **EST:** 1964
SQ FT: 40,000
SALES (est): 562.34K **Privately Held**
Web: www.sonicplatingco.com
SIC: 3471 Electroplating of metals or formed products

(P-6625)
GSP METAL FINISHING INC
16520 S Figueroa St (90248-2625)
PHONE..............................818 744-1328
Mike Palatas, *VP*
EMP: 35 **EST:** 2019
SALES (est): 2.66MM **Privately Held**
Web: www.gspmf.com
SIC: 3471 Electroplating of metals or formed products

(P-6626)
HIGHTOWER PLATING & MFG CO
Also Called: Anillo Industries
2090 N Glassell St (92865-3306)
P.O. Box 5586 (92863-5586)
PHONE..............................714 637-9110
Kurt Koch, *Pr*
Mark Koch, *
EMP: 50 **EST:** 1957
SQ FT: 8,000
SALES (est): 5.92MM **Privately Held**
SIC: 3471 Plating of metals or formed products

(P-6627)
HIXSON METAL FINISHING
829 Production Pl (92663-2809)
PHONE..............................800 900-9798
Carl Blazik, *Prin*
Douglas Greene, *
EMP: 116 **EST:** 1960
SQ FT: 38,000
SALES (est): 8.36MM **Privately Held**
Web: www.hmfgroup.com
SIC: 3471 Finishing, metals or formed products

(P-6628)
INDUSTRIAL METAL FINISHING INC
1941 Petra Ln (92870-6749)
PHONE..............................714 628-8808
Robert E Hayden, *Pr*
EMP: 19 **EST:** 1991
SQ FT: 12,000
SALES (est): 2.38MM **Privately Held**
Web: www.indmetfin.com
SIC: 3471 3398 Finishing, metals or formed products; Shot peening (treating steel to reduce fatigue)

(P-6629)
INTERNATIONAL PLATING SVC LLC (PA)
4045 Bonita Rd Ste 309 (91902-1337)
P.O. Box 210310 (91921-0310)
PHONE....................................619 454-2135
Guillermo A Fernandez, *Managing Member*
Jeffrey Robert Adams, *
EMP: 34 **EST:** 1996
SQ FT: 500
SALES (est): 8.51MM
SALES (corp-wide): 8.51MM **Privately Held**
Web: www.platinadorabaja.com
SIC: 3471 Electroplating of metals or formed products

(P-6630)
INTERNTIONAL PHOTO PLATES CORP
Also Called: Nanofilm
2641 Townsgate Rd Ste 100 (91361-2724)
PHONE....................................805 496-5031
Valdis Sneberg, *Pr*
Dorothy Cesari, *
Maria Flores, *
Dale Burow, *
▲ **EMP:** 25 **EST:** 1989
SQ FT: 8,000
SALES (est): 3.65MM **Privately Held**
SIC: 3471 2796 Plating and polishing; Platemaking services

(P-6631)
INVECO INC
Also Called: Mighty Green
440 Fair Dr Ste 200 (92626-6222)
PHONE....................................949 378-3850
Dennis D'alessio, *Pr*
EMP: 30 **EST:** 2013
SALES (est): 18MM **Privately Held**
SIC: 3471 Cleaning, polishing, and finishing

(P-6632)
JCR AIRCRAFT DEBURRING LLC
Also Called: Jcr Deburring
221 Foundation Ave (90631-6812)
PHONE....................................714 870-4427
Juan Carlos Ruiz, *CEO*
Juan Carlos Ruiz, *Managing Member*
Omar Ruiz, *
EMP: 80 **EST:** 1986
SALES (est): 10.46MM **Privately Held**
Web: www.jcrindustries.com
SIC: 3471 3541 3444 3542 Electroplating of metals or formed products; Deburring machines; Forming machine work, sheet metal; Machine tools, metal forming type

(P-6633)
JD PROCESSING INC
2220 Cape Cod Way (92703-3563)
PHONE....................................714 972-8161
Thomas Scimeca, *CEO*
EMP: 50 **EST:** 2014
SALES (est): 4.77MM **Privately Held**
Web: www.jdprocessinginc.com
SIC: 3471 3559 Anodizing (plating) of metals or formed products; Anodizing equipment

(P-6634)
KRYLER CORP
Also Called: Pacific Grinding
1217 E Ash Ave (92831-5019)
PHONE....................................714 871-9611
Chet Krygier Senior, *Pr*
Phyllis Krygier, *
EMP: 30 **EST:** 1977

SQ FT: 900
SALES (est): 2.37MM **Privately Held**
Web: www.krylercorporation.com
SIC: 3471 Electroplating of metals or formed products

(P-6635)
M & R PLATING CORPORATION
12375 Montague St (91331-2214)
PHONE....................................818 896-2700
Andres Rauda, *CEO*
EMP: 17 **EST:** 1976
SQ FT: 11,000
SALES (est): 1.88MM **Privately Held**
Web: www.m-rplatingcorp.com
SIC: 3471 Electroplating of metals or formed products

(P-6636)
M P C INDUSTRIAL PRODUCTS INC
Also Called: M P C Industries
2150 Mcgaw Ave (92614-0912)
PHONE....................................949 863-0106
Paul F Queyrel, *Ch*
John A Spencer, *
▲ **EMP:** 35 **EST:** 1952
SQ FT: 55,000
SALES (est): 787.5K **Privately Held**
Web: www.pmgrinding.net
SIC: 3471 3541 Polishing, metals or formed products; Grinding, polishing, buffing, lapping, and honing machines

(P-6637)
MAIN STEEL LLC
3100 Jefferson St (92504-4339)
PHONE....................................951 231-4949
Mike Folley, *Brnch Mgr*
EMP: 63
SALES (corp-wide): 1.54B **Privately Held**
SIC: 3471 Polishing, metals or formed products
HQ: Main Steel, Llc
2200 Pratt Blvd
Elk Grove Village IL
847 916-1220

(P-6638)
METAL CHEM INC
Also Called: Metal Chem
21514 Nordhoff St (91311-5822)
PHONE....................................818 727-9951
Carlos Pongo, *Pr*
EMP: 30 **EST:** 1997
SALES (est): 2.84MM **Privately Held**
Web: www.metalcheminc.com
SIC: 3471 3443 Plating of metals or formed products; Fabricated plate work (boiler shop)

(P-6639)
METAL SURFACES INTL LLC
6060 Shull St (90201-6297)
P.O. Box 5001 (90202-5001)
PHONE....................................562 927-1331
Olaf Schubert, *Pr*
Charles K Bell, *
Sam Bell, *
EMP: 150 **EST:** 1954
SQ FT: 85,000
SALES (est): 18.65MM **Privately Held**
Web: www.metalsurfaces.com
SIC: 3471 Electroplating of metals or formed products

(P-6640)
MORRELLS ELECTRO PLATING INC

Also Called: Morrell's Metal Finishing
432 E Euclid Ave (90222-2810)
P.O. Box 3085 (90223-3085)
PHONE....................................310 639-1024
Cyrus Gipoor, *Pr*
EMP: 30 **EST:** 1948
SQ FT: 20,000
SALES (est): 4.6MM **Privately Held**
Web: www.morrellsplating.com
SIC: 3471 Electroplating of metals or formed products

(P-6641)
MULTICHROME COMPANY INC (PA)
Also Called: Microplate
1013 W Hillcrest Blvd (90301-2019)
PHONE....................................310 216-1086
Steven A Peterman, *Pr*
EMP: 26 **EST:** 1962
SQ FT: 5,000
SALES (est): 2.46MM
SALES (corp-wide): 2.46MM **Privately Held**
Web: www.multiplate.com
SIC: 3471 Electroplating of metals or formed products

(P-6642)
NASMYTH TMF INC
29102 Hancock Pkwy (91355-1066)
PHONE....................................818 954-9504
Peter Smith, *CEO*
EMP: 54 **EST:** 2014
SQ FT: 10,000
SALES (est): 9.63MM
SALES (corp-wide): 244.12K **Privately Held**
Web: www.technicalmetalfinishing.com
SIC: 3471 3479 Anodizing (plating) of metals or formed products; Coating of metals and formed products
HQ: Ngl Realisations Limited
Nasmyth House
Coventry W MIDLANDS

(P-6643)
NEUTRON PLATING INC
2993 E Blue Star St (92806-2511)
PHONE....................................714 632-9241
Manuel Zavala, *Pr*
Manuel Zavala Junior, *VP*
Sylvia Cassillas, *
Glafira Zavala, *
EMP: 17 **EST:** 1983
SQ FT: 16,000
SALES (est): 468.31K **Privately Held**
SIC: 3471 Electroplating of metals or formed products

(P-6644)
OLD SPC INC
202 W 140th St (90061-1006)
PHONE....................................310 533-0748
Mary Mcmeans, *CEO*
Donna Martinez, *VP*
Jesus Diaz, *Sec*
EMP: 25 **EST:** 1999
SQ FT: 60,000
SALES (est): 5.33MM **Privately Held**
Web: www.spectrumplating.com
SIC: 3471 Electroplating of metals or formed products

(P-6645)
OMNI METAL FINISHING INC (PA)
11665 Coley River Cir (92708-4279)
PHONE....................................714 979-9414
Victor M Salazar, *Pr*

Ramiro Salazar, *
Filiberto Hernandez, *
EMP: 99 **EST:** 1980
SQ FT: 34,000
SALES (est): 15.79MM
SALES (corp-wide): 15.79MM **Privately Held**
Web: www.omnimetal.com
SIC: 3471 Electroplating of metals or formed products

(P-6646)
OPTI-FORMS INC
42310 Winchester Rd (92590-4810)
PHONE....................................951 296-1300
Kevin Thompson, *Pr*
Robert Brunson, *
Clint Tinker, *
EMP: 45 **EST:** 1984
SQ FT: 61,000
SALES (est): 10.3MM **Privately Held**
Web: www.optiforms.com
SIC: 3471 3827 Plating of metals or formed products; Optical instruments and lenses

(P-6647)
PENTRATE METAL PROCESSING
3517 E Olympic Blvd (90023-3976)
PHONE....................................323 269-2121
John J Grana, *Pr*
Vincent Grana, *
Nick Grana, *
Nick Gran, *Genl Mgr*
EMP: 30 **EST:** 1945
SQ FT: 18,000
SALES (est): 3.03MM **Privately Held**
Web: www.pentrate.com
SIC: 3471 Electroplating of metals or formed products

(P-6648)
PLASMA RGGEDIZED SOLUTIONS INC
5452 Business Dr (92649-1226)
PHONE....................................714 893-6063
Bob Marla, *Brnch Mgr*
EMP: 27
Web: www.plasmarugged.com
SIC: 3471 3479 Electroplating and plating; Coating of metals and formed products
PA: Plasma Ruggedized Solutions, Inc.
2284 Ringwood Ave Ste A
San Jose CA

(P-6649)
PLATERONICS PROCESSING INC
Also Called: Plateronics Processing
9164 Independence Ave (91311-5902)
PHONE....................................818 341-2191
Joseph Roter, *Pr*
Marvin Roter, *
Lee F Roter, *
EMP: 35 **EST:** 1959
SQ FT: 6,500
SALES (est): 2.48MM **Privately Held**
Web: www.plateronics.com
SIC: 3471 5051 Finishing, metals or formed products; Metals service centers and offices

(P-6650)
PRECISION ANODIZING & PLTG INC
Also Called: P A P
1601 N Miller St (92806-1469)
PHONE....................................714 996-1601
Jose A Salazar, *CEO*
EMP: 89 **EST:** 1971
SQ FT: 44,000

PRODUCTS & SVCS

SALES (est): 9.06MM **Privately Held**
Web:
www.precisionanodizingandplating.com
SIC: **3471** Electroplating of metals or formed
products

(P-6651)
PRIDE METAL POLISHING LLC
10822 Saint Louis Dr (91731-2030)
PHONE..................626 350-1326
Rod Lowell, *Pr*
EMP: 19 **EST:** 1984
SQ FT: 15,000
SALES (est): 848.04K **Privately Held**
Web: www.pridepolishing.com
SIC: **3471** Polishing, metals or formed
products

(P-6652)
QUAKER CITY PLATING
Also Called: Quaker City Plating & Silvrsm
11729 Washington Blvd (90606-2498)
P.O. Box 2406 (90610-2406)
PHONE..................562 945-3721
Michael Crain, *Mng Pt*
Angelo Dirado, *Mng Pt*
▲ **EMP:** 220 **EST:** 1937
SQ FT: 48,000
SALES (est): 23.36MM **Privately Held**
Web: www.qcpent.com
SIC: **3471** Plating of metals or formed
products

(P-6653)
QUALITY CONTROL PLATING
INC
4425 E Airport Dr Ste 113 (91761-7815)
PHONE..................909 605-0206
Jay J Singh, *VP*
Mona Singh, *Pr*
EMP: 22 **EST:** 1991
SQ FT: 3,500
SALES (est): 1.51MM **Privately Held**
SIC: **3471** Plating of metals or formed
products

(P-6654)
RAVLICH ENTERPRISES LLC
(PA)
Also Called: Neutronic Stamping & Plating
100 Business Center Dr (92878-3224)
PHONE..................714 964-8900
Anthony Ravlich, *CEO*
Nicholas Ravlich, *CFO*
EMP: 27 **EST:** 2003
SQ FT: 27,000
SALES (est): 10MM
SALES (corp-wide): 10MM **Privately Held**
Web: www.neutronicstamping.com
SIC: **3471** 3469 Electroplating of metals or
formed products; Metal stampings, nec

(P-6655)
RAVLICH ENTERPRISES LLC
Also Called: Spectrum Plating Company
202 W 140th St (90061-1006)
PHONE..................310 533-0748
Anthony Ravlich, *Brnch Mgr*
EMP: 41
SALES (corp-wide): 10MM **Privately Held**
Web: www.neutronicstamping.com
SIC: **3471** Plating and polishing
PA: Ravlich Enterprises, Llc
100 Business Center Dr
Corona CA
714 964-8900

(P-6656)
REAL PLATING INC
1245 W 2nd St (91766-1310)
PHONE..................909 623-2304
Juan Real, *CEO*
EMP: 25 **EST:** 2007
SQ FT: 5,264
SALES (est): 2.05MM **Privately Held**
Web: www.realplating.com
SIC: **3471** Electroplating of metals or formed
products

(P-6657)
ROSE MANUFACTURING
GROUP INC
Also Called: Elite Metal Finishing
2525 Jason Ct Ste 102 (92056-3000)
PHONE..................760 407-0232
Dan Rose, *Pr*
EMP: 26 **EST:** 2000
SQ FT: 3,300
SALES (est): 2.3MM **Privately Held**
Web: www.elite-metalfinishing.com
SIC: **3471** Plating of metals or formed
products

(P-6658)
SAFE PLATING INC
18001 Railroad St (91748-1215)
PHONE..................626 810-1872
Magdy Seif, *Pr*
Mario Gomez, *
EMP: 58 **EST:** 1979
SQ FT: 35,000
SALES (est): 9.53MM **Privately Held**
Web: www.safeplatinginc.com
SIC: **3471** Electroplating of metals or formed
products

(P-6659)
SANTA ANA PLATING (PA)
1726 E Rosslynn Ave (92831-5111)
PHONE..................310 923-8305
Tony Kakuk, *Pr*
EMP: 55 **EST:** 1954
SQ FT: 17,100
SALES (est): 6.29MM
SALES (corp-wide): 6.29MM **Privately Held**
SIC: **3471** Finishing, metals or formed
products

(P-6660)
SANTOSHI CORPORATION
Also Called: Entrance Tech
2439 Seaman Ave (91733-1936)
PHONE..................626 444-7118
Hershad Shah, *Pr*
Raksha Shah, *
EMP: 33 **EST:** 1971
SQ FT: 15,000
SALES (est): 4.63MM **Privately Held**
Web: www.alumacoat.com
SIC: **3471** Coloring and finishing of
aluminum or formed products

(P-6661)
SCHMIDT INDUSTRIES INC
Also Called: Prime Plating
11321 Goss St (91352-3206)
P.O. Box 1843 (91353-1843)
PHONE..................818 768-9100
Fred Schmidt, *Pr*
Jennifer Schmidt, *
EMP: 90 **EST:** 1986
SQ FT: 30,000
SALES (est): 10.57MM **Privately Held**
Web: www.prime-plating.com

SIC: **3471** Electroplating of metals or formed
products

(P-6662)
SHEFFIELD PLATERS INC
9850 Waples St (92121-2921)
PHONE..................858 546-8484
Dale Watkins Junior, *Pr*
Mark Watkins, *
Shelley Watkins, *Stockholder*
EMP: 85 **EST:** 1946
SQ FT: 20,000
SALES (est): 9.4MM **Privately Held**
Web: www.sheffieldplaters.com
SIC: **3471** Plating of metals or formed
products

(P-6663)
SHEILA STREET PROPERTIES
INC (PA)
5900 Sheila St (90040-2403)
P.O. Box 911458 (90091-1238)
PHONE..................323 838-9208
EMP: 51 **EST:** 1931
SALES (est): 9.63MM
SALES (corp-wide): 9.63MM **Privately
Held**
Web: www.valleyplating.com
SIC: **3471** Plating of metals or formed
products

(P-6664)
SOUTHERN CALIFORNIA
PLATING CO
3261 National Ave (92113-2636)
PHONE..................619 231-1481
Paul Hummell Junior, *Pr*
EMP: 30 **EST:** 1946
SQ FT: 13,000
SALES (est): 1.5MM **Privately Held**
Web: www.socalplating.com
SIC: **3471** Electroplating of metals or formed
products

(P-6665)
STABILE PLATING COMPANY
INC
1150 E Edna Pl (91724-2592)
PHONE..................626 339-9091
David Crest, *Pr*
Eric Crest, *VP*
Steven Crest, *VP*
EMP: 22 **EST:** 1959
SQ FT: 6,000
SALES (est): 2.3MM **Privately Held**
Web: www.stabileplating.com
SIC: **3471** 3444 3353 Plating of metals or
formed products; Sheet metalwork;
Aluminum sheet, plate, and foil

(P-6666)
STAINLESS MICRO-POLISH INC
Also Called: Micro-Polish
1286 N Grove St (92806-2113)
PHONE..................714 632-8903
Robert Maculsay, *Pr*
Elizabeth Maculsay, *Treas*
EMP: 17 **EST:** 1979
SQ FT: 10,000
SALES (est): 811.27K **Privately Held**
Web: www.stainlessmicropolish.com
SIC: **3471** Polishing, metals or formed
products

(P-6667)
STANDARD METAL PRODUCTS
INC
1541 W 132nd St (90249-2107)
P.O. Box 7636 (90504-9036)

PHONE..................310 532-9861
Danny Corrales Junior, *CEO*
Dan Corrales Senior, *Sec*
EMP: 24 **EST:** 1972
SQ FT: 24,000
SALES (est): 973.01K **Privately Held**
Web: www.sheet-metal.com
SIC: **3471** 3444 Cleaning, polishing, and
finishing; Sheet metalwork

(P-6668)
STUART-DEAN CO INC
14731 Franklin Ave Ste L (92780-7221)
PHONE..................714 544-4460
EMP: 22
SALES (corp-wide): 65.45MM **Privately
Held**
Web: www.stuartdean.com
SIC: **3471** Polishing, metals or formed
products
PA: Stuart-Dean Co. Inc.
4350 10th St
Long Island City NY
800 322-3180

(P-6669)
SUPERIOR CONNECTOR
PLATING INC
Also Called: Superior Plating
1901 E Cerritos Ave (92805-6427)
PHONE..................714 774-1174
Juan Martin, *Pr*
EMP: 22 **EST:** 1994
SQ FT: 7,500
SALES (est): 2.46MM **Privately Held**
Web: www.superiorplatingca.com
SIC: **3471** Electroplating of metals or formed
products

(P-6670)
SYMCOAT METAL PROCESSING
INC
7887 Dunbrook Rd Ste C (92126-4382)
PHONE..................858 451-3313
Sylvia Twiggs, *Pr*
Michelle Kanganis, *VP*
EMP: 24 **EST:** 1994
SQ FT: 12,000
SALES (est): 967.55K **Privately Held**
SIC: **3471** 3341 Finishing, metals or formed
products; Secondary nonferrous metals

(P-6671)
TECHNIC INC
1170 N Hawk Cir (92807-1789)
PHONE..................714 632-0200
Mike Chicos, *Mgr*
EMP: 30
SALES (corp-wide): 159.53MM **Privately
Held**
Web: www.technic.com
SIC: **3471** 2899 3678 3672 Plating of metals
or formed products; Plating compounds;
Electronic connectors; Printed circuit boards
PA: Technic, Inc.
47 Molter St
Cranston RI
401 781-6100

(P-6672)
TEMECULA QUALITY PLATING
INC
42147 Roick Dr (92590-3695)
PHONE..................951 296-9875
Duc Vo, *Pr*
Dat Vo, *
EMP: 32 **EST:** 2011
SALES (est): 1.82MM **Privately Held**
Web: www.temeculaplating.com

SIC: 3471 Electroplating of metals or formed products

(P-6673)
TRIDENT PLATING INC
10046 Romandel Ave (90670-3424)
PHONE....................562 906-2556
Maty Rodriguez, *Pr*
Juan Carlos Rodriguez, *
Ian Holmber, *
EMP: 28 EST: 1981
SQ FT: 18,197
SALES (est): 2.46MM **Privately Held**
Web: www.tridentplating.com
SIC: 3471 Electroplating of metals or formed products

(P-6674)
TRIUMPH PROC - EMBEE DIV INC
2158 S Hathaway St (92705-5249)
PHONE....................714 546-9842
EMP: 400
SALES (est): 10.75MM **Privately Held**
SIC: 3471 Electroplating and plating

(P-6675)
TRIUMPH PROCESSING INC
Also Called: Valence Lynwood
2605 Industry Way (90262-4007)
PHONE....................323 563-1338
Peter Labarbera, *CEO*
Richard C III, *
EMP: 103 EST: 1968
SQ FT: 140,000
SALES (est): 20.15MM
SALES (corp-wide): 138.9MM **Privately Held**
Web: www.valencesurfacetech.com
SIC: 3471 3398 3356 Anodizing (plating) of metals or formed products; Metal heat treating; Nonferrous rolling and drawing, nec
PA: Valence Surface Technologies Llc
300 Continental Blvd # 600
El Segundo CA
888 540-0878

(P-6676)
ULTRAMET
12173 Montague St (91331-2210)
PHONE....................818 899-0236
Andrew Duffy, *CEO*
Walter Abrams, *
Richard B Kaplan, *Stockholder*
James Kaplan, *Stockholder*
▲ EMP: 79 EST: 1970
SQ FT: 43,000
SALES (est): 16.07MM **Privately Held**
Web: www.ultrametcpt.com
SIC: 3471 8731 Electroplating and plating; Commercial physical research

(P-6677)
V & M COMPANY
14024 Avalon Blvd (90061-2636)
PHONE....................310 532-5633
Anthony Babiak, *Pr*
Timothy Babiak, *VP*
▲ EMP: 19 EST: 1948
SQ FT: 7,500
SALES (est): 1.29MM **Privately Held**
Web: www.vmplating.com
SIC: 3471 Electroplating of metals or formed products

(P-6678)
VALEX CORP (HQ)
6080 Leland St (93003-7605)
PHONE....................805 658-0944
▲ EMP: 83 EST: 1976
SALES (est): 24.07MM
SALES (corp-wide): 17.02B **Publicly Held**
SIC: 3471 3317 3494 Polishing, metals or formed products; Steel pipe and tubes; Valves and pipe fittings, nec
PA: Reliance Steel & Aluminum Co.
16100 N 71st St Ste 400
Scottsdale AZ
480 564-5700

(P-6679)
WE FIVE-R CORPORATION
Also Called: Bank C Plating Co
1507 S Sunol Dr (90023-4031)
PHONE....................323 263-6757
Dick Patel, *Pr*
◆ EMP: 17 EST: 1950
SQ FT: 8,000
SALES (est): 526.07K **Privately Held**
SIC: 3471 Electroplating of metals or formed products

(P-6680)
WEST COAST PVD INC
3280 Corporate Vw (92081-8528)
PHONE....................714 822-6362
Brian T Nevill, *CEO*
EMP: 21 EST: 2006
SALES (est): 1.41MM **Privately Held**
Web: www.westcoastpvd.com
SIC: 3471 Plating and polishing

3479 Metal Coating And Allied Services

(P-6681)
A-1 ENGRAVING CO INC
1230 N Jefferson St (92807-1631)
PHONE....................562 861-2216
Jack E Young, *Pr*
Grace Young, *Sec*
Don Schram, *VP*
EMP: 29 EST: 1966
SALES (est): 734.47K **Privately Held**
Web: www.a-1engraving.com
SIC: 3479 Engraving jewelry, silverware, or metal

(P-6682)
ABACUS POWDER COATING
1829 Tyler Ave (91733-3617)
PHONE....................626 443-7556
Esther Davidoff, *Pr*
EMP: 25 EST: 2006
SALES (est): 2.44MM **Privately Held**
Web: www.abacuspowder.com
SIC: 3479 Coating of metals and formed products

(P-6683)
ACTION POWDER COATING LLC
7949 Stromesa Ct Ste D (92126-6338)
PHONE....................858 566-2288
Chuck Dewent, *Managing Member*
EMP: 18 EST: 1993
SQ FT: 20,000
SALES (est): 1.37MM **Privately Held**
Web: www.actionpowdercoating.com
SIC: 3479 Coating of metals and formed products

(P-6684)
ADFA INCORPORATED
Also Called: A&A Jewelry Supply
319 W 6th St (90014-1703)
PHONE....................213 627-8004
Robert Adem, *Pr*
Naim Farah, *

▲ EMP: 45 EST: 1986
SALES (est): 4.4MM **Privately Held**
Web: www.aajewelry.com
SIC: 3479 3548 3172 Engraving jewelry, silverware, or metal; Electric welding equipment; Cases, jewelry

(P-6685)
AERO POWDER COATING INC
710 Monterey Pass Rd (91754-3607)
PHONE....................323 264-6405
Phillip Kontos, *Pr*
EMP: 28 EST: 1977
SQ FT: 27,000
SALES (est): 897.2K **Privately Held**
SIC: 3479 Coating of metals and formed products

(P-6686)
ALL SOURCE COATINGS INC
10625 Scripps Ranch Blvd Ste D (92131-1012)
PHONE....................858 586-0903
Jerry Zumbro, *Pr*
EMP: 21 EST: 2008
SQ FT: 2,000
SALES (est): 2.29MM **Privately Held**
Web: www.allsourceco.com
SIC: 3479 1721 Aluminum coating of metal products; Painting and paper hanging

(P-6687)
ALPHACOAT FINISHING LLC
9350 Cabot Dr (92126-4311)
PHONE....................949 748-7796
Vaishali Joshi, *
EMP: 28 EST: 2017
SALES (est): 2.67MM **Privately Held**
Web: www.alphacoatfinishing.com
SIC: 3479 Coating of metals and formed products

(P-6688)
AMADA AMERICA INC
100 S Puente St (92821-3813)
PHONE....................714 739-2111
EMP: 64
Web: www.amada.com
SIC: 3479 Aluminum coating of metal products
HQ: Amada America, Inc.
7025 Firestone Blvd
Buena Park CA
714 739-2111

(P-6689)
AMERICAN ETCHING & MFG
13730 Desmond St (91331-2706)
PHONE....................323 875-3910
Gary Kipka, *Pr*
EMP: 45 EST: 1972
SQ FT: 20,000
SALES (est): 4.21MM **Privately Held**
Web: www.aemetch.com
SIC: 3479 Etching on metals

(P-6690)
APPLIED COATINGS & LININGS
3224 Rosemead Blvd (91731-2807)
PHONE....................626 280-6354
EMP: 24
SQ FT: 150,000
SALES (est): 2.7MM **Privately Held**
Web: www.appliedcoatings.com
SIC: 3479 3471 Coating of metals and formed products; Plating and polishing

(P-6691)
APPLIED POWDERCOAT INC
3101 Camino Del Sol (93030-8999)
PHONE....................805 981-1991
Victor Anselmo, *Pr*
J Michael Hagan, *
Deborah Anselmo, *
EMP: 45 EST: 1989
SQ FT: 30,000
SALES (est): 4.86MM **Privately Held**
Web: www.appliedpowder.com
SIC: 3479 Coating of metals and formed products

(P-6692)
ARNACO INDUSTRIAL COATINGS
8445 Warvale St (90660-4316)
PHONE....................562 222-1022
Edawrd Gomez, *Pr*
Jose Vasquez, *Prin*
EMP: 20 EST: 2016
SALES (est): 2.26MM **Privately Held**
Web: www.aicindustrialcoatings.com
SIC: 3479 Coating of metals and formed products

(P-6693)
ASTRO CHROME AND POLSG CORP
8136 Lankershim Blvd (91605-1611)
PHONE....................818 781-1463
Jesse Gonzalez, *Pr*
EMP: 23 EST: 1981
SQ FT: 3,000
SALES (est): 1.34MM **Privately Held**
Web: www.astropowdercoating.com
SIC: 3479 Coating of metals and formed products

(P-6694)
ATLAS GALVANIZING LLC
2639 Leonis Blvd (90058-2203)
PHONE....................323 587-6247
Patricia New, *
EMP: 36 EST: 1936
SQ FT: 20,000
SALES (est): 2.53MM **Privately Held**
Web: www.atlasgalv.com
SIC: 3479 Coating of metals and formed products

(P-6695)
BJS&T ENTERPRISES INC
Also Called: San Diego Powder Coating
1702 N Magnolia Ave (92020-1287)
PHONE....................619 448-7795
Philip Johnson, *Pr*
Bob Johnson, *
Stephen Johnson, *
EMP: 50 EST: 2001
SQ FT: 7,000
SALES (est): 9.93MM **Privately Held**
Web: www.sandiegopowdercoating.com
SIC: 3479 Coating of metals and formed products

(P-6696)
CALWEST GALVANIZING CORP
Also Called: Calwest Galvanizing
2226 E Dominguez St (90810-1086)
PHONE....................310 549-2200
TOLL FREE: 888
Isaac Malbonado, *Genl Mgr*
▲ EMP: 35 EST: 1984
SQ FT: 20,000
SALES (est): 8.41MM
SALES (corp-wide): 4.35B **Publicly Held**
Web: www.valmontcoatings.com

P R O D U C T S & S V C S

SIC: **3479** 3317 Galvanizing of iron, steel, or end-formed products; Steel pipe and tubes
PA: Valmont Industries, Inc.
15000 Valmont Plz
Omaha NE
402 963-1000

(P-6697)
CERTIFIED ENAMELING INC (PA)
3342 Emery St (90023-3810)
PHONE..............................323 264-4403
Vicki Ziegel, *CEO*
Glenn Ziegel, *
EMP: 91 **EST:** 1953
SQ FT: 50,000
SALES (est): 9.55MM
SALES (corp-wide): 9.55MM **Privately Held**
Web: www.certifiedenameling.com
SIC: 3479 Coating of metals and formed products

(P-6698)
CREST COATING INC
1361 S Allec St (92805-6304)
PHONE..............................714 635-7090
TOLL FREE: 800
Michael D Erickson, *CEO*
Bonnie George, *
▲ **EMP:** 60 **EST:** 1968
SQ FT: 55,000
SALES (est): 9.3MM **Privately Held**
Web: www.crestcoating.com
SIC: 3479 Coating of metals and formed products

(P-6699)
DENMAC INDUSTRIES INC
7616 Rosecrans Ave (90723-2508)
P.O. Box 2144 (90723-8144)
PHONE..............................562 634-2714
Mark Plechot, *Pr*
Maurice Plechot, *
James Campagna, *
▲ **EMP:** 40 **EST:** 1974
SQ FT: 20,000
SALES (est): 5.76MM **Privately Held**
Web: www.denmac-ind.com
SIC: 3479 Coating of metals and formed products

(P-6700)
DURA COAT PRODUCTS INC (PA)
5361 Via Ricardo (92509-2414)
PHONE..............................951 341-6500
Myung K Hong, *CEO*
Lorrie Y Hong, *Sec*
Suzanne Faust, *CFO*
◆ **EMP:** 64 **EST:** 1986
SQ FT: 29,000
SALES (est): 45.96MM
SALES (corp-wide): 45.96MM **Privately Held**
Web: www.duracoatproducts.com
SIC: 3479 2851 Aluminum coating of metal products; Paints and allied products

(P-6701)
ELECTRO TECH COATINGS INC
Also Called: Electro Tech Powder Coating
836 Rancheros Dr Ste A (92069-7035)
PHONE..............................760 746-0292
EMP: 20 **EST:** 1994
SQ FT: 13,000
SALES (est): 3.36MM **Privately Held**
Web: www.electrotechcoatings.com

(P-6702)
ELYTE INC
Also Called: Quality Powder Coating
4516 District Blvd (93313-2314)
PHONE..............................661 832-1000
Marco Amavizca, *Pr*
Marco Amavizca, *Prin*
EMP: 18 **EST:** 2006
SALES (est): 1.97MM **Privately Held**
SIC: 3479 Coating of metals and formed products

(P-6703)
ETS EXPRESS LLC (DH)
Also Called: Ets Express
420 Lombard St (93030-5100)
PHONE..............................805 278-7771
Sharon Eyal, *Pr*
Taly Eyal, *CFO*
▲ **EMP:** 28 **EST:** 1998
SQ FT: 40,000
SALES (est): 24.8MM **Privately Held**
Web: www.etsexpress.com
SIC: 3479 3231 Etching and engraving; Cut and engraved glassware: made from purchased glass
HQ: Leedsworld, Inc.
400 Hunt Valley Rd
New Kensington PA
724 334-9000

(P-6704)
FLAME-SPRAY INC
4674 Alvarado Canyon Rd (92120-4304)
PHONE..............................619 283-2007
Larry Suhl, *Pr*
Darrel Suhl, *VP*
Roxy Suhl, *Dir*
Pam Scalzo, *Stockholder*
▲ **EMP:** 20 **EST:** 1969
SQ FT: 20,000
SALES (est): 3.27MM **Privately Held**
Web: www.flamesprayinc.com
SIC: 3479 Coating of metals and formed products

(P-6705)
FLETCHER COATING CO
Also Called: Fletcher Coating
426 W Fletcher Ave (92865-2612)
PHONE..............................714 637-4763
Kurtis Breeding, *CEO*
▲ **EMP:** 50 **EST:** 1971
SQ FT: 37,500
SALES (est): 4.78MM **Privately Held**
Web: www.fletcherkote.com
SIC: 3479 Coating of metals and formed products

(P-6706)
FVO SOLUTIONS INC
Also Called: Foothill Vctonal Opportunities
789 N Fair Oaks Ave (91103-3045)
PHONE..............................626 449-0218
▲ **EMP:** 75
Web: www.abilityfirst.org
SIC: 3479 3999 Coating of metals and formed products; Gold stamping, except books

(P-6707)
GEMTECH INDS GOOD EARTH MFG
Also Called: Gemtech International
2737 S Garnsey St (92707-3340)
P.O. Box 15506 (92735-0506)

PHONE..............................714 848-2517
Shig Shiwota, *Pr*
Maya Shiwota, *
David Shiwota, *
▲ **EMP:** 24 **EST:** 1971
SQ FT: 10,500
SALES (est): 2.38MM **Privately Held**
SIC: 3479 Coating of metals and formed products

(P-6708)
HALEY INDUS CTINGS LININGS INC
2919 Tanager Ave (90040-2723)
PHONE..............................323 588-8086
Yvonne P Haley, *Pr*
EMP: 21 **EST:** 1993
SALES (est): 3.33MM **Privately Held**
Web: www.haleyindustrial.com
SIC: 3479 1771 Coating of metals and formed products; Flooring contractor

(P-6709)
INLAND PACIFIC COATINGS INC
3556 Lytle Creek Rd (92358-9776)
PHONE..............................909 822-0594
Ciro Hernandez, *Prin*
EMP: 20 **EST:** 2012
SALES (est): 1.81MM **Privately Held**
SIC: 3479 1721 7389 Metal coating and allied services; Painting and paper hanging; Business Activities at Non-Commercial Site

(P-6710)
INLAND POWDER COATING CORP
Also Called: Prs Industries
1656 S Bon View Ave Ste F (91761-4419)
P.O. Box 3427 (91761-0943)
PHONE..............................909 947-1122
David Paul Flatten, *Pr*
Debbie Flatten, *
EMP: 104 **EST:** 1983
SQ FT: 83,000
SALES (est): 16.91MM **Privately Held**
Web: www.inlandpowder.com
SIC: 3479 3471 Coating of metals and formed products; Sand blasting of metal parts

(P-6711)
INNOVATIVE COATINGS TECHNOLOGY CORPORATION
Also Called: Incotec
1347 Poole St 106 (93501-1658)
PHONE..............................661 824-8101
EMP: 127 **EST:** 1992
SALES (est): 22.04MM **Privately Held**
Web: www.incoteccorp.com
SIC: 3479 8732 Coating of metals with plastic or resins; Research services, except laboratory

(P-6712)
ISLAND POWDER COATING
Also Called: Powder Coating
1830 Tyler Ave (91733-3618)
PHONE..............................626 279-2460
EMP: 30 **EST:** 1994
SALES (est): 2.17MM **Privately Held**
SIC: 3479 Coating of metals and formed products

(P-6713)
JAN-KENS ENAMELING COMPANY INC
715 E Cypress Ave (91016-4254)
PHONE..............................626 358-1849
EMP: 24

Web: www.jankens.com
SIC: 3479 Coating of metals and formed products

(P-6714)
KENNEDY NAME PLATE CO
4501 Pacific Blvd (90058-2207)
PHONE..............................323 585-0121
William J Kennedy Junior, *Pr*
Mike Kennedy, *
EMP: 25 **EST:** 1921
SQ FT: 36,000
SALES (est): 2.51MM **Privately Held**
Web: www.knpco.com
SIC: 3479 7336 3993 3444 Name plates: engraved, etched, etc.; Silk screen design; Signs and advertising specialties; Sheet metalwork

(P-6715)
KENS SPRAY EQUIPMENT INC
Also Called: Alloy Processing
1900 W Walnut St (90220-5019)
PHONE..............................310 635-9995
Joseph I Snowden, *Pr*
EMP: 133 **EST:** 1979
SALES (est): 20.95MM
SALES (corp-wide): 302.09B **Publicly Held**
Web: www.pccaero.com
SIC: 3479 Painting of metal products
HQ: Precision Castparts Corp.
5885 Meadows Rd Ste 620
Lake Oswego OR
503 946-4800

(P-6716)
LOS ANGELES GALVANIZING CO
2518 E 53rd St (90255-2505)
PHONE..............................323 583-2263
Lance Michael Rosenkranz, *CEO*
Jamie Rosenkranz, *
Tim Rosenkranz, *
Lance Rosenkranz, *
EMP: 58 **EST:** 1932
SQ FT: 26,000
SALES (est): 9.76MM **Privately Held**
Web: www.lagalvanizing.com
SIC: 3479 Coating of metals and formed products

(P-6717)
MABEL BAAS INC
Also Called: Royal Coatings
3960 Royal Ave (93063-3380)
PHONE..............................805 520-8075
Marilyn Teperson, *Pr*
EMP: 50 **EST:** 1991
SALES (est): 5.78MM **Privately Held**
Web: www.royalcoatings.com
SIC: 3479 Coating of metals and formed products

(P-6718)
METAL COATERS CALIFORNIA INC
Also Called: Metal Coaters System
9123 Center Ave (91730-5312)
PHONE..............................909 987-4681
Norman C Chambers, *CEO*
Dick Klein, *
Tom Scarinza, *
EMP: 75 **EST:** 1998
SALES (est): 28.22MM
SALES (corp-wide): 5.58B **Privately Held**
Web: www.bluescopecoatedproducts.com
SIC: 3479 Painting of metal products
HQ: Cornerstone Building Brands, Inc.
5020 Weston Pkwy Ste 400

▲ = Import ▼ = Export
◆ = Import/Export

Cary NC
866 419-0042

(P-6719)
**NELSON NAME PLATE
COMPANY (PA)**
Also Called: Nelson-Miller
708 Nogales St (91748-1306)
PHONE.................................323 663-3971
Jim Kaldem, *Pr*
▲ **EMP:** 95 **EST:** 1946
SALES (est): 43.25MM
SALES (corp-wide): 43.25MM **Privately
Held**
Web: www.nelson-miller.co
SIC: 3479 3993 Name plates: engraved,
etched, etc.; Signs and advertising
specialties

(P-6720)
NM HOLDCO INC
2800 Casitas Ave (90039-2942)
PHONE.................................323 663-3971
Mark Carroll, *Dir*
William Mckinley, *Dir*
EMP: 200 **EST:** 2011
SALES (est): 43.25MM **Privately Held**
SIC: 3479 3993 Name plates: engraved,
etched, etc.; Signs and advertising
specialties
PA: Superior Capital Partners Llc
418 N Main St
Royal Oak MI

(P-6721)
PAINT SPECIALISTS INC
8629 Bradley Ave (91352-3303)
P.O. Box 1124 (91353-1124)
PHONE.................................818 771-0552
Mike Kim, *Pr*
EMP: 18 **EST:** 1981
SQ FT: 15,000
SALES (est): 362.72K **Privately Held**
SIC: 3479 Coating of metals and formed
products

(P-6722)
**PARYLENE COATING SERVICES
INC**
Also Called: Polymer Coating Services
35 Argonaut (92656-4151)
PHONE.................................281 391-7665
EMP: 25
SIC: 3479 Coating of metals and formed
products

(P-6723)
PDU LAD CORPORATION (PA)
Also Called: Plastic Dress-Up
11165 Valley Spring Ln (91602-2646)
P.O. Box 3897 (91733-0897)
PHONE.................................626 442-7711
Loren Funk, *CEO*
Dennis Funk, *
Allen Greenblat, *
◆ **EMP:** 38 **EST:** 1990
SALES (est): 8.8MM **Privately Held**
Web: www.pducat.com
SIC: 3479 Name plates: engraved, etched,
etc.

(P-6724)
PELTEK HOLDINGS INC
35 Argonaut Ste A1 (92656-4151)
PHONE.................................949 855-8010
Jeffrey Stewart, *Pr*
Paul Stewart, *
Joyce Stewart, *
▲ **EMP:** 30 **EST:** 1974

SQ FT: 10,560
SALES (est): 2.98MM **Privately Held**
Web: www.peltekfab.com
SIC: 3479 5169 Bonderizing of metal or
metal products; Chemicals and allied
products, nec

(P-6725)
PERFORMANCE POWDER INC
2940 E La Jolla St Ste A (92806-1349)
PHONE.................................714 632-0600
Kevin Aaberg, *Pr*
Robert Goldberg, *
EMP: 29 **EST:** 1993
SALES (est): 4.71MM **Privately Held**
Web: www.performancepowder.com
SIC: 3479 Coating of metals and formed
products

(P-6726)
**PLASMA COATING
CORPORATION**
1900 W Walnut St (90220-5019)
PHONE.................................310 532-1951
James M Emery, *Pr*
Willard A Emery, *VP*
EMP: 22 **EST:** 1972
SALES (est): 9.54MM
SALES (corp-wide): 302.09B **Publicly
Held**
SIC: 3479 Coating of metals and formed
products
HQ: Southwest United Industries, Inc.
422 S Saint Louis Ave
Tulsa OK
918 587-4161

(P-6727)
**PLASMA TECHNOLOGY
INCORPORATED (PA)**
Also Called: P T I
1754 Crenshaw Blvd (90501-3384)
PHONE.................................310 320-3373
Robert Donald Dowell, *CEO*
Burnard Fosket, *
Malcom Jones, *
John Nikitich, *
▲ **EMP:** 73 **EST:** 1984
SQ FT: 40,000
SALES (est): 12.34MM
SALES (corp-wide): 12.34MM **Privately
Held**
Web: www.ptise.com
SIC: 3479 Coating of metals and formed
products

(P-6728)
POWDERCOAT SERVICES LLC
1747 W Lincoln Ave Ste K (92801-6770)
PHONE.................................714 533-2251
Ravi Rao, *Pr*
▲ **EMP:** 38 **EST:** 1981
SQ FT: 75,000
SALES (est): 5.73MM **Privately Held**
Web: www.powdercoatservices.com
SIC: 3479 7211 Coating of metals and
formed products; Power laundries, family
and commercial

(P-6729)
PROCESSES BY MARTIN INC
12150 Alameda St (90262-4005)
PHONE.................................310 637-1855
Irene Romero, *Pr*
Cathleen Fuentes, *
EMP: 45 **EST:** 1993
SQ FT: 200,000
SALES (est): 4.88MM **Privately Held**
Web: www.processesbymartin.com

SIC: 3479 Coating of metals and formed
products

(P-6730)
PVD COATINGS LLC
5271 Argosy Ave (92649-1015)
PHONE.................................714 899-4892
Red Silversterstein, *Managing Member*
EMP: 18 **EST:** 2001
SALES (est): 1.71MM **Privately Held**
Web: www.pvdcoatings.net
SIC: 3479 Coating of metals and formed
products

(P-6731)
RGF ENTERPRISES INC
220 Citation Cir (92878-5022)
PHONE.................................951 734-6922
Rodney G Fisher, *Pr*
EMP: 26 **EST:** 1976
SQ FT: 15,000
SALES (est): 2.15MM **Privately Held**
Web: www.rgfcoatings.com
SIC: 3479 Coating of metals and formed
products

(P-6732)
**RTS POWDER COATING INC
(PA)**
15121 Sierra Bonita Ln (91710-8904)
PHONE.................................909 393-5404
Donald D Reed Senior, *Pr*
EMP: 20 **EST:** 1991
SQ FT: 8,100
SALES (est): 3.67MM **Privately Held**
SIC: 3479 Coating of metals and formed
products

(P-6733)
S C COATINGS CORPORATION
41775 Elm St Ste 302 (92562-9267)
PHONE.................................951 461-9777
Michael Podratz, *Pr*
Victor Lopez, *
EMP: 48 **EST:** 2000
SALES (est): 7.3MM **Privately Held**
Web: www.sccoatingscorp.com
SIC: 3479 Coating of metals and formed
products

(P-6734)
SBIF INC
Also Called: Santa Barbara Indus Finshg
873 S Kellogg Ave (93117-3805)
PHONE.................................805 683-1711
Shelby See Junior, *Pr*
Rochelle See, *Sec*
EMP: 19 **EST:** 1971
SQ FT: 6,750
SALES (est): 969.93K **Privately Held**
Web: www.sbifin.com
SIC: 3479 7336 Painting of metal products;
Silk screen design

(P-6735)
SDC TECHNOLOGIES INC (HQ)
45 Parker Ste 100 (92618-1605)
PHONE.................................714 939-8300
Richard Chang, *Pr*
▲ **EMP:** 25 **EST:** 1986
SQ FT: 16,800
SALES (est): 46.26MM **Privately Held**
Web: www.sdctech.com
SIC: 3479 Coating of metals and formed
products
PA: Mitsui Chemicals, Inc.
2-2-1, Yaesu
Chuo-Ku TKY

(P-6736)
SHMAZE INDUSTRIES INC
Also Called: Shmaze Custom Coatings
20792 Canada Rd (92630-6732)
PHONE.................................949 583-1448
Michael Shamassian, *Pr*
Joanne Shamassian, *
EMP: 50 **EST:** 1987
SQ FT: 21,500
SALES (est): 5.64MM **Privately Held**
Web: www.shmaze.com
SIC: 3479 Coating of metals with plastic or
resins

(P-6737)
**SOCCO PLASTIC COATING
COMPANY**
11251 Jersey Blvd (91730-5147)
PHONE.................................909 987-4753
Peter M Smits, *Pr*
Peter M Smits Junior, *
Rose Smits, *
EMP: 25 **EST:** 1945
SQ FT: 60,000
SALES (est): 2.36MM **Privately Held**
Web: www.soccoplastics.com
SIC: 3479 3444 3088 2851 Coating of
metals with plastic or resins; Sheet
metalwork; Plastics plumbing fixtures;
Paints and allied products

(P-6738)
**SPECIALTY COATING SYSTEMS
INC**
4435 E Airport Dr Ste 100 (91761-7816)
PHONE.................................909 390-8818
Steven Frease, *Brnch Mgr*
EMP: 71
Web: www.scscoatings.com
SIC: 3479 Coating of metals and formed
products
HQ: Specialty Coating Systems, Inc.
7645 Woodland Dr
Indianapolis IN

(P-6739)
STEELSCAPE LLC
11200 Arrow Rte (91730-4805)
PHONE.................................909 987-4711
Ron Hurst, *Brnch Mgr*
EMP: 18
SALES (corp-wide): 127.33MM **Privately
Held**
Web: www.steelscape.com
SIC: 3479 Coating of metals and formed
products
PA: Steelscape, Llc
222 W Kalama River Rd
Kalama WA
360 673-8200

(P-6740)
SUNDIAL INDUSTRIES INC
Also Called: Powder Painting By Sundial
8421 Telfair Ave (91352-3926)
PHONE.................................818 767-4477
TOLL FREE: 866
Hasu Bhakta, *Pr*
Naseen Khan, *
Gurtreet Riaz, *
▲ **EMP:** 30 **EST:** 1980
SQ FT: 13,000
SALES (est): 4.36MM **Privately Held**
Web: www.sundialpowdercoating.com
SIC: 3479 Coating of metals and formed
products

(P-6741)
SUNDIAL POWDER COATINGS INC
Also Called: Bottle Coatings
8421 Telfair Ave (91352-3926)
PHONE....................818 767-4477
Hasu Bhakta, *CEO*
EMP: 25 **EST:** 1995
SALES (est): 2.61MM **Privately Held**
Web: www.sundialpowdercoating.com
SIC: 3479 Coating of metals and formed products

(P-6742)
THERM-O-NAMEL INC
2780 Martin Luther King Jr Blvd (90262-1857)
PHONE....................310 631-7866
Grant Kinsman, *Pr*
Byron Kinsman, *VP*
Sylvia Kinsman, *VP*
Colleen Kinsman, *Sec*
EMP: 27 **EST:** 1950
SQ FT: 15,000
SALES (est): 574.77K **Privately Held**
Web: www.thermonamel.com
SIC: 3479 3555 2851 2759 Painting of metal products; Printing trades machinery; Paints and allied products; Commercial printing, nec

(P-6743)
TIODIZE CO INC (PA)
5858 Engineer Dr (92649-1166)
PHONE....................714 898-4377
Thomas R Adams, *CEO*
EMP: 17 **EST:** 1966
SQ FT: 26,000
SALES (est): 9.73MM
SALES (corp-wide): 9.73MM **Privately Held**
Web: www.tiodize.com
SIC: 3479 Coating of metals and formed products

(P-6744)
TORTOISE INDUSTRIES INC
Also Called: Tortoise Tube
3052 Treadwell St (90065-1423)
PHONE....................323 258-7776
EMP: 40 **EST:** 1981
SALES (est): 4.31MM **Privately Held**
Web: www.tortoiseindustries.com
SIC: 3479 3498 1799 Painting, coating, and hot dipping; Tube fabricating (contract bending and shaping); Exterior cleaning, including sandblasting

(P-6745)
ULTIMATE METAL FINISHING CORP
6150 Sheila St (90040-2407)
PHONE....................323 890-9100
John Ondrasik, *Pr*
James M Sales, *Genl Mgr*
EMP: 49 **EST:** 1983
SQ FT: 4,800
SALES (est): 943.48K
SALES (corp-wide): 24.07MM **Privately Held**
SIC: 3479 Coating of metals and formed products
PA: Precision Wire Products, Inc.
6150 Sheila St
Commerce CA
323 890-9100

(P-6746)
UNITED WESTERN ENTERPRISES INC
Also Called: Uwe
850 Flynn Rd Ste 200 (93012-8783)
PHONE....................805 389-1077
Gerald Williams, *Pr*
Mike Lynch, *Pr*
EMP: 29 **EST:** 1969
SQ FT: 21,000
SALES (est): 4.18MM **Privately Held**
Web: www.uweinc.com
SIC: 3479 Etching, photochemical

3483 Ammunition, Except For Small Arms, Nec

(P-6747)
FIELD TIME TARGET TRAINING LLC
Also Called: Ft3 Tactical
8230 Electric Ave (90680-2640)
P.O. Box 1219 (90680-1219)
PHONE....................714 677-2841
Michael R Kaplan, *Managing Member*
EMP: 24 **EST:** 2010
SALES (est): 2.16MM **Privately Held**
Web: www.fieldtimetargetandtraining.com
SIC: 3483 7999 Ammunition, except for small arms, nec; Shooting range operation

3484 Small Arms

(P-6748)
SAI INDUSTRIES
Also Called: Standard Armament
631 Allen Ave (91201-2013)
PHONE....................818 842-6144
Curtis Correll, *CEO*
Gary Correll, *
Marcene Correll, *
Cathy Joens, *
Kriti Ahuja, *
◆ **EMP:** 40 **EST:** 1950
SQ FT: 24,000
SALES (est): 4.45MM **Privately Held**
Web: www.standardarmament.com
SIC: 3484 Guns (firearms) or gun parts, 30 mm. and below

3489 Ordnance And Accessories, Nec

(P-6749)
ARMTEC DEFENSE PRODUCTS CO (DH)
Also Called: Armtec Defense Technologies
85901 Avenue 53 (92236-2607)
PHONE....................760 398-0143
Robert W Cremin, *CEO*
◆ **EMP:** 330 **EST:** 1968
SQ FT: 108,000
SALES (est): 112.55MM
SALES (corp-wide): 6.58B **Publicly Held**
Web: www.armtecdefense.com
SIC: 3489 Artillery or artillery parts, over 30 mm.
HQ: Esterline Technologies Corp
1301 E 9th St Ste 3000
Cleveland OH
216 706-2960

(P-6750)
NETWORKS ELECTRONIC CO LLC
9750 De Soto Ave (91311-4409)
PHONE....................818 341-0440
Tamara Marie Christen, *Managing Member*
Andrew Campany, *
▼ **EMP:** 26 **EST:** 2005
SQ FT: 25,000
SALES (est): 5.44MM **Privately Held**
Web: www.networkselectronic.com
SIC: 3489 Ordnance and accessories, nec

(P-6751)
VECTOR LAUNCH LLC (PA)
Also Called: Vector
15261 Connector Ln (92649-1117)
PHONE....................202 888-3063
Jim Penrose, *CEO*
Robert Spalding, *Pr*
Robert Cleave, *CRO*
Stephanie Koster, *CFO*
Eric Besnard, *VP*
EMP: 246 **EST:** 2016
SALES (est): 13.87MM
SALES (corp-wide): 13.87MM **Privately Held**
Web: www.vector-launch.com
SIC: 3489 Rocket launchers

3491 Industrial Valves

(P-6752)
ADVANCED PROCESS SERVICES INC
4350 E Washington Blvd (90023-4410)
PHONE....................323 278-6530
Somjit Burdi, *CEO*
Thomas Burdi, *VP*
EMP: 25 **EST:** 2001
SALES (est): 1.68MM **Privately Held**
Web: www.advprocserv.com
SIC: 3491 Process control regulator valves

(P-6753)
AQUASYN LLC
9525 Owensmouth Ave Ste E (91311-8006)
PHONE....................818 350-0423
Dean Richards, *Brnch Mgr*
EMP: 19
SALES (corp-wide): 5.67MM **Privately Held**
Web: www.aquasyn.com
SIC: 3491 Industrial valves
PA: Aquasyn, Llc
1771 South Sutro Ter
Carson City NV
818 350-0423

(P-6754)
BERMINGHAM CNTRLS INC A CAL CO (PA)
11144 Business Cir (90703-5523)
PHONE....................562 860-0463
Gregory Gass, *Pr*
Edwin Bonner, *
Kevin Mulholland, *
EMP: 37 **EST:** 1961
SQ FT: 20,000
SALES (est): 8.41MM
SALES (corp-wide): 8.41MM **Privately Held**
Web: www.bermingham.com
SIC: 3491 3823 5084 Industrial valves; Process control instruments; Industrial machinery and equipment

(P-6755)
BVI INTERNATIONAL INC
4301 Yeager Way (93313-2018)
PHONE....................661 834-1775
◆ **EMP:** 20

SIC: 3491 Industrial valves

(P-6756)
C C I
22591 Avenida Empresa (92688-2003)
PHONE....................910 616-7426
Ed Villalva, *Mgr*
EMP: 25 **EST:** 2017
SALES (est): 2.15MM **Privately Held**
SIC: 3491 Industrial valves

(P-6757)
CIRCOR AEROSPACE INC (DH)
2301 Wardlow Cir (92878-5101)
P.O. Box 2824 (29304-2824)
PHONE....................951 270-6200
Carl Nasca, *Pr*
Christopher Celtruda, *VP*
Kathy Fazio, *Ex Sec*
Michael Dill, *VP*
Renuka Ayer, *VP*
◆ **EMP:** 245 **EST:** 1947
SQ FT: 100,000
SALES (est): 61.87MM **Publicly Held**
Web: www.circoraerospace.com
SIC: 3491 3494 3769 5085 Pressure valves and regulators, industrial; Plumbing and heating valves; Space vehicle equipment, nec; Seals, industrial
HQ: Circor International, Inc.
30 Corporate Dr Ste 200
Burlington MA
781 270-1200

(P-6758)
CURTISS-WRIGHT CORPORATION
Also Called: Defense Solutions
28965 Avenue Penn (91355-4185)
PHONE....................661 257-4430
EMP: 57
SALES (corp-wide): 2.56B **Publicly Held**
Web: www.curtisswright.com
SIC: 3491 Industrial valves
PA: Curtiss-Wright Corporation
130 Harbour Place Dr # 300
Davidson NC
704 869-4600

(P-6759)
CURTISS-WRIGHT CORPORATION
1675 Brandywine Ave Ste F (91911-6064)
PHONE....................619 482-3405
David Schurra, *Brnch Mgr*
EMP: 85
SALES (corp-wide): 2.56B **Publicly Held**
Web: www.curtisswright.com
SIC: 3491 Industrial valves
PA: Curtiss-Wright Corporation
130 Harbour Place Dr # 300
Davidson NC
704 869-4600

(P-6760)
CURTISS-WRIGHT FLOW CONTROL
Penny & Giles
28965 Avenue Penn (91355-4185)
PHONE....................626 851-3100
EMP: 160
SALES (corp-wide): 2.41B **Publicly Held**
SIC: 3491 Industrial valves
HQ: Curtiss-Wright Flow Control Corporation
1966 Broadhollow Rd Ste E
Farmingdale NY
631 293-3800

(P-6761)
CURTISS-WRIGHT FLOW CTRL CORP
Also Called: Collins Technologies
2950 E Birch St (92821-6246)
PHONE..................949 271-7500
Glenn Roberts, *Mgr*
EMP: 31
SALES (corp-wide): 2.56B **Publicly Held**
Web: www.curtisswright.com
SIC: 3491 Industrial valves
HQ: Curtiss-Wright Flow Control
  Corporation
  1966 Broadhollow Rd Ste E
  Farmingdale NY
  631 293-3800

(P-6762)
CURTISS-WRIGHT FLOW CTRL CORP
Also Called: Curtiss-Wrght Nclear Div Enrte
260 Ranger Ave (92821-6215)
PHONE..................714 528-2301
EMP: 68
SALES (corp-wide): 2.56B **Publicly Held**
Web: www.cwnuclear.com
SIC: 3491 Industrial valves
HQ: Curtiss-Wright Flow Control
  Corporation
  2950 E Birch St
  Brea CA
  714 528-1365

(P-6763)
DANCO VALVE COMPANY
15230 Lakewood Blvd (90706-4240)
PHONE..................562 925-2588
Mike Dante, *Pr*
EMP: 28 **EST:** 1985
SQ FT: 27,000
SALES (est): 1.11MM **Privately Held**
Web: www.dantevalve.com
SIC: 3491 5085 Industrial valves; Industrial
  supplies

(P-6764)
FCKINGSTON CO
Also Called: Storm Manufacturing
23201 Normandie Ave (90501-5050)
PHONE..................310 326-8287
Joe Taormina, *Pr*
▲ **EMP:** 21 **EST:** 1908
SQ FT: 32,500
SALES (est): 1.2MM **Privately Held**
Web: www.kingstonvalves.com
SIC: 3491 3494 Industrial valves; Plumbing
  and heating valves

(P-6765)
IMI CRITICAL ENGINEERING LLC (DH)
Also Called: IMI CCI
22591 Avenida Empresa (92688-2003)
PHONE..................949 858-1877
Kevin Mckown, *Pr*
Abhijit Rao, *CFO*
◆ **EMP:** 365 **EST:** 1961
SQ FT: 75,000
SALES (est): 126.11MM
SALES (corp-wide): 2.47B **Privately Held**
Web: www.imi-critical.com
SIC: 3491 Process control regulator valves
HQ: Imi Americas Inc.
  5400 S Delaware St
  Littleton CO
  763 488-5400

(P-6766)
INTERNTNAL PLYMR SOLUTIONS INC
Also Called: Ipolymer
5 Studebaker (92618-2013)
PHONE..................949 458-3731
Michael Siino, *Pr*
Patrick P Lee, *
Richard Ryan, *
Mark O'donnell, *Treas*
EMP: 48 **EST:** 1986
SQ FT: 18,000
SALES (est): 11.79MM
SALES (corp-wide): 2.14B **Publicly Held**
Web: www.ipolymer.com
SIC: 3491 3674 Industrial valves;
  Semiconductors and related devices
HQ: White Knight Fluid Handling, Llc
  187 E 670 S
  Kamas UT

(P-6767)
JAMES JONES COMPANY
1470 S Vintage Ave (91761-3646)
PHONE..................909 418-2558
Jerry Schnelzer, *Genl Mgr*
◆ **EMP:** 3988 **EST:** 1892
SQ FT: 68,000
SALES (est): 4.65MM
SALES (corp-wide): 1.25B **Publicly Held**
Web: www.joneswaterproducts.com
SIC: 3491 3494 Fire hydrant valves; Pipe
  fittings
HQ: Mueller Group, Llc
  1200 Abernathy Rd
  Atlanta GA
  770 206-4200

(P-6768)
PACIFIC SEISMIC PRODUCTS INC
233 E Avenue H8 (93535-1821)
PHONE..................661 942-4499
EMP: 24 **EST:** 1989
SQ FT: 10,000
SALES (est): 1.77MM **Privately Held**
Web: www.pspvalves.com
SIC: 3491 Industrial valves

(P-6769)
RELIANCE WORLDWIDE CORPORATION
2750 E Mission Blvd (91761-2909)
PHONE..................770 863-4005
EMP: 19
Web: www.rcw.com
SIC: 3491 Industrial valves
HQ: Reliance Worldwide Corporation
  2300 Defoor Hills Rd Nw
  Atlanta GA
  770 863-4005

(P-6770)
STORM MANUFACTURING GROUP INC
Also Called: Smg
23201 Normandie Ave (90501-5050)
PHONE..................310 326-8287
Dale Philippi, *CEO*
Russell Kneipp, *
Georgia S Claessens, *
Rick Ward, *
◆ **EMP:** 74 **EST:** 1908
SQ FT: 41,936
SALES (est): 13.88MM
SALES (corp-wide): 77.26MM **Privately Held**
Web: www.getsuperior.com

SIC: 3491 3494 Industrial valves; Sprinkler
  systems, field
PA: Storm Industries, Inc.
  23223 Normandie Ave
  Torrance CA
  310 534-5232

(P-6771)
WESTERN VALVE INC
Also Called: Western Valve
201 Industrial St (93307-2703)
P.O. Box 10628 (93389-0628)
PHONE..................661 327-7660
▲ **EMP:** 41 **EST:** 1991
SALES (est): 9.36MM **Privately Held**
Web: www.westernvalve.com
SIC: 3491 Industrial valves

3492 Fluid Power Valves And Hose Fittings

(P-6772)
ACOUSTICFAB LLC (DH)
28150 Industry Dr (91355-4100)
PHONE..................661 257-2242
EMP: 59 **EST:** 2008
SQ FT: 12,000
SALES (est): 5.64MM
SALES (corp-wide): 2.99B **Publicly Held**
SIC: 3492 3812 3728 Control valves,
  aircraft: hydraulic and pneumatic;
  Acceleration indicators and systems
  components, aerospace; Aircraft body and
  wing assemblies and parts
HQ: Itt Aerospace Controls Llc
  28150 Industry Dr
  Valencia CA
  315 568-7258

(P-6773)
CIRCOR INSTRMENTATION TECH INC
Also Called: CIRCOR INSTRUMENTATION
TECHNOLOGIES, INC.
2301 Wardlow Cir (92878-5101)
PHONE..................951 270-6200
Andy Brandenburg, *Genl Mgr*
EMP: 71
SALES (corp-wide): 3.37B **Publicly Held**
Web: www.circor.com
SIC: 3492 Control valves, fluid power:
  hydraulic and pneumatic
HQ: Crane Instrumentation & Sampling, Inc.
  405 Centura Ct
  Spartanburg SC
  864 574-7966

(P-6774)
CRANE CO
Also Called: CRANE CO.
3201 Walnut Ave (90755-5225)
PHONE..................562 426-2531
Kevin Mckown, *Mgr*
EMP: 110
SALES (corp-wide): 3.37B **Privately Held**
Web: www.craneco.com
SIC: 3492 Fluid power valves and hose
  fittings
HQ: Redco Corporation
  100 1st Stamford Pl
  Stamford CT
  203 363-7300

(P-6775)
ELECTROFILM MFG CO LLC
Also Called: Hartzell Aerospace
28150 Industry Dr (91355-4100)
PHONE..................661 257-2242
David Schmidt, *

Joseph W Brown, *
Simon Shackelton, *
EMP: 80 **EST:** 2008
SQ FT: 43,000
SALES (est): 20.02MM
SALES (corp-wide): 2.99B **Publicly Held**
Web: www.ef-heaters.com
SIC: 3492 3728 3812 Control valves,
  aircraft: hydraulic and pneumatic; Aircraft
  body and wing assemblies and parts;
  Acceleration indicators and systems
  components, aerospace
HQ: Itt Aerospace Controls Llc
  28150 Industry Dr
  Valencia CA
  315 568-7258

(P-6776)
FABER ENTERPRISES INC
14800 S Figueroa St (90248-1719)
PHONE..................310 323-6200
Kevin M Stein, *CEO*
Esther Faber, *
Ronald E Spencer, *
Marilyn Spencer, *
Loretta Appel, *
EMP: 110 **EST:** 1947
SALES (est): 9.68MM **Privately Held**
Web: www.pccfluidfittings.com
SIC: 3492 Control valves, aircraft: hydraulic
  and pneumatic

(P-6777)
GRISWOLD INDUSTRIES
Also Called: Soundcast
1731 Placentia Ave (92627-4416)
PHONE..................949 722-4831
EMP: 18
SALES (corp-wide): 75.13MM **Privately Held**
Web: www.cla-val.com
SIC: 3492 Control valves, fluid power:
  hydraulic and pneumatic
PA: Griswold Industries
  1701 Placentia Ave
  Costa Mesa CA
  949 722-4800

(P-6778)
INDUSTRIAL TUBE COMPANY LLC
Also Called: Industrial Tube Company
28150 Industry Dr (91355-4100)
PHONE..................661 295-4000
Farrokh Batliwala, *CEO*
EMP: 99 **EST:** 2008
SQ FT: 28,000
SALES (est): 25.05MM
SALES (corp-wide): 2.99B **Publicly Held**
SIC: 3492 3728 3812 Control valves,
  aircraft: hydraulic and pneumatic; Aircraft
  body and wing assemblies and parts;
  Acceleration indicators and systems
  components, aerospace
HQ: Itt Aerospace Controls Llc
  28150 Industry Dr
  Valencia CA
  315 568-7258

(P-6779)
S & H MACHINE INC
9928 Hayward Way (91733-3114)
PHONE..................626 448-5062
David Fisher, *Pr*
EMP: 23
SALES (corp-wide): 7.33MM **Privately Held**
Web: www.shmachine.com

SIC: 3492 3728 Fluid power valves and hose
fittings; Aircraft parts and equipment, nec
PA: S & H Machine, Inc.
900 N Lake St
Burbank CA
818 846-9847

3493 Steel Springs, Except Wire

(P-6780)
ARGO SPRING MFG CO INC
13930 Shoemaker Ave (90650-4534)
PHONE..............................800 252-2740
TOLL FREE: 800
Gene Fox, *Pr*
Michael Fox, *
Kay Greathouse, *
▲ EMP: 55 EST: 1966
SQ FT: 20,000
SALES (est): 7.24MM Privately Held
Web: www.argospringmfg.com
SIC: 3493 3495 3469 3599 Coiled flat springs
; Wire springs; Stamping metal for the trade
; Custom machinery

(P-6781)
EIBACH INC
Also Called: Eibach Springs, Inc.
264 Mariah Cir (92879-1706)
PHONE..............................951 256-8300
Greg Cooley, *Pr*
Gary Peek, *
Sieglinde Eibach, *
◆ EMP: 60 EST: 1987
SQ FT: 52,000
SALES (est): 15.49MM
SALES (corp-wide): 80.47MM Privately
Held
Web: www.eibach.com
SIC: 3493 Steel springs, except wire
HQ: Heinrich Eibach Gmbh
Am Lennedamm 1
Finnentrop NW
27215110

(P-6782)
JUENGERMANN INC
Also Called: Spring Industries
1899 Palma Dr Ste A (93003-5719)
PHONE..............................805 644-7165
Peter Juengermann, *Pr*
EMP: 40 EST: 1974
SQ FT: 21,600
SALES (est): 4.53MM Privately Held
Web: www.springind.com
SIC: 3493 3495 Steel springs, except wire;
Wire springs

(P-6783)
MATTHEW WARREN INC
Also Called: Helical Products
901 W Mccoy Ln (93455-1109)
P.O. Box 1069 (93456-1069)
PHONE..............................805 928-3851
Leroy Mcchesney, *Brnch Mgr*
EMP: 30
SALES (corp-wide): 1.05B Privately Held
Web: www.mwcomponents.com
SIC: 3493 Helical springs, hot wound:
railroad equip., etc.
HQ: Matthew Warren, Inc.
3426 Toringdon Way # 100
Charlotte NC
704 837-0331

(P-6784)
SCHELLINGER SPRING INC
8477 Utica Ave (91730-3809)

PHONE..............................909 373-0799
Dean Schellinger, *Pr*
EMP: 23 EST: 1954
SQ FT: 12,000
SALES (est): 2.26MM Privately Held
SIC: 3493 Steel springs, except wire

(P-6785)
SUPERSPRINGS INTERNATIONAL INC
5251 6th St (93013-2402)
PHONE..............................805 745-5553
Gerry Lamberti, *CEO*
Ryan Dougan, *
EMP: 32 EST: 1998
SALES (est): 4.73MM Privately Held
Web:
www.superspringsinternational.com
SIC: 3493 Automobile springs

3494 Valves And Pipe Fittings, Nec

(P-6786)
ALLAN AIRCRAFT SUPPLY CO LLC
11643 Vanowen St (91605-6128)
PHONE..............................818 765-4992
Robert Kahmann, *Managing Member*
Mary Katz, *Contrlr*
EMP: 45 EST: 1952
SQ FT: 30,000
SALES (est): 9.01MM Privately Held
Web: www.allanaircraft.com
SIC: 3494 Pipe fittings

(P-6787)
ANCO INTERNATIONAL INC
Also Called: Anco
19851 Cajon Blvd (92407-1828)
PHONE..............................909 887-2521
Marjorie A Nielsen, *Pr*
EMP: 36 EST: 1978
SQ FT: 13,500
SALES (est): 4.83MM Privately Held
Web: www.ancointernational.com
SIC: 3494 3599 3492 Valves and pipe
fittings, nec; Machine shop, jobbing and
repair; Fluid power valves and hose fittings

(P-6788)
BRASSCRAFT MANUFACTURING CO
Also Called: Brasscraft Corona
215 N Smith Ave (92878-3241)
PHONE..............................951 735-4375
Val Perillo, *Brnch Mgr*
EMP: 53
SALES (corp-wide): 8.68B Publicly Held
Web: www.brasscraft.com
SIC: 3494 3432 5074 Valves and pipe
fittings, nec; Plumbing fixture fittings and
trim; Plumbing fittings and supplies
HQ: Brasscraft Manufacturing Company
39600 Orchard Hill Pl
Novi MI
248 305-6000

(P-6789)
CURTISS-WRIGHT FLOW CTRL CORP (DH)
Also Called: Paul-Munroe Entertech Division
2950 E Birch St (92821-6246)
PHONE..............................714 528-1365
Frank U Erlach, *Pr*
Paul Mawn, *VP*
James Leachman, *VP*
Dan Miller, *Genl Mgr*

Jubel Easaw, *Prin*
▲ EMP: 80 EST: 1996
SQ FT: 30,550
SALES (est): 38.75MM
SALES (corp-wide): 2.56B Publicly Held
Web: www.curtisswright.com
SIC: 3494 3625 Valves and pipe fittings, nec;
Actuators, industrial
HQ: Curtiss-Wright Flow Control
Corporation
1966 Broadhollow Rd Ste E
Farmingdale NY
631 293-3800

(P-6790)
G-G DISTRIBUTION & DEV CO INC
Also Called: G/G Industries
28545 Livingston Ave (91355-4166)
PHONE..............................661 257-5700
John Gedney, *Pr*
Mary Ellen, *
Richard Greenberg, *
◆ EMP: 120 EST: 1974
SALES (est): 9.44MM Privately Held
SIC: 3494 3088 Plumbing and heating valves
; Plastics plumbing fixtures

(P-6791)
GRISWOLD CONTROLS LLC (PA)
Also Called: Griswold Controls
1700 Barranca Pkwy (92606-4824)
P.O. Box 19612 (92623-9612)
PHONE..............................949 559-6000
Brooks Sherman, *CEO*
◆ EMP: 100 EST: 1960
SALES (est): 21.09MM
SALES (corp-wide): 21.09MM Privately
Held
Web: www.griswoldcontrols.com
SIC: 3494 3491 Valves and pipe fittings, nec;
Industrial valves

(P-6792)
MISSION RUBBER COMPANY LLC
1660 Leeson Ln (92879-2061)
PHONE..............................951 736-1313
EMP: 185
SALES (corp-wide): 66.66MM Privately
Held
Web: www.missionrubber.com
SIC: 3494 Couplings, except pressure and
soil pipe
HQ: Mission Rubber Company Llc
1660 Leeson Ln
Corona CA
951 736-1313

(P-6793)
NELSON AERO SPACE INC
14800 S Figueroa St (90248-1719)
PHONE..............................310 323-6200
▲ EMP: 47 EST: 1962
SALES (est): 10MM
SALES (corp-wide): 302.09B Publicly
Held
Web: nelson.aerospace.mechdir.com
SIC: 3494 Valves and pipe fittings, nec
HQ: Designed Metal Connections, Inc.
14800 S Figueroa St
Gardena CA
310 323-6200

(P-6794)
RAIN BIRD CORPORATION (PA)
Also Called: Rain Bird
970 W Sierra Madre Ave (91702-1873)
PHONE..............................626 812-3400
Anthony La Fetra, *Pr*

◆ EMP: 125 EST: 1933
SALES (est): 433.78MM
SALES (corp-wide): 433.78MM Privately
Held
Web: www.rainbird.com
SIC: 3494 3432 3523 Sprinkler systems, field
; Lawn hose nozzles and sprinklers; Farm
machinery and equipment

(P-6795)
VACCO INDUSTRIES (DH)
10350 Vacco St (91733-3316)
PHONE..............................626 443-7121
Antonio E Gonzalez, *CEO*
Robert Mc Creadie, *
Paul Rowan, *
EMP: 248 EST: 1954
SALES (est): 97.3MM Publicly Held
Web: www.vacco.com
SIC: 3494 3492 3728 Valves and pipe
fittings, nec; Fluid power valves and hose
fittings; Aircraft parts and equipment, nec
HQ: Esco Technologies Holding Llc
9900 Clayton Rd Ste A
Saint Louis MO
314 213-7200

(P-6796)
VALTERRA PRODUCTS LLC (HQ)
15235 Brand Blvd Ste A101 (91345-1445)
PHONE..............................818 898-1671
Bryan Fletcher, *Managing Member*
▲ EMP: 20 EST: 1981
SQ FT: 50,000
SALES (est): 45.07MM
SALES (corp-wide): 2.84B Privately Held
Web: www.valterra.com
SIC: 3494 3088 3949 3432 Valves and pipe
fittings, nec; Plastics plumbing fixtures;
Skateboards; Plumbing fixture fittings and
trim
PA: Dometic Group Ab (Publ)
Hemvarnsgatan 15
Solna
101729780

3495 Wire Springs

(P-6797)
AARD INDUSTRIES INC
Also Called: Aard Spring & Stamping
42075 Avenida Alvarado (92590-3486)
PHONE..............................951 296-0844
William Verstegen, *Pr*
EMP: 22 EST: 1970
SQ FT: 5,000
SALES (est): 2.45MM Privately Held
Web: www.aard.com
SIC: 3495 3469 Wire springs; Metal
stampings, nec

(P-6798)
ATLAS SPRING MFGCORP
10635 Santa Monica Blvd Ste 320
(90025-8300)
PHONE..............................310 532-6200
Melvin Bayer, *Pr*
Stan Grietzer, *
Jeff Miller, *
EMP: 22 EST: 1932
SQ FT: 100,000
SALES (est): 694.15K Privately Held
SIC: 3495 Upholstery springs, unassembled

(P-6799)
BAL SEAL ENGINEERING LLC (DH)
19650 Pauling (92610-2610)

PHONE..............................949 460-2100
Richard Dawson, *CEO*
Peter J Balsells, *Ch*
Jacques Naviaux, *Vice Chairman*
Andrew Wiggins, *Contrlr*
▲ EMP: 202 EST: 1959
SQ FT: 325,000
SALES (est): 110.76MM
SALES (corp-wide): 687.96MM **Publicly Held**
Web: www.balseal.com
SIC: 3495 3053 Wire springs; Gaskets and sealing devices
HQ: Kaman Acquisition Usa, Inc.
1332 Blue Hills Ave
Bloomfield CT
860 243-7100

(P-6800)
BETTS COMPANY
Also Called: Betts Truck Parts
10771 Almond Ave Ste B (92337-7165)
PHONE..............................909 427-9988
TOLL FREE: 800
EMP: 30
SALES (corp-wide): 81.77MM **Privately Held**
Web: www.bettstruckparts.com
SIC: 3495 3493 Wire springs; Automobile springs
PA: Betts Company
2843 S Maple Ave
Fresno CA
559 498-3304

(P-6801)
C & M SPRING ENGRG CO INC
5244 Las Flores Dr (91710-9610)
P.O. Box 2559 (91708-2559)
PHONE..............................909 597-2030
Paul Lockhart, *Pr*
EMP: 17 EST: 1962
SQ FT: 15,000
SALES (est): 1.82MM **Privately Held**
Web: www.cmspring.com
SIC: 3495 3496 Mechanical springs, precision; Miscellaneous fabricated wire products

(P-6802)
CLIO INC
Also Called: B&B Spring Co
12981 166th St (90703-2104)
PHONE..............................562 926-3724
Jerome M Johnson, *Pr*
Reva J Johnson, *
Angela Christofferson, *
EMP: 39 EST: 1954
SQ FT: 2,000
SALES (est): 2.34MM **Privately Held**
Web: www.cliosprings.com
SIC: 3495 3679 Wire springs; Transducers, electrical

(P-6803)
ICONN ENGINEERING LLC
6882 Preakness Dr (92648-1567)
PHONE..............................714 696-8826
Jay Huang, *Pr*
EMP: 25 EST: 2011
SALES (est): 1.6MM **Privately Held**
Web: www.iconneng.com
SIC: 3495 Wire springs

(P-6804)
MATTHEW WARREN INC
Also Called: Century Spring
5959 Triumph St (90040-1609)
PHONE..............................800 237-5225
EMP: 75

SALES (corp-wide): 1.05B **Privately Held**
Web: www.mwcomponents.com
SIC: 3495 Wire springs
HQ: Matthew Warren, Inc.
3426 Toringdon Way # 100
Charlotte NC
704 837-0331

(P-6805)
NEWCOMB SPRING CORP
Also Called: Newcomb Spring of California
8380 Cerritos Ave (90680-2514)
PHONE..............................714 995-5341
Robert Guard, *Mgr*
EMP: 25
SALES (corp-wide): 60.18MM **Privately Held**
Web: www.newcombspring.com
SIC: 3495 3469 5085 Wire springs; Stamping metal for the trade; Springs
PA: Newcomb Spring Corp.
3155 North Point Pkwy G220
Alpharetta GA
770 981-2803

(P-6806)
ORLANDO SPRING CORP
5341 Argosy Ave (92649-1036)
PHONE..............................562 594-8411
Frank Mauro, *Pr*
Zachary Fischer, *
EMP: 40 EST: 1957
SQ FT: 20,000
SALES (est): 8.49MM **Privately Held**
Web: www.orlandospring.com
SIC: 3495 Wire springs

(P-6807)
PRECISION COIL SPRING COMPANY
10107 Rose Ave (91731-1801)
PHONE..............................626 444-0561
Albert H Goering, *CEO*
Bert Goering, *
Don Adkins, *
William Turek, *VP Mfg*
Gustavo Arenas, *VP Engg*
EMP: 111 EST: 1951
SQ FT: 45,000
SALES (est): 14.83MM **Privately Held**
Web: www.pcspring.com
SIC: 3495 Wire springs

(P-6808)
REV CO SPRING MFANUFACTURING
9915 Alburtis Ave (90670-3209)
PHONE..............................562 949-1958
Evelyn Valles, *Pr*
Vicky Garcia, *Sec*
Rudy Valles, *VP*
EMP: 18 EST: 1973
SQ FT: 6,000
SALES (est): 857.84K **Privately Held**
Web: www.revcospring.com
SIC: 3495 Precision springs

(P-6809)
SUPERIOR SPRING COMPANY
1260 S Talt Ave (92806-5533)
PHONE..............................714 490-0881
TOLL FREE: 800
Robert De Long Junior, *Pr*
EMP: 25 EST: 1958
SQ FT: 17,000
SALES (est): 4.62MM **Privately Held**
Web: www.superiorspring.com
SIC: 3495 Wire springs

3496 Miscellaneous Fabricated Wire Products

(P-6810)
AMERICAN WIRE INC
784 S Lugo Ave (92408-2236)
PHONE..............................909 884-9990
Bambang Rahardjanoto, *CEO*
▲ EMP: 19 EST: 1991
SQ FT: 12,000
SALES (est): 4.87MM **Privately Held**
Web: www.americanwirecorp.com
SIC: 3496 Mesh, made from purchased wire

(P-6811)
ANAHEIM WIRE PRODUCTS INC
1009 E Vermont Ave (92805-5618)
PHONE..............................714 563-8300
TOLL FREE: 800
Michael Lewis, *Pr*
▲ EMP: 20 EST: 1985
SQ FT: 14,000
SALES (est): 2.86MM **Privately Held**
Web: www.anaheimwire.com
SIC: 3496 Miscellaneous fabricated wire products

(P-6812)
ASSOCIATED COMPONENTS TECHNOLOGY INC
Also Called: A C T
13932 Nautilus Dr (92843-4027)
PHONE..............................714 265-4800
EMP: 22 EST: 1989
SALES (est): 2.17MM **Privately Held**
Web: www.act1.com
SIC: 3496 5065 3677 Wire winding; Electronic parts and equipment, nec; Electronic coils and transformers

(P-6813)
C M C STEEL FABRICATORS INC
Also Called: Fontana Steel
1455 Auto Center Dr Ste 200 (91761-2239)
P.O. Box 2219 (91729-2219)
PHONE..............................909 899-9993
Deborah Marshall, *Brnch Mgr*
EMP: 17
SALES (corp-wide): 8.8B **Publicly Held**
Web: www.cmc.com
SIC: 3496 3441 1791 Miscellaneous fabricated wire products; Fabricated structural metal; Concrete reinforcement, placing of
HQ: C M C Steel Fabricators, Inc.
1 Steel Mill Dr
Seguin TX
830 372-8200

(P-6814)
CALIFORNIA WIRE PRODUCTS CORP
Also Called: Cal-Monarch
1316 Railroad St (92882-1840)
PHONE..............................951 371-7730
John G Frei, *CEO*
Samuel A Agajanian, *
Sam Agajanian, *
▲ EMP: 30 EST: 1948
SQ FT: 34,000
SALES (est): 4.4MM **Privately Held**
Web: www.cawire.com
SIC: 3496 2542 Screening, woven wire: made from purchased wire; Partitions for floor attachment, prefabricated: except wood

(P-6815)
CIRCLE W ENTERPRISES INC
Also Called: Wirenetics Co
27737 Avenue Hopkins (91355-1223)
PHONE..............................661 257-2400
Howard Weiss, *CEO*
Michael Weiss, *
Phyllis G Weiss, *
Mark Lee, *
▲ EMP: 50 EST: 1969
SQ FT: 65,000
SALES (est): 10.73MM
SALES (corp-wide): 165.92MM **Privately Held**
SIC: 3496 Miscellaneous fabricated wire products
PA: B.J.G. Electronics, Inc.
141 Remington Blvd
Ronkonkoma NY
631 737-1234

(P-6816)
DHA AMERICA INC
5403 Harvest Run Dr (92130-4879)
PHONE..............................858 925-3246
▲ EMP: 54 EST: 1996
SALES (est): 9.64MM **Privately Held**
Web: www.dha-america.com
SIC: 3496 Wire winding
PA: Dae Ha Cable Co.,Ltd.
2022 Deogyeong-Daero, Giheung-Gu
Yongin-Gun

(P-6817)
EJAY FILTRATION INC
3036 Durahart St (92507-3446)
P.O. Box 5268 (92517-5268)
PHONE..............................951 683-0805
Jerry Green, *CEO*
Cheryl Young, *
Bob Rostig, *
EMP: 33 EST: 1988
SQ FT: 14,000
SALES (est): 4.46MM **Privately Held**
Web: www.ejayfiltration.com
SIC: 3496 Mesh, made from purchased wire

(P-6818)
INNOVIVE LLC (PA)
10019 Waples Ct (92121-2962)
PHONE..............................858 309-6620
Dee Conger, *CEO*
Joanna Xiong, *
◆ EMP: 40 EST: 2006
SQ FT: 50,000
SALES (est): 10.28MM **Privately Held**
Web: www.innovive.com
SIC: 3496 Cages, wire

(P-6819)
KEVIN WHALEY
Also Called: Whaley, Kevin Enterprises
9565 Pathway St (92071-4184)
PHONE..............................619 596-4000
Kevin M Whaley, *Owner*
▼ EMP: 30 EST: 1976
SQ FT: 24,000
SALES (est): 3.3MM **Privately Held**
Web: www.kwcages.com
SIC: 3496 Cages, wire

(P-6820)
LEXCO IMPORTS INC
1455 S Campus Ave (91761-4369)
P.O. Box 271 (91763-0271)
PHONE..............................800 883-1454
▲ EMP: 22 EST: 2001
SALES (est): 921.68K **Privately Held**
SIC: 3496 Miscellaneous fabricated wire products

PRODUCTS & SVCS

(P-6821)
NASHVILLE WIRE PDTS MFG CO LLC
10727 Commerce Way Ste C (92337-8246)
PHONE..............................714 736-0081
George Alvarez, *Asstg*
▲ **EMP:** 19 **EST:** 2006
SALES (est): 686.34K **Privately Held**
Web: www.nashvillewire.com
SIC: 3496 Miscellaneous fabricated wire products

(P-6822)
PACIFIC WIRE PRODUCTS INC
10725 Vanowen St (91605-6402)
PHONE..............................818 755-6400
Charles L Swick, *Pr*
EMP: 25 **EST:** 1984
SQ FT: 28,000
SALES (est): 3.75MM **Privately Held**
Web: www.prontoproducts.com
SIC: 3496 Miscellaneous fabricated wire products

(P-6823)
PRECISION WIRE PRODUCTS INC (PA)
6150 Sheila St (90040-2407)
PHONE..............................323 890-9100
Vladimir John Ondrasik Junior, *Prin*
V John Ondrasik, *
◆ **EMP:** 200 **EST:** 1946
SQ FT: 200,000
SALES (est): 24.07MM
SALES (corp-wide): 24.07MM **Privately Held**
Web: www.precisionwireproducts.com
SIC: 3496 Grocery carts, made from purchased wire

(P-6824)
R & B WIRE PRODUCTS INC
2902 W Garry Ave (92704-6510)
PHONE..............................714 549-3355
Richard G Rawlins, *Pr*
◆ **EMP:** 50 **EST:** 1948
SQ FT: 20,000
SALES (est): 9.06MM **Privately Held**
Web: www.rbwire.com
SIC: 3496 Miscellaneous fabricated wire products

(P-6825)
RAMPONE INDUSTRIES LLC
168 E Liberty Ave (92801-1011)
PHONE..............................714 265-0200
Horacio Rampone, *Managing Member*
▲ **EMP:** 30 **EST:** 2003
SALES (est): 4.37MM **Privately Held**
Web: www.ramponeindustries.com
SIC: 3496 Miscellaneous fabricated wire products

(P-6826)
RAPID MFG A CAL LTD PARTNR (PA)
Also Called: Rapid Manufacturing
8080 E Crystal Dr (92807-2524)
PHONE..............................714 974-2432
Patricia Engler Howard, *Genl Pt*
Ronald W Howard, *
EMP: 180 **EST:** 1986
SQ FT: 19,500
SALES (est): 98.54MM
SALES (corp-wide): 98.54MM **Privately Held**
Web: www.rapidmfg.com
SIC: 3496 Miscellaneous fabricated wire products

(P-6827)
RFC WIRE FORMS INC
Also Called: Rfc Wire Forms
525 Brooks St (91762-3702)
PHONE..............................909 467-0559
Donald C Kemby, *CEO*
Christine Kemby, *
▲ **EMP:** 70 **EST:** 1946
SQ FT: 29,000
SALES (est): 8.73MM **Privately Held**
Web: www.rfcwireforms.com
SIC: 3496 Miscellaneous fabricated wire products

(P-6828)
RPS INC
20331 Corisco St (91311-6120)
PHONE..............................818 350-8088
Travis Miller, *Pr*
EMP: 25 **EST:** 2017
SQ FT: 1,000
SALES (est): 2.03MM **Privately Held**
SIC: 3496 7389 Miscellaneous fabricated wire products; Design services

(P-6829)
TOP-SHELF FIXTURES LLC
5263 Schaefer Ave (91710-5554)
P.O. Box 2470 (91708-2470)
PHONE..............................909 627-7423
Alonso Munoz, *Managing Member*
EMP: 95 **EST:** 2002
SQ FT: 90,000
SALES (est): 20.98MM **Privately Held**
Web: www.topshelffixtures.com
SIC: 3496 Miscellaneous fabricated wire products

(P-6830)
TREE ISLAND WIRE (USA) INC
Also Called: Tree Island Wire USA
5080 Hallmark Pkwy (92407-1835)
P.O. Box 90100 (92427-1100)
PHONE..............................909 899-1673
Daryl Young Opts, *Mgr*
EMP: 115
SALES (corp-wide): 251.95MM **Privately Held**
Web: www.treeisland.com
SIC: 3496 Miscellaneous fabricated wire products
HQ: Tree Island Wire (Usa), Inc.
3880 Valley Blvd
Walnut CA

(P-6831)
UNITED SUNSHINE AMERICAN INDUSTRIES CORPORATION
Also Called: USA Industries
2808 E Marywood Ln (92867-1912)
EMP: 25 **EST:** 1948
SALES (est): 2.57MM **Privately Held**
Web: www.usa-industries.com
SIC: 3496 Fencing, made from purchased wire

(P-6832)
US RIGGING SUPPLY CORP
1600 E Mcfadden Ave (92705-4310)
PHONE..............................714 545-7444
Richard T Walker, *CEO*
▲ **EMP:** 50 **EST:** 1974
SQ FT: 20,000
SALES (est): 9.65MM **Privately Held**
Web: www.usrigging.com
SIC: 3496 5051 Miscellaneous fabricated wire products; Rope, wire (not insulated)

(P-6833)
WHITMOR PLSTIC WIRE CABLE CORP
Also Called: Whitmor Wirenetics
28420 Avenue Stanford (91355-3982)
PHONE..............................661 257-2400
EMP: 42
SALES (corp-wide): 9.37MM **Privately Held**
Web: www.wireandcable.com
SIC: 3496 5063 Cable, uninsulated wire: made from purchased wire; Electrical apparatus and equipment
PA: Whitmor Plastic Wire And Cable Corp.
27737 Avenue Hopkins
Santa Clarita CA
661 257-2400

(P-6834)
WHITMOR PLSTIC WIRE CABLE CORP (PA)
Also Called: Whitmor Wire and Cable
27737 Avenue Hopkins (91355-1223)
PHONE..............................661 257-2400
Michael Weiss, *Pr*
Jeff Siebert, *
Mark Lee, *
Dwight Van Lake, *
Stella Reaza, *
▼ **EMP:** 50 **EST:** 1959
SQ FT: 50,000
SALES (est): 9.37MM
SALES (corp-wide): 9.37MM **Privately Held**
Web: www.wireandcable.com
SIC: 3496 5063 3357 Cable, uninsulated wire: made from purchased wire; Electrical apparatus and equipment; Nonferrous wiredrawing and insulating

(P-6835)
WYREFAB INC
15711 S Broadway (90248-2401)
P.O. Box 3767 (90247-7467)
PHONE..............................310 523-2147
Charles Nick, *Pr*
John P Massey, *
EMP: 42 **EST:** 1948
SQ FT: 55,000
SALES (est): 4.42MM **Privately Held**
Web: www.wyrefab.com
SIC: 3496 Miscellaneous fabricated wire products

3498 Fabricated Pipe And Fittings

(P-6836)
AEROFIT LLC
1425 S Acacia Ave (92831-5317)
PHONE..............................714 521-5060
Jordan A Law, *Managing Member*
▲ **EMP:** 150 **EST:** 1968
SQ FT: 67,000
SALES (est): 51.23MM
SALES (corp-wide): 16.95B **Publicly Held**
Web: www.camaerospace.com
SIC: 3498 Pipe fittings, fabricated from purchased pipe
HQ: Consolidated Aerospace Manufacturing, Llc
1425 S Acacia Ave
Fullerton CA
714 989-2797

(P-6837)
AMERIFLEX INC
Also Called: Mw Components - Corona

2390 Railroad St (92878-5410)
PHONE..............................951 737-5557
John Bagnuolo, *CEO*
Chester Kwasniak, *CFO*
▲ **EMP:** 76 **EST:** 1981
SQ FT: 32,000
SALES (est): 18.34MM
SALES (corp-wide): 1.05B **Privately Held**
Web: www.mwcomponents.com
SIC: 3498 3494 3674 Fabricated pipe and fittings; Valves and pipe fittings, nec; Semiconductors and related devices
HQ: Mw Industries, Inc.
3426 Toringdon Way # 100
Charlotte NC
704 837-0331

(P-6838)
BAKER COUPLING COMPANY INC
2929 S Santa Fe Ave (90058-1425)
P.O. Box 7249 (91327-7249)
PHONE..............................323 583-3444
Ramendra Satyarthi, *Pr*
▲ **EMP:** 35 **EST:** 1982
SQ FT: 65,000
SALES (est): 3.73MM **Privately Held**
Web: www.bakercoupling.com
SIC: 3498 Couplings, pipe: fabricated from purchased pipe

(P-6839)
BASSANI MANUFACTURING
Also Called: Bassani Exhaust
2900 E La Jolla St (92806-1305)
PHONE..............................714 630-1821
Darryl Bassani, *Pr*
Becky Bassani, *
▲ **EMP:** 46 **EST:** 1969
SQ FT: 20,791
SALES (est): 9.45MM **Privately Held**
Web: www.bassani.com
SIC: 3498 3599 Fabricated pipe and fittings; Machine shop, jobbing and repair

(P-6840)
CAL PIPE MANUFACTURING INC (PA)
Also Called: Calpipe Security Bollards
12160 Woodruff Ave (90241-5606)
PHONE..............................562 803-4388
Dan Markus, *Pr*
Sheri Caine-markus, *VP*
▲ **EMP:** 37 **EST:** 1986
SQ FT: 125,000
SALES (est): 4.65MM
SALES (corp-wide): 4.65MM **Privately Held**
Web: www.atkore.com
SIC: 3498 Tube fabricating (contract bending and shaping)

(P-6841)
COTT TECHNOLOGIES INC
14923 Proctor Ave (91746-3206)
PHONE..............................626 961-3399
Gilbert L Decardenas, *Pr*
George C Salmas, *VP*
EMP: 17 **EST:** 1996
SALES (est): 509.96K **Privately Held**
SIC: 3498 Piping systems for pulp, paper, and chemical industries

(P-6842)
CRYOWORKS INC
3309 Grapevine St (91752-3503)
PHONE..............................951 360-0920
Timothy L Mast, *Pr*
Donna J Mast, *
Tamara Sipos, *

EMP: 58 **EST:** 2009
SALES (est): 10.35MM **Privately Held**
Web: www.cryoworks.net
SIC: 3498 1711 Fabricated pipe and fittings; Plumbing contractors

(P-6843)
CUNICO CORPORATION
1910 W 16th St (90813-1137)
P.O. Box 9010 (90810-0010)
PHONE..............................562 733-4600
▲ **EMP:** 45 **EST:** 1951
SALES (est): 9.45MM
SALES (corp-wide): 9.45MM **Privately Held**
Web: www.cunicocorp.com
SIC: 3498 Pipe fittings, fabricated from purchased pipe
PA: Citadel Capital Corporation
1910 W 16th St
Long Beach CA
562 733-4600

(P-6844)
CUSTOM PIPE & FABRICATION INC (HQ)
10560 Fern Ave (90680-2648)
P.O. Box 978 (90680-0978)
PHONE..............................800 553-3058
Danny Daniel, *CEO*
Leonard Shapiro, *Treas*
Jerry Witkow, *Sec*
▲ **EMP:** 60 **EST:** 1972
SQ FT: 8,000
SALES (est): 117.01MM
SALES (corp-wide): 134.62MM **Privately Held**
Web: www.custompipe.com
SIC: 3498 Tube fabricating (contract bending and shaping)
PA: Shapco Inc.
1666 20th St Ste 100
Santa Monica CA
310 264-1666

(P-6845)
EDMUND A GRAY CO (PA)
2277 E 15th St (90021-2852)
PHONE..............................213 625-0376
Lawrence Gray Junior, *CEO*
Lawrence Gray Iii, *VP*
Patricia Gray, *
▲ **EMP:** 75 **EST:** 1910
SQ FT: 50,000
SALES (est): 13.68MM
SALES (corp-wide): 13.68MM **Privately Held**
Web: www.eagray.com
SIC: 3498 Pipe fittings, fabricated from purchased pipe

(P-6846)
FLEXIBLE METAL INC
Also Called: FMI
1685 Brandywine Ave (91911-6020)
PHONE..............................734 516-3017
Michael Nocholson, *CEO*
▲ **EMP:** 180 **EST:** 1986
SALES (est): 40.23MM
SALES (corp-wide): 112.6MM **Privately Held**
Web: www.flexiblemetal.com
SIC: 3498 Fabricated pipe and fittings
PA: Hyspan Precision Products, Inc.
1685 Brandywine Ave
Chula Vista CA
619 421-1355

(P-6847)
ILCO INDUSTRIES INC
Also Called: Ilco Industries
1308 W Mahalo Pl (90220-5418)
PHONE..............................310 631-8655
Elias Awad, *Pr*
EMP: 35 **EST:** 1936
SQ FT: 23,000
SALES (est): 8.31MM **Privately Held**
Web: www.ilcoind.com
SIC: 3498 3492 Manifolds, pipe: fabricated from purchased pipe; Hose and tube fittings and assemblies, hydraulic/pneumatic

(P-6848)
MARK IV METAL PRODUCTS INC
544 W 132nd St (90248-1504)
PHONE..............................310 217-9700
David Viana, *Pr*
EMP: 22 **EST:** 1954
SQ FT: 20,000
SALES (est): 879.56K **Privately Held**
Web: www.markivmetal.com
SIC: 3498 Tube fabricating (contract bending and shaping)

(P-6849)
MD STAINLESS SERVICES
8241 Phlox St (90241-4841)
PHONE..............................562 904-7022
Marvin Davis, *Pr*
Sunshine Olsen, *Treas*
EMP: 20 **EST:** 1988
SQ FT: 15,000
SALES (est): 4.84MM **Privately Held**
Web: www.mdstainless.com
SIC: 3498 1711 Fabricated pipe and fittings; Process piping contractor

(P-6850)
ONE-WAY MANUFACTURING INC
1195 N Osprey Cir (92807-1709)
PHONE..............................714 630-8833
Sue Huang, *CEO*
Ike Huang, *COO*
EMP: 23 **EST:** 2005
SQ FT: 19,400
SALES (est): 4.32MM **Privately Held**
Web: www.onewaymfg.com
SIC: 3498 3599 1541 7692 Tube fabricating (contract bending and shaping); Machine and other job shop work; Truck and automobile assembly plant construction; Welding repair

(P-6851)
RIGHT MANUFACTURING LLC
7949 Stromesa Ct Ste G (92126-6338)
PHONE..............................858 566-7002
▲ **EMP:** 30 **EST:** 1971
SQ FT: 15,000
SALES (est): 2.65MM **Privately Held**
Web: www.rightmfg.com
SIC: 3498 3444 Tube fabricating (contract bending and shaping); Sheet metalwork

(P-6852)
RUSSELL FABRICATION CORP
Also Called: American Fabrication
4940 Gilmore Ave (93308-6150)
PHONE..............................661 861-8495
Kevin Russell, *Pr*
EMP: 45 **EST:** 1985
SALES (est): 9.51MM **Privately Held**
Web: www.americanfabandpowdercoating.com
SIC: 3498 3444 Fabricated pipe and fittings; Sheet metalwork

(P-6853)
TRINITY PROCESS SOLUTIONS INC
4740 E Bryson St (92807-1901)
PHONE..............................714 701-1112
Jack Brunner, *Pr*
Candace Brunner, *VP*
EMP: 20 **EST:** 2005
SQ FT: 13,000
SALES (est): 6.43MM
SALES (corp-wide): 700MM **Privately Held**
Web: www.trinityprocesssolutions.com
SIC: 3498 3317 8711 Fabricated pipe and fittings; Welded pipe and tubes; Engineering services
PA: Legence Holdings Llc
1601 Las Plumas Ave
San Jose CA
408 347-3400

(P-6854)
WESSEX INDUSTRIES INC
8619 Red Oak St (91730-4820)
PHONE..............................562 944-5760
Archie Castillo, *Pr*
Edward Mojica, *
Linne A Castillo, *
EMP: 25 **EST:** 1985
SQ FT: 30,000
SALES (est): 2.44MM **Privately Held**
SIC: 3498 8742 Pipe fittings, fabricated from purchased pipe; Management consulting services

---

3499 Fabricated Metal Products, Nec

(P-6855)
AMERICAN SECURITY PRODUCTS CO
Also Called: Amsec
11925 Pacific Ave (92337-8231)
P.O. Box 317001 (92331-7001)
PHONE..............................951 685-9680
Drew Meng, *Pr*
Thomas Cassutt, *CFO*
Robert Sallee, *
◆ **EMP:** 237 **EST:** 1946
SQ FT: 150,000
SALES (est): 44.62MM **Privately Held**
Web: www.americansecuritysafes.com
SIC: 3499 1731 Safes and vaults, metal; Safety and security specialization

(P-6856)
ARTISAN HOUSE INC
Also Called: Artisan House, Inc
8238 Lankershim Blvd (91605-1613)
PHONE..............................818 767-7476
Dennis Damore, *Brnch Mgr*
EMP: 30
SALES (corp-wide): 5.32MM **Privately Held**
SIC: 3499 Novelties and specialties, metal
PA: Artisan House, Inc.
3750 Cohasset St
Burbank CA
818 565-5030

(P-6857)
BEY-BERK INTERNATIONAL (PA)
9145 Deering Ave (91311-5802)
PHONE..............................818 773-7534
Kurken Y Berksanlar, *Pr*
Serop Beylerian, *
◆ **EMP:** 23 **EST:** 1980
SQ FT: 19,800

SALES (est): 2.56MM
SALES (corp-wide): 2.56MM **Privately Held**
Web: www.bey-berk.com
SIC: 3499 3873 Novelties and giftware, including trophies; Clocks, assembly of

(P-6858)
CHATSWORTH PRODUCTS INC (PA)
Also Called: C P I
4175 Guardian St (93063-3382)
PHONE..............................818 735-6100
Michael Custer, *CEO*
Larry Renaud, *
Larry Varblow, *
Tom Jorgenson, *
Ted Behrens, *
◆ **EMP:** 25 **EST:** 1990
SALES (est): 107.78MM **Privately Held**
Web: www.chatsworth.com
SIC: 3499 2542 Machine bases, metal; Partitions and fixtures, except wood

(P-6859)
CUSTOM IRON DESIGN
270 E Easy St Ste 1 (93065-1799)
PHONE..............................805 581-3763
Todd Van, *Brnch Mgr*
EMP: 21
SIC: 3499 Metal household articles
PA: Custom Iron Design
522 E Banning St
Compton CA

(P-6860)
DOT BLUE SAFES CORPORATION
2707 N Garey Ave (91767-1809)
PHONE..............................909 445-8888
Berge Jalakian, *CEO*
◆ **EMP:** 42 **EST:** 2004
SQ FT: 90,000
SALES (est): 9.01MM **Privately Held**
Web: www.bluedotsafes.com
SIC: 3499 8741 Safes and vaults, metal; Management services

(P-6861)
ECOOLTHING CORP
Also Called: Cool Things
1321 E Saint Gertrude Pl Ste A (92705-5241)
P.O. Box 6022 (92616-6022)
PHONE..............................714 368-4791
Connie Wang, *Pr*
Linda Wang, *
▲ **EMP:** 50 **EST:** 2001
SQ FT: 10,000
SALES (est): 4.38MM **Privately Held**
SIC: 3499 5199 Novelties and giftware, including trophies; Gifts and novelties

(P-6862)
EVANS INDUSTRIES INC
Darnell-Rose Div
17915 Railroad St (91748-1113)
PHONE..............................626 912-1688
Bob Batistic, *Mgr*
EMP: 73
SALES (corp-wide): 39.4MM **Privately Held**
Web: www.mmgmfg.com
SIC: 3499 5072 Wheels: wheelbarrow, stroller, etc.: disc, stamped metal; Casters and glides
HQ: Evans Industries, Inc.
3150 Livernois Rd Ste 170
Troy MI
313 259-2266

PRODUCTS & SVCS

(P-6863)
EXECUTIVE SAFE AND SEC CORP
Also Called: Amphion
10722 Edison Ct (91730-4845)
PHONE..............................909 947-7020
Scott C Denton, *Pr*
Robyn Denton, *
◆ **EMP:** 30 **EST:** 1999
SQ FT: 11,000
SALES (est): 6.24MM **Privately Held**
Web: www.amphion.biz
SIC: 3499 5072 7382 5099 Safes and vaults, metal; Security devices, locks; Confinement surveillance systems maintenance and monitoring; Locks and lock sets

(P-6864)
INTEGRATED TECH GROUP INC (PA)
11250 Playa Ct (90230-6127)
PHONE..............................310 391-7213
Anil Anji, *CEO*
EMP: 20 **EST:** 2006
SQ FT: 50,000
SALES (est): 46.01MM
SALES (corp-wide): 46.01MM **Privately Held**
Web: www.intetechgroup.com
SIC: 3499 Magnetic shields, metal

(P-6865)
INTRA STORAGE SYSTEMS INC
Also Called: Gibo/Kodama Chairs
7100 Honold Cir (92841-1424)
PHONE..............................714 373-2346
▲ **EMP:** 30 **EST:** 1983
SALES (est): 4MM **Privately Held**
Web: www.intrastorage.com
SIC: 3499 5084 3535 2599 Chair frames, metal; Materials handling machinery; Belt conveyor systems, general industrial use; Factory furniture and fixtures

(P-6866)
L A PROPOINT INC
10870 La Tuna Canyon Rd (91352-2009)
PHONE..............................818 767-6800
Mark Riddlesperger, *Pr*
James Hartman, *
▼ **EMP:** 30 **EST:** 2002
SQ FT: 28,000
SALES (est): 6.26MM **Privately Held**
Web: www.lapropoint.com
SIC: 3499 3449 Metal household articles; Miscellaneous metalwork

(P-6867)
LAMINATED SHIM COMPANY INC
1691 California Ave (92881-3375)
PHONE..............................951 273-3900
EMP: 25 **EST:** 1982
SALES (est): 3.45MM **Privately Held**
Web: www.laminatedshim.com
SIC: 3499 Shims, metal

(P-6868)
MAGNETIC COMPONENT ENGRG LLC (PA)
Also Called: M C E
2830 Lomita Blvd (90505-5101)
PHONE..............................310 784-3100
Linda Montgomerie, *CEO*
▲ **EMP:** 93 **EST:** 1973
SQ FT: 50,000
SALES (est): 13.38MM
SALES (corp-wide): 13.38MM **Privately Held**
Web: www.mceproducts.com

SIC: 3499 3677 Magnets, permanent: metallic; Electronic coils and transformers

(P-6869)
MATERIAL CONTROL INC
Also Called: Cotterman Company
6901 District Blvd Ste A (93313-2071)
PHONE..............................661 617-6033
Tony Ortiz, *Brnch Mgr*
EMP: 74
SALES (corp-wide): 49.54MM **Privately Held**
Web: www.materialcontrolinc.com
SIC: 3499 Metal ladders
PA: Material Control, Inc.
130 Seltzer Rd
Croswell MI
630 892-4274

(P-6870)
PAPPALECCO
3650 5th Ave Ste 104 (92103-4243)
PHONE..............................619 906-5566
Francesco Bucci, *Brnch Mgr*
EMP: 44
Web: www.pappalecco.com
SIC: 3499 Ice cream freezers, household, nonelectric; metal
PA: Pappalecco
1602 State St
San Diego CA

(P-6871)
PSM INDUSTRIES INC (PA)
14000 Avalon Blvd (90061-2636)
PHONE..............................888 663-8256
Craig Paullin, *CEO*
Susan Paullin, *
Mary Sherrill, *
▲ **EMP:** 60 **EST:** 1956
SALES (est): 43.79MM
SALES (corp-wide): 43.79MM **Privately Held**
Web: www.psmindustries.com
SIC: 3499 Friction material, made from powdered metal

(P-6872)
QUALITY MAGNETICS CORPORATION
18025 Adria Maru Ln (90746-1403)
P.O. Box 1238 (92240-0947)
PHONE..............................310 632-1941
William K Buckley, *CEO*
Chante Buckley, *CFO*
▲ **EMP:** 29 **EST:** 1991
SQ FT: 27,000
SALES (est): 1.14MM **Privately Held**
SIC: 3499 3299 Magnets, permanent: metallic; Ceramic fiber

(P-6873)
SPORTSMEN STEEL SAFE FABG CO (PA)
Also Called: Sportsman Steel Gun Safe
6311 N Paramount Blvd (90805-3301)
PHONE..............................562 984-0244
Kevin Hand, *CEO*
Chris Cude, *CFO*
▲ **EMP:** 20 **EST:** 1988
SQ FT: 30,000
SALES (est): 2.32MM
SALES (corp-wide): 2.32MM **Privately Held**
Web: www.sportsmansteelsafes.com
SIC: 3499 5999 Safes and vaults, metal; Safety supplies and equipment

(P-6874)
TROPI-CON FOODS INC
3691 Noakes St (90023-3244)
PHONE..............................949 472-2200
EMP: 24
SALES (corp-wide): 164.46K **Privately Held**
Web: www.tropicon.com
SIC: 3499 Novelties and specialties, metal
PA: Tropi-Con Foods, Inc.
17748 Sky Park Cir # 255
Irvine CA
949 472-2200

(P-6875)
VAULT PRO
13607 Pumice St (90670-5105)
PHONE..............................800 299-6929
Tony Darling, *Prin*
Dick Slater, *CFO*
▲ **EMP:** 17 **EST:** 2013
SALES (est): 1.63MM **Privately Held**
Web: www.vaultprousa.com
SIC: 3499 Fabricated metal products, nec

(P-6876)
VIGILANT DRONE DEFENSE INC
1055 W 7th St 33rd Fl (90017-2577)
PHONE..............................424 275-8282
Paul Tremaine, *Pr*
EMP: 20 **EST:** 2017
SALES (est): 1.39MM **Privately Held**
Web: www.vigilantdronedefense.com
SIC: 3499 3728 Target drones, for use by ships: metal; Target drones

3511 Turbines And Turbine Generator Sets

(P-6877)
ALTURDYNE POWER SYSTEMS INC
1405 N Johnson Ave (92020-1615)
PHONE..............................619 343-3204
Frank Verbeke, *Pr*
EMP: 30 **EST:** 2013
SQ FT: 3,000
SALES (est): 6.5MM **Privately Held**
Web: www.alturdyne.com
SIC: 3511 1731 Gas turbine generator set units, complete; Electric power systems contractors

(P-6878)
CAPSTONE GREEN ENERGY CORP (PA)
Also Called: Capstone
16640 Stagg St (91406-1630)
◆ **EMP:** 119 **EST:** 1988
SQ FT: 79,000
SALES (est): 69.64MM **Publicly Held**
Web: www.capstonegreenenergy.com
SIC: 3511 Turbines and turbine generator sets

(P-6879)
CLIPPER WINDPOWER PLC
Also Called: Clipper Windpower
6305 Carpinteria Ave Ste 300 (93013-2968)
PHONE..............................805 690-3275
Michael Keane, *
EMP: 740 **EST:** 2005
SALES (est): 66.33MM **Privately Held**
SIC: 3511 Turbines and turbine generator sets

(P-6880)
GE WIND ENERGY LLC
13681 Chantico Rd (93561-8188)
PHONE..............................661 823-6423
Gerlad Turk, *Mgr*
EMP: 213
SALES (corp-wide): 76.56B **Publicly Held**
SIC: 3511 Turbines and turbine generator sets
HQ: Ge Wind Energy, Llc
13000 Jameson Rd
Tehachapi CA
661 822-6835

(P-6881)
GE WIND ENERGY LLC (HQ)
13000 Jameson Rd (93561-8157)
PHONE..............................661 822-6835
◆ **EMP:** 400 **EST:** 2002
SALES (est): 494.82MM
SALES (corp-wide): 76.56B **Publicly Held**
SIC: 3511 Turbines and turbine generator sets
PA: General Electric Company
1 Financial Ctr Ste 3700
Boston MA
617 443-3000

(P-6882)
LA TURBINE (HQ)
28557 Industry Dr (91355-5424)
PHONE..............................661 294-8290
John Maskaluk, *CEO*
Danny Mascari, *
Christian Maskaluk, *
Idris Kebir, *
Richard Samson, *
▼ **EMP:** 69 **EST:** 2003
SQ FT: 90,000
SALES (est): 24.99MM **Publicly Held**
Web: www.chartindustries.com
SIC: 3511 Turbines and turbine generator sets and parts
PA: Chart Industries, Inc.
2200 Arprt Ind Dr Ste 1
Ball Ground GA

(P-6883)
MODULAR WIND ENERGY INC
1709 Apollo Ct (90740-5617)
PHONE..............................562 304-6782
EMP: 53 **EST:** 2007
SALES (est): 5.64MM **Privately Held**
Web: www.modwind.com
SIC: 3511 Turbines and turbine generator sets

(P-6884)
PRECISION ENGINE CONTROLS CORP (DH)
Also Called: Pecc
11661 Sorrento Valley Rd (92121-1083)
P.O. Box 7734 (44306-0734)
PHONE..............................858 792-3217
EMP: 102 **EST:** 1992
SALES (est): 48.47MM
SALES (corp-wide): 19.07B **Publicly Held**
SIC: 3511 Gas turbine generator set units, complete
HQ: Meggitt Limited
Pilot Way
Coventry W MIDLANDS
247 682-6900

(P-6885)
SOLAR TURBINES INCORPORATED (HQ)
2200 Pacific Hwy (92101-1773)
P.O. Box 85376 (92186-5376)

PHONE................................619 544-5352
Thomas Pellette, *Pr*
P Browning, *
Robert May, *
◆ **EMP:** 3890 **EST:** 1927
SQ FT: 1,080,000
SALES (est): 1.88B
SALES (corp-wide): 59.43B **Publicly Held**
Web: www.solarturbines.com
SIC: 3511 Gas turbine generator set units, complete
PA: Caterpillar Inc.
5205 N Ocnnor Blvd Ste 10 Connor
Irving TX
972 891-7700

(P-6886)
SOLAR TURBINES INCORPORATED
2660 Sarnen St (92154-6216)
PHONE................................619 544-5321
EMP: 25
SALES (corp-wide): 59.43B **Publicly Held**
Web: www.solarturbines.com
SIC: 3511 Gas turbine generator set units, complete
HQ: Solar Turbines Incorporated
2200 Pacific Hwy
San Diego CA
619 544-5352

(P-6887)
SOLAR TURBINES INCORPORATED
9330 Sky Park Ct (92123-4304)
PHONE................................858 694-6110
Stephen Kanyr, *Prin*
EMP: 200
SALES (corp-wide): 59.43B **Publicly Held**
Web: www.solarturbines.com
SIC: 3511 Gas turbine generator set units, complete
HQ: Solar Turbines Incorporated
2200 Pacific Hwy
San Diego CA
619 544-5352

(P-6888)
SOLAR TURBINES INCORPORATED
9250 Sky Park Ct A (92123-4302)
PHONE................................858 715-2060
EMP: 55
SQ FT: 60,155
SALES (corp-wide): 59.43B **Publicly Held**
Web: www.solarturbines.com
SIC: 3511 Gas turbine generator set units, complete
HQ: Solar Turbines Incorporated
2200 Pacific Hwy
San Diego CA
619 544-5352

(P-6889)
SOLAR TURBINES INTL CO (DH)
2200 Pacific Hwy (92101-1773)
P.O. Box 85376 (92186-5376)
PHONE................................619 544-5000
Thomas Pellette, *CEO*
Steve Gosslin, *Pr*
D M Lehmann, *VP*
D W Esbeck, *VP*
Greg Barr, *VP*
EMP: 20 **EST:** 1977
SALES (est): 45.19MM
SALES (corp-wide): 59.43B **Publicly Held**
SIC: 3511 Gas turbine generator set units, complete
HQ: Solar Turbines Incorporated
2200 Pacific Hwy

San Diego CA
619 544-5352

(P-6890)
TURBINE REPAIR SERVICES LLC (PA)
1838 E Cedar St (91761-7763)
PHONE................................909 947-2256
Victor M Sanchez, *Managing Member*
Dave Meyer, *
Michael Dorrel, *Managing Member*
Cesar Siordia, *
Danny Sanchez, *
EMP: 39 **EST:** 2000
SQ FT: 12,000
SALES (est): 16.3MM **Privately Held**
Web: www.turbinerepairservices.com
SIC: 3511 Turbines and turbine generator sets

(P-6891)
WEPOWER LLC
32 Journey Ste 250 (92656-5329)
PHONE................................866 385-9463
Marvin Winkler, *Managing Member*
Howard Makler, *Pr*
Kevin B Donovan, *Dir*
▲ **EMP:** 25 **EST:** 2008
SALES (est): 981.66K **Privately Held**
SIC: 3511 Turbines and turbine generator set units, complete

3519 Internal Combustion Engines, Nec

(P-6892)
CUMMINS PACIFIC LLC (HQ)
Also Called: Cummins
1939 Deere Ave (92606-4818)
PHONE................................949 253-6000
TOLL FREE: 800
Mark Yragui, *Pr*
▲ **EMP:** 85 **EST:** 2002
SALES (est): 87.89MM
SALES (corp-wide): 28.07B **Publicly Held**
Web: www.cummins.com
SIC: 3519 5063 7538 Internal combustion engines, nec; Generators; General automotive repair shops
PA: Cummins Inc.
500 Jackson St
Columbus IN
812 377-3842

(P-6893)
DETROIT DIESEL CORPORATION
10645 Studebaker Rd 2nd Fl (90241-3173)
PHONE................................562 929-7016
Glen Nutting, *VP*
EMP: 63
Web: www.demanddetroit.com
SIC: 3519 Engines, diesel and semi-diesel or dual-fuel
HQ: Detroit Diesel Corporation
13400 W Outer Dr
Detroit MI
313 592-5000

(P-6894)
GALE BANKS ENGINEERING
Also Called: Banks Power Products
546 S Duggan Ave (91702-5136)
PHONE................................626 969-9600
Gale C Banks Iii, *Pr*
Vicki L Banks, *
▲ **EMP:** 195 **EST:** 1970
SQ FT: 121,000
SALES (est): 39.37MM **Privately Held**
Web: www.bankspower.com

SIC: 3519 3714 Parts and accessories, internal combustion engines; Motor vehicle parts and accessories

(P-6895)
PACMET AEROSPACE LLC
Also Called: Pacmet Aerospace
224 Glider Cir (92878-5033)
PHONE................................909 218-8889
David Janes, *CEO*
David A Janes Junior, *Managing Member*
◆ **EMP:** 76 **EST:** 2005
SQ FT: 45,000
SALES (est): 14.87MM **Privately Held**
Web: www.pacmetaerospace.com
SIC: 3519 Jet propulsion engines

(P-6896)
TRACY INDUSTRIES INC
Also Called: Genuine Parts Distributors
3200 E Guasti Rd Ste 100 (91761-8661)
P.O. Box 1260 (91762-0260)
PHONE................................562 692-9034
Timothy Engvall, *CEO*
David Rosenberger, *
Erma Jean Tracy, *
Timothy Engvall, *Treas*
▲ **EMP:** 216 **EST:** 1946
SALES (est): 18.84MM **Privately Held**
SIC: 3519 7538 Internal combustion engines, nec; Engine rebuilding: automotive

(P-6897)
TRANSONIC COMBUSTION INC
461 Calle San Pablo (93012-8506)
PHONE................................805 465-5145
Wolfgang Bullmer, *Pr*
Timothy Noonan, *
Mike Cheiky, *
EMP: 40 **EST:** 2006
SALES (est): 7.15MM **Privately Held**
Web: www.tscombustion.com
SIC: 3519 Internal combustion engines, nec

3523 Farm Machinery And Equipment

(P-6898)
ALBERS MFG CO INC (PA)
Also Called: Albers Dairy Equipment. Inc
14323 Albers Way (91710-1134)
PHONE................................909 597-5537
Teo Albers Junior, *Pr*
◆ **EMP:** 21 **EST:** 1949
SQ FT: 10,000
SALES (est): 4.9MM
SALES (corp-wide): 4.9MM **Privately Held**
SIC: 3523 Barn stanchions and standards

(P-6899)
AQUANEERING INC
7960 Stromesa Ct (92126-4329)
PHONE................................858 578-2028
Mark Francis, *Pr*
Wendy Porter-francis, *VP*
EMP: 30 **EST:** 1984
SQ FT: 5,100
SALES (est): 7.88MM **Privately Held**
Web: www.aquaneering.com
SIC: 3523 Farm machinery and equipment

(P-6900)
B W IMPLEMENT CO
288 W Front St (93206)
P.O. Box 758 (93206-0758)
PHONE................................661 764-5254
John C Blair, *Pr*
Alene Parsons, *Sec*

Julien Parsons, *Treas*
EMP: 22 **EST:** 1948
SQ FT: 85,000
SALES (est): 2.5MM **Privately Held**
Web: www.bwimp.com
SIC: 3523 5083 5999 Tractors, farm; Farm implements; Farm machinery, nec

(P-6901)
BRAZEAU THOROUGHBRED FARMS LP
30500 State St (92543-9258)
PHONE................................951 201-2278
Nadine Anderson, *Brnch Mgr*
EMP: 25
SALES (corp-wide): 170.88K **Privately Held**
Web:
www.brazeauthoroughbredfarms.com
SIC: 3523 0291 0752 Harvesters, fruit, vegetable, tobacco, etc.; Animal specialty farm, general; Boarding services, horses: racing and non-racing
PA: Brazeau Thoroughbred Farms, L.P.
660 Camino De Los Mares
San Clemente CA

(P-6902)
CAGECO INC
16225 Beaver Rd (92301-3908)
PHONE................................800 605-4859
Mike Alexander, *Pr*
EMP: 38 **EST:** 2012
SALES (est): 3.48MM **Privately Held**
Web: www.cagecoinc.com
SIC: 3523 Barn, silo, poultry, dairy, and livestock machinery

(P-6903)
DIG CORPORATION
1210 Activity Dr (92081-8510)
PHONE................................760 727-0914
David Levy, *Pr*
Racquel Bibens, *
Greg Smith, *
Duy Johnson, *
◆ **EMP:** 43 **EST:** 1982
SQ FT: 45,000
SALES (est): 9.18MM **Privately Held**
Web: www.digcorp.com
SIC: 3523 Irrigation equipment, self-propelled

(P-6904)
DOUBLE K INDUSTRIES INC
9711 Mason Ave (91311-5208)
PHONE................................818 772-2887
Greg Crisp, *CEO*
▲ **EMP:** 19 **EST:** 2008
SALES (est): 2.18MM **Privately Held**
Web: www.doublekindustries.com
SIC: 3523 Farm machinery and equipment

(P-6905)
DRTS ENTERPRISES LTD
Also Called: Drip Research Technology Svcs
7979 Stromesa Ct Ste A (92126-4329)
PHONE................................858 270-7244
▲ **EMP:** 20
Web: www.drts.com
SIC: 3523 Irrigation equipment, self-propelled

(P-6906)
INVELOP INC
Also Called: Double K Industries
9711 Mason Ave (91311-5208)
PHONE................................818 772-2887
Gregory S Crisp, *Pr*
◆ **EMP:** 25 **EST:** 1982
SQ FT: 20,700
SALES (est): 827.43K **Privately Held**

Web: www.doublekindustries.com
SIC: **3523** 3999 3841 Clippers, for animal use: hand or electric; Pet supplies; Veterinarians' instruments and apparatus

(P-6907)
LYON TECHNOLOGIES INC
1690 Brandywine Ave Ste A (91911-6072)
P.O. Box 22758 (92192-2758)
▲ **EMP:** 25
Web: www.lyonvet.com
SIC: **3523** 3444 3841 Farm machinery and equipment; Sheet metalwork; Veterinarians' instruments and apparatus

(P-6908)
MARIE EDWARD VINEYARDS INC
6901 E Brundage Ln (93307-3057)
PHONE................................661 363-5038
Matthew E Brock, *Pr*
EMP: 35 **EST:** 1988
SALES (est): 3.35MM **Privately Held**
Web: www.brockstrailersinc.com
SIC: **3523** 5013 7539 5511 Trailers and wagons, farm; Trailer parts and accessories; Trailer repair; Trucks, tractors, and trailers: new and used

(P-6909)
NIKKEL IRON WORKS CORPORATION
17045 S Central Valley Hwy (93263-2704)
P.O. Box 1597 (93263-1597)
PHONE................................661 746-4904
Andrew Cummings, *Pr*
Shirley Cummings, *Sec*
EMP: 17 **EST:** 1924
SQ FT: 26,000
SALES (est): 3.57MM **Privately Held**
Web: www.nikkelironworks.com
SIC: **3523** Farm machinery and equipment

(P-6910)
OLSON IRRIGATION SYSTEMS
Also Called: Olson Industrial Systems
10910 Wheatlands Ave Ste A (92071-2857)
P.O. Box 711570 (92072-1570)
PHONE................................619 562-3100
Donald Olson, *Pr*
Kathleen Baldwin, *
▲ **EMP:** 28 **EST:** 1976
SQ FT: 17,000
SALES (est): 5.22MM **Publicly Held**
SIC: **3523** Sprayers and spraying machines, agricultural
HQ: Evoqua Water Technologies Llc
210 6th Ave Ste 3300
Pittsburgh PA
724 772-0044

(P-6911)
RAIN BIRD CORPORATION
9491 Ridgehaven Ct (92123-5601)
PHONE................................619 674-4068
Eileen Collins, *Mgr*
EMP: 28
SALES (corp-wide): 433.78MM **Privately Held**
Web: www.rainbird.com
SIC: **3523** Farm machinery and equipment
PA: Rain Bird Corporation
970 W Sierra Madre Ave
Azusa CA
626 812-3400

(P-6912)
RIVULIS IRRIGATION INC (HQ)
Also Called: John Deere Water
7545 Carroll Rd (92121-2401)
PHONE................................858 578-1860

◆ **EMP:** 20 **EST:** 1977
SALES (est): 97.26MM **Privately Held**
Web: www.rivulis.com
SIC: **3523** Fertilizing, spraying, dusting, and irrigation machinery
PA: Rivulis Irrigation Ltd
98 Alon Yigal
Tel Aviv-Jaffa

(P-6913)
SIGNATURE CONTROL SYSTEMS
16485 Laguna Canyon Rd Ste 130 (92618-3848)
PHONE................................949 580-3640
Brian Smith, *Pr*
◆ **EMP:** 100 **EST:** 2000
SQ FT: 7,000
SALES (est): 8.91MM **Privately Held**
Web: www.signaturecontrolsystems.com
SIC: **3523** Irrigation equipment, self-propelled

(P-6914)
SPECIALIZED DAIRY SERVICE INC
Also Called: S D S
1710 E Philadelphia St (91761-7705)
PHONE................................909 923-3420
Joe T Trujillo, *CEO*
Joe Trujillo, *VP*
EMP: 22 **EST:** 2004
SQ FT: 25,000
SALES (est): 5.02MM **Privately Held**
Web: www.sdsdairy.com
SIC: **3523** 3556 5083 Dairy equipment (farm), nec; Dairy and milk machinery; Dairy machinery and equipment

(P-6915)
STORM INDUSTRIES INC (PA)
Also Called: Storm
23223 Normandie Ave (90501-5050)
PHONE................................310 534-5232
Dale R Philippi, *CEO*
Guy E Marge, *
Georgia Claessens, *
▲ **EMP:** 100 **EST:** 1977
SALES (est): 77.26MM
SALES (corp-wide): 77.26MM **Privately Held**
Web: www.stormind.com
SIC: **3523** 6552 Irrigation equipment, self-propelled; Subdividers and developers, nec

(P-6916)
TORO COMPANY
1588 N Marshall Ave (92020-1523)
PHONE................................619 562-2950
Timothy Young, *Mgr*
EMP: 118
SQ FT: 86,578
SALES (corp-wide): 4.51B **Publicly Held**
Web: www.thetorocompany.com
SIC: **3523** Irrigation equipment, self-propelled
PA: The Toro Company
8111 Lyndale Ave S
Bloomington MN
952 888-8801

(P-6917)
TORO COMPANY
5825 Jasmine St (92504-1183)
P.O. Box 489 (92502-0489)
PHONE................................951 688-9221
Kendrick Melrose, *Mgr*
EMP: 86
SALES (corp-wide): 4.51B **Publicly Held**
Web: www.thetorocompany.com
SIC: **3523** Irrigation equipment, self-propelled
PA: The Toro Company
8111 Lyndale Ave S

Bloomington MN
952 888-8801

(P-6918)
UMBRLA INC
3242 Halladay St Ste 202 (92705-5648)
PHONE................................888 909-5564
Frank Knuettel Ii, *CEO*
EMP: 52 **EST:** 2019
SALES (est): 7.06MM **Publicly Held**
SIC: **3523** Farm machinery and equipment
PA: Unrivaled Brands, Inc.
3242 Halladay St Ste 202
Santa Ana CA

3524 Lawn And Garden Equipment

(P-6919)
MCLANE MANUFACTURING INC
6814 Foster Bridge Blvd (90201-2032)
PHONE................................562 633-8158
Elmer E Malchow, *Ch Bd*
Ronald Mc Lane, *
Olivia Osorio, *
▲ **EMP:** 65 **EST:** 1942
SALES (est): 9.46MM **Privately Held**
Web: www.mclaneedgers.com
SIC: **3524** Lawnmowers, residential: hand or power

(P-6920)
R&M SUPPLY INC
420 Harley Knox Blvd (92571-7566)
PHONE................................951 552-9860
◆ **EMP:** 100
Web: www.randmsupply.com
SIC: **3524** Lawn and garden equipment

(P-6921)
SCOTTS TEMECULA OPERATIONS LLC (DH)
42375 Remington Ave (92590-2512)
PHONE................................951 719-1700
Jim Hagedorn, *Ch*
Barry Sanders, *Pr*
▲ **EMP:** 41 **EST:** 2001
SQ FT: 400,000
SALES (est): 60.06MM
SALES (corp-wide): 3.55B **Publicly Held**
SIC: **3524** Lawn and garden equipment
HQ: The Scotts Company Llc
14111 Scottslawn Rd
Marysville OH
937 644-0011

(P-6922)
TRU-CUT INC
141 E 157th St (90248-2508)
P.O. Box 642475 (90064-8137)
PHONE................................310 630-0422
Nabi Merchant, *CEO*
▲ **EMP:** 35 **EST:** 1953
SQ FT: 28,620
SALES (est): 4.97MM **Privately Held**
Web: www.trucutmower.com
SIC: **3524** 5083 Lawn and garden mowers and accessories; Lawn and garden machinery and equipment

(P-6923)
WESTERN CACTUS GROWERS INC
1860 Monte Vista Dr (92084-7124)
P.O. Box 2018 (92085-2018)
PHONE................................760 726-1710
Thomas Hans Britsch, *CEO*
Margaret Britsch, *

▲ **EMP:** 25 **EST:** 1974
SQ FT: 6,000
SALES (est): 2.48MM **Privately Held**
SIC: **3524** 0181 Lawn and garden equipment ; Florists' greens and flowers

3531 Construction Machinery

(P-6924)
ALTEC INC
1127 Carrier Parkway Ave (93308-9666)
PHONE................................661 679-4177
EMP: 25
SALES (corp-wide): 1.21B **Privately Held**
Web: www.altec.com
SIC: **3531** Construction machinery
PA: Altec, Inc.
210 Inverness Center Dr
Birmingham AL
205 991-7733

(P-6925)
AMERICAN COMPACTION EQP INC
Also Called: Compaction American
29380 Hunco Way (92530-2757)
PHONE................................949 661-2921
Richard S Anderson, *CEO*
Monty Ihde, *
Darryl Kanell, *
Kelly Ihde, *
Mike Shoemaker, *
▲ **EMP:** 24 **EST:** 1987
SQ FT: 8,500
SALES (est): 15.33MM **Privately Held**
Web: www.acewheels.com
SIC: **3531** 7353 Soil compactors: vibratory; Heavy construction equipment rental
HQ: Cascade Corporation
2201 Ne 201st Ave
Fairview OR
503 669-6300

(P-6926)
BLACK DIAMOND BLADE COMPANY (PA)
Also Called: Cutting Edge Supply
234 E O St (92324-3466)
PHONE................................800 949-9014
John Brenner, *CEO*
Franklin J Brenner Senior, *Pr*
Hoby Brenner, *Treas*
◆ **EMP:** 35 **EST:** 1950
SQ FT: 16,000
SALES (est): 24.83MM
SALES (corp-wide): 24.83MM **Privately Held**
Web: www.cuttingedgesupply.com
SIC: **3531** Blades for graders, scrapers, dozers, and snow plows

(P-6927)
CAMLEVER INC
954 Se End Ave (91766-3837)
PHONE................................909 629-9669
John Z Harris, *Pr*
John Z Harris, *Pr*
Vanessa Rolden, *Sec*
EMP: 19 **EST:** 1965
SQ FT: 2,500
SALES (est): 2.56MM **Privately Held**
Web: www.camleverinc.com
SIC: **3531** 3799 3312 Construction machinery; Wheelbarrows; Blast furnaces and steel mills

(P-6928)
CAVOTEC INET US INC
5665 Corporate Ave (90630-4727)

PHONE..........................714 947-0005
▼ **EMP:** 70 **EST:** 2011
SALES (est): 25.72MM **Privately Held**
SIC: 3531 Airport construction machinery
HQ: Cavotec Us Holdings, Inc.
5665 Corporate Ave
Cypress CA
714 545-7900

(P-6929)
COUNTY OF LOS ANGELES
Also Called: Public Works, Dept of
14959 Proctor Ave (91746-3206)
PHONE..........................626 968-3312
Mike Lee, *Mgr*
EMP: 28
Web: www.lacounty.gov
SIC: 3531 9111 Road construction and
maintenance machinery; Executive offices
PA: County Of Los Angeles
500 W Temple St Ste 437
Los Angeles CA
213 974-1101

(P-6930)
COUNTY OF LOS ANGELES
Also Called: Public Works, Dept of
3637 Winter Canyon Rd (90265-4834)
PHONE..........................310 456-8014
Mark Sanchez, *Mgr*
EMP: 38
Web: www.lacounty.gov
SIC: 3531 9621 Graders, road (construction
machinery); Regulation, administration of
transportation
PA: County Of Los Angeles
500 W Temple St Ste 437
Los Angeles CA
213 974-1101

(P-6931)
CROWN PAVERS INC
Also Called: CROWN PAVERS INC
2434 W Valley Blvd Ste C (91803)
PHONE..........................323 636-3365
Manuel Corona, *Brnch Mgr*
EMP: 32
SALES (corp-wide): 203.78K **Privately
Held**
SIC: 3531 Pavers
PA: Crown Pavers, Inc.
429 S Hidalgo Ave
Alhambra CA

(P-6932)
EMPIRE SOUTHWEST LLC
Also Called: Caterpillar Authorized Dealer
3393 Us Highway 86 (92251-9527)
P.O. Box 936 (92251-0936)
PHONE..........................760 545-6200
Diane Madrigal, *Mgr*
EMP: 34
SALES (corp-wide): 641.54MM **Privately
Held**
Web: www.caterpillar.com
SIC: 3531 Construction machinery
PA: Empire Southwest, Llc
1725 S Country Club Dr
Mesa AZ
480 633-4000

(P-6933)
GROUND HOG INC
1470 Victoria Ct (92408-2831)
P.O. Box 290 (92402-0290)
PHONE..........................909 478-5700
Edward Carlson, *Pr*
Jack Carlson, *
▼ **EMP:** 25 **EST:** 1948
SQ FT: 52,000

SALES (est): 4.3MM **Privately Held**
Web: www.groundhoginc.com
SIC: 3531 Posthole diggers, powered

(P-6934)
H & L TOOTH COMPANY (PA)
Also Called: H & L Forge Company
1540 S Greenwood Ave (90640-6536)
P.O. Box 48 (74055-0048)
PHONE..........................323 721-5146
Richard L Launder, *Ch Bd*
Brian L Launder, *
▲ **EMP:** 85 **EST:** 1931
SQ FT: 220,000
SALES (est): 9.8MM
SALES (corp-wide): 9.8MM **Privately Held**
Web: www.hltooth.com
SIC: 3531 Bucket or scarifier teeth

(P-6935)
**HARCON PRECISION METALS
INC**
1790 Dornoch Ct (91910)
PHONE..........................619 423-5544
EMP: 50 **EST:** 1971
SALES (est): 6.49MM **Privately Held**
Web: www.harcon-precision.com
SIC: 3531 3444 Construction machinery;
Sheet metalwork

(P-6936)
HIROK INC
Also Called: Spitzlift
5644 Kearny Mesa Rd Ste H (92111-1311)
P.O. Box 3423 (92065-0959)
PHONE..........................619 713-5066
Michael Spitsbergen, *CEO*
Mark Spitsbergen, *VP*
EMP: 20 **EST:** 2005
SQ FT: 2,500
SALES (est): 3.7MM **Privately Held**
Web: www.spitzlist.com
SIC: 3531 Construction machinery

(P-6937)
JLG INDUSTRIES INC
Also Called: Jlg Serviceplus
7820 Lincoln Ave (92504-4443)
PHONE..........................951 358-1915
Eric Golden, *Mgr*
EMP: 56
Web: www.jlg.com
SIC: 3531 Cranes, nec
HQ: Jlg Industries, Inc.
1 Jlg Dr
Mc Connellsburg PA
717 485-5161

(P-6938)
MESA INDUSTRIES INC
Gunite Supplies & Equipment
1419 Palomares St (91750-5234)
PHONE..........................626 712-1708
EMP: 20
SQ FT: 18,286
SALES (corp-wide): 24.71MM **Privately
Held**
Web: www.mesa-intl.com
SIC: 3531 Concrete gunning equipment
PA: Mesa Industries, Inc.
4027 Eastern Ave
Cincinnati OH
513 321-2950

(P-6939)
MIXMOR INC
3131 Casitas Ave (90039-2499)
PHONE..........................323 664-1941
Michael K Mcnamara, *CEO*
Ann B Mc Namara, *Sec*

EMP: 19 **EST:** 1935
SQ FT: 17,000
SALES (est): 3.52MM **Privately Held**
Web: www.mixmor.com
SIC: 3531 Construction machinery

(P-6940)
QUIK MFG CO
Also Called: Q M C
18071 Mount Washington St (92708-6118)
PHONE..........................714 754-0337
Dannielle Schmidt, *Ch Bd*
Steve Schmidt, *
EMP: 28 **EST:** 1977
SQ FT: 25,000
SALES (est): 3.29MM **Privately Held**
Web: www.qmccranes.com
SIC: 3531 Cranes, nec

(P-6941)
SCHWING AMERICA INC
3351 Grapevine St Bldg A (91752-3510)
PHONE..........................909 681-6430
Albert Ornelas, *Mgr*
EMP: 26
SALES (corp-wide): 13.01B **Privately Held**
Web: www.schwing.com
SIC: 3531 Bituminous, cement and concrete
related products and equip.
HQ: Schwing America, Inc.
5900 Centerville Rd
Saint Paul MN
651 429-0999

(P-6942)
SILO CITY INC
1401 S Union Ave (93307-4141)
▲ **EMP:** 42 **EST:** 2001
SQ FT: 174,240
SALES (est): 2.11MM **Privately Held**
SIC: 3531 Bituminous, cement and concrete
related products and equip.

(P-6943)
STURGEON SERVICES INTL INC
Ssi
3511 Gilmore Ave (93308-6205)
P.O. Box 936 (93302-0936)
PHONE..........................661 322-4408
Ollie Sturgeon, *Brnch Mgr*
EMP: 400
Web: www.sturgeonservices.com
SIC: 3531 Construction machinery
PA: Sturgeon Services International, Inc.
3511 Gilmore Ave
Bakersfield CA

(P-6944)
TRAVIS SNYDER
Also Called: Advantage Backhoes
27248 Hwy 189 Ste Ab-06 (92317)
P.O. Box 647 (92325-0647)
PHONE..........................909 338-6302
Travis Snyder, *Prin*
EMP: 24 **EST:** 2006
SALES (est): 7.52MM **Privately Held**
Web: www.advantagebackhoes.com
SIC: 3531 Backhoes

(P-6945)
**TRIO ENGINEERED PRODUCTS
INC (HQ)**
Also Called: Trio
505 W Foothill Blvd (91702-2345)
PHONE..........................626 851-3966
Michael Francis Burke, *CEO*
Eugene Xue, *
◆ **EMP:** 25 **EST:** 2002
SALES (est): 10.27MM
SALES (corp-wide): 2.98B **Privately Held**

Web: www.global.weir
SIC: 3531 Construction machinery
attachments
PA: Weir Group Plc(The)
1 West Regent Street
Glasgow
141 637-7111

(P-6946)
US SAWS INC (PA)
Also Called: U S Saw & Blades
3702 W Central Ave (92704-5832)
PHONE..........................860 668-2402
Bruce Root, *CEO*
C W Duncan, *Pr*
Bill Glynn, *VP*
▲ **EMP:** 18 **EST:** 2004
SQ FT: 4,000
SALES (est): 10.96MM
SALES (corp-wide): 10.96MM **Privately
Held**
Web: www.ussaws.com
SIC: 3531 5082 Blades for graders,
scrapers, dozers, and snow plows; Road
construction and maintenance machinery

(P-6947)
WESTERN EQUIPMENT MFG INC
Also Called: Western Equipment Mfg
1160 Olympic Dr (92881-3390)
PHONE..........................951 284-2000
▲ **EMP:** 48 **EST:** 2010
SALES (est): 3.91MM **Privately Held**
Web: www.western-emi.com
SIC: 3531 Finishers and spreaders
(construction equipment)

3532 Mining Machinery

(P-6948)
**CAVOTEC US HOLDINGS INC
(HQ)**
Also Called: Cavotec Inet
5665 Corporate Ave (90630-4727)
PHONE..........................714 545-7900
Michael Larkin, *Pr*
EMP: 17 **EST:** 2008
SALES (est): 25.72MM **Privately Held**
SIC: 3532 3569 Drills, bits, and similar
equipment; Filters
PA: Cavotec Sa
Corso Elvezia 16
Lugano TI

(P-6949)
**POLYALLOYS INJECTED
METALS INC**
14000 Avalon Blvd (90061-2636)
PHONE..........................310 715-9800
Craig Paulin, *CEO*
EMP: 75 **EST:** 2001
SALES (est): 8.48MM
SALES (corp-wide): 43.79MM **Privately
Held**
Web: www.psmindustries.com
SIC: 3532 Amalgamators (metallurgical or
mining machinery)
PA: Psm Industries, Inc.
14000 Avalon Blvd
Los Angeles CA
888 663-8256

(P-6950)
SOTEC USA LLC
3076 S Edenglen Ave (91761-2626)
PHONE..........................909 525-5861
Gang Ye, *Managing Member*
EMP: 18
Web: www.sotecusa.com

SIC: 3532 Crushing, pulverizing, and screening equipment
HQ: Sotec Usa Llc
17870 Castleton St # 338
City Of Industry CA
909 930-2792

(P-6951)
SPAULDING EQUIPMENT COMPANY (PA)
Also Called: Spaulding Crusher Parts
75 Paseo Adelanto (92570-9343)
P.O. Box 1807 (92572-1807)
PHONE..................................951 943-4531
George E Spaulding, *Ch Bd*
James Michael Spaulding, *
Norman Vetter, *
Fred Stemrich, *
◆ EMP: 47 EST: 1966
SALES (est): 9.37MM
SALES (corp-wide): 9.37MM **Privately Held**
Web: www.spauldingequipment.com
SIC: 3532 5082 7699 Mineral beneficiation equipment; Mineral beneficiation machinery ; Industrial machinery and equipment repair

3533 Oil And Gas Field Machinery

(P-6952)
AQUEOS CORPORATION (PA)
418 Chapala St Ste E (93101-8056)
PHONE..................................805 364-0570
Theodore Roche Iv, *Pr*
Bradley Parro, *
Michael Pfau, *
Larry Barels, *
Eric Legendre, *
EMP: 50 EST: 2000
SQ FT: 23,000
SALES (est): 31.58MM
SALES (corp-wide): 31.58MM **Privately Held**
Web: www.aqueossubsea.com
SIC: 3533 Oil and gas field machinery

(P-6953)
AQUEOS CORPORATION
2550 Eastman Ave (93003-7714)
PHONE..................................805 676-4330
Theodore Roche, *Brnch Mgr*
EMP: 121
SALES (corp-wide): 31.58MM **Privately Held**
Web: www.aqueossubsea.com
SIC: 3533 Oil and gas field machinery
PA: Aqueos Corporation
418 Chapala St Ste E
Santa Barbara CA
805 364-0570

(P-6954)
CHANCELLOR OIL TOOLS INC
3521 Gulf St (93308-5210)
PHONE..................................661 324-2213
EMP: 40
SIC: 3533 Drilling tools for gas, oil, or water wells

(P-6955)
CONTROL SYSTEMS INTL INC
35 Parker (92618-1605)
PHONE..................................949 238-4150
Rob Lewis, *Genl Mgr*
EMP: 85
SALES (corp-wide): 6.73B **Privately Held**
Web: www.technipfmc.com

SIC: 3533 Oil and gas field machinery
HQ: Control Systems International, Inc.
8040 Nieman Rd
Shawnee Mission KS
913 599-5010

(P-6956)
DAWSON ENTERPRISES (PA)
Also Called: Cavins Oil Well Tools
2853 Cherry Ave (90755-1908)
P.O. Box 6039 (90806-0039)
PHONE..................................562 424-8564
James M Dawson, *CEO*
Harry Dawson, *
◆ EMP: 36 EST: 1928
SQ FT: 19,000
SALES (est): 9.61MM
SALES (corp-wide): 9.61MM **Privately Held**
Web: www.cavins.com
SIC: 3533 7359 Bits, oil and gas field tools: rock; Garage facility and tool rental

(P-6957)
DOWNHOLE STABILIZATION INC
3515 Thomas Way (93308-6215)
P.O. Box 2467 (93303-2467)
PHONE..................................661 631-1044
Jim Calanchini, *Pr*
Mike Jarboe, *
Jacob Banducci, *
Diane Calanchini, *
▲ EMP: 38 EST: 1989
SQ FT: 8,800
SALES (est): 9.91MM **Privately Held**
Web: www.downholestabilization.com
SIC: 3533 5082 3599 1389 Drilling tools for gas, oil, or water wells; Construction and mining machinery; Amusement park equipment; Construction, repair, and dismantling services

(P-6958)
GLOBAL ELASTOMERIC PDTS INC
5551 District Blvd (93313-2126)
PHONE..................................661 831-5380
Phil W Embury, *Pr*
Sandy Embury, *
▲ EMP: 55 EST: 1963
SQ FT: 20,000
SALES (est): 8.36MM **Privately Held**
Web: www.globaleee.com
SIC: 3533 5084 Oil and gas field machinery; Oil refining machinery, equipment, and supplies

(P-6959)
HYDRIL COMPANY
3237 Patton Way (93308-5717)
PHONE..................................661 588-9332
Ken Steinke, *Brnch Mgr*
EMP: 62
Web: www.tenaris.com
SIC: 3533 Oil field machinery and equipment
HQ: Hydril Company
302 Mccarty St
Houston TX

(P-6960)
JB ROGERS CONSULTING INC
7800 Davin Park Dr (93308-7230)
PHONE..................................661 397-4987
Paul J Farley, *Pr*
Winney Farley, *Sec*
J B Rogers, *VP*
EMP: 17 EST: 1977
SALES (est): 837.83K **Privately Held**
SIC: 3533 Oil field machinery and equipment

(P-6961)
KBA ENGINEERING LLC
2157 Mohawk St (93308-6020)
P.O. Box 1200 (93302-1200)
PHONE..................................661 323-0487
Richard C Jones, *Managing Member*
EMP: 95 EST: 1997
SQ FT: 45,000
SALES (est): 19.69MM **Privately Held**
Web: www.lufkin.com
SIC: 3533 3462 Oil and gas field machinery; Gear and chain forgings

(P-6962)
NOV INC
759 N Eckhoff St (92868-1005)
P.O. Box 6626 (92863-6626)
PHONE..................................714 978-1900
Owen Unruh, *Prin*
EMP: 52
SALES (corp-wide): 7.24B **Publicly Held**
Web: www.nov.com
SIC: 3533 Oil field machinery and equipment
PA: Nov Inc.
10353 Richmond Ave
Houston TX
346 223-3000

(P-6963)
SMITH INTERNATIONAL INC
Also Called: Omni Seals
11031 Jersey Blvd Ste A (91730-5150)
PHONE..................................909 906-7900
EMP: 130
Web: www.smithcodevelopment.com
SIC: 3533 Oil and gas field machinery
HQ: Smith International, Llc
5599 San Felipe St
Houston TX
281 443-3370

(P-6964)
TECHNIPFMC USA INC
6400 Oak Cyn Ste 100 (92618-5204)
PHONE..................................949 238-4150
EMP: 28
SALES (corp-wide): 6.73B **Privately Held**
Web: www.technipfmc.com
SIC: 3533 Oil field machinery and equipment
HQ: Technipfmc Usa, Inc.
13460 Lockwood Rd
Houston TX
281 591-4000

3534 Elevators And Moving Stairways

(P-6965)
ELEVATOR RESEARCH & MFG CO
1417 Elwood St (90021-2812)
PHONE..................................213 746-1914
Frank Edward Ed, *Park President*
Lynn Park, *
EMP: 49 EST: 1964
SQ FT: 5,000
SALES (est): 17.7MM
SALES (corp-wide): 67.62MM **Privately Held**
Web: www.elevatorresearch.com
SIC: 3534 Elevators and equipment
PA: Dewhurst Group Plc
Unit 9
Feltham MIDDX
208 744-8200

(P-6966)
GMS ELEVATOR SERVICES INC
Also Called: Gms Elevator Services
401 Borrego Ct (91773-2971)
PHONE..................................909 599-3904
G Matthew Simpkins, *Pr*
Pamela Simpkins, *
EMP: 35 EST: 1987
SQ FT: 4,000
SALES (est): 4.45MM **Privately Held**
Web: www.gmselevator.com
SIC: 3534 1796 Elevators and equipment; Elevator installation and conversion

(P-6967)
TL SHIELD & ASSOCIATES INC
Also Called: Inclinator of California
1030 Arroyo St (91340-1822)
P.O. Box 6845 (91359-6845)
PHONE..................................818 509-8228
Thomas Louis Shield, *Pr*
EMP: 35 EST: 1982
SQ FT: 2,000
SALES (est): 9.82MM **Privately Held**
Web: www.tlshield.com
SIC: 3534 1796 Elevators and equipment; Elevator installation and conversion

3535 Conveyors And Conveying Equipment

(P-6968)
AIR TUBE TRANSFER SYSTEMS INC
Also Called: A T T
715 N Cypress St (92867-6605)
PHONE..................................714 363-0700
Rick Blodgett, *Pr*
EMP: 31 EST: 1996
SQ FT: 10,000
SALES (est): 1.77MM **Privately Held**
Web: www.attsystems.com
SIC: 3535 1796 7699 3494 Pneumatic tube conveyor systems; Machinery installation; Industrial equipment services; Valves and pipe fittings, nec

(P-6969)
AMERICAN ULTRAVIOLET WEST INC
Also Called: Lesco
23555 Telo Ave (90505-4012)
PHONE..................................310 784-2930
Meredith C Stines, *Pr*
▲ EMP: 21 EST: 1978
SQ FT: 22,775
SALES (est): 4.71MM **Privately Held**
Web: www.americanultraviolet.com
SIC: 3535 5065 Conveyors and conveying equipment; Electronic parts

(P-6970)
APEX CONVEYOR CORP
40001 Via Caseta (92562-9114)
P.O. Box 812 (92564-0812)
PHONE..................................951 304-7808
EMP: 17 EST: 1995
SALES (est): 951.73K **Privately Held**
Web: www.apexconveyor.com
SIC: 3535 Conveyors and conveying equipment

(P-6971)
CONVEYOR SERVICE & ELECTRIC
9550 Ann St (90670-2616)
PHONE..................................562 777-1221
Patricia Moseley, *Pt*

Richard Moseley, *Pt*
Efren Alcantar, *Pt*
EMP: 23 **EST:** 1995
SQ FT: 13,000
SALES (est): 2.6MM **Privately Held**
Web: www.conserel.com
SIC: 3535 1796 Conveyors and conveying equipment; Machinery installation

(P-6972)
DEAMCO CORPORATION
6520 E Washington Blvd (90040-1822)
PHONE............................323 890-1190
Armen Hovannesian, *Pr*
Nick Kanian, *
◆ **EMP:** 21 **EST:** 1977
SQ FT: 55,000
SALES (est): 4.74MM **Privately Held**
Web: www.deamco.com
SIC: 3535 Conveyors and conveying equipment

(P-6973)
DEMATIC CORP
333 City Blvd W Ste 1820 (92868-2987)
PHONE............................714 388-8803
Pat Fitzpatrick, *Brnch Mgr*
EMP: 41
SALES (corp-wide): 11.57B **Privately Held**
SIC: 3535 Conveyors and conveying equipment
HQ: Dematic Corp.
756 W Peachtree St Nw
Atlanta GA

(P-6974)
INGALLS CONVEYORS INC
1005 W Olympic Blvd (90640-5121)
PHONE............................323 837-9900
TOLL FREE: 888
Maged Labib Nakla, *CEO*
Steve Ingalls, *Treas*
Colleen Ingalls, *Sec*
EMP: 21 **EST:** 1976
SQ FT: 174,000
SALES (est): 4.97MM **Privately Held**
Web: www.ingallsconveyors.com
SIC: 3535 8711 Conveyors and conveying equipment; Consulting engineer

(P-6975)
JOSE PEREZ ✪
Also Called: J&E Conveyor Services
5869 Silveira St (92880-4627)
PHONE............................920 318-6527
Jose Perez, *Owner*
EMP: 25 **EST:** 2022
SALES (est): 779.19K **Privately Held**
SIC: 3535 7389 Conveyors and conveying equipment; Business services, nec

(P-6976)
PNEUMATIC CONVEYING INC
960 E Grevillea Ct (91761-5612)
PHONE............................909 923-4481
EMP: 22 **EST:** 1978
SALES (est): 4.73MM **Privately Held**
Web:
www.pneumaticconveyingsolutions.com
SIC: 3535 Pneumatic tube conveyor systems

(P-6977)
SDI INDUSTRIES INC (DH)
Also Called: Autostore Integrator
24307 Magic Mountain Pkwy # 443 (91355-3402)
PHONE............................818 890-6002
Krish Nathan, *CEO*
Mark Conrad, *
▲ **EMP:** 150 **EST:** 1978

SALES (est): 51.1MM
SALES (corp-wide): 2.67MM **Privately Held**
Web: www.sdi.systems
SIC: 3535 3537 8748 8711 Conveyors and conveying equipment; Industrial trucks and tractors; Business consulting, nec; Engineering services
HQ: Element Logic As
Dyrskuevegen 26
Klofta

(P-6978)
TERRA NOVA TECHNOLOGIES INC
10770 Rockville St Ste A (92071)
PHONE............................619 596-7400
Ronald Kelly, *Pr*
EMP: 80 **EST:** 2019
SQ FT: 8,366
SALES (est): 12.41MM **Privately Held**
Web: www.tntinc.com
SIC: 3535 8742 Conveyors and conveying equipment; Management consulting services
HQ: Cementation Usa Inc.
10150 S Centennial Pkwy # 400
Sandy UT

(P-6979)
TIG/M LLC
9160 Jordan Ave (91311-5707)
PHONE............................818 709-8500
Alvaro Villa, *CEO*
Brad Read, *
David Hall, *
Bradley Read, *
EMP: 30 **EST:** 2005
SQ FT: 2,000
SALES (est): 4.94MM **Privately Held**
Web: www.tig-m.com
SIC: 3535 Trolley conveyors

3536 Hoists, Cranes, And Monorails

(P-6980)
CRANEVEYOR CORP (PA)
1524 Potrero Ave (91733-3017)
P.O. Box 3727 (91733-0727)
PHONE............................626 442-1524
Frank Gaetano Trimboli, *CEO*
Hector Valiente, *
John Lehman, *
Greg Bischoff, *
Michael Williams, *
▲ **EMP:** 67 **EST:** 1946
SQ FT: 41,200
SALES (est): 25.15MM
SALES (corp-wide): 25.15MM **Privately Held**
Web: www.craneveyor.com
SIC: 3536 3446 Cranes, overhead traveling; Railings, banisters, guards, etc: made from metal pipe

(P-6981)
KONECRANES INC
10310 Pioneer Blvd Ste 2 (90670-3732)
PHONE............................562 903-1371
Ari Ramo, *Brnch Mgr*
EMP: 45
Web: www.konecranes.com
SIC: 3536 Hoists, cranes, and monorails
HQ: Konecranes, Inc.
4401 Gateway Blvd
Springfield OH

(P-6982)
KONECRANES INC
1620 S Carlos Ave (91761-7601)
PHONE............................909 930-0108
Amy Gonzalez, *Brnch Mgr*
EMP: 24
Web: www.konecranes.com
SIC: 3536 Hoists, cranes, and monorails
HQ: Konecranes, Inc.
4401 Gateway Blvd
Springfield OH

(P-6983)
MOBILE EQUIPMENT COMPANY
Also Called: Mobile Equipment Appraisers
3610 Gilmore Ave (93308-6208)
P.O. Box 80776 (93380-0776)
PHONE............................661 327-8476
Evelyn Stanfill, *Pr*
Paul J Faulconer, *VP*
Gary Stanfill, *Genl Mgr*
Felecia Stanfill, *Sec*
EMP: 20 **EST:** 1960
SQ FT: 18,580
SALES (est): 2.64MM **Privately Held**
Web: www.mobile-equipment.com
SIC: 3536 8748 3559 Cranes, overhead traveling; Safety training service; Automotive related machinery

3537 Industrial Trucks And Tractors

(P-6984)
ANCRA INTERNATIONAL LLC
Aircraft Systems Division
601 S Vincent Ave (91702-5102)
PHONE............................626 765-4818
Ed Dugic, *Mgr*
EMP: 224
Web: www.ancra.com
SIC: 3537 2298 Industrial trucks and tractors ; Cargo nets
HQ: Ancra International Llc
601 S Vincent Ave
Azusa CA

(P-6985)
ANCRA INTERNATIONAL LLC (HQ)
601 S Vincent Ave (91702-5102)
PHONE............................626 765-4800
▲ **EMP:** 130 **EST:** 1996
SALES (est): 101MM **Privately Held**
Web: www.ancra.com
SIC: 3537 Lift trucks, industrial: fork, platform, straddle, etc.
PA: The Heico Companies, L.L.C.
70 W Madison St Ste 5600
Chicago IL

(P-6986)
ANTHONY WELDED PRODUCTS INC (PA)
1447 S Lexington St (93215-9700)
P.O. Box 299 (93062-0299)
PHONE............................661 721-7211
Frank S Salvucci Senior, *Ch*
Elsie Salvucci, *Pr*
EMP: 20 **EST:** 1958
SQ FT: 25,000
SALES (est): 5.87MM
SALES (corp-wide): 5.87MM **Privately Held**
Web: www.anthonycarts.com

SIC: 3537 3444 3443 Dollies (hand or power trucks), industrial,except mining; Sheet metalwork; Fabricated plate work (boiler shop)

(P-6987)
CRANEWORKS SOUTHWEST INC
1312 E Barham Dr (92078-4503)
PHONE............................760 735-9793
Marise Williams, *Off Mgr*
EMP: 18 **EST:** 2015
SALES (est): 2.51MM **Privately Held**
Web: www.crane-works.com
SIC: 3537 7353 Cranes, industrial truck; Cranes and aerial lift equipment, rental or leasing

(P-6988)
CROWN EQUIPMENT CORPORATION
Also Called: Crown Lift Trucks
4250 Greystone Dr (91761-3104)
PHONE............................909 923-8357
Mike Lammers, *Mgr*
EMP: 49
SALES (corp-wide): 7.04B **Privately Held**
Web: www.crown.com
SIC: 3537 Lift trucks, industrial: fork, platform, straddle, etc.
PA: Crown Equipment Corporation
44 S Washington St
New Bremen OH
419 629-2311

(P-6989)
CROWN EQUIPMENT CORPORATION
Also Called: Crown Lift Trucks
1300 Palomares St (91750-5232)
PHONE............................626 968-0556
Kevin Mccarthy, *Mgr*
EMP: 27
SQ FT: 28,000
SALES (corp-wide): 7.04B **Privately Held**
Web: www.crown.com
SIC: 3537 Lift trucks, industrial: fork, platform, straddle, etc.
PA: Crown Equipment Corporation
44 S Washington St
New Bremen OH
419 629-2311

(P-6990)
CROWN EQUIPMENT CORPORATION
Also Called: Crown Lift Trucks
4061 Via Oro Ave (90810-1458)
PHONE............................310 952-6600
Tom Labrador, *Brnch Mgr*
EMP: 64
SALES (corp-wide): 7.04B **Privately Held**
Web: www.crown.com
SIC: 3537 Lift trucks, industrial: fork, platform, straddle, etc.
PA: Crown Equipment Corporation
44 S Washington St
New Bremen OH
419 629-2311

(P-6991)
GLEASON INDUSTRIAL PDTS INC
Also Called: Milwaukee Hand Truck
10474 Santa Monica Blvd Ste 400 (90025-6929)
PHONE............................574 533-1141
Morton Kay, *CEO*
Shirley Kotler, *

PRODUCTS & SVCS

Howard Simon, *
▲ **EMP: 200 EST:** 1891
SQ FT: 200,000
SALES (est): 20.58MM **Privately Held**
SIC: 3537 Industrial trucks and tractors

(P-6992)
HYDRAULIC SHOP INC
2753 S Vista Ave (92316-3269)
PHONE...............................909 875-9336
Christopher O Kirk, *Pr*
EMP: 20 **EST:** 2006
SQ FT: 4,500
SALES (est): 4.85MM **Privately Held**
Web: www.hydraulicshopinc.com
SIC: 3537 Industrial trucks and tractors

(P-6993)
INDUSTRIAL DESIGN PRODUCTS INC
2700 Pomona Blvd (91768-3222)
P.O. Box 7846 (92860-8095)
PHONE...............................909 468-0693
Richard Fleischhacker Junior, *Pr*
Jose Pizarro, *Ex VP*
EMP: 21 **EST:** 1999
SQ FT: 14,000
SALES (est): 732.01K **Privately Held**
Web: www.idp-inc.com
SIC: 3537 5084 2542 Platforms, stands, tables, pallets, and similar equipment; Materials handling machinery; Pallet racks: except wood

(P-6994)
J&S GOODWIN INC (HQ)
5753 E Santa Ana Canyon Rd Ste G-355 (92807-3230)
PHONE...............................714 956-4040
Arthur J Goodwin, *CEO*
Sharon Goodwin, *
Mark Mcgregor, *CFO*
Scott Currie, *
Dan Broschak, *
◆ **EMP:** 65 **EST:** 1989
SQ FT: 3,000
SALES (est): 40.94MM
SALES (corp-wide): 8.59B **Publicly Held**
SIC: 3537 5088 5084 Trucks, tractors, loaders, carriers, and similar equipment; Golf carts; Materials handling machinery
PA: Polaris Inc.
2100 Highway 55
Medina MN
763 542-0500

(P-6995)
PAPE MATERIAL HANDLING INC
2600 Peck Rd (90601-1620)
P.O. Box 60007 (91716-0007)
PHONE...............................562 692-9311
Steve Smith, *Mgr*
EMP: 100
Web: www.papemh.com
SIC: 3537 5084 Forklift trucks; Industrial machinery and equipment
HQ: Pape' Material Handling, Inc.
355 Goodpasture Island Rd
Eugene OR

(P-6996)
POWER PT INC (PA)
Also Called: AAA Pallet
1500 Crafton Ave Bldg 100 (92359-1315)
PHONE...............................951 490-4149
Tyson Paulis, *CEO*
EMP: 32 **EST:** 2018
SALES (est): 4.32MM
SALES (corp-wide): 4.32MM **Privately Held**

SIC: 3537 Platforms, stands, tables, pallets, and similar equipment

(P-6997)
POWER PT INC
9292 Nancy St (90630-3318)
PHONE...............................714 826-7407
Tyson Paulis, *Brnch Mgr*
EMP: 36
SALES (corp-wide): 4.32MM **Privately Held**
SIC: 3537 Platforms, stands, tables, pallets, and similar equipment
PA: Power Pt Inc
1500 Crafton Ave Bldg 100
Mentone CA
951 490-4149

(P-6998)
SUPERIOR TRAILER WORKS
13700 Slover Ave (92337-7067)
PHONE...............................909 350-0185
Jack N Pocock, *CEO*
Jay Pocock, *
▲ **EMP:** 50 **EST:** 1935
SQ FT: 4,000
SALES (est): 7.64MM **Privately Held**
Web: www.superiortrailerworks.com
SIC: 3537 7539 Industrial trucks and tractors ; Trailer repair

(P-6999)
TAYLOR-DUNN MANUFACTURING LLC (HQ)
2114 W Ball Rd (92804-5498)
PHONE...............................714 956-4040
Keith Simon, *CEO*
◆ **EMP:** 100 **EST:** 1949
SQ FT: 145,000
SALES (est): 47.39MM
SALES (corp-wide): 50.11MM **Privately Held**
Web: www.taylor-dunn.com
SIC: 3537 Trucks, tractors, loaders, carriers, and similar equipment
PA: Waev Inc.
2114 W Ball Rd
Anaheim CA
714 956-4040

(P-7000)
WAEV INC (PA)
2114 W Ball Rd (92804-5417)
PHONE...............................714 956-4040
Keith Simon, *Pr*
Paul Vitrano, *Legal*
Cosmin Batrin, *Sr VP*
Jon Conlon, *Sr VP*
Luke Mulvaney, *Sr VP*
EMP: 26 **EST:** 2021
SALES (est): 50.11MM
SALES (corp-wide): 50.11MM **Privately Held**
Web: www.waevinc.com
SIC: 3537 Trucks, tractors, loaders, carriers, and similar equipment

(P-7001)
WIN-HOLT EQUIPMENT CORP
Also Called: Win-Holt Equip
2717 N Towne Ave (91767-2263)
PHONE...............................909 625-2624
Michael O'brien, *Mgr*
EMP: 21
SQ FT: 36,000
SALES (corp-wide): 49.88MM **Privately Held**
Web: www.winholt.com
SIC: 3537 Industrial trucks and tractors
PA: Win-Holt Equipment Corp.
20 Crossways Park Dr N # 205

Woodbury NY
516 222-0335

3541 Machine Tools, Metal Cutting Type

(P-7002)
AEROSPACE TOOL & GRINDING INC
14020 Shoemaker Ave (90650-4536)
P.O. Box 1536 (90651-1536)
PHONE...............................562 802-3339
Alonzo Burgos, *Pr*
Azzie Burgos, *VP*
EMP: 21 **EST:** 1987
SALES (est): 652.1K **Privately Held**
SIC: 3541 5251 Machine tools, metal cutting type; Tools

(P-7003)
AFFINITY LATH & PLASTER INC
1414 Tiffany Ln (92084-7265)
P.O. Box 362 (92085-0362)
PHONE...............................760 207-5311
Cynthia Michelle Bullard, *Brnch Mgr*
EMP: 27
SALES (corp-wide): 85.25K **Privately Held**
Web: www.southwestlathplaster.com
SIC: 3541 Lathes
PA: Affinity Lath & Plaster Inc.
818 Ora Avo Dr
Vista CA
760 453-3991

(P-7004)
APT MANUFACTURING LLC
Also Called: Stellar Engineering
2899 E Coronado St Ste E (92806-2535)
PHONE...............................714 632-0040
EMP: 18 **EST:** 2012
SALES (est): 2.15MM **Privately Held**
SIC: 3541 3451 Plasma process metal cutting machines; Screw machine products

(P-7005)
BERNHARDT AND BERNHARDT INC
Also Called: Protool Co
14771 Myford Rd Ste D (92780-7206)
PHONE...............................714 544-0708
Anton Bernhardt, *Pr*
Norbert Bernhardt, *Pr*
EMP: 21 **EST:** 1972
SQ FT: 4,600
SALES (est): 2.16MM **Privately Held**
Web: www.protoolco.com
SIC: 3541 Numerically controlled metal cutting machine tools

(P-7006)
CREMACH TECH INC
Also Called: Creative Machine Technology
400 E Parkridge Ave (92879-6618)
PHONE...............................951 735-3194
EMP: 74
Web: www.cmtus.com
SIC: 3541 Machine tools, metal cutting type
PA: Cremach Tech, Inc.
369 Meyer Cir
Corona CA

(P-7007)
CREMACH TECH INC (PA)
Also Called: Creative Machine Technology
369 Meyer Cir (92879-1078)
PHONE...............................951 735-3194
Mike Mcneeley, *CEO*
Mike Mcneeley, *Prin*

Jae Wan Choi, *
EMP: 66 **EST:** 1994
SQ FT: 34,000
SALES (est): 19.34MM **Privately Held**
Web: www.cmtus.com
SIC: 3541 8711 Machine tools, metal cutting type; Designing: ship, boat, machine, and product

(P-7008)
CTD MACHINES INC
7355 E Slauson Ave (90040-3626)
PHONE...............................213 689-4455
Kiwon Ban, *Genl Mgr*
Thomas Orlando, *Pr*
Seymour Lehrer, *VP*
Shirley Lehrer, *VP*
Ellen Orlando, *Sec*
EMP: 18 **EST:** 1967
SALES (est): 4.67MM **Privately Held**
Web: www.ctdsaw.com
SIC: 3541 Cutoff machines (metalworking machinery)

(P-7009)
DAC INTERNATIONAL INC
Also Called: D A C
6390 Rose Ln (93013-2922)
PHONE...............................805 684-8307
Kenneth R Payne, *Pr*
Joyce Kawachi, *
▲ **EMP:** 34 **EST:** 1999
SQ FT: 17,500
SALES (est): 6.66MM **Privately Held**
Web: www.dac-intl.com
SIC: 3541 Machine tools, metal cutting type

(P-7010)
DOLLAR SHAVE CLUB INC (HQ)
13335 Maxella Ave (90292-5619)
PHONE...............................310 975-8528
Jason Goldberger, *CEO*
Janet Song, *
Danny Miles, *
EMP: 104 **EST:** 2011
SALES (est): 94.1MM
SALES (corp-wide): 62.39B **Privately Held**
Web: www.dollarshaveclub.com
SIC: 3541 3991 2844 Shaving machines (metalworking); Shaving brushes; Shaving preparations
PA: Unilever Plc
Unilever House
London
207 572-1202

(P-7011)
DOWNEY GRINDING CO
12323 Bellflower Blvd (90242-2829)
P.O. Box 583 (90241-0583)
PHONE...............................562 803-5556
Larry Sequeira, *Pr*
Darla Sequeira, *
▲ **EMP:** 25 **EST:** 1960
SQ FT: 27,000
SALES (est): 2.29MM **Privately Held**
Web: www.downeygrindingpros.com
SIC: 3541 3599 Machine tools, metal cutting type; Machine shop, jobbing and repair

(P-7012)
ENSIGN US DRLG CAL INC (HQ)
7001 Charity Ave (93308-5824)
PHONE...............................661 589-0111
Selby Porter, *Pr*
Loys Honeycutt, *Prin*
EMP: 22 **EST:** 1962
SALES (est): 24.45MM
SALES (corp-wide): 1.17B **Privately Held**
Web: www.ensignusd.com

SIC: 3541 Drilling and boring machines
PA: Ensign Energy Services Inc
    400 5 Ave Sw Suite 1000
    Calgary AB
    403 262-1361

(P-7013)

HAAS AUTOMATION INC (PA)

2800 Sturgis Rd (93030-8901)
PHONE.................................805 278-1800
◆ **EMP:** 1521 **EST:** 1983
SALES (est): 437.22MM
SALES (corp-wide): 437.22MM **Privately Held**
Web: www.haascnc.com
SIC: 3541 Machine tools, metal cutting type

(P-7014)

K-V ENGINEERING INC

2411 W 1st St (92703-3509)
PHONE.................................714 229-9977
Duong Vu, *Pr*
Christie Vu,   *
EMP: 60 **EST:** 1984
SQ FT: 22,000
SALES (est): 10.2MM **Privately Held**
Web: www.kvengineering.com
SIC: 3541 3542 Milling machines; Machine tools, metal forming type

(P-7015)

KYOCERA TYCOM CORPORATION

Also Called: Kyoceara
3565 Cadillac Ave (92626-1401)
PHONE.................................714 428-3600
▲ **EMP:** 500
SIC: 3541 3845 3843 3841 Machine tools, metal cutting type; Endoscopic equipment, electromedical, nec; Cutting instruments, dental; Surgical and medical instruments

(P-7016)

MELFRED BORZALL INC

2712 Airpark Dr (93455-1418)
PHONE.................................805 614-4344
▲ **EMP:** 40 **EST:** 1946
SQ FT: 30,000
SALES (est): 7.79MM **Privately Held**
Web: www.melfredborzall.com
SIC: 3541 Machine tools, metal cutting type

(P-7017)

PRECISION DEBURRING SERVICES

4440 Manning Rd (90660-2164)
PHONE.................................562 944-4497
Darren Smith, *Pr*
▲ **EMP:** 24 **EST:** 1984
SALES (est): 810.31K **Privately Held**
Web: www.pdsdeburring.com
SIC: 3541 Machine tools, metal cutting type

(P-7018)

PRECON INC

Also Called: Precon Gage
3131 E La Palma Ave (92806-2895)
PHONE.................................714 630-7632
James Von Zabern, *Pr*
Audrey Von Zabern, *Sec*
EMP: 20 **EST:** 1970
SQ FT: 10,500
SALES (est): 476.33K **Privately Held**
Web: www.precon-inc.com
SIC: 3541 3545 3823 3471 Deburring machines; Gauges (machine tool accessories); Process control instruments; Plating and polishing

(P-7019)

R H STRASBAUGH (PA)

Also Called: Strasbaugh
    825 Buckley Rd (93401-8192)
PHONE.................................805 541-6424
Alan Strasbaugh, *CF*
Brad Diaz, *VP*
Eric Jacobson, *CUST SERV*
Michael Kirkpatrick, *S&M/Dir*
EMP: 72 **EST:** 1964
SQ FT: 135,000
SALES (est): 16.96MM
SALES (corp-wide): 16.96MM **Privately Held**
Web: www.gainliftoff.com
SIC: 3541 3559 5065 Grinding, polishing, buffing, lapping, and honing machines; Semiconductor manufacturing machinery; Electronic parts and equipment, nec

(P-7020)

REPUBLIC MACHINERY CO INC (PA)

Also Called: Lagun Engineering Solutions
    800 Sprucelake Dr (90710-1607)
PHONE.................................310 518-1100
Vivian Bezic, *CEO*
Joseph Bezic,   *
Nicole Bezic,   *
◆ **EMP:** 22 **EST:** 1969
SQ FT: 30,000
SALES (est): 4.3MM
SALES (corp-wide): 4.3MM **Privately Held**
Web: www.lagun.com
SIC: 3541 3542 3549 3545 Drilling and boring machines; Arbor presses; Metalworking machinery, nec; Machine knives, metalworking

(P-7021)

RYTAN INC

1648 W 134th St (90249-2014)
PHONE.................................310 328-6553
Carol J Silbaugh, *CEO*
▲ **EMP:** 18 **EST:** 1983
SQ FT: 20,400
SALES (est): 2.42MM **Privately Held**
Web: www.rytan.com
SIC: 3541 Keysetting machines

(P-7022)

S L FUSCO INC (PA)

1966 E Via Arado (90220-6100)
P.O. Box 5924 (90224-5924)
PHONE.................................310 868-1010
Jerald C Rosin, *CEO*
Eric Rosin, *Pr*
Arlene Rosin, *VP*
Barrie Williams, *Dir*
Tom Burke, *Dir*
◆ **EMP:** 45 **EST:** 1941
SQ FT: 40,000
SALES (est): 24.65MM
SALES (corp-wide): 24.65MM **Privately Held**
Web: www.slfusco.com
SIC: 3541 Machine tools, metal cutting type

(P-7023)

SAFETY PRODUCTS HOLDINGS LLC

170 Technology Dr (92618-2401)
PHONE.................................714 662-1033
Andreas Kieper, *of Glbl Sls*
EMP: 50 **EST:** 2016
SALES (est): 24.11MM **Privately Held**
SIC: 3541 3556 Machine tools, metal cutting type; Cutting, chopping, grinding, mixing, and similar machinery
PA: Bertram Capital Management, Llc
    950 Tower Ln Ste 1000
    Foster City CA

(P-7024)

SHERLINE PRODUCTS INCORPORATED

Also Called: Sherline Products
3235 Executive Rdg (92081-8527)
PHONE.................................760 727-5181
Joe Martin, *Pr*
Karl W Rohlin Iii, *CEO*
Charla Papp,   *
▲ **EMP:** 30 **EST:** 1973
SQ FT: 65,000
SALES (est): 4.54MM **Privately Held**
Web: www.sherlineipd.com
SIC: 3541 3545 Lathes, metal cutting and polishing; Machine tool accessories

(P-7025)

SOUTHWESTERN INDUSTRIES INC (PA)

Also Called: Trak Machine Tools
2615 Homestead Pl (90220-5610)
P.O. Box 9066 (90224-9066)
PHONE.................................310 608-4422
Stephen F Pinto, *CFO*
Richard W Leonhard,   *
John Arroues,   *
John Baumhauer,   *
Mark Eisen,   *
▲ **EMP:** 70 **EST:** 1951
SALES (est): 49.55MM
SALES (corp-wide): 49.55MM **Privately Held**
Web: www.southwesternindustries.com
SIC: 3541 Machine tools, metal cutting type

(P-7026)

TESCO PRODUCTS

25601 Avenue Stanford (91355-1103)
PHONE.................................661 257-0153
Mark Terry, *CEO*
EMP: 24 **EST:** 1946
SQ FT: 2,500
SALES (est): 793.21K **Privately Held**
Web: www.tescoproductsinc.com
SIC: 3541 5032 Grinding, polishing, buffing, lapping, and honing machines; Brick, stone, and related material

(P-7027)

US UNION TOOL INC (HQ)

1260 N Fee Ana St (92807-1817)
PHONE.................................714 521-6242
Hideo Hirano, *Pr*
Robert Smallwood,   *
▲ **EMP:** 45 **EST:** 1981
SQ FT: 44,000
SALES (est): 9.53MM **Privately Held**
Web: www.uniontool.co.jp
SIC: 3541 Machine tools, metal cutting type
PA: Union Tool Co.
    6-17-1, Minamioi
    Shinagawa-Ku TKY

3542 Machine Tools, Metal Forming Type

(P-7028)

ADDITION MANUFACTURING TECHNOLOGIES CA INC

1391 Specialty Dr Ste A (92081-8521)
PHONE.................................760 597-5220
▲ **EMP:** 35
SIC: 3542 Bending machines

(P-7029)

AMBRIT INDUSTRIES INC

432 Magnolia Ave (91204-2406)
PHONE.................................818 243-1224
Paul Yaussi, *Pr*
Louis A Yaussi,   *
Michelle Taylor,   *
EMP: 38 **EST:** 1946
SQ FT: 9,184
SALES (est): 3.07MM **Privately Held**
Web: www.ambritindustries.com
SIC: 3542 3363 Die casting machines; Aluminum die-castings

(P-7030)

AMERICAN PRECISION HYDRAULICS

5601 Research Dr (92649-1620)
PHONE.................................714 903-8610
Susan Smith, *Pr*
Steve Smith, *Pr*
EMP: 23 **EST:** 1996
SQ FT: 6,500
SALES (est): 2.69MM **Privately Held**
Web: www.americanprecisionassembly.com
SIC: 3542 Presses: hydraulic and pneumatic, mechanical and manual

(P-7031)

ANGELUS MACHINE CORP INTL

4900 Pacific Blvd (90058-2214)
PHONE.................................323 583-2171
Maurice Koeberle, *Ch Bd*
Chuck Deane,   *
EMP: 64 **EST:** 1910
SQ FT: 295,000
SALES (est): 3.52MM **Privately Held**
SIC: 3542 Metal container making machines: cans, etc.
HQ: Angelus Sanitary Can Machine Company
    4900 Pacific Blvd
    Vernon CA
    314 862-8000

(P-7032)

BROTHERS MACHINE & TOOL INC

11095 Inland Ave (91752-1155)
PHONE.................................951 361-9454
Jose E Razo, *Pr*
EMP: 20
SIC: 3542 Machine tools, metal forming type
PA: Brothers Machine & Tool, Inc.
    11098 Inland Ave
    Jurupa Valley CA

(P-7033)

MEDLIN RAMPS

14903 Marquardt Ave (90670-5128)
PHONE.................................877 463-3546
Mark Medlin, *Prin*
▲ **EMP:** 42 **EST:** 1990
SQ FT: 10,000
SALES (est): 5.96MM **Privately Held**
Web: www.medlinramps.com
SIC: 3542 5084 3441 Machine tools, metal forming type; Materials handling machinery; Fabricated structural metal

(P-7034)

MJC ENGINEERING AND TECH INC

15401 Assembly Ln (92649-1329)
PHONE.................................714 890-0618
Carl Lorentzen, *Pr*
Per Carlson, *VP*
Gro Jensen, *Treas*

Kristi Jensen, *Sec*
Bernd Hermann, *CFO*
◆ **EMP:** 18 **EST:** 1993
SQ FT: 10,000
SALES (est): 5.25MM **Privately Held**
Web: www.mjcengineering.com
SIC: **3542** Spinning machines, metal

(P-7035)
NUGIER PRESS COMPANY INC
Also Called: Nugier Hydraulics
18031 La Salle Ave (90248-3606)
PHONE..................................310 515-6025
Gary Livick, *Pr*
EMP: 17 **EST:** 1994
SALES (est): 806.05K **Privately Held**
SIC: **3542** 5084 Presses: hydraulic and
pneumatic, mechanical and manual;
Industrial machinery and equipment

(P-7036)
PHI (PA)
Also Called: PHI Hydraulics
14955 Salt Lake Ave (91746-3133)
PHONE..................................626 968-9680
Anthony Morrow, *Pr*
▼ **EMP:** 18 **EST:** 2010
SQ FT: 25,930
SALES (est): 4.98MM
SALES (corp-wide): 4.98MM **Privately
Held**
Web: www.phihydraulics.com
SIC: **3542** 3549 Presses: hydraulic and
pneumatic, mechanical and manual;
Metalworking machinery, nec

(P-7037)
PRECISION FASTENER
TOOLING INC
11530 Western Ave (90680-3490)
PHONE..................................714 898-8558
Charles Boyles, *Pr*
James Azevedo, *VP*
EMP: 29 **EST:** 1981
SQ FT: 10,000
SALES (est): 2.66MM **Privately Held**
Web: www.precisionfastenertooling.com
SIC: **3542** 3544 Bulldozers (metalworking
machinery); Special dies, tools, jigs, and
fixtures

(P-7038)
RAY CHINN CONSTRUCTION INC
424 24th St (93301-4104)
PHONE..................................661 327-2731
Raymond Dean Chinn, *Pr*
EMP: 22 **EST:** 2005
SALES (est): 919.91K **Privately Held**
SIC: **3542** Mechanical (pneumatic or
hydraulic) metal forming machines

(P-7039)
SAMTECH AUTOMOTIVE USA
INC
Also Called: Samtech International
1130 E Dominguez St (90746-3518)
PHONE..................................310 638-9955
▲ **EMP:** 50 **EST:** 1996
SQ FT: 27,812
SALES (est): 11.04MM **Privately Held**
Web: www.samtechintl.com
SIC: **3542** Machine tools, metal forming type
PA: Samtech Corp.
    1000-18, Emmyocho
    Kashiwara OSK

(P-7040)
UNIVERSAL PUNCH CORP
4001 W Macarthur Blvd (92704-6307)

P.O. Box 26879 (92799-6879)
PHONE..................................714 556-4488
Kenneth L Williams, *Pr*
Kevin Williams, *
Joan Williams, *
▲ **EMP:** 55 **EST:** 1974
SQ FT: 52,000
SALES (est): 8.7MM **Privately Held**
Web: www.universalpunch.com
SIC: **3542** 3545 3544 3452 Punching and
shearing machines; Machine tool
accessories; Special dies, tools, jigs, and
fixtures; Bolts, nuts, rivets, and washers

(P-7041)
US INDUSTRIAL TOOL & SUP CO
Also Called: Usit Co
14083 S Normandie Ave (90249-2614)
PHONE..................................310 464-8400
Keith Rowland, *CEO*
▲ **EMP:** 47 **EST:** 1955
SQ FT: 35,000
SALES (est): 8.82MM **Privately Held**
Web: www.ustool.com
SIC: **3542** 3546 Machine tools, metal
forming type; Power-driven handtools

(P-7042)
WEST COAST-ACCUDYNE INC
Also Called: Accudyne Engineering & Eqp
7180 Scout Ave (90201-3202)
P.O. Box 2159 (90202-2159)
PHONE..................................562 927-2546
George F Schofhauser, *Pr*
Kurt Anderegg, *VP*
Jill Wigney, *Sec*
▲ **EMP:** 20 **EST:** 1954
SALES (est): 3.35MM **Privately Held**
Web: www.accudyneeng.com
SIC: **3542** 5084 Presses: forming, stamping,
punching, sizing (machine tools); Machine
tools and accessories

3543 Industrial Patterns

(P-7043)
HP CORE CO INC
1264 Indian Springs Dr (91741-2336)
PHONE..................................323 582-1688
Ken Catalfo, *Pr*
Charles Catalfo, *VP*
EMP: 19 **EST:** 1964
SALES (est): 462.06K **Privately Held**
SIC: **3543** Foundry cores

(P-7044)
PATTERNS BEHAVIORAL
SERVICES I
3230 E Imperial Hwy Ste 203 (92821-1706)
PHONE..................................657 444-9002
EMP: 18 **EST:** 2015
SALES (est): 643.71K **Privately Held**
Web: www.patternsbehavior.com
SIC: **3543** Industrial patterns

3544 Special Dies, Tools,
Jigs, And Fixtures

(P-7045)
ACE CLEARWATER
ENTERPRISES INC
1614 Kona Dr (90220-5412)
PHONE..................................310 538-5380
James D Dodson, *Brnch Mgr*
EMP: 35
SALES (corp-wide): 46.01MM **Privately
Held**

Web: www.aceclearwater.com
SIC: **3544** 3728 3769 Special dies, tools,
jigs, and fixtures; Aircraft parts and
equipment, nec; Space vehicle equipment,
nec
PA: Ace Clearwater Enterprises, Inc.
    19815 Magellan Dr
    Torrance CA
    310 323-2140

(P-7046)
ADVANCED MACHINING
TOOLING INC
Also Called: C S C
13535 Danielson St (92064-6868)
PHONE..................................858 486-9050
Terry A Deane, *CEO*
Tony Cerda, *
Jodi Deane, *
EMP: 46 **EST:** 1989
SQ FT: 31,000
SALES (est): 7.47MM **Privately Held**
Web: www.amtmfg.com
SIC: **3544** 3599 Special dies, tools, jigs, and
fixtures; Machine shop, jobbing and repair

(P-7047)
ADVANCED MOLD
TECHNOLOGY INC
16507 Celadon Ct (91709-4611)
◆ **EMP:** 19 **EST:** 1984
SALES (est): 1.41MM **Privately Held**
Web: www.advancedmold.com
SIC: **3544** Special dies and tools

(P-7048)
AMBRIT ENGINEERING
CORPORATION
2640 Halladay St (92705-5649)
PHONE..................................714 557-1074
Terrence Saul, *CEO*
John F Mattimoe, *
Thomas W Vickers, *
▲ **EMP:** 65 **EST:** 1972
SQ FT: 32,000
SALES (est): 17.92MM **Privately Held**
Web: www.ambritengineering.com
SIC: **3544** Forms (molds), for foundry and
plastics working machinery

(P-7049)
AMERICAN PLASTIC
PRODUCTS INC
9243 Glenoaks Blvd (91352-2614)
PHONE..................................818 504-1073
Roupen Yegavian, *Pr*
Varosh Petrosian, *
▲ **EMP:** 75 **EST:** 1991
SQ FT: 35,000
SALES (est): 9.07MM **Privately Held**
SIC: **3544** Special dies and tools

(P-7050)
ART MOLD DIE CASTING INC
11872 Sheldon St (91352-1507)
PHONE..................................818 767-6464
Leo Benavides, *Pr*
Arman Sarkissian, *
EMP: 45 **EST:** 1965
SQ FT: 14,000
SALES (est): 976.47K **Privately Held**
Web: www.artmoldinc.com
SIC: **3544** 3369 3363 Industrial molds;
Nonferrous foundries, nec; Aluminum die-
castings

(P-7051)
ATS TOOL INC
Also Called: Ats Workholding
30222 Esperanza (92688-2121)
PHONE..................................949 888-1744
William Murphy, *Pr*
Sean Murphy, *VP*
▲ **EMP:** 25 **EST:** 1991
SALES (est): 2.03MM **Privately Held**
Web: www.atssystems.us
SIC: **3544** Jigs and fixtures

(P-7052)
AVIS ROTO DIE CO
1560 N San Fernando Rd (90065-1225)
P.O. Box 65617 (90065-0617)
PHONE..................................323 255-7070
Avetis Iskanian, *CEO*
EMP: 30 **EST:** 1982
SQ FT: 32,000
SALES (est): 4.62MM **Privately Held**
Web: www.avisrd.com
SIC: **3544** Paper cutting dies

(P-7053)
AW DIE ENGRAVING INC
8550 Roland St (90621-3199)
PHONE..................................714 521-7910
Arnold Werdin, *Pr*
Art Chavez, *
EMP: 30 **EST:** 1972
SQ FT: 9,000
SALES (est): 2.28MM **Privately Held**
Web: www.awdie.com
SIC: **3544** Dies and die holders for metal
cutting, forming, die casting

(P-7054)
BARROT CORPORATION
1881 Kaiser Ave (92614-5707)
PHONE..................................949 852-1640
Jesus Barrot, *Pr*
Carlos Barrot, *VP*
Robert Barrot, *Treas*
James Barrot, *Sec*
EMP: 22 **EST:** 1983
SQ FT: 15,000
SALES (est): 2.63MM **Privately Held**
Web: www.barrotcorp.com
SIC: **3544** 3769 Special dies and tools;
Space vehicle equipment, nec

(P-7055)
CACO-PACIFIC CORPORATION
(PA)
813 N Cummings Rd (91724-2597)
PHONE..................................626 331-3361
Robert G Hoffmann, *Pr*
Manfred Hoffman, *Ch Bd*
Thom Williams, *Sec*
◆ **EMP:** 142 **EST:** 1985
SQ FT: 45,000
SALES (est): 20.83MM
SALES (corp-wide): 20.83MM **Privately
Held**
Web: www.cacopacific.com
SIC: **3544** Industrial molds

(P-7056)
CAST-RITE CORPORATION
515 E Airline Way (90248-2593)
PHONE..................................310 532-2080
Donald De Haan, *Pr*
Wynn Chapman, *
Howard Watkins, *
▲ **EMP:** 98 **EST:** 1941
SQ FT: 74,712
SALES (est): 19.44MM
SALES (corp-wide): 24.75MM **Privately
Held**

338   2024 Southern California
Business Directory and Buyers Guide   ▲ = Import ▼ = Export
◆ = Import/Export

Web: www.cast-rite.com
SIC: **3544** 3471 3363 Special dies and tools;
Plating and polishing; Aluminum die-
castings
PA: Cast-Rite International, Inc.
515 E Airline Way
Gardena CA
310 532-2080

(P-7057)
CHARLES MEISNER INC
201 Sierra Pl Ste A (91786-5627)
PHONE.................909 946-8216
Charles Meisner, *Pr*
Carol Meisner, *
EMP: 25 **EST:** 1972
SQ FT: 19,000
SALES (est): 2.42MM **Privately Held**
Web: www.charlesmeisnerinc.com
SIC: **3544** 3599 Special dies and tools;
Machine shop, jobbing and repair

(P-7058)
**CHIP-MAKERS TOOLING
SUPPLY INC**
33867 Petunia St (92563-3491)
PHONE.................562 698-5840
Stephen Smith, *CEO*
Paul Hartman, *Pr*
Patty Rivera, *Treas*
EMP: 17 **EST:** 1990
SALES (est): 2.28MM **Privately Held**
Web: www.chip-makers.com
SIC: **3544** Special dies and tools

(P-7059)
CHRISTOS ENGINEERING INC
7626 Baldwin Pl (90602-1001)
PHONE.................562 907-4463
Eric Syndinos, *Pr*
EMP: 19 **EST:** 1992
SQ FT: 5,000
SALES (est): 975.4K **Privately Held**
SIC: **3544** Dies, steel rule

(P-7060)
COAST AEROSPACE MFG INC
Also Called: Coast Aerospace
950 Richfield Rd (92870-6732)
PHONE.................714 893-8066
Louis Ponce, *Pr*
Frank Fleck, *
Steven Castillo, *
David Rodriguez, *Design Vice President*
EMP: 43 **EST:** 1999
SALES (est): 8.93MM **Privately Held**
Web: www.coastaero.com
SIC: **3544** 3441 3728 3291 Special dies and
tools; Fabricated structural metal; Aircraft
parts and equipment, nec; Abrasive
products

(P-7061)
**COLBRIT MANUFACTURING CO
INC**
9666 Owensmouth Ave Ste G
(91311-8050)
PHONE.................818 709-3608
Gerardo Cruz, *Pr*
Marina Cruz, *
▲ **EMP:** 30 **EST:** 1979
SQ FT: 6,000
SALES (est): 4.92MM **Privately Held**
Web: www.colbrit.com
SIC: **3544** Special dies and tools

(P-7062)
COMPUTED TOOL & ENGRG INC
2910 E Ricker Way (92806-2526)

PHONE.................714 630-3911
Oscar Torres, *Pr*
Isabel Torres, *Sec*
EMP: 25 **EST:** 1983
SQ FT: 8,825
SALES (est): 363.62K **Privately Held**
Web: www.computedtool.com
SIC: **3544** Special dies and tools

(P-7063)
**CONCRETE MOLD
CORPORATION**
Also Called: Besser Company
2121 E Del Amo Blvd (90220-6301)
PHONE.................310 537-5171
Bradley Gardner, *Pr*
EMP: 54 **EST:** 1960
SQ FT: 30,000
SALES (est): 1MM
SALES (corp-wide): 213.44MM **Privately
Held**
Web: www.besser.com
SIC: **3544** Industrial molds
PA: Besser Company
801 Johnson St
Alpena MI
989 354-4111

(P-7064)
CRENSHAW DIE AND MFG CORP
7432 Prince Dr (92647-4553)
PHONE.................949 475-5505
TOLL FREE: 800
James V Ireland, *CEO*
Dale Congelliere, *
Sharon Piers, *
EMP: 55 **EST:** 1962
SQ FT: 38,000
SALES (est): 9.22MM **Privately Held**
Web: www.crenshawdiemfg.com
SIC: **3544** Special dies and tools

(P-7065)
DAUNTLESS INDUSTRIES INC
Also Called: Dauntless Molds
806 N Grand Ave (91724-2418)
PHONE.................626 966-4494
George R Payton, *Pr*
Norm Holt, *
EMP: 25 **EST:** 1975
SQ FT: 15,000
SALES (est): 5.03MM **Privately Held**
Web: www.dauntlessmolds.com
SIC: **3544** Special dies and tools

(P-7066)
**DAVID ENGINEERING &
MANUFACTURING INC**
1230 Quarry St (92879-1708)
PHONE.................951 735-5200
▲ **EMP:** 30
SIC: **3544** 3469 Special dies and tools;
Metal stampings, nec

(P-7067)
EDRO ENGINEERING LLC (DH)
Also Called: Voestalpine High Prfmce Mtls
20500 Carrey Rd (91789-2417)
PHONE.................909 594-5751
Terry Henn, *CEO*
Eric Henn, *
Mike Guscott, *
Laurinda Diaz, *Stockholder*
Kevin Ewing, *
◆ **EMP:** 36 **EST:** 1976
SQ FT: 60,000
SALES (est): 20.09MM
SALES (corp-wide): 19.29B **Privately Held**
Web: www.edro.com

SIC: **3544** 3599 Special dies and tools;
Machine shop, jobbing and repair
HQ: Voestalpine High Performance Metals
Llc
2505 Millennium Dr
Elgin IL
877 992-8764

(P-7068)
**ENSTROM MOLD &
ENGINEERING INC**
235 Trade St (92078-4373)
PHONE.................760 744-1880
Fred Enstrom, *Pr*
Janice Enstrom, *Sec*
Greg Metzger, *VP*
EMP: 17 **EST:** 1986
SQ FT: 12,500
SALES (est): 3.5MM **Privately Held**
Web: www.enstrommold.com
SIC: **3544** 3089 Industrial molds; Plastics
processing

(P-7069)
EXPRESS DIE SUPPLY INC
10020 Freeman Ave (90670-3406)
PHONE.................562 903-1700
Jeff Tsui, *Pr*
Jess Tsui, *Pr*
EMP: 20 **EST:** 2001
SALES (est): 1.62MM **Privately Held**
Web: www.expressdie.com
SIC: **3544** Special dies and tools

(P-7070)
**FAIRWAY INJECTION MOLDS
INC**
20109 Paseo Del Prado (91789-2665)
PHONE.................909 595-2201
Mark Gomulka, *CEO*
▲ **EMP:** 54 **EST:** 1977
SQ FT: 31,147
SALES (est): 12.14MM
SALES (corp-wide): 568.49MM **Privately
Held**
Web: www.fairwaymolds.com
SIC: **3544** Industrial molds
PA: Westfall Technik, Inc.
3883 Howard Hughes Pkwy # 590
Las Vegas NV
702 659-9898

(P-7071)
FLOTRON
2630 Progress St (92081-8412)
PHONE.................760 727-2700
Danny K Horrell, *Pr*
EMP: 24 **EST:** 1991
SQ FT: 25,000
SALES (est): 6.01MM **Privately Held**
Web: www.flotron.com
SIC: **3544** Special dies and tools

(P-7072)
FUSION PRODUCT MFG INC
24024 Humphries Rd Bldg 1 (91980-4008)
PHONE.................619 819-5521
Adalberto L Ramirez, *Pr*
Jose Ramirez, *
Simon Ramirez, *
▼ **EMP:** 72 **EST:** 2004
SQ FT: 36,000
SALES (est): 5.63MM **Privately Held**
Web: www.fusionpm.com
SIC: **3544** Forms (molds), for foundry and
plastics working machinery

(P-7073)
GEMINI MFG & ENGRG INC
1020 E Vermont Ave (92805-5617)
PHONE.................714 999-0010
Sandra Lowry, *Pr*
David Lowry, *VP*
EMP: 20 **EST:** 1979
SQ FT: 40,000
SALES (est): 2.58MM **Privately Held**
Web: www.geminimfg.com
SIC: **3544** 3599 Subpresses, metalworking;
Machine shop, jobbing and repair

(P-7074)
GRUBER SYSTEMS INC
29071 The Old Rd (91355-1083)
PHONE.................661 257-0464
John Hoskinson, *Ch Bd*
Jim Thiessen, *
Steve Miller, *
Diana Arima, *
Katherine Pavard, *
◆ **EMP:** 45 **EST:** 1968
SALES (est): 9.88MM **Privately Held**
Web: www.grubersystems.com
SIC: **3544** 3842 3531 3537 Industrial molds;
Whirlpool baths, hydrotherapy equipment;
Construction machinery; Industrial trucks
and tractors

(P-7075)
HIGHTOWER METAL PRODUCTS
2090 N Glassell St (92865-3306)
P.O. Box 5586 (92863-5586)
PHONE.................714 637-7000
Kurt Koch, *Pr*
Mark Koch, *
EMP: 66 **EST:** 1945
SQ FT: 20,000
SALES (est): 6.41MM **Privately Held**
SIC: **3544** Special dies and tools

(P-7076)
**HUGHES BROS AIRCRAFTERS
INC**
11010 Garfield Pl (90280-7512)
PHONE.................323 773-4541
Susan Hughes, *Pr*
James P Hughes, *
Michael Hall, *
EMP: 43 **EST:** 1947
SQ FT: 15,000
SALES (est): 4.72MM **Privately Held**
Web: www.hbai.com
SIC: **3544** 3449 3444 Die sets for metal
stamping (presses); Plastering accessories,
metal; Sheet metalwork

(P-7077)
IDEA TOOLING AND ENGRG INC
13915 S Main St (90061-2151)
PHONE.................310 608-7488
Peter Janner, *Pr*
Monica Janner, *
Moe Sumbulan, *
Inga Janner, *
▲ **EMP:** 56 **EST:** 1973
SALES (est): 6.93MM **Privately Held**
Web: www.ideatooling.com
SIC: **3544** 3061 Special dies and tools;
Mechanical rubber goods

(P-7078)
**KINGSON MOLD & MACHINE
INC**
1350 Titan Way (92821-3707)
PHONE.................714 871-0221
Gregory S Rex, *CEO*
EMP: 27 **EST:** 1977

PRODUCTS & SVCS

SQ FT: 8,500
SALES (est): 4.92MM **Privately Held**
Web: www.kingsonmold.com
SIC: **3544** 5031 Industrial molds; Molding, all
materials

(P-7079)
M I T INC
Also Called: Morin Industrial Technology
15202 Pipeline Ln (92649-1136)
PHONE.............................714 899-6066
Rene Morin, *Pr*
EMP: 38 **EST:** 1974
SQ FT: 12,000
SALES (est): 1.98MM **Privately Held**
SIC: **3544** Forms (molds), for foundry and
plastics working machinery

(P-7080)
MACDONALD CARBIDE CO
525 S Prospero Dr (91791-2931)
PHONE.............................626 960-4034
Amy Mac Donald, *Pr*
◆ **EMP:** 20 **EST:** 1967
SALES (est): 2.02MM **Privately Held**
Web: www.macdonaldcarbide.com
SIC: **3544** 3545 Special dies and tools;
Machine tool accessories

(P-7081)
MAGOR MOLD LLC
420 S Lone Hill Ave (91773-4600)
PHONE.............................909 592-3663
Wolfgang Buhler, *Pr*
Martin Schottli, *
▲ **EMP:** 68 **EST:** 1967
SQ FT: 15,000
SALES (est): 9.72MM **Privately Held**
Web: www.husky.co
SIC: **3544** Industrial molds

(P-7082)
MARMAN INDUSTRIES INC
1701 Earhart (91750-5827)
PHONE.............................909 392-2136
EMP: 90 **EST:** 1985
SALES (est): 15.08MM **Privately Held**
Web: www.marman.com
SIC: **3544** 3089 Industrial molds; Plastics
containers, except foam

(P-7083)
MR MOLD & ENGINEERING CORP
1150 Beacon St (92821-2936)
PHONE.............................714 996-5511
Richard Finnie Ii, *Pr*
Marilyn Finnie, *
EMP: 31 **EST:** 1985
SALES (est): 7.76MM **Privately Held**
Web: www.mrmold.com
SIC: **3544** Special dies and tools

(P-7084)
NIRON INC
20541 Earlgate St (91789-2909)
PHONE.............................909 598-1526
Glen Nieberle, *Pr*
Cheryl Nieberle, *
EMP: 17 **EST:** 1974
SQ FT: 17,000
SALES (est): 522.89K **Privately Held**
Web: www.niron.com
SIC: **3544** 3089 Industrial molds; Injection
molding of plastics

(P-7085)
PACE PUNCHES INC
297 Goddard (92618-4604)

PHONE.............................949 428-2750
Edward W Pepper, *Pr*
▲ **EMP:** 55 **EST:** 1978
SQ FT: 30,000
SALES (est): 8.95MM **Privately Held**
Web: www.pacepunches.com
SIC: **3544** Punches, forming and stamping

(P-7086)
PDC LLC
Also Called: Precision Diecut
4675 Vinita Ct (91710-5731)
PHONE.............................626 334-5000
EMP: 20 **EST:** 2010
SQ FT: 11,000
SALES (est): 4.49MM **Privately Held**
Web: www.teamtech.com
SIC: **3544** Special dies and tools

(P-7087)
PHILLIPS TOOL & DIE INC
Also Called: Busy Bee Tooling
1620 S Marigold Ave (91761-4551)
PHONE.............................909 947-8712
Robert F Phillips, *Prin*
EMP: 22 **EST:** 1970
SALES (est): 957.26K **Privately Held**
SIC: **3544** Special dies and tools

(P-7088)
PRECISE DIE AND FINISHING
9400 Oso Ave (91311-6020)
PHONE.............................818 773-9337
EMP: 27 **EST:** 2016
SQ FT: 15,000
SALES (est): 4.59MM **Privately Held**
Web: www.precisedf.com
SIC: **3544** Special dies and tools

(P-7089)
PRECISION FORGING DIES INC
Also Called: C&C Aerol Machining
10710 Sessler St (90280-7221)
PHONE.............................562 861-1878
Dan Kloss, *CEO*
Dan Kloss, *Pr*
EMP: 32 **EST:** 2001
SALES (est): 5.27MM **Privately Held**
Web: www.precisionforgingdies.com
SIC: **3544** Special dies and tools

(P-7090)
PRESTIGE MOLD INCORPORATED
11040 Tacoma Dr (91730-4857)
PHONE.............................909 980-6600
Donna C Pursell, *CEO*
Lance Spangler, *
▲ **EMP:** 98 **EST:** 1982
SQ FT: 28,500
SALES (est): 23.72MM
SALES (corp-wide): 23.72MM **Privately Held**
Web: www.prestigemold.com
SIC: **3544** Industrial molds
PA: Pres-Tek Plastics, Inc.
10700 7th St
Rancho Cucamonga CA
909 360-1600

(P-7091)
PRODUCT SLINGSHOT INC (DH)
Also Called: Forecast 3d
2221 Rutherford Rd (92008-8815)
PHONE.............................760 929-9380
Corey Douglas Weber, *Pr*
Donovan Weber, *
EMP: 24 **EST:** 1994
SQ FT: 28,000
SALES (est): 28.77MM

SALES (corp-wide): 1.51MM **Privately Held**
Web: www.forecast3d.com
SIC: **3544** 3082 3089 3555 Industrial molds;
Unsupported plastics profile shapes;
Casting of plastics; Printing trades
machinery
HQ: Gkn Powder Metallurgy Holdings
Limited
Unit 7 Chestnut Court
Redditch WORCS

(P-7092)
PUNCH PRESS PRODUCTS INC
Also Called: Auto Trend Products
2035 E 51st St (90058-2818)
PHONE.............................323 581-7151
Delmo Molinari, *Ch*
Cj Matiszik, *Pr*
Helen Wesley, *
Joseph Mcclure, *Genl Mgr*
▲ **EMP:** 67 **EST:** 1953
SQ FT: 150,000
SALES (est): 9.45MM **Privately Held**
Web: www.punch-press.com
SIC: **3544** 3469 3471 Special dies and tools;
Metal stampings, nec; Plating and polishing

(P-7093)
PYRAMID MOLD & TOOL
10155 Sharon Cir (91730-5300)
PHONE.............................909 476-2555
EMP: 62 **EST:** 1995
SQ FT: 30,300
SALES (est): 11.9MM
SALES (corp-wide): 53.65MM **Privately Held**
Web: www.pyramidmold.net
SIC: **3544** Industrial molds
PA: Sybridge Technologies U.S. Inc.
20700 Civic Center Dr # 430
Southfield MI
814 474-9100

(P-7094)
ROTO-DIE COMPANY INC
Also Called: Rotometrics
712 N Valley St Ste B (92801-3828)
PHONE.............................714 991-8701
Dick Townsend, *Mgr*
EMP: 32
SALES (corp-wide): 99.99MM **Privately Held**
Web: www.maxcessintl.com
SIC: **3544** Special dies and tools
PA: Roto-Die Company, Inc.
800 Howerton Ln
Eureka MO
636 587-3600

(P-7095)
S & S CARBIDE TOOL INC
2830 Via Orange Way Ste D (91978-1743)
PHONE.............................619 670-5214
Dennis Strong, *Pr*
Gary Stewart, *
EMP: 25 **EST:** 1986
SQ FT: 6,000
SALES (est): 3.11MM **Privately Held**
Web: www.apnglobal.ca
SIC: **3544** Special dies and tools

(P-7096)
SANTA FE ENTERPRISES INC
Also Called: SFE
11654 Pike St (90670-2938)
PHONE.............................562 692-7596
David Warner, *Pr*
Bob Becker, *
EMP: 27 **EST:** 1980

SQ FT: 20,000
SALES (est): 4.83MM **Privately Held**
Web: www.santafeenterprises.com
SIC: **3544** Special dies and tools

(P-7097)
SCHREY & SONS MOLD CO INC
24735 Avenue Rockefeller (91355-3466)
PHONE.............................661 294-2260
Walter Schrey, *Pr*
Thomas Schrey, *
William Schrey, *
Gertrude Schrey, *
EMP: 35 **EST:** 1969
SQ FT: 53,000
SALES (est): 6.38MM **Privately Held**
Web: www.schrey.com
SIC: **3544** Industrial molds

(P-7098)
STAINLESS INDUSTRIAL COMPANIES
11111 Santa Monica Blvd Ste 1120
(90025-3333)
PHONE.............................310 575-9400
Anthony Pritzker, *Pr*
▲ **EMP:** 47 **EST:** 1998
SALES (est): 11.17MM
SALES (corp-wide): 302.09B **Publicly Held**
Web: www.unitedrentals.com
SIC: **3544** Special dies and tools
HQ: The Marmon Group Llc
181 W Madison St Ste 3900
Chicago IL

(P-7099)
SUPERIOR JIG INC
1540 N Orangethorpe Way (92801-1289)
PHONE.............................714 525-4777
John Morrissey, *Pr*
Tracy Reed, *Sec*
EMP: 22 **EST:** 1960
SQ FT: 14,000
SALES (est): 5.23MM **Privately Held**
Web: www.superiorjiginc.com
SIC: **3544** 3599 Special dies and tools;
Machine shop, jobbing and repair

(P-7100)
TARPIN CORPORATION
Also Called: Western Forge Die
5361 Business Dr (92649-1223)
PHONE.............................714 891-6944
Harold Jermakian, *Pr*
EMP: 21 **EST:** 1981
SALES (est): 621.13K **Privately Held**
Web: www.westernforgedie.com
SIC: **3544** Dies, steel rule

(P-7101)
THUNDERBIRD INDUSTRIES INC
695 W Terrace Dr (91773-2917)
PHONE.............................909 394-1633
Donald Serio, *Pr*
EMP: 18 **EST:** 1985
SQ FT: 20,000
SALES (est): 873.46K **Privately Held**
SIC: **3544** 3089 Industrial molds; Injection
molding of plastics

(P-7102)
UNITED CALIFORNIA CORPORATION
12200 Woodruff Ave (90241-5608)
P.O. Box 4250 (90241-1250)
PHONE.............................562 803-1521
Dale L Bethke, *Pr*
Billie Huckins, *

EMP: 22 **EST:** 1974
SQ FT: 85,000
SALES (est): 862.71K **Privately Held**
Web: www.ucc-udb.com
SIC: 3544 Special dies and tools

(P-7103)
UPM INC
Also Called: Universal Plastic Mold
13245 Los Angeles St (91706-2295)
PHONE......................626 962-4001
Jason Dowling, *Pr*
Jason Dowling, *CEO*
Steve Dowling, *
Don Ashleigh, *
◆ **EMP:** 290 **EST:** 1962
SQ FT: 100,000
SALES (est): 29.13MM **Privately Held**
Web: www.upminc.com
SIC: 3544 3089 Forms (molds), for foundry
and plastics working machinery; Injection
molding of plastics

(P-7104)
VALCO PLANER WORKS INC
Also Called: Valco Precision Works
6131 Maywood Ave (90255-3213)
PHONE......................323 582-6355
Leonel F Valerio, *Pr*
Leonel G Valerio Junior, *VP*
Carlos Valerio, *
▼ **EMP:** 25 **EST:** 1953
SQ FT: 10,000
SALES (est): 4.65MM **Privately Held**
SIC: 3544 3545 Special dies, tools, jigs, and
fixtures; Machine tool accessories

(P-7105)
WAGNER DIE SUPPLY INC (PA)
2041 Elm Ct (91761-7619)
PHONE......................909 947-3044
Ellsworth Knutson, *Pr*
John Knutson, *
Tom Knutson, *
Mike Knutson, *
▲ **EMP:** 36 **EST:** 1947
SALES (est): 9.89MM
SALES (corp-wide): 9.89MM **Privately Held**
Web: www.wagnerdiesupply.com
SIC: 3544 Dies, steel rule

3545 Machine Tool Accessories

(P-7106)
AMERICAN QUALITY TOOLS INC
Also Called: American Quality Tools
12650 Magnolia Ave Ste B (92503-4690)
PHONE......................951 280-4700
Mukesh Aghi, *Pr*
Rakesh Aghi, *
▲ **EMP:** 45 **EST:** 1989
SQ FT: 22,000
SALES (est): 6.98MM **Privately Held**
Web: cobra-carbide.10web.me
SIC: 3545 Cutting tools for machine tools

(P-7107)
ATS WORKHOLDING LLC (PA)
Also Called: Ats Systems
30222 Esperanza (92688-2121)
PHONE......................800 321-1833
Kenneth Erkenbrack, *Pr*
Charles A Goad, *
Ken Erkenbrack, *
Carlos Hernandez, *
William V Nawn, *

▲ **EMP:** 43 **EST:** 1981
SQ FT: 22,840
SALES (est): 10.32MM
SALES (corp-wide): 10.32MM **Privately Held**
Web: www.atssystems.us
SIC: 3545 Milling machine attachments
(machine tool accessories)

(P-7108)
BARRANCA HOLDINGS LTD
Also Called: Barranca Diamond Products
22815 Frampton Ave (90501-5034)
PHONE......................310 523-5867
Brian Delahaut, *Pr*
▲ **EMP:** 104 **EST:** 1998
SALES (est): 889.86K
SALES (corp-wide): 44.8MM **Privately Held**
SIC: 3545 Diamond cutting tools for turning,
boring, burnishing, etc.
PA: Diamond Mk Products Inc
1315 Storm Pkwy
Torrance CA
310 539-5221

(P-7109)
CAMPBELL ENGINEERING INC
Also Called: Campbell Engineering
20412 Barents Sea Cir (92630-8807)
PHONE......................949 859-3306
James J Campbell, *CEO*
Carolyn Campbell, *
EMP: 24 **EST:** 1994
SQ FT: 3,800
SALES (est): 2.39MM **Privately Held**
Web: www.campbellcnc.com
SIC: 3545 3541 Precision measuring tools;
Lathes, metal cutting and polishing

(P-7110)
COASTAL CNTING INDUS SCALE INC
Also Called: Actionpac Scales & Automation
270 Quail Ct Ste 100 (93060-9205)
PHONE......................805 487-0403
John W Dishion, *Pr*
▲ **EMP:** 22 **EST:** 1982
SALES (est): 5.28MM **Privately Held**
Web: www.actionpacusa.com
SIC: 3545 3565 Machine tool accessories;
Packaging machinery

(P-7111)
COPLAN & COPLAN INC
Also Called: Speedpress Sign Supply
2270 Camino Vida Roble Ste H (92011)
PHONE......................760 268-0583
Jacob Coplan, *CEO*
◆ **EMP:** 20 **EST:** 1989
SQ FT: 14,000
SALES (est): 3.91MM **Privately Held**
Web: www.speedpress.com
SIC: 3545 Tools and accessories for
machine tools

(P-7112)
CRAIG TOOLS INC
142 Lomita St (90245-4113)
PHONE......................310 322-0614
William B Cleveland, *Pr*
Don Tripler, *
▼ **EMP:** 37 **EST:** 1958
SQ FT: 13,000
SALES (est): 5.6MM **Privately Held**
Web: www.craigtools.com
SIC: 3545 Precision tools, machinists'

(P-7113)
CRITERION MACHINE WORKS
765 W 16th St (92627-4302)
EMP: 40 **EST:** 1935
SALES (est): 4.53MM **Privately Held**
Web: www.criterionmachineworks.com
SIC: 3545 Machine tool attachments and
accessories

(P-7114)
CTE CALIFORNIA TL & ENGRG INC
Also Called: California Tool & Engineering
7801 Bolero Dr (92509-5219)
▲ **EMP:** 25 **EST:** 1987
SQ FT: 14,000
SALES (est): 1.77MM **Privately Held**
SIC: 3545 7389 2819 Cutting tools for
machine tools; Grinding, precision:
commercial or industrial; Carbides

(P-7115)
CURRY COMPANY LLC
Also Called: Carbro Company
15724 Condon Ave (90260-2531)
P.O. Box 278 (90260-0278)
PHONE......................310 643-8400
Patrick Curry, *Managing Member*
EMP: 40 **EST:** 2019
SALES (est): 4.88MM
SALES (corp-wide): 21MM **Privately Held**
Web: www.fullertontool.com
SIC: 3545 End mills
PA: Fullerton Tool Company, Inc.
121 Perry St
Saginaw MI
989 799-4550

(P-7116)
GUHRING INC
15581 Computer Ln (92649-1605)
PHONE......................714 841-3582
EMP: 50
SALES (corp-wide): 1.03B **Privately Held**
Web: www.guhring.com
SIC: 3545 Cutting tools for machine tools
HQ: Guhring, Inc.
1445 Commerce Ave
Brookfield WI
262 784-6730

(P-7117)
KARBIDE INC
12650 Magnolia Ave Ste B (92503-4690)
PHONE......................951 354-0900
▲ **EMP:** 23 **EST:** 2012
SALES (est): 2.31MM **Privately Held**
SIC: 3545 Cutting tools for machine tools

(P-7118)
KEMPTON MACHINE WORKS INC
4070 E Leaverton Ct (92807-1610)
PHONE......................714 990-0596
Greg Kempton, *Pr*
EMP: 26 **EST:** 1983
SQ FT: 14,000
SALES (est): 1.95MM **Privately Held**
Web:
www.kemptonmachineworksinc.com
SIC: 3545 3599 Tools and accessories for
machine tools; Machine shop, jobbing and
repair

(P-7119)
MERCURY BROACH CO INC
2546 Seaman Ave (91733-1986)
PHONE......................626 443-5904
Mark Eberlein, *Pr*

EMP: 19 **EST:** 1961
SQ FT: 7,000
SALES (est): 503.03K **Privately Held**
Web: mercurybroach.wordpress.com
SIC: 3545 Broaches (machine tool
accessories)

(P-7120)
MEYCO MACHINE AND TOOL INC
11579 Martens River Cir (92708-4201)
P.O. Box 9659 (92728-9659)
PHONE......................714 435-1546
Manuel Gomez, *CEO*
Victor Salazar, *
Max Gomez, *
Edith Martinez, *
Lorena Estrada, *
EMP: 38 **EST:** 1996
SQ FT: 12,500
SALES (est): 6.45MM **Privately Held**
Web: www.meycomachine.com
SIC: 3545 Tools and accessories for
machine tools

(P-7121)
MICRO TOOL & MANUFACTURING INC
6494 Federal Blvd (91945-1376)
PHONE......................619 582-2884
Fae Galea, *Pr*
Charles Galea, *VP*
Michael H Galea, *Sec*
Steve J Galea, *Asst VP*
John Galea, *Asst VP*
EMP: 22 **EST:** 1964
SQ FT: 10,000
SALES (est): 2.11MM **Privately Held**
Web: www.microtoolmfginc.com
SIC: 3545 3544 Precision tools, machinists';
Jigs: inspection, gauging, and checking

(P-7122)
NORANCO MANUFACTURING (USA) ACQUISITION CORP
Also Called: Noranco Corona Division
345 Cessna Cir Ste 102 (92880-2519)
PHONE......................951 721-8400
▲ **EMP:** 125 **EST:** 2013
SALES (est): 37.41MM
SALES (corp-wide): 302.09B **Publicly Held**
SIC: 3545 3728 Machine tool attachments
and accessories; Aircraft parts and
equipment, nec
HQ: Noranco Inc
710 Rowntree Dairy Rd
Woodbridge ON
905 264-2050

(P-7123)
PENNOYER-DODGE CO
6650 San Fernando Rd (91201-1745)
P.O. Box 5105 (91221-1017)
PHONE......................818 547-2100
Hazel Dodge, *Pr*
Karen Dodge, *
EMP: 40 **EST:** 1946
SALES (est): 4.96MM **Privately Held**
Web: www.pdgage.com
SIC: 3545 8734 5084 3643 Gauges
(machine tool accessories); Calibration and
certification; Instruments and control
equipment; Current-carrying wiring services

(P-7124)
PICOSYS INCORPORATED
Also Called: Invenios
320 N Nopal St (93103-3225)

PRODUCTS & SVCS

PHONE..............805 962-3333
EMP: 70
SIC: 3545 3821 Precision measuring tools;
    Micromanipulator

(P-7125)
PIONEER BROACH COMPANY (PA)
6434 Telegraph Rd (90040-2516)
PHONE..............323 728-1263
- Gary M Ezor, *CEO*
Robert Ezor, *
Karin Ezor, *
▲ **EMP:** 50 **EST:** 1939
SQ FT: 22,000
SALES (est): 7.85MM
SALES (corp-wide): 7.85MM **Privately Held**
Web: www.pioneerbroach.com
SIC: 3545 3599 3541 Broaches (machine tool accessories); Machine shop, jobbing and repair; Machine tools, metal cutting type

(P-7126)
PRECISION CUTTING TOOLS INC
5572 Fresca Dr (90623-1007)
PHONE..............562 921-7898
Audrey Sheth, *CEO*
▲ **EMP:** 30 **EST:** 1979
SALES (est): 4.37MM **Privately Held**
Web: www.pct-imc.com
SIC: 3545 3541 Cutting tools for machine tools; Drilling machine tools (metal cutting)

(P-7127)
PRECISION CUTTING TOOLS LLC
5572 Fresca Dr (90623-1007)
PHONE..............562 921-7898
Nikhil Sheth, *Prin*
Mehar Grewal, *Prin*
Audrey Sheth, *Prin*
Jacob Harpaz, *Prin*
EMP: 48 **EST:** 2018
SALES (est): 4.33MM **Privately Held**
Web: www.pct-imc.com
SIC: 3545 Cutting tools for machine tools

(P-7128)
PRO TOOL SERVICES INC
1704 Sunnyside Ct (93308-6859)
P.O. Box 80235 (93380-0235)
PHONE..............661 393-9222
Ron Jacobs, *Pr*
Mark Gardener, *
EMP: 28 **EST:** 2000
SQ FT: 4,000
SALES (est): 1.88MM **Privately Held**
Web: www.protoolservices.com
SIC: 3545 Tools and accessories for machine tools

(P-7129)
RAFCO-BRICKFORM LLC (PA)
Also Called: Rafco Products Brickform
11061 Jersey Blvd (91730-5135)
PHONE..............909 484-3399
Robert Freis, *Managing Member*
Matt Bissantti, *Managing Member*
▲ **EMP:** 72 **EST:** 1973
SQ FT: 79,000
SALES (est): 17.78MM
SALES (corp-wide): 17.78MM **Privately Held**
SIC: 3545 5169 Machine tool accessories; Adhesives, chemical

(P-7130)
SCIENTIFIC CUTTING TOOLS INC
220 W Los Angeles Ave (93065-1650)
PHONE..............805 584-9495
Dale Christopher, *Pr*
Jan Kaye, *
Gary Christopher, *
EMP: 37 **EST:** 1963
SALES (est): 4.71MM **Privately Held**
Web: www.sct-usa.com
SIC: 3545 Machine tool accessories

(P-7131)
SOUTHLAND MANUFACTURING INC
Also Called: Southland Enterprises
1311 Daisy St (92027-1121)
PHONE..............760 745-7913
Diana Young, *Pr*
Ruth E Young, *Pr*
Donald L Young, *Ch*
Diana Guminsky, *Sec*
EMP: 22 **EST:** 1979
SALES (est): 889.64K **Privately Held**
Web: www.southlandent.com
SIC: 3545 Tool holders

(P-7132)
STADCO (HQ)
Also Called: Standard Tool & Die Co
107 S Avenue 20 (90031-1709)
PHONE..............323 227-8888
Doug Paletz, *Pr*
Bob Parsi, *
Bret Matta, *
EMP: 33 **EST:** 1945
SQ FT: 15,000
SALES (est): 24.68MM **Publicly Held**
Web: www.stadco.com
SIC: 3545 3599 Precision tools, machinists'; Machine shop, jobbing and repair
PA: Techprecision Corporation
    1 Bella Dr
    Westminster MA

(P-7133)
STARRETT KINEMETRIC ENGRG INC
26052 Merit Cir Ste 103 (92653-7004)
PHONE..............949 348-1213
Douglas Starrett, *Pr*
EMP: 26 **EST:** 2007
SALES (est): 5.03MM
SALES (corp-wide): 256.18MM **Publicly Held**
Web: www.starrettmetrology.com
SIC: 3545 Machine tool accessories
PA: The L S Starrett Company
    121 Crescent St
    Athol MA
    978 249-3551

(P-7134)
SYGMA INC
Also Called: Sygma
13168 Flores St (90670-4023)
PHONE..............562 906-8880
Jimmy Fung, *CEO*
◆ **EMP:** 18 **EST:** 1992
SQ FT: 10,000
SALES (est): 935.85K **Privately Held**
Web: www.sygmatools.com
SIC: 3545 Machine tool accessories

(P-7135)
TOSCO - TOOL SPECIALTY COMPANY
Also Called: Tool Specialty Co
1011 E Slauson Ave (90011-5296)

P.O. Box 512157 (90051-0157)
PHONE..............323 232-3561
Jerry Tetzlaff, *Pr*
Ted Tetzlaff, *
▲ **EMP:** 25 **EST:** 1943
SQ FT: 19,500
SALES (est): 2.36MM **Privately Held**
Web: www.toolspecialty.com
SIC: 3545 Machine tool accessories

(P-7136)
UNITED DRILL BUSHING CORP
Also Called: United California
12200 Woodruff Ave (90241-5608)
P.O. Box 4250 (90241-1250)
PHONE..............562 803-1521
Dale L Bethke, *Pr*
Billie Huckins, *
EMP: 150 **EST:** 1964
SQ FT: 80,000
SALES (est): 24.96MM **Privately Held**
Web: www.ucc-udb.com
SIC: 3545 3544 Drill bushings (drilling jig); Special dies, tools, jigs, and fixtures

(P-7137)
VERIDIAM INC (DH)
1717 N Cuyamaca St (92020-1110)
PHONE..............619 448-1000
Brian Joyal, *CEO*
Jennifer Bowman, *
Robert Oevson, *
Scott Rogow, *
▲ **EMP:** 53 **EST:** 1996
SQ FT: 250,000
SALES (est): 64.67MM
SALES (corp-wide): 206.12MM **Privately Held**
Web: www.veridiam.com
SIC: 3545 3317 3354 3312 Precision tools, machinists'; Tubes, seamless steel; Tube, extruded or drawn, aluminum; Tubes, steel and iron
HQ: Whi Capital Partners
    191 N Wacker Dr Ste 1500
    Chicago IL

(P-7138)
VERTEX DIAMOND TOOL CO INC
940 W Cienega Ave (91773-2454)
PHONE..............909 599-1129
Tony Pontone, *CEO*
Loretta Pontone Houchin, *
Kenneth Houchin, *
EMP: 18 **EST:** 1977
SQ FT: 13,000
SALES (est): 999.78K **Privately Held**
Web: vertexdiamondtoom.mfgpages.com
SIC: 3545 Diamond cutting tools for turning, boring, burnishing, etc.

(P-7139)
VIKING PRODUCTS INC
20 Doppler (92618-4306)
PHONE..............949 379-5100
Marc Kaplan, *CEO*
EMP: 40 **EST:** 1981
SQ FT: 12,000
SALES (est): 3.72MM **Privately Held**
Web: www.vikingproducts.com
SIC: 3545 Precision measuring tools

(P-7140)
WESTERN GAGE CORPORATION
3316 Maya Linda Ste A (93012-8059)
PHONE..............805 445-1410
Donald E Moors, *Pr*
Nanette Moors, *
EMP: 24 **EST:** 1968
SQ FT: 22,000

SALES (est): 3.65MM **Privately Held**
Web: www.westerngage.com
SIC: 3545 Gauges (machine tool accessories)

(P-7141)
WETMORE TOOL AND ENGRG CO
Also Called: Wetmore Cutting Tools
5091 G St (91710-5141)
PHONE..............909 364-1000
Jerome David, *CEO*
Phil Kurtz, *Pr*
Mike Gallegos, *CFO*
Keith Rowland, *Ex VP*
▲ **EMP:** 75 **EST:** 1999
SQ FT: 32,000
SALES (est): 7.09MM
SALES (corp-wide): 11.77B **Privately Held**
Web: www.dormerpramet.com
SIC: 3545 5084 3544 3541 Cutting tools for machine tools; Industrial machinery and equipment; Special dies, tools, jigs, and fixtures; Machine tools, metal cutting type
HQ: Dormer Pramet Ab
    Tre Hjartans Vag 2
    Halmstad
    35165200

3546 Power-driven Handtools

(P-7142)
BLACK & DECKER CORPORATION
Also Called: Black & Decker
19701 Da Vinci (92610-2622)
PHONE..............949 672-4000
Chris Metz, *Mgr*
EMP: 33
SALES (corp-wide): 16.95B **Publicly Held**
Web: www.blackanddecker.com
SIC: 3546 3553 Power-driven handtools; Woodworking machinery
HQ: The Black & Decker Corporation
    701 E Joppa Rd
    Towson MD
    410 716-3900

(P-7143)
CALIFORNIA AIR TOOLS INC
8560 Siempre Viva Rd (92154-6270)
PHONE..............619 407-7905
Manuel Gonicman, *CEO*
Larry Cerneka, *Pr*
◆ **EMP:** 30 **EST:** 2002
SQ FT: 10,000
SALES (est): 5.07MM **Privately Held**
Web: www.californiaairtools.com
SIC: 3546 3563 5072 Cartridge-activated hand power tools; Air and gas compressors ; Power tools and accessories

(P-7144)
CHURCHILL AEROSPACE LLC
5091 G St (91710-5141)
PHONE..............909 266-3116
EMP: 19 **EST:** 1998
SALES (est): 230.72K **Privately Held**
Web: www.churchillaerospace.com
SIC: 3546 Power-driven handtools

(P-7145)
GEORGE JUE MFG CO INC
Also Called: Paramont Metal & Supply Co
8140 Rosecrans Ave (90723-2794)
PHONE..............562 634-8181
Vincent Jue, *CEO*
George Jue, *
Elenor Sylva, *

◆ **EMP:** 60 **EST:** 1946
SQ FT: 80,000
SALES (est): 9.27MM **Privately Held**
SIC: 3546 Drills and drilling tools

(P-7146)
MK DIAMOND PRODUCTS INC (PA)
1315 Storm Pkwy (90501-5041)
P.O. Box 2803 (90509-2803)
PHONE...........................310 539-5221
Robert J Delahaut, *Pr*
Brian Delahaut, *CFO*
David W Riley, *Sec*
◆ **EMP:** 96 **EST:** 1945
SQ FT: 35,000
SALES (est): 44.8MM
SALES (corp-wide): 44.8MM **Privately Held**
Web: www.mkdiamond.com
SIC: 3546 3425 Saws and sawing equipment ; Saw blades and handsaws

(P-7147)
SEESCAN INC (PA)
Also Called: Seektech
3855 Ruffin Rd (92123-1813)
PHONE...........................858 244-3300
Mark Olsson, *Pr*
John Chew, *
▲ **EMP:** 178 **EST:** 1983
SQ FT: 63,641
SALES (est): 41.5MM
SALES (corp-wide): 41.5MM **Privately Held**
Web: www.seescan.com
SIC: 3546 Power-driven handtools

(P-7148)
STANLEY BLACK & DECKER INC
15750 Jurupa Ave (92337-7329)
PHONE...........................909 491-6322
EMP: 18 **EST:** 2017
SALES (est): 1.86MM **Privately Held**
Web: www.stanleyblackanddecker.com
SIC: 3546 Power-driven handtools

(P-7149)
ZEPHYR MANUFACTURING CO INC
Also Called: Zephyr Tool Group
201 Hindry Ave (90301-1519)
PHONE...........................310 410-4907
Ray Chin, *VP Fin*
Earl Houston, *
Tom Houstan, *
Robert Szanter, *
▲ **EMP:** 100 **EST:** 1939
SQ FT: 60,000
SALES (est): 15.53MM **Privately Held**
Web: www.zephyrtoolgroup.com
SIC: 3546 3545 3423 Power-driven handtools; Machine tool accessories; Hand and edge tools, nec
PA: Shg Holdings Corp
201 Hindry Ave
Inglewood CA

3547 Rolling Mill Machinery

(P-7150)
ENGINEERED MACHINERY GROUP INC
Also Called: Macbee Engineering
1042 N Mountain Ave Ste B561 (91786-3695)
PHONE...........................909 579-0088

EMP: 17
Web: www.emc-wire.com
SIC: 3547 Steel rolling machinery

(P-7151)
JOHN LIST CORPORATION
Also Called: Protocast
9732 Cozycroft Ave (91311-4498)
PHONE...........................818 882-7848
John List, *Pr*
Susan List, *
EMP: 47 **EST:** 1966
SQ FT: 16,000
SALES (est): 8.39MM **Privately Held**
Web: www.protocastjlc.com
SIC: 3547 3365 3369 3366 Ferrous and nonferrous mill equipment, auxiliary; Aluminum and aluminum-based alloy castings; Nonferrous foundries, nec; Copper foundries

(P-7152)
OLD COUNTRY MILLWORK INC (PA)
Also Called: O C M
5855 Hooper Ave (90001-1280)
PHONE...........................323 234-2940
Gerard J Kilgallon, *CEO*
▲ **EMP:** 38 **EST:** 1984
SQ FT: 36,000
SALES (est): 10.07MM
SALES (corp-wide): 10.07MM **Privately Held**
Web: www.ocmcoil.com
SIC: 3547 3479 Rolling mill machinery; Painting, coating, and hot dipping

(P-7153)
ROBINSON ENGINEERING CORP
3575 Grapevine St (91752-3505)
PHONE...........................951 361-8000
Peter Robinson, *Pr*
Zora Robinson, *VP*
EMP: 17 **EST:** 1968
SQ FT: 20,000
SALES (est): 375.97K **Privately Held**
SIC: 3547 Rolling mill machinery

(P-7154)
VEST INC
6023 Alcoa Ave (90058-3954)
P.O. Box 58827 (90058-0827)
PHONE...........................800 421-6370
Yoshiki Murakami, *Pr*
Sean Mccaughan, *Pr*
Iwaki Sugimoto, *
Tomoya Shiraishi, *
Hideki Matsumoto, *
▲ **EMP:** 77 **EST:** 1970
SQ FT: 312,000
SALES (est): 24.31MM **Privately Held**
Web: www.vestinc.com
SIC: 3547 3317 Rolling mill machinery; Tubes, wrought: welded or lock joint
HQ: Shoji Jfe America Holdings Inc
301 E Ocean Blvd Ste 1750
Long Beach CA
562 637-3500

3548 Welding Apparatus

(P-7155)
AMADA WELD TECH INC (DH)
1820 S Myrtle Ave (91016-4833)
PHONE...........................626 303-5676
David Fawcett, *Pr*
Mark G Rodighiero, *
Kunio Minejima, *
James E Malloy, *

David Cielinski, *
◆ **EMP:** 33 **EST:** 1994
SQ FT: 70,000
SALES (est): 56.56MM **Privately Held**
Web: www.amadaweldtech.com
SIC: 3548 3699 3829 Soldering equipment, except hand soldering irons; Laser welding, drilling, and cutting equipment; Measuring and controlling devices, nec
HQ: Amada Weld Tech Co., Ltd.
200, Ishida
Isehara KNG

(P-7156)
BROCO INC
Also Called: Broco
400 S Rockefeller Ave (91761-8144)
PHONE...........................909 483-3222
◆ **EMP:** 25 **EST:** 1968
SALES (est): 5.2MM **Privately Held**
Web: www.broco-rankin.com
SIC: 3548 Welding and cutting apparatus and accessories, nec

(P-7157)
CREATIVE PATHWAYS INC
20815 Higgins Ct (90501-1830)
PHONE...........................310 530-1965
Timothy Rohrberg, *Pr*
Patrica Rohrberg, *
EMP: 35 **EST:** 1969
SQ FT: 29,000
SALES (est): 5.61MM **Privately Held**
Web: www.creativepaths.com
SIC: 3548 Welding and cutting apparatus and accessories, nec

(P-7158)
DIAMOND GROUND PRODUCTS INC
2651 Lavery Ct (91320-1502)
PHONE...........................805 498-3837
James C Elizarraz, *Pr*
▲ **EMP:** 30 **EST:** 1992
SQ FT: 40,000
SALES (est): 4.92MM **Privately Held**
Web: www.diamondground.com
SIC: 3548 Electrodes, electric welding

(P-7159)
M K PRODUCTS INC
Also Called: Mk Manufacturing
16882 Armstrong Ave (92606-4975)
PHONE...........................949 798-1234
Chris Westlake, *Pr*
Dana E Paquin, *
▲ **EMP:** 80 **EST:** 1966
SQ FT: 80,000
SALES (est): 18.57MM **Privately Held**
Web: www.mkproducts.com
SIC: 3548 Electric welding equipment

(P-7160)
OK INTERNATIONAL INC (DH)
Also Called: Metcal
10800 Valley View St (90630-5016)
PHONE...........................714 799-9910
◆ **EMP:** 224 **EST:** 1982
SALES (est): 45.72MM
SALES (corp-wide): 8.51B **Publicly Held**
Web: www.okinternational.com
SIC: 3548 Soldering equipment, except hand soldering irons
HQ: Dover Engineered Products Segment, Inc.
3005 Highland Pkwy # 200
Downers Grove IL
630 541-1540

(P-7161)
ONEX RF INC
1824 Flower Ave (91010-2931)
PHONE...........................626 358-6639
Onik Bogosyan, *Pr*
EMP: 18 **EST:** 1991
SALES (est): 2.38MM **Privately Held**
Web: www.onexrf.com
SIC: 3548 Welding apparatus

(P-7162)
SSCO MANUFACTURING INC
Also Called: ARC Products
8155 Mercury Ct Ste 100 (92111-1227)
PHONE...........................619 628-1022
Victor B Miller, *Pr*
Susan D Miller, *
Lane A Litke, *
EMP: 35 **EST:** 1988
SALES (est): 9.59MM
SALES (corp-wide): 3.76B **Publicly Held**
Web: mechanized.lincolnelectric.com
SIC: 3548 5085 7629 7699 Electric welding equipment; Welding supplies; Circuit board repair; Welding equipment repair
PA: Lincoln Electric Holdings, Inc.
22801 Saint Clair Ave
Cleveland OH
216 481-8100

(P-7163)
SUPER WELDING SOUTHERN CAL INC
1668 Newton Ave (92113-1013)
PHONE...........................619 239-8003
Roberto Victoria, *Pr*
Amelia Victoria, *VP*
Manuel Victoria, *Probation Officer*
EMP: 20 **EST:** 1987
SALES (est): 2.85MM **Privately Held**
Web: www.swsc-inc.com
SIC: 3548 1799 Arc welding generators, a.c. and d.c.; Welding on site

(P-7164)
TECHNICAL DEVICES COMPANY
560 Alaska Ave (90503-3904)
P.O. Box 329 (90507-0129)
PHONE...........................310 618-8437
Douglas N Winther, *CEO*
Rey Malazo, *
EMP: 48 **EST:** 1977
SQ FT: 35,000
SALES (est): 9.62MM
SALES (corp-wide): 9.62MM **Privately Held**
Web: www.technicaldev.com
SIC: 3548 3471 3544 3423 Soldering equipment, except hand soldering irons; Cleaning, polishing, and finishing; Special dies and tools; Hand and edge tools, nec
PA: Winther Technologies, Inc.
560 Alaska Ave
Torrance CA
310 618-8437

(P-7165)
WINTHER TECHNOLOGIES INC (PA)
Also Called: Technical Devices
560 Alaska Ave (90503-3904)
P.O. Box 329 (90507-0129)
PHONE...........................310 618-8437
Douglas N Winther, *Pr*
▲ **EMP:** 46 **EST:** 1986
SQ FT: 32,000
SALES (est): 9.62MM
SALES (corp-wide): 9.62MM **Privately Held**

(PA)=Parent Co (HQ)=Headquarters
✪ = New Business established in last 2 years

2024 Southern California
Business Directory and Buyers Guide

343

P R O D U C T S & S V C S

SIC: 3548 3544 3542 3471 Soldering equipment, except hand soldering irons; Special dies and tools; Machine tools, metal forming type; Cleaning and descaling metal products

3549 Metalworking Machinery, Nec

(P-7166)
ADAPT AUTOMATION INC
1661 Palm St Ste A (92701-5190)
PHONE.................................714 662-4454
Case Van Mechelen, *Prin*
Case V Mechelen, *
Tim Van Mechelen, *Prin*
Tia V Mechelen, *
Peter Smit, *
EMP: 34 **EST:** 1988
SQ FT: 50,000
SALES (est): 4.78MM **Privately Held**
Web: www.adaptautomation.com
SIC: 3549 Assembly machines, including robotic

(P-7167)
BMCI INC
Also Called: Bergandi Machinery Company
1689 S Parco Ave (91761-8308)
P.O. Box 3790 (91761-0977)
PHONE.................................951 361-8000
Scott Barsotti, *Pr*
Jose Garcia, *
Gary Costanzo, *
▼ **EMP:** 45 **EST:** 1994
SQ FT: 45,000
SALES (est): 8.33MM **Privately Held**
Web: www.bergandi.com
SIC: 3549 3548 Wiredrawing and fabricating machinery and equipment, ex. die; Welding apparatus

(P-7168)
EUBANKS ENGINEERING CO (PA)
1921 S Quaker Ridge Pl (91761-8041)
PHONE.................................909 483-2456
David C Eubanks, *Prin*
EMP: 21 **EST:** 1951
SQ FT: 34,000
SALES (est): 6.64MM
SALES (corp-wide): 6.64MM **Privately Held**
Web: www.eubanks.com
SIC: 3549 3825 Wiredrawing and fabricating machinery and equipment, ex. die; Test equipment for electronic and electrical circuits

(P-7169)
FOOMA AMERICA INC
12735 Stanhill Dr (90638-1937)
PHONE.................................310 921-0717
Soohyung Kim, *CEO*
EMP: 30 **EST:** 2019
SALES (est): 1.22MM **Privately Held**
SIC: 3549 Cutting and slitting machinery

(P-7170)
GOLDEN STATE ENGINEERING INC
15338 Garfield Ave (90723-4092)
PHONE.................................562 634-3125
Alexandra Rostovski, *CEO*
Mary Saguini, *
Eugenio Rostovski, *
Tom Scroggin, *
EMP: 120 **EST:** 1968

SQ FT: 65,000
SALES (est): 20.59MM **Privately Held**
Web: www.goldenstateeng.com
SIC: 3549 3541 3451 8711 Metalworking machinery, nec; Grinding, polishing, buffing, lapping, and honing machines; Screw machine products; Engineering services

(P-7171)
MASTERBILT ATMTN SOLUTIONS INC
12568 Kirkham Ct (92064-8899)
PHONE.................................858 748-6700
Robert Michalak, *CEO*
Charles D Ross, *Pr*
EMP: 22 **EST:** 1992
SQ FT: 12,000
SALES (est): 5.19MM **Privately Held**
Web: www.production-systems.com
SIC: 3549 Assembly machines, including robotic

(P-7172)
TELEDYNE SEABOTIX INC
2877 Historic Decatur Rd # 100 (92106-6177)
PHONE.................................619 239-5959
EMP: 68
SIC: 3549 Propeller straightening presses

(P-7173)
TRINITY ROBOTICS AUTOMTN LLC
4582 Brickell Privado St (91761-7827)
PHONE.................................562 690-4525
EMP: 18 **EST:** 2014
SALES (est): 1.79MM **Privately Held**
Web: www.trinityautomation.com
SIC: 3549 Assembly machines, including robotic

(P-7174)
UBTECH ROBOTICS CORP
767 S Alameda St (90021-1665)
PHONE.................................213 261-7153
John Rhee, *CEO*
EMP: 30 **EST:** 2015
SALES (est): 6MM **Privately Held**
Web: www.ubtrobot.com
SIC: 3549 Assembly machines, including robotic
PA: Ubtech Robotics Corp Ltd.
Room 2201, Building C1, Nanshan Zhiyuan, No. 1001 Xueyuan Avenue Shenzhen GD

(P-7175)
WALLNER EXPAC INC (PA)
Also Called: W T E
1274 S Slater Cir (91761-1522)
PHONE.................................909 481-8800
Sophia Wallner, *Ch Bd*
Michael Wallner, *
Paul Wallner, *
◆ **EMP:** 55 **EST:** 1959
SALES (est): 29.77MM
SALES (corp-wide): 29.77MM **Privately Held**
Web: www.expac.com
SIC: 3549 3542 Metalworking machinery, nec ; Machine tools, metal forming type

3552 Textile Machinery

(P-7176)
INNOVA DESIGN INC
13230 Evening Creek Dr S Ste 216 (92128-4106)

PHONE.................................858 535-9389
Adam Ziyun Chen, *CEO*
EMP: 17 **EST:** 2007
SALES (est): 966.75K **Privately Held**
SIC: 3552 3699 Spindles, textile; Laser systems and equipment

(P-7177)
LYTLE SCREEN PRINTING INC
21572 Surveyor Cir (92646-7067)
PHONE.................................714 969-2424
Tim Mcmillen, *Pr*
Mark Lytle, *Pr*
EMP: 18 **EST:** 1988
SQ FT: 6,000
SALES (est): 1.69MM **Privately Held**
Web: www.lysphb.com
SIC: 3552 7336 2759 Silk screens for textile industry; Silk screen design; Screen printing

(P-7178)
P&Y T-SHRTS SILK SCREENING INC
Also Called: American Printworks
2126 E 52nd St (90058-3448)
P.O. Box 58742 (90058-0742)
PHONE.................................323 585-4604
Yossi Zaga, *Pr*
EMP: 44 **EST:** 1984
SQ FT: 35,000
SALES (est): 2.13MM **Privately Held**
Web: www.apwla.com
SIC: 3552 5136 Silk screens for textile industry; Shirts, men's and boys'

(P-7179)
TAJIMA USA INC
19925 S Susana Rd (90221-5726)
PHONE.................................310 604-8200
Ron Krasnitz, *Pr*
▲ **EMP:** 35 **EST:** 1996
SQ FT: 25,000
SALES (est): 2.21MM **Privately Held**
SIC: 3552 Embroidery machines
PA: Tajima Industries Ltd.
1800, Ushiyamacho
Kasugai AIC

3554 Paper Industries Machinery

(P-7180)
ELLISON EDUCATIONAL EQP INC (PA)
Also Called: Sizzix
25862 Commercentre Dr (92630-8877)
PHONE.................................949 598-8822
Richard Birse, *CEO*
Kristin Highberg, *
▲ **EMP:** 38 **EST:** 1995
SQ FT: 132,000
SALES (est): 17.7MM
SALES (corp-wide): 17.7MM **Privately Held**
Web: www.ellison.com
SIC: 3554 Cutting machines, paper

3555 Printing Trades Machinery

(P-7181)
4L TECHNOLOGIES INC
Also Called: Catridge Return Center
325 Weakley St (92231-9659)
PHONE.................................817 538-0974
EMP: 137
SALES (corp-wide): 432.83MM **Privately Held**

Web: www.clovertech.com
SIC: 3555 Printing trades machinery
HQ: 4l Technologies Inc.
122 W Madison St
Ottawa IL
815 431-8100

(P-7182)
ANAJET LLC
1100 Valencia Ave (92780-6428)
PHONE.................................714 662-3200
▲ **EMP:** 20 **EST:** 2005
SALES (est): 5.49MM **Privately Held**
Web: www.ricohdtg.com
SIC: 3555 Printing trades machinery

(P-7183)
CAL PLATE (PA)
17110 Jersey Ave (90701-2694)
PHONE.................................562 403-3000
Richard Borelli, *Pr*
EMP: 63 **EST:** 1966
SQ FT: 33,000
SALES (est): 10.18MM
SALES (corp-wide): 10.18MM **Privately Held**
Web: www.calplate.com
SIC: 3555 3423 3544 Printing plates; Cutting dies, except metal cutting; Special dies, tools, jigs, and fixtures

(P-7184)
COUNT NUMBERING MACHINE INC
Also Called: Count Machinery Co
2128 Auto Park Way (92029-1344)
PHONE.................................760 739-9357
◆ **EMP:** 20
Web: www.count-usa.com
SIC: 3555 3554 Printing trades machinery; Folding machines, paper

(P-7185)
FABRIC8LABS INC
10788 Roselle St Ste 101 (92121-1562)
PHONE.................................858 215-1142
Jeff Herman, *CEO*
David Pain, *
EMP: 60 **EST:** 2016
SALES (est): 7.04MM **Privately Held**
Web: www.fabric8labs.com
SIC: 3555 Printing trades machinery

(P-7186)
IMPERIAL RUBBER PRODUCTS INC
5691 Gates St (91710-7603)
PHONE.................................909 393-0528
Ronald Hill, *CEO*
Bob Schwartz, *
Steve Huff, *
▲ **EMP:** 35 **EST:** 1989
SQ FT: 20,000
SALES (est): 5.18MM **Privately Held**
Web: www.imperialrubber.com
SIC: 3555 Printing trades machinery

(P-7187)
LITH-O-ROLL CORPORATION
9521 Telstar Ave (91731-2994)
P.O. Box 5328 (91734-1328)
PHONE.................................626 579-0340
Rita Sepe, *Pr*
EMP: 50 **EST:** 1957
SQ FT: 30,000
SALES (est): 9.49MM **Privately Held**
Web: www.lithoroll.com
SIC: 3555 Printing trades machinery

(P-7188)
PACIFIC BARCODE INC
27531 Enterprise Cir W Ste 201c
(92590-4864)
PHONE..................951 587-8717
Michael Meadors, *Pr*
Michael Meadors, *Pr*
Michelle Meadors, *
EMP: 37 EST: 1999
SQ FT: 8,600
SALES (est): 6.19MM Privately Held
Web: www.pacificbarcode.com
SIC: 3555 2759 3565 3577 Printing trades machinery; Commercial printing, nec; Labeling machines, industrial; Bar code (magnetic ink) printers

(P-7189)
PARA-PLATE & PLASTICS CO INC
Also Called: Para Plate
15910 Shoemaker Ave (90703-2200)
PHONE..................562 404-3434
Shane Pearson, *Pr*
Robert J Clapp, *
John Greenamyer, *
Steve Binnard, *
EMP: 27 EST: 1945
SQ FT: 17,000
SALES (est): 2.49MM Privately Held
Web: www.paraplate.com
SIC: 3555 7336 2796 Printing plates; Commercial art and graphic design; Platemaking services

(P-7190)
PIC MANUFACTURING INC
410 Sherwood Rd (93446-3554)
P.O. Box 665 (93447-0665)
PHONE..................805 238-5451
Michael D Camp, *Pr*
EMP: 17 EST: 1962
SQ FT: 9,000
SALES (est): 776.56K Privately Held
Web: www.picmanufacturing.com
SIC: 3555 Printing trade parts and attachments

(P-7191)
RIMA ENTERPRISES INC
Also Called: Rima-System
16417 Ladona Cir (92649-2133)
PHONE..................714 893-4534
Horst K Steinhart, *CEO*
▲ EMP: 62 EST: 1970
SALES (est): 7.41MM Privately Held
SIC: 3555 Bookbinding machinery

(P-7192)
THISTLE ROLLER CO INC
209 Van Norman Rd (90640-5393)
PHONE..................323 685-5322
Lizbeth Karpynec, *CEO*
Eric Karpynetz, *
▲ EMP: 35 EST: 1957
SQ FT: 45,000
SALES (est): 5.15MM Privately Held
Web: www.thistleroller.com
SIC: 3555 3312 2796 Printing trades machinery; Blast furnaces and steel mills; Platemaking services

---

3556 Food Products Machinery

(P-7193)
CAPNA FABRICATION
Also Called: Capna Systems

16501 Ventura Blvd Ste 400 (91436-2007)
PHONE..................888 416-6777
Vitaly Mekk, *CEO*
Gene Galyuk, *
EMP: 30 EST: 2017
SALES (est): 4.8MM Privately Held
SIC: 3556 Oilseed crushing and extracting machinery

(P-7194)
CASA HERRERA INC (PA)
2655 Pine St (91767-2115)
PHONE..................909 392-3930
Michael L Herrera, *CEO*
Ronald L Meade, *
Alfred J Herrera, *
Frank J Herrera, *
Susan A Herrera, *
◆ EMP: 100 EST: 1970
SQ FT: 100,000
SALES (est): 20.67MM
SALES (corp-wide): 20.67MM Privately Held
Web: www.casaherrera.com
SIC: 3556 Food products machinery

(P-7195)
FOODTOOLS CONSOLIDATED INC (PA)
315 Laguna St (93101-1716)
PHONE..................805 962-8383
Martin Grano, *Ch Bd*
Matt Browne, *
Doug Petrovich, *
◆ EMP: 20 EST: 1983
SQ FT: 8,500
SALES (est): 10.02MM
SALES (corp-wide): 10.02MM Privately Held
Web: www.foodtools.com
SIC: 3556 2679 Slicers, commercial, food; Paper products, converted, nec

(P-7196)
FOTIS AND SON IMPORTS INC (PA)
15451 Electronic Ln (92649-1333)
PHONE..................714 894-9022
Peter Georgatsos, *Pr*
Russ Hillas, *
Laura Georgatsos, *
Eleni Hillas, *
▲ EMP: 38 EST: 1976
SQ FT: 34,000
SALES (est): 9.53MM
SALES (corp-wide): 9.53MM Privately Held
Web: www.fotisandsonimports.com
SIC: 3556 Food products machinery

(P-7197)
FPEC CORPORATION A CAL CORP (PA)
Also Called: Food Processing Equipment Co
13623 Pumice St (90670-5105)
PHONE..................562 802-3727
Alan Davison, *CEO*
Ethel Davison, *Sec*
EMP: 18 EST: 1969
SQ FT: 18,000
SALES (est): 8.18MM
SALES (corp-wide): 8.18MM Privately Held
Web: www.fpec.com
SIC: 3556 Food products machinery

(P-7198)
FRESH VENTURE FOODS LLC
1205 Craig Dr (93458-4917)

P.O. Box 1023 (93456-1023)
PHONE..................805 928-3374
John Schaefer, *Managing Member*
Jeff Lundberg, *
EMP: 239 EST: 2012
SQ FT: 70
SALES (est): 22.38MM Privately Held
Web: www.freshventurefoods.com
SIC: 3556 Dehydrating equipment, food processing

(P-7199)
G & I ISLAS INDUSTRIES INC (PA)
Also Called: G & I Industries
12860 Schabarum Ave (91706-6801)
P.O. Box 1262 (91706-7262)
PHONE..................626 960-5020
Gonzalo R Islas, *CEO*
Sara Islas, *
▲ EMP: 23 EST: 1988
SQ FT: 12,500
SALES (est): 8.11MM
SALES (corp-wide): 8.11MM Privately Held
Web: www.giislasindustries.com
SIC: 3556 5084 Bakery machinery; Food industry machinery

(P-7200)
GOLDEN PACIFIC SEAFOODS INC
700 S Raymond Ave (92831-5233)
PHONE..................714 589-8888
Tony Zavala, *Pr*
EMP: 45 EST: 2016
SALES (est): 4.99MM Privately Held
SIC: 3556 Meat, poultry, and seafood processing machinery

(P-7201)
HAYWARD GORDON US INC
9351 Industrial Way (92301-3932)
PHONE..................760 246-3430
EMP: 254
Web: www.hayward-gordon.com
SIC: 3556 Cutting, chopping, grinding, mixing, and similar machinery
HQ: Hayward Gordon Us, Inc.
1541 S 92nd Pl
Seattle WA
206 767-5660

(P-7202)
INTERSTATE MEAT CO INC
Also Called: Sterling Pacific Meat Co.
6114 Scott Way (90040-3518)
PHONE..................323 838-9400
James T Asher, *Pr*
EMP: 100 EST: 1996
SALES (est): 10.65MM Privately Held
Web: www.sterlingpacificmeat.com
SIC: 3556 Meat processing machinery

(P-7203)
J C FORD COMPANY (HQ)
Also Called: JC Ford
901 S Leslie St (90631-6841)
PHONE..................714 871-7361
Scott D Ruhe, *CEO*
◆ EMP: 93 EST: 1945
SALES (est): 38.16MM Privately Held
Web: www.jcford.com
SIC: 3556 Food products machinery
PA: Ruhe Corporation
901 S Leslie St
La Habra CA

(P-7204)
JOHN BEAN TECHNOLOGIES CORP
1660 Iowa Ave Ste 100 (92507-0501)
P.O. Box 5710 (92517-5710)
PHONE..................951 222-2300
Thomas Brickweg, *Prin*
EMP: 51
Web: www.jbtc.com
SIC: 3556 3542 3523 Dairy and milk machinery; Nail heading machines; Dairy equipment (farm), nec
PA: John Bean Technologies Corporation
70 W Madison St Ste 4400
Chicago IL

(P-7205)
JUICY WHIP INC
1668 Curtiss Ct (91750-5848)
PHONE..................909 392-7500
TOLL FREE: 800
Gus Stratton, *Pr*
▲ EMP: 28 EST: 1981
SQ FT: 23,000
SALES (est): 5.4MM Privately Held
Web: www.juicywhip.com
SIC: 3556 2033 Beverage machinery; Fruit juices: fresh

(P-7206)
LAWRENCE EQUIPMENT LEASING INC (PA)
Also Called: Lawrence Equipment
2034 Peck Rd (91733-3727)
PHONE..................626 442-2894
John Lawrence, *CEO*
Linda Lawrence, *
Glenn Shelton, *
Jack Kirkpatrick, *Stockholder*
▲ EMP: 190 EST: 1981
SQ FT: 50,000
SALES (est): 48.01MM
SALES (corp-wide): 48.01MM Privately Held
Web: www.lawrenceequipment.com
SIC: 3556 Flour mill machinery

(P-7207)
MACHINE BUILDING SPC INC
Also Called: Conveyor Concepts
1977 Blake Ave (90039-3832)
PHONE..................323 666-8289
Charles Conaway, *Ch Bd*
Dennis James Conaway, *
Sandra Conaway, *
Sharon Conaway, *
EMP: 25 EST: 1960
SQ FT: 17,000
SALES (est): 3.09MM Privately Held
Web: www.machinebuildingspecialties.com
SIC: 3556 3535 Bakery machinery; Belt conveyor systems, general industrial use

(P-7208)
MEAT PACKERS BUTCHERS SUP INC
Also Called: Mpbs Industries
2820 E Washington Blvd (90023-4274)
PHONE..................323 268-8514
Jimmy Jin, *CEO*
Shaofa Jin, *Ch Bd*
▲ EMP: 17 EST: 1939
SQ FT: 16,000
SALES (est): 2.45MM Privately Held
Web: www.mpbs.com
SIC: 3556 Food products machinery

(P-7209)
MEMC LIQUIDATING CORPORATION

Also Called: Mc Cann's Engineering & Mfg Co
4570 Colorado Blvd (90638)
P.O. Box 39100 (90039-0100)
PHONE..................................818 637-7200
▲ EMP: 250
SIC: 3556 3586 3585 3581 Beverage machinery; Measuring and dispensing pumps; Refrigeration and heating equipment; Automatic vending machines

(P-7210)
NATIONAL BAND SAW COMPANY

1055 W Avenue L12 (93534-7045)
PHONE..................................661 294-9552
Harley Frank, Pr
Norman Frank, Ch Bd
▲ EMP: 17 EST: 1953
SQ FT: 12,000
SALES (est): 3.45MM Privately Held
Web: www.nbsparts.com
SIC: 3556 Meat processing machinery

(P-7211)
PACIFIC PACKAGING MCHY LLC

Also Called: Pack West Machinery
200 River Rd (92878-1435)
PHONE..................................951 393-2200
Gerald Carpino, CEO
Jerry Carpino, *
▲ EMP: 25 EST: 1962
SQ FT: 30,000
SALES (est): 7.55MM Privately Held
Web: www.pacificpak.com
SIC: 3556 3565 Food products machinery; Packaging machinery
HQ: Pro Mach, Inc.
50 E Rvrcnter Blvd Ste 18
Covington KY
513 831-8778

(P-7212)
RBM CONVEYOR SYSTEMS INC

1570 W Mission Blvd (91766-1247)
PHONE..................................909 620-1333
Roobik Kureghian, Pr
Armine Kureghian, Treas
▲ EMP: 20 EST: 1980
SALES (est): 2.48MM Privately Held
SIC: 3556 8711 3537 3535 Food products machinery; Engineering services; Industrial trucks and tractors; Conveyors and conveying equipment

(P-7213)
REXNORD INDUSTRIES LLC

Also Called: Industrial Components Div
2175 Union Pl (93065-1661)
PHONE..................................805 583-5514
Dave Kleinhaus, Mgr
EMP: 45
SALES (corp-wide): 1.37B Privately Held
SIC: 3556 3568 Food products machinery; Couplings, shaft: rigid, flexible, universal joint, etc.
PA: Rexnord Industries, Llc
111 W Michigan St
Milwaukee WI
414 643-3000

(P-7214)
RMJV LP (HQ)

Also Called: Fresh Creative Foods
3285 Corporate Vw (92081-8528)
PHONE..................................503 526-5752
Diana Robertson, Pt

EMP: 58 EST: 2011
SQ FT: 35,000
SALES (est): 45.19MM
SALES (corp-wide): 1.58B Privately Held
Web: www.freshcreativefoods.com
SIC: 3556 Food products machinery
PA: Reser's Fine Foods, Inc.
15570 Sw Jenkins Rd
Beaverton OR
503 643-6431

(P-7215)
SCOTT TURBON MIXER INC

9351 Industrial Way (92301-3932)
P.O. Box 160 (92301-0160)
PHONE..................................760 246-3430
EMP: 30 EST: 1980
SALES (est): 12.08MM Privately Held
Web: www.haywardgordon.com
SIC: 3556 Cutting, chopping, grinding, mixing, and similar machinery
HQ: Hayward Gordon Us, Inc.
1541 S 92nd Pl
Seattle WA
206 767-5660

(P-7216)
SHAVER SPECIALTY CO INC

20608 Earl St (90503-3009)
PHONE..................................310 370-6941
George Shaver, Pr
Ronald Shaver, VP
▲ EMP: 22 EST: 1937
SQ FT: 20,000
SALES (est): 2.44MM Privately Held
Web: www.shaverkeenkutter.com
SIC: 3556 3599 Choppers, commercial, food ; Machine shop, jobbing and repair

(P-7217)
SUPERIOR FOOD MACHINERY INC

8311 Sorensen Ave (90670-2125)
PHONE..................................562 949-0396
Danny Reyes, Pr
Polo Reyes, Pr
Marc Reyes, VP
EMP: 23 EST: 1975
SQ FT: 14,000
SALES (est): 4.96MM Privately Held
Web: www.superiorinc.com
SIC: 3556 Food products machinery

(P-7218)
WILLIAM BOUNDS LTD

23625 Madison St (90505-6004)
P.O. Box 1547 (90505-0547)
PHONE..................................310 375-0505
Helen Bounds, Pr
Sharon Bounds, *
◆ EMP: 19 EST: 1963
SQ FT: 18,000
SALES (est): 1.06MM Privately Held
Web: www.wmboundsltd.com
SIC: 3556 8733 Food products machinery; Noncommercial research organizations

---

3559 Special Industry Machinery, Nec

(P-7219)
ACME CRYOGENICS INC

Also Called: Cryogenic Experts
531 Sandy Cir (93036-0971)
PHONE..................................805 981-4500
Robert Worcester Junior, Brnch Mgr
EMP: 30
SALES (corp-wide): 8.51B Publicly Held
Web: www.acmecryo.com

SIC: 3559 Cryogenic machinery, industrial
HQ: Acme Cryogenics, Inc.
2801 Mitchell Ave
Allentown PA
610 966-4488

(P-7220)
AMERGENCE TECHNOLOGY INC

295 Brea Canyon Rd (91789-3049)
PHONE..................................909 859-8400
Shavonne Tran, Pr
▲ EMP: 29 EST: 2006
SQ FT: 40,000
SALES (est): 2.59MM Privately Held
Web: www.amergenceinc.com
SIC: 3559 Recycling machinery

(P-7221)
AMREP MANUFACTURING CO LLC

1555 S Cucamonga Ave (91761-4512)
PHONE..................................877 468-9278
Martin Bryant, CEO
EMP: 500 EST: 2019
SALES (est): 23.84MM Privately Held
Web: www.amrepproducts.com
SIC: 3559 Semiconductor manufacturing machinery

(P-7222)
AQUA PRO PROPERTIES VII LP

Also Called: Village Marine Technology
2000 W 135th St (90249-2456)
PHONE..................................310 516-9911
▲ EMP: 256
Web: www.villagemarine.com
SIC: 3559 Desalination equipment

(P-7223)
ASML US INC

Also Called: ASML US, Inc.
1 Viper Way Ste A (92081-7809)
PHONE..................................760 443-6244
Jenna Moggio, Prin
EMP: 480
SALES (corp-wide): 16.53B Privately Held
Web: www.asml.com
SIC: 3559 Semiconductor manufacturing machinery
HQ: Asml Us, Llc
2625 W Geronimo Pl
Chandler AZ
480 696-2888

(P-7224)
ASML US LLC

17075 Thornmint Ct (92127-2413)
PHONE..................................858 385-6500
EMP: 536
SALES (corp-wide): 16.53B Privately Held
Web: www.asml.com
SIC: 3559 Semiconductor manufacturing machinery
HQ: Asml Us, Llc
2625 W Geronimo Pl
Chandler AZ
480 696-2888

(P-7225)
AVANZATO TECHNOLOGY CORP

5335 Mcconnell Ave (90066-7025)
PHONE..................................312 509-0506
Carissa Davino, CEO
Jeremy Green, Dir Opers
EMP: 20 EST: 2016
SALES (est): 1.45MM Privately Held

SIC: 3559 5065 Electronic component making machinery; Electronic parts

(P-7226)
BARKENS HARDCHROME INC

Also Called: Bhc Industries
239 E Greenleaf Blvd (90220-4913)
PHONE..................................310 632-2000
Gary Barken, CEO
Carol Barken, VP
EMP: 25 EST: 1942
SQ FT: 60,000
SALES (est): 4.84MM Privately Held
Web: www.barkenshardchrome.com
SIC: 3559 5082 Metal finishing equipment for plating, etc.; Oil field equipment

(P-7227)
BENDPAK INC (PA)

30440 Agoura Rd (91301-2145)
PHONE..................................805 933-9970
Jeffrey Kritzer, Pr
Donald R Henthorn, *
◆ EMP: 138 EST: 1965
SALES (est): 39.83MM
SALES (corp-wide): 39.83MM Privately Held
Web: www.bendpak.com
SIC: 3559 3537 Automotive related machinery; Industrial trucks and tractors

(P-7228)
BOOM INDUSTRIAL INC

2010 Wright Ave (91750-5821)
PHONE..................................909 495-3555
Huiwen Chen, CEO
EMP: 60 EST: 2016
SALES (est): 2.56MM Privately Held
Web: www.boomindustrial.com
SIC: 3559 3069 Rubber working machinery, including tires; Rubber automotive products

(P-7229)
COSMODYNE LLC

Also Called: Nikkiso Cosmodyne
3010 Old Ranch Pkwy Ste 300 (90740-2750)
PHONE..................................562 795-5990
Peter Wagner, Pr
◆ EMP: 25 EST: 1997
SQ FT: 125,000
SALES (est): 9.77MM Privately Held
Web: www.nikkisoceig.com
SIC: 3559 3443 Smelting and refining machinery and equipment; Cryogenic tanks, for liquids and gases
HQ: Cryogenic Industries, Inc.
27710 Jefferson Ave # 301
Temecula CA
951 677-2081

(P-7230)
CP MANUFACTURING INC (HQ)

Also Called: CP Manufacturing
6795 Calle De Linea (92154-8017)
PHONE..................................619 477-3175
Robert M Davis, Pr
Ruth Davis, *
Theodora Davis Inman, *
Michael W Howard, *
John O Willis, General Vice President*
▲ EMP: 104 EST: 1977
SQ FT: 60,572
SALES (est): 29.25MM
SALES (corp-wide): 81.98MM Privately Held
Web: www.cpmfg.com
SIC: 3559 Recycling machinery
PA: Ims Recycling Services, Inc.
2697 Main St

San Diego CA
619 231-2521

(P-7231)
CRYOGENIC EXPERTS INC
Also Called: Cexi
531 Sandy Cir (93036-0971)
PHONE..................805 981-4500
EMP: 30
SIC: 3559 Cryogenic machinery, industrial

(P-7232)
CRYST MARK INC A SWAN TECHNO C
Also Called: Crystal Mark
613 Justin Ave (91201-2326)
PHONE..................818 240-7520
John Swan, *Pr*
Marko S Swan, *
E Michael Swan, *
Pauline Swan, *
EMP: 40 **EST:** 1968
SQ FT: 18,000
SALES (est): 9.62MM **Privately Held**
Web: www.crystalmarkinc.com
SIC: 3559 3471 Semiconductor manufacturing machinery; Sand blasting of metal parts

(P-7233)
CUSTOM METAL FINISHING INC
17804 S Western Ave (90248-3620)
P.O. Box 368 (90248-0368)
PHONE..................310 532-5075
David Alverez, *Pr*
Becky Martinez, *
Kelly Alverez, *
Lilly Alvarez, *
Larry Alvarez, *Stockholder*
EMP: 20 **EST:** 1978
SQ FT: 7,500
SALES (est): 830.56K **Privately Held**
Web: www.1800deburring.com
SIC: 3559 3471 Metal finishing equipment for plating, etc.; Plating and polishing

(P-7234)
EXCELLON ACQUISITION LLC (HQ)
Also Called: Excellon Automation Co
16130 Gundry Ave (90723-4831)
PHONE..................310 668-7700
EMP: 38 **EST:** 1962
SALES (est): 11.44MM
SALES (corp-wide): 11.44MM **Privately Held**
Web: www.excellon.com
SIC: 3559 Semiconductor manufacturing machinery
PA: Turning Point Capital, Llc
138 Del Prado St
Lake Oswego OR

(P-7235)
FC MANAGEMENT SERVICES
Also Called: PC Recycle
2001 Anchor Ct Ste B (91320-1616)
PHONE..................805 499-0050
Fulton Connor, *Pr*
EMP: 21 **EST:** 2017
SALES (est): 1.75MM **Privately Held**
Web: www.4tempus.com
SIC: 3559 Electronic component making machinery

(P-7236)
FLAT PLANET INC
618 Hampton Dr (90291-8625)
PHONE..................888 656-6872

Michael Lee Simpson, *CEO*
Erik Mickelson, *Contrlr*
EMP: 20 **EST:** 2006
SALES (est): 200K **Privately Held**
Web: www.flatplanetltd.com
SIC: 3559 Tobacco products machinery

(P-7237)
FLIGHT MICROWAVE CORPORATION
410 S Douglas St (90245-4628)
PHONE..................310 607-9819
Rolf Kich, *Pr*
Mike Callas, *
EMP: 26 **EST:** 2004
SQ FT: 8,000
SALES (est): 5.12MM **Publicly Held**
Web: www.flightmicrowave.com
SIC: 3559 Electronic component making machinery
HQ: Lucix Corporation
800 Avenida Acaso Ste E
Camarillo CA
805 987-6645

(P-7238)
FLIR MOTION CTRL SYSTEMS INC
6769 Hollister Ave (93117-3001)
PHONE..................650 692-3900
Philip Kahn, *Pr*
David Gaw, *VP*
▼ **EMP:** 33 **EST:** 1992
SQ FT: 6,000
SALES (est): 4.43MM
SALES (corp-wide): 5.46B **Publicly Held**
Web: www.flir.com
SIC: 3559 3541 Semiconductor manufacturing machinery; Robots for drilling, cutting, grinding, polishing, etc.
HQ: Teledyne Flir, Llc
27700 Sw Parkway Ave
Wilsonville OR
503 498-3547

(P-7239)
GLASTAR CORPORATION
Also Called: Glastar
8425 Canoga Ave (91304-2607)
PHONE..................818 341-0301
Lorie Mitchell, *Pr*
EMP: 20 **EST:** 1978
SQ FT: 14,000
SALES (est): 2.22MM **Privately Held**
Web: www.glastar.com
SIC: 3559 3563 3231 Glass making machinery: blowing, molding, forming, etc.; Spraying and dusting equipment; Products of purchased glass

(P-7240)
HEXCO INTERNATIONAL
Also Called: Cryogenic Industries
25720 Jefferson Ave (92562-6929)
PHONE..................951 677-2081
◆ **EMP:** 117
SIC: 3559 3561 3443 Cryogenic machinery, industrial; Pumps and pumping equipment; Fabricated plate work (boiler shop)

(P-7241)
INDUSTRIAL DYNAMICS CO LTD (PA)
Also Called: Filtec
3100 Fujita St (90505-4007)
P.O. Box 2945 (90509-2945)
PHONE..................310 325-5633
James Kearbey, *CEO*
▲ **EMP:** 105 **EST:** 1960

SQ FT: 155,000
SALES (est): 44.05MM
SALES (corp-wide): 44.05MM **Privately Held**
Web: www.filtec.com
SIC: 3559 3829 Screening equipment, electric; Measuring and controlling devices, nec

(P-7242)
INDUSTRIAL TOOLS INC
1800 Avenue Of The Stars (90067-4216)
PHONE..................805 483-1111
Donald O Murphy, *Pr*
John E Anderson, *
Kay Nolan, *
EMP: 50 **EST:** 1961
SALES (est): 8.81MM **Privately Held**
Web: www.iti-abrasives.com
SIC: 3559 3545 3544 3541 Semiconductor manufacturing machinery; Machine tool accessories; Special dies, tools, jigs, and fixtures; Machine tools, metal cutting type

(P-7243)
INTEGRTED CRYGNIC SLUTIONS LLC
Also Called: Nikkiso Cryoquip
2835 Progress Pl (92029-1516)
PHONE..................951 234-0899
Peter Wagner, *Managing Member*
EMP: 35 **EST:** 2014
SALES (est): 3.83MM **Privately Held**
SIC: 3559 Cryogenic machinery, industrial

(P-7244)
JGM AUTOMOTIVE TOOLING INC
Also Called: Motec USA
5355 Industrial Dr (92649-1516)
PHONE..................714 895-7001
James Munn, *CEO*
EMP: 18 **EST:** 1980
SQ FT: 8,000
SALES (est): 438.48K **Privately Held**
Web: www.jgm.com
SIC: 3559 5531 Automotive maintenance equipment; Auto and truck equipment and parts

(P-7245)
JOHN CURRIE PERFORMANCE GROUP
Also Called: Rockjock
1592 Jenks Dr (92878-5008)
PHONE..................714 367-1580
Stephen E Blaine, *Ch Bd*
EMP: 22 **EST:** 2019
SALES (est): 2.43MM **Privately Held**
SIC: 3559 Automotive maintenance equipment

(P-7246)
KVR INVESTMENT GROUP INC
Also Called: Pacific Plating
12113 Branford St (91352-5710)
PHONE..................818 896-1102
Rakesh Bajaria, *Pr*
Ken Pansuria, *
Harry Thummar, *
Benny Kadhrota, *
EMP: 60 **EST:** 1997
SALES (est): 5.31MM **Privately Held**
SIC: 3559 3471 Metal finishing equipment for plating, etc.; Plating and polishing

(P-7247)
MEGA MACHINERY INC
6688 Doolittle Ave (92503-1432)

PHONE..................951 300-9300
Richard Risch, *Pr*
Roger Blaney, *
EMP: 26 **EST:** 1991
SQ FT: 20,000
SALES (est): 582.6K **Privately Held**
SIC: 3559 Plastics working machinery

(P-7248)
MEI RIGGING & CRATING LLC
Also Called: Dunkel Bros. Machinery Moving
14555 Alondra Blvd (90638-5602)
P.O. Box 1630 (97321-0477)
PHONE..................714 712-5888
Dan Cappello, *Prin*
Sondra Ludwick, *
Seth Christensen, *
Patrick Moore, *
Terry Shain, *
EMP: 60 **EST:** 2018
SALES (est): 5.42MM **Privately Held**
Web: www.dunkelbros.com
SIC: 3559 Special industry machinery, nec

(P-7249)
MERITEK ELECTRONICS CORP (PA)
5160 Rivergrade Rd (91706-1406)
PHONE..................626 373-1728
Pa-shih Oliver Su, *CEO*
◆ **EMP:** 65 **EST:** 1993
SQ FT: 60,000
SALES (est): 20.99MM **Privately Held**
Web: www.meritekusa.com
SIC: 3559 5065 Electronic component making machinery; Electronic parts

(P-7250)
MOREHOUSE-COWLES LLC
Also Called: Epworth Morehouse Cowles
13930 Magnolia Ave (91710-7029)
PHONE..................909 627-7222
EMP: 25 **EST:** 2004
SALES (est): 8.14MM
SALES (corp-wide): 7.51B **Publicly Held**
Web: www.morehousecowles.com
SIC: 3559 Chemical machinery and equipment
HQ: Nusil Technology Llc
1050 Cindy Ln
Carpinteria CA
805 684-8780

(P-7251)
MORGAN POLYMER SEALS LLC
3303 2475a Paseo De Las Americas (92154)
PHONE..................619 498-9221
Kevin A Morgan, *CEO*
Todd Tesky, *VP Sls*
EMP: 400 **EST:** 1997
SALES (est): 11.09MM **Privately Held**
Web: www.morganpolymerseals.com
SIC: 3559 5211 3663 3365 Automotive related machinery; Energy conservation products; Space satellite communications equipment; Aerospace castings, aluminum

(P-7252)
NEWPORT ELECTRONICS INC
2229 S Yale St (92704-4401)
PHONE..................714 540-4914
▲ **EMP:** 90
SIC: 3559 3829 3822 3825 Electronic component making machinery; Temperature sensors, except industrial process and aircraft; Temperature controls, automatic; Measuring instruments and meters, electric

PRODUCTS & SVCS

(P-7253)
NORCHEM CORPORATION (PA)
5649 Alhambra Ave (90032-3107)
PHONE..............................323 221-0221
Gevork Minissian, *CEO*
▲ EMP: 50 EST: 1980
SQ FT: 50,000
SALES (est): 10.63MM
SALES (corp-wide): 10.63MM Privately Held
Web: www.norchemcorp.com
SIC: 3559 2842 2841 Chemical machinery and equipment; Laundry cleaning preparations; Soap and other detergents

(P-7254)
PALOMAR TECHNOLOGIES INC (PA)
6305 El Camino Real (92009-1606)
PHONE..............................760 931-3600
EMP: 47 EST: 1975
SQ FT: 40,000
SALES (est): 26.87MM Privately Held
Web: www.palomartechnologies.com
SIC: 3559 Semiconductor manufacturing machinery

(P-7255)
PEABODY ENGINEERING & SUP INC
Also Called: Peabody Engineering
13435 Estelle St (92879-1877)
PHONE..............................951 734-7711
Mark Peabody, *CEO*
Larry Peabody, *
◆ EMP: 25 EST: 1952
SQ FT: 32,400
SALES (est): 5.14MM Privately Held
Web: www.etanks.com
SIC: 3559 5084 Chemical machinery and equipment; Industrial machinery and equipment

(P-7256)
PHILLIPS 66 CO CARBON GROUP
2555 Willow Rd (93420-5731)
PHONE..............................805 489-4050
EMP: 28 EST: 2004
SALES (est): 5.76MM Privately Held
SIC: 3559 Petroleum refinery equipment

(P-7257)
PROLINE CONCRETE TOOLS INC
4645 North Ave Ste 102 (92056-3593)
PHONE..............................760 758-7240
Jeff Irwin, *CEO*
Paul Sowa, *
▼ EMP: 27 EST: 1990
SALES (est): 3.93MM Privately Held
Web: www.prolinestamps.com
SIC: 3559 Concrete products machinery

(P-7258)
RXSAFE LLC
Also Called: Rxsafe
2453 Cades Way Bldg A (92081-7831)
PHONE..............................760 593-7161
William Holmes, *Managing Member*
Shawn Orr, *
EMP: 68 EST: 2008
SALES (est): 23.02MM Privately Held
Web: www.rxsafe.com
SIC: 3559 Pharmaceutical machinery

(P-7259)
STARCO ENTERPRISES INC (PA)
Also Called: Four Star Chemical
3137 E 26th St (90058-8006)
PHONE..............................323 266-7111
George D Stroesenreuther, *CEO*
Ross Sklar, *
▲ EMP: 74 EST: 1973
SQ FT: 25,000
SALES (est): 16.32MM
SALES (corp-wide): 16.32MM Privately Held
Web: www.thestarcogroup.com
SIC: 3559 5169 5191 Degreasing machines, automotive and industrial; Specialty cleaning and sanitation preparations; Farm supplies

(P-7260)
SUSS MICROTEC INC (HQ)
2520 Palisades Dr (92882-0632)
PHONE..............................408 940-0300
Frank Averdung, *Pr*
Franz Richter, *
Peter Szafir, *
Stewart Mc C0naughy, *
Stefan Schneidewind, *
EMP: 130 EST: 1980
SALES (est): 40.01MM
SALES (corp-wide): 310.68MM Privately Held
Web: www.suss.com
SIC: 3559 3825 3674 Semiconductor manufacturing machinery; Instruments to measure electricity; Semiconductors and related devices
PA: SUss Microtec Se
SchleiBheimer Str. 90
Garching B. Munchen BY
89320070

(P-7261)
TIMEC COMPANIES INC
Also Called: Timec Southern California
6861 Charity Ave (93308-5918)
PHONE..............................661 322-8177
Will Nord, *Site Superintendent*
EMP: 50
Web: www.timec.com
SIC: 3559 Refinery, chemical processing, and similar machinery
HQ: Timec Companies Inc
473 E Channel Rd
Benicia CA
707 642-2222

(P-7262)
TRADEMARK PLASTICS INC
807 Palmyrita Ave (92507-1805)
PHONE..............................909 941-8810
Erin Carty, *Pr*
Kris Carty, *Sec*
David Carty, *COO*
◆ EMP: 150 EST: 1988
SQ FT: 100,000
SALES (est): 31.49MM Privately Held
Web: www.trademarkplastics.com
SIC: 3559 3089 Plastics working machinery; Injection molding of plastics
PA: Zhejiang Gongdong Medical Technology Co., Ltd.
No.10,Beiyuan Ave.,Huangyan Dist.
Taizhou ZJ

(P-7263)
TYSTAR CORPORATION
7050 Lampson Ave (92841-3912)
PHONE..............................310 781-9219
EMP: 20 EST: 1988

SALES (est): 4.16MM Privately Held
Web: en.tystar.com
SIC: 3559 3612 Semiconductor manufacturing machinery; Control transformers

(P-7264)
UNITED SURFACE SOLUTIONS LLC
11901 Burke St (90670-2507)
PHONE..............................562 693-0202
EMP: 27 EST: 2010
SQ FT: 20,000
SALES (est): 4.71MM Privately Held
Web: www.deburring.com
SIC: 3559 3541 Metal finishing equipment for plating, etc.; Deburring machines

(P-7265)
VECTRON INC
345 6th Ave (92101-7005)
PHONE..............................858 621-2400
Joseph L Vilella, *Pr*
EMP: 18 EST: 1992
SQ FT: 20,000
SALES (est): 651.76K Privately Held
SIC: 3559 Refinery, chemical processing, and similar machinery

(P-7266)
VIZUALOGIC LLC
1493 E Bentley Dr (92879-5102)
PHONE..............................407 509-3421
Janis Patterson, *
EMP: 200 EST: 2015
SQ FT: 3,000
SALES (est): 20MM Privately Held
Web: www.vizualogicdirect.com
SIC: 3559 Automotive related machinery

(P-7267)
ZAMBONI COMPANY USA INC
Also Called: Zamboni
15714 Colorado Ave (90723-4211)
PHONE..............................562 633-0751
▲ EMP: 35 EST: 1949
SALES (est): 6.1MM Privately Held
Web: www.zamboni.com
SIC: 3559 Ice resurfacing machinery

3561 Pumps And Pumping Equipment

(P-7268)
AQUASTAR POOL PRODUCTS INC
Also Called: Aquastar Pool Productions
2340 Palma Dr Ste 104 (93003-8091)
PHONE..............................877 768-2717
Olaf Mjelde, *CEO*
▲ EMP: 26 EST: 2003
SALES (est): 6.06MM Privately Held
Web: www.aquastarpoolproducts.com
SIC: 3561 Pumps, domestic: water or sump

(P-7269)
AQUATEC INTERNATIONAL INC
Also Called: Aquatec Water Systems
17422 Pullman St (92614-5527)
PHONE..............................949 225-2200
Bryan Hausner, *CEO*
Sami Levi, *
Isak Levi, *
Ivar Schoenmeyr, *
▲ EMP: 95 EST: 1986
SQ FT: 30,000
SALES (est): 22.79MM Privately Held
Web: www.aquatec.com

SIC: 3561 Pumps and pumping equipment

(P-7270)
BORIN MANUFACTURING INC
5741 Buckingham Pkwy Ste B (90230-6520)
PHONE..............................310 822-1000
Frank William Borin, *CEO*
Gregg Steele, *
EMP: 40 EST: 1976
SALES (est): 9.95MM Privately Held
Web: www.borin.com
SIC: 3561 3443 3317 3494 Pumps and pumping equipment; Fabricated plate work (boiler shop); Steel pipe and tubes; Valves and pipe fittings, nec

(P-7271)
CASCADE PUMP COMPANY
10107 Norwalk Blvd (90670-3354)
P.O. Box 2767 (90670-0767)
PHONE..............................562 946-1414
T W Summerfield, *CEO*
John Summerfield, *
EMP: 60 EST: 1948
SQ FT: 120,000
SALES (est): 9.97MM Privately Held
Web: www.cascadepump.com
SIC: 3561 3594 Pumps, domestic: water or sump; Fluid power pumps and motors

(P-7272)
CIRCOR NAVAL SOLUTIONS LLC (DH)
656 Marsat Ct Ste A (91911-4683)
P.O. Box 5020 (28111-5020)
PHONE..............................413 436-7711
Tony Najjar, *CEO*
Kelly J Ruscoe, *
Joshua Powell, *
◆ EMP: 86 EST: 1985
SQ FT: 200,000
SALES (est): 85MM Publicly Held
Web: www.warrenpumps.com
SIC: 3561 5084 Pumps and pumping equipment; Industrial machinery and equipment
HQ: Circor International, Inc.
30 Corporate Dr Ste 200
Burlington MA
781 270-1200

(P-7273)
CODYSALES INC
1393 Dodson Way Ste A (92507-2073)
P.O. Box 56099 (92517-0999)
PHONE..............................951 786-3650
Marius J A, *Pastor*
EMP: 17 EST: 2005
SALES (est): 958.63K Privately Held
SIC: 3561 Cylinders, pump

(P-7274)
CRYOSTAR USA LLC
13117 Meyer Rd (90605-3555)
PHONE..............................562 903-1290
▲ EMP: 56 EST: 2014
SALES (est): 9.21MM Privately Held
Web: www.cryostar.com
SIC: 3561 Pump jacks and other pumping equipment
HQ: Cryostar Sas
2 Rue De L Industrie
Hesingue
389702727

(P-7275)
CURLIN MEDICAL INC (HQ)
15662 Commerce Ln (92649-1604)
PHONE..............................714 897-9301

Martin Berarei, *Pr*
▲ **EMP:** 29 **EST:** 1998
SALES (est): 3.69MM
SALES (corp-wide): 3.32B **Publicly Held**
SIC: 3561 Pumps and pumping equipment
PA: Moog Inc.
400 Jamison Rd
Elma NY
716 652-2000

(P-7276)
FLOWSERVE CORPORATION
Flowserve
27455 Tierra Alta Way Ste C (92590-3498)
PHONE.................951 296-2464
Paul Cortenbach, *Brnch Mgr*
EMP: 62
SALES (corp-wide): 3.62B **Publicly Held**
Web: www.flowserve.com
SIC: 3561 3053 Industrial pumps and parts;
Gaskets; packing and sealing devices
PA: Flowserve Corporation
5215 N Ocnnor Blvd Ste 70 Connor
Irving TX
972 443-6500

(P-7277)
FLOWSERVE CORPORATION
Flowserve
2300 E Vernon Ave Stop 76 (90058-1609)
PHONE.................323 584-1890
Rick Soldo, *Brnch Mgr*
EMP: 342
SALES (corp-wide): 3.62B **Publicly Held**
Web: www.flowserve.com
SIC: 3561 Pumps and pumping equipment
PA: Flowserve Corporation
5215 N Ocnnor Blvd Ste 70 Connor
Irving TX
972 443-6500

(P-7278)
FLOWSERVE CORPORATION
Flowserve
1909 E Cashdan St (90220-6422)
PHONE.................310 667-4220
Dan Lattimore, *Mgr*
EMP: 63
SALES (corp-wide): 3.62B **Publicly Held**
Web: www.flowserve.com
SIC: 3561 Industrial pumps and parts
PA: Flowserve Corporation
5215 N Ocnnor Blvd Ste 70 Connor
Irving TX
972 443-6500

(P-7279)
GRISWOLD PUMP COMPANY
22069 Van Buren St (92313-5607)
PHONE.................909 422-1700
◆ **EMP:** 25 **EST:** 1996
SQ FT: 25,000
SALES (est): 13.48MM
SALES (corp-wide): 8.51B **Publicly Held**
Web: www.psgdover.com
SIC: 3561 5084 Industrial pumps and parts;
Industrial machinery and equipment
HQ: Psg California Llc
22069 Van Buren St
Grand Terrace CA
909 422-1700

(P-7280)
GROVER SMITH MFG CORP
Also Called: Grover Manufacturing
9717 Factorial Way (91733-1724)
P.O. Box 986 (90640-0986)
PHONE.................323 724-3444
Marilyn Schirmer, *Corporate President*
Marilyn Schirmer, *Pr*

Lino Paras, *
W Michael Meeker, *
EMP: 30 **EST:** 1925
SALES (est): 3.29MM **Privately Held**
Web: www.grovermfg.com
SIC: 3561 3569 Pumps and pumping
equipment; Lubrication equipment, industrial

(P-7281)
HASKEL INTERNATIONAL LLC (HQ)
100 E Graham Pl (91502-2027)
PHONE.................818 843-4000
Chris Krieps, *CEO*
Dave Alan Barta, *
Elmer Lee Doty, *
Maria Blase, *
▲ **EMP:** 125 **EST:** 1986
SQ FT: 78,000
SALES (est): 51MM
SALES (corp-wide): 5.92B **Publicly Held**
SIC: 3561 3594 5084 5085 Pumps and
pumping equipment; Fluid power pumps;
Hydraulic systems equipment and supplies;
Hose, belting, and packing
PA: Ingersoll Rand Inc.
525 Harbour Place Dr # 600
Davidson NC
704 896-4000

(P-7282)
LOS ANGLES PUMP VALVE PDTS INC
Also Called: Los Angeles Brass Products
2528 E 57th St (90255-2521)
P.O. Box 2007 (90255-1307)
PHONE.................323 277-7788
Santos J Pinto, *Pr*
Phil Pinto, *VP*
EMP: 20 **EST:** 1975
SQ FT: 11,000
SALES (est): 2.56MM **Privately Held**
Web: www.lapumpandvalve.com
SIC: 3561 Pump jacks and other pumping
equipment

(P-7283)
MJW INC
Also Called: American Lab and Systems
1328 W Slauson Ave (90044-2824)
PHONE.................323 778-8900
Mike Curry, *Pr*
Linda Curry, *
EMP: 65 **EST:** 1978
SQ FT: 30,000
SALES (est): 4.77MM **Privately Held**
Web: www.americanlabs.com
SIC: 3561 Industrial pumps and parts

(P-7284)
MOLEAER INC
3232 W El Segundo Blvd (90250-4823)
PHONE.................424 558-3567
Nicholas Dyner, *CEO*
Warren Russell, *
Bruce Scholten, *
Bryan Brister, *
Hoshang Subawalla, *Chief Business Officer**
EMP: 85 **EST:** 2016
SALES (est): 11.44MM **Privately Held**
Web: www.moleaer.com
SIC: 3561 Pumps and pumping equipment

(P-7285)
PENGUIN PUMPS INCORPORATED
Also Called: Filter Pump Industries
7932 Ajay Dr (91352-5315)

PHONE.................818 504-2391
Jerome S Hollander, *Pr*
▲ **EMP:** 50 **EST:** 1972
SQ FT: 20,000
SALES (est): 11.74MM
SALES (corp-wide): 11.74MM **Privately Held**
Web: www.filterpump.com
SIC: 3561 3569 Pumps and pumping
equipment; Filters, general line: industrial
PA: Finish Thompson, Inc.
921 Greengarden Rd
Erie PA
814 455-4478

(P-7286)
POLARIS E-COMMERCE INC
1941 E Occidental St (92705-5115)
PHONE.................714 907-0582
Insoo Hwang, *CEO*
▲ **EMP:** 25 **EST:** 2010
SALES (est): 2.35MM **Privately Held**
Web: www.bugkwikzap.com
SIC: 3561 Industrial pumps and parts

(P-7287)
PSG CALIFORNIA LLC (HQ)
Also Called: Wilden Pump
22069 Van Buren St (92313-5607)
PHONE.................909 422-1700
Denny L Buskirk, *Managing Member*
Daniel Anderson, *
◆ **EMP:** 295 **EST:** 1998
SQ FT: 153,000
SALES (est): 97.73MM
SALES (corp-wide): 8.51B **Publicly Held**
Web: www.psgdover.com
SIC: 3561 Industrial pumps and parts
PA: Dover Corporation
3005 Highland Pkwy # 200
Downers Grove IL
630 541-1540

(P-7288)
REED LLC
Also Called: Reed Manufacturing
13822 Oaks Ave (91710-7008)
PHONE.................909 287-2100
James W Shea, *Managing Member*
Cliff Kao, *VP*
◆ **EMP:** 40 **EST:** 1957
SQ FT: 69,000
SALES (est): 9.93MM **Privately Held**
Web: www.reedpumps.com
SIC: 3561 3531 Pumps and pumping
equipment; Bituminous, cement and
concrete related products and equip.

(P-7289)
SCHROFF INC
Also Called: Pep West, Inc.
7328 Trade St (92121-3435)
PHONE.................800 525-4682
Beth Wozniak, *CEO*
Bill Biancaniello, *Pr*
Judy Carle, *VP Fin*
Michael Meyer, *Treas*
▲ **EMP:** 800 **EST:** 2005
SALES (est): 79.63MM **Privately Held**
SIC: 3561 Pumps and pumping equipment
HQ: Schroff, Inc.
170 Commerce Dr
Warwick RI
763 204-7700

(P-7290)
SHURFLO LLC
Also Called: Pentair Water Treatment
3545 Harbor Gtwy S Ste 103 (92626-1457)
PHONE.................714 371-1550

▲ **EMP:** 430
Web: www.pentair.com
SIC: 3561 Pumps and pumping equipment

(P-7291)
SULZER PUMP SERVICES (US) INC
Also Called: Sulzer Bingham Pumps
9856 Jordan Cir (90670-3303)
P.O. Box 3904 (90670-1904)
PHONE.................562 903-1000
Tim Voyles, *Mgr*
EMP: 21
SQ FT: 18,968
SIC: 3561 Pumps and pumping equipment
HQ: Sulzer Pump Services (Us) Inc.
900 Threadneedle St # 700
Houston TX
281 417-7110

(P-7292)
TOTAL PROCESS SOLUTIONS LLC
1400 Norris Rd (93308-2232)
PHONE.................661 829-7910
Eddie L Rice, *Managing Member*
Stan Ellis, *Managing Member**
Travis Ellis, *Managing Member**
Joey L Taylor, *Managing Member**
EMP: 30 **EST:** 2012
SALES (est): 4.45MM **Privately Held**
SIC: 3561 3563 Cylinders, pump; Air and
gas compressors including vacuum pumps

(P-7293)
TRANE TECHNOLOGIES COMPANY LLC
Also Called: Ingersoll-Rand
2845 Pellissier Pl (90601-1512)
PHONE.................323 583-4771
EMP: 17
Web: www.trane.com
SIC: 3561 Pumps and pumping equipment
HQ: Trane Technologies Company Llc
800 Beaty St Ste E
Davidson NC
704 655-4000

(P-7294)
XYLEM WATER SOLUTIONS USA INC
17942 Cowan (92614-6026)
PHONE.................949 474-1679
EMP: 36
Web: www.xylem.com
SIC: 3561 Pumps and pumping equipment
HQ: Xylem Water Solutions U.S.A., Inc.
4828 Parkway Plaza Blvd # 200
Charlotte NC

(P-7295)
XYLEM WATER SYSTEMS (CALIFORNIA) INC
830 Bay Blvd Ste 101 (91911-1683)
PHONE.................619 575-7466
▲ **EMP:** 26
SIC: 3561 3443 Pumps and pumping
equipment; Fabricated plate work (boiler
shop)

3562 Ball And Roller Bearings

(P-7296)
AMERICAN METAL BEARING COMPANY
7191 Acacia Ave (92841-5297)
PHONE.................714 892-5527

Alfred A Anawati, *CEO*
Michael Litton, *VP*
Jim Demaio, *Sec*
▲ **EMP:** 21 **EST:** 1921
SQ FT: 40,000
SALES (est): 9.49MM
SALES (corp-wide): 29.51MM **Privately Held**
Web: www.ambco.net
SIC: 3562 7699 3568 Ball bearings and parts; Rebabbitting; Power transmission equipment, nec
PA: Marisco, Ltd.
91-607 Malakole St
Kapolei HI
808 682-1333

(P-7297)
CASTER CIVIL INC
1858 Rancho Janet (91901-2936)
PHONE...................626 201-1300
Danielle Caster, *Prin*
EMP: 26 **EST:** 2021
SALES (est): 2.26MM **Privately Held**
Web: www.castercivil.com
SIC: 3562 Casters

(P-7298)
CLEAN WAVE MANAGEMENT INC
Also Called: Impact Bearing
1291 Puerta Del Sol (92673-6310)
PHONE...................949 370-0740
Richard D Kay Junior, *CEO*
Michael Bartlett, *
◆ **EMP:** 30 **EST:** 1995
SQ FT: 20,000
SALES (est): 4.62MM **Privately Held**
Web: www.impactbearing.com
SIC: 3562 Ball bearings and parts

(P-7299)
INDUSTRIAL TCTNICS BRINGS CORP (DH)
18301 S Santa Fe Ave (90221-5519)
PHONE...................310 537-3750
Michael J Hartnett, *CEO*
EMP: 149 **EST:** 1990
SQ FT: 70,000
SALES (est): 51.59MM
SALES (corp-wide): 1.47B **Publicly Held**
Web: www.rbcbearings.com
SIC: 3562 5085 Roller bearings and parts; Bearings
HQ: Roller Bearing Company Of America, Inc.
102 Willenbrock Rd
Oxford CT
203 267-7001

(P-7300)
INTEGRATED ENERGY TECHNOLOGIES INC
Also Called: Doncasters Gce Integrated
1478 Santa Sierra Dr (91913-2862)
PHONE...................619 421-1151
EMP: 160
SIC: 3562 Casters

(P-7301)
NEXT POINT BEARING GROUP LLC
28364 Avenue Crocker (91355-1250)
PHONE...................818 988-1880
Mark Mickelson, *Managing Member*
John Burroughs, *
▲ **EMP:** 28 **EST:** 2012
SQ FT: 27,000
SALES (est): 8.29MM **Privately Held**

Web: www.nextpointbearing.com
SIC: 3562 5085 Ball and roller bearings; Bearings

(P-7302)
NMB (USA) INC (HQ)
Also Called: NMB Tech
9730 Independence Ave (91311-4323)
PHONE...................818 709-1770
◆ **EMP:** 50 **EST:** 1983
SALES (est): 451.49MM **Privately Held**
Web: www.nmbtc.com
SIC: 3562 5063 5084 3728 Ball bearings and parts; Motors, electric; Fans, industrial; Aircraft propellers and associated equipment
PA: Minebea Mitsumi Inc.
1-9-3, Higashishimbashi
Minato-Ku TKY

(P-7303)
SCHAEFFLER GROUP USA INC
34700 Pacific Coast Hwy Ste 203 (92624)
PHONE...................949 234-9799
Rich Peterson, *Brnch Mgr*
EMP: 32
SALES (corp-wide): 62.18B **Privately Held**
Web: www.schaeffler.us
SIC: 3562 Ball and roller bearings
HQ: Schaeffler Group Usa Inc.
308 Springhill Farm Rd
Fort Mill SC
803 548-8500

(P-7304)
SPECIALTY MOTIONS INC
5480 Smokey Mountain Way (92887-4247)
PHONE...................951 735-8722
Thomas Corey, *CEO*
Dorothy Corey, *Sec*
EMP: 20 **EST:** 1990
SQ FT: 13,000
SALES (est): 2.1MM **Privately Held**
SIC: 3562 5085 Ball and roller bearings; Bearings

(P-7305)
WEARTECH INTERNATIONAL INC
1177 N Grove St (92806-2110)
PHONE...................714 683-2430
▲ **EMP:** 43
Web: www.weartech.net
SIC: 3562 3313 3548 3496 Ball bearings and parts; Alloys, additive, except copper: not made in blast furnaces; Welding apparatus; Miscellaneous fabricated wire products

---

3563 Air And Gas Compressors

(P-7306)
ATLAS COPCO COMPRESSORS LLC
Also Called: Accurate Air Engineering
16207 Carmenita Rd (90703-2212)
PHONE...................562 484-6370
John T Lague, *Pr*
EMP: 35
SALES (corp-wide): 13.47B **Privately Held**
Web: www.accurateair.com
SIC: 3563 Air and gas compressors
HQ: Atlas Copco Compressors Llc
300 Technology Center Way # 550
Rock Hill SC
866 472-1015

(P-7307)
C M AUTOMOTIVE SYSTEMS INC (PA)
5646 W Mission Blvd (91762-4652)
PHONE...................909 869-7912
Chander Mittal, *Pr*
Sameer Mittal, *CFO*
▲ **EMP:** 23 **EST:** 1986
SALES (est): 4.47MM
SALES (corp-wide): 4.47MM **Privately Held**
Web: www.cmautomotive.com
SIC: 3563 Air and gas compressors

(P-7308)
DRESSER-RAND COMPANY
18502 Dominguez Hill Dr (90220-6415)
PHONE...................310 223-0600
EMP: 43
SALES (corp-wide): 73.09B **Privately Held**
SIC: 3563 Air and gas compressors
HQ: Dresser-Rand Company
500 Paul Clark Dr
Olean NY
716 375-3000

(P-7309)
KOBELCO COMPRESSORS AMER INC
301 N Smith Ave (92878-3242)
PHONE...................951 739-3030
EMP: 75
Web: www.kobelco-machinery-energy.com
SIC: 3563 Air and gas compressors
HQ: Kobelco Compressors America, Inc.
1450 W Rincon St
Corona CA

(P-7310)
KOBELCO COMPRESSORS AMER INC (DH)
1450 W Rincon St (92878-9205)
PHONE...................951 739-3030
Makoto Motoyoshi, *Pr*
◆ **EMP:** 260 **EST:** 1990
SALES (est): 55.25MM **Privately Held**
Web:
www.kobelco-machinery-energy.com
SIC: 3563 Air and gas compressors including vacuum pumps
HQ: Kobe Steel Usa Holdings Inc.
535 Madison Ave Fl 5
New York NY

(P-7311)
NORDSON CORPORATION
Also Called: Nordon Yestech
2765 Loker Ave W (92010-6601)
PHONE...................760 431-1919
Carla Loeffler, *Brnch Mgr*
EMP: 33
SALES (corp-wide): 2.59B **Publicly Held**
Web: www.nordson.com
SIC: 3563 Spraying outfits: metals, paints, and chemicals (compressor)
PA: Nordson Corporation
28601 Clemens Rd
Westlake OH
440 892-1580

(P-7312)
NORDSON CORPORATION
Also Called: Nordson Asymtek
2747 Loker Ave W (92010-6601)
PHONE...................760 431-1919
EMP: 212
SALES (corp-wide): 2.59B **Publicly Held**
Web: www.nordson.com

SIC: 3563 Air and gas compressors
PA: Nordson Corporation
28601 Clemens Rd
Westlake OH
440 892-1580

(P-7313)
NORDSON MARCH INC
2762 Loker Ave W (92010-6603)
PHONE...................925 827-1240
Jerry Wilder, *Brnch Mgr*
EMP: 75
SALES (corp-wide): 2.59B **Publicly Held**
Web: www.nordson.com
SIC: 3563 Air and gas compressors
HQ: March Nordson Inc
2470 Bates Ave Ste A
Concord CA
925 827-1240

(P-7314)
NORDSON TEST INSPTN AMRCAS INC
2765 Loker Ave W (92010-6601)
PHONE...................760 918-8471
Don Miller, *Pr*
Christine Schwarzmann, *
Robert E Veillette, *
EMP: 32 **EST:** 2002
SQ FT: 10,000
SALES (est): 11.12MM
SALES (corp-wide): 2.59B **Publicly Held**
Web: www.nordson.com
SIC: 3563 Air and gas compressors
PA: Nordson Corporation
28601 Clemens Rd
Westlake OH
440 892-1580

(P-7315)
NU VENTURE DIVING CO
Also Called: Nuvair
1600 Beacon Pl (93033-2433)
PHONE...................805 815-4044
Glenn Huebner, *CEO*
Glenn A Huebner, *CEO*
Janet Huebner, *VP*
◆ **EMP:** 22 **EST:** 1988
SQ FT: 27,000
SALES (est): 5.54MM **Privately Held**
Web: www.nuvair.com
SIC: 3563 Air and gas compressors

(P-7316)
SIEMENS ENERGY INC
18502 S Dominguez Hills Dr (90220-6415)
PHONE...................310 223-0660
EMP: 43
SALES (corp-wide): 33.81B **Privately Held**
Web: www.siemens-energy.com
SIC: 3563 Air and gas compressors
HQ: Siemens Energy, Inc.
4400 N Alafaya Trl
Orlando FL
407 736-2000

3564 Blowers And Fans

(P-7317)
ADWEST TECHNOLOGIES INC (HQ)
Also Called: Adwest
4222 E La Palma Ave (92807-1816)
PHONE...................714 632-8595
Brian Cannon, *VP*
Craig Bayer, *
Richard Whitford, *
Maryann Erickson, *
EMP: 35 **EST:** 1988

SQ FT: 23,500
SALES (est): 9.57MM **Publicly Held**
SIC: 3564 3585 3826 Air purification equipment; Heating equipment, complete; Thermal analysis instruments, laboratory type
PA: Ceco Environmental Corp.
14651 Dallas Pkwy Ste 500
Dallas TX

(P-7318)
AMERICAN METAL FILTER COMPANY
611 Marsat Ct (91911-4648)
PHONE..........................619 628-1917
Valentine C Deilgat, *Pr*
EMP: 17 **EST:** 1986
SALES (est): 2.59MM **Privately Held**
Web: www.amfco.com
SIC: 3564 Filters, air: furnaces, air conditioning equipment, etc.

(P-7319)
ATLAS COPCO MAFI-TRENCH CO LLC (DH)
Also Called: Atlas Copco
3037 Industrial Pkwy (93455-1807)
PHONE..........................805 928-5757
◆ **EMP:** 208 **EST:** 2007
SQ FT: 90,000
SALES (est): 101.25MM
SALES (corp-wide): 13.47B **Privately Held**
SIC: 3564 3533 8744 Turbo-blowers, industrial; Oil and gas field machinery; Facilities support services
HQ: Atlas Copco North America Llc
6 Century Dr Ste 310
Parsippany NJ

(P-7320)
CAMFIL FARR INC
3625 Del Amo Blvd Ste 260 (90503-1688)
PHONE..........................973 616-7300
Frank Shahin, *Prin*
EMP: 60 **EST:** 2010
SALES (est): 279.61K **Privately Held**
SIC: 3564 Blowers and fans

(P-7321)
CENTRAL BLOWER CO
3427 Pomona Blvd (91768-3260)
PHONE..........................626 330-3182
TOLL FREE: 800
David Roger Petersen, *Pr*
Eleanor Petersen, *VP*
Mary Petersen, *Stockholder*
EMP: 20 **EST:** 1979
SALES (est): 2.52MM **Privately Held**
Web: www.centralblower.com
SIC: 3564 Exhaust fans: industrial or commercial

(P-7322)
ENVION LLC
14724 Ventura Blvd Fl 200 (91403-3514)
PHONE..........................818 217-2500
▲ **EMP:** 85 **EST:** 2003
SQ FT: 36,000
SALES (est): 4.52MM
SALES (corp-wide): 20.39MM **Privately Held**
Web: www.envion.com
SIC: 3564 Air purification equipment
PA: Sylmark Inc.
7821 Orion Ave Ste 200
Van Nuys CA
818 217-2000

(P-7323)
HEPA CORPORATION
3071 E Coronado St (92806-2698)
PHONE..........................714 630-5700
EMP: 100 **EST:** 1968
SALES (est): 9.78MM **Privately Held**
Web: www.hepa.com
SIC: 3564 Air purification equipment

(P-7324)
IQAIR NORTH AMERICA INC
14351 Firestone Blvd (90638-5527)
PHONE..........................877 715-4247
Glory Z Dolphin, *CEO*
Frank Hammes, *
▲ **EMP:** 48 **EST:** 1991
SQ FT: 40,000
SALES (est): 22.9MM **Privately Held**
Web: www.iqair.com
SIC: 3564 8742 5999 Air cleaning systems; Materials mgmt. (purchasing, handling, inventory) consultant; Air purification equipment
PA: Icleen Entwicklungs- Und Vertriebsanstalt Fur Umweltprodukte C/O Jgt Treuunternehmen Reg. Vaduz

(P-7325)
M D H BURNER & BOILER CO INC
12106 Center St (90280-8046)
PHONE..........................562 630-2875
Mauro Donate, *CEO*
EMP: 18 **EST:** 1992
SQ FT: 5,000
SALES (est): 2.44MM **Privately Held**
SIC: 3564 7699 3443 3433 Air purification equipment; Boiler repair shop; Fabricated plate work (boiler shop); Heating equipment, except electric

(P-7326)
MACROAIR TECHNOLOGIES INC (PA)
Also Called: Macro Air Technologies
794 S Allen St (92408-2210)
P.O. Box 1467 (92324-0805)
PHONE..........................909 890-2270
TOLL FREE: 800
Edward Boyd, *CEO*
◆ **EMP:** 45 **EST:** 1979
SQ FT: 15,000
SALES (est): 19MM
SALES (corp-wide): 19MM **Privately Held**
Web: www.macroairfans.com
SIC: 3564 Ventilating fans: industrial or commercial

(P-7327)
MARS AIR SYSTEMS LLC
Also Called: Mars Air Curtains
14716 S Broadway (90248-1814)
PHONE..........................310 532-1555
▼ **EMP:** 75 **EST:** 1961
SALES (est): 16.28MM **Privately Held**
Web: www.marsair.com
SIC: 3564 Blowers and fans

(P-7328)
PACWEST AIR FILTER LLC
26550 Adams Ave (92562-7085)
PHONE..........................951 698-2228
Buddy Olds, *CEO*
EMP: 44 **EST:** 2009
SQ FT: 5,000
SALES (est): 4.55MM **Privately Held**
Web: www.pacwestfilter.com

SIC: 3564 5085 Filters, air: furnaces, air conditioning equipment, etc.; Filters, industrial

(P-7329)
QC MANUFACTURING INC
26040 Ynez Rd (92591-6033)
PHONE..........................951 325-6340
Dane Stevenson, *Pr*
▲ **EMP:** 65 **EST:** 2009
SALES (est): 20.16MM **Privately Held**
Web: www.quietcoolsystems.com
SIC: 3564 Blowers and fans

(P-7330)
ROTRON INCORPORATED
Ametek Rotron
474 Raleigh Ave (92020-3138)
PHONE..........................619 593-7400
Fred Taylor, *Mgr*
EMP: 120
SALES (corp-wide): 6.15B **Publicly Held**
Web: www.rotron.com
SIC: 3564 Blowers and fans
HQ: Rotron Incorporated
55 Hasbrouck Ln
Woodstock NY
845 679-2401

(P-7331)
STANDARD FILTER CORPORATION (PA)
3801 Ocean Ranch Blvd Ste 107 (92056-8603)
PHONE..........................866 443-3615
Tobey Wiik, *Pr*
◆ **EMP:** 26 **EST:** 1973
SALES (est): 4.34MM
SALES (corp-wide): 4.34MM **Privately Held**
Web: www.standardfilter.com
SIC: 3564 5199 Filters, air: furnaces, air conditioning equipment, etc.; Felt

(P-7332)
SUN INDUSTRIES CORPORATION
Also Called: Sun Industries
370 Amapola Ave Ste 101 (90501-7239)
PHONE..........................310 782-1188
▲ **EMP:** 21 **EST:** 1981
SALES (est): 2.58MM **Privately Held**
Web: www.sunindustries.com
SIC: 3564 5065 5013 3569 Filters, air: furnaces, air conditioning equipment, etc.; Electronic parts; Filters, air and oil; Filters

(P-7333)
SUNON INC (PA)
Also Called: Eme Fan & Motor
1075 W Lambert Rd Ste A (92821-2944)
PHONE..........................714 255-0208
Yin Su Hong, *CEO*
▲ **EMP:** 30 **EST:** 1998
SQ FT: 22,000
SALES (est): 3.34MM
SALES (corp-wide): 3.34MM **Privately Held**
Web: www.sunonusa.com
SIC: 3564 Blowers and fans

(P-7334)
TERRA UNIVERSAL INC
800 S Raymond Ave (92831-5234)
PHONE..........................714 526-0100
G H Sadaghiani, *CEO*
▲ **EMP:** 195 **EST:** 1975
SQ FT: 88,000
SALES (est): 41.62MM **Privately Held**

Web: www.terrauniversal.com
SIC: 3564 3567 3569 3572 Purification and dust collection equipment; Heating units and devices, industrial: electric; Filters; Computer storage devices

(P-7335)
TMC FLUID SYSTEMS INC
Also Called: Socal Cleaning & Insulation
1228 Village Way Ste H (92705-4747)
PHONE..........................714 553-0944
Dilva Mian, *Pr*
▲ **EMP:** 17 **EST:** 2011
SQ FT: 2,000
SALES (est): 1.68MM **Privately Held**
Web: www.tmcfluidsystems.com
SIC: 3564 Blowers and fans

(P-7336)
TRI-DIM FILTER CORPORATION
15271 Fairfield Ranch Rd Ste 150 (91709-8865)
PHONE..........................626 826-5893
Scott Breckenridge, *Mgr*
EMP: 30
SALES (corp-wide): 1.42MM **Privately Held**
Web: airfiltration.mann-hummel.com
SIC: 3564 Filters, air: furnaces, air conditioning equipment, etc.
HQ: Tri-Dim Filter Corporation
93 Industrial Dr
Louisa VA
540 967-2600

(P-7337)
US TOYO FAN CORPORATION
16025 Arrow Hwy Ste F (91706-2063)
P.O. Box 1941 (91507-1941)
PHONE..........................626 338-1111
William Jacobs, *Pr*
Robert Rosenthal, *VP*
Arnold Weisman, *Sec*
▲ **EMP:** 80 **EST:** 1981
SQ FT: 10,000
SALES (est): 9.92MM
SALES (corp-wide): 54.35MM **Privately Held**
Web: ustoyofan.descoindustries.com
SIC: 3564 Blowers and fans
PA: Desco Industries, Inc.
3651 Walnut Ave
Chino CA
909 627-8178

(P-7338)
VENTUREDYNE LTD
Climet Instruments Company
1320 W Colton Ave (92374-2864)
P.O. Box 1760 (92373-0543)
PHONE..........................909 793-2788
Ray Felbinger, *Mgr*
EMP: 65
SALES (corp-wide): 178 **Privately Held**
Web: www.venturedyne.com
SIC: 3564 3829 3825 3823 Blowing fans: industrial or commercial; Measuring and controlling devices, nec; Instruments to measure electricity; Process control instruments
PA: Venturedyne, Ltd.
600 College Ave
Pewaukee WI
262 691-9900

(P-7339)
VORTECH ENGINEERING INC
Also Called: Vortech
1650 Pacific Ave (93033-2746)
PHONE..........................805 247-0226

Jim Middlebrook, *CEO*
Randolf Riley, *
▲ **EMP:** 42 **EST:** 2001
SALES (est): 8.72MM **Privately Held**
Web: www.vortechsuperchargers.com
SIC: 3564 Blowing fans: industrial or commercial

(P-7340)
VORTOX AIR TECHNOLOGY INC
121 S Indian Hill Blvd (91711-4997)
PHONE..............................909 621-3843
EMP: 23 **EST:** 1917
SALES (est): 3.9MM **Privately Held**
Web: www.vortox.com
SIC: 3564 3444 3829 Air cleaning systems; Sheet metalwork; Measuring and controlling devices, nec

(P-7341)
WEMS INC (PA)
Also Called: Wems Electronics
4650 W Rosecrans Ave (90250-6841)
P.O. Box 528 (90251-0528)
PHONE..............................310 644-0251
Ronald Hood, *CEO*
Nancy Howe, *Information Technology**
Carroll Whitney, *
Charles Wilson, *
EMP: 84 **EST:** 1960
SQ FT: 78,000
SALES (est): 20.45MM
SALES (corp-wide): 20.45MM **Privately Held**
Web: www.wems.com
SIC: 3564 3612 6513 Blowers and fans; Transformers, except electric; Apartment building operators

3565 Packaging Machinery

(P-7342)
ACCU-SEAL SENCORPWHITE INC
225 Bingham Dr Ste B (92069-1418)
PHONE..............................760 591-9800
Lesly Jensen, *Pr*
EMP: 19 **EST:** 1971
SQ FT: 14,000
SALES (est): 5.16MM
SALES (corp-wide): 376.52MM **Privately Held**
Web: www.accu-seal.com
SIC: 3565 Packaging machinery
HQ: Sencorpwhite, Inc.
400 Kidds Hill Rd
Hyannis MA
508 771-9400

(P-7343)
ACCUTEK PACKAGING EQUIPMENT CO (PA)
Also Called: Kiss Packaging Systems
2980 Scott St (92081-8321)
PHONE..............................760 734-4177
Edward Chocholek, *Prin*
Drew Chocholek, *
Darren Chocholek, *
Drake Chocholek, *
◆ **EMP:** 25 **EST:** 1987
SALES (est): 18.18MM **Privately Held**
Web: www.accutekpackaging.com
SIC: 3565 Packaging machinery

(P-7344)
ALINE SYSTEMS CORPORATION
Also Called: Aline Systems
13844 Struikman Rd (90703-1032)
PHONE..............................562 229-9727

EMP: 20
SIC: 3565 Packaging machinery

(P-7345)
BELCO PACKAGING SYSTEMS INC
910 S Mountain Ave (91016-3641)
PHONE..............................626 357-9566
TOLL FREE: 800
Helen V Misik, *CEO*
A Michael Misik, *
▲ **EMP:** 25 **EST:** 1959
SQ FT: 35,000
SALES (est): 8.45MM **Privately Held**
Web: www.belcopackaging.com
SIC: 3565 Packing and wrapping machinery

(P-7346)
CAN LINES ENGINEERING INC (PA)
Also Called: C L E
9839 Downey Norwalk Rd (90241-5596)
PHONE..............................562 861-2996
Donald Koplien, *CEO*
Keenan Koplien, *
Erik Koplien, *
EMP: 89 **EST:** 1960
SQ FT: 40,000
SALES (est): 23.71MM
SALES (corp-wide): 23.71MM **Privately Held**
Web: www.canlines.com
SIC: 3565 3556 Canning machinery, food; Food products machinery

(P-7347)
CVC TECHNOLOGIES INC
10861 Business Dr (92337-8235)
PHONE..............................909 355-0311
Sheng Hui Yang, *CEO*
K Joe Yang, *Pr*
▲ **EMP:** 21 **EST:** 1998
SQ FT: 29,000
SALES (est): 5.77MM **Privately Held**
Web: www.cvctechnologies.com
SIC: 3565 Labeling machines, industrial
PA: Cvc Technologies Inc.
No. 190, Gongye 9th Rd.
Taichung City

(P-7348)
FUTURE COMMODITIES INTL INC
Also Called: Bestpack Packaging Systems
1425 S Campus Ave (91761-4366)
PHONE..............................888 588-2378
David L Lim, *Pr*
Chery Co Lim, *Ex VP*
▲ **EMP:** 27 **EST:** 1984
SQ FT: 27,500
SALES (est): 7.83MM **Privately Held**
Web: www.bestpack.com
SIC: 3565 Packaging machinery

(P-7349)
HIS INDUSTRIES INC
Also Called: Phoenix Engineering
1202 W Shelley Ct (92868-1239)
PHONE..............................949 383-4308
Lynn Worthington, *Pr*
▲ **EMP:** 20 **EST:** 1997
SQ FT: 6,000
SALES (est): 2.32MM **Privately Held**
Web: www.pouchmachines.com
SIC: 3565 Packaging machinery

(P-7350)
JACKSAM CORPORATION
Also Called: Jacksam Corp Blackout
4440 Von Karman Ave Ste 220 (92660-2011)

PHONE..............................800 605-3580
Mark Adams, *Pr*
Michael Sakala, *
EMP: 25 **EST:** 1989
SALES (est): 4.13MM **Privately Held**
Web: www.convectium.com
SIC: 3565 Bottling machinery: filling, capping, labeling

(P-7351)
LABEL-AIRE INC (PA)
Also Called: Label-Aire
550 Burning Tree Rd (92833-1449)
PHONE..............................714 449-5155
▲ **EMP:** 67 **EST:** 1968
SALES (est): 8.85MM
SALES (corp-wide): 8.85MM **Privately Held**
Web: www.label-aire.com
SIC: 3565 Labeling machines, industrial

(P-7352)
M & O PERRY INDUSTRIES INC
Also Called: Perry Industries
412 N Smith Ave (92878-4303)
PHONE..............................951 734-9838
Phillip Osterhaus, *CEO*
▲ **EMP:** 40 **EST:** 1987
SQ FT: 20,000
SALES (est): 7.67MM **Privately Held**
Web: www.moperry.com
SIC: 3565 8711 7629 5084 Packaging machinery; Engineering services; Electrical repair shops; Conveyor systems

(P-7353)
P R P MULTISOURCE INC
3836 Wacker Dr (91752-1147)
PHONE..............................951 681-6100
Phil Woss, *Pr*
Kurt Fisch, *Treas*
▲ **EMP:** 20 **EST:** 1994
SQ FT: 25,000
SALES (est): 2.47MM **Privately Held**
Web: www.multisource.us
SIC: 3565 5084 Vacuum packaging machinery; Packaging machinery and equipment

(P-7354)
SYSTEMS TECHNOLOGY INC
Also Called: Delaware Systems Technology
1350 Riverview Dr (92408-2944)
PHONE..............................909 799-9950
David R Landon, *CEO*
John G Stjohn, *
▲ **EMP:** 65 **EST:** 1998
SQ FT: 43,000
SALES (est): 9.47MM **Privately Held**
Web: www.systems-technology-inc.com
SIC: 3565 Packing and wrapping machinery

(P-7355)
UNITED BAKERY EQUIPMENT CO INC (PA)
Also Called: Hartman Slicer Div
15315 Marquardt Ave (90670-5709)
PHONE..............................310 635-8121
Dulce Sohm, *CFO*
◆ **EMP:** 99 **EST:** 1966
SALES (est): 19.16MM
SALES (corp-wide): 19.16MM **Privately Held**
Web: ube5.wpengine.com
SIC: 3565 3556 Packaging machinery; Bakery machinery

(P-7356)
W J ELLISON CO INC
Also Called: Pack West Machinery Co
200 River Rd (92878-1435)
PHONE..............................626 814-4766
William J Ellison, *Pr*
Janice K Ellison, *VP*
EMP: 45 **EST:** 1971
SQ FT: 20,000
SALES (est): 1.91MM **Privately Held**
Web: www.packwest.com
SIC: 3565 Packaging machinery

3566 Speed Changers, Drives, And Gears

(P-7357)
MARPLES GEARS INC
1310 Mountain View Cir (91702-1648)
PHONE..............................626 570-1744
TOLL FREE: 800
James A Phillips Iv, *CEO*
EMP: 23 **EST:** 1937
SALES (est): 4.54MM **Privately Held**
Web: www.marplesgears.com
SIC: 3566 Speed changers, drives, and gears

(P-7358)
MARTIN SPROCKET & GEAR INC
5920 Triangle Dr (90040-3688)
PHONE..............................323 728-8117
Gus Diaz, *Mgr*
EMP: 18
SQ FT: 8,500
SALES (corp-wide): 292.47MM **Privately Held**
Web: www.martinsprocket.com
SIC: 3566 5085 3568 Gears, power transmission, except auto; Sprockets; Power transmission equipment, nec
PA: Martin Sprocket & Gear, Inc.
3100 Sprocket Dr
Arlington TX
817 258-3000

(P-7359)
UNIVERSAL MOTION COMPONENTS CO INC
Also Called: U M C
2920 Airway Ave (92626-6008)
PHONE..............................714 437-9600
▲ **EMP:** 50 **EST:** 1978
SALES (est): 9.32MM **Privately Held**
Web: www.umcproducts.com
SIC: 3566 5013 3523 3429 Gears, power transmission, except auto; Truck parts and accessories; Irrigation equipment, self-propelled; Marine hardware

3567 Industrial Furnaces And Ovens

(P-7360)
ASC PROCESS SYSTEMS INC (PA)
Also Called: ASC
28402 Livingston Ave (91355-4172)
PHONE..............................818 833-0088
David C Mason, *Pr*
Dave Mason, *
Gudrun Mason, *
◆ **EMP:** 241 **EST:** 1988
SQ FT: 41,000
SALES (est): 39.43MM
SALES (corp-wide): 39.43MM **Privately Held**

Web: www.aschome.com
SIC: **3567** 3559 3443 Industrial furnaces and ovens; Sewing machines and hat and zipper making machinery; Fabricated plate work (boiler shop)

(P-7361)
BAKER FURNACE INC
Also Called: Baker Furnace
2680 Orbiter St (92821-6265)
PHONE..............................714 223-7262
Ernest E Bacon, *Pr*
Diane Bacon, *Sec*
▼ **EMP:** 19 **EST:** 1980
SALES (est): 2.31MM
SALES (corp-wide): 116.32MM **Privately Held**
Web: www.bakerfurnace.com
SIC: **3567** Heating units and devices, industrial: electric
HQ: Tps, Llc
2821 Old Route 15
New Columbia PA
570 538-7200

(P-7362)
CIRCLE INDUSTRIAL MFG CORP (PA)
Also Called: Cim Services
1613 W El Segundo Blvd (90222-1024)
PHONE..............................310 638-5101
Ronald M La Forest, *Pr*
John La Forest, *
Karen La Forest, *
EMP: 23 **EST:** 1953
SQ FT: 3,500
SALES (est): 4.83MM
SALES (corp-wide): 4.83MM **Privately Held**
Web: www.circleindustrial.com
SIC: **3567** 3542 3535 3444 Industrial furnaces and ovens; Sheet metalworking machines; Conveyors and conveying equipment; Sheet metalwork

(P-7363)
DICK FARRELL INDUSTRIES INC
Also Called: D.F. Industries
5071 Lindsay Ct (91710-5757)
PHONE..............................909 613-9424
Timothy Farrell, *Prin*
Richard Farrell, *VP*
Lisa Van Den Berg, *Sec*
▲ **EMP:** 17 **EST:** 1978
SQ FT: 25,000
SALES (est): 2.84MM **Privately Held**
Web: dickf.openfos.com
SIC: **3567** 3312 7699 Industrial furnaces and ovens; Ferroalloys, produced in blast furnaces; Industrial machinery and equipment repair

(P-7364)
DICKEN ENTERPRISES INC
22060 Bear Valley Rd (92308-7209)
PHONE..............................760 246-7333
Micahei T Dicken, *Pr*
Michael T Dicken, *Pr*
Marilyn Dicken, *Sec*
EMP: 21 **EST:** 1979
SQ FT: 25,000
SALES (est): 4.94MM **Privately Held**
Web: www.inductiontech.com
SIC: **3567** 7699 Induction heating equipment ; Industrial machinery and equipment repair

(P-7365)
DS FIBERTECH CORP
Also Called: Interntonal Thermoproducts Div
11015 Mission Park Ct (92071-5601)

PHONE..............................619 562-7001
Duong Minh Nguyen, *CEO*
Son Dinh Nguyen, *
Eric Ulrich, *
▲ **EMP:** 45 **EST:** 1993
SQ FT: 14,000
SALES (est): 9.59MM **Privately Held**
Web: www.dsfibertech.com
SIC: **3567** Heating units and devices, industrial: electric

(P-7366)
GREENBRIDGE TECHNOLOGY INC
1335 S Acacia Ave (92831-5315)
PHONE..............................714 991-0200
Mike Roth, *CEO*
James Clerk, *Pr*
Mercy Gingrich, *Treas*
EMP: 30 **EST:** 1972
SQ FT: 25,000
SALES (est): 3.3MM **Privately Held**
SIC: **3567** 7699 Industrial furnaces and ovens; Industrial machinery and equipment repair

(P-7367)
HEATER DESIGNS INC
2211 S Vista Ave (92316-2921)
PHONE..............................909 421-0971
James Fan, *Ch*
Tom Odendahl, *
EMP: 30 **EST:** 1986
SQ FT: 14,500
SALES (est): 2.58MM **Privately Held**
Web: www.heaterdesigns.com
SIC: **3567** Heating units and devices, industrial: electric

(P-7368)
JHAWAR INDUSTRIES LLC
525 Klug Cir (92878-5452)
PHONE..............................951 340-4646
Claudia Lujano, *
Larry Jackson, *
▼ **EMP:** 41 **EST:** 1975
SQ FT: 50,000
SALES (est): 20MM **Privately Held**
SIC: **3567** Vacuum furnaces and ovens

(P-7369)
L C MILLER COMPANY
717 Monterey Pass Rd (91754-3606)
PHONE..............................323 268-3611
Dolores Naimy, *Pr*
Victor De Lucia, *
Dave Vito, *
EMP: 27 **EST:** 1956
SQ FT: 14,000
SALES (est): 2.64MM **Privately Held**
Web: www.lcmiller.com
SIC: **3567** 3546 3625 3398 Heating units and devices, industrial: electric; Saws and sawing equipment; Industrial electrical relays and switches; Metal heat treating

(P-7370)
PACIFIC KILN INSULATIONS INC
Also Called: Pacific Kiln
14370 Veterans Way (92553-9058)
PHONE..............................951 697-4422
Joel Fritz, *Pr*
▲ **EMP:** 22 **EST:** 1978
SQ FT: 10,000
SALES (est): 3.53MM **Privately Held**
Web: www.pacifickiln.com
SIC: **3567** Fuel-fired furnaces and ovens

(P-7371)
PRIME HEAT INCORPORATED
1844 Friendship Dr Ste A (92020-1115)
PHONE..............................619 449-6623
Herb Boekamp, *Pr*
▲ **EMP:** 18 **EST:** 1988
SQ FT: 20,500
SALES (est): 4.3MM **Privately Held**
Web: www.primeheatsystems.com
SIC: **3567** Heating units and devices, industrial: electric

(P-7372)
RAMA CORPORATION
600 W Esplanade Ave (92583-4999)
PHONE..............................951 654-7351
Peggy Renshaw, *Pr*
EMP: 45 **EST:** 1947
SQ FT: 25,000
SALES (est): 8.78MM
SALES (corp-wide): 8.78MM **Privately Held**
Web: www.ramacorporation.com
SIC: **3567** 3634 Heating units and devices, industrial: electric; Electric housewares and fans
PA: Amark Industries, Inc.
600 W Esplanade Ave
San Jacinto CA
951 654-7351

(P-7373)
THERMTRONIX CORPORATION (PA)
17129 Muskrat Ave (92301-2260)
P.O. Box 100 (92301-0100)
PHONE..............................760 246-4500
Robert Nealon, *Pr*
Deborah Nealon, *Sec*
▲ **EMP:** 21 **EST:** 1984
SQ FT: 12,000
SALES (est): 2.74MM
SALES (corp-wide): 2.74MM **Privately Held**
Web: www.thermtronix.com
SIC: **3567** Metal melting furnaces, industrial: electric

(P-7374)
W P KEITH CO INC
Also Called: Keith Co
8323 Loch Lomond Dr (90660-2588)
PHONE..............................562 948-3636
Carol N Keith, *CEO*
Wendell P Keith Junior, *Pr*
▲ **EMP:** 25 **EST:** 1954
SQ FT: 19,200
SALES (est): 7.39MM **Privately Held**
Web: www.keithcompany.com
SIC: **3567** Kilns, nsk

3568 Power Transmission Equipment, Nec

(P-7375)
ANACO INC
311 Corporate Terrace Cir (92879-6028)
PHONE..............................951 372-2732
Leon Nolen Iii, *Pr*
▲ **EMP:** 140 **EST:** 1986
SALES (est): 18.95MM
SALES (corp-wide): 970.37MM **Privately Held**
Web: www.anaco-husky.com
SIC: **3568** Couplings, shaft: rigid, flexible, universal joint, etc.
PA: Mcwane, Inc.
2900 Highway 280 S # 300
Birmingham AL
205 414-3100

(P-7376)
ATR SALES INC
Also Called: Atra-Flex
110 E Garry Ave (92707-4201)
PHONE..............................714 432-8411
Jerry Hauck, *CEO*
Raymond Hoyt, *
EMP: 26 **EST:** 1980
SQ FT: 12,000
SALES (est): 4.65MM **Privately Held**
Web: www.atra-flex.com
SIC: **3568** Couplings, shaft: rigid, flexible, universal joint, etc.
HQ: U.S. Tsubaki Holdings, Inc.
301 E Marquardt Dr
Wheeling IL
847 459-9500

(P-7377)
HELICAL PRODUCTS COMPANY INC
901 W Mccoy Ln (93455-1196)
P.O. Box 1069 (93456-1069)
PHONE..............................805 928-3851
EMP: 120
SIC: **3568** 3495 3493 Couplings, shaft: rigid, flexible, universal joint, etc.; Instrument springs, precision; Steel springs, except wire

(P-7378)
HYSPAN PRECISION PRODUCTS INC (PA)
Also Called: Hyspan
1685 Brandywine Ave (91911-6020)
PHONE..............................619 421-1355
Eric Barnes, *CEO*
Donald R Heye, *
Phillip Ensz, *
Eric Barnes, *CFO*
◆ **EMP:** 100 **EST:** 1974
SQ FT: 54,000
SALES (est): 112.6MM
SALES (corp-wide): 112.6MM **Privately Held**
Web: www.hyspan.com
SIC: **3568** 3496 3441 Ball joints, except aircraft and auto; Woven wire products, nec ; Expansion joints (structural shapes), iron or steel

(P-7379)
INDU-ELECTRIC NORTH AMER INC (PA)
27756 Avenue Hopkins (91355-1222)
PHONE..............................310 578-2144
Martin Gerber, *CEO*
▲ **EMP:** 47 **EST:** 2002
SQ FT: 11,000
SALES (est): 8.89MM
SALES (corp-wide): 8.89MM **Privately Held**
Web: www.indu-electric.com
SIC: **3568** 5063 Power transmission equipment, nec; Power transmission equipment, electric

(P-7380)
INDUSTRIAL SPROCKETS GEARS INC
13650 Rosecrans Ave (90670-5025)
PHONE..............................323 233-7221
Max R Patridge, *CEO*
Monty Patridge, *VP*
Connie Patridge-eason, *Sec*
Mark Partridge, *Treas*
EMP: 21 **EST:** 1971
SQ FT: 18,000
SALES (est): 1.91MM **Privately Held**

PRODUCTS & SVCS

Web: www.industrialsprocketsandgears.com
SIC: **3568** 3566 3462 Chains, chains, and sprockets; Drives, high speed industrial, except hydrostatic; Iron and steel forgings

(P-7381)
WEST COAST YAMAHA INC
Also Called: West Coast Motor Sports
1622 Illinois Ave (92571-9374)
PHONE..................................951 943-2061
Gerald Morris Langston, *CEO*
Margret Mckinley, *Sec*
EMP: 25 EST: 1998
SALES (est): 2.47MM **Privately Held**
Web: www.yamaha.com
SIC: **3568** 5571 5561 Power transmission equipment, nec; Motorcycle dealers; Recreational vehicle dealers

---

3569 General Industrial Machinery,

(P-7382)
AVX FILTERS CORPORATION
11144 Penrose St (91352-2797)
PHONE..................................818 767-6770
John Gilbertson, *Pr*
▲ EMP: 90 EST: 1981
SQ FT: 25,000
SALES (est): 10.63MM **Privately Held**
Web: www.kyocera-avx.com
SIC: **3569** 3675 Filters; Electronic capacitors
HQ: Kyocera Avx Components Corporation
1 Avx Blvd
Fountain Inn SC
864 967-2150

(P-7383)
BLUELAB CORPORATION USA INC
437 S Cataract Ave (91773-2973)
PHONE..................................909 599-1940
Rick Jaries, *Pr*
EMP: 50 EST: 2010
SALES (est): 2.87MM **Privately Held**
SIC: **3569** Testing chambers for altitude, temperature, ordnance, power

(P-7384)
CAMPBELL MEMBRANE TECH INC
1168 N Johnson Ave (92020-1917)
PHONE..................................619 938-2481
Jeffrey Campbell, *CEO*
◆ EMP: 50 EST: 2007
SALES (est): 4.71MM **Privately Held**
Web: www.campbellsengineering.com
SIC: **3569** Filter elements, fluid, hydraulic line

(P-7385)
CAPSTONE FIRE MANAGEMENT INC (PA)
2240 Auto Park Way (92029-1249)
PHONE..................................760 839-2290
Jerry Dusa, *Pr*
Christopher Dusa, *
Matthew Dusa, *
EMP: 31 EST: 1989
SALES (est): 4.91MM
SALES (corp-wide): 4.91MM **Privately Held**
Web: www.capstonefire.com
SIC: **3569** Firefighting and related equipment

(P-7386)
CLAYTON MANUFACTURING COMPANY (PA)

Also Called: Clayton Industries
17477 Hurley St (91744-5106)
PHONE..................................626 443-9381
John Clayton, *Pr*
Boyd A Calvin, *
Phyllis Nielson, *
Alexander Smirnoff, *
Allen L Cluer, *
▲ EMP: 147 EST: 1930
SQ FT: 215,000
SALES (est): 88.12MM
SALES (corp-wide): 88.12MM **Privately Held**
Web: www.claytonindustries.com
SIC: **3569** 3829 3511 Generators: steam, liquid oxygen, or nitrogen; Dynamometer instruments; Turbines and turbine generator sets

(P-7387)
CLAYTON MANUFACTURING INC (HQ)
17477 Hurley St (91744-5106)
PHONE..................................626 443-9381
William Clayton Junior, *CEO*
Boyd A Calvin, *
Allen L Cluer, *
John Clayton, *
▼ EMP: 80 EST: 1930
SQ FT: 215,000
SALES (est): 22.22MM
SALES (corp-wide): 88.12MM **Privately Held**
Web: www.claytonindustries.com
SIC: **3569** 3829 Generators: steam, liquid oxygen, or nitrogen; Dynamometer instruments
PA: Clayton Manufacturing Company
17477 Hurley St
City Of Industry CA
626 443-9381

(P-7388)
DELTA DESIGN INC (HQ)
12367 Crosthwaite Cir (92064-6817)
PHONE..................................858 848-8000
Samer Aabbani, *Pr*
Charles A Schwan, *
James A Donahue, *
James Mcfarlane, *Sr VP*
Jeff Jose, *
▲ EMP: 400 EST: 1957
SQ FT: 334,000
SALES (est): 88.36MM
SALES (corp-wide): 812.77MM **Publicly Held**
Web: www.cohu.com
SIC: **3569** 3825 3674 Testing chambers for altitude, temperature, ordnance, power; Test equipment for electronic and electrical circuits; Semiconductors and related devices
PA: Cohu, Inc.
12367 Crosthwaite Cir
Poway CA
858 848-8100

(P-7389)
DELTA TAU DATA SYSTEMS INC CAL (HQ)
Also Called: Omron Delta Tau
21314 Lassen St (91311-4254)
PHONE..................................818 998-2095
Yasuto Ikuta, *Pr*
Tamara Dimitri, *
James Fornear, *
EMP: 129 EST: 1976
SALES (est): 46.56MM **Privately Held**
Web: automation.omron.com

SIC: **3569** 7372 3625 3577 Robots, assembly line: industrial and commercial; Prepackaged software; Relays and industrial controls; Computer peripheral equipment, nec
PA: Omron Corporation
801,
Horikawahigashiiruminamifudodocho,
Shiokojidoori, Shimogyo-
Kyoto KYO

(P-7390)
DESCHNER CORPORATION
3211 W Harvard St (92704-3976)
PHONE..................................714 557-1261
Joe Alessi, *Pr*
Toby Ryan, *
Frank Solis, *
EMP: 22 EST: 1958
SQ FT: 21,600
SALES (est): 1.44MM **Privately Held**
Web: www.deschner.com
SIC: **3569** 3594 Liquid automation machinery and equipment; Fluid power pumps and motors

(P-7391)
ENTEGRIS GP INC
4175 Santa Fe Rd (93401-8159)
PHONE..................................805 541-9299
Bertrand Loy, *Pr*
◆ EMP: 130 EST: 1975
SQ FT: 50,000
SALES (est): 23.09MM
SALES (corp-wide): 3.28B **Publicly Held**
Web: www.entegris.com
SIC: **3569** Gas producers, generators, and other gas related equipment
PA: Entegris, Inc.
129 Concord Rd
Billerica MA
978 436-6500

(P-7392)
FIREBLAST GLOBAL INC
Also Called: Fireblast
41633 Eastman Dr (92562-7054)
PHONE..................................951 277-8319
Richard Egelin, *CEO*
EMP: 25 EST: 2000
SALES (est): 4.62MM **Privately Held**
Web: www.fireblast.com
SIC: **3569** 8711 Firefighting apparatus; Engineering services

(P-7393)
HONEYBEE ROBOTICS LLC
2408 Lincoln Ave (91001-5436)
PHONE..................................303 774-7613
EMP: 43
Web: www.honeybeerobotics.com
SIC: **3569** Filters
HQ: Honeybee Robotics, Llc
1830 Lefthand Cir
Longmont CO
303 774-7613

(P-7394)
HONEYBEE ROBOTICS LLC
398 W Washington Blvd Ste 200 (91103-2000)
PHONE..................................510 207-4555
EMP: 43
Web: www.honeybeerobotics.com
SIC: **3569** Filters
HQ: Honeybee Robotics, Llc
1830 Lefthand Cir
Longmont CO
303 774-7613

(P-7395)
INDUSTRIAL FIRE SPRNKLR CO INC
3845 Imperial Ave (92113-1702)
PHONE..................................619 266-6030
L David Sandage, *Pr*
EMP: 35 EST: 1986
SALES (est): 4.67MM **Privately Held**
Web: www.indfire.net
SIC: **3569** 1731 Sprinkler systems, fire: automatic; Fire detection and burglar alarm systems specialization

(P-7396)
JEREMYWELL INTERNATIONAL INC
14 Vanderbilt (92618-2010)
PHONE..................................949 588-6888
Stephanie Chang, *Prin*
▲ EMP: 17 EST: 2013
SALES (est): 2.19MM **Privately Held**
Web: www.jeremywellindustry.com
SIC: **3569** 3714 General industrial machinery, nec; Fuel systems and parts, motor vehicle
PA: Hangzhou Fuhua Co., Ltd.
181, Fengqi Road
Hangzhou ZJ

(P-7397)
JOHNSTON INTERNATIONAL CORPORATION
Also Called: Kingman Industries
14272 Chambers Rd (92780-6994)
PHONE..................................714 542-4487
▲ EMP: 25 EST: 1970
SALES (est): 5MM **Privately Held**
Web:
johnston-international-corp-in-tustin-ca.cityfos.com
SIC: **3569** Assembly machines, non-metalworking

(P-7398)
KNIGHT LLC (HQ)
15340 Barranca Pkwy (92618-2215)
PHONE..................................949 595-4800
Don Julienne, *Dir*
Diane Peterson, *Dir*
▲ EMP: 100 EST: 1972
SQ FT: 46,000
SALES (est): 21.16MM
SALES (corp-wide): 3.18B **Publicly Held**
Web: www.knightequip.com
SIC: **3569** 3582 3589 Liquid automation machinery and equipment; Commercial laundry equipment; Dishwashing machines, commercial
PA: Idex Corporation
3100 Sanders Rd Ste 301
Northbrook IL
847 498-7070

(P-7399)
LUBRICATION SCIENTIFICS LLC
17651 Armstrong Ave (92614-5727)
PHONE..................................714 557-0664
Richard Hanley, *Managing Member*
EMP: 48 EST: 2014
SALES (est): 4.88MM **Privately Held**
Web: www.lubricationscientifics.com
SIC: **3569** Lubricating equipment

(P-7400)
MYERS MIXERS LLC
8376 Salt Lake Ave (90201-5817)
PHONE..................................323 560-4723
EMP: 41 EST: 2014
SALES (est): 5.44MM **Privately Held**

SIC: **3569** Centrifuges, industrial

(P-7401)
NEWLIFE2 (PA)
4855 Morabito Pl (93401-8748)
PHONE..........................805 549-8093
Kim Boege, *CEO*
EMP: 24 **EST:** 1954
SQ FT: 7,000
SALES (est): 2.97MM
SALES (corp-wide): 2.97MM **Privately Held**
Web: www.tankcleaningmachines.com
SIC: **3569** Liquid automation machinery and equipment

(P-7402)
NORCO INDUSTRIES INC (PA)
Also Called: Flo Dynamics
365 W Victoria St (90220-6062)
PHONE..........................310 639-4000
◆ **EMP:** 137 **EST:** 1964
SALES (est): 82.94MM
SALES (corp-wide): 82.94MM **Privately Held**
Web: www.norcoind.com
SIC: **3569** 2531 5085 3537 Jacks, hydraulic; Seats, automobile; Industrial supplies; Industrial trucks and tractors

(P-7403)
PACIFIC CONSOLIDATED INDS LLC
Also Called: PCI
12201 Magnolia Ave (92503-4820)
PHONE..........................951 479-0860
Bob Eng, *Managing Member*
Paul Stevens, *
Robert Eng, *
Alicia Fernandez, *
John Horton, *
◆ **EMP:** 77 **EST:** 2003
SQ FT: 85,000
SALES (est): 47.21MM
SALES (corp-wide): 47.21MM **Privately Held**
Web: www.pcigases.com
SIC: **3569** 1382 Gas separators (machinery); Oil and gas exploration services
PA: Pci Holding Company, Inc.
12201 Magnolia Ave
Riverside CA
951 479-0860

(P-7404)
PALL CORPORATION
4116 Sorrento Valley Blvd (92121-1407)
PHONE..........................858 455-7264
Richard Mc Donald, *Genl Mgr*
EMP: 136
SALES (corp-wide): 31.47B **Publicly Held**
Web: www.pall.com
SIC: **3569** Filters
HQ: Pall Corporation
25 Harbor Park Dr
Port Washington NY
516 484-5400

(P-7405)
PCI HOLDING COMPANY INC (PA)
12201 Magnolia Ave (92503-4820)
PHONE..........................951 479-0860
Bob Eng, *CEO*
EMP: 26 **EST:** 2012
SALES (est): 47.21MM
SALES (corp-wide): 47.21MM **Privately Held**
Web: www.pcigases.com

SIC: **3569** 1382 Gas separators (machinery); Oil and gas exploration services

(P-7406)
PHENIX TECHNOLOGY CORPORATION (PA)
Also Called: Phenix Technology
3453 Durahart St (92507-3452)
PHONE..........................951 272-4938
Raymond M Russell, *Ch Bd*
Angel Sanchez, *CEO*
EMP: 24 **EST:** 1971
SALES (est): 3.15MM
SALES (corp-wide): 3.15MM **Privately Held**
Web: www.phenixfirehelmets.com
SIC: **3569** Firefighting and related equipment

(P-7407)
PIPELINE PRODUCTS INC
1650 Linda Vista Dr Ste 110 (92078-3810)
PHONE..........................760 744-8907
Scott Higley, *Pr*
EMP: 17 **EST:** 1962
SQ FT: 20,000
SALES (est): 3.65MM **Privately Held**
Web: www.pipelineproducts.com
SIC: **3569** Filter elements, fluid, hydraulic line

(P-7408)
PREMIER FILTERS INC
Also Called: OEM
952 N Elm St (92867-5441)
PHONE..........................657 226-0091
Bob Singh, *Admn*
EMP: 23 **EST:** 2018
SALES (est): 2.24MM **Privately Held**
Web: www.premieremc.com
SIC: **3569** Filters, general line: industrial

(P-7409)
SEPARATION ENGINEERING INC
931 S Andreasen Dr Ste A (92029-1959)
PHONE..........................760 489-0101
Charles E Hull, *Pr*
▲ **EMP:** 34 **EST:** 1980
SQ FT: 20,000
SALES (est): 3.9MM **Privately Held**
SIC: **3569** Filters, general line: industrial

(P-7410)
STEARNS PRODUCT DEV CORP (PA)
Also Called: Doughpro
20281 Harvill Ave (92570-7235)
PHONE..........................951 657-0379
Steven Raio, *Pr*
▲ **EMP:** 91 **EST:** 1971
SQ FT: 50,000
SALES (est): 21.39MM
SALES (corp-wide): 21.39MM **Privately Held**
Web: www.proluxe.com
SIC: **3569** 3444 Assembly machines, non-metalworking; Sheet metalwork

(P-7411)
WALIN GROUP INC
Also Called: Brilliant AV
1117 Baker St Ste A (92626-4159)
P.O. Box 2074 (92859-0074)
PHONE..........................714 444-5980
Matthew James Walin, *CEO*
EMP: 20 **EST:** 2011
SALES (est): 5.06MM **Privately Held**
Web: www.brilliantav.com

SIC: **3569** 1382 Gas separators (machinery); Oil and gas exploration services

(P-7412)
WASSER FILTRATION INC (PA)
Also Called: Pacific Press
1215 N Fee Ana St (92807-1804)
PHONE..........................714 696-6450
Sean Duby, *Pr*
▲ **EMP:** 70 **EST:** 1987
SQ FT: 20,000
SALES (est): 9.49MM
SALES (corp-wide): 9.49MM **Privately Held**
Web: www.pacpress.com
SIC: **3569** 5084 Filters, general line: industrial; Industrial machinery and equipment

(P-7413)
WESTERN FILTER A DIVISION OF DONALDSON COMPANY INC
26235 Technology Dr (91355-1147)
P.O. Box 1299 (55440-1299)
PHONE..........................661 295-0800
▲ **EMP:** 100
Web: shop.donaldson.com
SIC: **3569** Filters

3571 Electronic Computers

(P-7414)
ACME PORTABLE MACHINES INC
1330 Mountain View Cir (91702-1648)
PHONE..........................626 610-1888
James Cheng, *Pr*
▲ **EMP:** 30 **EST:** 1994
SQ FT: 12,200
SALES (est): 7.21MM **Privately Held**
Web: www.acmeportable.com
SIC: **3571** Electronic computers

(P-7415)
ALERATEC INC
21722 Lassen St (91311-3623)
PHONE..........................818 678-6900
▲ **EMP:** 24 **EST:** 2000
SALES (est): 2.6MM **Privately Held**
Web: www.aleratec.com
SIC: **3571** 5045 Electronic computers; Computer peripheral equipment

(P-7416)
ALLHEALTH
515 S Figueroa St Ste 1300 (90071-3301)
PHONE..........................213 538-0762
John R Cochran, *CEO*
EMP: 24 **EST:** 1998
SALES (est): 1.24MM **Privately Held**
Web: www.allhealthinc.com
SIC: **3571** 7381 Electronic computers; Security guard service

(P-7417)
AMERICAN RELIANCE INC
Also Called: Amrel
789 N Fair Oaks Ave (91103-3045)
PHONE..........................626 443-6818
Edward Chen, *CEO*
Shelly Chen, *
▲ **EMP:** 45 **EST:** 1985
SALES (est): 8.83MM **Privately Held**
Web: www.amrel.com

SIC: **3571** Electronic computers

(P-7418)
APPLE TREE INTERNATIONAL CORP
1375 E Locust St Ste B (91761-4508)
PHONE..........................626 679-7025
Min Xiao, *CEO*
EMP: 18 **EST:** 2014
SALES (est): 2.38MM **Privately Held**
SIC: **3571** Electronic computers

(P-7419)
B-REEL FILMS INC
8383 Wilshire Blvd Ste 1000 (90211-2439)
PHONE..........................917 388-3836
Anders Wahlquist, *Pr*
EMP: 27 **EST:** 2007
SALES (est): 4.91MM **Privately Held**
Web: www.b-reel.com
SIC: **3571** Computers, digital, analog or hybrid

(P-7420)
BORSOS ENGINEERING INC
5924 Balfour Ct Ste 102 (92008-7378)
PHONE..........................760 930-0296
Steven D Borso, *Pr*
EMP: 19 **EST:** 1978
SQ FT: 5,600
SALES (est): 415K **Privately Held**
SIC: **3571** Electronic computers

(P-7421)
CONTINUOUS COMPUTING CORP
Also Called: Ccpu
10431 Wateridge Cir Ste 110 (92121)
PHONE..........................858 882-8800
Mike Dagenais, *CEO*
Ron Pyles, *
Erez Barnavon, *
Robert Telles, *
Michael Coward, *
EMP: 132 **EST:** 1998
SQ FT: 48,000
SALES (est): 25.78MM **Privately Held**
SIC: **3571** 3661 4812 5045 Computers, digital, analog or hybrid; Telephone and telegraph apparatus; Radiotelephone communication; Computers, peripherals, and software
HQ: Radisys Corporation
8900 Ne Walker Rd Ste 130
Hillsboro OR
503 615-1100

(P-7422)
CYBERNET MANUFACTURING INC
5 Holland Ste 201 (92618-2574)
PHONE..........................949 600-8000
◆ **EMP:** 720 **EST:** 1996
SALES (est): 74.53MM **Privately Held**
Web: www.cybernetman.com
SIC: **3571** 3577 Electronic computers; Computer peripheral equipment, nec

(P-7423)
DYNABOOK AMERICAS INC (HQ)
5241 California Ave Ste 100 (92617-3052)
PHONE..........................949 583-3000
Ikuaki Takayama, *Pr*
Takayuki Tono, *Sr VP*
James Robbins, *Genl Mgr*
EMP: 298 **EST:** 2018
SALES (est): 53.15MM **Privately Held**
Web: us.dynabook.com

SIC: **3569** 1382 Gas separators (machinery); Oil and gas exploration services

P R O D U C T S & S V C S

SIC: 3571 Electronic computers
PA: Sharp Corporation
1, Takumicho, Sakai-Ku
Sakai OSK

(P-7424)
EDGE SOLUTIONS CONSULTING INC (PA)
5126 Clareton Dr Ste 160 (91301-4529)
P.O. Box 661480 (91066-1480)
PHONE.............................818 591-3500
Marti Reeder, *Pr*
Marti R Hedge, *Pr*
EMP: 32 EST: 1999
SQ FT: 600
SALES (est): 8.62MM
SALES (corp-wide): 8.62MM Privately Held
Web:
www.edgesolutionsandconsulting.com
SIC: 3571 Mainframe computers

(P-7425)
GARNER HOLT PRODUCTIONS INC
Also Called: Garner Holt Productions
1255 Research Dr (92374-4541)
PHONE.............................909 799-3030
Garner L Holt, *Pr*
Michelle Berg, *
EMP: 50 EST: 1977
SQ FT: 50,000
SALES (est): 12.37MM Privately Held
Web: www.garnerholt.com
SIC: 3571 Electronic computers

(P-7426)
GATEWAY INC
Also Called: Gateway
12750 Gateway Park Rd # 124
(92064-2050)
PHONE.............................858 451-9933
EMP: 35
Web: www.acer.com
SIC: 3571 Personal computers
(microcomputers)
HQ: Gateway, Inc.
7565 Irvine Center Dr # 150
Irvine CA
949 471-7000

(P-7427)
GATEWAY INC (DH)
Also Called: Gateway
7565 Irvine Center Dr Ste 150
(92618-4933)
PHONE.............................949 471-7000
Ed Coleman, *CEO*
Neal E West, *Contrlr*
John Goldsberry, *CFO*
Craig Calle, *Treas*
◆ EMP: 250 EST: 1985
SQ FT: 98,000
SALES (est): 745.85MM Privately Held
Web: www.acer.com
SIC: 3571 3577 Personal computers
(microcomputers); Computer peripheral
equipment, nec
HQ: Acer American Holdings Corp.
1730 N 1st St Ste 400
San Jose CA

(P-7428)
GATEWAY US RETAIL INC
7565 Irvine Center Dr (92618-4918)
PHONE.............................949 471-7000
Wayne R Inouye, *Pr*
Brian Firestone, *Executive Strategy Vice President*
▲ EMP: 180 EST: 1998

SQ FT: 147,000
SALES (est): 9.97MM Privately Held
SIC: 3571 3577 5045 Electronic computers;
Computer peripheral equipment, nec;
Computers, peripherals, and software
HQ: Gateway, Inc.
7565 Irvine Center Dr # 150
Irvine CA
949 471-7000

(P-7429)
HP INC
Also Called: HP
16399 W Bernardo Dr Bldg 61
(92127-1801)
PHONE.............................858 924-5117
Philip Liebscher, *Brnch Mgr*
EMP: 350
SALES (corp-wide): 62.98B Publicly Held
Web: www.hp.com
SIC: 3571 Personal computers
(microcomputers)
PA: Hp Inc.
1501 Page Mill Rd
Palo Alto CA
650 857-1501

(P-7430)
I/O MAGIC CORPORATION
4 Marconi (92618-2525)
PHONE.............................949 707-4800
Tony Shahbaz, *CEO*
Steve Gillings, *CFO*
EMP: 39 EST: 2000
SALES (est): 733.61K Privately Held
SIC: 3571 3652 Computers, digital, analog
or hybrid; Compact laser discs, prerecorded

(P-7431)
INNERS TASKS LLC
Also Called: Remstek Corp
27708 Jefferson Ave Ste 201 (92590-2641)
PHONE.............................951 225-9696
Jason Patrick, *Managing Member*
James Stewart, *Managing Member*
Ryan Wetmore, *Managing Member*
EMP: 38 EST: 2015
SALES (est): 2.48MM Privately Held
SIC: 3571 Electronic computers

(P-7432)
INTERNATIONAL BUS MCHS CORP
IBM
600 Anton Blvd Ste 400 (92626-7677)
PHONE.............................714 472-2237
Jim Steele, *Genl Mgr*
EMP: 26
SALES (corp-wide): 60.53B Publicly Held
Web: www.ibm.com
SIC: 3571 5045 1731 Computers, digital,
analog or hybrid; Computers, nec;
Computer installation
PA: International Business Machines
Corporation
1 New Orchard Rd Ste 1 # 1
Armonk NY
914 499-1900

(P-7433)
INTERNATIONAL BUS MCHS CORP
Also Called: IBM
400 N Brand Blvd Fl 7 (91203-2364)
PHONE.............................818 553-8100
EMP: 700
SALES (corp-wide): 60.53B Publicly Held
Web: www.ibm.com
SIC: 3571 Minicomputers

PA: International Business Machines
Corporation
1 New Orchard Rd Ste 1 # 1
Armonk NY
914 499-1900

(P-7434)
IXI TECHNOLOGY INC
Also Called: Ixi Technology
22705 Savi Ranch Pkwy Ste 200
(92887-4604)
PHONE.............................714 221-5000
Michael Carter, *CEO*
Thomas Bell, *
EMP: 40 EST: 1986
SQ FT: 40,000
SALES (est): 7.59MM Privately Held
SIC: 3571 3672 Electronic computers;
Printed circuit boards

(P-7435)
KEY CODE MEDIA INC (PA)
270 S Flower St (91502-2101)
PHONE.............................818 303-3900
Michael Cavanagh, *CEO*
Ka Man Chan, *
EMP: 36 EST: 2001
SQ FT: 13,000
SALES (est): 48.61MM
SALES (corp-wide): 48.61MM Privately
Held
Web: www.keycodemedia.com
SIC: 3571 Computers, digital, analog or
hybrid

(P-7436)
KONTRON AMERICA INCORPORATED
9477 Waples St Ste 150 (92121-2937)
PHONE.............................800 822-7522
John Goode Junior, *Pr*
Ken Lowe, *
Thomas Sparrvik, *
▲ EMP: 75 EST: 1999
SQ FT: 40,000
SALES (est): 10.6MM Privately Held
Web: www.kontron.com
SIC: 3571 7373 Electronic computers;
Computer integrated systems design

(P-7437)
M2 MARKETPLACE INC
2555 W 190th St 201 (90504-6002)
EMP: 48 EST: 1994
SALES (est): 3.55MM Publicly Held
SIC: 3571 Electronic computers
HQ: Pcm, Inc.
200 N Pacific Coast Hwy # 1050
El Segundo CA
310 354-5600

(P-7438)
MATRI KART
448 W Market St (92101-6703)
PHONE.............................858 609-0933
EMP: 50 EST: 2020
SALES (est): 2.13MM Privately Held
SIC: 3571 Electronic computers

(P-7439)
MEDIATEK USA INC
1 Ada Ste 200 (92618-5341)
PHONE.............................408 526-1899
EMP: 124
SIC: 3571 3674 Electronic computers;
Semiconductors and related devices
HQ: Mediatek Usa Inc.
2840 Junction Ave
San Jose CA
408 526-1899

(P-7440)
MERCURY COMPUTER SYSTEM INC
1815 Aston Ave Ste 107 (92008-7340)
PHONE.............................760 494-9600
Lance Turner, *CEO*
EMP: 35 EST: 2007
SALES (est): 2.85MM Privately Held
SIC: 3571 Electronic computers

(P-7441)
MICRO/SYS INC
158 W Pomona Ave (91016-4558)
PHONE.............................818 244-4600
Susan Wooley, *Pr*
James K Finster, *
EMP: 30 EST: 1976
SALES (est): 4.33MM Privately Held
Web: www.embeddedsys.com
SIC: 3571 3674 Electronic computers;
Semiconductors and related devices

(P-7442)
MYRICOM INC
Also Called: Myricom
3871 E Colorado Blvd Ste 101 (91107)
PHONE.............................626 821-5555
Nanette Boden, *Pr*
Robert Henigson, *Ch Bd*
Rick Patton, *CFO*
Mike Mcpherson, *VP*
◆ EMP: 32 EST: 1994
SQ FT: 17,000
SALES (est): 1.34MM Privately Held
Web: www.cspi.com
SIC: 3571 Electronic computers

(P-7443)
ORACLE AMERICA INC
Also Called: Sun Microsystems
17901 Von Karman Ave Ste 800
(92614-6297)
PHONE.............................650 506-7000
Rick Kuhs, *Brnch Mgr*
EMP: 21
SALES (corp-wide): 49.95B Publicly Held
Web: www.oracle.com
SIC: 3571 Minicomputers
HQ: Oracle America, Inc.
500 Oracle Pkwy
Redwood City CA
650 506-7000

(P-7444)
ORANGE LOGIC LLC
29 Cezanne (92603-0207)
PHONE.............................914 361-9175
Charles Fakhreddine, *Prin*
EMP: 47
SALES (corp-wide): 4.79MM Privately
Held
Web: www.orangelogic.com
SIC: 3571 Electronic computers
PA: Orange Logic Llc
19100 Von Karman Ave # 900
Irvine CA
949 396-2233

(P-7445)
PREMIO INC (PA)
918 Radecki Ct (91748-1132)
PHONE.............................626 839-3100
Crystal Tsao, *CEO*
Tom Tsao, *
Ken Szeto, *
Eliza Leung, *
▲ EMP: 120 EST: 1989
SQ FT: 140,000
SALES (est): 41.5MM Privately Held
Web: www.premioinc.com

SIC: **3571** 7373 7378 Personal computers (microcomputers); Computer integrated systems design; Computer maintenance and repair

(P-7446)
PSITECH INC
18368 Bandilier Cir (92708-7001)
PHONE..............................714 964-7818
John T Kerr, *Ch Bd*
John S Kerr, *Stockholder*
EMP: 18 EST: 1980
SQ FT: 6,000
SALES (est): 833.89K **Privately Held**
Web: www.psitech.com
SIC: **3571** 3577 Personal computers (microcomputers); Computer peripheral equipment, nec

(P-7447)
ROSEWILL INC
17560 Rowland St (91748-1114)
PHONE..............................800 575-9885
EMP: 714
SALES (corp-wide): 2.38B **Publicly Held**
Web: www.rosewill.com
SIC: **3571** 5045 Electronic computers; Computers, peripherals, and software
HQ: Rosewill, Inc.
   17708 Rowland St
   City Of Industry CA

(P-7448)
RUGGED SYSTEMS INC
Also Called: Core Systems
13000 Danielson St Ste Q (92064-6827)
PHONE..............................858 391-1006
Chris O Brien, *CEO*
Chris Alan Schaffner, *
EMP: 156 EST: 2006
SQ FT: 63,000
SALES (est): 21.82MM **Privately Held**
Web: www.ruggedcomputersystems.com
SIC: **3571** 7373 Electronic computers; Computer integrated systems design

(P-7449)
SEPE INC
Also Called: Fax Star
245 Fischer Ave Ste C4 (92626-4538)
PHONE..............................714 241-7373
Michel J Remion, *Pr*
Patty King, *Sec*
EMP: 23 EST: 1984
SQ FT: 5,000
SALES (est): 1.28MM **Privately Held**
Web: www.faxstar.com
SIC: **3571** 7371 4822 Electronic computers; Computer software development; Facsimile transmission services

(P-7450)
SOLARFLARE COMMUNICATIONS INC (DH)
7505 Irvine Center Dr Ste 100 (92618-2930)
PHONE..............................949 581-6830
Russell Stern, *Pr*
Mary Jane Abalos, *
EMP: 97 EST: 2001
SQ FT: 22,097
SALES (est): 55.67MM
SALES (corp-wide): 23.6B **Publicly Held**
Web: www.solarflare.com
SIC: **3571** Electronic computers
HQ: Xilinx, Inc.
   2100 All Programable
   San Jose CA
   408 559-7778

(P-7451)
SOURCE CODE LLC
Also Called: Aberdeen
9808 Alburtis Ave (90670-3208)
PHONE..............................562 903-1500
EMP: 48
Web: www.thinkmate.com
SIC: **3571** 3572 Electronic computers; Computer storage devices
PA: Source Code, Llc
   232 Vanderbilt Ave
   Norwood MA

(P-7452)
SYNERGY MICROSYSTEMS INC (DH)
28965 Avenue Penn (91355-4185)
PHONE..............................858 452-0020
Chris Wiltsey, *Dir*
EMP: 70 EST: 1985
SALES (est): 24.36MM
SALES (corp-wide): 2.56B **Publicly Held**
Web: www.curtisswright.com
SIC: **3571** Computers, digital, analog or hybrid
HQ: Curtiss-Wright Controls, Inc.
   201 Old Boiling Sprng Rd
   Shelby NC
   704 869-4600

(P-7453)
TERADATA OPERATIONS INC (HQ)
17095 Via Del Campo (92127-1711)
PHONE..............................937 242-4030
Oliver Ratzesberger, *COO*
Stephen Brobst, *
Mark Culhane, *
Laura Nyquist, *
EMP: 100 EST: 2007
SALES (est): 877MM **Publicly Held**
Web: www.teradata.com
SIC: **3571** 7379 Electronic computers; Computer related consulting services
PA: Teradata Corporation
   17095 Via Del Campo
   San Diego CA

(P-7454)
THIS IS ROCKNROLL LLC
3950 Los Feliz Blvd Apt 208 (90027-2351)
PHONE..............................323 384-3966
EMP: 17
SALES (corp-wide): 211.31K **Privately Held**
Web: www.thisisrocknroll.com
SIC: **3571** 7389 Electronic computers; Business services, nec
PA: This Is Rock'n'roll, Llc
   527 Solano Ave
   Los Angeles CA
   323 384-3966

(P-7455)
TOSHIBA AMER INFO SYSTEMS INC
9740 Irvine Blvd Fl 1 (92618-1651)
PHONE..............................949 583-3000
Bill Goodwin, *Mgr*
EMP: 120
Web: www.toshiba.com
SIC: **3571** Electronic computers
HQ: Toshiba America Information Systems, Inc.
   1251 Ave Of The Amrcas St
   New York NY
   949 583-3000

(P-7456)
VINCI BRANDS LLC (PA)
1775 Flight Way Ste 300 (92782-1846)
PHONE..............................949 838-5111
Brian Stech, *CEO*
EMP: 168 EST: 2021
SALES (est): 9.46MM
SALES (corp-wide): 9.46MM **Privately Held**
SIC: **3571** 3676 Electronic computers; Electronic resistors

(P-7457)
VMC HOLDINGS GROUP CORP
9667 Owensmouth Ave Ste 202 (91311-4819)
P.O. Box 7396 (91327-7396)
PHONE..............................818 993-1466
Pierre Yenokian, *Pr*
Dorothy Yenokian, *
Chris Geudo, *
EMP: 31 EST: 1980
SQ FT: 8,500
SALES (est): 684.34K **Privately Held**
Web: www.vmcholdings.com
SIC: **3571** Electronic computers

(P-7458)
XMULTIPLE TECHNOLOGIES (PA)
Also Called: Xmultiple/Xrjax
1919 Williams St Ste 325 (93065-7848)
PHONE..............................805 579-1100
Alan Pocrass, *CEO*
Alan Pocrass, *Pr*
Drew Storberg, *VP*
▲ EMP: 22 EST: 1982
SALES (est): 7.37MM
SALES (corp-wide): 7.37MM **Privately Held**
Web: www.xmultiple.com
SIC: **3571** 3663 3661 3577 Electronic computers; Multiplex equipment; Telephone and telegraph apparatus; Computer peripheral equipment, nec

3572 Computer Storage Devices

(P-7459)
ADD-ON CMPT PERIPHERALS LLC
Also Called: Addon Networks
15775 Gateway Cir (92780-6470)
PHONE..............................949 546-8200
Matt Mccormick, *CEO*
Scott Krzywicki, *
Katie Patton Ctrl, *Prin*
▲ EMP: 73 EST: 1999
SALES (est): 19.59MM
SALES (corp-wide): 12.62B **Publicly Held**
Web: www.addonnetworks.com
SIC: **3572** 3577 5045 Computer storage devices; Computer peripheral equipment, nec; Computers and accessories, personal and home entertainment
PA: Amphenol Corporation
   358 Hall Ave
   Wallingford CT
   203 265-8900

(P-7460)
ADVANCED HPC INC
8228 Mercury Ct Ste 100 (92111-1232)
PHONE..............................858 716-8262
Toni Falcone, *CEO*
Toni Falcone, *Pr*
Jeff Tomlinson, *VP*

EMP: 18 EST: 2009
SALES (est): 4.44MM **Privately Held**
Web: www.advancedhpc.com
SIC: **3572** 3571 Computer storage devices; Electronic computers

(P-7461)
AFERIN LLC
9808 Alburtis Ave (90670-3208)
PHONE..............................562 903-1500
▲ EMP: 48
SIC: **3572** 3571 Computer storage devices; Electronic computers

(P-7462)
ALLSTAR MICROELECTRONICS INC
Also Called: Allstarshop.com
30191 Avenida De Las Bandera (92688)
PHONE..............................949 546-0888
Ming-chyi Chiang, *Pr*
EMP: 18 EST: 1995
SQ FT: 12,843
SALES (est): 2.5MM **Privately Held**
Web: www.allstarshop.com
SIC: **3572** Computer storage devices

(P-7463)
BNL TECHNOLOGIES INC
Also Called: Fantom Drives
22301 S Western Ave Ste 101 (90501)
PHONE..............................310 320-7272
Behzad Eshghieh, *CEO*
Hamid Khorsand, *
Nasser Ahdout, *
▲ EMP: 25 EST: 1998
SALES (est): 4.86MM **Privately Held**
Web: www.fantomdrives.com
SIC: **3572** Computer storage devices

(P-7464)
CAMEO TECHNOLOGIES INC
20511 Lake Forest Dr (92630-7741)
PHONE..............................949 672-7000
Matthew Massingel, *CEO*
EMP: 20 EST: 2012
SALES (est): 1.45MM
SALES (corp-wide): 12.32B **Publicly Held**
SIC: **3572** Disk drives, computer
HQ: Western Digital Technologies, Inc.
   5601 Great Oaks Pkwy
   San Jose CA

(P-7465)
CENTON ELECTRONICS INC (PA)
Also Called: Centon
27412 Aliso Viejo Pkwy (92656-3371)
PHONE..............................949 855-9111
Jennifer Miscione, *CEO*
Gene Miscione, *
Laura Miscione, *
◆ EMP: 60 EST: 1978
SQ FT: 20,000
SALES (est): 15.18MM
SALES (corp-wide): 15.18MM **Privately Held**
Web: www.centon.com
SIC: **3572** 5734 7379 Computer storage devices; Computer software and accessories; Computer related consulting services

(P-7466)
CERTANCE LLC (HQ)
Also Called: Quantum Corporation
141 Innovation Dr (92617-3211)
PHONE..............................949 856-7800
Howard L Matthews, *Pr*

Donald L Waite, *
EMP: 300 **EST:** 2000
SALES (est): 128.18MM
SALES (corp-wide): 412.75MM **Publicly Held**
Web: www.quantum.com
SIC: 3572 Computer tape drives and components
PA: Quantum Corporation
224 Airport Pkwy Ste 550
San Jose CA
408 944-4000

(P-7467)
CHENBRO MICOM (USA) INC
2800 Jurupa St (91761-2903)
PHONE....................909 937-0100
Mei Chi Chen, *Pr*
▲ **EMP:** 20 **EST:** 1983
SALES (est): 14.06MM **Privately Held**
SIC: 3572 Computer storage devices
PA: Chenbro Micom Co., Ltd.
18f, No. 558, Zhongyuan Rd.
New Taipei City TAP

(P-7468)
COMPUCASE CORPORATION
Also Called: Orion Tech
16720 Chestnut St Ste C (91748-1038)
PHONE....................626 336-6588
Doung Fu Hsu, *Pr*
Aaron Tao, *
Phillip Liu, *
▲ **EMP:** 1500 **EST:** 1995
SQ FT: 30,000
SALES (est): 90.86MM **Privately Held**
Web: www.hecgroupusa.com
SIC: 3572 Computer storage devices
PA: Compucase Enterprise Co., Ltd.
No. 225, Lane 54, Sec. 2, An Ho Rd.
Tainan City

(P-7469)
EP HOLDINGS INC
Also Called: Ep Memory
30442 Esperanza (92688-2144)
PHONE....................949 713-4600
Eric Krantz, *CEO*
EMP: 20 **EST:** 2005
SALES (est): 10.88MM **Privately Held**
Web: www.epholdingsinc.com
SIC: 3572 Computer storage devices

(P-7470)
GLOBAL SILICON ELECTRONICS INC
Also Called: Buslink Media
440 Cloverleaf Dr (91706-6500)
PHONE....................626 336-1888
James Djen, *CEO*
Jie Zhu, *
▲ **EMP:** 39 **EST:** 2004
SQ FT: 50,000
SALES (est): 4.77MM **Privately Held**
Web: www.buslink.com
SIC: 3572 Computer storage devices

(P-7471)
GLOBALVISION SYSTEMS INC
9401 Oakdale Ave Ste 100 (91311-6512)
PHONE....................888 227-7967
Oliver Song, *CEO*
EMP: 21 **EST:** 1996
SALES (est): 2.51MM **Privately Held**
Web: www.gv-systems.com
SIC: 3572 Computer disk and drum drives and components

(P-7472)
GST INC
3419 Via Lido Ste 164 (92663-3908)
PHONE....................949 510-1142
David Breisacher, *CEO*
▼ **EMP:** 42 **EST:** 2002
SQ FT: 10,000
SALES (est): 1.24MM **Privately Held**
SIC: 3572 Computer storage devices

(P-7473)
H CO COMPUTER PRODUCTS (PA)
Also Called: Thinkcp Technologies
16812 Hale Ave (92606-5021)
PHONE....................949 833-3222
Ali Hojreh, *CEO*
Mark Hojreh, *
Saed Hojreh, *
Mohammad Hojreh, *
◆ **EMP:** 25 **EST:** 1987
SQ FT: 15,600
SALES (est): 9.12MM **Privately Held**
Web: www.thinkcp.com
SIC: 3572 3577 Computer storage devices; Computer peripheral equipment, nec

(P-7474)
I/OMAGIC CORPORATION (PA)
20512 Crescent Bay Dr (92630-8847)
PHONE....................949 707-4800
Tony Shahbaz, *Ch Bd*
Tony Shahbaz, *Interim Chief Financial Officer*
Mary St George, *
▲ **EMP:** 30 **EST:** 1992
SQ FT: 52,000
SALES (est): 8.75MM **Privately Held**
Web: www.iomagic.com
SIC: 3572 3651 Computer storage devices; Home entertainment equipment, electronic, nec

(P-7475)
IN WIN DEVELOPMENT USA INC
188 Brea Canyon Rd (91789-3086)
PHONE....................909 348-0588
Wen Hsien Lai, *Pr*
Wen Hsien Lai, *Pr*
Paul Hao, *Ex VP*
▲ **EMP:** 20 **EST:** 1989
SQ FT: 50,000
SALES (est): 5.06MM **Privately Held**
Web: www.in-win.com
SIC: 3572 Computer tape drives and components
PA: In Win Development Inc.
57, Lane 350, Nan Shang Rd.,
Taoyuan City TAY

(P-7476)
LGARDE INC
15181 Woodlawn Ave (92780-6487)
PHONE....................714 259-0771
Gayle D Bilyeu, *Ch Bd*
Constantine Cassapakis, *Pr*
Gordon Veal, *Sec*
Alan R Hirasuna, *Treas*
Mitch Thomas, *Bd of Dir*
EMP: 24 **EST:** 1971
SQ FT: 19,000
SALES (est): 4.83MM **Privately Held**
Web: www.lgarde.com
SIC: 3572 8731 2822 3769 Tape recorders for computers; Engineering laboratory, except testing; Acrylic rubbers, polyacrylate ; Space vehicle equipment, nec

(P-7477)
MEMORY EXPERTS INTL USA INC (HQ)
2102 Business Center Dr (92612-1001)
PHONE....................714 258-3000
▲ **EMP:** 22 **EST:** 1996
SALES (est): 26.51MM
SALES (corp-wide): 35.77MM **Privately Held**
Web: www.memoryexpertsinc.com
SIC: 3572 3577 Computer storage devices; Computer peripheral equipment, nec
PA: Les Experts En Memoire Internationale Inc.
2321 Rue Cohen
Saint-Laurent QC
514 333-5010

(P-7478)
NGD SYSTEMS INC
3019 Wilshire Blvd (90403-2301)
PHONE....................949 870-9148
Mohammad Nader Salessi, *CEO*
EMP: 30 **EST:** 2016
SALES (est): 3.08MM **Privately Held**
Web: www.ngdsystems.com
SIC: 3572 Computer storage devices

(P-7479)
POSTVISION INC
Also Called: Archion
2605 E Foothill Blvd Ste 103 (91740)
PHONE....................818 840-0777
Reuben Lima, *CEO*
Mark Bianchi, *CEO*
Reuben Lima, *COO*
Daniel Stern, *Ex VP*
EMP: 17 **EST:** 1998
SQ FT: 6,000
SALES (est): 2.17MM **Privately Held**
SIC: 3572 Computer storage devices

(P-7480)
QUANTUM
220 S Glasgow Ave (90301-2102)
PHONE....................323 709-8880
EMP: 20 **EST:** 2018
SALES (est): 4.99MM **Privately Held**
SIC: 3572 Computer storage devices

(P-7481)
QUANTUM ALLIANCE INC
511 E Mountain St (91207-1421)
PHONE....................818 415-2085
Sabrina Tilimian, *Brnch Mgr*
EMP: 18
SALES (corp-wide): 304.55K **Privately Held**
SIC: 3572 Computer storage devices
PA: Quantum Alliance Inc.
700 N Central Ave Ste 560
Glendale CA

(P-7482)
QUANTUM CORPORATION
141 Innovation Dr Ste 100 (92617-3212)
PHONE....................949 856-7800
Lisa Ewbank, *Brnch Mgr*
EMP: 24
SALES (corp-wide): 412.75MM **Publicly Held**
Web: www.quantum.com
SIC: 3572 Computer storage devices
PA: Quantum Corporation
224 Airport Pkwy Ste 550
San Jose CA
408 944-4000

(P-7483)
RADIAN MEMORY SYSTEMS INC
5010 N Pkwy Ste 205 (91302)
PHONE....................818 222-4080
Michael Jadon, *CEO*
Brian Dexheimer, *Board Director**
Ted Samford, *Board Director**
EMP: 26 **EST:** 2011
SALES (est): 10MM **Privately Held**
Web: www.radianmemory.com
SIC: 3572 Computer storage devices

(P-7484)
SHAXON INDUSTRIES INC
337 W Freedom Ave (92865-2647)
PHONE....................714 779-1140
Ahmet Erdogan, *CEO*
Yuksel Acik, *
Bahadir Tulunay, *
Bekir Aydinoglu, *
Christina Rodriguez, *
▲ **EMP:** 85 **EST:** 1978
SALES (est): 15.45MM **Privately Held**
Web: www.shaxon.com
SIC: 3572 5045 3678 3661 Computer storage devices; Computers and accessories, personal and home entertainment; Electronic connectors; Telephone and telegraph apparatus

(P-7485)
SHOP4TECHCOM
Also Called: Leda Multimedia
13745 Seminole Dr (91710-5515)
PHONE....................909 248-2725
Danny Wang, *Pr*
▲ **EMP:** 45 **EST:** 1999
SQ FT: 25,500
SALES (est): 9.12MM
SALES (corp-wide): 9.12MM **Privately Held**
Web: www.shop4tech.com
SIC: 3572 5731 Computer tape drives and components; Video recorders, players, disc players, and accessories
PA: Plc Multimedia, Inc.
398 Lemon Creek Dr Ste K
Walnut CA
909 248-2680

(P-7486)
SILICON TECH INC
Also Called: Silicontech
3009 Daimler St (92705-5812)
PHONE....................949 476-1130
Manouch Moshayedi, *CEO*
Mike Moshayedi, *
Mark Moshayedi, *
EMP: 413 **EST:** 1998
SALES (est): 4.68MM
SALES (corp-wide): 12.32B **Publicly Held**
SIC: 3572 Computer storage devices
HQ: Stec, Inc.
3355 Michelson Dr Ste 100
Irvine CA

(P-7487)
STEC INC (HQ)
3355 Michelson Dr Ste 100 (92612-5694)
PHONE....................415 222-9996
Stephen D Milligan, *Pr*
▲ **EMP:** 340 **EST:** 1990
SQ FT: 73,100
SALES (est): 91.98MM
SALES (corp-wide): 12.32B **Publicly Held**
SIC: 3572 3674 3577 Computer storage devices; Semiconductors and related devices; Computer peripheral equipment, nec
PA: Western Digital Corporation
5601 Great Oaks Pkwy

▲ = Import ▼ = Export
◆ = Import/Export

San Jose CA
408 717-6000

(P-7488)
STEC INTERNATIONAL HOLDING INC
3001 Daimler St (92705-5812)
PHONE..............................949 476-1180
EMP: 169 **EST:** 2010
SALES (est): 2.45MM
SALES (corp-wide): 12.32B **Publicly Held**
SIC: 3572 Computer storage devices
HQ: Stec, Inc.
3355 Michelson Dr Ste 100
Irvine CA

(P-7489)
SYPRIS DATA SYSTEMS INC (HQ)
160 Via Verde (91773-3901)
PHONE..............................909 962-9400
Darrell Robertson, *Pr*
▲ **EMP:** 50 **EST:** 1957
SQ FT: 30,000
SALES (est): 241.14MM
SALES (corp-wide): 110.12MM **Publicly Held**
SIC: 3572 3651 Computer tape drives and components; Tape recorders: cassette, cartridge or reel: household use
PA: Sypris Solutions, Inc.
101 Bullitt Ln Ste 450
Louisville KY
502 329-2000

(P-7490)
US CRITICAL LLC (PA)
Also Called: US Critical
6 Orchard Ste 150 (92630-8352)
PHONE..............................949 916-9326
Thomas Horton, *Dir*
John Lightman, *CEO*
Kurt Dunteman, *VP*
Angela Lunt, *Opers Mgr*
EMP: 44 **EST:** 2013
SQ FT: 12,000
SALES (est): 7.87MM
SALES (corp-wide): 7.87MM **Privately Held**
Web: www.approvednetworks.com
SIC: 3572 Computer disk and drum drives and components

(P-7491)
US CRITICAL LLC
25422 Trabuco Rd # 320 (92630-2791)
PHONE..............................800 884-8945
Thomas Horton, *Dir*
EMP: 21
SALES (corp-wide): 7.87MM **Privately Held**
Web: www.approvednetworks.com
SIC: 3572 Computer disk and drum drives and components
PA: Us Critical Llc
6 Orchard Ste 150
Lake Forest CA
949 916-9326

(P-7492)
VIGOBYTE TAPE CORPORATION
2498 Roll Dr Ste 916 (92154-7213)
PHONE..............................866 803-8446
▲ **EMP:** 700
SIC: 3572 Magnetic storage devices, computer

(P-7493)
WESTERN DIGITAL CORPORATION
Also Called: Fremont Office
3337 Michelson Dr (92612-1699)
PHONE..............................949 672-7000
EMP: 23
SALES (corp-wide): 12.32B **Publicly Held**
Web: www.westerndigital.com
SIC: 3572 Disk drives, computer
PA: Western Digital Corporation
5601 Great Oaks Pkwy
San Jose CA
408 717-6000

(P-7494)
ZADARA STORAGE INC
6 Venture Ste 140 (92618-3314)
PHONE..............................949 251-0360
Nelson Nahum, *CEO*
Nir Ben Zvi, *
Yair Hershko, *
Vladimir Popovski, *
Doug Jury, *
▲ **EMP:** 93 **EST:** 2011
SALES (est): 13.57MM **Privately Held**
Web: www.zadara.com
SIC: 3572 Computer storage devices

3575 Computer Terminals

(P-7495)
GATEWAY MANUFACTURING LLC
7565 Irvine Center Dr (92618-4918)
PHONE..............................949 471-7000
Gary Fan, *Prin*
EMP: 92 **EST:** 2002
SALES (est): 2.27MM **Privately Held**
SIC: 3575 Computer terminals
HQ: Gateway, Inc.
7565 Irvine Center Dr # 150
Irvine CA
949 471-7000

(P-7496)
IMC NETWORKS CORP (PA)
25531 Commercentre Dr Ste 200 (92630-8873)
PHONE..............................949 465-3000
Jerry Roby, *Ch Bd*
Michael Dailey, *
▲ **EMP:** 40 **EST:** 1988
SQ FT: 35,000
SALES (est): 12.06MM
SALES (corp-wide): 12.06MM **Privately Held**
Web: www.opm25.com
SIC: 3575 3577 Computer terminals, monitors and components; Computer peripheral equipment, nec

(P-7497)
MTA MOVING TECH IN AMER INC
Also Called: MTA
10065 Via De La Amistad Ste A1 (92154-7286)
PHONE..............................619 651-7208
Edgar Vargas, *CEO*
Michelle Lynn Perez, *Pr*
James Stearrett, *CFO*
Alexandrina Perez, *Treas*
▼ **EMP:** 20 **EST:** 2004
SQ FT: 6,200
SALES (est): 56.68MM **Privately Held**
Web: www.mtaus.com

SIC: **3575** 5045 3571 7373 Computer terminals, monitors and components; Computer peripheral equipment; Electronic computers; Computer-aided engineering (CAE) systems service

(P-7498)
OCP GROUP INC
7130 Engineer Rd (92111-1422)
PHONE..............................858 279-7400
Neil Gleason, *Pr*
Tracy Sommer, *VP*
▲ **EMP:** 22 **EST:** 1989
SALES (est): 5.81MM **Privately Held**
Web: www.ocp.com
SIC: 3575 5051 7549 Computer terminals, monitors and components; Cable, wire; Automotive maintenance services

(P-7499)
SGB ENTERPRISES INC
24844 Anza Dr Ste A (91355-1286)
PHONE..............................661 294-8306
Joseph Padula, *Pr*
Joseph Padula, *CEO*
Chuck Burkholder, *CFO*
EMP: 22 **EST:** 1991
SQ FT: 9,600
SALES (est): 6.07MM **Privately Held**
Web: www.sgbent.com
SIC: 3575 5999 3728 3699 Cathode ray tube (CRT), computer terminal; Training materials, electronic; Aircraft training equipment; Flight simulators (training aids), electronic

(P-7500)
SMK MANUFACTURING INC
Also Called: SMK
1055 Tierra Del Rey Ste F (91910-7875)
PHONE..............................619 216-6400
Nobuyuki Suzuki, *CEO*
Naomasa Miyata, *VP*
Mathoru Hurukawa, *CFO*
▲ **EMP:** 50 **EST:** 1979
SQ FT: 14,688
SALES (est): 27.57MM **Privately Held**
Web: www.smkusa.com
SIC: 3575 Keyboards, computer, office machine
HQ: Smk Electronics Corporation Usa
1055 Tierra Del Rey Ste H
Chula Vista CA
619 216-6400

(P-7501)
TRANSPARENT PRODUCTS INC
28064 Avenue Stanford Unit E (91355-1160)
PHONE..............................661 294-9787
Fred Bonyadian, *Pr*
John Mcvay, *Pr*
▲ **EMP:** 50 **EST:** 1992
SQ FT: 18,000
SALES (est): 8.67MM **Privately Held**
Web: www.touchpage.com
SIC: 3575 7371 Computer terminals, monitors and components; Computer software systems analysis and design, custom

(P-7502)
VERTIV IT SYSTEMS INC
Also Called: Vertiv
970 W Valley Pkwy Ste 425 (92025-2554)
PHONE..............................760 504-5451
Bryan Kistler, *Prin*
EMP: 89
SALES (corp-wide): 5.69B **Publicly Held**
Web: www.vertiv.com

SIC: 3575 Computer terminals
HQ: Vertiv It Systems, Inc.
4991 Corporate Dr Nw
Huntsville AL
256 430-4000

3577 Computer Peripheral Equipment, Nec

(P-7503)
ACCES I/O PRODUCTS INC
10623 Roselle St (92121-1506)
PHONE..............................858 550-9559
John Persidok, *Pr*
Marty Wingett, *Quality*
EMP: 17 **EST:** 1984
SQ FT: 9,447
SALES (est): 4.49MM **Privately Held**
Web: www.accesio.com
SIC: 3577 Computer peripheral equipment, nec

(P-7504)
ADD-ON CMPT PERIPHERALS INC
15775 Gateway Cir (92780-6470)
PHONE..............................949 546-8200
James Patton, *CEO*
Matthew Mccormick, *VP*
Brent Loomis, *
Thomas Virden, *
▲ **EMP:** 130 **EST:** 2000
SQ FT: 11,000
SALES (est): 25.99MM **Privately Held**
Web: www.addonnetworks.com
SIC: 3577 5045 Computer peripheral equipment, nec; Computers, peripherals, and software

(P-7505)
AMAG TECHNOLOGY INC (DH)
2205 W 126th St Ste B (90250-3365)
PHONE..............................310 518-2380
Matt Barnette, *Ch Bd*
N Keith Whitelock, *
Robert A Sawyer Junior, *Pr*
Robert Causee, *
Gary Thorington-jones, *Treas*
▲ **EMP:** 48 **EST:** 1971
SALES (est): 24.89MM
SALES (corp-wide): 2.67MM **Privately Held**
Web: www.amag.com
SIC: 3577 Decoders, computer peripheral equipment
HQ: G4s Technology Limited
International Drive
Tewkesbury GLOS

(P-7506)
APEM INC (HQ)
970 Park Center Dr (92081-8301)
PHONE..............................978 372-1602
Peter Brouilette, *CEO*
Laurel Pittera, *
Marc Enjalbert, *
◆ **EMP:** 30 **EST:** 2008
SALES (est): 38MM **Privately Held**
Web: www.apem.com
SIC: 3577 3679 Computer peripheral equipment, nec; Electronic switches
PA: Idec Corporation
2-6-64, Nishimiyahara, Yodogawa-Ku
Osaka OSK

(P-7507)
APRICORN LLC
12191 Kirkham Rd (92064-6870)
PHONE..............................858 513-2000

PRODUCTS & SVCS

Paul Brown, *Pr*
Michael Gordon, *
▲ **EMP:** 29 **EST:** 1983
SQ FT: 21,000
SALES (est): 6.82MM **Privately Held**
Web: www.apricorn.com
SIC: 3577 5734 Computer peripheral
equipment, nec; Computer and software
stores

(P-7508)
BAR CODE SPECIALTIES INC
Also Called: Quest Solution
12272 Monarch St (92841-2907)
PHONE...................877 411-2633
EMP: 30
SIC: 3577 5045 Bar code (magnetic ink)
printers; Computer peripheral equipment

(P-7509)
BDR INDUSTRIES INC
Also Called: Rnd Enterprises
9700 Owensmouth Ave Lbby (91311-8073)
PHONE...................818 341-2112
Scott Riddle, *Brnch Mgr*
EMP: 20
SALES (corp-wide): 24.38MM **Privately
Held**
Web: www.rndcable.com
SIC: 3577 Computer peripheral equipment,
nec
PA: B.D.R. Industries, Inc.
820 E Avenue L12
Lancaster CA
661 940-8554

(P-7510)
BELKIN INTERNATIONAL INC
(DH)
Also Called: Belkin Components
555 S Aviation Blvd Ste 180 (90245)
PHONE...................310 751-5100
Steven Malony, *CEO*
Chester Pipkin, *
Jasjit Jay Singh, *
◆ **EMP:** 450 **EST:** 1983
SQ FT: 218,000
SALES (est): 473.4MM **Privately Held**
Web: www.belkin.com
SIC: 3577 5045 5065 Computer peripheral
equipment, nec; Computers and
accessories, personal and home
entertainment; Intercommunication
equipment, electronic
HQ: Foxconn Interconnect Technology
Limited
C/O Conyers Trust Company
(Cayman) Limited
George Town GR CAYMAN

(P-7511)
BEST DATA PRODUCTS INC
Also Called: Diamond Multimedia
9236 Deering Ave (91311-5803)
PHONE...................818 534-1414
Behrouz Zamanzadeh, *CEO*
Bruce Zaman, *
Shirley Zaman, *
▲ **EMP:** 85 **EST:** 1983
SALES (est): 9.88MM **Privately Held**
Web: www.diamondmm.com
SIC: 3577 Computer peripheral equipment,
nec

(P-7512)
BIXOLON AMERICA INC
2575 W 237th St (90505-5216)
PHONE...................858 764-4580
Chan Young Hwang, *CEO*
Yon H Son, *Pr*

◆ **EMP:** 44 **EST:** 2005
SALES (est): 11.34MM **Privately Held**
Web: www.bixolonusa.com
SIC: 3577 Printers, computer
PA: Bixolon Co., Ltd
344 Pangyo-Ro, Bundang-Gu
Seongnam

(P-7513)
C ENTERPRISES INC
Also Called: C Enterprises
16868 Via Del Campo Ct (92127-1771)
PHONE...................760 599-5111
Brian Tauber, *Pr*
Steven Yamasaki, *COO*
EMP: 64 **EST:** 1984
SALES (est): 15.15MM
SALES (corp-wide): 85.25MM **Publicly
Held**
Web: www.centerprises.com
SIC: 3577 5045 3357 3229 Computer
peripheral equipment, nec; Computers and
accessories, personal and home
entertainment; Nonferrous wiredrawing and
insulating; Pressed and blown glass, nec
PA: Rf Industries, Ltd.
16868 Via Del Campo Ct
San Diego CA
858 549-6340

(P-7514)
CALIFORNIA DIGITAL INC (PA)
6 Saddleback Rd (90274-5141)
P.O. Box 3399 (90510-3399)
PHONE...................310 217-0500
Terry Reiter, *Pr*
Wade Wood, *
Floyd Pothoven, *
EMP: 67 **EST:** 1973
SQ FT: 30,000
SALES (est): 5.02MM
SALES (corp-wide): 5.02MM **Privately
Held**
Web: www.florod.com
SIC: 3577 3571 3699 Computer peripheral
equipment, nec; Mainframe computers;
Electrical equipment and supplies, nec

(P-7515)
CIPHERTEX LLC
Also Called: Ciphertex Data Security
9301 Jordan Ave Ste 105a (91311-5863)
PHONE...................818 773-8989
Jerry Kaner, *CEO*
▲ **EMP:** 18 **EST:** 2009
SALES (est): 2.08MM **Privately Held**
Web: www.ciphertex.com
SIC: 3577 3572 Computer peripheral
equipment, nec; Computer storage devices

(P-7516)
CIRE GROUP INC
3579 E Foothill Blvd # 793 (91107-3119)
PHONE...................626 321-8822
Eric Hu, *Brnch Mgr*
EMP: 205
Web: www.tek-republic.com
SIC: 3577 Computer peripheral equipment,
nec
PA: Cire Group Inc.
18350 San Jose Ave
City Of Industry CA

(P-7517)
CMS PRODUCTS LLC
29620 Skyline Dr (93561-8571)
PHONE...................714 424-5520
Les Kristof, *Pr*
EMP: 22 **EST:** 2015
SALES (est): 760.48K **Privately Held**

Web: www.cmsproducts.com
SIC: 3577 Decoders, computer peripheral
equipment

(P-7518)
CONGATEC INC
6262 Ferris Sq (92121-3205)
PHONE...................858 457-2600
Ronald F Mazza, *Pr*
EMP: 33 **EST:** 2008
SALES (est): 5.11MM
SALES (corp-wide): 355.83K **Privately
Held**
Web: www.congatec.com
SIC: 3577 Computer peripheral equipment,
nec
HQ: Congatec Gmbh
Auwiesenstr. 5
Deggendorf BY
991 270-0100

(P-7519)
CS SYSTEMS INC
Also Called: Cs Electronics
16781 Noyes Ave (92606-5123)
PHONE...................949 475-9100
Christian Schwartz, *Pr*
Gayle Schwartz, *
▲ **EMP:** 25 **EST:** 1982
SQ FT: 33,200
SALES (est): 4.97MM **Privately Held**
Web: www.cs-electronics.com
SIC: 3577 3677 Computer peripheral
equipment, nec; Coil windings, electronic

(P-7520)
DATAMETRICS CORPORATION
Also Called: DMC
25 E Easy St (93065-7707)
PHONE...................805 577-9710
Carl Stella, *Pr*
Roger Lazer, *
Harry Altery, *
EMP: 45 **EST:** 1980
SQ FT: 45,000
SALES (est): 6.28MM
SALES (corp-wide): 12MM **Privately Held**
Web: www.datametrics.com
SIC: 3577 7373 Printers, computer; Value-
added resellers, computer systems
PA: Rugged Information Technology
Equipment Corporation
25 E Easy St
Simi Valley CA
805 577-9710

(P-7521)
DELKIN DEVICES INC (PA)
Also Called: Delkin Devices
13350 Kirkham Way (92064-7117)
PHONE...................858 391-1234
◆ **EMP:** 100 **EST:** 1986
SALES (est): 11.09MM
SALES (corp-wide): 11.09MM **Privately
Held**
Web: www.delkin.com
SIC: 3577 5734 3861 Computer peripheral
equipment, nec; Computer and software
stores; Photographic equipment and
supplies

(P-7522)
DELPHI DISPLAY SYSTEMS INC
3550 Hyland Ave (92626-1438)
PHONE...................714 825-3400
Ken Neeld, *CEO*
David Skinner, *VP Sls*
Doug Gordon, *Contrlr*
Michael Deson, *CEO*
▲ **EMP:** 55 **EST:** 1997

SQ FT: 10,000
SALES (est): 12.6MM
SALES (corp-wide): 2.73B **Publicly Held**
Web: www.delphidisplay.com
SIC: 3577 Computer peripheral equipment,
nec
PA: Toast, Inc.
401 Park Dr Ste 801
Boston MA
617 297-1005

(P-7523)
EFAXCOM (DH)
Also Called: Jetfax
6922 Hollywood Blvd Fl 5 (90028-6125)
PHONE...................323 817-3207
Ronald Brown, *Pr*
John H Harris, *INT'L Operations*
Gary P Kapner, *Vice President North
America*
EMP: 80 **EST:** 1988
SALES (est): 24.54MM
SALES (corp-wide): 1.39B **Publicly Held**
Web: www.ziffdavis.com
SIC: 3577 Computer peripheral equipment,
nec
HQ: J2 Cloud Services, Llc
700 S Flower St Fl 15
Los Angeles CA

(P-7524)
EFAXCOM
Also Called: J2 Global Communications
5385 Hollister Ave Ste 208 (93111-2389)
PHONE...................805 692-0064
EMP: 41
SALES (corp-wide): 1.39B **Publicly Held**
Web: www.ziffdavis.com
SIC: 3577 Computer peripheral equipment,
nec
HQ: Efax.Com
6922 Hollywood Blvd Fl 5
Los Angeles CA
323 817-3207

(P-7525)
EMULEX CORPORATION (DH)
5300 California Ave (92617-3038)
▲ **EMP:** 124 **EST:** 1979
SQ FT: 180,000
SALES (est): 291.56MM
SALES (corp-wide): 33.2B **Publicly Held**
Web: www.broadcom.com
SIC: 3577 3661 Input/output equipment,
computer; Telephone and telegraph
apparatus
HQ: Avago Technologies Wireless (U.S.A.)
Manufacturing Llc
4380 Ziegler Rd
Fort Collins CO

(P-7526)
ENCRYPTED ACCESS
CORPORATION
1730 Redhill Ave (92697-0001)
PHONE...................714 371-4125
Hirihisa Matsunaga, *Brnch Mgr*
EMP: 110
SIC: 3577 Punch card equipment: readers,
tabulators, sorters, etc.
PA: Encrypted Access Corporation
600 Anton Blvd Fl 11
Costa Mesa CA

(P-7527)
EPSON AMERICA INC (DH)
Also Called: Seiko Epson
3131 Katella Ave (90720-2335)
P.O. Box 93012 (90809-3012)
PHONE...................800 463-7766

John Lang, *Pr*
John D Lang, *
Genevieve Walker, *
◆ **EMP:** 510 **EST:** 1975
SQ FT: 163,000
SALES (est): 359.49MM **Privately Held**
Web: www.epson.com
SIC: 3577 Computer peripheral equipment, nec
HQ: U.S. Epson, Inc.
3131 Katella Ave
Los Alamitos CA

(P-7528)
FINIS LLC
3347 Michelson Dr Ste 100 (92612-0661)
P.O. Box 17192 (92623-7192)
PHONE...............................949 250-4929
EMP: 80 **EST:** 2015
SALES (est): 50.21MM
SALES (corp-wide): 59.98MM **Privately Held**
Web: www.incipio.com
SIC: 3577 Computer peripheral equipment, nec
PA: Incipio Technologies, Inc.
3347 Michelson Dr Ste 100
Irvine CA
888 893-1638

(P-7529)
FORESEESON CUSTOM DISPLAYS INC (PA)
2210 E Winston Rd (92806-5536)
PHONE...............................714 300-0540
Insik Kang, *Pr*
▲ **EMP:** 20 **EST:** 2000
SQ FT: 8,000
SALES (est): 5.71MM
SALES (corp-wide): 5.71MM **Privately Held**
Web: www.foreseesonusa.com
SIC: 3577 Computer peripheral equipment, nec

(P-7530)
GOODIX TECHNOLOGY INC
133 Technology Dr Ste 200 (92618-2465)
PHONE...............................858 554-0352
Fan Zhang, *CEO*
Bo Pi, *Sec*
EMP: 42 **EST:** 2014
SALES (est): 2.5MM **Privately Held**
SIC: 3577 Computer peripheral equipment, nec

(P-7531)
HP IT SERVICES INCORPORATED
1506 W Flower Ave (92833-3952)
PHONE...............................714 844-7737
Brian White, *CEO*
EMP: 25 **EST:** 2019
SALES (est): 250K **Privately Held**
SIC: 3577 7372 7382 Computer peripheral equipment, nec; Operating systems computer software; Confinement surveillance systems maintenance and monitoring

(P-7532)
INCIPIO TECHNOLOGIES INC (PA)
Also Called: Incipio Group
3347 Michelson Dr Ste 100 (92612-0661)
P.O. Box 17192 (92623-7192)
PHONE...............................888 893-1638
Brian Stech, *CEO*
Stephen Finney, *

◆ **EMP:** 28 **EST:** 2000
SALES (est): 59.98MM
SALES (corp-wide): 59.98MM **Privately Held**
Web: www.incipio.com
SIC: 3577 Computer peripheral equipment, nec

(P-7533)
INDUSTRIAL ELCTRNIC ENGNERS IN
Also Called: Iee
7723 Kester Ave (91405-1105)
PHONE...............................818 787-0311
Thomas Whinfrey, *Pr*
Thomas Whinfrey, *Pr*
Donald G Gumpertz, *Ch*
Alan R Wolen, *Sec*
▲ **EMP:** 100 **EST:** 1947
SQ FT: 131,000
SALES (est): 18.96MM **Privately Held**
Web: www.ieeinc.com
SIC: 3577 3575 Graphic displays, except graphic terminals; Keyboards, computer, office machine

(P-7534)
INFINEON TECH AMERICAS CORP
Interntnal Rctfier/Hexget Amer
41915 Business Park Dr (92590-3637)
PHONE...............................951 375-6008
Marc Rougee, *Brnch Mgr*
EMP: 710
SALES (corp-wide): 17.72B **Privately Held**
Web: www.infineon.com
SIC: 3577 3674 Computer peripheral equipment, nec; Semiconductor circuit networks
HQ: Infineon Technologies Americas Corp.
101 N Pacific Coast Hwy
El Segundo CA
310 726-8200

(P-7535)
INNOVATIVE TECH & ENGRG INC
Also Called: Innov8v
2691 Richter Ave Ste 124 (92606-5124)
PHONE...............................949 955-2501
EMP: 23 **EST:** 1997
SQ FT: 2,200
SALES (est): 728.92K **Privately Held**
Web: www.innov8v.com
SIC: 3577 5961 1731 5999 Computer peripheral equipment, nec; Computers and peripheral equipment, mail order; Safety and security specialization; Audio-visual equipment and supplies

(P-7536)
INPUT/OUTPUT TECHNOLOGY INC
28415 Industry Dr Ste 520 (91355-4161)
PHONE...............................661 257-1000
Ted Drapala, *Pr*
EMP: 20 **EST:** 1977
SALES (est): 2.32MM **Privately Held**
Web: www.iotechnology.com
SIC: 3577 3823 Input/output equipment, computer; Process control instruments

(P-7537)
INSTRUMENTATION TECH SYSTEMS
Also Called: Its
11949 Wood Ranch Rd (91344-2144)
PHONE...............................818 886-2034
Paul Hightower, *CEO*
Don C Janess, *VP*

▼ **EMP:** 19 **EST:** 1978
SALES (est): 1.66MM **Privately Held**
Web: www.itsamerica.com
SIC: 3577 Encoders, computer peripheral equipment

(P-7538)
INTERNET MACHINES CORPORATION (PA)
30501 Agoura Rd Ste 203 (91301-4389)
PHONE...............................818 575-2100
Christopher Hoogenboom, *CEO*
Christopher Hoogenboom, *Pr*
Frank Knuettel Ii, *CFO*
Chris Haywood, *VP Engg*
Aloke Gupta, *VP Mktg*
EMP: 70 **EST:** 1999
SQ FT: 18,500
SALES (est): 9.47MM
SALES (corp-wide): 9.47MM **Privately Held**
Web: www.internetmachines.com
SIC: 3577 Computer peripheral equipment, nec

(P-7539)
KINGSTON DIGITAL INC (HQ)
17600 Newhope St (92708-4220)
PHONE...............................714 435-2600
John Tu, *Pr*
David Sun, *Prin*
▲ **EMP:** 21 **EST:** 2007
SALES (est): 22.33MM
SALES (corp-wide): 418.24MM **Privately Held**
Web: www.kingston.com
SIC: 3577 Computer peripheral equipment, nec
PA: Kingston Technology Company, Inc.
17600 Newhope St
Fountain Valley CA
714 435-2600

(P-7540)
KINGSTON TECHNOLOGY CORP (PA)
17600 Newhope St (92708-4298)
PHONE...............................714 435-2600
John Tu, *CEO*
David Sun, *
▲ **EMP:** 500 **EST:** 1987
SALES (est): 479.84MM **Privately Held**
Web: www.kingston.com
SIC: 3577 Computer peripheral equipment, nec

(P-7541)
LASERGRAPHICS INC
Also Called: Lasergraphics General Business
20 Ada (92618-2303)
PHONE...............................949 753-8282
Mihai Demetrescu Ph.d., *Pr*
Stefan Demetrescu Ph.d., *Senior Vice President Research & Development*
Stefan Demetrescu, *Senior Vice President Research & Development*
David Boyd, *
▲ **EMP:** 40 **EST:** 1981
SQ FT: 20,000
SALES (est): 5.47MM **Privately Held**
Web: www.lasergraphics.com
SIC: 3577 7371 3823 Graphic displays, except graphic terminals; Custom computer programming services; Process control instruments

(P-7542)
LIVESCRIBE INC
930 Roosevelt (92620-3664)
▲ **EMP:** 50

Web: www.livescribe.com
SIC: 3577 3951 Computer peripheral equipment, nec; Pens and mechanical pencils

(P-7543)
LOGICUBE INC (PA)
Also Called: Logicube
19755 Nordhoff Pl (91311-6606)
PHONE...............................888 494-8832
Farid Emrani, *Pr*
Jack M Schuster, *Ch Bd*
Jeffrey Schuster, *CFO*
▲ **EMP:** 20 **EST:** 1993
SALES (est): 5.62MM **Privately Held**
Web: www.logicube.com
SIC: 3577 Computer peripheral equipment, nec

(P-7544)
LOGITECH INC
3 Jenner Ste 180 (92618-3835)
PHONE...............................510 795-8500
Darrell Bracken, *Brnch Mgr*
EMP: 713
Web: www.logitech.com
SIC: 3577 Computer peripheral equipment, nec
HQ: Logitech Inc.
3930 N 1st St
San Jose CA
510 795-8500

(P-7545)
LYNN PRODUCTS INC
Also Called: Pureformance Cables
2645 W 237th St (90505-5269)
PHONE...............................310 530-5966
Hsinyu Lin, *Pr*
Eric Tseng, *
Chen Huei Tseng, *
Chun Mei Shei, *Treas*
▲ **EMP:** 1000 **EST:** 1982
SQ FT: 35,000
SALES (est): 86.18MM **Privately Held**
Web: www.lynnprod.com
SIC: 3577 3357 Computer peripheral equipment, nec; Fiber optic cable (insulated)

(P-7546)
MAD CATZ INC
Also Called: Mad Catz
10680 Treena St Ste 500 (92131-2447)
PHONE...............................858 790-5008
▲ **EMP:** 250
SIC: 3577 5734 Computer peripheral equipment, nec; Software, computer games

(P-7547)
MAGMA INC
9918 Via Pasar (92126-4559)
PHONE...............................858 530-2511
▲ **EMP:** 30
Web: www.magma.com
SIC: 3577 Computer peripheral equipment, nec

(P-7548)
MAGTEK INC (PA)
1710 Apollo Ct (90740-5617)
PHONE...............................562 546-6400
Ann Marle Hart, *Pr*
Louis E Struett, *
▲ **EMP:** 200 **EST:** 1972
SQ FT: 48,000
SALES (est): 48.32MM
SALES (corp-wide): 48.32MM **Privately Held**
Web: www.magtek.com

PRODUCTS & SVCS

SIC: **3577** 3674 Readers, sorters, or inscribers, magnetic ink; Semiconductors and related devices

(P-7549)
MARWAY POWER SYSTEMS INC (PA)
Also Called: Marway Power Solutions
1721 S Grand Ave (92705-4808)
P.O. Box 30118 (92735-8118)
PHONE.................714 917-6200
TOLL FREE: 800 .
Paul Patel, *Pr*
Kevin Jacobs, *
◆ **EMP:** 39 **EST:** 1979
SQ FT: 33,400
SALES (est): 9.7MM
SALES (corp-wide): 9.7MM **Privately Held**
Web: www.marway.com
SIC: **3577** 8711 Computer peripheral equipment, nec; Engineering services

(P-7550)
METROMEDIA TECHNOLOGIES INC
311 Parkside Dr (91340-3036)
PHONE.................818 552-6500
Paul Havig, *Brnch Mgr*
EMP: 26
SALES (corp-wide): 20.45MM **Privately Held**
Web: www.mmt.com
SIC: **3577** Graphic displays, except graphic terminals
PA: Metromedia Technologies, Inc.
810 7th Ave Fl 29
New York NY
212 273-2100

(P-7551)
MISSION TECHNOLOGY GROUP INC
Also Called: Magma
9918 Via Pasar (92126-4559)
PHONE.................858 530-2511
▲ **EMP:** 30
Web: www.magma.com
SIC: **3577** Computer peripheral equipment, nec

(P-7552)
MITEK SYSTEMS INC (PA)
Also Called: Mitek
600 B St Ste 100 (92101-4505)
PHONE.................619 269-6800
Scipio Carnecchia, *CEO*
Scott Carter, *Ex Ch Bd*
Fuad Ahmad, *Interim Chief Financial Officer*
Jason L Gray, *CLO CCO*
Michael E Diamond, *Sr VP*
EMP: 113 **EST:** 1986
SQ FT: 29,000
SALES (est): 143.94MM
SALES (corp-wide): 143.94MM **Publicly Held**
Web: www.miteksystems.com
SIC: **3577** 7372 Computer peripheral equipment, nec; Business oriented computer software

(P-7553)
MOTION ENGINEERING INC (DH)
Also Called: M E I
33 S La Patera Ln (93117-3214)
PHONE.................805 696-1200
EMP: 60 **EST:** 1987
SQ FT: 21,000
SALES (est): 27.8MM
SALES (corp-wide): 5.22B **Publicly Held**

Web: www.motioneng.com
SIC: **3577** 8711 3823 Computer peripheral equipment, nec; Engineering services; Process control instruments
HQ: Altra Industrial Motion Corp.
300 Granite St Ste 201
Braintree MA
781 917-0600

(P-7554)
MOXA AMERICAS INC
601 Valencia Ave Ste 100 (92823-6357)
PHONE.................714 528-6777
Tein Shun, *CEO*
Ben Chen, *
Tein Shun Chen, *
▲ **EMP:** 50 **EST:** 2002
SQ FT: 8,000
SALES (est): 24.36MM **Privately Held**
Web: www.moxa.com
SIC: **3577** Input/output equipment, computer
PA: Moxa Inc.
13f, No. 3, Xinbei Blvd., Sec. 4,
New Taipei City TAP

(P-7555)
MPD HOLDINGS INC
Also Called: Mousepad Designs
16200 Commerce Way (90703-2324)
PHONE.................213 210-2591
Glenn M Boghosian, *Pr*
▲ **EMP:** 34 **EST:** 1993
SALES (est): 3.65MM **Privately Held**
Web: www.mpdholdings.com
SIC: **3577** 2822 Computer peripheral equipment, nec; Ethylene-propylene rubbers, EPDM polymers

(P-7556)
OLEA KIOSKS INC
13845 Artesia Blvd (90703-9000)
PHONE.................562 924-2644
Francisco Olea, *CEO*
Shauna Olea, *
▲ **EMP:** 54 **EST:** 1975
SQ FT: 50,000
SALES (est): 13.91MM **Privately Held**
Web: www.olea.com
SIC: **3577** Computer peripheral equipment, nec

(P-7557)
OMNIPRINT INC
1923 E Deere Ave (92705-5715)
PHONE.................949 833-0080
Fardin Mostafavi, *Pr*
▲ **EMP:** 24 **EST:** 1984
SQ FT: 22,000
SALES (est): 2.63MM **Privately Held**
Web: www.omniprintinc.com
SIC: **3577** 5045 Printers and plotters; Printers, computer

(P-7558)
ONE STOP SYSTEMS INC
Also Called: Magma
2235 Enterprise St Ste 110 (92029)
PHONE.................858 530-2511
Timothy Miller, *Prin*
EMP: 23
SALES (corp-wide): 72.42MM **Publicly Held**
Web: www.onestopsystems.com
SIC: **3577** Computer peripheral equipment, nec
PA: One Stop Systems, Inc.
2235 Entp St Ste 110
Escondido CA
760 745-9883

(P-7559)
ONE STOP SYSTEMS INC (PA)
Also Called: Oss
2235 Enterprise St Ste 110 (92029)
PHONE.................760 745-9883
David Raun, *Pr*
Kenneth Potashner, *
John W Morrison Junior, *CFO*
Jim Ison, *Chief Sales & Marketing Officer*
EMP: 34 **EST:** 1998
SQ FT: 29,342
SALES (est): 72.42MM
SALES (corp-wide): 72.42MM **Publicly Held**
Web: www.onestopsystems.com
SIC: **3577** Computer peripheral equipment, nec

(P-7560)
OPTIMA TECHNOLOGY CORPORATION
17062 Murphy Ave (92614-5914)
PHONE.................949 253-5768
Barry Eisler, *Brnch Mgr*
EMP: 343
Web: www.optimatech.com
SIC: **3577** Computer peripheral equipment, nec
PA: Optima Technology Corporation
2222 Michelson Dr # 1830
Irvine CA

(P-7561)
OWNZONES MEDIA NETWORK INC
315 S Beverly Dr Ste 315 (90212-4309)
PHONE.................855 466-9696
Dan Goman, *CEO*
Rick Capstraw, *CRO*
EMP: 21 **EST:** 2017
SALES (est): 642K **Privately Held**
SIC: **3577** Data conversion equipment, media-to-media: computer

(P-7562)
PHOTO SCIENCES INCORPORATED (PA)
301 9th St Ste 406 (92374-3403)
PHONE.................310 634-1500
Kyle Stogsdill, *CEO*
L J Stogsdill, *Ch*
Kathy Chambers, *Sec*
Wade Walsh, *Treas*
Jeff Platts, *VP Mktg*
EMP: 33 **EST:** 1972
SALES (est): 4.96MM
SALES (corp-wide): 4.96MM **Privately Held**
Web: www.photo-sciences.com
SIC: **3577** 7335 Computer output to microfilm units; Still and slide file production

(P-7563)
PRINCETON TECHNOLOGY INC
1691 Browning (92606-4808)
PHONE.................949 851-7776
Nasir Javed, *CEO*
▲ **EMP:** 30 **EST:** 1990
SQ FT: 14,000
SALES (est): 4.71MM **Privately Held**
Web: www.princetonusa.com
SIC: **3577** 5045 3674 Computer peripheral equipment, nec; Computers, peripherals, and software; Semiconductors and related devices

(P-7564)
PRINTRONIX LLC (PA)
7700 Irvine Center Dr Ste 700 (92618-2905)

PHONE.................714 368-2300
Werner Heid, *CEO*
Sean Irby, *
Bill Matthewes, *
▲ **EMP:** 54 **EST:** 1974
SALES (est): 24.32MM
SALES (corp-wide): 24.32MM **Privately Held**
Web: www.printronix.com
SIC: **3577** Printers, computer

(P-7565)
QUALITYLOGIC INC
2245 1st St Ste 103 (93065-0904)
PHONE.................208 424-1905
Joe Walker, *Mgr*
EMP: 109
SALES (corp-wide): 10.89MM **Privately Held**
Web: www.qualitylogic.com
SIC: **3577** 8748 Computer peripheral equipment, nec; Testing services
PA: Qualitylogic, Inc.
9576 W Emerald St
Boise ID
208 424-1905

(P-7566)
RAISE 3D TECHNOLOGIES INC
43 Tesla (92618-4603)
PHONE.................949 482-2040
Hua Feng, *CEO*
EMP: 23 **EST:** 2018
SALES (est): 4.21MM **Privately Held**
Web: www.raise3d.com
SIC: **3577** 7372 7336 Printers, computer; Prepackaged software; Graphic arts and related design
PA: Shanghai Fusion Tech Co., Ltd.
Room 402,403,404, No.68, 1688 Lane,
Guoquan N. Road, Yangpu Dist
Shanghai SH

(P-7567)
RGB SYSTEMS INC (PA)
Also Called: Extron Electronics
1025 E Ball Rd Ste 100 (92805-5957)
PHONE.................714 491-1500
Andrew C Edwards, *CEO*
◆ **EMP:** 185 **EST:** 1983
SQ FT: 160,000
SALES (est): 174.47MM
SALES (corp-wide): 174.47MM **Privately Held**
Web: www.extron.com
SIC: **3577** Computer output to microfilm units

(P-7568)
RICOH PRTG SYSTEMS AMER INC (HQ)
2390 Ward Ave Ste A (93065-1859)
PHONE.................805 578-4000
Osamu Namikawa, *Pr*
Leonard Stone, *VP*
Hiroyuki Kajiyama, *Pr*
◆ **EMP:** 400 **EST:** 1962
SQ FT: 97,000
SALES (est): 106.93MM **Privately Held**
Web: rpsa.ricoh.com
SIC: **3577** 3861 3955 Printers, computer; Toners, prepared photographic (not made in chemical plants); Ribbons, inked: typewriter, adding machine, register, etc.
PA: Ricoh Company, Ltd.
1-3-6, Nakamagome
Ota-Ku TKY

(P-7569)
RUGGED INFO TECH EQP CORP (PA)

Also Called: Ritec
25 E Easy St (93065-7707)
PHONE..............................805 577-9710
Carl C Stella, *Pr*
Harry P Alteri, *
Vincent Stella, *
Roger Lazer, *
◆ **EMP: 41 EST:** 1996
SQ FT: 25,000
SALES (est): 12MM
SALES (corp-wide): 12MM **Privately Held**
Web: www.ritecrugged.com
SIC: 3577 Computer peripheral equipment, nec

(P-7570)
SEMTEK INNVTIVE SOLUTIONS CORP
12777 High Bluff Dr Ste 225 (92130-2224)
PHONE..............................858 436-2270
John Sarkisian, *Ch Bd*
Patrick Hazel, *Pr*
▲ **EMP: 36 EST:** 1998
SQ FT: 10,000
SALES (est): 1.23MM **Privately Held**
Web: www.semtek.com
SIC: 3577 Readers, sorters, or inscribers, magnetic ink

(P-7571)
SYNAPTICS INC
1929 Main St Ste 105 (92614-6524)
PHONE..............................949 483-5594
EMP: 22 EST: 2018
SALES (est): 2.74MM **Privately Held**
Web: www.synaptics.com
SIC: 3577 Computer peripheral equipment, nec

(P-7572)
TOPAZ SYSTEMS INC (PA)
Also Called: Esign Emcee
875 Patriot Dr Ste A (93021-3351)
PHONE..............................805 520-8282
Anthony Zank, *Pr*
▲ **EMP: 25 EST:** 1995
SQ FT: 16,000
SALES (est): 9.79MM **Privately Held**
Web: www.topazsystems.com
SIC: 3577 7371 Graphic displays, except graphic terminals; Custom computer programming services

(P-7573)
TOYE CORPORATION
9230 Deering Ave (91311-5803)
P.O. Box 3997 (91313-3997)
PHONE..............................818 882-4000
Gordon Morris, *Pr*
▲ **EMP: 20 EST:** 1941
SQ FT: 5,000
SALES (est): 483.99K **Privately Held**
Web: www.toyecorp.com
SIC: 3577 Computer peripheral equipment, nec

(P-7574)
TRANSPARENT DEVICES INC
Also Called: Cybertouch
853 Lawrence Dr (91320-2232)
PHONE..............................805 499-5000
Abraham Gohari, *Pr*
EMP: 23 EST: 1982
SQ FT: 25,000
SALES (est): 3.35MM **Privately Held**
Web: www.cybertouch.com
SIC: 3577 Graphic displays, except graphic terminals

(P-7575)
TRI-NET TECHNOLOGY INC
21709 Ferrero (91789-5209)
PHONE..............................909 598-8818
Tom Chung, *CEO*
Tom Chung, *Pr*
Lisa Chung, *
Akinori Ogawa, *
▲ **EMP: 100 EST:** 1992
SQ FT: 35,000
SALES (est): 9.23MM **Privately Held**
Web: www.trinetusa.com
SIC: 3577 3571 Computer peripheral equipment, nec; Electronic computers

(P-7576)
UNITED TOTE COMPANY
4205 Ponderosa Ave (92123-1525)
PHONE..............................858 279-4250
Scott Pfennighausen, *Brnch Mgr*
EMP: 61
SALES (corp-wide): 1.81B **Publicly Held**
Web: www.unitedtote.com
SIC: 3577 Computer peripheral equipment, nec
HQ: United Tote Company
600 N Hurstbourne Pkwy # 400
Louisville KY
502 636-4520

(P-7577)
US COMPUTERS INC
Also Called: U S Technical Institute
181 W Orangethorpe Ave Ste C (92870-6931)
PHONE..............................714 528-0514
Uzma Sheikh, *Pr*
Saleem Sheikh, *VP*
EMP: 19 EST: 1997
SQ FT: 3,500
SALES (est): 3MM **Privately Held**
Web: www.uscomputersinc.com
SIC: 3577 8249 Computer peripheral equipment, nec; Vocational schools, nec

(P-7578)
VIEWSONIC CORPORATION (PA)
Also Called: Viewsonic
10 Pointe Dr Ste 200 (92821-7620)
PHONE..............................909 444-8888
James Chu, *Ch Bd*
Jeff Volpe, *
Brian Igoe, *
Sung Yi, *
Bonny Cheng, *
◆ **EMP: 140 EST:** 1987
SQ FT: 298,050
SALES (est): 171.21MM
SALES (corp-wide): 171.21MM **Privately Held**
Web: www.viewsonic.com
SIC: 3577 3575 5045 Computer peripheral equipment, nec; Computer terminals, monitors and components; Computer peripheral equipment

(P-7579)
VOYETRA TURTLE BEACH INC (DH)
Also Called: Turtle Beach
11011 Via Frontera Ste A (92127-1752)
PHONE..............................914 345-2255
▲ **EMP: 93 EST:** 1986
SALES (est): 59.9MM **Publicly Held**
SIC: 3577 7371 Computer peripheral equipment, nec; Computer software development
HQ: Vtb Holdings, Inc.
100 Summit Lake Dr
Valhalla NY
914 345-2255

(P-7580)
WESTERN TELEMATIC INC
5 Sterling (92618-2517)
PHONE..............................949 586-9950
Daniel Morrison, *CEO*
Herbert Hoover Iii, *Ch Bd*
▲ **EMP: 50 EST:** 1964
SQ FT: 24,000
SALES (est): 8.87MM **Privately Held**
Web: www.wti.com
SIC: 3577 5065 Computer peripheral equipment, nec; Electronic parts and equipment, nec

(P-7581)
WINIT AMERICA INC
381 Brea Canyon Rd (91789-3060)
PHONE..............................626 606-0308
EMP: 35
SALES (corp-wide): 8.83MM **Privately Held**
Web: www.winitamerica.com
SIC: 3577 Computer peripheral equipment, nec
PA: Win.It America, Inc.
18501 Arenth Ave
City Of Industry CA
626 328-0688

(P-7582)
ZEBRA TECHNOLOGIES CORPORATION
Also Called: Eltron International
30601 Agoura Rd (91301-2147)
PHONE..............................805 579-1800
Don Skinner, *Brnch Mgr*
EMP: 53
SALES (corp-wide): 5.78B **Publicly Held**
Web: www.zebra.com
SIC: 3577 Bar code (magnetic ink) printers
PA: Zebra Technologies Corporation
3 Overlook Pt
Lincolnshire IL
847 634-6700

3578 Calculating And Accounting Equipment

(P-7583)
ASTERES INC (PA)
10650 Treena St Ste 105 (92131-2436)
PHONE..............................858 777-8600
Linda Pinney, *CEO*
Martin Bridges, *
▲ **EMP: 27 EST:** 2003
SALES (est): 7.73MM
SALES (corp-wide): 7.73MM **Privately Held**
Web: www.asteres.com
SIC: 3578 Cash registers

(P-7584)
CAR ENTERPRISES INC
Also Called: C.A.R ENTERPRISES, INC.
13100 Main St (92345-4625)
PHONE..............................760 947-6411
Sam Anabi, *Pr*
EMP: 19
SALES (corp-wide): 116.84MM **Privately Held**
Web: www.shell.com
SIC: 3578 Automatic teller machines (ATM)
PA: C.A.R. Enterprises, Inc.
1450 N Benson Ave Unit A
Upland CA
909 932-9242

(P-7585)
SUZHOU SOUTH
18351 Colima Rd Ste 82 (91748-2791)
PHONE..............................626 322-0101
Joel Wynne, *Dir*
EMP: 300 EST: 2017
SALES (est): 14.96MM **Privately Held**
SIC: 3578 Banking machines

3579 Office Machines, Nec

(P-7586)
LYNDE-ORDWAY COMPANY INC
5402 Commercial Dr (92649-1232)
P.O. Box 8709 (92728-8709)
PHONE..............................714 957-1311
TOLL FREE: 800
Thomas Ordway, *Pr*
Penny Ordway, *Sec*
EMP: 18 EST: 1925
SALES (est): 3.46MM **Privately Held**
Web: www.lynde-ordway.com
SIC: 3579 5999 5044 7359 Paper handling machines; Business machines and equipment; Office equipment; Equipment rental and leasing, nec

(P-7587)
RICOH ELECTRONICS INC
17482 Pullman St (92614-5527)
PHONE..............................714 259-1220
Paul Bakonyi, *Mgr*
EMP: 153
SQ FT: 49,359
Web: rei.ricoh.com
SIC: 3579 3571 Mailing, letter handling, and addressing machines; Electronic computers
HQ: Ricoh Electronics, Inc.
1125 Hurricane Shoals Rd
Lawrenceville GA
714 566-2500

(P-7588)
SOLARIS PAPER INC
505 N Euclid St Ste 630 (92801-5506)
PHONE..............................714 687-6657
▲ **EMP: 197 EST:** 2005
SALES (est): 1.26MM **Privately Held**
Web: www.solarispaper.com
SIC: 3579 Paper handling machines
HQ: Solaris Paper, Inc.
770 The Cy Dr S Ste 3000
Orange CA

(P-7589)
WHITTIER MAILING PRODUCTS INC (PA)
13019 Park St (90670-4005)
PHONE..............................562 464-3000
Richard A Casford, *Pr*
EMP: 17 EST: 1991
SQ FT: 5,000
SALES (est): 4.39MM
SALES (corp-wide): 4.39MM **Privately Held**
Web: www.wmpwebstore.com
SIC: 3579 Mailing, letter handling, and addressing machines

3581 Automatic Vending Machines

(P-7590)
AVT INC
341 Bonnie Cir Ste 102 (92880-2895)
PHONE..............................951 737-1057
▲ **EMP:** 38

PRODUCTS & SVCS

Web: www.automatedretailingsystems.com
SIC: 3581 Automatic vending machines

(P-7591)
IMPULSE INDUSTRIES INC
Also Called: Impulse Amusement
9281 Borden Ave (91352-2034)
PHONE..........................818 767-4258
◆ EMP: 24 EST: 1986
SALES (est): 2.59MM Privately Held
Web: www.impulseindustries.com
SIC: 3581 3999 Automatic vending machines
; Coin-operated amusement machines

3582 Commercial Laundry Equipment

(P-7592)
DENIM-TECH LLC
375 E 2nd St Apt 604 (90012-4154)
PHONE..........................323 277-8998
▲ EMP: 100
Web: www.denim-tech.com
SIC: 3582 Commercial laundry equipment

3585 Refrigeration And Heating Equipment

(P-7593)
ACCO ENGINEERED SYSTEMS INC
3559 Landco Dr Ste B (93308-6169)
PHONE..........................661 631-1975
EMP: 24
SALES (corp-wide): 1.51B Privately Held
Web: www.accoes.com
SIC: 3585 Air conditioning equipment, complete
PA: Acco Engineered Systems, Inc.
    888 E Walnut St
    Pasadena CA
    818 244-6571

(P-7594)
ACE HEATERS LLC
130 Klug Cir (92878-5424)
PHONE..........................951 738-2230
Robin Cruse, CEO
William Newbauer Iii, Pr
EMP: 20 EST: 2016
SQ FT: 40,000
SALES (est): 3.43MM
SALES (corp-wide): 51.44MM Privately Held
Web: www.aceheaters.com
SIC: 3585 3443 Heating equipment, complete; Boiler and boiler shop work
PA: The Nudyne Group Llc
    45 Seymour St
    Stratford CT
    203 378-2659

(P-7595)
ADVANCED AEROSPACE
10781 Forbes Ave (92843-4977)
PHONE..........................714 265-6200
Steve Flowers, Pr
EMP: 20 EST: 1997
SALES (est): 459.25K Privately Held
SIC: 3585 Refrigeration equipment, complete

(P-7596)
ALLIANCE AIR PRODUCTS LLC (DH)
Also Called: Especializados Del Aire
2285 Michael Faraday Dr Ste 15 (92154-7926)

PHONE..........................619 428-9688
Luis Plascencia, Pr
EMP: 51 EST: 2004
SQ FT: 3,300
SALES (est): 133.9MM Privately Held
Web: www.allianceairproducts.com
SIC: 3585 Air conditioning units, complete: domestic or industrial
HQ: Daikin Applied Americas Inc.
    13600 Industrial Pk Blvd
    Minneapolis MN
    763 553-5330

(P-7597)
ALLIANCE AIR PRODUCTS LLC
9565 Heinrich Hertz Dr Ste 1 (92154-7920)
PHONE..........................619 664-0027
EMP: 409
Web: www.allianceairproducts.com
SIC: 3585 Refrigeration and heating equipment
HQ: Alliance Air Products, Llc.
    2285 Michael Faraday Dr
    San Diego CA
    619 428-9688

(P-7598)
AMERICAN CONDENSER & COIL LLC
Also Called: American Condenser
1628 W 139th St (90249-3003)
PHONE..........................310 327-8600
▲ EMP: 75
Web: www.americancondenser.com
SIC: 3585 Air conditioning condensers and condensing units

(P-7599)
ANTHONY INC (DH)
Also Called: Anthony International
12391 Montero Ave (91342-5370)
PHONE..........................818 365-9451
Jeffrey Clark, CEO
Michael Murth, *
David Lautenschaelger, *
Craig Little, *
◆ EMP: 850 EST: 2012
SQ FT: 350,000
SALES (est): 486.02MM
SALES (corp-wide): 8.51B Publicly Held
Web: www.anthonyintl.com
SIC: 3585 Refrigeration and heating equipment
HQ: Dover Refrigeration & Food Equipment, Inc.
    3005 Highland Pkwy # 200
    Downers Grove IL
    513 878-4400

(P-7600)
ARI INDUSTRIES INC
Also Called: Airdyne Refrigeration
17018 Edwards Rd (90703-2422)
PHONE..........................714 993-3700
R Tony Bedi, Pr
Ruth Lee Bedi, *
EMP: 80 EST: 1995
SQ FT: 20,000
SALES (est): 10.72MM Privately Held
Web: www.airdyne.com
SIC: 3585 Refrigeration equipment, complete

(P-7601)
BIGFOGG INC (PA)
30818 Wealth St (92563-2534)
PHONE..........................951 587-2460
Christopher Miehl, Pr
Chris Miehl, Pr
EMP: 17 EST: 2000
SALES (est): 4.56MM

SALES (corp-wide): 4.56MM Privately Held
Web: www.bigfogg.com
SIC: 3585 Air conditioning condensers and condensing units

(P-7602)
CLASSIC TENTS
Also Called: Classic Tents
19119 S Reyes Ave (90221-5811)
PHONE..........................310 328-5060
▲ EMP: 45
Web: www.bright.com
SIC: 3585 7359 1731 Air conditioning equipment, complete; Business machine and electronic equipment rental services; General electrical contractor

(P-7603)
COMMERCIAL DISPLAY SYSTEMS LLC
Also Called: C D S
17341 Sierra Hwy (91351-1625)
PHONE..........................818 361-8160
Fernando Calderon, Managing Member
John T Karnes, Managing Member*
Duane Beswick, *
EMP: 30 EST: 2002
SQ FT: 17,000
SALES (est): 5.04MM Privately Held
Web: www.cdsdoors.net
SIC: 3585 Refrigeration and heating equipment

(P-7604)
COMPU AIRE INC
8167 Byron Rd (90606-2615)
PHONE..........................562 945-8971
Balbir Narang, Pr
Robert Narang, *
▲ EMP: 150 EST: 1980
SQ FT: 75,000
SALES (est): 18MM Privately Held
Web: www.compu-aire.com
SIC: 3585 Air conditioning units, complete: domestic or industrial

(P-7605)
COOLTEC REFRIGERATION CORP
1250 E Franklin Ave Unit B (91766-5449)
P.O. Box 1150 (91769-1150)
PHONE..........................909 865-2229
Paul Bedi, CEO
George Share, Sec
EMP: 22 EST: 2005
SQ FT: 50,000
SALES (est): 5.06MM Privately Held
Web: www.cooltecrefrigeration.com
SIC: 3585 Refrigeration equipment, complete

(P-7606)
CROWNTONKA CALIFORNIA INC
Also Called: Thermal Rite
6514 E 26th St (90040-3240)
PHONE..........................909 230-6720
Dave Jett, Genl Mgr
EMP: 46
Web: www.everidge.com
SIC: 3585 Refrigeration and heating equipment
HQ: Crowntonka California, Inc.
    15600 37th Ave N Ste 100
    Minneapolis MN
    763 543-2386

(P-7607)
DAIKIN COMFORT TECH MFG LP
15024 Anacapa Rd (92392-2509)

PHONE..........................760 955-7770
Don Johnston, Brnch Mgr
EMP: 292
Web: www.goodmanmfg.com
SIC: 3585 Air conditioning equipment, complete
HQ: Daikin Comfort Technologies Manufacturing, L.P.
    19001 Kermier Rd
    Waller TX
    713 861-2500

(P-7608)
DATA AIRE INC (HQ)
230 W Blueridge Ave (92865-4225)
P.O. Box 7064 (92863-7064)
PHONE..........................800 347-2473
Duncan Moffatt, Pr
Edward J Altieri, *
▲ EMP: 60 EST: 1979
SALES (est): 24.07MM
SALES (corp-wide): 496.1MM Privately Held
Web: www.dataaire.com
SIC: 3585 Air conditioning units, complete: domestic or industrial
PA: Construction Specialties, Inc.
    3 Werner Way Ste 100
    Lebanon NJ
    908 236-0800

(P-7609)
ELCO RFRGN SOLUTIONS LLC
Also Called: Craft
2554 Commercial St (92113-1132)
PHONE..........................858 888-9447
Dean Rafiee, Ex Dir
EMP: 5000 EST: 2014
SALES (est): 88.97MM Privately Held
Web: www.icraft.us
SIC: 3585 3499 3999 Refrigeration and heating equipment; Fire- or burglary-resistive products; Barber and beauty shop equipment

(P-7610)
ENERGY LABS INC (DH)
Also Called: E L I
1695 Cactus Rd (92154-8102)
PHONE..........................619 671-0100
Ray Irani, Pr
▲ EMP: 400 EST: 1974
SQ FT: 150,000
SALES (est): 244.31MM
SALES (corp-wide): 5.69B Publicly Held
Web: energylabs.vertiv.com
SIC: 3585 Heating and air conditioning combination units
HQ: Vertiv Corporation
    505 N Cleveland Ave
    Westerville OH
    614 888-0246

(P-7611)
ENLINK GEOENERGY SERVICES INC
2630 Homestead Pl (90220-5610)
PHONE..........................424 242-1200
Mark Mizrahi, Pr
Howard Johnson, CIO
▲ EMP: 35 EST: 2004
SQ FT: 12,000
SALES (est): 728.35K Privately Held
SIC: 3585 Heat pumps, electric

(P-7612)
ENVIRO-INTERCEPT INC
7327 Varna Ave Unit 5 (91605-4183)
PHONE..........................818 982-6063
Fred Bonamici, Pr

Carlos Alverado, *VP*
Jim Watt, *Stockholder*
EMP: 20 **EST:** 1975
SQ FT: 11,500
SALES (est): 1.77MM **Privately Held**
SIC: 3585 Refrigeration and heating
equipment

(P-7613)
EVERIDGE INC
Also Called: Thermalrite
8886 White Oak Ave (91730-5106)
PHONE..........................909 605-6419
Chris Kahler, *Brnch Mgr*
EMP: 49
Web: www.everidge.com
SIC: 3585 Refrigeration and heating
equipment
PA: Everidge, Inc.
15600 37th Ave N Ste 100
Plymouth MN

(P-7614)
FERGUSON CO
6226 Cherry Ave (90805-3205)
P.O. Box 5849 (90721-5849)
PHONE..........................562 428-3300
Rosa Bermeo, *Prin*
EMP: 19 **EST:** 2006
SALES (est): 948.15K **Privately Held**
Web: www.fergusonpartners.com
SIC: 3585 5078 Refrigeration equipment,
complete; Refrigeration equipment and
supplies

(P-7615)
HUSSMANN CORPORATION
13770 Ramona Ave (91710-5423)
P.O. Box 5133 (91708-5133)
PHONE..........................909 590-4910
Mike Gleason, *Genl Mgr*
EMP: 350
Web: www.hussmann.com
SIC: 3585 7623 Refrigeration and heating
equipment; Refrigeration service and repair
HQ: Hussmann Corporation
12999 St Charles Rock Rd
Bridgeton MO
314 291-2000

(P-7616)
HUSSMANN TECH CORP AMER
Also Called: Panasnic Appls Rfrgn Systems C
2001 Sanyo Ave (92154-6212)
PHONE..........................619 661-1134
Shusaku Nagae, *CEO*
Kazuya Jinno, *
Shigeki Muneyasu, *
Akiko Woods, *
Hiroyuki Maotani, *
◆ **EMP:** 64 **EST:** 1978
SALES (est): 44.97MM **Privately Held**
SIC: 3585 3821 3632 Cabinets, show and
display, refrigerated; Freezers, laboratory;
Household refrigerators and freezers
HQ: Panasonic Corporation Of North
America
2 Riverfront Plz Ste 200
Newark NJ
201 348-7000

(P-7617)
LMW ENTERPRISES LLC
Also Called: Lrc Coil Company
10558 Norwalk Blvd (90670-3836)
PHONE..........................562 944-1969
EMP: 22
SALES (corp-wide): 3.65MM **Privately
Held**
Web: www.lrccoil.com

SIC: 3585 Refrigeration equipment, complete
PA: Lmw Enterprises Llc
3861 E 42nd Pl
Yuma AZ
562 944-1969

(P-7618)
**MANITWOC FDSRVICE
CMPANIES LLC**
Also Called: Chester Paul Company
1210 N Red Gum St (92806-1820)
PHONE..........................323 245-3761
EMP: 281
SALES (corp-wide): 2.67MM **Privately
Held**
Web: direct.welbilt.us
SIC: 3585 Refrigeration and heating
equipment
HQ: Manitowoc Foodservice Companies,
Llc
2227 Welbilt Blvd
Trinity FL

(P-7619)
MESTEK INC
Also Called: Anemostat Products
1220 E Watson Center Rd (90745-4206)
PHONE..........................310 835-7500
Chang Hung, *Mgr*
EMP: 200
SALES (corp-wide): 689.94MM **Privately
Held**
Web: www.mestek.com
SIC: 3585 3549 3542 3354 Heating
equipment, complete; Metalworking
machinery, nec; Punching, shearing, and
bending machines; Shapes, extruded
aluminum, nec
PA: Mestek, Inc.
260 N Elm St
Westfield MA
470 898-4533

(P-7620)
R-COLD INC
1221 S G St (92570-2477)
PHONE..........................951 436-5476
Michael Mulcahy, *Pr*
Ernest Gaston, *
EMP: 65 **EST:** 1982
SQ FT: 28,000
SALES (est): 10.84MM **Privately Held**
Web: www.r-cold.com
SIC: 3585 1541 Refrigeration and heating
equipment; Industrial buildings and
warehouses

(P-7621)
**RAHN INDUSTRIES
INCORPORATED (PA)**
Also Called: Rahn Industries
2630 Pacific Park Dr (90601-1611)
PHONE..........................562 908-0680
John Hancock, *Pr*
Jeff Meier, *
Claudia Maytum, *
▲ **EMP:** 46 **EST:** 1979
SQ FT: 25,000
SALES (est): 14.65MM
SALES (corp-wide): 14.65MM **Privately
Held**
Web: www.rahnindustries.com
SIC: 3585 Refrigeration and heating
equipment

(P-7622)
**REFRIGERATOR
MANUFACTURERS LLC**
Also Called: Airdyne Refrigeration

17018 Edwards Rd (90703-2422)
PHONE..........................562 926-2006
Tony Bedi, *Pr*
EMP: 47 **EST:** 2015
SALES (est): 5.99MM **Privately Held**
Web: www.rmi-econocold.com
SIC: 3585 Condensers, refrigeration

(P-7623)
SEAWARD PRODUCTS CORP
3721 Capitol Ave (90601-1732)
PHONE..........................562 699-7997
◆ **EMP:** 55 **EST:** 1975
SALES (est): 4.49MM **Privately Held**
SIC: 3585 3634 Heating equipment,
complete; Hot plates, electric

(P-7624)
TEAM AIR INC (PA)
Also Called: Team Air Conditioning Eqp
12771 Brown Ave (92509-1831)
PHONE..........................909 823-1957
Thirusenthil Nathan, *Pr*
Oliver Corbala, *
EMP: 35 **EST:** 1999
SALES (est): 8.24MM **Privately Held**
Web:
www.teamairconditionequipment.com
SIC: 3585 Air conditioning equipment,
complete

(P-7625)
THERMOCRAFT
2554 Commercial St (92113-1132)
PHONE..........................619 813-2985
Dean Rafiee, *Pr*
Dean Ideen Rafiee, *
EMP: 100 **EST:** 2016
SALES (est): 7.51MM **Privately Held**
SIC: 3585 5078 5031 Refrigeration and
heating equipment; Commercial
refrigeration equipment; Doors, garage

(P-7626)
**THREE STAR RFRGN ENGRG
INC**
Also Called: Kool Star
21720 S Wilmington Ave Ste 309
(90810-1641)
PHONE..........................310 327-9090
James Pak, *Pr*
Kyung Lee, *
William So, *
◆ **EMP:** 22 **EST:** 1989
SQ FT: 68,000
SALES (est): 765.41K **Privately Held**
SIC: 3585 4222 Air conditioning condensers
and condensing units; Refrigerated
warehousing and storage

(P-7627)
TRANE US INC
Also Called: Trane
3565 Corporate Ct Fl 1 (92123-2415)
PHONE..........................858 292-0833
Tyler Clemmer, *Brnch Mgr*
EMP: 80
Web: www.trane.com
SIC: 3585 Refrigeration and heating
equipment
HQ: Trane U.S. Inc.
800 Beaty St Ste E
Davidson NC
704 655-4000

(P-7628)
TRANE US INC
Also Called: Southern California Trane
3253 E Imperial Hwy (92821-6722)
PHONE..........................626 913-7123

John Clark, *Brnch Mgr*
EMP: 100
Web: www.trane.com
SIC: 3585 Heating and air conditioning
combination units
HQ: Trane U.S. Inc.
800 Beaty St Ste E
Davidson NC
704 655-4000

(P-7629)
TRANE US INC
Also Called: Trane
20450 E Walnut Dr N (91789-2921)
PHONE..........................626 913-7913
EMP: 27
Web: www.trane.com
SIC: 3585 Refrigeration and heating
equipment
HQ: Trane U.S. Inc.
800 Beaty St Ste E
Davidson NC
704 655-4000

(P-7630)
**TRUMED SYSTEMS
INCORPORATED**
4370 La Jolla Village Dr Ste 200
(92122-1233)
PHONE..........................844 878-6331
Jesper Jensen, *CEO*
Jesper Jensen, *Pr*
Joe Milkovits, *
Jim Martindale, *Field Operations Vice
President*
EMP: 29 **EST:** 2013
SALES (est): 4.99MM **Privately Held**
Web: www.trumedsystems.com
SIC: 3585 5078 Refrigeration and heating
equipment; Commercial refrigeration
equipment

(P-7631)
TURBO COIL INC
1532 Sinaloa Ave (91104-2744)
PHONE..........................626 644-6254
Hector Delgadillo, *CEO*
EMP: 20 **EST:** 2013
SQ FT: 2,000
SALES (est): 696.65K **Privately Held**
SIC: 3585 Compressors for refrigeration and
air conditioning equipment

(P-7632)
UTILITY REFRIGERATOR
12160 Sherman Way (91605-5501)
P.O. Box 570782 (91357-0782)
PHONE..........................818 764-6200
Michael Michrowski, *Pr*
▲ **EMP:** 20 **EST:** 2007
SALES (est): 4.14MM **Privately Held**
Web: www.utilityrefrigerator.com
SIC: 3585 Parts for heating, cooling, and
refrigerating equipment

(P-7633)
VEGE-MIST INC
Also Called: Alco Designs
407 E Redondo Beach Blvd (90248-2312)
PHONE..........................310 353-2300
Samuel Cohen, *CEO*
▲ **EMP:** 61 **EST:** 1988
SQ FT: 8,000
SALES (est): 14.91MM **Privately Held**
Web: www.alcodesigns.com
SIC: 3585 2541 5074 2542 Humidifying
equipment, except portable; Store and
office display cases and fixtures; Water
purification equipment; Partitions and
fixtures, except wood

(P-7634)
WILLIAMS FURNACE CO (DH)
Also Called: Williams Comfort Products
250 W Laurel St (92324-1435)
PHONE...................................562 450-3602
Michael Markowich, *Pr*
James Gidwitz, *
Joseph Sum, *
Mark Nichter, *
Ruth Ann Davis, *
▲ **EMP:** 173 **EST:** 1916
SQ FT: 400,000
SALES (est): 43.34MM
SALES (corp-wide): 113.28MM **Privately Held**
Web: www.williamscomfortprod.com
SIC: 3585 3433 Refrigeration and heating equipment; Heating equipment, except electric
HQ: Riverbend Industries Inc.
440 S La Salle St # 3100
Chicago IL
312 541-7200

3589 Service Industry Machinery, Nec

(P-7635)
ADVANCED UV INC (PA)
16350 Manning Way (90703-2224)
PHONE...................................562 407-0299
Kiyomitsu Kevin Toma, *CEO*
▲ **EMP:** 25 **EST:** 1996
SQ FT: 30,000
SALES (est): 9.4MM
SALES (corp-wide): 9.4MM **Privately Held**
Web: www.advanceduv.com
SIC: 3589 Water purification equipment, household type

(P-7636)
AMIAD USA INC
Also Called: West Coast Sales Office & Whse
1251 Maulhardt Ave (93030-7990)
PHONE...................................805 988-3323
EMP: 23
Web: www.amiad.com
SIC: 3589 Water treatment equipment, industrial
HQ: Amiad U.S.A., Inc.
120 Talbert Rd Ste J
Mooresville NC
704 662-3133

(P-7637)
AMIAD USA INC
Also Called: Amiad Filtration Systems
1251 Maulhardt Ave (93030-7990)
P.O. Box 5547 (93031-5547)
PHONE...................................805 988-3323
Tom Akehurst, *Pr*
Issac Orlans, *Stockholder**
▲ **EMP:** 35 **EST:** 1981
SQ FT: 30,000
SALES (est): 7.67MM **Privately Held**
Web: www.amiad.com
SIC: 3589 Water treatment equipment, industrial
PA: Amiad Water Systems Ltd
Kibbutz
Amiad

(P-7638)
AMPAC USA INC
5255 State St 5275 (91763)
PHONE...................................435 291-0961
Hunter Tyson, *Prin*
EMP: 50 **EST:** 2021
SALES (est): 3.01MM **Privately Held**

Web: www.ampac1.com
SIC: 3589 Water purification equipment, household type

(P-7639)
APPLIED MEMBRANES INC
Also Called: Wateranywhere
2450 Business Park Dr (92081-8847)
PHONE...................................760 727-3711
Gulshan Dhawan, *CEO*
◆ **EMP:** 178 **EST:** 1983
SQ FT: 55,000
SALES (est): 45.88MM **Privately Held**
Web: www.appliedmembranes.com
SIC: 3589 5074 Water purification equipment, household type; Water heaters and purification equipment

(P-7640)
AQUA PRODUCTS INC (DH)
2882 Whiptail Loop Ste 100 (92010-6758)
PHONE...................................973 857-2700
Giora Erlich, *Pr*
Joseph Porat, *
Kathleen A Mcclarnon, *Sec*
◆ **EMP:** 24 **EST:** 1964
SALES (est): 20.66MM
SALES (corp-wide): 322.15K **Privately Held**
Web: www.aquabot.com
SIC: 3589 Swimming pool filter and water conditioning systems
HQ: Foridra Srl
Strada Statale 16 Adriatica 16 17/A
Castelfidardo AN

(P-7641)
AQUAFINE CORPORATION (HQ)
29010 Avenue Paine (91355-4198)
PHONE...................................661 257-4770
Roberta Veloz, *Ch*
Michael Murphy, *
◆ **EMP:** 72 **EST:** 1949
SQ FT: 100,000
SALES (est): 24.33MM
SALES (corp-wide): 31.47B **Publicly Held**
Web: www.trojantechnologies.com
SIC: 3589 Water treatment equipment, industrial
PA: Danaher Corporation
2200 Penn Ave Nw Ste 800w
Washington DC
202 828-0850

(P-7642)
AQUAMOR LLC (PA)
Also Called: Watersentinel
42188 Rio Nedo (92590-3717)
PHONE...................................951 541-9517
▲ **EMP:** 100 **EST:** 2004
SALES (est): 14.91MM
SALES (corp-wide): 14.91MM **Privately Held**
Web: www.aquamor.com
SIC: 3589 Water filters and softeners, household type

(P-7643)
AQUEOUS TECHNOLOGIES CORP
1678 N Maple St (92878-3206)
PHONE...................................909 944-7771
Michael Konrad, *CEO*
▲ **EMP:** 23 **EST:** 1992
SQ FT: 15,000
SALES (est): 5.08MM **Privately Held**
Web: www.aqueoustech.com

SIC: 3589 3829 5084 7699 High pressure cleaning equipment; Physical property testing equipment; Cleaning equipment, high pressure, sand or steam; Industrial machinery and equipment repair

(P-7644)
AXEON WATER TECHNOLOGIES
40980 County Center Dr Ste 100 (92591-6052)
PHONE...................................760 723-5417
Augustin R Pavel, *Pr*
Jeanette Pavel, *
◆ **EMP:** 85 **EST:** 1989
SQ FT: 47,000
SALES (est): 24.17MM **Privately Held**
Web: www.axeonwater.com
SIC: 3589 5999 Water filters and softeners, household type; Water purification equipment

(P-7645)
B&W CUSTOM RESTAURANT EQP INC
541 E Jamie Ave (90631-6842)
PHONE...................................714 578-0332
Nathan Bojorquez, *Pr*
EMP: 20 **EST:** 1990
SALES (est): 2.24MM **Privately Held**
Web: www.bwcustom.com
SIC: 3589 8711 2599 Cooking equipment, commercial; Industrial engineers; Carts, restaurant equipment

(P-7646)
BLUE DESERT INTERNATIONAL INC
Also Called: Hydro Quip
510 N Sheridan St Ste A (92878-4024)
PHONE...................................951 273-7575
◆ **EMP:** 80 **EST:** 1994
SQ FT: 31,000
SALES (est): 9.71MM **Privately Held**
SIC: 3589 Swimming pool filter and water conditioning systems

(P-7647)
CHEMICAL METHODS ASSOC LLC (DH)
Also Called: CMA Dish Machines
12700 Knott St (92841-3904)
PHONE...................................714 898-8781
Fred G Palmer, *Pr*
▲ **EMP:** 30 **EST:** 1970
SQ FT: 50,000
SALES (est): 36.76MM
SALES (corp-wide): 2.67MM **Privately Held**
Web: www.cmadishmachines.com
SIC: 3589 Dishwashing machines, commercial
HQ: Ali Group North America Corporation
101 Corporate Woods Pkwy
Vernon Hills IL
847 215-6565

(P-7648)
CITY OF DELANO
Also Called: Delano Waste Water Treatment
1107 Lytle Ave (93215-9389)
PHONE...................................661 721-3352
Bill Hylton, *Mgr*
EMP: 42
SALES (corp-wide): 39.7MM **Privately Held**
Web: www.cityofdelano.org
SIC: 3589 Water treatment equipment, industrial
PA: City Of Delano
1015 11th Ave

Delano CA
661 721-3300

(P-7649)
CITY OF RIVERSIDE
Also Called: Water Treatment Plant
5950 Acorn St (92504-1036)
PHONE...................................951 351-6140
Richard Pallante, *Genl Mgr*
EMP: 129
SALES (corp-wide): 402.47MM **Privately Held**
Web: www.riversideca.gov
SIC: 3589 9111 Water treatment equipment, industrial; Mayors' office
PA: City Of Riverside
3900 Main St Fl 7
Riverside CA
951 826-5311

(P-7650)
CITY OF SANTA MONICA
Also Called: City Snta Mnica Wtr Trtmnt Pla
1228 S Bundy Dr (90025-1102)
PHONE...................................310 826-6712
Myriam Cardenas, *Brnch Mgr*
EMP: 235
SQ FT: 2,500
SALES (corp-wide): 502.49MM **Privately Held**
Web: www.santamonica.gov
SIC: 3589 Sewage and water treatment equipment
PA: City Of Santa Monica
1685 Main St
Santa Monica CA
310 458-8411

(P-7651)
COMCO INC
2151 N Lincoln St (91504-3344)
PHONE...................................818 333-8500
Colin Weightman, *Pr*
EMP: 36 **EST:** 1965
SQ FT: 12,500
SALES (est): 8.03MM **Privately Held**
Web: www.comcoinc.com
SIC: 3589 3291 Sandblasting equipment; Abrasive products

(P-7652)
COMPASS WATER SOLUTIONS INC (PA)
15542 Mosher Ave (92780-6425)
PHONE...................................949 222-5777
Thomas Farshler, *CEO*
Bill Tidmore, *
▲ **EMP:** 50 **EST:** 1983
SQ FT: 3,000
SALES (est): 11.08MM
SALES (corp-wide): 11.08MM **Privately Held**
Web: www.compasswater.com
SIC: 3589 Water treatment equipment, industrial

(P-7653)
DE NORA WATER TECHNOLOGIES LLC
1230 Rosecrans Ave Ste 300 (90266-2477)
PHONE...................................310 618-9700
Marwan Nesicolaci, *VP*
EMP: 19
SALES (corp-wide): 885.74MM **Privately Held**
SIC: 3589 Water treatment equipment, industrial
HQ: De Nora Water Technologies Llc
3000 Advance Ln
Colmar PA
215 997-4000

(P-7654)

DYNAMIC COOKING SYSTEMS INC

Also Called: Fisher & Paykel
695 Town Center Dr Ste 180 (92626-1924)
PHONE..............................714 372-7000
Laurence Mawhinney, *CEO*
Stuart Broadhurst, *
▲ **EMP: 700 EST: 1987**
SQ FT: 140,000
SALES (est): 95.31MM Privately Held
SIC: 3589 Cooking equipment, commercial
HQ: Fisher & Paykel Appliances Usa
    Holdings Inc.
    695 Town Center Dr # 180
    Costa Mesa CA

(P-7655)

ENAQUA

1350 Specialty Dr Ste D (92081-8522)
PHONE..............................760 599-2644
Manoj Kumar Jhawar, *CEO*
Mark Maki, *
Rudra Mishra, *
▲ **EMP: 30 EST: 1985**
SQ FT: 26,000
SALES (est): 9.18MM
SALES (corp-wide): 4.66B Privately Held
Web: www.enaqua.com
SIC: 3589 Water treatment equipment,
    industrial
HQ: Grundfos Ab
    Lunnagardsgatan 6
    MOlndal
    730958161

(P-7656)

ENGINEERED FOOD SYSTEMS

2490 Anselmo Dr (92879-8089)
P.O. Box 28321 (92809-0144)
PHONE..............................714 921-9913
Martin Olguin, *Pr*
Irma Olguin, *
▲ **EMP: 25 EST: 2008**
SQ FT: 18,000
SALES (est): 3.86MM Privately Held
Web: www.efs-eng.com
SIC: 3589 5084 Food warming equipment,
    commercial; Food product manufacturing
    machinery

(P-7657)

FILTRONICS INC

16872 Hale Ave Ste B (92606-5064)
PHONE..............................714 630-5040
EMP: 17 EST: 1974
SALES (est): 2.46MM Privately Held
Web: www.filtronics.com
SIC: 3589 Water treatment equipment,
    industrial

(P-7658)

FLUIDRA USA LLC (PA)

2882 Whiptail Loop Ste 100 (92010-6757)
PHONE..............................904 378-0999
Eloy P Corts, *Ch Bd*
Pere Ballart, *
Stephen B De Bever, *
Janice Hague, *
◆ **EMP: 20 EST: 1993**
SQ FT: 43,000
SALES (est): 9.77MM Privately Held
Web: www.fluidrausa.com
SIC: 3589 3561 5091 Swimming pool filter
    and water conditioning systems; Pumps
    and pumping equipment; Sporting and
    recreation goods

(P-7659)

G A SYSTEMS INC

226 W Carleton Ave (92867-3608)
PHONE..............................714 848-7529
Steven Anderson, *Pr*
EMP: 17 EST: 1968
SQ FT: 19,400
SALES (est): 3.08MM Privately Held
Web: www.gasystemsmfg.com
SIC: 3589 Commercial cooking and
    foodwarming equipment

(P-7660)

GORLITZ SEWER & DRAIN INC

10132 Norwalk Blvd (90670-3326)
PHONE..............................562 944-3060
James Kruger, *CEO*
Gerd Kruger, *
Elba Kruger, *
▲ **EMP: 30 EST: 1974**
SQ FT: 33,300
SALES (est): 4.34MM Privately Held
Web: www.gorlitz.com
SIC: 3589 Sewer cleaning equipment, power

(P-7661)

HYDRODEX LLC

31225 La Baya Dr (91362-4019)
PHONE..............................800 218-8813
EMP: 20 EST: 2019
SALES (est): 1.42MM Privately Held
Web: www.hydrodex.com
SIC: 3589 Water treatment equipment,
    industrial

(P-7662)

INNOVATIVE CONTROL SYSTEMS INC

20992 Bake Pkwy Ste 106 (92630-2170)
PHONE..............................800 246-3469
Cindy Penchishen, *Brnch Mgr*
EMP: 26
SALES (corp-wide): 8.51B Publicly Held
Web: www.icscarwashsystems.com
SIC: 3589 Car washing machinery
HQ: Innovative Control Systems, Inc.
    81 Highland Ave Ste 301
    Bethlehem PA

(P-7663)

J F DUNCAN INDUSTRIES INC (PA)

Also Called: Duray
4380 Ayers Ave (90058-4306)
PHONE..............................562 862-4269
Johnny F Wong, *CEO*
Don Durward, *
▲ **EMP: 86 EST: 1988**
SALES (est): 25.12MM Privately Held
Web: www.durayduncan.com
SIC: 3589 Cooking equipment, commercial

(P-7664)

J L WINGERT COMPANY

1298 N Blue Gum St (92806-2413)
P.O. Box 6207 (92846-6207)
PHONE..............................714 379-5519
Tommy Thomas, *CEO*
Reeve Thomas, *
EMP: 65 EST: 1965
SALES (est): 9.31MM Privately Held
Web: www.jlwingert.com
SIC: 3589 5084 Water treatment equipment,
    industrial; Industrial machinery and
    equipment

(P-7665)

JACUZZI INC (DH)

Also Called: Jacuzzi Outdoor Products

17872 Gillette Ave Ste 300 (92614-6502)
PHONE..............................909 606-7733
Roy A Jacuzzi, *Ch Bd*
Thomas Koos, *
Donald C Devine, *
◆ **EMP: 110 EST: 1979**
SALES (est): 457.27MM
SALES (corp-wide): 423.13K Privately Held
Web: www.jacuzzi.com
SIC: 3589 3088 Swimming pool filter and
    water conditioning systems; Hot tubs,
    plastics or fiberglass
HQ: Jacuzzi Brands Llc
    17872 Gillette Ave # 300
    Irvine CA
    909 606-1416

(P-7666)

JWC ENVIRONMENTAL INC

Also Called: Disposable Waste System
2600 S Garnsey St (92707-3339)
PHONE..............................714 662-5829
Steve Glomb, *CFO*
EMP: 100
SQ FT: 45,637
Web: www.jwce.com
SIC: 3589 Sewage treatment equipment
HQ: Jwc Environmental, Inc.
    2850 Redhill Ave Ste 125
    Santa Ana CA

(P-7667)

KELLERMYER BERGENSONS SVCS LLC (PA)

3605 Ocean Ranch Blvd Ste 200
(92056-2693)
PHONE..............................760 631-5111
Mark Minasian, *CEO*
Christian Cornelius-knudsen, *Pr*
Aj Long, *CFO*
Zulfiqar Rashid, *CIO*
Nathaniel Shaw, *Chief Commercial Officer*
EMP: 28 EST: 2001
SALES (est): 620.83MM
**SALES (corp-wide): 620.83MM Privately
Held**
Web: www.kbs-services.com
SIC: 3589 Commercial cleaning equipment

(P-7668)

LIFESOURCE WATER SYSTEMS INC (PA)

523 S Fair Oaks Ave (91105-2605)
PHONE..............................626 792-9996
B J Wright, *Pr*
EMP: 22 EST: 1984
SQ FT: 10,000
SALES (est): 10.7MM
**SALES (corp-wide): 10.7MM Privately
Held**
Web: www.lifesourcewater.com
SIC: 3589 5074 Water purification
    equipment, household type; Plumbing and
    hydronic heating supplies

(P-7669)

M D MANUFACTURING INC

34970 Mcmurtrey Ave (93308-9578)
P.O. Box 70277 (93387-0277)
PHONE..............................661 283-7550
Raymond Stewart, *Pr*
◆ **EMP: 19 EST: 1961**
SQ FT: 34,000
SALES (est): 4.67MM Privately Held
Web: www.builtinvacuum.com
SIC: 3589 Vacuum cleaners and sweepers,
    electric: industrial

(P-7670)

MANN+HMMEL WTR FLUID SLTONS IN (DH)

93 S La Patera Ln (93117-3246)
PHONE..............................805 964-8003
Peter Knappe, *Pr*
Kevin Edberg, *
◆ **EMP: 90 EST: 1990**
SQ FT: 40,000
SALES (est): 24.17MM
SALES (corp-wide): 5.01B Privately Held
Web:
water-fluid-filtration.mann-hummel.com
SIC: 3589 Water treatment equipment,
    industrial
HQ: Mann+Hummel Water & Fluid
    Solutions Gmbh
    Kasteler Str. 45
    Wiesbaden HE
    611 962-6001

(P-7671)

MAR COR PURIFICATION INC

6351 Orangethorpe Ave (90620-1340)
PHONE..............................800 633-3080
Sean West, *Brnch Mgr*
EMP: 29
SIC: 3589 Water treatment equipment,
    industrial
HQ: Mar Cor Purification, Inc.
    4450 Township Line Rd
    Skippack PA
    800 633-3080

(P-7672)

MAZZEI INJECTOR COMPANY LLC

500 Rooster Dr (93307-9555)
PHONE..............................661 363-6500
Angelo Mazzei, *CEO*
Geofffrey Whynot, *Pr*
Mary Mazzei, *Bd of Dir*
▲ **EMP: 24 EST: 1978**
SALES (est): 2.49MM
**SALES (corp-wide): 8.06MM Privately
Held**
Web: www.mazzei.net
SIC: 3589 Water treatment equipment,
    industrial
PA: Mazzei Injector Corporation
    500 Rooster Dr
    Bakersfield CA
    661 363-6500

(P-7673)

MEDIA BLAST & ABRASIVE INC

591 Apollo St (92821-3127)
PHONE..............................714 257-0484
Ronald Storer, *Pr*
EMP: 19 EST: 1997
SALES (est): 4.58MM Privately Held
Web: www.mediablast.com
SIC: 3589 3822 Sandblasting equipment;
    Environmental controls

(P-7674)

MEISSNER MFG CO INC (PA)

Also Called: Unicel
21701 Prairie St (91311-5835)
PHONE..............................818 678-0400
EMP: 53 EST: 1958
SALES (est): 7.84MM
**SALES (corp-wide): 7.84MM Privately
Held**
SIC: 3589 Swimming pool filter and water
    conditioning systems

PRODUCTS & SVCS

(P-7675)
MYTEE PRODUCTS INC
13655 Stowe Dr (92064-6873)
PHONE..............................858 679-1191
John La Barbera, *Pr*
Paul La Barbera, *
Gina La Barbera, *
◆ EMP: 43 EST: 1991
SQ FT: 45,000
SALES (est): 8.91MM Privately Held
Web: www.mytee.com
SIC: 3589 Commercial cleaning equipment

(P-7676)
N/S CORPORATION (PA)
Also Called: NS Wash Systems
235 W Florence Ave (90301-1293)
PHONE..............................310 412-7074
G Thomas Ennis Senior, *CEO*
Francis Penggardjaja, *
Lumen Ong, *
◆ EMP: 84 EST: 1967
SQ FT: 80,000
SALES (est): 20.74MM
SALES (corp-wide): 20.74MM Privately Held
Web: www.nswash.com
SIC: 3589 Car washing machinery

(P-7677)
NALCO WTR PRTRTMENT SLTONS LLC
Also Called: Nalco Water
1961 Petra Ln (92870-6749)
PHONE..............................714 792-0708
EMP: 28
SALES (corp-wide): 14.19B Publicly Held
SIC: 3589 Water treatment equipment, industrial
HQ: Nalco Water Pretreatment Solutions, Llc
1601 W Diehl Rd
Naperville IL
708 754-2550

(P-7678)
OSMOSIS TECHNOLOGY INC
Also Called: Osmotik
6900 Hermosa Cir (90620-1151)
PHONE..............................714 670-9303
Mike Joulakian, *Pr*
Sonia Joulakian, *VP*
EMP: 21 EST: 1984
SQ FT: 13,000
SALES (est): 2.9MM Privately Held
Web: www.osmotik.com
SIC: 3589 Water filters and softeners, household type

(P-7679)
PRODUCT SOLUTIONS INC
1182 N Knollwood Cir (92801-1307)
P.O. Box 6601 (92607-6601)
PHONE..............................714 545-9757
Robert Kreaton, *CEO*
Judith Keaton, *
▲ EMP: 50 EST: 1993
SQ FT: 25,000
SALES (est): 9.13MM Privately Held
Web: www.fastproductsolutions.com
SIC: 3589 3631 Commercial cooking and foodwarming equipment; Household cooking equipment

(P-7680)
PRONTO PRODUCTS CO (PA)
9850 Siempre Viva Rd (92154-7247)
PHONE..............................619 661-6995
Carlos Matos, *CEO*
William E Parrot, *

Martha J Wagner, *
Barbara Parrot, *
EMP: 39 EST: 1962
SALES (est): 4.42MM
SALES (corp-wide): 4.42MM Privately Held
Web: www.prontoproducts.com
SIC: 3589 3496 Commercial cooking and foodwarming equipment; Miscellaneous fabricated wire products

(P-7681)
PURI TECH INC
Also Called: Everfilt
3167 Progress Cir (91752-1112)
PHONE..............................951 360-8380
Barbara J Andrew, *Pr*
EMP: 22 EST: 1979
SQ FT: 10,600
SALES (est): 978.56K Privately Held
Web: www.everfilt.com
SIC: 3589 5074 Water treatment equipment, industrial; Water purification equipment

(P-7682)
QMP INC
25070 Avenue Tibbitts (91355-3447)
PHONE..............................661 294-6860
Freddy Vidal, *Pr*
Irma Vidal, *
▲ EMP: 45 EST: 1994
SQ FT: 40,000
SALES (est): 9.25MM Privately Held
Web: www.qmpusa.com
SIC: 3589 Sewage and water treatment equipment

(P-7683)
SEACO TECHNOLOGIES INC
280 El Cerrito Dr (93305-1328)
PHONE..............................661 326-1522
EMP: 28
Web: www.seacotech.com
SIC: 3589 Water treatment equipment, industrial
PA: Seaco Technologies, Inc.
3220 Patton Way
Bakersfield CA

(P-7684)
SEWER RODDING EQUIPMENT CO (PA)
Also Called: Flexible Video Systems
3217 Carter Ave (90292-5554)
PHONE..............................310 301-9009
Patrick Crane, *CEO*
EMP: 25 EST: 1932
SQ FT: 24,000
SALES (est): 9.75MM
SALES (corp-wide): 9.75MM Privately Held
SIC: 3589 Sewer cleaning equipment, power

(P-7685)
SHEPARD BROS INC (PA)
503 S Cypress St (90631-6126)
PHONE..............................562 697-1366
Ronald Shepard, *CEO*
Duane Shepard, *
Jon Wynkoop, *
▲ EMP: 119 EST: 1976
SQ FT: 57,830
SALES (est): 30.98MM
SALES (corp-wide): 30.98MM Privately Held
Web: www.shepardbros.com
SIC: 3589 5169 Sewage and water treatment equipment; Chemicals and allied products, nec

(P-7686)
SNOWPURE LLC
Also Called: Snowpure Water Technologies
130 Calle Iglesia Ste A (92672-7535)
P.O. Box 73368 (92673-0113)
PHONE..............................949 240-2188
Michael Snow, *Managing Member*
◆ EMP: 30 EST: 1979
SALES (est): 5.71MM Privately Held
Web: www.snowpure.com
SIC: 3589 5074 Water purification equipment, household type; Water purification equipment

(P-7687)
SPENUZZA INC
Also Called: Imperial Mfg Co
913 Oak Ave (91010-1951)
PHONE..............................626 358-8063
Peter Spenuzza Junior, *Pr*
EMP: 47
SALES (corp-wide): 4.03B Publicly Held
Web: www.imperialrange.com
SIC: 3589 Cooking equipment, commercial
HQ: Spenuzza, Inc.
1128 Sherborn St
Corona CA
951 281-1830

(P-7688)
SPENUZZA INC (HQ)
Also Called: Imperial Coml Cooking Eqp
1128 Sherborn St (92879-2089)
PHONE..............................951 281-1830
Peter Spenuzza, *CEO*
◆ EMP: 71 EST: 1957
SQ FT: 100,000
SALES (est): 25.31MM
SALES (corp-wide): 4.03B Publicly Held
Web: www.imperialrange.com
SIC: 3589 3556 Cooking equipment, commercial; Food products machinery
PA: The Middleby Corporation
1400 Toastmaster Dr
Elgin IL
847 741-3300

(P-7689)
TIMBUCKTOO MANUFACTURING INC
Also Called: T M I
1633 W 134th St (90249-2013)
PHONE..............................310 323-1134
Juen Lee, *CEO*
Kyu Lee, *
▲ EMP: 43 EST: 1974
SQ FT: 50,000
SALES (est): 4.69MM Privately Held
Web: www.timbucktoomfg.com
SIC: 3589 Car washing machinery

(P-7690)
VEOLIA WTS SERVICES USA INC
7777 Industry Ave (90660-4303)
PHONE..............................562 942-2200
Michael Dimick, *Bmch Mgr*
EMP: 60
SQ FT: 32,091
Web: www.suezwatertechnologies.com
SIC: 3589 Water treatment equipment, industrial
HQ: Veolia Wts Services Usa, Inc.
4545 Patent Rd
Norfolk VA
757 855-9000

(P-7691)
WATER WORKS INC
5490 Complex St Ste 601 (92123-1126)
PHONE..............................858 499-0119
John Warmes, *Pr*
EMP: 26 EST: 2006
SALES (est): 4.28MM Privately Held
Web: www.ultrapurewaterworks.com
SIC: 3589 Water treatment equipment, industrial

(P-7692)
WESFAC INC (HQ)
Also Called: Wespac
9300 Hall Rd (90241-5309)
PHONE..............................562 861-2160
Don Hyatt, *Pr*
Julie Hyatt, *
EMP: 17 EST: 1982
SQ FT: 55,000
SALES (est): 985.15K
SALES (corp-wide): 4.12MM Privately Held
Web: www.omniteaminc.com
SIC: 3589 3431 Commercial cooking and foodwarming equipment; Metal sanitary ware
PA: Omniment Industries, Inc
4380 Ayers Ave
Vernon CA
562 923-9660

(P-7693)
WHITTIER FILTRATION INC (DH)
120 S State College Blvd Ste 175 (92821-5834)
PHONE..............................714 986-5300
Jim Brown, *Pr*
John M Santelli, *Sec*
◆ EMP: 21 EST: 1977
SQ FT: 80,000
SALES (est): 9.84MM Privately Held
SIC: 3589 Water treatment equipment, industrial
HQ: Veolia Water Technologies, Inc.
4001 Weston Pkwy Ste 100
Cary NC

(P-7694)
YANCHEWSKI & WARDELL ENTPS INC
Also Called: Ecowater Systems
2241 La Mirada Dr (92081-8828)
PHONE..............................760 754-1960
Ryan Wardell, *Pr*
EMP: 95 EST: 2006
SALES (est): 8.15MM Privately Held
Web: www.ecowatersocal.com
SIC: 3589 3677 3639 Water purification equipment, household type; Filtration devices, electronic; Hot water heaters, household

(P-7695)
YARDNEY WATER MGT SYSTEMS INC (PA)
Also Called: Yardney Water MGT Systems
6666 Box Springs Blvd (92507-0736)
PHONE..............................951 656-6716
Chris Phillips, *Pr*
◆ EMP: 39 EST: 1948
SQ FT: 55,000
SALES (est): 7.15MM Privately Held
Web: www.yardneyfilters.com
SIC: 3589 Water treatment equipment, industrial

(P-7696)
Z P M INC
5770 Thornwood Dr Ste C (93117-3812)
PHONE................................805 681-3511
EMP: 22 **EST:** 1994
SQ FT: 2,400
SALES (est): 1.01MM **Privately Held**
SIC: 3589 5999 Water treatment equipment, industrial; Water purification equipment

(P-7697)
ZODIAC POOL SOLUTIONS LLC (PA)
2882 Whiptail Loop Ste 100 (92010-6757)
PHONE................................760 599-9600
Francois Mirallie, *Pr*
EMP: 47 **EST:** 2016
SALES (est): 455.34MM
SALES (corp-wide): 455.34MM **Privately Held**
Web: www.fluidrausa.com
SIC: 3589 Swimming pool filter and water conditioning systems

(P-7698)
ZODIAC POOL SYSTEMS LLC (HQ)
Also Called: Jandy Pool Products
2882 Whiptail Loop Ste 100 (92010-6757)
PHONE................................760 599-9600
Bruce Brooks, *CEO*
Anthony Prudhomme, *
Mike Allanc, *
◆ **EMP:** 250 **EST:** 1999
SALES (est): 455.34MM
SALES (corp-wide): 455.34MM **Privately Held**
Web: www.fluidrausa.com
SIC: 3589 3999 Swimming pool filter and water conditioning systems; Hot tub and spa covers
PA: Zodiac Pool Solutions Llc
     2882 Whiptail Loop # 100
     Carlsbad CA
     760 599-9600

3592 Carburetors, Pistons, Rings, Valves

(P-7699)
CP-CARRILLO INC (DH)
1902 Mcgaw Ave (92614-0910)
PHONE................................949 567-9000
▲ **EMP:** 160 **EST:** 2011
SQ FT: 31,840
SALES (est): 28.8MM
SALES (corp-wide): 3.39B **Privately Held**
Web: www.cp-carrillo.com
SIC: 3592 3714 Pistons and piston rings; Connecting rods, motor vehicle engine
HQ: Pankl Holdings, Inc.
     1902 Mcgaw Ave
     Irvine CA

(P-7700)
CP-CARRILLO INC
17401 Armstrong Ave (92614-5723)
PHONE................................949 567-9000
Barry Calvert, *Managing Member*
EMP: 30
SALES (corp-wide): 3.39B **Privately Held**
Web: www.cp-carrillo.com
SIC: 3592 3714 Pistons and piston rings; Connecting rods, motor vehicle engine
HQ: Cp-Carrillo, Inc.
     1902 Mcgaw Ave
     Irvine CA

(P-7701)
PACIFIC PISTON RING CO INC
3620 Eastham Dr (90232-2411)
P.O. Box 927 (90232-0927)
PHONE................................310 836-3322
Forest Shannon, *Pr*
Michael Shannon, *
Christina Davis, *
EMP: 58 **EST:** 1921
SQ FT: 35,000
SALES (est): 8.06MM **Privately Held**
Web: www.pacificpistonring.com
SIC: 3592 Pistons and piston rings

(P-7702)
PERFORMANCE MOTORSPORTS INC
5100 Campus Dr Ste 100 (92660-2191)
PHONE................................714 898-9763
▲ **EMP:** 265
SIC: 3592 Pistons and piston rings

(P-7703)
PROBE RACING COMPONENTS INC
Also Called: Kwikparts.com
5022 Onyx St (90503-2742)
PHONE................................310 784-2977
▲ **EMP:** 23 **EST:** 1987
SQ FT: 25,000
SALES (est): 2.35MM **Privately Held**
Web: www.vigilanteparts.com
SIC: 3592 3463 Pistons and piston rings; Engine or turbine forgings, nonferrous

(P-7704)
ROSS RACING PISTONS
625 S Douglas St (90245-4812)
PHONE................................310 536-0100
Ken Roble, *Pr*
J B Moe Mills, *VP*
Joy Roble, *
EMP: 55 **EST:** 1979
SQ FT: 25,000
SALES (est): 4.51MM **Privately Held**
Web: www.rosspistons.com
SIC: 3592 Pistons and piston rings

(P-7705)
RTR INDUSTRIES LLC (PA)
Also Called: Grant Piston Rings
4430 E Miraloma Ave Ste B (92807-1840)
PHONE................................714 996-0050
▲ **EMP:** 37 **EST:** 2002
SALES (est): 4.69MM
SALES (corp-wide): 4.69MM **Privately Held**
Web: www.grantpistonrings.com
SIC: 3592 Pistons and piston rings

(P-7706)
SEABISCUIT MOTORSPORTS INC
10800 Valley View St (90630-5016)
PHONE................................714 898-9763
EMP: 30
SALES (corp-wide): 195.05MM **Privately Held**
Web: www.wiseco.com
SIC: 3592 3714 Pistons and piston rings; Motor vehicle parts and accessories
HQ: Seabiscuit Motorsports, Inc.
     7201 Industrial Park Blvd
     Mentor OH
     440 951-6600

(P-7707)
SVF FLOW CONTROLS LLC
5595 Fresca Dr (90623-1006)
PHONE................................562 802-2255
Wayne Ulanski, *Pr*
EMP: 29 **EST:** 2018
SALES (est): 181.55K **Privately Held**
Web: www.svf.net
SIC: 3592 Valves, engine

3593 Fluid Power Cylinders And Actuators

(P-7708)
C & H MACHINE INC
Also Called: Support Equipment
943 S Andreasen Dr (92029)
PHONE................................760 746-6459
Lyle J Anderson, *Ex VP*
Charles Gohlich, *
EMP: 70 **EST:** 1964
SQ FT: 13,000
SALES (est): 9.9MM **Privately Held**
Web: www.c-hmachine.com
SIC: 3593 3599 Fluid power cylinders and actuators; Machine shop, jobbing and repair

(P-7709)
RTC ARSPACE - CHTSWRTH DIV INC (PA)
20409 Prairie St (91311-6029)
PHONE................................818 341-3344
James B Hart, *CEO*
Bj Schramm, *Pr*
Bill Hart, *
Elizabeth Hart, *
◆ **EMP:** 121 **EST:** 1958
SQ FT: 42,000
SALES (est): 27.44MM
SALES (corp-wide): 27.44MM **Privately Held**
Web: www.rtcaerospace.com
SIC: 3593 3594 3599 Fluid power cylinders and actuators; Fluid power pumps and motors; Machine shop, jobbing and repair

3594 Fluid Power Pumps And Motors

(P-7710)
BERNELL HYDRAULICS INC (PA)
8821 Etiwanda Ave (91739-9625)
P.O. Box 417 (91739-0417)
PHONE................................909 899-1751
TOLL FREE: 800
Terrance B Jones Senior, *Ch Bd*
Rhonda A Garness, *
John S Clemons, *
EMP: 28 **EST:** 1977
SALES (est): 9.48MM
SALES (corp-wide): 9.48MM **Privately Held**
Web: www.bernellhydraulics.com
SIC: 3594 5084 3621 3593 Pumps, hydraulic power transfer; Hydraulic systems equipment and supplies; Motors and generators; Fluid power cylinders and actuators

(P-7711)
CRISSAIR INC
28909 Avenue Williams (91355-4183)
PHONE................................661 367-3300
Michael Alfred, *Pr*
Patrick Lacanfora, *Sr VP*
Eric Grupp, *VP*
Beverly Miller, *VP*
EMP: 185 **EST:** 1954
SQ FT: 40,000
SALES (est): 45.98MM **Publicly Held**
Web: www.crissair.com
SIC: 3594 3492 Motors, pneumatic; Fluid power valves and hose fittings
PA: Esco Technologies Inc.
     9900 Clayton Rd Ste A
     Saint Louis MO

(P-7712)
HYPERION MOTORS LLC
1032 W Taft Ave (92865-4119)
PHONE................................714 363-5858
Angelo Kafantaris, *Prin*
EMP: 50 **EST:** 2011
SALES (est): 4.99MM **Privately Held**
Web: www.hyperion.inc
SIC: 3594 Fluid power pumps and motors

(P-7713)
PARKER-HANNIFIN CORPORATION
Also Called: Cylinder Division
221 Helicopter Cir (92878-5032)
PHONE................................951 280-3800
Donald P Szmania, *Brnch Mgr*
EMP: 88
SALES (corp-wide): 19.07B **Publicly Held**
Web: www.parker.com
SIC: 3594 3728 3593 Fluid power pumps and motors; Aircraft parts and equipment, nec; Fluid power cylinders and actuators
PA: Parker-Hannifin Corporation
     6035 Parkland Blvd
     Cleveland OH
     216 896-3000

(P-7714)
PARKER-HANNIFIN CORPORATION
Composite Sealing Systems Div
7664 Panasonic Way (92154-8206)
PHONE................................619 661-7000
Jim Rando, *Mgr*
EMP: 130
SALES (corp-wide): 19.07B **Publicly Held**
Web: www.parker.com
SIC: 3594 Fluid power pumps and motors
PA: Parker-Hannifin Corporation
     6035 Parkland Blvd
     Cleveland OH
     216 896-3000

(P-7715)
WESTERN HYDROSTATICS INC (PA)
1956 Keats Dr (92501-1747)
PHONE................................951 784-2133
TOLL FREE: 800
John Starke Scott, *Pr*
Tandy W Scott, *
Barnett Totten, *
▲ **EMP:** 28 **EST:** 1985
SALES (est): 4.44MM
SALES (corp-wide): 4.44MM **Privately Held**
Web: www.weshyd.com
SIC: 3594 7699 5084 Hydrostatic drives (transmissions); Hydraulic equipment repair ; Hydraulic systems equipment and supplies

3596 Scales And Balances, Except Laboratory

(P-7716)
JONEL ENGINEERING
500 E Walnut Ave (92832-2540)

P R O D U C T S   &   S V C S

P.O. Box 798 (92836-0798)
PHONE..............................714 879-2360
John Lawson, *Ch*
Mike Lawson, *Pr*
▼ **EMP:** 20 **EST:** 1963
SQ FT: 8,000
SALES (est): 3.23MM **Privately Held**
Web: www.jonel.com
SIC: 3596 5045 Weighing machines and
    apparatus; Computers, nec

3599 Industrial Machinery, Nec

(P-7717)
3-D PRECISION MACHINE INC
42132 Remington Ave (92590-2547)
PHONE..............................951 296-5449
Linda Luoma, *Pr*
Roy Luoma, *VP*
EMP: 30 **EST:** 2006
SQ FT: 14,000
SALES (est): 5.28MM **Privately Held**
Web: www.3dprecisionmachine.com
SIC: 3599 Machine shop, jobbing and repair

(P-7718)
3D MACHINE CO INC
4790 E Wesley Dr (92807-1941)
PHONE..............................714 777-8985
EMP: 30 **EST:** 1996
SQ FT: 3,300
SALES (est): 5.1MM **Privately Held**
Web: www.3dmachineco.com
SIC: 3599 Machine shop, jobbing and repair

(P-7719)
3DCAM INTERNATIONAL CORP
9801 Variel Ave (91311-4317)
PHONE..............................818 773-8777
Gary Vassighi, *Pr*
EMP: 18 **EST:** 2004
SALES (est): 2.65MM **Privately Held**
Web: www.3d-cam.com
SIC: 3599 3089 Machine shop, jobbing and
    repair; Injection molding of plastics

(P-7720)
5TH AXIS INC (PA)
7140 Engineer Rd (92111-1422)
PHONE..............................858 505-0432
▲ **EMP:** 200 **EST:** 2005
SQ FT: 21,000
SALES (est): 28MM
SALES (corp-wide): 28MM **Privately Held**
Web: www.5thaxis.com
SIC: 3599 Machine shop, jobbing and repair

(P-7721)
A & A MACHINE & DEV CO INC
16625 Gramercy Pl (90247-5201)
PHONE..............................310 532-7706
Arlene Hymovitz, *Pr*
Eric Hymovitz, *VP*
EMP: 18 **EST:** 1972
SQ FT: 12,000
SALES (est): 3.05MM **Privately Held**
Web: www.aamach.com
SIC: 3599 Machine shop, jobbing and repair

(P-7722)
A & B AEROSPACE INC
612 S Ayon Ave (91702-5122)
PHONE..............................626 334-2976
Kenneth Smith, *Pr*
Malcolm Smith, *
EMP: 35 **EST:** 1950
SQ FT: 23,000

SALES (est): 5.22MM **Privately Held**
Web: www.abaerospace.com
SIC: 3599 Machine shop, jobbing and repair

(P-7723)
A & D PRECISION MFG INC
4751 E Hunter Ave (92807-1940)
PHONE..............................714 779-2714
Phong Vo, *CEO*
Newton Pham, *CFO*
EMP: 21 **EST:** 1988
SQ FT: 9,000
SALES (est): 2.14MM **Privately Held**
Web: www.adprecisionmfg.com
SIC: 3599 3728 Machine shop, jobbing and
    repair; Aircraft parts and equipment, nec

(P-7724)
A & H ENGINEERING & MFG INC
Also Called: A & H Tool Engineering
17109 Edwards Rd (90703-2423)
PHONE..............................562 623-9717
Asher Sharoni, *Pr*
Tova Sharoni, *CFO*
EMP: 27 **EST:** 2005
SQ FT: 15,000
SALES (est): 777.29K **Privately Held**
SIC: 3599 Grinding castings for the trade

(P-7725)
A & M ENGINEERING INC
15854 Salvatiera St (91706-6603)
PHONE..............................626 813-2020
Boris Beljak Senior, *Pr*
Boris Beljak Senior, *Pr*
Boris Beljak Junior, *VP*
Roy Beljak, *
Anita Beljak, *
EMP: 80 **EST:** 1973
SQ FT: 25,000
SALES (est): 9.79MM **Privately Held**
Web: www.amengineeringinc.com
SIC: 3599 3812 3537 Machine shop, jobbing
    and repair; Search and navigation
    equipment; Industrial trucks and tractors

(P-7726)
A & R ENGINEERING CO INC
Also Called: A & R
1053 E Bedmar St (90746-3601)
PHONE..............................310 603-9060
Murat Sehidoglu, *Pr*
EMP: 72 **EST:** 1982
SQ FT: 23,334
SALES (est): 9.66MM **Privately Held**
Web: www.arengr.com
SIC: 3599 Machine shop, jobbing and repair

(P-7727)
A-Z MFG INC
Also Called: AZ Manufacturing
3101 W Segerstrom Ave (92704-5811)
PHONE..............................714 444-4446
Ann Lukas, *Prin*
Gary Lukas, *
EMP: 40 **EST:** 1993
SQ FT: 16,096
SALES (est): 6.37MM **Privately Held**
Web: www.azmfginc.com
SIC: 3599 Machine shop, jobbing and repair

(P-7728)
ABEN MACHINE PRODUCTS INC
Also Called: Aben
9550 Owensmouth Ave (91311-4801)
PHONE..............................818 960-4502
Nabeel Saoud, *Pr*
Nabeel Saoud, *Pr*
Esdras Giron, *Product Vice President*
EMP: 17 **EST:** 1998

SALES (est): 2.46MM **Privately Held**
Web: www.abenusa.com
SIC: 3599 Machine shop, jobbing and repair

(P-7729)
ACCU-TECH LASER PROCESSING INC
1175 Linda Vista Dr (92078-3811)
PHONE..............................760 744-6692
Michael C Gericke, *Pr*
Roger Underwood, *
EMP: 33 **EST:** 2006
SQ FT: 6,500
SALES (est): 2.67MM **Privately Held**
Web: www.accutechlaser.com
SIC: 3599 Machine shop, jobbing and repair

(P-7730)
ACCURATE PRFMCE MACHINING INC
2255 S Grand Ave (92705-5206)
PHONE..............................714 434-7811
Robert Keith Fischer, *CEO*
Larry Taylor, *VP*
Karen Fischer, *VP*
EMP: 21 **EST:** 1996
SQ FT: 3,200
SALES (est): 2.79MM **Privately Held**
Web: www.cncapm.com
SIC: 3599 Machine shop, jobbing and repair

(P-7731)
ACE INDUSTRIES INC
195 Mace St (91911-5820)
PHONE..............................619 482-2700
Bobby Yoo, *CEO*
Bobby Yoo, *Pr*
Joy Yoo, *Treas*
▲ **EMP:** 20 **EST:** 1998
SQ FT: 15,000
SALES (est): 2.52MM **Privately Held**
Web: www.aceindustriesinc.com
SIC: 3599 Machine shop, jobbing and repair

(P-7732)
ACE MACHINE SHOP INC
11200 Wright Rd (90262-3124)
PHONE..............................310 608-2277
Pedro Gallinucci, *Pr*
Lucia Gallinucci, *
EMP: 70 **EST:** 1956
SQ FT: 35,000
SALES (est): 7.04MM **Privately Held**
Web: www.isconcepts.com
SIC: 3599 Machine shop, jobbing and repair

(P-7733)
ACE TUBE BENDING
14 Journey (92656-3317)
PHONE..............................949 362-2220
EMP: 22 **EST:** 1978
SALES (est): 2.64MM **Privately Held**
Web: www.acetubebending.com
SIC: 3599 Machine shop, jobbing and repair

(P-7734)
ACKLEY METAL PRODUCTS INC
Also Called: Waco Products
1311 E Saint Gertrude Pl Ste B
(92705-5216)
PHONE..............................714 979-7431
Paul Ackley, *Pr*
EMP: 17 **EST:** 1985
SQ FT: 3,200
SALES (est): 881.81K **Privately Held**
Web: www.ackleymetal.com
SIC: 3599 Machine shop, jobbing and repair

(P-7735)
ADVANCED ENGINEERING & EDM INC
13007 Kirkham Way Ste A (92064-7152)
PHONE..............................858 679-6800
Norm Turoff, *CEO*
Lindy Bauer, *Contrlr*
EMP: 17 **EST:** 2013
SALES (est): 1.55MM **Privately Held**
Web: www.aeedm.com
SIC: 3599 Machine shop, jobbing and repair

(P-7736)
ADVANCED ENGINERING AND EDM
13007 Kirkham Way Ste A (92064-7152)
PHONE..............................858 679-6800
William J Bauer, *Mng Pt*
Norm Turoff, *Mng Pt*
EMP: 20 **EST:** 2011
SALES (est): 2.62MM **Privately Held**
Web: www.aeedm.com
SIC: 3599 Machine shop, jobbing and repair

(P-7737)
ADVANCED JOINING TECHNOLOGIES INC
3030 Red Hill Ave (92705-5823)
PHONE..............................949 756-8091
EMP: 25
Web: www.ajt-inc.com
SIC: 3599 Machine shop, jobbing and repair

(P-7738)
ADVANCED MCHNING SOLUTIONS INC
3523 Main St Ste 606 (91911-0803)
PHONE..............................619 671-3055
Pamela Yuhm, *Pr*
EMP: 35 **EST:** 2005
SALES (est): 3.8MM **Privately Held**
Web: www.amssd.com
SIC: 3599 Machine shop, jobbing and repair

(P-7739)
AERO CHIP INC
13563 Freeway Dr (90670-5633)
PHONE..............................562 404-6300
Solomon M Gavrila, *CEO*
Liviu Pribac, *
EMP: 50 **EST:** 1988
SQ FT: 17,000
SALES (est): 8.38MM **Privately Held**
Web: www.aerochip.com
SIC: 3599 Machine shop, jobbing and repair

(P-7740)
AERO DYNAMIC MACHINING INC
7472 Chapman Ave (92841-2106)
PHONE..............................714 379-1073
Wendy Nguyen, *Ch Bd*
David Nguyen, *
Wendy Nguyen, *VP*
Kevin Tran, *
▲ **EMP:** 65 **EST:** 1998
SALES (est): 10.52MM **Privately Held**
Web: www.aerodynamicinc.com
SIC: 3599 3499 Machine shop, jobbing and
    repair; Fire- or burglary-resistive products

(P-7741)
AERO INDUSTRIES LLC
139 Industrial Way (93427-9592)
P.O. Box 198 (93427-0198)
PHONE..............................805 688-6734
Dave Watkins, *Mgr*
EMP: 340 **EST:** 2007

SALES (est): 919.54K
SALES (corp-wide): 53.11MM **Privately Held**
Web: www.aero-cnc.com
SIC: **3599** Machine shop, jobbing and repair
PA: Gavial Holdings, Inc.
1435 W Mccoy Ln
Santa Maria CA
805 614-0060

(P-7742)
AERO MECHANISM PRECISION INC
21700 Marilla St (91311-4125)
PHONE..................................818 886-1855
Palminder Sehmbey, *Pr*
EMP: 34 **EST:** 1996
SQ FT: 8,000
SALES (est): 4.9MM **Privately Held**
Web: www.aeromechanism.com
SIC: **3599** Machine shop, jobbing and repair

(P-7743)
AERO-K
2040 E Dyer Rd (92705-5710)
PHONE..................................626 350-5125
Robert Krusic, *Pr*
EMP: 45 **EST:** 1983
SALES (est): 6.28MM **Privately Held**
Web: www.aero-k.com
SIC: **3599** Machine shop, jobbing and repair

(P-7744)
AERODYNAMIC ENGINEERING INC
15495 Graham St (92649-1205)
PHONE..................................714 891-2651
Bob Waddell, *
Alfred Mayer, *
Ewald Eisel, *
Mark Schultz, *Manager*
▲ **EMP:** 40 **EST:** 1968
SQ FT: 12,000
SALES (est): 5.4MM **Privately Held**
Web: www.aerodynamic.net
SIC: **3599** 3769 Machine shop, jobbing and repair; Space vehicle equipment, nec

(P-7745)
AERODYNE PRCSION MACHINING INC
5471 Argosy Ave (92649-1038)
PHONE..................................714 891-1311
Raymond Krispel, *Pr*
Otto Schulz, *
Veronica Schultz, *
▲ **EMP:** 25 **EST:** 1986
SQ FT: 20,000
SALES (est): 4.65MM **Privately Held**
Web: www.aerodyneprecision.com
SIC: **3599** Machine shop, jobbing and repair

(P-7746)
AEROLIANT MANUFACTURING INC
Also Called: Fordon Grind Industries
1613 Lockness Pl (90501-5119)
PHONE..................................310 257-1903
Patricia A Wiacek, *Pr*
Greg Wiacek, *VP*
EMP: 20 **EST:** 2009
SQ FT: 7,200
SALES (est): 4.89MM **Privately Held**
Web: www.amratec.com
SIC: **3599** Machine shop, jobbing and repair

(P-7747)
AEROTEK INC
2751 Park View Ct Ste 221 (93036-5450)
PHONE..................................805 604-3000
EMP: 1569
SALES (corp-wide): 15.88B **Privately Held**
Web: www.aerotek.com
SIC: **3599** Machine and other job shop work
HQ: Aerotek, Inc.
7301 Parkway Dr
Hanover MD
410 694-5100

(P-7748)
AGA PRECISION SYSTEMS INC
122 E Dyer Rd (92707-3732)
PHONE..................................714 540-3163
Ralph E Wilson, *Pr*
Wesley Wilson, *VP*
EMP: 39 **EST:** 1978
SQ FT: 14,100
SALES (est): 487.99K **Privately Held**
Web: www.agaprecisioninc.com
SIC: **3599** Machine shop, jobbing and repair

(P-7749)
ALCO ENGRG & TOOLING CORP
Also Called: Alco Metal Fab
3001 Oak St (92707-4235)
PHONE..................................714 556-6060
Frank Vallefuoco, *Pr*
Frank Vallefuoco, *CEO*
Tom Hare, *
Angelo D'eramo, *Sec*
EMP: 40 **EST:** 1944
SQ FT: 32,000
SALES (est): 3.9MM **Privately Held**
Web: www.alcoge.com
SIC: **3599** Machine shop, jobbing and repair

(P-7750)
ALDO FRAGALE
Also Called: Turner Precision
17813 S Main St Ste 111 (90248-3542)
PHONE..................................310 324-0050
Aldo Fragale, *Pr*
EMP: 26 **EST:** 1984
SQ FT: 2,500
SALES (est): 486.04K **Privately Held**
SIC: **3599** Machine shop, jobbing and repair

(P-7751)
ALL 4-PCB NORTH AMERICA INC
345 Mira Loma Ave (91204-2912)
PHONE..................................866 734-9403
Torsten Reckert, *Pr*
Roland Lacap, *VP*
▲ **EMP:** 17 **EST:** 2001
SQ FT: 4,000
SALES (est): 2.72MM **Privately Held**
Web: www.all4-pcb.us
SIC: **3599** 3545 3541 3672 Chemical milling job shop; Milling machine attachments (machine tool accessories); Chemical milling machines; Printed circuit boards

(P-7752)
ALL DIAMETER GRINDING INC
725 N Main St (92868-1105)
PHONE..................................714 744-1200
Marvin W Goodwin, *Pr*
Jeff Goodwin, *VP*
Barbara Goodwin, *Sec*
EMP: 22 **EST:** 1960
SQ FT: 9,500
SALES (est): 2.75MM **Privately Held**
Web: www.alldiametergrinding.com
SIC: **3599** Machine shop, jobbing and repair

(P-7753)
ALL STAR PRECISION
8739 Lion St (91730-4428)
PHONE..................................909 944-8373
Scott Jackson, *Owner*
Ron Jackson, *Pt*
EMP: 23 **EST:** 2004
SALES (est): 2.32MM **Privately Held**
Web: www.allstarprecision.com
SIC: **3599** Machine shop, jobbing and repair

(P-7754)
ALPHA AVIATION COMPONENTS INC (PA)
16772 Schoenborn St (91343-6108)
PHONE..................................818 894-8801
Lidia Gorko, *Pr*
William Tudor, *
EMP: 26 **EST:** 1954
SQ FT: 18,000
SALES (est): 4.33MM
SALES (corp-wide): 4.33MM **Privately Held**
Web: www.alphaaci.com
SIC: **3599** 3451 3728 Machine shop, jobbing and repair; Screw machine products; Aircraft parts and equipment, nec

(P-7755)
ALTS TOOL & MACHINE INC
10926 Woodside Ave N (92071-3272)
P.O. Box 712485 (92072-2485)
PHONE..................................619 562-6653
EMP: 55
Web: www.altstool.com
SIC: **3599** Machine shop, jobbing and repair

(P-7756)
AM-TEK ENGINEERING INC
1180 E Francis St Ste C (91761-4802)
PHONE..................................909 673-1633
Boone Bounyaseng, *CEO*
EMP: 18 **EST:** 1998
SQ FT: 10,000
SALES (est): 2.49MM **Privately Held**
Web: www.amtekeng.com
SIC: **3599** Machine shop, jobbing and repair

(P-7757)
AMERICAN DEBURRING INC
Also Called: A Fab
20742 Linear Ln (92630-7804)
PHONE..................................949 457-9790
Robert L Campbell, *Pr*
Theresa Cook, *
EMP: 25 **EST:** 1973
SQ FT: 11,000
SALES (est): 3.2MM **Privately Held**
Web: www.afabcnc.com
SIC: **3599** Machine shop, jobbing and repair

(P-7758)
ARAM PRECISION TOOL & DIE INC
9758 Cozycroft Ave (91311-4417)
P.O. Box 3696 (91313-3696)
PHONE..................................818 998-1000
Avi Amichai, *Pr*
Rona Amichai, *Sec*
EMP: 23 **EST:** 1979
SQ FT: 12,000
SALES (est): 332.43K **Privately Held**
SIC: **3599** 3451 Machine shop, jobbing and repair; Screw machine products

(P-7759)
ARANDA TOOLING INC
13950 Yorba Ave (91710-5520)
PHONE..................................714 379-6565

Pedro Aranda, *Pr*
Martha Aranda, *Sec*
▲ **EMP:** 70 **EST:** 1976
SQ FT: 60,000
SALES (est): 18.58MM **Privately Held**
Web: www.arandatooling.com
SIC: **3599** 3469 3544 3465 Machine shop, jobbing and repair; Metal stampings, nec; Special dies, tools, jigs, and fixtures; Automotive stampings

(P-7760)
AREMAC ASSOCIATES INC
2004 S Myrtle Ave (91016-4837)
PHONE..................................626 303-8795
Scott Sher, *CEO*
Mariela Vinas, *
EMP: 35 **EST:** 1963
SQ FT: 12,500
SALES (est): 2.21MM **Privately Held**
SIC: **3599** 3444 Machine shop, jobbing and repair; Sheet metalwork

(P-7761)
ARNOLD-GONSALVES ENGRG INC
5731 Chino Ave (91710-5226)
PHONE..................................909 465-1579
Manuel Gonsalves, *Pr*
Mike Arnold, *
EMP: 35 **EST:** 1969
SQ FT: 10,000
SALES (est): 2.79MM **Privately Held**
Web: www.arnoldgonsalveseng.com
SIC: **3599** 3444 Machine shop, jobbing and repair; Sheet metal specialties, not stamped

(P-7762)
ARROW ENGINEERING
4946 Azusa Canyon Rd (91706-1940)
PHONE..................................626 960-2806
John Beaman, *Pr*
Jim Ballantyne, *
EMP: 36 **EST:** 1974
SQ FT: 18,000
SALES (est): 5.13MM **Privately Held**
Web: www.arrow-engineering.com
SIC: **3599** Machine shop, jobbing and repair

(P-7763)
ARROW SCREW PRODUCTS INC
941 W Mccoy Ln (93455-1109)
PHONE..................................805 928-2269
Robert Vine, *CEO*
Tim Vine, *
Hoang Vine, *
EMP: 33 **EST:** 1956
SQ FT: 10,000
SALES (est): 4.05MM **Privately Held**
Web: www.aspsmca.com
SIC: **3599** 3541 Machine shop, jobbing and repair; Machine tools, metal cutting type

(P-7764)
ASSEMBLY AUTOMATION INDUSTRIES
Also Called: Assembly Automation
1849 Business Center Dr (91010-2902)
PHONE..................................626 303-2777
Francis E Frost, *CEO*
Elizabeth Frost, *
EMP: 21 **EST:** 1978
SQ FT: 10,000
SALES (est): 2.32MM **Privately Held**
Web: www.assemblyauto.com
SIC: **3599** Machine shop, jobbing and repair

PRODUCTS & SVCS

(P-7765)
AUGER INDUSTRIES INC
390 E Crowther Ave (92870-6419)
PHONE................................714 577-9350
John Auger, *Pr*
Francoise Auger, *Stockholder*
EMP: 17 **EST:** 1969
SQ FT: 12,000
SALES (est): 2.42MM **Privately Held**
Web: www.augerind.com
SIC: 3599 Machine shop, jobbing and repair

(P-7766)
AUTOMATION WEST INC
Also Called: Cameron Metal Cutting
1605 E Saint Gertrude Pl (92705-5311)
PHONE................................714 556-7381
George Danenhauer, *Pr*
David Roberts, *VP*
Linda Bingham, *Sec*
▲ **EMP:** 23 **EST:** 1977
SQ FT: 7,200
SALES (est): 648.83K **Privately Held**
SIC: 3599 7389 Machine shop, jobbing and repair; Metal cutting services

(P-7767)
AVATAR MACHINE LLC
18100 Mount Washington St (92708-6121)
PHONE................................714 434-2737
EMP: 23 **EST:** 2008
SALES (est): 9.4MM **Privately Held**
Web: www.avatarmachine.com
SIC: 3599 5049 Machine shop, jobbing and repair; Precision tools

(P-7768)
AXXIS CORPORATION
1535 Nandina Ave (92571-7010)
PHONE................................951 436-9921
Brandy Tidball, *Pr*
Brandy Tidball, *Pr*
Susan Tidball, *
Jo Olchawa, *
EMP: 35 **EST:** 2007
SALES (est): 5.16MM **Privately Held**
Web: www.axxiscorp.us
SIC: 3599 Machine shop, jobbing and repair

(P-7769)
AZURE MICRODYNAMICS INC
19652 Descartes (92610-2600)
PHONE................................949 699-3344
Stanislaw Sulek, *Pr*
Zyta Sulek, *Stockholder*
Oliver Sulek, *
Christopher Hughes, *
EMP: 77 **EST:** 1997
SALES (est): 15.2MM **Privately Held**
Web: www.azuremd.com
SIC: 3599 3544 Machine shop, jobbing and repair; Special dies, tools, jigs, and fixtures

(P-7770)
B & B PIPE AND TOOL CO
2301 Parker Ln (93308-6006)
PHONE................................661 323-8208
Joe Keller, *Genl Mgr*
EMP: 29
SALES (corp-wide): 11.4MM **Privately Held**
Web: www.bbpipe.com
SIC: 3599 Machine shop, jobbing and repair
PA: B & B Pipe And Tool Co.
3035 Walnut Ave
Long Beach CA
562 424-0704

(P-7771)
B S K T INC
Also Called: S & S Precision Sheetmetal
8447 Canoga Ave (91304-2607)
PHONE................................818 349-1566
Steve Kim, *Pr*
EMP: 17 **EST:** 1997
SQ FT: 12,000
SALES (est): 316.39K **Privately Held**
SIC: 3599 Machine shop, jobbing and repair

(P-7772)
B&B MANUFACTURING CO (PA)
27940 Beale Ct (91355-1210)
PHONE................................661 257-2161
Kenneth Gentry, *CEO*
Fred Duncan, *
▲ **EMP:** 192 **EST:** 1961
SQ FT: 180,000
SALES (est): 55.73MM
SALES (corp-wide): 55.73MM **Privately Held**
Web: www.bbmfg.com
SIC: 3599 Machine shop, jobbing and repair

(P-7773)
BAKERSFIELD MACHINE CO INC
Also Called: BMC Industries
5605 North Chester Ave Ext (93308)
P.O. Box 122 (93302-0122)
PHONE................................661 709-1992
John L Meyer, *Pr*
Alfred T Meyer Junior, *VP*
▲ **EMP:** 55 **EST:** 1924
SQ FT: 8,276
SALES (est): 8.97MM **Privately Held**
Web:
www.bakersfieldmachinerymovers.com
SIC: 3599 Machine shop, jobbing and repair

(P-7774)
BANNER AMERICAN PRODUCTS INC
42381 Rio Nedo (92590-3701)
PHONE................................951 296-9780
▲ **EMP:** 17 **EST:** 1974
SALES (est): 586.51K **Privately Held**
Web: www.klaico.com
SIC: 3599 Custom machinery

(P-7775)
BARBER WELDING AND MFG CO
7171 Scout Ave (90201-3201)
P.O. Box 635 (92885-0635)
PHONE................................562 928-2570
C Douglas Barber, *CEO*
Yvonne M Barber, *
EMP: 25 **EST:** 1943
SQ FT: 15,000
SALES (est): 2.25MM **Privately Held**
SIC: 3599 3443 Machine shop, jobbing and repair; Tanks for tank trucks, metal plate

(P-7776)
BAUMANN ENGINEERING
212 S Cambridge Ave (91711-4843)
PHONE................................909 621-4181
Fred Baumann, *Pr*
Isolde Doll, *
EMP: 85 **EST:** 1961
SQ FT: 18,057
SALES (est): 7.6MM **Privately Held**
Web: www.becontrols.com
SIC: 3599 Machine shop, jobbing and repair

(P-7777)
BAYLESS MANUFACTURING LLC
Also Called: Fabcon
26140 Avenue Hall (91355-4808)
PHONE................................661 257-3373
Robert Lummus, *Pr*
EMP: 235 **EST:** 1978
SALES (est): 22.26MM **Privately Held**
Web: www.baylessmfg.com
SIC: 3599 3444 Machine shop, jobbing and repair; Sheet metalwork

(P-7778)
BCI INC
Also Called: Advance Screw Products
1822 Belcroft Ave (91733-3703)
PHONE................................626 579-4234
Adam Bondra, *Pr*
June Bondra, *VP*
EMP: 28 **EST:** 1976
SQ FT: 6,500
SALES (est): 1.19MM **Privately Held**
Web: www.bostoncareer.org
SIC: 3599 5084 Machine shop, jobbing and repair; Welding machinery and equipment

(P-7779)
BENDER CCP INC (PA)
Also Called: Bender US
2150 E 37th St (90058-1417)
P.O. Box 847 (94510-0847)
PHONE................................707 745-9970
Randall Potter, *CEO*
▲ **EMP:** 31 **EST:** 2007
SALES (est): 14.64MM
SALES (corp-wide): 14.64MM **Privately Held**
Web: www.benderccp.com
SIC: 3599 3731 Custom machinery; Shipbuilding and repairing

(P-7780)
BENDICK PRECISION INC
56 La Porte St (91006-2827)
PHONE................................626 445-0217
Christie Joseph, *Pr*
Benny Joseph, *Sec*
EMP: 23 **EST:** 1975
SQ FT: 5,000
SALES (est): 2.38MM **Privately Held**
Web: www.bendick.com
SIC: 3599 3061 Machine shop, jobbing and repair; Medical and surgical rubber tubing (extruded and lathe-cut)

(P-7781)
BEONCA MACHINE INC
1680 Curtiss Ct (91750-5848)
PHONE................................909 392-9991
Johann Bock, *Pr*
Danny Bock, *Pr*
Dennis Bock, *VP*
Jame Bock, *Corporate Secretary*
EMP: 17 **EST:** 1973
SQ FT: 7,000
SALES (est): 2.44MM **Privately Held**
Web: www.beoncamachine.com
SIC: 3599 Machine shop, jobbing and repair

(P-7782)
BERANEK LLC
2340 W 205th St (90501-1436)
PHONE................................310 328-9094
Hector Beranek, *Pr*
Sean Holly, *
Christoper Lin, *
Tucker Cowden, *
Stephen Cook, *
EMP: 36 **EST:** 1978
SQ FT: 20,000
SALES (est): 10.87MM
SALES (corp-wide): 40.05MM **Privately Held**

Web: www.beranekinc.com
SIC: 3599 Machine shop, jobbing and repair
PA: J&E Precision Tool Holdings, Llc
107 Valley Rd
Southampton MA
413 527-8778

(P-7783)
BERNS BROS INC
Also Called: De Berns Company
1250 W 17th St (90813-1310)
PHONE................................562 437-0471
Steven Berns, *Pr*
Sue Porter, *VP*
▲ **EMP:** 17 **EST:** 1957
SQ FT: 20,000
SALES (est): 2.47MM **Privately Held**
Web: www.thebernscompany.com
SIC: 3599 Machine and other job shop work

(P-7784)
BLAGA PRECISION INC
11650 Seaboard Cir (90680-3426)
PHONE................................714 891-9509
Gavril Blaga, *Pr*
▲ **EMP:** 38 **EST:** 1983
SQ FT: 3,600
SALES (est): 934.19K **Privately Held**
Web: blagaprecisiont.mfgpages.com
SIC: 3599 Machine shop, jobbing and repair

(P-7785)
BMW PRECISION MACHINING INC
2379 Industry St (92054-4803)
PHONE................................760 439-6813
Richard Blakely, *Pr*
EMP: 25 **EST:** 1981
SQ FT: 17,400
SALES (est): 2.85MM **Privately Held**
Web: www.bmwprecision.com
SIC: 3599 Machine shop, jobbing and repair

(P-7786)
BOUDRAUX PRCSION MCHINING CORP
11762 Western Ave Ste G (90680-3481)
PHONE................................714 894-4523
Mike Boudreaux, *Pr*
Steve Boudreaux, *
EMP: 25 **EST:** 1990
SQ FT: 3,750
SALES (est): 1.72MM **Privately Held**
Web:
boudreaux-precision-machining-ca.hub.biz
SIC: 3599 Machine shop, jobbing and repair

(P-7787)
BREK MANUFACTURING CO (HQ)
1513 W 132nd St (90249-2107)
PHONE................................310 329-7638
▲ **EMP:** 61 **EST:** 1968
SALES (est): 56.04MM
SALES (corp-wide): 56.04MM **Privately Held**
Web: www.brek.aero
SIC: 3599 Machine shop, jobbing and repair
PA: Aernnova Engineering Us, Inc.
1513 W 132nd St
Gardena CA
310 329-7638

(P-7788)
BREK MANUFACTURING CO
2601 W Ball Rd Ste 105 (92804-5062)
PHONE................................310 329-7638
EMP: 108
SALES (corp-wide): 56.04MM **Privately Held**

Web: www.brek.aero
SIC: 3599 Machine shop, jobbing and repair
HQ: Brek Manufacturing Co.
1513 W 132nd St
Gardena CA
310 329-7638

(P-7789)
BTI AEROSPACE & ELECTRONICS
Also Called: B T I Areospace & Electronics
13546 Vintage Pl (91710-5243)
PHONE..............................909 465-1569
Gary Rindfleisch, *Pr*
▲ **EMP:** 20 **EST:** 1997
SQ FT: 25,000
SALES (est): 495.41K **Privately Held**
SIC: 3599 3444 3769 Machine shop, jobbing and repair; Sheet metalwork; Space vehicle equipment, nec

(P-7790)
BTL MACHINE
Also Called: Apex Design Tech.
1168 Sherborn St (92879-2089)
PHONE..............................951 808-9929
▲ **EMP:** 65
Web: www.btlmachine.com
SIC: 3599 Machine shop, jobbing and repair

(P-7791)
C & C DIE ENGRAVING
12510 Mccann Dr (90670-3337)
PHONE..............................562 944-3399
Salvador J Chavez, *Owner*
EMP: 23 **EST:** 1981
SQ FT: 10,000
SALES (est): 829.2K **Privately Held**
Web: www.cncdie.com
SIC: 3599 Machine shop, jobbing and repair

(P-7792)
C & D PRECISION COMPONENTS INC
Also Called: Trimatic
969 S Raymond Ave (91105-3241)
PHONE..............................626 799-7109
Coleen Ganguin, *Pr*
Daniel A Ganguin, *Sec*
EMP: 22 **EST:** 1964
SQ FT: 4,000
SALES (est): 460.69K **Privately Held**
SIC: 3599 Machine shop, jobbing and repair

(P-7793)
CARTER PUMP & MACHINE INC
635 G St (93280-2023)
P.O. Box 1258 (93280-8158)
PHONE..............................661 393-8620
Chet Grooman, *Pr*
EMP: 18 **EST:** 1987
SQ FT: 6,000
SALES (est): 453.8K **Privately Held**
SIC: 3599 7699 Machine shop, jobbing and repair; Pumps and pumping equipment repair

(P-7794)
CAVANAUGH MACHINE WORKS INC
1540 Santa Fe Ave (90813-1239)
PHONE..............................562 437-1126
John Wells, *Pr*
Michael Wells, *
EMP: 40 **EST:** 1946
SQ FT: 19,000
SALES (est): 4.9MM **Privately Held**
Web: www.cavmachine.com

SIC: 3599 3731 3441 Machine shop, jobbing and repair; Shipbuilding and repairing; Fabricated structural metal

(P-7795)
CENTERPOINT MFG CO INC
2625 N San Fernando Blvd (91504-3220)
PHONE..............................818 842-2147
John C Rotunno, *Pr*
Carmen Rotunno, *
EMP: 40 **EST:** 1966
SQ FT: 12,000
SALES (est): 6.81MM **Privately Held**
Web: www.centerpointmfgco.com
SIC: 3599 Machine shop, jobbing and repair

(P-7796)
CENTURY PRECISION ENGRG INC
2141 W 139th St (90249-2451)
PHONE..............................310 538-0015
Myron Yoo, *Pr*
Bruce Lee, *
EMP: 25 **EST:** 1980
SQ FT: 20,000
SALES (est): 4.67MM **Privately Held**
Web: www.centurype.com
SIC: 3599 Machine shop, jobbing and repair

(P-7797)
CHE PRECISION INC
2586 Calcite Cir (91320-1203)
PHONE..............................805 499-8885
Charles Holguin, *Pr*
Claude Holguin, *VP*
Charlie Holguin, *VP*
▲ **EMP:** 20 **EST:** 1989
SALES (est): 2.39MM **Privately Held**
Web: www.cheprecision.com
SIC: 3599 Machine shop, jobbing and repair

(P-7798)
CHEEK MACHINE CORP
1312 S Allec St (92805-6303)
PHONE..............................714 279-9486
EMP: 21 **EST:** 1994
SQ FT: 5,000
SALES (est): 3.39MM **Privately Held**
Web: www.cheekmachine.com
SIC: 3599 Machine shop, jobbing and repair

(P-7799)
CJ ADVISORS INC
6900 8th St (90620-1036)
PHONE..............................714 956-3388
Jason Cho, *CEO*
EMP: 23 **EST:** 1993
SALES (est): 1.74MM **Privately Held**
Web: www.hqmachine.com
SIC: 3599 Machine and other job shop work

(P-7800)
CJ PRECISION INDUSTRIES INC
2817 Cherry Ave (90755-1908)
PHONE..............................562 426-3708
Mike Vedder, *Pr*
Thomas Vedder, *VP*
Michael Vedder, *VP*
Cynthia Vedder, *Sec*
EMP: 20 **EST:** 1980
SQ FT: 10,000
SALES (est): 951.11K **Privately Held**
Web: www.cjprecisionindustries.com
SIC: 3599 Machine shop, jobbing and repair

(P-7801)
CLASSIC WIRE CUT COMPANY INC
28210 Constellation Rd (91355-5000)

PHONE..............................661 257-0558
Brett Bannerman, *Prin*
▲ **EMP:** 150 **EST:** 1984
SQ FT: 80,000
SALES (est): 19.19MM **Privately Held**
Web: www.classicwirecut.com
SIC: 3599 3841 Electrical discharge machining (EDM); Surgical instruments and apparatus

(P-7802)
CNC MACHINING INC
510 S Fairview Ave (93117-3617)
PHONE..............................805 681-8855
Gary Brous, *Pr*
Greg Brous, *VP*
Shirley Brous, *Sec*
EMP: 29 **EST:** 1985
SQ FT: 2,000
SALES (est): 2.04MM **Privately Held**
Web: www.cncmachining.com
SIC: 3599 Machine shop, jobbing and repair

(P-7803)
CNI MFG INC
Also Called: Computer-Nozzles
15627 Arrow Hwy (91706-2004)
PHONE..............................626 962-6646
Toby Argandona, *Pr*
David Argandona, *VP*
Yolanda Pullen, *Sec*
EMP: 18 **EST:** 1969
SQ FT: 32,200
SALES (est): 2.47MM **Privately Held**
Web: www.cni-mfg.com
SIC: 3599 3443 Custom machinery; Fabricated plate work (boiler shop)

(P-7804)
COAST COMPOSITES LLC
7 Burroughs (92618-2804)
PHONE..............................949 455-0665
Brendan Buckel, *Mgr*
EMP: 30
SALES (corp-wide): 21.65MM **Privately Held**
Web: www.ascentaerospace.com
SIC: 3599 Machine shop, jobbing and repair
PA: Coast Composites, Llc
5 Burroughs
Irvine CA
949 455-0665

(P-7805)
CODY CYLINDER SERVICE LLC
1393 Dodson Way Ste A (92507-2073)
P.O. Box 56099 (92517-0999)
PHONE..............................951 786-3650
Art Pastoor, *Pr*
Jolene Cody Patoor, *VP*
EMP: 21 **EST:** 2018
SALES (est): 3.5MM **Privately Held**
SIC: 3599 7379 Machine shop, jobbing and repair; Tape recertification service

(P-7806)
COMPUTER ASSISTED MFG TECH LLC
Also Called: Camtech
8710 Research Dr 8750 (92618)
PHONE..............................949 263-8911
Mike Dennis, *CEO*
EMP: 40 **EST:** 1982
SQ FT: 50,000
SALES (est): 9.23MM
SALES (corp-wide): 9.23MM **Privately Held**
SIC: 3599 Machine shop, jobbing and repair
HQ: Cam Holdco, Llc
8710 Research Dr

Irvine CA

(P-7807)
COMPUTER INTGRTED MCHINING INC
10940 Wheatlands Ave (92071-2857)
PHONE..............................619 596-9246
EMP: 21 **EST:** 1995
SQ FT: 20,000
SALES (est): 5.07MM **Privately Held**
Web: www.cimsd.com
SIC: 3599 Machine shop, jobbing and repair

(P-7808)
CONNELLY MACHINE WKS
Also Called: Acme Tool Grinding Company
420 N Terminal St (92701-4927)
PHONE..............................714 558-6855
Ray Connelly, *Pr*
Scott Connelly, *VP*
EMP: 22 **EST:** 1946
SQ FT: 17,000
SALES (est): 3.57MM **Privately Held**
Web: www.connellymachine.com
SIC: 3599 3492 Machine shop, jobbing and repair; Fluid power valves and hose fittings

(P-7809)
COZZA INC
9941 Prospect Ave (92071-4318)
PHONE..............................619 749-5663
Frank Charles Cozza, *Pr*
Gerry Tailor, *VP*
EMP: 19 **EST:** 2006
SQ FT: 10,000
SALES (est): 480.69K **Privately Held**
SIC: 3599 Machine and other job shop work

(P-7810)
CRESCO MANUFACTURING INC
Also Called: Crescomfg.com
1614 N Orangethorpe Way (92801-1227)
PHONE..............................714 525-2326
Jon Spielman, *Pr*
Alberta Spielman, *
EMP: 40 **EST:** 1981
SQ FT: 14,000
SALES (est): 5.25MM **Privately Held**
Web: petespielman.weebly.com
SIC: 3599 Machine shop, jobbing and repair

(P-7811)
CRUSH MASTER GRINDING CORP
755 Penarth Ave (91789-3028)
PHONE..............................909 595-2249
Sherman Durousseau, *Pr*
Jeanne Durousseau, *
EMP: 35 **EST:** 1976
SQ FT: 11,800
SALES (est): 2.92MM **Privately Held**
Web: www.crushmastergrinding.com
SIC: 3599 Machine shop, jobbing and repair

(P-7812)
D MILLS GRNDING MACHINING INC
1738 N Neville St (92865-4214)
PHONE..............................951 697-6847
Anthony Puccio, *Pr*
Gilles Madelmont, *
Joe Puccio, *
EMP: 150 **EST:** 1973
SALES (est): 1.73MM
SALES (corp-wide): 43.53MM **Privately Held**
Web: d-mills-grinding-machining-co-inc.hub.biz

SIC: 3599 Grinding castings for the trade
PA: Manufacturing Solutions, Inc.
1738 N Neville St
Orange CA
714 453-0100

(P-7813)
DARMARK CORPORATION
13225 Gregg St (92064-7120)
PHONE..................858 679-3970
Darwin Mark Zavadil, *Pr*
Martin T Drake, *
Lori Zavadil, *
Jackie Williams, *
EMP: 90 EST: 1979
SQ FT: 28,000
SALES (est): 17.49MM **Privately Held**
Web: www.darmark.com
SIC: 3599 Machine shop, jobbing and repair

(P-7814)
DELAFIELD CORPORATION (PA)
Also Called: Delafield Fluid Technology
1520 Flower Ave (91010-2925)
PHONE..................626 303-0740
Nik Ray, *Pr*
Jim Martin, *
Henry Custodia, *
◆ EMP: 120 EST: 1949
SQ FT: 90,000
SALES (est): 40.45MM
SALES (corp-wide): 40.45MM **Privately Held**
Web: www.dftcorp.com
SIC: 3599 5085 3498 3492 Hose, flexible metallic; Valves, pistons, and fittings; Tube fabricating (contract bending and shaping); Fluid power valves and hose fittings

(P-7815)
DELTA FABRICATION INC
9600 De Soto Ave (91311-5012)
PHONE..................818 407-4000
EMP: 90 EST: 1996
SQ FT: 20,000
SALES (est): 8.02MM **Privately Held**
Web: www.deltahi-tech.com
SIC: 3599 Machine shop, jobbing and repair

(P-7816)
DELTA HI-TECH
9600 De Soto Ave (91311-5012)
PHONE..................818 407-4000
Joe Ostrowsky, *CEO*
Ilan Ostrowsky, *
Gregory Elkhunovich, *
Chava Ostrowsky, *
▲ EMP: 130 EST: 1985
SQ FT: 40,000
SALES (est): 19.97MM **Privately Held**
Web: www.deltahi-tech.com
SIC: 3599 Machine shop, jobbing and repair

(P-7817)
DIAL PRECISION INC
17235 Darwin Ave (92345-5178)
P.O. Box 402259 (92340-2259)
PHONE..................760 947-3557
Darryl L Tarullo, *Ch Bd*
Jeff Marousek, *Prin*
Linda James, *Prin*
EMP: 95 EST: 1958
SQ FT: 15,000
SALES (est): 5.9MM **Privately Held**
Web: www.dialprecision.com
SIC: 3599 3545 Machine shop, jobbing and repair; Machine tool accessories

(P-7818)
DILIGENT SOLUTIONS INC
Also Called: Absolute EDM
3240 Grey Hawk Ct (92010-6651)
P.O. Box 985 (92564-0985)
PHONE..................760 814-8960
Stephen A Bowles, *Pr*
EMP: 20 EST: 2001
SALES (est): 2.36MM **Privately Held**
SIC: 3599 Machine shop, jobbing and repair

(P-7819)
DL HORTON ENTERPRISES INC
Also Called: Warmelin Precision Products
12705 Daphne Ave (90250-3311)
PHONE..................323 777-1700
EMP: 55
SIC: 3599 Machine shop, jobbing and repair

(P-7820)
DOW HYDRAULIC SYSTEMS INC
2895 Metropolitan Pl (91767-1853)
PHONE..................909 596-6602
Richard P Dow, *Pr*
Ryan K Dow, *
Bryan Dow, *
Keith Dow, *
EMP: 60 EST: 1968
SALES (est): 11.67MM **Privately Held**
Web: www.dowhydraulics.com
SIC: 3599 3594 Machine shop, jobbing and repair; Fluid power pumps and motors

(P-7821)
DUPLAN INDUSTRIES
Also Called: Gilbert Machine & Mfg
1265 Stone Dr (92078-4059)
PHONE..................760 744-4047
Nancy Duplan, *Pr*
Carlton Duplan, *Sec*
EMP: 23 EST: 1962
SQ FT: 15,000
SALES (est): 376.82K **Privately Held**
Web: www.gilbertmachine.com
SIC: 3599 Machine shop, jobbing and repair

(P-7822)
DYNAMIC ENTERPRISES INC
Also Called: D E I
2081 Rancho Hills Dr (91709-4763)
PHONE..................562 944-0271
Mildred Sudduth, *Pr*
Alan Sudduth, *VP*
Deanna Mansfield, *Sec*
◆ EMP: 21 EST: 1959
SALES (est): 2.44MM **Privately Held**
Web: www.dynamic-ent.com
SIC: 3599 Machine shop, jobbing and repair

(P-7823)
ED STIGLIC
Also Called: Stigtec Manufacturing
1125 Linda Vista Dr Ste 110 (92078-3819)
PHONE..................760 744-7239
Ed Stiglic, *Prin*
Teresa Stiglic, *Prin*
EMP: 19 EST: 1988
SQ FT: 10,000
SALES (est): 2.33MM **Privately Held**
Web: www.stigtec.com
SIC: 3599 Machine shop, jobbing and repair

(P-7824)
EJAYS MACHINE CO INC
1108 E Valencia Dr (92831-4627)
PHONE..................714 879-0558
Denise Eastin, *Pr*
Schuyler Eastin, *VP*
EMP: 20 EST: 1965

SALES (est): 2.31MM **Privately Held**
Web: www.ejaysmachine.com
SIC: 3599 Machine shop, jobbing and repair

(P-7825)
ELLINGSON INC
119 W Santa Fe Ave (92832-1831)
PHONE..................714 773-1923
Thomas Ellingson, *Pr*
T C Ellingson, *CEO*
Steven C Ellingson, *Sec*
EMP: 25 EST: 1946
SQ FT: 7,500
SALES (est): 896.24K **Privately Held**
Web: www.ellingson-inc.com
SIC: 3599 Machine shop, jobbing and repair

(P-7826)
ELY CO INC
3046 Kashiwa St (90505-4009)
PHONE..................310 539-5831
Walter Senff, *CEO*
Kurt Senff, *
Judith Senff, *
Bill Senff, *
EMP: 36 EST: 1953
SQ FT: 11,500
SALES (est): 5.06MM **Privately Held**
Web: www.elyco.com
SIC: 3599 Machine shop, jobbing and repair

(P-7827)
ENERGY LINK INDUS SVCS INC
11439 S Enos Ln (93311-9452)
P.O. Box 10716 (93389-0716)
PHONE..................661 765-4444
James R Miller Iii, *CEO*
Ray Miller, *
Matt Knight, *Stockholder**
West Moore, *Stockholder**
Joe Yrigoyen Stckhldrs, *Prin*
EMP: 34 EST: 2000
SALES (est): 8.23MM **Privately Held**
Web: www.energylink1.com
SIC: 3599 7699 Bellows, industrial: metal; Compressor repair

(P-7828)
EXPAND MACHINERY LLC
20869 Plummer St (91311-5005)
PHONE..................818 349-9166
EMP: 17 EST: 2012
SALES (est): 2.41MM **Privately Held**
Web: www.expandmachinery.com
SIC: 3599 Machine shop, jobbing and repair

(P-7829)
EXTRUDE HONE DEBURRING SVC INC
Also Called: Extrude Hone Abrsive Flow McHn
8800 Somerset Blvd (90723-4659)
PHONE..................562 531-2976
William Melendez, *Pr*
EMP: 21 EST: 1971
SQ FT: 11,000
SALES (est): 406.62K **Privately Held**
Web: www.extrudehoneafm.com
SIC: 3599 5084 Machine shop, jobbing and repair; Machine tools and accessories

(P-7830)
F & L TOOLS CORPORATION
Also Called: F & L Tls Precision Machining
245 Jason Ct (92879-6199)
PHONE..................951 279-1555
Tracey Pratt, *Pr*
Tracey Pratt, *VP*
Larry Pratt, *Prin*
EMP: 18 EST: 1972

SQ FT: 8,100
SALES (est): 5.61MM **Privately Held**
Web: www.fltcorp.com
SIC: 3599 Machine shop, jobbing and repair

(P-7831)
FIBREFORM ELECTRONICS INC
Also Called: Fibreform Precision Machining
5341 Argosy Ave (92649-1036)
PHONE..................714 898-9641
Zachary Fischer, *Ch Bd*
Zachary Fischer, *Ch Bd*
Frank Mauro, *
Todd Crow, *
EMP: 30 EST: 1945
SQ FT: 30,000
SALES (est): 4.57MM **Privately Held**
Web: www.fibreformprecision.com
SIC: 3599 Machine shop, jobbing and repair

(P-7832)
FORM GRIND CORPORATION
Also Called: Form Products
30062 Aventura (92688-2010)
PHONE..................949 858-7000
Ernest Treichler, *CEO*
Gary Treichler, *
Joan Treichler, *
EMP: 37 EST: 1963
SQ FT: 30,000
SALES (est): 3.58MM **Privately Held**
Web: www.formgrind.com
SIC: 3599 5084 Machine shop, jobbing and repair; Industrial machinery and equipment

(P-7833)
FORTNER ENG & MFG INC
2927 N Ontario St (91504-2017)
P.O. Box 30015 (84130-0015)
PHONE..................818 240-7740
David W Fortner, *Pr*
EMP: 30 EST: 1952
SQ FT: 24,000
SALES (est): 11.11MM **Publicly Held**
Web: www.fortnereng.com
SIC: 3599 Machine shop, jobbing and repair
HQ: Wencor Group, Llc
416 Dividend Dr
Peachtree City GA
678 490-0140

(P-7834)
FORTUNE MANUFACTURING INC
13849 Magnolia Ave (91710-7028)
PHONE..................909 591-1547
EMP: 45
SIC: 3599 Machine shop, jobbing and repair

(P-7835)
FRANK RUSSELL INC
341 Pacific Ave (93263-2046)
PHONE..................661 324-5575
Andrew Russell, *Pr*
EMP: 17 EST: 1939
SQ FT: 13,000
SALES (est): 2.41MM **Privately Held**
Web: www.frankrussellinc.com
SIC: 3599 5251 Machine shop, jobbing and repair; Hardware stores

(P-7836)
FRANKLINS INDS SAN DIEGO INC
12135 Dearborn Pl (92064-7111)
PHONE..................858 486-9399
Kelly Franklin, *Pr*
EMP: 44 EST: 1980
SQ FT: 20,000
SALES (est): 7.51MM **Privately Held**
Web: www.franklin-ind.com

▲ = Import ▼ = Export
◆ = Import/Export

SIC: 3599 Machine shop, jobbing and repair

(P-7837)
FRANS MANUFACTURING INC
126 N Vinewood St (92029-1332)
P.O. Box 461403 (92046-1403)
PHONE..............................760 741-9135
Frans Ketelaars, *Pr*
Michael Wibier, *VP*
EMP: 20 **EST:** 1980
SQ FT: 3,900
SALES (est): 431.73K **Privately Held**
Web: www.fransmfg.com
SIC: 3599 Machine shop, jobbing and repair

(P-7838)
FRONTIER ENGRG & MFG TECH INC
Also Called: Frontier Technologies
800 W 16th St (90813-1413)
PHONE..............................562 606-2655
John Tsai, *CEO*
Steve Hoekstra, *
▲ **EMP:** 46 **EST:** 1994
SQ FT: 30,000
SALES (est): 12.31MM **Privately Held**
Web: www.ftmfg.com
SIC: 3599 8711 Machine shop, jobbing and
repair; Engineering services

(P-7839)
FUTURE TECH METALS INC
719 Palmyrita Ave (92507-1811)
PHONE..............................951 781-4801
Tim Gearhardt, *Owner*
EMP: 20 **EST:** 1998
SALES (est): 4.33MM **Privately Held**
Web: www.futuretechmetals.com
SIC: 3599 Machine shop, jobbing and repair

(P-7840)
FUTURISTICS MACHINE INC
7014 Carroll Rd (92121-2213)
PHONE..............................858 450-0644
Mark Mcginn, *CEO*
EMP: 35 **EST:** 2016
SALES (est): 2.59MM **Privately Held**
Web: www.futuristicsmachine.com
SIC: 3599 Machine shop, jobbing and repair

(P-7841)
G V INDUSTRIES INC
1346 Cleveland Ave (91950-4207)
PHONE..............................619 474-3013
Gregory J Verdon, *Pr*
Joseph Verdon, *
Linda Verdon, *Corporate Vice President**
EMP: 38 **EST:** 1978
SQ FT: 14,000
SALES (est): 4.7MM **Privately Held**
Web: www.gvindustries.biz
SIC: 3599 Machine shop, jobbing and repair

(P-7842)
GAMMA AEROSPACE LLC
1461 S Balboa Ave (91761-7609)
PHONE..............................310 532-4480
Thomas C Hutton, *Managing Member*
EMP: 32
SALES (corp-wide): 46.4MM **Privately Held**
Web: www.gammaaero.com
SIC: 3599 Machine shop, jobbing and repair
PA: Gamma Aerospace Llc
601 Airport Dr
Mansfield TX
817 477-2193

(P-7843)
GARRETT PRECISION INC
25082 La Suen Rd (92653-5102)
PHONE..............................949 855-9710
Justin S Osborn, *CEO*
Dean Garrett, *Pr*
Lynn Sandra Garrett, *VP*
EMP: 19 **EST:** 1978
SQ FT: 6,500
SALES (est): 1.44MM **Privately Held**
SIC: 3599 Machine shop, jobbing and repair

(P-7844)
GBF ENTERPRISES INC
2709 Halladay St (92705-5618)
PHONE..............................714 979-7131
Cheryl Nowak, *Pr*
EMP: 25 **EST:** 1976
SQ FT: 17,000
SALES (est): 4.32MM **Privately Held**
Web: www.gbfenterprises.com
SIC: 3599 Machine shop, jobbing and repair

(P-7845)
GENERAL INDUSTRIAL REPAIR
6865 Washington Blvd (90640-5434)
PHONE..............................323 278-0873
EMP: 25 **EST:** 1995
SALES (est): 5.48MM **Privately Held**
Web: www.girepair.us
SIC: 3599 Machine shop, jobbing and repair

(P-7846)
GENERAL PRODUCTION SERVICES
670 Arroyo St (91340-2220)
PHONE..............................818 365-4211
Maria Hall, *Pr*
Loren S Hall, *VP*
EMP: 21 **EST:** 1975
SQ FT: 3,500
SALES (est): 508.42K **Privately Held**
SIC: 3599 Machine shop, jobbing and repair

(P-7847)
GEORGE FISCHER INC (HQ)
5462 Irwindale Ave Ste A (91706-2074)
PHONE..............................626 571-2770
Chris Blumer, *CEO*
Daniel Vaterlaus, *VP*
◆ **EMP:** 140 **EST:** 1954
SALES (est): 265.41MM **Privately Held**
Web: www.signet-gf.com
SIC: 3599 5074 3829 3559 Electrical
discharge machining (EDM); Pipes and
fittings, plastic; Testing equipment:
abrasion, shearing strength, etc.; Foundry
machinery and equipment
PA: Georg Fischer Ag
Amsler-Laffon-Strasse 9
Schaffhausen SH

(P-7848)
GERMAN MACHINED PRODUCTS INC
Also Called: German Machine Products
1415 W 178th St (90248-3201)
PHONE..............................310 532-4480
EMP: 32
SIC: 3599 Machine shop, jobbing and repair

(P-7849)
GLENDEE CORP
Also Called: Metalagraphics
5151 N Commerce Ave (93021-1763)
PHONE..............................805 523-2422
EMP: 20
SALES (corp-wide): 9.95MM **Privately Held**

Web: www.mgius.com
SIC: 3599 3444 Machine and other job shop
work; Sheet metalwork
PA: Glendee Corp.
5390 Gabbert Rd
Moorpark CA
805 523-2422

(P-7850)
GLENDEE CORP (PA)
Also Called: Metalagraphics
5390 Gabbert Rd (93021-1772)
PHONE..............................805 523-2422
EMP: 41 **EST:** 1975
SALES (est): 9.95MM
SALES (corp-wide): 9.95MM **Privately Held**
Web: www.mgius.com
SIC: 3599 3444 Machine and other job shop
work; Sheet metalwork

(P-7851)
GOEPPNER INDUSTRIES INC
22924 Lockness Ave (90501-5117)
PHONE..............................310 784-2800
Joanne Goeppner, *Pr*
EMP: 25 **EST:** 1972
SQ FT: 12,000
SALES (est): 774.91K **Privately Held**
Web: www.goeppnerindustries.com
SIC: 3599 Machine shop, jobbing and repair

(P-7852)
GOLDEN WEST MACHINE INC
9930 Jordan Cir (90670-3305)
PHONE..............................562 903-1111
Dan Goodman, *Prin*
Al Schlunegger, *
EMP: 35 **EST:** 1982
SQ FT: 25,000
SALES (est): 4.59MM **Privately Held**
Web: www.goldenwestmachine.com
SIC: 3599 7699 Machine shop, jobbing and
repair; Industrial machinery and equipment
repair

(P-7853)
GSP PRECISION INC
650 Town Center Dr Ste 950 (92626-1916)
PHONE..............................818 845-2212
George Gottardi, *Pr*
Walter D Prezioso, *CEO*
Pablo Prezioso, *Sec*
EMP: 46 **EST:** 1979
SQ FT: 6,000
SALES (est): 954.71K **Privately Held**
Web: www.gsp-precision.com
SIC: 3599 Machine shop, jobbing and repair

(P-7854)
GTR ENTERPRISES INCORPORATED
Also Called: Gtr
6352 Corte Del Abeto Ste E (92011-1408)
PHONE..............................760 931-1192
Kenneth Gray, *CEO*
Martin Randant, *
Mike Tedesco, *
EMP: 40 **EST:** 1992
SQ FT: 4,000
SALES (est): 4.97MM **Privately Held**
Web: www.gtrnet.com
SIC: 3599 5531 Machine shop, jobbing and
repair; Truck equipment and parts

(P-7855)
H & M FOUR-SLIDE INC
498 Melbourne Gln (92026-8565)
PHONE..............................951 461-8244
Hans Klahr, *Pr*

EMP: 25 **EST:** 1978
SALES (est): 429.02K **Privately Held**
Web: www.hmfourslide.com
SIC: 3599 Machine shop, jobbing and repair

(P-7856)
HALES ENGINEERING COINC
18 Wood Rd (93010-8327)
EMP: 49 **EST:** 1966
SALES (est): 6.22MM **Privately Held**
SIC: 3599 1791 3441 Machine shop, jobbing
and repair; Structural steel erection;
Fabricated structural metal

(P-7857)
HANSEN ENGINEERING CO
24020 Frampton Ave (90710-2102)
PHONE..............................310 534-3870
EMP: 86 **EST:** 1962
SALES (est): 8.94MM **Privately Held**
Web: www.hansenengineering.com
SIC: 3599 Machine shop, jobbing and repair

(P-7858)
HELFER ENTERPRISES
Also Called: Helfer Tool Co
3030 Oak St (92707-4236)
PHONE..............................714 557-2733
Bennie L Helfer, *Pr*
EMP: 32 **EST:** 1973
SQ FT: 12,000
SALES (est): 416.17K **Privately Held**
Web: www.helfertool.com
SIC: 3599 5084 3545 3544 Machine shop,
jobbing and repair; Industrial machinery
and equipment; Machine tool accessories;
Special dies, tools, jigs, and fixtures

(P-7859)
HERA TECHNOLOGIES LLC
1055 E Francis St (91761-5633)
PHONE..............................951 751-6191
Didi Truong, *CEO*
Aaron Evans, *
Eugene Chuck, *
EMP: 50 **EST:** 2015
SALES (est): 4.61MM **Privately Held**
Web: www.heratechnologies.com
SIC: 3599 Machine shop, jobbing and repair

(P-7860)
HI TEMP FORMING CO
315 Arden Ave Ste 28 (91203-1150)
PHONE..............................714 529-6556
Marvin Rosenberg, *Pr*
Doris Rosenberg, *
Jay Rosenberg, *
EMP: 24 **EST:** 1959
SQ FT: 36,000
SALES (est): 711.7K **Privately Held**
SIC: 3599 3812 3769 Machine shop, jobbing
and repair; Search and navigation
equipment; Space vehicle equipment, nec

(P-7861)
HI-TECH LABELS INCORPORATED
Also Called: Hi-Tech Products
8530 Roland St (90621-3124)
PHONE..............................714 670-2150
Jeffrey T Ruch, *CEO*
▲ **EMP:** 34 **EST:** 1983
SQ FT: 24,000
SALES (est): 6.75MM **Privately Held**
Web: www.hi-tech-products.com
SIC: 3599 Machine shop, jobbing and repair

(P-7862)

HI-TECH WELDING & FORMING INC

1327 Fayette St (92020-1512)
P.O. Box 1357 (92022-1357)
PHONE..............................619 562-5929
Aubrey Burer, *CEO*
John C Monsees, *
Amy Fitzgerald, *
EMP: 40 EST: 1984
SQ FT: 77,000
SALES (est): 1.27MM **Privately Held**
SIC: 3599 7692 3365 Machine shop, jobbing and repair; Welding repair; Aerospace castings, aluminum

(P-7863)

HIGH PRCSION GRNDING MCHNING I

1130 Pioneer Way (92020-1925)
PHONE..............................619 440-0303
Keith Brawner, *Pr*
Ken Gerhart, *
Shanda Brawner, *
EMP: 36 EST: 1971
SQ FT: 20,000
SALES (est): 1.54MM **Privately Held**
Web: www.highprecisiongrinding.com
SIC: 3599 Machine shop, jobbing and repair

(P-7864)

HMCOMPANY

4464 Mcgrath St Ste 111 (93003-7764)
PHONE..............................805 650-2651
Mark Woellert, *Owner*
EMP: 18 EST: 1977
SQ FT: 3,500
SALES (est): 458.36K **Privately Held**
Web: www.hm-company.net
SIC: 3599 Machine shop, jobbing and repair

(P-7865)

HOEFNER CORPORATION

9722 Rush St (91733-1777)
PHONE..............................626 443-3258
Gerald Hoefner, *Pr*
Karen Hoefner, *Sec*
EMP: 20 EST: 1946
SQ FT: 14,800
SALES (est): 2.55MM **Privately Held**
Web: www.hoefnercorp.com
SIC: 3599 3429 Machine shop, jobbing and repair; Hardware, nec

(P-7866)

HOLLAND & HERRING MFG INC

Also Called: H & H Manufacturing
661 E Monterey Ave (91767-5607)
PHONE..............................909 469-4700
Jerry C Holland, *Pr*
Lawrence P Saylor, *Sec*
Debbie Krakowe, *CFO*
Mark B Herring, *Stockholder*
Bruce N Herring, *Stockholder*
EMP: 35 EST: 1991
SQ FT: 15,000
SALES (est): 907.43K **Privately Held**
SIC: 3599 3471 Machine shop, jobbing and repair; Cleaning, polishing, and finishing

(P-7867)

HOUSTON ONTIC INC

20400 Plummer St (91311-5372)
PHONE..............................818 678-6555
EMP: 19 EST: 2016
SALES (est): 2.41MM **Privately Held**
Web: www.ontic.com
SIC: 3599 Machine shop, jobbing and repair

(P-7868)

HTE ACQUISITION LLC

Also Called: Hi-Tech Engineering
4610 Calle Quetzal (93012-8558)
PHONE..............................805 987-5449
Shaffiq Rahim, *Pr*
EMP: 20 EST: 2019
SQ FT: 15,000
SALES (est): 2.59MM **Privately Held**
Web: www.htemfg.com
SIC: 3599 Machine shop, jobbing and repair

(P-7869)

HYTRON MFG CO INC

15582 Chemical Ln (92649-1505)
PHONE..............................714 903-6701
James C Rehling, *Pr*
Robert Rehling, *
Cheryll Rehling, *
Deborah Strickland, *
EMP: 50 EST: 1963
SQ FT: 13,370
SALES (est): 7.91MM **Privately Held**
Web: www.hytronmfg.com
SIC: 3599 Machine shop, jobbing and repair

(P-7870)

I COPY INC

Also Called: Ibe Digital
11266 Monarch St Ste B (92841-1450)
PHONE..............................562 921-0202
Ronald Varing, *
EMP: 50 EST: 2001
SALES (est): 6.25MM **Privately Held**
Web: www.ibedigital.com
SIC: 3599 5044 5999 Amusement park equipment; Duplicating machines; Business machines and equipment

(P-7871)

INFINITE ENGINEERING INC

13682 Newhope St (92843-3712)
PHONE..............................714 534-4688
Simon Ho, *Pr*
Kelly Ho, *VP*
EMP: 17 EST: 2006
SALES (est): 537.37K **Privately Held**
Web: www.infinitecncshop.com
SIC: 3599 Machine shop, jobbing and repair

(P-7872)

INFOCUS CNC MACHINING INC

11245 Young River Ave (92708-4108)
PHONE..............................714 979-1253
EMP: 20 EST: 2007
SQ FT: 7,972
SALES (est): 1.71MM **Privately Held**
Web: www.infocuscnc.com
SIC: 3599 Machine shop, jobbing and repair

(P-7873)

INNO TECH MANUFACTURING INC

10109 Carroll Canyon Rd (92131-1109)
PHONE..............................858 565-4556
Marek Prochazka, *Pr*
Gail Prochazka, *CFO*
▲ **EMP: 19 EST:** 1996
SALES (est): 2.21MM **Privately Held**
Web: www.innotech-mfg.com
▪ **SIC: 3599** Machine shop, jobbing and repair

(P-7874)

INTERNATIONAL PRECISION INC

Also Called: I P
9526 Vassar Ave (91311-4168)
P.O. Box 4839 (91313-4839)
PHONE..............................818 882-3933

Renee M Brendel-konrad, *Pr*
Kalei Kaumaka Konrad, *VP*
◆ **EMP: 18 EST:** 1968
SQ FT: 12,000
SALES (est): 4.88MM **Privately Held**
Web: www.intlprecision.com
SIC: 3599 3728 Machine shop, jobbing and repair; Aircraft parts and equipment, nec

(P-7875)

INTRA AEROSPACE LLC

10671 Civic Center Dr (91730-3804)
PHONE..............................909 476-0343
Robert Sayig, *Prin*
EMP: 35 EST: 2018
SALES (est): 3.61MM **Privately Held**
Web: www.intra-aerospace.com
SIC: 3599 Machine shop, jobbing and repair

(P-7876)

INTRI-PLEX TECHNOLOGIES INC (HQ)

751 S Kellogg Ave (93117-3806)
PHONE..............................805 683-3414
Lawney J Falloon, *CEO*
David Janes, *
John Sullivan, *
Lawrence Ellis, *
▲ **EMP: 126 EST:** 1987
SQ FT: 46,000
SALES (est): 20.93MM
SALES (corp-wide): 21.69MM **Privately Held**
Web: www.intriplex.com
SIC: 3599 Machine shop, jobbing and repair
PA: Ipt Holding Inc
751 S Kellogg Ave
Goleta CA
805 683-3414

(P-7877)

ISI DETENTION CONTG GROUP INC

Also Called: Argyle Precision
577 N Batavia St (92868-1218)
PHONE..............................714 288-1770
Zach Greene, *Pr*
Joe Chavez, *
▲ **EMP: 90 EST:** 1993
SQ FT: 25,000
SALES (est): 9.98MM **Privately Held**
SIC: 3599 3444 Machine and other job shop work; Sheet metal specialties, not stamped

(P-7878)

J & F MACHINE INC

6401 Global Dr (90630-5227)
PHONE..............................714 527-3499
Micheline Varnum, *Pr*
Richard Varnum, *VP*
EMP: 22 EST: 1977
SQ FT: 8,500
SALES (est): 3.25MM **Privately Held**
Web: www.jandfmachine.com
SIC: 3599 Machine shop, jobbing and repair

(P-7879)

J & R MACHINE WORKS

45420 60th St W (93536-8322)
PHONE..............................661 945-8826
Jesse Alvarado, *Pt*
Rudy Alvarado, *Pt*
EMP: 21 EST: 1989
SQ FT: 3,500
SALES (est): 1.08MM **Privately Held**
Web: www.jrmachineworks.com
SIC: 3599 Machine shop, jobbing and repair

(P-7880)

J & S INC

229 E Gardena Blvd (90248-2800)
PHONE..............................310 719-7144
Joseph Brown, *Pr*
Margaret Brown, *
Sheryl Zamora, *
EMP: 33 EST: 1981
SQ FT: 6,141
SALES (est): 2.65MM **Privately Held**
SIC: 3599 Machine shop, jobbing and repair

(P-7881)

J AND K MANUFACTURING INC

14701 Garfield Ave (90723-3412)
PHONE..............................562 630-8417
▲ **EMP: 28 EST:** 1978
SALES (est): 3.99MM **Privately Held**
SIC: 3599 Machine shop, jobbing and repair

(P-7882)

J B TOOL INC

350 E Orangethorpe Ave Ste 6 (92870-6504)
PHONE..............................714 993-7173
Robert Barna, *Pr*
EMP: 17 EST: 1975
SQ FT: 12,000
SALES (est): 490.56K **Privately Held**
Web: www.jbtoolinc.com
SIC: 3599 Machine shop, jobbing and repair

(P-7883)

J FLYING MACHINE INC

701 S Andreasen Dr Ste C (92029-1950)
PHONE..............................760 504-0323
Jay Hegemann, *Owner*
EMP: 17 EST: 2001
SALES (est): 916.1K **Privately Held**
Web: www.flyingjmachine.com
SIC: 3599 Machine shop, jobbing and repair

(P-7884)

J I MACHINE COMPANY INC

9720 Distribution Ave (92121-2310)
PHONE..............................858 695-1787
Ila Ree Piel, *Pr*
James Piel, *
Mark Jay Piel, *VP*
Wendy Anne Piel, *VP*
▲ **EMP: 40 EST:** 1976
SQ FT: 15,400
SALES (est): 4.76MM **Privately Held**
Web: www.jimachine.com
SIC: 3599 3812 Machine shop, jobbing and repair; Search and navigation equipment

(P-7885)

JACO ENGINEERING

879 S East St (92805-5391)
PHONE..............................714 991-1680
H J Meagher, *Pr*
Barbara Meagher, *
EMP: 35 EST: 1964
SQ FT: 10,000
SALES (est): 5.18MM **Privately Held**
Web: www.jacoengineering.com
SIC: 3599 Machine shop, jobbing and repair

(P-7886)

JCPM INC

Also Called: J C Precision
8576 Red Oak St (91730-4822)
PHONE..............................909 484-9040
EMP: 23 EST: 1995
SQ FT: 5,200
SALES (est): 919.89K **Privately Held**
Web: www.jcpm-inc.com

SIC: 3599 Machine shop, jobbing and repair

(P-7887)
JET CUTTING SOLUTIONS INC
10853 Bell Ct (91730-4835)
PHONE.....................909 948-2424
Louis Mammolito, *Pr*
Thomas Ribas, *
Louis Mammooito, *
EMP: 45 EST: 2005
SALES (est): 5.35MM **Privately Held**
Web: www.jetcuttingsolutions.com
SIC: 3599 Machine shop, jobbing and repair

(P-7888)
JMG MACHINE INC
17037 Industry Pl (90638-5819)
PHONE.....................714 522-6221
EMP: 20 EST: 1994
SQ FT: 10,000
SALES (est): 2.2MM **Privately Held**
Web: www.jmgmachine.com
SIC: 3599 Machine shop, jobbing and repair

(P-7889)
JOHNSON MANUFACTURING INC
15201 Connector Ln (92649-1117)
PHONE.....................714 903-0393
Colleen Johnson, *CEO*
Allan Johnson, *
EMP: 35 EST: 1981
SQ FT: 13,000
SALES (est): 4.96MM **Privately Held**
Web: www.johnsonmfginc.com
SIC: 3599 Machine shop, jobbing and repair

(P-7890)
JOHNSON PRECISION PRODUCTS INC
1308 E Wakeham Ave (92705-4145)
PHONE.....................714 824-6971
Paul Cronin, *Pr*
EMP: 19 EST: 1961
SQ FT: 4,000
SALES (est): 4.97MM **Privately Held**
Web:
www.johnsonprecisionmachining.com
SIC: 3599 Machine shop, jobbing and repair

(P-7891)
JR MACHINE COMPANY INC
13245 Florence Ave (90670-4509)
PHONE.....................562 903-9477
Gilbert Reyes, *Pr*
EMP: 29 EST: 1973
SQ FT: 12,000
SALES (est): 2.47MM **Privately Held**
SIC: 3599 Machine shop, jobbing and repair

(P-7892)
K-P ENGINEERING CORP
2126 S Lyon St Ste A (92705-5328)
PHONE.....................714 545-7045
Kemal Pepic, *CEO*
EMP: 27 EST: 1980
SQ FT: 7,000
SALES (est): 887.72K **Privately Held**
Web: www.kpe.com
SIC: 3599 8711 Machine shop, jobbing and repair; Professional engineer

(P-7893)
K-TECH MACHINE INC
1377 Armorlite Dr (92069-1341)
PHONE.....................800 274-9424
Kenneth Russell, *Pr*
Stuart John Russell, *
EMP: 134 EST: 1990

SQ FT: 16,000
SALES (est): 24.39MM **Privately Held**
Web: www.k-techmachine.com
SIC: 3599 3444 Machine shop, jobbing and repair; Sheet metalwork

(P-7894)
KAP MANUFACTURING INC
327 W Allen Ave (91773-1441)
PHONE.....................909 599-2525
Michael D' Amato, *CFO*
Michael D Amato, *
Kathleen D Amato, *
Bryan D'amato, *VP*
EMP: 27 EST: 1999
SQ FT: 6,000
SALES (est): 5.46MM **Privately Held**
Web: www.kapmfg.com
SIC: 3599 Machine shop, jobbing and repair

(P-7895)
KAY & JAMES INC
Also Called: J&S Machine Works
14062 Balboa Blvd (91342-1005)
PHONE.....................818 998-0357
Kye Sook So, *CEO*
Jung M So, *
EMP: 75 EST: 1981
SQ FT: 25,000
SALES (est): 8.73MM **Privately Held**
SIC: 3599 Machine shop, jobbing and repair

(P-7896)
KEMAC TECHNOLOGY INC
503 S Vincent Ave (91702-5131)
PHONE.....................626 334-1519
EMP: 40
Web: www.tecometetch.com
SIC: 3599 3479 Chemical milling job shop; Etching and engraving

(P-7897)
KERLEYLEGACY63 INC
3000-3010 La Jolla St (92806)
PHONE.....................714 630-7286
EMP: 100
SIC: 3599 3469 3444 3061 Machine and other job shop work; Machine parts, stamped or pressed metal; Sheet metalwork ; Mechanical rubber goods

(P-7898)
KILGORE MACHINE COMPANY INC
2312 S Susan St (92704-4421)
PHONE.....................714 540-3659
Bryant Kilgore, *Pr*
Doree Kilgore, *VP*
Linda Mckenzie, *Prin*
Lisa Damico, *Prin*
EMP: 22 EST: 1968
SQ FT: 8,000
SALES (est): 2.78MM **Privately Held**
Web: www.kilgoremachinecompany.com
SIC: 3599 Machine shop, jobbing and repair

(P-7899)
KIMBERLY MACHINE INC
12822 Joy St (92840-6350)
PHONE.....................714 539-0151
Khanh Cao, *CEO*
Tam Nguyen, *
EMP: 35 EST: 1975
SQ FT: 10,300
SALES (est): 4.3MM **Privately Held**
Web: www.kimberlymachine.com
SIC: 3599 Machine shop, jobbing and repair

(P-7900)
KITCH ENGINEERING INC
12320 Montague St (91331-2213)
PHONE.....................818 897-7133
Steven Kitching, *Pr*
Terry Kitching, *
Kerri Kitching, *
EMP: 30 EST: 1984
SQ FT: 6,000
SALES (est): 5.28MM **Privately Held**
Web: www.kitchengineering.com
SIC: 3599 3751 Machine shop, jobbing and repair; Motorcycles, bicycles and parts

(P-7901)
L A GAUGE COMPANY INC
7440 San Fernando Rd (91352-4398)
PHONE.....................818 767-7193
Harbans Bawa, *Pr*
EMP: 74 EST: 1954
SQ FT: 26,682
SALES (est): 16.89MM **Privately Held**
Web: www.lagauge.com
SIC: 3599 Machine shop, jobbing and repair

(P-7902)
LANDMARK MFG INC
Also Called: Landmark Motor Cycle ACC
4112 Avenida De La Plata (92056-6099)
PHONE.....................760 941-6626
Tom Allen, *Pr*
Lowell Allen, *VP*
Pat Allen, *Sec*
EMP: 23 EST: 1979
SQ FT: 17,000
SALES (est): 2.51MM **Privately Held**
Web: www.landmarkmfg.com
SIC: 3599 3751 Machine shop, jobbing and repair; Motorcycle accessories

(P-7903)
LANGE PRECISION INC
1106 E Elm Ave (92831-5024)
PHONE.....................714 870-5420
Gregory R Lange, *Pr*
Lisa Lange, *CFO*
EMP: 18 EST: 1967
SQ FT: 35,000
SALES (est): 1.96MM **Privately Held**
Web: www.langeprecision.biz
SIC: 3599 Machine shop, jobbing and repair

(P-7904)
LANSAIR CORPORATION
25228 Anza Dr (91355-3496)
PHONE.....................661 294-9503
John Voshell, *Pr*
Eleanor Voshell, *VP*
EMP: 37 EST: 1966
SQ FT: 15,000
SALES (est): 910.2K **Privately Held**
Web: www.lansaircorp.com
SIC: 3599 Machine shop, jobbing and repair

(P-7905)
LASER INDUSTRIES INC
1351 Manhattan Ave (92831-5216)
PHONE.....................714 532-3271
Robert Karim, *Pr*
John Krickl, *
Joseph Butterly, *
Gary Nadau, *
EMP: 65 EST: 1986
SQ FT: 17,500
SALES (est): 11.52MM **Privately Held**
Web: www.laserindustries.com
SIC: 3599 Machine shop, jobbing and repair

(P-7906)
LASEROD TECHNOLOGIES LLC
20312 Gramercy Pl (90501-1511)
PHONE.....................310 328-5869
▼ EMP: 20 EST: 2011
SQ FT: 8,000
SALES (est): 1.9MM **Privately Held**
Web: www.laserod.com
SIC: 3599 Machine shop, jobbing and repair

(P-7907)
LAURELWOOD INDUSTRIES INC
Also Called: Automation Gt
1939 Palomar Oaks Way Ste B (92011-1311)
PHONE.....................760 705-1649
Simon Grant, *Pr*
EMP: 19 EST: 2009
SALES (est): 3MM **Privately Held**
SIC: 3599 8734 3545 Custom machinery; Product testing laboratory, safety or performance; Precision measuring tools

(P-7908)
LONG MACHINE INC
27450 Colt Ct (92590-3673)
PHONE.....................951 296-0194
Larry Long, *Pr*
Vicki Long, *VP*
EMP: 21 EST: 1979
SQ FT: 15,000
SALES (est): 2.66MM **Privately Held**
Web: www.longmachine.com
SIC: 3599 Machine shop, jobbing and repair

(P-7909)
LURAN INC
24927 Avenue Tibbitts Ste K (91355-1268)
PHONE.....................661 257-6303
Terry Decker Junior, *Pr*
Terry Decker, *
EMP: 18 EST: 1970
SQ FT: 20,000
SALES (est): 1.03MM **Privately Held**
Web: www.luraninc.com
SIC: 3599 Machine shop, jobbing and repair

(P-7910)
LUSK QUALITY MACHINE PRODUCTS
39457 15th St E (93550-3445)
P.O. Box 901030 (93590-1030)
PHONE.....................661 272-0630
Randall J Lusk, *CEO*
Lloyd Lusk, *
EMP: 27 EST: 1971
SQ FT: 25,000
SALES (est): 4.93MM **Privately Held**
Web: www.luskquality.com
SIC: 3599 3451 Machine shop, jobbing and repair; Screw machine products

(P-7911)
M & W MACHINE CORPORATION
Also Called: Capitol Machine Co
1642 E Edinger Ave Ste A (92705-5002)
PHONE.....................714 541-2652
George Nys, *Pr*
Sandra Nys, *Sec*
Jason Nys, *Sec*
EMP: 25 EST: 1965
SQ FT: 6,000
SALES (est): 403.5K **Privately Held**
SIC: 3599 Machine shop, jobbing and repair

(P-7912)
M-INDUSTRIAL ENTERPRISES LLC
Also Called: Project Management

PRODUCTS & SVCS

11 Via Onagro (92688-4126)
PHONE..............................949 413-7513
Zahid Nazarzai, *Owner*
EMP: 25 EST: 2001
SALES (est): 1.17MM **Privately Held**
SIC: 3599 Industrial machinery, nec

(P-7913)
MACHINE CRAFT OF SAN DIEGO
7204 Babilonia St (92009-6510)
PHONE..............................858 642-0509
Chinta M Sawh, *Pr*
Deo Sawh, *
Indra Starr, *
EMP: 19 EST: 1981
SALES (est): 440.46K **Privately Held**
SIC: 3599 3812 Machine shop, jobbing and
repair; Search and navigation equipment

(P-7914)
MACHINE PRECISION COMPONENTS
14014 Dinard Ave (90670-4923)
PHONE..............................562 404-0500
Mauro Michel, *CEO*
EMP: 18 EST: 2004
SALES (est): 1.97MM **Privately Held**
Web: www.mpcmachining.com
SIC: 3599 Machine shop, jobbing and repair

(P-7915)
MAGNA TOOL INC
5594 Market Pl (90630-4710)
PHONE..............................714 826-2500
Bob Melton, *Pr*
Cindy Melton, *CFO*
EMP: 20 EST: 1977
SQ FT: 8,500
SALES (est): 2.46MM **Privately Held**
Web: www.magnatoolinc.com
SIC: 3599 Machine shop, jobbing and repair

(P-7916)
MALMBERG ENGINEERING INC
655 Deep Valley Dr Ste 125 (90274-3688)
PHONE..............................925 606-6500
▼ EMP: 40
Web: www.malmbergeng.com
SIC: 3599 Custom machinery

(P-7917)
MANTI - MACHINE CO INC
11782 Western Ave Ste 15 (90680-3466)
PHONE..............................714 902-1465
William G Vlieland, *Pr*
Bj Vlieland, *Sec*
Dawn Harlow, *CFO*
EMP: 23 EST: 1966
SQ FT: 3,400
SALES (est): 396.49K **Privately Held**
SIC: 3599 Machine shop, jobbing and repair

(P-7918)
MAR ENGINEERING COMPANY
7350 Greenbush Ave (91605-4003)
PHONE..............................818 765-4805
Monte Markowitz, *CEO*
Samuel Markowitz, *
Barbara Markowitz, *
EMP: 25 EST: 1957
SQ FT: 12,000
SALES (est): 1.92MM **Privately Held**
Web: www.marengineering.com
SIC: 3599 Machine shop, jobbing and repair

(P-7919)
MARONEY COMPANY
9016 Winnetka Ave (91324-3235)
PHONE..............................818 882-2722

John C Maroney Senior, *Pr*
Francine L Maroney, *Sr VP*
EMP: 17 EST: 1955
SQ FT: 12,500
SALES (est): 2.37MM **Privately Held**
Web: www.maroneycompany.com
SIC: 3599 Machine shop, jobbing and repair

(P-7920)
MARTINEZ AND TUREK INC
Also Called: Martinez & Turek
300 S Cedar Ave (92376-9100)
PHONE..............................909 820-6800
Larry Tribe, *Pr*
Donald A Turek, *
Thomas J Martinez, *Testing Vice President*
Laurence Martinez, *
John Romero, *
EMP: 120 EST: 1980
SQ FT: 139,000
SALES (est): 19.02MM **Privately Held**
Web: www.mandtinc.com
SIC: 3599 Machine shop, jobbing and repair

(P-7921)
MATHY MACHINE INC
9315 Wheatlands Rd (92071-2860)
PHONE..............................619 448-0404
Jay Mathy, *Pr*
EMP: 30 EST: 1979
SQ FT: 14,000
SALES (est): 4.43MM **Privately Held**
Web: www.mathymachine.com
SIC: 3599 Machine shop, jobbing and repair

(P-7922)
MAUL MFG INC (PA)
3041 S Shannon St (92704-6320)
PHONE..............................714 641-0727
Tony Johnson, *Pr*
Lori Deorio, *
EMP: 20 EST: 1975
SQ FT: 10,080
SALES (est): 4.96MM
SALES (corp-wide): 4.96MM **Privately Held**
Web: www.ysc-mmi.com
SIC: 3599 3491 3492 Machine shop, jobbing
and repair; Solenoid valves; Control valves,
aircraft: hydraulic and pneumatic

(P-7923)
MCCOPPIN ENTERPRISES
Also Called: Accurate Manufacturing
Company
6641 San Fernando Rd (91201-1702)
PHONE..............................818 240-4840
Richard J Mc Coppin, *Pr*
Robert R Gagliardi, *VP*
John Gagliardi, *VP*
Carol Park, *Stockholder*
EMP: 22 EST: 1945
SQ FT: 25,000
SALES (est): 2.86MM **Privately Held**
Web: www.acc-mfg.com
SIC: 3599 3544 3441 Machine shop, jobbing
and repair; Dies and die holders for metal
cutting, forming, die casting; Fabricated
structural metal

(P-7924)
MD ENGINEERING INC
1550 Consumer Cir (92878-3225)
PHONE..............................951 736-5390
Mike Morgan, *Pr*
Ryan Cortes, *
Kurt Bryan Qco, *Prin*
EMP: 37 EST: 1999
SQ FT: 16,000
SALES (est): 4.82MM **Privately Held**

Web: www.mde-us.com
SIC: 3599 Machine shop, jobbing and repair

(P-7925)
MEDLIN AND SON ENGRG SVC INC
Also Called: Medlin & Sons
12484 Whittier Blvd (90602-1017)
PHONE..............................562 464-5889
George W Medlin Ii, *CEO*
Susan Medlin, *
EMP: 45 EST: 1959
SQ FT: 26,000
SALES (est): 3MM **Privately Held**
Web: www.medlinandson.com
SIC: 3599 Machine shop, jobbing and repair

(P-7926)
MELKES MACHINE INC
9928 Hayward Way (91733-3114)
PHONE..............................626 448-5062
Isabelle Melkesian, *Pr*
Brent Melkesian, *
EMP: 25 EST: 1960
SQ FT: 24,000
SALES (est): 497.53K **Privately Held**
Web: www.melkes.com
SIC: 3599 Machine shop, jobbing and repair

(P-7927)
MERCURY ENGINEERING CORP
5630 Imperial Hwy (90280-7420)
PHONE..............................562 861-7816
David Barker, *Pr*
EMP: 20 EST: 1949
SQ FT: 10,000
SALES (est): 679.64K **Privately Held**
Web: www.mercuryengineeringcorp.com
SIC: 3599 Machine shop, jobbing and repair

(P-7928)
MERRY AN CEJKA
Also Called: Scott Craft Co
4601 Cecilia St (90201-5813)
P.O. Box 430 (90201-0430)
PHONE..............................323 560-3949
Merry An Cejka, *Owner*
Amelia Leal-lee, *Prin*
Robert Cejka, *Prin*
Veronica Zazueta, *Prin*
EMP: 25 EST: 1966
SQ FT: 12,000
SALES (est): 2.39MM **Privately Held**
Web: www.scottcraftco.com
SIC: 3599 3544 Custom machinery; Special
dies, tools, jigs, and fixtures

(P-7929)
METAL CUTTING SERVICE
16233 Gale Ave (91745-1719)
PHONE..............................626 968-4764
David Viel, *Pr*
Milon Viel, *CEO*
Earl Viel, *Sec*
EMP: 18 EST: 1956
SQ FT: 32,000
SALES (est): 2.47MM **Privately Held**
Web: www.metalcut.com
SIC: 3599 Machine shop, jobbing and repair

(P-7930)
METALORE INC
750 S Douglas St (90245-4901)
PHONE..............................310 643-0360
Kenneth Hill, *Pr*
▲ EMP: 30 EST: 1961
SALES (est): 2.62MM **Privately Held**
Web: www.metalore.com

SIC: 3599 Machine shop, jobbing and repair

(P-7931)
METRIC MACHINING (PA)
Also Called: Master Machine Products
3263 Trade Center Dr (92507-3432)
PHONE..............................909 947-9222
David Parker, *Prin*
▲ EMP: 50 EST: 1973
SQ FT: 45,000
SALES (est): 41.2MM
SALES (corp-wide): 41.2MM **Privately Held**
Web: www.metricorp.com
SIC: 3599 Machine shop, jobbing and repair

(P-7932)
MEZIERE ENTERPRISES INC
220 S Hale Ave Ste A (92029-1719)
PHONE..............................800 208-1755
Michael Meziere, *Pr*
Don Meziere, *
Dave Meziere, *
▲ EMP: 30 EST: 1980
SQ FT: 15,000
SALES (est): 5.29MM **Privately Held**
Web: www.meziere.com
SIC: 3599 Machine shop, jobbing and repair

(P-7933)
MICRON MACHINE COMPANY
3337 Highway 67 (92065-7119)
PHONE..............................858 486-5900
Mark Conley, *CEO*
Donna Conley, *VP*
EMP: 22 EST: 1977
SALES (est): 2.05MM **Privately Held**
Web: www.micronmachine.com
SIC: 3599 8731 3462 3369 Machine shop,
jobbing and repair; Commercial physical
research; Iron and steel forgings;
Nonferrous foundries, nec

(P-7934)
MIKE DYELL MACHINE SHOP INC (PA)
160 S Linden Ave (92376-6204)
P.O. Box 974 (92377-0974)
PHONE..............................909 350-4101
Edith Dyell, *CEO*
Tom Bradley, *Pr*
EMP: 17 EST: 1968
SQ FT: 20,000
SALES (est): 3.87MM
SALES (corp-wide): 3.87MM **Privately Held**
Web: www.dyellmachine.com
SIC: 3599 5084 7699 Machine shop, jobbing
and repair; Hydraulic systems equipment
and supplies; Hydraulic equipment repair

(P-7935)
MIKE KENNEY TOOL INC
Also Called: Mkt Innovations
588 Porter Way (92870-6453)
PHONE..............................714 577-9262
Mike Kenney, *Pr*
Julie Kenney, *
▲ EMP: 37 EST: 1980
SALES (est): 3.65MM **Privately Held**
Web: www.mkti.com
SIC: 3599 Machine shop, jobbing and repair

(P-7936)
MIKELSON MACHINE SHOP INC
2546 Merced Ave (91733-1924)
PHONE..............................626 448-3920
James Michaelson, *Pr*
James M Mikelson, *
▼ EMP: 23 EST: 1967

SQ FT: 14,000
SALES (est): 4.32MM **Privately Held**
Web: www.mikelson.net
SIC: 3599 Machine shop, jobbing and repair

(P-7937)
MILCO WIRE EDM INC
Also Called: Milco Waterjet
15221 Connector Ln (92649-1117)
PHONE................................714 373-0098
Steven R Miller, *Pr*
EMP: 17 EST: 1990
SQ FT: 14,000
SALES (est): 2.48MM **Privately Held**
Web: www.milcowireedm.com
SIC: 3599 3541 Electrical discharge machining (EDM); Machine tools, metal cutting type

(P-7938)
MILLER MACHINE WORKS LLC
Also Called: Miller Cnc
789 Anita St (91911-3901)
PHONE................................619 501-9866
Todd Cuffaro, *CEO*
EMP: 17 EST: 2007
SQ FT: 7,500
SALES (est): 5.31MM **Privately Held**
Web: www.millercnc.com
SIC: 3599 Machine shop, jobbing and repair

(P-7939)
MILLIPART INC (PA)
412 W Carter Dr (91740-5998)
PHONE................................626 963-4101
Scot Jamison, *Pr*
EMP: 18 EST: 1954
SQ FT: 4,000
SALES (est): 2.94MM
SALES (corp-wide): 2.94MM **Privately Held**
Web: www.millipart.com
SIC: 3599 Machine shop, jobbing and repair

(P-7940)
MILLWORX PRCSION MACHINING INC
Also Called: Millworx
506 Malloy Ct (92878-4045)
PHONE................................951 371-2683
Stacy Wilson, *Pr*
Terry Windust, *VP*
Vince M, *Dir*
EMP: 22 EST: 2003
SQ FT: 3,500
SALES (est): 4.99MM **Privately Held**
Web: www.millworxprecision.com
SIC: 3599 Machine shop, jobbing and repair

(P-7941)
MITCO INDUSTRIES INC (PA)
2235 S Vista Ave (92316-2921)
PHONE................................909 877-0800
Larry Mitchell, *Pr*
Sammy Mitchell, *
EMP: 26 EST: 1972
SQ FT: 11,000
SALES (est): 4.51MM
SALES (corp-wide): 4.51MM **Privately Held**
Web: www.mitcoind.com
SIC: 3599 3533 Machine shop, jobbing and repair; Drilling tools for gas, oil, or water wells

(P-7942)
MKT INNOVATIONS
Also Called: Cooljet Systems
588 Porter Way (92870-6453)
PHONE................................714 524-7668

Mike Kenney, *CEO*
Kathy Jackson, *
▲ EMP: 68 EST: 2002
SALES (est): 7.56MM **Privately Held**
Web: www.mkti.com
SIC: 3599 3523 Machine shop, jobbing and repair; Farm machinery and equipment

(P-7943)
MODERN ENGINE INC
701 Sonora Ave (91201-2431)
PHONE................................818 409-9494
Vachagan Aslanian, *Pr*
Razmik Aslanian, *
Armond Aslanian, *
Nora Aslanian, *
▲ EMP: 43 EST: 1979
SQ FT: 26,000
SALES (est): 5.37MM **Privately Held**
Web: www.meparts.com
SIC: 3599 7539 Machine shop, jobbing and repair; Machine shop, automotive

(P-7944)
MOLNAR ENGINEERING INC
Also Called: Lee's Enterprise
20731 Marilla St (91311-4408)
PHONE................................818 993-3495
Laszlo Molnar, *CEO*
Linda D Molnar, *
Tom Molnar, *
Michael Molnar, *
▲ EMP: 37 EST: 1975
SQ FT: 12,000
SALES (est): 4.3MM **Privately Held**
Web: www.leesenterprise.com
SIC: 3599 Machine shop, jobbing and repair

(P-7945)
MOMENI ENGINEERING LLC
Also Called: Essex Industries
5451 Argosy Ave (92649-1038)
PHONE................................714 897-9301
Ahmad Momeni, *Managing Member*
EMP: 28 EST: 1982
SALES (est): 3.72MM **Privately Held**
Web: www.essexindustries.com
SIC: 3599 3841 Machine shop, jobbing and repair; Surgical and medical instruments

(P-7946)
MONO ENGINEERING CORP
20977 Knapp St (91311-5926)
PHONE................................818 772-4998
Siamak Morini, *CEO*
EMP: 50 EST: 1994
SQ FT: 40,000
SALES (est): 7.25MM **Privately Held**
Web: www.monoengineering.com
SIC: 3599 3444 8711 Machine shop, jobbing and repair; Sheet metalwork; Industrial engineers

(P-7947)
MOSEYS PRODUCTION MACHINISTS INC (PA)
1550 Lakeview Loop (92807)
PHONE................................714 693-4840
EMP: 42 EST: 1975
SALES (est): 5.92MM
SALES (corp-wide): 5.92MM **Privately Held**
Web: www.moseys.com
SIC: 3599 Machine shop, jobbing and repair

(P-7948)
MOTORVAC TECHNOLOGIES INC
1431 Village Way (92705-4714)

PHONE................................714 558-4822
Mark J Hallsman, *Pr*
John A Rome, *VP*
Gerry Quinn Bdmem, *Prin*
Ron Monark, *Ch Bd*
Stephen Greaves Bdmem, *Prin*
EMP: 30 EST: 1992
SQ FT: 24,360
SALES (est): 8.31MM **Privately Held**
Web: www.cpsproducts.com
SIC: 3599 2899 2842 5013 Gasoline filters, internal combustion engine, except auto; Fuel tank or engine cleaning chemicals; Polishes and sanitation goods; Automotive servicing equipment
PA: Erin Mills International Investment Corp.
C/O Dr. Trevor Carmichael
Bridgetown

(P-7949)
MUTH MACHINE WORKS (HQ)
8042 Katella Ave (90680-3207)
PHONE................................714 527-2239
Richard Muth, *Pr*
Lynn Muth, *VP*
Dwayne Gleason, *VP Opers*
Peter G Muth, *Treas*
▲ EMP: 20 EST: 1993
SQ FT: 2,000
SALES (est): 16.86MM
SALES (corp-wide): 49.61MM **Privately Held**
SIC: 3599 Machine shop, jobbing and repair
PA: Orco Block & Hardscape
11100 Beach Blvd
Stanton CA
714 527-2239

(P-7950)
NC DYNAMICS INCORPORATED
Also Called: Ncdi
6925 Downey Ave (90805-1823)
PHONE................................562 634-7392
Kevin Minter, *CEO*
Randall L Bazz, *
▲ EMP: 151 EST: 1979
SALES (est): 23.44MM
SALES (corp-wide): 92.77MM **Privately Held**
Web: www.ncdynamics.com
SIC: 3599 Machine shop, jobbing and repair
PA: Harlow Aerostructures Llc
1501 S Mclean Blvd
Wichita KS
316 265-5268

(P-7951)
NC DYNAMICS LLC
Also Called: NC Dynamics
3401 E 69th St (90805-1872)
PHONE................................562 634-7392
Phillip Friedman, *Prin*
EMP: 150 EST: 2017
SALES (est): 22.65MM
SALES (corp-wide): 92.77MM **Privately Held**
Web: www.ncdynamics.com
SIC: 3599 Machine shop, jobbing and repair
PA: Harlow Aerostructures Llc
1501 S Mclean Blvd
Wichita KS
316 265-5268

(P-7952)
NELGO INDUSTRIES INC
Also Called: Nelgo Manufacturing
598 Airport Rd (92058-1207)
PHONE................................760 433-6434
Peter Edward Goethel, *CEO*
EMP: 32 EST: 1966

SALES (est): 4.68MM **Privately Held**
Web: www.nelgo.com
SIC: 3599 Machine shop, jobbing and repair

(P-7953)
NELSON ENGINEERING LLC
11600 Monarch St (92841-1817)
PHONE................................714 893-7999
▲ EMP: 18 EST: 1986
SQ FT: 17,600
SALES (est): 642.02K **Privately Held**
SIC: 3599 Machine shop, jobbing and repair

(P-7954)
NEXT INTENT INC
Also Called: Next Intent
865 Via Esteban (93401-7178)
PHONE................................805 781-6755
EMP: 30 EST: 1996
SQ FT: 8,500
SALES (est): 5.11MM **Privately Held**
Web: www.nextintent.com
SIC: 3599 Machine shop, jobbing and repair

(P-7955)
NIEDWICK CORPORATION
Also Called: Niedwick Machine Co
967 N Eckhoff St (92867-5432)
P.O. Box 63851 (92602-6132)
PHONE................................714 771-9999
Theodore R Niedwick, *Pr*
EMP: 45 EST: 1992
SQ FT: 8,200
SALES (est): 5.2MM **Privately Held**
Web: www.niedwickmachine.com
SIC: 3599 Machine shop, jobbing and repair

(P-7956)
NOROTOS INC
201 E Alton Ave (92707-4416)
PHONE................................714 662-3113
Ronald Soto, *Pr*
John Soto, *
▲ EMP: 116 EST: 1985
SQ FT: 12,000
SALES (est): 9.36MM **Privately Held**
Web: www.norotos.com
SIC: 3599 3842 Machine shop, jobbing and repair; Surgical appliances and supplies

(P-7957)
NUSPACE INC (HQ)
4401 E Donald Douglas Dr (90808-1732)
PHONE................................562 497-3200
Ian Ballinger, *CEO*
Lili Zhou, *
◆ EMP: 26 EST: 1907
SQ FT: 60,000
SALES (est): 12.04MM
SALES (corp-wide): 12.04MM **Privately Held**
Web: www.keyengco.com
SIC: 3599 Air intake filters, internal combustion engine, except auto
PA: Ke Company Acquisition Corp.
4401 E Donald Douglas Dr
Long Beach CA
562 497-3200

(P-7958)
O & S PRECISION INC
20630 Nordhoff St (91311-6114)
PHONE................................818 718-8876
Scott Onasch, *CEO*
EMP: 20 EST: 1996
SQ FT: 5,000
SALES (est): 8.3MM **Privately Held**
Web: www.oands.com
SIC: 3599 Machine shop, jobbing and repair

PRODUCTS & SVCS

(P-7959)
ODONNELL MANUFACTURING INC

14811 Via Defrancesco Ave (92508-9005)
P.O. Box 6245 (92860-8041)
PHONE.............................562 944-9671
Steve O'donnell, *Pr*
▲ **EMP:** 25 **EST:** 1985
SQ FT: 10,000
SALES (est): 639.4K **Privately Held**
SIC: 3599 Machine shop, jobbing and repair

(P-7960)
OEM LLC

311 S Highland Ave (92832-2398)
PHONE.............................714 449-7500
John B Copp, *CEO*
▲ **EMP:** 23 **EST:** 1985
SQ FT: 40,000
SALES (est): 2.77MM **Privately Held**
Web: www.oempresssystems.com
SIC: 3599 Machine shop, jobbing and repair

(P-7961)
OMEGA PRECISION

13040 Telegraph Rd (90670-4078)
PHONE.............................562 946-2491
Richard Venegas, *CEO*
Joseph M Venegas, *
Richard M Venegas, *
Steve Venegas, *
EMP: 25 **EST:** 1965
SQ FT: 16,332
SALES (est): 4.91MM **Privately Held**
Web: www.omegaprecision.us
SIC: 3599 Machine shop, jobbing and repair

(P-7962)
ORANGE COUNTY SCREW PDTS INC

2993 E La Palma Ave (92806-2620)
PHONE.............................714 630-7433
Robert Andri, *Pr*
EMP: 20 **EST:** 1967
SQ FT: 8,000
SALES (est): 1.61MM **Privately Held**
SIC: 3599 3451 Machine shop, jobbing and repair; Screw machine products

(P-7963)
PACIFIC AEROSPACE MACHINE INC

3002 S Rosewood Ave (92707-3822)
PHONE.............................714 534-1444
Paul Nguyen, *CEO*
Kirk Nguyen, *
EMP: 21 **EST:** 1997
SQ FT: 50,000
SALES (est): 855.74K **Privately Held**
Web: www.pacificmachine.net
SIC: 3599 Machine shop, jobbing and repair

(P-7964)
PACIFIC BROACH & ENGRG ASSOC

1513 N Kraemer Blvd (92806-1407)
PHONE.............................714 632-5678
Steven R Yetzke, *Pr*
Michael Yetzke, *VP*
Elaine Montgomery, *Sec*
▲ **EMP:** 19 **EST:** 1943
SQ FT: 18,000
SALES (est): 1.72MM **Privately Held**
Web: www.bdlind.com
SIC: 3599 Machine shop, jobbing and repair

(P-7965)
PACIFIC MFG INC SAN DIEGO

1520 Corporate Center Dr (92154-6634)
PHONE.............................619 423-0316
Raymundo Montalvo, *Pr*
Maria A Montalvo, *VP*
EMP: 20 **EST:** 1977
SQ FT: 9,500
SALES (est): 2.48MM **Privately Held**
Web: www.pacmfginc.com
SIC: 3599 Machine shop, jobbing and repair

(P-7966)
PAMCO MACHINE WORKS INC

9359 Feron Blvd (91730-4516)
PHONE.............................909 941-7260
James Fredrick Wilkinson, *CEO*
Diane Wilkinson, *Sec*
EMP: 20 **EST:** 1956
SQ FT: 17,000
SALES (est): 4.45MM **Privately Held**
Web: www.pamcomachine.com
SIC: 3599 3462 Machine shop, jobbing and repair; Iron and steel forgings

(P-7967)
PARAMOUNT MACHINE CO INC

10824 Edison Ct (91730-3868)
P.O. Box 8068 (91701-0068)
PHONE.............................909 484-3600
Gregory A Harsen, *Pr*
Gail Harsen, *
EMP: 36 **EST:** 1964
SQ FT: 12,000
SALES (est): 5.7MM **Privately Held**
Web: www.paramountmachine.com
SIC: 3599 Machine shop, jobbing and repair

(P-7968)
PARK ENGINEERING AND MFG CO

Also Called: Pem
6430 Roland St (90621-3122)
P.O. Box 2275 (90621-0775)
PHONE.............................714 521-4660
Joanna Tenney, *CEO*
Jeff Tenney, *
EMP: 30 **EST:** 1959
SQ FT: 6,000
SALES (est): 2.4MM **Privately Held**
Web: www.park-engineering.com
SIC: 3599 Machine shop, jobbing and repair

(P-7969)
PDQ ENGINEERING INC

1199 Avenida Acaso Ste F (93012-8739)
PHONE.............................805 482-1334
Shannon Clark, *Pr*
Elmer Clark, *VP*
Scott Jenkins, *Mgr*
EMP: 24 **EST:** 1999
SQ FT: 10,000
SALES (est): 1.94MM **Privately Held**
SIC: 3599 Machine shop, jobbing and repair

(P-7970)
PEDAVENA MOULD AND DIE CO INC

12464 Mccann Dr (90670-3335)
PHONE.............................310 327-2814
Steve Scardenzan, *Pr*
Paul Weisbrich, *
▲ **EMP:** 28 **EST:** 1964
SQ FT: 12,000
SALES (est): 4.83MM **Privately Held**
Web: www.pmdprecision.com
SIC: 3599 Machine and other job shop work

(P-7971)
PENDARVIS MANUFACTURING INC

1808 N American St (92801-1001)
PHONE.............................714 992-0950
TOLL FREE: 800
Robert D Pendarvis, *CEO*
Brian Pendarvis, *
EMP: 25 **EST:** 1982
SQ FT: 8,000
SALES (est): 4.8MM **Privately Held**
Web: www.pendarvismanufacturing.com
SIC: 3599 Machine shop, jobbing and repair

(P-7972)
PERFORMANCE MACHINE TECH INC

25141 Avenue Stanford (91355-1227)
PHONE.............................661 294-8617
EMP: 38 **EST:** 1995
SQ FT: 10,000
SALES (est): 6.45MM **Privately Held**
Web: www.pmtinc.org
SIC: 3599 Machine shop, jobbing and repair

(P-7973)
PIEDRAS MACHINE CORPORATION

15154 Downey Ave Ste B (90723-4595)
PHONE.............................562 602-1500
Salvador Piedra, *Pr*
Ruben Piedra, *CFO*
Lucia Piedra, *Sec*
EMP: 19 **EST:** 2006
SALES (est): 1.53MM **Privately Held**
Web: www.piedrasmachine.com
SIC: 3599 Machine shop, jobbing and repair

(P-7974)
PL MACHINE CORPORATION

10716 Reagan St (90720-2431)
PHONE.............................714 892-1100
Andrew Dinh, *Ex Dir*
EMP: 22 **EST:** 2009
SALES (est): 3.41MM **Privately Held**
Web: www.plmachinecorp.com
SIC: 3599 Machine shop, jobbing and repair

(P-7975)
PLETHORA

2142 Beachwood Ter (90068-3449)
PHONE.............................323 851-1633
Ole Ostergard, *Prin*
EMP: 31 **EST:** 2014
SALES (est): 114.81K **Privately Held**
Web: www.plethora.world
SIC: 3599 Machine shop, jobbing and repair

(P-7976)
PRECISE ENGINEERING INC

11280 Turtleback Ct (92127-2007)
PHONE.............................858 345-7243
Ahmad S Rafiq, *Prin*
EMP: 21 **EST:** 2004
SALES (est): 305.54K **Privately Held**
Web: www.meggitt.com
SIC: 3599 Machine shop, jobbing and repair

(P-7977)
PRECISION ARCFT MACHINING INC

Also Called: Pamco
10640 Elkwood St (91352-4631)
PHONE.............................818 768-5900
Donald A Pisano, *Pr*
Joyce Pisano, *
Kimberly Pisano, *
▲ **EMP:** 50 **EST:** 1961

SQ FT: 6,500
SALES (est): 9.6MM **Privately Held**
Web: www.pamco-usa.com
SIC: 3599 3678 Machine shop, jobbing and repair; Electronic connectors

(P-7978)
PRECISION FRRITES CERAMICS INC

5432 Production Dr (92649-1525)
PHONE.............................714 901-7622
Myung Sook Hong, *CEO*
Sung Mo Hong, *Pr*
Ji Soo Lee, *General Vice President*
EMP: 90 **EST:** 1975
SQ FT: 23,811
SALES (est): 9.7MM **Privately Held**
Web: www.semiceramic.com
SIC: 3599 3264 3674 Machine shop, jobbing and repair; Porcelain electrical supplies; Semiconductors and related devices

(P-7979)
PRECISION WATERJET INC

Also Called: Precision Machining & Fab
4900 E Hunter Ave (92807-2057)
PHONE.............................888 538-9287
Shane Strowski, *Pr*
EMP: 39 **EST:** 2011
SALES (est): 7.83MM **Privately Held**
Web: www.h2ojet.com
SIC: 3599 Machine shop, jobbing and repair

(P-7980)
PRICE PRODUCTS INCORPORATED

106 State Pl (92029-1323)
PHONE.............................760 745-5602
John Price, *Pr*
Robert Price, *
Shirley L Price, *
EMP: 34 **EST:** 1968
SQ FT: 15,000
SALES (est): 4.91MM **Privately Held**
Web: www.priceproducts.com
SIC: 3599 Machine shop, jobbing and repair

(P-7981)
PROCESS FAB INC

13153 Lakeland Rd (90670-4520)
P.O. Box 314 (90670)
PHONE.............................562 921-1979
EMP: 180
SIC: 3599 8711 Machine shop, jobbing and repair; Industrial engineers

(P-7982)
PRONTO PRODUCTS CO

1801 W Olympic Blvd (91199-0001)
PHONE.............................800 377-6680
EMP: 21
SALES (corp-wide): 4.42MM **Privately Held**
Web: www.prontoproducts.com
SIC: 3599 Machine shop, jobbing and repair
PA: Pronto Products Co.
9850 Siempre Viva Rd
San Diego CA
619 661-6995

(P-7983)
PROTO SPACE ENGINEERING INC

2214 Loma Ave (91733-2518)
P.O. Box 1690 (91709-0057)
PHONE.............................626 442-8273
Linda Dabbs, *CEO*
Michael Dabbs, *
EMP: 26 **EST:** 1965

SQ FT: 24,000
SALES (est): 648.17K **Privately Held**
Web: www.psengr.com
SIC: 3599 Machine shop, jobbing and repair

(P-7984)
PSCMB REPAIRS INC
Also Called: Quality Industry Repair
12145 Slauson Ave (90670-2619)
PHONE..............................626 448-7778
Stephany Castellanos, *CEO*
EMP: 40 **EST:** 2012
SALES (est): 4.4MM **Privately Held**
Web: www.qir-usa.com
SIC: 3599 Machine shop, jobbing and repair

(P-7985)
PVA TEPLA AMERICA INC (HQ)
Also Called: Plasma Division
251 Corporate Terrace St (92879-6000)
PHONE..............................951 371-2500
Bill Marsh, *Pr*
EMP: 20 **EST:** 1971
SQ FT: 15,000
SALES (est): 8.51MM
SALES (corp-wide): 8.51MM **Privately Held**
Web: www.pvateplaamerica.com
SIC: 3599 Custom machinery
PA: Pva Holding, Llc
    251 Corporate Terrace St
    Corona CA
    951 270-3949

(P-7986)
PYRAMID PRECISION MACHINE INC
6721 Cobra Way (92121-4110)
PHONE..............................858 642-0713
Robert Taylor, *Pr*
Walter Gieffels, *
EMP: 100 **EST:** 1988
SQ FT: 23,800
SALES (est): 21.59MM **Privately Held**
Web: www.pyramidprecision.com
SIC: 3599 Machine shop, jobbing and repair

(P-7987)
QUALITASK INC
2840 E Gretta Ln (92806-2512)
PHONE..............................714 237-0900
Som Suntharaphat, *Pr*
Eduvigis Suntharaphat, *
Deb Beds, *
EMP: 26 **EST:** 1992
SQ FT: 13,100
SALES (est): 4.46MM **Privately Held**
Web: www.qualitask.com
SIC: 3599 Machine shop, jobbing and repair

(P-7988)
QUALITY CONTROLLED MFG INC
9429 Abraham Way (92071-2854)
PHONE..............................619 443-3997
William Grande, *Pr*
James Hiebing, *
Jane Currie, *
EMP: 70 **EST:** 1978
SQ FT: 25,000
SALES (est): 12.44MM **Privately Held**
Web:
www.qualitycontrolledmanufacturinginc.com
SIC: 3599 Machine shop, jobbing and repair

(P-7989)
QUALONTIME CORPORATION
19 Senisa (92612-2112)
PHONE..............................714 523-4751

Douglas J Siemer, *Pr*
EMP: 18 **EST:** 1968
SQ FT: 7,500
SALES (est): 487.85K **Privately Held**
SIC: 3599 Machine shop, jobbing and repair

(P-7990)
RA INDUSTRIES LLC
900 Glenneyre St (92651-2707)
PHONE..............................714 557-2322
Thomas Hyland, *
Carole A Follman, *
◆ **EMP:** 30 **EST:** 1969
SALES (est): 6.74MM **Privately Held**
Web: www.ra-industries.com
SIC: 3599 3593 Machine shop, jobbing and repair; Fluid power cylinders and actuators

(P-7991)
RALPH E AMES MACHINE WORKS
2301 Dominguez Way (90501-6200)
PHONE..............................310 328-8523
Mike Ames, *Pr*
Ron Ames, *
EMP: 45 **EST:** 1942
SQ FT: 11,000
SALES (est): 8.18MM **Privately Held**
Web: www.amesmachine.com
SIC: 3599 Machine shop, jobbing and repair

(P-7992)
RAMKO MFG INC
3500 Tanya Ave (92545-9410)
PHONE..............................951 652-3510
EMP: 100 **EST:** 1981
SALES (est): 19.17MM **Privately Held**
Web: www.ramko.com
SIC: 3599 Machine shop, jobbing and repair

(P-7993)
RAMP ENGINEERING INC
6850 Walthall Way (90723-2028)
PHONE..............................562 531-8030
Mark Scott, *CEO*
Robert C Scott, *
Lisa Scott, *
EMP: 24 **EST:** 1998
SQ FT: 12,000
SALES (est): 2.22MM **Privately Held**
Web: www.rampengineering.com
SIC: 3599 Machine shop, jobbing and repair

(P-7994)
RAPID PRODUCT SOLUTIONS INC
2240 Celsius Ave Ste D (93030-8015)
PHONE..............................805 485-7234
Max Gerdts, *Pr*
Douglas Wallis, *
Richard Fitch, *
▲ **EMP:** 30 **EST:** 1998
SQ FT: 10,000
SALES (est): 4.17MM **Privately Held**
Web: www.rapid-products.com
SIC: 3599 Machine shop, jobbing and repair

(P-7995)
REID PRODUCTS INC
Also Called: Reid Products
21430 Waalew Rd (92307-1026)
P.O. Box 1507 (92307-0028)
PHONE..............................760 240-1355
Kevin Reid, *Pr*
Shelby Reid, *
Lisa Grinser, *
Cliff R Carter, *
EMP: 48 **EST:** 1980
SQ FT: 15,000

SALES (est): 10.84MM **Privately Held**
Web: www.reidproducts.com
SIC: 3599 Machine shop, jobbing and repair

(P-7996)
REISNER ENTERPRISES INC
Also Called: Westcorp Engineering
1403 W Linden St (92507-6804)
PHONE..............................951 786-9478
Tom Reisner, *Pr*
EMP: 18 **EST:** 1983
SQ FT: 9,000
SALES (est): 410.66K **Privately Held**
SIC: 3599 Machine shop, jobbing and repair

(P-7997)
REMCO MCH & FABRICATION INC
1966 S Date Ave (92316-2442)
PHONE..............................909 877-3530
Jacque Lewis Russell, *CEO*
Jerry Gilson, *VP*
▲ **EMP:** 19 **EST:** 1979
SALES (est): 4.96MM **Privately Held**
SIC: 3599 3441 Machine shop, jobbing and repair; Fabricated structural metal

(P-7998)
RESEARCH METAL INDUSTRIES INC
1970 W 139th St (90249-2408)
PHONE..............................310 352-3200
Harish Brahmbhatt, *Pr*
◆ **EMP:** 35 **EST:** 1964
SQ FT: 24,000
SALES (est): 8.59MM **Privately Held**
Web: www.researchmetal.com
SIC: 3599 3469 Electrical discharge machining (EDM); Spinning metal for the trade

(P-7999)
RICAURTE PRECISION INC
1550 E Mcfadden Ave (92705-4308)
PHONE..............................714 667-0632
Luis Ricaurte, *CEO*
Marina Ricaurte, *Pr*
EMP: 22 **EST:** 1985
SQ FT: 72,000
SALES (est): 7.54MM **Privately Held**
Web: www.ricaurteprecision.com
SIC: 3599 Machine shop, jobbing and repair

(P-8000)
RINCON ENGINEERING CORPORATION
6325 Carpinteria Ave (93013-2901)
P.O. Box 87 (93014-0087)
PHONE..............................805 684-0935
Alberto Hugo, *CEO*
Roger Hugo, *
Richard Hugo, *
EMP: 43 **EST:** 1961
SQ FT: 12,000
SALES (est): 8.18MM **Privately Held**
Web: www.rinconengineering.com
SIC: 3599 3444 3441 Machine shop, jobbing and repair; Sheet metalwork; Fabricated structural metal

(P-8001)
RINCON ENGINEERING TECH
6325 Carpinteria Ave (93013-2901)
PHONE..............................805 684-4144
Edward Avetisian, *Prin*
EMP: 30
SALES (est): 3.16MM **Privately Held**
SIC: 3599 Machine shop, jobbing and repair

(P-8002)
ROBERT H OLIVA INC
Also Called: Romakk Engineering
19863 Nordhoff St (91324-3331)
PHONE..............................818 700-1035
Robert Oliva, *Pr*
Kim Oliva, *
EMP: 25 **EST:** 1975
SQ FT: 4,000
SALES (est): 2.45MM **Privately Held**
Web: www.romakk.com
SIC: 3599 Machine shop, jobbing and repair

(P-8003)
ROBERTS PRECISION ENGRG INC
Also Called: Robert's Engineering
1345 S Allec St (92805-6304)
PHONE..............................714 635-4485
Robert Flores Ii, *Pr*
EMP: 25 **EST:** 1979
SQ FT: 23,000
SALES (est): 4.2MM **Privately Held**
Web: www.roberts-eng.com
SIC: 3599 Machine shop, jobbing and repair

(P-8004)
ROC-AIRE CORP
2198 Pomona Blvd (91768-3332)
PHONE..............................909 784-3385
Thomas L Collins, *CEO*
Jason Collins, *Sec*
EMP: 22 **EST:** 1958
SQ FT: 52,000
SALES (est): 3.94MM **Privately Held**
Web: www.rocaire.com
SIC: 3599 Machine shop, jobbing and repair

(P-8005)
ROMEROS ENGINEERING INC
Also Called: American Turn-Key Fabricators
9175 Milliken Ave (91730-5509)
PHONE..............................909 481-1170
George Romero, *Pr*
EMP: 25 **EST:** 2005
SALES (est): 6.2MM **Privately Held**
Web: www.atf1.com
SIC: 3599 Machine and other job shop work

(P-8006)
RONCELLI PLASTICS INC
330 W Duarte Rd (91016-4519)
PHONE..............................800 250-6516
Gino Roncelli, *CEO*
Riley Cole, *
Bingo Roncelli, *
EMP: 151 **EST:** 1970
SQ FT: 11,000
SALES (est): 24.01MM **Privately Held**
Web: www.roncelli.com
SIC: 3599 Machine shop, jobbing and repair

(P-8007)
RONLO ENGINEERING LTD
955 Flynn Rd (93012-8704)
PHONE..............................805 388-3227
Ronnie Lowe, *CEO*
Rick Slaney, *
Karen Mc Master, *
Tracy Slaney, *
Patricia Lowe Stkhlr, *Prin*
EMP: 30 **EST:** 1969
SQ FT: 23,650
SALES (est): 5.44MM **Privately Held**
Web: www.ronlo.com
SIC: 3599 Machine shop, jobbing and repair

PRODUCTS & SVCS

(P-8008)
ROY & VAL TOOL GRINDING INC
10131 Canoga Ave (91311-3006)
PHONE..............................818 341-2434
Val Goelz, *Pr*
Jim Tweety, *VP*
Mark Goelz, *Sec*
EMP: 20 **EST:** 1966
SQ FT: 4,800
SALES (est): 348.89K **Privately Held**
SIC: 3599 7389 Machine shop, jobbing and repair; Grinding, precision: commercial or industrial

(P-8009)
S & S NUMERICAL CONTROL INC
Also Called: Satterfield Aerospace
19841 Nordhoff St (91324-3331)
PHONE..............................818 341-4141
John Satterfield, *Pr*
Roberta J Satterfield, *Sec*
EMP: 20 **EST:** 1982
SQ FT: 9,000
SALES (est): 2.45MM **Privately Held**
Web: www.ssnumerical.com
SIC: 3599 Machine shop, jobbing and repair

(P-8010)
S R MACHINING INC
640 Parkridge Ave (92860-3124)
PHONE..............................951 520-9486
Lawrence T Kaford, *Pr*
EMP: 22 **EST:** 2003
SALES (est): 1.82MM **Privately Held**
Web: www.srmachining.com
SIC: 3599 Machine shop -jobbing and repair

(P-8011)
S R MACHINING-PROPERTIES LLC
Also Called: S R Machining
640 Parkridge Ave (92860-3124)
PHONE..............................951 520-9486
Lawrence Kaford, *Pr*
▲ **EMP:** 134 **EST:** 1998
SQ FT: 28,000
SALES (est): 10.45MM **Privately Held**
Web: www.srmachining.com
SIC: 3599 3089 Machine shop, jobbing and repair; Injection molding of plastics

(P-8012)
S&S PRECISION MFG INC
2101 S Yale St (92704-4424)
PHONE..............................714 754-6664
David Mosier, *Pr*
EMP: 45 **EST:** 1987
SQ FT: 10,000
SALES (est): 8.45MM **Privately Held**
Web: www.ssprecisionmfg.com
SIC: 3599 Machine shop, jobbing and repair

(P-8013)
SANTA FE MACHINE WORKS INC
14578 Rancho Vista Dr (92335-4277)
PHONE..............................909 350-6877
Todd Kelly, *Pr*
Dennis Kelly, *
Gilbert Robinson, *
Patricia Kelly, *
Todd Kelly, *Sec*
EMP: 29 **EST:** 1923
SQ FT: 30,000
SALES (est): 4.95MM **Privately Held**
Web: www.santafemachine.com
SIC: 3599 Machine shop, jobbing and repair

(P-8014)
SANTOS PRECISION INC
2220 S Anne St (92704-4411)
PHONE..............................714 957-0299
Francisco Santos, *Pr*
Richard Santos, *
Evelyn Santos, *
EMP: 53 **EST:** 1979
SQ FT: 14,800
SALES (est): 2.4MM **Privately Held**
Web: www.santosprecision.com
SIC: 3599 Machine shop, jobbing and repair

(P-8015)
SARR INDUSTRIES INC
8975 Fullbright Ave (91311-6124)
PHONE..............................818 998-7735
Richard L Joice Junior, *Pr*
Angela Suszka, *Sec*
EMP: 20 **EST:** 1984
SQ FT: 5,500
SALES (est): 442.9K **Privately Held**
Web: www.sarrindustries.com
SIC: 3599 Machine shop, jobbing and repair

(P-8016)
SAVAGE MACHINING INC
2235 1st St Ste 116 (93065-0903)
PHONE..............................805 584-8047
Wade Savage, *Pr*
EMP: 23 **EST:** 2001
SALES (est): 5.35MM **Privately Held**
Web: www.savagemachininginc.com
SIC: 3599 Machine shop, jobbing and repair

(P-8017)
SCHNEIDERS MANUFACTURING INC
11122 Penrose St (91352-2724)
PHONE..............................818 771-0082
Nick Schneider, *Pr*
Tom Schneider, *
Trudy Schneider, *
EMP: 30 **EST:** 1967
SQ FT: 18,000
SALES (est): 2.35MM **Privately Held**
Web: www.schneidersmanufacturing.com
SIC: 3599 Machine shop, jobbing and repair

(P-8018)
SCREWMATIC INC
925 W 1st St (91702-4222)
P.O. Box 518 (91702-0518)
PHONE..............................626 334-7831
Louis E Zimmerli, *CEO*
Alice Zimmerli, *
Jeff Clow, *
EMP: 65 **EST:** 1953
SQ FT: 40,000
SALES (est): 9.84MM **Privately Held**
Web: www.screwmaticinc.com
SIC: 3599 Machine shop, jobbing and repair

(P-8019)
SDI LLC
21 Morgan Ste 150 (92618-2086)
PHONE..............................949 351-1866
Jon Korbonski, *Pr*
EMP: 20 **EST:** 2017
SALES (est): 1.64MM **Privately Held**
SIC: 3599 Custom machinery

(P-8020)
SEA RECOVERY CORPORATION
19610 S Rancho Way (90220-6039)
P.O. Box 5288 (90749-5288)
PHONE..............................310 608-5600
◆ **EMP:** 31 **EST:** 1981

SALES (est): 8.77MM
SALES (est): 19.07B **Publicly Held**
Web: www.parker.com
SIC: 3599 Custom machinery
PA: Parker-Hannifin Corporation
6035 Parkland Blvd
Cleveland OH
216 896-3000

(P-8021)
SENGA ENGINEERING INC
1525 E Warner Ave (92705-5419)
PHONE..............................714 549-8011
Roy Jones, *Pr*
EMP: 48 **EST:** 1976
SQ FT: 25,000
SALES (est): 9.27MM **Privately Held**
Web: www.senga-eng.com
SIC: 3599 Machine shop, jobbing and repair

(P-8022)
SENIOR AEROSPACE JET PDTS CORP
Senior Aerospace
9150 Balboa Ave (92123-1512)
PHONE..............................858 278-8400
EMP: 56
SALES (corp-wide): 1.02B **Privately Held**
Web: www.sajetproducts.com
SIC: 3599 Machine shop, jobbing and repair
HQ: Senior Operations, Llc
9106 Balboa Ave
San Diego CA
858 278-8400

(P-8023)
SENIOR OPERATIONS LLC
Also Called: Capo Industries Division
790 Greenfield Dr (92021-3101)
PHONE..............................909 627-2723
EMP: 70
SALES (corp-wide): 1.43B **Privately Held**
SIC: 3599 Hose, flexible metallic
HQ: Senior Operations Llc
300 E Devon Ave
Bartlett IL
630 372-3500

(P-8024)
SENIOR OPERATIONS LLC
Also Called: Jet Products
9106 Balboa Ave (92123-1512)
PHONE..............................858 278-8400
EMP: 97
SALES (corp-wide): 1.02B **Privately Held**
Web: www.sajetproducts.com
SIC: 3599 Hose, flexible metallic
HQ: Senior Operations Llc
300 E Devon Ave
Bartlett IL
630 372-3500

(P-8025)
SERAMPORE INDS PRIVATE LTD INC
8333 Almeria Ave (92335-3283)
PHONE..............................877 921-6111
EMP: 17
SALES (corp-wide): 22.77MM **Privately Held**
Web: www.sipindustries.com
SIC: 3599 Grinding castings for the trade
PA: Serampore Industries Private (Ltd.), Inc.
8876 Gulf Fwy Ste 500
Houston TX
713 923-6111

(P-8026)
SERRANO INDUSTRIES INC
9922 Tabor Pl (90670-3300)
PHONE..............................562 777-8180
Hoberto Serrano, *Pr*
Maria Serrano, *
Bobby Serrano, *
EMP: 34 **EST:** 1990
SQ FT: 30,000
SALES (est): 7.7MM **Privately Held**
Web: www.serrano-ind.com
SIC: 3599 Machine shop, jobbing and repair

(P-8027)
SHEFFIELD MANUFACTURING INC
9131 Glenoaks Blvd (91352-2692)
PHONE..............................310 320-1473
EMP: 70
SIC: 3599 3444 3548 3812 Machine shop, jobbing and repair; Sheet metalwork; Electric welding equipment; Search and navigation equipment

(P-8028)
SIMONZ MACHINE
4905 Morena Blvd Ste 1309 (92117-7376)
PHONE..............................858 692-5129
Dan Simonz, *Owner*
EMP: 17 **EST:** 1987
SQ FT: 6,000
SALES (est): 442.96K **Privately Held**
SIC: 3599 Machine shop, jobbing and repair

(P-8029)
SMI CA INC
Also Called: Saeilo Manufacturing Inds
14340 Iseli Rd (90670-5204)
PHONE..............................562 926-9407
Katsuhiko Tsukamoto, *CEO*
David Tsukamoto, *
Erik Kawakami, *
EMP: 26 **EST:** 1999
SQ FT: 10,000
SALES (est): 8.8MM
SALES (corp-wide): 34.71MM **Privately Held**
Web: www.smi-ca.com
SIC: 3599 Machine shop, jobbing and repair
PA: Saeilo Enterprises Inc
105 Kahr Ave
Greeley PA
845 735-6500

(P-8030)
SMITH BROTHERS MFG CORP
Also Called: Smith Brothers
5304 Banks St (92110-4008)
PHONE..............................619 296-3171
Larry D Smith, *Pr*
Billie L Mc Farland, *VP*
Karen Amberg, *Treas*
EMP: 18 **EST:** 1945
SQ FT: 5,700
SALES (est): 2.37MM **Privately Held**
Web: www.smithbrosmfg.com
SIC: 3599 3548 Machine shop, jobbing and repair; Electrodes, electric welding

(P-8031)
SOLO ENTERPRISE CORP
Also Called: Solo Golf
220 N California Ave (91744-4323)
P.O. Box 607 (91747-0607)
PHONE..............................626 961-3591
Richard F Mugica, *CEO*
Edward A Mugica, *
EMP: 50 **EST:** 1966
SQ FT: 20,000
SALES (est): 5.72MM **Privately Held**

Web: www.soloenterprisecorp.com
SIC: **3599** 3812 Machine shop, jobbing and repair; Search and navigation equipment

(P-8032)
SONSRAY INC
23935 Madison St (90505-6010)
PHONE..............................323 585-1271
Matthew Hoelscher, *Prin*
EMP: 60 **EST:** 2014
SALES (est): 6.94MM **Privately Held**
Web: www.sonsray.com
SIC: 3599 Industrial machinery, nec

(P-8033)
SOUTHERN CAL TCHNICAL ARTS INC
Also Called: Technical Arts
370 E Crowther Ave (92870-6419)
PHONE..............................714 524-2626
John H Robson Iv, *Pr*
John H Robson Iv, *Pr*
Christine Robson, *
Matt Robson, *
Kristi A Robson, *
EMP: 48 **EST:** 1970
SQ FT: 9,400
SALES (est): 11.84MM
SALES (corp-wide): 498.74MM **Publicly Held**
Web: www.technicalarts.net
SIC: **3599** 3827 Machine shop, jobbing and repair; Optical instruments and lenses
PA: Nn, Inc.
6210 Ardrey Kell Rd # 600
Charlotte NC
980 264-4300

(P-8034)
SPEC ENGINEERING COMPANY INC
13754 Saticoy St (91402-6518)
PHONE..............................818 780-3045
Gregory Viksman, *Pr*
Anna Viksman, *
EMP: 25 **EST:** 1987
SQ FT: 5,200
SALES (est): 2.74MM **Privately Held**
Web: www.specengco.com
SIC: **3599** 3412 Machine shop, jobbing and repair; Metal barrels, drums, and pails

(P-8035)
SPRAY SYSTEMS INC
1363 E Grand Ave (91766-3867)
PHONE..............................909 397-7511
▲ **EMP:** 20 **EST:** 1978
SALES (est): 2.24MM **Privately Held**
Web: www.spraysystems.com
SIC: **3599** 3444 Custom machinery; Sheet metalwork

(P-8036)
STINES MACHINE INC
2481 Coral St (92081-8431)
PHONE..............................760 599-9955
Edward L Huston, *Pr*
Tri Tran, *
EMP: 35 **EST:** 1969
SQ FT: 15,000
SALES (est): 3.41MM **Privately Held**
Web: www.stinesmachine.com
SIC: **3599** Machine shop, jobbing and repair

(P-8037)
SUN PRECISION MACHINING INC
1651 Market St Ste A (92880-1710)
PHONE..............................951 817-0056

EMP: 17
SALES (est): 2.68MM **Privately Held**
SIC: **3599** Machine shop, jobbing and repair

(P-8038)
SUPERIOR MACHINING MFG CO INC
322 Oak Pl (92821-4135)
PHONE..............................714 529-6000
Hussein Suheimat, *CEO*
EMP: 19 **EST:** 2015
SALES (est): 258.99K **Privately Held**
Web: www.smmcinc.com
SIC: **3599** Machine shop, jobbing and repair

(P-8039)
SUPERIOR THREAD ROLLING CO
12801 Wentworth St (91331-4332)
PHONE..............................818 504-3626
EMP: 80 **EST:** 1952
SALES (est): 11.25MM **Privately Held**
Web: www.superiorthread.com
SIC: **3599** 3542 3429 Machine shop, jobbing and repair; Thread rolling machines; Aircraft hardware

(P-8040)
SUPREME MACHINE PRODUCTS INC
302 Sequoia Ave (91761-1543)
PHONE..............................909 974-0349
Harold Hal Peterson, *Pr*
Isac Gomez, *VP*
EMP: 18 **EST:** 1955
SQ FT: 7,800
SALES (est): 4.92MM **Privately Held**
Web: www.suprememachineproducts.com
SIC: **3599** Machine shop, jobbing and repair

(P-8041)
T & M MACHINING
331 Irving Dr (93030-5172)
PHONE..............................805 983-6716
Mario Mangone, *Pr*
Kay Mangone, *Contrlr*
EMP: 20 **EST:** 1979
SALES (est): 2.43MM **Privately Held**
Web: www.tmmachining.com
SIC: **3599** 3544 Machine shop, jobbing and repair; Special dies, tools, jigs, and fixtures

(P-8042)
T I B INC
Also Called: B.T.i Tool Engineering
9525 Pathway St (92071-4170)
PHONE..............................619 562-3071
James W Jim Barnhill, *Pr*
James T Todd Barnhill, *VP*
Chris Barnhill, *VP*
EMP: 18 **EST:** 1967
SQ FT: 1,000
SALES (est): 2.24MM **Privately Held**
Web: www.bti-tool.com
SIC: **3599** Machine shop, jobbing and repair

(P-8043)
T/Q SYSTEMS INC
25131 Arctic Ocean Dr (92630-8852)
PHONE..............................949 455-0478
Victor Buytkus, *Pr*
Scott Moebius, *
EMP: 40 **EST:** 1988
SALES (est): 6.4MM **Privately Held**
Web: www.tqsystems.net
SIC: **3599** Machine shop, jobbing and repair

(P-8044)
TECHNIFORM INTERNATIONAL CORP
375 S Cactus Ave (92376-6320)
PHONE..............................909 877-6886
Richard S Jones, *Pr*
EMP: 176 **EST:** 1989
SQ FT: 60,000
SALES (est): 3.49MM **Privately Held**
Web: www.plantprefab.com
SIC: **3599** 3469 3444 Machine shop, jobbing and repair; Metal stampings, nec; Sheet metalwork

(P-8045)
TECNO INDUSTRIAL ENGRG INC
13528 Pumice St (90650-5249)
PHONE..............................562 623-4517
Juan Giner, *Pr*
Enrique Viano, *
EMP: 23 **EST:** 1979
SQ FT: 17,000
SALES (est): 710.71K **Privately Held**
Web: www.master-research.com
SIC: **3599** 3728 Machine shop, jobbing and repair; Aircraft parts and equipment, nec

(P-8046)
THIESSEN PRODUCTS INC
Also Called: Jim's Machining
555 Dawson Dr Ste A (93012-5085)
PHONE..............................805 482-6913
Jim Thiessen, *Pr*
Debra Thiessen, *
Jay R Thiessen, *
EMP: 130 **EST:** 1971
SQ FT: 44,000
SALES (est): 16.05MM **Privately Held**
Web: www.jimsusa.com
SIC: **3599** Machine shop, jobbing and repair

(P-8047)
THUNDERBOLT MANUFACTURING INC
641 S State College Blvd (92831-5115)
PHONE..............................714 632-0397
Minh Son To, *Pr*
EMP: 26 **EST:** 1990
SQ FT: 5,800
SALES (est): 2.93MM **Privately Held**
Web: www.thunderboltmfg.com
SIC: **3599** Machine shop, jobbing and repair

(P-8048)
TMX ENGINEERING AND MFG CORP
2141 S Standard Ave (92707-3034)
PHONE..............................714 641-5884
Souhil Toubia, *CEO*
Gus Toubia, *
Ali Ossaily, *
Steve Korn, *
Mauricio Escarcega, *
EMP: 75 **EST:** 1985
SQ FT: 23,000
SALES (est): 8.72MM **Privately Held**
Web: www.tmxengineering.com
SIC: **3599** 3728 3544 Machine shop, jobbing and repair; Aircraft parts and equipment, nec; Special dies, tools, jigs, and fixtures

(P-8049)
TOMI ENGINEERING INC
414 E Alton Ave (92707-4242)
PHONE..............................714 556-1474
Michael F Falbo, *CEO*
Anthony Falbo, *
EMP: 52 **EST:** 1975
SQ FT: 15,000

SALES (est): 10.2MM **Privately Held**
Web: www.tomiengineering.com
SIC: **3599** Machine shop, jobbing and repair

(P-8050)
TOWER INDUSTRIES INC
Also Called: Allied Mechanical Products
1720 S Bon View Ave (91761-4411)
PHONE..............................909 947-2723
Mark Slater, *Mgr*
EMP: 110
SQ FT: 60,794
SALES (corp-wide): 35.59MM **Privately Held**
Web: metal-stamping-companies.cmac.ws
SIC: **3599** Machine shop, jobbing and repair
PA: Tower Industries, Inc.
1518 N Endeavor Ln Ste C
Anaheim CA

(P-8051)
TREPANNING SPECIALITIES INC
Also Called: Trepanning Specialties
16201 Illinois Ave (90723-4996)
PHONE..............................562 633-8110
Donald B Laughlin, *Pr*
Patricia Laughlin, *VP*
▲ **EMP:** 23 **EST:** 1973
SQ FT: 7,000
SALES (est): 1.97MM **Privately Held**
Web: www.trepanningspec.com
SIC: **3599** Machine shop, jobbing and repair

(P-8052)
TRUE POSITION TECHNOLOGIES LLC
24900 Avenue Stanford (91355-1272)
PHONE..............................661 294-0030
Allen Sumian, *Pr*
EMP: 82 **EST:** 1990
SQ FT: 25,000
SALES (est): 12.9MM
SALES (corp-wide): 241.4MM **Privately Held**
Web: www.truepositiontech.com
SIC: **3599** Machine shop, jobbing and repair
PA: Hbd Industries, Inc.
5200 Upper Metro Pl # 110
Dublin OH
614 526-7000

(P-8053)
TRUE PRECISION MACHINING INC
175 Industrial Way (93427)
PHONE..............................805 964-4545
Todd Ackert, *Pr*
EMP: 22 **EST:** 1998
SQ FT: 17,000
SALES (est): 3.86MM **Privately Held**
Web: www.trueprecisionmachining.com
SIC: **3599** Machine shop, jobbing and repair

(P-8054)
TURRET LATHE SPECIALISTS INC
875 S Rose Pl (92805-5337)
PHONE..............................714 520-0058
Robert Mcbride, *Pr*
EMP: 18 **EST:** 1973
SQ FT: 6,000
SALES (est): 2.33MM **Privately Held**
Web: www.turretlathespecialists.com
SIC: **3599** Machine shop, jobbing and repair

(P-8055)
UNITED PRECISION CORP
20810 Plummer St (91311-5004)

PRODUCTS & SVCS

PHONE..................818 576-9540
Robert Hawrylo, *CEO*
Robert Stanley Hawrylo, *
EMP: 40 **EST:** 2014
SQ FT: 7,500
SALES (est): 5.86MM **Privately Held**
Web: www.upc-usa.com
SIC: 3599 3812 Machine shop, jobbing and repair; Defense systems and equipment

(P-8056)
UNIVERSAL PLANT SVCS CAL INC
20545 Belshaw Ave # A (90746-3505)
PHONE..................310 618-1600
Stewart Jones, *Brnch Mgr*
EMP: 92
SALES (corp-wide): 863.38MM **Privately Held**
Web: www.universalplant.com
SIC: 3599 Custom machinery
HQ: Universal Plant Services Of California, Inc.
20545a Belshaw Ave
Carson CA
310 618-1600

(P-8057)
UPLAND FAB INC
1445 Brooks St Ste L (91762-3665)
PHONE..................909 986-6565
Paul Sapra, *CEO*
Patsy Sapra, *
Steven Sapra, *
Jackson Sapra, *Stockholder**
EMP: 30 **EST:** 1970
SQ FT: 12,000
SALES (est): 4.7MM **Privately Held**
Web: www.uplandfab.com
SIC: 3599 2679 3083 Machine shop, jobbing and repair; Honeycomb core and board: made from purchased material; Plastics finished products, laminated

(P-8058)
V & S ENGINEERING COMPANY LTD
5766 Research Dr (92649-1617)
PHONE..................714 898-7869
Dino Dukovic, *Pr*
Dino Dokovic, *Pr*
EMP: 27 **EST:** 1979
SQ FT: 10,000
SALES (est): 581.03K **Privately Held**
Web: www.vseng.biz
SIC: 3599 Machine shop, jobbing and repair

(P-8059)
VALLEY PERFORATING LLC
3201 Gulf St (93308-4905)
PHONE..................661 324-4964
Mike Dover, *Pr*
Dorothy Reynolds, *
Alice Lomas, *
EMP: 65 **EST:** 1970
SQ FT: 10,440
SALES (est): 9.64MM **Privately Held**
Web: www.valleyperf.com
SIC: 3599 Machine shop, jobbing and repair

(P-8060)
VALLEY TOOL AND MACHINE CO INC
111 Explorer St (91768-3278)
PHONE..................909 595-2205
Chuck Rogers, *CEO*
Jim Rogers, *
Nancy Larson, *
EMP: 68 **EST:** 1982

SQ FT: 34,000
SALES (est): 3.61MM **Privately Held**
Web: www.valleytool-inc.com
SIC: 3599 7692 3544 Machine shop, jobbing and repair; Welding repair; Special dies, tools, jigs, and fixtures

(P-8061)
VANDERHORST BROTHERS INDUSTRIES INC
Also Called: V B I
1715 Surveyor Ave (93063-3374)
PHONE..................805 583-3333
EMP: 60 **EST:** 1973
SALES (est): 8.78MM **Privately Held**
Web: www.vbinc.com
SIC: 3599 3542 3728 Machine shop, jobbing and repair; Knurling machines; Aircraft parts and equipment, nec

(P-8062)
VANS MANUFACTURING INC
330 E Easy St Ste C (93065-7526)
PHONE..................805 522-6267
Louis Tignac, *Pr*
EMP: 19 **EST:** 1976
SQ FT: 8,500
SALES (est): 2.31MM **Privately Held**
SIC: 3599 Machine shop, jobbing and repair

(P-8063)
VEECO PROCESS EQUIPMENT INC
Slider Process Division
112 Robin Hill Rd (93117-3107)
PHONE..................805 967-2700
Ed Wagner, *Mgr*
EMP: 100
Web: www.veeco.com
SIC: 3599 3545 3544 3291 Machine shop, jobbing and repair; Machine tool accessories; Special dies, tools, jigs, and fixtures; Abrasive products
HQ: Veeco Process Equipment Inc.
1 Terminal Dr
Plainview NY

(P-8064)
VELLIOS MACHINE SHOP INC
Also Called: Vellios Automotive Machine Sp
4625 29th Manhattan Beach Blvd (90260)
PHONE..................310 643-8540
Harry Vellios, *Pr*
Carolyn Vellios, *Sec*
Mark Vellios, *VP*
EMP: 18 **EST:** 1975
SQ FT: 6,500
SALES (est): 432.78K **Privately Held**
Web: www.velliosmachineshop.com
SIC: 3599 3714 5013 Machine shop, jobbing and repair; Rebuilding engines and transmissions, factory basis; Automotive supplies and parts

(P-8065)
VENTURA HYDRULIC MCH WORKS INC
1555 Callens Rd (93003-5606)
PHONE..................805 656-1760
Fred H Malzacher, *Pr*
Elaine Z Malzacher, *VP*
EMP: 20 **EST:** 1965
SQ FT: 15,700
SALES (est): 4.56MM **Privately Held**
Web: www.venturahydraulics.com
SIC: 3599 Machine shop, jobbing and repair

(P-8066)
VESCIO THREADING CO
Also Called: Vescio Manufacturing Intl
14002 Anson Ave (90670-5202)
PHONE..................562 802-1868
Gregory Vescio, *CEO*
Greg Vescio, *
Robert Vescio, *
Verna Vescio, *
Bob Vescio, *
EMP: 73 **EST:** 1947
SQ FT: 13,000
SALES (est): 16.35MM **Privately Held**
Web: www.vesciothreading.com
SIC: 3599 Machine shop, jobbing and repair

(P-8067)
VIANH COMPANY INC
13841 A Better Way Ste 10c (92843-3930)
PHONE..................714 590-9808
EMP: 21 **EST:** 1989
SQ FT: 8,000
SALES (est): 2.32MM **Privately Held**
Web: www.vianhcompany.com
SIC: 3599 Machine shop, jobbing and repair

(P-8068)
VISTA INDUSTRIAL PRODUCTS INC
3210 Executive Rdg (92081-8527)
PHONE..................760 599-5050
EMP: 160 **EST:** 1991
SALES (est): 22.59MM **Privately Held**
Web: www.vista-industrial.com
SIC: 3599 Machine shop, jobbing and repair

(P-8069)
W MACHINE WORKS INC
13814 Del Sur St (91340-3440)
PHONE..................818 890-8049
Marzel Neckien, *Pr*
Randy Neckien, *
EMP: 45 **EST:** 1977
SQ FT: 25,000
SALES (est): 9.24MM **Privately Held**
Web: www.wmwcnc.com
SIC: 3599 Machine shop, jobbing and repair

(P-8070)
WAHLCO INC
Also Called: Wahlco
4774 Murrieta St Ste 3 (91710-5155)
PHONE..................714 979-7300
Alonso Munoz, *CEO*
Robert R Wahler, *
Barry J Southam, *
Dennis Nickel, *
◆ **EMP:** 106 **EST:** 1972
SALES (est): 17.33MM **Privately Held**
Web: www.wahlco.com
SIC: 3599 Custom machinery

(P-8071)
WALLACE E MILLER INC
Also Called: Micro-TEC
9155 Alabama Ave Ste B (91311-5867)
PHONE..................818 998-0444
Gary Case, *Pr*
Roxanne Case, *VP*
EMP: 26 **EST:** 1987
SQ FT: 8,000
SALES (est): 828.43K **Privately Held**
SIC: 3599 Machine shop, jobbing and repair

(P-8072)
WEBER DRILLING CO INC
4028 W 184th St (90504-4712)
PHONE..................310 670-7708
Marlene Wood, *Pr*

Ronald Wood, *
EMP: 25 **EST:** 1947
SALES (est): 2.35MM **Privately Held**
SIC: 3599 Machine shop, jobbing and repair

(P-8073)
WELDMAC MANUFACTURING COMPANY
1533 N Johnson Ave (92020-1683)
PHONE..................619 440-2300
Marshall J Rugg, *CEO*
EMP: 38 **EST:** 1969
SALES (est): 5.24MM **Privately Held**
Web: www.weldmac.com
SIC: 3599 Machine shop, jobbing and repair

(P-8074)
WELDMAC MANUFACTURING COMPANY
1451 N Johnson Ave (92020-1615)
PHONE..................619 440-2300
Marshall J Rugg, *Pr*
Barbara Bloomfield, *
Robert L Rugg, *
EMP: 122 **EST:** 1968
SQ FT: 100,000
SALES (est): 29.66MM **Privately Held**
Web: www.weldmac.com
SIC: 3599 3444 7692 Machine shop, jobbing and repair; Sheet metalwork; Brazing

(P-8075)
WEST BOND INC (PA)
1551 S Harris Ct (92806-5932)
PHONE..................714 978-1551
John C Price, *Pr*
Gary Phillips, *
Phyllis Eppig, *
▼ **EMP:** 47 **EST:** 1966
SQ FT: 38,000
SALES (est): 9.98MM
SALES (corp-wide): 9.98MM **Privately Held**
Web: www.westbond.com
SIC: 3599 Machine shop, jobbing and repair

(P-8076)
WESTERN CNC INC
1001 Park Center Dr (92081-8340)
PHONE..................760 597-7000
Danny Ashcraft, *Pr*
Carolyn Ashcraft, *
April Ashcraft Ramirez, *
EMP: 100 **EST:** 1980
SQ FT: 57,000
SALES (est): 17.22MM **Privately Held**
Web: www.westerncnc.com
SIC: 3599 Machine shop, jobbing and repair

(P-8077)
WESTERN PRECISION AERO LLC
11600 Monarch St (92841-1817)
PHONE..................714 893-7999
EMP: 37 **EST:** 2009
SQ FT: 16,000
SALES (est): 9.83MM
SALES (corp-wide): 1.47B **Publicly Held**
Web: www.rbcbearings.com
SIC: 3599 Machine shop, jobbing and repair
PA: Rbc Bearings Incorporated
102 Willenbrock Rd Bldg B
Oxford CT
203 267-7001

(P-8078)
WILCOX MACHINE CO
7180 Scout Ave (90201-3202)
P.O. Box 2159 (90202-2159)

PHONE...............................562 927-5353
George Schofhauser, Pr
Kurt Anderegg, *
Jill Wigney, *
Tom Anderegg, *
◆ EMP: 60 EST: 1955
SALES (est): 7.53MM Privately Held
Web: www.wilcoxmachine.com
SIC: 3599 Machine shop, jobbing and repair

(P-8079)
WILLIS MACHINE INC
11000 Alto Dr (93022-9569)
PHONE...............................805 604-4500
Harlan Willis, Pr
EMP: 23 EST: 1977
SALES (est): 3.59MM Privately Held
Web: www.willismachine.com
SIC: 3599 Machine shop, jobbing and repair

(P-8080)
WILMINGTON MACHINE INC
Also Called: Wilmington Ironworks
432 W C St (90744-5714)
PHONE...............................310 518-3213
Walter C Richards Iii, Pr
Elva Richards, Treas
J W Richards, Sec
EMP: 37 EST: 1920
SQ FT: 13,000
SALES (est): 834.1K Privately Held
Web: www.wilmingtonironworks.com
SIC: 3599 Machine shop, jobbing and repair

(P-8081)
WILSHIRE PRECISION PDTS INC
7353 Hinds Ave (91605-3704)
PHONE...............................818 765-4571
Thomas G Lewis, Pr
Wendy Lewis, *
Dana Lewis, *
Shoshona Lewis, *
EMP: 31 EST: 1951
SQ FT: 10,000
SALES (est): 5.13MM Privately Held
Web: www.wilshireprecision.com
SIC: 3599 3621 Machine shop, jobbing and repair; Motors, electric

(P-8082)
WIRE CUT COMPANY INC
6750 Caballero Blvd (90620-1134)
PHONE...............................714 994-1170
Sydney Omar, CEO
Milton M Thomas, *
Tina Thomas, *
EMP: 30 EST: 1978
SQ FT: 20,000
SALES (est): 4.48MM Privately Held
Web: www.wirecutcompany.com
SIC: 3599 Machine shop, jobbing and repair

(P-8083)
WMC PRCSION MCHNING GRNDNG
1234 E Ash Ave Ste A (92831-5013)
PHONE...............................714 773-0059
Richard Mourey, Pr
Leigh Thompson, Genl Mgr
EMP: 17 EST: 1951
SQ FT: 10,000
SALES (est): 429.25K Privately Held
SIC: 3599 Machine shop, jobbing and repair

(P-8084)
WOODRUFF CORPORATION
109 Calle Mayor (90277-6509)
PHONE...............................310 378-1611
Ronald D Woodruff, Pr
Dan Watts, *

EMP: 21 EST: 1961
SQ FT: 16,000
SALES (est): 268.88K Privately Held
SIC: 3599 Machine shop, jobbing and repair

(P-8085)
YOUNG MACHINE INC
Also Called: California Machine Specialties
12282 Colony Ave (91710-2095)
PHONE...............................909 464-0405
Anand Jagani, Pr
Gilbert Fresquez, Cnslt
EMP: 19 EST: 1970
SQ FT: 11,000
SALES (est): 2.29MM Privately Held
Web: www.calmachine.com
SIC: 3599 Machine shop, jobbing and repair

3612 Transformers, Except Electric

(P-8086)
ABBOTT TECHNOLOGIES INC
8203 Vineland Ave (91352-3956)
PHONE...............................818 504-0644
Kerima Marie Batte, CEO
EMP: 40 EST: 1961
SQ FT: 12,000
SALES (est): 8.24MM Privately Held
Web: www.abbott-tech.com
SIC: 3612 3559 3677 Transformers, except electric; Electronic component making machinery; Transformers power supply, electronic type

(P-8087)
ARNOLD MAGNETICS CORPORATION
Also Called: Arnold Magnetics
841 Avenida Acaso Ste A (93012-8798)
PHONE...............................805 484-4221
EMP: 52 EST: 1956
SALES (est): 9.92MM Privately Held
Web: www.amcpower.com
SIC: 3612 3679 Transformers, except electric; Power supplies, all types: static

(P-8088)
CALIFORNIA PAK INTL INC
17706 S Main St (90248-3517)
PHONE...............................310 223-2500
Byung Yull Kwon, Pr
Jeong Yang Kwon, CFO
▲ EMP: 20 EST: 1989
SQ FT: 15,000
SALES (est): 4MM Privately Held
Web: www.calpakusa.com
SIC: 3612 Distribution transformers, electric

(P-8089)
CALIFRNIA STATE UNIV CHNNEL IS
45 Rincon Dr Unit 104a (93012-8423)
PHONE...............................805 437-2670
EMP: 43 EST: 1996
SQ FT: 5,000
SALES (est): 1.14MM Privately Held
Web: www.csuci.edu
SIC: 3612 Power and distribution transformers

(P-8090)
CGR/THOMPSON INDUSTRIES INC
7155 Fenwick Ln (92683-5218)
PHONE...............................714 678-4200
Michael B Baughan, CEO
Vince Corti, *

Kevin Rowan, *
EMP: 45 EST: 2001
SQ FT: 10,000
SALES (est): 7.08MM
SALES (corp-wide): 67.07B Publicly Held
SIC: 3612 Machine tool transformers
HQ: B/E Aerospace, Inc.
1400 Corporate Center Way
Wellington FL

(P-8091)
CUSTOM MAGNETICS CAL INC
15142 Vista Del Rio Ave (91710-9694)
PHONE...............................909 620-3877
Christopher Cimino, CEO
▲ EMP: 27 EST: 2013
SALES (est): 5.27MM Privately Held
Web: www.cmi-power.com
SIC: 3612 Transformers, except electric

(P-8092)
DATATRONIC DISTRIBUTION INC
28151 Us Highway 74 (92585-8915)
P.O. Box 1580 (92585-1580)
▲ EMP: 19 EST: 2000
SQ FT: 8,200
SALES (est): 4.28MM Privately Held
Web: www.datatronics.com
SIC: 3612 Transformers, except electric
HQ: Datatronic Limited
19/F North Point Indl Bldg
North Point HK

(P-8093)
DATATRONICS ROMOLAND INC
Also Called: Datatronics
28151 Us Highway 74 (92585-8916)
P.O. Box 1579 (92585-1579)
PHONE...............................951 928-7700
Paul Y Siu, Pr
Wai M Siu Shui, *
▲ EMP: 70 EST: 1989
SQ FT: 38,800
SALES (est): 16.36MM Privately Held
Web: www.datatronics.com
SIC: 3612 3677 Transformers, except electric; Inductors, electronic

(P-8094)
DOW-ELCO INC
1313 W Olympic Blvd (90640-5010)
P.O. Box 669 (90640-0669)
PHONE...............................323 723-1288
Linda Su, Pr
Cecile Se Kay, VP
Grace Park, *
Ronald Cheung, *
Annie Su, *
EMP: 25 EST: 1946
SQ FT: 8,100
SALES (est): 2.45MM Privately Held
SIC: 3612 3829 3061 Vibrators, interrupter; Measuring and controlling devices, nec; Mechanical rubber goods

(P-8095)
ENERGY CNVRSION APPLCTIONS INC
Also Called: Eca
582 Explorer St (92821-3108)
PHONE...............................714 256-2166
Akbal Grewal, CEO
EMP: 17 EST: 1989
SQ FT: 10,000
SALES (est): 3.98MM Privately Held
Web: www.eca-mfg.com
SIC: 3612 8748 Transformers, except electric; Telecommunications consultant

(P-8096)
FULHAM CO INC
12705 S Van Ness Ave (90250-3322)
PHONE...............................323 779-2980
Antony Corrie, CEO
James Cooke, CFO
Harry Libby, VP
Mike Hu, VP
Deborah Knuckles, CFO
▲ EMP: 40 EST: 1994
SQ FT: 48,000
SALES (est): 11.46MM Privately Held
Web: www.fulham.com
SIC: 3612 Ballasts for lighting fixtures
HQ: Fulham Company Gmbh
Torstr. 138
Berlin BE

(P-8097)
GRAND GENERAL ACCESSORIES LLC
Also Called: Grand General
1965 E Vista Bella Way (90220-6106)
PHONE...............................310 631-2589
Shu-hui Sophia Lin Huang, CEO
Nan-huang Huang, Sec
▲ EMP: 39 EST: 1984
SALES (est): 7.68MM Privately Held
Web: www.grandgeneral.com
SIC: 3612 5531 3713 Transformers, except electric; Truck equipment and parts; Truck and bus bodies

(P-8098)
HIS COMPANY INC
Also Called: Hisco
2215 Paseo De Las Americas Ste 29 (92154-7908)
PHONE...............................858 513-7748
William Bland, Mgr
EMP: 17
SALES (corp-wide): 417.73MM Publicly Held
Web: www.hisco.com
SIC: 3612 5063 Distribution transformers, electric; Electronic wire and cable
HQ: His Company, Inc.
6650 Concord Park Dr
Houston TX
713 934-1600

(P-8099)
JACKSON ENGINEERING CO INC
9411 Winnetka Ave # A (91311-6035)
PHONE...............................818 886-9567
Ron Jackson, Pr
Dennis Elliott, *
EMP: 40 EST: 1951
SQ FT: 10,000
SALES (est): 3.04MM Privately Held
Web: www.jacksonengineering.com
SIC: 3612 Electronic meter transformers

(P-8100)
JUSTIN INC
Also Called: Justin
2663 Lee Ave (91733-1411)
PHONE...............................626 444-4516
Frank Justin Junior, Pr
Jeff Justin, *
Jeffrey Ross Justin, *
EMP: 50 EST: 1956
SQ FT: 4,000
SALES (est): 9.14MM Privately Held
Web: www.justininc.com
SIC: 3612 Specialty transformers

PRODUCTS & SVCS

(P-8101)
MGM TRANSFORMER CO
5701 Smithway St (90040-1583)
PHONE..................323 726-0888
Patrick Gogerchin, *CEO*
Patrick Gogerchin, *Pr*
Luis Otero, *
Bianca Kaveh, *
Sherry Boloury, *
◆ **EMP:** 70 **EST:** 1975
SQ FT: 40,000
SALES (est): 99.19MM **Privately Held**
Web: www.mgmtransformer.com
SIC: 3612 Transformers, except electric

(P-8102)
NUVVE HOLDING CORP (PA)
2488 Historic Decatur Rd Ste 200
(92106-6134)
PHONE..................619 456-5161
Gregory Poilasne, *Ch Bd*
Ted Smith, *Pr*
David G Robson, *CFO*
EMP: 24 **EST:** 1996
SALES (est): 5.37MM
SALES (corp-wide): 5.37MM **Publicly Held**
Web: www.nuvve.com
SIC: 3612 Power and distribution transformers

(P-8103)
OHMEGA SOLENOID CO INC
10912 Painter Ave (90670-4529)
P.O. Box 2747 (90670-0747)
PHONE..................562 944-7948
EMP: 47 **EST:** 1967
SALES (est): 6.66MM **Privately Held**
Web: www.ohmegasolenoid.com
SIC: 3612 3679 3677 Power and distribution transformers; Solenoids for electronic applications; Electronic coils and transformers

(P-8104)
ON-LINE POWER INCORPORATED (PA)
Also Called: Power Services
14000 S Broadway (90061-1018)
PHONE..................323 721-5017
Abbie Gougerchian, *CEO*
▲ **EMP:** 46 **EST:** 1980
SQ FT: 36,000
SALES (est): 10.25MM
SALES (corp-wide): 10.25MM **Privately Held**
Web: www.onlinepower.com
SIC: 3612 3621 3613 3677 Transformers, except electric; Motors and generators; Regulators, power; Electronic coils and transformers

(P-8105)
ONYX POWER INC
4011 W Carriage Dr (92704-6301)
PHONE..................714 513-1500
EMP: 104
SIC: 3612 Power and distribution transformers

(P-8106)
PACIFIC TRANSFORMER CORP
5399 E Hunter Ave (92807-2054)
PHONE..................714 779-0450
Patrick A Thomas, *CEO*
Justin Richardson, *
▲ **EMP:** 85 **EST:** 1981
SQ FT: 37,000
SALES (est): 38MM **Privately Held**
Web: www.pactran.com

(P-8107)
PIONEER CUSTOM ELEC PDTS CORP
10640 Springdale Ave (90670-3843)
PHONE..................562 944-0626
Geo Murickan, *Pr*
EMP: 68 **EST:** 2013
SALES (est): 19.53MM **Publicly Held**
Web: www.pioneercep.com
SIC: 3612 Electronic meter transformers
PA: Pioneer Power Solutions, Inc.
400 Kelby St Ste 1700
Fort Lee NJ

(P-8108)
PULSE ELECTRONICS INC (HQ)
15255 Innovation Dr Ste 100 (92128-3400)
PHONE..................858 674-8100
▲ **EMP:** 270 **EST:** 1955
SQ FT: 49,750
SALES (est): 311.53MM **Privately Held**
Web: www.pulseelectronics.com
SIC: 3612 3674 3677 Specialty transformers; Modules, solid state; Filtration devices, electronic
PA: Yageo Corporation
3f,No.233-1,Pao Chiao Rd.,
New Taipei City TAP

(P-8109)
RING LLC (HQ)
12515 Cerise Ave (90250-4801)
PHONE..................310 929-7085
Jamie Siminoff, *Managing Member*
▲ **EMP:** 300 **EST:** 2013
SQ FT: 40,000
SALES (est): 181.5MM **Publicly Held**
Web: www.ring.com
SIC: 3612 5065 Doorbell transformers, electric; Security control equipment and systems
PA: Amazon.Com, Inc.
410 Terry Ave N
Seattle WA

(P-8110)
RWNM INC
1240 Simpson Way (92029-1406)
▲ **EMP:** 33 **EST:** 1995
SQ FT: 2,200
SALES (est): 2.05MM **Privately Held**
SIC: 3612 Transformers, except electric

(P-8111)
SEMPRA GLOBAL (HQ)
488 8th Ave (92101-7123)
PHONE..................619 696-2000
Mark A Snell, *CEO*
EMP: 60 **EST:** 1997
SALES (est): 69.12MM
SALES (corp-wide): 14.44B **Publicly Held**
Web: www.sempra.com
SIC: 3612 Transformers, except electric
PA: Sempra
488 8th Ave
San Diego CA
619 696-2000

(P-8112)
STARLINEOEM INC
3183f Airway Ave Ste 112 (92626-4618)
PHONE..................949 342-8889
Rosario Pozzi, *Pr*
EMP: 20 **EST:** 2007
SALES (est): 178.31K **Privately Held**

(P-8113)
STREAMLINE AVIONICS INC
17672 Armstrong Ave (92614-5728)
PHONE..................949 861-8151
EMP: 22 **EST:** 2010
SALES (est): 2.5MM **Privately Held**
Web: www.streamlineavionics.com
SIC: 3612 Transformers, except electric

(P-8114)
TOCANW WHOLESALER
2801 Cmino Del Rio S Mssi (92108)
PHONE..................619 376-2860
EMP: 30 **EST:** 2020
SALES (est): 1.01MM **Privately Held**
SIC: 3612 Distribution transformers, electric

(P-8115)
ZETTLER MAGNETICS INC
2410 Birch St (92081-8472)
PHONE..................949 831-5000
▲ **EMP:** 190 **EST:** 1997
SQ FT: 80,000
SALES (est): 2.24MM **Privately Held**
Web: www.zettlercontrols.com
SIC: 3612 Transformers, except electric
PA: Zettler Components, Inc.
75 Columbia
Orange CA

3613 Switchgear And Switchboard Apparatus

(P-8116)
AEMI HOLDINGS LLC
6610 Cobra Way (92121-4107)
PHONE..................858 481-0210
Daniel H Chang, *Pr*
Xiang Ming Li, *Sr VP*
Caili Chang, *
▲ **EMP:** 77 **EST:** 1986
SQ FT: 45,000
SALES (est): 18.98MM **Privately Held**
Web: www.aem-usa.com
SIC: 3613 3677 7699 Fuses and fuse equipment; Inductors, electronic; Metal reshaping and replating services

(P-8117)
AGE INCORPORATED
14831 Spring Ave (90670-5109)
PHONE..................562 483-7300
Vasken Imasdounian, *Pr*
Daniel Imasdounian, *
Annie Imasdounian, *
▲ **EMP:** 35 **EST:** 1975
SALES (est): 4.2MM **Privately Held**
Web: www.agenameplate.com
SIC: 3613 3625 Control panels, electric; Electric controls and control accessories, industrial

(P-8118)
CROWN TECHNICAL SYSTEMS (PA)
13470 Philadelphia Ave (92337-7700)
PHONE..................951 332-4170
▲ **EMP:** 198 **EST:** 1996
SQ FT: 92,000
SALES (est): 89.73MM **Privately Held**
Web: www.crowntechnicalsystems.com
SIC: 3613 Control panels, electric

(P-8119)
CUSTOM CONTROL SENSORS LLC (PA)
Also Called: Custom Aviation Supply
21111 Plummer St (91311-4905)
P.O. Box 2516 (91313-2516)
PHONE..................818 341-4610
Henry P Acuff, *Pr*
Thomas Pilgrim, *
Joann D Acuff, *
EMP: 113 **EST:** 1957
SALES (est): 38.58MM
SALES (corp-wide): 38.58MM **Privately Held**
Web: www.ccsdualsnap.com
SIC: 3613 3643 3625 Switches, electric power except snap, push button, etc.; Current-carrying wiring services; Relays and industrial controls

(P-8120)
DATA LIGHTS RIGGING LLC
Also Called: Ratpac Dimmers
7508 Tyrone Ave (91405-1447)
PHONE..................818 786-0536
EMP: 17 **EST:** 2014
SALES (est): 990.82K **Privately Held**
Web: www.ratpaccontrols.com
SIC: 3613 Switchgear and switchboard apparatus

(P-8121)
ELECTRO SWITCH CORP
Also Called: Digitran
10410 Trademark St (91730-5826)
PHONE..................909 581-0855
Robert M Pineau, *Pr*
EMP: 69
SALES (corp-wide): 103.82MM **Privately Held**
Web: www.digitran-switches.com
SIC: 3613 3625 Switches, electric power except snap, push button, etc.; Industrial controls: push button, selector switches, pilot
HQ: Electro Switch Corp.
775 Pleasant St Ste 1
Weymouth MA
781 335-1195

(P-8122)
GENERAL SWITCHGEAR INC
14729 Spring Ave (90670-5107)
EMP: 30 **EST:** 1983
SALES (est): 2.27MM **Privately Held**
SIC: 3613 5063 Switchgear and switchgear accessories, nec; Electrical apparatus and equipment

(P-8123)
HYDRA-ELECTRIC COMPANY (PA)
3151 N Kenwood St (91505-1052)
PHONE..................818 843-6211
David E Schmidt, *CEO*
EMP: 178 **EST:** 1950
SQ FT: 90,000
SALES (est): 22.61MM
SALES (corp-wide): 22.61MM **Privately Held**
Web: www.hydraelectric.com
SIC: 3613 Switches, electric power except snap, push button, etc.

(P-8124)
ICONN INC
Also Called: Iconn Technologies
8909 Irvine Center Dr (92618-4249)
PHONE..................800 286-6742

Turker Hidirlar, *CEO*
▲ **EMP:** 56 **EST:** 2007
SQ FT: 9,920
SALES (est): 9.86MM **Privately Held**
Web: www.iconn-ems.com
SIC: 3613 3714 3678 3351 Power
connectors, electric; Booster (jump-start)
cables, automotive; Electronic connectors;
Wire, copper and copper alloy

(P-8125)

MARWELL CORPORATION

1094 Wabash Ave (92359)
P.O. Box 139 (92359-0139)
PHONE................................909 794-4192
Larry R Blackwell, *Pr*
Kelle A Blackwell, *Sec*
EMP: 18 **EST:** 1979
SQ FT: 3,500
SALES (est): 3.82MM **Privately Held**
Web: www.marwellcorp.com
SIC: 3613 Panel and distribution boards and
other related apparatus

(P-8126)

MYERS POWER PRODUCTS INC (PA)

Also Called: Myers FSI
2950 E Philadelphia St (91761-8545)
PHONE................................909 923-1800
Diana Grootonk, *CEO*
◆ **EMP:** 130 **EST:** 2003
SQ FT: 40,000
SALES (est): 172.09MM
SALES (corp-wide): 172.09MM **Privately Held**
Web: www.myerspower.com
SIC: 3613 Switchgear and switchboard
apparatus

(P-8127)

PANEL SHOP INC

Also Called: Electrical Systems
2800 Palisades Dr (92878-9427)
PHONE................................951 739-7000
Michael Hellmers, *Pr*
Carol Crawford, *
David Hellmers, *
EMP: 39 **EST:** 1974
SQ FT: 36,000
SALES (est): 4.75MM **Privately Held**
Web: www.pennecon.com
SIC: 3613 3625 Control panels, electric;
Relays and industrial controls

(P-8128)

PHAOSTRON INSTR ELECTRONIC CO

Also Called: Phaostron Instr Electronic Co
717 N Coney Ave (91702-2205)
PHONE................................626 969-6801
Paul R Mc Guirk, *Pr*
Andrew Mcguirk, *VP*
Jacqueline Cangialosi, *
EMP: 80 **EST:** 1937
SQ FT: 50,000
SALES (est): 12.17MM **Privately Held**
Web: www.phaostron.com
SIC: 3613 Metering panels, electric
PA: Westbase, Inc.
   717 N Coney Ave
   Azusa CA

(P-8129)

ROMAC SUPPLY CO INC

Also Called: Romac
17722 Neff Ranch Rd (92886-9013)
PHONE................................323 721-5810
TOLL FREE: 800
David B Rosenfield, *Pr*

Lisa R Podolsky, *
Phillip Rosenfield, *
Edith Rosenfield, *
Victoria Rosenfield, *
EMP: 60 **EST:** 1955
SALES (est): 20.89MM **Privately Held**
Web: www.tauberaronsinc.com
SIC: 3613 3621 3612 5063 Switchgear and
switchgear accessories, nec; Motors and
generators; Transformers, except electric;
Motors, electric

(P-8130)

STACO SYSTEMS INC (HQ)

Also Called: Staco Switch
7 Morgan (92618-2005)
PHONE................................949 297-8700
Patrick Hutchins, *Pr*
Jeffrey Nick, *VP*
Brett Meinsen, *VP Fin*
Tom Lanni, *VP*
Jeff Bowen, *VP Sls*
◆ **EMP:** 69 **EST:** 1957
SQ FT: 35,000
SALES (est): 17.22MM
SALES (corp-wide): 52.28MM **Privately Held**
Web: www.stacosystems.com
SIC: 3613 Switches, electric power except
snap, push button, etc.
PA: Components Corporation Of America
   5950 Berkshire Ln # 1500
   Dallas TX
   214 969-0166

(P-8131)

W A BENJAMIN ELECTRIC CO

1615 Staunton Ave (90021-3118)
PHONE................................213 749-7731
D E Benjamin, *Pr*
EMP: 50 **EST:** 1911
SALES (est): 10.64MM **Privately Held**
Web: www.benjaminelectric.com
SIC: 3613 Panelboards and distribution
boards, electric

(P-8132)

WEST COAST SWITCHGEAR (DH)

13837 Bettencourt St (90703-1009)
PHONE................................562 802-3441
Alfred P Cisternelli, *CEO*
▲ **EMP:** 93 **EST:** 2003
SQ FT: 20,000
SALES (est): 17.56MM **Privately Held**
Web: www.westcoastswitchgear.com
SIC: 3613 5063 Power circuit breakers;
Switchgear
HQ: Resa Power, Llc
   8723 Fallbrook Dr
   Houston TX
   832 900-8340

3621 Motors And Generators

(P-8133)

AC PROPULSION INC

441 Borrego Ct (91773-2971)
PHONE................................909 592-5399
▲ **EMP:** 20 **EST:** 1992
SALES (est): 3.67MM **Privately Held**
Web: www.acpropulsion.com
SIC: 3621 Electric motor and generator parts

(P-8134)

AIH LLC (DH)

Also Called: Astec International Holding
5810 Van Allen Way (92008-7300)
PHONE................................760 930-4600

Jay Geldmacher, *CEO*
Tom Rosenast, *CFO*
EMP: 47 **EST:** 2003
SALES (est): 376.93MM
SALES (corp-wide): 1.85B **Publicly Held**
Web: www.astecpower.com
SIC: 3621 3679 3629 Power generators;
Power supplies, all types: static; Power
conversion units, a.c. to d.c.: static-electric
HQ: Artesyn Embedded Technologies, Inc.
   2900 S Diablo Way B100
   Tempe AZ
   646 617-0186

(P-8135)

BARTA - SCHOENEWALD INC (PA)

Also Called: Advanced Motion Controls
3805 Calle Tecate (93012-5068)
PHONE................................805 389-1935
Sandor Barta, *Pr*
Daniel Schoenewald, *
▲ **EMP:** 116 **EST:** 1986
SQ FT: 86,000
SALES (est): 34.72MM
SALES (corp-wide): 34.72MM **Privately Held**
Web: www.a-m-c.com
SIC: 3621 3699 Servomotors, electric;
Electrical equipment and supplies, nec

(P-8136)

CALNETIX TECHNOLOGIES LLC (HQ)

16323 Shoemaker Ave (90703-2244)
PHONE................................562 293-1660
EMP: 67 **EST:** 2011
SALES (est): 22MM
SALES (corp-wide): 102.73MM **Privately Held**
Web: www.calnetix.com
SIC: 3621 Motors and generators
PA: Calnetix, Inc.
   16323 Shoemaker Ave
   Cerritos CA
   562 293-1660

(P-8137)

CHARGIE LLC

3947 Landmark St (90232-2315)
PHONE................................310 621-0024
Zach Jennings, *Managing Member*
EMP: 48 **EST:** 2020
SALES (est): 5.56MM **Privately Held**
Web: www.chargie.com
SIC: 3621 Electric motor and generator parts

(P-8138)

CMI INTEGRATED TECH INC

11248 Playa Ct (90230-6127)
EMP: 35 **EST:** 1989
SQ FT: 6,600
SALES (est): 3.48MM **Privately Held**
SIC: 3621 3825 Electric motor and generator
auxiliary parts; Instruments to measure
electricity

(P-8139)

COLE INSTRUMENT CORP

2650 S Croddy Way (92704-5238)
P.O. Box 25063 (92799-5063)
PHONE................................714 556-3100
Ric Garcia, *Pr*
Manuel Garcia, *
Muse Khawaja, *
EMP: 70 **EST:** 1965
SQ FT: 16,000
SALES (est): 14.19MM **Privately Held**
Web: www.cole-switches.com

SIC: 3621 3679 Motors and generators;
Electronic switches

(P-8140)

DIRECT DRIVE SYSTEMS INC

621 Burning Tree Rd (92833-1448)
PHONE................................714 872-5500
James Pribble, *CEO*
Michael Slater, *
Robert Clark, *
EMP: 57 **EST:** 2005
SALES (est): 23.72MM
SALES (corp-wide): 6.73B **Privately Held**
SIC: 3621 Electric motor and generator parts
HQ: Fmc Technologies, Inc.
   13460 Lockwood Rd
   Houston TX
   281 591-4000

(P-8141)

GLENTEK INC

208 Standard St (90245-3834)
PHONE................................310 322-3026
Richard Vasak, *CEO*
Helen Sysel, *
◆ **EMP:** 84 **EST:** 1964
SQ FT: 105,000
SALES (est): 12.57MM **Privately Held**
Web: www.glentek.com
SIC: 3621 Motors and generators

(P-8142)

GOHZ INC

23555 Golden Springs Dr Ste K1
(91765-2176)
PHONE................................800 603-1219
Zhuge Fusheng, *Pr*
EMP: 30 **EST:** 2015
SQ FT: 1,200
SALES (est): 5.1MM **Privately Held**
Web: www.gohz.com
SIC: 3621 Frequency converters (electric
generators)

(P-8143)

HI PERFRMNCE ELC VHCL SYSTEMS

620 S Magnolia Ave Ste B (91762-4030)
PHONE................................909 923-1973
Brian Guy Seymour, *CEO*
Toni Seymour, *Sec*
▲ **EMP:** 25 **EST:** 2002
SQ FT: 9,000
SALES (est): 1.71MM **Privately Held**
Web: www.hpevs.com
SIC: 3621 Motors, electric

(P-8144)

HITACHI AUTOMOTIVE SYSTEMS

Also Called: Los Angeles Plant
6200 Gateway Dr (90630-4842)
PHONE................................310 212-0200
EMP: 100
SIC: 3621 3714 Electric motor and generator
parts; Motor vehicle parts and accessories
HQ: Hitachi Automotive Systems Americas,
   Inc.
   955 Warwick Rd
   Harrodsburg KY
   859 734-9451

(P-8145)

IMAGE MICRO SPARE PARTS INC

7225 Oxford Way (90040-3644)
PHONE................................562 776-9808
Hassan Mohrekesh, *Pr*
EMP: 18 **EST:** 2015
SALES (est): 2.31MM **Privately Held**

(PA)=Parent Co (HQ)=Headquarters
✿ = New Business established in last 2 years

Web: www.imagemicro.com
SIC: **3621** Generating apparatus and parts, electrical

(P-8146)

INTEGRATED MAGNETICS INC
11250 Playa Ct (90230-6127)
PHONE.....................310 391-7213
Anil Nanji, *Pr*
*
EMP: 40 **EST:** 2012
SQ FT: 120,000
SALES (est): 10.59MM
SALES (corp-wide): 46.01MM **Privately Held**
Web: www.intemag.com
SIC: **3621 3679 3764** Rotors, for motors; Cores, magnetic; Rocket motors, guided missiles
PA: Integrated Technologies Group, Inc.
11250 Playa Ct
Culver City CA
310 391-7213

(P-8147)

KOLLMORGEN CORPORATION
33 S La Patera Ln (93117-3214)
PHONE.....................805 696-1236
EMP: 83
SALES (corp-wide): 5.22B **Publicly Held**
Web: www.kollmorgen.com
SIC: **3621** Servomotors, electric
HQ: Kollmorgen Corporation
203a W Rock Rd
Radford VA
540 639-9045

(P-8148)

LEOCH BATTERY CORPORATION (DH)
20322 Valencia Cir (92630-8158)
PHONE.....................949 588-5853
Hui Peng, *Pr*
Lili Shi, *
◆ **EMP:** 100 **EST:** 2003
SALES (est): 373MM **Privately Held**
Web: www.leochamericas.com
SIC: **3621** Storage battery chargers, motor and engine generator type
HQ: Leoch International Technology Limited
C/O Conyers Trust Company
(Cayman) Limited
George Town GR CAYMAN

(P-8149)

MAC M MC CULLY CORPORATION
Also Called: Mac M McCully Co
5316 Kazuko Ct (93021-1790)
PHONE.....................805 529-0661
Guy Mc Cully, *Pr*
Martha L Mccully, *Sec*
EMP: 35 **EST:** 1979
SALES (est): 3.35MM **Privately Held**
Web: www.mccullycorp.com
SIC: **3621** Motors, electric

(P-8150)

MAGICALL INC
4550 Calle Alto (93012-8509)
P.O. Box 3730 (93011-3730)
PHONE.....................805 484-4300
Joel Wacknov, *CEO*
▲ **EMP:** 26 **EST:** 2004
SALES (est): 5.33MM **Privately Held**
Web: www.magicall.biz
SIC: **3621 3612 3677 3679** Motors and generators; Power transformers, electric; Electronic coils and transformers; Static power supply converters for electronic applications

(P-8151)

MOTOR TECHNOLOGY INC
2301 Wardlow Cir (92878-5101)
PHONE.....................951 270-6200
Robert Buchwalder, *Pr*
Phyllis Buchwalder, *
George Teets, *
EMP: 67 **EST:** 1977
SQ FT: 12,600
SALES (est): 15.07MM **Publicly Held**
Web: www.circoraerospace.com
SIC: **3621** Motors, electric
HQ: Circor International, Inc.
30 Corporate Dr Ste 200
Burlington MA
781 270-1200

(P-8152)

NANTENERGY LLC
2040 E Mariposa Ave (90245-5027)
PHONE.....................310 905-4866
EMP: 75 **EST:** 2019
SALES (est): 3.1MM **Privately Held**
SIC: **3621 8731** Storage battery chargers, motor and engine generator type; Energy research

(P-8153)

POWERFLEX SYSTEMS LLC
15445 Innovation Dr (92128-3432)
P.O. Box 3155 (94024-0155)
PHONE.....................650 469-3392
George Lee, *CEO*
Steven Low, *
EMP: 24 **EST:** 2016
SALES (est): 3.04MM **Privately Held**
Web: www.powerflex.com
SIC: **3621** Generators for gas-electric or oil-electric vehicles

(P-8154)

RESMED MOTOR TECHNOLOGIES INC
Also Called: Resmed
9540 De Soto Ave (91311-5010)
PHONE.....................818 428-6400
David B Sears, *CEO*
▲ **EMP:** 170 **EST:** 2002
SQ FT: 35,000
SALES (est): 61.27MM **Publicly Held**
SIC: **3621 3714 3841** Coils, for electric motors or generators; Propane conversion equipment, motor vehicle; Surgical and medical instruments
PA: Resmed Inc.
9001 Spectrum Center Blvd
San Diego CA

(P-8155)

REULAND ELECTRIC CO (PA)
17969 Railroad St (91748-1192)
P.O. Box 1464 (91749-1464)
PHONE.....................626 964-6411
Noel C Reuland, *Pr*
William Kramer Iii, *VP*
▲ **EMP:** 130 **EST:** 1937
SQ FT: 100,000
SALES (est): 35.65MM
SALES (corp-wide): 35.65MM **Privately Held**
Web: www.reuland.com
SIC: **3621 3566 3363 3625** Motors, electric; Drives, high speed industrial, except hydrostatic; Aluminum die-castings; Electric controls and control accessories, industrial

(P-8156)

SEA ELECTRIC LLC
436 Alaska Ave (90503-3902)
PHONE.....................424 376-3660

EMP: 29
SALES (est): 10.75MM **Privately Held**
Web: www.sea-electric.com
SIC: **3621 3711** Motors and generators; Motor vehicles and car bodies

(P-8157)

SKURKA AEROSPACE INC (DH)
4600 Calle Bolero (93012-8575)
P.O. Box 2869 (93011-2869)
PHONE.....................805 484-8884
Michael Lisman, *CEO*
Lisa Sabol, *
Halle Terrion, *
EMP: 38 **EST:** 2004
SQ FT: 70,000
SALES (est): 32.59MM
SALES (corp-wide): 6.58B **Publicly Held**
Web: www.skurka-aero.com
SIC: **3621 3679** Motors, electric; Transducers, electrical
HQ: Transdigm, Inc.
1301 E 9th St Ste 3000
Cleveland OH

(P-8158)

SMI HOLDINGS INC
Also Called: Specialty Motors
28420 Witherspoon Pkwy (91355-4167)
PHONE.....................800 232-2612
▲ **EMP:** 25
SIC: **3621** Motors, electric

(P-8159)

SURE POWER INC
9255 Customhouse Plz (92154-7636)
PHONE.....................619 661-6292
EMP: 30
Web: www.sure-power.com
SIC: **3621** Motors and generators
HQ: Sure Power, Inc.
10955 Sw Avery St
Tualatin OR
503 692-5360

(P-8160)

THINGAP INC
Also Called: Thingap
4035 Via Pescador (93012-5050)
PHONE.....................805 477-9741
John Baumann, *CEO*
EMP: 33 **EST:** 2012
SALES (est): 5.73MM
SALES (corp-wide): 502.99MM **Publicly Held**
Web: www.thingap.com
SIC: **3621** Coils, for electric motors or generators
PA: Allient Inc.
495 Commerce Dr Ste 3
Amherst NY
716 242-8634

(P-8161)

VALLEY POWER SERVICES INC
425 S Hacienda Blvd (91745-1123)
PHONE.....................909 969-9345
Clark Lee, *Pr*
▲ **EMP:** 31 **EST:** 1999
SQ FT: 17,802
SALES (est): 3.98MM **Privately Held**
Web: www.valleypowersystems.com
SIC: **3621** Motor housings

3624 Carbon And Graphite Products

(P-8162)

ALLIANCE SPACESYSTEMS LLC
4398 Corporate Center Dr (90720-2537)
PHONE.....................714 226-1400
Rick Byrens, *Pr*
EMP: 155 **EST:** 1997
SQ FT: 101,000
SALES (est): 24.03MM
SALES (corp-wide): 189.21MM **Privately Held**
Web: www.appliedcomposites.com
SIC: **3624** Carbon and graphite products
PA: Applied Composites Holdings, Llc
25692 Atlantic Ocean Dr
Lake Forest CA
949 716-3511

(P-8163)

FRONTERA SOLUTIONS INC
1913 E 17th St Ste 210 (92705-8627)
PHONE.....................714 368-1631
Earl B Johnson, *Pr*
Ben Rawski, *
John Drake, *
EMP: 21 **EST:** 2001
SALES (est): 283.04K **Privately Held**
Web: www.fronterasolutionsinc.com
SIC: **3624 3231** Fibers, carbon and graphite; Insulating glass: made from purchased glass

(P-8164)

KBR INC
Also Called: Electro-Tech Machining Div
2000 W Gaylord St (90813-1032)
P.O. Box 92610 (14692-0610)
PHONE.....................562 436-9281
Ryan Mcmahon, *Pr*
▲ **EMP:** 32 **EST:** 1977
SQ FT: 39,000
SALES (est): 6.32MM **Privately Held**
Web: www.etmgraphite.com
SIC: **3624** Carbon and graphite products

(P-8165)

SPACESYSTEMS HOLDINGS LLC
4398 Corporate Center Dr (90720-2537)
PHONE.....................714 226-1400
Terence Lyons, *CEO*
Rick Byrens, *Pr*
Jeffrey David Lassiter, *CFO*
EMP: 20 **EST:** 2012
SQ FT: 101,000
SALES (est): 303.91K **Privately Held**
SIC: **3624** Carbon and graphite products

(P-8166)

TORAY PRFMCE MTLS CORP USA
Also Called: Toray PMC
1150 Calle Suerte (93012-8051)
PHONE.....................805 402-6664
EMP: 21 **EST:** 2020
SALES (est): 5.48MM **Privately Held**
Web: www.toraypmc.com
SIC: **3624** Fibers, carbon and graphite

▲ = Import ▼ = Export
◆ = Import/Export

3625 Relays And Industrial Controls

(P-8167)
ABSOLUTE GRAPHIC TECH USA INC
Also Called: Agt
235 Jason Ct (92879-6199)
PHONE..............................909 597-1133
Steven J Barberi, *Pr*
EMP: 49 **EST:** 2006
SQ FT: 25,800
SALES (est): 9.17MM **Privately Held**
Web: www.agt-usa.com
SIC: 3625 3577 Industrial electrical relays and switches; Printers and plotters

(P-8168)
ANAHEIM AUTOMATION INC
4985 E Landon Dr (92807-1972)
PHONE..............................714 992-6990
Faithe Reimbold, *VP*
Joann Witt, *
Nannette Israel, *
◆ **EMP:** 52 **EST:** 1966
SQ FT: 9,000
SALES (est): 8.73MM **Privately Held**
Web: www.anaheimautomation.com
SIC: 3625 3545 3566 Control equipment, electric; Machine tool accessories; Speed changers, drives, and gears

(P-8169)
AP PARPRO INC
2700 S Fairview St (92704-5947)
PHONE..............................619 498-9004
Hsiu Pi Wu, *Pr*
Po Ju Shih, *Sec*
EMP: 32 **EST:** 2005
SALES (est): 9.24MM **Privately Held**
Web: www.parpro.com
SIC: 3625 Relays and industrial controls

(P-8170)
BALBOA WATER GROUP LLC (HQ)
Also Called: Controlmyspa
3030 Airway Ave Ste B (92626-6036)
PHONE..............................714 384-0384
Eric Kownacki, *CEO*
David J Cline, *
Jean-pierre Parent, *Sr VP*
◆ **EMP:** 54 **EST:** 2007
SALES (est): 99.66MM
SALES (corp-wide): 885.4MM **Publicly Held**
Web: www.balboawater.com
SIC: 3625 3599 Electric controls and control accessories, industrial; Machine shop, jobbing and repair
PA: Helios Technologies, Inc.
7456 16th St E
Sarasota FL
941 362-1200

(P-8171)
CAL-COMP ELECTRONICS (USA) CO LTD
Also Called: Ccsd
9877 Waples St (92121-2922)
PHONE..............................858 587-6900
▲ **EMP:** 299
SIC: 3625 Actuators, industrial

(P-8172)
CALIFORNIA ECONOMIZER
Also Called: Zonex Systems
5622 Engineer Dr (92649-1124)
PHONE..............................714 898-9963
Jeff Osheroff, *Pr*
▲ **EMP:** 50 **EST:** 1988
SQ FT: 16,000
SALES (est): 5.32MM **Privately Held**
Web: www.zonexproducts.com
SIC: 3625 3822 Control equipment, electric; Environmental controls

(P-8173)
CONTROL SWITCHES INTL INC
2425 Mira Mar Ave (90815-1757)
P.O. Box 92349 (90809-2349)
PHONE..............................562 498-7331
Margerate Turner, *Ex VP*
Peggy Turner, *
Judith Steward, *
Susan Moore, *
Jane Armstrong, *
EMP: 25 **EST:** 1977
SQ FT: 10,000
SALES (est): 3.49MM
SALES (corp-wide): 11.85MM **Privately Held**
Web: www.controlswitches.com
SIC: 3625 Switches, electronic applications
PA: Control Switches, Inc.
2425 Mira Mar Ave
Long Beach CA
562 498-7331

(P-8174)
CRYDOM INC (DH)
2320 Paseo De Las Americas Ste 201 (92154-7273)
PHONE..............................619 210-1590
Bob Ciurczak, *Pr*
▲ **EMP:** 75 **EST:** 2005
SQ FT: 20,000
SALES (est): 112.36MM
SALES (corp-wide): 4.03B **Privately Held**
Web: www.sensata.com
SIC: 3625 5065 3674 3643 Control equipment, electric; Electronic parts and equipment, nec; Semiconductors and related devices; Current-carrying wiring services
HQ: Sensata Technologies, Inc.
529 Pleasant St
Attleboro MA

(P-8175)
CURTISS-WRGHT CNTRLS ELCTRNIC (DH)
Also Called: Curtiss-Wrght Cntrls Elctrnic
28965 Avenue Penn (91355-4185)
PHONE..............................661 702-1494
Thomas P Quinly, *CEO*
David Dietz, *
EMP: 172 **EST:** 1985
SQ FT: 18,700
SALES (est): 53.65MM
SALES (corp-wide): 2.56B **Publicly Held**
Web: www.curtisswright.com
SIC: 3625 8731 8711 3769 Relays and industrial controls; Commercial physical research; Consulting engineer; Space vehicle equipment, nec
HQ: Curtiss-Wright Controls, Inc.
201 Old Boiling Sprng Rd
Shelby NC
704 869-4600

(P-8176)
CUSTOM CONTROL SENSORS INC
21111 Plummer St (91311-4905)
PHONE..............................818 341-4610
EMP: 24 **EST:** 2015
SALES (est): 1.09MM **Privately Held**
Web: www.ccsdualsnap.com
SIC: 3625 Relays and industrial controls

(P-8177)
DOW-KEY MICROWAVE CORPORATION
Also Called: Dow-Key Microwave
4822 Mcgrath St (93003-7718)
PHONE..............................805 650-0260
David Wightman, *Pr*
EMP: 150 **EST:** 1970
SQ FT: 26,000
SALES (est): 28.88MM
SALES (corp-wide): 8.51B **Publicly Held**
Web: www.mpgdover.com
SIC: 3625 3678 3643 3613 Switches, electronic applications; Electronic connectors; Current-carrying wiring services; Switchgear and switchboard apparatus
PA: Dover Corporation
3005 Highland Pkwy # 200
Downers Grove IL
630 541-1540

(P-8178)
EAGLE ACCESS CTRL SYSTEMS INC
12953 Foothill Blvd (91342-4929)
PHONE..............................818 837-7900
Yossi Afriat, *CEO*
Avi Afriat, *VP Opers*
Oren Afriat, *CFO*
◆ **EMP:** 22 **EST:** 1996
SQ FT: 13,000
SALES (est): 8.85MM **Privately Held**
Web: www.eagleoperators.com
SIC: 3625 Control equipment, electric

(P-8179)
EATON ELECTRICAL INC
13201 Dahlia St (92337-6971)
PHONE..............................951 685-5788
EMP: 154
SIC: 3625 Motor controls and accessories
HQ: Eaton Electrical Inc.
1000 Cherrington Pkwy
Moon Township PA

(P-8180)
EMBEDDED SYSTEMS INC
Also Called: Esi Motion
2250a Union Pl (93065-1660)
PHONE..............................805 624-6030
Earnie Beem, *Pr*
Sheila D'angelo, *VP*
EMP: 40 **EST:** 2005
SALES (est): 11.54MM **Privately Held**
Web: www.esimotion.com
SIC: 3625 Motor starters and controllers, electric

(P-8181)
GENERAL DYNAMICS MISSION
General Dynamics Global
7603 Saint Andrews Ave Ste H (92154-8216)
PHONE..............................619 671-5400
Bud Jenkins, *Ofcr*
EMP: 83
SALES (corp-wide): 39.41B **Publicly Held**
Web: www.gdmissionsystems.com
SIC: 3625 3824 3825 3621 Relays and industrial controls; Fluid meters and counting devices; Instruments to measure electricity; Motors and generators
HQ: General Dynamics Mission Systems, Inc.
12450 Fair Lakes Cir
Fairfax VA
877 449-0600

(P-8182)
HONGFA AMERICA INC
Also Called: Xiamen Hongfa Electroacoustic
20381 Hermana Cir (92630-8701)
PHONE..............................714 669-2888
Guo Manjin, *CEO*
▲ **EMP:** 22 **EST:** 2015
SALES (est): 8.69MM **Privately Held**
Web: www.hongfa.com
SIC: 3625 6719 Electric controls and control accessories, industrial; Investment holding companies, except banks
HQ: Xiamen Hongfa Electroacoustic Co., Ltd.
No.91-101, Sunban South Road, Beibu Industrial Zone, Jimei
Xiamen FJ

(P-8183)
ITT CANNON LLC
Also Called: BIW Connector Systems
56 Technology Dr (92618-2301)
PHONE..............................714 557-4700
Farrokh Batliwala, *Prin*
Farrokh Batliwala, *Pr*
Mary Beth Gustafsson, *
Philip Bordages, *
John Capela, *CAO*
EMP: 132 **EST:** 2011
SALES (est): 45.75MM
SALES (corp-wide): 2.99B **Publicly Held**
Web: www.ittcannon.com
SIC: 3625 Control equipment, electric
HQ: Itt Industries Holdings, Inc
100 Wshington Blvd Fl 6 Flr 6
Stamford CT
914 641-2000

(P-8184)
ITT LLC
ITT Goulds Pumps
3951 Capitol Ave (90601-1734)
P.O. Box 1254 (91749-1254)
PHONE..............................562 908-4144
Shashank Patel, *Genl Mgr*
EMP: 75
SQ FT: 85,000
SALES (corp-wide): 2.99B **Publicly Held**
Web: www.itt.com
SIC: 3625 Control equipment, electric
HQ: Itt Llc
1133 Westchester Ave N-100
White Plains NY
914 641-2000

(P-8185)
M W SAUSSE & CO INC (PA)
Also Called: Vibrex
28744 Witherspoon Pkwy (91355-5425)
PHONE..............................661 257-3311
Torbjorn Helland, *Pr*
Dan Robinson, *
Paul Azevedo, *
Gregory Hall, *
▲ **EMP:** 59 **EST:** 1961
SQ FT: 12,000
SALES (est): 9.82MM
SALES (corp-wide): 9.82MM **Privately Held**
Web: www.vibrex.net
SIC: 3625 Control equipment, electric

(P-8186)
MICROSEMI CORP-POWER MGT GROUP
11861 Western Ave (92841-2119)
PHONE..............................714 994-6500
James J Peterson, *Pr*
John W Hohener, *
David Goren, *

Rob Warren, *General Vice President**
EMP: 249 **EST:** 1977
SQ FT: 135,000
SALES (est): 24.26MM
SALES (corp-wide): 8.44B **Publicly Held**
Web: www.microsemi.com
SIC: 3625 3677 3679 3613 Relays, for electronic use; Electronic transformers; Liquid crystal displays (LCD); Switchgear and switchboard apparatus
HQ: Microsemi Corp.-Power Management Group Holding
11861 Western Ave
Garden Grove CA
714 994-6500

(P-8187)
MOOG INC
Also Called: Moog Jon Street Warehouse
1218 W Jon St (90502-1208)
PHONE..................................310 533-1178
Alberto Bilalon, *Mgr*
EMP: 500
SALES (corp-wide): 3.32B **Publicly Held**
Web: www.moog.com
SIC: 3625 8711 3812 Relays and industrial controls; Aviation and/or aeronautical engineering; Aircraft/aerospace flight instruments and guidance systems
PA: Moog Inc.
400 Jamison Rd
Elma NY
716 652-2000

(P-8188)
RIGHT HAND MANUFACTURING INC
180 Otay Lakes Rd Ste 205 (91902-2444)
PHONE..................................619 819-5056
▲ **EMP:** 150 **EST:** 2003
SALES (est): 10.01MM **Privately Held**
Web: www.righthandmanufacturing.com
SIC: 3625 Control circuit devices, magnet and solid state

(P-8189)
ROSEMOUNT ANALYTICAL INC
2400 Barranca Pkwy (92606-5018)
Rural Route 22737 (60673-0001)
PHONE..................................713 396-8880
◆ **EMP:** 1100
SIC: 3625 3825 3823 3564 Relays and industrial controls; Instruments to measure electricity; Process control instruments; Blowers and fans

(P-8190)
S R C DEVICES INCCUSTOMER
6295 Ferris Sq Ste D (92121-3248)
PHONE..................................866 772-8668
Richard W Carlyle, *Pr*
Mark Mccabe, *Sr VP*
EMP: 303 **EST:** 2001
SQ FT: 2,000
SALES (est): 16.16MM **Privately Held**
SIC: 3625 3643 5065 Switches, electronic applications; Current-carrying wiring services; Electronic parts and equipment, nec

(P-8191)
SOUNDCOAT COMPANY INC
16901 Armstrong Ave (92606-4914)
PHONE..................................631 242-2200
Clay Simpson, *Brnch Mgr*
EMP: 69
SALES (corp-wide): 200.11MM **Privately Held**
Web: www.soundcoat.com

SIC: 3625 3086 3296 Noise control equipment; Plastics foam products; Mineral wool
HQ: The Soundcoat Company, Inc.
1 Burt Dr
Deer Park NY
631 242-2200

(P-8192)
SURFACE TECHNOLOGIES CORP
3170 Commercial St (92113-1427)
PHONE..................................619 564-8320
Bernard Meartz, *Mgr*
EMP: 30
SQ FT: 29,617
SALES (corp-wide): 24.92MM **Privately Held**
Web: www.surfacetechnologiescorp.com
SIC: 3625 Marine and navy auxiliary controls
PA: Surface Technologies Corporation
2440 Mayport Rd Ste 7
Jacksonville FL
904 241-1501

(P-8193)
SYSTEMS MCHS ATMTN CMPNNTS COR (PA)
Also Called: Smac
5807 Van Allen Way (92008-7309)
PHONE..................................760 929-7575
Ed Neff, *CEO*
Robert Berry, *
▲ **EMP:** 165 **EST:** 1990
SALES (est): 24.94MM **Privately Held**
Web: www.smac-mca.com
SIC: 3625 2822 3549 Actuators, industrial; Synthetic rubber; Assembly machines, including robotic

(P-8194)
TE CONNECTIVITY CORPORATION
Also Called: Kilovac
550 Linden Ave (93013-2038)
PHONE..................................805 684-4560
Mike Moschitto, *Brnch Mgr*
EMP: 30
Web: www.te.com
SIC: 3625 Relays, for electronic use
HQ: Te Connectivity Corporation
1050 Westlakes Dr
Berwyn PA
610 893-9800

(P-8195)
TEAL ELECTRONICS CORPORATION (PA)
10350 Sorrento Valley Rd (92121-1642)
PHONE..................................858 558-9000
Glen Kassan, *Ch Bd*
Donald Klein, *CEO*
William Bickel, *VP Fin*
David Nuzzo, *Treas*
◆ **EMP:** 79 **EST:** 1983
SQ FT: 36,059
SALES (est): 20.09MM
SALES (corp-wide): 20.09MM **Privately Held**
SIC: 3625 2631 3612 Noise control equipment; Transformer board; Transformers, except electric

(P-8196)
VISHAY TECHNO COMPONENTS LLC
Also Called: Vishay Spectro
4051 Greystone Dr (91761-3100)
PHONE..................................909 923-3313

Felix Zandman Ph.d., *Pr*
Robert A Freece, *
William J Spiers, *
▲ **EMP:** 89 **EST:** 1961
SQ FT: 30,000
SALES (est): 10.95MM
SALES (corp-wide): 3.5B **Publicly Held**
SIC: 3625 Resistors and resistor units
HQ: Vishay Dale Electronics, Llc
1122 23rd St
Columbus NE
605 665-9301

(P-8197)
WOODWARD HRT INC (HQ)
25200 Rye Canyon Rd (91355-1204)
PHONE..................................661 294-6000
Charles Blankenship, *CEO*
Tom Cromwell, *COO*
Bill Lacey, *CFO*
▲ **EMP:** 650 **EST:** 1954
SQ FT: 200,000
SALES (est): 224.82MM
SALES (corp-wide): 2.91B **Publicly Held**
SIC: 3625 3492 Actuators, industrial; Electrohydraulic servo valves, metal
PA: Woodward, Inc.
1081 Woodward Way
Fort Collins CO
970 482-5811

(P-8198)
ZBE INC
1035 Cindy Ln (93013-2905)
PHONE..................................805 576-1600
Zac Bogart, *Pr*
▲ **EMP:** 45 **EST:** 1980
SQ FT: 7,500
SALES (est): 7.55MM **Privately Held**
Web: www.zbe.com
SIC: 3625 3861 3577 Electric controls and control accessories, industrial; Photographic equipment and supplies; Computer peripheral equipment, nec

---

3629 Electrical Industrial Apparatus

(P-8199)
ADVANCED CHARGING TECH INC
Also Called: A C T
17260 Newhope St (92708-4210)
PHONE..................................877 228-5922
Robert J Istwan, *Pr*
Chris Oltman, *Coordtr*
Anthony Capalino, *Sec*
▲ **EMP:** 21 **EST:** 2008
SALES (est): 7.26MM **Privately Held**
Web: www.act-chargers.com
SIC: 3629 3691 Battery chargers, rectifying or nonrotating; Alkaline cell storage batteries

(P-8200)
ARECONT VISION LLC
425 E Colorado St Fl 7700 (91205-5117)
PHONE..................................818 937-0700
◆ **EMP:** 103
SIC: 3629 Electronic generation equipment

(P-8201)
AVEOX INC
2265 Ward Ave Ste A (93065-1864)
PHONE..................................805 915-0200
David Palombo, *Pr*
▲ **EMP:** 35 **EST:** 1992
SQ FT: 22,000
SALES (est): 10.4MM **Privately Held**

Web: www.aveox.com
SIC: 3629 Electronic generation equipment

(P-8202)
CAPAX TECHNOLOGIES INC
24842 Avenue Tibbitts (91355-3404)
PHONE..................................661 257-7666
Jagdish Patel, *Pr*
Nina Patel, *
EMP: 28 **EST:** 1988
SQ FT: 17,000
SALES (est): 2.24MM **Privately Held**
Web: www.capaxtechnologies.com
SIC: 3629 3675 Capacitors, fixed or variable; Electronic capacitors

(P-8203)
CONCURRENT HOLDINGS LLC
11150 Santa Monica Blvd Ste 825 (90025-3314)
PHONE..................................310 473-3065
Benjamin Teno, *Managing Member*
▲ **EMP:** 750 **EST:** 2012
SALES (est): 85.31MM
SALES (corp-wide): 406.38MM **Privately Held**
SIC: 3629 3679 Electronic generation equipment; Harness assemblies, for electronic use: wire or cable
PA: Balmoral Funds Llc
11150 Santa Monica Blvd
Los Angeles CA
310 473-3065

(P-8204)
DESCO INDUSTRIES INC (PA)
Also Called: Desco
3651 Walnut Ave (91710-2904)
PHONE..................................909 627-8178
◆ **EMP:** 75 **EST:** 1965
SALES (est): 54.35MM
SALES (corp-wide): 54.35MM **Privately Held**
Web: www.descoindustries.com
SIC: 3629 Static elimination equipment, industrial

(P-8205)
ENGINEERED MAGNETICS INC
Also Called: Aap Division
10524 S La Cienega Blvd (90304-1116)
PHONE..................................310 649-9000
Josh Shachar, *Ch Bd*
Kathy Tran, *
Maya Vu, *
Isabella Yi Sha Li, *Dir*
EMP: 26 **EST:** 2000
SQ FT: 57,000
SALES (est): 6.03MM **Privately Held**
Web: www.engineeredmagnetics.net
SIC: 3629 3812 3369 Power conversion units, a.c. to d.c.: static-electric; Missile guidance systems and equipment; Aerospace castings, nonferrous: except aluminum

(P-8206)
EPC POWER CORP (PA)
13250 Gregg St Ste A2 (92064-7164)
PHONE..................................858 748-5590
▼ **EMP:** 168 **EST:** 2010
SQ FT: 10,000
SALES (est): 38.82MM **Privately Held**
Web: www.epcpower.com
SIC: 3629 Battery chargers, rectifying or nonrotating

(P-8207)
IAMPLUS LLC
809 N Cahuenga Blvd (90038-3703)

PHONE.................................323 210-3852
Phil Molyneux, *Pr*
Chandrasekar Rathakrishnan, *Dir*
Rosemary Peschken, *CFO*
EMP: 56 **EST:** 2012
SQ FT: 3,900
SALES (est): 4.8MM
SALES (corp-wide): 10.01MM **Privately Held**
Web: www.iamplus.services
SIC: 3629 Electronic generation equipment
PA: I.Am.Plus Electronics, Inc.
809 N Cahuenga Blvd
Los Angeles CA
323 210-3852

(P-8208)
INTELLIGENT TECHNOLOGIES LLC
Also Called: Itech
9454 Waples St (92121-2919)
PHONE.................................858 458-1500
Rod Bolton, *Pr*
Frank Cooper, *
▲ **EMP:** 125 **EST:** 1997
SQ FT: 17,846
SALES (est): 49.82MM
SALES (corp-wide): 109.05MM **Privately Held**
Web: www.itecheng.com
SIC: 3629 3356 Battery chargers, rectifying or nonrotating; Battery metal
PA: Universal Power Group, Inc.
488 S Royal Ln
Coppell TX
469 892-1122

(P-8209)
INTERCONNECT SOLUTIONS CO LLC (PA)
17595 Mount Herrmann St (92708-4160)
PHONE.................................909 545-6140
Michael Engler, *CEO*
▲ **EMP:** 70 **EST:** 2018
SQ FT: 15,000
SALES (est): 26.91MM
SALES (corp-wide): 26.91MM **Privately Held**
Web: www.interconnectsolutions.com
SIC: 3629 Electronic generation equipment

(P-8210)
MAXWELL TECHNOLOGIES INC
3912 Calle Fortunada (92123-1827)
PHONE.................................858 503-3493
EMP: 100
SALES (corp-wide): 81.46B **Publicly Held**
Web: www.maxwell.com
SIC: 3629 Capacitors and condensers
HQ: Maxwell Technologies, Inc.
3888 Calle Fortunada
San Diego CA
858 503-3300

(P-8211)
Q C M INC
Also Called: Veris Manufacturing
285 Gemini Ave (92821-3704)
PHONE.................................714 414-1173
Jay Cadler, *CEO*
Larry Ching, *
▲ **EMP:** 45 **EST:** 2006
SALES (est): 20.65MM
SALES (corp-wide): 140.78MM **Privately Held**
Web: www.emeraldems.com
SIC: 3629 Electronic generation equipment
PA: Megatronics Us Ultimate Holdco Llc
1 Stiles Rd
Salem NH
888 706-0230

(P-8212)
SCIENTFIC APPLCTONS RES ASSOC (PA)
Also Called: Sara
6300 Gateway Dr (90630-4844)
PHONE.................................714 224-4410
Parviz Parhami, *CEO*
James Wes, *
Wes Addington, *
Amy Dockenhorf, *
EMP: 58 **EST:** 1989
SQ FT: 43,000
SALES (est): 57.09MM **Privately Held**
Web: www.sara.com
SIC: 3629 Electronic generation equipment

(P-8213)
SCOTT ENGINEERING INC
Also Called: Scott Manufacturing Solutions
5051 Edison Ave (91710-5716)
PHONE.................................909 594-9637
Luis Ernesto Lujan, *CEO*
Deborah N Davis, *
Jason J Huitrado, *
▲ **EMP:** 100 **EST:** 1967
SQ FT: 102,660
SALES (est): 35.59MM **Privately Held**
Web: www.scott-eng.com
SIC: 3629 3613 Electronic generation equipment; Switchgear and switchboard apparatus

(P-8214)
SEACOMP INC (PA)
1525 Faraday Ave (92008-7319)
PHONE.................................760 918-6722
Michael Szymanski, *CEO*
Terry Arbaugh, *
Robert Marshal, *
▲ **EMP:** 148 **EST:** 1989
SALES (est): 13.93MM
SALES (corp-wide): 13.93MM **Privately Held**
Web: www.seacomp.com
SIC: 3629 Battery chargers, rectifying or nonrotating

(P-8215)
SKYWORKS SOLUTIONS INC
1767 Carr Rd Ste 105 (92231-9506)
PHONE.................................301 874-6408
▲ **EMP:** 18
SALES (corp-wide): 4.77B **Publicly Held**
Web: www.skyworksinc.com
SIC: 3629 Capacitors and condensers
PA: Skyworks Solutions, Inc.
5260 California Ave # 100
Irvine CA
949 231-3000

(P-8216)
ZPOWER LLC
5171 Clareton Dr (91301-4523)
PHONE.................................805 445-7789
Herbert V Weigel Ii, *COO*
Dennis J Dugan, *
Barry A Freeman, *
Damon Mikoy, *
EMP: 210 **EST:** 1996
SALES (est): 47.95MM **Privately Held**
Web: www.riotenergy.com
SIC: 3629 Battery chargers, rectifying or nonrotating

3631 Household Cooking Equipment

(P-8217)
FUEGO LIVING LLC
1714 Alta Mura Rd (90272-2703)
PHONE.................................415 558-7151
EMP: 25
SALES (corp-wide): 488.06K **Privately Held**
SIC: 3631 Barbecues, grills, and braziers (outdoor cooking)
PA: Fuego Living Llc
5042 Wilshire Blvd
Los Angeles CA
415 558-7151

(P-8218)
JADE RANGE LLC
Also Called: Jade Products
2650 Orbiter St (92821-6265)
PHONE.................................714 961-2400
▲ **EMP:** 120 **EST:** 1998
SALES (est): 42MM
SALES (corp-wide): 4.03B **Publicly Held**
Web: www.jaderange.com
SIC: 3631 3589 Household cooking equipment; Commercial cooking and foodwarming equipment
PA: The Middleby Corporation
1400 Toastmaster Dr
Elgin IL
847 741-3300

(P-8219)
MAGMA PRODUCTS LLC
3940 Pixie Ave (90712-4136)
PHONE.................................562 627-0500
James Mashburn, *
◆ **EMP:** 70 **EST:** 1976
SQ FT: 22,000
SALES (est): 9.73MM **Privately Held**
Web: www.magmaproducts.com
SIC: 3631 3634 Barbecues, grills, and braziers (outdoor cooking); Griddles or grills, electric: household

(P-8220)
PACIFIC COAST MFG INC
5270 Edison Ave (91710-5719)
PHONE.................................909 627-7040
Bruce Doran, *Pr*
James Poremba, *
▲ **EMP:** 72 **EST:** 2011
SQ FT: 40,000
SALES (est): 13.98MM **Privately Held**
Web: www.pcmbbq.com
SIC: 3631 Barbecues, grills, and braziers (outdoor cooking)

(P-8221)
RH PETERSON CO (PA)
Also Called: Robert H Peterson Company
14724 Proctor Ave (91746-3202)
PHONE.................................626 369-5085
◆ **EMP:** 170 **EST:** 1949
SALES (est): 24.63MM
SALES (corp-wide): 24.63MM **Privately Held**
Web: www.rhpeterson.com
SIC: 3631 3433 Barbecues, grills, and braziers (outdoor cooking); Logs, gas fireplace

(P-8222)
ROYAL RANGE CALIFORNIA INC
Also Called: Royal Industries
3245 Corridor Dr (91752-1030)

PHONE.................................951 360-1600
▼ **EMP:** 65 **EST:** 1995
SQ FT: 52,000
SALES (est): 9.46MM **Privately Held**
Web: www.royalranges.com
SIC: 3631 Household cooking equipment

(P-8223)
SUNBEAM PRODUCTS INC
Also Called: Sunbeam
13052 Jurupa Ave (92337-6912)
PHONE.................................951 727-3901
EMP: 17
SALES (corp-wide): 9.46B **Publicly Held**
SIC: 3631 3634 3089 Barbecues, grills, and braziers (outdoor cooking); Electric housewares and fans; Plastics containers, except foam
HQ: Sunbeam Products, Inc.
2381 Nw Executive Ctr Dr
Boca Raton FL
770 418-7000

(P-8224)
SUPERIOR EQUIPMENT SOLUTIONS
1085 Bixby Dr (91745-1704)
PHONE.................................323 722-7900
Jeffrey Bernstein, *CEO*
Stephan Bernstein, *
▲ **EMP:** 60 **EST:** 2001
SQ FT: 45,000
SALES (est): 750MM **Privately Held**
Web: www.alfrescogrills.com
SIC: 3631 5046 Household cooking equipment; Restaurant equipment and supplies, nec

(P-8225)
TWIN EAGLES INC
13259 166th St (90703-2203)
PHONE.................................562 802-3488
Dante L Cantal, *Pr*
Epifania Cantal, *
▲ **EMP:** 101 **EST:** 1999
SQ FT: 45,000
SALES (est): 23.39MM
SALES (corp-wide): 2.84B **Privately Held**
Web: www.twineaglesgrills.com
SIC: 3631 Barbecues, grills, and braziers (outdoor cooking)
HQ: Dometic Corporation
5600 N River Rd Ste 250
Rosemont IL

(P-8226)
VIKING RANGE LLC
14680 Monte Vista Ave (91710-5744)
PHONE.................................909 662-3504
EMP: 22
SALES (corp-wide): 4.03B **Publicly Held**
Web: www.vikingrange.com
SIC: 3631 Household cooking equipment
HQ: Viking Range, Llc
111 W Front St
Greenwood MS
662 455-1200

3632 Household Refrigerators And Freezers

(P-8227)
REFRIDERATOR MANUFACTERS LLC
17018 Edwards Rd (90703-2422)
PHONE.................................562 229-0500
EMP: 42 **EST:** 2014
SQ FT: 40,000

PRODUCTS & SVCS

SALES (est): 4.68MM **Privately Held**
SIC: 3632 Freezers, home and farm

(P-8228)
REFRIGERATOR MANUFACTERS INC (PA)
Also Called: Econocold Refrigerators
17018 Edwards Rd (90703-2422)
PHONE....................................562 926-2006
Lawrence E Jaffe, *Pr*
Leo R Lewis, *Ex VP*
Russell E Anthony, *Ex VP*
EMP: 20 **EST:** 1945
SQ FT: 40,000
SALES (est): 3.94MM
SALES (corp-wide): 3.94MM **Privately Held**
Web: www.rmi-econocold.com
SIC: 3632 3585 Household refrigerators and freezers; Refrigeration and heating equipment

---

3634 Electric Housewares And Fans

(P-8229)
AG GLOBAL PRODUCTS LLC
Also Called: Fhi Brands
15408 Blackburn Ave (90650-6843)
PHONE....................................323 334-2900
◆ **EMP:** 18 **EST:** 2010
SALES (est): 844.68K **Privately Held**
SIC: 3634 3999 Hair curlers, electric; Hair and hair-based products

(P-8230)
BRANDS REPUBLIC INC
10333 Rush St (91733-3341)
PHONE....................................302 401-1195
Asif Kashif, *Prin*
EMP: 50
SALES (est): 1.6MM **Privately Held**
SIC: 3634 Electric housewares and fans

(P-8231)
CAPITAL BRANDS DISTRIBUTION L (PA)
10900 Wilshire Blvd Ste 900 (90024-6500)
PHONE....................................800 523-5993
Richard Krause, *CEO*
Lenny Sands, *
EMP: 62 **EST:** 2015
SALES (est): 65.12MM
SALES (corp-wide): 65.12MM **Privately Held**
Web: www.capitalbrands.com
SIC: 3634 Blenders, electric

(P-8232)
COSMO PRODUCTS LLC
Also Called: Cosmo
5431 Brooks St (91763-4563)
PHONE....................................626 416-5411
▲ **EMP:** 19 **EST:** 2014
SALES (est): 2.58MM **Privately Held**
Web: www.cosmoappliances.com
SIC: 3634 Electric household cooking appliances

(P-8233)
CRYOGENIC INDUSTRIES INC
25720 Jefferson Ave (92562-6929)
PHONE....................................951 677-2060
Peter Wagner, *CEO*
EMP: 200 **EST:** 2016
SALES (est): 16.68MM **Privately Held**
Web: www.nikkisoceig.com

SIC: 3634 Vaporizers, electric: household

(P-8234)
FELLOW INDUSTRIES INC
Also Called: Fellow
1342 1/2 Abbot Kinney Blvd (90291-3778)
PHONE....................................415 649-0361
Jacob Miller, *CEO*
EMP: 48
SALES (corp-wide): 9.92MM **Privately Held**
Web: www.fellowproducts.com
SIC: 3634 Electric housewares and fans
PA: Fellow Industries Inc.
820 Valencia St
San Francisco CA
415 649-0361

(P-8235)
FOLDIMATE INC
879 White Pine Ct (91377-4769)
PHONE....................................805 876-4418
Gal Rozov, *CEO*
Ori Kaplan, *COO*
EMP: 22 **EST:** 2012
SALES (est): 1.83MM **Privately Held**
Web: www.foldimate.com
SIC: 3634 Personal electrical appliances

(P-8236)
INSEAT SOLUTIONS LLC
1871 Wright Ave (91750-5817)
PHONE....................................562 447-1780
▲ **EMP:** 22 **EST:** 2000
SALES (est): 4.29MM **Privately Held**
Web: www.relaxor.com
SIC: 3634 Massage machines, electric, except for beauty/barber shops

(P-8237)
LUMA COMFORT LLC
Also Called: Luma Comfort
6600 Katella Ave (90630-5104)
PHONE....................................855 963-9247
Luke Peters, *Pr*
Luke Peters, *CEO*
Mariella Peters, *
▲ **EMP:** 50 **EST:** 2011
SQ FT: 30,000
SALES (est): 4.73MM **Privately Held**
Web: www.newair.com
SIC: 3634 Electric housewares and fans

(P-8238)
MJC AMERICA LTD (PA)
Also Called: Soleus International
20035 E Walnut Dr N (91789-2922)
P.O. Box 472 (91788-0472)
PHONE....................................888 876-5387
Simon Chu, *CEO*
◆ **EMP:** 35 **EST:** 1998
SQ FT: 100,000
SALES (est): 4.99MM
SALES (corp-wide): 4.99MM **Privately Held**
Web: www.soleusair.com
SIC: 3634 Electric housewares and fans

(P-8239)
T3 MICRO INC (PA)
880 Apollo St Ste 200 (90245-4701)
PHONE....................................310 452-2888
Kent Yu, *Pr*
▲ **EMP:** 17 **EST:** 2005
SALES (est): 8.95MM
SALES (corp-wide): 8.95MM **Privately Held**
Web: www.t3micro.com
SIC: 3634 5199 Hair dryers, electric; Hairbrushes

3639 Household Appliances, Nec

(P-8240)
BRENTWOOD APPLIANCES INC
Also Called: Import
3088 E 46th St (90058-2422)
PHONE....................................323 266-4600
Poorad Beni Panahi, *CEO*
Poorad Beni Panahi, *CEO*
Maurice Araghi, *
John Yadgari, *
◆ **EMP:** 36 **EST:** 2009
SQ FT: 65,000
SALES (est): 4.48MM **Privately Held**
Web: www.brentwoodus.com
SIC: 3639 Major kitchen appliances, except refrigerators and stoves

(P-8241)
BREVILLE USA INC
Also Called: Breville
19400 S Western Ave (90501-1119)
PHONE....................................310 755-3000
Stephen Krauss, *CEO*
Michelle Waters, *
Barbara Dirsa, *
◆ **EMP:** 50 **EST:** 1989
SQ FT: 135,000
SALES (est): 48.38MM **Privately Held**
Web: www.breville.com
SIC: 3639 3634 5722 Major kitchen appliances, except refrigerators and stoves; Coffee makers, electric: household; Microwave ovens
HQ: Breville Holdings Pty Limited
G Se 2 170 Bourke Rd
Alexandria NSW

(P-8242)
FISHER & PAYKEL APPLIANCES INC (DH)
695 Town Center Dr Ste 180 (92626-1902)
PHONE....................................949 790-8900
◆ **EMP:** 22 **EST:** 1996
SQ FT: 26,000
SALES (est): 52.15MM **Privately Held**
Web: www.fisherpaykel.com
SIC: 3639 3631 5064 5078 Dishwashing machines, household; Household cooking equipment; Electric household appliances, nec; Refrigeration equipment and supplies
HQ: Fisher & Paykel Appliances Usa Holdings Inc.
695 Town Center Dr # 180
Costa Mesa CA

(P-8243)
HESTAN COMMERCIAL CORPORATION
3375 E La Palma Ave (92806-2815)
PHONE....................................714 869-2380
Stanley Kin Sui Cheng, *CEO*
Eric Deng, *
Barry Needleman Ctrl, *Prin*
▲ **EMP:** 125 **EST:** 2013
SQ FT: 70,000
SALES (est): 28.18MM **Privately Held**
Web: commercial.hestan.com
SIC: 3639 Major kitchen appliances, except refrigerators and stoves
HQ: Meyer Corporation, U.S.
1 Meyer Plz
Vallejo CA
707 551-2800

3641 Electric Lamps

(P-8244)
CANDLE LAMP HOLDINGS LLC
949 S Coast Dr Ste 650 (92626)
PHONE....................................951 682-9600
Don Hinshaw, *CEO*
John Clark, *Managing Member**
EMP: 310 **EST:** 2006
SALES (est): 12.28MM **Privately Held**
SIC: 3641 3645 3589 3634 Electric lamps; Table lamps; Food warming equipment, commercial; Chafing dishes, electric

(P-8245)
DASOL INC
Also Called: Coronet Lighting
9004 Meredith Pl (90210-1841)
P.O. Box 2065 (90247-0010)
PHONE....................................310 327-6700
Sol Smith, *Ch Bd*
David Smith, *
Mark Smith, *
◆ **EMP:** 225 **EST:** 1944
SALES (est): 18.59MM **Privately Held**
SIC: 3641 Electric lamps and parts for generalized applications

(P-8246)
HOLLYWOOD LAMP & SHADE CO
Also Called: Kimberly Lighting
2838 E 54th St (90058-3632)
PHONE....................................323 585-3999
Fred Nadal, *Pr*
EMP: 22 **EST:** 1963
SALES (est): 961.37K **Privately Held**
Web: www.hollywoodlampandshade.com
SIC: 3641 3648 3645 Lamps, fluorescent, electric; Lighting equipment, nec; Lamp shades, metal

(P-8247)
IWORKS US INC
Also Called: Iworks
2501 S Malt Ave (90040-3203)
PHONE....................................323 278-8363
Eric Dortch, *CEO*
◆ **EMP:** 53 **EST:** 1988
SQ FT: 35,000
SALES (est): 9.44MM **Privately Held**
Web: www.iworksus.com
SIC: 3641 Electric lamps and parts for generalized applications

(P-8248)
LEDVANCE LLC
1651 S Archibald Ave (91761-7651)
PHONE....................................909 923-3003
Jane Running, *Owner*
EMP: 21 **EST:** 2017
SALES (est): 927.05K **Privately Held**
SIC: 3641 Electric lamps

(P-8249)
LITEGEAR INC
4406 W Vanowen St (91505-1134)
PHONE....................................818 358-8542
Albert M Demayo, *Pr*
EMP: 35 **EST:** 2006
SALES (est): 10.03MM **Privately Held**
Web: www.litegear.com
SIC: 3641 Electric lamps

(P-8250)
LITEPANELS INC
20600 Plummer St (91311-5111)
PHONE....................................818 752-7009

Rudy Pohlert, *Pr*
▲ **EMP:** 23 **EST:** 2008
SALES (est): 5.45MM
SALES (corp-wide): 543.23MM **Privately Held**
Web: www.litepanels.com
SIC: 3641 Electric lamps
HQ: Videndum Group Holdings Limited
   Bridge House
   Richmond
   208 332-4600

(P-8251)
OSRAM SYLVANIA INC
13350 Gregg St Ste 101 (92064-7137)
PHONE.................................858 748-5077
Dennis Cohen, *Brnch Mgr*
EMP: 86
SALES (corp-wide): 5B **Privately Held**
Web: www.sylvania-automotive.com
SIC: 3641 Electric lamps
HQ: Osram Sylvania Inc.
   200 Ballardvale St Bldg 2
   Wilmington MA
   978 570-3000

(P-8252)
TIVOLI LLC
17110 Armstrong Ave (92614-5718)
PHONE.................................714 957-6101
Jannhuan Jang, *CEO*
Targetti Poulsen, *Managing Member**
Eric Kramer, *Managing Member**
Susan Larson, *
▲ **EMP:** 50 **EST:** 2003
SALES (est): 11MM **Privately Held**
Web: www.tivolilighting.com
SIC: 3641 3646 Tubes, electric light; Ceiling systems, luminous

---

3643 Current-carrying Wiring Devices

(P-8253)
AERO-ELECTRIC CONNECTOR INC (PA)
2280 W 208th St (90501-1452)
PHONE.................................310 618-3737
Walter Neubauer, *Ch*
Walter Neubauer Junior, *CEO*
EMP: 344 **EST:** 1982
SQ FT: 65,000
SALES (est): 45.47MM
SALES (corp-wide): 45.47MM **Privately Held**
Web: www.aero-electric.com
SIC: 3643 3678 Connectors and terminals for electrical devices; Electronic connectors

(P-8254)
ALLAN KIDD
Also Called: AK Industries
3115 E Las Hermanas St (90221-5512)
PHONE.................................310 762-1600
Allan Kidd, *Owner*
EMP: 20 **EST:** 1995
SQ FT: 17,000
SALES (est): 4MM **Privately Held**
Web: www.ak-ind.com
SIC: 3643 Electric connectors

(P-8255)
AUTOSPLICE PARENT INC (PA)
Also Called: Autosplice
10431 Wateridge Cir Ste 110 (92121)
PHONE.................................858 535-0077
Santosh Rao, *CEO*
Ken Krone, *
Jeffrey Cartwright, *

Kevin Barry, *
▲ **EMP:** 200 **EST:** 1954
SQ FT: 20,000
SALES (est): 45.25MM
SALES (corp-wide): 45.25MM **Privately Held**
Web: www.autosplice.com
SIC: 3643 Electric connectors

(P-8256)
CELESTICA LLC
280 Campillo St Ste G (92231-3200)
PHONE.................................760 357-4880
Michael Garmon, *Brnch Mgr*
EMP: 19
SALES (corp-wide): 422MM **Privately Held**
Web: www.celestica.com
SIC: 3643 Current-carrying wiring services
HQ: Celestica Llc
   400 Galleria Pkwy Se # 1500
   Atlanta GA

(P-8257)
CONNECTEC COMPANY INC (PA)
1701 Reynolds Ave (92614-5711)
PHONE.................................949 252-1077
Rassool Kavezade, *CEO*
Lora Taleb, *
Mike Taleb, *
▲ **EMP:** 80 **EST:** 1988
SQ FT: 12,000
SALES (est): 26.36MM
SALES (corp-wide): 26.36MM **Privately Held**
Web: www.connectecco.com
SIC: 3643 3678 Electric connectors; Electronic connectors

(P-8258)
CTC GLOBAL CORPORATION (PA)
Also Called: Ctc Global
2026 Mcgaw Ave (92614-0911)
PHONE.................................949 428-8500
J D Sitton, *CEO*
Dean Hagen, *
Anne Mcdowell, *Commercial Vice President*
John Mansfield, *Strategy Vice President**
Eric Johnson, *OF FIELD Technology SRVS**
▲ **EMP:** 250 **EST:** 2011
SALES (est): 54.87MM
SALES (corp-wide): 54.87MM **Privately Held**
Web: www.ctcglobal.com
SIC: 3643 Power line cable

(P-8259)
DATA SOLDER INC
2915 Kilson Dr (92707-3716)
PHONE.................................714 429-9866
Irma Gomez, *Pr*
Guillermo Gomez, *VP*
EMP: 17 **EST:** 1997
SQ FT: 4,000
SALES (est): 1.02MM **Privately Held**
Web: www.datasolder.com
SIC: 3643 Solderless connectors (electric wiring devices)

(P-8260)
DDH ENTERPRISE INC (PA)
2220 Oak Ridge Way (92081-8341)
PHONE.................................760 599-0171
David Du, *CEO*
Danny Du, *
▲ **EMP:** 100 **EST:** 1988
SQ FT: 42,000
SALES (est): 97.89MM

SALES (corp-wide): 97.89MM **Privately Held**
Web: www.ddhent.com
SIC: 3643 3644 3699 Current-carrying wiring services; Noncurrent-carrying wiring devices; Electrical equipment and supplies, nec

(P-8261)
DMC POWER INC (PA)
623 E Artesia Blvd (90746-1201)
PHONE.................................310 323-1616
Tony Ward, *CEO*
Michael Yazdanpanah, *
Eben Kane, *
Ed Cox, *
▲ **EMP:** 50 **EST:** 2009
SQ FT: 40,000
SALES (est): 29.5MM **Privately Held**
Web: www.dmcpower.com
SIC: 3643 Current-carrying wiring services

(P-8262)
ELECTRO ADAPTER INC
Also Called: Plating
20640 Nordhoff St (91311-6114)
P.O. Box 2560 (91313-2560)
PHONE.................................818 998-1198
Ray Fish, *Pr*
Terrill Fish, *
EMP: 100 **EST:** 1969
SQ FT: 54,000
SALES (est): 12.11MM **Privately Held**
Web: www.electro-adapter.com
SIC: 3643 Electric connectors
PA: Intritec
   20640 Nordhoff St
   Chatsworth CA

(P-8263)
EMP CONNECTORS INC
2280 W 208th St (90501-1452)
PHONE.................................310 533-6799
Walter Neubauer, *Prin*
Walter Neubauer Junior, *Pr*
Erika Neubauer, *Prin*
EMP: 20 **EST:** 1987
SQ FT: 39,000
SALES (est): 2.5MM **Privately Held**
Web: www.conesys.com
SIC: 3643 3678 3612 Electric connectors; Electronic connectors; Transformers, except electric

(P-8264)
ESL POWER SYSTEMS INC
2800 Palisades Dr (92878-9427)
PHONE.................................800 922-4188
Michael Hellmers, *Pr*
David Hellmers, *
◆ **EMP:** 55 **EST:** 1995
SQ FT: 36,000
SALES (est): 15.95MM **Privately Held**
Web: www.eslpwr.com
SIC: 3643 Outlets, electric: convenience

(P-8265)
FOXLINK INTERNATIONAL INC (HQ)
3010 Saturn St Ste 200 (92821-6220)
PHONE.................................714 256-1777
Ching Fan Pu, *CEO*
James Lee, *
▲ **EMP:** 44 **EST:** 1994
SALES (est): 12.81MM **Privately Held**
SIC: 3643 3678 3679 3691 Current-carrying wiring services; Electronic connectors; Electronic circuits; Storage batteries
PA: Cheng Uei Precision Industry Co., Ltd.
   No.18, Chung Shan Rd.,
   New Taipei City TAP

(P-8266)
GLENAIR INC (PA)
Also Called: Papi Inc.
1211 Air Way (91201-2405)
PHONE.................................818 247-6000
EMP: 683 **EST:** 1956
SALES (est): 455.11MM
SALES (corp-wide): 455.11MM **Privately Held**
Web: www.glenair.com
SIC: 3643 3825 3357 Connectors and terminals for electrical devices; Test equipment for electronic and electrical circuits; Nonferrous wiredrawing and insulating

(P-8267)
HI REL CONNECTORS INC
Also Called: Hirel Connectors
760 Wharton Dr (91711-4800)
PHONE.................................909 626-1820
Fred Baumann, *CEO*
Frederick Bb Baumann, *
EMP: 300 **EST:** 1967
SQ FT: 25,000
SALES (est): 46.88MM **Privately Held**
Web: www.hirelco.com
SIC: 3643 3678 Connectors and terminals for electrical devices; Electronic connectors

(P-8268)
JUDCO MANUFACTURING INC (PA)
1429 240th St (90710-1306)
P.O. Box 487 (90710-0487)
PHONE.................................310 534-0959
▲ **EMP:** 200 **EST:** 1980
SALES (est): 21.81MM
SALES (corp-wide): 21.81MM **Privately Held**
Web: www.judco.net
SIC: 3643 Electric switches

(P-8269)
LYNCOLE GRUNDING SOLUTIONS LLC
Also Called: Lyncole Xit Grounding
3547 Voyager St Ste 204 (90503-1673)
PHONE.................................310 214-4000
EMP: 25 **EST:** 1985
SQ FT: 10,000
SALES (est): 3.52MM **Privately Held**
Web: www.vfclp.com
SIC: 3643 8711 Current-carrying wiring services; Consulting engineer

(P-8270)
MERCOTAC INC
6195 Corte Del Cedro Ste 100 (92011-1549)
PHONE.................................760 431-7723
Timothy Leslie, *Pr*
Dave Brunet, *VP*
Chris Rechlin, *Sec*
▼ **EMP:** 17 **EST:** 1978
SQ FT: 12,000
SALES (est): 2.51MM **Privately Held**
Web: www.mercotac.com
SIC: 3643 Connectors and terminals for electrical devices

(P-8271)
MICRO PLASTICS INC
20821 Dearborn St (91311-5916)
P.O. Box 189 (92079-0189)
PHONE.................................818 882-0244
Lynda Eurton, *Pr*
Agripina Eurton, *Sec*
Anacleto Gonzalez, *VP*

P R O D U C T S & S V C S

EMP: 19 **EST:** 1956
SQ FT: 11,000
SALES (est): 264.78K **Privately Held**
Web: www.micro-plastics.com
SIC: 3643 3089 Connectors and terminals for electrical devices; Molding primary plastics

(P-8272)
NIVEK INDUSTRIES INC
Also Called: International Component Tech
230 E Dyer Rd Ste K (92707-3751)
PHONE...................................714 545-8855
Kevin Pezzolla, *Pr*
EMP: 48 **EST:** 1987
SQ FT: 8,000
SALES (est): 5.03MM **Privately Held**
Web: www.intcomptech.com
SIC: 3643 Current-carrying wiring services

(P-8273)
PLT ENTERPRISES INC
Also Called: So-Cal Value Added
809 Calle Plano (93012-8516)
PHONE...................................805 389-5335
Pamela L Tunis, *Pr*
Peter L Tunis, *
Peter Tunis Junior, *Genl Mgr*
EMP: 75 **EST:** 1996
SQ FT: 41,000
SALES (est): 8.45MM **Privately Held**
SIC: 3643 3679 Current-carrying wiring services; Harness assemblies, for electronic use: wire or cable

(P-8274)
PRECISION STAMPINGS INC (PA)
Also Called: P S I
500 Egan Ave (92223-2132)
PHONE...................................951 845-1174
Herman Viets, *Ch Bd*
Steven Morgan, *
Frauke Roth, *Stockholder**
Peter Gailing, *Stockholder**
Herta Viets, *Stockholder**
EMP: 32 **EST:** 1966
SQ FT: 25,000
SALES (est): 8.74MM
SALES (corp-wide): 8.74MM **Privately Held**
Web: www.precisionstampingsinc.com
SIC: 3643 5084 7539 Contacts, electrical; Tool and die makers equipment; Machine shop, automotive

(P-8275)
SOURIAU USA INC (DH)
1740 Commerce Way (93446-3620)
PHONE...................................805 238-2840
Rob Hanes, *Pr*
◆ **EMP:** 46 **EST:** 2003
SQ FT: 55,000
SALES (est): 32.39MM **Privately Held**
SIC: 3643 Bus bars (electrical conductors)
HQ: Eaton Corporation
1000 Eaton Blvd
Cleveland OH
440 523-5000

(P-8276)
SULLINS ELECTRONICS CORP
Also Called: Sullins Connector Solutions
801 E Mission Rd # B (92069-3002)
PHONE...................................760 744-0125
Kayvan Sullins, *CEO*
▲ **EMP:** 75 **EST:** 1969
SQ FT: 33,000
SALES (est): 10.6MM **Privately Held**
Web: www.sullinscorp.com

SIC: 3643 3678 Connectors and terminals for electrical devices; Electronic connectors

(P-8277)
SUPERIOR GROUNDING SYSTEMS INC
Also Called: S G S
16021 Arrow Hwy Ste A (91706-2062)
P.O. Box 2171 (91706-1112)
PHONE...................................626 814-1981
Steve Phan, *Genl Pt*
Steve Phan, *Genl Mgr*
EMP: 21 **EST:** 1993
SQ FT: 15,000
SALES (est): 1.4MM **Privately Held**
SIC: 3643 Connectors and terminals for electrical devices

(P-8278)
T MCGEE ELECTRIC INC
12375 Mills Ave Ste 2 (91710-2082)
PHONE...................................909 591-6461
Trent Mcgee, *Pr*
EMP: 17 **EST:** 1950
SQ FT: 15,000
SALES (est): 1.6MM **Privately Held**
SIC: 3643 Solderless connectors (electric wiring devices)

(P-8279)
TECHNICAL RESOURCE INDUSTRIES (PA)
Also Called: T R I
12854 Daisy Ct (92399-2026)
PHONE...................................909 446-1109
Reinhard Thalmayer, *Pr*
EMP: 25 **EST:** 1988
SQ FT: 5,000
SALES (est): 1.59MM
SALES (corp-wide): 1.59MM **Privately Held**
SIC: 3643 Electric connectors

(P-8280)
TELEDYNE INSTRUMENTS INC
Also Called: Teledyne Impulse
9855 Carroll Canyon Rd (92131-1103)
PHONE...................................858 842-3100
Kenneth Mendoza, *Fin Mgr*
EMP: 79
SALES (corp-wide): 5.46B **Publicly Held**
Web: www.teledyne.com
SIC: 3643 Electric connectors
HQ: Teledyne Instruments, Inc.
16830 Chestnut St
City Of Industry CA
626 934-1500

(P-8281)
UNIVERSAL SWITCHING CORP
Also Called: U S C
7671 N San Fernando Rd (91505-1073)
PHONE...................................818 785-0200
EMP: 28 **EST:** 1992
SALES (est): 4.68MM **Privately Held**
Web: www.uswi.com
SIC: 3643 Electric switches

(P-8282)
WASCO SALES AND MARKETING INC
Also Called: Wasco Switches & Sensors
2245 A St (93455-1008)
PHONE...................................805 739-2747
Ronald Way, *Pr*
Dana Way, *Sec*
Dave Way, *Genl Mgr*
Carrie Way, *Mgr*
◆ **EMP:** 20 **EST:** 1987

SQ FT: 9,000
SALES (est): 7.34MM **Privately Held**
Web: www.wascoinc.com
SIC: 3643 Electric switches

3644 Noncurrent-carrying Wiring Devices

(P-8283)
SAF-T-CO SUPPLY
Also Called: All American Pipe Bending
1300 E Normandy Pl (92705-4138)
PHONE...................................714 547-9975
Patricia Mcdonald, *Pr*
Robyn Dague, *
Paul Mcdonald, *Sec*
EMP: 50 **EST:** 1987
SQ FT: 24,000
SALES (est): 24.58MM **Privately Held**
Web: www.saftco.com
SIC: 3644 5063 5032 5074 Noncurrent-carrying wiring devices; Electrical apparatus and equipment; Brick, stone, and related material; Pipes and fittings, plastic

(P-8284)
WESTERN TUBE & CONDUIT CORP (HQ)
2001 E Dominguez St (90810-1088)
P.O. Box 608 (16161-0608)
PHONE...................................310 537-6300
Barry Zekelman, *CEO*
▲ **EMP:** 88 **EST:** 2004
SQ FT: 420,000
SALES (est): 45.35MM **Privately Held**
Web: www.westerntube.com
SIC: 3644 3446 3317 Electric conduits and fittings; Fences or posts, ornamental iron or steel; Tubing, mechanical or hypodermic sizes: cold drawn stainless
PA: Zekelman Industries, Inc.
227 W Monroe St Ste 2600
Chicago IL

3645 Residential Lighting Fixtures

(P-8285)
ALGER-TRITON INC
Also Called: Alger International
5600 W Jefferson Blvd (90016-3131)
PHONE...................................310 229-9500
◆ **EMP:** 28 **EST:** 1993
SALES (est): 5.5MM **Privately Held**
Web: www.studio-at.com
SIC: 3645 Residential lighting fixtures

(P-8286)
AMERICAN NAIL PLATE LTG INC
Also Called: Anp Lighting
9044 Del Mar Ave (91763-1627)
PHONE...................................909 982-1807
Harry Foster, *CEO*
Joan Foster, *
Ron Foster, *
Bob Foster, *
▲ **EMP:** 70 **EST:** 1976
SQ FT: 13,000
SALES (est): 9.08MM **Privately Held**
Web: www.anplighting.com
SIC: 3645 3646 Residential lighting fixtures; Commercial lighting fixtures

(P-8287)
ANTHONY CALIFORNIA INC (PA)
14485 Monte Vista Ave (91710-5728)
PHONE...................................909 627-0351

Kuei-Ian Yeh, *CEO*
Cindy Chang, *
◆ **EMP:** 23 **EST:** 1983
SALES (est): 4.79MM
SALES (corp-wide): 4.79MM **Privately Held**
Web: www.anthonyshowrooms.com
SIC: 3645 5063 5023 Residential lighting fixtures; Lighting fixtures; Lamps: floor, boudoir, desk

(P-8288)
ARTIVA USA INC (PA)
Also Called: Artiva
13901 Magnolia Ave (91710-7030)
PHONE...................................909 628-1388
Po Y Webb, *Pr*
Gina Yeh, *VP*
▲ **EMP:** 35 **EST:** 2008
SQ FT: 20,000
SALES (est): 8.67MM **Privately Held**
Web: www.artivaus.com
SIC: 3645 5063 Residential lighting fixtures; Lighting fixtures

(P-8289)
ARTIVA USA INC
Also Called: Artiva
12866 Ann St Ste 1 (90670-3064)
PHONE...................................562 298-8968
Jane Wang, *Mgr*
EMP: 42
Web: www.artivaus.com
SIC: 3645 5063 Residential lighting fixtures; Lighting fixtures
PA: Artiva Usa Inc.
13901 Magnolia Ave
Chino CA

(P-8290)
BASE LITE CORPORATION
Also Called: Baselite
12260 Eastend Ave (91710-2008)
PHONE...................................909 444-2776
Moaaa A Teixeira, *CEO*
EMP: 38 **EST:** 1997
SQ FT: 10,000
SALES (est): 4.65MM **Privately Held**
Web: www.baselite.com
SIC: 3645 3646 Residential lighting fixtures; Commercial lighting fixtures

(P-8291)
DAB INC
Also Called: Spectrum Lighting
13415 Marquardt Ave (90670-5012)
PHONE...................................562 623-4773
David A Boose, *Pr*
▲ **EMP:** 52 **EST:** 1978
SQ FT: 31,000
SALES (est): 4.85MM **Privately Held**
Web: www.scll.com
SIC: 3645 3648 3646 Residential lighting fixtures; Decorative area lighting fixtures; Commercial lighting fixtures

(P-8292)
DMF INC
Also Called: Dmf Lighting
1118 E 223rd St Unit 1 (90745-4210)
PHONE...................................323 934-7779
Morteza Danesh, *Pr*
Fariba Danesh, *
Michael Danesh, *
▲ **EMP:** 51 **EST:** 1989
SQ FT: 8,000
SALES (est): 15.07MM **Privately Held**
Web: www.dmflighting.com

SIC: 3645 5063 Residential lighting fixtures; Lighting fixtures, commercial and industrial

(P-8293)
FEIT ELECTRIC COMPANY INC (PA)
Also Called: Feit Electric
4901 Gregg Rd (90660-2108)
PHONE..............................562 463-2852
Aaron Feit, *CEO*
Alan Feit, *
Toby S Feit, *
John Mcmillin, *CFO*
◆ **EMP: 182 EST:** 1978
SQ FT: 300,000
SALES (est): 65.67MM
SALES (corp-wide): 65.67MM **Privately Held**
Web: www.feit.com
SIC: 3645 3641 5023 3646 Residential lighting fixtures; Electric light bulbs, complete; Homefurnishings; Commercial lighting fixtures

(P-8294)
LIGHTS OF AMERICA INC (PA)
13602 12th St Ste B (91710-5200)
PHONE..............................909 594-7883
Usman Vakil, *CEO*
Farooq Vakil, *
◆ **EMP: 500 EST:** 1977
SQ FT: 210,000
SALES (est): 95.67MM
SALES (corp-wide): 95.67MM **Privately Held**
Web: www.lightsofamerica.com
SIC: 3645 3646 3641 Fluorescent lighting fixtures, residential; Fluorescent lighting fixtures, commercial; Electric lamps

(P-8295)
MAXIM LIGHTING INTL INC
247 Vineland Ave (91746-2319)
PHONE..............................626 956-4200
EMP: 23
SALES (corp-wide): 56.17MM **Privately Held**
Web: www.maximlighting.com
SIC: 3645 Residential lighting fixtures
PA: Maxim Lighting International, Inc.
253 Vineland Ave
City Of Industry CA
626 956-4200

(P-8296)
NL&A COLLECTIONS INC
Also Called: Nova
6323 Maywood Ave (90255-4531)
P.O. Box 661820 (90066-8820)
PHONE..............................323 277-6266
Daniel Edelist, *Pr*
◆ **EMP: 40 EST:** 1980
SQ FT: 48,675
SALES (est): 4.5MM **Privately Held**
Web: www.novaofcalifornia.com
SIC: 3645 5023 Boudoir lamps; Lamps: floor, boudoir, desk

(P-8297)
PHILIPS NORTH AMERICA LLC
11201 Iberia St Ste A (91752-3280)
PHONE..............................909 574-1800
Kenneth Parivar, *Brnch Mgr*
EMP: 135
SALES (corp-wide): 133.64MM **Privately Held**
Web: usa.philips.com
SIC: 3645 3648 3646 Residential lighting fixtures; Outdoor lighting equipment; Ceiling systems, luminous

HQ: Philips North America Llc
222 Jacobs St Fl 3
Cambridge MA
617 245-5900

(P-8298)
TROY-CSL LIGHTING INC
14508 Nelson Ave (91744-3514)
P.O. Box 514310 (90051-4310)
PHONE..............................626 336-4511
David Littman, *CEO*
Steve Nadell, *
Anne Wilcox, *
Ian Wilcox, *
◆ **EMP: 205 EST:** 1970
SALES (est): 40.47MM **Privately Held**
Web: www.csllighting.com
SIC: 3645 3646 Wall lamps; Ornamental lighting fixtures, commercial

(P-8299)
VIDESSENCE LLC (PA)
10768 Lower Azusa Rd (91731-1306)
PHONE..............................626 579-0943
Toni Swarens, *Pr*
▲ **EMP: 25 EST:** 1951
SQ FT: 35,000
SALES (est): 4.6MM
SALES (corp-wide): 4.6MM **Privately Held**
Web: www.videssence.tv
SIC: 3645 3648 Residential lighting fixtures; Stage lighting equipment

(P-8300)
WANGS ALLIANCE CORPORATION
Also Called: Wac Lighting
1750 S Archibald Ave (91761-1239)
PHONE..............................909 230-9401
Nina Chou, *Prin*
EMP: 20
SALES (corp-wide): 51.32MM **Privately Held**
Web: www.waclighting.com
SIC: 3645 Residential lighting fixtures
PA: Wangs Alliance Corporation
44 Harbor Park Dr
Port Washington NY
516 515-5000

(P-8301)
YAWITZ INC
Also Called: Evergreen Lighting
1379 Ridgeway St (91768-2701)
PHONE..............................909 865-5599
John Klena, *CEO*
George Cole Iii, *Marketing*
Victor Rosen, *
▲ **EMP: 42 EST:** 1997
SQ FT: 23,000
SALES (est): 8.88MM **Privately Held**
Web: www.evergreenlighting.com
SIC: 3645 3646 Fluorescent lighting fixtures, residential; Fluorescent lighting fixtures, commercial

---

3646 Commercial Lighting Fixtures

(P-8302)
A V POLES AND LIGHTING INC
43827 Division St (93535-4061)
P.O. Box 9054 (93539-9054)
PHONE..............................661 945-2731
Luis Romero, *CEO*
Roberta Wood, *Pr*
▼ **EMP: 20 EST:** 2013
SQ FT: 12,000
SALES (est): 2.35MM **Privately Held**

Web: www.avpolesandlighting.com
SIC: 3646 Commercial lighting fixtures

(P-8303)
ACCLAIM LIGHTING LLC
6122 S Eastern Ave (90040-3402)
PHONE..............................323 213-4626
Charles J Davies, *Prin*
▲ **EMP: 24 EST:** 2003
SALES (est): 3.74MM **Privately Held**
Web: www.acclaimlighting.com
SIC: 3646 3679 5063 Commercial lighting fixtures; Electronic loads and power supplies; Wire and cable

(P-8304)
ALCON LIGHTING INC
2845 S Robertson Blvd (90034-2439)
PHONE..............................310 733-1248
EMP: 20 EST: 2016
SALES (est): 2.22MM **Privately Held**
SIC: 3646 Commercial lighting fixtures

(P-8305)
ARTE DE MEXICO INC
Also Called: Arte De Mexico
5506 Riverton Ave (91601-2815)
PHONE..............................818 753-4510
David Staffers, *Mgr*
EMP: 71
SALES (corp-wide): 9.36MM **Privately Held**
Web: www.artedemexico.com
SIC: 3646 3446 Commercial lighting fixtures; Architectural metalwork
PA: Arte De Mexico, Inc.
1000 Chestnut St
Burbank CA
818 753-4559

(P-8306)
C W COLE & COMPANY INC
Also Called: Cole Lighting
2560 Rosemead Blvd (91733-1593)
PHONE..............................626 443-2473
Russell W Cole, *Ch Bd*
Stephen W Cole, *
Donald Cole, *
EMP: 41 EST: 1911
SQ FT: 25,000
SALES (est): 9.75MM **Privately Held**
Web: www.colelighting.com
SIC: 3646 Commercial lighting fixtures

(P-8307)
DECO ENTERPRISES INC
Also Called: Deco Lighting
2917 Vail Ave (90040-2615)
PHONE..............................323 726-2575
Saman Sinai, *Prin*
Saman Sinai, *CEO*
Ben Peterson, *
Benjamin Pouladian, *
▲ **EMP: 60 EST:** 2005
SQ FT: 100,000
SALES (est): 19.81MM **Privately Held**
Web: www.getdeco.com
SIC: 3646 Commercial lighting fixtures

(P-8308)
DM TECHNOLOGY & ENERGY INC
4615 State St (91763-6130)
PHONE..............................909 627-1600
Jia Deng, *CEO*
Jian Ma, *CFO*
▲ **EMP: 18 EST:** 1993
SQ FT: 10,000
SALES (est): 2.2MM **Privately Held**

SIC: 3646 3645 Commercial lighting fixtures; Residential lighting fixtures

(P-8309)
DSA PHOTOTECH LLC
Also Called: DSA Signage
2321 E Gladwick St (90220-6209)
PHONE..............................866 868-1602
▲ **EMP: 50 EST:** 1974
SALES (est): 8.71MM **Privately Held**
Web: www.dsasignage.com
SIC: 3646 3648 Commercial lighting fixtures; Lighting equipment, nec

(P-8310)
EDISON PRICE LIGHTING INC (PA)
Also Called: Epl
5424 E Slauson Ave (90040-2919)
PHONE..............................718 685-0700
Emma Price, *Pr*
Emma Price, *Ch Bd*
Joel R Siegel, *VP*
James D Vizzini, *VP*
▲ **EMP: 119 EST:** 1952
SALES (est): 21.49MM
SALES (corp-wide): 21.49MM **Privately Held**
Web: www.epl.com
SIC: 3646 Commercial lighting fixtures

(P-8311)
ENERTRON TECHNOLOGIES INC
3525 Del Mar Heights Rd (92130-2199)
PHONE..............................800 537-7649
Ronald Curley, *Pr*
EMP: 50 EST: 1985
SALES (est): 5.11MM **Privately Held**
SIC: 3646 3645 Fluorescent lighting fixtures, commercial; Fluorescent lighting fixtures, residential

(P-8312)
FLEXFIRE LEDS INC
Also Called: Evoralight
3554 Business Park Dr Ste F (92626-1423)
PHONE..............................925 273-9080
Brenton Mauriello, *CEO*
EMP: 24 EST: 2011
SQ FT: 4,600
SALES (est): 2.22MM **Privately Held**
Web: www.flexfireleds.com
SIC: 3646 5063 Commercial lighting fixtures; Lighting fixtures

(P-8313)
FLUORESCENT SUPPLY CO INC
Also Called: Fsc
9120 Center Ave (91730-5310)
PHONE..............................909 948-8878
Edward Yawitz, *CEO*
John Watkins, *Pr*
▲ **EMP: 48 EST:** 1969
SQ FT: 80,000
SALES (est): 22.04MM
SALES (corp-wide): 22.04MM **Privately Held**
Web: www.fsclighting.com
SIC: 3646 3645 Commercial lighting fixtures; Residential lighting fixtures
PA: Onward Capital Llc
525 W Monroe St Ste 22109
Chicago IL
847 983-0869

(P-8314)
FOCUS INDUSTRIES INC
Also Called: Focus Landscape
25301 Commercentre Dr (92630-8808)
PHONE..............................949 830-1350

Stan Shibata, *Pr*
June Shibata, *
▲ **EMP:** 100 **EST:** 1989
SQ FT: 40,000
SALES (est): 22.55MM **Privately Held**
Web: www.focusindustries.com
SIC: **3646** 5063 Commercial lighting fixtures; Electrical apparatus and equipment

(P-8315)
HALLMARK LIGHTING LLC
Also Called: Hallmark Lighting
1945 S Tubeway Ave (90040-1611)
PHONE..................818 885-5010
Christopher Larocca, *CEO*
Robert Godlewski, *
Julie Winfield, *
◆ **EMP:** 80 **EST:** 1978
SALES (est): 8.87MM **Privately Held**
Web: www.hallmarklighting.com
SIC: **3646** 3645 3641 Commercial lighting fixtures; Wall lamps; Electric lamps

(P-8316)
HI-LITE MANUFACTURING CO INC
13450 Monte Vista Ave (91710-5149)
PHONE..................909 465-1999
Dorothy A Ohai, *Pr*
◆ **EMP:** 90 **EST:** 1959
SQ FT: 157,000
SALES (est): 9.63MM **Privately Held**
Web: www.hilitemfg.com
SIC: **3646** 3645 Commercial lighting fixtures; Residential lighting fixtures

(P-8317)
INTENSE LIGHTING LLC
3340 E La Palma Ave (92806-2814)
PHONE..................714 630-9877
Roger Weisenaur, *
Kenneth Eidsvold, *
Tom Elam, *Prin*
Allan Gray, *Prin*
◆ **EMP:** 80 **EST:** 2001
SQ FT: 153,000
SALES (est): 22.26MM
SALES (corp-wide): 1.46B **Privately Held**
Web: www.intenselighting.com
SIC: **3646** 3645 Commercial lighting fixtures; Residential lighting fixtures
PA: Leviton Manufacturing Co., Inc.
201 N Service Rd
Melville NY
800 323-8920

(P-8318)
LAMPS PLUS INC
Also Called: Pacific Coast Lighting
4723 Telephone Rd (93003-5242)
PHONE..................805 642-9007
David Hillard, *Mgr*
EMP: 22
SALES (corp-wide): 490.53MM **Privately Held**
Web: www.lampsplus.com
SIC: **3646** 5719 5064 Commercial lighting fixtures; Lamps and lamp shades; Fans, household: electric
PA: Lamps Plus, Inc.
20250 Plummer St
Chatsworth CA
818 886-5267

(P-8319)
LF ILLUMINATION LLC
9200 Deering Ave (91311-5803)
PHONE..................818 885-1335
Loren Kessel, *Pr*
Eileen S Cheng, *

▲ **EMP:** 51 **EST:** 2013
SALES (est): 9.68MM **Privately Held**
Web: www.lfillumination.com
SIC: **3646** 3645 5719 Commercial lighting fixtures; Residential lighting fixtures; Lighting fixtures

(P-8320)
LIGHTWAY INDUSTRIES
28435 Industry Dr (91355-4107)
PHONE..................661 257-0286
Jeffrey Bargman, *Pr*
Gary N Patten, *
EMP: 23 **EST:** 1980
SQ FT: 22,300
SALES (est): 5MM **Privately Held**
Web: www.lightwayind.com
SIC: **3646** 3645 Commercial lighting fixtures; Residential lighting fixtures

(P-8321)
LUMIFICIENT CORPORATION
2280 Ward Ave (93065-1837)
PHONE..................763 424-3702
Carey Burkett, *Pr*
Stacie Braford, *VP*
◆ **EMP:** 31 **EST:** 2000
SALES (est): 3.79MM **Privately Held**
SIC: **3646** Commercial lighting fixtures
PA: Revolution Lighting Technologies, Inc.
177 Broad St Fl 12
Stamford CT

(P-8322)
MEDICAL ILLUMINATION INTERNATIONAL INC (PA)
Also Called: Nuvo
19749 Dearborn St (91311-6510)
PHONE..................818 838-3025
◆ **EMP:** 17 **EST:** 1978
SALES (est): 16.91MM
SALES (corp-wide): 16.91MM **Privately Held**
Web: www.medillum.com
SIC: **3646** 3841 Fluorescent lighting fixtures, commercial; Surgical and medical instruments

(P-8323)
NOMOFLO ENTERPRISES INC
Also Called: Kino Flo Lighting Systems
2840 N Hollywood Way (91505-1023)
PHONE..................818 767-6528
Frieder Hochheim, *Pr*
Gary Swink, *VP*
▲ **EMP:** 80 **EST:** 1987
SALES (est): 26.12MM **Privately Held**
Web: www.kinoflo.com
SIC: **3646** Commercial lighting fixtures

(P-8324)
OPTIC ARTS HOLDINGS INC
716 Monterey Pass Rd (91754-3607)
PHONE..................213 250-6069
Jason Mullen, *CEO*
Dorian L Hicklin, *
Mason Barker, *
EMP: 47 **EST:** 2011
SQ FT: 15,750
SALES (est): 10.42MM
SALES (corp-wide): 21.63MM **Privately Held**
Web: www.luminii.com
SIC: **3646** 3645 3648 Commercial lighting fixtures; Residential lighting fixtures; Decorative area lighting fixtures
PA: Luminii Llc
7777 N Merrimac Ave
Niles IL
224 333-6033

(P-8325)
ORION CHANDELIER INC
2202 S Wright St (92705-5316)
PHONE..................714 668-9668
Paul Depersis, *Pr*
Kirk Fisher, *Asst VP*
◆ **EMP:** 17 **EST:** 1998
SQ FT: 3,000
SALES (est): 2.49MM **Privately Held**
Web: www.orionchandelier.com
SIC: **3646** Commercial lighting fixtures

(P-8326)
PACIFIC LTG & STANDARDS CO
2815 Los Flores Blvd (90262-2416)
PHONE..................310 603-9344
Frank Munoz, *Pr*
Enrique Garcia, *
▲ **EMP:** 34 **EST:** 1982
SQ FT: 17,000
SALES (est): 4.57MM **Privately Held**
Web: www.pacificlighting.com
SIC: **3646** Commercial lighting fixtures

(P-8327)
PACLIGHTS LLC (PA)
Also Called: Paclights
15318 El Prado Rd (91710-7659)
P.O. Box 928 (91709-0031)
PHONE..................800 980-6386
Tommy Zhen, *CEO*
Fiona Zhao, *Pr*
▲ **EMP:** 19 **EST:** 2013
SQ FT: 20,000
SALES (est): 2.81MM
SALES (corp-wide): 2.81MM **Privately Held**
Web: www.paclights.com
SIC: **3646** Commercial lighting fixtures

(P-8328)
PRUDENTIAL LIGHTING CORP (PA)
Also Called: P L M
1774 E 21st St (90058-1007)
P.O. Box 58736 (90058-0736)
PHONE..................213 477-1694
Stanely J Ellis, *CEO*
Jeffrey Ellis, *
Elliot Ellis, *
Jolie Ellis, *
▲ **EMP:** 120 **EST:** 1955
SQ FT: 112,000
SALES (est): 35.97MM
SALES (corp-wide): 35.97MM **Privately Held**
Web: www.prulite.com
SIC: **3646** Fluorescent lighting fixtures, commercial

(P-8329)
R W SWARENS ASSOCIATES INC
Also Called: Engineered Lighting Products
10768 Lower Azusa Rd (91731-1306)
PHONE..................626 579-0943
Toni Swarens, *CEO*
Lauri Maines, *
▲ **EMP:** 33 **EST:** 1984
SALES (est): 2.08MM **Privately Held**
Web: www.elplighting.com
SIC: **3646** Commercial lighting fixtures

(P-8330)
SAPPHIRE CHANDELIER LLC
505 Porter Way (92870-6454)
PHONE..................714 879-3660
Hector Garibay, *Pt*
Hector Garibay, *Managing Member*
▲ **EMP:** 61 **EST:** 2009
SQ FT: 10,000

SALES (est): 6.88MM **Privately Held**
Web: www.sapphirechandelier.com
SIC: **3646** Commercial lighting fixtures

(P-8331)
SIGNIFY NORTH AMERICA CORP
3350 Enterprise Dr (92316-3538)
PHONE..................732 563-3000
EMP: 124
Web: www.signify.com
SIC: **3646** Commercial lighting fixtures
HQ: Signify North America Corporation
400 Crossing Blvd Ste 600
Bridgewater NJ
732 563-3000

(P-8332)
SPOTLITE POWER CORPORATION
9937 Jefferson Blvd Ste 110 (90232-3528)
PHONE..................310 838-2367
Halston Mikail, *Pr*
▲ **EMP:** 28 **EST:** 2016
SALES (est): 636.19K
SALES (corp-wide): 4.97MM **Privately Held**
SIC: **3646** Commercial lighting fixtures
PA: Spotlite America Corporation
9937 Jefferson Blvd # 110
Culver City CA
310 829-0200

(P-8333)
SUN & SUN INDUSTRIES INC
Also Called: Sun Industries
2101 S Yale St (92704-4424)
PHONE..................714 210-5141
Lynda Sun-frederick, *CEO*
Duncan Frederick, *
Ken Flockblower, *
EMP: 100 **EST:** 1995
SQ FT: 11,000
SALES (est): 15.91MM **Privately Held**
SIC: **3646** Fluorescent lighting fixtures, commercial

(P-8334)
SUN VALLEY LTG STANDARDS INC
Also Called: US Architectural Lighting
660 W Avenue O (93551-3610)
PHONE..................661 233-2000
Joseph Straus, *Pr*
Judith Straus, *VP*
EMP: 40 **EST:** 1984
SQ FT: 30,000
SALES (est): 2.4MM
SALES (corp-wide): 27.76MM **Privately Held**
Web: www.usaltg.com
SIC: **3646** 5063 3648 Ornamental lighting fixtures, commercial; Electrical apparatus and equipment; Lighting equipment, nec
PA: U.S. Pole Company, Inc.
660 W Avenue O
Palmdale CA
800 877-6537

(P-8335)
TOPAZ LIGHTING COMPANY LLC
225 Parkside Dr (91340-3033)
PHONE..................818 838-3123
EMP: 25
SALES (corp-wide): 1.7B **Privately Held**
Web: www.topaz-usa.com
SIC: **3646** Commercial lighting fixtures
HQ: Topaz Lighting Company Llc
3241 Route 112 Ste 7
Medford NY
800 666-2852

(P-8336)

TRITON CHANDELIER INC
Also Called: Triton
1301 Dove St Ste 900 (92660-2473)
PHONE...................................714 957-9600
Richard Cooley, *Pr*
▲ EMP: 18 EST: 1995
SQ FT: 10,000
SALES (est): 2.32MM Privately Held
SIC: 3646 Chandeliers, commercial

(P-8337)

TUJAYAR ENTERPRISES INC
Also Called: Tube Lighting Products
1346 Pioneer Way (92020-1626)
PHONE...................................619 442-0577
Rick Tempkin, *Pr*
▲ EMP: 21 EST: 1989
SQ FT: 9,000
SALES (est): 4.62MM Privately Held
Web: www.tubelightingproducts.com
SIC: 3646 3645 Commercial lighting fixtures;
  Residential lighting fixtures

(P-8338)

US ENERGY TECHNOLOGIES INC
Also Called: US Lighting Tech
14370 Myford Road Ste 100 (91789)
P.O. Box 365 (90621-0365)
PHONE...................................714 617-8800
◆ EMP: 50
Web: www.gelighting.com
SIC: 3646 Commercial lighting fixtures

(P-8339)

US POLE COMPANY INC (PA)
Also Called: U S Architectural Lighting
660 W Avenue O (93551-3610)
PHONE...................................800 877-6537
Joseph Straus, *Pr*
◆ EMP: 109 EST: 1984
SQ FT: 112,000
SALES (est): 27.76MM
SALES (corp-wide): 27.76MM Privately
Held
Web: www.usaltg.com
SIC: 3646 Commercial lighting fixtures

(P-8340)

VISION ENGRG MET STAMPING INC
Also Called: Vision Engineering
114 Grand Cypress Ave (93551-3617)
P.O. Box 901780 (93590-1780)
PHONE...................................661 575-0933
Joseph Avila, *CEO*
EMP: 100 EST: 1997
SQ FT: 72,000
SALES (est): 9.5MM Privately Held
Web: www.visionengineering.com
SIC: 3646 Ceiling systems, luminous

(P-8341)

VISIONAIRE LIGHTING LLC
Also Called: Visionaire Lighting
19645 S Rancho Way (90220-6028)
PHONE...................................310 512-6480
Bryan Fried, *CEO*
Cheryl Moorman, *
◆ EMP: 89 EST: 2000
SQ FT: 36,000
SALES (est): 21.64MM Privately Held
Web: www.visionairelighting.com
SIC: 3646 Commercial lighting fixtures

(P-8342)

WPMG INC
Also Called: Tempo Industries
1961 Mcgaw Ave (92614-0909)
PHONE...................................949 442-1601
Dennis Pearson, *CEO*
▲ EMP: 31 EST: 1986
SQ FT: 27,000
SALES (est): 7.81MM Privately Held
Web: www.tempollc.com
SIC: 3646 Commercial lighting fixtures

(P-8343)

YANKON INDUSTRIES INC (PA)
Also Called: Energetic Lighting
13445 12th St (91710-5206)
PHONE...................................909 591-2345
Wei Chen, *CEO*
David Liu, *CEO*
Kristen Tai, *CFO*
▲ EMP: 23 EST: 2009
SQ FT: 100,627
SALES (est): 4.71MM
SALES (corp-wide): 4.71MM Privately
Held
SIC: 3646 Commercial lighting fixtures

3647 Vehicular Lighting Equipment

(P-8344)

AMP PLUS INC
Also Called: Elco Lighting
2042 E Vernon Ave (90058-1613)
PHONE...................................323 231-2600
Steve Cohen, *Pr*
◆ EMP: 55 EST: 1991
SQ FT: 100,000
SALES (est): 9.51MM Privately Held
Web: www.elcolighting.com
SIC: 3647 5063 3645 Vehicular lighting
  equipment; Electrical apparatus and
  equipment; Residential lighting fixtures

(P-8345)

DELTA TECH INDUSTRIES LLC
13860 Benson Ave (91710-7007)
PHONE...................................909 673-1900
Bogdan G Durian, *Managing Member*
◆ EMP: 23 EST: 1978
SALES (est): 2.31MM Privately Held
Web: www.deltalights.com
SIC: 3647 Automotive lighting fixtures, nec

(P-8346)

EXCELLENCE OPTO INC (PA)
Also Called: E O I
21858 Garcia Ln (91789-0941)
PHONE...................................909 468-0550
Cheryl Huang, *Ch Bd*
Fang-yue Huang, *Pr*
▲ EMP: 21 EST: 2001
SQ FT: 18,000
SALES (est): 4.91MM
SALES (corp-wide): 4.91MM Privately
Held
Web: www.eoius.com
SIC: 3647 3669 3648 Automotive lighting
  fixtures, nec; Traffic signals, electric; Street
  lighting fixtures

(P-8347)

JKL COMPONENTS CORPORATION
13343 Paxton St (91331-2340)
PHONE...................................818 896-0019
Joseph Velas, *Pr*
Kent Koerting, *
EMP: 32 EST: 1974
SQ FT: 7,000
SALES (est): 4.46MM Privately Held
Web: www.jkllamps.com

SIC: 3647 3827 3699 Automotive lighting
  fixtures, nec; Optical instruments and lenses
  ; Electrical equipment and supplies, nec

(P-8348)

KC HILITES INC
13637 Cimarron Ave (90249-2461)
P.O. Box 155 (86046-0155)
PHONE...................................928 635-2607
Michael Dehaas, *Pr*
◆ EMP: 36 EST: 1970
SQ FT: 25,000
SALES (est): 7.65MM Privately Held
Web: www.kchilites.com
SIC: 3647 Vehicular lighting equipment

(P-8349)

SODERBERG MANUFACTURING CO INC
20821 Currier Rd (91789-3018)
PHONE...................................909 595-1291
B W Soderberg, *CEO*
Kathy Kirkeby, *
Rick Soderberg, *
Kari Levario, *
EMP: 85 EST: 1946
SALES (est): 9.55MM Privately Held
Web: www.soderberg.aero
SIC: 3647 3812 Aircraft lighting fixtures;
  Search and navigation equipment

3648 Lighting Equipment, Nec

(P-8350)

ALL ACCESS STGING PRDCTONS INC (PA)
1320 Storm Pkwy (90501-5041)
PHONE...................................310 784-2464
Clive Forrester, *CEO*
Erik Eastland, *
Robert Achlimbari, *
▲ EMP: 45 EST: 1997
SQ FT: 42,000
SALES (est): 13.74MM
SALES (corp-wide): 13.74MM Privately
Held
Web: www.allaccessinc.com
SIC: 3648 Stage lighting equipment

(P-8351)

AMERICAN GRIP INC
8468 Kewen Ave (91352-3118)
PHONE...................................818 768-8922
Lance Snoke, *Pr*
EMP: 25 EST: 1984
SQ FT: 15,000
SALES (est): 4.84MM Privately Held
Web: www.americangrip.com
SIC: 3648 3861 Stage lighting equipment;
  Stands, camera and projector

(P-8352)

AMERICAN POWER SOLUTIONS INC
14355 Industry Cir (90638-5810)
PHONE...................................714 626-0300
Bansik Yoon, *CEO*
▲ EMP: 20 EST: 2001
SALES (est): 5.04MM Privately Held
Web: www.americanpowersolutions.com
SIC: 3648 Lighting equipment, nec

(P-8353)

AMERILLUM LLC
Also Called: Alumen-8
3728 Maritime Way (92056-2702)
PHONE...................................760 727-7675
Ronald S Lancial, *Managing Member*

Serge Lambert, *
Guy St Pierre, *
▲ EMP: 54 EST: 2010
SQ FT: 27,000
SALES (est): 14.37MM
SALES (corp-wide): 3.95B Publicly Held
Web: www.alights.com
SIC: 3648 Lighting equipment, nec
PA: Acuity Brands, Inc.
  1170 Peachtree St Ne # 23
  Atlanta GA
  404 853-1400

(P-8354)

BEGA NORTH AMERICA INC
Also Called: Bega
1000 Bega Way (93013-2902)
PHONE...................................805 684-0533
Don Kinderdick, *CEO*
◆ EMP: 100 EST: 1985
SQ FT: 60,000
SALES (est): 28MM Privately Held
Web: www.bega-us.com
SIC: 3648 3646 Outdoor lighting equipment;
  Commercial lighting fixtures

(P-8355)

BIRCHWOOD LIGHTING INC
3340 E La Palma Ave (92806-2814)
PHONE...................................714 550-7118
EMP: 25 EST: 1993
SQ FT: 1,900
SALES (est): 9.06MM
SALES (corp-wide): 1.46B Privately Held
Web: www.birchwoodlighting.com
SIC: 3648 3646 3645 Decorative area
  lighting fixtures; Commercial lighting fixtures
  ; Residential lighting fixtures
PA: Leviton Manufacturing Co., Inc.
  201 N Service Rd
  Melville NY
  800 323-8920

(P-8356)

BIRNS OCEANOGRAPHICS INC
Also Called: Birns
1720 Fiske Pl (93033-1863)
PHONE...................................805 487-5393
▼ EMP: 19 EST: 1978
SALES (est): 2.68MM Privately Held
Web: www.birns.com
SIC: 3648 3643 Underwater lighting fixtures;
  Electric connectors

(P-8357)

BLISS HOLDINGS LLC
745 S Vinewood St (92029-1928)
PHONE...................................626 506-8696
▲ EMP: 50 EST: 2006
SALES (est): 5.93MM Privately Held
SIC: 3648 Lighting equipment, nec

(P-8358)

CLEAR BLUE ENERGY CORP
Also Called: Cbec
17150 Via Del Campo Ste 203
(92127-2139)
P.O. Box 532086 (92153-2086)
PHONE...................................858 451-1549
Paul Santina, *CEO*
Jim Kelly, *
EMP: 80 EST: 2009
SALES (est): 9.98MM Privately Held
Web: www.cbesco.com
SIC: 3648 1731 Lighting equipment, nec;
  Lighting contractor

(P-8359)

COOPER LIGHTING LLC
Also Called: Cooper Lighting

PRODUCTS & SVCS

3350 Enterprise Dr (92316-3538)
PHONE.....................909 605-6615
John Seiler, *Mgr*
EMP: 564
Web: www.cooperlighting.com
SIC: 3648 Lighting equipment, nec
HQ: Cooper Lighting, Llc
    1121 Highway 74 S
    Peachtree City GA
    770 486-4800

(P-8360)
DANA CREATH DESIGNS LTD
3030 Kilson Dr (92707-4203)
PHONE.....................714 662-0111
Dana E Creath, *Pt*
James K Creath, *
Raylene R Creath, *
EMP: 30 EST: 1968
SALES (est): 2.44MM Privately Held
Web: www.danacreath.com
SIC: 3648 3646 3645 Lighting equipment,
    nec; Commercial lighting fixtures;
    Residential lighting fixtures

(P-8361)
DEEPSEA POWER & LIGHT INC
4033 Ruffin Rd (92123-1817)
PHONE.....................858 576-1261
EMP: 23
SIC: 3648 Underwater lighting fixtures

(P-8362)
EEMA INDUSTRIES INC
Also Called: Liton Lighting
5461 W Jefferson Blvd (90016-3715)
PHONE.....................323 904-0200
Amir Esmail Zadeh, *Pr*
◆ EMP: 40 EST: 1998
SQ FT: 40,000
SALES (est): 7.33MM Privately Held
Web: www.liton.com
SIC: 3648 5063 Lighting equipment, nec;
    Electrical apparatus and equipment

(P-8363)
ELATION LIGHTING INC
Also Called: Elation Professional
6122 S Eastern Ave (90040-3402)
PHONE.....................323 582-3322
Toby Velazquez, *Pr*
Charles J Davies, *
▲ EMP: 60 EST: 1992
SQ FT: 50,000
SALES (est): 6.05MM Privately Held
Web: www.elationlighting.com
SIC: 3648 Lighting equipment, nec

(P-8364)
ELITE LIGHTING
Also Called: Elite Lighting
5424 E Slauson Ave (90040-2919)
PHONE.....................323 888-1973
Babak Rashididoust, *CEO*
◆ EMP: 200 EST: 1998
SQ FT: 25,000
SALES (est): 48.78MM Privately Held
Web: www.iuseelite.com
SIC: 3648 3646 3645 Lighting equipment,
    nec; Commercial lighting fixtures; Boudoir
    lamps

(P-8365)
EMAZING LIGHTS LLC
240 S Loara St (92802-1020)
PHONE.....................626 628-6482
Brian Lim, *Managing Member*
▲ EMP: 20 EST: 2010
SALES (est): 4.5MM Privately Held
Web: www.gloving.com

SIC: 3648 3229 Spotlights; Bulbs for electric
    lights

(P-8366)
FOXFURY LLC
Also Called: Foxfury Lighting Solution
3544 Seagate Way (92056-6041)
PHONE.....................760 945-4231
▲ EMP: 24 EST: 2005
SALES (est): 4.98MM Privately Held
Web: www.foxfury.com
SIC: 3648 Lighting equipment, nec

(P-8367)
GALLAGHER RENTAL INC
15701 Heron Ave (90638-5206)
PHONE.....................714 690-1559
Joseph Gallagher, *CEO*
Megan Gallagher, *
EMP: 30 EST: 2012
SALES (est): 3.89MM Privately Held
Web: www.gallagherstaging.com
SIC: 3648 Stage lighting equipment

(P-8368)
GREENSHINE NEW ENERGY LLC
23661 Birtcher Dr (92630-1770)
PHONE.....................949 609-9636
◆ EMP: 100 EST: 2010
SQ FT: 200
SALES (est): 13.02MM Privately Held
Web: www.streetlights-solar.com
SIC: 3648 Lighting equipment, nec

(P-8369)
JIMWAY INC
Also Called: Altair Lighting
20101 S Santa Fe Ave (90221-5917)
PHONE.....................310 886-3718
Hsing-min Keng, *CEO*
Irene Wang, *
▲ EMP: 100 EST: 1982
SQ FT: 200,000
SALES (est): 19.89MM Privately Held
Web: www.jimway.com
SIC: 3648 3221 5063 Lighting equipment,
    nec; Glass containers; Electrical apparatus
    and equipment

(P-8370)
KIM LIGHTING INC
Also Called: Kim Lighting & Mfg
16555 Gale Ave (91745-1713)
P.O. Box 1275 (91716)
PHONE.....................626 968-5666
▲ EMP: 550
SIC: 3648 3646 3317 Outdoor lighting
    equipment; Commercial lighting fixtures;
    Steel pipe and tubes

(P-8371)
LEDCONN CORP
Also Called: Ledconn
301 Thor Pl (92821-4133)
PHONE.....................714 256-2111
Tsanyu Wang, *Pr*
Wan Ting Huang, *
▲ EMP: 25 EST: 2008
SQ FT: 2,000
SALES (est): 4.82MM Privately Held
Web: www.ledconn.com
SIC: 3648 3993 7389 Lighting equipment,
    nec; Signs and advertising specialties;
    Interior decorating

(P-8372)
LG-LED SOLUTIONS LIMITED
15902 Halliburton Rd Ste A (91745-3500)
PHONE.....................626 587-8506

Zegao Hu, *CEO*
EMP: 50 EST: 2015
SALES (est): 2.73MM Privately Held
SIC: 3648 Lighting equipment, nec

(P-8373)
LIGHTING CONTROL & DESIGN INC
Also Called: LCD&d
9144 Deering Ave (91311-5801)
PHONE.....................323 226-0000
EMP: 46 EST: 1987
SALES (est): 11.58MM
SALES (corp-wide): 3.95B Publicly Held
Web: www.acuitybrands.com
SIC: 3648 3643 5719 Lighting equipment,
    nec; Current-carrying wiring services;
    Lighting fixtures
PA: Acuity Brands, Inc.
    1170 Peachtree St Ne # 23
    Atlanta GA
    404 853-1400

(P-8374)
MAG INSTRUMENT INC (PA)
2001 S Hellman Ave (91761-8019)
P.O. Box 50600 (91761-1083)
PHONE.....................909 947-1006
Anthony Maglica, *CEO*
James Zecchini, *
Thomas K Richardson, *
Malissa Peace, *
Brent Flaharty, *
▲ EMP: 810 EST: 1955
SQ FT: 1,000,000
SALES (est): 101.85MM
SALES (corp-wide): 101.85MM Privately Held
Web: www.maglite.com
SIC: 3648 Flashlights

(P-8375)
MOLE-RICHARDSON CO LTD (PA)
Also Called: Studio Depot
12154 Montague St (91331-2209)
PHONE.....................323 851-0111
▲ EMP: 100 EST: 1927
SALES (est): 9.65MM
SALES (corp-wide): 9.65MM Privately Held
Web: www.mole.com
SIC: 3648 3621 3861 3646 Lighting
    equipment, nec; Motors and generators;
    Photographic equipment and supplies;
    Commercial lighting fixtures

(P-8376)
NEW BEDFORD PANORAMEX CORP
Also Called: Nbp
1480 N Claremont Blvd (91711-3538)
PHONE.....................909 982-9806
Steven Robert Ozuna, *Pr*
James Casso, *
Bryce Nielsen, *
EMP: 35 EST: 1966
SQ FT: 65,000
SALES (est): 9.21MM Privately Held
Web: www.nbpcorp.com
SIC: 3648 Airport lighting fixtures: runway
    approach, taxi, or ramp

(P-8377)
NITERDER TCHNCAL LTG VDEO SYST
Also Called: Niterider
12255 Crosthwaite Cir Ste A (92064-8825)
PHONE.....................858 268-9316

Thomas Edward Carroll, *CEO*
Mark Schultz, *
▲ EMP: 35 EST: 1989
SALES (est): 5.59MM Privately Held
Web: www.niterider.com
SIC: 3648 3646 Lighting equipment, nec;
    Commercial lighting fixtures

(P-8378)
PACIFIC COAST LIGHTING INC (HQ)
Also Called: Pacific Coast Lighting Group
20238 Plummer St (91311-5449)
PHONE.....................800 709-9004
Clark Linstone, *CEO*
Dennis K Swanson, *Ch*
Manja Swanson, *Sec*
◆ EMP: 19 EST: 1979
SQ FT: 100,000
SALES (est): 41.3MM
SALES (corp-wide): 490.53MM Privately Held
Web: www.pacificcoastlighting.com
SIC: 3648 3641 5719 Lighting fixtures,
    except electric: residential; Electric lamp
    (bulb) parts; Lighting fixtures
PA: Lamps Plus, Inc.
    20250 Plummer St
    Chatsworth CA
    818 886-5267

(P-8379)
PELICAN PRODUCTS INC (PA)
Also Called: Pelican
23215 Early Ave (90505-4002)
PHONE.....................310 326-4700
James Curleigh, *CEO*
Scott Ermeti, *INTL Business*
Dave Pres Biothermal Div Willi ams, *Prin*
Chris Favreau, *
George Platisa, *
◆ EMP: 245 EST: 2007
SQ FT: 150,000
SALES (est): 485.3MM
SALES (corp-wide): 485.3MM Privately Held
Web: www.pelican.com
SIC: 3648 3161 3089 Flashlights; Luggage;
    Plastics containers, except foam

(P-8380)
REMOTE OCEAN SYSTEMS INC (PA)
Also Called: R O S
9581 Ridgehaven Ct (92123-1624)
PHONE.....................858 565-8500
Robert Acks, *CEO*
Christine Acks, *
EMP: 34 EST: 1975
SALES (est): 6.69MM
SALES (corp-wide): 6.69MM Privately Held
Web: www.rosys.com
SIC: 3648 3861 3812 3643 Underwater
    lighting fixtures; Photographic equipment
    and supplies; Search and navigation
    equipment; Current-carrying wiring services

(P-8381)
SHIMADA ENTERPRISES INC
Also Called: Celestial Lighting
14009 Dinard Ave (90670-4922)
PHONE.....................562 802-8811
Tak Shimada, *Pr*
Mick Shimada, *
▲ EMP: 30 EST: 1975
SQ FT: 11,000
SALES (est): 4.84MM Privately Held
Web: www.celestiallighting.com

SIC: **3648** Decorative area lighting fixtures

(P-8382)
STERIL-AIRE INC
25060 Avenue Stanford Ste 160 (91355)
PHONE..............................818 565-1128
◆ **EMP:** 23 **EST:** 1995
SALES (est): 4.73MM **Privately Held**
Web: www.steril-aire.com
SIC: **3648** Ultraviolet lamp fixtures

(P-8383)
SUREFIRE LLC (PA)
18300 Mount Baldy Cir (92708-6122)
PHONE..............................714 545-9444
Sean Vo, *
Joel Smith, *CAO**
◆ **EMP:** 175 **EST:** 2000
SQ FT: 45,000
SALES (est): 158.99MM
SALES (corp-wide): 158.99MM **Privately Held**
Web: www.surefire.com
SIC: **3648 3699** Flashlights; Laser systems and equipment

(P-8384)
THIN-LITE CORPORATION
530 Constitution Ave (93012-8595)
PHONE..............................805 987-5021
Alan Griffin, *Pr*
Lilian Cross Szymanek, *
▲ **EMP:** 47 **EST:** 1970
SQ FT: 27,000
SALES (est): 7.75MM **Privately Held**
Web: www.thinlite.com
SIC: **3648 3612 3646** Lighting equipment, nec; Transformers, except electric; Fluorescent lighting fixtures, commercial

(P-8385)
TIVOLI INDUSTRIES INC
1550 E Saint Gertrude Pl (92705-5310)
PHONE..............................714 957-6101
Peter Jang, *CEO*
▲ **EMP:** 20 **EST:** 1991
SALES (est): 376.47K **Privately Held**
SIC: **3648** Lighting equipment, nec

(P-8386)
TOTAL STRUCTURES INC
Also Called: Total Structures
1696 Walter St (93003-5619)
PHONE..............................805 676-3322
◆ **EMP:** 45 **EST:** 1995
SQ FT: 24,000
SALES (est): 10.74MM **Privately Held**
Web: www.totalstructures.com
SIC: **3648 3441** Lighting equipment, nec; Fabricated structural metal
HQ: Eurotruss B.V.
Castorweg 2
Leeuwarden FR
582158888

(P-8387)
TRULY GREEN SOLUTIONS LLC
9601 Variel Ave (91311-4914)
PHONE..............................818 206-4404
Rubina Jadwet, *CEO*
▲ **EMP:** 22 **EST:** 2010
SALES (est): 3.69MM **Privately Held**
Web: www.trulygreensolutions.com
SIC: **3648** Lighting equipment, nec

(P-8388)
UNIQUE LIGHTING SYSTEMS INC
5825 Jasmine St (92504-1144)
PHONE..............................800 955-4831
Randy Weisser, *Pr*
EMP: 18 **EST:** 2014
SALES (est): 714.08K **Privately Held**
Web: www.uniquelighting.com
SIC: **3648** Lighting equipment, nec

3651 Household Audio And Video Equipment

(P-8389)
ABSOLUTE USA INC
Also Called: Absolute Pro Music
1800 E Washington Blvd (90021-3127)
PHONE..............................213 744-0044
Mohammad K Razipour, *Pr*
Sasha Razipour, *
◆ **EMP:** 47 **EST:** 2002
SQ FT: 35,000
SALES (est): 16MM **Privately Held**
Web: www.absolutepromusic.com
SIC: **3651** Audio electronic systems

(P-8390)
ACTI CORPORATION INC
Also Called: California Acti
18 Technology Dr Ste 139 (92618-2311)
PHONE..............................949 753-0352
Juber Chu, *Pr*
Kelvin Wong, *CFO*
EMP: 20 **EST:** 2008
SALES (est): 5.25MM **Privately Held**
Web: www.acti.com
SIC: **3651 3663 3699** Household audio and video equipment; Cameras, television; Security devices
PA: Acti Corporation
7f, No. 1, Alley 20, Lane 407, Tiding Blvd., Sec. 2
Taipei City TAP

(P-8391)
ACTIVEON INC (PA)
10905 Technology Pl (92127-1811)
PHONE..............................858 798-3300
John Lee, *CEO*
Jonathan Zupnik, *VP*
▲ **EMP:** 49 **EST:** 2006
SALES (est): 4.74MM **Privately Held**
Web: www.activeon.com
SIC: **3651** Household audio and video equipment

(P-8392)
AL SHELLCO LLC (HQ)
9330 Scranton Rd Ste 600 (92121-7706)
PHONE..............................570 296-6444
Mark Lucas, *Managing Member*
Edward Anchel, *
Richard P Horner, *
Ross Gatlin, *
▲ **EMP:** 160 **EST:** 1953
SQ FT: 120,000
SALES (est): 106.36MM
SALES (corp-wide): 719.67MM **Privately Held**
SIC: **3651 3577** Radio receiving sets; Computer peripheral equipment, nec
PA: Prophet Equity Lp
1460 Main St Ste 200
Southlake TX
817 898-1500

(P-8393)
ANACOM GENERAL CORPORATION
Also Called: Anacom Medtek
1240 S Claudina St (92805-6232)
PHONE..............................714 774-8484
Daniel S Haines, *Pr*
William K Haines, *
▲ **EMP:** 48 **EST:** 1967
SQ FT: 20,000
SALES (est): 11.4MM **Privately Held**
Web: www.anacom-medtek.com
SIC: **3651 3577** Speaker monitors; Computer peripheral equipment, nec

(P-8394)
ANCHOR AUDIO INC
5931 Darwin Ct (92008-7302)
PHONE..............................760 827-7100
Janet Jacobs, *CEO*
David Jacobs, *
Dwight Garbe, *
▲ **EMP:** 58 **EST:** 1973
SQ FT: 31,200
SALES (est): 12.67MM **Privately Held**
Web: www.anchoraudio.com
SIC: **3651** Public address systems

(P-8395)
APOGEE ELECTRONICS CORPORATION
Also Called: Apogee Electronics
1715 Berkeley St (90404-4104)
PHONE..............................310 584-9394
Betty A Bennett, *CEO*
▲ **EMP:** 35 **EST:** 1985
SQ FT: 5,000
SALES (est): 8.28MM **Privately Held**
Web: www.apogeedigital.com
SIC: **3651 3621 8748** Audio electronic systems; Motors and generators; Communications consulting

(P-8396)
ARLO TECHNOLOGIES INC (PA)
Also Called: Arlo
2200 Faraday Ave Ste 150 (92008-7224)
PHONE..............................408 890-3900
Matthew Mcrae, *CEO*
Ralph E Faison, *Ch Bd*
Gordon Mattingly, *CFO*
Brian Busse, *Corporate Secretary*
EMP: 86 **EST:** 2014
SQ FT: 43,500
SALES (est): 490.41MM
SALES (corp-wide): 490.41MM **Publicly Held**
Web: www.arlo.com
SIC: **3651 7372** Household audio and video equipment; Application computer software

(P-8397)
AURASOUND INC
1801 E Edinger Ave Ste 190 (92705-4754)
PHONE..............................949 829-4000
EMP: 72
Web: www.aurasound.com
SIC: **3651** Household audio equipment

(P-8398)
BALTIC LTVIAN UNVRSAL ELEC LLC
Also Called: Blue Microphone
5706 Corsa Ave (91362-4057)
PHONE..............................818 879-5200
John Maier, *CEO*
Bart E Thielen, *
Bernard Wise, *
Martin Saulespurens, *
▲ **EMP:** 35 **EST:** 1998
SALES (est): 9.78MM **Privately Held**
SIC: **3651 5731** Microphones; Consumer electronic equipment, nec
PA: Logitech International S.A.
Route De Pampigny 20
Apples VD

(P-8399)
BEATS ELECTRONICS LLC
Also Called: Beats By Dre
8600 Hayden Pl (90232-2902)
PHONE..............................424 326-4679
▲ **EMP:** 500 **EST:** 2006
SALES (est): 97.89MM
SALES (corp-wide): 383.29B **Publicly Held**
SIC: **3651 3679** Speaker systems; Headphones, radio
PA: Apple Inc.
1 Apple Park Way
Cupertino CA
408 996-1010

(P-8400)
BELKIN INC
Also Called: Belkin
555 S Aviation Blvd (90245-4852)
PHONE..............................800 223-5546
Chester J Pipkin, *Pr*
George Platisa, *
◆ **EMP:** 515 **EST:** 2003
SALES (est): 30.63MM **Privately Held**
Web: www.belkin.com
SIC: **3651** Electronic kits for home assembly: radio, TV, phonograph
HQ: Belkin International, Inc.
555 S Avi Blvd Ste 180
El Segundo CA
310 751-5100

(P-8401)
BIG 5 ELECTRONICS INC
Also Called: Big Five Electronics
13452 Alondra Blvd (90703-2315)
PHONE..............................562 941-4669
Amina Bawaney, *CEO*
Latif Bawaney, *Pr*
Rizwan Bawaney, *CFO*
▲ **EMP:** 22 **EST:** 2003
SQ FT: 4,500
SALES (est): 4.85MM **Privately Held**
Web: www.big5electronics.com
SIC: **3651 5099 5065** Audio electronic systems; Video and audio equipment; Electronic parts and equipment, nec

(P-8402)
BOSS INTERNATIONAL LLC (PA)
Also Called: Boss Audio Systems
3451 Lunar Ct (93030-8976)
PHONE..............................805 988-0192
Soheil Rabbani, *Managing Member*
Sheila Rabbani, *VP*
▼ **EMP:** 35 **EST:** 2012
SALES (est): 10.88MM
SALES (corp-wide): 10.88MM **Privately Held**
Web: www.bossaudio.com
SIC: **3651** Audio electronic systems

(P-8403)
CUSTOM AUTOSOUND MFG INC
1030 Williamson Ave (92833-2746)
PHONE..............................714 535-1091
Carlton Sprague, *Pr*
▲ **EMP:** 18 **EST:** 1976
SQ FT: 18,000
SALES (est): 990.54K **Privately Held**
Web: www.customautosoundmfg.com
SIC: **3651** Audio electronic systems

(P-8404)
DANA INNOVATIONS (PA)
Also Called: Sonance
991 Calle Amanecer (92673-6212)
PHONE..............................949 492-7777
Ari Supran, *CEO*

Scott Struthers, *Pr*
Geoffrey L Spencer, *Sec*
Mike Simmons, *CFO*
◆ **EMP:** 156 **EST:** 1981
SQ FT: 42,320
SALES (est): 49.59MM
SALES (corp-wide): 49.59MM **Privately Held**
Web: www.sonance.com
SIC: 3651 5731 7629 Speaker systems; Radio, television, and electronic stores; Electrical repair shops

(P-8405)
DIGITAL PERIPH SOLUTIONS INC
Also Called: Q-See
160 S Old Springs Rd Ste 220 (92808-1260)
PHONE..............................714 998-3440
Priti Sharma, *Pr*
Rajeev Sharma, *
▲ **EMP:** 40 **EST:** 2002
SQ FT: 30,000
SALES (est): 9.04MM **Privately Held**
SIC: 3651 7382 Video camera-audio recorders, household use; Confinement surveillance systems maintenance and monitoring

(P-8406)
DOLBY LABORATORIES INC
Also Called: Doremi Labs
1020 Chestnut St (91506-1623)
PHONE..............................818 562-1101
EMP: 28
SALES (corp-wide): 1.3B **Publicly Held**
Web: www.dolby.com
SIC: 3651 Audio electronic systems
PA: Dolby Laboratories, Inc.
1275 Market St Fl 15
San Francisco CA
415 558-0200

(P-8407)
DOREMI LABS INC
Also Called: Doremi
1020 Chestnut St (91506-1623)
PHONE..............................818 562-1101
▲ **EMP:** 40
SIC: 3651 Audio electronic systems

(P-8408)
DWI ENTERPRISES
11081 Winners Cir Ste 100 (90720-2894)
PHONE..............................714 842-2236
Fred Delgleize, *Pr*
Dan Delgleize, *
Dave Dain, *
Amanda Delgleize, *
◆ **EMP:** 25 **EST:** 1980
SQ FT: 9,500
SALES (est): 2.02MM **Privately Held**
Web: www.dwienterprises.com
SIC: 3651 3669 Audio electronic systems; Visual communication systems

(P-8409)
ECOLINK INTELLIGENT TECH INC
2055 Corte Del Nogal (92011-1412)
PHONE..............................855 432-6546
Michael Lamb, *CEO*
EMP: 18 **EST:** 2007
SALES (est): 2.84MM **Publicly Held**
Web: www.discoverecolink.com
SIC: 3651 Video triggers (remote control TV devices)
PA: Universal Electronics Inc.
15147 N Scottsdale Rd

Scottsdale AZ

(P-8410)
ETI SOUND SYSTEMS INC
Also Called: Eti B Si Professional
5300 Harbor St (90040-3927)
PHONE..............................323 835-6660
Eli El-kiss, *Pr*
Avi El-kiss, *VP*
◆ **EMP:** 45 **EST:** 1989
SALES (est): 4.77MM **Privately Held**
Web: www.b-52pro.com
SIC: 3651 Speaker monitors

(P-8411)
FUNAI CORPORATION INC (HQ)
12489 Lakeland Rd (90670-3938)
PHONE..............................310 787-3000
Yoshihiro Sasaki, *CEO*
Hiroyuki Anabe, *
Ryo Fukuda, *
George Kanazawa, *
Yoichi Kanazawa, *
▲ **EMP:** 25 **EST:** 1991
SALES (est): 12.06MM **Privately Held**
Web: www.funai.us
SIC: 3651 3955 Television receiving sets; Print cartridges for laser and other computer printers
PA: Funai Electric Holdings Co., Ltd.
7-7-1, Nakagaito
Daito OSK

(P-8412)
FUNAI CORPORATION INC
Also Called: Funai Electric Co.
19900 Van Ness Ave (90501-1143)
PHONE..............................201 727-4560
◆ **EMP:** 77
SIC: 3651 Household audio and video equipment

(P-8413)
GENASYS INC (PA)
Also Called: Genasys
16262 W Bernardo Dr (92127-1879)
PHONE..............................858 676-1112
Richard S Danforth, *CEO*
Richard H Osgood Iii, *Ch Bd*
Dennis D Klahn, *CFO*
◆ **EMP:** 94 **EST:** 1980
SQ FT: 55,766
SALES (est): 46.66MM
SALES (corp-wide): 46.66MM **Publicly Held**
Web: www.genasys.com
SIC: 3651 Sound reproducing equipment

(P-8414)
HARMAN PROFESSIONAL INC
14780 Bar Harbor Rd (92336-4254)
PHONE..............................844 776-4899
EMP: 159
Web: www.jblpro.com
SIC: 3651 Audio electronic systems
HQ: Harman Professional, Inc.
8500 Balboa Blvd
Northridge CA
818 893-8411

(P-8415)
HARMAN PROFESSIONAL INC
24950 Grove View Rd (92551-9552)
PHONE..............................951 242-2927
EMP: 140
Web: www.jblpro.com
SIC: 3651 Household audio equipment
HQ: Harman Professional, Inc.
8500 Balboa Blvd
Northridge CA
818 893-8411

(P-8416)
HARMAN PROFESSIONAL INC (DH)
Also Called: Harman Professional
8500 Balboa Blvd (91325-5802)
P.O. Box 2200 (91328-2200)
PHONE..............................818 893-8411
Brian Divine, *CEO*
◆ **EMP:** 300 **EST:** 2006
SALES (est): 182.4MM **Privately Held**
Web: www.jblpro.com
SIC: 3651 Audio electronic systems
HQ: Harman International Industries Incorporated
400 Atlantic St Ste 15
Stamford CT
203 328-3500

(P-8417)
HENRYS ADIO VSUAL SLUTIONS INC
Also Called: Audio Images
18002 Cowan (92614-6812)
PHONE..............................714 258-7238
Mark Ontiveros, *CEO*
EMP: 30 **EST:** 1998
SALES (est): 5MM **Privately Held**
Web: www.audioimages.tv
SIC: 3651 Household audio and video equipment

(P-8418)
HONAV USA INC
3030 W Warner Ave (92704-5311)
PHONE..............................858 634-0617
David Jacobs, *Pr*
▲ **EMP:** 18 **EST:** 2013
SALES (est): 1.68MM **Privately Held**
SIC: 3651 Speaker systems
PA: Beijing Huajiang Culture Group Co., Ltd.
No.9, Chongwenmenwai Avenue, Chongwen District
Beijing BJ

(P-8419)
KSC INDUSTRIES INC
9771 Clairemont Mesa Blvd Ste E (92124-1300)
PHONE..............................619 671-0110
Jeffrey W King Junior, *Pr*
Malcolm Hollombe, *VP*
William Mccarty, *VP*
Lisa Michaud, *VP*
Mary Beth King-fuller, *Dir*
◆ **EMP:** 26 **EST:** 1973
SQ FT: 10,000
SALES (est): 1.95MM **Privately Held**
Web: www.kscind.com
SIC: 3651 Speaker systems

(P-8420)
M KLEMME TECHNOLOGY CORP
Also Called: K-Tek
1384 Poinsettia Ave Ste F (92081-8505)
PHONE..............................760 727-0593
Brenda L Parker, *Pr*
▲ **EMP:** 24 **EST:** 1996
SALES (est): 1.85MM **Privately Held**
Web: www.ktekpro.com
SIC: 3651 Audio electronic systems

(P-8421)
MAGNASYNC/MOVIOLA CORPORATION
Also Called: Magnasync-Moviola
1400 W Burbank Blvd (91506-1308)
PHONE..............................818 845-8066

EMP: 20
SALES (corp-wide): 22.49MM **Privately Held**
Web: www.filmtools.com
SIC: 3651 Household audio and video equipment
PA: Magnasync/Moviola Corporation
1015 N Hollywood Way
Burbank CA
818 845-8066

(P-8422)
MARSHALL ELECTRONICS INC (PA)
Also Called: Mogami
20608 Madrona Ave (90503-3715)
PHONE..............................310 333-0606
▲ **EMP:** 90 **EST:** 1979
SALES (est): 15.22MM
SALES (corp-wide): 15.22MM **Privately Held**
Web: www.marshall-usa.com
SIC: 3651 5961 Electronic kits for home assembly: radio, TV, phonograph; Electronic kits and parts, mail order

(P-8423)
MEDIAPOINTE INC
3952 Camino Ranchero (93012-5066)
PHONE..............................805 480-3700
Stephen Villoria, *CEO*
EMP: 20 **EST:** 2011
SALES (est): 730.22K **Privately Held**
Web: www.mediapointe.com
SIC: 3651 Audio electronic systems

(P-8424)
MJ BEST VIDEOGRAPHER LLC
14005 S Berendo Ave Apt 3 (90247-2248)
PHONE..............................209 208-8432
John S Morris, *CEO*
EMP: 209 **EST:** 2020
SALES (est): 6.5MM **Privately Held**
SIC: 3651 Video camera-audio recorders, household use

(P-8425)
MR DJ INC
1800 E Washington Blvd (90021-3127)
PHONE..............................213 744-0044
Mike Razipour, *CEO*
Shahzad Fatemi, *
▲ **EMP:** 50 **EST:** 2009
SALES (est): 3.1MM **Privately Held**
Web: www.mrdjusa.com
SIC: 3651 Audio electronic systems

(P-8426)
PHILIPS
3721 Valley Centre Dr Ste 500 (92130)
PHONE..............................916 337-8008
EMP: 29 **EST:** 2018
SALES (est): 2.61MM **Privately Held**
Web: usa.philips.com
SIC: 3651 Household audio and video equipment

(P-8427)
PIONEER SPEAKERS INC
2050 W 190th St Ste 100 (90504-6229)
PHONE..............................310 952-2000
◆ **EMP:** 1250
Web: www.pioneerspeakers.com
SIC: 3651 Speaker systems

(P-8428)
QSC LLC (PA)
Also Called: Qsc Audio
1675 Macarthur Blvd (92626-1440)

PHONE.............................800 854-4079
Joe Pham, *CEO*
Jatan Shah, *
Barry Ferrell, *
Ray Van Straten, *
Anna Csontos, *
◆ **EMP:** 163 **EST:** 1979
SQ FT: 180,000
SALES (est): 116.19MM
SALES (corp-wide): 116.19MM **Privately Held**
Web: www.qsc.com
SIC: 3651 Household audio equipment

(P-8429)
RENKUS-HEINZ INC (PA)
19201 Cook St (92610-3501)
PHONE.............................949 588-9997
Harro Heinz, *Ch*
Roscoe L Anthony Iii, *CEO*
Erika Heinz, *
▲ **EMP:** 79 **EST:** 1979
SQ FT: 48,500
SALES (est): 14.53MM
SALES (corp-wide): 14.53MM **Privately Held**
Web: www.renkus-heinz.com
SIC: 3651 Audio electronic systems

(P-8430)
ROBOT-GXG INC
8960 Toronto Ave (91730-5411)
PHONE.............................660 324-0030
Xiwen Xu, *Prin*
EMP: 20 **EST:** 2019
SALES (est): 1MM **Privately Held**
SIC: 3651 Home entertainment equipment, electronic, nec

(P-8431)
ROCK-OLA MANUFACTURING CORP
Also Called: Antique Apparatus Company
1445 Sepulveda Blvd (90501-5004)
PHONE.............................310 328-1306
Glenn S Streeter, *Pr*
◆ **EMP:** 80 **EST:** 1994
SALES (est): 11.5MM **Privately Held**
Web: www.rock-ola.com
SIC: 3651 Coin-operated phonographs, juke boxes

(P-8432)
RODE MICROPHONES LLC
2745 Raymond Ave (90755-2129)
P.O. Box 91028 (90809-1028)
PHONE.............................310 328-7456
Mark Ludmer, *CEO*
Peter Freedmon, *
Brian Swbaringen, *
▲ **EMP:** 140 **EST:** 2001
SALES (est): 21.22MM **Privately Held**
Web: www.rode.com
SIC: 3651 Microphones
HQ: Freedman Electronics Pty Ltd
107 Carnarvon St
Silverwater NSW

(P-8433)
SANYO MANUFACTURING CORPORATION
2055 Sanyo Ave (92154-6234)
P.O. Box 2000 (72336-2000)
PHONE.............................619 661-1134
◆ **EMP:** 100
SIC: 3651 Television receiving sets

(P-8434)
SCOSCHE INDUSTRIES INC
1550 Pacific Ave (93033-2451)
P.O. Box 2901 (93034-2901)
PHONE.............................805 486-4450
Roger J Alves, *CEO*
Scotia Alves, *
Kasidy Alves, *
Vincent Alves, *
Steven Klinger, *
◆ **EMP:** 180 **EST:** 1980
SQ FT: 83,000
SALES (est): 46.15MM **Privately Held**
Web: www.scosche.com
SIC: 3651 Audio electronic systems

(P-8435)
SONANCE ✪
212 Avenida Fabricante (92672-7538)
PHONE.............................949 492-7777
EMP: 25 **EST:** 2022
SALES (est): 1.13MM **Privately Held**
Web: iport.squarespace.com
SIC: 3651 Household audio and video equipment

(P-8436)
SONOS INC (PA)
Also Called: Sonos
614 Chapala St (93101-3312)
PHONE.............................805 965-3001
Patrick Spence, *Pr*
Michelangelo Volpi, *Ch Bd*
Edward Lazarus, *CLO*
Nicholas Millington, *CIO*
Shamayne Braman, *CPO*
◆ **EMP:** 91 **EST:** 2002
SALES (est): 1.66B
SALES (corp-wide): 1.66B **Publicly Held**
Web: www.sonos.com
SIC: 3651 Household audio and video equipment

(P-8437)
SONY ELECTRONICS INC
Also Called: Sony Style
16530 Via Esprillo (92127-1708)
PHONE.............................858 942-2400
Bill Lunger, *Prin*
EMP: 255
Web: www.sony.com
SIC: 3651 Household audio and video equipment
HQ: Sony Electronics Inc.
16535 Via Esprillo Bldg 1
San Diego CA
858 942-2400

(P-8438)
SONY ELECTRONICS INC (DH)
16535 Via Esprillo 1 (92127-1738)
PHONE.............................858 942-2400
Shigeki Ishizuka, *Pr*
Phil Molyneux, *
Hideki Komiyama, *
Rintaro Miyoshi, *
William A Glaser, *
◆ **EMP:** 1000 **EST:** 1988
SALES (est): 1.41B **Privately Held**
Web: www.sony.com
SIC: 3651 5064 3695 3671 Household audio and video equipment; Electrical appliances, television and radio; Video recording tape, blank; Television tubes
HQ: Sony Corporation Of America
25 Madison Ave Fl 27
New York NY

(P-8439)
SPEAKERCRAFT LLC
12471 Riverside Dr (91752-1007)
P.O. Box 9003 (91752)
PHONE.............................951 685-1759
◆ **EMP:** 100
Web: www.speakercraft.com
SIC: 3651 5731 Household audio equipment ; High fidelity stereo equipment

(P-8440)
SYNG INC (PA)
120 Mildred Ave (90291-4227)
PHONE.............................770 354-0915
Christopher Stringer, *CEO*
Damon Way, *
EMP: 60 **EST:** 2018
SALES (est): 9.56MM
SALES (corp-wide): 9.56MM **Privately Held**
Web: www.syngspace.com
SIC: 3651 Loudspeakers, electrodynamic or magnetic

(P-8441)
TECHNICOLOR USA INC
Also Called: Technicolor Connected USA
4049 Industrial Parkway Dr (93243-9719)
PHONE.............................661 496-1309
EMP: 445
SIC: 3651 Household audio and video equipment
HQ: Technicolor Usa, Inc.
6040 W Sunset Blvd
Hollywood CA
317 587-4287

(P-8442)
TECHNICOLOR USA INC (HQ)
Also Called: Technicolor
6040 W Sunset Blvd (90028-6402)
P.O. Box 1976 (46206-1976)
PHONE.............................317 587-4287
◆ **EMP:** 800 **EST:** 1987
SALES (est): 576.79MM **Privately Held**
SIC: 3651 3861 3661 Household audio and video equipment; Cameras, microfilm; Telephone sets, all types except cellular radio
PA: Vantiva
10 Boulevard De Grenelle
Paris

(P-8443)
TOSHIBA AMER ELCTRNIC CMPNNTS (DH)
Also Called: Toshiba
5231 California Ave (92617-3235)
PHONE.............................949 462-7700
Hideya Yamaguchi, *CEO*
Hitoshi Otsuka, *
Ichiro Hirata, *
Richard Tobias, *
Farhad Mafie, *
◆ **EMP:** 300 **EST:** 1998
SQ FT: 100,000
SALES (est): 412.02MM **Privately Held**
Web: www.toshiba.com
SIC: 3651 3631 3674 3679 Television receiving sets; Microwave ovens, including portable: household; Semiconductors and related devices; Electronic circuits
HQ: Toshiba America Inc
1251 Ave Of Amrcas Ste 41
New York NY
212 596-0600

(P-8444)
TOSHIBA AMERICA INC
5241 California Ave Ste 200 (92617-3052)
PHONE.............................212 596-0600
EMP: 2095
Web: www.toshiba.com
SIC: 3651 3631 5075 3571 Television receiving sets; Microwave ovens, including portable: household; Compressors, air conditioning; Personal computers (microcomputers)
HQ: Toshiba America Inc
1251 Ave Of Amrcas Ste 41
New York NY
212 596-0600

(P-8445)
ULTIMATE SOUND INC
1200 S Diamond Bar Blvd Ste 200 (91765-2298)
PHONE.............................909 861-6200
Robert Chiu, *Pr*
Cindy Chiu, *
◆ **EMP:** 300 **EST:** 1978
SQ FT: 20,000
SALES (est): 9.74MM **Privately Held**
SIC: 3651 5731 Loudspeakers, electrodynamic or magnetic; Radio, television, and electronic stores

(P-8446)
VANTAGE POINT PRODUCTS CORP (PA)
Also Called: Vpt Direct
9115 Dice Rd Ste 18 (90670-2538)
P.O. Box 2485 (90670-0485)
PHONE.............................562 946-1718
Donald R Burns, *CEO*
Mick Mulcahey, *Pr*
▲ **EMP:** 33 **EST:** 1988
SQ FT: 62,000
SALES (est): 4.74MM **Privately Held**
Web: www.thinkvp.com
SIC: 3651 Audio electronic systems

(P-8447)
VIZIO INC
2601 S Bdwy Unit B (90007-2731)
PHONE.............................213 746-7730
EMP: 122
SALES (corp-wide): 1.86B **Publicly Held**
Web: www.vizio.com
SIC: 3651 Television receiving sets
HQ: Vizio, Inc.
39 Tesla
Irvine CA
855 833-3221

(P-8448)
VIZIO INC (HQ)
39 Tesla (92618-4603)
PHONE.............................855 833-3221
William Wang, *CEO*
Adam Townsend, *
Jerry Huang, *
◆ **EMP:** 154 **EST:** 2002
SQ FT: 27,300
SALES (est): 189.78MM
SALES (corp-wide): 1.86B **Publicly Held**
Web: www.vizio.com
SIC: 3651 Television receiving sets
PA: Vizio Holding Corp.
39 Tesla
Irvine CA
949 428-2525

(P-8449)
VIZIO HOLDING CORP (PA)
Also Called: Vizio
39 Tesla (92618-4603)

PHONE..............................949 428-2525
William Wang, *Ch Bd*
Ben Wong, *Pr*
Adam Townsend, *CFO*
Michael O'donnell, *CRO*
EMP: 129 **EST:** 2003
SALES (est): 1.86B
SALES (corp-wide): 1.86B **Publicly Held**
Web: www.vizio.com
SIC: 3651 Household audio and video
　equipment

(P-8450)
VTL AMPLIFIERS INC
4774 Murietta St Ste 10 (91710-5155)
PHONE..............................909 627-5944
Luke Manley, *Pr*
▲ **EMP:** 24 **EST:** 2000
SQ FT: 6,000
SALES (est): 1.87MM **Privately Held**
Web: www.vtl.com
SIC: 3651 Audio electronic systems

(P-8451)
WIRELESS TECHNOLOGY INC
Also Called: Wti
2064 Eastman Ave Ste 113 (93003-7787)
PHONE..............................805 339-9696
EMP: 30 **EST:** 1987
SQ FT: 7,000
SALES (est): 4.74MM **Privately Held**
Web: www.gotowti.com
SIC: 3651 Household audio and video
　equipment

3652 Prerecorded Records
And Tapes

(P-8452)
CAPITOL-EMI MUSIC INC
Also Called: E M D
1750b Vine St (90028-5209)
PHONE..............................323 462-6252
EMP: 1500
SIC: 3652 Compact laser discs, prerecorded

(P-8453)
CMH RECORDS INC
Also Called: Dwell Records
2898 Rowena Ave Ste 201 (90039-2096)
P.O. Box 39439 (90039-0439)
PHONE..............................323 663-8098
David Haerle, *Pr*
EMP: 17 **EST:** 1975
SQ FT: 3,303
SALES (est): 1.52MM **Privately Held**
Web: www.cmhrecords.com
SIC: 3652 7929 Phonograph records,
　prerecorded; Entertainers and
　entertainment groups

(P-8454)
CPAPERLESS LLC
605 1/2 Orchid Ave (92625-2461)
P.O. Box 1113 (92625-6113)
PHONE..............................949 510-3365
EMP: 55 **EST:** 2018
SALES (est): 380.87K **Privately Held**
Web: www.safesend.com
SIC: 3652 Prerecorded records and tapes

(P-8455)
DIGITAL FLEX MEDIA INC
Also Called: CD Digital
11150 White Birch Dr (91730-3819)
PHONE..............................909 484-8440
EMP: 90
Web: www.digitalflexmedia.com

SIC: 3652 Compact laser discs, prerecorded

(P-8456)
DISCOPYLABS
Also Called: Dcl
4455 E Philadelphia St (91761-2329)
PHONE..............................909 390-3800
Larry Shaker, *Dir*
EMP: 20
SALES (corp-wide): 81.65MM **Privately
Held**
Web: www.dclcorp.com
SIC: 3652 4225 7379 7389 Prerecorded
　records and tapes; General warehousing
　and storage; Diskette duplicating service
PA: Discopylabs
　48641 Milmont Dr
　Fremont CA
　510 651-5100

(P-8457)
ENAS MEDIA INC
1316 Michillinda Ave (91006-1921)
PHONE..............................626 962-1115
Nagapet Keshishian, *Pr*
Avetis Keshishian, *
Serop Keshishian, *
EMP: 17 **EST:** 1985
SALES (est): 646.43K **Privately Held**
SIC: 3652 Phonograph records, prerecorded

(P-8458)
ERIKA RECORDS INC
6300 Caballero Blvd (90620-1126)
PHONE..............................714 228-5420
Liz Dunster, *Pr*
Erzsebet Dunster, *CEO*
▲ **EMP:** 20 **EST:** 1981
SALES (est): 4.93MM **Privately Held**
Web: www.erikarecords.com
SIC: 3652 5735 Phonograph records,
　prerecorded; Records

(P-8459)
**EXTREME GROUP HOLDINGS
LLC**
Also Called: Extreme Production Music
1531 14th St (90404-3302)
PHONE..............................310 899-3200
Emanuel Russell, *Brnch Mgr*
EMP: 20
Web: www.extrememusic.com
SIC: 3652 Prerecorded records and tapes
HQ: Extreme Group Holdings Llc
　25 Madison Ave
　New York NY

(P-8460)
GC INTERNATIONAL INC
Also Called: Al Johnson Company
4671 Calle Carga (93012-8560)
PHONE..............................805 389-4631
Mark Griffith, *Prin*
EMP: 20
SALES (corp-wide): 14.34MM **Privately
Held**
Web: www.aljcast.com
SIC: 3652 3369 Phonograph record blanks;
　Lead, zinc, and white metal
PA: Gc International, Inc.
　4671 Calle Carga
　Camarillo CA
　805 389-4631

(P-8461)
HOLLYWOOD RECORDS INC
Also Called: Andanov Music
500 S Buena Vista St (91521-0002)
PHONE..............................818 560-5670
Abbey Konowitch, *Genl Mgr*

EMP: 50 **EST:** 1990
SALES (est): 24.04MM
SALES (corp-wide): 88.9B **Publicly Held**
Web: www.hollywoodrecords.com
SIC: 3652 Prerecorded records and tapes
HQ: Walt Disney Music Company
　500 S Buena Vista St
　Burbank CA
　818 560-1000

(P-8462)
**PANASONIC DISC
MANUFACTURING
CORPORATION OF AMERICA**
20000 Mariner Ave Ste 200 (90503-1670)
PHONE..............................310 783-4800
▲ **EMP:** 200
Web: pdmc.panasonic.com
SIC: 3652 Compact laser discs, prerecorded

(P-8463)
PRECISE MEDIA SERVICES INC
Also Called: Precise-Full Service Media
888 Vintage Ave (91764-5392)
PHONE..............................909 481-3305
Choy Tim Lee, *CEO*
Robert Miller, *
▲ **EMP:** 25 **EST:** 1991
SQ FT: 112,000
SALES (est): 4.88MM **Privately Held**
Web: www.precisemedia.com
SIC: 3652 7819 Prerecorded records and
　tapes; Video tape or disk reproduction

(P-8464)
**RAINBO RECORD MFG CORP
(PA)**
Also Called: Rainbo Records & Cassettes
8960 Eton Ave (91304-1621)
P.O. Box 280700 (91328-0700)
PHONE..............................818 280-1100
Jack Brown, *Prin*
Steve Sheldon, *Prin*
▲ **EMP:** 50 **EST:** 1939
SQ FT: 50,000
SALES (est): 9.24MM
SALES (corp-wide): 9.24MM **Privately
Held**
Web: www.rainborecords.com
SIC: 3652 5099 Compact laser discs,
　prerecorded; Compact discs

(P-8465)
**RECORD TECHNOLOGY INC
(PA)**
486 Dawson Dr Ste 4s (93012-8049)
PHONE..............................805 484-2747
Don Mac Innis, *Pr*
Melodie Mac Innis, *
▲ **EMP:** 24 **EST:** 1972
SQ FT: 30,000
SALES (est): 2.48MM
SALES (corp-wide): 2.48MM **Privately
Held**
Web: www.recordtech.com
SIC: 3652 Master records or tapes,
　preparation of

(P-8466)
SUITECENTRIC LCC
5857 Owens Ave Ste 300 (92008-5507)
PHONE..............................760 520-1611
EMP: 17 **EST:** 2019
SALES (est): 1.83MM **Privately Held**
Web: www.suitecentric.com
SIC: 3652 Prerecorded records and tapes

(P-8467)
XR STUDIOS LLC
6700 Santa Monica Blvd (90038-1203)
PHONE..............................513 446-5621
EMP: 19 **EST:** 2021
SALES (est): 271.54K **Privately Held**
SIC: 3652 Prerecorded records and tapes

3661 Telephone And
Telegraph Apparatus

(P-8468)
BALAJI TRADING INC
Also Called: City of Industry
4850 Eucalyptus Ave (91710-9255)
PHONE..............................909 444-7999
Mukesh Batta, *CEO*
▲ **EMP:** 91 **EST:** 2010
SALES (est): 9.9MM **Privately Held**
SIC: 3661 Headsets, telephone

(P-8469)
**CALIENT TECHNOLOGIES INC
(PA)**
Also Called: Calient Technologies
120 Cremona Dr Ste 160 (93117-3168)
PHONE..............................805 695-4800
Arjun Gutpa, *Ofcr*
Kevin Welsh, *
Jitender Miglani, *
Daniel Tardent, *
Jag Setlur, *
▲ **EMP:** 30 **EST:** 1999
SQ FT: 150,000
SALES (est): 49.22MM
SALES (corp-wide): 49.22MM **Privately
Held**
Web: www.calient.net
SIC: 3661 Fiber optics communications
　equipment

(P-8470)
COASTAL CONNECTIONS
2085 Sperry Ave Ste B (93003-7452)
PHONE..............................805 644-5051
Andrew Devine, *Pr*
Nancy Devine, *
◆ **EMP:** 37 **EST:** 2002
SQ FT: 9,000
SALES (est): 3.93MM **Privately Held**
Web: www.coastalcon.com
SIC: 3661 Fiber optics communications
　equipment

(P-8471)
EPIC TECHNOLOGIES LLC
Also Called: Natel Engineering
9340 Owensmouth Ave (91311-6915)
PHONE..............................908 707-4085
Sudesh Arora, *Ch*
▲ **EMP:** 1750 **EST:** 2004
SQ FT: 52,000
SALES (est): 1.05B
SALES (corp-wide): 1.43B **Privately Held**
Web: www.neotech.com
SIC: 3661 3577 3679 Telephone and
　telegraph apparatus; Computer peripheral
　equipment, nec; Electronic circuits
PA: Natel Engineering Company, Llc
　9340 Owensmouth Ave
　Chatsworth CA
　818 495-8617

(P-8472)
**EXCELSUS A DIVISION OF
PULSE**
2875 Loker Ave E (92010-6626)
PHONE..............................760 476-1511

Alan Benjamin, *CEO*
John Kowalski, *
John Houston, *
Patrick Mccready, *VP*
Albert Thorp Iii, *Sec*
EMP: 42 **EST:** 1998
SALES (est): 2.05MM **Privately Held**
SIC: 3661 Telephone and telegraph apparatus
HQ: Pulse Electronics, Inc.
15255 Innovation Dr # 100
San Diego CA

(P-8473)
FRANKLIN WIRELESS CORP
Also Called: Franklin Wireless
9707 Waples St Ste 150 (92121-2954)
PHONE..............................858 623-0000
Ok Chae Kim, *Pr*
Gary Nelson, *
Yun J David Lee, *VP Sls*
Bill Bauer, *Interim Chief Financial Officer*
▲ **EMP:** 69 **EST:** 1981
SQ FT: 12,775
SALES (est): 45.95MM **Privately Held**
Web: www.franklinwireless.com
SIC: 3661 Fiber optics communications equipment

(P-8474)
GENERAL PHOTONICS CORP
Also Called: General Photonics
14351 Pipeline Ave (91710-5642)
PHONE..............................909 590-5473
▲ **EMP:** 51 **EST:** 1995
SQ FT: 20,000
SALES (est): 3.19MM **Publicly Held**
Web: www.lunainc.com
SIC: 3661 Fiber optics communications equipment
HQ: Luna Technologies, Inc.
301 1st St Sw Ste 200
Roanoke VA
540 769-8400

(P-8475)
INTERNTNAL CNNCTORS CABLE CORP
Also Called: I C C
2100 E Valencia Dr Ste D (92831-4811)
PHONE..............................888 275-4422
Mike Lin, *Pr*
Mike Lin, *Pr*
Eugene Chyun Tsai, *Stockholder*
▲ **EMP:** 110 **EST:** 1984
SQ FT: 38,720
SALES (est): 9.41MM **Privately Held**
SIC: 3661 5065 Telephone and telegraph apparatus; Telephone and telegraphic equipment

(P-8476)
LEADER ELECTRONICS (NA) INC
2901 S Harbor Blvd (92704-6428)
PHONE..............................714 435-0505
Grace Vhiu, *Pr*
▲ **EMP:** 19 **EST:** 2004
SALES (est): 869.58K **Privately Held**
SIC: 3661 Telephone cords, jacks, adapters, etc.
PA: Leader Electronics Inc.
8f, No. 138, Lane 235, Baoqiao Rd.
New Taipei City TAP

(P-8477)
LG-ERICSSON USA INC
20 Mason (92618-2706)
PHONE..............................877 828-2673
◆ **EMP:** 47
Web: www.lgericssonus.com

SIC: 3661 5065 Telephone sets, all types except cellular radio; Modems, computer

(P-8478)
LITTLEFEET INC
13000 Gregg St (92064-7151)
P.O. Box 3008 (91944-3008)
PHONE..............................858 375-6400
John Combs, *Pr*
John Combs, *Pr*
Carmen Genovse, *VP Opers*
Steve Domenik, *Dir*
EMP: 45 **EST:** 1999
SQ FT: 45,000
SALES (est): 4.67MM **Privately Held**
SIC: 3661 4812 Telegraph or telephone carrier and repeater equipment; Radiotelephone communication

(P-8479)
LYNX PHTNIC NTWORKS A DEL CORP
6303 Owensmouth Ave Fl 10 (91367-2262)
PHONE..............................818 802-0244
Daniel Tal, *CEO*
Michael Leigh, *Pr*
Beni Kopelovitz, *COO*
EMP: 18 **EST:** 1998
SQ FT: 30,000
SALES (est): 374.4K **Privately Held**
Web: www.lynxpn.com
SIC: 3661 Fiber optics communications equipment

(P-8480)
MOTOROLA SLTONS CNNCTIVITY INC (HQ)
42555 Rio Nedo (92590-3726)
P.O. Box 9007 (92589-9007)
PHONE..............................951 719-2100
Gino Bonanotte, *CEO*
John Jack Molloy, *Pr*
Andrew Sinclair, *
Uygar Gazioglu, *
Daniel Pekofske, *Care Vice President*
▲ **EMP:** 145 **EST:** 1967
SQ FT: 100,000
SALES (est): 64.12MM
SALES (corp-wide): 9.11B **Publicly Held**
Web: www.motorolasolutions.com
SIC: 3661 Telephone station equipment and parts, wire
PA: Motorola Solutions, Inc.
500 W Monroe St Ste 4400
Chicago IL
847 576-5000

(P-8481)
NOKIA OF AMERICA CORPORATION
Also Called: Alcatel-Lucent
2000 Corporate Center Dr (91320-1400)
PHONE..............................818 880-3500
Menandro Canelo, *Ofcr*
EMP: 24
SALES (corp-wide): 25.87B **Privately Held**
Web: www.nokia.com
SIC: 3661 Telephone and telegraph apparatus
HQ: Nokia Of America Corporation
600 Mountain Ave Ste 700
New Providence NJ

(P-8482)
OPTICAL ZONU CORPORATION
Also Called: Zonu
7510 Hazeltine Ave (91405-1419)
PHONE..............................818 780-9701
Meir Bartur, *Pr*

Frazad Ghadooshay, *VP*
Meir Bartur, *Prin*
▲ **EMP:** 18 **EST:** 2003
SALES (est): 4.3MM **Privately Held**
Web: www.opticalzonu.com
SIC: 3661 Fiber optics communications equipment

(P-8483)
QUINTRON SYSTEMS INC (PA)
Also Called: Quintron
1290 W Mccoy Ln (93455-1007)
PHONE..............................805 928-4343
Dominick Barry, *Pr*
James E Mc Glothlin, *
Elton L Hammers, *
David Wilhite, *
Sharon Lewis, *
EMP: 33 **EST:** 1970
SALES (est): 8.69MM
SALES (corp-wide): 8.69MM **Privately Held**
Web: www.quintron.com
SIC: 3661 1731 Telephone and telegraph apparatus; Telephone and telephone equipment installation

(P-8484)
RLH INDUSTRIES INC
936 N Main St (92867-5403)
PHONE..............................714 532-1672
James B Harris, *CEO*
Carol E Harris, *
Tristan Harris, *
▲ **EMP:** 40 **EST:** 1988
SQ FT: 16,000
SALES (est): 9.35MM **Privately Held**
Web: www.fiberopticlink.com
SIC: 3661 5065 5999 Telephone and telegraph apparatus; Communication equipment; Telephone equipment and systems

(P-8485)
SIEMENS MOBILITY INC
1026 E Lacy Ave (92805-5651)
PHONE..............................714 284-0206
David Hopping, *Brnch Mgr*
EMP: 32
SALES (corp-wide): 84.48B **Privately Held**
SIC: 3661 Telephones and telephone apparatus
HQ: Siemens Mobility, Inc.
1 Penn Plz Ste 1100
New York NY
212 672-4000

(P-8486)
U-BLOX SAN DIEGO INC
12626 High Bluff Dr Ste 200 (92130-2070)
PHONE..............................858 847-9611
David W Carey, *Pr*
EMP: 33 **EST:** 2009
SALES (est): 9.89MM **Privately Held**
SIC: 3661 3571 5045 Modems; Personal computers (microcomputers); Computers, peripherals, and software
HQ: U-Blox Ag
Zurcherstrasse 68
Thalwil ZH

3663 Radio And T.v. Communications Equipment

(P-8487)
24/7 STUDIO EQUIPMENT INC
Also Called: Hertz Entertainment Services
3111 N Kenwood St (91505-1041)
PHONE..............................818 840-8247

Lance Sorenson, *Pr*
Gary Mielke, *
EMP: 81 **EST:** 2006
SALES (est): 19.14MM
SALES (corp-wide): 8.69B **Publicly Held**
SIC: 3663 Studio equipment, radio and television broadcasting
PA: Hertz Global Holdings, Inc.
8501 Williams Rd Fl 3
Estero FL
239 301-7000

(P-8488)
ADAPTIVE DIGITAL SYSTEMS INC
20322 Sw Acacia St Ste 200 (92660-1702)
PHONE..............................949 955-3116
Attila W Mathe, *Pr*
Ralph Boehringer, *
Susan Cameron, *
▲ **EMP:** 27 **EST:** 1979
SQ FT: 6,500
SALES (est): 4.02MM **Privately Held**
Web: www.adaptivedigitalsystems.com
SIC: 3663 Marine radio communications equipment

(P-8489)
AETHERCOMM INC
3205 Lionshead Ave (92010-4710)
PHONE..............................760 208-6002
William Todd Thornton, *CEO*
Todd Thornton, *Pr*
Terri Thornton, *VP*
Richard Martinez, *CFO*
Mark Bahu, *Engr*
EMP: 125 **EST:** 1999
SQ FT: 46,000
SALES (est): 57.25MM **Privately Held**
Web: www.aethercomm.com
SIC: 3663 Radio and t.v. communications equipment
HQ: Frontgrade Technologies Llc
4350 Centennial Blvd
Colorado Springs CO

(P-8490)
AIR-TRAK
15090 Avenue Of Science Ste 103 (92128-3493)
PHONE..............................858 677-9950
Greg White, *Pr*
Marc Bernard, *VP*
Dennis Clark, *Ch*
Steve Porter, *VP Fin*
EMP: 21 **EST:** 1999
SQ FT: 5,600
SALES (est): 1.89MM **Privately Held**
Web: www.air-trak.com
SIC: 3663 Global positioning systems (GPS) equipment

(P-8491)
AIRGAIN INC (PA)
Also Called: AIRGAIN
3611 Valley Centre Dr Ste 150 (92130-3331)
PHONE..............................760 579-0200
Jacob Suen, *Pr*
James K Sims, *Ch Bd*
Morad Sbahi Senior, *Global Vice President*
Michael Elbaz, *CFO*
EMP: 34 **EST:** 1995
SQ FT: 10,300
SALES (est): 75.89MM
SALES (corp-wide): 75.89MM **Publicly Held**
Web: www.airgain.com
SIC: 3663 Antennas, transmitting and communications

(P-8492)
ALE USA INC
Also Called: Alcatel-Lucent Enterprise USA
2000 Corporate Center Dr (91320-1400)
PHONE..............................818 880-3500
Stephan Robineau, *Pr*
Louise Kuphal, *
EMP: 550 **EST:** 2014
SQ FT: 50,000
SALES (est): 195.9MM **Privately Held**
Web: www.al-enterprise.com
SIC: 3663 3613 Mobile communication
   equipment; Switchgear and switchboard
   apparatus
HQ: China Huaxin Post And Telecom
   Technologies Co., Ltd.
   04g, No. 4 Building, Yard 1, Naoshikou
   Street, Xicheng District
   Beijing BJ
   105 852-8866

(P-8493)
ALTINEX INC
Also Called: Air Gap International
500 S Jefferson St (92870-6617)
PHONE..............................714 990-0877
Jack Gershfeld, *Pr*
▲ **EMP:** 50 **EST:** 1993
SALES (est): 10.55MM **Privately Held**
Web: www.altinex.com
SIC: 3663 3577 3651 5099 Radio and t.v.
   communications equipment; Computer
   peripheral equipment, nec; Household
   audio and video equipment; Video and
   audio equipment

(P-8494)
**AMPLIFIER TECHNOLOGIES
INC (HQ)**
7133 Telegraph Rd (90640-6511)
PHONE..............................323 278-0001
Morris Kessler, *Pr*
▲ **EMP:** 25 **EST:** 1981
SQ FT: 84,000
SALES (est): 6.18MM
SALES (corp-wide): 10.16MM **Privately
Held**
Web: www.ati-amp.com
SIC: 3663 Television broadcasting and
   communications equipment
PA: Macey Investment Corp.
   1749 Chapin Rd
   Montebello CA
   323 278-0001

(P-8495)
ANTCOM CORPORATION
Also Called: Antcom
367 Van Ness Way Ste 602 (90501-6246)
PHONE..............................310 782-1076
Michael Ritter, *CEO*
Sean Huynh, *VP*
Doug Reid, *Genl Mgr*
Linda Cupchak, *Contrlr*
EMP: 45 **EST:** 1997
SQ FT: 15,000
SALES (est): 11.02MM
SALES (corp-wide): 491.93K **Privately
Held**
Web: www.antcom.com
SIC: 3663 Antennas, transmitting and
   communications
HQ: Novatel Inc.
   10921 14 St Ne
   Calgary AB
   403 295-4500

(P-8496)
ANYDATA CORPORATION
5405 Alton Pkwy (92604-3717)

PHONE..............................949 900-6040
EMP: 100
SIC: 3663 Mobile communication equipment

(P-8497)
ASTRA COMMUNICATIONS INC
1101 Chestnut St (91506-1624)
P.O. Box 391 (91503-0391)
PHONE..............................818 859-7305
Scott Bassett, *Pr*
Craig Bassett, *VP*
Kim Walsh, *Sec*
EMP: 18 **EST:** 1981
SQ FT: 11,000
SALES (est): 2.35MM **Privately Held**
Web: www.astracomm.com
SIC: 3663 Mobile communication equipment

(P-8498)
**ATX NETWORKS (SAN DIEGO)
CORP (DH)**
8880 Rehco Rd (92121-3265)
PHONE..............................858 546-5050
Dan Whalen, *Pr*
Ian A Lerner, *Chief Product Officer**
Carlos Shteremberg, *
Anthony Tibbs, *
Andrew Isherwood, *
◆ **EMP:** 27 **EST:** 1983
SQ FT: 7,000
SALES (est): 24.76MM
SALES (corp-wide): 107.62MM **Privately
Held**
Web: www.atx.com
SIC: 3663 5065 3678 Radio and t.v.
   communications equipment; Electronic
   parts and equipment, nec; Electronic
   connectors
HQ: Atx Networks Corp
   1602 Tricont Ave Unit 8
   Whitby ON
   905 428-6068

(P-8499)
BITTREE INCORPORATED
600 W Elk Ave (91204-1404)
P.O. Box 3764 (91221-0764)
PHONE..............................818 500-8142
▲ **EMP:** 29 **EST:** 1977
SALES (est): 2.12MM **Privately Held**
Web: www.bittree.com
SIC: 3663 Radio and t.v. communications
   equipment

(P-8500)
**BOEING SATELLITE SYSTEMS
INC (HQ)**
Also Called: Boeing
900 N Pacific Coast Hwy (90245-2710)
P.O. Box 92919 (90009-2919)
PHONE..............................310 791-7450
◆ **EMP:** 25 **EST:** 1995
SALES (est): 1.23B
SALES (corp-wide): 66.61B **Publicly Held**
Web: www.boeing.com
SIC: 3663 Satellites, communications
PA: The Boeing Company
   929 Long Bridge Dr
   Arlington VA
   703 414-6338

(P-8501)
**BROADCAST MICROWAVE
SVCS LLC (PA)**
Also Called: B M S
13475 Danielson St Ste 130 (92064-6825)
PHONE..............................858 391-3050
Harry Davoody, *CEO*
Mike Sieglen, *

Kristina Clark, *
EMP: 109 **EST:** 1982
SQ FT: 37,000
SALES (est): 23.63MM
SALES (corp-wide): 23.63MM **Privately
Held**
Web: www.bms-inc.com
SIC: 3663 Microwave communication
   equipment

(P-8502)
CALAMP CORP
1401 N Rice Ave (93030-7934)
PHONE..............................949 600-5600
EMP: 96
SALES (corp-wide): 294.95MM **Publicly
Held**
Web: www.calamp.com
SIC: 3663 Microwave communication
   equipment
PA: Calamp Corp.
   15635 Alton Pkwy Ste 250
   Irvine CA
   949 600-5600

(P-8503)
CALAMP CORP
2200 Faraday Ave Ste 220 (92008-7234)
PHONE..............................760 444-0952
EMP: 26
SALES (corp-wide): 294.95MM **Publicly
Held**
Web: www.calamp.com
SIC: 3663 Radio and t.v. communications
   equipment
PA: Calamp Corp.
   15635 Alton Pkwy Ste 250
   Irvine CA
   949 600-5600

(P-8504)
CENTRON INDUSTRIES INC
441 W Victoria St (90248-3528)
PHONE..............................310 324-6443
Yong W Kim, *CEO*
Hye S Kim, *Sec*
◆ **EMP:** 37 **EST:** 1984
SQ FT: 10,000
SALES (est): 8.95MM **Privately Held**
Web: www.centronind.com
SIC: 3663 Radio and t.v. communications
   equipment

(P-8505)
CPI MALIBU DIVISION
3623 Old Conejo Rd Ste 205 (91320-0803)
PHONE..............................805 383-1829
Joel Littman, *CFO*
EMP: 80 **EST:** 1975
SALES (est): 15.47MM **Privately Held**
SIC: 3663 Antennas, transmitting and
   communications
HQ: Communications & Power Industries
   Llc
   811 Hansen Way
   Palo Alto CA

(P-8506)
**CPI SATCOM & ANTENNA TECH
INC**
3111 Fujita St (90505-4006)
PHONE..............................310 539-6704
Sandra Seto, *Brnch Mgr*
EMP: 221
Web: www.cpii.com
SIC: 3663 Antennas, transmitting and
   communications
HQ: Cpi Satcom & Antenna Technologies
   Inc.
   1700 Cable Dr Ne

Conover NC
704 462-7330

(P-8507)
D X COMMUNICATIONS INC
Also Called: Tpl Communications
8160 Van Nuys Blvd (91402-4806)
PHONE..............................323 256-3000
Richard H Myers, *CEO*
Richard Myers, *
John Ehret, *
EMP: 28 **EST:** 1971
SALES (est): 4.22MM **Privately Held**
Web: www.tplcom.com
SIC: 3663 Satellites, communications

(P-8508)
**DENSO WIRELESS SYSTEMS
AMERICA INC**
2251 Rutherford Rd # 100 (92008-8815)
PHONE..............................760 734-4600
◆ **EMP:** 191
SIC: 3663 3714 Cellular radio telephone;
   Motor vehicle electrical equipment

(P-8509)
DJH ENTERPRISES
Also Called: Channel Vision Technology
23011 Moulton Pkwy Ste B6 (92653-1222)
PHONE..............................714 424-6500
◆ **EMP:** 35 **EST:** 1993
SALES (est): 4.8MM **Privately Held**
SIC: 3663 Radio and t.v. communications
   equipment

(P-8510)
DRACO BROADCAST INC
2000 N Lincoln St (91504-3333)
PHONE..............................818 736-5788
Aaron Street, *Genl Mgr*
EMP: 29
SALES (corp-wide): 965.03K **Privately
Held**
Web: www.dracobroadcast.com
SIC: 3663 Radio and t.v. communications
   equipment
PA: Draco Broadcast Inc
   9265 Commerce Hwy
   Pennsauken NJ
   856 324-2892

(P-8511)
DYNAMIC SCIENCES INTL INC
9400 Lurline Ave Unit B (91311-6022)
PHONE..............................818 226-6262
Eli Shiri, *Pr*
Robert Cook, *
Oren Shiri, *
EMP: 35 **EST:** 1972
SQ FT: 20,000
SALES (est): 3.24MM **Privately Held**
SIC: 3663 Radio receiver networks

(P-8512)
E-BAND COMMUNICATIONS LLC
17034 Camino San Bernardo (92127-5708)
PHONE..............................858 408-0660
Jamal Hamdani, *CEO*
Saul Umbrasas, *
Russ Kinsch, *
EMP: 30 **EST:** 2003
SALES (est): 5.74MM
SALES (corp-wide): 84.02MM **Privately
Held**
Web: www.e-band.com
SIC: 3663 Carrier equipment, radio
   communications
PA: Axxcss Wireless Solutions Inc
   82 Coromar Dr
   Goleta CA
   805 968-9621

▲ = Import ▼ = Export
◆ = Import/Export

(P-8513)
ECTRON CORPORATION
9340 Hazard Way Ste B2 (92123-1228)
PHONE..............................858 278-0600
E Earl Cunningham, *Pr*
Carol C Cunningham, *
Karl E Cunningham, *
EMP: 50 **EST:** 1964
SALES (est): 11.78MM **Privately Held**
Web: www.ectron.com
SIC: 3663 3829 3577 3823 Amplifiers, RF power and IF; Measuring and controlling devices, nec; Data conversion equipment, media-to-media: computer; Process control instruments

(P-8514)
EMPOWER RF SYSTEMS INC (PA)
Also Called: Empower Rf
316 W Florence Ave (90301-1104)
PHONE..............................310 412-8100
Barry Phelps, *Ch Bd*
Jon Jacocks, *
Larisa Stanisic, *
EMP: 76 **EST:** 1999
SQ FT: 30,000
SALES (est): 21MM
SALES (corp-wide): 21MM **Privately Held**
Web: www.empowerrf.com
SIC: 3663 Amplifiers, RF power and IF

(P-8515)
ENSEMBLE COMMUNICATIONS INC
2223 Avenida De La Playa (92037-3200)
PHONE..............................858 458-1400
Rami Hadar, *Pr*
Sheldon Gilbert, *
EMP: 140 **EST:** 1997
SQ FT: 63,000
SALES (est): 10.39MM **Privately Held**
SIC: 3663 Radio and t.v. communications equipment

(P-8516)
ESCAPE COMMUNICATIONS INC
2790 Skypark Dr Ste 203 (90505-5345)
PHONE..............................310 997-1300
Micheal Stewart, *Pr*
Gregory Caso Ph.D., *Ex VP*
James Nadeau, *Sec*
EMP: 17 **EST:** 1998
SQ FT: 5,300
SALES (est): 2.29MM **Privately Held**
Web: www.escapecom.com
SIC: 3663 8711 8731 Microwave communication equipment; Engineering services; Commercial physical research

(P-8517)
FEI-ZYFER INC (HQ)
7321 Lincoln Way (92841-1428)
PHONE..............................714 933-4000
Steve Strang, *Pr*
EMP: 31 **EST:** 1997
SQ FT: 50,000
SALES (est): 57.77MM
SALES (corp-wide): 40.78MM **Publicly Held**
Web: www.fei-zyfer.com
SIC: 3663 Television broadcasting and communications equipment
PA: Frequency Electronics, Inc.
55 Charles Lindbergh Blvd # 2
Uniondale NY
516 794-4500

(P-8518)
FLEET MANAGEMENT SOLUTIONS INC
310 Commerce Ste 100 (92602-1360)
PHONE..............................800 500-6009
Tony Eales, *CEO*
EMP: 26 **EST:** 2002
SALES (est): 8.53MM
SALES (corp-wide): 3.18B **Publicly Held**
Web:
www.fleetmanagementsolutions.com
SIC: 3663 4899 Radio and t.v. communications equipment; Satellite earth stations
HQ: Teletrac Navman (Uk) Ltd
First Floor
Milton Keynes BUCKS

(P-8519)
FLO TV INCORPORATED
5775 Morehouse Dr (92121-1714)
PHONE..............................858 651-1645
Gilbert P John, *Prin*
EMP: 45 **EST:** 2004
SALES (est): 4.09MM
SALES (corp-wide): 44.2B **Publicly Held**
Web: www.flotv.com
SIC: 3663 Transmitting apparatus, radio or television
PA: Qualcomm Incorporated
5775 Morehouse Dr
San Diego CA
858 587-1121

(P-8520)
GLOBAL MICROWAVE SYSTEMS INC
Also Called: G M S
1916 Palomar Oaks Way Ste 100 (92008-6510)
PHONE..............................760 496-0046
EMP: 47
SIC: 3663 7359 Microwave communication equipment; Business machine and electronic equipment rental services

(P-8521)
HADRIAN AUTOMATION INC
Also Called: Hadrian
19501 S Western Ave (90501-1116)
PHONE..............................503 807-4490
Christopher Power, *CEO*
Lars Lider, *
Sarah Annin, *
Dave Malcher, *Head OF Finance**
EMP: 100 **EST:** 2018
SALES (est): 9.58MM **Privately Held**
Web: www.hadrian.co
SIC: 3663 Space satellite communications equipment

(P-8522)
HBC SOLUTIONS HOLDINGS LLC
10877 Wilshire Blvd Fl 18 (90024-4373)
PHONE..............................321 727-9100
Daniel Abrams, *Managing Member*
EMP: 23 **EST:** 2013
SALES (est): 492.84K **Privately Held**
SIC: 3663 Radio broadcasting and communications equipment

(P-8523)
HILLSIDE CAPITAL INC
6222 Fallbrook Ave (91367-1601)
PHONE..............................650 367-2011
Becky Tran, *Pr*
EMP: 115 **EST:** 2008
SALES (est): 10.87MM **Privately Held**
SIC: 3663 Radio and t.v. communications equipment

(P-8524)
IMPAC TECHNOLOGIES INC
Also Called: Impac Technologies
3050 Red Hill Ave (92626-4524)
PHONE..............................714 427-2000
Louis Parker, *Pr*
EMP: 21 **EST:** 1992
SQ FT: 24,000
SALES (est): 585.02K **Privately Held**
Web: www.ozgift.com
SIC: 3663 Radio and t.v. communications equipment

(P-8525)
INGENU INC (PA)
Also Called: Ingenu
10301 Meanley Dr (92131-3011)
P.O. Box 22628 (92192-2628)
PHONE..............................858 ...
EMP: 20 **EST:** 2008
SALES (est): 10.41MM **Privately Held**
Web: www.ingenu.com
SIC: 3663 Radio and t.v. communications equipment

(P-8526)
INTERDIGITAL INC
Also Called: INTERDIGITAL, INC.
9276 Scranton Rd Ste 300 (92121-7700)
PHONE..............................858 210-4800
Julie Mcdonough, *Brnch Mgr*
EMP: 35
SALES (corp-wide): 457.79MM **Publicly Held**
Web: www.interdigital.com
SIC: 3663 Mobile communication equipment
HQ: Interdigital Wireless, Inc.
200 Bellevue Pkwy Ste 300
Wilmington DE

(P-8527)
KATZ MILLENNIUM SLS & MKTG INC
Also Called: Clear Channel Radio Sales
5700 Wilshire Blvd Ste 100 (90036-3659)
PHONE..............................323 966-5066
Nathan Brown, *Mgr*
EMP: 227
SIC: 3663 Radio receiver networks
HQ: Katz Millennium Sales & Marketing Inc.
125 W 55th St Frnt 3
New York NY

(P-8528)
KWORLD (USA) COMPUTER INC
499 Nibus Ste D (92821-3211)
PHONE..............................626 581-0867
Chung-chieh Wang, *Pr*
▲ **EMP:** 22 **EST:** 2002
SQ FT: 4,600
SALES (est): 4.51MM **Privately Held**
Web: www.kguardsecurity.com
SIC: 3663 Cable television equipment
PA: Kworld Computer Co.,Ltd
6f, 113, Chien 2nd Rd.,
New Taipei City TAP

(P-8529)
KYOCERA AVX CMPNNTS SAN DEGO I (DH)
Also Called: AVX Antenna, Inc.
5501 Oberlin Dr Ste 100 (92121-1718)
PHONE..............................858 550-3820
Laurent Desclos, *Pr*
Laurent Desclos, *CEO*
Vahid Manian, *COO*
Rick Johnson, *CFO*
Sebastian Rowson, *Chief Scientist*
▲ **EMP:** 21 **EST:** 2000
SALES (est): 9.59MM **Privately Held**
Web: www.kyocera-avx.com
SIC: 3663 Antennas, transmitting and communications
HQ: Kyocera Avx Components Corporation
1 Avx Blvd
Fountain Inn SC
864 967-2150

(P-8530)
L3 APPLIED TECHNOLOGIES INC (DH)
Also Called: Pulse Sciences
10180 Barnes Canyon Rd Ste 100 (92121-2724)
PHONE..............................858 404-7824
Michael T Strainese, *CEO*
Robert A Huffman, *
▼ **EMP:** 24 **EST:** 2011
SALES (est): 24.5MM
SALES (corp-wide): 17.06B **Publicly Held**
SIC: 3663 3669 3769 Telemetering equipment, electronic; Signaling apparatus, electric; Space vehicle equipment, nec
HQ: L3 Technologies, Inc.
600 3rd Ave Fl 34
New York NY
321 727-9100

(P-8531)
L3 TECHNOLOGIES INC
Also Called: L-3 Telemetry & Rf Products
9020 Balboa Ave (92123-1510)
PHONE..............................858 279-0411
Burt Smith, *Brnch Mgr*
EMP: 358
SALES (corp-wide): 17.06B **Publicly Held**
Web: www.l3harris.com
SIC: 3663 3669 3812 3679 Telemetering equipment, electronic; Signaling apparatus, electric; Search and navigation equipment; Microwave components
HQ: L3 Technologies, Inc.
600 3rd Ave Fl 34
New York NY
321 727-9100

(P-8532)
L3 TECHNOLOGIES INC
L3 Rccs
10180 Barnes Canyon Rd (92121-2724)
PHONE..............................858 552-9716
Jonathan Roy, *CFO*
EMP: 100
SALES (corp-wide): 17.06B **Publicly Held**
Web: www.l3harris.com
SIC: 3663 Telemetering equipment, electronic
HQ: L3 Technologies, Inc.
600 3rd Ave Fl 34
New York NY
321 727-9100

(P-8533)
L3 TECHNOLOGIES INC
Also Called: Communction Systms-Wst/ Lnkabit
9020 Balboa Ave (92123-1510)
PHONE..............................858 552-9500
Andrew Ivers, *Brnch Mgr*
EMP: 325
SALES (corp-wide): 17.06B **Publicly Held**
Web: www.l3harris.com
SIC: 3663 Space satellite communications equipment
HQ: L3 Technologies, Inc.
600 3rd Ave Fl 34
New York NY
321 727-9100

PRODUCTS & SVCS

(P-8534)
L3 TECHNOLOGIES INC
Also Called: Mariplro
7414 Hollister Ave (93117-2583)
PHONE...................................805 683-3881
EMP: 90
SALES (corp-wide): 17.06B **Publicly Held**
Web: www.l3harris.com
SIC: 3663 Telemetering equipment,
electronic
HQ: L3 Technologies, Inc.
600 3rd Ave Fl 34
New York NY
321 727-9100

(P-8535)
L3 TECHNOLOGIES INC
15825 Roxford St (91342-3537)
PHONE...................................818 367-0111
EMP: 142
SALES (corp-wide): 17.06B **Publicly Held**
Web: www.l3harris.com
SIC: 3663 Radio and t.v. communications
equipment
HQ: L3 Technologies, Inc.
600 3rd Ave Fl 34
New York NY
321 727-9100

(P-8536)
L3 TECHNOLOGIES INC
602 E Vermont Ave (92805-5607)
PHONE...................................714 758-4222
Robert Vanwechel, *Brnch Mgr*
EMP: 220
SALES (corp-wide): 17.06B **Publicly Held**
Web: www.l3harris.com
SIC: 3663 Telemetering equipment,
electronic
HQ: L3 Technologies, Inc.
600 3rd Ave Fl 34
New York NY
321 727-9100

(P-8537)
**L3HARRIS INTERSTATE ELEC
CORP**
604 E Vermont Ave (92805-5607)
PHONE...................................714 758-3395
Thomas Jackson, *Brnch Mgr*
EMP: 50
SALES (corp-wide): 17.06B **Publicly Held**
Web: www.l3harris.com
SIC: 3663 3621 Telemetering equipment,
electronic; Motors and generators
HQ: L3harris Interstate Electronics
Corporation
602 E Vermont Ave
Anaheim CA
714 758-0500

(P-8538)
LENNTEK CORPORATION
Also Called: Sonix
1610 Lockness Pl (90501-5119)
PHONE...................................310 534-2738
Danny Tsai, *Prin*
▲ EMP: 50 EST: 2007
SQ FT: 15,000
SALES (est): 6.18MM **Privately Held**
Web: www.shopsonix.com
SIC: 3663 Mobile communication equipment

(P-8539)
LIFESINNOVATIONS INC
6312 W 77th St (90045-1301)
PHONE...................................866 603-8456
Vic Hevoyan, *Pr*
EMP: 34
SALES (corp-wide): 400.15K **Privately
Held**

Web: www.lifesinnovations.com
SIC: 3663 Mobile communication equipment
PA: Lifesinnovations, Inc.
20938 Normandie Ave
Torrance CA
866 603-8456

(P-8540)
MAINLINE EQUIPMENT INC
Also Called: Mainline
20917 Higgins Ct (90501-1723)
PHONE...................................800 444-2288
EMP: 52 EST: 1986
SALES (est): 8.32MM **Privately Held**
Web: www.main-line-inc.com
SIC: 3663 7629 Satellites, communications;
Electrical equipment repair services

(P-8541)
MANLEY LABORATORIES INC
Also Called: Manufacturing
13880 Magnolia Ave (91710-7027)
PHONE...................................909 627-4256
Eveanna Manley, *Pr*
Eveanna Manley-collins, *Pr*
▲ EMP: 32 EST: 1992
SQ FT: 11,000
SALES (est): 6.53MM **Privately Held**
Web: www.manley.com
SIC: 3663 3651 Radio and t.v.
communications equipment; Audio
electronic systems

(P-8542)
**MARITIME TELECOM NETWRK
INC (DH)**
Also Called: Mtn Satellite Communications
6080 Center Dr Ste 1200 (90045-9209)
◆ EMP: 200 EST: 1990
SALES (est): 50.67MM **Privately Held**
SIC: 3663 Satellites, communications
HQ: Emerging Markets Communications,
Llc
1821 E Dyer Rd Ste 125
Santa Ana CA

(P-8543)
MARKETSPARK SUB INC ✪
Also Called: Marketspark
750 B St Ste 1630 (92101-8131)
PHONE...................................844 900-0599
Jeff Gower, *CEO*
Patrick Burns, *
Joe Kalinoski, *
EMP: 55 EST: 2023
SALES (est): 9.54MM **Privately Held**
SIC: 3663 Receivers, radio communications

(P-8544)
MICRO-MODE PRODUCTS INC
1870 John Towers Ave (92020-1193)
PHONE...................................619 449-3844
Vincent De Marco, *Pr*
Michael Cuban, *
Ruby Marco, *
EMP: 170 EST: 1971
SALES (est): 49.31MM
SALES (corp-wide): 2.99B **Publicly Held**
Web: www.micromode.com
SIC: 3663 3678 7389 Microwave
communication equipment; Electronic
connectors; Business services, nec
PA: Itt Inc.
100 Washington Blvd Fl 6
Stamford CT
914 641-2000

(P-8545)
MICROWAVE DYNAMICS LLC
16541 Scientific (92618-4356)
PHONE...................................949 679-7788
Shoja Peter Adel, *CEO*
Brian Adel, *Sec*
EMP: 18 EST: 1992
SQ FT: 10,000
SALES (est): 2.35MM **Privately Held**
Web: www.microwave-dynamics.com
SIC: 3663 5065 Microwave communication
equipment; Electronic parts and equipment,
nec

(P-8546)
**MILLENNIUM SPACE SYSTEMS
INC (HQ)**
2265 E El Segundo Blvd (90245-4608)
PHONE...................................310 683-5840
Stan Dubyn, *CEO*
Tiffany Guthrie, *COO*
Laura White, *CFO*
EMP: 32 EST: 2001
SQ FT: 10,000
SALES (est): 100.84MM
SALES (corp-wide): 66.61B **Publicly Held**
Web: www.millennium-space.com
SIC: 3663 Space satellite communications
equipment
PA: The Boeing Company
929 Long Bridge Dr
Arlington VA
703 414-6338

(P-8547)
MISSION MICROWAVE TECH LLC
6060 Phyllis Dr (90630-5243)
PHONE...................................951 893-4925
Francis Auricchio, *CEO*
Michael Delisio, *
John Ocampo, *
EMP: 70 EST: 2014
SALES (est): 10.1MM **Privately Held**
Web: www.missionmicrowave.com
SIC: 3663 Satellites, communications

(P-8548)
**MODULAR COMMUNICATIONS
SYSTEMS**
Also Called: Moducom
2629 Foothill Blvd (91214-3511)
PHONE...................................818 764-1333
Robert A Moesch, *Pr*
Bernard Brandt, *VP*
Peter Hong, *VP Opers*
EMP: 22 EST: 1978
SALES (est): 2.62MM **Privately Held**
Web: www.moducom.com
SIC: 3663 Radio and t.v. communications
equipment

(P-8549)
MOPHIE INC (DH)
15495 Sand Canyon Ave Ste 400
(92618-3153)
PHONE...................................888 866-7443
Daniel Huang, *CEO*
▲ EMP: 17 EST: 2005
SALES (est): 54.95MM
SALES (corp-wide): 521.92MM **Privately
Held**
Web: www.zagg.com
SIC: 3663 Mobile communication equipment
HQ: Zagg Inc
910 W Legacy Center Way # 5
Midvale UT

(P-8550)
**MOSELEY ASSOCIATES INC
(HQ)**
Also Called: Moseley
82 Coromar Dr (93117-3024)
PHONE...................................805 968-9621
Jamal N Hamdani, *Pr*
Bruce Tarr, *
▲ EMP: 76 EST: 1961
SQ FT: 56,000
SALES (est): 23.96MM
SALES (corp-wide): 79.92MM **Privately
Held**
Web: www.moseleysb.com
SIC: 3663 Radio and t.v. communications
equipment
PA: Axxcss Wireless Solutions Inc
82 Coromar Dr
Goleta CA
805 968-9621

(P-8551)
MTI LABORATORY INC
Also Called: Mtil
201 Continental Blvd Ste 300 (90245-4500)
PHONE...................................310 955-3700
Davis Kent, *Pr*
Alister Hsu, *CFO*
▼ EMP: 26 EST: 2006
SQ FT: 12,000
SALES (est): 6.7MM **Privately Held**
Web: www.mtigroup.com
SIC: 3663 Microwave communication
equipment
PA: Microelectronics Technology, Inc.
No. 1, Chuangxin 2nd Rd., Science-
Based Industrial Park,
Hsinchu City

(P-8552)
**NAVCOM TECHNOLOGY INC
(HQ)**
20780 Madrona Ave (90503-3777)
PHONE...................................310 381-2000
Tony Thelen, *CEO*
Craig Fawcept, *
Michael Linzy, *
EMP: 100 EST: 1997
SQ FT: 55,000
SALES (est): 20.38MM
SALES (corp-wide): 52.58B **Publicly Held**
Web: www.navcomtech.com
SIC: 3663 8748 Satellites, communications;
Communications consulting
PA: Deere & Company
1 John Deere Pl
Moline IL
309 765-8000

(P-8553)
NERDIST CHANNEL LLC
Also Called: Nerdist Industries
2900 W Alameda Ave Unit 1500
(91505-4220)
PHONE...................................818 333-2705
EMP: 30 EST: 2011
SALES (est): 5.93MM **Privately Held**
Web: www.nerdist.com
SIC: 3663 Digital encoders

(P-8554)
NEXTIVITY INC (PA)
16550 W Bernardo Dr Ste 550
(92127-1870)
PHONE...................................858 485-9442
Werner Sievers, *CEO*
Michiel Lotter, *
Carol Lee, *
George Lamb, *
Thomas Cooper, *Business Development**

▲ **EMP:** 49 **EST:** 2006
SALES (est): 52.55MM **Privately Held**
Web: www.cel-fi.com
SIC: 3663 Airborne radio communications
　equipment

(P-8555)
**NORTHROP GRUMMAN
SYSTEMS CORP**
Space Systems Division
1 Space Park Blvd (90278-1071)
PHONE.........................310 812-5149
EMP: 101
Web: www.northropgrumman.com
SIC: 3663 3674 3679 3761 Airborne radio
　communications equipment;
　Semiconductors and related devices;
　Antennas, satellite: household use; Guided
　missiles and space vehicles
HQ: Northrop Grumman Systems
　　Corporation
　　2980 Fairview Park Dr
　　Falls Church VA
　　703 280-2900

(P-8556)
OPHIR RF INC
Also Called: Ophir Rf
5300 Beethoven St Fl 3 (90066-7015)
PHONE.........................310 306-5556
Ilan Israely, *Pr*
Albert Barrios, *
EMP: 42 **EST:** 1992
SQ FT: 11,800
SALES (est): 9.04MM **Privately Held**
Web: www.ophirrf.com
SIC: 3663 Amplifiers, RF power and IF

(P-8557)
OPTODYNE INCORPORATION
21345 Hawthorne Blvd Unit 203
(90503-5656)
PHONE.........................310 635-7481
Charles Wang, *CEO*
Lichen Wang, *VP*
Lily Wang, *Sec*
▲ **EMP:** 20 **EST:** 1986
SALES (est): 848.39K **Privately Held**
SIC: 3663 3829 3827 Light communications
　equipment; Measuring and controlling
　devices, nec; Optical instruments and
　lenses

(P-8558)
OVATION R&G LLC (PA)
2850 Ocean Park Blvd Ste 225
(90405-2955)
PHONE.........................310 430-7575
Ken Solomon, *
Phil Gilligan, *
Liz Janneman, *
Brad Samuels, *
EMP: 19 **EST:** 2009
SALES (est): 3MM **Privately Held**
Web: www.ovationtv.com
SIC: 3663 Satellites, communications

(P-8559)
PACIFIC WAVE SYSTEMS INC
2525 W 190th St (90504-6002)
PHONE.........................714 893-0152
Carl Esposito, *CEO*
John J Tus, *
Victor Jay Miller, *
Robert B Topolski, *
EMP: 68 **EST:** 1992
SALES (est): 9.87MM **Privately Held**
Web: www.pacificwavesystems.com
SIC: 3663 Satellites, communications

(P-8560)
PEARPOINT INC
39740 Garand Ln Ste B (92211-7176)
PHONE.........................760 343-7350
Paul Tistai, *CEO*
Vince Monteleone, *
EMP: 46 **EST:** 1987
SQ FT: 15,000
SALES (est): 2.3MM
SALES (corp-wide): 30.44MM **Privately
Held**
Web: global.pearpoint.com
SIC: 3663 3829 5065 Television closed
　circuit equipment; Measuring and
　controlling devices, nec; Closed circuit TV
HQ: Radiodetection Limited
　　Western Drive
　　Bristol
　　117 976-7776

(P-8561)
PHONESUIT INC
1431 7th St Ste 201 (90401-2603)
PHONE.........................310 774-0282
Sumeet Gupta, *CEO*
EMP: 25 **EST:** 2012
SQ FT: 4,000
SALES (est): 2.42MM **Privately Held**
Web: www.phonesuit.com
SIC: 3663 Mobile communication equipment

(P-8562)
PROSHOT INVESTORS LLC
Also Called: Proshot Golf
14 Corporate Plaza Dr Ste 120
(92660-7995)
P.O. Box 9939 (92658-1939)
PHONE.........................949 586-9500
David Kuhn, *Pr*
▲ **EMP:** 18 **EST:** 2001
SALES (est): 1.41MM
SALES (corp-wide): 1.8MM **Privately Held**
Web: www.proshotgolf.com
SIC: 3663 Global positioning systems (GPS)
　equipment
PA: Prelude Financial, Inc.
　　2600 N Central Ave # 1700
　　Phoenix AZ
　　480 626-2423

(P-8563)
**QUALCOMM INCORPORATED
(PA)**
Also Called: Qualcomm
5775 Morehouse Dr (92121-1714)
PHONE.........................858 587-1121
Cristiano R Amon, *Pr*
Mark D Mclaughlin, *Ch Bd*
Akash Palkhiwala, *CFO*
James J Cathey, *CCO*
EMP: 1430 **EST:** 1985
SALES (est): 35.82B
SALES (corp-wide): 35.82B **Publicly Held**
Web: www.qualcomm.com
SIC: 3663 3674 7372 6794 Mobile
　communication equipment; Semiconductors
　and related devices; Business oriented
　computer software; Patent buying,
　licensing, leasing

(P-8564)
QUALCOMM INCORPORATED
Also Called: Qualcomm
4243 Campus Point Ct (92121-1513)
PHONE.........................858 587-1121
EMP: 41
SALES (corp-wide): 35.82B **Publicly Held**
Web: www.qualcomm.com
SIC: 3663 Radio and t.v. communications
　equipment

PA: Qualcomm Incorporated
　　5775 Morehouse Dr
　　San Diego CA
　　858 587-1121

(P-8565)
**RADIAN AUDIO ENGINEERING
INC**
2720 Kimball Ave (91767-2200)
PHONE.........................714 288-8900
Richard Kontrimas, *CEO*
Raimonda Kontrimas, *Sec*
◆ **EMP:** 20 **EST:** 1988
SALES (est): 2.26MM **Privately Held**
Web: www.radianaudio.com
SIC: 3663 5731 3651 Radio broadcasting
　and communications equipment; Radio,
　television, and electronic stores; Household
　audio and video equipment

(P-8566)
RAMONA RESEARCH INC
13741 Danielson St Ste J (92064-6895)
PHONE.........................858 679-0717
EMP: 19 **EST:** 2002
SALES (est): 5.63MM **Publicly Held**
Web: www.ramonaresearch.com
SIC: 3663 Microwave communication
　equipment
PA: Heico Corporation
　　3000 Taft St
　　Hollywood FL

(P-8567)
**RANTEC MICROWAVE
SYSTEMS INC**
Microwave Specialty Company
2066 Wineridge Pl (92029-1930)
PHONE.........................760 744-1544
Ben Walpole, *Pr*
EMP: 27
SALES (corp-wide): 12.58MM **Privately
Held**
Web: www.rantecantennas.com
SIC: 3663 Radio and t.v. communications
　equipment
PA: Rantec Microwave Systems, Inc.
　　31186 La Baya Dr
　　Westlake Village CA
　　818 223-5000

(P-8568)
RAVEON TECHNOLOGIES CORP
2320 Cousteau Ct (92081-8363)
PHONE.........................760 444-5995
John Richard Sonnenberg, *Pr*
EMP: 37 **EST:** 2003
SQ FT: 7,300
SALES (est): 6.18MM **Privately Held**
Web: www.raveon.com
SIC: 3663 Airborne radio communications
　equipment

(P-8569)
**RAYTHEON APPLIED SGNAL
TECH IN**
2000 E El Segundo Blvd (90245-4501)
PHONE.........................310 436-7000
John R Treichler, *CEO*
EMP: 72
SALES (corp-wide): 67.07B **Publicly Held**
Web: www.appsig.com
SIC: 3663 8711 Radio and t.v.
　communications equipment; Engineering
　services
HQ: Raytheon Applied Signal Technology,
　　Inc.
　　100 Headquarters Dr
　　San Jose CA
　　408 749-1888

(P-8570)
**REMEC BRDBAND WRLESS
NTWRKS LL**
17034 Camino San Bernardo (92127-5708)
PHONE.........................858 312-6900
Jamal Hamdani, *CEO*
Bruce Tarr, *
EMP: 180 **EST:** 2015
SALES (est): 46.57MM
SALES (corp-wide): 79.92MM **Privately
Held**
Web: www.remecbroadband.com
SIC: 3663 Mobile communication equipment
PA: Axxcss Wireless Solutions Inc
　　82 Coromar Dr
　　Goleta CA
　　805 968-9621

(P-8571)
**REMEC BROADBAND
WIRELESS LLC**
17034 Camino San Bernardo (92127-5708)
PHONE.........................858 312-6900
David K Newman, *Managing Member*
EMP: 102 **EST:** 2005
SALES (est): 19.75MM **Privately Held**
Web: www.remecbroadband.com
SIC: 3663 Radio and t.v. communications
　equipment

(P-8572)
ROSELM INDUSTRIES INC
2510 Seaman Ave (91733-1928)
PHONE.........................626 442-6840
Conrad Arguijo, *Pr*
EMP: 20 **EST:** 1965
SQ FT: 13,000
SALES (est): 2.19MM **Privately Held**
Web: www.roselmindustries.com
SIC: 3663 Radio and t.v. communications
　equipment

(P-8573)
**ROTATING PRCSION
MCHANISMS INC**
Also Called: RPM
8750 Shirley Ave (91324-3409)
PHONE.........................818 349-9774
Kathy Flynn-nikolai, *CEO*
Daniel P Flynn, *
Jerome Smith, *Stockholder**
EMP: 46 **EST:** 1986
SQ FT: 40,000
SALES (est): 11.33MM **Privately Held**
Web: www.rpm-psi.com
SIC: 3663 Radio and t.v. communications
　equipment

(P-8574)
SALEM MUSIC NETWORK INC
4880 Santa Rosa Rd Ste 300 (93012-5190)
PHONE.........................805 987-0400
Stuart W Epperson, *Prin*
EMP: 17 **EST:** 2001
SALES (est): 796.98K **Privately Held**
SIC: 3663 Radio broadcasting and
　communications equipment

(P-8575)
**SATELLITE SECURITY
CORPORATION**
6779 Mesa Ridge Rd Ste 100 (92121-2996)
PHONE.........................877 437-4199
John Phillips, *CEO*
EMP: 26 **EST:** 1998
SALES (est): 1.51MM **Privately Held**
SIC: 3663 Space satellite communications
　equipment

PRODUCTS & SVCS

(P-8576)
SEASPACE CORPORATION
9155 Brown Deer Rd (92121-2260)
PHONE.....................858 746-1100
Eric Park, *CEO*
Erik Park, *
Daniel Lee, *
Jihong Park, *
EMP: 25 **EST:** 1982
SALES (est): 5.26MM **Privately Held**
Web: www.seaspace.com
SIC: 3663 3829 Satellites, communications;
  Measuring and controlling devices. nec

(P-8577)
SECURE COMM SYSTEMS INC
(HQ)
Also Called: Benchmark Secure Technology
1740 E Wilshire Ave (92705-4615)
PHONE.....................714 547-1174
Edward Hanrahan, *Pr*
Michael Buseman, *
Roop Lakkaraju, *
Kenneth Dorfman, *
▲ **EMP:** 147 **EST:** 2014
SQ FT: 38,000
SALES (est): 111.48MM
SALES (corp-wide): 2.89B **Publicly Held**
Web: www.bench.com
SIC: 3663 3829 3577 3571 Encryption
  devices; Vibration meters, analyzers, and
  calibrators; Computer peripheral
  equipment, nec; Electronic computers
PA: Benchmark Electronics, Inc.
  56 S Rockford Dr
  Tempe AZ
  623 300-7000

(P-8578)
SEKAI ELECTRONICS INC (PA)
38 Waterworks Way (92618-3107)
PHONE.....................949 783-5740
Roland Soohoo, *CEO*
EMP: 25 **EST:** 1982
SQ FT: 7,000
SALES (est): 4.95MM
SALES (corp-wide): 4.95MM **Privately
Held**
Web: www.sekai-electronics.com
SIC: 3663 5065 Radio and t.v.
  communications equipment; Video
  equipment, electronic

(P-8579)
SIDUS SOLUTIONS LLC
7352 Trade St (92121-2422)
P.O. Box 420698 (92142-0698)
PHONE.....................619 275-5533
Leonard Pool, *Managing Member*
EMP: 19 **EST:** 2000
SQ FT: 1,000
SALES (est): 5.1MM **Privately Held**
Web: www.sidus-solutions.com
SIC: 3663 Radio and t.v. communications
  equipment

(P-8580)
**SIERRA AUTOMATED SYS/ENG
CORP**
Also Called: Sierra Automated Systems
2821 Burton Ave (91504-3224)
PHONE.....................818 840-6749
Edward O Fritz, *Pr*
Al Salci, *VP*
EMP: 20 **EST:** 1987
SALES (est): 3.99MM **Privately Held**
Web: www.sasaudio.com
SIC: 3663 Radio broadcasting and
  communications equipment

(P-8581)
**SILVUS TECHNOLOGIES INC
(PA)**
10990 Wilshire Blvd Ste 1500 (90024-3913)
PHONE.....................310 479-3333
Babak Daneshrad, *Ch*
Jimi Henderson, *
Weijun Zhu, *
Gorik Hossepian, *
Eduardo Iniguez, *
EMP: 56 **EST:** 2004
SQ FT: 7,200
SALES (est): 25.27MM
SALES (corp-wide): 25.27MM **Privately
Held**
Web: www.silvustechnologies.com
SIC: 3663 8731 Radio and t.v.
  communications equipment; Commercial
  physical research

(P-8582)
SOLECTEK CORPORATION
8375 Camino Santa Fe Ste A (92121)
PHONE.....................858 450-1220
Seung Joon Lee, *CEO*
Eric Lee, *Pr*
◆ **EMP:** 20 **EST:** 1997
SQ FT: 10,000
SALES (est): 2.38MM **Privately Held**
Web: www.solectek.com
SIC: 3663 Television broadcasting and
  communications equipment

(P-8583)
SPACE MICRO INC
15378 Avenue Of Science Ste 200
(92128-3451)
PHONE.....................858 332-0700
David Czajkowski, *CEO*
David J Strobel, *
David R Czajkowski, *
Patricia Ellison, *
Michael Jacox, *
EMP: 107 **EST:** 2002
SALES (est): 22.3MM **Privately Held**
Web: www.spacemicro.com
SIC: 3663 Space satellite communications
  equipment

(P-8584)
STM NETWORKS INC
Also Called: Stm Wireless
2 Faraday (92618-2737)
PHONE.....................949 273-6800
Emil Youssefzadeh, *CEO*
Faramarz Yousefzaheh, *
Albert Yousefzaheh, *
Umar Javed, *
Bjorn Platou, *
▲ **EMP:** 32 **EST:** 2001
SQ FT: 22,000
SALES (est): 2.57MM **Privately Held**
SIC: 3663 Satellites, communications

(P-8585)
SUNBRITETV LLC (DH)
2630 Townsgate Rd Ste F (91361-2780)
PHONE.....................805 214-7250
Cameron Hill, *Managing Member*
▲ **EMP:** 19 **EST:** 2010
SALES (est): 13.71MM
SALES (corp-wide): 1.12B **Publicly Held**
Web: www.sunbritetv.com
SIC: 3663 Transmitting apparatus, radio or
  television
HQ: Sunbrite Holding Corporation
  2001 Anchor Ct
  Thousand Oaks CA
  805 214-7250

(P-8586)
**TACHYON NETWORKS
INCORPORATED**
9339 Carroll Park Dr Ste 150 (92121-3247)
PHONE.....................858 882-8100
Peter A Carides, *CEO*
Laurence A Hinz, *
EMP: 48 **EST:** 1997
SQ FT: 18,000
SALES (est): 3.69MM **Privately Held**
Web: www.tachyon.com
SIC: 3663 Antennas, transmitting and
  communications

(P-8587)
**TATUNG COMPANY AMERICA
INC (HQ)**
2157 Mount Shasta Dr (90732-1334)
PHONE.....................310 637-2105
Huei-jihn Jih, *Pr*
Danny Huang, *
Christina Sun, *
▲ **EMP:** 98 **EST:** 1972
SALES (est): 25.45MM **Privately Held**
Web: www.tatungusa.com
SIC: 3663 3575 3944 3651 Television closed
  circuit equipment; Computer terminals,
  monitors and components; Video game
  machines, except coin-operated; Television
  receiving sets
PA: Tatung Company
  22 Chungshan North Road,3rd Sec.,
  Taipei City TAP

(P-8588)
**TELEMTRY CMMNCTONS
SYSTEMS INC**
Also Called: TCS
10020 Remmet Ave (91311-3854)
PHONE.....................818 718-6248
Sarin Michel Roy, *Pr*
Mihail Mateescu, *
EMP: 24 **EST:** 1999
SQ FT: 14,500
SALES (est): 7.08MM
SALES (corp-wide): 44.96MM **Privately
Held**
Web: www.tcs.la
SIC: 3663 Antennas, transmitting and
  communications
PA: Delta Information Systems, Inc.
  747 Dresher Rd Ste 125
  Horsham PA
  215 657-5270

(P-8589)
**THOMSON REUTERS
CORPORATION**
Also Called: Reuters Television La
5161 Lankershim Blvd # 250 (91601-4963)
PHONE.....................877 518-2761
Kevin Regan, *Brnch Mgr*
EMP: 31
SALES (corp-wide): 10.66B **Publicly Held**
Web: www.thomsonreuters.com
SIC: 3663 Satellites, communications
HQ: Thomson Reuters Corporation
  333 Bay St
  Toronto ON
  416 687-7500

(P-8590)
**TRANSCOM
TELECOMMUNICATION INC**
1390 E Burnett St Ste C (90755-3559)
PHONE.....................562 424-9616
EMP: 19 **EST:** 2019
SALES (est): 2.51MM **Privately Held**
Web: www.transcomla.com

SIC: 3663 Radio and t.v. communications
  equipment

(P-8591)
TRICOM RESEARCH INC
17791 Sky Park Cir Ste J (92614-6118)
PHONE.....................949 250-6024
◆ **EMP:** 64
SQ FT: 25,000
SALES (est): 4.22MM **Privately Held**
SIC: 3663 Radio and t.v. communications
  equipment

(P-8592)
TRICOM RESEARCH INC
17791 Sky Park Cir Ste J (92614-6150)
PHONE.....................949 250-6024
Paula Wright, *Pr*
John W Wright, *
EMP: 64 **EST:** 2012
SALES (est): 6.46MM **Privately Held**
Web: www.tricomresearch.com
SIC: 3663 Radio and t.v. communications
  equipment

(P-8593)
ULTIMATTE CORPORATION
5828 Calvin Ave (91356-1111)
PHONE.....................818 993-8007
Lynne Sauve, *Pr*
Paul Vlahos, *
Nina Michalko, *
Petro Vlahos, *Stockholder**
▲ **EMP:** 31 **EST:** 1976
SALES (est): 5.98MM **Privately Held**
Web: www.blackmagicdesign.com
SIC: 3663 3651 7371 Television
  broadcasting and communications
  equipment; Household audio and video
  equipment; Computer software
  development and applications
PA: Blackmagic Design Pty Ltd
  180 Bank St
  South Melbourne VIC

(P-8594)
VIASAT INC
2426 Town Garden Rd (92009-3029)
PHONE.....................760 476-2129
EMP: 35
SALES (corp-wide): 2.56B **Publicly Held**
Web: www.viasat.com
SIC: 3663 Space satellite communications
  equipment
PA: Viasat, Inc.
  6155 El Camino Real
  Carlsbad CA
  760 476-2200

(P-8595)
VIASAT INC (PA)
Also Called: Viasat
6155 El Camino Real (92009-1602)
PHONE.....................760 476-2200
Mark Dankberg, *Ch Bd*
K Guru Gowrappan, *Pr*
Kevin Harkenrider, *Ex VP*
Mark Miller, *Ex VP*
Shawn Duffy, *Sr VP*
▲ **EMP:** 711 **EST:** 1986
SALES (est): 2.56B
SALES (corp-wide): 2.56B **Publicly Held**
Web: www.viasat.com
SIC: 3663 4899 Space satellite
  communications equipment; Data
  communication services

(P-8596)
VIGOR SYSTEMS INC
4660 La Jolla Village Dr Ste 500
(92122-4601)

▲ = Import ▼ = Export
◆ = Import/Export

PHONE..............................866 748-4467
Magnus Sorlander, *CEO*
Shayna Smith, *
▲ **EMP:** 35 **EST:** 2002
SALES (est): 7.75MM **Privately Held**
Web: www.edisen.com
SIC: 3663 Studio equipment, radio and television broadcasting

(P-8597)
W B WALTON ENTERPRISES INC
4185 Hallmark Pkwy (92407-1832)
P.O. Box 9010 (92427-0010)
PHONE..............................951 683-0930
William B Walton Junior, *Pr*
Jane Walton, *
EMP: 26 **EST:** 1979
SQ FT: 30,000
SALES (est): 4.94MM **Privately Held**
Web: www.de-ice.com
SIC: 3663 1731 Satellites, communications; Electrical work

(P-8598)
WATER ASSOCIATES LLC
Also Called: Redtrac
5060 California Ave (93309-0728)
PHONE..............................661 281-6077
Jeff Young, *Managing Member*
EMP: 20 **EST:** 2002
SALES (est): 4.29MM **Privately Held**
Web: www.red-trac.com
SIC: 3663 3523 Radio and t.v. communications equipment; Irrigation equipment, self-propelled

(P-8599)
WV COMMUNICATIONS INC
1125 Business Center Cir Ste A (91320)
PHONE..............................805 376-1820
Uri Yulzari, *Pr*
Jim Tranovich, *
Ron Bosi, *
▲ **EMP:** 40 **EST:** 1998
SQ FT: 18,000
SALES (est): 6.96MM **Privately Held**
Web: www.wv-comm.com
SIC: 3663 Microwave communication equipment

(P-8600)
YAESU USA INC
6125 Phyllis Dr (90630-5242)
PHONE..............................714 827-7600
Jun Hasegawa, *CEO*
▲ **EMP:** 40 **EST:** 2012
SALES (est): 5.14MM **Privately Held**
Web: www.yaesu.com
SIC: 3663 Radio and t.v. communications equipment

3669 Communications Equipment, Nec

(P-8601)
BDFCO INC
Also Called: Damac
1926 Kauai Dr (92626-3542)
PHONE..............................714 228-2900
Frank J Kubat Junior, *CEO*
Daniel L Davis, *
Robert Mc Clory, *Stockholder*
▲ **EMP:** 80 **EST:** 1984
SQ FT: 120,000
SALES (est): 6.78MM **Privately Held**
SIC: 3669 Intercommunication systems, electric

(P-8602)
BITMAX LLC (PA)
6255 W Sunset Blvd Ste 1515 (90028-7416)
PHONE..............................323 978-7878
Nancy Bennett, *Managing Member*
EMP: 18 **EST:** 1998
SQ FT: 7,500
SALES (est): 5.03MM
SALES (corp-wide): 5.03MM **Privately Held**
Web: www.bitmax.net
SIC: 3669 7929 Visual communication systems; Entertainment service

(P-8603)
CANOGA PERKINS CORPORATION (HQ)
20600 Prairie St (91311-6008)
PHONE..............................818 718-6300
Alfred Tim Champion, *Pr*
James Heney, *
◆ **EMP:** 100 **EST:** 1965
SQ FT: 64,000
SALES (est): 23.98MM
SALES (corp-wide): 645.5MM **Privately Held**
Web: www.canoga.com
SIC: 3669 Intercommunication systems, electric
PA: Rowan Technologies, Inc.
     10 Indel Ave
     Rancocas NJ
     609 267-9000

(P-8604)
CARRIER FIRE SEC AMERICAS CORP
Also Called: Utc, Mas
2955 Red Hill Ave Ste 100 (92626-1207)
PHONE..............................949 737-7800
Shin Voeks, *Genl Mgr*
EMP: 115
SALES (corp-wide): 20.42B **Publicly Held**
Web: corporate.carrier.com
SIC: 3669 5063 Burglar alarm apparatus, electric; Alarm systems, nec
HQ: Carrier Fire & Security Americas Corporation
     13995 Pasteur Blvd
     Palm Beach Gardens FL

(P-8605)
COMPUTER SERVICE COMPANY
Also Called: Steiny & Company
210 N Delilah St (92879-1883)
PHONE..............................951 738-1444
EMP: 49
SALES (corp-wide): 4.98MM **Privately Held**
SIC: 3669 7629 Traffic signals, electric; Electrical repair shops
PA: Computer Service Company
     5463 Diaz St
     Baldwin Park CA
     951 738-1444

(P-8606)
D-TECH OPTOELECTRONICS INC
18062 Rowland St (91748-1205)
PHONE..............................626 956-1100
An Baoxin, *Pr*
EMP: 20 **EST:** 2007
SALES (est): 2.33MM **Privately Held**
Web: www.dtechopto.com
SIC: 3669 Intercommunication systems, electric
PA: Gcs Holdings, Inc.
     115 S 4th St W

Missoula MT

(P-8607)
DEI HEADQUARTERS INC
Also Called: Sound United
3002 Wintergreen Dr (92008-6883)
PHONE..............................760 598-6200
James E Minarik, *Pr*
Kevin P Duffy, *
Veysel P Goker, *
Crystal L Biggs, *
Josh Talge, *CMO*
▲ **EMP:** 385 **EST:** 2002
SALES (est): 58.44MM **Privately Held**
SIC: 3669 Burglar alarm apparatus, electric
HQ: Dei Holdings, Inc.
     5541 Fermi Ct
     Carlsbad CA
     760 598-6200

(P-8608)
DEI HOLDINGS INC (HQ)
Also Called: Masimo Consumer
5541 Fermi Ct (92008-7348)
PHONE..............................760 598-6200
Kevin Duffy, *CEO*
Veysel Goker, *
Michael Simmons, *
Michael Smith, *
Crystal Biggs, *
◆ **EMP:** 30 **EST:** 1999
SQ FT: 198,000
SALES (est): 108.47MM **Privately Held**
Web: www.masimo.com
SIC: 3669 3651 Burglar alarm apparatus, electric; Amplifiers: radio, public address, or musical instrument
PA: Viper Holdings Corporation
     200 Clarendon St Fl 54
     Boston MA

(P-8609)
ECONOLITE CONTROL PRODUCTS INC (PA)
1250 N Tustin Ave (92807-1617)
P.O. Box 6150 (92816-0150)
PHONE..............................714 630-3700
Michael C Doyle, *Ch*
Christian Haas, *CEO*
John Tracey, *CFO*
▼ **EMP:** 160 **EST:** 1933
SQ FT: 95,000
SALES (est): 127.41MM
SALES (corp-wide): 127.41MM **Privately Held**
Web: www.econolite.com
SIC: 3669 Traffic signals, electric

(P-8610)
ESCO TECHNOLOGIES INC
501 Del Norte Blvd (93030-7983)
PHONE..............................805 604-3875
EMP: 22
Web: www.escotechnologies.com
SIC: 3669 Intercommunication systems, electric
PA: Esco Technologies Inc.
     9900 Clayton Rd Ste A
     Saint Louis MO

(P-8611)
EXIGENT SENSORS LLC
11441 Markon Dr (92841-1404)
PHONE..............................949 439-1321
Jeff Buss, *Managing Member*
▲ **EMP:** 20 **EST:** 2007
SALES (est): 6.63MM **Privately Held**
SIC: 3669 Fire alarm apparatus, electric

(P-8612)
GENERAL MONITORS INC (DH)
16782 Von Karman Ave Ste 14 (92606-2417)
PHONE..............................949 581-4464
Nishan J Vartanian, *CEO*
Richard Lamishaw, *
◆ **EMP:** 110 **EST:** 1961
SALES (est): 49.75MM
SALES (corp-wide): 1.53B **Publicly Held**
Web: us.msasafety.com
SIC: 3669 1799 3812 Fire detection systems, electric; Gas leakage detection; Infrared object detection equipment
HQ: Msa Safety Sales, Llc
     1000 Cranberry Woods Dr
     Cranberry Township PA
     800 672-2222

(P-8613)
H M ELECTRONICS INC
Also Called: H. M. ELECTRONICS, INC.
2848 Whiptail Loop (92010-6708)
PHONE..............................858 535-6139
Mike Grell, *Brnch Mgr*
EMP: 21
SALES (corp-wide): 452.77MM **Privately Held**
Web: www.hme.com
SIC: 3669 Intercommunication systems, electric
PA: H.M. Electronics, Inc.
     2848 Whiptail Loop
     Carlsbad CA
     858 535-6000

(P-8614)
INDYME SOLUTIONS LLC
8295 Aero Pl Ste 260 (92123-2029)
PHONE..............................858 268-0717
Joe Joseph Eudano, *CEO*
Bill Kepner, *
James Doss, *
Philip Joostens, *
EMP: 50 **EST:** 1980
SQ FT: 18,000
SALES (est): 9.64MM **Privately Held**
Web: www.indyme.com
SIC: 3669 Burglar alarm apparatus, electric

(P-8615)
INDYME SOLUTIONS LLC
8295 Aero Pl Ste 260 (92123-2029)
PHONE..............................858 268-0717
Steve Deal, *CEO*
Dan Patton, *
Larry Cleary, *
Jay Standiford, *
Bill Kepner, *
▲ **EMP:** 80 **EST:** 1989
SQ FT: 20,000
SALES (est): 10.52MM **Privately Held**
Web: www.indyme.com
SIC: 3669 3663 Burglar alarm apparatus, electric; Airborne radio communications equipment

(P-8616)
JOHNSON CNTRLS FIRE PRTCTION L
Also Called: Simplexgrinnell
3568 Ruffin Rd (92123-2597)
P.O. Box 23080 (92193-3080)
PHONE..............................858 633-9100
Bob Jamieson, *Brnch Mgr*
EMP: 150

PRODUCTS & SVCS

SIC: **3669** 1731 1711 3873 Emergency alarms; Fire detection and burglar alarm systems specialization; Fire sprinkler system installation; Watches, clocks, watchcases, and parts
HQ: Johnson Controls Fire Protection Lp
6600 Congress Ave
Boca Raton FL
561 988-7200

(P-8617)
JTB SUPPLY COMPANY INC
1030 N Batavia St Ste A (92867-5541)
PHONE.................................714 639-9558
Jeff York, *Pr*
EMP: 17 **EST:** 1998
SQ FT: 10,000
SALES (est): 1.63MM **Privately Held**
Web: www.jtbsupplyco.com
SIC: **3669** Traffic signals, electric

(P-8618)
OPTEX INCORPORATED
10741 Walker St (90630-4720)
PHONE.................................800 966-7839
Makoto Kokobo, *CEO*
Tohru Kobayashi, *Ch Bd*
James Quick, *Pr*
Michael La Chere, *VP*
▲ **EMP:** 40 **EST:** 1992
SALES (est): 10.31MM **Privately Held**
Web: www.optexamerica.com
SIC: **3669** Emergency alarms
PA: Optex Group Company, Limited
4-7-5, Nionohama
Otsu SGA

(P-8619)
PALOMAR PRODUCTS INC
23042 Arroyo Vis (92688-2617)
PHONE.................................949 766-5300
Kevin Moschetti, *CEO*
Val Policky, *
Fred Ekstein, *
EMP: 79 **EST:** 1995
SQ FT: 35,000
SALES (est): 24.24MM
SALES (corp-wide): 6.58B **Publicly Held**
Web: www.palomar.com
SIC: **3669** Intercommunication systems, electric
PA: Transdigm Group Incorporated
1301 E 9th St Ste 3000
Cleveland OH
216 706-2960

(P-8620)
PETER PEPPER PRODUCTS INC (PA)
Also Called: CONTRACT FURNITURE AND ANCILLA
17929 S Susana Rd (90221-5520)
P.O. Box 5769 (90224-5769)
PHONE.................................310 639-0390
◆ **EMP:** 65 **EST:** 1952
SALES (est): 171.68K
SALES (corp-wide): 171.68K **Privately Held**
Web: www.peterpepper.com
SIC: **3669** Visual communication systems

(P-8621)
PI VARIABLES INC
Also Called: PI Variables
3002 Dow Ave Ste 138 (92780-7248)
PHONE.................................949 415-9411
James Selevan, *CEO*
Kathleen Selevan, *Pr*
EMP: 20 **EST:** 2013
SALES (est): 2.57MM **Privately Held**

Web: www.pi-lit.com
SIC: **3669** Traffic signals, electric

(P-8622)
QUALCOMM MEMS TECHNOLOGIES INC
5775 Morehouse Dr (92121-1714)
PHONE.................................858 587-1121
Greg Heinzinger, *Sr VP*
Derek Aberle, *
EMP: 97 **EST:** 1998
SQ FT: 9,000
SALES (est): 24.82MM
SALES (corp-wide): 35.82B **Publicly Held**
SIC: **3669** Visual communication systems
PA: Qualcomm Incorporated
5775 Morehouse Dr
San Diego CA
858 587-1121

(P-8623)
RAYTHEON APPLIED SGNAL TECH IN
160 N Riverview Dr Ste 300 (92808)
PHONE.................................714 917-0255
John Mcgrory, *Brnch Mgr*
EMP: 93
SALES (corp-wide): 67.07B **Publicly Held**
Web: www.appsig.com
SIC: **3669** Signaling apparatus, electric
HQ: Raytheon Applied Signal Technology, Inc.
100 Headquarters Dr
San Jose CA
408 749-1888

(P-8624)
RSG/AAMES SECURITY INC
3300 E 59th St (90805-4504)
PHONE.................................562 529-5100
Louis J Finkle, *Pr*
Michelle Reuven, *Off Mgr*
Danielle Roberts, *Stockholder*
▲ **EMP:** 28 **EST:** 1975
SQ FT: 17,000
SALES (est): 1.31MM **Privately Held**
Web: www.rsgsecurity.com
SIC: **3669** Fire alarm apparatus, electric

(P-8625)
SIEMENS RAIL AUTOMATION CORP
9568 Archibald Ave (91730-5744)
PHONE.................................909 532-5405
Jay Aslam, *Mgr*
EMP: 84
SALES (corp-wide): 84.48B **Privately Held**
Web: www.siemens.com
SIC: **3669** Railroad signaling devices, electric
HQ: Siemens Rail Automation Corporation
2400 Nelson Miller Pkwy
Louisville KY
800 626-2710

(P-8626)
SIGTRONICS CORPORATION
178 E Arrow Hwy (91773-3336)
PHONE.................................909 305-9399
Mark Kelley, *Pr*
Frank M Sigona, *Prin*
Jane Sigona, *Prin*
EMP: 20 **EST:** 1974
SQ FT: 12,000
SALES (est): 2.76MM **Privately Held**
Web: www.sigtronics.com
SIC: **3669** Intercommunication systems, electric

(P-8627)
STATEWIDE TRFFIC SFETY SGNS IN (HQ)
2722 S Fairview St Fl 2 (92704-5947)
PHONE.................................949 553-8272
Rob Sehnert, *CEO*
EMP: 44 **EST:** 1987
SALES (est): 49.93MM
SALES (corp-wide): 539.72MM **Privately Held**
Web: www.statewidess.com
SIC: **3669** Pedestrian traffic control equipment
PA: Awp, Inc.
4244 Mount Pleasant St Nw # 100
North Canton OH
330 677-7401

(P-8628)
SYSTECH CORPORATION
Also Called: Systech
118 State Pl Ste 101 (92029-1324)
PHONE.................................858 674-6500
D Mark Fowler, *Pr*
Don Armerding, *
Jon Goby, *
Cheri Houchin, *
Zenon Barelka, *
▲ **EMP:** 35 **EST:** 1980
SALES (est): 8.21MM **Privately Held**
Web: www.systech.com
SIC: **3669** 7371 3661 3577
Intercommunication systems, electric; Custom computer programming services; Telephone and telegraph apparatus; Computer peripheral equipment, nec

(P-8629)
TACTICAL COMMAND INDS INC (DH)
4700 E Airport Dr (91761-7875)
PHONE.................................925 219-1097
Scott O'brien, *CEO*
EMP: 23 **EST:** 1996
SALES (est): 11.32MM
SALES (corp-wide): 457.84MM **Publicly Held**
Web: www.safariland.com
SIC: **3669** Intercommunication systems, electric
HQ: Safariland, Llc
13386 International Pkwy
Jacksonville FL
904 741-5400

(P-8630)
TACTICAL COMMUNICATIONS CORP
473 Post St (93010-8553)
PHONE.................................805 987-4100
EMP: 25 **EST:** 2009
SQ FT: 11,000
SALES (est): 5.06MM **Privately Held**
Web: www.tacticalcommunications.com
SIC: **3669** 8999 Intercommunication systems, electric; Communication services

(P-8631)
TELLABS ACCESS LLC (HQ)
338 Pier Ave (90254-3617)
PHONE.................................630 798-8671
Mike Dagenais, *Pr*
Robb Warwick, *VP*
Doug Bayerd, *VP*
Jeff Carnes, *VP*
EMP: 44 **EST:** 2014
SALES (est): 27.25MM **Privately Held**
Web: www.tellabs.com

SIC: **3669** Intercommunication systems, electric
PA: Marlin Equity Partners, Llc
1301 Manhattan Ave
Hermosa Beach CA

(P-8632)
WALTON ELECTRIC CORPORATION
755 N Central Ave Ste A (91786-9475)
P.O. Box 1599 (91711-8599)
PHONE.................................909 981-5051
Tanyon D Dunkley, *CEO*
Don R Davis, *
Ron C Stickel, *
EMP: 150 **EST:** 1985
SQ FT: 10,150
SALES (est): 35.19MM **Privately Held**
Web: www.waltonelectriccorp.com
SIC: **3669** 1731 Fire alarm apparatus, electric ; Electrical work

(P-8633)
ZETTLER COMPONENTS INC (PA)
75 Columbia (92868)
PHONE.................................949 831-5000
Kurt Rexius, *Genl Mgr*
▲ **EMP:** 250 **EST:** 1996
SQ FT: 27,000
SALES (est): 65.75MM **Privately Held**
Web: www.zettlercomponents.com
SIC: **3669** 5065 5087 Intercommunication systems, electric; Intercommunication equipment, electronic; Firefighting equipment

3671 Electron Tubes

(P-8634)
ECOATM LLC (DH)
10121 Barnes Canyon Rd (92121-2725)
PHONE.................................858 999-3200
David Mersten, *
EMP: 250 **EST:** 2008
SALES (est): 103.88MM
SALES (corp-wide): 10.97B **Publicly Held**
Web: www.ecoatm.com
SIC: **3671** Electron tubes
HQ: Apollo Asset Management, Inc.
9 W 57th St Fl 42
New York NY

(P-8635)
NEWVAC LLC
Also Called: Newvac Division
9330 De Soto Ave (91311)
PHONE.................................310 990-0401
Garrett Hoffman, *Brnch Mgr*
EMP: 114
SALES (corp-wide): 96.54MM **Privately Held**
Web: www.newvac-llc.com
SIC: **3671** 3678 3679 Electron tubes; Electronic connectors; Harness assemblies, for electronic use: wire or cable
HQ: Newvac, Llc
9330 De Soto Ave
Chatsworth CA
310 525-1205

(P-8636)
NEWVAC LLC
Newvac Division
9330 De Soto Ave (91311-4926)
PHONE.................................747 202-7333
Garrett Hoffman, *Brnch Mgr*
EMP: 80
SALES (corp-wide): 96.54MM **Privately Held**

Web: www.newvac-llc.com
SIC: **3671** 3678 3679 3643 Electron tubes;
Electronic connectors; Harness assemblies,
for electronic use: wire or cable; Current-
carrying wiring services
HQ: Newvac, Llc
9330 De Soto Ave
Chatsworth CA
310 525-1205

3672 Printed Circuit Boards

(P-8637)
A & M ELECTRONICS INC
25018 Avenue Kearny (91355-1253)
PHONE..............................661 257-3680
Ron Simpson, *Pr*
Tiffiny Simpson, ***
EMP: 30 **EST:** 1977
SQ FT: 12,000
SALES (est): 4.82MM **Privately Held**
Web: www.aandmelectronics.com
SIC: **3672** Circuit boards, television and
radio printed

(P-8638)
ACCU-SEMBLY INC
1835 Huntington Dr (91010-2635)
PHONE..............................626 357-3447
John Hykes, *CEO*
Marilyn Hykes, ***
Jan Shimmin, *Stockholder**
John Shimmin, *Stockholder**
▲ **EMP:** 95 **EST:** 1983
SQ FT: 15,000
SALES (est): 22.18MM **Privately Held**
Web: www.accu-sembly.com
SIC: **3672** Printed circuit boards

(P-8639)
ACCURATE CIRCUIT ENGRG INC
Also Called: Ace
3019 Kilson Dr (92707-4202)
PHONE..............................714 546-2162
Charles Lowe, *CEO*
▲ **EMP:** 70 **EST:** 1984
SQ FT: 15,000
SALES (est): 9.13MM **Privately Held**
Web: www.ace-pcb.com
SIC: **3672** Printed circuit boards

(P-8640)
ACCURATE ENGINEERING INC
8710 Telfair Ave (91352-2530)
PHONE..............................818 768-3919
Shitalkumar Desai, *Pr*
Rush Patel, ***
Hiten Golakiea, ***
Suresh Jasani, ***
Gautam Jasani, ***
EMP: 25 **EST:** 1996
SQ FT: 15,000
SALES (est): 2.44MM **Privately Held**
Web: www.accueng.com
SIC: **3672** Printed circuit boards

(P-8641)
ACTION ELECTRONIC ASSEMBLY INC
Also Called: Prowave Manufacturing
2872 S Santa Fe Ave (92069-6046)
PHONE..............................760 510-0003
Salim Khalfan, *Pr*
Deborah A Walker, *Treas*
EMP: 25 **EST:** 1996
SQ FT: 4,000
SALES (est): 347.86K **Privately Held**
Web: www.prowavemfg.com

SIC: **3672** Printed circuit boards

(P-8642)
ADVANCED CIRCUITS INC
17067 Cantara St (91406-1112)
PHONE..............................818 345-1993
Ralph Richart, *Brnch Mgr*
EMP: 42
Web: www.4pcb.com
SIC: **3672** Printed circuit boards
PA: Advanced Circuits, Inc.
21101 E 32nd Pkwy
Aurora CO

(P-8643)
ALLIED ELECTRONIC SERVICES INC
1342 E Borchard Ave (92705-4413)
PHONE..............................714 245-2500
Dave Vadodaria, *Pr*
Bharati Vadodaria, *CFO*
EMP: 25 **EST:** 1988
SQ FT: 6,000
SALES (est): 470.54K **Privately Held**
Web: www.alliedelectronicsservices.com
SIC: **3672** Printed circuit boards

(P-8644)
ALMATRON ELECTRONICS INC
644 Young St (92705-5633)
PHONE..............................714 557-6000
Margarito Alvarez, *Pr*
EMP: 21 **EST:** 1984
SQ FT: 11,500
SALES (est): 1.75MM **Privately Held**
Web: www.almatron.com
SIC: **3672** Circuit boards, television and
radio printed

(P-8645)
AMBAY CIRCUITS INC
Also Called: Delta Dvh Circuits
16117 Leadwell St (91406-3417)
PHONE..............................818 786-8241
Kana Khunti, *Pr*
EMP: 20 **EST:** 1973
SQ FT: 5,500
SALES (est): 956.95K **Privately Held**
SIC: **3672** Circuit boards, television and
radio printed

(P-8646)
AMERICAN CIRCUIT TECH INC (PA)
5330 E Hunter Ave (92807-2053)
PHONE..............................714 777-2480
Ravi Kheni, *Pr*
Giradhar Butani, ***
Labheu Zalavadia, ***
Kanu Patel, ***
EMP: 36 **EST:** 1975
SQ FT: 22,000
SALES (est): 4.33MM
SALES (corp-wide): 4.33MM **Privately Held**
Web: www.excello.com
SIC: **3672** Circuit boards, television and
radio printed

(P-8647)
ANC TECHNOLOGY INC
Also Called: Shanghai Anc Electronic Tech
10195 Stockton Rd (93021-9755)
PHONE..............................805 530-3958
▲ **EMP:** 100 **EST:** 1994
SQ FT: 60,000
SALES (est): 6.91MM **Privately Held**
Web: www.anctech.com

SIC: **3672** 5083 Printed circuit boards;
Irrigation equipment

(P-8648)
APT ELECTRONICS INC
Also Called: APT Electronics
241 N Crescent Way (92801-6704)
PHONE..............................714 687-6760
Tae Myoung Kim, *CEO*
EMP: 112 **EST:** 1999
SQ FT: 20,000
SALES (est): 24.76MM **Privately Held**
Web: www.aptelectronics.com
SIC: **3672** Printed circuit boards

(P-8649)
ASROCK AMERICA INC
13848 Magnolia Ave (91710-7027)
PHONE..............................909 590-8308
James Teng, *Pr*
◆ **EMP:** 34 **EST:** 2003
SALES (est): 10.85MM **Privately Held**
Web: www.asrock.com
SIC: **3672** Printed circuit boards
HQ: Firstplace International Limited
C/O: Offshore Incorporations Limited
Road Town

(P-8650)
ASTRONIC
2 Orion (92656-4200)
PHONE..............................949 454-1180
Sang H Choi, *CEO*
Ok Kay Choi, *Sec*
▲ **EMP:** 143 **EST:** 1976
SQ FT: 41,000
SALES (est): 22.41MM **Privately Held**
SIC: **3672** 1742 Printed circuit boards;
Acoustical and insulation work

(P-8651)
AURUM ASSEMBLY PLUS INC
8829 Production Ave (92121-2220)
PHONE..............................858 578-8710
Karl Northwang, *Pr*
Robert Mosley, ***
Bobby Northwang, ***
EMP: 22 **EST:** 1994
SQ FT: 7,000
SALES (est): 829.95K **Privately Held**
Web: www.aurumassembly.com
SIC: **3672** 2298 Circuit boards, television
and radio printed; Wire rope centers

(P-8652)
AVANTEC MANUFACTURING INC
1811 N Case St (92865-4234)
PHONE..............................714 532-6197
Alan E Mcneeney, *CEO*
▲ **EMP:** 20 **EST:** 2003
SALES (est): 4.99MM **Privately Held**
Web: www.avantecusa.com
SIC: **3672** Printed circuit boards

(P-8653)
BENCHMARK ELEC MFG SLTONS MRPA
Also Called: Benchmark
200 Science Dr (93021-2003)
PHONE..............................805 532-2800
Jayne Desorcie, *Pr*
EMP: 523 **EST:** 1986
SALES (est): 96.38MM
SALES (corp-wide): 2.89B **Publicly Held**
Web: www.bench.com
SIC: **3672** Printed circuit boards

HQ: Benchmark Electronics Manufacturing
Solutions Inc.
5550 Hellyer Ave
San Jose CA
805 222-1303

(P-8654)
BENCHMARK ELEC PHOENIX INC
1659 Gailes Blvd (92154-8230)
PHONE..............................619 397-2402
Roberto Perez, *Brnch Mgr*
EMP: 300
SALES (corp-wide): 2.89B **Publicly Held**
Web: www.bench.com
SIC: **3672** 3577 Printed circuit boards;
Computer peripheral equipment, nec
HQ: Benchmark Electronics Phoenix, Inc.
56 S Rockford Dr
Tempe AZ
623 300-7000

(P-8655)
CAL-COMP USA (SAN DIEGO) INC
1940 Camino Vida Roble (92008-6516)
PHONE..............................858 587-6900
EMP: 215 **EST:** 1995
SQ FT: 65,000
SALES (est): 49.92MM **Privately Held**
Web: www.calcompusa.com
SIC: **3672** Circuit boards, television and
radio printed

(P-8656)
CALPAK USA INC
13748 Prairie Ave (90250-7359)
PHONE..............................310 937-7335
Danish Qureshi, *Pr*
▲ **EMP:** 20 **EST:** 1978
SALES (est): 2.62MM **Privately Held**
Web: www.calpak-usa.com
SIC: **3672** 3679 8742 4813 Printed circuit
boards; Commutators, electronic;
Management consulting services;
Telephone communication, except radio

(P-8657)
CARTEL ELECTRONICS LLC
Also Called: Apct Orange County
1900 Petra Ln Ste C (92870-6758)
PHONE..............................714 993-0270
▲ **EMP:** 85 **EST:** 1994
SALES (est): 1.24MM
SALES (corp-wide): 7MM **Privately Held**
Web: www.apct.com
SIC: **3672** Printed circuit boards
PA: Apct Holdings, Llc
3495 De La Cruz Blvd
Santa Clara CA
408 727-6442

(P-8658)
CELESTICA AEROSPACE TECH CORP
Also Called: Celestica-Aerospace
895 S Rockefeller Ave Ste 102
(91761-8145)
PHONE..............................512 310-7540
Jeffrey Bain, *Pr*
Thomas Lovelock, ***
Leslie K Sladek, ***
▲ **EMP:** 200 **EST:** 2002
SQ FT: 55,000
SALES (est): 50.93MM
SALES (corp-wide): 422MM **Privately Held**
Web: www.celestica.com

SIC: **3672** Printed circuit boards
HQ: Celestica Inc
1900-5140 Yonge St
North York ON
416 448-5800

(P-8659)
CHAD INDUSTRIES INCORPORATED
Also Called: Chad
1565 S Sinclair St (92806-5934)
PHONE..........................714 938-0080
Scott W Klimczak, *Pr*
Wayne Rapp, *
▲ **EMP: 40 EST:** 1973
SQ FT: 31,000
SALES (est): 5.11MM **Privately Held**
SIC: **3672** Printed circuit boards

(P-8660)
CHOOSE MANUFACTURING CO LLC
24 Passion Flower (92618-2252)
PHONE..........................714 327-1698
Herbert Chiu, *Managing Member*
▲ **EMP: 20 EST:** 2000
SALES (est): 2.26MM **Privately Held**
Web: www.choosemfg.com
SIC: **3672** Printed circuit boards

(P-8661)
CIRCUIT EXPRESS INC
67 W Easy St Ste 129 (93065-1601)
PHONE..........................805 581-2172
Himmat Desai, *CEO*
Vinny Kathrota, *Sec*
EMP: 20 EST: 1979
SQ FT: 5,000
SALES (est): 756.1K **Privately Held**
Web: www.circuitexpressinc.com
SIC: **3672** Circuit boards, television and radio printed

(P-8662)
CIRCUIT SERVICES LLC
Also Called: Career Tech Circuit Services
9134 Independence Ave (91311-5902)
PHONE..........................818 701-5391
Marc Haugen, *CEO*
EMP: 43 EST: 1998
SALES (est): 24.95MM
SALES (corp-wide): 147.68MM **Privately Held**
Web: www.careertech-usa.com
SIC: **3672** Printed circuit boards
PA: Fralock Holdings Llc
28525 Industry Dr
Valencia CA
661 702-6999

(P-8663)
CMS CIRCUIT SOLUTIONS INC
41549 Cherry St (92562-9193)
P.O. Box 1031 (92564-1031)
PHONE..........................951 698-4452
Clark M Steddom, *Pr*
Mark Chiang, *Prin*
EMP: 20 EST: 2005
SALES (est): 2.48MM **Privately Held**
Web: www.cmscircuits.com
SIC: **3672** Circuit boards, television and radio printed

(P-8664)
COAST TO COAST CIRCUITS INC (PA)
Also Called: Speedy Circuits
5331 Mcfadden Ave (92649-1204)
PHONE..........................714 891-9441

Edward Porter, *CEO*
Ronald Scott Lawhead, *
◆ **EMP: 41 EST:** 1985
SQ FT: 40,000
SALES (est): 13.55MM **Privately Held**
Web: www.c3circuits.com
SIC: **3672** Circuit boards, television and radio printed

(P-8665)
CONCEPT DEVELOPMENT LLC
Also Called: CDI
1881 Langley Ave (92614-5623)
PHONE..........................949 623-8000
James M Reardon, *Pr*
EMP: 20 EST: 1972
SQ FT: 12,880
SALES (est): 9.7MM
SALES (corp-wide): 72.42MM **Publicly Held**
Web: www.onestopsystems.com
SIC: **3672** Printed circuit boards
PA: One Stop Systems, Inc.
2235 Entp St Ste 110
Escondido CA
760 745-9883

(P-8666)
COPPER CLAD MLTILAYER PDTS INC
Also Called: C C M P
1150 N Hawk Cir (92807-1708)
PHONE..........................714 237-1388
Fred Ohanian, *Pr*
William Schwerter, *
▲ **EMP: 25 EST:** 1994
SQ FT: 13,200
SALES (est): 3.74MM **Privately Held**
Web: www.ccmpinc.com
SIC: **3672** Printed circuit boards

(P-8667)
CREATION TECH CALEXICO INC (HQ)
Also Called: Aisling Industries
1778 Zinetta Rd Ste F (92231-9511)
P.O. Box 1833 (92244-1833)
▲ **EMP: 25 EST:** 1985
SQ FT: 10,000
SALES (est): 85.94MM
SALES (corp-wide): 127.31MM **Privately Held**
SIC: **3672 3679** Printed circuit boards; Electronic circuits
PA: Creation Technologies Ltd
8999 Fraserton Crt
Burnaby BC
604 430-4336

(P-8668)
CROWN CIRCUITS INC
6070 Avenida Encinas (92011-1001)
PHONE..........................949 922-0144
Kamran A Saffari, *CEO*
Bert Arucnn, *
Nilofar Saffari, *
EMP: 33 EST: 1985
SQ FT: 20,000
SALES (est): 731.8K **Privately Held**
SIC: **3672** Printed circuit boards

(P-8669)
DE LEON ENTPS ELEC SPCLIST INC
Also Called: De Leon Enterprises
11934 Allegheny St (91352-1833)
PHONE..........................818 252-6690
Miguel De Leon, *Pr*
▲ **EMP: 24 EST:** 1994

SQ FT: 11,000
SALES (est): 2.46MM **Privately Held**
Web: www.deleonenterprises.com
SIC: **3672** Printed circuit boards

(P-8670)
DYNASTY ELECTRONIC COMPANY LLC
Also Called: Dec
1790 E Mcfadden Ave Ste 105 (92705-4638)
PHONE..........................714 550-1197
Fredrick Rodenhuis, *Managing Member*
Mark Clark, *
EMP: 65 EST: 2008
SQ FT: 10,000
SALES (est): 8.57MM **Privately Held**
Web: www.dec-assembly.com
SIC: **3672** Printed circuit boards

(P-8671)
ELECTRO SURFACE TECH INC
Also Called: E S T
2281 Las Palmas Dr # 101 (92011-1527)
PHONE..........................760 431-8306
Hiroo Kirpalani, *Pr*
EMP: 42 EST: 1989
SQ FT: 31,500
SALES (est): 2.54MM **Privately Held**
Web: www.est.com
SIC: **3672** Circuit boards, television and radio printed

(P-8672)
ELECTRONIC SURFC MOUNTED INDS
Also Called: Esmi
6731 Cobra Way (92121-4110)
PHONE..........................858 455-1710
Henry Kim, *Pr*
Lynn Kim, *
▼ **EMP: 40 EST:** 1986
SQ FT: 25,000
SALES (est): 5.59MM **Privately Held**
Web: www.esmiinc.com
SIC: **3672** Printed circuit boards

(P-8673)
ETI PARTNERS IV LLC
901 Wshngton Blvd Ste 208 (90292)
PHONE..........................949 273-4990
EMP: 20 EST: 2015
SALES (est): 1.07MM **Privately Held**
SIC: **3672** Printed circuit boards

(P-8674)
EXCELLO CIRCUITS INC
5330 E Hunter Ave (92807-2053)
PHONE..........................714 993-0560
Rax Ribadia, *Pr*
Sam Bhayani, *
Rax Ribadia, *VP*
Tushar Patel, *
EMP: 72 EST: 1992
SQ FT: 11,000
SALES (est): 9.11MM **Privately Held**
Web: www.excello.com
SIC: **3672** Printed circuit boards

(P-8675)
EXPERT ASSEMBLY SERVICES INC
Also Called: Expert Ems
14312 Chambers Rd Ste B (92780-6912)
PHONE..........................714 258-8880
Jack Quinn, *CEO*
EMP: 50 EST: 1997
SALES (est): 11.41MM **Privately Held**

SIC: **3672** Printed circuit boards

(P-8676)
FABRICATED COMPONENTS CORP
Also Called: Summit Interconnect Orange
130 W Bristol Ln (92865-2640)
PHONE..........................714 974-8590
Shane Whiteside, *Pr*
▼ **EMP: 140 EST:** 1979
SQ FT: 40,000
SALES (est): 24.05MM **Privately Held**
Web: www.fabricatedcomponents.com
SIC: **3672** Printed circuit boards

(P-8677)
FINE LINE CIRCUITS & TECH INC
594 Apollo St Ste A (92821-3134)
PHONE..........................714 529-2942
Rick Bajaria, *Pr*
Ken Pansuria, *
Vinny Kathrotia, *
EMP: 30 EST: 1995
SQ FT: 20,000
SALES (est): 4.47MM **Privately Held**
Web: www.finelinecircuits.com
SIC: **3672** Circuit boards, television and radio printed

(P-8678)
FINE PTCH ELCTRNIC ASSMBLY LLC
Also Called: Fine Pitch
5106 Azusa Canyon Rd (91706-1846)
PHONE..........................626 337-2800
Ashish Sheladiya, *Managing Member*
EMP: 20 EST: 2004
SQ FT: 15,000
SALES (est): 2.65MM **Privately Held**
Web: www.finepitchassembly.com
SIC: **3672** Printed circuit boards

(P-8679)
FTG CIRCUITS INC (DH)
20750 Marilla St (91311-4407)
PHONE..........................818 407-4024
Brad Bourne, *CEO*
Michael Labrador, *
Joe Ricci, *
Ed Hanna, *
▼ **EMP: 48 EST:** 1956
SQ FT: 38,000
SALES (est): 41.33MM
SALES (corp-wide): 65.73MM **Privately Held**
Web: www.ftgcorp.com
SIC: **3672 3644** Printed circuit boards; Terminal boards
HQ: Firan Technology Group (Usa) Corporation
20750 Marilla St
Chatsworth CA
818 407-4024

(P-8680)
GAVIAL ENGINEERING & MFG INC
1435 W Mccoy Ln (93455-1002)
PHONE..........................805 614-0060
Don Connors, *Pr*
Ken Hicks, *
Stanley D Connors, *
EMP: 50 EST: 2012
SQ FT: 25,000
SALES (est): 12.1MM
SALES (corp-wide): 53.11MM **Privately Held**
Web: www.gavial.com

▲ = Import ▼ = Export
◆ = Import/Export

SIC: **3672** 3679 Printed circuit boards;
Electronic circuits
PA: Gavial Holdings, Inc.
1435 W Mccoy Ln
Santa Maria CA
805 614-0060

(P-8681)
GEERIRAJ INC
Also Called: Mer-Mar Electronics
7042 Santa Fe Ave E Ste A1 (92345-5711)
PHONE..............................760 244-6149
Kanjibhai Ghadia, *Pr*
Suresh Patel, *
EMP: 28 **EST:** 1974
SQ FT: 22,000
SALES (est): 4.95MM **Privately Held**
SIC: 3672 Printed circuit boards

(P-8682)
GOLDEN WEST TECHNOLOGY
1180 E Valencia Dr (92831-4627)
PHONE..............................714 738-3775
Dan P Rieth, *Pr*
EMP: 60 **EST:** 1974
SQ FT: 30,000
SALES (est): 9.28MM **Privately Held**
Web: www.goldenwesttech.com
SIC: 3672 Printed circuit boards

(P-8683)
GRAPHIC RESEARCH INC
3339 Durham Ct (91504-1600)
PHONE..............................818 886-7340
Govind R Vaghashia, *Pr*
Pete Vaghashia, *
▲ **EMP:** 50 **EST:** 1966
SALES (est): 4.88MM **Privately Held**
Web: www.graphicresearch.com
SIC: 3672 Printed circuit boards

(P-8684)
HAMBY CORPORATION
27704 Avenue Scott (91355-1218)
PHONE..............................661 257-1924
EMP: 35 **EST:** 1956
SALES (est): 828.51K **Privately Held**
Web: www.hambycorp.com
SIC: 3672 Printed circuit boards

(P-8685)
HI TECH ELECTRONIC MFG CORP
Also Called: Hitem
1938 Avenida Del Oro (92056-5803)
PHONE..............................858 657-0908
Thai Nguyen, *CEO*
Vinh Lam, *
Tran Vu, *
▲ **EMP:** 82 **EST:** 1997
SALES (est): 11MM **Privately Held**
Web: www.hitem.com
SIC: 3672 Circuit boards, television and
radio printed

(P-8686)
HUGHES CIRCUITS INC
Also Called: Pcb Fabrication Facility
540 S Pacific St (92078-4050)
PHONE..............................760 744-0300
Barbara Hughes, *Brnch Mgr*
EMP: 126
SALES (corp-wide): 36.08MM **Privately
Held**
Web: www.hughescircuits.com
SIC: 3672 Circuit boards, television and
radio printed
PA: Hughes Circuits, Inc.
546 S Pacific St
San Marcos CA
760 744-0300

(P-8687)
HUGHES CIRCUITS INC (PA)
Also Called: Hci
546 S Pacific St (92078-4050)
PHONE..............................760 744-0300
Barbara Hughes, *CEO*
Jerry Hughes, *
Michelle Glatts, *
Joe Hughes, *
Steve Hughes, *
EMP: 99 **EST:** 1999
SQ FT: 50,000
SALES (est): 36.08MM
SALES (corp-wide): 36.08MM **Privately
Held**
Web: www.hughescircuits.com
SIC: 3672 3679 8711 3444 Printed circuit
boards; Electronic circuits; Engineering
services; Sheet metalwork

(P-8688)
IMPACT PROJECT MANAGEMENT INC
2872 S Santa Fe Ave (92069-6046)
PHONE..............................760 747-6616
Randy Scott Walker, *Pr*
Debbie Walker, *
▲ **EMP:** 24 **EST:** 2001
SALES (est): 2.78MM **Privately Held**
Web: www.impactprojects.com
SIC: 3672 Printed circuit boards

(P-8689)
IPC CAL FLEX INC
13337 South St 307 (90703-7308)
PHONE..............................714 952-0373
EMP: 26 **EST:** 1980
SQ FT: 25,000
SALES (est): 1.62MM **Privately Held**
SIC: 3672 Printed circuit boards

(P-8690)
IRVINE ELECTRONICS LLC
Also Called: Irvine Electronics Inc
1601 Alton Pkwy Ste A (92606-4801)
PHONE..............................949 250-0315
Jane Zerounian, *Pr*
Onnig Zerounian, *
EMP: 100 **EST:** 1969
SQ FT: 48,000
SALES (est): 25.34MM
SALES (corp-wide): 722.8MM **Privately
Held**
Web: www.irvine-electronics.com
SIC: 3672 Circuit boards, television and
radio printed
PA: Volex Plc
Unit C1
Basingstoke HANTS
203 370-8830

(P-8691)
ISU PETASYS CORP
12930 Bradley Ave (91342-3829)
PHONE..............................818 833-5800
Yong Kyoun Kim, *Pr*
▲ **EMP:** 95 **EST:** 1997
SQ FT: 50,000
SALES (est): 21.11MM **Privately Held**
Web: www.isupetasys.com
SIC: 3672 Printed circuit boards
PA: Isu Chemical Co., Ltd.
84 Sapyeong-Daero, Seocho-Gu
Seoul

(P-8692)
JABIL INC
Also Called: Jabil Chad Automation
1565 S Sinclair St (92806-5934)
PHONE..............................714 938-0080
Babak Naderi, *Dir Opers*
EMP: 50
SALES (corp-wide): 34.7B **Publicly Held**
Web: www.jabil.com
SIC: 3672 Printed circuit boards
PA: Jabil Inc.
10800 Roosevelt Blvd N
Saint Petersburg FL
727 577-9749

(P-8693)
JMP ELECTRONICS INC
2685 Dow Ave Ste A1 (92780-7241)
PHONE..............................714 730-2086
▲ **EMP:** 25 **EST:** 1992
SQ FT: 12,500
SALES (est): 2.02MM **Privately Held**
Web: www.jmpelectronics.com
SIC: 3672 Printed circuit boards

(P-8694)
K L ELECTRONIC INC
3083 S Harbor Blvd (92704-6448)
PHONE..............................714 751-5611
Khanh Ton, *Pr*
Luon Ton, *Sec*
Michael Ton, *CEO*
EMP: 21 **EST:** 1981
SQ FT: 4,000
SALES (est): 794.83K **Privately Held**
Web: www.klelectronics.com
SIC: 3672 Printed circuit boards

(P-8695)
KCA ELECTRONICS INC
Also Called: Summit Interconnect - Anaheim
223 N Crescent Way (92801-6704)
PHONE..............................714 239-2433
Shane Whiteside, *Pr*
▲ **EMP:** 180 **EST:** 1992
SQ FT: 60,000
SALES (est): 34.6MM
SALES (corp-wide): 1.77B **Privately Held**
Web: www.kcamerica.com
SIC: 3672 Circuit boards, television and
radio printed
HQ: Equity Hci Management L P
1730 Pennsylvania Ave Nw # 525
Washington DC

(P-8696)
LAMINATING COMPANY OF AMERICA
Also Called: Lcoa
20322 Windrow Dr Ste 100 (92630-8150)
PHONE..............................949 587-3300
Tim Redfern, *Pr*
Brad Biddol, *
▲ **EMP:** 20 **EST:** 1971
SALES (est): 2.25MM **Privately Held**
Web: www.lcoa.com
SIC: 3672 Printed circuit boards

(P-8697)
LARITECH INC
5898 Condor Dr (93021-2603)
PHONE..............................805 529-5000
William Larrick, *CEO*
Terry Gonzales, *
Joel Butler, *
EMP: 111 **EST:** 2001
SQ FT: 13,000
SALES (est): 32.82MM **Privately Held**
Web: www.laritech.com
SIC: 3672 Printed circuit boards

(P-8698)
LIFETIME MEMORY PRODUCTS INC
2505 Da Vinci Ste A (92614-0170)
P.O. Box 1207 (92652-1207)
PHONE..............................949 794-9000
Paul Columbus, *CEO*
Cameron Hum, *
◆ **EMP:** 40 **EST:** 1981
SQ FT: 16,000
SALES (est): 3.53MM **Privately Held**
Web: www.lifetimememory.com
SIC: 3672 5045 3674 Printed circuit boards;
Computers, peripherals, and software;
Semiconductors and related devices

(P-8699)
LORSER INDUSTRIES INC
9636 Arby Dr (90210-1202)
PHONE..............................619 917-4298
EMP: 21
SALES (corp-wide): 804.27K **Privately
Held**
Web: www.lorserindustries.com
SIC: 3672 Circuit boards, television and
radio printed
PA: Lorser Industries Inc
1959 Kellogg Ave
Carlsbad CA
760 438-6625

(P-8700)
MATRIX USA INC
2730 S Main St (92707-3435)
PHONE..............................714 825-0404
Kieran Healy, *Pr*
George Potocska, *
Sharon Nioson, *Branch Administrator*
▲ **EMP:** 25 **EST:** 2005
SALES (est): 5.17MM
SALES (corp-wide): 9.15MM **Privately
Held**
Web: www.matrixelectronics.com
SIC: 3672 Printed circuit boards
HQ: Matrix Electronics Limited
1124 Mid-Way Blvd
Mississauga ON
905 670-8400

(P-8701)
MAXTROL CORPORATION
1701 E Edinger Ave Ste B6 (92705-5010)
PHONE..............................714 245-0506
Uri Ranon, *Pr*
Leo Pardo, *
EMP: 40 **EST:** 1990
SQ FT: 5,000
SALES (est): 4.93MM **Privately Held**
Web: www.maxtrol.com
SIC: 3672 Printed circuit boards

(P-8702)
MERCURY SYSTEMS INC
400 Del Norte Blvd (93030-7997)
PHONE..............................805 388-1345
Deepak Alagh, *Brnch Mgr*
EMP: 110
SALES (corp-wide): 973.88MM **Publicly
Held**
Web: www.mrcy.com
SIC: 3672 Printed circuit boards
PA: Mercury Systems, Inc.
50 Minuteman Rd
Andover MA
978 256-1300

(P-8703)
MERCURY SYSTEMS INC
300 Del Norte Blvd (93030-7217)
PHONE..............................805 751-1100
Deepak Alagh, *Brnch Mgr*
EMP: 157
SALES (corp-wide): 973.88MM **Publicly
Held**

PRODUCTS & SVCS

Web: www.mrcy.com
SIC: 3672 Printed circuit boards
PA: Mercury Systems, Inc.
    50 Minuteman Rd
    Andover MA
    978 256-1300

(P-8704)
MFLEX DELAWARE INC
101 Academy Ste 250 (92617-3035)
PHONE.........................949 453-6800
Reza A Meshgin, *CEO*
EMP: 4933 EST: 2019
SALES (est): 1.1MM **Privately Held**
SIC: 3672 Printed circuit boards
HQ: Multi-Fineline Electronix, Inc.
    101 Academy Ste 250
    Irvine CA
    949 453-6800

(P-8705)
**MULTI-FINELINE ELECTRONIX
INC (HQ)**
Also Called: Mflex
101 Academy Ste 250 (92617-3035)
PHONE.........................949 453-6800
Reza Meshgin, *Pr*
Christine Besnard, *
Tom Kampfer, *
Neil Liu, *CIO*
Thomas Lee, *
EMP: 583 EST: 1984
SQ FT: 20,171
SALES (est): 468.31MM **Privately Held**
Web: www.mflex.com
SIC: 3672 Printed circuit boards
PA: Suzhou Dongshan Precision
    Manufacturing Co., Ltd.
    8 Fenghuangshan Road Dongshan
    Town, Wuzhong District
    Suzhou JS

(P-8706)
MULTILAYER PROTOTYPES INC
Also Called: Mpi
2320 Terra Bella Ln (93012-9080)
PHONE.........................805 498-9390
Steve Ferris, *Pr*
Dara Garza, *Sec*
EMP: 19 EST: 1981
SALES (est): 2.5MM **Privately Held**
Web: www.mpi-pcb.com
SIC: 3672 Circuit boards, television and
    radio printed

(P-8707)
MURRIETTA CIRCUITS
5000 E Landon Dr (92807-1978)
PHONE.........................714 970-2430
Andrew Murrietta, *CEO*
Albert G Murrieta, *
Albert A Murrieta, *
Josh Murrietta, *OK Vice President*
Helen Murrietta, *
EMP: 105 EST: 1992
SQ FT: 48,500
SALES (est): 22.67MM **Privately Held**
Web: www.murrietta.com
SIC: 3672 8711 Printed circuit boards;
    Engineering services

(P-8708)
**NASO INDUSTRIES
CORPORATION**
Also Called: Naso Technologies
3007 Bunsen Ave Ste Q (93003-7634)
PHONE.........................805 650-1231
Jahansooz Saleh, *CEO*
Namdar Saleh, *
Bryan Howe, *

Mike White, *
Soraya Saleh, *
EMP: 40 EST: 1990
SQ FT: 20,000
SALES (est): 8.71MM **Privately Held**
Web: www.naso.com
SIC: 3672 3599 Printed circuit boards;
    Machine shop, jobbing and repair

(P-8709)
**NATEL ENGINEERING
HOLDINGS INC**
9340 Owensmouth Ave (91311-6915)
PHONE.........................818 734-6500
EMP: 19 EST: 2015
SALES (est): 1.36MM **Privately Held**
Web: www.neotech.com
SIC: 3672 Printed circuit boards

(P-8710)
**NEW BRUNSWICK INDUSTRIES
INC**
1850 Gillespie Way (92020-1094)
PHONE.........................619 448-4900
Jim Krehbiel, *Pr*
Sue Harnack, *
Sue Krehbiel, *
EMP: 30 EST: 1982
SALES (est): 4.29MM **Privately Held**
Web: www.nbiinc.com
SIC: 3672 Circuit boards, television and
    radio printed

(P-8711)
NORTHWEST CIRCUITS CORP
8660 Avenida Costa Blanca (92154-6232)
PHONE.........................619 661-1701
Toribio Lobato, *Pr*
▲ EMP: 65 EST: 1991
SQ FT: 12,000
SALES (est): 7.72MM **Privately Held**
Web: www.nwcircuits.com
SIC: 3672 Printed circuit boards

(P-8712)
ONCORE MANUFACTURING LLC
Also Called: Oncore Velocity
237 Via Vera Cruz (92078-2617)
PHONE.........................760 737-6777
Arnulfo Villa, *Prin*
EMP: 110
SALES (corp-wide): 1.43B **Privately Held**
Web: www.neotech.com
SIC: 3672 Printed circuit boards
HQ: Oncore Manufacturing Llc
    9340 Owensmouth Ave
    Chatsworth CA

(P-8713)
**ONCORE MANUFACTURING
SVCS INC**
Also Called: Neo Tech Natel Epic Oncore
9340 Owensmouth Ave (91311-6915)
PHONE.........................510 360-2222
Sudesh Arora, *CEO*
David Brakenwagen, *Sr VP*
Sajjad Malik, *Ex VP*
Magdy Henry, *VP*
Zareen Mohta, *VP*
▲ EMP: 230 EST: 2007
SALES (est): 141.26MM
SALES (corp-wide): 1.43B **Privately Held**
Web: www.neotech.com
SIC: 3672 Printed circuit boards
PA: Natel Engineering Company, Llc
    9340 Owensmouth Ave
    Chatsworth CA
    818 495-8617

(P-8714)
OSI ELECTRONICS INC (HQ)
12533 Chadron Ave (90250-4807)
PHONE.........................310 978-0516
Paul Morben, *Pr*
Bruce Macdonald, *
Lou Campana, *
Alex Colquhoun, *
▲ EMP: 56 EST: 1995
SQ FT: 60,000
SALES (est): 139.26MM
SALES (corp-wide): 1.15B **Publicly Held**
Web: www.osielectronics.com
SIC: 3672 Printed circuit boards
PA: Osi Systems, Inc.
    12525 Chadron Ave
    Hawthorne CA
    310 978-0516

(P-8715)
PARPRO TECHNOLOGIES INC
Also Called: P T I
2700 S Fairview St (92704-5947)
PHONE.........................714 545-8886
Thomas Sparrvik, *CEO*
Keith Knight, *Pr*
Ngathuong Le, *COO*
Eduardo Serrano, *CFO*
EMP: 210 EST: 1998
SALES (est): 77.67MM **Privately Held**
Web: www.calquality.com
SIC: 3672 Printed circuit boards
PA: Parpro Corporation
    4f, No. 169, Jianxing Rd.
    Taoyuan City TAY

(P-8716)
PDM SOLUTIONS INC
Also Called: Protech Design & Manufacturing
8451 Miralani Dr Ste J (92126-4388)
PHONE.........................858 348-1000
James O'shea, *Pr*
Michelle Kim, *VP*
EMP: 20 EST: 1998
SQ FT: 5,700
SALES (est): 4.69MM **Privately Held**
Web: www.pdmsolutions.net
SIC: 3672 Printed circuit boards

(P-8717)
PHOTO FABRICATORS INC
7648 Burnet Ave (91405-1043)
PHONE.........................818 781-1010
Steve L Brooks, *Pr*
John R Brooks, *
Susan Brooks, *
▲ EMP: 75 EST: 1973
SQ FT: 14,000
SALES (est): 9.33MM **Privately Held**
Web: www.photofabricators.com
SIC: 3672 Circuit boards, television and
    radio printed

(P-8718)
PIONEER CIRCUITS INC
3021 S Shannon St (92704-6320)
PHONE.........................714 641-3132
Robert Lee, *CEO*
James Y Lee, *
EMP: 290 EST: 1981
SQ FT: 50,000
SALES (est): 58.9MM **Privately Held**
Web: www.pioneercircuits.com
SIC: 3672 3812 Printed circuit boards;
    Defense systems and equipment

(P-8719)
POWER CIRCUITS INC
2630 S Harbor Blvd (92704-5829)
PHONE.........................714 327-3000

Kenton K Alder, *Pr*
EMP: 87 EST: 1985
SALES (est): 11.96MM
SALES (corp-wide): 2.5B **Publicly Held**
Web: www.ttm.com
SIC: 3672 Printed circuit boards
PA: Ttm Technologies, Inc.
    200 Sandpointe Ave # 400
    Santa Ana CA
    714 327-3000

(P-8720)
Q-FLEX INC
1301 E Hunter Ave (92705-4133)
PHONE.........................714 664-0101
Nayna Uka, *Pr*
Nalini Celio, *Sec*
Pete Uka, *VP*
▲ EMP: 18 EST: 1988
SQ FT: 7,200
SALES (est): 4.73MM **Privately Held**
Web: www.q-flex.com
SIC: 3672 Printed circuit boards

(P-8721)
QUAL-PRO CORPORATION (HQ)
18510 S Figueroa St (90248-4519)
PHONE.........................310 329-7535
Brian Jeffrey Shane, *CEO*
Richard Fitzgerald, *
EMP: 200 EST: 1971
SQ FT: 55,000
SALES (est): 61.65MM **Privately Held**
Web: www.registrar-transfers.com
SIC: 3672 Circuit boards, television and
    radio printed
PA: Sfo Technologies Private Limited
    Plot No. 2, Cochin Special Economic
    Zone
    Kochi KL

(P-8722)
**QUALITY SYSTEMS INTGRATED
CORP**
7098 Miratech Dr Ste 170 (92121-3111)
PHONE.........................858 536-3128
EMP: 120
Web: www.qsic.com
SIC: 3672 Printed circuit boards
PA: Quality Systems Integrated Corporation
    6740 Top Gun St
    San Diego CA

(P-8723)
**QUALITY SYSTEMS INTGRATED
CORP (PA)**
Also Called: Quality Systems
6740 Top Gun St (92121-4114)
PHONE.........................858 587-9797
Kiem T Le, *CEO*
Minh Nguyen, *
Hai Bach, *
Thui Trong, *
Cecile Le, *
▲ EMP: 155 EST: 1994
SQ FT: 50,000
SALES (est): 47.28MM **Privately Held**
Web: www.qsic.com
SIC: 3672 Printed circuit boards

(P-8724)
ROYAL FLEX CIRCUITS INC
15505 Cornet St (90670-5511)
PHONE.........................562 404-0626
Milan Shah, *CEO*
EMP: 27 EST: 2013
SALES (est): 9.85MM
SALES (corp-wide): 1.77B **Privately Held**
Web: www.royalcircuits.com
SIC: 3672 Wiring boards

HQ: Royal Circuit Solutions, Llc
21 Hamilton Ct
Hollister CA
831 636-7789

(P-8725)
SAEHAN ELECTRONICS AMERICA INC (PA)
7880 Airway Rd Ste B5g (92154-8308)
PHONE....................858 496-1500
▲ **EMP:** 53 **EST:** 1994
SALES (est): 8.06MM **Privately Held**
Web: www.saehanusa.com
SIC: 3672 Printed circuit boards

(P-8726)
SAN DIEGO PCB DESIGN LLC
461 Whitby Gln (92027-2912)
PHONE....................858 271-5722
P Michael Stoehr, *Managing Member*
EMP: 18 **EST:** 2016
SALES (est): 1.25MM **Privately Held**
Web: www.sdpcb.com
SIC: 3672 Circuit boards, television and
radio printed

(P-8727)
SANMINA CORPORATION
2945 Airway Ave (92626-6007)
PHONE....................714 371-2800
Dox Scream, *Mgr*
EMP: 28
SQ FT: 60,580
Web: www.sanmina.com
SIC: 3672 Printed circuit boards
PA: Sanmina Corporation
2700 N 1st St
San Jose CA

(P-8728)
SANMINA CORPORATION
Viking Modular Solutions
2950 Red Hill Ave (92626-5935)
PHONE....................714 913-2200
Hamid Shokrgovar, *Pr*
EMP: 110
Web: www.sanmina.com
SIC: 3672 Printed circuit boards
PA: Sanmina Corporation
2700 N 1st St
San Jose CA

(P-8729)
SECURE TECHNOLOGY COMPANY
Also Called: Lark Engineering
2000 W Corporate Way (92801-5373)
PHONE....................714 991-6500
Patrick Huang, *Pr*
EMP: 24 **EST:** 2016
SALES (est): 4.54MM
SALES (corp-wide): 2.89B **Publicly Held**
Web: www.bench.com
SIC: 3672 Printed circuit boards
PA: Benchmark Electronics, Inc.
56 S Rockford Dr
Tempe AZ
623 300-7000

(P-8730)
SMART ELEC & ASSEMBLY INC
Also Called: Smart Electronics
2000 W Corporate Way (92801-5373)
PHONE....................714 772-2651
Robert Swelgin, *Pr*
Shou-lee Wang, *CEO*
James Wang, *
Dave Wopschall, *
Getaneh Bekele, *

▲ **EMP:** 120 **EST:** 1994
SQ FT: 34,500
SALES (est): 100.25MM
SALES (corp-wide): 2.89B **Publicly Held**
SIC: 3672 Printed circuit boards
HQ: Secure Communication Systems, Inc.
1740 E Wilshire Ave
Santa Ana CA
714 547-1174

(P-8731)
SOMACIS INC
13500 Danielson St (92064-6874)
PHONE....................858 513-2200
Giovanni Tridenti, *CEO*
▲ **EMP:** 120 **EST:** 1970
SQ FT: 76,000
SALES (est): 28.73MM
SALES (corp-wide): 2.67MM **Privately Held**
Web: www.somacis.com
SIC: 3672 Circuit boards, television and
radio printed
HQ: So.Ma.Ci.S. Spa
Via Jesina 17
Castelfidardo AN
071721531

(P-8732)
SOUTH COAST CIRCUITS INC
3506 W Lake Center Dr Ste A
(92704-6985)
PHONE....................714 966-2108
Charles R Benson, *CEO*
▲ **EMP:** 68 **EST:** 1982
SQ FT: 30,000
SALES (est): 9.13MM **Privately Held**
Web: www.sccircuits.com
SIC: 3672 Circuit boards, television and
radio printed

(P-8733)
SPECTRUM ASSEMBLY INC
Also Called: Spectrum Electronics
6300 Yarrow Dr Ste 100 (92011-1542)
PHONE....................760 930-4000
Ronald Topp, *Pr*
Ronald Tupp, *
Michael Baldwin, *
EMP: 147 **EST:** 1993
SQ FT: 20,000
SALES (est): 24.05MM **Privately Held**
Web: www.saicorp.com
SIC: 3672 3569 3315 3999 Printed circuit
boards; Assembly machines, non-
metalworking; Wire and fabricated wire
products; Barber and beauty shop
equipment

(P-8734)
SUMITRONICS USA INC
9335 Airway Rd Ste 212 (92154-7930)
PHONE....................619 661-0450
Jiro Hashiguchi, *CEO*
Ryuji Sumi, *CFO*
◆ **EMP:** 30 **EST:** 2007
SQ FT: 800
SALES (est): 23.21MM **Privately Held**
Web: www.sumitronics.com
SIC: 3672 Printed circuit boards
HQ: Sumitronics Corporation
1-2-2, Hitotsubashi
Chiyoda-Ku TKY

(P-8735)
SUMMIT INTERCONNECT INC (HQ)
223 N Crescent Way (92801-6704)
PHONE....................714 239-2433
Shane Whiteside, *Pr*

EMP: 150 **EST:** 2016
SALES (est): 154.36MM
SALES (corp-wide): 1.77B **Privately Held**
Web: www.summitinterconnect.com
SIC: 3672 Printed circuit boards
PA: Goldberg Lindsay & Co. Llc
630 5th Ave Fl 30
New York NY
212 651-1100

(P-8736)
TC COSMOTRONIC INC
Also Called: Cosmotronic
4663 E Guasti Rd Ste A (91761-8196)
PHONE....................949 660-0740
James R Savage, *CEO*
Tracyconrad Enriquez, *
EMP: 109 **EST:** 1969
SALES (est): 1.81MM **Privately Held**
SIC: 3672 Printed circuit boards

(P-8737)
TECHNOTRONIX INC
1381 N Hundley St (92806-1301)
PHONE....................714 630-9200
Jayshree Kapuria, *CEO*
EMP: 20 **EST:** 2012
SALES (est): 4.13MM **Privately Held**
Web: www.technotronix.us
SIC: 3672 Printed circuit boards

(P-8738)
TIGER BUSINESS HOLDINGS INC
32052 Sea Island Dr (92629-3629)
PHONE....................714 763-4180
Thomas Meeker, *Pr*
Masayuki Kojima, *VP*
Sherlene Meeker, *CFO*
◆ **EMP:** 18 **EST:** 1980
SALES (est): 2.46MM **Privately Held**
Web: www.taiyocircuitautomation.com
SIC: 3672 Printed circuit boards

(P-8739)
TRANSLINE TECHNOLOGY INC
1106 S Technology Cir (92805-6329)
PHONE....................714 533-8300
Kishor Patel, *Pr*
Larry Padmani, *
▲ **EMP:** 33 **EST:** 1996
SQ FT: 20,000
SALES (est): 4.83MM **Privately Held**
Web: www.translinetech.com
SIC: 3672 Printed circuit boards

(P-8740)
TRANTRONICS INC
1822 Langley Ave (92614-5624)
PHONE....................949 553-1234
Tom Tran, *Pr*
EMP: 32 **EST:** 1997
SALES (est): 6.89MM **Privately Held**
Web: www.trantronics.com
SIC: 3672 3599 Printed circuit boards;
Machine and other job shop work

(P-8741)
TRI-STAR LAMINATES INC
Also Called: Laminating Company of America
20322 Windrow Dr Ste 100 (92630-8150)
PHONE....................949 587-3200
Patrick Redfern, *Pr*
EMP: 33 **EST:** 2000
SQ FT: 50,000
SALES (est): 1.63MM **Privately Held**
SIC: 3672 Printed circuit boards

(P-8742)
TTM PRINTED CIRCUIT GROUP INC (HQ)
2630 S Harbor Blvd (92704-5829)
PHONE....................714 327-3000
Thomas T Edman, *Pr*
Steve Richards, *
▲ **EMP:** 156 **EST:** 2006
SALES (est): 122.88MM
SALES (corp-wide): 2.5B **Publicly Held**
Web: www.ttm.com
SIC: 3672 Printed circuit boards
PA: Ttm Technologies, Inc.
200 Sandpointe Ave # 400
Santa Ana CA
714 327-3000

(P-8743)
TTM TECHNOLOGIES INC (PA)
Also Called: Ttm
200 Sandpointe Ave Ste 400 (92707-5751)
PHONE....................714 327-3000
Thomas T Edman, *Pr*
Rex D Geveden, *Non-Executive Chairman
of the Board*
Daniel L Boehle, *Ex VP*
Philip Titterton, *Ex VP*
Douglas L Soder, *Ex VP*
EMP: 500 **EST:** 1978
SQ FT: 14,472
SALES (est): 2.5B
SALES (corp-wide): 2.5B **Publicly Held**
Web: www.ttm.com
SIC: 3672 Printed circuit boards

(P-8744)
TTM TECHNOLOGIES INC
2630 S Harbor Blvd (92704-5829)
PHONE....................714 241-0303
Dale Anderson, *Prin*
EMP: 300
SALES (corp-wide): 2.5B **Publicly Held**
Web: www.ttm.com
SIC: 3672 Printed circuit boards
PA: Ttm Technologies, Inc.
200 Sandpointe Ave # 400
Santa Ana CA
714 327-3000

(P-8745)
TTM TECHNOLOGIES INC
3140 E Coronado St (92806-1914)
PHONE....................714 688-7200
EMP: 290
SALES (corp-wide): 2.5B **Publicly Held**
Web: www.ttm.com
SIC: 3672 Printed circuit boards
PA: Ttm Technologies, Inc.
200 Sandpointe Ave # 400
Santa Ana CA
714 327-3000

(P-8746)
TTM TECHNOLOGIES INC
5037 Ruffner St (92111-1107)
PHONE....................858 874-2701
Mark Micale, *Mgr*
EMP: 242
SALES (corp-wide): 2.5B **Publicly Held**
Web: www.ttm.com
SIC: 3672 Printed circuit boards
PA: Ttm Technologies, Inc.
200 Sandpointe Ave # 400
Santa Ana CA
714 327-3000

(P-8747)
UNITED INTERNATIONAL TECH INC

9207 Deering Ave Ste B (91311-6960)
PHONE...................................818 772-9400
Edmundo Espindola, *CEO*
Edmundo Espindola, *
EMP: 36 **EST:** 2008
SALES (est): 2.75MM **Privately Held**
Web: www.uitpcb.com
SIC: 3672 7629 Circuit boards, television and radio printed; Circuit board repair

(P-8748)
VECTOR ELECTRONICS & TECH INC
11115 Vanowen St (91605-6371)
PHONE...................................818 985-8208
Rakesh Bajaria, *CEO*
Ken Pansuriah, *
Viny Kathrotia, *
▲ **EMP:** 25 **EST:** 2001
SALES (est): 4.06MM **Privately Held**
Web: www.vectorelect.com
SIC: 3672 Printed circuit boards

(P-8749)
VEECO ELECTRO FAB INC
1176 N Osprey Cir (92807-1709)
PHONE...................................714 630-8020
EMP: 21
SQ FT: 10,000
SALES (est): 2.57MM **Privately Held**
SIC: 3672 7629 Printed circuit boards; Circuit board repair

(P-8750)
VISION MANUFACTURING INC
1398 Poinsettia Ave # 101 (92081-8580)
PHONE...................................760 689-0020
Steven Truong, *Pr*
Kim Dang, *Sec*
▲ **EMP:** 70 **EST:** 2000
SQ FT: 10,000
SALES (est): 1.21MM **Privately Held**
SIC: 3672 Printed circuit boards

(P-8751)
WE IMAGINE INC
9371 Canoga Ave (91311-5879)
P.O. Box 5696 (91313-5696)
PHONE...................................818 709-0064
EMP: 53 **EST:** 1974
SALES (est): 5.46MM **Privately Held**
SIC: 3672 Printed circuit boards

(P-8752)
WFB ARCHIVES INC
13500 Danielson St (92064-6874)
EMP: 80
SIC: 3672 Printed circuit boards

(P-8753)
WINONICS INC
Also Called: Bench 2 Bench Technologies
1257 S State College Blvd (92831-5336)
PHONE...................................714 626-3755
EMP: 120
SALES (corp-wide): 35.2MM **Privately Held**
Web: www.winonics.com
SIC: 3672 Printed circuit boards
HQ: Winonics Llc
    660 N Puente St
    Brea CA
    714 256-8700

(P-8754)
YUN INDUSTRIAL CO LTD
Also Called: Y I C
161 Selandia Ln (90746-1412)
PHONE...................................310 715-1898

Ilun Yun, *Pr*
William Yun, *
Stephen Yun, *
◆ **EMP:** 40 **EST:** 1990
SQ FT: 16,000
SALES (est): 4.21MM **Privately Held**
Web: www.boardassembly.com
SIC: 3672 Printed circuit boards

3674 Semiconductors And Related Devices

(P-8755)
ABB ENTERPRISE SOFTWARE INC
Also Called: ABB ENTERPRISE SOFTWARE INC.
4600 Colorado Blvd (90039-1106)
PHONE...................................213 743-4819
Carol Clemons, *Brnch Mgr*
▲ **EMP:** 55
Web: new.abb.com
SIC: 3674 Microcircuits, integrated (semiconductor)
HQ: Abb Inc.
    305 Gregson Dr
    Cary NC

(P-8756)
ACCELERATED MEMORY PROD INC
Also Called: AMP
1317 E Edinger Ave (92705-4416)
PHONE...................................714 460-9800
Richard Mccauley, *Pr*
Cathleen Mccauley, *VP*
◆ **EMP:** 49 **EST:** 2007
SQ FT: 10,000
SALES (est): 5.66MM **Privately Held**
Web: www.ampinc.com
SIC: 3674 Semiconductors and related devices

(P-8757)
ADTECH PHOTONICS INC
Also Called: Adtech Optics
18007 Cortney Ct (91748-1203)
PHONE...................................626 956-1000
Mary Fong, *CEO*
EMP: 25 **EST:** 2012
SALES (est): 4.08MM **Privately Held**
Web: www.atoptics.com
SIC: 3674 Semiconductors and related devices

(P-8758)
ADVANCED SEMICONDUCTOR INC
Also Called: A S I
24955 Avenue Kearny (91355-1252)
PHONE...................................818 982-1200
Fred Golob, *CEO*
▲ **EMP:** 58 **EST:** 1979
SQ FT: 9,000
SALES (est): 4.93MM **Privately Held**
Web: www.advancedsemiconductor.com
SIC: 3674 Integrated circuits, semiconductor networks, etc.

(P-8759)
ADVANCED THERMAL SCIENCES CORP (DH)
3355 E La Palma Ave (92806-2815)
PHONE...................................714 688-4200
Bruce Thayer, *Pr*
Masashi Iwao, *
▲ **EMP:** 31 **EST:** 1997
SALES (est): 11.76MM

SALES (corp-wide): 67.07B **Publicly Held**
Web: www.atschiller.com
SIC: 3674 Semiconductors and related devices
HQ: B/E Aerospace, Inc.
    1400 Corporate Center Way
    Wellington FL

(P-8760)
ADVANTEST TEST SOLUTIONS INC
26211 Enterprise Way (92630-8402)
PHONE...................................949 523-6900
Jonathan Sinskie, *CEO*
Keith Sinskie, *CFO*
EMP: 52 **EST:** 2018
SALES (est): 22.4MM **Privately Held**
Web: www.advantest.com
SIC: 3674 Semiconductors and related devices
HQ: Advantest America, Inc.
    3061 Zanker Rd
    San Jose CA

(P-8761)
AEROFLEX INCORPORATED
15375 Barranca Pkwy Ste F106 (92618-2217)
PHONE...................................800 843-1553
Len Burrows, *Brnch Mgr*
EMP: 33
SALES (corp-wide): 2.67MM **Privately Held**
Web: www.caes.com
SIC: 3674 Semiconductors and related devices
HQ: Aeroflex Incorporated
    2121 Crystal Dr Ste 800
    Arlington VA
    516 694-6700

(P-8762)
AGILE TECHNOLOGIES INC
2 Orion (92656-4200)
PHONE...................................949 454-8030
Martin Munzer, *CEO*
David A Krohn, *Pr*
Rick Brooks, *VP*
EMP: 22 **EST:** 2002
SQ FT: 40,000
SALES (est): 977.71K **Privately Held**
Web: www.agiletech.org
SIC: 3674 Photoelectric magnetic devices

(P-8763)
AMERICAN ARIUM
Also Called: Arium
17791 Fitch (92614-6019)
PHONE...................................949 623-7090
Larry Traylor, *Pr*
Diane Dirks, *
EMP: 40 **EST:** 1977
SQ FT: 32,330
SALES (est): 6MM **Privately Held**
Web: www.asset-intertech.com
SIC: 3674 3577 Microprocessors; Computer peripheral equipment, nec

(P-8764)
AMERICAN SOLAR ADVANTAGE INC
Also Called: Asa Power BDH Engrg & Cnstr
13348 Monte Vista Ave (91710-5147)
PHONE...................................877 765-2388
Bobby D Harris, *Pr*
EMP: 20 **EST:** 2016
SALES (est): 3.5MM **Privately Held**
Web: www.asa.solar
SIC: 3674 1731 Solar cells; Electrical work

(P-8765)
AMONIX INC
1709 Apollo Ct (90740-5617)
PHONE...................................562 344-4750
▲ **EMP:** 120
SIC: 3674 Solar cells

(P-8766)
ANOKIWAVE INC (PA)
5355 Mira Sorrento Pl Ste 300 (92121-3802)
PHONE...................................858 792-9910
Nitin Jain, *Ch Bd*
Robert S Donahue, *
Deborah Dendy, *
Carl Frank, *
William Boecke, *
EMP: 44 **EST:** 1999
SALES (est): 11.36MM
SALES (corp-wide): 11.36MM **Privately Held**
Web: www.anokiwave.com
SIC: 3674 Semiconductors and related devices

(P-8767)
APIC CORPORATION
5800 Uplander Way (90230-6608)
PHONE...................................310 642-7975
James Chan, *VP*
Birendra Dutt, *
Koichi Sayano, *
Anguel Nikolov, *
EMP: 58 **EST:** 2001
SQ FT: 14,416
SALES (est): 9.48MM **Privately Held**
Web: www.apichip.com
SIC: 3674 Semiconductors and related devices

(P-8768)
ARM INC
5375 Mira Sorrento Pl Ste 540 (92121-3804)
PHONE...................................858 453-1900
Todd Vierra, *Brnch Mgr*
EMP: 678
SALES (corp-wide): 11.15B **Privately Held**
Web: www.arm.com
SIC: 3674 Integrated circuits, semiconductor networks, etc.
HQ: Arm, Inc.
    120 Rose Orchard Way
    San Jose CA

(P-8769)
ASC GROUP INC
12243 Branford St (91352-1010)
PHONE...................................818 896-1101
Chuck Rogers, *Pr*
EMP: 1119 **EST:** 1988
SQ FT: 80,000
SALES (est): 9.66MM
SALES (est): 1.71B **Privately Held**
Web: www.pmcglobalinc.com
SIC: 3674 Semiconductors and related devices
HQ: Pmc, Inc.
    12243 Branford St
    Sun Valley CA
    818 896-1101

(P-8770)
ASI SEMICONDUCTOR INC
Also Called: A S I
24955 Avenue Kearny (91355-1252)
PHONE...................................818 982-1200
Steve Golob, *Prin*
Mike Lincoln, *
Fred Golob, *

EMP: 25 EST: 2011
SALES (est): 4.18MM Privately Held
Web: www.advancedsemiconductor.com
SIC: 3674 Semiconductors and related
devices

(P-8771)
ATOMICA CORP
Also Called: IMT Analytical
75 Robin Hill Rd (93117-3108)
PHONE..............................805 681-2807
Eric Sigler, CEO
Jim Mcgibbon, CFO
Chris Gudeman, *
Dave Chrishna, *
▲ EMP: 115 EST: 1987
SQ FT: 130,000
SALES (est): 42.81MM Privately Held
Web: www.atomica.com
SIC: 3674 Semiconductors and related
devices

(P-8772)
AVID IDNTIFICATION SYSTEMS INC (PA)
Also Called: Avid
3185 Hamner Ave (92860-1937)
PHONE..............................951 371-7505
Hannis L Stoddard, CEO
Hannis L Stoddard, Pr
Peter Troesch, *
▲ EMP: 100 EST: 1986
SQ FT: 30,000
SALES (est): 12.93MM Privately Held
Web: www.avidid.com
SIC: 3674 5999 Semiconductors and related
devices; Pets and pet supplies

(P-8773)
BAYWA RE EPC LLC
17901 Von Karman Ave Ste 1050
(92614-5254)
PHONE..............................949 398-3915
Baywa R E Solar, Project LLC
EMP: 37 EST: 2015
SALES (est): 946.66K Privately Held
Web: us.baywa-re.com
SIC: 3674 Solar cells

(P-8774)
BAYWA RE SOLAR PROJECTS LLC (DH)
Also Called: Baywa R.E.renewable Energy
18575 Jamboree Rd Ste 850 (92612-2558)
PHONE..............................949 398-3915
▲ EMP: 211 EST: 2014
SALES (est): 1.03B
SALES (corp-wide): 28.11B Privately Held
Web: www.baywa-re.com
SIC: 3674 Solar cells
HQ: Baywa R.E. Ag
Arabellastr. 4
Munchen BY

(P-8775)
BROADCOM CORPORATION
15101 Alton Pkwy (92618-2372)
PHONE..............................949 926-5000
EMP: 76
SALES (corp-wide): 33.2B Publicly Held
Web: www.broadcom.com
SIC: 3674 Semiconductors and related
devices
HQ: Broadcom Corporation
1320 Ridder Park Dr
San Jose CA

(P-8776)
BROADCOM CORPORATION
Also Called: Broadcom Limited Bldg 2
15191 Alton Pkwy (92618-2300)
PHONE..............................714 376-5029
EMP: 29
SALES (corp-wide): 33.2B Publicly Held
Web: www.broadcom.com
SIC: 3674 Semiconductors and related
devices
HQ: Broadcom Corporation
1320 Ridder Park Dr
San Jose CA

(P-8777)
BROADCOM CORPORATION
16340 W Bernardo Dr Bldg A (92127-1802)
PHONE..............................858 385-8800
Bell Philip Andrew, Brnch Mgr
EMP: 116
SALES (corp-wide): 33.2B Publicly Held
Web: www.broadcom.com
SIC: 3674 Integrated circuits, semiconductor
networks, etc.
HQ: Broadcom Corporation
1320 Ridder Park Dr
San Jose CA

(P-8778)
CAELUX CORPORATION
404 N Halstead St (91107-3124)
PHONE..............................626 502-7033
Scott Graybeal, CEO
John Iannellli, Pr
Jeremy Ferrell, CFO
EMP: 27 EST: 2014
SALES (est): 3.39MM Privately Held
SIC: 3674 Semiconductors and related
devices

(P-8779)
CLARIPHY COMMUNICATIONS INC (DH)
15485 Sand Canyon Ave (92618-3154)
PHONE..............................949 861-3074
Nariman Yousefi, Pr
William J Ruehle, *
Norman L Swenson, *
EMP: 78 EST: 2004
SALES (est): 25.93MM
SALES (corp-wide): 5.92B Publicly Held
Web: www.marvell.com
SIC: 3674 Integrated circuits, semiconductor
networks, etc.
HQ: Inphi Corporation
110 Rio Robles
San Jose CA
408 217-7300

(P-8780)
CNT ACQUISITION CORP (DH)
1 Enterprise (92656-2606)
PHONE..............................949 380-6100
James J Peterson, Ch
EMP: 43 EST: 2014
SALES (est): 12.53MM
SALES (corp-wide): 8.44B Publicly Held
Web: www.microsemi.com
SIC: 3674 Rectifiers, solid state
HQ: Microsemi Corporation
11861 Western Ave
Garden Grove CA
949 380-6100

(P-8781)
CONEXANT HOLDINGS INC
4000 Macarthur Blvd (92660-2558)
PHONE..............................415 983-2706
EMP: 600

SIC: 3674 5065 Semiconductors and related
devices; Semiconductor devices

(P-8782)
CONEXANT SYSTEMS LLC (HQ)
1901 Main St Ste 300 (92614-0512)
PHONE..............................949 483-4600
Jan Johannessen, CEO
EMP: 23 EST: 2013
SQ FT: 140,000
SALES (est): 45.55MM
SALES (corp-wide): 1.36B Publicly Held
SIC: 3674 5065 Semiconductors and related
devices; Semiconductor devices
PA: Synaptics Incorporated
1109 Mckay Dr
San Jose CA
408 904-1100

(P-8783)
COOPER MICROELECTRONICS INC
Also Called: CMI
1671 Reynolds Ave (92614-5709)
PHONE..............................949 553-8352
Kenneth B Cooper Iii, Pr
Lily Cooper, *
▲ EMP: 37 EST: 1985
SQ FT: 10,000
SALES (est): 4.98MM Privately Held
Web: www.coopermicro.com
SIC: 3674 7371 Semiconductors and related
devices; Custom computer programming
services

(P-8784)
DATA CIRCLE INC
3333 Michelson Dr Ste 735 (92612-7679)
PHONE..............................949 260-6569
Steve Oren, CEO
EMP: 24 EST: 1991
SQ FT: 12,000
SALES (est): 248.42K Privately Held
SIC: 3674 Integrated circuits, semiconductor
networks, etc.

(P-8785)
DATA DEVICE CORPORATION
13000 Gregg St Ste C (92064-7151)
PHONE..............................858 503-3300
Dan Veenstra, Brnch Mgr
EMP: 35
SALES (corp-wide): 6.58B Publicly Held
Web: www.ddc-web.com
SIC: 3674 Semiconductors and related
devices
HQ: Data Device Corporation
105 Wilbur Pl
Bohemia NY
631 567-5600

(P-8786)
DAYLIGHT SOLUTIONS INC (DH)
Also Called: Drs Daylight Solutions
16845 Via Esprillo Ste 100 (92127-1701)
PHONE..............................858 432-7500
Timothy Day, CEO
Paul Larson, Pr
EMP: 167 EST: 2004
SALES (est): 40.72MM
SALES (corp-wide): 15.28B Publicly Held
Web: www.daylightsolutions.com
SIC: 3674 5084 3826 Molecular devices,
solid state; Instruments and control
equipment; Analytical instruments
HQ: Leonardo Drs, Inc.
2345 Crystal Dr Ste 1000
Arlington VA
703 416-8000

(P-8787)
DISPLAY PRODUCTS INC
Also Called: Data Display Products
445 S Douglas St (90245-4630)
PHONE..............................310 640-0442
EMP: 48 EST: 1970
SALES (est): 5MM Privately Held
Web: www.vcclite.com
SIC: 3674 3679 Semiconductors and related
devices; Electronic circuits

(P-8788)
DPA LABS INC
Also Called: Dpa Components International
2251 Ward Ave (93065-7556)
PHONE..............................805 581-9200
Douglas Young, Pr
Philip Young, VP
EMP: 50 EST: 1979
SQ FT: 38,000
SALES (est): 9.57MM Privately Held
Web: www.dpaci.com
SIC: 3674 8734 Semiconductors and related
devices; Testing laboratories

(P-8789)
DRS NTWORK IMAGING SYSTEMS LLC
Also Called: Drs Network & Imaging Systems
10600 Valley View St (90630-4833)
PHONE..............................714 220-3800
EMP: 100 EST: 2009
SALES (est): 23.98MM
SALES (corp-wide): 15.28B Publicly Held
Web: www.leonardodrs.com
SIC: 3674 8731 Infrared sensors, solid state;
Commercial physical research
HQ: Leonardo Drs, Inc.
2345 Crystal Dr Ste 1000
Arlington VA
703 416-8000

(P-8790)
EFFICIENT PWR CONVERSION CORP (PA)
909 N Pacific Coast Hwy (90245-2724)
PHONE..............................310 615-0279
Alexander Lidow, Pr
Robert Beach, *
Jianjun Cao, *
Bel Lazar, *
Massimo Marabotti, *
EMP: 60 EST: 2007
SQ FT: 2,700
SALES (est): 10.25MM Privately Held
Web: www.epc-co.com
SIC: 3674 Integrated circuits, semiconductor
networks, etc.

(P-8791)
EMCORE CORPORATION
Emcore-Ortel Division
2015 Chestnut St (91803-1542)
PHONE..............................626 293-3400
Hone Hu, VP
EMP: 175
SALES (corp-wide): 124.13MM Publicly
Held
Web: www.emcore.com
SIC: 3674 Semiconductors and related
devices
PA: Emcore Corporation
2015 Chestnut St
Alhambra CA
626 293-3400

(P-8792)
EMCORE CORPORATION (PA)
Also Called: Emcore

PRODUCTS & SVCS

2015 Chestnut St (91803-1542)
PHONE..............................626 293-3400
Jeffrey Rittichier, *CEO*
Stephen L Domenik, *
Tom Minichiello, *CFO*
Iain Black, *Sr VP*
▲ **EMP:** 230 **EST:** 1984
SQ FT: 68,000
SALES (est): 124.13MM
SALES (corp-wide): 124.13MM **Publicly Held**
Web: www.emcore.com
SIC: 3674 3559 Integrated circuits, semiconductor networks, etc.; Semiconductor manufacturing machinery

(P-8793)
EPSON ELECTRONICS AMERICA INC (DH)
3131 Katella Ave (90720-2335)
PHONE..............................408 922-0200
Koji Abe, *Pr*
Craig Hodowski, *Sec*
▲ **EMP:** 32 **EST:** 1997
SALES (est): 11.24MM **Privately Held**
SIC: 3674 5065 8731 Semiconductors and related devices; Electronic parts and equipment, nec; Commercial physical research
HQ: U.S. Epson, Inc.
3131 Katella Ave
Los Alamitos CA

(P-8794)
ESI INC
Also Called: Electronic Services
5710 W Manchester Ave Ste 109 (90045-4423)
P.O. Box 90772 (90009-0772)
PHONE..............................310 670-4974
Abraham Shiepe, *Pr*
B Colwell, *Sec*
L Dodzinksi, *CEO*
EMP: 32 **EST:** 1954
SQ FT: 5,000
SALES (est): 504.56K **Privately Held**
SIC: 3674 Integrated circuits, semiconductor networks, etc.

(P-8795)
ESSEX ELECTRONICS INC
1130 Mark Ave (93013-2918)
PHONE..............................805 684-7601
Stewart Frisch, *Ch Bd*
Jesse Moore, *CEO*
Fred Zimmermann, *Pr*
Garrett Kaufman, *Pr*
Dean Benjamin, *Prin*
▲ **EMP:** 23 **EST:** 1991
SQ FT: 7,000
SALES (est): 4.8MM **Privately Held**
Web: www.keyless.com
SIC: 3674 Semiconductors and related devices

(P-8796)
FALKOR PARTNERS LLC
Also Called: Semicoa
333 Mccormick Ave (92626-3422)
PHONE..............................714 721-8772
Allen Ronk, *CEO*
John Park, *
EMP: 21 **EST:** 2014
SQ FT: 24,000
SALES (est): 694.91K **Privately Held**
SIC: 3674 Semiconductors and related devices

(P-8797)
FORMER LUNA SUBSIDIARY INC (HQ)
EMP: 55 **EST:** 1998
SALES (est): 54.46MM **Publicly Held**
SIC: 3674 Semiconductors and related devices
PA: Luna Innovations Incorporated
301 1st St Sw Ste 200
Roanoke VA

(P-8798)
FULCRUM MICROSYSTEMS INC
26630 Agoura Rd (91302-1954)
PHONE..............................818 871-8100
Robert R Nunn, *CEO*
Dale Bartos, *
Mike Zeile, *
Uri Cummings, *
EMP: 58 **EST:** 1999
SQ FT: 17,077
SALES (est): 13.15MM
SALES (corp-wide): 63.05B **Publicly Held**
Web: www.fulcrummicro.com
SIC: 3674 Semiconductors and related devices
PA: Intel Corporation
2200 Mission College Blvd
Santa Clara CA
408 765-8080

(P-8799)
GLOBAL COMM SEMICONDUCTORS LLC
Also Called: G C S
23155 Kashiwa Ct (90505-4026)
PHONE..............................310 530-7274
Bau-hsing Brian Ann, *Pr*
Mark L Raggio, *Sec*
Ta-lun Darren Huang, *Ch*
EMP: 20 **EST:** 1997
SQ FT: 38,000
SALES (est): 10.12MM **Privately Held**
Web: www.gcsincorp.com
SIC: 3674 Semiconductors and related devices
PA: Gcs Holdings, Inc.
115 S 4th St W
Missoula MT

(P-8800)
GLOBAL LOCATE INC
5300 California Ave (92617-3038)
PHONE..............................949 926-5000
Anthony Maslowski, *Pr*
EMP: 42 **EST:** 2008
SALES (est): 2.12MM
SALES (corp-wide): 33.2B **Publicly Held**
SIC: 3674 Semiconductor diodes and rectifiers
HQ: Broadcom Corporation
1320 Ridder Park Dr
San Jose CA

(P-8801)
HALCYON MICROELECTRONICS INC
5467 2nd St (91706-2072)
PHONE..............................626 814-4688
Patricia Martin, *CEO*
Dennis Martin, *Pr*
EMP: 17 **EST:** 1981
SQ FT: 9,100
SALES (est): 585.17K **Privately Held**
Web: www.halcyonmicro.com
SIC: 3674 Microcircuits, integrated (semiconductor)

(P-8802)
HANWHA Q CELLS AMERICA INC (DH)
Also Called: Q Cells
400 Spectrum Center Dr Ste 1400 (92618-4934)
PHONE..............................949 748-5996
Dong In Shin, *CEO*
Sunghoon Kim, *Pr*
Hwal Noh, *CFO*
Goo Min, *Sls Mgr*
EMP: 17 **EST:** 2009
SALES (est): 17.87MM **Privately Held**
Web: www.q-cells.de
SIC: 3674 Solar cells
HQ: Hanwha Q Cells Americas Holdings Corp.
300 Spectrum Center Dr # 12
Irvine CA
949 748-5996

(P-8803)
HERMES-MICROVISION INC
17075 Thornmint Ct (92127-2413)
PHONE..............................858 385-6500
EMP: 23
SALES (corp-wide): 16.53B **Privately Held**
Web: www.asml.com
SIC: 3674 Semiconductors and related devices
HQ: Hermes-Microvision, Inc.
80 W Tasman Dr
San Jose CA
408 597-8600

(P-8804)
ICHIA USA INC
509 Telegraph Canyon Rd (91910-6436)
PHONE..............................619 482-2222
Simon Goh, *Genl Mgr*
◆ **EMP:** 57 **EST:** 1993
SQ FT: 3,000
SALES (est): 5.2MM **Privately Held**
SIC: 3674 Semiconductors and related devices
PA: Ichia Technologies, Inc.
268, Huaya 2nd Rd.,
Taoyuan City TAY

(P-8805)
IKANOS COMMUNICATIONS INC (DH)
5775 Morehouse Dr (92121-1714)
PHONE..............................858 587-1121
Rahul Patel, *Pr*
Sanjay Mehta, *
▲ **EMP:** 18 **EST:** 1999
SQ FT: 73,500
SALES (est): 72.36MM
SALES (corp-wide): 35.82B **Publicly Held**
SIC: 3674 Integrated circuits, semiconductor networks, etc.
HQ: Qualcomm Atheros, Inc.
1700 Technology Dr
San Jose CA
408 773-5200

(P-8806)
INDIE SEMICONDUCTOR INC (PA)
Also Called: Indie
32 Journey Ste 100 (92656-5329)
PHONE..............................949 608-0854
Donald Mcclymont, *CEO*
David Aldrich, *Ch Bd*
Ichiro Aoki, *Pr*
Steven Machuga, *COO*
EMP: 26 **EST:** 2019
SQ FT: 18,000

SALES (est): 110.8MM
SALES (corp-wide): 110.8MM **Publicly Held**
Web: www.indiesemi.com
SIC: 3674 Semiconductors and related devices

(P-8807)
INFINEON TECH AMERICAS CORP (HQ)
101 N Pacific Coast Hwy (90245-4318)
PHONE..............................310 726-8200
Oleg Khaykin, *CEO*
Ilan Daskal, *
▲ **EMP:** 900 **EST:** 1979
SALES (est): 1.07B
SALES (corp-wide): 17.72B **Privately Held**
Web: www.infineon.com
SIC: 3674 Integrated circuits, semiconductor networks, etc.
PA: Infineon Technologies Ag
Am Campeon 1-15
Neubiberg BY
892340

(P-8808)
INFINEON TECH AMERICAS CORP
1521 E Grand Ave (90245-4339)
P.O. Box 2788 (91729-2788)
PHONE..............................310 252-7116
EMP: 123
SALES (corp-wide): 17.72B **Privately Held**
Web: www.infineon.com
SIC: 3674 Semiconductors and related devices
HQ: Infineon Technologies Americas Corp.
101 N Pacific Coast Hwy
El Segundo CA
310 726-8200

(P-8809)
INFINEON TECH AMERICAS CORP
Crydom Controls
233 Kansas St (90245-4316)
PHONE..............................310 726-8000
Derek Lidow, *Mgr*
EMP: 47
SALES (corp-wide): 17.72B **Privately Held**
Web: www.infineon.com
SIC: 3674 Semiconductor circuit networks
HQ: Infineon Technologies Americas Corp.
101 N Pacific Coast Hwy
El Segundo CA
310 726-8200

(P-8810)
INFRAREDVISION TECHNOLOGY CORP
Also Called: I T C
140 Industrial Way (93427-9507)
PHONE..............................805 686-8848
James Giacobazzi, *Pr*
Kenneth Hay, *VP*
EMP: 85 **EST:** 2000
SALES (est): 4.56MM
SALES (corp-wide): 1.85B **Publicly Held**
SIC: 3674 Semiconductors and related devices
HQ: Lumasense Technologies, Inc.
888 Tasman Dr 100
Milpitas CA
408 727-1600

(P-8811)
INNOPHASE INC
Also Called: Innophase
5880 Oberlin Dr (92121-4762)

PHONE...............................619 541-8280
Yang Xu, *CEO*
Thomas Lee, *
EMP: 100 **EST:** 2011
SALES (est): 10MM **Privately Held**
Web: www.innophaseinc.com
SIC: 3674 Semiconductors and related
devices

(P-8812)
INPHI INTERNATIONAL PTE LTD
112 S Lakeview Canyon Rd (91362-3925)
PHONE...............................805 719-2300
Ford Tamer, *Pr*
John Edmunds, *CFO*
EMP: 21 **EST:** 2017
SALES (est): 1.29MM **Privately Held**
Web: www.marvell.com
SIC: 3674 Semiconductors and related
devices

(P-8813)
INTEGRA TECHNOLOGIES INC
321 Coral Cir (90245-4620)
PHONE...............................310 606-0855
Paul Aken, *Pr*
Jeff Burger, *
EMP: 50 **EST:** 1997
SQ FT: 15,000
SALES (est): 16.56MM **Privately Held**
Web: www.integratech.com
SIC: 3674 Modules, solid state

(P-8814)
INTERCONNECT SYSTEMS INTL LLC (DH)
Also Called: Interconnect Systems, Inc.
741 Flynn Rd (93012-8056)
PHONE...............................805 482-2870
Mark Gilliam, *Pr*
William P Miller, *
Glen Griswold, *
Louis Buldain, *
Thomas Casey, *
▲ **EMP:** 90 **EST:** 1987
SQ FT: 48,000
SALES (est): 30.05MM
SALES (corp-wide): 36.93B **Privately Held**
Web: www.isipkg.com
SIC: 3674 Computer logic modules
HQ: Molex, Llc
2222 Wellington Ct
Lisle IL
630 969-4550

(P-8815)
INVENLUX CORPORATION
168 Mason Way Ste B5 (91746-2339)
PHONE...............................626 277-4163
Chunhui Yan, *Pr*
EMP: 23 **EST:** 2008
SQ FT: 18,000
SALES (est): 519.39K **Privately Held**
SIC: 3674 Light emitting diodes

(P-8816)
IO SEMICONDUCTOR INCORPORATED
Also Called: Iosemi
4795 Eastgate Mall (92121-1971)
P.O. Box 910674 (92191-0674)
PHONE...............................858 362-4074
◆ **EMP:** 22
SIC: 3674 Semiconductors and related
devices

(P-8817)
IOG PRODUCTS LLC
9735 Lurline Ave (91311-4404)

PHONE...............................818 350-5077
EMP: 20 **EST:** 2010
SALES (est): 1.56MM **Privately Held**
Web: www.impactograph.com
SIC: 3674 Semiconductors and related
devices

(P-8818)
IQ-ANALOG CORPORATION
12348 High Bluff Dr Ste 110 (92130-3545)
PHONE...............................858 200-0388
Michael S Kappes, *Pr*
Randy Wayland, *
EMP: 25 **EST:** 2005
SALES (est): 5.39MM **Privately Held**
Web: www.iqanalog.com
SIC: 3674 Semiconductors and related
devices

(P-8819)
IRVINE SENSORS CORPORATION
3000 Airway Ave Ste A1 (92626-6003)
PHONE...............................714 444-8700
John C Carson, *Pr*
James Justice, *
Anthony Mastrangelo, *
EMP: 43 **EST:** 2013
SALES (est): 5.38MM **Privately Held**
Web: www.irvine-sensors.com
SIC: 3674 8731 Semiconductors and related
devices; Electronic research

(P-8820)
IXYS INTGRTED CRCITS DIV AV IN
145 Columbia (92656-1413)
PHONE...............................949 831-4622
Nathan Zommer, *Ch Bd*
Uzi Sasson, *
EMP: 559 **EST:** 1983
SQ FT: 28,000
SALES (est): 11.82MM
SALES (corp-wide): 2.51B **Publicly Held**
SIC: 3674 7389 Microcircuits, integrated
(semiconductor); Design services
HQ: Ixys, Llc
1590 Buckeye Dr
Milpitas CA
408 457-9000

(P-8821)
IXYS LONG BEACH INC (DH)
2500 Mira Mar Ave (90815-1758)
PHONE...............................562 296-6584
Nathan Zommer, *CEO*
Arnold Agbayani, *
▲ **EMP:** 25 **EST:** 1980
SQ FT: 20,000
SALES (est): 9.96MM
SALES (corp-wide): 2.51B **Publicly Held**
Web: www.littelfuse.com
SIC: 3674 5065 Semiconductors and related
devices; Electronic parts and equipment,
nec
HQ: Ixys, Llc
1590 Buckeye Dr
Milpitas CA
408 457-9000

(P-8822)
KTC-TU CORPORATION
17600 Newhope St (92708-4220)
PHONE...............................714 435-2600
John Tu, *Pr*
EMP: 20 **EST:** 2001
SALES (est): 505.3K **Privately Held**
Web: www.kingston.com
SIC: 3674 Magnetic bubble memory device

(P-8823)
KULR TECHNOLOGY CORPORATION
4863 Shawline St Ste B (92111-1435)
PHONE...............................408 675-7002
Michael Mo, *CEO*
Timothy Knowles, *
EMP: 25 **EST:** 2016
SALES (est): 2MM
SALES (corp-wide): 3.99MM **Publicly Held**
Web: www.kulrtechnology.com
SIC: 3674 3624 Semiconductors and related
devices; Carbon and graphite products
PA: Kulr Technology Group, Inc.
1999 S Bascom Ave Ste 700
Campbell CA
408 663-5247

(P-8824)
KYOCERA AMERICA INC
8611 Balboa Ave (92123-1580)
▲ **EMP:** 50
SIC: 3674 Integrated circuits, semiconductor
networks, etc.

(P-8825)
KYOCERA INTERNATIONAL INC (HQ)
8611 Balboa Ave (92123-1501)
PHONE...............................858 492-1456
Robert Whisler, *Vice Chairman*
Nick Huntalas, *
William Edwards, *VP*
George Woodworth, *VP*
Franklin Kim, *Div VP*
◆ **EMP:** 100 **EST:** 1969
SQ FT: 16,000
SALES (est): 113.45MM **Privately Held**
Web: global.kyocera.com
SIC: 3674 5023 5731 Semiconductors and
related devices; Kitchen tools and utensils,
nec; Radio, television, and electronic stores
PA: Kyocera Corporation
6, Takedatobadonocho, Fushimi-Ku
Kyoto KYO

(P-8826)
LABARGE/STC INC
200 Sandpointe Ave Ste 700 (92707-5751)
PHONE...............................281 207-1400
Anthony J Reardon, *Pr*
Samuel D Williams, *VP*
Weems Turner, *
James S Heiser, *Sec*
EMP: 362 **EST:** 1985
SALES (est): 5.03MM
SALES (corp-wide): 712.54MM **Publicly
Held**
SIC: 3674 Hybrid integrated circuits
HQ: Ducommun Labarge Technologies, Inc.
689 Craig Rd Ste 200
Saint Louis MO
314 997-0800

(P-8827)
LASER OPERATIONS LLC
Also Called: Qpc Laser
15632 Roxford St (91342-1265)
PHONE...............................818 986-0000
Morris Lichtenstein, *Managing Member*
Mikhail Leibov, *
Jeffrey Ungar, *
Elyahu Pendler, *Managing Member*
EMP: 27 **EST:** 2009
SQ FT: 40,320
SALES (est): 5.04MM **Privately Held**
Web: ygy.jsz.mybluehost.me

SIC: 3674 Semiconductors and related
devices

(P-8828)
LEDTRONICS INC (PA)
23105 Kashiwa Ct (90505-4026)
PHONE...............................310 534-1505
Pervaiz Lodhie, *Pr*
Almas Lodhie, *
▲ **EMP:** 40 **EST:** 1983
SQ FT: 60,000
SALES (est): 20.66MM
SALES (corp-wide): 20.66MM **Privately
Held**
Web: www.ledtronics.com
SIC: 3674 3825 3641 Light emitting diodes;
Instruments to measure electricity; Electric
lamps

(P-8829)
LOCKWOOD INDUSTRIES LLC (HQ)
Also Called: Fralock
28525 Industry Dr (91355-5424)
PHONE...............................661 702-6999
Marc Haugen, *CEO*
Bobbi Booher, *
EMP: 100 **EST:** 1966
SQ FT: 62,500
SALES (est): 42.73MM
SALES (corp-wide): 147.68MM **Privately
Held**
Web: www.fralock.com
SIC: 3674 3842 3089 2891 Semiconductors
and related devices; Prosthetic appliances;
Plastics containers, except foam; Sealants
PA: Fralock Holdings Llc
28525 Industry Dr
Valencia CA
661 702-6999

(P-8830)
LUMIO INC
6355 Topanga Canyon Blvd Ste 335
(91367-2102)
PHONE...............................586 861-2408
Freddy Raitan, *CEO*
Mario Neves, *VP Sls*
Dan Gunders, *VP Engg*
EMP: 22 **EST:** 2000
SALES (est): 1.39MM **Privately Held**
Web: www.lumio.com
SIC: 3674 Radiation sensors

(P-8831)
LUXTERA LLC
2320 Camino Vida Roble Ste 100
(92011-1562)
PHONE...............................760 448-3520
EMP: 162 **EST:** 2001
SALES (est): 48.58MM
SALES (corp-wide): 57B **Publicly Held**
Web: www.cisco.com
SIC: 3674 Semiconductors and related
devices
PA: Cisco Systems, Inc.
170 W Tasman Dr
San Jose CA
408 526-4000

(P-8832)
MACKENZIE LABORATORIES INC
1163 Nicole Ct (91740-5387)
P.O. Box 1416 (91740-1416)
PHONE...............................909 394-9007
Nagy Khattar, *Pr*
▲ **EMP:** 25 **EST:** 1952
SQ FT: 20,000
SALES (est): 4.91MM **Privately Held**

Web: www.macklabs.com
SIC: **3674** 3663 Semiconductors and related devices; Radio and t.v. communications equipment

(P-8833)
MARVELL SEMICONDUCTOR INC
15485 Sand Canyon Ave (92618-3154)
PHONE..........................949 614-7700
Robert E Romney, *Prin*
EMP: 674
SALES (corp-wide): 5.92B **Publicly Held**
Web: www.marvell.com
SIC: **3674** Semiconductors and related devices
HQ: Marvell Semiconductor, Inc.
     5488 Marvell Ln
     Santa Clara CA

(P-8834)
MASIMO SEMICONDUCTOR INC
52 Discovery (92618-3105)
PHONE..........................603 595-8900
Mark P De Raad, *Pr*
Gerry Hammarth, *VP*
EMP: 41 **EST:** 2012
SALES (est): 4.74MM **Publicly Held**
Web: www.masimo.com
SIC: **3674** Light emitting diodes
PA: Masimo Corporation
     52 Discovery
     Irvine CA

(P-8835)
MATERION PRCSION OPTICS THIN F
153 Industrial Way (93427-9592)
PHONE..........................805 688-4949
James Wafer, *CEO*
Connie G Kraft, *
▲ **EMP:** 94 **EST:** 1974
SQ FT: 15,000
SALES (est): 9.68MM **Publicly Held**
SIC: **3674** Thin film circuits
HQ: Materion Advanced Materials
     Technologies And Services Inc.
     2978 Main St
     Buffalo NY
     800 327-1355

(P-8836)
MAXLINEAR INC (PA)
5966 La Place Ct Ste 100 (92008-8830)
PHONE..........................760 692-0711
Kishore Seendripu, *Ch Bd*
Steven G Litchfield, *CORP*
Connie Kwong, *CAO*
Michael J Lachance, *VP Opers*
▲ **EMP:** 45 **EST:** 2003
SQ FT: 68,000
SALES (est): 1.12B
SALES (corp-wide): 1.12B **Publicly Held**
Web: www.maxlinear.com
SIC: **3674** Semiconductors and related devices

(P-8837)
MAXLINEAR TECHNOLOGIES LLC (HQ)
5966 La Place Ct Ste 100 (92008-8830)
PHONE..........................760 692-0711
EMP: 123
SALES (est): 2.56MM
SALES (corp-wide): 1.12B **Publicly Held**
Web: www.maxlinear.com
SIC: **3674** Semiconductors and related devices
PA: Maxlinear, Inc.
     5966 La Place Ct Ste 100

Carlsbad CA
760 692-0711

(P-8838)
MICRO ANALOG INC
Also Called: Analog
1861 Puddingstone Dr (91750-5825)
PHONE..........................909 392-8277
Hung T Nguyen, *CEO*
Khanh Van Nguyen, *
▲ **EMP:** 160 **EST:** 1991
SQ FT: 27,000
SALES (est): 24.75MM **Privately Held**
Web: www.micro-analog.com
SIC: **3674** Semiconductors and related devices

(P-8839)
MICROPLEX INC
1070 Ortega Way (92870-7124)
PHONE..........................714 630-8220
Clay Kucenas, *Pr*
EMP: 19 **EST:** 1986
SQ FT: 10,500
SALES (est): 861.1K **Privately Held**
Web: www.microplex-inc.com
SIC: **3674** Semiconductors and related devices

(P-8840)
MICROSEMI COMMUNICATIONS INC (DH)
Also Called: Catawba County Schools
4721 Calle Carga (93012-8560)
PHONE..........................805 388-3700
Christopher R Gardner, *Pr*
Martin S Mcdermut, *CFO*
Jacob Nielsen, *CIO*
EMP: 52 **EST:** 1987
SQ FT: 111,000
SALES (est): 49.44MM
SALES (corp-wide): 8.44B **Publicly Held**
Web: www.microsemi.com
SIC: **3674** Semiconductors and related devices
HQ: Microsemi Corporation
     11861 Western Ave
     Garden Grove CA
     949 380-6100

(P-8841)
MICROSEMI CORP - ANLOG MXED SG (DH)
Also Called: Linfinity Microelectronics
11861 Western Ave (92841-2119)
PHONE..........................714 898-8121
James Peterson, *CEO*
John Hohener, *CFO*
Paul Pickle, *COO*
Steve Litchfield, *CSO*
EMP: 78 **EST:** 1968
SALES (est): 141.9MM
SALES (corp-wide): 8.44B **Publicly Held**
Web: www.microsemi.com
SIC: **3674** Semiconductor circuit networks
HQ: Microsemi Corporation
     11861 Western Ave
     Garden Grove CA
     949 380-6100

(P-8842)
MICROSEMI CORP - HIGH PRFMCE T (DH)
11861 Western Ave (92841-2119)
PHONE..........................949 380-6100
James J Peterson, *CEO*
EMP: 56 **EST:** 2017
SALES (est): 37.01MM
SALES (corp-wide): 8.44B **Publicly Held**

Web: www.microsemi.com
SIC: **3674** Rectifiers, solid state
HQ: Microsemi Corporation
     11861 Western Ave
     Garden Grove CA
     949 380-6100

(P-8843)
MICROSEMI CORPORATION (HQ)
Also Called: Microsemi
11861 Western Ave (92841-2119)
PHONE..........................949 380-6100
Steve Sanghi, *Ch*
Eric Bjornholt, *
Ganesh Moorthy, *
EMP: 50 **EST:** 1960
SALES (est): 1.45B
SALES (corp-wide): 8.44B **Publicly Held**
Web: www.microsemi.com
SIC: **3674** Integrated circuits, semiconductor networks, etc.
PA: Microchip Technology Inc
     2355 W Chandler Blvd
     Chandler AZ
     480 792-7200

(P-8844)
MICROSEMI CORPORATION
Also Called: Microsemi Corp - Santa Ana
11861 Western Ave (92841-2119)
PHONE..........................714 898-7112
Lane Jorgensen, *Mgr*
EMP: 202
SQ FT: 93,000
SALES (corp-wide): 8.44B **Publicly Held**
Web: www.microsemi.com
SIC: **3674** Semiconductors and related devices
HQ: Microsemi Corporation
     11861 Western Ave
     Garden Grove CA
     949 380-6100

(P-8845)
MICROSS HOLDINGS INC
11150 Santa Monica Blvd (90025-3380)
PHONE..........................215 997-3200
EMP: 99 **EST:** 2010
SALES (est): 6.02MM **Privately Held**
SIC: **3674** Semiconductors and related devices

(P-8846)
MINDSPEED TECHNOLOGIES LLC (HQ)
Also Called: Mindspeed Technologies, Inc.
4000 Macarthur Blvd (92660-2507)
PHONE..........................949 579-3000
Raouf Y Halim, *CEO*
Stephen N Ananias, *Sr VP*
Gerald J Hamilton, *Senior Vice President Worldwide Sales*
Allison K Musetich, *Senior Vice President Human Resources*
Najabat H Bajwa, *Sr VP*
EMP: 88 **EST:** 2002
SQ FT: 97,000
SALES (est): 93.77MM **Publicly Held**
Web: www.macom.com
SIC: **3674** Semiconductors and related devices
PA: Macom Technology Solutions Holdings, Inc.
     100 Chelmsford St
     Lowell MA

(P-8847)
MORSE MICRO INC
40 Waterworks Way (92618-3107)
PHONE..........................949 501-7080

Michael De Nil, *CEO*
EMP: 85 **EST:** 2019
SALES (est): 5.25MM **Privately Held**
Web: www.morsemicro.com
SIC: **3674** Integrated circuits, semiconductor networks, etc.

(P-8848)
MRV COMMUNICATIONS INC
Also Called: Mrv
20520 Nordhoff St (91311-6113)
PHONE..........................818 773-0900
▲ **EMP:** 268
SIC: **3674** Integrated circuits, semiconductor networks, etc.

(P-8849)
NATEL ENGINEERING CO INC
Also Called: Neo Tech
6350 Palomar Oaks Ct (92011-1428)
PHONE..........................760 448-1500
Sudesh Arora, *Pr*
John Lowrey, *Chief*
EMP: 37 **EST:** 1969
SALES (est): 902.17K **Privately Held**
Web: www.neotech.com
SIC: **3674** 3679 Semiconductors and related devices; Antennas, receiving

(P-8850)
NETLIST INC (PA)
Also Called: Netlist
111 Academy Ste 100 (92617-3046)
PHONE..........................949 435-0025
Chun K Hong, *Ch Bd*
Gail Sasaki, *Ex VP*
EMP: 71 **EST:** 2000
SQ FT: 14,809
SALES (est): 161.64MM
SALES (corp-wide): 161.64MM **Publicly Held**
Web: www.netlist.com
SIC: **3674** Semiconductors and related devices

(P-8851)
NEWPORT FAB LLC
Also Called: Jazz Semiconductor
4321 Jamboree Rd (92660-3007)
PHONE..........................949 435-8000
EMP: 99 **EST:** 2002
SALES (est): 24.16MM **Privately Held**
Web: www.towersemi.com
SIC: **3674** Wafers (semiconductor devices)
HQ: Tower Semiconductor Newport Beach, Inc.
     4321 Jamboree Rd
     Newport Beach CA
     949 435-8000

(P-8852)
NEXT SEMICONDUCTOR TECH INC
4115 Sorrento Valley Blvd (92121-1406)
PHONE..........................858 707-7060
Mickey Rushing, *CEO*
Robert Kummer, *CFO*
EMP: 20 **EST:** 2020
SALES (est): 835.08K **Privately Held**
SIC: **3674** Semiconductors and related devices

(P-8853)
OMNISIL
5401 Everglades St (93003-6523)
PHONE..........................805 644-2514
David Clark, *Pr*
Dennis Strang, *VP*
Karin Clark, *Sec*
▲ **EMP:** 21 **EST:** 1986

▲ = Import ▼ = Export
◆ = Import/Export

SQ FT: 9,800
SALES (est): 1.9MM **Privately Held**
Web: www.omnisil.com
SIC: 3674 Silicon wafers, chemically doped

(P-8854)
ONEROOF ENERGY INC
4445 Eastgate Mall Ste 240 (92121)
PHONE..............................858 458-0533
EMP: 225
Web: www.oneroofenergy.com
SIC: 3674 Photovoltaic devices, solid state

(P-8855)
OPTO DIODE CORPORATION
750 Mitchell Rd (91320-2213)
PHONE..............................805 499-0335
EMP: 40
Web: www.optodiode.com
SIC: 3674 Diodes, solid state (germanium, silicon, etc.)

(P-8856)
OPTO DIODE CORPORATION
1260 Calle Suerte (93012-8053)
PHONE..............................805 465-8700
Mary Hagerty-goldberg, *Prin*
EMP: 26 **EST:** 1982
SALES (est): 7.45MM **Privately Held**
Web: www.optodiode.com
SIC: 3674 Semiconductors and related devices

(P-8857)
ORCA SYSTEMS INC
3990 Old Town Ave Ste C307 (92110-2930)
PHONE..............................858 679-9175
EMP: 18 **EST:** 2004
SALES (est): 1.64MM **Privately Held**
Web: www.orcasystems.com
SIC: 3674 Semiconductors and related devices

(P-8858)
OSI OPTOELECTRONICS INC
Also Called: Advanced Photonix
1240 Avenida Acaso (93012-8727)
PHONE..............................805 987-0146
Jean-pierre Maufras, *Genl Mgr*
EMP: 50
SALES (corp-wide): 1.15B **Publicly Held**
Web: www.osioptoelectronics.com
SIC: 3674 Semiconductors and related devices
HQ: Osi Optoelectronics, Inc.
12525 Chadron Ave
Hawthorne CA

(P-8859)
OSI OPTOELECTRONICS INC (HQ)
Also Called: United Detector Technology
12525 Chadron Ave (90250-4807)
PHONE..............................310 978-0516
▲ **EMP:** 113 **EST:** 1967
SALES (est): 103.42MM
SALES (corp-wide): 1.15B **Publicly Held**
Web: www.osioptoelectronics.com
SIC: 3674 3827 3812 3672 Photoconductive cells; Optical instruments and lenses; Search and navigation equipment; Printed circuit boards
PA: Osi Systems, Inc.
12525 Chadron Ave
Hawthorne CA
310 978-0516

(P-8860)
OSI SYSTEMS INC (PA)
12525 Chadron Ave (90250-4807)
PHONE..............................310 978-0516
Deepak Chopra, *Ch Bd*
Alan Edrick, *Ex VP*
Ajay Mehra, *OF OSI SOLUTIONS Business*
Victor Sze, *Ex VP*
Glenn Grindstaff, *Chief Human Resources Officer*
EMP: 325 **EST:** 1987
SQ FT: 88,000
SALES (est): 1.15B
SALES (corp-wide): 1.15B **Publicly Held**
Web: www.osi-systems.com
SIC: 3674 3845 Integrated circuits, semiconductor networks, etc.; Electromedical equipment

(P-8861)
OUTSOURCE MANUFACTURING INC
2460 Ash St (92081-8424)
PHONE..............................760 795-1295
▲ **EMP:** 60
Web: www.outsourcemanufacturing.com
SIC: 3674 Solid state electronic devices, nec

(P-8862)
PERMLIGHT PRODUCTS INC
Also Called: Perm Light
420 W 6th St (92780-4334)
PHONE..............................714 508-0729
▲ **EMP:** 20
Web: www.permlight.com
SIC: 3674 Light emitting diodes

(P-8863)
PHYSPEED CORPORATION
4055 Mission Oaks Blvd (93012-5156)
PHONE..............................805 259-3101
Yu Ruai, *Prin*
EMP: 55 **EST:** 2012
SALES (est): 470.7K
SALES (corp-wide): 1.12B **Publicly Held**
Web: www.physpeed.com
SIC: 3674 Semiconductors and related devices
PA: Maxlinear, Inc.
5966 La Place Ct Ste 100
Carlsbad CA
760 692-0711

(P-8864)
PIEZO-METRICS INC (PA)
Also Called: Micron Instruments
4584 Runway St (93063-3449)
PHONE..............................805 522-4676
Herbert Chelner, *Pr*
Sharon Chelner, *
EMP: 25 **EST:** 1967
SQ FT: 9,000
SALES (est): 4.54MM
SALES (corp-wide): 4.54MM **Privately Held**
Web: www.microninstruments.com
SIC: 3674 3829 Strain gages, solid state; Pressure transducers

(P-8865)
PLANSEE USA LLC
Also Called: E/G Electro-Graph
1491 Poinsettia Ave Ste 138 (92081-8541)
PHONE..............................760 438-9090
EMP: 60
SALES (corp-wide): 242.12K **Privately Held**
Web: www.plansee.com

SIC: 3674 Semiconductor diodes and rectifiers
HQ: Plansee Usa Llc
115 Constitution Blvd
Franklin MA
508 553-3800

(P-8866)
POLYFET RF DEVICES INC
1110 Avenida Acaso (93012-8725)
PHONE..............................805 484-9582
S K Leong, *Pr*
EMP: 25 **EST:** 1984
SQ FT: 7,500
SALES (est): 3.93MM **Privately Held**
Web: www.polyfet.com
SIC: 3674 Transistors

(P-8867)
PRIME SOLUTIONS INC
7235 Enclave Dr (92880-3827)
PHONE..............................702 354-7129
Gloria Shen, *Brnch Mgr*
EMP: 42
Web: www.primesolutions.com
SIC: 3674 Integrated circuits, semiconductor networks, etc.
PA: Prime Solutions, Inc.
48521 Warm Springs Blvd # 309
Fremont CA

(P-8868)
PRINTEC HT ELECTRONICS LLC
501 Sally Pl (92831-5014)
PHONE..............................714 484-7597
▲ **EMP:** 50 **EST:** 2011
SQ FT: 12,000
SALES (est): 11.49MM **Privately Held**
Web: www.printec-ht.com
SIC: 3674 3629 Modules, solid state; Electronic generation equipment
PA: Printec H. T. Electronics Corp.
No. 38, Liyan St.
New Taipei City TAP

(P-8869)
PSEMI CORPORATION (DH)
9369 Carroll Park Dr (92121-2257)
PHONE..............................858 731-9400
Tatsuo Bizen, *CEO*
James S Cable, *Ch Bd*
Takaki Muratajay C Biskupski, *CFO*
Takaki Murata, *HIGH PERFORMANCE ANALOG HP S UNIT*
▲ **EMP:** 70 **EST:** 1990
SQ FT: 96,384
SALES (est): 117.71MM **Privately Held**
Web: www.psemi.com
SIC: 3674 Silicon wafers, chemically doped
HQ: Murata Electronics North America, Inc.
2200 Lake Park Dr Se
Smyrna GA
770 436-1300

(P-8870)
QLOGIC LLC (DH)
15485 Sand Canyon Ave (92618-3154)
PHONE..............................949 389-6000
Arthur Chadwick, *
M Hussain, *
▲ **EMP:** 138 **EST:** 1992
SQ FT: 161,000
SALES (est): 83.84MM
SALES (corp-wide): 5.92B **Publicly Held**
Web: www.marvell.com
SIC: 3674 Integrated circuits, semiconductor networks, etc.
HQ: Cavium, Llc
5488 Marvell Ln
Santa Clara CA

(P-8871)
QUALCOMM DATACENTER TECH INC (HQ)
5775 Morehouse Dr (92121-1714)
PHONE..............................858 567-1121
Dileep Bhandarkar, *Pr*
Anand Chandrasekher, *VP*
EMP: 38 **EST:** 2016
SALES (est): 22.34MM
SALES (corp-wide): 35.82B **Publicly Held**
SIC: 3674 Integrated circuits, semiconductor networks, etc.
PA: Qualcomm Incorporated
5775 Morehouse Dr
San Diego CA
858 587-1121

(P-8872)
QUALCOMM INCORPORATED
Also Called: Qualcomm
2016 Palomar Airport Rd Ste 100 (92011-4400)
PHONE..............................858 651-8481
David Lieber, *Prin*
EMP: 19
SALES (corp-wide): 35.82B **Publicly Held**
Web: www.qualcomm.com
SIC: 3674 Integrated circuits, semiconductor networks, etc.
PA: Qualcomm Incorporated
5775 Morehouse Dr
San Diego CA
858 587-1121

(P-8873)
QUALCOMM INCORPORATED
Also Called: Qualcomm
5751 Pacific Center Blvd (92121-4252)
PHONE..............................858 909-0316
Margaret L Johnson, *Brnch Mgr*
EMP: 25
SALES (corp-wide): 35.82B **Publicly Held**
Web: www.qualcomm.com
SIC: 3674 Integrated circuits, semiconductor networks, etc.
PA: Qualcomm Incorporated
5775 Morehouse Dr
San Diego CA
858 587-1121

(P-8874)
QUALCOMM INCORPORATED
Also Called: Qualcomm
9393 Waples St Ste 150 (92121-3931)
PHONE..............................858 587-1121
EMP: 28
SALES (corp-wide): 35.82B **Publicly Held**
Web: www.qualcomm.com
SIC: 3674 7372 Integrated circuits, semiconductor networks, etc.; Prepackaged software
PA: Qualcomm Incorporated
5775 Morehouse Dr
San Diego CA
858 587-1121

(P-8875)
QUALCOMM INCORPORATED
Also Called: Qualcomm
10555 Sorrento Valley Rd (92121-1608)
PHONE..............................858 587-1121
Jim Callaghen, *Brnch Mgr*
EMP: 100
SALES (corp-wide): 35.82B **Publicly Held**
Web: www.qualcomm.com
SIC: 3674 Integrated circuits, semiconductor networks, etc.
PA: Qualcomm Incorporated
5775 Morehouse Dr
San Diego CA
858 587-1121

PRODUCTS & SVCS

(P-8876)
QUALCOMM LIMITED PARTNER INC
Also Called: Qualcomm
5775 Morehouse Dr (92121-1714)
PHONE..................................858 587-1121
Anthony Thornley, *Pr*
Richard Sulpivil, *Pr*
EMP: 75 **EST:** 1998
SALES (est): 13.75MM
SALES (corp-wide): 35.82B **Publicly Held**
SIC: 3674 Semiconductors and related devices
PA: Qualcomm Incorporated
5775 Morehouse Dr
San Diego CA
858 587-1121

(P-8877)
QUALCOMM TECHNOLOGIES INC (HQ)
5775 Morehouse Dr (92121-1714)
P.O. Box 919042 (92191-9042)
PHONE..................................858 587-1121
Cristiano Amon, *CEO*
James Thompson, *
Kevin Frizzell, *
Jim Cathey, *CCO*
▲ **EMP:** 298 **EST:** 2011
SALES (est): 1.88B
SALES (corp-wide): 35.82B **Publicly Held**
Web: www.qualcomm.com
SIC: 3674 7372 6794 Integrated circuits, semiconductor networks, etc.; Business oriented computer software; Patent buying, licensing, leasing
PA: Qualcomm Incorporated
5775 Morehouse Dr
San Diego CA
858 587-1121

(P-8878)
QUARTICS INC
15241 Laguna Canyon Rd Ste 200 (92618-3146)
P.O. Box 54648 (92619-4648)
PHONE..................................949 679-2672
Sherjil Ahmed, *Pr*
Adeel Ahmed, *
▲ **EMP:** 31 **EST:** 2005
SALES (est): 3.25MM **Privately Held**
Web: www.quartics.com
SIC: 3674 Semiconductors and related devices

(P-8879)
REVASUM INC
825 Buckley Rd (93401-8130)
PHONE..................................805 541-6424
Bill Kalenian, *Interim Chief Executive Officer*
Eric Jacobson, *OK Vice President*
Sarah Okada, *
Belinda Reyna, *
Dennis Riccio, *
EMP: 106 **EST:** 2016
SALES (est): 18.19MM **Privately Held**
Web: www.revasum.com
SIC: 3674 Semiconductors and related devices

(P-8880)
RF DIGITAL CORPORATION
1601 Pacific Coast Hwy Ste 290 (90254)
PHONE..................................949 610-0008
Armen Kazanchian, *Pr*
Rod Landers, *
EMP: 112 **EST:** 1999
SQ FT: 5,000
SALES (est): 6.51MM
SALES (corp-wide): 5B **Privately Held**

SIC: 3674 Modules, solid state
HQ: Heptagon Usa, Inc.
465 N Whisman Rd Ste 200
Mountain View CA
650 336-7990

(P-8881)
ROCKLEY PHOTONICS INC (HQ)
234 E Colorado Blvd Ste 600 (91101)
PHONE..................................626 304-9960
Andrew George Rickman, *CEO*
EMP: 192 **EST:** 2013
SALES (est): 76.99MM
SALES (corp-wide): 8.16MM **Privately Held**
Web: www.rockleyphotonics.com
SIC: 3674 Semiconductors and related devices
PA: Rockley Photonics Limited
57 Woodstock Road Clarendon
Business Centre Belsyre Court
Oxford OXON
186 529-2017

(P-8882)
SAC-TEC LABS INC (PA)
24311 Wilmington Ave (90745-6139)
PHONE..................................310 375-5295
Robert Kunesh, *Pr*
Bruce Kaufman, *Bd of Dir*
Marylin Hafermalz, *Stockholder*
EMP: 20 **EST:** 1991
SALES (est): 2.74MM **Privately Held**
Web: www.sactec.com
SIC: 3674 Semiconductors and related devices

(P-8883)
SANTIER INC
10103 Carroll Canyon Rd (92131-1109)
PHONE..................................858 271-1993
Kevin Cotner, *CEO*
Warren Bartholomew, *
▼ **EMP:** 64 **EST:** 1991
SQ FT: 23,000
SALES (est): 10.72MM
SALES (corp-wide): 16.39MM **Privately Held**
Web: www.santier.com
SIC: 3674 Semiconductors and related devices
HQ: Egide (Usa), Llc
4 Washington St
Cambridge MD
410 901-6100

(P-8884)
SEMICOA CORPORATION
333 Mccormick Ave (92626-3479)
PHONE..................................714 979-1900
Thomas E Epley, *CEO*
Ramesh Ramchandani, *
Gary B Joyce, *Interim Chief Financial Officer*
Perry Denning, *
▲ **EMP:** 60 **EST:** 2009
SALES (est): 8.69MM **Privately Held**
Web: www.semicoa.com
SIC: 3674 Semiconductors and related devices

(P-8885)
SEMICONDUCTOR PROCESS EQP LLC
Also Called: Spec
27963 Franklin Pkwy (91355-4110)
PHONE..................................661 257-0934
Arnold Gustin, *CEO*
Robin Douglas, *
Kevin Mcgillivray, *VP*

◆ **EMP:** 29 **EST:** 1986
SQ FT: 139,000
SALES (est): 7.28MM
SALES (corp-wide): 56.61MM **Privately Held**
Web: www.team-spec.com
SIC: 3674 Semiconductors and related devices
PA: Yield Engineering Systems, Inc.
3178 Laurelview Ct
Fremont CA
510 954-6889

(P-8886)
SEMTECH CORPORATION (PA)
Also Called: Semtech
200 Flynn Rd (93012-8790)
PHONE..................................805 498-2111
Paul H Pickle, *Pr*
Rockell N Hankin, *
Mark Lin, *Ex VP*
Asaf Silberstein, *Ex VP*
J Michael Wilson, *Co-Vice President*
▲ **EMP:** 180 **EST:** 1960
SQ FT: 88,000
SALES (est): 756.53MM
SALES (corp-wide): 756.53MM **Publicly Held**
Web: www.semtech.com
SIC: 3674 Semiconductors and related devices

(P-8887)
SEMTECH SAN DIEGO CORPORATION
10021 Willow Creek Rd (92131-1657)
PHONE..................................858 695-1808
Mark Drucker, *Pr*
EMP: 86 **EST:** 1994
SQ FT: 25,000
SALES (est): 14.97MM
SALES (corp-wide): 756.53MM **Publicly Held**
Web: www.semtech.com
SIC: 3674 Integrated circuits, semiconductor networks, etc.
PA: Semtech Corporation
200 Flynn Rd
Camarillo CA
805 498-2111

(P-8888)
SENSEMETRICS INC
750 B St Ste 1630 (92101-8131)
P.O. Box 16727 (80216-0727)
PHONE..................................619 738-8300
Cory Stewart Baldwin, *CEO*
EMP: 29 **EST:** 2014
SALES (est): 5.54MM
SALES (corp-wide): 965.05MM **Publicly Held**
Web: www.sensemetrics.com
SIC: 3674 Infrared sensors, solid state
PA: Bentley Systems, Incorporated
685 Stockton Dr
Exton PA
610 458-5000

(P-8889)
SILC TECHNOLOGIES INC
181 W Huntington Dr Ste 200 (91016-3456)
PHONE..................................626 375-1231
Bradley Luff, *Prin*
EMP: 38 **EST:** 2018
SALES (est): 4.9MM **Privately Held**
Web: www.silc.com
SIC: 3674 Semiconductors and related devices

(P-8890)
SKYWORKS SOLUTIONS INC
2427 W Hillcrest Dr (91320-2202)
PHONE..................................805 480-4400
Michael Gooch, *Mgr*
EMP: 43
SALES (corp-wide): 4.77B **Publicly Held**
Web: www.skyworksinc.com
SIC: 3674 Semiconductors and related devices
PA: Skyworks Solutions, Inc.
5260 California Ave # 100
Irvine CA
949 231-3000

(P-8891)
SKYWORKS SOLUTIONS INC
730 Lawrence Dr (91320-2207)
PHONE..................................805 480-4227
EMP: 42
SALES (corp-wide): 4.77B **Publicly Held**
Web: www.skyworksinc.com
SIC: 3674 Semiconductors and related devices
PA: Skyworks Solutions, Inc.
5260 California Ave # 100
Irvine CA
949 231-3000

(P-8892)
SKYWORKS SOLUTIONS INC (PA)
Also Called: SKYWORKS
5260 California Ave (92617-3228)
PHONE..................................949 231-3000
Liam K Griffin, *Ch Bd*
Kris Sennesael, *Sr VP*
Carlos S Bori, *S&M/VP*
Karilee A Durham, *Senior Vice President Human Resources*
Reza Kasnavi, *Senior Vice President Technology*
▲ **EMP:** 750 **EST:** 1962
SQ FT: 218,000
SALES (est): 4.77B
SALES (corp-wide): 4.77B **Publicly Held**
Web: www.skyworksinc.com
SIC: 3674 Integrated circuits, semiconductor networks, etc.

(P-8893)
SMT ELECTRONICS MFG INC
2630 S Shannon St (92704-5230)
PHONE..................................714 751-8894
EMP: 41 **EST:** 1995
SQ FT: 12,104
SALES (est): 1.25MM **Privately Held**
Web: www.smtelectronics.com
SIC: 3674 3672 Integrated circuits, semiconductor networks, etc.; Printed circuit boards

(P-8894)
SOLID STATE DEVICES INC
Also Called: Ssdi
14701 Firestone Blvd (90638-5918)
PHONE..................................562 404-4474
Arnold N Applebaum, *Pr*
David Franz, *
▲ **EMP:** 110 **EST:** 1967
SQ FT: 32,000
SALES (est): 20.29MM **Privately Held**
Web: www.ssdi-power.com
SIC: 3674 Diodes, solid state (germanium, silicon, etc.)

(P-8895)
SOURCE PHOTONICS USA INC (PA)

8521 Fallbrook Ave Ste 200 (91304)
PHONE..............................818 773-9044
Doug Wright, *CEO*
EMP: 249 **EST:** 1999
SALES (est): 24.59MM **Privately Held**
SIC: 3674 Semiconductors and related
   devices

(P-8896)
SOURCE PHOTONICS USA INC
8917 Fullbright Ave (91311-6124)
PHONE..............................818 407-5007
EMP: 19
SIC: 3674 Semiconductors and related
   devices
PA: Source Photonics Usa, Inc.
   8521 Fllbrook Ave Ste 200
   West Hills CA

(P-8897)
SST TECHNOLOGIES
Also Called: Sst Vacuum Reflow Systems
9801 Everest St (90242-3113)
PHONE..............................562 803-3361
Anthony Wilson, *Pr*
Ralph Burroughs, *
◆ **EMP:** 30 **EST:** 1969
SQ FT: 20,000
SALES (est): 7.42MM **Privately Held**
Web: www.palomartechnologies.com
SIC: 3674 Semiconductors and related
   devices
PA: Palomar Technologies, Inc.
   6305 El Camino Real
   Carlsbad CA

(P-8898)
**STELLAR MICROELECTRONICS
INC**
9340 Owensmouth Ave (91311-6915)
PHONE..............................661 775-3500
Sudesh Arora, *Pr*
EMP: 239 **EST:** 1974
SQ FT: 140,000
SALES (est): 52.21MM
SALES (corp-wide): 1.43B **Privately Held**
Web: www.neotech.com
SIC: 3674 Semiconductors and related
   devices
PA: Natel Engineering Company, Llc
   9340 Owensmouth Ave
   Chatsworth CA
   818 495-8617

(P-8899)
STRATEDGE CORPORATION
Also Called: Strat Edge
9424 Abraham Way Ste A (92071-5640)
PHONE..............................866 424-4962
Tim Going, *Pr*
Josie Santos, *
EMP: 40 **EST:** 1985
SALES (est): 7.22MM **Privately Held**
Web: www.stratedge.com
SIC: 3674 Semiconductors and related
   devices

(P-8900)
SUBSTANCE ABUSE PROGRAM
1370 S State St Ste A (92543)
PHONE..............................951 791-3350
Mark Thuve, *Mgr*
EMP: 30 **EST:** 2010
SALES (est): 1.33MM **Privately Held**
SIC: 3674 Semiconductors and related
   devices

(P-8901)
**SUMITOMO ELC SEMICDTR
MTLS INC**
915 Armorlite Dr (92069-1440)
PHONE..............................503 693-3100
Motoyoshi Tanaka, *Pr*
Scott Davis, *Sr VP*
Tetsuya Inoue, *VP*
▲ **EMP:** 60 **EST:** 2000
SQ FT: 90,000
SALES (est): 19.99MM **Privately Held**
Web: www.global-sei.com
SIC: 3674 Semiconductors and related
   devices
HQ: Sumitomo Electric U.S.A. Holdings, Inc.
   600 5th Ave Fl 18
   New York NY

(P-8902)
SUNCORE INC
15 Hubble Ste 200 (92618-4268)
PHONE..............................949 450-0054
Steven Brimmer, *Pr*
Donald A Nevins, *
Richard Sanett, *
Arthur Kozak, *
▲ **EMP:** 31 **EST:** 2004
SQ FT: 5,000
SALES (est): 2.93MM **Privately Held**
Web: www.suncoresolar.com
SIC: 3674 5063 5065 Solar cells; Batteries;
   Electronic parts and equipment, nec

(P-8903)
**SYMMETRY ELECTRONICS LLC
(DH)**
Also Called: Semiconductorstore.com
222 Pacific Coast Hwy (90245-5648)
PHONE..............................310 536-6190
Scott Wing, *Pr*
▲ **EMP:** 35 **EST:** 1997
SQ FT: 15,000
SALES (est): 21.09MM
SALES (corp-wide): 302.09B **Publicly
Held**
Web: www.symmetryelectronics.com
SIC: 3674 Semiconductors and related
   devices
HQ: Tti, Inc.
   2441 Northeast Pkwy
   Fort Worth TX
   817 740-9000

(P-8904)
SYNTIANT CORP (PA)
7555 Irvine Center Dr Ste 200
(92618-2912)
PHONE..............................949 774-4887
Kurt Busch, *CEO*
Paul Henderson, *
EMP: 50 **EST:** 2017
SALES (est): 10.22MM
SALES (corp-wide): 10.22MM **Privately
Held**
Web: www.syntiant.com
SIC: 3674 Semiconductors and related
   devices

(P-8905)
TALMO & CHINN INC
9537 Telstar Ave Ste 131 (91731-2912)
PHONE..............................626 443-1741
Bruce Talmo, *Pr*
Martin Chinn, *
EMP: 35 **EST:** 1972
SQ FT: 9,000
SALES (est): 3.06MM **Privately Held**
SIC: 3674 Semiconductors and related
   devices

(P-8906)
TELEDYNE DEFENSE ELEC LLC
Also Called: Teledyne Reynolds
1001 Knox St (90502-1030)
PHONE..............................310 823-5491
Mark Kotilinek, *Brnch Mgr*
EMP: 160
SALES (corp-wide): 5.46B **Publicly Held**
Web:
www.teledynedefenseelectronics.com
SIC: 3674 Semiconductors and related
   devices
HQ: Teledyne Defense Electronics, Llc
   1274 Terra Bella Ave
   Mountain View CA
   650 691-9800

(P-8907)
TELEDYNE INSTRUMENTS INC
Also Called: Teledyne
9855 Carroll Canyon Rd (92131-1103)
PHONE..............................858 842-3127
Mark Page, *Mgr*
EMP: 20
SALES (corp-wide): 5.46B **Publicly Held**
Web: www.teledyne.com
SIC: 3674 3678 3613 3423 Semiconductors
   and related devices; Electronic connectors;
   Switchgear and switchboard apparatus;
   Hand and edge tools, nec
HQ: Teledyne Instruments, Inc.
   16830 Chestnut St
   City Of Industry CA
   626 934-1500

(P-8908)
TENSORCOM INC
3530 John Hopkins Ct (92121-1121)
PHONE..............................760 496-3264
◆ **EMP:** 22 **EST:** 2007
SQ FT: 5,000
SALES (est): 5.8MM **Privately Held**
Web: www.tensorcom.com
SIC: 3674 Microcircuits, integrated
   (semiconductor)

(P-8909)
**TERIDIAN SEMICONDUCTOR
CORP (DH)**
6440 Oak Cyn Ste 100 (92618-5208)
PHONE..............................714 508-8800
EMP: 90 **EST:** 1996
SALES (est): 22.21MM
SALES (corp-wide): 12.31B **Publicly Held**
Web: www.teridian.com
SIC: 3674 Semiconductors and related
   devices
HQ: Teridian Semiconductor Holdings Corp.
   6440 Oak Cyn Ste 100
   Irvine CA

(P-8910)
**TOUCHDOWN TECHNOLOGIES
INC**
5188 Commerce Dr (91706-1450)
PHONE..............................626 472-6732
Haruo Matsuno, *Pr*
Patrick Flynn, *
Raffi Garabedian, *
Brian Flowers, *
▼ **EMP:** 30 **EST:** 1996
SQ FT: 30,000
SALES (est): 3.8MM **Privately Held**
SIC: 3674 Semiconductor diodes and
   rectifiers

(P-8911)
**TOWER SEMICDTR NEWPORT
BCH INC (DH)**
Also Called: Towerjazz
4321 Jamboree Rd (92660-3007)
PHONE..............................949 435-8000
Russell Ellwanger, *CEO*
Itzhak Edrei, *
Rafi Mor, *
Oren Shirazi, *
▲ **EMP:** 700 **EST:** 2002
SQ FT: 300,000
SALES (est): 221.47MM **Privately Held**
Web: www.towersemi.com
SIC: 3674 Wafers (semiconductor devices)
HQ: Tower Us Holdings Inc.
   4321 Jamboree Rd
   Newport Beach CA

(P-8912)
TRANSPHORM INC (PA)
75 Castilian Dr Ste 200 (93117-5580)
PHONE..............................805 456-1300
Primit Parikh, *Pr*
Umesh Mishra, *Ch Bd*
Cameron Mcaulay, *CFO*
EMP: 84 **EST:** 2017
SQ FT: 27,800
SALES (est): 16.51MM
SALES (corp-wide): 16.51MM **Publicly
Held**
Web: www.transphormusa.com
SIC: 3674 Microcircuits, integrated
   (semiconductor)

(P-8913)
**TRIDENT SPACE & DEFENSE
LLC**
Also Called: TCS Space & Component Tech
19951 Mariner Ave (90503-1738)
PHONE..............................310 214-5500
EMP: 47
Web: www.tridentsd.com
SIC: 3674 3812 8711 Semiconductors and
   related devices; Search and navigation
   equipment; Electrical or electronic
   engineering

(P-8914)
ULTRON SYSTEMS INC
5105 Maureen Ln (93021-1783)
PHONE..............................805 529-1485
Aki Egerer, *Pr*
Aaron Chan, *VP*
▲ **EMP:** 17 **EST:** 1982
SQ FT: 8,000
SALES (est): 2.38MM **Privately Held**
Web: www.ultronsystems.com
SIC: 3674 Semiconductors and related
   devices

(P-8915)
UNIREX CORP
Also Called: Unirex Technologies
2288 E 27th St (90058-1131)
PHONE..............................323 589-4000
Bijan Neman, *Pr*
Behzad Neman, *
▲ **EMP:** 25 **EST:** 1985
SQ FT: 33,000
SALES (est): 3.46MM **Privately Held**
Web: www.unirex.com
SIC: 3674 3572 Magnetic bubble memory
   device; Computer storage devices

(P-8916)
US SENSOR CORP
1832 W Collins Ave (92867-5425)
PHONE..............................714 639-1000
Roger W Dankert, *CEO*
EMP: 100 **EST:** 1989
SQ FT: 30,000
SALES (est): 26.8MM

(PA)=Parent Co (HQ)=Headquarters
✿ = New Business established in last 2 years

2024 Southern California
Business Directory and Buyers Guide

423

P R O D U C T S & S V C S

SALES (corp-wide): 2.51B **Publicly Held**
Web: www.littelfuse.com
SIC: 3674 3676 Semiconductors and related
devices; Thermistors, except temperature
sensors
PA: Littelfuse, Inc.
8755 W Higgins Rd Ste 500
Chicago IL
773 628-1000

(P-8917)
VENTURA TECHNOLOGY GROUP
855 E Easy St Ste 104 (93065-1825)
PHONE..................................805 581-0800
Douglas E Lafountaine, *Pr*
EMP: 26 **EST:** 1994
SQ FT: 7,400
SALES (est): 2.09MM **Privately Held**
Web: www.venturatech.com
SIC: 3674 Random access memory (RAM)

(P-8918)
VIRTIUM TECHNOLOGY INC
Also Called: Virtium
30052 Tomas (92688-2127)
PHONE..................................949 888-2444
▲ **EMP:** 35
SIC: 3674 Semiconductors and related
devices

(P-8919)
VISHAY THIN FILM LLC
Also Called: Vishay Spectoral Electronics
4051 Greystone Dr (91761-3100)
PHONE..................................909 923-3313
EMP: 23 **EST:** 2006
SALES (est): 461.2K **Privately Held**
SIC: 3674 Thin film circuits

(P-8920)
VITESSE MANUFACTURING & DEV
Also Called: Vitesse Semiconductor
11861 Western Ave (92841-2119)
PHONE..................................805 388-3700
Chris Gardner, *Pr*
EMP: 200 **EST:** 1984
SALES (est): 47.03MM
SALES (corp-wide): 8.44B **Publicly Held**
Web: www.microsemi.com
SIC: 3674 Microcircuits, integrated
(semiconductor)
HQ: Microsemi Communications, Inc.
4721 Calle Carga
Camarillo CA
805 388-3700

(P-8921)
W G HOLT INC
Also Called: Holt Integrated Circuits
101 Columbia (92656-1458)
PHONE..................................949 859-8800
David Mead, *CEO*
EMP: 65 **EST:** 1976
SALES (est): 12.73MM **Privately Held**
Web: www.holtic.com
SIC: 3674 Integrated circuits, semiconductor
networks, etc.

(P-8922)
WELDEX CORPORATION (PA)
6751 Katella Ave (90630-5105)
PHONE..................................714 761-2100
▲ **EMP:** 187 **EST:** 1992
SQ FT: 15,000
SALES (est): 20.1MM **Privately Held**
Web: cms.weldex.com

SIC: **3674** 3663 Light emitting diodes;
Television closed circuit equipment

(P-8923)
WORLDWIDE ENERGY AND MFG USA (PA)
Also Called: Worldwide
1800 S Myrtle Ave (91016-4833)
PHONE..................................650 692-7788
John Ballard, *Ch Bd*
Tiffany Margaret Shum, *Dir*
▲ **EMP:** 511 **EST:** 2000
SALES (est): 42.53MM
SALES (corp-wide): 42.53MM **Privately Held**
Web: www.wwmusa.com
SIC: 3674 Semiconductors and related
devices

(P-8924)
XEL USA INC
Also Called: XEL Group
23501 Ridge Route Dr Ste F (92653-1533)
PHONE..................................949 425-8686
EMP: 25 **EST:** 2008
SALES (est): 2.39MM **Privately Held**
Web: www.xelgroup.com
SIC: 3674 Magnetic bubble memory device

3675 Electronic Capacitors

(P-8925)
AMERICAN CAPACITOR CORPORATION
5367 3rd St (91706-2085)
PHONE..................................626 814-4444
Joseph Latourelle, *Pr*
EMP: 24 **EST:** 1979
SQ FT: 14,200
SALES (est): 457.66K **Privately Held**
Web: www.americancapacitor.com
SIC: 3675 5065 Electronic capacitors;
Electronic parts and equipment, nec

(P-8926)
CSI TECHNOLOGIES INC
2540 Fortune Way (92081-8441)
PHONE..................................760 682-2222
Gary W Greiser, *Pr*
Perry Sheth, *Stockholder*
Narendra C Soni, *Stockholder*
▲ **EMP:** 18 **EST:** 1969
SQ FT: 18,000
SALES (est): 4.41MM **Privately Held**
Web: www.csicapacitors.com
SIC: 3675 Electronic capacitors

(P-8927)
GENERAL ATOMICS ELECTRONIC SYSTEMS INC
4949 Greencraig Ln (92123-1675)
P.O. Box 85608 (92186-5608)
PHONE..................................858 522-8495
◆ **EMP:** 300
SIC: 3675 Electronic capacitors

(P-8928)
INCA ONE CORPORATION
1632 1/2 W 134th St (90249-2014)
PHONE..................................310 808-0001
Adriana Roberts, *Pr*
Tupac Roberts, *
▲ **EMP:** 35 **EST:** 1971
SALES (est): 4.87MM **Privately Held**
Web: www.inca-tvlifts.com
SIC: 3675 Electronic capacitors

(P-8929)
JOHANSON TECHNOLOGY INC
4001 Calle Tecate (93012-5087)
PHONE..................................805 575-0124
Justin Greene, *Ex Dir*
John Petrinec, *
▲ **EMP:** 130 **EST:** 1991
SQ FT: 30,000
SALES (est): 23.75MM **Privately Held**
Web: www.johansontechnology.com
SIC: 3675 5065 3674 Electronic capacitors;
Electronic parts and equipment, nec;
Semiconductors and related devices
PA: Johanson Ventures, Inc.
4001 Calle Tecate
Camarillo CA

(P-8930)
NEWMAR POWER LLC
1580 Sunflower Ave (92626-1511)
PHONE..................................800 854-3906
Wolfgang Hombrecher, *Managing Member*
EMP: 250 **EST:** 1979
SALES (est): 26.67MM
SALES (corp-wide): 95.13MM **Privately Held**
Web: www.poweringthenetwork.com
SIC: 3675 3678 3679 Electronic capacitors;
Electronic connectors; Electronic switches
PA: Mission Critical Electronics Llc
1580 Sunflower Ave
Costa Mesa CA
714 751-0488

3676 Electronic Resistors

(P-8931)
RIEDON INC (PA)
300 Cypress Ave (91801-3001)
▲ **EMP:** 150 **EST:** 1960
SQ FT: 12,000
SALES (est): 18.61MM **Privately Held**
Web: www.riedon.com
SIC: 3676 Electronic resistors

3677 Electronic Coils And Transformers

(P-8932)
A M I/COAST MAGNETICS INC
Also Called: Coast Magnetics
5333 W Washington Blvd (90016-1191)
PHONE..................................323 936-6188
Satya Dosaj, *CEO*
Dev Dosaj, *
Phillis Dosaj, *Stockholder*
EMP: 49 **EST:** 1965
SQ FT: 25,000
SALES (est): 5MM **Privately Held**
SIC: 3677 3549 Electronic transformers; Coil
winding machines for springs

(P-8933)
ALLIED COMPONENTS INTL
19671 Descartes (92610-2609)
PHONE..................................949 356-1780
Neal Mcdonald, *Pr*
Ruben Ramirez, *
▲ **EMP:** 25 **EST:** 1992
SQ FT: 9,000
SALES (est): 2.35MM **Privately Held**
Web: www.alliedcomponents.com
SIC: 3677 Electronic coils and transformers

(P-8934)
ASTRON CORPORATION
9 Autry (92618-2768)
PHONE..................................949 458-7277

Loren Pochirowski, *Pr*
William Pochirowski, *
▲ **EMP:** 40 **EST:** 1976
SQ FT: 18,000
SALES (est): 4.04MM **Privately Held**
Web: www.astroncorp.com
SIC: 3677 3679 Transformers power supply,
electronic type; Electronic circuits

(P-8935)
BECKER SPECIALTY CORPORATION
15310 Arrow Blvd (92335-3249)
PHONE..................................909 356-1095
Jack Mcgrew, *Brnch Mgr*
EMP: 99
SALES (corp-wide): 874.89MM **Privately Held**
SIC: 3677 Electronic coils and transformers
HQ: Becker Specialty Corporation
755 Il Route 83 Ste 223
Bensenville IL

(P-8936)
BOURNS INC (PA)
Also Called: Bourns
1200 Columbia Ave (92507-2129)
PHONE..................................951 781-5500
Gordon Bourns, *CEO*
Al Yost, *
James Heiken, *
Gregg Gibbons, *
◆ **EMP:** 171 **EST:** 1952
SQ FT: 205,000
SALES (est): 642.78MM
SALES (corp-wide): 642.78MM **Privately Held**
Web: www.bourns.com
SIC: 3677 3676 3661 3639 Electronic
transformers; Electronic resistors;
Telephone and telegraph apparatus; Major
kitchen appliances, except refrigerators and
stoves

(P-8937)
COAST/DVNCED CHIP MGNETICS INC
Also Called: Coast/A C M
4225 Spencer St (90503-2421)
PHONE..................................310 370-8188
Benjamin Nguyen, *CEO*
Ben Nguyen, *
Allen Adams, *Pr*
EMP: 19 **EST:** 1952
SQ FT: 3,000
SALES (est): 4.79MM **Privately Held**
Web: www.coastacm.com
SIC: 3677 Electronic coils and transformers

(P-8938)
COMPONETICS INC
600 Azure Hills Dr (93065-5528)
PHONE..................................805 498-0939
Oscar Maldonado, *Pr*
EMP: 25 **EST:** 2002
SALES (est): 830.86K **Privately Held**
SIC: 3677 Coil windings, electronic

(P-8939)
CORONA MAGNETICS INC
Also Called: C M I
201 Corporate Terrace St (92879-6000)
P.O. Box 1355 (92878-1355)
PHONE..................................951 735-7558
Jay Paasch, *CEO*
Heike Paasch, *
Cory Vila Managing, *Prin*
EMP: 120 **EST:** 1968
SQ FT: 17,000
SALES (est): 12.84MM **Privately Held**

Web: www.corona-magnetics.com
SIC: 3677 3679 Transformers power supply, electronic type; Electronic circuits

(P-8940)
CUSTOM SUPPRESSION INC
Also Called: Csi
26470 Ruether Ave Ste 106 (91350-2972)
PHONE..............................818 718-1040
Edward C Mcsweeney Junior, *Pr*
Genevieve Mc Sweeney, *Sec*
EMP: 17 EST: 1986
SQ FT: 7,000
SALES (est): 1.15MM Privately Held
SIC: 3677 3678 Filtration devices, electronic; Electronic connectors

(P-8941)
DSPM INC
Also Called: Digital Signal Power Mfg
439 S Stoddard Ave (92401-2025)
PHONE..............................714 970-2304
Milton Hanson, *Pr*
▲ EMP: 30 EST: 2003
SQ FT: 30,000
SALES (est): 5.14MM Privately Held
Web: www.dspmanufacturing.com
SIC: 3677 Transformers power supply, electronic type

(P-8942)
FILTER CONCEPTS INCORPORATED
22895 Eastpark Dr (92887-4653)
PHONE..............................714 545-7003
EMP: 38 EST: 1980
SALES (est): 8.04MM Privately Held
SIC: 3677 Filtration devices, electronic
PA: Astrodyne Corporation
36 Newburgh Rd
Hackettstown NJ

(P-8943)
FRONTIER ELECTRONICS CORP
667 Cochran St (93065-1939)
PHONE..............................805 522-9998
Jeannie Gu, *Pr*
Winston Gu, *VP*
Jay Valguna, *Contrlr*
Jean Pope, *Contrlr*
▲ EMP: 18 EST: 1985
SQ FT: 15,246
SALES (est): 3.36MM Privately Held
Web: dev.frontierusa.com
SIC: 3677 3674 Inductors, electronic; Semiconductors and related devices

(P-8944)
GENERAL LINEAR SYSTEMS INC
4332 Artesia Ave (92833-2523)
PHONE..............................714 994-4822
Jeffrey Steele, *Pr*
Garrett Hartney, *Pr*
Annette Hartney, *Sec*
James Mynatt, *VP*
EMP: 19 EST: 1972
SQ FT: 4,000
SALES (est): 2.48MM Privately Held
Web: www.coilwinder.com
SIC: 3677 Electronic coils and transformers

(P-8945)
MAGTECH & POWER CONVERSION INC
Also Called: Speciality Labs
1146 E Ash Ave (92831-5018)
PHONE..............................714 451-0106
Viet Pho, *Pr*

Linh Pho, *
EMP: 40 EST: 1981
SQ FT: 9,000
SALES (est): 4.99MM Privately Held
Web: www.magtechpower.com
SIC: 3677 Electronic transformers

(P-8946)
MEISSNER FILTRATION PDTS INC (PA)
1001 Flynn Rd (93012-8706)
PHONE..............................805 388-9911
Christopher Meissner, *Pr*
Laura Meissner, *VP*
▲ EMP: 20 EST: 1989
SQ FT: 45,000
SALES (est): 37.06MM Privately Held
Web: www.meissner.com
SIC: 3677 5047 8071 Filtration devices, electronic; Medical laboratory equipment; Testing laboratories

(P-8947)
MERCURY MAGNETICS INC
Also Called: Gulf Enterprises
10050 Remmet Ave (91311-3854)
PHONE..............................818 998-7791
Sergio Hamernik, *Pr*
Susan Hamernik, *VP*
▲ EMP: 20 EST: 1968
SQ FT: 21,000
SALES (est): 2.42MM Privately Held
Web: www.mercurymagnetics.com
SIC: 3677 Electronic transformers

(P-8948)
MIL-SPEC MAGNETICS INC
169 Pacific St (91768-3215)
PHONE..............................909 598-8116
Shelton Gunewardena, *CEO*
Tony Gunewardena, *
Andrew Gunewardena, *
EMP: 30 EST: 1990
SQ FT: 6,000
SALES (est): 6.05MM Privately Held
Web: www.milspecmag.com
SIC: 3677 3675 Electronic transformers; Electronic capacitors

(P-8949)
PARKER-HANNIFIN CORPORATION
Also Called: Water Purification
19610 S Rancho Way (90220-6039)
PHONE..............................310 608-5600
Jaime Garcia, *Prin*
EMP: 150
SALES (corp-wide): 19.07B Publicly Held
Web: www.parker.com
SIC: 3677 Filtration devices, electronic
PA: Parker-Hannifin Corporation
6035 Parkland Blvd
Cleveland OH
216 896-3000

(P-8950)
PAYNE MAGNETICS CORPORATION
854 W Front St (91722-3614)
PHONE..............................626 332-6207
George Payne, *Ch*
Jon S Payne, *
▲ EMP: 100 EST: 1982
SQ FT: 6,600
SALES (est): 4.48MM Privately Held
Web: www.payne-magnetics.com
SIC: 3677 3699 Electronic transformers; Electrical equipment and supplies, nec

(P-8951)
PREMIER MAGNETICS INC
20381 Barents Sea Cir (92630-8807)
PHONE..............................949 452-0511
James Earley, *Pr*
▲ EMP: 30 EST: 1991
SALES (est): 4.99MM Privately Held
Web: www.premiermag.com
SIC: 3677 3612 Electronic coils and transformers; Specialty transformers

(P-8952)
PUROFLUX CORPORATION
2121 Union Pl (93065-1661)
PHONE..............................805 579-0216
Henry Nmi Greenberg, *Pr*
▼ EMP: 17 EST: 1994
SQ FT: 25,000
SALES (est): 3.39MM Privately Held
Web: www.puroflux.com
SIC: 3677 3613 Filtration devices, electronic; Control panels, electric

(P-8953)
RAYCO ELECTRONIC MFG INC
1220 W 130th St (90247-1502)
PHONE..............................310 329-2660
Mahendra P Patel, *CEO*
Steve Mardani, *
Mayan Patel, *
EMP: 50 EST: 1941
SQ FT: 20,000
SALES (est): 9.57MM Privately Held
Web: www.raycoelectronics.com
SIC: 3677 3612 3621 Electronic transformers; Transformers, except electric; Motors and generators

(P-8954)
ROBERT M HADLEY COMPANY INC
4054 Transport St Ste B (93003-5680)
PHONE..............................805 658-7286
E Christopher Waian, *CEO*
Jim Hadley, *
Mary Hadley Waian, *
EMP: 80 EST: 1929
SQ FT: 28,000
SALES (est): 8.08MM Privately Held
Web: www.rmhco.com
SIC: 3677 Transformers power supply, electronic type

(P-8955)
SI MANUFACTURING INC
1440 S Allec St (92805-6305)
PHONE..............................714 956-7110
James R Reed, *Pr*
Ata Shafizadeh, *
▲ EMP: 50 EST: 2000
SALES (est): 9.67MM Privately Held
Web: www.simfg.com
SIC: 3677 8711 3612 3613 Electronic coils and transformers; Engineering services; Transformers, except electric; Switchgear and switchboard apparatus

(P-8956)
TUR-BO JET PRODUCTS CO INC
5025 Earle Ave (91770-1169)
PHONE..............................626 285-1294
Richard Bloom, *Pr*
Richard L Bloom, *
▲ EMP: 95 EST: 1945
SQ FT: 27,000
SALES (est): 12.97MM Privately Held
Web: www.tbj.aero
SIC: 3677 Coil windings, electronic

(P-8957)
TURBO COIL MANUFACTURING INC
1740 Evergreen St (91010-2845)
PHONE..............................626 599-7777
EMP: 33 EST: 2010
SALES (est): 2.8MM Privately Held
SIC: 3677 Electronic coils and transformers

(P-8958)
VANGUARD ELECTRONICS COMPANY (PA)
18292 Enterprise Ln (92648-1217)
PHONE..............................714 842-3330
EMP: 48 EST: 1952
SALES (est): 26.67MM
SALES (corp-wide): 26.67MM Privately Held
Web: www.ve1.com
SIC: 3677 Electronic transformers

3678 Electronic Connectors

(P-8959)
AEROFLITE ENTERPRISES INC
261 Gemini Ave (92821-3704)
PHONE..............................714 773-4251
◆ EMP: 52 EST: 1977
SALES (est): 8.71MM Privately Held
Web: www.aeroflite.com
SIC: 3678 Electronic connectors

(P-8960)
ALPHA PRODUCTS INC
351 Irving Dr (93030-5173)
PHONE..............................805 981-8666
Tony Gulrajani, *Pr*
◆ EMP: 33 EST: 1978
SQ FT: 12,000
SALES (est): 1.97MM Privately Held
Web: www.alpha-products.com
SIC: 3678 5065 Electronic connectors; Electronic parts and equipment, nec

(P-8961)
BRANTNER AND ASSOCIATES INC (DH)
Also Called: Te Connectivity MOG
1700 Gillespie Way (92020-1081)
PHONE..............................619 562-7070
Patrick G Simar, *Pr*
Denton Seilhan, *
▲ EMP: 142 EST: 1957
SQ FT: 35,000
SALES (est): 45.1MM Privately Held
Web: www.te.com
SIC: 3678 3643 Electronic connectors; Current-carrying wiring services
HQ: Brantner Holding Llc
501 Oakside Ave
Redwood City CA
650 361-5292

(P-8962)
CIRCUIT ASSEMBLY CORP (PA)
6 Autry Ste 150 (92618-2735)
PHONE..............................949 855-7887
Andrew Lang, *Pr*
Terri Lang, *
▲ EMP: 18 EST: 1969
SALES (est): 9.08MM
SALES (corp-wide): 9.08MM Privately Held
Web: www.circuitassembly.com
SIC: 3678 Electronic connectors

(P-8963)
CLEARPATHGPS LLC
Also Called: Clearpathgps
3463 State St # 494 (93105-2662)
PHONE....................805 979-3442
Christopher Fowler, *Managing Member*
Steve Wells, *Mng Pt*
EMP: 20 **EST:** 2013
SALES (est): 2.36MM **Privately Held**
Web: www.clearpathgps.com
SIC: 3678 Electronic connectors

(P-8964)
COMPONENT EQUIPMENT COINC
Also Called: Ceco
3050 Camino Del Sol (93030-7275)
P.O. Box 600 (93066-0600)
PHONE....................805 988-8004
Bill Rigby, *Pr*
Thomas Conway, *
EMP: 25 **EST:** 1979
SQ FT: 32,000
SALES (est): 2.47MM **Privately Held**
SIC: 3678 Electronic connectors

(P-8965)
CONESYS INC
548 Amapola Ave (90501-1472)
PHONE....................310 212-0065
Teresa Lynn De Foreest, *Admn*
EMP: 193
SALES (corp-wide): 58.29MM **Privately Held**
Web: www.conesys.com
SIC: 3678 Electronic connectors
PA: Conesys, Inc.
2280 W 208th St
Torrance CA
310 618-3737

(P-8966)
COOPER INTERCONNECT INC (DH)
750 W Ventura Blvd (93010-8382)
PHONE....................805 484-0543
Revathi Advaithi, *Pr*
EMP: 17 **EST:** 1945
SQ FT: 113,000
SALES (est): 54.17MM **Privately Held**
SIC: 3678 3643 Electronic connectors;
Electric connectors
HQ: Eaton Corporation
1000 Eaton Blvd
Cleveland OH
440 523-5000

(P-8967)
CORSAIR ELEC CONNECTORS INC
17100 Murphy Ave (92614-5916)
PHONE....................949 833-0273
Amir Saket, *Pr*
Steve Simmons, *Finance**
EMP: 140 **EST:** 2009
SQ FT: 34,554
SALES (est): 19.57MM **Privately Held**
Web:
www.corsairelectricalconnectors.com
SIC: 3678 Electronic connectors

(P-8968)
CRISTEK INTERCONNECTS LLC (DH)
Also Called: Cristek
5395 E Hunter Ave (92807-2054)
PHONE....................714 696-5200
Keith Barclay, *Pr*
EMP: 135 **EST:** 1985

SALES (est): 55.26MM
SALES (corp-wide): 152.91MM **Privately Held**
Web: www.cristek.com
SIC: 3678 Electronic connectors
HQ: Hermetic Solutions Group Inc.
16 Plains Rd
Essex CT
215 645-9420

(P-8969)
DETORONICS CORP
13071 Rosecrans Ave (90670-4930)
PHONE....................626 579-7130
Kenneth S Clark, *CEO*
Marcia Baroda, *
EMP: 37 **EST:** 1959
SQ FT: 20,000
SALES (est): 4.66MM **Privately Held**
Web: www.detoronics.com
SIC: 3678 Electronic connectors

(P-8970)
FLEXIBLE MANUFACTURING LLC
Also Called: F M I
1719 S Grand Ave (92705-4808)
PHONE....................714 259-7996
Carlos Cortes, *
Bart Pacetti, *
Tom Rendina, *
▲ **EMP:** 100 **EST:** 2001
SQ FT: 15,000
SALES (est): 13.49MM **Privately Held**
Web: www.4fmi.com
SIC: 3678 Electronic connectors

(P-8971)
GLEN - MAC SWISS CO
12848 Weber Way (90250-5537)
PHONE....................310 978-4555
Torkom Postajian, *Pr*
Armen Postajian, *Sec*
▲ **EMP:** 27 **EST:** 1963
SQ FT: 12,676
SALES (est): 849.31K **Privately Held**
Web: www.screwmachineshop.net
SIC: 3678 3429 3451 3599 Electronic connectors; Hardware, nec; Screw machine products; Machine shop, jobbing and repair

(P-8972)
HOLLAND ELECTRONICS LLC
Also Called: Holland Electronics
2935 Golf Course Dr (93003-7604)
PHONE....................805 339-9060
◆ **EMP:** 48 **EST:** 1998
SALES (est): 10.17MM
SALES (corp-wide): 12.62B **Publicly Held**
Web: www.hollandelectronics.com
SIC: 3678 5063 Electronic connectors; Electrical apparatus and equipment
PA: Amphenol Corporation
358 Hall Ave
Wallingford CT
203 265-8900

(P-8973)
I O INTERCONNECT LTD (PA)
Also Called: I/O Interconnect
1041 W 18th St Ste A101 (92627-4557)
PHONE....................714 564-1111
Gary Kung, *CEO*
▲ **EMP:** 50 **EST:** 1985
SALES (est): 49.62MM
SALES (corp-wide): 49.62MM **Privately Held**
Web: www.ioint.com

SIC: 3678 3679 Electronic connectors; Harness assemblies, for electronic use: wire or cable

(P-8974)
INFINITE ELECTRONICS INTL INC (DH)
17792 Fitch (92614-6020)
PHONE....................949 261-1920
Penny Cotner, *Pr*
Scott Rosner, *CFO*
Jim Dauw, *COO*
Terry G Jarniga, *Ofcr*
▲ **EMP:** 99 **EST:** 1972
SQ FT: 40,000
SALES (est): 231.46MM
SALES (corp-wide): 1.84B **Privately Held**
Web: www.infiniteelectronics.com
SIC: 3678 3357 3651 3643 Electronic connectors; Coaxial cable, nonferrous; Household audio and video equipment; Current-carrying wiring services
HQ: Infinite Electronics, Inc.
17792 Fitch
Irvine CA
949 261-1920

(P-8975)
J - T E C H
548 Amapola Ave (90501-1472)
PHONE....................310 533-6700
Walter Naubauer Junior, *CEO*
EMP: 136 **EST:** 1987
SALES (est): 14.17MM **Privately Held**
SIC: 3678 Electronic connectors

(P-8976)
JOSLYN SUNBANK COMPANY LLC
1740 Commerce Way (93446-3620)
PHONE....................805 238-2840
Mark Thek, *Genl Mgr*
Mike Ritter, *Dir Opers*
Kirsten Park, *VP*
EMP: 500 **EST:** 1997
SQ FT: 80,000
SALES (est): 61.75MM **Privately Held**
Web:
joslyn-sunbank-company-llc-in-paso-robles-ca.cityfos.com
SIC: 3678 3643 5065 Electronic connectors; Connectors and terminals for electrical devices; Connectors, electronic
HQ: Eaton Corporation
1000 Eaton Blvd
Cleveland OH
440 523-5000

(P-8977)
L & M MACHINING CORPORATION
550 S Melrose St (92870-6327)
PHONE....................714 414-0923
Mike Mai, *Pr*
EMP: 70 **EST:** 1985
SQ FT: 31,000
SALES (est): 14.46MM **Privately Held**
Web: www.lmcnc.com
SIC: 3678 Electronic connectors

(P-8978)
MIN-E-CON LLC
17312 Eastman (92614-5522)
PHONE....................949 250-0087
Wendell Jacob, *Managing Member*
John M Brown, *
Wendell P Jacob, *
▼ **EMP:** 60 **EST:** 1974
SALES (est): 9.99MM **Privately Held**
Web: www.min-e-con.com

SIC: 3678 Electronic connectors

(P-8979)
NEA ELECTRONICS INC
14370 White Sage Rd (93021-8720)
PHONE....................805 292-4010
EMP: 24 **EST:** 1995
SQ FT: 20,000
SALES (est): 5.76MM
SALES (corp-wide): 696.33MM **Privately Held**
Web: www.ebad.com
SIC: 3678 3629 3592 Electronic connectors; Battery chargers, rectifying or nonrotating; Valves
HQ: Ensign-Bickford Aerospace & Defense Co
640 Hopmeadow St
Simsbury CT
860 843-2289

(P-8980)
R KERN ENGINEERING & MFG CORP
Also Called: Kern Engineering
13912 Mountain Ave (91710-9018)
PHONE....................909 664-2440
Richard Kern, *CEO*
Roland A Kern, *
Helga Kern, *
Jose Nunez, *
▲ **EMP:** 54 **EST:** 1966
SQ FT: 34,000
SALES (est): 9.5MM **Privately Held**
Web: www.kerneng.com
SIC: 3678 3599 Electronic connectors; Machine shop, jobbing and repair

(P-8981)
RF INDUSTRIES LTD (PA)
16868 Via Del Campo Ct Ste 200 (92127-1771)
PHONE....................858 549-6340
Robert Dawson, *Pr*
Mark K Holdsworth, *
Peter Yin, *Corporate Secretary*
Ray Bibisi, *COO*
EMP: 89 **EST:** 1979
SQ FT: 21,908
SALES (est): 85.25MM
SALES (corp-wide): 85.25MM **Publicly Held**
Web: www.rfindustries.com
SIC: 3678 3643 3663 Electronic connectors; Electric connectors; Transmitter-receivers, radio

(P-8982)
SABRITEC
1550 Scenic Ave Ste 150 (92626-1465)
PHONE....................714 371-1100
EMP: 300
SIC: 3678 Electronic connectors

(P-8983)
TE CONNECTIVITY CORPORATION
Deutsch Engnred Intrcnnect Slt
3390 Alex Rd (92058-1319)
PHONE....................760 757-7500
Ken Watkins, *Brnch Mgr*
EMP: 81
Web: www.te.com
SIC: 3678 Electronic connectors
HQ: Te Connectivity Corporation
1050 Westlakes Dr
Berwyn PA
610 893-9800

▲ = Import ▼ = Export
◆ = Import/Export

(P-8984)
TEKTEST INC
Also Called: E-Z-Hook Test Products Div
5108 Azusa Canyon Rd (91706-1846)
P.O. Box 660729 (91066-0729)
PHONE.............................626 446-6175
Phelps M Wood, *Pr*
Beverly Wood, *VP*
EMP: 20 **EST:** 1970
SALES (est): 2.5MM **Privately Held**
Web: www.e-z-hook.com
SIC: 3678 Electronic connectors

(P-8985)
TIMCO/CAL RF INC
3910 Royal Ave Ste A (93063-3270)
PHONE.............................805 582-1777
EMP: 20 **EST:** 1960
SALES (est): 1.72MM **Privately Held**
SIC: 3678 Electronic connectors

(P-8986)
WINCHSTER INTRCNNECT MICRO LLC
1872 N Case St (92865-4233)
PHONE.............................714 637-7099
Ross Sealfon, *Pr*
Bruce I Billington, *
Thierry Pombart, *
Frank Malczyk Global, *Sls Mgr*
▲ **EMP:** 113 **EST:** 1977
SQ FT: 11,000
SALES (est): 23.35MM
SALES (corp-wide): 17.49B **Privately Held**
Web: www.winconn.com
SIC: 3678 Electronic connectors
HQ: Winchester Interconnect Corporation
68 Water St
Norwalk CT

3679 Electronic Components, Nec

(P-8987)
3Y POWER TECHNOLOGY INC
80 Bunsen (92618-4210)
PHONE.............................949 450-0152
Yuan Yu, *Pr*
▲ **EMP:** 17 **EST:** 1985
SQ FT: 13,800
SALES (est): 2.23MM **Privately Held**
Web: www.3ypower.com
SIC: 3679 Power supplies, all types: static

(P-8988)
A R ELECTRONICS INC
Also Called: Audiolink
31290 Plantation Dr (92276-6604)
PHONE.............................760 343-1200
Larry N Rich, *Pr*
Larry Rich, *Pr*
Cheryl Rich, *Sec*
EMP: 25 **EST:** 1985
SQ FT: 10,000
SALES (est): 887.47K **Privately Held**
SIC: 3679 5065 Electronic circuits;
Electronic parts and equipment, nec

(P-8989)
ABRACON
30332 Esperanza (92688-2118)
PHONE.............................949 546-8000
EMP: 25 **EST:** 2019
SALES (est): 778.36K **Privately Held**
Web: www.abracon.com
SIC: 3679 Electronic components, nec

(P-8990)
ACCRATRONICS SEALS CORPORATION
Also Called: A T S
2211 Kenmere Ave (91504-3416)
PHONE.............................818 843-1500
William Fisch, *CEO*
Corby Jones, *
Delbert Jones, *
Deken Jones, *
EMP: 72 **EST:** 1960
SQ FT: 10,000
SALES (est): 9.27MM **Privately Held**
Web: www.accratronics.com
SIC: 3679 Hermetic seals, for electronic equipment

(P-8991)
ADCO PRODUCTS INC
23091 Mill Creek Dr (92653-1258)
PHONE.............................937 339-6267
George Adkins, *Pr*
Randy Adkins, *
EMP: 77 **EST:** 1980
SQ FT: 12,500
SALES (est): 1.06MM **Privately Held**
Web: www.adcoprod.com
SIC: 3679 2499 Electronic circuits;
Surveyors' stakes, wood

(P-8992)
ADVANCED WAVEGUIDE TECH
23192 Alcalde Dr Ste E (92653-1451)
PHONE.............................949 297-3564
Garrett Biele, *CEO*
EMP: 30 **EST:** 2013
SALES (est): 4.05MM **Privately Held**
SIC: 3679 Waveguides and fittings

(P-8993)
AGILE RF INC
93 Castilian Dr (93117-3026)
PHONE.............................805 968-5159
Charles A Bischof, *Pr*
Tom Goodwin, *Pr*
EMP: 20 **EST:** 1999
SQ FT: 6,000
SALES (est): 2.03MM **Privately Held**
Web: www.agilerf.com
SIC: 3679 Microwave components

(P-8994)
ALYN INDUSTRIES INC
Also Called: Electronic Source Company
16028 Arminta St (91406-1808)
PHONE.............................818 988-7696
Scott J Alyn, *CEO*
▼ **EMP:** 100 **EST:** 1994
SALES (est): 30.05MM **Privately Held**
Web: www.electronic-source.com
SIC: 3679 Electronic circuits

(P-8995)
AMERICAN AUDIO COMPONENT INC
Also Called: AAC
20 Fairbanks Ste 198 (92618-1673)
PHONE.............................909 596-3788
▲ **EMP:** 26 **EST:** 1996
SALES (est): 8.98MM **Privately Held**
SIC: 3679 Transducers, electrical
HQ: Aac Acoustic Technologies
(Shenzhen) Co., Ltd.
Block A, Nanjing University Research
Center Shenzhen Branch, No.
Shenzhen GD

(P-8996)
AMSCO US INC
15341 Texaco Ave (90723-3946)
PHONE.............................562 630-0333
Mike Yazdi, *Pr*
EMP: 110 **EST:** 1998
SALES (est): 11.41MM **Privately Held**
Web: www.amscous.com
SIC: 3679 Harness assemblies, for
electronic use: wire or cable

(P-8997)
APEM INC
Also Called: Ch Products
970 Park Center Dr (92081-8301)
PHONE.............................760 598-2518
Peter Brouilette, *Pr*
EMP: 81
Web: www.chproducts.com
SIC: 3679 3577 Electronic switches;
Computer peripheral equipment, nec
HQ: Apem, Inc.
970 Park Center Dr
Vista CA

(P-8998)
ASTRO SEAL INC
827 Palmyrita Ave Ste B (92507-1820)
PHONE.............................951 787-6670
Michael Hammer, *Pr*
Roger Hammer, *
Karen Upfold, *
▲ **EMP:** 34 **EST:** 1964
SQ FT: 42,000
SALES (est): 4.75MM **Privately Held**
Web: www.astroseal.com
SIC: 3679 3678 Hermetic seals, for
electronic equipment; Electronic connectors

(P-8999)
AVR GLOBAL TECHNOLOGIES INC (PA)
Also Called: Avr Global Tech
500 La Terraza Blvd Ste 150 (92025)
P.O. Box 3814 (92629-8814)
PHONE.............................949 391-1180
Andy Bowman, *CEO*
Andy Bowman, *Pr*
Val Pontes, *Treas*
EMP: 197 **EST:** 2016
SALES (est): 11.13MM
SALES (corp-wide): 11.13MM **Privately Held**
Web: www.avrglobaltech.com
SIC: 3679 3714 5065 5063 Harness
assemblies, for electronic use: wire or cable
; Automotive wiring harness sets; Electronic
parts and equipment, nec; Wire and cable

(P-9000)
AZ DISPLAYS INC
2410 Birch St (92081-8472)
PHONE.............................949 831-5000
▲ **EMP:** 50 **EST:** 1996
SALES (est): 21.22MM **Privately Held**
Web: www.azdisplays.com
SIC: 3679 Liquid crystal displays (LCD)
HQ: American Zettler Inc.
2410 Birch St
Vista CA
949 831-5000

(P-9001)
B & G ELECTRONIC ASSEMBLY INC
10350 Regis Ct (91730-3055)
PHONE.............................909 608-2077
Robert M Odell, *CEO*
Lillian Odell, *VP*

EMP: 18 **EST:** 1998
SQ FT: 8,900
SALES (est): 2.97MM **Privately Held**
Web: www.bgelectronic.com
SIC: 3679 Harness assemblies, for
electronic use: wire or cable

(P-9002)
BASIC ELECTRONICS INC
11371 Monarch St (92841-1406)
PHONE.............................714 530-2400
Nancy Balzano, *Pr*
Al Balzano, *
EMP: 32 **EST:** 1967
SQ FT: 20,000
SALES (est): 6.17MM **Privately Held**
Web: www.basicelectronicsinc.com
SIC: 3679 3672 3613 Electronic circuits;
Printed circuit boards; Switchgear and
switchboard apparatus

(P-9003)
BE SERVICES COMPANY INC (HQ)
1200 Columbia Ave (92507-2129)
PHONE.............................626 284-9901
Gordon L Bourns, *CEO*
James G Heiken, *
Yuliya M Lyubovna, *
EMP: 25 **EST:** 2003
SALES (est): 3.47MM
SALES (corp-wide): 642.78MM **Privately Held**
SIC: 3679 Electronic circuits
PA: Bourns, Inc.
1200 Columbia Ave
Riverside CA
951 781-5500

(P-9004)
BE SERVICES COMPANY INC
300 Cypress Ave (91801-3001)
PHONE.............................626 284-9901
EMP: 322
SALES (corp-wide): 642.78MM **Privately Held**
SIC: 3679 Electronic circuits
HQ: Be Services Company, Inc.
1200 Columbia Ave
Riverside CA
626 284-9901

(P-9005)
BI TECHNOLOGIES CORPORATION (HQ)
Also Called: TT Electronics
120 S State College Blvd Ste 175
(92821-5834)
PHONE.............................714 447-2300
▲ **EMP:** 260 **EST:** 1984
SALES (est): 110.16MM
SALES (corp-wide): 742.85MM **Privately Held**
Web: www.ttelectronics.com
SIC: 3679 5065 8711 Electronic circuits;
Electronic parts and equipment, nec;
Engineering services
PA: Tt Electronics Plc
4th Floor
Woking
193 282-5300

(P-9006)
BI-SEARCH INTERNATIONAL INC
17550 Gillette Ave (92614-5610)
PHONE.............................714 258-4500
◆ **EMP:** 60 **EST:** 1996
SQ FT: 45,000

PRODUCTS & SVCS

SALES (est): 68.34MM **Privately Held**
Web: www.bisearch.com
SIC: 3679 Liquid crystal displays (LCD)

(P-9007)
BIVAR INC
Also Called: Bivar
4 Thomas (92618-2593)
PHONE..............................949 951-8808
Thomas Silber, *CEO*
▲ **EMP:** 40 **EST:** 1965
SQ FT: 26,040
SALES (est): 7.02MM **Privately Held**
Web: www.bivar.com
SIC: 3679 Electronic circuits

(P-9008)
BREE ENGINEERING CORP
135 Vallecitos De Oro Ste G (92069-1461)
PHONE..............................760 510-4950
Dan Bree, *Pr*
EMP: 30 **EST:** 1999
SALES (est): 2.76MM **Privately Held**
Web: www.breeeng.com
SIC: 3679 Electronic circuits

(P-9009)
C & S ASSEMBLY INC
1150 N Armando St (92806-2609)
PHONE..............................866 779-8939
Sandra A Foley, *Pr*
Sandra A Foley, *Pr*
Christopher Foley, *VP*
EMP: 48 **EST:** 1997
SQ FT: 12,000
SALES (est): 2.59MM **Privately Held**
Web: www.cnsassembly.com
SIC: 3679 5063 Harness assemblies, for electronic use: wire or cable; Electronic wire and cable

(P-9010)
CAC INC
Also Called: Cac
20322 Windrow Dr Ste 100 (92630-8150)
PHONE..............................949 587-3328
Patrick Redfern, *Pr*
▲ **EMP:** 23 **EST:** 1994
SALES (est): 2MM **Privately Held**
Web: www.cac-inc.com
SIC: 3679 Electronic circuits

(P-9011)
CAL SOUTHERN BRAIDING INC
Also Called: Scb Division
7450 Scout Ave (90201-4932)
PHONE..............................562 927-5531
Neal Castleman, *Pr*
EMP: 60 **EST:** 1976
SQ FT: 38,000
SALES (est): 14.02MM
SALES (corp-wide): 96.85MM **Privately Held**
SIC: 3679 Harness assemblies, for electronic use: wire or cable
PA: Dcx-Chol Enterprises, Inc.
12821 S Figueroa St
Los Angeles CA
310 516-1692

(P-9012)
CALI RESOURCES INC
Also Called: Brimes International
2310 Michael Faraday Dr (92154-7900)
PHONE..............................619 661-5741
Carlos Kelvin, *CEO*
◆ **EMP:** 45 **EST:** 1995
SQ FT: 30,000
SALES (est): 7.29MM **Privately Held**
Web: www.caliresources.com

SIC: 3679 Electronic circuits

(P-9013)
CARROS AMERICAS INC
Also Called: Innovista Sensors
2945 Townsgate Rd Ste 200 (91361-5802)
PHONE..............................805 267-7176
Eric Pilaud, *Pr*
Ben Watt, *
EMP: 150 **EST:** 2015
SALES: 39.36MM
SALES (corp-wide): 675.45K **Privately Held**
Web: www.crouzet.com
SIC: 3679 3577 Electronic circuits; Encoders, computer peripheral equipment
HQ: Lbo France Gestion
148 Rue De L Universite
Paris

(P-9014)
CCM ASSEMBLY & MFG INC (PA)
2275 Michael Faraday Dr Ste 6 (92154-7927)
PHONE..............................760 560-1310
Erika Marcela Murillo, *CEO*
Sergio Murillo, *Pr*
John Savage, *VP*
▲ **EMP:** 28 **EST:** 1997
SQ FT: 10,000
SALES: 4.94MM
SALES (corp-wide): 4.94MM **Privately Held**
Web: www.ccmassembly.com
SIC: 3679 3441 Harness assemblies, for electronic use: wire or cable; Fabricated structural metal

(P-9015)
CELESCO TRANSDUCER PRODUCTS
Also Called: Celesco Transducer Products
20630 Plummer St (91311-5111)
PHONE..............................818 701-2701
Hernan Cortez, *Prin*
▲ **EMP:** 25 **EST:** 2013
SALES (est): 563.72K **Privately Held**
SIC: 3679 1541 Transducers, electrical; Industrial buildings and warehouses

(P-9016)
CIAO WIRELESS INC
Also Called: Ciao
4000 Via Pescador (93012-5044)
PHONE..............................805 389-3224
Glen Wasylewski, *Pr*
▼ **EMP:** 70 **EST:** 2003
SQ FT: 42,000
SALES (est): 15.61MM **Privately Held**
Web: www.ciaowireless.com
SIC: 3679 3699 Microwave components; Pulse amplifiers

(P-9017)
CICON ENGINEERING INC (PA)
6633 Odessa Ave (91406-5746)
PHONE..............................818 909-6060
Ali Kolahi, *Pr*
Laurie Kertenian, *
Hamid Kolahi, *Stockholder**
Farah Kolahi, *Stockholder**
Abdi Kolahi, *
EMP: 169 **EST:** 1990
SQ FT: 50,000
SALES (est): 47.75MM
SALES (corp-wide): 47.75MM **Privately Held**
Web: www.cicon.com
SIC: 3679 Harness assemblies, for electronic use: wire or cable

(P-9018)
CKS SOLUTION INCORPORATED
556 Vanguard Way Ste C (92821-3929)
PHONE..............................714 292-6307
Patrick Park, *Mgr*
EMP: 34
SALES (corp-wide): 4.91MM **Privately Held**
Web: www.ckssolution.com
SIC: 3679 Liquid crystal displays (LCD)
PA: Cks Solution Incorporated
4293 Muhlhauser Rd
Fairfield OH
513 947-1277

(P-9019)
CLARY CORPORATION
150 E Huntington Dr (91016-3415)
PHONE..............................626 359-4486
John G Clary, *Ch Bd*
Donald G Ash, *
EMP: 40 **EST:** 1939
SQ FT: 26,000
SALES (est): 9.96MM **Privately Held**
Web: www.clary.com
SIC: 3679 3612 Electronic loads and power supplies; Transformers, except electric

(P-9020)
COASTAL COMPONENT INDS INC
Also Called: C C I
133 E Bristol Ln (92865-2749)
PHONE..............................714 685-6677
Mark Coe, *Pr*
Ronna Coe, *Ch*
Donald B Coe, *CEO*
Diana Romero, *VP*
EMP: 20 **EST:** 1990
SQ FT: 6,027
SALES (est): 4.97MM **Privately Held**
Web: www.ccicoastal.com
SIC: 3679 5065 3643 3678 Electronic circuits ; Electronic parts and equipment, nec; Electric connectors; Electronic connectors

(P-9021)
COOPER INTERCONNECT INC
13039 Crossroads Pkwy S (91746-3406)
PHONE..............................617 389-7080
Preston Shultz, *CEO*
EMP: 80
SIC: 3679 3643 3812 3672 Harness assemblies, for electronic use: wire or cable ; Current-carrying wiring services; Search and navigation equipment; Printed circuit boards
HQ: Cooper Interconnect, Inc.
750 W Ventura Blvd
Camarillo CA
805 484-0543

(P-9022)
CORELIS INC
13100 Alondra Blvd Ste 102 (90703-2262)
PHONE..............................562 926-6727
George Lafever, *CEO*
EMP: 25 **EST:** 1991
SQ FT: 15,000
SALES (est): 6.72MM
SALES (corp-wide): 92.53MM **Privately Held**
Web: www.corelis.com
SIC: 3679 Electronic circuits
PA: Electronic Warfare Associates, Inc.
13873 Park Center Rd 500s
Herndon VA
703 904-5700

(P-9023)
CRUCIAL POWER PRODUCTS
14000 S Broadway (90061-1018)
PHONE..............................323 721-5017
Abbie Gougerchian, *Prin*
EMP: 17 **EST:** 1992
SALES (est): 1.25MM **Privately Held**
Web: www.crucialpower.com
SIC: 3679 Electronic circuits

(P-9024)
CSR TECHNOLOGY INC
815 Alamo Ln (92025-7683)
PHONE..............................619 823-7919
EMP: 44
SALES (corp-wide): 6.77MM **Privately Held**
SIC: 3679 Electronic loads and power supplies
HQ: Csr Technology Inc.
1060 Rincon Cir
San Jose CA

(P-9025)
CUSTOM SENSORS & TECH INC
2475 Paseo De Las Americas (92154-7223)
PHONE..............................805 716-0322
Carlos Borboa, *Supervisor*
EMP: 567
SALES (corp-wide): 4.03B **Privately Held**
Web: www.cstsensors.com
SIC: 3679 Electronic circuits
HQ: Custom Sensors & Technologies, Inc.
1461 Lawrence Dr
Thousand Oaks CA
805 716-0322

(P-9026)
CUSTOM SENSORS & TECH INC (HQ)
Also Called: C S T
1461 Lawrence Dr (91320-1311)
PHONE..............................805 716-0322
Martha Sullivan, *CEO*
▲ **EMP:** 737 **EST:** 1997
SALES (est): 456.84MM
SALES (corp-wide): 4.03B **Privately Held**
Web: www.cstsensors.com
SIC: 3679 Electronic circuits
PA: Sensata Technologies Holding Plc
Interface House
Swindon WILTS
179 325-0031

(P-9027)
DAICO INDUSTRIES INC
1070 E 233rd St (90745-6205)
PHONE..............................310 507-3242
EMP: 90 **EST:** 1965
SALES (est): 9.91MM **Privately Held**
Web: www.daico.com
SIC: 3679 3674 Microwave components; Semiconductors and related devices

(P-9028)
DCX-CHOL ENTERPRISES INC (PA)
12821 S Figueroa St (90061-1157)
PHONE..............................310 516-1692
Neal Castleman, *Pr*
Brian Gamberg, *
Garret Hoffman, *
▲ **EMP:** 80 **EST:** 1997
SQ FT: 50,000
SALES (est): 96.85MM
SALES (corp-wide): 96.85MM **Privately Held**
Web: www.dcxchol.com

SIC: 3679 Electronic circuits

(P-9029)
DELTA GROUP ELECTRONICS INC
Also Called: Delta Group Electronics
10180 Scripps Ranch Blvd (92131-1234)
PHONE.............................858 569-1681
Bill West, *Genl Mgr*
EMP: 55
SALES (corp-wide): 116.76MM **Privately Held**
Web: www.deltagroupinc.com
SIC: 3679 3577 3672 Electronic circuits; Computer peripheral equipment, nec; Printed circuit boards
PA: Delta Group Electronics, Inc.
4521a Osuna Rd Ne
Albuquerque NM
505 883-7674

(P-9030)
DELTA MICROWAVE LLC
300 Del Norte Blvd (93030-7217)
PHONE.............................805 751-1100
▼ EMP: 66
Web: www.mrcy.com
SIC: 3679 Microwave components

(P-9031)
DXRAY INC
19355 Business Center Dr (91324-3503)
PHONE.............................818 280-0177
Jan Iwanczyk, *Pr*
Bradley Patt, *Ex VP*
Joseph Miller, *Dir*
EMP: 48 EST: 2003
SQ FT: 3,783
SALES (est): 869.01K **Privately Held**
Web: www.dxray.com
SIC: 3679 Electronic circuits

(P-9032)
DYNALLOY INC
2801 Mcgaw Ave (92614-5835)
PHONE.............................714 436-1206
Wayne Brown, *CEO*
Jess Brown, *VP*
EMP: 20 EST: 1989
SALES (est): 4.39MM **Privately Held**
Web: www.dynalloy.com
SIC: 3679 3357 5065 Electronic circuits; Nonferrous wiredrawing and insulating; Electronic parts

(P-9033)
DYTRAN INSTRUMENTS INC
21592 Marilla St (91311-4137)
PHONE.............................818 700-7818
Benjamin Bryson, *CEO*
Anne Hackney, *
David Cianciosi, *
EMP: 194 EST: 1980
SQ FT: 8,000
SALES (est): 38.19MM
SALES (corp-wide): 1.6B **Privately Held**
Web: www.dytran.com
SIC: 3679 3829 Transducers, electrical; Measuring and controlling devices, nec
HQ: Spectris Inc.
117 Flanders Rd
Westborough MA
508 768-6400

(P-9034)
EAGLERISE E&E INC
13405 Benson Ave (91710-5231)
PHONE.............................215 675-5953
Liangbin Lu, *Pr*
Tony Y Xu, *Treas*

Lucy Y Cheng, *Sec*
▲ EMP: 27 EST: 2006
SALES (est): 2.11MM **Privately Held**
Web: www.eaglerise.com
SIC: 3679 Electronic loads and power supplies
PA: Eaglerise Electric & Electronic (China) Co., Ltd
No.A3, Jianpinglu Guicheng Kejiyuan, Nanhai District
Foshan GD

(P-9035)
ECLIPTEK INC
24422 Avenida De La Carlota Ste 290 (92653)
PHONE.............................714 433-1200
Cary Rosen, *CEO*
EMP: 46 EST: 1987
SALES (est): 2.2MM **Privately Held**
Web: www.abracon.com
SIC: 3679 5065 3825 3677 Electronic crystals; Electronic parts and equipment, nec; Instruments to measure electricity; Electronic coils and transformers

(P-9036)
ELECTRO SWITCH CORP
Also Called: Arga Cntrls A Unit Elctro Swtc
10410 Trademark St (91730-5826)
PHONE.............................909 581-0855
EMP: 20
SALES (corp-wide): 103.82MM **Privately Held**
Web: www.digitran-es.com
SIC: 3679 Transducers, electrical
HQ: Electro Switch Corp.
775 Pleasant St Ste 1
Weymouth MA
781 335-1195

(P-9037)
ELECTRO-SUPPORT SYSTEMS CORP
Also Called: IMS-Ess
27449 Colt Ct (92590-3674)
P.O. Box 50067 (92619-0067)
PHONE.............................951 676-2751
EMP: 46 EST: 1977
SQ FT: 12,500
SALES (est): 846.43K **Privately Held**
Web: www.ims-ess.com
SIC: 3679 3845 3728 Electronic circuits; Electromedical equipment; Military aircraft equipment and armament

(P-9038)
ELECTRO-TECH PRODUCTS INC
Also Called: Electro-Tech Products
2001 E Gladstone St Ste A (91740-5381)
PHONE.............................909 592-1434
Ramzi Bader, *Pr*
▲ EMP: 30 EST: 1984
SQ FT: 11,000
SALES (est): 2.29MM **Privately Held**
Web: www.etp-inc.com
SIC: 3679 Electronic circuits

(P-9039)
ELECTROCUBE INC (PA)
Also Called: Southern Electronics
3366 Pomona Blvd (91768-3234)
PHONE.............................909 595-1821
Langdon Clay Parrill, *Pr*
Donald Duquette, *
Scott Wieland, *
◆ EMP: 47 EST: 1961
SQ FT: 27,000
SALES (est): 9.95MM

SALES (corp-wide): 9.95MM **Privately Held**
Web: www.electrocube.com
SIC: 3679 3675 Electronic circuits; Electronic capacitors

(P-9040)
EMI SOLUTIONS INC
13805 Alton Pkwy Ste B (92618-1690)
PHONE.............................949 206-9960
Julie Ydens, *Ch Bd*
Bob Ydens, *Pr*
▼ EMP: 18 EST: 1997
SQ FT: 6,500
SALES (est): 2.3MM **Privately Held**
Web: www.4emi.com
SIC: 3679 Electronic circuits

(P-9041)
ENFORA INC
9645 Scranton Rd Ste 205 (92121-17u4)
PHONE.............................972 234-1689
Mark Weinzierl, *Pr*
Kenneth Leddon, *
Slim S Souissi, *
Catherine F Ratcliffe, *
▲ EMP: 49 EST: 1999
SQ FT: 27,000
SALES (est): 8.83MM
SALES (corp-wide): 245.32MM **Publicly Held**
Web: www.inseego.com
SIC: 3679 Commutators, electronic
HQ: Inseego Wireless, Inc.
9710 Scranton Rd Ste 200
San Diego CA
858 812-3400

(P-9042)
ESP CORP
1175 W Victoria St (90220-5813)
PHONE.............................310 639-2535
Bayasouk Ounthaung, *Pr*
EMP: 23 EST: 2004
SALES (est): 755.96K **Privately Held**
SIC: 3679 Electronic components, nec

(P-9043)
EXPRESS MANUFACTURING INC (PA)
3519 W Warner Ave (92704-5214)
PHONE.............................714 979-2228
Chauk Pan Chin, *Pr*
Tony Chin, *
Catherine Lee Chin, *
C M Chin, *
▲ EMP: 475 EST: 1982
SQ FT: 96,000
SALES (est): 91.07MM
SALES (corp-wide): 91.07MM **Privately Held**
Web: www.eminc.com
SIC: 3679 3672 Electronic circuits; Printed circuit boards

(P-9044)
FABRICAST INC (PA)
2517 Seaman Ave (91733-1927)
P.O. Box 3176 (91733-0176)
PHONE.............................626 443-3247
H Phelps Wood Iii, *Pr*
EMP: 21 EST: 1960
SQ FT: 6,250
SALES (est): 2.26MM
SALES (corp-wide): 2.26MM **Privately Held**
Web: www.fabricast.com
SIC: 3679 3621 Electronic circuits; Motors and generators

(P-9045)
FEMA ELECTRONICS CORPORATION
22 Corporate Park (92606-3112)
PHONE.............................714 825-0140
Bob Cheng, *CEO*
Chinyun Cheng, *
▲ EMP: 30 EST: 2010
SQ FT: 3,000
SALES (est): 4MM **Privately Held**
Web: www.femacorp.com
SIC: 3679 Electronic crystals

(P-9046)
FOX ENTERPRISES LLC (HQ)
Also Called: Fox Electronics
24422 Avenida De La Carlota Ste 290 (92653)
PHONE.............................239 693-0099
Eugene Trefethen, *Pr*
EMP: 24 EST: 1979
SALES (est): 24.16MM **Privately Held**
SIC: 3679 5065 Quartz crystals, for electronic application; Electronic parts
PA: Abracon, Llc
5101 Hidden Creek Ln
Spicewood TX

(P-9047)
GAR ENTERPRISES
Also Called: K.G.S.electronics
1396 W 9th St (91786-5724)
PHONE.............................909 985-4575
Alex Morales, *Mgr*
EMP: 28
SALES (corp-wide): 23.35MM **Privately Held**
Web: www.kgselectronics.com
SIC: 3679 3621 3577 Electronic loads and power supplies; Motors and generators; Computer peripheral equipment, nec
PA: Gar Enterprises
418 E Live Oak Ave
Arcadia CA
626 574-1175

(P-9048)
GENERAL POWER SYSTEMS INC
Also Called: General Power Systems
955 E Ball Rd (92805-5916)
PHONE.............................714 956-9321
David Noyes, *Pr*
Frank Castle, *
David Noyes, *Ex VP*
EMP: 30 EST: 1984
SQ FT: 30,000
SALES (est): 7.38MM
SALES (corp-wide): 52.28MM **Privately Held**
SIC: 3679 Power supplies, all types: static
PA: Components Corporation Of America
5950 Berkshire Ln # 1500
Dallas TX
214 969-0166

(P-9049)
GES US (NEW ENGLAND) INC
1051 S East St (92805-5749)
PHONE.............................978 459-4434
Riachard Pelletier, *Genl Mgr*
EMP: 173 EST: 1986
SQ FT: 70,000
SALES (est): 8.17MM **Privately Held**
Web: www.41ststreetdelifl.com
SIC: 3679 3672 Electronic circuits; Printed circuit boards
HQ: Ges Investment Pte. Ltd.
28 Marsiling Lane
Singapore

PRODUCTS & SVCS

(P-9050)

GIGATERA COMMUNICATIONS

Also Called: KMW Communications
1818 E Orangethorpe Ave (92831-5324)
PHONE..................................714 515-1100
Duk Y Kim, *Ch Bd*
Duk Y Kim, *Pr*
Yeong Kim, *
Burton Calloway, *
▲ **EMP:** 65 **EST:** 1995
SQ FT: 4,500
SALES (est): 28.85MM **Privately Held**
Web: www.gteracom.com
SIC: 3679 5063 Electronic circuits; Electrical
apparatus and equipment
PA: Kmw Inc.
21 Dongtan-Daero 25-Gil
Hwaseong

(P-9051)

GTRAN INC (PA)

829 Flynn Rd (93012-8702)
PHONE..................................805 445-4500
Ray Yu, *Pr*
Deepak Mehrotra, *
Douglas Holmes, *
▲ **EMP:** 46 **EST:** 1999
SQ FT: 226,000
SALES (est): 7.13MM
SALES (corp-wide): 7.13MM **Privately
Held**
Web: www.gtran.net
SIC: 3679 Electronic circuits

(P-9052)

GUNJOY INC

22895 Eastpark Dr (92887-4653)
PHONE..................................714 289-0055
▲ **EMP:** 26
SIC: 3679 Power supplies, all types: static

(P-9053)

HANNSPREE NORTH AMERICA INC

13223 Black Mountain Rd (92129-2698)
PHONE..................................909 992-5025
▲ **EMP:** 60
SIC: 3679 Liquid crystal displays (LCD)

(P-9054)

HARPER & TWO INC (PA)

2937 Cherry Ave (90755-1910)
PHONE..................................562 424-3030
Dan Kilstofte, *Pr*
Jim Quilty, *Sec*
EMP: 18 **EST:** 1987
SALES (est): 2.36MM
SALES (corp-wide): 2.36MM **Privately
Held**
Web: www.harperandtwo.com
SIC: 3679 Electronic circuits

(P-9055)

HARWIL PRECISION PRODUCTS

Also Called: Harwil
541 Kinetic Dr (93030-7923)
PHONE..................................805 988-6800
Geoffrey Strand, *Pr*
Cynthia Strand, *
Teresa Bowmar, *
EMP: 35 **EST:** 1957
SQ FT: 33,000
SALES (est): 4.46MM **Privately Held**
Web: www.harwil.com
SIC: 3679 3625 3823 Electronic circuits;
Flow actuated electrical switches; Process
control instruments

(P-9056)

HERMETIC SEAL CORPORATION (DH)

Also Called: Ametek HCC
4232 Temple City Blvd (91770-1592)
PHONE..................................626 443-8931
Andrew Goldfarb, *Pr*
EMP: 200 **EST:** 1945
SQ FT: 36,000
SALES (est): 77MM
SALES (corp-wide): 6.15B **Publicly Held**
Web: www.ametek-ecp.com
SIC: 3679 3469 Hermetic seals, for
electronic equipment; Metal stampings, nec
HQ: Hcc Industries Leasing, Inc.
4232 Temple City Blvd
Rosemead CA
626 443-8933

(P-9057)

IJ RESEARCH INC

2919 S Tech Center Dr (92705-5657)
PHONE..................................714 546-8522
Rick Yoon, *Pr*
◆ **EMP:** 35 **EST:** 1988
SQ FT: 12,500
SALES (est): 8.8MM
SALES (corp-wide): 3.18B **Publicly Held**
Web: www.ijresearch.com
SIC: 3679 Hermetic seals, for electronic
equipment
HQ: Superior Technical Ceramics
Corporation
600 Industrial Park Rd
Saint Albans VT
802 527-7726

(P-9058)

IMPACT LLC

22521 Avenida Empresa Ste 107
(92688-2044)
PHONE..................................714 546-6000
EMP: 28 **EST:** 1998
SALES (est): 2.22MM **Privately Held**
Web: www.capitolimpact.org
SIC: 3679 3829 Electronic circuits;
Measuring and controlling devices, nec

(P-9059)

INFINITE ELECTRONICS INC (HQ)

Also Called: L-Com
17792 Fitch (92614-6020)
PHONE..................................949 261-1920
Penny Cotner, *Pr*
David Quinn, *CRO*
Emily Campbell, *CMO*
David Collier, *COO*
Alexander Arrieta, *Chief Human Resource
Officer*
EMP: 47 **EST:** 2007
SQ FT: 40,000
SALES (est): 369.37MM
SALES (corp-wide): 1.84B **Privately Held**
Web: www.infiniteelectronics.com
SIC: 3679 Electronic circuits
PA: Warburg Pincus Llc
450 Lexington Ave Fl 32
New York NY
212 878-0600

(P-9060)

INSTRMENT DSIGN ENGRG ASSOC IN

Also Called: Idea
2923 Saturn St Ste F (92821-6260)
PHONE..................................714 525-3302
Sabrina Lu, *Pr*
EMP: 22 **EST:** 1985

SALES (est): 781.15K **Privately Held**
SIC: 3679 3674 Electronic circuits;
Semiconductors and related devices

(P-9061)

INTEGRATED MICROWAVE CORP

Also Called: Imcsd
11353 Sorrento Valley Rd (92121-1303)
PHONE..................................858 259-2600
John F Anderson, *Pr*
Steven Porter, *CFO*
Robert J Perna, *Sec*
◆ **EMP:** 85 **EST:** 1982
SQ FT: 24,142
SALES (est): 20.77MM
SALES (corp-wide): 764.7MM **Publicly
Held**
Web: www.knowlescapacitors.com
SIC: 3679 Microwave components
HQ: Knowles Electronics, Llc
1151 Maplewood Dr
Itasca IL
630 250-5100

(P-9062)

INTERCONNECT SOLUTIONS CO LLC

Also Called: Tri-Tek Electronics
25358 Avenue Stanford (91355-1214)
PHONE..................................661 295-0020
Tony Lopez, *Brnch Mgr*
EMP: 62
SALES (corp-wide): 26.91MM **Privately
Held**
Web: www.interconnectsolutions.com
SIC: 3679 Harness assemblies, for
electronic use: wire or cable
PA: Interconnect Solutions Company, Llc
17595 Mount Herrmann St
Fountain Valley CA
909 545-6140

(P-9063)

INTERCTIVE DSPLAY SLUTIONS INC

Also Called: Interactive Display Solutions
490 Wald (92618-4638)
PHONE..................................949 727-1959
Brian Chung, *Pr*
Paul Kitzerow Senior V Press, *Prin*
Son Park V Press, *Prin*
Danny Lee, *
▲ **EMP:** 26 **EST:** 2004
SALES (est): 4.61MM **Privately Held**
Web: www.idsdisplay.com
SIC: 3679 Liquid crystal displays (LCD)

(P-9064)

INTERLINK ELECTRONICS INC (PA)

Also Called: KWJ ENGINEERING
1 Jenner Ste 200 (92618-3844)
PHONE..................................805 484-8855
Steven N Bronson, *Pr*
Ryan J Hoffman, *CFO*
Albert Lu, *Technology*
Peter Roussak, *VP*
▲ **EMP:** 48 **EST:** 1985
SQ FT: 4,351
SALES (est): 7.49MM
SALES (corp-wide): 7.49MM **Publicly
Held**
Web: www.interlinkelectronics.com
SIC: 3679 Electronic circuits

(P-9065)

INTERLOG CORPORATION

Also Called: Interlog Construction

1295 N Knollwood Cir (92801-1310)
PHONE..................................714 529-7808
Justin H Kwon, *CEO*
▲ **EMP:** 20 **EST:** 1989
SALES (est): 4.73MM **Privately Held**
Web: www.interlogcorp.com
SIC: 3679 Electronic circuits

(P-9066)

IQD FREQUENCY PRODUCTS INC

592 N Tercero Cir (92262-6243)
PHONE..................................408 250-1435
Neil Floodgate, *Pr*
EMP: 43 **EST:** 2010
SALES (est): 8.41MM
SALES (corp-wide): 20.7B **Privately Held**
Web: www.iqdfrequencyproducts.com
SIC: 3679 Microwave components
HQ: Iqd Frequency Products Limited
Station Road
Crewkerne
146 027-0200

(P-9067)

J L COOPER ELECTRONICS INC

Also Called: Jlcooper
142 Arena St (90245-3901)
PHONE..................................310 322-9990
James Loren Cooper, *Pr*
▲ **EMP:** 44 **EST:** 1981
SALES (est): 5.1MM **Privately Held**
SIC: 3679 Recording and playback
apparatus, including phonograph

(P-9068)

JANCO CORPORATION

Also Called: Esterline Mason
13955 Balboa Blvd (91342-1084)
P.O. Box 3038 (91508-3038)
PHONE..................................818 361-3366
▼ **EMP:** 120 **EST:** 1947
SALES (est): 26.52MM
SALES (corp-wide): 6.58B **Publicly Held**
Web: www.transdigm.com
SIC: 3679 3825 3643 5088 Electronic
switches; Shunts, electrical; Bus bars
(electrical conductors); Aircraft and parts,
nec
HQ: Esterline Technologies Corp
1301 E 9th St Ste 3000
Cleveland OH
216 706-2960

(P-9069)

JASPER ELECTRONICS

1580 N Kellogg Dr (92807-1902)
PHONE..................................714 917-0749
◆ **EMP:** 30 **EST:** 1995
SQ FT: 17,000
SALES (est): 5.63MM **Privately Held**
Web: www.jasperelectronics.com
SIC: 3679 Electronic loads and power
supplies

(P-9070)

JAXX MANUFACTURING INC

Also Called: Craig Kackert Design Tech
1912 Angus Ave (93063-3494)
PHONE..................................805 526-4979
Greg Liu, *Pr*
Veronica Liu, *
EMP: 45 **EST:** 2001
SALES (est): 7.91MM **Privately Held**
Web: www.jaxxmfg.com
SIC: 3679 Electronic circuits

▲ = Import ▼ = Export
◆ = Import/Export

(P-9071)
JAYCO INTERFACE
TECHNOLOGY INC
1351 Pico St (92881-3373)
PHONE.............................951 738-2000
Hemant Mistry, *Pr*
Shaila Rao, *Treas*
EMP: 33 EST: 1980
SQ FT: 23,000
SALES (est): 827.37K **Privately Held**
SIC: 3679 5065 Electronic circuits;
Electronic parts and equipment, nec

(P-9072)
JAYCO/MMI INC
1351 Pico St (92881-3373)
PHONE.............................951 738-2000
Shaila Mistry, *Pr*
Hemant Mistry, *
EMP: 42 EST: 1992
SQ FT: 24,000
SALES (est): 3.05MM **Privately Held**
Web: www.jaycopanels.com
SIC: 3679 5065 3577 2759 Electronic circuits
; Electronic parts and equipment, nec;
Computer peripheral equipment, nec;
Commercial printing, nec

(P-9073)
JOLO INDUSTRIES INC
10432 Brightwood Dr (92705-1591)
PHONE.............................714 554-6840
James S Giampiccolo, *Pr*
Theresa Giampiccolo, *Sec*
Chip Giampiccolo, *VP*
EMP: 19 EST: 1968
SQ FT: 8,000
SALES (est): 2.29MM **Privately Held**
Web: www.joneslogistics.com
SIC: 3679 3678 Electronic circuits;
Electronic connectors

(P-9074)
KATOLEC DEVELOPMENT INC
6120 Business Center Ct (92154-6652)
PHONE.............................619 710-0075
Eisuke Kato, *Pr*
▲ EMP: 45 EST: 2006
SALES (est): 2.61MM **Privately Held**
Web: www.katolec.com
SIC: 3679 Electronic circuits
PA: Katolec Corporation
2-8-7, Edagawa
Koto-Ku TKY

(P-9075)
KAVLICO CORPORATION (DH)
1461 Lawrence Dr (91320-1311)
PHONE.............................805 523-2000
Jeffrey J Cote, *CEO*
Martha Sullivan, *Pr*
▼ EMP: 1390 EST: 1962
SALES (est): 236.87MM
SALES (corp-wide): 4.03B **Privately Held**
Web: www.sensata.com
SIC: 3679 Transducers, electrical
HQ: Custom Sensors & Technologies, Inc.
1461 Lawrence Dr
Thousand Oaks CA
805 716-0322

(P-9076)
KEV-TON INC
925 Hale Pl Ste A10 (91914-3507)
PHONE.............................619 482-2600
Frank Sparling, *Ch Bd*
Bob Annette, *Pr*
David Briseno, *Stockholder*
EMP: 40 EST: 1983
SQ FT: 1,500
SALES (est): 3.67MM **Privately Held**
SIC: 3679 Electronic circuits

(P-9077)
LANDMARK ELECTRONICS INC
990 N Amelia Ave (91773-1401)
PHONE.............................626 967-2857
▲ EMP: 23
Web: www.landmarkelectronics.com
SIC: 3679 7699 5088 Static power supply
converters for electronic applications;
Aircraft flight instrument repair; Aircraft and
space vehicle supplies and parts

(P-9078)
LHV POWER CORPORATION
(PA)
10221 Buena Vista Ave Ste A
(92071-4484)
PHONE.............................619 258-7700
James Gevarges, *Pr*
▲ EMP: 25 EST: 1991
SQ FT: 20,000
SALES (est): 4.16MM **Privately Held**
Web: www.lhvpower.com
SIC: 3679 Power supplies, all types: static

(P-9079)
LUCIX CORPORATION (HQ)
Also Called: Lucix
800 Avenida Acaso Ste E (93012-8758)
PHONE.............................805 987-6645
Mark Shahriary, *Pr*
Cheryl Johnson, *
D Ick Fanucchi, *
▲ EMP: 83 EST: 1999
SQ FT: 48,000
SALES (est): 49.19MM **Publicly Held**
Web: www.lucix.com
SIC: 3679 8731 Microwave components;
Commercial physical research
PA: Heico Corporation
3000 Taft St
Hollywood FL

(P-9080)
MAGNETIC SENSORS
CORPORATION
1365 N Mccan St (92806-1316)
PHONE.............................714 630-8380
Charles Boudakian, *Pr*
Don Payne, *
EMP: 43 EST: 1983
SQ FT: 15,000
SALES (est): 8.88MM **Privately Held**
Web: www.magsensors.com
SIC: 3679 3677 Transducers, electrical; Coil
windings, electronic

(P-9081)
MAPLE IMAGING LLC (HQ)
1049 Camino Dos Rios (91360-2362)
PHONE.............................805 373-4545
Aldo Pichelli, *Pr*
EMP: 28 EST: 2019
SALES (est): 14.93MM
SALES (corp-wide): 5.46B **Publicly Held**
SIC: 3679 Electronic circuits
PA: Teledyne Technologies Inc
1049 Camino Dos Rios
Thousand Oaks CA
805 373-4545

(P-9082)
MASK TECHNOLOGY INC
2601 Oak St (92707-3720)
PHONE.............................714 557-3383
Andrew Holzmann, *Pr*
Joanne Deblis, *Dir*
EMP: 19 EST: 1983
SQ FT: 9,800
SALES (est): 708.45K **Privately Held**
Web: www.masktek.com
SIC: 3679 Electronic circuits

(P-9083)
MERCURY LLC - RF
INTEGRATED SOLUTIONS
1000 Avenida Acaso (93012-8712)
PHONE.............................805 388-1345
▲ EMP: 110
SIC: 3679 3663 Microwave components;
Amplifiers, RF power and IF

(P-9084)
MICROFABRICA INC
7911 Haskell Ave (91406-1909)
PHONE.............................888 964-2763
Eric Miller, *Prin*
Michael Lockard, *Prin*
Uri Frodis, *
Richard Chen, *
Greg Schmitz, *
EMP: 50 EST: 1999
SQ FT: 39,000
SALES (est): 23.8MM **Privately Held**
Web: www.microfabrica.com
SIC: 3679 Electronic circuits

(P-9085)
MICROMETALS INC (PA)
5615 E La Palma Ave (92807-2109)
PHONE.............................714 970-9400
Richard H Barden, *CEO*
◆ EMP: 143 EST: 1951
SQ FT: 50,000
SALES (est): 37.36MM
SALES (corp-wide): 37.36MM **Privately Held**
Web: www.micrometals.com
SIC: 3679 Cores, magnetic

(P-9086)
MITSUBSHI ELC VSUAL SLTONS
AME
Also Called: Mevsa
10833 Valley View St Ste 300 (90630-5046)
PHONE.............................800 553-7278
◆ EMP: 150 EST: 2011
SALES (est): 29.93MM **Privately Held**
Web: www.me-vis.com
SIC: 3679 Liquid crystal displays (LCD)
PA: Mitsubishi Electric Corporation
2-7-3, Marunouchi
Chiyoda-Ku TKY

(P-9087)
MUNEKATA AMERICA INC
2320 Paseo De Las Americas Ste 112
(92154-7281)
P.O. Box 15929 (92175-5929)
PHONE.............................619 661-8080
Nobumitsu Endo, *CEO*
Masayuki Sato, *
Naoharu Munekata, *
Koji Yanagida, *
▲ EMP: 500 EST: 1987
SQ FT: 700
SALES (est): 87.69MM **Privately Held**
Web: www.munekata.co.jp
SIC: 3679 Electronic circuits
PA: Munekata Co.,Ltd.
1-11-1, Horaicho
Fukushima FSM

(P-9088)
NATEL ENGINEERING
COMPANY LLC (PA)

Also Called: Neo Tech
9340 Owensmouth Ave (91311-6915)
PHONE.............................818 495-8617
Kunal Sharma, *
Laura Siegal, *
Victor Yamauchi, *
John Lowrey, *
▲ EMP: 210 EST: 1975
SQ FT: 200,000
SALES (est): 1.43B
SALES (corp-wide): 1.43B **Privately Held**
Web: www.neotech.com
SIC: 3679 3674 Antennas, receiving;
Semiconductors and related devices

(P-9089)
NEWVAC LLC
American Def Interconnect Div
9330 De Soto Ave (91311-4926)
PHONE.............................747 202-7333
Garrett Hoffman, *General Vice President*
EMP: 26
SALES (corp-wide): 96.54MM **Privately Held**
Web: www.newvac-llc.com
SIC: 3679 Harness assemblies, for
electronic use: wire or cable
HQ: Newvac, Llc
9330 De Soto Ave
Chatsworth CA
310 525-1205

(P-9090)
OASIS MATERIALS COMPANY
LLC (DH)
Also Called: Oasis Materials
12131 Community Rd (92064-8893)
PHONE.............................858 486-8846
Frank Polese, *Pr*
Stephen Nootens, *
Christopher Bateman, *
EMP: 22 EST: 2012
SQ FT: 22,000
SALES (est): 28.9MM
SALES (corp-wide): 147.68MM **Privately Held**
Web: www.fralock.com
SIC: 3679 Electronic circuits
HQ: Fralock Llc
28525 Industry Dr
Valencia CA
800 372-5625

(P-9091)
OCM PE HOLDINGS LP
333 S Grand Ave Fl 28 (90071-1530)
PHONE.............................213 830-6213
Mark C J Twaalfhoven, *CEO*
EMP: 10000 EST: 2012
SALES (est): 72.85MM **Privately Held**
SIC: 3679 3612 3663 Electronic circuits;
Transformers, except electric; Antennas,
transmitting and communications

(P-9092)
OMEGA LEADS INC
Also Called: Wire Harness & Cable Assembly
1509 Colorado Ave (90404-3316)
PHONE.............................310 394-6786
TOLL FREE: 800
Jeff Sweet Senior, *Pr*
EMP: 20 EST: 1960
SQ FT: 7,200
SALES (est): 4.03MM **Privately Held**
Web: www.omegaleads.com
SIC: 3679 Harness assemblies, for
electronic use: wire or cable

(P-9093)
OMNI CONNECTION INTL INC
126 Via Trevizio (92879-1772)
PHONE..........................951 898-6232
Henry Cheng, *Pr*
Phyllis Ting, *VP*
▲ **EMP:** 410 **EST:** 1992
SQ FT: 65,000
SALES (est): 68.37MM
SALES (corp-wide): 6.55B **Privately Held**
Web: www.omni-conn.com
SIC: 3679 Harness assemblies, for
electronic use: wire or cable
HQ: Electrical Components International,
Inc.
1 Cityplace Dr Ste 450
Saint Louis MO

(P-9094)
ONSHORE TECHNOLOGIES INC
2771 Plaza Del Amo Ste 802-803
(90503-9308)
PHONE..........................310 533-4888
EMP: 25 **EST:** 1992
SALES (est): 5.07MM **Privately Held**
Web: www.onshoretechnologies.com
SIC: 3679 Harness assemblies, for
electronic use: wire or cable

(P-9095)
OPTO 22
43044 Business Park Dr (92590-3614)
PHONE..........................951 695-3000
Mark Engman, *Pr*
Benson Hougland, *
Bob Sheffres, *
Kathleen Roe, *
◆ **EMP:** 200 **EST:** 1974
SQ FT: 135,000
SALES (est): 29.45MM **Privately Held**
Web: www.opto22.com
SIC: 3679 3823 3625 Electronic switches;
Process control instruments; Relays and
industrial controls

(P-9096)
ORBIT INTL INC
4965 Firenza Dr (90630-3569)
PHONE..........................909 468-5160
Teresa Chen, *Prin*
EMP: 24 **EST:** 2011
SALES (est): 1.71MM **Privately Held**
SIC: 3679 Electronic circuits

(P-9097)
ORMET CIRCUITS INC
6555 Nancy Ridge Dr Ste 200 (92121)
PHONE..........................858 831-0010
Till Langner, *CEO*
◆ **EMP:** 22 **EST:** 2001
SQ FT: 18,000
SALES (est): 4.86MM
SALES (corp-wide): 23.09B **Privately Held**
Web: www.emdgroup.com
SIC: 3679 Electronic circuits
HQ: Emd Performance Materials Corp.
1200 Intrepid Ave
Philadelphia PA
888 367-3275

(P-9098)
PIONEER MAGNETICS INC
1745 Berkeley St (90404-4104)
PHONE..........................310 829-6751
EMP: 110
Web: www.pioneermagnetics.com
SIC: 3679 Power supplies, all types: static

(P-9099)
PPST INC (PA)
17692 Fitch (92614-6022)
PHONE..........................800 421-1921
Kevin J Voelcker, *Pr*
▲ **EMP:** 35 **EST:** 2003
SALES (est): 30.94MM
SALES (corp-wide): 30.94MM **Privately
Held**
Web: www.adaptivepower.com
SIC: 3679 Power supplies, all types: static

(P-9100)
**PRECISION HERMETIC TECH
INC**
Also Called: Precision Hermetic
1940 W Park Ave (92373-8042)
PHONE..........................909 381-6011
Daniel B Schachtel, *Pr*
Sari Schachtel, *
EMP: 85 **EST:** 1989
SQ FT: 50,000
SALES (est): 15.55MM **Privately Held**
Web: www.precisionhermetic.com
SIC: 3679 Hermetic seals, for electronic
equipment

(P-9101)
PRED TECHNOLOGIES USA INC
Also Called: Pred
4901 Morena Blvd (92117-7319)
PHONE..........................858 999-2114
Charles Speidel, *CEO*
EMP: 70 **EST:** 2016
SALES (est): 5.3MM **Privately Held**
Web: www.tokktech.com
SIC: 3679 Headphones, radio

(P-9102)
PTB SALES INC (PA)
Also Called: Ptb
1361 Mountain View Cir (91702-1649)
PHONE..........................626 334-0500
Patrick T Blackwell, *CEO*
Brendan Riley, *
Dean Scarborough, *
Carmen Williams, *
▲ **EMP:** 28 **EST:** 1995
SQ FT: 16,000
SALES (est): 8.94MM
SALES (corp-wide): 8.94MM **Privately
Held**
Web: www.ptbsales.com
SIC: 3679 3563 Power supplies, all types:
static; Air and gas compressors including
vacuum pumps

(P-9103)
**PULSE ELECTRONICS
CORPORATION (HQ)**
Also Called: Pulse A Yageo Company
15255 Innovation Dr Ste 100 (92128-3400)
PHONE..........................858 674-8100
Mark C J Twaalfhoven, *CEO*
▲ **EMP:** 45 **EST:** 1947
SQ FT: 50,000
SALES (est): 516.12MM **Privately Held**
Web: www.pulseelectronics.com
SIC: 3679 3612 3663 Electronic circuits;
Transformers, except electric; Antennas,
transmitting and communications
PA: Yageo Corporation
3f,No.233-1,Pao Chiao Rd.,
New Taipei City TAP

(P-9104)
Q MICROWAVE INC
1591 Pioneer Way (92020-1637)
PHONE..........................619 258-7322

Eric Maat, *CEO*
Craig Higginson, *
Craig Shauan, *
EMP: 84 **EST:** 1998
SQ FT: 18,000
SALES (est): 14.9MM **Privately Held**
Web: www.qmicrowave.com
SIC: 3679 5065 Microwave components;
Electronic parts and equipment, nec

(P-9105)
QORVO CALIFORNIA INC
Also Called: Qorvo US
950 Lawrence Dr (91320-1522)
PHONE..........................805 480-5050
Charles J Abronson, *Ch Bd*
Ralph G Quinsey, *
Paul O Daughenbaugh, *
Mark Lampenfeld, *
Susan Liles, *
EMP: 49 **EST:** 1996
SQ FT: 11,000
SALES (est): 25.15MM
SALES (corp-wide): 3.57B **Publicly Held**
Web: www.qorvo.com
SIC: 3679 Electronic circuits
HQ: Qorvo Us, Inc.
2300 Ne Brookwood Pkwy
Hillsboro OR
336 664-1233

(P-9106)
REEDEX INC
15526 Commerce Ln (92649-1602)
PHONE..........................714 894-0311
Dan Reed, *Pr*
Ted Reed, *
▲ **EMP:** 49 **EST:** 1972
SALES (est): 9.83MM **Privately Held**
Web: www.reedex.com
SIC: 3679 Harness assemblies, for
electronic use: wire or cable

(P-9107)
RJA INDUSTRIES INC
Also Called: Automation Electronics
9640 Topanga Canyon Pl Ste J
(91311-0880)
PHONE..........................818 998-5124
Robert Aiani, *Pr*
Lynn Aiani, *Sec*
Chris Aiani, *VP*
Sandra Acnason, *Contrlr*
EMP: 26 **EST:** 1974
SQ FT: 10,000
SALES (est): 721.5K **Privately Held**
SIC: 3679 Harness assemblies, for
electronic use: wire or cable

(P-9108)
ROCKER SOLENOID COMPANY
Also Called: Rocker Industries
5492 Bolsa Ave (92649-1021)
PHONE..........................310 534-5660
John W Perry, *Pr*
Francis E Goodyear, *
Raymond Hatashita, *
Milton A Mather, *
▼ **EMP:** 88 **EST:** 1954
SQ FT: 23,000
SALES (est): 18.01MM **Privately Held**
Web: www.rockerindustries.com
SIC: 3679 3672 Solenoids for electronic
applications; Printed circuit boards

(P-9109)
ROGAR MANUFACTURING INC
Also Called: Ro Gar Mfg
866 E Ross Ave (92243-9652)
PHONE..........................760 335-3700

Pat Lewis, *Prin*
EMP: 126
SALES (corp-wide): 20.67MM **Privately
Held**
Web: www.rogarmfg.com
SIC: 3679 Electronic circuits
PA: Rogar Manufacturing Incorporated
866 E Ross Ave
El Centro CA
760 335-3700

(P-9110)
ROTECH ENGINEERING INC
Also Called: Rotech Engineering
1020 S Melrose St Ste A (92870-7169)
PHONE..........................714 632-0532
EMP: 20 **EST:** 1994
SQ FT: 10,000
SALES (est): 2.39MM **Privately Held**
Web: www.rotech-busbar.com
SIC: 3679 Electronic circuits

(P-9111)
RTIE HOLDINGS LLC
1800 E Via Burton (92806-1213)
PHONE..........................714 765-8200
EMP: 19 **EST:** 2010
SALES (est): 472.92K **Privately Held**
SIC: 3679 Electronic circuits

(P-9112)
S & C PRECISION INC
5045 Calmview Ave (91706-1802)
PHONE..........................626 338-7149
Jose Sanchez, *Pr*
EMP: 25 **EST:** 1987
SQ FT: 3,000
SALES (est): 988.88K **Privately Held**
SIC: 3679 3721 3599 Microwave
components; Aircraft; Machine shop,
jobbing and repair

(P-9113)
**SANDBERG INDUSTRIES INC
(PA)**
Also Called: E M S
2921 Daimler St (92705-5810)
PHONE..........................949 660-9473
J Sandberg, *CEO*
Steve Walker, *
Leo Boarts, *
John T Sandberg, *
Becky Tamblyn, *
EMP: 52 **EST:** 1978
SQ FT: 30,000
SALES (est): 9.69MM
SALES (corp-wide): 9.69MM **Privately
Held**
Web: www.unitindustriesgroup.com
SIC: 3679 3825 3672 3643 Electronic circuits
; Test equipment for electronic and
electrical circuits; Printed circuit boards;
Current-carrying wiring services

(P-9114)
SAS MANUFACTURING INC
405 N Smith Ave (92878-4305)
PHONE..........................951 734-1808
EMP: 45 **EST:** 1990
SQ FT: 24,000
SALES (est): 8.11MM **Privately Held**
Web: www.sasmanufacturing.com
SIC: 3679 Harness assemblies, for
electronic use: wire or cable

(P-9115)
SCEPTRE INC
Also Called: E-Scepter
16800 Gale Ave (91745-1804)
PHONE..........................626 369-3698

Stephen Liu, *CEO*
Cathy Liu, *
▲ **EMP:** 50 **EST:** 1984
SALES (est): 9.83MM **Privately Held**
Web: www.sceptre.com
SIC: 3679 Liquid crystal displays (LCD)

(P-9116)
SMITHS INTERCONNECT INC
375 Conejo Ridge Ave (91361-4928)
PHONE..............................805 267-0100
Dave Moorehouse, *Pr*
EMP: 68
SALES (corp-wide): 3.83B **Privately Held**
Web: www.smithsinterconnect.com
SIC: 3679 Microwave components
HQ: Smiths Interconnect, Inc.
4726 Eisenhower Blvd
Tampa FL
813 901-7200

(P-9117)
SMITHS INTRCNNECT AMERICAS INC
1231 E Dyer Rd Ste 235 (92705-5665)
PHONE..............................714 371-1100
Dom Matos, *Pr*
EMP: 300
SALES (corp-wide): 3.83B **Privately Held**
Web: www.smithsinterconnect.com
SIC: 3679 Microwave components
HQ: Smiths Interconnect Americas, Inc.
2001 Ne 46th St
Kansas City MO
913 342-5544

(P-9118)
SO-CAL VALUE ADDED LLC
809 Calle Plano (93012-8516)
PHONE..............................805 389-5335
Marco Muniz Day, *VP*
EMP: 35 **EST:** 2018
SQ FT: 40,000
SALES (est): 4MM **Privately Held**
Web: www.so-calvalueadded.com
SIC: 3679 3643 Harness assemblies, for electronic use: wire or cable; Current-carrying wiring services

(P-9119)
SPECTROLAB INC
12500 Gladstone Ave (91342-5373)
P.O. Box 9209 (91392-9209)
PHONE..............................818 365-4611
David Lillington, *Pr*
Edward Ringo, *
Jeff Peacock, *
Nasser Karam, *
Paul Ballew, *
EMP: 400 **EST:** 1956
SQ FT: 50,000
SALES (est): 89.89MM
SALES (corp-wide): 66.61B **Publicly Held**
Web: www.spectrolab.com
SIC: 3679 3674 Power supplies, all types: static; Solar cells
HQ: Boeing Satellite Systems, Inc.
900 N Pacific Coast Hwy
El Segundo CA

(P-9120)
STATEK CORPORATION
1449 W Orange Grove Ave (92868-1120)
PHONE..............................714 639-7810
EMP: 107
SALES (corp-wide): 82.77MM **Privately Held**
Web: www.statek.com
SIC: 3679 Electronic circuits
HQ: Statek Corporation
512 N Main St

Orange CA
714 639-7810

(P-9121)
STATEK CORPORATION (HQ)
Also Called: Statek
512 N Main St (92868-1102)
PHONE..............................714 639-7810
Michael Dastmalchian, *
Margaritha W Werren, *
▲ **EMP:** 143 **EST:** 1970
SQ FT: 71,000
SALES (est): 47.84MM
SALES (corp-wide): 82.77MM **Privately Held**
Web: www.statek.com
SIC: 3679 Electronic circuits
PA: Technicorp International Ii, Inc.
512 N Main St
Orange CA
714 639-7810

(P-9122)
STRIKE TECHNOLOGY INC
Also Called: Wilorco
24311 Wilmington Ave (90745-6139)
PHONE..............................562 437-3428
Robert Kunesh, *Ch Bd*
EMP: 25 **EST:** 2001
SQ FT: 9,800
SALES (est): 5.03MM **Privately Held**
Web: www.wilorco.com
SIC: 3679 Electronic circuits

(P-9123)
SUNTSU ELECTRONICS INC
Also Called: Suntsu
142 Technology Dr Ste 150 (92618-2429)
PHONE..............................949 783-7300
Casey Conlan, *Pr*
Jason Gann, *Sec*
▲ **EMP:** 30 **EST:** 2002
SQ FT: 14,000
SALES (est): 7.29MM **Privately Held**
Web: www.suntsu.com
SIC: 3679 5065 Electronic circuits; Electronic parts and equipment, nec

(P-9124)
SURE POWER INC
Also Called: Martek Power
1111 Knox St (90502-1034)
PHONE..............................310 542-8561
Maricela Sanchez, *Brnch Mgr*
EMP: 30
Web: www.sure-power.com
SIC: 3679 Power supplies, all types: static
HQ: Sure Power, Inc.
10955 Sw Avery St
Tualatin OR
503 692-5360

(P-9125)
TECHNICAL CABLE CONCEPTS INC
350 Lear Ave (92626-6015)
PHONE..............................714 835-1081
▲ **EMP:** 50 **EST:** 1989
SALES (est): 7.8MM **Privately Held**
Web: www.techcable.com
SIC: 3679 3229 Harness assemblies, for electronic use: wire or cable; Fiber optics strands

(P-9126)
TELEDYNE TECHNOLOGIES INC
Also Called: Teledyne Controls
501 Continental Blvd (90245-5036)
P.O. Box 1026 (90245-1026)
PHONE..............................310 765-3600

Masood Hassan, *Brnch Mgr*
EMP: 300
SALES (corp-wide): 5.46B **Publicly Held**
Web: www.teledyne.com
SIC: 3679 8731 3812 3519 Electronic circuits ; Commercial physical research; Search and navigation equipment; Internal combustion engines, nec
PA: Teledyne Technologies Inc
1049 Camino Dos Rios
Thousand Oaks CA
805 373-4545

(P-9127)
TELEDYNE TECHNOLOGIES INC
Also Called: Teledyne
12964 Panama St (90066-6534)
PHONE..............................310 822-8229
Bruce Gecks, *Mgr*
EMP: 360
SALES (corp-wide): 5.46B **Publicly Held**
Web: www.teledyne.com
SIC: 3679 Electronic circuits
PA: Teledyne Technologies Inc
1049 Camino Dos Rios
Thousand Oaks CA
805 373-4545

(P-9128)
TELEDYNE TECHNOLOGIES INC (PA)
Also Called: TELEDYNE TECHNOLOGIES
1049 Camino Dos Rios (91360-2362)
PHONE..............................805 373-4545
Aldo Pichelli, *Pr*
Robert Mehrabian, *
Jason Vanwees, *Ex VP*
Susan L Main, *Sr VP*
Melanie S Cibik, *CCO*
EMP: 250 **EST:** 1960
SALES (est): 5.46B
SALES (corp-wide): 5.46B **Publicly Held**
Web: www.teledyne.com
SIC: 3679 3761 3519 3724 Electronic circuits ; Guided missiles and space vehicles; Internal combustion engines, nec; Aircraft engines and engine parts

(P-9129)
TERADYNE INC
30701 Agoura Rd (91301-5928)
PHONE..............................818 991-2900
Greg Beecher, *Mgr*
EMP: 98
SALES (corp-wide): 3.16B **Publicly Held**
Web: www.teradyne.com
SIC: 3679 Electronic circuits
PA: Teradyne, Inc.
600 Riverpark Dr
North Reading MA
978 370-2700

(P-9130)
THOMPSON MAGNETICS INC
Also Called: Auto Doctor
42255 Baldaray Cir Ste C (92590-3632)
P.O. Box 2019 (92593-2019)
PHONE..............................951 676-0243
Howard M Thompson Senior, *Ch Bd*
Howard M Thompson Junior, *VP*
Betty J Thompson, *Sec*
David Thompson, *VP*
EMP: 21 **EST:** 1969
SQ FT: 16,000
SALES (est): 654.95K **Privately Held**
SIC: 3679 7538 Cores, magnetic; General automotive repair shops

(P-9131)
TRANSICO INC
Also Called: Eeco Switch
1240 Pioneer St Ste A (92821-3740)
PHONE..............................714 835-6000
▲ **EMP:** 24 **EST:** 1992
SALES (est): 1.8MM **Privately Held**
Web: www.eecoswitch.com
SIC: 3679 3672 3643 3577 Electronic switches; Printed circuit boards; Current-carrying wiring services; Computer peripheral equipment, nec

(P-9132)
TRIAD COMPONENTS GROUP INC (PA)
1675 Pioneer Way Ste C (92020-1642)
PHONE..............................619 993-3800
Jim Kalb, *Pr*
EMP: 18 **EST:** 1999
SALES (est): 1.77MM
SALES (corp-wide): 1.77MM **Privately Held**
Web: www.triadcomponentsgroup.com
SIC: 3679 Electronic components, nec

(P-9133)
TT ELCTRNICS PWR SLTONS US INC
1330 E Cypress St (91724-2103)
PHONE..............................626 967-6021
Michael Joseph Leahan, *CEO*
Matthew Alexander Sweaney, *Sec*
Kumen Rey Call, *CFO*
EMP: 120 **EST:** 2019
SALES (est): 24.32MM
SALES (corp-wide): 742.85MM **Privately Held**
Web: www.ttelectronics.com
SIC: 3679 Electronic circuits
PA: Tt Electronics Plc
4th Floor
Woking
193 282-5300

(P-9134)
U S CIRCUIT INC
2071 Wineridge Pl (92029-1931)
PHONE..............................760 489-1413
Michael Fariba, *Pr*
T J Sojitra, *Sr VP*
Mukesh Patel, *VP*
EMP: 80 **EST:** 1985
SQ FT: 40,000
SALES (est): 10.17MM
SALES (corp-wide): 11.64MM **Privately Held**
Web: www.uscircuit.com
SIC: 3679 3672 Electronic circuits; Printed circuit boards
PA: Ampel Incorporated
925 Estes Ave
Elk Grove Village IL
847 952-1900

(P-9135)
VAS ENGINEERING INC
4750 Viewridge Ave (92123-1640)
PHONE..............................858 569-1601
Rohak Vora, *CEO*
Greg Atzmiller, *
T J Sojitra, *Stockholder*
▲ **EMP:** 50 **EST:** 1979
SQ FT: 19,200
SALES (est): 23.17MM **Privately Held**
Web: www.vasengineering.com
SIC: 3679 3823 Electronic circuits; Temperature measurement instruments, industrial

PRODUCTS & SVCS

(P-9136)
VERTEX LCD INC
600 S Jefferson St Ste K (92870-6634)
P.O. Box 206 (92871-0206)
PHONE..............................714 223-7111
EMP: 35 **EST:** 1999
SALES (est): 3.92MM **Privately Held**
Web: www.vertexlcd.com
SIC: 3679 Liquid crystal displays (LCD)

(P-9137)
VISUAL COMMUNICATIONS COMPANY LLC
Also Called: Vcc
2173 Salk Ave Ste 175 (92008-7836)
PHONE..............................800 522-5546
EMP: 135 **EST:** 1976
SALES (est): 13.53MM **Privately Held**
Web: www.vcclite.com
SIC: 3679 Electronic circuits

(P-9138)
WAVESTREAM CORPORATION (HQ)
545 W Terrace Dr (91773-2915)
PHONE..............................909 599-9080
Robert Huffman, *CEO*
Nimrod Itach, *
Lanis Bell, *
James Rosenberg, *
EMP: 103 **EST:** 2006
SALES (est): 46.93MM **Privately Held**
Web: www.wavestream.com
SIC: 3679 8731 Microwave components;
    Commercial physical research
PA: Gilat Satellite Networks Ltd.
    21 Yegia Kapaim
    Petah Tikva

(P-9139)
WESTERN DIGITAL
19600 S Western Ave (90501-1117)
P.O. Box 5084 (92609-8584)
PHONE..............................510 557-7553
EMP: 24 **EST:** 2019
SALES (est): 2.91MM **Privately Held**
Web: www.westerndigital.com
SIC: 3679 Electronic components, nec

(P-9140)
WYVERN TECHNOLOGIES
1205 E Warner Ave (92705-5431)
PHONE..............................714 966-0710
James J Weber, *Pr*
EMP: 30 **EST:** 1984
SQ FT: 10,000
SALES (est): 4.5MM **Privately Held**
Web: www.wyverncorp.com
SIC: 3679 Microwave components

(P-9141)
XP POWER INC
Also Called: Switching Systems
1590 S Sinclair St (92806-5933)
PHONE..............................714 712-2642
Fred Mckirigan, *VP*
EMP: 64
Web: www.xppower.com
SIC: 3679 Power supplies, all types: static
HQ: Xp Power Inc.
    305 Foster St Ste 4
    Littleton MA
    800 253-0490

(P-9142)
Z-TRONIX INC
Also Called: Manufacturer
6327 Alondra Blvd (90723-3750)

PHONE..............................562 808-0800
Kamran Jahangard-mahboob, *CEO*
Roy R Jahangard, *Pr*
◆ **EMP:** 20 **EST:** 1997
SQ FT: 18,000
SALES (est): 6.18MM **Privately Held**
Web: www.z-tronix.com
SIC: 3679 5063 5065 Harness assemblies,
    for electronic use: wire or cable; Wire and
    cable; Connectors, electronic

3691 Storage Batteries

(P-9143)
BATTERY TECHNOLOGY INC (PA)
Also Called: B T I
16651 E Johnson Dr (91745-2413)
PHONE..............................626 336-6878
Christopher Chu, *Pr*
Andy Tong, *
▲ **EMP:** 60 **EST:** 1992
SQ FT: 20,000
SALES (est): 11.71MM **Privately Held**
Web: www.batterytech.com
SIC: 3691 Storage batteries

(P-9144)
EAST PENN MANUFACTURING
2709 Via Orange Way Ste B (91978-1708)
PHONE..............................619 660-0016
Kathy Broding, *Pr*
EMP: 32 **EST:** 1962
SQ FT: 1,600
SALES (est): 2.62MM **Privately Held**
Web: www.eastpennmanufacturing.com
SIC: 3691 Storage batteries

(P-9145)
ENERSYS
5580 Edison Ave (91710-6936)
PHONE..............................909 464-8251
Ken Hill, *Brnch Mgr*
EMP: 28
SALES (corp-wide): 3.71B **Publicly Held**
Web: www.enersys.com
SIC: 3691 Lead acid batteries (storage
    batteries)
PA: Enersys
    2366 Bernville Rd
    Reading PA
    610 208-1991

(P-9146)
ENEVATE CORPORATION
Also Called: Enevate
101 Theory Ste 200 (92617-3089)
PHONE..............................949 243-0399
Bob Kruse, *Pr*
Kirk Shockley, *
Doctor Benjamin Park, *Prin*
Jarvis Tou, *
Doug A Morris, *Quality Vice President*
▲ **EMP:** 62 **EST:** 2005
SQ FT: 17,000
SALES (est): 18.4MM **Privately Held**
Web: www.enevate.com
SIC: 3691 Storage batteries

(P-9147)
EREPLACEMENTS LLC
16885 W Bernardo Dr Ste 370
(92127-1618)
PHONE..............................714 361-2652
EMP: 30
Web: www.ereplacements.com
SIC: 3691 Storage batteries
PA: Ereplacements, Llc
    1300 Minters Chapel Rd # 100

Grapevine TX

(P-9148)
FLUX POWER HOLDINGS INC (PA)
2685 S Melrose Dr (92081-8783)
PHONE..............................877 505-3589
Ronald F Dutt, *Ch Bd*
Charles A Scheiwe, *CFO*
Jeffrey Mason, *VP Opers*
▲ **EMP:** 123 **EST:** 1998
SQ FT: 63,200
SALES (est): 66.34MM **Publicly Held**
Web: www.fluxpower.com
SIC: 3691 5063 Storage batteries; Storage
    batteries, industrial

(P-9149)
FRONT EDGE TECHNOLOGY INC
13455 Brooks Dr Ste A (91706-2254)
PHONE..............................626 856-8979
Simon Nieh, *Pr*
Roger Lin, *
EMP: 26 **EST:** 1994
SQ FT: 18,000
SALES (est): 4.7MM
SALES (corp-wide): 741.05MM **Publicly
Held**
Web: www.kla.com
SIC: 3691 Batteries, rechargeable
PA: Standex International Corporation
    23 Keewaydin Dr Ste 205
    Salem NH
    603 893-9701

(P-9150)
GOLD PEAK INDUSTRIES (NORTH AMERICA) INC
Also Called: GP Batteries
11245 W Bernardo Ct Ste 104
(92127-1676)
PHONE..............................858 674-6099
▲ **EMP:** 40
Web: www.gpina.com
SIC: 3691 Batteries, rechargeable

(P-9151)
INDUSTRIAL BATTERY ENGRG INC
Also Called: I B E
9121 De Garmo Ave (91352-2697)
PHONE..............................818 767-7067
Birger Holmquist, *CEO*
Michael Sloan, *
Ralph Holanov, *
Derek Sloan, *
Javier Sanchez, *
EMP: 47 **EST:** 1951
SQ FT: 20,000
SALES (est): 2.15MM **Privately Held**
Web: www.ibe-inc.com
SIC: 3691 3629 Storage batteries; Electronic
    generation equipment

(P-9152)
ONECHARGE INC
Also Called: Onecharge Biz
12472 Industry St (92841-2819)
PHONE..............................833 895-8624
Alexander Pisarev, *CEO*
Ashley Cooper, *
EMP: 50 **EST:** 2016
SQ FT: 8,500
SALES (est): 6.1MM **Privately Held**
Web: www.onecharge.biz
SIC: 3691 Storage batteries

(P-9153)
PALOS VERDES BUILDING CORP (PA)
Also Called: U S Battery Mfg Co
1675 Sampson Ave (92879-1889)
PHONE..............................951 371-8090
◆ **EMP:** 115 **EST:** 1949
SALES (est): 47.38MM
SALES (corp-wide): 47.38MM **Privately
Held**
Web: www.usbattery.com
SIC: 3691 Storage batteries

(P-9154)
SIMPLIPHI POWER INC
3100 Camino Del Sol (93030-7257)
PHONE..............................805 640-6700
Stephen P Andrews, *CEO*
Mark A Schwertfeger, *
▲ **EMP:** 34 **EST:** 2001
SQ FT: 5,300
SALES (est): 10.25MM
SALES (corp-wide): 2.04B **Privately Held**
Web: www.simpliphipower.com
SIC: 3691 Storage batteries
HQ: Briggs & Stratton, Llc
    12301 W Wirth St
    Wauwatosa WI
    414 259-5333

(P-9155)
SUNFUSION ENERGY SYSTEMS INC
9020 Kenamar Dr Ste 204 (92121-2431)
PHONE..............................800 544-0282
Walter Ellard, *Pr*
EMP: 24 **EST:** 2019
SQ FT: 6,000
SALES (est): 1.33MM **Privately Held**
Web: www.sunfusioness.com
SIC: 3691 Storage batteries

(P-9156)
TELEDYNE TECHNOLOGIES INC
Also Called: Teledyne Battery Products
840 W Brockton Ave (92374-2902)
P.O. Box 7950 (92375-1150)
PHONE..............................909 793-3131
Greg Donahey, *Brnch Mgr*
EMP: 58
SALES (corp-wide): 5.46B **Publicly Held**
Web: www.teledynebattery2.com
SIC: 3691 3692 Storage batteries; Primary
    batteries, dry and wet
PA: Teledyne Technologies Inc
    1049 Camino Dos Rios
    Thousand Oaks CA
    805 373-4545

(P-9157)
TROJAN BATTERY HOLDINGS LLC
12380 Clark St (90670-3804)
PHONE..............................800 423-6569
EMP: 44 **EST:** 2013
SALES (est): 5MM
SALES (corp-wide): 3.44B **Privately Held**
SIC: 3691 3692 Lead acid batteries (storage
    batteries); Primary batteries, dry and wet
HQ: Trojan Battery Company, Llc
    12380 Clark St
    Santa Fe Springs CA
    562 236-3000

3692 Primary Batteries, Dry And Wet

(P-9158)
B & B BATTERY (USA) INC (PA)
6415 Randolph St (90040-3511)
PHONE.....................323 278-1900
Jack Liu, *Pr*
George Liu, *VP*
▲ EMP: 18 EST: 1995
SQ FT: 20,000
SALES (est): 2.86MM Privately Held
SIC: 3692 Primary batteries, dry and wet

(P-9159)
QUALLION LLC
12744 San Fernando Rd Ste 100
(91342-3728)
PHONE.....................818 833-2000
Jackie York, *
▲ EMP: 155 EST: 1998
SALES (est): 42.93MM
SALES (corp-wide): 3.71B Publicly Held
Web: www.enersys.com
SIC: 3692 Primary batteries, dry and wet
PA: Enersys
2366 Bernville Rd
Reading PA
610 208-1991

(P-9160)
SPECTRUM BRANDS INC
Also Called: Spectrum Brands Hhi
19701 Da Vinci (92610-2622)
PHONE.....................949 672-4003
Phil Szuba, *Sr VP*
EMP: 700
SQ FT: 150,000
SALES (corp-wide): 558.24MM Privately Held
Web: www.spectrumbrands.com
SIC: 3692 Primary batteries, dry and wet
PA: Spectrum Brands, Inc.
3001 Deming Way
Middleton WI
608 275-3340

(P-9161)
TROJAN BATTERY COMPANY LLC (DH)
12380 Clark St (90670-3804)
PHONE.....................562 236-3000
TOLL FREE: 800
Richard A Heller, *CEO*
Alex Dimitrijevic, *CFO*
◆ EMP: 182 EST: 2013
SALES (est): 658.32MM
SALES (corp-wide): 3.44B Privately Held
Web: www.trojanbattery.com
SIC: 3692 3691 Primary batteries, dry and wet; Lead acid batteries (storage batteries)
HQ: C&D Technologies, Inc.
200 Precision Rd
Horsham PA
215 619-2700

3694 Engine Electrical Equipment

(P-9162)
AMERICAN INDUSTRIAL MANUFACTURING SERVICES INC
41673 Corning Pl (92562-7023)
PHONE.....................951 698-3379
▼ EMP: 107

SIC: 3694 Engine electrical equipment

(P-9163)
ARRIVER HOLDCO INC
5775 Morehouse Dr (92121-1714)
PHONE.....................858 587-1121
Jacob Svanberg, *CEO*
EMP: 7543 EST: 2017
SALES (est): 1.66B
SALES (corp-wide): 35.82B Publicly Held
Web: www.veoneer.com
SIC: 3694 3714 Automotive electrical equipment, nec; Motor vehicle parts and accessories
PA: Qualcomm Incorporated
5775 Morehouse Dr
San Diego CA
858 587-1121

(P-9164)
BATTERY-BIZ INC
Also Called: Ebatts.com
1380 Flynn Rd (93012-8016)
PHONE.....................800 848-6782
Ophir Marish, *CEO*
Yossi Jakubovits, *
▲ EMP: 63 EST: 1988
SQ FT: 60,000
SALES (est): 12.41MM Privately Held
Web: www.battery-biz.com
SIC: 3694 Battery charging generators, automobile and aircraft

(P-9165)
DSM&T CO INC
10609 Business Dr (92337-8212)
PHONE.....................909 357-7960
Sergio Corona, *CEO*
▲ EMP: 170 EST: 1982
SQ FT: 41,000
SALES (est): 24.97MM Privately Held
Web: www.dsmt.com
SIC: 3694 3357 3634 3643 Harness wiring sets, internal combustion engines; Nonferrous wiredrawing and insulating; Heating pads, electric; Cord connectors, electric

(P-9166)
ELECTRICAL REBUILDERS SLS INC (PA)
Also Called: Vapex-Genex-Precision
7603 Willow Glen Rd (90046-1608)
PHONE.....................323 249-7545
Mike Klapper, *Pr*
David Klapper, *
Mary Ann Klapper, *
▲ EMP: 75 EST: 1966
SALES (est): 4.89MM
SALES (corp-wide): 4.89MM Privately Held
SIC: 3694 3592 3714 Distributors, motor vehicle engine; Carburetors; Motor vehicle brake systems and parts

(P-9167)
LOOP INC
115 Eucalyptus Dr (90245-3839)
PHONE.....................888 385-6674
Dustin Cavanaugh, *CEO*
EMP: 30 EST: 2019
SALES (est): 4.41MM Privately Held
Web: www.evloop.io
SIC: 3694 Battery charging generators, automobile and aircraft

(P-9168)
LOW COST INTERLOCK INC
2038 W Park Ave (92373-6260)
P.O. Box 365 (92373-0121)

PHONE.....................844 387-0326
Michael E Lyon, *CEO*
EMP: 35 EST: 2010
SALES (est): 2.48MM Privately Held
Web: www.lowcostinterlock.com
SIC: 3694 Ignition apparatus and distributors

(P-9169)
M & H ELECTRIC FABRICATORS INC
13537 Alondra Blvd (90670-5602)
PHONE.....................562 926-9552
▲ EMP: 30 EST: 1985
SALES (est): 4.66MM Privately Held
Web: www.wiringharness.com
SIC: 3694 Automotive electrical equipment, nec

(P-9170)
MAXWELL TECHNOLOGIES INC (HQ)
Also Called: Maxwell
3888 Calle Fortunada (92123-1825)
PHONE.....................858 503-3300
Franz Fink, *Pr*
David Lyle, *
Emily Lough, *
▲ EMP: 94 EST: 1965
SQ FT: 30,500
SALES (est): 90.46MM
SALES (corp-wide): 81.46B Publicly Held
Web: www.maxwell.com
SIC: 3694 3629 Engine electrical equipment; Capacitors and condensers
PA: Tesla, Inc.
1 Tesla Rd
Austin TX
512 516-8177

(P-9171)
MYOTEK INDUSTRIES INCORPORATED (DH)
1278 Glenneyre St Ste 431 (92651-3103)
PHONE.....................949 502-3776
▲ EMP: 90 EST: 1998
SQ FT: 1,800
SALES (est): 29.51MM
SALES (corp-wide): 180.46MM Privately Held
Web: www.fordledfog.com
SIC: 3694 5013 Automotive electrical equipment, nec; Automotive servicing equipment
HQ: Myotek Holdings, Inc.
1176 Main St Ste B
Irvine CA
949 502-3776

(P-9172)
PERTRONIX INC
Also Called: Patriot Products
15601 Cypress Ave Unit B (91706-2120)
PHONE.....................909 599-5955
Jack Porter, *Mgr*
EMP: 26
SALES (corp-wide): 13.89MM Privately Held
Web: www.pertronixbrands.com
SIC: 3694 5013 Ignition apparatus, internal combustion engines; Automotive supplies and parts
PA: Pertronix, Llc
11414 W 79th St
Overland Park KS
909 599-5955

(P-9173)
POLAR POWER INC
Also Called: Polar Power

249 E Gardena Blvd (90248-2813)
PHONE.....................310 830-9153
EMP: 106 EST: 1979
SALES (est): 16.06MM Privately Held
Web: www.polarpower.com
SIC: 3694 Engine electrical equipment

(P-9174)
PRECO AIRCRAFT MOTORS INC
1133 Mission St (91030-3211)
P.O. Box 189 (91031-0189)
PHONE.....................626 799-3549
Peter Kingston Junior, *Pr*
Peter Kingston Senior, *Ch*
Linda D Kingston, *VP*
EMP: 20 EST: 1945
SQ FT: 10,000
SALES (est): 644.78K Privately Held
SIC: 3694 Motors, starting: automotive and aircraft

(P-9175)
TRADEMARK CONSTRUCTION CO INC (PA)
Also Called: Jmw Truss and Components
15916 Bernardo Center Dr (92127-1828)
PHONE.....................760 489-5647
Richard D Wilson, *Pr*
John Cao, *
Nancy Wilson, *
EMP: 60 EST: 1978
SQ FT: 12,000
SALES (est): 8.9MM
SALES (corp-wide): 8.9MM Privately Held
Web: www.jmwtruss.com
SIC: 3694 Engine electrical equipment

(P-9176)
URIMAN INC (HQ)
650 N Puente St (92821-2880)
PHONE.....................714 257-2080
Jinho Choi, *CEO*
Kyeong Ho Lee, *
Kyung Hoon Park, *
Young Hak Yun, *
Susie Chiang, *
◆ EMP: 18 EST: 1983
SQ FT: 42,144
SALES (est): 46.88MM Privately Held
SIC: 3694 3625 3714 Alternators, automotive; Starter, electric motor; Power steering equipment, motor vehicle
PA: HI D&I Halla Corporation
289 Olympic-Ro, Songpa-Gu
Seoul

(P-9177)
VANTAGE VEHICLE INTL INC
Also Called: Vantage Vehicle Group
1740 N Delilah St (92879-1893)
PHONE.....................951 735-1200
Michael Pak, *Pr*
◆ EMP: 30 EST: 2002
SQ FT: 50,000
SALES (est): 7.57MM Privately Held
Web: www.vantagevehicle.com
SIC: 3694 Distributors, motor vehicle engine

(P-9178)
XOS INC (PA)
Also Called: Xos
3550 Tyburn St Ste 100 (90065-1427)
PHONE.....................818 316-1890
Dakota Semler, *Ch Bd*
Giordano Sordoni, *COO*
Kingsley Afemikhe, *CFO*
EMP: 27 EST: 2020
SQ FT: 85,142
SALES (est): 36.38MM
SALES (corp-wide): 36.38MM Publicly Held

Web: www.xostrucks.com
SIC: **3694** Automotive electrical equipment, nec

3695 Magnetic And Optical Recording Media

(P-9179)
CD VIDEO MANUFACTURING INC
Also Called: C D Video
12650 Westminster Ave (92706-2139)
PHONE..................................714 265-0770
Minh T Nguyen, *Pr*
▲ **EMP:** 60 **EST:** 1995
SQ FT: 11,000
SALES (est): 13.55MM **Privately Held**
Web: www.cdvideomfg.com
SIC: **3695** 3652 7819 Video recording tape, blank; Compact laser discs, prerecorded; Services allied to motion pictures

(P-9180)
ELM SYSTEM INC
11622 El Camino Real Ste 100 (92130)
PHONE..................................408 694-2750
Ingyeom Kim, *CEO*
EMP: 18 **EST:** 2012
SALES (est): 1.12MM **Privately Held**
SIC: **3695** Computer software tape and disks: blank, rigid, and floppy

(P-9181)
FARSTONE TECHNOLOGY INC
184 Technology Dr Ste 205 (92618-2435)
PHONE.................................:.949 336-4321
EMP: 110
SALES (est): 3.1MM **Privately Held**
Web: www.farstone.com
SIC: **3695** Computer software tape and disks: blank, rigid, and floppy

(P-9182)
NORDSON CALIFORNIA INC
Also Called: Nordson Asymtek
2747 Loker Ave W (92010-6601)
PHONE..................................760 918-8490
◆ **EMP:** 94
SIC: **3695** 3561 Computer software tape and disks: blank, rigid, and floppy; Pump jacks and other pumping equipment

(P-9183)
REEL PICTURE PRODUCTIONS LLC
5330 Eastgate Mall (92121-2804)
PHONE..................................858 587-0301
Michael Ishayik, *Managing Member*
▲ **EMP:** 43 **EST:** 1997
SQ FT: 45,000
SALES (est): 4.92MM **Privately Held**
Web: www.reelpicture.com
SIC: **3695** Optical disks and tape, blank

(P-9184)
TARGET TECHNOLOGY COMPANY LLC
3420 Bristol St (92626-7133)
PHONE..................................949 788-0909
EMP: 50 **EST:** 1998
SALES (est): 4.43MM **Privately Held**
Web: www.targettechnology.com
SIC: **3695** Magnetic and optical recording media

(P-9185)
TECHNICOLOR DISC SERVICES CORP (HQ)
3601 Calle Tecate Ste 120 (93012-5097)
PHONE..................................805 445-1122
▲ **EMP:** 200 **EST:** 1996
SALES (est): 49.93MM **Privately Held**
SIC: **3695** 7361 Computer software tape and disks: blank, rigid, and floppy; Employment agencies
PA: Vantiva
10 Boulevard De Grenelle
Paris

(P-9186)
UNITED AUDIO VIDEO GROUP INC
7651 Densmore Ave (91406-2043)
PHONE..................................818 980-6700
Miriam Newman, *Pr*
Steven Newman, *VP*
Lauri Newman, *Sec*
▲ **EMP:** 24 **EST:** 1972
SALES (est): 720.39K **Privately Held**
Web: www.unitedavg.com
SIC: **3695** 5065 Audio range tape, blank; Tapes, audio and video recording

(P-9187)
UNITED MEDIA SERVICES INC
4955 E Hunter Ave (92807-2058)
PHONE..................................714 693-8168
David Lin, *Pr*
Louis Chase, *Stockholder**
EMP: 120 **EST:** 1992
SQ FT: 41,000
SALES (est): 6.99MM **Privately Held**
SIC: **3695** Video recording tape, blank

(P-9188)
VIDA LEASE CORPORATION
17807 Maclaren St Ste A (91744-5700)
PHONE..................................626 839-4912
Eva Chang Hsu, *Pr*
Tony Hsu, *VP*
Melody Paa, *Stockholder*
EMP: 23 **EST:** 1993
SQ FT: 40,000
SALES (est): 415.31K **Privately Held**
SIC: **3695** 5099 Magnetic tape; Video cassettes, accessories and supplies

3699 Electrical Equipment And Supplies, Nec

(P-9189)
A T PARKER INC (PA)
Also Called: Solar Electronics Company
10866 Chandler Blvd (91601-2945)
PHONE..................................818 755-1700
Tom A Parker, *Pr*
Jo Ann Dennis, *VP*
Sue Parker, *Sec*
▼ **EMP:** 22 **EST:** 1960
SQ FT: 7,500
SALES (est): 3.12MM
SALES (corp-wide): 3.12MM **Privately Held**
Web: www.solar-emc.com
SIC: **3699** Electrical equipment and supplies, nec

(P-9190)
A-Z EMISSIONS SOLUTIONS INC
Also Called: A-Z Bussales
1900 S Riverside Ave (92324-3344)
PHONE..................................951 781-1856
John Landherr, *Pr*

April Rosenquist, *Prin*
Joshua Pearson, *Prin*
Jeff Laliberte, *Prin*
David Goudeau, *Prin*
EMP: 26 **EST:** 1984
SALES (est): 274.15K **Privately Held**
Web: www.a-zbus.com
SIC: **3699** Heat emission operating apparatus

(P-9191)
AAMP OF AMERICA
2500 E Francis St (91761-7730)
PHONE..................................805 338-6800
Dennis Hill, *Owner*
▲ **EMP:** 23 **EST:** 2009
SALES (est): 2.22MM **Privately Held**
SIC: **3699** Electrical equipment and supplies, nec

(P-9192)
AGENTS WEST INC
Also Called: Electrical Products Rep
6 Hughes Ste 210 (92618-2063)
PHONE..................................949 614-0293
Aldo Pellicciotti, *Pr*
Stephen Benshoof, *VP*
Clyde Collins, *Treas*
Robert Rathburn, *Sec*
EMP: 45 **EST:** 1978
SQ FT: 30,000
SALES (est): 6.03MM **Privately Held**
Web: www.agentswest.com
SIC: **3699** 5063 Electrical equipment and supplies, nec; Electrical apparatus and equipment

(P-9193)
AITECH DEFENSE SYSTEMS INC
19756 Prairie St (91311-6531)
PHONE..................................818 700-2000
Moshe Tal, *CEO*
Erez Konfino, *CFO*
◆ **EMP:** 55 **EST:** 1990
SQ FT: 22,000
SALES (est): 22.56MM **Privately Held**
Web: www.aitechsystems.com
SIC: **3699** Electrical equipment and supplies, nec
PA: Aitech Rugged Group, Inc.
19756 Prairie St
Chatsworth CA

(P-9194)
AITECH RUGGED GROUP INC (PA)
19756 Prairie St (91311-6531)
PHONE..................................818 700-2000
Moshe Tal, *CEO*
Erez Konfino, ***
EMP: 50 **EST:** 2008
SALES (est): 29.92MM **Privately Held**
Web: www.aitechsystems.com
SIC: **3699** Electrical equipment and supplies, nec

(P-9195)
AMREX-ZETRON INC
Also Called: Amrex Electrotherapy Equipment
7034 Jackson St (90723-4835)
PHONE..................................310 527-6868
George Bell, *Pr*
▲ **EMP:** 17 **EST:** 1935
SQ FT: 20,000
SALES (est): 775.32K **Privately Held**
Web: www.amrexusa.com
SIC: **3699** 3845 High-energy particle physics equipment; Electromedical equipment

(P-9196)
BLISSLIGHTS INC
2625 Temple Heights Dr Ste A (92056-3590)
PHONE..................................888 868-4603
▲ **EMP:** 20 **EST:** 2007
SALES (est): 4.88MM **Privately Held**
Web: www.blisslights.com
SIC: **3699** Laser systems and equipment

(P-9197)
CALSTAR SYSTEMS GROUP INC
Also Called: Quikstor
6345 Balboa Blvd Ste 105 (91316-1517)
PHONE..................................818 922-2000
Dennis Levitt, *Pr*
▲ **EMP:** 22 **EST:** 1982
SALES (est): 2.29MM **Privately Held**
Web: www.quikstor.com
SIC: **3699** 7371 Security devices; Computer software development

(P-9198)
CARTTRONICS LLC (HQ)
90 Icon (92610-3000)
PHONE..................................888 696-2278
◆ **EMP:** 27 **EST:** 1997
SALES (est): 5.09MM
SALES (corp-wide): 79.48MM **Privately Held**
Web: www.gatekeepersystems.com
SIC: **3699** 7382 5065 Security devices; Security systems services; Security control equipment and systems
PA: Gatekeeper Systems, Inc.
90 Icon
Foothill Ranch CA
888 808-9433

(P-9199)
COAST WIRE & PLASTIC TECH LLC
1048 E Burgrove St (90746-3514)
PHONE..................................310 639-9473
George Lopez, *Co-Managing Member*
George Lopez, *Managing Member*
Mark Vanderwoude, ***
David Ibanez, ***
EMP: 750 **EST:** 1993
SQ FT: 60,000
SALES (est): 63.59MM
SALES (corp-wide): 2.61B **Publicly Held**
SIC: **3699** 3357 Electrical equipment and supplies, nec; Communication wire
PA: Belden Inc.
1 N Brentwood Blvd Fl 15
Saint Louis MO
314 854-8000

(P-9200)
CODA ENERGY HOLDINGS LLC
Also Called: Coda Energy
111 N Artsakh Ave Ste 300 (91206-4097)
PHONE..................................626 775-3900
Paul Detering, *CEO*
Peter Nortman, ***
John Bryan, ***
Davnette Librando, ***
Edward Solar, ***
▲ **EMP:** 19 **EST:** 2013
SALES (est): 2.44MM **Privately Held**
Web: www.codaenergy.com
SIC: **3699** Household electrical equipment

(P-9201)
COOPER CROUSE-HINDS LLC
Also Called: Cooper Interconnect
3350 Enterprise Dr (92316)
PHONE..................................951 241-8766
Morris Townsend, *Brnch Mgr*

EMP: 26
Web: www.coopercrouse-hinds.com
SIC: 3699 Fire control or bombing equipment, electronic
HQ: Cooper Crouse-Hinds, Llc
1201 Wolf St
Syracuse NY
315 477-7000

(P-9202)
COZZIA USA LLC (HQ)
861 S Oak Park Rd (91724-3624)
PHONE......................626 667-2272
▲ **EMP:** 19 **EST:** 2009
SQ FT: 5,500
SALES (est): 21MM **Privately Held**
Web: www.cozziausa.com
SIC: 3699 Electrical equipment and supplies, nec
PA: Xiamen Comfort Science&Technology Group Co., Ltd
Floor 8, No.31-37, Anling 2nd Road, Huli District
Xiamen FJ

(P-9203)
CUBIC DEFENSE APPLICATIONS INC (DH)
Also Called: Cubic Ground Training
9233 Balboa Ave (92123-1513)
P.O. Box 85587 (92186-5587)
PHONE......................858 776-5664
Steven Slijepcevic, *CEO*
John D Thomas, *
James R Edwards, *
Mark A Harrison, *
Norman R Bishop, *
▼ **EMP:** 589 **EST:** 1987
SQ FT: 130,000
SALES (est): 497.76MM
SALES (corp-wide): 1.48B **Privately Held**
Web: www.cubic.com
SIC: 3699 3663 3812 Flight simulators (training aids), electronic; Radio and t.v. communications equipment; Aircraft/ aerospace flight instruments and guidance systems
HQ: Cubic Corporation
9233 Balboa Ave
San Diego CA
858 277-6780

(P-9204)
CUBIC DEFENSE APPLICATIONS INC
CMS Secure Comms
9233 Balboa Ave (92123-1513)
PHONE......................858 505-2870
Jerry Madigan, *VP*
EMP: 200
SALES (corp-wide): 1.48B **Privately Held**
Web: www.cubic.com
SIC: 3699 7382 Security devices; Security systems services
HQ: Cubic Defense Applications, Inc.
9233 Balboa Ave
San Diego CA
858 776-5664

(P-9205)
CYMER LLC (HQ)
17075 Thornmint Ct (92127-2413)
PHONE......................858 385-7300
▲ **EMP:** 555 **EST:** 1996
SQ FT: 135,000
SALES (est): 659.74MM
SALES (corp-wide): 16.53B **Privately Held**
Web: www.cymer.com
SIC: 3699 3827 Laser systems and equipment; Lens mounts

PA: Asml Holding N.V.
De Run 6501
Veldhoven NB
853018496

(P-9206)
DISTRIBUTION ELECTRNICS VLUED
Also Called: Deva
2651 Dow Ave (92780-7207)
PHONE......................714 368-1717
Rodger Dale Baker, *CEO*
Ken Plock, *
◆ **EMP:** 23 **EST:** 1974
SQ FT: 13,800
SALES (est): 15.01MM **Privately Held**
Web: www.devainc.com
SIC: 3699 5065 Electrical equipment and supplies, nec; Electronic parts and equipment, nec
HQ: Deva, Inc.
555 Madison Ave Ste 1100
New York NY
212 223-2466

(P-9207)
DOORKING INC (PA)
Also Called: Doorking
120 S Glasgow Ave (90301-1502)
PHONE......................310 645-0023
Thomas Richmond, *Pr*
Pat Kochie, *
Susan Richmond, *
◆ **EMP:** 185 **EST:** 1948
SQ FT: 16,000
SALES (est): 98.13MM
SALES (corp-wide): 98.13MM **Privately Held**
Web: www.doorking.com
SIC: 3699 5065 3829 Security control equipment and systems; Security control equipment and systems; Measuring and controlling devices, nec

(P-9208)
DUTEK INCORPORATED
2228 Oak Ridge Way (92081-8341)
PHONE......................760 566-8888
David Du, *CEO*
Bill Marsh, *
EMP: 50 **EST:** 2000
SQ FT: 4,500
SALES (est): 20.57MM
SALES (corp-wide): 97.89MM **Privately Held**
Web: www.dutek.com
SIC: 3699 3629 3643 Electrical equipment and supplies, nec; Electronic generation equipment; Current-carrying wiring services
PA: Ddh Enterprise, Inc.
2220 Oak Ridge Way
Vista CA
760 599-0171

(P-9209)
ELECTRIC GATE STORE INC
15342 Chatsworth St (91345-2041)
PHONE......................818 361-6872
Jorge Nunez, *Pr*
EMP: 142
SALES (corp-wide): 8.83MM **Privately Held**
Web: www.gatestore.com
SIC: 3699 Security devices
PA: Electric Gate Store, Inc.
421 Park Ave
San Fernando CA
818 504-2300

(P-9210)
FEMTO BLANC INC
9267 Research Dr (92618-4286)
PHONE......................408 409-2900
Uri Abrams, *Brnch Mgr*
EMP: 59
SALES (corp-wide): 237.42K **Privately Held**
SIC: 3699 Laser systems and equipment
PA: Femto Blanc Inc.
243 N Union St
Lambertville NJ

(P-9211)
FREEDOM PHOTONICS LLC
41 Aero Camino (93117-3104)
PHONE......................805 967-4900
Leif Johansson, *
EMP: 50 **EST:** 2005
SQ FT: 14,500
SALES (est): 4.29MM
SALES (corp-wide): 31.94MM **Publicly Held**
Web: www.freedomphotonics.com
SIC: 3699 3827 3674 Laser systems and equipment; Optical test and inspection equipment; Light sensitive devices
PA: Luminar Technologies, Inc.
2603 Discovery Dr Ste 100
Orlando FL
407 900-5259

(P-9212)
GATEKEEPER SYSTEMS INC (PA)
90 Icon (92610-3000)
PHONE......................888 808-9433
Robert Harling, *CEO*
Jason Crowl, *
Keith Kato, *
Greg Meisenzahl, *
Robert Newbold, *
▲ **EMP:** 63 **EST:** 1998
SQ FT: 15,000
SALES (est): 79.48MM
SALES (corp-wide): 79.48MM **Privately Held**
Web: www.gatekeepersystems.com
SIC: 3699 Security devices

(P-9213)
GORES RADIO HOLDINGS LLC
10877 Wilshire Blvd Ste 1805 (90024-4373)
PHONE......................310 209-3010
Alex Gores, *Pr*
EMP: 56 **EST:** 2007
SALES (est): 7.41MM
SALES (corp-wide): 1.81B **Privately Held**
Web: www.gores.com
SIC: 3699 7382 Security devices; Security systems services
PA: The Gores Group Llc
9800 Wilshire Blvd
Beverly Hills CA
310 209-3010

(P-9214)
HC WEST LLC
7130 Convoy Ct (92111-1019)
PHONE......................858 277-3473
Robert Hunter, *Managing Member*
EMP: 300 **EST:** 2020
SALES (est): 20.19MM **Privately Held**
SIC: 3699 Security control equipment and systems

(P-9215)
HUNT ELECTRONIC USA INC
Also Called: Hunt Electronic
11790 Jersey Blvd (91730-4935)

PHONE......................909 987-6999
Ivan Lu, *CEO*
Karen Wang, *CFO*
◆ **EMP:** 19 **EST:** 1999
SQ FT: 23,000
SALES (est): 4.45MM **Privately Held**
Web: www.huntcctv.com
SIC: 3699 Security control equipment and systems

(P-9216)
INSTRUMENTS INCORPORATED
7263 Engineer Rd Ste G (92111-1493)
PHONE......................858 571-1111
EMP: 28 **EST:** 1941
SALES (est): 5.32MM **Privately Held**
Web: www.instrumentsinc.com
SIC: 3699 Electrical equipment and supplies, nec

(P-9217)
IRONWOOD ELECTRIC INC
13 Ashton (92692-4731)
PHONE......................714 630-2350
Raymond Chafe, *Prin*
EMP: 25 **EST:** 2011
SALES (est): 9.49MM **Privately Held**
Web: www.albdinc.com
SIC: 3699 1731 Electrical equipment and supplies, nec; Electrical work

(P-9218)
ISC8 INC
Also Called: Irvine Sensors
151 Kalmus Dr Ste A203 (92626-5999)
PHONE......................714 549-8211
EMP: 38
Web: www.isc8.com
SIC: 3699 3674 8731 Security control equipment and systems; Semiconductors and related devices; Electronic research

(P-9219)
IWERKS ENTERTAINMENT INC
Also Called: Simex-Iwerks
25040 Avenue Tibbitts Ste F (91355-3946)
PHONE......................661 678-1800
Gary Matus, *CEO*
Jeff Dahl, *
Mark Cornell, *
Donald Stults, *
EMP: 75 **EST:** 1986
SALES (est): 11.51MM
SALES (corp-wide): 17.76MM **Privately Held**
Web: www.simex-iwerks.com
SIC: 3699 7819 Electrical equipment and supplies, nec; Developing and printing of commercial motion picture film
PA: Simex Inc
600-210 King St E
Toronto ON
416 597-1585

(P-9220)
JACK J ENGEL MANUFACTURING INC
Also Called: Creative Automation
11641 Pendleton St (91352-2502)
PHONE......................818 767-6220
Jack Engel, *Pr*
Jack J Engel, *
Ilene Engel, *
EMP: 22 **EST:** 1968
SQ FT: 15,000
SALES (est): 891.67K **Privately Held**
Web: www.creativedispensing.com
SIC: 3699 5063 Electrical equipment and supplies, nec; Electrical supplies, nec

PRODUCTS & SVCS

(P-9221)
JBB INC
Also Called: Precision Waterjet
4900 E Hunter Ave (92807-2057)
PHONE..................888 538-9287
EMP: 22 **EST:** 1995
SALES (est): 2.13MM **Privately Held**
Web: www.h2ojet.com
SIC: 3699 Laser welding, drilling, and cutting
equipment

(P-9222)
KANEX
4295 Jurupa St Ste 111 (91761-1429)
PHONE..................714 332-1681
Kelvin Yan, CEO
▲ **EMP:** 25 **EST:** 1987
SALES (est): 4.31MM **Privately Held**
Web: www.kanex.com
SIC: 3699 5065 Electrical equipment and
supplies, nec; Electronic parts and
equipment, nec

(P-9223)
KELLY PNEUMATICS INC
1611 Babcock St (92663-2805)
PHONE..................800 704-7552
Ed Kelly, Pr
▲ **EMP:** 20 **EST:** 2003
SALES (est): 3.15MM **Privately Held**
Web: www.kellypneumatics.com
SIC: 3699 Electrical equipment and supplies,
nec

(P-9224)
**KULICKE SFFA WEDGE
BONDING INC**
Also Called: Kulicke & Soffa Industries
1821 E Dyer Rd Ste 200 (92705-5700)
PHONE..................949 660-0440
Scott Kulicke, Pr
▲ **EMP:** 200 **EST:** 2008
SALES (est): 43.75MM
SALES (corp-wide): 742.49MM **Publicly
Held**
Web: www.kns.com
SIC: 3699 Electrical equipment and supplies,
nec
PA: Kulicke And Soffa Industries, Inc.
1005 Virginia Dr
Fort Washington PA
215 784-6000

(P-9225)
KYOCERA SLD LASER INC (HQ)
Also Called: Sld Laser
485 Pine Ave (93117-3709)
PHONE..................805 696-6999
Steven Denbaars, CEO
Eric B Kim, *
Thomas Caulfield, *
George Stringer, *
Neal Woods, *
EMP: 46 **EST:** 2013
SQ FT: 3,000
SALES (est): 23.68MM **Privately Held**
Web: www.kyocera-sldlaser.com
SIC: 3699 Laser systems and equipment
PA: Kyocera Corporation
6, Takedatobadonocho, Fushimi-Ku
Kyoto KYO

(P-9226)
LASER SPECTRUM INC
15 Mira Mesa (92688-3418)
PHONE..................949 726-2978
EMP: 43
SALES (corp-wide): 253.91K **Privately
Held**
Web: www.laser-spectrum.com

SIC: 3699 Laser systems and equipment
PA: Laser Spectrum, Inc.
4605 Barranca Pkwy 101g
Irvine CA
949 551-8225

(P-9227)
LORENZ INC
Also Called: Karel Manufacturing
1749 Stergios Rd (92231-9657)
PHONE..................760 427-1815
▲ **EMP:** 47 **EST:** 1993
SQ FT: 73,000
SALES (est): 3.55MM **Privately Held**
SIC: 3699 Electrical equipment and supplies,
nec

(P-9228)
**MEGGITT SAFETY SYSTEMS
INC (DH)**
Also Called: Meggitt Ctrl Systms-Vntura Cnt
1785 Voyager Ave (93063-3363)
PHONE..................805 584-4100
Dennis Hutton, Pr
Dolores Watai, *
▲ **EMP:** 210 **EST:** 1999
SQ FT: 180,000
SALES (est): 118.2MM
SALES (corp-wide): 19.07B **Publicly Held**
Web: www.meggitt.com
SIC: 3699 3724 3728 7389 Betatrons;
Exhaust systems, aircraft; Aircraft parts and
equipment, nec; Fire protection service
other than forestry or public
HQ: Meggitt Limited
Pilot Way
Coventry W MIDLANDS
247 682-6900

(P-9229)
**MERCURY SECURITY
PRODUCTS LLC**
4811 Airport Plaza Dr Ste 300 (90815)
PHONE..................562 986-9105
Joseph Grillo, CEO
Hing Hung, Ex VP
▲ **EMP:** 19 **EST:** 2012
SALES (est): 4.98MM
SALES (corp-wide): 11.51B **Privately Held**
Web: www.mercury-security.com
SIC: 3699 8742 Security control equipment
and systems; Industry specialist consultants
HQ: Hid Global Corporation
611 Center Ridge Dr
Austin TX

(P-9230)
MYE TECHNOLOGIES INC
25060 Avenue Stanford (91355-3411)
PHONE..................661 964-0217
Anthony Garcia, Pr
▲ **EMP:** 45 **EST:** 2006
SALES (est): 5.84MM **Privately Held**
Web: www.myeinc.com
SIC: 3699 Electric sound equipment

(P-9231)
**NUPHOTON TECHNOLOGIES
INC**
41610 Corning Pl (92562-7023)
PHONE..................951 696-8366
Ramadas Pillai, CEO
Sindu Pillai, VP
Vish Govindan, CFO
Dan Vera, COO
EMP: 25 **EST:** 1996
SQ FT: 12,000
SALES (est): 13.25MM **Privately Held**
Web: www.nuphoton.com

SIC: 3699 Laser systems and equipment

(P-9232)
O & S CALIFORNIA INC
Also Called: Osca-Arcosa
9731 Siempre Viva Rd Ste E (92154-7200)
PHONE..................619 661-1800
Kazuo Murata, Pr
Jos Luis Furlong, *
▲ **EMP:** 400 **EST:** 1986
SQ FT: 4,676
SALES (est): 50.94MM **Privately Held**
Web: www.osca-arcosa.com
SIC: 3699 Electrical equipment and supplies,
nec
PA: Onamba Co.,Ltd.
3-1-27, Fukaekita, Higashinari-Ku
Osaka OSK

(P-9233)
OBRYANT ELECTRIC INC
3 Banting (92618-3601)
PHONE..................949 341-0025
EMP: 40
SALES (corp-wide): 46.42MM **Privately
Held**
Web: www.obryantelectric.com
SIC: 3699 1731 Electrical equipment and
supplies, nec; Electrical work
PA: O'bryant Electric, Inc.
9314 Eton Ave
Chatsworth CA
818 407-1986

(P-9234)
**ONESOURCE DISTRIBUTORS
LLC (DH)**
3951 Oceanic Dr (92056-5846)
PHONE..................760 966-4500
◆ **EMP:** 45 **EST:** 1983
SQ FT: 50,000
SALES (est): 296.02MM
SALES (corp-wide): 12.53MM **Privately
Held**
Web: www.1sourcedist.com
SIC: 3699 5063 5085 5084 Electrical
equipment and supplies, nec; Electrical
supplies, nec; Industrial supplies; Industrial
machinery and equipment
HQ: Sonepar Management Us, Inc.
510 Walnut St Ste 400
Philadelphia PA
215 399-5900

(P-9235)
**ORTHODYNE ELECTRONICS
CORPORATION (HQ)**
16700 Red Hill Ave (92606-4802)
PHONE..................949 660-0440
▲ **EMP:** 249 **EST:** 1960
SALES (est): 49.49MM
SALES (corp-wide): 742.49MM **Publicly
Held**
Web: www.orthodyneelectronics.com
SIC: 3699 Electrical equipment and supplies,
nec
PA: Kulicke And Soffa Industries, Inc.
1005 Virginia Dr
Fort Washington PA
215 784-6000

(P-9236)
OSI LASERSCAN INC
12525 Chadron Ave (90250-4807)
PHONE..................310 978-0516
Douglas Dillman, Contrlr
EMP: 27 **EST:** 2003
SALES (est): 4.45MM
SALES (corp-wide): 1.15B **Publicly Held**
Web: www.osilaserscan.com

SIC: 3699 3674 Laser systems and
equipment; Photoconductive cells
HQ: Osi Optoelectronics, Inc.
12525 Chadron Ave
Hawthorne CA

(P-9237)
OSI SUBSIDIARY INC
12525 Chadron Ave (90250-4807)
PHONE..................310 978-0516
EMP: 81 **EST:** 1995
SALES (est): 10.28MM
SALES (corp-wide): 1.15B **Publicly Held**
Web: www.osi-systems.com
SIC: 3699 Laser systems and equipment
PA: Osi Systems, Inc.
12525 Chadron Ave
Hawthorne CA
310 978-0516

(P-9238)
PACIFIC LASERTEC LLC (PA)
Also Called: Pacific Lasertec
215 Bingham Dr Ste 110 (92069-1403)
PHONE..................760 539-7169
Lynn Strickland, Managing Member
EMP: 20 **EST:** 2018
SQ FT: 19,000
SALES (est): 9.3MM
SALES (corp-wide): 9.3MM **Privately Held**
Web: www.pacificlasertec.com
SIC: 3699 Laser systems and equipment

(P-9239)
PACIFIC UTILITY PRODUCTS INC
2430 Railroad St (92880-5418)
PHONE..................951 493-8394
EMP: 20
SIC: 3699 Electrical equipment and supplies,
nec

(P-9240)
**PALOMAR TECH COMPANIES
(PA)**
6305 El Camino Real (92009-1606)
PHONE..................760 931-3600
EMP: 22 **EST:** 1995
SALES (est): 4.78MM **Privately Held**
Web: www.palomartechnologies.com
SIC: 3699 6512 Electrical equipment and
supplies, nec; Nonresidential building
operators

(P-9241)
**PHILATRON INTERNATIONAL
(PA)**
Also Called: Santa Fe Supply Company
15315 Cornet St (90670-5531)
PHONE..................562 802-0452
Phillip M Ramos Junior, CEO
Phillip M Ramos Senior, Ex VP
EMP: 99 **EST:** 1978
SQ FT: 100,000
SALES (est): 24.17MM
SALES (corp-wide): 24.17MM **Privately
Held**
Web: www.philatron.com
SIC: 3699 3694 3357 Electrical equipment
and supplies, nec; Engine electrical
equipment; Communication wire

(P-9242)
PILLER POWER SYSTEMS INC
5450 Kiowa Dr Unit 39 (91942-1314)
PHONE..................408 204-9578
Justin Jurek, Brnch Mgr
EMP: 34
SALES (corp-wide): 1.22B **Privately Held**
Web: www.piller.com

▲ = Import ▼ = Export
◆ = Import/Export

SIC: **3699** Electrical equipment and supplies, nec

HQ: Piller Power Systems Inc.
45 Wes Warren Dr
Middletown NY

(P-9243)
POWELL ELECTRIC
1314 7th St (90401-1608)
PHONE..............................310 394-6498
Rex Powell, *Brnch Mgr*
EMP: 27
Web: www.powell-electric.com
SIC: **3699 1731** Electrical equipment and supplies, nec; Electrical work
PA: Powell Electric
102 Labrea Way
San Rafael CA

(P-9244)
PRO SPOT INTERNATIONAL INC
5932 Sea Otter Pl (92010-6630)
PHONE..............................760 407-1414
Joran Olsson, *Pr*
Wendy Olsson, *Sec*
▲ **EMP:** 17 **EST:** 1986
SALES (est): 5.87MM **Privately Held**
Web: www.prospct.com
SIC: **3699** Electrical welding equipment

(P-9245)
PXISE ENERGY SOLUTIONS LLC
1455 Frazee Rd Ste 150 (92108-4436)
PHONE..............................619 696-2944
Patrick Lee, *CEO*
EMP: 36 **EST:** 2017
SALES (est): 8.89MM **Privately Held**
Web: www.pxise.com
SIC: **3699** Grids, electric
PA: Yokogawa Electric Corporation
2-9-32, Nakacho
Musashino TKY

(P-9246)
RAYTHEON COMPANY
Raytheon
6380 Hollister Ave (93117-3114)
PHONE..............................805 967-5511
Jack Gressingh, *Genl Mgr*
EMP: 200
SQ FT: 102,570
SALES (corp-wide): 67.07B **Publicly Held**
Web: www.rtx.com
SIC: **3699 3812** Countermeasure simulators, electric; Search and navigation equipment
HQ: Raytheon Company
870 Winter St
Waltham MA
781 522-3000

(P-9247)
RELDOM CORPORATION
3241 Industry Dr (90755-4013)
PHONE..............................562 498-3346
Peter Modler, *CEO*
EMP: 20 **EST:** 1979
SALES (est): 4.94MM **Privately Held**
Web: www.reldom.com
SIC: **3699** Security devices

(P-9248)
RIOT GLASS INC
17941 Brookshire Ln (92647-7132)
PHONE..............................800 580-2303
Brad Campbell, *CEO*
Pat Glass, *Pr*
EMP: 30 **EST:** 2017
SALES (est): 4.95MM **Privately Held**
Web: www.riotglass.com

SIC: **3699** Security devices

(P-9249)
RKS INC (HQ)
1955 Cordell Ct Ste 104 (92020-0901)
PHONE..............................858 571-4444
Russell Leonard Scheppmann, *CEO*
Allen Thomas, *COO*
Scott Skillman, *CFO*
Brian Shultz, *VP*
Mike Mcminn, *VP*
EMP: 18 **EST:** 2002
SQ FT: 7,747
SALES (est): 5.1MM **Privately Held**
SIC: **3699** Door opening and closing devices, electrical
PA: Abb Ltd
Affolternstrasse 44
ZUrich ZH

(P-9250)
ROMEO SYSTEMS INC
Also Called: Romeo Power Technology
514 Via De La Valle (92075-2717)
PHONE..............................323 675-2180
Michael Patterson, *Ch*
Lionel Selwood Junior, *CEO*
Lauren Webb, *
Criswell Choi, *
◆ **EMP:** 133 **EST:** 2014
SALES (est): 9.51MM
SALES (corp-wide): 50.83MM **Publicly Held**
SIC: **3699 8731** High-energy particle physics equipment; Energy research
HQ: Romeo Power, Inc.
514 Via De La Valle # 210
Solana Beach CA
833 467-2237

(P-9251)
ROSEMEAD ELECTRICAL SUPPLY
9150 Dice Rd (90670-2522)
PHONE..............................562 298-4190
Rony Perez, *CEO*
EMP: 50 **EST:** 2019
SALES (est): 2.8MM **Privately Held**
Web: www.rosemeadelectricalsupply.com
SIC: **3699** High-energy particle physics equipment

(P-9252)
SCHNEIDER ELC BUILDINGS LLC
Also Called: Invensys Climate Controls
100 W Victoria St (90805-2147)
PHONE..............................310 900-2385
Michael Utzman, *Prin*
EMP: 103
SALES (corp-wide): 82.05K **Privately Held**
SIC: **3699** Electrical equipment and supplies, nec
HQ: Schneider Electric Buildings, Llc
839 N Perryville Rd
Rockford IL
815 381-5000

(P-9253)
SCHNEIDER ELECTRIC
1660 Scenic Ave (92626-1410)
PHONE..............................949 713-9200
EMP: 27
SALES (est): 5.06MM **Privately Held**
Web: www.se.com
SIC: **3699** Electrical equipment and supplies, nec

(P-9254)
SERRA LASER AND WATERJET INC
1740 N Orangethorpe Park (92801-1138)
PHONE..............................714 680-6211
Glenn Kline, *CEO*
EMP: 30 **EST:** 2012
SALES (est): 3.08MM **Privately Held**
Web: www.serralaser.com
SIC: **3699** Laser welding, drilling, and cutting equipment

(P-9255)
SONNET TECHNOLOGIES INC
Also Called: Manufacturer
8 Autry (92618-2708)
PHONE..............................949 587-3500
Robert Farnsworth, *CEO*
Robert Farnsworth, *Pr*
Robert Rich, *
Angelia Farnsworth Magill, *
▲ **EMP:** 30 **EST:** 1986
SQ FT: 17,000
SALES (est): 7.87MM **Privately Held**
Web: www.sonnettech.com
SIC: **3699** Electrical equipment and supplies, nec

(P-9256)
SOUNDCRAFT INC
Also Called: Secura Key
20301 Nordhoff St (91311-6128)
PHONE..............................818 882-0020
Joel Smulson, *Pr*
Martin Casden, *
▲ **EMP:** 35 **EST:** 1971
SQ FT: 12,000
SALES (est): 7.91MM **Privately Held**
Web: www.securakey.com
SIC: **3699 1731 3829** Security control equipment and systems; Safety and security specialization; Measuring and controlling devices, nec

(P-9257)
STRACON INC
1672 Kaiser Ave Ste 1 (92614-5700) ✪
PHONE..............................949 851-2288
Son Pham, *Pr*
EMP: 17 **EST:** 1986
SQ FT: 10,000
SALES (est): 4.36MM **Privately Held**
Web: www.straconinc.com
SIC: **3699** Electrical equipment and supplies, nec

(P-9258)
SUMMIT ELECTRIC & DATA INC
27913 Smyth Dr (91355-4034)
PHONE..............................661 775-9901
Ray Vasquez, *Pr*
EMP: 18 **EST:** 2010
SALES (est): 4.76MM **Privately Held**
Web: www.summitelectservices.com
SIC: **3699 1731** Electrical equipment and supplies, nec; Electrical work

(P-9259)
SUSS MCRTEC PHTNIC SYSTEMS INC
2520 Palisades Dr (92882-0632)
PHONE..............................951 817-3700
Courtney T Sheets, *CEO*
Debora Blanchard, *
Debbie Brown, *
EMP: 90 **EST:** 1966
SALES (est): 18MM
SALES (corp-wide): 310.68MM **Privately Held**

Web: www.suss.com
SIC: **3699 7389** Electrical equipment and supplies, nec; Business services, nec
PA: SUss Microtec Se
SchleiBheimer Str. 90
Garching B. Munchen BY
89320070

(P-9260)
SWAG CORPORATION
Also Called: Ranger Patrol
1534 N Moorpark Rd Pmb 353 (91360-5129)
PHONE..............................805 499-6555
Scott Wagenseller, *CEO*
EMP: 45 **EST:** 2000
SALES (est): 3.03MM **Privately Held**
SIC: **3699 7381 7382 1731** Security control equipment and systems; Guard services; Burglar alarm maintenance and monitoring; Fire detection and burglar alarm systems specialization

(P-9261)
SYSTON CABLE TECHNOLOGY CORP
15278 El Prado Rd (91710-7623)
PHONE..............................888 679-7866
Daniel Wong, *Admn*
Yulin Wang, *Prin*
▲ **EMP:** 20 **EST:** 2014
SALES (est): 2.05MM **Privately Held**
Web: www.systoncable.com
SIC: **3699 4841 3351 3651** Electrical equipment and supplies, nec; Cable television services; Wire, copper and copper alloy; Household audio and video equipment

(P-9262)
TACTICAL MICRO INC (DH)
1740 E Wilshire Ave (92705-4615)
PHONE..............................714 547-1174
Ed Hanrahan, *Pr*
Allen Romk, *
John Moulton, *
Michael Hayden, *
▲ **EMP:** 18 **EST:** 2005
SQ FT: 14,000
SALES (est): 11.23MM
SALES (corp-wide): 2.89B **Publicly Held**
Web: www.bench.com
SIC: **3699** Electrical equipment and supplies, nec
HQ: Secure Communication Systems, Inc.
1740 E Wilshire Ave
Santa Ana CA
714 547-1174

(P-9263)
TRIGON ELECTRONICS INC
22865 Savi Ranch Pkwy Ste A (92887-4626)
PHONE..............................714 633-7442
Milton L Sneller, *CEO*
Lorna R Sneller, *Pr*
EMP: 18 **EST:** 1979
SALES (est): 5.1MM **Privately Held**
Web: www.trigonelectronics.com
SIC: **3699** Security control equipment and systems

(P-9264)
ULTRA-STEREO LABS INC
Also Called: U S L
181 Bonetti Dr (93401-7310)
PHONE..............................805 549-0161
James A Cashin, *Pr*
Jack Cashin, *Pr*
▲ **EMP:** 38 **EST:** 2016

PRODUCTS & SVCS

SQ FT: 15,000
SALES (est): 5.3MM
SALES (corp-wide): 116.19MM **Privately Held**
SIC: 3699 Electric sound equipment
PA: Qsc, Llc
 1675 Macarthur Blvd
 Costa Mesa CA
 800 854-4079

(P-9265)
UNDERSEA SYSTEMS INTL INC
Also Called: Ocean Technology Systems
3133 W Harvard St (92704-3912)
PHONE..............................714 754-7848
Michael R Pelissier, *Pr*
Jerry Peck, *
▲ **EMP:** 62 **EST:** 1987
SQ FT: 18,000
SALES (est): 12.95MM **Privately Held**
Web:
www.oceantechnologysystems.com
SIC: 3699 8711 Underwater sound
 equipment; Acoustical engineering

(P-9266)
UNITED SECURITY PRODUCTS INC
Also Called: Amtek
12675 Danielson Ct Ste 405 (92064-6835)
P.O. Box 785 (92074-0785)
PHONE..............................800 227-1592
Ted R Greene, *Pr*
▲ **EMP:** 32 **EST:** 1972
SALES (est): 4.58MM **Privately Held**
Web: www.unitedsecurity.com
SIC: 3699 5999 Security devices; Alarm
 signal systems

(P-9267)
UNIVERSAL SURVEILLANCE SYSTEMS LLC
Also Called: Universal Surveillance Systems
11172 Elm Ave (91730-7670)
PHONE..............................909 484-7870
▲ **EMP:** 80
SIC: 3699 Security control equipment and
 systems

(P-9268)
USA VISION SYSTEMS INC (HQ)
9301 Irvine Blvd (92618-1669)
PHONE..............................949 583-1519
Kuang Cheng Tai, *Pr*
▲ **EMP:** 40 **EST:** 2003
SALES (est): 17.35MM **Privately Held**
Web: www.geovision.com.tw
SIC: 3699 Security control equipment and
 systems
PA: Geovision, Inc.
 9f, 246, Nei Hu Rd., Sec. 1,
 Taipei City TAP

(P-9269)
VTI INSTRUMENTS CORPORATION (HQ)
2031 Main St (92614-6509)
PHONE..............................949 955-1894
Paul Dhillon, *CEO*
Jasdeep Dhillon, *
▲ **EMP:** 21 **EST:** 1990
SQ FT: 11,500
SALES (est): 10.41MM
SALES (corp-wide): 6.15B **Publicly Held**
Web: www.vtiinstruments.com
SIC: 3699 Electrical equipment and supplies,
 nec
PA: Ametek, Inc.
 1100 Cassatt Rd
 Berwyn PA
 610 647-2121

(P-9270)
WEST COAST CHAIN MFG CO
Also Called: Key-Bak
4245 Pacific Privado (91761-1588)
P.O. Box 9088 (91762-9088)
PHONE..............................909 923-7800
Boake Paugh, *Pr*
Mike Winegar, *
▲ **EMP:** 50 **EST:** 1948
SQ FT: 31,000
SALES (est): 9.51MM **Privately Held**
Web: www.keybak.com
SIC: 3699 Security devices

(P-9271)
WEST COAST CORPORATION
4245 Pacific Privado (91761-1588)
PHONE..............................909 923-7800
▲ **EMP:** 24 **EST:** 1986
SALES (est): 2.43MM **Privately Held**
Web: www.keybak.com
SIC: 3699 Security devices

(P-9272)
WESTGATE MFG INC
Also Called: Westgate Manufacturing
2462 E 28th St (90058-1402)
PHONE..............................323 826-9490
Isaac Hadjyan, *CEO*
Eryeh Hadjyan, *
Ebrahim Hadjyan, *
▲ **EMP:** 74 **EST:** 2008
SALES (est): 11.74MM **Privately Held**
Web: www.westgatemfg.com
SIC: 3699 5063 Electrical equipment and
 supplies, nec; Lighting fixtures

(P-9273)
XIRGO TECHNOLOGIES LLC
188 Camino Ruiz Fl 2 (93012-6700)
PHONE..............................805 319-4079
Roberto Piolanti, *CEO*
Mark Grout, *
Shawn Aleman, *CMO*
EMP: 62 **EST:** 2006
SALES (est): 14.96MM
SALES (corp-wide): 4.03B **Privately Held**
Web: www.sensatainsights.com
SIC: 3699 Electronic training devices
HQ: Sensata Technologies Limited
 2 Columbus Drive
 Farnborough HANTS

3711 Motor Vehicles And Car Bodies

(P-9274)
ALAN JOHNSON PRFMCE ENGRG INC
Also Called: Johnson Racing
1097 Foxen Canyon Rd (93454-9146)
PHONE..............................805 922-1202
Alan P Johnson, *Pr*
▲ **EMP:** 24 **EST:** 1985
SQ FT: 25,000
SALES (est): 4.89MM **Privately Held**
Web: www.alanjohnsonperformance.com
SIC: 3711 Motor vehicles and car bodies

(P-9275)
ALEPH GROUP INC
Also Called: Manufacturer
1900 E Alessandro Blvd Ste 105
(92508-2311)
PHONE..............................951 213-4815
Jales Mello, *CEO*
▼ **EMP:** 25 **EST:** 2012
SALES (est): 4.66MM **Privately Held**

Web: www.alephgroupinc.com
SIC: 3711 Motor vehicles and car bodies

(P-9276)
ALLIANZ SWEEPER COMPANY
5405 Industrial Pkwy (92407-1803)
▼ **EMP:** 180
SIC: 3711 Street sprinklers and sweepers
 (motor vehicles), assembly of

(P-9277)
AMERICAN HX AUTO TRADE INC
Also Called: U.S. Specialty Vehicles
4845 Via Del Cerro (92887-2641)
PHONE..............................909 484-1010
Amy Lin, *Managing Member*
▲ **EMP:** 72 **EST:** 2010
SALES (est): 5.31MM **Privately Held**
SIC: 3711 Automobile bodies, passenger
 car, not including engine, etc.

(P-9278)
ARTISAN VEHICLE SYSTEMS INC
742 Pancho Rd (93012-8576)
PHONE..............................805 402-6856
Michael Kasaba, *Pr*
EMP: 60 **EST:** 2010
SALES (est): 18.94MM
SALES (corp-wide): 11.77B **Privately Held**
Web: www.artisanvehicles.com
SIC: 3711 Personnel carriers (motor
 vehicles), assembly of
PA: Sandvik Ab
 Hogbovagen 45
 Sandviken
 26260000

(P-9279)
AZAA INVESTMENTS INC (PA)
6602 Convoy Ct Ste 200 (92111-1000)
P.O. Box 2198 (38101-2198)
PHONE..............................858 569-8111
William C Rhodes Iii, *Pr*
David Klein, *COO*
Jamere Jackson, *Sec*
Brian L Campbell, *Treas*
▼ **EMP:** 36 **EST:** 2012
SALES (est): 47.18MM
SALES (corp-wide): 47.18MM **Privately Held**
SIC: 3711 Motor vehicles and car bodies

(P-9280)
BAATZ ENTERPRISES INC
Also Called: Tow Industries
2223 W San Bernardino Rd (91790-1008)
PHONE..............................323 660-4866
Mark Ormonde Baatz, *CEO*
John O Baatz, *
Helen Baatz, *
▼ **EMP:** 38 **EST:** 1988
SALES (est): 5.13MM **Privately Held**
Web: www.towindustries.com
SIC: 3711 5013 7538 Motor vehicles and car
 bodies; Truck parts and accessories; Truck
 engine repair, except industrial

(P-9281)
BECKER AUTOMOTIVE DESIGNS INC
Also Called: Becker Automotive Design USA
1711 Ives Ave (93033-1866)
PHONE..............................805 487-5227
Howard Bernard Becker, *CEO*
Debra Becker, *
▲ **EMP:** 33 **EST:** 1996
SQ FT: 35,000
SALES (est): 5.04MM **Privately Held**

Web: www.beckerautodesign.com
SIC: 3711 Cars, armored, assembly of

(P-9282)
COACHWORKS HOLDINGS INC
1863 Service Ct (92507-2341)
PHONE..............................951 684-9585
Dale Carson, *Pr*
Terri L Carson, *Sec*
EMP: 18 **EST:** 2007
SALES (est): 4.66MM
SALES (corp-wide): 54.62MM **Privately Held**
SIC: 3711 Motor buses, except trackless
 trollies, assembly of
PA: D/T Carson Enterprises, Inc.
 42882 Ivy St
 Murrieta CA
 951 684-9585

(P-9283)
CZV INC
Also Called: Czinger Vehicles
19601 Hamilton Ave (90502-1309)
PHONE..............................424 603-1450
Kevin Czinger, *CEO*
Jens Sverdrup, *COO*
EMP: 77 **EST:** 2010
SALES (est): 9.93MM **Privately Held**
Web: www.czvinc.com
SIC: 3711 Automobile assembly, including
 specialty automobiles

(P-9284)
ELDORADO NATIONAL CAL INC (HQ)
9670 Galena St (92509-3089)
PHONE..............................951 727-9300
Peter Orthwein, *CEO*
◆ **EMP:** 350 **EST:** 1991
SQ FT: 62,000
SALES (est): 78.41MM **Publicly Held**
Web: www.eldorado-ca.com
SIC: 3711 Buses, all types, assembly of
PA: Rev Group, Inc.
 245 S Executive Dr # 100
 Brookfield WI

(P-9285)
FISKER AUTOMOTIVE INC
3080 Airway Ave (92626-6012)
▲ **EMP:** 53
SIC: 3711 7539 Motor vehicles and car
 bodies; Automotive repair shops, nec

(P-9286)
FISKER GROUP INC (HQ)
1888 Rosecrans Ave (90266-3795)
PHONE..............................833 434-7537
Henrik Fisker, *CEO*
John Finnucan, *Chief Accounting Officer*
EMP: 31 **EST:** 2016
SALES (corp-wide): 342K **Publicly Held**
Web: www.fiskerinc.com
SIC: 3711 Cars, electric, assembly of
PA: Fisker Inc.
 1888 Rosecrans Ave # 1000
 Manhattan Beach CA
 833 434-7537

(P-9287)
FISKER INC (PA)
Also Called: Fisker
1888 Rosecrans Ave (90266-3795)
PHONE..............................833 434-7537
Henrik Fisker, *Ch Bd*
Geeta Gupta, *CFO*
EMP: 27 **EST:** 2016
SQ FT: 72,649
SALES (est): 342K

SALES (corp-wide): 342K **Publicly Held**
Web: www.fiskerinc.com
SIC: **3711** Motor vehicles and car bodies

(P-9288)
FLYER DEFENSE LLC
151 W 135th St (90061-1645)
PHONE...............................310 324-5650
Oded Nechushtan, *CEO*
Steven Markowitz, *
▲ EMP: 75 EST: 2000
SALES (est): 12.4MM **Privately Held**
Web: www.flyerdefense.com
SIC: **3711 3714** Military motor vehicle
assembly; Motor vehicle parts and
accessories

(P-9289)
**GLOBAL ENVIRONMENTAL
PDTS INC**
Also Called: Global Sweeping Solutions
5405 Industrial Pkwy (92407-1803)
PHONE...............................909 713-1600
▲ EMP: 67 EST: 2011
SQ FT: 104,000
SALES (est): 10.94MM **Privately Held**
Web: www.globalsweeper.com
SIC: **3711** Street sprinklers and sweepers
(motor vehicles), assembly of

(P-9290)
GREENKRAFT INC
2530 S Birch St (92707-3444)
PHONE...............................714 545-7777
George Gemayel, *Ch Bd*
Sosi Bardakjian, *CFO*
EMP: 18 EST: 2008
SQ FT: 51,942
SALES (est): 434.17K **Privately Held**
Web: www.greenkraftinc.com
SIC: **3711 3519** Motor vehicles and car
bodies; Internal combustion engines, nec

(P-9291)
**GREENPOWER MOTOR
COMPANY INC**
8885 Haven Ave (91730-5199)
PHONE...............................909 308-0960
Fraser Atkinson, *CEO*
EMP: 51 EST: 2013
SALES (est): 9.68MM
SALES (corp-wide): 17.24MM **Privately
Held**
Web: www.greenpowermotor.com
SIC: **3711** Motor vehicles and car bodies
PA: Greenpower Motor Company Inc
240-209 Carrall St
Vancouver BC
604 563-4144

(P-9292)
HALCORE GROUP INC
Leader Industries
10941 Weaver Ave (91733-2752)
PHONE...............................626 575-0880
Gary Hunter, *Mgr*
EMP: 36
Web: www.hortonambulance.com
SIC: **3711** Motor vehicles and car bodies
HQ: Halcore Group, Inc.
3800 Mcdowell Rd
Grove City OH
614 539-8181

(P-9293)
HARBINGER MOTORS INC
15700 S Figueroa St (90248-2429)
PHONE...............................914 299-3998
John Harris, *CEO*

Phillip Weicker, *
Will Eberts, *
Gilbert Passin, *CPO*
Ben Dusastre, *
EMP: 42 EST: 2021
SALES (est): 4.47MM **Privately Held**
SIC: **3711** Chassis, motor vehicle

(P-9294)
KARMA AUTOMOTIVE LLC
9950 Jeronimo Rd (92618-2014)
PHONE...............................855 565-2762
Liang Zhou, *Managing Member*
Weiding Lu, *Managing Member*
John Maloney, *CRO*
Ashoka Achuthan, *CFO*
Marques Mccammon, *Pr*
EMP: 896 EST: 2014
SQ FT: 262,463
SALES (est): 243.13MM **Privately Held**
Web: www.karmaautomotive.com
SIC: **3711** Motor vehicles and car bodies
HQ: Wanxiang America Corporation
88 Airport Rd
Elgin IL

(P-9295)
**KOVATCH MOBILE EQUIPMENT
CORP**
Also Called: Kme Fire
14562 Manzanita Dr (92335-5377)
PHONE...............................951 685-1224
Ken Creese, *Brnch Mgr*
EMP: 33
SIC: **3711** Motor vehicles and car bodies
HQ: Kovatch Mobile Equipment Corp.
1 Industrial Complex
Nesquehoning PA
570 669-9461

(P-9296)
LIPPERT COMPONENTS INC
168 S Spruce Ave (92376-9005)
PHONE...............................909 873-0061
Andrew Zanschoick, *Mgr*
EMP: 21
SALES (corp-wide): 5.21B **Publicly Held**
Web: www.lci1.com
SIC: **3711 3469 3444 3714** Chassis, motor
vehicle; Stamping metal for the trade; Metal
roofing and roof drainage equipment; Motor
vehicle parts and accessories
HQ: Lippert Components, Inc.
3501 County Road 6 E
Elkhart IN
574 535-1125

(P-9297)
**MARTINS QUALITY TRUCK
BODY INC**
1831 W El Segundo Blvd (90222-1026)
PHONE...............................310 632-5978
Oscar Parra, *Prin*
Edith A Torres, *Prin*
EMP: 17 EST: 2012
SALES (est): 1.3MM **Privately Held**
Web: www.martinsqualitytruckbody.com
SIC: **3711** Motor vehicles and car bodies

(P-9298)
MARVIN LAND SYSTEMS INC
Also Called: Marvin Group The
261 W Beach Ave (90302-2904)
PHONE...............................310 674-5030
▲ EMP: 44 EST: 1995
SQ FT: 200,000
SALES (est): 28.54MM
SALES (corp-wide): 149.54MM **Privately
Held**
Web: www.marvinland.com

SIC: **3711** Military motor vehicle assembly
PA: Marvin Engineering Co., Inc.
261 W Beach Ave
Inglewood CA
310 674-5030

(P-9299)
**MAZDA MOTOR OF AMERICA
INC (HQ)**
Also Called: Mazda North Amercn Operations
200 Spectrum Center Dr Ste 100
(92618-5003)
P.O. Box 19734 (92623-9734)
PHONE...............................949 727-1990
◆ EMP: 400 EST: 1970
SALES (est): 519.77MM **Privately Held**
Web: www.mazdausa.com
SIC: **3711** Motor vehicles and car bodies
PA: Mazda Motor Corporation
3-1, Shinchi, Fuchucho
Aki-Gun HIR

(P-9300)
MILLENWORKS
1361 Valencia Ave (92780-6459)
PHONE...............................714 426-5500
▲ EMP: 75
SIC: **3711 5012 7549 8731** Military motor
vehicle assembly; Commercial vehicles;
Automotive customizing services,
nonfactory basis; Electronic research

(P-9301)
**MULLEN TECHNOLOGIES INC
(PA)**
Also Called: Mullen Auto Sales
1405 Pioneer St (92821-3721)
PHONE...............................714 613-1900
David Michery, *CEO*
Jerry Alban, *
William Johnston, *
EMP: 40 EST: 2014
SQ FT: 24,730
SALES (est): 10.3MM
SALES (corp-wide): 10.3MM **Privately
Held**
Web: www.mullenusa.com
SIC: **3711 5013** Motor vehicles and car
bodies; Motor vehicle supplies and new
parts

(P-9302)
NEW FLYER OF AMERICA INC
2880 Jurupa St (91761-2903)
P.O. Box 1464 (91743-1464)
PHONE...............................909 456-3566
EMP: 103
SALES (corp-wide): 2.05B **Privately Held**
Web: www.newflyer.com
SIC: **3711** Motor vehicles and car bodies
HQ: New Flyer Of America Inc.
6200 Glenn Carlson Dr
Saint Cloud MN

(P-9303)
PHOENIX CARS LLC
Also Called: Phoenix Motorcars
1500 Lakeview Loop (92807-1819)
PHONE...............................909 987-0815
▲ EMP: 39 EST: 2009
SQ FT: 40,000
SALES (est): 10.63MM **Publicly Held**
Web: www.phoenixmotorcars.com
SIC: **3711** Cars, electric, assembly of
HQ: Edisonfuture Inc.
4677 Old Ironsides Dr # 1
Santa Clara CA
408 919-8000

(P-9304)
**PROTERRA OPERATING
COMPANY INC**
393 Cheryl Ln (91789-3003)
PHONE...............................864 438-0000
EMP: 274
SALES (corp-wide): 309.36MM **Publicly
Held**
Web: www.proterra.com
SIC: **3711** Automobile assembly, including
specialty automobiles
HQ: Proterra Operating Company, Inc.
1815 Rollins Rd
Burlingame CA

(P-9305)
RIVIAN AUTOMOTIVE INC (PA)
Also Called: Rivian
14600 Myford Rd (92606-1005)
PHONE...............................888 748-4261
Robert J Scaringe, *Ch Bd*
Claire Mcdonough, *CFO*
Jiten Behl, *CGO*
Michael Callahan, *CLO*
Diane Lye, *CIO*
EMP: 361 EST: 2009
SALES (est): 1.66B
SALES (corp-wide): 1.66B **Publicly Held**
Web: www.rivian.com
SIC: **3711** Motor vehicles and car bodies

(P-9306)
RIVIAN AUTOMOTIVE LLC
1648 Ashley Way (92324-4000)
PHONE...............................309 249-8777
EMP: 129
SALES (corp-wide): 1.66B **Publicly Held**
Web: www.rivian.com
SIC: **3711 3714** Motor vehicles and car
bodies; Motor vehicle parts and accessories
HQ: Rivian Automotive, Llc
13250 N Haggerty Rd
Plymouth MI
888 748-4261

(P-9307)
SALEEN INCORPORATED (PA)
2735 Wardlow Rd (92882-2869)
PHONE...............................714 400-2121
Paul Wilbur, *Pr*
Stephen Saleen, *
Brian Walsh, *
Michael Simmons, *Chief Marketing*
◆ EMP: 200 EST: 1984
SALES (est): 24.23MM **Privately Held**
Web: www.saleen.com
SIC: **3711** Automobile assembly, including
specialty automobiles

(P-9308)
SHELBY CARROLL INTL INC (PA)
19021 S Figueroa St (90248-4510)
PHONE...............................310 538-2914
Carroll Shelby, *Prin*
EMP: 22 EST: 2009
SALES (est): 8.44MM **Privately Held**
Web: www.carrollshelby.com
SIC: **3711** Motor vehicles and car bodies

(P-9309)
SHYFT GROUP INC
1130 S Vail Ave (90640-6021)
PHONE...............................323 276-1933
EMP: 84
SALES (corp-wide): 1.03B **Publicly Held**
Web: www.theshyftgroup.com
SIC: **3711** Motor vehicles and car bodies
PA: The Shyft Group Inc
41280 Bridge St
Novi MI
517 543-6400

PRODUCTS & SVCS

(P-9310)
TCI ENGINEERING INC
Also Called: Total Cost Involved
1416 Brooks St (91762-3613)
PHONE...................................909 984-1773
Edward Moss, *Pr*
Edward Moss, *Pr*
Sherlly Prakarsa, *
EMP: 54 **EST:** 1974
SQ FT: 25,000
SALES (est): 8.82MM **Privately Held**
Web: www.totalcostinvolved.com
SIC: 3711 5531 3714 Chassis, motor vehicle
; Auto and home supply stores; Motor
vehicle parts and accessories

(P-9311)
TIFFANY COACHWORKS INC
Also Called: Tiffany Coachworks
420 N Mckinley St # 111-465 (92879-8099)
PHONE...................................951 657-2680
William Auden, *CEO*
James Powel, *
◆ **EMP:** 19 **EST:** 1992
SQ FT: 57,000
SALES (est): 241.79K **Privately Held**
Web: www.tiffanylimo.com
SIC: 3711 Motor vehicles and car bodies

(P-9312)
**VELASCO CARWASH SUPPLIES
CORP**
Also Called: Warner Chemicals Mfg
1601 Perrino Pl (90023-2675)
PHONE...................................310 715-3000
David Velasco, *CEO*
EMP: 25 **EST:** 1999
SALES (est): 2.13MM **Privately Held**
SIC: 3711 Automobile bodies, passenger
car, not including engine, etc.

(P-9313)
WARLOCK INDUSTRIES
Also Called: Tiffany Coach Builders
23129 Cajalco Rd Ste A (92570-7298)
PHONE...................................951 657-2680
▼ **EMP:** 46 **EST:** 2009
SALES (est): 2.32MM **Privately Held**
SIC: 3711 Motor vehicles and car bodies

(P-9314)
WEST COAST UNLIMITED
Also Called: West Coast Airlines
11161 Pierce St (92505-2713)
PHONE...................................951 352-1234
H J Manning Presgeneral, *Mgr*
L K Manning, *Pr*
EMP: 22 **EST:** 1953
SQ FT: 6,000
SALES (est): 604.91K **Privately Held**
SIC: 3711 7699 Fire department vehicles
(motor vehicles), assembly of; Fire control
(military) equipment repair

(P-9315)
XOS FLEET INC
Also Called: Xos Trucks
3550 Tyburn St Ste 100 (90065-1427)
PHONE...................................855 909-4407
Dakota Semler, *CEO*
Giordano Sordoni, *
Kingsley Afemikhe, *
Robert Ferber, *
EMP: 50 **EST:** 2015
SALES (est): 2.67MM
SALES (corp-wide): 36.38MM **Publicly
Held**
Web: www.xostrucks.com

SIC: 3711 3713 Truck and tractor truck
assembly; Truck bodies and parts
PA: Xos, Inc.
3550 Tyburn St Ste 100
Los Angeles CA
818 316-1890

3713 Truck And Bus Bodies

(P-9316)
**ARROW TRUCK BODIES & EQP
INC**
1639 S Campus Ave (91761-4364)
PHONE...................................909 947-3991
Raymond A Glaze, *Pr*
Keith Wysocki, *Pr*
Richard Rubio, *Sec*
EMP: 20 **EST:** 1963
SQ FT: 33,980
SALES (est): 698.51K **Privately Held**
SIC: 3713 Truck bodies (motor vehicles)

(P-9317)
**COMMERCIAL TRUCK EQP CO
LLC**
Also Called: Commercial Truck Equipment Co
12351 Bellflower Blvd (90242-2829)
PHONE...................................562 803-4466
James E Anderson, *Pr*
Lorena Anderson, *
EMP: 56 **EST:** 2008
SALES (est): 3.92MM **Privately Held**
Web: www.ctec-truckbody.com
SIC: 3713 Truck bodies (motor vehicles)

(P-9318)
**COMPLETE TRUCK BODY
REPAIR INC**
1217 N Alameda St (90222-4102)
P.O. Box 1792 (90723-1792)
PHONE...................................323 445-2675
Rodrigo Robles, *CEO*
EMP: 23 **EST:** 2012
SQ FT: 10,225
SALES (est): 2.45MM **Privately Held**
Web: www.completetruckbody.com
SIC: 3713 Truck bodies and parts

(P-9319)
CTBLA INC
1740 Albion St (90031-2520)
PHONE...................................323 276-1933
◆ **EMP:** 99 **EST:** 1995
SALES (est): 7.99MM **Privately Held**
SIC: 3713 Truck bodies (motor vehicles)

(P-9320)
**CUSTOM TRUCK ONE SOURCE
LP**
4500 State Rd (93308-4544)
PHONE...................................316 627-2608
EMP: 39
SALES (corp-wide): 1.57B **Publicly Held**
Web: www.customtruck.com
SIC: 3713 Truck and bus bodies
HQ: Custom Truck One Source, L.P.
7701 E 24 Hwy
Kansas City MO
855 931-1852

(P-9321)
DELTA STAG MANUFACTURING
Also Called: Delta-Stag Truck Body
1818 E Rosslynn Ave (92831-5140)
PHONE...................................562 904-6444
George Cashman Senior, *Pr*
EMP: 22 **EST:** 1997
SQ FT: 100,000

SALES (est): 1.28MM **Privately Held**
Web: www.deltastag.com
SIC: 3713 7549 Truck bodies (motor
vehicles); Automotive maintenance services

(P-9322)
DOUGLASS TRUCK BODIES INC
231 21st St (93301-4138)
PHONE...................................661 327-0258
TOLL FREE: 800
Rick Douglass, *Pr*
Deborah Douglass, *
Jean Raley, *
EMP: 24 **EST:** 1959
SQ FT: 5,000
SALES (est): 6.57MM **Privately Held**
Web: www.douglasstruckbodies.com
SIC: 3713 Truck bodies (motor vehicles)

(P-9323)
DYNAFLEX PRODUCTS (PA)
Also Called: Exhaust Tech
6466 Gayhart St (90040-2506)
PHONE...................................323 724-1555
Robert L Mcgovern, *Pr*
Denise Pehrsson, *CEO*
Robert L Mcgovern, *Prin*
Gil Contreras, *
EMP: 75 **EST:** 1971
SQ FT: 64,000
SALES (est): 16.78MM
SALES (corp-wide): 16.78MM **Privately
Held**
Web: www.dynaflexproducts.com
SIC: 3713 3498 3714 Truck and bus bodies;
Fabricated pipe and fittings; Exhaust
systems and parts, motor vehicle

(P-9324)
EBUS INC
9250 Washburn Rd (90242-2909)
PHONE...................................562 904-3474
Anders B Eklov, *Ch Bd*
EMP: 35 **EST:** 1983
SALES (est): 1.52MM **Privately Held**
Web: fcebus.wixsite.com
SIC: 3713 Bus bodies (motor vehicles)

(P-9325)
ERF ENTERPRISES INC
Also Called: Colton Truck Terminal Garage
863 E Valley Blvd (92324-3125)
PHONE...................................909 825-4080
Ed Doltar, *Pr*
Rich Doltar, *Prin*
Fran Fields, *Prin*
EMP: 18 **EST:** 2019
SALES (est): 1.25MM **Privately Held**
SIC: 3713 Truck bodies (motor vehicles)

(P-9326)
FLEMING METAL FABRICATORS
874 Camino De Los Mares (92673-3122)
PHONE...................................323 723-8203
Wade M Fleming, *Pr*
Marc Fleming, *
EMP: 30 **EST:** 1918
SALES (est): 4.56MM **Privately Held**
Web: www.flemingmetal.com
SIC: 3713 3441 3714 3577 Truck bodies and
parts; Fabricated structural metal; Motor
vehicle parts and accessories; Computer
peripheral equipment, nec

(P-9327)
HARBOR TRUCK BODIES INC
Also Called: Harbor Truck Body
255 Voyager Ave (92821-6223)
PHONE...................................714 996-0411
Ken Lindt, *Pr*

EMP: 79 **EST:** 1973
SQ FT: 50,000
SALES (est): 22.13MM **Privately Held**
Web: www.harbortruckandvan.com
SIC: 3713 7532 Truck bodies (motor
vehicles); Body shop, automotive

(P-9328)
HARDWARE IMPORTS INC
Also Called: Western Hardware Company
161 Commerce Way (91789-2719)
P.O. Box 4177 (91723-0577)
PHONE...................................909 595-6201
Gayle Pacheco, *Pr*
Robert Pacheco, *CFO*
◆ **EMP:** 22 **EST:** 1970
SQ FT: 6,000
SALES (est): 710.23K **Privately Held**
Web: www.westernhardware.com
SIC: 3713 3429 Truck and bus bodies;
Furniture hardware

(P-9329)
KRYSTAL INFINITY LLC
Also Called: Krystal Enterprises
6915 Arlington Ave (92504-1905)
EMP: 500
SIC: 3713 3711 Truck and bus bodies;
Automobile assembly, including specialty
automobiles

(P-9330)
LIMOS BY TIFFANY INC
Also Called: Tiffany Coachworks
23129 Cajalco Rd (92570-7298)
P.O. Box 46 (92572-0046)
PHONE...................................951 657-2680
EMP: 35 **EST:** 2001
SALES (est): 3.56MM **Privately Held**
SIC: 3713 Specialty motor vehicle bodies

(P-9331)
MCNEILUS TRUCK AND MFG INC
401 N Pepper Ave (92324-1817)
P.O. Box 1588 (92324-0849)
PHONE...................................909 370-2100
Liza Langley, *Brnch Mgr*
EMP: 33
Web: www.mcneiluscompanies.com
SIC: 3713 5511 3711 3531 Cement mixer
bodies; Pickups, new and used; Truck and
tractor truck assembly; Construction
machinery
HQ: Mcneilus Truck And Manufacturing, Inc.
524 E Highway St
Dodge Center MN
507 374-6321

(P-9332)
PHENIX ENTERPRISES INC (PA)
Also Called: Phenix Truck Bodies and Eqp
1785 Mount Vernon Ave (91768-3330)
PHONE...................................909 469-0411
Rick Albertini, *CEO*
Benjamin Albertini, *
Norma E Albertini, *
Paul Albertini, *
EMP: 39 **EST:** 1978
SQ FT: 100,000
SALES (est): 9.42MM
SALES (corp-wide): 9.42MM **Privately
Held**
Web: www.phenixent.com
SIC: 3713 3711 Truck bodies (motor
vehicles); Motor vehicles and car bodies

(P-9333)
SKAUG TRUCK BODY WORKS
1404 1st St (91340-2795)
PHONE...................................818 365-9123

▲ = Import ▼ = Export
◆ = Import/Export

George L Skaug, *Pr*
William Bill Reeves, *VP*
EMP: 18 **EST:** 1946
SQ FT: 3,200
SALES (est): 2.15MM **Privately Held**
Web: www.skaugtruckbody.com
SIC: 3713 Truck bodies (motor vehicles)

(P-9334)
SPARTAN TRUCK COMPANY INC
12266 Branford St (91352-1009)
PHONE..................818 899-1111
Myan Spaccarelli, *Pr*
EMP: 35 **EST:** 1972
SQ FT: 25,000
SALES (est): 5.22MM **Privately Held**
Web: www.spartantruck.com
SIC: 3713 7532 3537 Garbage, refuse truck bodies; Top and body repair and paint shops ; Industrial trucks and tractors

(P-9335)
TABC INC (DH)
6375 N Paramount Blvd (90805-3301)
PHONE..................562 984-3305
Michael Bafan, *CEO*
Yoshiaki Nishino, *
◆ **EMP:** 261 **EST:** 1974
SQ FT: 8,820
SALES (est): 113.12MM **Privately Held**
SIC: 3713 3469 3714 Truck beds; Metal stampings, nec; Motor vehicle parts and accessories
HQ: Toyota Motor Engineering & Manufacturing North America, Inc.
6565 Hdqtr Dr W1 3c 1 W
Plano TX

(P-9336)
TRADE LEASING INC
Also Called: Delta Stag Company
1818 E Rosslynn Ave (92831-5140)
PHONE..................714 538-4614
Carlos Arreola, *Pr*
Robert Cashman, *Sec*
EMP: 41 **EST:** 2011
SALES (est): 2.74MM
SALES (corp-wide): 2.74MM **Privately Held**
SIC: 3713 Truck and bus bodies
PA: Service Team Inc
1818 E Rosslynn Ave
Fullerton CA
562 904-6442

(P-9337)
VAHE ENTERPRISES INC
Also Called: Aa Leasing
750 E Slauson Ave (90011-5236)
PHONE..................323 235-6657
Vahe Karapetian, *CEO*
▲ **EMP:** 90 **EST:** 1976
SQ FT: 60,000
SALES (est): 9.89MM **Privately Held**
Web: www.aacatertruck.com
SIC: 3713 7513 Truck bodies (motor vehicles); Truck leasing, without drivers

---

3714 Motor Vehicle Parts And Accessories

(P-9338)
89908 INC
Also Called: AMP Research
15651 Mosher Ave (92780-6426)
PHONE..................949 221-0023
EMP: 35

SIC: 3714 Motor vehicle parts and accessories

(P-9339)
ACHATES POWER INC
4060 Sorrento Valley Blvd Ste A (92121-1428)
PHONE..................858 535-9920
David Crompton, *Pr*
David Johnson, *CEO*
John Koszewnik, *Prin*
Jerome Paye, *Dir Opers*
Carol Mottershead, *Finance*
EMP: 95 **EST:** 2003
SALES (est): 24.96MM **Privately Held**
Web: www.achatespower.com
SIC: 3714 8711 Motor vehicle engines and parts; Mechanical engineering

(P-9340)
ACME HEADLINING CO
Also Called: Acme Auto Headlining
550 W 16th St (90813-1510)
P.O. Box 847 (90801-0847)
PHONE..................562 432-0281
Bob Westmoreland, *VP*
Don Young, *
▲ **EMP:** 75 **EST:** 1948
SQ FT: 18,000
SALES (est): 5.83MM **Privately Held**
Web: www.acmeautoheadlining.com
SIC: 3714 Tops, motor vehicle

(P-9341)
ACSCO PRODUCTS INC
313 N Lake St (91502-1816)
PHONE..................818 953-2240
Thomas W Mc Intyre, *Pr*
EMP: 20 **EST:** 1963
SQ FT: 4,000
SALES (est): 3.93MM **Privately Held**
Web: www.acsco.net
SIC: 3714 Motor vehicle parts and accessories

(P-9342)
ADVANCE ADAPTERS INC
4320 Aerotech Center Way (93446-8529)
P.O. Box 247 (93447-0247)
PHONE..................805 238-7000
Mike Partridge, *Pr*
John Partridge, *
Angela Partridge, *Ofcr*
Randy Cronkright, *Pur Mgr*
▲ **EMP:** 44 **EST:** 1971
SQ FT: 44,000
SALES (est): 6.17MM **Privately Held**
Web: www.advanceadapters.com
SIC: 3714 Transmission housings or parts, motor vehicle

(P-9343)
ADVANCE ADAPTERS LLC
4320 Aerotech Center Way (93446-8529)
PHONE..................805 238-7000
John Upshur, *Prin*
EMP: 45 **EST:** 2017
SALES (est): 3.86MM **Privately Held**
Web: www.advanceadapters.com
SIC: 3714 Motor vehicle parts and accessories

(P-9344)
ADVANCED CLUTCH TECHNOLOGY INC
206 E Avenue K4 (93535-4685)
PHONE..................661 940-7555
▲ **EMP:** 30 **EST:** 1994
SQ FT: 18,000
SALES (est): 4.99MM **Privately Held**

Web: www.advancedclutch.com
SIC: 3714 Clutches, motor vehicle

(P-9345)
ADVANCED FLOW ENGINEERING INC (PA)
Also Called: Afe Power
252 Granite St (92879-1283)
PHONE..................951 493-7155
Shahriar Nick Niakan, *Pr*
Stuart Miyagishima, *
David Howey, *
Eric Griffith, *
Chris Barron, *
▲ **EMP:** 50 **EST:** 1999
SQ FT: 60,000
SALES (est): 21.62MM
SALES (corp-wide): 21.62MM **Privately Held**
Web: www.afepower.com
SIC: 3714 Motor vehicle engines and parts

(P-9346)
ADVANCED FLOW ENGINEERING INC
1375 Sampson Ave (92879-1748)
PHONE..................951 493-7100
EMP: 18
SALES (corp-wide): 21.62MM **Privately Held**
SIC: 3714 Motor vehicle engines and parts
PA: Advanced Flow Engineering, Inc.
252 Granite St
Corona CA
951 493-7155

(P-9347)
AGILITY FUEL SYSTEMS LLC (DH)
1815 Carnegie Ave (92705-5527)
PHONE..................949 236-5520
▲ **EMP:** 19 **EST:** 2010
SALES (est): 109.78MM **Privately Held**
Web: www.hexagonagility.com
SIC: 3714 Fuel systems and parts, motor vehicle
HQ: Agility Fuel Solutions Llc
3335 Susan St Ste 100
Costa Mesa CA
949 236-5520

(P-9348)
AIR FLOW RESEARCH HEADS INC
Also Called: Air Flow Research
28611 Industry Dr (91355-5413)
PHONE..................661 257-8124
Rick Sperling, *Pr*
▲ **EMP:** 40 **EST:** 1970
SQ FT: 14,000
SALES (est): 6.26MM **Privately Held**
Web: www.airflowresearch.com
SIC: 3714 Cylinder heads, motor vehicle

(P-9349)
AITA CLUTCH INC
960 S Santa Fe Ave (90221-4333)
PHONE..................323 585-4140
Guillermo Rios, *Pr*
Fred Rios, *
Albert Rios, *
EMP: 23 **EST:** 1982
SALES (est): 2.02MM **Privately Held**
SIC: 3714 5013 Clutches, motor vehicle; Automotive supplies and parts

(P-9350)
AMCOR INDUSTRIES INC
Also Called: Gorilla Automotive Products
6131 Knott Ave (90620-1031)
PHONE..................323 585-2852
Peter J Schermer, *Pr*
▲ **EMP:** 25 **EST:** 1983
SQ FT: 30,000
SALES (est): 5.31MM **Privately Held**
Web: www.gorilla-auto.com
SIC: 3714 3429 Motor vehicle wheels and parts; Hardware, nec
PA: Wheel Pros, Llc
5347 S Valentia Way # 200
Greenwood Village CO

(P-9351)
AMERICAN FABRICATION CORP (PA)
Also Called: American Best Car Parts
2891 E Via Martens (92806-1751)
PHONE..................714 632-1709
Greg Knox, *Pr*
Jodee Jensen Smith, *
▲ **EMP:** 70 **EST:** 1974
SALES (est): 9.23MM
SALES (corp-wide): 9.23MM **Privately Held**
Web: www.teamxenon.com
SIC: 3714 Motor vehicle parts and accessories

(P-9352)
AMERICAN RIM SUPPLY INC
1955 Kellogg Ave (92008-6582)
PHONE..................760 431-3666
Robert D Ward, *Pr*
▼ **EMP:** 40 **EST:** 1991
SQ FT: 20,000
SALES (est): 5.52MM **Privately Held**
Web: www.americanrim.com
SIC: 3714 Wheel rims, motor vehicle

(P-9353)
APEX PRECISION TECHNOLOGIES INC
23622 Calabasas Rd Ste 323 (91302-1549)
PHONE..................317 821-1000
EMP: 45 **EST:** 1951
SALES (est): 6.48MM **Privately Held**
SIC: 3714 3586 3498 3462 Motor vehicle parts and accessories; Measuring and dispensing pumps; Fabricated pipe and fittings; Iron and steel forgings

(P-9354)
ARIAS INDUSTRIES INC
Also Called: Arias Pistons
275 Roswell Ave (90803-1538)
PHONE..................310 532-9737
Nicholas Arias, *Pr*
Nicholas Arias Junior, *Pr*
Carmen Arias, *VP*
EMP: 27 **EST:** 1969
SQ FT: 20,000
SALES (est): 1.7MM **Privately Held**
Web: www.cp-carrillo.com
SIC: 3714 Motor vehicle engines and parts

(P-9355)
AUTO MOTIVE POWER INC
11643 Telegraph Rd (90670-3656)
PHONE..................800 894-7104
Anil Paryani, *Pr*
Lionel Selwood, *
Michael Rice, *CSO*
EMP: 120 **EST:** 2017
SALES (est): 10.02MM **Privately Held**
Web: www.amp.tech

SIC: 3714 Motor vehicle electrical equipment

(P-9356)
AUTOMAX STYLING INC
16833 Krameria Ave (92504-6118)
PHONE.................................951 530-1876
Guoxiang Zhou, *CEO*
EMP: 40 EST: 2005
SQ FT: 100,000
SALES (est): 3.22MM Privately Held
Web: www.automaxstyling.com
SIC: 3714 Motor vehicle parts and accessories

(P-9357)
AUTOMOCO LLC
Also Called: B & M Racing & Prfmce Pdts
9142 Independence Ave (91311-5902)
PHONE.................................707 544-4761
Brian Applegate, *Pr*
EMP: 21 EST: 1953
SALES (est): 904.9K Privately Held
SIC: 3714 Transmission housings or parts, motor vehicle

(P-9358)
AZUSA ENGINEERING INC
1542 W Industrial Park St (91722-3487)
P.O. Box 2909 (91722-8909)
PHONE.................................626 966-4071
James M Patronite, *CEO*
Tom Patronite, *Pr*
Janice M Patronite Esq, *Sec*
▲ EMP: 17 EST: 1960
SQ FT: 17,000
SALES (est): 2.38MM Privately Held
Web: www.azusaeng.com
SIC: 3714 Transmission housings or parts, motor vehicle

(P-9359)
B & I FENDER TRIMS INC
Also Called: B & I Fender
1401 Air Wing Rd (92154-7705)
PHONE.................................718 326-4323
Albert Sasson, *Pr*
Yzhak Faigenblat, *
▲ EMP: 45 EST: 1986
SQ FT: 80,000
SALES (est): 1.69MM Privately Held
Web: www.bitrim.com
SIC: 3714 Motor vehicle body components and frame

(P-9360)
BAB STEERING HYDRAULICS (PA)
Also Called: Bab Hydraulics
14554 Whittram Ave (92335-3108)
PHONE.................................208 573-4502
William Carlson, *Pr*
▲ EMP: 20 EST: 1989
SQ FT: 15,000
SALES (est): 4.49MM Privately Held
Web: www.babsteering.com
SIC: 3714 3713 5084 Hydraulic fluid power pumps, for auto steering mechanism; Truck and bus bodies; Hydraulic systems equipment and supplies

(P-9361)
BSST LLC
5462 Irwindale Ave Ste A (91706-2074)
PHONE.................................626 593-4500
Sandy Grouf, *CFO*
▲ EMP: 23 EST: 2000
SQ FT: 12,000
SALES (est): 1.54MM Publicly Held

SIC: 3714 Heaters, motor vehicle
PA: Gentherm Incorporated
21680 Haggerty Rd Ste 101
Northville MI

(P-9362)
BUNKER CORP (PA)
Also Called: Energy Suspension
1131 Via Callejon (92673-6230)
PHONE.................................949 361-3935
Donald Bunker, *CEO*
Boni Cambel, *
▼ EMP: 100 EST: 1985
SQ FT: 78,000
SALES (est): 22.12MM
SALES (corp-wide): 22.12MM Privately Held
Web: www.teamenergysuspension.com
SIC: 3714 Motor vehicle body components and frame

(P-9363)
BYD MOTORS LLC (HQ)
888 E Walnut St Fl 2 (91101-1897)
PHONE.................................213 748-3980
▲ EMP: 39 EST: 2010
SALES (est): 5.92MM
SALES (corp-wide): 2.43MM Privately Held
Web: en.byd.com
SIC: 3714 Motor vehicle electrical equipment
PA: Byd Us Holding Inc.
1800 S Figueroa St
Los Angeles CA
213 748-3980

(P-9364)
C R LAURENCE CO INC (HQ)
Also Called: Crl
2503 E Vernon Ave (90058-1826)
PHONE.................................323 588-1281
Arty Feles, *Pr*
Barbara Haaksma, *
Shirin Khosravi, *
Jacque Maples, *
Steve Whitcomb, *
◆ EMP: 380 EST: 1963
SQ FT: 170,000
SALES (est): 483.56MM
SALES (corp-wide): 32.72B Privately Held
Web: www.crlaurence.com
SIC: 3714 5072 5039 Sun roofs, motor vehicle; Hand tools; Glass construction materials
PA: Crh Public Limited Company
Stonemason S Way
Rathfarnham
14041000

(P-9365)
CANOO INC (PA)
19951 Mariner Ave (90503-1672)
PHONE.................................424 271-2144
Tony Aquila, *Ex Ch Bd*
Josette Sheeran, *Pr*
Greg Ethridge, *CFO*
Ramesh Murthy, *CAO*
Hector Ruiz, *Corporate Secretary*
EMP: 50 EST: 2017
SQ FT: 89,000
Web: www.canoo.com
SIC: 3714 Motor vehicle parts and accessories

(P-9366)
CAR SOUND EXHAUST SYSTEM INC
Also Called: Magnaslow
30142 Avenida De Las Bandera (92688-2116)

PHONE.................................949 858-5900
Don Billings, *Mgr*
EMP: 101
SALES (corp-wide): 122.75MM Privately Held
Web: www.magnaflow.com
SIC: 3714 Exhaust systems and parts, motor vehicle
PA: Car Sound Exhaust System, Inc.
1901 Corporate Ctr
Oceanside CA
949 858-5900

(P-9367)
CAR SOUND EXHAUST SYSTEM INC
23201 Antonio Pkwy (92688-2653)
PHONE.................................949 858-5900
Jerry Paolone, *Brnch Mgr*
EMP: 85
SALES (corp-wide): 122.75MM Privately Held
Web: www.magnaflow.com
SIC: 3714 Exhaust systems and parts, motor vehicle
PA: Car Sound Exhaust System, Inc.
1901 Corporate Ctr
Oceanside CA
949 858-5900

(P-9368)
CAR SOUND EXHAUST SYSTEM INC (PA)
Also Called: Magnaflow Performance
1901 Corporate Ctr (92056-5831)
PHONE.................................949 858-5900
Jerry Paolone, *CEO*
Scott Krog, *Prin*
◆ EMP: 20 EST: 1981
SQ FT: 45,000
SALES (est): 122.75MM
SALES (corp-wide): 122.75MM Privately Held
Web: www.magnaflow.com
SIC: 3714 Exhaust systems and parts, motor vehicle

(P-9369)
CARLSTAR GROUP LLC
10730 Production Ave (92337-8008)
PHONE.................................909 829-1703
EMP: 40
Web: www.carlstargroup.com
SIC: 3714 Motor vehicle parts and accessories
PA: The Carlstar Group Llc
725 Cool Springs Blvd # 5
Franklin TN

(P-9370)
CDC INTERNATIONAL INC
1925 E Puente St (91724-3375)
PHONE.................................626 347-7705
Co N Chuc, *Prin*
EMP: 20 EST: 2008
SALES (est): 822.74K Privately Held
SIC: 3714 Motor vehicle parts and accessories

(P-9371)
CENTER LINE WHEEL CORPORATION
Also Called: Center Line Performance Wheels
23 Corporate Plaza Dr Ste 150 (92660-7908)
PHONE.................................562 921-9637
Ray Lipper, *Pr*
▲ EMP: 42 EST: 1963
SALES (est): 5.09MM Privately Held

Web: www.centerlinewheels.com
SIC: 3714 Wheels, motor vehicle

(P-9372)
CODA AUTOMOTIVE INC
Also Called: CODA AUTOMOTIVE INC
14 Auto Center Dr (92618-2802)
PHONE.................................949 830-7000
EMP: 20
Web: www.codaautomotive.com
SIC: 3714 Motor vehicle parts and accessories
PA: Coda Automotive, Inc.
2340 S Fairfax Ave
Los Angeles CA

(P-9373)
CODA AUTOMOTIVE INC
Also Called: CODA AUTOMOTIVE INC
12101 W Olympic Blvd (90064-1017)
PHONE.................................310 820-3611
Phil Murtaugh, *CEO*
EMP: 20
Web: www.codaautomotive.com
SIC: 3714 Motor vehicle parts and accessories
PA: Coda Automotive, Inc.
2340 S Fairfax Ave
Los Angeles CA

(P-9374)
CODA AUTOMOTIVE INC
Also Called: CODA AUTOMOTIVE INC
1441 Camino Del Rio S (92108-3521)
PHONE.................................619 291-2040
EMP: 20
Web: www.codaautomotive.com
SIC: 3714 Motor vehicle parts and accessories
PA: Coda Automotive, Inc.
2340 S Fairfax Ave
Los Angeles CA

(P-9375)
CRAIG MANUFACTURING COMPANY (PA)
8129 Slauson Ave (90640-6621)
PHONE.................................323 726-7355
Craig Taslitt, *Pr*
Julie Taslitt Gross, *
EMP: 60 EST: 1976
SQ FT: 16,000
SALES (est): 4.81MM
SALES (corp-wide): 4.81MM Privately Held
Web: www.craigattachments.com
SIC: 3714 Radiators and radiator shells and cores, motor vehicle

(P-9376)
CROWER ENGRG & SLS CO INC
Also Called: Crower Cams
6180 Business Center Ct (92154-5604)
PHONE.................................619 661-6477
Barbara Crower, *Pr*
Loren Harris, *
Peter Harris, *
Donald Cave, *
Brett Cave, *
▲ EMP: 88 EST: 1955
SQ FT: 40,000
SALES (est): 23.44MM Privately Held
Web: www.crower.com
SIC: 3714 Camshafts, motor vehicle

(P-9377)
CURRIE ENTERPRISES
382 N Smith Ave (92878-4371)
PHONE.................................714 528-6957
Raymond Currie, *Pr*

Raymond Currie, *Pr*
Charles Currie, *
John Currie, *
◆ **EMP: 60 EST:** 1960
SQ FT: 13,000
SALES (est): 17.65MM **Privately Held**
Web: www.currieenterprises.com
SIC: 3714 3599 Differentials and parts, motor vehicle; Machine shop, jobbing and repair

(P-9378)
DANCHUK MANUFACTURING INC
3211 Halladay St (92705-5628)
PHONE..............................714 540-4363
Arthur Danchuk, *Pr*
Daniel Danchuk, *
▲ **EMP: 71 EST:** 1967
SALES (est): 9.4MM **Privately Held**
Web: www.danchuk.com
SIC: 3714 3465 Motor vehicle parts and accessories; Automotive stampings

(P-9379)
DEE ENGINEERING INC
6918 Ed Perkic St (92504-1001)
PHONE..............................909 947-5616
Gary Fulton, *VP*
EMP: 25
SALES (corp-wide): 7.59MM **Privately Held**
Web: www.prothane.com
SIC: 3714 Mufflers (exhaust), motor vehicle
PA: Dee Engineering, Inc.
1284 E 10 S
Lindon UT
714 979-4990

(P-9380)
DEL WEST ENGINEERING INC (PA)
Also Called: Del West USA
28128 Livingston Ave (91355-4115)
PHONE..............................661 295-5700
Al Sommer, *Ch*
Mark Sommer, *
Rosemarie Chegwin, *
Guido Keijzers, *
EMP: 120 **EST:** 1973
SQ FT: 50,000
SALES (est): 20.98MM
SALES (corp-wide): 20.98MM **Privately Held**
Web: www.delwestengineering.com
SIC: 3714 Motor vehicle parts and accessories

(P-9381)
DENSO PDTS & SVCS AMERICAS INC
41673 Corning Pl (92562-7023)
PHONE..............................951 698-3379
Yoshihiko Yamada, *Pr*
EMP: 150
Web: www.densorobotics.com
SIC: 3714 Motor vehicle parts and accessories
HQ: Denso Products And Services Americas, Inc.
3900 Via Oro Ave
Long Beach CA
310 834-6352

(P-9382)
DONALDSON COMPANY INC
26235 Technology Dr (91355-1147)
PHONE..............................661 295-0800
Paul Akian, *Pr*

EMP: 20
SALES (corp-wide): 3.43B **Publicly Held**
Web: www.donaldson.com
SIC: 3714 Mufflers (exhaust), motor vehicle
PA: Donaldson Company, Inc.
1400 W 94th St
Minneapolis MN
952 887-3131

(P-9383)
DOUGLAS TECHNOLOGIES GROUP INC (PA)
Also Called: Douglas Wheel
42092 Winchester Rd Ste B (92590-4805)
PHONE..............................760 758-5560
Johnny Leach, *Pr*
◆ **EMP:** 38 **EST:** 1982
SQ FT: 60,000
SALES (est): 7.79MM **Privately Held**
Web: www.dwtracing.com
SIC: 3714 Wheel rims, motor vehicle

(P-9384)
DRIVESHAFTPRO
7532 Anthony Ave (92841-4006)
PHONE..............................714 893-4585
Ronald Hart, *Pr*
EMP: 32 **EST:** 2016
SALES (est): 1.4MM **Privately Held**
Web: www.driveshaftpro.com
SIC: 3714 Motor vehicle parts and accessories

(P-9385)
DYNATRAC PRODUCTS LLC
7392 Count Cir (92647-4551)
PHONE..............................714 596-4461
Jim Mcgean, *Pr*
EMP: 27 **EST:** 2021
SALES (est): 2.55MM **Privately Held**
SIC: 3714 5013 5531 Motor vehicle transmissions, drive assemblies, and parts; Motor vehicle supplies and new parts; Truck equipment and parts

(P-9386)
EDELBROCK LLC
501 Amapola Ave (90501-1466)
PHONE..............................310 781-2290
EMP: 25
Web: www.edelbrock.com
SIC: 3714 Motor vehicle parts and accessories
HQ: Edelbrock, Llc
8649 Hacks Cross Rd
Olive Branch MS
310 781-2222

(P-9387)
EGR INCORPORATED (DH)
4000 Greystone Dr (91761-3101)
PHONE..............................909 923-7075
Rodney Horwill, *CEO*
John Whitten, *
Simon Mclellan, *CFO*
▲ **EMP:** 26 **EST:** 1993
SQ FT: 70,000
SALES (est): 24.8MM **Privately Held**
Web: www.egrusa.com
SIC: 3714 Motor vehicle parts and accessories
HQ: Oakmoore Pty. Ltd.
45 Machinery St
Darra QLD

(P-9388)
ENDERLE FUEL INJECTION
1830 Voyager Ave (93063-3348)
PHONE..............................805 526-3838
Kent H Enderle, *Pr*

Joan C Enderle, *Sec*
Jim Rehfeld, *VP*
EMP: 20 **EST:** 1966
SQ FT: 18,000
SALES (est): 2.36MM **Privately Held**
Web: www.enderlefuelsystems.com
SIC: 3714 Fuel systems and parts, motor vehicle

(P-9389)
ESSLINGER ENGINEERING INC
5946 Freedom Dr (91710-7014)
PHONE..............................909 539-0544
Dwaine E Esslinger, *Pr*
Elizabeth Esslinger, *Sec*
Dan Esslinger, *VP*
▲ **EMP:** 20 **EST:** 1969
SQ FT: 4,000
SALES (est): 2.37MM **Privately Held**
Web: www.esslingerracing.com
SIC: 3714 Motor vehicle engines and parts

(P-9390)
EVANS WALKER ENTERPRISES
Also Called: Evans, Walker Racing
2304 Fleetwood Dr (92509-2409)
P.O. Box 2469 (92516-2469)
PHONE..............................951 784-7223
Walker Evans, *Pr*
Randall Anderson, *VP*
Phyllis Evans, *Sec*
▲ **EMP:** 20 **EST:** 1978
SQ FT: 20,000
SALES (est): 12.15MM **Privately Held**
Web: www.walkerevansracing.com
SIC: 3714 Motor vehicle parts and accessories

(P-9391)
FOOTE AXLE & FORGE LLC
250 W Duarte Rd Ste A (91016-7460)
PHONE..............................323 268-4151
Michael F Denton Senior, *Managing Member*
Merrie N Denton, *
▲ **EMP:** 32 **EST:** 1937
SALES (est): 2.47MM **Privately Held**
Web: www.footeaxle.com
SIC: 3714 Differentials and parts, motor vehicle

(P-9392)
FORGIATO INC
Also Called: Forgiato
11915 Wicks St (91352-1908)
PHONE..............................818 771-9779
Norman Celik, *CEO*
Nisan G Celik, *
▲ **EMP:** 62 **EST:** 2006
SQ FT: 60,000
SALES (est): 9.14MM **Privately Held**
Web: www.forgiato.com
SIC: 3714 Motor vehicle wheels and parts

(P-9393)
GARRETT MOTION INC
290 E Cole Blvd (92231-3210)
PHONE..............................973 867-7016
EMP: 106
SALES (corp-wide): 3.63B **Privately Held**
Web: www.garrettmotion.com
SIC: 3714 Motor vehicle parts and accessories
PA: Garrett Motion Inc.
47548 Halyard Dr
Plymouth MI
734 359-5901

(P-9394)
GARRISON MANUFACTURING INC
3320 S Yale St (92704-6447)
PHONE..............................714 549-4880
Venu Shan, *Pr*
Jake Ralli, *
EMP: 30 **EST:** 1939
SQ FT: 26,000
SALES (est): 2.73MM **Privately Held**
Web: www.garrisonmfg.com
SIC: 3714 7699 5084 3593 Steering mechanisms, motor vehicle; Industrial machinery and equipment repair; Hydraulic systems equipment and supplies; Fluid power cylinders and actuators

(P-9395)
GEAR VENDORS INC
Also Called: Gear Vendors
1717 N Magnolia Ave (92020-1243)
PHONE..............................619 562-0060
Ken R Johnson, *CEO*
Rick Johnson, *
▲ **EMP:** 35 **EST:** 1981
SQ FT: 35,000
SALES (est): 3.09MM **Privately Held**
Web: www.gearvendors.com
SIC: 3714 Transmissions, motor vehicle

(P-9396)
GERHARDT GEAR CO INC
133 E Santa Anita Ave (91502-1926)
PHONE..............................818 842-6700
Ronald J Gerhardt, *CEO*
Mitch Gerhardt, *
John Kim, *
Kurht Gerhardt, *
EMP: 46 **EST:** 1937
SQ FT: 30,000
SALES (est): 8.14MM **Privately Held**
Web: www.gerhardtgear.com
SIC: 3714 3728 3769 3462 Gears, motor vehicle; Gears, aircraft power transmission; Space vehicle equipment, nec; Iron and steel forgings

(P-9397)
GIBSON PERFORMANCE CORPORATION
Also Called: Gibson Exhaust Systems
1270 Webb Cir (92879-5760)
PHONE..............................951 372-1220
Ronald Gibson, *Pr*
Julie Gibson, *
▲ **EMP:** 75 **EST:** 1990
SQ FT: 50,000
SALES (est): 9.72MM **Privately Held**
Web: www.gibsonperformance.com
SIC: 3714 5013 Exhaust systems and parts, motor vehicle; Motor vehicle supplies and new parts

(P-9398)
GRANATELLI MOTOR SPORTS INC
1000 Yarnell Pl (93033-2454)
PHONE..............................805 486-6644
Joseph R Granatelli, *CEO*
▲ **EMP:** 31 **EST:** 1998
SQ FT: 49,000
SALES (est): 2.85MM **Privately Held**
Web: www.granatellimotorsports.com
SIC: 3714 Fuel systems and parts, motor vehicle

(P-9399)
GROVER PRODUCTS CO
3424 E Olympic Blvd (90023-3000)

P.O. Box 23966 (90023-0966)
PHONE..............................323 263-9981
John A Roesch, *CEO*
▲ **EMP:** 100 **EST:** 1932
SQ FT: 60,000
SALES (est): 9.64MM **Privately Held**
Web: www.airhorns.com
SIC: 3714 3494 5999 Motor vehicle brake
systems and parts; Valves and pipe fittings,
nec; Plumbing and heating supplies

(P-9400)
HEATSHIELD PRODUCTS INC
1040 S Andreasen Dr Ste 110
(92029-1951)
P.O. Box 462500 (92046-2500)
PHONE..............................760 751-0441
Stephen Heye, *CEO*
Bruce Heye, *Pt*
Stephen J Heye, *Pt*
EMP: 20 **EST:** 1999
SQ FT: 500
SALES (est): 2.22MM **Privately Held**
Web: www.heatshieldproducts.com
SIC: 3714 Motor vehicle parts and
accessories

(P-9401)
HEDMAN MANUFACTURING (PA)
Also Called: Hedman Hedders
12438 Putnam St (90602-1002)
PHONE..............................562 204-1031
Robert Bandergriff, *Pr*
Ron Funfar, *
▲ **EMP:** 45 **EST:** 1978
SALES (est): 8.37MM
SALES (corp-wide): 8.37MM **Privately
Held**
Web: www.hedman.com
SIC: 3714 Exhaust systems and parts, motor
vehicle

(P-9402)
**HORSTMAN MANUFACTURING
CO INC**
1970 Peacock Blvd (92056-3538)
PHONE..............................760 598-2100
Allen Bourgeois, *Pr*
▲ **EMP:** 17 **EST:** 1963
SALES (est): 457.56K **Privately Held**
SIC: 3714 3944 Motor vehicle engines and
parts; Games, toys, and children's vehicles

(P-9403)
HT MULTINATIONAL INC
Also Called: Unisun Multinational
15780 El Prado Rd (91708-9154)
PHONE..............................909 325-8582
Chunli Zhao, *CEO*
▲ **EMP:** 21 **EST:** 2011
SALES (est): 6.64MM **Privately Held**
SIC: 3714 3429 5072 Motor vehicle brake
systems and parts; Hardware, nec;
Hardware
HQ: Sinatex, S.A. De C.V.
Industriales No. 1188 Pte.
Cajeme SON

(P-9404)
ICARCOVER INC
15529 Blackburn Ave (90650-6846)
PHONE..............................714 469-7759
Calvin Kim, *CEO*
EMP: 20 **EST:** 2019
SALES (est): 4.21MM **Privately Held**
Web: www.icarcover.com
SIC: 3714 Motor vehicle parts and
accessories

(P-9405)
**IMPCO TECHNOLOGIES INC
(HQ)**
Also Called: Impco
3030 S Susan St (92704-6435)
PHONE..............................714 656-1200
Massimo Fracchia, *Genl Mgr*
Peter Chase, *
◆ **EMP:** 160 **EST:** 1958
SQ FT: 108,000
SALES (est): 44.72MM
SALES (corp-wide): 305.7MM **Privately
Held**
Web: www.impcotechnologies.com
SIC: 3714 3592 7363 Fuel systems and
parts, motor vehicle; Carburetors;
Engineering help service
PA: Westport Fuel Systems Inc
1691 75th Ave
Vancouver BC
604 718-2000

(P-9406)
**INNOVA ELECTRONICS
CORPORATION**
Also Called: Equipment & Tool Institute
17352 Von Karman Ave (92614-6204)
PHONE..............................714 241-6800
Ieon C Chenn, *Pr*
EMP: 29 **EST:** 1990
SQ FT: 12,000
SALES (est): 9.16MM **Privately Held**
Web: www.innova.com
SIC: 3714 Motor vehicle electrical equipment

(P-9407)
K & G LATIROVIAN INC
Also Called: Kahgo Truck Parts
11182 Penrose St (91352-2724)
PHONE..............................818 319-2862
Kabrail Latirovian, *CEO*
EMP: 54
Web: www.kahgotruckparts.com
SIC: 3714 Motor vehicle parts and
accessories
PA: K & G Latirovian, Inc.
8277 Lankershim Blvd
North Hollywood CA

(P-9408)
KALAYDJAIN SHAHE INC
Also Called: Undercar Plus Company
7032 Valjean Ave (91406-3914)
PHONE..............................818 988-3700
EMP: 17 **EST:** 1991
SQ FT: 4,000
SALES (est): 731.31K **Privately Held**
Web: www.nexpart.com
SIC: 3714 Motor vehicle parts and
accessories

(P-9409)
**KENNEDY ENGINEERED PDTS
INC**
38830 17th St E (93550-3915)
PHONE..............................661 272-1147
Hobert Kennedy, *Owner*
▲ **EMP:** 17 **EST:** 1968
SQ FT: 5,900
SALES (est): 2.32MM **Privately Held**
Web: www.kennedyeng.com
SIC: 3714 Motor vehicle parts and
accessories

(P-9410)
KING SHOCK TECHNOLOGY INC
12472 Edison Way (92841-2821)
PHONE..............................719 394-3754
◆ **EMP:** 99 **EST:** 2001

SQ FT: 18,000
SALES (est): 17.87MM **Privately Held**
Web: www.registrar-transfers.com
SIC: 3714 Motor vehicle body components
and frame

(P-9411)
LAPCO WEST LLC
Also Called: Lapco West
13140 Midway Pl (90703-2233)
PHONE..............................562 348-4850
Graem Elliot, *CEO*
EMP: 20 **EST:** 2004
SALES (est): 2.13MM **Privately Held**
Web: www.lapcowest.com
SIC: 3714 Motor vehicle brake systems and
parts

(P-9412)
LEET TECHNOLOGY INC
1427 S Robertson Blvd (90035-3401)
PHONE..............................877 238-4492
Ding Jung Long, *CEO*
Kamal Hamidon, *Principal Accounting
Officer*
EMP: 17 **EST:** 2013
SALES (est): 151.98K **Privately Held**
SIC: 3714 Motor vehicle parts and
accessories

(P-9413)
**LENCO RACING
TRANSMISSIONS INC**
1326 E Francis St (91761-5714)
PHONE..............................909 673-9080
John Mihovetz, *Pr*
EMP: 17 **EST:** 2017
SALES (est): 475.46K **Privately Held**
Web: www.lencoracing.com
SIC: 3714 Motor vehicle parts and
accessories

(P-9414)
LLOYD DESIGN CORPORATION
Also Called: Lloyd Mats
19731 Nordhoff St (91324-3330)
PHONE..............................818 768-6001
Lloyd S Levine, *CEO*
Brendan Dooley, *
▲ **EMP:** 55 **EST:** 1974
SALES (est): 8.44MM **Privately Held**
Web: www.lloydmats.com
SIC: 3714 Motor vehicle parts and
accessories

(P-9415)
LOS ANGELES SLEEVE CO INC
Also Called: L.A. Sleeve
12051 Rivera Rd (90670-2211)
PHONE..............................562 945-7578
Nick G Metchkoff, *Pr*
David Metchkoff, *
James G Metchkoff, *
Sarah Metchkoff, *
▲ **EMP:** 29 **EST:** 1975
SQ FT: 33,000
SALES (est): 4.5MM **Privately Held**
Web: www.lasleeve.com
SIC: 3714 Exhaust systems and parts, motor
vehicle

(P-9416)
LSI PRODUCTS INC
12885 Wildflower Ln (92503-9772)
PHONE..............................951 343-9270
Alex Danze, *CEO*
▲ **EMP:** 19 **EST:** 1998
SALES (est): 476.11K **Privately Held**
Web: www.proarmor.com

SIC: 3714 Motor vehicle parts and
accessories

(P-9417)
LUND MOTION PRODUCTS INC
Also Called: AMP Research
3172 Nasa St (92821-6234)
PHONE..............................888 983-2204
Mitch Fogle, *Pr*
EMP: 35
SALES (corp-wide): 829.18MM **Privately
Held**
Web: www.realtruck.com
SIC: 3714 Motor vehicle parts and
accessories
HQ: Lund Motion Products, Inc.
4325 Hamilton Mill Rd # 4
Buford GA
678 804-3767

(P-9418)
M E D INC
14001 Marquardt Ave (90670-5018)
PHONE..............................562 921-0464
Steven Moore, *CEO*
Susan Lowe, *
EMP: 70 **EST:** 1974
SQ FT: 40,000
SALES (est): 16.03MM **Privately Held**
Web: www.dme-mfg.com
SIC: 3714 3429 Exhaust systems and parts,
motor vehicle; Clamps, couplings, nozzles,
and other metal hose fittings

(P-9419)
MAGNUSON PRODUCTS LLC
Also Called: Magnuson Superchargers
1990 Knoll Dr Ste A (93003-7309)
PHONE..............................805 642-8833
Kim Pendergast, *CEO*
Tim Krauskopf, *
EMP: 49 **EST:** 1970
SQ FT: 45,600
SALES (est): 10.59MM **Privately Held**
Web: www.magnusonsuperchargers.com
SIC: 3714 Motor vehicle parts and
accessories

(P-9420)
MAXON INDUSTRIES INC
11921 Slauson Ave (90670-2221)
P.O. Box 3434 (90078-3434)
PHONE..............................562 464-0099
Murray Lugash, *Pr*
Larry Lugash, *
Brenda Leung, *
EMP: 75 **EST:** 1957
SQ FT: 250,000
SALES (est): 9.82MM **Privately Held**
Web: www.maxonlift.com
SIC: 3714 Motor vehicle parts and
accessories

(P-9421)
MCLEOD RACING LLC
Also Called: McLeod Racing
1570 Lakeview Loop (92807-1819)
PHONE..............................714 630-2764
Paul Lee, *Pr*
Lana Chrisman, *VP*
EMP: 22 **EST:** 2009
SQ FT: 17,500
SALES (est): 3.73MM **Privately Held**
Web: www.mcleodracing.com
SIC: 3714 Clutches, motor vehicle

(P-9422)
MCO INC
13925 Benson Ave (91710-7024)
PHONE..............................909 627-3574

Leon O Martin, *Pr*
Vicki Martin, *Sec*
EMP: 21 **EST:** 1972
SQ FT: 10,000
SALES (est): 491.56K **Privately Held**
SIC: 3714 Frames, motor vehicle

(P-9423)
METRA ELECTRONICS CORPORATION
Also Called: Antenna Works
3201 E 59th St (90805-4501)
PHONE..............................562 470-6601
Steve Hertel, *Mgr*
EMP: 22
SALES (corp-wide): 98.4MM **Privately Held**
Web: www.metraonline.com
SIC: 3714 Motor vehicle body components and frame
PA: Metra Electronics Corporation
460 Walker St
Holly Hill FL
386 257-1186

(P-9424)
MGP EXHAUSTS USA INC
Also Called: MGP Exhausts USA, Inc.
2225 Meyers Ave (92029-1005)
PHONE..............................760 445-1235
EMP: 29
SALES (corp-wide): 1.05MM **Privately Held**
Web: www.hotbodiesracing.com
SIC: 3714 Acceleration equipment, motor vehicle
PA: Mgp Exhaust Usa, Inc.
12925 Brookprinter Pl
Poway CA
858 486-3838

(P-9425)
MID-WEST FABRICATING CO
Also Called: West Bent Bolt Division
8623 Dice Rd (90670-2511)
PHONE..............................562 698-9615
Steve Petersen, *Mgr*
EMP: 46
SQ FT: 40,000
SALES (corp-wide): 28.07MM **Privately Held**
Web: www.midwestfab.com
SIC: 3714 3452 3316 3312 Tie rods, motor vehicle; Bolts, nuts, rivets, and washers; Cold finishing of steel shapes; Wire products, steel or iron
PA: Mid-West Fabricating Co.
313 N Johns St
Amanda OH
740 969-4411

(P-9426)
MILODON INCORPORATED
2250 Agate Ct (93065-1842)
PHONE..............................805 577-5950
Steve Morrison, *Pr*
▲ **EMP:** 40 **EST:** 1957
SQ FT: 32,000
SALES (est): 5.42MM **Privately Held**
Web: www.milodon.com
SIC: 3714 Motor vehicle engines and parts

(P-9427)
MOBIS PARTS AMERICA LLC
Also Called: Mobis
10550 Talbert Ave # 4 (92708-6031)
PHONE..............................949 450-0014
EMP: 29
Web: www.mobisusa.com

SIC: 3714 Motor vehicle body components and frame
HQ: Mobis Parts America, Llc
10550 Talbert Ave Fl 4
Fountain Valley CA
786 515-1101

(P-9428)
MOTORCAR PARTS OF AMERICA INC (PA)
Also Called: MPA
2929 California St (90503-3914)
PHONE..............................310 212-7910
Selwyn Joffe, *Ch Bd*
David Lee, *CFO*
Kamlesh Shah, *CAO*
Douglas Schooner, *CMO*
Richard Mochulsky, *S&M/VP*
◆ **EMP:** 768 **EST:** 1968
SQ FT: 231,000
SALES (est): 683.07MM
SALES (corp-wide): 683.07MM **Publicly Held**
Web: www.motorcarparts.com
SIC: 3714 3694 3625 Motor vehicle parts and accessories; Alternators, automotive; Starter, electric motor

(P-9429)
MYGRANT GLASS COMPANY INC
10220 Camino Santa Fe (92121-3105)
PHONE..............................858 455-8022
EMP: 31
SQ FT: 32,185
SALES (corp-wide): 168.98MM **Privately Held**
Web: www.mygrantglassonline.com
SIC: 3714 5013 Motor vehicle parts and accessories; Motor vehicle supplies and new parts
PA: Mygrant Glass Company, Inc.
3271 Arden Rd
Hayward CA
510 785-4360

(P-9430)
N G K SPARK PLUGS USA INC
6 Whatney (92618-2805)
PHONE..............................949 855-8278
EMP: 20 **EST:** 2019
SALES (est): 789.37K **Privately Held**
Web: www.ngksparkplugs.com
SIC: 3714 Motor vehicle parts and accessories

(P-9431)
NEW CENTURY INDUSTRIES INC
7231 Rosecrans Ave (90723-2501)
P.O. Box 1845 (90723-1845)
PHONE..............................562 634-9551
Michael Mason, *CEO*
EMP: 50 **EST:** 1991
SQ FT: 32,000
SALES (est): 10.3MM **Privately Held**
SIC: 3714 3465 3469 Wheels, motor vehicle; Automotive stampings; Stamping metal for the trade

(P-9432)
NMSP INC (DH)
Also Called: A E M
2205 W 126th St Ste A (90250-3367)
PHONE..............................310 484-2322
Gregory Neuwirth, *Pr*
Peter Neuwirth, *
◆ **EMP:** 84 **EST:** 1997
SQ FT: 78,000

SALES (est): 24.18MM
SALES (corp-wide): 688.41MM **Publicly Held**
SIC: 3714 Motor vehicle engines and parts
HQ: Holley Performance Products Inc.
1801 Russellville Rd
Bowling Green KY
270 782-2900

(P-9433)
NMSP INC
1451 E 6th St (92879-1715)
PHONE..............................951 734-2453
Darrell Contreras, *Mgr*
EMP: 46
SALES (corp-wide): 688.41MM **Publicly Held**
SIC: 3714 Motor vehicle engines and parts
HQ: Nmsp, Inc.
2205 W 126th St Ste A
Hawthorne CA
310 484-2322

(P-9434)
NORTHROP GRMMN SPCE & MSSN SYS
2501 Santa Fe Ave (90278-1117)
PHONE..............................310 812-4321
EMP: 334
SIC: 3714 7373 3663 3661 Motor vehicle parts and accessories; Computer integrated systems design; Radio and t.v. communications equipment; Telephone and telegraph apparatus
HQ: Northrop Grumman Space & Mission Systems Corp.
6379 San Ignacio Ave
San Jose CA
703 280-2900

(P-9435)
NRG MOTORSPORTS INC
Also Called: Boyd Coddington Wheels
861 E Lambert Rd (90631-6143)
PHONE..............................714 541-1173
Boyd Coddington, *Pr*
▲ **EMP:** 55 **EST:** 1998
SALES (est): 4.27MM **Privately Held**
Web: www.nrgmotorsports.net
SIC: 3714 Wheels, motor vehicle

(P-9436)
OVERLAND VEHICLE SYSTEMS LLC
9830 Norwalk Blvd Ste 130 (90670-6104)
PHONE..............................833 226-4863
Sean Angues, *Managing Member*
EMP: 20 **EST:** 2018
SALES (est): 2.46MM **Privately Held**
Web: www.overlandvehiclesystems.com
SIC: 3714 Motor vehicle parts and accessories

(P-9437)
PANKL ENGINE SYSTEMS INC
Also Called: Sp Crankshaft
1902 Mcgaw Ave (92614-0910)
PHONE..............................949 428-8788
▲ **EMP:** 31
Web: www.spcrankshaft.com
SIC: 3714 Crankshaft assemblies, motor vehicle

(P-9438)
PARTS EXPEDITING AND DIST CO
Also Called: Pedco
10805 Artesia Blvd Ste 112 (90703-2678)
P.O. Box 59068 (90652-0068)

PHONE..............................562 944-3199
Virgil Cooley, *Pr*
Rachel Cooley, *
EMP: 18 **EST:** 1975
SQ FT: 32,000
SALES (est): 878.82K **Privately Held**
SIC: 3714 3519 Rebuilding engines and transmissions, factory basis; Internal combustion engines, nec

(P-9439)
PHOENIX MOTOR INC (DH)
Also Called: Phoenix Motorcars
1500 Lakeview Loop (92807-1819)
PHONE..............................909 987-0815
Xiaofeng Denton Peng, *Ch Bd*
Wenbing Chris Wang, *CFO*
Tarek Helou, *COO*
EMP: 30 **EST:** 2020
SALES (est): 4.33MM **Publicly Held**
Web: www.phoenixmotorcars.com
SIC: 3714 Motor vehicle electrical equipment
HQ: Edisonfuture Inc.
4677 Old Ironsides Dr # 1
Santa Clara CA
408 919-8000

(P-9440)
POWER-RIGHT INDUSTRIES LLC
4722 W Mission Blvd (91762-4413)
PHONE..............................909 628-4397
EMP: 18 **EST:** 2003
SALES (est): 1.29MM
SALES (corp-wide): 9.77MM **Privately Held**
SIC: 3714 Oil pump, motor vehicle
PA: Lloyd's Equipment, Inc.
4722 W Mission Blvd
Ontario CA
909 628-5586

(P-9441)
PRIME WHEEL CORPORATION
Also Called: Prime Wheel of Figueroa
17680 S Figueroa St (90248-3419)
PHONE..............................310 819-4123
Peter Liang, *Brnch Mgr*
EMP: 25
SALES (corp-wide): 315.67MM **Privately Held**
Web: www.primewheel.com
SIC: 3714 Wheels, motor vehicle
PA: Prime Wheel Corporation
17705 S Main St
Gardena CA
310 516-9126

(P-9442)
PRIME WHEEL CORPORATION
23920 Vermont Ave (90710-1602)
PHONE..............................310 326-5080
Eddie Chen, *Mgr*
EMP: 453
SQ FT: 200,000
SALES (corp-wide): 315.67MM **Privately Held**
Web: www.primewheel.com
SIC: 3714 3471 5013 Motor vehicle wheels and parts; Plating and polishing; Automotive supplies and parts
PA: Prime Wheel Corporation
17705 S Main St
Gardena CA
310 516-9126

(P-9443)
PRIME WHEEL CORPORATION (PA)
17705 S Main St (90248-3516)

PRODUCTS & SVCS

PHONE..........................310 516-9126
Philip Chen, *CEO*
Henry Chen, *
Mitchell M Tung, *
Albert Huang, *
Webb Carter, *Vice Chairman* *
◆ **EMP:** 600 **EST:** 1989
SQ FT: 320,000
SALES (est): 315.67MM
SALES (corp-wide): 315.67MM **Privately Held**
Web: www.primewheel.com
SIC: 3714 Wheels, motor vehicle

(P-9444)
QF LIQUIDATION INC (PA)
Also Called: Quantum Technologies
25242 Arctic Ocean Dr (92630-8821)
PHONE..........................949 930-3400
W Brian Olson, *Pr*
Bradley J Timon, *CFO*
Kenneth R Lombardo, *Corporate Secretary*
Mark Arold, *VP Opers*
David M Mazaika, *Development*
◆ **EMP:** 155 **EST:** 2000
SQ FT: 156,000
SALES (est): 24.78MM **Privately Held**
Web: www.qtww.com
SIC: 3714 3764 8711 Motor vehicle parts and accessories; Space propulsion units and parts; Engineering services

(P-9445)
R A PHILLIPS INDUSTRIES INC (PA)
Also Called: Phillips Industries
12012 Burke St (90670-2676)
PHONE..........................562 781-2121
◆ **EMP:** 35 **EST:** 1969
SALES (est): 71.29MM
SALES (corp-wide): 71.29MM **Privately Held**
Web: www.phillipsind.com
SIC: 3714 5531 Motor vehicle body components and frame; Truck equipment and parts

(P-9446)
RACEPAK LLC
30402 Esperanza (92688-2144)
PHONE..........................949 709-5555
Tom Tomlinson, *Pr*
EMP: 28 **EST:** 2014
SALES (est): 12.5MM
SALES (corp-wide): 688.41MM **Publicly Held**
Web: www.holley.com
SIC: 3714 Motor vehicle parts and accessories
HQ: Holley Performance Products Inc.
1801 Russellville Rd
Bowling Green KY
270 782-2900

(P-9447)
RACING POWER COMPANY
815 Tucker Ln (91789-2914)
PHONE..........................909 468-3690
Te Ming Chung, *CEO*
▲ **EMP:** 20 **EST:** 1955
SQ FT: 2,000
SALES (est): 3.99MM **Privately Held**
Web: www.usrpc.com
SIC: 3714 Motor vehicle parts and accessories

(P-9448)
RAM OFF ROAD ACCESSORIES INC
3901 Medford St (90063-1608)

PHONE..........................323 266-3850
Chris Foterek, *Pr*
William Longo, *VP*
EMP: 23 **EST:** 1989
SQ FT: 103,000
SALES (est): 713.22K **Privately Held**
SIC: 3714 Motor vehicle body components and frame

(P-9449)
RBW INDUSTRIES INC
5788 Schaefer Ave (91710-7003)
PHONE..........................909 591-5359
Larry Relevino, *Pr*
Marilyn Blodgett, *
Bob Arnett, *
▲ **EMP:** 65 **EST:** 1970
SQ FT: 72,000
SALES (est): 4.89MM **Privately Held**
Web: www.rbwindustries.com
SIC: 3714 3792 Fifth wheel, motor vehicle; Travel trailers and campers

(P-9450)
RICARDO DEFENSE INC (DH)
175 Cremona Dr Ste 140 (93117-3197)
PHONE..........................805 882-1884
Chester Gryzcan, *Pr*
Brian Smith, *
EMP: 22 **EST:** 1995
SALES (est): 17.5MM
SALES (corp-wide): 550.27MM **Privately Held**
SIC: 3714 8711 Motor vehicle brake systems and parts; Consulting engineer
HQ: Ricardo Defense Systems, Llc
300 E Big Beaver Rd # 180
Troy MI

(P-9451)
RLV TUNED EXHAUST PRODUCTS INC
2351 Thompson Way Bldg A (93455-1041)
PHONE..........................805 925-5461
Rodney L Verlengiere, *Pr*
Arthur R Verlengiere, *Sec*
▲ **EMP:** 26 **EST:** 1978
SQ FT: 5,000
SALES (est): 2.25MM **Privately Held**
Web: www.rlv.com
SIC: 3714 Exhaust systems and parts, motor vehicle

(P-9452)
ROLL ALONG VANS INC
1350 E Yorba Linda Blvd (92870-3833)
PHONE..........................714 528-9600
Dan Williams, *Mgr*
EMP: 34 **EST:** 1976
SQ FT: 40,400
SALES (est): 3MM **Privately Held**
Web: www.rollalongvans.com
SIC: 3714 Motor vehicle parts and accessories

(P-9453)
ROMEO POWER INC (HQ)
Also Called: Romeo Power
514 Via De La Valle (92075-2717)
PHONE..........................833 467-2237
Mark Russell, *Pr*
Kim Brady, *
Britton Worthen, *
EMP: 165 **EST:** 2018
SALES (est): 16.8MM
SALES (corp-wide): 50.83MM **Publicly Held**
Web: www.romeopower.com
SIC: 3714 Motor vehicle parts and accessories

PA: Nikola Corporation
4141 E Broadway Rd
Phoenix AZ
480 666-1038

(P-9454)
RYVID INC (PA)
12090 Carson St Ste H504 (90716-1142)
PHONE..........................650 515-6118
Jonathan Spira, *Prin*
EMP: 20 **EST:** 2021
SALES (est): 2.39MM
SALES (corp-wide): 2.39MM **Privately Held**
Web: www.ryvid.com
SIC: 3714 Motor vehicle parts and accessories

(P-9455)
S C I INDUSTRIES INC
Also Called: SCI
1433 Adelia Ave (91733-3002)
EMP: 25 **EST:** 1950
SALES (est): 2MM **Privately Held**
SIC: 3714 3599 Motor vehicle brake systems and parts; Machine shop, jobbing and repair

(P-9456)
S&B FILTERS INC
15461 Slover Ave Ste A (92337-1306)
PHONE..........................909 947-0015
Berry Carter, *Pr*
▲ **EMP:** 58 **EST:** 1981
SALES (est): 17.2MM **Privately Held**
Web: www.sandbfilters.com
SIC: 3714 3564 Filters: oil, fuel, and air, motor vehicle; Filters, air: furnaces, air conditioning equipment, etc.

(P-9457)
SANKO ELECTRONICS AMERICA INC (HQ)
2587 Otay Center Dr (92154-7612)
PHONE..........................310 618-1677
Hironori Saigusa, *CEO*
Akio Saigusa, *Pr*
Toshiaki Yamashita, *Pr*
▲ **EMP:** 19 **EST:** 1988
SALES (est): 11.1MM **Privately Held**
Web: www.sanko-grp.co.jp
SIC: 3714 Motor vehicle parts and accessories
PA: Sanko Electric Co.,Ltd.
7-23, Tamanoicho, Atsuta-Ku
Nagoya AIC

(P-9458)
SEDENQUIST-FRASER ENTPS INC
Also Called: Leisure Components
16730 Gridley Rd (90703-1730)
PHONE..........................562 924-5763
Jitu Patel, *Pr*
EMP: 36 **EST:** 1974
SQ FT: 22,000
SALES (est): 665.01K **Privately Held**
Web: www.sftech.com
SIC: 3714 3089 3544 Motor vehicle parts and accessories; Plastics processing; Special dies, tools, jigs, and fixtures

(P-9459)
SEYMOUR LEVINGER & CO
1455 Citrus St (92507-1603)
PHONE..........................909 673-9800
Amir Rosenbaum, *CEO*
▲ **EMP:** 32 **EST:** 1983
SQ FT: 16,000
SALES (est): 2.49MM **Privately Held**

Web: www.spectreperformance.com
SIC: 3714 Motor vehicle parts and accessories

(P-9460)
SHEPARD-THOMASON COMPANY
901 S Leslie St (90631-6841)
PHONE..........................714 773-5539
Thomas A Ruhe, *Pr*
Connie Ruhe, *
EMP: 71 **EST:** 1913
SQ FT: 25,000
SALES (est): 1.36MM **Privately Held**
SIC: 3714 Clutches, motor vehicle
PA: Ruhe Corporation
901 S Leslie St
La Habra CA

(P-9461)
SPECIAL DEVICES INCORPORATED
Also Called: Sdi
2655 1st St Ste 125 (93065-1548)
PHONE..........................805 387-1000
Yasuhiro Sakaki, *CEO*
Kenichi Tanaka, *
Kenichi Yamada, *
Harry Rector, *
Nicholas J Bruge, *CCO* *
▲ **EMP:** 600 **EST:** 1959
SALES (est): 77.79MM **Privately Held**
Web: www.daicelssa.com
SIC: 3714 Motor vehicle parts and accessories
PA: Daicel Corporation
3-1, Ofukacho, Kita-Ku
Osaka OSK

(P-9462)
SPECTRUM ACCESSORY DISTRS INC
9770 Carroll Centre Rd (92126-6504)
PHONE..........................858 653-6470
C Dwight Anderson, *Pr*
EMP: 19 **EST:** 1994
SALES (est): 265.34K **Privately Held**
SIC: 3714 5013 Motor vehicle body components and frame; Motor vehicle supplies and new parts

(P-9463)
STULL INDUSTRIES INC
1315 W Flint St (92530-3248)
PHONE..........................951 248-9789
William Stull, *Pr*
▲ **EMP:** 18 **EST:** 1974
SQ FT: 50,000
SALES (est): 478.51K **Privately Held**
Web: www.stullindustries.com
SIC: 3714 Motor vehicle body components and frame

(P-9464)
SUNNY AMER GLOBL AUTOTEC CORP
Also Called: SA & G Autotec
2681 Dow Ave Ste A (92780-7244)
PHONE..........................714 544-0400
Alex Han, *Owner*
▲ **EMP:** 22 **EST:** 2006
SALES (est): 472.59K **Privately Held**
Web: www.xlautocorp.com
SIC: 3714 Motor vehicle engines and parts

(P-9465)
SUPERIOR INDS INTL HLDINGS LLC (HQ)

7800 Woodley Ave (91406-1722)
PHONE..................................818 781-4973
Steven J Borick, *Ch Bd*
▲ **EMP:** 58 **EST:** 2008
SALES (est): 19.29MM
SALES (corp-wide): 1.64B **Publicly Held**
Web: www.superiorindustries.com
SIC: 3714 Motor vehicle wheels and parts
PA: Superior Industries International, Inc.
26600 Telg Rd Ste 400
Southfield MI
248 352-7300

(P-9466)
SWAY-A-WAY INC
9530 Cozycroft Ave (91311-5101)
PHONE..................................818 700-9712
▲ **EMP:** 31 **EST:** 1988
SALES (est): 4.57MM **Privately Held**
Web: www.swayaway.com
SIC: 3714 Motor vehicle parts and
accessories

(P-9467)
TAP MANUFACTURING LLC
Also Called: Pro Comp
2390 Boswell Rd (91914-3541)
PHONE..................................619 216-1444
Darren M Salvin, *Prin*
▲ **EMP:** 17 **EST:** 2009
SALES (est): 1.09MM **Privately Held**
SIC: 3714 Motor vehicle parts and
accessories

(P-9468)
THERMAL SOLUTIONS MFG INC
1390 S Tippecanoe Ave Ste B
(92408-2998)
PHONE..................................909 796-0754
Maureen Baker, *Brnch Mgr*
EMP: 33
SALES (corp-wide): 47.17MM **Privately
Held**
Web: www.thermalsolutionsmfg.com
SIC: 3714 Radiators and radiator shells and
cores, motor vehicle
PA: Thermal Solutions Manufacturing, Inc.
25 Century Blvd Ste 210
Nashville TN
800 359-9186

(P-9469)
THMX HOLDINGS LLC
Also Called: Thermal Dynamics
4850 E Airport Dr (91761-7818)
PHONE..................................909 390-3944
▲ **EMP:** 187
SIC: 3714 Motor vehicle parts and
accessories

(P-9470)
**THYSSENKRUPP BILSTEIN
AMER INC**
13225 Danielson St # 100 (92064-6843)
PHONE..................................858 386-5900
Doug Robertson, *VP*
EMP: 42
SALES (corp-wide): 40.78B **Privately Held**
Web: www.bilstein.com
SIC: 3714 5013 Motor vehicle parts and
accessories; Motor vehicle supplies and
new parts
HQ: Thyssenkrupp Bilstein Of America, Inc.
8685 Bilstein Blvd
Hamilton OH
513 881-7600

(P-9471)
TILTON ENGINEERING INC
25 Easy St (93427-9566)
P.O. Box 1787 (93427-1787)
PHONE..................................805 688-2353
Jason Wahl, *Pr*
Todd Cooper, *
▲ **EMP:** 50 **EST:** 1972
SQ FT: 15,000
SALES (est): 6.35MM **Privately Held**
Web: www.tiltonracing.com
SIC: 3714 Motor vehicle parts and
accessories

(P-9472)
TMI PRODUCTS INC
Also Called: TMI Visualogic
1493 E Bentley Dr Ste 102 (92879-5102)
PHONE..................................951 272-1996
▲ **EMP:** 150 **EST:** 1982
SALES (est): 28.31MM **Privately Held**
Web: www.tmiproducts.com
SIC: 3714 2399 Motor vehicle parts and
accessories; Seat covers, automobile

(P-9473)
TRANS-DAPT CALIFORNIA INC
12438 Putnam St (90602-1002)
PHONE..................................562 921-0404
Robert Vandergriff, *Pr*
Ron Funfar, *General Vice President**
Jan Garner, *
EMP: 40 **EST:** 1959
SQ FT: 37,000
SALES (est): 2.75MM **Privately Held**
Web: www.hedman.com
SIC: 3714 Motor vehicle parts and
accessories

(P-9474)
TRANSGO LLC
Also Called: Transco
2621 Merced Ave (91733-1905)
PHONE..................................626 443-7456
Gilbert W Younger, *Prin*
EMP: 27 **EST:** 1976
SQ FT: 4,560
SALES (est): 4.88MM **Privately Held**
Web: www.transgo.com
SIC: 3714 Motor vehicle parts and
accessories

(P-9475)
TRANSPORTATION POWER LLC
Also Called: Transpower
2057 Aldergrove Ave (92029-1902)
PHONE..................................858 248-4255
Michael C Simon, *Pr*
Paul Scott, *
James Burns, *
EMP: 45 **EST:** 2010
SALES (est): 12.77MM
SALES (corp-wide): 28.07B **Publicly Held**
Web: www.transpowerusa.com
SIC: 3714 Motor vehicle parts and
accessories
HQ: Meritor, Inc.
2135 W Maple Rd
Troy MI

(P-9476)
TUBE TECHNOLOGIES INC
Also Called: TTI Performance Exhaust
1555 Consumer Cir (92878-3226)
PHONE..................................951 371-4878
Sam Davis, *Pr*
Raul Rodriguez, *
Tom Nakawatase, *
Trini Respico, *
▲ **EMP:** 30 **EST:** 1988

SQ FT: 18,400
SALES (est): 2.69MM **Privately Held**
Web: www.ttiexhaust.com
SIC: 3714 3498 Exhaust systems and parts,
motor vehicle; Tube fabricating (contract
bending and shaping)
PA: Jindal Saw Limited
Jindal Centre, 12 Bhikaiji
New Delhi DL

(P-9477)
U S WHEEL CORPORATION
Also Called: US Wheel
15702 Producer Ln (92649-1303)
PHONE..................................714 892-0021
Eliot Mason, *Pr*
◆ **EMP:** 20 **EST:** 1986
SQ FT: 135,000
SALES (est): 8.18MM **Privately Held**
Web: www.uswheel.com
SIC: 3714 5013 Wheels, motor vehicle;
Wheels, motor vehicle

(P-9478)
UFO DESIGNS
Also Called: S F Technology
16730 Gridley Rd (90703-1730)
PHONE..................................562 924-5763
Jitu Patel, *Pr*
EMP: 22
SALES (corp-wide): 2.49MM **Privately
Held**
Web: www.ufodesign.com
SIC: 3714 3089 Motor vehicle parts and
accessories; Plastics processing
PA: U.F.O. Designs
5812 Machine Dr
Huntington Beach CA
714 892-4420

(P-9479)
ULTRA WHEEL COMPANY
Also Called: Platinum
586 N Gilbert St (92833-2549)
PHONE..................................714 449-7100
Sharon A Wood, *Pr*
Fred Dobler, *
James Smith, *Stockholder**
Jim Smith, *
▼ **EMP:** 25 **EST:** 1984
SQ FT: 65,000
SALES (est): 5.21MM **Privately Held**
Web: www.ultrawheel.com
SIC: 3714 Motor vehicle parts and
accessories

(P-9480)
UNI FILTER INC
1468 Manhattan Ave (92831-5222)
PHONE..................................714 535-6933
Lanny R Mitchell, *Pr*
Kathi Perry, *
Tom Gross, *
Robert A Nichols, *Stockholder**
Kenneth E Mitchell, *Stockholder**
EMP: 19 **EST:** 1971
SQ FT: 26,000
SALES (est): 2.17MM **Privately Held**
Web: www.unifilter.com
SIC: 3714 Filters: oil, fuel, and air, motor
vehicle

(P-9481)
US HYBRID CORPORATION (HQ)
2660 Columbia St (90503-3802)
PHONE..................................310 212-1200
Gordon Abas Goodarzi, *CEO*
▲ **EMP:** 24 **EST:** 1999
SALES (est): 12.61MM **Publicly Held**
Web: www.ushybrid.com

SIC: 3714 Motor vehicle engines and parts
PA: Ideanomics, Inc.
1441 Broadway Ste 5116
New York NY

(P-9482)
US MOTOR WORKS LLC (PA)
14722 Anson Ave (90670-5306)
PHONE..................................562 404-0488
◆ **EMP:** 43 **EST:** 1995
SQ FT: 37,000
SALES (est): 33.82MM **Privately Held**
Web: www.usmotorworks.com
SIC: 3714 Water pump, motor vehicle

(P-9483)
**US RADIATOR CORPORATION
(PA)**
4423 District Blvd (90058-3111)
P.O. Box 5486 (90255-9486)
PHONE..................................323 826-0965
Donald Armstrong, *Pr*
Tim Armstrong, *
William Zimmerman, *
▲ **EMP:** 29 **EST:** 1956
SQ FT: 35,000
SALES (est): 2.44MM
SALES (corp-wide): 2.44MM **Privately
Held**
Web: www.usradiator.com
SIC: 3714 Radiators and radiator shells and
cores, motor vehicle

(P-9484)
VETRONIX CORPORATION
2030 Alameda Padre Serra (93103-1716)
PHONE..................................805 966-2000
EMP: 152
SIC: 3714 3829 Motor vehicle parts and
accessories; Aircraft and motor vehicle
measurement equipment

(P-9485)
VINTIQUE INC
1828 W Sequoia Ave (92868-1018)
PHONE..................................714 634-1932
Chad Looney, *Pr*
Denise Looney, *VP*
Judy Looney, *Sec*
▲ **EMP:** 28 **EST:** 1973
SQ FT: 17,000
SALES (est): 2.17MM **Privately Held**
Web: www.vintique.com
SIC: 3714 Motor vehicle parts and
accessories

(P-9486)
WALKER PRODUCTS
Also Called: WALKER PRODUCTS
14291 Commerce Dr (92843-4944)
PHONE..................................714 554-5151
Chris Weaver, *Genl Mgr*
EMP: 50
SALES (corp-wide): 48.05MM **Privately
Held**
Web: www.walkerproducts.com
SIC: 3714 Motor vehicle parts and
accessories
PA: Walker Products, Inc.
525 W Congress St
Pacific MO
636 257-2400

(P-9487)
WILWOOD ENGINEERING (PA)
4700 Calle Bolero (93012-8561)
PHONE..................................805 388-1188
William H Wood, *Pr*
▲ **EMP:** 119 **EST:** 1977
SALES (est): 22.43MM

PRODUCTS & SVCS

SALES (corp-wide): 22.43MM **Privately Held**
Web: www.wilwood.com
SIC: 3714 Motor vehicle parts and accessories

(P-9488)
WSW CORP (PA)
Also Called: Waag
16000 Strathern St (91406-1316)
PHONE..............................818 989-5008
Gary Waagenaar, *CEO*
Mike Calka, *
Jennifer Waagenaar, *
▲ **EMP:** 45 EST: 1978
SQ FT: 55,000
SALES (est): 6.65MM
SALES (corp-wide): 6.65MM **Privately Held**
Web: www.waag.com
SIC: 3714 5712 Motor vehicle parts and accessories; Beds and accessories

3715 Truck Trailers

(P-9489)
ANDERSEN INDUSTRIES INC
17079 Muskrat Ave (92301-2259)
PHONE..............................760 246-8766
Steven Andersen, *CEO*
Wayne Andersen, *
Neil Andersen, *
EMP: 25 EST: 1980
SQ FT: 110,000
SALES (est): 4.88MM **Privately Held**
Web: www.andersenmp.com
SIC: 3715 3441 3444 Truck trailers; Fabricated structural metal; Hoppers, sheet metal

(P-9490)
BLACKSERIES CAMPERS INC
Also Called: Black Series Campers
19501 E Walnut Dr S (91748-2318)
PHONE..............................833 822-6737
Hongwei Qiu, *CEO*
Yichun Chen, *Sec*
EMP: 20 EST: 2017
SALES (est): 1.1MM **Privately Held**
Web: www.blackseries.net
SIC: 3715 Truck trailers

(P-9491)
CIE MANUFACTURING LLC
10530 Sessler St (90280-7252)
PHONE..............................877 711-0725
EMP: 29 EST: 2021
SALES (est): 9.08MM **Privately Held**
Web: www.ciemanufacturing.com
SIC: 3715 Truck trailers

(P-9492)
CIMC INTERMODAL EQUIPMENT LLC (HQ)
Also Called: Cimc Intermodal Equipment
10530 Sessler St (90280-7252)
PHONE..............................562 904-8600
▲ **EMP:** 70 EST: 2007
SALES (est): 43.48MM **Privately Held**
Web: www.ciemanufacturing.com
SIC: 3715 7539 Truck trailer chassis; Trailer repair
PA: China International Marine Containers (Group) Co., Ltd.
Floor 8, Zhongji Group Yanfa Center, No.2, Shekou Gangwan Avenue
Shenzhen GD

(P-9493)
DEXTER AXLE COMPANY
Also Called: Unique Functional Products
135 Sunshine Ln (92069-1733)
PHONE..............................760 744-1610
Steve Moore, *Dir*
EMP: 94
SALES (corp-wide): 1.41B **Privately Held**
Web: www.dexteraxle.com
SIC: 3715 3714 Trailer bodies; Motor vehicle parts and accessories
HQ: Dexter Axle Company Llc
2900 Industrial Pkwy
Elkhart IN

(P-9494)
OWEN TRAILERS INC
9020 Jurupa Rd (92509-3106)
P.O. Box 36 (90633-0036)
PHONE..............................951 361-4557
Loren Owen Junior, *Pr*
Angela P Owen, *
EMP: 25 EST: 1946
SQ FT: 34,000
SALES (est): 2.47MM **Privately Held**
Web: www.owentrailers.com
SIC: 3715 Truck trailers

(P-9495)
REFRIGRATED TRCK SOLUTIONS LLC
1115 E Dominguez St (90746-3517)
PHONE..............................323 594-4500
Frederick Lukken, *Pr*
EMP: 26 EST: 2015
SALES (est): 3.5MM **Privately Held**
Web: www.truckreefer.com
SIC: 3715 Truck trailers

(P-9496)
UNIQUE FUNCTIONAL PRODUCTS
Also Called: U F P
135 Sunshine Ln (92069-1733)
PHONE..............................760 744-1610
▲ **EMP:** 125
SIC: 3715 3714 Trailer bodies; Motor vehicle parts and accessories

(P-9497)
UNITED STATES LOGISTICS GROUP
Also Called: US Logistics
2700 Rose Ave Ste A (90755-1929)
P.O. Box 10129 (91209-3129)
PHONE..............................562 989-9555
Khachatur Khudikyan, *CEO*
EMP: 32 EST: 2009
SALES (est): 2.45MM **Privately Held**
Web: www.uslginc.com
SIC: 3715 Truck trailers

(P-9498)
UTILITY TRAILER MANUFACTURING (PA)
17295 Railroad St Ste A (91748-1043)
PHONE..............................626 965-1514
Paul F Bennett, *CEO*
Harold C Bennett, *
Craig M Bennett, *
Jeffrey J Bennett, *
Stephen F Bennett, *
◆ **EMP:** 300 EST: 1914
SQ FT: 50,000
SALES (est): 897.7MM
SALES (corp-wide): 897.7MM **Privately Held**
Web: www.utilitytrailer.com
SIC: 3715 Truck trailers

(P-9499)
UTILITY TRAILER MFG CO
Also Called: Utility Trlr Sls Southern Cal
15567 Valley Blvd (92335-6351)
PHONE..............................909 428-8300
TOLL FREE: 800
Thayne Stanger, *Brnch Mgr*
EMP: 178
SALES (corp-wide): 897.7MM **Privately Held**
Web: www.utilitytrailer.com
SIC: 3715 Semitrailers for truck tractors
PA: Utility Trailer Manufacturing Company, Llc
17295 Railroad St Ste A
City Of Industry CA
626 965-1514

(P-9500)
UTILITY TRAILER MFG CO
Tautliner Division
17295 Railroad St Ste A (91748-1043)
PHONE..............................909 594-6026
Linda Baker, *Mgr*
EMP: 141
SALES (corp-wide): 897.7MM **Privately Held**
Web: www.utilitytrailer.com
SIC: 3715 5199 Truck trailers; Tarpaulins
PA: Utility Trailer Manufacturing Company, Llc
17295 Railroad St Ste A
City Of Industry CA
626 965-1514

3716 Motor Homes

(P-9501)
FLEETWOOD MOTOR HOMES-CALIFINC (DH)
Also Called: Fleetwood Homes
3125 Myers St (92503-5527)
P.O. Box 7638 (92513-7638)
PHONE..............................951 354-3000
Edward B Caudill, *CEO*
Elden L Smith, *
Boyd R Plowman, *
Forrest D Theobald, *
Lyle N Larkin, *
▲ **EMP:** 210 EST: 1976
SQ FT: 262,900
SALES (est): 52.01MM **Privately Held**
SIC: 3716 Motor homes
HQ: Fleetwood Enterprises, Inc.
1351 Pomona Rd Ste 230
Corona CA
951 354-3000

(P-9502)
REXHALL INDUSTRIES INC
26857 Tannahill Ave (91387-3969)
PHONE..............................661 726-5470
William Jonathan Rex, *Ch Bd*
Cheryl Rex, *Corporate Secretary*
James C Rex, *General Vice President*
▲ **EMP:** 46 EST: 1986
SQ FT: 120,000
SALES (est): 4.99MM **Privately Held**
Web: www.rexhall.com
SIC: 3716 Motor homes

3721 Aircraft

(P-9503)
AEROVIRONMENT INC
825 S Myrtle Ave (91016-8600)
PHONE..............................626 357-9983
Stewart Hindle, *Mgr*

EMP: 42
SALES (corp-wide): 540.54MM **Publicly Held**
Web: www.avinc.com
SIC: 3721 Aircraft
PA: Aerovironment, Inc.
241 18th St S Ste 415
Arlington VA
805 520-8350

(P-9504)
AEROVIRONMENT INC
900 Innovators Way (93065-2072)
PHONE..............................805 520-8350
Wahid Nawabi, *Pr*
EMP: 25
SALES (corp-wide): 540.54MM **Publicly Held**
Web: www.avinc.com
SIC: 3721 Gliders (aircraft)
PA: Aerovironment, Inc.
241 18th St S Ste 415
Arlington VA
805 520-8350

(P-9505)
AEROVIRONMENT INC
1610 S Magnolia Ave (91016-4547)
PHONE..............................626 357-9983
EMP: 23
SALES (corp-wide): 540.54MM **Publicly Held**
Web: www.avinc.com
SIC: 3721 Aircraft
PA: Aerovironment, Inc.
241 18th St S Ste 415
Arlington VA
805 520-8350

(P-9506)
AEROVIRONMENT INC
222 E Huntington Dr Ste 118 (91016-8014)
P.O. Box 5130 (93062-5130)
PHONE..............................626 357-9983
EMP: 37
SALES (corp-wide): 540.54MM **Publicly Held**
Web: www.avinc.com
SIC: 3721 Aircraft
PA: Aerovironment, Inc.
241 18th St S Ste 415
Arlington VA
805 520-8350

(P-9507)
AIBOT US OPERATION INC
2883 E Spring St Ste 200 (90806-2467)
PHONE..............................562 283-3286
Jack Shen, *Off Mgr*
EMP: 21
SALES (est): 1.11MM **Privately Held**
SIC: 3721 Aircraft

(P-9508)
ALLCLEAR INC
200 N Pacific Coast Hwy Ste 1350 (90245)
PHONE..............................424 316-1596
Darryl Mayhorn, *CEO*
EMP: 42 EST: 2020
SALES (est): 944.16K **Privately Held**
Web: www.goallclear.com
SIC: 3721 Aircraft

(P-9509)
AMERICAN SCENCE TECH AS T CORP
2372 Morse Ave Ste 571 (92614-6234)
PHONE..............................310 773-1978
Kinda Assouad, *Brnch Mgr*
EMP: 85

SALES (corp-wide): 348MM **Privately Held**
SIC: **3721** 3724 3761 3764 Aircraft; Aircraft engines and engine parts; Guided missiles and space vehicles; Space propulsion units and parts
PA: American Science & Technology (As&T) Corporation
50 California St Fl 21
San Francisco CA
415 251-2800

(P-9510)
APM MANUFACTURING
341 W Blueridge Ave (92865-4201)
PHONE..............................714 453-0100
Gilles Madelmont, *Contrlr*
EMP: 105
SALES (corp-wide): 43.53MM **Privately Held**
Web: www.anaheimprecision.com
SIC: **3721** Aircraft
HQ: Apm Manufacturing
1738 N Neville St
Orange CA
714 453-0100

(P-9511)
BOEING
15320 Barranca Pkwy (92618-2215)
PHONE..............................949 623-2222
EMP: 42 EST: 2019
SALES (est): 578.95K **Privately Held**
Web: jobs.boeing.com
SIC: **3721** Airplanes, fixed or rotary wing

(P-9512)
BOEING COML SATELLITE SVCS INC (HQ)
900 N Pacific Coast Hwy (90245-2710)
PHONE..............................310 335-6682
Craig R Cooning, *CEO*
EMP: 17 EST: 2014
SALES (est): 1.25MM
SALES (corp-wide): 66.61B **Publicly Held**
Web: www.boeing.com
SIC: **3721** Aircraft
PA: The Boeing Company
929 Long Bridge Dr
Arlington VA
703 414-6338

(P-9513)
BOEING COMPANY
Also Called: Boeing
4000 N Lakewood Blvd (90808-1700)
PHONE..............................562 496-1000
Nan Bouchard, *VP*
EMP: 2000
SALES (corp-wide): 66.61B **Publicly Held**
Web: www.boeing.com
SIC: **3721** Airplanes, fixed or rotary wing
PA: The Boeing Company
929 Long Bridge Dr
Arlington VA
703 414-6338

(P-9514)
BOEING COMPANY
Also Called: Boeing
2220 E Carson St (90810-1226)
PHONE..............................310 522-2809
Jim Brown, *Mgr*
EMP: 125
SQ FT: 71,912
SALES (corp-wide): 66.61B **Publicly Held**
Web: www.boeing.com
SIC: **3721** Aircraft
PA: The Boeing Company
929 Long Bridge Dr

Arlington VA
703 414-6338

(P-9515)
BOEING COMPANY
Also Called: Boeing
4060 N Lakewood Blvd (90808-1700)
P.O. Box 200 (90801-0200)
PHONE..............................562 593-5511
Linda Van Reeden, *Mgr*
EMP: 1400
SALES (corp-wide): 66.61B **Publicly Held**
Web: www.boeing.com
SIC: **3721** Airplanes, fixed or rotary wing
PA: The Boeing Company
929 Long Bridge Dr
Arlington VA
703 414-6338

(P-9516)
BOEING COMPANY
Also Called: Boeing
Bldg-1454 Receiving (92135)
PHONE..............................619 545-8382
EMP: 996
SALES (corp-wide): 66.61B **Publicly Held**
Web: www.boeing.com
SIC: **3721** Airplanes, fixed or rotary wing
PA: The Boeing Company
929 Long Bridge Dr
Arlington VA
703 414-6338

(P-9517)
BOEING INTLLCTUAL PRPRTY LCNSI
14441 Astronautics Ln (92647-2080)
PHONE..............................562 797-2020
EMP: 321 EST: 2011
SALES (est): 52.95MM
SALES (corp-wide): 66.61B **Publicly Held**
SIC: **3721** Airplanes, fixed or rotary wing
PA: The Boeing Company
929 Long Bridge Dr
Arlington VA
703 414-6338

(P-9518)
BOEING SATELLITE SYSTEMS INC
Also Called: Boeing
2300 E Imperial Hwy (90245-2813)
P.O. Box 92919 (90009-2919)
PHONE..............................310 568-2735
Steve Tsukamoto, *Mgr*
EMP: 4161
SALES (corp-wide): 66.61B **Publicly Held**
Web: www.boeing.com
SIC: **3721** Aircraft
HQ: Boeing Satellite Systems, Inc.
900 N Pacific Coast Hwy
El Segundo CA

(P-9519)
CHIPTON-ROSS INC
420 Culver Blvd (90293-7706)
PHONE..............................310 414-7800
Judith Hinkley, *Pr*
EMP: 100 EST: 1983
SQ FT: 6,000
SALES (est): 9.01MM **Privately Held**
Web: www.chiptonross.com
SIC: **3721** 3731 8731 7363 Motorized aircraft ; Military ships, building and repairing; Commercial physical research; Temporary help service

(P-9520)
COMAC AMERICA CORPORATION
4350 Von Karman Ave Ste 400 (92660-2007)
PHONE..............................760 616-9614
Wei Ye, *CEO*
EMP: 31 EST: 2013
SALES (est): 4.31MM **Privately Held**
SIC: **3721** Aircraft
PA: Commercial Aircraft Corporation Of China,.Ltd.
No.1919, Shibo Avenue, Pudong New District
Shanghai SH

(P-9521)
EMPIRICAL SYSTEMS AROSPC INC (PA)
Also Called: Esaero
3580 Sueldo St (93401-7338)
P.O. Box 595 (93448-0595)
PHONE..............................805 474-5900
Andrew Gibson, *Pr*
Benjamin Schiltgen, *
EMP: 124 EST: 2003
SQ FT: 1,000
SALES (est): 22.49MM
SALES (corp-wide): 22.49MM **Privately Held**
Web: www.esaero.com
SIC: **3721** Aircraft

(P-9522)
FASTENER DIST HOLDINGS LLC
Also Called: Fdh Aero
5200 Sheila St (90040-3906)
PHONE..............................213 620-9950
EMP: 27
SALES (corp-wide): 470.7MM **Privately Held**
Web: www.aircraftfast.com
SIC: **3721** Aircraft
HQ: Fastener Distribution Holdings, Llc
5200 Sheila St
Commerce CA
213 620-9950

(P-9523)
GENERAL ATMICS ARNTCAL SYSTEMS (DH)
Also Called: Ga-Asi
14200 Kirkham Way (92064-7103)
PHONE..............................858 312-2810
Neal Blue, *Pr*
Brad Clark, *
Stacy Jakuttis, *
Tony Navarra, *
◆ EMP: 500 EST: 1992
SQ FT: 900,000
SALES (est): 1.59B **Privately Held**
Web: www.ga-asi.com
SIC: **3721** Aircraft
HQ: Aeronautical Systems Inc
16761 Via Del Campo Ct
San Diego CA

(P-9524)
GENERAL ATMICS ARNTCAL SYSTEMS
11906 Tech Center Ct (92064-7139)
PHONE..............................858 455-3358
EMP: 121
Web: www.ga-asi.com
SIC: **3721** Aircraft
HQ: General Atomics Aeronautical Systems, Inc.
14200 Kirkham Way
Poway CA

(P-9525)
GENERAL ATMICS ARNTCAL SYSTEMS
13330 Evening Creek Dr N (92128-4110)
PHONE..............................858 964-6700
Neal Blue, *Pr*
EMP: 459
Web: www.ga-asi.com
SIC: **3721** Aircraft
HQ: General Atomics Aeronautical Systems, Inc.
14200 Kirkham Way
Poway CA

(P-9526)
GENERAL ATMICS ARNTCAL SYSTEMS
13550 Stowe Dr (92064-6858)
PHONE..............................858 312-4247
EMP: 347
Web: www.ga-asi.com
SIC: **3721** Aircraft
HQ: General Atomics Aeronautical Systems, Inc.
14200 Kirkham Way
Poway CA

(P-9527)
GENERAL ATMICS ARNTCAL SYSTEMS
12220 Parkway Centre Dr (92064-6867)
PHONE..............................858 455-3000
Eric Jones, *Brnch Mgr*
EMP: 222
Web: www.ga-asi.com
SIC: **3721** Aircraft
HQ: General Atomics Aeronautical Systems, Inc.
14200 Kirkham Way
Poway CA

(P-9528)
GENERAL ATMICS ARNTCAL SYSTEMS
16761 Via Del Campo Ct (92127-1713)
PHONE..............................858 762-6700
EMP: 730
Web: www.ga-asi.com
SIC: **3721** Aircraft
HQ: General Atomics Aeronautical Systems, Inc.
14200 Kirkham Way
Poway CA

(P-9529)
GENERAL ATMICS ARNTCAL SYSTEMS
Also Called: General Atomics
3550 General Atomics Ct (92121-1122)
PHONE..............................858 455-2810
EMP: 500
Web: www.ga-asi.com
SIC: **3721** Aircraft
HQ: General Atomics Aeronautical Systems, Inc.
14200 Kirkham Way
Poway CA

(P-9530)
GENERAL ATMICS ARNTCAL SYSTEMS
12365 Crosthwaite Cir (92064-6817)
PHONE..............................858 762-6700
Cyndra Flanagen, *Dir*
EMP: 500
Web: www.ga-asi.com
SIC: **3721** Aircraft

PRODUCTS & SVCS

HQ: General Atomics Aeronautical
Systems, Inc.
14200 Kirkham Way
Poway CA

(P-9531)
GENERAL ATOMIC AERON
14040 Danielson St (92064-6857)
PHONE.................................858 455-4560
EMP: 232
Web: www.ga-asi.com
SIC: 3721 Aircraft
HQ: General Atomics Aeronautical
Systems, Inc.
14200 Kirkham Way
Poway CA

(P-9532)
GENERAL ATOMIC AERON
13950 Stowe Dr (92064-8803)
PHONE.................................858 312-3428
James N Blue, *Brnch Mgr*
EMP: 177
Web: www.ga-asi.com
SIC: 3721 Aircraft
HQ: General Atomics Aeronautical
Systems, Inc.
14200 Kirkham Way
Poway CA

(P-9533)
GENERAL ATOMIC AERON
14115 Stowe Dr (92064-7145)
PHONE.................................858 312-2543
EMP: 500
Web: www.ga-asi.com
SIC: 3721 Aircraft
HQ: General Atomics Aeronautical
Systems, Inc.
14200 Kirkham Way
Poway CA

(P-9534)
GENERAL ATOMIC AERON
Also Called: General Atomics
73 El Mirage Airport Rd Ste B (92301-9540)
PHONE.................................760 388-8208
Gary Bener, *Brnch Mgr*
EMP: 200
SQ FT: 34,425
Web: www.ga-asi.com
SIC: 3721 Aircraft
HQ: General Atomics Aeronautical
Systems, Inc.
14200 Kirkham Way
Poway CA

(P-9535)
GENERAL ELECTRIC COMPANY
Also Called: GE
18000 Phantom St (92394-7913)
PHONE.................................760 530-5200
John Hardell, *Prin*
EMP: 50
SALES (corp-wide): 76.56B **Publicly Held**
Web: www.ge.com
SIC: 3721 Aircraft
PA: General Electric Company
1 Financial Ctr Ste 3700
Boston MA
617 443-3000

(P-9536)
GKN AEROSPACE
12242 Western Ave (92841-2916)
PHONE.................................714 653-7531
EMP: 21 **EST:** 2016
SALES (est): 9.62MM **Privately Held**
Web: www.gknaerospace.com
SIC: 3721 Aircraft

(P-9537)
GULF STREAMS
4150 E Donald Douglas Dr (90808-1725)
PHONE.................................562 420-1818
Mike Kambourian, *Owner*
▲ **EMP:** 21 **EST:** 1960
SALES (est): 4.23MM **Privately Held**
SIC: 3721 Aircraft

(P-9538)
GULFSTREAM AEROSPACE CORP GA
4150 E Donald Douglas Dr (90808-1725)
PHONE.................................562 420-1818
Barry Russell, *Brnch Mgr*
EMP: 1015
SALES (corp-wide): 39.41B **Publicly Held**
SIC: 3721 Aircraft
HQ: Gulfstream Aerospace Corporation
(Georgia)
500 Gulfstream Rd
Savannah GA
912 965-3000

(P-9539)
GULFSTREAM AEROSPACE CORP GA
9818 Mina Ave (90605-3035)
PHONE.................................562 907-9300
EMP: 254
SALES (corp-wide): 39.41B **Publicly Held**
SIC: 3721 Airplanes, fixed or rotary wing
HQ: Gulfstream Aerospace Corporation
(Georgia)
500 Gulfstream Rd
Savannah GA
912 965-3000

(P-9540)
GULFSTREAM AEROSPACE CORP GA
Also Called: Gulfstream
16644 Roscoe Blvd (91406-1103)
PHONE.................................805 236-5755
EMP: 380
SALES (corp-wide): 39.41B **Publicly Held**
SIC: 3721 Aircraft
HQ: Gulfstream Aerospace Corporation
(Georgia)
500 Gulfstream Rd
Savannah GA
912 965-3000

(P-9541)
JETZERO INC
4301 E Donald Douglas Dr (90808-1730)
PHONE.................................949 474-8222
Thomas O'leary, *CEO*
EMP: 40 **EST:** 2021
SALES (est): 6.3MM **Privately Held**
Web: www.jetzero.aero
SIC: 3721 Aircraft

(P-9542)
JVR SHEETMETAL FABRICATION INC
Also Called: Talsco
7101 Patterson Dr (92841-1415)
PHONE.................................714 841-2464
EMP: 33 **EST:** 2003
SQ FT: 1,000
SALES (est): 4.58MM **Privately Held**
Web: www.talsco.com
SIC: 3721 Aircraft

(P-9543)
LEARJET INC
16750 Schoenborn St (91343-6108)

PHONE.................................818 894-8241
Tonya Sudduth, *Brnch Mgr*
EMP: 28
SALES (corp-wide): 6.91B **Privately Held**
Web: www.bombardier.com
SIC: 3721 Aircraft
HQ: Learjet Inc.
1 Learjet Way
Wichita KS
316 946-2000

(P-9544)
MADN AIRCRAFT HINGE
26911 Ruether Ave Ste Q (91351-6513)
PHONE.................................661 257-3430
Aroosh Shahbazian, *CEO*
EMP: 45 **EST:** 2020
SALES (est): 1.17MM **Privately Held**
Web: www.madnaircrafthinge.com
SIC: 3721 3728 Aircraft; Aircraft parts and
equipment, nec

(P-9545)
NORTHROP GRUMMAN SYSTEMS CORP
Northrop Grumman
1 Space Park Blvd # D1 1024 (90278-1071)
PHONE.................................310 812-4321
EMP: 305
Web: www.northropgrumman.com
SIC: 3721 3761 3728 Airplanes, fixed or
rotary wing; Guided missiles, complete;
Fuselage assembly, aircraft
HQ: Northrop Grumman Systems
Corporation
2980 Fairview Park Dr
Falls Church VA
703 280-2900

(P-9546)
NORTHROP GRUMMAN SYSTEMS CORP
Also Called: Aerospace Systems
1 Space Park Blvd (90278-1071)
PHONE.................................310 812-1089
EMP: 305
Web: www.northropgrumman.com
SIC: 3721 3761 3728 3812 Airplanes, fixed
or rotary wing; Guided missiles, complete;
Fuselage assembly, aircraft; Inertial
guidance systems
HQ: Northrop Grumman Systems
Corporation
2980 Fairview Park Dr
Falls Church VA
703 280-2900

(P-9547)
NORTHROP GRUMMAN SYSTEMS CORP
Also Called: Air Combat Systems
3520 E Avenue M (93550-7401)
PHONE.................................661 272-7000
David G Hogarth, *Mgr*
EMP: 300
Web: www.northropgrumman.com
SIC: 3721 3812 3761 Aircraft; Search and
navigation equipment; Guided missiles and
space vehicles
HQ: Northrop Grumman Systems
Corporation
2980 Fairview Park Dr
Falls Church VA
703 280-2900

(P-9548)
OVERAIR INC
3001 S Susan St (92704-6434)
PHONE.................................949 503-7503

Benjamin Tigner, *CEO*
Valerie Manning, *CCO**
EMP: 30 **EST:** 2019
SALES (est): 5.25MM **Privately Held**
Web: www.overair.com
SIC: 3721 Research and development on
aircraft by the manufacturer

(P-9549)
PCA AEROSPACE INC
15282 Newsboy Cir (92649-1202)
PHONE.................................714 901-5209
Ron Brandenburg, *Pr*
EMP: 26
SALES (corp-wide): 19.09MM **Privately
Held**
SIC: 3721 Research and development on
aircraft by the manufacturer
PA: Pca Aerospace, Inc.
17800 Gothard St
Huntington Beach CA
714 841-1750

(P-9550)
QUALITY TECH MFG INC
170 W Mindanao St (92316-2946)
PHONE.................................909 465-9565
EMP: 37 **EST:** 1996
SQ FT: 18,000
SALES (est): 4.63MM **Privately Held**
Web: www.qualitytechmfg.com
SIC: 3721 Aircraft

(P-9551)
SCALED COMPOSITES LLC
1624 Flight Line (93501-1663)
PHONE.................................661 824-4541
Greg Morris, *Pr*
Mark Taylor, *VP*
Jennifer Santiago, *Ex VP*
Ben Diachun, *VP*
Jason Kelley, *VP*
EMP: 500 **EST:** 2000
SQ FT: 160,000
SALES (est): 98.52MM **Publicly Held**
Web: www.scaled.com
SIC: 3721 3999 8711 Aircraft; Models,
except toy; Aviation and/or aeronautical
engineering
HQ: Northrop Grumman Systems
Corporation
2980 Fairview Park Dr
Falls Church VA
703 280-2900

(P-9552)
SHIELD AI INC (PA)
600 W Broadway Ste 250 (92101-3357)
PHONE.................................619 719-5740
Brandon Tseng, *Ch Bd*
Ryan Tseng, *CEO*
Jim Carlson, *Sec*
Kingsley Afemikhe, *CFO*
Thomas Tull, *Dir*
EMP: 601 **EST:** 2015
SQ FT: 20,000
SALES (est): 90.64MM
SALES (corp-wide): 90.64MM **Privately
Held**
Web: www.shield.ai
SIC: 3721 Aircraft

(P-9553)
SOARING AMERICA CORPORATION
Also Called: Mooney International
8354 Kimball Ave # F360 (91708-9267)
PHONE.................................909 270-2628
Cheng-yuan Jerry Chen, *CEO*
Albert Li, *CFO*

EMP: 45 EST: 2012
SALES (est): 3.71MM **Privately Held**
SIC: 3721 3728 Research and development on aircraft by the manufacturer; R and D by manuf., aircraft parts and auxiliary equipment

(P-9554)
SPACE EXPLORATION TECH CORP
731 Kelp Rd Slc-4 (93437)
PHONE..................310 848-4410
EMP: 45
SALES (corp-wide): 2.07B **Privately Held**
Web: www.spacex.com
SIC: 3721 Aircraft
PA: Space Exploration Technologies Corp.
1 Rocket Rd
Hawthorne CA
310 363-6000

(P-9555)
SPORT KITES INC
Also Called: Wills Wing
500 W Blueridge Ave (92865-4206)
PHONE..................714 998-6359
▲ EMP: 18 EST: 1973
SQ FT: 16,000
SALES (est): 2.52MM **Privately Held**
SIC: 3721 Hang gliders

(P-9556)
SWIFT TACTICAL SYSTEMS INC
1141 A Via Callejon (92673-6230)
PHONE..................800 547-9438
Richard Heise, *CEO*
EMP: 25 EST: 2019
SALES (est): 2.13MM **Privately Held**
Web: www.swiftautonomy.com
SIC: 3721 Aircraft

(P-9557)
TRI MODELS INC
5191 Oceanus Dr (92649-1026)
PHONE..................714 896-0823
Prince A Herzog Senior, *CEO*
Jeff Herzog, *
▲ EMP: 82 EST: 1972
SALES (est): 14.85MM **Privately Held**
Web: www.trimodels.com
SIC: 3721 Airplanes, fixed or rotary wing

(P-9558)
WORLDWIDE AEROS CORP
3971 Fredonia Dr (90068-1213)
PHONE..................818 344-3999
Igor Pasternak, *CEO*
▲ EMP: 82 EST: 1987
SALES (est): 8.84MM **Privately Held**
SIC: 3721 8711 Airships; Aviation and/or aeronautical engineering

3724 Aircraft Engines And Engine Parts

(P-9559)
AC&A ENTERPRISES LLC (HQ)
25671 Commercentre Dr (92630-8801)
PHONE..................949 716-3511
Justin Uchida, *CEO*
Justin Schultz, *
▲ EMP: 34 EST: 2004
SALES (est): 26.46MM
SALES (corp-wide): 189.21MM **Privately Held**
Web: www.appliedcomposites.com

SIC: 3724 3511 Aircraft engines and engine parts; Turbines and turbine generator sets
PA: Applied Composites Holdings, Llc
25692 Atlantic Ocean Dr
Lake Forest CA
949 716-3511

(P-9560)
ACCURATE GRINDING AND MFG CORP
807 E Parkridge Ave (92879-6609)
PHONE..................951 479-0909
Douglas Nilsen, *CEO*
Hans J Nilsen, *
David Nilsen, *
▲ EMP: 35 EST: 1950
SQ FT: 15,000
SALES (est): 8.5MM **Privately Held**
Web: shop.accuratefishing.com
SIC: 3724 3812 Aircraft engines and engine parts; Search and navigation equipment

(P-9561)
ADVANCED GRUND SYSTEMS ENGRG L (HQ)
Also Called: Agse
10805 Painter Ave (90670-4526)
PHONE..................562 906-9300
Diane Henderson, *CEO*
David Chetwood, *
▲ EMP: 40 EST: 1973
SALES (est): 23.69MM
SALES (corp-wide): 26.13MM **Privately Held**
Web: www.agsecorp.com
SIC: 3724 Aircraft engines and engine parts
PA: Westmont Industries Llc
10805 Painter Ave Uppr
Santa Fe Springs CA
562 944-6137

(P-9562)
AEROJET ROCKETDYNE DE INC
6633 Canoga Ave (91303-2703)
P.O. Box 7922 (91309-7922)
PHONE..................818 586-1000
Jerry Jackson, *Brnch Mgr*
EMP: 622
SALES (corp-wide): 17.06B **Publicly Held**
Web: www.l3harris.com
SIC: 3724 Aircraft engines and engine parts
HQ: Inc Aerojet Rocketdyne Of De
8900 De Soto Ave
Canoga Park CA
818 586-1000

(P-9563)
AMERICAN MTAL MFG RESOURCE INC
Also Called: American Metal
1989 W Holt Ave (91768-3352)
PHONE..................909 620-4500
EMP: 25 EST: 2007
SQ FT: 6,000
SALES (est): 2.52MM **Privately Held**
Web: www.ammrinc.com
SIC: 3724 3999 Aircraft engines and engine parts; Barber and beauty shop equipment

(P-9564)
CHROMALLOY COMPONENT SVCS INC
Precision Component Tech
7007 Consolidated Way (92121-2604)
PHONE..................858 877-2800
Nat Love, *Genl Mgr*
EMP: 41
SALES (corp-wide): 1.2B **Privately Held**
Web: www.chromalloy.com

SIC: 3724 Aircraft engines and engine parts
HQ: Chromalloy Component Services, Inc.
303 Industrial Park Rd
San Antonio TX
210 331-2300

(P-9565)
CHROMALLOY GAS TURBINE LLC
Also Called: Chromalloy Southwest
1749 Stergios Rd Ste 2 (92231-9657)
PHONE..................760 768-3723
EMP: 88
SALES (corp-wide): 1.2B **Privately Held**
Web: www.chromalloy.com
SIC: 3724 Aircraft engines and engine parts
HQ: Chromalloy Gas Turbine Llc
4100 Rca Blvd
Palm Beach Gardens FL
561 935-3571

(P-9566)
DUCOMMUN AEROSTRUCTURES INC (HQ)
268 E Gardena Blvd (90248-2814)
PHONE..................310 380-5390
Anthony Reardon, *CEO*
◆ EMP: 450 EST: 1949
SQ FT: 300,000
SALES (est): 378.08MM
SALES (corp-wide): 712.54MM **Publicly Held**
Web: www.ducommun.com
SIC: 3724 3812 3728 Aircraft engines and engine parts; Search and navigation equipment; Aircraft parts and equipment, nec
PA: Ducommun Incorporated
200 Sandpointe Ave # 700
Santa Ana CA
657 335-3665

(P-9567)
DUCOMMUN AEROSTRUCTURES INC
1885 N Batavia St (92865-4105)
PHONE..................714 637-4401
EMP: 106
SALES (corp-wide): 712.54MM **Publicly Held**
Web: www.ducommun.com
SIC: 3724 3812 3728 Aircraft engines and engine parts; Search and navigation equipment; Aircraft parts and equipment, nec
HQ: Ducommun Aerostructures, Inc.
268 E Gardena Blvd
Gardena CA
310 380-5390

(P-9568)
GARRETT MOTION INC
1778 Zinetta Rd Ste A (92231-9511)
PHONE..................760 357-3297
EMP: 59
SALES (corp-wide): 3.63B **Privately Held**
Web: www.garrettmotion.com
SIC: 3724 Aircraft engines and engine parts
PA: Garrett Motion Inc.
47548 Halyard Dr
Plymouth MI
734 359-5901

(P-9569)
GARRETT TRANSPORTATION I INC (HQ)
2525 W 190th St (90504-6002)
PHONE..................973 455-2000
Darius Adamczyk, *CEO*

EMP: 84 EST: 2018
SALES (est): 10.05MM
SALES (corp-wide): 3.63B **Privately Held**
SIC: 3724 Aircraft engines and engine parts
PA: Garrett Motion Inc.
47548 Halyard Dr
Plymouth MI
734 359-5901

(P-9570)
GKN AEROSPACE CHEM-TRONICS INC (DH)
Also Called: Chem-Tronics
1150 W Bradley Ave (92020-1504)
P.O. Box 1604 (92022-1604)
PHONE..................619 258-5000
Marcus J Bryson, *CEO*
Michael A Beck, *
Les Emanuel, *
Stacey Clapp, *
▲ EMP: 648 EST: 1953
SQ FT: 400,000
SALES (est): 194.63MM
SALES (corp-wide): 9.07B **Privately Held**
Web: www.gknaerospace.com
SIC: 3724 7699 Aircraft engines and engine parts; Aircraft and heavy equipment repair services
HQ: Gkn Limited
2nd Floor, One Central Boulevard
Solihull W MIDLANDS
121 210-9800

(P-9571)
HONEYWELL INTERNATIONAL INC
Also Called: Honeywell
233 Paulin Ave Box 8500 (92231-2615)
PHONE..................760 312-5300
William Bouscher, *Prin*
EMP: 17
SALES (corp-wide): 35.47B **Publicly Held**
Web: www.honeywell.com
SIC: 3724 Aircraft engines and engine parts
PA: Honeywell International Inc.
855 S Mint St
Charlotte NC
704 627-6200

(P-9572)
HONEYWELL INTERNATIONAL INC
Also Called: Honeywell
2525 W 190th St (90504-6002)
PHONE..................310 323-9500
Ken Defusco, *Brnch Mgr*
EMP: 1000
SALES (corp-wide): 35.47B **Publicly Held**
Web: www.honeywell.com
SIC: 3724 Aircraft engines and engine parts
PA: Honeywell International Inc.
855 S Mint St
Charlotte NC
704 627-6200

(P-9573)
INTERNATIONAL WIND INC (PA)
137 N Joy St (92879-1321)
PHONE..................562 240-3963
Cory Arendt, *Pr*
EMP: 49 EST: 2013
SALES (est): 7.67MM
SALES (corp-wide): 7.67MM **Privately Held**
Web: www.international-wind.com
SIC: 3724 8711 8742 Turbines, aircraft type; Engineering services; Management consulting services

PRODUCTS & SVCS

(P-9574)
IRISH INTERNATIONAL
5511 Skylab Rd (92647-2068)
PHONE..............................949 559-0930
Tom Mcfarland, *CEO*
Antonio Perez, *Corporate Secretary**
Jude Dozor, *
Mike Melancon, *
▲ EMP: 250 EST: 2015
SQ FT: 80,000
SALES (est): 9.35MM Privately Held
Web: www.encoregroup.aero
SIC: 3724 Aircraft engines and engine parts

(P-9575)
LOGISTICAL SUPPORT LLC
Also Called: RTC Aerospace
20409 Prairie St (91311-6029)
PHONE...............................818 341-3344
EMP: 125 EST: 1997
SQ FT: 14,600
SALES (est): 12.77MM Privately Held
Web: www.rtcaerospace.com
SIC: 3724 Aircraft engines and engine parts

(P-9576)
MARTON PRECISION MFG LLC
1365 S Acacia Ave (92831-5315)
PHONE...............................714 808-6523
Daniel J Marton, *Pr*
Mary Marton, *
EMP: 47 EST: 1986
SQ FT: 20,000
SALES (est): 12.27MM Privately Held
Web: www.martoninc.com
SIC: 3724 3599 3827 Aircraft engines and
engine parts; Machine and other job shop
work; Optical instruments and apparatus

(P-9577)
PARKER-HANNIFIN
CORPORATION
Fluid Systems Division
16666 Von Karman Ave (92606-4997)
PHONE...............................949 833-3000
Matthew Stafford, *Mgr*
EMP: 246
SALES (corp-wide): 19.07B Publicly Held
Web: www.parker.com
SIC: 3724 3728 Aircraft engines and engine
parts; Aircraft parts and equipment, nec
PA: Parker-Hannifin Corporation
6035 Parkland Blvd
Cleveland OH
216 896-3000

(P-9578)
PRINCETON TOOL INC
Also Called: Paragon Precision
25620 Rye Canyon Rd Ste A (91355-1139)
PHONE...............................661 257-1380
Kenneth Bevington Iii, *CEO*
EMP: 18
SALES (corp-wide): 20.3MM Privately
Held
Web: www.princetontool.com
SIC: 3724 Aircraft engines and engine parts
PA: Princeton Tool, Inc.
7830 Division Dr
Mentor OH
440 290-8666

(P-9579)
SAFRAN PWR UNITS SAN
DIEGO LLC
Also Called: Safran Power Units
4255 Ruffin Rd Ste 100 (92123-1247)
PHONE...............................858 223-2228
EMP: 70 EST: 2015

SQ FT: 22,000
SALES (est): 17.15MM
SALES (corp-wide): 650.78MM Privately
Held
Web: www.safran-group.com
SIC: 3724 Research and development on
aircraft engines and parts
HQ: Safran Power Units
8 Chemin Du Pont De Rupe
Toulouse
561375500

(P-9580)
SENIOR OPERATIONS LLC (HQ)
Also Called: Senior Aerospace Jet Products
9106 Balboa Ave (92123-1512)
PHONE...............................858 278-8400
Willis H Fletcher, *
Ronald R Blair, *
Steven Konold, *
John Shepherd, *
EMP: 142 EST: 1965
SQ FT: 125,000
SALES (est): 50.46MM
SALES (corp-wide): 1.02B Privately Held
Web: www.sajetproducts.com
SIC: 3724 3462 3444 Aircraft engines and
engine parts; Iron and steel forgings; Sheet
metalwork
PA: Senior Plc
59-61 High Street
Rickmansworth HERTS
192 377-5547

(P-9581)
THERMAL STRUCTURES INC
(DH)
2362 Railroad St (92878-5410)
PHONE...............................951 736-9911
Vaughn Barnes, *Pr*
▲ EMP: 270 EST: 1952
SQ FT: 175,000
SALES (est): 84.7MM Publicly Held
Web: www.thermalstructures.com
SIC: 3724 Aircraft engines and engine parts
HQ: Heico Aerospace Holdings Corp.
3000 Taft St
Hollywood FL
954 987-4000

(P-9582)
THERMAL STRUCTURES INC
2380 Railroad St (92878-5471)
PHONE...............................951 256-8051
EMP: 20
Web: www.thermalstructures.com
SIC: 3724 Aircraft engines and engine parts
HQ: Thermal Structures, Inc.
2362 Railroad St
Corona CA
951 736-9911

(P-9583)
VERTECHS ENTERPRISES INC
San Diego Welding and Forming
400 Raleigh Ave (92020)
PHONE...............................858 578-3900
Geosef Straza, *Pr*
EMP: 17
Web: www.vertechsusa.com
SIC: 3724 3728 Airfoils, aircraft engine;
Bodies, aircraft
PA: Vertechs Enterprises, Inc.
1071 Industrial Pl
El Cajon CA

3728 Aircraft Parts And Equipment, Nec

(P-9584)
A CDG BOEING COMPANY
4060 N Lakewood Blvd (90808-1700)
PHONE...............................562 608-2000
EMP: 225 EST: 2019
SALES (est): 700.81K Privately Held
SIC: 3728 Aircraft parts and equipment, nec

(P-9585)
A-INFO INC
60 Tesla (92618-4603)
PHONE...............................949 346-7326
Linda Williams, *Asst Mgr*
EMP: 35 EST: 2017
SALES (est): 2.5MM Privately Held
Web: www.ainfoinc.com
SIC: 3728 3812 5049 Aircraft parts and
equipment, nec; Antennas, radar or
communications; Analytical instruments

(P-9586)
ACE AIR MANUFACTURING
1430 W 135th St (90249-2218)
PHONE...............................310 323-7246
Aldo Lemus, *CEO*
EMP: 17 EST: 1957
SQ FT: 12,000
SALES (est): 2.34MM Privately Held
Web: www.aceairmfg.com
SIC: 3728 Aircraft parts and equipment, nec

(P-9587)
ACE CLEARWATER
ENTERPRISES INC (PA)
19815 Magellan Dr (90502-1107)
PHONE...............................310 323-2140
James D Dodson, *Pr*
Kellie Johnson, *
EMP: 100 EST: 1961
SALES (est): 46.01MM
SALES (corp-wide): 46.01MM Privately
Held
Web: www.aceclearwater.com
SIC: 3728 3544 7692 3812 Aircraft parts and
equipment, nec; Special dies, tools, jigs,
and fixtures; Welding repair; Search and
navigation equipment

(P-9588)
ACROMIL LLC
1168 Sherborn St (92879-2089)
PHONE...............................951 808-9929
David Nguyen, *Pr*
EMP: 60
SALES (corp-wide): 44.93MM Privately
Held
Web: www.acromil.com
SIC: 3728 Aircraft body and wing assemblies
and parts
HQ: Acromil, Llc
18421 Railroad St
City Of Industry CA
626 964-2522

(P-9589)
ACROMIL LLC (HQ)
18421 Railroad St (91748-1233)
PHONE...............................626 964-2522
Gerald A Niznick, *
Jon Konheim, *
EMP: 144 EST: 2015
SQ FT: 96,000
SALES (est): 44.93MM
SALES (corp-wide): 44.93MM Privately
Held

Web: www.acromil.com
SIC: 3728 Aircraft body and wing assemblies
and parts
PA: Acromil Corporation
18421 Railroad St
City Of Industry CA
626 964-2522

(P-9590)
ACROMIL CORPORATION (PA)
18421 Railroad St (91748-1281)
PHONE...............................626 964-2522
Gerald A Niznick, *Pr*
Jeanne Aguilera, *CFO*
Jon Konheim, *COO*
◆ EMP: 104 EST: 1961
SQ FT: 100,000
SALES (est): 44.93MM
SALES (corp-wide): 44.93MM Privately
Held
Web: www.acromil.com
SIC: 3728 Aircraft body and wing assemblies
and parts

(P-9591)
ACUFAST AIRCRAFT
PRODUCTS INC
12445 Gladstone Ave (91342-5321)
PHONE...............................818 365-7077
Art Dovlatian, *Pr*
Jaime Salazar, *
EMP: 40 EST: 2006
SALES (est): 9.41MM Privately Held
Web: www.acufastap.com
SIC: 3728 Aircraft parts and equipment, nec

(P-9592)
ADAMS RITE AEROSPACE INC
(DH)
4141 N Palm St (92835-1025)
PHONE...............................714 278-6500
John Schaefer, *Pr*
EMP: 83 EST: 1973
SQ FT: 100,000
SALES (est): 54.16MM
SALES (corp-wide): 6.58B Publicly Held
Web: www.araero.com
SIC: 3728 Aircraft parts and equipment, nec
HQ: Transdigm, Inc.
1301 E 9th St Ste 3000
Cleveland OH

(P-9593)
ADAPTIVE AEROSPACE
CORPORATION
501 Bailey Ave (93561-9012)
PHONE...............................661 300-0616
Bill Mccune, *CEO*
EMP: 25 EST: 2001
SALES (est): 3.45MM Privately Held
Web: www.adapt.aero
SIC: 3728 Aircraft parts and equipment, nec

(P-9594)
ADEPT FASTENERS INC (PA)
27949 Hancock Pkwy (91355-4116)
P.O. Box 579 (91310-0579)
PHONE...............................661 257-6600
Gary Young, *Pr*
Don List, *
EMP: 108 EST: 2001
SQ FT: 40,000
SALES (est): 65.06MM
SALES (corp-wide): 65.06MM Privately
Held
Web: www.adeptfasteners.com
SIC: 3728 Aircraft parts and equipment, nec

(P-9595)
ADVANCED DIGITAL MFG LLC
1343 E Wilshire Ave (92705-4420)
PHONE...............................714 245-0536
Javier Valdiveso, *Pr*
Javier J Valdiveso, *
Jimmy Garcia, *
EMP: 27 **EST:** 2003
SALES (est): 2.96MM **Privately Held**
Web: www.adm-works.com
SIC: 3728 R and D by manuf., aircraft parts
and auxiliary equipment

(P-9596)
**ADVANCED MTLS JOINING
CORP (PA)**
Also Called: Advanced Technology Co
2858 E Walnut St (91107-3755)
PHONE...............................626 449-2696
Jean L De Silvestri, *Pr*
Mohammed Islam, *
EMP: 41 **EST:** 1971
SQ FT: 23,000
SALES (est): 9.37MM
SALES (corp-wide): 9.37MM **Privately
Held**
Web: www.at-co.com
SIC: 3728 3724 Aircraft parts and
equipment, nec; Aircraft engines and
engine parts

(P-9597)
**AERO ENGINEERING & MFG CO
LLC**
Also Called: Aero Engineering
28217 Avenue Crocker (91355-1249)
PHONE...............................661 295-0875
Anthony Denogean, *Pr*
Dennis L Junker, *
Lance R Junker, *
Richard Jucksch, *
▼ **EMP:** 55 **EST:** 1948
SQ FT: 21,000
SALES (est): 10.42MM **Privately Held**
Web: www.aeroeng.com
SIC: 3728 5088 Aircraft assemblies,
subassemblies, and parts, nec; Aircraft and
parts, nec

(P-9598)
AERO PACIFIC CORPORATION
Also Called: Merco Manufacturing Co
20445 E Walnut Dr N (91789-2918)
PHONE...............................714 961-9200
Mark Heasley, *Pr*
EMP: 130 **EST:** 1961
SALES (est): 21.68MM **Privately Held**
Web: www.alignprecision.com
SIC: 3728 Aircraft parts and equipment, nec

(P-9599)
AERO-CRAFT HYDRAULICS INC
392 N Smith Ave (92878-4371)
PHONE...............................951 736-4690
Rod Guzman Senior, *Pr*
Brad Davidson, *
Cathy Norris, *
Suzane Treneer, *
EMP: 43 **EST:** 1963
SQ FT: 16,500
SALES (est): 5.34MM **Privately Held**
Web: www.aero-craft.com
SIC: 3728 5084 7699 Aircraft body and wing
assemblies and parts; Hydraulic systems
equipment and supplies; Aircraft and heavy
equipment repair services

(P-9600)
**AEROSHEAR AVIATION SVCS
INC (PA)**
7701 Woodley Ave 200 (91406-1732)
PHONE...............................818 779-1650
Lonnie Paschal, *CEO*
Christine Paschal, *
Ryan Hogan, *
EMP: 32 **EST:** 1996
SQ FT: 42,000
SALES (est): 4.92MM
SALES (corp-wide): 4.92MM **Privately
Held**
Web: www.aeroshearaviation.com
SIC: 3728 3599 1799 Aircraft parts and
equipment, nec; Machine shop, jobbing and
repair; Welding on site

(P-9601)
AEROSPACE DRIVEN TECH INC
Also Called: Driven Technologies
2807 Catherine Way (92705-5708)
PHONE...............................949 553-1606
Kathleen F Freeman, *CEO*
Roger H Gottfried, *Pr*
EMP: 18 **EST:** 2002
SQ FT: 10,000
SALES (est): 3.11MM **Privately Held**
Web: www.driven-technologies.com
SIC: 3728 Aircraft parts and equipment, nec

(P-9602)
**AEROSPACE DYNAMICS INTL
INC (DH)**
Also Called: ADI
25540 Rye Canyon Rd (91355-1169)
PHONE...............................661 257-3535
Joseph I Snowden, *CEO*
◆ **EMP:** 171 **EST:** 1989
SQ FT: 250,000
SALES (est): 97.53MM
SALES (corp-wide): 302.09B **Publicly
Held**
Web: www.pccaero.com
SIC: 3728 Aircraft parts and equipment, nec
HQ: Precision Castparts Corp.
5885 Meadows Rd Ste 620
Lake Oswego OR
503 946-4800

(P-9603)
**AEROSPACE DYNAMICS INTL
INC**
25575 Rye Canyon Rd (91355-1108)
PHONE...............................661 310-6986
EMP: 279
SALES (corp-wide): 302.09B **Publicly
Held**
Web: www.pccaero.com
SIC: 3728 Aircraft parts and equipment, nec
HQ: Aerospace Dynamics International, Inc.
25540 Rye Canyon Rd
Valencia CA

(P-9604)
**AEROSPACE ENGINEERING
LLC (PA)**
2632 Saturn St (92821-6701)
PHONE...............................714 996-8178
EMP: 89 **EST:** 2008
SALES (est): 22.35MM **Privately Held**
Web: www.karman-sd.com
SIC: 3728 3541 3599 Aircraft parts and
equipment, nec; Numerically controlled
metal cutting machine tools; Machine and
other job shop work

(P-9605)
**AEROSPACE ENGINEERING
LLC**
2141 S Standard Ave (92707-3034)
PHONE...............................714 641-5884
EMP: 31
Web: www.karman-sd.com
SIC: 3728 Aircraft parts and equipment, nec
PA: Aerospace Engineering, Llc
2632 Saturn St
Brea CA

(P-9606)
**AEROSPACE ENGRG SUPPORT
CORP**
Also Called: J and L Industries
645 Hawaii St (90245-4814)
P.O. Box 999 (90245-0999)
PHONE...............................310 297-4050
Asher Bartov, *CEO*
Abraham Wacht, *
EMP: 27 **EST:** 1987
SQ FT: 30,000
SALES (est): 4.95MM
SALES (corp-wide): 1.2B **Privately Held**
Web: www.aerospace.org
SIC: 3728 Aircraft parts and equipment, nec
PA: The Aerospace Corporation
2310 E El Segundo Blvd
El Segundo CA
310 336-5000

(P-9607)
**AEROSPACE PARTS HOLDINGS
INC**
Also Called: Cadence Aerospace
3150 E Miraloma Ave (92806-1906)
PHONE...............................949 877-3630
Olivier Jarrault, *CEO*
Ron Case, *
Don Devore, *
Mike Coburn, *
EMP: 1175 **EST:** 2012
SALES (est): 50.56MM **Privately Held**
Web: www.cadenceaerospace.com
SIC: 3728 Aircraft parts and equipment, nec

(P-9608)
**AHF-DUCOMMUN
INCORPORATED (HQ)**
Also Called: Ducommun Arostructures-
Gardena
268 E Gardena Blvd (90248-2814)
PHONE...............................310 380-5390
Joseph C Berenato, *Prin*
Eugene P Conese, *Prin*
Ralph D Crosby, *Prin*
Jay L Haberland, *Prin*
Robert D Paulson, *Prin*
◆ **EMP:** 250 **EST:** 1950
SQ FT: 105,000
SALES (est): 378.08MM
SALES (corp-wide): 712.54MM **Publicly
Held**
Web: www.ducommun.com
SIC: 3728 3812 3769 3469 Aircraft body and
wing assemblies and parts; Search and
navigation equipment; Space vehicle
equipment, nec; Metal stampings, nec
PA: Ducommun Incorporated
200 Sandpointe Ave # 700
Santa Ana CA
657 335-3665

(P-9609)
AIR CABIN ENGINEERING INC
231 W Blueridge Ave (92865-4226)
PHONE...............................714 637-4111
EMP: 25 **EST:** 1981

SALES (est): 3.64MM **Privately Held**
Web: www.aircabin.com
SIC: 3728 Aircraft parts and equipment, nec

(P-9610)
AIR COMPONENTS INC
10235 Indiana Ct (91730-5332)
PHONE...............................909 980-8224
David Blocker, *Pr*
Robert Ames, *VP*
EMP: 20 **EST:** 1987
SQ FT: 7,800
SALES (est): 4.55MM **Privately Held**
Web: www.aircomponentsinc.com
SIC: 3728 Aircraft parts and equipment, nec

(P-9611)
AIRBORNE TECHNOLOGIES INC
Also Called: Airborne Technologies
999 Avenida Acaso (93012-8700)
P.O. Box 2210 (93011-2210)
PHONE...............................805 389-3700
Greg Beason, *Pr*
Christopher Celtruda, *
Richard Drinkward, *
EMP: 232 **EST:** 1980
SQ FT: 40,000
SALES (est): 37.08MM
SALES (corp-wide): 89.67MM **Privately
Held**
Web: www.goallclear.com
SIC: 3728 5088 7699 3812 Aircraft parts and
equipment, nec; Aircraft equipment and
supplies, nec; Aircraft and heavy equipment
repair services; Search and navigation
equipment
PA: Kellstrom Holding Corporation
100 N Pcf Cast Hwy Ste 19
El Segundo CA
561 222-7455

(P-9612)
AIRCRAFT HINGE INC
28338 Constellation Rd Ste 970
(91355-5012)
PHONE...............................661 257-3434
Doug Silva, *Pr*
Terrina Arroyo, *Dir Fin*
Brianne Dautel, *Off Mgr*
▲ **EMP:** 20 **EST:** 1986
SQ FT: 11,000
SALES (est): 4.15MM **Privately Held**
Web: www.aircrafthinge.com
SIC: 3728 Aircraft parts and equipment, nec

(P-9613)
**AIRTECH INTERNATIONAL INC
(PA)**
Also Called: Airtech Advanced Mtls Group
5700 Skylab Rd (92647-2055)
PHONE...............................714 899-8100
Jeff Dahlgren, *Pr*
◆ **EMP:** 130 **EST:** 1973
SQ FT: 150,000
SALES (est): 95.6MM
SALES (corp-wide): 95.6MM **Privately
Held**
Web: www.airtechintl.com
SIC: 3728 3081 5088 2673 Aircraft parts and
equipment, nec; Unsupported plastics film
and sheet; Aeronautical equipment and
supplies; Bags: plastic, laminated, and
coated

(P-9614)
ALATUS AEROSYSTEMS
20415 E Walnut Dr N (91789-2959)
PHONE...............................909 217-9047
Michael Piceno, *Mgr*
EMP: 131

PRODUCTS & SVCS

SALES (corp-wide): 47.86MM **Privately Held**
Web: www.alatusaero.com
SIC: 3728 3489 Aircraft parts and equipment, nec; Artillery or artillery parts, over 30 mm.
PA: Alatus Aerosystems
9301 Mason Ave
Chatsworth CA
610 965-1630

(P-9615)
ALATUS AEROSYSTEMS
9301 Mason Ave (91311-5202)
PHONE..............................626 498-7376
Richard Oak, *Mgr*
EMP: 80
SALES (corp-wide): 47.86MM **Privately Held**
Web: www.alatusaero.com
SIC: 3728 3489 Aircraft parts and equipment, nec; Artillery or artillery parts, over 30 mm.
PA: Alatus Aerosystems
9301 Mason Ave
Chatsworth CA
610 965-1630

(P-9616)
ALATUS AEROSYSTEMS (PA)
9301 Mason Ave (91311-5202)
PHONE..............................610 965-1630
Scott Holland, *CEO*
Joe Zarrilli, *
◆ **EMP:** 20 **EST:** 1953
SALES (est): 47.86MM
SALES (corp-wide): 47.86MM **Privately Held**
Web: www.alatusaero.com
SIC: 3728 3489 Aircraft parts and equipment, nec; Artillery or artillery parts, over 30 mm.

(P-9617)
ALATUS AEROSYSTEMS
Also Called: Triumph Structures - Brea
9301 Mason Ave (91311-5202)
PHONE..............................714 732-0559
Manny Chacon, *Mgr*
EMP: 87
SALES (corp-wide): 47.86MM **Privately Held**
Web: www.alatusaero.com
SIC: 3728 3489 Aircraft parts and equipment, nec; Artillery or artillery parts, over 30 mm.
PA: Alatus Aerosystems
9301 Mason Ave
Chatsworth CA
610 965-1630

(P-9618)
ALIGN AEROSPACE LLC (PA)
9401 De Soto Ave (91311-4920)
PHONE..............................818 727-7800
EMP: 287 **EST:** 2011
SQ FT: 73,000
SALES (est): 120.97MM **Privately Held**
Web: www.alignaero.com
SIC: 3728 Aircraft parts and equipment, nec

(P-9619)
ALIGN PRECISION - ANAHEIM INC (DH)
7100 Belgrave Ave (92841-2809)
PHONE..............................714 961-9200
EMP: 80 **EST:** 2010
SALES (est): 30.72MM
SALES (corp-wide): 1.75B **Privately Held**
Web: www.alignprecision.com

SIC: 3728 Aircraft parts and equipment, nec
HQ: Align Precision Corp.
730 W 22nd St
Tempe AZ
480 968-1778

(P-9620)
ALL POWER MANUFACTURING CO
13141 Molette St (90670-5500)
PHONE..............................562 802-2640
Michael J Hartnett, *CEO*
▲ **EMP:** 130 **EST:** 1948
SALES (est): 34.54MM
SALES (corp-wide): 1.47B **Publicly Held**
Web: www.rbcbearings.com
SIC: 3728 2899 Aircraft assemblies, subassemblies, and parts, nec; Chemical preparations, nec
PA: Rbc Bearings Incorporated
102 Willenbrock Rd Bldg B
Oxford CT
203 267-7001

(P-9621)
ALVA MANUFACTURING INC
236 E Orangethorpe Ave (92870-6442)
PHONE..............................714 237-0925
Tam V Nguyen, *Pr*
EMP: 44 **EST:** 2011
SQ FT: 15,000
SALES (est): 5.14MM **Privately Held**
Web: www.alvamanufacturing.com
SIC: 3728 3599 Aircraft parts and equipment, nec; Machine and other job shop work

(P-9622)
AMERICAN AIRFRAME INC
Also Called: Pacific Airframe & Engineering
1201 Vanguard Dr (93033-2409)
PHONE..............................805 240-1608
EMP: 21
Web: www.pacificairframe.com
SIC: 3728 Airframe assemblies, except for guided missiles

(P-9623)
AMG TORRANCE LLC (DH)
Also Called: Metric Precision
5401 Business Dr (92649-1225)
PHONE..............................310 515-2584
EMP: 50 **EST:** 2009
SQ FT: 37,800
SALES (est): 22.44MM **Privately Held**
SIC: 3728 Ailerons, aircraft
HQ: Aerospace Manufacturing Group Inc
5401 Business Dr
Huntington Beach CA
714 894-9802

(P-9624)
AMRO FABRICATING CORPORATION (PA)
1430 Amro Way (91733-3046)
PHONE..............................626 579-2200
John Hammond, *Pr*
Michael Riley, *
EMP: 238 **EST:** 1977
SQ FT: 150,000
SALES (est): 45.24MM
SALES (corp-wide): 45.24MM **Privately Held**
Web: www.karman-sd.com
SIC: 3728 3769 3544 5088 Aircraft parts and equipment, nec; Space vehicle equipment, nec; Special dies, tools, jigs, and fixtures; Aircraft and space vehicle supplies and parts

(P-9625)
ANMAR PRECISION COMPONENTS INC
7424 Greenbush Ave (91605-4005)
PHONE..............................818 764-0901
Bruno Mudy, *Pr*
Teresa Mudy, *Sec*
Anthony Mudy, *VP*
EMP: 21 **EST:** 1983
SQ FT: 10,000
SALES (est): 821.61K **Privately Held**
SIC: 3728 Aircraft parts and equipment, nec

(P-9626)
APM MANUFACTURING (HQ)
Also Called: Anaheim Precision Mfg
1738 N Neville St (92865-4214)
PHONE..............................714 453-0100
Anthony Puccio, *CEO*
Gilles Madelmont, *
Joe Puccio, *
EMP: 45 **EST:** 1986
SQ FT: 57,000
SALES (est): 36.18MM
SALES (corp-wide): 43.53MM **Privately Held**
Web: www.anaheimprecision.com
SIC: 3728 3429 3599 3444 Aircraft parts and equipment, nec; Aircraft hardware; Machine shop, jobbing and repair; Sheet metalwork
PA: Manufacturing Solutions, Inc.
1738 N Neville St
Orange CA
714 453-0100

(P-9627)
APPLIED CMPSITE STRUCTURES INC (HQ)
1195 Columbia St (92821-2922)
PHONE..............................714 990-6300
David Horner, *CEO*
Jorge Garcia, *
Justin Uchida, *
EMP: 72 **EST:** 1975
SQ FT: 100,000
SALES (est): 51.48MM
SALES (corp-wide): 189.21MM **Privately Held**
Web: www.appliedcomposites.com
SIC: 3728 Aircraft parts and equipment, nec
PA: Applied Composites Holdings, Llc
25692 Atlantic Ocean Dr
Lake Forest CA
949 716-3511

(P-9628)
APPROVED AERONAUTICS LLC
Also Called: Manufacturer and Distributor
9130 Pulsar Ct (92883-4630)
PHONE..............................951 200-3730
Anthony Janes, *CEO*
EMP: 42 **EST:** 1999
SALES (est): 6.02MM **Privately Held**
Web: www.approvedaeronautics.com
SIC: 3728 Aircraft parts and equipment, nec

(P-9629)
ARDEN ENGINEERING INC (DH)
3130 E Miraloma Ave (92806-1906)
PHONE..............................949 877-3642
Thomas Hutton, *CEO*
John R Meisenbach Senior, *CEO*
Michael J Stow, *Pr*
▲ **EMP:** 21 **EST:** 1971
SQ FT: 25,000
SALES (est): 46.27MM
SALES (corp-wide): 666.39MM **Privately Held**
Web: www.cadenceaerospace.com

SIC: 3728 Aircraft body assemblies and parts
HQ: Arden Engineering Holdings, Inc.
1878 N Main St
Orange CA
714 998-6410

(P-9630)
ARDEN ENGINEERING INC
1878 N Main St (92865-4117)
Rural Route 3130 (92806)
PHONE..............................714 998-6410
Thorin Southworth, *of Corp*
EMP: 197
SALES (corp-wide): 666.39MM **Privately Held**
Web: www.cadenceaerospace.com
SIC: 3728 Aircraft body assemblies and parts
HQ: Arden Engineering, Inc.
3130 E Miraloma Ave
Anaheim CA
949 877-3642

(P-9631)
ARDEN ENGINEERING HOLDINGS INC (DH)
1878 N Main St (92865-4117)
PHONE..............................714 998-6410
EMP: 21 **EST:** 2010
SALES (est): 46.27MM
SALES (corp-wide): 666.39MM **Privately Held**
SIC: 3728 Aircraft body assemblies and parts
HQ: Cadence Aerospace, Llc
3150 E Miraloma Ave
Anaheim CA
949 877-3630

(P-9632)
ARROWHEAD PRODUCTS CORPORATION
Also Called: Arrowhead Products
4411 Katella Ave (90720-3599)
PHONE..............................714 822-2513
Andrew Whelan, *Pr*
Bill Gardner, *
Erick Reinhold, *
Pete Kraft, *
▲ **EMP:** 640 **EST:** 1968
SQ FT: 250,000
SALES (est): 166.38MM
SALES (corp-wide): 476.02MM **Privately Held**
Web: www.arrowheadproducts.net
SIC: 3728 Accumulators, aircraft propeller
HQ: Industrial Manufacturing Company Llc
8223 Brecksville Rd # 100
Brecksville OH
440 838-4700

(P-9633)
ASTOR MANUFACTURING
779 Anita St Ste B (91911-3937)
PHONE..............................661 645-5585
Erick Muschenheim, *Pr*
EMP: 25 **EST:** 2016
SQ FT: 3,500
SALES (est): 1.2MM **Privately Held**
Web: www.astormanufacturing.com
SIC: 3728 Aircraft body assemblies and parts

(P-9634)
ASTRO SPAR INC
3130 E Miraloma Ave (92806-1906)
PHONE..............................626 839-7858
▲ **EMP:** 42
Web: www.cadenceaerospace.com
SIC: 3728 Aircraft assemblies, subassemblies, and parts, nec

(P-9635)

ASTRO-TEK INDUSTRIES LLC

1198 N Kraemer Blvd (92806-1916)
PHONE.............................714 238-0022
Terry Smith, *
EMP: 80 EST: 2005
SQ FT: 50,000
SALES (est): 22.88MM Privately Held
Web: www.astro-tek.com
SIC: 3728 3599 3548 3449 Aircraft parts and equipment, nec; Electrical discharge machining (EDM); Welding apparatus; Miscellaneous metalwork

(P-9636)

ASTURIES MANUFACTURING CO INC

310 Cessna Cir (92878-5009)
PHONE.............................951 270-1766
Manuel Perez, Pr
Luis Perez, *
EMP: 25 EST: 1979
SQ FT: 50,850
SALES (est): 4.64MM Privately Held
SIC: 3728 3559 Aircraft parts and equipment, nec; Semiconductor manufacturing machinery

(P-9637)

AVANTUS AEROSPACE INC (DH)

29101 The Old Rd (91355-1014)
PHONE.............................661 295-8620
Brian Williams, CEO
Dennis Suedkamp, *
Scott Wilkinson, *
EMP: 125 EST: 2015
SQ FT: 75,000
SALES (est): 81.84MM
SALES (corp-wide): 123.82MM Privately Held
Web: www.avantusaerospace.com
HQ: Avantus Aerospace Limited
Unit 7 Millington Road
Hayes MIDDX

(P-9638)

AVCORP CMPSITE FABRICATION INC

1600 W 135th St (90249-2506)
P.O. Box 3580 (90247-7280)
PHONE.............................310 970-5658
Marcus Maria Van Rooij, Pr
EMP: 400 EST: 2015
SQ FT: 350,000
SALES (est): 90.75MM
SALES (corp-wide): 1.65MM Privately Held
SIC: 3728 Aircraft parts and equipment, nec
HQ: Avcorp Industries Inc
10025 River Way
Delta BC

(P-9639)

AVIBANK MFG INC (DH)

Also Called: Avibank
11500 Sherman Way (91605-5827)
P.O. Box 9909 (91609-1909)
PHONE.............................818 392-2100
Dan Welter, Pr
John Duran, *
▲ EMP: 115 EST: 1945
SALES (est): 90.28MM
SALES (corp-wide): 302.09B Publicly Held
Web: www.avibank.com
SIC: 3728 Aircraft parts and equipment, nec
HQ: Sps Technologies, Llc
301 Highland Ave
Jenkintown PA
215 572-3000

(P-9640)

B & E MANUFACTURING CO INC

12151 Monarch St (92841-2927)
PHONE.............................714 898-2269
Emmanuel Neildez, Pr
Jerome Guilloteau, Sec
EMP: 45 EST: 1981
SQ FT: 26,000
SALES (est): 14.22MM
SALES (corp-wide): 2.67MM Privately Held
Web: www.bandemfg.com
SIC: 3728 Aircraft parts and equipment, nec
HQ: Lisi
6 Rue Juvenal Viellard
Grandvillars

(P-9641)

B/E AEROSPACE INC

7155 Fenwick Ln (92683-5218)
PHONE.............................714 896-9001
Jim Melrose, Mgr
EMP: 136
SALES (corp-wide): 67.07B Publicly Held
Web: www.collinsaerospace.com
SIC: 3728 3647 Aircraft parts and equipment, nec; Aircraft lighting fixtures
HQ: B/E Aerospace, Inc.
1400 Corporate Center Way
Wellington FL

(P-9642)

B/E AEROSPACE MACROLINK

1500 N Kellogg Dr (92807-1902)
PHONE.............................714 777-8800
Mark Cordivari, Pr
EMP: 20 EST: 2015
SIC: 3728 Aircraft parts and equipment, nec

(P-9643)

BANDY MANUFACTURING LLC

3420 N San Fernando Blvd (91504-2532)
P.O. Box 7716 (91510-7716)
PHONE.............................818 846-9020
Tom Fulton, Pr
Kevin L Cummings, *
EMP: 93 EST: 1952
SQ FT: 60,000
SALES (est): 12.22MM Privately Held
Web: www.bandymanufacturing.com
SIC: 3728 Aircraft parts and equipment, nec

(P-9644)

BISH INC

2820 Via Orange Way Ste G (91978-1742)
PHONE.............................619 660-6220
William L Cary, Pr
Shane Nonthavet, VP
EMP: 23 EST: 1997
SQ FT: 16,000
SALES (est): 2.53MM Privately Held
SIC: 3728 Aircraft parts and equipment, nec

(P-9645)

BOEING ENCORE INTERIORS LLC

5511 Skylab Rd (92647-2068)
PHONE.............................949 559-0930
EMP: 21 EST: 2019
SALES (est): 5.5MM
SALES (corp-wide): 66.61B Publicly Held
Web: www.encoregroup.aero
SIC: 3728 1799 Aircraft parts and equipment, nec; Renovation of aircraft interiors
PA: The Boeing Company
929 Long Bridge Dr
Arlington VA
703 414-6338

(P-9646)

C&D ZODIAC AEROSPACE

7330 Lincoln Way (92841-1427)
PHONE.............................714 891-0683
▲ EMP: 37 EST: 2015
SALES (est): 185.44K Privately Held
SIC: 3728 Aircraft parts and equipment, nec

(P-9647)

C&H HYDRAULICS INC

Also Called: Acme Divac Industries
1585 Monrovia Ave (92663-2806)
PHONE.............................949 646-6230
James F Andreae, CEO
EMP: 24 EST: 1976
SQ FT: 8,000
SALES (est): 2.13MM Privately Held
Web: www.chhyd.com
SIC: 3728 8734 3769 3812 Aircraft parts and equipment, nec; Testing laboratories; Space vehicle equipment, nec; Search and navigation equipment

(P-9648)

CADENCE AEROSPACE LLC (HQ)

3150 E Miraloma Ave (92806-1906)
PHONE.............................949 877-3630
Olivier Jarrault, CEO
EMP: 105 EST: 2010
SQ FT: 5,000
SALES (est): 248.53MM
SALES (corp-wide): 666.39MM Privately Held
Web: www.cadenceaerospace.com
SIC: 3728 Aircraft body assemblies and parts
PA: Arlington Capital Partners Iv, L.P.
5425 Wisconsin Ave # 200
Chevy Chase MD
202 337-7500

(P-9649)

CADENCE AEROSPACE LLC

3130 E Miraloma Ave (92806-1906)
PHONE.............................425 353-0405
EMP: 18
SALES (est): 1.15MM Privately Held
Web: www.cadenceaerospace.com
SIC: 3728 Aircraft parts and equipment, nec

(P-9650)

CAL TECH PRECISION INC

1830 N Lemon St (92801-1000)
PHONE.............................714 992-4130
Guy Haarlammert, Pr
▲ EMP: 99 EST: 1989
SALES (est): 10.99MM Privately Held
Web: www.caltechprecision.com
SIC: 3728 Aircraft parts and equipment, nec

(P-9651)

CALIFORNIA COMPOSITES MGT INC

1935 E Occidental St (92705-5115)
PHONE.............................714 258-0405
Fred Good, Ch Bd
EMP: 22 EST: 1986
SQ FT: 30,000
SALES (est): 1.72MM Privately Held
SIC: 3728 3812 3624 Aircraft parts and equipment, nec; Search and navigation equipment; Carbon and graphite products

(P-9652)

CAMAR AIRCRAFT PARTS CO

Also Called: Camar Aircraft Parts Company
743 Flynn Rd (93012-8056)
P.O. Box 190 (93011-0190)
PHONE.............................805 389-8944

EMP: 22 EST: 2007
SALES (est): 4.5MM Privately Held
Web: www.camarac.com
SIC: 3728 Aircraft parts and equipment, nec

(P-9653)

CANYON COMPOSITES INCORPORATED

1548 N Gemini Pl (92801-1152)
PHONE.............................714 991-8181
EMP: 40 EST: 1996
SQ FT: 31,500
SALES (est): 8.17MM Privately Held
Web: www.canyoncomposites.com
SIC: 3728 8711 Aircraft parts and equipment, nec; Engineering services

(P-9654)

CANYON ENGINEERING PDTS INC

28909 Avenue Williams (91355-4183)
PHONE.............................661 294-0084
Todd Strickland, Pr
Paul Knerr, *
EMP: 88 EST: 1979
SQ FT: 70,000
SALES (est): 22.07MM Publicly Held
Web: www.crissair.com
SIC: 3728 Aircraft assemblies, subassemblies, and parts, nec
PA: Esco Technologies Inc.
9900 Clayton Rd Ste A
Saint Louis MO

(P-9655)

CARBON BY DESIGN LLC

1491 Poinsettia Ave Ste 136 (92081-8541)
PHONE.............................760 643-1300
EMP: 75 EST: 2003
SQ FT: 65,000
SALES (est): 10.29MM Publicly Held
Web: www.carbonbydesign.com
SIC: 3728 3761 Airframe assemblies, except for guided missiles; Guided missiles and space vehicles
HQ: Heico Flight Support Corp.
3000 Taft St
Hollywood FL
954 987-4000

(P-9656)

CARDONA MANUFACTURING CORP

1869 N Victory Pl (91504-3476)
PHONE.............................818 841-8358
Louis Cardona, Pr
Jo Ann Cardona, *
EMP: 26 EST: 1971
SQ FT: 10,000
SALES (est): 2.22MM Privately Held
Web: www.cardonamfg.com
SIC: 3728 3812 Aircraft parts and equipment, nec; Search and navigation equipment

(P-9657)

CAVOTEC DABICO US INC

5665 Corporate Ave (90630-4727)
PHONE.............................714 947-0005
Gary Matthews, Pr
Christian Bernadotte, *
Dorothy Chen, *
▲ EMP: 36 EST: 2008
SALES (est): 5.24MM Privately Held
Web: www.dabico.com
SIC: 3728 Aircraft parts and equipment, nec

(P-9658)
CHOL ENTERPRISES INC
12831 S Figueroa St (90061-1157)
PHONE..............................310 516-1328
Neal Castleman, *Pr*
Brian Gamberg, *VP*
EMP: 22 EST: 1991
SQ FT: 25,000
SALES (est): 764.47K **Privately Held**
Web: www.dcxchol.com
SIC: **3728** 3769 3678 3357 Aircraft
assemblies, subassemblies, and parts, nec;
Space vehicle equipment, nec; Electronic
connectors; Nonferrous wiredrawing and
insulating

(P-9659)
COAST COMPOSITES LLC (PA)
5 Burroughs (92618-2804)
PHONE..............................949 455-0665
Daniel Nowicki, *CFO*
◆ EMP: 80 EST: 1988
SQ FT: 60,000
SALES (est): 21.65MM
SALES (corp-wide): 21.65MM **Privately Held**
Web: www.ascentaerospace.com
SIC: **3728** 3544 3599 Aircraft parts and
equipment, nec; Special dies, tools, jigs,
and fixtures; Machine shop, jobbing and
repair

(P-9660)
COATING SPECIALTIES INC
Also Called: Aero Products Co.
815 E Rosecrans Ave (90059-3510)
PHONE..............................310 639-6900
Mitchell Grant, *Pr*
Mitchell Grant, *CEO*
William Johnson, *CEO*
EMP: 18 EST: 1973
SQ FT: 31,000
SALES (est): 4.82MM **Privately Held**
Web: www.coatingspecialties.com
SIC: **3728** 3812 Aircraft assemblies,
subassemblies, and parts, nec; Search and
navigation equipment

(P-9661)
COI CERAMICS INC
Also Called: Coic
7130 Miramar Rd Ste 100b (92121-2340)
PHONE..............................858 621-5700
David A Shanahan, *CEO*
Steve Atmur, *
Andy Szweda, *
EMP: 41 EST: 1999
SQ FT: 3,000
SALES (est): 21.95MM **Publicly Held**
Web: www.coiceramics.com
SIC: **3728** Aircraft parts and equipment, nec
HQ: Northrop Grumman Innovation
Systems, Inc.
2980 Fairview Park Dr
Falls Church VA

(P-9662)
COMPOSITES HORIZONS LLC
1471 W Industrial Park St (91722-3499)
PHONE..............................626 331-0861
EMP: 20
SALES (corp-wide): 302.09B **Publicly Held**
Web: www.pccstructurals.com
SIC: **3728** 3844 Aircraft parts and
equipment, nec; X-ray apparatus and tubes
HQ: Composites Horizons, Llc
1629 W Industrial Park St
Covina CA
626 331-0861

(P-9663)
COMPUCRAFT INDUSTRIES INC
Also Called: Cii
8787 Olive Ln (92071-4137)
P.O. Box 712529 (92072-2529)
PHONE..............................619 448-0787
Maurice Brear, *Pr*
Margarita Brear, *
EMP: 50 EST: 1972
SQ FT: 85,000
SALES (est): 7.5MM **Privately Held**
Web: www.ccind.com
SIC: **3728** Aircraft assemblies,
subassemblies, and parts, nec

(P-9664)
CONAX USA INC
31102 Via Cristal (92675-2916)
PHONE..............................949 690-4880
Erik Tordhol, *Brnch Mgr*
EMP: 181
SALES (corp-wide): 581.96K **Privately Held**
SIC: **3728** Aircraft parts and equipment, nec
PA: Conax Usa, Inc.
16870 W Bernardo Dr
San Diego CA
858 674-6668

(P-9665)
COPP INDUSTRIAL MFG INC
5510 Brooks St (91763-4522)
PHONE..............................909 593-7448
Sanjaya Amarasinghe, *CEO*
Sanjaya Amarasinghe, *Pr*
EMP: 20 EST: 1964
SALES (est): 4.99MM **Privately Held**
Web: www.coppmfg.com
SIC: **3728** 5088 3599 3444 Aircraft body and
wing assemblies and parts; Aeronautical
equipment and supplies; Machine shop,
jobbing and repair; Culverts, flumes, and
pipes

(P-9666)
CORONADO MANUFACTURING LLC
8991 Glenoaks Blvd (91352-2038)
PHONE..............................818 768-5010
Allen F Gowing, *Pr*
Phillip Belmonte, *
▼ EMP: 50 EST: 1959
SQ FT: 19,000
SALES (est): 13.3MM **Privately Held**
Web: www.coronadomfg.com
SIC: **3728** 5084 Military aircraft equipment
and armament; Industrial machine parts

(P-9667)
CRANE AEROSPACE INC
Crane Aerospace & Electronics
3000 Winona Ave (91504-2540)
PHONE..............................818 526-2600
Brendan Curran, *AERO GROUP*
EMP: 66
SALES (corp-wide): 3.37B **Publicly Held**
Web: www.craneae.com
SIC: **3728** Aircraft parts and equipment, nec
HQ: Crane Aerospace, Inc.
100 Stamford Pl
Stamford CT

(P-9668)
CTCOA LLC
Also Called: Consolidated Trading Co Amer
16818 Marquardt Ave (90703-1045)
PHONE..............................562 407-5375
Mark Robinson, *CEO*
Matthew Kuhnau, *
EMP: 36 EST: 2018

SALES (est): 7.39MM **Privately Held**
SIC: **3728** Aircraft parts and equipment, nec

(P-9669)
CURTISS-WRIGHT CONTROLS INC
6940 Farmdale Ave (91605-6210)
PHONE..............................818 503-0998
EMP: 30
SALES (corp-wide): 2.56B **Publicly Held**
Web: www.curtisswright.com
SIC: **3728** Aircraft assemblies,
subassemblies, and parts, nec
HQ: Curtiss-Wright Controls, Inc.
201 Old Boiling Sprng Rd
Shelby NC
704 869-4600

(P-9670)
D & D GEAR INCORPORATED
Also Called: Absolute Technologies
4890 E La Palma Ave (92807-1911)
PHONE..............................714 692-6570
Bill Beverage, *Pr*
▲ EMP: 210 EST: 1969
SQ FT: 82,500
SALES (est): 48.13MM **Privately Held**
Web: www.absolutetechnologies.com
SIC: **3728** Aircraft parts and equipment, nec

(P-9671)
DASCO ENGINEERING CORP
24747 Crenshaw Blvd (90505-5308)
PHONE..............................310 326-2277
Ward Olson, *Pr*
Glen Olson, *
John Karle, *
◆ EMP: 110 EST: 1964
SQ FT: 50,000
SALES (est): 19.53MM **Privately Held**
Web: www.dascoeng.com
SIC: **3728** Aircraft body and wing assemblies
and parts

(P-9672)
DELTA AIRLINES INC
Also Called: Delta Airlines
2357 Airlane Rd (92101-1055)
PHONE..............................619 491-2886
Margi Mitrea, *Mgr*
EMP: 23 EST: 2014
SALES (est): 452.79K **Privately Held**
Web: www.hawaiianairlines.com
SIC: **3728** Aircraft parts and equipment, nec

(P-9673)
DESIGNED METAL CONNECTIONS INC (DH)
Also Called: Permaswage USA
14800 S Figueroa St (90248-1719)
PHONE..............................310 323-6200
Thomas Mcdonnell, *VP*
▲ EMP: 500 EST: 2004
SQ FT: 175,000
SALES (est): 89.97MM
SALES (corp-wide): 302.09B **Publicly Held**
Web: www.pccfluidfittings.com
SIC: **3728** Aircraft parts and equipment, nec
HQ: Precision Castparts Corp.
5885 Meadows Rd Ste 620
Lake Oswego OR
503 946-4800

(P-9674)
DPI LABS INC
1350 Arrow Hwy (91750-5218)
PHONE..............................909 392-5777
Vicki Brown, *CEO*

Al Snow, *
Greg Desmet, *
Pam Archibald, *
EMP: 35 EST: 1984
SALES (est): 5.04MM **Privately Held**
Web: www.dpilabs.com
SIC: **3728** Aircraft parts and equipment, nec

(P-9675)
DUCOMMUN AEROSTRUCTURES INC
23301 Wilmington Ave (90745-6209)
PHONE..............................310 513-7200
EMP: 214
SALES (corp-wide): 712.54MM **Publicly Held**
Web: www.ducommun.com
SIC: **3728** Aircraft parts and equipment, nec
HQ: Ducommun Aerostructures, Inc.
268 E Gardena Blvd
Gardena CA
310 380-5390

(P-9676)
DUCOMMUN AEROSTRUCTURES INC
4001 El Mirage Rd (92301-9489)
PHONE..............................760 246-4191
Art Mcfarlan, *Mgr*
EMP: 68
SQ FT: 1,152
SALES (corp-wide): 712.54MM **Publicly Held**
Web: www.ducommun.com
SIC: **3728** Aircraft parts and equipment, nec
HQ: Ducommun Aerostructures, Inc.
268 E Gardena Blvd
Gardena CA
310 380-5390

(P-9677)
DUCOMMUN AEROSTRUCTURES INC
801 Royal Oaks Dr (91016-3630)
PHONE..............................626 358-3211
Maurice Harris, *Genl Mgr*
EMP: 30
SALES (corp-wide): 712.54MM **Publicly Held**
Web: www.ducommun.com
SIC: **3728** Aircraft parts and equipment, nec
HQ: Ducommun Aerostructures, Inc.
268 E Gardena Blvd
Gardena CA
310 380-5390

(P-9678)
DUCOMMUN INCORPORATED
801 Royal Oaks Dr (91016-3630)
PHONE..............................626 358-3211
Bradley W Spahr, *CEO*
EMP: 17
SALES (corp-wide): 712.54MM **Publicly Held**
Web: www.ducommun.com
SIC: **3728** Aircraft parts and equipment, nec
PA: Ducommun Incorporated
200 Sandpointe Ave # 700
Santa Ana CA
657 335-3665

(P-9679)
DUCOMMUN INCORPORATED (PA)
Also Called: Ducommun
200 Sandpointe Ave Ste 700 (92707-5751)
PHONE..............................657 335-3665
Stephen G Oswald, *Pr*
Jerry L Redondo, *VP Opers*

Rosalie F Rogers, *Chief Human Resources Officer*
Christopher D Wampler, *VP*
Rajiv A Tata, *Corporate Secretary*
▲ **EMP:** 216 **EST:** 1849
SALES (est): 712.54MM
SALES (corp-wide): 712.54MM **Publicly Held**
Web: www.ducommun.com
SIC: 3728 3679 Aircraft body and wing assemblies and parts; Microwave components

(P-9680)
DUCOMMUN LABARGE TECH INC (HQ)
Also Called: American Electronics
23301 Wilmington Ave (90745-6209)
PHONE..............................310 513-7200
Stephen G Oswald, *Pr*
Christopher Wampler, *VP*
Jerry Redondo, *VP*
Michelle Stein, *VP*
Rajiv Tata, *Sec*
▲ **EMP:** 180 **EST:** 1958
SQ FT: 117,000
SALES (est): 74.16MM
SALES (corp-wide): 712.54MM **Publicly Held**
Web: www.ducommun.com
SIC: 3728 3769 5065 3812 Aircraft parts and equipment, nec; Space vehicle equipment, nec; Electronic parts and equipment, nec; Search and navigation equipment
PA: Ducommun Incorporated
200 Sandpointe Ave # 700
Santa Ana CA
657 335-3665

(P-9681)
DYNAMIC FABRICATION INC
890 Mariner St (92821-3831)
PHONE..............................714 662-2440
Andrew Crook, *Pr*
Olga Garcia Crook, *
EMP: 25 **EST:** 1991
SQ FT: 22,000
SALES (est): 4.79MM **Privately Held**
Web: www.dynamicfab.com
SIC: 3728 3764 3761 3812 Aircraft parts and equipment, nec; Engines and engine parts, guided missile; Guided missiles and space vehicles; Defense systems and equipment

(P-9682)
EATON CORPORATION
Also Called: Ground Fueling
9650 Jeronimo Rd (92618-2024)
PHONE..............................714 272-4700
EMP: 18
Web: www.dix-eaton.com
SIC: 3728 3594 3561 3492 Aircraft parts and equipment, nec; Fluid power pumps and motors; Pumps and pumping equipment; Fluid power valves and hose fittings
HQ: Eaton Corporation
1000 Eaton Blvd
Cleveland OH
440 523-5000

(P-9683)
ENCORE SEATS INC
Also Called: Lift By Encore
5511 Skylab Rd (92647-2068)
PHONE..............................949 559-0930
Thomas Mcfarland, *CEO*
Mike Melancon, *
Aram Krikorian, *
EMP: 46 **EST:** 2015
SQ FT: 80,000

SALES (est): 5.94MM **Privately Held**
Web: www.encoregroup.aero
SIC: 3728 Aircraft assemblies, subassemblies, and parts, nec

(P-9684)
ENGINEERING JK AEROSPACE & DEF
23231 La Palma Ave (92887-4768)
PHONE..............................714 499-9092
Jonathan Crisan, *Pr*
EMP: 25 **EST:** 2012
SALES (est): 3.27MM **Privately Held**
Web: www.jke.aero
SIC: 3728 3724 Aircraft parts and equipment, nec; Aircraft engines and engine parts

(P-9685)
ESTERLINE TECHNOLOGIES CORP
1740 Commerce Way (93446-3620)
PHONE..............................805 238-2840
Preston Cole, *Brnch Mgr*
EMP: 25
SALES (corp-wide): 6.58B **Publicly Held**
Web: www.transdigm.com
SIC: 3728 Aircraft parts and equipment, nec
HQ: Esterline Technologies Corp
1301 E 9th St Ste 3000
Cleveland OH
216 706-2960

(P-9686)
FARRAR GRINDING COMPANY
347 E Beach Ave (90302-3191)
PHONE..............................323 678-4879
Clarke Farrar, *Pr*
EMP: 27 **EST:** 1957
SQ FT: 6,000
SALES (est): 1.75MM **Privately Held**
Web: www.farrar-grinding.com
SIC: 3728 3599 Aircraft parts and equipment, nec; Machine shop, jobbing and repair

(P-9687)
FERRA AEROSPACE INC
940 E Orangethorpe Ave Ste A (92801-1129)
PHONE..............................918 787-2220
EMP: 33
SALES (corp-wide): 53.02MM **Privately Held**
Web: www.ferra-group.com
SIC: 3728 Aircraft parts and equipment, nec
HQ: Ferra Aerospace, Inc.
64353 E 290 Rd
Grove OK
918 787-2220

(P-9688)
FLARE GROUP
Also Called: Aviation Equipment Processing
1571 Macarthur Blvd (92626-1407)
PHONE..............................714 850-2080
Dennis Heider, *Pr*
Steve Osorio, *
Daryl Silva, *
Jim Vinyard, *
Eric Trainor, *
EMP: 25 **EST:** 2010
SALES (est): 4.02MM **Privately Held**
Web: aveprocessing.elementor.cloud
SIC: 3728 Aircraft parts and equipment, nec

(P-9689)
FLEXCO INC
6855 Suva St (90201-1937)

PHONE..............................562 927-2525
Erik Moller, *Pr*
EMP: 36 **EST:** 1966
SQ FT: 14,000
SALES (est): 5.28MM **Privately Held**
Web: www.flexcoinc.com
SIC: 3728 3496 Aircraft parts and equipment, nec; Miscellaneous fabricated wire products

(P-9690)
FLIGHT ENVIRONMENTS INC
570 Linne Rd Ste 100 (93446-9460)
P.O. Box 3169 (93447-3169)
EMP: 25 **EST:** 1998
SALES (est): 2.25MM **Privately Held**
Web: www.luminary.aero
SIC: 3728 Aircraft parts and equipment, nec

(P-9691)
FLIGHT LINE PRODUCTS INC
Also Called: Flightways Manufacturing
28732 Witherspoon Pkwy (91355-5425)
PHONE..............................661 775-8366
▲ **EMP:** 40
SIC: 3728 5599 Aircraft parts and equipment, nec; Aircraft, self-propelled

(P-9692)
FMH AEROSPACE CORP
Also Called: F M H
17072 Daimler St (92614-5548)
PHONE..............................714 751-1000
Rick Busch, *CEO*
David Difranco, *Sec*
Valerie Gorman, *CFO*
▲ **EMP:** 100 **EST:** 1991
SQ FT: 15,000
SALES (est): 41.21MM
SALES (corp-wide): 6.15B **Publicly Held**
Web: www.fmhaerospace.com
SIC: 3728 Aircraft parts and equipment, nec
PA: Ametek, Inc.
1100 Cassatt Rd
Berwyn PA
610 647-2121

(P-9693)
FORMING SPECIALTIES INC
3262 Falkland Cir (92649-2812)
PHONE..............................310 639-1122
Darrell E Madole, *Pr*
EMP: 33 **EST:** 1976
SALES (est): 3.4MM **Privately Held**
Web: www.formingspecialties.com
SIC: 3728 3444 Aircraft parts and equipment, nec; Sheet metalwork

(P-9694)
FORREST MACHINING LLC
Also Called: Forrestmachining.com
27756 Avenue Mentry (91355-3453)
PHONE..............................661 257-0231
Tim Mickael, *CEO*
▲ **EMP:** 240 **EST:** 1979
SALES (est): 47.95MM
SALES (corp-wide): 47.95MM **Privately Held**
Web: www.fmiaerostructures.com
SIC: 3728 Aircraft parts and equipment, nec
PA: Dvsm, L.L.C.
760 Sw 9th Ave Ste 2300
Portland OR
503 223-2721

(P-9695)
FRAZIER AVIATION INC
445 N Fox St (91340-2501)
PHONE..............................818 898-1998
Robert L Frazier, *CEO*

Robert Frazier Iii, *Pr*
Charles E Ricard, *
Robert Frazier Iv, *Ex VP*
EMP: 44 **EST:** 1956
SQ FT: 44,000
SALES (est): 8.84MM **Privately Held**
Web: www.frazieraviation.com
SIC: 3728 5088 Aircraft body assemblies and parts; Transportation equipment and supplies

(P-9696)
GALI CORPORATION
Also Called: Dynamation Research
2301 Pontius Ave (90064-1809)
PHONE..............................310 477-1224
Gal Lipkin, *CEO*
EMP: 29 **EST:** 1983
SALES (est): 1.01MM **Privately Held**
Web: www.dynamationresearch.com
SIC: 3728 3812 Aircraft parts and equipment, nec; Aircraft control instruments

(P-9697)
GE AVIATION SYSTEMS LLC
Also Called: Mechancal Systm-Rial Refueling
23695 Via Del Rio (92887-2715)
PHONE..............................714 692-0200
Mary Normand, *Contrlr*
EMP: 21
SALES (corp-wide): 76.56B **Publicly Held**
Web: www.geaerospace.com
SIC: 3728 Aircraft assemblies, subassemblies, and parts, nec
HQ: Ge Aviation Systems Llc
1 Aviation Way
Cincinnati OH
937 898-9600

(P-9698)
GEAR MANUFACTURING INC
Also Called: G M I
3701 E Miraloma Ave (92806-2123)
PHONE..............................714 792-2895
Gary M Smith, *CEO*
EMP: 50 **EST:** 1989
SQ FT: 26,500
SALES (est): 10.44MM **Privately Held**
Web: www.gearmfg.com
SIC: 3728 3714 3566 3568 Gears, aircraft power transmission; Bearings, motor vehicle; Speed changers, drives, and gears; Power transmission equipment, nec

(P-9699)
GENERAL DYNAMICS OTS CAL INC
Also Called: GENERAL DYNAMICS OTS (CALIFORNIA), INC.
7603 Saint Andrews Ave Ste H (92154-8216)
PHONE..............................619 671-5411
EMP: 121
SALES (corp-wide): 39.41B **Publicly Held**
Web: www.gd-ots.com
SIC: 3728 Military aircraft equipment and armament
HQ: General Dynamics-Ots, Inc.
100 Carillon Pkwy Ste 100 # 100
Saint Petersburg FL
727 578-8100

(P-9700)
GIDDENS INDUSTRIES INC (DH)
3130 E Miraloma Ave (92806-1906)
PHONE..............................425 353-0405
Curt Schroeder, *Pr*
Kevin D Brown, *
Ron Case, *
Donald Devore, *

Michael F Finley, *
EMP: 150 **EST:** 1974
SALES (est): 52.45MM
SALES (corp-wide): 666.39MM **Privately Held**
Web: www.cadenceaerospace.com
SIC: 3728 Aircraft parts and equipment, nec
HQ: Giddens Holdings, Inc.
2600 94th St Sw Ste 150
Everett WA
425 353-0405

(P-9701)
GLEDHILL/LYONS INC
Also Called: Accurate Technology
1521 N Placentia Ave (92806-1236)
PHONE...............714 502-0274
David M Lyons, *Pr*
EMP: 43 **EST:** 2000
SQ FT: 31,200
SALES (est): 8.79MM **Privately Held**
Web: www.accuratetechnology.net
SIC: 3728 Aircraft parts and equipment, nec

(P-9702)
GLOBAL AEROSPACE TECH CORP
29077 Avenue Penn (91355-5426)
PHONE...............818 407-5600
Steve Cormier, *CEO*
EMP: 22 **EST:** 2006
SALES (est): 3.66MM **Privately Held**
Web: www.globalatcorp.com
SIC: 3728 Aircraft parts and equipment, nec

(P-9703)
GOODRICH CORPORATION
Goodrich Wheel and Brake Svcs
9920 Freeman Ave (90670-3421)
PHONE...............562 944-4441
Hosrow Bordbar, *Mgr*
EMP: 94
SALES (corp-wide): 67.07B **Publicly Held**
Web: www.collinsaerospace.com
SIC: 3728 Aircraft parts and equipment, nec
HQ: Goodrich Corporation
2730 W Tyvola Rd
Charlotte NC
704 423-7000

(P-9704)
GOODRICH CORPORATION
3355 E La Palma Ave (92806-2815)
PHONE...............714 984-1461
Rob Gibbs, *Genl Mgr*
EMP: 140
SALES (corp-wide): 67.07B **Publicly Held**
Web: www.collinsaerospace.com
SIC: 3728 Aircraft parts and equipment, nec
HQ: Goodrich Corporation
2730 W Tyvola Rd
Charlotte NC
704 423-7000

(P-9705)
GOODRICH CORPORATION
Also Called: Collins Aerospace
850 Lagoon Dr (91910-2001)
PHONE...............619 691-4111
David Gitlin, *Brnch Mgr*
EMP: 101
SALES (corp-wide): 67.07B **Publicly Held**
Web: www.collinsaerospace.com
SIC: 3728 Aircraft parts and equipment, nec
HQ: Goodrich Corporation
2730 W Tyvola Rd
Charlotte NC
704 423-7000

(P-9706)
HELICOPTER TECH CO LTD PARTNR
Also Called: Helicopter Technology Company
12902 S Broadway (90061-1118)
PHONE...............310 523-2750
Frank Palminteri, *Pr*
Gary Burdorf, *
◆ **EMP:** 24 **EST:** 1995
SQ FT: 197,000
SALES (est): 4.97MM **Privately Held**
Web: www.helicoptertech.com
SIC: 3728 3721 Aircraft parts and equipment, nec; Helicopters

(P-9707)
HUTCHINSON AROSPC & INDUST INC
Also Called: ARS
4510 W Vanowen St (91505-1135)
PHONE...............818 843-1000
Shano Cristilli, *Brnch Mgr*
EMP: 165
SALES (corp-wide): 788.22K **Publicly Held**
Web: www.hutchinsonai.com
SIC: 3728 Aircraft parts and equipment, nec
HQ: Hutchinson Aerospace & Industry, Inc.
82 South St
Hopkinton MA
508 417-7000

(P-9708)
HYDRAFLOW
Also Called: Hydraflow
1881 W Malvern Ave (92833-2403)
PHONE...............714 773-2600
EMP: 255 **EST:** 1961
SALES (est): 29.15MM **Privately Held**
Web: www.hydraflow.com
SIC: 3728 3492 Aircraft parts and equipment, nec; Fluid power valves for aircraft

(P-9709)
HYDRAULICS INTERNATIONAL INC (PA)
20961 Knapp St (91311-5926)
PHONE...............818 998-1231
Nicky Ghaemmaghami, *CEO*
Shah Banifazl, *
◆ **EMP:** 285 **EST:** 1976
SQ FT: 78,000
SALES (est): 107.64MM
SALES (corp-wide): 107.64MM **Privately Held**
Web: www.hiinet.com
SIC: 3728 Aircraft parts and equipment, nec

(P-9710)
HYDRAULICS INTERNATIONAL INC
9000 Mason Ave (91311-6178)
PHONE...............818 998-1236
Chuck Sherman, *Brnch Mgr*
EMP: 25
SALES (corp-wide): 107.64MM **Privately Held**
Web: www.hiinet.com
SIC: 3728 Aircraft parts and equipment, nec
PA: Hydraulics International, Inc.
20961 Knapp St
Chatsworth CA
818 998-1231

(P-9711)
HYDRAULICS INTERNATIONAL INC
9261 Independence Ave (91311-5905)
PHONE...............818 998-1231
EMP: 25
SALES (corp-wide): 107.64MM **Privately Held**
Web: www.hiigroup.com
SIC: 3728 Aircraft parts and equipment, nec
PA: Hydraulics International, Inc.
20961 Knapp St
Chatsworth CA
818 998-1231

(P-9712)
HYDRO-AIRE INC (HQ)
3000 Winona Ave (91504-2540)
PHONE...............818 526-2600
▲ **EMP:** 263 **EST:** 1947
SQ FT: 173,000
SALES (est): 184.7MM
SALES (corp-wide): 3.37B **Publicly Held**
Web: www.craneae.com
SIC: 3728 Aircraft parts and equipment, nec
PA: Crane Nxt, Co.
950 Winter St Fl 4
Waltham MA
610 430-2510

(P-9713)
HYDRO-AIRE AEROSPACE CORP
3000 Winona Ave (91504-2540)
PHONE...............818 526-2600
Jay Higgs, *Pr*
EMP: 200
SALES (corp-wide): 3.37B **Publicly Held**
SIC: 3728 Aircraft parts and equipment, nec
HQ: Hydro-Aire Aerospace Corp.
249 Abbe Rd S
Elyria OH
440 323-3211

(P-9714)
HYDROFORM USA INCORPORATED
2848 E 208th St (90810-1101)
PHONE...............310 632-6353
Chester K Jablonski, *CEO*
Mauricio Salazar, *
Jeffrey Lake, *Corporate Counsel**
▼ **EMP:** 154 **EST:** 1982
SQ FT: 95,000
SALES (est): 23.59MM **Privately Held**
Web: www.hydroformusa.com
SIC: 3728 Aircraft parts and equipment, nec

(P-9715)
ICE MANAGEMENT SYSTEMS INC
Also Called: IMS-Ess
27449 Colt Ct (92590-3674)
PHONE...............951 676-2751
EMP: 28
SIC: 3728 3694 3357 Deicing equipment, aircraft; Harness wiring sets, internal combustion engines; Aircraft wire and cable, nonferrous

(P-9716)
IKHANA GROUP LLC
Also Called: Ikhana Aircraft Services
37260 Sky Canyon Dr Hngr 20 (92563-2677)
PHONE...............951 600-0009
Brian Raduenz, *CEO*
▲ **EMP:** 120 **EST:** 2007
SALES (est): 24.83MM **Privately Held**
Web: www.ikhanagroup.com
SIC: 3728 Flaps, aircraft wing
PA: Aevex Aerospace, Llc
440 Stevens Ave Ste 150

Solana Beach CA

(P-9717)
IMPRESA AEROSPACE LLC
344 W 157th St (90248-2135)
PHONE...............310 354-1200
Steve Loye, *
Dennis Fitzgerald, *
Marco Barrantes, *
EMP: 169 **EST:** 1987
SQ FT: 26,000
SALES (est): 42MM
SALES (corp-wide): 42.24MM **Privately Held**
Web: www.impresaaerospace.com
SIC: 3728 3444 Aircraft parts and equipment, nec; Sheet metalwork
HQ: Impresa Acquisition Corporation
344 W 157th St
Gardena CA

(P-9718)
INET AIRPORT SYSTEMS INC
Also Called: Inet
5665 Corporate Ave (90630-4727)
PHONE...............714 888-2700
EMP: 50
SIC: 3728 4581 5088 Aircraft parts and equipment, nec; Aircraft servicing and repairing; Aircraft and parts, nec

(P-9719)
INFINITY AEROSPACE INC (PA)
9060 Winnetka Ave (91324-3235)
PHONE...............818 998-9811
Chet Huffman, *CEO*
R Lloyd Huffman, *
Steve Lonngren, *
EMP: 50 **EST:** 1958
SQ FT: 30,000
SALES (est): 9.05MM
SALES (corp-wide): 9.05MM **Privately Held**
SIC: 3728 Aircraft parts and equipment, nec

(P-9720)
INFLIGHT WARNING SYSTEMS INC
Also Called: Iws Predictive Technologies
3940 Prospect Ave Ste P (92886-1752)
PHONE...............714 993-9394
Joseph Barclay, *Pr*
George Orff, *Sec*
Jeff Bulkin, *CFO*
EMP: 19 **EST:** 2002
SQ FT: 6,000
SALES (est): 2.72MM **Privately Held**
Web: www.inflightwarningsystems.com
SIC: 3728 Aircraft assemblies, subassemblies, and parts, nec

(P-9721)
INTEGRAL AEROSPACE LLC
Also Called: Pcx Aerosystems - Santa Ana
2040 E Dyer Rd (92705-5710)
PHONE...............949 250-3123
Thomas Holzthum, *CEO*
John Kutler, *
Bryan Mclean, *VP*
Alan Guzik, *
EMP: 190 **EST:** 2016
SQ FT: 270,000
SALES (est): 50MM
SALES (corp-wide): 146.76MM **Privately Held**
Web: www.integralaerospace.com
SIC: 3728 Aircraft parts and equipment, nec
PA: Pcx Aerostructures, Llc
300 Fenn Rd
Newington CT
860 666-2471

(P-9722)

IRISH INTERIORS INC

5511 Skylab Rd Ste 101 (92647-2071)
PHONE...............................562 344-1700
Karl Jonson, *VP*
EMP: 200
SALES (corp-wide): 66.61B **Publicly Held**
Web: www.encoreaerospace.com
SIC: 3728 Aircraft parts and equipment, nec
HQ: Irish Interiors, Inc.
  5511 Skylab Rd Ste 101
  Huntington Beach CA
  949 559-0930

(P-9723)

IRISH INTERIORS INC (HQ)

Also Called: Lift By Encore
5511 Skylab Rd Ste 101 (92647-2071)
PHONE...............................949 559-0930
Thomas Mcfarland, *Pr*
Micheal Melancon, *
Karl Jonson, *
▲ **EMP:** 130 **EST:** 1972
SQ FT: 42,000
SALES (est): 81.25MM
SALES (corp-wide): 66.61B **Publicly Held**
Web: www.encoreaerospace.com
SIC: 3728 1799 Aircraft parts and
  equipment, nec; Renovation of aircraft
  interiors
PA: The Boeing Company
  929 Long Bridge Dr
  Arlington VA
  703 414-6338

(P-9724)

IRISH INTERIORS HOLDINGS INC

Also Called: IRISH INTERIORS HOLDINGS,
INC.
1729 Apollo Ct (90740-5617)
PHONE...............................949 559-0930
EMP: 20
SALES (corp-wide): 66.61B **Publicly Held**
Web: www.encoreaerospace.com
SIC: 3728 Aircraft parts and equipment, nec
HQ: Irish Interiors, Inc.
  5511 Skylab Rd Ste 101
  Huntington Beach CA
  949 559-0930

(P-9725)

IRWIN AVIATION INC

Also Called: Aero Performance
225 Airport Cir (92878-5027)
PHONE...............................951 372-9555
James Irwin, *CEO*
Nanci Irwin, *
EMP: 30 **EST:** 2014
SALES (est): 4.75MM **Privately Held**
Web: www.aeroperformance.com
SIC: 3728 Aircraft parts and equipment, nec

(P-9726)

ITT AEROSPACE CONTROLS LLC (HQ)

28150 Industry Dr (91355-4100)
PHONE...............................315 568-7258
Steven Giuliano, *
▲ **EMP:** 78 **EST:** 2011
SALES (est): 179.26MM
SALES (corp-wide): 2.99B **Publicly Held**
Web: www.ittaerospace.com
SIC: 3728 Aircraft parts and equipment, nec
PA: Itt Inc.
  100 Washington Blvd Fl 6
  Stamford CT
  914 641-2000

(P-9727)

ITT AEROSPACE CONTROLS LLC

ITT Aerospace Controls Unit S
28150 Industry Dr (91355-4101)
PHONE...............................661 295-4000
Robert Briggs, *Mgr*
EMP: 300
SALES (corp-wide): 2.99B **Publicly Held**
Web: www.ittaerospace.com
SIC: 3728 Aircraft parts and equipment, nec
HQ: Itt Aerospace Controls Llc
  28150 Industry Dr
  Valencia CA
  315 568-7258

(P-9728)

JET AIR FBO LLC

681 Kenney St (92020-1278)
PHONE...............................619 448-5991
EMP: 30 **EST:** 2005
SQ FT: 250,000
SALES (est): 2.76MM **Privately Held**
Web: www.jetairsystems.com
SIC: 3728 Refueling equipment for use in
  flight, airplane

(P-9729)

JOHNSON CALDRAUL INC

Also Called: Cal-Draulics
220 N Delilah St Ste 101 (92879-1883)
PHONE...............................951 340-1067
Douglas Johnson, *Pr*
Kenneth W Johnson, *
EMP: 30 **EST:** 1992
SQ FT: 12,000
SALES (est): 2.96MM **Privately Held**
SIC: 3728 3593 Aircraft parts and
  equipment, nec; Fluid power cylinders and
  actuators

(P-9730)

KAREM AIRCRAFT INC

1 Capital Dr (92630-2203)
PHONE...............................949 859-4444
EMP: 48 **EST:** 2004
SALES (est): 8.58MM **Privately Held**
Web: www.karemaircraft.com
SIC: 3728 Aircraft parts and equipment, nec

(P-9731)

KIRKHILL INC (HQ)

Also Called: Sfs
300 E Cypress St (92821-4007)
PHONE...............................714 529-4901
Kevin Stein, *Pr*
EMP: 103 **EST:** 2018
SALES (est): 94.99MM
SALES (corp-wide): 6.58B **Publicly Held**
Web: www.kirkhill.com
SIC: 3728 Aircraft parts and equipment, nec
PA: Transdigm Group Incorporated
  1301 E 9th St Ste 3000
  Cleveland OH
  216 706-2960

(P-9732)

KLUNE INDUSTRIES INC (DH)

Also Called: PCC Aerostructures
7323 Coldwater Canyon Ave (91605-4206)
PHONE...............................818 503-8100
Joseph I Snowden, *CEO*
Kenneth Ward, *
▲ **EMP:** 358 **EST:** 1972
SQ FT: 125,000
SALES (est): 131.11MM
SALES (corp-wide): 302.09B **Publicly
Held**
Web: www.pccaero.com

SIC: 3728 Aircraft parts and equipment, nec
HQ: Klune Holdings, Inc.
  7323 Coldwater Canyon Ave
  North Hollywood CA

(P-9733)

LANIC ENGINEERING INC (PA)

Also Called: Lanic Aerospace
12144 6th St (91730-6111)
PHONE...............................877 763-0411
S Robert Leaming, *CEO*
Shaun Arnold, *
Jason Arnold, *Prin*
EMP: 35 **EST:** 1984
SQ FT: 30,000
SALES (est): 17.35MM
SALES (corp-wide): 17.35MM **Privately
Held**
Web: www.lanicaerospace.com
SIC: 3728 3721 Aircraft parts and
  equipment, nec; Aircraft

(P-9734)

LAUNCHPINT ELC PRPLSION SLTONS

Also Called: Launchpoint Eps
320 Storke Rd (93117-2992)
PHONE...............................805 683-9659
Robert Reali, *CEO*
Robert Reali, *Prin*
Brian Clark, *Prin*
Christopher Grieco, *Prin*
Vicki Young, *Prin*
EMP: 20 **EST:** 2018
SALES (est): 2.82MM **Privately Held**
Web: www.launchpointeps.com
SIC: 3728 Aircraft parts and equipment, nec

(P-9735)

LEACH INTERNATIONAL CORP (DH)

6900 Orangethorpe Ave (90620-1390)
P.O. Box 5032 (90622-5032)
PHONE...............................714 736-7537
Richard Brad Lawrence, *CEO*
Mark Thek, *
Alain Durand, *
Carsten Muller, *
EMP: 500 **EST:** 1919
SALES (est): 175.58MM
SALES (corp-wide): 6.58B **Publicly Held**
Web: www.transdigm.com
SIC: 3728 Aircraft parts and equipment, nec
HQ: Esterline Technologies Corp
  1301 E 9th St Ste 3000
  Cleveland OH
  216 706-2960

(P-9736)

LEFIELL MANUFACTURING COMPANY

Also Called: Lefiell
13700 Firestone Blvd (90670-5652)
PHONE...............................562 921-3411
▲ **EMP:** 150 **EST:** 1930
SALES (est): 26.8MM **Privately Held**
Web: www.lefiell.com
SIC: 3728 3599 3724 Aircraft assemblies,
  subassemblies, and parts, nec; Machine
  shop, jobbing and repair; Aircraft engines
  and engine parts

(P-9737)

LLAMAS PLASTICS INC

12970 Bradley Ave (91342-3829)
PHONE...............................818 362-0371
Ricardo M Llamas, *CEO*
Oswald Llamas, *
Jeff Mabry, *

EMP: 105 **EST:** 1977
SQ FT: 37,000
SALES (est): 19.45MM **Privately Held**
Web: www.llamas-plastics.com
SIC: 3728 3089 3083 Aircraft parts and
  equipment, nec; Plastics containers, except
  foam; Laminated plastics plate and sheet

(P-9738)

LONG-LOK LLC

20531 Belshaw Ave (90746-3505)
PHONE...............................424 209-8726
EMP: 21
SALES (corp-wide): 9.6MM **Privately Held**
Web: www.longlok.com
SIC: 3728 R and D by manuf., aircraft parts
  and auxiliary equipment
PA: Long-Lok, Llc
  10630 Chester Rd
  Cincinnati OH
  336 343-7319

(P-9739)

LUXFER INC (DH)

Also Called: Luxfer Gas Cylinder
3016 Kansas Ave Bldg 1 (92507-3445)
PHONE...............................951 684-5110
John Rhodes, *Pr*
◆ **EMP:** 70 **EST:** 1973
SQ FT: 120,000
SALES (est): 110.24MM
SALES (corp-wide): 423.4MM **Privately
Held**
Web: www.luxfercylinders.com
SIC: 3728 3354 Aircraft parts and
  equipment, nec; Shapes, extruded
  aluminum, nec
HQ: Ba Holdings, Inc.
  3016 Kansas Ave Bldg 1
  Riverside CA

(P-9740)

MACHINETEK LLC

1985 Palomar Oaks Way (92011-1307)
PHONE...............................760 438-6644
EMP: 18 **EST:** 1992
SQ FT: 21,000
SALES (est): 4.94MM **Privately Held**
Web: www.machinetek.com
SIC: 3728 Aircraft assemblies,
  subassemblies, and parts, nec

(P-9741)

MANEY AIRCRAFT INC

Also Called: Maney Aircraft
1305 S Wanamaker Ave (91761-2237)
PHONE...............................909 390-2500
Martin T Bright, *CEO*
David A Ederer, *
Michael Neely, *
EMP: 30 **EST:** 1955
SQ FT: 14,700
SALES (est): 5.23MM **Privately Held**
Web: www.maneyaircraft.com
SIC: 3728 5088 3829 3812 Aircraft
  assemblies, subassemblies, and parts, nec;
  Aircraft and parts, nec; Aircraft and motor
  vehicle measurement equipment; Search
  and navigation equipment

(P-9742)

MARINO ENTERPRISES INC

Also Called: Gear Technology
10671 Civic Center Dr (91730-3804)
PHONE...............................909 476-0343
Thomas Marino, *Pr*
EMP: 35 **EST:** 1986
SQ FT: 16,320
SALES (est): 7.2MM **Privately Held**
Web: www.intra-aerospace.com

SIC: **3728** 3769 Gears, aircraft power transmission; Space vehicle equipment, nec

(P-9743)
MASON ELECTRIC CO
13955 Balboa Blvd (91342-1084)
PHONE..............................818 361-3366
Steven Brune, *Pr*
EMP: 350 **EST:** 1968
SQ FT: 105,000
SALES (est): 66.75MM
SALES (corp-wide): 6.58B **Publicly Held**
Web: www.masoncontrols.com
SIC: 3728 Aircraft parts and equipment, nec
HQ: Esterline Technologies Corp
1301 E 9th St Ste 3000
Cleveland OH
216 706-2960

(P-9744)
MASTER RESEARCH & MFG INC
13528 Pumice St (90650-5249)
PHONE..............................562 483-8789
Enrique Viano, *VP*
EMP: 52 **EST:** 1977
SQ FT: 31,200
SALES (est): 9.2MM **Privately Held**
Web: www.master-research.com
SIC: 3728 Aircraft body assemblies and parts

(P-9745)
MAVERICK AEROSPACE LLC
3718 Capitol Ave (90601-1731)
PHONE..............................714 578-1700
Steve Crisanti, *CEO*
Steve Crisanti, *Managing Member*
George Ono, *
Val Darie, *
Scott Curry, *
EMP: 100 **EST:** 2017
SQ FT: 40,000
SALES (est): 10.63MM **Privately Held**
Web: www.mavaero.com
SIC: 3728 3544 3761 3441 Aircraft parts and equipment, nec; Special dies, tools, jigs, and fixtures; Guided missiles and space vehicles; Fabricated structural metal

(P-9746)
MEGGITT (SAN DIEGO) INC (HQ)
Also Called: Meggitt Polymers & Composites
6650 Top Gun St (92121-4112)
PHONE..............................858 824-8976
EMP: 120 **EST:** 2008
SQ FT: 120,000
SALES (est): 51.8MM
SALES (corp-wide): 19.07B **Publicly Held**
Web: www.meggitt.com
SIC: 3728 Roto-blades for helicopters
PA: Parker-Hannifin Corporation
6035 Parkland Blvd
Cleveland OH
216 896-3000

(P-9747)
MEGGITT DEFENSE SYSTEMS INC
9801 Muirlands Blvd (92618-2521)
PHONE..............................949 465-7700
Roger Brum, *Pr*
Greg Brostek, *
Bob Bettwy, *
EMP: 353 **EST:** 1998
SQ FT: 153,000
SALES (est): 108.39MM
SALES (corp-wide): 19.07B **Publicly Held**
Web: www.meggittdefense.com
SIC: 3728 Military aircraft equipment and armament
HQ: Meggitt Limited
Pilot Way

Coventry W MIDLANDS
247 682-6900

(P-9748)
MEGGITT NORTH HOLLYWOOD INC (DH)
Also Called: Meggitt Control Systems
12838 Saticoy St (91605-3505)
PHONE..............................818 765-8160
Dennis Hutton, *CEO*
▲ **EMP:** 230 **EST:** 1969
SQ FT: 10,000
SALES (est): 100.51MM
SALES (corp-wide): 19.07B **Publicly Held**
Web: www.meggitt.com
SIC: 3728 Aircraft parts and equipment, nec
HQ: Meggitt Limited
Pilot Way
Coventry W MIDLANDS
247 682-6900

(P-9749)
MEGGITT NORTH HOLLYWOOD INC
10092 Foxrun Rd (92705-1407)
PHONE..............................818 691-6258
Jen Larsen, *Brnch Mgr*
EMP: 23
SALES (corp-wide): 19.07B **Publicly Held**
Web: www.meggitt.com
SIC: 3728 Aircraft parts and equipment, nec
HQ: Meggitt (North Hollywood), Inc.
12838 Saticoy St
North Hollywood CA

(P-9750)
MEGGITT SAFETY SYSTEMS INC
Also Called: Htl Manufacturing Div
1785 Voyager Ave (93063-3363)
PHONE..............................805 584-4100
Dennis Hutton, *Pr*
EMP: 90
SALES (corp-wide): 19.07B **Publicly Held**
Web: www.meggitt.com
SIC: 3728 Aircraft parts and equipment, nec
HQ: Meggitt Safety Systems, Inc.
1785 Voyager Ave
Simi Valley CA
805 584-4100

(P-9751)
MEGGITT SAFETY SYSTEMS INC
Meggitt Ctrl Systms-Vntura Cnt
1785 Voyager Ave (93063-3349)
PHONE..............................805 584-4100
Jim Healy, *Site Director*
EMP: 200
SALES (corp-wide): 19.07B **Publicly Held**
Web: www.meggitt.com
SIC: 3728 Aircraft parts and equipment, nec
HQ: Meggitt Safety Systems, Inc.
1785 Voyager Ave
Simi Valley CA
805 584-4100

(P-9752)
MEGGITT-USA INC (DH)
Also Called: Meggitt Polymers & Composites
1955 Surveyor Ave (93063-3369)
PHONE..............................805 526-5700
Eric Lardiere, *Sr VP*
Robert W Soukup, *
Greg Brostek, *
▲ **EMP:** 310 **EST:** 1980
SQ FT: 3,000
SALES (est): 663.26MM
SALES (corp-wide): 19.07B **Publicly Held**

Web: www.meggitt.com
SIC: 3728 3829 3679 Aircraft parts and equipment, nec; Vibration meters, analyzers, and calibrators; Electronic switches
HQ: Meggitt Limited
Pilot Way
Coventry W MIDLANDS
247 708-7211

(P-9753)
MISSION CRTICAL COMPOSITES LLC
15400 Graham St Ste 102 (92649-1257)
PHONE..............................714 831-2100
Robert Hartman, *Managing Member*
EMP: 22 **EST:** 2012
SALES (est): 3.87MM **Privately Held**
Web:
www.missioncriticalcomposites.com
SIC: 3728 3721 3724 3761 Aircraft assemblies, subassemblies, and parts, nec; Aircraft; Aircraft engines and engine parts; Guided missiles and space vehicles

(P-9754)
MULGREW ARCFT COMPONENTS INC
1810 S Shamrock Ave (91016-4251)
PHONE..............................626 256-1375
Mike Houshiar, *CEO*
EMP: 58 **EST:** 1979
SQ FT: 45,000
SALES (est): 9.25MM **Privately Held**
Web: www.mulgrewaircraft.com
SIC: 3728 Aircraft assemblies, subassemblies, and parts, nec

(P-9755)
NASCO AIRCRAFT BRAKE INC
Also Called: Meggitt Arcft Braking Systems
13300 Estrella Ave (90248-1519)
PHONE..............................310 532-4430
Daniel Aron, *CEO*
Phil Friedman, *
EMP: 100 **EST:** 1981
SQ FT: 25,000
SALES (est): 20.85MM
SALES (corp-wide): 19.07B **Publicly Held**
Web: www.nascoaircraft.com
SIC: 3728 Brakes, aircraft
HQ: Meggitt Aircraft Braking Systems Corporation
1204 Massillon Rd
Akron OH
330 796-4400

(P-9756)
NEILL AIRCRAFT CO
1260 W 15th St (90813-1302)
PHONE..............................562 432-7981
Judith L Carpenter, *Pr*
EMP: 275 **EST:** 1956
SQ FT: 150,000
SALES (est): 48.37MM **Privately Held**
Web: www.neillaircraft.com
SIC: 3728 Aircraft body and wing assemblies and parts

(P-9757)
NOTTHOFF ENGINEERING L A INC
5416 Argosy Ave (92649-1039)
PHONE..............................714 894-9802
Kelly Kaller, *CEO*
Karen Ewing, *
▲ **EMP:** 55 **EST:** 1941
SALES (est): 3.95MM **Privately Held**
Web: www.notthoff.com

SIC: **3728** 3599 Aircraft parts and equipment, nec; Machine shop, jobbing and repair

(P-9758)
OTTO INSTRUMENT SERVICE INC (PA)
1441 Valencia Pl (91761-7639)
PHONE..............................909 930-5800
William R Otto Junior, *Pr*
Lynne Amber Otto-miller, *BORN 1979 1999*
EMP: 45 **EST:** 1946
SQ FT: 36,800
SALES (est): 29.55MM
SALES (corp-wide): 29.55MM **Privately Held**
Web: www.ottoinstrument.com
SIC: 3728 5088 7699 Aircraft parts and equipment, nec; Aircraft equipment and supplies, nec; Aircraft flight instrument repair

(P-9759)
PACIFIC CONTOURS CORPORATION
5340 E Hunter Ave (92807-2053)
PHONE..............................714 693-1260
Tom Rapacz, *Pr*
Tim Anderson, *
Jon Stannard, *
EMP: 60 **EST:** 1997
SQ FT: 36,000
SALES (est): 11.75MM **Privately Held**
Web: www.pacificcontours.com
SIC: 3728 5088 Aircraft assemblies, subassemblies, and parts, nec; Aircraft and parts, nec

(P-9760)
PACIFIC PRECISION PRODUCTS MFG INC
Also Called: Pacific Precision Products
9671 Irvine Ctr Dr Koll Ctr Ii Bldg 6 (92618-4652)
PHONE..............................949 727-3844
EMP: 40 **EST:** 1973
SALES (est): 3.43MM **Privately Held**
SIC: 3728 3812 Oxygen systems, aircraft; Search and navigation equipment

(P-9761)
PACIFIC SKY SUPPLY INC
8230 San Fernando Rd (91352-3218)
PHONE..............................818 768-3700
Emilio B Perez, *CEO*
Emilio Perez, *
Kelly Anderson, *
EMP: 59 **EST:** 1954
SQ FT: 27,000
SALES (est): 9.14MM **Privately Held**
Web: www.pacsky.com
SIC: 3728 3724 5088 Aircraft parts and equipment, nec; Aircraft engines and engine parts; Transportation equipment and supplies

(P-9762)
PARKER-HANNIFIN CORPORATION
Also Called: Parker Aerospace
14300 Alton Pkwy (92618-1898)
PHONE..............................949 833-3000
Robert Bond, *Brnch Mgr*
EMP: 106
SQ FT: 180,000
SALES (corp-wide): 19.07B **Publicly Held**
Web: www.parker.com
SIC: 3728 Aircraft assemblies, subassemblies, and parts, nec

PA: Parker-Hannifin Corporation
6035 Parkland Blvd
Cleveland OH
216 896-3000

(P-9763)

PARKER-HANNIFIN CORPORATION

Also Called: Stratoflex Product Division
3800 Calle Tecate (93012-5070)
PHONE..............................805 484-8533
William Cartmill, *Brnch Mgr*
EMP: 81
SALES (corp-wide): 19.07B **Publicly Held**
Web: www.parker.com
SIC: 3728 3769 3568 Aircraft parts and equipment, nec; Space vehicle equipment, nec; Power transmission equipment, nec
PA: Parker-Hannifin Corporation
6035 Parkland Blvd
Cleveland OH
216 896-3000

(P-9764)

PCA AEROSPACE INC (PA)

17800 Gothard St (92647-6217)
PHONE..............................714 841-1750
Brian Murray, *CEO*
Gregory Ruffalo, *
▲ **EMP:** 71 **EST:** 1963
SQ FT: 58,000
SALES (est): 19.09MM
SALES (corp-wide): 19.09MM **Privately Held**
Web: www.lanicaero.com
SIC: 3728 3599 Aircraft parts and equipment, nec; Machine shop, jobbing and repair

(P-9765)

PERFORMANCE PLASTICS INC

7919 Saint Andrews Ave (92154-8224)
PHONE..............................714 343-3928
Jim Renaud, *Pr*
EMP: 99 **EST:** 1977
SQ FT: 50,000
SALES (est): 22.56MM **Privately Held**
Web: www.perf-plastics.com
SIC: 3728 Aircraft parts and equipment, nec
PA: Rock West Composites, Inc.
7625 Panasonic Way
San Diego CA

(P-9766)

PMC INC (HQ)

12243 Branford St (91352-1010)
PHONE..............................818 896-1101
Christopher Lette, *Pr*
EMP: 88 **EST:** 1962
SALES (est): 541.32MM
SALES (corp-wide): 1.71B **Privately Held**
Web: www.pmcglobalinc.com
SIC: 3728 3724 Bodies, aircraft; Engine mount parts, aircraft
PA: Pmc Global, Inc.
12243 Branford St
Sun Valley CA
818 896-1101

(P-9767)

PMD INC

12464 Mccann Dr (90670-3335)
PHONE..............................925 765-0629
Peter D Gillis, *CEO*
EMP: 18 **EST:** 2017
SALES (est): 2.24MM **Privately Held**
Web: www.pmdprecision.com
SIC: 3728 Gears, aircraft power transmission

(P-9768)

PRECISION AEROSPACE CORP

11155 Jersey Blvd Ste A (91730-5148)
PHONE..............................909 945-9604
Jim Hudson, *Pr*
EMP: 70 **EST:** 1989
SQ FT: 50,000
SALES (est): 9.42MM **Privately Held**
Web: www.pac.cc
SIC: 3728 Aircraft assemblies, subassemblies, and parts, nec

(P-9769)

PRECISION TUBE BENDING

13626 Talc St (90670-5114)
PHONE..............................562 921-6723
Diane M Williams, *CEO*
EMP: 98 **EST:** 1957
SQ FT: 60,000
SALES (est): 18.84MM **Privately Held**
Web: www.precision-tube-bending.com
SIC: 3728 3498 Aircraft parts and equipment, nec; Tube fabricating (contract bending and shaping)

(P-9770)

PTI TECHNOLOGIES INC (DH)

501 Del Norte Blvd (93030-7983)
PHONE..............................805 604-3700
Rowland Ellis, *Pr*
Beth Kozlowski, *
▲ **EMP:** 212 **EST:** 1979
SQ FT: 225,000
SALES (est): 57.5MM **Publicly Held**
Web: www.ptitechnologies.com
SIC: 3728 Aircraft parts and equipment, nec
HQ: Esco Technologies Holding Llc
9900 Clayton Rd Ste A
Saint Louis MO
314 213-7200

(P-9771)

Q1 TEST INC

1100 S Grove Ave Ste B2 (91761-4574)
PHONE..............................909 390-9718
Allen Riley, *CEO*
Jason Riley, *Pr*
EMP: 21 **EST:** 2005
SQ FT: 10,500
SALES (est): 4.14MM **Privately Held**
Web: www.q1testinc.com
SIC: 3728 Turret test fixtures, aircraft

(P-9772)

QPI HOLDINGS INC (DH)

22906 Frampton Ave (90501-5035)
PHONE..............................310 539-2855
David J Hammond, *Prin*
EMP: 22 **EST:** 2014
SALES (est): 21.34MM
SALES (corp-wide): 666.39MM **Privately Held**
Web: www.cadenceaerospace.com
SIC: 3728 Aircraft assemblies, subassemblies, and parts, nec
HQ: Cadence Aerospace, Llc
3150 E Miraloma Ave
Anaheim CA
949 877-3630

(P-9773)

QUALITY FORMING LLC

Also Called: Qfi Prv Aerospace
22906 Frampton Ave (90501-5035)
PHONE..............................310 539-2855
Mark Severns, *Pr*
▲ **EMP:** 100 **EST:** 1972
SALES (est): 21.34MM
SALES (corp-wide): 666.39MM **Privately Held**

Web: www.cadenceaerospace.com
SIC: 3728 Aircraft assemblies, subassemblies, and parts, nec
HQ: Qpi Holdings, Inc.
22906 Frampton Ave
Torrance CA
310 539-2855

(P-9774)

QUATRO COMPOSITES LLC

Also Called: Quatro Composites
13250 Gregg St Ste A1 (92064-7164)
PHONE..............................712 707-9200
EMP: 160
Web: www.sekisuiaerospace.com
SIC: 3728 Aircraft parts and equipment, nec
HQ: Quatro Composites, L.L.C.
403 14th St Se
Orange City IA
712 707-9200

(P-9775)

ROBINSON HELICOPTER CO INC

2901 Airport Dr (90505-6115)
PHONE..............................310 539-0508
Kurt L Robinson, *CEO*
Frank Robinson, *
Tim Goetz, *
P Wayne Walden, *
◆ **EMP:** 970 **EST:** 1973
SQ FT: 260,000
SALES (est): 171.82MM **Privately Held**
Web: www.robinsonheli.com
SIC: 3728 Aircraft parts and equipment, nec

(P-9776)

ROCKWELL COLLINS INC

1733 Alton Pkwy (92606-4901)
PHONE..............................714 929-3000
EMP: 51
SALES (corp-wide): 67.07B **Publicly Held**
Web: www.rtx.com
SIC: 3728 Aircraft parts and equipment, nec
HQ: Rockwell Collins, Inc.
400 Collins Rd Ne
Cedar Rapids IA

(P-9777)

ROCKWELL COLLINS INC

1757 Carr Rd Ste 100 (92231-9781)
PHONE..............................760 768-4732
Nicolas Pineda, *Mgr*
EMP: 25
SALES (corp-wide): 67.07B **Publicly Held**
Web: www.rockwellcollins.com
SIC: 3728 Aircraft parts and equipment, nec
HQ: Rockwell Collins, Inc.
400 Collins Rd Ne
Cedar Rapids IA

(P-9778)

ROGERS HOLDING COMPANY INC

Also Called: V & M Precision Grinding Co.
1130 Columbia St (92821-2921)
PHONE..............................714 257-4850
Aldo Devile, *Prin*
Tom Rogers, *
EMP: 60 **EST:** 1946
SQ FT: 65,000
SALES (est): 4.69MM **Privately Held**
Web: www.vmprecision.com
SIC: 3728 Alighting (landing gear) assemblies, aircraft

(P-9779)

ROHR INC (HQ)

Also Called: Collins Aerospace
850 Lagoon Dr (91910-2001)
PHONE..............................619 691-4111

Greg Peters, *Pr*
Curtis Reusser, *
Kenneth Wood, *
Robert A Gustafson, *General Vice President**
Brian Broderick, *
▲ **EMP:** 2100 **EST:** 1969
SQ FT: 2,770,000
SALES (est): 901.28MM
SALES (corp-wide): 67.07B **Publicly Held**
SIC: 3728 Nacelles, aircraft
PA: Rtx Corporation
1000 Wilson Blvd
Arlington VA
781 522-3000

(P-9780)

RSA ENGINEERED PRODUCTS LLC

Also Called: Trimas Aerospace
110 W Cochran St Ste A (93065-6228)
PHONE..............................805 584-4150
Ray Scarcello, *CEO*
◆ **EMP:** 90 **EST:** 2012
SQ FT: 43,000
SALES (est): 27.89MM
SALES (corp-wide): 883.83MM **Publicly Held**
Web: www.rsaeng.com
SIC: 3728 Aircraft parts and equipment, nec
PA: Trimas Corporation
38505 Woodward Ave # 200
Bloomfield Hills MI
248 631-5450

(P-9781)

SABRIN CORPORATION

Also Called: Astronics Company
2836 E Walnut St (91107-3755)
PHONE..............................626 792-3813
Julian Doherty, *CEO*
▲ **EMP:** 19 **EST:** 1961
SQ FT: 8,000
SALES (est): 3.02MM **Privately Held**
Web: www.sabrin.com
SIC: 3728 3444 3544 3499 Aircraft parts and equipment, nec; Sheet metalwork; Special dies, tools, jigs, and fixtures; Shims, metal

(P-9782)

SAFRAN CABIN GALLEYS US INC (HQ)

17311 Nichols Ln (92647-5721)
PHONE..............................714 861-7300
Matthew Stafford, *CEO*
Vincent Kozar, *CFO*
◆ **EMP:** 717 **EST:** 1986
SQ FT: 90,000
SALES (est): 289.68MM
SALES (corp-wide): 650.78MM **Privately Held**
SIC: 3728 Aircraft parts and equipment, nec
PA: Safran
2 Bd Du General Martial Valin
Paris

(P-9783)

SAFRAN CABIN INC (HQ)

5701 Bolsa Ave (92647-2063)
PHONE..............................714 934-0000
Jorge Ortega, *CEO*
Norman Jordan, *
Scott Savian, *
Daniel Edmundson, *
Arnault Dumont Lauret, *
▲ **EMP:** 500 **EST:** 1972
SQ FT: 150,000
SALES (est): 508.16MM
SALES (corp-wide): 650.78MM **Privately Held**

PRODUCTS & SVCS

Web: www.safran-group.com
SIC: 3728 Aircraft assemblies,
  subassemblies, and parts, nec
PA: Safran
  2 Bd Du General Martial Valin
  Paris

(P-9784)
SAFRAN CABIN INC
11240 Warland Dr (90630-5035)
PHONE..............................562 344-4780
Gary Reese, *Brnch Mgr*
EMP: 248
SALES (corp-wide): 650.78MM **Privately Held**
Web: www.safran-group.com
SIC: 3728 Aircraft assemblies,
  subassemblies, and parts, nec
HQ: Safran Cabin Inc.
  5701 Bolsa Ave
  Huntington Beach CA
  714 934-0000

(P-9785)
SAFRAN CABIN INC
Also Called: C & D Aerospace
7330 Lincoln Way (92841-1427)
PHONE..............................714 891-1906
Alec Azarian, *Brnch Mgr*
EMP: 140
SALES (corp-wide): 650.78MM **Privately Held**
Web: www.safran-group.com
SIC: 3728 3443 Aircraft assemblies,
  subassemblies, and parts, nec; Fabricated
  plate work (boiler shop)
HQ: Safran Cabin Inc.
  5701 Bolsa Ave
  Huntington Beach CA
  714 934-0000

(P-9786)
SAFRAN CABIN INC
12472 Industry St (92841-2819)
PHONE..............................714 901-2672
Mike Boyd, *Brnch Mgr*
EMP: 137
SALES (corp-wide): 650.78MM **Privately Held**
Web: www.safran-group.com
SIC: 3728 Aircraft parts and equipment, nec
HQ: Safran Cabin Inc.
  5701 Bolsa Ave
  Huntington Beach CA
  714 934-0000

(P-9787)
SAFRAN CABIN INC
1500 Glenn Curtiss St (90746-4012)
PHONE..............................714 934-0000
EMP: 119
SALES (corp-wide): 650.78MM **Privately Held**
Web: www.safran-group.com
SIC: 3728 Aircraft assemblies,
  subassemblies, and parts, nec
HQ: Safran Cabin Inc.
  5701 Bolsa Ave
  Huntington Beach CA
  714 934-0000

(P-9788)
SAFRAN CABIN INC
2850 Skyway Dr (93455-1410)
PHONE..............................805 922-3013
Jude F Dozor, *Brnch Mgr*
EMP: 140
SALES (corp-wide): 650.78MM **Privately Held**
Web: www.safran-group.com

SIC: 3728 Aircraft parts and equipment, nec
HQ: Safran Cabin Inc.
  5701 Bolsa Ave
  Huntington Beach CA
  714 934-0000

(P-9789)
SAFRAN CABIN INC
Also Called: 4 Flight
8595 Milliken Ave Ste 101 (91730-4942)
PHONE..............................909 652-9700
Tom Mcfarland, *CEO*
EMP: 158
SALES (corp-wide): 650.78MM **Privately Held**
Web: www.safran-group.com
SIC: 3728 Aircraft parts and equipment, nec
HQ: Safran Cabin Inc.
  5701 Bolsa Ave
  Huntington Beach CA
  714 934-0000

(P-9790)
SAFRAN CABIN INC
Also Called: Safran Cabin Tijuana S.a De Cv
2695 Customhouse Ct Ste 111
(92154-7645)
PHONE..............................619 661-6292
EMP: 173
SALES (corp-wide): 650.78MM **Privately Held**
Web: www.safran-group.com
SIC: 3728 Aircraft assemblies,
  subassemblies, and parts, nec
HQ: Safran Cabin Inc.
  5701 Bolsa Ave
  Huntington Beach CA
  714 934-0000

(P-9791)
SAFRAN CABIN INC
Also Called: C&D Aerodesign
6754 Calle De Linea Ste 111 (92154-8021)
PHONE..............................619 671-0430
Jose Martinez, *Mgr*
EMP: 223
SALES (corp-wide): 650.78MM **Privately Held**
Web: www.safran-group.com
SIC: 3728 Aircraft parts and equipment, nec
HQ: Safran Cabin Inc.
  5701 Bolsa Ave
  Huntington Beach CA
  714 934-0000

(P-9792)
SAFRAN CABIN MATERIALS LLC
5701 Bolsa Ave (92647-2063)
PHONE..............................909 947-4115
Lek Makpaiboon, *Pr*
EMP: 24 EST: 2013
SALES (est): 2.44MM
SALES (corp-wide): 650.78MM **Privately Held**
SIC: 3728 Aircraft parts and equipment, nec
PA: Safran
  2 Bd Du General Martial Valin
  Paris

(P-9793)
SAFRAN SEATS SANTA MARIA LLC
2641 Airpark Dr (93455-1415)
PHONE..............................805 922-5995
▲ EMP: 638 EST: 2012
SALES (est): 132.09MM
SALES (corp-wide): 650.78MM **Privately Held**
Web: weber.zodiac.com

SIC: 3728 Aircraft parts and equipment, nec
HQ: Safran Seats Usa Llc
  2000 Weber Dr
  Gainesville TX
  940 668-4825

(P-9794)
SANDERS COMPOSITES INC (HQ)
Also Called: Sanders Composites Industries
3701 E Conant St (90808-1783)
PHONE..............................562 354-2800
Larry O'toole, *CEO*
EMP: 49 EST: 1988
SQ FT: 44,400
SALES (est): 12.3MM
SALES (corp-wide): 137.12MM **Privately Held**
Web: www.sanderscomposites.com
SIC: 3728 Aircraft assemblies,
  subassemblies, and parts, nec
PA: Sanders Industries Holdings, Inc.
  3701 E Conant St
  Long Beach CA
  562 354-2920

(P-9795)
SEHANSON INC
2121 E Via Burton (92806-1220)
PHONE..............................714 778-1900
Stanley E Hanson, *Pr*
Christopher J Jones, *
EMP: 47 EST: 2000
SQ FT: 18,000
SALES (est): 2.03MM **Privately Held**
Web: www.acraaerospace.com
SIC: 3728 3429 Aircraft parts and
  equipment, nec; Hardware, nec

(P-9796)
SENIOR OPERATIONS LLC
Senior Aerospace SSP
2980 N San Fernando Blvd (91504-2522)
PHONE..............................818 260-2900
Launie Flemning, *Mgr*
EMP: 380
SALES (corp-wide): 1.02B **Privately Held**
Web: www.seniorssp.com
SIC: 3728 3599 Aircraft parts and
  equipment, nec; Bellows, industrial: metal
HQ: Senior Operations Llc
  300 E Devon Ave
  Bartlett IL
  630 372-3500

(P-9797)
SKYLOCK INDUSTRIES
1290 W Optical Dr (91702-3249)
PHONE..............................201 637-9505
Jim Pease, *Prin*
Jeff Crevoiserat, *Prin*
EMP: 50 EST: 1973
SALES (est): 3.2MM **Privately Held**
Web: www.skylock.com
SIC: 3728 Aircraft parts and equipment, nec

(P-9798)
SKYLOCK INDUSTRIES LLC
1290 W Optical Dr (91702-3249)
PHONE..............................626 334-2391
Jeff Creoiserat, *Ch Bd*
Jim Pease, *
EMP: 70 EST: 1973
SQ FT: 14,000
SALES (est): 19.69MM **Privately Held**
Web: www.skylock.com
SIC: 3728 Aircraft parts and equipment, nec

(P-9799)
SOUTHWEST MACHINE & PLASTIC CO
Also Called: Southwest Plastics Co
620 W Foothill Blvd (91741-2403)
PHONE..............................626 963-6919
W Thomas Jorgensen, *Pr*
Alfred D Jorgensen, *
▲ EMP: 30 EST: 1937
SALES (est): 4.82MM **Privately Held**
Web: www.southwestplastics.com
SIC: 3728 3089 3544 Aircraft parts and
  equipment, nec; Injection molding of plastics
  ; Special dies, tools, jigs, and fixtures

(P-9800)
SPACE-LOK INC
13306 Halldale Ave (90249-2204)
P.O. Box 2919 (90247-1119)
PHONE..............................310 527-6150
Scott F Wade, *Pr*
Jeffrey Wade, *
EMP: 138 EST: 1962
SALES (est): 31.84MM
SALES (corp-wide): 218.18MM **Privately Held**
Web: space-lok.herokuapp.com
SIC: 3728 3542 3812 3452 Aircraft
  assemblies, subassemblies, and parts, nec;
  Machine tools, metal forming type; Search
  and navigation equipment; Bolts, nuts,
  rivets, and washers
HQ: Novaria Fastening Systems, Llc
  6300 Ridglea Pl Ste 800
  Fort Worth TX
  817 381-3810

(P-9801)
SPEC TOOL COMPANY
Also Called: Alice G Fink-Painter
11805 Wakeman St (90670-2130)
P.O. Box 1056 (90660-1056)
PHONE..............................323 723-9533
Alice G Fink-painter, *Pr*
D B Fink, *
Albert G Fink Junior, *VP*
EMP: 50 EST: 1954
SALES (est): 8.85MM **Privately Held**
Web: www.spectoolgse.com
SIC: 3728 Aircraft parts and equipment, nec

(P-9802)
SPS TECHNOLOGIES LLC
Air Industries
12570 Knott St (92841-3932)
PHONE..............................714 892-5571
Michael Wu, *Contrlr*
EMP: 50
SALES (corp-wide): 302.09B **Publicly Held**
Web: www.pccfasteners.com
SIC: 3728 Aircraft parts and equipment, nec
HQ: Sps Technologies, Llc
  301 Highland Ave
  Jenkintown PA
  215 572-3000

(P-9803)
SUMMIT MACHINE LLC
2880 E Philadelphia St (91761-8523)
PHONE..............................909 923-2744
▼ EMP: 120 EST: 2003
SQ FT: 103,000
SALES (est): 27.25MM
SALES (corp-wide): 302.09B **Publicly Held**
Web: www.summitmachining.com
SIC: 3728 3599 Aircraft parts and
  equipment, nec; Machine shop, jobbing and
  repair

HQ: Precision Castparts Corp.
5885 Meadows Rd Ste 620
Lake Oswego OR
503 946-4800

(P-9804)
SUNGEAR INC
8535 Arjons Dr Ste G (92126-4360)
PHONE....................858 549-3166
Lee Miramontes, *Managing Member*
Glenn Wilcox, *Mfg Mgr*
Paul Scott, *QA*
EMP: 42 **EST:** 1982
SQ FT: 16,000
SALES (est): 7.85MM
SALES (corp-wide): 101.1MM **Privately Held**
Web: www.sungearinc.com
SIC: 3728 Gears, aircraft power transmission
PA: H-D Advanced Manufacturing
Company
2418 Greens Rd
Houston TX
346 219-0320

(P-9805)
SUNVAIR INC (HQ)
Also Called: Sunvair
29145 The Old Rd (91355-1015)
PHONE....................661 294-3777
Robert Dann, *Pr*
Edward Waschak, *
Melba Waschak, *
EMP: 32 **EST:** 1956
SQ FT: 26,000
SALES (est): 17.73MM
SALES (corp-wide): 30.27MM **Privately Held**
Web: www.sunvair.com
SIC: 3728 7699 Aircraft landing assemblies and heavy equipment repair services
PA: Sunvair Aerospace Group, Inc.
29145 The Old Rd
Valencia CA
661 294-3777

(P-9806)
SUNVAIR OVERHAUL INC
Also Called: A H Plating
29145 The Old Rd (91355-1015)
PHONE....................661 257-6123
John Waschak, *CEO*
Timothy Waschak, *
Robert Waschak, *
John Waschak, *Ch Bd*
EMP: 20 **EST:** 1978
SQ FT: 35,000
SALES (est): 407.12K **Privately Held**
Web: www.sunvair.com
SIC: 3728 5088 Alighting (landing gear) assemblies, aircraft; Aircraft and parts, nec

(P-9807)
SWIFT ENGINEERING INC
Also Called: Swift Engineering
1141a Via Callejon (92673-6230)
PHONE....................949 492-6608
▲ **EMP:** 83 **EST:** 1982
SALES (est): 20.32MM **Privately Held**
Web: www.swiftengineering.com
SIC: 3728 3714 3624 Aircraft body and wing assemblies and parts; Motor vehicle parts and accessories; Fibers, carbon and graphite
PA: Matsushita International Corp
1141 Via Callejon
San Clemente CA

(P-9808)
SYMBOLIC DISPLAYS INC
1917 E Saint Andrew Pl (92705-5143)
PHONE....................714 258-2811
Candy Suits, *CEO*
▼ **EMP:** 76 **EST:** 1964
SQ FT: 15,860
SALES (est): 14.07MM **Privately Held**
Web: www.symbolicdisplays.com
SIC: 3728 3812 3577 Aircraft parts and equipment, nec; Search and navigation equipment; Computer peripheral equipment, nec

(P-9809)
SYNERGETIC TECH GROUP INC
1712 Earhart (91750-5826)
PHONE....................909 305-4711
Tony Espinoza, *CEO*
Mary Jones, *
Kevin Jones, *
Michelle Valdez, *
EMP: 27 **EST:** 1997
SQ FT: 2,400
SALES (est): 4.9MM **Privately Held**
Web: www.synergetic-us.com
SIC: 3728 Aircraft parts and equipment, nec

(P-9810)
TALSCO INC
7101 Patterson Dr (92841-1415)
PHONE....................714 841-2464
EMP: 36
SIC: 3728 Aircraft assemblies, subassemblies, and parts, nec

(P-9811)
TDG AEROSPACE INC
2180 Chablis Ct Ste 106 (92029-2076)
PHONE....................760 466-1040
Virginia Richard, *Ch Bd*
Virginia Richard, *Ch*
Gerry Bench, *Pr*
Fred Bond, *CFO*
EMP: 18 **EST:** 1991
SALES (est): 2.64MM **Privately Held**
Web: www.tdgaerospace.com
SIC: 3728 Aircraft parts and equipment, nec

(P-9812)
THALES AVIONICS INC
48 Discovery (92618-3170)
PHONE....................949 381-3033
Dominique Giannoni, *Owner*
EMP: 37
SALES (corp-wide): 277.29MM **Privately Held**
SIC: 3728 Aircraft parts and equipment, nec
HQ: Thales Avionics, Inc.
7415 Emerald Dunes Dr # 2000
Orlando FL
407 812-2600

(P-9813)
THALES AVIONICS INC
Also Called: Inflight Entrmt & Connectivity
51 Discovery Ste 100 (92618-3120)
PHONE....................949 790-2500
Brad Foreman, *Mgr*
EMP: 37
SALES (corp-wide): 277.29MM **Privately Held**
SIC: 3728 3663 Aircraft parts and equipment, nec; Radio and t.v. communications equipment
HQ: Thales Avionics, Inc.
7415 Emerald Dunes Dr # 2000
Orlando FL
407 812-2600

(P-9814)
THALES AVIONICS INC
9975 Toledo Way (92618-1826)
PHONE....................949 829-5808
EMP: 37
SALES (corp-wide): 277.29MM **Privately Held**
SIC: 3728 Aircraft parts and equipment, nec
HQ: Thales Avionics, Inc.
7415 Emerald Dunes Dr # 2000
Orlando FL
407 812-2600

(P-9815)
THOMPSON INDUSTRIES LTD
Also Called: Thompson ADB Industries
7155 Fenwick Ln (92683-5218)
PHONE....................310 679-9193
Werner Lieberherr, *CEO*
EMP: 96 **EST:** 1965
SQ FT: 52,000
SALES (est): 8.33MM
SALES (corp-wide): 67.07B **Publicly Held**
SIC: 3728 Aircraft parts and equipment, nec
HQ: B/E Aerospace, Inc.
1400 Corporate Center Way
Wellington FL

(P-9816)
TJ AEROSPACE INC
Also Called: Tj Aerospace
12601 Monarch St (92841-3918)
PHONE....................714 891-3564
Tien Dang, *CEO*
Tien N Dang, *CEO*
EMP: 23 **EST:** 2007
SQ FT: 6,000
SALES (est): 9.7MM **Privately Held**
Web: www.tjaerospace.com
SIC: 3728 3541 Aircraft parts and equipment, nec; Machine tools, metal cutting type

(P-9817)
TMW CORPORATION (PA)
Also Called: Crown Discount Tools
15148 Bledsoe St (91342-3807)
PHONE....................818 362-5665
William Windette, *Pr*
Gary Berger, *
EMP: 110 **EST:** 1973
SQ FT: 115,000
SALES (est): 9.77MM
SALES (corp-wide): 9.77MM **Privately Held**
SIC: 3728 Aircraft landing assemblies and brakes

(P-9818)
TRANSDIGM INC
Adel Wggins Grp-Commercial Div
5000 Triggs St (90022-4833)
P.O. Box 22228 (90022-0228)
PHONE....................323 269-9181
Cindy Terakawa, *Brnch Mgr*
EMP: 96
SALES (corp-wide): 6.58B **Publicly Held**
Web: www.transdigm.com
SIC: 3728 3365 Aircraft parts and equipment, nec; Aerospace castings, aluminum
HQ: Transdigm, Inc.
1301 E 9th St Ste 3000
Cleveland OH

(P-9819)
TRI-TECH PRECISION INC
1863 N Case St (92865-4234)
PHONE....................714 970-1363
Ernie Husted, *Pr*

EMP: 17 **EST:** 1989
SALES (est): 2MM **Privately Held**
Web: www.tri-techprecision.com
SIC: 3728 3544 Aircraft parts and equipment, nec; Special dies, tools, jigs, and fixtures

(P-9820)
TRIO MANUFACTURING INC
601 Lairport St (90245-5005)
PHONE....................310 640-6123
Michael Hunkins, *Pr*
Michael Hunkins, *Pr*
Brian Hunkins, *
▲ **EMP:** 125 **EST:** 1943
SALES (est): 23.01MM **Privately Held**
Web: www.triomfg.com
SIC: 3728 3829 3812 3663 Aircraft parts and equipment, nec; Measuring and controlling devices, nec; Search and navigation equipment; Radio and t.v. communications equipment

(P-9821)
TRIUMPH ACTTION SYSTEMS - VLNC
Also Called: Triumph Group
28150 Harrison Pkwy (91355-4109)
PHONE....................661 702-7537
Daniel J Crowley, *Pr*
Jim Mccabe, *Sr VP*
Dan Ostrosky, *VP*
Gary Tenison, *
John B Wright Ii, *Sr VP*
EMP: 250 **EST:** 2001
SALES (est): 50.42MM **Publicly Held**
SIC: 3728 Aircraft parts and equipment, nec
PA: Triumph Group, Inc.
555 E Lancaster Ave # 400
Radnor PA

(P-9822)
TRIUMPH INSULATION SYSTEMS LLC
Also Called: Triumph Group
1754 Carr Rd Ste 103 (92231-9509)
PHONE....................760 618-7543
▲ **EMP:** 900 **EST:** 1976
SALES (est): 206.87MM **Publicly Held**
SIC: 3728 Aircraft parts and equipment, nec
HQ: Triumph Aerospace Systems Group, Inc.
899 Cassatt Rd Ste 210
Berwyn PA

(P-9823)
TRIUMPH STRUCTURES - EVERETT INC
Also Called: Triumph Structures
17055 Gale Ave (91745-1808)
PHONE....................425 348-4100
▲ **EMP:** 202
SIC: 3728 Aircraft parts and equipment, nec

(P-9824)
VANTAGE ASSOCIATES INC
Also Called: Vantage Master Machine Company
12333 Los Nietos Rd (90670-2911)
PHONE....................562 968-1400
Paul Roy, *Brnch Mgr*
EMP: 40
SALES (corp-wide): 21.95MM **Privately Held**
Web: www.vantageassoc.com
SIC: 3728 Aircraft assemblies, subassemblies, and parts, nec
PA: Vantage Associates Inc.
12333 Los Nietos Rd

(PA)=Parent Co (HQ)=Headquarters
✪ = New Business established in last 2 years

2024 Southern California
Business Directory and Buyers Guide

465

PRODUCTS & SVCS

Santa Fe Springs CA
619 477-6940

(P-9825)
VISION AEROSPACE LLC
Also Called: Romakk Engineering
19863 Nordhoff St (91324-3331)
PHONE....................818 700-1035
EMP: 24 **EST:** 2018
SALES (est): 3.13MM **Privately Held**
SIC: 3728 Aircraft parts and equipment, nec

(P-9826)
WESANCO INC
14870 Desman Rd (90638-5746)
PHONE....................714 739-4989
Brain Szymanski, *CFO*
▲ **EMP:** 30 **EST:** 1973
SQ FT: 30,000
SALES (est): 12MM
SALES (corp-wide): 237.86MM **Privately Held**
Web: www.wesanco.com
SIC: 3728 Oleo struts, aircraft
HQ: Zsi-Foster, Inc.
1751 Summit Dr
Auburn Hills MI

(P-9827)
WESTERN METHODS MACHINERY CORPORATION
Also Called: Western Methods
2344 Pullman St (92705-5507)
PHONE....................949 252-6600
EMP: 120 **EST:** 1977
SALES (est): 10.34MM **Privately Held**
SIC: 3728 3769 Aircraft parts and equipment, nec; Space vehicle equipment, nec

(P-9828)
WHITTAKER CORPORATION
1955 Surveyor Ave Fl 2 (93063-3369)
PHONE....................805 526-5700
Erick Lardiere, *Pr*
▲ **EMP:** 40 **EST:** 1942
SQ FT: 276,000
SALES (est): 9.26MM
SALES (corp-wide): 19.07B **Publicly Held**
Web: www.whittakercorp.com
SIC: 3728 3669 7373 Aircraft parts and equipment, nec; Fire detection systems, electric; Systems integration services
HQ: Meggitt Limited
Pilot Way
Coventry W MIDLANDS
247 682-6900

(P-9829)
WOODWARD HRT INC
Also Called: Woodward Duarte
1700 Business Center Dr (91010-2859)
PHONE....................626 359-9211
Don Grimes, *Mgr*
EMP: 250
SALES (corp-wide): 2.91B **Publicly Held**
SIC: 3728 5084 Aircraft parts and equipment, nec; Hydraulic systems equipment and supplies
HQ: Woodward Hrt, Inc.
25200 Rye Canyon Rd
Santa Clarita CA
661 294-6000

(P-9830)
ZENITH MANUFACTURING INC
Also Called: Zipco
3087 12th St (92507-4904)
PHONE....................818 767-2106
James Phoung, *Pr*

EMP: 25 **EST:** 2006
SQ FT: 47,000
SALES (est): 3MM **Privately Held**
SIC: 3728 Aircraft parts and equipment, nec

(P-9831)
ZODIAC AEROSPACE
11340 Jersey Blvd (91730-4919)
PHONE....................909 652-9700
EMP: 17 **EST:** 2018
SALES (est): 857.17K **Privately Held**
SIC: 3728 Aircraft parts and equipment, nec

(P-9832)
ZODIAC WTR WASTE AERO SYSTEMS
Also Called: Monogram Systems
1500 Glenn Curtiss St (90746-4012)
PHONE....................310 884-7000
EMP: 83 **EST:** 1958
SALES (est): 15.32MM
SALES (corp-wide): 650.78MM **Privately Held**
SIC: 3728 Aircraft parts and equipment, nec
PA: Safran
2 Bd Du General Martial Valin
Paris

3731 Shipbuilding And Repairing

(P-9833)
APR ENGINEERING INC
Also Called: Oceanwide Repairs
1812 W 9th St (90813-2614)
P.O. Box 9100 (90810-0100)
PHONE....................562 983-3800
Roy Herington, *Pr*
Trina Young, *
▲ **EMP:** 33 **EST:** 1997
SALES (est): 4.74MM **Privately Held**
Web: www.oceanwiderepair.com
SIC: 3731 Shipbuilding and repairing

(P-9834)
BAE SYSTEMS SAN DEGO SHIP REPR
2205 Belt St (92113-3634)
P.O. Box 13308 (92170-3308)
PHONE....................619 238-1000
David Thomas, *Pr*
James M Blue, *
Alice M Eldridge, *
◆ **EMP:** 1278 **EST:** 1976
SALES (est): 228.87MM
SALES (corp-wide): 25.59B **Privately Held**
SIC: 3731 Shipbuilding and repairing
HQ: Bae Systems Ship Repair Inc.
750 W Berkley Ave
Norfolk VA
757 494-4000

(P-9835)
COLONNAS SHIPYARD WEST LLC
2890 Faivre St Ste 150 (91911-4983)
PHONE....................757 545-2414
Robert Boyd, *Prin*
Ana Nowland, *Ofcr*
EMP: 30 **EST:** 2017
SALES (est): 2.39MM **Privately Held**
Web: www.colonnaship.com
SIC: 3731 Shipbuilding and repairing

(P-9836)
CONTINENTAL MARITIME INDS INC

1995 Bay Front St (92113-2122)
PHONE....................619 234-8851
David H Mc Queary, *Pr*
Lee E Wilson, *
EMP: 429 **EST:** 1990
SQ FT: 90,000
SALES (est): 94.63MM **Publicly Held**
Web: www.cmsd-msr.com
SIC: 3731 Shipbuilding and repairing
PA: Huntington Ingalls Industries, Inc.
4101 Washington Ave
Newport News VA

(P-9837)
CRAFT LABOR & SUPPORT SVCS LLC
1545 Tidelands Ave Ste C (91950-4240)
PHONE....................619 336-9977
Michael Greene, *Brnch Mgr*
EMP: 169
SALES (corp-wide): 8.27MM **Privately Held**
Web: www.craftlabor.com
SIC: 3731 Shipbuilding and repairing
PA: Craft Labor And Support Services, Llc
7636 230th St Sw Apt B
Edmonds WA
206 304-4543

(P-9838)
HII SAN DIEGO SHIPYARD INC
1995 Bay Front St (92101-1951)
PHONE....................619 234-8851
Christopher Joseph Miner, *CEO*
Ronald Sugar, *
EMP: 325 **EST:** 1981
SQ FT: 90,000
SALES (est): 73.83MM **Publicly Held**
Web: www.cmsd-msr.com
SIC: 3731 Military ships, building and repairing
PA: Huntington Ingalls Industries, Inc.
4101 Washington Ave
Newport News VA

(P-9839)
INTEGRATED MARINE SERVICES INC
Also Called: IMS
2320 Main St (91911-4610)
PHONE....................619 429-0300
Larry Samano, *Pr*
EMP: 55 **EST:** 2003
SALES (est): 9.4MM **Privately Held**
Web: www.imships.com
SIC: 3731 Shipbuilding and repairing

(P-9840)
LARSON AL BOAT SHOP
1046 S Seaside Ave (90731-7334)
PHONE....................310 514-4100
Jack Wall, *CEO*
Gloria Wall, *
George Wall, *
▲ **EMP:** 70 **EST:** 1903
SQ FT: 65,000
SALES (est): 23.56MM **Privately Held**
Web: www.larsonboat.com
SIC: 3731 4493 Military ships, building and repairing; Marinas

(P-9841)
MILLER MARINE
2275 Manya St (92154-4713)
PHONE....................619 791-1500
Pauline Senter, *CEO*
Edward Senter, *
Miller Marine, *
EMP: 45 **EST:** 1989
SQ FT: 13,500

SALES (est): 9.51MM **Privately Held**
Web: www.millermarine.us
SIC: 3731 7389 Shipbuilding and repairing; Grinding, precision: commercial or industrial

(P-9842)
NATIONAL STL & SHIPBUILDING CO (HQ)
2798 Harbor Dr (92113-3650)
P.O. Box 85278 (92186-5278)
PHONE....................619 544-3400
Michael Toner, *Ch Bd*
David Carver, *
Phebe Novakoviz, *
Blaise Brennan, *
Andrew Chen, *
◆ **EMP:** 477 **EST:** 1892
SQ FT: 100,000
SALES (est): 513.58MM
SALES (corp-wide): 39.41B **Publicly Held**
Web: www.nassco.com
SIC: 3731 Military ships, building and repairing
PA: General Dynamics Corporation
11011 Sunset Hills Rd
Reston VA
703 876-3000

(P-9843)
NAVIGATIONAL SERVICES
34 E 17th St Ste C (91950-4501)
P.O. Box 2444 (91951-2444)
PHONE....................619 477-1564
Frank Soto, *Pr*
Frank Soto Senior, *Pr*
EMP: 18 **EST:** 1998
SQ FT: 3,800
SALES (est): 459.64K **Privately Held**
Web: www.navigationalservices.com
SIC: 3731 Commercial passenger ships, building and repairing

(P-9844)
NAVY UNITED STATES DEPARTMENT
Also Called: Supervision of Shipbuilding
32nd St Naval Sta (92136-0001)
P.O. Box 368119 (92136-0001)
PHONE....................619 556-6033
EMP: 712
Web: www.navy.mil
SIC: 3731 9711 Shipbuilding and repairing; Navy
HQ: United States Department Of The Navy
1200 Navy Pentagon
Washington DC

(P-9845)
PACIFIC SHIP REPR FBRCTION INC (PA)
1625 Rigel St (92113-3887)
P.O. Box 13428 (92170-3428)
PHONE....................619 232-3200
David J Moore, *CEO*
Gary N Thomas, *Contracts Director*
EMP: 287 **EST:** 1969
SQ FT: 136,000
SALES (est): 46.49MM
SALES (corp-wide): 46.49MM **Privately Held**
Web: www.pacship.com
SIC: 3731 3444 Combat vessels, building and repairing; Sheet metalwork

(P-9846)
PAIGE SITTA & ASSOCIATES INC (PA)
Also Called: Paige Floor Cvg Specialists
2050 Wilson Ave Ste B (91950-6500)

PHONE..............................619 233-5912
Scott Nicholson, *Pr*
Peter Sitta, *
Debbie Kelley, *
EMP: 22 **EST:** 1989
SQ FT: 9,000
SALES (est): 4.21MM
SALES (corp-wide): 4.21MM **Privately Held**
Web: www.paigefc.com
SIC: 3731 1752 Shipbuilding and repairing; Floor laying and floor work, nec

(P-9847)
PYR PRESERVATION SERVICES
Also Called: Pyr
2393 Newton Ave Ste B (92113-3648)
PHONE..............................619 338-8395
Daniel R Cummins, *CEO*
▲ **EMP:** 30 **EST:** 1997
SQ FT: 12,500
SALES (est): 2.5MM **Privately Held**
Web: www.pyrsd.com
SIC: 3731 3589 3479 2851 Commercial cargo ships, building and repairing; Sandblasting equipment; Etching and engraving; Epoxy coatings

(P-9848)
TRIDENT MARITIME SYSTEMS INC
651 Drucker Ln (92154)
PHONE..............................619 346-3800
EMP: 32
SALES (corp-wide): 513.66MM **Privately Held**
Web: www.tridentllc.com
SIC: 3731 Shipbuilding and repairing
HQ: Trident Maritime Systems, Inc.
2011 Crystal Dr Ste 1102
Arlington VA
703 236-1590

(P-9849)
VALIANT TECHNICAL SERVICES INC
1785 Utah Ave (93437-6020)
PHONE..............................757 628-9500
Danny Schanick, *Mgr*
EMP: 57
SQ FT: 5,734
SALES (corp-wide): 417.01MM **Privately Held**
SIC: 3731 Shipbuilding and repairing
HQ: Valiant Technical Services Inc.
4465 Guthrie Hwy
Clarksville TN

(P-9850)
WALASHEK INDUSTRIAL & MAR INC
1428 Mckinley Ave (91950-4217)
PHONE..............................619 498-1711
Frank Walashek, *Mgr*
EMP: 42
SALES (corp-wide): 24.59MM **Privately Held**
Web: www.walashek.com
SIC: 3731 Shipbuilding and repairing
HQ: Walashek Industrial & Marine, Inc.
3411 Amherst St
Norfolk VA

(P-9851)
WALKER DESIGN INC
Also Called: Walker Engineering Enterprises
9255 San Fernando Rd (91352-1416)
PHONE..............................818 252-7788
Robert A Walker Junior, *CEO*

Shari Goodgame, *
Michael Delillo, *
▲ **EMP:** 33 **EST:** 1976
SQ FT: 29,800
SALES (est): 5.11MM **Privately Held**
Web: www.walkerairsep.com
SIC: 3731 Lighters, marine: building and repairing

3732 Boatbuilding And Repairing

(P-9852)
ADEPT PROCESS SERVICES INC
Also Called: APS Marine
609 Anita St (91911-4619)
P.O. Box 2130 (91933-2130)
PHONE..............................619 434-3194
Gary Southerland, *Pr*
EMP: 34 **EST:** 2005
SALES (est): 4.22MM **Privately Held**
Web: www.adeptworks.net
SIC: 3732 4493 7699 Boatbuilding and repairing; Boat yards, storage and incidental repair; Boat repair

(P-9853)
AIR & GAS TECH INC
Also Called: Cem
11433 Woodside Ave (92071-4725)
PHONE..............................619 955-5980
Anthony Greenwell, *Pr*
Berenice Cossio, *
Jacob Meek, *
EMP: 25 **EST:** 1979
SQ FT: 18,000
SALES (est): 4.81MM **Privately Held**
Web: www.cemcorp.net
SIC: 3732 Boatbuilding and repairing

(P-9854)
ANACAPA MARINE SERVICES (PA)
Also Called: Anacapa Boatyard
151 Shipyard Way Ste 5 (92663-4460)
PHONE..............................805 985-1818
Richard Fairchild, *Pr*
EMP: 17 **EST:** 1973
SQ FT: 8,000
SALES (est): 2.24MM
SALES (corp-wide): 2.24MM **Privately Held**
SIC: 3732 5088 Boatbuilding and repairing; Marine supplies

(P-9855)
BASIN MARINE INC
Also Called: Basin Marine Shipyard
829 Harbor Island Dr Ste A (92660-7235)
PHONE..............................949 673-0360
Paul Smith, *Pr*
▲ **EMP:** 23 **EST:** 1956
SQ FT: 44,000
SALES (est): 2.13MM **Privately Held**
Web: www.basinmarine.com
SIC: 3732 5551 Boatbuilding and repairing; Marine supplies, nec

(P-9856)
CATALINA YACHTS INC (PA)
Also Called: Morgan Marine
2259 Ward Ave (93065-1863)
PHONE..............................818 884-7700
Frank W Butler, *Pr*
Sharon Day, *
◆ **EMP:** 50 **EST:** 1968
SALES (est): 23.05MM

SALES (corp-wide): 23.05MM **Privately Held**
Web: www.catalinayachts.com
SIC: 3732 5551 Sailboats, building and repairing; Boat dealers

(P-9857)
DRISCOLL INC
Also Called: Driscoll Boat Works
2500 Shelter Island Dr (92106-3114)
PHONE..............................619 226-2500
Thomas Driscoll, *Pr*
John Gerald Driscoll, *
Joseph E Driscoll, *
Mary-carol Driscoll, *Sec*
▲ **EMP:** 50 **EST:** 1947
SQ FT: 2,400
SALES (est): 9.5MM **Privately Held**
Web: www.driscollinc.com
SIC: 3732 Boatbuilding and repairing

(P-9858)
GAMBOL INDUSTRIES INC
1880 Century Park E Ste 950 (90067-1612)
PHONE..............................562 901-2470
Robert A Stein, *Pr*
John Bridwell, *
▲ **EMP:** 45 **EST:** 1992
SALES (est): 8.37MM **Privately Held**
Web: www.gambolindustries.com
SIC: 3732 7699 4493 Yachts, building and repairing; Boat repair; Boat yards, storage and incidental repair

(P-9859)
HOBIE CAT COMPANY (PA)
4925 Oceanside Blvd (92056-3044)
PHONE..............................760 758-9100
Richard Rogers, *CEO*
Doug Skidmore, *
Bill Baldwin, *
◆ **EMP:** 140 **EST:** 1995
SQ FT: 60,000
SALES (est): 48.95MM
SALES (corp-wide): 48.95MM **Privately Held**
Web: www.hobie.com
SIC: 3732 Sailboats, building and repairing

(P-9860)
INDEL ENGINEERING INC
Also Called: Marina Shipyard
6400 E Marina Dr (90803-4618)
PHONE..............................562 594-0995
D E Bud Tretter, *Pr*
Jerry Tretter, *
Kurt Tretter, *
EMP: 35 **EST:** 1964
SQ FT: 3,000
SALES (est): 2.61MM **Privately Held**
Web: www.marinashipyard.com
SIC: 3732 Houseboats, building and repairing

(P-9861)
MACGREGOR YACHT CORPORATION
1631 Placentia Ave (92627-4355)
PHONE..............................310 621-2206
Roger Mac Gregor, *Pr*
Mary Lou Gregor Mac, *Sec*
EMP: 24 **EST:** 1963
SQ FT: 10,000
SALES (est): 461.36K **Privately Held**
SIC: 3732 5551 Sailboats, building and repairing; Boat dealers

(P-9862)
MATTHEW SMITH CRAMPTON
Also Called: Marine Outfitters
300 Carlsbad Village Dr # 10 (92008-2900)

PHONE..............................760 840-8404
EMP: 22 **EST:** 1996
SQ FT: 15,000
SALES (est): 1.62MM **Privately Held**
SIC: 3732 7699 Boatbuilding and repairing; Boat repair

(P-9863)
MAURER MARINE INC
873 W 17th St (92627-4308)
PHONE..............................949 645-7673
Craig Maurer, *Pr*
Jay S Maurer, *VP*
EMP: 18 **EST:** 1979
SALES (est): 2.57MM **Privately Held**
Web: www.maurermarine.com
SIC: 3732 7389 Yachts, building and repairing; Yacht brokers

(P-9864)
NAVIGATOR YACHTS AND PDTS INC
Also Called: Navigator Yachts
364 Malbert St (92570-8336)
PHONE..............................951 657-2117
Xia Wang, *CEO*
Jule Marshall, *
EMP: 20 **EST:** 1988
SQ FT: 30,000
SALES (est): 429.44K **Privately Held**
Web: www.navigatoryachts.com
SIC: 3732 Yachts, building and repairing

(P-9865)
OCEAN PROTECTA INCORPORATED
14708 Biola Ave (90638-4450)
PHONE..............................714 891-2628
Edgar Chong Tan, *CEO*
Myron Reyes, *
EMP: 50 **EST:** 2014
SALES (est): 2.45MM **Privately Held**
Web: www.oceanprotecta.com
SIC: 3732 Boatbuilding and repairing

(P-9866)
SHELTER ISLAND YCHTWAYS LTD A
Also Called: Shelter Island Boatyard
2330 Shelter Island Dr Ste 1 (92106-3126)
PHONE..............................619 222-0481
William Roberts, *Genl Pt*
▲ **EMP:** 21 **EST:** 1953
SQ FT: 20,000
SALES (est): 2.38MM **Privately Held**
Web: www.siyc.com
SIC: 3732 6512 Boatbuilding and repairing; Lessors of piers, docks, associated buildings and facilities

(P-9867)
VENTURA HARBOR BOATYARD INC
1415 Spinnaker Dr (93001-4339)
PHONE..............................805 654-1433
Robert Bartosh, *Pr*
Stephen James, *
Kim Morris, *
Dale Morris, *
EMP: 35 **EST:** 1986
SQ FT: 2,000
SALES (est): 4.57MM **Privately Held**
Web: www.vhby.com
SIC: 3732 4493 Boatbuilding and repairing; Boat yards, storage and incidental repair

---

(PA)=Parent Co (HQ)=Headquarters
✪ = New Business established in last 2 years

(P-9868)
WILLARD MARINE INC
4602 North Ave (92056-3509)
PHONE................................714 666-2150
Jordan Angle, *CEO*
Joseph Nangle, *
Justin Law, *
▲ **EMP:** 55 **EST:** 1957
SALES (est): 14.3MM **Privately Held**
Web: www.willardmarine.com
SIC: 3732 Boats, fiberglass: building and repairing

3743 Railroad Equipment

(P-9869)
KINKISHARYO (USA) INC
300 Continental Blvd Ste 300 (90245)
PHONE................................424 276-1803
▲ **EMP:** 146
Web: www.kinkisharyo.com
SIC: 3743 Train cars and equipment, freight or passenger

(P-9870)
KINKISHARYO INT LLC (HQ)
1960 E Grand Ave Ste 1210 (90245-5061)
PHONE................................424 276-1803
Hideki Hatai, *Managing Member*
▲ **EMP:** 19 **EST:** 1999
SQ FT: 6,000
SALES (est): 72MM **Privately Held**
Web: www.kinkisharyo.com
SIC: 3743 3321 Train cars and equipment, freight or passenger; Railroad car wheels and brake shoes, cast iron
PA: Kinki Sharyo Co., Ltd., The
2-2-46, Inadauemachi
Higashi-Osaka OSK

3751 Motorcycles, Bicycles, And Parts

(P-9871)
ALL AMERICAN RACERS INC
Also Called: Dan Gurneys All Amercn Racers
2334 S Broadway (92707-3250)
P.O. Box 2186 (92707-0186)
PHONE................................714 540-1771
Daniel S Gurney, *CEO*
Justin B Gurney, *
Kathy Weida, *
EMP: 162 **EST:** 1962
SQ FT: 25,000
SALES (est): 24.1MM **Privately Held**
Web: www.allamericanracers.com
SIC: 3751 Motorcycles and related parts

(P-9872)
AMERICAN EAGLE MFG CO
Also Called: American Eagle Motorcycles
18301 Von Karman Ave Ste 1000
(92612-1009)
PHONE................................949 251-0722
EMP: 24 **EST:** 1989
SQ FT: 40,000
SALES (est): 210K **Privately Held**
Web:
www.americaneaglemanufacturing.com
SIC: 3751 Motorcycles and related parts

(P-9873)
BARNETT TOOL & ENGINEERING
Also Called: Barnett Performance Products
2238 Palma Dr (93003-8068)
PHONE................................805 642-9435

Michael Taylor, *Pr*
Colleen Taylor, *
EMP: 60 **EST:** 1948
SQ FT: 43,000
SALES (est): 10.37MM **Privately Held**
Web: www.barnettclutches.com
SIC: 3751 Motorcycle accessories

(P-9874)
BELT DRIVES LTD
Also Called: B D L
505 W Lambert Rd (92821-3909)
PHONE................................714 693-1313
EMP: 21 **EST:** 1990
SQ FT: 30,000
SALES (est): 4.02MM **Privately Held**
Web: www.beltdrives.com
SIC: 3751 Motorcycles and related parts

(P-9875)
C C I REDLANDS INC
Also Called: CCI
721 Nevada St Ste 308 (92373-8053)
P.O. Box 365 (92373-0121)
PHONE................................909 307-6500
EMP: 24 **EST:** 1988
SALES (est): 497.98K **Privately Held**
Web: www.redlands.edu
SIC: 3751 5091 Bicycles and related parts; Bicycle equipment and supplies

(P-9876)
FMF RACING
Also Called: Flying Machine Factory
18033 S Santa Fe Ave (90221-5514)
PHONE................................310 631-4363
Don Emler, *CEO*
▲ **EMP:** 150 **EST:** 1985
SALES (est): 24.53MM **Privately Held**
Web: www.fmfracing.com
SIC: 3751 5571 Motorcycle accessories; Motorcycle parts and accessories

(P-9877)
K & N ENGINEERING INC (PA)
Also Called: K&N
1455 Citrus St (92507-1603)
P.O. Box 1329 (92502-1329)
PHONE................................951 826-4000
Randy Bays, *CEO*
◆ **EMP:** 565 **EST:** 1964
SQ FT: 270,000
SALES (est): 140.52MM
SALES (corp-wide): 140.52MM **Privately Held**
Web: www.knfilters.com
SIC: 3751 3599 3714 Handle bars, motorcycle and bicycle; Air intake filters, internal combustion engine, except auto; Filters: oil, fuel, and air, motor vehicle

(P-9878)
LOADED BOARDS INC
10575 Virginia Ave (90232-3520)
PHONE................................310 839-1800
Don Tashman, *CEO*
◆ **EMP:** 17 **EST:** 2002
SQ FT: 5,500
SALES (est): 1.82MM **Privately Held**
Web: www.loadedboards.com
SIC: 3751 Bicycles and related parts

(P-9879)
MARKLAND INDUSTRIES INC (PA)
1111 E Mcfadden Ave (92705-4103)
PHONE................................714 245-2850
Donald R Markland, *Pr*
▲ **EMP:** 53 **EST:** 1978
SQ FT: 100,000

SALES (est): 10.4MM
SALES (corp-wide): 10.4MM **Privately Held**
Web: www.marklandindustries.com
SIC: 3751 Motorcycle accessories

(P-9880)
PERFORMANCE MACHINE INC
Also Called: Performance Machine
6892 Marlin Cir (90623-1017)
PHONE................................714 523-3000
▲ **EMP:** 200
SIC: 3751 3714 Motorcycle accessories; Brake drums, motor vehicle

(P-9881)
RAZOR USA LLC (PA)
Also Called: Razor
12723 166th St (90703-2102)
P.O. Box 3610 (90703-3610)
PHONE................................562 345-6000
Carlton Calvin, *Managing Member*
Robert Chen, *Managing Member*
◆ **EMP:** 60 **EST:** 2000
SQ FT: 50,000
SALES (est): 61.54MM **Privately Held**
Web: global.razor.com
SIC: 3751 Motor scooters and parts

(P-9882)
SEGWAY INC
405 E Santa Clara St Ste 100 (91006-7219)
PHONE................................603 222-6000
Luke Gao, *CEO*
Chen Huang, *
Ye Wang, *
◆ **EMP:** 120 **EST:** 2000
SALES (est): 22.39MM
SALES (corp-wide): 5.09MM **Privately Held**
Web: www.segway.com
SIC: 3751 Motor scooters and parts
HQ: Nunn Bo (Tianjin) Technology Co., Ltd.
No.3, Tianrui Road, Qiche Industries Park, Wu Qing District
Tianjin TJ

(P-9883)
SONDORS INC
2710 Yates Ave (90040-2624)
PHONE................................323 372-3000
Storm Sondors, *CEO*
EMP: 20 **EST:** 2017
SALES (est): 3.24MM **Privately Held**
Web: www.sondors.com
SIC: 3751 Gears, motorcycle and bicycle

(P-9884)
SPINERGY INC
1709 La Costa Meadows Dr (92078-5105)
PHONE................................760 496-2121
Martin Connolly, *Pr*
▲ **EMP:** 80 **EST:** 1977
SQ FT: 63,000
SALES (est): 14.86MM **Privately Held**
Web: www.spinergy.com
SIC: 3751 3949 7389 Bicycles and related parts; Exercise equipment; Design services

(P-9885)
SUPER73 INC (PA)
16591 Noyes Ave (92606-5102)
PHONE................................949 649-4607
Legrand Crewse, *CEO*
▼ **EMP:** 22 **EST:** 2018
SALES (est): 4.92MM
SALES (corp-wide): 4.92MM **Privately Held**
Web: www.super73.com

SIC: 3751 5012 Motorcycles, bicycles and parts; Motorcycles

(P-9886)
TOLEMAR INC
Also Called: Tolemar Manufacturing
5221 Oceanus Dr (92649-1028)
PHONE................................714 362-8166
Steve Ramelot, *CEO*
▲ **EMP:** 21 **EST:** 1994
SQ FT: 25,000
SALES (est): 1.84MM **Privately Held**
Web: www.tolemar.com
SIC: 3751 Motorcycles and related parts

(P-9887)
TWO BROTHERS RACING INC
3474 Niki Way (92507-6811)
PHONE................................714 550-6070
Craig A Erion, *Pr*
◆ **EMP:** 18 **EST:** 1985
SALES (est): 4.98MM **Privately Held**
Web: www.twobros.com
SIC: 3751 5013 Motorcycles and related parts; Motorcycle parts

(P-9888)
V&H PERFORMANCE LLC
Also Called: Vance & Hines
13861 Rosecrans Ave (90670-5207)
PHONE................................562 921-7461
Andrew Graves, *CEO*
Mike Kennedy, *
Terry Vance, *
Byron Hines, *Stockholder*
▼ **EMP:** 65 **EST:** 2010
SQ FT: 12,000
SALES (est): 31.63MM
SALES (corp-wide): 251.1MM **Privately Held**
Web: www.vanceandhines.com
SIC: 3751 5013 Motorcycles, bicycles and parts; Motorcycle parts
PA: Motorsport Aftermarket Group, Inc.
13861 Rosecrans Ave
Santa Fe Springs CA
917 838-4002

(P-9889)
WESTERN MFG & DISTRG LLC
Also Called: I.V. League Medical
835 Flynn Rd (93012-8702)
P.O. Box 7192 (92067-7192)
PHONE................................805 988-1010
EMP: 40 **EST:** 1970
SQ FT: 25,000
SALES (est): 4.82MM **Privately Held**
Web:
www.westernmanufacturinganddistributing.com
SIC: 3751 3841 3599 Motorcycles and related parts; Surgical and medical instruments; Machine shop, jobbing and repair

3761 Guided Missiles And Space Vehicles

(P-9890)
ABL SPACE SYSTEMS COMPANY
224 Oregon St (90245-4214)
P.O. Box 1608 (90245-6608)
PHONE................................424 321-5049
Harrison O'hanley, *CEO*
Daniel Piemont, *
EMP: 60 **EST:** 2017
SALES (est): 22.47MM **Privately Held**
Web: www.ablspacesystems.com

SIC: **3761** Guided missiles and space vehicles

(P-9891)
ASTROBOTIC TECHNOLOGY INC
1570 Sabovich St (93501-1681)
PHONE..................888 488-8455
David Masten, *Engr*
EMP: 92
SALES (corp-wide): 44.28MM Privately Held
Web: www.astrobotic.com
SIC: **3761** Guided missiles and space vehicles
PA: Astrobotic Technology, Inc.
503 Martindale St
Pittsburgh PA
412 682-3282

(P-9892)
BOEING COMPANY
Also Called: Boeing
14441 Astronautics Ln (92647-2080)
PHONE..................714 896-3311
James Mcnerney, *Brnch Mgr*
EMP: 368
SQ FT: 2,200,000
SALES (corp-wide): 66.61B Publicly Held
Web: www.boeing.com
SIC: **3761 3769** Guided missiles and space vehicles; Space vehicle equipment, nec
PA: The Boeing Company
929 Long Bridge Dr
Arlington VA
703 414-6338

(P-9893)
GALACTIC CO LLC (DH)
Also Called: Spaceship Company, The
16555 Spaceship Landing Way (93501-1534)
PHONE..................661 824-6600
Michael Colglazier, *CEO*
Enrico Palermo, *
EMP: 19 **EST:** 2006
SQ FT: 200,000
SALES (est): 50.95MM Publicly Held
Web: www.virgingalactic.com
SIC: **3761** Rockets, space and military, complete
HQ: Galactic Enterprises, Llc
166 N Roadrunner Pkwy
Las Cruces NM

(P-9894)
IMPULSE SPACE INC
2651 Manhattan Beach Blvd (90278-1604)
PHONE..................949 315-5540
Thomas Mueller, *CEO*
EMP: 25 **EST:** 2021
SALES (est): 2.77MM Privately Held
Web: www.impulsespace.com
SIC: **3761** Guided missiles and space vehicles

(P-9895)
KRATOS DEF & SEC SOLUTIONS INC (PA)
Also Called: Kratos
10680 Treena St Ste 600 (92131-2440)
PHONE..................858 812-7300
Eric Demarco, *Pr*
William Hoglund, *
Deanna Hom Lund, *
Marie Mendoza, *Sr VP*
Benjamin Goodwin, *Senior Vice President Corporate Development*
EMP: 166 **EST:** 1995
SALES (est): 898.3MM Publicly Held

Web: www.kratosdefense.com
SIC: **3761 3663 7382 8711** Guided missiles and space vehicles; Microwave communication equipment; Security systems services; Engineering services

(P-9896)
MASTEN SPACE SYSTEMS INC
Also Called: Masten Space
1570 Sabovich St 25 (93501-1681)
PHONE..................888 488-8455
EMP: 38 **EST:** 2004
SQ FT: 6,000
SALES (est): 5.11MM Privately Held
Web: www.masten.aero
SIC: **3761** Guided missiles and space vehicles

(P-9897)
ROCKET LAB USA INC (PA)
3881 Mcgowen St (90808-1702)
PHONE..................714 465-5737
Peter Beck, *Ch Bd*
Adam Spice, *CFO*
Shaun O'donnell, *Executive Global Operations Vice President*
Arjun Kampani, *Corporate Secretary*
EMP: 80 **EST:** 2006
SALES (est): 211MM
SALES (corp-wide): 211MM Publicly Held
Web: www.rocketlabusa.com
SIC: **3761** Guided missiles and space vehicles

(P-9898)
SPACE EXPLORATION TECH CORP (PA)
Also Called: Spacex
1 Rocket Rd (90250-6844)
PHONE..................310 363-6000
Elon Musk, *CEO*
Gwynne Shotwell, *
Bret Johnsen, *
◆ **EMP:** 1544 **EST:** 2002
SQ FT: 964,000
SALES (est): 2.07B
SALES (corp-wide): 2.07B Privately Held
Web: www.spacex.com
SIC: **3761** Rockets, space and military, complete

(P-9899)
SPACE EXPLORATION TECH CORP
Also Called: Spacex
2700 Miner St (90731)
PHONE..................714 330-8668
EMP: 45
SALES (corp-wide): 2.07B Privately Held
Web: www.spacex.com
SIC: **3761** Rockets, space and military, complete
PA: Space Exploration Technologies Corp.
1 Rocket Rd
Hawthorne CA
310 363-6000

(P-9900)
SPACE EXPLORATION TECH CORP
Also Called: Spacex Wilkie
12520 Wilkie Ave (90249)
PHONE..................323 754-1285
EMP: 45
SALES (corp-wide): 2.07B Privately Held
Web: www.spacex.com
SIC: **3761** Rockets, space and military, complete
PA: Space Exploration Technologies Corp.
1 Rocket Rd

Hawthorne CA
310 363-6000

(P-9901)
SPACE EXPLORATION TECH CORP
Also Called: Spacex
3976 Jack Northrop Ave (90250-4441)
PHONE..................310 889-4968
EMP: 45
SALES (corp-wide): 2.07B Privately Held
Web: www.spacex.com
SIC: **3761** Rockets, space and military, complete
PA: Space Exploration Technologies Corp.
1 Rocket Rd
Hawthorne CA
310 363-6000

(P-9902)
SPACEX LLC
12533 Crenshaw Blvd (90250-3302)
PHONE..................310 970-5845
EMP: 5286 **EST:** 2004
SALES (est): 8.31MM
SALES (corp-wide): 2.07B Privately Held
Web: www.spacex.com
SIC: **3761** Guided missiles and space vehicles
PA: Space Exploration Technologies Corp.
1 Rocket Rd
Hawthorne CA
310 363-6000

(P-9903)
STELLAR EXPLORATION INC
835 Airport Dr (93401-8370)
PHONE..................805 459-1425
Tomas Svitek, *Pr*
Tomas Svitek, *Pr*
Iva Svitek, *
EMP: 24 **EST:** 2001
SQ FT: 3,000
SALES (est): 3.17MM Privately Held
Web: www.stellar-exploration.com
SIC: **3761** Space vehicles, complete

(P-9904)
TAYCO ENGINEERING INC
10874 Hope St (90630-5214)
P.O. Box 6034 (90630-0034)
PHONE..................714 952-2240
Jay Chung, *Pr*
Ann Taylor, *
Sheri T Nikolakopulos, *
EMP: 130 **EST:** 1971
SQ FT: 55,600
SALES (est): 15.87MM Privately Held
Web: www.taycoeng.com
SIC: **3761** Guided missiles and space vehicles

(P-9905)
TYVAK NN-SATELLITE SYSTEMS INC (DH)
15330 Barranca Pkwy (92618-2215)
PHONE..................949 753-1020
EMP: 75 **EST:** 2011
SALES (est): 25.19MM
SALES (corp-wide): 94.24MM Publicly Held
Web: www.terranorbital.com
SIC: **3761 3764** Space vehicles, complete; Space propulsion units and parts
HQ: Terran Orbital Operating Corporation
6800 Broken Sound Pkwy Nw S
Boca Raton FL
561 988-1704

(P-9906)
UNITED LAUNCH ALLIANCE LLC
1579 Utah Ave, Bldg. 7525 (93437)
PHONE..................303 269-5876
Deborah Settit, *Prin*
EMP: 347
Web: www.ulalaunch.com
SIC: **3761** Guided missiles and space vehicles
PA: United Launch Alliance, L.L.C.
9501 E Panorama Cir
Centennial CO

(P-9907)
VARDA SPACE INDUSTRIES INC
225 S Aviation Blvd (90245-4604)
PHONE..................833 707-0020
Delian Asparouhov, *Pr*
EMP: 70 **EST:** 2020
SALES (est): 9.13MM Privately Held
Web: www.varda.com
SIC: **3761** Space vehicles, complete

(P-9908)
XCOR AEROSPACE INC
Also Called: Xcor
1314 Flight Line (93501-1665)
P.O. Box 61310 (93501)
PHONE..................661 824-4714
▲ **EMP:** 87
Web: www.xcor.com
SIC: **3761** Guided missiles and space vehicles, research and development

3764 Space Propulsion Units And Parts

(P-9909)
MICROCOSM INC
3111 Lomita Blvd (90505-5108)
PHONE..................310 219-2700
James Wertz, *Pr*
Alice Wertz, *
Doctor Robert E Conger, *VP*
EMP: 40 **EST:** 1984
SQ FT: 50,000
SALES (est): 6.04MM Privately Held
Web: www.smad.com
SIC: **3764 2731 3769** Space propulsion units and parts; Book publishing; Space vehicle equipment, nec

(P-9910)
MORPHEUS SPACE INC (PA)
300 Continental Blvd Ste 350 (90245-5077)
PHONE..................562 766-8470
Daniel Bock, *CEO*
Istvan Lorincz, *
Istan Lorincz, *
EMP: 17 **EST:** 2019
SALES (est): 3.77MM
SALES (corp-wide): 3.77MM Privately Held
Web: www.morpheus-space.com
SIC: **3764** Space propulsion units and parts

(P-9911)
PHASE FOUR INC
12605 S Van Ness Ave (90250-3321)
PHONE..................310 648-8454
Jonathan Jarvis, *CEO*
EMP: 17 **EST:** 2015
SALES (est): 2.6MM Privately Held
Web: www.phasefour.io
SIC: **3764** Space propulsion units and parts

(P-9912)
RELATIVITY SPACE INC (PA)
3500 E Burnett St (90815-1730)
PHONE..............................424 393-4309
Timothy Ellis, *CEO*
Jordan Noone, *
Alexander Kwan, *
Muhammad Shahzad, *
Roxanne Fung, *Corporate Controller*
EMP: 337 **EST:** 2015
SQ FT: 10,000
SALES (est): 135.25MM
SALES (corp-wide): 135.25MM **Privately Held**
Web: www.relativityspace.com
SIC: 3764 Space propulsion units and parts

(P-9913)
SPINLAUNCH INC
4350 E Conant St (90808-1868)
PHONE..............................650 516-7746
Jonathan Yaney, *Pr*
Domhnal Slattery, *Ch Bd*
EMP: 88 **EST:** 2015
SALES (est): 10.78MM **Privately Held**
Web: www.spinlaunch.com
SIC: 3764 Propulsion units for guided missiles and space vehicles

3769 Space Vehicle Equipment, Nec

(P-9914)
AMERICAN AUTOMATED ENGRG INC
Also Called: A A E Aerospace & Coml Tech
5382 Argosy Ave (92649-1037)
PHONE..............................714 898-9951
Kenneth Christensen, *Pr*
EMP: 85 **EST:** 1967
SQ FT: 48,000
SALES (est): 9.5MM **Privately Held**
SIC: 3769 Space vehicle equipment, nec

(P-9915)
CLIFFDALE MANUFACTURING LLC
Also Called: RTC Aerospace
20409 Prairie St (91311-6029)
PHONE..............................818 341-3344
Brad Hart, *CEO*
EMP: 200 **EST:** 1943
SQ FT: 42,000
SALES (est): 16.88MM **Privately Held**
Web: www.rtcaerospace.com
SIC: 3769 3599 Space vehicle equipment, nec; Machine shop, jobbing and repair

(P-9916)
COMPOSITE OPTICS INCORPORATED
Also Called: Atk
7130 Miramar Rd Ste 100b (92121-2340)
PHONE..............................937 490-4145
EMP: 800
SIC: 3769 Space vehicle equipment, nec

(P-9917)
DW AND BB CONSULTING INC
11381 Bradley Ave (91331-2358)
PHONE..............................818 896-9899
David Wyckoff, *Pr*
Lee Brown, *
Ben Bensal, *
EMP: 70 **EST:** 1989
SQ FT: 10,000
SALES (est): 8.85MM **Privately Held**
Web: www.kdlprecision.com

SIC: 3769 2822 3061 Space vehicle equipment, nec; Silicone rubbers; Oil and gas field machinery rubber goods (mechanical)

(P-9918)
HYDROMACH INC
20400 Prairie St (91311-8129)
PHONE..............................818 341-0915
Norberto A Cusinato, *CEO*
Jose Nicosia, *
Anna M Cusinato, *
EMP: 40 **EST:** 1976
SQ FT: 23,000
SALES (est): 5.61MM **Privately Held**
Web: www.hydromach.com
SIC: 3769 3599 Space vehicle equipment, nec; Machine shop, jobbing and repair

(P-9919)
LEDA CORPORATION
7080 Kearny Dr (92648-6254)
PHONE..............................714 841-7821
Joseph K Tung, *Pr*
Dorothy Tung, *
David Tung, *
EMP: 30 **EST:** 1985
SQ FT: 15,000
SALES (est): 6.83MM **Privately Held**
Web: www.ledacorp.net
SIC: 3769 Guided missile and space vehicle parts and aux. equip., R&D

(P-9920)
MICRO STEEL INC
7850 Alabama Ave (91304-4905)
PHONE..............................818 348-8701
Lazar Hersko, *Pr*
Claudia Sceelo, *
Tova Hersko, *
EMP: 25 **EST:** 1986
SQ FT: 14,500
SALES (est): 3.5MM **Privately Held**
Web: www.microsteel.net
SIC: 3769 Space vehicle equipment, nec

(P-9921)
STANFORD MU CORPORATION
Also Called: Airborne Components
20725 Annalee Ave (90746-3503)
PHONE..............................310 605-2888
Stanford Mu, *Pr*
Lynn Price, *
Robert Friend, *
EMP: 40 **EST:** 1992
SALES (est): 7.57MM **Privately Held**
Web: www.stanfordmu.com
SIC: 3769 3764 7699 Space vehicle equipment, nec; Space propulsion units and parts; Aircraft and heavy equipment repair services

(P-9922)
VANTAGE ASSOCIATES INC (PA)
12333 Los Nietos Rd (90670-2911)
PHONE..............................619 477-6940
Mary Normand, *CEO*
Eric Clack, *
Andrea Alpinieri Glover, *
EMP: 35 **EST:** 1980
SQ FT: 15,000
SALES (est): 21.95MM
SALES (corp-wide): 21.95MM **Privately Held**
Web: www.vantageassoc.com
SIC: 3769 2821 3728 3083 Space vehicle equipment, nec; Plastics materials and resins; Aircraft parts and equipment, nec; Laminated plastics plate and sheet

3792 Travel Trailers And Campers

(P-9923)
CUSTOM FIBREGLASS MFG CO
Also Called: Custom Hardtops
1711 Harbor Ave (90813-1300)
PHONE..............................562 432-5454
Hartmut W Schroeder, *Pr*
Joel Thiefburg, *
Robert L Edwards, *
◆ **EMP:** 165 **EST:** 1966
SQ FT: 135,000
SALES (est): 31.71MM
SALES (corp-wide): 1.62B **Privately Held**
Web: www.snugtop.com
SIC: 3792 Pickup covers, canopies or caps
HQ: Truck Accessories Group, Llc
28858 Ventura Dr
Elkhart IN
574 522-5337

(P-9924)
FLEETWOOD TRAVEL TRLRS IND INC (DH)
3125 Myers St (92503-5527)
P.O. Box 7638 (92513-7638)
PHONE..............................951 354-3000
Edward B Caudill, *Pr*
Edward B Caudill, *Pr*
Boyd R Plowman, *Ex VP*
Forrest D Theobald, *Sr VP*
Lyle N Larkin, *VP*
EMP: 143 **EST:** 1971
SQ FT: 262,900
SALES (est): 10.22MM **Privately Held**
SIC: 3792 Travel trailers and campers
HQ: Fleetwood Enterprises, Inc.
1351 Pomona Rd Ste 230
Corona CA
951 354-3000

(P-9925)
FLEETWOOD TRAVEL TRLRS OF MD (DH)
3125 Myers St (92503-5527)
P.O. Box 7638 (92513-7638)
PHONE..............................951 351-3500
Elden L Smith, *Pr*
Forrest D Theobald, *Sr VP*
Lyle N Larkin, *VP*
Christopher J Braun, *Sr VP*
▲ **EMP:** 26 **EST:** 1969
SQ FT: 262,900
SALES (est): 5.03MM **Privately Held**
SIC: 3792 Travel trailers and campers
HQ: Fleetwood Enterprises, Inc.
1351 Pomona Rd Ste 230
Corona CA
951 354-3000

(P-9926)
MVP RV INC
40 E Verdugo Ave (91502-1931)
PHONE..............................951 848-4288
Brad Williams, *Pr*
Roger Humeston, *CFO*
Pablo Carmona, *COO*
▲ **EMP:** 17 **EST:** 1996
SALES (est): 1.62MM **Privately Held**
SIC: 3792 Travel trailer chassis

(P-9927)
PACIFIC COACHWORKS INC
3411 N Perris Blvd Bldg 1 (92571-3100)
PHONE..............................951 686-7294
Brett Bashaw, *CEO*
Michael Rhodes, *

EMP: 155 **EST:** 2006
SALES (est): 15.62MM **Privately Held**
Web: www.pacificcoachworks.com
SIC: 3792 Travel trailers and campers

(P-9928)
PROTO HOMES LLC
11301 W Olympic Blvd (90064-1615)
PHONE..............................310 271-7544
EMP: 40 **EST:** 2009
SALES (est): 5.15MM **Privately Held**
Web: www.protohomes.com
SIC: 3792 House trailers, except as permanent dwellings

3795 Tanks And Tank Components

(P-9929)
DN TANKS INC
Also Called: Dyk
351 Cypress Ln (92020-1603)
P.O. Box 696 (92022-0696)
PHONE..............................619 440-8181
EMP: 147
Web: www.dntanks.com
SIC: 3795 Tanks and tank components
PA: Dn Tanks, Inc.
11 Teal Rd
Wakefield MA

(P-9930)
DYK INCORPORATED (HQ)
Also Called: Dyk Prestressed Tanks
351 Cypress Ln (92020-1603)
P.O. Box 696 (92022-0696)
PHONE..............................619 440-8181
Charles Crowley, *CEO*
Max R Dykmans, *
Bill Hendrickson, *
Bill Crowley, *
David Gourley, *
◆ **EMP:** 24 **EST:** 1989
SALES (est): 6.03MM **Privately Held**
Web: www.dntanks.com
SIC: 3795 8711 1542 Tanks and tank components; Engineering services; Nonresidential construction, nec
PA: Dn Tanks, Inc.
11 Teal Rd
Wakefield MA

(P-9931)
TIGER TANKS INC
3397 Edison Hwy (93307-2234)
P.O. Box 21041 (93390-1041)
PHONE..............................661 363-8335
TOLL FREE: 888
Robert E Bimat, *Ch Bd*
Darryck Selk, *
Bryan Lewis, *
Carol Bimat, *
Roger Burns, *
EMP: 30 **EST:** 1997
SQ FT: 55,000
SALES (est): 4.78MM **Privately Held**
Web: www.tigertanksinc.com
SIC: 3795 3443 Tanks and tank components ; Fabricated plate work (boiler shop)

3799 Transportation Equipment, Nec

(P-9932)
CLUB CAR LLC
Also Called: Engersall
1203 Hall Ave (92509-2214)
PHONE..............................951 735-4675

Adam Burke, *Mgr*
EMP: 29
SALES (corp-wide): 434.77MM **Privately Held**
Web: www.clubcar.com
SIC: 3799 5088 Golf carts, powered; Golf carts
PA: Club Car, Llc
    4125 Washington Rd
    Evans GA
    706 863-3000

(P-9933)
DG PERFORMANCE SPC INC
4100 E La Palma Ave (92807-1818)
PHONE..............................714 961-8850
Mark W Dooley, *Pr*
William J Dooley, *
Joan K Dooley, *
EMP: 100 **EST:** 1972
SQ FT: 25,000
SALES (est): 8.68MM **Privately Held**
Web: www.dgperformance.com
SIC: 3799 3751 5012 5961 Recreational vehicles; Motorcycles and related parts; Recreation vehicles, all-terrain; Fitness and sporting goods, mail order

(P-9934)
HALL ASSOCIATES RACG PDTS INC
2711 Plaza Del Amo Ste 503 (90503-7344)
PHONE..............................310 326-4111
Ammie Armstrong, *CEO*
Kennith C Hall, *Pr*
EMP: 17 **EST:** 1995
SALES (est): 2.47MM **Privately Held**
Web: www.hallass.com
SIC: 3799 8733 3699 Recreational vehicles; Research institute; Security devices

(P-9935)
NATIONAL SIGNAL INC
2440 Artesia Ave (92833-2543)
PHONE..............................714 441-7707
◆ **EMP:** 50 **EST:** 1971
SQ FT: 55,000
SALES (est): 9.24MM **Privately Held**
Web: www.nationalsignalinc.net
SIC: 3799 Trailers and trailer equipment

3812 Search And Navigation Equipment

(P-9936)
ACCUTURN CORPORATION
7189 Old 215 Frontage Rd Ste 101 (92553-7903)
PHONE..............................951 656-6621
Ignatius C Araujo, *CEO*
Iggy Araujo, *
Mark Sayegh, *Stockholder*
Henri Rahmon, *Stockholder*
EMP: 26 **EST:** 1974
SQ FT: 15,000
SALES (est): 4.82MM **Privately Held**
Web: www.accuturninc.com
SIC: 3812 3089 3599 Acceleration indicators and systems components, aerospace; Automotive parts, plastic; Machine shop, jobbing and repair

(P-9937)
AEROANTENNA TECHNOLOGY INC
20732 Lassen St (91311-4507)
PHONE..............................818 993-3842
Yosef Klein, *Pr*

Joe Klein, *
Carmela Klein, *
▲ **EMP:** 140 **EST:** 1991
SALES (est): 26.21MM **Publicly Held**
Web: www.aeroantenna.com
SIC: 3812 3663 Antennas, radar or communications; Antennas, transmitting and communications
HQ: Heico Electronic Technologies Corp.
    3000 Taft St
    Hollywood FL
    954 987-6101

(P-9938)
AEROJET RCKETDYNE HOLDINGS INC (HQ)
222 N Pacific Coast Hwy Ste 500 (90245)
P.O. Box 537012 (95853-7012)
PHONE..............................310 252-8100
Ross Niebergall, *Pr*
Joseph Chontos, *VP*
EMP: 75 **EST:** 1915
SALES (est): 2.24B
Web: www.l3harris.com
SIC: 3812 3764 3769 6552 Defense systems and equipment; Propulsion units for guided missiles and space vehicles; Space vehicle equipment, nec; Subdividers and developers, nec
PA: L3harris Technologies, Inc.
    1025 W Nasa Blvd
    Melbourne FL
    321 727-9100

(P-9939)
ALLIANT TCHSYSTEMS OPRTONS LLC
9401 Corbin Ave (91324-2400)
PHONE..............................818 887-8195
Ronald Hill, *Prin*
EMP: 400 **EST:** 2002
SALES (est): 67.19MM **Publicly Held**
SIC: 3812 Search and navigation equipment
HQ: Northrop Grumman Innovation Systems, Inc.
    2980 Fairview Park Dr
    Falls Church VA

(P-9940)
ALLIANT TCHSYSTEMS OPRTONS LLC
21250 Califa St (91367-5001)
PHONE..............................818 887-8185
EMP: 18
Web: www.northropgrumman.com
SIC: 3812 Search and navigation equipment
HQ: Alliant Techsystems Operations Llc
    2980 Fairview Park Dr
    Falls Church VA

(P-9941)
ALLIANT TCHSYSTEMS OPRTONS LLC
9401 Corbin Ave (91324-2400)
PHONE..............................818 887-8195
Albert Calabrese, *Pr*
EMP: 24
Web: www.northropgrumman.com
SIC: 3812 Search and navigation equipment
HQ: Alliant Techsystems Operations Llc
    2980 Fairview Park Dr
    Falls Church VA

(P-9942)
ANDURIL INDUSTRIES INC
2910 S Tech Center Dr (92705-5657)
PHONE..............................949 891-1607
EMP: 50

SALES (corp-wide): 508.23MM **Privately Held**
Web: www.anduril.com
SIC: 3812 Search and navigation equipment
PA: Anduril Industries, Inc.
    1400 Anduril
    Costa Mesa CA
    949 891-1607

(P-9943)
ANDURIL INDUSTRIES INC (PA)
1400 Anduril (92626-1548)
PHONE..............................949 891-1607
Brian Schimpf, *CEO*
Matthew Grimm, *COO*
EMP: 43 **EST:** 2017
SQ FT: 155,000
SALES: 508.23MM
SALES (corp-wide): 508.23MM **Privately Held**
Web: www.anduril.com
SIC: 3812 Search and navigation equipment

(P-9944)
APEX TECHNOLOGY HOLDINGS INC
Also Called: Apex Design Technology
2850 E Coronado St (92806-2503)
PHONE..............................321 270-3630
Lance Schroeder, *Pr*
EMP: 513 **EST:** 2005
SQ FT: 80,000
SALES (est): 48.87MM **Privately Held**
Web: www.apexdt.com
SIC: 3812 Acceleration indicators and systems components, aerospace

(P-9945)
AQUA-LUNG AMERICA INC (DH)
Also Called: Aqualung Group
2105 Rutherford Rd (92008-7329)
PHONE..............................760 376-9813
Andrew Gritzbaugh, *CEO*
Graham Church, *
Ligaya Bowman, *
James Hay, *
◆ **EMP:** 135 **EST:** 1990
SQ FT: 135,000
SALES (est): 96.07MM
SALES (corp-wide): 1.46MM **Privately Held**
Web: us.aqualung.com
SIC: 3812 3949 Search and navigation equipment; Sporting and athletic goods, nec
HQ: Aqualung International
    Les Vaisseaux Batiment C Sophia
    Antipolis
    Valbonne

(P-9946)
ARETE ASSOCIATES (PA)
Also Called: Arete Associates
9301 Corbin Ave Ste 2000 (91324-2508)
PHONE..............................818 885-2200
David Campion, *Pr*
Doug Deprospo, *CSO*
Christopher Choi, *
Sallie Di Vincenzo, *CAO*
EMP: 125 **EST:** 1975
SQ FT: 170,000
SALES: 100MM
SALES (corp-wide): 100MM **Privately Held**
Web: www.arete.com
SIC: 3812 3827 Aircraft/aerospace flight instruments and guidance systems; Sighting and fire control equipment, optical

(P-9947)
ARGON ST INC
6696 Mesa Ridge Rd Ste A (92121-2950)
PHONE..............................703 270-6927
Matthew Hoff, *Brnch Mgr*
EMP: 66
SALES (corp-wide): 66.61B **Publicly Held**
Web: www.argonst.com
SIC: 3812 Search and navigation equipment
HQ: Argon St, Inc.
    12701 Fair Lkes Cir Ste 8
    Fairfax VA
    703 322-0881

(P-9948)
ARMTEC COUNTERMEASURES CO (DH)
85901 Avenue 53 (92236-2607)
PHONE..............................760 398-0143
Paul Heidenreich, *VP*
◆ **EMP:** 17 **EST:** 2002
SQ FT: 100,000
SALES (est): 112.55MM
SALES (corp-wide): 6.58B **Publicly Held**
Web: www.armtecdefense.com
SIC: 3812 Defense systems and equipment
HQ: Armtec Defense Products Co.
    85901 Avenue 53
    Coachella CA

(P-9949)
ASCENT AEROSPACE
1395 S Lyon St (92705-4608)
PHONE..............................586 726-0500
EMP: 65 **EST:** 2020
SALES (est): 11.29MM **Privately Held**
Web: www.ascentaerospace.com
SIC: 3812 Search and navigation equipment

(P-9950)
ATK LAUNCH SYSTEMS LLC
16707 Via Del Campo Ct (92127-1713)
PHONE..............................858 592-2509
EMP: 464
Web: www.northropgrumman.com
SIC: 3812 Search and navigation equipment
HQ: Atk Launch Systems Llc
    9160 N Highway 83
    Corinne UT
    801 251-2512

(P-9951)
ATK SPACE SYSTEMS LLC
Also Called: Atk Arspace Strctres Test Fclt
16707 Via Del Campo Ct (92127-1713)
PHONE..............................858 487-0970
Brian Welge, *Mgr*
EMP: 95
Web: www.northropgrumman.com
SIC: 3812 Search and navigation equipment
HQ: Atk Space Systems Llc
    6033 Bandini Blvd
    Commerce CA
    323 722-0222

(P-9952)
ATK SPACE SYSTEMS LLC
Also Called: Space Components Division
7130 Miramar Rd Ste 100b (92121-2340)
PHONE..............................858 621-5700
EMP: 79
Web: www.northropgrumman.com
SIC: 3812 Search and navigation equipment
HQ: Atk Space Systems Llc
    6033 Bandini Blvd
    Commerce CA
    323 722-0222

PRODUCTS & SVCS

(P-9953)
ATK SPACE SYSTEMS LLC
600 Pine Ave (93117-3803)
PHONE....................805 685-2262
Blake Larson, *CEO*
EMP: 95
Web: www.northropgrumman.com
SIC: 3812 Search and navigation equipment
HQ: Atk Space Systems Llc
6033 Bandini Blvd
Commerce CA
323 722-0222

(P-9954)
ATK SPACE SYSTEMS LLC (DH)
Also Called: Space Components
6033 Bandini Blvd (90040-2968)
PHONE....................323 722-0222
Blake Larson, *Pr*
Daniel J Murphy, *
Ronald D Dittemore, *
James Armor, *
Thomas R Wilson, *
◆ **EMP:** 50 **EST:** 1963
SQ FT: 104,000
SALES (est): 293.63MM **Publicly Held**
Web: www.northropgrumman.com
SIC: 3812 Search and navigation equipment
HQ: Northrop Grumman Innovation
Systems, Inc.
2980 Fairview Park Dr
Falls Church VA

(P-9955)
ATK SPACE SYSTEMS LLC
1960 E Grand Ave Ste 1150 (90245-5166)
PHONE....................310 343-3799
Dale Woolheater, *Brnch Mgr*
EMP: 63
Web: www.northropgrumman.com
SIC: 3812 Search and navigation equipment
HQ: Atk Space Systems Llc
6033 Bandini Blvd
Commerce CA
323 722-0222

(P-9956)
ATK SPACE SYSTEMS LLC
370 N Halstead St (91107-3122)
PHONE....................626 351-0205
Joe Tellegrino, *Mgr*
EMP: 95
Web: www.northropgrumman.com
SIC: 3812 3826 8711 Search and navigation equipment; Instruments measuring thermal properties; Engineering services
HQ: Atk Space Systems Llc
6033 Bandini Blvd
Commerce CA
323 722-0222

(P-9957)
BAE SYSTEMS LAND ARMAMENTS LP
1650 Industrial Blvd (91911-3922)
PHONE....................619 455-0213
Todd Eden, *Brnch Mgr*
EMP: 42
SALES (corp-wide): 25.59B **Privately Held**
Web: www.baesystems.com
SIC: 3812 Search and navigation equipment
HQ: Bae Systems Land & Armaments L.P.
2941 Frview Pk Dr Ste 100
Falls Church VA
571 461-6000

(P-9958)
BAE SYSTEMS TECH SLTONS SVCS I

9650 Chesapeake Dr (92123-1307)
PHONE....................858 278-3042
David Davis, *Brnch Mgr*
EMP: 42
SALES (corp-wide): 25.59B **Privately Held**
SIC: 3812 Navigational systems and instruments
HQ: Bae Systems Technology Solutions & Services Inc.
520 Gaither Rd
Rockville MD
703 847-5820

(P-9959)
BAE SYSTEMS TECH SOL SRVC INC
Acreage 56 & 66 Bldg 70 (93501)
PHONE....................661 816-3474
Brad Thiele, *III*
EMP: 628
SALES (corp-wide): 25.59B **Privately Held**
SIC: 3812 Navigational systems and instruments
HQ: Bae Systems Technology Solutions & Services Inc.
520 Gaither Rd
Rockville MD
703 847-5820

(P-9960)
BIOSPHERICAL INSTRUMENTS INC
5340 Riley St (92110-2621)
PHONE....................619 686-1888
Charles Booth, *CEO*
Doctor John Morrow, *Pr*
EMP: 23 **EST:** 1977
SQ FT: 7,000
SALES (est): 4.34MM **Privately Held**
Web: www.biospherical.com
SIC: 3812 8733 3826 Light or heat emission operating apparatus; Research institute; Photometers

(P-9961)
CAES SYSTEMS LLC
9404 Chesapeake Dr (92123-1303)
PHONE....................858 560-1301
Dave Young, *Brnch Mgr*
EMP: 208
SALES (corp-wide): 2.44B **Privately Held**
Web: www.caes.com
SIC: 3812 Search and navigation equipment
HQ: Caes Systems Llc
305 Richardson Rd
Lansdale PA

(P-9962)
CHANNEL TECHNOLOGIES GROUP LLC
Also Called: Ctg
879 Ward Dr (93111-2920)
P.O. Box 90326 (93190-0326)
PHONE....................805 967-0171
EMP: 1356
SIC: 3812 Search and navigation equipment

(P-9963)
COHERENT AEROSPACE & DEFENSE INC (HQ)
Also Called: Ii-VI Aerospace & Defense Inc
36570 Briggs Rd (92563-2387)
PHONE....................951 926-2994
EMP: 121 **EST:** 1961
SALES (est): 63.97MM
SALES (corp-wide): 5.16B **Publicly Held**
Web: www.iiviad.com

SIC: 3812 3827 Infrared object detection equipment; Optical instruments and apparatus
PA: Coherent Corp.
375 Saxonburg Blvd
Saxonburg PA
724 352-4455

(P-9964)
CONDOR PACIFIC INDUSTRIES INC (PA)
905 Rancho Conejo Blvd (91320-1716)
PHONE....................818 889-2150
Sidney Meltzner, *Pr*
EMP: 21 **EST:** 2006
SALES (est): 4.92MM **Privately Held**
Web: www.condorpacific.com
SIC: 3812 3728 Gyroscopes; Aircraft parts and equipment, nec

(P-9965)
CONSOLIDATED AEROSPACE MFG LLC (HQ)
Also Called: CAM
1425 S Acacia Ave (92831-5317)
PHONE....................714 989-2797
Dave Werner, *Managing Member*
EMP: 46 **EST:** 2012
SALES (est): 312.2MM
SALES (corp-wide): 16.95B **Publicly Held**
Web: www.stanleyblackanddecker.com
SIC: 3812 Search and navigation equipment
PA: Stanley Black & Decker, Inc.
1000 Stanley Dr
New Britain CT
860 225-5111

(P-9966)
CUBIC CORPORATION (HQ)
Also Called: Cubic
9233 Balboa Ave (92123-1513)
PHONE....................858 277-6780
Stevan Slijepcevic, *Pr*
Anshooman Aga, *Ex VP*
Mark A Harrison, *CAO*
Grace G Lee, *Chief Human Resources Officer*
Hilary L Hageman, *Corporate Secretary*
EMP: 1243 **EST:** 1951
SQ FT: 265,000
SALES (est): 1.48B
SALES (corp-wide): 1.48B **Privately Held**
Web: www.cubic.com
SIC: 3812 3699 7372 3724 Defense systems and equipment; Flight simulators (training aids), electronic; Application computer software; Aircraft engines and engine parts
PA: Atlas Cc Acquisition Corp.
850 New Burton Rd Ste 201
Dover DE
858 277-6780

(P-9967)
CUMMINS AEROSPACE LLC (PA)
Also Called: Cummins Aerospace
2320 E Orangethorpe Ave (92806-1223)
PHONE....................714 879-2800
Sean Beriah Cummins, *CEO*
William Beriah Cummins, *
Tina Marie Cummins, *
Mary Ellen Cummins, *
Sean Beriah Cummins, *Dir*
EMP: 30 **EST:** 1978
SQ FT: 35,000
SALES (est): 10.61MM
SALES (corp-wide): 10.61MM **Privately Held**
Web: www.cumminsaerospace.com

SIC: 3812 3519 3728 Search and navigation equipment; Internal combustion engines, nec; Aircraft parts and equipment, nec

(P-9968)
DECA INTERNATIONAL CORP
Also Called: Golf Buddy
10700 Norwalk Blvd (90670-3824)
PHONE....................714 367-5900
▲ **EMP:** 28 **EST:** 2005
SQ FT: 3,000
SALES (est): 4.96MM **Privately Held**
SIC: 3812 Navigational systems and instruments

(P-9969)
DECATUR ELECTRONICS INC (HQ)
15890 Bernardo Center Dr (92127-2320)
PHONE....................888 428-4315
Brian Brown, *CEO*
Luisa Nechodom, *
◆ **EMP:** 70 **EST:** 1955
SQ FT: 10,000
SALES (est): 28.88MM **Privately Held**
Web: www.decaturelectronics.com
SIC: 3812 Radar systems and equipment
PA: D & K Engineering
16990 Goldentop Rd
San Diego CA

(P-9970)
DG ENGINEERING CORP (PA)
Also Called: Schulz Engineering
13326 Ralston Ave (91342-7608)
PHONE....................818 364-9024
Gary Gilmore, *Ch Bd*
Aret Demiral, *
▲ **EMP:** 20 **EST:** 1973
SQ FT: 7,000
SALES (est): 5.56MM
SALES (corp-wide): 5.56MM **Privately Held**
Web: www.dge-corp.com
SIC: 3812 3845 Aircraft control systems, electronic; Electromedical equipment

(P-9971)
EATON AEROSPACE LLC
Also Called: Eaton
9650 Jeronimo Rd (92618-2024)
PHONE....................949 452-9500
Lily Bridenbaker, *Mgr*
EMP: 25
SIC: 3812 3365 Acceleration indicators and systems components, aerospace; Aerospace castings, aluminum
HQ: Eaton Aerospace Llc
1000 Eaton Blvd
Cleveland OH
216 523-5000

(P-9972)
EDGE AUTONOMY SLO LLC
831 Buckley Rd (93401-8130)
PHONE....................805 544-0932
John Purvis, *CEO*
Gordon Jennings, *
EMP: 41 **EST:** 1989
SQ FT: 19,000
SALES (est): 10.38MM
SALES (corp-wide): 1.05B **Privately Held**
Web: www.edgeautonomy.io
SIC: 3812 7371 3721 Electronic detection systems (aeronautical); Computer software development and applications; Aircraft
HQ: Edge Autonomy Bend, Llc
2789 Nw Lolo Dr
Bend OR
541 678-0515

(P-9973)

EDO COMMUNICATIONS AND COUNTERMEASURES SYSTEMS INC

Also Called: Force Protection Systems
7821 Orion Ave (91406-2029)
PHONE..................818 464-2475
EMP: 60
SIC: 3812 3663 3612 7371 Search and navigation equipment; Radio and t.v. communications equipment; Signaling transformers, electric; Custom computer programming services

(P-9974)

EMPLOYER DEFENSE GROUP

2390 E Orangewood Ave Ste 520 (92806-6188)
PHONE..................949 200-0137
Michelle Oelhafen, *Prin*
EMP: 19 **EST:** 2017
SALES (est): 4.35MM **Privately Held**
Web: www.edglaw.com
SIC: 3812 Defense systems and equipment

(P-9975)

ENSIGN-BICKFORD AROSPC DEF CO

14370 White Sage Rd (93021-8720)
P.O. Box 429 (93020-0429)
PHONE..................805 292-4000
EMP: 153
SALES (corp-wide): 696.33MM **Privately Held**
Web: www.ebad.com
SIC: 3812 Search and navigation equipment
HQ: Ensign-Bickford Aerospace & Defense Co
640 Hopmeadow St
Simsbury CT
860 843-2289

(P-9976)

FIRAN TECH GROUP USA CORP (HQ)

20750 Marilla St (91311-4407)
PHONE..................818 407-4024
Brad Bourne, *Pr*
EMP: 61 **EST:** 2004
SALES (est): 98.57MM
SALES (corp-wide): 65.73MM **Privately Held**
Web: www.ftgcorp.com
SIC: 3812 Aircraft control systems, electronic
PA: Firan Technology Group Corporation
250 Finchdene Sq
Toronto ON
416 299-4000

(P-9977)

GARMIN INTERNATIONAL INC

135 S State College Blvd Ste 110 (92821-5823)
PHONE..................909 444-5000
EMP: 370
Web: www.garmin.com
SIC: 3812 Navigational systems and instruments
HQ: Garmin International, Inc.
1200 E 151st St
Olathe KS

(P-9978)

GENERAL FORMING CORPORATION

640 Alaska Ave (90503-5100)
PHONE..................310 326-0624
Ward Olson, *CEO*

EMP: 43 **EST:** 1956
SALES (est): 9.33MM **Privately Held**
Web: www.generalformingcorporation.com
SIC: 3812 3769 3444 3728 Search and navigation equipment; Space vehicle equipment, nec; Sheet metal specialties, not stamped; Aircraft parts and equipment, nec

(P-9979)

GLOBAL A LGISTICS TRAINING INC

Also Called: Galt
3860 Calle Fortunada Ste 100 (92123-4800)
PHONE..................760 688-0365
John Kohut, *CEO*
Bayne Bunce, *COO*
Lili Topchev, *CFO*
John Kohut, *Ch Bd*
EMP: 30 **EST:** 2015
SALES (est): 7.43MM **Privately Held**
Web: www.galt.aero
SIC: 3812 3721 3728 Aircraft/aerospace flight instruments and guidance systems; Research and development on aircraft by the manufacturer; Military aircraft equipment and armament

(P-9980)

GOLDAK INC

15835 Monte St Ste 104 (91342-7674)
P.O. Box 1988 (91209-1988)
PHONE..................818 240-2666
Dan Mulcahey, *Pr*
Dan Mulcahey, *Pr*
Butch Mulcahey, *
Thomas Mulcahey, *
Jeanie Mulcahey, *
EMP: 25 **EST:** 1970
SQ FT: 3,000
SALES (est): 2.57MM **Privately Held**
Web: www.goldak.com
SIC: 3812 Detection apparatus: electronic/magnetic field, light/heat

(P-9981)

INTELLISENSE SYSTEMS INC

21041 S Western Ave (90501-1711)
PHONE..................310 320-1827
Frank Willis, *CEO*
Frank Willis, *Pr*
Selvy Utama, *
EMP: 146 **EST:** 2017
SQ FT: 43,000
SALES (est): 53.57MM **Privately Held**
Web: www.intellisenseinc.com
SIC: 3812 Search and navigation equipment

(P-9982)

INTEROCEAN INDUSTRIES INC

Also Called: Interocean Systems
9201 Isaac St Ste C (92071-5627)
PHONE..................858 292-0808
Michael Pearlman, *CEO*
Stephen Pearlman, *
▼ **EMP:** 31 **EST:** 1945
SALES (est): 4.48MM **Privately Held**
Web: www.interoceansystems.com
SIC: 3812 3699 3826 3531 Search and navigation equipment; Underwater sound equipment; Environmental testing equipment; Marine related equipment

(P-9983)

INTEROCEAN SYSTEMS LLC

9201 Isaac St Ste C (92071-5627)
PHONE..................858 565-8400
Michael D Pearlman, *Pr*

EMP: 35 **EST:** 2005
SALES (est): 7.03MM
SALES (corp-wide): 47.28MM **Privately Held**
Web: www.interoceansystems.com
SIC: 3812 3699 Search and navigation equipment; Underwater sound equipment
PA: Delmar Systems, Inc.
8114 Highway 90 E
Broussard LA
337 365-0180

(P-9984)

JARIET TECHNOLOGIES INC

103 W Torrance Blvd (90277-3633)
PHONE..................310 698-1001
Charles Harper, *CEO*
David Clark, *
Monica Gilbert, *
Matthew Hoppe, *
Craig Hornbuckle, *
EMP: 35 **EST:** 2015
SQ FT: 20,000
SALES (est): 5.8MM **Privately Held**
Web: www.jariettech.com
SIC: 3812 Search and navigation equipment

(P-9985)

L3 TECHNOLOGIES INC

Also Called: Photonics Division
5957 Landau Ct (92008-8803)
PHONE..................760 431-6800
Tim Call, *VP*
EMP: 131
SALES (corp-wide): 17.06B **Publicly Held**
Web: www.l3harris.com
SIC: 3812 Search and navigation equipment
HQ: L3 Technologies, Inc.
600 3rd Ave Fl 34
New York NY
321 727-9100

(P-9986)

L3 TECHNOLOGIES INC

Datron Advanced Tech Div
200 W Los Angeles Ave (93065-1650)
PHONE..................805 584-1717
John Digioia, *Brnch Mgr*
EMP: 100
SALES (corp-wide): 17.06B **Publicly Held**
Web: www.l3harris.com
SIC: 3812 Search and navigation equipment
HQ: L3 Technologies, Inc.
600 3rd Ave Fl 34
New York NY
321 727-9100

(P-9987)

L3 TECHNOLOGIES INC

901 E Ball Rd (92805-5916)
PHONE..................714 956-9200
EMP: 23
SALES (corp-wide): 17.06B **Publicly Held**
Web: www.l3harris.com
SIC: 3812 Search and navigation equipment
HQ: L3 Technologies, Inc.
600 3rd Ave Fl 34
New York NY
321 727-9100

(P-9988)

L3 TECHNOLOGIES INC

Ocean Systems Division
28022 Industry Dr (91355-4191)
PHONE..................818 367-0111
David Defranco, *Brnch Mgr*
EMP: 200
SALES (corp-wide): 17.06B **Publicly Held**
Web: www.l3harris.com

SIC: 3812 Search and navigation equipment
HQ: L3 Technologies, Inc.
600 3rd Ave Fl 34
New York NY
321 727-9100

(P-9989)

L3HARRIS TECHNOLOGIES INC

Also Called: Harris
7821 Orion Ave (91406-2029)
P.O. Box 7713 (91409-7713)
PHONE..................818 901-2523
EMP: 350
SALES (corp-wide): 17.06B **Publicly Held**
Web: www.l3harris.com
SIC: 3812 Search and navigation equipment
PA: L3harris Technologies, Inc.
1025 W Nasa Blvd
Melbourne FL
321 727-9100

(P-9990)

L3HARRIS TECHNOLOGIES INC

Also Called: Harris
12121 Wilshire Blvd Ste 910 (90025-1123)
PHONE..................310 481-6000
EMP: 42
SALES (corp-wide): 17.06B **Publicly Held**
Web: www.l3harris.com
SIC: 3812 7371 Search and navigation equipment; Computer software development
PA: L3harris Technologies, Inc.
1025 W Nasa Blvd
Melbourne FL
321 727-9100

(P-9991)

L3HARRIS TECHNOLOGIES INC

1400 S Shamrock Ave (91016-4267)
PHONE..................626 305-6230
Pat Carr, *Brnch Mgr*
EMP: 88
SALES (corp-wide): 17.06B **Publicly Held**
Web: www.l3harris.com
SIC: 3812 Search and navigation equipment
PA: L3harris Technologies, Inc.
1025 W Nasa Blvd
Melbourne FL
321 727-9100

(P-9992)

LAIRD R & F PRODUCTS INC (DH)

2091 Rutherford Rd (92008-7316)
PHONE..................760 916-9410
▲ **EMP:** 49 **EST:** 1996
SQ FT: 62,000
SALES (est): 23.82MM
SALES (corp-wide): 13.02B **Publicly Held**
SIC: 3812 Radar systems and equipment
HQ: Laird Technologies, Inc.
16401 Swingley Ridge Rd
Chesterfield MO
636 898-6000

(P-9993)

LOCKHEED MARTIN CORPORATION

Also Called: Helendale Lckheed Plant Prtcti
17452 Wheeler Rd (92342-9677)
PHONE..................760 952-4200
EMP: 51
Web: www.gyrocamsystems.com
SIC: 3812 Search and navigation equipment
PA: Lockheed Martin Corporation
6801 Rockledge Dr
Bethesda MD

(P-9994)
LOCKHEED MARTIN CORPORATION
Also Called: Lockheed Martin
Nas North Island (92118)
PHONE..................................619 437-7230
EMP: 232
Web: www.gyrocamsystems.com
SIC: 3812 Search and navigation equipment
PA: Lockheed Martin Corporation
6801 Rockledge Dr
Bethesda MD

(P-9995)
LOCKHEED MARTIN CORPORATION
Santa Barbara Focal Plane
346 Bollay Dr (93117-5550)
PHONE..................................805 571-2346
Bryan Butler, *Mgr*
EMP: 25
SQ FT: 8,500
Web: www.lockheedmartin.com
SIC: 3812 Infrared object detection equipment
PA: Lockheed Martin Corporation
6801 Rockledge Dr
Bethesda MD

(P-9996)
LOCKHEED MARTIN CORPORATION
Also Called: Lockheed Martin Aeronautics Co
1011 Lockheed Way (93599-0001)
PHONE..................................661 572-7428
Rick Baker, *VP*
EMP: 4000
Web: www.lockheedmartin.com
SIC: 3812 Search and navigation equipment
PA: Lockheed Martin Corporation
6801 Rockledge Dr
Bethesda MD

(P-9997)
LOCKHEED MARTIN ORINCON CORP (HQ)
10325 Meanley Dr (92131-3011)
PHONE..................................858 455-5530
Daniel Alspach, *Ch Bd*
EMP: 200 **EST:** 1973
SQ FT: 41,000
SALES (est): 55.37MM **Publicly Held**
SIC: 3812 Search and navigation equipment
PA: Lockheed Martin Corporation
6801 Rockledge Dr
Bethesda MD

(P-9998)
LYTX INC (PA)
9785 Towne Centre Dr (92121-1968)
PHONE..................................858 430-4000
Brandon Nixon, *CEO*
Paul J Pucino, *CFO*
Tom Fisher, *VP*
Drew Martin, *Ex VP*
David Riordan, *Ex VP*
EMP: 300 **EST:** 1998
SQ FT: 100,000
SALES (est): 123.43MM
SALES (corp-wide): 123.43MM **Privately Held**
Web: www.lytx.com
SIC: 3812 Search and detection systems and instruments

(P-9999)
MISSION RESEARCH CORPORATION (DH)

Also Called: Atk Mission Research
6750 Navigator Way Ste 200 (93117-3657)
PHONE..................................805 690-2447
Kevin Vogel, *Prin*
EMP: 98 **EST:** 1987
SQ FT: 40,000
SALES (est): 46.03MM **Publicly Held**
SIC: 3812 Search and navigation equipment
HQ: Northrop Grumman Innovation Systems, Inc.
2980 Fairview Park Dr
Falls Church VA

(P-10000)
MOOG INC
7406 Hollister Ave (93117-2583)
PHONE..................................805 618-3900
Robert W Urban, *Genl Mgr*
EMP: 300
SALES (corp-wide): 3.32B **Publicly Held**
Web: www.moog.com
SIC: 3812 3492 3625 3769 Aircraft control systems, electronic; Electrohydraulic servo valves, metal; Relays and industrial controls ; Space vehicle equipment, nec
PA: Moog Inc.
400 Jamison Rd
Elma NY
716 652-2000

(P-10001)
MOOG INC
21339 Nordhoff St (91311-5819)
PHONE..................................818 341-5156
Ruben Nalbandian, *Sls Mgr*
EMP: 150
SALES (corp-wide): 3.32B **Publicly Held**
Web: www.moog.com
SIC: 3812 Aircraft control systems, electronic
PA: Moog Inc.
400 Jamison Rd
Elma NY
716 652-2000

(P-10002)
MOOG INC
Also Called: Moog Aircraft Group
20263 S Western Ave (90501-1310)
PHONE..................................310 533-1178
Alberto Bilalon, *Mgr*
EMP: 450
SALES (corp-wide): 3.32B **Publicly Held**
Web: www.moog.com
SIC: 3812 Search and navigation equipment
PA: Moog Inc.
400 Jamison Rd
Elma NY
716 652-2000

(P-10003)
MP SOLUTIONS INC
21818 S Wilmington Ave Ste 411 (90810-1642)
EMP: 20 **EST:** 1999
SALES (est): 4.76MM **Privately Held**
Web: www.simulatorps.com
SIC: 3812 Aircraft control instruments

(P-10004)
MTI DE BAJA INC
915 Industrial Way (92582-3890)
PHONE..................................951 654-2333
Monty Merkin, *CEO*
EMP: 24 **EST:** 2009
SALES (est): 1.69MM **Privately Held**
Web: www.mtibaja.com
SIC: 3812 Acceleration indicators and systems components, aerospace

(P-10005)
NEVWEST INC
1225 Exposition Way Ste 140 (92154)
PHONE..................................619 420-8100
Alfredo Liburd, *Pr*
Virginia Burd, *
EMP: 18 **EST:** 2004
SALES (est): 1.59MM **Privately Held**
Web: www.nevwestinc.com
SIC: 3812 Warfare counter-measure equipment

(P-10006)
NORTHROP GRMMAN INNVTION SYSTE
Also Called: Ca75 Atk
9617 Distribution Ave (92121-2307)
PHONE..................................858 621-5700
David W Thompson, *Pr*
EMP: 300
Web: www.northropgrumman.com
SIC: 3812 Search and navigation equipment
HQ: Northrop Grumman Innovation Systems, Inc.
2980 Fairview Park Dr
Falls Church VA

(P-10007)
NORTHROP GRMMAN INNVTION SYSTE
9401 Corbin Ave (91324-2400)
PHONE..................................818 887-8100
EMP: 100
Web: www.northropgrumman.com
SIC: 3812 Search and navigation equipment
HQ: Northrop Grumman Innovation Systems, Inc.
2980 Fairview Park Dr
Falls Church VA

(P-10008)
NORTHROP GRUMMAN CORPORATION
Also Called: Northrop Grmman Arospc Systems
3520 E Avenue M (93550-7401)
PHONE..................................661 272-7334
EMP: 31
Web: www.northropgrumman.com
SIC: 3812 Search and navigation equipment
PA: Northrop Grumman Corporation
2980 Fairview Park Dr
Falls Church VA

(P-10009)
NORTHROP GRUMMAN CORPORATION
18701 Caminito Pasadero (92128-6162)
PHONE..................................858 967-1221
Dagnall Barry, *Brnch Mgr*
EMP: 735
Web: www.northropgrumman.com
SIC: 3812 Search and detection systems and instruments
PA: Northrop Grumman Corporation
2980 Fairview Park Dr
Falls Church VA

(P-10010)
NORTHROP GRUMMAN CORPORATION
198 Willow Grove Pl (92027-5348)
PHONE..................................310 864-7342
EMP: 37
Web: www.northropgrumman.com
SIC: 3812 Search and navigation equipment
PA: Northrop Grumman Corporation
2980 Fairview Park Dr

Falls Church VA

(P-10011)
NORTHROP GRUMMAN CORPORATION
Northrop Grumman Aviation
1 Hornet Way (90245-2804)
PHONE..................................310 332-1000
Ray Pollok, *Mgr*
EMP: 200
Web: www.northropgrumman.com
SIC: 3812 Search and navigation equipment
PA: Northrop Grumman Corporation
2980 Fairview Park Dr
Falls Church VA

(P-10012)
NORTHROP GRUMMAN CORPORATION
19782 Macarthur Blvd (92612-2452)
PHONE..................................949 260-9800
Jeffrey Smith, *Mgr*
EMP: 46
Web: www.northropgrumman.com
SIC: 3812 Search and navigation equipment
PA: Northrop Grumman Corporation
2980 Fairview Park Dr
Falls Church VA

(P-10013)
NORTHROP GRUMMAN INTL TRDG INC
21240 Burbank Blvd (91367-6680)
PHONE..................................818 715-3607
David Perry, *CEO*
EMP: 44 **EST:** 2014
SALES (est): 7.03MM **Publicly Held**
SIC: 3812 Search and navigation equipment
HQ: Northrop Grumman International, Inc.
2980 Fairview Park Dr
Falls Church VA

(P-10014)
NORTHROP GRUMMAN SYSTEMS CORP
California Microwave Systems
21200 Burbank Blvd (91367-6675)
PHONE..................................818 715-2597
Roy Medlin, *Brnch Mgr*
EMP: 184
Web: www.northropgrumman.com
SIC: 3812 Search and navigation equipment
HQ: Northrop Grumman Systems Corporation
2980 Fairview Park Dr
Falls Church VA
703 280-2900

(P-10015)
NORTHROP GRUMMAN SYSTEMS CORP
Also Called: Weapons System Division
9401 Corbin Ave (91324-2400)
PHONE..................................818 887-8110
Richard Nolan, *Brnch Mgr*
EMP: 368
Web: www.northropgrumman.com
SIC: 3812 Search and navigation equipment
HQ: Northrop Grumman Systems Corporation
2980 Fairview Park Dr
Falls Church VA
703 280-2900

(P-10016)
NORTHROP GRUMMAN SYSTEMS CORP
6033 Bandini Blvd (90040-2968)

PHONE..................................714 240-6521
EMP: 145
Web: www.northropgrumman.com
SIC: 3812 Aircraft/aerospace flight
instruments and guidance systems
HQ: Northrop Grumman Systems
Corporation
2980 Fairview Park Dr
Falls Church VA
703 280-2900

(P-10017)
**NORTHROP GRUMMAN
SYSTEMS CORP**
400 Continental Blvd (90245-5076)
PHONE..................................480 355-7716
EMP: 79
Web: www.northropgrumman.com
SIC: 3812 Aircraft/aerospace flight
instruments and guidance systems
HQ: Northrop Grumman Systems
Corporation
2980 Fairview Park Dr
Falls Church VA
703 280-2900

(P-10018)
**NORTHROP GRUMMAN
SYSTEMS CORP**
2550 Honolulu Ave (91020-1858)
PHONE..................................818 249-5252
Arthur F Brown, *Mgr*
EMP: 69
Web: www.northropgrumman.com
SIC: 3812 Search and navigation equipment
HQ: Northrop Grumman Systems
Corporation
2980 Fairview Park Dr
Falls Church VA
703 280-2900

(P-10019)
**NORTHROP GRUMMAN
SYSTEMS CORP**
Also Called: Northrop Grmman Elctrnic Syste
1100 W Hollyvale St (91702-3305)
P.O. Box 296 (91702-0296)
PHONE..................................626 812-1000
Carl Fischer, *Mgr*
EMP: 5136
Web: www.northropgrumman.com
SIC: 3812 Search and navigation equipment
HQ: Northrop Grumman Systems
Corporation
2980 Fairview Park Dr
Falls Church VA
703 280-2900

(P-10020)
**NORTHROP GRUMMAN
SYSTEMS CORP**
Western Region
3520 E Avenue M (93550-7401)
PHONE..................................661 540-0446
Jim Pace, *Brnch Mgr*
EMP: 53
Web: www.northropgrumman.com
SIC: 3812 Search and navigation equipment
HQ: Northrop Grumman Systems
Corporation
2980 Fairview Park Dr
Falls Church VA
703 280-2900

(P-10021)
**NORTHROP GRUMMAN
SYSTEMS CORP**
Defense Systems Sector
1 Space Park Blvd (90278-1071)

PHONE..................................855 737-8364
Jack Distaso, *Brnch Mgr*
EMP: 140
SQ FT: 500,000
Web: www.northropgrumman.com
SIC: 3812 Search and navigation equipment
HQ: Northrop Grumman Systems
Corporation
2980 Fairview Park Dr
Falls Church VA
703 280-2900

(P-10022)
**NORTHROP GRUMMAN
SYSTEMS CORP**
2477 Manhattan Beach Blvd (90278-1544)
PHONE..................................310 812-4321
Bruce R Gerding, *VP*
EMP: 79
Web: www.northropgrumman.com
SIC: 3812 Search and navigation equipment
HQ: Northrop Grumman Systems
Corporation
2980 Fairview Park Dr
Falls Church VA
703 280-2900

(P-10023)
**NORTHROP GRUMMAN
SYSTEMS CORP**
1111 W 3rd St (91702-3328)
PHONE..................................626 812-1464
Michael Clayton, *Mgr*
EMP: 763
Web: www.northropgrumman.com
SIC: 3812 Search and navigation equipment
HQ: Northrop Grumman Systems
Corporation
2980 Fairview Park Dr
Falls Church VA
703 280-2900

(P-10024)
**NORTHROP GRUMMAN
SYSTEMS CORP**
1 Hornet Way (90245-2804)
PHONE..................................310 332-1000
EMP: 395
Web: www.northropgrumman.com
SIC: 3812 Search and navigation equipment
HQ: Northrop Grumman Systems
Corporation
2980 Fairview Park Dr
Falls Church VA
703 280-2900

(P-10025)
**NORTHROP GRUMMAN
SYSTEMS CORP**
6411 W Imperial Hwy (90045-6307)
PHONE..................................310 556-4911
Shea Mark, *Prin*
EMP: 303
Web: www.northropgrumman.com
SIC: 3812 Search and navigation equipment
HQ: Northrop Grumman Systems
Corporation
2980 Fairview Park Dr
Falls Church VA
703 280-2900

(P-10026)
**NORTHROP GRUMMAN
SYSTEMS CORP**
Litton Navigation Systems Div
21240 Burbank Blvd Ms 29 (91367-6680)
PHONE..................................818 715-4040
Bill Allison, *Div Pres*
EMP: 1000

Web: www.northropgrumman.com
SIC: 3812 Search and navigation equipment
HQ: Northrop Grumman Systems
Corporation
2980 Fairview Park Dr
Falls Church VA
703 280-2900

(P-10027)
**NORTHROP GRUMMAN
SYSTEMS CORP**
Also Called: Northrop Grumman CMS
21240 Burbank Blvd (91367-6680)
PHONE..................................818 715-4854
Roy Medland, *Brnch Mgr*
EMP: 276
Web: www.northropgrumman.com
SIC: 3812 Search and navigation equipment
HQ: Northrop Grumman Systems
Corporation
2980 Fairview Park Dr
Falls Church VA
703 280-2900

(P-10028)
**NORTHROP GRUMMAN
SYSTEMS CORP**
Also Called: Northrop Grmman Def Mssion
Sys
9326 Spectrum Center Blvd (92123-1443)
PHONE..................................410 765-5589
Steve Appel, *Brnch Mgr*
EMP: 1539
Web: www.northropgrumman.com
SIC: 3812 7379 Search and navigation
equipment; Computer related consulting
services
HQ: Northrop Grumman Systems
Corporation
2980 Fairview Park Dr
Falls Church VA
703 280-2900

(P-10029)
**NORTHROP GRUMMAN
SYSTEMS CORP**
15120 Innovation Dr (92128-3402)
PHONE..................................858 592-4518
Chris Willenborg, *Brnch Mgr*
EMP: 408
SQ FT: 211,000
Web: www.northropgrumman.com
SIC: 3812 8711 7373 Search and navigation
equipment; Engineering services;
Computer integrated systems design
HQ: Northrop Grumman Systems
Corporation
2980 Fairview Park Dr
Falls Church VA
703 280-2900

(P-10030)
**NORTHROP GRUMMAN
SYSTEMS CORP**
17066 Goldentop Rd (92127-2412)
PHONE..................................858 618-4349
Gerald Dufresne, *Mgr*
EMP: 223
Web: www.northropgrumman.com
SIC: 3812 3761 7373 3721 Search and
detection systems and instruments; Guided
missiles, complete; Computer integrated
systems design; Airplanes, fixed or rotary
wing
HQ: Northrop Grumman Systems
Corporation
2980 Fairview Park Dr
Falls Church VA
703 280-2900

(P-10031)
**NORTHROP GRUMMAN
SYSTEMS CORP**
9112 Spectrum Center Blvd (92123-1439)
PHONE..................................858 514-9020
EMP: 79
Web: www.northropgrumman.com
SIC: 3812 Search and navigation equipment
HQ: Northrop Grumman Systems
Corporation
2980 Fairview Park Dr
Falls Church VA
703 280-2900

(P-10032)
**NORTHROP GRUMMAN
SYSTEMS CORP**
Also Called: Aerontics Systems Arspc Strctr
16707 Via Del Campo Ct (92127-1713)
PHONE..................................858 592-2535
Audrey Clark, *Brnch Mgr*
EMP: 18
Web: www.northropgrumman.com
SIC: 3812 Search and navigation equipment
HQ: Northrop Grumman Systems
Corporation
2980 Fairview Park Dr
Falls Church VA
703 280-2900

(P-10033)
**NORTHROP GRUMMAN
SYSTEMS CORP**
7130 Miramar Rd Ste 100b (92121-2340)
PHONE..................................858 621-7395
EMP: 66
Web: www.northropgrumman.com
SIC: 3812 Aircraft/aerospace flight
instruments and guidance systems
HQ: Northrop Grumman Systems
Corporation
2980 Fairview Park Dr
Falls Church VA
703 280-2900

(P-10034)
**NORTHROP GRUMMAN
SYSTEMS CORP**
Also Called: Northrop Grumman Space
9326 Spectrum Center Blvd (92123-1443)
PHONE..................................858 514-9000
Mike Twyman, *Brnch Mgr*
EMP: 79
Web: www.northropgrumman.com
SIC: 3812 Search and navigation equipment
HQ: Northrop Grumman Systems
Corporation
2980 Fairview Park Dr
Falls Church VA
703 280-2900

(P-10035)
**NORTHROP GRUMMAN
SYSTEMS CORP**
2700 Camino Del Sol (93030-7967)
PHONE..................................805 278-2074
Pierre Courduroux, *Brnch Mgr*
EMP: 92
Web: www.northropgrumman.com
SIC: 3812 Aircraft/aerospace flight
instruments and guidance systems
HQ: Northrop Grumman Systems
Corporation
2980 Fairview Park Dr
Falls Church VA
703 280-2900

PRODUCTS & SVCS

(P-10036)
NORTHROP GRUMMAN SYSTEMS CORP
760 Paseo Camarillo Ste 200 (93010-6000)
PHONE......................805 987-8831
Steve Crans, *Mgr*
EMP: 170
Web: www.northropgrumman.com
SIC: 3812 Search and navigation equipment
HQ: Northrop Grumman Systems
    Corporation
    2980 Fairview Park Dr
    Falls Church VA
    703 280-2900

(P-10037)
NORTHROP GRUMMAN SYSTEMS CORP
5161 Verdugo Way (93012-8603)
PHONE......................805 987-9739
Jim Lueck, *Brnch Mgr*
EMP: 39
Web: www.northropgrumman.com
SIC: 3812 8731 8711 7371 Search and
    navigation equipment; Commercial physical
    research; Engineering services; Custom
    computer programming services
HQ: Northrop Grumman Systems
    Corporation
    2980 Fairview Park Dr
    Falls Church VA
    703 280-2900

(P-10038)
NORTHROP GRUMMAN SYSTEMS CORP
2601 Camino Del Sol (93030-7996)
PHONE......................805 684-6641
Kathy Warden, *CEO*
Richard Nelson, *
Alice Reed, *
EMP: 110 EST: 1999
SQ FT: 70,000
SALES (est): 35.8MM Publicly Held
Web: www.northropgrumman.com
SIC: 3812 Search and navigation equipment
HQ: Northrop Grumman Systems
    Corporation
    2980 Fairview Park Dr
    Falls Church VA
    703 280-2900

(P-10039)
NORTHROP GRUMMAN SYSTEMS CORP
Building 806 (92310)
PHONE......................760 380-4268
EMP: 53
Web: www.northropgrumman.com
SIC: 3812 Search and navigation equipment
HQ: Northrop Grumman Systems
    Corporation
    2980 Fairview Park Dr
    Falls Church VA
    703 280-2900

(P-10040)
NORTHROP GRUMMAN SYSTEMS CORP
Also Called: Technical Services
862 E Hospitality Ln (92408-3530)
PHONE......................703 713-4096
EMP: 39
Web: www.northropgrumman.com
SIC: 3812 Search and navigation equipment
HQ: Northrop Grumman Systems
    Corporation
    2980 Fairview Park Dr
    Falls Church VA
    703 280-2900

(P-10041)
NORTHROP GRUMMAN SYSTEMS CORP
600 Pine Ave (93117-3803)
PHONE......................714 240-6521
EMP: 79
Web: www.northropgrumman.com
SIC: 3812 Aircraft/aerospace flight
    instruments and guidance systems
HQ: Northrop Grumman Systems
    Corporation
    2980 Fairview Park Dr
    Falls Church VA
    703 280-2900

(P-10042)
NORTHROP GRUMMAN SYSTEMS CORP
Strategic Deterrent Systems
1467 Fairway Dr (93455-1404)
PHONE......................805 315-5728
EMP: 53
Web: www.northropgrumman.com
SIC: 3812 Inertial guidance systems
HQ: Northrop Grumman Systems
    Corporation
    2980 Fairview Park Dr
    Falls Church VA
    703 280-2900

(P-10043)
ONE STEP GPS LLC
675 Glenoaks Blvd Unit C (91340-4803)
PHONE......................818 659-2031
Kevin Kenneth Dale, *
EMP: 28 EST: 2017
SALES (est): 3.22MM Privately Held
Web: www.onestepgps.com
SIC: 3812 Search and navigation equipment

(P-10044)
ORBITAL SCIENCES LLC
Talo Rd Bldg 1555 (93437)
P.O. Box 5159 (93437-0159)
PHONE......................805 734-5400
Eric Denbrook, *Mgr*
EMP: 294
Web: www.orbitalsciencesllc.com
SIC: 3812 Search and navigation equipment
HQ: Orbital Sciences Llc
    2980 Fairview Park Dr
    Falls Church VA
    703 552-8203

(P-10045)
ORBITAL SCIENCES LLC
16707 Via Del Campo Ct (92127-1713)
PHONE......................858 618-1847
Brian Welge, *Brnch Mgr*
EMP: 210
Web: www.orbitalsciencesllc.com
SIC: 3812 Search and navigation equipment
HQ: Orbital Sciences Llc
    2980 Fairview Park Dr
    Falls Church VA
    703 552-8203

(P-10046)
ORBITAL SCIENCES LLC
Also Called: Space Systems Division
2401 E El Segundo Blvd Ste 200
(90245-4631)
PHONE......................703 406-5000
Antonio Elias, *Ex VP*
EMP: 210
Web: www.orbitalsciencesllc.com
SIC: 3812 Search and navigation equipment
HQ: Orbital Sciences Llc
    2980 Fairview Park Dr

Falls Church VA
703 552-8203

(P-10047)
ORBITAL SCIENCES LLC
1151 W Reeves Ave (93555-2313)
PHONE......................818 887-8345
David Rocca, *Brnch Mgr*
EMP: 210
Web: www.orbitalsciencesllc.com
SIC: 3812 Search and navigation equipment
HQ: Orbital Sciences Llc
    2980 Fairview Park Dr
    Falls Church VA
    703 552-8203

(P-10048)
PACIFIC DEFENSE STRATEGIES INC (PA)
Also Called: Pacific Defense
400 Continental Blvd Ste 100 (90245-5076)
PHONE......................310 722-6050
Travis Slocumb, *CEO*
Scott Hoffman, *CFO*
Kent Mader, *COO*
EMP: 23 EST: 2020
SALES (est): 7.07MM
SALES (corp-wide): 7.07MM Privately
Held
Web: www.pacific-defense.com
SIC: 3812 Defense systems and equipment

(P-10049)
PACIFIC SCIENTIFIC COMPANY (DH)
Also Called: Electro Kinetics Division
1785 Voyager Ave (93063-3363)
PHONE......................805 526-5700
James Simpkins, *Prin*
David Penner, *
James Healey, *
◆ EMP: 23 EST: 1998
SALES (est): 102.16MM
SALES (corp-wide): 19.07B Publicly Held
Web: www.hachultra.com
SIC: 3812 3669 3621 3694 Aircraft control
    systems, electronic; Fire detection systems,
    electric; Generators and sets, electric;
    Alternators, automotive
HQ: Meggitt-Usa, Inc.
    1955 Surveyor Ave
    Simi Valley CA
    805 526-5700

(P-10050)
PNEUDRAULICS INC
8575 Helms Ave (91730-4591)
PHONE......................909 980-5366
Michael Saville, *CEO*
Dain Miller, *
▼ EMP: 275 EST: 1956
SQ FT: 48,000
SALES (est): 46.54MM
SALES (corp-wide): 6.58B Publicly Held
Web: www.pneudraulics.com
SIC: 3812 Acceleration indicators and
    systems components, aerospace
PA: Transdigm Group Incorporated
    1301 E 9th St Ste 3000
    Cleveland OH
    216 706-2960

(P-10051)
RANTEC MICROWAVE SYSTEMS INC (PA)
31186 La Baya Dr (91362-4003)
PHONE......................818 223-5000
Carl Grindle, *CEO*
Carl E Grindle, *

Graham R Wilson, *
Steven B Chegwin, *
Steven Chegwin, *
EMP: 55 EST: 2000
SQ FT: 35,000
SALES (est): 12.58MM
SALES (corp-wide): 12.58MM Privately
Held
Web: www.rantecantennas.com
SIC: 3812 Antennas, radar or
    communications

(P-10052)
RAYTHEON COMPANY
Also Called: Raytheon
8650 Balboa Ave (92123-1502)
PHONE......................858 571-6598
EMP: 47
SALES (corp-wide): 67.07B Publicly Held
Web: www.rtx.com
SIC: 3812 Sonar systems and equipment
HQ: Raytheon Company
    870 Winter St
    Waltham MA
    781 522-3000

(P-10053)
RAYTHEON COMPANY
Also Called: Raytheon
75 Coromar Dr (93117-3023)
PHONE......................805 562-4611
EMP: 75
SALES (corp-wide): 67.07B Publicly Held
Web: www.rtx.com
SIC: 3812 8731 3845 3825 Sonar systems
    and equipment; Commercial research
    laboratory; Electromedical equipment;
    Instruments to measure electricity
HQ: Raytheon Company
    870 Winter St
    Waltham MA
    781 522-3000

(P-10054)
RAYTHEON COMPANY
Raytheon
1801 Hughes Dr (92833-2200)
P.O. Box 3310 (92834-3310)
PHONE......................714 732-0119
EMP: 30
SALES (corp-wide): 67.07B Publicly Held
Web: www.rtx.com
SIC: 3812 7371 Sonar systems and
    equipment; Computer software
    development and applications
HQ: Raytheon Company
    870 Winter St
    Waltham MA
    781 522-3000

(P-10055)
RAYTHEON COMPANY
Also Called: Raytheon
1921 E Mariposa Ave (90245)
PHONE......................310 647-1000
David Wajsgras, *Brnch Mgr*
EMP: 100
SALES (corp-wide): 67.07B Publicly Held
Web: www.rtx.com
SIC: 3812 4899 Sonar systems and
    equipment; Satellite earth stations
HQ: Raytheon Company
    870 Winter St
    Waltham MA
    781 522-3000

(P-10056)
RAYTHEON COMPANY
Also Called: Raytheon
2000 E El Segundo Blvd (90245-4501)

P.O. Box 925 (90245-0925)
PHONE..............................310 647-9438
EMP: 25
SALES (corp-wide): 67.07B **Publicly Held**
Web: www.rtx.com
SIC: 3812 Aircraft/aerospace flight
instruments and guidance systems
HQ: Raytheon Company
870 Winter St
Waltham MA
781 522-3000

(P-10057)
RAYTHEON COMPANY
Also Called: Raytheon
2000 E El Segundo Blvd (90245-4501)
P.O. Box 902 (90245-0902)
PHONE..............................310 647-9438
EMP: 10000
SALES (corp-wide): 67.07B **Publicly Held**
Web: www.rtx.com
SIC: 3812 Defense systems and equipment
HQ: Raytheon Company
870 Winter St
Waltham MA
781 522-3000

(P-10058)
RAYTHEON COMPANY
Also Called: Raytheon
2000 E El Segundo Blvd (90245-4501)
PHONE..............................310 647-1000
John Jones, *Mgr*
EMP: 500
SALES (corp-wide): 67.07B **Publicly Held**
Web: www.rtx.com
SIC: 3812 Defense systems and equipment
HQ: Raytheon Company
870 Winter St
Waltham MA
781 522-3000

(P-10059)
RAYTHEON DGITAL FORCE TECH LLC (DH)
Also Called: Digital Force Technologies
6779 Mesa Ridge Rd Ste 150 (92121-2909)
PHONE..............................858 546-1244
EMP: 38 **EST:** 2000
SQ FT: 14,500
SALES (est): 14.41MM
SALES (corp-wide): 67.07B **Publicly Held**
Web: www.digitalforcetech.com
SIC: 3812 8711 Defense systems and
equipment; Engineering services
HQ: Raytheon Bbn Technologies Corp.
10 Moulton St
Cambridge MA
617 873-8000

(P-10060)
REMEC DEFENSE & SPACE INC
Also Called: Cobham
9404 Chesapeake Dr (92123-1388)
PHONE..............................858 560-1301
EMP: 1000
SALES (corp-wide): 67.07B **Publicly Held**
SIC: 3812 Search and navigation equipment

(P-10061)
REVEAL IMAGING TECH INC
10260 Campus Point Dr Ste 6130
(92121-1522)
PHONE..............................571 526-6000
EMP: 72
Web: www.leidos.com
SIC: 3812 Search and navigation equipment
HQ: Reveal Imaging Technologies, Inc.
10260 Campus Point Dr # 6130
San Diego CA
571 526-6000

(P-10062)
REVEAL IMAGING TECH INC (DH)
10260 Campus Point Dr Rm 6130
(92121-1522)
PHONE..............................571 526-6000
Joseph S Secker, *CEO*
David Reissfelder, *CFO*
Bill Aitkenhead Ph.d., *VP Engg*
James Buckley, *VP Sls*
▲ **EMP:** 25 **EST:** 2002
SQ FT: 2,000
SALES (est): 1.99MM **Publicly Held**
Web: www.leidos.com
SIC: 3812 7372 Search and detection
systems and instruments; Application
computer software
HQ: Leidos, Inc.
1750 Presidents St
Reston VA
571 526-6000

(P-10063)
ROCKWELL COLLINS INC
1733 Alton Pkwy (92606-4901)
PHONE..............................714 929-3000
EMP: 26
SALES (corp-wide): 67.07B **Publicly Held**
Web: www.rockwellcollins.com
SIC: 3812 Search and navigation equipment
HQ: Rockwell Collins, Inc.
400 Collins Rd Ne
Cedar Rapids IA

(P-10064)
ROGERSON AIRCRAFT CORPORATION (PA)
16940 Von Karman Ave (92606-4923)
PHONE..............................949 660-0666
Michael J Rogerson, *Pr*
Milton R Pizinger, *
Jonathan C Smith, *
EMP: 80 **EST:** 1975
SALES (est): 35.65MM
SALES (corp-wide): 35.65MM **Privately Held**
Web: www.rogerson.com
SIC: 3812 3545 3492 3728 Aircraft flight
instruments; Machine tool accessories;
Fluid power valves and hose fittings; Fuel
tanks, aircraft

(P-10065)
ROGERSON KRATOS
403 S Raymond Ave (91105-2609)
PHONE..............................626 449-3090
Lawrence Smith, *CEO*
Michael Rogerson, *
Milton R Pizinger, *
Cannon Mathews, *
Alice Williams Cstr Srv, *Prin*
EMP: 160 **EST:** 1981
SQ FT: 28,000
SALES (est): 25.66MM
SALES (corp-wide): 35.65MM **Privately Held**
Web: www.rogersonkratos.com
SIC: 3812 3825 3699 Aircraft flight
instruments; Instruments to measure
electricity; Electrical equipment and
supplies, nec
PA: Rogerson Aircraft Corporation
16940 Von Karman Ave
Irvine CA
949 660-0666

(P-10066)
SANDEL AVIONICS INC (PA)
Also Called: Sandel
1370 Decision St Ste D (92081-8551)

PHONE..............................760 727-4900
Steven Jeppson, *Pr*
Grant Miller, *
EMP: 31 **EST:** 1997
SALES (est): 22.51MM
SALES (corp-wide): 22.51MM **Privately Held**
Web: www.nighthawkfs.com
SIC: 3812 Aircraft control instruments

(P-10067)
SANDEL AVIONICS INC
Also Called: Sandel Avionics
2405 Dogwood Way (92081-8409)
PHONE..............................760 727-4900
Gerald Block, *Brnch Mgr*
EMP: 169
SALES (corp-wide): 22.51MM **Privately Held**
Web: www.nighthawkfs.com
SIC: 3812 Aircraft control instruments
PA: Sandel Avionics, Inc.
1370 Decision St Ste D
Vista CA
760 727-4900

(P-10068)
SANTA BARBARA INFRARED INC (DH)
Also Called: Sbir
30 S Calle Cesar Chavez Ste D
(93103-5652)
PHONE..............................805 965-3669
EMP: 90 **EST:** 1986
SALES (est): 15.79MM **Publicly Held**
Web: www.sbir.com
SIC: 3812 Infrared object detection
equipment
HQ: Heico Electronic Technologies Corp.
3000 Taft St
Hollywood FL
954 987-6101

(P-10069)
SCIENTIFIC-ATLANTA LLC
Scientific Atlanta
13112 Evening Creek Dr S (92128-4108)
PHONE..............................619 679-6000
Richard Lapointe, *Contrlr*
EMP: 25
SALES (corp-wide): 57B **Publicly Held**
SIC: 3812 Navigational systems and
instruments
HQ: Scientific-Atlanta, Llc
5030 Sugarloaf Pkwy 1
Lawrenceville GA
678 277-1000

(P-10070)
SENSOR SYSTEMS INC
8929 Fullbright Ave (91311-6179)
PHONE..............................818 341-5366
Mary E Bazar, *CEO*
Si Robin, *
Dennis E Bazar, *
EMP: 258 **EST:** 1961
SQ FT: 60,000
SALES (est): 49.82MM **Publicly Held**
Web: www.sensorantennas.com
SIC: 3812 Aircraft flight instruments
HQ: Heico Electronic Technologies Corp.
3000 Taft St
Hollywood FL
954 987-6101

(P-10071)
SIMULATOR PDT SOLUTIONS LLC
Also Called: Panel Products
21818 S Wilmington Ave Ste 411
(90810-1642)

PHONE..............................310 830-3331
Nabil Abdou, *Pr*
EMP: 26 **EST:** 2021
SQ FT: 5,200
SALES (est): 7.03MM
SALES (corp-wide): 49.31MM **Publicly Held**
SIC: 3812 Aircraft control instruments
PA: Orbit International Corp.
80 Cabot Ct
Hauppauge NY
631 435-8300

(P-10072)
SPACE VECTOR CORPORATION
20520 Nordhoff St (91311-6113)
PHONE..............................818 734-2600
EMP: 36 **EST:** 1969
SALES (est): 7.45MM **Privately Held**
SIC: 3812 3691 3663 3761 Defense systems
and equipment; Batteries, rechargeable;
Global positioning systems (GPS)
equipment; Guided missiles and space
vehicles

(P-10073)
STELLANT SYSTEMS INC (DH)
Also Called: Electron Devices
3100 Lomita Blvd (90505-5104)
P.O. Box 2999 (90509-2999)
PHONE..............................310 517-6000
Paul Russell, *CEO*
Steve Shpock, *
▲ **EMP:** 508 **EST:** 2000
SALES (est): 115.74MM
SALES (corp-wide): 296.08MM **Privately Held**
Web: www.stellantsystems.com
SIC: 3812 3764 3671 Navigational systems
and instruments; Space propulsion units
and parts; Traveling wave tubes
HQ: Stellant Midco, Llc
Torrance CA

(P-10074)
TECHNOVATIVE APPLICATIONS
3160 Enterprise St Ste A (92821-6288)
PHONE..............................714 996-0104
EMP: 61 **EST:** 1987
SALES (est): 10.92MM **Privately Held**
Web: www.tnov.com
SIC: 3812 Radar systems and equipment

(P-10075)
TECNOVA ADVANCED SYSTEMS INC
Also Called: Tecnadyne
9770 Carroll Centre Rd Ste A (92126)
P.O. Box 676086 (92067-6086)
PHONE..............................858 586-9660
Andrew Bazeley, *Pr*
Ute Pelzer, *CFO*
EMP: 20 **EST:** 1984
SQ FT: 17,150
SALES (est): 4.64MM **Privately Held**
Web: www.tecnadyne.com
SIC: 3812 Search and navigation equipment

(P-10076)
TELEDYNE CONTROLS LLC
501 Continental Blvd (90245-5036)
P.O. Box 1026 (90245-1026)
PHONE..............................310 765-3600
George C Bobb Iii, *CEO*
Robert Mehrabian, *Ch Bd*
Masood Hassan, *Pr*
Susan L Main, *Sr VP*
Melanie S Cibik, *Sr VP*
EMP: 616 **EST:** 2015
SALES (est): 123.25MM

SALES (corp-wide): 5.46B **Publicly Held**
Web: www.teledynecontrols.com
SIC: **3812** Search and navigation equipment
PA: Teledyne Technologies Inc
1049 Camino Dos Rios
Thousand Oaks CA
805 373-4545

(P-10077)
TELEDYNE FLIR LLC
6769 Hollister Ave (93117-3001)
PHONE.....................................805 964-9797
James Woolaway, *CEO*
EMP: 68
SALES (corp-wide): 5.46B **Publicly Held**
Web: www.flir.com
SIC: **3812** Aircraft/aerospace flight instruments and guidance systems
HQ: Teledyne Flir, Llc
27700 Sw Parkway Ave
Wilsonville OR
503 498-3547

(P-10078)
TELEDYNE INSTRUMENTS INC
Also Called: Teledyne Rd Instruments
14020 Stowe Dr (92064-6846)
PHONE.....................................858 842-2600
Dennis Klahn, *Brnch Mgr*
EMP: 140
SALES (corp-wide): 5.46B **Publicly Held**
Web: www.teledyne.com
SIC: **3812** 3829 Search and navigation equipment; Measuring and controlling devices, nec
HQ: Teledyne Instruments, Inc.
16830 Chestnut St
City Of Industry CA
626 934-1500

(P-10079)
TELEDYNE RD INSTRUMENTS INC
14020 Stowe Dr (92064-6846)
PHONE.....................................858 842-2600
EMP: 200
SIC: **3812** 3829 Search and navigation equipment; Measuring and controlling devices, nec

(P-10080)
TELETRAC NAVMAN US LTD (HQ)
310 Commerce Ste 100 (92602-1360)
PHONE.....................................866 527-9896
Tj Chung, *Pr*
Mike Henn, *CFO*
▲ EMP: 38 EST: 2007
SALES (est): 18.55MM
SALES (corp-wide): 3.18B **Publicly Held**
Web: www.teletracnavman.com
SIC: **3812** Navigational systems and instruments
PA: Vontier Corporation
5438 Wade Park Blvd # 601
Raleigh NC
984 275-6000

(P-10081)
TELETRONICS TECHNOLOGY CORP
Also Called: I A D S
190 Sierra Ct Ste A3 (93550-7608)
PHONE.....................................661 273-7033
EMP: 22
SALES (corp-wide): 2.56B **Publicly Held**
Web: www.curtisswright.com
SIC: **3812** Aircraft/aerospace flight instruments and guidance systems

HQ: Teletronics Technology Corp
15 Terry Dr
Newtown PA

(P-10082)
TINKER & RASOR
791 S Waterman Ave (92408-2331)
P.O. Box 1667 (92402-1667)
PHONE.....................................909 890-0700
Theodore Byerley, *Pr*
Denise Byerley, *
Mary Butcher, *
▲ EMP: 23 EST: 1948
SQ FT: 15,000
SALES (est): 2.37MM **Privately Held**
Web: www.tinker-rasor.com
SIC: **3812** 3829 Detection apparatus: electronic/magnetic field, light/heat; Measuring and controlling devices, nec

(P-10083)
TMC ICE PROTECTION SYSTEMS LLC (PA)
Also Called: TMC Aero
10850 Wilshire Blvd Ste 1250 (90024-4305)
PHONE.....................................951 677-6934
Bob Yari, *CEO*
Edward Rigney, *COO*
Michael Heaton, *Ofcr*
EMP: 20 EST: 2014
SQ FT: 10,000
SALES (est): 4.52MM
SALES (corp-wide): 4.52MM **Privately Held**
SIC: **3812** 8711 Acceleration indicators and systems components, aerospace; Aviation and/or aeronautical engineering

(P-10084)
TMC ICE PROTECTION SYSTEMS LLC
Also Called: TMC Aero
25775 Jefferson Ave (92562-6903)
PHONE.....................................951 677-6934
Edward Rigney, *COO*
EMP: 20
SALES (corp-wide): 4.52MM **Privately Held**
SIC: **3812** 8711 Aircraft/aerospace flight instruments and guidance systems; Aviation and/or aeronautical engineering
PA: Tmc Ice Protection Systems Llc
10850 Wilshire Blvd # 12
Los Angeles CA
951 677-6934

(P-10085)
TOWER MECHANICAL PRODUCTS INC
Also Called: Allied Mechanical Products
1720 S Bon View Ave (91761-4411)
PHONE.....................................714 947-2723
Richard B Slater, *Pr*
James W Longcrier, *
Susan J Hardy, *
EMP: 126 EST: 1953
SQ FT: 148,000
SALES (est): 20.52MM
SALES (corp-wide): 35.59MM **Privately Held**
Web: www.alliedmech.com
SIC: **3812** Acceleration indicators and systems components, aerospace
PA: Tower Industries, Inc.
1518 N Endeavor Ln Ste C
Anaheim CA

(P-10086)
TUFFER MANUFACTURING CO INC
163 E Liberty Ave (92801-1012)
PHONE.....................................714 526-3077
Cathy Kim, *Pr*
Ken Kim, *
EMP: 39 EST: 1977
SQ FT: 12,000
SALES (est): 6.16MM **Privately Held**
Web: www.tuffermfg.com
SIC: **3812** 3599 Search and navigation equipment; Machine shop, jobbing and repair

(P-10087)
VIRGIN ORBIT HOLDINGS INC (HQ)
4022 E Conant St (90808-1777)
PHONE.....................................562 388-4400
Daniel M Hart, *CEO*
Evan Lovell, *Ch Bd*
Brita O'rear, *CFO*
Jim Simpson, *CSO*
Derrick Boston, *CLO*
EMP: 19 EST: 2017
SQ FT: 151,000
SALES (est): 33.11MM **Publicly Held**
Web: www.virginorbit.com
SIC: **3812** 3761 Space vehicle guidance systems and equipment; Space vehicles, complete
PA: Virgin Investments Limited
C/O Harney Corporate Services Limited
Road Town

(P-10088)
VOTAW PRECISION TECHNOLOGIES
Also Called: Votaw
13153 Lakeland Rd (90670-4542)
P.O. Box 314 (90740-0314)
PHONE.....................................562 944-0661
Steve Lamb, *CEO*
David Takes, *Pr*
Jonathan Miller, *CFO*
▲ EMP: 140 EST: 1964
SQ FT: 240,000
SALES (est): 40MM **Privately Held**
Web: www.votaw.com
SIC: **3812** Acceleration indicators and systems components, aerospace

3821 Laboratory Apparatus And Furniture

(P-10089)
CERA INC
14180 Live Oak Ave Ste I (91706-1350)
P.O. Box 1608 (91706-7608)
PHONE.....................................626 814-2688
Philip Dimson, *Pr*
◆ EMP: 21 EST: 1987
SQ FT: 2,000
SALES (est): 2.45MM **Privately Held**
Web: www.cerasalonoc.com
SIC: **3821** Chemical laboratory apparatus, nec

(P-10090)
CHEMAT TECHNOLOGY INC
Also Called: Chemat Vision
9036 Winnetka Ave (91324-3235)
PHONE.....................................818 727-9786
Haixing Zheng, *CEO*
▲ EMP: 32 EST: 1990
SQ FT: 30,000

SALES (est): 5MM **Privately Held**
Web: www.chemat.com
SIC: **3821** 3827 Chemical laboratory apparatus, nec; Optical test and inspection equipment

(P-10091)
CLEATECH LLC
Also Called: Global Lab Supply
2106 N Glassell St (92865-3308)
PHONE.....................................714 754-6668
EMP: 27 EST: 2010
SALES (est): 3.96MM **Privately Held**
Web: www.cleatech.com
SIC: **3821** Laboratory apparatus and furniture

(P-10092)
EVERGREEN INDUSTRIES INC (DH)
Also Called: Evergreen Scientific
2254 E 49th St (90058-2823)
PHONE.....................................323 583-1331
◆ EMP: 73 EST: 1969
SALES (est): 12.69MM
SALES (corp-wide): 2.13B **Privately Held**
Web: www.evergreensci.com
SIC: **3821** Laboratory equipment: fume hoods, distillation racks, etc.
HQ: Caplugs, Inc.
2150 Elmwood Ave
Buffalo NY
716 876-9855

(P-10093)
GENETRONICS INC
11494 Sorrento Valley Rd Ste A (92121-1318)
PHONE.....................................858 597-6006
James Heppell, *Ch*
Avtar Dhillon, *
Peter Kies, *
Douglas Murdock, *
EMP: 26 EST: 1983
SQ FT: 25,000
SALES (est): 841.7K **Publicly Held**
SIC: **3821** 8731 3826 Laboratory apparatus, except heating and measuring; Biotechnical research, commercial; Analytical instruments
PA: Inovio Pharmaceuticals, Inc.
660 W Germantown Pike # 1
Plymouth Meeting PA

(P-10094)
HANSON LAB SOLUTIONS INC
747 Calle Plano (93012-8556)
PHONE.....................................805 498-3121
Mike Hanson, *Pr*
Joe Matta, *
Joseph F Matta, *
▲ EMP: 30 EST: 1971
SQ FT: 40,000
SALES (est): 7.02MM **Privately Held**
Web: www.hansonlab.com
SIC: **3821** Laboratory furniture

(P-10095)
ISEC INCORPORATED
5735 Kearny Villa Rd Ste 105 (92123)
PHONE.....................................858 279-9085
Don Shaw, *Pr*
EMP: 86
SALES (corp-wide): 317.22MM **Privately Held**
Web: www.isecinc.com
SIC: **3821** Laboratory apparatus and furniture
PA: Isec, Incorporated
6000 Greenwood Plaza Blvd # 200
Greenwood Village CO
303 790-1444

▲ = Import ▼ = Export
◆ = Import/Export

(P-10096)
NEWPORT CORPORATION (HQ)
Also Called: Newport
1791 Deere Ave (92606-4814)
P.O. Box 19607 (92623-9607)
PHONE.....................949 863-3144
Seth Bagshaw, *Pr*
Kathleen Burke, *
Derek D'antilio, *Treas*
◆ **EMP:** 536 **EST:** 1938
SALES (est): 518.58MM
SALES (corp-wide): 3.55B **Publicly Held**
Web: go.newport.com
SIC: 3821 3699 3827 3826 Worktables, laboratory; Laser systems and equipment; Optical instruments and lenses; Analytical optical instruments
PA: Mks Instruments, Inc.
2 Tech Dr Ste 201
Andover MA
978 645-5500

(P-10097)
PROCISEDX INC
9449 Carroll Park Dr (92121-5202)
PHONE.....................858 382-4598
Peter Westlake, *Pr*
Larry Mimms, *
EMP: 30 **EST:** 2019
SALES (est): 4.19MM **Privately Held**
Web: www.procisedx.com
SIC: 3821 Balances, laboratory

(P-10098)
QUALIGEN INC (HQ)
2042 Corte Del Nogal Ste B (92011-1438)
PHONE.....................760 918-9165
EMP: 21 **EST:** 1996
SQ FT: 23,000
SALES (est): 9.82MM
SALES (corp-wide): 49.52MM **Privately Held**
Web: www.qlgntx.com
SIC: 3821 3841 Laboratory apparatus and furniture; Surgical and medical instruments
PA: Chembio Diagnostics, Inc.
555 Wireless Blvd
Hauppauge NY
631 924-1135

(P-10099)
ROMAR INNOVATIONS INC
Also Called: Romar Innovations
42371 Avenida Alvarado (92590-3446)
PHONE.....................951 296-3480
EMP: 100 **EST:** 1998
SALES (est): 8.77MM **Privately Held**
Web: www.aquaultraviolet.com
SIC: 3821 Sterilizers

3822 Environmental Controls

(P-10100)
CATALYTIC SOLUTIONS INC (HQ)
1700 Fiske Pl (93033-1863)
PHONE.....................805 486-4649
▲ **EMP:** 24 **EST:** 1996
SQ FT: 75,000
SALES (est): 22.43MM **Privately Held**
Web: www.cdti.com
SIC: 3822 Environmental controls
PA: Cdti Advanced Materials, Inc.
1641 Fiske Pl
Oxnard CA

(P-10101)
CHRONOMITE LABORATORIES INC
17451 Hurley St (91744-5106)
P.O. Box 3527 (91744-0527)
PHONE.....................310 534-2300
Donald E Morris, *CEO*
▲ **EMP:** 34 **EST:** 1967
SALES (est): 7MM
SALES (corp-wide): 99.15MM **Privately Held**
Web: www.chronomite.com
SIC: 3822 8731 3432 Water heater controls; Commercial physical research; Plumbing fixture fittings and trim
PA: Acorn Engineering Company
15125 Proctor Ave
City Of Industry CA
800 488-8999

(P-10102)
CONTRCTOR CMPLIANCE MONITORING
2343 Donnington Way (92139-2927)
PHONE.....................619 472-9065
Deborah Wilder, *Brnch Mgr*
EMP: 27
SALES (corp-wide): 862.02K **Privately Held**
Web: www.ccmilcp.com
SIC: 3822 5082 Building services monitoring controls, automatic; General construction machinery and equipment
PA: Contractor Compliance & Monitoring Inc
635 Mariners Island Blvd
San Mateo CA
650 522-4403

(P-10103)
ELECTRASEM CORP
372 Elizabeth Ln (92878-5028)
PHONE.....................951 371-6140
Don S Edwards, *Pr*
▲ **EMP:** 115 **EST:** 1980
SALES (est): 2.19MM
SALES (corp-wide): 1.53B **Publicly Held**
SIC: 3822 Electric heat proportioning controls, modulating controls
HQ: General Monitors, Inc.
16782 Von Karman Ave # 14
Irvine CA
949 581-4464

(P-10104)
HONEYWELL INTERNATIONAL INC
Also Called: Honeywell
2055 Dublin Dr (92154-8203)
PHONE.....................619 671-5612
Virgel Mccormick, *Mgr*
EMP: 110
SALES (corp-wide): 35.47B **Publicly Held**
Web: www.honeywell.com
SIC: 3822 3494 Environmental controls; Valves and pipe fittings, nec
PA: Honeywell International Inc.
855 S Mint St
Charlotte NC
704 627-6200

(P-10105)
MEGGITT WESTERN DESIGN INC
Also Called: Western Design
9801 Muirlands Blvd (92618-2521)
PHONE.....................949 465-7700
▲ **EMP:** 104
SIC: 3822 3483 Environmental controls; Ammunition components

(P-10106)
ROBERTSHAW CONTROLS COMPANY
1751 3rd St # 102 (92860-2670)
PHONE.....................951 893-6233
Jeff From, *Mgr*
EMP: 47
Web: www.robertshaw.com
SIC: 3822 3823 Environmental controls; Process control instruments
HQ: Robertshaw Controls Company
1222 Hamilton Pkwy
Itasca IL

(P-10107)
TELLKAMP SYSTEMS INC (PA)
15523 Carmenita Rd (90670-5609)
PHONE.....................562 802-1621
◆ **EMP:** 49 **EST:** 1971
SALES (est): 4.39MM
SALES (corp-wide): 4.39MM **Privately Held**
Web: www.tellkamp.com
SIC: 3822 3564 Environmental controls; Air purification equipment

(P-10108)
TRUE FRESH HPP LLC
6535 Caballero Blvd Unit B (90620-8106)
PHONE.....................949 922-8801
EMP: 34 **EST:** 2015
SALES (est): 5.92MM **Privately Held**
Web: www.truefreshhpp.com
SIC: 3822 Refrigeration controls (pressure)

(P-10109)
WESTERN ENVIRONMENTAL INC
62150 Gene Welmas Dr (92254-6550)
PHONE.....................760 396-0222
Ed Kennon, *Pt*
EMP: 30 **EST:** 2002
SALES (est): 3.6MM **Privately Held**
Web: www.wei-mecca.com
SIC: 3822 Environmental controls

(P-10110)
XPOWER MANUFACTURE INC
668 S 6th Ave (91746-3025)
PHONE.....................626 285-3301
Keidy Gu, *CEO*
Guogen Cui, *
▲ **EMP:** 40 **EST:** 2011
SALES (est): 11.4MM **Privately Held**
Web: www.xpower.com
SIC: 3822 3999 3564 Air flow controllers, air conditioning and refrigeration; Pet supplies; Blowing fans: industrial or commercial
PA: Xinshengyuan Electrical Appliances Co., Ltd.
No.3, East Area No.3 Road, Xiantang Industrial Zone, Longjiang T
Foshan GD

3823 Process Control Instruments

(P-10111)
3D INFOTECH (PA)
7 Hubble (92618-4209)
PHONE.....................949 988-0200
Rohit Khanna, *Pr*
EMP: 30 **EST:** 2006
SALES (est): 6.56MM **Privately Held**
Web: www.3dinfotech.com
SIC: 3823 Temperature measurement instruments, industrial

(P-10112)
3D INSTRUMENTS LLC
Also Called: Sierra Precision
4990 E Hunter Ave (92807-2057)
PHONE.....................714 399-9200
EMP: 100
Web: www.wika.com
SIC: 3823 Pressure gauges, dial and digital

(P-10113)
ADVANCED ELECTROMAGNETICS INC
Also Called: Aemi
1320 Air Wing Rd Ste 101 (92154-7707)
PHONE.....................619 449-9492
Per Iversen, *Pr*
◆ **EMP:** 37 **EST:** 1980
SQ FT: 16,000
SALES (est): 16.61MM
SALES (corp-wide): 10.71MM **Privately Held**
Web: www.mvg-world.com
SIC: 3823 3825 Absorption analyzers: infrared, x-ray, etc.: industrial; Instruments to measure electricity
HQ: Orbit/Fr, Inc.
650 Louis Dr Ste 100
Warminster PA

(P-10114)
ALPHA SENSORS INC
Also Called: Alpha Technics
24024 Humphries Rd (91980-4008)
PHONE.....................949 250-6578
Daniel M O'brien, *CEO*
Lisa Marie Ryan, *
Linda Lee, *
EMP: 24 **EST:** 1979
SALES (est): 4.82MM **Privately Held**
Web: www.te.com
SIC: 3823 Temperature measurement instruments, industrial

(P-10115)
ALPHA TECHNICS INC
24024 Humphries Rd (91980-4008)
PHONE.....................949 250-6578
Lisa Marie Ryan, *Pr*
Dan Obrien, *
EMP: 200 **EST:** 2011
SALES (est): 52.79MM **Privately Held**
SIC: 3823 Process control instruments
HQ: Te Connectivity Ltd.
601 13th St Nw Ste 850s
Washington DC
800 522-6752

(P-10116)
AMETEK AMERON LLC (HQ)
Also Called: Mass Systems
4750 Littlejohn St (91706-2274)
PHONE.....................626 856-0101
Keith Marsicola, *Managing Member*
Steve Tanner, *Managing Member*
EMP: 55 **EST:** 1988
SQ FT: 2,600
SALES (est): 23.05MM
SALES (corp-wide): 6.15B **Publicly Held**
Web: www.ametekmro.com
SIC: 3823 3999 3728 8711 Pressure gauges, dial and digital; Fire extinguishers, portable; Aircraft parts and equipment, nec; Industrial engineers
PA: Ametek, Inc.
1100 Cassatt Rd
Berwyn PA
610 647-2121

(P-10117)
ANALYTICAL INDUSTRIES INC
Also Called: Advanced Instruments
2855 Metropolitan Pl (91767-1853)
PHONE..............................909 392-6900
EMP: 45 **EST:** 1994
SQ FT: 15,000
SALES (est): 9.3MM **Privately Held**
Web: www.aii1.com
SIC: **3823** Process control instruments

(P-10118)
BAMBECK SYSTEMS INC (PA)
1921 Carnegie Ave Ste 3a (92705-5510)
PHONE..............................949 250-3100
Robert J Bambeck, *Pr*
Robert Deweerd, *VP*
EMP: 19 **EST:** 1980
SQ FT: 6,100
SALES (est): 3.23MM
SALES (corp-wide): 3.23MM **Privately Held**
Web: www.bambecksystems.com
SIC: **3823** Boiler controls: industrial, power, and marine type

(P-10119)
BIODOT INC (HQ)
2852 Alton Pkwy (92606-5104)
PHONE..............................949 440-3685
Anthony Lemmo, *CEO*
EMP: 93 **EST:** 1994
SQ FT: 24,000
SALES (est): 21.44MM
SALES (corp-wide): 1.9B **Privately Held**
Web: www.biodot.com
SIC: **3823** 3826 Process control instruments; Analytical instruments
PA: Ats Corporation
730 Fountain St N Bldg 2
Cambridge ON
604 332-2666

(P-10120)
BLUERIDGE TECHNOLOGY INC
3375 E Hill St Ste 1 (90755-1219)
PHONE..............................562 762-5914
John O Low, *Brnch Mgr*
EMP: 20
SIC: **3823** Process control instruments
PA: Blueridge Technology Inc
4541 Montair Ave Apt B23
Long Beach CA

(P-10121)
CALIFRNIA ANLYTICAL INSTRS INC
Also Called: Cai
1312 W Grove Ave (92865-4136)
PHONE..............................714 974-5560
R Pete Furton, *Ch*
Harold J Peper, *
Loren T Mathews, *
EMP: 61 **EST:** 1992
SQ FT: 26,400
SALES (est): 11.34MM **Privately Held**
Web: www.gasanalyzers.com
SIC: **3823** Process control instruments

(P-10122)
CAMERON TECHNOLOGIES US LLC
Also Called: Cameron's Measurement Systems
4040 Capitol Ave (90601-1735)
PHONE..............................562 222-8440
Victor Hart, *Manager*
EMP: 33
SIC: **3823** Industrial flow and liquid measuring instruments
HQ: Cameron Technologies Us, Llc
1000 Mcclaren Woods Dr
Coraopolis PA

(P-10123)
CK TECHNOLOGIES INC (PA)
Also Called: Ckt
3629 Vista Mercado (93012-8055)
PHONE..............................805 987-4801
Karl F Zimmermann, *Pr*
Heidi Zimmerman, *VP*
EMP: 20 **EST:** 1987
SQ FT: 34,000
SALES (est): 5.65MM
SALES (corp-wide): 5.65MM **Privately Held**
Web: www.ckt.com
SIC: **3823** 3825 5065 Water quality monitoring and control systems; Instruments to measure electricity; Electronic parts and equipment, nec

(P-10124)
COMPUTATIONAL SYSTEMS INC
4301 Resnik Ct (93313-4851)
PHONE..............................661 832-5306
Shannon Romine, *Brnch Mgr*
EMP: 80
SALES (corp-wide): 15.16B **Publicly Held**
Web: www.emerson.com
SIC: **3823** Process control instruments
HQ: Computational Systems, Incorporated
8000 West Florissant Ave
Saint Louis MO
314 553-2000

(P-10125)
CONTINENTAL CONTROLS CORP
Also Called: Manufacturing
7710 Kenamar Ct (92121-2425)
PHONE..............................858 453-9880
David Fisher, *Pr*
Richard Fisher, *
Judith Fisher, *
Ross Fisher, *
▲ **EMP:** 28 **EST:** 1989
SQ FT: 17,000
SALES (est): 4.38MM **Privately Held**
Web: www.continentalcontrols.com
SIC: **3823** 3533 Process control instruments; Oil and gas field machinery

(P-10126)
COSASCO INC
11841 Smith Ave (90670-3226)
PHONE..............................562 949-0123
EMP: 97 **EST:** 2015
SALES (est): 6.75MM **Privately Held**
Web: www.cosasco.com
SIC: **3823** Process control instruments

(P-10127)
CRYSTAL ENGINEERING CORP
708 Fiero Ln Ste 9 (93401-7945)
P.O. Box 3033 (93403-3033)
PHONE..............................805 595-5477
David Porter, *Pr*
▲ **EMP:** 38 **EST:** 1981
SALES (est): 11.97MM
SALES (corp-wide): 6.15B **Publicly Held**
Web: www.ametekcalibration.com
SIC: **3823** Pressure gauges, dial and digital
PA: Ametek, Inc.
1100 Cassatt Rd
Berwyn PA
610 647-2121

(P-10128)
DIGIVISION INC
9830 Summers Ridge Rd (92121-3083)
PHONE..............................858 530-0100
Randy Millar, *Ex VP*
Randy Millar, *VP*
Richard Hier, *VP*
EMP: 24 **EST:** 1982
SQ FT: 10,000
SALES (est): 720.08K **Privately Held**
SIC: **3823** 8731 Digital displays of process variables; Commercial physical research

(P-10129)
E D Q INC
2920 Halladay St (92705-5623)
PHONE..............................714 546-6010
Erik K Moller, *CEO*
Randy Heartfield, *
Mary C Heartfield, *
▲ **EMP:** 39 **EST:** 1960
SQ FT: 14,000
SALES (est): 7.24MM **Privately Held**
Web: www.qedaero.com
SIC: **3823** 3829 3812 Pressure gauges, dial and digital; Accelerometers; Aircraft/aerospace flight instruments and guidance systems

(P-10130)
EMBEDDED DESIGNS INC
Also Called: K I C
16120 W Bernardo Dr Ste A (92127-1875)
PHONE..............................858 673-6050
Casey Kazmierowicz, *Ch*
Bjorn Dahle, *
Henryk J Kazmier, *
Miles Moreau, *
Phil Kazmierowicz, *
EMP: 32 **EST:** 1984
SQ FT: 9,500
SALES (est): 6.05MM **Privately Held**
Web: www.kicthermal.com
SIC: **3823** Temperature measurement instruments, industrial

(P-10131)
ETI SYSTEMS
Also Called: Polaris Music
1800 Century Park E Ste 600 (90067-1501)
PHONE..............................310 684-3664
Bill Tice, *Pr*
Gayle Tice, *
EMP: 60 **EST:** 1962
SQ FT: 8,200
SALES (est): 4.25MM **Privately Held**
Web: www.etisystems.com
SIC: **3823** Potentiometric self-balancing inst., except X-Y plotters

(P-10132)
FLUID COMPONENTS INTL LLC (PA)
Also Called: F C I
1755 La Costa Meadows Dr (92078-5187)
PHONE..............................760 744-6950
Dan Mcqueen, *CEO*
Daniel M Mcqueen, *Pr*
Ronald E Ogle, *
Barbara Succetti, *
▲ **EMP:** 183 **EST:** 1992
SQ FT: 49,000
SALES (est): 23.63MM **Privately Held**
Web: www.fluidcomponents.com
SIC: **3823** Process control instruments

(P-10133)
FUNDAMENTAL TECH INTL INC
Also Called: F T I
2900 E 29th St (90806-2315)

PHONE..............................562 595-0661
▼ **EMP:** 24 **EST:** 1996
SQ FT: 20,000
SALES (est): 3.16MM **Privately Held**
SIC: **3823** Liquid analysis instruments, industrial process type

(P-10134)
FUTEK ADVANCED SENSOR TECH INC
Also Called: Futek Advanced Sensor Tech
10 Thomas (92618-2702)
PHONE..............................949 465-0900
Javad Mokhberi, *CEO*
Javad Mokhbery, *
▼ **EMP:** 140 **EST:** 1988
SQ FT: 23,000
SALES (est): 30MM **Privately Held**
Web: www.futek.com
SIC: **3823** 8711 Process control instruments; Engineering services

(P-10135)
GEORG FISCHER SIGNET LLC
5462 Irwindale Ave Ste A (91706-2048)
PHONE..............................626 571-2770
Charlotte Hill, *Managing Member*
James Jackson, *Prin*
John Pregenzer, *Prin*
▲ **EMP:** 90 **EST:** 1953
SALES (est): 20.69MM **Privately Held**
SIC: **3823** Process control instruments
HQ: Georg Fischer Spa
Via Eugenio Villoresi 2/4
Agrate Brianza MB

(P-10136)
GET ENGINEERING CORP
Also Called: Get Engineering
9350 Bond Ave (92021-2850)
PHONE..............................619 443-8295
Roger Kuroda, *CEO*
Leslie Adams, *CEO*
Rodney Tuttle, *Prin*
EMP: 18 **EST:** 1982
SQ FT: 14,500
SALES (est): 5.01MM **Privately Held**
Web: www.gethdio.com
SIC: **3823** 7373 3812 3679 Computer interface equipment, for industrial process control; Computer integrated systems design; Search and navigation equipment; Electronic circuits

(P-10137)
GRAPHTEC AMERICA INC (DH)
Also Called: Graphtec
17462 Armstrong Ave (92614-5724)
PHONE..............................949 770-6010
◆ **EMP:** 49 **EST:** 1949
SQ FT: 35,000
SALES (est): 16.5MM **Privately Held**
Web: www.graphtecamerica.com
SIC: **3823** 5064 Process control instruments; Video cassette recorders and accessories
HQ: Graphtec Corp.
503-10, Shinanocho, Totsuka-Ku
Yokohama KNG

(P-10138)
GUIDED WAVE INC
2121 Aviation Dr (91786-2195)
PHONE..............................919 264-9651
Mark Morano, *Mgr*
EMP: 25
SALES (corp-wide): 23.17MM **Privately Held**
Web: www.process-insights.com
SIC: **3823** Process control instruments
HQ: Guided Wave Inc.
3033 Gold Canal Dr

Rancho Cordova CA
916 638-4944

(P-10139)

HARDY PROCESS SOLUTIONS

Also Called: Hardy Process Solutions
10075 Mesa Rim Rd (92121-2913)
PHONE..............................858 278-2900
Eric Schellenberger, *Pr*
Steve Hanes, *
◆ **EMP:** 50 **EST:** 1980
SALES (est): 19.57MM
SALES (corp-wide): 5.37B **Publicly Held**
Web: www.hardysolutions.com
SIC: 3823 3829 3596 Process control
instruments; Measuring and controlling
devices, nec; Scales and balances, except
laboratory
HQ: Dynamic Instruments, Inc.
10737 Lexington Dr
Knoxville TN
858 278-4900

(P-10140)

INNOVATIVE INTEGRATION INC

741 Flynn Rd (93012-8056)
PHONE..............................805 520-3300
Jim Henderson, *Pr*
Dan Mclane, *VP*
▲ **EMP:** 30 **EST:** 1988
SQ FT: 11,000
SALES (est): 4.96MM **Privately Held**
Web: www.isipkg.com
SIC: 3823 3571 Process control instruments;
Electronic computers

(P-10141)

ITI ELECTRO-OPTIC CORPORATION

1500 Olympia Blvd Ste 400 (90021-1900)
PHONE..............................310 312-4526
EMP: 20
SALES (corp-wide): 4.65MM **Privately Held**
Web: www.itieo.com
SIC: 3823 Infrared instruments, industrial
process type
PA: Iti Electro-Optic Corporation
11500 W Olympic Blvd
Los Angeles CA
310 445-8900

(P-10142)

ITI ELECTRO-OPTIC CORPORATION (PA)

Also Called: Ccd
11500 W Olympic Blvd Ste 400
(90064-1524)
PHONE..............................310 445-8900
Mei Shi, *Ch Bd*
Robert Nevins, *Pr*
John Sun, *Ex VP*
James Wang, *VP Fin*
Richard Caserio, *VP Mktg*
▲ **EMP:** 20 **EST:** 1985
SQ FT: 5,000
SALES (est): 4.65MM
SALES (corp-wide): 4.65MM **Privately
Held**
Web: www.itieo.com
SIC: 3823 Infrared instruments, industrial
process type

(P-10143)

KING INSTRUMENT COMPANY INC

12700 Pala Dr (92841-3924)
PHONE..............................714 891-0008
Clyde F King, *Pr*

EMP: 50 **EST:** 1983
SQ FT: 46,000
SALES (est): 9.38MM **Privately Held**
Web: www.kinginstrumentco.com
SIC: 3823 Flow instruments, industrial
process type

(P-10144)

KING NUTRONICS LLC

Also Called: King Nutronics Corporation
6421 Independence Ave (91367-2608)
PHONE..............................818 887-5460
Robert Welther, *Pr*
EMP: 34 **EST:** 1960
SQ FT: 21,000
SALES (est): 6.62MM
SALES (corp-wide): 9.39MM **Privately
Held**
Web: www.kingnutronics.com
SIC: 3823 3825 Pressure measurement
instruments, industrial; Instruments to
measure electricity
PA: Raptor Scientific
81 Fuller Way
Berlin CT
860 829-0001

(P-10145)

MCCROMETER INC (HQ)

3255 W Stetson Ave (92545-7763)
PHONE..............................951 652-6811
Stephen Bell, *Pr*
Ian Rule, *
◆ **EMP:** 214 **EST:** 1996
SQ FT: 9,090
SALES (est): 65.05MM
SALES (corp-wide): 751.76MM **Publicly
Held**
Web: www.mccrometer.com
SIC: 3823 Process control instruments
PA: Veralto Enterprise Llc
225 Wyman St Ste 250
Waltham MA
603 860-7300

(P-10146)

MOORE INDUSTRIES-INTERNATIONAL INC (PA)

Also Called: Moore Industries
16650 Schoenborn St (91343-6106)
PHONE..............................818 894-7111
▲ **EMP:** 200 **EST:** 1965
SALES (est): 39.36MM
SALES (corp-wide): 39.36MM **Privately
Held**
Web: www.miinet.com
SIC: 3823 5084 Process control instruments;
Industrial machinery and equipment

(P-10147)

MYRON L COMPANY

2450 Impala Dr (92010-7226)
PHONE..............................760 438-2021
Gary O Robinson, *Pr*
Jerry Adams, *
◆ **EMP:** 80 **EST:** 1957
SQ FT: 43,000
SALES (est): 23.98MM **Privately Held**
Web: www.myronl.com
SIC: 3823 3825 3613 Electrodes used in
industrial process measurement;
Instruments to measure electricity;
Switchgear and switchboard apparatus

(P-10148)

NORDSON ASYMTEK INC

Also Called: Nordson Asymtek
2747 Loker Ave W (92010-6601)
PHONE..............................760 431-1919
▲ **EMP:** 250

SIC: 3823 Industrial flow and liquid
measuring instruments

(P-10149)

NUMATIC ENGINEERING INC

7915 Ajay Dr (91352-5315)
P.O. Box 1477 (35201-1477)
PHONE..............................818 768-1200
▲ **EMP:** 38
SIC: 3823 Process control instruments

(P-10150)

OLEUMTECH CORPORATION

19762 Pauling (92610-2611)
PHONE..............................949 305-9009
Paul Gregory, *CEO*
Vrej Isa, *COO*
EMP: 57 **EST:** 2002
SQ FT: 55,000
SALES (est): 12.62MM **Privately Held**
Web: www.oleumtech.com
SIC: 3823 Process control instruments

(P-10151)

PRESSURE PROFILE SYSTEMS INC

5757 W Century Blvd Ste 600
(90045-6429)
PHONE..............................310 641-8100
Denis A O'connor, *CEO*
Jae S Son, *CEO*
Steven Sanchez, *Treas*
David Ables, *Sec*
EMP: 17 **EST:** 1996
SALES (est): 2.61MM **Privately Held**
Web: www.pressureprofile.com
SIC: 3823 Process control instruments

(P-10152)

PRIMORDIAL DIAGNOSTICS INC

Also Called: Pulse Instruments
3233 Mission Oaks Blvd Ste P
(93012-5134)
PHONE..............................800 462-1926
Karan Khurana, *Pr*
Mridula Khurana, *
EMP: 25 **EST:** 1985
SALES (est): 2.47MM **Privately Held**
SIC: 3823 5063 5074 Water quality
monitoring and control systems; Electrical
apparatus and equipment; Water
purification equipment

(P-10153)

PROMACH FILLING SYSTEMS LLC

200 River Rd (92878-1435)
PHONE..............................951 393-2200
EMP: 20 **EST:** 2018
SALES (est): 1.8MM **Privately Held**
Web: www.pacificpak.com
SIC: 3823 Process control instruments

(P-10154)

RAIN MSTR IRRGTION SYSTEMS INC

5825 Jasmine St (92504-1144)
P.O. Box 489 (92502-0489)
PHONE..............................805 527-4498
Jim Sieminski, *Pr*
John Torosiani, *
EMP: 42 **EST:** 1982
SQ FT: 13,000
SALES (est): 4.84MM
SALES (corp-wide): 4.51B **Publicly Held**
Web: www.rainmaster.com
SIC: 3823 Process control instruments
PA: The Toro Company
8111 Lyndale Ave S

Bloomington MN
952 888-8801

(P-10155)

RENAU CORPORATION

Also Called: Renau Electronic Laboratories
9309 Deering Ave (91311-5858)
PHONE..............................818 341-1994
Karol Renau, *CEO*
Christine Renau, *Sec*
▲ **EMP:** 20 **EST:** 1981
SQ FT: 10,000
SALES (est): 6.69MM **Privately Held**
Web: www.renau.com
SIC: 3823 Controllers, for process variables,
all types

(P-10156)

REOTEMP INSTRUMENT CORPORATION (PA)

10656 Roselle St (92121-1524)
PHONE..............................858 784-0710
▲ **EMP:** 55 **EST:** 1965
SALES (est): 14.45MM
SALES (corp-wide): 14.45MM **Privately
Held**
Web: www.reotemp.com
SIC: 3823 3829 3585 Thermometers, filled
system: industrial process type;
Thermometers and temperature sensors;
Heating equipment, complete

(P-10157)

ROHRBACK COSASCO SYSTEMS INC (DH)

11841 Smith Ave (90670-3226)
PHONE..............................562 949-0123
Bryan Sanderlin, *CEO*
▼ **EMP:** 71 **EST:** 1977
SQ FT: 37,000
SALES (est): 17.49MM
SALES (corp-wide): 2.23B **Privately Held**
Web: www.cosasco.com
SIC: 3823 8742 Process control instruments;
Industry specialist consultants
HQ: Halma Investment Holdings Limited
Misbourne Court Rectory Way
Amersham BUCKS

(P-10158)

RONAN ENGINEERING COMPANY (PA)

Also Called: Ronan Engnrng/Rnan Msrment
Div
28209 Avenue Stanford (91355-3984)
P.O. Box 129 (91310-0129)
PHONE..............................661 702-1344
John A Hewitson, *CEO*
▼ **EMP:** 56 **EST:** 1962
SQ FT: 50,000
SALES (est): 12.79MM
SALES (corp-wide): 12.79MM **Privately
Held**
Web: www.ronan.com
SIC: 3823 3825 Process control instruments;
Measuring instruments and meters, electric

(P-10159)

SABIA INCORPORATED (PA)

Also Called: Sabia
10919 Technology Pl Ste A (92127-1882)
PHONE..............................858 217-2200
Steve Foster, *CEO*
Clinton L Lingren, *
James Miller, *
Craig Belnap, *
Edward Nunn, *
EMP: 24 **EST:** 2000
SALES (est): 6.41MM

SALES (corp-wide): 6.41MM **Privately Held**
Web: www.sabiainc.com
SIC: 3823 Process control instruments

(P-10160)
SANTA BARBARA CONTROL SYSTEMS
Also Called: Chemtrol
5375 Overpass Rd (93111-3015)
PHONE..............................805 683-8833
Pablo Navarro, *Pr*
Jacques Steininger, *CEO*
Joe Osuna, *Acctnt*
EMP: 19 **EST:** 1976
SQ FT: 8,000
SALES (est): 5.61MM **Privately Held**
Web: www.sbcontrol.com
SIC: 3823 3589 7699 Water quality monitoring and control systems; Swimming pool filter and water conditioning systems; Cash register repair

(P-10161)
SENSOREX CORPORATION
11751 Markon Dr (92841-1812)
PHONE..............................714 895-4344
▲ **EMP:** 62 **EST:** 1972
SALES (est): 14.59MM
SALES (corp-wide): 2.23B **Privately Held**
Web: www.sensorex.com
SIC: 3823 3826 Process control instruments; PH meters, except industrial process type
HQ: Halma Holdings Inc.
535 Sprngfeld Ave Ste 110
Summit NJ
513 772-5501

(P-10162)
SENSOSCIENTIFIC LLC
685 Cochran St Ste 200 (93065-1921)
PHONE..............................800 279-3101
Mike Zarei, *
Ramin Rostami, *
Masoud Zarei, *Sec*
▲ **EMP:** 43 **EST:** 2005
SQ FT: 4,000
SALES (est): 9.53MM
SALES (corp-wide): 179.34MM **Privately Held**
Web: www.sensoscientific.com
SIC: 3823 Process control instruments
HQ: Process Sensing Technologies Corp.
135 Engineers Rd Ste 150
Hauppauge NY
631 427-3898

(P-10163)
SOFFA ELECTRIC INC
5901 Corvette St (90040-1601)
PHONE..............................323 728-0230
EMP: 48 **EST:** 1971
SALES (est): 24.57MM **Privately Held**
Web: www.soffaelectric.com
SIC: 3823 1731 8711 8742 Process control instruments; General electrical contractor; Engineering services; Automation and robotics consultant

(P-10164)
SUEZ WATER INDIANA LLC
Also Called: West Bsin Wtr Rclamation Plant
1935 S Hughes Way (90245-4729)
PHONE..............................310 414-0183
EMP: 68
SIC: 3823 Water quality monitoring and control systems
HQ: Suez Water Indiana Llc
461 From Rd Ste F
Paramus NJ
201 767-9300

(P-10165)
TERN DESIGN LTD
Also Called: Oceanscience
14020 Stowe Dr (92064-6846)
PHONE..............................760 754-2400
Ronald George, *Pr*
EMP: 25 **EST:** 1995
SQ FT: 4,800
SALES (est): 4.83MM **Privately Held**
Web: www.teledynemarine.com
SIC: 3823 Buoyancy instruments, industrial process type

(P-10166)
THERMOMETRICS CORPORATION (PA)
18714 Parthenia St (91324-3813)
PHONE..............................818 886-3755
Jorge Hernandez, *Pr*
Robert Hernandez, *
EMP: 19 **EST:** 1965
SQ FT: 16,897
SALES (est): 7.31MM
SALES (corp-wide): 7.31MM **Privately Held**
Web: www.thermometricscorp.com
SIC: 3823 Process control instruments

(P-10167)
TRANSLOGIC INCORPORATED
5641 Engineer Dr (92649-1123)
PHONE..............................714 890-0058
Donald Ross, *CEO*
Gregory Ross, *
EMP: 41 **EST:** 1979
SALES (est): 5.38MM **Privately Held**
Web: www.translogicinc.com
SIC: 3823 3829 Temperature instruments: industrial process type; Measuring and controlling devices, nec

(P-10168)
VERTIV CORPORATION
Also Called: Vertiv
35 Parker (92618-1605)
PHONE..............................949 457-3600
Anita Golden, *Brnch Mgr*
EMP: 52
SALES (corp-wide): 5.69B **Publicly Held**
Web: www.vertiv.com
SIC: 3823 Process control instruments
HQ: Vertiv Corporation
505 N Cleveland Ave
Westerville OH
614 888-0246

(P-10169)
WORLD WATER INC
9848 Everest St (90242-3114)
P.O. Box 2331 (90662-2331)
PHONE..............................562 940-1964
Fernando Guerrero, *CEO*
EMP: 40 **EST:** 2006
SQ FT: 1,000
SALES (est): 5.62MM **Privately Held**
Web: www.worldwaterinc.com
SIC: 3823 Water quality monitoring and control systems

(P-10170)
WORLDWIDE ENVMTL PDTS INC (PA)
Also Called: Imperials Sand Dunes
1100 Beacon St (92821-2936)
PHONE..............................714 990-2700
EMP: 90 **EST:** 1991
SQ FT: 23,000
SALES (est): 20.12MM **Privately Held**
Web: www.wep-inc.com

SIC: 3823 3694 Process control instruments; Automotive electrical equipment, nec

(P-10171)
XIRRUS INC
2545 W Hillcrest Dr Ste 220 (91320-2217)
PHONE..............................805 262-1600
Shane Buckley, *CEO*
Dirk Gates, *Ofcr*
Patrick Parker, *CDO*
Sam Bass, *VP*
◆ **EMP:** 42 **EST:** 2004
SALES (est): 3.45MM **Privately Held**
Web: www.cambiumnetworks.com
SIC: 3823 Computer interface equipment, for industrial process control

(P-10172)
YOUNG ENGINEERING & MFG INC (PA)
560 W Terrace Dr (91773-2914)
P.O. Box 3984 (91773-7984)
PHONE..............................909 394-3225
Winston Young, *Pr*
Joanne Young, *
◆ **EMP:** 21 **EST:** 1980
SQ FT: 55,000
SALES (est): 8.57MM
SALES (corp-wide): 8.57MM **Privately Held**
Web: www.youngeng.com
SIC: 3823 5084 8711 5074 Process control instruments; Industrial machinery and equipment; Consulting engineer; Water purification equipment

3824 Fluid Meters And Counting Devices

(P-10173)
BLUE-WHITE INDUSTRIES LTD (PA)
5300 Business Dr (92649-1224)
PHONE..............................714 893-8529
Robert E Gledhill, *Pr*
Robert E Gledhill Iii, *VP*
Jeanne Hendrickson, *
Cindy Henderson, *
▲ **EMP:** 69 **EST:** 1957
SQ FT: 48,000
SALES (est): 19.72MM
SALES (corp-wide): 19.72MM **Privately Held**
Web: www.blue-white.com
SIC: 3824 3561 3589 Water meters; Industrial pumps and parts; Sewage and water treatment equipment

(P-10174)
D & K ENGINEERING (PA)
Also Called: Decatur Electronics
16990 Goldentop Rd (92127-2415)
PHONE..............................858 451-8999
Jeffrey Moss, *CEO*
Alex Kunczynski, *
Diane Law, *
Bill Suttner, *
Peter Ma, *VP*
▲ **EMP:** 92 **EST:** 2000
SQ FT: 60,000
SALES (est): 141.94MM **Privately Held**
Web: www.dkengineering.com
SIC: 3824 8711 Mechanical and electromechanical counters and devices; Acoustical engineering

(P-10175)
EMCOR FACILITIES SERVICES INC
2 Cromwell (92618-1816)
PHONE..............................949 475-6020
EMP: 200
SALES (corp-wide): 11.08B **Publicly Held**
Web: www.emcorfacilities.com
SIC: 3824 Fluid meters and counting devices
HQ: Emcor Facilities Services, Inc.
9655 Reading Rd
Cincinnati OH
888 846-9462

(P-10176)
INTERSCAN CORPORATION
4590 Ish Dr Ste 110 (93063-7666)
PHONE..............................805 823-8301
Richard Shaw, *Pr*
Michael Shaw, *VP*
Lorienne Shaw, *VP*
EMP: 23 **EST:** 1975
SQ FT: 10,000
SALES (est): 3.8MM **Privately Held**
Web: www.gasdetection.com
SIC: 3824 3829 Gasmeters, domestic and large capacity: industrial; Measuring and controlling devices, nec
PA: Chen Instrument Design Inc.
1554 Ne 3rd Ave
Camas WA

(P-10177)
MINDRUM PRECISION INC
Also Called: Mindrum Precision Products
10000 4th St (91730-5723)
PHONE..............................909 989-1728
Diane Mindrum, *CEO*
Daniel Mindrum, *
Matt Wade, *
EMP: 49 **EST:** 1956
SQ FT: 30,000
SALES (est): 10.06MM **Privately Held**
Web: www.mindrum.com
SIC: 3824 3827 3823 3264 Fluid meters and counting devices; Optical instruments and lenses; Process control instruments; Porcelain electrical supplies

(P-10178)
SPARLING INSTRUMENTS LLC
4097 Temple City Blvd (91731-1046)
PHONE..............................626 444-0571
▲ **EMP:** 25 **EST:** 1996
SQ FT: 56,000
SALES (est): 4.8MM **Privately Held**
Web: www.sparlinginstruments.com
SIC: 3824 3823 5084 Fluid meters and counting devices; Process control instruments; Industrial machinery and equipment

(P-10179)
ZENNER USA INC
1910 E Westward Ave (92220-6366)
P.O. Box 895 (92220-0019)
PHONE..............................951 849-8822
Ron Gallon, *CEO*
▲ **EMP:** 34 **EST:** 2012
SALES (est): 3.69MM **Privately Held**
Web: www.zenner.com
SIC: 3824 Water meters

3825 Instruments To Measure Electricity

(P-10180)
AGILENT TECHNOLOGIES INC

1170 Mark Ave (93013-2918)
PHONE..............................805 566-6655
Britt Meelby Jensen, *Genl Mgr*
EMP: 44
SALES (corp-wide): 6.85B **Publicly Held**
Web: www.agilent.com
SIC: 3825 Instruments to measure electricity
PA: Agilent Technologies, Inc.
  5301 Stevens Creek Blvd
  Santa Clara CA
  800 227-9770

(P-10181)
AGILENT TECHNOLOGIES INC
Also Called: Agilent Technologies
6392 Via Real (93013-2921)
PHONE..............................805 566-1405
EMP: 94
SALES (corp-wide): 6.85B **Publicly Held**
Web: www.agilent.com
SIC: 3825 Instruments to measure electricity
PA: Agilent Technologies, Inc.
  5301 Stevens Creek Blvd
  Santa Clara CA
  800 227-9770

(P-10182)
AGILENT TECHNOLOGIES INC
11011 N Torrey Pines Rd (92037-1007)
PHONE..............................858 373-6300
Janet King, *Prin*
EMP: 29
SALES (corp-wide): 6.85B **Publicly Held**
Web: www.agilent.com
SIC: 3825 Instruments to measure electricity
PA: Agilent Technologies, Inc.
  5301 Stevens Creek Blvd
  Santa Clara CA
  800 227-9770

(P-10183)
AMETEK PROGRAMMABLE POWER INC (HQ)
Also Called: Ametek Programmable Power
9250 Brown Deer Rd (92121-2267)
PHONE..............................858 450-0085
Matthew Mannell, *CEO*
Dalip Puri, *CFO*
▲ **EMP:** 350 **EST:** 2006
SQ FT: 110,000
SALES (est): 114.65MM
SALES (corp-wide): 6.15B **Publicly Held**
Web: www.programmablepower.com
SIC: 3825 Instruments to measure electricity
PA: Ametek, Inc.
  1100 Cassatt Rd
  Berwyn PA
  610 647-2121

(P-10184)
ARBITER SYSTEMS INCORPORATED (PA)
1324 Vendels Cir Ste 121 (93446-3806)
PHONE..............................805 237-3831
Craig Armstrong, *Pr*
Bruce Roeder, *
EMP: 30 **EST:** 1973
SQ FT: 15,000
SALES (est): 5.59MM
SALES (corp-wide): 5.59MM **Privately Held**
Web: www.arbiter.com
SIC: 3825 3829 3663 Test equipment for electronic and electric measurement; Measuring and controlling devices, nec; Radio and t.v. communications equipment

(P-10185)
ASTRONICS TEST SYSTEMS INC (HQ)
2652 Mcgaw Ave (92614-5840)
PHONE..............................800 722-2528
James Mulato, *Pr*
David Burney, *
Brian Price, *
◆ **EMP:** 130 **EST:** 2014
SQ FT: 98,600
SALES (est): 73.5MM
SALES (corp-wide): 534.89MM **Publicly Held**
Web: www.astronics.com
SIC: 3825 Test equipment for electronic and electric measurement
PA: Astronics Corporation
  130 Commerce Way
  East Aurora NY
  716 805-1599

(P-10186)
B&K PRECISION CORPORATION (PA)
22820 Savi Ranch Pkwy (92887-4610)
PHONE..............................714 921-9095
▲ **EMP:** 19 **EST:** 1951
SQ FT: 17,000
SALES (est): 7.69MM **Privately Held**
Web: www.bkprecision.com
SIC: 3825 5063 Instruments to measure electricity; Electrical apparatus and equipment

(P-10187)
BAE SYSTEMS INFO ELCTRNIC SYST
Also Called: Bae Systems
10920 Technology Pl (92127-1874)
PHONE..............................858 592-5000
Mark Gist, *Brnch Mgr*
EMP: 699
SALES (corp-wide): 25.59B **Privately Held**
Web: www.baesystems.com
SIC: 3825 7373 3812 Test equipment for electronic and electric measurement; Computer integrated systems design; Search and navigation equipment
HQ: Bae Systems Information And Electronic Systems Integration Inc.
  65 Spit Brook Rd
  Nashua NH
  603 885-4321

(P-10188)
BAE SYSTEMS NATIONAL SECURITY SOLUTIONS INC
10920 Technology Pl (92127-1874)
P.O. Box 509008 (92150-9008)
PHONE..............................858 592-5000
▲ **EMP:** 2200
SIC: 3825 7373 3812 Test equipment for electronic and electric measurement; Computer integrated systems design; Search and navigation equipment

(P-10189)
CHILICON POWER LLC (PA)
15415 W Sunset Blvd Ste 102 (90272-3546)
PHONE..............................310 800-1396
▲ **EMP:** 24 **EST:** 2011
SALES (est): 2.48MM
SALES (corp-wide): 2.48MM **Privately Held**
Web: www.chiliconpower.com
SIC: 3825 Power measuring equipment, electrical

(P-10190)
CHROMA SYSTEMS SOLUTIONS INC (HQ)
19772 Pauling (92610-2611)
PHONE..............................949 297-4848
Fred Sabatine, *Pr*
▲ **EMP:** 21 **EST:** 2001
SQ FT: 25,000
SALES (est): 27.28MM **Privately Held**
Web: www.chromausa.com
SIC: 3825 Measuring instruments and meters, electric
PA: Chroma Ate Inc.
  No. 88, Wenmao Rd.,
  Taoyuan City TAY

(P-10191)
COHU INC (PA)
Also Called: Cohu
12367 Crosthwaite Cir (92064-6817)
PHONE..............................858 848-8100
Luis A Muller, *Pr*
James A Donahue, *Non-Executive Chairman of the Board*
Christopher G Bohrson Senior, *Global Vice President*
Ian P Lawee, *Sr VP*
Jeffrey D Jones, *VP Fin*
▲ **EMP:** 220 **EST:** 1947
SQ FT: 147,000
SALES (est): 812.77MM
SALES (corp-wide): 812.77MM **Publicly Held**
Web: www.cohu.com
SIC: 3825 Semiconductor test equipment

(P-10192)
COHU INTERFACE SOLUTIONS LLC (HQ)
Also Called: Factron Test Fixtures
12367 Crosthwaite Cir (92064-6817)
PHONE..............................858 848-8000
Luis Muller, *CEO*
▲ **EMP:** 75 **EST:** 1965
SALES (est): 25.01MM
SALES (corp-wide): 812.77MM **Publicly Held**
Web: www.cohu.com
SIC: 3825 3678 Test equipment for electronic and electrical circuits; Electronic connectors
PA: Cohu, Inc.
  12367 Crosthwaite Cir
  Poway CA
  858 848-8100

(P-10193)
CONCISYS
5452 Oberlin Dr (92121-1715)
PHONE..............................858 292-5888
Giao Huu Nguyen, *Managing Member*
Vu Wing, *
▲ **EMP:** 40 **EST:** 2000
SALES (est): 9.85MM **Privately Held**
Web: www.concisys.com
SIC: 3825 Digital test equipment, electronic and electrical circuits

(P-10194)
DELTA DESIGN (LITTLETON) INC
12367 Crosthwaite Cir (92064-6817)
PHONE..............................858 848-8100
Charles A Schwan, *Ch Bd*
Nicholas J Cedrone, *
▲ **EMP:** 570 **EST:** 1994
SQ FT: 102,000
SALES (est): 88.71MM
SALES (corp-wide): 812.77MM **Publicly Held**

SIC: 3825 Test equipment for electronic and electrical circuits
PA: Cohu, Inc.
  12367 Crosthwaite Cir
  Poway CA
  858 848-8100

(P-10195)
DIVERSFIED TCHNCAL SYSTEMS INC (HQ)
1720 Apollo Ct (90740-5617)
PHONE..............................562 493-0158
Stephen D Pruitt, *CEO*
Steve Pruitt, *
George M Beckage, *
Tim Kippen, *
Kirsten Larsen, *
▲ **EMP:** 29 **EST:** 1990
SQ FT: 55,000
SALES (est): 23.29MM
SALES (corp-wide): 362.58MM **Publicly Held**
Web: www.dtsweb.com
SIC: 3825 3679 3495 8731 Instruments to measure electricity; Electronic circuits; Clock springs, precision; Commercial physical research
PA: Vishay Precision Group, Inc.
  3 Great Valley Pkwy # 150
  Malvern PA
  484 321-5300

(P-10196)
ENERSPONSE INC
1148 Manhattan Ave (90266-5323)
PHONE..............................949 829-3901
EMP: 23 **EST:** 2016
SALES (est): 601.81K **Privately Held**
Web: www.enersponse.com
SIC: 3825 8748 1731 Electrical energy measuring equipment; Energy conservation consultant; Energy management controls

(P-10197)
EQUUS PRODUCTS INC
17352 Von Karman Ave (92614-6204)
PHONE..............................714 424-6779
Ieon C Chen, *CEO*
Cynthia H Tsai, *
Duke Chen Skthldr, *Prin*
Michael Chen Skthldr, *Prin*
◆ **EMP:** 31 **EST:** 1982
SQ FT: 36,000
SALES (est): 4.7MM **Privately Held**
Web: www.equus.com
SIC: 3825 3545 3714 Electrical power measuring equipment; Machine tool accessories; Motor vehicle parts and accessories

(P-10198)
ERP POWER LLC (PA)
2625 Townsgate Rd (91361-5758)
PHONE..............................805 517-1300
Jeffrey Frank, *CEO*
Abdul Sher-jan, *COO*
Andy Williams, *Ex VP*
EMP: 17 **EST:** 2005
SALES (est): 16.45MM **Privately Held**
Web: www.erp-power.com
SIC: 3825 Energy measuring equipment, electrical

(P-10199)
FIELDPIECE INSTRUMENTS INC (PA)
Also Called: Fieldpiece
1636 W Collins Ave (92867-5421)
PHONE..............................714 634-1844
Cameron Rouns, *CEO*

PRODUCTS & SVCS

Tim J Way, *
▲ **EMP:** 52 **EST:** 1990
SQ FT: 4,000
SALES (est): 12.02MM **Privately Held**
Web: www.fieldpiece.com
SIC: 3825 3829 3826 3823 Instruments for measuring electrical quantities; Measuring and controlling devices, nec; Analytical instruments; Process control instruments

(P-10200)
FIRST LEGAL NETWORK
1517 Beverly Blvd (90026-5704)
PHONE..................213 250-1111
Alex Martinez, *CEO*
EMP: 23 **EST:** 2015
SALES (est): 3.41MM **Privately Held**
Web: www.firstlegalnetwork.com
SIC: 3825 4899 Network analyzers; Communication signal enhancement network services

(P-10201)
FISCHER CSTM CMMUNICATIONS INC (PA)
19220 Normandie Ave Unit B (90502-1011)
PHONE..................310 303-3300
David Fischer, *Pr*
Allen Fischer, *
EMP: 21 **EST:** 1971
SALES (est): 9.01MM
SALES (corp-wide): 9.01MM **Privately Held**
Web: www.fischercc.com
SIC: 3825 Digital test equipment, electronic and electrical circuits

(P-10202)
GOULD & BASS COMPANY INC
1431 W 2nd St (91766-1299)
PHONE..................909 623-6793
John S Bass, *CEO*
EMP: 32 **EST:** 1971
SQ FT: 66,000
SALES (est): 5.46MM **Privately Held**
Web: www.gould-bass.net
SIC: 3825 3535 3556 Test equipment for electronic and electric measurement; Belt conveyor systems, general industrial use; Packing house machinery

(P-10203)
HEXAGON MFG INTELLIGENCE INC
Romer Cimcore
3536 Seagate Way Ste 100 (92056-2672)
PHONE..................760 994-1401
Steve Ilmrud, *Genl Mgr*
EMP: 60
Web: www.hexagon.com
SIC: 3825 Instruments to measure electricity
HQ: Hexagon Manufacturing Intelligence, Inc.
　250 Circuit Dr
　North Kingstown RI
　401 886-2000

(P-10204)
HID GLOBAL CORPORATION
15370 Barranca Pkwy (92618-2215)
PHONE..................949 732-2000
EMP: 49
SALES (corp-wide): 11.51B **Privately Held**
Web: www.hidglobal.com
SIC: 3825 Instruments to measure electricity
HQ: Hid Global Corporation
　611 Center Ridge Dr
　Austin TX

(P-10205)
INTELLIGENT CMPT SOLUTIONS INC (PA)
8968 Fullbright Ave (91311-6123)
PHONE..................818 998-5805
Uzi Kohavi, *Pr*
Gonen Ravid, *
▲ **EMP:** 25 **EST:** 1989
SQ FT: 21,000
SALES (est): 6.12MM **Privately Held**
Web: www.ics-iq.com
SIC: 3825 3577 3572 Test equipment for electronic and electrical circuits; Computer peripheral equipment, nec; Computer storage devices

(P-10206)
INTERNATIONAL TRANDUCER CORP
Also Called: Channel Technologies Group
869 Ward Dr (93111-2920)
PHONE..................805 683-2575
Robert F Carlson, *
Kevin Ruelas, *
Brian Dolan, *
EMP: 160 **EST:** 1966
SALES (est): 23.37MM
SALES (corp-wide): 53.11MM **Privately Held**
SIC: 3825 3812 Transducers for volts, amperes, watts, vars, frequency, etc.; Search and navigation equipment
PA: Gavial Holdings, Inc.
　1435 W Mccoy Ln
　Santa Maria CA
　805 614-0060

(P-10207)
IXIA
Also Called: Ixia Communications
26701 Agoura Rd (91302-1960)
PHONE..................818 871-1800
EMP: 37
SALES (corp-wide): 5.42B **Publicly Held**
Web: www.keysight.com
SIC: 3825 Network analyzers
HQ: Ixia
　26601 Agoura Rd
　Calabasas CA
　818 871-1800

(P-10208)
IXIA (HQ)
26601 Agoura Rd (91302-1959)
PHONE..................818 871-1800
Neil Dougherty, *Pr*
Jeffrey Li, *VP*
Jason Kary, *
Matthew S Alexander, *Corporate Secretary**
Stephen Williams, *
EMP: 275 **EST:** 1997
SQ FT: 116,000
SALES (est): 443.72MM
SALES (corp-wide): 5.42B **Publicly Held**
Web: www.keysight.com
SIC: 3825 7371 Network analyzers; Custom computer programming services
PA: Keysight Technologies, Inc.
　1400 Fountaingrove Pkwy
　Santa Rosa CA
　800 829-4444

(P-10209)
L3HARRIS INTERSTATE ELEC CORP
3033 Science Park Rd (92121-1167)
PHONE..................858 552-9500
Andrew Leuthe, *Prin*
EMP: 74

SALES (corp-wide): 17.06B **Publicly Held**
Web: www.l3harris.com
SIC: 3825 7379 5045 Test equipment for electronic and electric measurement; Computer related consulting services; Computer software
HQ: L3harris Interstate Electronics Corporation
　602 E Vermont Ave
　Anaheim CA
　714 758-0500

(P-10210)
L3HARRIS INTERSTATE ELEC CORP
Also Called: Human Resources
708 E Vermont Ave (92805-5611)
PHONE..................714 758-0500
EMP: 50
SALES (corp-wide): 17.06B **Publicly Held**
Web: www.l3harris.com
SIC: 3825 Test equipment for electronic and electric measurement
HQ: L3harris Interstate Electronics Corporation
　602 E Vermont Ave
　Anaheim CA
　714 758-0500

(P-10211)
L3HARRIS INTERSTATE ELEC CORP
Also Called: Integrated Technical Services
600 E Vermont Ave (92805-5607)
PHONE..................714 758-0500
Robert Schembre, *Brnch Mgr*
EMP: 50
SALES (corp-wide): 17.06B **Publicly Held**
Web: www.l3harris.com
SIC: 3825 Instruments to measure electricity
HQ: L3harris Interstate Electronics Corporation
　602 E Vermont Ave
　Anaheim CA
　714 758-0500

(P-10212)
L3HARRIS INTERSTATE ELEC CORP (DH)
Also Called: L-3 Interstate Electronics
602 E Vermont Ave (92805-5607)
P.O. Box 3117 (92803-3117)
PHONE..................714 758-0500
Christopher E Kubasik, *CEO*
Arthur H Lim, *Treas*
Scott T Mikuen, *Dir*
Kristene E Schumacher, *Dir*
EMP: 275 **EST:** 1955
SQ FT: 235,700
SALES (est): 185.65MM
SALES (corp-wide): 17.06B **Publicly Held**
Web: www.l3harris.com
SIC: 3825 3812 3679 Test equipment for electronic and electric measurement; Navigational systems and instruments; Liquid crystal displays (LCD)
HQ: L3 Technologies, Inc.
　600 3rd Ave Fl 34
　New York NY
　321 727-9100

(P-10213)
LITEL INSTRUMENTS INC
10650 Scripps Ranch Blvd Ste 105 (92131-2471)
PHONE..................858 546-3788
Robert O Hunter Junior, *Pr*
EMP: 20 **EST:** 1990
SALES (est): 925.62K **Privately Held**
Web: www.litel.net

SIC: 3825 Instruments to measure electricity

(P-10214)
MAGNEBIT HOLDING CORP
9474 La Cuesta Dr (91941-5634)
PHONE..................858 573-0727
Catherine Jacobson, *Pr*
Peter Jacobson, *
EMP: 25 **EST:** 1981
SALES (est): 2.07MM **Privately Held**
Web: www.magnebit.com
SIC: 3825 3471 Instruments to measure electricity; Plating and polishing

(P-10215)
MARVIN TEST SOLUTIONS INC
1770 Kettering (92614-5616)
PHONE..................949 263-2222
Loofie Gutterman, *Pr*
Leon Tsimmerman, *
Gerald Friedman, *
EMP: 96 **EST:** 1987
SQ FT: 31,000
SALES (est): 17.55MM
SALES (corp-wide): 149.54MM **Privately Held**
Web: www.marvintest.com
SIC: 3825 Instruments to measure electricity
PA: Marvin Engineering Co., Inc.
　261 W Beach Ave
　Inglewood CA
　310 674-5030

(P-10216)
MEREX INC
1283 Flynn Rd (93012-8013)
P.O. Box 3474 (91313-3474)
PHONE..................805 446-2700
Chester J Dopler, *CEO*
Ahmad Shams, *Pr*
Nathan Skop, *Ex VP*
EMP: 24 **EST:** 1984
SALES (est): 1.04MM **Privately Held**
Web: www.goallclear.com
SIC: 3825 Instruments to measure electricity

(P-10217)
MRV SYSTEMS LLC
6370 Lusk Blvd Ste F100 (92121-2754)
PHONE..................800 645-7114
EMP: 20 **EST:** 2010
SALES (est): 3.51MM **Privately Held**
Web: www.mrvsys.com
SIC: 3825 3823 Instruments to measure electricity; Temperature measurement instruments, industrial

(P-10218)
N H RESEARCH LLC
16601 Hale Ave (92606-5049)
PHONE..................949 474-3900
Eric H Starkloff, *Pr*
▲ **EMP:** 68 **EST:** 1965
SQ FT: 29,000
SALES (est): 25.65MM
SALES (corp-wide): 1.66B **Privately Held**
Web: www.nhresearch.com
SIC: 3825 3829 Test equipment for electronic and electrical circuits; Measuring and controlling devices, nec
PA: National Instruments Corporation
　11500 N Mopac Expy
　Austin TX
　512 683-0100

(P-10219)
NEARFIELD SYSTEMS INC
19730 Magellan Dr (90502-1104)
PHONE..................310 525-7000
Greg Hindman, *Pr*

▲ = Import ▼ = Export
◆ = Import/Export

Dan Slater, *
Rod Douglass, *
▼ **EMP:** 62 **EST:** 1988
SALES (est): 16.98MM
SALES (corp-wide): 6.15B **Publicly Held**
Web: www.nearfield.com
SIC: 3825 3829 Test equipment for electronic and electric measurement; Measuring and controlling devices, nec
HQ: Nsi-Mi Technologies Inc.
   1125 Satellit Blvd Nw # 100
   Suwanee GA
   678 475-8300

(P-10220)
NEOLOGY INC (PA)
Also Called: Neology
1917 Palomar Oaks Way Ste 110 (92008-5512)
PHONE..................858 391-0260
Bradley Feldmann, *CEO*
Neil Jadhav, *CDO**
Steve Haddix, *
◆ **EMP:** 85 **EST:** 1986
SALES (est): 38.17MM
SALES (corp-wide): 38.17MM **Privately Held**
Web: www.neology.net
SIC: 3825 Integrated circuit testers

(P-10221)
PULSE INSTRUMENTS
22301 S Western Ave Ste 107 (90501)
PHONE..................310 515-5330
Sylvia Kan, *Pr*
David Kan, *VP Engg*
EMP: 23 **EST:** 1975
SALES (est): 4.75MM **Privately Held**
Web: www.pulseinstruments.com
SIC: 3825 3823 Pulse (signal) generators; Process control instruments

(P-10222)
ROHDE & SCHWARZ USA INC
2255 N Ontario St Ste 150 (91504-3120)
PHONE..................818 846-3600
EMP: 22
SALES (corp-wide): 2.7B **Privately Held**
Web: www.rohde-schwarz.com
SIC: 3825 Instruments to measure electricity
HQ: Rohde & Schwarz Usa, Inc.
   6821 Benjamin Franklin Dr
   Columbia MD
   410 910-7800

(P-10223)
STS INSTRUMENTS INC
2802 Kelvin Ave Ste 100 (92614-5897)
P.O. Box 1805 (73402-1805)
PHONE..................580 223-4773
Kevin Voelcker, *Pr*
William D Long, *Treas*
Barbara J Stinnett, *Sec*
▲ **EMP:** 47 **EST:** 1954
SALES (est): 2.08MM
SALES (corp-wide): 30.94MM **Privately Held**
Web: www.stsinstruments.com
SIC: 3825 Test equipment for electronic and electrical circuits
PA: Ppst, Inc.
   17692 Fitch
   Irvine CA
   800 421-1921

(P-10224)
SURFACE OPTICS CORPORATION
11555 Rancho Bernardo Rd (92127-1441)
PHONE..................858 675-7404

Jonathan Dummer, *CEO*
James C Jafolla, *
Mark Dombrowski, *
Marian Geremia, *
James Jafolla, *
EMP: 50 **EST:** 1977
SQ FT: 18,000
SALES (est): 12.16MM **Privately Held**
Web: www.surfaceoptics.com
SIC: 3825 8748 3829 8731 Instruments to measure electricity; Business consulting, nec; Measuring and controlling devices, nec ; Commercial physical research

(P-10225)
TASEON INC
515 S Flower St Fl 25 (90071-2228)
PHONE..................408 240-7800
▲ **EMP:** 18 **EST:** 2007
SQ FT: 21,000
SALES (est): 766.56K **Privately Held**
SIC: 3825 Network analyzers

(P-10226)
TELEDYNE LECROY INC
1049 Camino Dos Rios (91360-2362)
PHONE..................434 984-4500
EMP: 18
SALES (corp-wide): 5.46B **Publicly Held**
Web: www.teledynelecroy.com
SIC: 3825 Oscillographs and oscilloscopes
HQ: Teledyne Lecroy, Inc.
   700 Chestnut Ridge Rd
   Chestnut Ridge NY
   845 425-2000

(P-10227)
TESCO CONTROLS INC
Also Called: TESCO CONTROLS, INC.
42015 Remington Ave Ste 102 (92590-2563)
PHONE..................916 395-8800
Tracy Adams, *Pr*
EMP: 50
SALES (corp-wide): 100MM **Privately Held**
Web: www.tescocontrols.com
SIC: 3825 3571 3625 Meters: electric, pocket, portable, panelboard, etc.; Minicomputers; Relays and industrial controls
PA: Tesco Controls, Llc
   8440 Florin Rd
   Sacramento CA
   916 395-8800

(P-10228)
TRI-NET INC
14721 Hilton Dr (92336-4013)
PHONE..................909 483-3555
Rosemarie V Hall, *Pr*
EMP: 46 **EST:** 1991
SQ FT: 7,500
SALES (est): 1.89MM **Privately Held**
Web: www.trinet.com
SIC: 3825 Test equipment for electronic and electric measurement

(P-10229)
VELHER LLC
350 10th Ave Ste 1000 (92101-8705)
PHONE..................619 494-6310
Luis Velazquez, *Managing Member*
EMP: 50 **EST:** 2019
SALES (est): 4.18MM **Privately Held**
Web: www.velher.net
SIC: 3825 Energy measuring equipment, electrical

(P-10230)
VITREK LLC (PA)
Also Called: Xitron Technologies
12169 Kirkham Rd Ste C (92064-8835)
PHONE..................858 689-2755
Kevin Clark, *CEO*
Don Millstein, *
▲ **EMP:** 25 **EST:** 1990
SQ FT: 4,000
SALES (est): 23.73MM **Privately Held**
Web: www.vitrek.com
SIC: 3825 Test equipment for electronic and electric measurement

(P-10231)
WILCOMPUTE
38713 Tierra Subida Ave Ste 200 (93551-4562)
PHONE..................818 674-0506
Paul Wilson, *CEO*
EMP: 24 **EST:** 2001
SALES (est): 1.23MM **Privately Held**
SIC: 3825 7389 Network analyzers

3826 Analytical Instruments

(P-10232)
AFFYMETRIX INC
5893 Oberlin Dr (92121-3773)
PHONE..................858 642-2058
EMP: 39
SALES (corp-wide): 44.91B **Publicly Held**
Web: www.affymetrix.com
SIC: 3826 Analytical instruments
HQ: Affymetrix, Inc.
   3380 Central Expy
   Santa Clara CA

(P-10233)
ANALYTIK JENA US LLC
2066 W 11th St (91786-3509)
PHONE..................781 376-9899
Chris Griffith, *Mgr*
EMP: 18
Web: www.uvp.com
SIC: 3826 Analytical instruments
HQ: Analytik Jena Us Llc
   3 Highwood Dr Ste 103e
   Tewksbury MA

(P-10234)
APPLIED INSTRUMENT TECH INC
2121 Aviation Dr (91786-2195)
PHONE..................909 204-3700
EMP: 40 **EST:** 2010
SALES (est): 10.46MM
SALES (corp-wide): 82.05K **Privately Held**
SIC: 3826 Analytical instruments
HQ: Schneider Electric Usa, Inc.
   1 Boston Pl Ste 2700
   Boston MA
   978 975-9600

(P-10235)
AUTONOMOUS MEDICAL DEVICES INC
10524 S La Cienega Blvd (90304-1116)
PHONE..................310 641-2700
EMP: 43
SALES (corp-wide): 9.87MM **Privately Held**
Web: www.amdilabs.com
SIC: 3826 Analytical instruments

PA: Autonomous Medical Devices Incorporated
   3511 W Sunflower Ave
   Santa Ana CA
   657 660-6800

(P-10236)
AUTONOMOUS MEDICAL DEVICES INC (PA)
3511 W Sunflower Ave (92704-6944)
P.O. Box 28404 (92799-8404)
PHONE..................657 660-6800
David Okrongly, *CEO*
Christopher Bissell, *
EMP: 28 **EST:** 2013
SQ FT: 3,750
SALES (est): 9.87MM
SALES (corp-wide): 9.87MM **Privately Held**
Web: www.amdilabs.com
SIC: 3826 Analytical instruments

(P-10237)
BECKMAN COULTER INC
2470 Faraday Ave (92010-7224)
PHONE..................760 438-9151
Claire O'donadan, *Mgr*
EMP: 125
SALES (corp-wide): 31.47B **Publicly Held**
Web: www.beckmancoulter.com
SIC: 3826 Analytical instruments
HQ: Beckman Coulter, Inc.
   250 S Kraemer Blvd
   Brea CA
   714 993-5321

(P-10238)
BECKMAN COULTER INC (HQ)
250 S Kraemer Blvd (92821-6232)
P.O. Box 2268 (92822-2268)
PHONE..................714 993-5321
◆ **EMP:** 1200 **EST:** 1935
SALES (est): 274.59K
SALES (corp-wide): 31.47B **Publicly Held**
Web: www.beckmancoulter.com
SIC: 3826 3841 3821 Analytical instruments; Diagnostic apparatus, medical; Chemical laboratory apparatus, nec
PA: Danaher Corporation
   2200 Penn Ave Nw Ste 800w
   Washington DC
   202 828-0850

(P-10239)
BECKMAN INSTRUMENTS INC
2500 N Harbor Blvd (92835-2600)
PHONE..................714 871-4848
EMP: 24 **EST:** 1934
SALES (est): 935.83K **Privately Held**
SIC: 3826 Analytical instruments

(P-10240)
BECKMAN INSTRUMENTS INC
8733 Scott St (91770-1363)
PHONE..................626 309-0110
J Cendejas, *Pr*
EMP: 51 **EST:** 2003
SALES (est): 609.21K **Privately Held**
Web: www.beckman.com
SIC: 3826 Analytical instruments

(P-10241)
BECTON DICKINSON AND COMPANY
Also Called: Bdc Distribution Center
2200 W San Bernardino Ave (92374-5008)
PHONE..................909 748-7300
Ricardo Frias, *Brnch Mgr*
EMP: 58

PRODUCTS & SVCS

SALES (corp-wide): 19.37B **Publicly Held**
Web: www.bd.com
SIC: 3826 Elemental analyzers
PA: Becton, Dickinson And Company
   1 Becton Dr
   Franklin Lakes NJ
   201 847-6800

(P-10242)
BEMCO INC (PA)
2255 Union Pl (93065-1661)
PHONE..........................805 583-4970
Randy Jean Bruskrud, *Pr*
Brian Bruskrud, *
EMP: 24 **EST:** 1951
SQ FT: 50,000
SALES (est): 4.95MM
SALES (corp-wide): 4.95MM **Privately Held**
Web: www.bemcoinc.com
SIC: 3826 Environmental testing equipment

(P-10243)
BIONANO GENOMICS INC (PA)
Also Called: BIONANO GENOMICS
9540 Towne Centre Dr Ste 100 (92121)
PHONE.............................858 888-7600
R Erik Holmlin, *Pr*
David L Barker, *
Christopher Stewart, *CFO*
Mark Oldakowski, *COO*
Alka Chaubey, *CMO*
EMP: 90 **EST:** 2003
SQ FT: 35,823
SALES (est): 27.8MM
SALES (corp-wide): 27.8MM **Publicly Held**
Web: www.bionano.com
SIC: 3826 Analytical instruments

(P-10244)
BIOPAC SYSTEMS INC
42 Aero Camino (93117-3105)
PHONE.............................805 685-0066
Alan Macy, *CEO*
William Mcmullen, *VP*
Marc Wester, .*
EMP: 40 **EST:** 1986
SQ FT: 16,000
SALES (est): 9.16MM **Privately Held**
Web: www.biopac.com
SIC: 3826 Analytical instruments

(P-10245)
BIORAD INC
9500 Jeronimo Rd (92618-2017)
PHONE.............................949 598-1200
EMP: 30
SALES (est): 2.52MM **Privately Held**
Web: www.bio-rad.com
SIC: 3826 Analytical instruments

(P-10246)
BROADLEY-JAMES CORPORATION
19 Thomas (92618-2704)
PHONE.............................949 829-5555
Scott Broadley, *Pr*
Leighton S Broadley, *
Scott T Broadley, *Prin*
Catherine A Broadley, *
EMP: 79 **EST:** 1967
SQ FT: 24,000
SALES (est): 16.17MM **Privately Held**
Web: www.broadleyjames.com
SIC: 3826 3823 Analytical instruments;
   Industrial process measurement equipment

(P-10247)
BRUKER CORPORATION
3601 Calle Tecate Ste C (93012-5069)
PHONE.............................805 388-3326
Steve Minne, *Brnch Mgr*
EMP: 18
SALES (corp-wide): 2.53B **Publicly Held**
Web: www.bruker.com
SIC: 3826 Analytical instruments
PA: Bruker Corporation
   40 Manning Rd
   Billerica MA
   978 663-3660

(P-10248)
CAPILLARY BIOMEDICAL INC
2 Wrigley Ste 101 (92618-2759)
PHONE.............................949 317-1701
Paul Strasma, *Pr*
EMP: 28 **EST:** 2014
SALES (est): 5.45MM **Publicly Held**
Web: www.tandemdiabetes.com
SIC: 3826 3841 Analytical instruments;
   Surgical and medical instruments
PA: Tandem Diabetes Care, Inc.
   12400 High Bluff Dr # 100
   San Diego CA

(P-10249)
CITY OF SAN DIEGO
Also Called: Public Utilites Emts
2392 Kincaid Rd (92101-0811)
PHONE.............................619 758-2310
Steve Meyer, *Mgr*
EMP: 159
SQ FT: 92,782
SALES (corp-wide): 2.67B **Privately Held**
Web: www.sandiego.gov
SIC: 3826 Sewage testing apparatus
PA: City Of San Diego
   202 C St
   San Diego CA
   619 236-6330

(P-10250)
COMBIMATRIX CORPORATION (HQ)
310 Goddard Ste 150 (92618-4601)
PHONE.............................949 753-0624
EMP: 34 **EST:** 1995
SQ FT: 12,200
SALES (est): 9.55MM **Publicly Held**
Web: www.combimatrix.com
SIC: 3826 8731 8071 Analytical instruments;
   Biotechnical research, commercial; Medical
   laboratories
PA: Invitae Corporation
   1400 16th St
   San Francisco CA

(P-10251)
CONDITION MONITORING SVCS INC
Also Called: Condition Monitoring Services
855 San Ysidro Ln (93444-8500)
P.O. Box 278 (93444-0278)
PHONE.............................888 359-3277
Kirk F Cormany, *Pr*
EMP: 21 **EST:** 2006
SALES (est): 2.59MM **Privately Held**
Web:
www.conditionmonitoringservices.com
SIC: 3826 Infrared analytical instruments

(P-10252)
CUE HEALTH INC
Also Called: Cue Health
4980 Carroll Canyon Rd Ste 110
(92121-1732)

PHONE..........................858 412-8151
Ayub Khattak, *Ch Bd*
Chris Achar, *CSO*
John Gallagher, *CFO*
Clint Sever, *CPO*
EMP: 775 **EST:** 2010
SQ FT: 21,000
SALES (est): 483.48MM **Privately Held**
Web: www.cuehealth.com
SIC: 3826 Analytical instruments

(P-10253)
DOE & INGALLS CAL OPER LLC
1060 Citrus St (92507-1730)
PHONE.............................951 801-7175
John Hollenbach, *Managing Member*
EMP: 36 **EST:** 2008
SQ FT: 43,000
SALES (est): 9.88MM
SALES (corp-wide): 44.91B **Publicly Held**
SIC: 3826 Analytical instruments
HQ: Doe & Ingalls Management, Llc
   4813 Emperor Blvd Ste 300
   Durham NC

(P-10254)
EMD MILLIPORE CORPORATION
28835 Single Oak Dr (92590-5501)
PHONE.............................951 676-8080
Patrick Schneider, *Mgr*
EMP: 56
SALES (corp-wide): 23.09B **Privately Held**
Web: www.millipore.com
SIC: 3826 Analytical instruments
HQ: Emd Millipore Corporation
   400 Summit Dr
   Burlington MA
   800 645-5476

(P-10255)
EMD MILLIPORE CORPORATION
26578 Old Julian Hwy (92065-6733)
PHONE.............................760 788-9692
Haizhen Liu, *Mgr*
EMP: 36
SQ FT: 9,694
SALES (corp-wide): 23.09B **Privately Held**
Web: www.millipore.com
SIC: 3826 Analytical instruments
HQ: Emd Millipore Corporation
   400 Summit Dr
   Burlington MA
   800 645-5476

(P-10256)
ENDRESS & HAUSER CONDUCTA INC
Also Called: Endresshauser Conducta
4123 E La Palma Ave St200 (92807-1813)
PHONE.............................800 835-5474
Manfred A Jagiella, *CEO*
Claude Genswein, *
EMP: 50 **EST:** 1976
SQ FT: 31,000
SALES (est): 12.5MM **Privately Held**
Web: www.analysis-oem.com
SIC: 3826 3823 Water testing apparatus;
   Process control instruments
HQ: Endress+Hauser Conducta Gmbh+Co.
   Kg
   Dieselstr. 24
   Gerlingen BW
   715620915387

(P-10257)
ENDRESS+HSER OPTCAL ANALIS INC
11027 Arrow Rte (91730-4866)
PHONE.............................909 477-2329
EMP: 28 **EST:** 2001

SALES (est): 798.85K **Privately Held**
SIC: 3826 Analytical instruments
PA: Endress+Hauser Ag
   Kagenstrasse 2
   Reinach BL

(P-10258)
ENTECH INSTRUMENTS INC
2207 Agate Ct (93065-1839)
PHONE.............................805 527-5939
Daniel B Cardin, *CEO*
▲ **EMP:** 55 **EST:** 1989
SQ FT: 25,000
SALES (est): 9.34MM **Privately Held**
Web: www.entechinst.com
SIC: 3826 Environmental testing equipment

(P-10259)
FILMETRICS INC (HQ)
10655 Roselle St Ste 200 (92121-1557)
PHONE.............................858 573-9300
EMP: 20 **EST:** 1993
SQ FT: 2,691
SALES (est): 9.07MM
SALES (corp-wide): 741.05MM **Publicly Held**
Web: www.filmetrics.com
SIC: 3826 Analytical optical instruments
PA: Standex International Corporation
   23 Keewaydin Dr Ste 205
   Salem NH
   603 893-9701

(P-10260)
FOCUS TECHNOLOGIES HOLDING CO
10703 Progress Way (90630-4714)
PHONE.............................800 838-4548
Charles C Harwood, *Pr*
Don Mooney, *VP*
Edward Caffrey, *VP*
EMP: 25 **EST:** 1985
SQ FT: 28,000
SALES (est): 446.63K **Privately Held**
Web: molecular.diasorin.com
SIC: 3826 8071 Analytical instruments;
   Testing laboratories

(P-10261)
HAMILTON SUNDSTRAND CORP
Collins Aerospace
960 Overland Ct (91773-1742)
P.O. Box 2801 (91769-2801)
PHONE.............................909 593-5300
Bob Hertel, *Brnch Mgr*
EMP: 240
SALES (corp-wide): 67.07B **Publicly Held**
Web: www.collinsaerospace.com
SIC: 3826 3861 3812 Spectrometers;
   Cameras, still and motion picture (all types)
   ; Search and navigation equipment
HQ: Hamilton Sundstrand Corporation
   1 Hamilton Rd
   Windsor Locks CT
   619 714-9442

(P-10262)
HORIBA AMERICAS HOLDING INC (HQ)
9755 Research Dr (92618-4626)
PHONE.............................949 250-4811
Juichi Saito, *CEO*
EMP: 1055 **EST:** 2017
SALES (est): 438.93MM **Privately Held**
Web: www.horiba.com
SIC: 3826 Analytical instruments
PA: Horiba, Ltd.
   2, Kisshoimmiyanohigashicho, Minami-
   Ku
   Kyoto KYO

▲ = Import ▼ = Export
◆ = Import/Export

(P-10263)
HORIBA INSTRUMENTS INC (DH)
Also Called: Horiba Automotive Test Systems
9755 Research Dr (92618-4626)
PHONE..................................949 250-4811
Jai Hakhu, *Ch Bd*
▲ **EMP**: 195 **EST**: 1998
SQ FT: 80,000
SALES (est): 194.11MM **Privately Held**
Web: www.horiba.com
SIC: **3826** 3829 3511 3825 Analytical
instruments; Measuring and controlling
devices, nec; Turbines and turbine
generator sets; Instruments to measure
electricity
HQ: Horiba Americas Holding Incorporated
9755 Research Dr
Irvine CA
949 250-4811

(P-10264)
ILLUMINA INC
9885 Towne Centre Dr (92121-1975)
PHONE..................................800 809-4566
William Rastetter, *Ch*
EMP: 20
SALES (corp-wide): 4.58B **Publicly Held**
Web: www.illumina.com
SIC: **3826** Analytical instruments
PA: Illumina, Inc.
5200 Illumina Way
San Diego CA
858 202-4500

(P-10265)
ILLUMINA INC (PA)
Also Called: Illumina
5200 Illumina Way (92122-4616)
PHONE..................................858 202-4500
Charles E Dadswell, *Interim Chief
Executive Officer*
Stephen P Macmillan, *Non-Executive
Chairman of the Board*
Robert Ragusa, *COO*
Sam Samad, *CFO*
▲ **EMP**: 559 **EST**: 1998
SQ FT: 1,176,000
SALES (est): 4.58B
SALES (corp-wide): 4.58B **Publicly Held**
Web: www.illumina.com
SIC: **3826** 3821 Analytical instruments;
Clinical laboratory instruments, except
medical and dental

(P-10266)
INTERGLOBAL WASTE MGT INC
820 Calle Plano (93012-8557)
PHONE..................................805 388-1588
Harold Katersky, *Ch Bd*
Thomas Williams, *Stockholder*
EMP: 80 **EST**: 2000
SALES (est): 5.52MM **Privately Held**
SIC: **3826** Analytical instruments

(P-10267)
**INVITROGEN IP HOLDINGS INC
(DH)**
5791 Van Allen Way (92008-7321)
PHONE..................................760 603-7200
Stuart Hepburn, *Pr*
EMP: 64 **EST**: 2003
SALES (est): 60.24MM
SALES (corp-wide): 44.91B **Publicly Held**
SIC: **3826** Analytical instruments
HQ: Life Technologies Corporation
5781 Van Allen Way
Carlsbad CA
760 603-7200

(P-10268)
**LAMBDA RESEARCH OPTICS
INC**
1695 Macarthur Blvd (92626-1440)
PHONE..................................714 327-0600
Mark Youn, *Pr*
▲ **EMP**: 65 **EST**: 1991
SQ FT: 3,500
SALES (est): 8.77MM **Privately Held**
Web: www.lambda.cc
SIC: **3826** 3827 3229 Laser scientific and
engineering instruments; Optical
instruments and lenses; Pressed and blown
glass, nec

(P-10269)
**LEICA BIOSYSTEMS IMAGING
INC (HQ)**
Also Called: Aperio
1360 Park Center Dr (92081-8300)
PHONE..................................760 539-1100
James F O'reilly, *VP*
Dirk G Soenksen, *
Greg Crandall, *
Jared N Schwartz, *Chief Medical Officer*
Keith B Hagen, *
EMP: 127 **EST**: 2011
SQ FT: 37,000
SALES (est): 55.77MM
SALES (corp-wide): 31.47B **Publicly Held**
Web: www.leicabiosystems.com
SIC: **3826** Analytical instruments
PA: Danaher Corporation
2200 Penn Ave Nw Ste 800w
Washington DC
202 828-0850

(P-10270)
**LIFE TECHNOLOGIES
CORPORATION**
Also Called: Life Technologies
5791 Van Allen Way (92008-7321)
PHONE..................................760 918-0135
EMP: 216
SALES (corp-wide): 44.91B **Publicly Held**
Web: www.thermofisher.com
SIC: **3826** Analytical instruments
HQ: Life Technologies Corporation
5781 Van Allen Way
Carlsbad CA
760 603-7200

(P-10271)
**LIFE TECHNOLOGIES
CORPORATION**
Also Called: Supplier Diversity Program
5791 Van Allen Way (92008-7321)
PHONE..................................760 918-4259
EMP: 28
SALES (corp-wide): 44.91B **Publicly Held**
Web: www.thermofisher.com
SIC: **3826** Analytical instruments
HQ: Life Technologies Corporation
5781 Van Allen Way
Carlsbad CA
760 603-7200

(P-10272)
MAKO INDUSTRIES SC INC
1280 N Red Gum St (92806-1820)
PHONE..................................714 632-1400
John Tittelfitz, *CEO*
▲ **EMP**: 22 **EST**: 2007
SALES (est): 861.15K **Privately Held**
Web: www.makoindustries.com
SIC: **3826** Environmental testing equipment

(P-10273)
MEANS ENGINEERING INC
5927 Geiger Ct (92008-7305)
PHONE..................................760 931-9452
David William Means, *CEO*
Lisa Means, *
EMP: 70 **EST**: 1996
SQ FT: 34,000
SALES (est): 16.4MM **Privately Held**
Web: www.meanseng.com
SIC: **3826** 3699 3559 Analytical instruments;
Electrical equipment and supplies, nec;
Semiconductor manufacturing machinery

(P-10274)
**MOLECULAR BIOPRODUCTS
INC (DH)**
9389 Waples St (92121-3903)
PHONE..................................858 453-7551
Seth H Hoogasian, *CEO*
Gary J Marmontello, *
R Jeffrey Harris, *
Michael K Bresson, *
John Buono, *
◆ **EMP**: 110 **EST**: 1978
SQ FT: 45,000
SALES (est): 110.71MM
SALES (corp-wide): 44.91B **Publicly Held**
Web: www.thermofisher.com
SIC: **3826** Analytical instruments
HQ: Fisher Scientific International Llc
81 Wyman St
Waltham MA

(P-10275)
MOTIONLOFT INC
13681 Newport Ave Ste 8 (92780-7815)
PHONE..................................415 580-7671
Joyce Reitman, *CEO*
Chris Garrison, *
EMP: 39 **EST**: 2010
SALES (est): 6.07MM **Privately Held**
Web: www.motionloft.com
SIC: **3826** 7372 Analytical instruments;
Application computer software

(P-10276)
MP BIOMEDICALS LLC (HQ)
Also Called: Mp Biomedicals
9 Goddard (92618-4600)
PHONE..................................949 833-2500
Huanjie Wang, *CEO*
Tom Stankovich, *CFO*
▲ **EMP**: 20 **EST**: 2003
SALES (est): 103.31MM
SALES (corp-wide): 704.65MM **Privately
Held**
Web: www.mpbio.com
SIC: **3826** Analytical instruments
PA: Valiant Co., Ltd
No.11, Wuzhishan Road, Economic
Technology Development Zone, Fus
Yantai SD
535 637-8873

(P-10277)
NANOVEA INC (PA)
6 Morgan Ste 156 (92618-1922)
PHONE..................................949 461-9292
Pierre Leroux, *CEO*
Pierre Leroux, *Pr*
EMP: 23 **EST**: 2008
SALES (est): 9.2MM **Privately Held**
Web: www.nanovea.com
SIC: **3826** Analytical instruments

(P-10278)
NDC TECHNOLOGIES INC
5314 Irwindale Ave (91706-2086)
PHONE..................................626 960-3300

▲ **EMP**: 20
SALES (corp-wide): 2.59B **Publicly Held**
Web: www.ndc.com
SIC: **3826** Analytical instruments
HQ: Ndc Technologies, Inc.
8001 Technology Blvd
Dayton OH
937 233-9935

(P-10279)
**OXFORD INSTRS ASYLUM RES
INC (HQ)**
Also Called: Asylum Research
7416 Hollister Ave (93117-2583)
PHONE..................................805 696-6466
Jason Cleveland, *CEO*
Roger Proksch, *
John Green, *
Richard Clark, *
Dick Clark, *
EMP: 55 **EST**: 2012
SALES (est): 11.73MM
SALES (corp-wide): 534.42MM **Privately
Held**
Web: afm.oxinst.com
SIC: **3826** Analytical instruments
PA: Oxford Instruments Plc
Magnetic Resonance
Abingdon OXON
186 539-3200

(P-10280)
OXFORD NANOIMAGING INC
11045 Roselle St Ste 3 (92121-1218)
PHONE..................................650 690-2708
Bo Jing, *CEO*
Feyo Sickinghe, *
James Smobry, *
Nick Dobbs, *
EMP: 90 **EST**: 2019
SALES (est): 4.95MM **Privately Held**
Web: www.oni.bio
SIC: **3826** Microscopes, electron and proton

(P-10281)
PHENOMENEX INC (HQ)
411 Madrid Ave (90501-1430)
PHONE..................................310 212-0555
Farshad Mahjoor, *Pr*
James F O Reilly, *
Frank T Mcfaden, *CFO*
▲ **EMP**: 250 **EST**: 1982
SQ FT: 100,000
SALES (est): 132.13MM
SALES (corp-wide): 31.47B **Publicly Held**
Web: www.phenomenex.com
SIC: **3826** Analytical instruments
PA: Danaher Corporation
2200 Penn Ave Nw Ste 800w
Washington DC
202 828-0850

(P-10282)
QUANTUM DESIGN INC (PA)
Also Called: Quantum Design International
10307 Pacific Center Ct (92121-4340)
PHONE..................................858 481-4400
Greg Degeller, *Pr*
Michael B Simmonds, *
David Schultz, *
Martin Kugler, *
▲ **EMP**: 217 **EST**: 1982
SQ FT: 118,000
SALES (est): 52.1MM
SALES (corp-wide): 52.1MM **Privately
Held**
Web: www.qdusa.com
SIC: **3826** Laser scientific and engineering
instruments

(P-10283)

QUANTUM MAGNETICS LLC

1251 E Dyer Rd Ste 140 (92705-5677)
PHONE...............................714 258-4400
EMP: 609
SIC: 3826 3812 Magnetic resonance
imaging apparatus; Search and navigation
equipment

(P-10284)

QUEST DIAGNOSTICS NICHOLS INST (HQ)

Also Called: Quest Diagnostics
33608 Ortega Hwy (92675-2042)
PHONE...............................949 728-4000
Catherine T Doherty, *CEO*
Nicholas Conti, *
Timothy Sharpe, *
Dan Haemmerle, *
Mark Garawitz, *
EMP: 1000 **EST:** 1971
SQ FT: 240,000
SALES (est): 240.87MM
SALES (corp-wide): 9.88B **Publicly Held**
Web: www.questdiagnostics.com
SIC: 3826 8071 Analytical instruments;
Testing laboratories
PA: Quest Diagnostics Incorporated
500 Plaza Dr Ste G
Secaucus NJ
973 520-2700

(P-10285)

SAFEGUARD ENVIROGROUP INC

153 Lowell Ave (91741-2449)
PHONE...............................626 512-7585
EMP: 24
SALES (est): 2.77MM **Privately Held**
Web: www.safeguardenviro.com
SIC: 3826 Moisture analyzers

(P-10286)

SCREENING SYSTEMS INC (PA)

36 Blackbird Ln (92656-1765)
P.O. Box 3931 (92654-3931)
PHONE...............................949 855-1751
Susan L Baker, *Pr*
Susan Baker, *
EMP: 25 **EST:** 1979
SQ FT: 34,000
SALES (est): 2.42MM
SALES (corp-wide): 2.42MM **Privately Held**
Web: www.scrsys.com
SIC: 3826 3829 Environmental testing
equipment; Measuring and controlling
devices, nec

(P-10287)

SHORE WESTERN MANUFACTURING

19888 Quiroz Ct (91789-2828)
PHONE...............................626 357-3251
Donald Schroeder, *Pr*
Alice Schroeder, *
▲ **EMP:** 34 **EST:** 1967
SALES (est): 4.23MM **Privately Held**
SIC: 3826 Environmental testing equipment

(P-10288)

SINGULAR GENOMICS SYSTEMS INC

Also Called: SINGULAR GENOMICS
3010 Science Park Rd (92121-1102)
PHONE...............................858 333-7830
Andrew Spaventa, *Ch Bd*
David Daly, *Pr*
Dalen Meeter, *VP Fin*

Jorge Velarde, *Senior Vice President Corporate Development & Strategy*
Eli Glezer, *CSO*
EMP: 138 **EST:** 2016
SALES (est): 765K **Privately Held**
Web: www.singulargenomics.com
SIC: 3826 Analytical instruments

(P-10289)

SPRITE INDUSTRIES INCORPORATED

Also Called: Sprite Showers
1791 Railroad St (92878-5011)
PHONE...............................951 735-1015
David K Farley, *Pr*
Sherry Farley, *VP Sls*
Kathleen Farley, *Admn Execs*
Doris Farley, *Sec*
▲ **EMP:** 20 **EST:** 1974
SQ FT: 25,000
SALES (est): 2.41MM **Privately Held**
Web: www.spritewater.com
SIC: 3826 3589 Water testing apparatus;
Water filters and softeners, household type

(P-10290)

TELEDYNE FLIR COML SYSTEMS INC (DH)

6769 Hollister Ave (93117-3001)
PHONE...............................805 964-9797
▲ **EMP:** 350 **EST:** 1996
SALES (est): 253.99MM
SALES (corp-wide): 5.46B **Publicly Held**
Web: www.flir.com
SIC: 3826 Analytical instruments
HQ: Teledyne Flir, Llc
27700 Sw Parkway Ave
Wilsonville OR
503 498-3547

(P-10291)

TELEDYNE HANSON RESEARCH INC

9810 Variel Ave (91311-4316)
PHONE...............................818 882-7266
▲ **EMP:** 31
SIC: 3826 Analytical instruments

(P-10292)

TELEDYNE INSTRUMENTS INC

Teledyne Hanson Research
9810 Variel Ave (91311-4316)
PHONE...............................818 882-7266
Thomas Reslewic, *Mgr*
EMP: 31
SALES (corp-wide): 5.46B **Publicly Held**
Web: www.teledyne.com
SIC: 3826 Analytical instruments
HQ: Teledyne Instruments, Inc.
16830 Chestnut St
City Of Industry CA
626 934-1500

(P-10293)

TELEDYNE REDLAKE MASD LLC (DH)

1049 Camino Dos Rios (91360-2362)
PHONE...............................805 373-4545
Edwin Roks, *Pr*
EMP: 21 **EST:** 1999
SQ FT: 50,000
SALES (est): 13.16MM
SALES (corp-wide): 5.46B **Publicly Held**
SIC: 3826 3861 3822 3812 Analytical
instruments; Photographic equipment and
supplies; Environmental controls; Search
and navigation equipment
HQ: Teledyne Digital Imaging Us, Inc.
700 Technology Park Dr # 2

Billerica MA
978 670-2000

(P-10294)

TELESIS BIO INC

10431 Wateridge Cir Ste 150 (92121)
PHONE...............................858 526-3080
Todd R Nelson, *Pr*
Franklin R Witney, *
Jennifer I Mcnealey, *CFO*
EMP: 226 **EST:** 2011
SQ FT: 28,000
SALES (est): 27.43MM **Privately Held**
Web: www.codexdna.com
SIC: 3826 Analytical instruments

(P-10295)

TERUMO AMERICAS HOLDING INC

Also Called: Cardiovascular Systems
1311 Valencia Ave (92780-6447)
PHONE...............................714 258-8001
EMP: 19
Web: www.terumomedical.com
SIC: 3826 Hemoglobinometers
HQ: Terumo Americas Holding, Inc.
265 Davidson Ave Ste 320
Somerset NJ
732 302-4900

(P-10296)

TETRA TECH EC INC

17885 Von Karman Ave # 500
(92614-5227)
PHONE...............................949 809-5000
Andrew Brack, *Brnch Mgr*
EMP: 50
SALES (corp-wide): 3.5B **Publicly Held**
SIC: 3826 Environmental testing equipment
HQ: Tetra Tech Ec, Inc.
6 Century Dr Ste 3
Parsippany NJ
973 630-8000

(P-10297)

THERMO FISHER SCIENTIFIC INC

5823 Newton Dr (92008-7361)
PHONE...............................781 622-1000
EMP: 32
SALES (corp-wide): 44.91B **Publicly Held**
Web: www.thermofisher.com
SIC: 3826 Analytical instruments
PA: Thermo Fisher Scientific Inc.
168 3rd Ave
Waltham MA
781 622-1000

(P-10298)

THERMO FISHER SCIENTIFIC INC

Also Called: Molecular Bio Products
9389 Waples St (92121-3903)
PHONE...............................858 453-7551
Cesar Ramirez, *Brnch Mgr*
EMP: 70
SALES (corp-wide): 44.91B **Publicly Held**
Web: www.thermofisher.com
SIC: 3826 Analytical instruments
PA: Thermo Fisher Scientific Inc.
168 3rd Ave
Waltham MA
781 622-1000

(P-10299)

THERMO FISHER SCIENTIFIC INC

5791 Van Allen Way (92008-7321)
PHONE...............................760 603-7200

EMP: 26
SALES (corp-wide): 44.91B **Publicly Held**
Web: www.thermofisher.com
SIC: 3826 Analytical instruments
PA: Thermo Fisher Scientific Inc.
168 3rd Ave
Waltham MA
781 622-1000

(P-10300)

THERMO FISHER SCIENTIFIC INC

Also Called: Thermo Fisher Scientific
5781 Van Allen Way (92008-7321)
PHONE...............................760 268-8641
Heather Schultheisz, *Brnch Mgr*
EMP: 38
SALES (corp-wide): 44.91B **Publicly Held**
Web: www.thermofisher.com
SIC: 3826 Analytical instruments
PA: Thermo Fisher Scientific Inc.
168 3rd Ave
Waltham MA
781 622-1000

(P-10301)

THERMO FSHER SCNTIFIC PSG CORP (HQ)

5791 Van Allen Way (92008-7321)
PHONE...............................760 603-7200
Marc N Casper, *Pr*
EMP: 214 **EST:** 2020
SALES (est): 99.19MM
SALES (corp-wide): 44.91B **Publicly Held**
SIC: 3826 Analytical instruments
PA: Thermo Fisher Scientific Inc.
168 3rd Ave
Waltham MA
781 622-1000

(P-10302)

V & P SCIENTIFIC INC

9823 Pacific Heights Blvd Ste T (92121)
PHONE...............................858 455-0643
Patrick H Cleveland, *Pr*
Victoria L Cleveland, *Sec*
▲ **EMP:** 19 **EST:** 1982
SQ FT: 7,000
SALES (est): 3.77MM **Privately Held**
Web: www.vp-sci.com
SIC: 3826 Analytical instruments

(P-10303)

VEECO PROCESS EQUIPMENT INC

Digital Instruments Div
112 Robin Hill Rd (93117-3107)
PHONE...............................805 967-1400
Don Kenia, *CEO*
EMP: 91
Web: www.veeco.com
SIC: 3826 3827 Microscopes, electron and
proton; Optical instruments and lenses
HQ: Veeco Process Equipment Inc.
1 Terminal Dr
Plainview NY

(P-10304)

W R GRACE & CO-CONN

Also Called: Grace Dvson Discovery Sciences
17434 Mojave St (92345-7611)
PHONE...............................760 244-6107
EMP: 18
SALES (corp-wide): 6.27B **Privately Held**
Web: www.grace.com
SIC: 3826 Chromatographic equipment,
laboratory type
HQ: W. R. Grace & Co.-Conn.
7500 Grace Dr

Columbia MD

(P-10305)
WYATT TECHNOLOGY LLC (HQ)
Also Called: Wyatt Technology
6330 Hollister Ave (93117-3115)
PHONE.....................................805 681-9009
Philip J Wyatt, *CEO*
Geofrey K Wyatt, *
Clifford D Wyatt, *
Carolyn Walton, *
EMP: 118 EST: 1982
SQ FT: 30,000
SALES (est): 37.98MM **Publicly Held**
Web: www.wyatt.com
SIC: 3826 Laser scientific and engineering
instruments
PA: Waters Corporation
34 Maple St
Milford MA

3827 Optical Instruments And Lenses

(P-10306)
AAREN SCIENTIFIC INC (DH)
Also Called: Carl Zeiss Meditec,
1040 S Vintage Ave Ste A (91761-3608)
PHONE.....................................909 937-1033
Hans-joachim Miesner, *Pr*
Stevens Chevillotte, *
James Thornton, *
Victor Garcia, *
Jan Willem De Cler, *
▲ **EMP: 94 EST: 2008**
SQ FT: 15,000
SALES (est): 13.22MM **Privately Held**
Web: www.aareninc.com
SIC: 3827 3851 Optical instruments and
lenses; Ophthalmic goods
HQ: Carl Zeiss Meditec, Inc.
5300 Central Pkwy
Dublin CA
925 557-4100

(P-10307)
ABRISA INDUSTRIAL GLASS INC (HQ)
200 Hallock Dr (93060-9646)
P.O. Box 85055 (60680-0851)
PHONE.....................................805 525-4902
Rajiv Ahuja, *CEO*
▲ **EMP: 90 EST: 1980**
SQ FT: 93,000
SALES (est): 25.13MM **Privately Held**
Web: www.abrisatechnologies.com
SIC: 3827 Optical instruments and lenses
PA: Graham Partners, Inc.
3811 West Chester Pike # 200
Newtown Square PA

(P-10308)
ABRISA TECHNOLOGIES
200 Hallock Dr (93060-9646)
P.O. Box 489 (93061-0489)
PHONE.....................................805 525-4902
Blake Fennell, *CEO*
Maartin Ostendorp, *CFO*
EMP: 50 EST: 2013
SALES (est): 9.75MM **Privately Held**
Web: www.abrisatechnologies.com
SIC: 3827 Optical instruments and lenses

(P-10309)
BUK OPTICS INC
Also Called: Precision Glass & Optics
3600 W Moore Ave (92704-6835)
PHONE.....................................714 384-9620
Daniel S Bukaty, *CEO*

Daniel Bukaty Junior, *Pr*
▲ **EMP: 42 EST: 1985**
SQ FT: 25,000
SALES (est): 6.16MM **Privately Held**
Web: www.pgo.com
SIC: 3827 Optical instruments and apparatus

(P-10310)
CARL ZEISS MEDITEC PROD LLC
1040 S Vintage Ave Ste A (91761-3631)
PHONE.....................................877 644-4657
Hans-joachim Miesner, *Pr*
James Thornton, *
Paul Yun, *
Min Qu, *
EMP: 99 EST: 2017
SQ FT: 67,000
SALES (est): 12.59MM **Privately Held**
Web: www.zeiss.com
SIC: 3827 Optical instruments and lenses
HQ: Carl Zeiss Meditec, Inc.
5300 Central Pkwy
Dublin CA
925 557-4100

(P-10311)
COHERENT AEROSPACE & DEF INC
14192 Chambers Rd (92780-6908)
PHONE.....................................714 247-7100
Mark Maiberger, *Genl Mgr*
EMP: 60
SALES (corp-wide): 5.16B **Publicly Held**
Web: www.iiviad.com
SIC: 3827 7389 8748 Optical instruments
and apparatus; Design services; Business
consulting, nec
HQ: Coherent Aerospace & Defense, Inc.
36570 Briggs Rd
Murrieta CA
951 926-2994

(P-10312)
DELTRONIC CORPORATION
Also Called: Hi-Precision Grinding
3900 W Segerstrom Ave (92704-6312)
PHONE.....................................714 545-5800
Robert C Larzelere, *Pr*
Diane Larzelere, *
Sterling Sander, *
▼ **EMP: 73 EST: 1955**
SQ FT: 40,000
SALES (est): 15.24MM **Privately Held**
Web: www.deltronic.com
SIC: 3827 3545 Optical comparators;
Gauges (machine tool accessories)

(P-10313)
ELECTRO-OPTICAL INDUSTRIES LLC
859 Ward Dr (93111-2960)
PHONE.....................................805 964-6701
EMP: 20
SIC: 3827 Optical instruments and apparatus

(P-10314)
ENHANCED VISION SYSTEMS INC (HQ)
15301 Springdale St (92649-1140)
PHONE.....................................800 440-9476
◆ **EMP: 66 EST: 1996**
SALES (est): 21.72MM
SALES (corp-wide): 36.83MM **Privately Held**
Web: www.enhancedvision.com
SIC: 3827 Optical instruments and lenses
PA: Freedom Scientific Blv Group, Llc
17757 Us Highway 19 N # 200

Clearwater FL
727 803-8000

(P-10315)
GMTO CORPORATION
Also Called: Giant Mgllan Tlscope Orgnztion
300 N Lake Ave Fl 14 (91101-4164)
PHONE.....................................626 204-0500
Robert Shelton, *Pr*
Alan Gordon, *
Amy Honbo, *
Doctor Robert N Shelton, *Pr*
Sara Lee Keller, *
▲ **EMP: 70 EST: 2007**
SALES (est): 8.77MM **Privately Held**
Web: www.giantmagellan.org
SIC: 3827 8733 Telescopes: elbow,
panoramic, sighting, fire control, etc.;
Noncommercial research organizations

(P-10316)
GOOCH AND HOUSEGO CAL LLC
5390 Kazuko Ct (93021-1790)
PHONE.....................................805 529-3324
EMP: 80 EST: 2008
SALES (est): 9.52MM
SALES (corp-wide): 146.6MM **Privately Held**
Web: www.gandh.com
SIC: 3827 3823 Optical instruments and
lenses; Process control instruments
PA: Gooch & Housego Plc
Dowlish Ford
Ilminster
146 025-6440

(P-10317)
HOYA HOLDINGS INC
Hoya Corporation USA
425 E Huntington Dr (91016-3632)
PHONE.....................................626 739-5200
Al Benzoni, *VP*
EMP: 97
Web: www.hoya.com
SIC: 3827 Optical instruments and lenses
HQ: Hoya Holdings, Inc.
820 N Mccarthy Blvd # 220
Milpitas CA

(P-10318)
I-COAT COMPANY LLC
12020 Mora Dr Ste 2 (90670-6082)
PHONE.....................................562 941-9989
Arman Bernardi, *CEO*
▲ **EMP: 50 EST: 2003**
SQ FT: 6,000
SALES (est): 10.09MM
SALES (corp-wide): 2.55MM **Privately Held**
Web: www.icoatcompany.com
SIC: 3827 Optical instruments and lenses
HQ: Essilor Of America, Inc.
13555 N Stemmons Fwy
Dallas TX

(P-10319)
IDEX HEALTH & SCIENCE LLC
2051 Palomar Airport Rd Ste 200 (92011-1461)
PHONE.....................................760 438-2131
Blake Fennell, *Brnch Mgr*
EMP: 114
SALES (corp-wide): 3.18B **Publicly Held**
Web: www.idex-hs.com
SIC: 3827 3699 Optical instruments and
lenses; Laser systems and equipment
HQ: Idex Health & Science Llc
600 Park Ct
Rohnert Park CA
707 588-2000

(P-10320)
INFINITE OPTICS INC
1712 Newport Cir Ste F (92705-5118)
PHONE.....................................714 557-2299
Geza Keller, *Pr*
Daniel Houston, *
Joseph Goodhand, *
Steven Crawford, *
Denise Banionis, *
EMP: 24 EST: 2003
SQ FT: 12,860
SALES (est): 4.21MM **Privately Held**
Web: www.infiniteoptics.com
SIC: 3827 Lens coating and grinding
equipment

(P-10321)
INTEVAC PHOTONICS INC
Also Called: Intevac Vision Systems
5909 Sea Lion Pl Ste A (92010-6634)
PHONE.....................................760 476-0339
EMP: 22
SALES (corp-wide): 95.11MM **Publicly Held**
SIC: 3827 Optical instruments and lenses
HQ: Intevac Photonics, Inc.
3560 Bassett St
Santa Clara CA

(P-10322)
IRCAMERA LLC
30 S Calle Cesar Chavez (93103-5652)
PHONE.....................................805 965-9650
EMP: 20 EST: 2011
SALES (est): 5.09MM **Publicly Held**
Web: www.ircameras.com
SIC: 3827 3812 Optical test and inspection
equipment; Infrared object detection
equipment
HQ: Santa Barbara Infrared, Inc.
30 S Calle Cesar Chavez D
Santa Barbara CA
805 965-3669

(P-10323)
LIGHTWORKS OPTICS INC
14192 Chambers Rd (92780-6908)
PHONE.....................................714 247-7100
EMP: 60
Web: www.iiviad.com
SIC: 3827 7389 8748 Optical instruments
and apparatus; Design services; Business
consulting, nec

(P-10324)
LUMINIT LLC (PA)
1850 W 205th St (90501-1526)
PHONE.....................................310 320-1066
Engin Arik, *Managing Member*
Linh Whitaker, *
▲ **EMP: 41 EST: 2005**
SALES (est): 9.47MM **Privately Held**
Web: www.luminitco.com
SIC: 3827 Optical instruments and lenses

(P-10325)
MACHINE VISION PRODUCTS INC (PA)
3270 Corporate Vw Ste D (92081-8570)
PHONE.....................................760 438-1138
George T Ayoub, *CEO*
▲ **EMP: 40 EST: 1993**
SQ FT: 60,000
SALES (est): 10.51MM **Privately Held**
Web: www.visionpro.com
SIC: 3827 7371 3229 Optical instruments
and lenses; Custom computer
programming services; Pressed and blown
glass, nec

(P-10326)
MARK OPTICS INC
1424 E Saint Gertrude Pl (92705-5271)
PHONE...................714 545-6684
Julie A Houser, *Pr*
Judy A Chapman, *CFO*
▲ **EMP:** 20 **EST:** 1994
SALES (est): 2.34MM **Privately Held**
Web: www.markoptics.com
SIC: 3827 Optical elements and assemblies,
except ophthalmic

(P-10327)
MELLES GRIOT INC
2072 Corte Del Nogal (92011-1427)
PHONE...................760 438-2131
Marcus Barber, *Mgr*
EMP: 21 **EST:** 1984
SALES (est): 435.47K **Privately Held**
Web: www.idex-hs.com
SIC: 3827 Optical instruments and lenses

(P-10328)
MELLES GRIOT INC
2051 Palomar Airport Rd # 200
(92011-1462)
PHONE...................760 438-2254
EMP: 85
SIC: 3827 3699 Optical instruments and
lenses; Laser systems and equipment

(P-10329)
NCSTAR INC
18031 Cortney Ct (91748-1203)
PHONE...................866 627-8278
EMP: 18 **EST:** 2014
SALES (est): 4.61MM **Privately Held**
Web: www.ncstar.com
SIC: 3827 Optical instruments and lenses

(P-10330)
**NEWPORT OPTCAL INDS
HLDNGS LTD (PA)**
Also Called: Newport Glassworks
10564 Fern Ave (90680-2648)
P.O. Box 127 (90680-0127)
PHONE...................714 484-8100
Ray Larsen, *Pr*
▲ **EMP:** 20 **EST:** 1979
SQ FT: 12,000
SALES (est): 2.31MM
SALES (corp-wide): 2.31MM **Privately
Held**
SIC: 3827 5049 Lenses, optical: all types
except ophthalmic; Optical goods

(P-10331)
NIPRO OPTICS INC
7 Marconi (92618-2701)
PHONE...................949 215-1151
Tom Gross, *Pr*
EMP: 30 **EST:** 2005
SQ FT: 3,500
SALES (est): 2.88MM **Privately Held**
Web: www.niprooptics.com
SIC: 3827 Reflectors, optical

(P-10332)
OPTICAL CORPORATION (DH)
9731 Topanga Canyon Pl (91311-4135)
PHONE...................818 725-9750
Francis Dominic, *Pr*
EMP: 23 **EST:** 1932
SQ FT: 14,000
SALES (est): 12.07MM **Publicly Held**
Web: www.theopticianllc.com
SIC: 3827 Optical instruments and lenses
HQ: Excel Technology, Inc.
125 Middlesex Tpke

Bedford MA
781 266-5700

(P-10333)
OPTOSIGMA CORPORATION
3210 S Croddy Way (92704-6348)
PHONE...................949 851-5881
EMP: 25 **EST:** 1995
SQ FT: 13,000
SALES (est): 5.08MM **Privately Held**
Web: www.optosigma.com
SIC: 3827 Optical instruments and lenses
PA: Sigma Koki Co.,Ltd.
1-19-9, Midori
Sumida-Ku TKY

(P-10334)
PHOTO RESEARCH INC
Also Called: Photo Research
9731 Topanga Canyon Pl (91311-4135)
PHONE...................818 341-5151
EMP: 24
SIC: 3827 Optical instruments and lenses

(P-10335)
**PVP ADVANCED EO SYSTEMS
INC (DH)**
14312 Franklin Ave Ste 100 (92780-7011)
PHONE...................714 508-2740
Bruce E Ferguson, *CEO*
John Le Blanc, *
▲ **EMP:** 48 **EST:** 1997
SQ FT: 21,000
SALES (est): 14.7MM **Privately Held**
Web: www.advancedeo.systems
SIC: 3827 Optical instruments and apparatus
HQ: Rafael U.S.A., Inc.
6903 Rockledge Dr Ste 850
Bethesda MD

(P-10336)
REYNARD CORPORATION
1020 Calle Sombra (92673-6227)
PHONE...................949 366-8866
Forrest Reynard, *Pr*
Jean Reynard, *
Randy Reynard, *
EMP: 32 **EST:** 1984
SQ FT: 28,000
SALES (est): 7.91MM **Privately Held**
Web: www.reynardcorp.com
SIC: 3827 Mirrors, optical

(P-10337)
**SANTEC CALIFORNIA
CORPORATION**
Also Called: Optotest Corp.
4750 Calle Quetzal (93012-8534)
PHONE...................805 987-1700
Taihei Miyakoshi, *CEO*
Richard Buerli, *Pr*
Ursula Buerli, *Sec*
EMP: 20 **EST:** 2002
SQ FT: 3,000
SALES (est): 7.67MM **Privately Held**
Web: inst.santec.com
SIC: 3827 Optical test and inspection
equipment
PA: Santec Holdings Corporation
5823, Toshiuesaka, Okusa
Komaki AIC

(P-10338)
SCOPE CITY (PA)
2978 Topaz Ave (93063-2168)
P.O. Box 1630 (93062-1630)
PHONE...................805 522-6646
Maurice Sweiss, *CEO*
▲ **EMP:** 35 **EST:** 1980

SQ FT: 35,000
SALES: 4.84MM
SALES (corp-wide): 4.84MM **Privately
Held**
Web: www.scopecity.com
SIC: 3827 Optical instruments and lenses

(P-10339)
SELLERS OPTICAL INC
Also Called: Precision Optical
320 Kalmus Dr (92626-6013)
PHONE...................949 631-6800
Alan Mixon Lambert, *Ch Bd*
Paul Dimeck, *
Rod Randolph, *
Janice Lambert, *
Alan Lambert Junior, *VP*
EMP: 57 **EST:** 1981
SQ FT: 17,000
SALES (est): 11.54MM **Privately Held**
Web: www.precisionoptical.com
SIC: 3827 Optical instruments and apparatus

(P-10340)
SPECTRUM SCIENTIFIC INC
16692 Hale Ave Ste A (92606-5052)
PHONE...................949 260-9900
Daphnie Chakran, *Pr*
EMP: 27 **EST:** 2004
SALES (est): 2.84MM **Privately Held**
Web: www.ssioptics.com
SIC: 3827 Optical instruments and lenses

(P-10341)
SYNERGEYES INC (PA)
Also Called: Synergeyes
2236 Rutherford Rd Ste 115 (92008-8836)
PHONE...................760 476-9410
James K Kirchner, *Pr*
Thomas M Crews, *
David Voris, *
James Gorechner, *
David Fancher, *
▲ **EMP:** 98 **EST:** 2005
SALES (est): 24.15MM
SALES (corp-wide): 24.15MM **Privately
Held**
Web: www.synergeyes.com
SIC: 3827 Optical instruments and lenses

(P-10342)
**TELEDYNE SCENTIFIC IMAGING
LLC**
Also Called: Teledyne Optmum Optcal
Systems
4153 Calle Tesoro (93012-8760)
EMP: 46
SALES (corp-wide): 5.46B **Publicly Held**
Web: www.teledyne-si.com
SIC: 3827 Optical instruments and lenses
HQ: Teledyne Scientific & Imaging, Llc
1049 Camino Dos Rios
Thousand Oaks CA

(P-10343)
TFD INCORPORATED
Also Called: Thin Film Devices
1180 N Tustin Ave (92807-1732)
PHONE...................714 630-7127
Saleem Shaikh, *CEO*
Joy Shaikh, *
▲ **EMP:** 25 **EST:** 1984
SQ FT: 20,000
SALES (est): 4.95MM **Privately Held**
Web: www.tfdinc.com
SIC: 3827 Optical instruments and lenses

(P-10344)
**TOUCH INTERNATIONAL
DISPLAY ENHANCEMENTS
CORP**
11231 Jola Ln (92843-3515)
PHONE...................512 646-0310
EMP: 28
SIC: 3827 Optical instruments and lenses

(P-10345)
UNITED SCOPE LLC (HQ)
Also Called: Amscope
14370 Myford Rd Ste 150 (92606-1016)
PHONE...................714 942-3202
Frank Dai, *CEO*
Andrew Wu, *VP*
Mandy J Liu, *CFO*
Nathaniel Fasnacht, *CFO*
▲ **EMP:** 18 **EST:** 2013
SQ FT: 58,000
SALES (est): 11.57MM
SALES (corp-wide): 333.76MM **Privately
Held**
Web: www.unitedscope.com
SIC: 3827 5049 Optical instruments and
lenses; Optical goods
PA: L Squared Capital Partners Llc
3434 Via Lido Ste 300
Newport Beach CA
949 398-0168

(P-10346)
WINTRISS ENGINEERING CORP
9010 Kenamar Dr Ste 101 (92121-3437)
PHONE...................858 550-7300
Andrew W Ash, *CEO*
Vic Wintriss, *Pr*
Pete Burggren, *Sls Dir*
▲ **EMP:** 23 **EST:** 1986
SQ FT: 11,576
SALES (est): 5.01MM **Privately Held**
Web: www.weco.com
SIC: 3827 Optical test and inspection
equipment

(P-10347)
**Z C & R COATING FOR OPTICS
INC**
1401 Abalone Ave (90501-2889)
PHONE...................310 381-3060
Rajiv Ahuja, *CEO*
EMP: 43 **EST:** 1979
SQ FT: 21,781
SALES (est): 8.64MM **Privately Held**
Web: www.abrisatechnologies.com
SIC: 3827 Lens coating equipment
HQ: Abrisa Industrial Glass, Inc.
200 Hallock Dr
Santa Paula CA
805 525-4902

(P-10348)
ZYGO CORPORATION
Also Called: Zygo Optical Systems
2031 Main St (92614-6509)
PHONE...................714 918-7433
Eric D'Ippolito, *Mgr*
EMP: 22
SALES (corp-wide): 6.15B **Publicly Held**
Web: www.zygo.com
SIC: 3827 Optical instruments and lenses
HQ: Zygo Corporation
21 Laurel Brook Rd
Middlefield CT
860 347-8506

3829 Measuring And Controlling Devices, Nec

(P-10349)
ADVANCED MICRO INSTRUMENTS INC
Also Called: AMI
225 Paularino Ave (92626-3313)
PHONE..............................714 848-5533
EMP: 23 **EST:** 1999
SQ FT: 2,500
SALES (est): 5.38MM **Privately Held**
Web: www.amio2.com
SIC: 3829 Measuring and controlling devices, nec

(P-10350)
AES NDT
1821 W 213th St Ste L (90501-2847)
P.O. Box 239 (90507-0239)
PHONE..............................310 947-6755
Adolfo Velasco, *Brnch Mgr*
EMP: 20
SALES (corp-wide): 2.16MM **Privately Held**
Web: www.aesndt.com
SIC: 3829 Measuring and controlling devices, nec
PA: Aes Ndt
1821 W 213th St Ste L
Torrance CA
310 953-9822

(P-10351)
ALVARADO MANUFACTURING CO INC
12660 Colony Ct (91710-2975)
PHONE..............................909 591-8431
Bret Armatas, *CEO*
◆ **EMP:** 108 **EST:** 1955
SQ FT: 69,000
SALES (est): 23.33MM **Privately Held**
Web: www.alvaradomfg.com
SIC: 3829 Turnstiles, equipped with counting mechanisms

(P-10352)
APPLIED TECHNOLOGIES ASSOC INC (HQ)
Also Called: A T A
3025 Buena Vista Dr (93446-8555)
PHONE..............................805 239-9100
William B Wade, *Pr*
William B Wade, *Pr*
George Walker, *
▲ **EMP:** 127 **EST:** 1981
SALES (est): 32.25MM
SALES (corp-wide): 400.64MM **Privately Held**
Web: secure.scientificdrilling.com
SIC: 3829 1381 Surveying instruments and accessories; Drilling oil and gas wells
PA: Scientific Drilling International, Inc.
16071 Grnspint Pk Dr Ste
Houston TX
281 443-3300

(P-10353)
BARKSDALE INC (DH)
3211 Fruitland Ave (90058-3717)
P.O. Box 58843 (90058-0843)
PHONE..............................323 583-6243
Subramanya Prasad, *Pr*
▲ **EMP:** 148 **EST:** 1946
SQ FT: 115,000
SALES (est): 65.75MM
SALES (corp-wide): 3.37B **Publicly Held**
Web: www.barksdale.com

SIC: 3829 3491 3823 3643 Measuring and controlling devices, nec; Industrial valves; Process control instruments; Current-carrying wiring services
HQ: Crane Controls, Inc.
100 Stamford Pl
Stamford CT

(P-10354)
BEI NORTH AMERICA LLC (DH)
1461 Lawrence Dr (91320-1303)
PHONE..............................805 716-0642
Martha Sullivan, *Pr*
Jeffrey Cote, *VP*
Alison Roelke, *VP*
EMP: 103 **EST:** 2015
SALES (est): 25.19MM
SALES (corp-wide): 4.03B **Privately Held**
SIC: 3829 Measuring and controlling devices, nec
HQ: Custom Sensors & Technologies, Inc.
1461 Lawrence Dr
Thousand Oaks CA
805 716-0322

(P-10355)
BRENNER-FIEDLER & ASSOC INC (PA)
Also Called: B F
4059 Flat Rock Dr (92505-5859)
P.O. Box 7938 (92513-7938)
PHONE..............................562 404-2721
James Kloman, *CEO*
EMP: 39 **EST:** 1957
SQ FT: 28,669
SALES (est): 12.74MM
SALES (corp-wide): 12.74MM **Privately Held**
Web: www.brenner-fiedler.com
SIC: 3829 5085 Accelerometers; Hydraulic and pneumatic pistons and valves

(P-10356)
C J INSTRUMENTS INCORPORATED
Also Called: Pace Transducer Co
P.O. Box 570430 (91357-0430)
PHONE..............................818 996-4131
Charles Tucker, *Pr*
Marshal Canter, *Genl Mgr*
Joe Bisera, *Prin*
EMP: 20 **EST:** 1968
SQ FT: 1,500
SALES (est): 2MM **Privately Held**
SIC: 3829 3641 3679 2819 Pressure transducers; Lead-in wires, electric lamp made from purchased wire; Transducers, electrical; Aluminum oxide

(P-10357)
CALIFORNIA DYNAMICS CORP (PA)
Also Called: Caldyn
20500 Prairie St (91311-6006)
PHONE..............................323 223-3882
Donald Benkert, *Pr*
Adell Benkert, *VP*
▲ **EMP:** 24 **EST:** 1966
SALES (est): 4.97MM
SALES (corp-wide): 4.97MM **Privately Held**
Web: www.caldyn.com
SIC: 3829 Vibration meters, analyzers, and calibrators

(P-10358)
CALIFORNIA SENSOR CORPORATION
2075 Corte Del Nogal Ste P (92011-1413)

PHONE..............................760 438-0525
Adrianus Van De Ven, *CEO*
Ralph Miller, *
David L Byma, *
Robert Destremps, *
Richard Wilkinson, *
EMP: 43 **EST:** 1986
SQ FT: 6,000
SALES (est): 4.21MM **Privately Held**
Web: www.calsense.com
SIC: 3829 5083 Measuring and controlling devices, nec; Irrigation equipment

(P-10359)
CARROS SENSORS SYSTEMS CO LLC (DH)
Also Called: BEI Industrial Encoders
1461 Lawrence Dr (91320-1303)
PHONE..............................805 968-0782
Eric Pilaud, *CEO*
Jean-yves Mouttet, *Treas*
Victor Copeland, *
▲ **EMP:** 125 **EST:** 1990
SALES (est): 98.44MM
SALES (corp-wide): 4.03B **Privately Held**
SIC: 3829 Measuring and controlling devices, nec
HQ: Sensata Technologies, Inc.
529 Pleasant St
Attleboro MA

(P-10360)
DAVIDSON OPTRONICS INC
Also Called: Doi Venture
9087 Arrow Rte Ste 180 (91730-4451)
PHONE..............................626 962-5181
Eugene Dumitrascu, *Ch Bd*
Debra Richards, *Sec*
EMP: 22 **EST:** 1932
SQ FT: 40,000
SALES (est): 9.62MM
SALES (corp-wide): 1.02B **Privately Held**
Web: www.trioptics.com
SIC: 3829 3827 Measuring and controlling devices, nec; Optical instruments and apparatus
HQ: Trioptics Llc
9087 Arrow Rte Ste 180
Rancho Cucamonga CA
626 962-5181

(P-10361)
ECKERT ZEGLER ISOTOPE ✪ PDTS INC (HQ)
Also Called: Isotope Products Lab
24937 Avenue Tibbitts (91355-3427)
PHONE..............................661 309-1010
Frank Yeager, *CEO*
Joe Hathcock, *
Karen Haskins, *
EMP: 45 **EST:** 1967
SQ FT: 40,000
SALES (est): 28.27MM
SALES (corp-wide): 230.84MM **Privately Held**
SIC: 3829 Nuclear radiation and testing apparatus
PA: Eckert & Ziegler Strahlen- Und Medizintechnik Ag
Robert-Rossle-Str. 10
Berlin BE
309410840

(P-10362)
ECKERT ZEGLER ISOTOPE PDTS INC
1800 N Keystone St (91504-3417)
PHONE..............................661 309-1010
Karl Amlauer, *Brnch Mgr*
EMP: 33

SALES (corp-wide): 230.84MM **Privately Held**
SIC: 3829 Nuclear radiation and testing apparatus
HQ: Eckert & Ziegler Isotope Products, Inc.
24937 Avenue Tibbitts
Valencia CA
661 309-1010

(P-10363)
F & D FLORES ENTERPRISES INC
Also Called: Hardware Specialties
761 E Francis St (91761-5514)
PHONE..............................909 975-4853
Frank Flores, *Pr*
▲ **EMP:** 22 **EST:** 1921
SQ FT: 20,000
SALES (est): 2.48MM **Privately Held**
Web: www.hardwarespecialties.com
SIC: 3829 5031 3446 Automatic turnstiles and related apparatus; Lumber, plywood, and millwork; Architectural metalwork

(P-10364)
FAR WEST TECHNOLOGY INC
330 S Kellogg Ave Ste B (93117-3814)
PHONE..............................805 964-3615
John D Rickey, *CEO*
John Handloser Junior, *Ex VP*
▼ **EMP:** 17 **EST:** 1971
SQ FT: 6,100
SALES (est): 2.42MM **Privately Held**
Web: www.fwt.com
SIC: 3829 Nuclear radiation and testing apparatus

(P-10365)
FITBIT INC
Also Called: Fitbit, Inc.
15255 Innovation Dr Ste 200 (92128-3410)
PHONE..............................415 513-1000
EMP: 81
SALES (corp-wide): 282.84B **Publicly Held**
Web: www.fitbit.com
SIC: 3829 Measuring and controlling devices, nec
HQ: Fitbit Llc
199 Fremont St Fl 14
San Francisco CA

(P-10366)
FLOWLINE INC
Also Called: Flowline Liquid Intelligence
10500 Humbolt St (90720-2439)
PHONE..............................562 598-3015
Stephen E Olson, *Ch Bd*
Scott Olson, *
EMP: 25 **EST:** 1990
SQ FT: 8,000
SALES (est): 3.25MM **Privately Held**
Web: www.flowline.com
SIC: 3829 5084 Measuring and controlling devices, nec; Industrial machinery and equipment

(P-10367)
GAMMA SCIENTIFIC INC
Also Called: Road Vista
9925 Carroll Canyon Rd (92131-1105)
PHONE..............................858 635-9008
Kong G Loh, *CEO*
▲ **EMP:** 48 **EST:** 1961
SQ FT: 20,000
SALES (est): 10.91MM **Privately Held**
Web: www.gamma-sci.com

SIC: **3829** 3648 3821 Measuring and controlling devices, nec; Reflectors, for lighting equipment: metal; Calibration tapes, for physical testing machines

(P-10368)
GANTNER INSTRUMENTS INC
402 W Broadway Ste 400 (92101-3554)
PHONE..................888 512-5788
Ravi Shukla, *CEO*
EMP: 50 **EST:** 2010
SALES (est): 9.12MM
SALES (corp-wide): 22.73MM **Privately Held**
Web: www.gantner-instruments.com
SIC: 3829 Measuring and controlling devices, nec
PA: Gantner Instruments Gmbh
　Montafoner StraBe 4
　Schruns
　555 677-4630

(P-10369)
H2SCAN CORPORATION (PA)
27215 Turnberry Ln Unit A (91355-1068)
PHONE..................661 775-9575
Michael Allman, *CEO*
Dennis W Reid, *
EMP: 22 **EST:** 2002
SQ FT: 10,000
SALES (est): 6.07MM
SALES (corp-wide): 6.07MM **Privately Held**
Web: www.h2scan.com
SIC: 3829 Hydrometers, except industrial process type

(P-10370)
HAMILTON SUNDSTRAND SPC SYSTMS
Also Called: Hsssi
960 Overland Ct (91773-1742)
PHONE..................909 288-5300
Edward Francis, *Ex Dir*
Lawrence R Mcnamara, *Pr*
Daniel C Lee, *
Clinton Gardiner, *
Eugene Dougherty, *
EMP: 76 **EST:** 2002
SQ FT: 134,000
SALES (est): 20.27MM
SALES (corp-wide): 67.07B **Publicly Held**
SIC: 3829 Measuring and controlling devices, nec
HQ: Goodrich Corporation
　2730 W Tyvola Rd
　Charlotte NC
　704 423-7000

(P-10371)
HORIBA INTERNATIONAL CORP
9755 Research Dr (92618-4626)
PHONE..................949 250-4811
▲ **EMP:** 930
SIC: 3829 Measuring and controlling devices, nec

(P-10372)
IMAGEGRID INC
5010 Campus Dr (92660-2120)
PHONE..................949 852-1000
EMP: 20 **EST:** 2006
SALES (est): 2.74MM **Privately Held**
SIC: 3829 Thermometers, including digital: clinical

(P-10373)
IMDEX TECHNOLOGY USA LLC
179 Cross St (93401-7597)
PHONE..................805 540-2017

EMP: 20 **EST:** 2011
SALES (est): 9.4MM **Privately Held**
SIC: 3829 8711 Surveying instruments and accessories; Engineering services
PA: Imdex Ltd
　216 Balcatta Rd
　Balcatta WA

(P-10374)
INTERNATIONAL SENSOR TECH
3 Whatney Ste 100 (92618-2836)
PHONE..................949 452-9000
Thomas Jack Chou, *Pr*
Doris Chou, *
Daniel R Chuo, *
Tai Cam Luu, *Sec*
▲ **EMP:** 21 **EST:** 1972
SQ FT: 20,000
SALES (est): 4.68MM **Privately Held**
Web: www.intlsensor.com
SIC: 3829 Gas detectors

(P-10375)
IRROMETER COMPANY INC
Also Called: Watermark
1425 Palmyrita Ave (92507-1600)
PHONE..................951 682-9505
Jeremy Sullivan, *Pr*
Thomas C Penning, *Pr*
Samuel Legget, *Treas*
Jeremy Sullivan, *VP*
EMP: 19 **EST:** 1951
SQ FT: 9,000
SALES (est): 3.64MM **Privately Held**
Web: www.irrometer.com
SIC: 3829 Measuring and controlling devices, nec

(P-10376)
J L SHEPHERD AND ASSOC INC
1010 Arroyo St (91340-1822)
PHONE..................818 898-2361
Dorothy Shepherd, *Pr*
Joseph L Shepherd, *
Diana Shepherd, *
Mary Shepherd, *
Dorothy Shepherd, *Sec*
▲ **EMP:** 27 **EST:** 1967
SQ FT: 15,000
SALES (est): 4.55MM **Privately Held**
Web: www.jlshepherd.com
SIC: 3829 3844 Nuclear radiation and testing apparatus; Irradiation equipment, nec

(P-10377)
KAP MEDICAL
1395 Pico St (92881-3373)
PHONE..................951 340-4360
Raj K Gowda, *Pr*
Dave Lewis, *
Dan Rosenmayer, *
◆ **EMP:** 35 **EST:** 1999
SQ FT: 20,000
SALES (est): 7.42MM **Privately Held**
Web: www.kapmedical.com
SIC: 3829 8711 Medical diagnostic systems, nuclear; Consulting engineer

(P-10378)
KARL STORZ IMAGING INC (HQ)
Also Called: Optronics
1 S Los Carneros Rd (93117-5506)
PHONE..................805 968-5563
Miles Hartfield, *Genl Mgr*
EMP: 344 **EST:** 1984
SQ FT: 105,000
SALES (est): 136.58MM
SALES (corp-wide): 2.24B **Privately Held**
Web: www.karlstorz.com

SIC: **3829** 3841 Measuring and controlling devices, nec; Surgical and medical instruments
PA: Karl Storz Se & Co. Kg
　Dr.-Karl-Storz-Str. 34
　Tuttlingen BW
　74617080

(P-10379)
MEASURE UAS INC
Also Called: Pilatus Unmanned
5862 Bolsa Ave Ste 104 (92649-1169)
PHONE..................714 916-6166
Josh Kornoff, *Mgr*
EMP: 25
SALES (corp-wide): 7.66MM **Privately Held**
Web: www.ageagle.com
SIC: 3829 Surveying instruments and accessories
PA: Measure Uas, Inc.
　1701 Rhode Island Ave Nw
　Washington DC
　202 793-3052

(P-10380)
MEASUREMENT SPECIALTIES INC
9131 Oakdale Ave Ste 170 (91311-6502)
PHONE..................818 701-2750
Robert Simon, *Brnch Mgr*
EMP: 52
Web: www.te.com
SIC: 3829 Measuring and controlling devices, nec
HQ: Measurement Specialties, Inc.
　1000 Lucas Way
　Hampton VA
　757 766-1500

(P-10381)
MECHANIZED SCIENCE SEALS INC
Also Called: Ms Bellows
5322 Mcfadden Ave (92649-1239)
PHONE..................714 898-5602
Jon Hamren, *Pr*
Robin Hamren, *Sec*
Victoria Hamren, *Treas*
EMP: 22 **EST:** 1964
SQ FT: 10,000
SALES (est): 2.35MM **Privately Held**
Web: www.msbellows.com
SIC: 3829 Measuring and controlling devices, nec

(P-10382)
MEGGITT (ORANGE COUNTY) INC (DH)
Also Called: Meggitt Sensing Systems
4 Marconi (92618-2525)
PHONE..................949 493-8181
▲ **EMP:** 264 **EST:** 1947
SALES (est): 101.8MM
SALES (corp-wide): 19.07B **Publicly Held**
SIC: 3829 Vibration meters, analyzers, and calibrators
HQ: Meggitt Limited
　Pilot Way
　Coventry W MIDLANDS
　247 682-6900

(P-10383)
MEPS REAL-TIME INC
Also Called: Intellgard Inventory Solutions
12220 World Trade Dr Ste 210 (92128-3900)
PHONE..................760 448-9500
EMP: 50 **EST:** 2000

SALES (est): 9.23MM **Privately Held**
Web: www.ig.solutions
SIC: 3829 Accelerometers

(P-10384)
MINUS K TECHNOLOGY INC
460 Hindry Ave Ste C (90301-2044)
PHONE..................310 348-9656
David L Platus, *Pr*
Nancee Schwartz, *
EMP: 110 **EST:** 1991
SQ FT: 2,500
SALES (est): 5.25MM **Privately Held**
Web: www.minusk.com
SIC: 3829 Measuring and controlling devices, nec

(P-10385)
NDT SYSTEMS INC
5542 Buckingham Dr Ste A (92649-1158)
PHONE..................714 893-2438
Grant Johnston, *CEO*
Gregory Smith, *Pr*
EMP: 22 **EST:** 1974
SALES (est): 9.85MM
SALES (corp-wide): 5.43B **Privately Held**
Web: www.ndtsystems.com
SIC: 3829 Ultrasonic testing equipment
HQ: Amec Foster Wheeler Limited
　23rd Floor
　London
　203 215-1700

(P-10386)
OMNI OPTICAL PRODUCTS INC (PA)
17282 Eastman (92614)
PHONE..................714 634-5700
Ken Panique, *Pr*
▲ **EMP:** 25 **EST:** 1986
SALES (est): 5.02MM
SALES (corp-wide): 5.02MM **Privately Held**
SIC: 3829 Surveying instruments and accessories

(P-10387)
OPTIVUS PROTON THERAPY INC
1475 Victoria Ct (92408-2831)
P.O. Box 608 (92354-0608)
PHONE..................909 799-8300
Jon W Slater, *CEO*
Daryl L Anderson, *
EMP: 75 **EST:** 1992
SQ FT: 35,000
SALES (est): 15.85MM **Privately Held**
Web: www.optivus.com
SIC: 3829 7371 8742 3699 Nuclear radiation and testing apparatus; Custom computer programming services; Maintenance management consultant; Electrical equipment and supplies, nec

(P-10388)
OPTRON SCIENTIFIC COMPANY INC
Also Called: Technical Associates
7051 Eton Ave (91303-2112)
PHONE..................818 883-6103
Robert Goldstein, *Pr*
EMP: 31 **EST:** 1947
SQ FT: 10,000
SALES (est): 4.98MM **Privately Held**
Web: www.tech-associates.com
SIC: 3829 Nuclear radiation and testing apparatus

▲ = Import ▼ = Export
◆ = Import/Export

(P-10389)

PACIFIC DIVERSIFIED CAPITAL CO

101 Ash St (92101-3017)
PHONE..................619 696-2000
Steve Baum, *Ch Bd*
Thomas Page, *
Henry Huta, *
Michael Lowell, *
EMP: 121 **EST:** 1983
SALES (est): 7.11MM
SALES (corp-wide): 14.44B **Publicly Held**
SIC: 3829 Measuring and controlling devices, nec
HQ: San Diego Gas & Electric Company
   8330 Century Park Ct
   San Diego CA
   619 696-2000

(P-10390)

PROPRIETARY CONTROLS SYSTEMS

Also Called: P C S C
3830 Del Amo Blvd # 102 (90503-2119)
PHONE..................310 303-3600
Masami Kosaka, *Pr*
Robert K Takahashi, *
▲ **EMP:** 45 **EST:** 1983
SALES (est): 5.49MM
SALES (corp-wide): 9.94MM **Privately Held**
SIC: 3829 3669 Measuring and controlling devices, nec; Burglar alarm apparatus, electric
PA: Ttik, Inc.
   3541 Challenger St
   Torrance CA
   310 303-3600

(P-10391)

QUALITY CONTROL SOLUTIONS INC

43339 Business Park Dr Ste 101 (92590-3636)
PHONE..................951 676-1616
EMP: 22 **EST:** 1979
SQ FT: 7,500
SALES (est): 4.6MM **Privately Held**
Web: www.qc-solutions.com
SIC: 3829 5084 Measuring and controlling devices, nec; Instruments and control equipment

(P-10392)

QUANTUM GROUP INC

6827 Nancy Ridge Dr (92121-2233)
PHONE..................858 566-9959
Mark K Goldstein, *Pr*
Ivan Nelson, *Stockholder**
Robert Banach, *
▲ **EMP:** 35 **EST:** 1982
SALES (est): 1.62MM **Privately Held**
Web: store.qginc.com
SIC: 3829 8732 7389 Fire detector systems, non-electric; Research services, except laboratory; Fire protection service other than forestry or public

(P-10393)

RADCAL CORPORATION

Also Called: M D H
426 W Duarte Rd (91016-4544)
PHONE..................626 357-7921
Curt Harkless, *CEO*
Kenneth Mettler, *
J Howard Marshall Iii, *Ch Bd*
Timothy M Harrington, *
Patrick Pyers, *
▲ **EMP:** 35 **EST:** 1973
SQ FT: 10,000
SALES (est): 8.19MM **Privately Held**
Web: www.radcal.com
SIC: 3829 Nuclear radiation and testing apparatus

(P-10394)

REDLINE DETECTION LLC (PA)

828 W Taft Ave (92865-4232)
PHONE..................714 579-6961
Zachary Parker, *CEO*
▲ **EMP:** 23 **EST:** 2004
SQ FT: 21,000
SALES (est): 14.62MM
SALES (corp-wide): 14.62MM **Privately Held**
Web: www.redlinedetection.com
SIC: 3829 Liquid leak detection equipment

(P-10395)

SEMCO

1495 S Gage St (92408-2835)
PHONE..................909 799-9666
Shawn Martin, *Owner*
▲ **EMP:** 25 **EST:** 1994
SQ FT: 5,400
SALES (est): 2.35MM **Privately Held**
Web: www.semco.com
SIC: 3829 3599 Physical property testing equipment; Machine shop, jobbing and repair

(P-10396)

SKF CONDITION MONITORING INC (DH)

Also Called: SKF Aptitude Exchange
9444 Balboa Ave Ste 150 (92123-4377)
PHONE..................858 496-3400
Mark Mcginn, *CEO*
EMP: 120 **EST:** 1983
SQ FT: 31,000
SALES (est): 46.03MM
SALES (corp-wide): 9.24B **Privately Held**
SIC: 3829 Vibration meters, analyzers, and calibrators
HQ: Skf Usa Inc.
   890 Forty Foot Rd
   Lansdale PA
   267 436-6000

(P-10397)

SOILMOISTURE EQUIPMENT CORP

801 S Kellogg Ave (93117-3886)
P.O. Box 30025 (93130-0025)
PHONE..................805 964-3525
Whitney Skaling, *CEO*
Percy E Skaling, *
Jan Skaling, *
Kenneth Macaulay, *
▲ **EMP:** 23 **EST:** 1950
SQ FT: 14,000
SALES (est): 4.86MM **Privately Held**
Web: www.soilmoisture.com
SIC: 3829 Measuring and controlling devices, nec

(P-10398)

SPECTRAL LABS INCORPORATED

Also Called: Spectral Labs
15920 Bernardo Center Dr (92127-1828)
PHONE..................858 451-0540
James H Winso, *Pr*
Eric Ackermann, *VP*
John Rolando, *Stockholder*
James Adams, *Proj Mgr*
EMP: 20 **EST:** 2008
SQ FT: 2,000
SALES (est): 3.32MM **Privately Held**
Web: www.spectrallabs.com
SIC: 3829 Measuring and controlling devices, nec

(P-10399)

STRUCTURAL DIAGNOSTICS INC

Also Called: S D I
650 Via Alondra (93012-8733)
PHONE..................805 987-7755
EMP: 33 **EST:** 1994
SQ FT: 30,000
SALES (est): 4MM **Privately Held**
Web: www.sdindt.com
SIC: 3829 Measuring and controlling devices, nec

(P-10400)

SYSTEMS INTEGRATED LLC

2200 N Glassell St (92865-2702)
PHONE..................714 998-0900
John Holbrook, *Dir*
EMP: 19 **EST:** 1999
SQ FT: 7,000
SALES (est): 992.15K **Privately Held**
Web: www.systemsintegrated.com
SIC: 3829 Measuring and controlling devices, nec

(P-10401)

TELEDYNE INSTRUMENTS INC

Also Called: Teledyne API
9970 Carroll Canyon Rd Ste A (92131-1106)
PHONE..................619 239-5959
Jeff Franks, *Brnch Mgr*
EMP: 100
SALES (corp-wide): 5.46B **Publicly Held**
Web: www.teledyne-api.com
SIC: 3829 3823 Measuring and controlling devices, nec; Process control instruments
HQ: Teledyne Instruments, Inc.
   16830 Chestnut St
   City Of Industry CA
   626 934-1500

(P-10402)

TELEDYNE INSTRUMENTS INC

Teledyne Advnced Plltion Instr
9970 Carroll Canyon Rd (92131-1106)
PHONE..................858 657-9800
Robert Mehrabian, *CEO*
EMP: 61
SALES (corp-wide): 5.46B **Publicly Held**
Web: www.teledyne.com
SIC: 3829 Measuring and controlling devices, nec
HQ: Teledyne Instruments, Inc.
   16830 Chestnut St
   City Of Industry CA
   626 934-1500

(P-10403)

TELEDYNE INSTRUMENTS INC

Also Called: Teledyne Analytical Instrs
16830 Chestnut St (91748-1017)
PHONE..................626 934-1500
Tom Compas, *Brnch Mgr*
EMP: 170
SQ FT: 70,000
SALES (corp-wide): 5.46B **Publicly Held**
Web: www.teledyne-ai.com
SIC: 3829 Measuring and controlling devices, nec
HQ: Teledyne Instruments, Inc.
   16830 Chestnut St
   City Of Industry CA
   626 934-1500

(P-10404)

TEMPTRON ENGINEERING INC

7823 Deering Ave (91304-5006)
PHONE..................818 346-4900
Edward Skei, *Pr*
Beverly Skei, *
EMP: 35 **EST:** 1971
SQ FT: 13,000
SALES (est): 2.92MM **Privately Held**
Web: www.temptronengineeringinc.com
SIC: 3829 3769 3823 Measuring and controlling devices, nec; Space vehicle equipment, nec; Temperature instruments: industrial process type

(P-10405)

TRANSDUCER TECHNIQUES LLC

42480 Rio Nedo (92590-3734)
PHONE..................951 719-3965
Randy A Baker, *Managing Member*
EMP: 37 **EST:** 1978
SQ FT: 27,000
SALES (est): 8.4MM **Privately Held**
Web: www.transducertechniques.com
SIC: 3829 Measuring and controlling devices, nec

(P-10406)

VALIDYNE ENGINEERING CORP

8626 Wilbur Ave (91324-4438)
P.O. Box 8626 (91327-8626)
PHONE..................818 886-8488
▲ **EMP:** 21 **EST:** 1968
SALES (est): 3.27MM **Privately Held**
Web: www.validyne.com
SIC: 3829 3669 3823 Pressure transducers; Signaling apparatus, electric; Process control instruments

(P-10407)

VANTARI MEDICAL LLC

15440 Laguna Canyon Rd # 26 (92618-2138)
PHONE..................949 783-5300
Nick Arroyo, *CEO*
Phil Lamb, *CFO*
EMP: 32 **EST:** 2015
SALES (est): 621.75K **Privately Held**
SIC: 3829 Medical diagnostic systems, nuclear

3841 Surgical And Medical Instruments

(P-10408)

AALTO SCIENTIFIC LTD

1959 Kellogg Ave (92008-6582)
PHONE..................800 748-6674
R Reynolds, *Director of Information*
EMP: 25 **EST:** 2018
SALES (est): 1.19MM **Privately Held**
Web: www.aaltoscientific.com
SIC: 3841 Surgical and medical instruments

(P-10409)

ABBOTT RAPID DX NORTH AMER LLC

Also Called: Abbott Rapid Diagnos
5995 Pacific Center Blvd (92121-6309)
PHONE..................858 805-3804
Arnold Valdez, *Prin*
EMP: 39
SALES (corp-wide): 43.65B **Publicly Held**
SIC: 3841 Surgical and medical instruments
HQ: Abbott Rapid Dx North America, Llc
   30 S Keller Rd Ste 100
   Orlando FL

PRODUCTS & SVCS

(P-10410)
ABBOTT VASCULAR INC
Also Called: Abbott Vascular
30590 Cochise Cir (92563-2501)
P.O. Box 3020 (60064-9320)
PHONE..................................408 845-3186
EMP: 568
SALES (corp-wide): 43.65B **Publicly Held**
Web: www.abbott.com
SIC: 3841 Surgical instruments and
apparatus
HQ: Abbott Vascular Inc.
3200 Lakeside Dr
Santa Clara CA
408 845-3000

(P-10411)
ABBOTT VASCULAR INC
42301 Zevo Dr Ste D (92590-3731)
P.O. Box 9018 (92589-9018)
PHONE..................................951 914-2400
Rhonda Reddick, *Mgr*
EMP: 665
SALES (corp-wide): 43.65B **Publicly Held**
Web: www.cardiovascular.abbott
SIC: 3841 Catheters
HQ: Abbott Vascular Inc.
3200 Lakeside Dr
Santa Clara CA
408 845-3000

(P-10412)
ACCESS SCIENTIFIC INC
1042 N El Camino Real Ste B-349 (92024)
PHONE..................................858 354-8761
EMP: 18 **EST:** 2004
SQ FT: 2,700
SALES (est): 756.46K **Privately Held**
Web: www.smiths-medical.com
SIC: 3841 Surgical and medical instruments

(P-10413)
ACCLARENT INC
31 Technology Dr Ste 200 (92618-2302)
PHONE..................................650 687-5888
David Shepherd, *Pr*
Cristina Todasco, *
EMP: 400 **EST:** 2004
SALES (est): 97.46MM
SALES (corp-wide): 94.94B **Publicly Held**
Web: www.acclarent.com
SIC: 3841 Surgical and medical instruments
HQ: Ethicon Inc.
1000 Route 202
Raritan NJ
800 384-4266

(P-10414)
ACCRIVA DGNOSTICS
HOLDINGS INC (DH)
Also Called: Itc Nexus Holding Company
6260 Sequence Dr (92121-4358)
PHONE..................................858 404-8203
Scott Cramer, *CEO*
Greg Tibbitts, *CFO*
Tom Whalen, *CSO*
EMP: 350 **EST:** 2010
SALES (est): 92.51MM **Privately Held**
Web: www.werfen.com
SIC: 3841 2835 6719 Diagnostic apparatus,
medical; Blood derivative diagnostic agents
; Investment holding companies, except
banks
HQ: Instrumentation Laboratory Company
180 Hartwell Rd
Bedford MA

(P-10415)
ACI MEDICAL LLC
1857 Diamond St Ste A (92078-5129)
PHONE..................................760 744-4400
EMP: 47 **EST:** 1984
SALES (est): 5.69MM **Privately Held**
Web: www.acimedical.com
SIC: 3841 Diagnostic apparatus, medical

(P-10416)
ACUTUS MEDICAL INC
Also Called: ACUTUS MEDICAL
2210 Faraday Ave Ste 100 (92008-7225)
PHONE..................................442 232-6080
David Roman, *Pr*
R Scott Huennekens, *
Takeo Mukai, *Sr VP*
Steven Mcquillan, *Sr VP*
EMP: 338 **EST:** 2011
SQ FT: 50,800
SALES (est): 16.36MM **Privately Held**
Web: www.acutusmedical.com
SIC: 3841 Surgical and medical instruments

(P-10417)
ADVANCED STERLIZATION (HQ)
Also Called: A S P
33 Technology Dr (92618-2346)
PHONE..................................800 595-0200
EMP: 104 **EST:** 1991
SALES (est): 21.23MM
SALES (corp-wide): 5.83B **Publicly Held**
Web: www.asp.com
SIC: 3841 Surgical and medical instruments
PA: Fortive Corporation
6920 Seaway Blvd
Everett WA
425 446-5000

(P-10418)
AJINOMOTO ALTHEA INC (HQ)
Also Called: Ajinomoto Bio-Pharma Services
11040 Roselle St (92121-1205)
PHONE..................................858 882-0123
David Enloe Junior, *Pr*
Martha J Demski, *
Chris Duffy, *
Ej Brandreth, *Regional*
Jack Wright, *
EMP: 164 **EST:** 1998
SALES (est): 88.12MM **Privately Held**
Web: www.ajibio-pharma.com
SIC: 3841 2836 Hypodermic needles and
syringes; Coagulation products
PA: Ajinomoto Co., Inc.
1-15-1, Kyobashi
Chuo-Ku TKY

(P-10419)
ALCON LENSX INC (DH)
Also Called: Alcon
15800 Alton Pkwy (92618-3818)
PHONE..................................949 753-1393
Kevin J Buehler, *CEO*
Elaine Whitbeck, *CLO*
EMP: 99 **EST:** 2006
SQ FT: 20,000
SALES (est): 34.47MM **Privately Held**
SIC: 3841 Surgical lasers
HQ: Alcon, Inc.
1132 Ferris Rd
Amelia OH
513 722-1037

(P-10420)
ALCON RESEARCH LTD
Also Called: ALCON RESEARCH, LTD.
15800 Alton Pkwy (92618-3818)
PHONE..................................949 387-2142
EMP: 54

Web: www.alcon.com
SIC: 3841 Surgical instruments and
apparatus
HQ: Alcon Research, Llc
6201 South Fwy
Fort Worth TX
817 551-4555

(P-10421)
ALCON VISION LLC
24514 Sunshine Dr (92677-7826)
PHONE..................................949 753-6218
EMP: 348
Web: www.alcon.com
SIC: 3841 Surgical and medical instruments
HQ: Alcon Vision, Llc
6201 South Fwy
Fort Worth TX
817 293-0450

(P-10422)
ALCON VISION LLC
Also Called: Alcon Surgical
15800 Alton Pkwy (92618-3818)
P.O. Box 19587 (92623-9587)
PHONE..................................949 753-6488
Kenneth Lickel, *Mgr*
EMP: 600
SQ FT: 32,000
Web: www.alcon.com
SIC: 3841 3851 5049 Surgical and medical
instruments; Ophthalmic goods; Optical
goods
HQ: Alcon Vision, Llc
6201 South Fwy
Fort Worth TX
817 293-0450

(P-10423)
ALL MANUFACTURERS INC
Also Called: Allied Harbor Aerospace Fas
1831 Commerce St Ste 101 (92878-5026)
PHONE..................................951 280-4200
Jon R Gerwin, *CEO*
Ron Gerwin, *
EMP: 197 **EST:** 1993
SALES (est): 14.53MM **Privately Held**
Web: www.allied1.com
SIC: 3841 3694 Surgical and medical
instruments; Motors, starting: automotive
and aircraft

(P-10424)
ALLIANCE MEDICAL
PRODUCTS INC
Also Called: Siegfried Irvine
9292 Jeronimo Rd (92618-1905)
PHONE..................................949 664-9616
EMP: 45
Web: www.siegfried.ch
SIC: 3841 Medical instruments and
equipment, blood and bone work
HQ: Alliance Medical Products, Inc.
9342 Jeronimo Rd
Irvine CA
949 768-4690

(P-10425)
ALLIANCE MEDICAL
PRODUCTS INC (DH)
Also Called: Siegfried Irvine
9342 Jeronimo Rd (92618-1903)
PHONE..................................949 768-4690
Robert Hughes, *CEO*
Brian Jones, *
Frank Pham, *
▲ **EMP:** 41 **EST:** 2001
SQ FT: 55,000
SALES (est): 45.27MM **Privately Held**
Web: www.siegfried.ch

SIC: 3841 7819 Medical instruments and
equipment, blood and bone work;
Laboratory service, motion picture
HQ: Siegfried Usa Holding , Inc.
33 Industrial Park Rd
Pennsville NJ
856 678-3601

(P-10426)
ALPHATEC HOLDINGS INC (PA)
Also Called: Alphatec
1950 Camino Vida Roble (92008-6505)
PHONE..................................760 431-9286
Patrick S Miles, *Pr*
J Todd Koning, *Ex VP*
Eric Dasso, *ADJUNCTIVE
TECHNOLOGIES*
Kelli M Howell, *Clinical Vice President*
Craig E Hunsaker, *PEOPLE CULTURE*
EMP: 231 **EST:** 1990
SQ FT: 121,541
SALES (est): 350.87MM **Publicly Held**
Web: www.atecspine.com
SIC: 3841 Surgical and medical instruments

(P-10427)
AMADA WELD TECH INC
245 E El Norte St (91016-4828)
PHONE..................................626 303-5676
EMP: 40
Web: www.amadaweldtech.com
SIC: 3841 Surgical and medical instruments
HQ: Amada Weld Tech Inc.
1820 S Myrtle Ave
Monrovia CA

(P-10428)
AMEDITECH INC
9940 Mesa Rim Rd (92121-2910)
PHONE..................................858 535-1968
Robert Joel, *Prin*
▲ **EMP:** 118 **EST:** 1999
SQ FT: 47,000
SALES (est): 29.54MM
SALES (corp-wide): 43.65B **Publicly Held**
SIC: 3841 Medical instruments and
equipment, blood and bone work
HQ: Alere Inc.
51 Sawyer Rd Ste 200
Waltham MA
781 647-3900

(P-10429)
AMO USA INC
1700 E Saint Andrew Pl (92705-4933)
PHONE..................................714 247-8200
Tom Frinzi, *Pr*
EMP: 200 **EST:** 2002
SQ FT: 100,000
SALES (est): 54.13MM
SALES (corp-wide): 94.94B **Publicly Held**
SIC: 3841 3845 Surgical and medical
instruments; Laser systems and equipment,
medical
HQ: Johnson & Johnson Surgical Vision,
Inc.
31 Technology Dr Bldg 29a
Irvine CA
949 581-5799

(P-10430)
APEX MEDICAL
TECHNOLOGIES INC
10064 Mesa Ridge Ct Ste 202
(92121-2948)
PHONE..................................858 535-0012
▲ **EMP:** 20 **EST:** 1985
SALES (est): 2.35MM **Privately Held**
Web: www.apexmedtech.com

SIC: **3841** 8731 Surgical and medical instruments; Medical research, commercial

(P-10431)
APPLIED CARDIAC SYSTEMS INC
1 Hughes Ste A (92618-2021)
PHONE...................949 855-9366
Loren A Manera, *CEO*
Tricia Meads, *
Susan Marcus, *
Robert Wilks, *
▲ **EMP:** 64 **EST:** 1981
SQ FT: 18,000
SALES (est): 8.82MM **Privately Held**
Web: www.acsd4u.com
SIC: 3841 Diagnostic apparatus, medical

(P-10432)
APPLIED MANUFACTURING LLC
22872 Avenida Empresa (92688-2650)
PHONE...................949 713-8000
Tom Wachli, *Pr*
EMP: 1200 **EST:** 2017
SALES (est): 116.16MM
SALES (corp-wide): 699.84MM **Privately Held**
Web: www.appliedmed.com
SIC: 3841 Surgical and medical instruments
HQ: Applied Medical Resources Corporation
22872 Avenida Empresa
Rcho Sta Marg CA
949 713-8000

(P-10433)
APPLIED MEDICAL CORPORATION (PA)
Also Called: Applied Medical Resources
22872 Avenida Empresa (92688-2650)
PHONE...................949 713-8000
Said Hilal, *CEO*
EMP: 247 **EST:** 1987
SALES (est): 699.84MM
SALES (corp-wide): 699.84MM **Privately Held**
Web: www.appliedmedical.com
SIC: 3841 Surgical and medical instruments

(P-10434)
APPLIED MEDICAL CORPORATION
30152 Aventura (92688-2019)
PHONE...................949 713-2174
Jeff Bechtold, *Brnch Mgr*
EMP: 1269
SALES (corp-wide): 699.84MM **Privately Held**
Web: www.appliedmedical.com
SIC: 3841 Surgical and medical instruments
PA: Applied Medical Corporation
22872 Avenida Empresa
Rcho Sta Marg CA
949 713-8000

(P-10435)
APPLIED MEDICAL DIST CORP
22872 Avenida Empresa (92688-2650)
PHONE...................949 713-8000
Said Hilal, *CEO*
Stephen Stanley, *
EMP: 700 **EST:** 1998
SALES (est): 108.5MM
SALES (corp-wide): 699.84MM **Privately Held**
Web: www.appliedmedical.com
SIC: 3841 Surgical and medical instruments

HQ: Applied Medical Resources Corporation
22872 Avenida Empresa
Rcho Sta Marg CA
949 713-8000

(P-10436)
APPLIED MEDICAL RESOURCES
30152 Esperanza (92688-2120)
PHONE...................949 459-1042
EMP: 24 **EST:** 2013
SALES (est): 951.85K **Privately Held**
Web: www.appliedmedical.com
SIC: 3841 Surgical and medical instruments

(P-10437)
APPLIED MEDICAL RESOURCES CORP (HQ)
Also Called: Applied Medical Distribution
22872 Avenida Empresa (92688-2650)
PHONE...................949 713-8000
Said S Hilal, *Pr*
Stephen E Stanley, *Group President*
Nabil Hilal, *Group President*
Samir Tall, *
Gary Johnson, *Group President*
▲ **EMP:** 51 **EST:** 1987
SQ FT: 800,000
SALES (est): 649.89MM
SALES (corp-wide): 699.84MM **Privately Held**
Web: www.appliedmedical.com
SIC: 3841 Surgical and medical instruments
PA: Applied Medical Corporation
22872 Avenida Empresa
Rcho Sta Marg CA
949 713-8000

(P-10438)
APRICOT DESIGNS INC
677 Arrow Grand Cir (91722-2146)
PHONE...................626 966-3299
▲ **EMP:** 66 **EST:** 1989
SQ FT: 6,200
SALES (est): 10.79MM **Privately Held**
Web: www.sptlabtech.com
SIC: 3841 Surgical and medical instruments
HQ: Spt Labtech Limited
Cambridge Road
Royston
122 362-7555

(P-10439)
ARCH MED SLTONS - ESCNDIDO LLC
950 Borra Pl (92029-2011)
PHONE...................760 432-9785
Eli Crotzer, *CEO*
EMP: 209 **EST:** 2020
SALES (est): 2.29MM
SALES (corp-wide): 24.46MM **Privately Held**
SIC: 3841 Surgical and medical instruments
PA: Arch Cutting Tools, Llc
2600 S Telegraph Rd
Bloomfield Hills MI
734 266-6900

(P-10440)
ARTHREX INC
Also Called: Arthrex California Technology
460 Ward Dr Ste C (93111-2351)
PHONE...................805 964-8104
Bob Weber, *Brnch Mgr*
EMP: 163
SALES (corp-wide): 501.69MM **Privately Held**
Web: www.arthrex.com
SIC: 3841 Diagnostic apparatus, medical
PA: Arthrex, Inc.
1370 Creekside Blvd

Naples FL
239 643-5553

(P-10441)
ASPEN MEDICAL PRODUCTS LLC
6481 Oak Cyn (92618-5202)
P.O. Box 22116 (91185-0001)
PHONE...................949 681-0200
Jim Cloar, *Pr*
▲ **EMP:** 70 **EST:** 1993
SQ FT: 52,000
SALES (est): 28.19MM
SALES (corp-wide): 182.7MM **Privately Held**
Web: www.aspenmp.com
SIC: 3841 Surgical and medical instruments
PA: Cogr, Inc.
140 E 45th St Fl 43
New York NY
212 370-5600

(P-10442)
AVITA THERAPEUTICS INC
28159 Avenue Stanford Ste 220 (91355)
PHONE...................661 367-9170
Kathy Mcgee, *COO*
EMP: 18 **EST:** 2020
SALES (est): 99.59K **Privately Held**
SIC: 3841 Surgical and medical instruments

(P-10443)
AXIOM MEDICAL INCORPORATED
19320 Van Ness Ave (90501-1103)
PHONE...................310 533-9020
EMP: 40 **EST:** 1976
SALES (est): 5.01MM **Privately Held**
Web: www.axiommed.com
SIC: 3841 3842 Surgical and medical instruments; Surgical appliances and supplies

(P-10444)
B BRAUN MEDICAL INC
2525 Mcgaw Ave (92614-5841)
P.O. Box 19791 (92623-9791)
PHONE...................610 691-5400
Keith Klaes, *Mgr*
EMP: 1300
SALES (corp-wide): 2.67MM **Privately Held**
Web: www.bbraunusa.com
SIC: 3841 Catheters
HQ: B. Braun Medical Inc.
824 12th Ave
Bethlehem PA
610 691-5400

(P-10445)
B BRAUN MEDICAL INC
Also Called: B Braun Medical
2206 Alton Pkwy (92606-5000)
PHONE...................949 660-3151
EMP: 34
SALES (corp-wide): 2.67MM **Privately Held**
Web: www.bbraunusa.com
SIC: 3841 Surgical and medical instruments
HQ: B. Braun Medical Inc.
824 12th Ave
Bethlehem PA
610 691-5400

(P-10446)
B BRAUN MEDICAL INC
2488 Alton Pkwy (92606-5037)
PHONE...................949 660-2581
EMP: 28

SALES (corp-wide): 2.67MM **Privately Held**
Web: www.bbraunusa.com
SIC: 3841 Surgical and medical instruments
HQ: B. Braun Medical Inc.
824 12th Ave
Bethlehem PA
610 691-5400

(P-10447)
B BRAUN MEDICAL INC
1151 Mildred St Ste B (91761-3504)
PHONE...................909 906-7575
EMP: 143
SALES (corp-wide): 2.67MM **Privately Held**
Web: www.bbraunusa.com
SIC: 3841 Surgical and medical instruments
HQ: B. Braun Medical Inc.
824 12th Ave
Bethlehem PA
610 691-5400

(P-10448)
BAXALTA US INC
1700 Rancho Conejo Blvd (91320-1424)
PHONE...................805 498-8664
Paul Marshall, *Mgr*
EMP: 466
SIC: 3841 2835 2389 3842 Surgical and medical instruments; Blood derivative diagnostic agents; Hospital gowns; Surgical appliances and supplies
HQ: Baxalta Us Inc.
1200 Lakeside Dr
Bannockburn IL
224 948-2000

(P-10449)
BAXTER HEALTHCARE CORPORATION
Also Called: Baxter Medication Delivery
17511 Armstrong Ave (92614-5725)
PHONE...................949 474-6301
Michael Mussallem, *Mgr*
EMP: 250
SALES (corp-wide): 15.11B **Publicly Held**
Web: www.baxter.com
SIC: 3841 Surgical and medical instruments
HQ: Baxter Healthcare Corporation
1 Baxter Pkwy
Deerfield IL
224 948-2000

(P-10450)
BEAUTY HEALTH COMPANY (PA)
2165 E Spring St (90806-2114)
PHONE...................800 603-4996
Andrew Stanleick, *Pr*
Brenton L Saunders, *
Michael Monahan, *CFO*
Brad Hauser, *COO*
Daniel Watson, *CRO*
EMP: 350 **EST:** 1997
SQ FT: 23,000
SALES (est): 365.88MM
SALES (corp-wide): 365.88MM **Publicly Held**
SIC: 3841 Surgical and medical instruments

(P-10451)
BECKMAN COULTER INC
Beckman Coulter Diagnostics
250 S Kraemer Blvd (92821-6232)
P.O. Box 8000 (92822-8000)
PHONE...................818 970-2161
Albert Ziegler, *Mgr*
EMP: 200
SALES (corp-wide): 31.47B **Publicly Held**
Web: www.beckmancoulter.com

SIC: 3841 3821 Surgical and medical instruments; Clinical laboratory instruments, except medical and dental
HQ: Beckman Coulter, Inc.
250 S Kraemer Blvd
Brea CA
714 993-5321

(P-10452)
BECTON DICKINSON AND COMPANY
Also Called: Care Fusion Products
3750 Torrey View Ct (92130-2622)
PHONE................................888 876-4287
EMP: 68
SALES (corp-wide): 19.37B **Publicly Held**
Web: www.bd.com
SIC: 3841 Medical instruments and equipment, blood and bone work
PA: Becton, Dickinson And Company
1 Becton Dr
Franklin Lakes NJ
201 847-6800

(P-10453)
BIO-MEDICAL DEVICES INC
Also Called: Maxair Systems
17171 Daimler St (92614-5508)
PHONE................................949 752-9642
Nick Herbert, *Pr*
Alan Davidner, *Stockholder**
Harry N Herbert, *
▲ **EMP:** 37 **EST:** 1988
SQ FT: 40,000
SALES (est): 9.52MM **Privately Held**
Web: www.maxair-systems.com
SIC: 3841 2353 Surgical and medical instruments; Hats, caps, and millinery

(P-10454)
BIO-MEDICAL DEVICES INTL INC
17171 Daimler St (92614-5508)
PHONE................................949 752-9642
Nicholas Herbert, *Pr*
Allan Schultz, *
EMP: 25 **EST:** 1998
SALES (est): 5.35MM **Privately Held**
Web: www.maxair-systems.com
SIC: 3841 2353 Surgical and medical instruments; Hats, caps, and millinery

(P-10455)
BIOFILM INC
3225 Executive Rdg (92081-8527)
PHONE................................760 727-9030
Lisa A O'carroll, *CEO*
Daniel Wray, *
Mike Adams, *
Lois Wray, *
Natalie Garcia, *
EMP: 54 **EST:** 1991
SQ FT: 61,000
SALES (est): 13.28MM **Privately Held**
Web: www.astroglide.com
SIC: 3841 Surgical and medical instruments

(P-10456)
BIOGENERAL INC
9925 Mesa Rim Rd (92121-2911)
PHONE................................858 453-4451
Victor Wild, *Pr*
▲ **EMP:** 30 **EST:** 1986
SALES (est): 4.55MM **Privately Held**
Web: www.biogeneral.com
SIC: 3841 Surgical and medical instruments

(P-10457)
BIOJECT INC
6769 Mesa Ridge Rd Ste 99 (92121-2995)
PHONE................................503 692-8001

EMP: 20
SIC: 3841 Surgical instruments and apparatus

(P-10458)
BIOPLATE INC
570 S Melrose St (92870-6327)
PHONE................................310 815-2100
Thomas Hopson, *Pr*
Tadeusz Wellisz, *Ch Bd*
EMP: 21 **EST:** 1994
SALES (est): 5.03MM **Privately Held**
Web: www.bioplate.com
SIC: 3841 Surgical and medical instruments

(P-10459)
BIOSEAL
167 W Orangethorpe Ave (92870-6922)
PHONE................................714 528-4695
Bill Runion, *Pr*
Robert C Kopple, *
Jeff Myers, *
▲ **EMP:** 40 **EST:** 1988
SQ FT: 8,500
SALES (est): 9.44MM **Privately Held**
Web: www.biosealnet.com
SIC: 3841 5047 Surgical and medical instruments; Hospital equipment and furniture

(P-10460)
BOLT MEDICAL INC
5993 Avenida Encinas Ste 100 (92008-4459)
PHONE................................949 287-3207
Keegan Harper, *CEO*
Katie Walker, *
EMP: 58 **EST:** 2019
SALES (est): 4.89MM **Privately Held**
SIC: 3841 8731 Surgical and medical instruments; Biological research

(P-10461)
BOSTON SCIENTIFIC CORPORATION
Also Called: Boston Scientific - Valencia
25155 Rye Canyon Loop (91355-5004)
PHONE................................800 678-2575
Phill Tarves, *Mgr*
EMP: 45
SALES (corp-wide): 12.68B **Publicly Held**
Web: www.bostonscientific.com
SIC: 3841 Surgical and medical instruments
PA: Boston Scientific Corporation
300 Boston Scientific Way
Marlborough MA
508 683-4000

(P-10462)
BRANAN MEDICAL CORPORATION (PA)
9940 Mesa Rim Rd (92121-2910)
PHONE................................949 598-7166
Cindy Horton, *CEO*
Raphael Wong, *
Beckie Chien, *
▲ **EMP:** 25 **EST:** 1998
SQ FT: 8,400
SALES (est): 4.07MM
SALES (corp-wide): 4.07MM **Privately Held**
SIC: 3841 Diagnostic apparatus, medical

(P-10463)
BREG INC (HQ)
2382 Faraday Ave (92008-7220)
PHONE................................760 599-3000
Brad Lee, *Pr*
Stuart M Essig, *

Aaron Heisler, *
Tom Sohn, *
Steve Paul, *COMMERCIAL Operations**
◆ **EMP:** 171 **EST:** 1989
SALES (est): 24K **Privately Held**
Web: www.breg.com
SIC: 3841 Surgical and medical instruments
PA: Water Street Healthcare Partners Llc
444 W Lake St Ste 1800
Chicago IL

(P-10464)
BRUIN BIOMETRICS LLC
10877 Wilshire Blvd Ste 1600 (90024-4371)
PHONE................................310 268-9494
EMP: 17 **EST:** 2009
SQ FT: 3,000
SALES (est): 4MM
SALES (corp-wide): 7.13B **Privately Held**
Web: www.bruinbiometrics.com
SIC: 3841 Diagnostic apparatus, medical
HQ: Arjo Ab (Publ)
MalmO
103354500

(P-10465)
CALBIOTECH EXPORT INC
1935 Cordell Ct (92020-0911)
PHONE................................619 660-6162
Noori Barka, *Pr*
▼ **EMP:** 38 **EST:** 1998
SQ FT: 22,500
SALES (est): 9.43MM **Privately Held**
Web: www.calbiotech.com
SIC: 3841 8731 8071 Diagnostic apparatus, medical; Medical research, commercial; Medical laboratories
HQ: Erba Diagnostics Mannheim Gmbh
Mallaustr. 69-73
Mannheim BW

(P-10466)
CALDERA MEDICAL INC
4360 Park Terrace Dr Ste 140 (91361-4634)
PHONE................................818 879-6555
Bryon L Merade, *Pr*
Jeff Hubauer, *COO*
John Pitstick, *CFO*
EMP: 70 **EST:** 2002
SQ FT: 25,000
SALES (est): 20.41MM **Privately Held**
Web: www.calderamedical.com
SIC: 3841 Surgical and medical instruments

(P-10467)
CAMINO NEUROCARE
5955 Pacific Center Blvd (92121-4309)
PHONE................................858 455-1115
Tony Andrasfay, *Mgr*
EMP: 50 **EST:** 1981
SQ FT: 35,000
SALES (est): 1.7MM **Publicly Held**
SIC: 3841 Diagnostic apparatus, medical
PA: Integra Lifesciences Holdings Corporation
1100 Campus Rd
Princeton NJ

(P-10468)
CANARY MEDICAL USA LLC
2710 Loker Ave W Ste 350 (92010-6645)
PHONE................................760 448-5066
William Hunter, *CEO*
Jeffrey M Gross, *
EMP: 100 **EST:** 2018
SALES (est): 4.86MM **Privately Held**
Web: www.canarymedical.com
SIC: 3841 Surgical and medical instruments

(P-10469)
CAPISTRANO LABS INC
150 Calle Iglesia Ste B (92672-7550)
PHONE................................949 492-0390
Paul Meyers, *Pr*
Matt Stabley, *Treas*
EMP: 19 **EST:** 1986
SQ FT: 8,000
SALES (est): 2.19MM **Privately Held**
Web: www.capolabs.com
SIC: 3841 Diagnostic apparatus, medical

(P-10470)
CAREFUSION 207 INC
1100 Bird Center Dr (92262-8000)
PHONE................................760 778-7200
Edward Borkowski, *CFO*
Carol Zilm, *INFUS & RESP**
Cathy Cooney, *
Neil Ryding, *GLOBAL MFG SUPPLY**
Joan Stafslien, *
▲ **EMP:** 327 **EST:** 2005
SALES (est): 55.32MM
SALES (corp-wide): 1.8B **Privately Held**
SIC: 3841 8741 Surgical and medical instruments; Nursing and personal care facility management
PA: Vyaire Holding Company
26125 N Riverwoods Blvd
Mettawa IL
872 757-0114

(P-10471)
CAREFUSION 213 LLC (DH)
3750 Torrey View Ct (92130-2622)
PHONE................................800 523-0502
David L Schlotterbeck, *CEO*
Edward Borkowski, *
Dwight Windstead, *
◆ **EMP:** 450 **EST:** 2008
SALES (est): 133.71MM
SALES (corp-wide): 19.37B **Publicly Held**
Web: www.bd.com
SIC: 3841 Surgical and medical instruments
HQ: Carefusion Corporation
3750 Torrey View Ct
San Diego CA

(P-10472)
CAREFUSION CORPORATION
10020 Pacific Mesa Blvd Bldg A (92121)
PHONE................................858 617-4271
EMP: 52
SALES (corp-wide): 19.37B **Publicly Held**
Web: www.bd.com
SIC: 3841 Surgical and medical instruments
HQ: Carefusion Corporation
3750 Torrey View Ct
San Diego CA

(P-10473)
CAREFUSION CORPORATION
1100 Bird Center Dr (92262-8000)
PHONE................................760 778-7200
Carol Zilm, *Pr*
EMP: 59
SALES (corp-wide): 19.37B **Publicly Held**
Web: www.bd.com
SIC: 3841 Surgical and medical instruments
HQ: Carefusion Corporation
3750 Torrey View Ct
San Diego CA

(P-10474)
CAREFUSION CORPORATION
22745 Savi Ranch Pkwy (92887-4668)
PHONE................................800 231-2466
Bill Ross, *Brnch Mgr*
EMP: 73
SALES (corp-wide): 19.37B **Publicly Held**

Web: www.bd.com
SIC: 3841 Surgical and medical instruments
HQ: Carefusion Corporation
3750 Torrey View Ct
San Diego CA

(P-10475)
CAREFUSION SOLUTIONS LLC (DH)
3750 Torrey View Ct (92130-2622)
PHONE..............................858 617-2100
Keiran Gallahue, CEO
Tom Leonard, Pr
James Hinrichs, CFO
Don Abbey, Ex VP
Scott Bostick, Sr VP
EMP: 600 EST: 2007
SALES (est): 487.4MM
SALES (corp-wide): 19.37B Publicly Held
Web: www.bd.com
SIC: 3841 Surgical and medical instruments
HQ: Carefusion Corporation
3750 Torrey View Ct
San Diego CA

(P-10476)
CAROL COLE COMPANY
Also Called: Nuface
1325 Sycamore Ave Ste A (92081-7810)
PHONE..............................888 360-9171
Carol Cole, CEO
Ted Schwarz, *
EMP: 123 EST: 1989
SQ FT: 3,000
SALES (est): 32.02MM Privately Held
Web: www.mynuface.com
SIC: 3841 Skin grafting equipment

(P-10477)
CAROLINA LQUID CHMISTRIES CORP
510 W Central Ave Ste C (92821-3032)
P.O. Box 92249 (92822)
PHONE..............................336 722-8910
Phil Shugart, Brnch Mgr
EMP: 25
Web: www.carolinachemistries.com
SIC: 3841 Surgical and medical instruments
PA: Carolina Liquid Chemistries
Corporation
313 Gallimore Dairy Rd
Greensboro NC

(P-10478)
CAS MEDICAL SYSTEMS INC (HQ)
1 Edwards Way (92614-5688)
PHONE..............................203 488-6056
Thomas Patton, Pr
Jeffery Baird, *
Paul Benni, CSO*
EMP: 49 EST: 2018
SALES (est): 21.92MM
SALES (corp-wide): 5.38B Publicly Held
Web: www.edwards.com
SIC: 3841 Diagnostic apparatus, medical
PA: Edwards Lifesciences Corp
1 Edwards Way
Irvine CA
949 250-2500

(P-10479)
CHART SEQUAL TECHNOLOGIES INC
12230 World Trade Dr Ste 100
(92128-3796)
PHONE..............................858 202-3100
▲ EMP: 90
Web: www.caireinc.com

SIC: 3841 Diagnostic apparatus, medical

(P-10480)
CHEN-TECH INDUSTRIES INC (DH)
Also Called: ATI Forged Products
9 Wrigley (92618-2711)
PHONE..............................949 855-6716
Richard Harshman, CEO
Shannon Ko, *
EMP: 38 EST: 1979
SQ FT: 18,000
SALES (est): 12.39MM Publicly Held
Web: www.atimaterials.com
SIC: 3841 3769 3724 3463 Surgical and
medical instruments; Space vehicle
equipment, nec; Aircraft engines and
engine parts; Aluminum forgings
HQ: Ati Ladish Llc
5481 S Packard Ave
Cudahy WI
414 747-2611

(P-10481)
CHROMOLOGIC LLC
Also Called: Chromologic
1225 S Shamrock Ave (91016-4244)
PHONE..............................626 381-9974
Naresh Menon, Managing Member
EMP: 28 EST: 2008
SALES (est): 3.25MM Privately Held
Web: www.chromologic.com
SIC: 3841 Diagnostic apparatus, medical

(P-10482)
CLEARPOINT NEURO INC (PA)
120 S Sierra Ave Ste 100 (92075-1874)
PHONE..............................949 900-6833
EMP: 51 EST: 1998
SALES (est): 20.55MM Publicly Held
Web: www.clearpointneuro.com
SIC: 3841 Surgical and medical instruments

(P-10483)
COMPANION MEDICAL INC
11011 Via Frontera Ste D (92127-1752)
PHONE..............................858 522-0252
Sean Saint, CEO
Michael Mensinger, *
EMP: 58 EST: 2015
SALES (est): 7.1MM Privately Held
Web: www.medtronicdiabetes.com
SIC: 3841 Surgical and medical instruments
PA: Medtronic Public Limited Company
20 Hatch Street Lower
Dublin

(P-10484)
COMPOSITE MANUFACTURING INC
Also Called: CMI
970 Calle Amanecer Ste D (92673-6250)
PHONE..............................949 361-7580
EMP: 36 EST: 1995
SQ FT: 16,000
SALES (est): 6.55MM Privately Held
Web: www.carbonfiber.com
SIC: 3841 3624 Operating tables; Carbon
and graphite products

(P-10485)
COVIDIEN HOLDING INC
2101 Faraday Ave (92008-7205)
PHONE..............................760 603-5020
EMP: 151
Web: www.covidien.com
SIC: 3841 Surgical and medical instruments
HQ: Covidien Holding Inc.
710 Medtronic Pkwy

Minneapolis MN

(P-10486)
COVIDIEN HOLDING INC
Also Called: Covidien Kenmex
2475 Paseo De Las Americas Ste A
(92154-7255)
PHONE..............................619 690-8500
Javira Gonzales, Mgr
EMP: 151
Web: www.covidien.com
SIC: 3841 Surgical and medical instruments
HQ: Covidien Holding Inc.
710 Medtronic Pkwy
Minneapolis MN

(P-10487)
COVIDIEN LP
Also Called: Vascular Therapies
9775 Toledo Way (92618-1811)
PHONE..............................949 837-3700
Hal Hurwitz, CFO
EMP: 174
Web: www.forcetriad.com
SIC: 3841 Surgical and medical instruments
HQ: Covidien Lp
15 Hampshire St
Mansfield MA
763 514-4000

(P-10488)
CYTORI THERAPEUTICS INC
5764 Pacific Center Blvd Ste 110 (92121)
PHONE..............................858 458-0900
EMP: 23 EST: 2019
SALES (est): 1.23MM Privately Held
Web: www.cytori.com
SIC: 3841 Surgical and medical instruments

(P-10489)
DAVID KOPF INSTRUMENTS
7324 Elmo St (91042-2205)
P.O. Box 636 (91043-0636)
PHONE..............................818 352-3274
Carl Koph, CEO
J David Kopf, *
Carol Kopf, *
EMP: 28 EST: 1959
SQ FT: 13,836
SALES (est): 3.55MM Privately Held
Web: www.kopfinstruments.com
SIC: 3841 Veterinarians' instruments and
apparatus

(P-10490)
DEVAX INC
13900 Alton Pkwy Ste 125 (92618-1621)
PHONE..............................949 461-0450
Jeff Theil, CEO
EMP: 32 EST: 1999
SQ FT: 5,000
SALES (est): 2.43MM Privately Held
SIC: 3841 Surgical and medical instruments

(P-10491)
DEXCOM INC (PA)
Also Called: DEXCOM
6340 Sequence Dr (92121-4356)
PHONE..............................858 200-0200
Kevin R Sayer, Ch Bd
Jereme M Sylvain, CAO
Jacob S Leach, Ex VP
Michael Brown, CLO
Girish Naganathan, Ex VP
EMP: 568 EST: 1999
SALES (est): 2.91B
SALES (corp-wide): 2.91B Publicly Held
Web: www.dexcom.com
SIC: 3841 Surgical and medical instruments

(P-10492)
DIAGNOSTIXX OF CALIFORNIA CORP
Also Called: Immunalysis
829 Towne Center Dr (91767-5901)
PHONE..............................909 482-0840
▲ EMP: 22
Web: www.soht.org
SIC: 3841 2835 Diagnostic apparatus,
medical; Diagnostic substances

(P-10493)
DIALITY INC
181 Technology Dr Ste 150 (92618-2484)
PHONE..............................949 916-5851
Osman Khawar, CEO
Aaron Mishkin, Sec
Ather Khan, CFO
EMP: 64 EST: 2015
SALES (est): 3.49MM Privately Held
Web: www.diality.com
SIC: 3841 Hemodialysis apparatus

(P-10494)
DIGITAL SURGERY SYSTEMS INC
Also Called: True Digital Surgery
125 Cremona Dr Pmb 110 (93117-3083)
PHONE..............................805 978-5400
Aidan Foley, Pr
Arthur Rice, *
Simon Raab, *
Kevin Foley, *
J Flagg Flanagan, *
EMP: 34 EST: 2018
SALES (est): 3.67MM Privately Held
Web: www.truedigitalsurgery.com
SIC: 3841 Surgical and medical instruments

(P-10495)
DUPACO INC
4144 Avenida De La Plata Ste B (92056)
PHONE..............................760 758-4550
Gregory Jordan, Pr
EMP: 43 EST: 1962
SQ FT: 30,000
SALES (est): 4.35MM Privately Held
Web: www.dupacoinc.com
SIC: 3841 3845 Medical instruments and
equipment, blood and bone work;
Electromedical equipment

(P-10496)
EAGLE LABS LLC
Also Called: Eagle Labs
10201a Trademark St Ste A (91730-5849)
PHONE..............................909 481-0011
Richard J De Camp, Pr
EMP: 65 EST: 1988
SQ FT: 30,000
SALES (est): 10.25MM
SALES (corp-wide): 39.92MM Privately
Held
Web: www.eaglelabs.com
SIC: 3841 Surgical and medical instruments
HQ: Summit Medical, Llc
815 Northwest Pkwy # 100
Saint Paul MN
651 789-3939

(P-10497)
EASYDIAL INC
181 Technology Dr Ste 150 (92618-2484)
PHONE..............................949 916-5851
Philippe Faurie, CEO
EMP: 24 EST: 2015
SALES (est): 2.11MM Privately Held
Web: www.easydialhdbs.com

SIC: 3841 Hemodialysis apparatus

(P-10498)
ECA MEDICAL INSTRUMENTS (DH)
1107 Tourmaline Dr (91320-1208)
PHONE....................805 376-2509
John J Nino, *Pr*
EMP: 21 EST: 1979
SQ FT: 14,982
SALES (est): 10.87MM **Publicly Held**
Web: www.ecamedical.com
SIC: 3841 Surgical and medical instruments
HQ: Acas, Llc
2 Bethesda Metro Ctr # 1200
Bethesda MD
301 951-6122

(P-10499)
EDWARDS LFSCIENCES CARDIAQ LLC
1 Edwards Way (92614-5688)
PHONE....................949 387-2615
Robrecht Michiels, *CEO*
J Brent Ratz, *Pr*
EMP: 56 EST: 2007
SALES (est): 1.68MM
SALES (corp-wide): 5.38B **Publicly Held**
Web: www.edwards.com
SIC: 3841 Surgical and medical instruments
PA: Edwards Lifesciences Corp
1 Edwards Way
Irvine CA
949 250-2500

(P-10500)
EKLIN MEDICAL SYSTEMS INC
6359 Paseo Del Lago (92011-1317)
PHONE....................760 918-9626
Robert Antin, *Pr*
EMP: 43 EST: 2002
SQ FT: 16,000
SALES (est): 4.17MM
SALES (corp-wide): 42.84B **Privately Held**
SIC: 3841 5047 Medical instruments and
equipment, blood and bone work; Medical
and hospital equipment
HQ: Vca Inc.
12401 W Olympic Blvd
Los Angeles CA
310 571-6500

(P-10501)
ELECTRONIC WAVEFORM LAB INC
5702 Bolsa Ave (92649-1128)
PHONE....................714 843-0463
Ryan Haney, *Pr*
William Jim Heaney, *Pr*
Patricia Heaney, *
Ryan Haney, *Pr*
EMP: 25 EST: 1981
SALES (est): 5.17MM **Privately Held**
Web: www.h-wave.com
SIC: 3841 Anesthesia apparatus

(P-10502)
ENCHANNEL MEDICAL LTD
555 Corporate Dr Ste 165 (92694-2170)
PHONE....................949 694-6802
Jun Feng, *CEO*
EMP: 25 EST: 2021
SALES (est): 938.57K **Privately Held**
SIC: 3841 Diagnostic apparatus, medical

(P-10503)
ENDOLOGIX INC (PA)
Also Called: Endologix
2 Musick (92618-1631)

PHONE....................949 595-7200
John Onopchenko, *CEO*
Daniel Lemaitre, *
Matthew Thompson, *CMO*
Jeff Fecho Cqo, *Prin*
Cindy Pinto, *Interim Vice President*
▲ EMP: 58 EST: 1992
SQ FT: 129,000
SALES (est): 143.37MM **Privately Held**
Web: www.endologix.com
SIC: 3841 Surgical and medical instruments

(P-10504)
ENDOLOGIX CANADA LLC
2 Musick (92618-1631)
PHONE....................949 595-7200
EMP: 79 EST: 2014
SALES (est): 10.39MM **Privately Held**
SIC: 3841 Catheters
HQ: Trivascular, Inc.
2 Musick
Irvine CA

(P-10505)
ENVVENO MEDICAL CORPORATION
70 Doppler (92618-4306)
PHONE....................949 261-2900
Robert A Berman, *CEO*
Craig Glynn, *CFO*
Marc H Glickman, *CMO*
EMP: 19 EST: 1987
SQ FT: 14,507
Web: www.envveno.com
SIC: 3841 Surgical and medical instruments

(P-10506)
EPICA MEDICAL INNOVATIONS LLC
901 Calle Amanecer Ste 150 (92673-4219)
PHONE....................949 238-6323
▲ EMP: 24 EST: 2012
SQ FT: 4,441
SALES (est): 4.72MM
SALES (corp-wide): 9.92MM **Privately Held**
Web: www.epicaanimalhealth.com
SIC: 3841 5047 Medical instruments;
Medical equipment and supplies
PA: Epica International, Inc.
901 Calle Amanecer # 150
San Clemente CA
949 238-6323

(P-10507)
FLUID LINE TECHNOLOGY CORP
4590 Ish Dr (93063-7678)
P.O. Box 3116 (91313-3116)
PHONE....................818 998-8848
Joseph Marcilese, *Pr*
Phillip Jaramilla, *
▼ EMP: 25 EST: 1989
SALES (est): 4.14MM **Privately Held**
Web: www.fluidlinetech.com
SIC: 3841 2833 Surgical and medical
instruments; Medicinals and botanicals

(P-10508)
FLUXERGY INC
15 Musick (92618-1638)
PHONE....................949 305-4201
Tej Patel, *Brnch Mgr*
EMP: 18
SALES (corp-wide): 10.44MM **Privately Held**
Web: www.fluxergy.com
SIC: 3841 Surgical and medical instruments
PA: Fluxergy, Inc.
30 Fairbanks

Irvine CA
949 305-4201

(P-10509)
FLUXERGY INC
13766 Alton Pkwy (92618-1639)
PHONE....................949 305-4201
Tej Patel, *Brnch Mgr*
EMP: 18
SALES (corp-wide): 10.44MM **Privately Held**
Web: www.fluxergy.com
SIC: 3841 Surgical and medical instruments
PA: Fluxergy, Inc.
30 Fairbanks
Irvine CA
949 305-4201

(P-10510)
FOUNDRY MED INNOVATIONS INC
Also Called: Toolbox Medical Innovations
1965 Kellogg Ave (92008-6582)
PHONE....................888 445-2333
John K Zeis, *Pr*
EMP: 17 EST: 2014
SALES (est): 4.48MM **Privately Held**
SIC: 3841 Diagnostic apparatus, medical
PA: Te Connectivity Ltd.
Muhlenstrasse 26
Schaffhausen SH

(P-10511)
FREUDENBERG MEDICAL LLC
5050 Rivergrade Rd (91706-1405)
PHONE....................626 814-9684
Coburn Pharr, *Brnch Mgr*
EMP: 149
SALES (corp-wide): 12.23B **Privately Held**
Web: www.inhealth.com
SIC: 3841 Surgical and medical instruments
HQ: Freudenberg Medical, Llc
1110 Mark Ave
Carpinteria CA
805 684-3304

(P-10512)
FUSION BIOTEC INC
160 S Cypress St Ste 400 (92866-1314)
PHONE....................949 264-3437
Bruce Alan Sargeant, *CEO*
EMP: 26 EST: 2016
SQ FT: 3,000
SALES (est): 4.74MM **Privately Held**
Web: www.fusion-biotec.com
SIC: 3841 Surgical and medical instruments

(P-10513)
FZIOMED INC (PA)
231 Bonetti Dr (93401-7376)
PHONE....................805 546-0610
EMP: 39 EST: 1996
SQ FT: 36,000
SALES (est): 6.37MM **Privately Held**
Web: www.fziomed.com
SIC: 3841 Surgical and medical instruments

(P-10514)
GENALYTE INC (PA)
6620 Mesa Ridge Rd (92121-3917)
PHONE....................858 956-1200
Cary Gunn, *CEO*
Kevin Lo, *Pr*
Martin Gleeson, *VP*
William A Hagstrom, *Prin*
EMP: 17 EST: 2007
SALES (est): 8.42MM **Privately Held**
Web: www.genalyte.com

SIC: 3841 Diagnostic apparatus, medical

(P-10515)
GENBODY AMERICA LLC
3420 De Forest Cir (91752-1165)
PHONE....................949 561-0664
David Yoo, *CEO*
EMP: 34 EST: 2020
SALES (est): 2.5MM **Privately Held**
Web: www.genbodyamerica.com
SIC: 3841 5047 2835 Diagnostic apparatus,
medical; Medical equipment and supplies;
Microbiology and virology diagnostic
products

(P-10516)
GENMARK DIAGNOSTICS INC (DH)
Also Called: Genmark
5964 La Place Ct Ste 100 (92008-8829)
PHONE....................760 448-4300
EMP: 449 EST: 2020
SALES (est): 171.55MM **Privately Held**
Web: diagnostics.roche.com
SIC: 3841 Surgical and medical instruments
HQ: Roche Holdings, Inc.
1 Dna Way
South San Francisco CA
650 225-1000

(P-10517)
GLAUKOS CORPORATION (PA)
1 Glaukos Way (92656-2704)
PHONE....................949 367-9600
Thomas W Burns, *Ch Bd*
Joseph E Gilliam, *Pr*
Tomas Navratil, *CDO*
Alex R Thurman, *Sr VP*
EMP: 208 EST: 1998
SQ FT: 160,000
SALES (est): 282.86MM
SALES (corp-wide): 282.86MM **Publicly Held**
Web: www.glaukos.com
SIC: 3841 Eye examining instruments and
apparatus

(P-10518)
GLYSENS INCORPORATED
3931 Sorrento Valley Blvd Ste 110 (92121-1402)
PHONE....................858 638-7708
Bill Markle, *CEO*
Timothy Routh, *
EMP: 30 EST: 1997
SALES (est): 4.84MM **Privately Held**
Web: www.glysens.com
SIC: 3841 Surgical and medical instruments

(P-10519)
HAEMONETICS MANUFACTURING INC (HQ)
1630 W Industrial Park St (91722-3419)
PHONE....................626 339-7388
Neil Ryding, *CEO*
◆ EMP: 42 EST: 2012
SQ FT: 61,313
SALES (est): 24.06MM
SALES (corp-wide): 1.17B **Publicly Held**
Web: www.haemonetics.com
SIC: 3841 Surgical and medical instruments
PA: Haemonetics Corporation
125 Summer St Ste 1800
Boston MA
781 848-7100

(P-10520)
HEMODIALYSIS INC
Also Called: Hunnington Dialysis Center

806 S Fair Oaks Ave (91105-2601)
PHONE..............................626 792-0548
Susan Burkhart, *Mgr*
EMP: 75
SALES (corp-wide): 8.93MM **Privately Held**
Web: www.hemodialysis-inc.com
SIC: 3841 8011 Hemodialysis apparatus; Hematologist
PA: Hemodialysis, Inc.
710 W Wilson Ave
Glendale CA
818 500-8736

(P-10521)
HOYA SURGICAL OPTICS INC
110 Progress (92618-0390)
PHONE..............................909 680-3900
Yasuro Mori, *CFO*
Bruno Chermette, *Pr*
EMP: 23 **EST:** 2007
SALES (est): 6.08MM **Privately Held**
Web: www.hoyasurgicaloptics.com
SIC: 3841 Surgical and medical instruments

(P-10522)
HYCOR BIOMEDICAL LLC
Also Called: Hycor
7272 Chapman Ave Ste A (92841-2103)
PHONE..............................714 933-3000
Dick Aderman, *Pr*
Richard Hockins, *
Phil Crusco, *
Mark Van Cleve, *
Eric Whitters, *
▲ **EMP:** 120 **EST:** 1985
SQ FT: 76,000
SALES (est): 45.37MM
SALES (corp-wide): 188.16MM **Privately Held**
Web: www.hycorbiomedical.com
SIC: 3841 2835 Surgical and medical instruments; Diagnostic substances
PA: Linden, Llc
111 S Wacker Dr Ste 3350
Chicago IL
312 506-5657

(P-10523)
HYDRAFACIAL LLC (HQ)
Also Called: Hydrafacial Company, The
2165 E Spring St (90806-2114)
PHONE..............................800 603-4996
Clint Carnell, *CEO*
Jeff Nardoci, *
Randy Sieve, *
▲ **EMP:** 88 **EST:** 2012
SQ FT: 22,515
SALES (est): 20.44MM
SALES (corp-wide): 365.88MM **Publicly Held**
Web: www.hydrafacial.com
SIC: 3841 Surgical and medical instruments
PA: The Beauty Health Company
2165 E Spring St
Long Beach CA
800 603-4996

(P-10524)
I-FLOW LLC
43 Discovery Ste 100 (92618-3150)
PHONE..............................800 448-3569
Donald Earhart, *Pr*
James J Dal Porto, *
James R Talevich, *
EMP: 1100 **EST:** 1985
SQ FT: 66,675
SALES (est): 118.36MM
SALES (corp-wide): 20.18B **Publicly Held**
Web: www.avanospainmanagement.com

SIC: 3841 Surgical instruments and apparatus
PA: Kimberly-Clark Corporation
351 Phelps Dr
Irving TX
972 281-1200

(P-10525)
ICU MEDICAL INC (PA)
Also Called: ICU MEDICAL
951 Calle Amanecer (92673-6212)
PHONE..............................949 366-2183
Vivek Jain, *Ch Bd*
Christian B Voigtlander, *COO*
Brian Bonnell, *CFO*
Daniel Woolson, *Corporate Vice President*
Virginia Sanzone, *Corporate Vice President*
▲ **EMP:** 303 **EST:** 1984
SQ FT: 39,000
SALES (est): 2.28B
SALES (corp-wide): 2.28B **Publicly Held**
Web: www.icumed.com
SIC: 3841 3845 IV transfusion apparatus; Pacemaker, cardiac

(P-10526)
ICU MEDICAL SALES INC (HQ)
951 Calle Amanecer (92673-6212)
PHONE..............................949 366-2183
Vivek Jain, *CEO*
EMP: 84 **EST:** 2001
SQ FT: 39,000
SALES (est): 13.88MM
SALES (corp-wide): 2.28B **Publicly Held**
Web: www.icumed.com
SIC: 3841 IV transfusion apparatus
PA: Icu Medical, Inc.
951 Calle Amanecer
San Clemente CA
949 366-2183

(P-10527)
IGENOMIX USA LLC
Also Called: Ivigen
383 Van Ness Ave Ste 1605 (90501-7225)
PHONE..............................818 919-1657
Refik Kayali, *Mgr*
EMP: 34
SALES (corp-wide): 308.28MM **Privately Held**
Web: www.igenomix.com
SIC: 3841 8071 Biopsy instruments and equipment; Medical laboratories
HQ: Igenomix Usa, Inc.
7955 Nw 12th St Ste 415
Doral FL
305 501-4948

(P-10528)
IMPEDIMED INC (HQ)
5900 Pasteur Ct Ste 125 (92008-7334)
PHONE..............................760 585-2100
Richard Carreon, *CEO*
Don Myll, *CFO*
EMP: 20 **EST:** 2002
SQ FT: 15,000
SALES (est): 10.64MM **Privately Held**
Web: www.impedimed.com
SIC: 3841 Surgical and medical instruments
PA: Impedimed Limited
U 1 50 Parker Ct
Pinkenba QLD

(P-10529)
INARI MEDICAL INC (PA)
Also Called: Inari
6001 Oak Cyn Ste 100 (92618-5200)
PHONE..............................877 927-4747
William Hoffman, *CEO*
Mitchell Hill, *CFO*

Thomas Tu, *CMO*
Drew Hykes, *COO*
Janet Byk, *Finance*
EMP: 90 **EST:** 2011
SQ FT: 38,200
SALES (est): 383.47MM
SALES (corp-wide): 383.47MM **Publicly Held**
Web: www.inarimedical.com
SIC: 3841 Surgical and medical instruments

(P-10530)
INNOVATIVE PRODUCT BRANDS INC
Also Called: Ipb
7045 Palm Ave (92346-3291)
PHONE..............................909 864-7477
Bryan Joe Tapocik, *Ch*
Stacy Kristine Tapocik, *Sec*
Shane Nielsen, *CEO*
▲ **EMP:** 20 **EST:** 2001
SALES (est): 2.5MM **Privately Held**
Web: www.innovativeproductbrands.com
SIC: 3841 Surgical and medical instruments

(P-10531)
INOGEN INC (PA)
301 Coromar Dr (93117-3286)
PHONE..............................805 562-0500
Kevin Smith, *Pr*
Elizabeth Mora, *
Alison Bauerlein, *Corporate Secretary*
George Parr, *CCO*
Jason M Somer, *Ex VP*
◆ **EMP:** 208 **EST:** 2001
SQ FT: 46,000
SALES (est): 377.24MM
SALES (corp-wide): 377.24MM **Publicly Held**
Web: www.inogen.com
SIC: 3841 3842 7352 Surgical and medical instruments; Surgical appliances and supplies; Medical equipment rental

(P-10532)
INOVA LABS INC
9001 Spectrum Center Blvd Ste 200 (92123-1438)
P.O. Box 18536 (78760-8536)
PHONE..............................866 647-0691
Brooke Harding, *CEO*
John B Rush, *
Phil Martin, *
Randy Williams, *
Dragan Nebrigic, *
▲ **EMP:** 55 **EST:** 2008
SALES (est): 11.82MM **Publicly Held**
Web: www.lifechoiceoxygen.com
SIC: 3841 Surgical and medical instruments
PA: Resmed Inc.
9001 Spectrum Center Blvd
San Diego CA

(P-10533)
INTEGER HOLDINGS CORPORATION
Also Called: Greatbatch Medical
8830 Siempre Viva Rd Ste 100 (92154-6278)
PHONE..............................619 498-9448
Raul Mata, *Brnch Mgr*
EMP: 60
SALES (corp-wide): 1.38B **Publicly Held**
Web: www.integer.net
SIC: 3841 Surgical and medical instruments
PA: Integer Holdings Corporation
5830 Gran Pkwy Ste 1150
Plano TX
214 618-5243

(P-10534)
INTEGRA LFSCNCES HOLDINGS CORP
5955 Pacific Center Blvd (92121-4309)
PHONE..............................609 529-9748
Peter Arduini, *CEO*
EMP: 25
Web: www.integralife.com
SIC: 3841 3845 Surgical and medical instruments; Electromedical equipment
PA: Integra Lifesciences Holdings Corporation
1100 Campus Rd
Princeton NJ

(P-10535)
INTERFACE ASSOCIATES INC
Also Called: Interface Catheter Solutions
27721 La Paz Rd (92677-3948)
PHONE..............................949 448-7056
EMP: 175
Web: www.interfaceusa.com
SIC: 3841 5047 Surgical and medical instruments; Hospital equipment and furniture

(P-10536)
INTERNATIONAL TECHNIDYNE CORP (DH)
Also Called: Itc
6260 Sequence Dr (92121-4358)
PHONE..............................858 263-2300
Scott Cramer, *Pr*
Greg Tibbitts, *
Tom Whalen, *
Matt Bastardi, *
Kimberly Ballard, *
EMP: 250 **EST:** 1969
SQ FT: 130,000
SALES (est): 65.89MM **Privately Held**
Web: www.werfen.com
SIC: 3841 3829 Diagnostic apparatus, medical; Medical diagnostic systems, nuclear
HQ: Accriva Diagnostics Holdings, Inc.
6260 Sequence Dr
San Diego CA
858 404-8203

(P-10537)
IRVINE BIOMEDICAL INC
2375 Morse Ave (92614-6233)
PHONE..............................949 851-3053
EMP: 200
SIC: 3841 Catheters

(P-10538)
ISSAC MEDICAL INC
2761 Walnut Ave (92780-7051)
PHONE..............................805 239-4284
EMP: 320
SIC: 3841 2822 2821 Surgical and medical instruments; Synthetic rubber; Plastics materials and resins

(P-10539)
IVERA MEDICAL LLC
10805 Rancho Bernardo Rd Ste 100 (92127)
PHONE..............................888 861-8228
Bobby E Rogers, *Pr*
EMP: 31 **EST:** 2007
SALES (est): 3.71MM
SALES (corp-wide): 34.23B **Publicly Held**
Web: www.curos.com
SIC: 3841 IV transfusion apparatus
PA: 3m Company
3m Center
Saint Paul MN
651 733-1110

(P-10540)
JIT MANUFACTURING INC
1610 Commerce Way (93446-3699)
PHONE..............................805 238-5000
Sharon Smith, *CEO*
EMP: 50
SALES (est): 4.69MM **Privately Held**
Web: www.jitmfginc.com
SIC: 3841 Medical instruments and
equipment, blood and bone work

(P-10541)
KARL STORZ ENDSCPY-
AMERICA INC
1 N Los Carneros Dr (93117)
PHONE..............................800 964-5563
EMP: 67
SALES (corp-wide): 2.24B **Privately Held**
Web: www.karlstorz.com
SIC: 3841 3845 Suction therapy apparatus;
Endoscopic equipment, electromedical, nec
HQ: Karl Storz Endoscopy-America, Inc.
2151 E Grand Ave
El Segundo CA
424 218-8100

(P-10542)
KARL STORZ ENDSCPY-
AMERICA INC (HQ)
2151 E Grand Ave (90245-5025)
PHONE..............................424 218-8100
Charles Wilhelm, *CEO*
Mark Green, *VP*
Sken Huang, *CFO*
Sonal Matai, *Mng Dir*
▲ **EMP:** 415 **EST:** 1971
SQ FT: 90,000
SALES (est): 280.88MM
SALES (corp-wide): 2.24B **Privately Held**
Web: www.karlstorz.com
SIC: 3841 5047 Surgical and medical
instruments; Medical equipment and
supplies
PA: Karl Storz Se & Co. Kg
Dr.-Karl-Storz-Str. 34
Tuttlingen BW
74617080

(P-10543)
KARL STORZ IMAGING INC
32 Aero Camino (93117-3105)
PHONE..............................805 968-5563
EMP: 28
SALES (corp-wide): 2.24B **Privately Held**
Web: www.karlstorz.com
SIC: 3841 Surgical and medical instruments
HQ: Karl Storz Imaging, Inc.
1 S Los Carneros Rd
Goleta CA

(P-10544)
KONIGSBERG INSTRUMENTS
INC
1017 S Mountain Ave (91016-3642)
PHONE..............................626 775-6500
▼ **EMP:** 35
SIC: 3841 Surgical and medical instruments

(P-10545)
KOROS USA INC
610 Flinn Ave (93021-2008)
PHONE..............................805 529-0825
Tibor Koros, *Pr*
▲ **EMP:** 25 **EST:** 1974
SQ FT: 12,000
SALES (est): 4.93MM **Privately Held**
Web: www.korosusa.com
SIC: 3841 Diagnostic apparatus, medical

(P-10546)
LIFE SCIENCE OUTSOURCING
INC
Also Called: Medical Device Manufacturing
830 Challenger St (92821-2946)
PHONE..............................714 672-1090
Barry Kazemi, *Pr*
Charlie Ricci, *
Neil A Goldman, *
◆ **EMP:** 80 **EST:** 1997
SQ FT: 56,000
SALES (est): 30.24MM **Privately Held**
Web: www.lso-inc.com
SIC: 3841 Surgical instruments and
apparatus

(P-10547)
LINKS MEDICAL PRODUCTS INC
(PA)
9249 Research Dr (92618-4286)
PHONE..............................949 753-0001
Thomas L Buckley, *CEO*
Patrick Buckley, *
▲ **EMP:** 22 **EST:** 1996
SALES (est): 3.6MM **Privately Held**
Web: www.linksmed.com
SIC: 3841 Medical instruments and
equipment, blood and bone work

(P-10548)
LISI AEROSPACE
2600 Skypark Dr (90505-5314)
PHONE..............................310 326-8110
EMP: 30 **EST:** 2019
SALES (est): 13.84MM **Privately Held**
Web: www.lisi-medical.com
SIC: 3841 Surgical and medical instruments

(P-10549)
MAGNABIOSCIENCES LLC
6325 Lusk Blvd (92121-3733)
PHONE..............................858 481-4400
Ronald E Sager, *
Dave Cox, *
David M Shultx, *
Greg Degeller, *
EMP: 23 **EST:** 2001
SQ FT: 2,200
SALES (est): 2.35MM
SALES (corp-wide): 52.1MM **Privately**
Held
Web: www.magnabiosciences.com
SIC: 3841 5047 5999 Diagnostic apparatus,
medical; Diagnostic equipment, medical;
Medical apparatus and supplies
PA: Quantum Design, Inc.
10307 Pacific Center Ct
San Diego CA
858 481-4400

(P-10550)
MARLEE MANUFACTURING INC
4711 E Guasti Rd (91761-8106)
PHONE..............................909 390-3222
Russell Wells, *Pr*
Patricia Wells, *
Shawn Cory, *
EMP: 39 **EST:** 1984
SQ FT: 41,000
SALES (est): 4.53MM **Privately Held**
Web: www.marleemanufacturing.com
SIC: 3841 3599 Surgical and medical
instruments; Machine shop, jobbing and
repair

(P-10551)
MASIMO AMERICAS INC
52 Discovery (92618-3105)
PHONE..............................949 297-7000

Rick Fishel, *CEO*
EMP: 68 **EST:** 2004
SALES (est): 10.37MM **Publicly Held**
Web: www.masimo.com
SIC: 3841 Surgical and medical instruments
PA: Masimo Corporation
52 Discovery
Irvine CA

(P-10552)
MAST BIOSURGERY USA INC
Also Called: Mast Biosurgery
6749 Top Gun St Ste 108 (92121-4151)
PHONE..............................858 550-8050
Thomas Brooas, *Pr*
Thoms Brooas, *
EMP: 30 **EST:** 2004
SQ FT: 10,000
SALES (est): 2.96MM **Privately Held**
Web: www.mastbio.com
SIC: 3841 Surgical and medical instruments

(P-10553)
MED-SAFE SYSTEMS INC
10975 Torreyana Rd (92121-1106)
PHONE..............................855 236-2772
Joseph Taylor, *Genl Mgr*
◆ **EMP:** 40 **EST:** 1982
SQ FT: 90,000
SALES (est): 2.44MM
SALES (corp-wide): 19.37B **Publicly Held**
SIC: 3841 Surgical instruments and
apparatus
PA: Becton, Dickinson And Company
1 Becton Dr
Franklin Lakes NJ
201 847-6800

(P-10554)
MEDICAL DEPOT INC
Also Called: Drive Devilbiss Healthcare
548 W Merrill Ave (92376-9101)
PHONE..............................877 224-0946
EMP: 46
SALES (corp-wide): 409.99MM **Privately**
Held
Web: www.drivemedical.com
SIC: 3841 Surgical and medical instruments
HQ: Medical Depot, Inc.
99 Seaview Blvd Ste 210
Port Washington NY

(P-10555)
MEDICAL TACTILE INC
5500 W Rosecrans Ave Ste A
(90250-6642)
PHONE..............................310 641-8228
Jae Son, *Ch*
Steven Sanchez, *Sec*
Denis O'connor, *CEO*
▼ **EMP:** 20 **EST:** 2004
SALES (est): 1.36MM **Privately Held**
Web: www.mybexa.com
SIC: 3841 Diagnostic apparatus, medical

(P-10556)
MEDICOOL INC
20460 Gramercy Pl (90501-1513)
PHONE..............................310 782-2200
Steve Yeager, *Prin*
▲ **EMP:** 17 **EST:** 1986
SQ FT: 15,000
SALES (est): 2.34MM **Privately Held**
Web: www.medicool.com
SIC: 3841 Inhalators, surgical and medical

(P-10557)
MEDTRONIC INC
Also Called: Medtronic
1659 Gailes Blvd (92154-8230)

PHONE..............................949 798-3934
Araceli Rodriguez, *Brnch Mgr*
EMP: 35
Web: www.medtronic.com
SIC: 3841 Surgical and medical instruments
HQ: Medtronic, Inc.
710 Medtronic Pkwy
Minneapolis MN
763 514-4000

(P-10558)
MEDTRONIC INC
Also Called: Medtronic
2101 Faraday Ave (92008-7205)
PHONE..............................760 214-3009
EMP: 25
Web: www.medtronic.com
SIC: 3841 Surgical and medical instruments
HQ: Medtronic, Inc.
710 Medtronic Pkwy
Minneapolis MN
763 514-4000

(P-10559)
MEDTRONIC INC
Also Called: Medtronic
9775 Toledo Way (92618-1811)
PHONE..............................949 837-3700
Geoff Martha, *Ch Bd*
EMP: 200
Web: www.medtronic.com
SIC: 3841 Surgical and medical instruments
HQ: Medtronic, Inc.
710 Medtronic Pkwy
Minneapolis MN
763 514-4000

(P-10560)
MEDTRONIC INC
Medtronic
1851 E Deere Ave (92705-5720)
PHONE..............................949 474-3943
Walter Cuevas, *Mgr*
EMP: 455
SQ FT: 47,000
Web: www.medtronic.com
SIC: 3841 Surgical and medical instruments
HQ: Medtronic, Inc.
710 Medtronic Pkwy
Minneapolis MN
763 514-4000

(P-10561)
MEDTRONIC ATS MEDICAL INC
1851 E Deere Ave (92705-5720)
PHONE..............................949 380-9333
Walter Cuevas, *Brnch Mgr*
EMP: 133
Web: www.medtronic.com
SIC: 3841 Surgical instruments and
apparatus
HQ: Medtronic Ats Medical, Inc.
710 Medtronic Pkwy
Minneapolis MN
763 553-7736

(P-10562)
MEDTRONIC MINIMED INC (DH)
Also Called: Medtronic
18000 Devonshire St (91325-1219)
PHONE..............................800 646-4633
Sean Salmon, *Pr*
Austin Domenici, *
Eric P Geismar, *
George J Montague, *
▲ **EMP:** 1200 **EST:** 1993
SQ FT: 250,000
SALES (est): 455.06MM **Privately Held**
Web: www.medtronicdiabetes.com

SIC: **3841** Surgical and medical instruments
HQ: Medtronic, Inc.
710 Medtronic Pkwy
Minneapolis MN
763 514-4000

(P-10563)
MEDTRONIC PS MEDICAL INC (DH)
Also Called: Medtronic
5290 California Ave # 100 (92617-3229)
PHONE...............................805 571-3769
◆ **EMP: 200 EST:** 1978
SALES (est): 102.71MM **Privately Held**
Web: www.medtronic.com
SIC: **3841** Surgical and medical instruments
HQ: Medtronic, Inc.
710 Medtronic Pkwy
Minneapolis MN
763 514-4000

(P-10564)
MERIT MEDICAL SYSTEMS INC
6 Journey Ste 125 (92656-5319)
PHONE...............................801 208-4793
Judy Wagner, *Brnch Mgr*
EMP: 20
SALES (corp-wide): 1.15B **Publicly Held**
Web: www.merit.com
SIC: **3841** Surgical and medical instruments
PA: Merit Medical Systems, Inc.
1600 W Merit Pkwy
South Jordan UT
801 253-1600

(P-10565)
METTLER ELECTRONICS CORP
1333 S Claudina St (92805-6266)
PHONE...............................714 533-2221
Stephen C Mettler, *CEO*
Mark Mettler, *
Donna Mettler, *
Matthew Ferrari, *
▲ **EMP: 42 EST:** 1957
SQ FT: 22,500
SALES (est): 6.35MM **Privately Held**
Web: www.mettlerelectronics.com
SIC: **3841** Surgical and medical instruments

(P-10566)
MICRO THERAPEUTICS INC (HQ)
Also Called: Ev3 Neurovascular
9775 Toledo Way (92618-1811)
PHONE...............................949 837-3700
Thomas C Wilder Iii, *Pr*
Thomas Berryman, *CFO*
EMP: 38 **EST:** 1993
SQ FT: 43,000
SALES (est): 48.82MM **Privately Held**
Web: www.medtronic.com
SIC: **3841** Surgical and medical instruments
PA: Medtronic Public Limited Company
20 Hatch Street Lower
Dublin

(P-10567)
MICROVENTION INC (DH)
Also Called: Microvention Terumo
35 Enterprise (92656-2601)
PHONE...............................714 258-8000
Carsten Schroeder, *Pr*
Kazuaki Kitabatake, *
Bruce Canter, *
Thierry De Bosson, *
Jacques Dion, *
▲ **EMP: 190 EST:** 1997
SQ FT: 35,000
SALES (est): 222.49MM **Privately Held**
Web: microvention.herokuapp.com

SIC: **3841** Surgical and medical instruments
HQ: Terumo Americas Holding, Inc.
265 Davidson Ave Ste 320
Somerset NJ
732 302-4900

(P-10568)
MICROVENTION INC
1311 Valencia Ave (92780-6447)
PHONE...............................714 258-8001
EMP: 28
Web: microvention.herokuapp.com
SIC: **3841** Surgical and medical instruments
HQ: Microvention, Inc.
35 Enterprise
Aliso Viejo CA
714 258-8000

(P-10569)
MODULAR MEDICAL INC
Also Called: MODULAR MEDICAL
10740 Thornmint Rd (92127-2700)
PHONE...............................858 800-3500
James Besser, *CEO*
Paul Diperna, *
Kevin Schmid, *COO*
EMP: 38 EST: 2015
SQ FT: 24,000
Web: www.modular-medical.com
SIC: **3841** Surgical and medical instruments

(P-10570)
MONOBIND SALES INC (PA)
100 N Pointe Dr (92630-2270)
PHONE...............................949 951-2665
Frederick Jerome, *Pr*
Doctor Jay Singh, *VP*
▲ **EMP: 25 EST:** 1977
SQ FT: 18,000
SALES (est): 4.88MM
SALES (corp-wide): 4.88MM **Privately Held**
Web: www.monobind.com
SIC: **3841** Diagnostic apparatus, medical

(P-10571)
MPS MEDICAL INC
785 Challenger St (92821-2948)
PHONE...............................714 672-1090
Barry A Kazemi, *CEO*
EMP: 37 EST: 2014
SALES (est): 5.64MM
SALES (corp-wide): 25.61MM **Privately Held**
Web: www.innovamedgroup.com
SIC: **3841** Surgical and medical instruments
PA: Innova Medical Group, Inc.
800 E Colo Blvd Ste 288
Pasadena CA
760 330-6123

(P-10572)
NELLIX INC
2 Musick (92618-1631)
PHONE...............................650 213-8700
Robert D Mitchell, *Pr*
Doug Hughes, *
EMP: 29 EST: 2001
SQ FT: 7,500
SALES (est): 9.84MM **Privately Held**
SIC: **3841** Surgical and medical instruments
PA: Endologix, Inc.
2 Musick
Irvine CA

(P-10573)
NEOMEND INC
60 Technology Dr (92618-2301)
PHONE...............................949 783-3300
David Renzi, *Pr*

Kevin Cousins, *
David Hanson, *
Pete Davis, *
▼ **EMP: 90 EST:** 1999
SQ FT: 21,000
SALES (est): 23.51MM
SALES (corp-wide): 18.87B **Publicly Held**
SIC: **3841** Surgical and medical instruments
HQ: C. R. Bard, Inc.
1 Becton Dr
Franklin Lakes NJ
201 847-6800

(P-10574)
NEUROPTICS INC
9223 Research Dr (92618-4286)
PHONE...............................949 250-9792
▲ **EMP: 45 EST:** 1995
SALES (est): 7.57MM **Privately Held**
Web: www.neuroptics.com
SIC: **3841** Surgical and medical instruments

(P-10575)
NEUROVASC TECHNOLOGIES INC
3 Jenner Ste 100 (92618-3827)
PHONE...............................949 258-9946
EMP: 18 **EST:** 2016
SALES (est): 5.17MM **Privately Held**
Web: www.neurovasctechnologies.com
SIC: **3841** Surgical and medical instruments

(P-10576)
NEW WORLD MEDICAL INCORPORATED
10763 Edison Ct (91730-4844)
PHONE...............................909 466-4304
A Mateen Ahmed, *Pr*
Omar Ahmed, *VP*
EMP: 17 **EST:** 1990
SQ FT: 10,000
SALES (est): 5.09MM **Privately Held**
Web: www.newworldmedical.com
SIC: **3841** Ophthalmic instruments and apparatus

(P-10577)
NEWPORT MEDICAL INSTRS INC
Also Called: Covidien
1620 Sunflower Ave (92626-1513)
PHONE...............................949 642-3910
Philippe Negre, *Pr*
◆ **EMP: 89 EST:** 1981
SQ FT: 33,328
SALES (est): 10.73MM **Privately Held**
Web: www.allenstethoscopes.com
SIC: **3841 3842 3845** Surgical and medical instruments; Respirators; Electromedical equipment
HQ: Covidien Limited
20 Lower Hatch Street
Dublin

(P-10578)
NEXUS DX INC
6759 Mesa Ridge Rd (92121-4902)
PHONE...............................858 410-4600
Nam Shin, *CEO*
▼ **EMP: 34 EST:** 2009
SQ FT: 39,000
SALES (est): 8.02MM
SALES (corp-wide): 310.54K **Privately Held**
Web: www.nexus-dx.com
SIC: **3841** Diagnostic apparatus, medical
HQ: Polaris Medinet, Llc
13571 Zinnia Hills Pl
San Diego CA
858 410-4600

(P-10579)
NOBLES MEDICAL TECH INC
17080 Newhope St (92708-4206)
PHONE...............................714 427-0398
Anthony A Nobles, *Prin*
EMP: 42 **EST:** 2009
SALES (est): 2.32MM **Privately Held**
SIC: **3841** Medical instruments and equipment, blood and bone work

(P-10580)
NORDSON MEDICAL (CA) LLC
7612 Woodwind Dr (92647-7164)
PHONE...............................657 215-4200
David Zgonc, *Managing Member*
EMP: 51 EST: 1991
SQ FT: 40,000
SALES (est): 21.84MM
SALES (corp-wide): 2.59B **Publicly Held**
Web: www.nordsonmedical.com
SIC: **3841** Surgical and medical instruments
PA: Nordson Corporation
28601 Clemens Rd
Westlake OH
440 892-1580

(P-10581)
NU-HOPE LABORATORIES INC
12640 Branford St (91331-3451)
P.O. Box 331150 (91333-1150)
PHONE...............................818 899-7711
Bradley Johnson Galindo, *CEO*
Estelle Galindo, *
▲ **EMP: 38 EST:** 1959
SQ FT: 25,000
SALES (est): 4.78MM **Privately Held**
Web: www.nu-hope.com
SIC: **3841** Surgical and medical instruments

(P-10582)
NUVASIVE INC
4223 Ponderosa Ave Ste C (92123-1529)
PHONE...............................858 909-1800
EMP: 18
SALES (corp-wide): 958.1MM **Publicly Held**
Web: www.nuvasive.com
SIC: **3841** Surgical and medical instruments
HQ: Nuvasive, Inc.
7475 Lusk Blvd
San Diego CA
858 909-1800

(P-10583)
NUVASIVE INC (HQ)
7475 Lusk Blvd (92121-5707)
PHONE...............................858 909-1800
J Christopher Barry, *CEO*
Daniel J Wolterman, *
Rajesh J Asarpota, *CAO*
Carol A Cox, *External Affairs Vice President*
Joan B Stafslien, *Corporate Secretary*
▲ **EMP: 75 EST:** 1997
SQ FT: 152,000
SALES (est): 403.72MM
SALES (corp-wide): 958.1MM **Publicly Held**
Web: www.nuvasive.com
SIC: **3841** Surgical and medical instruments
PA: Globus Medical, Inc.
2560 Gen Armistead Ave
West Norriton PA
610 930-1800

(P-10584)
NUVASIVE SPCLZED ORTHPDICS INC
101 Enterprise Ste 100 (92656-2604)
PHONE...............................949 837-3600
Edmund Roschak, *CEO*

Robert Krist, *
Jeff Rydin, *CSO**
EMP: 100 **EST:** 2007
SQ FT: 52,741
SALES (est): 21.37MM
SALES (corp-wide): 958.1MM **Publicly Held**
Web: www.nuvasive.com
SIC: 3841 Inhalation therapy equipment
HQ: Nuvasive, Inc.
7475 Lusk Blvd
San Diego CA
858 909-1800

(P-10585)
ORCHID MPS
3233 W Harvard St (92704-3917)
PHONE..................714 549-9203
Mark Deischter, *VP*
EMP: 100 **EST:** 2005
SALES (est): 4.6MM **Privately Held**
Web: www.orchid-ortho.com
SIC: 3841 Surgical and medical instruments

(P-10586)
PACIFIC INTEGRATED MFG INC
4364 Bonita Rd Ste 454 (91902-1421)
PHONE..................619 921-3464
Stephen F Keane, *CEO*
Charles Peinado, *
EMP: 200 **EST:** 2000
SALES (est): 8.98MM **Privately Held**
Web: www.pacific-im.com
SIC: 3841 Diagnostic apparatus, medical

(P-10587)
PETER BRASSELER HOLDINGS LLC
4837 Mcgrath St (93003-6442)
PHONE..................805 658-2643
Laura Kriese, *Brnch Mgr*
EMP: 74
SALES (corp-wide): 47.53MM **Privately Held**
Web: www.brasselerusamedical.com
SIC: 3841 Surgical and medical instruments
PA: Peter Brasseler Holdings, Llc
1 Brasseler Blvd
Savannah GA
912 925-8525

(P-10588)
PHARMACO-KINESIS CORPORATION
10604 S La Cienega Blvd (90304-1115)
PHONE..................310 641-2700
Frank Adell, *Prin*
Thomas Chen, *
Peter Hirshfield, *
John Muthew, *
EMP: 26 **EST:** 2006
SALES (est): 4.94MM **Privately Held**
Web: www.pharmaco-kinesis.com
SIC: 3841 Surgical and medical instruments

(P-10589)
PHILLPS-MDISIZE COSTA MESA LLC
3545 Harbor Blvd (92626-1406)
PHONE..................949 477-9495
Bob Frank, *Genl Mgr*
EMP: 240 **EST:** 1997
SQ FT: 45,000
SALES (est): 50.36MM
SALES (corp-wide): 36.93B **Privately Held**
Web: www.phillipsmedisize.com
SIC: 3841 Surgical and medical instruments
HQ: Molex, Llc
2222 Wellington Ct

Lisle IL
630 969-4550

(P-10590)
PLANET INNOVATION INC
2720 Loker Ave W Ste P (92010-6606)
PHONE..................847 943-7270
Anthony White, *Pr*
EMP: 30 **EST:** 2013
SALES (est): 9.4MM **Privately Held**
Web: www.planetinnovation.com
SIC: 3841 Surgical and medical instruments
PA: Planet Innovation Holdings Ltd
436 Elgar Rd
Box Hill VIC

(P-10591)
PRO-DEX INC (PA)
Also Called: Pro-Dex
2361 Mcgaw Ave (92614-5831)
PHONE..................949 769-3200
Richard L Van Kirk, *Pr*
Nicholas J Swenson, *
Alisha K Charlton, *CFO*
EMP: 120 **EST:** 1978
SQ FT: 28,000
SALES (est): 46.09MM **Publicly Held**
Web: www.pro-dex.com
SIC: 3841 3843 7372 3594 Surgical and medical instruments; Dental equipment; Business oriented computer software; Motors, pneumatic

(P-10592)
PROVIDIEN MACHINING & METALS CORPORATION
Also Called: Dynaroll
12840 Bradley Ave (91342-3827)
PHONE..................818 367-3161
◆ **EMP:** 70 **EST:** 1987
SALES (est): 13.34MM **Privately Held**
Web: www.providienmedical.com
SIC: 3841 Surgical and medical instruments
PA: Providien, Llc
6740 Nancy Ridge Dr
San Diego CA

(P-10593)
PRYOR PRODUCTS
1819 Peacock Blvd (92056-3578)
PHONE..................760 724-8244
Jeffrey Pryor, *CEO*
Paul Pryor, *
▲ **EMP:** 50 **EST:** 1971
SQ FT: 29,000
SALES (est): 9.08MM **Privately Held**
Web: www.pryorproducts.com
SIC: 3841 IV transfusion apparatus

(P-10594)
RADIOLOGY SUPPORT DEVICES INC
1904 E Dominguez St (90810-1002)
PHONE..................310 518-0527
Matthew Alderson, *CEO*
EMP: 29 **EST:** 1989
SQ FT: 16,000
SALES (est): 4.2MM **Privately Held**
Web: www.rsdphantoms.com
SIC: 3841 3844 Diagnostic apparatus, medical; X-ray apparatus and tubes

(P-10595)
REBOUND THERAPEUTICS CORP
13900 Alton Pkwy Ste 120 (92618-1621)
PHONE..................949 305-8111
Jeffrey Valko, *CEO*
EMP: 26 **EST:** 2015

SALES (est): 4.61MM **Publicly Held**
SIC: 3841 Surgical and medical instruments
PA: Integra Lifesciences Holdings Corporation
1100 Campus Rd
Princeton NJ

(P-10596)
RESMED CORP
14040 Danielson St (92064-6857)
PHONE..................858 746-2400
EMP: 30 **EST:** 2019
SALES (est): 1.68MM **Privately Held**
Web: www.resmed.co.in
SIC: 3841 Surgical and medical instruments

(P-10597)
RESMED INC (PA)
Also Called: Resmed
9001 Spectrum Center Blvd (92123-1438)
PHONE..................858 836-5000
Michael Farrell, *Ch Bd*
Rob Douglas, *Pr*
Brett Sandercock, *CFO*
EMP: 702 **EST:** 1989
SQ FT: 230,000
SALES (est): 4.22B **Publicly Held**
Web: www.resmed.com
SIC: 3841 7372 Diagnostic apparatus, medical; Application computer software

(P-10598)
REVERSE MEDICAL CORPORATION
Also Called: Reverse Medical
13700 Alton Pkwy Ste 167 (92618-1618)
PHONE..................949 215-0660
EMP: 47 **EST:** 2007
SALES (est): 2.76MM **Privately Held**
Web: www.reversemed.com
SIC: 3841 Surgical and medical instruments
HQ: Covidien Limited
20 Lower Hatch Street
Dublin

(P-10599)
RF SURGICAL SYSTEMS LLC
5927 Landau Ct (92008-8803)
PHONE..................855 522-7027
John Buhler, *Pr*
Ron Wangerin, *CFO*
▲ **EMP:** 55 **EST:** 2008
SQ FT: 24,000
SALES (est): 20.94MM **Privately Held**
SIC: 3841 Surgical and medical instruments
HQ: Medtronic, Inc.
710 Medtronic Pkwy
Minneapolis MN
763 514-4000

(P-10600)
RMS/ENDLGIX SDWAYS MERGER CORP
2 Musick (92618-1631)
PHONE..................949 595-7200
John Onopchenko, *CEO*
EMP: 55 **EST:** 2002
SALES (est): 2.27MM **Privately Held**
Web: www.endologix.com
SIC: 3841 Catheters
PA: Endologix, Inc.
2 Musick
Irvine CA

(P-10601)
ROX MEDICAL INC (PA)
150 Calle Iglesia Ste A (92672-7550)
P.O. Box 4078 (92629-9078)
PHONE..................949 276-8968

Mike Mackinnon, *CEO*
Keegan Harper, *Ch Bd*
Jonathan Sackner-bernstein, *CMO*
EMP: 19 **EST:** 2003
SQ FT: 3,500
SALES (est): 2.48MM
SALES (corp-wide): 2.48MM **Privately Held**
Web: www.roxmedical.com
SIC: 3841 Surgical and medical instruments

(P-10602)
SECHRIST INDUSTRIES INC
4225 E La Palma Ave (92807-1815)
PHONE..................714 579-8400
Edward Pulwer, *CEO*
John Razzano, *
◆ **EMP:** 2336 **EST:** 1973
SQ FT: 74,000
SALES (est): 24.01MM
SALES (corp-wide): 240.92MM **Privately Held**
Web: www.sechristusa.com
SIC: 3841 Surgical and medical instruments
HQ: Wound Care Holdings, Llc
5220 Belfort Rd Ste 130
Jacksonville FL
800 379-9774

(P-10603)
SENDX MEDICAL INC
1945 Palomar Oaks Way Ste 100 (92011-1300)
PHONE..................760 930-6300
Henrik Schimmell, *Pr*
▲ **EMP:** 116 **EST:** 1998
SQ FT: 35,000
SALES (est): 33.44MM
SALES (corp-wide): 31.47B **Publicly Held**
SIC: 3841 Surgical and medical instruments
HQ: Radiometer America Inc.
250 S Kraemer Blvd Msb1sw
Brea CA
800 736-0600

(P-10604)
SEQUENT MEDICAL INC
35 Enterprise (92656-2601)
PHONE..................949 830-9600
Thomas C Wilder, *Pr*
Kevin J Cousins, *
EMP: 65 **EST:** 2006
SALES (est): 10.95MM **Privately Held**
Web: microvention.herokuapp.com
SIC: 3841 Surgical and medical instruments
HQ: Microvention, Inc.
35 Enterprise
Aliso Viejo CA
714 258-8000

(P-10605)
SIEMENS HLTHCARE DGNOSTICS INC
Also Called: Siemens Medical Solutions
5210 Pacific Concourse Dr (90045-6900)
PHONE..................310 645-8200
Anthony Bihl, *Brnch Mgr*
EMP: 55
SALES (corp-wide): 84.48B **Privately Held**
Web: new.siemens.com
SIC: 3841 5047 8011 8734 Diagnostic apparatus, medical; Diagnostic equipment, medical; Hematologist; X-ray inspection service, industrial
HQ: Siemens Healthcare Diagnostics Inc.
511 Benedict Ave
Tarrytown NY
914 631-8000

(P-10606)
SOURCE SCIENTIFIC LLC
2144 Michelson Dr (92612-1304)
PHONE.....................949 231-5096
▲ **EMP:** 39
Web: www.bit-group.com
SIC: 3841 8711 Surgical and medical
instruments; Engineering services

(P-10607)
SPECIALTEAM MEDICAL SVC INC
22445 La Palma Ave Ste F (92887-3811)
PHONE.....................714 694-0348
EMP: 17 **EST:** 1996
SQ FT: 7,000
SALES (est): 713.9K **Privately Held**
Web: www.specialteam.com
SIC: 3841 Surgical and medical instruments

(P-10608)
SPECTRUM INC
Also Called: Spectrum Laboratories
18617 S Broadwick St (90220-6435)
P.O. Box 512939 (90051-0939)
PHONE.....................310 885-4600
▲ **EMP:** 200
SIC: 3841 3821 3842 Surgical and medical
instruments; Laboratory apparatus and
furniture; Surgical appliances and supplies

(P-10609)
SPINAL ELEMENTS HOLDINGS INC
Also Called: Spinal Elements
3115 Melrose Dr Ste 200 (92010-6690)
PHONE.....................877 774-6255
Ronald Lloyd, *Pr*
Steven J Healy, *
Steve Mcgowan, *CFO*
Ricardo J Simmons, *CMO*
Paul Graveline, *Ex VP*
EMP: 120 **EST:** 2016
SQ FT: 42,000
SALES (est): 95.92MM **Privately Held**
Web: www.spinalelements.com
SIC: 3841 Surgical and medical instruments

(P-10610)
SURGISTAR INC (PA)
Also Called: Sabel
2310 La Mirada Dr (92081-7862)
PHONE.....................760 598-2480
Jonathan Woodward, *Pr*
Hema Chaudhary, *
◆ **EMP:** 35 **EST:** 1992
SQ FT: 12,000
SALES (est): 4.99MM **Privately Held**
Web: www.surgistar.com
SIC: 3841 Surgical and medical instruments

(P-10611)
SWEDEN & MARTINA INC
600 Anton Blvd Ste 1134 (92626-1920)
PHONE.....................844 862-7846
Elisabetta Martina, *Pr*
EMP: 33 **EST:** 2014
SALES (est): 1.59MM **Privately Held**
SIC: 3841 Medical instruments and
equipment, blood and bone work

(P-10612)
SYNERGY HEALTH AST LLC (DH)
Also Called: Americas Regional Division
9020 Activity Rd Ste D (92126-4454)
PHONE.....................858 586-1166
▲ **EMP:** 44 **EST:** 2004

SALES (est): 11.65MM **Privately Held**
SIC: 3841 Surgical and medical instruments
HQ: Steris Corporation
5960 Heisley Rd
Mentor OH
440 354-2600

(P-10613)
TANDEM DIABETES CARE INC (PA)
Also Called: Tandem Diabetes Care
12400 High Bluff Dr (92130-3077)
PHONE.....................877 801-6901
John F Sheridan, *Pr*
Rebecca Robertson, *
David B Berger, *Ex VP*
Leigh A Vosseller, *Ex VP*
EMP: 2549 **EST:** 2006
SQ FT: 77,458
SALES (est): 801.22MM **Publicly Held**
Web: www.tandemdiabetes.com
SIC: 3841 2833 Surgical and medical
instruments; Insulin: bulk, uncompounded

(P-10614)
TANDEM MEDICAL INC
535 Encinitas Blvd Ste 109 (92024-3742)
PHONE.....................858 673-3900
Marc S Lieberman, *Pr*
EMP: 30 **EST:** 1998
SALES (est): 1.76MM **Privately Held**
Web: www.tanmed.com
SIC: 3841 IV transfusion apparatus

(P-10615)
TECOMET INC
Also Called: Tecomet
503 S Vincent Ave (91702-5131)
PHONE.....................626 334-1519
EMP: 547
SALES (corp-wide): 832.81MM **Privately Held**
Web: www.tecomet.com
SIC: 3841 3444 Diagnostic apparatus,
medical; Sheet metalwork
HQ: Tecomet Inc.
115 Eames St
Wilmington MA
978 642-2400

(P-10616)
TENEX HEALTH INC
26902 Vista Ter (92630-8123)
PHONE.....................949 454-7500
William Maya, *Pr*
Bernard Morrey, *Chief Medical Officer*
Ivan Mijatovic, *
Jagi Gill, *
▲ **EMP:** 70 **EST:** 2011
SQ FT: 15,000
SALES (est): 8MM **Privately Held**
Web: www.tenexhealth.com
SIC: 3841 Surgical and medical instruments

(P-10617)
THI INC
1525 E Edinger Ave (92705-4907)
PHONE.....................714 444-4643
Jim Willett, *CEO*
▲ **EMP:** 100 **EST:** 2000
SQ FT: 35,000
SALES (est): 21.72MM **Privately Held**
Web: www.tenacore.com
SIC: 3841 7699 Surgical instruments and
apparatus; Surgical instrument repair

(P-10618)
TMJ SOLUTIONS LLC
Also Called: TMJ Concepts
6059 King Dr (93003-7607)

PHONE.....................805 650-3391
Heather Wise, *Pr*
EMP: 54 **EST:** 1989
SQ FT: 7,280
SALES (est): 9.73MM
SALES (corp-wide): 18.45B **Publicly Held**
SIC: 3841 Surgical and medical instruments
PA: Stryker Corporation
2825 Airview Blvd
Portage MI
269 385-2600

(P-10619)
TRELLBORG SLING SLTIONS US INC (DH)
Also Called: Issac
2761 Walnut Ave (92780-7051)
PHONE.....................714 415-0280
William Reising, *CEO*
Tom Mazelin, *
Ron Fraleigh, *
Kevin Beatty, *
Fiona Guo, *
EMP: 150 **EST:** 1993
SQ FT: 1,600
SALES (est): 43.74MM
SALES (corp-wide): 4.26B **Privately Held**
SIC: 3841 Surgical and medical instruments
HQ: Trelleborg Corporation
200 Veterans Blvd Ste 3
South Haven MI
269 639-9891

(P-10620)
TRELLEBORG SEALING SOLUTIONS
Also Called: TRELLEBORG SEALING
SOLUTIONS TUSTIN, INC.
3034 Propeller Dr (93446-9519)
PHONE.....................805 239-4284
William E Reising, *Brnch Mgr*
EMP: 85
SALES (corp-wide): 4.26B **Privately Held**
SIC: 3841 Surgical and medical instruments
HQ: Trelleborg Sealing Solutions Us, Inc.
2761 Walnut Ave
Tustin CA

(P-10621)
TRIVASCULAR INC (DH)
2 Musick (92618-1631)
PHONE.....................707 543-8800
John Onopchenko, *CEO*
EMP: 36 **EST:** 1998
SALES (est): 38.18MM **Privately Held**
Web: www.endologix.com
SIC: 3841 Surgical and medical instruments
HQ: Trivascular Technologies, Inc.
2 Musick
Irvine CA
707 543-8800

(P-10622)
TRIVASCULAR TECHNOLOGIES INC (HQ)
2 Musick (92618-1631)
PHONE.....................707 543-8800
John Onopchenko, *CEO*
Christopher G Chavez, *Pr*
Michael R Kramer, *CFO*
EMP: 188 **EST:** 2008
SQ FT: 110,000
SALES (est): 47.3MM **Privately Held**
Web: www.endologix.com
SIC: 3841 Surgical and medical instruments
PA: Endologix, Inc.
2 Musick
Irvine CA

(P-10623)
TRUEVISION SYSTEMS INC
Also Called: Truevision 3d Surgical
315 Bollay Dr Ste 101 (93117-2948)
PHONE.....................805 963-9700
A Burton Tripathi, *CEO*
Robert Reali, *
▲ **EMP:** 43 **EST:** 2003
SQ FT: 10,549
SALES (est): 13.65MM **Privately Held**
Web: www.myalcon.com
SIC: 3841 Surgical and medical instruments
HQ: Alcon, Inc.
1132 Ferris Rd
Amelia OH
513 722-1037

(P-10624)
U S MEDICAL INSTRUMENTS INC (PA)
888 Prospect St Ste 100 (92037-8200)
P.O. Box 928439 (92192-8439)
PHONE.....................619 661-5500
Matthew Mazur, *Ch*
George A Schapiro, *Sec*
Carlos H Manjarrez, *VP Opers*
Eldridge Fridge, *Dir*
A R Moosa, *Dir*
EMP: 33 **EST:** 1991
SQ FT: 60,000
SALES (est): 4.11MM **Privately Held**
SIC: 3841 Surgical and medical instruments

(P-10625)
UNITED MEDICAL DEVICES LLC
16250 Ventura Blvd (91436-2204)
PHONE.....................310 551-4100
EMP: 24 **EST:** 2010
SALES (est): 878.74K **Privately Held**
Web: www.playboycondoms.com
SIC: 3841 Surgical and medical instruments

(P-10626)
UOC USA INC
Also Called: United Orthopedic Corp USA
15251 Alton Pkwy Ste 100 (92618-2307)
PHONE.....................949 328-3366
Calvin Lin, *Pr*
▲ **EMP:** 17 **EST:** 2012
SALES (est): 4.79MM **Privately Held**
Web: us.unitedorthopedic.com
SIC: 3841 Surgical and medical instruments
PA: United Orthopedic Corporation
No. 57, Park Ave. 2 Science Park
Hsinchu City

(P-10627)
VERTIFLEX INC
25155 Rye Canyon Loop (91355-5004)
PHONE.....................442 325-5900
Earl Fender, *CEO*
EMP: 40 **EST:** 2004
SALES (est): 14.83MM
SALES (corp-wide): 12.68B **Publicly Held**
Web: www.bostonscientific.com
SIC: 3841 Surgical and medical instruments
PA: Boston Scientific Corporation
300 Boston Scientific Way
Marlborough MA
508 683-4000

(P-10628)
VERTOS MEDICAL INC LLC
95 Enterprise Ste 325 (92656-2612)
PHONE.....................949 349-0008
James M Corbett, *CEO*
Rebecca Colbert, *CFO*
Stephen E Paul, *Chief Commercial Officer*
EMP: 62 **EST:** 2005
SQ FT: 25,000

PRODUCTS & SVCS

SALES (est): 10.28MM **Privately Held**
Web: www.vertosmed.com
SIC: 3841 3842 Medical instruments and
  equipment, blood and bone work; Surgical
  appliances and supplies

(P-10629)
VIASYS RESPIRATORY CARE INC
Also Called: Biosys Healthcare
22745 Savi Ranch Pkwy (92887-4668)
PHONE..............................714 283-2228
William B Ross, *Pr*
EMP: 56 EST: 1961
SQ FT: 120,000
SALES (est): 2.6MM
SALES (corp-wide): 19.37B **Publicly Held**
Web: www.viasyshealthcare.com
SIC: 3841 Diagnostic apparatus, medical
HQ: Carefusion Corporation
  3750 Torrey View Ct
  San Diego CA

(P-10630)
VYAIRE MEDICAL INC
510 Technology Dr Ste 100 (92618-1346)
PHONE..............................714 919-3265
Gaurav Agarwal, *CEO*
EMP: 30
SALES (corp-wide): 1.8B **Privately Held**
Web: www.vyaire.com
SIC: 3841 Surgical and medical instruments
HQ: Vyaire Medical, Inc.
  26125 N Riverwoods Blvd
  Mettawa IL
  833 327-3284

3842 Surgical Appliances And Supplies

(P-10631)
ADVANCED ARM DYNAMICS (PA)
123 W Torrance Blvd Ste 203 (90277-3614)
PHONE..............................310 372-3050
John Miguelez, *Pr*
Creighton Uyechi, *
Dan Conyers, *
Tiffany Ryan, *
Misty Carver, *
EMP: 21 EST: 1998
SALES (est): 9.94MM
SALES (corp-wide): 9.94MM **Privately Held**
Web: www.armdynamics.com
SIC: 3842 Prosthetic appliances

(P-10632)
ADVANCED BIONICS LLC (HQ)
Also Called: A B
12740 San Fernando Rd (91342-3700)
PHONE..............................661 362-1400
Rainer Platz, *CEO*
EMP: 450 EST: 1997
SALES (est): 91.6MM **Privately Held**
Web: www.advancedbionics.com
SIC: 3842 Hearing aids
PA: Sonova Holding Ag
  Laubisrutistrasse 28
  StAfa ZH

(P-10633)
ADVANCED BIONICS CORPORATION (HQ)
28515 Westinghouse Pl (91355-4833)
PHONE..............................661 362-1400
Rainer Platz, *CEO*
Alfred Mann, *

Jeffrey Goldberg, *
▲ EMP: 154 EST: 2007
SALES (est): 130.03MM **Privately Held**
Web: www.advancedbionics.com
SIC: 3842 Hearing aids
PA: Sonova Holding Ag
  Laubisrutistrasse 28
  StAfa ZH

(P-10634)
ALPHATEC SPINE INC (HQ)
Also Called: Atec Spine
1950 Camino Vida Roble (92008-6505)
PHONE..............................760 431-9286
James M Corbett, *CEO*
Patrick Ryan, *
Thomas Mcleer, *Sr VP*
Ebun S Garner, *
Michael O'neill, *CFO*
▲ EMP: 250 EST: 1990
SALES (est): 93.43MM **Publicly Held**
Web: www.atecspine.com
SIC: 3842 8711 5047 Surgical appliances
  and supplies; Engineering services;
  Medical equipment and supplies
PA: Alphatec Holdings, Inc.
  1950 Camino Vida Roble
  Carlsbad CA

(P-10635)
AMERICAN MED O & P CLINIC INC
4955 Van Nuys Blvd (91403-1801)
PHONE..............................818 281-5747
Konstandin Kumuryan, *CEO*
EMP: 20 EST: 2020
SALES (est): 1.33MM **Privately Held**
SIC: 3842 Prosthetic appliances

(P-10636)
AMERICH CORPORATION (PA)
13222 Saticoy St (91605-3404)
PHONE..............................818 982-1711
Edward Richmond, *Pr*
Dino Pacifici, *
Greg Richmond, *
▲ EMP: 120 EST: 1982
SALES (est): 23.68MM
SALES (corp-wide): 23.68MM **Privately Held**
Web: www.americh.com
SIC: 3842 3432 3431 3261 Whirlpool baths,
  hydrotherapy equipment; Plumbing fixture
  fittings and trim; Metal sanitary ware;
  Vitreous plumbing fixtures

(P-10637)
ANSELL SNDEL MED SOLUTIONS LLC
9301 Oakdale Ave Ste 300 (91311-6539)
PHONE..............................818 534-2500
Anthony B Lopez, *Pr*
Wendell Franke, *Associate Director Global Training*
Stephanie Barth, *
◆ EMP: 32 EST: 2002
SQ FT: 14,600
SALES (est): 6.94MM **Privately Held**
Web: www.ansell.com
SIC: 3842 Surgical appliances and supplies
PA: Ansell Limited
  678 Victoria St
  Richmond VIC

(P-10638)
BIOMET INC
181 Technology Dr (92618-2484)
PHONE..............................949 453-3200
EMP: 29
SALES (corp-wide): 6.94B **Publicly Held**

Web: www.zimmerbiomet.com
SIC: 3842 Orthopedic appliances
HQ: Biomet, Inc.
  345 E Main St
  Warsaw IN
  574 267-6639

(P-10639)
BOSTON SCNTFIC NRMDLATION CORP (HQ)
25155 Rye Canyon Loop (91355-5004)
PHONE..............................661 949-4310
Michael F Mahoney, *CEO*
Kevin Ballinger, *
Wendy Carruthers, *
Supratim Bose, *
Jeffrey D Capello, *
▲ EMP: 450 EST: 1993
SQ FT: 26,000
SALES (est): 92.78MM
SALES (corp-wide): 12.68B **Publicly Held**
SIC: 3842 3841 5047 Hearing aids; Surgical
  and medical instruments; Medical and
  hospital equipment
PA: Boston Scientific Corporation
  300 Boston Scientific Way
  Marlborough MA
  508 683-4000

(P-10640)
BOYD CHATSWORTH INC
9959 Canoga Ave (91311-3002)
PHONE..............................818 998-1477
Douglas Britt, *CEO*
Jeremiah Shives, *
Kelly Weber, *
▲ EMP: 59 EST: 1972
SQ FT: 14,000
SALES (est): 14.47MM **Privately Held**
Web: www.boydcorp.com
SIC: 3842 Adhesive tape and plasters,
  medicated or non-medicated
HQ: Boyd Corporation
  5960 Inglewood Dr Ste 115
  Pleasanton CA
  209 236-1111

(P-10641)
BREATHE TECHNOLOGIES INC
15091 Bake Pkwy (92618-2501)
PHONE..............................949 988-7700
Lawrence A Mastrovich, *Pr*
Paul J Lytle, *
John L Miclot, *
Rebecca Mabry, *
Gary Berman, *Chief Business Officer*
EMP: 39 EST: 2005
SALES (est): 24.46MM
SALES (corp-wide): 15.11B **Publicly Held**
Web: www.hillrom.com
SIC: 3842 Respirators
HQ: Hill-Rom, Inc.
  1069 State Route 46 E
  Batesville IN
  812 934-7777

(P-10642)
CURTISS-WRGHT CNTRLS INTGRTED
Also Called: Penny & Giles Drive Technology
210 Ranger Ave (92821-6215)
PHONE..............................714 982-1860
John Camp, *Pr*
EMP: 69
SALES (corp-wide): 2.56B **Publicly Held**
Web: www.curtisswright.com
SIC: 3842 Braces, elastic
HQ: Curtiss-Wright Controls Integrated
  Sensing, Inc.
  28965 Avenue Penn

Valencia CA
661 257-4430

(P-10643)
DIAMOND GLOVES
1100 S Linwood Ave Ste A (92705-4345)
PHONE..............................714 667-0506
John Te, *CEO*
▲ EMP: 22 EST: 2009
SALES (est): 2.4MM **Privately Held**
Web: www.diamondglove.com
SIC: 3842 Gloves, safety

(P-10644)
DJO LLC
3151 Scott St (92081-8365)
PHONE..............................760 727-1280
Andi Donner, *Brnch Mgr*
EMP: 55
SALES (corp-wide): 1.56B **Publicly Held**
Web: www.djoglobal.com
SIC: 3842 Surgical appliances and supplies
HQ: Djo, Llc
  2900 Lake Vista Dr # 200
  Lewisville TX
  760 727-1283

(P-10645)
DJO LLC
1430 Decision St (92081-8553)
PHONE..............................800 321-9549
EMP: 41
SALES (corp-wide): 1.56B **Publicly Held**
Web: www.djoglobal.com
SIC: 3842 Surgical appliances and supplies
HQ: Djo, Llc
  2900 Lake Vista Dr # 200
  Lewisville TX
  760 727-1283

(P-10646)
DJO LLC
5919 Sea Otter Pl Ste 200 (92010-6750)
PHONE..............................800 321-9549
EMP: 26
SALES (corp-wide): 1.56B **Publicly Held**
Web: www.djoglobal.com
SIC: 3842 Surgical appliances and supplies
HQ: Djo, Llc
  2900 Lake Vista Dr # 200
  Lewisville TX
  760 727-1283

(P-10647)
DJO CONSUMER LLC
Also Called: Enovis Consumer
1430 Decision St (92081-8553)
PHONE..............................760 727-1280
EMP: 18
SALES (est): 502.08K **Privately Held**
SIC: 3842 Surgical appliances and supplies

(P-10648)
DJO HOLDINGS LLC (DH)
1430 Decision St (92081-8553)
PHONE..............................760 727-1280
Brady R Shirley, *Pr*
▼ EMP: 22 EST: 2006
SALES (est): 1.19B
SALES (corp-wide): 1.56B **Publicly Held**
Web: www.djoglobal.com
SIC: 3842 Surgical appliances and supplies
HQ: Djo Global, Inc.
  2900 Lake Vista Dr
  Lewisville TX

(P-10649)
DRS OWN INC (PA)
Also Called: Good Feet

5923 Farnsworth Ct (92008-7303)
PHONE............................760 804-0751
David E Workman, *Pr*
◆ **EMP:** 20 **EST:** 1995
SQ FT: 18,400
SALES (est): 5.9MM
SALES (corp-wide): 5.9MM **Privately Held**
Web: www.goodfeet.com
SIC: 3842 Abdominal supporters, braces, and trusses

(P-10650)
DYNAMICS ORTHTICS PRSTHTICS IN
Also Called: Dynamics O&P
1830 W Olympic Blvd Ste 123
(90006-3734)
PHONE............................213 383-9212
Peter J Sean, *CEO*
EMP: 34 **EST:** 1988
SQ FT: 20,662
SALES (est): 5.24MM **Privately Held**
Web: www.walkagain.com
SIC: 3842 Orthopedic appliances

(P-10651)
EDWARDS LIFESCIENCES
11811 Landon Dr (91752-4002)
PHONE............................951 749-3316
EMP: 23
SALES (est): 585.13K **Privately Held**
Web: www.edwards.com
SIC: 3842 Surgical appliances and supplies

(P-10652)
EDWARDS LIFESCIENCES CORP
1402 Alton Pkwy (92606-4838)
PHONE............................949 250-3522
Diane Nguyen, *Brnch Mgr*
EMP: 17
SALES (corp-wide): 5.38B **Publicly Held**
Web: www.edwards.com
SIC: 3842 Surgical appliances and supplies
PA: Edwards Lifesciences Corp
1 Edwards Way
Irvine CA
949 250-2500

(P-10653)
EDWARDS LIFESCIENCES CORP (PA)
Also Called: EDWARDS
1 Edwards Way (92614-5688)
PHONE............................949 250-2500
Bernard J Zovighian, *Pr*
Michael A Mussallem, *Non-Executive Chairman of the Board*
Scott B Ullem, *Corporate Vice President*
Donald E Bobo Junior, *Corporate Vice President*
Daveen Chopra, *Corporate Vice President*
EMP: 1600 **EST:** 1958
SALES (est): 5.38B
SALES (corp-wide): 5.38B **Publicly Held**
Web: www.edwards.com
SIC: 3842 Surgical appliances and supplies

(P-10654)
EDWARDS LIFESCIENCES CORP
Also Called: Edwards Life Sciences Cardio V
17221 Red Hill Ave (92614-5688)
PHONE............................949 250-2500
EMP: 124
SALES (corp-wide): 5.38B **Publicly Held**
Web: www.edwards.com
SIC: 3842 Surgical appliances and supplies
PA: Edwards Lifesciences Corp
1 Edwards Way
Irvine CA
949 250-2500

(P-10655)
EDWARDS LIFESCIENCES CORP PR
1 Edwards Way (92614-5688)
PHONE............................949 250-2500
Michael A Mussallem, *Ch*
Dirksen J Lehman, *VP*
Christine Z Mccauley, *VP*
Stanton J Rowe, *VP*
Scott B Ullem, *VP*
EMP: 47 **EST:** 1999
SALES (est): 2.14MM
SALES (corp-wide): 5.38B **Publicly Held**
Web: www.edwards.com
SIC: 3842 Orthopedic appliances
PA: Edwards Lifesciences Corp
1 Edwards Way
Irvine CA
949 250-2500

(P-10656)
EMERGENT GROUP INC (DH)
10939 Pendleton St (91352-1522)
PHONE............................818 394-2800
Bruce J Haber, *CEO*
Louis Buther, *Pr*
William M Mckay, *CFO*
EMP: 55 **EST:** 1996
SQ FT: 13,000
SALES (est): 20.18MM
SALES (corp-wide): 1.12B **Publicly Held**
SIC: 3842 7352 Surgical appliances and supplies; Medical equipment rental
HQ: Agiliti Health, Inc.
6625 W 78th St Ste 300
Minneapolis MN
952 893-3200

(P-10657)
ENDOTEC INC
14525 Valley View Ave Ste H (90670-5237)
PHONE............................714 681-6306
Young B Shim, *CEO*
EMP: 39 **EST:** 1999
SQ FT: 5,900
SALES (est): 11.25MM **Privately Held**
SIC: 3842 Orthopedic appliances
PA: Cellumed Co., Ltd.
Rm 402
Seoul

(P-10658)
ETHICON INC
33 Technology Dr (92618-2346)
PHONE............................949 581-5799
Charles Austin, *Brnch Mgr*
EMP: 300
SALES (corp-wide): 94.94B **Publicly Held**
Web: www.jnj.com
SIC: 3842 Sutures, absorbable and non-absorbable
HQ: Ethicon Inc.
1000 Route 202
Raritan NJ
800 384-4266

(P-10659)
FERRACO INC (HQ)
Also Called: Human Dsgns Prsthtic Orthtic L
2933 Long Beach Blvd (90806-1517)
PHONE............................562 988-2414
Natalie Rose Cronin, *CEO*
Eric Ferraco, *
Brian Cronin, *
EMP: 23 **EST:** 1991
SALES (est): 8MM
SALES (corp-wide): 16MM **Privately Held**
Web: www.humandesigns.com
SIC: 3842 Surgical appliances and supplies
PA: Arc-V, Inc.
1639 N Hollywood Way

Burbank CA
626 445-7797

(P-10660)
FINEST HOUR HOLDINGS INC
Also Called: Aos
3203 Kashiwa St (90505-4020)
PHONE............................310 533-9966
Gary Sohngen, *CEO*
Paul Doner, *
Barry Hubbard, *
Michael Payne, *
EMP: 34 **EST:** 2001
SALES (est): 5.22MM **Privately Held**
Web: www.aosortho.com
SIC: 3842 Implants, surgical

(P-10661)
FRANK STUBBS CO INC
1830 Eastman Ave (93030-8935)
PHONE............................805 278-4300
Glenn Soensker, *CFO*
David Paul Pearson, *
Glenn Alan Slensker, *
EMP: 23 **EST:** 1966
SQ FT: 50,100
SALES (est): 1.16MM **Privately Held**
Web: www.fstubbs.com
SIC: 3842 Supports: abdominal, ankle, arch, kneecap, etc.

(P-10662)
FREEDOM DESIGNS INC
2241 N Madera Rd (93065-1762)
PHONE............................805 582-0077
Kathleen Leneghan, *Pr*
▲ **EMP:** 120 **EST:** 1981
SQ FT: 40,000
SALES (est): 20.93MM
SALES (corp-wide): 741.73MM **Publicly Held**
Web: www.freedomdesigns.com
SIC: 3842 Wheelchairs
PA: Invacare Corporation
1 Invacare Way
Elyria OH
440 329-6000

(P-10663)
FREUDENBERG MEDICAL LLC (DH)
Also Called: Helix Medical
1110 Mark Ave (93013-2918)
PHONE............................805 684-3304
Jorg Schneewind, *CEO*
Thomas Vassalo, *
▲ **EMP:** 177 **EST:** 1984
SQ FT: 66,000
SALES (est): 130.52MM
SALES (corp-wide): 12.23B **Privately Held**
Web: www.freudenbergmedical.com
SIC: 3842 Prosthetic appliances
HQ: Freudenberg North America Limited Partnership
47774 W Anchor Ct
Plymouth MI

(P-10664)
FREUDENBERG MEDICAL LLC
6385 Rose Ln Ste A (93013-2941)
PHONE............................805 576-5308
Belinda Jackson, *Mgr*
EMP: 66
SALES (corp-wide): 12.23B **Privately Held**
Web: www.freudenbergmedical.com
SIC: 3842 Prosthetic appliances
HQ: Freudenberg Medical, Llc
1110 Mark Ave
Carpinteria CA
805 684-3304

(P-10665)
FREUDENBERG MEDICAL LLC
1009 Cindy Ln (93013-2905)
PHONE............................805 684-3304
Lorena Lundeen, *Mgr*
EMP: 49
SALES (corp-wide): 12.23B **Privately Held**
Web: www.freudenbergmedical.com
SIC: 3842 Prosthetic appliances
HQ: Freudenberg Medical, Llc
1110 Mark Ave
Carpinteria CA
805 684-3304

(P-10666)
HANGER PRSTHTICS ORTHTICS W IN
1127 Wilshire Blvd Ste 310 (90017-3901)
PHONE............................213 250-7850
Rafael Bibbens, *Mgr*
EMP: 77
SALES (corp-wide): 1.12B **Privately Held**
SIC: 3842 5999 Orthopedic appliances; Orthopedic and prosthesis applications
HQ: Hanger Prosthetics & Orthotics West, Inc.
4155 E La Palma Ave B4
Anaheim CA
714 961-2112

(P-10667)
HANGER PRSTHTICS ORTHTICS W IN (HQ)
4155 E La Palma Ave Ste 400 (92807-1857)
PHONE............................714 961-2112
Vinit K Asar, *CEO*
EMP: 21 **EST:** 1970
SALES (est): 7.06MM
SALES (corp-wide): 1.12B **Privately Held**
SIC: 3842 Orthopedic appliances
PA: Hanger, Inc.
10910 Domain Dr Ste 300
Austin TX
512 777-3800

(P-10668)
HONEYWELL SAFETY PDTS USA INC
7828 Waterville Rd (92154-8205)
PHONE............................619 661-8383
Dave M Cote, *CEO*
EMP: 110
SALES (corp-wide): 35.47B **Publicly Held**
Web: www.honeywell.com
SIC: 3842 Ear plugs
HQ: Honeywell Safety Products Usa, Inc.
2711 Centerville Rd
Wilmington DE
302 636-5401

(P-10669)
HOWMEDICA OSTEONICS CORP
6885 Flanders Dr Ste G (92121-2933)
PHONE............................800 621-6104
EMP: 92
SALES (corp-wide): 18.45B **Publicly Held**
SIC: 3842 Surgical appliances and supplies
HQ: Howmedica Osteonics Corp.
325 Corporate Dr
Mahwah NJ
201 831-5000

(P-10670)
IMPLANTECH ASSOCIATES INC
Also Called: Allied Bio Medical
6025 Nicolle St Ste B (93003-7602)
P.O. Box 392 (93002-0392)
PHONE............................805 289-1665

PRODUCTS & SVCS

William Binder, *Pr*
EMP: 30 **EST:** 1989
SQ FT: 11,000
SALES (est): 4.96MM **Privately Held**
Web: www.implantech.com
SIC: 3842 Implants, surgical

(P-10671)
INFAB LLC
1040 Avenida Acaso (93012-8712)
PHONE.................................805 987-5255
Brittany Lepley, *CEO*
Donald J Cusick, *
Justine Peterson, *
Daren Dickerson, *
◆ **EMP:** 57 **EST:** 1980
SQ FT: 40,000
SALES (est): 19.05MM **Privately Held**
Web: www.infabcorp.com
SIC: 3842 Radiation shielding aprons,
　　gloves, sheeting, etc.

(P-10672)
INHEALTH TECHNOLOGIES
1110 Mark Ave (93013-2918)
PHONE.................................800 477-5969
Ed Munoz, *Prin*
EMP: 21 **EST:** 2005
SALES (est): 1.29MM **Privately Held**
Web: www.inhealth.com
SIC: 3842 Surgical appliances and supplies

(P-10673)
INTERPORE CROSS INTL INC (DH)
181 Technology Dr (92618-2484)
PHONE.................................949 453-3200
Dan Hann, *Pr*
Greg Hartman, *CFO*
▲ **EMP:** 58 **EST:** 1975
SALES (est): 27.27MM
SALES (corp-wide): 6.94B **Publicly Held**
Web: www.interpore.org
SIC: 3842 3843 Orthopedic appliances;
　　Dental equipment and supplies
HQ: Biomet, Inc.
　　345 E Main St
　　Warsaw IN
　　574 267-6639

(P-10674)
ISOMEDIX OPERATIONS INC
Also Called: Steris Isomedix
43425 Business Park Dr (92590-3647)
PHONE.................................951 694-9340
EMP: 57
Web: www.steris.com
SIC: 3842 Surgical appliances and supplies
HQ: Isomedix Operations Inc.
　　5960 Heisley Rd
　　Mentor OH

(P-10675)
ISOMEDIX OPERATIONS INC
Also Called: A Steris Company
1000 Sarah Pl (91761-8621)
PHONE.................................909 390-9942
Michael Au, *Brnch Mgr*
EMP: 40
Web: www.steris.com
SIC: 3842 Surgical appliances and supplies
HQ: Isomedix Operations Inc.
　　5960 Heisley Rd
　　Mentor OH

(P-10676)
JOHNSON & JOHNSON
Also Called: Johnson & Johnson
15715 Arrow Hwy (91706-2006)
PHONE.................................909 839-8650

Cathy Somalis, *Mgr*
EMP: 300
SALES (corp-wide): 94.94B **Publicly Held**
Web: www.jnj.com
SIC: 3842 Dressings, surgical
PA: Johnson & Johnson
　　1 Johnson And Johnson Plz
　　New Brunswick NJ
　　732 524-0400

(P-10677)
JOHNSON WILSHIRE INC
17343 Freedom Way (91748-1001)
PHONE.................................562 777-0088
David W Pang, *Pr*
EMP: 25 **EST:** 2007
SQ FT: 120,000
SALES (est): 1.23MM **Privately Held**
Web: www.johnsonwilshire.com
SIC: 3842 Personal safety equipment

(P-10678)
KINAMED INC
820 Flynn Rd (93012-8701)
PHONE.................................805 384-2748
Clyde R Pratt, *Pr*
Vineet Sarin, *
Bob Bruce, *
EMP: 26 **EST:** 1987
SQ FT: 28,828
SALES (est): 8.41MM **Privately Held**
Web: www.kinamed.com
SIC: 3842 Implants, surgical
PA: Vme Acquisition Corp.
　　820 Flynn Rd
　　Camarillo CA

(P-10679)
KYOCERA MEDICAL TECH INC
1200 California St Ste 210 (92374-2945)
PHONE.................................909 557-2360
Takahiro Kobayashi, *CEO*
EMP: 48 **EST:** 2019
SALES (est): 3.76MM **Privately Held**
Web: www.kyocera-medical.com
SIC: 3842 Prosthetic appliances

(P-10680)
MEDICAL PACKAGING CORPORATION
Also Called: Hygenia
941 Avenida Acaso (93012-8700)
PHONE.................................805 388-2383
Frederic L Nason, *Pr*
Susan J Nason, *
EMP: 100 **EST:** 1974
SQ FT: 45,000
SALES (est): 8.75MM **Privately Held**
Web: www.medicalpackaging.com
SIC: 3842 2835 Surgical appliances and
　　supplies; Diagnostic substances

(P-10681)
MEDLINE INDUSTRIES LP
42500 Winchester Rd (92590-2570)
PHONE.................................951 296-2600
EMP: 30
SALES (corp-wide): 7.75B **Privately Held**
Web: www.medline.com
SIC: 3842 Surgical appliances and supplies
PA: Medline Industries, Lp
　　3 Lakes Dr
　　Northfield IL
　　847 949-5500

(P-10682)
MEGIDDO GLOBAL LLC
17101 Central Ave Ste 1c (90746-1360)
PHONE.................................844 477-7007
EMP: 25 **EST:** 2017

SALES (est): 1.2MM **Privately Held**
Web: www.megiddo-global.com
SIC: 3842 2393 2329 3728 Bulletproof vests;
　　Textile bags; Field jackets, military; Military
　　aircraft equipment and armament

(P-10683)
MENTOR WORLDWIDE LLC (DH)
31 Technology Dr Ste 200 (92618-2302)
PHONE.................................800 636-8678
David Shepherd, *Pr*
Joshua H Levine, *Managing Member*
Flavia Pease, *
▲ **EMP:** 250 **EST:** 1969
SALES (est): 455.62MM
SALES (corp-wide): 94.94B **Publicly Held**
Web: www.mentordirect.com
SIC: 3842 3845 3841 Surgical appliances
　　and supplies; Ultrasonic medical
　　equipment, except cleaning; Medical
　　instruments and equipment, blood and
　　bone work
HQ: Ethicon Inc.
　　1000 Route 202
　　Raritan NJ
　　800 384-4266

(P-10684)
MOLDEX-METRIC INC
Also Called: Moldex
10111 Jefferson Blvd (90232-3509)
PHONE.................................310 837-6500
Mark Magidson, *CEO*
Debra Magidson, *
◆ **EMP:** 500 **EST:** 1960
SQ FT: 80,000
SALES (est): 92.25MM **Privately Held**
Web: www.moldex.com
SIC: 3842 Personal safety equipment

(P-10685)
MPS ANZON LLC
Also Called: Orchid Orthopedis
11911 Clark St (91006-6026)
PHONE.................................626 471-3553
EMP: 136
SALES (est): 2.29MM
SALES (corp-wide): 496.98MM **Privately Held**
SIC: 3842 Orthopedic appliances
PA: Tulip Us Holdings, Inc.
　　1489 Cedar St
　　Holt MI
　　517 694-2300

(P-10686)
NOBBE ORTHOPEDICS INC
3010 State St (93105-3304)
PHONE.................................805 687-7508
Ralph W Nobbe, *Pr*
Rolf Schiefel, *
Erwin Nobbe, *
EMP: 77 **EST:** 1964
SQ FT: 2,850
SALES (est): 2.49MM
SALES (corp-wide): 1.12B **Privately Held**
Web: www.hangerclinic.com
SIC: 3842 2342 Cosmetic restorations;
　　Corsets and allied garments
PA: Hanger, Inc.
　　10910 Domain Dr Ste 300
　　Austin TX
　　512 777-3800

(P-10687)
ORTHO ENGINEERING INC (PA)
17402 Chatsworth St Ste 200 (91344-7620)
PHONE.................................310 559-5996
Avo Ashkharikian, *Pr*
EMP: 22 **EST:** 1991

SQ FT: 4,000
SALES (est): 3.67MM **Privately Held**
Web: www.orthoengineering.com
SIC: 3842 Braces, orthopedic

(P-10688)
ORTHOTIC HOLDINGS INC
8665 Miralani Dr Ste 300 (92126-4398)
PHONE.................................858 368-8873
Jason Kraus, *Brnch Mgr*
EMP: 42
SALES (corp-wide): 23.91MM **Privately Held**
Web: www.ohi.net
SIC: 3842 Foot appliances, orthopedic
PA: Orthotic Holdings, Inc.
　　4825 E Ingram St
　　Mesa AZ
　　416 479-8609

(P-10689)
OSSUR AMERICAS INC (HQ)
200 Spectrum Center Dr (92618-5005)
PHONE.................................800 233-6263
Mahesh Mansukhani, *CEO*
Avanindra Chaturvedi, *
◆ **EMP:** 40 **EST:** 1984
SALES (est): 98.04MM
SALES (corp-wide): 718.65MM **Privately Held**
SIC: 3842 Braces, orthopedic
PA: Ossur Hf.
　　Grjothalsi 5
　　Reykjavik
　　4253400

(P-10690)
OSSUR AMERICAS INC
19762 Pauling (92610-2611)
PHONE.................................949 382-3883
Edward Castillo, *Brnch Mgr*
EMP: 41
SALES (corp-wide): 718.65MM **Privately Held**
SIC: 3842 Prosthetic appliances
HQ: Ossur Americas, Inc.
　　200 Spectrum Center Dr # 700
　　Irvine CA
　　800 233-6263

(P-10691)
PASSY-MUIR INC (PA)
17992 Mitchell S Ste 200 (92614-6813)
PHONE.................................949 833-8255
Cameron Jolly, *Pr*
EMP: 30 **EST:** 1985
SQ FT: 1,200
SALES (est): 6.69MM
SALES (corp-wide): 6.69MM **Privately Held**
Web: www.passy-muir.com
SIC: 3842 Orthopedic appliances

(P-10692)
PATIENT SAFETY TECHNOLOGIES INC
15440 Laguna Canyon Rd Ste 150 (92618-2143)
PHONE.................................949 387-2277
EMP: 25
Web: www.safeor.com
SIC: 3842 Surgical appliances and supplies

(P-10693)
PAULSON MANUFACTURING CORP (PA)
46752 Rainbow Canyon Rd (92592-5927)
PHONE.................................951 676-2451
Roy Paulson, *Pr*

Thomas V Paulson, *
Joyce Paulson, *
▲ **EMP:** 95 **EST:** 1947
SQ FT: 42,000
SALES (est): 24.76MM
SALES (corp-wide): 24.76MM **Privately Held**
Web: www.paulsonmfg.com
SIC: 3842 Personal safety equipment

(P-10694)
PSYONIC INC
9999 Businesspark Ave Ste B (92131-1174)
PHONE..............................888 779-6642
Aadeel Akhtar, *CEO*
EMP: 20 **EST:** 2015
SQ FT: 400
SALES (est): 1.6MM **Privately Held**
Web: www.psyonic.io
SIC: 3842 3821 Limbs, artificial; Incubators, laboratory

(P-10695)
REVA MEDICAL INC (PA)
5751 Copley Dr Ste B (92111-7912)
PHONE..............................858 966-3000
Jeffrey Anderson, *CEO*
Jeff Anderson, *Pr*
C Raymond Larkin Junior, *Ch Bd*
Leigh F Elkolli, *Corporate Secretary*
EMP: 41 **EST:** 1998
SQ FT: 37,000
SALES (est): 7.88MM
SALES (corp-wide): 7.88MM **Privately Held**
Web: www.revamedical.com
SIC: 3842 Surgical appliances and supplies

(P-10696)
RIZZO INC
Also Called: Om Tactical
7720 Airport Business Pkwy (91406)
PHONE..............................818 781-6891
▲ **EMP:** 23
Web: www.omtactical.com
SIC: 3842 Personal safety equipment

(P-10697)
ROLLING SALS WHLCHAIR LACROSSE
5333 Mission Center Rd Ste 115 (92108-1302)
PHONE..............................619 677-1431
Bill Lundstrom, *Prin*
EMP: 29 **EST:** 2018
SALES (est): 188.04K **Privately Held**
Web: www.wheelchairlacrosse.com
SIC: 3842 Wheelchairs

(P-10698)
SAFARILAND LLC
4700 E Airport Dr (91761-7875)
PHONE..............................909 923-7300
Warren B Kanders, *Brnch Mgr*
EMP: 354
SALES (corp-wide): 457.84MM **Publicly Held**
Web: www.safariland.com
SIC: 3842 Bulletproof vests
HQ: Safariland, Llc
13386 International Pkwy
Jacksonville FL
904 741-5400

(P-10699)
SAS SAFETY CORPORATION
Also Called: Sas Safety
3031 Gardenia Ave (90807-5215)
PHONE..............................562 427-2775

James Anthony Mccool, *Pr*
Daniel M Deambrosio, *
Daniel J Lett, *
Anh Phuong Katy Vu, *Treas*
◆ **EMP:** 60 **EST:** 1983
SQ FT: 90,000
SALES (est): 14.75MM **Privately Held**
Web: www.sassafety.com
SIC: 3842 Personal safety equipment

(P-10700)
SEASPINE INC
Also Called: Integra Lifesciences
5770 Armada Dr (92008-4608)
PHONE..............................760 727-8399
Keith Valentine, *CEO*
EMP: 80 **EST:** 2002
SQ FT: 22,000
SALES (est): 24.54MM
SALES (corp-wide): 191.45MM **Privately Held**
Web: www.seaspine.com
SIC: 3842 5999 Orthopedic appliances; Orthopedic and prosthesis applications
HQ: Seaspine Orthopedics Corporation
5770 Armada Dr
Carlsbad CA
866 942-8698

(P-10701)
SEASPINE ORTHOPEDICS CORP (HQ)
5770 Armada Dr (92008-4608)
PHONE..............................866 942-8698
Keith Valentine, *CEO*
EMP: 20 **EST:** 2015
SALES (est): 28.05MM
SALES (corp-wide): 191.45MM **Privately Held**
Web: www.seaspine.com
SIC: 3842 5999 Orthopedic appliances; Orthopedic and prosthesis applications
PA: Seaspine Holdings Corporation
5770 Armada Dr
Carlsbad CA
760 727-8399

(P-10702)
SIENTRA INC (PA)
Also Called: Sientra
3333 Michelson Dr Ste 650 (92612-0681)
PHONE..............................805 562-3500
Ronald Menezes, *Pr*
Caroline Van Hove, *
Oliver Bennett, *CCO*
Andrew Schmidt, *Sr VP*
Valerie Miller, *Corporate Controller*
EMP: 80 **EST:** 2003
SQ FT: 14,000
SALES (est): 90.55MM
SALES (corp-wide): 90.55MM **Publicly Held**
Web: www.sientra.com
SIC: 3842 Surgical appliances and supplies

(P-10703)
ST JUDE MEDICAL LLC
101 E Valencia Mesa Dr (92835-3809)
PHONE..............................714 992-3000
Daniel J Starks, *Brnch Mgr*
EMP: 48
SALES (corp-wide): 43.65B **Publicly Held**
Web: www.stjudemedicalcenter.org
SIC: 3842 8099 Surgical appliances and supplies; Blood related health services
HQ: St. Jude Medical, Llc
1 Saint Jude Medical Dr
Saint Paul MN
651 756-2000

(P-10704)
STERIS CORPORATION
Also Called: Steris
9020 Activity Rd Ste D (92126-4454)
PHONE..............................858 586-1166
Walt Rosebrough, *Mgr*
EMP: 110
Web: www.steris.com
SIC: 3842 Surgical appliances and supplies
HQ: Steris Corporation
5960 Heisley Rd
Mentor OH
440 354-2600

(P-10705)
SUNRISE MEDICAL INC
2382 Faraday Ave Ste 200 (92008-7220)
PHONE..............................619 930-1500
Thomas Rossnagel, *CEO*
Peter Riley, *
Randi Binstock, *
EMP: 24 **EST:** 1983
SALES (est): 835.09K **Privately Held**
Web: www.sunrisemedical.com
SIC: 3842 Orthopedic appliances

(P-10706)
SUREFIRE LLC
17680 Newhope St Ste B (92708-4220)
PHONE..............................714 545-9444
Daniel Fischer, *Pdt Mgr*
EMP: 45
SALES (corp-wide): 158.99MM **Privately Held**
Web: www.surefire.com
SIC: 3842 3484 3648 Ear plugs; Guns (firearms) or gun parts, 30 mm. and below; Flashlights
PA: Surefire, Llc
18300 Mount Baldy Cir
Fountain Valley CA
714 545-9444

(P-10707)
SUREFIRE LLC
17760 Newhope St Ste A (92708-5401)
PHONE..............................714 545-9444
Daniel Fischer, *Pdt Mgr*
EMP: 45
SALES (corp-wide): 158.99MM **Privately Held**
Web: www.surefire.com
SIC: 3842 3484 3648 Ear plugs; Guns (firearms) or gun parts, 30 mm. and below; Flashlights
PA: Surefire, Llc
18300 Mount Baldy Cir
Fountain Valley CA
714 545-9444

(P-10708)
SUREFIRE LLC
2110 S Anne St (92704-4409)
PHONE..............................714 641-0483
Gustav Bonse, *Mfg Mgr*
EMP: 45
SALES (corp-wide): 158.99MM **Privately Held**
Web: www.surefire.com
SIC: 3842 3484 3648 Ear plugs; Guns (firearms) or gun parts, 30 mm. and below; Flashlights
PA: Surefire, Llc
18300 Mount Baldy Cir
Fountain Valley CA
714 545-9444

(P-10709)
SUREFIRE LLC
18300 Mount Baldy Cir (92708-6122)

PHONE..............................714 545-9444
Joel Smith, *Brnch Mgr*
EMP: 45
SALES (corp-wide): 158.99MM **Privately Held**
Web: www.surefire.com
SIC: 3842 Surgical appliances and supplies
PA: Surefire, Llc
18300 Mount Baldy Cir
Fountain Valley CA
714 545-9444

(P-10710)
SUREFIRE LLC
2121 S Yale St (92704-4437)
PHONE..............................714 545-9444
John D Matthews, *Brnch Mgr*
EMP: 45
SALES (corp-wide): 158.99MM **Privately Held**
Web: www.surefire.com
SIC: 3842 Ear plugs
PA: Surefire, Llc
18300 Mount Baldy Cir
Fountain Valley CA
714 545-9444

(P-10711)
SUREFIRE LLC
2300 S Yale St (92704-5330)
PHONE..............................714 641-0483
EMP: 45
SALES (corp-wide): 158.99MM **Privately Held**
Web: www.surefire.com
SIC: 3842 3484 3648 Ear plugs; Guns (firearms) or gun parts, 30 mm. and below; Flashlights
PA: Surefire, Llc
18300 Mount Baldy Cir
Fountain Valley CA
714 545-9444

(P-10712)
TOTAL RESOURCES INTL INC (PA)
420 S Lemon Ave (91789-2956)
PHONE..............................909 594-1220
George Rivera, *CEO*
Gregg Rivera, *
Merlyn Rivera, *
▲ **EMP:** 49 **EST:** 1993
SQ FT: 115,000
SALES (est): 21.16MM **Privately Held**
Web: www.trikits.com
SIC: 3842 First aid, snake bite, and burn kits

(P-10713)
TOWNSEND INDUSTRIES INC
4401 Stine Rd (93313-2306)
PHONE..............................661 837-1795
EMP: 65
SALES (corp-wide): 1.25MM **Privately Held**
SIC: 3842 Braces, orthopedic
HQ: Townsend Industries, Inc.
4615 Shepard St
Bakersfield CA
661 837-1795

(P-10714)
TOWNSEND INDUSTRIES INC
4833 N Hills Dr (93308-1186)
PHONE..............................661 837-1795
Rick Riley, *Brnch Mgr*
EMP: 65
SALES (corp-wide): 1.25MM **Privately Held**
Web: www.thuasneusa.com

PRODUCTS & SVCS

SIC: **3842** Braces, orthopedic
HQ: Townsend Industries, Inc.
4615 Shepard St
Bakersfield CA
661 837-1795

(P-10715)
TOWNSEND INDUSTRIES INC (DH)
Also Called: Townsend Design
4615 Shepard St (93313-2339)
PHONE................................661 837-1795
EMP: 130 EST: 1984
SALES (est): 31.67MM
SALES (corp-wide): 1.25MM **Privately Held**
SIC: **3842** Braces, orthopedic
HQ: Thuasne North America Inc.
4615 Shepard St
Bakersfield CA
800 432-3466

(P-10716)
ULTIMATE EARS CONSUMER LLC
3 Jenner Ste 180 (92618-3835)
PHONE................................949 502-8340
Mindy Harvey, *Owner*
▲ EMP: 756 EST: 2004
SALES (est): 12.09MM **Privately Held**
SIC: **3842** Hearing aids
HQ: Logitech Inc.
3930 N 1st St
San Jose CA
510 795-8500

(P-10717)
UNITED BIOLOGICS INC
2871 Pullman St (92705-5713)
PHONE................................949 345-7490
Craig Johnson, *CEO*
John Barnhill, *
EMP: 37 EST: 2002
SALES (est): 4.88MM **Privately Held**
Web: www.unitedbiologics.com
SIC: **3842** Models, anatomical

(P-10718)
US ARMOR CORPORATION
10715 Bloomfield Ave (90670-3913)
PHONE................................562 207-4240
Stephen Armellino, *Pr*
Susan L Armellino, *
Jana Armellino, *CFO*
▲ EMP: 45 EST: 1986
SQ FT: 14,000
SALES (est): 8.14MM **Privately Held**
Web: www.usarmor.com
SIC: **3842** 2326 5999 Bulletproof vests; Men's and boy's work clothing; Safety supplies and equipment

(P-10719)
VALEDA COMPANY LLC
Also Called: Safe Haven
13571 Vaughn St Unit E (91340-3006)
PHONE................................800 421-8700
EMP: 45
SALES (corp-wide): 12.36MM **Privately Held**
SIC: **3842** Wheelchairs
PA: Valeda Company, Llc
4031 Ne 12th Ter
Oakland Park FL
954 986-6665

(P-10720)
VCP MOBILITY HOLDINGS INC
Also Called: Sunrise Med HM Hlth Care Group

745 Design Ct Ste 602 (91911-6165)
PHONE................................619 213-6500
Steve Winston, *Mgr*
EMP: 25
SALES (corp-wide): 702.31MM **Privately Held**
SIC: **3842** Wheelchairs
HQ: Vcp Mobility Holdings, Inc.
7477 Dry Creek Pkwy
Niwot CO
303 218-4600

(P-10721)
VISION QUEST INDUSTRIES INC
Also Called: V Q Orthocare
1390 Decision St Ste A (92081-8578)
PHONE................................949 261-6382
James W Knape, *CEO*
Kevin Lunau, *
Bob Blachford, *
▲ EMP: 175 EST: 1989
SALES (est): 24.66MM **Privately Held**
SIC: **3842** 5999 Braces, orthopedic; Medical apparatus and supplies

(P-10722)
WEBER ORTHOPEDIC LP (PA)
Also Called: Hely & Weber Orthopedic
1185 E Main St (93060-2954)
P.O. Box 832 (93061-0832)
PHONE................................800 221-5465
Jim Weber, *Pt*
Jim Weber, *Pr*
John P Hely, *
▲ EMP: 62 EST: 1982
SQ FT: 28,000
SALES (est): 9.25MM
SALES (corp-wide): 9.25MM **Privately Held**
Web: www.hely-weber.com
SIC: **3842** 5047 Braces, orthopedic; Orthopedic equipment and supplies

(P-10723)
XR LLC
15251 Pipeline Ln (92649-1135)
PHONE................................714 847-9292
Ari Suss, *Managing Member*
Kelly Eberhard Allen, *
▲ EMP: 27 EST: 2002
SQ FT: 68,000
SALES (est): 5.04MM **Privately Held**
Web: www.xrllc.com
SIC: **3842** Personal safety equipment

(P-10724)
ZIMMER DENTAL INC
1900 Aston Ave (92008-7308)
PHONE................................800 854-7019
EMP: 440 EST: 1981
SALES (est): 51.96MM
SALES (corp-wide): 6.94B **Publicly Held**
SIC: **3842** 8021 3843 Implants, surgical; Offices and clinics of dentists; Dental equipment and supplies
HQ: Zimmer, Inc.
1800 W Center St
Warsaw IN
800 348-9500

(P-10725)
ZIMMER MELIA & ASSOCIATES INC (PA)
6832 Presidio Dr (92648-3025)
PHONE................................615 377-0118
K Michael Melia, *Pr*
EMP: 25 EST: 2005
SALES (est): 4.47MM **Privately Held**
SIC: **3842** Orthopedic appliances

3843 Dental Equipment And Supplies

(P-10726)
3M COMPANY
3M
2111 Mcgaw Ave (92614-0908)
PHONE................................949 863-1360
David Goldinger, *Brnch Mgr*
EMP: 294
SQ FT: 77,656
SALES (corp-wide): 34.23B **Publicly Held**
Web: www.3m.com
SIC: **3843** 5047 Dental equipment and supplies; Dental equipment and supplies
PA: 3m Company
3m Center
Saint Paul MN
651 733-1110

(P-10727)
3M UNITEK CORPORATION
Also Called: 3M Unitek
2724 Peck Rd (91016-5005)
PHONE................................626 445-7960
Mary Jo Abler, *CEO*
Fred Palensky, *
▲ EMP: 480 EST: 1948
SQ FT: 249,000
SALES (est): 83.7MM
SALES (corp-wide): 34.23B **Publicly Held**
SIC: **3843** Orthodontic appliances
PA: 3m Company
3m Center
Saint Paul MN
651 733-1110

(P-10728)
ALPHA DENTAL OF UTAH INC
12898 Towne Center Dr (90703-8546)
PHONE................................562 467-7759
Anthony S Barth, *Prin*
EMP: 57 EST: 2010
SALES (est): 591.95K **Privately Held**
Web: www.delta.org
SIC: **3843** Dental equipment and supplies

(P-10729)
AURIDENT INCORPORATED
610 S State College Blvd (92831-5138)
P.O. Box 7200 (92834-7200)
PHONE................................714 870-1851
Howard M Hoffman, *Pr*
David H Fell, *
Fredelle G Hoffman, *
EMP: 30 EST: 1974
SQ FT: 2,700
SALES (est): 3.1MM **Privately Held**
Web: www.aurident.com
SIC: **3843** Dental alloys for amalgams

(P-10730)
BELPORT COMPANY INC (PA)
Also Called: Gingi Pak
4825 Calle Alto (93012-8530)
P.O. Box 240 (93011-0240)
PHONE................................805 484-1051
Jo Pennington, *Pr*
EMP: 19 EST: 1954
SQ FT: 22,000
SALES (est): 5MM
SALES (corp-wide): 5MM **Privately Held**
Web: www.gingi-pak.com
SIC: **3843** Dental hand instruments, nec

(P-10731)
BIEN AIR USA INC
Also Called: Bien Air

8861 Research Dr Ste 100 (92618-4255)
PHONE................................949 477-6050
Arhur Mateen, *Pr*
Jean Claude Maeier, *
Arthur Mateen, *
EMP: 65 EST: 1959
SALES (est): 39.95MM **Privately Held**
Web: dental.bienair.com
SIC: **3843** 7699 5047 Dental equipment; Dental instrument repair; Hospital equipment and furniture
HQ: Bien-Air Dental Sa
Langgasse 60
Biel-Bienne BE

(P-10732)
BIOLASE INC
4225 Prado Rd Ste 102 (92878-7443)
PHONE................................949 361-1200
Richard Whitt, *Mgr*
EMP: 75
SALES (corp-wide): 48.46MM **Publicly Held**
Web: www.biolase.com
SIC: **3843** Dental equipment and supplies
PA: Biolase, Inc.
27042 Twne Cntre Dr Ste 2
Lake Forest CA
949 361-1200

(P-10733)
CONAMCO SA DE CV
3008 Palm Hill Dr (92084-6555)
PHONE................................760 586-4356
Jane Mitchell, *VP*
Herman Mitchell, *VP*
Alfredo Mobarak, *Ch Bd*
EMP: 75 EST: 2017
SQ FT: 20,000
SALES (est): 2.06MM **Privately Held**
SIC: **3843** Cement, dental

(P-10734)
CYBER MEDICAL IMAGING INC
Also Called: Xdr Radiology
11300 W Olympic Blvd Ste 710 (90064-1637)
PHONE................................888 937-9729
Douglas Yoon, *CEO*
Adam Chen, *
Joel Karafin, *
EMP: 25 EST: 2003
SQ FT: 2,800
SALES (est): 3.66MM **Privately Held**
Web: www.xdrradiology.com
SIC: **3843** Dental equipment and supplies

(P-10735)
DANSEREAU HEALTH PRODUCTS
1581 Commerce St (92878-3230)
PHONE................................951 549-1400
▲ EMP: 36 EST: 1957
SALES (est): 3.5MM **Privately Held**
Web: www.dhpdental.com
SIC: **3843** Dental equipment and supplies

(P-10736)
DANVILLE MATERIALS LLC
4020 E Leaverton Ct (92807-1610)
PHONE................................714 399-0334
Greg Dorsman, *Mgr*
EMP: 20
SALES (corp-wide): 27.48MM **Privately Held**
Web: www.zestdent.com
SIC: **3843** Dental materials
HQ: Danville Materials, Llc
2875 Loker Ave E
Carlsbad CA

▲ = Import ▼ = Export
◆ = Import/Export

(P-10737)

DCII NORTH AMERICA LLC (HQ)
200 S Kraemer Blvd Bldg E (92821-6208)
PHONE................................714 817-7000
John Bedford, *VP*
EMP: 50 EST: 2018
SALES (est): 656.9K
SALES (corp-wide): 2.57B **Publicly Held**
SIC: 3843 Dental equipment and supplies
PA: Envista Holdings Corporation
    200 S Kraemer Blvd Bldg E
    Brea CA
    714 817-7000

(P-10738)

DENOVO DENTAL INC
Also Called: Denovo
5130 Commerce Dr (91706-1450)
P.O. Box 548 (91706-0548)
PHONE................................626 480-0182
Richard R Parker, *Pr*
Joseph Parker, *VP*
Jeanette Parker, *Sec*
▼ EMP: 20 EST: 1981
SQ FT: 10,000
SALES (est): 2.35MM **Privately Held**
Web: www.denovodental.com
SIC: 3843 5047 Dental equipment and
    supplies; Dental equipment and supplies

(P-10739)

DENTIS USA CORPORATION
11095 Knott Ave Ste B (90630-5136)
PHONE................................323 677-4363
Sim Gibong, *CEO*
Kichul Sim, *CFO*
▲ EMP: 18 EST: 2010
SALES (est): 1.73MM **Privately Held**
Web: www.dentisusa.com
SIC: 3843 Dental materials

(P-10740)

**DH DENTAL BUSINESS SVCS
LLC (HQ)**
200 S Kraemer Blvd Bldg E (92821-6208)
PHONE................................714 817-7000
Amir Aghdaei, *CEO*
EMP: 106 EST: 2013
SALES (est): 24.51MM
SALES (corp-wide): 2.57B **Publicly Held**
Web: www.kerrdental.com
SIC: 3843 Dental engines
PA: Envista Holdings Corporation
    200 S Kraemer Blvd Bldg E
    Brea CA
    714 817-7000

(P-10741)

DIAMODENT INC
1580 N Harmony Cir (92807-2092)
PHONE................................888 281-8850
Kazem Jeff Rassoli, *Pr*
EMP: 25 EST: 2000
SALES (est): 717.05K **Privately Held**
Web: www.diamodent.com
SIC: 3843 Dental equipment and supplies

(P-10742)

DUX INDUSTRIES INC
Also Called: Dux Dental Products
1717 W Collins Ave (92867-5422)
P.O. Box 14247 (92863-1447)
PHONE................................805 488-1122
▲ EMP: 65
Web: www.duxdental.com
SIC: 3843 Dental equipment and supplies

(P-10743)

**ENVISTA HOLDINGS
CORPORATION (PA)**
Also Called: Envista
200 S Kraemer Blvd Bldg E (92821-6208)
PHONE................................714 817-7000
Amir Aghdaei, *Pr*
Scott Huennekens, *Ch Bd*
Howard H Yu, *Sr VP*
Mark E Nance, *Sr VP*
Mischa M Reis Senior, *Strategy Vice
President*
EMP: 80 EST: 2018
SALES (est): 2.57B
SALES (corp-wide): 2.57B **Publicly Held**
Web: www.envistaco.com
SIC: 3843 Dental equipment and supplies

(P-10744)

**EVOLVE DENTAL
TECHNOLOGIES INC**
5 Vanderbilt (92618-2011)
PHONE................................949 713-0909
Rodger Kurthy, *CEO*
Sharon Kurthy, *Pr*
EMP: 26 EST: 2007
SALES (est): 9.02MM **Privately Held**
Web: www.korwhitening.com
SIC: 3843 Dental equipment and supplies

(P-10745)

**HANDPIECE PARTS &
PRODUCTS INC**
707 W Angus Ave (92868-1305)
PHONE................................714 997-4331
Steve Bowen, *Pr*
Lyla Bowen, *
EMP: 30 EST: 1992
SQ FT: 18,000
SALES (est): 2.22MM **Privately Held**
Web: www.handpieceparts.com
SIC: 3843 Dental materials

(P-10746)

**IMPLANT DIRECT SYBRON INTL
LLC (HQ)**
3050 E Hillcrest Dr Ste 100 (91362-3195)
PHONE................................818 444-3000
EMP: 49 EST: 2010
SALES (est): 15.2MM
SALES (corp-wide): 31.47B **Publicly Held**
Web: www.implantdirect.com
SIC: 3843 Dental equipment and supplies
PA: Danaher Corporation
    2200 Penn Ave Nw Ste 800w
    Washington DC
    202 828-0850

(P-10747)

**IMPLANT DIRECT SYBRON MFG
LLC**
Also Called: Implant Direct
3050 E Hillcrest Dr (91362-3154)
PHONE................................818 444-3300
Gerald A Niznick, *Managing Member*
EMP: 200 EST: 2010
SQ FT: 45,622
SALES (est): 62.91MM
SALES (corp-wide): 31.47B **Publicly Held**
Web: www.implantdirect.com
SIC: 3843 Dental equipment and supplies
PA: Danaher Corporation
    2200 Penn Ave Nw Ste 800w
    Washington DC
    202 828-0850

(P-10748)

**JENERIC/PENTRON
INCORPORATED (HQ)**
1717 W Collins Ave (92867-5422)
PHONE................................203 265-7397
Gordon Cohen, *Pr*
Martin Schulman, *
EMP: 200 EST: 1977
SQ FT: 46,000
SALES (est): 37.08MM
SALES (corp-wide): 48.87MM **Privately
Held**
SIC: 3843 Dental equipment
PA: Pentron Corporation
    53 N Plains Industrial Rd
    Wallingford CT
    203 265-7397

(P-10749)

KERR CORPORATION (HQ)
1717 W Collins Ave (92867-5422)
P.O. Box 14247 (92863-1447)
PHONE................................714 516-7400
Damien Mcdonald, *CEO*
Steve Semmelmayer, *
Steve Dunkerken, *
Leo Pranitis, *
◆ EMP: 218 EST: 1891
SQ FT: 105,000
SALES (est): 314.59MM **Privately Held**
Web: www.kerrdental.com
SIC: 3843 Dental materials
PA: Sybron Dental Specialties, Inc.
    1717 W Collins Ave
    Orange CA

(P-10750)

KETTENBACH LP
16052 Beach Blvd Ste 221 (92647-3855)
PHONE................................877 532-2123
Daniel Parrilli, *Dir*
EMP: 49 EST: 2007
SALES (est): 2.87MM **Privately Held**
Web: www.kettenbach-dental.us
SIC: 3843 5047 Dental equipment and
    supplies; Dental equipment and supplies

(P-10751)

KEYSTONE DENTAL INC
5 Holland Ste 209 (92618-2576)
PHONE................................781 328-3324
Michael Nealon, *Owner*
EMP: 37
Web: www.keystonedental.com
SIC: 3843 Dental equipment and supplies
PA: Keystone Dental, Inc.
    154 Middlesex Tpke Ste 2
    Burlington MA

(P-10752)

KEYSTONE DENTAL INC
13645 Alton Pkwy Ste A (92618-1693)
PHONE................................781 328-3382
Michael Nealon, *Brnch Mgr*
EMP: 37
Web: www.keystonedental.com
SIC: 3843 Enamels, dentists'
PA: Keystone Dental, Inc.
    154 Middlesex Tpke Ste 2
    Burlington MA

(P-10753)

LACLEDE INC
Also Called: Laclede Research Center
2103 E University Dr (90220-6413)
PHONE................................310 605-4280
Michael Pellico, *Pr*
Stephen Pellico, *
◆ EMP: 35 EST: 1978
SQ FT: 25,000

SALES (est): 9.1MM **Privately Held**
Web: www.laclede.com
SIC: 3843 Dental equipment

(P-10754)

**LANCER ORTHODONTICS INC
(PA)**
2726 Loker Ave W (92010-6603)
PHONE................................760 744-5585
Giorgio Beretta, *CEO*
Janet Moore, *Sec*
Lisa Li, *CFO*
▲ EMP: 20 EST: 1967
SALES (est): 11.24MM
SALES (corp-wide): 11.24MM **Privately
Held**
Web: www.lancerortho.com
SIC: 3843 5047 Orthodontic appliances;
    Dental equipment and supplies

(P-10755)

ORMCO CORPORATION
200 S Kraemer Blvd (92821-6208)
PHONE................................909 962-5705
EMP: 39
SALES (corp-wide): 2.57B **Publicly Held**
Web: www.ormco.com
SIC: 3843 Orthodontic appliances
HQ: Ormco Corporation
    1717 W Collins Ave
    Orange CA
    714 516-7400

(P-10756)

ORMCO CORPORATION (HQ)
Also Called: Sybron Endo
1717 W Collins Ave (92867-5422)
PHONE................................714 516-7400
Patrik Eriksson, *CEO*
Jason R Davis, *VP*
◆ EMP: 100 EST: 1975
SQ FT: 104,000
SALES (est): 126.01MM
SALES (corp-wide): 2.57B **Publicly Held**
Web: www.ormco.com
SIC: 3843 Orthodontic appliances
PA: Envista Holdings Corporation
    200 S Kraemer Blvd Bldg E
    Brea CA
    714 817-7000

(P-10757)

ORTHO ORGANIZERS INC
1822 Aston Ave (92008-7306)
PHONE................................760 448-8600
David Parker, *Ch*
Russell J Bonafede, *
Robert Riley, *
Ted Dreifuss, *
Alison Weber, *
▲ EMP: 226 EST: 1975
SQ FT: 65,000
SALES (est): 33.76MM
SALES (corp-wide): 12.65B **Publicly Held**
Web: www.henryscheinortho.com
SIC: 3843 5047 Orthodontic appliances;
    Dental equipment and supplies
PA: Henry Schein, Inc.
    135 Duryea Rd
    Melville NY
    631 843-5500

(P-10758)

**ORTHODENTAL
INTERNATIONAL INC**
280 Campillo St Ste J (92231-3200)
PHONE................................760 357-8070
Armando Lozano, *Pr*
▲ EMP: 57 EST: 1994
SALES (est): 10.75MM

PRODUCTS & SVCS

SALES (corp-wide): 3.92B **Publicly Held**
SIC: **3843** Orthodontic appliances
PA: Dentsply Sirona Inc.
13320 Balntyn Corp Pl
Charlotte NC
844 848-0137

(P-10759)
PAC-DENT INC
670 Endeavor Cir (92821-2949)
PHONE..............................909 839-0888
Daniel Wang, *CEO*
EMP: 49 EST: 2003
SALES (est): 4.22MM **Privately Held**
Web: www.pac-dent.com
SIC: **3843** Dental equipment and supplies

(P-10760)
PANADENT CORPORATION
580 S Rancho Ave (92324-3252)
PHONE..............................909 783-1841
Arlene Lee, *Ch Bd*
Thomas E Lee, *Pr*
EMP: 20 EST: 1966
SQ FT: 1,200
SALES (est): 3.11MM **Privately Held**
Web: www.panadent.com
SIC: **3843** Dental hand instruments, nec

(P-10761)
PDMA VENTURES INC
Also Called: Zet-Tek Precision Machining
22951 La Palma Ave (92887-6701)
PHONE..............................714 777-8770
Charles Platt, *Pr*
Mark Deischter, *
EMP: 35 EST: 2016
SALES (est): 3.11MM **Privately Held**
SIC: **3843** 3842 3841 Dental equipment and
supplies; Surgical appliances and supplies;
Surgical and medical instruments

(P-10762)
PRECISION ONE MEDICAL INC
3923 Oceanic Dr Ste 200 (92056-5866)
PHONE..............................760 945-7966
J Todd Strong, *CEO*
David P Dutil, *
Mike Mills, *
EMP: 80 EST: 2009
SQ FT: 10,000
SALES (est): 8.66MM **Privately Held**
Web: www.precisiononemedical.com
SIC: **3843** Dental equipment and supplies

(P-10763)
PROMA INC
730 Kingshill Pl (90746-1219)
PHONE..............................310 327-0035
Raymond Tai, *CEO*
Harold Tai, *
▲ EMP: 40 EST: 1967
SQ FT: 37,000
SALES (est): 4.55MM **Privately Held**
Web: www.proma.us
SIC: **3843** Dental equipment and supplies

(P-10764)
RANIR LLC
Also Called: Dr. Fresh
6 Centerpointe Dr Ste 640 (90623-2587)
PHONE..............................866 373-7374
Kevin Parekh, *Brnch Mgr*
EMP: 34
Web: www.perrigo.com
SIC: **3843** Dental equipment and supplies
HQ: Ranir, Llc
4701 East Paris Ave Se
Grand Rapids MI
616 698-8880

(P-10765)
REPLACEMENT PARTS INDS INC
Also Called: RPI
625 Cochran St (93065-1939)
P.O. Box 940250 (93094-0250)
PHONE..............................818 882-8611
Ira Lapides, *Pr*
Albert M Lapides, *Ch*
Sherry Lapides, *Sec*
◆ EMP: 25 EST: 1972
SQ FT: 15,000
SALES (est): 6.32MM **Privately Held**
Web: www.rpiparts.com
SIC: **3843** 3841 3821 Dental equipment;
Surgical and medical instruments;
Laboratory apparatus, except heating and
measuring

(P-10766)
**SCIENTIFIC
PHARMACEUTICALS INC**
Also Called: SCI-Pharm
3221 Producer Way (91768-3916)
PHONE..............................909 595-9922
▲ EMP: 40 EST: 1979
SALES (est): 5.21MM **Privately Held**
Web: www.scipharm.com
SIC: **3843** 2891 Dental materials; Adhesives
and sealants

(P-10767)
SELANE PRODUCTS INC (PA)
Also Called: Sml Space Maintainers Labs
9129 Lurline Ave (91311-5922)
P.O. Box 2101 (91313-2101)
PHONE..............................818 998-7460
Rob Veis, *CEO*
▲ EMP: 60 EST: 1957
SQ FT: 12,000
SALES (est): 9.83MM
SALES (corp-wide): 9.83MM **Privately
Held**
Web: www.smldent.com
SIC: **3843** 8072 Orthodontic appliances;
Dental laboratories

(P-10768)
SONENDO INC (PA)
26061 Merit Cir Ste 102 (92653-7010)
PHONE..............................949 766-3636
Bjarne Bergheim, *Pr*
Anthony P Bihl Iii, *Non-Executive Chairman
of the Board*
Michael P Watts, *CFO*
Roy T Chen, *Chief Talent Officer*
EMP: 234 EST: 2006
SQ FT: 55,000
SALES (est): 41.66MM **Publicly Held**
Web: www.sonendo.com
SIC: **3843** Dental equipment and supplies

(P-10769)
SPRINTRAY INC (PA)
2705 Media Center Dr # 2 (90065-1700)
PHONE..............................800 914-8004
Amir Mansouri, *CEO*
Jing Zhang, *
Erich Kreidler, *
Arun Subramony, *
Jessie Zhang, *
EMP: 187 EST: 2017
SALES (est): 23.24MM
SALES (corp-wide): 23.24MM **Privately
Held**
Web: www.sprintray.com
SIC: **3843** Dental equipment and supplies

(P-10770)
STRAIGHT SMILE LLC (HQ)
Also Called: Byte
3435 Ocean Park Blvd Ste 107-252
(90405-3301)
PHONE..............................424 389-4551
Neeraj Gunsagar, *CEO*
EMP: 17 EST: 2017
SQ FT: 1,900
SALES (est): 1.2MM
SALES (corp-wide): 3.92B **Publicly Held**
Web: www.byteme.com
SIC: **3843** Dental equipment and supplies
PA: Dentsply Sirona Inc.
13320 Balntyn Corp Pl
Charlotte NC
844 848-0137

(P-10771)
**SYBRON DENTAL SPECIALTIES
INC**
1332 S Lone Hill Ave (91740-5339)
PHONE..............................909 596-0276
Andy Astadurian, *Brnch Mgr*
EMP: 47
Web: www.kerrdental.com
SIC: **3843** Dental equipment and supplies
PA: Sybron Dental Specialties, Inc.
1717 W Collins Ave
Orange CA

(P-10772)
**SYBRON DENTAL SPECIALTIES
INC (PA)**
Also Called: Analytic Endodontics
1717 W Collins Ave (92867-5422)
PHONE..............................714 516-7400
Damien Mcdonald, *CEO*
◆ EMP: 250 EST: 1993
SQ FT: 16,000
SALES (est): 915.77MM **Privately Held**
Web: www.kerrdental.com
SIC: **3843** 2834 Dental laboratory equipment
; Pharmaceutical preparations

(P-10773)
TALLADIUM INC (PA)
27360 Muirfield Ln (91355-1010)
PHONE..............................661 295-0900
Eddie Harms, *CEO*
Geoff Harms, *
◆ EMP: 26 EST: 1980
SQ FT: 9,000
SALES (est): 6.45MM
SALES (corp-wide): 6.45MM **Privately
Held**
Web: www.talladium.com
SIC: **3843** 3541 5047 Investment material,
dental; Milling machines; Dental equipment
and supplies

(P-10774)
TRUABUTMENT INC
17666 Fitch (92614-6022)
PHONE..............................714 956-1488
Hyungick Kim, *CEO*
Sangho Yoo, *
EMP: 59 EST: 2013
SQ FT: 1,800
SALES (est): 12MM **Privately Held**
Web: www.truabutment.com
SIC: **3843** Dental equipment and supplies

(P-10775)
**UNIVERSAL ORTHODONTIC
LAB INC**
11917 Front St (90650-2900)
PHONE..............................562 484-0500
Young Paul Kim, *Owner*

EMP: 18 EST: 1995
SALES (est): 936.16K **Privately Held**
Web: www.uniortholab.com
SIC: **3843** Dental equipment

(P-10776)
US DENTAL INC
Also Called: Young Dental
13043 166th St (90703-2201)
PHONE..............................562 404-3500
Young Hoon Park, *CEO*
EMP: 20 EST: 2015
SALES (est): 1.23MM **Privately Held**
Web: www.usdentalinc.com
SIC: **3843** Dental equipment and supplies

(P-10777)
VIADE PRODUCTS INC
354 Dawson Dr (93012-8008)
PHONE..............................805 484-2114
Keith Zinser, *Pr*
Sandra Zinser, *Sec*
John Menzie, *VP*
EMP: 18 EST: 1968
SQ FT: 8,000
SALES (est): 548.35K **Privately Held**
Web: www.viade.com
SIC: **3843** 5047 5999 Dental laboratory
equipment; Dental laboratory equipment;
Medical apparatus and supplies

(P-10778)
WESTSIDE RESOURCES INC
Also Called: Crystal Tip
8850 Research Dr (92618-4223)
PHONE..............................800 944-3939
Donovan Berkely, *CEO*
Derek Jenkins, *
▲ EMP: 40 EST: 2000
SQ FT: 18,000
SALES (est): 3.66MM **Privately Held**
SIC: **3843** 5047 Dental equipment and
supplies; Medical and hospital equipment

(P-10779)
ZYRIS INC
6868 Cortona Dr Ste A (93117-1362)
PHONE..............................805 560-9888
Sandra Hirsch, *CEO*
Sandra Y Hirsch, *
James Hirsch, *
Rolando Mia, *
Catherine Gloster Vv, *Pr*
▲ EMP: 50 EST: 2001
SQ FT: 10,200
SALES (est): 11.84MM **Privately Held**
Web: www.zyris.com
SIC: **3843** 5047 Dental equipment; Dental
equipment and supplies

3844 X-ray Apparatus And Tubes

(P-10780)
ASHTEL STUDIOS INC
Also Called: Ashtel Dental
1610 E Philadelphia St (91761-5759)
PHONE..............................909 434-0911
Anish Patel, *CEO*
◆ EMP: 25 EST: 2006
SQ FT: 40,000
SALES (est): 132.27MM **Privately Held**
Web: www.ashtelstudios.com
SIC: **3844** 3991 5122 X-ray apparatus and
tubes; Toothbrushes, except electric;
Toothbrushes, except electric

(P-10781)

ASTROPHYSICS INC (PA)
21481 Ferrero (91789-5233)
PHONE..............................909 598-5488
Francois Zayek, *CEO*
Francois Zayek, *Pr*
John Pan, *
▼ **EMP:** 129 **EST:** 2002
SQ FT: 65,376
SALES (est): 59.64MM
SALES (corp-wide): 59.64MM **Privately Held**
Web: www.astrophysicsinc.com
SIC: 3844 X-ray apparatus and tubes

(P-10782)

CARR CORPORATION (PA)
1547 11th St (90401-2999)
PHONE..............................310 587-1113
John Carr, *Pr*
Paul Carr, *
Reese Carr, *
EMP: 25 **EST:** 1946
SQ FT: 25,000
SALES (est): 5.41MM
SALES (corp-wide): 5.41MM **Privately Held**
Web: www.carrcorporation.com
SIC: 3844 3861 3842 X-ray apparatus and tubes; Processing equipment, photographic; Surgical appliances and supplies

(P-10783)

IMMPORT THERAPEUTICS INC
Also Called: Antigen Discovery
1 Technology Dr Ste E309 (92618-2343)
PHONE..............................949 679-4068
Philip Felgner, *Pr*
EMP: 17 **EST:** 2002
SALES (est): 3.33MM **Privately Held**
Web: www.antigendiscovery.com
SIC: 3844 Therapeutic X-ray apparatus and tubes

(P-10784)

NORDSON DAGE INC
Also Called: Nordson
2747 Loker Ave W (92010-6601)
PHONE..............................440 985-4496
John J Keane, *CEO*
Robert E Veillette, *
Phil Vere, *
▲ **EMP:** 30 **EST:** 1977
SQ FT: 6,000
SALES (est): 9.76MM
SALES (corp-wide): 2.59B **Publicly Held**
Web: www.nordson.com
SIC: 3844 3544 5065 3823 X-ray apparatus and tubes; Special dies, tools, jigs, and fixtures; Electronic parts; Process control instruments
PA: Nordson Corporation
28601 Clemens Rd
Westlake OH
440 892-1580

(P-10785)

RAPISCAN SYSTEMS INC (HQ)
2805 Columbia St (90503-3804)
PHONE..............................310 978-1457
Deepak Chopra, *CEO*
Ajay Mehra, *
Eric Luiz, *
Andy Kotowski, *
◆ **EMP:** 115 **EST:** 1993
SQ FT: 93,000
SALES (est): 150.66MM
SALES (corp-wide): 1.15B **Publicly Held**
Web: www.rapiscansystems.com

SIC: 3844 X-ray apparatus and tubes
PA: Osi Systems, Inc.
12525 Chadron Ave
Hawthorne CA
310 978-0516

(P-10786)

ZIEHM INSTRUMENTARIUM
4181 Latham St (92501-1729)
PHONE..............................407 615-8560
Wolfram Klawitter, *Pr*
Lars Nillson, *VP*
Richard Westrick, *VP*
Stan Talaba, *VP*
EMP: 33 **EST:** 1980
SQ FT: 11,000
SALES (est): 486.58K **Privately Held**
Web: www.ziehm.com
SIC: 3844 X-ray apparatus and tubes

3845 Electromedical Equipment

(P-10787)

ADVANCED BIONICS LLC
26081 Avenue Hall (91355-1241)
PHONE..............................310 819-4004
EMP: 48
Web: www.advancedbionics.com
SIC: 3845 Electromedical equipment
HQ: Advanced Bionics, Llc
12740 San Fernando Rd
Sylmar CA

(P-10788)

ALERE CONNECT LLC
9975 Summers Ridge Rd (92121-2997)
PHONE..............................888 876-3327
Kent E Dicks, *CEO*
Lyle Scritsmier, *CFO*
Ellen Chiniars, *Sec*
David Teitel, *Treas*
EMP: 24 **EST:** 2006
SALES (est): 1.9MM
SALES (corp-wide): 43.65B **Publicly Held**
SIC: 3845 Electromedical equipment
PA: Abbott Laboratories
100 Abbott Park Rd
Abbott Park IL
224 667-6100

(P-10789)

AMPRONIX LLC
15 Whatney (92618-2808)
PHONE..............................949 273-8000
Burton Tripathi, *Managing Member*
◆ **EMP:** 62 **EST:** 1982
SQ FT: 58,000
SALES (est): 19.01MM **Privately Held**
Web: www.ampronix.com
SIC: 3845 5047 Electrotherapeutic apparatus; Diagnostic equipment, medical

(P-10790)

AXELGAARD MANUFACTURING CO (PA)
Also Called: Axelgaard
520 Industrial Way (92028-2244)
PHONE..............................760 723-7554
Jens Axelgaard, *CSO*
Dan Jeffery, *
▲ **EMP:** 92 **EST:** 1985
SQ FT: 33,000
SALES (est): 30.44MM
SALES (corp-wide): 30.44MM **Privately Held**
Web: www.axelgaard.com
SIC: 3845 Electromedical equipment

(P-10791)

AXELGAARD MANUFACTURING CO
Also Called: Axelgaard Manufacturing
329 W Aviation Rd (92028-3201)
PHONE..............................760 723-7554
EMP: 23
SALES (corp-wide): 30.44MM **Privately Held**
Web: www.axelgaard.com
SIC: 3845 Electromedical equipment
PA: Axelgaard Manufacturing Co., Ltd
520 Industrial Way
Fallbrook CA
760 723-7554

(P-10792)

BETA BIONICS INC
11 Hughes (92618-1902)
PHONE..............................949 297-6635
Edward Damiano, *CEO*
EMP: 85 **EST:** 2016
SALES (est): 7.37MM **Privately Held**
Web: www.betabionics.com
SIC: 3845 Patient monitoring apparatus, nec

(P-10793)

BIONESS INC
25103 Rye Canyon Loop (91355-5004)
PHONE..............................661 362-4850
Todd Cushman, *Pr*
Alfred E Mann, *Ch*
Jim Mchargue, *COO*
Dan Lutz, *Sr VP*
Perry Payne, *VP Opers*
▲ **EMP:** 190 **EST:** 2004
SQ FT: 29,000
SALES (est): 50.97MM
SALES (corp-wide): 512.12MM **Publicly Held**
Web: www.bionessrehab.com
SIC: 3845 5047 Transcutaneous electrical nerve stimulators (TENS); Medical and hospital equipment
PA: Bioventus Inc.
4721 Emperor Blvd Ste 100
Durham NC
919 474-6700

(P-10794)

BIOSENSE WEBSTER INC (HQ)
31 Technology Dr Ste 200 (92618-2302)
PHONE..............................909 839-8500
Uri Yaron, *CEO*
Jasmina Brooks, *
Kevin Robert Costello, *
Gerianne T Sarte, *
▲ **EMP:** 150 **EST:** 1980
SALES (est): 146.03MM
SALES (corp-wide): 94.94B **Publicly Held**
Web: www.jnj.com
SIC: 3845 3841 Electromedical apparatus; Surgical and medical instruments
PA: Johnson & Johnson
1 Johnson And Johnson Plz
New Brunswick NJ
732 524-0400

(P-10795)

CAREFUSION CORPORATION (HQ)
Also Called: Bd Carefusion
3750 Torrey View Ct (92130-2622)
PHONE..............................858 617-2000
Thomas E Polen Junior, *Pr*
Christopher R Reidy, *
▲ **EMP:** 420 **EST:** 2009
SALES (est): 2.32B
SALES (corp-wide): 19.37B **Publicly Held**
Web: www.bd.com

SIC: 3845 8742 3841 Electromedical equipment; Hospital and health services consultant; Surgical instruments and apparatus
PA: Becton, Dickinson And Company
1 Becton Dr
Franklin Lakes NJ
201 847-6800

(P-10796)

CHRISTIE MEDICAL HOLDINGS INC
Also Called: Veinviewer
10550 Camden Dr (90630-4600)
PHONE..............................714 236-8610
George Pinho, *Pr*
Chris Schnee, *S&M/VP*
EMP: 20 **EST:** 2009
SALES (est): 1.95MM **Privately Held**
SIC: 3845 Electromedical equipment
HQ: Christie Digital Systems Usa, Inc.
10550 Camden Dr
Cypress CA
714 236-8610

(P-10797)

COASTLINE INTERNATIONAL
1207 Bangor St (92106-2407)
PHONE..............................888 748-7177
Larry Angione, *CEO*
▲ **EMP:** 250 **EST:** 1981
SQ FT: 32,000
SALES (est): 13.07MM **Privately Held**
Web: www.coastlineintl.com
SIC: 3845 3841 Electromedical equipment; Surgical and medical instruments

(P-10798)

DAYLIGHT DEFENSE LLC
Also Called: Drs Daylight Defense
16465 Via Esprillo Ste 100 (92127-1701)
PHONE..............................858 432-7500
EMP: 175 **EST:** 2009
SALES (est): 24.48MM
SALES (corp-wide): 15.28B **Publicly Held**
SIC: 3845 Laser systems and equipment, medical
HQ: Daylight Solutions, Inc.
16465 Via Esprillo # 100
San Diego CA
858 432-7500

(P-10799)

DECISION SCIENCES MED CO LLC
Also Called: Decision Medical
12345 First American Way Ste 100 (92064-6828)
PHONE..............................858 602-1600
Stuart J Rabin, *Managing Member*
Jed A Palmacci, *CEO*
EMP: 20 **EST:** 2012
SALES (est): 2.47MM **Privately Held**
Web: www.dsmedco.com
SIC: 3845 3841 Electromedical equipment; Surgical and medical instruments

(P-10800)

DOLPHIN MEDICAL INC (HQ)
12525 Chadron Ave (90250-4807)
PHONE..............................800 448-6506
Deepak Chopra, *Pr*
Thomas Scharf, *
▲ **EMP:** 100 **EST:** 2001
SALES (est): 49.64MM
SALES (corp-wide): 1.15B **Publicly Held**
SIC: 3845 Ultrasonic medical equipment, except cleaning
PA: Osi Systems, Inc.
12525 Chadron Ave

PRODUCTS & SVCS

Hawthorne CA
310 978-0516

(P-10801)
EDWARDS LIFESCIENCES US INC (HQ)
Also Called: Edwards
1 Edwards Way (92614-5688)
PHONE...............................949 250-2500
Michael A Mussallem, *Ch*
Dirksen J Lehman, *
Christine Z Mccauley, *VP*
Stanton J Rowe, *
Scott B Ullem, *
EMP: 80 **EST:** 2011
SALES (est): 25.44MM
SALES (corp-wide): 5.38B **Publicly Held**
Web: www.edwards.com
SIC: 3845 Patient monitoring apparatus, nec
PA: Edwards Lifesciences Corp
1 Edwards Way
Irvine CA
949 250-2500

(P-10802)
FLEXICARE INCORPORATED
15281 Barranca Pkwy Ste D (92618-2202)
PHONE...............................949 450-9999
Ghassem Poormand, *Pr*
▲ **EMP:** 37 **EST:** 2006
SALES (est): 5.31MM **Privately Held**
Web: www.flexicare.com
SIC: 3845 Electromedical equipment

(P-10803)
GEN-PROBE SALES & SERVICE INC
10210 Genetic Center Dr (92121-4394)
PHONE...............................858 410-8000
EMP: 35 **EST:** 2010
SALES (est): 9.12MM
SALES (corp-wide): 3.91B **Publicly Held**
Web: www.hologic.com
SIC: 3845 Electromedical equipment
PA: Hologic, Inc.
250 Campus Dr
Marlborough MA
508 263-2900

(P-10804)
GIVEN IMAGING LOS ANGELES LLC
5860 Uplander Way (90230-6608)
PHONE...............................310 641-8492
Ron Mcintyre, *Business Operations Vice President*
Eric Finkelman, *ENGG*
Jeffrey Sawyer, *Global Marketing Director*
◆ **EMP:** 175 **EST:** 2003
SALES (est): 44.22MM **Privately Held**
SIC: 3845 Electromedical equipment
HQ: Given Imaging Ltd.
2 Hacarmel
Yokneam Illit

(P-10805)
HOLOGIC INC
9393 Waples St (92121-3907)
PHONE...............................858 410-8792
EMP: 23 **EST:** 1995
SALES (est): 1.25MM **Privately Held**
Web: www.hologic.com
SIC: 3845 Electromedical equipment

(P-10806)
HOLOGIC INC
10210 Genetic Center Dr (92121-4362)
PHONE...............................858 410-8000
Gonzalo Martinez, *Brnch Mgr*

EMP: 229
SALES (est): 3.91B **Publicly Held**
Web: www.hologic.com
SIC: 3845 Ultrasonic medical equipment, except cleaning
PA: Hologic, Inc.
250 Campus Dr
Marlborough MA
508 263-2900

(P-10807)
HYGEIA II MEDICAL GROUP INC
Also Called: A Breast Pump and More
6241 Yarrow Dr Ste A (92011-1541)
PHONE...............................714 515-7571
Brett Nakfoor, *CEO*
Mark Engler, *
Brett Nakfoor, *Pr*
▲ **EMP:** 40 **EST:** 2007
SALES (est): 5.19MM **Privately Held**
Web: www.hygeiahealth.com
SIC: 3845 Electromedical equipment

(P-10808)
HYPERBARIC TECHNOLOGIES INC
3224 Hoover Ave (91950-7224)
PHONE...............................619 336-2022
W T Gurnee, *Pr*
EMP: 80 **EST:** 1992
SQ FT: 15,000
SALES (est): 7.61MM **Privately Held**
SIC: 3845 3841 7352 3443 Electromedical equipment; Medical instruments and equipment, blood and bone work; Medical equipment rental; Fabricated plate work (boiler shop)

(P-10809)
JOHNSON JHNSON SRGCAL VSION IN (HQ)
Also Called: Johnson & Johnson Vision
31 Technology Dr Bldg 29a (92618-2302)
P.O. Box 25929 (92799-5929)
PHONE...............................949 581-5799
Warren C Foust, *CEO*
Craig S Virgil, *
Christian A Cuzick, *
▲ **EMP:** 300 **EST:** 2001
SALES (est): 468.84MM
SALES (corp-wide): 94.94B **Publicly Held**
Web: www.jnjvisionpro.com
SIC: 3845 3841 Laser systems and equipment, medical; Ophthalmic instruments and apparatus
PA: Johnson & Johnson
1 Johnson And Johnson Plz
New Brunswick NJ
732 524-0400

(P-10810)
LOBUE LASER & EYE MEDICAL CTRS
40740 California Oaks Rd (92562-5727)
PHONE...............................951 696-1135
EMP: 21
SALES (corp-wide): 7.12MM **Privately Held**
Web: www.lobue2020eyes.com
SIC: 3845 Laser systems and equipment, medical
PA: Lobue Laser & Eye Medical Ctrs Inc
40700 California Oaks Rd
Murrieta CA
951 696-1135

(P-10811)
MASIMO CORPORATION (PA)
Also Called: Masimo

52 Discovery (92618-3105)
PHONE...............................949 297-7000
Joseph E Kiani, *Ch Bd*
Bilal Muhsin, *COO*
Micah Young, *Ex VP*
Tao Levy, *Ex VP*
Tom Mcclenahan, *Corporate Secretary*
▲ **EMP:** 350 **EST:** 1989
SQ FT: 314,400
SALES (est): 2.04B **Publicly Held**
Web: www.masimo.com
SIC: 3845 Electromedical equipment

(P-10812)
MASIMO CORPORATION
40 Parker (92618-1604)
PHONE...............................949 297-7000
Joe Kiani, *Brnch Mgr*
EMP: 50
Web: www.masimo.com
SIC: 3845 Electromedical equipment
PA: Masimo Corporation
52 Discovery
Irvine CA

(P-10813)
MASIMO CORPORATION
9600 Jeronimo Rd (92618-2024)
PHONE...............................949 297-7000
Joe Kiani, *Brnch Mgr*
EMP: 50
Web: www.masimo.com
SIC: 3845 Electromedical equipment
PA: Masimo Corporation
52 Discovery
Irvine CA

(P-10814)
MASIMO CORPORATION
15776 Laguna Canyon Rd (92618-3111)
PHONE...............................949 297-7000
EMP: 18
Web: www.masimo.com
SIC: 3845 Patient monitoring apparatus, nec
PA: Masimo Corporation
52 Discovery
Irvine CA

(P-10815)
MEDTRONIC 3F THERAPEUTICS INC
1851 E Deere Ave (92705-5720)
PHONE...............................949 399-1675
Donna Saito, *Brnch Mgr*
EMP: 165
Web: www.medtronic.com
SIC: 3845 3842 3841 Electromedical equipment; Surgical appliances and supplies; Surgical and medical instruments
HQ: Medtronic 3f Therapeutics, Inc.
710 Medtronic Pkwy
Minneapolis MN
763 514-4000

(P-10816)
NATUS MEDICAL INCORPORATED
5955 Pacific Center Blvd (92121-4309)
PHONE...............................858 260-2590
Stephen Dirocco, *Dir Opers*
EMP: 71
SALES (corp-wide): 28.49MM **Privately Held**
Web: www.natus.com
SIC: 3845 3841 Electromedical equipment; Surgical instruments and apparatus
HQ: Natus Medical Incorporated
6701 Koll Center Pkwy # 12
Pleasanton CA
925 223-6700

(P-10817)
NEURASIGNAL INC
Also Called: Novasignal
1109 Westwood Blvd (90024-3411)
PHONE...............................877 638-7251
Robert Hamilton, *CEO*
EMP: 35
SALES (est): 3.74MM **Privately Held**
Web: www.novasignal.com
SIC: 3845 Electromedical equipment

(P-10818)
NUVASIVE MANUFACTURING LLC (DH)
7475 Lusk Blvd (92121-5707)
PHONE...............................858 909-1800
EMP: 29 **EST:** 2013
SALES (est): 10.3MM
SALES (corp-wide): 958.1MM **Publicly Held**
Web: www.nuvasive.com
SIC: 3845 Ultrasonic scanning devices, medical
HQ: Nuvasive, Inc.
7475 Lusk Blvd
San Diego CA
858 909-1800

(P-10819)
PACESETTER INC (DH)
Also Called: Ventritex
15900 Valley View Ct (91342-3585)
P.O. Box 9221 (91392-9221)
PHONE...............................818 362-6822
Eric S Fain, *CEO*
Ronald A Matricaria, *
▲ **EMP:** 725 **EST:** 1994
SALES (est): 398.03MM
SALES (corp-wide): 43.65B **Publicly Held**
SIC: 3845 Defibrillator
HQ: St. Jude Medical, Llc
1 Saint Jude Medical Dr
Saint Paul MN
651 756-2000

(P-10820)
PACESETTER INC
13150 Telfair Ave (91342-3573)
PHONE...............................818 493-2715
Ignacio Machuca, *Brnch Mgr*
▲ **EMP:** 268
SALES (corp-wide): 43.65B **Publicly Held**
SIC: 3845 Defibrillator
HQ: Pacesetter, Inc.
15900 Valley View Ct
Sylmar CA

(P-10821)
PACESETTER INC
4946 Florence Ave (90201-4319)
PHONE...............................323 773-0591
EMP: 259
SALES (corp-wide): 43.65B **Publicly Held**
SIC: 3845 Electromedical equipment
HQ: Pacesetter, Inc.
15900 Valley View Ct
Sylmar CA

(P-10822)
PALYON MEDICAL CORPORATION
28432 Constellation Rd (91355-5081)
P.O. Box 2091 (85646-2091)
EMP: 25 **EST:** 2009
SALES (est): 3.95MM **Privately Held**
Web: www.palyonmedical.com
SIC: 3845 Ultrasonic scanning devices, medical

(P-10823)

PHILIPS IMAGE GDED THRAPY CORP (DH)

Also Called: Volcano
3721 Valley Centre Dr Ste 500 (92130)
PHONE....................................800 228-4728
Ronald A Matricaria, *Ch Bd*
R Scott Huennekens, *
John T Dahldorf, *
Darin M Lippoldt, *Chief Compliance Officer*
John Onopchenko, *Executive Strategy Vice President*
▲ **EMP:** 300 **EST:** 2000
SQ FT: 92,602
SALES (est): 477.97MM
SALES (corp-wide): 133.64MM **Privately Held**
SIC: 3845 Ultrasonic medical equipment, except cleaning
HQ: Philips Holding U.S.A., Inc.
222 Jacobs St
Cambridge MA

(P-10824)

RESHAPE WEIGHTLOSS INC (HQ)

1001 Calle Amanecer (92673-6260)
PHONE....................................949 429-6680
Barton P Bandy, *Pr*
Thomas Stankovich, *CFO*
EMP: 32 **EST:** 2002
SQ FT: 14,479
SALES (est): 11.3MM
SALES (corp-wide): 11.24MM **Publicly Held**
Web: www.dfrlawri.com
SIC: 3845 Electromedical equipment
PA: Reshape Lifesciences Inc.
18 Technology Dr Ste 110
Irvine CA
949 429-6680

(P-10825)

SOTERA WIRELESS INC

5841 Edison Pl Ste 140 (92008-6500)
PHONE....................................858 427-4620
Tom Watlington, *CEO*
Benjamin Kanter, *CMO*
Mark Spring, *CFO*
Jim Welch, *Ex VP*
EMP: 104 **EST:** 2002
SALES (est): 19.07MM **Privately Held**
Web: www.soteradigitalhealth.com
SIC: 3845 Electromedical equipment

(P-10826)

STRAND PRODUCTS INC (PA)

2233 Knoll Dr (93003-7398)
P.O. Box 4610 (93140-4610)
PHONE....................................800 343-7985
Wesley Prunckle, *CEO*
James Wilson, *
Susana Loewe, *
John Hottinger, *
▲ **EMP:** 20 **EST:** 1972
SQ FT: 6,000
SALES (est): 5.79MM **Privately Held**
Web: www.strandproducts.com
SIC: 3845 5063 Ultrasonic scanning devices, medical; Wire and cable

(P-10827)

SYNERON INC (DH)

Also Called: Syneron Candela
3 Goodyear Ste A (92618-2050)
PHONE....................................866 259-6661
Doctor Shimon Eckhouse, *Ch Bd*
Shimon Eckhouse, *
Doctor Opher Shapira, *VP*
Doron Gerstel, *

Leslie Rigali, *
EMP: 87 **EST:** 2000
SALES (est): 102.55MM **Privately Held**
Web: www.candelamedical.com
SIC: 3845 Laser systems and equipment, medical
HQ: Syneron Medical Ltd
26 Hakidma
Yokneam Illit

(P-10828)

TEK84 INC (PA)

13495 Gregg St (92064-7135)
PHONE....................................858 676-5382
Steven Smith, *CEO*
Kevin Russeth, *Pr*
Richard Wagner, *VP*
Eduardo Parodi, *VP*
Jonathan Shultz, *CFO*
EMP: 51 **EST:** 2009
SALES (est): 8.17MM **Privately Held**
Web: www.tek84.com
SIC: 3845 Electromedical apparatus

(P-10829)

TENSYS MEDICAL INC

12625 High Bluff Dr Ste 213 (92130-2052)
PHONE....................................858 552-1941
Stuart Gallant, *CEO*
EMP: 32 **EST:** 1995
SQ FT: 25,370
SALES (est): 2.74MM **Privately Held**
Web: www.tensysmedical.com
SIC: 3845 3841 Ultrasonic scanning devices, medical; Surgical and medical instruments

(P-10830)

VIVOMETRICS INC

16030 Ventura Blvd # 470 (91436-2731)
PHONE....................................805 667-2225
Howard R Baker, *Pr*
EMP: 17 **EST:** 1999
SQ FT: 8,220
SALES (est): 494.07K **Privately Held**
SIC: 3845 3842 Patient monitoring apparatus, nec; Surgical appliances and supplies

---

3851 Ophthalmic Goods

(P-10831)

ADVANCED VISION SCIENCE INC

5743 Thornwood Dr (93117-3801)
PHONE....................................805 683-3851
Cynthia Bentley, *Pr*
EMP: 40 **EST:** 1976
SQ FT: 30,000
SALES (est): 8.67MM **Privately Held**
Web: www.advancedvisionscience.com
SIC: 3851 3841 8011 Intraocular lenses; Surgical and medical instruments; Offices and clinics of medical doctors
PA: Santen Pharmaceutical Co., Ltd.
4-20, Ofukacho, Kita-Ku
Osaka OSK

(P-10832)

BARTON PERREIRA LLC

459 Wald (92618-4639)
PHONE....................................949 305-5360
Patty Jo L Perreira, *
▲ **EMP:** 25 **EST:** 2006
SALES (est): 4.24MM **Privately Held**
Web: www.bartonperreira.com
SIC: 3851 Protective eyeware

(P-10833)

BAUSCH & LOMB INCORPORATED

Also Called: Bausch & Lomb
15273 Alton Pkwy Ste 100 (92618-2609)
PHONE....................................949 788-6000
Ron Zarella, *Brnch Mgr*
EMP: 200
SALES (corp-wide): 8.05B **Privately Held**
Web: www.bausch.com
SIC: 3851 Ophthalmic goods
HQ: Bausch & Lomb Incorporated
400 Somerset Corp Blvd
Bridgewater NJ
866 246-8245

(P-10834)

BLENDERS EYEWEAR LLC

Also Called: Blenders Eyewear
4683 Cass St (92109-2808)
PHONE....................................858 490-2178
Chase Fisher, *CEO*
EMP: 75 **EST:** 2012
SALES (est): 10.15MM **Privately Held**
Web: www.blenderseyewear.com
SIC: 3851 Glasses, sun or glare
HQ: Safilo America, Inc.
300 Lighting Way Ste 400
Secaucus NJ

(P-10835)

COSTCO WHOLESALE CORPORATION

Also Called: Costco Optical Location 908
1001 W 19th St (91950-5435)
PHONE....................................619 336-3412
EMP: 197
SALES (corp-wide): 242.29B **Publicly Held**
SIC: 3851 Eyeglasses, lenses and frames
PA: Costco Wholesale Corporation
999 Lake Dr Ste 200
Issaquah WA
425 313-8100

(P-10836)

DRAGON ALLIANCE INC

Also Called: Dragon Alliance
971 Calle Amanecer (92673-4228)
PHONE....................................760 931-4900
William H Howard, *Pr*
Ryan Vance, *Sec*
▲ **EMP:** 83 **EST:** 1993
SQ FT: 3,500
SALES (est): 21.55MM
SALES (corp-wide): 1.89B **Privately Held**
Web: www.dragonalliance.com
SIC: 3851 Glasses, sun or glare
HQ: Marchon Eyewear, Inc.
35 Hub Dr
Melville NY
631 755-2020

(P-10837)

ELECTRIC VISUAL EVOLUTION LLC (PA)

Also Called: Electric
950 Calle Amanecer Ste 101 (92673-6211)
PHONE....................................949 940-9125
Eric Crane, *CEO*
◆ **EMP:** 28 **EST:** 1999
SQ FT: 2,000
SALES (est): 8.8MM
SALES (corp-wide): 8.8MM **Privately Held**
Web: www.electriccalifornia.com
SIC: 3851 5094 5136 Glasses, sun or glare; Watchcases; Apparel belts, men's and boys'

(P-10838)

ESSILOR LABORATORIES AMER INC

Also Called: Meridian Optical
9560 Ridgehaven Ct Ste B (92123-1668)
PHONE....................................858 565-0751
Cheryl Jacobson, *Prin*
EMP: 34
SALES (corp-wide): 2.55MM **Privately Held**
Web: www.essilorinstrumentsusa.com
SIC: 3851 Ophthalmic goods
HQ: Essilor Laboratories Of America, Inc.
13515 N Stemmons Fwy
Dallas TX
972 241-4141

(P-10839)

ESSILOR LABORATORIES AMER INC

Also Called: Elite Optical
1450 W Walnut St (90220-5013)
PHONE....................................310 604-8668
Real Goulet, *Prin*
EMP: 28
SALES (corp-wide): 2.55MM **Privately Held**
Web: www.signetarmorlite.com
SIC: 3851 Eyeglasses, lenses and frames
HQ: Essilor Laboratories Of America, Inc.
13515 N Stemmons Fwy
Dallas TX
972 241-4141

(P-10840)

EYEONICS INC

Also Called: Bausch & Lomb Surgical Div
15273 Alton Pkwy Ste 100 (92618-2609)
PHONE....................................949 788-6000
Joseph F Gordon, *CEO*
EMP: 50 **EST:** 1998
SALES (est): 8.83MM
SALES (corp-wide): 8.05B **Privately Held**
SIC: 3851 Ophthalmic goods
HQ: Bausch & Lomb Incorporated
400 Somerset Corp Blvd
Bridgewater NJ
866 246-8245

(P-10841)

HOYA CORPORATION

Also Called: Hoya San Diego
4255 Ruffin Rd (92123-1232)
PHONE....................................858 309-6050
Charlie Pendrell, *Prin*
EMP: 45
Web: www.hoyavision.com
SIC: 3851 Ophthalmic goods
HQ: Hoya Corporation
651 E Corporate Dr
Lewisville TX
972 221-4141

(P-10842)

KAZAK-MARS INC

Also Called: K Mars
16430 Vanowen St (91406-4729)
PHONE....................................818 375-1033
Dan Sadovsky, *Pr*
▲ **EMP:** 29 **EST:** 1995
SQ FT: 7,000
SALES (est): 2.29MM **Privately Held**
Web: www.kmarsoptical.com
SIC: 3851 Ophthalmic goods

(P-10843)

MARCH VISION CARE INC

6701 Center Dr W Ste 790 (90045-1563)
PHONE....................................310 665-0975

PRODUCTS & SVCS

EMP: 42 **EST:** 2005
SALES (est): 14.16MM
SALES (corp-wide): 324.16B **Publicly Held**
Web: www.marchvisioncare.com
SIC: 3851 Frames, lenses, and parts, eyeglass and spectacle
HQ: March Holdings, Inc.
6701 Center Dr W Ste 790
Los Angeles CA

(P-10844)
MEDENNIUM INC (PA)
9 Parker Ste 150 (92618-1691)
PHONE..............................949 789-9000
Jacob Feldman, *Pr*
James R Zullo, *
EMP: 40 **EST:** 1998
SQ FT: 20,000
SALES (est): 5.1MM
SALES (corp-wide): 5.1MM **Privately Held**
Web: www.medennium.com
SIC: 3851 Intraocular lenses

(P-10845)
OAKLEY INC (DH)
1 Icon (92610-3000)
PHONE..............................949 951-0991
Colin Baden, *Pr*
D Scott Olivet, *
Jim Jannard, *
Gianluca Tagliabue, *
Jon Krause, *
◆ **EMP:** 900 **EST:** 1994
SQ FT: 550,000
SALES (est): 984.07MM
SALES (corp-wide): 2.55MM **Privately Held**
Web: www.oakley.com
SIC: 3851 2339 3873 3143 Ophthalmic goods; Women's and misses' outerwear, nec; Watches, clocks, watchcases, and parts; Men's footwear, except athletic
HQ: Luxottica Of America Inc.
4000 Luxottica Pl
Mason OH

(P-10846)
OAKLEY SALES CORP
1 Icon (92610-3000)
PHONE..............................949 672-6925
Link Newcomb, *Pr*
◆ **EMP:** 247 **EST:** 2001
SQ FT: 400,000
SALES (est): 10.04MM
SALES (corp-wide): 2.55MM **Privately Held**
SIC: 3851 Glasses, sun or glare
HQ: Oakley, Inc.
1 Icon
Foothill Ranch CA
949 951-0991

(P-10847)
OASIS MEDICAL INC (PA)
510 S Vermont Ave 528 (91741)
P.O. Box 1137 (91740-1137)
PHONE..............................909 305-5400
Norman Delgado, *Ch Bd*
Craig Delgado, *
Arlene Delgado, *
◆ **EMP:** 55 **EST:** 1987
SQ FT: 14,000
SALES (est): 18.37MM
SALES (corp-wide): 18.37MM **Privately Held**
Web: www.oasismedical.com
SIC: 3851 5048 Ophthalmic goods; Ophthalmic goods

(P-10848)
OPHTHONIX INC
900 Glenneyre St (92651-2707)
PHONE..............................760 842-5600
Stephen J Osbaldeston, *CEO*
▲ **EMP:** 29 **EST:** 2000
SQ FT: 50,000
SALES (est): 2.21MM **Privately Held**
Web: www.ophthonix.com
SIC: 3851 Eyes, glass and plastic

(P-10849)
PRESBIBIO LLC
Also Called: Presbia
36 Plateau (92656-8026)
PHONE..............................949 502-7010
EMP: 45 **EST:** 2008
SALES (est): 4.68MM **Privately Held**
SIC: 3851 Frames, lenses, and parts, eyeglass and spectacle

(P-10850)
RXSIGHT INC (PA)
Also Called: Rxsight
100 Columbia Ste 120 (92656-4114)
PHONE..............................949 521-7830
Ron Kurtz, *Pr*
J Andy Corley, *
Shelley Thunen, *CFO*
Ilya Goldshleger, *COO*
Eric Weinberg, *CCO*
▼ **EMP:** 86 **EST:** 1997
SQ FT: 109,822
SALES (est): 49.01MM
SALES (corp-wide): 49.01MM **Publicly Held**
Web: www.rxsight.com
SIC: 3851 Ophthalmic goods

(P-10851)
SIGNET ARMORLITE INC (DH)
5803 Newton Dr Ste A (92008-7312)
P.O. Box 3309 (60132-3309)
PHONE..............................760 744-4000
Brad Staley, *Pr*
Bruno Salvadori, *
Andrea Moscatelli, *
M Kathryn Bernard, *
John Hingey, *
▲ **EMP:** 400 **EST:** 1969
SQ FT: 138,000
SALES (est): 26.59MM
SALES (corp-wide): 2.55MM **Privately Held**
Web: www.signetarmorlite.com
SIC: 3851 Ophthalmic goods
HQ: Essilor Of America, Inc.
13555 N Stemmons Fwy
Dallas TX

(P-10852)
SPORTIFEYE OPTICS INC
1854 Business Center Dr (91010-2901)
PHONE..............................877 742-5000
Tom Pfeiffer, *CEO*
EMP: 20 **EST:** 2017
SALES (est): 1.2MM **Privately Held**
Web: www.sportifeye.com
SIC: 3851 Frames, lenses, and parts, eyeglass and spectacle

(P-10853)
SPY INC (PA)
1896 Rutherford Rd (92008-7326)
PHONE..............................760 804-8420
▲ **EMP:** 69 **EST:** 1994
SQ FT: 32,551
SALES (est): 13.91MM **Privately Held**
Web: www.spyoptic.com

SIC: 3851 5099 Glasses, sun or glare; Sunglasses

(P-10854)
STAAR SURGICAL COMPANY (PA)
Also Called: Staar
25651 Atlantic Ocean Dr Ste A1 (92630-8835)
PHONE..............................626 303-7902
Thomas G Frinzi, *CEO*
Scott Barnes, *CMO*
Patrick Williams, *CFO*
Samuel Gesten, *CLO*
▲ **EMP:** 632 **EST:** 1982
SALES (est): 284.39MM
SALES (corp-wide): 284.39MM **Publicly Held**
Web: www.staar.com
SIC: 3851 Ophthalmic goods

(P-10855)
TEKIA INC
17 Hammond Ste 414 (92618-1635)
PHONE..............................949 699-1300
Gene Currie, *Pr*
Larry Blake, *VP Engg*
EMP: 20 **EST:** 1995
SQ FT: 5,000
SALES (est): 2.44MM **Privately Held**
Web: www.tekia.com
SIC: 3851 8742 Intraocular lenses; Hospital and health services consultant

(P-10856)
VISIONARY CONTACT LENS INC
2940 E Miraloma Ave (92806-1811)
PHONE..............................714 237-1900
Richard Belliveau, *Pr*
Cindy Belliveau, *Treas*
EMP: 37 **EST:** 1992
SQ FT: 16,000
SALES (est): 555.06K **Privately Held**
Web: www.visionarylens.com
SIC: 3851 5048 Contact lenses; Contact lenses

(P-10857)
YOUNGER MFG CO (PA)
Also Called: Younger Optics
2925 California St (90503-3914)
PHONE..............................310 783-1533
Joseph David Rips, *CEO*
Tom Balch, *
Roshan Seresinhe, *
◆ **EMP:** 280 **EST:** 1955
SQ FT: 130,000
SALES (est): 84.79MM
SALES (corp-wide): 84.79MM **Privately Held**
Web: www.youngeroptics.com
SIC: 3851 Lenses, ophthalmic

3861 Photographic Equipment And Supplies

(P-10858)
ANSCHUTZ FILM GROUP LLC (HQ)
10201 W Pico Blvd # 52 (90064-2606)
PHONE..............................310 887-1000
Michael Bostick, *CEO*
▲ **EMP:** 30 **EST:** 2004
SALES (est): 8.03MM **Privately Held**
Web: www.walden.com
SIC: 3861 Motion picture film
PA: The Anschutz Corporation
555 17th St Ste 2400

Denver CO

(P-10859)
AVID TECHNOLOGY INC
Also Called: Avid
101 S 1st St Ste 200 (91502-1938)
PHONE..............................818 557-2520
Kristin Bedient, *Mgr*
EMP: 45
SALES (corp-wide): 417.41MM **Privately Held**
Web: www.avid.com
SIC: 3861 Editing equipment, motion picture: viewers, splicers, etc.
PA: Avid Technology, Inc.
75 Blue Sky Dr
Burlington MA
978 640-3000

(P-10860)
CAROLENSE ENTRMT GROUP LLC ✪
506 S Spring St (90013-3200)
PHONE..............................405 493-1120
Danesha Barber, *Managing Member*
EMP: 60 **EST:** 2022
SALES (est): 2.94MM **Privately Held**
SIC: 3861 7389 Film, sensitized motion picture, X-ray, still camera, etc.; Business services, nec

(P-10861)
CDS CALIFORNIA LLC
3330 Cahuenga Blvd W Ste 200 (90068-1354)
PHONE..............................818 766-5000
EMP: 19 **EST:** 2012
SALES (est): 4.76MM **Privately Held**
SIC: 3861 Photographic equipment and supplies

(P-10862)
CHRISTIE DIGITAL SYSTEMS INC (HQ)
10550 Camden Dr (90630-4600)
PHONE..............................714 236-8610
Hideaki Onishi, *CEO*
Michael Phipps, *
EMP: 83 **EST:** 1999
SALES (est): 99.79MM **Privately Held**
Web: www.christiedigital.com
SIC: 3861 6719 Projectors, still or motion picture, silent or sound; Investment holding companies, except banks
PA: Ushio Inc.
1-6-5, Marunouchi
Chiyoda-Ku TKY

(P-10863)
CLOVER ENVMTL SOLUTIONS LLC
Also Called: Distribution Cente
315 Weakley St Bldg 3 (92231-9659)
PHONE..............................760 357-9277
EMP: 50
SALES (corp-wide): 173.68MM **Privately Held**
Web: www.cloverimaging.com
SIC: 3861 Printing equipment, photographic
PA: Clover Environmental Solutions Llc
4200 Columbus St
Ottawa IL
866 734-6548

(P-10864)
DJI TECHNOLOGY INC
17301 Edwards Rd (90703-2427)
PHONE..............................818 235-0789
Jie Shen, *CEO*

EMP: 71 EST: 2015
SALES (est): 7.83MM **Privately Held**
SIC: 3861 Aerial cameras

(P-10865)
ELITE SCREENS INC
12282 Knott St (92841-2825)
PHONE..............................877 511-1211
Jeff Chen, *Pr*
Henry Yoh, *
◆ **EMP:** 30 **EST:** 2004
SALES (est): 7.56MM **Privately Held**
Web: www.elitescreens.com
SIC: 3861 Photographic equipment and
supplies

(P-10866)
FASTEC IMAGING CORPORATION
17150 Via Del Campo Ste 301
(92127-2111)
PHONE..............................858 592-2342
Stephen W Ferrell, *Pr*
Charles Mrdjenovich, *
EMP: 25 **EST:** 2003
SALES (est): 3.47MM **Privately Held**
Web: www.fastecimaging.com
SIC: 3861 Cameras and related equipment

(P-10867)
FPC INC
1017 N Las Palmas Ave (90038-2400)
PHONE..............................323 468-5778
◆ **EMP:** 40
SIC: 3861 7829 Photographic equipment
and supplies; Motion picture distribution
services

(P-10868)
HF GROUP INC (PA)
Also Called: Houston Fearless 76
203 W Artesia Blvd (90220-5517)
PHONE..............................310 605-0755
Myung S Lee, *Ch Bd*
James H Lee, *
Scott Mccormack, *VP Fin*
Virginia C Clark, *
EMP: 40 **EST:** 1929
SQ FT: 45,000
SALES (est): 16.68MM
SALES (corp-wide): 16.68MM **Privately
Held**
Web: www.hf76.com
SIC: 3861 Processing equipment,
photographic

(P-10869)
HOLLYWOOD FILM COMPANY
Also Called: Hav Holdings & Subsidiaries
9265 Borden Ave (91352-2034)
PHONE..............................818 683-1130
Vincent Carabello, *Pr*
Antonia L Carabello, *
◆ **EMP:** 22 **EST:** 1937
SQ FT: 79,000
SALES (est): 1.56MM **Privately Held**
Web: www.tommylentsch.com
SIC: 3861 7819 Editing equipment, motion
picture: viewers, splicers, etc.; Services
allied to motion pictures

(P-10870)
JONDO LTD (HQ)
22700 Savi Ranch Pkwy (92887-4608)
PHONE..............................714 279-2300
John Stuart Doe, *CEO*
EMP: 60 **EST:** 1989
SQ FT: 50,000
SALES (est): 8MM
SALES (corp-wide): 516MM **Privately
Held**

Web: www.jondo.com
SIC: 3861 Photographic equipment and
supplies
PA: Circle Graphics, Inc.
120 9th Ave
Longmont CO
303 532-2370

(P-10871)
KALAP INC
401 N Brand Blvd Ste 814 (91203-4434)
PHONE..............................818 332-6916
Karen Petrosyan, *CEO*
EMP: 18 **EST:** 2021
SALES (est): 1.25MM **Privately Held**
SIC: 3861 Sound recording and reproducing
equipment, motion picture

(P-10872)
LASER TECHNOLOGIES & SERVICES LLC
Also Called: Laser Technologies
1175 Aviation Pl (91340-1460)
▲ **EMP:** 100
SIC: 3861 5999 Reproduction machines and
equipment; Telephone and communication
equipment

(P-10873)
MATTHEWS STUDIO EQUIPMENT INC
Also Called: M S E
15148 Bledsoe St (91342-3807)
PHONE..............................818 843-6715
Edward Phillips Iii, *Pr*
▲ **EMP:** 38 **EST:** 1960
SALES (est): 937.39K **Privately Held**
SIC: 3861 Motion picture apparatus and
equipment

(P-10874)
MODERN STUDIO EQUIPMENT INC
16200 Stagg St (91406-1715)
PHONE..............................818 764-8574
Seno Mousally, *Pr*
Rina Mousally, *VP*
EMP: 19 **EST:** 1980
SALES (est): 2.47MM **Privately Held**
Web: www.modernstudio.com
SIC: 3861 Motion picture apparatus and
equipment

(P-10875)
MOVING IMAGE TECHNOLOGIES LLC
17760 Newhope St Ste B (92708-5442)
PHONE..............................714 751-7998
Glenn Sherman, *Managing Member*
Bevan Wright, *
Joe Delgado, *
Phil Rassnon, *
David Richards, *
▲ **EMP:** 32 **EST:** 2003
SQ FT: 18,000
SALES (est): 9.19MM
SALES (corp-wide): 20.21MM **Publicly
Held**
Web: www.movingimagetech.com
SIC: 3861 Motion picture apparatus and
equipment
PA: Moving Image Technologies, Inc.
17760 Newhope St Ste B
Fountain Valley CA
714 751-7998

(P-10876)
MPO VIDEOTRONICS INC (PA)
5069 Maureen Ln (93021-7148)
PHONE..............................805 499-8513
Larry Kaiser, *Pr*
Julius Barron, *
Don Gaston, *
EMP: 75 **EST:** 1947
SALES (est): 9.6MM
SALES (corp-wide): 9.6MM **Privately Held**
Web: www.mpo-video.com
SIC: 3861 5065 7819 3823 Motion picture
apparatus and equipment; Video
equipment, electronic; Equipment rental,
motion picture; Process control instruments

(P-10877)
PANAVISION INC
Also Called: Panavision Hollywood
6735 Selma Ave (90028-6134)
PHONE..............................323 464-3800
Lisa Harp, *VP*
EMP: 24
Web: www.panavision.com
SIC: 3861 Photographic equipment and
supplies
PA: Panavision Inc.
6101 Variel Ave
Woodland Hills CA

(P-10878)
PANAVISION INTERNATIONAL LP (HQ)
6101 Variel Ave (91367-3722)
P.O. Box 4360 (91365-4360)
PHONE..............................818 316-1080
Robert Beitcher, *Pr*
Ross Landfbuam, *
▲ **EMP:** 380 **EST:** 1991
SQ FT: 150,000
SALES (est): 92.42MM **Privately Held**
Web: www.panavision.com
SIC: 3861 Cameras and related equipment
PA: Panavision Inc.
6101 Variel Ave
Woodland Hills CA

(P-10879)
PHOTO-SONICS INC (PA)
9131 Independence Ave (91311-5903)
PHONE..............................818 842-2141
EMP: 33 **EST:** 1928
SALES (est): 14.13MM
SALES (corp-wide): 14.13MM **Privately
Held**
Web: www.photosonics.com
SIC: 3861 3827 3663 7819 Photographic
equipment and supplies; Lenses, optical: all
types except ophthalmic;
Phototransmission equipment; Equipment
rental, motion picture

(P-10880)
PHOTRONICS INC
1760 Arroyo Gln (92026-1859)
PHONE..............................760 294-1896
Bob Rhodes, *Mgr*
EMP: 160
SALES (corp-wide): 824.55MM **Publicly
Held**
Web: www.photronics.com
SIC: 3861 Photographic equipment and
supplies
HQ: Photronics Inc
2428 N Ontario St
Burbank CA
203 740-5653

(P-10881)
PHOTRONICS INC (DH)
Also Called: Photronics California
2428 N Ontario St (91504-3119)
PHONE..............................203 740-5653
James Mac Donald Junior, *Ch Bd*
Constantine Maristos, *
EMP: 280 **EST:** 1970
SQ FT: 30,000
SALES (est): 109.87MM
SALES (corp-wide): 824.55MM **Publicly
Held**
Web: www.photronics.com
SIC: 3861 Photographic equipment and
supplies
HQ: Align-Rite International Limited
1 Technology Dr
Bridgend M GLAM

(P-10882)
REDCOM INC
94 Icon (92610-3000)
PHONE..............................949 206-7900
EMP: 18 **EST:** 2006
SALES (est): 554.6K **Privately Held**
Web: www.red.com
SIC: 3861 Photographic equipment and
supplies

(P-10883)
REDCOM LLC
Also Called: Red Digital Cinema Camera Co
94 Icon (92610-3000)
PHONE..............................949 404-4084
James H Jannard, *CEO*
Mike D Executive, *
Vince Hassel, *
Greg Weeks, *
Scott Olivet, *
▲ **EMP:** 498 **EST:** 1999
SALES (est): 143.28MM
SALES (corp-wide): 10.25MM **Privately
Held**
Web: www.red.com
SIC: 3861 Motion picture apparatus and
equipment
HQ: Red Europe Limited
Pinewood Road
Iver BUCKS
175 378-5454

(P-10884)
RICOH ELECTRONICS INC
2310 Redhill Ave (92705-5538)
PHONE..............................714 566-6079
EMP: 250
Web: rei.ricoh.com
SIC: 3861 3695 Photocopy machines;
Magnetic and optical recording media
HQ: Ricoh Electronics, Inc.
1125 Hurricane Shoals Rd
Lawrenceville GA
714 566-2500

(P-10885)
SANTA BARBARA INSTRUMENT GP INC
Also Called: Sbig Astronomical Instruments
150 Castilian Dr (93117-3028)
PHONE..............................925 463-3410
EMP: 23 **EST:** 1991
SALES (est): 2.11MM **Privately Held**
Web: www.diffractionlimited.com
SIC: 3861 Cameras and related equipment

(P-10886)
STEWART FILMSCREEN CORP (PA)
1161 Sepulveda Blvd (90502-2754)

PHONE..............................310 784-5300
Donald R Stewart, *Ex VP*
Thomas E Stewart, *
Adrian Silva, *
◆ **EMP:** 160 **EST:** 1947
SQ FT: 43,000
SALES (est): 23.69MM
SALES (corp-wide): 23.69MM **Privately Held**
Web: www.stewartfilmscreen.com
SIC: 3861 Screens, projection

(P-10887)
THERMAPRINT CORPORATION
11 Autry Ste B (92618-2766)
PHONE..............................949 583-0800
Natalie J Hochner, *Pr*
Gary Larsen, *
▲ **EMP:** 25 **EST:** 1985
SQ FT: 14,500
SALES (est): 2.38MM **Privately Held**
Web: www.thermaprint.com
SIC: 3861 3443 3585 2759 Graphic arts plates, sensitized; Fabricated plate work (boiler shop); Parts for heating, cooling, and refrigerating equipment; Screen printing

(P-10888)
UNITY SALES INTERNATIONAL INC
Also Called: Unity Digital
2950 Airway Ave Ste A12 (92626-6019)
PHONE..............................714 800-1700
Timothy Mccanna, *Pr*
EMP: 18 **EST:** 1998
SQ FT: 4,000
SALES (est): 870.95K **Privately Held**
Web: www.unitydigital.com
SIC: 3861 Cameras and related equipment

(P-10889)
VITEK INDUS VIDEO PDTS INC
28492 Constellation Rd (91355-5081)
PHONE..............................661 294-8043
Greg Alan Bier, *CEO*
◆ **EMP:** 20 **EST:** 1998
SQ FT: 9,200
SALES (est): 2.32MM **Privately Held**
Web: www.vitekcctv.com
SIC: 3861 5099 Cameras and related equipment; Video and audio equipment

(P-10890)
WBI INC
8201 Woodley Ave (91406-1231)
PHONE..............................800 673-4968
◆ **EMP:** 600
SIC: 3861 Toners, prepared photographic (not made in chemical plants)

3873 Watches, Clocks, Watchcases, And Parts

(P-10891)
AMG EMPLOYEE MANAGEMENT INC
Also Called: Time Masters
1220 S Central Ave Ste 203 (91204-2547)
PHONE..............................323 254-7448
TOLL FREE: 800
Tigran Galstyan, *Pr*
▲ **EMP:** 17 **EST:** 1998
SALES (est): 2.92MM **Privately Held**
Web: www.amgtime.com

SIC: 3873 7371 7372 3579 Timers for industrial use, clockwork mechanism only; Computer software development; Business oriented computer software; Time clocks and time recording devices

(P-10892)
CHASE-DURER LTD (PA)
8455 Fountain Ave Unit 515 (90069)
PHONE..............................310 550-7280
Brandon Chase, *Pr*
▲ **EMP:** 19 **EST:** 1997
SALES (est): 1.26MM
SALES (corp-wide): 1.26MM **Privately Held**
Web: www.chase-durer.com
SIC: 3873 Watches, clocks, watchcases, and parts

(P-10893)
MOD-ELECTRONICS INC
Also Called: Ese
142 Sierra St (90245-4117)
PHONE..............................310 322-2136
William Kaiser, *Pr*
Brian Way, *
▲ **EMP:** 26 **EST:** 1971
SQ FT: 7,500
SALES (est): 4.51MM **Privately Held**
Web: www.ese-web.com
SIC: 3873 3663 3651 3625 Clocks, assembly of; Radio and t.v. communications equipment; Household audio and video equipment; Relays and industrial controls

---

3911 Jewelry, Precious Metal

(P-10894)
ALLISON-KAUFMAN CO
7640 Haskell Ave (91406-2005)
PHONE..............................818 373-5100
Bart Kaufman, *CEO*
Jay A Kaufman, *
▲ **EMP:** 36 **EST:** 1946
SQ FT: 21,000
SALES (est): 2.78MM **Privately Held**
Web: www.allisonkaufman.com
SIC: 3911 Jewelry, precious metal

(P-10895)
ALOR INTERNATIONAL LTD
Also Called: Philippe Charriol USA
11722 Sorrento Valley Rd (92121-1021)
PHONE..............................858 454-0011
Jack Zemer, *CEO*
Sandy Zemer, *
Ori Zemer, *
Tal Zemer, *
▲ **EMP:** 45 **EST:** 1975
SALES (est): 3.72MM **Privately Held**
Web: www.alor.com
SIC: 3911 3172 3915 Vanity cases, precious metal; Personal leather goods, nec; Jewel preparing: instruments, tools, watches, and jewelry

(P-10896)
AMERICAS GOLD INC
Also Called: Americas Gold - Amrcas Damonds
650 S Hill St Ste 224 (90014-1769)
PHONE..............................213 688-4904
Rafi M Siddiqui, *Pr*
Samina Siddiqui, *
EMP: 30 **EST:** 1999
SQ FT: 4,500
SALES (est): 2.23MM **Privately Held**
Web: www.americasgold.com

SIC: 3911 Jewelry, precious metal

(P-10897)
AMINCO INTERNATIONAL USA INC
Also Called: California Premium Incentives
20571 Crescent Bay Dr (92630-8825)
PHONE..............................949 457-3261
Ann Wu, *Ex Dir*
William Wu, *
Ann Wu, *Treas*
▲ **EMP:** 62 **EST:** 1978
SQ FT: 35,000
SALES (est): 9.62MM **Privately Held**
Web: www.amincousa.com
SIC: 3911 5099 Jewelry, precious metal; Brass goods

(P-10898)
ARTS ELEGANCE INC
154 W Bellevue Dr (91105-2504)
PHONE..............................626 793-4794
Arutiun Mikaelian, *Pr*
EMP: 45
SALES (corp-wide): 4.46MM **Privately Held**
SIC: 3911 Jewelry, precious metal
PA: Art's Elegance, Inc.
739 E Walnut St Ste 200
Pasadena CA
626 405-1522

(P-10899)
BESTSIO LLC
1230 Santa Anita Ave Ste D (91733-3861)
PHONE..............................626 841-8543
Maggie Qin, *Managing Member*
EMP: 18
SALES (est): 828.41K **Privately Held**
SIC: 3911 Jewelry apparel

(P-10900)
CRISLU CORP
20916 Higgins Ct (90501-1722)
PHONE..............................310 322-3444
◆ **EMP:** 30 **EST:** 1961
SALES (est): 4.78MM **Privately Held**
Web: www.crislu.com
SIC: 3911 Jewel settings and mountings, precious metal

(P-10901)
ELBA JEWELRY INC
Also Called: Elba Company
910 N Amelia Ave (91773-1401)
PHONE..............................909 394-5803
Edouard Bachoura, *Pr*
▼ **EMP:** 19 **EST:** 1994
SQ FT: 10,000
SALES (est): 2.55MM **Privately Held**
Web: www.sophiafiori.com
SIC: 3911 Jewelry, precious metal

(P-10902)
GIVING KEYS INC
836 Traction Ave (90013-1816)
PHONE..............................213 935-8791
Caitlin Crosby, *CEO*
Brit Gilmore, *
▲ **EMP:** 20 **EST:** 2012
SQ FT: 8,000
SALES (est): 1.47MM **Privately Held**
Web: www.thegivingkeys.com
SIC: 3911 Jewelry, precious metal

(P-10903)
KESMOR ASSOCIATES
Also Called: American Designs
610 S Broadway Ste 717 (90014-1814)

PHONE..............................213 629-2300
Joseph Keshoyan, *Pr*
Hasmik Keshoyan, *VP*
EMP: 20 **EST:** 1985
SQ FT: 6,000
SALES (est): 1.45MM **Privately Held**
SIC: 3911 Jewelry, precious metal

(P-10904)
KRYSTAL VENTURES LLC
Also Called: Gracek Jewelry
17 Shell Bch (92657-2151)
PHONE..............................213 507-2215
Daniel Kang, *Managing Member*
Krystal Kang, *
EMP: 30 **EST:** 2016
SALES (est): 1.57MM **Privately Held**
SIC: 3911 4813 5734 Jewelry, precious metal ; Online service providers; Software, business and non-game

(P-10905)
L SPARK
1140 Kendall Rd Ste A (93401-8047)
PHONE..............................805 626-0511
Courtney Bonzi, *CEO*
EMP: 40 **EST:** 2016
SALES (est): 2.88MM **Privately Held**
SIC: 3911 Jewelry apparel

(P-10906)
LA GEM AND JEWELRY DESIGN (PA)
Also Called: La Rocks
659 S Broadway Fl 7 (90014-2291)
PHONE..............................213 488-1290
Ashish Arora, *CEO*
Elsa Behney, *Sec*
▲ **EMP:** 37 **EST:** 2002
SALES (est): 9.6MM
SALES (corp-wide): 9.6MM **Privately Held**
Web: www.la-rocks.com
SIC: 3911 5094 Jewelry, precious metal; Jewelry

(P-10907)
LA GEM AND JWLY DESIGN INC
Also Called: L.a. Gem And Jewelry Design, Inc.
3232 E Washington Blvd (90058-8022)
PHONE..............................213 488-1290
Joseph W Behney, *CEO*
EMP: 63
SALES (corp-wide): 9.6MM **Privately Held**
Web: www.la-rocks.com
SIC: 3911 Jewelry, precious metal
PA: L.A. Gem And Jewelry Design, Inc
659 S Broadway Fl 7
Los Angeles CA
213 488-1290

(P-10908)
LEONARD CRAFT CO LLC
1815 Ritchey St Ste B (92705-5124)
PHONE..............................714 549-0678
Stephen D Leonard, *CEO*
Stephen D Leonard, *Managing Member*
EMP: 95 **EST:** 2017
SALES (est): 4.64MM **Privately Held**
SIC: 3911 5947 Jewelry, precious metal; Gift shop

(P-10909)
RASTACLAT LLC
100 W Broadway Ste 3000 (90802-4467)
PHONE..............................424 287-0902
EMP: 36 **EST:** 2010
SALES (est): 5.04MM **Privately Held**
Web: www.rastaclat.com

SIC: **3911** Bracelets, precious metal

(P-10910)
SAGE GODDESS INC
21010 Figueroa St (90745-1937)
PHONE............................650 733-6639
Athena I Perrakis, *CEO*
David Maeizlik, *
EMP: 42 **EST:** 2013
SALES (est): 2.51MM **Privately Held**
Web: www.sagegoddess.com
SIC: **3911** 5944 5999 Jewelry apparel; Jewelry, precious stones and precious metals; Perfumes and colognes

(P-10911)
SAGE MACHADO INC
Also Called: Sage
133 N Gramercy Pl (90004-4013)
PHONE............................323 931-0595
EMP: 25 **EST:** 1995
SQ FT: 2,600
SALES (est): 849.8K **Privately Held**
Web: www.thesagelifestyle.com
SIC: **3911** 5944 5999 5621 Jewelry, precious metal; Jewelry stores; Perfumes and colognes; Boutiques

(P-10912)
SUNRISE JEWELRY MFG CORP
Also Called: Anjolee
4425 Convoy St Ste 226 (92111-3731)
PHONE............................619 270-5624
Sol Levy, *Pr*
EMP: 18 **EST:** 1977
SALES (est): 420.71K **Privately Held**
Web: www.thejewelrydomain.com
SIC: **3911** Jewelry, precious metal

(P-10913)
TEMPLE CUSTOM JEWELERS LLC
1640 Camino Del Rio N Ste 220 (92108)
PHONE............................800 988-3844
Anthony Temple, *CEO*
EMP: 50 **EST:** 2016
SALES (est): 2.89MM **Privately Held**
SIC: **3911** 5094 Jewelry mountings and trimmings; Jewelry and precious stones

(P-10914)
US GOLD TRADING INC
117 E Providencia Ave (91502-1922)
PHONE............................818 558-7766
Sarkis Adamian, *CEO*
EMP: 18 **EST:** 1975
SQ FT: 25,000
SALES (est): 1.26MM **Privately Held**
SIC: **3911** Jewelry, precious metal

3914 Silverware And Plated Ware

(P-10915)
CAL SIMBA INC (PA)
1283 Flynn Rd (93012-8013)
PHONE............................805 240-1177
Jay Schechter, *CEO*
Stuart Seeler, *
John Stout, *
▲ **EMP:** 38 **EST:** 1974
SALES (est): 10.33MM
SALES (corp-wide): 10.33MM **Privately Held**
Web: www.simbaline.com

SIC: **3914** 2672 3452 2821 Trophies, plated (all metals); Labels (unprinted), gummed: made from purchased materials; Pins; Polyurethane resins

3915 Jewelers' Materials And Lapidary Work

(P-10916)
AM CASTENADA INC
1450 University Ave Ste P (92507-4432)
PHONE............................951 686-3966
EMP: 28
SALES (corp-wide): 1.08MM **Privately Held**
SIC: **3915** Lapidary work and diamond cutting and polishing
PA: Am Castenada Inc.
1090 Third Ave Ste 19
Chula Vista CA
619 498-1042

(P-10917)
CGM INC
Also Called: Cgm Findings
19611 Ventura Blvd Ste 211 (91356-2907)
PHONE............................818 609-7088
TOLL FREE: 800
Devinder Bindra, *CEO*
▲ **EMP:** 25 **EST:** 1984
SQ FT: 12,000
SALES (est): 2.36MM **Privately Held**
Web: www.cgmfindings.com
SIC: **3915** 5094 Jewelers' materials and lapidary work; Precious metals

(P-10918)
LUCENT DIAMONDS INC
6303 Owensmouth Ave Fl 10 (91367-2262)
PHONE............................424 781-7127
Alex Grizenko, *
EMP: 31 **EST:** 2000
SALES (est): 2.01MM **Privately Held**
Web: www.lucentdiamonds.com
SIC: **3915** 5094 5999 Diamond cutting and polishing; Diamonds (gems); Gems and precious stones

(P-10919)
QUADRTECH CORPORATION
Also Called: Studex
521 W Rosecrans Ave (90248-1514)
PHONE............................310 523-1697
Vladimir Reil, *Pr*
▲ **EMP:** 29 **EST:** 1999
SALES (est): 5.02MM **Privately Held**
Web: www.earpiercing.com
SIC: **3915** 3423 Jewelers' materials and lapidary work; Jewelers' hand tools

(P-10920)
STARDUST DIAMOND CORP
Also Called: Diamonds By Design
550 S Hill St Ste 1420 (90013-2415)
PHONE............................213 239-9999
EMP: 22 **EST:** 1995
SQ FT: 3,600
SALES (est): 864.13K **Privately Held**
Web: www.stardustdiamonds.com
SIC: **3915** 5094 Jewelers' findings and materials; Diamonds (gems)

3931 Musical Instruments

(P-10921)
BBE SOUND INC (PA)
Also Called: G & L Musical Instruments
2548 Fender Ave Ste G (92831-4439)

PHONE............................714 897-6766
David Mclaren, *CEO*
Shailesh Karia, *CFO*
Robert Ruzzito, *VP Sls*
John Mclaren, *Prin*
John T Davey, *Prin*
▲ **EMP:** 22 **EST:** 1984
SQ FT: 10,000
SALES (est): 5.71MM
SALES (corp-wide): 5.71MM **Privately Held**
Web: www.bbesound.com
SIC: **3931** 3651 Guitars and parts, electric and nonelectric; Amplifiers: radio, public address, or musical instrument

(P-10922)
DUNCAN CARTER CORPORATION (PA)
Also Called: Seymour Duncan
5427 Hollister Ave (93111-2307)
PHONE............................805 964-9749
Seymour Duncan, *Ch*
Cathy Carter Duncan, *
▲ **EMP:** 99 **EST:** 1976
SQ FT: 20,000
SALES (est): 21.03MM
SALES (corp-wide): 21.03MM **Privately Held**
Web: www.seymourduncan.com
SIC: **3931** 5736 3674 3651 Guitars and parts, electric and nonelectric; Musical instrument stores; Semiconductors and related devices; Household audio and video equipment

(P-10923)
ERNIE BALL INC (PA)
Also Called: Ernie Ball
4117 Earthwood Ln (93401-7541)
PHONE............................805 544-7726
Brian Ball, *CEO*
Sterling C Ball, *VP*
▲ **EMP:** 29 **EST:** 1965
SQ FT: 50,000
SALES (est): 25.27MM
SALES (corp-wide): 25.27MM **Privately Held**
Web: www.ernieball.com
SIC: **3931** Guitars and parts, electric and nonelectric

(P-10924)
FENDER MUSICAL INSTRS CORP
311 Cessna Cir (92878-5021)
PHONE............................480 596-9690
EMP: 800
SALES (corp-wide): 1.87B **Privately Held**
Web: www.fender.com
SIC: **3931** 3651 Musical instruments; Amplifiers: radio, public address, or musical instrument
HQ: Fender Musical Instruments Corporation
17600 N Perimeter Dr # 100
Scottsdale AZ
480 596-9690

(P-10925)
HARRIS ORGANS INC
Also Called: Harris' Precision Products
7047 Comstock Ave (90602-1399)
PHONE............................562 693-3442
David C Harris, *Pr*
EMP: 21 **EST:** 1971
SQ FT: 12,000
SALES (est): 1.72MM **Privately Held**
Web: www.harrisorgans.com

SIC: **3931** 3599 Pipes, organ; Machine shop, jobbing and repair

(P-10926)
KANSTUL MUSICAL INSTRS INC
Also Called: K M I
23772 Perth Bay (92629-4203)
PHONE............................714 563-1000
Zigmant J Kanstul, *Pr*
EMP: 42 **EST:** 1982
SALES (est): 4.48MM **Privately Held**
Web: www.kanstul.com
SIC: **3931** Brass instruments and parts

(P-10927)
LR BAGGS CORPORATION
483 N Frontage Rd (93444-9596)
PHONE............................805 929-3545
Lloyd R Baggs, *CEO*
▲ **EMP:** 22 **EST:** 1975
SALES (est): 4.5MM **Privately Held**
Web: www.lrbaggs.com
SIC: **3931** 3825 3651 Guitars and parts, electric and nonelectric; Transducers for volts, amperes, watts, vars, frequency, etc.; Household audio and video equipment

(P-10928)
PALADAR MFG INC
53973 Polk St (92236-3816)
P.O. Box 4117 (93403-4117)
PHONE............................760 775-4222
Sterling C Ball, *Pr*
Roland S Ball, *
▲ **EMP:** 52 **EST:** 1979
SQ FT: 6,000
SALES (est): 4.77MM **Privately Held**
Web: www.bigpoppasmokers.com
SIC: **3931** Strings, musical instrument

(P-10929)
QUILTER LABORATORIES LLC
1791 Reynolds Ave (92614-5711)
PHONE............................714 519-6114
Patrick H Quilter, *Prin*
▲ **EMP:** 17 **EST:** 2011
SALES (est): 727.38K **Privately Held**
Web: www.quilterlabs.com
SIC: **3931** Guitars and parts, electric and nonelectric

(P-10930)
REMO INC (PA)
28101 Industry Dr (91355-4102)
PHONE............................661 294-5600
Remo D Belli, *Pr*
Fredy Shen, *
Douglas Sink, *
◆ **EMP:** 300 **EST:** 1957
SQ FT: 216,000
SALES (est): 99.5MM
SALES (corp-wide): 99.5MM **Privately Held**
Web: www.remo.com
SIC: **3931** Heads, drum

(P-10931)
RICKENBACKER INTERNATIONAL CORPORATION
Also Called: Ric
3895 S Main St (92707-5710)
PHONE............................714 545-5574
EMP: 75 **EST:** 1931
SALES (est): 4.55MM **Privately Held**
Web: www.pixeljar.site
SIC: **3931** Guitars and parts, electric and nonelectric

PRODUCTS & SVCS

(P-10932)
RICO CORPORATION (HQ)
Also Called: Rico Products
8484 San Fernando Rd (91352-3227)
PHONE..................................818 394-2700
James D Addario, *CEO*
◆ **EMP:** 169 **EST:** 1928
SALES (est): 38.66MM
SALES (corp-wide): 169.13MM **Privately Held**
Web: www.daddario.com
SIC: 3931 5099 Reeds for musical instruments; Musical instruments
PA: D'addario & Company, Inc.
595 Smith St
Farmingdale NY
631 439-3300

(P-10933)
SCHECTER GUITAR RESEARCH INC
10953 Pendleton St (91352-1522)
PHONE..................................818 767-1029
Michael Ciravolo, *Pr*
◆ **EMP:** 43 **EST:** 1987
SQ FT: 11,000
SALES (est): 4.85MM **Privately Held**
Web: www.schecterguitars.com
SIC: 3931 Musical instruments

(P-10934)
TOM ANDERSON GUITARWORKS
845 Rancho Conejo Blvd (91320-1794)
PHONE..................................805 498-1747
Tom Anderson, *Owner*
Rachel Williams, *Off Mgr*
EMP: 17 **EST:** 2012
SALES (est): 981.21K **Privately Held**
Web: www.andersonguitarworks.com
SIC: 3931 Guitars and parts, electric and nonelectric

(P-10935)
YAMAHA GUITAR GROUP INC (HQ)
26580 Agoura Rd (91302-1921)
PHONE..................................818 575-3600
Joe Bentivegna, *Pr*
Christine Hagemann, *
◆ **EMP:** 120 **EST:** 1988
SQ FT: 20,000
SALES (est): 51.74MM **Privately Held**
Web: www.yamahaguitargroup.com
SIC: 3931 Musical instruments
PA: Yamaha Corporation
10-1, Nakazawacho, Naka-Ku
Hamamatsu SZO

(P-10936)
YAMAHA GUITAR GROUP INC
26664 Agoura Rd (91302-1954)
PHONE..................................818 575-3900
Paul Foeckler, *Pr*
EMP: 38
Web: www.line6.com
SIC: 3931 Musical instruments
HQ: Yamaha Guitar Group, Inc.
26580 Agoura Rd
Calabasas CA
818 575-3600

3942 Dolls And Stuffed Toys

(P-10937)
CLOUD B INC
150 W Walnut St Ste 100 (90248-3145)
PHONE..................................310 781-3833

Linda Suh, *CEO*
◆ **EMP:** 22 **EST:** 2002
SQ FT: 4,100
SALES (est): 4.68MM
SALES (corp-wide): 9.79MM **Publicly Held**
Web: www.cloudb.com
SIC: 3942 5099 Stuffed toys, including animals; Baby carriages, strollers and related products
PA: Vinco Ventures, Inc.
6 N Main St
Fairport NY
866 900-0992

(P-10938)
FAR OUT TOYS INC
300 N Pacific Coast Hwy Ste 1050 (90245)
PHONE..................................310 480-7554
Keith Meggs, *CEO*
EMP: 20 **EST:** 2017
SQ FT: 3,700
SALES (est): 4.14MM **Privately Held**
Web: www.farouttoysinc.com
SIC: 3942 5092 Dolls and stuffed toys; Toys and games
HQ: Far Out Toys (Hk) Co., Limited
Rm 805 8/F Inter-Continental Plz
Tsim Sha Tsui KLN

(P-10939)
MAHAR MANUFACTURING CORP (PA)
Also Called: Fiesta Concession
2834 E 46th St (90058-2404)
PHONE..................................323 581-9988
Donald Mcintyre, *CEO*
Carol Reynolds, *
◆ **EMP:** 39 **EST:** 1971
SQ FT: 100,000
SALES (est): 8.08MM
SALES (corp-wide): 8.08MM **Privately Held**
Web: www.fiestatoy.com
SIC: 3942 Stuffed toys, including animals

(P-10940)
MATTEL INC (PA)
Also Called: MATTEL
333 Continental Blvd (90245-5032)
PHONE..................................310 252-2000
Ynon Kreiz, *Ch Bd*
Steve Totzke, *CCO*
Anthony Disilvestro, *CFO*
Jonathan Anschell, *CLO*
Yoon Hugh, *CAO*
◆ **EMP:** 1700 **EST:** 1945
SQ FT: 360,000
SALES (est): 5.43B
SALES (corp-wide): 5.43B **Publicly Held**
Web: about.mattel.com
SIC: 3942 3944 Dolls and stuffed toys; Games, toys, and children's vehicles

(P-10941)
MATTEL INVESTMENT INC
333 Continental Blvd (90245-5032)
PHONE..................................310 252-2000
EMP: 25 **EST:** 1997
SALES (est): 6.15MM
SALES (corp-wide): 5.43B **Publicly Held**
SIC: 3942 Dolls and stuffed toys
PA: Mattel, Inc.
333 Continental Blvd
El Segundo CA
310 252-2000

(P-10942)
MOOSE TOYS LLC
Also Called: Moose

737 Campus Sq W (90245-2567)
PHONE..................................310 341-4642
Manny Stul, *Ch*
EMP: 95 **EST:** 2018
SALES (est): 24.17MM **Privately Held**
Web: www.moosetoys.com
SIC: 3942 3944 5092 7389 Dolls and stuffed toys; Electronic games and toys; Toys and hobby goods and supplies; Business services, nec
HQ: Moose Toys Pty Ltd
29 Grange Road
Cheltenham VIC

(P-10943)
STROTTMAN INTERNATIONAL INC (PA)
Also Called: Strottman
36 Executive Park Ste 200 (92614-4717)
PHONE..................................949 623-7900
◆ **EMP:** 25 **EST:** 1983
SALES (est): 10.13MM
SALES (corp-wide): 10.13MM **Privately Held**
Web: www.strottman.com
SIC: 3942 5092 5145 Dolls and stuffed toys; Toy novelties and amusements; Confectionery

(P-10944)
UPD INC
Also Called: United Pacific Designs
4507 S Maywood Ave (90058-2610)
PHONE..................................323 588-8811
Shahin Dardashty, *Pr*
Fred Dardashty, *
Ben Hooshim, *
◆ **EMP:** 60 **EST:** 1990
SQ FT: 140,000
SALES (est): 15.45MM **Privately Held**
Web: www.updinc.net
SIC: 3942 5112 3944 Dolls and stuffed toys; Pens and/or pencils; Puzzles

3944 Games, Toys, And Children's Vehicles

(P-10945)
ALIQUANTUM INTERNATIONAL INC
Also Called: Aqi
2009 S Parco Ave (91761-5700)
PHONE..................................909 773-0880
▲ **EMP:** 40 **EST:** 2010
SQ FT: 15,000
SALES (est): 5.17MM **Privately Held**
Web: www.aqi-intl.com
SIC: 3944 Games, toys, and children's vehicles

(P-10946)
ASSOCIATED ELECTRICS INC (HQ)
21062 Bake Pkwy Ste 100 (92630-2183)
PHONE..................................949 544-7500
Shawn Ireland, *CEO*
Chung L Lai, *Pr*
Clifton Lett, *VP*
▲ **EMP:** 17 **EST:** 1965
SALES (est): 4.75MM **Privately Held**
Web: www.associatedelectrics.com
SIC: 3944 Automobile and truck models, toy and hobby
PA: Thunder Tiger Corporation
No. 7, 6th Rd., Industry Park
Taichung City

(P-10947)
BANDAI NMCO TOYS CLLCTBLES AME (DH)
23 Odyssey (92618-3144)
PHONE..................................949 271-6000
Shusuke Takahara, *CEO*
Atsushi Takeuchi, *
Katsushi Murakami, *
Takeshi Nojima, *
Brian Goldner, *
▲ **EMP:** 53 **EST:** 1978
SQ FT: 75,000
SALES (est): 25.82MM **Privately Held**
Web: www.bandai.com
SIC: 3944 Games, toys, and children's vehicles
HQ: Bandai Namco Holdings Usa Inc.
2120 Park Pl Ste 120
El Segundo CA

(P-10948)
BRAINSTORMPRODUCTS LLC
1011 S Andreasen Dr Ste 100 (92029-1962)
PHONE..................................760 871-1135
Randal W Joe, *Pr*
Ryan Marsh, *Dir Opers*
◆ **EMP:** 22 **EST:** 2006
SQ FT: 4,000
SALES (est): 20.77MM **Privately Held**
Web: www.xkites.com
SIC: 3944 Kites

(P-10949)
DREAMGEAR LLC
Also Called: Isound
20001 S Western Ave (90501-1306)
P.O. Box 478 (90508-0478)
PHONE..................................310 222-5522
Yahya Ahdout, *CEO*
Richard Weston, *
◆ **EMP:** 49 **EST:** 2002
SQ FT: 60,000
SALES (est): 17.32MM **Privately Held**
Web: www.dreamgear.com
SIC: 3944 Electronic games and toys

(P-10950)
DT MATTSON ENTERPRISES INC
Also Called: Protoform
201 W Lincoln St (92220-4933)
P.O. Box 456 (92223-0456)
PHONE..................................951 849-9781
Todd Mattson, *CEO*
▲ **EMP:** 40 **EST:** 1983
SQ FT: 20,000
SALES (est): 8MM **Privately Held**
Web: www.prolineracing.com
SIC: 3944 5521 Games, toys, and children's vehicles; Trucks, tractors, and trailers: used

(P-10951)
ERGO BABY CARRIER INC (HQ)
680 Knox St Ste 125 (90502-1342)
PHONE..................................213 283-2090
Bill Chiasson, *CEO*
Karin A Frost, *
Svea Frost, *
Elias Sabo, *
◆ **EMP:** 44 **EST:** 2003
SALES (est): 52.56MM **Publicly Held**
Web: www.ergobaby.com
SIC: 3944 Baby carriages and restraint seats
PA: Compass Diversified Holdings
301 Riverside Ave Fl 2
Westport CT

(P-10952)
EXPLODING KITTENS LLC
101 S La Brea Ave Ste A (90036-2998)
PHONE...................................310 788-8699
Matthew Inman, *
EMP: 29 EST: 2015
SALES (est): 5.26MM **Privately Held**
Web: www.explodingkittens.com
SIC: 3944 7371 Board games, children's and
adults'; Computer software development
and applications
PA: Asmodee Group
     Quartier Villaroy
     Guyancourt

(P-10953)
HORIZON HOBBY LLC
4710 E Guasti Rd Ste A (91761-8121)
PHONE...................................909 390-9595
Yolanda Perry, *Brnch Mgr*
EMP: 67
SALES (corp-wide): 94.6MM **Privately
Held**
Web: www.horizonhobby.com
SIC: 3944 5092 Automobile and truck
models, toy and hobby; Hobby goods
PA: Horizon Hobby, Llc
     2904 Research Rd
     Champaign IL
     217 352-1913

(P-10954)
IMPERIAL TOY LLC (PA)
16641 Roscoe Pl (91343-6104)
PHONE...................................818 536-6500
Peter Tiger, *Managing Member*
Arthur Hirsch, *
◆ **EMP:** 115 **EST:** 1969
SQ FT: 400,000
SALES (est): 25.12MM
SALES (corp-wide): 25.12MM **Privately
Held**
Web: www.jaru.com
SIC: 3944 Games, toys, and children's
vehicles

(P-10955)
INSOMNIAC GAMES INC (PA)
2255 N Ontario St Ste 550 (91504-3120)
PHONE...................................818 729-2400
Theodore C Price, *Pr*
Alex Hastings, *VP*
Brian Hastings, *Sec*
EMP: 73 **EST:** 1994
SALES (est): 42.13MM
SALES (corp-wide): 42.13MM **Privately
Held**
Web: www.insomniac.games
SIC: 3944 Electronic games and toys

(P-10956)
JADA GROUP INC (DH)
Also Called: Jada Toys
18521 Railroad St (91748-1316)
PHONE...................................626 810-8382
William Anthony Simons, *CEO*
Wai Han Ko, *
Manfred Duschl, *
◆ **EMP:** 20 **EST:** 1999
SALES (est): 28.53MM
SALES (corp-wide): 143.22MM **Privately
Held**
Web: www.jadatoys.com
SIC: 3944 Games, toys, and children's
vehicles
HQ: Simba-Dickie-Group Gmbh
     Werkstr. 1
     Furth BY
     911976501

(P-10957)
JAKKS PACIFIC INC (PA)
Also Called: Jakks
2951 28th St (90405-2961)
PHONE...................................424 268-9444
EMP: 66 **EST:** 1995
SQ FT: 65,858
SALES (est): 796.19MM **Publicly Held**
Web: www.jakks.com
SIC: 3944 Games, toys, and children's
vehicles

(P-10958)
JAKKS PACIFIC INC
Also Called: Flying Colors
21749 Baker Pkwy (91789-5234)
PHONE...................................909 594-7771
Michelle Tromp, *Brnch Mgr*
EMP: 30
Web: www.jakks.com
SIC: 3944 5092 Games, toys, and children's
vehicles; Toys, nec
PA: Jakks Pacific, Inc.
     2951 28th St
     Santa Monica CA

(P-10959)
**MATTEL DIRECT IMPORT INC
(HQ)**
Also Called: Mattel
333 Continental Blvd (90245-5032)
PHONE...................................310 252-2000
Kevin Farr, *CEO*
Bryan G Stockton, *Pr*
EMP: 48 **EST:** 2007
SALES (est): 11.32MM
SALES (corp-wide): 5.43B **Publicly Held**
SIC: 3944 3942 3949 Games, toys, and
children's vehicles; Dolls, except stuffed toy
animals; Sporting and athletic goods, nec
PA: Mattel, Inc.
     333 Continental Blvd
     El Segundo CA
     310 252-2000

(P-10960)
MATTEL OPERATIONS INC
333 Continental Blvd (90245-5032)
PHONE...................................310 252-2000
EMP: 22 **EST:** 1946
SALES (est): 1.76MM
SALES (corp-wide): 5.43B **Publicly Held**
SIC: 3944 Games, toys, and children's
vehicles
PA: Mattel, Inc.
     333 Continental Blvd
     El Segundo CA
     310 252-2000

(P-10961)
**MEGA BRANDS AMERICA INC
(DH)**
Also Called: Rose Art Industries
333 Continental Blvd (90245-5032)
PHONE...................................949 727-9009
Marc Bertrand, *CEO*
Vic Bertrand, *
◆ **EMP:** 80 **EST:** 1923
SALES (est): 179.23MM
SALES (corp-wide): 5.43B **Publicly Held**
SIC: 3944 Blocks, toy
HQ: Mega Brands Inc.
     4505 Rue Hickmore
     Saint-Laurent QC
     514 333-5555

(P-10962)
**MOORES IDEAL PRODUCTS
LLC**

Also Called: M I P
830 W Golden Grove Way (91722-3257)
PHONE...................................626 339-9007
Eustace Moore Junior, *Managing Member*
EMP: 20 **EST:** 1978
SQ FT: 8,600
SALES (est): 851.82K **Privately Held**
Web: www.miponline.com
SIC: 3944 Automobile and truck models, toy
and hobby

(P-10963)
NINJA JUMP INC
3221 N San Fernando Rd (90065-1414)
PHONE...................................323 255-5418
◆ **EMP:** 75 **EST:** 1984
SQ FT: 35,000
SALES (est): 5.23MM **Privately Held**
Web: www.ninjajump.com
SIC: 3944 Games, toys, and children's
vehicles

(P-10964)
PLAYHUT INC
18560 San Jose Ave (91748-1365)
PHONE...................................909 869-8083
Yu Zheng, *CEO*
▲ **EMP:** 20 **EST:** 1992
SALES (est): 5.17MM **Privately Held**
Web: www.basicfun.com
SIC: 3944 Games, toys, and children's
vehicles
PA: Basic Fun, Inc.
     301 E Yamato Rd Ste 4200
     Boca Raton FL

(P-10965)
ROAD CHAMPS INC
22619 Pacific Coast Hwy Ste 250 (90265)
PHONE...................................310 456-7799
Stephen Berman, *Pr*
EMP: 150 **EST:** 1960
SQ FT: 51,000
SALES (est): 22.7MM **Publicly Held**
SIC: 3944 Automobiles and trucks, toy
PA: Jakks Pacific, Inc.
     2951 28th St
     Santa Monica CA

(P-10966)
SHELCORE INC (PA)
Also Called: Shelcore Toys
7811 Lemona Ave (91405-1139)
PHONE...................................818 883-2400
Arnold Rubin, *Pr*
◆ **EMP:** 29 **EST:** 1975
SQ FT: 20,000
SALES (est): 61.17MM
SALES (corp-wide): 61.17MM **Privately
Held**
Web: www.funrise.com
SIC: 3944 Blocks, toy

(P-10967)
**TOYMAX INTERNATIONAL INC
(HQ)**
22619 Pacific Coast Hwy (90265-5054)
PHONE...................................310 456-7799
Jack Friedman, *CEO*
Stephen G Berman, *
Joel M Bennett, *CFO*
◆ **EMP:** 56 **EST:** 1990
SQ FT: 30,000
SALES (est): 45.61MM **Publicly Held**
SIC: 3944 5092 Games, toys, and children's
vehicles; Toys and games
PA: Jakks Pacific, Inc.
     2951 28th St
     Santa Monica CA

(P-10968)
USAOPOLY INC
Also Called: Op Games, The
5999 Avenida Encinas Ste 150
(92008-4431)
PHONE...................................760 431-5910
Dane S Chapin, *CEO*
Tom Nirschel, *
▲ **EMP:** 94 **EST:** 1994
SQ FT: 10,000
SALES (est): 17.94MM **Privately Held**
Web: www.theop.games
SIC: 3944 Board games, puzzles, and
models, except electronic

3949 Sporting And Athletic Goods, Nec

(P-10969)
ABSOLUTE BOARD CO INC
4040 Calle Platino Ste 102 (92056-5833)
P.O. Box 4098 (92052-4098)
PHONE...................................760 295-2201
▲ **EMP:** 19 **EST:** 2011
SALES (est): 2.04MM **Privately Held**
Web: www.absoluteboardco.com
SIC: 3949 Skateboards

(P-10970)
ACUSHNET COMPANY
Also Called: Titleist
2819 Loker Ave E (92010-6626)
PHONE...................................760 804-6500
John Worster, *Brnch Mgr*
EMP: 300
Web: www.titleist.com
SIC: 3949 Shafts, golf club
HQ: Acushnet Company
     333 Bridge St
     Fairhaven MA
     508 979-2000

(P-10971)
ADDADAY INC
12304 Santa Monica Blvd Ste 355
(90025-1542)
P.O. Box 163 (90274-0163)
PHONE...................................424 259-3368
Victor Yang, *CEO*
EMP: 20 **EST:** 2010
SALES (est): 6.9MM **Privately Held**
Web: www.experiencelyric.com
SIC: 3949 3634 Sporting and athletic goods,
nec; Massage machines, electric, except
for beauty/barber shops

(P-10972)
ALDILA GOLF CORP
13450 Stowe Dr (92064-6860)
PHONE...................................858 513-1801
EMP: 104
Web: www.aldila.com
SIC: 3949 Shafts, golf club
HQ: Aldila Golf Corp.
     1945 Kellogg Ave
     Carlsbad CA

(P-10973)
ALDILA GOLF CORP (DH)
1945 Kellogg Ave (92008-6582)
PHONE...................................858 513-1801
Peter R Mathewson, *CEO*
Scott Bier, *
Sue-wei Yeh, *Contrlr*
▲ **EMP:** 78 **EST:** 1991
SQ FT: 52,156
SALES (est): 25.16MM **Privately Held**
Web: www.aldila.com

PRODUCTS & SVCS

SIC: 3949 Shafts, golf club
HQ: Aldila, Inc.
1945 Kellogg Ave
Carlsbad CA
858 513-1801

(P-10974)
AMRON INTERNATIONAL INC (PA)
Also Called: Amron
1380 Aspen Way (92081-8349)
PHONE..............................760 208-6500
Debra L Ritchie, *CEO*
◆ **EMP: 69 EST:** 1979
SQ FT: 40,000
SALES (est): 10.62MM
SALES (corp-wide): 10.62MM **Privately Held**
Web: www.amronintl.com
SIC: 3949 5091 Skin diving equipment, scuba type; Diving equipment and supplies

(P-10975)
ASPHALT FABRIC AND ENGRG INC
2683 Lime Ave (90755-2718)
PHONE..............................562 997-4129
Bill Goldsmith, *Pr*
Doug Coulter, *
Joe Salamone, *
EMP: 90 EST: 1998
SQ FT: 5,000
SALES (est): 16.65MM **Privately Held**
Web: www.afesports.com
SIC: 3949 Sporting and athletic goods, nec

(P-10976)
AZA INDUSTRIES INC (PA)
1410 Vantage Ct (92081-8509)
PHONE..............................760 560-0440
David H Brown, *Pr*
Jim Passamonte, *
Bill Pierce, *
▲ **EMP: 40 EST:** 1977
SQ FT: 27,000
SALES (est): 9.14MM **Privately Held**
SIC: 3949 Skateboards

(P-10977)
BELL FOUNDRY CO (PA)
5310 Southern Ave (90280-3690)
P.O. Box 1070 (90280-1070)
PHONE..............................323 564-5701
Cesar Capallini, *Pr*
Wanda De Wald, *
Dimitry Rabyy, *
▲ **EMP: 54 EST:** 1924
SQ FT: 140,000
SALES (est): 4.86MM
SALES (corp-wide): 4.86MM **Privately Held**
Web: www.bfco.com
SIC: 3949 3321 Dumbbells and other weightlifting equipment; Gray and ductile iron foundries

(P-10978)
BLACK BOX DISTRIBUTION LLC
371 2nd St Ste 1 (92024-3524)
PHONE..............................760 268-1174
◆ **EMP: 70 EST:** 2009
SALES (est): 5.56MM **Privately Held**
SIC: 3949 Skateboards

(P-10979)
BRAVO HIGHLINE LLC ✪
3101 Ocean Park Blvd Ste 100 (90405-3022)
PHONE..............................562 484-5100

Bart Thielen, *CEO*
Nicholas Schultz, *Managing Member**
Dinesh Mirchandani, *
EMP: 25 EST: 2023
SALES (est): 1.01MM **Privately Held**
SIC: 3949 3944 Skateboards; Scooters, children's

(P-10980)
BRAVO SPORTS
Also Called: Sector9
4370 Jutland Dr (92117-3642)
PHONE..............................858 408-0083
Derek Oneill, *CEO*
EMP: 23
SALES (corp-wide): 43.64MM **Privately Held**
Web: www.bravosportscorp.com
SIC: 3949 Skateboards
HQ: Bravo Sports
12801 Carmenita Rd
Santa Fe Springs CA
562 484-5100

(P-10981)
BRAVO SPORTS (HQ)
12801 Carmenita Rd (90670-4805)
P.O. Box 2967 (90670-0967)
PHONE..............................562 484-5100
Nicholas R Schultz, *Pr*
◆ **EMP: 80 EST:** 1987
SQ FT: 100,000
SALES (est): 38.75MM
SALES (corp-wide): 43.64MM **Privately Held**
Web: www.bravosportscorp.com
SIC: 3949 Sporting and athletic goods, nec
PA: Transom Bravo Holdings Corp.
12801 Carmenita Rd
Santa Fe Springs CA
562 484-5100

(P-10982)
C PREME LIMITED LLC
Also Called: C-Preme
1250 E 223rd St (90745-4266)
PHONE..............................310 355-0498
▲ **EMP: 21 EST:** 2010
SQ FT: 40,000
SALES (est): 2.78MM
SALES (corp-wide): 3.08B **Publicly Held**
Web: www.c-preme.com
SIC: 3949 5091 5571 5099 Skateboards; Bicycles; Motor scooters; Luggage
PA: Vista Outdoor Inc.
1 Vista Way
Anoka MN
763 433-1000

(P-10983)
CASA DE HERMANDAD (PA)
Also Called: West Area Opportunity Center
1639 11th St (90404-3727)
PHONE..............................310 477-8272
David Abelar, *Pr*
EMP: 25 EST: 1970
SALES (est): 80.05K
SALES (corp-wide): 80.05K **Privately Held**
SIC: 3949 Driving ranges, golf, electronic

(P-10984)
CONDOR OUTDOOR PRODUCTS INC (PA)
Also Called: Condor
5268 Rivergrade Rd (91706-1336)
PHONE..............................626 358-3270
Spencer Tien, *Pr*
Neil Chen, *
◆ **EMP: 38 EST:** 1994
SQ FT: 11,000

SALES (est): 8.26MM
SALES (corp-wide): 8.26MM **Privately Held**
Web: www.condoroutdoor.com
SIC: 3949 Sporting and athletic goods, nec

(P-10985)
CRAZY INDUSTRIES
Also Called: Savi Customs
8675 Avenida Costa Norte (92154-6253)
PHONE..............................619 270-9090
Jane Roe, *CEO*
Don Roe, *CFO*
EMP: 45 EST: 2018
SALES (est): 4.49MM **Privately Held**
Web: www.savicustoms.com
SIC: 3949 2339 2329 Sporting and athletic goods, nec; Sportswear, women's; Men's and boys' sportswear and athletic clothing

(P-10986)
DIAMOND BASEBALL COMPANY INC
Also Called: Diamond Sports
1880 E Saint Andrew Pl (92705-5043)
P.O. Box 55090 (92619-5090)
PHONE..............................800 366-2999
Jay Hicks, *CEO*
Andrea Gordon, *Pr*
Robert W Ezell, *VP*
◆ **EMP: 23 EST:** 1977
SQ FT: 120,000
SALES (est): 4.88MM **Privately Held**
Web: www.diamond-sports.com
SIC: 3949 5091 Baseball equipment and supplies, general; Athletic goods

(P-10987)
DIVING UNLIMITED INTL INC
Also Called: Diving Unlimited Int.
1148 Delevan Dr (92102-2436)
PHONE..............................619 236-1203
Susan Long, *CEO*
Richard Long, *
◆ **EMP: 75 EST:** 1963
SQ FT: 14,500
SALES (est): 16.61MM **Privately Held**
Web: www.divedui.com
SIC: 3949 Skin diving equipment, scuba type

(P-10988)
EASTON HOCKEY INC
Also Called: Eastern Sports
3500 Willow Ln (91361-4921)
PHONE..............................818 782-6445
◆ **EMP:** 1500
Web: www.eastonhockey.com
SIC: 3949 Sporting and athletic goods, nec

(P-10989)
FAIRWAY IMPORT-EXPORT INC
Also Called: Lift Aviation
2130 E Gladwick St (90220-6203)
PHONE..............................262 788-7313
Guido Rietdyk, *Pr*
Kevin Hinyub, *
◆ **EMP: 35 EST:** 1987
SQ FT: 17,000
SALES (est): 5.39MM **Privately Held**
Web: www.liftsafety.com
SIC: 3949 Protective sporting equipment

(P-10990)
FASTHOUSE INC
28757 Industry Dr (91355-5414)
PHONE..............................661 775-5963
Kenneth Alexander, *CEO*
Dan Worrell, *Prin*
Jason Fonzy, *Prin*
EMP: 23 EST: 2013

SALES (est): 5.31MM **Privately Held**
Web: www.fasthouse.com
SIC: 3949 Team sports equipment

(P-10991)
FITNESS WAREHOUSE LLC (PA)
Also Called: Hoist Fitness Systems
9990 Alesmith Ct Ste 130 (92126-4200)
PHONE..............................858 578-7676
Jeffrey Partrick, *Pt*
◆ **EMP: 30 EST:** 1999
SALES (est): 4.65MM
SALES (corp-wide): 4.65MM **Privately Held**
SIC: 3949 Sporting and athletic goods, nec

(P-10992)
FUJIKURA COMPOSITE AMERICA INC
Also Called: Fujikuria Composits
1819 Aston Ave Ste 101 (92008-7338)
PHONE..............................760 598-6060
Peter Sanchez, *Pr*
Kenji Morita, *CFO*
▲ **EMP: 20 EST:** 1994
SALES (est): 6.32MM **Privately Held**
Web: www.fujikuragolf.com
SIC: 3949 Shafts, golf club
PA: Fujikura Composites Inc.
3-5-7, Ariake
Koto-Ku TKY

(P-10993)
GAMEBREAKER INC (PA)
31324 Via Colinas Ste 102 (91362-6750)
PHONE..............................818 224-7424
Michael Juels, *Pr*
Dina Juels, *Sec*
EMP: 20 EST: 2011
SQ FT: 5,000
SALES (est): 4.61MM
SALES (corp-wide): 4.61MM **Privately Held**
Web: www.gamebreaker.com
SIC: 3949 2329 2339 Guards: football, basketball, soccer, lacrosse, etc.; Men's and boys' athletic uniforms; Uniforms, athletic: women's, misses', and juniors'

(P-10994)
GOLF SALES WEST INC
Also Called: Golf Sales West
1901 Eastman Ave (93030-5171)
PHONE..............................805 988-3363
▲ **EMP: 50 EST:** 1988
SALES (est): 2.7MM **Privately Held**
Web: www.golfsaleswest.com
SIC: 3949 Bags, golf

(P-10995)
GOLF SUPPLY HOUSE USA INC
Also Called: Eagle One Golf Products
1340 N Jefferson St (92807-1614)
PHONE..............................714 983-0050
◆ **EMP:** 70
SIC: 3949 5941 Golf equipment; Golf goods and equipment

(P-10996)
HEART RATE INC
Also Called: Versaclimber
1411 E Wilshire Ave (92705-4422)
PHONE..............................714 850-9716
Richard D Charnitski, *Pr*
Dan Charnitski, *
▲ **EMP: 38 EST:** 1978
SQ FT: 18,000
SALES (est): 75.04K **Privately Held**
Web: www.versaclimber.com

SIC: **3949** Exercise equipment

(P-10997)

HOBIE CAT COMPANY II LLC

4925 Oceanside Blvd (92056-3099)
PHONE................................760 758-9100
EMP: 200 **EST:** 2021
SALES (est): 17.31MM **Privately Held**
Web: www.hobie.com
SIC: **3949** Water sports equipment

(P-10998)

HOIST FITNESS SYSTEMS INC

Also Called: Hoist Fitness
11900 Community Rd (92064-7143)
PHONE................................858 578-7676
Jeffrey Partrick, *CEO*
Billy Kim, *
◆ **EMP:** 81 **EST:** 1977
SQ FT: 105,000
SALES (est): 23.09MM **Privately Held**
Web: www.hoistfitness.com
SIC: **3949** 5941 Exercise equipment;
Exercise equipment

(P-10999)

HUPA INTERNATIONAL INC

Also Called: Body Flex Sports
21717 Ferrero (91789-5209)
PHONE................................909 598-9876
Bob Hsiung, *Pr*
▲ **EMP:** 21 **EST:** 1996
SQ FT: 30,000
SALES (est): 2.3MM **Privately Held**
Web: www.hupa.net
SIC: **3949** Exercise equipment

(P-11000)

HYPER ICE INC (PA)

Also Called: Hyperice
525 Technology Dr Ste 100 (92618-1389)
PHONE................................949 565-4994
Jim Huether, *CEO*
Robert Marton, *
▲ **EMP:** 44 **EST:** 2010
SALES (est): 13.68MM
SALES (corp-wide): 13.68MM **Privately Held**
Web: www.hyperice.com
SIC: **3949** 5136 5621 5699 Sporting and
athletic goods, nec; Sportswear, men's and
boys'; Women's sportswear; Sports apparel

(P-11001)

HYPERFLY INC

2251 Las Palmas Dr (92011-1527)
PHONE................................760 300-0909
Kerstin Pakter, *CEO*
EMP: 25 **EST:** 2019
SALES (est): 1.26MM **Privately Held**
Web: www.hyperfly.com
SIC: **3949** Sporting and athletic goods, nec

(P-11002)

I & I SPORTS SUPPLY COMPANY (PA)

435 W Alondra Blvd (90248-2424)
PHONE................................310 715-6800
Alan Iba, *Pr*
▲ **EMP:** 20 **EST:** 1984
SALES (est): 4.28MM
SALES (corp-wide): 4.28MM **Privately Held**
Web: www.iisports.com
SIC: **3949** 5091 5941 Sporting and athletic
goods, nec; Sporting and recreation goods;
Martial arts equipment and supplies

(P-11003)

IFIT INC

2220 Almond Ave (92374-2073)
PHONE................................909 335-2888
EMP: 1333
SALES (corp-wide): 1.75B **Privately Held**
Web: www.ifit.com
SIC: **3949** Treadmills
HQ: Ifit Inc.
1500 S 1000 W
Logan UT
435 750-5000

(P-11004)

ILLAH SPORTS INC

Also Called: Belding Golf Bag Company, The
1610 Fiske Pl (93033-1849)
PHONE................................805 240-7790
Brien Patermo, *CEO*
Steve Perrin, *
Jackie Perrin, *
▲ **EMP:** 50 **EST:** 2003
SALES (est): 4.12MM **Privately Held**
SIC: **3949** Sporting and athletic goods, nec

(P-11005)

IRON GRIP BARBELL COMPANY INC

11377 Markon Dr (92841-1402)
PHONE................................714 850-6900
▼ **EMP:** 85 **EST:** 1993
SALES (est): 15.86MM **Privately Held**
Web: www.irongrip.com
SIC: **3949** Exercise equipment

(P-11006)

JBL ENTERPRISES INC

3219 Roymar Rd (92058-1311)
P.O. Box 1105 (92856-0105)
PHONE................................760 754-2727
Guy Skinner, *Pr*
▲ **EMP:** 21 **EST:** 1978
SQ FT: 10,000
SALES (est): 784.42K **Privately Held**
Web: www.jblspearguns.com
SIC: **3949** Fishing equipment

(P-11007)

JOHNSON OUTDOORS INC

Scuba Pro
1166 Fesler St Ste A (92020-1813)
PHONE................................619 402-1023
Joe Stella, *Brnch Mgr*
EMP: 114
SALES (corp-wide): 743.36MM **Publicly Held**
Web: www.johnsonoutdoors.com
SIC: **3949** 5091 Skin diving equipment,
scuba type; Diving equipment and supplies
PA: Johnson Outdoors Inc.
555 Main St
Racine WI
262 631-6600

(P-11008)

L A STEEL CRAFT PRODUCTS (PA)

1975 Lincoln Ave (91103-1321)
P.O. Box 90365 (91109-0365)
PHONE................................626 798-7401
Beverly Holt, *Pr*
John C Gaudesi, *COO*
▲ **EMP:** 21 **EST:** 1951
SQ FT: 200,000
SALES (est): 1.92MM
SALES (corp-wide): 1.92MM **Privately Held**
Web: www.lasteelcraft.com

SIC: **3949** Playground equipment

(P-11009)

LIQUID FORCE WAKEBOARDS

Also Called: Free Motion Wakeboards
1815 Aston Ave Ste 105 (92008-7340)
PHONE................................760 943-8364
Tony Finn, *Owner*
◆ **EMP:** 24 **EST:** 1995
SALES (est): 1.5MM **Privately Held**
Web: www.liquidforce.com
SIC: **3949** Water sports equipment

(P-11010)

LUCITE INTL PRTNR HOLDINGS INC

MRC Composite Product
5441 Avenida Encinas Ste B (92008-4412)
PHONE................................760 929-0001
Hikaro Shikashi, *VP*
EMP: 99
SIC: **3949** Golf equipment
PA: Lucite International Partnership
Holdings, Inc.
1403 Foulk Rd
Wilmington DE

(P-11011)

LUCKY STRIKE ENTERTAINMENT INC (PA)

Also Called: Lucky Strike
15260 Ventura Blvd Ste 1110 (91403-5346)
PHONE................................818 933-3752
Steven Foster, *Pr*
EMP: 50 **EST:** 2004
SALES (est): 279.66MM **Privately Held**
Web: www.luckystrikeent.com
SIC: **3949** 5812 5813 Bowling alleys and
accessories; American restaurant; Bar
(drinking places)

(P-11012)

MARTIN SPORTS INC (PA)

Also Called: Martin Archery
1100 Glendon Ave Ste 920 (90024-3513)
PHONE................................509 529-2554
Rich Weatherford, *Prin*
Tracy Reiff, *
Richard Weatherford, *
Kevin Ma, *VP*
Tim Larkin, *
▲ **EMP:** 21 **EST:** 2013
SQ FT: 28,000
SALES (est): 4.88MM
SALES (corp-wide): 4.88MM **Privately Held**
SIC: **3949** Sporting and athletic goods, nec

(P-11013)

MED-FIT SYSTEMS INC

3553 Rosa Way (92028-2663)
PHONE................................760 723-3618
Dean Sbragia, *Pr*
Juergen Kopf, *VP*
Alex Sbragia, *Sec*
▲ **EMP:** 18 **EST:** 1993
SQ FT: 1,500
SALES (est): 1.28MM **Privately Held**
Web: www.medfitsystems.com
SIC: **3949** 5047 Exercise equipment;
Therapy equipment

(P-11014)

MELIN LLC

10 Faraday (92618-2714)
PHONE................................323 489-3274
Hoang Tu, *Prin*
EMP: 31 **EST:** 2019
SALES (est): 1.25MM **Privately Held**

Web: www.melin.com
SIC: **3949** Sporting and athletic goods, nec

(P-11015)

MISSION HOCKEY COMPANY (PA)

12 Goodyear Ste 100 (92618-3764)
PHONE................................949 585-9390
▲ **EMP:** 17 **EST:** 1994
SQ FT: 10,000
SALES (est): 1.97MM **Privately Held**
Web: inhaler.missionhockey.com
SIC: **3949** Hockey equipment and supplies,
general

(P-11016)

NORBERTS ATHLETIC PRODUCTS INC

354 W Gardena Blvd (90248-2739)
P.O. Box 1890 (90733-1890)
PHONE................................310 830-6672
Loren Dill, *Pr*
▲ **EMP:** 19 **EST:** 1977
SQ FT: 4,000
SALES (est): 2.91MM **Privately Held**
Web: www.norberts.com
SIC: **3949** Sporting and athletic goods, nec

(P-11017)

ORCA ARMS LLC

Also Called: Orca Arms
9825 Carroll Centre Rd Ste 100 (92126)
PHONE................................858 586-0503
Hamid R Ray Akhavan, *Managing Member*
Ardeshir Akhavan, *
▲ **EMP:** 68 **EST:** 2012
SQ FT: 5,500
SALES (est): 4.23MM **Privately Held**
Web: www.orcaarms.com
SIC: **3949** 5099 Sporting and athletic goods,
nec; Firearms and ammunition, except
sporting

(P-11018)

OUTDOOR SPORTS GEAR INC

2320 Cousteau Ct Ste 100 (92081-8363)
◆ **EMP:** 49 **EST:** 1959
SQ FT: 77,000
SALES (est): 4.54MM
SALES (corp-wide): 9.46B **Publicly Held**
SIC: **3949** 3069 2339 2329 Winter sports
equipment; Life jackets, inflatable:
rubberized fabric; Women's and misses'
athletic clothing and sportswear; Men's and
boys' athletic uniforms
HQ: Jarden Llc
221 River St
Hoboken NJ

(P-11019)

RIP CURL INC (DH)

Also Called: Rip Curl USA
3030 Airway Ave (92626-6036)
PHONE................................714 422-3600
Kelly Gibson, *CEO*
Matt Szot, *CFO*
◆ **EMP:** 60 **EST:** 1992
SALES (est): 75.34MM **Privately Held**
Web: www.ripcurl.com
SIC: **3949** Surfboards
HQ: Rip Curl International Pty Ltd
101 Surf Coast Hwy
Torquay VIC

(P-11020)

ROSEN & ROSEN INDUSTRIES INC

Also Called: R & R Industries
204 Avenida Fabricante (92672-7538)

PRODUCTS & SVCS

PHONE..................949 361-9238
Richard Rosen, *Pr*
Daniel Rosen, *
▲ **EMP:** 80 **EST:** 1979
SQ FT: 22,500
SALES (est): 6.33MM **Privately Held**
Web: www.rrind.com
SIC: 3949 7389 Sporting and athletic goods, nec; Embroidery advertising

(P-11021)
RPSZ CONSTRUCTION LLC
1201 W 5th St Ste T340 (90017-1489)
PHONE..................314 677-5831
Rick Platt, *Managing Member*
EMP: 43 **EST:** 2008
SQ FT: 3,500
SALES (est): 407.11K
SALES (corp-wide): 37.75MM **Privately Held**
SIC: 3949 Trampolines and equipment
HQ: Sky Zone, Llc
    1201 W 5th St Ste T340
    Los Angeles CA
    310 734-0300

(P-11022)
SAFER SPORTS INC
Also Called: Light Helmets
5670 El Camino Real Ste B (92008-7125)
PHONE..................760 444-0082
Nick Esayian, *CEO*
Justin Bert, *
EMP: 30 **EST:** 2017
SALES (est): 2.72MM **Privately Held**
Web: www.lighthelmets.com
SIC: 3949 Helmets, athletic

(P-11023)
SAINT NINE AMERICA INC
10700 Norwalk Blvd (90670-3824)
PHONE..................562 921-5300
Timothy Chae, *CEO*
Terry Kim, *
Max Kim, *
EMP: 40 **EST:** 2018
SALES (est): 2.98MM **Privately Held**
Web: www.saintnineamerica.com
SIC: 3949 Team sports equipment

(P-11024)
SEIRUS INNOVATIVE ACC INC
Also Called: Seirus Innovation
13975 Danielson St (92064-6889)
PHONE..................858 513-1212
Michael Carey, *Pr*
Joseph H Edwards, *
Wendy Carey, *
Robert Murphy, *
▲ **EMP:** 65 **EST:** 1984
SQ FT: 11,000
SALES (est): 8.53MM **Privately Held**
Web: www.seirus.com
SIC: 3949 Sporting and athletic goods, nec

(P-11025)
SHOCK DOCTOR INC (PA)
Also Called: Shock Doctor Sports
11488 Slater Ave (92708-5440)
PHONE..................800 233-6956
Michael Magerman, *CEO*
Kevin Johnson, *CFO*
▲ **EMP:** 82 **EST:** 2008
SALES (est): 74.86MM **Privately Held**
Web: www.shockdoctor.com
SIC: 3949 Protective sporting equipment

(P-11026)
SHOCK DOCTOR INC
Also Called: United Sports Brands

11488 Slater Ave (92708-5440)
PHONE..................657 383-4400
EMP: 40
Web: www.shockdoctor.com
SIC: 3949 Sporting and athletic goods, nec
PA: Doctor Shock Inc
    11488 Slater Ave
    Fountain Valley CA

(P-11027)
SKATE ONE CORP
Also Called: Roller Bones
6860 Cortona Dr Ste B (93117-3021)
PHONE..................805 964-1330
George Powell, *Pr*
▲ **EMP:** 80 **EST:** 1976
SALES (est): 20.58MM **Privately Held**
Web: www.skateone.com
SIC: 3949 Skateboards

(P-11028)
STANDARD SALES LLC (PA)
Also Called: Stansport
2801 E 12th St (90023-3621)
PHONE..................323 269-0510
Max Wartnik, *Ch*
Victor Preisler, *
Eva Wartnik, *
◆ **EMP:** 35 **EST:** 1964
SQ FT: 100,000
SALES (est): 7.75MM
SALES (corp-wide): 7.75MM **Privately Held**
Web: www.stansport.com
SIC: 3949 Camping equipment and supplies

(P-11029)
STAR TRAC HEALTH & FITNESS INC
Also Called: Star Trac
14410 Myford Rd (92606-1001)
Rural Route 300 (98662)
PHONE..................714 669-1660
▲ **EMP:** 20
Web: www.corehandf.com
SIC: 3949 Exercise equipment

(P-11030)
STAR TRAC STRENGTH INC
Also Called: Star Trac Fitness
14410 Myford Rd (92606-1001)
Rural Route 300 (98662)
PHONE..................714 669-1660
▲ **EMP:** 405
SIC: 3949 5091 Exercise equipment; Exercise equipment

(P-11031)
SURE GRIP INTERNATIONAL
5519 Rawlings Ave (90280-7495)
PHONE..................562 923-0724
James Ball, *VP*
Ione L Ball, *
▲ **EMP:** 60 **EST:** 1937
SQ FT: 30,000
SALES (est): 4.61MM **Privately Held**
Web: www.suregrip.com
SIC: 3949 Skates and parts, roller

(P-11032)
SURF TO SUMMIT INC
Also Called: Photo Printing Pros
7234 Hollister Ave (93117-2807)
PHONE..................805 964-1896
▲ **EMP:** 18 **EST:** 1993
SALES (est): 1.9MM **Privately Held**
Web: www.surftosummit.com
SIC: 3949 Sporting and athletic goods, nec

(P-11033)
TACTICOMBAT INC
11640 Mcbean Dr (91732-1105)
PHONE..................626 315-4433
Daisy Chan, *Pr*
Tik Yan Tse, *CEO*
EMP: 19 **EST:** 2014
SQ FT: 2,500
SALES (est): 1MM **Privately Held**
Web: www.tacticombat.com
SIC: 3949 2389 Golf equipment; Men's miscellaneous accessories

(P-11034)
TOPGOLF CALLAWAY BRANDS CORP (PA)
2180 Rutherford Rd (92008-7328)
PHONE..................760 931-1771
Oliver G Brewer Iii, *Pr*
John F Lundgren, *
Erik J Anderson, *
Rebecca Fine, *CPO*
Brian P Lynch, *CLO*
◆ **EMP:** 349 **EST:** 1982
SALES (est): 4B
SALES (corp-wide): 4B **Publicly Held**
Web: www.topgolfcallawaybrands.com
SIC: 3949 2329 2339 6794 Golf equipment; Men's and boys' sportswear and athletic clothing; Women's and misses' athletic clothing and sportswear; Patent buying, licensing, leasing

(P-11035)
TOTAL GYM COMMERCIAL LLC
100 Chesterfield Dr # G (92007-1922)
PHONE..................858 586-6080
▲ **EMP:** 18 **EST:** 2011
SALES (est): 1.34MM **Privately Held**
Web: www.totalgym.com
SIC: 3949 5091 Exercise equipment; Exercise equipment

(P-11036)
TUFFSTUFF FITNESS INTL INC
155 N Riverview Dr (92808-1225)
PHONE..................909 629-1600
Richard M Reyes Junior, *Ch Bd*
Cammie Grider, *
◆ **EMP:** 66 **EST:** 1992
SALES (est): 12.82MM
SALES (corp-wide): 12.82MM **Privately Held**
Web: www.tuffstufffitness.com
SIC: 3949 Exercise equipment
PA: Brooks Industrial Marketplace
    23401 Mount Ashland Ct
    Murrieta CA
    714 269-1689

(P-11037)
TWIN PEAK INDUSTRIES INC
Also Called: Jungle Jumps
12420 Montague St Ste E (91331-2140)
PHONE..................800 259-5906
Edmond K Keshishian, *Pr*
Raffi Sepanian, *
EMP: 32 **EST:** 2008
SALES (est): 2.39MM **Privately Held**
SIC: 3949 3069 Playground equipment; Air-supported rubber structures

(P-11038)
UKE CORPORATION
Also Called: Underwater Kinetics
13400 Danielson St (92064-8830)
PHONE..................858 513-9100
◆ **EMP:** 95 **EST:** 1971
SALES (est): 9.05MM **Privately Held**

SIC: 3949 3648 3646 3161 Water sports equipment; Flashlights; Commercial lighting fixtures; Luggage

(P-11039)
UNISEN INC
Also Called: Star Trac
14410 Myford Rd (92606-1001)
Rural Route 300 (98662)
PHONE..................714 669-1660
◆ **EMP:** 20 **EST:** 1975
SALES (est): 2.2MM **Privately Held**
SIC: 3949 Exercise equipment

(P-11040)
US DIVERS CO INC
2340 Cousteau Ct (92081-8346)
PHONE..................760 597-5000
Graham Church, *Sec*
EMP: 79 **EST:** 1947
SALES (est): 1.07MM
SALES (corp-wide): 1.46MM **Privately Held**
Web: www.usdivers.com
SIC: 3949 Water sports equipment
HQ: Aqua-Lung America, Inc.
    2105 Rutherford Rd
    Carlsbad CA
    760 376-9813

(P-11041)
WEST COAST TRENDS INC
Also Called: Train Reaction
17811 Jamestown Ln (92647-7136)
PHONE..................714 843-9288
Jeffrey C Herold, *CEO*
Vivienne Herold, *
▲ **EMP:** 50 **EST:** 1990
SQ FT: 26,000
SALES (est): 5.75MM **Privately Held**
Web: www.clubglove.com
SIC: 3949 Golf equipment

(P-11042)
WESTERN GOLF CAR MFG INC
Also Called: Western Golf Car Sales Co
69391 Dillon Rd (92241-8433)
PHONE..................760 671-6691
Scott Stevens, *Pr*
Robert W Thomas, *
EMP: 55 **EST:** 1981
SQ FT: 60,000
SALES (est): 4.57MM **Privately Held**
SIC: 3949 3799 Sporting and athletic goods, nec; Golf carts, powered

(P-11043)
WORLD CLASS CHEERLEADING INC
20212 Hart St (91306-3520)
PHONE..................877 923-2645
Akram Hemaidan, *CEO*
EMP: 33 **EST:** 2009
SALES (est): 1.73MM **Privately Held**
Web: www.worldclasscheerleading.com
SIC: 3949 Sporting and athletic goods, nec

(P-11044)
XS SCUBA INC (PA)
4040 W Chandler Ave (92704-5202)
PHONE..................714 424-0434
Daniel F Babcock, *Pr*
◆ **EMP:** 24 **EST:** 2002
SALES (est): 4.88MM
SALES (corp-wide): 4.88MM **Privately Held**
Web: www.xsscuba.com

SIC: **3949** 5091 Skin diving equipment, scuba type; Diving equipment and supplies

(P-11045)
ZONSON COMPANY INC
3197 Lionshead Ave (92010-4702)
PHONE..............................760 597-0338
Jeff Yearours, *VP*
▲ **EMP:** 26 **EST:** 2001
SALES (est): 1.96MM **Privately Held**
Web: www.zonson.com
SIC: **3949** Bags, golf

3951 Pens And Mechanical Pencils

(P-11046)
HARTLEY COMPANY
Also Called: Hartley-Racon
1987 Placentia Ave (92627-6265)
P.O. Box 10999 (92627-0999)
PHONE..............................949 646-9643
Ed Kuder, *Pr*
Mike Quinley, *VP*
▲ **EMP:** 22 **EST:** 1947
SQ FT: 75,000
SALES (est): 2.36MM **Privately Held**
Web: www.shopcarpetsdirect.com
SIC: **3951** Cartridges, refill: ball point pens

(P-11047)
NATIONAL PEN CO LLC (DH)
Also Called: National Pen Company
12121 Scripps Summit Dr Ste 200
(92131-4607)
P.O. Box 502380 (92150-2380)
PHONE..............................866 900-7367
Peter Kelly, *CEO*
Richard Obrigawitch, *CFO*
◆ **EMP:** 150 **EST:** 1966
SQ FT: 40,000
SALES (est): 252.48MM **Privately Held**
Web: www.pens.com
SIC: **3951** 3993 Pens and mechanical pencils ; Advertising novelties
HQ: Cimpress Usa Incorporated
170 Data Dr
Waltham MA
781 652-6300

3952 Lead Pencils And Art Goods

(P-11048)
AARDVARK CLAY & SUPPLIES INC (PA)
1400 E Pomona St (92705-4858)
PHONE..............................714 541-4157
George Johnston, *Pr*
Daniel T Carreon, *
Richard Mac Pherson, *General Vice President**
K Douglas Pherson Mac, *Sec*
▲ **EMP:** 30 **EST:** 1972
SQ FT: 25,000
SALES (est): 4.84MM
SALES (corp-wide): 4.84MM **Privately Held**
Web: www.aardvarkclay.com
SIC: **3952** 5945 Modeling clay; Arts and crafts supplies

(P-11049)
CONVERSION TECHNOLOGY CO INC (PA)
5360 N Commerce Ave (93021-1762)
PHONE..............................805 378-0033

Jim Newkirk, *Pr*
Russell Greenhouse, *
▲ **EMP:** 50 **EST:** 1994
SQ FT: 28,000
SALES (est): 15.86MM **Privately Held**
SIC: **3952** 2893 2899 Ink, drawing: black and colored; Printing ink; Ink or writing fluids

(P-11050)
SALIS INTERNATIONAL INC
3921 Oceanic Dr Ste 802 (92056-5857)
PHONE..............................303 384-3588
Lawrence R Salis, *Pr*
◆ **EMP:** 38 **EST:** 1934
SQ FT: 10,000
SALES (est): 2.22MM **Privately Held**
Web: www.docmartins.com
SIC: **3952** Water colors, artists'

(P-11051)
WESTECH PRODUCTS INC (PA)
Also Called: Westech Wax Products
1242 Enterprise Ct (92882-7125)
PHONE..............................951 279-4496
Lawrence Dahlin, *Pr*
Erik Dahlin, *
Barry Dahlin, *
▲ **EMP:** 24 **EST:** 1980
SQ FT: 31,000
SALES (est): 4.83MM
SALES (corp-wide): 4.83MM **Privately Held**
Web: www.westechwax.com
SIC: **3952** 5169 Crayons: chalk, gypsum, charcoal, fusains, pastel, wax, etc.; Waxes, except petroleum

---

3953 Marking Devices

(P-11052)
JOY PRODUCTS CALIFORNIA INC
Also Called: Coastal Enterprises
17281 Mount Wynne Cir (92708-4107)
PHONE..............................714 437-7250
Shayne Perkins, *Pr*
Jay Kollins, *Off Mgr*
▲ **EMP:** 24 **EST:** 1981
SQ FT: 12,000
SALES (est): 859.45K **Privately Held**
SIC: **3953** 2759 Screens, textile printing; Screen printing

---

3955 Carbon Paper And Inked Ribbons

(P-11053)
BUSHNELL RIBBON CORPORATION
300 W Brookdale Pl (92832-1465)
P.O. Box 2543 (90670-0543)
PHONE..............................562 948-1410
Jim Kinmartin, *Pr*
James C Kinmartin, *
Mary Alice Milward, *
Paul C Kinmartin, *
EMP: 22 **EST:** 1903
SQ FT: 24,000
SALES (est): 1.1MM **Privately Held**
Web: www.himado.com
SIC: **3955** Ribbons, inked: typewriter, adding machine, register, etc.

(P-11054)
CALIFORNIA RIBBON CARBN CO INC
8420 Quinn St (90241-2624)

▲ **EMP:** 100 **EST:** 1939
SALES (est): 4.02MM **Privately Held**
SIC: **3955** Ribbons, inked: typewriter, adding machine, register, etc.

(P-11055)
E ALKO INC
Also Called: Laser Imaging International
8201 Woodley Ave (91406-1231)
PHONE..............................818 587-8700
Eyal Alkoby, *Pr*
Eyal Alkoby, *CEO*
Beth Alkoby, *Prin*
▲ **EMP:** 39 **EST:** 1992
SQ FT: 45,000
SALES (est): 1.02MM **Privately Held**
SIC: **3955** 3861 Print cartridges for laser and other computer printers; Photographic equipment and supplies

(P-11056)
ECMM SERVICES INC
1320 Valley Vista Dr # 204 (91765-3956)
PHONE..............................714 988-9388
Vincent Yang, *Pr*
Donald Sung, *
EMP: 250 **EST:** 2010
SALES (est): 23.4MM **Privately Held**
SIC: **3955** 5045 Print cartridges for laser and other computer printers; Printers, computer
PA: Hon Hai Precision Industry Co., Ltd.
No. 2, Ziyou St.
New Taipei City TAP

(P-11057)
GENERAL RIBBON CORP
Also Called: G R C
5775 E Los Angeles Ave Ste 230 (91311)
PHONE..............................818 709-1234
Stephen R Morgan, *Pr*
Robert W Daggs, *
▲ **EMP:** 500 **EST:** 1946
SQ FT: 110,000
SALES (est): 29.88MM **Privately Held**
Web: www.printgrc.com
SIC: **3955** 3861 Ribbons, inked: typewriter, adding machine, register, etc.; Photographic equipment and supplies

(P-11058)
KEYTONEX INC
5957 Pat Ave (91367-1058)
PHONE..............................310 828-2207
EMP: 24
Web: www.monroe-systems.com
SIC: **3955** Carbon paper and inked ribbons
PA: Keytonex Inc.
7900 Alabama Ave
Canoga Park CA

(P-11059)
LASERCARE TECHNOLOGIES INC (PA)
Also Called: Lasercare
14370 Myford Rd Ste 100 (92606-1015)
PHONE..............................310 202-4200
TOLL FREE: 800
Paul Wilhelm, *Pr*
EMP: 34 **EST:** 1993
SALES (est): 5MM
SALES (corp-wide): 5MM **Privately Held**
Web: www.lasercare.com
SIC: **3955** 7378 5734 Print cartridges for laser and other computer printers; Computer peripheral equipment repair and maintenance; Printers and plotters: computers

(P-11060)
PLANET GREEN CARTRIDGES INC
Also Called: Planet Green
20724 Lassen St (91311-4507)
PHONE..............................818 725-2596
Sean Levi, *Pr*
Natalya Levi, *
◆ **EMP:** 84 **EST:** 2000
SQ FT: 29,699
SALES (est): 10.14MM **Privately Held**
Web: www.pginkjets.com
SIC: **3955** 5093 Print cartridges for laser and other computer printers; Plastics scrap

(P-11061)
RAYZIST PHOTOMASK INC (PA)
Also Called: Honor Life
955 Park Center Dr (92081-8312)
PHONE..............................760 727-8561
Randy S Willis, *CEO*
▲ **EMP:** 54 **EST:** 1984
SQ FT: 28,000
SALES (est): 9.76MM
SALES (corp-wide): 9.76MM **Privately Held**
Web: www.rayzist.com
SIC: **3955** 3281 3589 Stencil paper, gelatin or spirit process; Cut stone and stone products; Sandblasting equipment

(P-11062)
SERCOMP LLC (PA)
5401 Tech Cir Ste 200 (93021-1713)
P.O. Box 92728 (91715-2728)
PHONE..............................805 299-0020
EMP: 89 **EST:** 2003
SQ FT: 67,000
SALES (est): 4.93MM
SALES (corp-wide): 4.93MM **Privately Held**
Web: www.sercomp.com
SIC: **3955** 3577 Print cartridges for laser and other computer printers; Computer peripheral equipment, nec

(P-11063)
US PRINT & TONER INC
Also Called: National Copy Cartridge
14751 Franklin Ave Ste B (92780-7272)
PHONE..............................619 562-6995
James Meyers, *Pr*
▲ **EMP:** 22 **EST:** 2011
SALES (est): 2.06MM **Privately Held**
SIC: **3955** Print cartridges for laser and other computer printers

(P-11064)
VISION IMAGING SUPPLIES INC
9540 Cozycroft Ave (91311-5101)
PHONE..............................818 885-4515
Bernard Khachi, *CEO*
Benard Khachi, *
Raymond Khachi, *
▲ **EMP:** 40 **EST:** 2004
SALES (est): 4.84MM **Privately Held**
Web: www.vis-llc.com
SIC: **3955** Print cartridges for laser and other computer printers

---

3961 Costume Jewelry

(P-11065)
BOB SIEMON DESIGNS INC
3501 W Segerstrom Ave (92704-6449)
PHONE..............................714 549-0678
▲ **EMP:** 95
Web: www.bobsiemon.com

SIC: 3961 3911 Costume jewelry, ex. precious metal and semiprecious stones; Jewelry, precious metal

(P-11066)
LOUNGEFLY LLC
Also Called: Lounge Fly
108 S Mayo Ave (91789-3090)
PHONE..................................818 718-5600
Dale Schultz, *
▲ EMP: 25 EST: 1998
SALES (est): 5.52MM
SALES (corp-wide): 1.32B **Publicly Held**
Web: www.loungefly.com
SIC: 3961 Costume jewelry
PA: Funko, Inc.
2802 Wetmore Ave Ste 100
Everett WA
425 783-3616

(P-11067)
PINCRAFT INC
Also Called: Pin Concepts
7933 Ajay Dr (91352-5315)
PHONE..................................818 248-0077
Vahe Asatourian, Pr
▲ EMP: 27 EST: 1999
SALES (est): 2.37MM **Privately Held**
Web: www.pincraft.com
SIC: 3961 Pins (jewelry), except precious metal

3965 Fasteners, Buttons, Needles, And Pins

(P-11068)
ALCOA FASTENING SYSTEMS
11711 Arrow Rte (91730-4902)
PHONE..................................909 483-2333
EMP: 33 EST: 2014
SALES (est): 249.46K **Privately Held**
Web: www.alcoa.com
SIC: 3965 Fasteners

(P-11069)
CATAME INC (PA)
Also Called: Ucan Zippers
1930 Long Beach Ave (90058-1020)
PHONE..................................213 749-2610
Liz Lai, CEO
Liz H Lai, CEO
Paul Lai, CFO
Floyd Lai, Sec
▲ EMP: 17 EST: 1995
SQ FT: 50,000
SALES (est): 2.11MM
SALES (corp-wide): 2.11MM **Privately Held**
Web: www.ucanzippers.com
SIC: 3965 5131 Zipper; Zippers

(P-11070)
HENWAY INC
Also Called: Anatase Products
1314 Goodrick Dr (93561-1508)
PHONE..................................661 822-6873
David Benhan, VP
Scott D Baker, Sec
EMP: 18 EST: 1977
SQ FT: 18,500
SALES (est): 2MM **Privately Held**
Web: www.aircraftbolts.com
SIC: 3965 3452 Fasteners; Bolts, nuts, rivets, and washers

(P-11071)
LABELTEX MILLS INC (PA)
5301 S Santa Fe Ave (90058-3519)

PHONE..................................323 582-0228
Torag Pourshamtobi, CEO
Shahrokh Shamtobi, *
Ben Younessi, *
Babak Younessi, *
◆ EMP: 200 EST: 1994
SALES (est): 21.09MM **Privately Held**
Web: www.labeltexusa.com
SIC: 3965 2253 2241 Fasteners, buttons, needles, and pins; Collar and cuff sets, knit; Labels, woven

(P-11072)
MATTHEW WARREN INC
Also Called: Mw Compnnts - Anheim Ideal Fas
3850 E Miraloma Ave (92806-2108)
PHONE..................................714 630-7840
Simon Newman, CEO
EMP: 50 EST: 2021
SALES (est): 2.82MM **Privately Held**
SIC: 3965 Fasteners, buttons, needles, and pins

(P-11073)
MORTON GRINDING INC
Also Called: Morton Manufacturing
201 E Avenue K15 (93535-4572)
PHONE..................................661 298-0895
Yolanda A Morton, Ch Bd
Wallace Morton, *
John Morton, *
Patrick Dansby, *
EMP: 110 EST: 1967
SQ FT: 45,000
SALES (est): 15.62MM **Privately Held**
Web: www.mortonmanufacturing.com
SIC: 3965 3769 3452 Fasteners; Space vehicle equipment, nec; Bolts, nuts, rivets, and washers

(P-11074)
PAIHO NORTH AMERICA CORP
16051 El Prado Rd (91708-9144)
PHONE..................................661 257-6611
Yi Ming Lin, Pr
Shu-ching Hsieh, CFO
▲ EMP: 22 EST: 2003
SQ FT: 52,000
SALES (est): 4.13MM **Privately Held**
Web: www.paiho-usa.com
SIC: 3965 Fasteners, hooks and eyes

(P-11075)
ROSE LILLA INC
1050 S Cypress St (90631-6862)
PHONE..................................888 519-8889
EMP: 22 EST: 2015
SALES (est): 4.33MM **Privately Held**
Web: www.lillarose.biz
SIC: 3965 Hairpins, except rubber

(P-11076)
SPS TECHNOLOGIES LLC
Also Called: Aerospace Fasteners Group
1224 E Warner Ave (92705-5414)
PHONE..................................714 545-9311
Mike Kleene, Brnch Mgr
EMP: 500
SQ FT: 40,000
SALES (corp-wide): 302.09B **Publicly Held**
Web: www.pccfasteners.com
SIC: 3965 3728 3452 3714 Fasteners; Aircraft parts and equipment, nec; Bolts, nuts, rivets, and washers; Motor vehicle parts and accessories
HQ: Sps Technologies, Llc
301 Highland Ave
Jenkintown PA
215 572-3000

(P-11077)
SPS TECHNOLOGIES LLC
Cherry Aerospace Div
1224 E Warner Ave (92705-5414)
PHONE..................................714 371-1925
Michael Harhen, Brnch Mgr
EMP: 500
SALES (corp-wide): 302.09B **Publicly Held**
Web: www.pccfasteners.com
SIC: 3965 3452 Fasteners; Bolts, nuts, rivets, and washers
HQ: Sps Technologies, Llc
301 Highland Ave
Jenkintown PA
215 572-3000

(P-11078)
TOLEETO FASTENER INTERNATIONAL
1580 Jayken Way (91911-4644)
PHONE..................................619 662-1355
David Deavenport, Pr
Tom V Oss, *
Sara Davenport, *
EMP: 26 EST: 1985
SQ FT: 10,000
SALES (est): 2.41MM **Privately Held**
Web: www.tfifab.com
SIC: 3965 Fasteners

(P-11079)
TWO LADS INC (PA)
5001 Hampton St (90058-2133)
P.O. Box 58572 (90058-0572)
PHONE..................................323 584-0064
Lee R Adams, Pr
David Scharf, *
▼ EMP: 30 EST: 1991
SQ FT: 6,300
SALES (est): 2.25MM **Privately Held**
Web: www.2lads.com
SIC: 3965 5131 2241 Buttons and parts; Buttons; Narrow fabric mills

(P-11080)
WCBM COMPANY (PA)
Also Called: West Coast Button Mfg Co
1812 W 135th St (90249-2520)
PHONE..................................323 262-3274
Keith Tanabe, CEO
Grace Kadoya, *
▲ EMP: 32 EST: 1976
SQ FT: 19,000
SALES (est): 2.4MM
SALES (corp-wide): 2.4MM **Privately Held**
SIC: 3965 Buttons and parts

(P-11081)
WEST COAST AEROSPACE INC (PA)
220 W E St (90744-5502)
PHONE..................................310 518-3167
Kenneth L Wagner Junior, Pr
Thomas Lieb, *
▲ EMP: 90 EST: 1977
SQ FT: 7,200
SALES (est): 9.94MM
SALES (corp-wide): 9.94MM **Privately Held**
Web: www.westcoastaerospace.com
SIC: 3965 3452 Fasteners; Bolts, nuts, rivets, and washers

(P-11082)
YKK (USA) INC
Also Called: Y K K U S A
5001 E La Palma Ave (92807-1926)
PHONE..................................714 701-1200

Mike Blunt, Mgr
EMP: 27
Web: www.ykkamericas.com
SIC: 3965 5131 Fasteners; Zippers
HQ: Ykk (U.S.A.), Inc.
1300 Cobb Industrial Dr
Marietta GA
770 427-5521

3991 Brooms And Brushes

(P-11083)
A & B BRUSH MFG CORP
1150 3 Ranch Rd (91010-2751)
PHONE..................................626 303-8856
Donn Anawalt, Pr
Donn D J Anawalt Junior, VP
▲ EMP: 18 EST: 1963
SQ FT: 26,500
SALES (est): 654.64K **Privately Held**
Web: www.abbrush.com
SIC: 3991 Brushes, household or industrial

(P-11084)
AMERICAN ROTARY BROOM CO INC
688 New York Dr (91768-3311)
PHONE..................................909 629-9117
Joe Baeskens, Brnch Mgr
EMP: 23
SALES (corp-wide): 2.27MM **Privately Held**
Web: www.united-rotary.com
SIC: 3991 3711 4959 Brooms; Motor vehicles and car bodies; Sweeping service: road, airport, parking lot, etc.
PA: American Rotary Broom Co., Inc.
181 Pawnee St Ste B
San Marcos CA
760 591-4025

(P-11085)
BRUSH RESEARCH MFG CO INC
Also Called: Brm Manufacturing
4642 Floral Dr (90022-1244)
PHONE..................................323 261-2193
Tara L Rands, CEO
Robert Fowlie, *
Grant Fowlie, *
Heather Jones, *
▲ EMP: 130 EST: 1962
SALES (est): 21.15MM **Privately Held**
Web: www.brushresearch.com
SIC: 3991 Brushes, household or industrial

(P-11086)
BUTLER HOME PRODUCTS LLC
9409 Buffalo Ave (91730-6012)
PHONE..................................909 476-3884
Paul Anton, Brnch Mgr
EMP: 176
SALES (corp-wide): 642.04MM **Privately Held**
Web: www.cleanerhomeliving.com
SIC: 3991 2392 Brooms; Mops, floor and dust
HQ: Butler Home Products, Llc
2 Cabot Rd Ste 102
Hudson MA
508 597-8000

(P-11087)
EASY REACH SUPPLY LLC
3737 Capitol Ave (90601-1732)
PHONE..................................601 582-7866
EMP: 22
SALES (corp-wide): 14.37MM **Privately Held**
Web: www.easyreachinc.com

SIC: 3991 Brooms and brushes
HQ: Easy Reach Supply, Llc
32 Raspberry Ln
Hattiesburg MS
601 582-7866

(P-11088)
FOAMPRO MFG INC
Also Called: Foampro Manufacturing
1781 Langley Ave (92614-5621)
P.O. Box 18888 (92623-8888)
PHONE...............................949 252-0112
Gregory Isaac, *Ch Bd*
Chad Coil, *
▲ EMP: 80 EST: 1952
SQ FT: 25,000
SALES (est): 7.9MM **Privately Held**
Web: www.foampromfg.com
SIC: 3991 Paint rollers

(P-11089)
GORDON BRUSH MFG CO INC (PA)
3737 Capitol Ave (90601-1732)
PHONE...............................323 724-7777
TOLL FREE: 800
Kenneth L Rakusin, *Pr*
William E Loitz, *
▲ EMP: 20 EST: 1951
SQ FT: 51,600
SALES (est): 14.37MM
SALES (corp-wide): 14.37MM **Privately Held**
Web: www.gordonbrush.com
SIC: 3991 Brushes, household or industrial

(P-11090)
KINGSOLVER INC
Also Called: Supreme Enterprise
8417 Secura Way (90670-2215)
P.O. Box 3106 (90670-0106)
PHONE...............................562 945-7590
Keith Kingsolver, *Pr*
Christina Kingsolver, *Sec*
▲ EMP: 19 EST: 1994
SQ FT: 22,000
SALES (est): 2.4MM **Privately Held**
SIC: 3991 5199 Brooms; Broom, mop, and paint handles

(P-11091)
LAKIM INDUSTRIES INCORPORATED (PA)
Also Called: Quali-Tech Manufacturing
389 Rood Rd (92231-9763)
PHONE...............................310 637-8900
Song B Kim, *CEO*
▲ EMP: 20 EST: 1974
SALES (est): 6.44MM
SALES (corp-wide): 6.44MM **Privately Held**
Web: www.quali-tech.com
SIC: 3991 Paint rollers

(P-11092)
WESTCOAST BRUSH MFG INC
1330 Philadelphia St (91766-5563)
PHONE...............................909 627-7170
Heriberto Guerrero, *Pr*
Concepcion Guerrero, *VP*
▲ EMP: 22 EST: 1979
SQ FT: 20,000
SALES (est): 2.27MM **Privately Held**
Web: www.westcoastbrush.com
SIC: 3991 Brushes, household or industrial

3993 Signs And Advertising Specialties

(P-11093)
3S SIGN SERVICES INC
Also Called: P.S. Services
1320 N Red Gum St (92806-1317)
PHONE...............................714 683-1120
Michael W Schmidt, *CEO*
EMP: 25 EST: 2018
SALES (est): 1.42MM **Privately Held**
Web: www.psserv.com
SIC: 3993 Signs and advertising specialties

(P-11094)
ABIS SIGNS INC
Also Called: ABIS SIGNS INC
14240 Don Julian Rd Ste E (91746-3040)
PHONE...............................626 818-4329
Eddie Takahashi, *Prin*
EMP: 17
SALES (corp-wide): 350.75K **Privately Held**
SIC: 3993 Neon signs
PA: Abis Signs, Inc.
12223 Highland Ave # 106
Rancho Cucamonga CA
626 818-4303

(P-11095)
ADTI MEDIA LLC
Also Called: Advanced Digital Tech Intl
1257 Simpson Way (92029-1403)
PHONE...............................951 795-4446
◆ EMP: 20 EST: 2010
SALES (est): 1.71MM **Privately Held**
Web: www.adtimedia.com
SIC: 3993 Signs and advertising specialties

(P-11096)
AMERICAN FLEET & RET GRAPHICS
Also Called: Amgraph
2091 Del Rio Way (91761-8038)
PHONE...............................909 937-7570
Kristin Stewart, *CEO*
Brian Stewart, *
EMP: 37 EST: 2006
SALES (est): 5.7MM **Privately Held**
Web: www.theamgraphgroup.com
SIC: 3993 Signs and advertising specialties

(P-11097)
ARCHITECTURAL DESIGN SIGNS INC (PA)
Also Called: Ad/S Companies
1160 Railroad St (92882-1835)
PHONE...............................951 278-0680
EMP: 95 EST: 1995
SQ FT: 630,000
SALES (est): 23.4MM **Privately Held**
Web: www.ad-s.com
SIC: 3993 Signs and advertising specialties

(P-11098)
ASTRO DISPLAY COMPANY INC
4247 E Airport Dr (91761-1565)
PHONE...............................909 605-2875
TOLL FREE: 800
Thomas Andric, *Ch Bd*
EMP: 20 EST: 1946
SQ FT: 16,000
SALES (est): 1.5MM **Privately Held**
Web: www.astrodisplay.com
SIC: 3993 7319 3089 Displays and cutouts, window and lobby; Display advertising service; Plastics processing

(P-11099)
BK SIGNS INC
1028 W Kirkwall Rd (91702-5126)
PHONE...............................626 334-5600
Brian Scott Kanner, *CEO*
EMP: 18 EST: 1992
SQ FT: 16,000
SALES (est): 1.96MM **Privately Held**
Web: www.bksigns.com
SIC: 3993 1731 Signs and advertising specialties; General electrical contractor

(P-11100)
CAL-SIGN WHOLESALE INC
2110 S Anne St (92704-4409)
PHONE...............................209 523-7446
Greg Johnson, *Pr*
Mark Johnson, *VP*
Roger Johnson, *Sec*
EMP: 17 EST: 1974
SALES (est): 2.13MM **Privately Held**
Web: www.calsignwholesale.com
SIC: 3993 Electric signs

(P-11101)
CALIFORNIA NEON PRODUCTS
Also Called: C N P Signs & Graphics
9944 Blossom Valley Rd (92021-2203)
PHONE...............................619 283-2191
Peter Mccarter, *CEO*
Robert Mccarter, *VP*
Richard Mccarter, *Sec*
EMP: 70 EST: 1939
SALES (est): 9.63MM **Privately Held**
Web: www.cnpsigns.com
SIC: 3993 1799 Electric signs; Sign installation and maintenance

(P-11102)
CALIFORNIA SIGNS INC
Also Called: CA Signs
10280 Glenoaks Blvd (91331-1604)
PHONE...............................818 899-1888
Matthew Miller, *Pr*
Yvette Miller, *
EMP: 35 EST: 1962
SQ FT: 21,000
SALES (est): 4.73MM **Privately Held**
Web: www.casigns.com
SIC: 3993 Signs, not made in custom sign painting shops

(P-11103)
CLEGG INDUSTRIES INC
Also Called: Clegg Promo
19032 S Vermont Ave (90248-4412)
PHONE...............................310 225-3800
Timothy P Clegg, *CEO*
Kevin Clegg, *
Michael Bistocchi, *
Michael Amar, *
Los Angeles, *
▲ EMP: 175 EST: 1987
SQ FT: 31,000
SALES (est): 23.17MM **Privately Held**
SIC: 3993 3648 2542 Advertising novelties; Lighting equipment, nec; Partitions and fixtures, except wood

(P-11104)
COAST SIGN INCORPORATED
Also Called: Coast Sign Display
1500 W Embassy St (92802-1016)
PHONE...............................714 520-9144
Afshan Alemi, *CEO*
S Charlie Alemi, *
Bonnie Metz, *
▲ EMP: 250 EST: 1964
SQ FT: 130,000
SALES (est): 45.23MM **Privately Held**

Web: www.coastsign.com
SIC: 3993 Signs, not made in custom sign painting shops

(P-11105)
CORNERSTONE DISPLAY GROUP INC
Also Called: Cornerstone
28340 Avenue Crocker (91355-1238)
PHONE...............................661 705-1700
▲ EMP: 45 EST: 1995
SQ FT: 20,000
SALES (est): 9.65MM **Privately Held**
Web: www.cornerstonedisplay.com
SIC: 3993 Advertising artwork

(P-11106)
COWBOY DIRECT RESPONSE
Also Called: Synergy Direct Response
130 E Alton Ave (92707-4415)
PHONE...............................714 824-3780
Cynthia Rogers, *CEO*
John T Rogers, *
Cynthia Rogers, *Pr*
EMP: 35 EST: 2004
SQ FT: 10,000
SALES (est): 5.41MM **Privately Held**
Web: www.synergydr.com
SIC: 3993 8999 2759 Advertising artwork; Advertising copy writing; Promotional printing

(P-11107)
CUMMINGS RESOURCES LLC
1495 Columbia Ave (92507-2021)
PHONE...............................951 248-1130
EMP: 39
SQ FT: 50,000
SALES (corp-wide): 719.67MM **Privately Held**
Web: www.harborpipe.com
SIC: 3993 Signs and advertising specialties
HQ: Cummings Resources Llc
15 Century Blvd Ste 200
Nashville TN

(P-11108)
CUMMINGS RESOURCES LLC
330 W Citrus St (92324-1417)
PHONE...............................951 248-1130
EMP: 39
SALES (corp-wide): 719.67MM **Privately Held**
Web: www.cummingsbrandnew.com
SIC: 3993 Signs and advertising specialties
HQ: Cummings Resources Llc
15 Century Blvd Ste 200
Nashville TN

(P-11109)
DG-DISPLAYS LLC
355 Parkside Dr (91340-3036)
PHONE...............................877 358-5976
Zachary Blumenfeld, *
EMP: 30 EST: 2016
SQ FT: 25,000
SALES (est): 1.27MM **Privately Held**
SIC: 3993 Signs and advertising specialties

(P-11110)
DUNBAR ELECTRIC SIGN COMPANY
Also Called: City Crane
4020 Rosedale Hwy (93308-6131)
P.O. Box 10717 (93389-0717)
PHONE...............................661 323-2600
Clayton Dunbar, *CEO*
EMP: 25 EST: 1972
SALES (est): 422.57K **Privately Held**

PRODUCTS & SVCS

SIC: 3993 7629 5999 1799 Electric signs;
Electrical equipment repair services;
Banners; Sign installation and maintenance

(P-11111)
EDELMANN USA INC (DH)
Also Called: Bert-Co. of Ontario CA
2150 S Parco Ave (91761-5768)
P.O. Box 4150 (91761-1068)
PHONE..............................323 669-5700
Constantin Karl Schuetz, *CEO*
EMP: 18 **EST:** 2016
SALES (est): 6.56MM
SALES (corp-wide): 350.51MM **Privately Held**
Web: www.edelmannusa.com
SIC: 3993 Signs and advertising specialties
HQ: Edelmann Gmbh
Steinheimer Str. 45
Heidenheim An Der Brenz BW
73213400

(P-11112)
ELRO MANUFACTURING COMPANY (PA)
Also Called: Elro Sign Company
400 W Walnut St (90248-3137)
PHONE..............................310 380-7444
Max R Rhodes, *CEO*
Frank J Rhodes, *VP*
EMP: 20 **EST:** 1948
SQ FT: 18,000
SALES (est): 5.21MM
SALES (corp-wide): 5.21MM **Privately Held**
Web: www.elrosigns.com
SIC: 3993 Electric signs

(P-11113)
ENCORE IMAGE INC
303 W Main St (91762-3843)
P.O. Box 9297 (91762-9297)
PHONE..............................909 986-4632
Terry Wilkins, *CEO*
EMP: 27 **EST:** 2006
SQ FT: 30,000
SALES (est): 7.42MM
SALES (corp-wide): 14.8MM **Privately Held**
Web: www.encoreimage.com
SIC: 3993 1799 Electric signs; Sign installation and maintenance
PA: Encore Image Group, Inc.
1445 Sepulveda Blvd
Torrance CA
310 534-7500

(P-11114)
ENCORE IMAGE GROUP INC (PA)
Also Called: Encore Image
1445 Sepulveda Blvd (90501-5004)
PHONE..............................310 534-7500
Kozell Boren, *Ch Bd*
Tom Johnson, *
Tommy K Boren, *Prin*
▲ **EMP:** 90 **EST:** 1959
SQ FT: 70,000
SALES (est): 14.8MM
SALES (corp-wide): 14.8MM **Privately Held**
Web: www.encoreimagegroup.com
SIC: 3993 Electric signs

(P-11115)
ENHANCE AMERICA INC
3463 Grapevine St (91752-3504)
PHONE..............................951 361-3000
Jackson Ling, *Pr*
◆ **EMP:** 20 **EST:** 2002

SALES (est): 2.44MM **Privately Held**
Web: www.enhanceamerica.com
SIC: 3993 Signs and advertising specialties

(P-11116)
EVANS MANUFACTURING INC (HQ)
Also Called: Evans Manufacturing
7422 Chapman Ave (92841-2106)
P.O. Box 5669 (92846-0669)
PHONE..............................714 379-6100
Alan Vaught, *CEO*
▲ **EMP:** 185 **EST:** 1990
SQ FT: 17,000
SALES (est): 54.67MM
SALES (corp-wide): 94.31MM **Privately Held**
Web: www.evans-mfg.com
SIC: 3993 3089 Signs and advertising specialties; Injection molding of plastics
PA: Hub Pen Company, Llc
1525 Washington St Ste 1
Braintree MA
781 535-5500

(P-11117)
EXPO-3 INTERNATIONAL INC
12350 Edison Way 60 (92841-2810)
PHONE..............................714 379-8383
Daniel J Mills, *Ch Bd*
Chris Smith, *Pr*
EMP: 21 **EST:** 1974
SQ FT: 60,000
SALES (est): 871.25K **Privately Held**
Web: www.expo3.com
SIC: 3993 Displays and cutouts, window and lobby

(P-11118)
FAN FAVE INC
Also Called: Fanfave
10329 Dorset St (91730-3067)
PHONE..............................909 975-4999
EMP: 20 **EST:** 2012
SQ FT: 17,000
SALES (est): 2.49MM **Privately Held**
Web: www.fanfave.com
SIC: 3993 Advertising artwork

(P-11119)
FEDERAL HEATH SIGN COMPANY LLC
3609 Ocean Ranch Blvd Ste 204 (92056-8601)
PHONE..............................760 941-0715
Tim O'donald, *Brnch Mgr*
EMP: 120
SALES (corp-wide): 1.84B **Privately Held**
Web: www.federalheath.com
SIC: 3993 Neon signs
HQ: Federal Heath Sign Company, Llc
2300 St Hwy 121
Euless TX

(P-11120)
FEDERAL PRISON INDUSTRIES
Also Called: Unicor
3901 Klein Blvd (93436-2706)
PHONE..............................805 735-2771
Steve Southall, *Mgr*
EMP: 19
Web: www.bop.gov
SIC: 3993 2759 3315 2521 Signs and advertising specialties; Commercial printing, nec; Cable, steel: insulated or armored; Wood office furniture
HQ: Federal Prison Industries, Inc
320 Frst St N W Fncl Mgt
Washington DC

(P-11121)
FOVELL ENTERPRISES INC
Also Called: Southwest Sign Company
1852 Pomona Rd (92878-3277)
PHONE..............................951 734-6275
Jack Fovell, *CEO*
▲ **EMP:** 26 **EST:** 1991
SQ FT: 12,500
SALES (est): 4.34MM **Privately Held**
Web: www.southwestsign.com
SIC: 3993 Electric signs

(P-11122)
FUSION SIGN & DESIGN INC (PA)
680 Columbia Ave (92507-2144)
PHONE..............................877 477-8777
Loren Hanson, *CEO*
Dave Haffter, *Prin*
▲ **EMP:** 17 **EST:** 2006
SALES (est): 21.69MM **Privately Held**
Web: www.fusionsign.com
SIC: 3993 Electric signs

(P-11123)
GEORGE P JOHNSON COMPANY
18500 Crenshaw Blvd (90504-5055)
PHONE..............................310 965-4300
Chris Meyer, *CEO*
EMP: 38
SALES (corp-wide): 281.93MM **Privately Held**
Web: sg.gpj.com
SIC: 3993 Signs and advertising specialties
HQ: George P. Johnson Company
1914 Taylor Pt
Auburn Hills MI
248 475-2500

(P-11124)
INFINITY WATCH CORPORATION
Also Called: Iwcus
21078 Commerce Point Dr (91789-3051)
PHONE..............................626 289-9878
Patrick Tam, *Pr*
Brenda Tam, *
▲ **EMP:** 25 **EST:** 1990
SQ FT: 12,000
SALES (est): 1.95MM **Privately Held**
Web: www.infinitywatch.com
SIC: 3993 Signs and advertising specialties

(P-11125)
INTEGRATED SIGN ASSOCIATES
1160 Pioneer Way Ste M (92020-1944)
PHONE..............................619 579-2229
Aaron Coippinger, *Pr*
EMP: 30 **EST:** 1982
SQ FT: 15,000
SALES (est): 4.54MM **Privately Held**
Web: www.isasign.com
SIC: 3993 Neon signs

(P-11126)
JOHN BISHOP DESIGN INC
Also Called: J B3d
731 N Main St (92868-1105)
PHONE..............................714 744-2300
EMP: 38 **EST:** 1989
SQ FT: 1,000
SALES (est): 3.33MM **Privately Held**
Web: www.jb3d.com
SIC: 3993 Signs and advertising specialties

(P-11127)
JONES SIGN CO INC
Also Called: Ultrasigns Electrical Advg
9474 Chesapeake Dr Ste 902 (92123-1027)

PHONE..............................858 569-1400
John Mortensen, *Pr*
EMP: 135
SALES (corp-wide): 119.49MM **Privately Held**
Web: www.jonessign.com
SIC: 3993 Signs and advertising specialties
PA: Jones Sign Co., Inc.
1711 Scheuring Rd
De Pere WI
920 983-6700

(P-11128)
K S DESIGNS INC
Also Called: Cal West Designs
9515 Sorensen Ave (90670-2650)
PHONE..............................562 929-3973
Robin Shelton, *Pr*
EMP: 32 **EST:** 1979
SQ FT: 49,000
SALES (est): 2.29MM **Privately Held**
SIC: 3993 Displays and cutouts, window and lobby

(P-11129)
LA6721 LLC
1275 E 6th St (90021-1209)
PHONE..............................323 484-4070
Maria Endoza, *Pr*
EMP: 19 **EST:** 2015
SALES (est): 7.14MM **Privately Held**
SIC: 3993 Signs and advertising specialties

(P-11130)
LOCAL NEON COMPANY INC
12536 Chadron Ave (90250-4850)
PHONE..............................310 978-2000
Scott Blakely, *Pr*
Jeanne Blakely, *
Cassius C Blakely, *Stockholder*
EMP: 24 **EST:** 1953
SQ FT: 20,000
SALES (est): 370.06K **Privately Held**
SIC: 3993 Signs and advertising specialties

(P-11131)
LOREN INDUSTRIES
Also Called: Loren Electric Sign & Lighting
12226 Coast Dr (90601-1607)
PHONE..............................562 699-1122
Daniel Marc Lorenzon, *CEO*
Michelle Lornezon, *
EMP: 45 **EST:** 1996
SQ FT: 8,000
SALES (est): 6.78MM **Privately Held**
Web: www.lorenindustries.com
SIC: 3993 3648 1799 Electric signs; Outdoor lighting equipment; Sign installation and maintenance

(P-11132)
LUXURY SIGNS INC
7525 Jurupa Ave Ste E (92504-1046)
PHONE..............................951 446-9303
EMP: 28
SALES (corp-wide): 406.43K **Privately Held**
SIC: 3993 Signs and advertising specialties
PA: Luxury Signs Inc
1700 Hamner Ave Ste 211
Norco CA

(P-11133)
MANERI SIGN CO INC
1928 W 135th St (90249-2452)
PHONE..............................310 327-6261
Don Nicholas, *Pr*
EMP: 35 **EST:** 1980
SQ FT: 20,000
SALES (est): 2.3MM

▲ = Import ▼ = Export
◆ = Import/Export

SALES (corp-wide): 48.27MM **Privately Held**
Web: www.statewidess.com
SIC: **3993** Signs and advertising specialties
PA: Traffic Solutions Corporation
4000 Westerly Pl Ste 100
Newport Beach CA
949 553-8272

(P-11134)
MAXWELL ALARM SCREEN MFG INC
Also Called: Maxwell Sign and Decal Div
20327 Nordhoff St (91311-6128)
PHONE.................................818 773-5533
Michael A Kagen, *CEO*
Patty Kagen, *
EMP: 28 EST: 1977
SQ FT: 28,000
SALES (est): 2.36MM **Privately Held**
Web: www.maxwellmfg.com
SIC: **3993** 3442 Signs and advertising specialties; Screens, window, metal

(P-11135)
MEDIA NATION ENTERPRISES LLC
Also Called: Media Nation
25361 Commercentre Dr Ste 100 (92630)
PHONE.................................714 371-9494
Navin Narang, *Brnch Mgr*
EMP: 21
SALES (corp-wide): 4.83MM **Privately Held**
Web: www.medianationoutdoor.com
SIC: **3993** Signs and advertising specialties
PA: Media Nation Enterprises, Llc
15271 Barranca Pkwy
Irvine CA
888 502-8222

(P-11136)
MEDIA NATION ENTERPRISES LLC (PA)
Also Called: Media Nation USA
15271 Barranca Pkwy (92618-2201)
PHONE.................................888 502-8222
Navin D Narang, *Managing Member*
EMP: 24 EST: 2009
SALES (est): 4.83MM
SALES (corp-wide): 4.83MM **Privately Held**
Web: www.medianationoutdoor.com
SIC: **3993** 5699 7371 Signs and advertising specialties; Customized clothing and apparel; Software programming applications

(P-11137)
METAL ART OF CALIFORNIA INC (PA)
Also Called: Sign Mart
640 N Cypress St (92867-6604)
PHONE.................................714 532-7100
Gene S Sobel, *Pr*
Calvin Larson, *
◆ EMP: 91 EST: 1974
SQ FT: 22,000
SALES (est): 19.07MM
SALES (corp-wide): 19.07MM **Privately Held**
Web: metalart.openfos.com
SIC: **3993** Signs and advertising specialties

(P-11138)
MMXVIII HOLDINGS INC
20251 Sw Acacia St Ste 120 (92660-0768)
PHONE.................................800 672-3974
EMP: 24 EST: 2016
SQ FT: 7,500

SALES (est): 2.56MM **Privately Held**
SIC: **3993** Signs and advertising specialties

(P-11139)
MYERS & SONS HI-WAY SAFETY INC (PA)
Also Called: Hi-Way Safety
13310 5th St (91710-5125)
P.O. Box 1030 (91708-1030)
PHONE.................................909 591-1781
TOLL FREE: 800
Michael Rodgers, *CEO*
Brandon Myer, *
▲ EMP: 80 EST: 1970
SQ FT: 36,400
SALES (est): 23.43MM
SALES (corp-wide): 23.43MM **Privately Held**
SIC: **3993** Signs, not made in custom sign painting shops

(P-11140)
NATIONAL SIGN & MARKETING CORP
Also Called: Visual Information Systems Co
13580 5th St (91710-5113)
P.O. Box 2409 (91708-2409)
PHONE.................................909 591-4742
John J Kane, *Pr*
Jeffrey Fredrickson, *
EMP: 70 EST: 1997
SQ FT: 46,000
SALES (est): 12.65MM **Privately Held**
Web: www.nsmc.com
SIC: **3993** Neon signs

(P-11141)
NEIMAN/HOELLER INC
Also Called: Neiman & Company
6842 Valjean Ave (91406-4712)
PHONE.................................818 781-8600
Harry J Neiman, *CEO*
Robert R Hoeller Iii, *Pr*
EMP: 56 EST: 1965
SQ FT: 17,000
SALES (est): 7.11MM **Privately Held**
Web: www.neimanandco.com
SIC: **3993** 3646 Electric signs; Ornamental lighting fixtures, commercial

(P-11142)
OPTEC DISPLAYS INC
1700 S De Soto Pl Ste A (91761-8060)
PHONE.................................866 924-5239
◆ EMP: 64 EST: 1996
SALES (est): 21.51MM **Privately Held**
Web: www.optec.com
SIC: **3993** Signs and advertising specialties

(P-11143)
ORANGE CNTY NAME PLATE CO INC
13201 Arctic Cir (90670-5509)
P.O. Box 2764 (90670-0764)
PHONE.................................714 522-7693
Elias Rodriguez, *Pr*
Ben L Rodriguez, *
Sam Rodriguez, *
EMP: 85 EST: 1965
SQ FT: 31,000
SALES (est): 6.97MM **Privately Held**
Web: www.ocnameplates.com
SIC: **3993** Name plates: except engraved, etched, etc.: metal

(P-11144)
PD GROUP
Also Called: Sign-A-Rama
41945 Boardwalk Ste L (92211-9099)

PHONE.................................760 674-3028
EMP: 22 EST: 1995
SQ FT: 11,500
SALES (est): 1.61MM **Privately Held**
Web: www.pdsignarama.com
SIC: **3993** 7389 5999 Signs and advertising specialties; Sign painting and lettering shop ; Banners

(P-11145)
PRIMUS INC
Also Called: Western Highway Products
17901 Jamestown Ln (92647-7138)
P.O. Box 534 (92648-0534)
PHONE.................................714 527-2261
Steve Ellsworth, *Pr*
Timothy M Riordan, *
▲ EMP: 80 EST: 1926
SQ FT: 120,000
SALES (est): 9.81MM **Privately Held**
Web: www.primus.us
SIC: **3993** Signs, not made in custom sign painting shops

(P-11146)
PRO-LITE INC
Also Called: Advanced Products
3505 Cadillac Ave Ste D (92626-1464)
PHONE.................................714 668-9988
Kuo-fong Kaoh, *Pr*
◆ EMP: 17 EST: 1986
SQ FT: 7,200
SALES (est): 3.06MM **Privately Held**
Web: www.pro-lite.com
SIC: **3993** Signs and advertising specialties

(P-11147)
QUIEL BROS ELC SIGN SVC CO INC
272 S I St (92410-2408)
PHONE.................................909 885-4476
Larry R Quiel, *Pr*
Raymond Quiel, *
Jerry Quiel, *
Gary Quiel, *
▲ EMP: 40 EST: 1962
SQ FT: 8,000
SALES (est): 4.44MM **Privately Held**
Web: www.quielsigns.com
SIC: **3993** 7353 1731 7629 Electric signs; Cranes and aerial lift equipment, rental or leasing; General electrical contractor; Electrical equipment repair, high voltage

(P-11148)
R&M DEESE INC
Also Called: Electro-Tech's
1875 Sampson Ave (92879-6009)
P.O. Box 2317 (92878-2317)
PHONE.................................951 734-7342
Raymond Deese, *Pr*
Mary Deese, *Sec*
▲ EMP: 22 EST: 1976
SQ FT: 20,000
SALES (est): 2.47MM **Privately Held**
Web: www.electro-techs.net
SIC: **3993** 3679 Signs and advertising specialties; Liquid crystal displays (LCD)

(P-11149)
RICHARDS NEON SHOP INC
Also Called: RNS Channel Letters
4375 Prado Rd Ste 102 (92878-7444)
PHONE.................................951 279-6767
EMP: 24 EST: 1991
SALES (est): 2.35MM **Privately Held**
Web: www.rnsletters.com
SIC: **3993** Electric signs

(P-11150)
ROSS NAME PLATE COMPANY
2 Red Plum Cir (91755-7486)
PHONE.................................323 725-6812
Michael Ross, *Pr*
EMP: 37 EST: 1957
SQ FT: 25,000
SALES (est): 2.08MM **Privately Held**
Web: www.rossnameplate.com
SIC: **3993** 2754 Name plates: except engraved, etched, etc.: metal; Labels: gravure printing

(P-11151)
S2K GRAPHICS INC
Also Called: S 2 K
4686 Industrial St (93063-3413)
PHONE.................................818 885-3900
Dan C Pulos, *CEO*
Jack Wilson, *Ch Bd*
Dana Rosellini, *Sec*
EMP: 35 EST: 1989
SALES (est): 10.81MM **Privately Held**
Web: www.s2kgraphics.com
SIC: **3993** 7532 2759 Signs and advertising specialties; Truck painting and lettering; Screen printing
HQ: Franke Usa Holding, Inc.
800 Aviation Pkwy
Smyrna TN

(P-11152)
SAFETY SYSTEMS HAWAII
P.O. Box 5299 (92616-5299)
PHONE.................................808 847-4017
EMP: 18 EST: 2011
SALES (est): 438.97K **Privately Held**
SIC: **3993** Signs and advertising specialties

(P-11153)
SAFEWAY SIGN COMPANY
9875 Yucca Rd (92301-2282)
PHONE.................................760 246-7070
Michael F Moore, *Pr*
David C Moore, *
Andrea M Gutierrez, *
EMP: 49 EST: 1948
SQ FT: 60,000
SALES (est): 9.43MM **Privately Held**
Web: www.safewaysign.com
SIC: **3993** Signs, not made in custom sign painting shops

(P-11154)
SAN DIEGO ELECTRIC SIGN INC
Also Called: SD Electric Sign
1890 Cordell Ct Ste 105 (92020-0913)
P.O. Box 103 (91908-0103)
PHONE.................................619 258-1775
Greg Ballard, *Pr*
Jayne Ballard, *VP*
Lelsie Crosby, *Sec*
EMP: 17 EST: 2001
SALES (est): 2.51MM **Privately Held**
Web: www.sdelectricsign.com
SIC: **3993** Electric signs

(P-11155)
SANTA CLARITA SIGNS
26330 Diamond Pl (91350-5820)
PHONE.................................661 291-1188
EMP: 38 EST: 2009
SALES (est): 283.28K **Privately Held**
Web: www.signalscv.com
SIC: **3993** Signs and advertising specialties

(P-11156)
SCHEA HOLDINGS INC
Also Called: Signgroup/Karman

9812 Independence Ave (91311-4319)
PHONE..................................818 998-3636
Michael Schackne, *Pr*
Kathy Schackne, *VP*
EMP: 22 **EST:** 1993
SQ FT: 10,000
SALES (est): 3.86MM **Privately Held**
Web: www.sgksigns.net
SIC: 3993 Electric signs

(P-11157)
SHYE WEST INC (PA)
Also Called: Imagine This
43 Corporate Park Ste 102 (92606-5148)
PHONE..................................949 486-4598
Patrick Papaccio, *Pr*
Shawn Keep, *
Amy French, *
▲ **EMP:** 27 **EST:** 1999
SQ FT: 6,000
SALES (est): 10.17MM
SALES (corp-wide): 10.17MM **Privately Held**
Web: www.imaginethis.com
SIC: 3993 5099 Advertising novelties;
Novelties, durable

(P-11158)
SIGN IMAGE INC
20440 Corisco St (91311-6121)
PHONE..................................818 772-1393
Renee Serkin, *Pr*
EMP: 25 **EST:** 1994
SALES (est): 488.09K **Privately Held**
Web: www.signimageinc.com
SIC: 3993 Signs and advertising specialties

(P-11159)
SIGN INDUSTRIES INC
2101 Carrillo Privado (91761-7600)
PHONE..................................909 930-0303
Maria Saavedra, *Pr*
Enrique Saavedra, *
▲ **EMP:** 30 **EST:** 1994
SQ FT: 4,500
SALES (est): 4.87MM **Privately Held**
Web: www.signindustries.tv
SIC: 3993 Neon signs

(P-11160)
SIGN POST BYWAY INC
901 Cossa Ct (93454-3406)
PHONE..................................949 566-3016
Diane E Herman, *Brnch Mgr*
EMP: 17
SALES (corp-wide): 79.87K **Privately Held**
SIC: 3993 Signs and advertising specialties
PA: Sign Post Byway, Inc.
1130 E Clark Ave Ste 150
Santa Maria CA

(P-11161)
SIGN SPECIALISTS CORPORATION
111 W Dyer Rd Ste F (92707-3425)
PHONE..................................714 641-0064
Garrick Batt, *CEO*
EMP: 22 **EST:** 2001
SALES (est): 5.25MM **Privately Held**
Web: www.signspecialists.com
SIC: 3993 Signs, not made in custom sign
painting shops

(P-11162)
SIGNAGE SOLUTIONS CORPORATION
2231 S Dupont Dr (92806-6105)
PHONE..................................714 491-0299
Chris Deruyter, *CEO*

Jim Gledhill, *
EMP: 30 **EST:** 1990
SQ FT: 14,000
SALES (est): 4.97MM **Privately Held**
Web: www.signage-solutions.com
SIC: 3993 7389 Signs and advertising
specialties; Sign painting and lettering shop

(P-11163)
SIGNRESOURCE LLC (DH)
6135 District Blvd (90270-3449)
P.O. Box 549 (90270-0549)
PHONE..................................323 771-2098
EMP: 157 **EST:** 1969
SALES (est): 73.44MM
SALES (corp-wide): 269.26MM **Privately Held**
Web: www.signresource.com
SIC: 3993 Signs and advertising specialties
HQ: Royston Llc
1 Pickroy Rd
Jasper GA
800 334-1766

(P-11164)
SIGNS AND SERVICES COMPANY
10980 Boatman Ave (90680-2602)
PHONE..................................714 761-8200
Jacob Deryuyter, *CEO*
Matt De Ruyter, *
EMP: 33 **EST:** 1986
SQ FT: 16,000
SALES (est): 4.61MM **Privately Held**
Web: www.signsandservicesco.com
SIC: 3993 Signs, not made in custom sign
painting shops

(P-11165)
SIGNTECH ELECTRICAL ADVG INC
Also Called: Signtech
4444 Federal Blvd (92102-2505)
PHONE..................................619 527-6100
Harold E Schauer Junior, *CEO*
David E Schauer, *
Kimra Schauer, *
Art Navarro, *
Patty Soria, *
EMP: 120 **EST:** 1984
SQ FT: 25,000
SALES (est): 19.82MM **Privately Held**
Web: www.signtech.com
SIC: 3993 1799 Electric signs; Sign
installation and maintenance

(P-11166)
SIGNTRONIX INC
Also Called: Gulf Development
1445 Sepulveda Blvd (90501-5004)
PHONE..................................310 534-7500
▲ **EMP:** 100
Web: www.signtronix.com
SIC: 3993 Signs and advertising specialties

(P-11167)
STANDARDVISION LLC
3370 N San Fernando Rd Ste 206 (90065-1440)
PHONE..................................323 222-3630
Alberto Garcia, *Prin*
Kevin Bartanian, *Prin*
Hs Moon, *Prin*
▲ **EMP:** 34 **EST:** 2007
SQ FT: 25,000
SALES (est): 5.92MM **Privately Held**
Web: www.standardvision.com
SIC: 3993 7336 Signs and advertising
specialties; Commercial art and graphic
design

(P-11168)
STANFORD SIGN & AWNING INC (PA)
2556 Faivre St (91911-4604)
PHONE..................................619 423-6200
David Lesage, *Pr*
EMP: 50 **EST:** 1974
SQ FT: 35,000
SALES (est): 7.74MM
SALES (corp-wide): 7.74MM **Privately Held**
Web: www.stanfordsign.com
SIC: 3993 2394 Electric signs; Canvas
awnings and canopies

(P-11169)
STATEWIDE TRFFIC SFETY SGNS IN
2722 S Fairview St (92704-5947)
PHONE..................................714 468-1919
Don Nicholas, *Owner*
EMP: 25
SALES (corp-wide): 539.72MM **Privately Held**
Web: www.statewidess.com
SIC: 3993 Signs and advertising specialties
HQ: Statewide Traffic Safety And Signs, Inc.
2722 S Fairview St Fl 2
Santa Ana CA
949 553-8272

(P-11170)
STATEWIDE TRFFIC SFETY SGNS IN
1100 Main St Ste 100 (92614-6737)
P.O. Box 5299 (92616-5299)
PHONE..................................949 553-8272
EMP: 26
SALES (corp-wide): 539.72MM **Privately Held**
Web: www.statewidess.com
SIC: 3993 Signs and advertising specialties
HQ: Statewide Traffic Safety And Signs, Inc.
2722 S Fairview St Fl 2
Santa Ana CA
949 553-8272

(P-11171)
SUNSET SIGNS AND PRINTING INC
Also Called: Contractor
2906 E Coronado St (92806-2501)
PHONE..................................714 255-9104
EMP: 50 **EST:** 1992
SALES (est): 9.44MM **Privately Held**
Web: www.sunsetsignsoc.com
SIC: 3993 Signs and advertising specialties

(P-11172)
SUPERIOR ELECTRICAL ADVG INC (PA)
1700 W Anaheim St (90813-1102)
PHONE..................................562 495-3808
Jim Sterk, *CEO*
Patti Skoglundadams, *
Doug Tokeshi, *
Stan Janocha, *
▲ **EMP:** 85 **EST:** 1962
SQ FT: 100,000
SALES (est): 15.72MM
SALES (corp-wide): 15.72MM **Privately Held**
Web: www.superiorsigns.com
SIC: 3993 7629 Electric signs; Electrical
equipment repair services

(P-11173)
TDI SIGNS
13158 Arctic Cir (90670-5508)
PHONE..................................562 436-5188
Arthur Rivas, *Pr*
EMP: 25 **EST:** 2003
SALES (est): 2.01MM **Privately Held**
Web: www.tdisigns.com
SIC: 3993 Electric signs

(P-11174)
TEMEKA INCORPORATED
150 W Walnut Ave (92571-3262)
PHONE..................................951 296-3570
EMP: 23 **EST:** 1991
SALES (est): 1.11MM **Privately Held**
SIC: 3993 2431 Signs and advertising
specialties; Millwork

(P-11175)
TFN ARCHITECTURAL SIGNAGE INC (PA)
Also Called: Third Floor North Company
527 Fee Ana St (92870-6702)
PHONE..................................714 556-0990
Brian L Burnett, *Pr*
Ellen Vaughn, *
Teresa Burnett, *
Catherine Burnett, *Stockholder**
Jeff Burnett, *Stockholder**
EMP: 44 **EST:** 1980
SALES (est): 5.45MM
SALES (corp-wide): 5.45MM **Privately Held**
Web: www.thirdfloornorth.com
SIC: 3993 Signs, not made in custom sign
painting shops

(P-11176)
TRADENET ENTERPRISE INC
Also Called: Vantage Led
1580 Magnolia Ave (92879-2073)
PHONE..................................888 595-3956
Chris Ma, *CEO*
▲ **EMP:** 60 **EST:** 1997
SALES (est): 11.46MM **Privately Held**
Web: www.vantageled.com
SIC: 3993 Electric signs

(P-11177)
TRAFFIC CONTROL & SAFETY CORP
13755 Blaisdell Pl (92064-6837)
PHONE..................................858 679-7292
EMP: 18
Web: www.statewidess.com
SIC: 3993 5088 7359 5082 Signs, not made
in custom sign painting shops;
Transportation equipment and supplies;
Work zone traffic equipment (flags, cones,
barrels, etc.); Contractor's materials
PA: Traffic Control And Safety Corporation
1100 Main St
Irvine CA

(P-11178)
VALLEY ENERPRISES INC
18600 Van Buren Blvd (92508-9111)
PHONE..................................951 789-0843
EMP: 19 **EST:** 2011
SALES (est): 478.36K **Privately Held**
Web: www.vesigns.com
SIC: 3993 Signs and advertising specialties

(P-11179)
VOGUE SIGN INC
Also Called: Vogue Sign Company
715 Commercial Ave (93030-7233)
PHONE..................................805 487-7222

Jack Woodruff, *Pr*
EMP: 20 **EST:** 1955
SQ FT: 11,000
SALES (est): 1.78MM **Privately Held**
Web: www.voguesigns.com
SIC: 3993 Electric signs

(P-11180)
WESTERN SIGN SYSTEMS INC
Also Called: Western Sign Systems
261 S Pacific St (92078-2429)
PHONE...........................760 736-6070
David Lesage, *Pr*
EMP: 25 **EST:** 1993
SQ FT: 6,000
SALES (est): 2.21MM **Privately Held**
Web: www.western-sign.com
SIC: 3993 Signs and advertising specialties

(P-11181)
WOLFPACK INC
Also Called: Wolfpack Sign Group
2440 Grand Ave Ste B (92081-7829)
P.O. Box 3620 (92085-3620)
PHONE...........................760 736-4500
Carolyn Wolf, *CEO*
Ryan Meyer, *VP*
Peter Wolf, *Sec*
EMP: 48 **EST:** 1995
SQ FT: 15,000
SALES (est): 2.57MM **Privately Held**
Web: www.wolfpackllc.com
SIC: 3993 Signs, not made in custom sign
   painting shops

(P-11182)
**YOUNG ELECTRIC SIGN
COMPANY**
Also Called: Yesco
10235 Bellegrave Ave (91752-1919)
PHONE...........................909 923-7668
Duane Wardle, *Brnch Mgr*
EMP: 206
SQ FT: 8,500
SALES (corp-wide): 498.12MM **Privately
Held**
Web: www.yesco.com
SIC: 3993 1799 Electric signs; Sign
   installation and maintenance
PA: Young Electric Sign Company Inc
   2401 S Foothill Dr
   Salt Lake City UT
   801 464-4600

3996 Hard Surface Floor Coverings, Nec

(P-11183)
ALTRO USA INC
Also Called: Compass Flooring
12648 Clark St (90670-3950)
PHONE...........................562 944-8292
Al Boegh, *Prin*
EMP: 73
SALES (corp-wide): 194.81MM **Privately
Held**
Web: www.altro.com
SIC: 3996 5023 Hard surface floor
   coverings, nec; Resilient floor coverings:
   tile or sheet
HQ: Altro Usa, Inc.
   80 Industrial Way Ste 1
   Wilmington MA
   800 377-5597

(P-11184)
RAM BOARD INC
27460 Avenue Scott Unit A (91355-3472)
PHONE...........................818 848-0400

◆ **EMP:** 30 **EST:** 2008
SALES (est): 4.91MM **Privately Held**
Web: www.ramboard.com
SIC: 3996 5023 Hard surface floor
   coverings, nec; Floor coverings

3999 Manufacturing Industries, Nec

(P-11185)
**ABOVE & BEYOND BALLOONS
INC**
Also Called: Above and Beyond
1 Wrigley (92618-2711)
PHONE...........................949 586-8470
Michael Chaklos, *CEO*
Karen Chaklos, *
▲ **EMP:** 44 **EST:** 2002
SALES (est): 4.51MM **Privately Held**
Web: www.advertisingballoons.com
SIC: 3999 Advertising display products

(P-11186)
**ADVANCED BUILDING
SYSTEMS INC**
11905 Regentview Ave (90241-5515)
PHONE...........................818 652-4252
Alex Youssef, *Pr*
EMP: 20 **EST:** 2018
SALES (est): 1.42MM **Privately Held**
SIC: 3999 Manufacturing industries, nec

(P-11187)
**ADVANCED COSMETIC RES
LABS INC**
Also Called: Acrl
20550 Prairie St (91311-6006)
PHONE...........................818 709-9945
Kitty Hunter, *Pr*
▲ **EMP:** 50 **EST:** 1994
SQ FT: 48,000
SALES (est): 9.45MM **Privately Held**
Web: www.acrl.com
SIC: 3999 2844 Barber and beauty shop
   equipment; Perfumes, cosmetics and other
   toilet preparations

(P-11188)
AMARETTO ORCHARDS LLC
Also Called: Famoso Nut
32331 Famoso Woody Rd (93250-9771)
PHONE...........................661 399-9697
◆ **EMP:** 20 **EST:** 1990
SALES (est): 2MM **Privately Held**
Web: www.famosonut.com
SIC: 3999 2068 Nut shells, grinding, from
   purchased nuts; Salted and roasted nuts
   and seeds

(P-11189)
**AMGEN MANUFACTURING
LIMITED**
1 Amgen Center Dr (91320-1799)
PHONE...........................787 656-2000
Victoria H Blatter, *Prin*
EMP: 34 **EST:** 2008
SALES (est): 9.85MM
SALES (corp-wide): 26.32B **Publicly Held**
Web: www.amgen.com
SIC: 3999 Atomizers, toiletry
PA: Amgen Inc.
   1 Amgen Center Dr
   Thousand Oaks CA
   805 447-1000

(P-11190)
ARAMARK UNIFORM MFG CO
115 N First St (91502-1856)
PHONE...........................800 999-8989
EMP: 25 **EST:** 2013
SALES (est): 5.34MM **Publicly Held**
SIC: 3999 Manufacturing industries, nec
HQ: Aramark Services, Inc.
   2400 Market St
   Philadelphia PA
   215 238-3000

(P-11191)
ARTBOXX FRAMING INC
Also Called: Intercontinental Art
555 W Victoria St (90220-5513)
PHONE...........................310 604-6933
EMP: 26
SIC: 3999 5999 Framed artwork; Art, picture
   frames, and decorations

(P-11192)
**ARTIFICIAL GRASS
LIQUIDATORS**
Also Called: Agl
42505 Rio Nedo (92590-3726)
PHONE...........................951 677-3377
Dillon Georgian, *Pr*
Vicky Hernandez, *Prin*
EMP: 30 **EST:** 2015
SALES (est): 2.2MM **Privately Held**
Web: www.artificialgrassliquidators.com
SIC: 3999 Grasses, artificial and preserved

(P-11193)
BCD INDUSTRIES CORP
24298 Via Vargas Dr (92553-6231)
PHONE...........................760 927-8988
Juan Briseno, *Prin*
EMP: 18 **EST:** 2017
SALES (est): 498.25K **Privately Held**
SIC: 3999 Manufacturing industries, nec

(P-11194)
BEACH HOUSE GROUP LLC
Also Called: Beach House Group
222 N Pacific Coast Hwy Fl 10
(90245-5615)
PHONE...........................310 356-6180
Lance Kalish, *
Shaun Neff, *
Ido Leffler, *
Sachin Harneja, *
EMP: 54 **EST:** 2014
SALES (est): 6.29MM **Privately Held**
Web: www.beachhousegrp.com
SIC: 3999 Advertising display products

(P-11195)
BEAUTY TENT INC
1131 N Kenmore Ave Apt 6 (90029-1525)
PHONE...........................323 717-7131
Naira Harutyunyan, *Pr*
EMP: 25 **EST:** 2019
SALES (est): 735.9K **Privately Held**
Web: www.beautytent.com
SIC: 3999 Hair curlers, designed for beauty
   parlors

(P-11196)
BIO-REIGNS INC
1451 Edinger Ave Ste D (92780-6250)
PHONE...........................949 922-2032
Bryan Reed, *Pr*
EMP: 65 **EST:** 2018
SALES (est): 2.73MM **Privately Held**
Web: www.bioreigns.com
SIC: 3999

(P-11197)
BLOOMIOS INC
201 W Montecito St (93101-3824)
PHONE...........................805 222-6330
Michael Hill, *CEO*
Barrett Evans, *CSO*
John Bennett, *
EMP: 30 **EST:** 2001
SALES (est): 6.08MM **Privately Held**
Web: www.bloomios.com
SIC: 3999 5159

(P-11198)
**BRIGHT GLOW CANDLE
COMPANY INC (PA)**
Also Called: Bright Glow
20591 E Via Verde St (91724-3715)
PHONE...........................909 469-4733
Richard Alcedo, *Pr*
◆ **EMP:** 24 **EST:** 1990
SALES (est): 4.56MM
SALES (corp-wide): 4.56MM **Privately
Held**
Web: www.brightglowcandle.com
SIC: 3999 Candles

(P-11199)
**CAL AM MANUFACTURING CO
INC**
1939 Friendship Dr Ste E (92020-1138)
P.O. Box 819 (91944-0819)
PHONE...........................800 992-0499
W Sidney Aitken, *CEO*
EMP: 23 **EST:** 1979
SALES (est): 2.64MM **Privately Held**
Web: www.calam.net
SIC: 3999 Atomizers, toiletry

(P-11200)
CALIFORNIA EXOTIC NOVLT LLC
1455 E Francis St (91761-8329)
P.O. Box 50400 (91761-1078)
PHONE...........................909 606-1950
Susan Colvin, *Managing Member*
Jackie White, *
▲ **EMP:** 88 **EST:** 1994
SQ FT: 66,000
SALES (est): 9.47MM **Privately Held**
Web: www.calexotics.com
SIC: 3999 5947 Novelties, bric-a-brac, and
   hobby kits; Novelties

(P-11201)
**CAMBRO MANUFACTURING
COMPANY**
21558 Ferrero (91789-5216)
PHONE...........................909 354-8962
EMP: 104
SALES (corp-wide): 307.89MM **Privately
Held**
Web: www.cambro.com
SIC: 3999 Barber and beauty shop
   equipment
PA: Cambro Manufacturing Company Inc
   5801 Skylab Rd
   Huntington Beach CA
   714 848-1555

(P-11202)
CANNALOGIC
5404 Whitsett Ave # 219 (91607-1615)
PHONE...........................619 458-0775
Jasmine Savoy, *Pr*
EMP: 17 **EST:** 2017
SALES (est): 558.55K **Privately Held**
SIC: 3999 Manufacturing industries, nec

(P-11203)
CARBERRY LLC
3645 Long Beach Blvd (90807-4018)
PHONE.................................562 264-5078
EMP: 24
SALES (corp-wide): 4.32MM **Privately Held**
SIC: 3999 2064
; Chewing candy, not chewing gum
HQ: Carberry Llc
17130 Muskrat Ave Ste B
Adelanto CA
800 564-0842

(P-11204)
CARBERRY LLC (HQ)
Also Called: Plus Products
17130 Muskrat Ave Ste B (92301-2473)
PHONE.................................800 564-0842
EMP: 24 **EST:** 2017
SQ FT: 12,000
SALES (est): 4.32MM
SALES (corp-wide): 4.32MM **Privately Held**
SIC: 3999 2064
; Chewing candy, not chewing gum
PA: Plus Products Holdings Inc.
340 S Lemon Ave Ste 9392
Walnut CA
800 564-0842

(P-11205)
CBDSD INC
1844 Mission Rd (92029-1112)
PHONE.................................760 738-4200
Sandra Tierney, *Brnch Mgr*
EMP: 28
SALES (corp-wide): 147.81K **Privately Held**
SIC: 3999
PA: Cbdsd, Inc.
2054 Rorex Dr
Escondido CA

(P-11206)
CDM COMPANY INC
12 Corporate Plaza Dr Ste 200
(92660-7986)
PHONE.................................949 644-2820
Mitchella Jankins, *Pr*
▲ **EMP:** 23 **EST:** 1990
SQ FT: 7,000
SALES (est): 2.86MM **Privately Held**
Web: www.thecdmco.com
SIC: 3999 3944 8742 5112 Novelties, bric-a-brac, and hobby kits; Games, toys, and children's vehicles; Marketing consulting services; Pens and/or pencils

(P-11207)
CHRIS PUTRIMAS
1930 E Carson St Ste 102 (90810-1246)
PHONE.................................877 434-1666
Chris Putrimas, *Owner*
EMP: 50
SALES (est): 1.14MM **Privately Held**
SIC: 3999 Manufacturing industries, nec

(P-11208)
CJ FOODS MFG BEAUMONT CORP
415 Nicholas Rd (92223-2612)
PHONE.................................951 916-9300
Geon Il Lee, *CEO*
EMP: 25 **EST:** 2018
SALES (est): 4.94MM **Privately Held**
SIC: 3999 Chairs, hydraulic, barber and beauty shop
PA: Cj Cheiljedang Corporation
330 Dongho-Ro, Jung-Gu
Seoul

(P-11209)
CLAYBOURNE INDUSTRIES INC
5055 Western Way (92571-7420)
P.O. Box 2231 (92516-2231)
PHONE.................................951 675-4508
Nicholas Ortega, *Pr*
EMP: 24 **EST:** 2017
SALES (est): 903.17K **Privately Held**
Web: www.claybourneco.com
SIC: 3999

(P-11210)
COMMERCE ON DEMAND LLC
Also Called: Good Tree
7121 Telegraph Rd (90640-6511)
PHONE.................................562 360-4819
Rashaan Everett, *Managing Member*
EMP: 60 **EST:** 2020
SALES (est): 10MM **Privately Held**
SIC: 3999 Manufacturing industries, nec

(P-11211)
DEVELOPLUS INC
1575 Magnolia Ave (92879-2073)
PHONE.................................951 738-8595
▲ **EMP:** 140 **EST:** 1990
SQ FT: 40,000
SALES (est): 32.67MM **Privately Held**
Web: www.developlus.com
SIC: 3999 5087 Hair and hair-based products
; Beauty parlor equipment and supplies

(P-11212)
DMA ENTERPRISES INC (PA)
Also Called: Thermasol Steam Bath
2255 Union Pl (93065-1661)
PHONE.................................805 520-2468
▲ **EMP:** 18 **EST:** 1989
SALES (est): 5.27MM **Privately Held**
SIC: 3999 3431 Hot tubs; Bathroom fixtures, including sinks

(P-11213)
DO IT RIGHT PRODUCTS LLC
Also Called: DO IT RIGHT PRODUCTS LLC
1838 N Case St (92865-4233)
PHONE.................................714 998-8152
Elana Sherve, *Brnch Mgr*
EMP: 43
SALES (corp-wide): 2.29MM **Privately Held**
SIC: 3999 Models, general, except toy
PA: Do It Right Products, Llc
44321 62nd St W
Lancaster CA
661 722-9664

(P-11214)
EDWARDS LIFESCIENCES FING LLC
1 Edwards Way (92614-5688)
PHONE.................................949 250-3480
Mike Mussaollem, *Pr*
EMP: 36 **EST:** 2003
SALES (est): 2.38MM
SALES (corp-wide): 5.38B **Publicly Held**
Web: www.edwards.com
SIC: 3999 Advertising curtains
PA: Edwards Lifesciences Corp
1 Edwards Way
Irvine CA
949 250-2500

(P-11215)
FLAME AND WAX INC
Also Called: Voluspa
2900 Mccabe Way (92614-6239)
PHONE.................................949 752-4000
Troy C Arntsen, *CEO*
Troy C Arntsen, *CEO*
Traci Arntsen, *
▲ **EMP:** 134 **EST:** 2001
SALES (est): 18.59MM **Privately Held**
Web: www.voluspa.com
SIC: 3999 2844 Candles; Perfumes, cosmetics and other toilet preparations

(P-11216)
FORRESTER EASTLAND CORPORATION
Also Called: Versa Stage
1320 Storm Pkwy (90501-5041)
PHONE.................................310 784-2464
Clive Forrester, *CEO*
Erik Eastland, *
EMP: 36 **EST:** 1991
SQ FT: 17,900
SALES (est): 2.47MM **Privately Held**
SIC: 3999 7819 Stage hardware and equipment, except lighting; Equipment and prop rental, motion picture production

(P-11217)
FOUNTAINHEAD INDUSTRIES
700 N San Vicente Blvd Ste G410
(90069-5060)
PHONE.................................310 248-2444
Hal Kline, *Pr*
EMP: 20 **EST:** 2005
SALES (est): 1.13MM **Privately Held**
SIC: 3999 Chairs, hydraulic, barber and beauty shop

(P-11218)
FRINGE STUDIO LLC
17909 Fitch (92614-6016)
P.O. Box 3663 (90231-3663)
PHONE.................................310 390-9900
Scott Kingsland, *Managing Member*
▲ **EMP:** 30 **EST:** 2004
SALES (est): 5.22MM **Privately Held**
Web: www.fringestudio.com
SIC: 3999 2621 Pet supplies; Stationary, envelope and tablet papers
PA: Punch Studio, Llc
6025 W Slauson Ave
Culver City CA

(P-11219)
GENERAL WAX CO INC (PA)
Also Called: General Wax & Candle Co
6863 Beck Ave (91605-6206)
P.O. Box 9398 (91609-1398)
PHONE.................................818 765-5800
Carol Lazar, *CEO*
Mike Tapp, *
Colton Lazar, *
Keith Tapp, *
J C Edmond, *
◆ **EMP:** 85 **EST:** 1949
SQ FT: 120,000
SALES (est): 11.31MM
SALES (corp-wide): 11.31MM **Privately Held**
Web: www.generalwax.com
SIC: 3999 Candles

(P-11220)
GLOBAL UXE INC
Also Called: Aquiesse
405 Science Dr (93021-2247)
PHONE.................................805 583-4600
▲ **EMP:** 20 **EST:** 2011
SALES (est): 1.09MM **Privately Held**
SIC: 3999 Candles

(P-11221)
GLOBALUXE INC
Also Called: Candle Crafters
405 Science Dr (93021-2093)
PHONE.................................805 583-4600
Michael Joseph Horn, *CEO*
▲ **EMP:** 20 **EST:** 2003
SALES (est): 2.43MM **Privately Held**
Web: www.aquiesse.com
SIC: 3999 5199 5999 Candles; Candles; Candle shops

(P-11222)
GOLDEN SUPREME INC
12304 Mccann Dr (90670-3333)
PHONE.................................562 903-1063
Ross Stillwagon, *Pr*
Fernando Fischbach, *
Ricardo J Fischbach, *
▲ **EMP:** 30 **EST:** 1990
SQ FT: 13,000
SALES (est): 2.14MM **Privately Held**
Web: www.goldensupreme.com
SIC: 3999 5087 Hair curlers, designed for beauty parlors; Beauty parlor equipment and supplies

(P-11223)
GUZZLER MANUFACTURING INC
1510 Hayes Ave (90813-1126)
PHONE.................................562 436-0250
Mark Brockman, *Mgr*
EMP: 45
SALES (corp-wide): 1.43B **Publicly Held**
Web: www.fssolutionsgroup.com
SIC: 3999 Atomizers, toiletry
HQ: Guzzler Manufacturing, Inc.
8584 Borden Ave
Leeds AL

(P-11224)
H & H SPECIALTIES INC
14850 Don Julian Rd Ste B (91746-3122)
PHONE.................................626 575-0776
Reid Neslage, *Owner*
Mary Louise Higgins, *
EMP: 31 **EST:** 1967
SQ FT: 30,000
SALES (est): 4.81MM **Privately Held**
Web: www.hhspecialties.com
SIC: 3999 3625 Stage hardware and equipment, except lighting; Relays and industrial controls

(P-11225)
HALONUS INC
6855 E Swarthmore Dr (92807-5118)
PHONE.................................714 345-0822
Steve Newhouse, *CEO*
EMP: 336 **EST:** 2018
SALES (est): 707.36K **Privately Held**
SIC: 3999 5099 5999 Fire extinguishers, portable; Fire extinguishers; Fire extinguishers
HQ: A-Gas Us Inc.
1100 Haskins Rd
Bowling Green OH
800 372-1301

(P-11226)
HEXODEN HOLDINGS INC (PA)
1219 Linda Vista Dr (92078-3809)
PHONE.................................858 201-3412
Donna Razzoli, *Pr*
EMP: 89 **EST:** 2017
SALES (est): 2.55MM
SALES (corp-wide): 2.55MM **Privately Held**

SIC: **3999** Manufacturing industries, nec

(P-11227)
HOLIDAY FOLIAGE INC
Also Called: Holiday Foliage
2592 Otay Center Dr (92154-7611)
PHONE..................619 661-9094
Kristine Vanzutphen, *CEO*
Juanita Keller, *VP*
William Vanzutphen Junior, *CFO*
▲ **EMP:** 38 **EST:** 1994
SQ FT: 18,000
SALES (est): 9.46MM **Privately Held**
Web: www.holidayfoliage.com
SIC: **3999** Artificial trees and flowers

(P-11228)
HUNTINGTON INGALLS INDUSTRIES
9444 Balboa Ave Ste 400 (92123-4378)
PHONE..................858 522-6000
EMP: 24 **EST:** 2011
SALES (est): 2.43MM **Privately Held**
Web: www.hii.com
SIC: **3999** Manufacturing industries, nec

(P-11229)
ICON LINE INC
Also Called: I.C.O.N. Salon
20600 Ventura Blvd Ste C (91364-6691)
PHONE..................818 709-4266
Chiara Scudieri, *Pr*
▲ **EMP:** 18 **EST:** 2001
SQ FT: 1,800
SALES (est): 1.27MM **Privately Held**
Web: www.iconproducts.com
SIC: **3999** **5999** Hair, dressing of, for the trade; Hair care products

(P-11230)
INNOVATIVE CASEWORK MFG INC
12261 Industry St (92841-2815)
PHONE..................714 890-9100
Valerie Perez, *Prin*
EMP: 25 **EST:** 2017
SALES (est): 1.03MM **Privately Held**
SIC: **3999** Manufacturing industries, nec

(P-11231)
INTEGRATED MFG SOLUTIONS LLC
2590 Pioneer Ave Ste C (92081-8427)
PHONE..................760 599-4300
Baophuong Nguyen, *Pr*
EMP: 24 **EST:** 2007
SQ FT: 2,000
SALES (est): 1.61MM **Privately Held**
Web: www.integratedmfg.net
SIC: **3999** Chairs, hydraulic, barber and beauty shop

(P-11232)
INTERSTATE CABINET INC
Also Called: Interstate Design Industry
1631 Pomona Rd Ste B (92874-4327)
PHONE..................951 736-0777
James L Fago, *Pr*
Nancy Fago-fleer, *Sec*
▲ **EMP:** 20 **EST:** 1975
SQ FT: 56,000
SALES (est): 438.05K **Privately Held**
Web: interstatecabinet.openfos.com
SIC: **3999** Barber and beauty shop equipment

(P-11233)
JACUZZI BRANDS LLC
Also Called: Sundance Spas
14525 Monte Vista Ave (91710-5721)
P.O. Box 2900 (91708-2900)
PHONE..................909 606-1416
Diana Fox, *Mgr*
EMP: 47
SALES (corp-wide): 423.13K **Privately Held**
Web: www.jacuzzi.com
SIC: **3999** Hot tubs
HQ: Jacuzzi Brands Llc
17872 Gillette Ave # 300
Irvine CA
909 606-1416

(P-11234)
JOE BLASCO ENTERPRISES INC
Also Called: Joe Blasco Cosmetics
1285 N Valdivia Way # A (92262-5428)
PHONE..................323 467-4949
Joseph D Blasco, *Pr*
▲ **EMP:** 43 **EST:** 1986
SQ FT: 13,788
SALES (est): 690.4K
SALES (corp-wide): 2.21MM **Privately Held**
Web: www.joeblasco.com
SIC: **3999** **7231** **2844** Barber and beauty shop equipment; Cosmetology school; Perfumes, cosmetics and other toilet preparations
PA: Joe Blasco Make-Up Center West, Inc.
1285 N Valdivia Way A
Palm Springs CA
323 467-4949

(P-11235)
JORGE ULLOA
Also Called: Jem Unlimited Iron
3162 E La Palma Ave Ste F (92806-2810)
PHONE..................714 630-0499
Martha Ulloa, *Pr*
EMP: 18 **EST:** 2002
SQ FT: 4,000
SALES (est): 1.19MM **Privately Held**
SIC: **3999** Lawn ornaments

(P-11236)
K31 ROAD ENGINEERING LLC
Also Called: K31
1968 S Coast Hwy Pmb 593 (92651-3681)
PHONE..................305 928-1968
Rainer Piel, *CEO*
EMP: 35 **EST:** 2014
SALES (est): 1.43MM **Privately Held**
Web: www.k31.org
SIC: **3999** **5039** Manufacturing industries, nec; Construction materials, nec

(P-11237)
KAIROS MANUFACTURING INC
Also Called: Architectural Iron Works
201 Bridge St (93401-5510)
PHONE..................805 544-2216
EMP: 17 **EST:** 2017
SALES (est): 882.83K **Privately Held**
SIC: **3999** Manufacturing industries, nec

(P-11238)
KURZ TRANSFER PRODUCTS LP
415 N Smith Ave (92878-4305)
PHONE..................951 738-9521
Hastings Kurz, *Prin*
EMP: 71
SALES (corp-wide): 1.02B **Privately Held**

Web: www.kurzusa.com
SIC: **3999** Atomizers, toiletry
HQ: Kurz Transfer Products, Lp
11836 Patterson Rd
Huntersville NC
704 927-3700

(P-11239)
L A HQ INC
5363 Wilshire Blvd (90036-4213)
PHONE..................310 880-7433
Amiel Fonkou, *CEO*
EMP: 20 **EST:** 2018
SALES (est): 1.3MM **Privately Held**
SIC: **3999** Hair and hair-based products

(P-11240)
LA SPAS INC
1325 N Blue Gum St (92806-1750)
PHONE..................714 630-1150
▲ **EMP:** 130
Web: www.maaxspas.com
SIC: **3999** **5091** Hot tubs; Fitness equipment and supplies

(P-11241)
LDI OPERATIONS LLC
450 N Brand Blvd Ste 900 (91203-2397)
PHONE..................818 240-7500
Brendan Mcloughlin, *CMO*
Lon Osmond, *Executive Editor**
▲ **EMP:** 120 **EST:** 1954
SQ FT: 35,000
SALES (est): 758.35K
SALES (corp-wide): 5.4B **Privately Held**
SIC: **3999** Education aids, devices and supplies
HQ: Wolters Kluwer Health, Inc.
2001 Market St Ste 5
Philadelphia PA
215 521-8300

(P-11242)
LEARNING RESOURCES INC
Also Called: Educational Insights
19700 S Vermont Ave (90502-1100)
PHONE..................800 995-4436
EMP: 20
SALES (corp-wide): 27.82MM **Privately Held**
Web: www.rappahannock.edu
SIC: **3999** **3944** Education aids, devices and supplies; Games, toys, and children's vehicles
PA: Learning Resources, Inc.
380 N Fairway Dr
Vernon Hills IL
800 333-8281

(P-11243)
LEOBEN COMPANY
16692 Burke Ln (92647-4536)
PHONE..................951 284-9653
Samir Tabikha, *Pr*
EMP: 26 **EST:** 2017
SALES (est): 2.88MM **Privately Held**
SIC: **3999** Barber and beauty shop equipment

(P-11244)
LEXOR INC
7400 Hazard Ave (92683-5031)
PHONE..................714 444-4144
Marianna Magos, *CEO*
Christopher L Long, *
▲ **EMP:** 90 **EST:** 2007
SALES (est): 15.54MM **Privately Held**
Web: www.lexor.com
SIC: **3999** Chairs, hydraulic, barber and beauty shop

(P-11245)
LOTUS AND LUNA
5780 Chesapeake Ct Ste 5 (92123-1030)
PHONE..................805 216-4451
Jannel Sisting, *Pr*
EMP: 28 **EST:** 2017
SALES (est): 4.17MM **Privately Held**
Web: www.lotusandluna.com
SIC: **3999** Manufacturing industries, nec

(P-11246)
MACRO INDUSTRIES INC
14178 Albers Way (91710-6938)
PHONE..................909 606-2218
Eric Zhang, *Prin*
EMP: 17 **EST:** 2019
SALES (est): 956.21K **Privately Held**
Web: www.macroindustries.com
SIC: **3999** Manufacturing industries, nec

(P-11247)
MACS LIFT GATE INC (PA)
2801 E South St (90805-3736)
PHONE..................562 529-3465
Michael Macdonald, *CEO*
Richard Mac Donald, *
Lawrence Mac Donald, *
Gerald J Donald Mac, *VP*
EMP: 24 **EST:** 1957
SALES (est): 3.65MM
SALES (corp-wide): 3.65MM **Privately Held**
Web: www.macsliftgate.com
SIC: **3999** **5013** Wheelchair lifts; Motor vehicle supplies and new parts

(P-11248)
MANUFACTURED SOLUTIONS LLC
9601 Janice Cir (92861-2705)
PHONE..................714 548-6915
Marcela Cortes, *Pr*
EMP: 40 **EST:** 2020
SALES (est): 1.73MM **Privately Held**
SIC: **3999** **3444** Manufacturing industries, nec; Sheet metalwork

(P-11249)
MARCH PRODUCTS INC
Also Called: Astella
4645 Troy Ct (92509-2003)
PHONE..................909 622-4800
Yungcheng Ma, *Pr*
◆ **EMP:** 72 **EST:** 2001
SQ FT: 70,000
SALES (est): 17.5MM **Privately Held**
Web: www.californiaumbrella.com
SIC: **3999** **2211** Umbrellas, garden or wagon ; Umbrella cloth, cotton

(P-11250)
MEDICAL BRKTHRUGH MSSAGE CHIRS
24971 Avenue Stanford (91355-1278)
PHONE..................408 677-7702
Max Lun, *CEO*
EMP: 24 **EST:** 2016
SALES (est): 4.61MM **Privately Held**
Web: www.medicalbreakthrough.org
SIC: **3999** Massage machines, electric: barber and beauty shops

(P-11251)
MERCADO LATINO INC
Continental Candle Company
1420 W Walnut St (90220-5013)
PHONE..................310 537-1062
EMP: 72
SALES (corp-wide): 87.08MM **Privately Held**

Web: www.continentalcandle.com
SIC: **3999** 3641 7699 3645 Candles; Electric lamps; Restaurant equipment repair; Residential lighting fixtures
PA: Mercado Latino, Inc.
  245 Baldwin Park Blvd
  City Of Industry CA
  626 333-6862

(P-11252)
MGR DESIGN INTERNATIONAL INC
1950 Williams Dr (93036-2630)
PHONE.................................805 981-6400
Rony Haviv, *CEO*
◆ **EMP: 200 EST:** 2001
SQ FT: 80,000
SALES (est): 24.82MM **Privately Held**
Web: www.mgrdesign.com
SIC: **3999** Potpourri

(P-11253)
NANO FILTER INC
22310 Bonita St (90745-4103)
PHONE.................................949 316-8866
Bennett Koo, *Pr*
EMP: 60 **EST:** 2020
SALES (est): 4.57MM **Privately Held**
SIC: **3999** Manufacturing industries, nec

(P-11254)
NATUREMAKER INC
6225 El Camino Real (92009-1604)
PHONE.................................760 438-4244
Gary Hanick, *Pr*
Bennett Abrams, *
EMP: 30 **EST:** 1979
SQ FT: 40,000
SALES (est): 2.62MM **Privately Held**
Web: www.naturemaker.com
SIC: **3999** Artificial trees and flowers

(P-11255)
NEIGHBRHOOD BUS ADVRTSMENT LTD ✪
14752 Crenshaw Blvd (90249-3602)
PHONE.................................442 300-1803
EMP: 26 **EST:** 2022
SALES (est): 1.05MM **Privately Held**
SIC: **3999** Advertising display products

(P-11256)
NEW DIMENSION ONE SPAS INC (DH)
1819 Aston Ave Ste 105 (92008-7338)
P.O. Box 2600 (92051-2600)
PHONE.................................800 345-7727
Robert Hallam, *Pr*
Linda Hallam, *
Chris Theriot, *CIO**
Phil Sandner, *PROC**
Terry Hauser, *
◆ **EMP: 160 EST:** 1977
SQ FT: 125,000
SALES (est): 35.24MM
SALES (corp-wide): 423.13K **Privately Held**
Web: www.d1spas.com
SIC: **3999** 3088 Hot tubs; Plastics plumbing fixtures
HQ: Jacuzzi Brands Llc
  17872 Gillette Ave # 300
  Irvine CA
  909 606-1416

(P-11257)
NORLAINE INC
Also Called: Patina V
1449 W Industrial Park St (91722-3414)

PHONE.................................626 961-2471
◆ **EMP:** 200
Web: www.cnlmannequins.com
SIC: **3999** Mannequins

(P-11258)
OMD REMANUFACTURING INC
4395 E Olympic Blvd (90023-4140)
PHONE.................................213 220-3851
Delmy Y Lopez, *Brnch Mgr*
EMP: 21
SALES (corp-wide): 114.91K **Privately Held**
SIC: **3999** Barber and beauty shop equipment
PA: Omd Remanufacturing, Inc.
  2405 Linn Ave Ste B
  El Monte CA

(P-11259)
ORIGIN LLC
119 E Graham Pl (91502-2028)
PHONE.................................818 848-1648
▲ **EMP:** 35
SIC: **3999** Advertising display products

(P-11260)
PACIFICA BEAUTY LLC
Also Called: Pacifica International
1090 Eugenia Pl Ste 200 (93013-2011)
PHONE.................................844 332-8440
Nathalie Kristo, *
▲ **EMP: 100 EST:** 1997
SQ FT: 58,000
SALES (est): 15.24MM **Privately Held**
Web: www.pacificabeauty.com
SIC: **3999** 2844 Candles; Perfumes, cosmetics and other toilet preparations

(P-11261)
PACMIN INCORPORATED (PA)
Also Called: Pacific Miniatures
2021 Raymer Ave (92833-2664)
PHONE.................................714 447-4478
Frederick Ouweleen Junior, *Pr*
Flora Ouweleen, *
Daniel Ouweleen, *
▲ **EMP: 96 EST:** 1981
SQ FT: 35,400
SALES (est): 9.9MM
SALES (corp-wide): 9.9MM **Privately Held**
Web: www.pacmin.com
SIC: **3999** Models, general, except toy

(P-11262)
PAUL FERRANTE INC
Also Called: Ferrante Paul Cstm Lmps & Shds
8464 Melrose Pl (90069-5308)
PHONE.................................310 854-4412
Thomas Raynor, *Pr*
▲ **EMP: 40 EST:** 1962
SQ FT: 2,000
SALES (est): 4.78MM **Privately Held**
Web: www.paulferrante.com
SIC: **3999** 5099 3645 Shades, lamp or candle; Antiques; Residential lighting fixtures

(P-11263)
PCI INDUSTRIES INC
700 S Vail Ave (90640-4954)
PHONE.................................323 889-6770
Jack Scilley, *Owner*
EMP: 27
SALES (corp-wide): 46.63MM **Privately Held**
Web: www.pottorff.com
SIC: **3999** Atomizers, toiletry
PA: Pci Industries, Inc.
  5101 Blue Mound Rd

Fort Worth TX
817 509-2300

(P-11264)
PCI INDUSTRIES INC
6490 Fleet St (90040-1710)
PHONE.................................323 728-0004
Jim Turner, *Mgr*
EMP: 27
SALES (corp-wide): 46.63MM **Privately Held**
Web: www.pottorff.com
SIC: **3999** Atomizers, toiletry
PA: Pci Industries, Inc.
  5101 Blue Mound Rd
  Fort Worth TX
  817 509-2300

(P-11265)
PERFECT CHOICE MFRS INC
Also Called: West Coast Metal Stamping
17819 Gillette Ave (92614-6501)
PHONE.................................714 792-0322
Kevin Price, *CEO*
EMP: 42 EST: 2021
SALES (est): 2.49MM **Privately Held**
SIC: **3999** Manufacturing industries, nec

(P-11266)
PET PARTNERS INC (PA)
Also Called: North American Pet Products
450 N Sheridan St (92878-4020)
PHONE.................................951 279-9888
▲ **EMP: 170 EST:** 1995
SQ FT: 120,000
SALES (est): 24.86MM **Privately Held**
Web: www.petpartners.org
SIC: **3999** Pet supplies

(P-11267)
PF CANDLE CO
2213 W Sunset Blvd (90026-3053)
PHONE.................................323 284-8431
EMP: 26 EST: 2018
SALES (est): 520.77K **Privately Held**
Web: www.pfcandleco.com
SIC: **3999** Candles

(P-11268)
PHIARO INCORPORATED
9016 Research Dr (92618-4215)
PHONE.................................949 727-1261
Takeichiro Iwasaki, *Pr*
▲ **EMP: 32 EST:** 1988
SQ FT: 35,000
SALES (est): 7.97MM **Privately Held**
Web: www.phiaro.jp
SIC: **3999** Models, general, except toy
PA: Phiaro Corporation, Inc.
  8-2-3, Nobitome
  Niiza STM

(P-11269)
PICNIC TIME INC
Also Called: Beach State
5131 Maureen Ln (93021-1783)
PHONE.................................805 529-7400
Gustavo Cosaro, *CEO*
◆ **EMP: 77 EST:** 1982
SQ FT: 20,000
SALES (est): 23.12MM **Privately Held**
Web: www.picnictime.com
SIC: **3999** 5199 Handles, handbag and luggage; Bags, baskets, and cases

(P-11270)
PLUS CBD LLC
591 Camino De La Reina Ste 1200 (92108)
PHONE.................................855 758-7223

EMP: 25 EST: 2015
SALES (est): 463.73K
SALES (corp-wide): 16.2MM **Privately Held**
Web: www.pluscbdoil.com
SIC: **3999**
PA: Cv Sciences, Inc.
  9530 Padgett St Ste 107
  San Diego CA
  866 290-2157

(P-11271)
POMMES FRITES CANDLE CO
Also Called: Pf Candle Co
7300 E Slauson Ave (90040-3627)
PHONE.................................213 488-2016
Kristen Pumphrey, *CEO*
Thomas Neuberger, *
EMP: 30 EST: 2014
SALES (est): 4.62MM **Privately Held**
Web: www.pfcandleco.com
SIC: **3999** 5149 5199 5999 Candles; Flavorings and fragrances; Candles; Candle shops

(P-11272)
PRESERVED TREESCAPES INTERNATIONAL INC
Also Called: Preserved Treescapes Intl
180 Vallecitos De Oro (92069-1435)
PHONE.................................760 631-6789
◆ **EMP:** 75
Web: www.treescapes.com
SIC: **3999** Artificial trees and flowers

(P-11273)
QUALITY RESOURCES DIST LLC
16254 Beaver Rd (92301-3906)
PHONE.................................510 378-6861
Wesley Staley, *Managing Member*
EMP: 21 EST: 2018
SALES (est): 993.41K **Privately Held**
SIC: **3999**

(P-11274)
REAPS COMPANY LLC
Also Called: Caravan Distribution
1950 S Santa Fe Ave (90021-2935)
PHONE.................................212 256-1186
Michael Hurt, *Owner*
EMP: 21 EST: 2015
SALES (est): 1.5MM **Privately Held**
SIC: **3999**

(P-11275)
REEL EFX INC
5539 Riverton Ave (91601-2816)
PHONE.................................818 762-1710
Jim Gill, *Pr*
Susan Gill, *
Rosy Romano, *
Susan Milliken, *
EMP: 25 EST: 1982
SQ FT: 34,000
SALES (est): 2.71MM **Privately Held**
Web: www.reelefx.com
SIC: **3999** Stage hardware and equipment, except lighting

(P-11276)
RICON CORP
1135 Aviation Pl (91340-1460)
PHONE.................................818 267-3000
William Baldwin, *Pr*
Raymond T Betler, *
Jason Moore, *
◆ **EMP: 135 EST:** 1971
SQ FT: 225,000
SALES (est): 28.66MM **Publicly Held**
Web: www.riconcorp.com

SIC: 3999 Wheelchair lifts
PA: Westinghouse Air Brake Technologies
Corporation
30 Isabella St
Pittsburgh PA

(P-11277)
RUCCI INC
6700 11th Ave (90043-4730)
PHONE...............................323 778-9000
Ramin Lavian, *Pr*
Elsie Lavian, *VP*
▲ **EMP:** 20 **EST:** 1990
SQ FT: 17,000
SALES (est): 531.42K **Privately Held**
Web: www.juliasbeauty.com
SIC: 3999 5087 Barber and beauty shop
equipment; Beauty parlor equipment and
supplies

(P-11278)
SCRIPTO-TOKAI CORPORATION
(HQ)
2055 S Haven Ave (91761-0736)
PHONE...............................909 930-5000
Tomoyuki Kurata, *Pr*
Tokiharu Murofushi, *
Fred Ashley, *
▲ **EMP:** 80 **EST:** 1923
SQ FT: 120,000
SALES (est): 10.45MM **Privately Held**
Web: www.calicobrands.com
SIC: 3999 3951 Cigarette lighters, except
precious metal; Ball point pens and parts
PA: Tokai Corporation
6-21-1, Nishishinjuku
Shinjuku-Ku TKY

(P-11279)
SEGA HOLDINGS USA INC
9737 Lurline Ave (91311-4404)
PHONE...............................415 701-6000
◆ **EMP:** 1880
SIC: 3999 5045 Coin-operated amusement
machines; Computers and accessories,
personal and home entertainment

(P-11280)
SGPS INC
Also Called: Show Group Production Services
15823 S Main St (90248-2548)
PHONE...............................310 538-4175
Barrie Owen, *CEO*
Katy Marx, *
EMP: 85 **EST:** 1991
SQ FT: 40,000
SALES (est): 11.56MM **Privately Held**
Web: www.sgpsshowrig.com
SIC: 3999 Theatrical scenery

(P-11281)
SHAPELL INDUSTRIES
1990 S Bundy Dr Ste 500 (90025-5245)
PHONE...............................323 655-7330
EMP: 45 **EST:** 2018
SALES (est): 929.32K **Privately Held**
SIC: 3999 Manufacturing industries, nec

(P-11282)
SILVESTRI STUDIO INC (PA)
Also Called: Silvester California
8125 Beach St (90001-3426)
P.O. Box 512198 (90051-0198)
PHONE...............................323 277-4420
E Alain Levi, *CEO*
▲ **EMP:** 80 **EST:** 1934
SQ FT: 130,000
SALES (est): 9.73MM
SALES (corp-wide): 9.73MM **Privately**
Held

Web: www.silvestricalifornia.com
SIC: 3999 2542 3993 Mannequins; Office
and store showcases and display fixtures;
Signs and advertising specialties

(P-11283)
SOFTUB INC (PA)
24700 Avenue Rockefeller (91355-3465)
PHONE...............................858 602-1920
Liberte Chan, *CEO*
Tom Thornbury, *
▲ **EMP:** 85 **EST:** 1983
SALES (est): 22.38MM
SALES (corp-wide): 22.38MM **Privately**
Held
Web: www.softub.com
SIC: 3999 Hot tubs

(P-11284)
SPARKS EXHBITS
ENVRNMENTS CORP
Also Called: Sparks Los Angeles
3143 S La Cienega Blvd (90016-3110)
PHONE...............................562 941-0101
EMP: 84
SALES (corp-wide): 1.56B **Privately Held**
Web: www.wearesparks.com
SIC: 3999 Advertising display products
HQ: Sparks Exhibits & Environments Pa Llc
2828 Charter Rd
Philadelphia PA
215 676-1100

(P-11285)
STANG INDUSTRIES INC
Also Called: Stang Industrial Products
8778 Kimball Ave (91708-9613)
PHONE...............................914 479-9810
Charles Ronie, *CEO*
Abdul Kashif, *CFO*
◆ **EMP:** 19 **EST:** 1943
SALES (est): 5.67MM **Privately Held**
Web: www.stangindustries.com
SIC: 3999 3492 3561 Fire extinguishers,
portable; Control valves, aircraft: hydraulic
and pneumatic; Pumps and pumping
equipment

(P-11286)
STEELDECK INC
13147 S Western Ave (90249-1921)
PHONE...............................323 290-2100
Phil Parsons, *Pr*
Adrian Funnell, *
▲ **EMP:** 25 **EST:** 1993
SALES (est): 4.03MM **Privately Held**
Web: www.steeldeck.com
SIC: 3999 2541 2531 Stage hardware and
equipment, except lighting; Partitions for
floor attachment, prefabricated: wood;
Theater furniture

(P-11287)
SUN BADGE CO
2248 S Baker Ave (91761-7710)
PHONE...............................909 930-1444
Rick Hamilton, *Pr*
Chris Hamilton, *
▲ **EMP:** 35 **EST:** 1957
SQ FT: 24,000
SALES (est): 3.53MM **Privately Held**
Web: www.sunbadgeorders.com
SIC: 3999 Badges, metal: policemen,
firemen, etc.

(P-11288)
SUNDANCE SPAS INC (DH)
Also Called: Sundance Spas
17872 Gillette Ave Ste 300 (92614-6573)
PHONE...............................909 606-7733

David Jackson, *CEO*
Rich Strong, *
◆ **EMP:** 31 **EST:** 1998
SALES (est): 38.04MM
SALES (corp-wide): 423.13K **Privately**
Held
Web: www.sundancespas.com
SIC: 3999 1799 5999 Hot tubs; Swimming
pool construction; Spas and hot tubs
HQ: Jacuzzi Brands Llc
17872 Gillette Ave # 300
Irvine CA
909 606-1416

(P-11289)
SUNDERSTORM LLC
1146 N Central Ave (91202-2506)
PHONE...............................818 605-6682
Cameron Clark, *CEO*
Keith Cich, *Pr*
EMP: 17 **EST:** 2015
SALES (est): 1.38MM **Privately Held**
Web: www.sunderstorm.com
SIC: 3999

(P-11290)
SUNSTAR SPA COVERS INC
(HQ)
26074 Avenue Hall Ste 13 (91355-1240)
PHONE...............................858 602-1950
Tom Thornbury, *Ch Bd*
Edward Mcgarry, *Pr*
▲ **EMP:** 40 **EST:** 2000
SALES (est): 9.61MM
SALES (corp-wide): 22.38MM **Privately**
Held
SIC: 3999 Hot tub and spa covers
PA: Softub, Inc.
24700 Avenue Rockefeller
Valencia CA
858 602-1920

(P-11291)
SUPERIOR-STUDIO SPC INC
2239 Yates Ave (90040-1913)
PHONE...............................323 278-0100
TOLL FREE: 800
Jean-pierre Fournier, *Pr*
◆ **EMP:** 20 **EST:** 1995
SQ FT: 60,000
SALES (est): 2.06MM **Privately Held**
Web: www.studiospecialties.ca
SIC: 3999 Advertising display products

(P-11292)
TAG TOYS INC
1810 S Acacia Ave (90220-4927)
PHONE...............................310 639-4566
Lawrence Mestyanek, *CEO*
Judy Mestyanek, *
EMP: 65 **EST:** 1976
SQ FT: 60,000
SALES (est): 4.65MM **Privately Held**
Web: www.tagtoys.com
SIC: 3999 8351 3944 Education aids,
devices and supplies; Child day care
services; Games, toys, and children's
vehicles

(P-11293)
TANDEM DESIGN INC
Also Called: Tandem Exhibit
1846 W Sequoia Ave (92868-1018)
PHONE...............................714 978-7272
Maury Bonas, *Pr*
Susan Bonas, *VP*
EMP: 23 **EST:** 1975
SQ FT: 20,000
SALES (est): 1.41MM **Privately Held**
Web: www.tandemexhibits.com

SIC: 3999 Preparation of slides and exhibits

(P-11294)
TAOTAO MANUFACTURER INC
9073 Arcadia Ave (91775-1401)
PHONE...............................626 688-9880
Paul Tao, *Brnch Mgr*
EMP: 19
SALES (corp-wide): 172K **Privately Held**
Web: www.taotaomanufacturer.com
SIC: 3999 Barber and beauty shop
equipment
PA: Taotao Manufacturer, Inc.
9833 Garibaldi Ave
Temple City CA
626 688-9880

(P-11295)
TECHNICAL MANUFACTURING
W LLC
24820 Avenue Tibbitts (91355-3404)
PHONE...............................661 295-7226
EMP: 29 **EST:** 2010
SALES (est): 5.23MM **Privately Held**
Web: www.tmwmedical.com
SIC: 3999 Barber and beauty shop
equipment

(P-11296)
TOM LEONARD INVESTMENT
CO INC
Also Called: Peak Seasons
7240 Sycamore Canyon Blvd (92508-2331)
PHONE...............................951 351-7778
Tom Leonard, *CEO*
Greg Szuba, *
Arlene Leonard, *
▲ **EMP:** 24 **EST:** 1992
SQ FT: 35,000
SALES (est): 873.35K **Privately Held**
Web: www.peakseasons.store
SIC: 3999 3399 Christmas tree ornaments,
except electrical and glass; Paste, metal

(P-11297)
TOPLINE MANUFACTURING INC
7032 Alondra Blvd (90723-3926)
PHONE...............................562 633-0605
Byungs Chae, *CEO*
EMP: 17 **EST:** 2020
SALES (est): 994.38K **Privately Held**
SIC: 3999 Manufacturing industries, nec

(P-11298)
TRAXX CORPORATION
1201 E Lexington Ave (91766-5520)
PHONE...............................909 623-8032
Craig Silvers, *CEO*
Jon Hall, *
▲ **EMP:** 100 **EST:** 2007
SQ FT: 52,000
SALES (est): 17.47MM **Privately Held**
Web: www.traxxcorp.com
SIC: 3999 Carpet tackles

(P-11299)
TRE MILANO LLC
Also Called: Instyler
2730 Monterey St Ste 101 (90503-7206)
PHONE...............................310 260-8888
▲ **EMP:** 21 **EST:** 2007
SALES (est): 4.17MM **Privately Held**
Web: www.instyler.com
SIC: 3999 Hair and hair-based products

(P-11300)
TRNLWB LLC
Also Called: Trinity Lighweight
17410 Lockwood Valley Rd (93225-9318)

PRODUCTS & SVCS

PHONE..............................661 245-3736
EMP: 4900
SALES (corp-wide): 86.82MM Privately Held
Web: www.trinityesc.com
SIC: 3999 Barber and beauty shop equipment
PA: Trnlwb, Llc
1112 E Cpeland Rd Ste 500
Arlington TX
800 581-3117

(P-11301)
TTT INNOVATIONS LLC
Also Called: TTT Innovations
20850 Plummer St (91311-5004)
P.O. Box 86 (91365-0086)
PHONE..............................818 201-8828
Thomas Bruggemann, CEO
EMP: 20 EST: 2016
SALES (est): 1.59MM Privately Held
Web: www.tomstumbletrimmer.com
SIC: 3999 Atomizers, toiletry

(P-11302)
VAL USA MANUFACTURER INC
1050 W Central Ave Ste A (92821-2200)
PHONE..............................626 839-8069
Lijuan Zhen, Mgr
▲ EMP: 30 EST: 2014
SALES (est): 1.84MM Privately Held
SIC: 3999 Manufacturing industries, nec

(P-11303)
VBX LABS LLC
9631 Topanga Canyon Pl (91311-4118)
PHONE..............................747 256-0103
Claudia Lopez, Prin
EMP: 23 EST: 2017
SALES (est): 492.99K Privately Held
Web: www.vbxlabs.com
SIC: 3999

(P-11304)
VITAVET LABS INC
Also Called: Nuvet Labs
5717 Corsa Ave (91362-4001)
PHONE..............................818 865-2600
Blake Kirschbaum, Pr
Doctor Raymond Kirschbaum, CFO
▼ EMP: 20 EST: 1997
SALES (est): 2.73MM Privately Held
Web: www.nuvet.com
SIC: 3999 Pet supplies

(P-11305)
WALLY & PAT ENTERPRISES
Also Called: Complete Aquatic Systems
13530 S Budlong Ave (90247-2030)
PHONE..............................310 532-2031
Shareen King, Pr
EMP: 48 EST: 2000
SALES (est): 4.72MM Privately Held
SIC: 3999 Barber and beauty shop equipment

(P-11306)
WATKINS MANUFACTURING CORP (HQ)
Also Called: Watkins Wellness
1280 Park Center Dr (92081-8398)
PHONE..............................760 598-6464
Vijaikrishna Teenarsipur, CEO
Christopher Peavey, *
◆ EMP: 127 EST: 1977
SQ FT: 430,000
SALES (est): 164.33MM
SALES (corp-wide): 8.68B Publicly Held
Web: jobs.masco.com
SIC: 3999 Hot tubs

PA: Masco Corporation
17450 College Pkwy
Livonia MI
313 274-7400

(P-11307)
WBT GROUP LLC
Also Called: Wbt Industries
1401 S Shamrock Ave (91016-4246)
PHONE..............................323 735-1201
▲ EMP: 40 EST: 2009
SALES (est): 4.44MM Privately Held
Web: www.wbtindustries.com
SIC: 3999 Buttons: Red Cross, union, identification

(P-11308)
WHITLOCK INDUSTRIES INC
Also Called: Whitlock Surfboards
609 Mission Ave (92054-2831)
PHONE..............................760 231-9262
Cory Whitlock, CEO
Robert Whitlock, Owner
Cory Whitlock, VP
EMP: 17 EST: 2002
SALES (est): 1.59MM Privately Held
Web: www.whitlocksurfexperience.com
SIC: 3999 3949 2759 7999 Manufacturing industries, nec; Sporting and athletic goods, nec; Screen printing; Amusement and recreation, nec

(P-11309)
WOOD CANDLE WICK TECH INC
Also Called: Makesy
9750 Irvine Blvd Ste 106 (92618-1676)
PHONE..............................310 488-5885
Dayna Marie Decker, CEO
EMP: 21 EST: 2015
SALES (est): 540.46K Privately Held
SIC: 3999 Candles

(P-11310)
ZOO MED LABORATORIES INC
3650 Sacramento Dr (93401-7113)
PHONE..............................805 542-9988
▲ EMP: 133 EST: 1977
SALES (est): 11.15MM Privately Held
Web: www.zoomed.com
SIC: 3999 5199 Pet supplies; Pets and pet supplies

4011 Railroads, Line-haul Operating

(P-11311)
LOS ANGELES JUNCTION RLWY CO
4433 Exchange Ave (90058-2622)
PHONE..............................323 277-2004
Chuck Potempa, CEO
Rob Rellyl, *
Rm Reilly, *
EMP: 103 EST: 1922
SALES (est): 5.84MM
SALES (corp-wide): 302.09B Publicly Held
SIC: 4011 Railroads, line-haul operating
HQ: Bnsf Railway Company
2650 Lou Menk Dr
Fort Worth TX
800 795-2673

(P-11312)
TRONA RAILWAY COMPANY
13068 Main St (93562-1911)
PHONE..............................760 372-2312
EMP: 590 EST: 1913

SQ FT: 30,000
SALES (est): 3.74MM Privately Held
SIC: 4011 Railroads, line-haul operating
HQ: Searles Valley Minerals Inc.
9401 Indian Creek Pkwy
Overland Park KS

(P-11313)
UNION PACIFIC RAILROAD COMPANY
Also Called: Union Pacific Lines
2401 E Sepulveda Blvd (90810-1945)
PHONE..............................562 490-7000
EMP: 300
SALES (corp-wide): 24.88B Publicly Held
Web: www.up.com
SIC: 4011 Railroads, line-haul operating
HQ: Union Pacific Railroad Company Inc
1400 Douglas St
Omaha NE
402 544-5000

4111 Local And Suburban Transit

(P-11314)
ACCESS SERVICES
Also Called: ACCESS PARATRANSIT
3449 Santa Anita Ave (91731-2424)
P.O. Box 5728 (91734-1728)
PHONE..............................213 270-6000
Doran J Barnes, CEO
Shelly Verrinder, *
EMP: 80 EST: 1994
SALES (est): 176.28MM Privately Held
Web: www.accessla.org
SIC: 4111 Local and suburban transit

(P-11315)
AIRPORT CONNECTION INC
Also Called: Roadrunner Shuttle
95 Dawson Dr (93012-8001)
PHONE..............................805 389-8196
Sumaia Sandlin, CEO
Desmond P Sandlin, *
EMP: 180 EST: 1991
SQ FT: 3,500
SALES (est): 18.98MM Privately Held
SIC: 4111 4119 Airport transportation; Limousine rental, with driver

(P-11316)
FIRST STUDENT INC
Also Called: Community Transit Services
4337 Rowland Ave (91731-1119)
PHONE..............................626 448-9446
John Desmond, Brnch Mgr
EMP: 119
Web: www.firststudentinc.com
SIC: 4111 4119 Bus line operations; Local passenger transportation, nec
PA: First Student, Inc.
600 Vine St Ste 1400
Cincinnati OH

(P-11317)
FIRST TRANSIT INC
15730 S Figueroa St (90248-2429)
P.O. Box Figueroa (90248)
PHONE..............................323 222-0010
John Britt, Brnch Mgr
EMP: 87
SALES (corp-wide): 4.23MM Privately Held
Web: www.transdevna.com
SIC: 4111 Local and suburban transit
HQ: First Transit, Inc.
600 Vine St Ste 1400
Cincinnati OH
513 241-2200

(P-11318)
FIRST TRANSIT INC
Also Called: First Group
1213 W Arbor Vitae St (90301-2903)
PHONE..............................310 216-9584
EMP: 87
SALES (corp-wide): 4.23MM Privately Held
Web: www.transdevna.com
SIC: 4111 Local and suburban transit
HQ: First Transit, Inc.
600 Vine St Ste 1400
Cincinnati OH
513 241-2200

(P-11319)
FIRST TRANSIT INC
29 Prado Rd (93401-7314)
PHONE..............................805 544-2730
Kim Blakeman, Mgr
EMP: 160
SALES (corp-wide): 4.23MM Privately Held
Web: www.transdevna.com
SIC: 4111 Bus transportation
HQ: First Transit, Inc.
600 Vine St Ste 1400
Cincinnati OH
513 241-2200

(P-11320)
FORREST GROUP LLC (PA)
1422 N Curson Ave Apt 9 (90046-4037)
PHONE..............................619 808-9798
Allen Forrest, CEO
EMP: 64 EST: 2016
SALES (est): 1.86MM
SALES (corp-wide): 1.86MM Privately Held
Web: www.tfgla.com
SIC: 4111 8742 7319 3532 Airport transportation; Food and beverage consultant; Display advertising service; Shuttle cars, underground

(P-11321)
GOLDEN EMPIRE TRANSIT DISTRICT (PA)
Also Called: Get-A-Lift Handicap Bus Trnsp
1830 Golden State Ave (93301-1012)
PHONE..............................661 869-2438
Steven Woods, CEO
Karen King, *
EMP: 232 EST: 1973
SALES (est): 49.74MM
SALES (corp-wide): 49.74MM Privately Held
Web: www.getbus.org
SIC: 4111 Bus line operations

(P-11322)
KEOLIS TRANSIT AMERICA INC
14663 Keswick St (91405-1204)
PHONE..............................818 616-5254
Steve Shaw, Pr
EMP: 175
SALES (corp-wide): 4.23MM Privately Held
Web: www.keolisna.com
SIC: 4111 Local and suburban transit
HQ: Keolis Transit America, Inc.
53 State St Fl 11
Boston MA

(P-11323)
KEOLIS TRANSIT AMERICA INC
660 W Avenue L (93534-7117)
PHONE..............................661 341-3910
Steve Shaw, Pr
EMP: 90

SALES (corp-wide): 4.23MM **Privately Held**
Web: www.keolisna.com
SIC: 4111 Local and suburban transit
HQ: Keolis Transit America, Inc.
53 State St Fl 11
Boston MA

(P-11324)
LONG BEACH PUBLIC TRNSP CO
1300 Gardenia Ave (90804-3220)
PHONE..................562 591-2301
Laurence Jackson, *Brnch Mgr*
EMP: 80
SALES (corp-wide): 57.81MM **Privately Held**
Web: www.ridelbt.com
SIC: 4111 Bus line operations
PA: Long Beach Public Transportation Co Inc
1963 E Anaheim St
Long Beach CA
562 599-8571

(P-11325)
LONG BEACH PUBLIC TRNSP CO (PA)
Also Called: Long Beach Transit
1963 E Anaheim St (90813-3907)
PHONE..................562 599-8571
Kenneth A Mcdonald, *CEO*
Kenneth A Mcdonald, *CEO*
Laurence W Jackson, *
EMP: 570 **EST:** 1963
SQ FT: 10,000
SALES (est): 57.81MM
SALES (corp-wide): 57.81MM **Privately Held**
Web: www.ridelbt.com
SIC: 4111 Local and suburban transit

(P-11326)
LOS ANGLES CNTY MTRO TRNSP AUT (PA)
Also Called: Metro
1 Gateway Plz Fl 25 (90012-3745)
P.O. Box 512296 (90051-0296)
PHONE..................323 466-3876
Stephanie Wiggins, *CEO*
Rick Thorpe, *CEO*
Nalini Ahuja, *Dir*
Brian Boudreau, *Ex Dir*
Greg Kildare, *Ex Dir*
EMP: 900 **EST:** 1964
SALES (est): 628.29MM
SALES (corp-wide): 628.29MM **Privately Held**
Web: www.metro.net
SIC: 4111 Local and suburban transit

(P-11327)
LOS ANGLES CNTY MTRO TRNSP AUT
9201 Canoga Ave (91311-5839)
PHONE..................213 922-6308
Pat Orr, *Mgr*
EMP: 716
SALES (corp-wide): 628.29MM **Privately Held**
Web: www.metro.net
SIC: 4111 Bus line operations
PA: Los Angeles County Metropolitan Transportation Authority
1 Gateway Plz Fl 25
Los Angeles CA
323 466-3876

(P-11328)
LOS ANGLES CNTY MTRO TRNSP AUT
900 Lyon St (90012-2913)
PHONE..................213 922-5887
John Drayton, *Mgr*
EMP: 536
SALES (corp-wide): 628.29MM **Privately Held**
Web: www.metro.net
SIC: 4111 Bus line operations
PA: Los Angeles County Metropolitan Transportation Authority
1 Gateway Plz Fl 25
Los Angeles CA
323 466-3876

(P-11329)
LOS ANGLES CNTY MTRO TRNSP AUT
Also Called: Division 1
1130 E 6th St (90021-1108)
PHONE..................213 922-6301
Ron Reedy, *Brnch Mgr*
EMP: 355
SALES (corp-wide): 628.29MM **Privately Held**
Web: www.metro.net
SIC: 4111 Bus line operations
PA: Los Angeles County Metropolitan Transportation Authority
1 Gateway Plz Fl 25
Los Angeles CA
323 466-3876

(P-11330)
LOS ANGLES CNTY MTRO TRNSP AUT
630 W Avenue 28 (90065-1502)
PHONE..................213 922-6203
Cheryl Brown, *Mgr*
EMP: 387
SALES (corp-wide): 628.29MM **Privately Held**
Web: www.metro.net
SIC: 4111 Bus line operations
PA: Los Angeles County Metropolitan Transportation Authority
1 Gateway Plz Fl 25
Los Angeles CA
323 466-3876

(P-11331)
LOS ANGLES CNTY MTRO TRNSP AUT
1 Gateway Plaza Dr (90012-3745)
PHONE..................213 922-6202
Maria Japardi, *Brnch Mgr*
EMP: 536
SALES (corp-wide): 628.29MM **Privately Held**
Web: www.metro.net
SIC: 4111 Bus line operations
PA: Los Angeles County Metropolitan Transportation Authority
1 Gateway Plz Fl 25
Los Angeles CA
323 466-3876

(P-11332)
LOS ANGLES CNTY MTRO TRNSP AUT
8800 Santa Monica Blvd (90069-4536)
PHONE..................213 922-6207
Grant Myers, *Mgr*
EMP: 718
SALES (corp-wide): 628.29MM **Privately Held**
Web: www.metro.net

SIC: 4111 Bus line operations
PA: Los Angeles County Metropolitan Transportation Authority
1 Gateway Plz Fl 25
Los Angeles CA
323 466-3876

(P-11333)
LOS ANGLES CNTY MTRO TRNSP AUT
Also Called: Metro
11900 Branford St (91352-1003)
PHONE..................213 922-6215
Gary Stivack, *Mgr*
EMP: 899
SALES (corp-wide): 628.29MM **Privately Held**
Web: www.metro.net
SIC: 4111 Bus line operations
PA: Los Angeles County Metropolitan Transportation Authority
1 Gateway Plz Fl 25
Los Angeles CA
323 466-3876

(P-11334)
LOS ANGLES CNTY MTRO TRNSP AUT
Also Called: Metro
720 E 15th St (90021-2122)
PHONE..................213 533-1506
Carla Aleman, *Brnch Mgr*
EMP: 356
SALES (corp-wide): 628.29MM **Privately Held**
Web: www.metro.net
SIC: 4111 Bus line operations
PA: Los Angeles County Metropolitan Transportation Authority
1 Gateway Plz Fl 25
Los Angeles CA
323 466-3876

(P-11335)
LOS ANGLES CNTY MTRO TRNSP AUT
Also Called: Green Line Rail Eqp Maint
14724 Aviation Blvd (90260-1122)
PHONE..................310 643-3804
Ed Smith, *Mgr*
EMP: 354
SALES (corp-wide): 628.29MM **Privately Held**
Web: www.metro.net
SIC: 4111 Local and suburban transit
PA: Los Angeles County Metropolitan Transportation Authority
1 Gateway Plz Fl 25
Los Angeles CA
323 466-3876

(P-11336)
LOS ANGLES CNTY MTRO TRNSP AUT
Also Called: Lacmta
470 Bauchet St (90012-2907)
PHONE..................213 922-5012
Jim Montoya, *Brnch Mgr*
EMP: 2168
SALES (corp-wide): 628.29MM **Privately Held**
Web: www.metro.net
SIC: 4111 Bus transportation
PA: Los Angeles County Metropolitan Transportation Authority
1 Gateway Plz Fl 25
Los Angeles CA
323 466-3876

(P-11337)
LOS ANGLES CNTY MTRO TRNSP AUT
Also Called: Division 7
100 Sunset Ave (90291-2517)
PHONE..................310 392-8636
John Adams, *Mgr*
EMP: 537
SALES (corp-wide): 628.29MM **Privately Held**
Web: www.metro.net
SIC: 4111 Bus transportation
PA: Los Angeles County Metropolitan Transportation Authority
1 Gateway Plz Fl 25
Los Angeles CA
323 466-3876

(P-11338)
LOS ANGLES CNTY MTRO TRNSP AUT
Also Called: Office of Inspector General
818 W 7th St Ste 500 (90017-3463)
PHONE..................213 244-6783
Arthur Sinai, *Mgr*
EMP: 537
SALES (corp-wide): 628.29MM **Privately Held**
Web: www.metro.net
SIC: 4111 Bus line operations
PA: Los Angeles County Metropolitan Transportation Authority
1 Gateway Plz Fl 25
Los Angeles CA
323 466-3876

(P-11339)
LOS ANGLES CNTY MTRO TRNSP AUT
320 S Santa Fe Ave (90013-1812)
P.O. Box 194 (90078-0194)
PHONE..................213 626-4455
EMP: 783
SALES (corp-wide): 628.29MM **Privately Held**
Web: www.metro.net
SIC: 4111 Bus line operations
PA: Los Angeles County Metropolitan Transportation Authority
1 Gateway Plz Fl 25
Los Angeles CA
323 466-3876

(P-11340)
MV TRANSPORTATION INC
13690 Vaughn St (91340-3017)
PHONE..................323 666-0856
EMP: 242
SALES (corp-wide): 1.31B **Privately Held**
Web: www.mvtransit.com
SIC: 4111 Local and suburban transit
PA: Mv Transportation, Inc.
2711 N Haskell Ave # 150
Dallas TX
972 391-4600

(P-11341)
MV TRANSPORTATION INC
1242 Los Angeles St (91204-2404)
PHONE..................818 409-3387
Jesse Saavedra, *Brnch Mgr*
EMP: 241
SALES (corp-wide): 1.31B **Privately Held**
Web: www.mvtransit.com
SIC: 4111 Local and suburban transit
PA: Mv Transportation, Inc.
2711 N Haskell Ave # 150
Dallas TX
972 391-4600

PRODUCTS & SVCS

(P-11342)
MV TRANSPORTATION INC
15677 Phoebe Ave (90638-5214)
PHONE...........................562 943-6776
EMP: 241
SALES (corp-wide): 1.31B Privately Held
Web: www.mvtransit.com
SIC: 4111 Local and suburban transit
PA: Mv Transportation, Inc.
　　2711 N Haskell Ave # 150
　　Dallas TX
　　972 391-4600

(P-11343)
MV TRANSPORTATION INC
5420 W Jefferson Blvd (90016-3716)
PHONE...........................323 936-9783
EMP: 282
SALES (corp-wide): 1.31B Privately Held
Web: www.mvtransit.com
SIC: 4111 Local and suburban transit
PA: Mv Transportation, Inc.
　　2711 N Haskell Ave # 150
　　Dallas TX
　　972 391-4600

(P-11344)
MV TRANSPORTATION INC
14011 S Central Ave (90059-3622)
PHONE...........................310 638-0556
EMP: 282
SALES (corp-wide): 1.31B Privately Held
Web: www.mvtransit.com
SIC: 4111 Local and suburban transit
PA: Mv Transportation, Inc.
　　2711 N Haskell Ave # 150
　　Dallas TX
　　972 391-4600

(P-11345)
MV TRANSPORTATION INC
16738 Stagg St (91406-1635)
PHONE...........................818 374-9145
Judy Smith, Mgr
EMP: 241
SALES (corp-wide): 1.31B Privately Held
Web: www.mvtransit.com
SIC: 4111 Local and suburban transit
PA: Mv Transportation, Inc.
　　2711 N Haskell Ave # 150
　　Dallas TX
　　972 391-4600

(P-11346)
MV TRANSPORTATION INC
1612 State St (92311-4107)
PHONE...........................760 255-3330
Tom Conlon, Mgr
EMP: 241
SALES (corp-wide): 1.31B Privately Held
Web: www.mvtransit.com
SIC: 4111 Local and suburban transit
PA: Mv Transportation, Inc.
　　2711 N Haskell Ave # 150
　　Dallas TX
　　972 391-4600

(P-11347)
MV TRANSPORTATION INC
303 Via Del Norte (92058-1231)
PHONE...........................760 400-0300
EMP: 241
SALES (corp-wide): 1.31B Privately Held
Web: www.mvtransit.com
SIC: 4111 Local and suburban transit
PA: Mv Transportation, Inc.
　　2711 N Haskell Ave # 150
　　Dallas TX
　　972 391-4600

(P-11348)
MV TRANSPORTATION INC
755 Norlak Ave (92025-2514)
PHONE...........................760 520-0118
EMP: 201
SALES (corp-wide): 1.31B Privately Held
Web: www.mvtransit.com
SIC: 4111 Local and suburban transit
PA: Mv Transportation, Inc.
　　2711 N Haskell Ave # 150
　　Dallas TX
　　972 391-4600

(P-11349)
MV TRANSPORTATION INC
265 S Rancho Rd (91361-5222)
PHONE...........................805 557-7372
Cheryl Seafert, Brnch Mgr
EMP: 201
SALES (corp-wide): 1.31B Privately Held
Web: www.mvtransit.com
SIC: 4111 Local and suburban transit
PA: Mv Transportation, Inc.
　　2711 N Haskell Ave # 150
　　Dallas TX
　　972 391-4600

(P-11350)
MV TRANSPORTATION INC
Also Called: Mv Transportation
670 Lawrence Dr (91320-2205)
PHONE...........................805 375-5467
EMP: 201
SALES (corp-wide): 1.31B Privately Held
Web: www.mvtransit.com
SIC: 4111 Local and suburban transit
PA: Mv Transportation, Inc.
　　2711 N Haskell Ave # 150
　　Dallas TX
　　972 391-4600

(P-11351)
OMNITRANS
4748 Arrow Hwy (91763-1208)
PHONE...........................909 379-7100
John Steffon, Brnch Mgr
EMP: 219
SALES (corp-wide): 8.48MM Privately Held
Web: www.omnitrans.org
SIC: 4111 Bus line operations
PA: Omnitrans
　　1700 W 5th St
　　San Bernardino CA
　　909 379-7100

(P-11352)
OMNITRANS (PA)
1700 W 5th St (92411-2499)
PHONE...........................909 379-7100
TOLL FREE: 800
EMP: 212 EST: 1976
SALES (est): 8.48MM
SALES (corp-wide): 8.48MM Privately Held
Web: www.omnitrans.org
SIC: 4111 Bus line operations

(P-11353)
ORANGE CNTY TRNSP AUTH SCHLRSH
11790 Cardinal Cir (92843-3839)
P.O. Box 14184 (92863-1584)
PHONE...........................714 560-6282
Arthur Leahy, CEO
EMP: 82
SALES (corp-wide): 761.4MM Privately Held
Web: www.octa.net

SIC: 4111 Bus line operations
PA: Orange County Transportation
　　Authority Scholarship Foundation, Inc.
　　550 S Main St
　　Orange CA
　　714 636-7433

(P-11354)
ORANGE CNTY TRNSP AUTH SCHLRSH
Also Called: Octa
600 S Main St Ste 910 (92868-4689)
PHONE...........................714 999-1726
EMP: 600
SALES (corp-wide): 761.4MM Privately Held
Web: www.octa.net
SIC: 4111 Bus line operations
PA: Orange County Transportation
　　Authority Scholarship Foundation, Inc.
　　550 S Main St
　　Orange CA
　　714 636-7433

(P-11355)
ORANGE CNTY TRNSP AUTH SCHLRSH (PA)
Also Called: Orange County Trnsp Auth
550 S Main St (92868-4506)
P.O. Box 14184 (92863-1584)
PHONE...........................714 636-7433
Darrell Johnson, CEO
Don Hansen, *
John Dunning Junior, COO
Amy Wu, *
EMP: 350 EST: 1972
SQ FT: 77,000
SALES (est): 761.4MM
SALES (corp-wide): 761.4MM Privately Held
Web: www.octa.net
SIC: 4111 8711 Bus line operations;
　　Construction and civil engineering

(P-11356)
PRIVATE SUITE LAX LLC
Also Called: PS
6871 W Imperial Hwy (90045-6311)
PHONE...........................310 907-9950
Joshua Gausman, Managing Member
Amina Belouizdad, Managing Member*
Jordi Mena, *
EMP: 140 EST: 2017
SQ FT: 57,590
SALES (est): 22MM Privately Held
Web: www.reserveps.com
SIC: 4111 Airport transportation

(P-11357)
RIVERSIDE TRANSIT AGENCY (PA)
Also Called: R T A
1825 3rd St (92507-3484)
P.O. Box 59968 (92517-1968)
PHONE...........................951 565-5000
Larry Rubio, CEO
EMP: 350 EST: 1977
SQ FT: 10,400
SALES (est): 3.22MM
SALES (corp-wide): 3.22MM Privately Held
Web: www.riversidetransit.com
SIC: 4111 Bus transportation

(P-11358)
SAN BERNARDINO CNTY TRNSP AUTH
Also Called: SANBAG
1170 W 3rd St Fl 2 (92410-1724)

PHONE...........................909 884-8276
Raymond Wolfe, Ex Dir
EMP: 125 EST: 1973
SALES (est): 672.67MM Privately Held
Web: www.gosbcta.com
SIC: 4111 Local and suburban transit

(P-11359)
SAN DIEGO METRO TRNST SYS
1255 Imperial Ave Ste 1000 (92101-7490)
PHONE...........................619 231-1466
Sharon Cooney, CEO
Paul Jadlonski, *
Stan Abrams, *
EMP: 1600 EST: 1976
SQ FT: 40,000
SALES (est): 112.66MM Privately Held
Web: www.sandiego.com
SIC: 4111 Bus line operations

(P-11360)
SAN DIEGO TRANSIT CORPORATION (PA)
Also Called: SAN DIEGO METROPOLITAN TRANSIT
100 16th St (92101-7694)
PHONE...........................619 238-0100
Langley Powell, Ex Dir
EMP: 650 EST: 1967
SQ FT: 20,000
SALES (est): 87.04MM
SALES (corp-wide): 87.04MM Privately Held
Web: www.sdmts.com
SIC: 4111 Commuter bus operation

(P-11361)
SAN DIEGO TROLLEY INC
Also Called: SAN DIEGO TROLLEY INC
1341 Commercial St (92113-1021)
PHONE...........................619 595-4933
Bill Brown, Brnch Mgr
EMP: 483
SALES (corp-wide): 149MM Privately Held
Web: www.sdmts.com
SIC: 4111 Trolley operation
HQ: San Diego Trolley, Inc.
　　1255 Imperial Ave Ste 900
　　San Diego CA
　　619 595-4949

(P-11362)
SAN GABRIEL TRANSIT INC (PA)
Also Called: San Gabriel Valley Cab Co
3650 Rockwell Ave (91731-2322)
PHONE...........................626 258-1310
Timmy Mardirossian, Pr
Sedik Mardirossian, *
Eda Aghajanian, *
EMP: 220 EST: 1953
SQ FT: 8,000
SALES (est): 47.41MM
SALES (corp-wide): 47.41MM Privately Held
Web: www.sgtransit.com
SIC: 4111 Local and suburban transit

(P-11363)
SAN LUIS OBSPO RGNAL TRNST AUT
Also Called: Slorta
253 Elks Ln (93401-5410)
PHONE...........................805 781-4465
Omar Mcpherson, Prin
Geoff Straw, *
Tania Arnold, *
EMP: 90 EST: 1989

SALES (est): 9.01MM **Privately Held**
Web: www.slorta.org
SIC: 4111 Local and suburban transit

(P-11364)
SANTA BARBARA METRO TRNST DST (PA)
Also Called: M T D
550 Olive St (93101-1610)
PHONE......................805 963-3364
David Davis, *Ch*
John Britton, *
Chuck Mcquary, *Vice Chairman*
Bill Shelor, *
Roger Aceves, *
EMP: 85 EST: 1967
SQ FT: 8,500
SALES (est): 22.76MM
SALES (corp-wide): 22.76MM **Privately Held**
Web: www.sbmtd.gov
SIC: 4111 Bus line operations

(P-11365)
SHUTTLE SMART INC
6150 W 96th St (90045-5218)
PHONE......................310 338-9466
Brian Clark, *Brnch Mgr*
EMP: 130
SALES (corp-wide): 1.8MM **Privately Held**
Web: www.shuttlesmart.net
SIC: 4111 Airport transportation
PA: Shuttle Smart, Inc.
25923 Washington Blvd Ne
Kingston WA
303 757-4870

(P-11366)
SMS TRANSPORTATION SVCS INC
865 S Figueroa St Ste 2750 (90017-2627)
PHONE......................213 489-5367
John Harris, *CEO*
Delilah Lanoix, *
Danielle Wiltz, *
Jennifer Wiltz, *
EMP: 150 EST: 1994
SQ FT: 3,000
SALES (est): 14.74MM **Privately Held**
Web: www.smstransportation.net
SIC: 4111 Airport transportation

(P-11367)
SOUTHERN CAL RGIONAL RAIL AUTH
Also Called: Metrolink Doc
2704 N Garey Ave (91767-1810)
PHONE......................213 808-7043
EMP: 143
Web: www.metrolinktrains.com
SIC: 4111 Commuter rail passenger operation
PA: Southern California Regional Rail Authority
900 Wilshire Blvd # 1500
Los Angeles CA

(P-11368)
SOUTHERN CAL RGIONAL RAIL AUTH (PA)
Also Called: Metrolink
900 Wilshire Blvd Ste 1500 (90017-3402)
P.O. Box 812060 (90081-0018)
PHONE......................213 452-0200
Darren M Kettle, *CEO*
Stephanie Wiggins, *
Elissa Konove, *
Gary Lettengarver, *
Ronnie Campbell, *

EMP: 128 EST: 1991
SALES (est): 93.97MM **Privately Held**
Web: www.metrolinktrains.com
SIC: 4111 Commuter rail passenger operation

(P-11369)
SUNLINE TRANSIT AGENCY (PA)
Also Called: STA
32505 Harry Oliver Trl (92276-3501)
PHONE......................760 343-3456
Glenn Miller, *Ch*
Caroline Rude, *
Greg Pettis, *
EMP: 160 EST: 1977
SQ FT: 19,006
SALES (est): 48.63MM
SALES (corp-wide): 48.63MM **Privately Held**
Web: www.sunline.org
SIC: 4111 Local and suburban transit

4119 Local Passenger Transportation, Nec

(P-11370)
AMBULNZ HEALTH LLC
12531 Vanowen St (91605-5321)
PHONE......................877 311-5555
EMP: 261
SALES (corp-wide): 18.79MM **Privately Held**
Web: www.ambulnz.com
SIC: 4119 Ambulance service
PA: Ambulnz Health, Llc
3550 N Academy Blvd
Colorado Springs CO
877 311-5555

(P-11371)
AMERICAN MED RSPNSE INLAND EMP (HQ)
879 Marlborough Ave (92507-2133)
PHONE......................951 782-5200
Bill Fanger, *Pr*
EMP: 80 EST: 1962
SALES (est): 21.62MM **Privately Held**
SIC: 4119 Ambulance service
PA: Global Medical Response, Inc.
6363 S Fiddlers Green Cir
Greenwood Village CO

(P-11372)
AMERICAN MEDICAL RESPONSE INC
Also Called: American Medical Response
1111 Montalvo Way (92262-5440)
PHONE......................760 883-5000
Wayne Dennis, *Prin*
EMP: 160
Web: www.amr.net
SIC: 4119 8099 Ambulance service; Medical rescue squad
HQ: American Medical Response, Inc.
6363 S Fiddlers Green Cir
Greenwood Village CO

(P-11373)
AMERICAN PROF AMBULANCE CORP
16945 Sherman Way (91406-3614)
P.O. Box 7263 (91409-7263)
PHONE......................818 996-2200
Lyubov Popok, *Pr*
EMP: 85 EST: 2002
SALES (est): 5.2MM **Privately Held**
Web: www.apa-ems.com

SIC: 4119 Ambulance service

(P-11374)
AMERICARE AMBULANCE
Also Called: AMERICARE AMBULANCE
10730 Thornmint Rd (92127-2700)
PHONE......................760 739-9723
Mark Ewing, *Brnch Mgr*
EMP: 129
SALES (corp-wide): 458.99K **Privately Held**
SIC: 4119 Ambulance service
PA: Americare Ambulance Llc
6524 Fremont Cir
Huntington Beach CA
310 835-9390

(P-11375)
ATLANTIC EXPRESS TRNSP
Also Called: Atlantic Express of California
2450 Long Beach Blvd (90806-3125)
PHONE......................562 997-6868
Darinda Garnett, *Mgr*
EMP: 167
SALES (corp-wide): 301.19MM **Privately Held**
SIC: 4119 8748 4151 Local passenger transportation, nec; Traffic consultant; School buses
HQ: Atlantic Express Transportation Corp
7 North St
Staten Island NY
718 442-7000

(P-11376)
BLS LMSINE SVC LOS ANGELES INC
Also Called: B L S Limousine Service
2860 Fletcher Dr (90039-2452)
PHONE......................323 644-7166
Jay D Okon, *Pr*
Phyllis Okon, *
EMP: 350 EST: 1988
SQ FT: 20,000
SALES (est): 8.7MM **Privately Held**
Web: www.blsco.com
SIC: 4119 Limousine rental, with driver

(P-11377)
CALIFORNIA MED RESPONSE INC
Also Called: Cal-Med Ambulance
1557 Santa Anita Ave (91733-3313)
PHONE......................562 968-1818
Ronald A Marks, *Pr*
Ronald A Marks, *Pr*
Linda Marks, *
EMP: 80 EST: 2009
SALES (est): 7.05MM **Privately Held**
Web: www.calmedambulance.com
SIC: 4119 Ambulance service

(P-11378)
CALL-THE-CAR
21950 Copley Dr (91765-4461)
P.O. Box 4114 (90640-9302)
PHONE......................855 282-6968
Michelle Tyson, *CEO*
EMP: 89 EST: 2012
SALES (est): 9.5MM **Privately Held**
Web: www.callthecar.com
SIC: 4119 Local passenger transportation, nec

(P-11379)
CARE MEDICAL TRNSP INC
Also Called: Care Ambulance
9770 Candida St (92126-4536)
PHONE......................858 653-4520

EMP: 190 EST: 1995
SQ FT: 14,000
SALES (est): 4.37MM **Privately Held**
SIC: 4119 Ambulance service

(P-11380)
CLS TRNSPRTTION LOS ANGLES LLC (HQ)
Also Called: Empire Cls Wrldwide Chffred Sv
600 S Allied Way (90245-4727)
PHONE......................310 414-8189
David Singler, *Managing Member*
William Minich, *
EMP: 150 EST: 1987
SALES (est): 22.82MM **Privately Held**
Web: www.empirecls.com
SIC: 4119 Limousine rental, with driver
PA: Gts Holdings, Inc.
225 Meadowlands Pkwy
Secaucus NJ

(P-11381)
EASTWESTPROTO INC
Also Called: Lifeline Ambulance
6605 E Washington Blvd (90040-1813)
PHONE......................888 535-5728
Genady Gorin, *CEO*
Genia Gorin, *
EMP: 275 EST: 2002
SQ FT: 10,000
SALES (est): 28.48MM **Privately Held**
Web: www.lifeline-ems.com
SIC: 4119 Ambulance service

(P-11382)
EMERGENCY AMBULANCE SVC INC
3200 E Birch St Ste A (92821-6287)
PHONE......................714 990-1331
Phillip E Davis, *Pr*
EMP: 80 EST: 1977
SALES (est): 15.3MM **Privately Held**
Web: www.emergencyambulance.com
SIC: 4119 Ambulance service

(P-11383)
EXECUTIVE NETWORK ENTPS INC (PA)
Also Called: Malibu Limousine Service
13440 Beach Ave (90292-5624)
PHONE......................310 447-2759
EMP: 80 EST: 2003
SQ FT: 5,000
SALES (est): 4.74MM **Privately Held**
SIC: 4119 Limousine rental, with driver

(P-11384)
EXECUTIVE NETWORK ENTPS INC
1224 21st St Apt E (90404-1390)
PHONE......................310 457-8822
Patricia Stephenson, *Mgr*
EMP: 520
SIC: 4119 Limousine rental, with driver
PA: Executive Network Enterprises, Inc.
13440 Beach Ave
Marina Del Rey CA

(P-11385)
FALCK MOBILE HEALTH CORP
212 S Atlantic Blvd Ste 102 (90022)
PHONE......................323 720-1578
EMP: 444
SALES (corp-wide): 4.95B **Privately Held**
Web: www.falck.us
SIC: 4119 Ambulance service
HQ: Falck Mobile Health Corp.
1517 W Braden Ct
Orange CA
714 288-3800

P
R
O
D
U
C
T
S
&
S
V
C
S

(P-11386)
FALCK MOBILE HEALTH CORP
8932 Katella Ave Ste 201 (92804-6299)
PHONE..................714 828-7750
Dan Richardson, *Prin*
EMP: 444
SALES (corp-wide): 4.95B **Privately Held**
Web: www.falck.us
SIC: **4119** Ambulance service
HQ: Falck Mobile Health Corp.
1517 W Braden Ct
Orange CA
714 288-3800

(P-11387)
FILYN CORPORATION
Also Called: Lynch Ambulance Service
2950 E La Jolla St (92806-1307)
PHONE..................714 632-0225
Walter John Lynch, *CEO*
Nancy Lynch, *
EMP: 200 **EST:** 1986
SALES (est): 19.48MM **Privately Held**
Web: www.lynchambulance.com
SIC: **4119** Ambulance service

(P-11388)
FLIXBUS INC
12575 Beatrice St (90066-7001)
PHONE..................925 577-4164
Pierre Gourdain, *CEO*
EMP: 104 **EST:** 2017
SALES (est): 6.73MM
SALES (corp-wide): 611.17MM **Privately Held**
Web: www.flixbus.com
SIC: **4119** Local rental transportation
HQ: Flix North America Inc.
315 Continental Ave
Dallas TX
214 564-8215

(P-11389)
GARY CARDIFF ENTERPRISES INC
Also Called: Cardiff Transportation
75255 Sheryl Ave (92211-5129)
PHONE..................760 568-1403
Gary Cardiff, *CEO*
Sharon Cardiff, *
EMP: 89 **EST:** 1990
SQ FT: 10,000
SALES (est): 8.46MM **Privately Held**
Web: www.cardifflimo.com
SIC: **4119** Limousine rental, with driver

(P-11390)
GLOBAL PARATRANSIT INC
400 W Compton Blvd (90248-1700)
PHONE..................310 715-7550
Reza Nasrollahy, *Pr*
EMP: 300 **EST:** 2000
SQ FT: 17,000
SALES (est): 25.4MM **Privately Held**
Web: www.global-paratransit.com
SIC: **4119** Ambulance service

(P-11391)
LANDJET (PA)
1090 Hall Ave (92509-1800)
PHONE..................909 873-4636
Kevin Sacalas, *CEO*
EMP: 131 **EST:** 2018
SALES (est): 5.9MM
SALES (corp-wide): 5.9MM **Privately Held**
Web: www.landjet-inc.com
SIC: **4119** Local rental transportation

(P-11392)
LEADER INDUSTRIES INC
Also Called: Leader Emergency Vehicles
10941 Weaver Ave (91733-2752)
PHONE..................626 575-0880
EMP: 160 **EST:** 2001
SALES (est): 16.12MM **Privately Held**
Web: www.leaderambulance.com
SIC: **4119** 5046 3711 Ambulance service;
Commercial equipment, nec; Motor
vehicles and car bodies

(P-11393)
LIBERTY AMBULANCE LLC
9441 Washburn Rd (90242-2912)
PHONE..................562 741-6230
EMP: 103 **EST:** 2008
SALES (est): 11.35MM **Privately Held**
Web: www.libertyambulance.com
SIC: **4119** Ambulance service

(P-11394)
MEDIC-1 AMBULANCE SERVICE INC
1305 W Arrow Hwy Ste 206 (91773-2338)
PHONE..................909 592-8840
Gordon Shipp, *Pr*
Todd Duprey, *
Gary Sylvester, *
EMP: 92 **EST:** 2001
SALES (est): 4.53MM **Privately Held**
SIC: **4119** Ambulance service

(P-11395)
MEDIX AMBULANCE SERVICE INC (PA)
26021 Pala (92691-2705)
P.O. Box 1000 (92609-1000)
PHONE..................949 470-8915
EMP: 157 **EST:** 1978
SALES (est): 9.17MM
SALES (corp-wide): 9.17MM **Privately Held**
SIC: **4119** Ambulance service

(P-11396)
MEDRESPONSE (PA)
7040 Hayvenhurst Ave (91406-3801)
P.O. Box 8379 (91409-8379)
PHONE..................818 442-9222
Andrew Stepansky, *CEO*
EMP: 113 **EST:** 2002
SALES (est): 2.46MM
SALES (corp-wide): 2.46MM **Privately Held**
Web: www.medresponseinc.com
SIC: **4119** Ambulance service

(P-11397)
MERCY MEDICAL TRNSP INC
27350 Valley Center Rd Ste A
(92082-7220)
P.O. Box 530 (92082-0530)
PHONE..................760 739-8026
Richard Roesch, *Pr*
EMP: 188 **EST:** 1993
SALES (est): 8.69MM **Privately Held**
Web: www.mercymedtrans.com
SIC: **4119** 8062 Ambulance service; General
medical and surgical hospitals

(P-11398)
MISSION AMBULANCE INC
400 Ramona Ave (92879-1443)
P.O. Box 3111 (92878-3111)
PHONE..................951 272-2300
Daniel Gold, *Pr*
EMP: 81 **EST:** 1999
SALES (est): 8.67MM **Privately Held**
Web: www.missionsafetyservices.com
SIC: **4119** Ambulance service

(P-11399)
MUSIC EXPRESS INC (PA)
2601 W Empire Ave (91504-3225)
PHONE..................818 845-1502
EMP: 171 **EST:** 1973
SALES (est): 24.71MM
SALES (corp-wide): 24.71MM **Privately Held**
Web: www.musicexpress.com
SIC: **4119** Limousine rental, with driver

(P-11400)
PREMIER MEDICAL TRANSPORT INC
Also Called: Premier Ambulance
260 N Palm St # 200 (92821-2870)
PHONE..................805 340-5191
Adrian Dehghanmanesh, *CEO*
EMP: 117 **EST:** 2007
SALES (est): 12.93MM **Privately Held**
Web: www.premieramb.com
SIC: **4119** Ambulance service

(P-11401)
PRN AMBULANCE LLC
8928 Sepulveda Blvd (91343-4306)
PHONE..................818 810-3600
Mike Sechrist, *CEO*
Avo Avetisyan, *Pr*
Elena Whorton, *Pr*
Kevin Gorman, *CFO*
Michael Gorman, *COO*
EMP: 300 **EST:** 2001
SQ FT: 3,000
SALES (est): 58.95MM
SALES (corp-wide): 249.05MM **Privately Held**
Web: www.prnambulance.com
SIC: **4119** Ambulance service
PA: Pt-1 Holdings, Llc
720 Portal St
Cotati CA
707 665-4295

(P-11402)
RYANS EXPRESS TRNSP SVCS INC (PA)
Also Called: Ryan's Express
19500 Mariner Ave (90503-1644)
PHONE..................310 219-2960
John Busskohl, *CEO*
Chris Sanchez, *
George Cohen, *
Alexander E Hansen, *
Daniel Azar, *
EMP: 80 **EST:** 1999
SQ FT: 20,000
SALES (est): 19.99MM
SALES (corp-wide): 19.99MM **Privately Held**
Web: www.ryanstransportation.com
SIC: **4119** Limousine rental, with driver

(P-11403)
SAN LUIS AMBULANCE SERVICE INC
3546 S Higuera St (93401-7304)
P.O. Box 954 (93406-0954)
PHONE..................805 543-2626
Frank I Kelton, *Pr*
Betsy Kelton, *
EMP: 124 **EST:** 1967
SQ FT: 7,500
SALES (est): 9.65MM **Privately Held**
Web: www.sanluisambulance.info

SIC: **4119** Ambulance service

(P-11404)
SCHAEFER AMBULANCE SERVICE INC
Also Called: Gold Cross Ambulance
4627 Beverly Blvd (90004-3101)
P.O. Box 74609 (90004-0609)
PHONE..................323 468-1642
TOLL FREE: 800
EMP: 463
Web: www.schaeferamb.com
SIC: **4119** Ambulance service

(P-11405)
SUNLINE TRANSIT AGENCY
790 Vine Ave (92236-1736)
PHONE..................760 972-4059
EMP: 119
SALES (corp-wide): 48.63MM **Privately Held**
Web: www.sunline.org
SIC: **4119** Local passenger transportation, nec
PA: Sunline Transit Agency
32505 Harry Oliver Trl
Thousand Palms CA
760 343-3456

(P-11406)
TRANSDEV SERVICES INC
5640 Peck Rd (91006-5850)
PHONE..................626 357-7912
EMP: 745
SALES (corp-wide): 4.23MM **Privately Held**
Web: www.transdevna.com
SIC: **4119** 4121 Local passenger
transportation, nec; Taxicabs
HQ: Transdev Services, Inc.
720 E Bttrfeld Rd Ste 300
Lombard IL
630 571-7070

(P-11407)
TRANSDEV SERVICES INC
544 Vernon Way (92020-1935)
PHONE..................619 401-4503
EMP: 169
SALES (corp-wide): 4.23MM **Privately Held**
Web: www.transdevna.com
SIC: **4119** Local passenger transportation, nec
HQ: Transdev Services, Inc.
720 E Bttrfeld Rd Ste 300
Lombard IL
630 571-7070

(P-11408)
TRIPLE R TRANSPORTATION INC
978 Rd 192 (93215)
P.O. Box 38 (93216-0038)
PHONE..................661 725-6494
Joe Rodriguez, *Pr*
EMP: 80 **EST:** 2008
SALES (est): 3.89MM **Privately Held**
SIC: **4119** Local rental transportation

(P-11409)
VIRGIN FISH INC (PA)
Also Called: Avalon Transportation Co
1000 Corporate Pointe Ste 150
(90230-7690)
PHONE..................310 391-6161
Jeff Brush, *Prin*
Jeff Brush, *Pr*
David Dinwiddie, *

EMP: 150 EST: 1990
SQ FT: 3,000
SALES (est): 23.41MM Privately Held
Web: www.avalontrans.com
SIC: 4119 Limousine rental, with driver

(P-11410)
WESTMED AMBULANCE INC
Also Called: WESTMED AMBULANCE, INC
3872 Las Flores Canyon Rd (90265-5264)
PHONE..................................310 456-3830
EMP: 155
Web: www.westmedambulance.com
SIC: 4119 Ambulance service
PA: Westmed Ambulance, Inc.
13933 Crenshaw Blvd
Hawthorne CA

(P-11411)
WESTMED AMBULANCE INC
Also Called: WESTMED AMBULANCE, INC
2537 Old San Pasqual Rd (92027-4753)
PHONE..................................310 219-1779
Allen Cress, Prin
EMP: 155
Web: www.westmedambulance.com
SIC: 4119 Ambulance service
PA: Westmed Ambulance, Inc.
13933 Crenshaw Blvd
Hawthorne CA

4121 Taxicabs

(P-11412)
ADMINISTRATIVE SVCS COOP INC
1515 W 190th St Ste 200 (90249-2933)
PHONE..................................310 715-1968
Martiros Manukyan, CEO
Raymond Mcgreevy, Pr
EMP: 200 EST: 1992
SALES (est): 7.5MM Privately Held
SIC: 4121 Taxicabs

4131 Intercity And Rural Bus Transportation

(P-11413)
SANTA BARBARA TRNSP CORP
Also Called: Student Transportation America
26501 Ruether Ave (91350-2600)
PHONE..................................661 259-7285
Richard Varner, Dir
EMP: 100
SALES (corp-wide): 2.01B Privately Held
SIC: 4131 4151 Intercity and rural bus transportation; School buses
HQ: Santa Barbara Transportation Corporation
3349 Hwy 138 Ste C
Wall Township NJ
732 280-4200

(P-11414)
SANTA MONICA CITY OF
Santa Monica Big Blue Bus
1685 Main St (90401-3248)
PHONE..................................310 458-1975
Edward King, Mgr
EMP: 271
SALES (corp-wide): 502.49MM Privately Held
Web: www.santamonica.gov
SIC: 4131 Intercity and rural bus transportation
PA: City Of Santa Monica
1685 Main St
Santa Monica CA
310 458-8411

4141 Local Bus Charter Service

(P-11415)
EMPIRE TRANSPORTATION INC
8800 Park St (90706-5529)
PHONE..................................562 529-2676
Miguel Oliver, CEO
Bertha Aguirre, *
Monica Escorza Oliver, *
EMP: 425 EST: 2005
SQ FT: 25,000
SALES (est): 35.8MM Privately Held
Web: www.emptransportation.com
SIC: 4141 7521 4111 Local bus charter service; Indoor parking services; Bus transportation

4142 Bus Charter Service, Except Local

(P-11416)
COACH USA INC
Also Called: Foothill Transit West Covina
5640 Peck Rd (91006-5850)
PHONE..................................626 357-7912
Keith Whalen, Brnch Mgr
EMP: 100
Web: www.coachusa.com
SIC: 4142 Bus charter service, except local
HQ: Coach Usa, Inc.
160 S Route 17 N
Paramus NJ

(P-11417)
HOT DOGGER TOURS INC
Also Called: Gold Coast Tours
105 Gemini Ave (92821-3702)
PHONE..................................714 988-4088
TOLL FREE: 800
John Hartley, Pr
Mark Wilkerson, *
EMP: 120 EST: 1976
SQ FT: 955
SALES (est): 14.23MM Privately Held
Web: www.goldcoasttours.com
SIC: 4142 4725 4141 Bus charter service, except local; Tours, conducted; Local bus charter service

(P-11418)
SURERIDE CHARTER INC
Also Called: Sun Diego Charter
522 W 8th St (91950-1004)
PHONE..................................619 336-9200
EMP: 120 EST: 1994
SQ FT: 60,000
SALES (est): 16.23MM Privately Held
Web: www.sundiegocharter.com
SIC: 4142 Bus charter service, except local

4151 School Buses

(P-11419)
ANTELOPE VLY SCHL TRNSP AGCY
670 W Avenue L8 (93534-7100)
PHONE..................................661 952-3106
Morris Fuselier Iii, CEO
Gary Russell, *
Joanne Downen, *
EMP: 206 EST: 1980
SALES (est): 21.01MM Privately Held
Web: www.avsta.com
SIC: 4151 School buses

(P-11420)
COUNTY OF LOS ANGELES
Also Called: Pupil Transportation
9402 Greenleaf Ave (90605-2700)
PHONE..................................562 945-2581
Dan Ibarra, Dir
EMP: 218
Web: www.lacounty.gov
SIC: 4151 9621 School buses; Regulation, administration of transportation
PA: County Of Los Angeles
500 W Temple St Ste 437
Los Angeles CA
213 974-1101

(P-11421)
DURHAM SCHOOL SERVICES L P
723 S Alameda St (90220-3809)
PHONE..................................310 767-5820
Raphael Balonos, Mgr
EMP: 200
Web: www.durhamschoolservices.com
SIC: 4151 School buses
HQ: Durham School Services, L. P.
2601 Navistar Dr
Lisle IL
630 836-0292

(P-11422)
DURHAM SCHOOL SERVICES L P
8555 Flower Ave (90723-5602)
PHONE..................................562 408-1206
Paul Wiggins, Genl Mgr
EMP: 114
Web: www.durhamschoolservices.com
SIC: 4151 School buses
HQ: Durham School Services, L. P.
2601 Navistar Dr
Lisle IL
630 836-0292

(P-11423)
DURHAM SCHOOL SERVICES L P
4029 Las Virgenes Rd (91302-3505)
PHONE..................................818 880-4257
Nanette Nanzini, Genl Mgr
EMP: 171
Web: www.durhamschoolservices.com
SIC: 4151 School buses
HQ: Durham School Services, L. P.
2601 Navistar Dr
Lisle IL
630 836-0292

(P-11424)
DURHAM SCHOOL SERVICES L P
2713 River Ave (91770-3303)
PHONE..................................626 573-3769
David Gonzales, Genl Mgr
EMP: 1000
Web: www.durhamschoolservices.com
SIC: 4151 School buses
HQ: Durham School Services, L. P.
2601 Navistar Dr
Lisle IL
630 836-0292

(P-11425)
DURHAM SCHOOL SERVICES L P
Also Called: Lidlaw Educational Services
12999 Victoria St (91739-9532)
PHONE..................................909 899-1809
Laura Randals, Mgr

EMP: 114
Web: www.durhamschoolservices.com
SIC: 4151 School buses
HQ: Durham School Services, L. P.
2601 Navistar Dr
Lisle IL
630 836-0292

(P-11426)
DURHAM SCHOOL SERVICES L P
3151 W 5th St Ste A (93030-6415)
PHONE..................................805 483-6076
Lee Philips, Genl Mgr
EMP: 200
Web: www.durhamschoolservices.com
SIC: 4151 School buses
HQ: Durham School Services, L. P.
2601 Navistar Dr
Lisle IL
630 836-0292

(P-11427)
DURHAM SCHOOL SERVICES L P
2003 Laguna Canyon Rd (92651-1123)
PHONE..................................949 376-0376
EMP: 114
Web: www.durhamschoolservices.com
SIC: 4151 School buses
HQ: Durham School Services, L. P.
2601 Navistar Dr
Lisle IL
630 836-0292

(P-11428)
FIRST STUDENT INC
Also Called: Laidlaw Educational Services
5006 E Calle San Raphael (92264-3452)
PHONE..................................760 320-4659
Mike Robertson, Mgr
EMP: 323
Web: www.firststudentinc.com
SIC: 4151 School buses
PA: First Student, Inc.
600 Vine St Ste 1400
Cincinnati OH

(P-11429)
FIRST STUDENT INC
Also Called: Cardinal Transportation
14800 S Avalon Blvd (90248-2012)
PHONE..................................310 769-2400
Ray Borales, Pr
Roy J Weber, *
▲ EMP: 5056 EST: 1987
SQ FT: 18,000
SALES (est): 10.01MM
SALES (corp-wide): 5.71B Privately Held
Web: www.firststudentinc.com
SIC: 4151 School buses
HQ: Firstgroup America, Inc.
191 Rosa Parks St
Cincinnati OH
513 241-2200

(P-11430)
LONG BEACH UNIFIED SCHOOL DST
Also Called: Transportation Department
2700 Pine Ave (90806-2617)
PHONE..................................562 426-6176
Paul Bailey, Dir
EMP: 167
SALES (corp-wide): 788.46MM Privately Held
Web: www.lbschools.net
SIC: 4151 School buses
PA: Long Beach Unified School District
1515 Hughes Way

PRODUCTS & SVCS

Long Beach CA
562 997-8000

(P-11431)
SANTA BARBARA TRNSP CORP
42138 7th St W (93534-7145)
PHONE..............................661 510-0566
EMP: 138
SALES (corp-wide): 2.01B **Privately Held**
SIC: 4151 School buses
HQ: Santa Barbara Transportation
    Corporation
    3349 Hwy 138 Ste C
    Wall Township NJ
    732 280-4200

(P-11432)
SANTA BARBARA TRNSP CORP
Also Called: Student Transportation America
6500 Hollister Ave Ste 100 (93117-3011)
PHONE..............................805 928-0402
EMP: 188
SALES (corp-wide): 2.01B **Privately Held**
SIC: 4151 4121 School buses; Taxicabs
HQ: Santa Barbara Transportation
    Corporation
    3349 Hwy 138 Ste C
    Wall Township NJ
    732 280-4200

(P-11433)
SANTA BARBARA TRNSP CORP
Also Called: Student Transportation America
520 Gannon Pl (92025-2513)
PHONE..............................760 746-0850
EMP: 206
SALES (corp-wide): 2.01B **Privately Held**
SIC: 4151 School buses
HQ: Santa Barbara Transportation
    Corporation
    3349 Hwy 138 Ste C
    Wall Township NJ
    732 280-4200

4173 Bus Terminal And Service Facilities

(P-11434)
DURHAM SCHOOL SERVICES L P
2818 W 5th St (92703-1824)
PHONE..............................714 542-8989
Debbie Williams, *Mgr*
EMP: 257
SQ FT: 4,843
Web: www.durhamschoolservices.com
SIC: 4173 4151 Maintenance facilities for
    motor vehicle passenger transport; School
    buses
HQ: Durham School Services, L. P.
    2601 Navistar Dr
    Lisle IL
    630 836-0292

(P-11435)
GREYHOUND LINES INC
1716 E 7th St (90021-1202)
PHONE..............................213 629-8400
Mark Jacobson, *Prin*
EMP: 97
SQ FT: 100,000
SALES (corp-wide): 611.17MM **Privately
Held**
Web: www.greyhound.com
SIC: 4173 Bus terminal operation
HQ: Greyhound Lines, Inc.
    350 N Saint Paul St # 300
    Dallas TX
    214 849-8000

4212 Local Trucking, Without Storage

(P-11436)
365 DELIVERY INC
440 E Huntington Dr Ste 300 (91006-3776)
PHONE..............................818 815-5005
Bernardo Anders, *Pr*
Ariana Barrera, *
EMP: 100 **EST:** 2017
SALES (est): 2.52MM **Privately Held**
SIC: 4212 Delivery service, vehicular

(P-11437)
A G HACIENDA INCORPORATED
32794 Sherwood Ave (93250-9626)
P.O. Box 367 (93250-0367)
PHONE..............................661 792-2418
Xochilht Gonzalez, *Pr*
EMP: 400 **EST:** 1997
SALES (est): 9.77MM **Privately Held**
SIC: 4212 0761 4214 Local trucking, without
    storage; Farm labor contractors; Local
    trucking with storage

(P-11438)
A-TEAM DELIVERS LLC
12127 Mall Blvd Ste A322 (92392-7665)
PHONE..............................858 254-8401
Steve Ford, *CEO*
EMP: 80 **EST:** 2020
SALES (est): 2.55MM **Privately Held**
SIC: 4212 Delivery service, vehicular

(P-11439)
ADVANCED CHEMICAL TRNSPT INC
600 Iowa St (92373-8047)
PHONE..............................951 790-7989
EMP: 196
SALES (corp-wide): 95.12MM **Privately
Held**
Web: www.actenviro.com
SIC: 4212 Hazardous waste transport
PA: Advanced Chemical Transport, Inc.
    967 Mabury Rd
    San Jose CA
    408 548-5050

(P-11440)
AJR TRUCKING INC
435 E Weber Ave (90222-1424)
PHONE..............................310 707-1120
Khachatur Khudikyan, *CEO*
Angel Reyes, *
Hakop Khudikyan, *
EMP: 84 **EST:** 1989
SQ FT: 12,000
SALES (est): 10.01MM **Privately Held**
Web: www.ajrtrucking.com
SIC: 4212 Mail carriers, contract

(P-11441)
ANCON MARINE LLC
Also Called: Ancon Services
2735 Rose Ave (90755-1927)
PHONE..............................562 326-5900
EMP: 102
SALES (corp-wide): 113.73MM **Privately
Held**
Web: www.anconservices.com
SIC: 4212 Local trucking, without storage
PA: Ancon Marine, Llc
    10571 Los Alamitos Blvd
    Los Alamitos CA
    707 756-0286

(P-11442)
APEX BULK COMMODITIES INC (PA)
Also Called: Apex Bulk Commodities
12531 Violet Rd Ste A (92301-2731)
PHONE..............................760 246-6077
EMP: 200 **EST:** 1967
SALES (est): 41.54MM
SALES (corp-wide): 41.54MM **Privately
Held**
Web: www.apexbulk.com
SIC: 4212 4213 Liquid haulage, local;
    Trucking, except local

(P-11443)
ARAKELIAN ENTERPRISES INC
Also Called: Athens Services
11121 Pendleton St (91352-1513)
PHONE..............................818 768-2644
Ron Arakelian Junior, *CEO*
EMP: 164
SALES (corp-wide): 199.65MM **Privately
Held**
Web: www.athensservices.com
SIC: 4212 Garbage collection and transport,
    no disposal
PA: Arakelian Enterprises, Inc.
    14048 Valley Blvd
    City Of Industry CA
    626 336-3636

(P-11444)
BELSHIRE TRNSP SVCS INC
Also Called: Belshire
25971 Towne Centre Dr (92610-2462)
PHONE..............................949 460-5200
Karen Cass, *Pr*
EMP: 125 **EST:** 2002
SALES (est): 9.48MM **Privately Held**
Web: www.belshire.com
SIC: 4212 Hazardous waste transport

(P-11445)
BURNS AND SONS TRUCKING INC
Also Called: Dependable Disposal and Recycl
9210 Olive Dr (91977-2305)
P.O. Box 1640 (91979-1640)
PHONE..............................619 460-5394
TOLL FREE: 800
Eva N Burns, *CEO*
Jack Burns Senior, *Pr*
Tom Mcfarlane, *Genl Mgr*
Jim Burns, *
Jack Burns Junior, *VP*
EMP: 85 **EST:** 1977
SQ FT: 6,000
SALES (est): 15.08MM **Privately Held**
Web: www.burnsandsons.com
SIC: 4212 4214 Local trucking, without
    storage; Local trucking with storage

(P-11446)
C P S EXPRESS
4375 E Lowell St Ste G (91761-2227)
P.O. Box 248 (91752-0248)
PHONE..............................951 685-1041
Kurt Allen, *CEO*
Timothy Pollock, *
Paul Anderson, *
EMP: 115 **EST:** 1980
SQ FT: 7,000
SALES (est): 23.73MM
SALES (corp-wide): 23.73MM **Privately
Held**
Web: www.cpsexpress.com
SIC: 4212 4213 4214 Local trucking, without
    storage; Trucking, except local; Local
    trucking with storage
PA: Haddy, J G Sales Co, Inc
    4375 E Lowell St Ste G

Ontario CA
951 685-4100

(P-11447)
CARGO SOLUTION BROKERAGE INC
14587 Valley Blvd (92335-6248)
PHONE..............................909 350-1644
Yudvinder S Kang, *CEO*
EMP: 200 **EST:** 2004
SALES (est): 4.61MM **Privately Held**
SIC: 4212 Local trucking, without storage

(P-11448)
CATERED FIT CORP
13631 Saticoy St (91402-6301)
PHONE..............................855 400-2348
Adam Friden, *Genl Mgr*
EMP: 102
SALES (corp-wide): 6.72MM **Privately
Held**
Web: www.cateredfit.com
SIC: 4212 5812 Baggage transfer; Caterers
PA: Catered Fit Corp
    5150 N State Road 7
    Fort Lauderdale FL
    954 549-4693

(P-11449)
CENTRAL STATES LOGISTICS INC
Also Called: Diligent Delivery Systems
28338 Constellation Rd Ste 940
(91355-5012)
PHONE..............................661 295-7222
Larry Browne, *Brnch Mgr*
EMP: 181
SALES (corp-wide): 36.79MM **Privately
Held**
Web: www.diligentusa.com
SIC: 4212 Delivery service, vehicular
PA: Central States Logistics, Inc.
    9200 Derrington Rd # 100
    Houston TX
    888 374-3354

(P-11450)
CJ LOGISTICS AMERICA LLC
12350 Philadelphia Ave (91752-3228)
PHONE..............................909 605-7233
EMP: 187
Web: america.cjlogistics.com
SIC: 4212 4213 4225 4731 Local trucking,
    without storage; Trucking, except local;
    General warehousing and storage; Freight
    consolidation
HQ: Cj Logistics America, Llc
    1750 S Wolf Rd
    Des Plaines IL

(P-11451)
CNET EXPRESS
15134 Indiana Ave Apt 38 (90723-3582)
PHONE..............................949 357-5475
Diana Diaz Vargas, *CEO*
Tamara Lupoe, *Prin*
Allen E Lupoe Junior, *Prin*
EMP: 102 **EST:** 2018
SALES (est): 3.08MM **Privately Held**
SIC: 4212 Delivery service, vehicular

(P-11452)
DLF LOGISTICS LLC
Also Called: Dlf Logistics
1019 S Rimpau Blvd (90019-1810)
P.O. Box 1929 (90801-1929)
PHONE..............................626 387-3797
Durran Felton, *Managing Member*
EMP: 81 **EST:** 2019

SALES (est): 2.42MM **Privately Held**
SIC: **4212** Local trucking, without storage

(P-11453)
GALE/TRIANGLE INC (PA)
Also Called: Triangle West
12816 Shoemaker Ave (90670-6346)
PHONE..................................562 741-1300
Michael Kaplan, *CEO*
Bob Kaplan, *Pr*
Craig Kaplan, *CEO*
▲ **EMP:** 94 **EST:** 1994
SQ FT: 40,000
SALES (est): 6.54MM **Privately Held**
SIC: **4212 4214** Local trucking, without storage; Local trucking with storage

(P-11454)
GATEWAY LOGISTICS TECH LLC
11400 W Olympic Blvd (90064-1579)
PHONE..................................732 750-9000
Jim Deveau, *CEO*
EMP: 156 **EST:** 2020
SALES (est): 935.41K
SALES (corp-wide): 42.44MM **Privately Held**
SIC: **4212 4213** Local trucking, without storage; Trucking, except local
PA: Taylored Services Parent Co. Inc.
1495 E Locust St
Ontario CA
909 510-4800

(P-11455)
GAZELLE TRANSPORTATION LLC
34915 Gazelle Ct (93308-9618)
PHONE..................................661 322-8868
EMP: 193 **EST:** 1992
SALES (est): 20.08MM **Privately Held**
Web: www.gazelletrans.com
SIC: **4212** Local trucking, without storage

(P-11456)
GENERAL LGSTICS SYSTEMS US INC
12300 Bell Ranch Dr (90670-3356)
PHONE..................................562 577-6037
EMP: 171
SALES (corp-wide): 14.47B **Privately Held**
Web: www.gls-us.com
SIC: **4212** Delivery service, vehicular
HQ: General Logistics Systems Us, Inc.
4000 Executive Pkwy # 295
San Ramon CA

(P-11457)
GENERAL LGSTICS SYSTEMS US INC
24305 Prielipp Rd (92595-7425)
PHONE..................................951 677-3972
EMP: 128
SALES (corp-wide): 14.47B **Privately Held**
Web: www.gls-us.com
SIC: **4212** Delivery service, vehicular
HQ: General Logistics Systems Us, Inc.
4000 Executive Pkwy # 295
San Ramon CA

(P-11458)
GRIMMWAY ENTERPRISES INC
11646 Malaga Rd (93203-9641)
PHONE..................................307 302-0090
EMP: 94
SALES (corp-wide): 1.86B **Privately Held**
Web: www.grimmway.com
SIC: **4212** Farm to market haulage, local
PA: Grimmway Enterprises, Inc.
14141 Di Giorgio Rd

Arvin CA
800 301-3101

(P-11459)
HANSON AGGRGTES MD-PACIFIC INC
50 S Kellogg Ave (93117-3417)
PHONE..................................805 967-2371
EMP: 18
SALES (corp-wide): 21.19B **Privately Held**
SIC: **4212 3281** Local trucking, without storage; Stone, quarrying and processing of own stone products
HQ: Hanson Aggregates Mid-Pacific, Inc.
12667 Alcosta Blvd # 400
San Ramon CA

(P-11460)
HF COX INC
Also Called: Cox Petroleum Transport
8330 Atlantic Ave (90201-5808)
PHONE..................................323 587-2359
Diane Judge, *Brnch Mgr*
EMP: 290
SALES (corp-wide): 683.25K **Privately Held**
Web: www.coxpetroleum.com
SIC: **4212** Petroleum haulage, local
PA: H.F. Cox, Inc.
118 Cox Transport Way
Bakersfield CA
661 366-3236

(P-11461)
HUB GROUP TRUCKING INC
13867 Valley Blvd (92335-5230)
PHONE..................................909 770-8950
Roy Sheredon, *Brnch Mgr*
EMP: 500
SALES (corp-wide): 5.34B **Publicly Held**
Web: www.hubgroup.com
SIC: **4212** Local trucking, without storage
HQ: Hub Group Trucking, Inc.
2001 Hub Group Way
Oak Brook IL
630 271-3600

(P-11462)
MULECHAIN INC
2901 W Coast Hwy Ste 200 (92663-4045)
PHONE..................................888 456-8881
Ralph Liu, *CEO*
EMP: 56 **EST:** 2017
SALES (est): 1MM **Privately Held**
Web: www.mulechain.com
SIC: **4212 7372** Delivery service, vehicular; Application computer software

(P-11463)
ROY MILLER FREIGHT LINES LLC (PA)
3165 E Coronado St (92806-1915)
P.O. Box 18419 (92817-8419)
PHONE..................................714 632-5511
Danny Miller, *Mng*
Danny Miller, *CEO*
Wiley R Miller Junior, *Managing Member*
EMP: 100 **EST:** 1942
SALES (est): 19.14MM
SALES (corp-wide): 19.14MM **Privately Held**
Web: www.roymiller.com
SIC: **4212** Local trucking, without storage

(P-11464)
SAVAGE SERVICES CORPORATION
8636 Sorensen Ave (90670-2633)
PHONE..................................562 400-2044

EMP: 80
SALES (corp-wide): 1.73B **Privately Held**
Web: www.savageco.com
SIC: **4212** Local trucking, without storage
HQ: Savage Services Corporation
901 W Legacy Center Way
Midvale UT

(P-11465)
SOUTHERN COUNTIES TERMINALS
Also Called: Griley Air Freight
5341 W 104th St (90045-6009)
P.O. Box 92940 (90009-2940)
PHONE..................................310 642-0462
EMP: 90 **EST:** 1973
SALES (est): 15.35MM **Privately Held**
Web: www.grileyair.com
SIC: **4212** Local trucking, without storage

(P-11466)
TRANSPRTTION BRKG SPCLISTS INC
Also Called: Tbs
3151 Airway Ave Ste F208 (92626-4621)
PHONE..................................714 754-4236
Ben Haeri, *CEO*
Steve Kennedy, *
Mike Owens, *
Lee Mayer, *
Fred Khac, *
EMP: 450 **EST:** 2016
SALES (est): 16.39MM **Privately Held**
SIC: **4212** Local trucking, without storage

(P-11467)
ULS EXPRESS INC
2850 E Del Amo Blvd (90221-6007)
P.O. Box 7547 (90807-0547)
PHONE..................................310 631-0800
EMP: 157 **EST:** 1987
SQ FT: 220,000
SALES (est): 4.62MM **Privately Held**
Web: www.uwc-net.com
SIC: **4212** Local trucking, without storage
HQ: Universal Logistics System, Inc.
2850 Del Amo Blvd
Carson CA
310 631-0800

(P-11468)
UNITED PUMPING SERVICE INC
14000 Valley Blvd (91746-2801)
PHONE..................................626 961-9326
Eduardo T Perry Senior, *Pr*
Daniel C Perry, *
Margaret Perry, *
Eduardo Perry Junior, *Sec*
EMP: 95 **EST:** 1970
SQ FT: 25,000
SALES (est): 21.71MM **Privately Held**
Web: www.unitedpumping.com
SIC: **4212** Hazardous waste transport

(P-11469)
WASTE MANAGEMENT RECYCLING
Also Called: Waste Management
9227 Tujunga Ave (91352-1542)
P.O. Box 7400 (91109-7400)
PHONE..................................818 767-6180
EMP: 97 **EST:** 1955
SALES (est): 35.42MM
SALES (corp-wide): 19.7B **Publicly Held**
SIC: **4212 4953** Garbage collection and transport, no disposal; Sanitary landfill operation
PA: Waste Management, Inc.
800 Capitol St Ste 3000

Houston TX
713 512-6200

(P-11470)
XPO CARTAGE INC
Also Called: Pacer
5800 Sheila St (90040-2322)
PHONE..................................800 837-7584
EMP: 83
SIC: **4212** Local trucking, without storage

4213 Trucking, Except Local

(P-11471)
ARDWIN INC
Also Called: Ardwin Freight
2940 N Hollywood Way (91505-1024)
P.O. Box 1609 (91507-1609)
PHONE..................................818 767-7777
Edwin Sahakian, *Pr*
EMP: 130 **EST:** 1988
SQ FT: 10,000
SALES (est): 20.98MM **Privately Held**
Web: www.ardwin.com
SIC: **4213** Contract haulers

(P-11472)
BEST OVERNITE EXPRESS INC (PA)
Also Called: Best Overnight Express
406 Live Oak Ave (91706-1314)
P.O. Box 90816 (91715-0816)
PHONE..................................626 256-6340
William K Applebee, *Pr*
Mike White, *
Micah Applebee, *
EMP: 100 **EST:** 1988
SQ FT: 25,000
SALES (est): 32.1MM **Privately Held**
Web: www.bestovernite.com
SIC: **4213** Trucking, except local

(P-11473)
CARGO SOLUTION EXPRESS INC (PA)
14587 Valley Blvd # 89 (92335-6248)
PHONE..................................909 350-1644
Balwinder Kaur Kang, *Pr*
EMP: 250 **EST:** 2002
SQ FT: 10,000
SALES (est): 99.15MM
SALES (corp-wide): 99.15MM **Privately Held**
Web: www.cargosolutionexpress.com
SIC: **4213** Trucking, except local

(P-11474)
CERTIFIED FRT LOGISTICS INC (PA)
1344 White Ct (93458-3732)
P.O. Box 5668 (93456-5668)
PHONE..................................800 592-5906
James O Nelson, *Pr*
Edwin F Nelson Junior, *VP*
Jon Cramer, *
Scott Cramer, *
EMP: 120 **EST:** 1963
SQ FT: 40,000
SALES (est): 42.02MM
SALES (corp-wide): 42.02MM **Privately Held**
Web: www.certifiedfreightlogistics.com
SIC: **4213** Refrigerated products transport

(P-11475)
CJ LOGISTICS AMERICA LLC
1895 Marigold Ave (92374-5028)
PHONE..................................909 363-4354

Greg Hart, *Genl Pt*
EMP: 93
Web: america.cjlogistics.com
SIC: 4213 4212 Trucking, except local; Local trucking, without storage
HQ: Cj Logistics America, Llc
1750 S Wolf Rd
Des Plaines IL

(P-11476)
CONTRACTORS CARGO COMPANY (PA)
Also Called: Contractors Rigging & Erectors
7223 Alondra Blvd (90723-3901)
P.O. Box 5290 (90224-5290)
PHONE..............................310 609-1957
Carla Ann Wheeler, *CEO*
Gerald D Wheeler, *
Kimberly Dorio, *
◆ **EMP:** 80 **EST:** 1959
SALES (est): 24.28MM
SALES (corp-wide): 24.28MM **Privately Held**
Web: www.contractorscargo.com
SIC: 4213 4731 1623 4741 Contract haulers; Freight transportation arrangement; Water, sewer, and utility lines; Rental of railroad cars

(P-11477)
COVENANT TRANSPORT INC
Also Called: Covenant Transport
1300 E Franklin Ave (91766-5416)
PHONE..............................909 469-0130
EMP: 660
Web: www.covenantlogistics.com
SIC: 4213 Contract haulers
HQ: Covenant Transport, Inc.
400 Birmingham Hwy
Chattanooga TN
423 821-1212

(P-11478)
CRST EXPEDITED INC
Also Called: Gardner Logistics
9032 Merrill Ave (91708)
P.O. Box 747 (91708-0747)
PHONE..............................909 563-5606
EMP: 188
SALES (corp-wide): 980.15MM **Privately Held**
Web: www.crst.com
SIC: 4213 Contract haulers
HQ: Crst Expedited, Inc.
201 1st St Se
Cedar Rapids IA
800 443-0940

(P-11479)
CRST EXPEDITED INC
1219 E Elm St (91761-4585)
PHONE..............................909 563-5606
John Smith, *Brnch Mgr*
EMP: 500
SALES (corp-wide): 980.15MM **Privately Held**
Web: www.crst.com
SIC: 4213 4212 Trucking, except local; Local trucking, without storage
HQ: Crst Expedited, Inc.
201 1st St Se
Cedar Rapids IA
800 443-0940

(P-11480)
D C SHOWER DOORS INC
Also Called: Image Transfer
26121 Avenue Hall (91355-3490)
PHONE..............................661 257-1177
Jason Shepard, *Pr*

EMP: 191 **EST:** 1996
SQ FT: 125,000
SALES (est): 1.04MM
SALES (corp-wide): 136.14MM **Privately Held**
Web: www.cwdoors.com
SIC: 4213 Trucking, except local
PA: Contractors Wardrobe, Inc.
26121 Avenue Hall
Valencia CA
661 257-1177

(P-11481)
DEPENDABLE COMPANIES
2555 E Olympic Blvd (90023-2605)
PHONE..............................800 548-8608
Ron Massman, *CEO*
EMP: 129 **EST:** 2015
SALES (est): 10.47MM **Privately Held**
Web: www.godependable.com
SIC: 4213 Trucking, except local

(P-11482)
DEPENDABLE HIGHWAY EXPRESS INC (PA)
Also Called: Dependable Logistics Services
2555 E Olympic Blvd (90023-2605)
P.O. Box 58047 (90058-0047)
PHONE..............................323 526-2200
Ronald Massman, *Pr*
Robert Massman, *VP*
Michael Dougan, *CFO*
◆ **EMP:** 300 **EST:** 1984
SQ FT: 1,680,000
SALES (est): 206.32MM
SALES (corp-wide): 206.32MM **Privately Held**
Web: www.godependable.com
SIC: 4213 4225 Contract haulers; General warehousing and storage

(P-11483)
DOUBLE EAGLE TRNSP CORP
12135 Scarbrough Ct (92344-9200)
PHONE..............................760 956-3770
Gerald E Butcher, *Pr*
EMP: 140 **EST:** 1992
SQ FT: 10,125
SALES (est): 8.43MM **Privately Held**
SIC: 4213 4212 Contract haulers; Local trucking, without storage

(P-11484)
ESPARZA ENTERPRISES INC
500 Workman St (93307-6871)
PHONE..............................661 631-0347
EMP: 792
SALES (corp-wide): 135MM **Privately Held**
Web: www.esparzainc.com
SIC: 4213 Trucking, except local
PA: Esparza Enterprises, Inc.
3851 Fruitvale Ave
Bakersfield CA
661 831-0002

(P-11485)
ESTES EXPRESS LINES
14727 Alondra Blvd (90638-5617)
PHONE..............................714 994-3770
Benjamin J Torman, *Brnch Mgr*
EMP: 147
SALES (corp-wide): 3.56B **Privately Held**
Web: www.estes-express.com
SIC: 4213 Contract haulers
PA: Estes Express Lines
3901 W Broad St
Richmond VA
804 353-1900

(P-11486)
ESTES EXPRESS LINES
Also Called: Estes
13327 Temple Ave (91746-1513)
PHONE..............................626 333-9090
Kieran O'carroll, *Mgr*
EMP: 85
SQ FT: 6,156
SALES (corp-wide): 3.56B **Privately Held**
Web: www.estes-express.com
SIC: 4213 4212 Less-than-truckload (LTL); Local trucking, without storage
PA: Estes Express Lines
3901 W Broad St
Richmond VA
804 353-1900

(P-11487)
ESTES EXPRESS LINES
10736 Cherry Ave (92337-7196)
PHONE..............................909 427-9850
Mark Brown, *Mgr*
EMP: 110
SALES (corp-wide): 3.56B **Privately Held**
Web: www.estes-express.com
SIC: 4213 4212 Less-than-truckload (LTL); Local trucking, without storage
PA: Estes Express Lines
3901 W Broad St
Richmond VA
804 353-1900

(P-11488)
ESTES EXPRESS LINES
120 Press Ln (91910-1012)
PHONE..............................619 425-4040
Craig Buker, *Brnch Mgr*
EMP: 86
SALES (corp-wide): 3.56B **Privately Held**
Web: www.estes-express.com
SIC: 4213 Contract haulers
PA: Estes Express Lines
3901 W Broad St
Richmond VA
804 353-1900

(P-11489)
H RAUVEL INC
Also Called: Nova Transportation Services
501 W Walnut St (90220-5221)
PHONE..............................562 989-3333
Hector Velasco, *Mgr*
EMP: 180
SALES (corp-wide): 23.11MM **Privately Held**
Web: www.novafreight.net
SIC: 4213 Trucking, except local
PA: H. Rauvel, Inc.
1710 E Sepulveda Blvd
Carson CA
310 604-0060

(P-11490)
HEARTLAND EXPRESS INC IOWA
Also Called: Heartland Express
10131 Redwood Ave (92335-6236)
PHONE..............................319 626-3600
Matthew Gonzalez, *Supervisor*
EMP: 566
SALES (corp-wide): 968MM **Publicly Held**
Web: www.heartlandexpress.com
SIC: 4213 Trucking, except local
HQ: Heartland Express, Inc. Of Iowa
901 Heartland Way
North Liberty IA
319 626-3600

(P-11491)
HI PRO INC
4584 Adobe Rd (92277-1671)
P.O. Box 148 (92277-0148)
PHONE..............................760 367-7734
Joshua Stoneback, *CEO*
EMP: 200 **EST:** 2012
SALES (est): 9.74MM **Privately Held**
Web: www.hiproinc.com
SIC: 4213 7389 4212 Trucking, except local; Brokers, contract services; Delivery service, vehicular

(P-11492)
JACK JONES TRUCKING INC
1090 E Belmont St (91761-4501)
PHONE..............................909 456-2500
Valerie Liese, *Pr*
Erin Craig, *
Bob Liese, *
Kristy Richardson, *
Robert Liese, *
EMP: 100 **EST:** 1971
SQ FT: 3,000
SALES (est): 10.29MM **Privately Held**
Web: www.jjtinc.com
SIC: 4213 Trucking, except local

(P-11493)
LANDFORCE CORPORATION
17201 N D St (92394-1401)
PHONE..............................760 843-7839
Rajinder Bhangu, *CEO*
EMP: 120 **EST:** 2000
SALES (est): 8.63MM **Privately Held**
Web: www.landforcecorp.com
SIC: 4213 Trucking, except local

(P-11494)
LAS VEGAS / LA EXPRESS INC (PA)
1000 S Cucamonga Ave (91761-3461)
PHONE..............................909 972-3100
Ronald Cain Junior, *CEO*
Beverly A Adley, *
Michael P Adley, *
EMP: 170 **EST:** 1988
SQ FT: 163,000
SALES (est): 18.9MM **Privately Held**
Web: www.vegasexpress.com
SIC: 4213 Trucking, except local

(P-11495)
LOAD DELIVERED LOGISTICS LLC
214 Main St (90291-2522)
PHONE..............................310 822-0215
Michael Cherney, *Mgr*
EMP: 109
SALES (corp-wide): 1.18B **Privately Held**
SIC: 4213 Trucking, except local
HQ: Load Delivered Logistics Llc
640 N Lasalle Ste 555
Chicago IL
877 930-5623

(P-11496)
LTL PROS INC
13610 S Archibald Ave (91761-7930)
PHONE..............................909 350-1600
Manuel Vargas, *Pr*
EMP: 80 **EST:** 2017
SALES (est): 2.78MM **Privately Held**
Web: www.ltlpros.com
SIC: 4213 Trucking, except local

(P-11497)
MARK CLEMONS
Also Called: Mtc Transportation

4584 Adobe Rd (92277-1671)
P.O. Box 148 (92277-0148)
PHONE..............................760 361-1531
Mark Clemons, *Owner*
Genevieve Clemons, *Mgr*
EMP: 200 **EST:** 1978
SALES (est): 7.35MM **Privately Held**
SIC: 4213 4212 4513 4522 Heavy
machinery transport; Local trucking, without
storage; Air courier services; Air
transportation, nonscheduled

(P-11498)
MASHBURN TRNSP SVCS INC
1423 Kern St (93268-4607)
P.O. Box 66 (93268-8066)
PHONE..............................661 763-5724
Denise Mashburn, *Pr*
Michael Mashburn, *
EMP: 120 **EST:** 1987
SQ FT: 2,000
SALES (est): 16.63MM **Privately Held**
Web: www.mashburntransportation.com
SIC: 4213 4212 Contract haulers; Local
trucking, without storage

(P-11499)
NATIONAL RETAIL TRNSP INC
400 Harley Knox Blvd (92571-7566)
PHONE..............................951 243-6110
EMP: 81
SALES (corp-wide): 496.65MM **Privately
Held**
SIC: 4213 Trucking, except local
HQ: National Retail Transportation, Inc.
2820 16th St
North Bergen NJ
201 866-0462

(P-11500)
NEW LEGEND INC
8613 Etiwanda Ave (91739-9611)
PHONE..............................855 210-2300
EMP: 231
Web: www.newlegendinc.com
SIC: 4213 4212 Trucking, except local; Local
trucking, without storage
PA: New Legend, Inc.
811 S 59th Ave
Phoenix AZ

(P-11501)
**PACIFIC DRAYAGE SERVICES
LLC**
Also Called: Pds
550 W Artesia Blvd (90220-5524)
PHONE..............................833 334-4622
Mark George, *Managing Member*
EMP: 210 **EST:** 2019
SALES (est): 13.69MM
SALES (corp-wide): 488.55MM **Privately
Held**
Web: www.imcc.com
SIC: 4213 Trucking, except local
PA: Imc Companies - National Accounts,
Llc
1305 Schilling Blvd W
Collierville TN
901 746-3700

(P-11502)
**PAN PACIFIC PETROLEUM CO
INC (PA)**
9302 Garfield Ave (90280-3805)
P.O. Box 1966 (90280-1966)
PHONE..............................562 928-0100
Robert Roth, *CEO*
Dale Snyder, *
Steven Roth, *
EMP: 100 **EST:** 1962

SQ FT: 600
SALES (est): 7.33MM
SALES (corp-wide): 7.33MM **Privately
Held**
SIC: 4213 5172 Liquid petroleum transport,
non-local; Petroleum brokers

(P-11503)
POINTDIRECT TRANSPORT INC
19083 Mermack Ave (92532-2256)
PHONE..............................909 371-0837
Adolfo De La Herran, *Pr*
EMP: 100 **EST:** 2014
SALES (est): 2.46MM **Privately Held**
Web: www.point-direct.com
SIC: 4213 Trucking, except local

(P-11504)
**RPM TRANSPORTATION INC
(DH)**
11660 Arroyo Ave (92705-3057)
PHONE..............................714 388-3500
Shawn Duke, *Pr*
Andrew Lewes, *
▲ **EMP:** 110 **EST:** 1985
SQ FT: 175,000
SALES (est): 17.69MM
SALES (corp-wide): 1.16B **Privately Held**
Web: www.odysseylogistics.com
SIC: 4213 4225 4214 Trailer or container on
flat car (TOFC/COFC); General
warehousing; Local trucking with storage
HQ: Rpm Consolidated Services, Inc.
1901 Raymer Ave
Fullerton CA
714 388-3500

(P-11505)
**STANLEY G ALEXANDER INC
(PA)**
Also Called: Alexander's Moving & Storage
2942 Dow Ave (92780-7220)
PHONE..............................714 731-1658
EMP: 130 **EST:** 1953
SALES (est): 53.18MM
SALES (corp-wide): 53.18MM **Privately
Held**
Web: www.alexanders.net
SIC: 4213 Trucking, except local

(P-11506)
**STEVENS TRANSPORTATION
INC**
Also Called: Stevens Trucking
7100 E Brundage Ln (93307-3060)
PHONE..............................661 366-3286
EMP: 150 **EST:** 1984
SALES (est): 23.69MM **Privately Held**
Web: www.stibk.com
SIC: 4213 Refrigerated products transport

(P-11507)
SWIFT LEASING CO LLC
14392 Valley Blvd (92335-5240)
PHONE..............................909 347-0500
EMP: 287
Web: www.swifttrans.com
SIC: 4213 Contract haulers
HQ: Swift Leasing Co., Llc
2200 S 75th Ave
Phoenix AZ
602 269-9700

(P-11508)
**TCI TRANSPORTATION
SERVICES**
14561 Merrill Ave Bldg B (92335-4219)
PHONE..............................909 355-8545
EMP: 194

SALES (corp-wide): 29.25MM **Privately
Held**
Web: www.tcitransportation.com
SIC: 4213 Trucking, except local
PA: Tci Transportation Services
4950 Triggs St
Commerce CA
323 269-3033

(P-11509)
U C L INCORPORATED (PA)
Also Called: United Cargo Logistics
620 S Hacienda Blvd (91745-1126)
PHONE..............................323 235-0099
Byung Y Chang, *CEO*
Chris Chang, *
Yong Ku, *
EMP: 100 **EST:** 1998
SQ FT: 16,000
SALES (est): 27.76MM
SALES (corp-wide): 27.76MM **Privately
Held**
Web: www.uclinc.com
SIC: 4213 Trucking, except local

(P-11510)
U S XPRESS INC
363 Nina Lee Rd (92231-9527)
PHONE..............................760 768-6707
EMP: 299
Web: www.usxpress.com
SIC: 4213 Trucking, except local
HQ: U. S. Xpress, Inc.
4080 Jenkins Rd
Chattanooga TN
866 266-7270

(P-11511)
VALLEY BULK INC
17649 Turner Rd (92394-8716)
P.O. Box 1100 (92393-1100)
PHONE..............................760 843-0574
Jeff W Golson, *Pr*
EMP: 85 **EST:** 1995
SALES (est): 7.83MM **Privately Held**
Web: www.valleybulkinc.com
SIC: 4213 Contract haulers

(P-11512)
XPO LOGISTICS FREIGHT INC
13364 Marlay Ave (92337-6919)
PHONE..............................951 685-1244
EMP: 100
SALES (corp-wide): 7.72B **Publicly Held**
Web: www.xpo.com
SIC: 4213 Contract haulers
HQ: Xpo Logistics Freight, Inc.
2211 Old Earhart Rd # 100
Ann Arbor MI
800 755-2728

(P-11513)
XPO LOGISTICS FREIGHT INC
1955 E Washington Blvd (90021-3206)
PHONE..............................213 744-0664
Todd Liverman, *Brnch Mgr*
EMP: 166
SQ FT: 39,842
SALES (corp-wide): 7.72B **Publicly Held**
Web: www.xpo.com
SIC: 4213 4212 4731 Contract haulers;
Local trucking, without storage; Freight
forwarding
HQ: Xpo Logistics Freight, Inc.
2211 Old Earhart Rd # 100
Ann Arbor MI
800 755-2728

(P-11514)
XPO LOGISTICS FREIGHT INC
12903 Lakeland Rd (90670-4516)
PHONE..............................562 946-8331
EMP: 92
SALES (corp-wide): 7.72B **Publicly Held**
Web: www.xpo.com
SIC: 4213 Contract haulers
HQ: Xpo Logistics Freight, Inc.
2211 Old Earhart Rd # 100
Ann Arbor MI
800 755-2728

(P-11515)
XPO LOGISTICS FREIGHT INC
2102 N Batavia St (92865-3104)
PHONE..............................714 282-7717
Tim Worner, *Mgr*
EMP: 87
SALES (corp-wide): 7.72B **Publicly Held**
Web: www.xpo.com
SIC: 4213 Contract haulers
HQ: Xpo Logistics Freight, Inc.
2211 Old Earhart Rd # 100
Ann Arbor MI
800 755-2728

4214 Local Trucking With
Storage

(P-11516)
COROVAN CORPORATION (PA)
12302 Kerran St (92064-6884)
PHONE..............................858 762-8100
Richard R Schmitz, *CEO*
Robert J Schmitz, *
Thomas A Schmitz, *
EMP: 175 **EST:** 1994
SQ FT: 80,000
SALES (est): 98.92MM **Privately Held**
Web: www.corovan.com
SIC: 4214 Local trucking with storage

(P-11517)
**COROVAN MOVING & STORAGE
CO (HQ)**
12302 Kerran St (92064-6884)
PHONE..............................858 748-1100
Richard R Schmitz, *Pr*
Robert J Schmitz, *
Thomas A Schmitz, *
Jerry P Brothers, *
▲ **EMP:** 100 **EST:** 1948
SQ FT: 600,000
SALES (est): 65.6MM **Privately Held**
Web: www.corovan.com
SIC: 4214 4213 Household goods moving
and storage, local; Household goods
transport
PA: Corovan Corporation
12302 Kerran St
Poway CA

(P-11518)
CRUZ MODULAR INC (PA)
Also Called: Systechs
249 W Baywood Ave Ste B (92865-2604)
PHONE..............................714 283-2890
Linda Galleran, *CEO*
Vince Schlachter, *Pr*
Malcolm Craycroft, *VP*
EMP: 90 **EST:** 1991
SALES (est): 4.45MM **Privately Held**
Web: cruzmodulard.openfos.com
SIC: 4214 7641 4226 1799 Furniture moving
and storage, local; Reupholstery and
furniture repair; Special warehousing and
storage, nec; Office furniture installation

PRODUCTS & SVCS

(P-11519)
FN LOGISTICS LLC
12588 Florence Ave (90670-3919)
PHONE....................213.625-5900
Richard Saghian, *Pr*
EMP: 941
SIC: 4214 Local trucking with storage
HQ: Fn Logistics, Llc.
　　2801 E 46th St
　　Vernon CA
　　213 625-5900

(P-11520)
FOX TRANSPORTATION INC
18408 S Laurel Park Rd (90220-6015)
PHONE..............................310 971-0867
Luke Shire, *Mgr*
EMP: 227
Web: www.foxtransportationinc.com
SIC: 4214 4225 Local trucking with storage;
　　General warehousing and storage
PA: Fox Transportation, Inc.
　　8610 Helms Ave
　　Rancho Cucamonga CA

(P-11521)
**GREAT AMRCN LOGISTICS DIST
INC**
13565 Larwin Cir (90670-5032)
PHONE..............................562 229-3601
TOLL FREE: 800
EMP: 85 **EST:** 1993
SQ FT: 120,000
SALES (est): 13.49MM **Privately Held**
Web: www.greatamerican-logistics.com
SIC: 4214 4212 4213 6719 Household
　　goods moving and storage, local; Moving
　　services; Trucking, except local; Investment
　　holding companies, except banks

(P-11522)
**SCHICK MOVING & STORAGE
CO (PA)**
2721 Michelle Dr (92780-7018)
P.O. Box 3627 (92781-3627)
PHONE..............................714 731-5500
TOLL FREE: 800
Gordon C Schick, *Pr*
Arthur C Schick Junior, *VP*
Beverly C Schick, *
Gordon Schick, *
Lynne M Larson, *
EMP: 100 **EST:** 1956
SQ FT: 113,000
SALES (est): 6.9MM
SALES (corp-wide): 6.9MM **Privately Held**
Web: www.schickusa.com
SIC: 4214 Household goods moving and
　　storage, local

(P-11523)
**VAN TORRANCE & STORAGE
COMPANY (PA)**
Also Called: S & M Moving Systems
12128 Burke St (90670-2678)
TOLL FREE: 800
◆ **EMP:** 100 **EST:** 1918
SQ FT: 95,000
SALES (est): 48.8MM
SALES (corp-wide): 48.8MM **Privately
Held**
Web: www.unitedvanlines.com
SIC: 4214 4213 Local trucking with storage;
　　Trucking, except local

(P-11524)
**VERNON CENTRAL
WAREHOUSE INC**
Also Called: Vernon Warehouse Co

2050 E 38th St (90058-1615)
P.O. Box 58426 (90058-0426)
PHONE..............................323 234-2200
Joseph E Tack, *CEO*
Robert L Shipp, *
Joe Tack, *
Jim Boltinghouse, *
Steve Shanklin, *
EMP: 125 **EST:** 1933
SQ FT: 100,000
SALES (est): 20.6MM **Privately Held**
Web: www.sweetenerproducts.com
SIC: 4214 5149 Local trucking with storage;
　　Natural and organic foods

4215 Courier Services,
Except By Air

(P-11525)
ALL COUNTIES COURIER INC
1900 S State College Blvd Ste 450
(92806-6163)
PHONE..............................714 599-9300
Patricia Cochran, *Pr*
EMP: 200 **EST:** 1984
SALES (est): 20.26MM **Privately Held**
SIC: 4215 Package delivery, vehicular

(P-11526)
**BATTLE-TESTED STRATEGIES
LLC**
650 Commerce Ave Ste E (93551-3884)
PHONE..............................661 802-6509
Johnathon Ervin, *CEO*
EMP: 90 **EST:** 2018
SALES (est): 2.72MM **Privately Held**
SIC: 4215 7379 Package delivery, vehicular;
　　Computer related services, nec

(P-11527)
DHB DELIVERY LLC
1134 N Chestnut Ln (91702-6867)
PHONE..............................626 588-7562
Daniel R Bourgault, *Managing Member*
EMP: 84 **EST:** 2019
SALES (est): 2.68MM **Privately Held**
SIC: 4215 Package delivery, vehicular

(P-11528)
DI OVERNITE LLC
Also Called: Deliver-It
1900 S State College Blvd Ste 450
(92806-6163)
PHONE..............................877 997-7447
EMP: 89 **EST:** 2013
SALES (est): 12.11MM **Privately Held**
Web: www.deliver-it.com
SIC: 4215 Package delivery, vehicular

(P-11529)
FUNNELCLOUDSALES
21758 Placeritos Blvd (91321-1830)
PHONE..............................661 284-6032
Timothy Kane, *Pr*
EMP: 90
SALES (est): 1.34MM **Privately Held**
SIC: 4215 7389 Package delivery, vehicular;
　　Business services, nec

(P-11530)
**INTEGRATED PARCEL
NETWORK**
Also Called: Pacific Couriers
11135 Rush St Ste A (91733-3520)
PHONE..............................714 278-6100
Nadia Youssef, *CEO*
EMP: 275 **EST:** 1985
SALES (est): 4.49MM **Privately Held**

Web: www.iparcelnetwork.com
SIC: 4215 4214 7389 Package delivery,
　　vehicular; Local trucking with storage;
　　Courier or messenger service

(P-11531)
JET DELIVERY INC (PA)
2169 Wright Ave (91750-5835)
PHONE..............................800 716-7177
Michael Barbata, *Pr*
Jason Barbata, *CIO**
Mark Sur, *
EMP: 90 **EST:** 1950
SQ FT: 34,000
SALES (est): 24.73MM
SALES (corp-wide): 24.73MM **Privately
Held**
Web: www.jetdelivery.com
SIC: 4215 4231 4212 4213 Package
　　delivery, vehicular; Trucking terminal
　　facilities; Local trucking, without storage;
　　Trucking, except local

(P-11532)
KXP CARRIER SERVICES LLC
Also Called: Expak Logistics
11777 San Vicente Blvd (90049-5011)
PHONE..............................424 320-5300
Michael S Kraus, *CEO*
EMP: 140 **EST:** 2014
SQ FT: 1,500
SALES (est): 1.01MM
SALES (corp-wide): 24.03MM **Privately
Held**
Web: www.expak.com
SIC: 4215 Parcel delivery, vehicular
PA: Kxp Advantage Services, Llc
　　11777 San Vicente Blvd # 747
　　Los Angeles CA
　　424 320-5300

(P-11533)
MADDEN CORPORATION
Also Called: Pam's Delivery Svc & Nat Msgnr
2301 E Pacifica Pl (90220-6210)
PHONE..............................714 922-1670
Donald L Madden, *Pr*
EMP: 100 **EST:** 2003
SALES (est): 13.18MM **Privately Held**
SIC: 4215 Courier services, except by air

(P-11534)
MESSENGER EXPRESS (PA)
5435 Cahuenga Blvd Ste C (91601-2948)
PHONE..............................213 614-0475
Gilbert Kort, *Pr*
EMP: 143 **EST:** 1976
SALES (est): 4.48MM
SALES (corp-wide): 4.48MM **Privately
Held**
Web:
www.lightningmessengerexpress.com
SIC: 4215 7389 4212 Package delivery,
　　vehicular; Courier or messenger service;
　　Delivery service, vehicular

(P-11535)
**NATIONAL LOGISTICS TEAM
LLC**
21496 Main St (92313-5806)
P.O. Box 75 (92572-0075)
PHONE..............................951 369-5841
Eric Meza, *Managing Member*
EMP: 20 **EST:** 2013
SALES (est): 1.23MM **Privately Held**
Web: www.nlt-llc.com
SIC: 4215 2448 Package delivery, vehicular;
　　Pallets, wood

(P-11536)
ONTRAC LOGISTICS INC
Ontrac
11085 Olinda St (91352-3302)
PHONE..............................818 504-9043
EMP: 85
SALES (corp-wide): 735.78MM **Privately
Held**
Web: www.ontrac.com
SIC: 4215 Courier services, except by air
HQ: Ontrac Logistics, Inc.
　　8401 Greensboro Dr Fl 7
　　Mc Lean VA

(P-11537)
PEACH INC
Also Called: Action Messenger Service
1311 N Highland Ave (90028-7608)
P.O. Box 69763 (90069-0763)
PHONE..............................323 654-2333
Arthur P Ruben, *Pr*
EMP: 125 **EST:** 1990
SQ FT: 3,500
SALES (est): 9.7MM **Privately Held**
Web: www.actionmessenger.com
SIC: 4215 7389 Courier services, except by
　　air; Courier or messenger service

(P-11538)
SPEEDY EXPRESS LLC
4401 W Slauson Ave Ste A (90043-2267)
PHONE..............................818 300-7785
Kentrice Jones, *Prin*
EMP: 96 **EST:** 2020
SALES (est): 2.72MM **Privately Held**
SIC: 4215 Courier services, except by air

(P-11539)
UNITED PARCEL SERVICE INC
Also Called: UPS
17115 S Western Ave (90247-5299)
PHONE..............................310 217-2646
Randy Hulhellt, *Mgr*
EMP: 120
SALES (corp-wide): 100.34B **Publicly
Held**
Web: www.ups.com
SIC: 4215 4513 Parcel delivery, vehicular;
　　Air courier services
HQ: United Parcel Service, Inc.
　　55 Glenlake Pkwy
　　Atlanta GA
　　404 828-6000

(P-11540)
UNITED PARCEL SERVICE INC
Also Called: UPS
16000 Arminta St (91406-1895)
PHONE..............................404 828-6000
EMP: 293
SALES (corp-wide): 100.34B **Publicly
Held**
Web: www.ups.com
SIC: 4215 Parcel delivery, vehicular
HQ: United Parcel Service, Inc.
　　55 Glenlake Pkwy
　　Atlanta GA
　　404 828-6000

(P-11541)
UNITED PARCEL SERVICE INC
Also Called: UPS
13233 Moore St (90703-2276)
PHONE..............................562 404-3236
Gary Mieredos, *Mgr*
EMP: 320
SALES (corp-wide): 100.34B **Publicly
Held**
Web: www.ups.com

SIC: **4215** Parcel delivery, vehicular
HQ: United Parcel Service, Inc.
55 Glenlake Pkwy
Atlanta GA
404 828-6000

(P-11542)
UNITED PARCEL SERVICE INC
Also Called: UPS
1100 Baldwin Park Blvd (91706-5895)
PHONE..............................626 814-6216
EMP: 466
SALES (corp-wide): 100.34B **Publicly Held**
Web: www.ups.com
SIC: **4215** 4513 Parcel delivery, vehicular; Air courier services
HQ: United Parcel Service, Inc.
55 Glenlake Pkwy
Atlanta GA
404 828-6000

(P-11543)
UNITED PARCEL SERVICE INC
Also Called: UPS
3140 Jurupa St (91761)
PHONE..............................909 974-7212
Richard Ricardo, *Prin*
EMP: 958
SALES (corp-wide): 100.34B **Publicly Held**
Web: www.ups.com
SIC: **4215** Parcel delivery, vehicular
HQ: United Parcel Service, Inc.
55 Glenlake Pkwy
Atlanta GA
404 828-6000

(P-11544)
UNITED PARCEL SERVICE INC
Also Called: UPS
7925 Ronson Rd (92111-1997)
PHONE..............................909 279-5111
EMP: 546
SALES (corp-wide): 100.34B **Publicly Held**
Web: www.ups.com
SIC: **4215** Parcel delivery, vehicular
HQ: United Parcel Service, Inc.
55 Glenlake Pkwy
Atlanta GA
404 828-6000

(P-11545)
UNITED PARCEL SERVICE INC
Also Called: UPS
2300 Boswell Ct (91914-3520)
PHONE..............................619 482-8119
EMP: 120
SALES (corp-wide): 100.34B **Publicly Held**
Web: www.ups.com
SIC: **4215** Parcel delivery, vehicular
HQ: United Parcel Service, Inc.
55 Glenlake Pkwy
Atlanta GA
404 828-6000

(P-11546)
UNITED PARCEL SERVICE INC
Also Called: UPS
22 Brookline (92656-1461)
PHONE..............................949 643-6634
EMP: 732
SALES (corp-wide): 100.34B **Publicly Held**
Web: www.ups.com
SIC: **4215** Parcel delivery, vehicular
HQ: United Parcel Service, Inc.
55 Glenlake Pkwy

Atlanta GA
404 828-6000

(P-11547)
UNITY COURIER SERVICE INC (DH)
3231 Fletcher Dr (90065-2919)
P.O. Box 10909 (91510-0909)
PHONE..............................323 255-9800
Ali Sharifi, *CEO*
Larry Lum, *
EMP: 200 **EST:** 1984
SQ FT: 11,000
SALES (est): 58.7MM
SALES (corp-wide): 8.81B **Privately Held**
SIC: **4215** Package delivery, vehicular
HQ: Tforce Tl Holdings Usa, Inc.
4701 E 32nd St
Joplin MO
877 396-2639

4221 Farm Product Warehousing And Storage

(P-11548)
HONEYVILLE INC
11600 Dayton Dr (91730-5525)
PHONE..............................909 980-9500
EMP: 85
SALES (corp-wide): 188.43MM **Privately Held**
Web: www.honeyville.com
SIC: **4221** 5153 2045 2041 Grain elevator, storage only; Grains; Prepared flour mixes and doughs; Flour and other grain mill products
PA: Honeyville, Inc.
1040 W 600 N
Ogden UT
435 494-4193

4222 Refrigerated Warehousing And Storage

(P-11549)
AMERICOLD LOGISTICS LLC
5401 Santa Ana St (91761-8626)
PHONE..............................909 937-2200
Chris Mckeon, *Brnch Mgr*
EMP: 112
SALES (corp-wide): 2.91B **Publicly Held**
Web: www.americold.com
SIC: **4222** Warehousing, cold storage or refrigerated
HQ: Americold Logistics, Llc
10 Glenlake Pkwy Ste 600
Atlanta GA
678 441-1400

(P-11550)
AMERICOLD LOGISTICS LLC
Also Called: Americold Realty
700 Malaga St (91761-8627)
P.O. Box 3967 (91761-0989)
PHONE..............................909 390-4950
Jeff Canfield, *Mgr*
EMP: 91
SALES (corp-wide): 2.91B **Publicly Held**
Web: www.americold.com
SIC: **4222** Warehousing, cold storage or refrigerated
HQ: Americold Logistics, Llc
10 Glenlake Pkwy Ste 600
Atlanta GA
678 441-1400

(P-11551)
EXETER PACKERS INC
Also Called: Sun Pacific Cold Storage
33374 Lerdo Hwy (93308-9782)
PHONE..............................661 399-0416
Richard Peters, *Mgr*
EMP: 118
SALES (corp-wide): 41.55MM **Privately Held**
Web: www.sunpacific.com
SIC: **4222** 0172 Warehousing, cold storage or refrigerated; Grapes
PA: Exeter Packers, Inc.
1250 E Myer Ave
Exeter CA
559 592-5168

(P-11552)
MIKE CAMPBELL & ASSOCIATES LTD
Also Called: Mike Campbell Assoc Logistics
10907 Downey Ave Ste 203 (90241-3737)
PHONE..............................626 369-3981
Vickie J Campbell, *CEO*
James Heermans, *
Paul Trump, *
EMP: 100 **EST:** 1983
SALES (est): 50.19MM **Privately Held**
SIC: **4222** 4225 4214 4213 Storage, frozen or refrigerated goods; General warehousing and storage; Local trucking with storage; Trucking, except local

(P-11553)
MOUNTAIN WATER ICE COMPANY
2843 Benet Rd (92058-1245)
PHONE..............................760 722-7611
Steven Gabriel, *Pr*
EMP: 26
SALES (corp-wide): 4.83MM **Privately Held**
SIC: **4222** 2097 5999 Warehousing, cold storage or refrigerated; Block ice; Ice
PA: Mountain Water Ice Company Inc
17011 Central Ave
Carson CA
310 638-0321

(P-11554)
POWERED BY FULFILLMENT INC
20880 Krameria Ave (92518-1512)
PHONE..............................626 825-9841
Caleb Alexander Lee, *CEO*
EMP: 100 **EST:** 2020
SALES (est): 3.66MM **Privately Held**
SIC: **4222** Warehousing, cold storage or refrigerated

(P-11555)
PREFERRED FRZR SVCS - LBF LLC
4901 Bandini Blvd (90058-5400)
PHONE..............................323 263-8811
Brian Beattie, *CEO*
▲ **EMP:** 1000 **EST:** 2013
SALES (est): 2.57MM **Privately Held**
SIC: **4222** Warehousing, cold storage or refrigerated

(P-11556)
PREMIER COLD STORAGE & PKG LLC ✪
1071 E 233rd St (90745-6206)
PHONE..............................949 444-8859
Steve Karo, *Pr*
EMP: 205 **EST:** 2022
SALES (est): 9.55MM **Privately Held**

SIC: **4222** 3053 Warehousing, cold storage or refrigerated; Packing materials

(P-11557)
STANDARD-SOUTHERN CORPORATION
Also Called: Los Angeles Cold Storage Co
400 S Central Ave (90013-1712)
P.O. Box 54244 (90054-0244)
PHONE..............................213 624-1831
Larry Rauch, *Mgr*
EMP: 80
SALES (corp-wide): 30.46MM **Privately Held**
Web: www.lacold.com
SIC: **4222** Warehousing, cold storage or refrigerated
PA: Standard-Southern Corporation
4635 Suthwest Fwy Ste 910
Houston TX
713 627-1700

(P-11558)
STANDARD-SOUTHERN CORPORATION
Also Called: L.A. Cold Storage
440 S Central Ave (90013-1712)
PHONE..............................213 624-1831
Larry Rauch, *Pr*
EMP: 181
SALES (corp-wide): 30.46MM **Privately Held**
Web: www.standardsouthern.com
SIC: **4222** Warehousing, cold storage or refrigerated
PA: Standard-Southern Corporation
4635 Suthwest Fwy Ste 910
Houston TX
713 627-1700

(P-11559)
STANDARD-SOUTHERN CORPORATION
Also Called: Los Angeles Cold Storage
715 E 4th St (90013-1727)
PHONE..............................213 624-1831
Thom Thomas, *Brnch Mgr*
EMP: 109
SALES (corp-wide): 30.46MM **Privately Held**
Web: www.standardsouthern.com
SIC: **4222** Warehousing, cold storage or refrigerated
PA: Standard-Southern Corporation
4635 Suthwest Fwy Ste 910
Houston TX
713 627-1700

4225 General Warehousing And Storage

(P-11560)
ACT FULFILLMENT INC (PA)
3155 Universe Dr (91752-3252)
PHONE..............................909 930-9083
Randolph Cox, *CEO*
Randolph Cox, *Pr*
Lydiann Cox, *CFO*
▲ **EMP:** 220 **EST:** 2004
SALES (est): 24.03MM **Privately Held**
Web: www.actfulfillment.com
SIC: **4225** General warehousing

(P-11561)
ADVANCED STRLZTION PDTS SVCS I
Also Called: Advanced Strlztion Pdts Lgstic
13135 Napa St (92335-2961)

PRODUCTS & SVCS

PHONE..................909 350-6987
EMP: 445
SALES (corp-wide): 5.83B **Publicly Held**
Web: www.asp.com
SIC: 4225 General warehousing and storage
HQ: Advanced Sterlization Products
Services Inc.
33 Technology Dr
Irvine CA

(P-11562)
ADVANTAGE MEDIA SERVICES INC
Also Called: AMS Fulfillment
28220 Industry Dr (91355-4105)
PHONE..................661 705-7588
John Bevacqua, *VP*
EMP: 210
SALES (corp-wide): 39.78MM **Privately Held**
Web: www.amsfulfillment.com
SIC: 4225 General warehousing
PA: Advantage Media Services, Inc.
29010 Commerce Center Dr
Valencia CA
661 775-0611

(P-11563)
ALBERTSONS LLC
Also Called: Albertson's Distribution Ctr
9300 Toledo Way (92618-1802)
PHONE..................949 855-2465
EMP: 80
SALES (corp-wide): 77.65B **Publicly Held**
Web: www.albertsons.com
SIC: 4225 General warehousing and storage
HQ: Albertson's Llc
250 E Parkcenter Blvd
Boise ID
208 395-6200

(P-11564)
AMAZONCOM INC
Also Called: Amazon.Com
1910 E Central Ave (92408-0123)
PHONE..................626 260-6954
EMP: 89
Web: www.amazon.com
SIC: 4225 General warehousing and storage
PA: Amazon.Com, Inc.
410 Terry Ave N
Seattle WA

(P-11565)
ASHLEY FURNITURE INDS LLC
Also Called: Ashley Furniture
2250 W Lugonia Ave (92374-5050)
PHONE..................909 825-4900
EMP: 470
SALES (corp-wide): 4.17B **Privately Held**
Web: www.ashleyfurniture.com
SIC: 4225 5021 General warehousing;
Furniture
PA: Ashley Furniture Industries, Llc
1 Ashley Way
Arcadia WI
608 323-3377

(P-11566)
C & B DELIVERY SERVICE
Also Called: Temco
1405 E Franklin Ave (91766-5453)
PHONE..................909 623-4708
Virginia Templeton, *Pr*
EMP: 85 **EST:** 1967
SQ FT: 91,000
SALES (est): 2.58MM **Privately Held**
SIC: 4225 General warehousing

(P-11567)
COASTAL PACIFIC FD DISTRS INC
Also Called: Coastal Pacific Foods
1520 E Mission Blvd Ste B (91761-2124)
PHONE..................909 947-2066
EMP: 84
SALES (corp-wide): 496.11MM **Privately Held**
Web: www.cpfd.com
SIC: 4225 General warehousing and storage
PA: Coastal Pacific Food Distributors, Inc.
1015 Performance Dr
Stockton CA
909 947-2066

(P-11568)
COSTCO WHOLESALE CORPORATION
Also Called: Mira Loma Dry Depot
11600 Riverside Dr Ste A (91752-3700)
PHONE..................951 361-3606
Rachell Aguire, *Brnch Mgr*
EMP: 613
SALES (corp-wide): 242.29B **Publicly Held**
Web: www.costco-locations.org
SIC: 4225 General warehousing and storage
PA: Costco Wholesale Corporation
999 Lake Dr Ste 200
Issaquah WA
425 313-8100

(P-11569)
COUNTY OF LOS ANGELES
Also Called: Public Works, Dept of
1537 Alcazar St (90033-1001)
PHONE..................626 458-1707
Shirely Gist, *Mgr*
EMP: 82
SALES (corp-wide): 31.7B **Privately Held**
Web: www.lacounty.gov
SIC: 4225 9511 General warehousing and
storage; Air, water, and solid waste
management
PA: County Of Los Angeles
500 W Temple St Ste 437
Los Angeles CA
213 974-1101

(P-11570)
CRYOMAX USA INC (HQ)
127 N California Ave Ste B (91744-4313)
PHONE..................626 330-3388
Yen T Liu, *Pr*
James Ho, *CFO*
James Ting, *COO*
EMP: 17 **EST:** 2006
SQ FT: 55,000
SALES (est): 9.8MM **Privately Held**
Web: www.cryomaxusa.com
SIC: 4225 3443 3714 General warehousing;
Heat exchangers: coolers (after, inter),
condensers, etc.; Radiators and radiator
shells and cores, motor vehicle
PA: Cryomax Cooling System Corp.
No. 28, Gongqu Rd., Fangyuan
Industrial Park
Fangyuan Township CHA

(P-11571)
DALTON TRUCKING INC (PA)
13560 Whittram Ave (92335-2951)
P.O. Box 5025 (92334-5025)
PHONE..................909 823-0663
Terry Klenske, *CEO*
Mathew Klenske, *
Eleanor Klenske, *
Roszetta Bautista, *
EMP: 159 **EST:** 1970

SQ FT: 11,000
SALES (est): 37.99MM
SALES (corp-wide): 37.99MM **Privately Held**
Web: www.daltontrucking.com
SIC: 4225 General warehousing and storage

(P-11572)
DART INTERNATIONAL A CORP (HQ)
Also Called: Dart Entities
1430 S Eastman Ave (90023-4006)
P.O. Box 23944 (90023-0944)
PHONE..................323 264-8746
Terence Dedeaux, *CEO*
Paul Martin, *
William J Smollen, *
EMP: 110 **EST:** 1979
SQ FT: 50,000
SALES (est): 26.55MM
SALES (corp-wide): 114.71MM **Privately Held**
Web: www.dartentities.com
SIC: 4225 General warehousing
PA: Dart Transportation Service, A
Corporation
1430 S Eastman Ave Ste 1
Commerce CA
323 981-8205

(P-11573)
DART WAREHOUSE CORPORATION (HQ)
1430 S Eastman Ave (90023-4006)
PHONE..................323 264-1011
Robert Anthony Santich, *CEO*
Raoul Dedeaux, *
Eileen Takahashi, *
Ashok Agarwal, *
Don Brown, *
▲ **EMP:** 255 **EST:** 1938
SALES (est): 57.34MM
SALES (corp-wide): 114.71MM **Privately Held**
Web: www.dartentities.com
SIC: 4225 General warehousing
PA: Dart Transportation Service, A
Corporation
1430 S Eastman Ave Ste 1
Commerce CA
323 981-8205

(P-11574)
DISTRIBUTION ALTERNATIVES INC
10621 6th St (91730-5900)
PHONE..................909 746-5600
EMP: 100
SALES (corp-wide): 95.6MM **Privately Held**
Web: www.daserv.com
SIC: 4225 General warehousing
PA: Distribution Alternatives, Inc.
6870 21st Ave
Lino Lakes MN
651 636-9167

(P-11575)
EDMUND A GRAY CO
1901 Imperial St (90021-2830)
PHONE..................213 625-2725
Lawrence Gray Junior, *Brnch Mgr*
EMP: 35
SALES (corp-wide): 13.68MM **Privately Held**
Web: www.eagray.com
SIC: 4225 3498 General warehousing and
storage; Pipe fittings, fabricated from
purchased pipe
PA: Edmund A. Gray Co.
2277 E 15th St

Los Angeles CA
213 625-0376

(P-11576)
F R T INTERNATIONAL INC (PA)
Also Called: Frontier Logistics Services
1700 N Alameda St (90222-4128)
PHONE..................310 604-8208
Brian Chung, *CEO*
Joyce Chung, *
◆ **EMP:** 80 **EST:** 1983
SQ FT: 200,000
SALES (est): 26.2MM
SALES (corp-wide): 26.2MM **Privately Held**
SIC: 4225 4731 4412 4214 General
warehousing; Customhouse brokers; Deep
sea foreign transportation of freight; Local
trucking with storage

(P-11577)
FASHION LOGISTICS INC
20550 Denker Ave (90501-1645)
PHONE..................424 201-4100
EMP: 130
SALES (corp-wide): 32.95MM **Privately Held**
Web: www.fashionlogistics.com
SIC: 4225 General warehousing
PA: Fashion Logistics, Inc.
621 Us Highway 46 W
Hasbrouck Heights NJ
201 596-0040

(P-11578)
FLOWSPACE INC
660 Baker St Ste B201 (92626-4409)
PHONE..................323 741-1325
Joseph Benjamin Eachus Junior, *CEO*
Jason Harbert, *
Anne Hallock, *CRO*
EMP: 90 **EST:** 2016
SALES (est): 10.57MM **Privately Held**
Web: www.flow.space
SIC: 4225 General warehousing

(P-11579)
FOAMEX LP
Foamex
19201 S Reyes Ave (90221-5807)
PHONE..................323 774-5600
Dean Offerman, *Brnch Mgr*
EMP: 150
Web: www.fxi.com
SIC: 4225 General warehousing and storage
PA: Foamex L.P.
100 W Matsonford Rd # 5
Wayne PA

(P-11580)
FTDI WEST INC
3375 Enterprise Dr (92316-3539)
PHONE..................909 473-1111
Alan Baum, *Pr*
Steve Rocha, *
EMP: 80 **EST:** 2008
SALES (est): 19.26MM **Privately Held**
Web: www.ftdiwest.com
SIC: 4225 Warehousing, self storage

(P-11581)
GENERAL ELECTRIC COMPANY
Also Called: GE
20005 Business Pkwy (91789-2944)
PHONE..................909 869-7404
Gary Anderson, *Mgr*
EMP: 95
SALES (corp-wide): 76.56B **Publicly Held**
Web: www.geappliances.com

SIC: **4225** 4226 General warehousing;
Special warehousing and storage, nec
PA: General Electric Company
1 Financial Ctr Ste 3700
Boston MA
617 443-3000

(P-11582)
GENERATIONAL PROPERTIES INC
3141 E 44th St (90058-2405)
PHONE...................................323 583-3163
Angelo V Antoci, *Prin*
Angelo V Antoci, *Prin*
Sam Perricone, *
EMP: 291 **EST:** 1950
SQ FT: 4,000
SALES (est): 22.29MM **Privately Held**
SIC: 4225 General warehousing and storage

(P-11583)
GXO LOGISTICS SUPPLY CHAIN INC
3520 S Cactus Ave (92316-3816)
PHONE...................................336 309-6201
Christopher Cotto, *Mgr*
EMP: 1000
SALES (corp-wide): 8.99B **Publicly Held**
Web: www.gxo.com
SIC: 4225 General warehousing and storage
HQ: Gxo Logistics Supply Chain, Inc.
4043 Piedmont Pkwy
High Point NC
336 232-4100

(P-11584)
GXO LOGISTICS SUPPLY CHAIN INC
2163 S Riverside Ave (92324-3355)
PHONE...................................951 512-1201
Miguel Moreno, *Brnch Mgr*
EMP: 100
SALES (corp-wide): 8.99B **Publicly Held**
Web: www.gxo.com
SIC: 4225 General warehousing
HQ: Gxo Logistics Supply Chain, Inc.
4043 Piedmont Pkwy
High Point NC
336 232-4100

(P-11585)
HAULAWAY STORAGE CNTRS INC
11292 Western Ave (90680-2912)
P.O. Box 125 (90680-0125)
PHONE...................................800 826-9040
Clifford Robert Ronnenberg, *CEO*
Daniel Letto, *
Joyce Amato, *
EMP: 440 **EST:** 2000
SALES (est): 18.56MM
SALES (corp-wide): 335.28MM **Privately Held**
Web: www.haulaway.com
SIC: 4225 General warehousing and storage
PA: Cr&R Incorporated
11292 Western Ave
Stanton CA
714 826-9049

(P-11586)
HOME DEPOT USA INC
Also Called: Home Depot, The
11650 Venture Dr (91752-3209)
PHONE...................................951 361-1235
John Lawson, *Brnch Mgr*
EMP: 133
SALES (corp-wide): 157.4B **Publicly Held**
Web: www.homedepot.com

SIC: **4225** General warehousing and storage
HQ: Home Depot U.S.A., Inc.
2455 Paces Ferry Rd Se
Atlanta GA

(P-11587)
HOME DEPOT USA INC
Also Called: Home Depot, The
8535 Oakwood Pl Ste B (91730-4864)
PHONE...................................909 483-8115
Rose Navares, *Mgr*
EMP: 104
SALES (corp-wide): 157.4B **Publicly Held**
Web: www.homedepot.com
SIC: 4225 General warehousing and storage
HQ: Home Depot U.S.A., Inc.
2455 Paces Ferry Rd Se
Atlanta GA

(P-11588)
HOME DEPOT USA INC
Also Called: Home Depot, The
13250 Gregg St Ste A2 (92064-7164)
PHONE...................................858 859-4143
Greg Williams, *Prin*
EMP: 118
SALES (corp-wide): 157.4B **Publicly Held**
Web: www.homedepot.com
SIC: 4225 General warehousing and storage
HQ: Home Depot U.S.A., Inc.
2455 Paces Ferry Rd Se
Atlanta GA

(P-11589)
HOME DEPOT USA INC
Also Called: Home Depot, The
14659 Alondra Blvd Ste B (90638-5629)
PHONE...................................714 522-8651
EMP: 91
SALES (corp-wide): 157.4B **Publicly Held**
Web: www.homedepot.com
SIC: 4225 General warehousing and storage
HQ: Home Depot U.S.A., Inc.
2455 Paces Ferry Rd Se
Atlanta GA

(P-11590)
HYDRAFACIAL LLC
Also Called: Hydrafacial Company, The
3600 E Burnett St (90815-1749)
PHONE...................................562 391-2052
Evan Hoover, *Brnch Mgr*
EMP: 30
SALES (corp-wide): 365.88MM **Publicly Held**
Web: www.hydrafacial.com
SIC: 4225 2844 General warehousing and storage; Toilet preparations
HQ: Hydrafacial Llc
2165 E Spring St
Long Beach CA
800 603-4996

(P-11591)
KAIR HARBOR EXPRESS LLC (PA)
1129 Canal Ave (90813-2623)
PHONE...................................562 432-6800
Peter Wu, *Managing Member*
EMP: 80 **EST:** 2015
SQ FT: 50,000
SALES (est): 21.96MM
SALES (corp-wide): 21.96MM **Privately Held**
Web: www.kairharborexpress.com
SIC: 4225 4214 General warehousing and storage; Local trucking with storage

(P-11592)
KKW TRUCKING INC (PA)
3100 Pomona Blvd (91768-3230)
P.O. Box 2960 (91769-2960)
PHONE...................................909 869-1200
Dennis W Firestone, *CEO*
Lynnette Brown, *
EMP: 550 **EST:** 1962
SQ FT: 150,000
SALES (est): 101.18MM
SALES (corp-wide): 101.18MM **Privately Held**
Web: www.kkwtrucks.com
SIC: 4225 4231 4226 4214 General warehousing and storage; Trucking terminal facilities; Special warehousing and storage, nec; Local trucking with storage

(P-11593)
KROGER CO
Also Called: Ralphs Logistics - Compton DC
2201 S Wilmington Ave (90220-5448)
PHONE...................................859 630-6959
Lisa Allen, *Brnch Mgr*
EMP: 500
SALES (corp-wide): 148.26B **Publicly Held**
Web: www.thekrogerco.com
SIC: 4225 General warehousing and storage
PA: The Kroger Co
1014 Vine St Ste 1000
Cincinnati OH
513 762-4000

(P-11594)
LOCKHEED MARTIN CORPORATION
Also Called: Rotary and Miission Systems
Bldg 821 South Loop (92310)
PHONE...................................760 386-2572
Kurt Pinkerton, *Mgr*
EMP: 142
Web: www.gyrocamsystems.com
SIC: 4225 General warehousing and storage
PA: Lockheed Martin Corporation
6801 Rockledge Dr
Bethesda MD

(P-11595)
LOWES HOME CENTERS LLC
Also Called: Lowe's
3984 Indian Ave (92571-3154)
PHONE...................................951 443-2500
Thomas Tucker, *Brnch Mgr*
EMP: 347
SALES (corp-wide): 97.06B **Publicly Held**
Web: www.lowes.com
SIC: 4225 General warehousing and storage
HQ: Lowe's Home Centers, Llc
1000 Lowes Blvd
Mooresville NC
336 658-4000

(P-11596)
MAKESPACE LABS INC
3526 Hayden Ave (90232-2413)
PHONE...................................800 920-9440
Rahul Gandhi, *CEO*
Chang Paik, *
EMP: 200 **EST:** 2013
SALES (est): 8.62MM **Privately Held**
Web: www.clutter.com
SIC: 4225 General warehousing and storage

(P-11597)
MCR PRINTING AND PACKG CORP
8830 Siempre Viva Rd (92154-6278)
PHONE...................................619 488-3012

EMP: 170
SALES (corp-wide): 10.12MM **Privately Held**
Web: www.mcrprintingandpackaging.com
SIC: 4225 General warehousing
PA: Mcr Printing And Packaging, Corp.
113 W G St Pmb 438
San Diego CA
619 488-3169

(P-11598)
MIDAS EXPRESS LOS ANGELES INC
11854 Alameda St (90262-4019)
PHONE...................................310 609-0366
Jack Wu, *Pr*
Jacky Strong, *Stockholder**
▲ **EMP:** 200 **EST:** 1995
SQ FT: 90,000
SALES (est): 9.58MM **Privately Held**
Web: www.midasexpress.com
SIC: 4225 4731 4226 General warehousing and storage; Freight forwarding; Textile warehousing

(P-11599)
MOULTON LOGISTICS MANAGEMENT
7855 Hayvenhurst Ave (91406-1712)
P.O. Box 8191 (91409-8191)
PHONE...................................818 997-1800
◆ **EMP:** 175
Web: www.amwarelogistics.com
SIC: 4225 4822 General warehousing and storage; Electronic mail

(P-11600)
MSBLOUS LLC
11671 Dayton Dr (91730-5526)
PHONE...................................909 929-9689
Jiayi CU, *Mgr*
EMP: 84
SALES (corp-wide): 2.22MM **Privately Held**
SIC: 4225 General warehousing and storage
PA: Msblous Llc
8 The Grn Ste 7360
Dover DE
909 908-1889

(P-11601)
MULHOLLAND BROTHERS
11840 Dorothy St Apt 301 (90049-7902)
PHONE...................................510 280-5485
John Holland, *Prin*
EMP: 48
SALES (corp-wide): 8.17MM **Privately Held**
Web: www.shopmulholland.com
SIC: 4225 3161 2512 General warehousing; Luggage; Upholstered household furniture
PA: Mulholland Brothers
1710 4th St
Berkeley CA
415 824-5995

(P-11602)
NEOVIA LOGISTICS DIST LP
5750 E Francis St (91761-3607)
PHONE...................................909 657-4900
EMP: 96
SALES (corp-wide): 672.55MM **Privately Held**
Web: www.neovialogistics.com
SIC: 4225 General warehousing and storage
HQ: Neovia Logistics Distribution, Lp
6363 N State Highway # 700
Irving TX

PRODUCTS & SVCS

(P-11603)
NORDSTROM INC
Also Called: Nordstrom
1600 S Milliken Ave (91761-2301)
PHONE.............................909 390-1040
Pat Smith, *Mgr*
EMP: 300
SALES (corp-wide): 15.53B **Publicly Held**
Web: www.nordstrom.com
SIC: 4225 4226 General warehousing and storage; Special warehousing and storage, nec
PA: Nordstrom, Inc.
1617 6th Ave
Seattle WA
206 628-2111

(P-11604)
OSRAM SYLVANIA INC
1651 S Archibald Ave (91761-7651)
PHONE.............................909 923-3003
Wayne Cansford, *Brnch Mgr*
EMP: 99
SALES (corp-wide): 5B **Privately Held**
Web: www.sylvania-automotive.com
SIC: 4225 Warehousing, self storage
HQ: Osram Sylvania Inc.
200 Ballardvale St Bldg 2
Wilmington MA
978 570-3000

(P-11605)
QUICK BOX LLC
13838 S Figueroa St (90061-1026)
PHONE.............................310 436-6444
EMP: 107
SALES (corp-wide): 26.2MM **Privately Held**
Web: www.quickbox.com
SIC: 4225 General warehousing and storage
PA: Quick Box, Llc
11551 E 45th Ave Unit C
Denver CO
303 757-6500

(P-11606)
QUILL LLC
Also Called: Quill Distribution Center
1500 S Dupont Ave (91761-1406)
PHONE.............................909 390-0600
Rocky Velasquez, *Mgr*
EMP: 249
Web: www.quill.com
SIC: 4225 General warehousing and storage
HQ: Quill Llc
300 Tri State Intl
Lincolnshire IL
800 982-3400

(P-11607)
RADIAL SOUTH LP
Also Called: Radial
2225 Alder Ave (92377-8513)
PHONE.............................610 491-7000
EMP: 418
SALES (corp-wide): 2.34B **Privately Held**
Web: www.radial.com
SIC: 4225 General warehousing
HQ: Radial South, L.P.
935 1st Ave
King Of Prussia PA
610 491-7000

(P-11608)
ROADEX AMERICA INC
2132 E Dominguez St Ste B (90810-1006)
PHONE.............................310 878-9800
Nicholas Sim, *Pr*
Russle Loh, *
Johnny Kwan, *

▲ EMP: 100 EST: 2001
SALES (est): 24.54MM **Privately Held**
Web: www.roadexamerica.com
SIC: 4225 5113 4789 General warehousing and storage; Industrial and personal service paper; Cargo loading and unloading services

(P-11609)
RPM CONSOLIDATED SERVICES INC (HQ)
1901 Raymer Ave (92833-2512)
PHONE.............................714 388-3500
Shawn K Duke, *CEO*
Dan Laporte, *
▲ EMP: 100 EST: 2002
SQ FT: 15,000
SALES (est): 95.99MM
SALES (corp-wide): 1.16B **Privately Held**
Web: www.odysseylogistics.com
SIC: 4225 4214 General warehousing and storage; Local trucking with storage
PA: Odyssey Logistics & Technology Corporation
100 Reserve Rd Ste Cc210
Danbury CT
203 448-3900

(P-11610)
SAN DIEGO GAS & ELECTRIC CO
Mirimar Storage
6875c Consolidated Way (92121-2602)
PHONE.............................858 547-2086
EMP: 101
SALES (corp-wide): 14.44B **Publicly Held**
Web: www.sdge.com
SIC: 4225 4932 4924 4911 General warehousing and storage; Gas and other services combined; Natural gas distribution; Electric services
HQ: San Diego Gas & Electric Company
8330 Century Park Ct
San Diego CA
619 696-2000

(P-11611)
SCHNEIDER ELECTRIC USA INC
Also Called: Pelco By Schneider Electric
14725 Monte Vista Ave (91710-5732)
PHONE.............................909 438-2295
EMP: 100
SALES (corp-wide): 82.05K **Privately Held**
Web: www.se.com
SIC: 4225 General warehousing and storage
HQ: Schneider Electric Usa, Inc.
1 Boston Pl Ste 2700
Boston MA
978 975-9600

(P-11612)
SMART & FINAL STORES LLC
5500 Sheila St (90040-1425)
PHONE.............................323 725-0791
Tom Bullici, *Mgr*
EMP: 206
SIC: 4225 General warehousing and storage
HQ: Smart & Final Stores Llc
600 Citadel Dr
Commerce CA

(P-11613)
SPROUTS FARMERS MARKET INC
280 De Berry St (92324-4404)
PHONE.............................888 577-7688
EMP: 190
SALES (corp-wide): 6.4B **Publicly Held**
Web: www.sprouts.com

SIC: 4225 5411 General warehousing and storage; Grocery stores
PA: Sprouts Farmers Market, Inc.
5455 E High St Ste 111
Phoenix AZ
480 814-8016

(P-11614)
SST IV 8020 LAS VGAS BLVD S LL
Also Called: Smartstop Self Storage
10 Terrace Rd (92694-1182)
PHONE.............................949 429-6600
H Michael Schwartz, *Managing Member*
Paula Mathews, *
Wayne Johnson, *
Michael Terjung, *
EMP: 99 EST: 2018
SALES (est): 2.45MM **Privately Held**
Web: www.smartstopselfstorage.com
SIC: 4225 Warehousing, self storage

(P-11615)
TAKANE USA INC
2055 S Haven Ave (91761-0736)
PHONE.............................909 923-5511
Masahiko Yamada, *Manager*
EMP: 129
Web: www.calicobrands.com
SIC: 4225 General warehousing and storage
HQ: Takane U.S.A., Inc.
369 Van Ness Way Ste 715
Torrance CA
310 212-1411

(P-11616)
TANIMURA ANTLE FRESH FOODS INC
761 Commercial Ave (93030-7233)
PHONE.............................805 483-2358
Sergio Romero, *Mgr*
EMP: 150
SALES (corp-wide): 321.47MM **Privately Held**
Web: www.taproduce.com
SIC: 4225 Warehousing, self storage
PA: Tanimura & Antle Fresh Foods, Inc.
1 Harris Rd
Salinas CA
831 455-2950

(P-11617)
TARGET CORPORATION
Also Called: T.com Ontario Fc T-9479
1505 S Haven Ave (91761-2928)
PHONE.............................909 937-5500
Jacqueline Yee, *Brnch Mgr*
EMP: 177
SALES (corp-wide): 50.09B **Publicly Held**
Web: www.target.com
SIC: 4225 General warehousing and storage
PA: Target Corporation
1000 Nicollet Mall
Minneapolis MN
612 304-6073

(P-11618)
TARGET CORPORATION
Also Called: Target
14750 Miller Ave (92336-1685)
PHONE.............................909 355-6000
George Spreiser, *Genl Mgr*
EMP: 103
SALES (corp-wide): 50.09B **Publicly Held**
Web: www.target.com
SIC: 4225 General warehousing and storage
PA: Target Corporation
1000 Nicollet Mall
Minneapolis MN
612 304-6073

(P-11619)
TAYLORED FMI LLC
1495 E Locust St (91761-4570)
PHONE.............................909 510-4800
Jim Deveau, *CEO*
EMP: 140 EST: 2020
SALES (est): 937.12K
SALES (corp-wide): 42.44MM **Privately Held**
Web: www.tayloredservices.com
SIC: 4225 General warehousing
PA: Taylored Services Parent Co. Inc.
1495 E Locust St
Ontario CA
909 510-4800

(P-11620)
TAYLORED SERVICES LLC (DH)
Also Called: Taylored Services
1495 E Locust St (91761-4570)
PHONE.............................909 510-4800
Jim Deveau, *CEO*
▲ EMP: 80 EST: 1992
SQ FT: 330,000
SALES (est): 96.45MM **Privately Held**
Web: www.tayloredservices.com
SIC: 4225 4731 General warehousing and storage; Agents, shipping
HQ: Taylored Services Holdings, Llc
1495 E Locust St
Ontario CA
909 510-4800

(P-11621)
TAYLORED SERVICES HOLDINGS LLC (DH)
Also Called: Taylored Services
1495 E Locust St (91761-4570)
PHONE.............................909 510-4800
Mikhail Kholyavenko, *CEO*
EMP: 80 EST: 2008
SQ FT: 330,000
SALES (est): 106.04MM **Privately Held**
Web: www.tayloredservices.com
SIC: 4225 General warehousing and storage
HQ: Yusen Logistics (Americas) Inc.
300 Lighting Way Ste 100
Secaucus NJ
201 553-3800

(P-11622)
TONYS EXPRESS INC (PA)
10613 Jasmine St (92337-8241)
PHONE.............................909 427-8700
John Ohle, *CEO*
▲ EMP: 127 EST: 1954
SQ FT: 180,000
SALES (est): 28.76MM
SALES (corp-wide): 28.76MM **Privately Held**
Web: www.tonysexpress.com
SIC: 4225 4214 4212 General warehousing and storage; Local trucking with storage; Local trucking, without storage

(P-11623)
TOTAL WAREHOUSE INC
2895 E Miraloma Ave (92806-1804)
PHONE.............................480 582-3954
Boyd Kiefus, *CEO*
Dawn Koopmann, *
EMP: 119 EST: 2017
SALES (est): 8.29MM **Privately Held**
Web: www.totalwarehouse.com
SIC: 4225 7699 3537 5046 Miniwarehouse, warehousing; Industrial equipment services ; Forklift trucks; Commercial equipment, nec

▲ = Import ▼ = Export
◆ = Import/Export

(P-11624)
TRI-MODAL DIST SVCS INC
22560 Lucerne St (90745-4303)
PHONE..............................310 522-1844
▲ **EMP:** 91
SALES (corp-wide): 29.27MM **Privately Held**
Web: www.abilitytrimodal.com
SIC: 4225 General warehousing and storage
PA: Tri-Modal Distribution Services, Inc.
2011 E Carson St
Carson CA
310 522-5506

(P-11625)
UNIFIED GROCERS INC
Also Called: U W G Southern California Div
457 E Martin Luther King Jr Blvd
(90011-5650)
PHONE..............................323 232-6124
Maurice Ochua, *Brnch Mgr*
EMP: 83
Web: www.unfi.com
SIC: 4225 8742 2051 General warehousing and storage; Marketing consulting services; Bread, cake, and related products
HQ: Unfi Grocers Distribution, Inc.
2500 S Atlantic Blvd
Commerce CA
323 264-5200

(P-11626)
UNIS LLC
19914 S Via Baron (90220-6104)
PHONE..............................310 747-7388
Omar Garcia, *Brnch Mgr*
EMP: 90
SALES (corp-wide): 194.54MM **Privately Held**
Web: www.unisco.com
SIC: 4225 General warehousing and storage
PA: Unis, Llc
218 Machlin Ct Ste A
Walnut CA
909 839-2600

(P-11627)
UNIVERSAL PACKG SYSTEMS INC
Also Called: Paklab
14570 Monte Vista Ave (91710-5743)
PHONE..............................909 517-2442
EMP: 125
SALES (corp-wide): 359.71MM **Privately Held**
SIC: 4225 General warehousing
PA: Universal Packaging Systems, Inc.
380 Townline Rd Ste 130
Hauppauge NY
631 543-2277

(P-11628)
WALMART INC
Also Called: Walmart
1001 Columbia Ave (92507-2135)
PHONE..............................951 320-5722
EMP: 107
SALES (corp-wide): 611.29B **Publicly Held**
Web: corporate.walmart.com
SIC: 4225 General warehousing and storage
PA: Walmart Inc.
702 Sw 8th St
Bentonville AR
479 640-8287

(P-11629)
WEBER DISTRIBUTION LLC
Also Called: Weber Distribution
15301 Shoemaker Ave (90650-6859)

PHONE..............................562 404-9996
John Nutt, *VP*
EMP: 118
Web: www.weberlogistics.com
SIC: 4225 4214 General warehousing; Local trucking with storage
PA: Weber Distribution, Llc
13530 Rosecrans Ave
Santa Fe Springs CA

(P-11630)
WILSONART LLC
Also Called: Ralph Wilson Plastics
13911 Gannet St (90670-5326)
P.O. Box 2336 (90670-0336)
PHONE..............................562 921-7426
Carl Stephens, *Mgr*
EMP: 23
SQ FT: 72,000
SALES (corp-wide): 979.84MM **Privately Held**
Web: www.wilsonart.com
SIC: 4225 5162 3083 2891 General warehousing and storage; Plastics materials and basic shapes; Laminated plastics plate and sheet; Adhesives and sealants
HQ: Wilsonart Llc
2501 Wilsonart Dr
Temple TX
254 207-7000

4226 Special Warehousing And Storage, Nec

(P-11631)
ACCESS INFO HOLDINGS LLC
12135 Davis St (92557-6369)
PHONE..............................909 459-1417
EMP: 724
SALES (corp-wide): 46.95MM **Privately Held**
Web: www.accesscorp.com
SIC: 4226 Document and office records storage
PA: Access Information Holdings, Llc
500 Unicorn Park Dr # 500
Woburn MA
925 583-0100

(P-11632)
DSV SOLUTIONS LLC
Also Called: DSV
13032 Slover Ave Ste 200 (92337-6901)
PHONE..............................909 829-5804
EMP: 101
SALES (corp-wide): 32.91B **Privately Held**
Web: www.go2uti.com
SIC: 4226 Textile warehousing
HQ: Dsv Solutions, Llc
200 Wood Ave S 300
Iselin NJ
732 850-8000

(P-11633)
EXPRESS IMAGING SERVICES INC
1805 W 208th St Ste 202 (90501-1808)
PHONE..............................888 846-8804
Paul Terry, *Pr*
Kenny Ly, *
Tan Ly, *CIO*
Anni Ly, *Leasing Manager*
EMP: 100 **EST:** 2004
SQ FT: 10,000
SALES (est): 8.71MM **Privately Held**
Web: www.eiscallcenter.com
SIC: 4226 Document and office records storage

(P-11634)
PACIFIC CHEMICAL DIST CORP (HQ)
Also Called: Pacific Chemical
6250 Caballero Blvd (90620-1124)
PHONE..............................714 521-7161
James N Tausz, *Pr*
James Banister, *
Rhonda Tausz, *
◆ **EMP:** 100 **EST:** 1978
SQ FT: 144,000
SALES (est): 24.92MM
SALES (corp-wide): 552.56MM **Privately Held**
Web: www.pacchem.com
SIC: 4226 Special warehousing and storage, nec
PA: Quantix Scs, Llc
24 Waterway Ave Ste 450
The Woodlands TX
800 542-8058

(P-11635)
WOOD SPACE INDUSTRIES INC
Also Called: Ariana Air Freight
429 W Levers Pl (92867-3620)
PHONE..............................714 996-4552
David E Reed, *Pr*
Gary Broyles, *Stockholder*
Jeff Horn, *Stockholder*
EMP: 18 **EST:** 1970
SALES (est): 868.39K **Privately Held**
Web: www.amexport.net
SIC: 4226 2441 4731 2449 Special warehousing and storage, nec; Nailed wood boxes and shook; Freight forwarding; Wood containers, nec

4424 Deep Sea Domestic Transportation Of Freight

(P-11636)
POLAR TANKERS INC
60 Berth (90731-7252)
PHONE..............................310 519-8260
Chris Adams, *Brnch Mgr*
EMP: 210
SALES (corp-wide): 82.16B **Publicly Held**
Web: polartankers.conocophillips.com
SIC: 4424 Deep sea domestic transportation of freight
HQ: Polar Tankers, Inc.
300 Oceangate
Long Beach CA
562 388-1400

4481 Deep Sea Passenger Transportation, Except Ferry

(P-11637)
PRINCESS CRUISE LINES LTD (HQ)
Also Called: Princess Cruises
24305 Town Center Dr (91355-1329)
P.O. Box 959 (91380-9059)
PHONE..............................661 753-0000
Jan Swartz, *CEO*
John Padgett, *
Natalya Leahy, *
◆ **EMP:** 2000 **EST:** 1965
SALES (est): 1.52B
SALES (corp-wide): 3.94B **Privately Held**
Web: www.princess.com
SIC: 4481 4725 7011 Deep sea passenger transportation, except ferry; Tour operators; Hotels
PA: Carnival Plc
Carnival House

Southampton HANTS
238 065-6666

4489 Water Passenger Transportation

(P-11638)
CATALINA CHANNEL EXPRESS INC (HQ)
Also Called: Catalina Express Cruises
385 E Swinford St (90731-1002)
PHONE..............................310 519-7971
Greg Bombard, *Pr*
Douglas Bombard, *
EMP: 200 **EST:** 1981
SQ FT: 20,000
SALES (est): 54.13MM
SALES (corp-wide): 54.13MM **Privately Held**
Web: www.catalinaexpress.com
SIC: 4489 Excursion boat operators
PA: Bombard Marine & Resort Management Services, Inc.
95 Berth
San Pedro CA
310 519-7971

(P-11639)
HORNBLOWER YACHTS LLC
Also Called: Hornblower Cruises & Events
2825 5th Ave (92103-6326)
PHONE..............................619 686-8700
Jim Unger, *Brnch Mgr*
EMP: 95
SALES (corp-wide): 495.57MM **Privately Held**
Web: www.cityexperiences.com
SIC: 4489 7299 4499 Excursion boat operators; Banquet hall facilities; Chartering of commercial boats
PA: Hornblower Yachts, Llc
The Embarcadero Pier 3 St Pier
San Francisco CA
415 424-4309

(P-11640)
SO CAL SHIP SERVICES
Also Called: Ship Services
971 S Seaside Ave (90731-7331)
PHONE..............................310 519-8411
Michael A Lanham, *Pr*
EMP: 85 **EST:** 1982
SQ FT: 10,000
SALES (est): 12.25MM **Privately Held**
SIC: 4489 Water taxis

4491 Marine Cargo Handling

(P-11641)
INTERNATIONAL TRNSP SVC LLC (PA)
1281 Pier G Way (90802-6353)
P.O. Box 22704 (90801-5704)
PHONE..............................562 435-7781
Kim Holtermand, *CEO*
Sean Lindsay, *COO*
Louis Paul, *Bd of Dir*
Richard Nicholson, *Bd of Dir*
▲ **EMP:** 114 **EST:** 1971
SQ FT: 10,000
SALES (est): 26.45MM
SALES (corp-wide): 26.45MM **Privately Held**
Web: www.itslb.com
SIC: 4491 Marine loading and unloading services

(P-11642)
LBCT LLC
1171 Pier F Ave (90802-6252)
PHONE....................562 951-6000
Anthony Otto, *Mgr*
EMP: 90 **EST:** 1980
SALES (est): 4.83MM **Privately Held**
Web: www.lbct.com
SIC: 4491 Marine terminals

(P-11643)
MARINE TERMINALS CORPORATION
389 Terminal Way (90731-7430)
PHONE....................310 519-2300
◆ **EMP:** 300 **EST:** 1931
SALES (est): 48.68MM
SALES (corp-wide): 251B **Privately Held**
Web: www.portsamerica.com
SIC: 4491 Stevedoring
HQ: Mtc Holdings
3 Embarcadero Ctr Ste 550
San Francisco CA
912 651-4000

(P-11644)
PORT OF LONG BEACH
415 W Ocean Blvd (90802-4511)
P.O. Box 570 (90801-0570)
PHONE....................562 283-7000
Paula Grond, *Sec*
EMP: 452 **EST:** 2014
SALES (est): 31.27MM **Privately Held**
Web: www.polb.com
SIC: 4491 Docks, piers and terminals
PA: City Of Long Beach
1800 E Wardlow Rd
Long Beach CA
562 570-6450

(P-11645)
PORT OF LOS ANGELES
425 S Palos Verdes St (90731-3309)
PHONE....................310 732-3508
Gene Seroka, *Ex Dir*
EMP: 264 **EST:** 2017
SALES (est): 627.84MM **Privately Held**
Web: www.portoflosangeles.org
SIC: 4491 Waterfront terminal operation

(P-11646)
SAN DIEGO UNIFIED PORT DST
1400 Tidelands Ave (91950-6200)
PHONE....................619 686-6200
EMP: 115
SALES (corp-wide): 167.04MM **Privately Held**
Web: www.portofsandiego.org
SIC: 4491 Marine cargo handling
PA: San Diego Unified Port District
3165 Pacific Hwy
San Diego CA
619 686-6200

(P-11647)
SAN DIEGO UNIFIED PORT DST (PA)
Also Called: PORT OF SAN DIEGO
3165 Pacific Hwy (92101-1128)
P.O. Box 120488 (92112-0488)
PHONE....................619 686-6200
John Bolduc, *CEO*
Robert Deangelis, *
Karen Porteous, *
Randa Coniglio, *
Thomas Russell, *
EMP: 240 **EST:** 1962
SQ FT: 120,000
SALES (est): 167.04MM

SALES (corp-wide): 167.04MM **Privately Held**
Web: www.portofsandiego.org
SIC: 4491 Marine cargo handling

(P-11648)
SUDERMAN CONTG STEVEDORES INC (PA)
Also Called: Metro Ports
3806 Worsham Ave (90808-1896)
PHONE....................409 762-8131
EMP: 100 **EST:** 1987
SQ FT: 4,500
SALES (est): 9.92MM **Privately Held**
Web: www.metroports.com
SIC: 4491 Stevedoring

(P-11649)
TOTAL INTERMODAL SERVICES INC (PA)
7101 Jackson St (90723-4836)
PHONE....................562 427-6300
Amador Sanchez Junior, *Pr*
▲ **EMP:** 50 **EST:** 1991
SALES (est): 18.62MM **Privately Held**
Web: www.totalintermodal.com
SIC: 4491 4213 7534 4731 Marine cargo handling; Trucking, except local; Tire retreading and repair shops; Freight forwarding

4492 Towing And Tugboat Service

(P-11650)
BRUSCO TUG & BARGE INC
170 E Port Hueneme Rd (93041-3213)
PHONE....................805 986-1600
David Brusco, *Brnch Mgr*
EMP: 125
SALES (corp-wide): 20.45MM **Privately Held**
Web: www.bruscotug.com
SIC: 4492 Tugboat service
PA: Brusco Tug & Barge, Inc.
548 14th Ave
Longview WA
360 423-9856

(P-11651)
PACIFIC MARITIME FREIGHT INC
Also Called: PACIFIC MARITIME FREIGHT, INC.
1512 Pier C St (90813-4043)
PHONE....................562 590-8188
EMP: 95
SALES (corp-wide): 41.59MM **Privately Held**
Web: www.pacificmaritimegroup.com
SIC: 4492 Tugboat service
PA: Pacific Maritime Group, Inc.
1444 Cesar E Chavez Pkwy
San Diego CA
619 533-7932

4493 Marinas

(P-11652)
SHELTER POINTE LLC
Also Called: Shelter Pointe Hotel & Marina
1551 Shelter Island Dr (92106-3102)
PHONE....................619 221-8000
Jeff Foster, *Managing Member*
EMP: 229 **EST:** 1993
SALES (est): 10.8MM
SALES (corp-wide): 98.27MM **Privately Held**

Web: www.resortkonakai.com
SIC: 4493 7011 7997 5812 Marinas; Resort hotel; Country club, membership; American restaurant
HQ: Pacifica Hotel Company
39 Argonaut
Aliso Viejo CA
805 957-0095

4499 Water Transportation Services, Nec

(P-11653)
BLUE OCEAN MARINE LLC
2060 Knoll Dr Ste 100 (93003-7391)
PHONE....................805 658-2628
EMP: 30 **EST:** 2010
SALES (est): 3.81MM **Privately Held**
SIC: 4499 1389 7359 Boat rental, commercial; Oil field services, nec; Equipment rental and leasing, nec

(P-11654)
C & C BOATS INC
2124 Main St Ste 145 (92648-6471)
P.O. Box 1279 (92647-1279)
PHONE....................714 969-0900
Thomas Croft, *Pr*
Don Croft, *
EMP: 18 **EST:** 1960
SALES (est): 438.96K **Privately Held**
Web: www.cccrewboats.com
SIC: 4499 3731 Chartering of commercial boats; Shipbuilding and repairing

(P-11655)
HANJIN SHIPPING CO LTD
301 Hanjin Rd (90802)
PHONE....................201 291-4600
Taisoo Suk, *Ex Dir*
◆ **EMP:** 691 **EST:** 1994
SALES (est): 31.81MM **Privately Held**
SIC: 4499 Steamship leasing

4512 Air Transportation, Scheduled

(P-11656)
AEROTRANSPORTE DE CARGE UNION
Also Called: Aerounion
5625 W Imperial Hwy (90045-6323)
PHONE....................310 649-0069
Luis Ramo, *Pr*
Steven Connolly, *VP*
EMP: 400 **EST:** 2006
SALES (est): 9.64MM **Privately Held**
Web: pcola.gulf.net
SIC: 4512 Air cargo carrier, scheduled

(P-11657)
AIR NEW ZEALAND LIMITED
222 N Pacific Coast Hwy Ste 900 (90245-5629)
PHONE....................310 648-7000
Roger Poulton, *VP*
EMP: 100
Web: www.airnewzealand.com
SIC: 4512 Air passenger carrier, scheduled
PA: Air New Zealand Limited
185 Fanshawe St
Auckland AUK

(P-11658)
AMERICAN AIRLINES INC
400 World Way Ste F (90045-5863)
P.O. Box 92246 (90009-2246)

PHONE....................310 646-4553
Sally Rabideau, *Owner*
EMP: 298
SALES (corp-wide): 48.97B **Publicly Held**
Web: www.aacreditunion.org
SIC: 4512 Air passenger carrier, scheduled
HQ: American Airlines, Inc.
1 Skyview Dr
Fort Worth TX
682 278-9000

(P-11659)
AMERIFLIGHT LLC
4700 W Empire Ave (91505-1098)
PHONE....................818 847-0000
EMP: 130
SALES (corp-wide): 98.21MM **Privately Held**
Web: www.ameriflight.com
SIC: 4512 Air cargo carrier, scheduled
PA: Ameriflight, Llc
1515 W 20th St
Dfw Airport TX
800 800-4538

(P-11660)
CHINA AIRLINES LTD
5651 W 96th St (90045-5539)
PHONE....................310 484-1818
EMP: 107
Web: www.china-airlines.com
SIC: 4512 Air passenger carrier, scheduled
HQ: China Airlines, Ltd.
11201 Aviation Blvd
Los Angeles CA

(P-11661)
CHINA AIRLINES LTD
Also Called: Baggage Service
380 World Way Ste S14 (90045-5890)
PHONE....................310 646-4293
Tim Chan, *Mgr*
EMP: 107
Web: www.china-airlines.com
SIC: 4512 Air passenger carrier, scheduled
HQ: China Airlines, Ltd.
11201 Aviation Blvd
Los Angeles CA

(P-11662)
JETBLUE AIRWAYS INC
Also Called: Jet Blue
4100 E Donald Douglas Dr (90808-1754)
PHONE....................562 394-4397
Alex Wilcox, *Dir*
EMP: 93 **EST:** 2004
SALES (est): 6.35MM
SALES (corp-wide): 9.16B **Publicly Held**
SIC: 4512 Air passenger carrier, scheduled
PA: Jetblue Airways Corporation
2701 Queens Plz N
Long Island City NY
718 286-7900

(P-11663)
KOREAN AIR LINES CO LTD
Also Called: Korean Air
380 World Way Ste S4 (90045-5847)
PHONE....................310 646-4866
EMP: 175
Web: www.koreanair.com
SIC: 4512 Air passenger carrier, scheduled
PA: Korean Airlines Co., Ltd.
260 Haneul-Gil, Gangseo-Gu
Seoul

(P-11664)
KOREAN AIRLINES CO LTD
Also Called: Korean Arln Crgo Reservations
6101 W Imperial Hwy (90045-6305)

PHONE..................310 410-2000
Jinkul Lee, *Pr*
EMP: 250
Web: www.koreanair.com
SIC: 4512 4513 Air passenger carrier, scheduled; Package delivery, private air
PA: Korean Airlines Co., Ltd.
260 Haneul-Gil, Gangseo-Gu
Seoul

(P-11665)
KOREAN AIRLINES CO LTD
Also Called: Korean Air
1813 Wilshire Blvd Ste 400 (90057-3600)
PHONE..................213 484-1900
Kyung Kim, *Brnch Mgr*
EMP: 100
Web: www.koreanair.com
SIC: 4512 4729 Air passenger carrier, scheduled; Airline ticket offices
PA: Korean Airlines Co., Ltd.
260 Haneul-Gil, Gangseo-Gu
Seoul

(P-11666)
L A AIR INC
5933 W Century Blvd 500 (90045-5471)
PHONE..................310 215-8245
Dennis W Altbrandt, *CEO*
Wayne Schoenfeld, ***
Tim Clary, *MARKET PLANNING**
William J Wolf, ***
EMP: 134 **EST:** 1980
SQ FT: 6,119
SALES (est): 4.08MM **Privately Held**
SIC: 4512 Air passenger carrier, scheduled

(P-11667)
NIPPON CARGO AIRLINES CO LTD
6501 W Imperial Hwy Hngr 8 (90045-6308)
PHONE..................310 417-0801
EMP: 84
Web: www.nca.aero
SIC: 4512 Air passenger carrier, scheduled
HQ: Nippon Cargo Airlines Co., Ltd.
663 N Access Rd
Chicago IL

(P-11668)
PIEDMONT AIRLINES INC
Also Called: American Airlines/Eagle
4100 E Donald Douglas Dr (90808-1754)
PHONE..................562 421-1806
Sean Lucas, *Mgr*
EMP: 147
SALES (corp-wide): 48.97B **Publicly Held**
Web: www.piedmont-airlines.com
SIC: 4512 Air passenger carrier, scheduled
HQ: Piedmont Airlines, Inc.
5443 Airport Terminal Rd
Salisbury MD
410 572-5100

(P-11669)
POLAR AIR CARGO LP
100 Oceangate Fl 15 (90802-4347)
PHONE..................310 568-4551
FAX: 562 436-9333
EMP: 480
SALES (est): 13.37MM
SALES (corp-wide): 1.84B **Publicly Held**
SIC: 4512 Air cargo carrier, scheduled
PA: Atlas Air Worldwide Holdings, Inc.
2000 Westchester Ave
Purchase NY
914 701-8000

(P-11670)
SINGAPORE AIRLINES LIMITED
222 N Pacific Coast Hwy Ste 1600 (90245)
PHONE..................310 647-1922
Tee Hooi Teoh, *Mgr*
EMP: 135
Web: www.singaporeair.com
SIC: 4512 Air passenger carrier, scheduled
PA: Singapore Airlines Limited
25 Airline Road
Singapore

(P-11671)
SOUTHWEST AIRLINES CO
Also Called: Southwest Airlines
18601 Airport Way Ste 237 (92707-5257)
PHONE..................949 252-5200
Larry Pits, *Mgr*
EMP: 80
SALES (corp-wide): 23.81B **Publicly Held**
Web: www.southwest.com
SIC: 4512 Air passenger carrier, scheduled
PA: Southwest Airlines Co.
2702 Love Field Dr
Dallas TX
214 792-4000

(P-11672)
UNITED AIRLINES INC
Also Called: Continental Airlines
7300 World Way W Rm 144 (90045-5829)
PHONE..................310 258-3319
Ken Jaminson, *Mgr*
EMP: 89
SALES (corp-wide): 44.95B **Publicly Held**
SIC: 4512 Air passenger carrier, scheduled
HQ: United Airlines, Inc.
233 S Wacker Dr Ste 710
Chicago IL
872 825-4000

(P-11673)
UNITED COURIERS INC (DH)
Also Called: U C I Distribution Plus
3280 E Foothill Blvd (91107-3148)
PHONE..................213 383-3611
Stephan Cretier, *CEO*
Richard R Irvin, ***
Robert G Irvin, ***
EMP: 200 **EST:** 1957
SQ FT: 25,000
SALES (est): 47.99MM
SALES (corp-wide): 175.11MM **Privately Held**
SIC: 4512 4215 4212 7381 Air cargo carrier, scheduled; Courier services, except by air; Local trucking, without storage; Armored car services
HQ: Ati Systems International, Inc.
2000 Nw Corp Blvd Ste 101
Boca Raton FL
561 939-7000

(P-11674)
UNITED PARCEL SERVICE INC
Also Called: UPS
1457 E Victoria Ave (92408-2923)
PHONE..................800 742-5877
EMP: 106
SALES (corp-wide): 100.34B **Publicly Held**
Web: www.ups.com
SIC: 4512 Air cargo carrier, scheduled
HQ: United Parcel Service, Inc.
55 Glenlake Pkwy
Atlanta GA
404 828-6000

(P-11675)
UNITED PARCEL SERVICE INC
Also Called: UPS
3110 Jurupa St (91761-2902)
PHONE..................909 605-7740
EMP: 120
SALES (corp-wide): 100.34B **Publicly Held**
Web: www.ups.com
SIC: 4512 Air cargo carrier, scheduled
HQ: United Parcel Service, Inc.
55 Glenlake Pkwy
Atlanta GA
404 828-6000

4513 Air Courier Services

(P-11676)
FEDERAL EXPRESS CORPORATION
Also Called: Fedex
3333 S Grand Ave (90007-4116)
PHONE..................800 463-3339
EMP: 100
SALES (corp-wide): 90.16B **Publicly Held**
Web: www.fedex.com
SIC: 4513 Package delivery, private air
HQ: Federal Express Corporation
3610 Hacks Cross Rd
Memphis TN
901 369-3600

(P-11677)
MEJICO EXPRESS INC (PA)
Also Called: Grupoex
14849 Firestone Blvd Fl 1 (90638)
PHONE..................714 690-8300
Jose Leon, *Pr*
EMP: 150 **EST:** 1988
SALES (est): 7.7MM **Privately Held**
SIC: 4513 Letter delivery, private air

(P-11678)
UNITED PARCEL SERVICE INC
Also Called: UPS
3333 S Downey Rd (90058-4116)
PHONE..................323 260-8957
Tony Peralta, *Mgr*
EMP: 226
SALES (corp-wide): 100.34B **Publicly Held**
Web: www.ups.com
SIC: 4513 4215 Air courier services; Courier services, except by air
HQ: United Parcel Service, Inc.
55 Glenlake Pkwy
Atlanta GA
404 828-6000

4522 Air Transportation, Nonscheduled

(P-11679)
ADVANCED AIR LLC
Also Called: Advanced Air
12101 Crenshaw Blvd Ste 100 (90250-3369)
PHONE..................310 644-3344
Levi Stockton, *Pr*
EMP: 150 **EST:** 2005
SQ FT: 2,500
SALES (est): 24.34MM **Privately Held**
Web: www.advancedairlines.com
SIC: 4522 4512 Air transportation, nonscheduled; Air transportation, scheduled

(P-11680)
AVJET CORPORATION (DH)
4301 W Empire Ave (91505-1109)
PHONE..................818 841-6190
EMP: 80 **EST:** 1979
SALES (est): 15.66MM
SALES (corp-wide): 39.41B **Publicly Held**
Web: www.avjet.com
SIC: 4522 5599 4581 Flying charter service; Aircraft, self-propelled; Aircraft cleaning and janitorial service
HQ: Jet Aviation Of America, Inc.
112 Chrles A Lndbrgh Dr T
Teterboro NJ
201 288-8400

(P-11681)
NAVAJO INVESTMENTS INC (PA)
17962 Cowan (92614-6026)
PHONE..................949 863-9200
William Langston, *Pr*
EMP: 98 **EST:** 1985
SQ FT: 17,000
SALES (est): 4.65MM
SALES (corp-wide): 4.65MM **Privately Held**
Web: www.snyderlangston.com
SIC: 4522 Air transportation, nonscheduled

(P-11682)
PEGASUS ELITE AVIATION INC
7943 Woodley Ave (91406-1232)
PHONE..................818 742-6666
EMP: 162 **EST:** 2007
SALES (est): 27.45MM
SALES (corp-wide): 27.45MM **Privately Held**
Web: www.pegjet.com
SIC: 4522 Flying charter service
PA: Prima Air Group Llc
800 E Colo Blvd Ste 888
Pasadena CA

(P-11683)
SUN AIR JETS LLC
855 Aviation Dr Ste 200 (93010-8595)
PHONE..................805 389-9301
Brian Counsil, *Pr*
Steve Maloney, ***
Rob Cox, *OF Maintenance**
Ed Fares, ***
EMP: 114 **EST:** 1999
SQ FT: 10,000
SALES (est): 25.12MM **Privately Held**
Web: www.sunairjets.com
SIC: 4522 4581 Flying charter service; Aircraft servicing and repairing

4581 Airports, Flying Fields, And Services

(P-11684)
ADIENT AEROSPACE LLC (PA)
2850 Skyway Dr (93455-1410)
PHONE..................949 514-1851
Tony Guy, *CEO*
Michael Rowen, *COO*
EMP: 122 **EST:** 2018
SALES (est): 85MM
SALES (corp-wide): 85MM **Privately Held**
SIC: 4581 Aircraft servicing and repairing

(P-11685)
AIR 88 INC
Also Called: Crownair Aviation
3753 John J Montgomery Dr (92123-1751)
PHONE..................858 277-1453
David Ryan, *Pr*

PRODUCTS & SVCS

Laura Cagliero, *
EMP: 51 **EST:** 1951
SQ FT: 53,600
SALES (est): 5.16MM **Privately Held**
Web: www.crownairaviation.com
SIC: 4581 3829 Aircraft maintenance and repair services; Fuel system instruments, aircraft

(P-11686)
AIRCRAFT REPAIR & OVERHAUL SVC (PA)
Also Called: A R O Service
1186 N Grove St (92806-2109)
PHONE..................714 630-9494
Thomas Haefele, *CEO*
Robert C Haefele, *Pr*
Mark Haefele, *VP*
Shirley M Haefele, *Sec*
EMP: 20 **EST:** 1975
SQ FT: 90,000
SALES (est): 4.59MM
SALES (corp-wide): 4.59MM **Privately Held**
Web: www.aroservice.com
SIC: 4581 3728 Airports, flying fields, and services; Aircraft parts and equipment, nec

(P-11687)
AIRPORT TERMINAL MGT INC
6851 W Imperial Hwy (90045-6311)
PHONE..................310 988-1492
EMP: 321
SALES (corp-wide): 22.92MM **Privately Held**
Web: www.atmlax.com
SIC: 4581 Airport terminal services
PA: Airport Terminal Management, Inc.
216 W Florence Ave
Inglewood CA
310 590-1650

(P-11688)
ALLIANCE GROUND INTL LLC
6181 W Imperial Hwy (90045-6305)
PHONE..................310 646-2446
EMP: 1231
SALES (corp-wide): 478.27MM **Privately Held**
Web: www.allianceground.com
SIC: 4581 Airfreight loading and unloading services
HQ: Alliance Ground International, Llc
9130 S Ddland Blvd Ste 18
Miami FL
305 740-3252

(P-11689)
AVIATION & DEFENSE INC
Also Called: ADI
255 S Leland Norton Way (92408-0103)
PHONE..................909 382-3487
Daniel M Scanlon, *CEO*
Mike Scanlon, *Pr*
Dan Scanlon, *VP*
Kathy Meza, *Contrlr*
Jim Anderson, *Sls Dir*
EMP: 180 **EST:** 2011
SQ FT: 180,000
SALES (est): 24.47MM **Privately Held**
Web: www.adi.aero
SIC: 4581 Aircraft maintenance and repair services

(P-11690)
AVIATION MAINTENANCE GROUP INC
8352 Kimball Ave Hngr 3 (91708-9267)
PHONE..................714 469-0515
Jeremy G Schuster, *Pr*

Doug Crowther, *
EMP: 85 **EST:** 1995
SALES (est): 4.85MM **Privately Held**
SIC: 4581 Aircraft maintenance and repair services

(P-11691)
CLAY LACY AVIATION INC (PA)
Also Called: C L A
7435 Valjean Ave (91406-2901)
PHONE..................818 989-2900
TOLL FREE: 800
Brian Kirkdoffer, *Pr*
Hershel Clay Lacy, *
EMP: 317 **EST:** 1969
SQ FT: 18,000
SALES (est): 157.17MM
SALES (corp-wide): 157.17MM **Privately Held**
Web: www.claylacy.com
SIC: 4581 Airport terminal services

(P-11692)
COMAV LLC
Also Called: Comav Aviation
18260 Phantom W (92394-7971)
PHONE..................760 523-5100
EMP: 103
SALES (corp-wide): 83.02MM **Privately Held**
Web: www.comav.com
SIC: 4581 Aircraft maintenance and repair services
PA: Comav, Llc
18499 Phantom St Ste 17
Victorville CA
760 523-5100

(P-11693)
COMAV TECHNICAL SERVICES LLC
Also Called: S C A
18438 Readiness St (92394-7945)
PHONE..................760 530-2400
Craig Garrick, *CEO*
Jon Day, *
▲ **EMP:** 223 **EST:** 1999
SQ FT: 47,625
SALES (est): 48.55MM
SALES (corp-wide): 83.02MM **Privately Held**
Web: www.comav.com
SIC: 4581 Aircraft maintenance and repair services
PA: Comav, Llc
18499 Phantom St Ste 17
Victorville CA
760 523-5100

(P-11694)
COUNTY OF ORANGE
Also Called: John Wayne Airport
3160 Airway Ave (92626-4608)
PHONE..................949 252-5006
Loan Leblow, *Brnch Mgr*
EMP: 135
SALES (corp-wide): 5.2B **Privately Held**
Web: www.ocgov.com
SIC: 4581 9621 Airport; Aircraft regulating agencies
PA: County Of Orange
400 W Civic Center Dr G36
Santa Ana CA
714 834-6200

(P-11695)
DEPARTMENT OF ARPRTS OF THE CY
1 World Way (90045-5803)
PHONE..................855 463-5252

EMP: 1507
SALES (est): 1.43MM
SALES (corp-wide): 1.38B **Privately Held**
Web: www.lawa.org
SIC: 4581 Airport
PA: Los Angeles World Airports
1 World Way
Los Angeles CA
855 463-5252

(P-11696)
DSD TRUCKING INC
2411 Santa Fe Ave (90278-1125)
PHONE..................310 338-3395
Dan Cuevas, *Pr*
EMP: 100 **EST:** 1984
SQ FT: 300,000
SALES (est): 15.56MM **Privately Held**
Web: www.dsdcompanies.com
SIC: 4581 Air freight handling at airports

(P-11697)
F & E ARCFT MINT LOS ANGELES LL
531 Main St Ste 672 (90245-3006)
PHONE..................310 338-0063
EMP: 350 **EST:** 1992
SALES (est): 17.58MM **Privately Held**
Web: www.feairmaintenance.com
SIC: 4581 7699 Aircraft servicing and repairing; Aircraft and heavy equipment repair services

(P-11698)
GAT - ARLN GROUND SUPPORT INC
2627 N Hollywood Way (91505-1062)
PHONE..................818 847-9127
EMP: 221
Web: www.wearegat.net
SIC: 4581 Airports, flying fields, and services
PA: Gat - Airline Ground Support, Inc.
246 City Cir Ste 2000
Peachtree City GA

(P-11699)
LOS ANGELES WORLD AIRPORTS
5312 W 99th Pl (90045-5722)
PHONE..................424 646-9118
EMP: 226
SALES (corp-wide): 1.38B **Privately Held**
Web: www.lawa.org
SIC: 4581 Airport
PA: Los Angeles World Airports
1 World Way
Los Angeles CA
855 463-5252

(P-11700)
LOS ANGELES WORLD AIRPORTS
Also Called: Human Resources Services
7301 World Way W Fl 5 (90045-5828)
PHONE..................424 646-5900
EMP: 452
SALES (corp-wide): 1.38B **Privately Held**
Web: www.lawa.org
SIC: 4581 Airport
PA: Los Angeles World Airports
1 World Way
Los Angeles CA
855 463-5252

(P-11701)
LOS ANGELES WORLD AIRPORTS (PA)
1 World Way (90045-5803)

P.O. Box 92216 (90009-2216)
PHONE..................855 463-5252
Justin Erbacci, *CEO*
Michael Cummings, *
Robert L Gilbert, *Chief Development Officer*
Arif Alikhan, *
EMP: 222 **EST:** 2010
SALES (est): 1.38B
SALES (corp-wide): 1.38B **Privately Held**
Web: www.lawa.org
SIC: 4581 Airport

(P-11702)
PACIFIC AVIATION CORPORATION (PA)
201 Continental Blvd Ste 220 (90245-4500)
PHONE..................310 646-4015
EMP: 200 **EST:** 1995
SALES (est): 30.47MM **Privately Held**
Web: www.pacificaviation.com
SIC: 4581 Airport terminal services

(P-11703)
PACIFIC OIL COOLER SERVICE INC
1677 Curtiss Ct (91750-5848)
PHONE..................909 593-8400
Paul Saurenman Senior, *Pr*
Jan Saurenman, *Prin*
◆ **EMP:** 20 **EST:** 1988
SALES (est): 3.37MM **Privately Held**
Web: www.oilcoolers.com
SIC: 4581 3443 Aircraft servicing and repairing; Fabricated plate work (boiler shop)

(P-11704)
PHS / MWA
Also Called: Phs/Mwa Aviation Services
42374 Avenida Alvarado # A (92590)
PHONE..................951 695-1008
Mary Bale, *CEO*
Bill Voetsch, *
EMP: 147 **EST:** 2003
SALES (est): 25.51MM **Publicly Held**
Web: www.wencor.com
SIC: 4581 3492 7629 Aircraft servicing and repairing; Control valves, aircraft: hydraulic and pneumatic; Electrical repair shops
HQ: Wencor Group, Llc
416 Dividend Dr
Peachtree City GA
678 490-0140

(P-11705)
REPAIRTECH INTERNATIONAL INC
Also Called: Repair Tech International
7850 Gloria Ave (91406-1821)
PHONE..................818 989-2681
Stanley H Bennett, *Pr*
Patricia J Bennett, *
EMP: 30 **EST:** 1978
SALES (est): 4.06MM **Privately Held**
Web: www.repairtechinternational.com
SIC: 4581 3721 3999 Aircraft servicing and repairing; Aircraft; Atomizers, toiletry

(P-11706)
SAN DEGO CNTY RGNAL ARPRT AUTH (PA)
Also Called: Sdcraa
3225 N Harbor Dr Fl 3 (92101-1045)
P.O. Box 82776 (92138-2776)
PHONE..................619 400-2400
Thella F Bowens, *CEO*
EMP: 229 **EST:** 2003
SALES (est): 215.94MM
SALES (corp-wide): 215.94MM **Privately Held**

▲ = Import ▼ = Export
◆ = Import/Export

Web: www.san.org
SIC: **4581** Airport

(P-11707)
SIERRA GROUP INC
1129 N Calvert Blvd China Lake
(93555-7815)
P.O. Box 1628 (93527-1628)
PHONE............................760 377-1000
Tyrrell Richards-o'tyrrell, *Prin*
Pheadar Diarmuid Diogenes O'ty rrell, *Prin*
Mary K Jacobs, *Sr VP*
◆ **EMP:** 18 **EST:** 1957
SQ FT: 4,800
SALES (est): 334.36K **Privately Held**
SIC: **4581 7379 3429 8711** Aircraft servicing
and repairing; Computer related
maintenance services; Parachute hardware
; Consulting engineer

(P-11708)
SWISSPORT CARGO SERVICES LP
Also Called: Cargo Service Center
11001 Aviation Blvd (90045-6123)
PHONE............................310 910-9541
Mark Wood, *Genl Mgr*
EMP: 157
SALES (corp-wide): 2.67MM **Privately Held**
Web: www.swissport.com
SIC: **4581** Airport terminal services
HQ: Swissport Cargo Services, L.P.
23723 Air Frt Ln Bldg 5
Dulles VA
703 742-4300

(P-11709)
WORLD SVC WST/LA INFLGHT SVC L
Also Called: L.A. Inflight Service Company
1812 W 135th St (90249-2520)
PHONE............................310 538-7000
Steven H Yoon, *Managing Member*
◆ **EMP:** 170 **EST:** 1988
SQ FT: 13,572
SALES (est): 2.08MM **Privately Held**
SIC: **4581** Aircraft cleaning and janitorial
service

4613 Refined Petroleum Pipelines

(P-11710)
SFPP LP (DH)
1100 W Town And Country Rd Ste 600
(92868-4647)
PHONE............................714 560-4400
Park Shaper, *Genl Pt*
Richard D Kinder, *Genl Pt*
EMP: 150 **EST:** 1998
SQ FT: 75,000
SALES (est): 319.91MM **Publicly Held**
Web: www.kindermorgan.com
SIC: **4613** Gasoline pipelines (common
carriers)
HQ: Kinder Morgan Energy Partners, L.P.
1001 La St Ste 1000
Houston TX
713 369-9000

4724 Travel Agencies

(P-11711)
ALTOUR INTERNATIONAL INC
Also Called: Altour Travel Master
10635 Santa Monica Blvd Ste 200
(90025-8300)
PHONE............................310 571-6000
EMP: 259
Web: www.altour.com
SIC: **4724** Travel agencies
PA: Altour International, Inc.
1270 Avenue Of The Flr 15
New York NY

(P-11712)
ALTOUR INTERNATIONAL INC (PA)
12100 W Olympic Blvd Ste 300
(90064-1051)
PHONE............................310 571-6000
Alexander Chemla, *Pr*
David Sefton, *
EMP: 80 **EST:** 1995
SQ FT: 8,000
SALES (est): 25.7MM **Privately Held**
Web: www.altour.com
SIC: **4724** Travel agencies

(P-11713)
AMAWATERWAYS LLC (PA)
4500 Park Granada # 200 (91302-1677)
PHONE............................800 626-0126
EMP: 245 **EST:** 2008
SALES (est): 86.22MM **Privately Held**
Web: www.amawaterways.com
SIC: **4724** Travel agencies

(P-11714)
AMERICANTOURS INTL LLC (HQ)
6053 W Century Blvd Ste 700
(90045-6430)
PHONE............................310 641-9953
Michael Fitzpatrick, *
EMP: 105 **EST:** 2003
SQ FT: 20,000
SALES (est): 29.11MM
SALES (corp-wide): 29.11MM **Privately Held**
Web: www.americantours.com
SIC: **4724 4725** Travel agencies; Tour
operators
PA: Americantours International Inc.
6053 W Century Blvd # 70
Los Angeles CA
310 641-9953

(P-11715)
HELLOWORLD TRAVEL SVCS USA INC
Also Called: Qantas Vctons Nwmans
Vacations
6171 W Century Blvd Ste 160
(90045-5300)
PHONE............................310 535-1005
Ross Webster, *Pr*
Gary Goeldner, *
EMP: 100 **EST:** 1985
SALES (est): 21.7MM **Privately Held**
Web: www.qantasvacations.com
SIC: **4724** Tourist agency arranging
transport, lodging and car rental
PA: Helloworld Travel Limited
179 Normanby Rd
South Melbourne VIC

(P-11716)
HORNBLOWER YACHTS LLC
Also Called: Hornblower Cruisers and Events
2527 W Coast Hwy (92663-4709)
PHONE............................949 650-2412
Kevin Lorton, *Brnch Mgr*
EMP: 552
SALES (corp-wide): 495.57MM **Privately Held**

Web: www.cityexperiences.com
SIC: **4724** Travel agencies
PA: Hornblower Yachts, Llc
The Embarcadero Pier 3 St Pier
San Francisco CA
415 424-4309

(P-11717)
IDS INC
Also Called: IDS Technology
20300 Ventura Blvd Ste 200 (91364-2448)
PHONE............................866 297-5757
Nathan Morad, *CEO*
Alberto Gamez, *CMO**
John Ledo, *
Gary Kurtz, *Legal Counsel**
EMP: 97 **EST:** 2009
SQ FT: 9,000
SALES (est): 4.25MM **Privately Held**
Web: www.idscontrols.com
SIC: **4724 7372** Travel agencies; Business
oriented computer software

(P-11718)
JTB AMERICAS LTD (HQ)
3625 Del Amo Blvd Ste 260 (90503-1688)
PHONE............................310 406-3121
Tsuneo Irita, *Pr*
Benny Harrell, *
EMP: 100 **EST:** 1963
SALES (est): 196.64MM **Privately Held**
Web: www.jtbamericas.com
SIC: **4724** Travel agencies
PA: Jtb Corp.
2-3-11, Higashishinagawa
Shinagawa-Ku TKY

(P-11719)
LBF TRAVEL INC
Also Called: Travelerhelpdesk.com
4545 Murphy Canyon Rd Ste 210
(92123-4318)
PHONE............................858 429-7599
Michael H Thomas, *CEO*
Adrian Myram, *
EMP: 300 **EST:** 2010
SALES (est): 41.74MM **Privately Held**
Web: www.lbftravel.com
SIC: **4724** Tourist agency arranging
transport, lodging and car rental

(P-11720)
NIPPON TRAVEL AGENCY PCF INC (DH)
Also Called: Nta Pacific
1411 W 190th St Ste 650 (90248-4369)
PHONE............................310 768-0017
Tadashi Wakayama, *Pr*
Akio Tsuna, *
▲ **EMP:** 80 **EST:** 1973
SQ FT: 20,000
SALES (est): 48.73MM **Privately Held**
Web: www.ntaamerica.com
SIC: **4724** Tourist agency arranging
transport, lodging and car rental
HQ: Nippon Travel Agency Co., Ltd.
1-19-1, Nihombashi
Chuo-Ku TKY

(P-11721)
OXY INC
Also Called: OXY-World Travel
10889 Wilshire Blvd (90024-4200)
PHONE............................310 824-1315
Donald L Moore, *Pr*
EMP: 104 **EST:** 1974
SALES (est): 12.39MM
SALES (corp-wide): 37.09B **Publicly Held**
Web: www.oxy.com

SIC: **4724** Tourist agency arranging
transport, lodging and car rental
PA: Occidental Petroleum Corporation
5 Greenway Plz Ste 110
Houston TX
713 215-7000

(P-11722)
PINNACLE TRAVEL SERVICES LLC
390 N Pacific Coast Hwy (90245-4475)
PHONE............................310 414-1787
Robert G Singh, *CEO*
EMP: 151 **EST:** 1999
SQ FT: 15,000
SALES (est): 23.23MM **Privately Held**
Web: www.ptsla.com
SIC: **4724** Tourist agency arranging
transport, lodging and car rental

(P-11723)
PLEASANT HOLIDAYS LLC (HQ)
Also Called: Pleasant Hawaiian Holiday
2404 Townsgate Rd (91361-2505)
PHONE............................818 991-3390
Jack E Richards, *CEO*
Duke Ah Moo, *
Bruce Rosenberg, *
EMP: 300 **EST:** 1998
SQ FT: 55,000
SALES (est): 154.34MM
SALES (corp-wide): 1.08B **Privately Held**
Web: beta.pleasantholidays.com
SIC: **4724** Tourist agency arranging
transport, lodging and car rental
PA: Automobile Club Of Southern California
2601 S Figueroa St
Los Angeles CA
213 741-3686

(P-11724)
PRINCESS CRUISE LINES LTD
Also Called: Princess Cruises
24833 Anza Dr (91355-1259)
P.O. Box 966 (91380-9066)
PHONE............................661 753-2197
Princess Cruise, *Prin*
EMP: 1114
SALES (corp-wide): 3.94B **Privately Held**
Web: www.princess.com
SIC: **4724** Travel agencies
HQ: Princess Cruise Lines, Ltd.
24305 Town Center Dr
Santa Clarita CA
661 753-0000

(P-11725)
PROTRAVEL INTERNATIONAL LLC
345 N Maple Dr (90210-3869)
PHONE............................310 271-9566
Sara Sessa, *Brnch Mgr*
EMP: 100
SALES (corp-wide): 97.32MM **Privately Held**
Web: www.protravelinc.com
SIC: **4724** Travel agencies
PA: Protravel International Llc
1633 Broadway Fl 35
New York NY
212 755-4550

(P-11726)
SKYLINK TRAVEL INC
18000 Studebaker Rd Ste 330
(90703-2674)
PHONE............................212 380-2438
Moon K Lee, *Prin*
EMP: 103
SALES (corp-wide): 159.48MM **Publicly Held**

PRODUCTS & SVCS

Web: www.skylinkus.com
SIC: 4724 Travel agencies
HQ: Skylink Travel Inc.
15 W 36th St Fl 4
New York NY
212 380-2438

4725 Tour Operators

(P-11727)
ANTENNA AUDIO INC (PA)
Also Called: Antenna International
555 W 5th St Ste 3725 (90013-2670)
PHONE..............................203 523-0320
Janet Matricciani, *CEO*
Ira Morgenstern, *
▲ **EMP:** 796 **EST:** 1997
SALES (est): 20.98MM
SALES (corp-wide): 20.98MM **Privately Held**
Web: www.antenna-international.com
SIC: 4725 Tour operators

(P-11728)
PACIFIC COAST SIGHTSEEING TOUR
2001 S Manchester Ave (92802-3803)
PHONE..............................714 507-1157
Kristin Martinez, *General Mng*
Luis Silva, *
EMP: 230 **EST:** 2012
SALES (est): 23MM **Privately Held**
Web: www.anaheimoc.org
SIC: 4725 4173 Arrangement of travel tour packages, wholesale; Bus terminal operation
HQ: Coach Usa, Inc.
160 S Route 17 N
Paramus NJ

(P-11729)
PRINCESS CRUISE LINES LTD
24200 Magic Mountain Pkwy (91355-4886)
PHONE..............................661 753-0000
Barbara Potter, *Brnch Mgr*
EMP: 13077
SALES (corp-wide): 3.94B **Privately Held**
Web: www.princess.com
SIC: 4725 7011 4481 Tours, conducted; Hotels; Deep sea passenger transportation, except ferry
HQ: Princess Cruise Lines, Ltd.
24305 Town Center Dr
Santa Clarita CA
661 753-0000

(P-11730)
SANTA CATALINA ISLAND COMPANY (PA)
Also Called: Scico
4 Park Plz Ste 420 (92614-5259)
P.O. Box 737 (90704-0737)
PHONE..............................310 510-2000
Randall Herrel Senior, *CEO*
Paxson H Offield, *
John T Dravinski, *
Ronald C Doutt, *
EMP: 114 **EST:** 1959
SALES (est): 78.14MM
SALES (corp-wide): 78.14MM **Privately Held**
Web: www.visitcatalinaisland.com
SIC: 4725 Sightseeing tour companies

(P-11731)
SCREAMLINE INVESTMENT CORP
Also Called: Tourcoach Transportation
2130 S Tubeway Ave (90040-1614)

PHONE..............................323 201-0114
Kamrouz Farhadi, *CEO*
Vahid Sapir, *
Farima Akopians, *
Shoeleh Sapir, *
▲ **EMP:** 120 **EST:** 1992
SQ FT: 8,000
SALES (est): 24.5MM **Privately Held**
Web: www.tourcoach.com
SIC: 4725 Sightseeing tour companies

4729 Passenger Transportation Arrangement

(P-11732)
KOREAN AIRLINES CO LTD
Also Called: Korean Air
900 Wilshire Blvd Ste 1100 (90017-4701)
PHONE..............................213 484-5700
Kitaek Kang, *Genl Mgr*
EMP: 489
Web: www.koreanair.com
SIC: 4729 Airline ticket offices
PA: Korean Airlines Co., Ltd.
260 Haneul-Gil, Gangseo-Gu
Seoul

(P-11733)
MATRIX AVIATION SERVICES INC
6171 W Century Blvd Ste 100 (90045-5300)
PHONE..............................310 337-3037
Ramez Reno, *CEO*
Borseen Oushana, *
EMP: 175 **EST:** 2008
SQ FT: 3,000
SALES (est): 21.24MM **Privately Held**
Web: www.matrix-aviation.com
SIC: 4729 Airline ticket offices

4731 Freight Transportation Arrangement

(P-11734)
ABLE FREIGHT SERVICES LLC (PA)
5340 W 104th St (90045-6010)
PHONE..............................310 568-8883
◆ **EMP:** 90 **EST:** 1992
SALES (est): 30.82MM **Privately Held**
Web: www.ablefreight.com
SIC: 4731 Freight forwarding

(P-11735)
AGILITY HOLDINGS INC (DH)
Also Called: Agility Logistics
310 Commerce Ste 250 (92602-1399)
PHONE..............................714 617-6300
◆ **EMP:** 80 **EST:** 1996
SALES (est): 1.01B
SALES (corp-wide): 32.91B **Privately Held**
SIC: 4731 4213 4214 Domestic freight forwarding; Household goods transport; Household goods moving and storage, local
HQ: Agility Logistics International B.V.
Incheonweg 17
Rozenburg Nh NH
884360105

(P-11736)
AGILITY LOGISTICS CORP (DH)
Also Called: Global Integrated Logistics
310 Commerce Ste 250 (92602-1399)
PHONE..............................714 617-6300
◆ **EMP:** 90 **EST:** 1973
SALES (est): 426.24MM

SALES (corp-wide): 32.91B **Privately Held**
Web: www.agility.com
SIC: 4731 7372 1381 Freight transportation arrangement; Prepackaged software; Drilling oil and gas wells
HQ: Agility Holdings, Inc.
310 Commerce Ste 250
Irvine CA

(P-11737)
AIR EXPRESS INTL USA INC
Also Called: Dhl Global Forwarding
19900 S Vermont Ave Ste A (90502-1147)
PHONE..............................310 297-4401
Tim Robertson, *Mgr*
EMP: 85
SALES (corp-wide): 98.08B **Privately Held**
SIC: 4731 Freight forwarding
HQ: Air Express International Usa, Inc.
1210 S Pine Island Rd
Plantation FL
786 264-3500

(P-11738)
AIR GROUP LEASING INC
1111 E Watson Center Rd Ste C (90745-4217)
PHONE..............................310 684-4095
Victor Leigh, *Pr*
Thomas Bowling, *
▲ **EMP:** 1560 **EST:** 1992
SQ FT: 2,900
SALES (est): 5.93MM
SALES (corp-wide): 9.65B **Publicly Held**
SIC: 4731 4513 Freight forwarding; Package delivery, private air
PA: Alaska Air Group, Inc
19300 International Blvd
Seatac WA
206 392-5040

(P-11739)
AMERITRANS EXPRESS INC
15130 Ventura Blvd # 313 (91403-3301)
PHONE..............................818 201-0524
Chunlei Hou, *CEO*
EMP: 19 **EST:** 2014
SALES (est): 820.49K **Privately Held**
SIC: 4731 3799 Freight transportation arrangement; Transportation equipment, nec

(P-11740)
APEX LOGISTICS INTL INC (PA)
Also Called: Apex USA
18554 S Susana Rd (90221-5620)
PHONE..............................310 665-0288
Elsie Qian, *CEO*
Hui Qian, *
▲ **EMP:** 227 **EST:** 2003
SALES (est): 2.72B
SALES (corp-wide): 2.72B **Privately Held**
Web: www.apexglobe.com
SIC: 4731 Freight forwarding

(P-11741)
APM TERMINALS PACIFIC LLC
Also Called: Mearsk
2500 Navy Way Pier 400 (90731-7554)
PHONE..............................310 221-4000
Milan D.o.s., *Brnch Mgr*
EMP: 401
SALES (corp-wide): 2.41MM **Privately Held**
Web: www.apmterminals.com
SIC: 4731 Agents, shipping
HQ: Apm Terminals Pacific Llc
9300 Arrowpoint Blvd
Charlotte NC

(P-11742)
BLACKROCK LOGISTICS INC
Also Called: Blackrock Logistics
14601 Slover Ave (92337-7163)
PHONE..............................909 259-5357
Larry T James, *Pr*
EMP: 114
SALES (corp-wide): 44.52MM **Privately Held**
Web: www.blackrock-logistics.net
SIC: 4731 Freight forwarding
PA: Blackrock Logistics Inc.
7031 Koll Center Pkwy # 250
Pleasanton CA
925 523-3878

(P-11743)
CARGOMATIC INC (PA)
211 E Ocean Blvd Ste 350 (90802-4808)
PHONE..............................866 513-2343
Richard Gerstein, *CEO*
Andrew Straub, *
Matt Hogan, *
Steve Jackson, *CAO**
EMP: 129 **EST:** 2013
SALES (est): 95.65MM
SALES (corp-wide): 95.65MM **Privately Held**
Web: www.cargomatic.com
SIC: 4731 Transportation agents and brokers

(P-11744)
CARMICHAEL INTERNATIONAL SVC (DH)
Also Called: C I Container Line
1200 Corporate Center Dr Ste 200 (91754)
PHONE..............................213 353-0800
John Salvo, *Pr*
Vince Salvo, *
Jim Ryan, *
◆ **EMP:** 100 **EST:** 1961
SQ FT: 19,000
SALES (est): 94.64MM **Privately Held**
Web: www.carmnet.com
SIC: 4731 Customhouse brokers
HQ: Kintetsu World Express, Inc.
2-15-1, Konan
Minato-Ku TKY

(P-11745)
CARROLL FULMER LOGISTICS CORP
13773 Algranti Ave (91342-2607)
PHONE..............................626 435-9940
Josh Quijano, *Brnch Mgr*
EMP: 294
SALES (corp-wide): 182.11MM **Privately Held**
Web: www.cfulmer.com
SIC: 4731 Truck transportation brokers
HQ: Carroll Fulmer Logistics Corporation
8340 American Way
Groveland FL
352 429-5000

(P-11746)
CEVA LOGISTICS LLC
19600 S Western Ave (90501-1117)
PHONE..............................310 223-6500
Marvin O Schlanger, *Mgr*
EMP: 300
SALES (corp-wide): 31.16K **Privately Held**
Web: www.cevalogistics.com
SIC: 4731 Domestic freight forwarding
HQ: Ceva Logistics, Llc
15350 Vickery Dr
Houston TX
281 618-3100

(P-11747)
CJ LOGISTICS AMERICA LLC
5690 Industrial Pkwy (92407-1885)
PHONE.....................540 377-2302
EMP: 187
Web: america.cjlogistics.com
SIC: 4731 Freight forwarding
HQ: Cj Logistics America, Llc
1750 S Wolf Rd
Des Plaines IL

(P-11748)
CROWLEY MARINE SERVICES INC
86 Berth 300 S Harbor Blvd (90731-3353)
PHONE.....................310 732-6500
Andrew Gauphier, *Mgr*
EMP: 394
Web: www.crowley.com
SIC: 4731 Freight transportation arrangement
HQ: Crowley Marine Services, Inc.
9487 Regency Square Blvd
Jacksonville FL

(P-11749)
DCW DCW INC
20500 Denker Ave (90501-1645)
PHONE.....................310 324-3147
Henry Mandil, *CEO*
EMP: 100 EST: 2020
SALES (est): 5.71MM Privately Held
SIC: 4731 4225 Freight transportation arrangement; General warehousing and storage

(P-11750)
DE WELL CONTAINER SHIPPING INC
Also Called: Logistics
5553 Bandini Blvd Unit A (90201-6421)
PHONE.....................310 735-8600
Yang Shi, *CEO*
▲ EMP: 90 EST: 2004
SALES (est): 27.42MM Privately Held
Web: www.de-well.com
SIC: 4731 Freight forwarding
PA: De Well Container Shipping Corp.
No.1568, Gangcheng Road, Pudong
New District
Shanghai SH

(P-11751)
DEPENDABLE GLOBAL EXPRESS INC (PA)
Also Called: D G X
19201 S Susana Rd (90221-5710)
P.O. Box 513370 (90051-3370)
PHONE.....................310 537-2000
Ronald Massman, *CEO*
Bradley Dechter, *
Tim Rice, *
◆ EMP: 144 EST: 2004
SALES (est): 24.8MM Privately Held
Web: www.dgxglobal.com
SIC: 4731 Freight forwarding

(P-11752)
DFDS INTERNATIONAL CORPORATION
Also Called: Dfds Transport US
898 Sepulveda Blvd, 6th Floor
(90245-2705)
PHONE.....................310 414-1516
Tina Larsen, *Genl Mgr*
EMP: 80
SALES (corp-wide): 3.75B Privately Held
Web: www.dfdstransportusa.com
SIC: 4731 Foreign freight forwarding
HQ: Dfds International Corporation
100 Walnut Ave Ste 405

Clark NJ

(P-11753)
DHX-DEPENDABLE HAWAIIAN EX INC (PA)
19201 S Susana Rd (90221-5710)
PHONE.....................310 537-2000
Ronald Massman, *Ch*
Annette Massman, *
Bradley Dechter, *
◆ EMP: 150 EST: 1980
SQ FT: 106,000
SALES (est): 94.57MM
SALES (corp-wide): 94.57MM Privately Held
Web: www.dhx.com
SIC: 4731 Foreign freight forwarding

(P-11754)
DIRECTED LLC
1 Viper Way Ste 1 (92081-7811)
PHONE.....................800 876-0800
Robert Struble, *CEO*
James Wiesen, *
Joseph Tristani, *
David Meisels, *
EMP: 164 EST: 2014
SQ FT: 83,057
SALES (est): 80MM Privately Held
Web: www.directed.com
SIC: 4731 Domestic freight forwarding

(P-11755)
DSV SOLUTIONS LLC
Also Called: Corp., R.g Barry
13230 San Bernardino Ave (92335-5229)
PHONE.....................909 349-6100
EMP: 116
SALES (corp-wide): 32.91B Privately Held
Web: www.go2uti.com
SIC: 4731 Freight forwarding
HQ: Dsv Solutions, Llc
200 Wood Ave S 300
Iselin NJ
732 850-8000

(P-11756)
DSV SOLUTIONS LLC
1670 Etiwanda Ave Ste A (91761-3641)
PHONE.....................909 390-4563
Bob Mccullough, *Mgr*
EMP: 101
SQ FT: 400,000
SALES (corp-wide): 32.91B Privately Held
Web: www.go2uti.com
SIC: 4731 Freight forwarding
HQ: Dsv Solutions, Llc
200 Wood Ave S 300
Iselin NJ
732 850-8000

(P-11757)
DSV SOLUTIONS LLC
3454 E Miraloma Ave (92806-2101)
PHONE.....................714 630-0110
EMP: 87
SALES (corp-wide): 32.91B Privately Held
Web: www.go2uti.com
SIC: 4731 Freight forwarding
HQ: Dsv Solutions, Llc
200 Wood Ave S 300
Iselin NJ
732 850-8000

(P-11758)
EMPIRE MED TRANSPORTATIONS LLC
Also Called: Unicare Medical Transportation
1433 W Linden St Ste M (92507-6816)

PHONE.....................877 473-6029
EMP: 83 EST: 2017
SALES (est): 800K Privately Held
SIC: 4731 Freight forwarding

(P-11759)
EXPEDITORS INTL WASH INC
19701 Hamilton Ave (90502-1352)
PHONE.....................310 343-6200
Eric Mooney, *Brnch Mgr*
EMP: 300
SALES (corp-wide): 17.07B Publicly Held
Web: www.expeditors.com
SIC: 4731 Freight forwarding
PA: Expeditors International Of Washington, Inc.
1015 3rd Ave
Seattle WA
206 674-3400

(P-11760)
EXPEDITORS INTL WASH INC
Also Called: Expeditors International
12200 Wilkie Ave # 100 (90250-1838)
PHONE.....................310 343-6200
EMP: 96
SALES (corp-wide): 17.07B Publicly Held
Web: www.expeditors.com
SIC: 4731 Foreign freight forwarding
PA: Expeditors International Of Washington, Inc.
1015 3rd Ave
Seattle WA
206 674-3400

(P-11761)
FLOCK FREIGHT INC
Also Called: Auptix and Flock Freight
701 S Coast Highway 101 (92024-4441)
PHONE.....................855 744-7585
Oren Zaslansky, *CEO*
Pete Price, *
Luis Saenz, *
EMP: 120 EST: 2015
SALES (est): 58.1MM Privately Held
Web: www.flockfreight.com
SIC: 4731 Freight forwarding

(P-11762)
FNS INC (PA)
Also Called: FNS
1545 Francisco St (90501-1330)
PHONE.....................661 615-2300
◆ EMP: 100 EST: 1995
SQ FT: 100,000
SALES (est): 511.46MM Privately Held
Web: www.fnsusa.com
SIC: 4731 Freight forwarding

(P-11763)
GLOBAL MAIL INC
921 W Artesia Blvd (90220-5105)
PHONE.....................310 735-0800
Eric Ricardo, *Brnch Mgr*
EMP: 225
SALES (corp-wide): 98.08B Privately Held
SIC: 4731 Freight transportation arrangement
HQ: Global Mail, Inc.
2700 S Comm Pkwy Ste 300
Weston FL
800 805-9306

(P-11764)
GLOVIS AMERICA INC (HQ)
17305 Von Karman Ave Ste 200
(92614-6674)
PHONE.....................714 427-0944
Bong Jeong Ko, *CEO*
Scott Cornell, *
◆ EMP: 185 EST: 2002

SQ FT: 34,700
SALES (est): 856.58MM Privately Held
Web: www.glovisusa.com
SIC: 4731 Freight forwarding
PA: Hyundai Glovis Co.,Ltd
83-21 Wangsimni-Ro, Seongdong-Gu
Seoul

(P-11765)
GOLDEN HOUR DATA SYSTEMS INC
10052 Mesa Ridge Ct Ste 200
(92121-2971)
P.O. Box 19786 (92159-0786)
PHONE.....................858 768-2500
Kevin Hutton, *Pr*
Charles Haczewski, *
Peter Goutmann, *
Bill Dow, *
Eric Fleming, *CSO*
EMP: 120 EST: 1997
SQ FT: 14,000
SALES (est): 47.91MM Privately Held
Web: www.goldenhour.com
SIC: 4731 Transportation agents and brokers
HQ: Zoll Medical Corporation
269 Mill Rd
Chelmsford MA
978 421-9655

(P-11766)
GXO LOGISTICS SUPPLY CHAIN INC
7140 Cajon Blvd (92407-1898)
PHONE.....................909 838-5631
Luis Gonzales, *Mgr*
EMP: 100
SALES (corp-wide): 8.99B Publicly Held
Web: www.gxo.com
SIC: 4731 Freight forwarding
HQ: Gxo Logistics Supply Chain, Inc.
4043 Piedmont Pkwy
High Point NC
336 232-4100

(P-11767)
HANJIN TRANSPORTATION CO LTD
Also Called: Hanjin Global Logistics
15913 S Main St (90248-2550)
PHONE.....................310 522-5030
Bryce Dalziel, *Pr*
J B Park, *
EMP: 90 EST: 1996
SALES (est): 16.11MM Privately Held
Web: www.hanjinusa.com
SIC: 4731 Transportation agents and brokers

(P-11768)
HAPAG-LLOYD (AMERICA) LLC
555 E Ocean Blvd Ste 300 (90802-5052)
PHONE.....................562 435-0771
Oli Reichol, *Brnch Mgr*
EMP: 124
SQ FT: 5,000
SALES (corp-wide): 35.88B Privately Held
Web: www.hapag-lloyd.com
SIC: 4731 4412 4729 Agents, shipping; Deep sea foreign transportation of freight; Steamship ticket offices
HQ: Hapag-Lloyd (America) Llc
3 Ravinia Dr Ste 1600
Atlanta GA
732 562-1800

(P-11769)
HITACHI TRANSPORT SYSTEM (AMERICA) LTD
21061 S Wstn Ave Ste 300 (90501)

P.O. Box 512046 (90051-0046)
PHONE..............................310 787-3420
▲ EMP: 283
SIC: **4731** Freight forwarding

(P-11770)
HOME EXPRESS DELIVERY SVC LLC
Also Called: Temco Logistics
25361 Commercentre Dr Ste 250 (92630)
PHONE..............................949 715-9844
EMP: 1000 EST: 2013
SALES (est): 35MM **Privately Held**
SIC: **4731** Freight transportation arrangement

(P-11771)
HUB GROUP LOS ANGELES LLC
Also Called: Hub City
1400 N Harbor Blvd # 300 (92835-4126)
P.O. Box 71357 (60694-1357)
PHONE..............................714 449-6300
▲ EMP: 85
SIC: **4731** Agents, shipping

(P-11772)
INLOG INC
6765 Westminster Blvd Ste 424
(92683-3769)
PHONE..............................949 212-3867
EMP: 85
SALES (corp-wide): 6.8MM **Privately Held**
SIC: **4731** Freight transportation arrangement
PA: Inlog, Inc.
    4760 Preston Rd
    Frisco TX
    949 212-5241

(P-11773)
INNOVEL SOLUTIONS INC
Also Called: Sears
5691 E Philadelphia St Ste 200
(91761-2805)
PHONE..............................909 605-1446
EMP: 592
SALES (corp-wide): 4.18B **Privately Held**
Web: marketplace.sears.com
SIC: **4731** Agents, shipping
HQ: Innovel Solutions, Inc.
    3333 Beverly Rd
    Hoffman Estates IL
    847 286-2500

(P-11774)
INNOVEL SOLUTIONS INC
Also Called: Sears
960 Sherman St (92110-4013)
PHONE..............................619 497-1123
Steve Tiger, *Mgr*
EMP: 592
SALES (corp-wide): 4.18B **Privately Held**
Web: marketplace.sears.com
SIC: **4731** Agents, shipping
HQ: Innovel Solutions, Inc.
    3333 Beverly Rd
    Hoffman Estates IL
    847 286-2500

(P-11775)
IRON MOUNTAIN INFO MGT LLC
441 N Oak St (90302-3314)
PHONE..............................818 848-9766
Jesse Ascencio, *Mgr*
EMP: 85
Web: www.bondednj.com
SIC: **4731** Freight forwarding
HQ: Iron Mountain Information
    Management, Llc
    3205 Burton Ave
    Burbank CA

(P-11776)
KUEHNE + NAGEL INC
20000 S Western Ave (90501-1305)
PHONE..............................310 641-5500
Horst Gerjets, *Mgr*
EMP: 243
Web: home.kuehne-nagel.com
SIC: **4731** Freight forwarding
HQ: Kuehne + Nagel Inc.
    10 Exchange Pl Fl 19-20
    Jersey City NJ
    201 413-5500

(P-11777)
L E COPPERSMITH INC (PA)
Also Called: Coppersmith Global Logistics
525 S Douglas St Ste 100 (90245-4810)
PHONE..............................310 607-8000
Jeffrey Craig Coppersmith, *Pr*
Lew E Coppersmith Ii, *Sec*
Douglas S Walkley, *
Jim Rowley, *
◆ EMP: 80 EST: 1948
SQ FT: 40,000
SALES (est): 61.97MM
SALES (corp-wide): 61.97MM **Privately Held**
Web: www.coppersmith.com
SIC: **4731** 4789 Customhouse brokers;
    Cargo loading and unloading services

(P-11778)
LOGISTEED AMERICA INC
Also Called: Logisteed Monterey Park
1000 Corporate Center Dr Ste 400 (91754)
PHONE..............................323 263-8100
Tomoyuki Miyazaki, *Pr*
EMP: 100
Web: www.logisteed-america.com
SIC: **4731** Customhouse brokers
HQ: Logisteed America, Inc.
    21061 S Wstn Ave Ste 300
    Torrance CA
    310 787-3420

(P-11779)
M-7 CONSOLIDATION INC
475 W Apra St (90220-5527)
PHONE..............................310 898-3456
John J Brown, *Pr*
Harald Niehenke, *
John Brown, *
Kathleen Hogan, *
Harvey Turner, *
▼ EMP: 140 EST: 1994
SQ FT: 2,000
SALES (est): 24MM **Privately Held**
SIC: **4731** Foreign freight forwarding

(P-11780)
MAERSK WHSNG DIST SVCS USA LLC (HQ)
Also Called: Performance Team
2240 E Maple Ave (90245-6507)
PHONE..............................562 345-2200
Cliff Katab, *
Michael B Kaplan, *
Tracy Kaplan, *
Linda Kaplan, *
◆ EMP: 200 EST: 1987
SALES (est): 507.16MM
SALES (corp-wide): 77.53B **Privately Held**
Web: www.performanceteam.net
SIC: **4731** 4225 4213 Freight forwarding;
    General warehousing and storage;
    Trucking, except local
PA: A.P. Moller - Marsk A/S
    Esplanaden 50
    Kobenhavn K
    33142990

(P-11781)
MAERSK WHSNG DIST SVCS USA LLC
1651 California St Ste A (92374-2904)
PHONE..............................801 301-1732
EMP: 148
SALES (corp-wide): 2.41MM **Privately Held**
Web: www.performanceteam.net
SIC: **4731** Freight forwarding
HQ: Maersk Warehousing & Distribution
    Services Usa Llc
    2240 E Maple Ave
    El Segundo CA
    562 345-2200

(P-11782)
MAINFREIGHT INC (HQ)
1400 Glenn Curtiss St (90746-4030)
PHONE..............................310 900-1974
John Hepworth, *Pr*
Ron Frady, *
◆ EMP: 90 EST: 1970
SQ FT: 100,000
SALES (est): 493.9MM **Privately Held**
Web: www.mainfreight.com
SIC: **4731** Domestic freight forwarding
PA: Mainfreight Limited
    2 Railway Lane
    Auckland AUK

(P-11783)
MAPCARGO GLOBAL LOGISTICS (PA)
2501 Santa Fe Ave (90278-1117)
PHONE..............................310 297-8300
Marek Adam Panasewicz, *Pr*
◆ EMP: 74 EST: 1990
SQ FT: 20,000
SALES (est): 38.58MM **Privately Held**
Web: www.mapcargo.com
SIC: **4731** 2448 Domestic freight forwarding;
    Cargo containers, wood and wood with
    metal

(P-11784)
MIRAMAR TRANSPORTATION INC
Also Called: Pilot Freight Services
9340 Cabot Dr Ste I (92126-4397)
P.O. Box 502850 (92150-2850)
PHONE..............................858 693-0071
Richard Evan Fore, *Pr*
Richard Evan Fore, *Pr*
Bob Mirinda, *
Carrie Jones, *
EMP: 100 EST: 1993
SALES (est): 22.16MM **Privately Held**
Web: www.miramartrans.com
SIC: **4731** Freight forwarding

(P-11785)
MODIVCARE SOLUTIONS LLC
7441 Lincoln Way # 225 (92841-1452)
PHONE..............................714 503-6871
Kymblyn Brown, *Prin*
EMP: 123
SALES (corp-wide): 2.51B **Publicly Held**
Web: www.modivcare.com
SIC: **4731** Freight transportation arrangement
HQ: Modivcare Solutions, Llc
    6900 E Layton Ave # 1200
    Denver CO

(P-11786)
NATIONWIDE TRANS INC (PA)
11727 Eastend Ave (91710-1560)
P.O. Box 2558 (91708-2558)
PHONE..............................909 355-3211

Kong Lee, *Pr*
Chris Bendigo, *
Max Paul, *
EMP: 100 EST: 2006
SALES (est): 9.47MM
SALES (corp-wide): 9.47MM **Privately Held**
SIC: **4731** Freight transportation arrangement

(P-11787)
NEXT TRUCKING INC
301 E Ocean Blvd Ste 1950 (90802-4878)
P.O. Box 7849 (90504-9249)
PHONE..............................213 444-2250
Abhishek Kapur, *CEO*
EMP: 160 EST: 2016
SALES (est): 32.23MM **Privately Held**
Web: www.nexttrucking.com
SIC: **4731** 4225 Freight forwarding; General
    warehousing and storage

(P-11788)
NIPPON EXPRESS
Also Called: Co Ltd, All Nippon Airways
21250 Hawthorne Blvd Fl 2 (90503-5513)
PHONE..............................310 782-3000
EMP: 108 EST: 2011
SALES (est): 9MM **Privately Held**
Web: www.nipponexpress.com
SIC: **4731** Freight forwarding

(P-11789)
NOATUM LOGISTICS USA LLC
1100 W Walnut St (90220-5114)
PHONE..............................310 527-2104
▼ EMP: 242
Web: www.miq.com
SIC: **4731** Freight forwarding
HQ: Noatum Logistics Usa, Llc
    11501 Outlook St Ste 500
    Overland Park KS

(P-11790)
NRI USA LLC (PA)
Also Called: Nri Distribution
13200 S Broadway (90061-1124)
PHONE..............................323 345-6456
▲ EMP: 100 EST: 2011
SQ FT: 65,000
SALES (est): 60.01MM
SALES (corp-wide): 60.01MM **Privately Held**
Web: www.nri3pl.com
SIC: **4731** Freight forwarding

(P-11791)
PACIFIC LOGISTICS CORP (PA)
Also Called: Paclo
7255 Rosemead Blvd (90660-4047)
PHONE..............................562 478-4700
Douglas E Hockersmith, *Pr*
Timothy K Hewey, *
Diane J Hockersmith, *
▲ EMP: 208 EST: 1999
SQ FT: 206,000
SALES (est): 112.27MM
SALES (corp-wide): 112.27MM **Privately Held**
Web: www.pacific-logistics.com
SIC: **4731** Freight forwarding

(P-11792)
PATRIOT BROKERAGE INC
7840 Foothill Blvd Ste H (91040-2907)
PHONE..............................910 227-4142
Ross Tsarukyan, *Managing Member*
Liyan Tsarukyan, *
EMP: 84 EST: 2014
SQ FT: 13,000
SALES (est): 8.85MM **Privately Held**

SIC: 4731 Freight forwarding

(P-11793)
PORT LOGISTICS GROUP INC
19801 S Santa Fe Ave (90221-5915)
PHONE.............................310 669-2551
Timothy Page, *Prin*
EMP: 373
Web: www.whiplash.com
SIC: 4731 Freight transportation arrangement
PA: Port Logistics Group, Inc.
    288 S Mayo Ave
    City Of Industry CA

(P-11794)
PREMIERE CUSTOMS BROKERS INC
5951 Skylab Rd (92647-2062)
PHONE.............................310 410-6825
Richard K Lowery, *CEO*
EMP: 835 EST: 1994
SALES (est): 9.68MM
SALES (corp-wide): 1.44B **Publicly Held**
Web: www.premierechb.com
SIC: 4731 Customhouse brokers
HQ: Smart Modular Technologies Inc.
    39870 Eureka Dr
    Newark CA

(P-11795)
PRO LOADERS INC
14032 Santa Ana Ave (92337-7035)
PHONE.............................909 355-5531
Bruce Degler, *Pr*
Kim Pugmire, *
Christopher Ebert, *
EMP: 200 EST: 1981
SQ FT: 600
SALES (est): 23.87MM **Privately Held**
SIC: 4731 1629 7359 7519 Truck
transportation brokers; Earthmoving
contractor; Equipment rental and leasing,
nec; Trailer rental

(P-11796)
QUIK PICK EXPRESS LLC
23610 Banning Blvd (90745-6220)
PHONE.............................310 763-3000
Tom Boyle, *Managing Member*
EMP: 193
SALES (corp-wide): 50.91MM **Privately Held**
Web: www.quikpickexpress.com
SIC: 4731 Freight transportation arrangement
PA: Quik Pick Express Llc
    1021 E 233rd St
    Carson CA
    310 763-3000

(P-11797)
R L JONES-SAN DIEGO INC (PA)
1778 Zinetta Rd Ste A (92231-9511)
P.O. Box 472 (92232-0472)
PHONE.............................760 357-3177
Russell L Jones, *Pr*
Earl Roberts, *
EMP: 100 EST: 1952
SALES (est): 46.48MM
SALES (corp-wide): 46.48MM **Privately Held**
Web: www.rljones.com
SIC: 4731 4225 Customhouse brokers;
General warehousing and storage

(P-11798)
RED ROCK PALLET COMPANY
81153 Red Rock Rd (92253-9334)
P.O. Box 1231 (95763-1231)
PHONE.............................530 852-7744
Mark John Allen, *CEO*

EMP: 41 EST: 2008
SQ FT: 2,000
SALES (est): 2.12MM **Privately Held**
Web: www.redrockcompany.com
SIC: 4731 2448 Freight transportation
arrangement; Pallets, wood

(P-11799)
ROCK-IT CARGO USA LLC
5343 W Imperial Hwy Ste 900
(90045-6241)
PHONE.............................310 410-0935
EMP: 185
Web: www.rockit.global
SIC: 4731 Freight forwarding
PA: Rock-It Cargo Usa Llc
    201 Rock Lititz Blvd
    Lititz PA

(P-11800)
SALSON LOGISTICS INC
1331 Torrance Blvd (90501-2351)
PHONE.............................973 986-0200
Brian Howver, *Brnch Mgr*
EMP: 137
Web: www.salson.com
SIC: 4731 Freight forwarding
HQ: Salson Logistics, Inc.
    888 Doremus Ave
    Newark NJ
    973 986-0200

(P-11801)
SEAWORLD GLOBAL LOGISTICS
9350 Wilshire Blvd Ste 203 (90212-3214)
PHONE.............................310 579-9164
Dhakshitha Gabriel, *Pr*
EMP: 385 EST: 2017
SALES (est): 20.62MM **Privately Held**
SIC: 4731 Foreign freight forwarding

(P-11802)
SELECT AIRCARGO SERVICES INC
12801 S Figueroa St (90061-1157)
PHONE.............................310 851-8500
◆ EMP: 80
SIC: 4731 Foreign freight forwarding

(P-11803)
SILVER HAWK FREIGHT INC
Also Called: Titan Woirldwide
16410 Bloomfield Ave (90703)
PHONE.............................562 404-0226
Amar Durrani, *Pr*
EMP: 96 EST: 2011
SALES (est): 6.02MM **Privately Held**
Web: www.titan-worldwide.com
SIC: 4731 Freight forwarding

(P-11804)
STATES LOGISTICS SERVICES INC (PA)
5650 Dolly Ave (90621-1872)
PHONE.............................714 521-6520
Daniel Monson, *CEO*
William Donovan, *
Kirk Hellofs, *
Jennifer Monson, *
▲ EMP: 140 EST: 1958
SQ FT: 900,000
SALES (est): 182.96MM **Privately Held**
Web: www.stateslogistics.com
SIC: 4731 Freight transportation arrangement

(P-11805)
STEVENS GLOBAL LOGISTICS INC (PA)

Also Called: Steven Global Freight Services
3700 Redondo Beach Ave (90278-1108)
P.O. Box 729 (90260-0729)
PHONE.............................800 229-7284
Thomas J Petrizzio, *CEO*
Karl Chambers, *
Gary Hooper, *
◆ EMP: 95 EST: 1985
SQ FT: 48,000
SALES (est): 57.42MM
SALES (corp-wide): 57.42MM **Privately Held**
Web: www.stevensglobal.com
SIC: 4731 Freight forwarding

(P-11806)
STRAIGHT FORWARDING INC
Also Called: Meow Logistics
20275 Business Pkwy (91789-2974)
PHONE.............................909 594-3400
Yihsiang Wu, *CEO*
EMP: 100 EST: 2011
SALES (est): 78.88MM **Privately Held**
Web: www.sfi.com
SIC: 4731 Foreign freight forwarding

(P-11807)
SUPRA NATIONAL EXPRESS INC
1421 Charles Willard St (90746-4025)
PHONE.............................310 549-7105
Daniel Linares, *CEO*
EMP: 125 EST: 2014
SALES (est): 25.32MM **Privately Held**
Web: www.snecorp.com
SIC: 4731 Truck transportation brokers

(P-11808)
TAYLORED SVCS PARENT CO INC (PA)
1495 E Locust St (91761-4570)
PHONE.............................909 510-4800
Bill Butler, *CEO*
Michael Yusko, *
EMP: 80 EST: 2012
SQ FT: 330,000
SALES (est): 42.44MM
SALES (corp-wide): 42.44MM **Privately Held**
Web: www.tayloredservices.com
SIC: 4731 Agents, shipping

(P-11809)
TOLL GLOBAL FWDG SCS USA INC
Also Called: FMI International West 2
400 Westmont Dr 450 (90731)
PHONE.............................732 750-9000
Gary Hecht, *Mgr*
EMP: 95
SIC: 4731 Freight forwarding
HQ: Toll Global Forwarding Scs (Usa) Inc.
    800 Federal Blvd Ste 2
    Carteret NJ
    732 750-9000

(P-11810)
TOLL GLOBAL FWDG SCS USA INC
Also Called: TOLL GLOBAL FORWARDING SCS (USA) INC.
3355 Dulles Dr (91752-3244)
PHONE.............................951 360-8310
Bryan Howber, *Sr VP*
EMP: 100
SIC: 4731 Freight forwarding
HQ: Toll Global Forwarding Scs (Usa) Inc.
    800 Federal Blvd Ste 2
    Carteret NJ
    732 750-9000

(P-11811)
TRANSIT AIR CARGO INC
2204 E 4th St (92705-3868)
P.O. Box 10053 (92711-0053)
PHONE.............................714 571-0393
Gulnawaz Khodayar, *CEO*
Christy Colton, *
Michelle Nguyen, *
◆ EMP: 94 EST: 1989
SQ FT: 10,000
SALES (est): 24.63MM **Privately Held**
Web: www.transitair.com
SIC: 4731 Foreign freight forwarding

(P-11812)
TRI-TECH LOGISTICS LLC
1370 Brea Blvd Ste 200 (92835-4128)
PHONE.............................855 373-7049
Gurdeep Singh Dhaliwal, *
Jeremy Engstrom, *
EMP: 210 EST: 2014
SALES (est): 23.13MM
SALES (corp-wide): 6.55MM **Privately Held**
Web: www.tritechlogistics.com
SIC: 4731 Freight forwarding
PA: Tri-Tech Logistics Ltd
    17660 65a Ave Unit 208
    Surrey BC
    604 415-9898

(P-11813)
UNIS LLC (PA)
Also Called: United Network Info Svcs
218 Machlin Ct Ste A (91789-3057)
PHONE.............................909 839-2600
James Lin, *Pr*
Gracie Leung, *CFO*
EMP: 200 EST: 2012
SALES (est): 194.54MM
SALES (corp-wide): 194.54MM **Privately Held**
Web: www.unisco.com
SIC: 4731 Freight forwarding

(P-11814)
VANGUARD LGISTICS SVCS USA INC (HQ)
Also Called: Brennan International Trnspt
5000 Airport Plaza Dr Ste 200 (90815)
PHONE.............................310 847-3000
Charles Brennan, *Ch*
J Thurso Barendse, *VP*
Therese Groff, *VP*
Derek Moore, *TAX*
Ank Deroos, *Dir*
◆ EMP: 100 EST: 1978
SALES (est): 227.78MM
SALES (corp-wide): 478.07MM **Privately Held**
Web: www.vanguardlogistics.com
SIC: 4731 Freight consolidation
PA: Naca Holdings, Inc.
    5000 Arprt Plz Dr Ste 200
    Long Beach CA
    310 847-3000

(P-11815)
VEG FRESH LOGISTICS LLC ✪
1400 W Rincon St (92878-9205)
PHONE.............................714 446-8800
EMP: 220 EST: 2022
SALES (est): 56.1MM **Privately Held**
Web: www.vegfresh.com
SIC: 4731 Transportation agents and brokers
PA: Veg-Fresh Farms, Llc
    1400 W Rincon St
    Corona CA

PRODUCTS & SVCS

(P-11816)
XPO LOGISTICS SUPPLY CHAIN INC
5200b E Airport Dr (91761-8601)
PHONE...........................909 390-9799
FAX: 909 937-6089
EMP: 156
SALES (corp-wide): 14.62B **Publicly Held**
SIC: 4731 Freight transportation arrangement
HQ: Xpo Logistics Supply Chain, Inc.
    4035 Piedmont Pkwy
    High Point NC
    336 232-4100

(P-11817)
XPORT FORWARDING LLC
620 Newport Center Dr Ste 1100 (92660)
PHONE...........................949 354-0609
Mario Bruendel, *Brnch Mgr*
EMP: 85
SALES (corp-wide): 3.37MM **Privately Held**
Web: www.xportforwarding.com
SIC: 4731 Freight forwarding
PA: Xport Forwarding, Llc
    2323 Main St
    Irvine CA
    949 668-1010

(P-11818)
YUSEN LOGISTICS AMERICAS INC
2417 E Carson St Ste 100 (90810-1252)
PHONE...........................310 518-3008
P Smith, *Brnch Mgr*
EMP: 200
SIC: 4731 Freight forwarding
HQ: Yusen Logistics (Americas) Inc.
    300 Lighting Way Ste 100
    Secaucus NJ
    201 553-3800

4783 Packing And Crating

(P-11819)
CHANDLER PACKAGING A TRANSPAK COMPANY
Also Called: Fragile Handle With Care
7595 Raytheon Rd (92111-1506)
P.O. Box 421110 (92142-1110)
PHONE...........................858 292-5674
EMP: 64
Web: www.chanpack.com
SIC: 4783 2449 3081 3086 Packing and crating; Wood containers, nec; Packing materials, plastics sheet; Packaging and shipping materials, foamed plastics

(P-11820)
DIVERSIFIED LOGISTIC SVCS INC
13033 Telegraph Rd (90670-4011)
PHONE...........................562 941-3600
Anthony Dellaquila, *Pr*
EMP: 22 **EST:** 2008
SQ FT: 11,000
SALES (est): 2.42MM **Privately Held**
Web: www.dlspro1.com
SIC: 4783 2449 1796 4214 Packing and crating; Rectangular boxes and crates, wood; Machine moving and rigging; Household goods moving and storage, local

(P-11821)
L&L FOODS HOLDINGS LLC
333 N Euclid Way (92801-6738)
PHONE...........................714 254-1430
EMP: 200

SIC: 4783 Packing goods for shipping

(P-11822)
MEK ENTERPRISES INC
3517 Camino Del Rio S Ste 215 (92108)
PHONE...........................619 527-0957
Marc Kranz, *CEO*
EMP: 100 **EST:** 2012
SALES (est): 10.36MM **Privately Held**
Web: www.4mek.com
SIC: 4783 4214 Packing and crating; Furniture moving and storage, local

(P-11823)
PETCO ANIMAL SUPPLIES INC (DH)
Also Called: Petco
10850 Via Frontera (92127-1705)
PHONE...........................858 453-7845
Ron Coughlin, *
Brad Weston, *Pr*
Charlie Piscitello, *
Michael M Nuzzo, *
Michael W Zuna, *Chief Marketing DIGITAL* *
◆ **EMP:** 500 **EST:** 1965
SQ FT: 164,000
SALES (est): 2.15B
SALES (corp-wide): 298.11K **Privately Held**
Web: www.petco.com
SIC: 4783 5999 5199 Crating goods for shipping; Pet supplies; Pet supplies
HQ: Petco Holdings, Inc. Llc
    10850 Via Frontera
    San Diego CA
    858 453-7845

(P-11824)
WHALING PACKAGING CO
21020 S Wilmington Ave (90810-1232)
P.O. Box 4547 (90749-4547)
PHONE...........................310 518-6021
Thomas Whaling, *Pr*
Michelle Whaling, *
EMP: 27 **EST:** 1978
SQ FT: 12,973
SALES (est): 2.21MM **Privately Held**
Web: www.whalingpackaging.com
SIC: 4783 2653 2441 Packing and crating; Corrugated and solid fiber boxes; Nailed wood boxes and shook

4785 Inspection And Fixed Facilities

(P-11825)
COFIROUTE USA LLC
Also Called: Cofiroute
100 Progress Ste 110 (92618-0353)
PHONE...........................949 754-0198
Gary Hausdorfer, *CEO*
Darla Casby, *
▲ **EMP:** 112 **EST:** 2002
SALES (est): 30.25MM
SALES (corp-wide): 16.98MM **Privately Held**
Web: www.cofirouteusa.com
SIC: 4785 Toll road operation
HQ: Vinci Concessions
    1973 Boulevard De La Defense
    Nanterre

4789 Transportation Services, Nec

(P-11826)
ADVANCED MULTIMODAL DIST INC

Also Called: Preferred Carrier California
14822 Central Ave (91710-9509)
PHONE...........................800 838-3058
Fredy Salvador Funes, *CEO*
EMP: 150 **EST:** 2017
SALES (est): 4.95MM **Privately Held**
SIC: 4789 4731 Cargo loading and unloading services; Freight forwarding

(P-11827)
AMBIANCE TRANSPORTATION LLC
6901 San Fernando Rd (91201-1608)
PHONE...........................818 955-5757
EMP: 90 **EST:** 2018
SALES (est): 4.54MM **Privately Held**
SIC: 4789 Transportation services, nec

(P-11828)
AMERICAN TRANSPORTATION CO LLC
635 W Colorado St Ste 108a (91204)
PHONE...........................818 660-2343
Isaac Albekyan, *Prin*
EMP: 88 **EST:** 2012
SALES (est): 1.79MM **Privately Held**
SIC: 4789 Transportation services, nec

(P-11829)
CAPSTONE LOGISTICS LLC
Also Called: Capstone Logistics
12661 Aldi Pl (92555-6703)
PHONE...........................770 414-1929
EMP: 148
SALES (corp-wide): 1.18B **Privately Held**
Web: www.capstonelogistics.com
SIC: 4789 Cargo loading and unloading services
PA: Capstone Logistics, Llc
    30 Technology Pkwy S # 2
    Peachtree Corners GA
    770 414-1929

(P-11830)
COMPREHENSIVE DIST SVCS INC
18726 S Western Ave Ste 300 (90248)
PHONE...........................310 523-1546
Sam Lee, *Pr*
EMP: 150 **EST:** 2010
SALES (est): 9.49MM **Privately Held**
SIC: 4789 Freight car loading and unloading

(P-11831)
FLUOR FLTRON BLFOUR BTTY DRGDO
5901 W Century Blvd (90045-5411)
PHONE...........................949 420-5000
Kenneth Isett, *Prin*
Terry Gohde, *Prin*
EMP: 99 **EST:** 2018
SALES (est): 4.24MM **Privately Held**
Web: www.lalinxs.com
SIC: 4789 Transportation services, nec

(P-11832)
FULL SCALE LOGISTICS LLC
2722 Rocky Point Ct (91362-4943)
PHONE...........................805 279-6799
Kristen Infeld, *CEO*
EMP: 85 **EST:** 2020
SALES (est): 3.24MM **Privately Held**
SIC: 4789 Transportation services, nec

(P-11833)
GUNDERSON RAIL SERVICES LLC
Also Called: Greenbrier Rail Services

1475 Cooley Ct (92408-2830)
P.O. Box 1715 (92402-1715)
PHONE...........................909 478-0541
Kevin Johnson, *Contrlr*
EMP: 132
SQ FT: 64,248
SALES (corp-wide): 3.94B **Publicly Held**
Web: www.gbrx.com
SIC: 4789 Railroad car repair
HQ: Gunderson Rail Services Llc
    1 Centerpointe Dr Ste 200
    Lake Oswego OR
    503 684-7000

(P-11834)
HYPERLOOP TECHNOLOGIES INC
Also Called: Hyperloop One
777 S Alameda St Ste 400 (90021-1657)
PHONE...........................213 800-3270
Sultan Ahmed Bin Sulayem, *Ch Bd*
Jay Walder, *
William Mulholland, *
Josh Giegel, *
Brent Callinicos, *
EMP: 197 **EST:** 2014
SALES (est): 99.68MM **Privately Held**
Web: www.virginhyperloop.com
SIC: 4789 Pipeline terminal facilities, independently operated

(P-11835)
KAYDAN LOGISTICS LLC
45562 Ponderosa Ct (92592-2829)
PHONE...........................951 961-9000
Kirk Morrison, *CEO*
EMP: 91 **EST:** 2020
SALES (est): 4.99MM **Privately Held**
SIC: 4789 Transportation services, nec

(P-11836)
MERIDIAN RAIL ACQUISITION
Also Called: Greenbrier Rail
1475 Cooley Ct (92408-2830)
P.O. Box 1715 (92402-1715)
PHONE...........................909 478-0541
EMP: 203
SALES (corp-wide): 3.94B **Publicly Held**
Web: www.gbrx.com
SIC: 4789 Railroad car repair
HQ: Meridian Rail Acquisition Corp
    1 Centerpointe Dr Ste 400
    Lake Oswego OR
    503 684-7000

(P-11837)
NERYS LOGISTICS INC
9925 Airway Rd (92154-7932)
PHONE...........................619 616-2124
EMP: 124
SALES (corp-wide): 12.26MM **Privately Held**
SIC: 4789 Cargo loading and unloading services
PA: Nery's Logistics, Inc.
    774 Mays Blvd
    Incline Village NV
    775 338-7060

(P-11838)
PATRIOT LOGISTICS SERVICES LLC
1520 Independence Way (92084-3616)
PHONE...........................443 994-9660
Joshua Schraeder, *Prin*
Kenneth Dinsmore, *
EMP: 80 **EST:** 2020
SALES (est): 3.23MM **Privately Held**
SIC: 4789 Transportation services, nec

(P-11839)
RIOLO TRANSPORTATION INC
2725 Jefferson St Ste 2d (92008-1705)
PHONE..................760 729-4405
Gail Phipps, *Brnch Mgr*
EMP: 378
Web: www.riolo.com
SIC: 4789 Pipeline terminal facilities,
independently operated
PA: Riolo Transportation, Inc.
759 N Vulcan Ave
Encinitas CA

(P-11840)
TAYLORED TRANSLOAD LLC
1495 E Locust St (91761-4570)
PHONE..................909 510-4800
Jim Deveau, *Prin*
EMP: 140 **EST:** 2020
SALES (est): 1.13MM
SALES (corp-wide): 42.44MM **Privately Held**
SIC: 4789 Cargo loading and unloading services
PA: Taylored Services Parent Co. Inc.
1495 E Locust St
Ontario CA
909 510-4800

(P-11841)
TW SERVICES INC
1801 W Romneya Dr Ste 601 (92801-1828)
PHONE..................714 441-2400
Charles An, *Pr*
Thomas Hwang, *
EMP: 300 **EST:** 2009
SALES (est): 23.73MM **Privately Held**
Web: www.twserviceinc.com
SIC: 4789 Freight car loading and unloading

4812 Radiotelephone Communication

(P-11842)
20/20 MOBILE CORP
3380 La Sierra Ave (92503-5271)
PHONE..................909 587-2973
EMP: 83
SALES (corp-wide): 4.96MM **Privately Held**
SIC: 4812 Cellular telephone services
PA: 20/20 Mobile Corp
10050 Magnolia Ave
Riverside CA
951 354-8100

(P-11843)
AT&T CORP
Rm 620 (92805)
PHONE..................714 284-2878
EMP: 311
SALES (corp-wide): 120.74B **Publicly Held**
Web: www.att.com
SIC: 4812 Cellular telephone services
HQ: At&t Corp.
1 At&T Way
Bedminster NJ
800 403-3302

(P-11844)
AT&T CORP
2260 E Imperial Hwy (90245-3501)
PHONE..................303 596-8431
Anne Chow, *CEO*
EMP: 94
SALES (corp-wide): 120.74B **Publicly Held**

Web: www.att.com
SIC: 4812 Cellular telephone services
HQ: At&T Corp.
28 Liberty St
New York NY

(P-11845)
BLACK DOT WIRELESS LLC
23456 Madero Ste 210 (92691-2783)
PHONE..................949 502-3800
Marc Anthony, *Managing Member*
Gary Arnett, *
EMP: 85 **EST:** 2004
SALES (est): 24.14MM **Privately Held**
Web: www.blackdotwireless.com
SIC: 4812 Cellular telephone services

(P-11846)
CUBIC SECURE COMMUNICATIONS I
9233 Balboa Ave (92123-1513)
PHONE..................858 505-2000
Steve Slijepcevic, *Managing Member*
EMP: 275
SALES (est): 10.8MM **Privately Held**
Web: www.cubic.com
SIC: 4812 Radiotelephone communication

(P-11847)
DIRECTV GROUP HOLDINGS LLC (HQ)
Also Called: Directv
2260 E Imperial Hwy (90245-3501)
PHONE..................310 964-5000
Michael White, *Pr*
Patrick Doyle, *Ex VP*
Larry Hunter, *Ex VP*
Joseph Bosch, *Chief Human Resources Officer*
Steven Adams, *CAO*
▲ **EMP:** 170 **EST:** 1977
SALES (est): 2.53B
SALES (corp-wide): 120.74B **Publicly Held**
SIC: 4812 Cellular telephone services
PA: At&t Inc.
208 S Akard St
Dallas TX
210 821-4105

(P-11848)
EA MOBILE INC
5510 Lincoln Blvd (90094-2034)
PHONE..................310 754-7125
EMP: 96 **EST:** 2000
SQ FT: 23,000
SALES (est): 5.64MM
SALES (corp-wide): 7.43B **Publicly Held**
SIC: 4812 Cellular telephone services
PA: Electronic Arts Inc.
209 Redwood Shores Pkwy
Redwood City CA
650 628-1500

(P-11849)
ESCHAT ✪
3450 Broad St Ste 106 (93401-7214)
PHONE..................805 541-5044
EMP: 100 **EST:** 2023
SALES (est): 3.37MM **Privately Held**
SIC: 4812 Radiotelephone communication

(P-11850)
MBIT WIRELESS INC (PA)
4340 Von Karman Ave Ste 140 (92660-1201)
PHONE..................949 205-4559
Bhasker Patel, *Pr*
Mw Sohn, *

EMP: 131 **EST:** 2005
SALES (est): 9.98MM **Privately Held**
Web: www.mbitwireless.com
SIC: 4812 Cellular telephone services

(P-11851)
NEW CINGULAR WIRELESS SVCS INC
Also Called: AT&T
252 Broadway (92101-5004)
PHONE..................619 238-3638
Jason Cid, *Brnch Mgr*
EMP: 87
SALES (corp-wide): 120.74B **Publicly Held**
Web: www.att.com
SIC: 4812 5999 Cellular telephone services; Mobile telephones and equipment
HQ: New Cingular Wireless Services, Inc.
7277 164th Ave Ne
Redmond WA
425 827-4500

(P-11852)
NEXTEL COMMUNICATIONS INC
Also Called: Nextel
330 Commerce (92602-1398)
PHONE..................714 368-4509
Don Girkis, *VP*
EMP: 150
SALES (corp-wide): 79.57B **Publicly Held**
Web: www.sprint.com
SIC: 4812 Cellular telephone services
HQ: Nextel Communications, Inc.
12502 Sunrise Valley Dr
Reston VA
833 639-8353

(P-11853)
PACIFIC BELL TELEPHONE COMPANY
3847 Cardiff Ave (90232-2613)
PHONE..................310 515-2898
EMP: 4444
SALES (corp-wide): 120.74B **Publicly Held**
Web: www.att.com
SIC: 4812 Cellular telephone services
HQ: Pacific Bell Telephone Company
430 Bush St Fl 3
San Francisco CA
415 542-9000

(P-11854)
SPRINT COMMUNICATIONS CO LP
15582 Whittwood Ln (90603-2355)
PHONE..................562 943-8907
EMP: 148
SALES (corp-wide): 79.57B **Publicly Held**
SIC: 4812 Cellular telephone services
HQ: Sprint Communications Company L.P.
6391 Sprint Pkwy
Overland Park KS
800 829-0965

(P-11855)
SPRINT COMMUNICATIONS CO LP
5381 W Centinela Ave (90045-2003)
PHONE..................310 216-9093
EMP: 201
SALES (corp-wide): 79.57B **Publicly Held**
SIC: 4812 4813 Cellular telephone services; Local and long distance telephone communications
HQ: Sprint Communications Company L.P.
6391 Sprint Pkwy
Overland Park KS
800 829-0965

(P-11856)
SPRINT COMMUNICATIONS CO LP
44416 Valley Central Way (93536-6528)
PHONE..................661 951-8927
EMP: 188
SALES (corp-wide): 79.57B **Publicly Held**
SIC: 4812 Cellular telephone services
HQ: Sprint Communications Company L.P.
6391 Sprint Pkwy
Overland Park KS
800 829-0965

(P-11857)
SPRINT COMMUNICATIONS CO LP
1270 W Redondo Beach Blvd (90247-3411)
PHONE..................310 515-0293
EMP: 148
SALES (corp-wide): 79.57B **Publicly Held**
SIC: 4812 Cellular telephone services
HQ: Sprint Communications Company L.P.
6391 Sprint Pkwy
Overland Park KS
800 829-0965

(P-11858)
SPRINT COMMUNICATIONS CO LP
4225 Oceanside Blvd (92056-3472)
PHONE..................760 941-4535
EMP: 188
SALES (corp-wide): 79.57B **Publicly Held**
SIC: 4812 Cellular telephone services
HQ: Sprint Communications Company L.P.
6391 Sprint Pkwy
Overland Park KS
800 829-0965

(P-11859)
SPRINT COMMUNICATIONS CO LP
Also Called: Sprint
31754 Temecula Pkwy Ste A (92592-6805)
PHONE..................951 303-8501
EMP: 161
SALES (corp-wide): 79.57B **Publicly Held**
SIC: 4812 5065 4813 Cellular telephone services; Telephone and telegraphic equipment; Local and long distance telephone communications
HQ: Sprint Communications Company L.P.
6391 Sprint Pkwy
Overland Park KS
800 829-0965

(P-11860)
SPRINT COMMUNICATIONS CO LP
23865 Clinton Keith Rd (92595-9829)
PHONE..................951 461-9786
EMP: 148
SALES (corp-wide): 79.57B **Publicly Held**
SIC: 4812 Cellular telephone services
HQ: Sprint Communications Company L.P.
6391 Sprint Pkwy
Overland Park KS
800 829-0965

(P-11861)
SPRINT COMMUNICATIONS CO LP
3580 Grand Oaks (92881-4656)
PHONE..................951 340-1924
EMP: 161
SALES (corp-wide): 79.57B **Publicly Held**

PRODUCTS & SVCS

SIC: **4812** 4813 Cellular telephone services; Local and long distance telephone communications
HQ: Sprint Communications Company L.P.
6391 Sprint Pkwy
Overland Park KS
800 829-0965

(P-11862)
SPRINT CORPORATION
Also Called: Sprint
432 S Broadway (90013-1103)
PHONE...............................213 613-4200
EMP: 118
SALES (corp-wide): 79.57B **Publicly Held**
Web: www.sprint.com
SIC: **4812** Cellular telephone services
HQ: Sprint Llc
6200 Sprint Pkwy
Overland Park KS
855 848-3280

(P-11863)
SPRINT CORPORATION
Also Called: Sprint
4707 Firestone Blvd (90280-3403)
PHONE...............................323 357-0797
EMP: 118
SALES (corp-wide): 79.57B **Publicly Held**
Web: www.sprint.com
SIC: **4812** Cellular telephone services
HQ: Sprint Llc
6200 Sprint Pkwy
Overland Park KS
855 848-3280

(P-11864)
TRELLISWARE TECHNOLOGIES INC (HQ)
10641 Scripps Summit Ct Ste 100 (92131-3918)
PHONE...............................858 753-1600
Metin Bayram, *Pr*
Steve Fisher, *CFO*
Paul Konopka, *CCO*
Anna Kochka, *Pers/VP*
Matt Fallows, *Vice-President Global Business Development*
EMP: 125 **EST:** 2000
SQ FT: 46,000
SALES (est): 50.16MM
SALES (corp-wide): 2.56B **Publicly Held**
Web: www.trellisware.com
SIC: **4812** 4813 3663 Radiotelephone communication; Local and long distance telephone communications; Airborne radio communications equipment
PA: Viasat, Inc.
6155 El Camino Real
Carlsbad CA
760 476-2200

(P-11865)
VERIZON SERVICES CORP
Also Called: Verizon
2530 Wilshire Blvd Fl 1 (90403-4616)
PHONE...............................310 315-1100
EMP: 332
SALES (corp-wide): 136.84B **Publicly Held**
Web: www.sitestar.net
SIC: **4812** Cellular telephone services
HQ: Verizon Services Corp.
22011 Loudoun County Pkwy 125-100
Ashburn VA
703 729-5931

(P-11866)
VERIZON SOUTH INC
Also Called: Verizon

424 S Patterson Ave (93111-2404)
PHONE...............................805 681-8527
Dennis Candini, *Mgr*
EMP: 207
SALES (corp-wide): 136.84B **Publicly Held**
Web: www.verizon.com
SIC: **4812** Cellular telephone services
HQ: Verizon South Inc.
600 Hidden Rdg
Irving TX
972 718-5600

4813 Telephone Communication, Except Radio

(P-11867)
3H COMMUNICATION SYSTEMS INC
3 Winterbranch (92604-4604)
PHONE...............................949 529-1583
Purna Subedi, *CEO*
Michael Giarratano, *
EMP: 47 **EST:** 2014
SALES (est): 4.82MM **Privately Held**
Web:
www.3hcommunicationsystems.com
SIC: **4813** 4812 3663 3761 Voice telephone communications; Radiotelephone communication; Radio and t.v. communications equipment; Rockets, space and military, complete

(P-11868)
AB CELLULAR HOLDING LLC
Also Called: At & T Wireless Service
1452 Edinger Ave (92780-6246)
PHONE...............................562 468-6846
EMP: 2100
SIC: **4813** Local and long distance telephone communications

(P-11869)
ADICIO INC
5857 Owens Ave Ste 300 (92008-5507)
PHONE...............................760 602-9502
Richard Miller, *Pr*
Richette Lock, *
Mike Cavallo, *
EMP: 90 **EST:** 1997
SALES (est): 14.52MM **Privately Held**
Web: www.adicio.com
SIC: **4813** Internet host services

(P-11870)
AT&T SERVICES INC
Also Called: SBC
1010 Wilshire Blvd (90017-5662)
PHONE...............................213 975-4089
Cathy Bazieto, *Brnch Mgr*
EMP: 20
SALES (corp-wide): 120.74B **Publicly Held**
SIC: **4813** 2741 7331 4812 Local and long distance telephone communications; Directories, telephone: publishing only, not printed on site; Direct mail advertising services; Radiotelephone communication
HQ: At&T Services, Inc.
208 S Akard St Ste 110
Dallas TX
210 821-4105

(P-11871)
AT&T SERVICES INC
Also Called: SBC
950 W Washington Ave (92025-1637)

PHONE...............................760 489-3187
George Rivera, *Prin*
EMP: 20
SALES (corp-wide): 120.74B **Publicly Held**
SIC: **4813** 2741 4822 7331 Local and long distance telephone communications; Directories, telephone: publishing only, not printed on site; Telegraph and other communications; Direct mail advertising services
HQ: At&T Services, Inc.
208 S Akard St Ste 110
Dallas TX
210 821-4105

(P-11872)
BOLDYN NETWORKS US SERVICES LL
Also Called: Mobilitie Services, LLC
121 Innovation Dr Ste 200 (92617-3094)
PHONE...............................877 999-7070
Gary Jabara, *Ch*
Christos Karmis, *
Dissy Sarabosing, *
Dana Tardelli, *
EMP: 350 **EST:** 2015
SALES (est): 56.13MM
SALES (corp-wide): 72.96MM **Privately Held**
Web: www.boldyn.com
SIC: **4813** Local telephone communications
PA: Boardwalk Ig Management, Llc
1945 Placentia Ave Ste D
Costa Mesa CA

(P-11873)
BOLDYN NTWRKS US OPRATIONS LLC
121 Innovation Dr (92617-3091)
PHONE...............................949 515-1500
EMP: 145 **EST:** 2021
SALES (est): 7.87MM **Privately Held**
Web: www.boldyn.com
SIC: **4813** Online service providers

(P-11874)
BROADVIEW NETWORKS INC
7731 Hayvenhurst Ave (91406-1735)
PHONE...............................818 939-0015
EMP: 86
SALES (corp-wide): 6.51B **Privately Held**
SIC: **4813** Local and long distance telephone communications
HQ: Broadview Networks, Inc.
4001 N Rodney Parham Rd
Little Rock AR

(P-11875)
CALIFORNIA INTERNET LP (PA)
Also Called: Geolinks
251 Camarillo Ranch Rd (93012-5082)
PHONE...............................805 225-4638
Skyler Ditchfield, *Pt*
Ryan Adams, *
Phil Oseas, *
Ryan Hauf, *
EMP: 164 **EST:** 2011
SALES (est): 46.21MM
SALES (corp-wide): 46.21MM **Privately Held**
Web: www.geolinks.com
SIC: **4813** Internet connectivity services

(P-11876)
CONNEXITY INC (DH)
Also Called: Shopzilla.com
2120 Colorado Ave Ste 400 (90404-3504)
PHONE...............................310 571-1235
William Glass, *CEO*

Aaron Young, *CFO*
Blythe Holden, *Sr VP*
EMP: 203 **EST:** 2012
SALES (est): 94.72MM
SALES (corp-wide): 694.97MM **Privately Held**
Web: www.connexity.com
SIC: **4813** 7383 7331 Online service providers; News syndicates; Direct mail advertising services
HQ: Symphony Technology Group, L.L.C.
428 University Ave
Palo Alto CA
650 935-9500

(P-11877)
FORTITUDE TECHNOLOGY INC
Also Called: Carinet
8929 Complex Dr Ste A (92123-1454)
PHONE...............................858 974-5080
Tim Caulfield, *CEO*
Joe Mcmillen, *Prin*
Michael C Robert, *
EMP: 85 **EST:** 1997
SQ FT: 40,000
SALES (est): 7.4MM **Privately Held**
SIC: **4813** Internet connectivity services

(P-11878)
FOX INTERACTIVE MEDIA INC
6100 Center Dr Ste 800 (90045-9201)
PHONE...............................310 969-7000
EMP: 128
SIC: **4813** Online service providers

(P-11879)
FREE CONFERENCING CORPORATION
Also Called: Freeconferencecall.com
4300 E Pacific Coast Hwy (90804-2114)
P.O. Box 41069 (90853-1069)
PHONE...............................562 437-1411
EMP: 116 **EST:** 2004
SQ FT: 10,000
SALES (est): 17.46MM **Privately Held**
Web: www.freeconferencecall.com
SIC: **4813** 7389 Voice telephone communications

(P-11880)
FRONTIER CALIFORNIA INC
Also Called: Verizon
510 Park Ave (91340-2527)
PHONE...............................818 365-0542
Gloria Caudill, *Brnch Mgr*
EMP: 373
SALES (corp-wide): 5.79B **Publicly Held**
SIC: **4813** Telephone communication, except radio
HQ: Frontier California Inc.
401 Merritt 7
Norwalk CT
203 614-5600

(P-11881)
FRONTIER CALIFORNIA INC
Also Called: Verizon
1 Wellpoint Way (91362-3893)
PHONE...............................805 372-6000
Alex Stadler, *Prin*
EMP: 298
SALES (corp-wide): 5.79B **Publicly Held**
SIC: **4813** Telephone communication, except radio
HQ: Frontier California Inc.
401 Merritt 7
Norwalk CT
203 614-5600

(P-11882)
FRONTIER CALIFORNIA INC
Also Called: Verizon
200 W Church St (93458-5005)
PHONE......................805 925-0000
Carrie Ramsey, *Mgr*
EMP: 335
SALES (corp-wide): 5.79B **Publicly Held**
SIC: 4813 Long distance telephone
communications
HQ: Frontier California Inc.
401 Merritt 7
Norwalk CT
203 614-5600

(P-11883)
FRONTIER CALIFORNIA INC
Also Called: Verizon
7352 Slater Ave (92647-6227)
PHONE......................714 375-6713
Patrick Dillon, *Mgr*
EMP: 335
SALES (corp-wide): 5.79B **Publicly Held**
SIC: 4813 8721 5065 8711 Local and long
distance telephone communications; Billing
and bookkeeping service; Telephone and
telegraphic equipment; Electrical or
electronic engineering
HQ: Frontier California Inc.
401 Merritt 7
Norwalk CT
203 614-5600

(P-11884)
FRONTIER CALIFORNIA INC
Also Called: Verizon
83793 Doctor Carreon Blvd (92201-7035)
PHONE......................760 342-0500
EMP: 298
SALES (corp-wide): 5.79B **Publicly Held**
SIC: 4813 Local and long distance telephone
communications
HQ: Frontier California Inc.
401 Merritt 7
Norwalk CT
203 614-5600

(P-11885)
**GOOGLE INTERNATIONAL LLC
(DH)**
35018 Avenue D (92399-4407)
PHONE......................650 253-0000
Eric Schmidt, *Ch Bd*
Larry Page, *
David C Drummond, *
▼ **EMP:** 83 **EST:** 2014
SALES (est): 48.19MM
SALES (corp-wide): 282.84B **Publicly
Held**
Web: www.google.com
SIC: 4813 7375 Internet connectivity services
; Information retrieval services
HQ: Google Llc
1600 Amphitheatre Pkwy
Mountain View CA
650 253-0000

(P-11886)
HULU LLC
12312 W Olympic Blvd (90064)
PHONE......................888 631-4858
Mike Hopkins, *CEO*
EMP: 738
SALES (corp-wide): 88.9B **Publicly Held**
Web: www.hulu.com
SIC: 4813 4833 Internet host services;
Television translator station
HQ: Hulu, Llc
2500 Broadway Ste 200
Santa Monica CA

(P-11887)
HULU LLC (HQ)
2500 Broadway Ste 200 (90404-3071)
PHONE......................310 571-4700
Randy Freer, *CEO*
Joe Earley, *Pr*
EMP: 252 **EST:** 2007
SALES (est): 1.88B
SALES (corp-wide): 88.9B **Publicly Held**
Web: www.hulu.com
SIC: 4813 4833 Internet host services;
Television translator station
PA: The Walt Disney Company
500 S Buena Vista St
Burbank CA
818 560-1000

(P-11888)
**INCOMNET COMMUNICATIONS
CORP**
2801 Main St (92614-5027)
PHONE......................949 251-8000
George P Blanco, *Pr*
John Hill, *Ch Bd*
Stephen A Garcia, *CFO*
Andrew Kalinowski, *VP Mktg*
EMP: 80 **EST:** 1983
SQ FT: 68,000
SALES (est): 7.73MM **Privately Held**
SIC: 4813 Long distance telephone
communications

(P-11889)
**INFONET SERVICES
CORPORATION (DH)**
Also Called: BT Infonet
2160 E Grand Ave (90245-5024)
PHONE......................310 335-2600
David Andrew, *CEO*
Jose A Collazo, *
Paul Galleberg, *
Akbar H Firdosy, *
John C Hoffman, *
▲ **EMP:** 600 **EST:** 1988
SQ FT: 150,000
SALES (est): 202.89MM
SALES (corp-wide): 24.85B **Privately Held**
Web: www.infonet.com
SIC: 4813 7373 7375 Data telephone
communications; Computer integrated
systems design; Information retrieval
services
HQ: British Telecommunications Public
Limited Company
1 Braham Street
London
800 917-1017

(P-11890)
JYNORMUS LLC
19800 Macarthur Blvd 3rd Fl (92612-2421)
PHONE......................949 436-2112
EMP: 17 **EST:** 2006
SQ FT: 5,000
SALES (est): 1.22MM **Privately Held**
SIC: 4813 2741 Internet connectivity services
; Racing forms and programs: publishing
and printing

(P-11891)
MEDIA TEMPLE INC
12655 W Jefferson Blvd # 400
(90066-7008)
PHONE......................877 578-4000
Russell P Reeder, *CEO*
Marc Dumont, *
John Carey, *
Albert Lopez, *
Rod Stoddard, *
EMP: 203 **EST:** 1998

SALES (est): 48.87MM
SALES (corp-wide): 4.09B **Publicly Held**
Web: www.mediatemple.net
SIC: 4813 7371 Internet host services;
Computer software development and
applications
HQ: Godaddy.Com, Llc
2155 E Godaddy Way
Tempe AZ

(P-11892)
MIS SCIENCES CORP
2550 N Hollywood Way Ste 404
(91505-1055)
PHONE......................818 847-0213
EMP: 125 **EST:** 1996
SQ FT: 7,500
SALES (est): 9.67MM **Privately Held**
Web: www.mis-sciences.com
SIC: 4813 8748 7376 8742 Internet
connectivity services; Systems engineering
consultant, ex. computer or professional;
Computer facilities management;
Management information systems
consultant

(P-11893)
MP3COM INC
4790 Eastgate Mall (92121-2060)
PHONE......................858 623-7000
Derrick Oien, *COO*
Michael Robertson, *Prin*
EMP: 82 **EST:** 1998
SQ FT: 61,000
SALES (est): 1.72MM
SALES (corp-wide): 30.15B **Publicly Held**
SIC: 4813 Internet host services
HQ: Cbs Interactive Inc.
680 Folsom St
San Francisco CA

(P-11894)
**MPOWER HOLDING
CORPORATION (HQ)**
Also Called: Tpx Communications
515 S Flower St Fl 36 (90071-2201)
PHONE......................866 699-8242
Richard A Jalkut, *CEO*
Richard A Jalkut, *Ch Bd*
Timothy J Medina, *
EMP: 89 **EST:** 1996
SALES (est): 437.41MM **Privately Held**
SIC: 4813 Internet connectivity services
PA: U.S. Telepacific Holdings Corp.
515 S Flower St Fl 47
Los Angeles CA

(P-11895)
NEXTPOINT INC (PA)
Also Called: Break Media
8750 Wilshire Blvd Ste 200 (90211-2700)
PHONE......................310 360-5904
Keith Richman, *Pr*
Andrew Doyle, *
David Subar, *
EMP: 80 **EST:** 2005
SALES (est): 22.65MM **Privately Held**
Web: www.breakmedia.com
SIC: 4813 Internet connectivity services

(P-11896)
PAYCHEX BENEFIT TECH INC
Also Called: Benetrac
2385 Northside Dr Ste 100 (92108-2716)
PHONE......................800 322-7292
Martin Mucci, *CEO*
B Thomas Golisano, *
Jan Hawthorne, *
Susan Short, *
John B Gibson, *

EMP: 110 **EST:** 1986
SALES (est): 24.46MM
SALES (corp-wide): 5.01B **Publicly Held**
SIC: 4813 Online service providers
PA: Paychex, Inc.
911 Panorama Trl S
Rochester NY
585 385-6666

(P-11897)
PCS MOBILE SOLUTIONS LLC
3534 Tweedy Blvd (90280-6026)
PHONE......................323 567-2490
EMP: 80
SALES (corp-wide): 48.68MM **Privately
Held**
Web: www.pcsmobilesolutions.com
SIC: 4813 4812 Local and long distance
telephone communications; Cellular
telephone services
PA: Pcs Mobile Solutions, Llc
32000 Northwestern Hwy # 279
Farmington Hills MI
248 539-2221

(P-11898)
PHONECOM INC
14288 Danielson St (92064-8891)
PHONE......................973 577-6380
EMP: 93 **EST:** 2013
SALES (est): 624.3K **Privately Held**
Web: www.phone.com
SIC: 4813 Internet connectivity services

(P-11899)
**PUBLIC COMMUNICATIONS
SVCS INC**
11859 Wilshire Blvd Ste 600 (90025-6616)
P.O. Box 2868 (36652-2868)
PHONE......................310 231-1000
Paul Jennings, *CEO*
Tommie Joe, *
Dennis Komai, *
EMP: 150 **EST:** 1987
SQ FT: 15,000
SALES (est): 16.92MM **Privately Held**
SIC: 4813 Local and long distance telephone
communications

(P-11900)
QWEST CYBERSOLUTIONS LLC
Also Called: Qwest
3015 Winona Ave (91504-2541)
PHONE......................818 729-2100
Gino Roa, *Dir*
EMP: 141
SALES (corp-wide): 17.48B **Publicly Held**
SIC: 4813 Telephone communication, except
radio
HQ: Qwest Cyber.Solutions Llc
931 14th St
Denver CO
303 296-2787

(P-11901)
SCALEFAST INC (PA)
Also Called: Pepitastore
2100 E Grand Ave (90245-5024)
PHONE......................310 595-4040
Nicolas Stehle, *CEO*
Yanick Turgeon, *
Olivier Schott, *
EMP: 103 **EST:** 2014
SALES (est): 41.9MM
SALES (corp-wide): 41.9MM **Privately
Held**
Web: www.scalefast.com
SIC: 4813 Proprietary online service
networks

PRODUCTS & SVCS

(P-11902)
SPOKEO INC
556 S Fair Oaks Ave Ste 1 (91105-2656)
PHONE...............................877 913-3088
EMP: 214
Web: www.spokeo.com
SIC: 4813 Internet host services
PA: Spokeo, Inc.
199 S Los Robles Ave # 711
Pasadena CA

(P-11903)
SPRINT COMMUNICATIONS CO LP
1316 N Azusa Ave (91722-1259)
PHONE...............................626 339-0430
EMP: 148
SALES (corp-wide): 79.57B Publicly Held
SIC: 4813 4812 Local and long distance telephone communications; Cellular telephone services
HQ: Sprint Communications Company L.P.
6391 Sprint Pkwy
Overland Park KS
800 829-0965

(P-11904)
SPRINT COMMUNICATIONS CO LP
111 Universal Hollywood Dr (91608-1054)
PHONE...............................818 755-7100
Bill Henry, Mgr
EMP: 148
SALES (corp-wide): 79.57B Publicly Held
SIC: 4813 4812 Long distance telephone communications; Radiotelephone communication
HQ: Sprint Communications Company L.P.
6391 Sprint Pkwy
Overland Park KS
800 829-0965

(P-11905)
SPRINT COMMUNICATIONS CO LP
Also Called: Sprint
12913 Harbor Blvd Ste Q4 (92840-5856)
PHONE...............................714 534-2107
EMP: 188
SALES (corp-wide): 79.57B Publicly Held
SIC: 4813 4812 Local and long distance telephone communications; Cellular telephone services
HQ: Sprint Communications Company L.P.
6391 Sprint Pkwy
Overland Park KS
800 829-0965

(P-11906)
SPRINT COMMUNICATIONS CO LP
1505 E Enterprise Dr (92408-0159)
PHONE...............................909 382-6030
Bill Neece, Mgr
EMP: 148
SALES (corp-wide): 79.57B Publicly Held
SIC: 4813 4812 Long distance telephone communications; Radiotelephone communication
HQ: Sprint Communications Company L.P.
6391 Sprint Pkwy
Overland Park KS
800 829-0965

(P-11907)
SYDATA INC
6494 Weathers Pl Ste 100 (92121-2938)
PHONE...............................760 444-4368
Sindhura Thummalasetty, CEO

EMP: 125 EST: 2018
SALES (est): 9.03MM Privately Held
Web: www.sydatainc.com
SIC: 4813 7371 Internet connectivity services; Custom computer programming services

(P-11908)
TELISIMO INTERNATIONAL CORP
2330 Shelter Island Dr Ste 210a (92106-3126)
PHONE...............................619 325-1593
Linda G Noda Hobbs, Pr
Mark D Wooster, *
▲ EMP: 400 EST: 1990
SQ FT: 15,000
SALES (est): 25.71MM Privately Held
Web: www.wirelessweb.com
SIC: 4813 Telephone communication, except radio

(P-11909)
TEMPO COMMUNICATIONS INC (PA)
1390 Aspen Way (92081-8349)
PHONE...............................800 642-2155
Jason Edward Butchko, CEO
John Parizek, *
David Collmann, *
EMP: 85 EST: 2019
SALES (est): 21.19MM
SALES (corp-wide): 21.19MM Privately Held
Web: www.tempocom.com
SIC: 4813 3823 Telephone communication, except radio; Absorption analyzers: infrared, x-ray, etc.: industrial

(P-11910)
TRUCONNECT COMMUNICATIONS INC (PA)
Also Called: Telescape
1149 S Hill St Ste 400 (90015-2207)
PHONE...............................512 919-2641
Mathew Johnson, CEO
Robert A Yap, *
Nathan Johnson, *
EMP: 201 EST: 2001
SALES (est): 38.01MM
SALES (corp-wide): 38.01MM Privately Held
Web: www.truconnect.com
SIC: 4813 Internet host services

(P-11911)
ULTRA COMMUNICATIONS INC
990 Park Center Dr Ste H (92081-8352)
PHONE...............................760 652-0011
Charles Kuznia, Pr
EMP: 17 EST: 2004
SALES (est): 11.9MM
SALES (corp-wide): 178.24MM Privately Held
Web: www.ultracomm-inc.com
SIC: 4813 2653 Telephone communication, except radio; Corrugated and solid fiber boxes
PA: Samtec Inc
520 Park East Blvd
New Albany IN
812 944-6733

(P-11912)
XSOLLA (USA) INC (PA)
Also Called: Xsolla
15260 Ventura Blvd Ste 2230 (91403-5356)
PHONE...............................818 435-6613
EMP: 540 EST: 2009
SQ FT: 30,000

SALES (est): 66.15MM Privately Held
Web: www.xsolla.com
SIC: 4813 Internet connectivity services

(P-11913)
YTEL INC
26632 Towne Centre Dr Ste 300 (92610)
PHONE...............................800 382-4913
Nick Newsom, CEO
EMP: 100 EST: 2012
SALES (est): 11.42MM Privately Held
Web: www.ytel.com
SIC: 4813 Internet host services

(P-11914)
ZENLAYER INC
21680 Gateway Center Dr Ste 350 (91765-2456)
P.O. Box 5709 (91765-7709)
PHONE...............................909 718-3558
Joe Zhu, CEO
EMP: 408 EST: 2016
SALES (est): 48.05MM Privately Held
Web: www.zenlayer.com
SIC: 4813 Internet connectivity services

(P-11915)
ZYXEL COMMUNICATIONS INC
Also Called: Zyxel
1130 N Miller St (92806-2001)
PHONE...............................714 632-0882
Howie Chu, Pr
◆ EMP: 80 EST: 1989
SQ FT: 32,000
SALES (est): 21.33MM Privately Held
Web: www.zyxel.com
SIC: 4813 Internet host services
HQ: Zyxel Communications Corporation
No. 2, Gongye E. 9th Rd.,
Baoshan Township HSI

4822 Telegraph And Other Communications

(P-11916)
DELUXE ENCORE INC
Also Called: A Deluxe Entrmt Svcs Group Co
2400 W Empire Ave Ste 400 (91504-3355)
PHONE...............................323 466-7663
Warren Stein, CEO
EMP: 178 EST: 2013
SALES (est): 2.32MM Privately Held
SIC: 4822 Cable, telegram, and telex services

(P-11917)
J2 CLOUD SERVICES LLC (HQ)
Also Called: Efax Corporate
700 S Flower St Fl 15 (90017-4101)
PHONE...............................323 860-9200
EMP: 80 EST: 1995
SQ FT: 40,000
SALES (est): 668.5MM
SALES (corp-wide): 1.39B Publicly Held
Web: enterprise.efax.com
SIC: 4822 Telegraph and other communications
PA: Ziff Davis, Inc.
114 5th Ave Fl 14
New York NY
212 503-3500

4832 Radio Broadcasting Stations

(P-11918)
ABC CABLE NETWORKS GROUP (HQ)

Also Called: ABC
500 S Buena Vista St (91521-0007)
PHONE...............................818 460-7477
Gary K Marsh, CEO
Anne M Sweeney, *
Patrick Lopker, *
▲ EMP: 200 EST: 1969
SALES (est): 490.92MM
SALES (corp-wide): 88.9B Publicly Held
Web: www.thewaltdisneycompany.com
SIC: 4832 4833 Radio broadcasting stations; Television broadcasting stations
PA: The Walt Disney Company
500 S Buena Vista St
Burbank CA
818 560-1000

(P-11919)
AGM CALIFORNIA INC
1400 Easton Dr Ste 144 (93309-9404)
P.O. Box 2700 (93303-2700)
PHONE...............................661 328-0118
Lawrence Rogers Brandon, Pr
EMP: 126 EST: 2010
SALES (est): 5.79MM Privately Held
Web: www.americangeneralmedia.com
SIC: 4832 Radio broadcasting stations

(P-11920)
BUCK OWENS PRODUCTION CO INC (PA)
Also Called: Kuzz FM
2800 Buck Owens Blvd (93308-6314)
PHONE...............................661 326-1011
Buck Owens Junior, Pr
Michael Owens, VP
EMP: 21 EST: 1966
SQ FT: 32,000
SALES (est): 8.44MM
SALES (corp-wide): 8.44MM Privately Held
Web: www.buckowens.com
SIC: 4832 4833 2741 Radio broadcasting stations; Television broadcasting stations; Miscellaneous publishing

(P-11921)
DASH RADIO INC
Also Called: Dash Radio
6230 Wilshire Blvd # 118 (90048-5126)
PHONE...............................310 456-9993
Scott Keeney, Pr
Ron Goldie, Sec
EMP: 81 EST: 2014
SALES (est): 1.24MM Privately Held
Web: www.dashradio.com
SIC: 4832 Radio broadcasting stations

(P-11922)
DISNEY ENTERPRISES INC (DH)
Also Called: Disney
500 S Buena Vista St (91521-0001)
P.O. Box 3232 (92803-3232)
PHONE...............................818 560-1000
Christine M Mccarthy, Pr
◆ EMP: 561 EST: 1986
SALES (est): 40.66B
SALES (corp-wide): 88.9B Publicly Held
Web: www.disney.com
SIC: 4832 6794 5331 7996 Radio broadcasting stations; Copyright buying and licensing; Variety stores; Theme park, amusement
HQ: Twdc Enterprises 18 Corp.
500 S Buena Vista St
Burbank CA

(P-11923)
EL DORADO BROADCASTERS LLC

11920 Hesperia Rd (92345-1851)
PHONE..................760 241-1313
Tim Anderson, *Prin*
EMP: 92 **EST:** 2007
SALES (est): 4.28MM **Privately Held**
Web: www.edbroadcasters.com
SIC: 4832 Radio broadcasting stations,
music format

(P-11924)
ENTERCOM MEDIA CORP
Also Called: CBS
900 E Washington St Ste 315 (92324-7111)
PHONE..................909 825-9525
Kevin Murphy, *Genl Mgr*
EMP: 85
SALES (corp-wide): 1.25B **Publicly Held**
Web: www.audacyinc.com
SIC: 4832 Radio broadcasting stations
HQ: Entercom Media Corp.
345 Hudson St
New York NY
212 314-9200

(P-11925)
ENTERCOM MEDIA CORP
Also Called: CBS
5670 Wilshire Blvd Ste 200 (90036-5679)
PHONE..................323 930-7317
Sials Marshall, *Brnch Mgr*
EMP: 126
SALES (corp-wide): 1.25B **Publicly Held**
Web: www.audacy.com
SIC: 4832 Radio broadcasting stations,
music format
HQ: Entercom Media Corp.
345 Hudson St
New York NY
212 314-9200

(P-11926)
KIFM SMOOTH JAZZ 981 INC
1615 Murray Canyon Rd (92108-4314)
PHONE..................619 297-3698
Mike Stafford, *Pr*
EMP: 110 **EST:** 1999
SQ FT: 12,000
SALES (est): 19.54MM
SALES (corp-wide): 1.25B **Publicly Held**
SIC: 4832 Radio broadcasting stations
HQ: Abe Entercom Holdings Llc
401 E City Ave Ste 809
Bala Cynwyd PA
404 239-7211

(P-11927)
KRCA LICENSE LLC
1845 W Empire Ave (91504-9922)
PHONE..................818 840-1400
EMP: 105 **EST:** 2001
SALES (est): 4.55MM
SALES (corp-wide): 283.69MM **Privately
Held**
SIC: 4832 Radio broadcasting stations
HQ: Krca Television Llc
1 Estrella Way
Burbank CA

(P-11928)
LBI MEDIA HOLDINGS INC
3101 W 5th St (92703-1829)
PHONE..................714 554-5000
Jesus Mar, *Brnch Mgr*
EMP: 334
SALES (corp-wide): 283.69MM **Privately
Held**
SIC: 4832 Radio broadcasting stations
HQ: Lbi Media Holdings, Inc.
1 Estrella Way
Burbank CA

(P-11929)
**LIBERMAN BROADCASTING
INC (PA)**
1845 W Empire Ave (91504-9922)
PHONE..................818 729-5300
Lenard D Liberman, *CEO*
Jose Liberman, *
Frederic T Boyer, *
Eduardo Leon, *
Winter Horton, *
EMP: 83 **EST:** 2004
SALES (est): 283.69MM
SALES (corp-wide): 283.69MM **Privately
Held**
Web: www.estrellamedia.com
SIC: 4832 Radio broadcasting stations

(P-11930)
LOCAL MEDIA SAN DIEGO LLC
Also Called: Magic 92.5
6160 Cornerstone Ct E Ste 150
(92121-3720)
PHONE..................858 888-7000
Norman Mckee, *CFO*
EMP: 100 **EST:** 2009
SALES (est): 6.91MM **Privately Held**
Web: www.magic925.com
SIC: 4832 Radio broadcasting stations,
music format

(P-11931)
**MULTICULTURAL RDO
BRDCSTG INC**
747 E Green St (91101-2145)
PHONE..................626 844-8882
EMP: 99
SALES (corp-wide): 49.85MM **Privately
Held**
Web: www.mrbi.net
SIC: 4832 Radio broadcasting stations,
music format
PA: Multicultural Radio Broadcasting, Inc.
207 William St Fl 11 Flr 11
New York NY
212 966-1059

(P-11932)
NBCUNIVERSAL MEDIA LLC
Also Called: Universal Pictures Intl
100 Universal City Plz Bldg 2160 (91608)
PHONE..................818 777-1000
EMP: 534
SALES (corp-wide): 121.43B **Publicly
Held**
Web: www.nbc.com
SIC: 4832 7812 Radio broadcasting stations;
Motion picture production and distribution
HQ: Nbcuniversal Media, Llc
30 Rockefeller Plz Fl 2
New York NY

(P-11933)
PANDORA MEDIA LLC
3000 Ocean Park Blvd Ste 3050
(90405-3020)
PHONE..................424 653-6803
EMP: 237
SALES (corp-wide): 12.16B **Publicly Held**
Web: www.pandora.com
SIC: 4832 Radio broadcasting stations
HQ: Pandora Media, Llc
2100 Franklin St Ste 700
Oakland CA
510 451-4100

(P-11934)
RADIO DISNEY GROUP LLC
3800 W Alameda Ave Ste 1150
(91505-4331)
PHONE..................818 569-5000
EMP: 102 **EST:** 2003
SALES (est): 25.54MM
SALES (corp-wide): 88.9B **Publicly Held**
Web: radio.disney.com
SIC: 4832 Radio broadcasting stations
HQ: Abc Cable Networks Group
500 S Buena Vista St
Burbank CA
818 460-7477

(P-11935)
**SAN BRNRDINO CMNTY
COLLEGE DST**
Also Called: Kvcr, TV & FM
701 S Mount Vernon Ave (92410-2705)
PHONE..................909 384-4444
Larry Ciecalone, *Pr*
EMP: 107
SALES (corp-wide): 46.53MM **Privately
Held**
Web: www.sbccd.cc.ca.us
SIC: 4832 4833 Radio broadcasting stations;
Television broadcasting stations
PA: San Bernardino Community College
District
550 E Hospitality Ln # 200
San Bernardino CA
909 382-4000

(P-11936)
SIRIUS XM RADIO INC
953 N Sycamore Ave (90038-2373)
PHONE..................323 802-1100
EMP: 127
SALES (corp-wide): 12.16B **Publicly Held**
Web: www.siriusxm.com
SIC: 4832 Radio broadcasting stations
HQ: Sirius Xm Radio Inc.
1221 Ave Of The Amrcas 35
New York NY

4833 Television Broadcasting
Stations

(P-11937)
ABC SIGNATURE STUDIOS INC
500 S Buena Vista St (91521-0001)
PHONE..................818 560-1000
Linda A Bagley, *CEO*
EMP: 86 **EST:** 1989
SALES (est): 20.58MM
SALES (corp-wide): 88.9B **Publicly Held**
SIC: 4833 Television broadcasting stations
PA: The Walt Disney Company
500 S Buena Vista St
Burbank CA
818 560-1000

(P-11938)
AMERICAN MULTIMEDIA TV USA
Also Called: Amtv USA
530 S Lake Ave Unit 368 (91101-3515)
PHONE..................626 466-1038
Jason Quin, *Pr*
EMP: 67 **EST:** 2004
SALES (est): 2.31MM **Privately Held**
Web: www.amtvusa.com
SIC: 4833 7372 Television broadcasting
stations; Application computer software

(P-11939)
BAY CITY TELEVISION INC (PA)
8253 Ronson Rd (92111-2004)
P.O. Box 880083 (92168-0083)
PHONE..................858 279-6666
Jose Antonio Baston Patino, *CEO*
Robert Taylor, *
EMP: 100 **EST:** 1953

SQ FT: 12,000
SALES (est): 17.4MM
SALES (corp-wide): 17.4MM **Privately
Held**
Web: www.sandiego6.com
SIC: 4833 7311 Television broadcasting
stations; Advertising agencies

(P-11940)
CBS BROADCASTING INC
Also Called: CBS
4024 Radford Ave Bldg 4 (91604)
PHONE..................818 655-8500
Michael Klausman, *Pr*
EMP: 123
SALES (corp-wide): 30.15B **Publicly Held**
Web: www.cbsnews.com
SIC: 4833 Television broadcasting stations
HQ: Cbs Broadcasting Inc.
524 W 57th St
New York NY
212 975-4321

(P-11941)
CBS STUDIOS INC
Also Called: Csi Vegas
27420 Avenue Scott Ste A (91355-3450)
PHONE..................661 964-6020
EMP: 469
SALES (corp-wide): 30.15B **Publicly Held**
Web: www.paramount.com
SIC: 4833 Television broadcasting stations
HQ: Cbs Studios Inc.
6100 Wilshire Blvd # 1000
Los Angeles CA

(P-11942)
CNN AMERICA INC
Also Called: Cnn
6430 W Sunset Blvd Ste 300 (90028-7901)
PHONE..................323 993-5000
Suzanne Spurgeon, *Prin*
EMP: 186
Web: www.cnn.com
SIC: 4833 Television broadcasting stations
HQ: Cnn America Inc.
190 Marietta St Nw 12s
Atlanta GA

(P-11943)
CW NETWORK LLC (HQ)
Also Called: Cwtv
3300 W Olive Ave Fl 3 (91505-4640)
PHONE..................818 977-2500
Dennis Miller, *Pr*
John Maatta, *
Mitchell Nedick, *
Tom Martin, *
Ashley Hovey, *Chief Digital Officer**
EMP: 210 **EST:** 2006
SALES (est): 112.21MM
SALES (corp-wide): 5.21MM **Publicly
Held**
Web: www.cwtv.com
SIC: 4833 Television broadcasting stations
PA: Nexstar Media Group, Inc.
545 E John Carpenter Fwy
Irving TX
972 373-8800

(P-11944)
**DISNEY NETWORKS GROUP
LLC (DH)**
Also Called: Fox Network Center
10201 W Pico Blvd Bldg 101 (90064-2606)
P.O. Box 900 (90213-0900)
PHONE..................310 369-1000
Brian Sullivan, *Pr*
EMP: 86 **EST:** 1996
SALES (est): 41.5MM

PRODUCTS & SVCS

SALES (corp-wide): 88.9B **Publicly Held**
SIC: 4833 Television broadcasting stations
HQ: Fox Entertainment Group, Llc
   1211 Ave Of The Americas
   New York NY
   212 852-7000

(P-11945)
ENTRAVSION COMMUNICATIONS CORP (PA)
2425 Olympic Blvd Ste 6000w (90404-4030)
PHONE..............................310 447-3870
EMP: 114 **EST:** 1996
SQ FT: 16,000
SALES (est): 956.21MM **Publicly Held**
Web: www.entravision.com
SIC: 4833 4832 Television broadcasting stations; Radio broadcasting stations

(P-11946)
ENTRAVSION COMMUNICATIONS CORP
Also Called: K S S C - F M
5700 Wilshire Blvd Ste 250 (90036-3659)
PHONE..............................323 900-6100
Jeff Liberman, *Pr*
EMP: 100
Web: www.entravision.com
SIC: 4833 4832 Television broadcasting stations; Radio broadcasting stations
PA: Entravision Communications Corporation
   2425 Olympic Blvd Ste 600
   Santa Monica CA

(P-11947)
EW SCRIPPS COMPANY
Also Called: Kgtv
4600 Air Way (92102-2528)
PHONE..............................619 237-1010
Derek Dalton, *VP*
EMP: 217
SALES (corp-wide): 2.45B **Publicly Held**
Web: www.10news.com
SIC: 4833 Television broadcasting stations
PA: The E W Scripps Company
   312 Walnut St Ste 2800
   Cincinnati OH
   513 977-3000

(P-11948)
FOX INC (DH)
Also Called: Home Entertainment Div
10201 W Pico Blvd (90064-2606)
P.O. Box 900 (90213-0900)
PHONE..............................310 369-1000
K Rupert Murdoch, *Ch Bd*
Mike Dunn, *
Jay Itzkowitz, *
▲ **EMP:** 2000 **EST:** 1984
SQ FT: 25,000
SALES (est): 881.26MM
SALES (corp-wide): 88.9B **Publicly Held**
Web: www.fox.com
SIC: 4833 7812 Television broadcasting stations; Motion picture production and distribution
HQ: News America Incorporated
   1211 Ave Of The Americas
   New York NY
   212 852-7000

(P-11949)
FOX BROADCASTING COMPANY LLC (HQ)
10201 W Pico Blvd Bldg 1003220 (90064-2606)
P.O. Box 900 (90213-0900)

PHONE..............................310 369-1000
David F Devoe Junior, *CEO*
Nancy Utley, *
Sang Gong, *
Del Mayberry, *
Joe Earley, *
EMP: 200 **EST:** 1986
SQ FT: 41,000
SALES (est): 115.56MM
SALES (corp-wide): 14.91B **Publicly Held**
Web: www.fox.com
SIC: 4833 Television broadcasting stations
PA: Fox Corporation
   1211 Ave Of The Americas
   New York NY
   212 852-7000

(P-11950)
FOX SPORTS INC (DH)
Also Called: F O X
10201 W Pico Blvd (90064-2606)
PHONE..............................310 369-1000
EMP: 131 **EST:** 1995
SALES (est): 192.62MM
SALES (corp-wide): 88.9B **Publicly Held**
Web: www.foxsports.com
SIC: 4833 Television broadcasting stations
HQ: Fox Entertainment Group, Llc
   1211 Ave Of The Americas
   New York NY
   212 852-7000

(P-11951)
FOX TELEVISION STATIONS INC (HQ)
Also Called: Fox Television Center
1999 S Bundy Dr (90025-5203)
PHONE..............................310 584-2000
Roger Ailes, *Ch Bd*
Murdock Lachlan, *
Bill Lamb, *
Amy Carney, *
Dick Slenker, *Operations*
▲ **EMP:** 300 **EST:** 1998
SALES (est): 871.03MM
SALES (corp-wide): 14.91B **Publicly Held**
Web: www.foxla.com
SIC: 4833 7313 Television broadcasting stations; Radio, television, publisher representatives
PA: Fox Corporation
   1211 Ave Of The Americas
   New York NY
   212 852-7000

(P-11952)
FOX US PRODUCTIONS 27 INC
1600 Rosecrans Ave Bldg 5a (90266-3708)
PHONE..............................310 727-2550
EMP: 139
SALES (est): 887.75K
SALES (corp-wide): 88.9B **Publicly Held**
SIC: 4833 Television broadcasting stations
HQ: Fox Entertainment Group, Llc
   1211 Ave Of The Americas
   New York NY
   212 852-7000

(P-11953)
HALLMARK MEDIA US LLC (DH)
Also Called: Hallmark Channel
12700 Ventura Blvd Ste 100 (91604-2469)
PHONE..............................818 755-2400
EMP: 95 **EST:** 1995
SALES (est): 46.99MM
SALES (corp-wide): 2.72B **Privately Held**
Web: www.hallmark.com
SIC: 4833 Television broadcasting stations
HQ: Crown Media Holdings, Inc.
   12700 Ventura Blvd # 100

Studio City CA
888 390-7474

(P-11954)
HERRING NETWORKS INC
Also Called: Awe
4757 Morena Blvd (92117-3462)
PHONE..............................858 270-6900
Charles P Herring, *Pr*
EMP: 130 **EST:** 2003
SALES (est): 13.6MM **Privately Held**
Web: www.awetv.com
SIC: 4833 Television broadcasting stations

(P-11955)
KING WORLD PRODUCTIONS INC
Also Called: King World
1575 N Gower St Ste 100 (90028-6488)
PHONE..............................310 264-3549
EMP: 154
SALES (corp-wide): 30.15B **Publicly Held**
Web: www.paramount.com
SIC: 4833 Television broadcasting stations
HQ: King World Productions, Inc
   51 W 52nd St Fl 24
   New York NY
   212 315-4000

(P-11956)
KSBY COMMUNICATIONS LLC
1772 Calle Joaquin (93405-7210)
PHONE..............................805 541-6666
Kathleen Choal, *Pr*
EMP: 173 **EST:** 2005
SALES (est): 7.37MM
SALES (corp-wide): 2.45B **Publicly Held**
Web: www.ksby.com
SIC: 4833 Television broadcasting stations
PA: The E W Scripps Company
   312 Walnut St Ste 2800
   Cincinnati OH
   513 977-3000

(P-11957)
LIFETIME ENTRMT SVCS LLC
Also Called: Lifetime TV Network
2049 Century Park E Ste 840 (90067-3101)
PHONE..............................310 556-7500
Maryann Harris, *Genl Mgr*
EMP: 300
SALES (corp-wide): 88.9B **Publicly Held**
Web: www.mylifetime.com
SIC: 4833 5942 Television broadcasting stations; Book stores
HQ: Lifetime Entertainment Services, Llc
   235 E 45th St
   New York NY
   212 424-7000

(P-11958)
MCKINNON PUBLISHING COMPANY
4575 Viewridge Ave (92123-1623)
PHONE..............................858 571-5151
Michael Mckinnon, *Pr*
EMP: 599 **EST:** 1993
SALES (est): 1.93MM **Privately Held**
Web: www.kusi.com
SIC: 4833 Television broadcasting stations
HQ: Mckinnon Broadcasting Company
   565 Gage Ln
   San Diego CA
   858 571-5151

(P-11959)
NBC SUBSIDIARY (KNBC-TV) LLC
Also Called: NBC

100 Universal City Plz Bldg 2120 (91608)
P.O. Box 66132 (90066-0132)
PHONE..............................818 684-5746
Todd Mokhtari, *Pr*
Jenik Badalian, *
EMP: 250 **EST:** 2009
SALES (est): 76.11MM
SALES (corp-wide): 121.43B **Publicly Held**
Web: www.nbcuniversal.com
SIC: 4833 Television broadcasting stations
PA: Comcast Corporation
   1 Comcast Ctr
   Philadelphia PA
   215 286-1700

(P-11960)
NEWPORT TELEVISION LLC
Kget-TV
2120 L St (93301-2331)
PHONE..............................661 283-1700
Sandy Dipasquale, *Pr*
EMP: 671
SALES (corp-wide): 20.65MM **Privately Held**
Web: www.kget.com
SIC: 4833 Television translator station
PA: Newport Television Llc
   460 Nichols Rd Ste 250
   Kansas City MO
   816 751-0200

(P-11961)
PUBLIC MDIA GROUP SOUTHERN CAL (PA)
2900 W Alameda Ave Unit 600 (91505-4216)
PHONE..............................714 241-4100
Andrew Russell, *Pr*
Jamie Myers, *
Paul Nelson, *
Dawn Ariza, *
EMP: 100 **EST:** 1960
SQ FT: 50,000
SALES (est): 54.29MM
SALES (corp-wide): 54.29MM **Privately Held**
Web: www.pbssocal.org
SIC: 4833 Television broadcasting stations

(P-11962)
REVOLT MEDIA AND TV LLC
Also Called: Revolt
9200 W Sunset Blvd Fl 3 (90069-3502)
PHONE..............................323 645-3000
Detavio Samuels, *CEO*
Keith Clinkscales, *
EMP: 120 **EST:** 2010
SALES (est): 21.93MM **Privately Held**
Web: www.revolt.tv
SIC: 4833 Television broadcasting stations

(P-11963)
SF BROADCASTING WISCONSIN INC
2425 Olympic Blvd (90404-4030)
PHONE..............................310 586-2410
EMP: 151 **EST:** 1994
SALES (est): 27.41MM
SALES (corp-wide): 3.19B **Publicly Held**
SIC: 4833 Television broadcasting stations
PA: Match Group, Inc.
   8750 N Cntl Expy Ste 1400
   Dallas TX
   214 576-9352

(P-11964)
SMITH BROADCASTING GROUP INC

Also Called: Keyt Television
730 Miramonte Dr (93109-1417)
P.O. Box 729 (93102-0729)
PHONE...............................805 882-3933
Michael Granados, *Genl Mgr*
EMP: 332
SALES (corp-wide): 6.69MM **Privately Held**
Web: www.keyt.com
SIC: **4833** 7313 Television broadcasting stations; Television and radio time sales
PA: Smith Broadcasting Group, Inc
2315 Red Rose Way
Santa Barbara CA
805 965-0400

(P-11965)
TRINITY BRDCSTG NETWRK INC
Also Called: Trinity Christn Ctr Santa Ana
2442 Michelle Dr (92780-7015)
PHONE...............................714 665-3619
Paul F Crouch, *Pr*
EMP: 150 EST: 1987
SALES (est): 25.74MM
SALES (corp-wide): 120.98MM **Privately Held**
Web: www.tbn.org
SIC: **4833** Television broadcasting stations
PA: Trinity Christian Center Of Santa Ana, Inc.
13600 Heritage Pkwy # 200
Fort Worth TX
714 665-3619

(P-11966)
TWDC ENTERPRISES 18 CORP (HQ)
Also Called: Disney Financial Services
500 S Buena Vista St (91521-0001)
PHONE...............................818 560-1000
◆ EMP: 521 EST: 1925
SALES (est): 46.53B
SALES (corp-wide): 88.9B **Publicly Held**
Web: www.thewaltdisneycompany.com
SIC: **4833** 4841 7011 7996 Television broadcasting stations; Cable television services; Resort hotel; Amusement parks
PA: The Walt Disney Company
500 S Buena Vista St
Burbank CA
818 560-1000

(P-11967)
TWENTETH CNTURY FOX INTL TV IN
10201 W Pico Blvd (90064-2606)
PHONE...............................310 369-1000
Peter Chernin, *Ch Bd*
EMP: 5980 EST: 1996
SALES (est): 20.44MM
SALES (corp-wide): 88.9B **Publicly Held**
SIC: **4833** Television broadcasting stations
HQ: Fox Entertainment Group, Llc
1211 Ave Of The Americas
New York NY
212 852-7000

(P-11968)
VALLEYCREST PRODUCTIONS LTD
500 S Buena Vista St (91521-0001)
PHONE...............................818 560-5391
Joseph Santaniello, *CEO*
EMP: 100 EST: 1999
SALES (est): 47.48MM
SALES (corp-wide): 88.9B **Publicly Held**
SIC: **4833** Television broadcasting stations
HQ: Twdc Enterprises 18 Corp.
500 S Buena Vista St
Burbank CA

4841 Cable And Other Pay Television Services

(P-11969)
BDR INDUSTRIES INC (PA)
Also Called: R N D Enterprises
820 E Avenue L12 (93535-5403)
PHONE...............................661 940-8554
Scott Riddle, *Pr*
Edward Donovan, *
▲ EMP: 95 EST: 1984
SQ FT: 30,000
SALES (est): 24.38MM
SALES (corp-wide): 24.38MM **Privately Held**
Web: www.rndcable.com
SIC: **4841** Cable television services

(P-11970)
CALIFORNIA BROADCAST CTR LLC
3800 Via Oro Ave (90810-1866)
PHONE...............................310 233-2425
Bruce Churchill, *CEO*
EMP: 91 EST: 1955
SALES (est): 7.16MM
SALES (corp-wide): 120.74B **Publicly Held**
SIC: **4841** Cable and other pay television services
HQ: Directv Latin America, Llc
1 Rockefeller Plz
New York NY
212 205-0500

(P-11971)
CCO HOLDINGS LLC
3106 San Gabriel Blvd (91770-2579)
PHONE...............................626 500-1214
Steve Stannard, *Brnch Mgr*
EMP: 112
SALES (corp-wide): 54.02B **Publicly Held**
SIC: **4841** Cable television services
HQ: Cco Holdings, Llc
400 Atlantic St
Stamford CT
203 905-7801

(P-11972)
CCO HOLDINGS LLC
23841 Malibu Rd (90265-4644)
PHONE...............................310 589-3008
EMP: 112
SALES (corp-wide): 54.02B **Publicly Held**
SIC: **4841** Cable television services
HQ: Cco Holdings, Llc
400 Atlantic St
Stamford CT
203 905-7801

(P-11973)
CCO HOLDINGS LLC
12319 Norwalk Blvd (90650-2039)
PHONE...............................562 239-2761
EMP: 112
SALES (corp-wide): 54.02B **Publicly Held**
SIC: **4841** Cable television services
HQ: Cco Holdings, Llc
400 Atlantic St
Stamford CT
203 905-7801

(P-11974)
CCO HOLDINGS LLC
1151 N Azusa Ave (91702-2005)
PHONE...............................626 513-0204
EMP: 112
SALES (corp-wide): 54.02B **Publicly Held**

SIC: **4841** Cable television services
HQ: Cco Holdings, Llc
400 Atlantic St
Stamford CT
203 905-7801

(P-11975)
CCO HOLDINGS LLC
Also Called: Charter Communications
2310 N Bellflower Blvd (90815-2019)
PHONE...............................562 228-1262
EMP: 112
SALES (corp-wide): 54.02B **Publicly Held**
SIC: **4841** Cable television services
HQ: Cco Holdings, Llc
400 Atlantic St
Stamford CT
203 905-7801

(P-11976)
CCO HOLDINGS LLC
2684 N Tustin St (92865-2438)
PHONE...............................714 509-5861
EMP: 112
SALES (corp-wide): 54.02B **Publicly Held**
SIC: **4841** 3663 3651 Cable television services; Radio and t.v. communications equipment; Household audio and video equipment
HQ: Cco Holdings, Llc
400 Atlantic St
Stamford CT
203 905-7801

(P-11977)
CCO HOLDINGS LLC
1128 W Branch St (93420-1906)
PHONE...............................805 904-1047
EMP: 112
SALES (corp-wide): 54.02B **Publicly Held**
SIC: **4841** Cable television services
HQ: Cco Holdings, Llc
400 Atlantic St
Stamford CT
203 905-7801

(P-11978)
CCO HOLDINGS LLC
1131 Creston Rd (93446-3031)
PHONE...............................805 400-1002
EMP: 112
SALES (corp-wide): 54.02B **Publicly Held**
SIC: **4841** Cable television services
HQ: Cco Holdings, Llc
400 Atlantic St
Stamford CT
203 905-7801

(P-11979)
CCO HOLDINGS LLC
Also Called: Charter Communications
51 W Main St Ste F (93001-2566)
PHONE...............................805 232-5887
EMP: 112
SALES (corp-wide): 54.02B **Publicly Held**
SIC: **4841** Cable television services
HQ: Cco Holdings, Llc
400 Atlantic St
Stamford CT
203 905-7801

(P-11980)
CCO HOLDINGS LLC
21898 Us Highway 18 (92307-3916)
PHONE...............................760 810-4076
EMP: 150
SALES (corp-wide): 54.02B **Publicly Held**
SIC: **4841** Cable television services
HQ: Cco Holdings, Llc
400 Atlantic St

Stamford CT
203 905-7801

(P-11981)
CCO HOLDINGS LLC
26827 Baseline St (92346-3059)
PHONE...............................909 742-8273
EMP: 112
SALES (corp-wide): 54.02B **Publicly Held**
SIC: **4841** 3663 3651 Cable television services; Radio and t.v. communications equipment; Household audio and video equipment
HQ: Cco Holdings, Llc
400 Atlantic St
Stamford CT
203 905-7801

(P-11982)
COMCAST CORPORATION
Also Called: Comcast
1205 S Dupont Ave (91761-1536)
PHONE...............................909 890-0886
Mike Shanter, *Brnch Mgr*
EMP: 100
SQ FT: 23,318
SALES (corp-wide): 121.43B **Publicly Held**
Web: corporate.comcast.com
SIC: **4841** Cable television services
PA: Comcast Corporation
1 Comcast Ctr
Philadelphia PA
215 286-1700

(P-11983)
COX COMMUNICATIONS CAL LLC
5159 Federal Blvd (92105-5428)
PHONE...............................619 262-1122
James Robbins, *CEO*
EMP: 380
SALES (corp-wide): 16.61B **Privately Held**
SIC: **4841** Cable television services
HQ: Cox Communications California, Llc
6205 Pachtree Dunwoody Rd
Atlanta GA
404 843-5000

(P-11984)
DIRECTV
1655 W 110th Pl (90047-4826)
PHONE...............................323 810-2032
Geron Flynn, *Prin*
EMP: 99 EST: 2010
SALES (est): 762.77K **Privately Held**
Web: www.directv.com
SIC: **4841** Direct broadcast satellite services (DBS)

(P-11985)
DIRECTV INC
2260 E Imperial Hwy (90245-3501)
P.O. Box 105249 (30348-5249)
PHONE...............................888 388-4249
EMP: 476 EST: 2015
SALES (est): 45.31MM **Privately Held**
Web: www.directv.com
SIC: **4841** Cable and other pay television services

(P-11986)
DIRECTV ENTERPRISES LLC
2230 E Imperial Hwy (90245-3504)
P.O. Box 956 (90245-0956)
PHONE...............................310 535-5000
EMP: 16229 EST: 1995
SQ FT: 75,000
SALES (est): 9.31MM
SALES (corp-wide): 120.74B **Publicly Held**

PRODUCTS & SVCS

SIC: **4841** Direct broadcast satellite services (DBS)
HQ: Directv Holdings Llc
2230 E Imperial Hwy
El Segundo CA
310 964-5000

(P-11987)
DIRECTV GROUP HOLDINGS LLC
715 E Avenue L8 Ste 101 (93535-5405)
PHONE.................................661 632-6562
EMP: 116
SALES (corp-wide): 120.74B **Publicly Held**
SIC: **4841** Direct broadcast satellite services (DBS)
HQ: Directv Group Holdings, Llc
2260 E Imperial Hwy
El Segundo CA

(P-11988)
DIRECTV GROUP HOLDINGS LLC
140 Station Ave (93555-3838)
PHONE.................................760 375-8300
EMP: 144
SALES (corp-wide): 120.74B **Publicly Held**
SIC: **4841** Cable and other pay television services
HQ: Directv Group Holdings, Llc
2260 E Imperial Hwy
El Segundo CA

(P-11989)
DIRECTV GROUP HOLDINGS LLC
360 Cortez Cir (93012-8630)
PHONE.................................805 207-6675
EMP: 116
SALES (corp-wide): 120.74B **Publicly Held**
SIC: **4841** Cable television services
HQ: Directv Group Holdings, Llc
2260 E Imperial Hwy
El Segundo CA

(P-11990)
DIRECTV GROUP INC (DH)
Also Called: Directv
2260 E Imperial Hwy (90245-3501)
PHONE.................................310 964-5000
Michael White, *CEO*
Patrick T Doyle, *
Romulo Pontual, *
John F Murphy, *CAO**
J William Little, *
▲ **EMP:** 128 **EST:** 1977
SALES (est): 1.87B
SALES (corp-wide): 120.74B **Publicly Held**
SIC: **4841** 6794 Direct broadcast satellite services (DBS); Franchises, selling or licensing
HQ: Directv Group Holdings, Llc
2260 E Imperial Hwy
El Segundo CA

(P-11991)
DIRECTV INTERNATIONAL INC (DH)
2230 E Imperial Hwy Fl 10 (90245-3504)
PHONE.................................310 964-6460
EMP: 150 **EST:** 1996
SALES (est): 494.29MM
SALES (corp-wide): 120.74B **Publicly Held**

(P-11992)
E ENTERTAINMENT TELEVISION INC
Also Called: Style Network
5750 Wilshire Blvd # 500 (90036-3697)
PHONE.................................323 954-2400
EMP: 900
SIC: **4841** 4833 Cable television services; Television broadcasting stations

(P-11993)
FX NETWORKS LLC
10201 W Pico Blvd Bldg 103 (90064-2606)
P.O. Box 900 (90213-0900)
PHONE.................................310 369-1000
John Landgraf, *Managing Member*
Stephanie Gibbons, *
EMP: 150 **EST:** 1997
SALES (est): 53.25MM
SALES (corp-wide): 88.9B **Publicly Held**
Web: www.fxnetworks.com
SIC: **4841** Cable television services
HQ: Fox Entertainment Group, Llc
1211 Ave Of The Americas
New York NY
212 852-7000

(P-11994)
GAME SHOW NETWORK MUSIC LLC (DH)
Also Called: G S N
2150 Colorado Ave Ste 100 (90404-5514)
PHONE.................................310 255-6800
Mark Seldman, *Managing Member*
EMP: 244 **EST:** 1992
SALES (est): 89.95MM **Privately Held**
SIC: **4841** Cable television services
HQ: Sony Pictures Entertainment, Inc.
10202 Washington Blvd
Culver City CA
310 244-4000

(P-11995)
GLOBECAST AMERICA INCORPORATED
10525 Washington Blvd (90232-3311)
PHONE.................................310 845-3900
EMP: 205
SALES (corp-wide): 23.35B **Privately Held**
Web: www.globecast.com
SIC: **4841** Satellite master antenna systems services (SMATV)
HQ: Globecast America Incorporated
10525 Washington Blvd
Culver City CA
310 845-3900

(P-11996)
INTERNATIONAL FMLY ENTRMT INC (DH)
Also Called: Fox Family Channel
3800 W Alameda Ave (91505-4300)
PHONE.................................818 560-1000
Mel Woods, *Pr*
EMP: 144 **EST:** 1990
SALES (est): 102.39MM
SALES (corp-wide): 88.9B **Publicly Held**
SIC: **4841** 7812 7922 7999 Cable television services; Television film production; Theatrical producers; Recreation services
HQ: Abc Family Worldwide, Inc.
500 S Buena Vista St

Burbank CA
818 560-1000

(P-11997)
NDS AMERICAS INC (DH)
3500 Hyland Ave (92626-1459)
PHONE.................................714 434-2100
Abe Peled, *Pr*
Dov Rubin, *
Alex Gersh, *
EMP: 90 **EST:** 1992
SALES (est): 42.68MM
SALES (corp-wide): 57B **Publicly Held**
Web: www.synamedia.com
SIC: **4841** Cable television services
HQ: Nds Group Limited
9-11 New Square
Feltham MIDDX

(P-11998)
OWN LLC
Also Called: Oprah Winfrey Network
4000 Warner Blvd (91522-0001)
PHONE.................................323 602-5500
Oprah Winfrey, *CRO*
Oprah Winfrey, *Chief Creative Officer*
Erik Logan, *
Sheri Salata, *
EMP: 140 **EST:** 2008
SALES (est): 97.31MM
SALES (corp-wide): 189.98MM **Privately Held**
Web: www.oprah.com
SIC: **4841** Cable television services
PA: Discovery Communications, Inc.
10100 Santa Monica Blvd
Los Angeles CA
310 975-5906

(P-11999)
SPECTRUM MGT HOLDG CO LLC
Also Called: Time Warner
3550 Wilshire Blvd (90010-2401)
PHONE.................................323 657-0899
EMP: 84
SALES (corp-wide): 54.02B **Publicly Held**
Web: www.spectrum.com
SIC: **4841** Cable television services
HQ: Spectrum Management Holding Company, Llc
400 Atlantic St
Stamford CT
203 905-7801

(P-12000)
SPECTRUM MGT HOLDG CO LLC
Also Called: Time Warner
5865 Friars Rd (92110-6009)
PHONE.................................619 684-6106
EMP: 86
SALES (corp-wide): 54.02B **Publicly Held**
Web: www.spectrum.com
SIC: **4841** Cable television services
HQ: Spectrum Management Holding Company, Llc
400 Atlantic St
Stamford CT
203 905-7801

(P-12001)
TIME WARNER COMPANIES INC
Also Called: Time Warner
2939 Nebraska Ave (90404-4108)
PHONE.................................310 315-4437
Pauline Thomke, *Brnch Mgr*
EMP: 649
Web: www.wbd.com

SIC: **4841** Cable television services
HQ: Time Warner Companies, Inc.
1 Time Warner Ctr
New York NY
212 484-8000

(P-12002)
VIDEO VICE DATA COMMUNICATIONS (PA)
Also Called: Vvd Communications
7391 Lincoln Way (92841-1428)
P.O. Box 91421 (90809-1421)
PHONE.................................714 897-6300
Bantofin Montoya, *Pr*
Annie Yonemura, *
EMP: 201 **EST:** 2002
SQ FT: 30,000
SALES (est): 36.81MM
SALES (corp-wide): 36.81MM **Privately Held**
Web: www.vvdservices.com
SIC: **4841** 1731 Cable and other pay television services; Electrical work

(P-12003)
VUBIQUITY HOLDINGS INC (DH)
Also Called: Vubiquity
15301 Ventura Blvd Ste 3000 (91403-5837)
PHONE.................................818 526-5000
Darcy Antonellis, *CEO*
Doug Sylvester, *
William G Arendt, *
James P Riley, *
Stephen Holsten, *
EMP: 185 **EST:** 2006
SALES (est): 120.51MM
SALES (corp-wide): 4.58B **Privately Held**
Web: www.amdocs.com
SIC: **4841** Cable and other pay television services
HQ: Amdocs, Inc.
625 Mryvlle Cntre Dr Ste
Saint Louis MO
314 212-7000

4899 Communication Services, Nec

(P-12004)
COMMUNICATIONS SUPPLY CORP
6251 Knott Ave (90620-1010)
PHONE.................................714 670-7711
Michael Davis, *Genl Mgr*
EMP: 70
Web: www.wesco.com
SIC: **4899** 1731 3577 3357 Data communication services; Communications specialization; Computer peripheral equipment, nec; Nonferrous wiredrawing and insulating
HQ: Communications Supply Corp
225 W Station Square Dr # 700
Pittsburgh PA
630 221-6400

(P-12005)
CTEK INC
2425 Golden Hill Rd Ste 106 (93446-7038)
PHONE.................................310 241-2973
Phil Sutter, *Pr*
EMP: 25 **EST:** 2003
SALES (est): 5.28MM
SALES (corp-wide): 388.23MM **Publicly Held**
Web: www.ctekproducts.com
SIC: **4899** 3661 Communication signal enhancement network services; Fiber optics communications equipment

PA: Digi International Inc.
9350 Excelsior Blvd # 700
Hopkins MN
952 912-3444

(P-12006)
DISCOVERY COMMUNICATIONS INC (PA)
10100 Santa Monica Blvd Ste 1500
(90067-4002)
PHONE....................310 975-5906
David Zazlov, *CEO*
EMP: 260 **EST:** 2014
SALES (est): 189.98MM
SALES (corp-wide): 189.98MM **Privately Held**
Web: www.discovery.com
SIC: 4899 Data communication services

(P-12007)
HORIZON COMMUNICATION TECH INC
Also Called: Horizon Communication
13700 Alton Pkwy Ste 154-278
(92618-1628)
PHONE....................714 982-3900
Nicolle Degraw, *CEO*
Micheal Degraw, *
Anthony Turrentine, *
Alex Hisa, *
EMP: 80 **EST:** 1998
SALES (est): 21.63MM **Privately Held**
SIC: 4899 Data communication services

(P-12008)
INTELSAT US LLC
Also Called: Intell Set
1600 Forbes Way (90810-1830)
PHONE....................310 525-5500
EMP: 105
SALES (corp-wide): 754.17MM **Privately Held**
Web: www.intelsat.com
SIC: 4899 Satellite earth stations
HQ: Intelsat Us Llc
7900 Tysons One Pl
Mc Lean VA

(P-12009)
IPS GROUP INC (PA)
7737 Kenamar Ct (92121-2425)
PHONE....................858 404-0607
David W King, *CEO*
Amir Sedadi, *VP*
Dario Paduano, *CFO*
Chad Randall, *COO*
▲ **EMP:** 37 **EST:** 2000
SALES (est): 58.9MM
SALES (corp-wide): 58.9MM **Privately Held**
Web: www.ipsgroupinc.com
SIC: 4899 3824 Communication signal enhancement network services; Parking meters

(P-12010)
NEXUS IS INC
27202 Turnberry Ln Ste 100 (91355-1022)
PHONE....................704 969-2200
EMP: 340
SIC: 4899 Data communication services

(P-12011)
PROSOFT TECHNOLOGY INC (HQ)
9201 Camino Media Ste 200 (93311-1362)
PHONE....................661 716-5100
Thomas Crone, *Pr*
EMP: 101 **EST:** 1990

SALES (est): 51.24MM
SALES (corp-wide): 2.61B **Publicly Held**
Web: www.prosoft-technology.com
SIC: 4899 Data communication services
PA: Belden Inc.
1 N Brentwood Blvd Fl 15
Saint Louis MO
314 854-8000

(P-12012)
SIEGE MEDIA LLC
624 Broadway Ste 301 (92101-5421)
PHONE....................858 751-4439
Ross Hudgens, *Prin*
EMP: 89 **EST:** 2016
SALES (est): 1.62MM **Privately Held**
Web: www.siegemedia.com
SIC: 4899 Communication services, nec

(P-12013)
TELETRAC INC (PA)
Also Called: Fleet Mangement Solutions
310 Commerce Ste 100 (92602-1360)
PHONE....................714 897-0877
Tj Chung, *Pr*
Tim Van Cleve, *
▲ **EMP:** 143 **EST:** 1995
SALES (est): 84.77MM
SALES (corp-wide): 84.77MM **Privately Held**
Web: www.teletracnavman.com
SIC: 4899 Data communication services

(P-12014)
THINKOM SOLUTIONS INC
4881 W 145th St (90250-6701)
PHONE....................310 371-5486
Mark Silk, *CEO*
William W Milroy, *
Michael Burke, *
Stuart Coppedge, *
Matthew Turk, *
EMP: 116 **EST:** 2000
SQ FT: 74,000
SALES (est): 30.05MM **Privately Held**
Web: www.thinkom.com
SIC: 4899 Satellite earth stations

(P-12015)
WOVEXX HOLDINGS INC (DH)
Also Called: Redwood
10381 Jefferson Blvd (90232-3511)
PHONE....................310 424-2080
EMP: 90 **EST:** 2010
SQ FT: 12,000
SALES (est): 46.91MM **Publicly Held**
SIC: 4899 7929 Data communication services; Entertainment service
HQ: Warner Music Group Corp.
1633 Broadway
New York NY
212 275-2000

4911 Electric Services

(P-12016)
AES ALAMITOS LLC
Also Called: AES
690 N Studebaker Rd (90803-2221)
PHONE....................562 493-7891
Weikko Wirta, *Managing Member*
EMP: 90 **EST:** 1997
SALES (est): 56.57MM
SALES (corp-wide): 12.62B **Publicly Held**
Web: www.aes.com
SIC: 4911 Generation, electric power
PA: The Aes Corporation
4300 Wilson Blvd Ste 1100
Arlington VA
703 522-1315

(P-12017)
CHESTNUT RIDGE ENERGY COMPANY
18101 Von Karman Ave Ste 920
(92612-1012)
▲ **EMP:** 185 **EST:** 1998
SALES (est): 2.29MM
SALES (corp-wide): 408.14MM **Privately Held**
SIC: 4911 Generation, electric power
HQ: Edison Mission Holdings Co.
18101 Von Karman Ave # 1700
Irvine CA
949 752-5588

(P-12018)
COMBUSTION ASSOCIATES INC
Also Called: Cai
555 Monica Cir (92878-5447)
PHONE....................951 272-6999
Mukund Kavia, *Pr*
Kusum Kavia, *
Prajesh Kavia, *
▼ **EMP:** 50 **EST:** 1991
SQ FT: 40,000
SALES (est): 48.76MM **Privately Held**
Web: www.cai3.com
SIC: 4911 3443 Fossil fuel electric power generation; Boiler and boiler shop work

(P-12019)
CYPRESS CREEK HOLDINGS LLC
3250 Ocean Park Blvd Ste 355
(90405-3208)
PHONE....................310 581-6299
Ben Van De Bunt, *Ch*
Matthew Mcgovern, *CEO*
Michael Cohen, *
EMP: 100 **EST:** 2014
SALES (est): 7.97MM **Privately Held**
SIC: 4911

(P-12020)
ECOFLOW TECHNOLOGY INC
245 E Main St Ste 107 (91801-7506)
PHONE....................407 247-6023
Yun Zhang, *CEO*
EMP: 32 **EST:** 2017
SALES (est): 607.29K **Privately Held**
Web: www.ecoflow.com
SIC: 4911 3674
; Solar cells

(P-12021)
EDF RENEWABLES INC (PA)
15445 Innovation Dr (92128-3432)
P.O. Box 504080 (92150-4080)
PHONE....................858 521-3300
Tristan Grimbert, *Pr*
Luis Silva, *CFO*
▲ **EMP:** 225 **EST:** 1987
SALES (est): 678.73MM **Privately Held**
Web: www.edf-re.com
SIC: 4911 Electric services

(P-12022)
EDISON CAPITAL
18101 Von Karman Ave Ste 1700
(92612-1012)
PHONE....................909 594-3789
Thomas Mc Daniel, *Pr*
Larry Mount, *
Jim Phillipsen, *
Richard E Lucey, *
Phillip Dandridge, *
EMP: 103 **EST:** 1987
SQ FT: 12,000
SALES (est): 47.31MM

SALES (corp-wide): 17.22B **Publicly Held**
SIC: 4911 Electric services
HQ: Edison Mission Group Inc.
2244 Walnut Grove Ave
Rosemead CA
626 302-2222

(P-12023)
EDISON INTERNATIONAL (PA)
2244 Walnut Grove Ave (91770-3714)
P.O. Box 976 (91770-0976)
PHONE....................626 302-2222
Pedro J Pizarro, *Pr*
Maria Rigatti, *Ex VP*
Adam S Umanoff, *Ex VP*
Caroline Choi Senior, *Corporate Affairs Vice President*
Jacqueline Trapp, *Senior Vice President Human Resources*
EMP: 1092 **EST:** 1987
SALES (est): 17.22B
SALES (corp-wide): 17.22B **Publicly Held**
Web: www.edison.com
SIC: 4911 Electric services

(P-12024)
EDISON MISSION ENERGY (PA)
Also Called: Edison Mission
2244 Walnut Grove Ave (91770-3714)
PHONE....................626 302-5778
Theodore F Craver Junior, *Dir*
Raymond W Vickers, *Dir*
John P Finneran Junior, *Dir*
Paul Jacob, *Dir*
W James Scilacci, *Dir*
▲ **EMP:** 143 **EST:** 2001
SQ FT: 71,000
SALES (est): 408.14MM
SALES (corp-wide): 408.14MM **Privately Held**
Web: www.edisonenergy.com
SIC: 4911 Electric services

(P-12025)
EDISON MSSION MIDWEST HOLDINGS
2244 Walnut Grove Ave (91770-3714)
PHONE....................626 302-2222
Guy F Gorney, *Pr*
EMP: 1844 **EST:** 1999
SALES (est): 23.82MM
SALES (corp-wide): 17.22B **Publicly Held**
Web: www.edison.com
SIC: 4911 Electric services
HQ: Edison Mission Group Inc.
2244 Walnut Grove Ave
Rosemead CA
626 302-2222

(P-12026)
HANWHA Q CELLS USA CORP
300 Spectrum Center Dr Ste 1250
(92618-4925)
PHONE....................949 748-5996
Jae Kyu Lee, *Pr*
EMP: 95 **EST:** 2000
SALES (est): 12.87MM **Privately Held**
Web: www.qcellsusa.com
SIC: 4911

(P-12027)
IMPERIAL IRRIGATION DISTRICT (PA)
Also Called: I I D
333 E Barioni Blvd (92251-1773)
P.O. Box 937 (92251-0937)
PHONE....................800 303-7756
Stephen Benson, *Pr*
Anthony Sanchez, *
Stella Mendoza, *

PRODUCTS & SVCS

Mike Abatti, *
Keven Kelly, *
▲ **EMP: 700 EST:** 1911
SQ FT: 10,000
SALES (est): 859.47MM
SALES (corp-wide): 859.47MM **Privately Held**
Web: www.iid.com
SIC: 4911 4971 4931 Hydro electric power generation; Water distribution or supply systems for irrigation; Electric and other services combined

(P-12028)
INSPIRE ENERGY HOLDINGS LLC
Also Called: Inspire Energy
3402 Pico Blvd Ste 300 (90405-2118)
PHONE..................866 403-2620
Patrick Maloney, *CEO*
EMP: 138 **EST:** 2013
SALES (est): 55.21MM
SALES (corp-wide): 381.31B **Privately Held**
Web: www.inspirecleanenergy.com
SIC: 4911 Distribution, electric power
PA: Shell Plc
　　Shell Centre
　　London
　　800 731-8888

(P-12029)
NRG CALIFORNIA SOUTH LP
Also Called: Etiwanda Power Plant
8996 Etiwanda Ave (91739-9662)
PHONE..................909 899-7241
Lee Moore, *Brnch Mgr*
EMP: 217
SIC: 4911 Generation, electric power
HQ: Nrg California South Lp
　　804 Carnegie Ctr
　　Princeton NJ

(P-12030)
NRG CALIFORNIA SOUTH LP
Also Called: Coolwater Generating Station
37000 E Santa Fe St (92327)
PHONE..................760 254-5241
Bob Ott, *Mgr*
EMP: 124
SIC: 4911 Generation, electric power
HQ: Nrg California South Lp
　　804 Carnegie Ctr
　　Princeton NJ

(P-12031)
NRG CALIFORNIA SOUTH LP
Also Called: Mandalay Generating Station
393 Harbor Blvd (93035-1108)
PHONE..................805 984-5241
Thomas Di Ciolli, *Mgr*
EMP: 226
SIC: 4911 Fossil fuel electric power generation
HQ: Nrg California South Lp
　　804 Carnegie Ctr
　　Princeton NJ

(P-12032)
NRG SOLAR LLC
5790 Fleet St (92008-4703)
PHONE..................760 710-2140
EMP: 129 **EST:** 2012
SALES (est): 13.44MM **Publicly Held**
SIC: 4911 Generation, electric power
HQ: Nrg Repowering Holdings Llc
　　211 Carnegie Ctr
　　Princeton NJ
　　760 710-2140

(P-12033)
OUTSOURCE UTILITY CONTR CORP
17115 Alburtis Ave (90701-2616)
PHONE..................714 238-9263
Heather Morgan, *Pr*
Joe Morgan, *
Josh Stewart, *
EMP: 200 **EST:** 2010
SALES (est): 47.03MM **Privately Held**
Web: www.outsourceucc.com
SIC: 4911 Distribution, electric power

(P-12034)
PACIFIC GAS AND ELECTRIC CO
Also Called: PG&e
4340 Old Santa Fe Rd (93401-8160)
PHONE..................805 545-4562
Del Richie, *Mgr*
EMP: 163
Web: www.pge.com
SIC: 4911 Transmission, electric power
HQ: Pacific Gas And Electric Company
　　300 Lakeside Dr Ste 210
　　Oakland CA
　　415 973-7000

(P-12035)
PACIFIC GAS AND ELECTRIC CO
Also Called: PG&e
9 Mi Nw Of Avila Bch (93424)
P.O. Box 56 (93424-0056)
PHONE..................805 506-5280
David Oatley, *Brnch Mgr*
EMP: 1400
Web: www.pge.com
SIC: 4911 Transmission, electric power
HQ: Pacific Gas And Electric Company
　　300 Lakeside Dr Ste 210
　　Oakland CA
　　415 973-7000

(P-12036)
PACIFIC GAS AND ELECTRIC CO
Also Called: PG&e
800 Price Canyon Rd (93449-2722)
PHONE..................805 546-5267
Don Boatman, *Brnch Mgr*
EMP: 190
Web: www.pge.com
SIC: 4911 Transmission, electric power
HQ: Pacific Gas And Electric Company
　　300 Lakeside Dr Ste 210
　　Oakland CA
　　415 973-7000

(P-12037)
PACIFIC GAS AND ELECTRIC CO
Also Called: PG&e
160 Cow Meadow Pl (93465)
PHONE..................805 434-4418
EMP: 95
Web: www.pge.com
SIC: 4911 Transmission, electric power
HQ: Pacific Gas And Electric Company
　　300 Lakeside Dr Ste 210
　　Oakland CA
　　415 973-7000

(P-12038)
PACIFIC GAS AND ELECTRIC CO
Also Called: PG&e
35863 Fairview Rd (92347-9710)
PHONE..................760 253-2925
Dan Lytle, *Mgr*
EMP: 176
Web: www.pge.com
SIC: 4911 Transmission, electric power
HQ: Pacific Gas And Electric Company
　　300 Lakeside Dr Ste 210

Oakland CA
415 973-7000

(P-12039)
PACIFIC GAS AND ELECTRIC CO
Also Called: PG&e
145453 National Trails Hway (92363)
P.O. Box 337 (92363-0337)
PHONE..................760 326-2615
Felix Vasquez, *Mgr*
EMP: 122
Web: www.pge.com
SIC: 4911 Transmission, electric power
HQ: Pacific Gas And Electric Company
　　300 Lakeside Dr Ste 210
　　Oakland CA
　　415 973-7000

(P-12040)
PACIFIC GAS AND ELECTRIC CO
Also Called: PG&e
4201 Arrow St (93308-4938)
PHONE..................661 398-5918
EMP: 190
Web: www.pge.com
SIC: 4911 Transmission, electric power
HQ: Pacific Gas And Electric Company
　　300 Lakeside Dr Ste 210
　　Oakland CA
　　415 973-7000

(P-12041)
RRI ENERGY COOLWATER INC
37000 E Santa Fe St (92327)
PHONE..................760 254-5290
Mark Jacobs, *Pr*
EMP: 98 **EST:** 1997
SALES (est): 5.75MM **Publicly Held**
SIC: 4911 Generation, electric power
HQ: Reliant Energy Retail Holdings, Llc
　　1000 Main St
　　Houston TX
　　713 497-3000

(P-12042)
SAN DIEGO GAS & ELECTRIC CO
Also Called: Eastern District Office
104 N Johnson Ave (92020-3181)
PHONE..................619 441-3834
Allan Marchart, *Mgr*
EMP: 267
SALES (corp-wide): 14.44B **Publicly Held**
Web: www.sdge.com
SIC: 4911 Distribution, electric power
HQ: San Diego Gas & Electric Company
　　8330 Century Park Ct
　　San Diego CA
　　619 696-2000

(P-12043)
SAN DIEGO GAS & ELECTRIC CO
Also Called: SDG&ec
5488 Overland Ave (92123-1205)
P.O. Box 129007 (92112-9007)
PHONE..................858 541-5920
Patrick Lee, *Mgr*
EMP: 146
SALES (corp-wide): 14.44B **Publicly Held**
Web: www.sdge.com
SIC: 4911 4924 Generation, electric power; Natural gas distribution
HQ: San Diego Gas & Electric Company
　　8330 Century Park Ct
　　San Diego CA
　　619 696-2000

(P-12044)
SAN DIEGO GAS & ELECTRIC CO
Project Construction Metro
701 33rd St (92102-3341)
PHONE..................619 699-1018
Scott Furgerson, *Mgr*
EMP: 166
SALES (corp-wide): 14.44B **Publicly Held**
Web: www.sdge.com
SIC: 4911 Distribution, electric power
HQ: San Diego Gas & Electric Company
　　8330 Century Park Ct
　　San Diego CA
　　619 696-2000

(P-12045)
SAN DIEGO GAS & ELECTRIC CO
Also Called: SDG&e
2300 Harveson Pl (92029-1965)
PHONE..................760 432-2508
Carl La Peter, *Prin*
EMP: 292
SALES (corp-wide): 14.44B **Publicly Held**
Web: www.sdge.com
SIC: 4911 Distribution, electric power
HQ: San Diego Gas & Electric Company
　　8330 Century Park Ct
　　San Diego CA
　　619 696-2000

(P-12046)
SAN DIEGO GAS & ELECTRIC CO
Also Called: SDG&e
5488 Overland Ave (92123-1205)
PHONE..................858 654-6377
E Dimuzio, *Brnch Mgr*
EMP: 322
SALES (corp-wide): 14.44B **Publicly Held**
Web: www.sdge.com
SIC: 4911 Distribution, electric power
HQ: San Diego Gas & Electric Company
　　8330 Century Park Ct
　　San Diego CA
　　619 696-2000

(P-12047)
SAN DIEGO GAS & ELECTRIC CO
Also Called: SDG&e
10975 Technology Pl (92127-1811)
PHONE..................858 613-3216
EMP: 111
SALES (corp-wide): 14.44B **Publicly Held**
Web: www.sdge.com
SIC: 4911 Distribution, electric power
HQ: San Diego Gas & Electric Company
　　8330 Century Park Ct
　　San Diego CA
　　619 696-2000

(P-12048)
SAN DIEGO GAS & ELECTRIC CO
Also Called: SDG&e
8306 Century Park Ct # Cp42c (92123-1530)
PHONE..................858 654-1289
Eric Llewellyn, *Brnch Mgr*
EMP: 80
SALES (corp-wide): 14.44B **Publicly Held**
Web: www.sdge.com
SIC: 4911 Distribution, electric power
HQ: San Diego Gas & Electric Company
　　8330 Century Park Ct
　　San Diego CA
　　619 696-2000

▲ = Import ▼ = Export
◆ = Import/Export

(P-12049)
SAN DIEGO GAS & ELECTRIC CO
Also Called: SDG&e
1801 S Atlantic Blvd (91754-5207)
PHONE..............................619 696-2000
J Walker Martin, *CEO*
EMP: 161
SALES (corp-wide): 14.44B **Publicly Held**
Web: www.sdge.com
SIC: **4911** Distribution, electric power
HQ: San Diego Gas & Electric Company
8330 Century Park Ct
San Diego CA
619 696-2000

(P-12050)
SEMPRA ENERGY
Also Called: Sempra Energy
9305 Lightwave Ave (92123-6463)
PHONE..............................619 696-2000
Sean Luko, *Brnch Mgr*
EMP: 1000
SALES (corp-wide): 14.44B **Publicly Held**
Web: www.sempra.com
SIC: **4911** 4923 Distribution, electric power;
Gas transmission and distribution
PA: Sempra
488 8th Ave
San Diego CA
619 696-2000

(P-12051)
SEMPRA ENERGY GLOBAL ENTPS
101 Ash St (92101-3017)
PHONE..............................619 696-2000
Mark Snell, *Pr*
Mark Fisher, *
Michael Allman, *
EMP: 1000 EST: 1997
SQ FT: 10,000
SALES (est): 480.01MM
SALES (corp-wide): 14.44B **Publicly Held**
Web: www.sempra.com
SIC: **4911** 4924 Generation, electric power;
Natural gas distribution
PA: Sempra
488 8th Ave
San Diego CA
619 696-2000

(P-12052)
SEMPRA ENERGY INTERNATIONAL
Also Called: Sempra Energy Utilities
101 Ash St (92101-3017)
PHONE..............................619 696-2000
Luis Eduardo Pawluszek, *CEO*
Donald E Felsinger, *
Mark A Snell, *
Javade Chaudhri, *
Randall L Clark, *
EMP: 1200 EST: 1998
SALES (est): 576.02MM
SALES (corp-wide): 14.44B **Publicly Held**
Web: www.sempra.com
SIC: **4911** Electric services
PA: Sempra
488 8th Ave
San Diego CA
619 696-2000

(P-12053)
SERVITEK ELECTRIC INC
Also Called: Servitek Electric Hawaii
618 Brea Canyon Rd Ste J (91789-3022)
PHONE..............................626 227-1650
Geoffrey Reyes, *Pr*

EMP: 20 EST: 2018
SALES (est): 641.61K **Privately Held**
Web: www.servitekelectric.com
SIC: **4911** 3612 Electric services; Voltage
regulating transformers, electric power

(P-12054)
SOLARRESERVE INC
520 Broadway Fl 6 (90401-2420)
PHONE..............................310 315-2200
Kevin B Smith, *CEO*
Stephen Mullennix, *
EMP: 99 EST: 2008
SQ FT: 20,000
SALES (est): 19.38MM **Privately Held**
SIC: **4911** Distribution, electric power

(P-12055)
SOLV ENERGY LLC (HQ)
16680 W Bernardo Dr (92127-1900)
PHONE..............................858 251-4888
George Hershman, *CEO*
Ben Catalano, *CFO*
EMP: 159 EST: 2015
SALES (est): 30.23MM **Privately Held**
Web: www.solvenergy.com
SIC: **4911**
PA: American Securities Llc
590 Madison Ave Fl 38
New York NY

(P-12056)
SOUTHERN CALIFORNIA EDISON CO
Also Called: Thousand Oaks Service Center
3589 Foothill Dr (91361-2475)
PHONE..............................818 999-1880
Jerry Willaferd, *Brnch Mgr*
EMP: 87
SALES (corp-wide): 17.22B **Publicly Held**
Web: www.sce.com
SIC: **4911** 8741 Electric services; Business
management
HQ: Southern California Edison Company
2244 Walnut Grove Ave
Rosemead CA
626 302-1212

(P-12057)
SOUTHERN CALIFORNIA EDISON CO
Also Called: Lighthipe Substation
6900 Orange Ave (90805-1599)
PHONE..............................562 529-7301
Jim Hill, *Mgr*
EMP: 87
SQ FT: 38,928
SALES (corp-wide): 17.22B **Publicly Held**
Web: www.sce.com
SIC: **4911** Electric services
HQ: Southern California Edison Company
2244 Walnut Grove Ave
Rosemead CA
626 302-1212

(P-12058)
SOUTHERN CALIFORNIA EDISON CO
13025 Los Angeles St (91706-2241)
PHONE..............................626 814-4212
EMP: 292
SQ FT: 21,000
SALES (corp-wide): 17.22B **Publicly Held**
Web: www.sce.com
SIC: **4911** Electric services
HQ: Southern California Edison Company
2244 Walnut Grove Ave
Rosemead CA
626 302-1212

(P-12059)
SOUTHERN CALIFORNIA EDISON CO
Also Called: Covina Service Center
800 W Cienega Ave (91773-2490)
PHONE..............................909 592-3757
EMP: 219
SALES (corp-wide): 17.22B **Publicly Held**
Web: www.sce.com
SIC: **4911** Electric services
HQ: Southern California Edison Company
2244 Walnut Grove Ave
Rosemead CA
626 302-1212

(P-12060)
SOUTHERN CALIFORNIA EDISON CO
Also Called: Whittier Service Center
9901 Geary Ave (90670-3251)
PHONE..............................562 903-3191
EMP: 297
SALES (corp-wide): 17.22B **Publicly Held**
Web: www.sce.com
SIC: **4911** Electric services
HQ: Southern California Edison Company
2244 Walnut Grove Ave
Rosemead CA
626 302-1212

(P-12061)
SOUTHERN CALIFORNIA EDISON CO
Also Called: Western Division Regional Off
125 Elm Ave (90802-4918)
PHONE..............................562 491-3803
EMP: 255
SALES (corp-wide): 17.22B **Publicly Held**
Web: www.sce.com
SIC: **4911** Generation, electric power
HQ: Southern California Edison Company
2244 Walnut Grove Ave
Rosemead CA
626 302-1212

(P-12062)
SOUTHERN CALIFORNIA EDISON CO
Also Called: Ctac Research 60901
6090 N Irwindale Ave (91702-3207)
PHONE..............................626 812-7380
EMP: 246
SALES (corp-wide): 17.22B **Publicly Held**
Web: www.sce.com
SIC: **4911** Electric services
HQ: Southern California Edison Company
2244 Walnut Grove Ave
Rosemead CA
626 302-1212

(P-12063)
SOUTHERN CALIFORNIA EDISON CO
Alhambra Combined Facility
501 S Marengo Ave (91803-1640)
P.O. Box 700 (91770-0700)
PHONE..............................626 308-6193
EMP: 593
SALES (corp-wide): 17.22B **Publicly Held**
Web: www.sce.com
SIC: **4911** Generation, electric power
HQ: Southern California Edison Company
2244 Walnut Grove Ave
Rosemead CA
626 302-1212

(P-12064)
SOUTHERN CALIFORNIA EDISON CO
Also Called: Southern Cal Edson - Prvate Ch
2131 Walnut Grove Ave (91770-3769)
PHONE..............................626 302-1212
Grant Thomas, *Brnch Mgr*
EMP: 301
SALES (corp-wide): 17.22B **Publicly Held**
Web: www.sce.com
SIC: **4911** Distribution, electric power
HQ: Southern California Edison Company
2244 Walnut Grove Ave
Rosemead CA
626 302-1212

(P-12065)
SOUTHERN CALIFORNIA EDISON CO
2 Innovation Way Fl 1 (91768-2560)
PHONE..............................909 274-1925
EMP: 493
SALES (corp-wide): 17.22B **Publicly Held**
Web: www.sce.com
SIC: **4911** Electric services
HQ: Southern California Edison Company
2244 Walnut Grove Ave
Rosemead CA
626 302-1212

(P-12066)
SOUTHERN CALIFORNIA EDISON CO
Also Called: Ridgecrest Service Center
510 S China Lake Blvd (93555-5006)
PHONE..............................760 375-1821
EMP: 119
SALES (corp-wide): 17.22B **Publicly Held**
Web: www.sce.com
SIC: **4911** Electric services
HQ: Southern California Edison Company
2244 Walnut Grove Ave
Rosemead CA
626 302-1212

(P-12067)
SOUTHERN CALIFORNIA EDISON CO
Also Called: Monrovia Service Center
1440 S California Ave (91016-4211)
PHONE..............................626 303-8480
Robert Robinson, *Prin*
EMP: 187
SQ FT: 31,603
SALES (corp-wide): 17.22B **Publicly Held**
Web: www.sce.com
SIC: **4911** Electric services
HQ: Southern California Edison Company
2244 Walnut Grove Ave
Rosemead CA
626 302-1212

(P-12068)
SOUTHERN CALIFORNIA EDISON CO
Also Called: Irwindale 6000
6000 N Irwindale Ave Ste A (91702-3200)
PHONE..............................626 815-7296
Ray Maese, *Brnch Mgr*
EMP: 91
SALES (corp-wide): 17.22B **Publicly Held**
Web: www.sce.com
SIC: **4911** Electric services
HQ: Southern California Edison Company
2244 Walnut Grove Ave
Rosemead CA
626 302-1212

PRODUCTS & SVCS

(P-12069)
SOUTHERN CALIFORNIA EDISON CO
265 Ne End Ave (91767-5803)
PHONE.................909 469-0251
John Risen, *Brnch Mgr*
EMP: 607
SALES (corp-wide): 17.22B **Publicly Held**
Web: www.sce.com
SIC: 4911 Electric services
HQ: Southern California Edison Company
2244 Walnut Grove Ave
Rosemead CA
626 302-1212

(P-12070)
SOUTHERN CALIFORNIA EDISON CO
Also Called: Compton Service Center
1924 E Cashdan St (90220-6403)
PHONE.................310 608-5029
Floyd Rich, *Brnch Mgr*
EMP: 269
SALES (corp-wide): 17.22B **Publicly Held**
Web: www.sce.com
SIC: 4911 Electric services
HQ: Southern California Edison Company
2244 Walnut Grove Ave
Rosemead CA
626 302-1212

(P-12071)
SOUTHERN CALIFORNIA EDISON CO
Also Called: N Trans/Sub Regional Office
28250 Gateway Village Dr (91355-1177)
PHONE.................661 607-0207
EMP: 192
SALES (corp-wide): 17.22B **Publicly Held**
Web: www.sce.com
SIC: 4911 Electric services
HQ: Southern California Edison Company
2244 Walnut Grove Ave
Rosemead CA
626 302-1212

(P-12072)
SOUTHERN CALIFORNIA EDISON CO (HQ)
Also Called: SCE
2244 Walnut Grove Ave (91770-3714)
P.O. Box 976 (91770-0976)
PHONE.................626 302-1212
Kevin M Payne, *Pr*
Steven D Powell, *Ofcr*
William M Petmecky Iii, *Sr VP*
Caroline Choi Senior, *Corporate Affairs Vice President*
Jacqueline Trapp, *Senior Vice President Human Resources*
▲ **EMP:** 1200 **EST:** 1909
SALES (est): 17.17B
SALES (corp-wide): 17.22B **Publicly Held**
Web: www.sce.com
SIC: 4911 Generation, electric power
PA: Edison International
2244 Walnut Grove Ave
Rosemead CA
626 302-2222

(P-12073)
SOUTHERN CALIFORNIA EDISON CO
Also Called: North Orange County Svc Ctr
1851 W Valencia Dr (92833-3215)
PHONE.................714 870-3225
David Kama, *Dist Mgr*
EMP: 411
SALES (corp-wide): 17.22B **Publicly Held**

Web: www.sce.com
SIC: 4911 Distribution, electric power
HQ: Southern California Edison Company
2244 Walnut Grove Ave
Rosemead CA
626 302-1212

(P-12074)
SOUTHERN CALIFORNIA EDISON CO
Also Called: Valley Substation
26125 Menifee Rd (92585-9441)
PHONE.................800 336-2822
Henry Herrea, *Brnch Mgr*
EMP: 96
SALES (corp-wide): 17.22B **Publicly Held**
Web: www.sce.com
SIC: 4911 Generation, electric power
HQ: Southern California Edison Company
2244 Walnut Grove Ave
Rosemead CA
626 302-1212

(P-12075)
SOUTHERN CALIFORNIA EDISON CO
Also Called: Southeastern Westminster
7300 Fenwick Ln (92683-5238)
PHONE.................714 895-0420
Dee Pak Nanda, *VP*
EMP: 648
SALES (corp-wide): 17.22B **Publicly Held**
Web: www.sce.com
SIC: 4911 Electric services
HQ: Southern California Edison Company
2244 Walnut Grove Ave
Rosemead CA
626 302-1212

(P-12076)
SOUTHERN CALIFORNIA EDISON CO
Also Called: Saddleback Valley Service Ctr
14155 Bake Pkwy (92618-1818)
PHONE.................949 587-5416
Robert Torres, *Mgr*
EMP: 132
SALES (corp-wide): 17.22B **Publicly Held**
Web: www.sce.com
SIC: 4911 Electric services
HQ: Southern California Edison Company
2244 Walnut Grove Ave
Rosemead CA
626 302-1212

(P-12077)
SOUTHERN CALIFORNIA EDISON CO
Also Called: Orange Coast Service Center
7333 Bolsa Ave (92683-5210)
PHONE.................714 895-0163
EMP: 100
SALES (corp-wide): 17.22B **Publicly Held**
Web: www.sce.com
SIC: 4911 Electric services
HQ: Southern California Edison Company
2244 Walnut Grove Ave
Rosemead CA
626 302-1212

(P-12078)
SUNNOVA ENERGY CORPORATION
6531 Irvine Center Dr Ste 200
(92618-2146)
PHONE.................877 757-7697
EMP: 720
SALES (corp-wide): 176.35MM **Privately Held**

Web: www.sunnova.com
SIC: 4911
PA: Sunnova Energy Corporation
20 Greenway Plz Ste 540
Houston TX
281 985-9900

(P-12079)
TWIN OAKS POWER LP (HQ)
101 Ash St Hq10b (92101-3017)
PHONE.................619 696-2034
EMP: 100 **EST:** 2002
SALES (est): 72MM
SALES (corp-wide): 14.44B **Publicly Held**
SIC: 4911 4924 Generation, electric power; Natural gas distribution
PA: Sempra
488 8th Ave
San Diego CA
619 696-2000

4922 Natural Gas Transmission

(P-12080)
SOUTHERN CALIFORNIA GAS CO
9400 Oakdale Ave (91311-6511)
P.O. Box 513249 (90051-1249)
PHONE.................818 701-2592
EMP: 264
SALES (corp-wide): 14.44B **Publicly Held**
Web: www.socalgas.com
SIC: 4922 4923 Pipelines, natural gas; Gas transmission and distribution
HQ: Southern California Gas Company
555 W 5th St Ste 14h1
Los Angeles CA
213 244-1200

4924 Natural Gas Distribution

(P-12081)
CLEAN ENERGY
4675 Macarthur Ct Ste 800 (92660-1895)
PHONE.................949 437-1000
EMP: 832 **EST:** 1996
SALES (est): 323.67MM
SALES (corp-wide): 420.16MM **Publicly Held**
Web: www.cleanenergyfuels.com
SIC: 4924 Natural gas distribution
PA: Clean Energy Fuels Corp.
4675 Macarthur Ct Ste 800
Newport Beach CA
949 437-1000

(P-12082)
SAN DIEGO GAS & ELECTRIC CO
Also Called: SDG&e
14601 Virginia St (92555-8100)
PHONE.................951 243-2241
John Garcia, *Mgr*
EMP: 241
SALES (corp-wide): 14.44B **Publicly Held**
Web: www.sdge.com
SIC: 4924 Natural gas distribution
HQ: San Diego Gas & Electric Company
8330 Century Park Ct
San Diego CA
619 696-2000

(P-12083)
SOUTHERN CALIFORNIA GAS CO
25200 Trumble Rd (92585-9664)

PHONE.................213 244-1200
EMP: 89
SALES (corp-wide): 14.44B **Publicly Held**
Web: www.socalgas.com
SIC: 4924 Natural gas distribution
HQ: Southern California Gas Company
555 W 5th St Ste 14h1
Los Angeles CA
213 244-1200

(P-12084)
SOUTHERN CALIFORNIA GAS CO (HQ)
Also Called: Gas Company, The
555 W 5th St Ste 14h1 (90013-1010)
PHONE.................213 244-1200
Debra L Reed, *Ch*
Scott D Drury, *CEO*
Maryam Sabbaghian Brown, *Pr*
Steven D Davis, *Ex VP*
Joseph A Householder, *Ex VP*
EMP: 505 **EST:** 1910
SALES (est): 6.84B
SALES (corp-wide): 14.44B **Publicly Held**
Web: www.socalgas.com
SIC: 4924 4922 4932 Natural gas distribution ; Natural gas transmission; Gas and other services combined
PA: Sempra
488 8th Ave
San Diego CA
619 696-2000

(P-12085)
SOUTHERN CALIFORNIA GAS CO
1 Liberty (92656-3830)
PHONE.................714 634-7221
Bill Jameson, *Brnch Mgr*
EMP: 89
SALES (corp-wide): 14.44B **Publicly Held**
Web: www.socalgas.com
SIC: 4924 Natural gas distribution
HQ: Southern California Gas Company
555 W 5th St Ste 14h1
Los Angeles CA
213 244-1200

(P-12086)
SOUTHERN CALIFORNIA GAS CO
Also Called: La Jolla Station
3050 E La Jolla St (92806)
PHONE.................213 244-1200
EMP: 124
SALES (corp-wide): 14.44B **Publicly Held**
Web: www.socalgas.com
SIC: 4924 4922 4932 Natural gas distribution ; Natural gas transmission; Gas and other services combined
HQ: Southern California Gas Company
555 W 5th St Ste 14h1
Los Angeles CA
213 244-1200

(P-12087)
SOUTHERN CALIFORNIA GAS CO
Also Called: Honor Rancho Station
23130 Valencia Blvd (91355-1716)
PHONE.................800 427-2200
Dan Skope, *VP*
EMP: 132
SALES (corp-wide): 14.44B **Publicly Held**
Web: www.socalgas.com
SIC: 4924 Natural gas distribution
HQ: Southern California Gas Company
555 W 5th St Ste 14h1
Los Angeles CA
213 244-1200

(P-12088)
SOUTHERN CALIFORNIA GAS CO
333 E Main St Ste J (91801-3914)
PHONE..............................323 881-3587
G H Chavez, *Brnch Mgr*
EMP: 89
SALES (corp-wide): 14.44B **Publicly Held**
Web: www.socalgas.com
SIC: 4924 Natural gas distribution
HQ: Southern California Gas Company
555 W 5th St Ste 14h1
Los Angeles CA
213 244-1200

(P-12089)
SOUTHERN CALIFORNIA GAS CO
6738 Bright Ave (90601-4306)
PHONE..............................562 803-3341
Richard Duran, *Brnch Mgr*
EMP: 89
SALES (corp-wide): 14.44B **Publicly Held**
Web: www.socalgas.com
SIC: 4924 Natural gas distribution
HQ: Southern California Gas Company
555 W 5th St Ste 14h1
Los Angeles CA
213 244-1200

(P-12090)
SOUTHERN CALIFORNIA GAS CO
8141 Gulana Ave (90293-7930)
PHONE..............................310 823-7945
James Wine, *Mgr*
EMP: 391
SALES (corp-wide): 14.44B **Publicly Held**
Web: www.socalgas.com
SIC: 4924 Natural gas distribution
HQ: Southern California Gas Company
555 W 5th St Ste 14h1
Los Angeles CA
213 244-1200

(P-12091)
SOUTHERN CALIFORNIA GAS CO
1600 Corporate Center Dr (91754-7607)
P.O. Box C (91756-0001)
PHONE..............................213 244-1200
Joe M Rivera, *Rgnl Mgr*
EMP: 223
SALES (corp-wide): 14.44B **Publicly Held**
Web: www.socalgas.com
SIC: 4924 Natural gas distribution
HQ: Southern California Gas Company
555 W 5th St Ste 14h1
Los Angeles CA
213 244-1200

(P-12092)
SOUTHERN CALIFORNIA GAS CO
1050 Overland Ct (91773-1704)
P.O. Box 513249 (90051-1249)
PHONE..............................909 305-8297
Janet Yee, *Mgr*
EMP: 231
SQ FT: 39,344
SALES (corp-wide): 14.44B **Publicly Held**
Web: www.socalgas.com
SIC: 4924 Natural gas distribution
HQ: Southern California Gas Company
555 W 5th St Ste 14h1
Los Angeles CA
213 244-1200

(P-12093)
SOUTHERN CALIFORNIA GAS CO
Also Called: Northern Reg. Sub Base
1510 N Chester Ave (93308-2559)
PHONE..............................661 399-4431
James Pina, *Mgr*
EMP: 107
SALES (corp-wide): 14.44B **Publicly Held**
Web: www.socalgas.com
SIC: 4924 Natural gas distribution
HQ: Southern California Gas Company
555 W 5th St Ste 14h1
Los Angeles CA
213 244-1200

(P-12094)
SOUTHERN CALIFORNIA GAS CO
Also Called: Socalgas
12801 Tampa Ave (91326-1045)
PHONE..............................818 363-8542
EMP: 320
SALES (corp-wide): 14.44B **Publicly Held**
Web: www.socalgas.com
SIC: 4924 Natural gas distribution
HQ: Southern California Gas Company
555 W 5th St Ste 14h1
Los Angeles CA
213 244-1200

(P-12095)
SOUTHERN CALIFORNIA GAS CO
Also Called: Gas Company, The
9240 Firestone Blvd (90241-5388)
PHONE..............................562 803-7500
EMP: 510
SALES (corp-wide): 14.44B **Publicly Held**
Web: www.socalgas.com
SIC: 4924 Natural gas distribution
HQ: Southern California Gas Company
555 W 5th St Ste 14h1
Los Angeles CA
213 244-1200

(P-12096)
SOUTHERN CALIFORNIA GAS CO
1801 S Atlantic Blvd (91754-5207)
PHONE..............................213 244-1200
W J Torres, *Brnch Mgr*
EMP: 995
SALES (corp-wide): 14.44B **Publicly Held**
Web: www.sempra.com
SIC: 4924 Natural gas distribution
HQ: Southern California Gas Company
555 W 5th St Ste 14h1
Los Angeles CA
213 244-1200

(P-12097)
SOUTHERN CALIFORNIA GAS CO
Also Called: Industry Station
920 S Stimson Ave (91745-1640)
PHONE..............................213 244-1200
EMP: 113
SALES (corp-wide): 14.44B **Publicly Held**
Web: www.socalgas.com
SIC: 4924 Natural gas distribution
HQ: Southern California Gas Company
555 W 5th St Ste 14h1
Los Angeles CA
213 244-1200

(P-12098)
SOUTHERN CALIFORNIA GAS CO
Also Called: Regional Office
1981 W Lugonia Ave (92374-9720)
P.O. Box 513249 (90051-1249)
PHONE..............................909 335-7802
James Boland, *Mgr*
EMP: 340
SALES (corp-wide): 14.44B **Publicly Held**
Web: www.socalgas.com
SIC: 4924 Natural gas distribution
HQ: Southern California Gas Company
555 W 5th St Ste 14h1
Los Angeles CA
213 244-1200

(P-12099)
SOUTHERN CALIFORNIA GAS CO
155 S G St (92410-3317)
PHONE..............................909 335-7941
Al Garcia, *Brnch Mgr*
EMP: 245
SALES (corp-wide): 14.44B **Publicly Held**
Web: www.socalgas.com
SIC: 4924 Natural gas distribution
HQ: Southern California Gas Company
555 W 5th St Ste 14h1
Los Angeles CA
213 244-1200

(P-12100)
SOUTHERN CALIFORNIA GAS TOWER
555 W 5th St (90013-1010)
PHONE..............................213 244-1200
Ed Guiles, *Pr*
EMP: 1000 EST: 1987
SALES (est): 133.19MM
SALES (corp-wide): 14.44B **Publicly Held**
SIC: 4924 Natural gas distribution
HQ: Southern California Gas Company
555 W 5th St Ste 14h1
Los Angeles CA
213 244-1200

4931 Electric And Other Services Combined

(P-12101)
AMERICAN GREEN LIGHTS LLC
Also Called: American Green Lights
10755 Scripps Poway Pkwy Ste 419 (92131)
PHONE..............................858 547-8837
EMP: 25 EST: 2008
SQ FT: 25,000
SALES (est): 4.8MM **Privately Held**
Web: www.americangreenlights.com
SIC: 4931 3648 3646 Electric and other services combined; Outdoor lighting equipment; Commercial lighting fixtures

(P-12102)
CALPINE ENERGY SOLUTIONS LLC (DH)
401 W A St Ste 500 (92101-7991)
PHONE..............................877 273-6772
EMP: 104 EST: 2006
SALES (est): 403.3MM
SALES (corp-wide): 10.07B **Privately Held**
Web: www.calpinesolutions.com
SIC: 4931 4932 Electric and other services combined; Gas and other services combined
HQ: Calpine Corporation
717 Texas St Ste 1000

Houston TX
713 830-2000

(P-12103)
CITY OF BURBANK
Also Called: Burbank Water & Power
164 W Magnolia Blvd (91502-1772)
PHONE..............................818 238-3550
Ronald E Davis, *Brnch Mgr*
EMP: 315
SALES (corp-wide): 259.01MM **Privately Held**
Web: www.burbankwaterandpower.com
SIC: 4931 4941 4911 7389 Electric and other services combined; Water supply; Electric services; Interior design services
PA: City Of Burbank
275 E Olive Ave
Burbank CA
818 238-5800

(P-12104)
CITY OF CORONADO
Also Called: Public Services
101 B Ave (92118-1510)
PHONE..............................619 522-7380
EMP: 118
SALES (corp-wide): 62.19MM **Privately Held**
Web: www.coronado.ca.us
SIC: 4931 9111 Electric and other services combined; Mayors' office
PA: City Of Coronado
1825 Strand Way
Coronado CA
619 522-7300

(P-12105)
SAN DIEGO GAS & ELECTRIC CO
Also Called: Supplier Diversity
8315 Century Park Ct Ste Cp-21d (92123-1548)
PHONE..............................866 616-5565
EMP: 131
SALES (corp-wide): 14.44B **Publicly Held**
Web: www.sdge.com
SIC: 4931 4911 Electric and other services combined; Generation, electric power
HQ: San Diego Gas & Electric Company
8330 Century Park Ct
San Diego CA
619 696-2000

(P-12106)
SAN DIEGO GAS & ELECTRIC CO (DH)
Also Called: SDG&E
8330 Century Park Ct (92123-1530)
PHONE..............................619 696-2000
TOLL FREE: 800
Caroline A Winn, *CEO*
Jessie J Knight Junior, *Ch Bd*
Scott D Drury, *
Steven D Davis, *
J Chris Baker, *Chief Information Technology Officer**
◆ EMP: 254 EST: 1905
SALES (est): 5.84B
SALES (corp-wide): 14.44B **Publicly Held**
Web: www.sdge.com
SIC: 4931 4911 4924 Electric and other services combined; Generation, electric power; Natural gas distribution
HQ: Enova Corporation
101 Ash St
San Diego CA

(P-12107)

SAN DIEGO GAS & ELECTRIC CO

Also Called: Orange County Service Center
662 Camino De Los Mares (92673-2827)
PHONE..................................949 361-8090
James Valentine, *Brnch Mgr*
EMP: 126
SALES (corp-wide): 14.44B **Publicly Held**
Web: www.sdge.com
SIC: **4931** 4911 Electric and other services combined; Electric services
HQ: San Diego Gas & Electric Company
8330 Century Park Ct
San Diego CA
619 696-2000

4932 Gas And Other Services Combined

(P-12108)

SEMPRA (PA)

488 8th Ave (92101-7123)
PHONE..................................619 696-2000
Jeffrey W Martin, *Ch Bd*
Karen L Sedgwick, *Chief Human Resources Officer*
Trevor I Mihalik, *Ex VP*
Kevin C Sagara, *Group President*
Peter R Wall, *CAO*
EMP: 1000 **EST:** 1998
SALES (est): 14.44B
SALES (corp-wide): 14.44B **Publicly Held**
Web: www.sempra.com
SIC: **4932** 4911 5172 4922 Gas and other services combined; Electric services; Petroleum products, nec; Natural gas transmission

4939 Combination Utilities, Nec

(P-12109)

AGILE SOURCING PARTNERS INC

Also Called: Agile
2385 Railroad St (92878-5411)
PHONE..................................951 279-4154
Jeff Giffen, *CEO*
Maria Thompson, *
EMP: 225 **EST:** 2006
SQ FT: 2,300
SALES (est): 77.04MM **Privately Held**
Web: www.agilesourcingpartners.com
SIC: **4939** Combination utilities, nec

(P-12110)

IMPERIAL IRRIGATION DISTRICT

81600 58th Ave (92253-7663)
P.O. Box 1080 (92247-1080)
PHONE..................................760 398-5811
Charles Haskin, *Genl Mgr*
EMP: 108
SALES (corp-wide): 859.47MM **Privately Held**
Web: www.iid.com
SIC: **4939** 4911 Combination utilities, nec; Electric services
PA: Imperial Irrigation District
333 E Barioni Blvd
Imperial CA
800 303-7756

(P-12111)

LOS ANGELES DEPT WTR & PWR

Also Called: Scattergood Generation Plant

12700 Vista Del Mar (90293-8502)
PHONE..................................310 524-8500
EMP: 1050
Web: www.ladwp.com
SIC: **4939** Combination utilities, nec
HQ: Los Angeles Department Of Water And Power
111 N Hope St
Los Angeles CA
213 367-1320

(P-12112)

SAN DIEGO GAS & ELECTRIC CO

North Coast O & M Center
5016 Carlsbad Blvd (92008-4303)
PHONE..................................760 438-6200
Jim Boland, *Dir*
EMP: 196
SALES (corp-wide): 14.44B **Publicly Held**
Web: www.sdge.com
SIC: **4939** 4924 4911 Combination utilities, nec; Natural gas distribution; Electric services
HQ: San Diego Gas & Electric Company
8330 Century Park Ct
San Diego CA
619 696-2000

(P-12113)

SAN DIEGO GAS & ELECTRIC CO

Also Called: SDG&e
436 H St (91910-4308)
PHONE..................................858 654-1135
Charles Johnson, *Crdt Mgr*
EMP: 241
SALES (corp-wide): 14.44B **Publicly Held**
Web: www.sdge.com
SIC: **4939** Combination utilities, nec
HQ: San Diego Gas & Electric Company
8330 Century Park Ct
San Diego CA
619 696-2000

4941 Water Supply

(P-12114)

AMERICAN STATES WATER COMPANY (PA)

Also Called: AWR
630 E Foothill Blvd (91773-1207)
PHONE..................................909 394-3600
Robert J Sprowls, *Pr*
Anne M Holloway, *
Eva G Tang, *Corporate Secretary*
EMP: 568 **EST:** 1929
SALES (est): 491.53MM
SALES (corp-wide): 491.53MM **Publicly Held**
Web: americanstateswatercompany.gcs-web.com
SIC: **4941** 4911 Water supply; Electric services

(P-12115)

COACHLLA VLY WTR DST PUB FCLTI

75525 Hovley Ln E (92260)
PHONE..................................760 398-2651
Steve Robins, *Brnch Mgr*
EMP: 172
SALES (corp-wide): 185.22MM **Privately Held**
Web: www.cvwd.org
SIC: **4941** 4952 4971 Water supply; Sewerage systems; Irrigation systems

PA: Coachella Valley Water District Public Facilities Corporation
75515 Hovley Ln E
Palm Desert CA
760 398-2651

(P-12116)

COACHLLA VLY WTR DST PUB FCLTI (PA)

Also Called: Coachella Valley Water Dst
75515 Hovley Ln E (92211-5104)
P.O. Box 1058 (92236-1058)
PHONE..................................760 398-2651
TOLL FREE: 888
James M Barrett, *Genl Mgr*
Steve Robbins, *Interim General Manager**
Amy Ammons, *Finance**
Jim Barrett, *
Isabel Luna, *
▲ EMP: 225 **EST:** 1918
SALES (est): 185.22MM
SALES (corp-wide): 185.22MM **Privately Held**
Web: www.cvwd.org
SIC: **4941** 4971 4952 7389 Water supply; Water distribution or supply systems for irrigation; Sewerage systems; Water softener service

(P-12117)

COUNTY OF LOS ANGELES

Also Called: Water & Power Department
6801 E 2nd St (90803-4324)
PHONE..................................213 367-3176
Victor Barra, *Dir*
EMP: 91
SALES (corp-wide): 31.7B **Privately Held**
Web: www.lacounty.gov
SIC: **4941** 9511 9631 4939 Water supply; Air, water, and solid waste management; Regulation, administration of utilities; Combination utilities, nec
PA: County Of Los Angeles
500 W Temple St Ste 437
Los Angeles CA
213 974-1101

(P-12118)

COUNTY OF LOS ANGELES

Also Called: Department of Public Works
900 S Fremont Ave (91803-1331)
P.O. Box 1460 (91802-2460)
PHONE..................................626 458-4000
Gail Farber, *Dir*
EMP: 300
Web: www.ladpw.org
SIC: **4941** 9511 4971 Water supply; Air, water, and solid waste management; Irrigation systems
PA: County Of Los Angeles
500 W Temple St Ste 437
Los Angeles CA
213 974-1101

(P-12119)

CUCAMONGA VALLEY WATER DST

10440 Ashford St (91730-3057)
P.O. Box 638 (91729-0638)
PHONE..................................909 987-2591
Martin Zvirbulis, *CEO*
Kathleen Tiegs, *
Oscar Gonzalez, *
EMP: 100 **EST:** 1955
SQ FT: 15,000
SALES (est): 105.19MM **Privately Held**
Web: www.cvwdwater.com
SIC: **4941** Water supply

(P-12120)

DESERT WATER AGENCY FING CORP

Also Called: DWA
1200 S Gene Autry Trl (92264-3533)
P.O. Box 1710 (92263-1710)
PHONE..................................760 323-4971
Patricia G Oyga, *CEO*
Craig Ewing Undetermined, *Prin*
EMP: 88 **EST:** 2007
SQ FT: 38,000
SALES (est): 41.87MM **Privately Held**
Web: www.dwa.org
SIC: **4941** Water supply

(P-12121)

EASTERN MUNICIPAL WATER DST

19750 Evans Rd (92571-7469)
PHONE..................................951 657-7469
Paul D Jones Ii, *Brnch Mgr*
EMP: 200
SALES (corp-wide): 298.85MM **Privately Held**
Web: www.emwd.org
SIC: **4941** Water supply
PA: Eastern Municipal Water District
2270 Trumble Rd
Perris CA
951 928-3777

(P-12122)

EASTERN MUNICIPAL WATER DST (PA)

2270 Trumble Rd (92572)
P.O. Box 8300 (92572-8300)
PHONE..................................951 928-3777
Paul D Jones Ii, *CEO*
▲ EMP: 420 **EST:** 1950
SQ FT: 160,000
SALES (est): 298.85MM
SALES (corp-wide): 298.85MM **Privately Held**
Web: www.emwd.org
SIC: **4941** 4952 Water supply; Sewerage systems

(P-12123)

INLAND EMPIRE UTLTIES AGCY A M (PA)

6075 Kimball Ave (91708-9174)
P.O. Box 9020 (91709-0902)
PHONE..................................909 993-1600
Shivaji Deshmukh, *CEO*
Kati Parker, *
John Anderson, *
Michael Camacho, *
Wyatt Troxel, *
EMP: 92 **EST:** 1950
SQ FT: 60,000
SALES (est): 160.44MM
SALES (corp-wide): 160.44MM **Privately Held**
Web: www.ieua.org
SIC: **4941** Water supply

(P-12124)

IRVINE RANCH WATER DISTRICT

3512 Michelson Dr (92612-1757)
P.O. Box 14128 (92623-4128)
PHONE..................................949 453-5300
Carl Ballard, *Dir*
EMP: 205
SALES (corp-wide): 88.94MM **Privately Held**
Web: www.irwd.com
SIC: **4941** 4952 Water supply; Sewerage systems
PA: Irvine Ranch Water District Inc
15600 Sand Canyon Ave

Irvine CA
949 453-5300

(P-12125)
IRVINE RANCH WATER DISTRICT (PA)
15600 Sand Canyon Ave (92618-3100)
P.O. Box 57000 (92619-7000)
PHONE..................................949 453-5300
Paul Jones, *Genl Mgr*
Robert Jacobson, *
EMP: 110 **EST:** 1961
SQ FT: 52,000
SALES (est): 88.94MM
SALES (corp-wide): 88.94MM **Privately Held**
Web: www.irwd.com
SIC: 4941 4952 Water supply; Sewerage systems

(P-12126)
JURUPA COMMUNITY SERVICES DST
11201 Harrel St (92509)
PHONE..................................951 685-7073
EMP: 89
SALES (corp-wide): 13.88MM **Privately Held**
SIC: 4941 4952 Water supply; Sewerage systems
PA: Jurupa Community Services District
11201 Harrel St
Jurupa Valley CA
951 360-5770

(P-12127)
LAS VIRGENES MUNICIPAL WTR DST
4232 Las Virgenes Rd Lbby (91302-3594)
PHONE..................................818 251-2100
Glen Peterson, *Pr*
Charles Caspary, *
Lee Renger, *
Jay Lewitt, *
Leonard E Polan, *
EMP: 125 **EST:** 1958
SQ FT: 10,000
SALES (est): 67.09MM **Privately Held**
Web: www.lvmwd.com
SIC: 4941 Water supply

(P-12128)
LOS ANGELES DEPT WTR & PWR (HQ)
Also Called: Ladwp
111 N Hope St (90012-2607)
P.O. Box 51111 (90051-5700)
PHONE..................................213 367-1320
Martin Adams, *Genl Mgr*
David H Wright, *
Joseph A Brajevich, *
▲ **EMP:** 897 **EST:** 1902
SALES (est): 1.06B **Privately Held**
Web: www.ladwp.com
SIC: 4941 4911 Water supply; Electric services
PA: City Of Los Angeles
200 N Spring St Ste 303
Los Angeles CA
213 978-0600

(P-12129)
LOS ANGELES DEPT WTR & PWR
1141 W 2nd St Bldg D (90012-2007)
PHONE..................................213 367-5706
Carol Tharp, *Brnch Mgr*
EMP: 1050
Web: www.ladwp.com

SIC: 4941 Water supply
HQ: Los Angeles Department Of Water And Power
111 N Hope St
Los Angeles CA
213 367-1320

(P-12130)
LOS ANGELES DEPT WTR & PWR
4030 Crenshaw Blvd (90008-2533)
P.O. Box 51211 (90051-5511)
PHONE..................................323 256-8079
EMP: 1576
Web: www.ladwp.com
SIC: 4941 4911 Water supply; Electric services
HQ: Los Angeles Department Of Water And Power
111 N Hope St
Los Angeles CA
213 367-1320

(P-12131)
LOS ANGELES DEPT WTR & PWR
11801 Sheldon St (91352-1508)
PHONE..................................213 367-1342
Kirk Bergland, *Brnch Mgr*
EMP: 1050
Web: www.ladwp.com
SIC: 4941 Water supply
HQ: Los Angeles Department Of Water And Power
111 N Hope St
Los Angeles CA
213 367-1320

(P-12132)
LOS ANGELES DEPT WTR & PWR
1630 N Main St (90012-1936)
PHONE..................................213 367-4211
Paul Abram, *Mgr*
▲ **EMP:** 875
Web: www.ladwp.com
SIC: 4941 4911 Water supply; Electric services
HQ: Los Angeles Department Of Water And Power
111 N Hope St
Los Angeles CA
213 367-1320

(P-12133)
METROPLTAN WTR DST OF STHERN C
Also Called: Metropolitan Water Lavern
700 Moreno Ave (91750-3303)
P.O. Box 54153 (90054-0153)
PHONE..................................909 593-7474
Wendell Williams, *Brnch Mgr*
EMP: 370
SALES (corp-wide): 597.83MM **Privately Held**
Web: www.mwdh2o.com
SIC: 4941 Water supply
PA: The Metropolitan Water District Of Southern California
700 N Alameda St
Los Angeles CA
213 217-6000

(P-12134)
METROPLTAN WTR DST OF STHERN C
Also Called: Robert B Diemer Trtmnt Plant
3972 Valley View Ave (92886-1828)
PHONE..................................714 577-5031

Trudi Loy, *Mgr*
EMP: 83
SALES (corp-wide): 597.83MM **Privately Held**
Web: www.mwdh2o.com
SIC: 4941 Water supply
PA: The Metropolitan Water District Of Southern California
700 N Alameda St
Los Angeles CA
213 217-6000

(P-12135)
MOULTON NGUEL WTR DST PUB FCLT
Also Called: Moulton Niguel Water District
26161 Gordon Rd (92653-8224)
P.O. Box 30203 (92607-0203)
PHONE..................................949 831-2500
Richard Fiore, *Pr*
David Cain, *
John V Foley, *
EMP: 97 **EST:** 1960
SALES (est): 72.49MM **Privately Held**
Web: www.mnwd.com
SIC: 4941 4959 Water supply; Sanitary services, nec

(P-12136)
OTAY WATER DISTRICT
2554 Sweetwater Springs Blvd (91978-2004)
PHONE..................................619 670-2222
Gary Croucher, *Pr*
Jose Lopez, *
Mark Watton, *
German Alvarez, *
Manny Magana, *
EMP: 170 **EST:** 1956
SQ FT: 6,000
SALES (est): 108.75MM **Privately Held**
Web: www.otaywater.gov
SIC: 4941 1623 Water supply; Water, sewer, and utility lines

(P-12137)
PALMDALE WATER DISTRICT
2029 E Avenue Q (93550-4050)
PHONE..................................661 947-4111
Michael Williams, *CFO*
Dennis Hoffmeyer, *
EMP: 93 **EST:** 1991
SALES (est): 31.32MM **Privately Held**
Web: www.palmdalewater.org
SIC: 4941 Water supply

(P-12138)
PUBLIC AUTHORITY
401 Mile Of Cars Way Ste 200 (91950-6612)
PHONE..................................619 731-3705
Andrea Villa, *Prin*
EMP: 100 **EST:** 2016
SALES (est): 955.28K **Privately Held**
Web: www.sdihsspa.com
SIC: 4941 Water supply

(P-12139)
RANCHO CALIFORNIA WATER DST (PA)
Also Called: RCWD
42135 Winchester Rd (92590-4800)
P.O. Box 9017 (92589-9017)
PHONE..................................951 296-6900
William E Plummer, *Prin*
Bennet Drake, *Pr*
Stephen J Corona, *Pr*
Ralph Daily, *Pr*
John E Hoagland, *VP*
EMP: 143 **EST:** 1965

SQ FT: 71,000
SALES (est): 72.48MM
SALES (corp-wide): 72.48MM **Privately Held**
Web: www.ranchowater.com
SIC: 4941 Water supply

(P-12140)
SAN DIEGO COUNTY WATER AUTH
610 W 5th Ave (92025-4093)
PHONE..................................760 480-1991
Brendan Sheehan, *Pr*
EMP: 184
SALES (corp-wide): 105.74MM **Privately Held**
Web: www.sdcwa.org
SIC: 4941 Water supply
PA: San Diego County Water Authority
4677 Overland Ave
San Diego CA
858 522-6600

(P-12141)
SAN DIEGO COUNTY WATER AUTH (PA)
4677 Overland Ave (92123-1233)
PHONE..................................858 522-6600
Maureen Stapleton, *Genl Mgr*
Dennis Cushman, *
Eric Sandler, *
Sandy Kerl, *
Mark Muir, *
▲ **EMP:** 96 **EST:** 1944
SQ FT: 26,000
SALES (est): 105.74MM
SALES (corp-wide): 105.74MM **Privately Held**
Web: www.sdcwa.org
SIC: 4941 Water supply

(P-12142)
SAN GABRIEL VALLEY WATER ASSN
725 N Azusa Ave (91702-2528)
PHONE..................................626 815-1305
EMP: 100 **EST:** 1955
SALES (est): 251.12K **Privately Held**
Web: www.sgvwa.org
SIC: 4941 Water supply

(P-12143)
SAN GABRIEL VALLEY WATER CO
8440 Nuevo Ave (92335-3824)
P.O. Box 987 (92334-0987)
PHONE..................................909 822-2201
Mike Mcgraw, *Mgr*
EMP: 116
SQ FT: 2,727
SALES (corp-wide): 48.82MM **Privately Held**
Web: www.sgvwater.com
SIC: 4941 Water supply
PA: San Gabriel Valley Water Co.
11142 Garvey Ave
El Monte CA
626 448-6183

(P-12144)
SAN GABRIEL VALLEY WATER CO (PA)
Also Called: Fontana Water Company
11142 Garvey Ave (91733-2425)
P.O. Box 6010 (91734-2010)
PHONE..................................626 448-6183
R H Nicholson Junior, *Ch Bd*
Michael L Whitehead, *Pr*
David Batt, *VP*

PRODUCTS & SVCS

Frank A Lo Guidice, *VP Opers*
T J Ryan, *Sec*
EMP: 125 **EST:** 1936
SQ FT: 30,000
SALES (est): 48.82MM
SALES (corp-wide): 48.82MM **Privately Held**
Web: www.sgvwater.com
SIC: 4941 Water supply

(P-12145)
SANTA CLARITA VALLEY WTR AGCY
Also Called: Santa Clarita Water Division
26521 Summit Cir (91350-3049)
PHONE.................661 259-2737
Mauricio E Guardado Junior, *Prin*
EMP: 160
SALES (corp-wide): 87.54MM **Privately Held**
Web: www.yourscvwater.com
SIC: 4941 Water supply
PA: Santa Clarita Valley Water Agency
27234 Bouquet Canyon Rd
Santa Clarita CA
661 297-1600

(P-12146)
SANTA CLRITA VLY WTR AGCY FING
27234 Bouquet Canyon Rd (91350-2173)
PHONE.................661 259-2737
Tom Campbell, *CEO*
Ronald J Kelly, *
April Jacobs, *
Dan Masnada, *
William Cooper, *
EMP: 120 **EST:** 1962
SQ FT: 1,000
SALES (est): 30.93MM **Privately Held**
Web: www.yourscvwater.com
SIC: 4941 Water supply

(P-12147)
SANTA MARGARITA WATER DISTRICT
26101 Antonio Pkwy (92688-5505)
P.O. Box 7005 (92690-7005)
PHONE.................949 459-6400
EMP: 135
Web: www.smwd.com
SIC: 4941 Water supply
PA: Santa Margarita Water District
26111 Antonio Pkwy
Rcho Sta Marg CA
949 459-6400

(P-12148)
SWEETWTER AUTH EMPLYEES CMMTTE (PA)
505 Garrett Ave (91910-5505)
P.O. Box 2328 (91912-2328)
PHONE.................619 420-1413
Mark Rogers, *Ex Dir*
James Smyth, *
Teresa Thomas, *
W D Pocklington, *
Margaret C Welsh, *
EMP: 112 **EST:** 2004
SALES (est): 55.39MM
SALES (corp-wide): 55.39MM **Privately Held**
Web: www.sweetwater.org
SIC: 4941 Water supply

(P-12149)
SWWC UTILITIES INC (DH)
1325 N Grand Ave Ste 100 (91724-4044)
EMP: 173 **EST:** 2007

SQ FT: 32,000
SALES (est): 94.48MM **Privately Held**
Web: www.swwc.com
SIC: 4941 4952 Water supply; Sewerage systems
HQ: Southwest Water Company
1325 N Grand Ave Ste 100
Covina CA
626 543-2500

(P-12150)
THE METROPOLITAN WATER DISTRICT OF SOUTHERN CALIFORNIA (PA)
Also Called: Mwd
700 N Alameda St (90012-2944)
P.O. Box 54153 (90054-0153)
PHONE.................213 217-6000
EMP: 850 **EST:** 1928
SALES (est): 597.83MM
SALES (corp-wide): 597.83MM **Privately Held**
Web: www.mwdh2o.com
SIC: 4941 Water supply

(P-12151)
VALLECITOS WATER DISTRICT FINANCING CORPORATION (HQ)
Also Called: Vallecitos Water District
201 Vallecitos De Oro (92069-1453)
PHONE.................760 744-0460
EMP: 96 **EST:** 1955
SALES (est): 69.93MM **Privately Held**
Web: www.vwd.org
SIC: 4941 4952 Water supply; Sewerage systems
PA: Vallecitos Water District
201 Vallecitos De Oro
San Marcos CA

4952 Sewerage Systems

(P-12152)
HADRONEX INC
Also Called: Smartcover Systems
2110 Enterprise St (92029-2000)
PHONE.................760 291-1980
David Drake, *Pr*
Gregory Quist, *
EMP: 33 **EST:** 2006
SALES (est): 11.83MM **Privately Held**
Web: www.smartcoversystems.com
SIC: 4952 3594 Sewerage systems; Fluid power motors

4953 Refuse Systems

(P-12153)
AGRI SERVICE INC
3720 Oceanic Way Ste 204 (92056-2653)
PHONE.................760 295-6255
Mary Matava, *Pr*
Francesca San Diego, *
EMP: 24 **EST:** 1979
SQ FT: 1,700
SALES (est): 6.6MM **Privately Held**
Web: www.agriserviceinc.com
SIC: 4953 2875 Recycling, waste materials; Potting soil, mixed

(P-12154)
ARACO ENTERPRISES LLC
Also Called: Athens Environmental Services
9189 De Garmo Ave (91352-2609)
PHONE.................818 767-0675
Michael R Arakelian, *
EMP: 400 **EST:** 2017
SALES (est): 24.71MM **Privately Held**

SIC: 4953 Garbage: collecting, destroying, and processing

(P-12155)
ARAKELIAN ENTERPRISES INC
Also Called: Athens Services
15045 Salt Lake Ave (91746-3315)
PHONE.................626 336-3636
Ron Arakelian Junior, *Owner*
EMP: 377
SALES (corp-wide): 199.65MM **Privately Held**
Web: www.athensservices.com
SIC: 4953 Rubbish collection and disposal
PA: Arakelian Enterprises, Inc.
14048 Valley Blvd
City Of Industry CA
626 336-3636

(P-12156)
ARAKELIAN ENTERPRISES INC (PA)
Also Called: Athens Services
14048 Valley Blvd (91746-2801)
P.O. Box 60009 (91716-0009)
PHONE.................626 336-3636
Ron Arakelian Junior, *CEO*
Michael Arakelian, *
Kevin Hanifin, *
Gary Clifford, *
Dennis Chiappetta, *
EMP: 311 **EST:** 1958
SQ FT: 10,000
SALES (est): 199.65MM
SALES (corp-wide): 199.65MM **Privately Held**
Web: www.athensservices.com
SIC: 4953 Recycling, waste materials

(P-12157)
ARAKELIAN ENTERPRISES INC
687 Iowa Ave (92507-1610)
PHONE.................951 342-3300
Sal Orozco, *Mgr*
EMP: 119
SALES (corp-wide): 199.65MM **Privately Held**
Web: www.athensservices.com
SIC: 4953 Recycling, waste materials
PA: Arakelian Enterprises, Inc.
14048 Valley Blvd
City Of Industry CA
626 336-3636

(P-12158)
ATHENS DISPOSAL COMPANY INC (PA)
14048 Valley Blvd (91746-2801)
P.O. Box 60009 (91716-0009)
PHONE.................626 336-3636
Ron Arakelian Senior, *Pr*
Ron Arakelian Junior, *VP*
EMP: 350 **EST:** 1958
SALES (est): 78.22MM
SALES (corp-wide): 78.22MM **Privately Held**
SIC: 4953 Recycling, waste materials

(P-12159)
BEST WAY DISPOSAL CO INC
Also Called: Advance Disposal Company
17105 Mesa St (92345-5155)
P.O. Box 400997 (92340-0997)
PHONE.................760 244-9773
Robert Bath, *Ch Bd*
Sheila Bath, *
EMP: 103 **EST:** 1965
SALES (est): 12.66MM **Privately Held**
Web: www.advancedisposal.com

SIC: 4953 Garbage: collecting, destroying, and processing

(P-12160)
BURRTEC WASTE INDUSTRIES INC (HQ)
Also Called: Burrtec
9890 Cherry Ave (92335-5202)
PHONE.................909 429-4200
Cole Burr, *Pr*
▲ **EMP:** 150 **EST:** 1978
SQ FT: 10,000
SALES (est): 307.49MM
SALES (corp-wide): 320.11MM **Privately Held**
Web: www.burrtec.com
SIC: 4953 4212 Rubbish collection and disposal; Local trucking, without storage
PA: Burrtec Waste Group, Inc.
9890 Cherry Ave
Fontana CA
909 429-4200

(P-12161)
BURRTEC WASTE INDUSTRIES INC
Also Called: Jack's Disposal Inc
5455 Industrial Pkwy (92407-1803)
PHONE.................909 889-1969
Cole Burr, *Pr*
James Avakian, *
Jack Avakian Junior, *Sec*
Joseph Avakian, *
EMP: 215 **EST:** 1951
SQ FT: 500
SALES (est): 3.38MM
SALES (corp-wide): 3.38MM **Privately Held**
Web: www.burrtec.com
SIC: 4953 Rubbish collection and disposal
PA: Burr Group, Inc.
9890 Cherry Ave
Fontana CA
909 429-4200

(P-12162)
CALIFORNIA MARINE CLEANING INC (PA)
2049 Main St (92113-2216)
P.O. Box 13653 (92170-3653)
PHONE.................619 231-8788
Matthew R Carr, *Pr*
Hazel Carr, *
EMP: 110 **EST:** 1985
SQ FT: 10,000
SALES (est): 41.23MM
SALES (corp-wide): 41.23MM **Privately Held**
Web: www.marinecleaning.com
SIC: 4953 Hazardous waste collection and disposal

(P-12163)
CALIFORNIA WASTE SERVICES LLC
621 W 152nd St (90247-2732)
PHONE.................310 538-5998
Eric Casper, *Pr*
EMP: 120 **EST:** 1999
SQ FT: 20,000
SALES (est): 24.33MM **Privately Held**
Web: www.californiawasteservices.com
SIC: 4953 Refuse collection and disposal services

(P-12164)
CALMET INC (PA)
Also Called: Metropolitan Waste Disposal
7202 Petterson Ln (90723-2022)

PHONE.............................323 721-8120
Thomas K Blackman, *Pr*
William Kalpakoff, *VP*
Kris Kazarian, *Sec*
Gary Kazarian, *Treas*
EMP: 180 **EST:** 1953
SQ FT: 38,000
SALES (est): 14.63MM
SALES (corp-wide): 14.63MM **Privately Held**
Web: www.calmet.com
SIC: 4953 4212 Rubbish collection and disposal; Local trucking, without storage

(P-12165)
CEDARWOOD-YOUNG COMPANY (PA)
Also Called: Allan Company
14620 Joanbridge St (91706-1750)
PHONE.............................626 962-4047
Jason Young, *Pr*
Stephen Young, *Ch*
Michael Ochniak, *CFO*
Richard Hubbard, *VP Opers*
Don Rogers, *VP Mktg*
◆ **EMP:** 175 **EST:** 1963
SQ FT: 4,350
SALES (est): 252.16MM
SALES (corp-wide): 252.16MM **Privately Held**
Web: www.allancompany.com
SIC: 4953 Recycling, waste materials

(P-12166)
COVANTA LONG BCH RNWBLE ENRGY
118 Pier S Ave (90802-1039)
PHONE.............................562 436-0636
▲ **EMP:** 124 **EST:** 2013
SALES (est): 9.81MM
SALES (corp-wide): 1.91B **Privately Held**
SIC: 4953 Recycling, waste materials
HQ: Covanta Energy, Llc
445 South St
Morristown NJ
862 345-5000

(P-12167)
E J HARRISON & SONS INC
Also Called: Harrison, E J & Sons Recycling
1589 Lirio Ave (93004-3227)
PHONE.............................805 647-1414
TOLL FREE: 800
Ken Keys, *Genl Mgr*
EMP: 173
SALES (corp-wide): 24.61MM **Privately Held**
Web: www.ejharrison.com
SIC: 4953 2611 Rubbish collection and disposal; Pulp mills
PA: E. J. Harrison & Sons, Inc.
5275 Colt St
Ventura CA
805 647-1414

(P-12168)
ECOLOGY RECYCLING SERVICES LLC
785 E M St (92324-3911)
PHONE.............................909 370-1318
EMP: 168
SALES (corp-wide): 12.79B **Publicly Held**
SIC: 4953 Recycling, waste materials
HQ: Ecology Recycling Services, Llc
16700 Valley View Ave # 340
La Mirada CA
562 921-9975

(P-12169)
EDCO DISPOSAL CORPORATION (PA)
Also Called: La Mesa Disposal
2755 California Ave (90755-3304)
PHONE.............................619 287-7555
Steve South, *CEO*
Edward Burr, *
Sandra Burr, *
EMP: 250 **EST:** 1967
SQ FT: 8,000
SALES (est): 134.33MM
SALES (corp-wide): 134.33MM **Privately Held**
Web: www.edcodisposal.com
SIC: 4953 Rubbish collection and disposal

(P-12170)
FLAT WHITE ECONOMY INV USA LLC
5151 California Ave Ste 100 (92626)
PHONE.............................949 344-5013
EMP: 165 **EST:** 2016
SALES (est): 1MM **Privately Held**
SIC: 4953 Recycling, waste materials

(P-12171)
IMS ELECTRONICS RECYCLING INC
Also Called: I M S Electonics Recycling
12455 Kerran St Ste 300 (92064-8834)
PHONE.............................858 679-1555
▼ **EMP:** 102
SIC: 4953 Recycling, waste materials

(P-12172)
MARBORG INDUSTRIES (PA)
728 E Yanonali St (93103-3233)
P.O. Box 4127 (93140-4127)
PHONE.............................805 963-1852
Mario Borgatello Junior, *Pr*
David Borgatello, *
EMP: 250 **EST:** 1974
SALES (est): 52.32MM
SALES (corp-wide): 52.32MM **Privately Held**
Web: www.marborg.com
SIC: 4953 7359 7699 4212 Rubbish collection and disposal; Portable toilet rental; Septic tank cleaning service; Local trucking, without storage

(P-12173)
MARBORG RECOVERY LP
14470 Calle Real (93117-9732)
PHONE.............................805 963-1852
Brian Borgatello, *Pt*
EMP: 250 **EST:** 2016
SALES (est): 51.57MM
SALES (corp-wide): 52.32MM **Privately Held**
Web: www.marborg.com
SIC: 4953 Recycling, waste materials
PA: Marborg Industries
728 E Yanonali St
Santa Barbara CA
805 963-1852

(P-12174)
MP ENVIRONMENTAL SVCS INC (PA)
3400 Manor St (93308-1451)
P.O. Box 80358 (93380-0358)
PHONE.............................800 458-3036
Dawn Calderwood, *Pr*
▲ **EMP:** 117 **EST:** 1991
SQ FT: 8,000
SALES (est): 92.88MM **Privately Held**
Web: www.mpenviro.com

SIC: 4953 4213 8748 7699 Hazardous waste collection and disposal; Trucking, except local; Environmental consultant; Tank repair and cleaning services

(P-12175)
NORCAL WASTE SERVICES INC
3514 Emery St (90023-3908)
PHONE.............................626 357-8666
John Harabedian, *Genl Mgr*
EMP: 100 **EST:** 1982
SALES (est): 6.11MM **Privately Held**
SIC: 4953 Rubbish collection and disposal

(P-12176)
ORANGE COUNTY SANITATION (PA)
10844 Ellis Ave (92708-7018)
P.O. Box 8127 (92728-8127)
PHONE.............................714 962-2411
James Herberg, *Genl Mgr*
James Ruth, *
▲ **EMP:** 300 **EST:** 1954
SALES (est): 315.43MM
SALES (corp-wide): 315.43MM **Privately Held**
Web: www.ocsan.gov
SIC: 4953 Waste materials, disposal at sea

(P-12177)
PALM SPRINGS DISPOSAL SERVICES
4690 E Mesquite Ave (92264-3510)
P.O. Box 2711 (92263-2711)
PHONE.............................760 327-1351
Frederic Wade, *CEO*
James Cunningham, *
Ray Wade, *
Mike Jaycox, *
EMP: 82 **EST:** 1972
SQ FT: 2,000
SALES (est): 14.08MM **Privately Held**
Web: www.palmspringsdisposal.com
SIC: 4953 Recycling, waste materials

(P-12178)
PAVEMENT COATINGS CO
Also Called: Pavement Coatings Co
736 Mission Rock Rd (93060-9762)
PHONE.............................805 647-0693
EMP: 233
SALES (corp-wide): 53.85MM **Privately Held**
Web: www.pavementrecycling.com
SIC: 4953 Recycling, waste materials
PA: Pavement Coatings Co.
10240 San Sevaine Way
Jurupa Valley CA
714 826-3011

(P-12179)
POTENTIAL INDUSTRIES INC (PA)
720 East E St (90744-6014)
P.O. Box 293 (90748-0293)
PHONE.............................310 549-5901
Anthony J Fan, *Pr*
Phillip C Chen, *Vice Chairman*
Daniel J Domonoske, *
Henry J Chen, *
Jessie Chen, *
◆ **EMP:** 149 **EST:** 1975
SQ FT: 45,000
SALES (est): 42.15MM
SALES (corp-wide): 42.15MM **Privately Held**
Web: www.potentialindustries.com
SIC: 4953 5093 Recycling, waste materials; Scrap and waste materials

(P-12180)
R PLANET EARTH LLC
3200 Fruitland Ave (90058-3718)
PHONE.............................213 320-0601
EMP: 135 **EST:** 2013
SALES (est): 11.7MM **Privately Held**
Web: www.rplanetearth.com
SIC: 4953 2611 Recycling, waste materials; Pulp mills, mechanical and recycling processing

(P-12181)
RAINBOW DISPOSAL CO INC (HQ)
Also Called: Rainbow Refuse Recycling
17121 Nichols Ln (92647-5719)
P.O. Box 1026 (92647-1026)
PHONE.............................714 847-3581
Jerry Moffatt, *CEO*
Stan Tkaczyck, *
EMP: 115 **EST:** 1956
SQ FT: 6,000
SALES (est): 48.28MM
SALES (corp-wide): 13.51B **Publicly Held**
SIC: 4953 Garbage: collecting, destroying, and processing
PA: Republic Services, Inc.
18500 N Allied Way # 100
Phoenix AZ
480 627-2700

(P-12182)
RECOLOGY LOS ANGELES
Also Called: Recology
9189 De Garmo Ave (91352-2609)
PHONE.............................818 767-0675
EMP: 400 **EST:** 2006
SALES (est): 22.28MM **Privately Held**
SIC: 4953 Garbage: collecting, destroying, and processing

(P-12183)
RECYCLER CORE COMPANY INC
Also Called: Northwest Recycler Core
2727 Kansas Ave (92507-2638)
PHONE.............................951 276-1687
Kenneth Meier, *Pr*
Gisela Meier, *
Ruth Harris, *
▲ **EMP:** 100 **EST:** 1984
SQ FT: 280,000
SALES (est): 16.01MM **Privately Held**
Web: www.rccauto.com
SIC: 4953 Recycling, waste materials

(P-12184)
RERUBBER LLC
115 N Del Rosa Dr Ste C (92408-0192)
PHONE.............................909 786-2811
▲ **EMP:** 19 **EST:** 2007
SALES (est): 4.11MM **Privately Held**
Web: www.rerubber.com
SIC: 4953 3069 Recycling, waste materials; Type, rubber
PA: Enertech Solutions, Llc
30515 7th Ave
Redlands CA

(P-12185)
SA RECYCLING LLC (PA)
Also Called: SA Recycling
2411 N Glassell St (92865-2717)
PHONE.............................714 632-2000
George Adams, *CEO*
George Adams, *Managing Member*
Mark Sweetman, *
◆ **EMP:** 160 **EST:** 2007
SQ FT: 40,000

P R O D U C T S & S V C S

SALES (est): 742.73MM **Privately Held**
Web: www.sarecycling.com
SIC: 4953 Recycling, waste materials

(P-12186)
SANITTION DSTRCTS LOS ANGLES C
1955 Workman Mill Rd (90601-1415)
P.O. Box 4998 (90607-4998)
PHONE..................................562 908-4288
Steve Mcguin, *Mgr*
Grace Robinson Chan, *Genl Mgr*
EMP: 1698 EST: 2007
SALES (est): 467.68MM
SALES (corp-wide): 726.8MM **Privately Held**
Web: www.lacsd.org
SIC: 4953 Sanitary landfill operation
PA: Los Angeles County Sanitation Districts
1955 Workman Mill Rd
Whittier CA
562 699-7411

(P-12187)
SMC GREASE SPECIALIST INC
1600 W Pellisier Rd (92324-3301)
P.O. Box 79200 (92877-0173)
PHONE..................................951 788-6042
Salvatore Coco, *Pr*
EMP: 27 EST: 2003
SQ FT: 2,500
SALES (est): 4.48MM **Privately Held**
Web: www.smcgrease.com
SIC: 4953 2992 Recycling, waste materials;
Oils and greases, blending and
compounding

(P-12188)
SOLAG INCORPORATED
Also Called: Solag Disposal Co
31641 Ortege Hwy (92675)
PHONE..................................949 728-1206
Clifford Ronnenberg, *Ch Bd*
Patricia Leyes, *
EMP: 523 EST: 1958
SALES (est): 1.73MM
SALES (corp-wide): 335.28MM **Privately Held**
SIC: 4953 4212 Rubbish collection and
disposal; Local trucking, without storage
PA: Cr&R Incorporated
11292 Western Ave
Stanton CA
714 826-9049

(P-12189)
TALCO PLASTICS INC (PA)
1000 W Rincon St (92878-9228)
PHONE..................................951 531-2000
John L Shedd Senior, *Ch*
John L Shedd Junior, *Pr*
Bob Shedd, *
Ron Petty, *
William O'grady, *VP*
EMP: 85 EST: 1972
SQ FT: 110,000
SALES (est): 22.23MM
SALES (corp-wide): 22.23MM **Privately Held**
Web: www.talcoplastics.com
SIC: 4953 2821 Recycling, waste materials;
Plastics materials and resins

(P-12190)
USA WASTE OF CALIFORNIA INC
Also Called: Los Angeles City Hauling
9081 Tujunga Ave (91352-1516)
P.O. Box 541 (90078-0541)
PHONE..................................818 252-3112

Jim Fish, *CEO*
EMP: 100
SALES (corp-wide): 19.7B **Publicly Held**
SIC: 4953 Recycling, waste materials
HQ: Usa Waste Of California, Inc.
11931 Foundation Pl # 200
Gold River CA
916 387-1400

(P-12191)
VALLEY GARBAGE RUBBISH CO INC
Also Called: Healtth Sanitation Services
1850 W Betteravia Rd (93455-1065)
PHONE..................................805 614-1131
Keith Ramsey, *Prin*
EMP: 138 EST: 1957
SQ FT: 3,000
SALES (est): 50.39MM
SALES (corp-wide): 19.7B **Publicly Held**
Web: wmhss.wm.com
SIC: 4953 Garbage: collecting, destroying,
and processing
PA: Waste Management, Inc.
800 Capitol St Ste 3000
Houston TX
713 512-6200

(P-12192)
VARNER BROS INC
1808 Roberts Ln (93308-2228)
P.O. Box 80427 (93380-0427)
PHONE..................................661 399-2944
Vernon Varner, *Sec*
Elvey L Varner, *
EMP: 124 EST: 1959
SQ FT: 12,000
SALES (est): 13.72MM **Privately Held**
SIC: 4953 Garbage: collecting, destroying,
and processing

(P-12193)
VERDECO RECYCLING INC
8685 Bowers Ave (90280-3317)
PHONE..................................323 537-4617
Robert Bindner, *CEO*
Alexander Delnik, *
Carmen Chivu, *
◆ EMP: 25 EST: 2011
SALES (est): 48.46MM
SALES (corp-wide): 1.3MM **Privately Held**
Web: www.verdecorecycling.com
SIC: 4953 3089 Recycling, waste materials;
Plastics containers, except foam
HQ: Verdeco Recycling Holdings Llc
8685 Bowers Ave
South Gate CA
323 537-4617

(P-12194)
WARE DISPOSAL INC
1451 Manhattan Ave (92831-5221)
PHONE..................................714 834-0234
Judith Helaine Ware, *CEO*
Ben Ware, *
Jay Ware, *
EMP: 120 EST: 1970
SQ FT: 48,900
SALES (est): 30.3MM **Privately Held**
Web: www.waredisposal.com
SIC: 4953 Refuse collection and disposal
services

(P-12195)
WASTE MANAGEMENT CAL INC
Also Called: Waste Management
10910 Dawson Canyon Rd (92883-5020)
PHONE..................................951 277-1740
Damon De Frates, *Brnch Mgr*
EMP: 115

SALES (corp-wide): 19.7B **Publicly Held**
SIC: 4953 Garbage: collecting, destroying,
and processing
HQ: Waste Management Of California, Inc.
9081 Tujunga Ave
Sun Valley CA
877 836-6526

(P-12196)
WASTE MANAGEMENT CAL INC (HQ)
Also Called: Waste Management
9081 Tujunga Ave (91352-1516)
PHONE..................................877 836-6526
EMP: 230 EST: 1953
SQ FT: 35,000
SALES (est): 439.26MM
SALES (corp-wide): 19.7B **Publicly Held**
SIC: 4953 Garbage: collecting, destroying,
and processing
PA: Waste Management, Inc.
800 Capitol St Ste 3000
Houston TX
713 512-6200

(P-12197)
WASTE MANAGEMENT CAL INC
Also Called: Waste Management
2801 N Madera Rd (93065-6208)
PHONE..................................805 522-7023
Scott Tignac, *Mgr*
EMP: 195
SALES (corp-wide): 19.7B **Publicly Held**
SIC: 4953 Recycling, waste materials
HQ: Waste Management Of California, Inc.
9081 Tujunga Ave
Sun Valley CA
877 836-6526

(P-12198)
WASTE MANAGEMENT CAL INC
Also Called: Waste Management
1001 W Bradley Ave (92020-1501)
PHONE..................................619 596-5100
TOLL FREE: 800
Rex Buck, *Prin*
EMP: 160
SQ FT: 2,000
SALES (corp-wide): 19.7B **Publicly Held**
SIC: 4953 Recycling, waste materials
HQ: Waste Management Of California, Inc.
9081 Tujunga Ave
Sun Valley CA
877 836-6526

(P-12199)
WASTE MANAGEMENT CAL INC
Also Called: Waste Management
2141 Oceanside Blvd (92054-4405)
PHONE..................................760 439-2824
John Lusignan, *Mgr*
EMP: 126
SQ FT: 4,500
SALES (corp-wide): 19.7B **Publicly Held**
SIC: 4953 4212 Garbage: collecting,
destroying, and processing; Local trucking,
without storage
HQ: Waste Management Of California, Inc.
9081 Tujunga Ave
Sun Valley CA
877 836-6526

(P-12200)
WASTE MANAGEMENT CAL INC
Also Called: Waste Management
1200 W City Ranch Rd (93551-4456)
PHONE..................................661 947-7197
Carl Mccarthy, *Mgr*
EMP: 126
SALES (corp-wide): 19.7B **Publicly Held**

SIC: 4953 Rubbish collection and disposal
HQ: Waste Management Of California, Inc.
9081 Tujunga Ave
Sun Valley CA
877 836-6526

(P-12201)
WASTE MGT COLLECTN RECYCL INC
Also Called: Waste Management
1449 W Rosecrans Ave (90249-2639)
P.O. Box 1428 (90249-0428)
PHONE..................................310 532-6511
Dave Hauser, *Prin*
EMP: 92
SALES (corp-wide): 19.7B **Publicly Held**
SIC: 4953 5064 Garbage: collecting,
destroying, and processing; Garbage
disposals
HQ: Waste Management Collection And
Recycling, Inc.
1001 Fannin St Ste 4000
Houston TX

(P-12202)
WASTE MGT COLLECTN RECYCL INC
Also Called: Waste Management
13940 Live Oak Ave (91706-1321)
PHONE..................................626 960-7551
Rick Decaiva, *Mgr*
EMP: 132
SALES (corp-wide): 19.7B **Publicly Held**
SIC: 4953 4212 Rubbish collection and
disposal; Local trucking, without storage
HQ: Waste Management Collection And
Recycling, Inc.
1001 Fannin St Ste 4000
Houston TX

(P-12203)
WASTE MGT COLLECTN RECYCL INC
Also Called: Waste Management
17700 Indian St (92551-9511)
PHONE..................................951 242-0421
Scott Jenkins, *Mgr*
EMP: 116
SALES (corp-wide): 19.7B **Publicly Held**
SIC: 4953 Recycling, waste materials
HQ: Waste Management Collection And
Recycling, Inc.
1001 Fannin St Ste 4000
Houston TX

(P-12204)
WASTE MGT COLLECTN RECYCL INC
Also Called: Waste Management
16122 Construction Cir E (92606-4498)
PHONE..................................949 451-2600
EMP: 125
SALES (corp-wide): 19.7B **Publicly Held**
SIC: 4953 4212 Recycling, waste materials;
Garbage collection and transport, no
disposal
HQ: Waste Management Collection And
Recycling, Inc.
1001 Fannin St Ste 4000
Houston TX

(P-12205)
YUCAIPA DISPOSAL INC
9890 Cherry Ave (92335-5202)
PHONE..................................909 429-4200
Cole Burr, *Pr*
David R Marriner, *CFO*
EMP: 95 EST: 1959
SQ FT: 1,500

SALES (est): 1.74MM
SALES (corp-wide): 320.11MM **Privately Held**
Web: www.burrtec.com
SIC: 4953 4212 Rubbish collection and disposal; Local trucking, without storage
PA: Burrtec Waste Group, Inc.
9890 Cherry Ave
Fontana CA
909 429-4200

(P-12206)
ZEREP MANAGEMENT CORPORATION (PA)
17445 Railroad St (91748-1026)
PHONE..............................626 855-5522
Manuel Perez, *CEO*
EMP: 245 **EST:** 1970
SQ FT: 4,000
SALES (est): 37.94MM
SALES (corp-wide): 37.94MM **Privately Held**
Web: www.valleyvistaservices.com
SIC: 4953 4212 Refuse collection and disposal services; Local trucking, without storage

4959 Sanitary Services, Nec

(P-12207)
AMPCO CONTRACTING INC
17991 Cowan (92614-6025)
PHONE..............................949 955-2255
Andrew Pennor, *Ch*
Tim Vitta, *
Reggie Kama, *
Joe Ha, *
EMP: 220 **EST:** 2004
SALES (est): 53.13MM **Privately Held**
Web: www.ampcocontracting.com
SIC: 4959 1795 1794 Environmental cleanup services; Wrecking and demolition work; Excavation and grading, building construction

(P-12208)
CLEANSTREET LLC
1918 W 169th St (90247-5254)
PHONE..............................800 225-7316
TOLL FREE: 800
Christopher Valerian, *Pr*
EMP: 194 **EST:** 1965
SALES (est): 25.56MM
SALES (corp-wide): 536.39MM **Privately Held**
Web: www.sweepingcorp.com
SIC: 4959 Sweeping service: road, airport, parking lot, etc.
HQ: Sca Of Ca, Llc
4141 Rockside Rd Ste 100
Seven Hills OH
216 777-2750

(P-12209)
JONSET LLC
Also Called: Sunset Property Services
16251 Construction Cir W (92606-4412)
PHONE..............................949 551-5151
John Howhannesian, *Pr*
EMP: 96 **EST:** 1968
SQ FT: 6,000
SALES (est): 9.64MM
SALES (corp-wide): 536.39MM **Privately Held**
SIC: 4959 7349 Sweeping service: road, airport, parking lot, etc.; Janitorial service, contract basis
HQ: Sca Of Ca, Llc
4141 Rockside Rd Ste 100
Seven Hills OH
216 777-2750

(P-12210)
LOS ANGLES CNTY SNTTION DSTRCT (PA)
Also Called: L.A.cO.
1955 Workman Mill Rd (90601-1415)
P.O. Box 4998 (90607-4998)
PHONE..............................562 699-7411
Stephen Maguin, *Genl Mgr*
EMP: 850 **EST:** 1924
SALES (est): 726.8MM
SALES (corp-wide): 726.8MM **Privately Held**
Web: www.lacsd.org
SIC: 4959 Sanitary services, nec

(P-12211)
SULLIVAN INTERNATIONAL GROUP INC
Also Called: Sullivan
2750 Womble Rd Ste 100 (92106-6111)
PHONE..............................619 260-1432
EMP: 132
SIC: 4959 Toxic or hazardous waste cleanup

4971 Irrigation Systems

(P-12212)
CITY OF ANAHEIM
Anaheim City Utilities Div
201 S Anaheim Blvd (92805-3826)
P.O. Box 3069 (92803-3069)
PHONE..............................714 254-0125
Ed Aghjayan, *Brnch Mgr*
EMP: 100
Web: www.anaheim.net
SIC: 4971 9111 Water distribution or supply systems for irrigation; Mayors' office
PA: City Of Anaheim
200 S Anaheim Blvd
Anaheim CA
714 765-5162

(P-12213)
HUNTER INDUSTRIES INCORPORATED (PA)
Also Called: Hunter
1940 Diamond St (92078-5190)
PHONE..............................760 744-5240
Gregory R Hunter, *CEO*
Stephanie C Brownell, *
◆ **EMP:** 193 **EST:** 1993
SQ FT: 450,000
SALES (est): 538.15MM **Privately Held**
Web: www.hunterindustries.com
SIC: 4971 3089 Irrigation systems; Fittings for pipe, plastics

(P-12214)
OAK SPRINGS NURSERY INC
13761 Eldridge Ave (91342-1764)
P.O. Box 922906 (91392-2906)
PHONE..............................818 367-5832
Manuel Cacho, *Pr*
EMP: 90 **EST:** 1993
SALES (est): 9.37MM **Privately Held**
SIC: 4971 0781 Irrigation systems; Landscape services

(P-12215)
PALO VERDE IRRIGATION DISTRICT
180 W 14th Ave (92225-2714)
PHONE..............................760 922-3144
Ed Smith, *Genl Mgr*
Janice Love, *CLLTR*
EMP: 85 **EST:** 1923
SQ FT: 8,125
SALES (est): 14.02MM **Privately Held**

Web: www.pvid.org
SIC: 4971 Water distribution or supply systems for irrigation

(P-12216)
VISTA IRRIGATION DISTRICT
Also Called: Vid
1391 Engineer St (92081-8836)
PHONE..............................760 597-3100
John Amodeo, *Genl Mgr*
Roy Coox, *
EMP: 99 **EST:** 1923
SQ FT: 2,500
SALES (est): 43.19MM **Privately Held**
Web: www.vidwater.org
SIC: 4971 Water distribution or supply systems for irrigation

5012 Automobiles And Other Motor Vehicles

(P-12217)
A-Z BUS SALES INC (PA)
Also Called: John Deere Authorized Dealer
1900 S Riverside Ave (92324-3344)
PHONE..............................951 781-7188
Edwin John Landherr, *CEO*
James Reynolds, *
▼ **EMP:** 90 **EST:** 1984
SQ FT: 20,000
SALES (est): 49.64MM
SALES (corp-wide): 49.64MM **Privately Held**
Web: www.a-zbus.com
SIC: 5012 5082 Busses; Construction and mining machinery

(P-12218)
ABC BUS INC
1485 Dale Way (92626-3918)
PHONE..............................714 444-5888
Dane Cornell, *CEO*
EMP: 86
SALES (corp-wide): 182.45MM **Privately Held**
SIC: 5012 4173 Busses; Bus terminal and service facilities
HQ: Abc Bus, Inc.
1506 30th St Nw
Faribault MN
507 334-1871

(P-12219)
ADESA CORPORATION LLC
2175 Cactus Rd (92154-8002)
PHONE..............................619 661-5565
EMP: 92
Web: www.adesa.com
SIC: 5012 5521 Automobile auction; Used car dealers
HQ: Adesa Corporation, Llc
11299 Illinois St
Carmel IN

(P-12220)
ALEXANDER DENNIS INCORPORATED
31566 Railroad Canyon Rd Ste 3 (92587-9446)
PHONE..............................951 244-9429
Colin Robertson, *CEO*
Stephen Walsh, *
▲ **EMP:** 2000 **EST:** 2004
SALES (est): 56.4MM
SALES (corp-wide): 2.05B **Privately Held**
Web: www.alexander-dennis.com
SIC: 5012 Busses
HQ: Alexander Dennis Limited
9 Central Boulevard

Larbert

(P-12221)
AMERICAN HONDA MOTOR CO INC (HQ)
Also Called: American Honda
1919 Torrance Blvd (90501-2722)
P.O. Box 2200 (90509-2200)
PHONE..............................310 783-2000
Noriya Kaihara, *CEO*
Lyle Shroyer, *VP*
Yuichi Shimizu, *Sec*
Mikio Himuro, *CFO*
◆ **EMP:** 2375 **EST:** 1959
SALES (est): 12.82B **Privately Held**
Web: www.honda.com
SIC: 5012 3732 Automobiles; Jet skis
PA: Honda Motor Co., Ltd.
2-1-1, Minamiaoyama
Minato-Ku TKY

(P-12222)
AQUIRECORPS NORWALK AUTO AUCTN
Also Called: Aquire
12405 Rosecrans Ave (90650-5056)
PHONE..............................562 864-7464
Rj Romero, *Ch Bd*
Lou Rudich, *
Chuck Doskow, *
Steve Fleurant, *
EMP: 125 **EST:** 1979
SQ FT: 55,000
SALES (est): 34.08MM **Privately Held**
Web: www.norwalkautoauction.com
SIC: 5012 Automobile auction

(P-12223)
CALIFRNIA AUTO DALERS EXCH LLC
Also Called: Riverside Auto Auction
1320 N Tustin Ave (92807-1619)
PHONE..............................714 996-2400
Tim Van Dam, *Genl Mgr*
EMP: 400 **EST:** 1985
SALES (est): 47.32MM
SALES (corp-wide): 16.61B **Privately Held**
SIC: 5012 Automobile auction
HQ: Manheim Investments, Inc.
6205 Pachtree Dunwoody Rd
Atlanta GA
866 626-4346

(P-12224)
HYUNDAI MOTOR AMERICA (HQ)
10550 Talbert Ave (92708-6032)
P.O. Box 20850 (92728-0850)
PHONE..............................714 965-3000
Randy Parker, *CEO*
Jerry Flannery, *Legal*
Brian Smith, *COO*
Youngil Ko, *CFO*
Angela Zepeda, *CMO*
◆ **EMP:** 454 **EST:** 1985
SQ FT: 469,000
SALES (est): 1.1B **Privately Held**
Web: www.hyundaiusa.com
SIC: 5012 5511 Automobiles and other motor vehicles; Automobiles, new and used
PA: Hyundai Motor Company
12 Heolleung-Ro, Seocho-Gu
Seoul

(P-12225)
INLAND KENWORTH INC (HQ)
9730 Cherry Ave (92335-5257)
PHONE..............................909 823-9955
TOLL FREE: 800
Leigh Parker, *Ch*

William Currie, *
Les Ziegler, *
Jim Beidrwieden, *
▼ **EMP:** 105 **EST:** 1934
SQ FT: 60,000
SALES (est): 104.26MM
SALES (corp-wide): 1.1MM **Privately Held**
Web: www.inland-group.com
SIC: **5012** 7538 5013 7513 Trucks, commercial; Diesel engine repair: automotive; Truck parts and accessories; Truck rental and leasing, no drivers
PA: Inland Industries Ltd
2482 Douglas Rd
Burnaby BC
604 291-6021

(P-12226)
LOS ANGELES TRUCK CENTERS LLC
Also Called: Los Angeles Freightliner
13800 Valley Blvd (92335-5216)
PHONE..............................909 510-4000
Ricardo Flores, *Mgr*
EMP: 200
SALES (corp-wide): 233.56MM **Privately Held**
Web: www.velocitytruckcenters.com
SIC: **5012** 7538 5531 5511 Trucks, commercial; General automotive repair shops; Auto and home supply stores; New and used car dealers
PA: Los Angeles Truck Centers, Llc
2429 Peck Rd
Whittier CA
562 447-1200

(P-12227)
MARATHON INDUSTRIES INC
Also Called: Marathon Truck Bodies
25597 Springbrook Ave (91350-2427)
P.O. Box 800279 (91380-0279)
PHONE..............................661 286-1520
Chad Hess, *Pr*
Roger K Hess, *
Tom Garcia, *
EMP: 145 **EST:** 1993
SQ FT: 75,000
SALES (est): 27.5MM **Privately Held**
Web: www.marathontruckbody.com
SIC: **5012** 3713 Automobiles and other motor vehicles; Truck and bus bodies

(P-12228)
NISSAN NORTH AMERICA INC
Nissan Division
1683 Sunflower Ave (92626-1540)
P.O. Box 5555 (92628-5555)
PHONE..............................714 433-3700
FAX: 714 433-3746
EMP: 150
SALES (corp-wide): 103.12B **Privately Held**
SIC: **5012** Automotive brokers
HQ: Nissan North America Inc
1 Nissan Way
Franklin TN
615 725-1000

(P-12229)
UTILITY TRLR SLS STHERN CAL LL (PA)
15567 Valley Blvd (92335-6351)
PHONE..............................877 275-4887
Craig M Bennett, *
Stephen F Bennet, *
Harold C Bennett, *
Jeffrey J Bennett, *
EMP: 100 **EST:** 2007
SALES (est): 20.94MM **Privately Held**

Web: www.utilitytrailersales.com
SIC: **5013** 5531 5561 Trailers for passenger vehicles; Automotive supplies and parts; Auto and truck equipment and parts; Travel trailers: automobile, new and used

5013 Motor Vehicle Supplies And New Parts

(P-12230)
4 WHEEL PARTS WHOLESALERS LLC
400 W Artesia Blvd (90220-5501)
PHONE..............................310 900-7725
▼ **EMP:** 452 **EST:** 2010
SALES (est): 10.42MM **Privately Held**
Web: www.4wheelparts.com
SIC: **5013** Automotive supplies and parts

(P-12231)
APW KNOX-SEEMAN WAREHOUSE INC (HQ)
1073 E Artesia Blvd (90746-1601)
PHONE..............................310 604-4373
Tong Y Suhr, *CEO*
Susan Suhr, *
▲ **EMP:** 98 **EST:** 1972
SQ FT: 32,000
SALES (est): 47.91MM
SALES (corp-wide): 48.2MM **Privately Held**
Web: www.apwks.com
SIC: **5013** 5531 Automotive supplies and parts; Automotive parts
PA: Auto Parts Warehouse, Inc.
16941 Keegan Ave
Carson CA
800 913-6119

(P-12232)
ASIAN EUROPEAN PRODUCTS INC
Also Called: E P I
18071 Fitch Fl 250 (92614-6085)
P.O. Box 28989 (92799-8989)
PHONE..............................949 553-3900
▲ **EMP:** 150
SIC: **5013** Automotive supplies and parts

(P-12233)
AZIMC INVESTMENTS INC
Also Called: IMC
8901 Canoga Ave (91304-1512)
PHONE..............................818 678-1200
Kristen Wright, *Sec*
Thomas Kliman, *
William Giles, *
◆ **EMP:** 250 **EST:** 1962
SALES (est): 87.59MM
SALES (corp-wide): 495MM **Privately Held**
SIC: **5013** Automotive supplies and parts
HQ: Interamerican Motor, Llc
8901 Canoga Ave
Canoga Park CA
800 874-8925

(P-12234)
BATTERY SYSTEMS INC
12322 Monarch St (92841-2909)
PHONE..............................714 667-9320
EMP: 106
SALES (corp-wide): 545.41MM **Privately Held**
Web: www.batterysystems.net
SIC: **5013** Motor vehicle supplies and new parts

PA: Battery Systems, Inc.
8585 N Stemmons Fwy # 60
Dallas TX
310 667-9320

(P-12235)
BRAGG INVESTMENT COMPANY INC
Also Called: Coastline Equipment
1930 Lockwood St (93036-2679)
PHONE..............................805 485-2106
Buck Baird, *Mgr*
EMP: 97
SQ FT: 17,900
SALES (corp-wide): 489.53MM **Privately Held**
Web: www.braggcompanies.com
SIC: **5013** 7629 7359 5082 Trailer parts and accessories; Business machine repair, electric; Lawn and garden equipment rental ; Construction and mining machinery
PA: Bragg Investment Company, Inc.
6251 N Paramount Blvd
Long Beach CA
562 984-2400

(P-12236)
CAL-STATE AUTO PARTS INC (PA)
Also Called: Auto Pride
1361 N Red Gum St (92806-1318)
PHONE..............................714 630-5950
Richard J Deblasi, *CEO*
Steven Brooker, *
John Mcmillin, *CFO*
▲ **EMP:** 105 **EST:** 1971
SQ FT: 76,000
SALES (est): 44.73MM
SALES (corp-wide): 44.73MM **Privately Held**
Web: www.calstateautoparts.com
SIC: **5013** Automotive supplies and parts

(P-12237)
DENSO PDTS & SVCS AMERICAS INC (DH)
Also Called: Dsca
3900 Via Oro Ave (90810-1868)
PHONE..............................310 834-6352
Yoshihiko Yamada, *CEO*
Hirokatsu Yamashita, *Pr*
Roy Nakaue, *Ex VP*
Peter Clotz, *VP Sls*
Eugene Stark, *VP Prd*
◆ **EMP:** 452 **EST:** 1971
SQ FT: 235,000
SALES (est): 221.87MM **Privately Held**
Web: www.densorobotics.com
SIC: **5013** 7361 5075 3714 Automotive supplies and parts; Employment agencies; Warm air heating and air conditioning; Motor vehicle parts and accessories
HQ: Denso International America, Inc.
24777 Denso Dr
Southfield MI
248 350-7500

(P-12238)
DNA SPECIALTY INC
200 W Artesia Blvd (90220-5500)
PHONE..............................310 767-4070
James Choi, *Pr*
▲ **EMP:** 90 **EST:** 1984
SQ FT: 80,000
SALES (est): 24.13MM **Privately Held**
Web: www.dnaspecialty.com
SIC: **5013** 3714 Wheels, motor vehicle; Wheels, motor vehicle

(P-12239)
EGGE MACHINE COMPANY INC (PA)
8403 Allport Ave (90670-2109)
PHONE..............................562 945-3419
Robert Egge, *Pr*
Kathy Weaver, *
Judy Egge, *
▲ **EMP:** 29 **EST:** 1915
SQ FT: 10,000
SALES (est): 8.12MM
SALES (corp-wide): 8.12MM **Privately Held**
Web: www.egge.com
SIC: **5013** 3592 5531 Automotive supplies and parts; Valves; Automotive parts

(P-12240)
EMPI INC
301 E Orangethorpe Ave (92801-1032)
PHONE..............................714 446-9606
Peter Guile, *CEO*
Todd Tyler, *CFO*
EMP: 89 **EST:** 2018
SQ FT: 127,000
SALES (est): 28.78MM **Privately Held**
Web: www.empius.com
SIC: **5013** 3713 Automotive supplies and parts; Specialty motor vehicle bodies

(P-12241)
HANSON DISTRIBUTING COMPANY (PA)
975 W 8th St (91702-2246)
PHONE..............................626 224-9800
Daniel Hanson, *CEO*
EMP: 115 **EST:** 1954
SQ FT: 160,000
SALES (est): 64.25MM
SALES (corp-wide): 64.25MM **Privately Held**
Web: www.hansondistributing.com
SIC: **5013** Automotive supplies and parts

(P-12242)
HIGHLINE AFTERMARKET LLC
Also Called: Atlantic Pacific Automotive
10385 San Sevaine Way Ste B (91752-3272)
PHONE..............................951 361-0331
Scott Hultman, *Mgr*
EMP: 53
SQ FT: 37,000
SALES (corp-wide): 741.18MM **Privately Held**
Web: www.highlinewarren.com
SIC: **5013** 6512 2992 3519 Automotive supplies and parts; Commercial and industrial building operation; Lubricating oils ; Parts and accessories, internal combustion engines
HQ: Highline Aftermarket, Llc
4500 Malone Rd Ste 2
Memphis TN

(P-12243)
HINO MOTORS MFG USA INC
4550 Wineville Ave (91752-3723)
PHONE..............................951 727-0286
Debra Martinas, *Brnch Mgr*
EMP: 93
Web: www.hmmusa.com
SIC: **5013** Truck parts and accessories
HQ: Hino Motors Manufacturing U.S.A., Inc.
45501 W 12 Mile Rd
Novi MI

(P-12244)
INNOVATIVE METAL DESIGNS INC
12691 Monarch St (92841-3918)
PHONE.....................714 799-6700
Carlos Danze, *CEO*
Marcelo Danze, *Pr*
▲ EMP: 20 EST: 1983
SQ FT: 6,000
SALES (est): 4.33MM **Privately Held**
Web: www.innovativemetals.com
SIC: 5013 3841 3827 Motorcycle parts;
Surgical and medical instruments; Optical
instruments and lenses

(P-12245)
KEYSTONE AUTOMOTIVE WAREHOUSE
Also Called: KEYSTONE AUTOMOTIVE
WAREHOUSE
15640 Cantu Galleano Ranch Rd
(91752-1404)
PHONE.....................951 277-5237
Michael Decicco, *Prin*
EMP: 100
SALES (corp-wide): 12.79B **Publicly Held**
Web: www.keystoneautomotive.com
SIC: 5013 Radiators
HQ: Keystone Automotive Warehouse, Inc.
44 Tunkhannock Ave
Exeter PA
570 655-4514

(P-12246)
MAXZONE VEHICLE LIGHTING CORP (HQ)
Also Called: Depo Auto Parts
15889 Slover Ave Unit A (92337-7299)
PHONE.....................909 822-3288
Polo Hsu, *Pr*
◆ EMP: 50 EST: 1997
SQ FT: 32,000
SALES (est): 32.22MM **Privately Held**
Web: www.maxzone.com
SIC: 5013 3714 Automotive supplies and
parts; Motor vehicle electrical equipment
PA: Depo Auto Parts Ind. Co., Ltd.
No. 20-3, Nanshi Ln.
Lukang Township CHA

(P-12247)
MERIDIAN RACK & PINION INC
Also Called: Meridian
9980 Huennekens St Ste 200 (92121-2968)
PHONE.....................888 875-0026
Renee Thomas-jacobs, *CEO*
Dara Greaney, *VP*
Matt Glauber, *Pr*
Chris Struempler, *CFO*
▲ EMP: 130 EST: 1989
SALES (est): 24.98MM **Privately Held**
Web: www.buyautoparts.com
SIC: 5013 5961 Automotive supplies and
parts; Mail order house, order taking office
only

(P-12248)
METROPOLITAN AUTOMOTIVE WAREHOUSE
Also Called: Auto Value
535 Tennis Court Ln (92408-1615)
P.O. Box 1529 (92402-1529)
PHONE.....................909 885-2886
▼ EMP: 700
SIC: 5013 Automotive supplies and parts

(P-12249)
MOBIS PARTS AMERICA LLC (HQ)
Also Called: Mobis Ventures Sv
10550 Talbert Ave 4th Fl (92708-6031)
PHONE.....................786 515-1101
Yun Dong Park, *Managing Member*
Tae Hwan Chung, *
Beomseo Koo, *
◆ EMP: 90 EST: 2003
SALES (est): 224.39MM **Privately Held**
Web: www.mobisusa.com
SIC: 5013 Automotive supplies and parts
PA: Hyundai Mobis Co., Ltd.
203 Teheran-Ro, Gangnam-Gu
Seoul

(P-12250)
NSV INTERNATIONAL CORP
1250 E 29th St (90755-1800)
P.O. Box 14660 (90853-4660)
PHONE.....................562 438-3836
Victor Harris, *CEO*
Stephan Humphries, *
Isabel Palafox, *
EMP: 100 EST: 2011
SQ FT: 1,200
SALES (est): 5.02MM **Privately Held**
Web: www.nsvauto.com
SIC: 5013 Automotive supplies

(P-12251)
PARTS AUTHORITY LLC
Also Called: Fast Undercar
4277 Transport St (93003-5657)
PHONE.....................805 676-3410
Randy Buller, *Pr*
EMP: 110
SALES (corp-wide): 495MM **Privately Held**
Web: www.fastundercar.com
SIC: 5013 Automotive supplies and parts
PA: Parts Authority, Llc
3 Dakota Dr Ste 110
New Hyde Park NY
833 380-8511

(P-12252)
PHOENIX WHEEL COMPANY INC
Also Called: Hre Performance Wheels
2611 Commerce Way Ste D (92081-8455)
PHONE.....................760 598-1960
Christian J Luhnow, *CEO*
Alan Peltier, *
Phillip Hillhouse, *
▲ EMP: 40 EST: 1993
SQ FT: 58,000
SALES (est): 17.47MM **Privately Held**
Web: www.hrewheels.com
SIC: 5013 3714 Wheels, motor vehicle;
Motor vehicle wheels and parts

(P-12253)
PREVOST CAR (US) INC
3384 De Forest Cir (91752)
PHONE.....................951 360-2550
Tim Willmuth, *Brnch Mgr*
EMP: 58
SALES (corp-wide): 45.13B **Privately Held**
Web: www.prevostcar.com
SIC: 5013 4173 5012 3711 Automotive
supplies and parts; Maintenance facilities,
buses; Busses; Buses, all types, assembly
of
HQ: Prevost Car (Us) Inc.
7817 National Service Rd
Greensboro NC
908 222-7211

(P-12254)
R1 CONCEPTS INC (PA)
Also Called: Zion Automotive Group
13140 Midway Pl (90703-2233)
PHONE.....................714 777-2323
Phouc Martin Trinh, *Pr*
Thang Trinh, *COO*
◆ EMP: 25 EST: 2004
SALES (est): 24.97MM
SALES (corp-wide): 24.97MM **Privately Held**
Web: www.r1concepts.com
SIC: 5013 3714 Automotive engines and
engine parts; Motor vehicle brake systems
and parts

(P-12255)
RALCO HOLDINGS INC (DH)
13861 Rosecrans Ave (90670-5207)
PHONE.....................949 440-5094
Michael Moore, *CEO*
EMP: 159 EST: 2009
SALES (est): 305.57MM **Privately Held**
SIC: 5013 3751 Motorcycle parts;
Motorcycle accessories
HQ: Velocity Pooling Vehicle, Llc
651 Canyon Dr Ste 100
Coppell TX

(P-12256)
RALLY HOLDINGS LLC
17771 Mitchell N (92614-6028)
PHONE.....................817 919-6833
EMP: 1151 EST: 2006
SALES (est): 305.57MM **Privately Held**
SIC: 5013 3751 Motorcycle parts;
Motorcycle accessories
HQ: Ralco Holdings, Inc.
13861 Rosecrans Ave
Santa Fe Springs CA
949 440-5094

(P-12257)
RAMCAR BATTERIES INC
2700 Carrier Ave (90040-2572)
PHONE.....................323 726-1212
Clifford J Crowe, *CEO*
Jaime Agustines, *VP*
◆ EMP: 42 EST: 1919
SQ FT: 90,000
SALES (est): 12.31MM **Privately Held**
Web: www.ramcarbattery.com
SIC: 5013 3691 Automotive batteries; Lead
acid batteries (storage batteries)

(P-12258)
REELS INC
Also Called: Mr Bug
301 E Orangethorpe Ave (92801-1032)
PHONE.....................714 446-9606
▲ EMP: 80 EST: 1971
SALES (est): 10.48MM **Privately Held**
Web: www.empius.com
SIC: 5013 Automotive supplies and
parts; Motor vehicle parts and accessories

(P-12259)
SADDLEMEN CORPORATION
Also Called: Saddlemen
17801 S Susana Rd (90221-5411)
PHONE.....................310 638-1222
David Echert, *CEO*
▲ EMP: 140 EST: 1987
SQ FT: 20,000
SALES (est): 12.75MM **Privately Held**
Web: www.saddlemen.com
SIC: 5013 3751 Motorcycle parts;
Motorcycle accessories

(P-12260)
SCAT ENTERPRISES INC
1400 Kingsdale Ave (90278-3927)
PHONE.....................310 370-5501
Philip T Lieb, *Pr*
Craig Schenasi, *
◆ EMP: 65 EST: 1960
SQ FT: 42,000
SALES (est): 24.68MM **Privately Held**
Web: www.scatenterprises.com
SIC: 5013 3714 Automotive supplies and
parts; Motor vehicle parts and accessories

(P-12261)
SHRIN LLC
Also Called: Coverking
900 E Arlee Pl (92805-5645)
P.O. Box 9860 (92812-7860)
PHONE.....................714 850-0303
Narendra Gupta, *Managing Member*
◆ EMP: 100 EST: 1988
SQ FT: 90,000
SALES (est): 24.35MM **Privately Held**
Web: www.coverking.com
SIC: 5013 3714 Automotive supplies and
parts; Motor vehicle parts and accessories

(P-12262)
SILLA AUTOMOTIVE LLC
Also Called: Silla Cooling Systems
1217 W Artesia Blvd (90220-5305)
PHONE.....................800 624-1499
▲ EMP: 200
SIC: 5013 Radiators

(P-12263)
SPECIALTY INTERIOR MFG INC
Also Called: Sim Ideation
16751 Millikan Ave (92606-5009)
PHONE.....................714 296-8618
Courtney Tassie, *CEO*
EMP: 35 EST: 2012
SQ FT: 4,500
SALES (est): 3.5MM **Privately Held**
SIC: 5013 2531 Automotive supplies and
parts; Seats, aircraft

(P-12264)
VGP HOLDINGS LLC
9520 John St (90670-2904)
PHONE.....................562 906-6200
EMP: 288
SIC: 5013 Automotive engines and engine
parts
HQ: Vgp Holdings Llc
100 Valvoline Way Pmb 200
Lexington KY
859 357-7777

(P-12265)
WABASH NATIONAL TRLR CTRS INC
16025 Slover Ave (92337-7368)
PHONE.....................765 771-5300
Joe Newfield, *Mgr*
EMP: 47
SALES (corp-wide): 2.5B **Publicly Held**
Web: www.onewabash.com
SIC: 5013 5012 7539 3715 Motor vehicle
supplies and new parts; Automobiles and
other motor vehicles; Automotive repair
shops, nec; Truck trailers
HQ: Wabash National Trailer Centers, Inc.
1000 Sagamore Pkwy S
Lafayette IN
765 771-5300

PRODUCTS & SVCS

(P-12266)
WEBASTO CHARGING SYSTEMS INC (DH)
1333 S Mayflower Ave Ste 100 (91016-4066)
PHONE..................................626 415-4000
John Thomas, *CEO*
Doug Mcelroy, *CFO*
EMP: 85 **EST:** 2018
SALES (est): 22.44MM
SALES (corp-wide): 4.2B **Privately Held**
SIC: 5013 Automobile service station equipment
HQ: Webasto Roof Systems Inc.
2500 Executive Hills Dr
Auburn Hills MI
248 997-5100

(P-12267)
YOSHIMURA RES & DEV AMER INC
5420 Daniels St Ste A (91710-9012)
PHONE..................................909 628-4722
Fujio Yoshimura, *Pr*
Suehiro Watanabe, *
Don Sakakura, *
▲ **EMP:** 100 **EST:** 1975
SQ FT: 12,000
SALES (est): 24.8MM **Privately Held**
Web: www.yoshimura-rd.com
SIC: 5013 Motorcycle parts

5014 Tires And Tubes

(P-12268)
FALKEN TIRE HOLDINGS INC
Also Called: Falken Tires
8656 Haven Ave (91730-9103)
PHONE..................................800 723-2553
Richard Smallwood, *Pr*
▲ **EMP:** 80 **EST:** 2006
SALES (est): 22.76MM **Privately Held**
SIC: 5014 Automobile tires and tubes
PA: Sumitomo Rubber Industries, Ltd.
3-6-9, Wakinohamacho, Chuo-Ku
Kobe HYO

(P-12269)
GREENBALL CORP (PA)
Also Called: Towmaster Tire & Wheel
222 S Harbor Blvd Ste 700 (92805-3702)
PHONE..................................714 782-3060
Chris S H Tsai, *CEO*
Jenny Tsai, *
◆ **EMP:** 50 **EST:** 1976
SQ FT: 80,000
SALES (est): 48.5MM
SALES (corp-wide): 48.5MM **Privately Held**
Web: www.greenballtires.com
SIC: 5014 5013 3999 Automobile tires and tubes; Wheels, motor vehicle; Atomizers, toiletry

(P-12270)
ITD ARIZONA INC
6737 E Washington Blvd (90040-1801)
PHONE..................................323 722-8542
◆ **EMP:** 98
SIC: 5014 Tires and tubes

(P-12271)
LAKIN TIRE WEST INCORPORATED (PA)
Also Called: Lakin Tire of Calif
15305 Spring Ave (90670-5645)
PHONE..................................562 802-2752
Robert Lakin, *CEO*
David Lakin, *
◆ **EMP:** 164 **EST:** 1973
SQ FT: 50,000
SALES (est): 52.31MM
SALES (corp-wide): 52.31MM **Privately Held**
Web: www.lakintire.com
SIC: 5014 5531 Tires, used; Auto and home supply stores

(P-12272)
PETES ROAD SERVICE INC (PA)
2230 E Orangethorpe Ave (92831-5329)
PHONE..................................714 446-1207
▲ **EMP:** 55 **EST:** 1954
SALES (est): 35.91MM
SALES (corp-wide): 35.91MM **Privately Held**
Web: www.petesrs.com
SIC: 5014 7534 7539 Tires and tubes; Tire retreading and repair shops; Wheel alignment, automotive

(P-12273)
SUMITOMO RUBBER NORTH AMER INC (HQ)
Also Called: Falken Tire
8656 Haven Ave (91730-9107)
PHONE..................................909 466-1116
Richard Smallwood, *CEO*
Toby Beiner, *
◆ **EMP:** 120 **EST:** 1963
SQ FT: 190,000
SALES (est): 101.56MM **Privately Held**
Web: www.falkentire.com
SIC: 5014 Automobile tires and tubes
PA: Sumitomo Rubber Industries, Ltd.
3-6-9, Wakinohamacho, Chuo-Ku
Kobe HYO

(P-12274)
TIRECO INC (PA)
500 W 190th St Ste 600 (90248-4269)
PHONE..................................310 767-7990
Justin R Liu, *
Mimi Liu, *
◆ **EMP:** 150 **EST:** 2000
SALES (est): 112.53MM
SALES (corp-wide): 112.53MM **Privately Held**
Web: www.tireco.com
SIC: 5014 5013 5051 Tires, used; Wheels, motor vehicle; Tubing, metal

(P-12275)
YOKOHAMA TIRE CORPORATION (DH)
Also Called: Yokohama Tire USA
1 Macarthur Pl Ste 800 (92707-5948)
P.O. Box 4550 (92834-4550)
PHONE..................................714 870-3800
◆ **EMP:** 150 **EST:** 1969
SALES (est): 497.5MM **Privately Held**
Web: www.yokohamaotr.com
SIC: 5014 3011 Automobile tires and tubes; Automobile tires, pneumatic
HQ: Yokohama Corporation Of North America
1 Macarthur Pl
Santa Ana CA

5021 Furniture

(P-12276)
ABBYSON LIVING CORP
Also Called: Yellow Luxury
26500 Agoura Rd Ste 102 (91302-3571)
PHONE..................................805 465-5500
Yavar Rafieha, *Pr*
EMP: 112 **EST:** 2008
SALES (est): 15.03MM **Privately Held**
Web: www.abbyson.com
SIC: 5021 Household furniture

(P-12277)
BENCHPRO INC
Also Called: Bench Depot
23949 Tecate Mission Rd (91980)
P.O. Box G (91980-0958)
PHONE..................................619 478-9400
Jay David Lissner, *Pr*
▲ **EMP:** 188 **EST:** 2001
SQ FT: 155,000
SALES (est): 24.92MM **Privately Held**
Web: www.benchpro.com
SIC: 5021 Furniture

(P-12278)
BLUMENTHAL DISTRIBUTING INC (PA)
Also Called: Office Star Products
1901 S Archibald Ave (91761-8548)
P.O. Box 3520 (91761-0952)
PHONE..................................909 930-2000
Richard Blumenthal, *CEO*
Richard Blumenthal, *Pr*
Rose Blumenthal, *Stockholder*
Jennifer Blumenthal, *
◆ **EMP:** 150 **EST:** 1983
SQ FT: 200,000
SALES (est): 54.5MM
SALES (corp-wide): 54.5MM **Privately Held**
Web: www.officestar.net
SIC: 5021 2522 Office furniture, nec; Chairs, office: padded or plain: except wood

(P-12279)
CAMBIUM BUSINESS GROUP INC (PA)
Also Called: Fairmont Designs
6950 Noritsu Ave (90620-1311)
PHONE..................................714 670-1171
George Tsai, *Ch*
Jason Liu, *
Kevin Fitzgerald, *
Mark Klingensmith, *
◆ **EMP:** 120 **EST:** 1984
SQ FT: 200,000
SALES (est): 39.46MM
SALES (corp-wide): 39.46MM **Privately Held**
Web: www.fairmontdesigns.com
SIC: 5021 2511 Household furniture; Wood household furniture

(P-12280)
EC GROUP INC (PA)
Also Called: Dennis & Leen
5960 Bowcroft St (90016-4302)
PHONE..................................310 815-2700
Richard Hallberg, *Pr*
Daniel Cuevas, *
Barbara Wiseley, *
▲ **EMP:** 80 **EST:** 1985
SQ FT: 18,000
SALES (est): 23.58MM **Privately Held**
Web: www.dennisandleen.com
SIC: 5021 Furniture

(P-12281)
FURNITURE AMERICA CAL INC (PA)
Also Called: Import Direct
20300 Business Pkwy (91789-2940)
PHONE..................................866 923-8500
George Wells, *CEO*
Rocky Yang, *
Jean Chen, *
◆ **EMP:** 36 **EST:** 2005
SALES (est): 24.73MM **Privately Held**
Web: www.foagroup.com
SIC: 5021 2512 Furniture; Upholstered household furniture

(P-12282)
FURNITURE AMERICA CAL INC
19635 E Walnut Dr N (91789-2815)
PHONE..................................909 718-7276
EMP: 22
Web: www.foagroup.com
SIC: 5021 2512 Furniture; Upholstered household furniture
PA: Furniture Of America California, Inc.
20300 Business Pkwy
City Of Industry CA

(P-12283)
GOFORTH & MARTI (PA)
Also Called: G/M Business Interiors
110 W A St Ste 140 (92101-3702)
PHONE..................................800 686-6583
Stephen L Easley, *Pr*
Laurinda Easley, *
Stephen W Easley, *CIO*
Josie Donley, *
▲ **EMP:** 90 **EST:** 1944
SQ FT: 38,000
SALES (est): 110MM
SALES (corp-wide): 110MM **Privately Held**
Web: www.gmbi.net
SIC: 5021 Office furniture, nec

(P-12284)
HWOOD GROUP
9229 W Sunset Blvd Ste 305 (90069-3402)
PHONE..................................310 859-1011
John Terzian, *Prin*
EMP: 95 **EST:** 2015
SALES (est): 10.08MM **Privately Held**
Web: www.hwoodgroup.com
SIC: 5021 Restaurant furniture, nec

(P-12285)
INTEX RECREATION CORP
4001 Via Oro Ave (90810-1400)
PHONE..................................310 549-5400
Tien P Zee, *CEO*
Jim Lai, *
Bill Smith, *
Bob Howe, *
◆ **EMP:** 100 **EST:** 1966
SQ FT: 330,000
SALES (est): 22.14MM **Privately Held**
Web: www.intexcorp.com
SIC: 5021 5092 5091 5162 Waterbeds; Toys, nec; Watersports equipment and supplies; Plastics materials and basic shapes
PA: Intex Corp.
4001 Via Oro Ave Ste 210
Long Beach CA

(P-12286)
JANUS ET CIE (PA)
12310 Greenstone Ave (90670-4737)
PHONE..................................310 601-2958
Janice K Feldman, *CEO*
Paul Warren, *
Greg Buscher, *
◆ **EMP:** 110 **EST:** 1977
SQ FT: 154,000
SALES (est): 53.47MM
SALES (corp-wide): 53.47MM **Privately Held**
Web: www.janusetcie.com

▲ = Import ▼ = Export
◆ = Import/Export

SIC: 5021 5712 Outdoor and lawn furniture, nec; Furniture stores

(P-12287)
NEW TANGRAM LLC
Also Called: BKM Total Office of Texas
9200 Sorensen Ave (90670-2645)
PHONE..................................562 365-5000
Joseph P Lozowski, *Brnch Mgr*
EMP: 177
SALES (corp-wide): 185.06MM **Privately Held**
Web: www.tangraminteriors.com
SIC: 5021 Office furniture, nec
PA: New Tangram, Llc
9200 Sorensen Ave
Santa Fe Springs CA
562 365-5000

(P-12288)
OFFICE MASTER INC
Also Called: Om Smart Seating
1110 Mildred St (91761-3512)
PHONE..................................909 392-5678
◆ **EMP:** 60 **EST:** 1986
SALES (est): 17.98MM **Privately Held**
Web: www.omseating.com
SIC: 5021 2522 Office furniture, nec; Benches, office: except wood

(P-12289)
OMNIA ITALIAN DESIGN LLC
4900 Edison Ave (91710-5713)
PHONE..................................909 393-4400
Peter Zolferino, *Managing Member*
Luie Nastri, *
◆ **EMP:** 200 **EST:** 1989
SQ FT: 110,000
SALES (est): 37.72MM **Privately Held**
Web: www.omnialeather.com
SIC: 5021 Household furniture

(P-12290)
POUNDEX ASSOCIATES CORPORATION
21490 Baker Pkwy (91789-5239)
PHONE..................................909 444-5878
Lionel Chen, *Ch*
◆ **EMP:** 100 **EST:** 1988
SQ FT: 55,000
SALES (est): 23.85MM **Privately Held**
Web: www.poundex.com
SIC: 5021 Household furniture

(P-12291)
SITONIT SEATING INC
6415 Katella Ave (90630-5245)
PHONE..................................714 995-4800
Paul Devries, *CEO*
EMP: 83 **EST:** 2008
SALES (est): 11.93MM **Privately Held**
Web: www.sitonit.net
SIC: 5021 Office furniture, nec
PA: Exemplis Llc
6415 Katella Ave Ste 100
Cypress CA

(P-12292)
UNISOURCE SOLUTIONS INC (PA)
8350 Rex Rd (90660-3785)
PHONE..................................562 654-3500
James Kastner, *CEO*
Ken Kastner, *Pr*
Jim Kastner, *Ch*
Clem Nieto, *CFO*
▲ **EMP:** 105 **EST:** 1987
SQ FT: 186,000
SALES (est): 48.15MM

SALES (corp-wide): 48.15MM **Privately Held**
Web: www.unisourceit.com
SIC: 5021 Office furniture, nec

(P-12293)
VIRCO INC (HQ)
2027 Harpers Way (90501-1524)
PHONE..................................310 533-0474
Robert Virtue, *CEO*
Robert Dose, *
▼ **EMP:** 249 **EST:** 1998
SQ FT: 560,000
SALES (est): 48.89MM
SALES (corp-wide): 231.06MM **Publicly Held**
Web: www.virco.com
SIC: 5021 2599 Furniture; Factory furniture and fixtures
PA: Virco Mfg. Corporation
2027 Harpers Way
Torrance CA
310 533-0474

(P-12294)
WINNERS ONLY INC
1365 Park Center Dr (92081-8338)
PHONE..................................760 599-0300
Alex Shu, *Ch*
Sheue-wen Lee, *CEO*
Fred Dizon, *
◆ **EMP:** 200 **EST:** 1989
SALES (est): 26.11MM **Privately Held**
Web: www.winnersonly.com
SIC: 5021 Office furniture, nec

5023 Homefurnishings

(P-12295)
AMERICAN FAUCET COATINGS CORP
3280 Corporate Vw (92081-8528)
PHONE..................................760 598-5895
Susan E Butler, *Pr*
◆ **EMP:** 50 **EST:** 1993
SALES (est): 16MM **Privately Held**
Web: www.newwavehendersonville.com
SIC: 5023 3432 Homefurnishings; Plumbing fixture fittings and trim

(P-12296)
BRADSHAW INTERNATIONAL INC (PA)
Also Called: Bradshaw Home
9409 Buffalo Ave (91730-6012)
PHONE..................................909 476-3884
James Hair, *CEO*
Steve Molineaux, *
Robert Michelson, *
Jeff Megorden, *
Gary Appel, *
◆ **EMP:** 280 **EST:** 2010
SQ FT: 313,048
SALES (est): 642.04MM
SALES (corp-wide): 642.04MM **Privately Held**
Web: www.bradshawhome.com
SIC: 5023 Kitchenware

(P-12297)
BUSTER AND PUNCH INC
10844 Burbank Blvd (91601-2519)
PHONE..................................818 392-3827
David Schlocker, *CEO*
EMP: 25 **EST:** 2020
SALES (est): 3.16MM **Privately Held**
Web: www.busterandpunch.com

SIC: 5023 5063 5719 3429 Homefurnishings ; Lighting fixtures, residential; Lighting fixtures; Cabinet hardware

(P-12298)
CONTRACTORS FLRG SVC CAL INC
300 E Dyer Rd (92707-3740)
P.O. Box 15106 (92735-0106)
PHONE..................................714 556-6100
EMP: 110 **EST:** 1996
SQ FT: 10,000
SALES (est): 19.98MM **Privately Held**
Web: www.cfsofca.com
SIC: 5023 Floor coverings

(P-12299)
ELIJAH TEXTILES INC
Also Called: Sharp Fabric
1251 E Olympic Blvd Ste 108 (90021-1859)
PHONE..................................310 666-3443
Kourosh Amirianfar, *Pr*
EMP: 82 **EST:** 2001
SQ FT: 100,000
SALES (est): 34MM **Privately Held**
SIC: 5023 5949 Sheets, textile; Fabric stores piece goods

(P-12300)
EV RAY INC
6400 Variel Ave (91367-2577)
PHONE..................................818 346-5381
Lee Brown, *Pr*
EMP: 50 **EST:** 1962
SQ FT: 22,000
SALES (est): 6.97MM **Privately Held**
Web: www.rayev.com
SIC: 5023 2211 2591 2391 Draperies; Draperies and drapery fabrics, cotton; Drapery hardware and window blinds and shades; Curtains and draperies

(P-12301)
GA GERTMENIAN AND SONS LLC (PA)
300 W Avenue 33 (90031-3503)
PHONE..................................213 250-7777
▲ **EMP:** 149 **EST:** 1896
SALES (est): 24.13MM
SALES (corp-wide): 24.13MM **Privately Held**
Web: www.gertmenian.com
SIC: 5023 Rugs

(P-12302)
GALLEHER LLC (PA)
Also Called: Galleher
9303 Greenleaf Ave (90670-3029)
PHONE..................................562 944-8885
Ted Kozikowski, *CEO*
Jeff Hamar, *Ofcr*
Todd Hamar, *Sr VP*
Rick Coates, *Sr VP*
Russell Rumley, *CFO*
▲ **EMP:** 110 **EST:** 1937
SQ FT: 100,000
SALES (est): 110.9MM
SALES (corp-wide): 110.9MM **Privately Held**
Web: www.galleher.com
SIC: 5023 Homefurnishings

(P-12303)
GIBSON OVERSEAS INC (PA)
Also Called: Gibson Homeware
2410 Yates Ave (90040-1918)
PHONE..................................323 832-8900
Sol Gabbay, *CEO*
Darioush Gabbay, *

Soloman Gabbay, *
◆ **EMP:** 325 **EST:** 1979
SQ FT: 850,000
SALES (est): 221.89MM
SALES (corp-wide): 221.89MM **Privately Held**
Web: www.gibsonusa.com
SIC: 5023 3269 2511 Glassware; Kitchen and table articles, coarse earthenware; Kitchen and dining room furniture

(P-12304)
GTT INTERNATIONAL INC
1615 Eastridge Ave (92507-7111)
PHONE..................................951 788-8729
Mohammed Arshad, *Pr*
Hafiz Ur Rahaman, *
▲ **EMP:** 35 **EST:** 1991
SALES (est): 5.15MM **Privately Held**
SIC: 5023 2258 Bedspreads; Lace and warp knit fabric mills

(P-12305)
KATZIRS FLOOR & HM DESIGN INC (PA)
Also Called: National Hrdwood Flrg Moulding
14959 Delano St (91411-2123)
PHONE..................................818 988-9663
Omer Katzir, *CEO*
Jeannette Katzir, *
▲ **EMP:** 22 **EST:** 1982
SQ FT: 19,270
SALES (est): 9.19MM
SALES (corp-wide): 9.19MM **Privately Held**
Web: www.nationalhardwood.com
SIC: 5023 2435 Wood flooring; Hardwood veneer and plywood

(P-12306)
LEDRA BRANDS INC
Also Called: Bruck Lighting Systems
88 Maxwell (92618-4641)
PHONE..................................714 259-9959
Alex Ladjevardi, *Pr*
Jade Turney, *
Farah Emami, *
David Derk, *
Jorg Westerheide, *
▲ **EMP:** 112 **EST:** 1993
SALES (est): 26.55MM **Privately Held**
Web: www.ledrabrands.com
SIC: 5023 Lamps: floor, boudoir, desk

(P-12307)
MARIAK INDUSTRIES INC
Also Called: Mariak Window Fashion
879 W 190th St Ste 1050 (90248-4224)
PHONE..................................310 661-4400
Leo Elinson, *CEO*
▲ **EMP:** 269 **EST:** 1986
SALES (est): 48.04MM
SALES (corp-wide): 1.56B **Privately Held**
Web: www.mariak.com
SIC: 5023 2591 Vertical blinds; Blinds vertical
PA: Springs Window Fashions, Llc
7549 Graber Rd
Middleton WI
608 836-1011

(P-12308)
MSRS INC
Also Called: Vm International
945 E Church St (92507-1103)
PHONE..................................310 952-9000
Moe Vazin, *CEO*
Roya Vazin, *CFO*
◆ **EMP:** 120 **EST:** 1996
SQ FT: 250,000
SALES (est): 33.12MM **Privately Held**

PRODUCTS & SVCS

SIC: **5023** 2821 Kitchenware; Plastics
materials and resins

(P-12309)
NEW CLASSIC HM FURNISHING INC (PA)
Also Called: New Classic Furniture
7351 Mcguire Ave (92336-1668)
PHONE..........................909 484-7676
Jean Tong, *CEO*
◆ **EMP:** 42 **EST:** 2001
SALES (est): 104.06MM
SALES (corp-wide): 104.06MM **Privately Held**
Web: www.newclassicfurniture.com
SIC: **5023** 2512 Homefurnishings; Upholstered household furniture

(P-12310)
NEXGRILL INDUSTRIES INC (PA)
Also Called: Nexgrill Industries
14050 Laurelwood Pl (91710-5454)
PHONE..........................909 598-8799
Sherman Lin, *CEO*
◆ **EMP:** 98 **EST:** 1993
SQ FT: 50,000
SALES (est): 27.26MM
SALES (corp-wide): 27.26MM **Privately Held**
Web: www.nexgrill.com
SIC: **5023** 3631 Grills, barbecue; Barbecues, grills, and braziers (outdoor cooking)

(P-12311)
NORCAL POTTERY PRODUCTS INC
5700 E Airport Dr (91761-8620)
PHONE..........................909 390-3745
Carrie Roberts, *Mgr*
EMP: 135
SALES (corp-wide): 3.31B **Publicly Held**
SIC: **5023** Pottery
HQ: Norcal Pottery Products, Inc.
1000 Washington St
Foxboro MA
510 895-5966

(P-12312)
OMEGA MOULDING WEST LLC
Also Called: Omega
5500 Lindbergh Ln (90201-6410)
PHONE..........................323 261-3510
Bernard Portnoy, *Managing Member*
◆ **EMP:** 130 **EST:** 1998
SQ FT: 130,000
SALES (est): 18.25MM **Privately Held**
Web: www.omegamoulding.com
SIC: **5023** Frames and framing, picture and mirror

(P-12313)
PACIFIC HERITG HM FASHION INC
Also Called: Home Decor Wholesaler
901 Lawson St (91748-1121)
PHONE..........................909 598-5200
Meng Lan Liu, *Pr*
Frank Hsu, *
▲ **EMP:** 25 **EST:** 2002
SALES (est): 4.95MM **Privately Held**
SIC: **5023** 2392 Window shades; Blankets, comforters and beddings

(P-12314)
REU DISTRIBUTION LLC
Also Called: Republic Floor
7227 Telegraph Rd (90640-6512)
PHONE..........................323 201-4200
Eliyahu Shuat, *

EMP: 700 **EST:** 2015
SALES (est): 175MM **Privately Held**
SIC: **5023** 5211 2426 Wood flooring; Flooring, wood; Flooring, hardwood

(P-12315)
SIDS CARPET BARN (PA)
Also Called: Abbey Carpet
132 W 8th St (91950-1197)
PHONE..........................619 477-7000
Allan W Ziman, *Pr*
Allan W Ziman, *Pr*
Don Pasquill, *
Stacy B Ziman, *
Robert Wood, *
EMP: 24 **EST:** 1950
SQ FT: 7,800
SALES (est): 30.14MM
SALES (corp-wide): 30.14MM **Privately Held**
Web: www.sidscarpet.com
SIC: **5023** 1771 5713 1389 Carpets; Flooring contractor; Carpets; Construction, repair, and dismantling services

(P-12316)
TEST-RITE PRODUCTS CORP (DH)
1900 Burgundy Pl (91761-2308)
PHONE..........................909 605-9899
Kelly Ho, *Pr*
Jack Ho, *
◆ **EMP:** 80 **EST:** 1975
SQ FT: 400,000
SALES (est): 67.23MM **Privately Held**
SIC: **5023** Homefurnishings
HQ: Test-Rite International (U.S.) Co., Ltd.
1900 Burgundy Pl Ste X
Ontario CA

(P-12317)
THREE WISE MEN INC
Also Called: Max Windsor Floors
11818 San Marino St Ste B (91730-6015)
PHONE..........................909 477-6698
▲ **EMP:** 20
Web: www.epochnetwork.com
SIC: **5023** 3996 Wood flooring; Hard surface floor coverings, nec

(P-12318)
TIFFANY DALE INC (PA)
14765 Firestone Blvd (90638-5918)
PHONE..........................714 739-2700
Ye H Chung, *CEO*
Connie Chung, *
▲ **EMP:** 83 **EST:** 1979
SALES (est): 12.37MM
SALES (corp-wide): 12.37MM **Privately Held**
Web: www.daletiffany.com
SIC: **5023** Lamps: floor, boudoir, desk

(P-12319)
TRI-WEST LTD (PA)
12005 Pike St (90670-6100)
PHONE..........................562 692-9166
Allen Gage, *Pr*
Randy Sims, *Pt*
John Lubinxki, *Pt*
▲ **EMP:** 200 **EST:** 1976
SQ FT: 300,000
SALES (est): 100.68MM
SALES (corp-wide): 100.68MM **Privately Held**
Web: www.triwestltd.com
SIC: **5023** Floor coverings

(P-12320)
UNIQUE CARPETS LTD
7360 Jurupa Ave (92504-1025)
PHONE..........................951 352-8125
Bill D Graves, *Pr*
Robert L Binford, *
Martin Lopez, *
▲ **EMP:** 55 **EST:** 1985
SALES (est): 9.88MM **Privately Held**
Web: www.uniquecarpetsltd.com
SIC: **5023** 2273 Carpets; Carpets and rugs

(P-12321)
UNIVERSAL WOOD MOULDING INC (PA)
Also Called: Universal Framing Products
21139 Centre Pointe Pkwy (91350-2994)
PHONE..........................661 362-6262
Jon M Bromberg, *CEO*
Avi Feibenlatt, *Ch Bd*
Mark Gottlieb, *
▲ **EMP:** 50 **EST:** 1995
SALES (est): 24.32MM
SALES (corp-wide): 24.32MM **Privately Held**
Web: www.universalarquati.com
SIC: **5023** 3999 Frames and framing, picture and mirror; Atomizers, toiletry

(P-12322)
VENUS GROUP INC (PA)
Also Called: Venus Textiles
25861 Wright St (92610-3504)
PHONE..........................949 609-1299
Kirit D Patel, *CEO*
Rajni D Patel, *VP*
◆ **EMP:** 78 **EST:** 1971
SALES (est): 35.59MM
SALES (corp-wide): 35.59MM **Privately Held**
Web: www.venusgroup.com
SIC: **5023** 2392 5719 Towels; Towels, fabric and nonwoven: made from purchased materials; Towels

(P-12323)
ZWILLING JA HENCKELS LLC
Also Called: Z Willing J A Henckels
100 Citadel Dr Ste 575 (90040-1571)
PHONE..........................323 597-1421
EMP: 244
SALES (corp-wide): 4.45B **Privately Held**
Web: www.zwilling.com
SIC: **5023** Kitchenware
HQ: Zwilling J.A. Henckels, Llc
270 Marble Ave
Pleasantville NY
914 749-3400

5031 Lumber, Plywood, And Millwork

(P-12324)
ATRIUM DOOR & WIN CO ARIZ INC
5455 E La Palma Ave Ste A (92807-2006)
PHONE..........................714 693-0601
Gregory T Faherty, *Pr*
Jeff Hull, *
Randall S Fojtasek, *
EMP: 144 **EST:** 1960
SQ FT: 220,000
SALES (est): 11.79MM
SALES (corp-wide): 5.58B **Privately Held**
SIC: **5031** Windows
HQ: Atrium Windows And Doors, Inc.
9001 Ambassador Row
Dallas TX
214 583-1840

(P-12325)
BUILDERS FENCE COMPANY INC (PA)
8937 San Fernando Rd (91352-1410)
P.O. Box 125 (91353-0125)
PHONE..........................818 768-5500
Marshall K Frankel, *Pr*
▲ **EMP:** 35 **EST:** 1959
SQ FT: 6,400
SALES (est): 48.82MM
SALES (corp-wide): 48.82MM **Privately Held**
Web: www.buildersfence.com
SIC: **5031** 1799 3446 Fencing, wood; Ornamental metal work; Architectural metalwork

(P-12326)
CRYSTAL PCF WIN & DOOR SYS LLC
Also Called: Crystal
1850 Atlanta Ave (92507-2476)
PHONE..........................951 779-9300
EMP: 32 **EST:** 2010
SALES (est): 23.79MM **Privately Held**
Web: www.crystalpacificwindow.com
SIC: **5031** 2431 5039 Windows; Doors and door parts and trim, wood; Doors, sliding

(P-12327)
DECWOOD INC
Also Called: Decorative Woods Lbr & Molding
3 Oldfield (92618-2800)
PHONE..........................949 588-9663
Peter Juteau, *CEO*
Elise Juteau, *CFO*
EMP: 19 **EST:** 1979
SQ FT: 22,200
SALES (est): 2.06MM **Privately Held**
Web: www.decorativewoods.com
SIC: **5031** 5211 2431 Building materials, exterior; Millwork and lumber; Doors and door parts and trim, wood

(P-12328)
EXPO INDUSTRIES INC
Also Called: Expo Builders Supply
7455 Carroll Rd (92121-2303)
P.O. Box 711 (92121)
PHONE..........................858 566-3110
EMP: 95
Web: www.expostucco.com
SIC: **5031** 3299 Building materials, exterior; Stucco

(P-12329)
FLEETWOOD ALUMINUM PRODUCTS INC
Also Called: Fleetwood Windows and Doors
1 Fleetwood Way (92879-5101)
P.O. Box 1086 (92878-1086)
PHONE..........................800 736-7363
EMP: 250 **EST:** 1960
SALES (est): 40.89MM **Privately Held**
Web: www.fleetwoodusa.com
SIC: **5031** 3442 Doors and windows; Metal doors, sash, and trim

(P-12330)
FOUNDATION BUILDING MTLS INC (HQ)
Also Called: Foundation Building Materials
2520 Redhill Ave (92705-5542)
PHONE..........................714 380-3127
Ruben Mendoza, *Pr*
John Gorey, *
Pete Welly, *
Onur Demirkaya, *
Richard J Tilley, *

EMP: 237 **EST:** 2016
SALES (est): 2.06B **Privately Held**
Web: www.fbmsales.com
SIC: 5031 5033 5039 Building materials, interior; Roofing, siding, and insulation; Ceiling systems and products
PA: American Securities Llc
590 Madison Ave Fl 38
New York NY

(P-12331)
GROVE LUMBER & BLDG SUPS INC (PA)
27126 Watson Rd (92585-9792)
PHONE..............................909 947-0277
Raymond G Croll Junior, *CEO*
EMP: 190 **EST:** 1979
SQ FT: 3,000
SALES (est): 100.98MM
SALES (corp-wide): 100.98MM **Privately Held**
Web: www.grovelumber.com
SIC: 5031 5211 Lumber: rough, dressed, and finished; Lumber products

(P-12332)
HARDY WINDOW COMPANY (PA)
1639 E Miraloma Ave (92870-6623)
PHONE..............................714 996-1807
Chance P Hardy, *Pr*
EMP: 141 **EST:** 1998
SQ FT: 14,000
SALES (est): 33.55MM
SALES (corp-wide): 33.55MM **Privately Held**
Web:
www.orangecountywindowanddoor.com
SIC: 5031 Windows

(P-12333)
JAMES HARDIE BUILDING PDTS INC
10901 Elm Ave (92337-7327)
PHONE..............................909 355-6500
Bob Mussleman, *Brnch Mgr*
EMP: 130
Web: www.jameshardie.com
SIC: 5031 3272 Building materials, exterior; Areaways, basement window: concrete
HQ: James Hardie Building Products Inc.
231 S La Salle St # 2000
Chicago IL
312 291-5072

(P-12334)
JELD-WEN INC
Also Called: American Building Supply
120 S Cedar Ave (92376-9010)
PHONE..............................909 879-8700
Carlos Duran, *Brnch Mgr*
EMP: 104
Web: www.abs-abs.com
SIC: 5031 Doors, nec
HQ: Jeld-Wen, Inc.
2645 Silver Crescent Dr
Charlotte NC
800 535-3936

(P-12335)
JELD-WEN INC
Also Called: Jeld-Wen Windows
2760 Progress St Ste B (92081-8449)
PHONE..............................760 597-4201
Clint Honeycutt, *Genl Mgr*
EMP: 300
Web: www.jeld-wen.com
SIC: 5031 Doors and windows
HQ: Jeld-Wen, Inc.
2645 Silver Crescent Dr
Charlotte NC
800 535-3936

(P-12336)
KELLY-WRIGHT HARDWOODS INC
450 Delta Ave (92821-2935)
P.O. Box 728 (90637-0728)
PHONE..............................714 632-9930
Harold J Wright, *CEO*
EMP: 19 **EST:** 1982
SQ FT: 60,000
SALES (est): 1.05MM **Privately Held**
Web: www.kelly-wright.com
SIC: 5031 2431 2426 Hardboard; Millwork; Hardwood dimension and flooring mills

(P-12337)
NICHOLS LUMBER & HARDWARE CO
Also Called: Ace Hardware
13470 Dalewood St (91706-5883)
PHONE..............................626 960-4802
Judith A Nichols, *Pr*
Charles Nichols, *
EMP: 75 **EST:** 1958
SALES (est): 24.91MM **Privately Held**
Web: www.nicholslumber.com
SIC: 5031 5251 2421 Lumber: rough, dressed, and finished; Hardware stores; Sawmills and planing mills, general

(P-12338)
OREGON PCF BLDG PDTS MAPLE INC
Also Called: Orepac Millwork Products
2401 E Philadelphia St (91761-7743)
PHONE..............................909 627-4043
Douglas Hart, *Pr*
▲ **EMP:** 125 **EST:** 1992
SALES (est): 23.89MM
SALES (corp-wide): 471.9MM **Privately Held**
Web: www.orepac.com
SIC: 5031 5032 Building materials, exterior; Brick, stone, and related material
PA: Orepac Holding Company
30170 Sw Ore Pac Ave
Wilsonville OR
503 685-5499

(P-12339)
PANORAMIC DOORS LLC
3265 Production Ave Ste A (92058-1361)
PHONE..............................760 722-1300
Raffy Timonian, *VP*
EMP: 103
SALES (corp-wide): 23.63MM **Privately Held**
Web: www.panoramicdoors.com
SIC: 5031 Windows
PA: Panoramic Doors Llc
15050 Frye Rd
Fort Worth TX
817 952-3500

(P-12340)
POTTER ROEMER LLC (HQ)
17451 Hurley St (91744-5106)
P.O. Box 3527 (91744-0527)
PHONE..............................626 855-4890
Donald E Morris, *Managing Member*
▲ **EMP:** 55 **EST:** 1937
SQ FT: 110,000
SALES (est): 27MM
SALES (corp-wide): 99.15MM **Privately Held**
Web: www.potterroemer.com
SIC: 5031 3569 2542 Skylights, all materials; Firefighting and related equipment; Partitions and fixtures, except wood
PA: Acorn Engineering Company
15125 Proctor Ave

City Of Industry CA
800 488-8999

(P-12341)
RELIABLE WHOLESALE LUMBER INC (PA)
7600 Redondo Cir (92648-1303)
P.O. Box 191 (92648-0191)
PHONE..............................714 848-8222
Jerome M Higman, *Pr*
Jerome M Higman, *Pr*
David Higman, *
Will Higman, *
Jerry Higman, *Prin*
EMP: 90 **EST:** 1970
SQ FT: 4,500
SALES (est): 101.05MM
SALES (corp-wide): 101.05MM **Privately Held**
Web: www.rwli.net
SIC: 5031 2421 Lumber: rough, dressed, and finished; Sawmills and planing mills, general

(P-12342)
ROBERTS LUMBER SALES INC
Also Called: Robert's Lumber
2661 S Lilac Ave (92316-3211)
PHONE..............................909 350-9164
Robert Cantero Junior, *CEO*
Lori Cantero, *
EMP: 57 **EST:** 1997
SALES (est): 18.37MM **Privately Held**
Web: www.robertslumbersales.com
SIC: 5031 2448 Lumber: rough, dressed, and finished; Wood pallets and skids

(P-12343)
SHAPP INTERNATIONAL TRDG INC
Also Called: Shapp Internatioonal
6000 Reseda Blvd (91356-1571)
P.O. Box 893 (91365-0893)
PHONE..............................818 348-3000
Allan Shapiro, *Pr*
Louis Justin, *
EMP: 118 **EST:** 1991
SQ FT: 8,000
SALES (est): 10.27MM **Privately Held**
SIC: 5031 5064 5112 5021 Lumber, plywood, and millwork; Electrical appliances, major; Stationery and office supplies; Furniture

(P-12344)
WALNUT INVESTMENT CORP
Also Called: AMS
2940 E White Star Ave (92806-2627)
PHONE..............................714 238-9240
▲ **EMP:** 550
SIC: 5031 5039 5072 Building materials, exterior; Ceiling systems and products; Hardware

(P-12345)
WEST WOOD PRODUCTS INC (PA)
2943 E Las Hermanas St (90221-5508)
PHONE..............................310 631-8978
Golan Levy, *Pr*
Shrone Levy, *VP*
Orly Levy, *Sec*
▲ **EMP:** 18 **EST:** 1988
SQ FT: 91,000
SALES (est): 21.66MM **Privately Held**
Web: www.west-wood.net
SIC: 5031 2499 Lumber, plywood, and millwork; Decorative wood and woodwork

(P-12346)
WESTSIDE BLDG SAN DIEGO LLC
Also Called: Westside Building Materials
11620 Sorrento Valley Rd (92121-1011)
PHONE..............................858 566-4343
EMP: 48 **EST:** 2007
SALES (est): 9.64MM **Privately Held**
Web: www.westsidebmc.com
SIC: 5031 3299 Building materials, exterior; Mica products

5032 Brick, Stone, And Related Material

(P-12347)
ATLAS CONSTRUCTION SUPPLY INC
7550 Stage Rd (90621-1224)
PHONE..............................714 441-9500
Pat Kelley, *Mgr*
EMP: 32
SALES (corp-wide): 49.08MM **Privately Held**
Web: www.atlasform.com
SIC: 5032 5211 5082 3444 Concrete building products; Masonry materials and supplies; Contractor's materials; Concrete forms, sheet metal
PA: Atlas Construction Supply, Inc.
4640 Brinnell St
San Diego CA
858 277-2100

(P-12348)
BEST CHEER STONE INC (PA)
3190 E Miraloma Ave (92806-1906)
PHONE..............................714 399-1588
Chung Lun Ko, *CEO*
Yanlin K Xu, *CFO*
▲ **EMP:** 22 **EST:** 2005
SALES (est): 23.93MM **Privately Held**
Web: www.bestcheerstone.com
SIC: 5032 3281 Granite building stone; Stone, quarrying and processing of own stone products

(P-12349)
CEMEX CEMENT INC
1201 W Gladstone St (91702-5142)
P.O. Box 575 (91702-0575)
PHONE..............................626 969-1747
Steve Hayes, *Mgr*
EMP: 99
SIC: 5032 3273 3251 1411 Concrete mixtures; Ready-mixed concrete; Brick and structural clay tile; Dimension stone
HQ: Cemex Cement, Inc.
10100 Katy Fwy Ste 300
Houston TX
713 650-6200

(P-12350)
CEMEX CONSTRUCTION MTLS INC (DH)
3990 Concours Ste 200 (91764)
PHONE..............................909 974-5500
Deborah Sue Politte, *Pr*
Gilberto Perez, *
Thomas Edgeller, *
◆ **EMP:** 35 **EST:** 1990
SQ FT: 20,419
SALES (est): 44.12MM **Privately Held**
SIC: 5032 1423 Cement; Crushed and broken granite
HQ: Cemex, Inc.
10100 Katy Fwy Ste 300
Houston TX
713 650-6200

(P-12351)
COAST ROCK PRODUCTS INC
1625 E Donovan Rd (93454-2582)
P.O. Box 1280 (93456-1280)
PHONE..................................805 925-2505
Ron Root, *Pr*
Steve Will, *
John Will, *
George Hamel, *
EMP: 45 **EST:** 1955
SQ FT: 5,000
SALES (est): 6.78MM **Privately Held**
SIC: 5032 3273 3241 2951 Cement; Ready-mixed concrete; Cement, hydraulic; Asphalt paving mixtures and blocks

(P-12352)
CONCRETE TIE INDUSTRIES INC (PA)
Also Called: Concrete Tie
130 E Oris St (90222-2714)
P.O. Box 5406 (90224-5406)
PHONE..................................310 628-2328
Paul J Schoendienst, *Pr*
Steve Sim, *
EMP: 70 **EST:** 1981
SQ FT: 280,000
SALES (est): 9.21MM
SALES (corp-wide): 9.21MM **Privately Held**
SIC: 5032 3452 Concrete and cinder building products; Bolts, nuts, rivets, and washers

(P-12353)
ELDORADO STONE LLC
24100 Orange Ave (92570-8791)
PHONE..................................951 601-3838
EMP: 700
Web: www.eldoradostone.com
SIC: 5032 Brick, stone, and related material
HQ: Eldorado Stone Llc
3817 Ocean Ranch Blvd # 114
Oceanside CA
800 925-1491

(P-12354)
EMSER TILE LLC (PA)
Also Called: Design Made Easy
8431 Santa Monica Blvd (90069-4209)
PHONE..................................323 650-2000
◆ **EMP:** 275 **EST:** 1968
SALES (est): 273.97MM
SALES (corp-wide): 273.97MM **Privately Held**
Web: www.emser.com
SIC: 5032 5211 Ceramic wall and floor tile, nec; Tile, ceramic

(P-12355)
KRETUS GROUP INC (PA)
1129 N Patt St (92801-2568)
PHONE..................................714 738-6640
Ron Webber, *Pr*
EMP: 21 **EST:** 2005
SQ FT: 8,800
SALES (est): 4.92MM **Privately Held**
Web: www.kretus.com
SIC: 5032 3569 Concrete building products; Assembly machines, non-metalworking

(P-12356)
M S INTERNATIONAL INC (PA)
Also Called: MSI Orange Showroom & Dist Ctr
2095 N Batavia St (92865-3101)
PHONE..................................714 685-7500
Manahar Shah, *CEO*
Rajesh Shah, *
Rutesh Shah, *

Chandrika Shah, *
◆ **EMP:** 266 **EST:** 1983
SQ FT: 500,000
SALES (est): 513.97MM
SALES (corp-wide): 513.97MM **Privately Held**
Web: www.msisurfaces.com
SIC: 5032 5023 Granite building stone; Floor coverings

(P-12357)
MARJAN STONE INC
2758 Via Orange Way (91978-1744)
PHONE..................................619 825-6000
Hikmet Pauls, *CEO*
EMP: 25 **EST:** 2006
SQ FT: 1,600
SALES (est): 5.2MM **Privately Held**
Web: www.marjanstone.com
SIC: 5032 3281 Granite building stone; Cut stone and stone products

(P-12358)
NEW GENERATION ENGRG CNSTR INC
22815 Frampton Ave (90501-5034)
PHONE..................................424 329-3950
Raul Ocegueda, *Pr*
EMP: 25 **EST:** 2016
SALES (est): 8.27MM **Privately Held**
Web: www.tngec.com
SIC: 5032 1459 3317 3531 Brick, stone, and related material; Clays (common) quarrying; Steel pipe and tubes; Construction machinery

(P-12359)
PACIFIC CLAY PRODUCTS INC
14741 Lake St (92530-1610)
PHONE..................................661 857-1401
Barry Coley, *Pr*
Kai Chin, *
Dale Kline, *
▲ **EMP:** 160 **EST:** 1930
SQ FT: 200,000
SALES (est): 48.16MM **Privately Held**
Web: www.pacificclay.com
SIC: 5032 3251 Tile and clay products; Paving brick, clay

(P-12360)
PATRICK INDUSTRIES INC
Also Called: Custom Vinyls
13414 Slover Ave (92337-6977)
PHONE..................................909 350-4440
Vince Fergan, *Brnch Mgr*
EMP: 41
SALES (corp-wide): 4.88B **Publicly Held**
Web: www.patrickind.com
SIC: 5032 1799 2435 3083 Brick, stone, and related material; Building site preparation; Hardwood veneer and plywood; Laminated plastics plate and sheet
PA: Patrick Industries, Inc.
107 W Franklin St
Elkhart IN
574 294-7511

(P-12361)
ROBERTSONS READY MIX LTD
16952 S D St (92395-3302)
PHONE..................................702 798-0568
EMP: 94
Web: www.rrmca.com
SIC: 5032 Gravel
HQ: Robertson's Ready Mix, Ltd., A California Limited Partnership
200 S Main St Ste 200 # 200
Corona CA
951 493-6500

(P-12362)
UGM CITATAH INC (PA)
Also Called: Ugmc
13220 Cambridge St (90670-4902)
PHONE..................................562 921-9549
Viken Dave Yaghjian, *Pr*
Bruce Feaster, *
Irmen Yaghjian, *
▲ **EMP:** 125 **EST:** 1987
SQ FT: 46,000
SALES (est): 19.08MM
SALES (corp-wide): 19.08MM **Privately Held**
Web: www.ugmcstone.com
SIC: 5032 1741 1743 Marble building stone; Stone masonry; Terrazzo, tile, marble and mosaic work

(P-12363)
VALORI SAND & GRAVEL COMPANY
Also Called: Thompson Building Materials
11027 Cherry Ave (92337-7118)
P.O. Box 950 (92334-0950)
PHONE..................................909 350-3000
EMP: 250
SALES (est): 23.42MM **Privately Held**
Web: www.thompsonbldg.com
SIC: 5032 5211 Brick, stone, and related material; Cement
PA: Valori Sand & Gravel Company Inc
141 W Taft Ave
Orange CA
714 637-0104

(P-12364)
WESTERN PACIFIC DISTRG LLC
Also Called: Westpac Materials
341 W Meats Ave (92865-2623)
PHONE..................................714 974-6837
Mark Hamilton, *Managing Member*
EMP: 157 **EST:** 2001
SALES (est): 48.62MM **Privately Held**
Web: www.westpacmaterials.com
SIC: 5032 Drywall materials

(P-12365)
WHITEWATER ROCK & SUP CO INC
58645 Old Highway 60 (92282-7600)
PHONE..................................760 325-2747
Allan E Bankus Junior, *Pr*
Irene Bankus, *
▲ **EMP:** 33 **EST:** 1962
SQ FT: 4,500
SALES (est): 5.93MM **Privately Held**
Web: www.whitewater-rock.com
SIC: 5032 3281 Building stone; Stone, quarrying and processing of own stone products

---

5033 Roofing, Siding, And Insulation

(P-12366)
BEACON PACIFIC INC
Also Called: Pacific Supply
675 N Batavia St (92868-1220)
PHONE..................................714 288-1974
EMP: 110
SIC: 5033 5211 Roofing, asphalt and sheet metal; Roofing material

(P-12367)
INSUL-THERM INTERNATIONAL INC (PA)
Also Called: Insul-Therm

6651 E 26th St (90040-3215)
PHONE..................................323 728-0558
▲ **EMP:** 28 **EST:** 1982
SALES (est): 23.24MM
SALES (corp-wide): 23.24MM **Privately Held**
Web: www.insultherm.com
SIC: 5033 2899 3296 Insulation, thermal; Insulating compounds; Mineral wool

(P-12368)
PACIFIC AWARD METALS INC
Also Called: Gibraltar
10302 Birtcher Dr (91752-1829)
PHONE..................................909 390-9880
Brian Lipke, *Brnch Mgr*
EMP: 55
SALES (corp-wide): 1.39B **Publicly Held**
Web: www.gibraltarbuildingproducts.com
SIC: 5033 2952 3444 Roofing and siding materials; Roofing materials; Sheet metalwork
HQ: Pacific Award Metals, Inc.
1450 Virginia Ave
Baldwin Park CA
626 814-4410

(P-12369)
STANDARD INDUSTRIES INC
Also Called: GAF Materials
6505 Zerker Rd (93263-9614)
PHONE..................................661 387-1110
Phil Halpin, *Genl Mgr*
EMP: 100
SALES (corp-wide): 6.27B **Privately Held**
Web: www.gaf.com
SIC: 5033 Roofing and siding materials
HQ: Standard Building Solutions Inc.
1 Campus Dr
Parsippany NJ

5039 Construction Materials, Nec

(P-12370)
BAKERSFIELD SHINGLES WHOLESALE INC
Also Called: Bsw Roofing Contractors
4 P St (93304-3192)
P.O. Box 70272 (93387-0272)
PHONE..................................661 327-3727
EMP: 85 **EST:** 1971
SALES (est): 11.25MM **Privately Held**
Web: www.bswroofing.com
SIC: 5039 1761 Eavestroughing, parts and supplies; Roofing contractor

(P-12371)
LSF9 CYPRESS LP (PA)
2741 Walnut Ave Ste 200 (92780-7063)
PHONE..................................714 380-3127
Ruben Mendoza, *Pr*
EMP: 156 **EST:** 2015
SALES (est): 153.99MM
SALES (corp-wide): 153.99MM **Privately Held**
SIC: 5039 5031 5033 Ceiling systems and products; Wallboard; Insulation materials

(P-12372)
LSF9 CYPRESS PARENT 2 LLC
2741 Walnut Ave Ste 200 (92780-7063)
PHONE..................................714 380-3127
EMP: 3500 **EST:** 2016
SALES (est): 153.99MM
SALES (corp-wide): 153.99MM **Privately Held**

SIC: 5039 5031 5033 Ceiling systems and products; Wallboard; Insulation materials
PA: Lsf9 Cypress L.P.
2741 Walnut Ave Ste 200
Tustin CA
714 380-3127

(P-12373)
ULTRAGLAS INC
3392 Hampton Ct (91362-1130)
PHONE.............................818 772-7744
Jane Skeeter, *Pr*
▼ **EMP:** 23 **EST:** 1972
SALES (est): 4.63MM **Privately Held**
Web: www.ultraglas.com
SIC: 5039 3231 3211 5231 Glass construction materials; Products of purchased glass; Flat glass; Glass, leaded or stained

(P-12374)
WHITE CAP SUPPLY GROUP INC
Also Called: White Cap 301
28255 Kelly Johnson Pkwy (91355-5080)
PHONE.............................661 294-7737
Julia Laguardia, *Brnch Mgr*
EMP: 3596
SALES (corp-wide): 7.35B **Privately Held**
SIC: 5039 5072 Air ducts, sheet metal; Hardware
HQ: White Cap Supply Group, Inc.
6250 Brook Hllow Pkwy Ste
Norcross GA

5043 Photographic Equipment And Supplies

(P-12375)
AAA IMAGING & SUPPLIES INC
Also Called: AAA Imaging Solutions
2313 S Susan St (92704-4420)
PHONE.............................714 431-0570
Robert G Noterman, *CEO*
Lou Burgess, *VP*
◆ **EMP:** 25 **EST:** 1998
SALES (est): 9.57MM **Privately Held**
Web: www.aaaimaging.com
SIC: 5043 3861 7699 Photographic processing equipment; Processing equipment, photographic; Photographic equipment repair

(P-12376)
CANON USA INC
15955 Alton Pkwy (92618-3731)
PHONE.............................949 753-4000
Glen Takahashi, *Mgr*
EMP: 350
Web: usa.canon.com
SIC: 5043 5044 5045 8741 Photographic cameras, projectors, equipment and supplies; Office equipment; Computers, nec ; Management services
HQ: Canon U.S.A., Inc.
1 Canon Park
Melville NY
516 328-5000

(P-12377)
DIAKONT ADVANCED TECH INC
Also Called: Diakont
3193 Lionshead Ave (92010-4702)
PHONE.............................858 551-5551
Edward Petit De Mange, *CEO*
Mikhail Fedosovskiy, *
◆ **EMP:** 30 **EST:** 2011
SQ FT: 11,000
SALES (est): 6.77MM **Privately Held**
Web: www.diakont.com

SIC: 5043 7389 3625 Photographic equipment and supplies; Patrol of electric transmission or gas lines; Actuators, industrial

(P-12378)
JK IMAGING LTD
17239 S Main St (90248-3129)
PHONE.............................310 755-6848
Joe Atick, *CEO*
Mike Feng, *
Shu-ping Wu, *CFO*
▲ **EMP:** 100 **EST:** 2012
SQ FT: 6,000
SALES (est): 9.04MM **Privately Held**
SIC: 5043 Cameras and photographic equipment

(P-12379)
NORITSU-AMERICA CORPORATION (HQ)
6900 Noritsu Ave (90620-1372)
P.O. Box 5039 (90622-5039)
PHONE.............................714 521-9040
Michiro Niikura, *CEO*
Kanichi Nishimoto, *
Akihiko Kuwabara, *
◆ **EMP:** 115 **EST:** 1978
SQ FT: 27,500
SALES (est): 69.13MM **Privately Held**
Web: www.noritsu.com
SIC: 5043 Photographic processing equipment
PA: Noritsu Koki Co., Ltd.
1-10-10, Azabujuban
Minato-Ku TKY

(P-12380)
PILGRIM OPERATIONS LLC
Also Called: Tailbroom Media Grop
12020 Chandler Blvd Ste 200 (91607)
PHONE.............................818 478-4500
Douglas Liechty, *Managing Member*
EMP: 400 **EST:** 2012
SALES (est): 22.06MM **Privately Held**
SIC: 5043 Motion picture studio and theater equipment

5044 Office Equipment

(P-12381)
ALLSTATE IMAGING INC (PA)
21621 Nordhoff St (91311-5828)
PHONE.............................818 678-4550
Alan Jurick, *Pr*
Richard Shapiro, *
Russel Leventhal, *
EMP: 80 **EST:** 1990
SALES (est): 14.98MM **Privately Held**
SIC: 5044 Office equipment

(P-12382)
CANON BUSINESS SOLUTIONS-WEST INC
110 W Walnut St (90248-3100)
P.O. Box 51075 (90074-1075)
PHONE.............................310 217-3000
EMP: 450
SIC: 5044 Office equipment

(P-12383)
CANON SOLUTIONS AMERICA INC
Also Called: Canon
6435 Ventura Blvd Ste C007 (93003-7228)
PHONE.............................844 443-4636
Suzanne Alpizar, *Mgr*
EMP: 37

Web: csa.canon.com
SIC: 5044 7699 3861 Copying equipment; Photocopy machine repair; Photographic equipment and supplies
HQ: Canon Solutions America, Inc.
1 Canon Park
Melville NY
631 330-5000

(P-12384)
INTEGRUS LLC
Also Called: Advanced Office
14370 Myford Rd Ste 100 (92606-1015)
PHONE.............................949 538-9211
Mike Dixon, *CEO*
Richard Van Dyke, *Pr*
Tim Wickers, *VP*
EMP: 100 **EST:** 2011
SALES (est): 23.07MM **Privately Held**
SIC: 5044 Office equipment

(P-12385)
KYOCERA DCMENT SOLUTIONS W LLC
14101 Alton Pkwy (92618-1815)
PHONE.............................800 996-9591
Norihiko Ina, *Managing Member*
Mike Graves, *
EMP: 150 **EST:** 2008
SALES (est): 24.47MM **Privately Held**
SIC: 5044 Office equipment
HQ: Kyocera Document Solutions America, Inc.
225 Sand Rd
Fairfield NJ
973 808-8444

(P-12386)
MICROTEK LAB INC (HQ)
13337 South St (90703-7308)
PHONE.............................310 687-4823
Clark Hsu, *Pr*
Stewart Chow, *
▲ **EMP:** 110 **EST:** 1980
SQ FT: 126,000
SALES (est): 61.04MM **Privately Held**
Web: www.microtekusa.com
SIC: 5044 Copying equipment
PA: Microtek International Inc.
No.6 Industry E. Road 3 Science-Based Industrial Park
Hsinchu City

(P-12387)
NEW AGE ELECTRONICS INC
21950 Arnold Center Rd (90810-1646)
PHONE.............................310 549-0000
▲ **EMP:** 130
SIC: 5044 5045 Office equipment; Computers, peripherals, and software

(P-12388)
RICOH ELECTRONICS INC
1920 W Base Line Rd (92376-3016)
PHONE.............................714 566-2500
EMP: 94
Web: rei.ricoh.com
SIC: 5044 Photocopy machines
HQ: Ricoh Electronics, Inc.
1125 Hurricane Shoals Rd
Lawrenceville GA
714 566-2500

(P-12389)
TOSHIBA AMER BUS SOLUTIONS INC (DH)
Also Called: Toshiba
25530 Commercentre Dr (92630-8855)
PHONE.............................949 462-6000

Scott Maccabe, *CEO*
Desmond Allen, *
Mark Mathews, *
Bill Lombard, *
Larry White, *
◆ **EMP:** 350 **EST:** 1999
SQ FT: 90,000
SALES (est): 1.38B **Privately Held**
Web: business.toshiba.com
SIC: 5044 Copying equipment
HQ: Toshiba Tec Corporation
1-11-1, Osaki
Shinagawa-Ku TKY

(P-12390)
UNITED RIBBON COMPANY INC
Also Called: United Imaging
21201 Oxnard St (91367-5015)
PHONE.............................818 716-1515
TOLL FREE: 800
Michael Cohen, *Pr*
Yigal Avrahamy, *
EMP: 85 **EST:** 1973
SQ FT: 22,000
SALES (est): 51.7MM **Privately Held**
Web: www.unitedimaging.com
SIC: 5044 5943 5021 7699 Office equipment ; Office forms and supplies; Office and public building furniture; Office equipment and accessory customizing

(P-12391)
XEROX EDUCATION SERVICES LLC (DH)
2277 E 220th St (90810-1639)
PHONE.............................310 830-9847
J Michael Peffer, *Managing Member*
Mike R Festa, *Managing Member**
EMP: 90 **EST:** 1970
SALES (est): 247.08MM
SALES (corp-wide): 3.86B **Publicly Held**
Web: www.afsa.com
SIC: 5044 Office equipment
HQ: Conduent Business Services, Llc
100 Campus Dr Ste 200
Florham Park NJ
973 261-7100

5045 Computers, Peripherals, And Software

(P-12392)
ADESSO INC
Also Called: ADS Techonlogy
20659 Valley Blvd (91789-2731)
PHONE.............................909 839-2929
Allen Ku, *Pr*
▲ **EMP:** 200 **EST:** 1994
SALES (est): 21.78MM **Privately Held**
Web: www.adesso.com
SIC: 5045 Computer peripheral equipment

(P-12393)
ALTAMETRICS HOSTING LLC
Also Called: Altametrics
3191 Red Hill Ave Ste 100 (92626-3451)
PHONE.............................800 676-1281
Mitesh Gala, *Pr*
Anand Gala, *
Ajay Shiv, *CIO**
EMP: 140 **EST:** 2001
SQ FT: 6,000
SALES (est): 34.92MM **Privately Held**
Web: www.altametrics.com
SIC: 5045 Computer software

PRODUCTS & SVCS

(P-12394)

ALURATEK INC

Also Called: Aluratek
15241 Barranca Pkwy (92618-2201)
PHONE..................................866 580-1978
John P Wolikow, *CEO*
Akash Patel, *CFO*
Victor Wang, *Prin*
▲ **EMP:** 20 **EST:** 2006
SQ FT: 5,000
SALES (est): 4.62MM **Privately Held**
Web: www.aluratek.com
SIC: 5045 3651 Computers, peripherals, and software; Home entertainment equipment, electronic, nec

(P-12395)

AMERICAN FUTURE TECH CORP

Also Called: Ibuypower
529 Baldwin Park Blvd (91746-1419)
PHONE..................................888 462-3899
Alex Hou, *CEO*
Darren Su, *
▲ **EMP:** 120 **EST:** 1997
SQ FT: 25,000
SALES (est): 133.76MM **Privately Held**
Web: www.ibuypower.com
SIC: 5045 Computer peripheral equipment

(P-12396)

AMERICAN SCALE CO INC

Also Called: Scales
21326 E Arrow Hwy (91724-1442)
P.O. Box 158 (91773-0158)
PHONE..................................800 773-7225
David William Eccles Iii, *CEO*
EMP: 24 **EST:** 1946
SQ FT: 4,150
SALES (est): 4.8MM **Privately Held**
Web: www.americanscale.com
SIC: 5045 3596 7699 Computers, peripherals, and software; Scales and balances, except laboratory; Scale repair service

(P-12397)

ATEN TECHNOLOGY INC

Also Called: Iogear
15365 Barranca Pkwy (92618-2216)
PHONE..................................949 453-8782
▲ **EMP:** 80 **EST:** 1996
SALES (est): 29.99MM **Privately Held**
Web: www.iogear.com
SIC: 5045 Computer peripheral equipment
PA: Aten International Co., Ltd.
3f, No. 125, Sec. 2, Datong Rd.
New Taipei City TAP

(P-12398)

AVATAR TECHNOLOGY INC

339 Cheryl Ln (91789-3003)
PHONE..................................909 598-7696
Juanito Pangalilingan, *CEO*
Toresa Lou, *
▲ **EMP:** 30 **EST:** 1999
SQ FT: 48,000
SALES (est): 4.94MM **Privately Held**
Web: www.v4me.com
SIC: 5045 3571 Computers, nec; Electronic computers

(P-12399)

BAKER & TAYLOR HOLDINGS LLC

Also Called: Baker & Taylor Marketing Svc
10350 Barnes Canyon Rd (92121-2708)
PHONE..................................858 457-2500
EMP: 1436
SALES (corp-wide): 2.52B **Privately Held**

SIC: 5045 5065 5192 7822 Computer software; Tapes, audio and video recording; Books; Television tape distribution
HQ: Baker & Taylor Holdings, Llc
2810 Coliseum Centre Dr # 300
Charlotte NC
704 998-3100

(P-12400)

BRAINSTORM CORPORATION

Also Called: Skytech Gaming
1620 Proforma Ave (91761-7605)
PHONE..................................888 370-8882
Kevin Hsu, *CEO*
◆ **EMP:** 200 **EST:** 2005
SALES (est): 79.31MM **Privately Held**
Web: www.brainstormco.com
SIC: 5045 5065 Computer peripheral equipment; Electronic parts and equipment, nec
PA: Dfi Inc.
10f, No. 97, Xintai 5th Rd., Sec. 1
New Taipei City TAP

(P-12401)

BROADWAY TYPEWRITER CO INC

Also Called: Arey Jones Eductl Solutions
1055 6th Ave Ste 101 (92101-5201)
PHONE..................................800 998-9199
Michael Scarpella, *Pr*
Peter Scarpella, *
David Scarpella, *
Margaret Scarpella, *
EMP: 80 **EST:** 1968
SQ FT: 40,000
SALES (est): 139.47MM **Privately Held**
Web: www.areyjones.com
SIC: 5045 7378 Computers, peripherals, and software; Computer maintenance and repair

(P-12402)

CURVATURE LLC (DH)

7418 Hollister Ave Ste 110 (93117-2675)
PHONE..................................800 230-6638
Christopher Adams, *Pr*
Betsy Dellinger, *
Andrew Gehrlein, *
◆ **EMP:** 300 **EST:** 2001
SALES (est): 251.01MM **Privately Held**
Web: www.curvature.com
SIC: 5045 7379 Computer peripheral equipment; Computer related maintenance services
HQ: Nhr Newco Holdings Llc
6500 Hollister Ave # 210
Santa Barbara CA
805 964-9975

(P-12403)

D-LINK SYSTEMS INCORPORATED

Also Called: D - Link
14420 Myford Rd Ste 100 (92606-1019)
PHONE..................................714 885-6000
William Brown, *Pr*
▲ **EMP:** 164 **EST:** 1986
SQ FT: 120,000
SALES (est): 52.65MM **Privately Held**
Web: us.dlink.com
SIC: 5045 3577 Computers, nec; Computer peripheral equipment, nec
PA: D-Link Corporation
No. 289, Xinhu 3rd Rd.
Taipei City TAP

(P-12404)

DANE ELEC CORP USA (HQ)

Also Called: Gigastone America
17520 Von Karman Ave (92614-6208)

PHONE..................................949 450-2900
◆ **EMP:** 32 **EST:** 1985
SQ FT: 25,000
SALES (est): 1MM **Privately Held**
Web: en.gigastone.com
SIC: 5045 3577 8731 Computer software; Computer peripheral equipment, nec; Computer (hardware) development
PA: Gigastone Corporation
4f, No. 166, Xinhu 2nd Rd.
Taipei City TAP

(P-12405)

DATA EXCHANGE CORPORATION (PA)

Also Called: D E X
3600 Via Pescador (93012-5035)
PHONE..................................805 388-1711
Sheldon Malchicoff, *CEO*
Alan Kheel, *
Burcak Sungur, *
▲ **EMP:** 300 **EST:** 1980
SQ FT: 100,000
SALES (est): 70.96MM
SALES (corp-wide): 70.96MM **Privately Held**
Web: www.dex.com
SIC: 5045 7378 Computers, peripherals, and software; Computer and data processing equipment repair/maintenance

(P-12406)

DATALLEGRO INC

85 Enterprise Ste 200 (92656-2614)
PHONE..................................949 680-3000
Stuart Frost, *Ch Bd*
Mark Theissen, *
EMP: 100 **EST:** 2003
SQ FT: 16,000
SALES (est): 26.35MM
SALES (corp-wide): 211.91B **Publicly Held**
Web: www.datallegro.com
SIC: 5045 Computer software
PA: Microsoft Corporation
1 Microsoft Way
Redmond WA
425 882-8080

(P-12407)

ELOTEK SYSTEMS INC (PA)

216 Avenida Fabricante Ste 112 (92672)
PHONE..................................949 366-4404
Michael Elovitz, *Pr*
Adam Elovitz, *VP*
David Elovitz, *VP*
Judith Elovitz, *VP*
EMP: 20 **EST:** 1981
SQ FT: 4,500
SALES (est): 8.09MM
SALES (corp-wide): 8.09MM **Privately Held**
Web: www.elotek.com
SIC: 5045 3825 Computers, nec; Instruments to measure electricity

(P-12408)

EN POINTE TECHNOLOGIES SLS LLC

200 N Pacific Coast Hwy Ste 1050 (90245-4340)
PHONE..................................310 337-6151
Frank Khulusi, *CEO*
Robert Miley, *
Brandon Laverne, *
EMP: 200 **EST:** 2015
SALES (est): 182.57MM **Publicly Held**
SIC: 5045 Computer peripheral equipment
HQ: Pcm, Inc.
200 N Pacific Coast Hwy # 1050

El Segundo CA
310 354-5600

(P-12409)

ENVIRONMENTAL SYSTEMS RESEARCH INSTITUTE INC (PA)

Also Called: Esri
380 New York St (92373-8118)
P.O. Box 7661 (92375-0661)
PHONE..................................909 793-2853
EMP: 1900 **EST:** 1973
SALES (est): 490.13MM
SALES (corp-wide): 490.13MM **Privately Held**
Web: www.esri.com
SIC: 5045 7371 Computer software; Computer software development and applications

(P-12410)

ESET LLC (HQ)

Also Called: Eset North America
610 W Ash St Ste 1700 (92101-3345)
PHONE..................................619 876-5400
Anton Zajac, *Pr*
Andrew Lee, *
Brett Stapleton, *
Brent Mccarty, *VP*
EMP: 123 **EST:** 1999
SQ FT: 57,000
SALES (est): 72.67MM **Privately Held**
SIC: 5045 Computer software
PA: Eset, Spol. S R.O. .
Einsteinova 3541/24
Bratislava-Petrzalka

(P-12411)

ESRI INTERNATIONAL LLC

380 New York St (92373-8118)
PHONE..................................909 793-2853
EMP: 48 **EST:** 2002
SALES (est): 971.86K
SALES (corp-wide): 490.13MM **Privately Held**
Web: www.esri.com
SIC: 5045 7371 7372 7373 Computer software; Custom computer programming services; Prepackaged software; Computer integrated systems design
PA: Environmental Systems Research Institute, Inc.
380 New York St
Redlands CA
909 793-2853

(P-12412)

EWORKPLACE MANUFACTURING INC

Also Called: Batchmaster Software
9861 Irvine Center Dr (92618-4307)
PHONE..................................949 583-1646
Sahib Dudani, *Pr*
EMP: 200 **EST:** 1999
SQ FT: 5,000
SALES (est): 45.18MM **Privately Held**
Web: www.batchmaster.com
SIC: 5045 Computer software

(P-12413)

GAR ENTERPRISES (PA)

Also Called: Kgs Electronics
418 E Live Oak Ave (91006-5619)
PHONE..................................626 574-1175
Nathan Sugimoto, *CEO*
Pastor Kazuo G Sugimoto, *Prin*
EMP: 70 **EST:** 1960
SALES (est): 23.35MM
SALES (corp-wide): 23.35MM **Privately Held**
Web: www.kgselectronics.com

▲ = Import ▼ = Export
◆ = Import/Export

SIC: **5045** 3728 Anti-static equipment and devices; Aircraft assemblies, subassemblies, and parts, nec

(P-12414)

GBT INC

Also Called: Gigabyte Technology
17358 Railroad St (91748-1023)
PHONE....................626 854-9338
Eric C Lu, *Pr*
Eric C Lu, *Pr*
James Liao, *
▲ **EMP:** 130 **EST:** 1990
SQ FT: 35,000
SALES (est): 634.41MM **Privately Held**
SIC: **5045** Computers and accessories, personal and home entertainment
PA: Giga-Byte Technology Co., Ltd.
No. 6, Baoqiang Rd.,
New Taipei City TAP

(P-12415)

GENERAL PROCUREMENT INC (PA)

Also Called: Connect Computers
1964 W Corporate Way (92801-5373)
PHONE....................949 679-7960
▲ **EMP:** 84 **EST:** 1991
SALES (est): 92.18MM **Privately Held**
Web: www.generalprocurement.com
SIC: **5045** 5065 Computers, peripherals, and software; Electronic parts

(P-12416)

GENESIS COMPUTER SYSTEMS INC

4055 E La Palma Ave Ste C (92807-1750)
PHONE....................714 632-3648
▼ **EMP:** 20 **EST:** 1994
SQ FT: 3,500
SALES (est): 4.74MM **Privately Held**
Web: www.usgenesis.com
SIC: **5045** 3571 Computers, peripherals, and software; Electronic computers

(P-12417)

GENICA CORPORATION

43195 Business Park Dr (92590-3629)
PHONE....................855 433-5747
▲ **EMP:** 334
Web: www.genica.com
SIC: **5045** 5734 Computer peripheral equipment; Modems, monitors, terminals, and disk drives: computers

(P-12418)

GETAC INC

Also Called: Getac North America
15495 Sand Canyon Ave Ste 350 (92618-3152)
PHONE....................949 681-2900
▲ **EMP:** 90 **EST:** 1994
SQ FT: 12,000
SALES (est): 56.22MM **Privately Held**
Web: www.getac.com
SIC: **5045** Mainframe computers
PA: Getac Holdings Corporation
Building A, 5f, No. 209. Sec. 1.
Nangang Rd.
Taipei City TAP

(P-12419)

HITACHI SOLUTIONS AMERICA LTD (DH)

100 Spectrum Center Dr Ste 350 (92618-4967)
PHONE....................949 242-1300
Keiho Akiyama, *CEO*
▲ **EMP:** 30 **EST:** 1990

SQ FT: 12,000
SALES (est): 266.41MM **Privately Held**
Web: global.hitachi-solutions.com
SIC: **5045** 7372 Computer software; Prepackaged software
HQ: Hitachi Solutions, Ltd.
4-12-7, Higashishinagawa
Shinagawa-Ku TKY

(P-12420)

INGRAM MICRO INC (HQ)

Also Called: Im-Logstics An Ingram McRo Div
3351 Michelson Dr Ste 100 (92612-0697)
PHONE....................714 566-1000
Paul Bay, *CEO*
Mike Zilis, *
Augusto Aragone, *
◆ **EMP:** 4000 **EST:** 1979
SALES (est): 32.76B **Privately Held**
Web: corp.ingrammicro.com
SIC: **5045** Computer software
PA: Platinum Equity, Llc
360 N Crescent Dr Bldg S
Beverly Hills CA

(P-12421)

INGRAM MICRO SERVICES LLC

3351 Michelson Dr Ste 100 (92612-0697)
PHONE....................714 566-1000
EMP: 82 **EST:** 2014
SALES (est): 828.67K **Privately Held**
Web: www.ingrammicroservices.com
SIC: **5045** Computer software

(P-12422)

JAL AVIONET USA (HQ)

300 Continental Blvd # 190 (90245-5045)
PHONE....................310 606-1000
◆ **EMP:** 30 **EST:** 1985
SQ FT: 13,375
SALES (est): 10.17MM **Privately Held**
Web: www.jalavionet.com
SIC: **5045** 7372 5065 7377 Computer software; Prepackaged software; Communication equipment; Computer rental and leasing
PA: Japan Airlines Co.,Ltd.
2-4-11, Higashishinagawa
Shinagawa-Ku TKY

(P-12423)

K-MICRO INC

Also Called: Corpinfo Services
1618 Stanford St (90404-5368)
PHONE....................310 442-3200
Michael Sabourian, *Pr*
Ahmad Gramian, *
EMP: 96 **EST:** 1984
SQ FT: 25,000
SALES (est): 16.68MM **Privately Held**
Web: www.corpinfo.com
SIC: **5045** 7378 7373 7371 Computers and accessories, personal and home entertainment; Computer maintenance and repair; Computer integrated systems design ; Custom computer programming services

(P-12424)

KINGSTON TECHNOLOGY COMPANY INC (PA)

17600 Newhope St (92708-4220)
PHONE....................714 435-2600
◆ **EMP:** 780 **EST:** 1987
SALES (est): 418.24MM
SALES (corp-wide): 418.24MM **Privately Held**
Web: www.kingston.com
SIC: **5045** 3674 Computer peripheral equipment; Random access memory (RAM)

(P-12425)

MAGNELL ASSOCIATE INC (DH)

Also Called: A B S
17560 Rowland St (91748-1114)
PHONE....................800 685-3471
Robert Chang, *CEO*
◆ **EMP:** 130 **EST:** 1990
SALES (est): 472.79MM
SALES (corp-wide): 2.38B **Publicly Held**
Web: www.absgamingpc.com
SIC: **5045** Computers and accessories, personal and home entertainment
HQ: Newegg Inc.
17560 Rowland St
City Of Industry CA
626 271-9700

(P-12426)

MEDIATEK USA INC

10188 Telesis Ct Ste 500 (92121-4761)
PHONE....................858 731-9200
EMP: 124
SIC: **5045** Computer software
HQ: Mediatek Usa Inc.
2840 Junction Ave
San Jose CA
408 526-1899

(P-12427)

MICRO-TECHNOLOGY CONCEPTS INC

Also Called: M T C
17837 Rowland St (91748-1122)
PHONE....................626 839-6800
Roy Han, *Pr*
▲ **EMP:** 85 **EST:** 1989
SQ FT: 42,500
SALES (est): 17.71MM
SALES (corp-wide): 39.29MM **Privately Held**
Web: www.mtcusa.com
SIC: **5045** Computer peripheral equipment
PA: Mtc Direct, Inc.
17837 Rowland St
City Of Industry CA
626 839-6800

(P-12428)

MSI COMPUTER CORP (HQ)

901 Canada Ct (91748-1136)
PHONE....................626 913-0828
Andy Tung, *CEO*
Connie Chang, *
◆ **EMP:** 90 **EST:** 1998
SQ FT: 77,500
SALES (est): 62.13MM **Privately Held**
Web: www.msicomputer.com
SIC: **5045** Computer peripheral equipment
PA: Micro-Star International Co., Ltd.
No.69, Lide St.,
New Taipei City TAP

(P-12429)

MTC WORLDWIDE CORP

17837 Rowland St (91748-1122)
PHONE....................626 839-6800
Roy Han, *CEO*
▲ **EMP:** 79 **EST:** 1989
SQ FT: 42,500
SALES (est): 21.57MM
SALES (corp-wide): 39.29MM **Privately Held**
Web: www.mtcusa.com
SIC: **5045** 3577 Computer peripheral equipment; Computer peripheral equipment, nec
PA: Mtc Direct, Inc.
17837 Rowland St
City Of Industry CA
626 839-6800

(P-12430)

PAYDARFAR INDUSTRIES INC

Also Called: Saratech
26054 Acero (92691-2768)
PHONE....................949 481-3267
Saeed Paydarfar Ph.d., *CEO*
EMP: 60 **EST:** 2002
SQ FT: 5,930
SALES (est): 21.9MM **Privately Held**
Web: www.saratech.com
SIC: **5045** 8711 7372 7373 Computer software; Engineering services; Prepackaged software; Value-added resellers, computer systems

(P-12431)

PC SPECIALISTS INC (DH)

Also Called: Technology Integration Group
10620 Treena St Ste 300 (92131-1141)
PHONE....................858 566-1900
EMP: 117 **EST:** 1983
SALES (est): 517.23MM
SALES (corp-wide): 831.25MM **Privately Held**
Web: www.tig.com
SIC: **5045** 3571 7371 Computers, peripherals, and software; Electronic computers; Custom computer programming services
HQ: Converge Technology Solutions Corp
85 Rue Victoria etage 2eme
Gatineau QC
416 360-3995

(P-12432)

PREMIER SYSTEMS USA INC (PA)

Also Called: Olloclip
16291 Gothard St (92647-3612)
PHONE....................657 204-9861
Patrick O'neill, *CEO*
Anne O'neill, *Opers Mgr*
▲ **EMP:** 18 **EST:** 2010
SQ FT: 6,000
SALES (est): 4.45MM
SALES (corp-wide): 4.45MM **Privately Held**
SIC: **5045** 3841 Computer peripheral equipment; Surgical and medical instruments

(P-12433)

PRINTSAFE INC

11895 Community Rd Ste B (92064-7125)
PHONE....................858 748-8600
Thomas Hittle, *CEO*
Linda Hittle, *
EMP: 25 **EST:** 1988
SQ FT: 15,000
SALES (est): 4.98MM **Privately Held**
Web: www.printsafe.com
SIC: **5045** 3953 5084 Printers, computer; Marking devices; Printing trades machinery, equipment, and supplies

(P-12434)

PRIVATE LABEL PC LLC

Also Called: Private Label
748 Epperson Dr (91748-1336)
PHONE....................626 965-8686
▲ **EMP:** 120 **EST:** 1987
SALES (est): 24.39MM **Privately Held**
Web: www.plpc.com
SIC: **5045** Computer peripheral equipment

(P-12435)

QUARTIC SOLUTIONS LLC

1427 Chalcedony St (92109-2127)
PHONE....................858 377-8470
Timo Luostarinen, *Mgr*

Jodi Luostarinen, *
EMP: 35 **EST:** 2004
SALES (est): 2.62MM **Privately Held**
Web: www.quarticsolutions.com
SIC: 5045 7372 7389 7371 Computer software; Application computer software; Mapmaking services; Custom computer programming services

(P-12436)

SAMSUNG RESEARCH AMERICA INC

18500 Von Karman Ave Ste 700 (92612-0504)
PHONE..............................949 468-1143
David Swanson, *Brnch Mgr*
EMP: 432
Web: sra.samsung.com
SIC: 5045 Computers, peripherals, and software
HQ: Samsung Research America, Inc.
665 Clyde Ave
Mountain View CA

(P-12437)

SERVERS DIRECT LLC

20480 Business Pkwy (91789-2938)
PHONE..............................800 576-7931
Andy Juang, *CEO*
Howard Gilles, *
EMP: 104 **EST:** 2003
SALES (est): 2.39MM **Privately Held**
Web: www.serversdirect.com
SIC: 5045 Computers, peripherals, and software
PA: Equus Computer Systems, Inc.
201 General Mills Blvd
Minneapolis MN

(P-12438)

SMC NETWORKS INC (HQ)

Also Called: Ignitenet
20 Mason (92618-2706)
PHONE..............................949 679-8029
Alex Kim, *CEO*
Frank Kuo, *
Inho Kim, *
Lane Ruoff, *
◆ **EMP:** 80 **EST:** 1971
SQ FT: 22,650
SALES (est): 23.84MM **Privately Held**
Web: www.smc.com
SIC: 5045 Computer peripheral equipment
PA: Accton Technology Corporation
1 Creation 3rd Rd., Hsinchu Science Park,
Hsinchu City

(P-12439)

SOLID OAK SOFTWARE INC (PA)

319 W Mission St (93101-2822)
P.O. Box 6826 (93160-6826)
PHONE..............................805 568-5415
Brian P Milburn Senior, *Pr*
Brian Milburn, *
Mark Kanter, *
EMP: 25 **EST:** 1990
SALES (est): 9.27MM **Privately Held**
Web: www.27labs.com
SIC: 5045 7372 Computer software; Prepackaged software

(P-12440)

SOUTHLAND TECHNOLOGY INC

8053 Vickers St (92111-1917)
PHONE..............................858 694-0932
Grace Pedigo, *CEO*
Robert Pedigo, *
EMP: 65 **EST:** 2001

SQ FT: 16,000
SALES (est): 64.89MM **Privately Held**
Web: www.southlandtechnology.com
SIC: 5045 8748 7373 7379 Computer peripheral equipment; Systems engineering consultant, ex. computer or professional; Computer integrated systems design; Computer related maintenance services

(P-12441)

SPIRENT COMMUNICATIONS INC (HQ)

Also Called: Spirent Calabasas
27349 Agoura Rd (91301-2413)
PHONE..............................818 676-2300
Eric G Hutchinson, *CEO*
Bill Burns, *Pr*
▲ **EMP:** 350 **EST:** 1988
SALES (est): 598.51MM
SALES (corp-wide): 607.5MM **Privately Held**
Web: www.spirent.com
SIC: 5045 3663 3829 3825 Computers, peripherals, and software; Radio and t.v. communications equipment; Measuring and controlling devices, nec; Instruments to measure electricity
PA: Spirent Communications Plc
Origin One
Crawley W SUSSEX
129 376-7676

(P-12442)

SQUARE ENIX INC

999 N Pacific Coast Hwy Fl 3 (90245)
PHONE..............................310 846-0400
Mike Fischer, *Pr*
Clinton Foy, *COO*
Koichiro Hyashi, *Sec*
▲ **EMP:** 110 **EST:** 1998
SALES (est): 49.93MM **Privately Held**
Web: www.square-enix.com
SIC: 5045 7372 Computer software; Publisher's computer software
HQ: Square Enix Of America Holdings, Inc.
999 N Pacific Coast Hwy # 3
El Segundo CA

(P-12443)

SYSPRO IMPACT SOFTWARE INC

Also Called: Syspro
1775 Flight Way Ste 150 (92782-1844)
PHONE..............................714 437-1000
Brian Stein, *CEO*
Joey Benadretti, *
Kristin Valentyn, *CRO**
EMP: 200 **EST:** 1991
SALES (est): 47.65MM **Privately Held**
Web: us.syspro.com
SIC: 5045 7372 7371 Computer software; Prepackaged software; Custom computer programming services

(P-12444)

TEAC AMERICA INC (HQ)

Also Called: Teac
10410 Pioneer Blvd Ste 1 (90670-3734)
PHONE..............................323 726-0303
Koichiro Nakamura, *Pr*
H Derek Davis, *
Patericia Wallace, *
Derek Davis, *
▲ **EMP:** 19 **EST:** 1967
SALES (est): 17.64MM **Privately Held**
Web: www.teac.co.jp
SIC: 5045 5064 5065 3651 Computer peripheral equipment; Electrical entertainment equipment; Magnetic recording tape; Household audio and video equipment

PA: Teac Corporation
1-47, Ochiai
Tama TKY

(P-12445)

TECHNOSYLVA INC

2261 Caminito Preciosa Norte (92037)
PHONE..............................858 729-3648
Joaquin Ramirez, *Pr*
EMP: 17 **EST:** 2012
SALES (est): 1.36MM **Privately Held**
Web: www.technosylva.com
SIC: 5045 7372 7379 Computer software; Application computer software; Computer related consulting services

(P-12446)

TP-LINK USA CORPORATION

3760 Kilroy Airport Way Ste 600 (90806-2443)
PHONE..............................562 528-7700
Dana Knight, *Mktg Dir*
EMP: 86
Web: www.tp-link.com
SIC: 5045 Computer peripheral equipment
HQ: Tp-Link Usa Corporation
10 Mauchly
Irvine CA
626 333-0234

(P-12447)

TREY ARCH LLC

3420 Ocean Park Blvd Ste 2000 (90405-3304)
PHONE..............................310 581-4700
EMP: 399 **EST:** 1996
SALES (est): 29.26MM
SALES (corp-wide): 211.91B **Publicly Held**
SIC: 5045 5092 Computer software; Video games
HQ: Activision Blizzard, Inc.
2701 Olympic Blvd Bldg B
Santa Monica CA
310 255-2000

(P-12448)

TW SECURITY CORP (DH)

5 Park Plz Ste 400 (92614-8524)
PHONE..............................949 932-1000
EMP: 120 **EST:** 2008
SQ FT: 28,000
SALES (est): 110.53MM **Privately Held**
SIC: 5045 Computer software
HQ: Trustwave Holdings, Inc.
70 W Madison St Ste 600
Chicago IL
312 750-0950

(P-12449)

UBIQ SECURITY INC

Also Called: Ubiq
4660 La Jolla Village Dr Ste 100 (92122-4604)
PHONE..............................888 434-6674
Wias Issa, *CEO*
Eric Tobias, *
Linda Eigner, *
EMP: 27 **EST:** 2012
SALES (est): 5.11MM **Privately Held**
Web: www.ubiqsecurity.com
SIC: 5045 7372 Computer software; Prepackaged software

(P-12450)

VIRTIUM LLC

30052 Tomas (92688-2127)
PHONE..............................949 888-2444
Robert P Healy, *Managing Member*
Sean P Barrette, *

EMP: 100 **EST:** 2015
SALES (est): 23.85MM **Privately Held**
Web: www.virtium.com
SIC: 5045 Computers, peripherals, and software

(P-12451)

WHI SOLUTIONS INC

Also Called: D S T Macdonald
28470 Avenue Stanford Ste 200 (91355)
PHONE..............................661 257-2120
Bruce Adamson, *Brnch Mgr*
EMP: 140
Web: www.whisolutions.com
SIC: 5045 7371 Computers, nec; Computer software development
HQ: Whi Solutions, Inc.
2145 Hamilton Ave
San Jose CA
914 697-9301

5046 Commercial Equipment, Nec

(P-12452)

BUYEFFICIENT LLC

903 Calle Amanecer Ste 200 (92673-6251)
PHONE..............................949 382-3129
Dennis Baker, *Pr*
EMP: 130 **EST:** 2000
SALES (est): 7.3MM **Publicly Held**
Web: www.avendra.com
SIC: 5046 Hotel equipment and supplies
HQ: Avendra, Llc
540 Gaither Rd Ste 200
Rockville MD
301 825-0500

(P-12453)

DEPENDBLE BREAK RM SLTIONS INC

1431 W 9th St Ste B (91786-5698)
PHONE..............................909 982-5933
Zachary Oliver, *Pr*
Mark Oliver, *
EMP: 80 **EST:** 1987
SALES (est): 10.79MM **Privately Held**
Web: www.dependablevend.com
SIC: 5046 7389 5963 5078 Vending machines, coin-operated; Coffee service; Bottled water delivery; Drinking water coolers, mechanical

(P-12454)

GEMCO DISPLAY AND STR FIXS LLC (PA)

Also Called: Victory Display & Store Fixs
2640 E Del Amo Blvd (90221-6004)
PHONE..............................800 262-1126
TOLL FREE: 800
David Nutel, *Pr*
Fred Berman, *Ch Bd*
▲ **EMP:** 20 **EST:** 1999
SALES (est): 5.87MM **Privately Held**
Web: www.victorydisplay.com
SIC: 5046 3089 Store fixtures; Plastics processing

(P-12455)

HANNAM CHAIN USA INC (PA)

Also Called: Hannam Chain Super 1 Market
2740 W Olympic Blvd (90006-2633)
PHONE..............................213 382-2922
Kee W Ha, *CEO*
Kee W Ha, *CEO*
Jeong Wan Koo, *Pr*
▲ **EMP:** 105 **EST:** 1987
SQ FT: 22,000

SALES (est): 24.41MM
SALES (corp-wide): 24.41MM **Privately Held**
SIC: 5046 5411 Restaurant equipment and supplies, nec; Supermarkets, independent

(P-12456)
HEC ASSET MANAGEMENT INC
29341 Kimberlina Rd (93280-7617)
P.O. Box 1200 (93280-8100)
PHONE...............................661 587-2250
Keith B Gardiner, *CEO*
EMP: 100 **EST:** 2011
SALES (est): 13.66MM **Privately Held**
SIC: 5046 Commercial equipment, nec

(P-12457)
INNOVATIVE DISPLAYWORKS INC
Also Called: I D W
8825 Boston Pl (91730-4922)
PHONE...............................909 447-8254
Leo Wills, *CEO*
Nathan W Linder, *
◆ **EMP:** 40 **EST:** 2000
SQ FT: 5,000
SALES (est): 26.42MM
SALES (corp-wide): 54.9MM **Privately Held**
Web: www.idw.global
SIC: 5046 3441 2541 5078 Display equipment, except refrigerated; Fabricated structural metal; Display fixtures, wood; Beverage coolers
PA: Oxford Financial Group, Ltd.
11711 N Meridian St # 600
Carmel IN
317 843-5678

(P-12458)
INTERSTATE ELECTRIC CO INC
Also Called: IEC
2240 Yates Ave (90040-1914)
PHONE...............................800 225-5432
Edward Urlik, *CEO*
▲ **EMP:** 85 **EST:** 1946
SQ FT: 72,000
SALES (est): 24.22MM **Privately Held**
Web: www.iecdelivers.com
SIC: 5046 Signs, electrical

(P-12459)
JETRO HOLDINGS LLC
1611 E Washington Blvd (90021-3133)
PHONE...............................213 516-0301
Javier Gomez, *Brnch Mgr*
EMP: 268
Web: www.restaurantdepot.com
SIC: 5046 Restaurant equipment and supplies, nec
HQ: Jetro Holdings, Llc
1710 Whitestone Expy
Whitestone NY

(P-12460)
JETRO HOLDINGS LLC
7466 Carroll Rd Ste 100 (92121-2356)
PHONE...............................858 564-0466
Dan Camacho, *Brnch Mgr*
EMP: 268
Web: www.restaurantdepot.com
SIC: 5046 Restaurant equipment and supplies, nec
HQ: Jetro Holdings, Llc
1710 Whitestone Expy
Whitestone NY

(P-12461)
JONES SIGNS CO INC
Also Called: Ultrasigns Electrical Advg
9025 Balboa Ave Ste 150 (92123-1522)
PHONE...............................858 569-1400
EMP: 120
Web: www.ultrasign.com
SIC: 5046 Signs, electrical

(P-12462)
JUSTMAN PACKAGING & DISPLAY (PA)
5819 Telegraph Rd (90040-1515)
PHONE...............................323 728-8888
Morley Justman, *Pr*
Russell Justman, *VP*
Barbara Cabaret, *CFO*
▲ **EMP:** 65 **EST:** 1989
SALES (est): 23.76MM
SALES (corp-wide): 23.76MM **Privately Held**
SIC: 5046 5113 2752 Display equipment, except refrigerated; Corrugated and solid fiber boxes; Commercial printing, lithographic

(P-12463)
SHOPPER INC
2655 Park Center Dr Ste B (93065-6333)
PHONE...............................805 527-6700
Bill Bieda, *CEO*
Elliot Bieda, *
Eta Bieda, *
◆ **EMP:** 300 **EST:** 1992
SALES (est): 47.15MM **Privately Held**
SIC: 5046 Store fixtures

(P-12464)
TRIMARK RAYGAL LLC
Also Called: Trimark Orange County
210 Commerce (92602-1318)
PHONE...............................949 474-1000
Michael Anthony Costanzo, *Pr*
Eric Smith, *
Dirk Hallett, *Corporate Secretary*
EMP: 220 **EST:** 1971
SQ FT: 62,850
SALES (est): 153MM **Privately Held**
Web: www.trimarkusa.com
SIC: 5046 Restaurant equipment and supplies, nec
PA: Trimark Usa, Llc
9 Hampshire St
Mansfield MA

(P-12465)
TRUST 1 SALES INC
Also Called: Sam Sung Fixtures
1737 S Vermont Ave (90006-4523)
PHONE...............................323 732-3300
▲ **EMP:** 100 **EST:** 1984
SQ FT: 12,000
SALES (est): 8.16MM **Privately Held**
Web: www.trust1sales.com
SIC: 5046 7699 Restaurant equipment and supplies, nec; Restaurant equipment repair

---

5047 Medical And Hospital Equipment

(P-12466)
A PLUS INTERNATIONAL INC (PA)
5138 Eucalyptus Ave (91710-9254)
PHONE...............................909 591-5168
Wayne Lin, *Pr*
David Lee, *VP*
◆ **EMP:** 73 **EST:** 1988

SQ FT: 150,000
SALES (est): 22.69MM
SALES (corp-wide): 22.69MM **Privately Held**
Web: www.aplusgroup.net
SIC: 5047 3842 Medical equipment and supplies; Surgical appliances and supplies

(P-12467)
ALPHAEON CORPORATION
17901 Von Karman Ave Ste 150 (92614-6297)
PHONE...............................949 284-4555
Murthy Simhambhatla, *CEO*
Murthy Simhambhatla, *Pr*
Robert E Grant, *Vice Chairman*
Bob Rhatigan, *
William Link, *
EMP: 105 **EST:** 2012
SALES (est): 42.24MM
SALES (corp-wide): 44.5MM **Privately Held**
Web: www.alphaeon.com
SIC: 5047 Hospital equipment and furniture
PA: Strathspey Crown Holdings Llc
4040 Macarthur Blvd # 210
Newport Beach CA
949 260-1700

(P-12468)
AMERICAN MED & HOSP SUP CO INC
Also Called: Am-Touch Dental
28703 Industry Dr (91355-5414)
PHONE...............................661 294-1213
Harish Khetarpal, *CEO*
Roma Khetarpal, *
▲ **EMP:** 32 **EST:** 1987
SQ FT: 25,000
SALES (est): 16.16MM **Privately Held**
Web: www.amtouch.com
SIC: 5047 3843 3842 Medical equipment and supplies; Dental equipment and supplies; Surgical appliances and supplies

(P-12469)
AMERICAN MEDICAL TECH INC
17595 Cartwright Rd (92614-5847)
PHONE...............................949 553-0359
Jean Signore, *Pr*
Jerry Signore, *VP*
EMP: 100 **EST:** 1989
SALES (est): 24.34MM **Privately Held**
Web: www.amtwoundcare.com
SIC: 5047 Medical equipment and supplies

(P-12470)
AMERICAN TOOTH INDUSTRIES
1200 Stellar Dr (93033-2404)
PHONE...............................805 487-9868
Emilio Pozzi, *CEO*
Bruno Pozzi, *
Victoria Pozzi, *
Roberto Trada, *
Minda Darimbang, *
▲ **EMP:** 98 **EST:** 1985
SQ FT: 28,000
SALES (est): 20.55MM **Privately Held**
Web: www.americantooth.com
SIC: 5047 Dental equipment and supplies

(P-12471)
ARJO INC
17502 Fabrica Way (90703-7014)
PHONE...............................714 412-1170
Harald Stock, *Brnch Mgr*
EMP: 278
SALES (corp-wide): 7.13B **Privately Held**
Web: www.arjo.com

SIC: 5047 Medical equipment and supplies
HQ: Arjo, Inc.
2349 W Lake St Ste 250
Addison IL
630 785-4490

(P-12472)
ATG - DESIGNING MOBILITY INC (DH)
Also Called: Numotion
11075 Knott Ave Ste B (90630-5150)
PHONE...............................562 921-0258
TOLL FREE: 800
Mike Swinford, *CEO*
EMP: 26 **EST:** 1996
SQ FT: 10,500
SALES (est): 8.86MM
SALES (corp-wide): 491.33MM **Privately Held**
Web: www.numotion.com
SIC: 5047 5999 3842 Medical equipment and supplies; Medical apparatus and supplies; Wheelchairs
HQ: Atg Holdings, Inc.
805 Brook St Ste 2
Rocky Hill CT

(P-12473)
AVENUE MEDICAL EQUIPMENT INC
38062 Encanto Rd (92563-3208)
PHONE...............................949 680-7444
Myo Tun, *Pr*
EMP: 35 **EST:** 2015
SALES (est): 3.14MM **Privately Held**
Web: www.avenueme.com
SIC: 5047 5021 3842 5048 Medical equipment and supplies; Furniture; Orthopedic appliances; Ophthalmic goods

(P-12474)
AVITA MEDICAL AMERICAS LLC
Also Called: Avita Medical
28159 Avenue Stanford Ste 220 (91355)
PHONE...............................661 367-9170
Michael Perry, *Managing Member*
▲ **EMP:** 114 **EST:** 2005
SQ FT: 23,000
SALES (est): 34.42MM **Privately Held**
Web: www.avitamedical.com
SIC: 5047 Medical and hospital equipment
HQ: Avita Medical Pty Limited
L 7 330 Collins St
Melbourne VIC

(P-12475)
BALT USA LLC
Also Called: Blockade Medical
29 Parker Ste 100 (92618-1667)
PHONE...............................949 788-1443
EMP: 90 **EST:** 2011
SQ FT: 47,000
SALES (est): 37.79MM
SALES (corp-wide): 2.4MM **Privately Held**
Web: www.baltgroup.com
SIC: 5047 3841 Medical equipment and supplies; Surgical and medical instruments
HQ: Balt International
10 Rue De La Croix Vigneron
Montmorency
139894641

(P-12476)
BETTER NIGHT LLC
5471 Kearny Villa Rd Ste 200 (92123)
PHONE...............................619 299-6299
EMP: 90 **EST:** 2017
SALES (est): 8.67MM **Privately Held**
Web: www.betternightsolutions.com

SIC: 5047 Medical and hospital equipment

(P-12477)

BIONIME USA CORPORATION
1450 E Spruce St Ste B (91761-8313)
PHONE.............................909 781-6969
Chun-mu Huang, *Prin*
Alex Wang, *
▲ EMP: 25 EST: 2008
SALES (est): 2.47MM **Privately Held**
Web: www.bionimeusa.com
SIC: 5047 2835 Diagnostic equipment,
medical; In vitro diagnostics

(P-12478)

BIOSITE INC
9975 Summers Ridge Rd (92121-2997)
PHONE.............................510 683-9063
Yonkin John, *Pr*
EMP: 103 EST: 2011
SALES (est): 6.05MM **Privately Held**
Web: www.biositesystems.com
SIC: 5047 Medical equipment and supplies

(P-12479)

CAMERON HEALTH INC
905 Calle Amanecer # 300 (92673-6277)
PHONE.............................949 940-4000
EMP: 100
SIC: 5047 Medical equipment and supplies

(P-12480)

**CANON MEDICAL SYSTEMS
USA INC (DH)**
Also Called: Video Sensing Division
2441 Michelle Dr (92780-7047)
P.O. Box 2068 (92781-2068)
PHONE.............................714 730-5000
Shuzo Yamamoto, *Pr*
Nader Rad, *VP*
Calum G Cunningham, *VP*
Scott Goodwin, *VP*
John Patterson, *CFO*
◆ EMP: 300 EST: 1989
SQ FT: 135,000
SALES (est): 496.54MM **Privately Held**
Web: us.medical.canon
SIC: 5047 X-ray machines and tubes
HQ: Canon Medical Systems Corporation
1385, Shimoishigami
Otawara TCG

(P-12481)

**CARLSBAD INTERNATIONAL
EXPORT INC**
Also Called: Carlsbad Medical Supply
1954 Kellogg Ave (92008-6581)
PHONE.............................760 438-5323
▲ EMP: 20
SIC: 5047 3841 Medical equipment and
supplies; Surgical and medical instruments

(P-12482)

CONVAID PRODUCTS LLC
2830 California St (90503-3908)
P.O. Box 4209 (90274-9571)
PHONE.............................310 618-0111
Chris Braun, *CEO*
Mervyn M Watkins, *
◆ EMP: 89 EST: 1976
SALES (est): 30.7MM **Privately Held**
Web: www.etac.com
SIC: 5047 Medical equipment and supplies

(P-12483)

DISCUS DENTAL LLC (PA)
1700 S Baker Ave (91761-7707)
PHONE.............................310 845-8600
◆ EMP: 150 EST: 2007

SALES (est): 31.14MM **Privately Held**
Web: www.discusdental.com
SIC: 5047 Dental equipment and supplies

(P-12484)

DURASAFE INC
Also Called: Life Guard Gloves
18999 Railroad St (91748-1322)
PHONE.............................626 965-1588
Chin Shing Hung, *CEO*
Pat Hung, *CFO*
▲ EMP: 19 EST: 1988
SQ FT: 35,000
SALES (est): 4.62MM **Privately Held**
Web: www.lifeguardgloves.com
SIC: 5047 3069 Medical equipment and
supplies; Medical sundries, rubber

(P-12485)

ELECTROMED INC
4590 Ish Dr (93063-7678)
PHONE.............................805 523-7500
Terry Belford, *Brnch Mgr*
EMP: 86
SALES (corp-wide): 48.07MM **Publicly
Held**
Web: www.smartvest.com
SIC: 5047 Medical equipment and supplies
PA: Electromed, Inc.
500 6th Ave Nw
New Prague MN
952 758-9299

(P-12486)

ELERS MEDICAL USA INC
21707 Hawthorne Blvd Ste 206
(90503-7009)
PHONE.............................858 336-4900
Donald Mccormick, *Pr*
EMP: 20 EST: 2020
SALES (est): 4.86MM
SALES (corp-wide): 8.08MM **Privately
Held**
SIC: 5047 5999 3841 Medical equipment
and supplies; Medical apparatus and
supplies; Surgical and medical instruments
PA: Elers Medical Finland Oy
Niittytaival 13
Espoo
207305010

(P-12487)

**FISHER & PAYKEL
HEALTHCARE INC**
17400 Laguna Canyon Rd Ste 300
(92618-5425)
PHONE.............................949 453-4000
▲ EMP: 150 EST: 1995
SQ FT: 5,000
SALES (est): 90.27MM **Privately Held**
Web: www.fphcare.com
SIC: 5047 Medical equipment and supplies
HQ: Fisher & Paykel Healthcare
Corporation Limited
15 Maurice Paykel Pl
Auckland AUK

(P-12488)

**GOLDEN STATE MEDICAL SUP
INC**
5187 Camino Ruiz (93012-8601)
PHONE.............................805 477-9866
Benjamin Hall, *
Thomas S Weaver, *
Shiela Curran, *
Anita Wrublevski, *
Jim Mcmanimie, *Sr VP*
EMP: 150 EST: 1989
SQ FT: 95,500
SALES (est): 47.53MM

SALES (corp-wide): 47.53MM **Privately
Held**
Web: www.gsms.us
SIC: 5047 Medical equipment and supplies
PA: Gsms, Inc.
5187 Camino Ruiz
Camarillo CA
805 477-9866

(P-12489)

GORDIAN MEDICAL INC
Also Called: Restorixhealth
17595 Cartwright Rd (92614-5847)
PHONE.............................714 556-0200
EMP: 290 EST: 2007
SALES (est): 46.64MM **Privately Held**
Web: www.amtwoundcare.com
SIC: 5047 Medical equipment and supplies

(P-12490)

GRIFOLS USA LLC
13111 Temple Ave (91746-1500)
PHONE.............................626 435-2600
EMP: 515
Web: www.grifols.com
SIC: 5047 Diagnostic equipment, medical
HQ: Grifols Usa, Llc
2410 Grifols Way
Los Angeles CA
323 225-2221

(P-12491)

H AND H DRUG STORES INC
Also Called: Western Drug Medical Supply
114 E Airport Dr (92408-3473)
PHONE.............................909 890-9700
EMP: 80
SALES (corp-wide): 61.72MM **Privately
Held**
Web: www.westerndrug.com
SIC: 5047 Medical equipment and supplies
PA: H And H Drug Stores, Inc.
3604 San Fernando Rd
Glendale CA
818 956-6691

(P-12492)

HARDY DIAGNOSTICS INC (PA)
1430 W Mccoy Ln (93455-1005)
P.O. Box 645264 (45264-5264)
PHONE.............................805 346-2766
Jay R Hardy, *Pr*
Jeff Schroder, *
◆ EMP: 300 EST: 1980
SQ FT: 75,000
SALES (est): 95.87MM
SALES (corp-wide): 95.87MM **Privately
Held**
Web: www.hardydiagnostics.com
SIC: 5047 2836 Medical equipment and
supplies; Agar culture media

(P-12493)

HORIBAABX INC
Also Called: Horiba Medical
34 Bunsen (92618-4210)
PHONE.............................949 453-0500
▲ EMP: 108
Web: www.horiba.com
SIC: 5047 Medical and hospital equipment

(P-12494)

IHEALTH MANUFACTURING INC
✪
15715 Arrow Hwy (91706-2006)
PHONE.............................216 785-0107
EMP: 80 EST: 2022
SALES (est): 10.11MM **Privately Held**
Web: www.ihealthlabs.com

SIC: 5047 Medical and hospital equipment

(P-12495)

**JB DENTAL SUPPLY CO INC
(PA)**
17000 Kingsview Ave (90746-1230)
PHONE.............................310 202-8855
TOLL FREE: 800
Joseph Berman, *Pr*
Manny Chada, *
EMP: 120 EST: 1973
SQ FT: 26,000
SALES (est): 22.86MM
SALES (corp-wide): 22.86MM **Privately
Held**
SIC: 5047 Dental equipment and supplies

(P-12496)

KLM LABORATORIES INC
Also Called: Klm Orthotic
28280 Alta Vista Ave (91355-0958)
PHONE.............................661 295-2600
Kirk Marshall, *Pr*
Scott Marshall, *
Kent Marshall, *
EMP: 100 EST: 1974
SQ FT: 35,000
SALES (est): 24.34MM **Privately Held**
Web: www.klmlabstore.com
SIC: 5047 3842 Medical laboratory
equipment; Foot appliances, orthopedic

(P-12497)

LEVLAD LLC
9200 Mason Ave (91311-6005)
PHONE.............................818 882-2951
◆ EMP: 215 EST: 1973
SALES (est): 47.42MM **Privately Held**
Web: www.levlad.com
SIC: 5047 5122 Incontinent care products
and supplies; Cosmetics
PA: Natural Products Group, Llc
9400 Jeronimo Rd
Irvine CA

(P-12498)

**MCKESSON MDCL-SRGCAL
TOP HLDNG**
Also Called: Physician Sales & Service
1938 W Malvern Ave (92833-2105)
PHONE.............................800 300-4350
Mike Baker, *Brnch Mgr*
EMP: 292
SALES (corp-wide): 276.71B **Publicly
Held**
Web: mms.mckesson.com
SIC: 5047 Medical equipment and supplies
HQ: Mckesson Medical-Surgical Top
Holdings Inc.
2054 Vista Pkwy Ste 400
West Palm Beach FL
904 332-3000

(P-12499)

MENTOR WORLDWIDE LLC
5425 Hollister Ave (93111-3341)
PHONE.............................805 681-6000
Diane Becker, *Mgr*
EMP: 500
SALES (corp-wide): 94.94MM **Publicly Held**
Web: www.mentordirect.com
SIC: 5047 Medical and hospital equipment
HQ: Mentor Worldwide Llc
31 Technology Dr Ste 200
Irvine CA
800 636-8678

(P-12500)
MOBILITY SOLUTIONS INC (PA)
7895 Convoy Ct Ste 11 (92111-1215)
PHONE..............................858 278-0591
▲ EMP: 25 EST: 1994
SALES (est): 8.58MM Privately Held
Web: www.mobility-solutions.com
SIC: 5047 3842 Medical equipment and
supplies; Wheelchairs

(P-12501)
NIHON KOHDEN AMERICA LLC (HQ)
Also Called: Nihon Kohden America, Inc.
15353 Barranca Pkwy (92618-2216)
PHONE..............................949 580-1555
Eiichi Tanaka, CEO
Shinya Hama, CCO*
Ken Kanzler, *
▲ EMP: 130 EST: 1979
SQ FT: 35,000
SALES (est): 166.95MM Privately Held
Web: us.nihonkohden.com
SIC: 5047 Electro-medical equipment
PA: Nihon Kohden Corporation
1-31-4, Nishiochiai
Shinjuku-Ku TKY

(P-12502)
OWENS & MINOR DISTRIBUTION INC
452 Sespe Ave (93015-2042)
PHONE..............................805 524-0243
Michael Guelzow, Brnch Mgr
EMP: 631
Web: www.owens-minor.com
SIC: 5047 Medical equipment and supplies
HQ: Owens & Minor Distribution, Inc.
9120 Lockwood Blvd
Mechanicsville VA
804 723-7000

(P-12503)
P M D HOLDING CORP
Also Called: Peerigon Medical Distribution
26672 Towne Centre Dr Ste 310
(92610-2818)
PHONE..............................949 595-4777
Frank Schyving, Pr
Charles Kruger, *
Rick Hayes, *
Mike Shaunessy Technical Servi ces, Prin
EMP: 259 EST: 1996
SALES (est): 14.79MM Privately Held
SIC: 5047 Medical equipment and supplies

(P-12504)
PACIFIC MEDICAL GROUP INC
Also Called: Avante Health Solutions
212 Avenida Fabricante (92672-7538)
PHONE..............................949 493-1030
Sterling Peloso, Pr
EMP: 100 EST: 2005
SALES (est): 24.49MM Privately Held
Web: www.pacificmedicalsupply.com
SIC: 5047 Medical equipment and supplies

(P-12505)
PARTER MEDICAL PRODUCTS INC
17015 Kingsview Ave (90746-1220)
PHONE..............................310 327-4417
Hormonz Foroughi, Pr
Parviz Hassanzadeh, Stockholder*
▲ EMP: 160 EST: 1984
SQ FT: 40,000
SALES (est): 24.44MM Privately Held
Web: www.partermedical.com

SIC: 5047 Medical equipment and supplies

(P-12506)
PEARSON DENTAL SUPPLIES INC (PA)
Also Called: Pearson Surgical Supply Co
13161 Telfair Ave (91342-3574)
PHONE..............................818 362-2600
Keyhan Kashfian, Pr
Parviz Kashfian, *
Nader Kashfian, *
▲ EMP: 105 EST: 1983
SQ FT: 88,000
SALES (est): 71.98MM
SALES (corp-wide): 71.98MM Privately
Held
Web: www.pearsondental.com
SIC: 5047 Dental equipment and supplies

(P-12507)
PETER BRASSELER HOLDINGS LLC
Also Called: Comet Medical
4837 Mcgrath St Ste J (93003-8077)
PHONE..............................805 650-5209
Orlando Deleon, Mgr
EMP: 73
SALES (corp-wide): 47.53MM Privately
Held
Web: www.brasselerusa.com
SIC: 5047 3841 3843 Dental equipment and
supplies; Surgical and medical instruments;
Dental equipment
PA: Peter Brasseler Holdings, Llc
1 Brasseler Blvd
Savannah GA
912 925-8525

(P-12508)
PMB GROUP INC
Also Called: Pmb Group
12778 Brookprinter Pl (92064-6810)
PHONE..............................619 690-7300
Fatih Buyuksonmez, Pr
▲ EMP: 17 EST: 2007
SALES (est): 6.96MM Privately Held
Web: www.conquerscientific.com
SIC: 5047 3826 Medical laboratory
equipment; Amino acid analyzers

(P-12509)
POM MEDICAL LLC
5456 Endeavour Ct (93021-1705)
PHONE..............................805 306-2105
EMP: 99 EST: 2012
SALES (est): 4.9MM Privately Held
Web: www.proceduraloxygenmask.com
SIC: 5047 Oxygen therapy equipment

(P-12510)
QUAD-C JH HOLDINGS INC
4593 Ish Dr Ste 320 (93063-7696)
PHONE..............................800 966-6662
EMP: 230
SALES (corp-wide): 101.03MM Privately
Held
SIC: 5047 Medical equipment and supplies
PA: Quad-C Jh Holdings Inc.
2430 Whthall Pk Dr Ste 10
Charlotte NC
800 826-0270

(P-12511)
QUAD-C JH HOLDINGS INC
1055 E Discovery Ln (92801-1147)
PHONE..............................502 741-0421
EMP: 230
SALES (corp-wide): 101.03MM Privately
Held

SIC: 5047 Medical equipment and supplies
PA: Quad-C Jh Holdings Inc.
2430 Whthall Pk Dr Ste 10
Charlotte NC
800 826-0270

(P-12512)
SAKURA FINETEK USA INC (HQ)
1750 W 214th St (90501-2857)
PHONE..............................310 972-7800
Takashi Tsuzuki, Ch Bd
Anthony C Marotti, *
Kam Patel, *
▲ EMP: 109 EST: 1986
SQ FT: 68,000
SALES (est): 98.64MM Privately Held
Web: www.sakuraus.com
SIC: 5047 Medical laboratory equipment
PA: Sakura Global Holding Co., Ltd.
3-1-9, Nihombashihoncho
Chuo-Ku TKY

(P-12513)
SHIELD-DENVER HEALTH CARE CTR (HQ)
Also Called: Shield Healthcare
27911 Franklin Pkwy (91355-4110)
PHONE..............................661 294-4200
Jim Snell, Pr
Jeffery Thompson, *
Cheryl Hornberger, *
EMP: 200 EST: 1983
SQ FT: 95,000
SALES (est): 43.74MM Privately Held
SIC: 5047 Medical equipment and supplies
PA: Dharma Ventures Group, Inc
24700 Ave Rockefeller
Valencia CA

(P-12514)
SHIMADZU PRECISION INSTRS INC
Shimadzu Medical Systems
20101 S Vermont Ave (90502-1328)
PHONE..............................310 217-8855
Akinori Yamaguchi, Pr
EMP: 80
Web: www.spi-inc.com
SIC: 5047 Medical equipment and supplies
HQ: Shimadzu Precision Instruments, Inc.
3645 N Lakewood Blvd
Long Beach CA
562 420-6226

(P-12515)
SIGMA SUPPLY & DIST INC
701 W Harvard St (91204-1142)
PHONE..............................818 246-4624
Arthur Keshishyan, CEO
▲ EMP: 18 EST: 1998
SQ FT: 6,500
SALES (est): 4.49MM Privately Held
SIC: 5047 3841 Medical equipment and
supplies; Surgical and medical instruments

(P-12516)
STARZ INC
Also Called: Starz Tipz
23016 Lake Forest Dr Ste D303 (92653)
PHONE..............................877 595-6789
Donovan Berkely, CEO
EMP: 18 EST: 2008
SQ FT: 6,000
SALES (est): 1.21MM Privately Held
Web: www.starztipz.com
SIC: 5047 3843 Dental equipment and
supplies; Dental equipment and supplies

(P-12517)
SUNRISE RESPIRATORY CARE INC
1881 Langley Ave (92614-5523)
PHONE..............................949 398-6555
Oscar Munoz, CEO
Oscar L Munoz, *
EMP: 110 EST: 2010
SALES (est): 17.26MM Privately Held
Web: www.sunriseresp.com
SIC: 5047 Medical equipment and supplies

(P-12518)
TEAM POST-OP INC
Also Called: Team Post-Op
17256 Red Hill Ave (92614-5628)
PHONE..............................949 253-5500
Jeffrey Salamon, Pr
Lisa Salamon, *
EMP: 105 EST: 1988
SQ FT: 1,400
SALES (est): 14.01MM
SALES (corp-wide): 1.12B Privately Held
Web: www.orthokinetix.net
SIC: 5047 Orthopedic equipment and
supplies
HQ: Hanger Prosthetics & Orthotics, Inc.
10910 Domain Dr Ste 300
Austin TX
512 777-3800

(P-12519)
THORWEAR INC
Also Called: Elevate Dynamics
5674 El Camino Real (92008-7130)
PHONE..............................760 224-3393
Jason Thorne, CEO
Kelly Mcgee, VP
Efrain Navarette, Prin
Matt Hollister, VP Opers
EMP: 19 EST: 2019
SALES (est): 2.37MM Privately Held
Web: www.elevatemovement.com
SIC: 5047 3845 Medical equipment and
supplies; Electromedical apparatus

(P-12520)
TOTAL HEALTH ENVIRONMENT LLC
743 W Taft Ave (92865-4229)
PHONE..............................714 637-1010
EMP: 30 EST: 2014
SALES (est): 3.74MM Privately Held
Web: www.the-gsc.net
SIC: 5047 3843 5021 Medical and hospital
equipment; Dental equipment; Office
furniture, nec

(P-12521)
TWIN MED INC
5900 Wilshire Blvd Ste 2600 (90036-5013)
▲ EMP: 500
SIC: 5047 Medical equipment and supplies

(P-12522)
WALK VASCULAR LLC
17171 Daimler St (92614-5508)
PHONE..............................949 752-9642
Dave Look, Managing Member
EMP: 20 EST: 2010
SALES (est): 8.62MM
SALES (corp-wide): 43.65B Publicly Held
Web: www.cardiovascular.abbott
SIC: 5047 3841 Medical equipment and
supplies; Surgical and medical instruments
PA: Abbott Laboratories
100 Abbott Park Rd
Abbott Park IL
224 667-6100

PRODUCTS & SVCS

(P-12523)
ZEST ANCHORS LLC
Also Called: Zest Dental Solutions
2230 Enterprise St (92029-2004)
PHONE....................................760 743-7744
EMP: 90
SALES (corp-wide): 14.24MM **Privately Held**
Web: www.zestdent.com
• **SIC: 5047** Dental equipment and supplies
PA: Zest Anchors, Llc
2875 Loker Ave E
Carlsbad CA
760 743-7744

5048 Ophthalmic Goods

(P-12524)
ESSILOR LABORATORIES AMER INC
Also Called: Bartley Optical
1300 W Optical Dr (91702-3282)
PHONE....................................626 969-6181
Robert Babcock, *Mgr*
EMP: 38
SALES (corp-wide): 2.55MM **Privately Held**
Web: www.essilorinstrumentsusa.com
SIC: 5048 3851 Frames, ophthalmic; Ophthalmic goods
HQ: Essilor Laboratories Of America, Inc.
13515 N Stemmons Fwy
Dallas TX
972 241-4141

5049 Professional Equipment, Nec

(P-12525)
ABC SCHOOL EQUIPMENT INC
Also Called: Platinum Visual Systems
1451 E 6th St (92879-1715)
PHONE....................................951 817-2200
Gary P Stell Junior, *CEO*
Thomas Mendez, *
EMP: 70 **EST:** 1964
SQ FT: 35,000
SALES (est): 20.5MM **Privately Held**
Web: www.abcse.com
SIC: 5049 3861 2531 School supplies; Photographic equipment and supplies; Public building and related furniture

(P-12526)
EXCEL SCIENTIFIC LLC
18350 George Blvd (92394-7930)
PHONE....................................760 246-4545
▲ **EMP:** 23 **EST:** 2001
SQ FT: 27,000
SALES (est): 27.49MM **Privately Held**
Web: www.excelscientific.com
SIC: 5049 3821 Scientific and engineering equipment and supplies; Laboratory apparatus, except heating and measuring
PA: Vance Street Capital Llc
15304 W Sunset Blvd # 200
Pacific Palisades CA

(P-12527)
INDIO PRODUCTS INC (PA)
Also Called: Seven Sisters of New Orleans
12910 Mulberry Dr Unit A (90602-3455)
PHONE....................................323 720-1188
▲ **EMP:** 130 **EST:** 2010
SALES (est): 25.3MM
SALES (corp-wide): 25.3MM **Privately Held**
Web: www.indioproducts.com

SIC: 5049 3999 Religious supplies; Candles

(P-12528)
LEXICON MARKETING (USA) INC (PA)
Also Called: Lexicon Marketing
640 S San Vicente Blvd (90048-4654)
PHONE....................................323 782-8282
Valeria Rico, *Pr*
EMP: 81 **EST:** 1979
SALES (est): 62.07MM **Privately Held**
SIC: 5049 5999 School supplies; Education aids, devices and supplies

(P-12529)
MCBAIN SYSTEMS A CAL LTD PRTNR
810 Lawrence Dr (91320-2208)
PHONE....................................805 581-6800
Michael Crump, *Pr*
▲ **EMP:** 20 **EST:** 1965
SALES (est): 5.8MM **Privately Held**
Web: www.mcbainsystems.com
SIC: 5049 3827 7699 Scientific and engineering equipment and supplies; Optical instruments and apparatus; Optical instrument repair

(P-12530)
MOLECULAR BIOPRODUCTS SVC CORP (HQ)
Also Called: Pgc Scientiifics
10636 Scripps Summit Ct (92131-3965)
PHONE....................................858 875-7696
Paul Nowak, *Pr*
Ron Perkins, *CFO*
◆ **EMP:** 20 **EST:** 1988
SALES (est): 23.77MM **Privately Held**
SIC: 5049 3089 3821 Laboratory equipment, except medical or dental; Injection molded finished plastics products, nec; Laboratory apparatus and furniture
PA: Biotix Holdings, Inc.
10636 Scripps Summit Ct
San Diego CA

(P-12531)
REM OPTICAL COMPANY INC
Also Called: REM Eye Wear
10941 La Tuna Canyon Rd (91352-2012)
PHONE....................................818 504-3950
Alessandro Baronti, *Pr*
Donna Gindy, *COO*
Donna Nakawaki, *CFO*
Claudio Ninotti, *VP*
◆ **EMP:** 149 **EST:** 1977
SQ FT: 42,000
SALES (est): 49.15MM
SALES (corp-wide): 525.12MM **Privately Held**
Web: www.derigo.us
SIC: 5049 Optical goods
HQ: De Rigo Vision Spa
Zona Industriale Villanova 12
Longarone BL

(P-12532)
SAPPHIRE CLEAN ROOMS LLC
2810 E Coronado St (92806-2503)
PHONE....................................714 316-5036
Hector Garibay, *Pr*
EMP: 136
SALES (corp-wide): 8.61MM **Privately Held**
Web: www.sapphirecleanrooms.com
SIC: 5049 Laboratory equipment, except medical or dental
PA: Sapphire Clean Rooms, Llc
505 Porter Way

Placentia CA
714 316-5036

(P-12533)
TECAN SP INC
14180 Live Oak Ave (91706-1350)
P.O. Box 1608 (91706-7608)
PHONE....................................626 962-0010
▲ **EMP:** 84 **EST:** 1997
SALES (est): 46.32MM **Privately Held**
Web: www.tecan.com
SIC: 5049 Laboratory equipment, except medical or dental
PA: Tecan Group Ag
Seestrasse 103
MAnnedorf ZH

5051 Metals Service Centers And Offices

(P-12534)
ALUMINUM PRECISION PDTS INC
1001 Mcwane Blvd (93033-9016)
PHONE....................................805 488-4401
Richard Hayes, *Brnch Mgr*
EMP: 125
SQ FT: 15,000
SALES (corp-wide): 80.17MM **Privately Held**
Web: www.aluminumprecision.com
SIC: 5051 Steel
PA: Aluminum Precision Products, Inc.
3333 W Warner Ave
Santa Ana CA
714 546-8125

(P-12535)
BERGSEN INC
12241 Florence Ave (90670-3805)
PHONE....................................562 236-9787
Thomas Sharpe, *CEO*
◆ **EMP:** 25 **EST:** 1971
SQ FT: 27,000
SALES (est): 14MM **Privately Held**
Web: www.bergsen.com
SIC: 5051 3317 Steel; Boiler tubes (wrought)

(P-12536)
BLUE CHIP STAMPS INC
301 E Colorado Blvd Ste 300 (91101)
PHONE....................................626 585-6700
Robert H Bird, *COO*
Charles T Munger, *CEO*
Jeffrey L Jacobson, *
Kenneth E Wittmeyer, *VP*
EMP: 3074 **EST:** 1956
SQ FT: 123,732
SALES (est): 221.89MM
SALES (corp-wide): 302.09B **Publicly Held**
SIC: 5051 Steel
PA: Berkshire Hathaway Inc.
3555 Farnam St Ste 1440
Omaha NE
402 346-1400

(P-12537)
CALIFORNIA STEEL AND TUBE
16049 Stephens St (91745-1717)
PHONE....................................626 968-5511
TOLL FREE: 800
Rick Hirsch, *Pr*
Ron Prichard, *VP*
EMP: 108 **EST:** 1952
SQ FT: 108,000
SALES (est): 27.37MM
SALES (corp-wide): 9.74B **Privately Held**
Web: www.californiasteelandtube.com

SIC: 5051 Steel
HQ: Kloeckner Metals Corporation
500 Colonial Center Pkwy # 500
Roswell GA

(P-12538)
CALIFORNIA STEEL SERVICES INC
Also Called: California Steel Services
1212 S Mountain View Ave (92408-3001)
PHONE....................................909 796-2222
Parviz Razavian, *CEO*
EMP: 49 **EST:** 1983
SQ FT: 78,000
SALES (est): 22.09MM **Privately Held**
Web: www.calsteel.com
SIC: 5051 3444 3443 Steel; Sheet metalwork ; Fabricated plate work (boiler shop)

(P-12539)
CENTURY TUBES INC
7910 Dunbrook Rd (92126-4371)
PHONE....................................858 586-0550
Christine Young, *Pr*
Conrad M Young, *VP*
▲ **EMP:** 22 **EST:** 1980
SQ FT: 10,000
SALES (est): 5.16MM **Privately Held**
Web: www.centurytubes.com
SIC: 5051 3312 3356 3351 Pipe and tubing, steel; Tubes, steel and iron; Nonferrous rolling and drawing, nec; Copper rolling and drawing

(P-12540)
CKKM INC (PA)
Also Called: Nova Steel Company
265 Radio Rd (92879-1725)
PHONE....................................951 371-8484
Bernard Smokowski, *Pr*
Jacqueline Lowery, *
Mary Jo Thometz, *
EMP: 21 **EST:** 1991
SQ FT: 50,000
SALES (est): 27.22MM **Privately Held**
Web: www.adp-ca.com
SIC: 5051 3444 Steel; Pipe, sheet metal

(P-12541)
CMC REBAR WEST
5425 Industrial Pkwy (92407-1803)
PHONE....................................909 713-1130
Lee Albright, *Mgr*
EMP: 101
SIC: 5051 Steel
HQ: Cmc Rebar West
3880 Murphy Canyon Rd # 100
San Diego CA

(P-12542)
COAST ALUMINUM INC (PA)
Also Called: Coast Aluminum
10628 Fulton Wells Ave (90670-3740)
P.O. Box 2144 (90670-0440)
PHONE....................................562 946-6061
TOLL FREE: 800
Thomas C Clark, *Pr*
Bonnie Clark, *Stockholder**
▲ **EMP:** 125 **EST:** 1982
SQ FT: 112,000
SALES (est): 482.99MM **Privately Held**
Web: www.coastaluminum.com
SIC: 5051 Miscellaneous nonferrous products

(P-12543)
CONQUEST INDUSTRIES INC
12740 Lakeland Rd (90670-4633)
PHONE....................................562 906-1111
▲ **EMP:** 25 **EST:** 1979

SALES (est): 8.78MM **Privately Held**
Web: www.conquestind.com
SIC: 5051 3559 Nonferrous metal sheets, bars, rods, etc., nec; Jewelers' machines

(P-12544)
COONER SALES COMPANY LLC (PA)
Also Called: Cooner Wire Company
9265 Owensmouth Ave (91311-5854)
PHONE..............................818 882-8311
Patrick G Weir, *Pr*
▲ **EMP:** 19 **EST:** 1957
SQ FT: 17,825
SALES (est): 9.68MM
SALES (corp-wide): 9.68MM **Privately Held**
Web: www.coonerwire.com
SIC: 5051 3679 Wire, nec; Harness assemblies, for electronic use: wire or cable

(P-12545)
CREST STEEL CORPORATION
Also Called: Crest Steel
6580 General Rd (92509-0103)
PHONE..............................951 727-2600
James Hoffman, *CEO*
Kris Farris, *
Dave Zertuche, *
Paul Worden, *
▲ **EMP:** 90 **EST:** 1964
SQ FT: 12,000
SALES (est): 60.93MM
SALES (corp-wide): 17.02B **Publicly Held**
Web: www.creststeel.com
SIC: 5051 Steel
PA: Reliance Steel & Aluminum Co.
16100 N 71st St Ste 400
Scottsdale AZ
480 564-5700

(P-12546)
DANIEL GERARD WORLDWIDE INC
Also Called: City Wire Cloth
13055 Jurupa Ave (92337-6982)
PHONE..............................951 361-1111
TOLL FREE: 800
Todd Snelbaker, *Mgr*
EMP: 71
SQ FT: 50,000
SALES (corp-wide): 52.43MM **Privately Held**
Web: www.gerarddaniel.com
SIC: 5051 3496 3356 3315 Wire, nec; Mesh, made from purchased wire; Nonferrous rolling and drawing, nec; Steel wire and related products
PA: Gerard Daniel Worldwide, Inc.
34 Barnhart Dr
Hanover PA
800 232-3332

(P-12547)
DOUGLAS STEEL SUPPLY INC (PA)
Also Called: DOUGLAS STEEL SUPPLY CO.
4804 Laurel Canyon Blvd (91607-3717)
PHONE..............................323 587-7676
Douglas Stein, *CEO*
Donal Hecht, *
EMP: 86 **EST:** 1972
SQ FT: 100,000
SALES (est): 88.5K
SALES (corp-wide): 88.5K **Privately Held**
SIC: 5051 Steel

(P-12548)
EARLE M JORGENSEN COMPANY
350 S Grand Ave Ste 5100 (90071-3421)
PHONE..............................323 567-1122
Janice Day, *Mgr*
EMP: 90
SALES (corp-wide): 17.02B **Publicly Held**
Web: www.emjmetals.com
SIC: 5051 Steel
HQ: Earle M. Jorgensen Company
10650 Alameda St
Lynwood CA
323 567-1122

(P-12549)
EARLE M JORGENSEN COMPANY (HQ)
Also Called: EMJ Corporate
10650 Alameda St (90262-1754)
PHONE..............................323 567-1122
◆ **EMP:** 120 **EST:** 2006
SALES (est): 544.68MM
SALES (corp-wide): 17.02B **Publicly Held**
Web: www.emjmetals.com
SIC: 5051 Metals service centers and offices
PA: Reliance Steel & Aluminum Co.
16100 N 71st St Ste 400
Scottsdale AZ
480 564-5700

(P-12550)
ENDURA STEEL INC (HQ)
Also Called: Smith Ironworks
17671 Bear Valley Rd (92345-4902)
PHONE..............................760 244-9325
Jonathan D Hove, *Pr*
Robert E Hove, *Ch Bd*
Dan Such, *VP*
Lori A Clifton, *Sec*
EMP: 18 **EST:** 1972
SQ FT: 6,500
SALES (est): 34.01MM
SALES (corp-wide): 63.93MM **Privately Held**
Web: www.robar.com
SIC: 5051 3441 Steel; Fabricated structural metal
PA: Robar Enterprises, Inc.
17671 Bear Valley Rd
Hesperia CA
760 244-5456

(P-12551)
FRY STEEL COMPANY
13325 Molette St (90670-5568)
P.O. Box 4028 (90670-1028)
PHONE..............................562 802-2721
◆ **EMP:** 115 **EST:** 1945
SALES (est): 39.99MM
SALES (corp-wide): 17.02B **Publicly Held**
Web: www.frysteel.com
SIC: 5051 5099 Steel; Brass goods
PA: Reliance Steel & Aluminum Co.
16100 N 71st St Ste 400
Scottsdale AZ
480 564-5700

(P-12552)
GVS ITALY
8616 La Tijera Blvd (90045-3944)
PHONE..............................424 382-4343
Bruno Montesano, *Mgr*
EMP: 100 **EST:** 2016
SALES (est): 9.12MM **Privately Held**
SIC: 5051 Aluminum bars, rods, ingots, sheets, pipes, plates, etc.

(P-12553)
HARBOR PIPE AND STEEL INC
Also Called: James Metals
1495 Columbia Ave Bldg 10 (92507-2074)
PHONE..............................951 369-3990
Joseph W Beattie, *Pr*
Martha Fournier, *
Teri Stevens, *
P Jay Peterson, *
Tom Liljegren, *
▲ **EMP:** 150 **EST:** 1962
SALES (est): 47.54MM **Privately Held**
Web: www.harborpipe.com
SIC: 5051 Steel

(P-12554)
JACK RUBIN & SONS INC (PA)
13103 S Alameda St (90222-2806)
P.O. Box 3005 (90223-3005)
PHONE..............................310 635-5407
Bruce Rubin, *CEO*
Phillip Mandel, *
Michael Rubin, *
◆ **EMP:** 25 **EST:** 1945
SQ FT: 30,000
SALES (est): 25.09MM
SALES (corp-wide): 25.09MM **Privately Held**
Web: www.wirerope.net
SIC: 5051 3496 3999 Rope, wire (not insulated); Woven wire products, nec; Atomizers, toiletry

(P-12555)
JFE SHOJI AMERICA HOLDINGS INC (DH)
301 E Ocean Blvd Ste 1750 (90802-4827)
PHONE..............................562 637-3500
Naosuke Oda, *Pr*
Hidehiko Ogawa, *
Toshihiro Kabasawa, *
◆ **EMP:** 85 **EST:** 1965
SQ FT: 7,500
SALES (est): 286.74MM **Privately Held**
Web: www.jfe-shoji-steel-america.com
SIC: 5051 Steel
HQ: Jfe Shoji Corporation
1-9-5, Otemachi
Chiyoda-Ku TKY

(P-12556)
JIMS SUPPLY CO INC (PA)
3500 Buck Owens Blvd (93308-4920)
P.O. Box 668 (93302-0668)
PHONE..............................661 616-6977
TOLL FREE: 800
Clay Watson, *CEO*
Jennifer Drake, *
Jennice Boylan, *
Dan Drake, *
Bryan Boylan, *
▲ **EMP:** 82 **EST:** 1959
SQ FT: 25,300
SALES (est): 39.16MM
SALES (corp-wide): 39.16MM **Privately Held**
Web: www.jimssupply.com
SIC: 5051 Steel

(P-12557)
JOOR BROS WELDING INC
Also Called: Joor Bros Metal Supply
2818 Garretson Ave (92881-3509)
PHONE..............................951 737-3950
William Joor, *CEO*
Garrett Joor, *Sec*
EMP: 21 **EST:** 1949
SQ FT: 20,000
SALES (est): 1.89MM **Privately Held**

SIC: 5051 3443 Steel; Tanks, standard or custom fabricated: metal plate

(P-12558)
M-H IRONWORKS INC
1000 S Seaward Ave (93001-3735)
P.O. Box 58364 (90058-0364)
▲ **EMP:** 52 **EST:** 1947
SALES (est): 4.39MM **Privately Held**
SIC: 5051 3312 Steel; Blast furnaces and steel mills

(P-12559)
MCNICHOLS COMPANY
Also Called: McNichols
14108 Arbor Pl (90703-2404)
PHONE..............................562 921-3344
Pat Roche, *Mgr*
EMP: 17
SQ FT: 20,000
SALES (corp-wide): 191.36MM **Privately Held**
Web: www.mcnichols.com
SIC: 5051 3496 3446 Steel; Wire cloth and woven wire products; Open flooring and grating for construction
PA: Mcnichols Company
2502 N Rocky Point Dr # 750
Tampa FL
877 884-4653

(P-12560)
MWS PRECISION WIRE INDS INC
Also Called: Mws Wire Industries
3000 Camino Del Sol (93030-7275)
PHONE..............................818 991-8553
TOLL FREE: 888
Benjamin Konrad, *Pr*
Darrell H Friedman, *
Alan Friedman, *
Lois J Friedman, *
EMP: 52 **EST:** 1968
SQ FT: 32,000
SALES (est): 27.17MM **Privately Held**
Web: www.mwswire.com
SIC: 5051 3351 3357 Copper sheets, plates, bars, rods, pipes, etc., nec; Wire, copper and copper alloy; Nonferrous wiredrawing and insulating

(P-12561)
NEIGHBORHOOD STEEL LLC (HQ)
Also Called: Maas-Hansen Steel
5555 Garden Grove Blvd Ste 250 (92683-1886)
P.O. Box 58307 (90058-0307)
PHONE..............................714 236-8700
Gary Stein, *Managing Member*
EMP: 30 **EST:** 2015
SALES (est): 37.84MM
SALES (corp-wide): 634.65MM **Privately Held**
Web: www.sss-steel.com
SIC: 5051 3312 Steel; Blast furnaces and steel mills
PA: Triple-S Steel Holdings, Inc.
6000 Jensen Dr
Houston TX
713 697-7105

(P-12562)
NORMAN INDUSTRIAL MTLS INC
Also Called: Industrial Metal Supply Co
2481 Alton Pkwy (92606-5030)
PHONE..............................949 250-3343
Jerry Entin, *VP*
EMP: 69
SQ FT: 40,000
SALES (corp-wide): 150.06MM **Privately Held**

PRODUCTS & SVCS

Web: www.industrialmetalsupply.com
SIC: 5051 5099 3366 Steel; Brass goods; Bronze foundry, nec
PA: Norman Industrial Materials, Inc.
8300 San Fernando Rd
Sun Valley CA
818 729-3333

(P-12563)
NORMAN INDUSTRIAL MTLS INC (PA)
Also Called: Industrial Metal Supply Co
8300 San Fernando Rd (91352-3222)
PHONE..............................818 729-3333
TOLL FREE: 800
Eric Steinhauer, *CEO*
David Pace, *
David Berkey, *
Dave Cohen, *
▲ **EMP:** 125 **EST:** 1945
SQ FT: 70,000
SALES (est): 150.06MM
SALES (corp-wide): 150.06MM **Privately Held**
Web: www.industrialmetalsupply.com
SIC: 5051 3441 3449 Metals service centers and offices; Fabricated structural metal; Miscellaneous metalwork

(P-12564)
PACIFIC STEEL GROUP
2755 S Willow Ave (92316-3260)
PHONE..............................858 449-7219
EMP: 417
SALES (corp-wide): 119.78MM **Privately Held**
Web: www.pacificsteelgroup.com
SIC: 5051 Iron and steel (ferrous) products
PA: Pacific Steel Group
4805 Murphy Canyon Rd
San Diego CA
858 251-1100

(P-12565)
PUSAN PIPE AMERICA INC
Also Called: Seah Steel America
2100 Main St Ste 100 (92614-6238)
PHONE..............................949 655-8000
Byung Joon Lee, *CEO*
Jun Lee, *
▲ **EMP:** 357 **EST:** 1978
SALES (est): 34.64MM **Privately Held**
SIC: 5051 Steel

(P-12566)
RAMCAST ORNAMENTAL SUP CO INC
Also Called: Ramcast Steel
1450 E Mission Blvd (91766-2229)
PHONE..............................909 469-4767
Ismael Ramirez, *Brnch Mgr*
EMP: 30
SQ FT: 5,478
SALES (corp-wide): 47.95MM **Privately Held**
Web: www.ramcaststeel.net
SIC: 5051 3312 Steel; Stainless steel
PA: Ramcast Ornamental Supply Company, Inc.
2201 Firestone Blvd
Los Angeles CA
323 585-1625

(P-12567)
RAPID CONN INC
6 Goddard (92618-4600)
PHONE..............................949 951-3722
Chuang Juay Ang, *CEO*
Balaji Raghunathan, *VP*
◆ **EMP:** 24 **EST:** 2000

SALES (est): 3.18MM **Privately Held**
Web: www.thelumicharge.com
SIC: 5051 3643 5085 Wire, nec; Connectors and terminals for electrical devices; Twine

(P-12568)
RELIANCE STEEL & ALUMINUM CO
Metal Center
12034 Greenstone Ave (90670-4727)
P.O. Box 2101 (90670-0013)
PHONE..............................562 944-3322
Jay Rose, *Brnch Mgr*
EMP: 80
SQ FT: 142,000
SALES (corp-wide): 17.02B **Publicly Held**
Web: www.rsac.com
SIC: 5051 Steel
PA: Reliance Steel & Aluminum Co.
16100 N 71st St Ste 400
Scottsdale AZ
480 564-5700

(P-12569)
RELIANCE STEEL & ALUMINUM CO
Also Called: Reliance Steel Company
2537 E 27th St (90058-1284)
PHONE..............................323 583-6111
John Becknell, *Brnch Mgr*
EMP: 200
SALES (corp-wide): 17.02B **Publicly Held**
Web: www.rsac.com
SIC: 5051 Steel
PA: Reliance Steel & Aluminum Co.
16100 N 71st St Ste 400
Scottsdale AZ
480 564-5700

(P-12570)
RELIANCE STEEL & ALUMINUM CO
Bralco Metals
15090 Northam St (90638-5757)
PHONE..............................714 736-4800
TOLL FREE: 800
Michael Hubbart, *Brnch Mgr*
EMP: 118
SALES (corp-wide): 17.02B **Publicly Held**
Web: www.rsac.com
SIC: 5051 Steel
PA: Reliance Steel & Aluminum Co.
16100 N 71st St Ste 400
Scottsdale AZ
480 564-5700

(P-12571)
ROSSIN STEEL INC
9102 Birch St (91977-4109)
PHONE..............................619 656-9200
Ted F Rossin, *CEO*
Jeffrey Clinkscleas, *
EMP: 110 **EST:** 2005
SALES (est): 30.59MM **Privately Held**
Web: www.rossinsteelinc.com
SIC: 5051 Steel

(P-12572)
STAUB METALS LLC
7747 Rosecrans Ave (90723-2509)
P.O. Box 1425 (90723-1425)
PHONE..............................562 602-2200
EMP: 85 **EST:** 1980
SALES (est): 25.44MM **Privately Held**
Web: www.staubmetals.com
SIC: 5051 Steel

(P-12573)
STREUTER TECHNOLOGIES
Also Called: Streuter Fastel Timtel
208 Avenida Fabricante Ste 200 (92672)
PHONE..............................949 369-7676
Bart Streuter, *Pr*
Bart S Streuter, *Pr*
Brad Streuter, *VP*
▲ **EMP:** 18 **EST:** 2005
SQ FT: 13,000
SALES (est): 4.83MM **Privately Held**
Web: www.streuter.com
SIC: 5051 2891 Ferrous metals; Adhesives and sealants

(P-12574)
TA CHEN INTERNATIONAL INC (HQ)
Also Called: Sunland Shutters
5855 Obispo Ave (90805-3715)
PHONE..............................562 808-8000
Johnny Hsieh, *CEO*
James Chang, *
John Hellighausen, *
Andrew Chang, *
◆ **EMP:** 172 **EST:** 1989
SQ FT: 200,000
SALES (est): 917.07MM **Privately Held**
Web: www.tachen.com
SIC: 5051 Steel
PA: Ta Chen Stainless Pipe Co., Ltd.
No. 125, Xintian 2nd St.
Tainan City

(P-12575)
TMX AEROSPACE
12821 Carmenita Rd Unit F (90670-4805)
PHONE..............................562 215-4410
EMP: 120 **EST:** 2006
SALES (est): 14.04MM **Privately Held**
Web: www.thyssenkrupp-aerospace.com
SIC: 5051 Steel

(P-12576)
TOOL COMPONENTS INC (PA)
Also Called: E-Z Lok Division
240 E Rosecrans Ave (90248-1942)
P.O. Box 2069 (90247-0069)
PHONE..............................310 323-5613
TOLL FREE: 800
▲ **EMP:** 38 **EST:** 1956
SALES (est): 21.33MM
SALES (corp-wide): 21.33MM **Privately Held**
Web: www.tciprecision.com
SIC: 5051 3429 Aluminum bars, rods, ingots, sheets, pipes, plates, etc.; Metal fasteners

(P-12577)
TOTTEN TUBES INC (PA)
500 W Danlee St (91702-2341)
PHONE..............................626 812-0220
Tracy N Totten, *CEO*
David Totten, *
Linda Furse, *
Jeffrey Totten, *
EMP: 60 **EST:** 1955
SQ FT: 73,000
SALES (est): 48.57MM
SALES (corp-wide): 48.57MM **Privately Held**
Web: www.tottentubes.com
SIC: 5051 3498 Pipe and tubing, steel; Coils, pipe; fabricated from purchased pipe

(P-12578)
TRANSTAR METALS CORP
Also Called: Castle Metals Aerospace
14001 Orange Ave (90723-2017)
PHONE..............................562 630-1400

▲ **EMP:** 450
SIC: 5051 Aluminum bars, rods, ingots, sheets, pipes, plates, etc.

(P-12579)
TRI-TECH METALS INC
9039 Charles Smith Ave (91730-5566)
PHONE..............................909 948-1401
Sam Allen, *Pr*
Richard Lee Hiromoto, *CEO*
Rock Hargus, *VP*
Sam Allen, *Sec*
Margo Beltran, *Treas*
EMP: 18 **EST:** 1998
SQ FT: 10,000
SALES (est): 9.25MM **Privately Held**
Web: www.tri-techmetals.com
SIC: 5051 3499 3291 Steel; Aerosol valves, metal; Steel wool

(P-12580)
VER SALES INC (PA)
2509 N Naomi St (91504-3236)
PHONE..............................818 567-3000
TOLL FREE: 800
Gloria Ryan, *CEO*
James J Ryan, *CEO*
Craig Ryan, *VP*
Paul Ryan, *VP*
Patrick Ryan, *VP*
▲ **EMP:** 45 **EST:** 1972
SQ FT: 30,000
SALES (est): 25.33MM
SALES (corp-wide): 25.33MM **Privately Held**
Web: www.versales.com
SIC: 5051 5099 3357 Metal wires, ties, cables, and screening; Safety equipment and supplies; Nonferrous wiredrawing and insulating

5063 Electrical Apparatus And Equipment

(P-12581)
AAA ELECTRIC MOTOR SALES & SVC (PA)
1346 Venice Blvd (90006-5595)
PHONE..............................213 749-2367
Brian A Maloney, *Pr*
Robert A Maloney, *Pr*
Nancy Maloney, *Sec*
EMP: 19 **EST:** 1971
SQ FT: 3,500
SALES (est): 10.34MM
SALES (corp-wide): 10.34MM **Privately Held**
Web: www.aaa-electric.net
SIC: 5063 7694 Motors, electric; Electric motor repair

(P-12582)
ADJ PRODUCTS LLC (PA)
6122 S Eastern Ave (90040-3402)
PHONE..............................323 582-2650
Toby Velasquez, *Managing Member*
EMP: 120 **EST:** 2012
SALES (est): 15.41MM
SALES (corp-wide): 15.41MM **Privately Held**
Web: www.adj.com
SIC: 5063 Lighting fixtures

(P-12583)
ADVANTAGE MANUFACTURING INC
Also Called: Electric Motors
616 S Santa Fe St (92705-4109)

PHONE..................714 505-1166
Lyann Courant, *CEO*
Michael Collins, *
◆ **EMP:** 30 **EST:** 1992
SQ FT: 25,000
SALES (est): 11.9MM **Privately Held**
Web: www.advantageman.com
SIC: 5063 5091 3621 5999 Motors, electric;
Swimming pools, equipment and supplies;
Motors, electric; Swimming pools, hot tubs,
and sauna equipment and supplies

(P-12584)
AQ LIGHTING GROUP TEXAS
INC
Also Called: Aq Lighting Group
28486 Westinghouse Pl Ste 120 (91355)
PHONE..................818 534-5300
Cynthia Piana, *Pr*
Tom Piana, *
EMP: 25 **EST:** 2017
SQ FT: 16,000
SALES (est): 21MM **Privately Held**
SIC: 5063 3645 3612 2599 Light bulbs and
related supplies; Light shades, metal;
Distribution transformers, electric; Factory
furniture and fixtures

(P-12585)
BARTCO LIGHTING INC
5761 Research Dr (92649-1616)
PHONE..................714 230-3200
Robert Barton, *CEO*
Dana B Mcke, *Ex VP*
Brian Labbe, *
▲ **EMP:** 70 **EST:** 1998
SALES (est): 23.98MM **Privately Held**
Web: www.bartcolighting.com
SIC: 5063 3648 Lighting fixtures, commercial
and industrial; Airport lighting fixtures:
runway approach, taxi, or ramp

(P-12586)
BATTERY SYSTEMS INC
16725 Roscoe Blvd (91343-6110)
PHONE..................818 474-1500
EMP: 86
SALES (corp-wide): 545.41MM **Privately**
Held
Web: www.batterysystems.net
SIC: 5063 Batteries
PA: Battery Systems, Inc.
8585 N Stemmons Fwy # 60
Dallas TX
310 667-9320

(P-12587)
BAY CITY EQUIPMENT INDS INC
Also Called: John Deere Authorized Dealer
13625 Danielson St (92064-6829)
PHONE..................619 938-8200
Mark Loftin, *CEO*
Rodney Lee, *
Charles Loftin, *
EMP: 100 **EST:** 1932
SQ FT: 20,000
SALES (est): 56.26MM **Privately Held**
Web: www.bcew.com
SIC: 5063 5082 Generators; Construction
and mining machinery

(P-12588)
BRITHINEE ELECTRIC
620 S Rancho Ave (92324-3243)
PHONE..................909 825-7971
Wallace B Brithinee, *Pr*
Donald P Brithinee, *VP*
EMP: 57 **EST:** 1963
SALES (est): 17.39MM **Privately Held**
Web: www.brithinee.com

SIC: 5063 7694 Motors, electric; Electric
motor repair

(P-12589)
CABLECONN INDUSTRIES INC
Also Called: Cableconn
7198 Convoy Ct (92111-1019)
PHONE..................858 571-7111
Lisa Coffman, *Pr*
Roger Newman, *
Rod Coffman, *
EMP: 65 **EST:** 1991
SQ FT: 20,000
SALES (est): 22.72MM **Privately Held**
Web: www.cableconn.com
SIC: 5063 3678 3643 Building wire and cable
; Electronic connectors; Current-carrying
wiring services

(P-12590)
CALIFORNIA BREAKERS INC
Also Called: Cbione
2490 Grand Ave (92081-7804)
PHONE..................760 598-1528
Carlos Trevino, *CEO*
EMP: 22 **EST:** 1977
SQ FT: 18,000
SALES (est): 7MM **Privately Held**
Web: www.cbione.com
SIC: 5063 1731 3823 Electrical supplies, nec
; Electric power systems contractors;
Industrial process measurement equipment

(P-12591)
CORDELIA LIGHTING INC
20101 S Santa Fe Ave (90221-5917)
PHONE..................310 886-3490
James Keng, *Pr*
Li-wei Wang, *VP*
▲ **EMP:** 106 **EST:** 1985
SQ FT: 200,000
SALES (est): 23.82MM **Privately Held**
Web: www.cordelia.com
SIC: 5063 Lighting fixtures

(P-12592)
EATON AEROSPACE LLC
Eaton Aerospace
4690 Colorado Blvd (90039-1106)
PHONE..................818 409-0200
Stephanie Stewart, *Brnch Mgr*
EMP: 256
SQ FT: 41,117
SIC: 5063 3492 Electrical apparatus and
equipment; Fluid power valves and hose
fittings
HQ: Eaton Aerospace Llc
1000 Eaton Blvd
Cleveland OH
216 523-5000

(P-12593)
ECOSENSE LIGHTING INC (PA)
837 N Spring St Ste 103 (90012-2323)
PHONE..................855 632-6736
Mark Reynoso, *CEO*
George Mueller, *
Neil Gamble, *
Steven Gelsomini, *
Robert T Mcculley, *VP*
▲ **EMP:** 95 **EST:** 2008
SALES (est): 45.79MM
SALES (corp-wide): 45.79MM **Privately**
Held
Web: www.ecosenselighting.com
SIC: 5063 Lighting fixtures

(P-12594)
ECOSENSE LIGHTING INC
14811 Myford Rd (92780-7227)

PHONE..................714 823-1014
EMP: 129
SALES (corp-wide): 45.79MM **Privately**
Held
Web: www.ecosenselighting.com
SIC: 5063 Lighting fixtures
PA: Ecosense Lighting Inc.
837 N Spring St Ste 103
Los Angeles CA
855 632-6736

(P-12595)
EXPO POWER SYSTEMS INC
Also Called: Enviroguard
5534 Olive St (91763-1649)
PHONE..................800 506-9884
Doug Frazier, *Pr*
EMP: 34 **EST:** 1993
SQ FT: 15,000
SALES (est): 18.79MM **Privately Held**
Web: www.enviroguard.com
SIC: 5063 3444 Batteries; Sheet metalwork

(P-12596)
GRAYBAR ELECTRIC
COMPANY INC
Also Called: Graybar
1370 Valley Vista Dr Ste 100 (91765-3921)
PHONE..................909 451-4300
Bruce Spencer, *Brnch Mgr*
EMP: 153
SALES (corp-wide): 8.77B **Privately Held**
Web: www.graybar.com
SIC: 5063 5065 Electrical supplies, nec;
Telephone equipment
PA: Graybar Electric Company, Inc.
34 N Meramec Ave
Saint Louis MO
314 573-9200

(P-12597)
GRAYBAR ELECTRIC
COMPANY INC
8606 Miralani Dr (92126-4353)
PHONE..................858 578-8606
Chris Ruperto, *Mgr*
EMP: 89
SQ FT: 42,973
SALES (corp-wide): 8.77B **Privately Held**
Web: www.graybar.com
SIC: 5063 Electrical supplies, nec
PA: Graybar Electric Company, Inc.
34 N Meramec Ave
Saint Louis MO
314 573-9200

(P-12598)
HOCHIKI AMERICA
CORPORATION (HQ)
Also Called: Hochiki
7051 Village Dr Ste 100 (90621-2262)
P.O. Box 514689 (90051-4689)
PHONE..................714 522-2246
Hisham Harake, *CEO*
Hiroshi Kamei, *
Sunichi Shoji V Pes, *Prin*
Michel Nader, *
◆ **EMP:** 95 **EST:** 1972
SQ FT: 30,000
SALES (est): 48.18MM **Privately Held**
Web: www.hochikiamerica.com
SIC: 5063 3669 Fire alarm systems; Fire
detection systems, electric
PA: Hochiki Corporation
2-10-43, Kamiosaki
Shinagawa-Ku TKY

(P-12599)
JME INC (PA)
Also Called: T M B
527 Park Ave (91340-2557)
PHONE..................201 896-8600
Colin R Waters, *CEO*
Thomas M Bissett, *
◆ **EMP:** 80 **EST:** 1982
SQ FT: 34,000
SALES (est): 38.15MM
SALES (corp-wide): 38.15MM **Privately**
Held
Web: www.tmb.com
SIC: 5063 Lighting fittings and accessories

(P-12600)
KOBERT & COMPANY INC
Also Called: L.H. Dottie Co
6131 Garfield Ave (90040-3610)
PHONE..................323 725-1000
▲ **EMP:** 90 **EST:** 1965
SALES (est): 29.43MM **Privately Held**
Web: www.lhdottie.com
SIC: 5063 5074 Electrical supplies, nec;
Plumbing fittings and supplies

(P-12601)
LIGHTING TECHNOLOGIES INTL
LLC
13700 Live Oak Ave (91706-1319)
PHONE..................626 480-0755
▲ **EMP:** 190 **EST:** 2016
SALES (est): 24.12MM **Privately Held**
Web: www.ltilighting.com
SIC: 5063 3648 Lighting fixtures; Lighting
equipment, nec

(P-12602)
LOS ANGELES LTG MFG CO INC
Also Called: L A Lighting
10141 Olney St (91731-2311)
PHONE..................626 454-8300
William D Shapiro, *Pr*
Mieko Shapiro, *VP*
◆ **EMP:** 70 **EST:** 1988
SQ FT: 50,000
SALES (est): 22.27MM **Privately Held**
Web: www.lalighting.com
SIC: 5063 3646 Lighting fixtures; Ceiling
systems, luminous

(P-12603)
MAGNETIKA INC (PA)
2041 W 139th St (90249-2409)
PHONE..................310 527-8100
Francis Ishida, *Pr*
Basil P Caloyeras, *
EMP: 80 **EST:** 1960
SQ FT: 40,000
SALES (est): 31.93MM
SALES (corp-wide): 31.93MM **Privately**
Held
Web: www.magnetika.com
SIC: 5063 3612 Transformers, electric;
Ballasts for lighting fixtures

(P-12604)
MAIN ELECTRIC SUPPLY CO
LLC
8146 Byron Rd (90606-2616)
PHONE..................323 753-5131
Darrin Gunter, *Brnch Mgr*
EMP: 20
SALES (corp-wide): 464.19MM **Privately**
Held
Web: www.mainelectricsupply.com
SIC: 5063 3699 Electrical supplies, nec;
Electrical equipment and supplies, nec
PA: Main Electric Supply Company Llc
3600 W Segerstrom Ave

PRODUCTS & SVCS

Santa Ana CA
949 833-3052

(P-12605)
MAIN ELECTRIC SUPPLY CO
LLC
4674 Cardin St (92111-1419)
PHONE..............................858 737-7000
EMP: 33
SALES (corp-wide): 464.19MM **Privately Held**
Web: www.mainelectricsupply.com
SIC: 5063 3699 Electrical supplies, nec; Electrical equipment and supplies, nec
PA: Main Electric Supply Company Llc
3600 W Segerstrom Ave
Santa Ana CA
949 833-3052

(P-12606)
MAXIM LIGHTING INTL INC (PA)
Also Called: Maxim Lighting
253 Vineland Ave (91746-2319)
PHONE..............................626 956-4200
Jacob Sperling, *CEO*
Zvi Sperling, *
Michael S Andrews, *
▲ **EMP:** 200 **EST:** 1999
SQ FT: 26,000
SALES (est): 56.17MM
SALES (corp-wide): 56.17MM **Privately Held**
Web: www.maximlighting.com
SIC: 5063 Lighting fixtures

(P-12607)
MOTIVE ENERGY INC (PA)
17260 Newhope St (92708-4210)
PHONE..............................714 888-2525
Robert J Istwan, *Pr*
▼ **EMP:** 80 **EST:** 1979
SQ FT: 35,000
SALES (est): 43.24MM
SALES (corp-wide): 43.24MM **Privately Held**
Web: www.motiveenergy.com
SIC: 5063 Storage batteries, industrial

(P-12608)
MULTIQUIP INC (DH)
Also Called: Mq Power
6141 Katella Ave Ste 200 (90630-5202)
PHONE..............................310 537-3700
Robert J Graydon, *CEO*
James Henehan, *
◆ **EMP:** 300 **EST:** 1973
SALES (est): 214.36MM **Privately Held**
Web: www.multiquip.com
SIC: 5063 5082 3645 Generators; General construction machinery and equipment; Garden, patio, walkway and yard lighting fixtures: electric
HQ: Itochu International Inc.
1251 Ave Of The Amrcas Fl
New York NY
212 818-8000

(P-12609)
MURCAL INC
Also Called: Murcal
41343 12th St W (93551-1442)
PHONE..............................661 272-4700
Robert J Murphy, *Pr*
John H Murphy, *
Essie Murphy, *Stockholder*
EMP: 26 **EST:** 1958
SQ FT: 20,000
SALES (est): 9.75MM **Privately Held**
Web: www.murcal.com

SIC: 5063 3621 3694 Motor controls, starters and relays: electric; Storage battery chargers, motor and engine generator type; Ignition apparatus, internal combustion engines

(P-12610)
NORA LIGHTING INC
6505 Gayhart St (90040-2507)
PHONE..............................323 767-2600
Fred Farzan, *CEO*
Jill Farzan, *
Neda Farzan, *
◆ **EMP:** 150 **EST:** 1989
SQ FT: 150,000
SALES (est): 90MM **Privately Held**
Web: www.noralighting.com
SIC: 5063 3648 5719 Lighting fixtures; Lighting fixtures, except electric: residential; Lighting fixtures

(P-12611)
ORBIT INDUSTRIES INC
7533 Garfield Ave (90201-4817)
PHONE..............................213 745-8884
Saeed Nikayin, *CEO*
John Alexandrovic, *
▲ **EMP:** 98 **EST:** 1965
SALES (est): 35.87MM **Privately Held**
Web: www.orbitelectric.com
SIC: 5063 Electrical apparatus and equipment
HQ: Element Materials Technology Group Limited
Davidson Building, 5 Southampton Street
London
800 470-3598

(P-12612)
PACIFIC POWER SYSTEMS
INTEGRATION INC
14729 Spring Ave (90670-5107)
PHONE..............................562 281-0500
EMP: 23
SIC: 5063 3826 Transformers, electric; Petroleum product analyzing apparatus

(P-12613)
PLC IMPORTS INC
Also Called: P L C Lighting
9667 Owensmouth Ave Ste 201
(91311-4819)
PHONE..............................818 349-1600
Daniel Gilardi, *Pr*
Robert Gilardi, *
▲ **EMP:** 25 **EST:** 1992
SALES (est): 4.63MM **Privately Held**
Web: www.plclighting.com
SIC: 5063 3646 Light bulbs and related supplies; Commercial lighting fixtures

(P-12614)
QUANTUM AUTOMATION (PA)
4400 E La Palma Ave (92807-1807)
P.O. Box 18687 (92817-8687)
PHONE..............................714 854-0800
Brian Gallogly, *Pr*
EMP: 35 **EST:** 1991
SQ FT: 11,000
SALES (est): 13.12MM **Privately Held**
Web: www.quantumautomation.com
SIC: 5063 3825 3613 Electrical apparatus and equipment; Electrical power measuring equipment; Control panels, electric

(P-12615)
REGENCY ENTERPRISES INC
(PA)

Also Called: Regency Supply
9261 Jordan Ave (91311-5739)
PHONE..............................818 901-0255
Ron Regenstreif, *CEO*
Scott Anderson, *
Isaac Regenstreif, *
Judah Regenstreif, *
Mike Goldstone, *
◆ **EMP:** 272 **EST:** 1981
SALES (est): 104.14MM
SALES (corp-wide): 104.14MM **Privately Held**
Web: www.regencysupply.com
SIC: 5063 Light bulbs and related supplies

(P-12616)
ROS ELECTRICAL SUP EQP CO
LLC
9529 Slauson Ave (90660-4749)
PHONE..............................562 695-9000
EMP: 20 **EST:** 2008
SALES (est): 2.74MM **Privately Held**
Web: www.rps-powersystems.com
SIC: 5063 3699 Electrical supplies, nec; Electrical equipment and supplies, nec

(P-12617)
SGGH LLC
15301 Ventura Blvd Ste 400 (91403-6629)
PHONE..............................805 435-1255
EMP: 838 **EST:** 2014
SALES (est): 1.04MM
SALES (corp-wide): 133.24MM **Publicly Held**
SIC: 5063 6162 Circuit breakers; Mortgage bankers and loan correspondents
PA: Elah Holdings, Inc.
8214 Westchester Dr # 950
Dallas TX
805 435-1255

(P-12618)
SIEMENS INDUSTRY INC
6141 Katella Ave (90630-5202)
PHONE..............................714 761-2200
Eric Ackerman, *Genl Mgr*
EMP: 80
SALES (corp-wide): 84.48B **Privately Held**
Web: new.siemens.com
SIC: 5063 Electrical apparatus and equipment
HQ: Siemens Industry, Inc.
100 Technology Dr
Alpharetta GA
847 215-1000

(P-12619)
SLOAN ELECTRIC
CORPORATION
3520 Main St (92113-3804)
PHONE..............................619 239-5174
EMP: 28 **EST:** 1985
SALES (est): 9.54MM **Privately Held**
Web: www.sloanelectric.com
SIC: 5063 7694 7629 Motor controls, starters and relays: electric; Electric motor repair; Generator repair

(P-12620)
SUNCO LIGHTING INC
27811 Hancock Pkwy Ste A (91355-4187)
PHONE..............................844 334-9938
Sorush Tahour, *CEO*
EMP: 44 **EST:** 2014
SALES (est): 8.93MM **Privately Held**
Web: www.sunco.com
SIC: 5063 3699 Electrical supplies, nec; Electrical equipment and supplies, nec

(P-12621)
UNS ELECTRIC INC
6565 Valley View St (90623-1060)
PHONE..............................714 690-3660
EMP: 26
SALES (corp-wide): 8.22B **Privately Held**
Web: www.uesaz.com
SIC: 5063 3691 Storage batteries, industrial; Storage batteries
HQ: Uns Electric, Inc.
88 E Broadway Blvd 901
Tucson AZ
928 681-8966

(P-12622)
US ELECTRICAL SERVICES INC
Also Called: Wiedenbach-Brown
1501 E Orangethorpe Ave Ste 140
(92831-5252)
PHONE..............................714 982-1534
Scott King, *Mgr*
EMP: 27
SALES (corp-wide): 1.5B **Privately Held**
Web: www.usesi.com
SIC: 5063 3645 Lighting fixtures; Residential lighting fixtures
HQ: U.S. Electrical Services, Inc.
701 Middle St
Middletown CT

(P-12623)
USHIO AMERICA INC (HQ)
5440 Cerritos Ave (90630-4567)
PHONE..............................714 236-8600
William Mackenzie, *CEO*
Shinji Kameda, *CFO*
Ako Shimada, *Sec*
Yuichi Asaka, *Prin*
◆ **EMP:** 90 **EST:** 1967
SQ FT: 70,000
SALES (est): 57.83MM **Privately Held**
Web: www.ushio.com
SIC: 5063 Lighting fixtures, commercial and industrial
PA: Ushio Inc.
1-6-5, Marunouchi
Chiyoda-Ku TKY

(P-12624)
VET NATIONAL INC
Also Called: Vet National Mail
3621 State St (93105-2521)
PHONE..............................805 692-8487
EMP: 20 **EST:** 1996
SALES (est): 3.91MM **Privately Held**
Web: www.vetnational.com
SIC: 5063 3088 3541 7331 Electrical apparatus and equipment; Plastics plumbing fixtures; Machine tools, metal cutting type; Mailing service

(P-12625)
WALTERS WHOLESALE
ELECTRIC CO (HQ)
18626 S Susana Rd (90221-5621)
PHONE..............................562 988-3100
John L Walter, *
Bill Durkee, *
Roland Wood, *
Nancy Nielsen, *
▼ **EMP:** 50 **EST:** 1953
SALES (est): 374.7MM
SALES (corp-wide): 1.5B **Privately Held**
Web: www.walterswholesale.com
SIC: 5063 3699 1731 Wire and cable; Electrical equipment and supplies, nec; Lighting contractor

PA: Consolidated Electrical Distributors, Inc.
1920 Westridge Dr
Irving TX
972 582-5300

(P-12626)
WAMCO INC (PA)
17752 Fitch (92614-6033)
PHONE.................................714 545-5560
Michael Matthews, *CEO*
Chris Matthews, *Pr*
Eric Lemay, *VP*
Michael Phillips, *VP*
Steve Dunkerken, *CFO*
▲ **EMP:** 19 **EST:** 1968
SQ FT: 30,000
SALES (est): 12.95MM
SALES (corp-wide): 12.95MM **Privately Held**
Web: www.wamcoinc.com
SIC: 5063 3647 5088 Electrical supplies, nec ; Vehicular lighting equipment; Transportation equipment and supplies

(P-12627)
WESTERN LIGHTING INDS INC
Also Called: Orgatech Omegalux
12203 Magnolia Ave Ste 1 (92503-4890)
PHONE.................................626 969-6820
Lawrence St Ives, *CEO*
▲ **EMP:** 22 **EST:** 1983
SALES (est): 4.84MM **Privately Held**
SIC: 5063 3646 Lighting fixtures; Fluorescent lighting fixtures, commercial

5064 Electrical Appliances, Television And Radio

(P-12628)
DATABYTE TECHNOLOGY INC (PA)
Also Called: Databyte
2300 Peck Rd (90601-1601)
PHONE.................................626 305-0500
Lawrence Ho, *Pr*
▲ **EMP:** 20 **EST:** 1980
SQ FT: 32,000
SALES (est): 4.21MM
SALES (corp-wide): 4.21MM **Privately Held**
SIC: 5064 3651 Electrical entertainment equipment; Household audio equipment

(P-12629)
DRAGON TRADE INTL CORP
1205 Highland Ave (91950-3536)
PHONE.................................619 816-6062
Jorge Petit, *CEO*
Carlos Hermida, *
Manuel Hermida Rodriguez, *
EMP: 200 **EST:** 2014
SALES (est): 55MM **Privately Held**
SIC: 5064 Electrical appliances, major

(P-12630)
E & S INTERNATIONAL ENTPS INC (PA)
Also Called: Import Direct
7801 Hayvenhurst Ave (91406-1712)
PHONE.................................818 887-0700
Philip Asherian, *CEO*
Farshad Asherian, *Pr*
Mike Rad, *COO*
Mark Barron, *CFO*
◆ **EMP:** 168 **EST:** 1983
SQ FT: 60,000
SALES (est): 81.89MM

SALES (corp-wide): 81.89MM **Privately Held**
Web: www.esintl.com
SIC: 5064 Electrical appliances, major

(P-12631)
ETEKCITY CORPORATION
Also Called: Etekcity
1202 N Miller St Unit A (92806-1956)
PHONE.................................855 686-3835
Grace Yang, *CEO*
Phillip Chen, *
Sean Yang, *CIO*
EMP: 125 **EST:** 2011
SALES (est): 41.51MM **Privately Held**
Web: www.vesync.com
SIC: 5064 Electrical appliances, television and radio

(P-12632)
HARMAN-KARDON INCORPORATED
Also Called: Harman-Kardon
8500 Balboa Blvd (91329-0003)
P.O. Box 2200 (91328-2200)
PHONE.................................818 841-4600
Tom Mcloughlin, *
Chet Simon, *VP Fin*
▲ **EMP:** 275 **EST:** 1949
SALES (est): 62.81MM **Privately Held**
Web: www.harman.com
SIC: 5064 3651 High fidelity equipment; Household audio and video equipment
HQ: Harman International Industries Incorporated
400 Atlantic St Ste 15
Stamford CT
203 328-3500

(P-12633)
HOMELAND HOUSEWARES LLC
Also Called: Magic Bullet
10900 Wilshire Blvd Ste 900 (90024-6500)
PHONE.................................310 996-7200
Rich Krause, *CEO*
▲ **EMP:** 80 **EST:** 2003
SALES (est): 14.8MM
SALES (corp-wide): 65.12MM **Privately Held**
Web: homeland-housewares.pissedconsumer.com
SIC: 5064 5963 Electrical appliances, major; Appliance sales, house-to-house
HQ: Capital Brands, Llc
10900 Wilshire Blvd # 900
Los Angeles CA

(P-12634)
MEMOREX PRODUCTS INC
17777 Center Court Dr N Ste 800 (90703-9320)
PHONE.................................562 653-2800
Michael Golacinski, *Pr*
Allan Yap, *
Mae Higa, *
Kevin Mcdonnell, *Sr VP*
▲ **EMP:** 159 **EST:** 1993
SQ FT: 212,000
SALES (est): 7.95MM **Publicly Held**
SIC: 5064 5065 5045 3652 Electrical entertainment equipment; Radio and television equipment and parts; Computer peripheral equipment; Prerecorded records and tapes
PA: Glassbridge Enterprises, Inc.
18 E 50th St Ste 700
New York NY

(P-12635)
PHILIPS NORTH AMERICA LLC
Also Called: Innercool Therapies
3721 Valley Centre Dr (92130-3329)
PHONE.................................858 677-6390
EMP: 90
SALES (corp-wide): 133.64MM **Privately Held**
Web: usa.philips.com
SIC: 5064 Television sets
HQ: Philips North America Llc
222 Jacobs St Fl 3
Cambridge MA
617 245-5900

(P-12636)
PIONEER NORTH AMERICA INC (DH)
970 W 190th St Ste 360 (90502-1001)
P.O. Box 1720 (90801-1720)
PHONE.................................310 952-2000
Masao Kawabata, *CEO*
Kazunori Yamamoto, *Pr*
◆ **EMP:** 19 **EST:** 1978
SQ FT: 4,855
SALES (est): 565.91MM **Privately Held**
Web: www.pioneerelectronics.com
SIC: 5064 3651 High fidelity equipment; Household audio and video equipment
HQ: Pioneer Corporation
2-28-8, Honkomagome
Bunkyo-Ku TKY

(P-12637)
SAMSUNG ELECTRONICS AMER INC
5601 E Slauson Ave Ste 200 (90040-2953)
PHONE.................................323 374-6300
EMP: 224
Web: www.samsung.com
SIC: 5064 Electrical appliances, television and radio
HQ: Samsung Electronics America, Inc.
85 Challenger Rd
Ridgefield Park NJ
201 229-4000

(P-12638)
TTE TECHNOLOGY INC
Also Called: Tcl Electronics
189 Technology Dr (92618-2402)
PHONE.................................877 300-8837
Mark Zhang, *Pr*
Nicole Feng, *Dir Fin*
▲ **EMP:** 150 **EST:** 2004
SQ FT: 50,000
SALES (est): 169.46MM
SALES (corp-wide): 4.15MM **Privately Held**
Web: www.tcl.com
SIC: 5064 Television sets
HQ: Tcl Electronics Holdings Limited
C/O Maples Corporate Services Limited
George Town GR CAYMAN

(P-12639)
TV GUIDE ENTRMT GROUP LLC
2700 Colorado Ave Ste 200 (90404-5502)
PHONE.................................310 360-1441
EMP: 82 **EST:** 1998
SALES (est): 78.41MM
SALES (corp-wide): 30.15B **Publicly Held**
SIC: 5064 Electrical entertainment equipment
HQ: Cbs Interactive Inc.
680 Folsom St
San Francisco CA

5065 Electronic Parts And Equipment, Nec

(P-12640)
ACE WIRELESS & TRADING INC
3031 Orange Ave Ste B (92707-4246)
PHONE.................................949 748-5700
◆ **EMP:** 375
SIC: 5065 Electronic parts

(P-12641)
ADVANCED MP TECHNOLOGY LLC (DH)
27271 Las Ramblas Ste 300 (92691-8042)
PHONE.................................800 492-3113
Homayoun Shorooghi, *Pr*
◆ **EMP:** 126 **EST:** 1994
SALES (est): 51.24MM
SALES (corp-wide): 410.29MM **Privately Held**
Web: www.a2globalelectronics.com
SIC: 5065 Electronic parts
HQ: America Ii Electronics, Llc
2500 118th Ave N
Saint Petersburg FL
727 573-0900

(P-12642)
AIR ELECTRO INC (PA)
9452 De Soto Ave (91311-4910)
P.O. Box 2231 (91313-2231)
PHONE.................................818 407-5400
EMP: 104 **EST:** 1951
SALES (est): 26.76MM
SALES (corp-wide): 26.76MM **Privately Held**
Web: www.airelectro.com
SIC: 5065 3674 Electronic parts; Computer logic modules

(P-12643)
BATTERY SYSTEMS INC
26151 Jefferson Ave Ste A (92562-9560)
PHONE.................................951 894-2960
Mikel Sides, *Brnch Mgr*
EMP: 85
SALES (corp-wide): 545.41MM **Privately Held**
Web: www.batterysystems.net
SIC: 5065 Electronic parts and equipment, nec
PA: Battery Systems, Inc.
8585 N Stemmons Fwy # 60
Dallas TX
310 667-9320

(P-12644)
BEAR COMMUNICATIONS INC
Also Called: Bearcom Wireless Worldwide
8290 Vickers St Ste D (92111-2116)
PHONE.................................619 263-2159
Rick Andrews, *Brnch Mgr*
EMP: 85
SALES (corp-wide): 809.13MM **Privately Held**
Web: www.bearcom.com
SIC: 5065 Communication equipment
HQ: Bear Communications, Inc.
4009 Dist Dr Ste 200
Garland TX

(P-12645)
BEAR COMMUNICATIONS INC
Also Called: Bearcom Wireless Worldwide
8584 Venice Blvd (90034-2549)
PHONE.................................310 854-2327
TOLL FREE: 800
Stan Cameron, *Brnch Mgr*

EMP: 85
SALES (corp-wide): 809.13MM **Privately Held**
Web: www.bearcom.com
SIC: 5065 Communication equipment
HQ: Bear Communications, Inc.
4009 Dist Dr Ste 200
Garland TX

(P-12646)
BIP CORPORATION
2951 Norman Strasse Rd (92069-5933)
PHONE..................760 591-9822
▲ **EMP:** 19 **EST:** 1988
SQ FT: 3,000
SALES (est): 4.81MM **Privately Held**
Web: www.bipcorp.com
SIC: 5065 3663 Communication equipment; Radio and t.v. communications equipment

(P-12647)
BISCO INC
5065 E Hunter Ave (92807-6001)
P.O. Box 3005 (90408-3005)
PHONE..................714 693-2901
Michael Levinrad, *Pr*
EMP: 144 **EST:** 2010
SALES (est): 13.53MM **Privately Held**
Web: www.biscoind.com
SIC: 5065 Electronic parts

(P-12648)
BISCO INDUSTRIES INC (HQ)
Also Called: Fastcor
5065 E Hunter Ave (92807-6001)
PHONE..................800 323-1232
▲ **EMP:** 85 **EST:** 1973
SALES (est): 160.95MM
SALES (corp-wide): 319.4MM **Publicly Held**
Web: www.biscoind.com
SIC: 5065 Electronic parts
PA: Eaco Corporation
5065 E Hunter Ave
Anaheim CA
714 876-2490

(P-12649)
BITCENTRAL INC
Also Called: Bitcentral
4340 Von Karman Ave # 410 (92660-2085)
PHONE..................949 253-9000
EMP: 85
SIC: 5065 Communication equipment

(P-12650)
BROWNSTONE COMPANIES INC
Also Called: Brownstone Security
2629 Manhattan Beach Blvd # 100 (90278-1604)
PHONE..................310 297-3600
EMP: 700
SIC: 5065 Security control equipment and systems

(P-12651)
CAL SOUTHERN SOUND IMAGE INC (PA)
Also Called: Sound Image
2425 Auto Park Way (92029-1222)
PHONE..................760 737-3900
David R Shadoan, *CEO*
Ralph Wagner, *
EMP: 65 **EST:** 1984
SQ FT: 28,000
SALES (est): 49.52MM
SALES (corp-wide): 49.52MM **Privately Held**
Web: www.sound-image.com

SIC: 5065 3651 5064 Sound equipment, electronic; Speaker systems; Electrical appliances, television and radio

(P-12652)
CALRAD ELECTRONICS INC
819 N Highland Ave (90038-3416)
PHONE..................323 465-2131
Robert Shupper, *Pr*
▲ **EMP:** 20 **EST:** 1939
SALES (est): 4.62MM **Privately Held**
Web: www.calrad.com
SIC: 5065 3678 3663 3661 Electronic parts; Electronic connectors; Radio and t.v. communications equipment; Telephone and telegraph apparatus

(P-12653)
CBOL CORPORATION
19850 Plummer St (91311-5652)
PHONE..................818 704-8200
Howard Nam, *COO*
Kenneth Cheung, *
Lynn Turk, *
Spencer H Kim, *
◆ **EMP:** 131 **EST:** 1987
SQ FT: 69,820
SALES (est): 99.45MM **Privately Held**
Web: www.cbol.com
SIC: 5065 5072 5013 5088 Electronic parts and equipment, nec; Hardware; Motor vehicle supplies and new parts; Transportation equipment and supplies

(P-12654)
CICOIL LLC
24960 Avenue Tibbitts (91355-3426)
PHONE..................661 295-1295
Jeffrey T Crane, *CEO*
John Palahnuk, *
Patrick H Albert, *
EMP: 120 **EST:** 1956
SQ FT: 16,000
SALES (est): 31.3MM **Privately Held**
Web: www.cicoil.com
SIC: 5065 Electronic parts and equipment, nec

(P-12655)
CYNERGY PROF SYSTEMS LLC
23187 La Cadena Dr Ste 102 (92653-1481)
PHONE..................800 776-7978
Cynthia Mason, *Managing Member*
EMP: 30 **EST:** 2009
SALES (est): 87.49MM **Privately Held**
Web: www.cynergy.pro
SIC: 5065 7379 3663 3661 Communication equipment; Computer related maintenance services; Radio and t.v. communications equipment; Communication headgear, telephone

(P-12656)
ELECTRONIC HARDWARE LIMITED (PA)
13257 Saticoy St (91605-3486)
PHONE..................818 982-6100
R E Vudrogivic, *CEO*
Richard Degn, *Pr*
EMP: 32 **EST:** 1973
SQ FT: 10,000
SALES (est): 4.48MM
SALES (corp-wide): 4.48MM **Privately Held**
Web: www.electronichardware.com
SIC: 5065 5072 3541 Electronic parts; Hardware; Machine tools, metal cutting type

(P-12657)
ENERPRO INC
99 Aero Camino (93117-3822)
PHONE..................805 683-2114
Thomas Bourbeau, *Pr*
Frank J Bourbeau, *
Ilse Bourbeau, *
Thomas Bourbeau, *VP*
◆ **EMP:** 25 **EST:** 1983
SQ FT: 27,000
SALES (est): 9.71MM **Privately Held**
Web: www.enerpro-inc.com
SIC: 5065 3699 Electronic parts and equipment, nec; Accelerating waveguide structures

(P-12658)
EQUITY INTERNATIONAL INC
Also Called: B & W
5541 Fermi Ct (92008-7348)
PHONE..................978 664-2712
Joseph Atkins, *Pr*
Stephen Curran, *
Cindy Hughes, *
EMP: 574 **EST:** 1993
SALES (est): 107.37MM **Privately Held**
Web: www.bowerswilkins.com
SIC: 5065 Radio and television equipment and parts
HQ: B & W Group Ltd
Dale Road
Worthing W SUSSEX
190 322-1500

(P-12659)
EVERFOCUS ELECTRONICS CORP (HQ)
324 W Blueridge Ave (92865-4202)
PHONE..................626 844-8888
◆ **EMP:** 20 **EST:** 1996
SALES (est): 12.26MM **Privately Held**
Web: www.everfocus.com
SIC: 5065 3699 Security control equipment and systems; Security control equipment and systems
PA: Everfocus Electronics Corp.
2f, 8, Lane 270, Beishen Rd., Sec. 3
New Taipei City TAP

(P-12660)
FOREIGN TRADE CORPORATION
Also Called: Technocel
685 Cochran St Ste 200 (93065-1921)
PHONE..................805 823-8400
▲ **EMP:** 115
SIC: 5065 Mobile telephone equipment

(P-12661)
GENERAL TRANSISTOR CORPORATION (PA)
Also Called: G T C
12449 Putnam St (90602-1023)
PHONE..................310 578-7344
Albert A Barrios, *Pr*
Ilan Israely, *
EMP: 30 **EST:** 1976
SALES (est): 9.06MM
SALES (corp-wide): 9.06MM **Privately Held**
Web: www.gtcelectronics.com
SIC: 5065 3674 Semiconductor devices; Semiconductor circuit networks

(P-12662)
HARMAN INTERNATIONAL INDS INC
Also Called: Los Angeles Sales Office
8500 Balboa Blvd (91325-5802)
PHONE..................818 893-8411

Jan Quaglia, *Brnch Mgr*
EMP: 2591
Web: www.harman.com
SIC: 5065 Radio parts and accessories, nec
HQ: Harman International Industries Incorporated
400 Atlantic St Ste 15
Stamford CT
203 328-3500

(P-12663)
HEC INC
Also Called: Total Garments
30961 Agoura Rd Ste 311 (91361-5607)
PHONE..................818 879-7414
Shaukat H Zaidi, *CEO*
Shamim Zaidi, *VP*
EMP: 338 **EST:** 1996
SQ FT: 4,500
SALES (est): 21.84MM **Privately Held**
Web: www.hoorayusa.com
SIC: 5065 Electronic parts

(P-12664)
HIGH TECH PET PRODUCTS
2111 Portola Rd # A (93003-7723)
PHONE..................805 644-1797
Nicholas Donge, *Pr*
▲ **EMP:** 60 **EST:** 1980
SALES (est): 5.07MM **Privately Held**
Web: www.hitecpet.com
SIC: 5065 2399 Electronic parts and equipment, nec; Pet collars, leashes, etc.: non-leather

(P-12665)
HIRSCH ELECTRONICS LLC
1900 Carnegie Ave Ste B (92705-5557)
PHONE..................949 250-8888
John Picc, *Managing Member*
John Piccininni, *Managing Member**
Stephen D Healy, *Managing Member**
EMP: 85 **EST:** 1981
SQ FT: 34,600
SALES (est): 17.44MM **Publicly Held**
Web: www.identiv.com
SIC: 5065 Security control equipment and systems
PA: Identiv, Inc.
2201 Walnut Ave Ste 100
Fremont CA

(P-12666)
HM ELECTRONICS INC (PA)
Also Called: H M E
2848 Whiptail Loop (92010-6708)
PHONE..................858 535-6000
Harrison Y Miyahira, *Ch Bd*
Charles Miyahira, *CEO*
◆ **EMP:** 315 **EST:** 1971
SQ FT: 73,000
SALES (est): 452.77MM
SALES (corp-wide): 452.77MM **Privately Held**
Web: www.hme.com
SIC: 5065 Electronic parts and equipment, nec

(P-12667)
HOME SECURITY STORES INC
Also Called: Norco Alarms
12660 Magnolia Ave (92503-4636)
PHONE..................951 782-8494
◆ **EMP:** 34
Web: www.homesecuritystore.com
SIC: 5065 3699 Security control equipment and systems; Security control equipment and systems

(P-12668)

I C CLASS COMPONENTS CORP (PA)
Also Called: Classic Components
23605 Telo Ave (90505-4028)
PHONE.....................310 539-5500
Jeffrey Klein, *Pr*
Kris Klein, *Ex VP*
Daniel Lee, *VP*
Mike Thomas, *VP*
▲ EMP: 100 EST: 1985
SQ FT: 53,000
SALES (est): 95.8MM
SALES (corp-wide): 95.8MM **Privately Held**
Web: www.class-ic.com
SIC: 5065 Electronic parts

(P-12669)

IMPACT COMPONENTS A CALIFORNIA LIMITED PARTNERSHIP
6010 Cornerstone Ct W Ste 200 (92121-3746)
PHONE.....................858 634-4800
▲ EMP: 30 EST: 1897
SALES (est): 9.59MM **Privately Held**
SIC: 5065 3674 Electronic parts; Integrated circuits, semiconductor networks, etc.

(P-12670)

INTELLIPOWER INC
Also Called: Ametek Intellipower
1746 N Saint Thomas Cir (92865-4247)
PHONE.....................714 921-1580
G W Bill Shipman, *CEO*
Dan Rieth, *
Oscar Tang, *
Dan Johnson, *
EMP: 100 EST: 1988
SQ FT: 22,000
SALES (est): 44.08MM
SALES (corp-wide): 6.15B **Publicly Held**
Web: www.intellipower.com
SIC: 5065 Electronic parts and equipment, nec
PA: Ametek, Inc.
1100 Cassatt Rd
Berwyn PA
610 647-2121

(P-12671)

INTERNTIONAL TECH SYSTEMS CORP
Also Called: Itsco
10721 Walker St (90630-4720)
PHONE.....................714 761-8886
Stanley Ning, *Pr*
▲ EMP: 48 EST: 1985
SQ FT: 40,000
SALES (est): 25.33MM **Privately Held**
Web: www.itsco.net
SIC: 5065 3578 Electronic parts and equipment, nec; Point-of-sale devices

(P-12672)

JAE ELECTRONICS INC (HQ)
142 Technology Dr Ste 100 (92618-2430)
PHONE.....................949 753-2600
Noriyuki Konishi, *Pr*
Shinjiro Ando, *Treas*
◆ EMP: 36 EST: 1977
SQ FT: 20,000
SALES (est): 154.52MM **Privately Held**
Web: www.jaeusa.com
SIC: 5065 3679 3829 3678 Connectors, electronic; Electronic circuits; Measuring and controlling devices, nec; Electronic connectors

PA: Japan Aviation Electronics Industry, Limited
1-21-1, Dogenzaka
Shibuya-Ku TKY

(P-12673)

JRI INC
Also Called: J R Industries
31280 La Baya Dr (91362-4005)
PHONE.....................818 706-2424
Craig Pfefferman, *CEO*
▲ EMP: 50 EST: 1987
SQ FT: 20,000
SALES (est): 23.72MM **Privately Held**
Web: www.jri.com
SIC: 5065 3679 Electronic parts; Harness assemblies, for electronic use: wire or cable

(P-12674)

JVCKENWOOD USA CORPORATION (HQ)
4001 Worsham Ave (90808-1976)
P.O. Box 22745 (90801-5745)
PHONE.....................310 639-9000
Shinya Niina, *Pr*
Joseph Glassett, *
Mark Jasin, *
Craig Geiger, *
Harvey D Mitnick, *
▲ EMP: 160 EST: 1961
SQ FT: 238,000
SALES (est): 80.58MM **Privately Held**
Web: us.jvckenwood.com
SIC: 5065 Electronic parts and equipment, nec
PA: Jvckenwood Corporation
3-12, Moriyacho, Kanagawa-Ku
Yokohama KNG

(P-12675)

KLEIN ELECTRONICS INC
Also Called: Klein Electronics
349 N Vinewood St (92029-1338)
PHONE.....................760 781-3220
▲ EMP: 26 EST: 1992
SQ FT: 13,700
SALES (est): 4.94MM **Privately Held**
Web: www.kleinelectronics.com
SIC: 5065 3663 Electronic parts and equipment, nec; Radio broadcasting and communications equipment

(P-12676)

L3HARRIS INTERSTATE ELEC CORP
707 E Vermont Ave A (92805-5612)
PHONE.....................714 758-0500
EMP: 149
SALES (corp-wide): 17.06B **Publicly Held**
Web: www.l3harris.com
SIC: 5065 Electronic parts
HQ: L3harris Interstate Electronics Corporation
602 E Vermont Ave
Anaheim CA
714 758-0500

(P-12677)

LIGHTPOINTE COMMUNICATIONS INC
Also Called: Lightpointe Wireless
8515 Arjons Dr Ste G (92126-4358)
PHONE.....................858 834-4083
Heinz A Willerbrand, *Ch Bd*
Lorian Sanders, *
▲ EMP: 25 EST: 2000
SALES (est): 5.2MM **Privately Held**
Web: www.lightpointe.com

SIC: 5065 3661 Communication equipment; Fiber optics communications equipment

(P-12678)

LINKSYS LLC
120 Theory (92617-3210)
PHONE.....................408 526-4000
EMP: 156
Web: www.linksys.com
SIC: 5065 Electronic parts and equipment, nec
HQ: Linksys Llc
121 Theory Ste 150
Irvine CA
310 751-5100

(P-12679)

LINKSYS LLC
121 Theory Ste 150 (92617-3204)
PHONE.....................310 751-5100
EMP: 194
Web: www.linksys.com
SIC: 5065 Electronic parts and equipment, nec
HQ: Linksys Llc
121 Theory Ste 150
Irvine CA
310 751-5100

(P-12680)

LINKSYS USA INC
121 Theory (92617-3209)
PHONE.....................949 270-8500
Harry Dewhirst, *CEO*
EMP: 100 EST: 2018
SALES (est): 27.07MM
SALES (corp-wide): 4.42B **Publicly Held**
Web: www.linksys.com
SIC: 5065 3577 Communication equipment; Data conversion equipment, media-to-media: computer
PA: Fortinet, Inc.
899 Kifer Rd
Sunnyvale CA
408 235-7700

(P-12681)

MATRIX-FOCALSPOT INC
2747 Loker Ave W (92010-6601)
PHONE.....................858 536-5050
Fred Schlieper, *Pr*
Frank Silva, *VP*
▲ EMP: 38 EST: 2003
SQ FT: 7,100
SALES (est): 9.44MM
SALES (corp-wide): 2.67MM **Privately Held**
Web: www.nordsonmatrix.com
SIC: 5065 3844 Electronic parts; X-ray apparatus and tubes
HQ: Matrix Technologies Gmbh
Kapellenstr. 12
Feldkirchen BY
892000338200

(P-12682)

MAURY MICROWAVE INC (PA)
2900 Inland Empire Blvd (91764-4804)
PHONE.....................909 987-4715
Michael Howo, *CEO*
▲ EMP: 200 EST: 1957
SQ FT: 6,000
SALES (est): 61.84MM
SALES (corp-wide): 61.84MM **Privately Held**
Web: www.maurymw.com
SIC: 5065 Electronic parts and equipment, nec

(P-12683)

MITSUBISHI ELECTRIC US INC (DH)
Also Called: Meus
5900 Katella Ave Ste A (90630-5019)
P.O. Box 6007 (90630-0007)
PHONE.....................714 220-2500
Mike Corbo, *Pr*
Masahiro Oya, *
Mike Corbo, *Pr*
Jared Baker, *
Perry Pappous, *
◆ EMP: 200 EST: 2000
SQ FT: 10,400
SALES (est): 931.5MM **Privately Held**
Web: us.mitsubishielectric.com
SIC: 5065 3534 1796 3669 Electronic parts; Escalators, passenger and freight; Elevator installation and conversion; Visual communication systems
HQ: Mitsubishi Electric Us Holdings, Inc.
5900 Katella Ave Ste A
Cypress CA
714 220-2500

(P-12684)

MOTOROLA MOBILITY LLC
Also Called: Motorola
6450 Sequence Dr (92121-4376)
PHONE.....................858 455-1500
Rick Neal, *Brnch Mgr*
EMP: 73
SQ FT: 30,000
Web: www.motorola.com
SIC: 5065 3663 Communication equipment; Radio and t.v. communications equipment
HQ: Motorola Mobility Llc
222 Mdse Mart Plz # 1800
Chicago IL

(P-12685)

MOTORS & CONTROLS WHSE INC
Also Called: Sabina Motors & Controls
1440 N Burton Pl (92806-1204)
PHONE.....................714 956-0480
Vincent Tjelmeland, *Pr*
◆ EMP: 29 EST: 1969
SQ FT: 35,000
SALES (est): 8.99MM **Privately Held**
Web: www.sabinadrives.com
SIC: 5065 3621 Electronic parts; Motors, electric

(P-12686)

MTROIZ INTERNATIONAL
150 S Kenmore Ave (90004-5603)
PHONE.....................661 998-8013
Eun H Chae, *CEO*
Hong Chae, *
Stephen Banks, *
EMP: 32 EST: 2011
SALES (est): 2.31MM **Privately Held**
Web: www.mtroiz.com
SIC: 5065 2844 5023 5047 Communication equipment; Perfumes, cosmetics and other toilet preparations; Homefurnishings; Medical and hospital equipment

(P-12687)

NISCAYAH INC
Hamilton Pacific
751 N Todd Ave (91702-2244)
PHONE.....................626 683-8167
Diane Frank, *Brnch Mgr*
EMP: 95
SALES (corp-wide): 16.95B **Publicly Held**
SIC: 5065 Security control equipment and systems
HQ: Niscayah, Inc.
2400 Commerce Ave Ste 500

PRODUCTS & SVCS

Duluth GA
678 474-1720

(P-12688)
NORTH AMERICAN VIDEO CORP (PA)
Also Called: Navco Security Systems
1335 S Acacia Ave (92831-5315)
PHONE..................................714 779-7499
Jason Oakley, *CEO*
William Augustus Groves, *
Margaret Groves, *
William Groves, *
Sharon Bryant, *
◆ **EMP:** 45 **EST:** 1975
SALES (est): 81.67MM
SALES (corp-wide): 81.67MM **Privately Held**
Web: www.navco.com
SIC: 5065 3812 Video equipment, electronic; Acceleration indicators and systems components, aerospace

(P-12689)
NOVACAP LLC
25111 Anza Dr (91355-3416)
PHONE..................................661 295-5920
Mark Skoog, *CEO*
Shelley Mears, *
▲ **EMP:** 280 **EST:** 1980
SQ FT: 38,000
SALES (est): 55.8MM
SALES (corp-wide): 764.7MM **Publicly Held**
Web: www.novacap.ca
SIC: 5065 Electronic parts and equipment, nec
PA: Knowles Corporation
1151 Maplewood Dr
Itasca IL
630 250-5100

(P-12690)
P C A ELECTRONICS INC
16799 Schoenborn St (91343-6194)
PHONE..................................818 892-0761
Morris Weinberg, *Pr*
Benjamin Weinberg, *
EMP: 44 **EST:** 1949
SQ FT: 30,000
SALES (est): 8.04MM **Privately Held**
Web: www.pca.com
SIC: 5065 3674 Electronic parts; Semiconductors and related devices

(P-12691)
PRESIDIO COMPONENTS INC
7169 Construction Ct (92121-2615)
PHONE..................................858 578-9390
Violet Devoe, *Pr*
Daniel Devoe, *
Alan Devoe, *
Lambert Devoe, *
▲ **EMP:** 120 **EST:** 1980
SQ FT: 35,000
SALES (est): 55.32MM **Privately Held**
Web: www.presidiocomponents.com
SIC: 5065 Electronic parts and equipment, nec

(P-12692)
Q TECH CORPORATION
6161 Chip Ave (90630-5213)
PHONE..................................310 836-7900
Sally Phillips, *Pr*
Richard Taylor, *
EMP: 200 **EST:** 1972
SALES (est): 42.77MM **Privately Held**
Web: www.q-tech.com

SIC: 5065 Electronic parts and equipment, nec

(P-12693)
QUINSTAR TECHNOLOGY INC
24085 Garnier St (90505-5319)
PHONE..................................310 320-1111
Leo Fong, *Pr*
John Kuno, *
▲ **EMP:** 72 **EST:** 1993
SALES (est): 37.82MM **Privately Held**
Web: www.quinstar.com
SIC: 5065 3671 Electronic parts and equipment, nec; Cathode ray tubes, including rebuilt

(P-12694)
RANTEC POWER SYSTEMS INC (HQ)
1173 Los Olivos Ave (93402-3230)
PHONE..................................805 596-6000
Michael C Bickel, *Pr*
Michael C Bickel, *Pr*
Frank Janku, *
EMP: 97 **EST:** 1963
SQ FT: 40,000
SALES (est): 49.58MM
SALES (corp-wide): 56.3MM **Privately Held**
Web: www.rantec.com
SIC: 5065 Electronic parts and equipment, nec
PA: Rps Holdings, Inc.
1173 Los Olivos Ave
Los Osos CA
805 596-6000

(P-12695)
RAYTHEON CMMAND CTRL SLTONS LL (DH)
1801 Hughes Dr (92833-2200)
P.O. Box 34055 (92834-9455)
PHONE..................................714 446-3118
Alex Cresswell, *
Don Johnson, *
▲ **EMP:** 700 **EST:** 2001
SALES (est): 312.6K
SALES (corp-wide): 67.07B **Publicly Held**
SIC: 5065 Security control equipment and systems
HQ: Raytheon Company
870 Winter St
Waltham MA
781 522-3000

(P-12696)
RECOM GROUP
449 Borrego Ct (91773-2971)
PHONE..................................909 599-1370
Robert Norden, *CEO*
◆ **EMP:** 20 **EST:** 1997
SALES (est): 4.6MM **Privately Held**
Web: www.recomgroup.com
SIC: 5065 3679 5046 Electronic parts; Liquid crystal displays (LCD); Store fixtures and display equipment

(P-12697)
SAMSUNG INTERNATIONAL INC (DH)
333 H St Ste 6000 (91910-5565)
PHONE..................................619 671-6001
Byaong Gueon Jeon, *CEO*
Wonchul Song, *
Hak Seob Shim, *
◆ **EMP:** 50 **EST:** 1983
SALES (est): 82.13MM **Privately Held**
Web: www.samsung.com

SIC: 5065 3663 Mobile telephone equipment ; Mobile communication equipment
HQ: Samsung Electronics America, Inc.
85 Challenger Rd
Ridgefield Park NJ
201 229-4000

(P-12698)
STEREN ELECTRONICS INTL LLC (PA)
Also Called: Steren Electronic Solutions
8445 Camino Santa Fe (92121-2650)
PHONE..................................800 266-3333
David Shteremberg, *
Vick Soffer, *
Jose Zyman, *
◆ **EMP:** 100 **EST:** 1956
SALES (est): 22.01MM
SALES (corp-wide): 22.01MM **Privately Held**
Web: www.sterenusa.com
SIC: 5065 Connectors, electronic

(P-12699)
SUPERIOR COMMUNICATIONS INC (PA)
Also Called: Puregear
5027 Irwindale Ave Ste 900 (91706-2187)
PHONE..................................877 522-4727
Solomon Chen, *
Jeffrey Banks, *CEO*
Robert Chen, *
Keith Kam, *
Jennifer Ju, *Legal Counsel**
▲ **EMP:** 248 **EST:** 1991
SQ FT: 11,000
SALES (est): 93.98MM **Privately Held**
Web: www.superiorcommunications.com
SIC: 5065 Communication equipment

(P-12700)
TALLEY INC (PA)
Also Called: Talley & Associates
12976 Sandoval St (90670-4061)
P.O. Box 3123 (90670-0123)
PHONE..................................562 906-8000
John R Talley, *CEO*
Mark D Talley, *
Elizabeth J Talley, *
Jeffrey R Talley, *
Richard M Talley, *
◆ **EMP:** 110 **EST:** 1968
SQ FT: 80,000
SALES (est): 100.18MM
SALES (corp-wide): 100.18MM **Privately Held**
Web: www.talleycom.com
SIC: 5065 Communication equipment

(P-12701)
TAMURA CORPORATION OF AMERICA (HQ)
277 Rancheros Dr Ste 190 (92069-2982)
PHONE..................................800 472-6624
Norihiko Nanjo, *CEO*
Junko Walker, *Sec*
Tony Shinonuma, *CFO*
Takatoshi Nakakaryia, *Chief Operating Officer Sales*
▲ **EMP:** 26 **EST:** 1976
SQ FT: 10,801
SALES (est): 28.13MM **Privately Held**
Web: www.tamuracorp.com
SIC: 5065 5063 3677 Electronic parts; Electrical apparatus and equipment; Electronic coils and transformers
PA: Tamura Corporation
1-19-43, Higashioizumi
Nerima-Ku TKY

(P-12702)
TAPE SPECIALTY INC
Also Called: T S I
24831 Avenue Tibbitts (91355-3405)
PHONE..................................661 702-9030
Steve Feldman, *Pr*
Stu Feldman, *
Peggy James, *
▲ **EMP:** 28 **EST:** 1976
SQ FT: 19,000
SALES (est): 4.76MM **Privately Held**
Web: www.tsidm.com
SIC: 5065 3652 7389 Magnetic recording tape; Magnetic tape (audio): prerecorded; Music and broadcasting services

(P-12703)
TDK-LAMBDA AMERICAS INC
401 Mile Of Cars Way Ste 325 (91950-6610)
PHONE..................................619 575-4400
Pascal Shauson, *CEO*
EMP: 200
Web: us.tdk-lambda.com
SIC: 5065 Electronic parts and equipment, nec
HQ: Tdk-Lambda Americas Inc.
405 Essex Rd
Tinton Falls NJ
732 795-4100

(P-12704)
TECH SYSTEMS INC
7372 Walnut Ave Ste J (90620-1718)
PHONE..................................714 523-5404
Raymond Downs, *Mgr*
EMP: 210
SALES (corp-wide): 50.19MM **Privately Held**
Web: www.techsystemsinc.com
SIC: 5065 Closed circuit TV
PA: Tech Systems, Inc.
4942 Summer Oak Dr
Buford GA
770 495-8700

(P-12705)
TECOM INDUSTRIES INCORPORATED
375 Conejo Ridge Ave (91361-4928)
PHONE..................................805 267-0100
◆ **EMP:** 160
Web: www.smithsinterconnect.com
SIC: 5065 Electronic parts

(P-12706)
TELIT WIRELESS SOLUTIONS INC
7700 Irvine Center Dr (92618-2923)
PHONE..................................949 461-7150
EMP: 131
Web: www.telit.com
SIC: 5065 Electronic parts
PA: Telit Wireless Solutions, Inc.
5425 Page Rd Ste 120
Durham NC

(P-12707)
TV EARS INC
2701 Via Orange Way Ste 1 (91978-1702)
PHONE..................................619 797-1600
George Dennis, *CEO*
Nancy Nelson, *
Steffens Meeks, *CPO**
▲ **EMP:** 30 **EST:** 1998
SALES (est): 9.56MM **Privately Held**
Web: www.tvears.com
SIC: 5065 3651 Sound equipment, electronic ; Television receiving sets

(P-12708)
UNION TECHNOLOGY CORP
718 Monterey Pass Rd (91754-3607)
PHONE..............................323 266-6871
David I Chu, *CEO*
Robert Boughrum, *
Raj Amin, *
Gary Koniow, *
Benha Choonhauri, *
◆ **EMP:** 50 **EST:** 1991
SQ FT: 21,800
SALES (est): 15.01MM **Privately Held**
Web: www.quanticutc.com
SIC: 5065 3675 Electronic parts; Electronic
capacitors

(P-12709)
WATERFI LLC
4379 30th St Ste 2 (92104-1323)
PHONE..............................619 438-0058
Royce Nicholas, *Managing Member*
EMP: 18 **EST:** 2011
SALES (est): 2.49MM **Privately Held**
Web: www.waterfi.com
SIC: 5065 2899 Electronic parts and
equipment, nec; Waterproofing compounds

(P-12710)
WEXLER CORPORATION
Also Called: Wexler Video
1111 S Victory Blvd (91502-2550)
PHONE..............................818 846-9381
EMP: 1630 **EST:** 1980
SALES (est): 45.67MM **Privately Held**
Web: www.reesewexler.com
SIC: 5065 7359 Video equipment, electronic;
Equipment rental and leasing, nec
HQ: H.I.G. Capital, Inc.
1450 Brickell Ave Fl 31
Miami FL
305 379-2322

(P-12711)
WINCHESTER INTERCONNECT EC LLC
Also Called: Elrob LLC
12691 Monarch St (92841-3918)
PHONE..............................714 230-6122
Arik Vrobel, *Pr*
Roberto Ortega, *Finance CTRL* *
▲ **EMP:** 54 **EST:** 1960
SQ FT: 38,500
SALES (est): 85.79MM
SALES (corp-wide): 17.49B **Privately Held**
Web: www.el-comsystems.com
SIC: 5065 3679 3613 3643 Electronic parts;
Harness assemblies, for electronic use:
wire or cable; Switchgear and switchboard
apparatus; Current-carrying wiring services
HQ: Winchester Interconnect Corporation
68 Water St
Norwalk CT

5072 Hardware

(P-12712)
ALLIED INTERNATIONAL LLC
Also Called: Allied International
28955 Avenue Sherman (91355-5446)
PHONE..............................818 364-2333
Timothy Florian, *CEO*
Melissa Berninger, *
▲ **EMP:** 50 **EST:** 1962
SQ FT: 106,000
SALES (est): 14.87MM **Privately Held**
Web: www.alliedtools.com
SIC: 5072 3499 Hand tools; Stabilizing bars
(cargo), metal

(P-12713)
AMERICAN KAL ENTERPRISES INC (PA)
Also Called: Pro America Premium Tools
4265 Puente Ave (91706-3420)
PHONE..............................626 338-7308
John Toshima, *Pr*
Mila Bierotte, *
▲ **EMP:** 90 **EST:** 1966
SQ FT: 32,000
SALES (est): 17.71MM
SALES (corp-wide): 17.71MM **Privately Held**
SIC: 5072 3546 3463 3462 Hand tools;
Power-driven handtools; Nonferrous
forgings; Iron and steel forgings

(P-12714)
ASSA ABLOY RSDENTIAL GROUP INC
600 Baldwin Park Blvd (91746)
PHONE..............................626 369-4718
Birk Sorennsen, *Mgr*
EMP: 597
SALES (corp-wide): 4.72B **Publicly Held**
Web: www.emtek.com
SIC: 5072 Hardware
HQ: Assa Abloy Residential Group, Inc.
12801 Schabarum Ave
Irwindale CA
626 961-0413

(P-12715)
ASSA ABLOY RSDENTIAL GROUP INC (HQ)
Also Called: Emtek Products
12801 Schabarum Ave (91706-6808)
PHONE..............................626 961-0413
Lucas Boselli, *CEO*
Thomas Millar, *
◆ **EMP:** 200 **EST:** 1979
SALES (est): 157.72MM
SALES (corp-wide): 4.72B **Publicly Held**
Web: www.emtek.com
SIC: 5072 Hardware
PA: Fortune Brands Innovations, Inc.
520 Lake Cook Rd
Deerfield IL
847 484-4400

(P-12716)
B & B SPECIALTIES INC
G S Aerospace Division
4321 E La Palma Ave (92807-1887)
PHONE..............................714 985-3075
Tom Rutan, *Mgr*
EMP: 100
SALES (corp-wide): 22.69MM **Privately Held**
Web: www.bbspecialties.com
SIC: 5072 3429 Miscellaneous fasteners;
Hardware, nec
PA: B & B Specialties, Inc.
4321 E La Palma Ave
Anaheim CA
714 985-3000

(P-12717)
CHUAOLSON ENTERPRISES INC
1274 N Grove St (92806-2113)
P.O. Box 1240 (92871-1240)
PHONE..............................714 630-4751
Terry Olson, *CEO*
John Chua, *VP*
EMP: 22 **EST:** 1984
SQ FT: 11,785
SALES (est): 4.39MM **Privately Held**

SIC: 5072 3429 Builders' hardware, nec;
Hardware, nec

(P-12718)
CLARENDON SPECIALTY FAS INC
2180 Temple Ave (90804-1020)
PHONE..............................714 842-2603
Arnaud Zemmour, *Admn*
Michael Lang, *
Jeff Heywood, *
▲ **EMP:** 90 **EST:** 1985
SQ FT: 4,000
SALES (est): 23.06MM **Privately Held**
Web: www.clarendonsf.com
SIC: 5072 3444 Miscellaneous fasteners;
Sheet metalwork

(P-12719)
CORONA CLIPPER INC
Also Called: Corona Tools
22440 Temescal Canyon Rd Ste 102
(92883-4200)
PHONE..............................951 737-6515
Stephen J Erickson, *CEO*
Al Schulten, *
John Reisveck, *
◆ **EMP:** 86 **EST:** 1927
SQ FT: 85,000
SALES (est): 45.24MM
SALES (corp-wide): 26.64MM **Privately Held**
Web: www.coronatoolsusa.com
SIC: 5072 3524 Hand tools; Lawn and
garden equipment
PA: Natt Tools Group Inc
460 Sherman Ave N
Hamilton ON
905 549-7433

(P-12720)
DH CASTER INTERNATIONAL INC
2260 S Haven Ave Ste C (91761-0740)
PHONE..............................909 930-6400
Mary Lyn Baker, *CEO*
Richard J Baker, *Pr*
▲ **EMP:** 18 **EST:** 1996
SQ FT: 10,000
SALES (est): 2.83MM **Privately Held**
Web: www.dhcasters.com
SIC: 5072 3999 Hardware; Atomizers, toiletry

(P-12721)
E B BRADLEY CO (PA)
5602 Bickett St (90058-3606)
P.O. Box 58548 (90058-0548)
PHONE..............................323 585-9917
Don Lorey, *Pr*
Scott Simons, *
Ramn Miramontes, *
David Jackson, *
▲ **EMP:** 48 **EST:** 1946
SQ FT: 45,000
SALES (est): 154.3MM
SALES (corp-wide): 154.3MM **Privately Held**
Web: www.ebbradley.com
SIC: 5072 2452 Hardware; Panels and
sections, prefabricated, wood

(P-12722)
E B BRADLEY CO
10903 Vanowen St (91605-6408)
PHONE..............................800 533-3030
Earl Bertrand Bradley, *Brnch Mgr*
EMP: 19
SALES (corp-wide): 154.3MM **Privately Held**
Web: www.ebbradley.com

SIC: 5072 2452 Hardware; Panels and
sections, prefabricated, wood
PA: E. B. Bradley Co.
5602 Bickett St
Vernon CA
323 585-9917

(P-12723)
HAMPTON PRODUCTS INTL CORP (PA)
50 Icon (92610-3000)
PHONE..............................949 472-4256
Gregory J Gluchowski, *Junior President*
Gregory J Gluchowski Junior, *Pr*
▲ **EMP:** 100 **EST:** 1973
SQ FT: 160,000
SALES (est): 87.89MM
SALES (corp-wide): 87.89MM **Privately Held**
Web: www.hamptonproducts.com
SIC: 5072 Hardware

(P-12724)
HD SUPPLY DISTRIBUTION SERVICES LLC
Also Called: Crown Bolt
26940 Aliso Viejo Pkwy (92656-2622)
PHONE..............................949 643-4700
◆ **EMP:** 1078
Web: www.hdsupplyhardwaresolutions.com
SIC: 5072 Screws

(P-12725)
LONG-LOK FASTENERS CORPORATION
20531 Belshaw Ave (90746-3505)
PHONE..............................424 213-4570
Sarah Melendez, *Brnch Mgr*
EMP: 19
SALES (corp-wide): 23.95MM **Privately Held**
Web: www.longlok.com
SIC: 5072 3452 5085 Bolts; Bolts, nuts,
rivets, and washers; Fasteners, industrial:
nuts, bolts, screws, etc.
HQ: Long-Lok Fasteners Corporation
14755 Preston Rd Ste 520
Dallas TX
888 656-9450

(P-12726)
MACPHERSON WSTN TL SUP CO LLC
1160 N Tustin Ave (92807-1735)
PHONE..............................714 666-4100
Jerry Gerardot, *Brnch Mgr*
EMP: 17
SALES (corp-wide): 50.43MM **Privately Held**
Web: www.westtool.com
SIC: 5072 3423 Hand tools; Hand and edge
tools, nec
PA: Macpherson Western Tool & Supply
Co. Llc
203 Lawrence Dr Ste D
Livermore CA
925 443-8665

(P-12727)
MAKITA USA INC (HQ)
Also Called: Makita
14930 Northam St (90638-5753)
PHONE..............................714 522-8088
Sean Okada, *Pr*
Yuhei Iwanaga, *CFO*
◆ **EMP:** 250 **EST:** 1970
SQ FT: 130,000
SALES (est): 468.51MM **Privately Held**
Web: www.makitatools.com

SIC: 5072　Power handtools
PA: Makita Corporation
3-11-8, Sumiyoshicho
Anjo AIC

(P-12728)
PBB INC
1311 E Philadelphia St (91761-5719)
PHONE..................................909 923-6250
Jeff Wood, *Pr*
R C Kung, *VP*
▲ **EMP:** 20 **EST:** 1987
SQ FT: 30,000
SALES (est): 4.34MM **Privately Held**
Web: www.pbbinc.com
SIC: 5072 3429　Builders' hardware, nec;
Builders' hardware

(P-12729)
PENN ELCOM INC (HQ)
Also Called: Penn Elcom Hardware
7465 Lampson Ave (92841-2903)
PHONE..................................714 230-6200
Philip John Stratford, *CEO*
Roger Willems, *
◆ **EMP:** 35 **EST:** 1993
SQ FT: 28,000
SALES (est): 27MM **Privately Held**
Web: www.penn-elcom.com
SIC: 5072 3429　Hardware; Hardware, nec
PA: Penn Elcom Corporation
C/O Maples Corporate Services (Bvi)
Limited
Road Town

(P-12730)
PENN ENGINEERING COMPONENTS
29045 Avenue Penn (91355-5426)
PHONE..................................818 503-1511
Robert Washburn, *Pr*
Jane Washburn, *Sec*
Bill Down, *VP*
EMP: 20 **EST:** 1971
SQ FT: 10,500
SALES (est): 4.77MM **Privately Held**
Web: www.pennengineering.com
SIC: 5072 3679　Hardware; Microwave
components

(P-12731)
PORTEOUS ENTERPRISES INC (DH)
1040 E Watson Center Rd (90745-4202)
PHONE..................................310 549-9180
◆ **EMP:** 175 **EST:** 1969
SALES (est): 48.34MM **Privately Held**
SIC: 5072　Nuts (hardware)
HQ: Brighton-Best International, Inc.
5855 Obispo Ave
Long Beach CA
562 808-8000

(P-12732)
RIEF ENTERPRISES INC (PA)
Also Called: South Bay Abrams Mfg & Dist
15662 Producer Ln (92649-1310)
P.O. Box 2118 (92647-0118)
PHONE..................................714 934-3400
TOLL FREE: 800
▼ **EMP:** 23 **EST:** 1959
SALES (est): 8.66MM
SALES (corp-wide): 8.66MM **Privately Held**
Web: www.southbayabrams.com
SIC: 5072 5149 3315 3089　Cutlery; Spices
and seasonings; Wire carts: grocery,
household, and industrial; Holders: paper
towel, grocery bag, etc.: plastics

(P-12733)
SEVILLE CLASSICS INC (PA)
19401 Harborgate Way (90501-1322)
PHONE..................................310 533-3800
Jackson Yang, *CEO*
Julie Yang, *
◆ **EMP:** 157 **EST:** 1979
SQ FT: 10,000
SALES (est): 35.66MM
SALES (corp-wide): 35.66MM **Privately Held**
Web: www.sevilleclassics.com
SIC: 5072 5199　Hardware; General
merchandise, non-durable

(P-12734)
SHAMROCK SUPPLY COMPANY INC (PA)
Also Called: Shamrock Companies, The
3366 E La Palma Ave (92806-2814)
PHONE..................................714 575-1800
John J O'connor, *Co-Secretary*
Michael O'connor, *Pr*
▲ **EMP:** 52 **EST:** 1975
SQ FT: 45,000
SALES (est): 50.12MM
SALES (corp-wide): 50.12MM **Privately Held**
Web: www.shamrocksupply.com
SIC: 5072 5084 3842　Hand tools; Industrial
machinery and equipment; Personal safety
equipment

(P-12735)
SUNCOAST POST-TENSION LTD
Also Called: Suncoast Post
1528 E Cedar St (91761-5761)
PHONE..................................909 673-0490
Ken Douglas, *Mgr*
EMP: 18
Web: www.suncoast-pt.com
SIC: 5072 3316 3315 5211　Builders'
hardware, nec; Cold finishing of steel
shapes; Cable, steel: insulated or armored;
Masonry materials and supplies
HQ: Suncoast Post-Tension, Ltd.
16825 Northchase Dr # 1100
Houston TX
281 445-8886

(P-12736)
WURTH LOUIS AND COMPANY (DH)
895 Columbia St (92821-2917)
P.O. Box 2253 (92822-2253)
PHONE..................................714 529-1771
Vito Mancini, *Pr*
Tom Mauss, *
Ed Mcgraw, *VP*
▲ **EMP:** 90 **EST:** 1975
SQ FT: 116,000
SALES (est): 84.42MM
SALES (corp-wide): 20.7B **Privately Held**
Web: www.wurthlac.com
SIC: 5072 5198　Furniture hardware, nec;
Stain
HQ: Wurth Group Of North America Inc.
93 Grant St
Ramsey NJ

5074 Plumbing And Hydronic Heating Supplies

(P-12737)
BURKE ENGINEERING CO
9700 Factorial Way (91733-1725)
P.O. Box 928 (92075-0928)
PHONE..................................626 579-6763
EMP: 100
Web: www.burkehvacr.com
SIC: 5074 5084 5075　Heating equipment
(hydronic); Controlling instruments and
accessories; Warm air heating and air
conditioning

(P-12738)
ELMCO SALES INC (PA)
15070 Proctor Ave (91746-3305)
P.O. Box 3787 (91744-0787)
PHONE..................................626 855-4831
Donald E Morris, *Ch Bd*
Kristin E Kahle, *
EMP: 90 **EST:** 1944
SQ FT: 49,650
SALES (est): 23.24MM
SALES (corp-wide): 23.24MM **Privately Held**
Web: www.elmcoaz.com
SIC: 5074　Plumbing fittings and supplies

(P-12739)
EPS CORPORATE HOLDINGS INC
12468 Lambert Rd (90606-2710)
PHONE..................................562 698-7774
Len Erickson, *Brnch Mgr*
EMP: 19
SIC: 5074 3498　Plumbing fittings and
supplies; Pipe fittings, fabricated from
purchased pipe
HQ: Eps Corporate Holdings, Inc.
3100 Dnald Dglas Loop Hng
Santa Monica CA

(P-12740)
FERGUSON FIRE FABRICATION INC (DH)
Also Called: Pacific Fire Safety
2750 S Towne Ave (91766-6205)
PHONE..................................909 517-3085
Leo J Klien, *Pr*
Leo J Klien, *
Dave Keltner, *
▲ **EMP:** 100 **EST:** 1987
SQ FT: 120,000
SALES (est): 232.98MM
SALES (corp-wide): 2.67MM **Privately Held**
Web: www.ferguson.com
SIC: 5074 5099　Plumbing fittings and
supplies; Safety equipment and supplies
HQ: Ferguson Enterprises, Llc
751 Lakefront Cmns
Newport News VA
757 969-4011

(P-12741)
GLOBAL PLUMBING & FIRE SUPPLY
723 Sonora Ave (91201-2431)
PHONE..................................818 550-8444
Armond Sarkissian, *CEO*
EMP: 112 **EST:** 2016
SALES (est): 9.5MM **Privately Held**
Web: www.firesprinklerstore.com
SIC: 5074　Plumbing fittings and supplies

(P-12742)
GREEN CONVERGENCE (PA)
Also Called: Sunpower By Green
Convergence
28476 Westinghouse Pl (91355-0929)
PHONE..................................661 294-9495
Mark Clinton Figearo, *CEO*
Donald Schramm, *
Stacy Hitt, *
EMP: 52 **EST:** 2008

SQ FT: 6,000
SALES (est): 24.79MM
SALES (corp-wide): 24.79MM **Privately Held**
Web: www.greenconvergence.com
SIC: 5074 1711 2493 2621　Heating
equipment and panels, solar; Solar energy
contractor; Roofing board, unsaturated;
Roofing felt stock

(P-12743)
H2O INNOVATION USA HOLDING INC
Also Called: H2o Innovation Operation Maint
1048 La Mirada Ct (91355-1013)
PHONE..................................418 688-0170
Coley Ali, *Brnch Mgr*
EMP: 86
SALES (corp-wide): 119.63MM **Privately Held**
SIC: 5074 7389　Water softeners; Water
softener service
HQ: H2o Innovation Usa Holding, Inc.
8900 109th Ave N Ste 1000
Champlin MN
763 566-8961

(P-12744)
HARRINGTON INDUSTRIAL PLAS LLC (PA)
14480 Yorba Ave (91710-5766)
P.O. Box 5128 (91708-5128)
PHONE..................................909 597-8641
Eben Lenderking, *CEO*
Dave Abercrombie, *Pr*
Mike Tourtelot, *CFO*
▼ **EMP:** 85 **EST:** 1959
SQ FT: 50,000
SALES (est): 600.66MM
SALES (corp-wide): 600.66MM **Privately Held**
Web: www.hipco.com
SIC: 5074　Pipes and fittings, plastic

(P-12745)
KEYLINE SALES INC
9768 Firestone Blvd (90241-5510)
PHONE..................................562 904-3910
Richard Banner, *Pr*
John Shaw, *
Mike Powers, *
EMP: 42 **EST:** 1974
SQ FT: 3,500
SALES (est): 9.77MM **Privately Held**
Web: www.keylinesales.com
SIC: 5074 3822　Plumbing fittings and
supplies; Environmental controls

(P-12746)
LARSEN SUPPLY CO (PA)
Also Called: Lasco
12055 Slauson Ave (90670-2601)
PHONE..................................562 698-0731
John Palumbo, *CEO*
Rella Bodinus, *
Ruth Larsen, *Stockholder*
◆ **EMP:** 100 **EST:** 1930
SQ FT: 60,000
SALES (est): 22.97MM
SALES (corp-wide): 22.97MM **Privately Held**
Web: www.lasco.net
SIC: 5074 5075　Plumbing fittings and
supplies; Warm air heating and air
conditioning

(P-12747)
MITTAL RAM
100 E Hillcrest Blvd (90301-2415)
PHONE..................................310 769-6669

Ram Mittal, *Owner*
Lillian Mittal, *Prin*
EMP: 95 **EST:** 1989
SALES (est): 5.43MM **Privately Held**
SIC: 5074 Heating equipment and panels, solar

(P-12748)
TA INDUSTRIES INC (HQ)
Also Called: Truaire
11130 Bloomfield Ave (90670-4603)
P.O. Box 4448 (90670-1460)
PHONE...............................562 466-1000
Yongki Yi, *Prin*
Elizabeth Yi, *VP*
▲ **EMP:** 28 **EST:** 1996
SQ FT: 86,000
SALES (est): 25.67MM
SALES (corp-wide): 757.9MM **Publicly Held**
Web: www.rectorseal.com
SIC: 5074 5075 3567 Heating equipment (hydronic); Air conditioning and ventilation equipment and supplies; Heating units and devices, industrial: electric
PA: Csw Industrials, Inc.
5420 Lyndon B Johnson Fwy
Dallas TX
214 884-3777

(P-12749)
WATERSTONE FAUCETS LLC
Also Called: Waterstone Faucets
41180 Raintree Ct (92562-7020)
P.O. Box 1240 (92593-1240)
PHONE...............................951 304-0520
Christopher G Kuran, *Managing Member*
Steve Kliewer, *
Bob Santella, *
▲ **EMP:** 131 **EST:** 1999
SQ FT: 42,000
SALES (est): 23.78MM **Privately Held**
Web: www.waterstoneco.com
SIC: 5074 3432 Plumbing fittings and supplies; Faucets and spigots, metal and plastic

---

5075 Warm Air Heating And Air Conditioning

(P-12750)
AC PRO INC (PA)
Also Called: MSI Hvac
11700 Industry Ave (92337-6934)
PHONE...............................951 360-7849
Dion Quinn, *CEO*
EMP: 250 **EST:** 1986
SQ FT: 80,000
SALES (est): 107.01MM
SALES (corp-wide): 107.01MM **Privately Held**
Web: www.acpro.com
SIC: 5075 3444 Air conditioning and ventilation equipment and supplies; Sheet metalwork

(P-12751)
DUST COLLECTOR SERVICES INC
1280 N Sunshine Way (92806-1746)
PHONE...............................714 237-1690
TOLL FREE: 800
Timothy Schlentz, *Pr*
Jannie Schlentz, *VP*
Jeff Schlentz, *VP*
Gregory Schlentz, *VP*
EMP: 20 **EST:** 1994
SQ FT: 10,000
SALES (est): 4.86MM **Privately Held**

Web: www.dustcollectorservices.com
SIC: 5075 3564 Warm air heating and air conditioning; Purification and dust collection equipment

(P-12752)
ESPECIAL T HVAC SHTMTL FTTNGS
1239 E Franklin Ave (91766-5450)
PHONE...............................909 869-9150
Gerardo Tavarez, *Pr*
Maria Tavarez, *
▲ **EMP:** 30 **EST:** 2001
SQ FT: 12,000
SALES (est): 10.99MM **Privately Held**
Web: www.especialt.com
SIC: 5075 3444 Air conditioning and ventilation equipment and supplies; Sheet metalwork

(P-12753)
FLORENCE FILTER CORPORATION
530 W Manville St (90220-5510)
PHONE...............................310 637-1137
Adrian M Anhood, *CEO*
Floriana A Anhood, *
Erika A Anhood, *
▲ **EMP:** 60 **EST:** 1971
SQ FT: 55,000
SALES (est): 10.68MM **Privately Held**
Web: www.florencefilter.com
SIC: 5075 3564 5211 Air filters; Filters, air: furnaces, air conditioning equipment, etc.; Lumber and other building materials

(P-12754)
GEORGE T HALL CO INC (PA)
Also Called: California Control Solutions
1605 E Gene Autry Way (92805-6730)
P.O. Box 25269 (92825-5269)
PHONE...............................909 825-9751
Charles Niemann, *Pr*
James Martin, *
Marlyn Niemann, *
▲ **EMP:** 30 **EST:** 1932
SQ FT: 15,000
SALES (est): 25.5MM
SALES (corp-wide): 25.5MM **Privately Held**
Web: www.georgethall.com
SIC: 5075 5085 3613 Warm air heating and air conditioning; Industrial supplies; Control panels, electric

(P-12755)
HEAT TRANSFER PDTS GROUP LLC
Also Called: Htpghnl
1933 S Vineyard Ave (91761-7747)
PHONE...............................909 786-3669
EMP: 145
Web: www.htpg.com
SIC: 5075 Warm air heating and air conditioning
HQ: Heat Transfer Products Group, Llc
3885 Crestwood Pkwy Nw # 50
Duluth GA

(P-12756)
HKF INC (PA)
Also Called: Therm Pacific
5983 Smithway St (90040-1607)
PHONE...............................323 225-1318
James P Hartfield, *Pr*
▲ **EMP:** 57 **EST:** 1990
SALES (est): 46.71MM
SALES (corp-wide): 46.71MM **Privately Held**

SIC: 5075 3873 5064 3567 Warm air heating and air conditioning; Watches, clocks, watchcases, and parts; Electrical appliances, television and radio; Industrial furnaces and ovens

(P-12757)
INJEN TECHNOLOGY COMPANY LTD
244 Pioneer Pl (91768-3275)
PHONE...............................909 839-0706
Ron Delgado, *CEO*
▲ **EMP:** 30 **EST:** 1998
SALES (est): 15.64MM **Privately Held**
Web: www.injen.com
SIC: 5075 3714 Air filters; Filters: oil, fuel, and air, motor vehicle

(P-12758)
PURE PROCESS FILTRATION INC
Also Called: Ppf
7429 Lampson Ave (92841)
PHONE...............................714 891-6527
Melinda Limas, *Pr*
Melinda James, *Pr*
Heather Stewart, *VP*
EMP: 17 **EST:** 2006
SQ FT: 5,000
SALES (est): 4.54MM **Privately Held**
Web: www.pureprocessfiltration.com
SIC: 5075 3569 3599 Air filters; Filters; Air intake filters, internal combustion engine, except auto

(P-12759)
US AIRCONDITIONING DISTRIBUTORS INC (PA)
Also Called: U.S. Airconditioning Distrs
16900 Chestnut St (91748-1012)
P.O. Box 1111 (91749-1111)
PHONE...............................626 854-4500
◆ **EMP:** 150 **EST:** 1964
SALES (est): 87.8MM **Privately Held**
Web: www.us-ac.com
SIC: 5075 1711 Air conditioning equipment, except room units, nec; Plumbing, heating, air-conditioning

---

5078 Refrigeration Equipment And Supplies

(P-12760)
BEVERAGES & MORE INC
6820 Katella Ave (90630-5108)
PHONE...............................714 891-1242
Jeff Ruffelo, *Brnch Mgr*
EMP: 113
SALES (corp-wide): 1.61B **Privately Held**
Web: www.bevmo.com
SIC: 5078 Refrigerated beverage dispensers
HQ: Beverages & More, Inc.
1401 Willow Pass Rd # 90
Concord CA

(P-12761)
BRIO WATER TECHNOLOGY INC
Also Called: Dtwusa
768 Turnbull Canyon Rd (91745-1401)
PHONE...............................800 781-1680
Frank Melkonian, *CEO*
Gerard A Thompson, *Sec*
Arman Melkonian, *Dir*
▲ **EMP:** 30 **EST:** 2013
SALES (est): 9.98MM **Privately Held**
Web: www.dtwusa.com

SIC: 5078 3589 Drinking water coolers, mechanical; Water filters and softeners, household type

(P-12762)
HILL PHOENIX INC
Walk-Ins Western Operations
14680 Monte Vista Ave (91710-5744)
PHONE...............................909 592-8830
Sangyup Steve Lee, *Mgr*
EMP: 83
SALES (corp-wide): 8.51B **Publicly Held**
Web: www.hillphoenix.com
SIC: 5078 Refrigeration equipment and supplies
HQ: Hill Phoenix, Inc.
2016 Gees Mill Rd Ne
Conyers GA

(P-12763)
OMNITEAM INC
4380 Ayers Ave (90058-4306)
PHONE...............................562 923-9660
Kans Haasis Junior, *CEO*
Robert Davis, *
Don Hyatt Senior, *VP*
EMP: 125 **EST:** 1999
SALES (est): 24.11MM **Privately Held**
Web: www.omniteaminc.com
SIC: 5078 Commercial refrigeration equipment

(P-12764)
PEPSI-COLA METRO BTLG CO INC
Also Called: Pepsi-Cola
6659 Sycamore Canyon Blvd (92507-0733)
PHONE...............................951 697-3200
EMP: 28
SALES (corp-wide): 86.39B **Publicly Held**
Web: www.pepsico.com
SIC: 5078 2086 5149 Refrigerated beverage dispensers; Bottled and canned soft drinks; Soft drinks
HQ: Pepsi-Cola Metropolitan Bottling Company, Inc.
700 Anderson Hill Rd
Purchase NY
914 767-6000

(P-12765)
REFRIGERATION HDWR SUP CORP
9255 Deering Ave (91311-5804)
PHONE...............................800 537-8300
TOLL FREE: 800
EMP: 52
SALES (corp-wide): 22.94MM **Privately Held**
Web: www.rhsparts.com
SIC: 5078 5722 3585 7699 Refrigeration equipment and supplies; Household appliance stores; Refrigeration and heating equipment; Restaurant equipment repair
PA: Refrigeration Hardware Supply Corporation
632 Foresight Cir
Grand Junction CO
970 241-2800

5082 Construction And Mining Machinery

(P-12766)
CAMERON WEST COAST INC
Also Called: Cameron Surface Systems
4315 Yeager Way (93313-2018)
▲ **EMP:** 90 **EST:** 1992

SQ FT: 48,000
SALES (est): 22.56MM **Publicly Held**
SIC: 5082 1389 7353 Oil field equipment; Oil field services, nec; Oil field equipment, rental or leasing
HQ: Cameron International Corporation
1333 West Loop S Ste 1700
Houston TX

(P-12767)
DENARDI MACHINERY INC
Also Called: D3 Equipment
1475 Pioneer Way (92020-1627)
PHONE..............................619 749-0039
EMP: 102
SIC: 5082 7699 General construction machinery and equipment; Construction equipment repair

(P-12768)
GAMA CONTRACTING SERVICES INC
1835 Floradale Ave (91733-3605)
PHONE..............................626 442-7200
Jose Sergio Duenas, *Pr*
EMP: 140 **EST:** 2008
SALES (est): 19.35MM **Privately Held**
Web: www.gamacsi.com
SIC: 5082 1795 8744 General construction machinery and equipment; Wrecking and demolition work; Environmental remediation

(P-12769)
GOTTSTEIN CORPORATION
3500 Chester Ave (93301-1630)
PHONE..............................661 322-8934
Scott Gottstein, *Brnch Mgr*
EMP: 210
SALES (corp-wide): 57MM **Privately Held**
Web: www.gottsteincorporation.com
SIC: 5082 General construction machinery and equipment
PA: Gottstein Corporation
39 Elm Rd
Hazle Township PA
570 454-7162

(P-12770)
HERCA TELECOMM SERVICES INC
Also Called: Herca Construction Services
18610 Beck St (92570-9185)
PHONE..............................951 940-5941
Hector R Castellon, *Pr*
Tracy Hertel, *
Raul Castellon, *
Alfredo Castellon, *
Alfonso Catellon, *
EMP: 56 **EST:** 2005
SQ FT: 67,900
SALES (est): 20.06MM **Privately Held**
Web: www.hercatelecomm.com
SIC: 5082 1623 1731 3663 General construction machinery and equipment; Communication line and transmission tower construction; General electrical contractor; Antennas, transmitting and communications

(P-12771)
HULSEY CONTRACTING INC
1740 Howard Pl (92373-8090)
PHONE..............................951 549-3665
Roberto Hulsey, *CEO*
EMP: 20 **EST:** 2012
SALES (est): 4.82MM **Privately Held**
Web: www.hulseycontracting.com
SIC: 5082 2493 2851 General construction machinery and equipment; Insulation and roofing material, reconstituted wood; Polyurethane coatings

(P-12772)
JOHNSON MACHINERY CO (PA)
Also Called: Caterpillar Authorized Dealer
800 E La Cadena Dr (92507-8715)
P.O. Box 351 (92502-0351)
PHONE..............................951 686-4560
William Johnson Junior, *Pr*
Kevin Kelly, *
Matt Merickel, *
◆ **EMP:** 175 **EST:** 1940
SQ FT: 70,000
SALES (est): 49.45MM
SALES (corp-wide): 49.45MM **Privately Held**
Web: www.johnson-machinery.com
SIC: 5082 General construction machinery and equipment

(P-12773)
JPL GLOBAL LLC
Also Called: Iq Power Tools
4635 Wade Ave (92571-7494)
P.O. Box 7449 (92552-7449)
PHONE..............................888 274-7744
Paul Guth, *Managing Member*
Scott Craft, *Genl Mgr*
▲ **EMP:** 23 **EST:** 2009
SALES (est): 15MM **Privately Held**
Web: www.iqpowertools.us
SIC: 5082 1741 3541 Masonry equipment and supplies; Masonry and other stonework; Machine tools, metal cutting type

(P-12774)
MALOOF NAMAN BUILDERS
Also Called: Heavy Civil - Gen Engrg Cnstr
9614 Cozycroft Ave (91311-5116)
PHONE..............................818 775-0040
Omar G Maloof, *Pr*
EMP: 52 **EST:** 2009
SALES (est): 6.02MM **Privately Held**
SIC: 5082 3531 1629 8711 Road construction equipment; Road construction and maintenance machinery; Dams, waterways, docks, and other marine construction; Building construction consultant

(P-12775)
NAUMANN/HOBBS MTL HDLG CORP II
Also Called: Hawthorne Lift Systems
86998 Avenue 52 (92236-2710)
PHONE..............................866 266-2244
EMP: 105
SALES (corp-wide): 90MM **Privately Held**
SIC: 5082 5084 General construction machinery and equipment; Industrial machinery and equipment
PA: Naumann/Hobbs Material Handling Corporation Ii, Inc.
4336 S 43rd Pl
Phoenix AZ
602 437-1331

(P-12776)
OAKCROFT ASSOCIATES INC (PA)
Also Called: American Assod Roofg Distrs
750 Monterey Pass Rd (91754-3607)
P.O. Box 63309 (90063-0309)
PHONE..............................323 261-5122
James D Yundt, *Pr*
James S Yundt, *VP*
Joellen Yundt, *Sec*
John Carmack, *Dir*
Jonathan Yundt, *VP*
▲ **EMP:** 31 **EST:** 1950
SQ FT: 14,500
SALES (est): 13.82MM

SALES (corp-wide): 13.82MM **Privately Held**
Web: www.roofmaster.com
SIC: 5082 3531 5199 General construction machinery and equipment; Roofing equipment; Broom, mop, and paint handles

(P-12777)
QUINN COMPANY
Also Called: Caterpillar Authorized Dealer
2200 Pegasus Dr (93308-6801)
PHONE..............................661 393-5800
Steve Eucce, *Brnch Mgr*
EMP: 88
SALES (corp-wide): 472.61MM **Privately Held**
Web: www.quinncompany.com
SIC: 5082 5083 5084 7353 General construction machinery and equipment; Farm and garden machinery; Industrial machinery and equipment; Heavy construction equipment rental
HQ: Quinn Company
10006 Rose Hills Rd
City Of Industry CA
562 463-4000

(P-12778)
QUINN SHEPHERD MACHINERY
Also Called: Caterpillar Authorized Dealer
10006 Rose Hills Rd (90601-1702)
P.O. Box 226789 (90022-6789)
PHONE..............................562 463-6000
Blake Quinn, *Pr*
▲ **EMP:** 287 **EST:** 1924
SQ FT: 163,000
SALES (est): 97.6MM
SALES (corp-wide): 472.61MM **Privately Held**
Web: www.quinncompany.com
SIC: 5082 5084 General construction machinery and equipment; Industrial machinery and equipment
PA: Quinn Group, Inc.
10006 Rose Hills Rd
City Of Industry CA
562 463-4000

(P-12779)
THOMPCO INC
899 Mission Rock Rd (93060-9800)
PHONE..............................805 933-8048
EMP: 27 **EST:** 2008
SALES (est): 3.25MM **Privately Held**
SIC: 5082 1389 Oil field equipment; Oil and gas field services, nec

5083 Farm And Garden Machinery

(P-12780)
EURODRIP USA INC
7545 Carroll Rd (92121-2401)
PHONE..............................559 674-2670
◆ **EMP:** 80 **EST:** 1996
SALES (est): 32.77MM **Privately Held**
Web: www.eurodripusa.com
SIC: 5083 3084 Irrigation equipment; Plastics pipe
HQ: Rivulis S.A.
Athinon - Lamias National Rd (55th Km), P.O. Box 34
Oinofyta

(P-12781)
I BRANDS LLC
2617 N Sepulveda Blvd (90266-2737)
PHONE..............................424 336-5216
EMP: 140 **EST:** 2010

SALES (corp-wide): 8.7MM **Privately Held**
Web: www.tomaro.com
SIC: 5083 Agricultural machinery and equipment

(P-12782)
SPEARS MANUFACTURING CO (PA)
15853 Olden St (91342-1293)
P.O. Box 9203 (91392-9203)
PHONE..............................818 364-1611
Robert Wayne Spears, *CEO*
Wayne Spears, *
Michael Valasquez, *General Vice President**
Ken Ruggles, *
◆ **EMP:** 134 **EST:** 1970
SQ FT: 119,088
SALES (est): 1.37B
SALES (corp-wide): 1.37B **Privately Held**
Web: www.spearsmanufacturing.com
SIC: 5083 3494 Irrigation equipment; Valves and pipe fittings, nec

5084 Industrial Machinery And Equipment

(P-12783)
ACE HYDRAULIC SALES & SVC INC
2901 Gibson St (93308-6107)
P.O. Box 5097 (93388-5097)
PHONE..............................661 327-0571
Gary Chambers, *CEO*
Claus Bjorneboe, *VP*
EMP: 18 **EST:** 1976
SQ FT: 20,000
SALES (est): 4.53MM **Privately Held**
Web: www.acehydraulic.net
SIC: 5084 7699 3561 Hydraulic systems equipment and supplies; Hydraulic equipment repair; Cylinders, pump

(P-12784)
AIRGAS SAFETY INC
Also Called: Airgas
2355 Workman Mill Rd (90601-1459)
PHONE..............................562 699-5239
Olaya Rivera, *Brnch Mgr*
EMP: 21
SALES (corp-wide): 109.44MM **Privately Held**
Web: www.airgas.com
SIC: 5084 5085 3561 3841 Safety equipment; Welding supplies; Cylinders, pump; Surgical and medical instruments
HQ: Airgas Safety, Inc.
2501 Green Ln
Levittown PA

(P-12785)
AIRGAS USA LLC
3737 Worsham Ave (90808-1774)
P.O. Box 7423 (91109-7423)
PHONE..............................562 497-1991
Douglas L Jones, *Reg Pr*
EMP: 1726
SALES (corp-wide): 109.44MM **Privately Held**
Web: www.airgas.com
SIC: 5084 Welding machinery and equipment
HQ: Airgas Usa, Llc
259 N Radnor Chester Rd
Radnor PA
216 642-6600

(P-12786)
ALS GROUP INC
Also Called: Capri Tools

1788 W 2nd St (91766-1206)
PHONE..............................909 622-7555
Anderson Cheung, *CEO*
▲ **EMP**: 25 **EST**: 2005
SALES (est): 10.67MM **Privately Held**
SIC: 5084 3545 3546 3423 Pneumatic tools and equipment; Precision measuring tools; Power-driven handtools; Wrenches, hand tools

(P-12787)
CDS MOVING EQUIPMENT INC (PA)
Also Called: Cds Packing Solutions
375 W Manville St (90220-5617)
PHONE..............................310 631-1100
TOLL FREE: 800
Allen J Sidor, *Pr*
▲ **EMP**: 80 **EST**: 1981
SQ FT: 100,000
SALES (est): 57.92MM
SALES (corp-wide): 57.92MM **Privately Held**
Web: www.cds-usa.com
SIC: 5084 Materials handling machinery

(P-12788)
CENTERLINE INDUSTRIAL INC
2530 Southport Way Ste D (91950-6676)
PHONE..............................858 505-0838
EMP: 29 **EST**: 1996
SQ FT: 15,000
SALES (est): 1.5MM **Privately Held**
SIC: 5084 3544 Machine tools and accessories; Special dies, tools, jigs, and fixtures

(P-12789)
DSI PROCESS SYSTEMS LLC
Also Called: Statco
7595 Reynolds Cir (92647-6787)
PHONE..............................314 382-1525
EMP: 136 **EST**: 2010
SALES (est): 19.92MM **Privately Held**
Web: www.statco-dsi.com
SIC: 5084 Industrial machinery and equipment

(P-12790)
EQUIPMENT DEPOT INC
Also Called: Southern California Mtl Hdlg
12393 Slauson Ave (90606-2824)
PHONE..............................562 949-1000
David Turner, *Pr*
EMP: 150
Web: www.eqdepot.com
SIC: 5084 Conveyor systems
HQ: Equipment Depot, Inc.
16330 Air Center Blvd
Houston TX
713 365-2530

(P-12791)
INDUSTRIAL DATA COMMUNICATIONS
Also Called: I D C
4000 Fruitvale Ave Ste 16 (93308-5176)
P.O. Box 13155 (93389-3155)
PHONE..............................661 589-4477
Lisa Sanli, *CEO*
EMP: 22 **EST**: 1989
SALES (est): 1.83MM **Privately Held**
Web: www.ese-corp.com
SIC: 5084 7371 3663 Measuring and testing equipment, electrical; Custom computer programming services; Digital encoders

(P-12792)
INDUSTRIAL PARTS DEPOT LLC (HQ)
Also Called: Ipd
1550 Charles Willard St (90746-4039)
PHONE..............................310 530-1900
Michael Badar, *Pr*
Russell Kneipp, *Managing Member**
◆ **EMP**: 70 **EST**: 1955
SALES (est): 26.55MM
SALES (corp-wide): 77.26MM **Privately Held**
Web: www.ipdparts.com
SIC: 5084 3519 Engines and parts, diesel; Parts and accessories, internal combustion engines
PA: Storm Industries, Inc.
23223 Normandie Ave
Torrance CA
310 534-5232

(P-12793)
JOHN TILLMAN COMPANY (DH)
1300 W Artesia Blvd (90220-5307)
PHONE..............................310 764-0110
Phillip Mcgreevy, *Pr*
▲ **EMP**: 100 **EST**: 1928
SQ FT: 25,000
SALES (est): 37.94MM
SALES (corp-wide): 14.5B **Privately Held**
Web: www.jtillman.com
SIC: 5084 3842 3548 Safety equipment; Personal safety equipment; Welding apparatus
HQ: Bunzl Distribution Inc.
1 Cityplace Dr Ste 200
Saint Louis MO

(P-12794)
JWC ENVIRONMENTAL INC (DH)
Also Called: Windjmmer Capitl Investors III
2850 Redhill Ave Ste 125 (92705-5541)
PHONE..............................949 833-3888
Ken Biele, *CEO*
Joe Ruiz, *CFO*
◆ **EMP**: 30 **EST**: 1989
SALES (est): 66.19MM **Privately Held**
Web: www.jwce.com
SIC: 5084 3589 Industrial machinery and equipment; Commercial cleaning equipment
HQ: Sulzer Management Ag
Neuwiesenstrasse 15
Winterthur ZH

(P-12795)
KAFCO SALES COMPANY
2300 E 37th St (90058-1405)
P.O. Box 58563 (90058-0563)
PHONE..............................323 588-7141
Akira Urakawa, *CEO*
▲ **EMP**: 26 **EST**: 1978
SQ FT: 15,500
SALES (est): 4.83MM **Privately Held**
Web: www.kafcodemexico.com
SIC: 5084 3842 Safety equipment; Surgical appliances and supplies

(P-12796)
KECO INC
Also Called: Pump-A-Head
3475 Kurtz St (92110-4430)
P.O. Box 80308 (92138-0308)
PHONE..............................619 298-3800
Anne Bleier, *Prin*
Anne Kenton Bleier, *Pr*
Andrew Bleier, *VP*
▼ **EMP**: 20 **EST**: 1954
SQ FT: 2,000
SALES (est): 4.69MM **Privately Held**
Web: www.pumpahead.com

SIC: 5084 3594 3561 3589 Pumps and pumping equipment, nec; Fluid power pumps; Pumps and pumping equipment; Sewage and water treatment equipment

(P-12797)
MATERIAL HANDLING SUPPLY INC (HQ)
12900 Firestone Blvd (90670-5405)
PHONE..............................800 921-7715
TOLL FREE: 800
Alexander Stephen Lynn, *CEO*
Donn C Lynn Junior, *Ch Bd*
John Hanson, *
EMP: 80 **EST**: 1962
SQ FT: 85,000
SALES (est): 19.08MM
SALES (corp-wide): 19.08MM **Privately Held**
Web: www.mhs-ca.com
SIC: 5084 7629 5046 Food industry machinery; Electrical repair shops; Commercial equipment, nec
PA: Envicor
12900 Firestone Blvd
Santa Fe Springs CA
562 921-7715

(P-12798)
MAXON LIFT CORP (PA)
11921 Slauson Ave (90670-2221)
PHONE..............................562 464-0099
Casey Lugash, *Pr*
Brenda Leung, *VP Fin*
▲ **EMP**: 110 **EST**: 1957
SQ FT: 30,000
SALES (est): 66.93MM **Privately Held**
Web: www.maxonlift.com
SIC: 5084 3537 3534 Lift trucks and parts; Industrial trucks and tractors; Elevators and moving stairways

(P-12799)
MEASURMENT INSTRMNTTION CNTRLS
Also Called: Electrcal Instrmnttion Cntrls
2960 Pacini St (93314-8796)
PHONE..............................661 401-0070
Robert Smith, *Pr*
EMP: 29 **EST**: 2012
SALES (est): 4.57MM **Privately Held**
SIC: 5084 1623 3825 3823 Industrial machinery and equipment; Electric power line construction; Instruments for measuring electrical quantities; Industrial process measurement equipment

(P-12800)
MENKE MARKING DEVICES INC
Also Called: Menke Marketing Devices
10440 Pioneer Blvd Ste 4 (90670-5574)
P.O. Box 2986 (90670-0986)
PHONE..............................562 921-1380
Stephen Menke, *Pr*
EMP: 29 **EST**: 1943
SALES (est): 4.56MM **Privately Held**
Web: www.menkemarking.com
SIC: 5084 3953 Industrial machinery and equipment; Marking devices

(P-12801)
MUTUAL LIQUID GAS & EQP CO INC (PA)
Also Called: Mutual Propane
17117 S Broadway (90248-3191)
PHONE..............................310 515-0553
Melvin Moore, *CEO*
Steve Moore, *
EMP: 30 **EST**: 1934

SQ FT: 3,100
SALES (est): 18.67MM
SALES (corp-wide): 18.67MM **Privately Held**
Web: www.mutualpropane.com
SIC: 5084 3549 Propane conversion equipment; Metalworking machinery, nec

(P-12802)
OLIVER HEALTHCARE PACKAGING CO
Also Called: Clean Cut Technologies
1145 N Ocean Cir (92806-1939)
PHONE..............................714 864-3500
Mike Benevento, *Pr*
EMP: 100
SALES (corp-wide): 2.13B **Privately Held**
Web: www.oliverhcp.com
SIC: 5084 5199 3053 Processing and packaging equipment; Packaging materials; Packing materials
HQ: Oliver Healthcare Packaging Company
445 6th St Nw
Grand Rapids MI
616 456-7711

(P-12803)
ONEIL DATA SYSTEMS LLC
12655 Beatrice St (90066-7300)
PHONE..............................310 448-6400
▲ **EMP**: 150
SIC: 5084 Fans, industrial

(P-12804)
OTIS ELEVATOR COMPANY
512 Paula Ave Ste A (91201-2363)
PHONE..............................818 241-2828
Sam Goe, *Brnch Mgr*
EMP: 250
SQ FT: 15,000
SALES (corp-wide): 13.69B **Publicly Held**
Web: www.otis.com
SIC: 5084 7699 Elevators; Elevators: inspection, service, and repair
HQ: Otis Elevator Company
1 Carrier Pl
Farmington CT
860 674-3000

(P-12805)
OTIS ELEVATOR COMPANY
Also Called: United Technologies
711 E Ball Rd Ste 200 (92805-5960)
PHONE..............................714 758-9593
Bob Mcleese, *Brnch Mgr*
EMP: 101
SALES (corp-wide): 13.69B **Publicly Held**
Web: www.otis.com
SIC: 5084 1796 Elevators; Elevator installation and conversion
HQ: Otis Elevator Company
1 Carrier Pl
Farmington CT
860 674-3000

(P-12806)
OTIS ELEVATOR COMPANY
3949 Viewridge Ave (92123)
PHONE..............................858 560-5881
Brian Petler, *Mgr*
EMP: 34
SQ FT: 1,400
SALES (corp-wide): 13.69B **Publicly Held**
Web: www.otis.com
SIC: 5084 5082 7699 3534 Elevators; General construction machinery and equipment; Door and window repair; Elevators and moving stairways
HQ: Otis Elevator Company
1 Carrier Pl

Farmington CT
860 674-3000

(P-12807)
PAPE MATERIAL HANDLING INC
2615 Pellissier Pl (90601-1508)
PHONE..................................562 463-8000
Jordan Pape, *Brnch Mgr*
EMP: 200
Web: www.papemh.com
SIC: 5084 7699 7359 Lift trucks and parts; Industrial machinery and equipment repair; Industrial truck rental
HQ: Pape' Material Handling, Inc.
355 Goodpasture Island Rd
Eugene OR

(P-12808)
PARKER-HANNIFIN CORPORATION
Customer Support Military Div
14300 Alton Pkwy (92618-1898)
PHONE..................................949 465-4519
Edwin Feick, *Brnch Mgr*
EMP: 119
SALES (corp-wide): 19.07B **Publicly Held**
Web: www.parker.com
SIC: 5084 Hydraulic systems equipment and supplies
PA: Parker-Hannifin Corporation
6035 Parkland Blvd
Cleveland OH
216 896-3000

(P-12809)
POWELL WORKS INC
Also Called: Powell Works
17807 Maclaren St Ste B (91744-5700)
PHONE..................................909 861-6699
Jerry Wang, *Pr*
▲ EMP: 256 EST: 2015
SQ FT: 2,500
SALES (est): 18.54MM **Privately Held**
SIC: 5084 Compressors, except air conditioning

(P-12810)
POWER GENERATION ENTPS INC
26764 Oak Ave (91351-2409)
PHONE..................................818 484-8550
Vartan Seropian, *CEO*
EMP: 110 EST: 2014
SALES (est): 9.39MM **Privately Held**
Web: www.powergenenterprises.com
SIC: 5084 Industrial machinery and equipment

(P-12811)
PRO SAFETY INC
20503 Belshaw Ave (90746-3505)
PHONE..................................562 364-7450
Catherina Zember, *Pr*
EMP: 148 EST: 2015
SQ FT: 88,000
SALES (est): 22.88MM **Privately Held**
Web: www.airprotarservices.com
SIC: 5084 8331 Industrial machinery and equipment; Job training and related services

(P-12812)
QUALLS STUD WELDING PDTS INC
Also Called: Stud Welding Products
9459 Washburn Rd (90242-2912)
PHONE..................................562 923-7883
Robert Butcher, *Brnch Mgr*
EMP: 18
SALES (corp-wide): 8.81MM **Privately Held**

Web: www.studweldprod.com
SIC: 5084 7692 1799 Welding machinery and equipment; Welding repair; Welding on site
PA: Quall's Stud Welding Products, Inc.
7820 S 210th St Ste C103
Kent WA
425 656-9787

(P-12813)
R & J MATERIAL HANDLING INC
345 Adams Cir (92882-1896)
PHONE..................................951 735-0000
John Lessing Junior, *CEO*
John Lessing Junior, *Pr*
John Lessing Senior, *Pr*
Jason Lessing, *CFO*
EMP: 19 EST: 2006
SQ FT: 14,100
SALES (est): 7.78MM **Privately Held**
Web: www.rjforklift.com
SIC: 5084 7692 Materials handling machinery; Welding repair

(P-12814)
RAJYSAN INCORPORATED (PA)
Also Called: Mmd Equipment
4175 Guardian St (93063-3382)
P.O. Box 1360 (93062-1360)
PHONE..................................661 775-4920
Gurpreet Sahani, *Pr*
Amarjit S Sahani, *Ch Bd*
Gurpreet Sahani, *CEO*
Rajinder Sahani, *Sec*
▲ EMP: 20 EST: 1984
SALES (est): 19.81MM
SALES (corp-wide): 19.81MM **Privately Held**
Web: www.rajysan.com
SIC: 5084 3715 Lift trucks and parts; Truck trailers

(P-12815)
RAYMOND HANDLING SOLUTIONS INC (DH)
9939 Norwalk Blvd (90670-3321)
P.O. Box 3683 (90670-1683)
PHONE..................................562 944-8067
James Wilcox, *CEO*
EMP: 188 EST: 2002
SQ FT: 5,000
SALES (est): 118.87MM **Privately Held**
Web: www.raymondwest.com
SIC: 5084 7699 7359 Materials handling machinery; Industrial machinery and equipment repair; Industrial truck rental
HQ: The Raymond Corporation
22 S Canal St
Greene NY
607 656-2311

(P-12816)
RDM INDUSTRIES
14310 Gannet St (90638-5221)
PHONE..................................714 690-0380
Jaz Manak, *CEO*
Jaz Manak, *Pr*
Dan Gilmore, *Stockholder**
◆ EMP: 28 EST: 2011
SALES (est): 8.76MM **Privately Held**
Web: www.rdmindustriesinc.com
SIC: 5084 3565 5162 2671 Industrial machinery and equipment; Aerating machines, for beverages; Plastics materials, nec; Plastic film, coated or laminated for packaging

(P-12817)
REBAS INC
Also Called: Toyota Material Hdlg Solutions

12907 Imperial Hwy (90670-4715)
PHONE..................................562 941-4155
Shankar Basu, *Ch Bd*
Simon Walker, *
▲ EMP: 104 EST: 1990
SQ FT: 103,000
SALES (est): 37.91MM **Privately Held**
Web: www.toyotamhs.com
SIC: 5084 Materials handling machinery

(P-12818)
REPLANET LLC
800 N Haven Ave Ste 120 (91764-4951)
P.O. Box 2893 (95344-0893)
PHONE..................................951 520-1700
EMP: 600
Web: www.replanet.com
SIC: 5084 4953 Recycling machinery and equipment; Refuse systems

(P-12819)
SCHURMAN FINE PAPERS
3333 Bristol St (92626-1873)
PHONE..................................714 549-0212
EMP: 24
SALES (corp-wide): 101.03MM **Privately Held**
Web: www.srgretail.com
SIC: 5084 2621 Industrial machinery and equipment; Paper mills
PA: Schurman Fine Papers
300 Oak Bluff Ln
Goodlettsville TN
707 425-8006

(P-12820)
SHARP INDUSTRIES INC (PA)
Also Called: Sharp
3501 Challenger St Fl 2 (90503-1697)
PHONE..................................310 370-5990
James Chen, *Ch Bd*
Nicholas Chen, *CEO*
George Lee, *Sr VP*
Roger Lee, *VP*
▲ EMP: 23 EST: 1976
SQ FT: 40,000
SALES (est): 8.2MM
SALES (corp-wide): 8.2MM **Privately Held**
Web: www.sharp-industries.com
SIC: 5084 3542 Machine tools and accessories; Arbor presses

(P-12821)
SHIP & SHORE ENVIRONMENTAL INC
2474 N Palm Dr (90755-4007)
PHONE..................................562 997-0233
Anoosheh Mostafaei, *Pr*
Anu D Vij, *
▲ EMP: 38 EST: 2000
SQ FT: 4,000
SALES (est): 12.29MM **Privately Held**
Web: www.shipandshore.com
SIC: 5084 3444 Pollution control equipment, air (environmental); Awnings and canopies

(P-12822)
SOUTHERN CAL HYDRLIC ENGRG COR
Also Called: S C Hydraulic Engineering
1130 Columbia St (92821-2921)
PHONE..................................714 257-4800
Donna Perez, *Pr*
David Vedder, *
Manuel Perez, *
EMP: 40 EST: 1953
SQ FT: 65,000
SALES (est): 9.96MM **Privately Held**
Web: www.schydraulic.com

SIC: 5084 3594 Pumps and pumping equipment, nec; Pumps, hydraulic power transfer

(P-12823)
SOUTHERN CALIFORNIA MATERIAL HANDLING INC
Also Called: Scmh
12393 Slauson Ave (90606-2824)
P.O. Box 80770 (91118-8770)
PHONE..................................562 949-1006
▲ EMP: 150
SIC: 5084 Conveyor systems

(P-12824)
STAINLESS STL FABRICATORS INC
Also Called: Cook King
15120 Desman Rd (90638-5737)
PHONE..................................714 739-9904
Craig Miller, *Pr*
Dave Hart, *
Glenna Miller, *
Jennifer Arcos, *Prin*
EMP: 60 EST: 1985
SQ FT: 11,204
SALES (est): 23.48MM **Privately Held**
Web: www.ssfab.net
SIC: 5084 3444 Industrial machinery and equipment; Restaurant sheet metalwork

(P-12825)
STATCO ENGRG & FABRICATORS LLC (PA)
Also Called: Interstate Mnroe McHy Sups Div
7595 Reynolds Cir (92647-6752)
PHONE..................................714 375-6300
Andrew W Moeder, *Managing Member*
EMP: 20 EST: 1982
SQ FT: 11,000
SALES (est): 108.11MM
SALES (corp-wide): 108.11MM **Privately Held**
Web: www.statco-engineering.com
SIC: 5084 3556 Processing and packaging equipment; Food products machinery

(P-12826)
SURFACE PUMPS INC (PA)
3301 Unicorn Rd (93308-6852)
P.O. Box 5757 (93388-5757)
PHONE..................................661 393-1545
Steven J Durrett, *Pr*
David Cook, *
Marty Rushing, *
EMP: 51 EST: 1970
SQ FT: 14,000
SALES (est): 24.34MM
SALES (corp-wide): 24.34MM **Privately Held**
Web: www.surfacepumps.com
SIC: 5084 7699 8711 3519 Pumps and pumping equipment, nec; Pumps and pumping equipment repair; Engineering services; Parts and accessories, internal combustion engines

(P-12827)
SVF FLOW CONTROLS INC
5595 Fresca Dr (90623-1006)
PHONE..................................562 802-2255
Wayne Ulanski, *Pr*
David Steel, *
Russell Stern, *Stockholder**
▲ EMP: 40 EST: 1993
SQ FT: 20,000
SALES (est): 13.04MM **Privately Held**
Web: www.svf.net

▲ = Import ▼ = Export
◆ = Import/Export

SIC: **5084** 3491 3494 **5085** Instruments and control equipment; Industrial valves; Valves and pipe fittings, nec; Valves and fittings

(P-12828)
SWARCO MCCAIN INC (DH)
2365 Oak Ridge Way (92081-8348)
PHONE................................760 727-8100
Jo Ann Mills, *CEO*
▲ **EMP:** 250 **EST:** 1987
SQ FT: 6,700
SALES (est): 157.67MM
SALES (corp-wide): 2.67MM **Privately Held**
Web: www.mccain-inc.com
SIC: 5084 3444 3669 Industrial machinery and equipment; Sheet metalwork; Traffic signals, electric
HQ: Swarco Ag
Blattenwaldweg 8
Wattens
522458770

(P-12829)
TESTEQUITY INC
Also Called: Testequity
6100 Condor Dr (93021-2608)
PHONE................................805 498-9933
EMP: 85
SIC: 5084 Measuring and testing equipment, electrical

(P-12830)
TK ELEVATOR CORPORATION
1965 Gillespie Way Ste 101 (92020-0505)
PHONE................................619 596-7220
Jeff Hansen, *Mgr*
EMP: 105
SALES (corp-wide): 2.67MM **Privately Held**
Web: www.tkelevator.com
SIC: 5084 Elevators
HQ: Tk Elevator Corporation
788 Cir 75 Pkwy Se # 500
Atlanta GA
678 319-3240

(P-12831)
VALLEY POWER SYSTEMS INC
Also Called: Valley Detriot Diesel
4000 Rosedale Hwy (93308-6131)
PHONE................................661 325-9001
Ken Relyea, *Brnch Mgr*
EMP: 100
SALES (corp-wide): 178.72MM **Privately Held**
Web: www.valleypowersystems.com
SIC: 5084 Engines and parts, diesel
PA: Valley Power Systems, Inc.
425 S Hacienda Blvd
City Of Industry CA
626 333-1243

(P-12832)
VALLEY POWER SYSTEMS INC (PA)
Also Called: John Deere Authorized Dealer
425 S Hacienda Blvd (91745-1123)
PHONE................................626 333-1243
TOLL FREE: 800
Hampton Clark Lee, *Ch Bd*
Michael Barnett, *Pr*
Robert K Humphryes, *CFO*
Richard Kickliter, *VP*
Bruce Noble, *Marketing*
◆ **EMP:** 100 **EST:** 1949
SQ FT: 49,000
SALES (est): 178.72MM
SALES (corp-wide): 178.72MM **Privately Held**

Web: www.valleypowersystems.com
SIC: 5084 Engines and parts, diesel

(P-12833)
VAUGHANS INDUSTRIAL REPAIR INC
16224 Garfield Ave (90723-4804)
P.O. Box 1898 (90723-1898)
PHONE................................562 633-2660
Thomas Vaughan, *Pr*
Patricia Vaughan, *
David Newton, *
John L Smith, *
Keven Vaughan, *
EMP: 35 **EST:** 1978
SQ FT: 20,000
SALES (est): 9.22MM
SALES (corp-wide): 9.22MM **Privately Held**
Web: www.virc1.com
SIC: 5084 1711 3599 Oil refining machinery, equipment, and supplies; Mechanical contractor; Machine and other job shop work
PA: Vss Sales, Inc.
16220 Garfield Ave
Paramount CA
562 630-0606

(P-12834)
WASSCO
Also Called: Wassco Sales
12778 Brookprinter Pl (92064-6810)
P.O. Box 856 (60076-0856)
PHONE................................858 679-0444
EMP: 106
SIC: 5084 Machine tools and metalworking machinery

(P-12835)
WASTECH CONTROLS & ENGRG INC
20600 Nordhoff St (91311-6114)
PHONE................................818 998-3500
Paul Nicolas, *Pr*
▲ **EMP:** 58 **EST:** 1987
SQ FT: 30,000
SALES (est): 24.8MM **Privately Held**
Web: www.wastechengineering.com
SIC: 5084 3561 3823 3559 Waste compactors; Pumps, domestic: water or sump; Industrial flow and liquid measuring instruments; Anodizing equipment

(P-12836)
WCS DISTRIBUTING INC
Also Called: Pro Spray Equipment
268 W Orange Show Ln (92408-2037)
PHONE................................909 888-2015
Steve Sykes, *Pr*
◆ **EMP:** 21 **EST:** 1990
SQ FT: 20,000
SALES (est): 11.73MM **Privately Held**
Web: www.wcsdistributinginc.com
SIC: 5084 3499 5083 Engines and transportation equipment; Nozzles, spray: aerosol, paint, or insecticide; Lawn machinery and equipment

(P-12837)
WESTAIR GASES & EQUIPMENT INC
Also Called: Westair Gases & Equipment
3901 Buck Owens Blvd (93308-4927)
PHONE................................661 387-6800
Steve Castiglione, *Mgr*
EMP: 160
SALES (corp-wide): 100.78MM **Privately Held**

Web: www.westairgases.com
SIC: 5084 Welding machinery and equipment
PA: Westair Gases & Equipment, Inc.
2505 Congress St
San Diego CA
866 937-8247

(P-12838)
WESTCOAST ROTOR INC
119 W 154th St (90248-2201)
PHONE................................310 327-5050
TOLL FREE: 800
Vehan Mahdessian, *Pr*
Krikor Mahdessian, *CFO*
▲ **EMP:** 21 **EST:** 1982
SQ FT: 15,625
SALES (est): 4.7MM **Privately Held**
Web: www.westcoastrotor.com
SIC: 5084 3561 Pumps and pumping equipment, nec; Pumps and pumping equipment

(P-12839)
WESTERN REFINING INC
1201 Baker St (92626-3916)
PHONE................................714 708-2200
EMP: 45
Web: www.wnr.com
SIC: 5084 2911 Metalworking machinery; Petroleum refining
HQ: Western Refining, Inc.
212 N Clark Dr
El Paso TX

(P-12840)
WESTERN REFINING INC
22232 Wilmington Ave (90745-4308)
PHONE................................310 834-1297
EMP: 23
Web: www.wnr.com
SIC: 5084 2911 Metalworking machinery; Petroleum refining
HQ: Western Refining, Inc.
212 N Clark Dr
El Paso TX

(P-12841)
WESTERN REFINING INC
4357 E Cesar E Chavez Ave (90022-1401)
PHONE................................323 264-8500
EMP: 34
Web: www.wnr.com
SIC: 5084 2911 Metalworking machinery; Petroleum refining
HQ: Western Refining, Inc.
212 N Clark Dr
El Paso TX

(P-12842)
YALE/CHASE EQUIPMENT AND SERVICES INC
2615 Pellissier Pl (90601-1508)
P.O. Box 1231 (91749-1231)
PHONE................................562 463-8000
TOLL FREE: 800
◆ **EMP:** 200
Web: www.papemh.com
SIC: 5084 7699 7359 Lift trucks and parts; Industrial machinery and equipment repair; Industrial truck rental

---

5085 Industrial Supplies

(P-12843)
A ROYAL WOLF PORTABLE STOR INC
400 E Compton Blvd (90248-2017)
PHONE................................310 719-1048

Sherry Nocachuma, *Brnch Mgr*
EMP: 28
SALES (corp-wide): 2.14B **Publicly Held**
Web: www.getacoolbox.com
SIC: 5085 7359 2448 Commercial containers ; Shipping container leasing; Cargo containers, wood and wood with metal
HQ: A Royal Wolf Portable Storage, Inc.
23422 Clawiter Rd
Hayward CA
510 264-3321

(P-12844)
AMERICAN INDUSTRIAL SOURCE INC
15759 Strathern St Ste 1 (91406-1345)
P.O. Box 8011 (91409-8011)
PHONE................................800 661-0622
Boris Kofsman, *Pr*
EMP: 90 **EST:** 2005
SALES (est): 8MM **Privately Held**
Web:
www.americanindustrialsource.com
SIC: 5085 Industrial supplies

(P-12845)
BRIDGESTONE HOSEPOWER LLC
Also Called: Hose Power USA
2865 Pellissier Pl (90601-1512)
PHONE................................562 699-9500
Alfonso Sanchez, *Genl Mgr*
EMP: 20
Web: www.hosepower.com
SIC: 5085 3492 Hose, belting, and packing; Hose and tube fittings and assemblies, hydraulic/pneumatic
HQ: Bridgestone Hosepower, Llc
50 Industrial Loop N
Orange Park FL

(P-12846)
CARPENTER GROUP
Also Called: American Rigging & Supply
2380 Main St (92113-3643)
PHONE................................619 233-5625
Bruce Yoder, *Brnch Mgr*
EMP: 30
SQ FT: 10,000
SALES (corp-wide): 24.59MM **Privately Held**
Web: www.americanriggingsd.com
SIC: 5085 5084 3537 Industrial supplies; Industrial machinery and equipment; Industrial trucks and tractors
PA: The Carpenter Group
222 Napoleon St
San Francisco CA
415 285-1954

(P-12847)
CENTRAL PURCHASING LLC (HQ)
Also Called: Harbor Freight Tools
26677 Agoura Rd (91302-1959)
P.O. Box 6010 (93011-6010)
PHONE................................800 444-3353
Allan Smidt, *
◆ **EMP:** 500 **EST:** 1968
SQ FT: 277,000
SALES (est): 1.85B
SALES (corp-wide): 1.99B **Privately Held**
Web: go.harborfreight.com
SIC: 5085 5961 5251 Tools, nec; Tools and hardware, mail order; Tools
PA: Harbor Freight Tools Usa, Inc.
26677 Agoura Rd
Calabasas CA
818 836-5001

(P-12848)
CLOVER ENVMTL SOLUTIONS LLC
Also Called: Color Laser R&D
9414 Eton Ave (91311-5862)
PHONE..................................815 431-8100
EMP: 691
SALES (corp-wide): 173.68MM **Privately Held**
Web: www.cloverimaging.com
SIC: 5085 Ink, printer's
PA: Clover Environmental Solutions Llc
4200 Columbus St
Ottawa IL
866 734-6548

(P-12849)
CURIOSITY INK MEDIA LLC
478 Ellis St (91105-1617)
PHONE..................................561 287-5776
EMP: 127 **EST:** 2017
SALES (est): 157.49K
SALES (corp-wide): 5.43MM **Publicly Held**
SIC: 5085 Ink, printer's
PA: Grom Social Enterprises, Inc.
2060 Nw Boca Raton Blvd
Boca Raton FL
561 287-5776

(P-12850)
CUSTOM BUILDING PRODUCTS LLC
1900 Norris Rd (93308-2229)
PHONE..................................661 393-0422
Kevin Odell, *Brnch Mgr*
EMP: 52
Web: www.custombuildingproducts.com
SIC: 5085 5211 3531 Adhesives, tape and plasters; Masonry materials and supplies; Construction machinery
HQ: Custom Building Products Llc
7711 Center Ave Ste 500
Huntington Beach CA
800 272-8786

(P-12851)
D & D SAW WORKS INC
Also Called: D & D Tool & Supply
1445 Engineer St Ste 110 (92081-8846)
EMP: 126
SIC: 5085 Industrial supplies

(P-12852)
DHV INDUSTRIES INC
3451 Pegasus Dr (93308-6827)
PHONE..................................661 392-8948
Tingchun Huang, *Pr*
◆ **EMP:** 52 **EST:** 1996
SQ FT: 180,000
SALES (est): 9.09MM **Privately Held**
Web: www.dhvindustries.com
SIC: 5085 3491 Valves and fittings; Industrial valves

(P-12853)
DUHIG AND CO INC
Also Called: Duhig Stainless
5071 Telegraph Rd (90022-4997)
P.O. Box 226966 (90022-0666)
◆ **EMP:** 48
Web: www.fergusonindustrial.com
SIC: 5085 5051 3441 Valves and fittings; Pipe and tubing, steel; Fabricated structural metal

(P-12854)
FASTENER DIST HOLDINGS LLC (HQ)
5200 Sheila St (90040-3906)
PHONE..................................213 620-9950
Scott Tucker, *Pr*
EMP: 20 **EST:** 2014
SALES (est): 470.7MM
SALES (corp-wide): 470.7MM **Privately Held**
Web: www.aircraftfast.com
SIC: 5085 3721 Fasteners, industrial: nuts, bolts, screws, etc.; Aircraft
PA: Fdh Aero, Llc
5200 Sheila St
Commerce CA
213 620-9950

(P-12855)
FASTENER TECHNOLOGY CORP
7415 Fulton Ave (91605-4116)
PHONE..................................818 764-6467
Dennis Suedkamp, *CEO*
Thomas Boat, *
EMP: 125 **EST:** 1979
SQ FT: 24,000
SALES (est): 23.09MM
SALES (corp-wide): 123.82MM **Privately Held**
Web: www.ftc-usa.com
SIC: 5085 3812 5251 Fasteners, industrial: nuts, bolts, screws, etc.; Aircraft/aerospace flight instruments and guidance systems; Tools
HQ: Avantus Aerospace, Inc.
29101 The Old Rd
Valencia CA
661 295-8620

(P-12856)
GENERAL TOOL INC
Also Called: Gt Diamond
2025 Alton Pkwy (92606-4904)
PHONE..................................949 261-2322
Jae Woo Kim, *CEO*
▲ **EMP:** 90 **EST:** 1984
SQ FT: 40,000
SALES (est): 24.47MM **Privately Held**
Web: www.gtdiamond.com
SIC: 5085 Diamonds, industrial: natural, crude

(P-12857)
GRISWOLD INDUSTRIES
Also Called: Griswald Industries
24100 Water Ave (92570-6738)
PHONE..................................951 657-1718
Fred Zimmer, *Mgr*
EMP: 17
SQ FT: 25,000
SALES (corp-wide): 75.13MM **Privately Held**
Web: www.cla-val.com
SIC: 5085 3494 Valves and fittings; Valves and pipe fittings, nec
PA: Griswold Industries
1701 Placentia Ave
Costa Mesa CA
949 722-4800

(P-12858)
HOWMET GLOBL FSTNING SYSTEMS I (HQ)
Also Called: Howmet Fastening Systems
3990a Heritage Oak Ct (93063-6711)
PHONE..................................805 426-2270
Vagner Finelli, *Pr*
▲ **EMP:** 120 **EST:** 1977
SQ FT: 37,000
SALES (est): 1.11B
SALES (corp-wide): 5.66B **Publicly Held**

SIC: 5085 5072 5065 Fasteners and fastening equipment; Hardware; Electronic parts and equipment, nec
PA: Howmet Aerospace Inc.
201 Isabella St Ste 200
Pittsburgh PA
412 553-1950

(P-12859)
INDEX FASTENERS INC (PA)
Also Called: Distribution
945 E Grevillea Ct (91761-5612)
PHONE..................................909 923-5002
Shane Bearly, *CEO*
▲ **EMP:** 19 **EST:** 1977
SQ FT: 30,000
SALES (est): 14.58MM
SALES (corp-wide): 14.58MM **Privately Held**
Web: www.indexthermoplastics.com
SIC: 5085 2821 3081 Fasteners, industrial: nuts, bolts, screws, etc.; Plastics materials and resins; Plastics film and sheet

(P-12860)
INDUSTRIAL VALCO INC (PA)
Also Called: Industrial Valco
3135 E Ana St (90221-5606)
PHONE..................................310 635-0711
Rob C Raban, *Pr*
▲ **EMP:** 20 **EST:** 1983
SQ FT: 62,000
SALES (est): 27.25MM
SALES (corp-wide): 27.25MM **Privately Held**
Web: www.ivalco.com
SIC: 5085 3498 Valves and fittings; Pipe fittings, fabricated from purchased pipe

(P-12861)
LIBERTY SYNERGISTICS INC
Also Called: Liberty Photo Products
1041 Calle Trepadora (92673-6204)
PHONE..................................949 361-1100
▲ **EMP:** 55
Web: www.ivokenow.com
SIC: 5085 3861 Industrial supplies; Photographic equipment and supplies

(P-12862)
LONESTAR SIERRA LLC
1820 W Orangewood Ave (92868-2043)
PHONE..................................866 575-5680
EMP: 225 **EST:** 2016
SALES (est): 19.81MM **Privately Held**
Web: www.lonestarsierra.com
SIC: 5085 Refractory material

(P-12863)
LORD & SONS INC
10504 Pioneer Blvd (90670-3704)
PHONE..................................562 529-2500
Lawrence James, *Mgr*
EMP: 97
SALES (corp-wide): 355.83K **Privately Held**
Web: www.lordandsons.com
SIC: 5085 Fasteners, industrial: nuts, bolts, screws, etc.
HQ: Lord & Sons, Inc.
430 E Trimble Rd
San Jose CA
408 293-4841

(P-12864)
MCMASTER-CARR SUPPLY COMPANY
9630 Norwalk Blvd (90670-2932)
P.O. Box 54960 (90054-0960)
PHONE..................................562 692-5911

EMP: 471
SALES (corp-wide): 621.02MM **Privately Held**
Web: www.mcmaster.com
SIC: 5085 Industrial supplies
PA: Mcmaster-Carr Supply Company
600 N County Line Rd
Elmhurst IL
630 834-9600

(P-12865)
MIDLAND INDUSTRIES
659 E Ball Rd (92805-5910)
PHONE..................................800 821-5725
Vince Hodes, *Owner*
EMP: 100 **EST:** 2020
SALES (est): 5.12MM **Privately Held**
SIC: 5085 Valves, pistons, and fittings

(P-12866)
MOTION INDUSTRIES INC
Also Called: F & L Industrial Solutions
12550 Stowe Dr (92064-6804)
PHONE..................................858 602-1500
Lori Lefeuvre, *Brnch Mgr*
EMP: 23
SALES (corp-wide): 22.1B **Publicly Held**
Web: www.fandl8020.com
SIC: 5085 3355 Bearings; Extrusion ingot, aluminum: made in rolling mills
HQ: Motion Industries, Inc.
1605 Alton Rd
Birmingham AL
205 956-1122

(P-12867)
NELSON STUD WELDING INC
Also Called: Automatic Screw Mch Pdts Co
630 E Lambert Rd (92821-4119)
P.O. Box 1608 (35602-1608)
PHONE..................................256 353-1931
Mike Selby, *Genl Mgr*
EMP: 113
SALES (corp-wide): 16.95B **Publicly Held**
Web: www.stanleyengineeredfastening.com
SIC: 5085 Fasteners, industrial: nuts, bolts, screws, etc.
HQ: Nelson Stud Welding, Inc.
7900 W Ridge Rd
Elyria OH
440 329-0400

(P-12868)
NMC GROUP INC
Also Called: Nylon Molding
300 E Cypress St (92821-4007)
PHONE..................................714 223-3525
Michael Johnson, *Pr*
Wolfgang Hombrecher, *
▲ **EMP:** 24 **EST:** 1972
SALES (est): 27.17MM
SALES (corp-wide): 6.58B **Publicly Held**
Web: www.nylonmoldingcorp.com
SIC: 5085 3089 Fasteners and fastening equipment; Injection molding of plastics
HQ: Ta Aerospace Co.
28065 Franklin Pkwy
Valencia CA
661 775-1100

(P-12869)
NSK PRECISION AMERICA INC
Also Called: NSK Prcsion Amer Snta Fe Sprng
13921 Bettencourt St (90703-1011)
PHONE..................................562 968-1000
EMP: 84
SIC: 5085 Bearings
HQ: Nsk Precision America, Inc.
3450 Bearing Dr

Franklin IN
317 738-5000

(P-12870)
PACIFIC ECHO INC
23540 Telo Ave (90505-4098)
PHONE..................................310 539-1822
Takeo Ogami, *CEO*
▲ **EMP:** 90 **EST:** 1967
SQ FT: 110,000
SALES (est): 40.15MM **Privately Held**
Web: www.pacificecho.com
SIC: 5085 Hose, belting, and packing
HQ: Kakuichi Co., Ltd.
1415, Midoricho, Tsuruga
Nagano NAG

(P-12871)
PCBC HOLDCO INC
12748 Florence Ave (90670-3906)
PHONE..................................562 944-9549
Robert Gardner, *Pr*
▲ **EMP:** 38 **EST:** 1989
SQ FT: 47,000
SALES (est): 12MM **Privately Held**
Web: www.pacificcoastbolt.com
SIC: 5085 3965 3452 5072 Fasteners,
industrial: nuts, bolts, screws, etc.;
Fasteners; Bolts, nuts, rivets, and washers;
Bolts, nuts, and screws

(P-12872)
PENTACON INC
21123 Nordhoff St (91311-5816)
PHONE..................................818 727-8000
EMP: 300
SIC: 5085 5063 Fasteners and fastening
equipment; Electrical fittings and
construction materials

(P-12873)
**PINNACLE INDUSTRIAL SUPPLY
INC**
1612 Pacific Rim Ct (92154-7501)
PHONE..................................619 710-4255
Daniel Halecky, *CEO*
Brian Chin, *
EMP: 32 **EST:** 1984
SQ FT: 6,226
SALES (est): 22.37MM **Privately Held**
Web: www.pinnacleca.com
SIC: 5085 3312 3317 3494 Valves and
fittings; Pipes, iron and steel; Pipes,
seamless steel; Pipe fittings

(P-12874)
**RBC TRANSPORT DYNAMICS
CORP**
3131 W Segerstrom Ave (92704-5811)
PHONE..................................203 267-7001
Michael Harnett, *Pr*
▲ **EMP:** 185 **EST:** 1992
SQ FT: 75,000
SALES (est): 51.24MM
SALES (corp-wide): 1.47B **Publicly Held**
Web: www.rbcbearings.com
SIC: 5085 3728 Bearings; Aircraft
assemblies, subassemblies, and parts, nec
HQ: Roller Bearing Company Of America,
Inc.
102 Willenbrock Rd
Oxford CT
203 267-7001

(P-12875)
REVCO INDUSTRIES INC (PA)
10747 Norwalk Blvd (90670-3823)
PHONE..................................562 777-1588
C Edward Chu, *Ch Bd*

Steve Hwang, *
Hong Brian Choi, *
Thomas Han, *
Jimmy Wu, *
◆ **EMP:** 28 **EST:** 1974
SQ FT: 24,000
SALES (est): 10.33MM
SALES (corp-wide): 10.33MM **Privately
Held**
Web: www.blackstallion.com
SIC: 5085 5136 3842 Valves and fittings;
Work clothing, men's and boys'; Personal
safety equipment

(P-12876)
**RUTLAND TOOL & SUPPLY CO
(HQ)**
Also Called: MSC Metalworking
2225 Workman Mill Rd (90601-1437)
PHONE..................................562 566-5000
TOLL FREE: 800
Thomas J Neri, *CEO*
Andrew Verey, *
◆ **EMP:** 140 **EST:** 2005
SALES (est): 56.07MM **Publicly Held**
SIC: 5085 5251 Industrial supplies; Tools
PA: Msc Industrial Direct Co., Inc.
515 Broadhollow Rd # 1000
Melville NY

(P-12877)
SAN DIEGO SIGN COMPANY INC
Also Called: Wholesale Displays
5960 Pascal Ct (92008-8808)
PHONE..................................888 748-7446
Eric Steven Van Velzer, *CEO*
Vance Rodney Van Velzer, *
Eric Christopher Van Velzer, *
▲ **EMP:** 28 **EST:** 1963
SQ FT: 15,000
SALES (est): 13.98MM **Privately Held**
Web: www.sdsign.com
SIC: 5085 3993 Signmaker equipment and
supplies; Signs and advertising specialties

(P-12878)
SAW DAILY SERVICE INC
4481 Firestone Blvd (90280-3320)
P.O. Box 3458 (92834-3458)
PHONE..................................323 564-1791
▲ **EMP:** 50
SIC: 5085 7699 3546 Knives, industrial;
Industrial machinery and equipment repair;
Saws and sawing equipment

(P-12879)
SHAR-CRAFT INC (PA)
Also Called: Seal & Packing Supply
1103 33rd St (93301-2121)
PHONE..................................661 324-4985
James L Craft, *Pr*
Chris Craft, *VP*
Sharon Craft, *Sec*
EMP: 22 **EST:** 1966
SQ FT: 14,000
SALES (est): 9.75MM
SALES (corp-wide): 9.75MM **Privately
Held**
Web: www.sharcraftinc.com
SIC: 5085 3599 3479 Packing, industrial;
Machine shop, jobbing and repair; Coating
of metals and formed products

(P-12880)
SO CAL SANDBAGS INC
12620 Bosley Ln (92883-6358)
PHONE..................................951 277-3404
Peter Rasinski, *Pr*
EMP: 100 **EST:** 1986
SALES (est): 29.1MM **Privately Held**

Web: www.socalsandbags.com
SIC: 5085 5999 Industrial supplies; Safety
supplies and equipment

(P-12881)
**SOLAR LINK INTERNATIONAL
INC**
4652 E Brickell St Ste A (91761-1593)
P.O. Box 56 (91773-0056)
PHONE..................................909 605-7789
Chien Hui Liu Eeo, *Prin*
Johnny Tsai, *
▲ **EMP:** 218 **EST:** 1998
SALES (est): 22.43MM **Privately Held**
Web: www.solar-link.com
SIC: 5085 Industrial supplies

(P-12882)
SPS TECHNOLOGIES LLC
Shur-Lok Company
2541 White Rd (92614-6235)
PHONE..................................949 474-6000
Damian Moreau, *Mgr*
EMP: 424
SALES (corp-wide): 302.09B **Publicly
Held**
Web: www.shur-lok.com
SIC: 5085 Fasteners, industrial: nuts,
screws, etc.
HQ: Sps Technologies, Llc
301 Highland Ave
Jenkintown PA
215 572-3000

(P-12883)
SPS TECHNOLOGIES LLC
Also Called: Pb Fasteners
1700 W 132nd St (90249-2008)
PHONE..................................310 323-6222
EMP: 260
SALES (corp-wide): 302.09B **Publicly
Held**
Web: www.pccfasteners.com
SIC: 5085 Fasteners, industrial: nuts, bolts,
screws, etc.
HQ: Sps Technologies, Llc
301 Highland Ave
Jenkintown PA
215 572-3000

(P-12884)
**THALASINOS ENTERPRISES
INC**
Also Called: T & T Enterprises
1220 Railroad St (92882-1837)
PHONE..................................951 340-0911
Brent Thalasinos, *CEO*
John Thalasinos, *Ch Bd*
Alison Siedler, *VP*
▲ **EMP:** 23 **EST:** 1993
SQ FT: 54,000
SALES (est): 8.83MM **Privately Held**
Web: www.ttenterprises.com
SIC: 5085 3452 Fasteners, industrial: nuts,
bolts, screws, etc.; Nuts, metal

(P-12885)
TONNAGE INDUSTRIAL LLC
2130 W Cowles St (90813-1022)
PHONE..................................800 893-9681
EMP: 25 **EST:** 2018
SALES (est): 3.89MM **Privately Held**
Web: www.tonnageindustrial.com
SIC: 5085 3312 5051 Industrial supplies;
Bars and bar shapes, steel, hot-rolled;
Structural shapes, iron or steel

(P-12886)
TRICO LEASING COMPANY LLC
30154 Rhone Dr (90275-5736)
PHONE..................................877 259-9997
EMP: 52
SALES (corp-wide): 880.76K **Privately
Held**
SIC: 5085 3792 Commercial containers;
Travel trailer chassis
PA: Trico Leasing Company, Llc
30154 Rhone Dr
Rancho Palos Verdes CA
877 259-9997

(P-12887)
**TSC AUTO ID TECHNOLOGY
AMERICA (HQ)**
3040 Saturn St Ste 200 (92821-6231)
PHONE..................................909 468-0100
Hank Wang, *Pr*
▲ **EMP:** 120 **EST:** 2008
SALES (est): 21.93MM **Privately Held**
SIC: 5085 Ink, printer's
PA: Tsc Auto Id Technology Co., Ltd.
9f, No. 95, Minquan Rd.
New Taipei City TAP

(P-12888)
WEST COAST AEROSPACE INC
24224 Broad St (90745-6006)
PHONE..................................310 518-0633
Ken Wagner, *Pr*
EMP: 18
SQ FT: 26,456
SALES (corp-wide): 9.94MM **Privately
Held**
Web: www.westcoastaerospace.com
SIC: 5085 3545 3541 3452 Fasteners,
industrial: nuts, bolts, screws, etc.; Machine
tool accessories; Machine tools, metal
cutting type; Bolts, nuts, rivets, and washers
PA: West Coast Aerospace, Inc.
220 W E St
Wilmington CA
310 518-3167

5087 Service Establishment Equipment

(P-12889)
CHIRO INC (PA)
Also Called: Mr Clean Maintenance Systems
2260 S Vista Ave (92316-2908)
P.O. Box 31 (92324-0031)
PHONE..................................909 879-1160
Arthur Rose, *Pr*
Timothy Russell, *
EMP: 130 **EST:** 1980
SQ FT: 10,000
SALES (est): 47.97MM
SALES (corp-wide): 47.97MM **Privately
Held**
Web: www.mrcleansystems.com
SIC: 5087 7349 5169 Cleaning and
maintenance equipment and supplies;
Cleaning service, industrial or commercial;
Chemicals and allied products, nec

(P-12890)
EXTENSIONS PLUS INC
Also Called: Extensions Plus
5428 Reseda Blvd (91356-2606)
PHONE..................................818 881-5611
Helene Stahl, *Pr*
EMP: 30 **EST:** 1994
SALES (est): 4.61MM **Privately Held**
Web: www.extensions-plus.com

PRODUCTS & SVCS

SIC: **5087** 3999 Beauty parlor equipment and supplies; Hair and hair-based products

(P-12891)
GLAMOUR INDUSTRIES CO
100 Wilshire Blvd Ste 700 (90401-3602)
PHONE................................213 687-8600
EMP: 100
SALES (corp-wide): 110.3MM **Privately Held**
Web: www.aiibeauty.com
SIC: **5087** Beauty parlor equipment and supplies
PA: Glamour Industries, Co.
2220 Gaspar Ave
Commerce CA
323 728-2999

(P-12892)
HYDRO TEK SYSTEMS INC
Also Called: Hydro Tek
2353 Almond Ave (92374-2035)
PHONE................................909 799-9222
TOLL FREE: 800
John S Koen, *Pr*
Andrea S Koen, *
◆ **EMP:** 63 **EST:** 1985
SQ FT: 45,000
SALES (est): 19.71MM
SALES (corp-wide): 1.11B **Privately Held**
Web: www.hydrotek.us
SIC: **5087** 3589 5084 Service establishment equipment; Commercial cleaning equipment ; Industrial machinery and equipment
HQ: Nilfisk A/S
Marmorvej 8
Kobenhavn O
43238100

(P-12893)
MALYS OF CALIFORNIA INC
28145 Harrison Pkwy (91355-4165)
PHONE................................661 295-8317
EMP: 500
SIC: **5087** Barber shop equipment and supplies

(P-12894)
NIKKEN GLOBAL INC (HQ)
18301 Von Karman Ave Ste 120 (92612-1009)
PHONE................................949 789-2000
Tom Toshizo Watanabe, *Ch Bd*
Kendall Cho, *
▲ **EMP:** 155 **EST:** 1996
SALES (est): 92.01MM **Privately Held**
SIC: **5087** 5023 5013 5122 Stress reducing equipment, electric; Bedspreads; Seat covers; Vitamins and minerals
PA: Nikken International, Inc.
18301 Von Karman Ave
Irvine CA

(P-12895)
SPILO WORLDWIDE INC
Also Called: Spilo Worldwide
100 Wilshire Blvd Ste 700 (90401-3602)
PHONE................................213 687-8600
Marc Spilo, *CEO*
◆ **EMP:** 100 **EST:** 1977
SALES (est): 9.65MM
SALES (corp-wide): 1.56B **Publicly Held**
SIC: **5087** Beauty parlor equipment and supplies
PA: Enovis Corporation
2711 Centerville Rd # 400
Wilmington DE
301 252-9160

(P-12896)
SWEIS INC (PA)
20000 Mariner Ave (90503-7140)
PHONE................................310 375-0558
EMP: 70 **EST:** 2000
SALES (est): 23.12MM **Privately Held**
Web: www.sweisinc.com
SIC: **5087** 2844 Beauty parlor equipment and supplies; Hair preparations, including shampoos

(P-12897)
WAXIES ENTERPRISES LLC (DH)
Also Called: Waxie Sanitary Supply
9353 Waxie Way (92123-1350)
P.O. Box 60227 (90060-0227)
PHONE................................800 995-4466
TOLL FREE: 800
EMP: 140 **EST:** 1945
SALES (est): 250.63MM **Privately Held**
Web: info.waxie.com
SIC: **5087** Janitors' supplies
HQ: Envoy Solutions, Llc
2101 Claire Ct
Glenview IL
847 832-4000

5088 Transportation Equipment And Supplies

(P-12898)
AIR FRAME MFG & SUPPLY CO INC
Also Called: Air Frame Mfg. & Supply Co.
26135 Technology Dr (91355-1138)
PHONE................................661 257-7728
Yoshinobu Kawamura, *CEO*
Ray Wong, *
Howard Miyoshi, *
Yoshimi Sussan, *
▼ **EMP:** 35 **EST:** 1964
SQ FT: 30,000
SALES (est): 13.13MM **Privately Held**
Web: www.afmsupply.com
SIC: **5088** 3999 3728 Aircraft and parts, nec; Atomizers, toiletry; Accumulators, aircraft propeller

(P-12899)
AIRCRAFT HARDWARE WEST
Also Called: Ahw
2180 Temple Ave (90804-1020)
PHONE................................562 961-9324
Frank Ioffrida, *CEO*
Krista Wildermuth, *
▲ **EMP:** 30 **EST:** 2002
SQ FT: 15,000
SALES (est): 14.34MM **Privately Held**
Web: www.ahw-corp.com
SIC: **5088** 3993 5072 Aircraft and parts, nec; Name plates: except engraved, etched, etc.: metal; Hardware

(P-12900)
AIREY ENTERPRISES LLC
Also Called: A Transportation
5530 Corbin Ave Ste 325 (91356-6037)
P.O. Box 17328 (91416-7328)
PHONE................................818 530-3362
EMP: 160 **EST:** 2015
SALES (est): 10.01MM **Privately Held**
SIC: **5088** Transportation equipment and supplies

(P-12901)
AM MACHINING INC
Also Called: APV Manufacturing & Engrg Co
7422 Walnut Ave (90620-1762)
PHONE................................714 367-0830
Frank T Amador Junior, *Pr*
Jay Conlon, *Gen'l Mgr*
Stella Mermingez, *CFO*
EMP: 19 **EST:** 1993
SQ FT: 24,000
SALES (est): 5.05MM **Privately Held**
Web: www.apvmfg.com
SIC: **5088** 3541 Aeronautical equipment and supplies; Machine tool replacement & repair parts, metal cutting types

(P-12902)
APICAL INDUSTRIES INC
Also Called: Dart Aerospace
3030 Enterprise Ct Ste A (92081-8358)
PHONE................................760 724-5300
EMP: 100 **EST:** 1995
SQ FT: 30,000
SALES (est): 35.53MM
SALES (corp-wide): 6.58B **Publicly Held**
Web: www.apicalindustries.com
SIC: **5088** 3728 Helicopter parts; Aircraft landing assemblies and brakes
HQ: Dart Aerospace Company
9900 Boul Cavendish Suite 310
Saint-Laurent QC
514 907-5959

(P-12903)
BOEING STLLITE SYSTEMS INTL IN (HQ)
Also Called: Boeing Company, The
2260 E Imperial Hwy (90245-3501)
P.O. Box 92919 (90009-2919)
PHONE................................310 364-4000
Randy Brinkley, *Pr*
Craig R Cooning, *
David Lillington, *
Danny Howard, *
▲ **EMP:** 40 **EST:** 1967
SALES (est): 106.54MM
SALES (corp-wide): 66.61B **Publicly Held**
SIC: **5088** 4899 3663 Aircraft and space vehicle supplies and parts; Satellite earth stations; Radio and t.v. communications equipment
PA: The Boeing Company
929 Long Bridge Dr
Arlington VA
703 414-6338

(P-12904)
COM DEV USA LLC
2333 Utah Ave (90245-4818)
PHONE................................424 456-8000
EMP: 100
Web: www.comdev-usa.com
SIC: **5088** 3679 Aircraft equipment and supplies, nec; Microwave components

(P-12905)
COMAV LLC (PA)
18499 Phantom St Ste 17 (92394-7962)
PHONE................................760 523-5100
Craig Garrick, *Pr*
Jon Day, *CFO*
EMP: 52 **EST:** 2012
SQ FT: 58,732
SALES (est): 83.02MM
SALES (corp-wide): 83.02MM **Privately Held**
Web: www.comav.com
SIC: **5088** 4581 3599 Aircraft and parts, nec; Aircraft maintenance and repair services; Machine and other job shop work

(P-12906)
DESSER TIRE & RUBBER CO LLC
Also Called: Cee Baileys Aircraft Plastics
6900 W Acco St (90640-5435)
PHONE................................323 837-1497
Brian Elliott, *Contrlr*
EMP: 30
SALES (corp-wide): 949.76MM **Publicly Held**
Web: www.desser.com
SIC: **5088** 3728 Aircraft and space vehicle supplies and parts; Aircraft parts and equipment, nec
HQ: Desser Tire & Rubber Co., Llc
6900 W Acco St
Montebello CA
323 721-4900

(P-12907)
FALCON AEROSPACE HOLDINGS LLC
Also Called: Wesco Aircraft
27727 Avenue Scott (91355-1219)
PHONE................................661 775-7200
Randy J Snyder, *Ch Bd*
Gregory A Hann, *
Tommy Lee, *
EMP: 1250 **EST:** 2006
SALES (est): 221.89MM **Privately Held**
Web: www.incora.com
SIC: **5088** Aircraft and parts, nec

(P-12908)
INTEGRATED PROCUREMENT TECH (PA)
Also Called: Ipt
7230 Hollister Ave (93117-2807)
PHONE................................805 682-0842
◆ **EMP:** 85 **EST:** 1996
SQ FT: 26,000
SALES (est): 82.14MM **Privately Held**
Web: www.iptsb.com
SIC: **5088** 5065 Aircraft and parts, nec; Communication equipment

(P-12909)
ITOCHU AVIATION INC (DH)
222 N Pacific Coast Hwy Ste 2200 (90245)
P.O. Box 997 (90245-0997)
PHONE................................310 640-2770
Naoya Osaki, *CEO*
Takehiko Yamada, *
▲ **EMP:** 25 **EST:** 1973
SALES (est): 28.12MM **Privately Held**
SIC: **5088** 3728 Aircraft and parts, nec; Aircraft parts and equipment, nec
HQ: Itochu International Inc.
1251 Ave Of The Amrcas Fl
New York NY
212 818-8000

(P-12910)
JCM ENGINEERING CORP
2690 E Cedar St (91761-8533)
PHONE................................909 923-3730
Robert Schenkkan, *Pr*
Myrna Lamar, *
Ken Safford, *
EMP: 85 **EST:** 1979
SQ FT: 140,000
SALES (est): 23.33MM **Privately Held**
Web: www.jcmcorp.com
SIC: **5088** Aeronautical equipment and supplies

(P-12911)
KETTENBURG MARINE CORPORATION
2810 Carleton St (92106-2792)
P.O. Box 6448 (92166-0448)
PHONE................................619 224-8211

▲ = Import ▼ = Export
◆ = Import/Export

Tom Fetter, *Pr*
Jane T Fetter, *
▼ **EMP:** 140 **EST:** 1919
SQ FT: 30,000
SALES (est): 12.93MM **Privately Held**
SIC: 5088 7699 Marine supplies; Boat repair

(P-12912)
LOGISTICAL SUPPORT LLC
20409 Prairie St (91311-6029)
PHONE..............................818 341-3344
Joseph Lucan, *
Jerry Hill, *
EMP: 120 **EST:** 1997
SQ FT: 14,600
SALES (est): 26.24MM
SALES (corp-wide): 39.34MM **Privately Held**
Web: www.rtcaerospace.com
SIC: 5088 Aircraft and parts, nec
PA: Rtc Aerospace Llc
7215 45th Street Ct E
Fife WA
918 407-0291

(P-12913)
ONTIC ENGINEERING AND MFG INC (PA)
20400 Plummer St (91311-5372)
P.O. Box 2424 (91313-2424)
PHONE..............................818 678-6555
Gareth Hall, *CEO*
Peg Billson, *Pr*
Toby Richard Woolrych, *CFO*
Susan Coates Kroll, *Sec*
EMP: 95 **EST:** 1986
SQ FT: 54,000
SALES (est): 450.6MM
SALES (corp-wide): 450.6MM **Privately Held**
Web: www.ontic.com
SIC: 5088 3728 3812 3563 Aircraft equipment and supplies, nec; Aircraft parts and equipment, nec; Search and navigation equipment; Air and gas compressors

(P-12914)
PROPONENT INC (PA)
Also Called: Proponent
3120 Enterprise St (92821-6236)
PHONE..............................714 223-5400
Andrew Todhunter, *Pr*
Steven Frields, *
Corey Yarnell, *
▲ **EMP:** 175 **EST:** 1972
SALES (est): 127.06MM
SALES (corp-wide): 127.06MM **Privately Held**
Web: www.proponent.com
SIC: 5088 3728 Aircraft and parts, nec; Aircraft parts and equipment, nec

(P-12915)
RAYTHEON LGSTICS SPPORT TRNING
2000 E El Segundo Blvd (90245-4501)
PHONE..............................310 647-9438
EMP: 337
SALES (corp-wide): 67.07B **Publicly Held**
SIC: 5088 Aeronautical equipment and supplies
HQ: Raytheon Logistics Support & Training Company
180 Hartwell Rd
Bedford MA
310 647-9438

(P-12916)
REGENT AEROSPACE CORPORATION (PA)
Also Called: Regent
28110 Harrison Pkwy (91355-4109)
PHONE..............................661 257-3000
Reza Soltanianzadeh, *CEO*
Reza Soltanian, *
Tim Garvin, *
▲ **EMP:** 200 **EST:** 1993
SQ FT: 90,000
SALES (est): 100.28MM **Privately Held**
Web: www.regentaerospace.com
SIC: 5088 3728 Aircraft and parts, nec; Aircraft parts and equipment, nec

(P-12917)
STRECH PLASTICS INCORPORATED
900 John St Ste J (92220-6204)
PHONE..............................951 922-2224
James M Strech, *CEO*
▲ **EMP:** 50 **EST:** 1974
SQ FT: 52,000
SALES (est): 20.55MM **Privately Held**
Web: www.strechplastics.com
SIC: 5088 3949 Golf carts; Sporting and athletic goods, nec

(P-12918)
SUNDANCE CUSTOM GOLF CARTS INC
Also Called: Sundance Custom Golf Carts
1240 Vernon Way (92020-1839)
PHONE..............................619 449-0822
Michael Matheny, *CEO*
EMP: 19 **EST:** 2010
SALES (est): 2.51MM **Privately Held**
Web: www.sundancegolfcars.com
SIC: 5088 3799 Golf carts; Golf carts, powered

(P-12919)
TELEDYNE RESON INC
5212 Verdugo Way (93012-8662)
PHONE..............................805 964-6260
Robert Mehrabian, *CEO*
EMP: 33 **EST:** 1985
SALES (est): 18.69MM
SALES (corp-wide): 5.46B **Publicly Held**
Web: www.teledynemarine.com
SIC: 5088 3812 Navigation equipment and supplies; Sonar systems and equipment
PA: Teledyne Technologies Inc
1049 Camino Dos Rios
Thousand Oaks CA
805 373-4545

(P-12920)
THORNTON TECHNOLOGY CORP
Also Called: Thornton Technologies
2608 Temple Heights Dr (92056-3512)
PHONE..............................760 471-9969
William S Thornton, *Prin*
EMP: 23
SALES (est): 5.18MM **Privately Held**
Web: www.thorntontech.com
SIC: 5088 4581 3812 Aircraft equipment and supplies, nec; Aircraft cleaning and janitorial service; Search and navigation equipment
PA: Thornton Technology Corp
5410 Us Highway 2 W
Columbia Falls MT
406 257-7223

(P-12921)
UNITED AERONAUTICAL CORP
7360 Laurel Canyon Blvd (91605-3710)
P.O. Box 7102 (91615-0102)
PHONE..............................818 764-2102
Lawrence P Holt, *CEO*
Bradford T Beck, *
◆ **EMP:** 32 **EST:** 1988
SQ FT: 200,000
SALES (est): 16.39MM **Privately Held**
Web: www.unitedaero.com
SIC: 5088 3812 Aeronautical equipment and supplies; Search and navigation equipment

(P-12922)
UNITED STATES MARINE CORPS
Also Called: Marine Aviation Logistics
Marine Corps Air Stn Bldg 23122 (Camp Pendleton) (92049)
PHONE..............................760 725-3564
EMP: 100
Web: www.marines.mil
SIC: 5088 9711 Marine supplies; Marine Corps
HQ: United States Marine Corps
Branch Hlth Clnic Bldg 5
Beaufort SC

(P-12923)
WESCO AIRCRAFT HARDWARE CORP
27727 Avenue Scott (91355-3909)
PHONE..............................661 775-7200
Steve Halford, *Brnch Mgr*
EMP: 400
SALES (corp-wide): 1.7B **Privately Held**
Web: www.incora.com
SIC: 5088 Aircraft and parts, nec
HQ: Wesco Aircraft Hardware Corp.
2601 Meacham Blvd Ste 400
Fort Worth TX
817 284-4449

(P-12924)
WILLIAMS AEROSPACE & MFG INC (HQ)
999 Avenida Acaso (93012-8700)
PHONE..............................805 586-8699
Greg Beason, *CEO*
Richard Drinkward, *CFO*
▲ **EMP:** 23 **EST:** 1982
SQ FT: 9,910
SALES (est): 9.5MM
SALES (corp-wide): 89.67MM **Privately Held**
Web: www.goallclear.com
SIC: 5088 3728 3724 Aircraft equipment and supplies, nec; Aircraft parts and equipment, nec; Aircraft engines and engine parts
PA: Kellstrom Holding Corporation
100 N Pcf Cast Hwy Ste 19
El Segundo CA
561 222-7455

5091 Sporting And Recreation Goods

(P-12925)
AQUA PERFORMANCE INC
Also Called: A.J. Metal Manufacturing
425 N Smith Ave (92878-4305)
P.O. Box 370 (92878-0370)
PHONE..............................951 340-2056
EMP: 34 **EST:** 1990
SQ FT: 20,000
SALES (est): 9.16MM **Privately Held**
Web: www.aquaperformance.com

SIC: 5091 3339 3444 Watersports equipment and supplies; Primary nonferrous metals, nec; Sheet metalwork

(P-12926)
BIKES ONLINE INC
2711 Loker Ave W (92010-6601)
PHONE..............................650 272-3378
Andre Batista, *Dir Opers*
EMP: 95 **EST:** 2019
SALES (est): 9.96MM **Privately Held**
Web: www.bikesonline.com
SIC: 5091 Bicycles

(P-12927)
EASTON BASEBALL / SOFTBALL INC
3500 Willow Ln (91361-4921)
PHONE..............................800 632-7866
Maria Easton, *Prin*
▲ **EMP:** 22 **EST:** 2014
SALES (est): 1.73MM **Privately Held**
Web: easton.rawlings.com
SIC: 5091 3949 Sporting and recreation goods; Sporting and athletic goods, nec

(P-12928)
EASTON DIAMOND SPORTS LLC
3500 Willow Ln (91361-4921)
PHONE..............................800 632-7866
Ed Kinnaly, *CEO*
EMP: 100 **EST:** 2017
SALES (est): 20.36MM **Privately Held**
Web: easton.rawlings.com
SIC: 5091 Sporting and recreation goods

(P-12929)
FULL-SWING GOLF INC
1905 Aston Ave Ste 100 (92008-7393)
PHONE..............................858 675-1100
▲ **EMP:** 30 **EST:** 1986
SALES (est): 28.59MM **Privately Held**
Web: www.fullswinggolf.com
SIC: 5091 3949 Golf equipment; Golf equipment

(P-12930)
INTEX PROPERTIES S BAY CORP (PA)
4001 Via Oro Ave Ste 210 (90810-1400)
PHONE..............................310 549-5400
Tien P Zee, *Pr*
◆ **EMP:** 97 **EST:** 1970
SQ FT: 80,000
SALES (est): 91.03MM
SALES (corp-wide): 91.03MM **Privately Held**
Web: www.intexcorp.com
SIC: 5091 5092 5021 3081 Watersports equipment and supplies; Toys, nec; Waterbeds; Vinyl film and sheet

(P-12931)
SHIMANO NORTH AMER HOLDG INC (HQ)
Also Called: Shimano North America Bicycle
1 Holland (92618-2506)
PHONE..............................949 951-5003
Hiroshi Matsui, *CEO*
Jim Lafrance, *
Gerriet O'neill, *Contrlr*
▲ **EMP:** 150 **EST:** 1986
SQ FT: 122,000
SALES (est): 91.38MM **Privately Held**
SIC: 5091 Bicycle parts and accessories
PA: Shimano Inc.
77, 3cho, Oimatsucho, Sakai-Ku
Sakai OSK

PRODUCTS & SVCS

(P-12932)
TEA FINANCIAL SERVICES
Also Called: Inland Sports Group
32100 Menifee Rd (92584-9015)
PHONE..............................951 301-8884
EMP: 20
SIC: 5091 2759 Sporting and recreation goods; Letterpress and screen printing

---

5092 Toys And Hobby Goods And Supplies

(P-12933)
ANATEX ENTERPRISES INC
Also Called: Anatex
15911 Arminta St (91406-1807)
PHONE..............................818 908-1888
Fleur Chesler, *Pr*
Mark Chesler, *
▲ **EMP:** 25 **EST:** 1982
SALES (est): 4.94MM **Privately Held**
Web: www.anatex.com
SIC: 5092 3944 Toys, nec; Games, toys, and children's vehicles

(P-12934)
AURORA WORLD INC
Also Called: Aurora
8820 Mercury Ln (90660-6706)
PHONE..............................562 205-1222
TOLL FREE: 800
Heui-yul Noh, *CEO*
Kee Sun Hong, *
◆ **EMP:** 110 **EST:** 1991
SQ FT: 100,000
SALES (est): 49.38MM **Privately Held**
Web: www.auroragift.com
SIC: 5092 Toys, nec
PA: Aurora World Corporation
624 Teheran-Ro, Gangnam-Gu
Seoul

(P-12935)
BANDAI NAMCO ENTRMT AMER INC
Also Called: Ndga
23 Odyssey (92618-3144)
PHONE..............................408 235-2000
Naoki Katashima, *CEO*
Masaaki Tsuji, *
Graeme Bayless, *
Shuji Nakata, *
Hide Irie, *
▲ **EMP:** 200 **EST:** 1990
SQ FT: 51,118
SALES (est): 96.33MM **Privately Held**
Web: www.bandainamcoent.com
SIC: 5092 Video games
HQ: Bandai Namco Holdings Usa Inc.
2120 Park Pl Ste 120
El Segundo CA

(P-12936)
CREATIVE BABY INC
2222 Lee Ave (91733-2500)
PHONE..............................626 330-2289
Charles P C Hsieh, *CEO*
Bruce Hsieh, *VP*
Nancy Hsieh, *Sec*
Andy Hsieh, *Treas*
◆ **EMP:** 20 **EST:** 2013
SALES (est): 2.81MM **Privately Held**
Web: www.creativebabyinc.com
SIC: 5092 3999 Toys and hobby goods and supplies; Models, except toy

(P-12937)
DELTA CREATIVE INC
2690 Pellissier Pl (90601-1507)
PHONE..............................800 423-4135
William B George, *Pr*
Alexander Ritchie, *
Martina Mueller, *
▲ **EMP:** 105 **EST:** 1974
SQ FT: 112,000
SALES (est): 29.21MM **Privately Held**
Web: www.plaidonline.com
SIC: 5092 5198 Arts and crafts equipment and supplies; Paints
HQ: Dk Household Brands Holding Ag
Muhlebachstrasse 20
ZUrich ZH

(P-12938)
DESIGN INTERNATIONAL GROUP INC
755 Epperson Dr (91748-1335)
PHONE..............................626 369-2289
William Yeh, *Pr*
Julie Hwang, *
◆ **EMP:** 25 **EST:** 2003
SALES (est): 8.8MM **Privately Held**
Web: www.luckydig.com
SIC: 5092 5947 2678 Toys and hobby goods and supplies; Gifts and novelties; Stationery products

(P-12939)
ME & MY BIG IDEAS LLC
Also Called: Happy Planner, The
6261 Katella Ave (90630-5249)
PHONE..............................240 348-5240
Tom Shaw, *CEO*
Stephanie Rahmatulla, *
▲ **EMP:** 101 **EST:** 1998
SALES (est): 26.31MM **Privately Held**
Web: www.thehappyplanner.com
SIC: 5092 Arts and crafts equipment and supplies

(P-12940)
MERCHSOURCE LLC (DH)
Also Called: Threesixty Group
7755 Irvine Center Dr (92618-2903)
PHONE..............................800 374-2744
Johann Clapp, *Managing Member*
Mike Roberts, *
◆ **EMP:** 115 **EST:** 2011
SALES (est): 97.9MM
SALES (corp-wide): 1.44MM **Privately Held**
Web: www.merchsource.com
SIC: 5092 Toys and hobby goods and supplies
HQ: Threesixty Group Limited
28/F Harbourside Hq
Kowloon Bay KLN

(P-12941)
MGA ENTERTAINMENT INC
9220 Winnetka Ave (91311-8172)
PHONE..............................800 222-4685
Isaac Larian, *CEO*
Steve Schultz, *
Elizabeth Risha, *
◆ **EMP:** 2100 **EST:** 1980
SALES (est): 310.11MM **Privately Held**
SIC: 5092 Toys, nec

(P-12942)
PC WOO INC (PA)
Also Called: Mega Toys
6443 E Slauson Ave (90040-3107)
PHONE..............................323 887-8138
Tak Kwan Woo, *Prin*
Peter Tak Kwan Woo, *

Liwen Kao, *OF SEASONAL DIV*
Charlie Woo, *Head Secretary*
◆ **EMP:** 83 **EST:** 1989
SQ FT: 120,000
SALES (est): 26.38MM **Privately Held**
SIC: 5092 Toys, nec

(P-12943)
SEGA OF AMERICA INC
250 E Olive Ave Ste 200 (91502-1211)
PHONE..............................747 477-3708
EMP: 270
Web: www.sega.com
SIC: 5092 Video games
HQ: Sega Of America, Inc.
140 Progress Ste 100
Irvine CA
949 788-0455

(P-12944)
SEGA OF AMERICA INC (DH)
140 Progress Ste 100 (92618-0338)
PHONE..............................949 788-0455
Shuji Utsumi, *CEO*
Mitsuhiro Tanaka, *
Jeffrey Shieh, *
▲ **EMP:** 45 **EST:** 1985
SALES (est): 90.88MM **Privately Held**
Web: www.sega.com
SIC: 5092 3999 Video games; Coin-operated amusement machines
HQ: Sega Corporation
1-1-1, Nishishinagawa
Shinagawa-Ku TKY

(P-12945)
SMC PRODUCTS INC
Also Called: Hpi Racing
22651 Lambert St Ste 105 (92630-1611)
PHONE..............................949 753-1099
▲ **EMP:** 68
SIC: 5092 3944 Toys and hobby goods and supplies; Electronic toys

(P-12946)
ULTRA PRO INTERNATIONAL LLC
Also Called: Jolly Roger Games
6049 E Slauson Ave (90040-3007)
PHONE..............................323 890-2100
Marc Lieberman, *
Herman Lee, *
▲ **EMP:** 122 **EST:** 2011
SALES (est): 53.46MM **Privately Held**
Web: www.ultrapro.com
SIC: 5092 3944 Toys and hobby goods and supplies; Games, toys, and children's vehicles

(P-12947)
VICTORY INTL GROUP LLC
Also Called: M Z J
14748 Pipeline Ave Ste B (91709-6024)
PHONE..............................949 407-5888
Dawson Fan, *Pr*
▲ **EMP:** 230 **EST:** 2001
SQ FT: 4,960
SALES (est): 896MM **Privately Held**
Web: www.victoryintlgroup.com
SIC: 5092 3843 2389 3842 Toys and hobby goods and supplies; Dental equipment and supplies; Hospital gowns; Respiratory protection equipment, personal

(P-12948)
WHAM-O INC
6301 Owensmouth Ave Ste 700 (91367-2265)
PHONE..............................818 963-4200
Raylin Hsieh, *CEO*

Jeff Hsieh, *
Blake Wong, *
◆ **EMP:** 59 **EST:** 1997
SALES (est): 15.78MM **Privately Held**
Web: www.wham-o.com
SIC: 5092 5091 3944 3949 Toys and games; Surfing equipment and supplies; Toy trains, airplanes, and automobiles; Sporting and athletic goods, nec

---

5093 Scrap And Waste Materials

(P-12949)
75S CORP
Also Called: FMC Metals
800 E 62nd St (90001-1506)
PHONE..............................323 234-7708
Kevin Armstrong, *CEO*
Octavio Cabrerra, *OK Vice President*
◆ **EMP:** 42 **EST:** 1959
SALES (est): 9.28MM **Privately Held**
Web: www.fmcmet.com
SIC: 5093 3341 Nonferrous metals scrap; Recovery and refining of nonferrous metals

(P-12950)
ATLAS PACIFIC CORPORATION (PA)
2803 Industrial Dr (92316-3249)
P.O. Box 726 (92324-0726)
PHONE..............................909 421-1200
Gregory Woolfson, *Pr*
▼ **EMP:** 25 **EST:** 1980
SQ FT: 10,000
SALES (est): 9.64MM
SALES (corp-wide): 9.64MM **Privately Held**
Web: www.atlaspacific.net
SIC: 5093 3341 3339 Nonferrous metals scrap; Brass smelting and refining (secondary); Zinc refining (primary), including slabs & dust

(P-12951)
B & B PLASTICS RECYCLERS INC (PA)
3040 N Locust Ave (92377-3706)
PHONE..............................909 829-3606
Baltasar Mejia, *Pr*
Bacilio Mejia, *
EMP: 46 **EST:** 1998
SQ FT: 100,000
SALES (est): 23.15MM
SALES (corp-wide): 23.15MM **Privately Held**
Web: www.bbplasticsinc.com
SIC: 5093 2673 Plastics scrap; Bags: plastic, laminated, and coated

(P-12952)
CEDARWOOD-YOUNG COMPANY
Also Called: Allan Company
14618 Arrow Hwy (91706-1733)
PHONE..............................626 962-4047
EMP: 55
SQ FT: 10,664
SALES (corp-wide): 252.16MM **Privately Held**
Web: www.allancompany.com
SIC: 5093 2611 Waste paper; Pulp mills
PA: Cedarwood-Young Company
14620 Joanbridge St
Baldwin Park CA
626 962-4047

▲ = Import ▼ = Export
◆ = Import/Export

(P-12953)
FIRMA PLASTIC CO INC
9309 Rayo Ave (90280-3612)
PHONE..............................323 567-7767
David A Carpenter, *VP*
EMP: 244 **EST:** 1990
SALES (est): 1.48MM **Privately Held**
SIC: 5093 Metal scrap and waste materials
HQ: Metal Management, Inc.
2425 S Wood St
Chicago IL
773 890-4210

(P-12954)
GLOBAL PLASTICS INC
145 Malbert St (92570-8624)
PHONE..............................951 657-5466
Nadim Salim Bahou, *Pr*
Patti Gilmour, *
▲ **EMP:** 120 **EST:** 1996
SQ FT: 55,000
SALES (est): 24.21MM **Privately Held**
Web: www.globalpetinc.com
SIC: 5093 4953 3053 Plastics scrap; Recycling, waste materials; Packing materials

(P-12955)
GREENPATH RECOVERY WEST INC
Also Called: Greenpath Recovery Recycl Svcs
330 W Citrus St Ste 250 (92324-1422)
PHONE..............................909 954-0686
Joe Castro, *Pr*
EMP: 60 **EST:** 2012
SQ FT: 90,000
SALES (est): 8.01MM **Privately Held**
Web: www.greenpathrecovery.com
SIC: 5093 3089 2821 Scrap and waste materials; Plastics processing; Plastics materials and resins

(P-12956)
PAVEMENT RECYCLING SYSTEMS INC (PA)
Also Called: Prsi
10240 San Sevaine Way (91752-1100)
PHONE..............................951 682-1091
Richard W Gove, *Pr*
Stephen Concannon, *
Nathan Beyler, *Prin*
▲ **EMP:** 125 **EST:** 1989
SQ FT: 40,000
SALES (est): 72.5MM **Privately Held**
Web: www.pavementrecycling.com
SIC: 5093 1611 Scrap and waste materials; Surfacing and paving

(P-12957)
SELF SERVE AUTO DISMANTLERS (PA)
Also Called: Adams Steel
3200 E Frontera St (92806-2822)
P.O. Box 6258 (92816-0258)
PHONE..............................714 630-8901
George Adams Junior, *Pr*
Mike Adams, *
Terry Adams, *
Wendy Adams, *
◆ **EMP:** 120 **EST:** 1987
SQ FT: 41,000
SALES (est): 21.73MM **Privately Held**
SIC: 5093 Ferrous metal scrap and waste

(P-12958)
TST INC
Standards Metals
2132 E Dominguez St (90810-1022)

PHONE..............................310 835-0115
Andrew G Stein, *CEO*
EMP: 28
SALES (corp-wide): 45.96MM **Privately Held**
Web: www.tst-inc.com
SIC: 5093 3354 Metal scrap and waste materials; Aluminum extruded products
PA: Tst, Inc.
13428 Benson Ave
Chino CA
951 685-2155

5094 Jewelry And Precious Stones

(P-12959)
A-MARK PRECIOUS METALS INC (PA)
Also Called: A-Mark
2121 Rosecrans Ave Ste 6300 (90245-4743)
PHONE..............................310 587-1477
Gregory N Roberts, *CEO*
Jeffrey D Benjamin, *Ch Bd*
Thor G Gjerdrum, *Pr*
Brian Aquilino, *COO*
Kathleen Simpson Taylor, *Ex VP*
▲ **EMP:** 92 **EST:** 1965
SQ FT: 9,000
SALES (est): 9.29B
SALES (corp-wide): 9.29B **Publicly Held**
Web: www.amark.com
SIC: 5094 Jewelry

(P-12960)
C&C JEWELRY MFG INC
323 W 8th St Fl 4 (90014-3109)
PHONE..............................213 623-6800
Mikhail Chekhman, *Pr*
Robert Connolly, *
Dmitriy Moskalenko Ctrl, *Prin*
▲ **EMP:** 75 **EST:** 2001
SQ FT: 3,000
SALES (est): 28.36MM **Privately Held**
SIC: 5094 3915 Jewelry; Jewel preparing: instruments, tools, watches, and jewelry

(P-12961)
CITIZEN WATCH COMPANY OF AMERICA INC (HQ)
Also Called: Citizen Watch America
1000 W 190th St (90502-1040)
PHONE..............................800 321-1023
▲ **EMP:** 150 **EST:** 1975
SALES (est): 97.29MM **Privately Held**
SIC: 5094 Watches and parts
PA: Citizen Watch Co., Ltd.
6-1-12, Tanashicho
Nishitokyo TKY

(P-12962)
GOLDCO DIRECT LLC
Also Called: Goldco
24025 Park Sorrento Ste 210 (91302-4025)
PHONE..............................818 343-0186
EMP: 80 **EST:** 2006
SALES (est): 40MM **Privately Held**
Web: www.goldco.com
SIC: 5094 Precious metals

(P-12963)
INDUSTRIAL STRENGTH CORP
6115 Corte Del Cedro (92011-1516)
PHONE..............................760 795-1068
EMP: 17 **EST:** 1995
SALES (est): 3.75MM **Privately Held**
Web: www.isbodyjewelry.com

SIC: 5094 3961 3911 Jewelry; Costume jewelry; Jewelry, precious metal

(P-12964)
MAURICE KRAIEM & COMPANY
Also Called: Mk Luxury Group
228 S Beverly Dr (90212-3805)
PHONE..............................213 629-0038
Moshe Kraiem, *CEO*
▲ **EMP:** 24 **EST:** 1978
SALES (est): 4.78MM **Privately Held**
Web: www.mkdiamonds.com
SIC: 5094 3911 Jewelry; Jewelry, precious metal

(P-12965)
MEL BERNIE AND COMPANY INC (PA)
Also Called: 1928 Jewelry Company
3000 W Empire Ave (91504-3109)
PHONE..............................818 841-1928
Melvyn Bernie, *CEO*
▲ **EMP:** 250 **EST:** 1968
SQ FT: 65,000
SALES (est): 46.13MM
SALES (corp-wide): 46.13MM **Privately Held**
Web: www.1928.com
SIC: 5094 Jewelry

(P-12966)
NIXON INC (PA)
Also Called: Nixon Watches
2810 Whiptail Loop Ste 1 (92010-6754)
Rural Route 2810 Whiptail (92010)
PHONE..............................888 455-9200
Andrew Laats, *
▲ **EMP:** 120 **EST:** 1997
SALES (est): 49.35MM
SALES (corp-wide): 49.35MM **Privately Held**
Web: www.nixon.com
SIC: 5094 5611 5136 Watches and parts; Clothing accessories: men's and boys'; Leather and sheep lined clothing, men's and boys'

(P-12967)
SIMON G JEWELRY INC
Also Called: Zeghani
528 State St (91203-1524)
PHONE..............................818 500-8595
Zaven Ghanimian, *CEO*
Simon Ghanimian, *
Hratch Shahbazian, *
▲ **EMP:** 48 **EST:** 1994
SQ FT: 10,000
SALES (est): 9.85MM **Privately Held**
Web: www.simongjewelry.com
SIC: 5094 3911 Jewelry; Jewelry, precious metal

(P-12968)
SIMON GOLUB & SONS INC (DH)
Also Called: Lorenzo USA
514 Via De La Valle Ste 210 (92075)
▲ **EMP:** 90 **EST:** 1923
SQ FT: 40,000
SALES (est): 37.92MM **Privately Held**
Web: www.portlandjewelrysupplies.com
SIC: 5094 3911 Jewelry; Jewelry, precious metal
HQ: Astral Holdings Inc
5506 6th Ave S
Seattle WA

(P-12969)
SWEDA COMPANY LLC
Also Called: Sweda
17411 E Valley Blvd (91744-5159)

PHONE..............................626 357-9999
Brandon Mackay, *CEO*
Seidler Sweda, *
Paul Beck, *
Scott Pearson, *
Kellie Claudio, *
◆ **EMP:** 273 **EST:** 1976
SQ FT: 350,000
SALES (est): 56.55MM **Privately Held**
SIC: 5094 5044 Watches and parts; Calculators, electronic

5099 Durable Goods, Nec

(P-12970)
C D LISTENING BAR INC
Also Called: Super D Phantom Distribution
17822 Gillette Ave Ste A (92614-0527)
PHONE..............................949 225-1170
EMP: 730
Web: www.criticschoiceonline.com
SIC: 5099 Compact discs

(P-12971)
CENTERLINE WOOD PRODUCTS
15447 Anacapa Rd Ste 102 (92392-2481)
PHONE..............................760 246-4530
Michael Rodriguez, *Pr*
EMP: 99 **EST:** 2017
SALES (est): 5.8MM **Privately Held**
Web: www.cwp.cab
SIC: 5099 Wood and wood by-products

(P-12972)
D J AMERICAN SUPPLY INC
Also Called: American Dj Group of Companies
6122 S Eastern Ave (90040-3402)
PHONE..............................323 582-2650
Charles J Davies, *CEO*
Charles Davies, *
Toby B Velazquez, *Sec*
◆ **EMP:** 126 **EST:** 1985
SQ FT: 100,000
SALES (est): 24.32MM **Privately Held**
Web: www.americandjsupply.com
SIC: 5099 5719 5999 Firearms and ammunition, except sporting; Lighting fixtures; Theatrical equipment and supplies

(P-12973)
DENNIS FOLAND INC (PA)
Also Called: Logo Expressions
1500 S Hellman Ave (91761-7634)
P.O. Box 4591 (91761-0822)
PHONE..............................909 930-9900
Dennis Foland, *CEO*
Beverly Foland, *
▲ **EMP:** 50 **EST:** 1979
SQ FT: 140,000
SALES (est): 23.66MM
SALES (corp-wide): 23.66MM **Privately Held**
Web: www.folandgroup.com
SIC: 5099 3944 Souvenirs; Games, toys, and children's vehicles

(P-12974)
FAM PPE LLC
5553-B Bandini Blvd B (90201)
PHONE..............................323 888-7755
Frank M Zarabi, *Managing Member*
EMP: 223 **EST:** 2020
SALES (est): 327.37K **Privately Held**
SIC: 5099 Safety equipment and supplies
PA: Fam, Llc
5553 B Bandini Blvd
Bell CA

PRODUCTS & SVCS

(P-12975)

FT 2 INC

1211 N Miller St (92806-1933)
PHONE..............................714 765-5555
◆ **EMP:** 170
SIC: 5099 2393 3161 Carrying cases; Textile bags; Luggage

(P-12976)

GENIUS PRODUCTS INC

3301 Exposition Blvd Ste 100 (90404)
PHONE..............................310 453-1222
Trevor Drinkwater, *Pr*
Stephen K Bannon, *
Edward J Byrnes, *
▲ **EMP:** 222 **EST:** 2005
SQ FT: 40,520
SALES (est): 25.76MM **Privately Held**
Web: www.geniusproducts.com
SIC: 5099 3652 7819 Video and audio equipment; Prerecorded records and tapes; Video tape or disk reproduction

(P-12977)

GOLDEN STATE MEDICAL SUPPLY

5247 Camino Ruiz (93012-8602)
PHONE..............................805 477-8966
Benjamin Hall, *CEO*
Thomas Weaver, *CFO*
EMP: 99 **EST:** 2017
SALES (est): 2.42MM **Privately Held**
Web: www.gsms.us
SIC: 5099 Durable goods, nec

(P-12978)

GUTHY-RENKER LLC

Also Called: Guthy-Renker Direct
3340 Ocean Park Blvd Fl 2 (90405-3204)
PHONE..............................310 581-6250
EMP: 80
Web: www.guthy-renker.com
SIC: 5099 7812 5999 Tapes and cassettes, prerecorded; Commercials, television: tape or film; Cosmetics
PA: Guthy-Renker Llc
100 N Pcf Cast Hwy Ste 16
El Segundo CA

(P-12979)

H2W

Also Called: Iced Out Gear
7660 Alabama Ave (91304-4902)
PHONE..............................800 578-3088
Dan Gershon, *CEO*
Eric Liberman, *Sec*
David Levich, *CFO*
▲ **EMP:** 22 **EST:** 2002
SQ FT: 8,000
SALES (est): 4.34MM **Privately Held**
Web: www.noveltysunglasses.com
SIC: 5099 3052 Sunglasses; Air line or air brake hose, rubber or rubberized fabric

(P-12980)

MIZARI ENTERPRISES INC (PA)

5455 Wilshire Blvd Ste 1410 (90036-4201)
PHONE..............................323 549-9400
Alan Mizrahi, *CEO*
EMP: 20 **EST:** 1997
SQ FT: 2,000
SALES (est): 8.15MM **Privately Held**
Web: catalog.mizari.com
SIC: 5099 3639 Video and audio equipment; Major kitchen appliances, except refrigerators and stoves

(P-12981)

OLIVET INTERNATIONAL INC (PA)

11015 Hopkins St (91752-3248)
PHONE..............................951 681-8888
Sean Lin, *Managing Member*
Lydia Hsu, *
David Yu, *
Pei Te Lin, *
▲ **EMP:** 89 **EST:** 1984
SQ FT: 456,000
SALES (est): 172.9MM
SALES (corp-wide): 172.9MM **Privately Held**
Web: www.olivetintl.com
SIC: 5099 3161 Luggage; Luggage

(P-12982)

PLATINUM DISC LLC

Also Called: Echo Bridge Home Entertainment
10203 Santa Monica Blvd Fl 5 (90067-6416)
PHONE..............................608 784-6620
Nate Hart, *Pr*
Nathan Hart, *
▼ **EMP:** 91 **EST:** 1995
SALES (est): 24.03MM
SALES (corp-wide): 24.03MM **Privately Held**
SIC: 5099 Compact discs
PA: Echo Bridge Entertainment, Llc
75 2nd Ave Ste 500
Needham MA
781 444-6767

(P-12983)

RGGD INC (PA)

Also Called: Crystal Art Gallery
4950 S Santa Fe Ave (90058-2106)
PHONE..............................323 581-6617
Randy Greenberg, *CEO*
Douglas Song, *
◆ **EMP:** 79 **EST:** 1994
SQ FT: 120,000
SALES (est): 26.79MM
SALES (corp-wide): 26.79MM **Privately Held**
Web: www.crystalartgallery.com
SIC: 5099 3441 Wood and wood by-products; Fabricated structural metal

(P-12984)

ROLAND CORPORATION US (HQ)

5100 S Eastern Ave (90040-2938)
P.O. Box 910921 (90091-0921)
PHONE..............................323 890-3700
Christopher Bristol, *CEO*
Dennis M Houlihan, *
Mark S Malbon, *
Charles L Wright, *
Junpei Yamato, *
◆ **EMP:** 165 **EST:** 1953
SQ FT: 50,000
SALES (est): 70.96MM **Privately Held**
Web: www.roland.com
SIC: 5099 5045 3931 Musical instruments; Computer peripheral equipment; Organs, all types: pipe, reed, hand, electronic, etc.
PA: Roland Corporation
2036-1, Hosoechonakagawa, Kita-Ku
Hamamatsu SZO

(P-12985)

ROSEN ELECTRONICS LLC

Also Called: Rosen Electronics
2500 E Francis St (91761-7730)
PHONE..............................951 898-9808
W Thomas Clements, *Pr*
▲ **EMP:** 75 **EST:** 2003

SALES (est): 21.56MM
SALES (corp-wide): 75.4MM **Privately Held**
SIC: 5099 3679 Video and audio equipment; Liquid crystal displays (LCD)
PA: Aamp Of Florida, Inc.
15500 Lightwave Dr # 202
Clearwater FL
727 572-9255

(P-12986)

SAMICK MUSIC CORP

Also Called: Health Mate
10541 Calle Lee Ste 119los (90720-6782)
PHONE..............................800 946-6001
Baik Lee, *CEO*
Kuhn Sung Kim, *
▲ **EMP:** 60 **EST:** 1983
SQ FT: 8,000
SALES (est): 20.44MM **Privately Held**
Web: www.smcmusic.com
SIC: 5099 3931 Musical instruments; Musical instruments
PA: Samick Musical Instruments Co.,Ltd
313 Soi-Ro, Soi-Myeon
Eumseong

(P-12987)

SUN COAST MERCHANDISE CORP

6405 Randolph St (90040-3511)
PHONE..............................323 720-9700
Kumar C Bhavnani, *Pr*
Dilip Bhavnani, *
Vidya Bhavnani, *
◆ **EMP:** 250 **EST:** 1943
SQ FT: 120,000
SALES (est): 24.59MM **Privately Held**
Web: www.sunscopeusa.com
SIC: 5099 Brass goods

(P-12988)

TAYLOR-LISTUG INC (PA)

Also Called: Taylor Guitars
1980 Gillespie Way (92020-1096)
PHONE..............................619 258-1207
Kurt Listug, *CEO*
Robert Taylor, *
▲ **EMP:** 245 **EST:** 1968
SQ FT: 86,000
SALES (est): 180.56MM
SALES (corp-wide): 180.56MM **Privately Held**
Web: www.taylorguitars.com
SIC: 5099 5736 3931 Musical instruments; Musical instrument stores; Guitars and parts, electric and nonelectric

(P-12989)

YAMAHA CORPORATION OF AMERICA (HQ)

Also Called: Yamaha Music Corporation U S A
6600 Orangethorpe Ave (90620-1396)
PHONE..............................714 522-9011
Hitoshi Fukutome, *CEO*
Terry Lewis, *
Brian Jemelian, *
◆ **EMP:** 300 **EST:** 1958
SALES (est): 427.4MM **Privately Held**
Web: usa.yamaha.com
SIC: 5099 5065 5091 3931 Musical instruments; Sound equipment, electronic; Sporting and recreation goods; Musical instruments
PA: Yamaha Corporation
10-1, Nakazawacho, Naka-Ku
Hamamatsu SZO

5111 Printing And Writing Paper

(P-12990)

KELLY SPICERS INC (HQ)

Also Called: Kelly Spicers Packaging North
12310 Slauson Ave (90670-2629)
PHONE..............................562 698-1199
Janice Gotteseman, *Pr*
Rick Anderson, *
▲ **EMP:** 180 **EST:** 1965
SQ FT: 365,000
SALES (est): 606.41MM
SALES (corp-wide): 1.33B **Privately Held**
Web: www.kellyspicers.com
SIC: 5111 5199 5087 Fine paper; Packaging materials; Janitors' supplies
PA: Central National Gottesman Inc.
3 Manhattanville Rd # 301
Purchase NY
914 696-9000

5112 Stationery And Office Supplies

(P-12991)

BLUE SKY THE CLOR IMGNTION LLC

Also Called: Day Designer
410 Exchange Ste 250 (92602-1392)
PHONE..............................714 389-7700
James E Freeman Iii, *CEO*
Warren Vidovich, *Managing Member*
Jeannie M Alich, *
Dennis Marquardt, *
▲ **EMP:** 85 **EST:** 2002
SALES (est): 42.98MM **Privately Held**
Web: www.bluesky.com
SIC: 5112 5943 Stationery and office supplies; Stationery stores

(P-12992)

CENVEO WORLDWIDE LIMITED

705 Baldwin Park Blvd (91746-1504)
PHONE..............................626 369-4921
Timothy Hollywood, *Brnch Mgr*
EMP: 410
SALES (corp-wide): 1.04B **Privately Held**
Web: www.cenveo.com
SIC: 5112 Stationery and office supplies
HQ: Cenveo Worldwide Limited
200 First Stamford Pl
Stamford CT
203 595-3000

(P-12993)

ESSENDANT CO

Also Called: United Stationers
918 S Stimson Ave (91745-1640)
PHONE..............................626 961-0011
Terry Deines, *Mgr*
EMP: 134
Web: www.essendant.com
SIC: 5112 5044 5021 5943 Office supplies, nec; Office equipment; Furniture; Office forms and supplies
HQ: Essendant Co.
1 Parkway North Blvd # 100
Deerfield IL
847 627-7000

(P-12994)

GRAPHIC BUSINESS SOLUTIONS INC

Also Called: House of Magnets
1912 John Towers Ave (92020-1158)
PHONE..............................619 258-4081

▲ **EMP:** 39 **EST:** 1994
SQ FT: 10,000
SALES (est): 16.89MM **Privately Held**
Web: www.gogbs.com
SIC: 5112 2752 Business forms; Commercial printing, lithographic

(P-12995)
IMAGE SOURCE INC (PA)
Also Called: Bluebird Office Supplies
2110 Pontius Ave (90025-5726)
P.O. Box 642380 (90064-8094)
PHONE...........................310 477-0700
Faramarz Sadeghi, *CEO*
Ramin Sadeghi, *Treas*
▲ **EMP:** 181 **EST:** 1982
SQ FT: 5,000
SALES (est): 19.23MM
SALES (corp-wide): 19.23MM **Privately Held**
Web: imagesourceusa.visualedgeit.com
SIC: 5112 5943 Office supplies, nec; Office forms and supplies

(P-12996)
PENTEL OF AMERICA LTD (HQ)
2715 Columbia St (90503-3861)
PHONE...........................310 320-3831
Chotaro Koumi, *Pr*
Norikazu Hasegama, *
Nobuo Aihara, *CMO**
Toshiro Hemmi, *
◆ **EMP:** 132 **EST:** 1966
SQ FT: 46,000
SALES (est): 97.63MM **Privately Held**
Web: www.pentel.com
SIC: 5112 3951 5199 3952 Pens and/or pencils; Pens and mechanical pencils; Artists' materials; Artists' materials, except pencils and leads
PA: Pentel Co., Ltd.
7-2, Nihombashikoamicho
Chuo-Ku TKY

(P-12997)
PRESTIGE GRAPHICS INC
9630 Ridgehaven Ct Ste B (92123-5605)
PHONE...........................858 560-8213
Mark Grantham, *Pr*
▲ **EMP:** 30 **EST:** 1988
SALES (est): 11.38MM **Privately Held**
SIC: 5112 2752 Business forms; Offset printing
PA: Pgac Corp.
9630 Ridgehaven Ct Ste B
San Diego CA

(P-12998)
PUNCH STUDIO LLC (PA)
6025 W Slauson Ave (90230-6507)
P.O. Box 3663 (90231-3663)
PHONE...........................310 390-9900
Todd Brian Kirshner, *CEO*
Nathalie Carrer, *
◆ **EMP:** 230 **EST:** 2001
SQ FT: 106,000
SALES (est): 57.91MM **Privately Held**
Web: www.punchstudio.com
SIC: 5112 Greeting cards

(P-12999)
R R DONNELLEY & SONS COMPANY
Also Called: Moore Business Forms
40610 County Center Dr Ste 100 (92591-6021)
PHONE...........................951 296-2890
Rick Budge, *Mgr*
EMP: 53
SALES (corp-wide): 15B **Privately Held**

Web: www.rrd.com
SIC: 5112 2761 2752 Business forms; Manifold business forms; Color lithography
HQ: R. R. Donnelley & Sons Company
35 W Wacker Dr
Chicago IL
800 782-4892

(P-13000)
SYSTEM SUPPLY STATIONERY CORP
1251 E Walnut St (90746-1318)
PHONE...........................310 223-0880
Enrico Ventura, *Pr*
▲ **EMP:** 18 **EST:** 1949
SQ FT: 30,000
SALES (est): 9.9MM **Privately Held**
Web: www.3scorp.com
SIC: 5112 5021 2752 Office supplies, nec; Office furniture, nec; Billheads, lithographed

(P-13001)
VIKING OFFICE PRODUCTS INC (DH)
3366 E Willow St (90755-2311)
PHONE...........................562 490-1000
M Bruce Nelson, *Pr*
Mark R Brown, *Vice-President Information Systems**
Ronald W Weissman, *Senior Vice President Logistics**
▲ **EMP:** 292 **EST:** 1960
SQ FT: 187,000
SALES (est): 349.49MM
SALES (corp-wide): 8.49B **Publicly Held**
Web: www.officedepot.com
SIC: 5112 5021 5045 5087 Office supplies, nec; Office furniture, nec; Computers, peripherals, and software; Janitors' supplies
HQ: Office Depot, Llc
6600 N Military Trl
Boca Raton FL
561 438-4800

(P-13002)
XSE GROUP INC
92 Argonaut Ste 235 (92656-4112)
PHONE...........................888 272-8340
EMP: 199
SALES (corp-wide): 96.92MM **Privately Held**
Web: www.xsegroup.com
SIC: 5112 Office supplies, nec
PA: Xse Group, Inc.
35 Phil Mack Dr
Middletown CT
888 272-8340

5113 Industrial And Personal Service Paper

(P-13003)
ANDWIN CORPORATION (PA)
Also Called: Andwin Scientific
167 W Cochran St (93065-6217)
P.O. Box 689 (91365-0689)
PHONE...........................818 999-2828
Natalie Sarraf, *CEO*
Jesse Palaganas, *
▲ **EMP:** 62 **EST:** 1950
SALES (est): 59.75MM
SALES (corp-wide): 59.75MM **Privately Held**
Web: www.andwinclinical.com
SIC: 5113 5199 5087 5047 Shipping supplies; Art goods and supplies; Janitors' supplies; Hospital equipment and furniture

(P-13004)
BUNZL DISTRIBUTION CAL LLC (DH)
Also Called: Bunzl
3310 E Miraloma Ave (92806-1911)
PHONE...........................714 688-1900
Derek R Goodin, *
Scot Gregory, *
◆ **EMP:** 98 **EST:** 1989
SQ FT: 150,000
SALES (est): 87.38MM
SALES (corp-wide): 14.5B **Privately Held**
Web: www.bunzldistribution.com
SIC: 5113 Paper, wrapping or coarse, and products
HQ: Bunzl Distribution Usa, Llc
1 Cityplace Dr Ste 200
Saint Louis MO

(P-13005)
CALIFORNIA BOX II
8949 Toronto Ave (91730-5412)
PHONE...........................909 944-9202
John Widera, *CEO*
Mackey Davis, *
EMP: 80 **EST:** 1990
SQ FT: 100,000
SALES (est): 10.58MM
SALES (corp-wide): 33.56MM **Privately Held**
Web: www.calbox.com
SIC: 5113 2653 Corrugated and solid fiber boxes; Boxes, corrugated: made from purchased materials
PA: California Box Company
13901 Carmenita Rd
Santa Fe Springs CA
562 921-1223

(P-13006)
E & S PAPER CO
Also Called: Delta Packaging Products
14110 S Broadway (90061-1019)
PHONE...........................310 538-8700
TOLL FREE: 800
Spencer Pritkin, *Pr*
Richard Hemmer, *
Rosalind Pritikin, *
EMP: 28 **EST:** 1964
SQ FT: 21,000
SALES (est): 4.99MM **Privately Held**
Web: www.deltapackaging.com
SIC: 5113 5085 2679 3086 Paperboard and products; Packing, industrial; Paperboard products, converted, nec; Packaging and shipping materials, foamed plastics

(P-13007)
FRICK PAPER COMPANY LLC
Also Called: Paper Mart Indus & Ret Packg
2164 N Batavia St (92865-3104)
PHONE...........................714 787-4900
Tom Frick, *Managing Member*
John Frick, *
◆ **EMP:** 106 **EST:** 1921
SQ FT: 210,000
SALES (est): 83.52MM **Privately Held**
Web: www.papermart.com
SIC: 5113 Paper, wrapping or coarse, and products

(P-13008)
GEORGIA-PACIFIC LLC
Also Called: Georgia-Pacific
9206 Santa Fe Springs Rd (90670-2618)
PHONE...........................562 861-6226
EMP: 275
SALES (corp-wide): 36.93B **Privately Held**
Web: www.gp.com

SIC: 5113 2653 Corrugated and solid fiber boxes; Boxes, corrugated: made from purchased materials
HQ: Georgia-Pacific Llc
133 Peachtree St Nw
Atlanta GA
404 652-4000

(P-13009)
GOLDEN EYE MEDIA USA INC
Also Called: Lotus Trolley Bags
1000 Camino De Las Ondas (92011-3402)
PHONE...........................760 688-9962
Farzan Dehmoubed, *CEO*
◆ **EMP:** 17 **EST:** 2009
SQ FT: 2,000
SALES (est): 2.85MM **Privately Held**
Web: www.lotus-sustainables.com
SIC: 5113 2394 Bags, paper and disposable plastic; Air cushions and mattresses, canvas

(P-13010)
IMPERIAL BAG & PAPER CO LLC
Also Called: Paper Company, The
2825 Warner Ave (92606-4443)
PHONE...........................800 834-6248
Julie Scheibe, *VP Opers*
EMP: 98
SALES (corp-wide): 1.63B **Privately Held**
Web: www.imperialdade.com
SIC: 5113 5199 Containers, paper and disposable plastic; Packaging materials
PA: Imperial Bag & Paper Co. Llc
255 Route 1 And 9
Jersey City NJ
201 437-7440

(P-13011)
OAK PAPER PRODUCTS CO INC (PA)
Also Called: Acorn Paper Products Co.
3686 E Olympic Blvd (90023-3146)
P.O. Box 23965 (90023-0965)
PHONE...........................323 268-0507
TOLL FREE: 800
David Weissberg, *CEO*
Max Weissberg, *
▲ **EMP:** 174 **EST:** 1959
SQ FT: 250,000
SALES (est): 91.84MM
SALES (corp-wide): 91.84MM **Privately Held**
Web: www.acorn-paper.com
SIC: 5113 5199 5087 2653 Shipping supplies; Packaging materials; Janitors' supplies; Corrugated and solid fiber boxes

(P-13012)
ORORA PACKAGING SOLUTIONS
Also Called: Corru Kraft Buena Pk Div 5058
6200 Caballero Blvd (90620-1124)
PHONE...........................714 562-6002
EMP: 149
Web: www.ororapackagingsolutions.com
SIC: 5113 2653 Paper, wrapping or coarse, and products; Boxes, corrugated: made from purchased materials
HQ: Orora Packaging Solutions
6600 Valley View St
Buena Park CA
714 562-6000

(P-13013)
ORORA PACKAGING SOLUTIONS (HQ)
Also Called: Orora North America
6600 Valley View St (90620-1145)
PHONE...........................714 562-6000

PRODUCTS & SVCS

Bernardino Salvatore, *Pr*
Bernardino Salvatorre, *
David Conley, *
Lara Coons, *
◆ **EMP:** 100 **EST:** 1951
SQ FT: 300,000
SALES (est): 1.88B **Privately Held**
Web: www.ororapackagingsolutions.com
SIC: 5113 2653 Paper, wrapping or coarse, and products; Boxes, corrugated: made from purchased materials
PA: Orora Limited
109 Burwood Rd
Hawthorn VIC

(P-13014)
ORORA PACKAGING SOLUTIONS
Also Called: Landsberg Flfilment Sltons Div
13397 Marlay Ave Ste A (92337-6946)
PHONE..............................909 770-5400
EMP: 41
Web: www.ororagroup.com
SIC: 5113 2653 Paper, wrapping or coarse, and products; Boxes, corrugated: made from purchased materials
HQ: Orora Packaging Solutions
6600 Valley View St
Buena Park CA
714 562-6000

(P-13015)
ORORA PACKAGING SOLUTIONS
Also Called: Mpp San Diego Div 6064
664 N Twin Oaks Valley Rd (92069-1712)
PHONE..............................760 510-7170
Scott Romagnoli, *Mgr*
EMP: 25
Web: www.ororagroup.com
SIC: 5113 2653 Paper, wrapping or coarse, and products; Boxes, corrugated: made from purchased materials
HQ: Orora Packaging Solutions
6600 Valley View St
Buena Park CA
714 562-6000

(P-13016)
ORORA PACKAGING SOLUTIONS
Also Called: Landsberg Snta Brbara Div 1046
2146 Eastman Ave (93030-5168)
PHONE..............................805 278-5040
Terry Mayfield, *Mgr*
EMP: 22
Web: www.ororagroup.com
SIC: 5113 2653 Paper, wrapping or coarse, and products; Boxes, corrugated: made from purchased materials
HQ: Orora Packaging Solutions
6600 Valley View St
Buena Park CA
714 562-6000

(P-13017)
ORORA PACKAGING SOLUTIONS
Also Called: Landsberg Los Angeles Div 1001
1640 S Greenwood Ave (90640-6538)
P.O. Box 800 (90640-0800)
PHONE..............................323 832-2000
Jed Wockenfuss, *Mgr*
EMP: 168
Web: www.ororagroup.com
SIC: 5113 2653 Paper, wrapping or coarse, and products; Boxes, corrugated: made from purchased materials
HQ: Orora Packaging Solutions
6600 Valley View St

Buena Park CA
714 562-6000

(P-13018)
ORORA PACKAGING SOLUTIONS
Mpp Los Angeles Div 6060
3201 W Mission Rd (91803-1113)
PHONE..............................626 284-9524
Marc Fenster, *Mgr*
EMP: 26
Web: www.ororapackagingsolutions.com
SIC: 5113 2653 Paper, wrapping or coarse, and products; Boxes, corrugated: made from purchased materials
HQ: Orora Packaging Solutions
6600 Valley View St
Buena Park CA
714 562-6000

(P-13019)
ORORA PACKAGING SOLUTIONS
Also Called: Landsberg Orange Cnty Div 1025
7001 Village Dr Ste 155 (90621-2276)
PHONE..............................714 525-4900
Jerry Mejia, *Mgr*
EMP: 26
Web: www.ororagroup.com
SIC: 5113 2653 Paper, wrapping or coarse, and products; Boxes, corrugated: made from purchased materials
HQ: Orora Packaging Solutions
6600 Valley View St
Buena Park CA
714 562-6000

(P-13020)
ORORA PACKAGING SOLUTIONS
Also Called: Mpp Fullerton Div 6061
1901 E Rosslynn Ave (92831-5141)
PHONE..............................714 278-6000
Carol Hortick, *Brnch Mgr*
EMP: 45
Web: www.ororapackagingsolutions.com
SIC: 5113 2653 Paper, wrapping or coarse, and products; Boxes, corrugated: made from purchased materials
HQ: Orora Packaging Solutions
6600 Valley View St
Buena Park CA
714 562-6000

(P-13021)
P & R PAPER SUPPLY CO INC (HQ)
1898 E Colton Ave (92374-9798)
P.O. Box 590 (92373-0201)
PHONE..............................909 389-1807
Robert Tillis, *CEO*
Joe Maiberger, *
Luke Maiberger, *
Chris Dirx, *
Paul Cervino, *
▼ **EMP:** 90 **EST:** 1965
SQ FT: 75,000
SALES (est): 81.69MM
SALES (corp-wide): 1.63B **Privately Held**
Web: www.prpaper.com
SIC: 5113 5169 5149 5072 Paper, wrapping or coarse, and products; Chemicals and allied products, nec; Groceries and related products, nec; Hardware
PA: Imperial Bag & Paper Co. Llc
255 Route 1 And 9
Jersey City NJ
201 437-7440

(P-13022)
PERRIN BERNARD SUPOWITZ LLC (HQ)
Also Called: Fergadis Enterprises
5496 Lindbergh Ln (90201-6409)
PHONE..............................323 981-2800
Ken Sweder, *Ch*
Ron Margolis, *CFO*
EMP: 132 **EST:** 1926
SQ FT: 175,000
SALES (est): 276.73MM
SALES (corp-wide): 1.01B **Privately Held**
Web: www.individualfoodservice.com
SIC: 5113 Industrial and personal service paper
PA: Kelso & Company, L.P.
299 Park Ave Fl 30
New York NY
212 350-7700

(P-13023)
PIONEER PACKING INC (PA)
2430 S Grand Ave (92705-5211)
PHONE..............................714 540-9751
Michael S Blower, *Pr*
Ronald Scagliotti, *
▲ **EMP:** 30 **EST:** 1976
SQ FT: 170,000
SALES (est): 50.82MM
SALES (corp-wide): 50.82MM **Privately Held**
Web: www.pioneerpackinginc.com
SIC: 5113 2653 Shipping supplies; Boxes, corrugated: made from purchased materials

(P-13024)
SAN DIEGO DIE CUTTING INC
3112 Moore St (92110-4480)
PHONE..............................619 297-4453
George Thomas Christian, *Pr*
James Roche, *
◆ **EMP:** 34 **EST:** 1956
SQ FT: 12,000
SALES (est): 9.96MM **Privately Held**
Web: www.sddiecutting.com
SIC: 5113 3544 7319 2759 Corrugated and solid fiber boxes; Special dies and tools; Display advertising service; Embossing on paper

(P-13025)
USED CARDBOARD BOXES INC
4032 Wilshire Blvd Ste 402 (90010-3413)
PHONE..............................323 724-2500
Marty Metro, *CEO*
▲ **EMP:** 125 **EST:** 2006
SALES (est): 48.27MM **Privately Held**
Web: www.usedcardboardboxes.com
SIC: 5113 Corrugated and solid fiber boxes

(P-13026)
VALLEY BOX CO INC
10611 Prospect Ave (92071-4532)
PHONE..............................619 449-2882
Robert Eschwege, *Pr*
EMP: 40 **EST:** 1966
SQ FT: 7,000
SALES (est): 16.55MM **Privately Held**
Web: www.valleybox.com
SIC: 5113 2448 2653 2449 Corrugated and solid fiber boxes; Cargo containers, wood; Corrugated and solid fiber boxes; Wood containers, nec

5122 Drugs, Proprietaries, And Sundries

(P-13027)
ADVANCED PHRM SVCS INC
Also Called: JBA Brands
11555 Monarch St Ste B (92841-1814)
PHONE..............................714 903-1006
Tracy Nguyen, *CEO*
Dennis Ngo, *CEO*
▲ **EMP:** 19 **EST:** 2005
SALES (est): 2.43MM **Privately Held**
SIC: 5122 2833 Pharmaceuticals; Medicinals and botanicals

(P-13028)
AMERISOURCEBERGEN DRUG CORP
Also Called: ABC Valencia
1851 California Ave (92881-6477)
PHONE..............................951 371-2000
Ron Green, *Mgr*
EMP: 150
SALES (corp-wide): 262.17B **Publicly Held**
Web: www.amerisourcebergendrug.com
SIC: 5122 4225 Pharmaceuticals; General warehousing and storage
HQ: Amerisourcebergen Drug Corporation
1 W 1st Ave
Conshohocken PA
610 727-7000

(P-13029)
BAXTER HEALTHCARE CORPORATION
1 Baxter Way Ste 100 (91362-3813)
PHONE..............................805 372-3000
John Bacich, *Pr*
EMP: 96
SALES (corp-wide): 15.11B **Publicly Held**
Web: www.baxter.com
SIC: 5122 2834 2836 5047 Drugs, proprietaries, and sundries; Solutions, pharmaceutical; Biological products, except diagnostic; Medical equipment and supplies
HQ: Baxter Healthcare Corporation
1 Baxter Pkwy
Deerfield IL
224 948-2000

(P-13030)
BEAUTY 21 COSMETICS INC
Also Called: L A Girl
2021 S Archibald Ave (91761-8535)
PHONE..............................909 945-2220
Lan Jack Yu, *CEO*
Chafe Yu Trinh, *
Mahon So Yu, *
◆ **EMP:** 175 **EST:** 1985
SQ FT: 250,000
SALES (est): 45.25MM **Privately Held**
Web: www.lagirlusa.com
SIC: 5122 2844 Cosmetics; Perfumes, cosmetics and other toilet preparations

(P-13031)
CENCORA INC
1368 Metropolitan Dr (92868)
P.O. Box 247 (08086-0247)
PHONE..............................610 727-7000
Daniel Ramirez, *Mgr*
EMP: 249
SALES (corp-wide): 262.17B **Publicly Held**
Web: www.amerisourcebergen.com
SIC: 5122 Pharmaceuticals
PA: Cencora, Inc.
1 W 1st Ave

Conshohocken PA
610 727-7000

(P-13032)
CHEMI-SOURCE INC
Also Called: Metabolic Response Modifiers
2665 Vista Pacific Dr (92056-3500)
PHONE.................................760 477-8177
▲ **EMP:** 38 **EST:** 1996
SQ FT: 24,000
SALES (est): 19.32MM **Privately Held**
Web: www.mrmnutrition.com
SIC: 5122 2833 5499 Vitamins and minerals;
Medicinals and botanicals; Health and
dietetic food stores

(P-13033)
COLORESCIENCE INC
2141 Palomar Airport Rd Ste 200
(92011-1423)
PHONE.................................866 426-5673
Mary Fisher, *CEO*
Josie Juncal, *CCO**
Ted Ebel, *Chief Business Officer**
Steve P Loomis, *
▲ **EMP:** 111 **EST:** 2000
SQ FT: 15,000
SALES (est): 31.05MM **Privately Held**
Web: www.colorescience.com
SIC: 5122 2844 Cosmetics; Cosmetic
preparations

(P-13034)
**CONQUISTADOR
INTERNATIONAL LLC**
Also Called: Posh'n Bae
21200 Oxnard St Ste 492 (91365-7301)
PHONE.................................424 249-9304
Andrew Andrew, *Managing Member*
EMP: 100 **EST:** 2018
SALES (est): 10.19MM **Privately Held**
SIC: 5122 Cosmetics

(P-13035)
COPAN DIAGNOSTICS INC (DH)
26055 Jefferson Ave (92562-6983)
PHONE.................................951 696-6957
◆ **EMP:** 18 **EST:** 1994
SQ FT: 28,000
SALES (est): 162.8MM **Privately Held**
Web: www.copanusa.com
SIC: 5122 5049 3826 Biologicals and allied
products; Laboratory equipment, except
medical or dental; Analytical instruments
HQ: Copan Italia Spa
Via Francesco Perotti 10
Brescia BS
030 268-7211

(P-13036)
DAKO NORTH AMERICA INC
6392 Via Real (93013-2921)
P.O. Box 58059 (93013)
PHONE.................................805 566-6655
◆ **EMP:** 325
SIC: 5122 3841 Biologicals and allied
products; Diagnostic apparatus, medical

(P-13037)
**DANNE MONTAGUE-KING CO
(PA)**
Also Called: Dmk
10420 Pioneer Blvd (90670-3734)
PHONE.................................562 944-0230
Danne King, *Pr*
Randy Larsen, *
▲ **EMP:** 17 **EST:** 1996
SQ FT: 30,000
SALES (est): 9.02MM **Privately Held**

Web: www.dannemking.com
SIC: 5122 5999 2844 Cosmetics; Toiletries,
cosmetics, and perfumes; Cosmetic
preparations

(P-13038)
DERM COSMETIC LABS INC (PA)
Also Called: Derm Cosmetic Labs
6370 Altura Blvd (90620-1001)
PHONE.................................714 562-8873
Loksarang D Hardas, *Pr*
▲ **EMP:** 21 **EST:** 1988
SQ FT: 60,000
SALES (est): 4.96MM
SALES (corp-wide): 4.96MM **Privately
Held**
Web: www.lastotallyawesome.com
SIC: 5122 2844 Cosmetics, perfumes, and
hair products; Cosmetic preparations

(P-13039)
**DHOUSE BRANDS INC //
COMUNE**
Also Called: Comune
2301 E 7th St Ste F103 (90023-1037)
PHONE.................................213 291-7576
John Inn, *CEO*
EMP: 20 **EST:** 2021
SALES (est): 1.09MM **Privately Held**
SIC: 5122 2389 2339 2335 Cosmetics;
Apparel and accessories, nec; Women's
and misses' accessories; Women's,
junior's, and misses' dresses

(P-13040)
**DISTRIBUTION ALTERNATIVES
INC**
1979 Renaissance Pkwy (92376-2403)
PHONE.................................909 770-8900
EMP: 100
SALES (corp-wide): 95.6MM **Privately
Held**
Web: www.daserv.com
SIC: 5122 Cosmetics
PA: Distribution Alternatives, Inc.
6870 21st Ave
Lino Lakes MN
651 636-9167

(P-13041)
FFF ENTERPRISES INC (PA)
44000 Winchester Rd (92590-2578)
PHONE.................................951 296-2500
Patrick M Schmidt, *CEO*
Wayne Talleur, *CFO*
Chris Ground, *COO*
Jonathan Hahn, *CIO*
Michael J Alkire, *Bd of Dir*
EMP: 300 **EST:** 1988
SQ FT: 162,000
SALES (est): 539.81MM
SALES (corp-wide): 539.81MM **Privately
Held**
Web: www.fffenterprises.com
SIC: 5122 Pharmaceuticals

(P-13042)
GLAMOUR INDUSTRIES CO (PA)
Also Called: American International Inds
2220 Gaspar Ave (90040-1516)
PHONE.................................323 728-2999
Zvi Ryzman, *Pr*
Theresa Cooper, *Ex VP*
Charlie Loveless, *VP*
Betty Ryzman, *Sec*
EMP: 400 **EST:** 1971
SQ FT: 224,000
SALES (est): 110.3MM
SALES (corp-wide): 110.3MM **Privately
Held**

Web: www.aiibeauty.com
SIC: 5122 2844 Cosmetics; Cosmetic
preparations

(P-13043)
GLOVES IN A BOTTLE INC
3720 Park Pl (91020-1623)
P.O. Box 615 (91021-0615)
PHONE.................................818 248-9980
▲ **EMP:** 20 **EST:** 1994
SQ FT: 4,000
SALES (est): 4.81MM **Privately Held**
Web: www.glovesinabottle.com
SIC: 5122 2844 5999 Cosmetics; Perfumes,
cosmetics and other toilet preparations;
Toiletries, cosmetics, and perfumes

(P-13044)
H D SMITH LLC
1370 E Victoria St (90746-7501)
P.O. Box 6231 (90749-6231)
PHONE.................................310 641-1885
Bob Schwartz, *Mgr*
EMP: 100
SALES (corp-wide): 262.17B **Publicly
Held**
SIC: 5122 5047 Pharmaceuticals; Medical
and hospital equipment
HQ: H. D. Smith, Llc
1 W 1st Ave Ste 100
Conshohocken PA
866 232-1222

(P-13045)
HARD CANDY LLC
833 W 16th St (92663-2801)
PHONE.................................949 515-3923
EMP: 30 **EST:** 1995
SQ FT: 12,200
SALES (est): 2.54MM **Privately Held**
SIC: 5122 2844 Cosmetics; Perfumes,
cosmetics and other toilet preparations

(P-13046)
**HATCHBEAUTY PRODUCTS
LLC (PA)**
Also Called: Hatchbeauty
355 S Grand Ave (90071-3152)
P.O. Box 641415 (90064-6415)
PHONE.................................310 396-7070
Tracy Holland, *Managing Member*
Benjamin Bennett, *
◆ **EMP:** 83 **EST:** 2009
SALES (est): 38.75MM
SALES (corp-wide): 38.75MM **Privately
Held**
Web: www.hatchcltv.com
SIC: 5122 Cosmetics, perfumes, and hair
products

(P-13047)
IRISYS INC
6828 Nancy Ridge Dr Ste 100 (92121)
PHONE.................................858 623-1520
EMP: 86 **EST:** 2001
SQ FT: 10,000
SALES (est): 20.33MM **Privately Held**
Web: www.societalcdmo.com
SIC: 5122 8748 Pharmaceuticals; Business
consulting, nec

(P-13048)
JARROW FORMULAS INC (PA)
15233 Ventura Blvd Fl 900 (91403-2250)
PHONE.................................310 204-6936
Ojesh Bhalla, *CEO*
Jarrow L Rogovin, *
Michael Jacobs, *
Peilin Guo, *
Clayton Dubose, *

◆ **EMP:** 80 **EST:** 1977
SQ FT: 37,000
SALES (est): 52.95MM
SALES (corp-wide): 52.95MM **Privately
Held**
Web: www.jarrow.com
SIC: 5122 Vitamins and minerals

(P-13049)
JLO BEAUTY & LIFESTYLE LLC
100 N Pacific Coast Hwy Ste 1900 (90245)
PHONE.................................888 853-3169
Richard Odum, *Managing Member*
EMP: 27 **EST:** 2019
SALES (est): 5.87MM **Privately Held**
SIC: 5122 2844 Cosmetics; Perfumes,
cosmetics and other toilet preparations

(P-13050)
KUSH SUPPLY CO LLC
7375 Chapman Ave (92841-2104)
PHONE.................................714 243-4023
EMP: 97
SALES (corp-wide): 10.04MM **Privately
Held**
Web: www.kushco.com
SIC: 5122 Pharmaceuticals
PA: Kush Supply Co. Llc
6261 Katella Ave Ste 250
Cypress CA
714 243-4098

(P-13051)
LIFETECH RESOURCES LLC
Also Called: International Research Labs
700 Science Dr (93021-2012)
PHONE.................................805 944-1199
Richard Carieri, *Ch Bd*
Susan Mccarthy, *Pr*
Anna Carieri, *
▲ **EMP:** 85 **EST:** 1990
SQ FT: 152,000
SALES (est): 46MM **Privately Held**
Web: www.lifetechresources.com
SIC: 5122 5149 Cosmetics; Health foods

(P-13052)
**MARKWINS BEAUTY BRANDS
INC (PA)**
22067 Ferrero (91789-5214)
PHONE.................................909 595-8898
Lina Chen, *CEO*
John Chen, *
◆ **EMP:** 150 **EST:** 1984
SQ FT: 320,000
SALES (est): 270.93MM
SALES (corp-wide): 270.93MM **Privately
Held**
Web: www.markwinsbeauty.com
SIC: 5122 Cosmetics

(P-13053)
MCKESSON CORPORATION
Also Called: McKesson Drug Company
9501 Norwalk Blvd (90670-2929)
P.O. Box 2116 (90670-0116)
PHONE.................................562 463-2100
Todd Kleinow, *Mgr*
EMP: 108
SALES (corp-wide): 276.71B **Publicly
Held**
Web: www.mckesson.com
SIC: 5122 Pharmaceuticals
PA: Mckesson Corporation
6555 State Highway 161
Irving TX
972 446-4800

PRODUCTS & SVCS

(PA)=Parent Co (HQ)=Headquarters
✪ = New Business established in last 2 years

(P-13054)
MEDICAL RESEARCH INSTITUTE
Also Called: M R I
21411 Prairie St (91311-5829)
PHONE....................................818 739-6000
Chirag Patel, *CEO*
Patrick S Mccullough, *Pr*
Jenia G Khudagulyan, *
Alfred Baumeler, *CMO*
Kevin J Dwyer, *
EMP: 243 **EST:** 1997
SALES (est): 3.67MM
SALES (corp-wide): 121.68MM **Privately Held**
SIC: 5122 Vitamins and minerals
PA: Natrol Llc
    21411 Prairie St
    Chatsworth CA
    818 739-6000

(P-13055)
METAGENICS LLC (PA)
25 Enterprise Ste 200 (92656-2713)
PHONE....................................949 366-0818
Pat Smallcombe, *Pr*
Jean M Bellin, *
Dave Tuit, *
John Troup, *CSO*
Sara Gottfried, *CMO*
◆ **EMP:** 150 **EST:** 1983
SQ FT: 88,000
SALES (est): 188.55MM
SALES (corp-wide): 188.55MM **Privately Held**
Web: www.metagenics.com
SIC: 5122 Vitamins and minerals

(P-13056)
MURAD LLC
1340 Storm Pkwy (90501-5041)
PHONE....................................310 726-3300
EMP: 108
SALES (corp-wide): 62.39B **Privately Held**
Web: www.murad.com
SIC: 5122 Cosmetics
HQ: Murad, Llc
    2121 Park Pl Fl 1
    El Segundo CA

(P-13057)
N QIAGEN AMERCN HOLDINGS INC (HQ)
27220 Turnberry Ln Ste 200 (91355-1005)
PHONE....................................800 426-8157
Peer Schatz, *Pr*
EMP: 250 **EST:** 2000
SALES (est): 476.32MM **Privately Held**
SIC: 5122 Biologicals and allied products
PA: Qiagen N.V.
    Hulsterweg 82
    Venlo LI

(P-13058)
NATUREWARE INC
6590 Darin Way (90630-5121)
PHONE....................................714 251-4510
Eun Ah Shin, *CEO*
Han C Shin, *
EMP: 96 **EST:** 2006
SALES (est): 22.65MM **Privately Held**
SIC: 5122 Vitamins and minerals

(P-13059)
NEW MILANI GROUP LLC
Also Called: Milani Cosmetics
10000 Washington Blvd Ste 210
(90232-2782)
P.O. Box 58585 (90058-0585)
PHONE....................................323 582-9404
Mary Van Praag, *CEO*

Lindsay Shumlas, *CFO*
Evelyn Wang, *CMO*
▲ **EMP:** 93 **EST:** 2001
SQ FT: 11,893
SALES (est): 32.98MM **Privately Held**
Web: www.milanicosmetics.com
SIC: 5122 Cosmetics

(P-13060)
ONCOR CORP
Also Called: ONCOR CORP
13115 Barton Rd Ste G-H (90605-2762)
PHONE....................................562 944-0230
Danne King, *Brnch Mgr*
EMP: 19
Web: www.dannemking.com
SIC: 5122 2844 Toilet preparations; Perfumes, cosmetics and other toilet preparations
PA: Danne Montague-King Co
    10420 Pioneer Blvd
    Santa Fe Springs CA

(P-13061)
PAUL MITCHELL JOHN SYSTEMS (PA)
Also Called: Paul Mitchell
20705 Centre Pointe Pkwy (91350-2967)
P.O. Box 10597 (90213-3597)
PHONE....................................800 793-8790
John Paul Dejoria, *Ch Bd*
Michaeline Dejoria, *CEO*
◆ **EMP:** 80 **EST:** 1980
SQ FT: 90,000
SALES (est): 100.53MM
SALES (corp-wide): 100.53MM **Privately Held**
Web: www.paulmitchell.com
SIC: 5122 5999 Hair preparations; Hair care products

(P-13062)
PLATINUM PERFORMANCE INC (HQ)
90 Thomas Rd (93427-9657)
P.O. Box 990 (93427-0990)
PHONE....................................800 553-2400
Mark J Herthel, *Pr*
EMP: 27 **EST:** 1996
SQ FT: 7,000
SALES (est): 27.11MM
SALES (corp-wide): 8.08B **Publicly Held**
Web: www.platinumperformance.com
SIC: 5122 2023 Vitamins and minerals; Dietary supplements, dairy and non-dairy based
PA: Zoetis Inc.
    10 Sylvan Way Ste 100
    Parsippany NJ
    973 822-7000

(P-13063)
PPHM INC
Also Called: Avid Bioservices
14282 Franklin Ave (92780-7009)
PHONE....................................714 508-6100
Nicholas Green, *CEO*
Daniel Hart, *CFO*
Jeffrey Masten, *VP*
EMP: 100 **EST:** 2002
SALES (est): 40.96MM
SALES (corp-wide): 149.27MM **Publicly Held**
SIC: 5122 Pharmaceuticals
PA: Avid Bioservices, Inc.
    14191 Myford Rd
    Tustin CA
    714 508-6100

(P-13064)
PRIMAL ELEMENTS INC
Also Called: Primal Elements
18062 Redondo Cir (92648-1326)
PHONE....................................714 899-0757
▲ **EMP:** 99 **EST:** 1993
SQ FT: 56,500
SALES (est): 25.37MM **Privately Held**
Web: www.primalelements.com
SIC: 5122 2841 Cosmetics; Detergents, synthetic organic or inorganic alkaline

(P-13065)
QYK BRANDS LLC
12821 Western Ave (92841-4027)
PHONE....................................949 312-7119
EMP: 189 **EST:** 2017
SALES (est): 20.76MM **Privately Held**
Web: www.qyk.us
SIC: 5122 2842 3842 2023 Pharmaceuticals; Disinfectants, household or industrial plant; Respiratory protection equipment, personal; Dietary supplements, dairy and non-dairy based

(P-13066)
RUGBY LABORATORIES INC (DH)
311 Bonnie Cir (92878-5182)
PHONE....................................951 270-1400
David C Hsia Ph.d., *Pr*
Michael E Boser, *
Chato Abad, *
Frederick Wilkinson, *
Michel J Feldman, *
EMP: 90 **EST:** 1961
SALES (est): 92.61MM
SALES (corp-wide): 205.01B **Publicly Held**
SIC: 5122 2834 Pharmaceuticals; Pharmaceutical preparations
HQ: The Harvard Drug Group L L C
    341 Mason Rd
    La Vergne TN
    800 616-2471

(P-13067)
SCIENCE OF SKINCARE LLC
Also Called: Innovative Skin Care
3333 N San Fernando Blvd (91504-2531)
PHONE....................................818 254-7961
C Bryan Johns, *Managing Member*
Alec Call, *
◆ **EMP:** 84 **EST:** 2003
SQ FT: 36,000
SALES (est): 26.51MM **Privately Held**
Web: www.isclinical.com
SIC: 5122 Cosmetics

(P-13068)
SGII INC (PA)
Also Called: Senegence International
19651 Alter (92610-2507)
PHONE....................................949 521-6161
Joni Rogers Kante, *CEO*
Philippe Guerreau, *
Ben Kante, *
▲ **EMP:** 244 **EST:** 1997
SQ FT: 49,415
SALES (est): 89.75MM
SALES (corp-wide): 89.75MM **Privately Held**
Web: web.senegence.com
SIC: 5122 Cosmetics

(P-13069)
SOS BEAUTY INC
9100 Wilshire Blvd (90212-3415)
PHONE....................................424 285-1405
Dustin Cash, *CEO*

Charlene Valledor, *
EMP: 38 **EST:** 2017
SALES (est): 5.25MM **Privately Held**
Web: www.sosbty.com
SIC: 5122 3221 7389 3172 Cosmetics, perfumes, and hair products; Cosmetic jars, glass; Cosmetic kits, assembling and packaging; Cosmetic bags

(P-13070)
SPA DE SOLEIL INC
Also Called: Pharmaskincare
10443 Arminta St (91352-4109)
PHONE....................................818 504-3200
Rena Revivo, *CEO*
▲ **EMP:** 20 **EST:** 1994
SALES (est): 6MM **Privately Held**
Web: www.spadesoleil.com
SIC: 5122 2844 Cosmetics; Cosmetic preparations

(P-13071)
STAR NAIL PRODUCTS INC
Also Called: Star Nail International
29120 Avenue Paine (91355-5402)
PHONE....................................661 257-3376
Tony Cuccio, *CEO*
Elaine Watson, *
Christina Jahn, *
Anthony Cuccio, *
Roberta Cuccio, *
◆ **EMP:** 55 **EST:** 1982
SQ FT: 14,000
SALES (est): 11.65MM **Privately Held**
Web: www.starnail.com
SIC: 5122 2844 7231 Cosmetics; Perfumes, cosmetics and other toilet preparations; Beauty shops

(P-13072)
UNITE EUROTHERAPY INC
2870 Whiptail Loop Ste 100 (92010-6709)
PHONE....................................760 585-1800
Andrew Dale, *Pr*
Andrew Dale, *CEO*
Jerry Trombetta, *
▲ **EMP:** 80 **EST:** 2002
SALES (est): 23MM **Privately Held**
Web: www.unitehair.com
SIC: 5122 Hair preparations

(P-13073)
URBAN DECAY COSMETICS LLC
Also Called: Urban Decay
833 W 16th St (92663-2801)
PHONE....................................949 631-4504
▲ **EMP:** 370 **EST:** 2000
SALES (est): 5.57MM
SALES (corp-wide): 5.95B **Privately Held**
SIC: 5122 Cosmetics
PA: L'oreal
    Mugler Beaute
    Paris
    140206000

(P-13074)
VALLEY OF SUN COSMETICS LLC
Also Called: Valley of The Sun Labs
535 Patrice Pl (90248-4232)
PHONE....................................310 327-9062
Ajmal Shehzad, *
◆ **EMP:** 156 **EST:** 1994
SQ FT: 10,000
SALES (est): 22.79MM **Privately Held**
Web: www.hollywoodstyleusa.com
SIC: 5122 Cosmetics

(P-13075)
VIVA LIFE SCIENCE INC
350 Paularino Ave (92626-4616)
PHONE....................................949 645-6100
David Fan, *Pr*
EMP: 220 **EST:** 1987
SQ FT: 60,000
SALES (est): 2.43MM
SALES (corp-wide): 22.12MM **Privately Held**
Web: www.vivalife.com
SIC: 5122 2833 Vitamins and minerals; Medicinals and botanicals
PA: Westar Nutrition Corp.
350 Paularino Ave
Costa Mesa CA
949 645-6100

(P-13076)
WECKERLE COSMETICS USA INC
Also Called: Weckerle Cosmetic
525 Maple Ave (90503-3905)
PHONE....................................310 328-7000
Thomas Weckerle, *Pr*
Petra Webersberger, *
▲ **EMP:** 35 **EST:** 1979
SQ FT: 20,000
SALES (est): 24.79MM
SALES (corp-wide): 90.77MM **Privately Held**
Web: www.weckerle.com
SIC: 5122 5084 2844 Cosmetics; Packaging machinery and equipment; Lipsticks
PA: Weckerle Holding Gmbh
Holzhofstr. 26
Weilheim I. Ob BY
88192930

(P-13077)
WELLA OPERATIONS US LLC
4500 Park Granada Ste 100 (91302-1665)
PHONE....................................818 999-5112
Sennen Pamich, *Sr VP*
EMP: 500 **EST:** 2020
SALES (est): 106.83MM
SALES (corp-wide): 261.21MM **Privately Held**
SIC: 5122 Cosmetics, perfumes, and hair products
PA: Wella Germany Gmbh
Berliner Allee 65-65a
Darmstadt HE
61513020

5131 Piece Goods And Notions

(P-13078)
A W CHANG CORPORATION (PA)
Also Called: Excalibur International
6945 Atlantic Ave (90805-1415)
PHONE....................................310 764-2000
William Chang, *CEO*
Abraham K Chang, *
William Chang, *VP*
▲ **EMP:** 27 **EST:** 1989
SQ FT: 12,000
SALES (est): 27.29MM **Privately Held**
SIC: 5131 5632 2211 Silk piece goods, woven; Apparel accessories; Apparel and outerwear fabrics, cotton

(P-13079)
ALEXANDER HENRY FABRICS INC
1550 Flower St (91201-2356)
PHONE....................................818 562-8200

Marcus De Leon, *Pr*
Kim Dunn, *
EMP: 40 **EST:** 1992
SALES (est): 6.14MM **Privately Held**
Web: www.ahfabrics.com
SIC: 5131 2211 Cotton goods; Broadwoven fabric mills, cotton

(P-13080)
BLUE RIDGE HOME FASHIONS INC
15761 Tapia St (91706-2177)
PHONE....................................626 960-6069
◆ **EMP:** 39 **EST:** 1994
SALES (est): 12.49MM **Privately Held**
Web: www.blueridgehome.com
SIC: 5131 3999 2392 Textiles, woven, nec; Feathers and feather products; Blankets, comforters and beddings

(P-13081)
CHARMING TRIM & PACKAGING
5889 Rickenbacker Rd (90040-3027)
PHONE....................................415 302-7021
Richard Ringeisen, *Pr*
Barry Chan, *
EMP: 1000 **EST:** 2011
SALES (est): 40.49MM **Privately Held**
Web: www.charmingtrim.com
SIC: 5131 3111 Trimmings, apparel; Garment leather

(P-13082)
J ROBERT SCOTT INC (PA)
722 N La Cienega Blvd (90069-5086)
▲ **EMP:** 120 **EST:** 1972
SALES (est): 24.19MM
SALES (corp-wide): 24.19MM **Privately Held**
Web: www.jrobertscott.com
SIC: 5131 2512 2511 Textiles, woven, nec; Upholstered household furniture; Wood household furniture

(P-13083)
L & R DISTRIBUTORS INC
9292 9th St (91730-4407)
PHONE....................................909 980-3807
EMP: 266
SALES (corp-wide): 465.97MM **Privately Held**
Web: www.lrdist.com
SIC: 5131 Notions, nec
PA: L. & R. Distributors, Inc.
88 35th St Ste 4
Brooklyn NY
718 272-2100

(P-13084)
M M FAB INC
Also Called: South Seas Imports
2300 E Gladwick St (90220-6208)
PHONE....................................310 763-3800
Richard Friedman, *Prin*
▲ **EMP:** 85 **EST:** 1988
SQ FT: 110,000
SALES (est): 14.94MM **Privately Held**
Web: www.southseasimports.com
SIC: 5131 Textiles, woven, nec

(P-13085)
MATRIX INTERNATIONAL TEX INC
Also Called: Matrix
1363 S Bonnie Beach Pl (90023-4001)
P.O. Box 23484 (90023-0409)
PHONE....................................323 582-9100
Kourosh Neman, *Prin*
Kourosh Neman, *CEO*

Chris Neman, *
Kevin Neman, *
Simin Neman, *
◆ **EMP:** 28 **EST:** 1997
SQ FT: 60,000
SALES (est): 8.66MM **Privately Held**
Web: www.matrixtextiles.com
SIC: 5131 2299 Broadwoven fabrics; Apparel filling: cotton waste, kapok, and related material

(P-13086)
MOMENTUM TEXTILES LLC (PA)
Also Called: Momentum Textiles Wallcovering
17811 Fitch (92614-6001)
PHONE....................................949 833-8886
David Krakoff, *CEO*
Joanne Corrao, *
◆ **EMP:** 40 **EST:** 1987
SQ FT: 20,000
SALES (est): 99.65MM
SALES (corp-wide): 99.65MM **Privately Held**
Web: www.momentumtextilesandwalls.com
SIC: 5131 2221 Upholstery fabrics, woven; Broadwoven fabric mills, manmade

(P-13087)
MORGAN FABRICS CORPORATION (PA)
Also Called: Morgan Fabrics
4265 Exchange Ave (90058-2604)
P.O. Box 58523 (90058-0523)
PHONE....................................323 583-9981
Arnold Gittelson, *Ch*
Michael Gittelson, *Pr*
Robert Gittelson, *VP*
Ken Yang, *CFO*
◆ **EMP:** 60 **EST:** 1956
SQ FT: 50,000
SALES (est): 23.53MM
SALES (corp-wide): 23.53MM **Privately Held**
Web: www.morgan-fabrics.com
SIC: 5131 2759 Textiles, woven, nec; Commercial printing, nec

(P-13088)
PHOENIX TEXTILE INC (PA)
Also Called: Level 99
14600 S Broadway (90248-1812)
PHONE....................................310 715-7090
Dominic Poon, *Pr*
Joseph Tse, *Treas*
◆ **EMP:** 87 **EST:** 1984
SQ FT: 39,000
SALES (est): 23.57MM
SALES (corp-wide): 23.57MM **Privately Held**
Web: www.phoenixla.com
SIC: 5131 7389 Textiles, woven, nec; Sewing contractor

(P-13089)
PINDLER & PINDLER INC (PA)
Also Called: Pindler
11910 Poindexter Ave (93021-1748)
P.O. Box 8007 (93020-8007)
PHONE....................................805 531-9090
Curt R Pindler, *Pr*
S L Crawford Junior, *Ex VP*
Barbara Bick, *
▲ **EMP:** 95 **EST:** 1939
SQ FT: 75,000
SALES (est): 46.18MM
SALES (corp-wide): 46.18MM **Privately Held**
Web: www.pindler.com

SIC: 5131 Drapery material, woven

(P-13090)
RADIX TEXTILE INC
Also Called: Radix
600 E Washington Blvd Ste C2 (90015-3739)
PHONE....................................323 234-1667
Arad Shemirani, *CEO*
▲ **EMP:** 99 **EST:** 2007
SALES (est): 9.27MM **Privately Held**
SIC: 5131 2211 Piece goods and other fabrics; Broadwoven fabric mills, cotton

(P-13091)
RDMM LEGACY INC
Also Called: Fabri Cote
724 E 60th St (90001-1013)
P.O. Box 1856 (90001-0856)
PHONE....................................323 232-2147
▲ **EMP:** 30 **EST:** 1957
SALES (est): 4.78MM **Privately Held**
Web: www.fabricote.com
SIC: 5131 2295 Coated fabrics; Coated fabrics, not rubberized

(P-13092)
ROMEX TEXTILES INC (PA)
1430 Griffith Ave (90021-2127)
PHONE....................................213 749-9090
Shawn Binafard, *CEO*
▲ **EMP:** 39 **EST:** 1993
SALES (est): 17.35MM **Privately Held**
Web: www.romextex.com
SIC: 5131 2211 Textiles, woven, nec; Apparel and outerwear fabrics, cotton

(P-13093)
SO TECH/SPCL OP TECH INC (PA)
Also Called: Special Operations Tech
206 Star Of India Ln (90746-1418)
PHONE....................................310 202-9007
James W Cragg V, *Pr*
▲ **EMP:** 32 **EST:** 1997
SQ FT: 12,000
SALES (est): 9.63MM
SALES (corp-wide): 9.63MM **Privately Held**
Web: www.sotechtactical.com
SIC: 5131 2396 Nylon piece goods, woven; Apparel findings and trimmings

(P-13094)
SOFTLINE HOME FASHIONS INC
13130 S Normandie Ave (90249-2128)
PHONE....................................310 630-4848
Jason Carr, *Pr*
Jason Carr, *CEO*
Rodney Carr, *Pr*
◆ **EMP:** 20 **EST:** 2000
SALES (est): 4.84MM **Privately Held**
Web: www.softlinehome.com
SIC: 5131 2391 Piece goods and other fabrics; Curtains and draperies

(P-13095)
SPECIALTY TEXTILE SERVICES LLC
1333 30th St Ste A (92154-3484)
PHONE....................................619 476-8750
Mark Wilstine, *Mgr*
EMP: 155
Web: www.specialtytextileservices.com
SIC: 5131 Textiles, woven, nec
PA: Specialty Textile Services Llc
737 W Buchanan St
Phoenix AZ

P
R
O
D
U
C
T
S

&

S
V
C
S

(P-13096)
STEVEN LABEL CORPORATION (PA)
11926 Burke St (90670-2546)
P.O. Box 3688 (90670-1688)
PHONE..............................562 698-9971
EMP: 119 **EST:** 1954
SALES (est): 25.1MM
SALES (corp-wide): 25.1MM **Privately Held**
Web: www.stevenlabel.com
SIC: 5131 3643 Labels; Electric switches

(P-13097)
TALON INTERNATIONAL INC (PA)
21900 Burbank Blvd Ste 101 (91367-6469)
PHONE..............................818 444-4100
Mark Dyne, *Ch Bd*
Larry Dyne, *Interim Chief Financial Officer*
Daniel Ryu, *CSO*
Gary Dyne, *Executive Global Sales Vice President*
Peter Vaz, *Area Vice President*
EMP: 96 **EST:** 1997
SALES (est): 48.88MM **Privately Held**
Web: www.taloninternational.com
SIC: 5131 3965 Sewing supplies and notions ; Zipper

5136 Men's And Boy's Clothing

(P-13098)
BLACK BOX INC
371 2nd St Ste 1 (92024-3524)
PHONE..............................760 804-3300
▲ **EMP:** 100
SIC: 5136 5137 Men's and boy's clothing; Women's and children's clothing

(P-13099)
CHEF WORKS INC (PA)
12325 Kerran St # A (92064-6801)
PHONE..............................858 643-5600
Neil R Gross, *CEO*
Joshua C Gross, *Pr*
David Roth, *COO*
David Forster, *CFO*
▲ **EMP:** 137 **EST:** 1994
SQ FT: 50,000
SALES (est): 113.26MM **Privately Held**
Web: www.chefworks.com
SIC: 5136 5137 Uniforms, men's and boys'; Uniforms, women's and children's

(P-13100)
COLOSSEUM ATHLETICS CORP
Also Called: Colosseum Athletics
2400 S Wilmington Ave (90220-5403)
PHONE..............................310 667-8341
Stuart Whang, *CEO*
◆ **EMP:** 85 **EST:** 1992
SQ FT: 64,227
SALES (est): 36.14MM **Privately Held**
Web: www.colosseumusa.com
SIC: 5136 5137 Sportswear, men's and boys' ; Sportswear, women's and children's

(P-13101)
ELIEL & CO
Also Called: Eliel Cycling
2215 La Mirada Dr (92081-8828)
PHONE..............................760 877-8469
Ryan Eliel Cady, *CEO*
EMP: 23 **EST:** 2014
SALES (est): 4.43MM **Privately Held**
Web: www.elielcycling.com

SIC: 5136 2389 Sportswear, men's and boys' ; Men's miscellaneous accessories

(P-13102)
FASHION WORLD INCORPORATED
Also Called: Bijan
420 N Rodeo Dr (90210-4502)
PHONE..............................310 273-6544
Manigeh Messa, *Mgr*
EMP: 128
SALES (corp-wide): 4.71MM **Privately Held**
SIC: 5136 Men's and boy's clothing
PA: Fashion World, Incorporated
421 N Rodeo Dr Ph
Beverly Hills CA
310 273-6544

(P-13103)
FORIA INTERNATIONAL INC
18689 Arenth Ave (91748-1302)
PHONE..............................626 912-8836
◆ **EMP:** 111
Web: www.foria.com
SIC: 5136 Men's and boy's clothing

(P-13104)
HELMET HOUSE LLC (PA)
Also Called: Tour Master
26855 Malibu Hills Rd (91301-5100)
PHONE..............................800 421-7247
Robert M Miller, *CEO*
Philip Bellomy, *
Randy Hutchings, *
◆ **EMP:** 84 **EST:** 1969
SQ FT: 80,000
SALES (est): 40.34MM
SALES (corp-wide): 40.34MM **Privately Held**
Web: www.helmethouse.com
SIC: 5136 3949 3751 Men's and boy's clothing; Helmets, athletic; Motorcycle accessories

(P-13105)
HYBRID PROMOTIONS LLC (PA)
Also Called: Hybrid Promotions
10700 Valley View St (90630-4835)
PHONE..............................714 952-3866
William Scott Hutchison, *CEO*
Faith Garcia-ross, *COO*
Ed Massura Csco, *Prin*
◆ **EMP:** 135 **EST:** 1999
SALES (est): 252.15MM
SALES (corp-wide): 252.15MM **Privately Held**
Web: www.hybridapparel.com
SIC: 5136 5137 5611 Sportswear, men's and boys'; Women's and children's clothing; Men's and boys' clothing stores

(P-13106)
MICHAEL GERALD LTD
Also Called: Mgl
1852 Carnegie Ave (92705-5545)
PHONE..............................562 921-9611
Gerald D Barnes, *CEO*
▲ **EMP:** 23 **EST:** 1983
SALES (est): 4.91MM **Privately Held**
SIC: 5136 2329 3999 Sweaters, men's and boys'; Men's and boys' sportswear and athletic clothing; Atomizers, toiletry

(P-13107)
MOUNTAIN GEAR CORPORATION
Also Called: Tri-Mountain
4889 4th St (91706-2194)

PHONE..............................626 851-2488
Daniel Tsai, *CEO*
Rosie Tsai, *
▲ **EMP:** 125 **EST:** 1994
SQ FT: 300,000
SALES (est): 21.76MM **Privately Held**
Web: www.trimountain.com
SIC: 5136 Sportswear, men's and boys'

(P-13108)
PRANA LIVING LLC (HQ)
Also Called: Prana
3209 Lionshead Ave (92010-4710)
PHONE..............................866 915-6457
Monica Mirro, *Pr*
▲ **EMP:** 89 **EST:** 1992
SALES (est): 27.64MM
SALES (corp-wide): 3.46B **Publicly Held**
Web: www.prana.com
SIC: 5136 5137 Men's and boy's clothing; Women's and children's clothing
PA: Columbia Sportswear Company
14375 Nw Science Park Dr
Portland OR
503 985-4000

(P-13109)
QUAKE CITY CASUALS INC
Also Called: Quake City Caps
1800 S Flower St (90015-3424)
PHONE..............................213 746-0540
John Glucksman, *CEO*
▲ **EMP:** 125 **EST:** 1977
SQ FT: 11,500
SALES (est): 20.32MM **Privately Held**
Web: www.capstoneheadwear.com
SIC: 5136 Men's and boy's clothing

(P-13110)
SAYARI SHAHRZAD
Also Called: Blue Bay Industries
4822 Aqueduct Ave (91436-1621)
PHONE..............................310 903-6368
Shahrzad Sayari, *Owner*
EMP: 25 **EST:** 2017
SALES (est): 1.69MM **Privately Held**
SIC: 5136 2339 2329 5651 Men's and boys' sportswear and work clothing; Women's and misses' athletic clothing and sportswear ; Ski and snow clothing: men's and boys'; Unisex clothing stores

(P-13111)
SPORTEK INTERNATIONAL INC
Also Called: Sport Tek
2425 S Eastern Ave (90040-1414)
PHONE..............................213 239-6700
Joseph Hanasabzadeh, *Pr*
Manouchehr Satirian, *VP*
Ben Hanasabzadeh, *CEO*
◆ **EMP:** 18 **EST:** 2003
SQ FT: 50,000
SALES (est): 5.69MM **Privately Held**
Web: www.sportek.com
SIC: 5136 5137 2254 Sportswear, men's and boys'; Sportswear, women's and children's; Underwear, knit

(P-13112)
STR WORLDWIDE INC
Also Called: Silver Star Distribution
17462 Von Karman Ave (92614-6206)
PHONE..............................949 276-5990
Luke Burrett, *Pr*
▲ **EMP:** 5035 **EST:** 1991
SQ FT: 2,000
SALES (est): 5.43MM **Privately Held**
SIC: 5136 Sportswear, men's and boys'
PA: Authentic Brands Group Llc
1411 Broadway Fl 4

New York NY

(P-13113)
STUSSY INC
Also Called: Stussy
17426 Daimler St (92614-5514)
PHONE..............................949 474-9255
Frank Sinatra, *CEO*
▲ **EMP:** 90 **EST:** 1985
SQ FT: 30,000
SALES (est): 60.88MM **Privately Held**
Web: www.stussy.com
SIC: 5136 Men's and boy's clothing

(P-13114)
TEE TOP OF CALIFORNIA INC (PA)
Also Called: Procelebrity
11801 Goldring Rd (91006-5880)
PHONE..............................626 303-1868
Herbert Huang, *CEO*
Frances Huang, *Treas*
Balentina Huang, *VP Sls*
▲ **EMP:** 20 **EST:** 1977
SQ FT: 2,000
SALES (est): 4.47MM
SALES (corp-wide): 4.47MM **Privately Held**
Web: www.goprocelebrity.com
SIC: 5136 2396 2395 Shirts, men's and boys' ; Automotive and apparel trimmings; Pleating and stitching

(P-13115)
TRLGGC SERVICES LLC
1888 Rosecrans Ave (90266-3712)
PHONE..............................323 266-3072
EMP: 256 **EST:** 2015
SALES (est): 1.49MM
SALES (corp-wide): 350MM **Privately Held**
SIC: 5136 5137 Work clothing, men's and boys'; Women's and children's dresses, suits, skirts, and blouses
HQ: True Religion Sales, Llc
500 W 190th St Ste 300
Gardena CA

(P-13116)
UNI HOSIERY CO INC (PA)
1911 E Olympic Blvd (90021-2421)
PHONE..............................213 228-0100
Harry Hayog Chung, *CEO*
◆ **EMP:** 120 **EST:** 1988
SQ FT: 500,000
SALES (est): 24.55MM
SALES (corp-wide): 24.55MM **Privately Held**
Web: www.unihosiery.com
SIC: 5136 5137 Hosiery, men's and boys'; Hosiery: women's, children's, and infants'

(P-13117)
VANTAGE CUSTOM CLASSICS INC
Also Called: Vantage Apparel
3321 S Susan St (92704-6858)
PHONE..............................714 755-1133
Patty Venny, *Mgr*
EMP: 117
SALES (corp-wide): 45.64MM **Privately Held**
Web: www.vantageapparel.com
SIC: 5136 2397 2395 Sportswear, men's and boys'; Schiffli machine embroideries; Pleating and stitching
PA: Vantage Custom Classics, Inc.
100 Vantage Dr
Avenel NJ
732 340-3000

▲ = Import ▼ = Export
◆ = Import/Export

5137 Women's And Children's Clothing

(P-13118)
ALSTYLE AP & ACTIVEWEAR MGT CO (HQ)
1501 E Cerritos Ave (92805-6400)
PHONE.....................714 765-0400
Rauf Gajiani, *CEO*
Amin Amdani, *
◆ **EMP:** 1800 **EST:** 2001
SQ FT: 715,000
SALES (est): 447.65MM
SALES (corp-wide): 3.24B **Privately Held**
SIC: 5137 Women's and children's clothing
PA: Les Vetements De Sport Gildan Inc
  600 Boul De Maisonneuve O 33eme
  Etage
  Montreal QC
  514 735-2023

(P-13119)
BP CLOTHING LLC
Also Called: Baby Phat
3424 Garfield Ave (90040-3104)
▲ **EMP:** 150
SIC: 5137 Women's and children's clothing

(P-13120)
CALIFORNIA RAIN COMPANY INC
Also Called: California Rain
1213 E 14th St (90021-2215)
PHONE.....................213 623-6061
Jack Jhy C Jang, *Pr*
◆ **EMP:** 90 **EST:** 1986
SQ FT: 8,600
SALES (est): 15.82MM **Privately Held**
Web: www.californiarainla.com
SIC: 5137 5136 5699 Sportswear, women's
  and children's; Sportswear, men's and boys'
  ; Customized clothing and apparel

(P-13121)
DAMO TEXTILE INC
Also Called: Damo Clothing Company
12121 Wilshire Blvd Ste 1120 (90025-1164)
PHONE.....................213 741-1323
James Min, *CEO*
Paul Eeahn, *
Edwin Min, *
▲ **EMP:** 40 **EST:** 1999
SALES (est): 9.24MM **Privately Held**
Web: www.damoclothing.com
SIC: 5137 3999 Women's and children's
  clothing; Atomizers, toiletry

(P-13122)
DC SHOES INC
Also Called: Quiksilver/Dc Shoes
11310 Cantu Galleano Ranch Rd
(91752-3717)
PHONE.....................951 361-7712
EMP: 36
Web: www.dcshoes.com
SIC: 5137 5136 5139 2329 Women's and
  children's clothing; Men's and boy's clothing
  ; Footwear; Men's and boys' sportswear
  and athletic clothing
HQ: Dc Shoes, Inc.
  5600 Argosy Ave Ste 100
  Huntington Beach CA

(P-13123)
DELTA GALIL USA INC
Also Called: Loomworks Apparel
16912 Von Karman Ave (92606-4972)
PHONE.....................949 296-0380

EMP: 247
Web: www.deltagalil.com
SIC: 5137 Women's and children's lingerie
  and undergarments
HQ: Delta Galil Usa Inc.
  1 Harmon Plz Fl 5
  Secaucus NJ
  201 902-0055

(P-13124)
EDGEMINE INC
Also Called: Mine
1801 E 50th St (90058-1940)
PHONE.....................323 267-8222
Kevin Chang Kang, *CEO*
Kristen Han, *Pr*
Sarah King, *VP*
Daniel Kang, *CFO*
▲ **EMP:** 130 **EST:** 1994
SQ FT: 200,000
SALES (est): 95MM **Privately Held**
Web: www.edgemine.com
SIC: 5137 5621 5961 Women's and
  children's clothing; Women's specialty
  clothing stores; Electronic shopping

(P-13125)
FIESTA FASHION CO INC (PA)
1100 Wall St Ste 106 (90015-2326)
PHONE.....................213 748-5775
Edward Kim, *Pr*
Peter Choi, *VP*
▲ **EMP:** 20 **EST:** 1996
SQ FT: 1,000
SALES (est): 10MM
SALES (corp-wide): 10MM **Privately Held**
Web: www.fiestafashionla.com
SIC: 5137 2339 Women's and children's
  clothing; Athletic clothing: women's,
  misses', and juniors'

(P-13126)
FLIRT INC
Also Called: Belldini
141 E Jefferson Blvd (90011-2330)
PHONE.....................213 748-4442
▲ **EMP:** 20
SIC: 5137 2339 Women's and children's
  sportswear and swimsuits; Sportswear,
  women's

(P-13127)
FOX HEAD INC (HQ)
Also Called: Fox Racing
16752 Armstrong Ave (92606-4912)
PHONE.....................949 757-9500
Jeff Mcguane, *CEO*
Tanya Fischesser, *
◆ **EMP:** 492 **EST:** 1974
SALES (est): 211.34MM
SALES (corp-wide): 3.08B **Publicly Held**
Web: www.foxracing.com
SIC: 5137 5699 5136 5961 Sportswear,
  women's and children's; Sports apparel;
  Sportswear, men's and boys'; Mail order
  house, nec
PA: Vista Outdoor Inc.
  1 Vista Way
  Anoka MN
  763 433-1000

(P-13128)
JOHNNY WAS LLC
395 Santa Monica Pl Ste 124 (90401-3477)
PHONE.....................310 656-0600
Eli Levite, *Brnch Mgr*
EMP: 98
SALES (corp-wide): 1.41B **Publicly Held**
Web: www.johnnywas.com

SIC: 5137 2339 Women's and children's
  clothing; Women's and misses' accessories
HQ: Johnny Was, Llc
  999 Peachtree St Ne # 688
  Atlanta GA
  323 582-1005

(P-13129)
KAREN KANE INC (PA)
2275 E 37th St (90058-1427)
PHONE.....................323 588-0000
Michael Kane, *CEO*
Lonnie Kane, *CFO*
Karen Kane, *Sec*
Cecelia Jenkins, *Treas*
▲ **EMP:** 130 **EST:** 1979
SQ FT: 96,000
SALES (est): 92.98MM
SALES (corp-wide): 92.98MM **Privately Held**
Web: www.karenkane.com
SIC: 5137 Women's and children's clothing

(P-13130)
LA DYE & PRINT INC
13416 Estrella Ave (90248-1513)
PHONE.....................310 327-3200
George Chaghouri, *CEO*
EMP: 35 **EST:** 2011
SQ FT: 1,800
SALES (est): 4.79MM **Privately Held**
Web: www.ladyeandprint.com
SIC: 5137 2269 Women's and children's
  dresses, suits, skirts, and blouses; Linen
  fabrics: dyeing, finishing, and printing

(P-13131)
LILY BLEU INC
Also Called: Jessie & Jenna
1406 W 178th St (90248-3202)
PHONE.....................310 225-2522
Michael Weis, *CEO*
Barbara Cambilargiu, *VP*
▲ **EMP:** 20 **EST:** 2002
SQ FT: 8,700
SALES (est): 4.82MM **Privately Held**
Web: www.leahzawadzki.com
SIC: 5137 2339 Women's and children's
  clothing; Sportswear, women's

(P-13132)
LOVIN ENTERPRISES INC
Also Called: Dreamgirl International
5548 Lindbergh Ln (90201-6410)
PHONE.....................323 268-0220
▲ **EMP:** 55 **EST:** 1978
SALES (est): 24.03MM **Privately Held**
Web: www.dreamgirldirect.com
SIC: 5137 2389 2329 Lingerie; Costumes;
  Athletic clothing, except uniforms: men's,
  youths' and boys'

(P-13133)
LYMI INC (PA)
Also Called: Reformation, The
2744 E 11th St (90023-3404)
PHONE.....................855 756-0560
Hali Borenstein, *CEO*
Jennifer Maclellan, *
Yael Alfalo, *
▲ **EMP:** 100 **EST:** 2013
SQ FT: 120,000
SALES (est): 272.4MM
SALES (corp-wide): 272.4MM **Privately Held**
Web: www.thereformation.com
SIC: 5137 Women's and children's clothing

(P-13134)
MAD ENGINE GLOBAL LLC
6740 Cobra Way Ste 100 (92121-4102)
PHONE.....................858 558-5270
EMP: 306 **EST:** 2020
SALES (est): 33.73MM **Privately Held**
SIC: 5137 Women's and children's clothing

(P-13135)
MARIKA GROUP INC
Also Called: Shiva-Shakthi
8960 Carroll Way (92121-2429)
PHONE.....................858 537-5300
Donald Schumacher, *Prin*
Donald Schumacher, *CEO*
Scott Kalman, *
Lew Corpuz, *
▲ **EMP:** 25 **EST:** 1983
SQ FT: 60,000
SALES (est): 1.04MM **Privately Held**
SIC: 5137 2339 Sportswear, women's and
  children's; Women's and misses' outerwear,
  nec

(P-13136)
MATESTA CORPORATION
5620 Knott Ave (90621-1808)
P.O. Box 5395 (90622-5395)
PHONE.....................949 874-6052
Salim Saeed, *CEO*
Robert Abraham, *CFO*
EMP: 106 **EST:** 2017
SALES (est): 62MM **Privately Held**
Web: www.matesta.com
SIC: 5137 5136 Women's and children's
  clothing; Men's and boy's clothing

(P-13137)
MIAS FASHION MFG CO INC
Also Called: California Basic
12623 Cisneros Ln (90670-3373)
PHONE.....................562 906-1060
Peter D Anh, *Pr*
Brian Song, *
◆ **EMP:** 252 **EST:** 1999
SALES (est): 83MM **Privately Held**
Web: www.miasfashion.com
SIC: 5137 Women's and children's clothing

(P-13138)
NEW PRIDE CORPORATION
Also Called: Belinda
5101 Pacific Blvd (90058-2217)
PHONE.....................323 584-6608
Miran Byun, *CEO*
Ho Lee, *Pr*
EMP: 55 **EST:** 2007
SQ FT: 5,000
SALES (est): 4.66MM **Privately Held**
SIC: 5137 2331 Women's and children's
  clothing; Women's and misses' blouses and
  shirts

(P-13139)
NHN GLOBAL INC (HQ)
Also Called: Fashiongo.com
2250 Maple Ave (90011-1190)
PHONE.....................424 672-1177
Daniel Lee, *CEO*
EMP: 109 **EST:** 2005
SALES (est): 50.67MM **Privately Held**
Web: www.nhnglobal.com
SIC: 5137 7389 Women's and children's
  clothing
PA: Nhn Corporation
  16 Daewangpangyo-Ro 645beon-Gil,
  Bundang-Gu
  Seongnam

PRODUCTS & SVCS

(P-13140)
NYDJ APPAREL LLC
Also Called: Not Your Daughters Jeans
5401 S Soto St (90058-3618)
PHONE..................................323 581-9040
Lisa Collier, *Pr*
Steve Brink, *
▲ **EMP:** 200 **EST:** 2003
SQ FT: 6,000
SALES (est): 44.59MM **Privately Held**
Web: www.nydj.com
SIC: 5137 Women's and children's clothing

(P-13141)
O & K INC (PA)
Also Called: One Clothing
2121 E 37th St (90058-1416)
PHONE..................................323 846-5700
Chang Ho Ok, *CEO*
Seongeun Kim, *
Chang Ho, *
▲ **EMP:** 134 **EST:** 1989
SQ FT: 55,000
SALES (est): 23.69MM **Privately Held**
Web: www.oneclothing.com
SIC: 5137 Women's and children's clothing

(P-13142)
PIEGE CO (PA)
Also Called: Buffalo
20120 Plummer St (91311-5448)
PHONE..................................818 727-9100
Kambiz Zarabi, *CEO*
Morad Zarabi, *
Michael Zarabi, *
Nara Estpanian, *
▲ **EMP:** 95 **EST:** 1981
SQ FT: 48,000
SALES (est): 41.83MM
SALES (corp-wide): 41.83MM **Privately Held**
Web: www.felina.com
SIC: 5137 5136 5632 Lingerie; Men's and boys' suits and trousers; Lingerie and corsets (underwear)

(P-13143)
PRINCESS CRUISE LINES LTD
1242 E 25th St (90011-1708)
PHONE..................................213 745-0314
Delcino Fernandez, *Brnch Mgr*
EMP: 165
SALES (corp-wide): 3.94B **Privately Held**
Web: www.princess.com
SIC: 5137 Infants' wear
HQ: Princess Cruise Lines, Ltd.
24305 Town Center Dr
Santa Clarita CA
661 753-0000

(P-13144)
RCRV INC (PA)
Also Called: Rock Revival
4715 S Alameda St (90058-2014)
PHONE..................................323 235-7300
Eric S Choi, *Pr*
Young S Cho, *
Kheim Nguyen, *Design Vice President**
◆ **EMP:** 23 **EST:** 2008
SQ FT: 70,000
SALES (est): 51.19MM
SALES (corp-wide): 51.19MM **Privately Held**
Web: www.rockrevival.com
SIC: 5137 2673 Women's and children's clothing; Garment and wardrobe bags, (plastic film)

(P-13145)
RUBY RIBBON INC
4607 Lakeview Canyon Rd Pmb 405 (91361)
PHONE..................................650 449-4470
▲ **EMP:** 25 **EST:** 2012
SALES (est): 2.7MM **Privately Held**
Web: www.rubyribbon.com
SIC: 5137 5632 5699 2254 Underwear: women's, children's, and infants'; Lingerie and corsets (underwear); Sports apparel; Shorts, shirts, slips, and panties (underwear): knit

(P-13146)
RUNWAY LIQUIDATION LLC (HQ)
2761 Fruitland Ave (90058-3607)
PHONE..................................323 589-2224
Martine Melloul, *
Brian Fleming, *
Bernd Kroeber, *
◆ **EMP:** 29 **EST:** 1989
SQ FT: 500,000
SALES (est): 254.75MM
SALES (corp-wide): 357.89MM **Privately Held**
SIC: 5137 5621 2335 Women's and children's clothing; Women's clothing stores ; Women's, junior's, and misses' dresses
PA: Marquee Brands Llc
330 W 34th St Fl 15
New York NY
212 203-8135

(P-13147)
SAME SWIM LLC
2333 E 49th St (90058-2820)
PHONE..................................323 582-2588
EMP: 90 **EST:** 2015
SALES (est): 4.07MM **Privately Held**
SIC: 5137 Women's and children's sportswear and swimsuits

(P-13148)
SEVEN LICENSING COMPANY LLC
Also Called: Seven7 Brands
801 S Figueroa St Ste 2500 (90017-5504)
PHONE..................................323 780-8250
▲ **EMP:** 102 **EST:** 2002
SALES (est): 38.76MM **Privately Held**
Web: www.sunrisebrands.com
SIC: 5137 Women's and children's accessories
PA: Sunrise Brands, Llc
801 S Figueroa St # 2500
Los Angeles CA

(P-13149)
SIGNAL PRODUCTS INC (PA)
Also Called: Signal Products/Guess Handbags
5600 W Adams Blvd Ste 200 (90016-2563)
PHONE..................................213 748-0990
▲ **EMP:** 90 **EST:** 1992
SALES (est): 21.8MM **Privately Held**
Web: www.signalbrands.com
SIC: 5137 Handbags

(P-13150)
SNOWMASS APPAREL INC (PA)
Also Called: County Clothing Company
15225 Alton Pkwy (92618-2354)
PHONE..................................949 788-0617
George Wong, *CEO*
Edmond Wong, *
Harry Yip, *
▲ **EMP:** 45 **EST:** 1984
SALES (est): 7.76MM
SALES (corp-wide): 7.76MM **Privately Held**

SIC: 5137 5136 2339 Women's and children's outerwear; Men's and boys' outerwear; Women's and misses' outerwear, nec

(P-13151)
STANCE INC (PA)
Also Called: Stance
197 Avenida La Pata (92673-6307)
PHONE..................................949 391-9030
John Wilson, *CEO*
Brian Shea, *
▲ **EMP:** 215 **EST:** 2009
SALES (est): 84.98MM
SALES (corp-wide): 84.98MM **Privately Held**
Web: www.stance.com
SIC: 5137 Women's and children's clothing

(P-13152)
SWATFAME INC (PA)
Also Called: Kut From The Kloth
16425 Gale Ave (91745-1722)
PHONE..................................626 961-7928
Mitchell Quaranta, *CEO*
Jonathan Greenberg, *
Brian Min, *
Bruce Stern, *
▲ **EMP:** 290 **EST:** 1978
SQ FT: 233,000
SALES (est): 88.04MM
SALES (corp-wide): 88.04MM **Privately Held**
Web: www.swatfame.com
SIC: 5137 2211 2339 Dresses; Denims; Women's and misses' outerwear, nec

(P-13153)
TARRANT APPAREL GROUP
Also Called: Fashion Resources
5401 S Soto St (90058-3618)
PHONE..................................323 780-8250
Gerard Guez, *Ch Bd*
Todd Kay, *
Peter Akaradian, *
▲ **EMP:** 94 **EST:** 1988
SALES (est): 14.26MM **Privately Held**
Web: www.sunrisebrands.com
SIC: 5137 Women's and children's clothing
PA: Sunrise Brands, Llc
5401 S Soto St
Vernon CA

(P-13154)
THE TIMING INC
Also Called: Timing Fashion
2807 S Santa Fe Ave (90058-1408)
PHONE..................................323 589-5577
Kevin Kim, *CEO*
Bowhan Kim, *
Alice Kang, *
◆ **EMP:** 40 **EST:** 1989
SALES (est): 9.88MM **Privately Held**
Web: www.timingfashion.com
SIC: 5137 2331 2335 2339 Women's and children's clothing; Women's and misses' blouses and shirts; Women's, junior's, and misses' dresses; Women's and misses' outerwear, nec

(P-13155)
TYR SPORT INC (HQ)
Also Called: T Y R
1790 Apollo Ct (90740-5617)
P.O. Box 1930 (92647-1930)
PHONE..................................714 897-0799
Matt Dilorenzo, *CEO*
◆ **EMP:** 17 **EST:** 1984
SQ FT: 80,000
SALES (est): 49.29MM

SALES (corp-wide): 49.29MM **Privately Held**
Web: www.tyr.com
SIC: 5137 5136 5091 2329 Sportswear, women's and children's; Beachwear, men's and boys'; Sporting and recreation goods; Bathing suits and swimwear: men's and boys'
PA: Swimwear Anywhere, Inc.
85 Sherwood Ave
Farmingdale NY
631 420-1400

(P-13156)
WALL STREET ALLEY T-SHIRT CO
4125 E Brundage Ln (93307-2387)
PHONE..................................661 324-6207
Dominic S Webby, *Pt*
Stella Webby, *Pt*
EMP: 29 **EST:** 1980
SQ FT: 4,400
SALES (est): 830.15K **Privately Held**
Web: www.wsimp.com
SIC: 5137 5136 2395 2331 Sportswear, women's and children's; Sportswear, men's and boys'; Emblems, embroidered; Women's and misses' blouses and shirts

5139 Footwear

(P-13157)
ACI INTERNATIONAL (PA)
844 Moraga Dr (90049-1632)
PHONE..................................310 889-3400
Steven Jackson, *CEO*
David Mankowitz, *
Anna Liau, *
▲ **EMP:** 80 **EST:** 1952
SQ FT: 40,000
SALES (est): 62.71MM
SALES (corp-wide): 62.71MM **Privately Held**
Web: www.acifootwear.com
SIC: 5139 3021 Shoes; Rubber and plastics footwear

(P-13158)
ASICS AMERICA CORPORATION (HQ)
Also Called: Asics Tiger
7755 Irvine Center Dr Ste 400 (92618-2904)
PHONE..................................949 453-8888
Gene Mccarthy, *Pr*
Seiho Gohashi, *
Kenji Sakai, *
◆ **EMP:** 109 **EST:** 1973
SALES (est): 882.54MM **Privately Held**
Web: www.asics.com
SIC: 5139 5136 5137 2369 Footwear, athletic ; Sportswear, men's and boys'; Sportswear, women's and children's; Girl's and children's outerwear, nec
PA: Asics Corporation
7-1-1, Minatojimanakamachi, Chuo-Ku
Kobe HYO

(P-13159)
AYLESVA INC
14537 Garfield Ave (90723-3425)
PHONE..................................562 688-0592
Jose Luis Solorcano, *Pr*
EMP: 120 **EST:** 2013
SALES (est): 4.55MM **Privately Held**
Web: aylesva-com-inc.hub.biz
SIC: 5139 5661 5651 5137 Shoes; Shoe stores; Family clothing stores; Coordinate sets: women's, children's, and infants'

(P-13160)
CAPE ROBBIN INC
1943 W Mission Blvd (91766-1037)
PHONE...................................626 810-8080
Michael Chen, *CEO*
▲ **EMP:** 50 **EST:** 2011
SQ FT: 20,000
SALES (est): 9.62MM **Privately Held**
Web: www.caperobbin.com
SIC: 5139 3171 Shoes; Handbags, women's

(P-13161)
CONVERSE INC
1437 3rd Street Promenade 39 (90401)
PHONE...................................310 451-0314
EMP: 89
SALES (corp-wide): 51.22B **Publicly Held**
Web: www.converse.com
SIC: 5139 5661 Footwear, athletic;
   Footwear, athletic
HQ: Converse Inc.
   1 Lovejoy Wharf
   Boston MA
   617 248-9530

(P-13162)
FORTUNE DYNAMIC INC
21923 Ferrero (91789-5210)
PHONE...................................909 979-8318
Carol Lee, *Pr*
James Lee, *
◆ **EMP:** 90 **EST:** 1986
SQ FT: 150,000
SALES (est): 19.78MM **Privately Held**
Web: www.fortunedynamic.com
SIC: 5139 Shoes

(P-13163)
OSATA ENTERPRISES INC
Also Called: Globe Shoes
18105 Bishop Ave (90746-4020)
PHONE...................................888 445-6237
Matthew Hill, *Pr*
Gary Valentine, *
▲ **EMP:** 100 **EST:** 1997
SQ FT: 30,000
SALES (est): 32.67MM **Privately Held**
SIC: 5139 Shoes
PA: Globe International Limited
   1 Fennell St
   Port Melbourne VIC

(P-13164)
PRIMA ROYALE ENTERPRISES LTD
Also Called: Prima Royale
150 S Los Robles Ave Ste 100
(91101-2456)
PHONE...................................626 960-8388
Ing Nan Yu, *CEO*
Harry K T Chow, *
Bobby Bruce Levy, *
◆ **EMP:** 22 **EST:** 1988
SQ FT: 55,000
SALES (est): 1.7MM **Privately Held**
SIC: 5139 3143 Shoes; Men's footwear,
   except athletic

(P-13165)
SKECHERS USA INC
Also Called: Skechers Factory Outlet 335
29800 Eucalyptus Ave (92555-6738)
PHONE...................................951 242-4307
Carlette Moore, *Mgr*
EMP: 23
Web: local.skechers.com
SIC: 5139 3021 Footwear; Shoes, rubber or
   plastic molded to fabric
PA: Skechers U.S.A., Inc.
   228 Manhattan Beach Blvd # 200

Manhattan Beach CA

(P-13166)
SOUTH CONE INC
Also Called: Reef
5935 Darwin Ct (92008-7302)
PHONE...................................760 431-2300
Mike Jensen, *CEO*
◆ **EMP:** 120 **EST:** 1984
SQ FT: 37,583
SALES (est): 26.68MM
SALES (corp-wide): 11.61B **Publicly Held**
Web: www.reef.com
SIC: 5139 3144 3143 Shoes; Women's
   footwear, except athletic; Men's footwear,
   except athletic
PA: V.F. Corporation
   1551 Wewatta St
   Denver CO
   720 778-4000

5141 Groceries, General Line

(P-13167)
ACOSTA INC
Also Called: Acosta Sales & Marketing
480 Apollo St Ste C (92821-3121)
PHONE...................................714 988-1500
Rick Nist, *Brnch Mgr*
EMP: 150
SALES (corp-wide): 1.88B **Privately Held**
Web: www.acosta.com
SIC: 5141 Food brokers
HQ: Acosta Remainco, Inc.
   6600 Corporate Ctr Pkwy
   Jacksonville FL
   904 281-9800

(P-13168)
ADVANTAGE-CROWN SLS & MKTG LLC (DH)
1400 S Douglass Rd Ste 200 (92806-6904)
P.O. Box 66010 (92816-6010)
PHONE...................................714 780-3000
Bob Vesley, *CFO*
▲ **EMP:** 1100 **EST:** 1995
SALES (est): 340.5MM
SALES (corp-wide): 4.71B **Publicly Held**
SIC: 5141 Food brokers
HQ: Advantage Sales & Marketing Llc
   15310 Barranca Pkwy # 100
   Irvine CA
   949 797-2900

(P-13169)
AFC DISTRIBUTION CORP
19205 S Laurel Park Rd (90220-6032)
PHONE...................................310 604-3630
Sadamu Taniguch, *CEO*
EMP: 250 **EST:** 2016
SALES (est): 89.31MM **Privately Held**
Web: www.afcsushi.com
SIC: 5141 Groceries, general line
PA: Zensho Holdings Co., Ltd.
   2-18-1, Konan
   Minato-Ku TKY

(P-13170)
AFC TRADING & WHOLESALE INC
Also Called: American Food Co
4738 Valley Blvd (90032-3834)
PHONE...................................323 223-7738
Jackson K H Wu, *Pr*
◆ **EMP:** 20 **EST:** 1985
SQ FT: 20,000
SALES (est): 4.92MM **Privately Held**
Web: www.afcsoyfoods.com

SIC: 5141 2099 Food brokers; Tofu, except
frozen desserts

(P-13171)
AMK FOODSERVICES INC
Also Called: Kaney Foods
830 Capitolio Way (93401-7122)
P.O. Box 1188 (93406-1188)
PHONE...................................805 544-7600
John P Kaney, *CEO*
EMP: 130 **EST:** 1988
SQ FT: 35,000
SALES (est): 25.36MM **Privately Held**
SIC: 5141 Food brokers

(P-13172)
ANSAR GALLERY INC
2505 El Camino Rd (92782)
PHONE...................................949 220-0000
Ali Akbar Feroozesh, *Prin*
Hussein Saadat, *
▲ **EMP:** 200 **EST:** 2013
SQ FT: 120,000
SALES (est): 36.44MM **Privately Held**
Web: www.ansargallery.us
SIC: 5141 Food brokers
PA: Ansar Gallery Llc Branch
   Office No M, Al-Ittihad Street-Ansar
   Mall, Al-Nahda
   Sharjah

(P-13173)
BROOKS RESTAURANT GROUP INC (PA)
Also Called: Dynaco Equipment Co
220 Five Cities Dr (93449-3004)
PHONE...................................559 485-8520
EMP: 35 **EST:** 1973
SALES (est): 23.06MM
SALES (corp-wide): 23.06MM **Privately Held**
SIC: 5141 5087 2011 5812 Groceries,
   general line; Restaurant supplies; Meat
   packing plants; Steak restaurant

(P-13174)
BUFFALO MARKET INC
Also Called: Buffalo Market
1439 N Highland Ave (90028-7622)
PHONE...................................650 337-0078
Adam Olejniczak, *CEO*
Charmaine Button, *
Sean Howell, *
EMP: 140 **EST:** 2019
SALES (est): 22MM **Privately Held**
Web: www.buffalomarket.com
SIC: 5141 Groceries, general line

(P-13175)
CANTON FOOD CO INC
750 S Alameda St (90021-1624)
PHONE...................................213 688-7707
Shiu Lit Kwan, *CEO*
Shui Lit Kwan, *
Cho W Kwan, *
Wai Kam Kwan, *
▲ **EMP:** 106 **EST:** 1979
SQ FT: 96,000
SALES (est): 29.65MM **Privately Held**
Web: www.cantonfoodco.com
SIC: 5141 5146 5411 5421 Food brokers;
   Seafoods; Grocery stores; Seafood markets

(P-13176)
CONCORD FOODS INC (HQ)
4601 E Guasti Rd (91761-8105)
PHONE...................................909 975-2000
Nick J Sciortino Junior, *Pr*
John Sciortino, *
Roy Sciortino, *

EMP: 89 **EST:** 1985
SQ FT: 67,000
SALES (est): 49.54MM
SALES (corp-wide): 76.32MM **Publicly Held**
Web: www.concordfoodsinc.com
SIC: 5141 Food brokers
PA: Sysco Corporation
   1390 Enclave Pkwy
   Houston TX
   281 584-1390

(P-13177)
DELIVERR INC
307 S Wilson Ave Apt 6 (91106-3238)
PHONE...................................213 534-8686
EMP: 415
SALES (corp-wide): 504.44MM **Privately Held**
Web: www.deliveer.com
SIC: 5141 Groceries, general line
HQ: Deliverr, Inc.
   110 Sutter St Fl 9
   San Francisco CA
   415 475-9175

(P-13178)
DPI SPECIALTY FOODS WEST INC (DH)
Also Called: Dpi Specialty Foods
601 S Rockefeller Ave (91761-7871)
PHONE...................................909 975-1019
John Jordan, *CEO*
Donna Robbins, *
James De Keyser, *
Larry Noble, *
Conor Crowley, *
◆ **EMP:** 102 **EST:** 1951
SQ FT: 250,000
SALES (est): 477.21MM
SALES (corp-wide): 2.4B **Privately Held**
Web: www.dpispecialtyfoods.com
SIC: 5141 Food brokers
HQ: Dpi Specialty Foods, Inc.
   601 S Rockefeller Ave
   Ontario CA

(P-13179)
DPI SPECIALTY FOODS WEST INC
Also Called: Dpi West
930 S Rockefeller Ave (91761-8149)
PHONE...................................909 975-1019
EMP: 233
SALES (corp-wide): 2.4B **Privately Held**
Web: www.dpispecialtyfoods.com
SIC: 5141 Food brokers
HQ: Dpi Specialty Foods West, Inc.
   601 S Rockefeller Ave
   Ontario CA
   909 975-1019

(P-13180)
FOOD SALES WEST INC
235 Baker St (92626-4504)
P.O. Box 19738 (92623-9738)
PHONE...................................714 966-2900
David Lyons, *CEO*
Carl Scharffenberger, *
Mary Ellen Scharffenberger, *
Robert Watkins, *
Michael Berkson, *
EMP: 85 **EST:** 1973
SQ FT: 12,000
SALES (est): 18.88MM **Privately Held**
SIC: 5141 Food brokers

PRODUCTS & SVCS

(P-13181)
FOOTHILL PACKING INC
2255 S Broadway (93454-7871)
PHONE...............................805 925-7900
Jorge Rivera, *Pr*
EMP: 489
SALES (corp-wide): 46.83MM **Privately Held**
Web: www.foothillpacking.com
SIC: 5141 Food brokers
PA: Foothill Packing, Inc.
1582 Moffett St
Salinas CA
831 784-1453

(P-13182)
GOURMET FOODS INC (PA)
2910 E Harcourt St (90221-5502)
PHONE...............................310 632-3300
Marcel Lagnaz, *Managing Member*
Mitch Rosen, *Managing Member*
◆ **EMP:** 81 **EST:** 1986
SQ FT: 35,000
SALES (est): 48.76MM
SALES (corp-wide): 48.76MM **Privately Held**
Web: www.gourmetfoodsinc.com
SIC: 5141 5812 2099 Food brokers; Eating places; Food preparations, nec

(P-13183)
GRAND SUPERCENTER INC
8550 Chetle Ave Ste B (90606-2662)
PHONE...............................562 318-3451
Ilyeon Kwon, *CEO*
EMP: 90
SALES (corp-wide): 485.87MM **Privately Held**
SIC: 5141 5499 Groceries, general line; Juices, fruit or vegetable
HQ: Grand Supercenter Inc.
300 Chubb Ave
Lyndhurst NJ
201 507-9900

(P-13184)
ICPK CORPORATION
Also Called: Hpp Food Services
1130 W C St (90744-5102)
PHONE...............................310 830-8020
EMP: 70
SALES (corp-wide): 17.78MM **Privately Held**
Web: www.hppfs.com
SIC: 5141 2035 Groceries, general line; Dressings, salad: raw and cooked (except dry mixes)
PA: Icpk Corporation
16700 Valley View Ave # 170
La Mirada CA
714 321-7025

(P-13185)
MARQUEZ BROTHERS ENTPS INC
15480 Valley Blvd (91746-3325)
PHONE...............................626 330-3310
Gustavo Marquez, *Pr*
Juan Marquez, *
Jaime Marquez, *
◆ **EMP:** 200 **EST:** 1993
SQ FT: 200,000
SALES (est): 22.87MM **Privately Held**
SIC: 5141 Food brokers

(P-13186)
MCLANE FOODSERVICE INC
Also Called: McLane Riverside
14813 Meridian Pkwy (92518-3004)
PHONE...............................951 867-3727

Eric Polk, *Brnch Mgr*
EMP: 205
SALES (corp-wide): 302.09B **Publicly Held**
Web: www.mclaneco.com
SIC: 5141 Food brokers
HQ: Mclane Foodservice, Inc.
4747 Mclane Pkwy
Temple TX
254 771-7500

(P-13187)
MERCADO LATINO INC (PA)
245 Baldwin Park Blvd (91746-1404)
P.O. Box 6168 (91734-6168)
PHONE...............................626 333-6862
Roberto Rodriguez, *CEO*
Richard Rodriguez, *
Jorge Rodriguez, *
Angelita Rodriguez, *
◆ **EMP:** 100 **EST:** 1963
SQ FT: 105,000
SALES (est): 87.08MM
SALES (corp-wide): 87.08MM **Privately Held**
Web: www.mercadolatinoinc.com
SIC: 5141 5148 Food brokers; Fresh fruits and vegetables

(P-13188)
NONGSHIM AMERICA INC (HQ)
Also Called: Nongshim
12155 6th St (91730-6115)
PHONE...............................909 481-3698
Dong Y Shin, *CEO*
Joon Park, *
Jongmin Chung, *
Chris Gepford, *
◆ **EMP:** 250 **EST:** 1994
SALES (est): 83.03MM **Privately Held**
Web: www.nongshimusa.com
SIC: 5141 2098 Food brokers; Noodles (e.g. egg, plain, and water), dry
PA: Nongshim Co., Ltd.
112 Yeouidaebang-Ro, Dongjak-Gu
Seoul

(P-13189)
OTASTY FOODS INC
160 S Hacienda Blvd (91745-1101)
PHONE...............................626 330-1229
Ming Chao Huang, *Pr*
Ken Chen, *
◆ **EMP:** 91 **EST:** 1994
SQ FT: 58,000
SALES (est): 27.82MM **Privately Held**
Web: www.otastyfoods.com
SIC: 5141 Food brokers

(P-13190)
PALISADES RANCH INC
Also Called: Goldberg and Solovy Foods Inc
5925 Alcoa Ave (90058-3920)
PHONE...............................323 581-6161
Paul Paget, *CEO*
Earl Goldberg, *Pr*
EMP: 285 **EST:** 1974
SQ FT: 70,000
SALES (est): 93.67MM
SALES (corp-wide): 76.32MM **Publicly Held**
Web: www.gsfoods.com
SIC: 5141 5149 5046 5169 Food brokers; Groceries and related products, nec; Restaurant equipment and supplies, nec; Chemicals and allied products, nec
PA: Sysco Corporation
1390 Enclave Pkwy
Houston TX
281 584-1390

(P-13191)
PIVEG INC
3525 Del Mar Heights Rd Ste 1069 (92130-2199)
PHONE...............................858 436-3070
Roberto L Espinoza, *CEO*
▲ **EMP:** 220 **EST:** 2004
SALES (est): 57.3MM **Privately Held**
Web: www.piveg.com
SIC: 5141 Food brokers

(P-13192)
PREMIER FOOD SERVICES INC
14359 Amargosa Rd Ste F (92392-2334)
PHONE...............................760 843-8000
David Lopez, *Brnch Mgr*
EMP: 515
SALES (corp-wide): 422MM **Privately Held**
Web: www.premierfoodservices.com
SIC: 5141 Groceries, general line
HQ: Premier Food Services, Inc.
9500 Gilman Dr
La Jolla CA

(P-13193)
REAL MEX FOODS INC
Also Called: El Torito Franchising Company
5660 Katella Ave Ste 200 (90630-5059)
PHONE...............................714 523-0031
EMP: 100
SIC: 5141 5182 5087 2099 Food brokers; Wine and distilled beverages; Restaurant supplies; Food preparations, nec

(P-13194)
SMART & FINAL STORES INC
Also Called: SMART & FINAL STORES, INC.
1308 W Edinger Ave (92704-4306)
PHONE...............................714 549-2362
EMP: 325
SALES (corp-wide): 4.74B **Privately Held**
SIC: 5141 Groceries, general line
HQ: Smart Stores Operations Llc
600 Citadel Dr
Commerce CA
323 869-7500

(P-13195)
SMART & FINAL STORES INC
Also Called: SMART & FINAL STORES, INC.
26911 Trabuco Rd (92691-3506)
PHONE...............................949 581-1212
EMP: 325
SALES (corp-wide): 4.74B **Privately Held**
SIC: 5141 Groceries, general line
HQ: Smart Stores Operations Llc
600 Citadel Dr
Commerce CA
323 869-7500

(P-13196)
SMART & FINAL STORES INC
Also Called: SMART & FINAL STORES, INC.
13346 Limonite Ave (92880-3360)
PHONE...............................909 773-1813
EMP: 217
SALES (corp-wide): 4.74B **Privately Held**
SIC: 5141 Groceries, general line
HQ: Smart Stores Operations Llc
600 Citadel Dr
Commerce CA
323 869-7500

(P-13197)
SMART & FINAL STORES INC
Also Called: SMART & FINAL STORES, INC.
2121 Spring St (93446-1455)
PHONE...............................805 237-0323

EMP: 325
SALES (corp-wide): 4.74B **Privately Held**
SIC: 5141 Groceries, general line
HQ: Smart Stores Operations Llc
600 Citadel Dr
Commerce CA
323 869-7500

(P-13198)
SMART & FINAL STORES INC
Also Called: SMART & FINAL STORES, INC.
850 Linden Ave (93013-2043)
PHONE...............................805 566-2174
EMP: 325
SALES (corp-wide): 4.74B **Privately Held**
SIC: 5141 Groceries, general line
HQ: Smart Stores Operations Llc
600 Citadel Dr
Commerce CA
323 869-7500

(P-13199)
SMART & FINAL STORES INC
Also Called: SMART & FINAL STORES, INC.
9870 N Magnolia Ave (92071-1901)
PHONE...............................619 449-2396
EMP: 325
SALES (corp-wide): 4.74B **Privately Held**
SIC: 5141 Groceries, general line
HQ: Smart Stores Operations Llc
600 Citadel Dr
Commerce CA
323 869-7500

(P-13200)
SMART & FINAL STORES INC
Also Called: SMART & FINAL STORES, INC.
150 B Ave (92118-1511)
PHONE...............................619 522-2014
EMP: 217
SALES (corp-wide): 4.74B **Privately Held**
SIC: 5141 Groceries, general line
HQ: Smart Stores Operations Llc
600 Citadel Dr
Commerce CA
323 869-7500

(P-13201)
SMART & FINAL STORES INC
Also Called: SMART & FINAL STORES, INC.
13439 Camino Canada (92021-8811)
PHONE...............................619 390-1738
EMP: 325
SALES (corp-wide): 4.74B **Privately Held**
SIC: 5141 Groceries, general line
HQ: Smart Stores Operations Llc
600 Citadel Dr
Commerce CA
323 869-7500

(P-13202)
SMART & FINAL STORES INC
Also Called: SMART & FINAL STORES, INC.
1845 W Vista Way (92083-6119)
PHONE...............................760 732-1480
EMP: 325
SALES (corp-wide): 4.74B **Privately Held**
SIC: 5141 Groceries, general line
HQ: Smart Stores Operations Llc
600 Citadel Dr
Commerce CA
323 869-7500

(P-13203)
SMART & FINAL STORES INC
Also Called: SMART & FINAL STORES, INC.
955 Carlsbad Village Dr (92008-1802)
PHONE...............................760 434-2449
EMP: 217
SALES (corp-wide): 4.74B **Privately Held**

SIC: 5141 Groceries, general line
HQ: Smart Stores Operations Llc
600 Citadel Dr
Commerce CA
323 869-7500

(P-13204)
SMART & FINAL STORES INC
Also Called: SMART & FINAL STORES, INC.
933 Sweetwater Rd (91977-4837)
PHONE..............................619 668-9039
EMP: 325
SALES (corp-wide): 4.74B Privately Held
SIC: 5141 Groceries, general line
HQ: Smart Stores Operations Llc
600 Citadel Dr
Commerce CA
323 869-7500

(P-13205)
SMART & FINAL STORES INC
Also Called: SMART & FINAL STORES, INC.
2235 University Ave (92104-2717)
PHONE..............................619 291-1842
EMP: 325
SALES (corp-wide): 4.74B Privately Held
SIC: 5141 Groceries, general line
HQ: Smart Stores Operations Llc
600 Citadel Dr
Commerce CA
323 869-7500

(P-13206)
SMART & FINAL STORES INC
Also Called: SMART & FINAL STORES, INC.
2800 Fletcher Pkwy (92020-2111)
PHONE..............................619 589-7000
EMP: 325
SALES (corp-wide): 4.74B Privately Held
SIC: 5141 Groceries, general line
HQ: Smart Stores Operations Llc
600 Citadel Dr
Commerce CA
323 869-7500

(P-13207)
SMART & FINAL STORES INC
Also Called: SMART & FINAL STORES, INC.
10740 Westview Pkwy (92126-2962)
PHONE..............................858 578-7343
EMP: 325
SALES (corp-wide): 4.74B Privately Held
SIC: 5141 Groceries, general line
HQ: Smart Stores Operations Llc
600 Citadel Dr
Commerce CA
323 869-7500

(P-13208)
SMART & FINAL STORES INC
Also Called: SMART & FINAL STORES, INC.
5770 Lindero Canyon Rd (91362-4088)
PHONE..............................818 889-8253
EMP: 217
SALES (corp-wide): 4.74B Privately Held
SIC: 5141 Groceries, general line
HQ: Smart Stores Operations Llc
600 Citadel Dr
Commerce CA
323 869-7500

(P-13209)
SMART & FINAL STORES INC
Also Called: SMART & FINAL STORES, INC.
7800 Telegraph Rd (93004-1503)
PHONE..............................805 647-4276
Brian Gillman, *Brnch Mgr*
EMP: 325
SALES (corp-wide): 4.74B Privately Held

SIC: 5141 Groceries, general line
HQ: Smart Stores Operations Llc
600 Citadel Dr
Commerce CA
323 869-7500

(P-13210)
SMART & FINAL STORES INC
Also Called: SMART & FINAL STORES, INC.
5135 E Los Angeles Ave (93063-3431)
PHONE..............................805 520-6035
EMP: 217
SALES (corp-wide): 4.74B Privately Held
SIC: 5141 Groceries, general line
HQ: Smart Stores Operations Llc
600 Citadel Dr
Commerce CA
323 869-7500

(P-13211)
SMART & FINAL STORES INC
Also Called: SMART & FINAL STORES, INC.
4550 W Pico Blvd (90019-4257)
PHONE..............................323 549-9586
EMP: 217
SALES (corp-wide): 4.74B Privately Held
SIC: 5141 Groceries, general line
HQ: Smart Stores Operations Llc
600 Citadel Dr
Commerce CA
323 869-7500

(P-13212)
SMART & FINAL STORES INC
Also Called: SMART & FINAL STORES, INC.
1005 W Arrow Hwy (91773-2422)
PHONE..............................909 592-2190
EMP: 325
SALES (corp-wide): 4.74B Privately Held
SIC: 5141 Groceries, general line
HQ: Smart Stores Operations Llc
600 Citadel Dr
Commerce CA
323 869-7500

(P-13213)
SMART & FINAL STORES INC
Also Called: SMART & FINAL STORES, INC.
15427 Amar Rd (91744-2803)
PHONE..............................626 330-2495
Robert Terry, *Brnch Mgr*
EMP: 325
SALES (corp-wide): 4.74B Privately Held
SIC: 5141 Groceries, general line
HQ: Smart Stores Operations Llc
600 Citadel Dr
Commerce CA
323 869-7500

(P-13214)
SMART & FINAL STORES INC
Also Called: SMART & FINAL STORES, INC.
18555 Devonshire St (91324-1308)
PHONE..............................818 368-6409
Marie Teolis, *Brnch Mgr*
EMP: 325
SALES (corp-wide): 4.74B Privately Held
SIC: 5141 Groceries, general line
HQ: Smart Stores Operations Llc
600 Citadel Dr
Commerce CA
323 869-7500

(P-13215)
SMART & FINAL STORES INC
Also Called: SMART & FINAL STORES, INC.
644 Redondo Ave (90814-1453)
PHONE..............................562 438-0450
EMP: 217
SALES (corp-wide): 4.74B Privately Held

SIC: 5141 Groceries, general line
HQ: Smart Stores Operations Llc
600 Citadel Dr
Commerce CA
323 869-7500

(P-13216)
SMART & FINAL STORES INC
Also Called: SMART & FINAL STORES, INC.
615 N Pacific Coast Hwy (90277-2107)
PHONE..............................323 497-8528
EMP: 325
SALES (corp-wide): 4.74B Privately Held
SIC: 5141 Groceries, general line
HQ: Smart Stores Operations Llc
600 Citadel Dr
Commerce CA
323 869-7500

(P-13217)
SMART & FINAL STORES INC
Also Called: SMART & FINAL STORES, INC.
240 S Diamond Bar Blvd (91765-1605)
PHONE..............................323 855-8434
EMP: 217
SALES (corp-wide): 4.74B Privately Held
SIC: 5141 Groceries, general line
HQ: Smart Stores Operations Llc
600 Citadel Dr
Commerce CA
323 869-7500

(P-13218)
SMART & FINAL STORES INC
Also Called: SMART & FINAL STORES, INC.
3830 W Verdugo Ave (91505-3441)
PHONE..............................818 954-8631
EMP: 217
SALES (corp-wide): 4.74B Privately Held
SIC: 5141 Groceries, general line
HQ: Smart Stores Operations Llc
600 Citadel Dr
Commerce CA
323 869-7500

(P-13219)
SMART & FINAL STORES INC
Also Called: SMART & FINAL STORES, INC.
5038 W Avenue N (93551-5729)
PHONE..............................661 722-6210
Danny Omada, *Brnch Mgr*
EMP: 325
SALES (corp-wide): 4.74B Privately Held
SIC: 5141 Groceries, general line
HQ: Smart Stores Operations Llc
600 Citadel Dr
Commerce CA
323 869-7500

(P-13220)
SMART & FINAL STORES INC
Also Called: SMART & FINAL STORES, INC.
13003 Whittier Blvd (90602-3046)
PHONE..............................562 907-7037
David Hirs, *Brnch Mgr*
EMP: 325
SALES (corp-wide): 4.74B Privately Held
SIC: 5141 Groceries, general line
HQ: Smart Stores Operations Llc
600 Citadel Dr
Commerce CA
323 869-7500

(P-13221)
SMART & FINAL STORES INC
Also Called: SMART & FINAL STORES, INC.
303 E Foothill Blvd (91702-2516)
PHONE..............................626 334-5189
EMP: 217
SALES (corp-wide): 4.74B Privately Held

(P-13222)
SMART & FINAL STORES LLC
Also Called: Smart & Final
10113 Venice Blvd (90034-5809)
PHONE..............................310 559-1722
Eddie Preciado, *Mgr*
EMP: 121
SQ FT: 19,886
SIC: 5141 Groceries, general line
HQ: Smart & Final Stores Llc
600 Citadel Dr
Commerce CA

(P-13223)
SMART & FINAL STORES LLC
Also Called: Smart & Final
939 N Western Ave (90029-3246)
PHONE..............................323 466-9289
Joe Simmons, *Mgr*
EMP: 96
SQ FT: 30,381
SIC: 5141 Groceries, general line
HQ: Smart & Final Stores Llc
600 Citadel Dr
Commerce CA

(P-13224)
SMART & FINAL STORES LLC
Also Called: Smart & Final 341
1125 E El Segundo Blvd (90059-3101)
PHONE..............................323 569-7148
Rodney Peete, *Mgr*
EMP: 96
SIC: 5141 Groceries, general line
HQ: Smart & Final Stores Llc
600 Citadel Dr
Commerce CA

(P-13225)
SMART & FINAL STORES LLC
Also Called: Smart & Final
12210 Santa Monica Blvd (90025-2518)
PHONE..............................310 207-8688
Jerry Miyamoto, *Mgr*
EMP: 217
SQ FT: 18,263
SIC: 5141 Groceries, general line
HQ: Smart & Final Stores Llc
600 Citadel Dr
Commerce CA

(P-13226)
SMART & FINAL STORES LLC
Also Called: Smart & Final
2308 E 4th St (90033-4306)
PHONE..............................323 268-9179
Juan Garcia, *Mgr*
EMP: 133
SQ FT: 11,648
SIC: 5141 Groceries, general line
HQ: Smart & Final Stores Llc
600 Citadel Dr
Commerce CA

(P-13227)
SMART & FINAL STORES LLC
1216 Compton Ave (90021-2331)
PHONE..............................213 747-6697
Lisa Mesias, *Mgr*
EMP: 97
SQ FT: 14,160
SIC: 5141 Groceries, general line
HQ: Smart & Final Stores Llc
600 Citadel Dr

PRODUCTS & SVCS

Commerce CA

(P-13228)
SMART & FINAL STORES LLC (DH)
Also Called: Smart & Final
600 Citadel Dr (90040-1562)
PHONE....................323 869-7500
David G Hirz, *Pr*
EMP: 97 **EST:** 1991
SALES (est): 1.53B **Privately Held**
SIC: 5141 Groceries, general line
HQ: Chedraui Usa, Inc.
600 Citadel Dr
Commerce CA
323 869-7500

(P-13229)
SMART STORES OPERATIONS LLC (DH)
Also Called: Smart & Final
600 Citadel Dr (90040-1562)
PHONE....................323 869-7500
David B Kaplan, *Ch Bd*
David G Hirz, *Pr*
Richard N Phegley, *
Leland P Smith, *
Edward Wong, *Senior Vice President Supply Chain**
EMP: 447 **EST:** 1900
SQ FT: 81,000
SALES (est): 4.74B
SALES (corp-wide): 4.74B **Privately Held**
SIC: 5141 Groceries, general line
HQ: Smart & Final Holdings, Inc.
600 Citadel Dr
Commerce CA
800 894-0511

(P-13230)
SMART STORES OPERATIONS LLC
12339 Poway Rd (92064-4218)
PHONE....................858 748-0101
EMP: 217
SALES (corp-wide): 4.74B **Privately Held**
SIC: 5141 Groceries, general line
HQ: Smart Stores Operations Llc
600 Citadel Dr
Commerce CA
323 869-7500

(P-13231)
SOUTHWEST TRADERS INCORPORATED (PA)
Also Called: Swt Stockton
27565 Diaz Rd (92590-3411)
PHONE....................951 699-7800
Ken Smith, *CEO*
Lynne Bredemeier, *
▲ **EMP:** 180 **EST:** 1977
SQ FT: 130,000
SALES (est): 398.79MM
SALES (corp-wide): 398.79MM **Privately Held**
Web: www.southwesttraders.com
SIC: 5141 Food brokers

(P-13232)
SYGMA NETWORK INC
Also Called: Sygma
46905 47th St W (93536-8527)
PHONE....................661 723-0405
Mike Wren, *Brnch Mgr*
EMP: 162
SALES (corp-wide): 76.32MM **Publicly Held**
Web: www.sygmanetwork.com
SIC: 5141 Food brokers

HQ: The Sygma Network Inc
5550 Blazer Pkwy Ste 300
Dublin OH

(P-13233)
SYSCO LOS ANGELES INC
Also Called: Sysco
20701 Currier Rd (91789-2904)
PHONE....................909 595-9595
TOLL FREE: 800
Daniel S Haag, *CEO*
John Kao, *Sr VP*
Sal Adelberg, *
◆ **EMP:** 1000 **EST:** 1988
SALES (est): 305.77MM
SALES (corp-wide): 76.32MM **Publicly Held**
Web: www.sysco.com
SIC: 5141 5084 Groceries, general line; Food industry machinery
PA: Sysco Corporation
1390 Enclave Pkwy
Houston TX
281 584-1390

(P-13234)
SYSCO RIVERSIDE INC
15750 Meridian Pkwy (92518-3001)
PHONE....................951 601-5300
Saul Adelsberg, *CEO*
EMP: 375 **EST:** 2009
SALES (est): 198.23MM
SALES (corp-wide): 76.32MM **Publicly Held**
Web: www.sysco-riverside.com
SIC: 5141 5142 5143 5144 Food brokers; Packaged frozen goods; Dairy products, except dried or canned; Poultry and poultry products
PA: Sysco Corporation
1390 Enclave Pkwy
Houston TX
281 584-1390

(P-13235)
SYSCO SAN DIEGO INC
Also Called: Sysco
12180 Kirkham Rd (92064-6879)
PHONE....................858 513-7300
Kevin Mangan, *CEO*
Debra Morey, *
◆ **EMP:** 370 **EST:** 1996
SQ FT: 250,000
SALES (est): 204.66MM
SALES (corp-wide): 76.32MM **Publicly Held**
Web: www.sysco.com
SIC: 5141 5142 5147 5148 Food brokers; Packaged frozen goods; Meats and meat products; Fresh fruits and vegetables
PA: Sysco Corporation
1390 Enclave Pkwy
Houston TX
281 584-1390

(P-13236)
SYSCO VENTURA INC
Also Called: Sysco
3100 Sturgis Rd (93030-7276)
PHONE....................805 205-7000
Jerry L Barash, *Pr*
Manny Fernandez, *
Bill Delaney, *
Brian Beach, *
Twila Day, *
EMP: 300 **EST:** 2003
SQ FT: 370,000
SALES (est): 105.14MM
SALES (corp-wide): 76.32MM **Publicly Held**
Web: www.sysco.com

SIC: 5141 Food brokers
PA: Sysco Corporation
1390 Enclave Pkwy
Houston TX
281 584-1390

(P-13237)
TAPIA ENTERPRISES INC (PA)
Also Called: Tapia Brothers Co
6067 District Blvd (90270-3560)
PHONE....................323 560-7415
Raul Tapia, *CEO*
Francisco Tapia, *Treas*
Ramon Tapia, *Sec*
▲ **EMP:** 95 **EST:** 1985
SQ FT: 40,000
SALES (est): 86.67MM
SALES (corp-wide): 86.67MM **Privately Held**
Web: www.tapiabrothers.com
SIC: 5141 Groceries, general line

(P-13238)
UNION SUP COMSY SOLUTIONS INC
2301 E Pacifica Pl (90220-6210)
PHONE....................785 357-5005
Guy Steele, *CFO*
Kyle Deere, *
EMP: 325 **EST:** 2012
SALES (est): 53.74MM **Publicly Held**
Web: www.unionsupply.com
SIC: 5141 5661 2252 Food brokers; Footwear, athletic; Men's, boys', and girls' hosiery
HQ: Union Supply Group, Inc.
2500 Regent Blvd Ste 100
Dallas TX

(P-13239)
US FOODS INC
15155 Northam St (90638-5754)
P.O. Box 29283 (85038-9283)
PHONE....................714 670-3500
EMP: 172
Web: www.usfoods.com
SIC: 5141 5046 3556 2099 Food brokers; Commercial equipment, nec; Food products machinery; Food preparations, nec
HQ: Us Foods, Inc.
9399 W Higgins Rd # 100
Rosemont IL

(P-13240)
VIELE & SONS INC (PA)
Also Called: Viele & Sons Instnl Groc
1820 E Valencia Dr (92831-4847)
PHONE....................714 447-3663
TOLL FREE: 800
Anthony J Viele, *Pr*
Anthony Viele Junior, *VP*
Mike Viele, *VP*
Joseph Viele, *Treas*
Frances Viele, *Sec*
EMP: 90 **EST:** 1958
SQ FT: 95,000
SALES (est): 48.93MM
SALES (corp-wide): 48.93MM **Privately Held**
Web: www.vieleandsons.com
SIC: 5141 Food brokers

(P-13241)
VITCO DISTRIBUTORS INC
Also Called: Vitco Food Service
715 E California St (91761-1814)
PHONE....................909 355-1300
Kostas Vitakis, *Pr*
Emmanuel Vitakis, *
EMP: 199 **EST:** 2001

SQ FT: 20,000
SALES (est): 98.58MM **Privately Held**
Web: www.vitcofoods.com
SIC: 5141 Food brokers

(P-13242)
WISMETTAC ASIAN FOODS INC (HQ)
Also Called: Wismettac Fresh Fish
13409 Orden Dr (90670-6336)
PHONE....................562 802-1900
Yoshiro Susaki, *Ch*
Yuji Sasa, *
Hiroyuki Shinkai, *
Toshiyuki Nishikawa, *
◆ **EMP:** 200 **EST:** 1960
SQ FT: 225,000
SALES (est): 496.09MM **Privately Held**
Web: www.wismettacusa.com
SIC: 5141 Groceries, general line
PA: Nishimoto Co., Ltd.
3-2-1, Nihombashimuromachi
Chuo-Ku TKY

5142 Packaged Frozen Goods

(P-13243)
CONTESSA LIQUIDATING CO INC
222 W 6th St Fl 8 (90731-3345)
P.O. Box 1950 (90733-1950)
◆ **EMP:** 113
SIC: 5142 5146 Packaged frozen goods; Seafoods

(P-13244)
CONTESSA PREMIUM FOODS INC
5980 Alcoa Ave (90058-3925)
PHONE....................310 832-8000
EMP: 250
SIC: 5142 5146 Packaged frozen goods; Fish and seafoods

(P-13245)
EL PRIMO FOODS INC
608 Monterey Pass Rd (91754-2419)
PHONE....................626 289-5054
EMP: 225
SIC: 5142 Packaged frozen goods

(P-13246)
GOLDEN WEST TRADING INC
Also Called: Royal Poultry
4401 S Downey Rd (90058-2518)
P.O. Box 58161 (90058-0161)
PHONE....................323 581-3663
Erik Litmanovich, *CEO*
Tony Cimolino, *
Levi Litmanovich, *
Josh Solovy, *
Zack Levenson, *
▲ **EMP:** 180 **EST:** 1992
SQ FT: 40,000
SALES (est): 205.16MM
SALES (corp-wide): 452.76MM **Privately Held**
Web: www.gwfg.com
SIC: 5142 Meat, frozen: packaged
PA: Golden West Food Group, Inc.
4401 S Downey Rd
Vernon CA
888 807-3663

(P-13247)
JON-LIN FROZEN FOODS (PA)
Also Called: Jon-Lin Foods
1620 N 8th St (92324-1302)

PHONE.....................909 825-8542
Russell H Burch, *Pr*
Mary Kate Burch, *Sec*
Joseph Burch, *VP*
Jan Burch, *Treas*
EMP: 85 **EST:** 1962
SALES (est): 20.26MM
SALES (corp-wide): 20.26MM **Privately Held**
SIC: 5142 Packaged frozen goods

(P-13248)
MARIE CLLENDER WHOLESALERS INC
170 E Rincon St (92879-1327)
PHONE.....................951 737-6760
Phillip Ratner, *Pr*
Gerald Tanaka, *
Kurt Schweickhart, *
EMP: 4031 **EST:** 1968
SQ FT: 28,000
SALES (est): 22.84MM
SALES (corp-wide): 421.81MM **Privately Held**
SIC: 5142 Bakery products, frozen
HQ: Castle Harlan Partners Iii Lp
150 E 58th St Fl 38
New York NY
212 644-8600

(P-13249)
WEI-CHUAN USA INC (PA)
13031 Temple Ave (91746-1418)
PHONE.....................626 225-7168
Steve Lin, *Pr*
William Huang, *Treas*
Benny Chang, *Sec*
◆ **EMP:** 120 **EST:** 1972
SQ FT: 38,000
SALES (est): 92.64MM
SALES (corp-wide): 92.64MM **Privately Held**
Web: www.weichuanusa.com
SIC: 5142 2038 Packaged frozen goods;
Dinners, frozen and packaged

(P-13250)
WEST PICO FOODS INC
5201 S Downey Rd (90058-3703)
P.O. Box 58107 (90058-0107)
PHONE.....................323 586-9050
Elias Naghi, *Pr*
Don Lubitz, *
▲ **EMP:** 125 **EST:** 1969
SQ FT: 42,000
SALES (est): 34.78MM **Privately Held**
Web: www.westpicofoods.com
SIC: 5142 5144 Packaged frozen goods;
Poultry: live, dressed or frozen
(unpackaged)

5143 Dairy Products, Except Dried Or Canned

(P-13251)
CACIQUE DISTRIBUTORS US
Also Called: Cacique
14923 Proctor Ave (91746-3206)
P.O. Box 1047 (91017-1047)
PHONE.....................626 961-3399
EMP: 240
SIC: 5143 Cheese

(P-13252)
CACIQUE FOODS LLC
Also Called: Cacique
14923 Proctor Ave (91746-3206)
P.O. Box 1047 (91017-1047)
PHONE.....................626 961-3399

EMP: 240
SALES (corp-wide): 129.03MM **Privately Held**
Web: www.caciquefoods.com
SIC: 5143 Cheese
PA: Cacique Foods Llc
1410 Westridge Cir N
Irving TX
626 961-3399

(P-13253)
CLEMSON DISTRIBUTION INC (PA)
20722 Currier Rd (91789-2903)
PHONE.....................909 595-2770
Rolando T Santos, *Pr*
Emeline Santos, *
▲ **EMP:** 23 **EST:** 1994
SQ FT: 32,000
SALES (est): 48.49MM
SALES (corp-wide): 48.49MM **Privately Held**
Web: www.clemsondistribution.com
SIC: 5143 2013 Ice cream and ices;
Prepared beef products, from purchased beef

(P-13254)
DFA DAIRY BRANDS FLUID LLC
17851 Railroad St (91748-1118)
PHONE.....................800 395-7004
EMP: 326
SALES (corp-wide): 24.52B **Privately Held**
Web: www.dfamilk.com
SIC: 5143 Dairy products, except dried or canned
HQ: Dfa Dairy Brands Fluid, Llc
1405 N 98th St
Kansas City KS
816 801-6455

(P-13255)
LOS ALTOS FOOD PRODUCTS LLC
Also Called: Los Altos
450 Baldwin Park Blvd (91746-1407)
PHONE.....................626 330-6555
Raul Andrade, *Pr*
Raul Andrade, *Pr*
Gloria Andrade, *
EMP: 105 **EST:** 1988
SQ FT: 38,000
SALES (est): 91.8MM **Privately Held**
Web: www.losaltosfoods.com
SIC: 5143 Cheese

(P-13256)
MCCONNELLS FINE ICE CREAMS LLC
800 Del Norte Blvd (93030-8971)
PHONE.....................805 963-8813
Briana Gray, *Managing Member*
Charlie Price, *Managing Member*
Michael Palmer, *Managing Member*
Eva Ein, *Managing Member*
EMP: 38 **EST:** 2011
SQ FT: 184,000
SALES (est): 20.28MM **Privately Held**
Web: www.mcconnells.com
SIC: 5143 2024 Ice cream and ices; Ice cream, bulk

(P-13257)
NESTLE ICE CREAM COMPANY
7301 District Blvd (93313-2042)
PHONE.....................661 398-3500
James L Dintaman, *CEO*
▲ **EMP:** 1920 **EST:** 1993
SALES (est): 396.25K **Privately Held**

SIC: 5143 5451 Ice cream and ices; Ice cream (packaged)
HQ: Nestle Usa, Inc.
1812 N Moore St
Arlington VA
703 682-4600

5144 Poultry And Poultry Products

(P-13258)
HIDDEN VILLA RANCH PRODUCE INC (HQ)
Also Called: Hidden Villa Ranch
310 N Harbor Blvd Ste 205 (92832-1954)
P.O. Box 34001 (92834-9411)
PHONE.....................714 680-3447
Tim E Luberski, *Pr*
Don Lawson, *
Greg Schneider, *
Michael Sencer, *
Robert J Kelly Bob, *Ex VP*
◆ **EMP:** 270 **EST:** 1995
SQ FT: 21,619
SALES (est): 410MM
SALES (corp-wide): 410MM **Privately Held**
Web: www.hiddenvilla.com
SIC: 5144 Eggs
PA: Luberski, Inc.
310 N Harbor Blvd Ste 205
Fullerton CA
714 680-3447

(P-13259)
INTERSTATE FOODS INC
310 S Long Beach Blvd (90221-3400)
PHONE.....................310 635-2442
Carlos Velasco, *CEO*
EMP: 145 **EST:** 1999
SQ FT: 13,000
SALES (est): 42.59MM **Privately Held**
SIC: 5144 Poultry products, nec

(P-13260)
ROGERS POULTRY CO (PA)
5050 S Santa Fe Ave (90058-2124)
PHONE.....................323 585-0802
TOLL FREE: 800
George V Saffarrans, *CEO*
John C Butler, *
EMP: 100 **EST:** 1979
SQ FT: 15,000
SALES (est): 40.15MM
SALES (corp-wide): 40.15MM **Privately Held**
Web: www.rogerspoultry.com
SIC: 5144 Poultry products, nec

(P-13261)
ROGERS POULTRY CO
2020 E 67th St (90001-2169)
PHONE.....................800 585-0802
John C Butler, *COO*
EMP: 80
SALES (corp-wide): 40.15MM **Privately Held**
Web: www.rogerspoultry.com
SIC: 5144 Poultry products, nec
PA: Roger's Poultry Co.
5050 S Santa Fe Ave
Vernon CA
323 585-0802

5145 Confectionery

(P-13262)
AMERICAN NUTS LLC (HQ)
12950 San Fernando Rd (91342-3601)
PHONE.....................818 364-8855
Jim Duatte, *Pr*
Aamir Chinoy, *CFO*
Karrie Brooks Ctrl, *Prin*
EMP: 138 **EST:** 2018
SALES (est): 64.78MM
SALES (corp-wide): 132.47MM **Privately Held**
Web: www.americannuts.com
SIC: 5145 2034 Nuts, salted or roasted;
Dried and dehydrated fruits
PA: Gauge Capital Llc
1256 Main St Ste 256
Southlake TX
682 334-5800

(P-13263)
B B G MANAGEMENT GROUP (PA)
Also Called: Granlund Candies
12164 California St (92399-4333)
PHONE.....................909 797-9581
R Scott Burkle, *Pr*
Margie Rogan, *
EMP: 50 **EST:** 1961
SQ FT: 10,000
SALES (est): 9.48MM
SALES (corp-wide): 9.48MM **Privately Held**
SIC: 5145 2064 Candy; Candy and other confectionery products

(P-13264)
BALANCE FOODS INC
5743 Smithway St Ste 103 (90040-1548)
PHONE.....................323 838-5555
Florencia Cuetara, *CEO*
Theia D Ainlle Esq, *Sr VP*
EMP: 38 **EST:** 2014
SALES (est): 9.07MM **Privately Held**
Web: www.balancefoods.net
SIC: 5145 2096 Snack foods; Potato chips and similar snacks

(P-13265)
CANTEEN VENDING - SAN DIEGO
Also Called: Rainbow Vending & Distributing
5515 Market St (92114-2218)
PHONE.....................619 527-1900
Greg Karron, *Pr*
Greg Carron, *
Don Martin, *
EMP: 1790 **EST:** 1968
SQ FT: 10,300
SALES (est): 9.28MM
SALES (corp-wide): 29.97B **Privately Held**
Web: www.canteensd.com
SIC: 5145 5149 5962 Snack foods; Soft drinks; Candy and snack food vending machines
HQ: Compass Group Usa, Inc.
2400 Yorkmont Rd
Charlotte NC

(P-13266)
CENTURY SNACKS LLC
5560 E Slauson Ave (90040-2921)
PHONE.....................323 278-9578
Valerie Oswalt, *CEO*
David Lowe, *Ch*
Tiffany Obenchain, *VP*
Mel Deane, *Vice Chairman*
Stephen Famolaro, *CFO*

EMP: 330 **EST:** 1999
SQ FT: 280,000
SALES (est): 102.08MM
SALES (corp-wide): 177.61MM **Privately Held**
Web: www.centurysnacks.com
SIC: 5145 2064 Nuts, salted or roasted; Nuts, candy covered
HQ: Scncs, Llc
5560 E Slauson Ave
Commerce CA
323 278-9578

(P-13267)
CONSOLIDATED SVC DISTRS INC
Also Called: Jacks Candy
777 S Central Ave (90021-1507)
PHONE..............................908 687-5800
Steven Simon, *Pr*
Herbert Lefkowitz, *
Mark Leskowitz, *
Bill German, *
▲ **EMP:** 85 **EST:** 1937
SALES (est): 23.93MM **Privately Held**
Web: www.jackscandy.com
SIC: 5145 5194 Candy; Tobacco and tobacco products

(P-13268)
ENERGY CLUB INC
Also Called: Energy Club
12950 Pierce St (91331-2526)
▲ **EMP:** 80 **EST:** 1984
SALES (est): 25.51MM
SALES (corp-wide): 25.51MM **Privately Held**
SIC: 5145 2099 Confectionery; Food preparations, nec
PA: Shackleton Equity Partners Llc
4119 Guardian St
Simi Valley CA
310 733-5658

(P-13269)
FRITO-LAY NORTH AMERICA INC
Also Called: Frito-Lay
28801 Highway 58 (93314-9584)
PHONE..............................661 328-6034
Jason Audler, *Mgr*
EMP: 245
SALES (corp-wide): 86.39B **Publicly Held**
Web: www.fritolay.com
SIC: 5145 Snack foods
HQ: Frito-Lay North America, Inc.
7701 Legacy Dr
Plano TX

(P-13270)
FRITO-LAY NORTH AMERICA INC
Also Called: Frito-Lay
1500 Francisco St (90501-1329)
PHONE..............................310 224-5600
Dexter Matt, *Genl Mgr*
EMP: 30
SQ FT: 75,861
SALES (corp-wide): 86.39B **Publicly Held**
Web: www.fritolay.com
SIC: 5145 2099 2096 Snack foods; Food preparations, nec; Potato chips and similar snacks
HQ: Frito-Lay North America, Inc.
7701 Legacy Dr
Plano TX

(P-13271)
FRITO-LAY NORTH AMERICA INC
Also Called: Frito-Lay
9535 Archibald Ave (91730-5737)
PHONE..............................909 941-6214
Brian Birrell, *Mgr*
EMP: 500
SALES (corp-wide): 86.39B **Publicly Held**
Web: www.fritolay.com
SIC: 5145 Snack foods
HQ: Frito-Lay North America, Inc.
7701 Legacy Dr
Plano TX

(P-13272)
FRITO-LAY NORTH AMERICA INC
Also Called: Frito-Lay
9846 4th St (91730-5720)
PHONE..............................909 941-6218
George Smith, *Mgr*
EMP: 42
SALES (corp-wide): 86.39B **Publicly Held**
Web: www.fritolay.com
SIC: 5145 2099 2096 Snack foods; Food preparations, nec; Potato chips and similar snacks
HQ: Frito-Lay North America, Inc.
7701 Legacy Dr
Plano TX

(P-13273)
LAYMON CANDY CO INC
276 Commercial Rd (92408-4149)
PHONE..............................909 825-4408
Kenneth Laymon, *Pr*
Paul T Applen, *
▲ **EMP:** 27 **EST:** 1927
SQ FT: 43,000
SALES (est): 8.21MM **Privately Held**
Web: www.laymoncandy.com
SIC: 5145 2064 Candy; Candy and other confectionery products

(P-13274)
S&E GOURMET CUTS INC
Also Called: Country Archer Jerky
1055 E Cooley Ave (92408-2819)
PHONE..............................909 370-0155
Eugene Kang, *CEO*
Susan Kang, *
EMP: 150 **EST:** 2011
SALES (est): 45.02MM **Privately Held**
Web: www.countryarcher.com
SIC: 5145 2013 Snack foods; Cured meats, from purchased meat

(P-13275)
SUPERIOR NUT CO INC
5200 Valley Blvd (90032-3929)
PHONE..............................323 223-2431
Laura Rosen, *CEO*
Jacqueline Rosen, *Stockholder*
EMP: 18 **EST:** 1964
SQ FT: 22,000
SALES (est): 9.65MM **Privately Held**
Web: www.superiornutla.com
SIC: 5145 2068 Nuts, salted or roasted; Nuts: dried, dehydrated, salted or roasted

(P-13276)
YOUBAR INC (PA)
445 Wilson Way (91744-3935)
PHONE..............................626 537-1851
EMP: 53 **EST:** 2007
SALES (est): 30.25MM **Privately Held**
Web: www.youbars.com

SIC: 5145 5812 2064 Snack foods; Food bars; Granola and muesli, bars and clusters

5146 Fish And Seafoods

(P-13277)
CATALINA OFFSHORE PRODUCTS INC
5202 Lovelock St (92110-4011)
PHONE..............................619 297-9797
EMP: 90 **EST:** 1975
SALES (est): 14.1MM **Privately Held**
Web: www.catalinaop.com
SIC: 5146 Seafoods

(P-13278)
CENTRAL COAST SEAFOODS
5495 Traffic Way (93422-4246)
PHONE..............................805 462-3474
Giovanni Comin, *Pr*
Molly Comin, *
EMP: 135 **EST:** 1973
SQ FT: 10,000
SALES (est): 2.5MM
SALES (corp-wide): 105.89MM **Privately Held**
Web: www.ccseafood.com
SIC: 5146 Seafoods
PA: Santa Monica Seafood Company
18531 S Broadwick St
Rancho Dominguez CA
310 886-7900

(P-13279)
DEL MAR SEAFOODS INC
1449 Spinnaker Dr (93001-4355)
PHONE..............................805 850-0421
EMP: 185
Web: www.delmarseafoods.com
SIC: 5146 Seafoods
PA: Del Mar Seafoods, Inc.
331 Ford St
Watsonville CA

(P-13280)
H & N FOODS INTERNATIONAL INC (HQ)
Also Called: H & N Fish Co.
5580 S Alameda St (90058-3426)
PHONE..............................323 586-9300
Hua Thanh Ngo, *Pr*
Christine Ngo, *
Bobby Ngo, *
Dat Trieu, *
◆ **EMP:** 125 **EST:** 1981
SQ FT: 45,000
SALES (est): 48.37MM
SALES (corp-wide): 57.39MM **Privately Held**
Web: www.hngroup.com
SIC: 5146 Seafoods
PA: H & N Group, Inc.
5580 S Alameda St
Vernon CA
323 586-9388

(P-13281)
H & T SEAFOOD INC
5598 Lindbergh Ln (90201-6410)
PHONE..............................323 526-0888
◆ **EMP:** 41 **EST:** 1994
SQ FT: 120,000
SALES (est): 26MM **Privately Held**
Web: www.htseafood.com
SIC: 5146 2092 Fish and seafoods; Fresh or frozen fish or seafood chowders, soups, and stews

(P-13282)
KINGS SEAFOOD COMPANY LLC
7691 Edinger Ave (92647-3604)
PHONE..............................714 793-1177
Malia Cappuccio, *Brnch Mgr*
EMP: 556
Web: www.kingsseafood.com
SIC: 5146 Seafoods
PA: King's Seafood Company, Llc
3185 Airway Ave Ste J
Costa Mesa CA

(P-13283)
PROSPECT ENTERPRISES INC (PA)
Also Called: American Fish and Seafood
625 Kohler St (90021-1023)
PHONE..............................213 599-5700
Ernest Y Doizaki, *Ch Bd*
Jack King, *
Paula Eberhardt, *
◆ **EMP:** 160 **EST:** 1947
SQ FT: 20,000
SALES (est): 99.24MM
SALES (corp-wide): 99.24MM **Privately Held**
Web: www.kansasmarine.com
SIC: 5146 2092 Fish, fresh; Fresh or frozen packaged fish

(P-13284)
QUALY PAK SPECIALTY FOODS INC
2208 Signal Pl (90731-7227)
PHONE..............................310 541-3023
◆ **EMP:** 85
Web: www.qualypak.com
SIC: 5146 5142 Fish, fresh; Fish, frozen: packaged

(P-13285)
RED CHAMBER CO (PA)
1912 E Vernon Ave (90058-1611)
PHONE..............................323 234-9000
Shan Chun Kou, *Ch Bd*
Shu Chin Kou, *Ch Bd*
Ming Bin Kou, *CEO*
◆ **EMP:** 341 **EST:** 1974
SQ FT: 15,000
SALES (est): 94.16MM
SALES (corp-wide): 94.16MM **Privately Held**
Web: www.redchamber.com
SIC: 5146 4222 Seafoods; Warehousing, cold storage or refrigerated

(P-13286)
SEAFOOD FAMILY PARTNERS LP
1123 Cory Ave (90069-1701)
PHONE..............................310 761-1500
Anthony J Cigliano, *Prin*
EMP: 165 **EST:** 2008
SALES (est): 10.35MM **Privately Held**
SIC: 5146 Seafoods

(P-13287)
SHINING OCEAN INC
10888 7th St (91730-5421)
PHONE..............................253 826-3700
Daryl Gormley, *CEO*
Michael Beauregard, *
Matthew Lacki, *
◆ **EMP:** 140 **EST:** 1985
SALES (est): 22.52MM
SALES (corp-wide): 22.52MM **Privately Held**
Web: www.kanimi.com

SIC: **5146** Seafoods
PA: Aquamar Holdings, Inc.
10888 7th St
Rancho Cucamonga CA
909 481-4700

(P-13288)
TRI-UNION SEAFOODS LLC (DH)
Also Called: Chicken of Sea International
2150 E Grand Ave (90245-5024)
P.O. Box 85568 (92186-5568)
PHONE..............................424 397-8556
Valentin Ramirez, *CEO*
Christie Fleming, *
Jim Cox, *
Ignatius Dharma, *
David E Roszmann, *
◆ **EMP:** 69 **EST:** 1996
SQ FT: 24,000
SALES (est): 75.25MM **Privately Held**
SIC: **5146 2091** Seafoods; Tuna fish:
packaged in cans, jars, etc.
HQ: Thai Union North America, Inc.
2150 E Grand Ave
El Segundo CA
424 397-8556

5147 Meats And Meat Products

(P-13289)
AI FOODS CORPORATION (PA)
1700 N Soto St (90033-1127)
PHONE..............................323 222-0827
Clarissa Takakawa, *CEO*
▲ **EMP:** 25 **EST:** 1995
SALES (est): 9.11MM
SALES (corp-wide): 9.11MM **Privately Held**
Web: www.aifoodscorp.com
SIC: **5147 2013** Meats, fresh; Cured meats,
from purchased meat

(P-13290)
BICARA LTD
318 Avenue I Ste 65 (90277-5601)
PHONE..............................310 316-6222
William Jeffrey Hughes, *CEO*
William D Hughes, *
Raymond Rosenthal, *
◆ **EMP:** 300 **EST:** 1948
SQ FT: 105,000
SALES (est): 24.62MM **Privately Held**
SIC: **5147 5146 5141** Meats and meat
products; Seafoods; Groceries, general line

(P-13291)
BRIDGFORD MARKETING COMPANY (DH)
1308 N Patt St (92801-2551)
P.O. Box 3773 (92803-3773)
PHONE..............................714 526-5533
Allan L Bridgford, *Ch*
Allan L Bridgford Senior, *Ch*
William L Bridgford, *
John Simmons, *
Ray Lancey, *
EMP: 89 **EST:** 1957
SQ FT: 100,000
SALES (est): 84.74MM
SALES (corp-wide): 265.9MM **Publicly Held**
Web: www.bridgford.com
SIC: **5147 5149** Meats and meat products;
Bakery products
HQ: Bridgford Foods Corporation
1707 S Good Latimer Expy
Dallas TX
714 526-5533

(P-13292)
DEL MAR HOLDING LLC
1022 Bay Marina Dr 10 (91950-6398)
PHONE..............................313 659-7300
Leon Bergmann, *CEO*
Joel Jorgensen, *
EMP: 1600 **EST:** 2016
SALES (est): 86.51MM **Privately Held**
SIC: **5147** Meats and meat products

(P-13293)
EASTLAND CORPORATION
Also Called: C & H Meat Company
3017 Bandini Blvd (90058-4109)
PHONE..............................323 261-5388
Young Yoo, *Pr*
Young Won, *VP*
EMP: 23 **EST:** 1973
SQ FT: 10,000
SALES (est): 4.57MM **Privately Held**
Web: www.candhmeatco.com
SIC: **5147 2013** Meats, fresh; Cooked
meats, from purchased meat

(P-13294)
HARVEST MEAT COMPANY INC
Also Called: HARVEST MEAT COMPANY, INC.
1022 Bay Marina Dr Ste 106 (91950-6327)
PHONE..............................619 477-0185
Jonathan Leavy, *Brnch Mgr*
EMP: 100
SALES (corp-wide): 535.73MM **Privately Held**
Web: www.harvestfooddistributors.com
SIC: **5147** Meats, fresh
HQ: Harvest Meat Company Inc
1000 Bay Marina Dr
National City CA

(P-13295)
HARVEST MEAT COMPANY INC (HQ)
Also Called: Harvest Food Distributors
1000 Bay Marina Dr (91950-6302)
PHONE..............................619 477-0185
Leon Bergmann, *CEO*
◆ **EMP:** 80 **EST:** 1994
SQ FT: 60,000
SALES (est): 226.66MM
SALES (corp-wide): 535.73MM **Privately Held**
Web: www.harvestfooddistributors.com
SIC: **5147** Meats, fresh
PA: Del Mar Holdings, L.L.C.
12499 Evergreen Ave
Detroit MI
313 659-7300

(P-13296)
HEARTLAND MEAT COMPANY INC
Also Called: H M C
3461 Main St (91911-5828)
PHONE..............................619 407-3668
TOLL FREE: 800
Joseph E Stidman, *CEO*
James Methey, *
Stephanie Stidman, *
EMP: 70 **EST:** 1971
SQ FT: 49,000
SALES (est): 23.4MM **Privately Held**
Web: www.heartlandmeat.com
SIC: **5147 2013** Meats, fresh; Sausages and
other prepared meats

(P-13297)
HV RANDALL FOODS LLC
2900 Ayers Ave (90058-4304)

P.O. Box 2669 (90255-8069)
PHONE..............................323 261-6565
M Scott Dineen, *CEO*
Alan Cutler, *
EMP: 140 **EST:** 2020
SALES (est): 27.17MM **Privately Held**
Web: www.randallfoods.com
SIC: **5147** Meats and meat products

(P-13298)
JENSEN MEAT COMPANY INC
2550 Britannia Blvd Ste 101 (92154-7404)
PHONE..............................619 754-6400
Abel Olivera, *CEO*
Sam Acuna, *
Jeff Hamann, *
EMP: 95 **EST:** 1958
SQ FT: 25,000
SALES (est): 95.16MM **Privately Held**
Web: www.jensenmeat.com
SIC: **5147** Meats, fresh

(P-13299)
JETRO CASH AND CARRY ENTPS LLC
Also Called: Restaurant Depot
1709 Main St (92113-1025)
PHONE..............................619 233-0200
Frank Shapiro, *Brnch Mgr*
EMP: 100
Web: www.restaurantdepot.com
SIC: **5147 5141 5142 5181** Meats, fresh;
Groceries, general line; Packaged frozen
goods; Beer and other fermented malt
liquors
HQ: Jetro Cash And Carry Enterprises, Llc
1710 Whitestone Expy
Whitestone NY
718 762-8700

(P-13300)
L & T MEAT CO
3050 E 11th St (90023-3606)
PHONE..............................323 262-2815
EMP: 80 **EST:** 1995
SQ FT: 20,000
SALES (est): 23.02MM **Privately Held**
Web: www.ltmeat.com
SIC: **5147** Meats, fresh

(P-13301)
MPCI HOLDINGS INC
Also Called: Monterrey The Natural Choice
7850 Waterville Rd (92154-8219)
P.O. Box 81046 (92138-1046)
PHONE..............................619 294-2222
TOLL FREE: 800
▲ **EMP:** 130
SIC: **5147 5143 5148 5113** Meats, fresh;
Cheese; Fresh fruits and vegetables;
Disposable plates, cups, napkins, and
eating utensils

(P-13302)
NEWPORT MEAT SOUTHERN CAL INC
Also Called: Newport Meat Company
16691 Hale Ave (92606-5025)
PHONE..............................949 399-4200
Timothy K Hussman, *CEO*
Denise Van Voorhis, *
EMP: 227 **EST:** 1976
SQ FT: 92,000
SALES (est): 94.5MM
SALES (corp-wide): 76.32MM **Publicly Held**
Web: www.newportmeat.com
SIC: **5147 5142** Meats, fresh; Packaged
frozen goods
PA: Sysco Corporation
1390 Enclave Pkwy

Houston TX
281 584-1390

(P-13303)
PONTRELLI & LARRICCHIA LTD
Also Called: Pontrlli-Laricchia Sausage Mfg
6080 Malburg Way (90058-3946)
PHONE..............................323 583-6690
Dominic T Pontrelli, *Pt*
Vito Pontrelli, *Pt*
EMP: 21 **EST:** 1925
SQ FT: 20,000
SALES (est): 9.57MM **Privately Held**
Web: www.maestrosausage.com
SIC: **5147 2013** Meats and meat products;
Sausages and other prepared meats

(P-13304)
PRODUCERS MEAT AND PROV INC
Also Called: Tarantino Wholesale Fd Distrs
7651 Saint Andrews Ave (92154-8209)
PHONE..............................619 232-7593
Rose M Tarantino, *CEO*
▲ **EMP:** 35 **EST:** 1961
SQ FT: 10,000
SALES (est): 24.3MM **Privately Held**
SIC: **5147 2013** Meats, fresh; Sausages and
other prepared meats

(P-13305)
RANCHO FOODS INC
2528 E 37th St (90058-1725)
P.O. Box 58504 (90058-0504)
PHONE..............................323 585-0503
Annette Mac Donald, *Pr*
John Mac Donald, *VP*
EMP: 100 **EST:** 1972
SQ FT: 26,000
SALES (est): 29.1MM **Privately Held**
Web: www.ranchofoods.com
SIC: **5147 2013** Meats, fresh; Sausages and
other prepared meats

(P-13306)
RW ZANT LLC (DH)
1470 E 4th St (90033-4236)
PHONE..............................323 980-5457
Robert W Zant, *Pr*
William Zant, *
▲ **EMP:** 90 **EST:** 1950
SQ FT: 42,000
SALES (est): 47.3MM
SALES (corp-wide): 1.24B **Privately Held**
Web: www.rwzant.com
SIC: **5147 5146 5144 4222** Meats, fresh;
Fish and seafoods; Poultry and poultry
products; Cheese warehouse
HQ: Honor Holdings Inc.
5505 Tacony St
Philadelphia PA
215 236-1700

(P-13307)
STROUK GROUP LLC
Also Called: Monsieur Marcel
6333 W 3rd St Ste 150 (90036-3154)
PHONE..............................323 939-7792
Stephane Strouk, *Pr*
Katrin Strouk, *
EMP: 105 **EST:** 1998
SALES (est): 13.9MM **Privately Held**
Web: www.mrmarcel.com
SIC: **5147 5143 5812** Meats and meat
products; Cheese; French restaurant

(P-13308)
SYDNEY & ANNE BLOOM FARMS INC

Also Called: Randall Farms
2900 Ayers Ave (90058-4304)
P.O. Box 2669 (90255-8069)
PHONE.................................323 261-6565
EMP: 545 **EST:** 1952
SALES (est): 98.62MM **Privately Held**
Web: www.randallfoods.com
SIC: 5147 7299 Meats and meat products;
Butcher service, processing only - does not
sell meat

(P-13309)
THREE SONS INC
Also Called: Merit Day Food Service
5201 Industry Ave (90660-2505)
P.O. Box 6 (90660-0006)
PHONE.................................562 801-4100
Michael Shannon Day, *CEO*
John Brenan, *
David Day, *Stockholder**
Mariellen Day, *Stockholder**
Michael Day, *Stockholder**
▲ **EMP:** 87 **EST:** 1975
SQ FT: 40,000
SALES (est): 21.29MM **Privately Held**
Web: www.americanmeatcompanies.com
SIC: 5147 2013 2011 Meats, cured or
smoked; Sausages and other prepared
meats; Meat packing plants

(P-13310)
WAYNE PROVISION CO INC (PA)
Also Called: Premier Meat Company
5030 Gifford Ave (90058-2726)
P.O. Box 58183 (90058-0183)
PHONE.................................323 277-5888
Naftali Greenberg, *CEO*
Eldad Hadar, *
Terry Hanks, *
▼ **EMP:** 92 **EST:** 1975
SQ FT: 7,822
SALES (est): 49.99MM
SALES (corp-wide): 49.99MM **Privately
Held**
Web: www.premiermeatcompany.com
SIC: 5147 5144 Meats, fresh; Poultry and
poultry products

5148 Fresh Fruits And Vegetables

(P-13311)
4 EARTH FARMS LLC (PA)
Also Called: McL Fresh
5555 E Olympic Blvd (90022-5129)
PHONE.................................323 201-5800
David Lake, *CEO*
Robert Lake, *
◆ **EMP:** 329 **EST:** 1993
SQ FT: 165,000
SALES (est): 69.45MM **Privately Held**
Web: www.4earthfarms.com
SIC: 5148 4783 Fresh fruits and vegetables;
Containerization of goods for shipping

(P-13312)
AGRI-EMPIRE
630 W 7th St (92583-4015)
P.O. Box 490 (92581-0490)
PHONE.................................951 654-7311
Larry J Minor, *Pr*
EMP: 120 **EST:** 1943
SQ FT: 5,000
SALES (est): 25.97MM **Privately Held**
Web: www.agri-empire.com
SIC: 5148 Potatoes, fresh

(P-13313)
BORG PRODUCE SALES LLC
1601 E Olympic Blvd Ste 100 (90021-1940)
P.O. Box 21008 (90021-0008)
PHONE.................................213 624-2674
▲ **EMP:** 170
SIC: 5148 Fresh fruits and vegetables

(P-13314)
BOSKOVICH FRESH CUT LLC
711 Diaz Ave (93030-7247)
P.O. Box 1272 (93032-1272)
PHONE.................................805 487-2299
George Boskovich, *CEO*
George Boskovich, *Managing Member*
Lina Perez, *
EMP: 250 **EST:** 2018
SALES (est): 24.49MM **Privately Held**
SIC: 5148 Vegetables, fresh

(P-13315)
BUY FRESH PRODUCE INC
6636 E 26th St (90040-3216)
PHONE.................................323 796-0127
Ted Kasnetsis, *Pr*
Traci Kasnetsis, *
EMP: 80 **EST:** 2005
SQ FT: 23,500
SALES (est): 22.65MM **Privately Held**
Web: www.buyfreshproduceinc.com
SIC: 5148 Fruits, fresh

(P-13316)
COAST CITRUS DISTRIBUTORS (PA)
Also Called: Coast Tropical
7597 Bristow Ct (92154-7419)
P.O. Box 530369 (92153-0369)
PHONE.................................619 661-7950
James M Alvarez, *Ch Bd*
Margarita Alvarez, *
◆ **EMP:** 100 **EST:** 1950
SQ FT: 80,000
SALES (est): 122.73MM
SALES (corp-wide): 122.73MM **Privately
Held**
Web: www.coasttropical.com
SIC: 5148 Fruits, fresh

(P-13317)
COAST PRODUCE COMPANY (PA)
1791 Bay St (90021-1655)
P.O. Box 86468 (90086-0468)
PHONE.................................213 955-4900
Mike Ito, *CEO*
John K Dunn, *
Rick Uyeno, *
▲ **EMP:** 165 **EST:** 1955
SQ FT: 80,000
SALES (est): 47.07MM
SALES (corp-wide): 47.07MM **Privately
Held**
Web: www.coastproduce.com
SIC: 5148 Fruits, fresh

(P-13318)
D&D WHOLESALE DISTRIBUTORS LLC
777 Baldwin Park Blvd (91746-1504)
PHONE.................................626 333-2111
Joe Dupree, *Pr*
Pamela Dupree, *
EMP: 90 **EST:** 1979
SQ FT: 20,000
SALES (est): 31.09MM **Privately Held**
Web: www.ddwholesale.com
SIC: 5148 5143 Fruits, fresh; Dairy products,
except dried or canned

(P-13319)
DAVALAN SALES INC
Also Called: Davalan Fresh
1601 E Olympic Blvd Ste 325 (90021-1957)
PHONE.................................213 623-2500
Alan Frick, *Pr*
Dave Bouton, *
▲ **EMP:** 200 **EST:** 1983
SQ FT: 15,000
SALES (est): 23.92MM **Privately Held**
Web: www.davalanfresh.com
SIC: 5148 Fruits, fresh

(P-13320)
EVOLUTION FRESH INC
Also Called: Evolution Juice
11655 Jersey Blvd Ste A (91730-4903)
PHONE.................................800 794-9986
Chris Bruzzo, *CEO*
Ricki Reves, *
▲ **EMP:** 180 **EST:** 2010
SQ FT: 70,000
SALES (est): 72.22MM
SALES (corp-wide): 1.33B **Privately Held**
Web: www.evolutionfresh.com
SIC: 5148 2037 Fruits, fresh; Frozen fruits
and vegetables
HQ: Wm. Bolthouse Farms, Inc.
7200 E Brundage Ln
Bakersfield CA
661 366-7209

(P-13321)
FAMILY TREE PRODUCE INC
5510 E La Palma Ave (92807-2108)
PHONE.................................714 693-5688
Fidel Guzman, *Pr*
Christy Guzman, *
EMP: 115 **EST:** 1975
SQ FT: 33,000
SALES (est): 37.41MM **Privately Held**
Web: www.familytreeproduce.com
SIC: 5148 Fruits, fresh

(P-13322)
FARMERS LINK INC
2858 E 26th St (90058-8005)
P.O. Box 86223 (90086-0223)
PHONE.................................213 623-5242
Saul G Pinon, *Pr*
EMP: 82
SALES (corp-wide): 4.67MM **Privately
Held**
SIC: 5148 Vegetables
PA: Farmers Link, Inc
1601 E Olympic Blvd
Los Angeles CA
213 623-5242

(P-13323)
FIELD FRESH FOODS INCORPORATED
14805 S San Pedro St (90248-2030)
P.O. Box 3877 (90247-7577)
PHONE.................................310 719-8422
EMP: 600 **EST:** 1994
SALES (est): 70.34MM **Privately Held**
Web: www.fieldfresh.com
SIC: 5148 Vegetables, fresh

(P-13324)
FRESHPOINT INC
Also Called: Freshpoint Las Vegas
155 N Orange Ave (91744-3432)
PHONE.................................626 855-1400
Terry Owen, *Pr*
EMP: 191
SALES (corp-wide): 76.32MM **Publicly
Held**
Web: www.freshpoint.com

SIC: 5148 Fresh fruits and vegetables
HQ: Freshpoint, Inc.
1390 Enclave Pkwy
Houston TX

(P-13325)
FRESHPOINT SOUTHERN CAL INC
Also Called: Freshpoint Southern California
155 N Orange Ave (91744-3432)
PHONE.................................626 855-1400
Verne L Lusby Junior, *CEO*
Robert Gordon, *
Jim Procuniar, *
Rich Dachman, *
Jeff Ronk, *
EMP: 208 **EST:** 1921
SQ FT: 97,000
SALES (est): 67.52MM
SALES (corp-wide): 76.32MM **Publicly
Held**
Web: www.freshpoint.com
SIC: 5148 5142 Fruits, fresh; Packaged
frozen goods
PA: Sysco Corporation
1390 Enclave Pkwy
Houston TX
281 584-1390

(P-13326)
GIUMARRA AGRICOM INTL LLC
15651 Old Milky Way (92027-7104)
PHONE.................................760 480-8502
Don Corsaro, *Brnch Mgr*
EMP: 1829
SALES (corp-wide): 134.67MM **Privately
Held**
Web: www.giumarra.com
SIC: 5148 Fruits
HQ: Giumarra Agricom International Llc
1601 E Olympic Blvd
Los Angeles CA

(P-13327)
GREEN FARMS INC
Also Called: Worldwide Produce
2652 Long Beach Ave (90058-1323)
PHONE.................................858 831-7701
Abbas Ghulam, *Brnch Mgr*
EMP: 89
SALES (corp-wide): 115.73MM **Privately
Held**
Web: www.wwproduce.com
SIC: 5148 Fresh fruits and vegetables
HQ: Green Farms California, Llc
2652 Long Beach Ave Ste 2
Los Angeles CA

(P-13328)
GREEN THUMB PRODUCE INC
2648 W Ramsey St (92220-3716)
P.O. Box 1357 (92220-0010)
PHONE.................................951 849-4711
EMP: 250 **EST:** 1996
SALES (est): 45.31MM **Privately Held**
Web: www.greenthumbproduce.com
SIC: 5148 Fresh fruits and vegetables

(P-13329)
GRIMMWAY ENTERPRISES INC
Also Called: Cal-Organic Farms
12000 Main St (93241-2836)
P.O. Box 81498 (93380-1498)
PHONE.................................661 845-3758
EMP: 278
SALES (corp-wide): 1.86B **Privately Held**
Web: www.calorganicfarms.com
SIC: 5148 Vegetables, fresh
PA: Grimmway Enterprises, Inc.
14141 Di Giorgio Rd

Arvin CA
800 301-3101

(P-13330)
INDEX FRESH INC (PA)
1250 Corona Pointe Ct Ste 401
(92879-1781)
PHONE...............................909 877-0999
TOLL FREE: 800
Dana L Thomas, *Pr*
Merrill Causey, *
Giovanni Cavaletto, *
◆ **EMP:** 52 **EST:** 1914
SQ FT: 40,000
SALES (est): 48.66MM
SALES (corp-wide): 48.66MM **Privately Held**
Web: www.indexfresh.com
SIC: 5148 2099 Fruits, fresh; Vegetables, peeled for the trade

(P-13331)
INGARDIA BROS PRODUCE INC
700 S Hathaway St (92705-4126)
PHONE...............................949 645-1365
EMP: 190 **EST:** 1973
SALES (est): 36.47MM **Privately Held**
Web: www.ingardiabros.com
SIC: 5148 5146 Fresh fruits and vegetables; Seafoods

(P-13332)
LA SPECIALTY PRODUCE CO (PA)
Also Called: Vesta Foodservice
13527 Orden Dr (90670-6338)
P.O. Box 2293 (90670-0293)
PHONE...............................562 741-2200
Michael Glick, *CEO*
Scott Parra-matthews, *CFO*
EMP: 375 **EST:** 1985
SQ FT: 188,000
SALES (est): 210.39MM
SALES (corp-wide): 210.39MM **Privately Held**
Web: www.vestafoodservice.com
SIC: 5148 Fruits, fresh

(P-13333)
LEGACY FARMS LLC
1765 W Penhall Way (92801-6728)
PHONE...............................714 736-1800
Nick Cancellieri, *Managing Member*
Ron Shimizu, *Managing Member*
Michael Sanders, *Managing Member*
▲ **EMP:** 100 **EST:** 1991
SQ FT: 95,000
SALES (est): 50.51MM **Privately Held**
Web: www.legacyproduce.com
SIC: 5148 Fruits, fresh

(P-13334)
NATURES PRODUCE
3305 Bandini Blvd (90058-4130)
P.O. Box 58366 (90058-0366)
PHONE...............................323 235-4343
Rick Polisky, *CEO*
▲ **EMP:** 110 **EST:** 2000
SALES (est): 48.11MM **Privately Held**
Web: www.naturesproduce.com
SIC: 5148 Fruits, fresh

(P-13335)
PACIFIC TRELLIS FRUIT LLC (PA)
Also Called: Borg Produce Sales
2301 E 7th St Ste C200 (90023-1041)
PHONE...............................323 859-9600
Josh Leichter, *CEO*

David Sullivan, *
▲ **EMP:** 130 **EST:** 1999
SQ FT: 10,000
SALES (est): 90.36MM
SALES (corp-wide): 90.36MM **Privately Held**
Web: www.dulcinea.com
SIC: 5148 Fruits, fresh

(P-13336)
PRIMETIME INTERNATIONAL INC
47110 Washington St Ste 103
(92253-2186)
PHONE...............................760 399-4166
Mark Nickerson, *Managing Member*
Mike Way, *Managing Member*
Jeff Taylor, *Managing Member*
▲ **EMP:** 95 **EST:** 1994
SALES (est): 19.81MM **Privately Held**
Web: www.primetimeproduce.com
SIC: 5148 4783 Vegetables, fresh; Packing goods for shipping
PA: Sun And Sands Enterprises, Llc
47110 Washington St # 103
La Quinta CA

(P-13337)
PROFESSIONAL PRODUCE
2570 E 25th St (90058-1211)
P.O. Box 58308 (90058-0308)
PHONE...............................323 277-1550
Ted Kaplan, *CEO*
Maribel Reyes, *
◆ **EMP:** 99 **EST:** 1994
SQ FT: 5,000
SALES (est): 40.35MM **Privately Held**
Web: www.profproduce.com
SIC: 5148 Fruits, fresh

(P-13338)
READY PAC PRODUCE INC (DH)
Also Called: Ready Pac Foods
4401 Foxdale St (91706-2161)
PHONE...............................800 800-4088
Tony Sarsam, *CEO*
Jay Ellis, *Sls Mgr*
Bob Estes, *CIO*
Dan Redfern, *CFO*
Tristan Simpson, *CMO*
▲ **EMP:** 239 **EST:** 1969
SQ FT: 480,000
SALES (est): 256.43MM
SALES (corp-wide): 2.67MM **Privately Held**
Web: www.readypac.com
SIC: 5148 2099 Fresh fruits and vegetables; Salads, fresh or refrigerated
HQ: Ready Pac Foods, Inc.
4401 Foxdale St
Irwindale CA
626 856-8686

(P-13339)
SEASON PRODUCE CO INC
1601 E Olympic Blvd Ste 315 (90021-1942)
PHONE...............................213 689-0008
Patrick R Horwath, *Pr*
Daniel Horwath, *
Timothy R Horwath, *
EMP: 353 **EST:** 1958
SQ FT: 20,000
SALES (est): 23.87MM
SALES (corp-wide): 23.87MM **Privately Held**
SIC: 5148 Fresh fruits and vegetables
PA: S & H Packing & Sales Co., Inc.
2590 Harriet St
Vernon CA
323 581-7172

(P-13340)
SHAPIRO-GILMAN-SHANDLER CO
Also Called: S G S Produce
739 Decatur St (90021-1649)
PHONE...............................213 593-1200
Minyi Xu, *CEO*
Carol C Shandler, *
Morris Shander, *
Muriel Shandler, *
▲ **EMP:** 101 **EST:** 1907
SQ FT: 50,000
SALES (est): 44.42MM
SALES (corp-wide): 297.68MM **Privately Held**
Web: www.sgsproduce.com
SIC: 5148 Fruits, fresh
PA: Grubmarket, Inc.
1925 Jerrold Ave
San Francisco CA
415 986-0523

(P-13341)
SUN PACIFIC MARKETING COOP INC
Also Called: Sun Pacific Farming
31452 Old River Rd (93311-9621)
PHONE...............................661 847-1015
Bob Dipiazza, *Brnch Mgr*
EMP: 395
SALES (corp-wide): 92.65MM **Privately Held**
Web: www.sunpacific.com
SIC: 5148 Fresh fruits and vegetables
PA: Sun Pacific Marketing Cooperative, Inc.
1095 E Green St
Pasadena CA
213 612-9957

(P-13342)
SUNKIST GROWERS INC (PA)
27770 Entertainment Dr (91355-1091)
PHONE...............................661 290-8900
Russell Hanlin Ii, *Pr*
Richard G French, *VP*
Michael Wootton, *Sr VP*
John Mc Guigan, *VP*
Russell L Hanlin Ii, *VP*
◆ **EMP:** 223 **EST:** 1893
SQ FT: 50,000
SALES (est): 1.15B
SALES (corp-wide): 1.15B **Privately Held**
Web: www.sunkist.com
SIC: 5148 2033 2037 2899 Fruits, fresh; Fruit juices: packaged in cans, jars, etc.; Fruit juice concentrates, frozen; Lemon oil (edible)

(P-13343)
SUNRISE GROWERS INC
701 W Kimberly Ave # 210 (92870-6330)
PHONE...............................714 706-6090
EMP: 140
SIC: 5148 Fruits

(P-13344)
V & L PRODUCE INC
Also Called: General Produce
2550 E 25th St (90058-1211)
PHONE...............................323 589-3125
Victor Mendoza, *Pr*
▲ **EMP:** 140 **EST:** 1984
SQ FT: 12,000
SALES (est): 29.6MM **Privately Held**
Web: www.vlproduce.com
SIC: 5148 Fresh fruits and vegetables

(P-13345)
VAL-PRO INC (PA)
Also Called: Valley Fruit & Produce Co
1601 E Olympic Blvd Ste 300 (90021-1942)
PHONE...............................213 627-8736
◆ **EMP:** 170 **EST:** 1920
SALES (est): 35.49MM
SALES (corp-wide): 35.49MM **Privately Held**
Web: www.valleyproduce.com
SIC: 5148 Fruits, fresh

(P-13346)
VEG-FRESH FARMS LLC (PA)
Also Called: Veg Fresh
1400 W Rincon St (92878-9205)
PHONE...............................800 422-5535
EMP: 134 **EST:** 1989
SQ FT: 94,000
SALES (est): 56.1MM **Privately Held**
Web: www.vegfresh.com
SIC: 5148 Vegetables, fresh

(P-13347)
VENTURA COUNTY LEMON COOP
Also Called: Ventura Pacific Co
2620 Sakioka Dr (93030-5647)
P.O. Box 6986 (93031-6986)
PHONE...............................805 385-3345
Donald Dames, *Pr*
Milton Daily, *Ch Bd*
James H Gill, *Sec*
Jim Waters, *Treas*
EMP: 80 **EST:** 1943
SALES (est): 19.98MM **Privately Held**
Web: www.venturapacific.com
SIC: 5148 4783 3999 Fruits, fresh; Containerization of goods for shipping; Fruits, artificial and preserved

(P-13348)
WEST CENTRAL PRODUCE INC
Also Called: West Central Food Service
12840 Leyva St (90650-6852)
P.O. Box 4664 (90607-4664)
PHONE...............................213 629-3600
Michael Dodo, *CEO*
Jamie Purcell, *
Lance Shiring, *
▲ **EMP:** 400 **EST:** 1970
SQ FT: 34,000
SALES (est): 92.57MM **Privately Held**
Web: www.westcentralfoodservice.com
SIC: 5148 5147 5149 5146 Fruits, fresh; Meats and meat products; Dairy products, dried or canned; Seafoods

(P-13349)
WORLD VARIETY PRODUCE INC
Also Called: Melissas World Variety Produce
5325 S Soto St (90058-3624)
P.O. Box 514599 (90051-2599)
PHONE...............................800 588-0151
Joe V Hernandez, *Prin*
Joe V Hernandez, *Pr*
Sharon Hernandez, *
David Shafer, *
◆ **EMP:** 325 **EST:** 1983
SQ FT: 244,000
SALES (est): 80.3MM **Privately Held**
Web: www.melissas.com
SIC: 5148 Fruits, fresh

5149 Groceries And Related Products, Nec

(P-13350)
APP WHOLESALE LLC
3686 E Olympic Blvd (90023-3146)
PHONE...............................323 980-8315
EMP: 500 **EST:** 2013
SQ FT: 220,000
SALES (est): 84.69MM **Privately Held**
Web: www.app-wholesale.com
SIC: 5149 2741 Specialty food items;
Business service newsletters: publishing
and printing

(P-13351)
ASPIRE BAKERIES LLC
Also Called: Fresh Start Bakeries
1220 S Baker Ave (91761-7739)
P.O. Box 1283 (91802-1283)
PHONE...............................909 472-3500
Rob Crawford, *Genl Mgr*
EMP: 197
SALES (corp-wide): 1.77B **Privately Held**
Web: www.aspirebakeries.com
SIC: 5149 Bakery products
HQ: Aspire Bakeries Llc
6701 Center Dr W Ste 850
Los Angeles CA
844 992-7747

(P-13352)
ASPIRE BAKERIES LLC
6501 District Blvd (93313-2000)
PHONE...............................661 832-0409
EMP: 189
SALES (corp-wide): 1.77B **Privately Held**
Web: www.aspirebakeries.com
SIC: 5149 Bakery products
HQ: Aspire Bakeries Llc
6701 Center Dr W Ste 850
Los Angeles CA
844 992-7747

(P-13353)
BAKEMARK USA LLC (PA)
Also Called: Bakemark
7351 Crider Ave (90660-3705)
PHONE...............................562 949-1054
Jim Parker, *Managing Member*
◆ **EMP:** 100 **EST:** 1928
SQ FT: 275,000
SALES (est): 578.75MM
SALES (corp-wide): 578.75MM **Privately
Held**
Web: www.bakemark.com
SIC: 5149 2045 3556 2099 Bakery products;
Flours and flour mixes, from purchased flour
; Food products machinery; Food
preparations, nec

(P-13354)
**BAKERY EX SOUTHERN CAL
LLC**
1910 W Malvern Ave (92833-2105)
PHONE...............................714 446-9470
EMP: 100 **EST:** 2001
SQ FT: 28,000
SALES (est): 23.54MM **Privately Held**
SIC: 5149 Bakery products

(P-13355)
BLUETRITON BRANDS INC
Also Called: Arrowhead Water
619 N Main St (92868-1103)
PHONE...............................714 532-6220
Dan Miller, *Mgr*
EMP: 105

SQ FT: 16,312
SALES (corp-wide): 1.3B **Privately Held**
Web: local.readyrefresh.com
SIC: 5149 5499 5963 5078 Water, distilled;
Water: distilled mineral or spring; Bottled
water delivery; Refrigeration equipment and
supplies
HQ: Bluetriton Brands, Inc.
900 Long Ridge Rd Bldg 2
Stamford CT

(P-13356)
**BUENA VISTA FOOD PRODUCTS
INC (DH)**
823 W 8th St (91702-2247)
PHONE...............................626 815-8859
Laura Trujillo, *Pr*
Michelle Reitzin-bass, *Prin*
Peter Woods, *Prin*
Mike Likovich, *Prin*
EMP: 115 **EST:** 1991
SALES (est): 50.51MM **Privately Held**
Web: www.bvfoods.com
SIC: 5149 Bakery products
HQ: Sterling Foods, Llc
1075 Arion Pkwy
San Antonio TX
210 490-1669

(P-13357)
CABO FOODS INC (PA)
Also Called: Cabo Foods
303 Broadway St Ste 104-105
(92651-1816)
PHONE...............................949 463-2373
Brady D Bunte, *Pr*
EMP: 24 **EST:** 2003
SALES (est): 12.57MM
SALES (corp-wide): 12.57MM **Privately
Held**
SIC: 5149 2086 2096 5145 Natural and
organic foods; Carbonated beverages,
nonalcoholic: pkged. in cans, bottles;
Tortilla chips; Snack foods

(P-13358)
CALIFORNIA BAKING COMPANY
Also Called: California Bread Co.
681 Anita St (91911-4663)
PHONE...............................619 591-8289
Abraham Levy, *Pr*
EMP: 300 **EST:** 2002
SALES (est): 24.87MM **Privately Held**
Web: www.californiabaking.com
SIC: 5149 2051 Bakery products; Sponge
goods, bakery: except frozen

(P-13359)
CIBARIA INTERNATIONAL INC
705 Columbia Ave (92507-2141)
PHONE...............................951 823-8490
Kathy Griset, *Pr*
Karen Moore, *
▲ **EMP:** 30 **EST:** 1998
SQ FT: 55,000
SALES (est): 41.11MM **Privately Held**
Web: www.cibaria-intl.com
SIC: 5149 2899 Cooking oils; Essential oils

(P-13360)
CJ AMERICA INC (HQ)
Also Called: C J Foods
300 S Grand Ave Ste 1100 (90071-3173)
PHONE...............................213 338-2700
Hyunsoo Shin, *CEO*
Jae Kyung Jeon, *
◆ **EMP:** 54 **EST:** 1984
SALES (est): 485.8MM **Privately Held**
Web: www.cjamerica.com

SIC: 5149 1541 3556 5169 Groceries and
related products, nec; Food products
manufacturing or packing plant construction
; Food products machinery; Food additives
and preservatives
PA: Cj Cheiljedang Corporation
330 Dongho-Ro, Jung-Gu
Seoul

(P-13361)
COASTAL COCKTAILS INC (PA)
Also Called: Modern Gourmet Foods
1920 E Deere Ave Ste 100 (92705-5717)
PHONE...............................949 250-8951
Boaz Shonfeld, *CEO*
▲ **EMP:** 60 **EST:** 2009
SALES (est): 39MM **Privately Held**
Web: www.coastalcocktails.com
SIC: 5149 2086 Food gift baskets; Bottled
and canned soft drinks

(P-13362)
**COMPLETELY FRESH FOODS
INC**
4401 S Downey Rd (90058-2518)
P.O. Box 58667 (90058-0667)
PHONE...............................323 722-9136
Josh Solovy, *Pr*
Levi Litmanovich, *
Eric Litmanovich, *
EMP: 200 **EST:** 2006
SQ FT: 15,000
SALES (est): 46.35MM
SALES (corp-wide): 452.76MM **Privately
Held**
Web: www.gwfg.com
SIC: 5149 5046 Specialty food items;
Commercial equipment, nec
PA: Golden West Food Group, Inc.
4401 S Downey Rd
Vernon CA
888 807-3663

(P-13363)
**CORE-MARK INTERNATIONAL
INC**
200 Coremark Ct (93307-8402)
P.O. Box 70458 (93387-0458)
PHONE...............................661 366-2673
Caral Parker, *Pr*
EMP: 211
SALES (corp-wide): 57.25B **Publicly Held**
Web: www.core-mark.com
SIC: 5149 Groceries and related products,
nec
HQ: Core-Mark International, Inc.
1500 Solana Blvd Ste 3400
Westlake TX
650 589-9445

(P-13364)
**CORE-MARK INTERNATIONAL
INC**
2311 E 48th St (90058-2007)
PHONE...............................323 583-6531
Julian Puentes, *Brnch Mgr*
EMP: 174
SALES (corp-wide): 57.25B **Publicly Held**
Web: www.core-mark.com
SIC: 5149 5194 5145 Groceries and related
products, nec; Tobacco and tobacco
products; Confectionery
HQ: Core-Mark International, Inc.
1500 Solana Blvd Ste 3400
Westlake TX
650 589-9445

(P-13365)
**CULINARY HISPANIC FOODS
INC**
Also Called: Productos Chata
805 Bow St (91914)
PHONE...............................619 955-6101
Jorge Aguilar, *CEO*
Carlos Machado, *
▲ **EMP:** 1458 **EST:** 2011
SQ FT: 4,000
SALES (est): 70.89MM **Privately Held**
SIC: 5149 Canned goods: fruit, vegetables,
seafood, meats, etc.

(P-13366)
DESERT VALLEY DATE LLC
86740 Industrial Way (92236-2718)
PHONE...............................760 398-0999
Greg Willsey, *Managing Member*
EMP: 85 **EST:** 2020
SALES (est): 10.1MM **Privately Held**
Web: www.desertvalleydate.com
SIC: 5149 5148 Organic and diet food; Fruits

(P-13367)
EL GUAPO SPICES INC (PA)
Also Called: El Guapo Spices and Herbs Pkg
6200 E Slauson Ave (90040-3012)
PHONE...............................213 312-1300
Dan Terrazas, *Pr*
EMP: 100 **EST:** 1982
SALES (est): 9.18MM
SALES (corp-wide): 9.18MM **Privately
Held**
SIC: 5149 Spices and seasonings

(P-13368)
GALASSOS BAKERY (PA)
Also Called: Galasso's Bakery
10820 San Sevaine Way (91752-1116)
PHONE...............................951 360-1211
Jeannette Galasso, *Pr*
Mark Bailey, *
Pearl Denault, *
Rick Vargas, *Operations*
EMP: 180 **EST:** 1923
SQ FT: 110,000
SALES (est): 95.32MM
SALES (corp-wide): 95.32MM **Privately
Held**
Web: www.galassos.com
SIC: 5149 Bakery products

(P-13369)
**GOGLANIAN BAKERIES INC
(HQ)**
Also Called: Goglanian
3401 W Segerstrom Ave (92704-6404)
PHONE...............................714 338-1145
◆ **EMP:** 300 **EST:** 1978
SQ FT: 71,500
SALES (est): 55.7MM
SALES (corp-wide): 4.81B **Privately Held**
Web: www.richsusa.com
SIC: 5149 Bakery products
PA: Rich Products Corporation
1 Robert Rich Way
Buffalo NY
716 878-8000

(P-13370)
**HARRIS FREEMAN & CO INC
(PA)**
Also Called: Harris Tea Company
3110 E Miraloma Ave (92806-1906)
PHONE...............................714 765-7525
Anil J Shah, *CEO*
Kevin Shah, *
Meena Shah, *

◆ **EMP:** 500 **EST:** 1981
SQ FT: 58,000
SALES (est): 150K
SALES (corp-wide): 150K **Privately Held**
Web: www.harrisfreeman.com
SIC: **5149** 2099 Tea; Spices, including grinding

(P-13371)
JANS ENTERPRISES CORPORATION
Also Called: Wira Co
4181 Temple City Blvd Ste A (91731-1030)
PHONE...................626 575-2000
Anthony Kartawinata, *Pr*
Nila Prawirawidjaja, *
◆ **EMP:** 25 **EST:** 1998
SQ FT: 50,000
SALES (est): 6.45MM **Privately Held**
Web: www.jansfood.com
SIC: **5149** 2026 2096 Specialty food items; Milk, ultra-high temperature (longlife); Potato chips and similar snacks

(P-13372)
JFC INTERNATIONAL INC (HQ)
7101 E Slauson Ave (90040-3622)
P.O. Box 875349 (90087-0449)
PHONE...................323 721-6100
Yoshiyuki Ishigaki, *CEO*
Hiroyuki Enomoto, *
◆ **EMP:** 203 **EST:** 1948
SALES (est): 604.95MM **Privately Held**
Web: www.jfc.com
SIC: **5149** 7389 Specialty food items; Labeling bottles, cans, cartons, etc.
PA: Kikkoman Corporation
2-1-1, Nishishimbashi
Minato-Ku TKY

(P-13373)
JFC INTERNATIONAL INC
Also Called: Los Angeles Branch
7140 Bandini Blvd (90040-3325)
PHONE...................323 721-6900
Tamaki Saijo, *Brnch Mgr*
EMP: 165
Web: www.jfc.com
SIC: **5149** Specialty food items
HQ: Jfc International Inc
7101 E Slauson Ave
Commerce CA
323 721-6100

(P-13374)
KIDS HEALTHY FOODS LLC
2030 Main St Ste 1300 (92614-7220)
PHONE...................949 260-4950
Jeff Mcclelland, *CEO*
EMP: 25 **EST:** 2010
SALES (est): 9.94MM **Privately Held**
Web: www.kidshealthyfoods.com
SIC: **5149** 2099 Beverages, except coffee and tea; Tea blending

(P-13375)
LA PROVENCE INC
Also Called: La Provence Bakery
1370 W San Marcos Blvd Ste 130 (92078-1601)
PHONE...................760 736-3299
Philip Dardaine, *CEO*
Thierry Bouchereau, *
Karen Dardaine, *
EMP: 95 **EST:** 1990
SQ FT: 6,000
SALES (est): 26.31MM **Privately Held**
Web: www.laprovenceinc.com
SIC: **5149** Bakery products

(P-13376)
LEE KUM KEE (USA) INC (DH)
Also Called: Lee's Kitchen
14841 Don Julian Rd (91746-3110)
PHONE...................626 709-1888
Simon Wu, *CEO*
David H W Lee, *
◆ **EMP:** 44 **EST:** 1983
SQ FT: 50,000
SALES (est): 177.39MM **Privately Held**
Web: usa.lkk.com
SIC: **5149** 2099 2035 Sauces; Food preparations, nec; Pickles, sauces, and salad dressings
HQ: Lee Kum Kee International Holdings Limited
Tai Po Indl Est
Tai Po NT

(P-13377)
LENORE JOHN & CO (PA)
1250 Delevan Dr (92102-2437)
PHONE...................619 232-6136
John G Lenore, *CEO*
Jamie Lenore, *
Karl Hurlbert, *
◆ **EMP:** 120 **EST:** 1966
SQ FT: 50,000
SALES (est): 45.4MM
SALES (corp-wide): 45.4MM **Privately Held**
Web: www.johnlenore.com
SIC: **5149** 5182 5181 Soft drinks; Wine; Beer and other fermented malt liquors

(P-13378)
MHH HOLDINGS INC
5653 Alton Pkwy (92618-4058)
PHONE...................949 651-9903
Cynthia Espere, *Brnch Mgr*
EMP: 216
SALES (corp-wide): 23.68MM **Privately Held**
SIC: **5149** Tea
PA: Mhh Holdings, Inc.
4580 Calle Alto
Camarillo CA
805 484-7924

(P-13379)
MHH HOLDINGS INC
415 S Lake Ave Ste 108 (91101-5047)
PHONE...................626 744-9370
Xiomara Bellido, *Prin*
EMP: 217
SALES (corp-wide): 23.68MM **Privately Held**
SIC: **5149** Tea
PA: Mhh Holdings, Inc.
4580 Calle Alto
Camarillo CA
805 484-7924

(P-13380)
MONDELEZ GLOBAL LLC
Also Called: Nabisco
5815 Clark St (91761-3676)
PHONE...................909 605-0140
Botie Magee, *Brnch Mgr*
EMP: 61
Web: www.mondelezinternational.com
SIC: **5149** 2099 2052 Crackers, cookies, and bakery products; Food preparations, nec; Cookies and crackers
HQ: Mondelez Global Llc
905 W Fulton Market # 200
Chicago IL
847 943-4000

(P-13381)
MONSTER ENERGY COMPANY (HQ)
Also Called: Monster Energy
1 Monster Way (92879-7101)
PHONE...................866 322-4466
Rodney C Sacks, *CEO*
Hilton H Scholsberg, *V Ch Bd*
Thomas J Kelly, *CFO*
◆ **EMP:** 258 **EST:** 1992
SQ FT: 300,000
SALES (est): 577.37K
SALES (corp-wide): 6.31B **Publicly Held**
Web: www.monsterbevcorp.com
SIC: **5149** Juices
PA: Monster Beverage Corporation
1 Monster Way
Corona CA
951 739-6200

(P-13382)
MUTUAL TRADING CO INC (DH)
4200 Shirley Ave (91731-1130)
PHONE...................213 626-9458
Masatoshi Ohata, *Dir*
Atsuko Kanai, *
Yoshihiro Sakata, *
Ami Nakanishi, *Dir*
Minori Mori, *
◆ **EMP:** 105 **EST:** 1926
SALES (est): 191.56MM **Privately Held**
Web: www.lamtc.com
SIC: **5149** 5141 5023 Groceries and related products, nec; Groceries, general line; Homefurnishings
HQ: Takara Shuzo International Co., Ltd.
20, Naginatabokocho, Higashiiru, Karasuma, Shijodoori, Shimogyo-Kyoto KYO

(P-13383)
NATURES BEST
6 Pointe Dr Ste 300 (92821-6323)
P.O. Box 2248 (92822-2248)
PHONE...................714 255-4600
▲ **EMP:** 360
SIC: **5149** Health foods

(P-13384)
NEUROBRANDS LLC
Also Called: Neuro Drinks
15303 Ventura Blvd Ste 675 (91403-6608)
P.O. Box 55245 (91413-0245)
PHONE...................310 393-6444
Diana Jenkins, *CEO*
Scott Laporta, *
Greg Buscher, *
▲ **EMP:** 125 **EST:** 2009
SALES (est): 42.36MM **Privately Held**
Web: www.drinkneuro.com
SIC: **5149** Soft drinks

(P-13385)
NIITAKAYA USA INC (PA)
1801 Aeros Way (90640-6505)
PHONE...................323 720-5050
Katsutoshi Suda, *Pr*
Hideo Nakagawa, *
▲ **EMP:** 23 **EST:** 1981
SQ FT: 17,000
SALES (est): 23.24MM **Privately Held**
Web: www.niitakaya.com
SIC: **5149** 2099 Pickles, preserves, jellies, and jams; Food preparations, nec

(P-13386)
OLDE THOMPSON LLC
2300 Celsius Ave (93030-5572)
PHONE...................805 983-0388
EMP: 49

SALES (corp-wide): 476.62MM **Privately Held**
Web: www.oldethompson.com
SIC: **5149** 2099 Groceries and related products, nec; Food preparations, nec
HQ: Olde Thompson, Llc
3250 Camino Del Sol
Oxnard CA
805 983-0388

(P-13387)
PASTA PICCININI INC
950 N Fair Oaks Ave (91103-3009)
PHONE...................626 798-0841
Stefano Piccinini, *CEO*
▲ **EMP:** 37 **EST:** 1971
SQ FT: 30,000
SALES (est): 21.54MM **Privately Held**
Web: www.pastapiccinini.com
SIC: **5149** 5812 2045 Pasta and rice; Eating places; Biscuit dough, prepared: from purchased flour

(P-13388)
PERFECT BAR LLC
Also Called: Perfect Snacks
3931 Sorrento Valley Blvd Ste 100 (92121-1402)
PHONE...................866 628-8548
Bill Keith, *CEO*
EMP: 200 **EST:** 2005
SQ FT: 16,000
SALES (est): 96.39MM **Publicly Held**
Web: www.perfectsnacks.com
SIC: **5149** Health foods
PA: Mondelez International, Inc.
905 W Fulton Market # 200
Chicago IL

(P-13389)
PF BAKERIES LLC
Also Called: P-Tabun
1375 Fayette St (92020-1512)
PHONE...................858 263-4863
Elad Primosher Mbrprin, *Owner*
▲ **EMP:** 20 **EST:** 2013
SALES (est): 1.76MM **Privately Held**
Web: www.pfbakeries.com
SIC: **5149** 2051 Bakery products; Rolls, bread type: fresh or frozen

(P-13390)
QUALITY NATURALLY FOODS INC (PA)
Also Called: Yum Yum Donut Shop
18830 San Jose Ave (91748-1325)
PHONE...................626 854-6363
◆ **EMP:** 42 **EST:** 1971
SALES (est): 30.56MM
SALES (corp-wide): 30.56MM **Privately Held**
Web: www.qnfoods.com
SIC: **5149** 2099 2045 Bakery products; Food preparations, nec; Prepared flour mixes and doughs

(P-13391)
REYES COCA-COLA BOTTLING LLC
Also Called: Coca-Cola
12925 Bradley Ave (91342-3830)
PHONE...................818 362-4307
Larry Campbell, *Brnch Mgr*
EMP: 54
SALES (corp-wide): 850.14MM **Privately Held**
Web: www.reyescocacola.com
SIC: **5149** 4225 2086 Soft drinks; General warehousing; Bottled and canned soft drinks
PA: Reyes Coca-Cola Bottling, L.L.C.
3 Park Plz Ste 600

Irvine CA
213 744-8616

(P-13392)
ROCKVIEW DAIRIES INC (PA)
Also Called: Motive Nation
7011 Stewart And Gray Rd (90241-4347)
P.O. Box 668 (90241-0668)
PHONE..................................562 927-5511
Egbert Jim Degroot, *CEO*
Ted De Groot, *
Joe Valadez, *
◆ **EMP:** 188 **EST:** 1966
SALES (est): 87.42MM
SALES (corp-wide): 87.42MM **Privately Held**
Web: www.rockviewfarms.com
SIC: 5149 5143 2026 Dried or canned foods; Milk; Fluid milk

(P-13393)
ROYAL CROWN ENTERPRISES INC
780 Epperson Dr (91748-1336)
PHONE..................................626 854-8080
◆ **EMP:** 150
SIC: 5149 5141 Canned goods: fruit, vegetables, seafood, meats, etc.; Groceries, general line

(P-13394)
SHAMROCK FOODS COMPANY
12400 Riverside Dr (91752-1004)
PHONE..................................951 685-6314
EMP: 696
SALES (corp-wide): 5.7B **Privately Held**
Web: www.shamrockfoods.com
SIC: 5149 Groceries and related products, nec
PA: Shamrock Foods Company
3900 E Camelback Rd # 300
Phoenix AZ
602 233-6400

(P-13395)
SUN TEN LABS LIQUIDATION CO
9250 Jeronimo Rd (92618-1905)
PHONE..................................949 587-0509
▲ **EMP:** 18 **EST:** 1986
SALES (est): 2.39MM **Privately Held**
Web: www.sunten.com
SIC: 5149 2834 2833 Spices and seasonings; Pharmaceutical preparations; Medicinals and botanicals

(P-13396)
SUNFOOD CORPORATION
Also Called: Sunfood Superfoods
1830 Gillespie Way Ste 101 (92020-0922)
PHONE..................................619 596-7979
Robert Deupree, *CEO*
▲ **EMP:** 95 **EST:** 2009
SALES (est): 48.45MM **Privately Held**
Web: www.sunfood.com
SIC: 5149 Natural and organic foods

(P-13397)
SURGE GLOBL BKRIES HLDINGS LLC (PA)
Also Called: Global Bakeries
13336 Paxton St (91331-2339)
PHONE..................................818 896-0525
Chris Botticella, *CEO*
Ash Aghasi, *COO*
EMP: 98 **EST:** 2018
SQ FT: 44,000
SALES (est): 22.62MM
SALES (corp-wide): 22.62MM **Privately Held**

Web: www.globalbakeriesllc.com
SIC: 5149 Bakery products

(P-13398)
SWEETENER PRODUCTS INC (PA)
Also Called: Sweetener Products Company
2050 E 38th St (90058-1615)
P.O. Box 58426 (90058-0426)
PHONE..................................323 234-2200
Dale Jabour, *Pr*
EMP: 20 **EST:** 1923
SALES (est): 85.89MM
SALES (corp-wide): 85.89MM **Privately Held**
Web: www.sweetenerproducts.com
SIC: 5149 2062 Groceries and related products, nec; Cane sugar refining

(P-13399)
SWELL COFFEE ROASTING CO LP
Also Called: Swell Cafe, The
501 W Broadway Ste 290 (92101-8651)
PHONE..................................619 504-9244
John Vallas, *CEO*
EMP: 20 **EST:** 2015
SALES (est): 1.7MM **Privately Held**
SIC: 5149 5046 8742 2095 Specialty food items; Commercial cooking and food service equipment; Restaurant and food services consultants; Roasted coffee

(P-13400)
TADIN INC
Also Called: Tadin Herb & Tea Co.
3345 E Slauson Ave (90058-3914)
PHONE..................................213 406-8880
▲ **EMP:** 95
Web: www.tadin.com
SIC: 5149 Tea

(P-13401)
TL MONTGOMERY & ASSOCIATES INC
2833 Leonis Blvd Ste 205 (90058-2909)
PHONE..................................323 583-1645
▼ **EMP:** 110
SIC: 5149 Pet foods

(P-13402)
TLD ACQUISITION CO LLC
Also Called: Tld Distribution Co
505 S 7th Ave (91746-3121)
▲ **EMP:** 150
SIC: 5149 5023 5145 5046 Beverages, except coffee and tea; Glassware; Snack foods; Restaurant equipment and supplies, nec

(P-13403)
US FOODS INC
Also Called: General Cold Stg 4145
8457 Eastern Ave (90201-7137)
PHONE..................................562 806-2445
EMP: 159
Web: www.usfoods.com
SIC: 5149 Dried or canned foods
HQ: Us Foods, Inc.
9399 W Higgins Rd # 100
Rosemont IL

(P-13404)
US FOODS INC
Also Called: Central Prcss 4140
636 Stanford Ave (90021-1006)
PHONE..................................213 623-4150
EMP: 159

Web: www.usfoods.com
SIC: 5149 Dried or canned foods
HQ: Us Foods, Inc.
9399 W Higgins Rd # 100
Rosemont IL

(P-13405)
US FOODS INC
Also Called: P&O Stg-Carson 4150
1610 E Sepulveda Blvd (90745-6120)
PHONE..................................310 632-6265
EMP: 159
Web: www.usfoods.com
SIC: 5149 Dried or canned foods
HQ: Us Foods, Inc.
9399 W Higgins Rd # 100
Rosemont IL

5153 Grain And Field Beans

(P-13406)
GRAIN TO GREEN INC
301 N El Camino Real (92672-4716)
P.O. Box 1697 (92018-1697)
PHONE..................................760 845-6107
Gina Marsaglia, *Prin*
EMP: 111
SALES (corp-wide): 6.27MM **Privately Held**
Web: www.pizzaport.com
SIC: 5153 Grains
PA: Grain To Green Inc
2730 Gateway Rd Ste 100
Carlsbad CA
760 707-1655

5159 Farm-product Raw Materials, Nec

(P-13407)
FLUIDS MANUFACTURING INC
11941 Vose St (91605-5750)
P.O. Box 16297 (91615-6297)
PHONE..................................818 264-4657
Stephan Sutton, *CEO*
EMP: 150 **EST:** 2015
SALES (est): 12.29MM **Privately Held**
SIC: 5159

(P-13408)
IMPERIAL WESTERN PRODUCTS INC A CALIFORNIA CORPORATION (HQ)
86600 Avenue 54 (92236-3812)
P.O. Box 1110 (92236-1110)
PHONE..................................760 398-0815
▼ **EMP:** 50 **EST:** 1966
SALES (est): 102.96MM
SALES (corp-wide): 458.01MM **Privately Held**
Web: www.imperialwesternproducts.com
SIC: 5159 2841 2869 Cotton merchants and products; Glycerin, crude or refined: from fats; Industrial organic chemicals, nec
PA: Denali Water Solutions Llc
3308 Bernice Ave
Russellville AR
479 498-0500

(P-13409)
SOUTH VALLEY ALMOND CO LLC
Also Called: South Valley Farms
15443 Beech Ave (93280-7604)
PHONE..................................661 391-9000
Paul C Genho, *Managing Member*
Merrill Dibble, *Managing Member*

◆ **EMP:** 200 **EST:** 2007
SQ FT: 4,000
SALES (est): 25.63MM **Privately Held**
Web: www.southvalleyfarms.com
SIC: 5159 Nuts and nut by-products

5162 Plastics Materials And Basic Shapes

(P-13410)
CIRRUS ENTERPRISES LLC
Also Called: E.V. Roberts
18027 Bishop Ave (90746-4019)
PHONE..................................310 204-6159
Tracey H Cloud, *
▲ **EMP:** 52 **EST:** 1938
SQ FT: 26,000
SALES (est): 24.84MM **Privately Held**
Web: www.evroberts.com
SIC: 5162 2821 2891 5198 Plastics products, nec; Epoxy resins; Adhesives and sealants; Paints, varnishes, and supplies

(P-13411)
COAST PLASTICS INC (PA)
4711 E Guasti Rd (91761-8106)
PHONE..................................626 812-9174
Matt Humphries, *Pr*
EMP: 17 **EST:** 1979
SALES (est): 3.79MM
SALES (corp-wide): 3.79MM **Privately Held**
Web: www.coastplasticsinc.com
SIC: 5162 3089 Plastics materials, nec; Plastics processing

(P-13412)
CONSOLIDATED PLASTICS CORP (PA)
Also Called: Paragon Plastics Co Div
14954 La Palma Dr (91710-9695)
PHONE..................................909 393-8222
Jean Bouris, *Pr*
Gloria Jean Bouris, *
EMP: 50 **EST:** 1973
SQ FT: 45,000
SALES (est): 9.97MM
SALES (corp-wide): 9.97MM **Privately Held**
Web: www.planetplastics.com
SIC: 5162 3599 Plastics sheets and rods; Machine shop, jobbing and repair

(P-13413)
ELKAY PLASTICS CO INC (PA)
6000 Sheila St (90040-2405)
PHONE..................................323 722-7073
Louis Chertkow, *Pr*
Geoffrey Pankau, *
▲ **EMP:** 100 **EST:** 1966
SQ FT: 175,000
SALES (est): 101.9MM
SALES (corp-wide): 101.9MM **Privately Held**
Web: www.lkpkg.com
SIC: 5162 Plastics products, nec

(P-13414)
LAIRD PLASTICS INC
12991 Marquardt Ave (90670-4828)
PHONE..................................562 464-9929
TOLL FREE: 800
Andy Boyle, *Brnch Mgr*
EMP: 38
Web: www.lairdplastics.com
SIC: 5162 3089 Plastics materials, nec; Windows, plastics
HQ: Laird Plastics, Inc.
5800 Campus Circle Dr E # 1

Irving TX
469 299-7000

(P-13415)
ORANGE COUNTY INDUS PLAS INC (PA)
Also Called: Ocip
4811 E La Palma Ave (92807-1954)
PHONE......................714 632-9450
Robert Robinson, *Pr*
▲ **EMP:** 25 **EST:** 1985
SQ FT: 70,198
SALES (est): 27.79MM
SALES (corp-wide): 27.79MM **Privately Held**
Web: www.ocip.com
SIC: 5162 2821 Plastics products, nec; Plastics materials and resins

(P-13416)
PLASTIC SALES SOUTHERN INC
Also Called: Plastic Sales
425 Havana Ave (90814-1928)
PHONE......................714 375-7900
James Quinn, *Pr*
EMP: 23 **EST:** 1980
SALES (est): 2.49MM **Privately Held**
SIC: 5162 3089 Plastics sheets and rods; Injection molding of plastics

(P-13417)
REGAL-PIEDMONT PLASTICS LLC
Also Called: Piedmont Plastics
17000 Valley View Ave (90638-5827)
P.O. Box 1274 (90308-1274)
PHONE......................562 404-4014
TOLL FREE: 800
Carlos Bennett, *Brnch Mgr*
EMP: 34
SALES (corp-wide): 201.65MM **Privately Held**
Web: www.regalpiedmontplastics.com
SIC: 5162 2396 5169 Plastics sheets and rods; Furniture trimmings, fabric; Silicon lubricants
HQ: Regal-Piedmont Plastics, Llc
5010 W W T Harris Blvd
Charlotte NC

(P-13418)
S & W PLASTIC STORES INC (PA)
Also Called: S & W Plastics Supply
14270 Albers Way (91710-6940)
PHONE......................909 390-0090
William B Goldstein, *CEO*
David Goldstein, *
▲ **EMP:** 35 **EST:** 1964
SQ FT: 25,000
SALES (est): 8.16MM
SALES (corp-wide): 8.16MM **Privately Held**
Web: www.sandwplastics.com
SIC: 5162 5719 3089 Plastics products, nec; Housewares, nec; Plastics kitchenware, tableware, and houseware

(P-13419)
TRANSCENDIA INC
Also Called: Transilwrap Company
9000 9th St Ste 140 (91730-4499)
PHONE......................909 944-9981
Jorge Zaldivar, *Brnch Mgr*
EMP: 44
SQ FT: 41,400
SALES (corp-wide): 290.26MM **Privately Held**

Web: www.transcendia.com
SIC: 5162 3081 3089 Plastics materials and basic shapes; Unsupported plastics film and sheet; Plastics processing
PA: Transcendia, Inc.
9201 Belmont Ave Ste 100a
Franklin Park IL
847 678-1800

5169 Chemicals And Allied Products, Nec

(P-13420)
ACCESS BUSINESS GROUP LLC
Also Called: Access Logistics
12825 Leffingwell Ave (90670-6339)
PHONE......................808 422-9482
Hee Douglas, *Brnch Mgr*
EMP: 282
Web: www.amwayglobal.com
SIC: 5169 Chemicals and allied products, nec
HQ: Access Business Group Llc
7575 Fulton St E
Ada MI

(P-13421)
ACCESS BUSINESS GROUP LLC
5600 Beach Blvd (90621-2007)
P.O. Box 5940 (90622-5940)
PHONE......................714 562-6200
Steve Vanandel, *BD*
EMP: 477
Web: www.amwayglobal.com
SIC: 5169 Chemicals and allied products, nec
HQ: Access Business Group Llc
7575 Fulton St E
Ada MI

(P-13422)
ACCESS BUSINESS GROUP LLC
Also Called: Nutrilite
5609 River Way (90621-1709)
PHONE......................714 562-7914
EMP: 293
Web: www.amwayglobal.com
SIC: 5169 Chemicals and allied products, nec
HQ: Access Business Group Llc
7575 Fulton St E
Ada MI

(P-13423)
ADVANTAGE CHEMICAL LLC
27375 Via Industria (92590-3699)
PHONE......................951 225-4631
EMP: 22 **EST:** 2010
SQ FT: 20,000
SALES (est): 4.97MM **Privately Held**
Web: www.advantagechemical.com
SIC: 5169 2842 Specialty cleaning and sanitation preparations; Sanitation preparations

(P-13424)
APPLIED SILICONE COMPANY LLC
Also Called: Applied Silicone
1050 Cindy Ln (93013-2906)
PHONE......................805 525-5657
Ralph Alastair Winn, *Pr*
Phil Galarnau, *
▲ **EMP:** 81 **EST:** 1987
SQ FT: 20,000
SALES (est): 42.8MM
SALES (corp-wide): 7.51B **Publicly Held**
SIC: 5169 Chemicals and allied products, nec

HQ: Nusil Technology Llc
1050 Cindy Ln
Carpinteria CA
805 684-8780

(P-13425)
BRENNTAG PACIFIC INC (DH)
10747 Patterson Pl (90670-4043)
PHONE......................562 903-9626
David Eckelbarger, *CEO*
Steven Pozzi, *Pr*
H Edward Boyadjian, *Ex VP*
Julia Tu, *Contrlr*
Leslie Lenhardt, *Sec*
▲ **EMP:** 102 **EST:** 2003
SALES (est): 391.54MM **Privately Held**
SIC: 5169 Chemicals, industrial and heavy
HQ: Brenntag North America, Inc.
5083 Pottsville Pike
Reading PA
610 926-6100

(P-13426)
CALWAX LLC (DH)
16511 Knott Ave (90638-6011)
PHONE......................626 969-4334
John Paraszczak, *Managing Member*
▲ **EMP:** 37 **EST:** 1955
SQ FT: 40,000
SALES (est): 21.79MM **Privately Held**
Web: www.calwax.com
SIC: 5169 2842 Waxes, except petroleum; Waxes for wood, leather, and other materials
HQ: Remet Corporation
210 Commons Rd
Utica NY
315 797-8700

(P-13427)
CHAMPION CHEMICAL CO CAL INC
Also Called: Champion Chemical Co
8319 Greenleaf Ave (90602-2912)
P.O. Box 5429 (90607-5429)
PHONE......................562 945-1456
Andrew L Ellis, *Pr*
Andrew L Ellis, *CEO*
David C Ellis, *Cnslt*
Dennis C Hall, *VP*
EMP: 32 **EST:** 1960
SQ FT: 8,000
SALES (est): 11.76MM **Privately Held**
SIC: 5169 2841 2842 2843 Specialty cleaning and sanitation preparations; Soap and other detergents; Polishes and sanitation goods; Surface active agents

(P-13428)
CHEMBRIDGE CORPORATION (PA)
11199 Sorrento Valley Rd Ste 206 (92121-1334)
PHONE......................858 451-7400
Eugene Vaisberg, *CEO*
Sergey Altshteyn, *Pr*
EMP: 260 **EST:** 1993
SQ FT: 26,000
SALES (est): 29.83MM **Privately Held**
Web: www.chembridge.com
SIC: 5169 Chemicals and allied products, nec

(P-13429)
CHEMSIL SILICONES INC
21900 Marilla St (91311-4129)
PHONE......................818 700-0302
Williams S Patrick, *CEO*
Patrick S Williams, *
Bruce Mcdonald, *General Vice President*

Ian Cleminson, *
Tom Martin, *
◆ **EMP:** 26 **EST:** 2000
SQ FT: 32,789
SALES (est): 24.6MM
SALES (corp-wide): 1.96B **Publicly Held**
Web: www.chemsil.com
SIC: 5169 2869 Chemicals and allied products, nec; Silicones
PA: Innospec Inc.
8310 S Valley Hwy Ste 350
Englewood CO
303 792-5554

(P-13430)
CHEROKEE CHEMICAL CO INC (PA)
Also Called: CCI
3540 E 26th St (90058-4103)
PHONE......................323 265-1112
Da Criswell, *CEO*
EMP: 47 **EST:** 1964
SQ FT: 30,000
SALES (est): 28.76MM
SALES (corp-wide): 28.76MM **Privately Held**
Web: www.ccichemical.com
SIC: 5169 2842 2819 Specialty cleaning and sanitation preparations; Polishes and sanitation goods; Industrial inorganic chemicals, nec

(P-13431)
EMBEE PERFORMANCE LLC
Also Called: Embee Powder Coating
2100 Ritchey St (92705-5134)
PHONE......................714 540-1354
David Dahlberg, *Managing Member*
EMP: 20 **EST:** 2000
SALES (est): 2.26MM **Privately Held**
Web: www.embeeperformance.com
SIC: 5169 3471 Polishes, nec; Plating of metals or formed products

(P-13432)
ESE INC
Also Called: Ese
1111 S Central Ave (90021-2041)
PHONE......................213 614-0102
David Kazemi, *CEO*
▲ **EMP:** 25 **EST:** 1993
SALES (est): 5MM **Privately Held**
Web: www.realklean.com
SIC: 5169 5065 Alcohols and anti-freeze compounds; Soap and other detergents; Electronic parts and equipment, nec

(P-13433)
GENERAL ELECTRIC COMPANY
Also Called: GE
4045 Cheyenne Ct (91710-5468)
PHONE......................909 517-2560
Linda Nguyen, *Mgr*
EMP: 19
SALES (corp-wide): 76.56B **Publicly Held**
Web: www.ge.com
SIC: 5169 2869 Silicon lubricants; Industrial organic chemicals, nec
PA: General Electric Company
1 Financial Ctr Ste 3700
Boston MA
617 443-3000

(P-13434)
GEO DRILLING FLUIDS INC (PA)
Also Called: Industrial Minerals Company
1431 Union Ave (93305-5732)
P.O. Box 1478 (93302-1478)
PHONE......................661 325-5919

Jim Clifford, *Pr*
Dan Bauman, *
Bob French, *
Don Boulet, *
Tom Needham, *
▲ **EMP:** 30 **EST:** 1950
SQ FT: 7,500
SALES (est): 33.93MM
SALES (corp-wide): 33.93MM **Privately Held**
Web: www.geodf.com
SIC: 5169 1389 7389 Chemicals and allied products, nec; Servicing oil and gas wells; Grinding, precision: commercial or industrial

(P-13435)
HILL BROTHERS CHEMICAL COMPANY (PA)
Also Called: Hill Brothers Chemical
3000 E Birch St Ste 108 (92821-6261)
PHONE..............................714 998-8800
Adam Hill, *Pr*
Matthew Thorne, *
Thomas F James, *
Kathryn J Waters, *
▲ **EMP:** 150 **EST:** 1935
SALES (est): 125.44MM
SALES (corp-wide): 125.44MM **Privately Held**
Web: www.hillbrothers.com
SIC: 5169 2819 Acids; Calcium chloride and hypochlorite

(P-13436)
NORMAN FOX & CO
5511 S Boyle Ave (90058-3932)
P.O. Box 58727 (90058-0727)
PHONE..............................323 973-4900
Alex Kirby, *Brnch Mgr*
EMP: 23
SALES (corp-wide): 44.88MM **Privately Held**
Web: www.norfoxchem.com
SIC: 5169 2841 Industrial chemicals; Soap: granulated, liquid, cake, flaked, or chip
PA: Norman, Fox & Co.
    14970 Don Julian Rd
    City Of Industry CA
    800 632-1777

(P-13437)
NORMAN FOX & CO (PA)
Also Called: Norfox
14970 Don Julian Rd (91746-3111)
PHONE..............................800 632-1777
Stephen Halpin, *CEO*
Bob Code, *
◆ **EMP:** 40 **EST:** 1971
SQ FT: 5,000
SALES (est): 44.88MM
SALES (corp-wide): 44.88MM **Privately Held**
Web: www.norfoxchem.com
SIC: 5169 2841 Chemicals and allied products, nec; Soap: granulated, liquid, cake, flaked, or chip

(P-13438)
R D ABBOTT CO INC
11958 Monarch St (92841-2112)
PHONE..............................562 944-5354
Keith Arthur Thomas, *CEO*
▲ **EMP:** 91 **EST:** 1949
SALES (est): 57.75MM **Privately Held**
Web: www.rdabbott.com
SIC: 5169 Chemicals and allied products, nec

(P-13439)
SPECTRUM LABORATORY PDTS INC
Also Called: Spectrum Lab & Phrm Pdts
14422 S San Pedro St (90248-2027)
PHONE..............................520 292-3103
Elizabeth Brown, *CEO*
EMP: 31
SALES (corp-wide): 126.91MM **Privately Held**
Web: www.spectrumrx.com
SIC: 5169 2869 2819 Organic chemicals, synthetic; Laboratory chemicals, organic; Industrial inorganic chemicals, nec
PA: Spectrum Laboratory Products, Inc.
    769 Jersey Ave
    New Brunswick NJ
    732 214-1300

(P-13440)
UNIVAR SOLUTIONS USA INC
2600 Garfield Ave (90040-2608)
P.O. Box 512062 (90040)
PHONE..............................323 727-7005
Gary Cramer, *Brnch Mgr*
EMP: 175
SALES (corp-wide): 11.48B **Privately Held**
Web: www.univarsolutions.com
SIC: 5169 Industrial chemicals
HQ: Univar Solutions Usa Inc.
    3075 Highland Pkwy # 200
    Downers Grove IL
    331 777-6000

(P-13441)
VALEANT BIOMEDICALS INC (DH)
1 Enterprise (92656-2606)
PHONE..............................949 461-6000
Tim Tyson, *Pr*
EMP: 100 **EST:** 1983
SQ FT: 55,000
SALES (est): 101.77MM
SALES (corp-wide): 8.05B **Privately Held**
SIC: 5169 2835 8731 3826 Chemicals and allied products, nec; Diagnostic substances ; Biotechnical research, commercial; Analytical instruments
HQ: Bausch Health Americas, Inc.
    400 Somerset Corp Blvd
    Bridgewater NJ
    908 927-1400

(P-13442)
VALUDOR PRODUCTS LLC
179 Calle Magdalena Ste 100 (92024-3779)
PHONE..............................760 635-8500
Alberto Machado, *CEO*
EMP: 17 **EST:** 2018
SALES (est): 36.56MM
SALES (corp-wide): 204.72MM **Privately Held**
Web: www.valudor.com
SIC: 5169 5191 2851 Adhesives, chemical; Fertilizers and agricultural chemicals; Paints and paint additives
PA: Monroe Capital Management Advisors, Llc
    311 S Wacker Dr Ste 6400
    Chicago IL
    312 258-8300

(P-13443)
VIJALL INC
Also Called: Chemtec Chemical Company
21900 Marilla St (91311-4129)
PHONE..............................818 700-0071
Patrick S Williams, *Pr*
Bruce Mcdonald, *Pr*

Ian Cleminson, *
Tom Martin, *
David E Williams, *
▲ **EMP:** 26 **EST:** 1987
SQ FT: 32,789
SALES (est): 9.39MM
SALES (corp-wide): 1.96B **Publicly Held**
Web: www.chemteccc.com
SIC: 5169 2819 Industrial chemicals; Industrial inorganic chemicals, nec
HQ: Innospec Active Chemicals Llc
    510 W Grimes Ave
    High Point NC
    336 882-3308

(P-13444)
ZEP INC
Selig Chemical Industries
1000 Railroad St (92882-1947)
PHONE..............................877 428-9937
Mike Saults, *Mgr*
EMP: 163
SALES (corp-wide): 978.45MM **Privately Held**
Web: www.zep.com
SIC: 5169 Industrial chemicals
HQ: Zep Inc.
    600 Galleria Pkwy Se # 1500
    Atlanta GA
    877 428-9937

5171 Petroleum Bulk Stations And Terminals

(P-13445)
SOUTHERN COUNTIES OIL CO (DH)
Also Called: SC Fuels
1800 W Katella Ave Ste 210 (92867-3417)
P.O. Box 4159 (92863-4159)
PHONE..............................714 744-7140
TOLL FREE: 800
Shameek Konar, *CEO*
Mimi Taylor, *
David Larimer, *
▲ **EMP:** 95 **EST:** 1969
SALES (est): 960.53MM
SALES (corp-wide): 3.84B **Privately Held**
Web: www.scfuels.com
SIC: 5171 5541 5172 Petroleum bulk stations ; Gasoline service stations; Petroleum products, nec
HQ: Pilot Travel Centers Llc
    5508 Lonas Dr
    Knoxville TN
    877 866-7378

(P-13446)
ZECO SYSTEMS INC
Also Called: Greenlots
767 S Alameda St Ste 200 (90021-1660)
PHONE..............................888 751-8560
Andreas Lips, *CEO*
Brett Hauser, *
Lin-dhuang Khoo, *Sr VP*
Harmeet Singh, *
Ron Mahabir, *
EMP: 95 **EST:** 2012
SQ FT: 10,000
SALES (est): 53.36MM
SALES (corp-wide): 381.31B **Privately Held**
Web: www.shellrecharge.com
SIC: 5171 Petroleum bulk stations and terminals
HQ: Zeco Holdings, Inc.
    925 N La Brea Ave
    West Hollywood CA
    888 751-8560

5172 Petroleum Products, Nec

(P-13447)
ASTRA OIL COMPANY INC
301 Main St Ste 201 (92648-5171)
PHONE..............................714 969-6569
◆ **EMP:** 160
Web: www.astraoil.com
SIC: 5172 Petroleum products, nec

(P-13448)
CASEY COMPANY (PA)
180 E Ocean Blvd Ste 1010 (90802-4711)
PHONE..............................562 436-9685
Larry Delpit Senior, *Ch*
Betty Jane Blanchette, *
Barbara Odom, *
EMP: 129 **EST:** 1982
SQ FT: 4,000
SALES (est): 101.77MM
SALES (corp-wide): 101.77MM **Privately Held**
SIC: 5172 Petroleum products, nec

(P-13449)
CLIPPER OIL INC
Also Called: Clipper Oil Company
2040 Harbor Island Dr Ste 203 (92101-1018)
PHONE..............................619 692-9701
Kevin Alameda, *VP*
Sandi Myers, *Contrlr*
Tony Maude, *Sls Dir*
Zheng Intr Sales Bunker Tian T rader, *Prin*
◆ **EMP:** 20 **EST:** 1979
SQ FT: 1,100
SALES (est): 22.16MM **Privately Held**
Web: www.clipperoil.com
SIC: 5172 2873 5169 Diesel fuel; Anhydrous ammonia; Salts, industrial

(P-13450)
EFUEL LLC
Also Called: Easy Fuel
65 Enterprise 3rd Fl (92656-2601)
PHONE..............................949 330-7145
Donald Harper, *CEO*
EMP: 90 **EST:** 2016
SALES (est): 43.99MM
SALES (corp-wide): 175.7B **Publicly Held**
Web: www.efuelco.com
SIC: 5172 Petroleum products, nec
PA: Phillips 66
    2331 Citywest Blvd
    Houston TX
    832 765-3010

(P-13451)
EMPIRE OIL CO
2756 S Riverside Ave (92316-3500)
PHONE..............................909 877-0226
Richard Alden Senior, *CEO*
Richard Scott Alden Junior, *Pr*
Donald Welker, *
EMP: 132 **EST:** 1961
SQ FT: 2,300
SALES (est): 2.42MM **Publicly Held**
SIC: 5172 Diesel fuel
HQ: Northern Tier Energy Lp
    1250 W Washington St # 300
    Tempe AZ
    602 302-5450

(P-13452)
GENERAL PETROLEUM LLC (HQ)
Also Called: G P Resources

▲ = Import ▼ = Export
◆ = Import/Export

19501 S Santa Fe Ave (90221-5913)
P.O. Box 2136 (76099-2136)
PHONE.................................562 983-7300
James A Halsam Iii, *CEO*
Michael Ruehring, *
Sean Kha, *
▲ **EMP:** 150 **EST:** 1946
SQ FT: 5,000
SALES (est): 46.98MM
SALES (corp-wide): 66.45MM **Privately Held**
SIC: 5172 Crude oil
PA: Pecos, Inc.
19501 S Santa Fe Ave
Compton CA
310 356-2300

(P-13453)
POMA HOLDING COMPANY INC
571 W Slover Ave (92316-2454)
PHONE.................................909 877-2441
EMP: 118
Web: www.pomacos.com
SIC: 5172 Petroleum products, nec

(P-13454)
PREMIER FUEL DISTRIBUTORS INC
Also Called: Premier Fuel Delivery Service
156 E La Cadena Dr (92507-8699)
PHONE.................................760 423-3610
Hugo Rodriguez, *CEO*
EMP: 150 **EST:** 2013
SALES (est): 19.06MM **Privately Held**
SIC: 5172 2869 Petroleum products, nec; Fuels

(P-13455)
TESORO REFINING & MKTG CO LLC
2101 E Pacific Coast Hwy (90744-2914)
PHONE.................................877 837-6762
James Nichols, *Brnch Mgr*
EMP: 238
SIC: 5172 Service station supplies, petroleum
HQ: Tesoro Refining & Marketing Company Llc
19100 Ridgewood Pkwy
San Antonio TX
210 626-6000

(P-13456)
TIODIZE CO INC
15701 Industry Ln (92649-1569)
PHONE.................................714 898-4377
Thomas Adams, *Pr*
EMP: 38
SALES (corp-wide): 9.73MM **Privately Held**
Web: www.tiodize.com
SIC: 5172 3471 Lubricating oils and greases ; Anodizing (plating) of metals or formed products
PA: Tiodize Co., Inc.
5858 Engineer Dr
Huntington Beach CA
714 898-4377

5181 Beer And Ale

(P-13457)
ADVANCE BEVERAGE CO INC
5200 District Blvd (93313-2330)
P.O. Box 9517 (93389-9517)
PHONE.................................661 833-3783
William K Lazzerini Senior, *Ch Bd*
William K Lazzerini Junior, *Pr*
Anthony Lazzerini, *

◆ **EMP:** 90 **EST:** 1952
SQ FT: 93,000
SALES (est): 41.54MM **Privately Held**
Web: www.advancebeverage.com
SIC: 5181 5182 Beer and other fermented malt liquors; Wine

(P-13458)
ALLIED COMPANY HOLDINGS INC
28311 Constellation Rd (91355-5048)
P.O. Box 129 (92398-0129)
PHONE.................................661 510-6533
Kevin R Williams, *Brnch Mgr*
EMP: 186
SALES (corp-wide): 47.07MM **Privately Held**
SIC: 5181 Beer and other fermented malt liquors
PA: Allied Company Holdings, Inc.
13235 Golden State Rd
Sylmar CA
818 493-6400

(P-13459)
ALLIED COMPANY HOLDINGS INC (PA)
Also Called: Best-Way Distributing Co
13235 Golden State Rd (91342-1129)
PHONE.................................818 493-6400
Kevin Williams, *CEO*
William L Larson, *
Erin S Gabler, *
Earl J Whitehead, *
◆ **EMP:** 98 **EST:** 1953
SQ FT: 240,000
SALES (est): 47.07MM
SALES (corp-wide): 47.07MM **Privately Held**
Web: www.alliedbeverages.com
SIC: 5181 Beer and other fermented malt liquors

(P-13460)
BEAUCHAMP DISTRIBUTING COMPANY
1911 S Santa Fe Ave (90221-5306)
PHONE.................................310 639-5320
Patrick L Beauchamp, *Pr*
Mary S Beauchamp, *
Stacee L Beauchamp, *
Peter J Gumpert, *
▲ **EMP:** 100 **EST:** 1971
SQ FT: 100,000
SALES (est): 47.24MM **Privately Held**
Web: www.beauchampdist.com
SIC: 5181 5149 Beer and other fermented malt liquors; Groceries and related products, nec

(P-13461)
BENNY ENTERPRISES INC
Also Called: Quality Distributor
1100 N Johnson Ave Ste 110 (92020-1917)
PHONE.................................619 592-4455
Raad Benny, *CEO*
EMP: 40 **EST:** 1994
SQ FT: 8,000
SALES (est): 15.84MM **Privately Held**
SIC: 5181 5141 5087 5015 Beer and ale; Groceries, general line; Cleaning and maintenance equipment and supplies; Automotive parts and supplies, used

(P-13462)
CENTRAL COAST DISTRIBUTING LLC
815 S Blosser Rd (93458-4915)
PHONE.................................805 922-2108

▲ **EMP:** 90 **EST:** 2001
SQ FT: 51,651
SALES (est): 19.29MM **Privately Held**
Web: www.greatbeer.us
SIC: 5181 Beer and other fermented malt liquors

(P-13463)
CLASSIC BEV SOUTHERN CAL LLC
120 Puente Ave (91746-2301)
PHONE.................................626 934-3700
Carlos Joseph Sanchez, *CEO*
John Thomas, *
▲ **EMP:** 261 **EST:** 1978
SQ FT: 102,000
SALES (est): 49.29MM **Privately Held**
Web: www.classicdist.com
SIC: 5181 Beer and other fermented malt liquors

(P-13464)
CREST BEVERAGE LLC
1348 47th St (92102-2510)
PHONE.................................858 452-2300
Steven S Sourapas, *Managing Member*
▲ **EMP:** 400 **EST:** 2009
SALES (est): 49.99MM **Privately Held**
Web: www.crestbeverage.com
SIC: 5181 Beer and other fermented malt liquors

(P-13465)
CREST BEVERAGE COMPANY INC
3840 Via De La Valle Ste 300 (92014-4268)
P.O. Box 9160 (92067-4160)
PHONE.................................858 452-2300
Steven S Sourapas Senior, *Pr*
▲ **EMP:** 170 **EST:** 1956
SQ FT: 160,000
SALES (est): 19.82MM **Privately Held**
Web: www.crestbeverage.com
SIC: 5181 5182 5149 Beer and other fermented malt liquors; Wine; Groceries and related products, nec

(P-13466)
GATE CITY BEVERAGE DISTRS (PA)
2505 Steele Rd (92408-3913)
PHONE.................................909 799-0281
Leona Aronoff, *Pr*
Barry Aronoff, *
▲ **EMP:** 294 **EST:** 1940
SQ FT: 280,000
SALES (est): 47.89MM
SALES (corp-wide): 47.89MM **Privately Held**
Web: www.gatecitybeverage.com
SIC: 5181 5149 5145 Beer and other fermented malt liquors; Soft drinks; Confectionery

(P-13467)
HARALAMBOS BEVERAGE CO
26717 Palmetto Ave (92374-1513)
PHONE.................................562 347-4300
H T Haralambos, *CEO*
Anthony Haralambos, *
Thomas Haralambos, *
Sally Haralambos, *
▲ **EMP:** 300 **EST:** 1933
SALES (est): 56.73MM **Privately Held**
SIC: 5181 5149 Beer and other fermented malt liquors; Beverages, except coffee and tea

(P-13468)
HARBOR DISTRIBUTING LLC (HQ)
Also Called: Golden Brands
5901 Bolsa Ave (92647-2053)
PHONE.................................714 933-2400
Jude Reyes, *
Chris Reyes, *
▲ **EMP:** 200 **EST:** 1989
SQ FT: 150,000
SALES (est): 893.68MM **Privately Held**
Web: www.harbordistributingllc.com
SIC: 5181 Beer and other fermented malt liquors
PA: Reyes Holdings, L.L.C.
6250 N River Rd Ste 9000
Rosemont IL

(P-13469)
HARBOR DISTRIBUTING LLC
Also Called: Harbor Distributing Co
16407 S Main St (90248-2823)
PHONE.................................310 538-5483
David Reyes, *Brnch Mgr*
EMP: 81
Web: www.reyesholdings.com
SIC: 5181 Beer and other fermented malt liquors
HQ: Harbor Distributing, L.L.C
5901 Bolsa Ave
Huntington Beach CA
714 933-2400

(P-13470)
JORDANOS INC (PA)
Also Called: Jordano's Food Service
550 S Patterson Ave (93111-2498)
P.O. Box 6803 (93160-6803)
PHONE.................................805 964-0611
Peter Jordano, *CEO*
Michael F Sieckowski, *VP*
Jeffrey S Jordano, *Ex VP*
▲ **EMP:** 250 **EST:** 1915
SQ FT: 80,000
SALES (est): 315.61MM
SALES (corp-wide): 315.61MM **Privately Held**
Web: www.jordanos.com
SIC: 5181 5182 5149 5141 Beer and other fermented malt liquors; Wine; Soft drinks; Groceries, general line

(P-13471)
LIQUID INVESTMENTS INC (PA)
3840 Via De La Valle Ste 300 (92014-4268)
PHONE.................................858 509-8510
Ron L Fowler, *CEO*
Terry L Harris, *
Mark Herculson, *
▲ **EMP:** 170 **EST:** 1981
SQ FT: 190,000
SALES (est): 44.89MM
SALES (corp-wide): 44.89MM **Privately Held**
Web: www.nextsolutions.us
SIC: 5181 5145 5182 Beer and other fermented malt liquors; Fountain supplies; Wine

(P-13472)
STRAUB DISTRIBUTING CO LTD (PA)
4633 E La Palma Ave (92807-1909)
PHONE.................................714 779-4000
Michael L Cooper, *Genl Pt*
Don Beightol, *Pt*
Robert K Adams, *Pt*
▲ **EMP:** 150 **EST:** 1948
SQ FT: 32,000
SALES (est): 55.82MM

PRODUCTS & SVCS

SALES (corp-wide): 55.82MM **Privately Held**
Web: www.straubdistributing.com
SIC: 5181 Beer and other fermented malt liquors

(P-13473)
TRIANGLE DISTRIBUTING CO
Also Called: Heimark Distributing
12065 Pike St (90670-2964)
PHONE................................562 699-3424
▲ **EMP:** 270
SIC: 5181 Beer and other fermented malt liquors

5182 Wine And Distilled Beverages

(P-13474)
BREAKTHRU BEVERAGE CAL LLC (HQ)
6550 E Washington Blvd (90040-1822)
P.O. Box 910900 (90091-0900)
PHONE................................800 331-2829
James P Myerson, *Pr*
◆ **EMP:** 350 **EST:** 1966
SQ FT: 135,000
SALES (est): 363.76MM
SALES (corp-wide): 2.8B **Privately Held**
Web: www.breakthrubevca.com
SIC: 5182 Wine
PA: Breakthru Beverage Group, Llc
60 E 42nd St Ste 1915
New York NY
212 699-7000

(P-13475)
CUSHMAN WINERY CORPORATION
Also Called: Zaca Mesa Winery
6905 Foxen Canyon Rd (93441-4530)
P.O. Box 899 (93441-0899)
PHONE................................805 688-9339
Brook Williams, *Pr*
Susan English, *
▲ **EMP:** 21 **EST:** 1972
SALES (est): 11.98MM **Privately Held**
Web: www.zacamesa.com
SIC: 5182 2084 0172 Wine; Wines; Grapes

(P-13476)
FARM STREET DESIGNS INC
Also Called: Van's Gifts
2520 Mira Mar Ave (90815-1758)
PHONE................................562 985-0026
Howard Colover, *CEO*
Reva Colover, *
▲ **EMP:** 33 **EST:** 1984
SQ FT: 39,000
SALES (est): 9.66MM **Privately Held**
SIC: 5182 2033 2035 5023 Wine; Tomato sauce: packaged in cans, jars, etc.; Dressings, salad: raw and cooked (except dry mixes); Kitchenware

(P-13477)
GUARACHI WINE PARTNERS INC
Also Called: Parker Station
27001 Agoura Rd Ste 285 (91301-5141)
PHONE................................818 225-5100
Alejandro Guarachi, *CEO*
▲ **EMP:** 80 **EST:** 1988
SQ FT: 5,000
SALES (est): 23.23MM **Privately Held**
Web: www.guarachiwinepartners.com
SIC: 5182 Wine

(P-13478)
LUCAS & LEWELLEN VINEYARDS INC (PA)
Also Called: Lucas Lwllen Vnyrds Tasting Rm
1645 Copenhagen Dr (93463-3742)
P.O. Box 648 (93440-0648)
PHONE................................805 686-9336
Royce R Lewellen, *Pr*
Louis A Lucas, *
EMP: 25 **EST:** 1996
SALES (est): 9.3MM
SALES (corp-wide): 9.3MM **Privately Held**
Web: www.llwine.com
SIC: 5182 2084 Wine; Wines

(P-13479)
MONTESQUIEU CORP
Also Called: Montesquieu Vins & Domaines
888 W E St (92101-5915)
PHONE................................877 705-5669
Fonda Hopkins, *Pr*
Frank Kryger, *
▲ **EMP:** 100 **EST:** 1991
SALES (est): 18.49MM **Privately Held**
Web: www.montesquieu.com
SIC: 5182 8743 Wine; Promotion service

(P-13480)
REPUBLIC NAT DISTRG CO LLC (PA)
Also Called: Rndc
14402 Franklin Ave (92780-7013)
P.O. Box 37100 (40233-7100)
PHONE................................714 368-4615
Jay Johnson, *Managing Member*
Nicholas Mehall, *
Robert Hendrickson, *
Robert Cornella, *
Sean Halligan, *Co-Executive Vice President*
▲ **EMP:** 144 **EST:** 1998
SALES (est): 1.4B
SALES (corp-wide): 1.4B **Privately Held**
Web: www.rndc-usa.com
SIC: 5182 Wine

(P-13481)
SOUTHERN GLZERS WINE SPRITS LL
Also Called: Southern Glzers Wine Sprits Ca
17101 Valley View Ave (90703-2413)
PHONE................................562 926-2000
EMP: 500
SALES (corp-wide): 7.22B **Privately Held**
Web: www.southernglazers.com
SIC: 5182 5181 Wine; Beer and ale
PA: Southern Glazer's Wine And Spirits, Llc
1600 Nw 163rd St
Miami FL
866 375-9555

(P-13482)
YOUNGS HOLDINGS INC (PA)
15 Enterprise Ste 100 (92656-2654)
PHONE................................714 368-4615
Chris Underwood, *Pr*
Vernon Underwood Junior, *Ch Bd*
EMP: 100 **EST:** 1973
SALES (est): 439.37MM
SALES (corp-wide): 439.37MM **Privately Held**
Web: www.youngsholdings.com
SIC: 5182 Wine

(P-13483)
YOUNGS MARKET COMPANY LLC (HQ)
14402 Franklin Ave (92780-7013)
PHONE................................800 317-6150
Chris Underwood, *CEO*
Dennis Hamann, *
◆ **EMP:** 350 **EST:** 1888
SQ FT: 250,000
SALES (est): 1.06B
SALES (corp-wide): 1.4B **Privately Held**
Web: www.rndc-usa.com
SIC: 5182 Wine
PA: Republic National Distributing Company, Llc
14402 Franklin Ave
Tustin CA
714 368-4615

(P-13484)
YOUNGS MARKET COMPANY LLC
Also Called: Wine Dept
500 S Central Ave (90013-1715)
PHONE................................213 629-3929
Mark Sneed, *Brnch Mgr*
EMP: 495
SALES (corp-wide): 1.4B **Privately Held**
Web: www.rndc-usa.com
SIC: 5182 Wine
HQ: Young's Market Company, Llc
14402 Franklin Ave
Tustin CA
800 317-6150

5191 Farm Supplies

(P-13485)
ACX INTERMODAL INC
920 E Pacific Coast Hwy (90744-2725)
PHONE................................310 241-6229
John Gombos, *Pr*
▼ **EMP:** 114 **EST:** 1983
SALES (est): 4.11MM **Privately Held**
Web: www.acxintermodal.com
SIC: 5191 Animal feeds
HQ: Al Dahra Acx, Inc.
920 E Pacific Coast Hwy
Wilmington CA

(P-13486)
AG RX (PA)
Also Called: Mountain View Transportation
751 S Rose Ave (93030-5146)
P.O. Box 2008 (93034-2008)
PHONE................................805 487-0696
Ken Burdullis, *Pr*
EMP: 92 **EST:** 1993
SQ FT: 45,000
SALES (est): 54.03MM **Privately Held**
Web: www.agrx.com
SIC: 5191 Fertilizer and fertilizer materials

(P-13487)
BROMA APPLICATORS LLC
322 W J St (92227-3116)
PHONE................................760 351-0101
EMP: 20 **EST:** 1997
SQ FT: 1,200
SALES (est): 4.34MM **Privately Held**
SIC: 5191 2879 Pesticides; Fungicides, herbicides

(P-13488)
L & L NURSERY SUPPLY INC (HQ)
Also Called: Unigro
2552 Shenandoah Way (92407-1845)
PHONE................................909 591-0461
Lloyd Swindell, *Ch Bd*
Tom Medhurst, *Pr*
▲ **EMP:** 150 **EST:** 1953
SQ FT: 107,000
SALES (est): 98.18MM

SALES (corp-wide): 183.31MM **Privately Held**
Web: www.bfgsupply.com
SIC: 5191 2875 2449 5193 Insecticides; Potting soil, mixed; Wood containers, nec; Flowers and florists supplies
PA: Bfg Supply Co., Llc
14500 Kinsman Rd
Burton OH
800 883-0234

(P-13489)
LEACH GRAIN & MILLING CO INC
8131 Pivot St (90241-4853)
PHONE................................562 869-4451
Willis R Leach Senior, *Pr*
Roy Leach, *
Willis R Leach Junior, *Sec*
Bruce Leach, *Stockholder*
EMP: 26 **EST:** 1934
SQ FT: 20,000
SALES (est): 4.75MM **Privately Held**
Web: www.leachgrain.com
SIC: 5191 2047 2048 Farm supplies; Dog and cat food; Bird food, prepared

(P-13490)
SEEDS OF CHANGE INC
Also Called: Sustainable Agriculture
31 Mountain Laurel (92679-4216)
P.O. Box 4908 (90224-4908)
PHONE................................310 764-7700
Will Righeimer, *CEO*
◆ **EMP:** 120 **EST:** 1997
SALES (est): 21.91MM
SALES (corp-wide): 42.84B **Privately Held**
Web: www.seedsofchange.com
SIC: 5191 0723 Seeds: field, garden, and flower; Crop preparation services for market
HQ: Mars Food Us, Llc
2001 E Cashdan St Ste 201
Rancho Dominguez CA
310 933-0670

(P-13491)
SEMINIS VEGETABLE SEEDS INC (DH)
Also Called: Seminis
2700 Camino Del Sol (93030-7967)
PHONE................................855 733-3834
Michael J Frank, *CEO*
Kerry Preete, *
◆ **EMP:** 600 **EST:** 1962
SQ FT: 370,000
SALES (est): 463.76MM
SALES (corp-wide): 52.7B **Privately Held**
Web: www.seminis-us.com
SIC: 5191 0723 Seeds: field, garden, and flower; Crop preparation services for market
HQ: Bayer Northern Production Co., Llc
800 N Lindbergh Blvd
Saint Louis MO
314 694-1000

(P-13492)
TARGET SPECIALTY PRODUCTS INC
15415 Marquardt Ave (90670-5711)
P.O. Box 3408 (90670-1408)
PHONE................................562 865-9541
EMP: 100
Web: www.target-specialty.com
SIC: 5191 Chemicals, agricultural

5192 Books, Periodicals, And Newspapers

(P-13493)
BAKER & TAYLOR LLC
10350 Barnes Canyon Rd Ste 100 (92121-2708)
PHONE...............................858 457-2500
James Leidich, *Dir*
EMP: 184
Web: www.baker-taylor.com
SIC: 5192 5099 5199 5045 Books; Tapes and cassettes, prerecorded; Calendars; Computer software
PA: Baker & Taylor, Llc
2810 Clseum Cntre Dr Ste
Charlotte NC

(P-13494)
EL AVISO MAGAZINE
4850 Gage Ave (90201-1409)
P.O. Box 3360 (90202-3360)
PHONE...............................323 586-9199
Jose Zepeda, *CEO*
EMP: 83 **EST:** 1988
SALES (est): 2.47MM **Privately Held**
Web: www.elaviso.com
SIC: 5192 2721 Magazines; Magazines: publishing and printing

(P-13495)
GREAT ATLANTIC NEWS LLC
Also Called: News Group, The
1575 N Main St (92867-3439)
PHONE...............................770 863-9000
EMP: 109
SALES (corp-wide): 10.3B **Privately Held**
SIC: 5192 5994 Periodicals; Magazine stand
HQ: Great Atlantic News L.L.C.
1962 Highway 160 W # 102
Fort Mill SC

(P-13496)
MADER NEWS INC
508 S Varney St (91502-2126)
PHONE...............................818 551-5000
Avan Mader, *Pr*
EMP: 100 **EST:** 1972
SALES (est): 12.28MM **Privately Held**
Web: www.madernews.com
SIC: 5192 Newspapers

(P-13497)
PENTON OVERSEAS INC
2310 Camino Vida Roble Ste 105 (92011)
PHONE...............................760 809-6030
Hugh V Penton, *CEO*
Hugh V Penton Senior, *Ch*
George Stroesenreuther, *
Annette Norris, *
▲ **EMP:** 19 **EST:** 1986
SQ FT: 40,000
SALES (est): 1.27MM **Privately Held**
SIC: 5192 2731 Books; Books, publishing only

(P-13498)
WHITE DIGITAL MEDIA INC
Also Called: Wdm Group
3394 Carmel Mountain Rd Ste 250 (92121-1065)
PHONE...............................760 827-7800
Brian Smith, *CEO*
Glen White, *
Matthew P Melucci, *Chief Content Officer*
EMP: 150 **EST:** 2007
SALES (est): 19.03MM **Privately Held**
SIC: 5192 Magazines

5193 Flowers And Florists Supplies

(P-13499)
ALTMAN SPECIALTY PLANTS LLC
Also Called: Altman Flowers
2575 Olive Hill Rd (92028-9557)
PHONE...............................800 348-4881
EMP: 433
SALES (corp-wide): 865.96MM **Privately Held**
Web: www.altmanplants.com
SIC: 5193 Nursery stock
PA: Altman Specialty Plants, Llc
3742 Blue Bird Canyon Rd
Vista CA
800 348-4881

(P-13500)
ALTMAN SPECIALTY PLANTS LLC (PA)
Also Called: Altman Plants
3742 Blue Bird Canyon Rd (92084-7432)
PHONE...............................800 348-4881
Ken Altman, *CEO*
Deena Altman, *
▲ **EMP:** 800 **EST:** 1973
SQ FT: 4,000
SALES (est): 865.96MM
SALES (corp-wide): 865.96MM **Privately Held**
Web: www.altmanplants.com
SIC: 5193 3999 Nursery stock; Atomizers, toiletry

(P-13501)
B & B NURSERIES INC
Also Called: Landscape Center
9505 Cleveland Ave (92503-6241)
P.O. Box 7399 (92513-7399)
PHONE...............................951 352-8383
Mark Barrett, *CEO*
EMP: 109 **EST:** 1985
SALES (est): 13.18MM **Privately Held**
Web: www.tlcnurseries.com
SIC: 5193 0781 Flowers and nursery stock; Landscape counseling services

(P-13502)
BANDY RANCH FLORAL CORP
2755 Dos Aarons Way Ste B (92081-8359)
PHONE...............................805 757-9905
Steve Dodge, *CEO*
EMP: 115 **EST:** 2015
SALES (est): 32.25MM **Privately Held**
Web: www.bandyranchfloral.com
SIC: 5193 Flowers, fresh

(P-13503)
BELLA TERRA NURSERY INC
Also Called: Terra Bella Nursery
302 Hollister St (92154-4700)
P.O. Box 551 (91912-0551)
PHONE...............................619 585-1118
EMP: 100 **EST:** 2007
SALES (est): 9.7MM **Privately Held**
Web: www.terrabellanursery.com
SIC: 5193 Flowers and florists supplies

(P-13504)
BOUQS COMPANY
Also Called: Thebouqs.com
4094 Glencoe Ave (90292-5608)
PHONE...............................888 320-2687
Kimberly Tobman, *CEO*
John Tabis, *Ch Bd*
Jp Montfar, *COO*
EMP: 87 **EST:** 2012
SALES (est): 14.66MM **Privately Held**
Web: www.bouqs.com
SIC: 5193 Flowers, fresh

(P-13505)
COUNTRY FLORAL SUPPLY INC (PA)
Also Called: Country Furnishings
3802 Weatherly Cir (91361-3821)
PHONE...............................805 520-8026
Mark Reese, *Pr*
Debbie Reese, *
▲ **EMP:** 80 **EST:** 1982
SQ FT: 60,000
SALES (est): 8.94MM
SALES (corp-wide): 8.94MM **Privately Held**
SIC: 5193 5999 Artificial flowers; Artificial flowers

(P-13506)
DELTA FLORAL DISTRIBUTORS INC
6810 West Blvd (90043-4668)
PHONE...............................323 751-8116
Foti Defterios, *Pr*
▲ **EMP:** 200 **EST:** 1984
SQ FT: 30,000
SALES (est): 23.13MM **Privately Held**
SIC: 5193 Flowers, fresh

(P-13507)
GREEN THUMB INTERNATIONAL INC
21812 Sherman Way (91303-1940)
PHONE...............................818 340-6400
Del Berquist, *Prin*
EMP: 87
SALES (corp-wide): 24.03MM **Privately Held**
Web: www.greenthumb.com
SIC: 5193 5261 0782 0181 Nursery stock; Retail nurseries and garden stores; Lawn and garden services; Ornamental nursery products
PA: Green Thumb International Inc
7105 Jordan Ave
Canoga Park CA
818 340-6400

(P-13508)
GRINGO VENTURES LLC
Also Called: Dos Gringos
3260 Corporate Vw (92081-8528)
PHONE...............................760 477-7999
EMP: 354 **EST:** 1995
SALES (est): 47.6MM **Privately Held**
Web: www.dosgringos.com
SIC: 5193 0181 Flowers and florists supplies ; Ornamental nursery products

(P-13509)
GROLINK PLANT COMPANY INC (PA)
Also Called: Grolink
4107 W Gonzales Rd (93036-7783)
P.O. Box 5506 (93031-5506)
PHONE...............................805 984-7958
Anthony Vollering, *CEO*
Art Gordijin, *
Jerry Van Wingerden, *
Harry Van Wingerden, *Stockholder*
Ton Vallering, *
▲ **EMP:** 149 **EST:** 1985
SQ FT: 400,000
SALES (est): 17.87MM
SALES (corp-wide): 17.87MM **Privately Held**
Web: www.grolink.com
SIC: 5193 0181 Nursery stock; Ornamental nursery products

(P-13510)
JENNY SILKS INC
Also Called: Jenny Silks
2101 S Grand Ave (92705-5231)
PHONE...............................714 597-7272
Jennifer Cheng, *Pr*
EMP: 17 **EST:** 1985
SALES (est): 3.36MM **Privately Held**
Web: www.jennysilks.com
SIC: 5193 3999 Flowers, fresh; Artificial flower arrangements

(P-13511)
KENDAL FLORAL SUPPLY LLC (PA)
Also Called: Kendal North Bouquet Co
1960 Kellogg Ave (92008-6581)
PHONE...............................888 828-9875
Kenneth X Baca, *Pr*
▲ **EMP:** 80 **EST:** 1973
SALES (est): 51.67MM
SALES (corp-wide): 51.67MM **Privately Held**
Web: www.sheilafrankllc.com
SIC: 5193 Flowers, fresh

(P-13512)
LA VERNE NURSERY INC
3653 Center St (93040-8051)
PHONE...............................805 521-0111
EMP: 90
Web: www.everde.com
SIC: 5193 Nursery stock
PA: La Verne Nursery, Inc.
1025 N Todd Ave
Azusa CA

(P-13513)
MELLANO & CO
Also Called: Melano Enterprises
734 Wilshire Rd (92057-2111)
P.O. Box 100 (92068-0100)
PHONE...............................760 433-9550
Harry M Mellano, *Owner*
EMP: 108
SALES (corp-wide): 49.4MM **Privately Held**
Web: www.mellano.com
SIC: 5193 Flowers, fresh
PA: Mellano & Company
766 Wall St
Los Angeles CA
213 622-0796

(P-13514)
NAKASE BROTHERS WHL NURS LP (PA)
9441 Krepp Dr (92646-2799)
PHONE...............................949 855-4388
Shigeo Gary Nakase, *Managing Member*
▲ **EMP:** 100 **EST:** 1965
SALES (est): 22.88MM
SALES (corp-wide): 22.88MM **Privately Held**
Web: www.nakasebros.com
SIC: 5193 Nursery stock

(P-13515)
NAKASE BROTHERS WHOLESALE NURS
Also Called: NAKASE BROTHERS WHOLESALE NURSERY
20621 Lake Forest Dr (92630-7743)
PHONE...............................949 855-4388
Joann Shurlock, *Mgr*

EMP: 180
SALES (corp-wide): 22.88MM **Privately Held**
Web: www.nakasebros.com
SIC: 5193 Nursery stock
PA: Nakase Brothers Wholesale Nursery Lp
9441 Krepp Dr
Huntington Beach CA
949 855-4388

(P-13516)
NORMANS NURSERY INC
5800 Via Real (93013-2610)
PHONE..............................805 684-5442
EMP: 142
SALES (corp-wide): 95.85MM **Privately Held**
Web: www.nngrower.com
SIC: 5193 Nursery stock
PA: Norman's Nursery, Inc.
8665 Duarte Rd
San Gabriel CA
626 285-9795

(P-13517)
NORMANS NURSERY INC
Also Called: Norman's Nursery
20500 Ramona Blvd (91706)
PHONE..............................626 285-9795
Ricardo Goodman, *Mgr*
EMP: 143
SALES (corp-wide): 95.85MM **Privately Held**
Web: www.nngrower.com
SIC: 5193 Nursery stock
PA: Norman's Nursery, Inc.
8665 Duarte Rd
San Gabriel CA
626 285-9795

(P-13518)
PYRAMID FLOWERS INC
3813 Doris Ave (93030-4706)
PHONE..............................805 382-8070
Fred Van Wingerden, *Pr*
Edith Van Wingerden, *
▲ **EMP:** 120 **EST:** 1991
SQ FT: 900,000
SALES (est): 16.07MM **Privately Held**
Web: www.pyramidflowers.com
SIC: 5193 Flowers, fresh

(P-13519)
SPECTRUM EQUIPMENT LLC
Also Called: Spectrum Floral Service
2505 Commerce Way (92081-8420)
PHONE..............................760 599-8849
Gene Aschbrenner, *Managing Member*
Sarah Aschbrenner, *
William Simon, *
EMP: 80 **EST:** 2017
SQ FT: 16,000
SALES (est): 10.24MM **Privately Held**
SIC: 5193 Flowers, fresh

(P-13520)
T - Y NURSERY INC
15335 Highway 76 (92061-9583)
P.O. Box 424 (92061-0424)
PHONE..............................760 742-2151
Alfonso Ramos, *Mgr*
EMP: 200
SALES (corp-wide): 23.67MM **Privately Held**
Web: www.tynursery.com
SIC: 5193 5261 Plants, potted; Retail nurseries
PA: T - Y Nursery, Inc.
5221 Arvada St
Torrance CA
310 370-2561

(P-13521)
VILLAGE NURSERIES WHL LLC
20099 Santa Rosa Mine Rd (92570-7774)
PHONE..............................951 657-3940
Joseph Jensen, *Brnch Mgr*
EMP: 272
SALES (corp-wide): 47.24MM **Privately Held**
Web: www.everde.com
SIC: 5193 Nursery stock
PA: Village Nurseries Wholesale, Llc
1589 N Main St
Orange CA
714 279-3100

5194 Tobacco And Tobacco Products

(P-13522)
KRETEK INTERNATIONAL INC (DH)
5449 Endeavour Ct (93021-1712)
PHONE..............................805 531-8888
Hugh R Cassar, *CEO*
Lynn K Cassar, *
Sean Cassar, *
Donald Gormley, *
Eliot Suied, *
◆ **EMP:** 90 **EST:** 1983
SQ FT: 80,000
SALES (est): 76.31MM **Privately Held**
Web: www.kretek.com
SIC: 5194 Cigarettes
HQ: Pt. Djarum
Jl. Ahmad Yani No. 28
Kabupaten Kudus JT

5198 Paints, Varnishes, And Supplies

(P-13523)
BERG LACQUER CO (PA)
Also Called: Pacific Coast Lacquer
3150 E Pico Blvd (90023-3632)
PHONE..............................323 261-8114
Sandra Berg, *Pr*
Robert O Berg, *
Donna Berg, *
▲ **EMP:** 65 **EST:** 1934
SQ FT: 85,000
SALES (est): 23.85MM
SALES (corp-wide): 23.85MM **Privately Held**
SIC: 5198 2851 Paints; Paints and paint additives

5199 Nondurable Goods, Nec

(P-13524)
99 CENTS ONLY STORES LLC (HQ)
Also Called: 99 Cents Only Stores
4000 Union Pacific Ave (90023-3202)
PHONE..............................323 980-8145
Barry J Feld, *CEO*
Felicia Thornton, *V Ch Bd*
Michael Kvitko, *CMO*
Ashok Walia, *CFO*
◆ **EMP:** 500 **EST:** 1965
SALES (est): 730.02MM
SALES (corp-wide): 730.02MM **Privately Held**
Web: www.99only.com
SIC: 5199 5331 4225 General merchandise, non-durable; Variety stores; General warehousing and storage
PA: Number Holdings, Inc.
4000 Union Pacific Ave

Commerce CA
323 980-8145

(P-13525)
AHI INVESTMENT INC (DH)
Also Called: Linzer Products
675 Glenoaks Blvd (91340-1471)
P.O. Box 310 (91341-0310)
PHONE..............................818 979-0030
Hisatoshi Ohtsuka, *Prin*
Mark Saji, *Ex VP*
Yuko Waki, *Prin*
◆ **EMP:** 25 **EST:** 1989
SQ FT: 75,000
SALES (est): 120MM **Privately Held**
Web: www.linzerproducts.com
SIC: 5199 3991 Broom, mop, and paint handles; Paintbrushes
HQ: Ohtsuka Brush Mfg.Co., Ltd.
4-1, Yotsuya
Shinjuku-Ku TKY

(P-13526)
AMERICAN PAPER & PLASTICS LLC
Also Called: American Paper & Provisions
550 S 7th Ave (91746-3120)
PHONE..............................626 444-0000
Daniel Emrani, *CEO*
EMP: 119 **EST:** 1982
SQ FT: 300,000
SALES (est): 48.7MM
SALES (corp-wide): 1.63B **Privately Held**
Web: www.appinc.com
SIC: 5199 Packaging materials
PA: Imperial Bag & Paper Co. Llc
255 Route 1 And 9
Jersey City NJ
201 437-7440

(P-13527)
ANNS TRADING COMPANY INC
Also Called: Urban Concepts
5333 S Downey Rd (90058-3725)
PHONE..............................323 585-4702
Hyung Don Kim, *CEO*
Daniel Im, *
Mi H Kim, *Sec*
◆ **EMP:** 30 **EST:** 1981
SALES (est): 4.88MM **Privately Held**
Web: www.annstrading.com
SIC: 5199 2335 Gifts and novelties; Women's, junior's, and misses' dresses

(P-13528)
ATLANTIS ENTERPRISES INC
8100 Remmet Ave Ste 1 (91304-6413)
PHONE..............................818 712-0572
Vartan Schaljian, *Pr*
▲ **EMP:** 24 **EST:** 1998
SALES (est): 2.32MM **Privately Held**
Web: www.atlantistime.com
SIC: 5199 3993 Advertising specialties; Advertising novelties

(P-13529)
BIO HAZARD INC
6247 Randolph St (90040-3514)
PHONE..............................213 625-2116
EMP: 30 **EST:** 2007
SALES (est): 8.38MM **Privately Held**
Web: www.biohazardinc.com
SIC: 5199 3221 Smokers' supplies; Glass containers

(P-13530)
BLISTERPAK INC
Also Called: Blisterpak
3020 Supply Ave (90040-2710)
PHONE..............................323 728-5555

Steven C Mattis, *CEO*
▲ **EMP:** 20 **EST:** 1974
SQ FT: 15,000
SALES (est): 5.21MM **Privately Held**
Web: www.blisterpak.com
SIC: 5199 3089 3069 Packaging materials; Air mattresses, plastics; Floor coverings, rubber

(P-13531)
BLUEMARK INC
27909 Hancock Pkwy (91355-4116)
PHONE..............................323 230-0770
Joseph Shusterman, *CEO*
Yosef Shusterman, *
EMP: 112 **EST:** 2009
SALES (est): 24.7MM **Privately Held**
Web: www.bluemark.com
SIC: 5199 Advertising specialties

(P-13532)
BTG S CORP (PA)
Also Called: Four Seasons General Mdse
2801 E Vernon Ave (90058-1803)
PHONE..............................323 582-4444
◆ **EMP:** 85 **EST:** 1985
SALES (est): 37.58MM
SALES (corp-wide): 37.58MM **Privately Held**
Web: www.4sgm.com
SIC: 5199 General merchandise, non-durable

(P-13533)
CHUS PACKAGING SUPPLIES INC
10011 Santa Fe Springs Rd (90670-2921)
PHONE..............................562 944-6411
Pao Chang Chu, *CEO*
Julie Chieh Yu Chu, *Pr*
▲ **EMP:** 22 **EST:** 1985
SQ FT: 30,000
SALES (est): 23.19MM **Privately Held**
Web: www.chuspkg.com
SIC: 5199 2653 Packaging materials; Boxes, corrugated: made from purchased materials

(P-13534)
CLOUDRADIANT CORP (PA)
Also Called: Enbiz International
12 Fuchsia (92630-1431)
PHONE..............................408 256-1527
Anil Rao, *Pr*
◆ **EMP:** 128 **EST:** 2010
SALES (est): 23.69MM
SALES (corp-wide): 23.69MM **Privately Held**
SIC: 5199 8748 7371 8711 General merchandise, non-durable; Business consulting, nec; Computer software systems analysis and design, custom; Consulting engineer

(P-13535)
ERNEST PACKAGING (PA)
Also Called: Ernest Paper
5777 Smithway St (90040-1507)
PHONE..............................800 233-7788
Charles Wilson, *Ch Bd*
Timothy Wilson, *
▲ **EMP:** 130 **EST:** 1947
SQ FT: 300,000
SALES (est): 189.32MM
SALES (corp-wide): 189.32MM **Privately Held**
Web: www.ernestpackaging.com
SIC: 5199 7389 5113 Packaging materials; Cosmetic kits, assembling and packaging; Shipping supplies

(P-13536)

EUROW AND OREILLY CORP
Also Called: Equine Comfort Products
51 Moreland Rd (93065-1662)
PHONE........................800 747-7452
Donna O'reilly, *CEO*
Patrice Bonnefoi, *
◆ **EMP:** 32 **EST:** 2000
SQ FT: 60,000
SALES (est): 14.38MM **Privately Held**
Web: www.eurow.com
SIC: 5199 2392 General merchandise, non-durable; Towels, dishcloths and dust cloths

(P-13537)

EVE HAIR INC (PA)
Also Called: Eve
3935 Paramount Blvd (90712-4100)
PHONE........................562 377-1020
◆ **EMP:** 37 **EST:** 1990
SQ FT: 44,000
SALES (est): 4.97MM **Privately Held**
Web: www.evehairinc.com
SIC: 5199 3999 Wigs; Hair and hair-based products

(P-13538)

EZCARETECH USA INC
21081 S Western Ave Ste 130 (90501)
PHONE........................424 558-3191
Justin Chung, *CEO*
Kyungho Min, *
Justin Park, *
EMP: 350 **EST:** 2019
SALES (est): 10.82MM **Privately Held**
Web: www.ezcaretech.com
SIC: 5199 Nondurable goods, nec

(P-13539)

GAJU MARKET CORPORATION
450 S Western Ave (90020-4120)
PHONE........................213 382-9444
David Rhee, *CEO*
EMP: 135 **EST:** 2015
SQ FT: 2,000
SALES (est): 25MM **Privately Held**
Web: www.gajumarketplace.com
SIC: 5199 General merchandise, non-durable

(P-13540)

GRAPHIC PACKAGING INTL LLC
1600 Barranca Pkwy (92606-4823)
PHONE........................949 250-0900
Wendy Shute, *Brnch Mgr*
EMP: 100
Web: www.graphicpkg.com
SIC: 5199 Packaging materials
HQ: Graphic Packaging International, Llc
1500 Riveredge Pkwy # 100
Atlanta GA

(P-13541)

HIPPO CORPORATION
Also Called: Displays & Holders
2535 W Via Palma (92801-2624)
PHONE........................714 229-9152
Aloysius Aaron, *Pr*
Maureen Aaron, *VP*
Dawnna Aaron, *Sec*
EMP: 18 **EST:** 1986
SQ FT: 1,800
SALES (est): 2.22MM **Privately Held**
Web: www.displaysandholders.com
SIC: 5199 2754 2396 7319 Advertising specialties; Imprinting: gravure; Screen printing on fabric articles; Display advertising service

(P-13542)

JEWELSCENT INC
955 W Imperial Hwy Ste 120 (92821-3812)
P.O. Box 8965 (92822-5965)
PHONE........................800 550-1762
Nga Nguyen, *CEO*
EMP: 86 **EST:** 2013
SALES (est): 2.49MM **Privately Held**
Web: www.jewelscent.com
SIC: 5199 Candles

(P-13543)

KATZKIN LEATHER INC (PA)
6868 W Acco St (90640-5441)
PHONE........................323 725-1243
Brook Mayberry, *Pr*
Scott Briskie, *
▲ **EMP:** 200 **EST:** 1998
SQ FT: 50,000
SALES (est): 48.6MM
SALES (corp-wide): 48.6MM **Privately Held**
Web: www.katzkin.com
SIC: 5199 2531 Leather and cut stock; Seats, automobile

(P-13544)

LEE-MAR AQUARIUM & PET SUPS
Also Called: Lee Mar Aquarium & Pet Sups
2459 Dogwood Way (92081-8421)
PHONE........................760 727-1300
Terran R Boyd, *Pr*
▲ **EMP:** 100 **EST:** 1971
SQ FT: 67,000
SALES (est): 8.82MM **Privately Held**
Web: www.leemarpet.com
SIC: 5199 3999 Pet supplies; Pet supplies

(P-13545)

LOGOMARK INC
Also Called: Valumark
1201 Bell Ave (92780-6420)
PHONE........................714 675-6100
Trevor Gnesin, *Pr*
▲ **EMP:** 250 **EST:** 1992
SQ FT: 200,000
SALES (est): 92.77MM **Privately Held**
Web: www.logomark.com
SIC: 5199 Advertising specialties

(P-13546)

M M S TRADING INC
100 Corporate Pointe (90230-7612)
PHONE........................323 587-1082
Sumir Kaytee, *CEO*
▲ **EMP:** 39 **EST:** 2005
SALES (est): 3.11MM **Privately Held**
Web: www.mmstradinginc.com
SIC: 5199 3171 Yarns, nec; Women's handbags and purses

(P-13547)

MACK PACKAGING INC
1239 Linda Vista Dr (92078-3809)
PHONE........................760 752-3500
Kevin Mackinnon, *Pr*
EMP: 22 **EST:** 2009
SALES (est): 4.87MM **Privately Held**
Web: www.mackpacbranding.com
SIC: 5199 2759 Advertising specialties; Commercial printing, nec

(P-13548)

MIDWAY INTERNATIONAL INC
Also Called: Bobbi Boss
13131 166th St (90703-2202)
PHONE........................800 826-2383
Ha Chung, *CEO*
◆ **EMP:** 97 **EST:** 1985
SQ FT: 32,700
SALES (est): 31.59MM **Privately Held**
Web: www.bobbiboss.com
SIC: 5199 5047 Wigs; Medical equipment and supplies

(P-13549)

MISA IMPORTS INC
2343 Saybrook Ave (90040-1721)
PHONE........................562 281-6773
EMP: 100
SALES (corp-wide): 345.56MM **Privately Held**
Web: www.misaimports.com
SIC: 5199 Art goods and supplies
PA: Misa Imports Inc.
1502 Viceroy Dr
Dallas TX
972 235-3834

(P-13550)

MODERN CANDLE CO INC
Also Called: Modern Candles
12884 Bradley Ave (91342-3827)
PHONE........................323 441-0104
Armik Pirijanian, *CEO*
Nora Pirijanian, *
▲ **EMP:** 45 **EST:** 1995
SALES (est): 17.5MM **Privately Held**
Web: www.moderncandle.com
SIC: 5199 3999 Candles; Candles

(P-13551)

NIFTY PACKAGE CO INC
175 S Cambridge St (92866-1634)
PHONE........................714 863-6058
Michelle Hensley, *CEO*
EMP: 20 **EST:** 2015
SALES (est): 1.47MM **Privately Held**
Web: www.niftypackage.co
SIC: 5199 2679 5947 7299 Packaging materials; Gift wrap and novelties, paper; Gifts and novelties; Gift wrapping services

(P-13552)

NW PACKAGING LLC (PA)
Also Called: NW Packaging
1201 E Lexington Ave (91766-5520)
P.O. Box 357 (92871-0357)
PHONE........................909 706-3627
Robert E Sliter, *Admn*
EMP: 100 **EST:** 2012
SALES (est): 19.33MM
SALES (corp-wide): 19.33MM **Privately Held**
Web: www.nwpackagingonline.com
SIC: 5199 Packaging materials

(P-13553)

PCF GROUP LLC
Also Called: Pacific Coast Foam
8585 Miramar Pl (92121-2529)
PHONE........................858 455-1274
EMP: 29 **EST:** 1995
SQ FT: 15,000
SALES (est): 2.86MM **Privately Held**
Web: www.pcfconstructiongroup.com
SIC: 5199 3086 Foams and rubber; Plastics foam products

(P-13554)

POLYCELL PACKAGING CORPORATION
12851 Midway Pl (90703-2141)
PHONE........................562 483-6000
▲ **EMP:** 35 **EST:** 1995
SALES (est): 13.92MM **Privately Held**
Web: www.polycellpkg.com

SIC: 5199 3089 Packaging materials; Blister or bubble formed packaging, plastics

(P-13555)

REDBARN PET PRODUCTS INC (PA)
Also Called: Redbarn Premium Pet Products
3229 E Spring St Ste 310 (90806-2478)
PHONE........................562 495-7315
◆ **EMP:** 236 **EST:** 1994
SQ FT: 50,000
SALES (est): 57.4MM **Privately Held**
Web: www.redbarn.com
SIC: 5199 2047 Pet supplies; Dog and cat food

(P-13556)

REVOLTION CNSMR SLTIONS CA LLC (DH)
Also Called: Command Packaging
3840 E 26th St (90058-4107)
PHONE........................323 980-0918
◆ **EMP:** 112 **EST:** 1989
SQ FT: 170,000
SALES (est): 84.55MM
SALES (corp-wide): 803.37MM **Privately Held**
Web: www.commandpackaging.com
SIC: 5199 Packaging materials
HQ: Delta Plastics Of The South, Llc
8801 Frazier Pike
Little Rock AR

(P-13557)

ROCKWELL ENTERPRISES INC
20327 Regina Ave (90503-2513)
PHONE........................626 796-1511
Frank Giovinazzo, *Pr*
Akemi Giovinazzo, *Sec*
EMP: 20 **EST:** 1967
SALES (est): 2.48MM **Privately Held**
Web: www.rockwellenterprises.com
SIC: 5199 3581 Maps and charts; Automatic vending machines

(P-13558)

ROYAL PAPER BOX CO CALIFORNIA (PA)
1105 S Maple Ave (90640-6007)
P.O. Box 458 (90640-0458)
PHONE........................323 728-7041
Jim Hodges, *CEO*
Darryl Carlson, *VP*
Scott Larson, *VP*
Andy Polanco, *VP*
Steve Perez, *VP*
▲ **EMP:** 197 **EST:** 1940
SQ FT: 172,500
SALES (est): 900.5K
SALES (corp-wide): 900.5K **Privately Held**
Web: www.royalpaperbox.com
SIC: 5199 Packaging materials

(P-13559)

RYL INC
2738 Supply Ave (90040-2704)
PHONE........................213 503-7968
Ronald Lee, *Pr*
Sandra Lee, *
▲ **EMP:** 55 **EST:** 1996
SQ FT: 31,000
SALES (est): 8.72MM **Privately Held**
Web: www.colorglasstube.com
SIC: 5199 3221 General merchandise, non-durable; Glass containers

(P-13560)

SCHROFF INC
7328 Trade St (92121-3435)

PHONE..............................858 740-2400
Robert Bradley, *Brnch Mgr*
EMP: 1409
Web: schroff.nvent.com
SIC: 5199 Packaging materials
HQ: Schroff, Inc.
170 Commerce Dr
Warwick RI
763 204-7700

(P-13561)
SHIMS BARGAIN INC (PA)
Also Called: J C Sales
2600 S Soto St (90058-8015)
PHONE..............................323 881-0099
Sesilia Song, *CEO*
Kenneth Suh, *
James Shim, *
Bj Chang, *CFO*
◆ **EMP:** 100 **EST:** 1993
SQ FT: 420,000
SALES (est): 90.41MM **Privately Held**
Web: www.jcsalesweb.com
SIC: 5199 General merchandise, non-durable

(P-13562)
SMITH PACKING INC
680 S Simas Rd (93455-9700)
P.O. Box 1338 (93456-1338)
PHONE.............................:.805 348-1817
Alvaro Quesada, *Prin*
EMP: 118
SALES (corp-wide): 9.23MM **Privately Held**
Web: www.smithpacking.com
PA: Smith Packing, Inc.
111 W Chapel St
Santa Maria CA
805 348-1818

(P-13563)
TARGUS INTERNATIONAL LLC (PA)
Also Called: Targus
1211 N Miller St (92806-1933)
PHONE..............................714 765-5555
Mikel H Williams, *CEO*
Bill Oppenlander, *
Victor C Streufert, *
◆ **EMP:** 175 **EST:** 1995
SQ FT: 200,656
SALES (est): 97.3MM
SALES (corp-wide): 97.3MM **Privately Held**
Web: us.targus.com
SIC: 5199 5065 Bags, baskets, and cases; Electronic parts and equipment, nec

(P-13564)
THORO--PACKAGING (DH)
1467 Davril Cir (92878-4357)
PHONE..............................951 278-2100
Janet Dabek Steiner, *Pr*
EMP: 125 **EST:** 1967
SQ FT: 56,000
SALES (est): 48.87MM **Privately Held**
Web: www.autajon.com
SIC: 5199 Packaging materials
HQ: Autajon Cs
Chemin De Fontjarus Pt Pelican
Montelimar
475002000

(P-13565)
UNIX PACKAGING LLC
5361 Alexander St (90040-3062)
PHONE..............................213 627-5050
EMP: 278
SALES (corp-wide): 93.6MM **Privately Held**

Web: www.unixpackaging.com
SIC: 5199 Packaging materials
PA: Unix Packaging, Llc
9 Minson Way
Montebello CA
213 627-5050

(P-13566)
VICTORY FOAM INC (PA)
3 Holland (92618-2506)
PHONE..............................949 474-0690
Frank M Comerford, *CEO*
Myles Comerford, *
Helen Comerford, *
▲ **EMP:** 94 **EST:** 1982
SQ FT: 53,000
SALES (est): 37.51MM
SALES (corp-wide): 37.51MM **Privately Held**
Web: www.victoryfoam.com
SIC: 5199 3086 Packaging materials; Cups and plates, foamed plastics

(P-13567)
VICTORY SPORTSWEAR INC
Also Called: Victory Sportswear
2381 Buena Vista St (91010-3301)
PHONE..............................866 308-0798
Victor Ju, *CEO*
Xiao Can Zhang, *CFO*
▲ **EMP:** 22 **EST:** 1999
SQ FT: 22,000
SALES (est): 4.91MM **Privately Held**
Web: www.victorysportswearinc.com
SIC: 5199 5949 2321 2326 Automobile fabrics; Knitting goods and supplies; Men's and boys' dress shirts; Men's and boy's work clothing

(P-13568)
WEST BAY IMPORTS INC
7245 Oxford Way (90040-3644)
PHONE..............................323 720-5777
Yong Kyu Yi, *CEO*
◆ **EMP:** 30 **EST:** 1981
SALES (est): 7MM **Privately Held**
Web: www.westbayinc.com
SIC: 5199 2389 Wigs; Masquerade costumes

5211 Lumber And Other Building Materials

(P-13569)
BOISE CASCADE COMPANY
Also Called: Boise Cascade
7145 Arlington Ave (92503-1508)
PHONE..............................951 343-3000
Mike Bland, *Mgr*
EMP: 93
SALES (corp-wide): 8.39B **Publicly Held**
Web: www.bc.com
SIC: 5211 5031 Lumber products; Lumber: rough, dressed, and finished
PA: Boise Cascade Company
1111 W Jefferson St # 100
Boise ID
208 384-6161

(P-13570)
COASTAL DOORS
21818 S Wilmington Ave Ste 407 (90810-1642)
PHONE..............................562 665-5585
Brock William Livesey, *CEO*
EMP: 24 **EST:** 2019
SQ FT: 2,200
SALES (est): 2.42MM **Privately Held**
Web: www.coastal-corp.com

SIC: 5211 3442 Garage doors, sale and installation; Garage doors, overhead: metal

(P-13571)
DIXIELINE LUMBER COMPANY LLC
2625 Durahart St (92507-2654)
PHONE..............................951 224-8491
EMP: 628
SALES (corp-wide): 22.73B **Publicly Held**
Web: www.dixieline.com
SIC: 5211 5251 2439 5072 Lumber and other building materials; Builders' hardware ; Trusses, wooden roof; Hardware
HQ: Dixieline Lumber Company Llc
3250 Sports Arena Blvd
San Diego CA
619 224-4120

(P-13572)
DIXIELINE LUMBER COMPANY LLC (DH)
Also Called: Dixieline Probuild
3250 Sports Arena Blvd (92110-4588)
P.O. Box 85307 (92186-5307)
PHONE..............................619 224-4120
William S Cowling Ii, *Ch Bd*
Joe Laurence, *
Don Polich, *
▲ **EMP:** 55 **EST:** 1913
SQ FT: 12,000
SALES (est): 86.38MM
SALES (corp-wide): 22.73B **Publicly Held**
Web: www.dixieline.com
SIC: 5211 5251 2439 5072 Lumber and other building materials; Builders' hardware ; Trusses, wooden roof; Hardware
HQ: Lanoga Corporation
17946 Ne 65th St
Redmond WA
425 883-4125

(P-13573)
EMSER TILE LLC
42092 Winchester Rd (92590-4805)
PHONE..............................951 296-3671
Ed Combs, *Mgr*
EMP: 29
SALES (corp-wide): 273.97MM **Privately Held**
Web: www.emser.com
SIC: 5211 5032 5023 3272 Tile, ceramic; Tile and clay products; Floor coverings; Floor tile, precast terrazzo
PA: Emser Tile, Llc
8431 Santa Monica Blvd
Los Angeles CA
323 650-2000

(P-13574)
EMSER TILE LLC
4546 Stine Rd (93313-2300)
PHONE..............................661 837-4400
Ghodsian Sah, *Mgr*
EMP: 39
SALES (corp-wide): 273.97MM **Privately Held**
Web: www.emser.com
SIC: 5211 5032 3253 Tile, ceramic; Ceramic wall and floor tile, nec; Ceramic wall and floor tile
PA: Emser Tile, Llc
8431 Santa Monica Blvd
Los Angeles CA
323 650-2000

(P-13575)
G & G DOOR PRODUCTS INC
7600 Stage Rd (90621-1226)
PHONE..............................714 228-2008

EMP: 35 **EST:** 1995
SQ FT: 13,500
SALES (est): 8.43MM **Privately Held**
Web: www.ggdoor.net
SIC: 5211 3442 Doors, storm: wood or metal ; Metal doors, sash, and trim

(P-13576)
GANAHL LUMBER COMPANY
Also Called: Benjamin Moore Authorized Ret
150 W Blaine St (92878-4047)
P.O. Box 1326 (92878-1326)
PHONE..............................951 278-4000
Mark Ganahl, *Prin*
EMP: 67
SALES (corp-wide): 781.96MM **Privately Held**
Web: www.ganahllumber.com
SIC: 5211 2431 5031 1751 Millwork and lumber; Millwork; Lumber: rough, dressed, and finished; Window and door (prefabricated) installation
PA: Ganahl Lumber Company
1220 E Ball Rd
Anaheim CA
714 772-5444

(P-13577)
GEORGE L THROOP CO
Also Called: Do It Best
444 N Fair Oaks Ave (91103-3619)
P.O. Box 92405 (91109-2405)
PHONE..............................626 796-0285
TOLL FREE: 800
Jeffrey Throop, *Pr*
George L Throop Iii, *VP*
Ann T Comey, *
▲ **EMP:** 32 **EST:** 1921
SQ FT: 10,500
SALES (est): 9.67MM **Privately Held**
Web: www.throop.com
SIC: 5211 5251 3272 Millwork and lumber; Hardware stores; Concrete products, nec

(P-13578)
HIGHLANDER HOME INC
Also Called: You Should Have It
6679 Tierra Vista Ct (92130-1382)
PHONE..............................858 261-4068
Zhongyuan Wang, *CEO*
EMP: 24
SALES (corp-wide): 202.9K **Privately Held**
SIC: 5211 2511 Wallboard (composition) and paneling; Garden furniture: wood
PA: Highlander Home Inc.
1515 Fayette St
El Cajon CA
858 261-4068

(P-13579)
HOME DEPOT USA INC
Also Called: Home Depot, The
3323 Madison St (92504-4132)
PHONE..............................951 358-1370
Brian Lay, *Mgr*
EMP: 127
SALES (corp-wide): 157.4B **Publicly Held**
Web: www.homedepot.com
SIC: 5211 7359 Home centers; Tool rental
HQ: Home Depot U.S.A., Inc.
2455 Paces Ferry Rd Se
Atlanta GA

(P-13580)
HOME DEPOT USA INC
Also Called: Home Depot, The
6140 Hamner Ave (91752-3121)
PHONE..............................951 727-0324
Otto Torres, *Mgr*
EMP: 94

▲ = Import ▼ = Export
◆ = Import/Export

SALES (corp-wide): 157.4B **Publicly Held**
Web: www.homedepot.com
SIC: 5211 7359 Home centers; Tool rental
HQ: Home Depot U.S.A., Inc.
2455 Paces Ferry Rd Se
Atlanta GA

(P-13581)
HOME DEPOT USA INC
Also Called: Home Depot, The
15975 Perris Blvd (92551-4692)
PHONE..............................951 485-5400
Maribel Reyes, *Mgr*
EMP: 98
SALES (corp-wide): 157.4B **Publicly Held**
Web: www.homedepot.com
SIC: 5211 7359 Home centers; Tool rental
HQ: Home Depot U.S.A., Inc.
2455 Paces Ferry Rd Se
Atlanta GA

(P-13582)
HOME DEPOT USA INC
Also Called: Home Depot, The
25100 Madison Ave (92562-8907)
PHONE..............................951 698-1555
Maria Tub, *Mgr*
EMP: 128
SALES (corp-wide): 157.4B **Publicly Held**
Web: www.homedepot.com
SIC: 5211 7359 Home centers; Tool rental
HQ: Home Depot U.S.A., Inc.
2455 Paces Ferry Rd Se
Atlanta GA

(P-13583)
HOME DEPOT USA INC
Also Called: Home Depot, The
1355 E Ontario Ave (92881-6604)
PHONE..............................951 808-0327
Vanessa Muenoz, *Brnch Mgr*
EMP: 126
SALES (corp-wide): 157.4B **Publicly Held**
Web: www.homedepot.com
SIC: 5211 7359 Home centers; Tool rental
HQ: Home Depot U.S.A., Inc.
2455 Paces Ferry Rd Se
Atlanta GA

(P-13584)
HOME DEPOT USA INC
Also Called: Home Depot, The
27401 La Paz Rd (92677-3739)
PHONE..............................949 831-3698
Dan Schneid, *Brnch Mgr*
EMP: 137
SALES (corp-wide): 157.4B **Publicly Held**
Web: www.homedepot.com
SIC: 5211 7359 Home centers; Tool rental
HQ: Home Depot U.S.A., Inc.
2455 Paces Ferry Rd Se
Atlanta GA

(P-13585)
HOME DEPOT USA INC
Also Called: Home Depot, The
625 S Placentia Ave (92831-5199)
PHONE..............................714 459-4909
Pete Canscale, *Mgr*
EMP: 115
SALES (corp-wide): 157.4B **Publicly Held**
Web: www.homedepot.com
SIC: 5211 7359 Home centers; Tool rental
HQ: Home Depot U.S.A., Inc.
2455 Paces Ferry Rd Se
Atlanta GA

(P-13586)
HOME DEPOT USA INC
Also Called: Home Depot, The

1095 N Pullman St (92807-2516)
PHONE..............................714 921-1215
Rob Sholte, *Mgr*
EMP: 98
SALES (corp-wide): 157.4B **Publicly Held**
Web: www.homedepot.com
SIC: 5211 7359 Home centers; Tool rental
HQ: Home Depot U.S.A., Inc.
2455 Paces Ferry Rd Se
Atlanta GA

(P-13587)
HOME DEPOT USA INC
Also Called: Home Depot, The
600 S Harbor Blvd (90631-6166)
PHONE..............................562 690-6006
Merna Rosas, *Mgr*
EMP: 99
SALES (corp-wide): 157.4B **Publicly Held**
Web: www.homedepot.com
SIC: 5211 7359 Home centers; Tool rental
HQ: Home Depot U.S.A., Inc.
2455 Paces Ferry Rd Se
Atlanta GA

(P-13588)
HOME DEPOT USA INC
Also Called: Home Depot, The
3500 W Macarthur Blvd (92704-6808)
PHONE..............................714 966-8551
Beatrice Celazeo, *Genl Mgr*
EMP: 110
SALES (corp-wide): 157.4B **Publicly Held**
Web: www.homedepot.com
SIC: 5211 7359 Home centers; Tool rental
HQ: Home Depot U.S.A., Inc.
2455 Paces Ferry Rd Se
Atlanta GA

(P-13589)
HOME DEPOT USA INC
Also Called: Home Depot, The
435 W Katella Ave (92867-4603)
PHONE..............................714 538-9600
Michelle Fromholz, *Mgr*
EMP: 120
SALES (corp-wide): 157.4B **Publicly Held**
Web: www.homedepot.com
SIC: 5211 1752 1751 Home centers; Carpet laying; Window and door installation and erection
HQ: Home Depot U.S.A., Inc.
2455 Paces Ferry Rd Se
Atlanta GA

(P-13590)
HOME DEPOT USA INC
Also Called: Home Depot, The
2300 Harbor Blvd Ste F (92626-6200)
PHONE..............................949 646-4220
Marcella Kinsey, *Mgr*
EMP: 118
SALES (corp-wide): 157.4B **Publicly Held**
Web: www.homedepot.com
SIC: 5211 7359 Home centers; Tool rental
HQ: Home Depot U.S.A., Inc.
2455 Paces Ferry Rd Se
Atlanta GA

(P-13591)
HOME DEPOT USA INC
Also Called: Home Depot, The
20021 Lake Forest Dr (92630-8703)
PHONE..............................949 609-0221
Elizabeth Capippi, *Mgr*
EMP: 107
SALES (corp-wide): 157.4B **Publicly Held**
Web: www.homedepot.com
SIC: 5211 7359 Home centers; Tool rental
HQ: Home Depot U.S.A., Inc.
2455 Paces Ferry Rd Se

Atlanta GA

(P-13592)
HOME DEPOT USA INC
Also Called: Home Depot, The
27952 Hillcrest (92692-3637)
PHONE..............................949 364-1900
EMP: 94
SALES (corp-wide): 157.4B **Publicly Held**
Web: www.homedepot.com
SIC: 5211 7359 Home centers; Tool rental
HQ: Home Depot U.S.A., Inc.
2455 Paces Ferry Rd Se
Atlanta GA

(P-13593)
HOME DEPOT USA INC
Also Called: Home Depot, The
10801 Garden Grove Blvd (92843-1201)
PHONE..............................714 539-0319
Chris Murray, *Mgr*
EMP: 121
SALES (corp-wide): 157.4B **Publicly Held**
Web: www.homedepot.com
SIC: 5211 7359 Home centers; Tool rental
HQ: Home Depot U.S.A., Inc.
2455 Paces Ferry Rd Se
Atlanta GA

(P-13594)
HOME DEPOT USA INC
Also Called: Home Depot, The
1750 E Edinger Ave (92705-5031)
PHONE..............................714 259-1030
Rudy Teralta, *Mgr*
EMP: 90
SALES (corp-wide): 157.4B **Publicly Held**
Web: www.homedepot.com
SIC: 5211 7359 Home centers; Tool rental
HQ: Home Depot U.S.A., Inc.
2455 Paces Ferry Rd Se
Atlanta GA

(P-13595)
HOME DEPOT USA INC
Also Called: Home Depot, The
355 Marketplace Ave (92113-1960)
PHONE..............................619 263-1533
Brian Farwell, *Mgr*
EMP: 94
SALES (corp-wide): 157.4B **Publicly Held**
Web: www.homedepot.com
SIC: 5211 7359 Home centers; Tool rental
HQ: Home Depot U.S.A., Inc.
2455 Paces Ferry Rd Se
Atlanta GA

(P-13596)
HOME DEPOT USA INC
Also Called: Home Depot, The
1475 E Valley Pkwy (92027-2313)
PHONE..............................760 233-1285
Marco Bernardino, *Mgr*
EMP: 143
SALES (corp-wide): 157.4B **Publicly Held**
Web: www.homedepot.com
SIC: 5211 7359 Home centers; Tool rental
HQ: Home Depot U.S.A., Inc.
2455 Paces Ferry Rd Se
Atlanta GA

(P-13597)
HOME DEPOT USA INC
Also Called: Home Depot, The
1320 Eastlake Pkwy (91915-4116)
PHONE..............................619 421-0639
Emil Isvanca, *Mgr*
EMP: 106
SALES (corp-wide): 157.4B **Publicly Held**
Web: www.homedepot.com

SIC: 5211 7359 Home centers; Tool rental
HQ: Home Depot U.S.A., Inc.
2455 Paces Ferry Rd Se
Atlanta GA

(P-13598)
HOME DEPOT USA INC
Also Called: Home Depot, The
298 Fletcher Pkwy (92020-2506)
PHONE..............................619 401-6610
Bill Walker, *Brnch Mgr*
EMP: 100
SALES (corp-wide): 157.4B **Publicly Held**
Web: www.homedepot.com
SIC: 5211 7359 Home centers; Tool rental
HQ: Home Depot U.S.A., Inc.
2455 Paces Ferry Rd Se
Atlanta GA

(P-13599)
HOME DEPOT USA INC
Also Called: Home Depot, The
7530 Broadway (91945-1604)
PHONE..............................619 589-2999
EMP: 137
SALES (corp-wide): 157.4B **Publicly Held**
Web: www.homedepot.com
SIC: 5211 7359 Home centers; Tool rental
HQ: Home Depot U.S.A., Inc.
2455 Paces Ferry Rd Se
Atlanta GA

(P-13600)
HOME DEPOT USA INC
Also Called: Home Depot, The
401 W Ventura Blvd (93010-9122)
PHONE..............................805 389-9918
Michael Curbelo, *Mgr*
EMP: 297
SALES (corp-wide): 157.4B **Publicly Held**
Web: www.homedepot.com
SIC: 5211 7359 Home centers; Tool rental
HQ: Home Depot U.S.A., Inc.
2455 Paces Ferry Rd Se
Atlanta GA

(P-13601)
HOME DEPOT USA INC
Also Called: Home Depot, The
401 W Esplanade Dr (93036-1298)
PHONE..............................805 983-0653
Chris Barajas, *Mgr*
EMP: 121
SALES (corp-wide): 157.4B **Publicly Held**
Web: www.homedepot.com
SIC: 5211 7359 Home centers; Tool rental
HQ: Home Depot U.S.A., Inc.
2455 Paces Ferry Rd Se
Atlanta GA

(P-13602)
HOME DEPOT USA INC
Also Called: Home Depot, The
1151 W Lugonia Ave (92374-2000)
PHONE..............................909 748-0505
Kade Kasner, *Brnch Mgr*
EMP: 129
SALES (corp-wide): 157.4B **Publicly Held**
Web: www.homedepot.com
SIC: 5211 7359 Home centers; Tool rental
HQ: Home Depot U.S.A., Inc.
2455 Paces Ferry Rd Se
Atlanta GA

(P-13603)
HOME DEPOT USA INC
Also Called: Home Depot, The
15150 Bear Valley Rd (92395-8709)
PHONE..............................760 955-2999
EMP: 127

PRODUCTS & SVCS

SALES (corp-wide): 157.4B **Publicly Held**
Web: www.homedepot.com
SIC: **5211** 7359 Home centers; Tool rental
HQ: Home Depot U.S.A., Inc.
2455 Paces Ferry Rd Se
Atlanta GA

(P-13604)
HOME DEPOT USA INC
Also Called: Home Depot, The
14549 Ramona Ave (91710-5647)
PHONE...............................909 393-5205
EMP: 138
SALES (corp-wide): 157.4B **Publicly Held**
Web: www.homedepot.com
SIC: **5211** 7359 Home centers; Tool rental
HQ: Home Depot U.S.A., Inc.
2455 Paces Ferry Rd Se
Atlanta GA

(P-13605)
HOME DEPOT USA INC
Also Called: Home Depot, The
11884 Foothill Blvd (91730-3900)
PHONE...............................909 948-9200
EMP: 120
SALES (corp-wide): 157.4B **Publicly Held**
Web: www.homedepot.com
SIC: **5211** 7359 Home centers; Tool rental
HQ: Home Depot U.S.A., Inc.
2455 Paces Ferry Rd Se
Atlanta GA

(P-13606)
HOME DEPOT USA INC
Also Called: Home Depot, The
1830 W Slauson Ave (90047-1126)
PHONE...............................323 292-1397
John Cruz, *Mgr*
EMP: 214
SQ FT: 110,000
SALES (corp-wide): 157.4B **Publicly Held**
Web: www.homedepot.com
SIC: **5211** 7359 Home centers; Tool rental
HQ: Home Depot U.S.A., Inc.
2455 Paces Ferry Rd Se
Atlanta GA

(P-13607)
HOME DEPOT USA INC
Also Called: Home Depot, The
2055 N Figueroa St (90065-1021)
PHONE...............................323 342-9495
Laud Ashbar, *Mgr*
EMP: 203
SQ FT: 107,880
SALES (corp-wide): 157.4B **Publicly Held**
Web: www.homedepot.com
SIC: **5211** 7359 Home centers; Tool rental
HQ: Home Depot U.S.A., Inc.
2455 Paces Ferry Rd Se
Atlanta GA

(P-13608)
HOME DEPOT USA INC
Also Called: Home Depot, The
6400 Alondra Blvd (90723-3726)
PHONE...............................562 272-8055
Raul M Rodriguez, *Brnch Mgr*
EMP: 120
SALES (corp-wide): 157.4B **Publicly Held**
Web: www.homedepot.com
SIC: **5211** 7359 Home centers; Tool rental
HQ: Home Depot U.S.A., Inc.
2455 Paces Ferry Rd Se
Atlanta GA

(P-13609)
HOME DEPOT USA INC
Also Called: Home Depot, The

3200 Puente Ave (91706-5526)
PHONE...............................626 813-7131
Chip Dazies, *Mgr*
EMP: 107
SQ FT: 105,920
SALES (corp-wide): 157.4B **Publicly Held**
Web: www.homedepot.com
SIC: **5211** 7359 Home centers; Tool rental
HQ: Home Depot U.S.A., Inc.
2455 Paces Ferry Rd Se
Atlanta GA

(P-13610)
HOME DEPOT USA INC
Also Called: Home Depot, The
110 E Sepulveda Blvd (90745-6301)
PHONE...............................310 835-7547
Emily R Simpson, *Mgr*
EMP: 139
SALES (corp-wide): 157.4B **Publicly Held**
Web: www.homedepot.com
SIC: **5211** 7359 Home centers; Tool rental
HQ: Home Depot U.S.A., Inc.
2455 Paces Ferry Rd Se
Atlanta GA

(P-13611)
HOME DEPOT USA INC
Also Called: Home Depot, The
12322 Washington Blvd (90606-2503)
PHONE...............................562 789-4121
Ben Deardudin, *Mgr*
EMP: 122
SALES (corp-wide): 157.4B **Publicly Held**
Web: www.homedepot.com
SIC: **5211** 7359 Home centers; Tool rental
HQ: Home Depot U.S.A., Inc.
2455 Paces Ferry Rd Se
Atlanta GA

(P-13612)
HOME DEPOT USA INC
Also Called: Home Depot, The
14603 Ocean Gate Ave (90250-6744)
PHONE...............................310 644-9600
Jason Oaks, *Mgr*
EMP: 115
SALES (corp-wide): 157.4B **Publicly Held**
Web: www.homedepot.com
SIC: **5211** 7359 Home centers; Tool rental
HQ: Home Depot U.S.A., Inc.
2455 Paces Ferry Rd Se
Atlanta GA

(P-13613)
HOME DEPOT USA INC
Also Called: Home Depot, The
7015 Telegraph Rd (90040-3225)
PHONE...............................323 727-9600
EMP: 223
SALES (corp-wide): 157.4B **Publicly Held**
Web: www.homedepot.com
SIC: **5211** 7359 Home centers; Tool rental
HQ: Home Depot U.S.A., Inc.
2455 Paces Ferry Rd Se
Atlanta GA

(P-13614)
HOME DEPOT USA INC
Also Called: Home Depot, The
12975 W Jefferson Blvd (90066-7023)
PHONE...............................310 822-3330
EMP: 148
SALES (corp-wide): 157.4B **Publicly Held**
Web: www.homedepot.com
SIC: **5211** 7359 Home centers; Tool rental
HQ: Home Depot U.S.A., Inc.
2455 Paces Ferry Rd Se
Atlanta GA

(P-13615)
HOME DEPOT USA INC
Also Called: Home Depot, The
12960 Foothill Blvd (91342-4928)
PHONE...............................818 365-7662
EMP: 128
SALES (corp-wide): 157.4B **Publicly Held**
Web: www.homedepot.com
SIC: **5211** 7359 Home centers; Tool rental
HQ: Home Depot U.S.A., Inc.
2455 Paces Ferry Rd Se
Atlanta GA

(P-13616)
HOME DEPOT USA INC
Also Called: Home Depot, The
20642 Golden Triangle Rd (91351-2419)
PHONE...............................661 252-7800
EMP: 148
SALES (corp-wide): 157.4B **Publicly Held**
Web: www.homedepot.com
SIC: **5211** 7359 Home centers; Tool rental
HQ: Home Depot U.S.A., Inc.
2455 Paces Ferry Rd Se
Atlanta GA

(P-13617)
HOME DEPOT USA INC
Also Called: Home Depot, The
2450 Cherry Ave (90755-3706)
PHONE...............................562 595-9200
EMP: 87
SALES (corp-wide): 157.4B **Publicly Held**
Web: www.homedepot.com
SIC: **5211** 7359 Home centers; Tool rental
HQ: Home Depot U.S.A., Inc.
2455 Paces Ferry Rd Se
Atlanta GA

(P-13618)
HOME DEPOT USA INC
Also Called: Home Depot, The
575 N China Lake Blvd (93555-3581)
PHONE...............................760 375-4614
Garbriel Garcia, *Mgr*
EMP: 114
SALES (corp-wide): 157.4B **Publicly Held**
Web: www.homedepot.com
SIC: **5211** 7359 Home centers; Tool rental
HQ: Home Depot U.S.A., Inc.
2455 Paces Ferry Rd Se
Atlanta GA

(P-13619)
HOME DEPOT USA INC
Also Called: Home Depot, The
7121 Firestone Blvd (90241-4104)
PHONE...............................562 776-2200
Max Hernandez, *Mgr*
EMP: 238
SALES (corp-wide): 157.4B **Publicly Held**
Web: www.homedepot.com
SIC: **5211** 7359 Home centers; Tool rental
HQ: Home Depot U.S.A., Inc.
2455 Paces Ferry Rd Se
Atlanta GA

(P-13620)
HOME DEPOT USA INC
Also Called: Home Depot, The
16800 Roscoe Blvd (91406-1105)
PHONE...............................818 780-5448
John Cruz, *Mgr*
EMP: 120
SALES (corp-wide): 157.4B **Publicly Held**
Web: www.homedepot.com
SIC: **5211** 7359 Home centers; Tool rental
HQ: Home Depot U.S.A., Inc.
2455 Paces Ferry Rd Se
Atlanta GA

(P-13621)
HOME DEPOT USA INC
Also Called: Home Depot, The
3040 E Slauson Ave (90255-3138)
PHONE...............................323 587-5520
Ross Manzo, *Mgr*
EMP: 143
SALES (corp-wide): 157.4B **Publicly Held**
Web: www.homedepot.com
SIC: **5211** 7359 Home centers; Tool rental
HQ: Home Depot U.S.A., Inc.
2455 Paces Ferry Rd Se
Atlanta GA

(P-13622)
HOME DEPOT USA INC
Also Called: Home Depot, The
3363 W Century Blvd (90303-1366)
PHONE...............................310 677-1944
Kim Dixon, *Mgr*
EMP: 111
SQ FT: 107,421
SALES (corp-wide): 157.4B **Publicly Held**
Web: www.homedepot.com
SIC: **5211** 7359 Home centers; Tool rental
HQ: Home Depot U.S.A., Inc.
2455 Paces Ferry Rd Se
Atlanta GA

(P-13623)
HOME DEPOT USA INC
Also Called: Home Depot, The
1625 S Mountain Ave (91016-4205)
PHONE...............................626 256-0580
Mako Kapaska, *Mgr*
EMP: 151
SALES (corp-wide): 157.4B **Publicly Held**
Web: www.homedepot.com
SIC: **5211** 7359 Home centers; Tool rental
HQ: Home Depot U.S.A., Inc.
2455 Paces Ferry Rd Se
Atlanta GA

(P-13624)
INDUSTRIAL WOOD PRODUCTS INC
5123 Brooks St (91763-4806)
P.O. Box 3121 (91763-9221)
PHONE...............................909 625-1247
Jaime Ramirez, *Pr*
Lydia Ramrez, *VP*
EMP: 18 **EST**: 1984
SALES (est): 2.43MM **Privately Held**
SIC: **5211** 2448 2449 2441 Millwork and
lumber; Pallets, wood; Rectangular boxes
and crates, wood; Nailed wood boxes and
shook

(P-13625)
LOWES HOME CENTERS LLC
Also Called: Lowe's
2053 N Imperial Ave (92243-1324)
PHONE...............................760 337-6700
Chad Manley, *Mgr*
EMP: 100
SALES (corp-wide): 97.06B **Publicly Held**
Web: www.lowes.com
SIC: **5211** 5031 5722 5064 Home centers;
Building materials, exterior; Household
appliance stores; Electrical appliances,
television and radio
HQ: Lowe's Home Centers, Llc
1000 Lowes Blvd
Mooresville NC
336 658-4000

(P-13626)
LOWES HOME CENTERS LLC
Also Called: Lowe's
1601 Columbus St (93305-2133)

PHONE..............................661 889-9000
Francisco Dubon, *Brnch Mgr*
EMP: 142
SALES (corp-wide): 97.06B **Publicly Held**
Web: www.lowes.com
SIC: **5211** 5031 5722 5064   Home centers;
  Building materials, exterior; Household
  appliance stores; Electrical appliances,
  television and radio
HQ: Lowe's Home Centers, Llc
  1000 Lowes Blvd
  Mooresville NC
  336 658-4000

(P-13627)
LOWES HOME CENTERS LLC
Also Called: Lowe's
13500 Paxton St (91331-2352)
PHONE..............................818 686-4300
Mario Garza, *Brnch Mgr*
EMP: 124
SALES (corp-wide): 97.06B **Publicly Held**
Web: www.lowes.com
SIC: **5211** 5031 5722 5064   Home centers;
  Building materials, exterior; Household
  appliance stores; Electrical appliances,
  television and radio
HQ: Lowe's Home Centers, Llc
  1000 Lowes Blvd
  Mooresville NC
  336 658-4000

(P-13628)
LOWES HOME CENTERS LLC
Also Called: Lowe's
8383 Topanga Canyon Blvd (91304-2343)
PHONE..............................818 610-1960
Pete Reed, *Brnch Mgr*
EMP: 90
SALES (corp-wide): 97.06B **Publicly Held**
Web: www.lowes.com
SIC: **5211** 5031 5722 5064   Home centers;
  Building materials, exterior; Household
  appliance stores; Electrical appliances,
  television and radio
HQ: Lowe's Home Centers, Llc
  1000 Lowes Blvd
  Mooresville NC
  336 658-4000

(P-13629)
LOWES HOME CENTERS LLC
Also Called: Lowe's
2000 W Empire Ave (91504-3434)
PHONE..............................818 557-2300
Chris Mcgilroy, *Mgr*
EMP: 135
SALES (corp-wide): 97.06B **Publicly Held**
Web: www.lowes.com
SIC: **5211** 5031 5722 5064   Home centers;
  Building materials, exterior; Household
  appliance stores; Electrical appliances,
  television and radio
HQ: Lowe's Home Centers, Llc
  1000 Lowes Blvd
  Mooresville NC
  336 658-4000

(P-13630)
LOWES HOME CENTERS LLC
Also Called: Hawthorne Lowe's
2800 W 120th St (90250-3338)
PHONE..............................323 327-4000
Mike Bryant, *Mgr*
EMP: 149
SALES (corp-wide): 97.06B **Publicly Held**
Web: www.lowes.com
SIC: **5211** 5031 5722 5064   Home centers;
  Building materials, exterior; Household
  appliance stores; Electrical appliances,
  television and radio

HQ: Lowe's Home Centers, Llc
  1000 Lowes Blvd
  Mooresville NC
  336 658-4000

(P-13631)
LOWES HOME CENTERS LLC
Also Called: Lowe's
8600 Washington Blvd (90660-3790)
PHONE..............................562 942-9909
Jose Rodriquez, *Brnch Mgr*
EMP: 138
SALES (corp-wide): 97.06B **Publicly Held**
Web: www.lowes.com
SIC: **5211** 5031 5722 5064   Home centers;
  Building materials, exterior; Household
  appliance stores; Electrical appliances,
  television and radio
HQ: Lowe's Home Centers, Llc
  1000 Lowes Blvd
  Mooresville NC
  336 658-4000

(P-13632)
LOWES HOME CENTERS LLC
Also Called: Lowe's
39500 Lowes Dr (93551-3754)
PHONE..............................661 267-9888
Veronica Pinkui, *Mgr*
EMP: 90
SQ FT: 133,410
SALES (corp-wide): 97.06B **Publicly Held**
Web: www.lowes.com
SIC: **5211** 5031 5722 5064   Home centers;
  Building materials, exterior; Household
  appliance stores; Electrical appliances,
  television and radio
HQ: Lowe's Home Centers, Llc
  1000 Lowes Blvd
  Mooresville NC
  336 658-4000

(P-13633)
LOWES HOME CENTERS LLC
Also Called: Lowe's
22255 S Western Ave (90501-4106)
PHONE..............................310 787-1469
Ricky Garcia, *Mgr*
EMP: 114
SALES (corp-wide): 97.06B **Publicly Held**
Web: www.lowes.com
SIC: **5211** 5031 5722 5064   Home centers;
  Building materials, exterior; Household
  appliance stores; Electrical appliances,
  television and radio
HQ: Lowe's Home Centers, Llc
  1000 Lowes Blvd
  Mooresville NC
  336 658-4000

(P-13634)
LOWES HOME CENTERS LLC
Also Called: Lowe's
19601 Nordhoff St (91324-2422)
PHONE..............................818 477-9022
Mark Harrison, *Store Mgr*
EMP: 179
SALES (corp-wide): 97.06B **Publicly Held**
Web: www.lowes.com
SIC: **5211** 5031 5722 5064   Home centers;
  Building materials, exterior; Household
  appliance stores; Electrical appliances,
  television and radio
HQ: Lowe's Home Centers, Llc
  1000 Lowes Blvd
  Mooresville NC
  336 658-4000

(P-13635)
LOWES HOME CENTERS LLC
Also Called: Lowe's
14873 Carmenita Rd (90650-5232)
PHONE..............................562 926-0826
Patrick Cosley, *Mgr*
EMP: 92
SALES (corp-wide): 97.06B **Publicly Held**
Web: www.lowes.com
SIC: **5211** 5031 5722 5064   Home centers;
  Building materials, exterior; Household
  appliance stores; Electrical appliances,
  television and radio
HQ: Lowe's Home Centers, Llc
  1000 Lowes Blvd
  Mooresville NC
  336 658-4000

(P-13636)
LOWES HOME CENTERS LLC
Also Called: Lowe's
19001 Golden Valley Rd (91387-1471)
PHONE..............................661 678-4430
Veronica January, *Brnch Mgr*
EMP: 109
SALES (corp-wide): 97.06B **Publicly Held**
Web: www.lowes.com
SIC: **5211** 5031 5722 5064   Home centers;
  Building materials, exterior; Household
  appliance stores; Electrical appliances,
  television and radio
HQ: Lowe's Home Centers, Llc
  1000 Lowes Blvd
  Mooresville NC
  336 658-4000

(P-13637)
LOWES HOME CENTERS LLC
Also Called: Lowe's
11399 Foothill Blvd (91730-7626)
PHONE..............................909 476-9697
Jeniffer Lang, *Mgr*
EMP: 129
SALES (corp-wide): 97.06B **Publicly Held**
Web: www.lowes.com
SIC: **5211** 5031 5722 5064   Home centers;
  Building materials, exterior; Household
  appliance stores; Electrical appliances,
  television and radio
HQ: Lowe's Home Centers, Llc
  1000 Lowes Blvd
  Mooresville NC
  336 658-4000

(P-13638)
LOWES HOME CENTERS LLC
Also Called: Lowe's
14333 Bear Valley Rd (92392-5403)
PHONE..............................760 949-9565
Shawn Pierson, *Mgr*
EMP: 90
SALES (corp-wide): 97.06B **Publicly Held**
Web: www.lowes.com
SIC: **5211** 5031 5722 5064   Home centers;
  Building materials, exterior; Household
  appliance stores; Electrical appliances,
  television and radio
HQ: Lowe's Home Centers, Llc
  1000 Lowes Blvd
  Mooresville NC
  336 658-4000

(P-13639)
LOWES HOME CENTERS LLC
Also Called: Lowe's
1659 W Foothill Blvd (91786-3533)
PHONE..............................909 982-4795
Dan Caganap, *Mgr*
EMP: 105
SALES (corp-wide): 97.06B **Publicly Held**

Web: www.lowes.com
SIC: **5211** 5031 5722 5064   Home centers;
  Building materials, exterior; Household
  appliance stores; Electrical appliances,
  television and radio
HQ: Lowe's Home Centers, Llc
  1000 Lowes Blvd
  Mooresville NC
  336 658-4000

(P-13640)
LOWES HOME CENTERS LLC
Also Called: Lowe's
16851 Sierra Lakes Pkwy (92336-1226)
PHONE..............................909 350-7900
Jan Hardy, *Mgr*
EMP: 118
SALES (corp-wide): 97.06B **Publicly Held**
Web: www.lowes.com
SIC: **5211** 5031 5722 5064   Home centers;
  Building materials, exterior; Household
  appliance stores; Electrical appliances,
  television and radio
HQ: Lowe's Home Centers, Llc
  1000 Lowes Blvd
  Mooresville NC
  336 658-4000

(P-13641)
LOWES HOME CENTERS LLC
Also Called: Lowe's
1725 W Redlands Blvd (92373-8012)
PHONE..............................909 307-8883
Jim Riley, *Mgr*
EMP: 92
SALES (corp-wide): 97.06B **Publicly Held**
Web: www.lowes.com
SIC: **5211** 5031 5722 5064   Home centers;
  Building materials, exterior; Household
  appliance stores; Electrical appliances,
  television and radio
HQ: Lowe's Home Centers, Llc
  1000 Lowes Blvd
  Mooresville NC
  336 658-4000

(P-13642)
LOWES HOME CENTERS LLC
Also Called: Lowe's
12189 Apple Valley Rd (92308-6702)
PHONE..............................760 961-3000
Chris Horan, *Mgr*
EMP: 107
SALES (corp-wide): 97.06B **Publicly Held**
Web: www.lowes.com
SIC: **5211** 5031 5722 5064   Home centers;
  Building materials, exterior; Household
  appliance stores; Electrical appliances,
  television and radio
HQ: Lowe's Home Centers, Llc
  1000 Lowes Blvd
  Mooresville NC
  336 658-4000

(P-13643)
LOWES HOME CENTERS LLC
Also Called: Lowe's
2390 S Grove Ave (91761-4808)
PHONE..............................909 969-9053
Myarna Zega, *Mgr*
EMP: 120
SALES (corp-wide): 97.06B **Publicly Held**
Web: www.lowes
SIC: **5211** 5031 5722 5064   Home centers;
  Building materials, exterior; Household
  appliance stores; Electrical appliances,
  television and radio
HQ: Lowe's Home Centers, Llc
  1000 Lowes Blvd
  Mooresville NC
  336 658-4000

PRODUCTS & SVCS

(P-13644)
LOWES HOME CENTERS LLC
Also Called: Lowe's
4777 Chino Hills Pkwy (91709-5849)
PHONE..................................909 438-9000
EMP: 138
SALES (corp-wide): 97.06B **Publicly Held**
Web: www.lowes.com
SIC: 5211 5031 5722 5064 Home centers;
Building materials, exterior; Household
appliance stores; Electrical appliances,
television and radio
HQ: Lowe's Home Centers, Llc
1000 Lowes Blvd
Mooresville NC
336 658-4000

(P-13645)
LOWES HOME CENTERS LLC
Also Called: Lowe's
27847 Greenspot Rd (92346-4381)
PHONE..................................909 557-9010
EMP: 92
SALES (corp-wide): 97.06B **Publicly Held**
Web: www.lowes.com
SIC: 5211 5031 5722 5064 Home centers;
Building materials, exterior; Household
appliance stores; Electrical appliances,
television and radio
HQ: Lowe's Home Centers, Llc
1000 Lowes Blvd
Mooresville NC
336 658-4000

(P-13646)
LOWES HOME CENTERS LLC
Also Called: Lowe's
155 Old Grove Rd (92057-1216)
PHONE..................................760 966-7140
Mike Shratz, *Mgr*
EMP: 105
SALES (corp-wide): 97.06B **Publicly Held**
Web: www.lowes.com
SIC: 5211 5031 5722 5064 Home centers;
Building materials, exterior; Household
appliance stores; Electrical appliances,
television and radio
HQ: Lowe's Home Centers, Llc
1000 Lowes Blvd
Mooresville NC
336 658-4000

(P-13647)
LOWES HOME CENTERS LLC
Also Called: Lowe's
151 Vista Village Dr (92083-4974)
PHONE..................................760 631-6255
Bill Mobley, *Brnch Mgr*
EMP: 92
SALES (corp-wide): 97.06B **Publicly Held**
Web: www.lowes.com
SIC: 5211 5031 5722 5064 Home centers;
Building materials, exterior; Household
appliance stores; Electrical appliances,
television and radio
HQ: Lowe's Home Centers, Llc
1000 Lowes Blvd
Mooresville NC
336 658-4000

(P-13648)
LOWES HOME CENTERS LLC
Also Called: Lowe's
2225 Otay Lakes Rd (91915-1001)
PHONE..................................619 739-9060
EMP: 118
SALES (corp-wide): 97.06B **Publicly Held**
Web: www.lowes.com

SIC: 5211 5031 5722 5064 Home centers;
Building materials, exterior; Household
appliance stores; Electrical appliances,
television and radio
HQ: Lowe's Home Centers, Llc
1000 Lowes Blvd
Mooresville NC
336 658-4000

(P-13649)
LOWES HOME CENTERS LLC
Also Called: Lowe's
9416 Mission Gorge Rd (92071-3847)
P.O. Box 710909 (92072-0909)
PHONE..................................619 212-4100
Jim Andrews, *Mgr*
EMP: 110
SALES (corp-wide): 97.06B **Publicly Held**
Web: www.lowes.com
SIC: 5211 5031 5722 5064 Home centers;
Building materials, exterior; Household
appliance stores; Electrical appliances,
television and radio
HQ: Lowe's Home Centers, Llc
1000 Lowes Blvd
Mooresville NC
336 658-4000

(P-13650)
LOWES HOME CENTERS LLC
Also Called: Lowe's
620 W Mission Ave (92025-1611)
PHONE..................................760 484-5113
Bill Mobley, *Mgr*
EMP: 92
SALES (corp-wide): 97.06B **Publicly Held**
Web: www.lowes.com
SIC: 5211 5031 5722 5064 Home centers;
Building materials, exterior; Household
appliance stores; Electrical appliances,
television and radio
HQ: Lowe's Home Centers, Llc
1000 Lowes Blvd
Mooresville NC
336 658-4000

(P-13651)
LOWES HOME CENTERS LLC
Also Called: Lowe's
500 S Mills Rd (93003-3459)
PHONE..................................805 675-8800
Glen Sueishi, *Mgr*
EMP: 122
SALES (corp-wide): 97.06B **Publicly Held**
Web: www.lowes.com
SIC: 5211 5031 5722 5064 Home centers;
Building materials, exterior; Household
appliance stores; Electrical appliances,
television and radio
HQ: Lowe's Home Centers, Llc
1000 Lowes Blvd
Mooresville NC
336 658-4000

(P-13652)
LOWES HOME CENTERS LLC
Also Called: Lowe's
1275 Simi Town Center Way (93065-0513)
PHONE..................................805 426-2780
Bob Derr, *Mgr*
EMP: 101
SALES (corp-wide): 97.06B **Publicly Held**
Web: www.lowes.com
SIC: 5211 5031 5722 5064 Home centers;
Building materials, exterior; Household
appliance stores; Electrical appliances,
television and radio
HQ: Lowe's Home Centers, Llc
1000 Lowes Blvd
Mooresville NC
336 658-4000

(P-13653)
LOWES HOME CENTERS LLC
Also Called: Lowe's
2445 Golden Hill Rd (93446-6385)
PHONE..................................805 602-9051
EMP: 124
SALES (corp-wide): 97.06B **Publicly Held**
Web: www.lowes.com
SIC: 5211 5031 5722 5064 Home centers;
Building materials, exterior; Household
appliance stores; Electrical appliances,
television and radio
HQ: Lowe's Home Centers, Llc
1000 Lowes Blvd
Mooresville NC
336 658-4000

(P-13654)
LOWES HOME CENTERS LLC
Also Called: Lowe's
2318 Northside Dr (92108-2704)
PHONE..................................619 584-5500
Rebecca Young, *Mgr*
EMP: 145
SALES (corp-wide): 97.06B **Publicly Held**
Web: www.lowes.com
SIC: 5211 5031 5722 5064 Home centers;
Building materials, exterior; Household
appliance stores; Electrical appliances,
television and radio
HQ: Lowe's Home Centers, Llc
1000 Lowes Blvd
Mooresville NC
336 658-4000

(P-13655)
LOWES HOME CENTERS LLC
Also Called: Lowe's
907 Avenida Pico (92673-3908)
PHONE..................................949 369-4644
Sonya Olmedo, *Mgr*
EMP: 98
SALES (corp-wide): 97.06B **Publicly Held**
Web: www.lowes.com
SIC: 5211 5031 5722 5064 Home centers;
Building materials, exterior; Household
appliance stores; Electrical appliances,
television and radio
HQ: Lowe's Home Centers, Llc
1000 Lowes Blvd
Mooresville NC
336 658-4000

(P-13656)
LOWES HOME CENTERS LLC
Also Called: Lowe's
1500 N Lemon St (92801-1204)
PHONE..................................714 447-6140
Brian Hefel, *Brnch Mgr*
EMP: 175
SALES (corp-wide): 97.06B **Publicly Held**
Web: www.lowes.com
SIC: 5211 5031 5722 5064 Home centers;
Building materials, exterior; Household
appliance stores; Electrical appliances,
television and radio
HQ: Lowe's Home Centers, Llc
1000 Lowes Blvd
Mooresville NC
336 658-4000

(P-13657)
LOWES HOME CENTERS LLC
Also Called: Lowe's
1380 S Beach Blvd (90631-6374)
PHONE..................................562 690-5122
Ken Konkel, *Mgr*
EMP: 109
SALES (corp-wide): 97.06B **Publicly Held**
Web: www.lowes.com

SIC: 5211 5031 5722 5064 Home centers;
Building materials, exterior; Household
appliance stores; Electrical appliances,
television and radio
HQ: Lowe's Home Centers, Llc
1000 Lowes Blvd
Mooresville NC
336 658-4000

(P-13658)
LOWES HOME CENTERS LLC
Also Called: Lowe's
2500 Park Ave (92782-2712)
PHONE..................................714 913-2663
Nico Zavala, *Mgr*
EMP: 110
SALES (corp-wide): 97.06B **Publicly Held**
Web: www.lowes.com
SIC: 5211 5031 5722 5064 Home centers;
Building materials, exterior; Household
appliance stores; Electrical appliances,
television and radio
HQ: Lowe's Home Centers, Llc
1000 Lowes Blvd
Mooresville NC
336 658-4000

(P-13659)
LOWES HOME CENTERS LLC
Also Called: Lowe's
30472 Haun Rd (92584-6810)
PHONE..................................951 723-1930
Dave Jenkins, *Brnch Mgr*
EMP: 112
SALES (corp-wide): 97.06B **Publicly Held**
Web: www.lowes.com
SIC: 5211 5031 5722 5064 Home centers;
Building materials, exterior; Household
appliance stores; Electrical appliances,
television and radio
HQ: Lowe's Home Centers, Llc
1000 Lowes Blvd
Mooresville NC
336 658-4000

(P-13660)
LOWES HOME CENTERS LLC
Also Called: Lowe's
9851 Magnolia Ave (92503-3528)
PHONE..................................951 509-5500
Daniel Mergio, *Brnch Mgr*
EMP: 142
SALES (corp-wide): 97.06B **Publicly Held**
Web: www.lowes.com
SIC: 5211 5031 5722 5064 Home centers;
Building materials, exterior; Household
appliance stores; Electrical appliances,
television and radio
HQ: Lowe's Home Centers, Llc
1000 Lowes Blvd
Mooresville NC
336 658-4000

(P-13661)
LOWES HOME CENTERS LLC
Also Called: Lowe's
78865 Highway 111 (92253-2003)
PHONE..................................760 771-5566
Ron Stewart, *Mgr*
EMP: 112
SALES (corp-wide): 97.06B **Publicly Held**
Web: www.lowes.com
SIC: 5211 5031 5722 5064 Home centers;
Building materials, exterior; Household
appliance stores; Electrical appliances,
television and radio
HQ: Lowe's Home Centers, Llc
1000 Lowes Blvd
Mooresville NC
336 658-4000

(P-13662)
LOWES HOME CENTERS LLC
Also Called: Lowe's
5201 E Ramon Rd (92264-3600)
PHONE................................760 866-1901
Robert Richmond, *Brnch Mgr*
EMP: 129
SALES (corp-wide): 97.06B **Publicly Held**
Web: www.lowes.com
SIC: 5211 5031 5722 5064 Home centers;
Building materials, exterior; Household
appliance stores; Electrical appliances,
television and radio
HQ: Lowe's Home Centers, Llc
1000 Lowes Blvd
Mooresville NC
336 658-4000

(P-13663)
LOWES HOME CENTERS LLC
Also Called: Lowe's
24701 Madison Ave (92562-9763)
PHONE................................951 461-8916
Scott Holland, *Mgr*
EMP: 101
SALES (corp-wide): 97.06B **Publicly Held**
Web: www.lowes.com
SIC: 5211 5031 5722 5064 Home centers;
Building materials, exterior; Household
appliance stores; Electrical appliances,
television and radio
HQ: Lowe's Home Centers, Llc
1000 Lowes Blvd
Mooresville NC
336 658-4000

(P-13664)
LOWES HOME CENTERS LLC
Also Called: Lowe's
12400 Day St (92553-7501)
PHONE................................951 656-1859
David Jenkins, *Mgr*
EMP: 85
SALES (corp-wide): 97.06B **Publicly Held**
Web: www.lowes.com
SIC: 5211 5031 5722 5064 Home centers;
Building materials, exterior; Household
appliance stores; Electrical appliances,
television and radio
HQ: Lowe's Home Centers, Llc
1000 Lowes Blvd
Mooresville NC
336 658-4000

(P-13665)
LOWES HOME CENTERS LLC
Also Called: Lowe's
40390 Winchester Rd (92591-5519)
PHONE................................951 296-1618
Rose Burns, *Mgr*
EMP: 105
SALES (corp-wide): 97.06B **Publicly Held**
Web: www.lowes.com
SIC: 5211 5031 5722 5064 Home centers;
Building materials, exterior; Household
appliance stores; Electrical appliances,
television and radio
HQ: Lowe's Home Centers, Llc
1000 Lowes Blvd
Mooresville NC
336 658-4000

(P-13666)
LOWES HOME CENTERS LLC
Also Called: Lowe's
1285 Magnolia Ave (92879-2092)
PHONE................................951 256-9004
Jeff Fowler, *Brnch Mgr*
EMP: 101
SALES (corp-wide): 97.06B **Publicly Held**

Web: www.lowes.com
SIC: 5211 5031 5722 5064 Home centers;
Building materials, exterior; Household
appliance stores; Electrical appliances,
television and radio
HQ: Lowe's Home Centers, Llc
1000 Lowes Blvd
Mooresville NC
336 658-4000

(P-13667)
LOWES HOME CENTERS LLC
Also Called: Lowe's
29335 Central Ave (92532-2212)
PHONE................................951 253-6000
A Nuseibtel, *Prin*
EMP: 120
SALES (corp-wide): 97.06B **Publicly Held**
Web: www.lowes.com
SIC: 5211 5031 5722 5064 Home centers;
Building materials, exterior; Household
appliance stores; Electrical appliances,
television and radio
HQ: Lowe's Home Centers, Llc
1000 Lowes Blvd
Mooresville NC
336 658-4000

(P-13668)
PARAGON INDUSTRIES INC
Also Called: Bedrosian's Tiles & Stone
1515 E Winston Rd (92805-6445)
PHONE................................714 778-1800
Diana Kelly, *Pr*
EMP: 100
SALES (corp-wide): 251.57MM **Privately
Held**
Web: www.bedrosians.com
SIC: 5211 5032 Tile, ceramic; Brick, stone,
and related material
PA: Paragon Industries, Inc.
4285 N Golden State Blvd
Fresno CA
559 275-5000

(P-13669)
PAREX USA INC
Also Called: La Habra Stucco
2150 Eastridge Ave (92507-0720)
PHONE................................951 653-3549
Brian Carrier, *Mgr*
EMP: 18
Web: www.parexusa.com
SIC: 5211 3299 Lumber and other building
materials; Stucco
HQ: Parex Usa, Inc.
2150 Eastridge Ave
Riverside CA
714 778-2266

(P-13670)
**SMI ARCHITECTURAL
MILLWORK INC**
Also Called: SMI Millwork
2116 W Chestnut Ave (92703-4306)
PHONE................................714 567-0112
Robert Stolo, *Pr*
Karen Kawasaki, *
Timothy J Stolo, *
EMP: 35 **EST:** 1997
SQ FT: 1,500
SALES (est): 4.48MM **Privately Held**
Web: www.smimillwork.com
SIC: 5211 2431 Millwork and lumber;
Millwork

(P-13671)
**SUPERIOR READY MIX
CONCRETE LP**
Also Called: San Diego Ready Mix

9245 Camino Santa Fe (92121-2201)
PHONE................................858 695-0666
J Frederickson, *Brnch Mgr*
EMP: 71
SALES (corp-wide): 205.26MM **Privately
Held**
Web: superiorrm.cloudflareaccess.com
SIC: 5211 3273 Concrete and cinder block;
Ready-mixed concrete
PA: Superior Ready Mix Concrete L.P.
1564 Mission Rd
Escondido CA
760 745-0556

(P-13672)
SWAN FENCE INCORPORATED
600 W Manville St (90220-5508)
PHONE................................310 669-8000
Shigehiro Hatake, *Pr*
Jun Ando, *
EMP: 25 **EST:** 1988
SQ FT: 50,000
SALES (est): 5.69MM **Privately Held**
Web: www.swanfence.com
SIC: 5211 3315 Fencing; Fence gates,
posts, and fittings: steel
PA: Koiwa Kanaami Co., Ltd.
3-20-14, Nishiasakusa
Taito-Ku TKY

5231 Paint, Glass, And Wallpaper Stores

(P-13673)
**DUNN-EDWARDS
CORPORATION (DH)**
Also Called: Dunn-Dwrds Pints Wallcoverings
6119 E Washington Blvd (90040-2436)
P.O. Box 30389 (90030-0389)
PHONE................................888 337-2468
Karl Altergott, *Pr*
◆ **EMP:** 150 **EST:** 1925
SALES (est): 325.93MM **Privately Held**
Web: www.dunnedwards.com
SIC: 5231 2851 Paint; Lacquer: bases,
dopes, thinner
HQ: Nippon Paint Holdings Co., Ltd.
2-1-2, Oyodokita, Kita-Ku
Osaka OSK

(P-13674)
SWARTZ GLASS CO INC (PA)
821 Lincoln Blvd (90291-2846)
PHONE................................310 392-0001
Raphael Swartz, *CEO*
Michael Swartz, *Treas*
Mark Swartz, *VP*
EMP: 18 **EST:** 1933
SQ FT: 2,500
SALES (est): 1.92MM
SALES (corp-wide): 1.92MM **Privately
Held**
Web: www.swartzglassvenice.com
SIC: 5231 1793 7536 3231 Glass, leaded or
stained; Glass and glazing work;
Automotive glass replacement shops;
Products of purchased glass   ,

(P-13675)
**VISTA PAINT CORPORATION
(PA)**
2020 E Orangethorpe Ave (92831-5327)
PHONE................................714 680-3800
Eddie R Fischer, *Pr*
Eddie R Fischer, *Pr*
Jerome Fischer, *
Joe Wittenberg, *Marketing**
▲ **EMP:** 150 **EST:** 1956
SQ FT: 140,000

SALES (est): 96.51MM
SALES (corp-wide): 96.51MM **Privately
Held**
Web: www.vistapaint.com
SIC: 5231 2851 Paint; Paints and paint
additives

5251 Hardware Stores

(P-13676)
**CONSOLIDATED DEVICES INC
(HQ)**
Also Called: CDI Torque Products
19220 San Jose Ave (91748-1417)
PHONE................................626 965-0668
Michael King, *Pr*
Gary Keefe, *
▲ **EMP:** 25 **EST:** 1968
SQ FT: 90,000
SALES (est): 24.2MM
SALES (corp-wide): 4.49B **Publicly Held**
Web: www.cditorque.com
SIC: 5251 3679 3625 5072 Tools;
Transducers, electrical; Control equipment,
electric; Hardware
PA: Snap-On Incorporated
2801 80th St
Kenosha WI
262 656-5200

(P-13677)
**COORDNTED WIRE ROPE
RGGING INC (HQ)**
Also Called: Coordinated Companies
1707 E Anaheim St (90744-4706)
PHONE................................310 834-8535
Phiip T Gibson, *CEO*
Kristin Burgett, *VP*
▲ **EMP:** 20 **EST:** 1962
SQ FT: 8,640
SALES (est): 9.57MM
SALES (corp-wide): 14.95MM **Privately
Held**
Web: www.coordinatedcompanies.com
SIC: 5251 2298 Hardware stores; Wire rope
centers
PA: Coordinated Equipment Co.
1707 E Anaheim St
Wilmington CA
310 834-8535

(P-13678)
HERBERT RIZZARDINI
Also Called: Gateway Hardware
6259 Highway 178 (93527)
P.O. Box 1180 (93527-1180)
PHONE................................760 377-4571
Herbert Rizzardini, *Owner*
EMP: 18 **EST:** 1987
SQ FT: 7,000
SALES (est): 2.41MM **Privately Held**
SIC: 5251 2048 Hardware stores; Livestock
feeds

5261 Retail Nurseries And Garden Stores

(P-13679)
**GREEN THUMB
INTERNATIONAL INC**
Also Called: Green Thumb Nurseries
23734 Newhall Ave (91321-3125)
PHONE................................661 259-1071
Bryan Payne, *Mgr*
EMP: 86
SALES (corp-wide): 24.03MM **Privately
Held**
Web: www.greenthumb.com

PRODUCTS & SVCS

SIC: 5261 5712 5193 0782 Nursery stock, seeds and bulbs; Outdoor and garden furniture; Nursery stock; Sodding contractor
PA: Green Thumb International Inc
7105 Jordan Ave
Canoga Park CA
818 340-6400

(P-13680)
TREASURE GARDEN INC (PA)
13401 Brooks Dr (91706-2294)
PHONE..............................626 814-0168
Oliver Ma, *Pr*
Margaret Chang, *
◆ **EMP:** 50 **EST:** 1984
SQ FT: 45,000
SALES (est): 23.25MM
SALES (corp-wide): 23.25MM **Privately Held**
Web: www.treasuregarden.com
SIC: 5261 2514 Retail nurseries and garden stores; Lawn furniture: metal

5311 Department Stores

(P-13681)
PENNEY OPCO LLC
Also Called: JC Penney
400 S Baldwin Ave Lowr (91007-1909)
PHONE..............................626 445-6454
Jeff Paige, *Mgr*
EMP: 104
SALES (corp-wide): 1.93B **Privately Held**
SIC: 5311 7231 Department stores, non-discount; Beauty shops
HQ: Penney Opco Llc
6501 Legacy Dr Ste B100
Plano TX
972 431-4746

(P-13682)
PENNEY OPCO LLC
Also Called: JC Penney 1505
1203 Plaza Dr (91790-2885)
PHONE..............................626 960-3711
Bob Watanabe, *Brnch Mgr*
EMP: 170
SALES (corp-wide): 1.93B **Privately Held**
SIC: 5311 7231 5995 Department stores, non-discount; Beauty shops; Optical goods stores
HQ: Penney Opco Llc
6501 Legacy Dr Ste B100
Plano TX
972 431-4746

(P-13683)
PENNEY OPCO LLC
Also Called: JC Penney
280 W Hillcrest Dr (91360-4210)
PHONE..............................805 497-6811
M Kline, *Brnch Mgr*
EMP: 143
SALES (corp-wide): 1.93B **Privately Held**
SIC: 5311 7231 5995 Department stores, non-discount; Beauty shops; Optical goods stores
HQ: Penney Opco Llc
6501 Legacy Dr Ste B100
Plano TX
972 431-4746

(P-13684)
WALMART INC
Also Called: Walmart
1366 S Riverside Ave (92376-7608)
PHONE..............................909 820-9912
EMP: 243
SQ FT: 180,839

SALES (corp-wide): 611.29B **Publicly Held**
Web: corporate.walmart.com
SIC: 5311 7384 Department stores, discount ; Film developing services
PA: Walmart Inc.
702 Sw 8th St
Bentonville AR
479 640-8287

5331 Variety Stores

(P-13685)
CPL HOLDINGS LLC
12181 Bluff Creek Dr Ste 250 (90094-2992)
PHONE..............................310 348-6800
Patrick Gregory, *CFO*
Stephen Krenzer, *
EMP: 200 **EST:** 2012
SQ FT: 40,000
SALES (est): 22.35MM **Privately Held**
Web: www.coredigitalmedia.com
SIC: 5331 6719 5961 Variety stores; Investment holding companies, except banks; Electronic shopping

(P-13686)
GOODWILL INDS SOUTHERN CAL (PA)
342 N San Fernando Rd (90031-1730)
PHONE..............................323 223-1211
Patrick Mcclenahan, *Pr*
Michelle Tan, *
▲ **EMP:** 880 **EST:** 1919
SQ FT: 200,000
SALES (est): 279.59MM
SALES (corp-wide): 279.59MM **Privately Held**
Web: www.goodwillsocal.org
SIC: 5331 8331 Variety stores; Vocational rehabilitation agency

(P-13687)
NUMBER HOLDINGS INC (PA)
4000 Union Pacific Ave (90023-3202)
PHONE..............................323 980-8145
Frank J Schools, *
▲ **EMP:** 175 **EST:** 2011
SALES (est): 730.02MM
SALES (corp-wide): 730.02MM **Privately Held**
Web: www.99only.com
SIC: 5331 5199 Variety stores; General merchandise, non-durable

(P-13688)
PG USA LLC
Also Called: Pricegrabber.com
5150 W Goldleaf Cir (90056-1662)
PHONE..............................310 954-1040
◆ **EMP:** 85 **EST:** 1999
SALES (est): 11.82MM
SALES (corp-wide): 694.97MM **Privately Held**
SIC: 5331 4813 Variety stores; Online service providers
HQ: Connexity, Inc.
2120 Colorado Ave Ste 400
Santa Monica CA

5399 Miscellaneous General Merchandise

(P-13689)
COSTCO WHOLESALE CORPORATION
Also Called: Costco

1345 N Montebello Blvd (90640-2585)
PHONE..............................323 890-1904
EMP: 205
SIC: 5399 5014 Warehouse club stores; Automobile tires and tubes

(P-13690)
EGGS WEST
13610 S Archibald Ave (91761-7930)
PHONE..............................909 947-6207
H Dean Foster, *Pr*
Jeff Foster, *
Ann Foster, *
EMP: 18 **EST:** 1969
SALES (est): 945.74K **Privately Held**
SIC: 5399 2015 Warehouse club stores; Poultry slaughtering and processing

(P-13691)
SMART & FINAL STORES LLC
Also Called: Smart & Final
10935 Firestone Blvd (90650-2242)
PHONE..............................562 868-0794
Jackie Turcios, *Mgr*
EMP: 85
SIC: 5399 4225 Warehouse club stores; General warehousing
HQ: Smart & Final Stores Llc
600 Citadel Dr
Commerce CA

5411 Grocery Stores

(P-13692)
ALBERTSONS LLC
Also Called: Albertsons 6514
8938 Trautwein Rd Ste A (92508-9191)
PHONE..............................951 656-6603
Bill Brown, *Mgr*
EMP: 68
SALES (corp-wide): 77.65B **Publicly Held**
Web: www.starbucks.com
SIC: 5411 2051 Supermarkets, chain; Bread, cake, and related products
HQ: Albertson's Llc
250 E Parkcenter Blvd
Boise ID
208 395-6200

(P-13693)
ALBERTSONS LLC
Also Called: Albertsons 6798
30901 Riverside Dr (92530-4934)
PHONE..............................951 245-4461
Brad Sharp, *Mgr*
EMP: 24
SALES (corp-wide): 77.65B **Publicly Held**
Web: www.starbucks.com
SIC: 5411 5992 2052 2051 Supermarkets, chain; Florists; Cookies and crackers; Bread, cake, and related products
HQ: Albertson's Llc
250 E Parkcenter Blvd
Boise ID
208 395-6200

(P-13694)
ARRIETTA INCORPORATED
Also Called: La Tolteca Mexican Foods
429 N Azusa Ave (91702-3442)
PHONE..............................626 334-0302
Benjamin E Arrietta, *Pr*
Jean Arrietta, *
Tim Arrietta, *
Ben D Arrietta, *
EMP: 33 **EST:** 1948
SQ FT: 19,000
SALES (est): 4.43MM **Privately Held**

SIC: 5411 2099 5812 Delicatessen stores; Tortillas, fresh or refrigerated; Mexican restaurant

(P-13695)
COUSINS FOODS LLC
Also Called: Jericho Foods
2021 1st St (91340-2611)
PHONE..............................818 767-3842
Zadi Janah, *CEO*
Moshe Sarid, *Managing Member*
EMP: 20 **EST:** 2011
SALES (est): 2.69MM **Privately Held**
SIC: 5411 2035 1541 Grocery stores, independent; Dressings, salad: raw and cooked (except dry mixes); Food products manufacturing or packing plant construction

(P-13696)
DIANAS MEXICAN FOOD PDTS INC
Also Called: Labonita Diana's Mexican Food
300 E Sepulveda Blvd (90745-5923)
PHONE..............................310 834-4886
Carlos Andres, *Mgr*
EMP: 44
SQ FT: 1,660
SALES (corp-wide): 26.49MM **Privately Held**
Web: www.dianas.net
SIC: 5411 2099 5812 Delicatessen stores; Food preparations, nec; Mexican restaurant
PA: Diana's Mexican Food Products, Inc.
16330 Pioneer Blvd
Norwalk CA
562 926-5802

(P-13697)
EL NOPALITO INC (PA)
Also Called: El Nopalito Mexican Food
560 Santa Fe Dr (92024-4640)
PHONE..............................760 436-5775
Kia Garcia, *Pr*
Hilcias Garcia, *VP*
EMP: 20 **EST:** 1974
SQ FT: 4,000
SALES (est): 4.18MM
SALES (corp-wide): 4.18MM **Privately Held**
Web: www.el-nopalito.com
SIC: 5411 5812 2099 Grocery stores; Mexican restaurant; Tortillas, fresh or refrigerated

(P-13698)
EL TIGRE INC
Also Called: El Tigre Warehouse 2
2909 Coronado Ave (92154-2150)
PHONE..............................619 429-8212
M Rodriguez, *Genl Mgr*
EMP: 109
SALES (corp-wide): 26.75MM **Privately Held**
SIC: 5411 2051 Grocery stores, independent ; Bread, cake, and related products
PA: El Tigre, Inc.
1002 Mission Creek Rd
Fallbrook CA
760 728-8800

(P-13699)
GELSONS MARKETS
13455 Maxella Ave (90292-5682)
PHONE..............................310 306-3192
Romel Montero, *Genl Mgr*
EMP: 87
SALES (corp-wide): 384.74MM **Privately Held**
Web: www.gelsons.com

SIC: **5411** 2051 5461 Supermarkets, chain; Bread, cake, and related products; Retail bakeries
HQ: Gelson's Markets
13833 Freeway Dr
Santa Fe Springs CA
310 638-2842

(P-13700)
HOLZHEUS EL RANCHO MARKET INC
2886 Mission Dr (93463-9408)
PHONE..................805 688-4300
EMP: 100 **EST:** 1966
SALES (est): 9.8MM **Privately Held**
Web: www.californiafreshmarket.com
SIC: 5411 5147 Grocery stores, independent ; Meats, fresh

(P-13701)
MAJOR MARKET INC
Also Called: Major Market-Ftd Florist
845 S Main Ave (92028-3347)
PHONE..................760 723-0857
John Elkon, *Mgr*
EMP: 122
SALES (corp-wide): 24.34MM **Privately Held**
Web: www.majormarketgrocery.com
SIC: 5411 7336 Supermarkets, chain; Commercial art and graphic design
PA: Major Market, Inc.
845 S Main Ave
Fallbrook CA
760 723-0857

(P-13702)
PRESTIGE STATIONS INC (DH)
Also Called: Am/PM Mini Market
4 Centerpointe Dr (90623-1015)
PHONE..................714 670-5145
John Lannan, *VP*
EMP: 200 **EST:** 1974
SQ FT: 7,000
SALES (est): 270.65MM
SALES (corp-wide): 241.39B **Privately Held**
Web: www.ampm.com
SIC: 5411 7549 5541 Convenience stores, chain; Automotive maintenance services; Filling stations, gasoline
HQ: Atlantic Richfield Company Inc
4 Centerpointe Dr Ste 200
La Palma CA
800 333-3991

(P-13703)
STATER BROS MARKETS
10114 Adams Ave (92646-4907)
PHONE..................714 963-0949
Kevin Wagner, *Mgr*
EMP: 36
SALES (corp-wide): 1.5B **Privately Held**
Web: www.staterbros.com
SIC: 5411 5912 5992 2052 Supermarkets, chain; Drug stores; Florists; Cookies and crackers
HQ: Stater Bros. Markets
301 S Tippecanoe Ave
San Bernardino CA
909 733-5000

(P-13704)
STATER BROS MARKETS
1131 N State College Blvd (92806-2704)
PHONE..................714 991-5310
Scott Jefferson, *Mgr*
EMP: 35
SALES (corp-wide): 1.5B **Privately Held**
Web: www.staterbros.com

SIC: **5411** 5912 5992 2051 Supermarkets, chain; Drug stores; Florists; Bread, cake, and related products
HQ: Stater Bros. Markets
301 S Tippecanoe Ave
San Bernardino CA
909 733-5000

(P-13705)
SUPER CENTER CONCEPTS INC
Also Called: Superior Super Warehouse
7300 Atlantic Ave (90201-4305)
PHONE..................323 562-8980
Peter Buyn, *Brnch Mgr*
EMP: 118
Web: www.superiorgrocers.com
SIC: 5411 5421 2052 2051 Grocery stores, independent; Meat and fish markets; Cookies and crackers; Bread, cake, and related products
PA: Super Center Concepts, Inc.
15510 Carmenita Rd
Santa Fe Springs CA

(P-13706)
SUPER CENTER CONCEPTS INC
Also Called: Superior Warehouse
10211 Avalon Blvd (90003-4819)
PHONE..................323 241-6789
Mat Kovacs, *Brnch Mgr*
EMP: 79
Web: www.superiorgrocers.com
SIC: 5411 2051 5812 5461 Supermarkets, independent; Bread, cake, and related products; Carry-out only (except pizza) restaurant; Retail bakeries
PA: Super Center Concepts, Inc.
15510 Carmenita Rd
Santa Fe Springs CA

(P-13707)
VONS COMPANIES INC
Also Called: Vons 2124
7789 Foothill Blvd (91042-2195)
PHONE..................818 353-4917
Kevin Micalles, *Mgr*
EMP: 132
SQ FT: 39,200
SALES (corp-wide): 77.65B **Publicly Held**
SIC: 5411 5912 5992 2051 Supermarkets, chain; Drug stores; Florists; Bread, cake, and related products
HQ: The Vons Companies Inc
5918 Stoneridge Mall Rd
Pleasanton CA
925 467-3000

(P-13708)
VONS COMPANIES INC
Also Called: Vons 2111
24160 Lyons Ave (91321-2442)
PHONE..................661 259-9214
Phil Nakamura, *Mgr*
EMP: 132
SALES (corp-wide): 77.65B **Publicly Held**
SIC: 5411 5912 2051 Supermarkets, chain; Drug stores; Bread, cake, and related products
HQ: The Vons Companies Inc
5918 Stoneridge Mall Rd
Pleasanton CA
925 467-3000

(P-13709)
VONS COMPANIES INC
Also Called: Vons 2381
535 N Mckinley St (92879-1297)
PHONE..................951 278-8284
Rick Williams, *Mgr*
EMP: 132

SALES (corp-wide): 77.65B **Publicly Held**
Web: www.starbucks.com
SIC: 5411 5912 2051 5461 Supermarkets, chain; Drug stores; Bread, cake, and related products; Retail bakeries
HQ: The Vons Companies Inc
5918 Stoneridge Mall Rd
Pleasanton CA
925 467-3000

(P-13710)
VONS COMPANIES INC
Also Called: Vons 2560
1758 W Grand Ave (93433-2293)
PHONE..................805 481-2492
Jim Clark, *Mgr*
EMP: 132
SALES (corp-wide): 77.65B **Publicly Held**
SIC: 5411 5912 3556 Supermarkets, chain; Drug stores; Food products machinery
HQ: The Vons Companies Inc
5918 Stoneridge Mall Rd
Pleasanton CA
925 467-3000

(P-13711)
VONS COMPANIES INC
Also Called: Vons 2030
25850 The Old Rd (91381-1710)
PHONE..................661 254-3570
Brian Flaherty, *Mgr*
EMP: 132
SALES (corp-wide): 77.65B **Publicly Held**
Web: www.starbucks.com
SIC: 5411 5912 2051 5461 Supermarkets, chain; Drug stores; Bread, cake, and related products; Retail bakeries
HQ: The Vons Companies Inc
5918 Stoneridge Mall Rd
Pleasanton CA
925 467-3000

(P-13712)
VONS COMPANIES INC
Also Called: Vons 2407
475 W Main St (92227-2244)
PHONE..................760 351-3002
Frank Huerta, *Mgr*
EMP: 132
SALES (corp-wide): 77.65B **Publicly Held**
SIC: 5411 5912 2051 7384 Supermarkets, chain; Drug stores; Bread, cake, and related products; Photofinish laboratories
HQ: The Vons Companies Inc
5918 Stoneridge Mall Rd
Pleasanton CA
925 467-3000

(P-13713)
WORLD OIL MARKETING COMPANY (PA)
9302 Garfield Ave (90280-3805)
P.O. Box 1966 (90280-1966)
PHONE..................562 928-0100
Robert S Roth, *Pr*
Florence Roth, *VP*
Steven Roth, *VP*
Richard Roth, *VP*
EMP: 20 **EST:** 1977
SQ FT: 60,000
SALES (est): 128.17MM
SALES (corp-wide): 128.17MM **Privately Held**
Web: www.worldoilcorp.com
SIC: 5411 2951 5541 4213 Convenience stores; Paving mixtures; Gasoline service stations; Liquid petroleum transport, non-local

5431 Fruit And Vegetable Markets

(P-13714)
LINNS FRUIT BIN INC (PA)
Also Called: Linn's Main Bin
2535 Village Ln Ste A (93428-3428)
PHONE..................805 927-1499
Maureen Linn, *Pr*
Renee Linn, *
John Linn, *
Aaron Linn, *
EMP: 35 **EST:** 1995
SQ FT: 16,000
SALES (est): 8.88MM
SALES (corp-wide): 8.88MM **Privately Held**
Web: www.linnsfruitbin.com
SIC: 5431 2053 5812 Fruit and vegetable markets; Frozen bakery products, except bread; Eating places

5461 Retail Bakeries

(P-13715)
DUDLEYS BAKERY INC
30218 Hwy 78 (92070-9733)
P.O. Box 67 (92070-0067)
PHONE..................760 765-0488
Barry Burnye, *Mgr*
EMP: 38 **EST:** 1946
SQ FT: 6,000
SALES (est): 2.47MM **Privately Held**
Web: www.dudleysbakery.com
SIC: 5461 5149 2051 Bread; Bakery products ; Bread, cake, and related products

(P-13716)
JESSIE LORD BAKERY LLC
Also Called: Jessie Lord
21100 S Western Ave (90501-1705)
PHONE..................310 533-6010
Tracy Lee, *
▲ **EMP:** 50 **EST:** 2003
SQ FT: 130,000
SALES (est): 25.28MM **Privately Held**
Web: www.jessielordbakery.com
SIC: 5461 2051 Retail bakeries; Cakes, bakery: except frozen

(P-13717)
JULIAN BAKERY INC
624 Garrison St Ste1-2 (92054-4844)
PHONE..................760 721-5200
Heath Squier, *CEO*
EMP: 40 **EST:** 1990
SQ FT: 35,000
SALES (est): 30MM **Privately Held**
Web: www.julianbakery.com
SIC: 5461 2053 2023 5149 Bread; Frozen bakery products, except bread; Dietary supplements, dairy and non-dairy based; Organic and diet food

(P-13718)
KAYLAS CAKE CORPORATION
1311 S Gilbert St (92833-4302)
PHONE..................714 869-1522
Kayla Lee, *CEO*
EMP: 30 **EST:** 2014
SALES (est): 1.11MM **Privately Held**
Web: www.thekaylascake.com
SIC: 5461 5149 2024 Cakes; Bakery products; Ice cream and frozen deserts

(P-13719)

LA FE TORTILLA FACTORY INC (PA)
Also Called: La Fe Tortilleria Factory
1512 Linda Vista Dr (92078-3808)
P.O. Box 787 (92079-0787)
PHONE..............................760 752-8350
Isabel Delgado, *CEO*
Hoxsie Smith, *Pr*
Andrea Smith, *VP*
EMP: 30 **EST:** 1985
SQ FT: 4,000
SALES (est): 2.39MM
SALES (corp-wide): 2.39MM **Privately Held**
Web: www.lafetortilleria.com
SIC: 5461 2099 5812 5046 Retail bakeries; Tortillas, fresh or refrigerated; Mexican restaurant; Bakery equipment and supplies

(P-13720)

MADONNA INN INC
100 Madonna Rd (93405-5408)
PHONE..............................805 543-3000
Phyllis Madonna, *CEO*
EMP: 200 **EST:** 1951
SQ FT: 9,200
SALES (est): 24.31MM **Privately Held**
Web: www.madonnainn.com
SIC: 5461 5812 5813 7991 Retail bakeries; Cafe; Bar (drinking places); Spas

(P-13721)

MAMOLOS CNTNTL BAILEY BAKERIES
Also Called: Viktor Benes Bakeries
2734 Townsgate Rd (91361-2906)
PHONE..............................805 496-0045
Manigeh Tabataba, *Mgr*
EMP: 141
SALES (corp-wide): 9.89MM **Privately Held**
Web: www.viktorbenesbakery.com
SIC: 5461 5149 Cakes; Bakery products
PA: Mamolo's Continental & Bailey Bakeries Inc
703 S Main St
Burbank CA
818 841-9347

(P-13722)

PORTOS BAKERY BURBANK INC
Also Called: Portos Bakery & Cafe
3614 W Magnolia Blvd (91505-2913)
PHONE..............................818 846-9100
Raul R Porto, *CEO*
EMP: 50 **EST:** 2006
SALES (est): 11.7MM **Privately Held**
Web: www.portosbakery.com
SIC: 5461 2051 Cakes; Bread, cake, and related products

(P-13723)

SONORA BAKERY INC
4484 Whittier Blvd (90022-1534)
PHONE..............................323 269-2253
Hector Oratowski, *Pr*
Theresa Oratowski, *
Dennis Oratowski, *
EMP: 30 **EST:** 1986
SQ FT: 6,000
SALES (est): 1MM **Privately Held**
Web: www.sonorabakery.com
SIC: 5461 2051 5812 Retail bakeries; Bread, cake, and related products; Caterers

(P-13724)

WETZELS PRETZELS LLC
Also Called: Store 3
525 Parkway Plz Unit 525 (92020-2531)
PHONE..............................619 588-1074
EMP: 29
SALES (corp-wide): 23.55MM **Privately Held**
Web: www.wetzels.com
SIC: 5461 2099 Pretzels; Food preparations, nec
HQ: Wetzel's Pretzels, Llc
35 Hugus Aly Ste 300
Pasadena CA

(P-13725)

YAMAZAKI CALIFORNIA INC
123 Japanese Village Plaza Mall (90012-3908)
PHONE..............................213 624-2773
Kazumasa Tsugita, *Pr*
Shinichi Suzuki, *
▲ **EMP:** 20 **EST:** 1977
SQ FT: 6,600
SALES (est): 980.94K **Privately Held**
SIC: 5461 2051 Bakery: wholesale or wholesale/retail combined
PA: Yamazaki Baking Co., Ltd.
3-10-1, Iwamotocho
Chiyoda-Ku TKY

5499 Miscellaneous Food Stores

(P-13726)

COROMEGA COMPANY INC (PA)
2525 Commerce Way (92081-8420)
P.O. Box 131135 (92013-1135)
PHONE..............................760 599-6088
Frank Morley, *Pr*
Alice Chen, *
▲ **EMP:** 30 **EST:** 1999
SALES (est): 6.9MM
SALES (corp-wide): 6.9MM **Privately Held**
Web: www.coromega.com
SIC: 5499 2099 Health foods; Food preparations, nec

(P-13727)

HARRIS SPICE COMPANY INC (HQ)
Also Called: Spice Products Company
3110 E Miraloma Ave (92806-1906)
PHONE..............................714 507-1919
▼ **EMP:** 37 **EST:** 2010
SALES (est): 1.6MM
SALES (corp-wide): 150K **Privately Held**
Web: www.harrisspice.com
SIC: 5499 2099 Tea; Food preparations, nec
PA: Harris Freeman & Co., Inc.
3110 E Miraloma Ave
Anaheim CA
714 765-7525

(P-13728)

IHERB LLC (PA)
Also Called: Iherb House Brands
22780 Harley Knox Blvd Unit 101 (92570)
PHONE..............................951 616-3600
Emun Zabihi, *
◆ **EMP:** 1501 **EST:** 2001
SQ FT: 336,000
SALES (est): 1.64B
SALES (corp-wide): 1.64B **Privately Held**
Web: www.iherb.com
SIC: 5499 5122 Vitamin food stores; Drugs, proprietaries, and sundries

(P-13729)

LA COSTA COFFEE ROASTING CO (PA)
6965 El Camino Real Ste 208 (92009-4113)
PHONE..............................760 438-8160
Douglas Novak, *Owner*
Douglas Novak, *Mng Pt*
Paul Novak, *Pt*
Linda Novak, *Pt*
EMP: 25 **EST:** 1991
SALES (est): 2.02MM **Privately Held**
Web: www.lacostacoffee.com
SIC: 5499 5149 2095 Coffee; Coffee, green or roasted; Coffee roasting (except by wholesale grocers)

(P-13730)

LANGER JUICE COMPANY INC
Also Called: Langers Juice
16195 Stephens St (91745-1718)
PHONE..............................626 336-3100
Bruce Langer, *CEO*
David Langer, *
◆ **EMP:** 260 **EST:** 1960
SQ FT: 140,000
SALES (est): 71.84MM **Privately Held**
Web: www.langers.com
SIC: 5499 2033 Juices, fruit or vegetable; Vegetable juices: fresh

(P-13731)

NAKED JUICE CO GLENDORA INC
1333 S Mayflower Ave # 100 (91016-5265)
PHONE..............................626 873-2600
Monty Sharma, *CEO*
Tom Hicks, *
Paul Travis, *
EMP: 400 **EST:** 1976
SALES (est): 24.28MM
SALES (corp-wide): 86.39B **Publicly Held**
SIC: 5499 2033 Juices, fruit or vegetable; Fruit juices: fresh
PA: Pepsico, Inc.
700 Anderson Hill Rd
Purchase NY
914 253-2000

(P-13732)

TEALOVE INC
9810 Sierra Ave Ste A (92335-6779)
PHONE..............................714 408-8245
Elli Nguyen, *CFO*
EMP: 20 **EST:** 2018
SALES (est): 250K **Privately Held**
Web: tealove.smartonlineorder.com
SIC: 5499 2099 2086 5812 Tea; Tea blending ; Tea, iced: packaged in cans, bottles, etc.; Coffee shop

(P-13733)

TONE IT UP INC
1110 Manhattan Ave (90266-5313)
P.O. Box 323 (90245-0323)
PHONE..............................310 376-7645
Russell Sternlicht, *CEO*
Christine Sana, *
▲ **EMP:** 31 **EST:** 2009
SQ FT: 3,000
SALES (est): 6.88MM **Privately Held**
Web: my.toneitup.com
SIC: 5499 2099 5149 Health and dietetic food stores; Food preparations, nec; Groceries and related products, nec

(P-13734)

VITA-HERB NUTRICEUTICALS INC
172 E La Jolla St (92870-7111)

PHONE..............................714 632-3726
M Bing Baksh, *CEO*
▲ **EMP:** 35 **EST:** 1999
SQ FT: 11,000
SALES (est): 6.82MM **Privately Held**
Web: www.vhni.com
SIC: 5499 2834 Vitamin food stores; Pharmaceutical preparations

5511 New And Used Car Dealers

(P-13735)

ADVANTAGE FORD LINCOLN MERCURY
Also Called: Advantage Ford
1031 Central Ave (91010-2424)
PHONE..............................626 305-9188
Gary W Hoecker, *Pr*
EMP: 97 **EST:** 1997
SQ FT: 20,280
SALES (est): 21.57MM **Privately Held**
Web: www.fordofduarte.com
SIC: 5511 7532 Automobiles, new and used; Top and body repair and paint shops

(P-13736)

AL ASHER & SONS INC
5301 Valley Blvd (90032-3930)
PHONE..............................800 896-2480
James A Asher, *CEO*
James A Asher, *Pr*
Robert L Asher, *
◆ **EMP:** 25 **EST:** 1914
SQ FT: 80,000
SALES (est): 9.55MM **Privately Held**
Web: www.alasher.com
SIC: 5511 7353 3531 Trucks, tractors, and trailers: new and used; Heavy construction equipment rental; Construction machinery

(P-13737)

ALHAMBRA MOTORS INC
Also Called: Goudy Honda
1400 W Main St (91801-1952)
PHONE..............................626 576-1114
TOLL FREE: 800
EMP: 156 **EST:** 1958
SALES (est): 45.89MM **Privately Held**
Web: www.goudyhonda.com
SIC: 5511 7521 Automobiles, new and used; Automobile parking

(P-13738)

AMERICAN SUZUKI MOTOR CORPORATION
3251 E Imperial Hwy (92821-6722)
P.O. Box 1100 (92822-1100)
PHONE..............................714 996-7040
◆ **EMP:** 382
SIC: 5511 5571 5091 5013 Automobiles, new and used; Motorcycle dealers; Outboard motors; Motor vehicle supplies and new parts

(P-13739)

BARGAIN RENT-A-CAR
Also Called: Lexus of Cerritos
18800 Studebaker Rd (90703-5339)
PHONE..............................562 865-7447
Afshin Kahensohayegh, *Mgr*
Lewis M Webb, *
Jerry Heuer, *Acting Secretary*
EMP: 130 **EST:** 1960
SALES (est): 50.96MM
SALES (corp-wide): 26.98B **Publicly Held**
Web: www.cerritoslexus.com

SIC: **5511** 5521 5012 Automobiles, new and used; Used car dealers; Automobiles and other motor vehicles
HQ: Webb Automotive Group, Inc.
200 Sw 1st Ave
Fort Lauderdale FL
954 769-7000

(P-13740)
BOB BAKER VOLKSWAGEN
Also Called: Bob Baker Chrysler-Plymouth
5500 Paseo Del Norte (92008-4428)
P.O. Box 2129 (92067-2129)
PHONE.................................760 438-2200
Michael Baker, *Pr*
Micheal Baker, *
Tom Solomon, *
William Kornik, *General Vice President*
Michelle Wagstaff, *
EMP: 90 **EST:** 1975
SALES (est): 22.65MM
SALES (corp-wide): 109.29MM **Privately Held**
Web:
www.autonationvolkswagencarlsbad.com
SIC: **5511** 7538 5531 Automobiles, new and used; General automotive repair shops; Automotive parts
PA: Bob Baker Enterprises, Inc.
591 Camino De La Reina
San Diego CA
619 683-5591

(P-13741)
BOB STALL CHEVROLET
7601 Alvarado Rd (91942-8211)
P.O. Box 339 (91944-0339)
PHONE.................................619 460-1311
John Stall, *CEO*
Thomas Stall, *
EMP: 110 **EST:** 1958
SALES (est): 23.38MM **Privately Held**
Web: www.bobstall.com
SIC: **5511** 7538 Automobiles, new and used; General automotive repair shops

(P-13742)
BOULEVARD AUTOMOTIVE GROUP (PA)
Also Called: Boulevard Collision Center
2850 Cherry Ave (90755-1909)
PHONE.................................562 492-1000
EMP: 83 **EST:** 1961
SALES (est): 16.05MM
SALES (corp-wide): 16.05MM **Privately Held**
Web: www.boulevard4u.com
SIC: **5511** 7538 Automobiles, new and used; General automotive repair shops

(P-13743)
BRECHT ENTERPRISES INC
Also Called: Brecht BMW
1555 Auto Park Way (92029-2003)
P.O. Box 461089 (92046-1089)
PHONE.................................760 745-3000
TOLL FREE: 888
EMP: 100 **EST:** 1985
SQ FT: 56,000
SALES (est): 33.49MM **Privately Held**
Web: www.bmwofescondido.com
SIC: **5511** 5571 6159 5013 Automobiles, new and used; Motorcycle dealers; Equipment and vehicle finance leasing companies; Automotive supplies and parts

(P-13744)
CABE BROTHERS
Also Called: Cabe Toyota
2895 Long Beach Blvd (90806-1533)

PHONE.................................562 595-7411
John Cabe, *Pr*
Marilyn Gidden, *
Glenda Favilla, *
Myra Cabe, *
EMP: 81 **EST:** 1956
SQ FT: 11,080
SALES (est): 40.6MM **Privately Held**
Web: www.cabetoyota.com
SIC: **5511** 7538 Automobiles, new and used; General automotive repair shops

(P-13745)
CADILLAC MOTOR DIV AREA
30930 Russell Ranch Rd (91362-7378)
PHONE.................................805 373-9575
Mike Jackson, *Mgr*
EMP: 175 **EST:** 1955
SALES (est): 67.71MM **Publicly Held**
Web: www.cadillac.com
SIC: **5511** 3711 Automobiles, new and used; Motor vehicles and car bodies
HQ: General Motors Llc
300 Renaissance Ctr L1
Detroit MI

(P-13746)
CENTER AUTOMOTIVE INC
Also Called: Center B M W
5201 Van Nuys Blvd (91401-5618)
P.O. Box 3870 (91031-6870)
PHONE.................................818 907-9995
EMP: 85 **EST:** 1968
SQ FT: 50,000
SALES (est): 27.92MM **Privately Held**
Web: www.bmwshermanoaks.com
SIC: **5511** 5012 Automobiles, new and used; Automobiles and other motor vehicles

(P-13747)
CENTURY WEST LLC
4245 Lankershim Blvd (91602-2802)
PHONE.................................818 432-5800
Dennis Lin, *Pr*
EMP: 92 **EST:** 1995
SALES (est): 30.88MM **Privately Held**
Web: www.centurywestbmw.com
SIC: **5511** 7538 Automobiles, new and used; General automotive repair shops

(P-13748)
CITRUS MOTORS ONTARIO INC (PA)
Also Called: Citrus Ford
1375 S Woodruff Way (91761-2233)
P.O. Box 4270 (91761-8970)
PHONE.................................909 390-0930
Dennis Shannon, *Pr*
Alice Van Dentoorn, *
EMP: 211 **EST:** 1950
SALES (est): 49.18MM
SALES (corp-wide): 49.18MM **Privately Held**
Web: www.citrusmotors.com
SIC: **5511** 7538 Automobiles, new and used; General automotive repair shops

(P-13749)
COUNTY FORD NORTH INC (PA)
Also Called: North County GMC
450 W Vista Way (92083-5829)
PHONE.................................760 945-9900
James E Crowley, *Pr*
Sean Crowley, *
Jeffrey Friestedt, *
Joseph Weir, *
Scott Crowley, *
▼ **EMP:** 213 **EST:** 1992
SALES (est): 62.08MM **Privately Held**
Web: www.northcountyford.net

SIC: **5511** 5521 7538 7515 Automobiles, new and used; Used car dealers; General automotive repair shops; Passenger car leasing

(P-13750)
COURTESY CHEVROLET CENTER
Also Called: Geo Sales-Courtesy Chevrolet
750 Camino Del Rio N (92108-3207)
PHONE.................................619 297-4321
TOLL FREE: 877
William R Gruwell, *Pr*
EMP: 86 **EST:** 1961
SQ FT: 60,000
SALES (est): 18.97MM **Privately Held**
Web: www.courtesysandiego.com
SIC: **5511** 7538 5531 7515 Automobiles, new and used; General automotive repair shops; Auto and home supply stores; Passenger car leasing

(P-13751)
CREVIER CLASSICS LLC
1500 Auto Mall Dr (92705-4743)
PHONE.................................714 835-3171
EMP: 320 **EST:** 1971
SALES (est): 32.76MM **Privately Held**
Web: www.crevierbmw.com
SIC: **5511** 5521 5531 7538 Automobiles, new and used; Automobiles, used cars only ; Auto and home supply stores; General automotive repair shops

(P-13752)
D LONGO INC
Also Called: Longo Scion
3534 Peck Rd (91731-3526)
PHONE.................................626 580-6000
Greg Penske, *Pr*
EMP: 380 **EST:** 1967
SALES (est): 168.53MM
SALES (corp-wide): 5.16B **Privately Held**
Web: www.longotoyota.com
SIC: **5511** 7538 Automobiles, new and used; General automotive repair shops
PA: Penske Corporation
2555 S Telegraph Rd
Bloomfield Hills MI
248 648-2000

(P-13753)
DAVID A CAMPBELL CORPORATION
Also Called: B M W of Riverside
3060 Adams St (92504-4014)
P.O. Box 4007 (92514-4007)
PHONE.................................951 785-4444
Allen David Franklin, *CEO*
Steven Campbell, *
Patrick Campbell, *
EMP: 150 **EST:** 1975
SQ FT: 45,000
SALES (est): 28.19MM **Privately Held**
Web: www.bmwofriverside.com
SIC: **5511** 7538 Automobiles, new and used; General automotive repair shops

(P-13754)
DCH ACURA OF TEMECULA
Also Called: Lithia
26705 Ynez Rd (92591-4693)
P.O. Box 9043 (92589-9043)
PHONE.................................877 847-9532
Kenneth Colson, *VP*
EMP: 100 **EST:** 2014
SALES (est): 10.98MM **Privately Held**
Web: www.ohacura.com

SIC: **5511** 7539 5531 Automobiles, new and used; Automotive repair shops, nec; Automotive parts

(P-13755)
DCH CALIFORNIA MOTORS INC
Also Called: Toyota of Oxnard
1631 Auto Center Dr (93036-8972)
PHONE.................................805 988-7900
Shau-wai Lam, *Pr*
Scott Borg, *
EMP: 95 **EST:** 1991
SALES (est): 23.52MM
SALES (corp-wide): 28.19B **Publicly Held**
Web: www.toyotaofoxnard.com
SIC: **5511** 7538 7532 Automobiles, new and used; General automotive repair shops; Top and body repair and paint shops
HQ: Dch North America Inc.
955 Rte 9 N
South Amboy NJ
732 727-9168

(P-13756)
DCH GARDENA HONDA
Also Called: Gardena Honda
15541 S Western Ave (90249-4320)
P.O. Box 3220 (90247-1420)
PHONE.................................310 515-5700
TOLL FREE: 800
Shauwai Lam, *Prin*
EMP: 140 **EST:** 1979
SQ FT: 290,000
SALES (est): 45.27MM
SALES (corp-wide): 28.19B **Publicly Held**
Web: www.gardenahonda.com
SIC: **5511** 7538 Automobiles, new and used; General automotive repair shops
HQ: Dch North America Inc.
955 Rte 9 N
South Amboy NJ
732 727-9168

(P-13757)
DICK DEWESE CHEVROLET INC
Also Called: Tom Bell Chevrolet
800 Alabama St (92374-2806)
PHONE.................................909 793-2681
Tom O Bell, *Pr*
Derek Hanson, *
Lynn Drysdale, *
EMP: 102 **EST:** 1951
SQ FT: 10,000
SALES (est): 32.85MM **Privately Held**
Web: www.tombellchevrolet.com
SIC: **5511** 7538 5531 5521 Automobiles, new and used; General automotive repair shops; Auto and home supply stores; Used car dealers

(P-13758)
DREW FORD
Also Called: Drew Hyundai
8970 La Mesa Blvd (91942-0849)
P.O. Box 188 (91944-0188)
PHONE.................................619 464-7777
William J Drew, *Pr*
EMP: 250 **EST:** 1927
SQ FT: 90,000
SALES (est): 51.99MM **Privately Held**
Web: www.drewauto.com
SIC: **5511** 7538 Automobiles, new and used; General automotive repair shops

(P-13759)
EL CENTRO MOTORS
Also Called: Ford Lincoln Mercury
1520 Ford Dr (92243-1603)
P.O. Box 3250 (92244-3250)
PHONE.................................760 336-2100

EMP: 95 **EST:** 1901
SALES (est): 39.31MM **Privately Held**
Web: www.elcentromotors.net
SIC: 5511 7538 5531 Automobiles, new and used; General automotive repair shops; Automotive parts

(P-13760)
EL MONTE AUTOMOTIVE GROUP INC
Also Called: Longo Lexus
3530 Peck Rd (91731-3526)
PHONE..................................626 580-6200
Greg Penske, *Pr*
EMP: 104 **EST:** 1989
SALES (est): 33.75MM **Privately Held**
Web: www.longolexus.com
SIC: 5511 7532 7515 5521 Automobiles, new and used; Top and body repair and paint shops; Passenger car leasing; Used car dealers

(P-13761)
EL MONTE AUTOMOTIVE GROUP LLC
Also Called: Nelson Honda
3464 Peck Rd (91731-3253)
PHONE..................................626 444-0321
TOLL FREE: 800
EMP: 80 **EST:** 1960
SALES (est): 19.43MM **Privately Held**
SIC: 5511 7538 7515 5531 Automobiles, new and used; General automotive repair shops; Passenger car leasing; Auto and home supply stores

(P-13762)
EMERGENCY VEHICLE GROUP INC
Also Called: E V G
2883 E Coronado St Ste A (92806-2552)
PHONE..................................714 238-0110
Travis Grinstead, *Pr*
EMP: 25 **EST:** 2005
SQ FT: 15,000
SALES (est): 9.53MM **Privately Held**
Web: www.evginc.net
SIC: 5511 5012 3569 5013 Trucks, tractors, and trailers: new and used; Ambulances; Firefighting apparatus; Motor vehicle supplies and new parts

(P-13763)
ESCONDIDO MOTORS LLC
Also Called: Mercedes Benz of Escondido
1101 W 9th Ave (92025-3843)
PHONE..................................760 745-5000
Simon Sarriedine, *CEO*
Jack Manukyan, *
EMP: 80 **EST:** 1988
SALES (est): 25.03MM **Privately Held**
Web: www.mbescondido.com
SIC: 5511 7515 5531 Automobiles, new and used; Automobiles, used cars only ; Passenger car leasing; Auto and home supply stores

(P-13764)
EUROPA AUTO IMPORTS INC
Also Called: Mercedes Benz of San Diego
4750 Kearny Mesa Rd (92111-2405)
PHONE..................................858 569-6900
Ora Smith, *Pr*
Judy Antrim, *
Duayne Hancock, *
▼ **EMP:** 116 **EST:** 1957
SQ FT: 10,000
SALES (est): 30.76MM **Privately Held**
Web: www.mbsd.com

SIC: 5511 5521 7538 Automobiles, new and used; Used car dealers; General automotive repair shops

(P-13765)
FAA BEVERLY HILLS INC
Also Called: Beverly Hills BMW
5070 Wilshire Blvd (90036-4381)
PHONE..................................323 801-1430
Step Jones, *Genl Mgr*
EMP: 85 **EST:** 1991
SQ FT: 4,000
SALES (est): 33.27MM
SALES (corp-wide): 14B **Publicly Held**
Web: www.bmwofbeverlyhills.com
SIC: 5511 7538 Automobiles, new and used; General automotive repair shops
PA: Sonic Automotive, Inc.
      4401 Colwick Rd
      Charlotte NC
      704 566-2400

(P-13766)
FELIX CHEVROLET LP (PA)
Also Called: Felix Chevrolet
714 W Olympic Blvd Ste 1124 (90015-1425)
PHONE..................................213 748-6141
Nicholas N Shammas, *Pt*
George Damaa, *Pt*
EMP: 113 **EST:** 1921
SALES (est): 52.74MM
SALES (corp-wide): 52.74MM **Privately Held**
Web: www.felixchevrolet.com
SIC: 5511 7538 7532 5531 Automobiles, new and used; General automotive repair shops; Top and body repair and paint shops ; Auto and home supply stores

(P-13767)
FIESTA FORD INC
Also Called: Fiesta Ford Lincoln-Mercury
79015 Avenue 40 (92203-9499)
PHONE..................................760 775-7777
Paul J Thiel, *CEO*
EMP: 126 **EST:** 1966
SQ FT: 304,920
SALES (est): 49.21MM **Privately Held**
Web: www.quicklane.com
SIC: 5511 7538 Automobiles, new and used; General automotive repair shops

(P-13768)
FORD OF SANTA MONICA INC
Also Called: Ford
1402 Santa Monica Blvd (90404-1710)
PHONE..................................310 451-1588
Ron Davis, *Pr*
EMP: 92 **EST:** 1948
SALES (est): 36.46MM **Privately Held**
Web: www.smford.com
SIC: 5511 5012 Automobiles, new and used; Ambulances

(P-13769)
FOX HILLS AUTO INC (PA)
Also Called: Airport Marina Ford
5880 W Centinela Ave (90045-1504)
PHONE..................................310 649-3673
Norris J Bishton Junior, *CEO*
▲ **EMP:** 140 **EST:** 1989
SQ FT: 35,000
SALES (est): 70.01MM **Privately Held**
Web: www.ford.com
SIC: 5511 7538 5531 5521 Automobiles, new and used; General automotive repair shops; Auto and home supply stores; Used car dealers

(P-13770)
GALPIN MOTORS INC (PA)
Also Called: Galpin Ford
15505 Roscoe Blvd (91343-6503)
PHONE..................................818 787-3800
Herbert F Boeckman Ii, *Pr*
Karl L Boeckmann, *
Bradley M Boeckmann, *
Alan J Skobin, *
Jane Boeckmann, *
▼ **EMP:** 500 **EST:** 1946
SQ FT: 175,000
SALES (est): 372.23MM
SALES (corp-wide): 372.23MM **Privately Held**
Web: www.galpin.com
SIC: 5511 5521 7538 7515 Automobiles, new and used; Used car dealers; General automotive repair shops; Passenger car leasing

(P-13771)
GENERAL MOTORS LLC
Also Called: General Motors
3050 Lomita Blvd Ste 237 (90505-5103)
PHONE..................................313 556-5000
Nicholas Herron, *Brnch Mgr*
EMP: 26
Web: www.gm.com
SIC: 5511 3711 Automobiles, new and used; Automobile assembly, including specialty automobiles
HQ: General Motors Llc
      300 Renaissance Ctr L1
      Detroit MI

(P-13772)
GEORGE CHEVROLET
Also Called: George Chevrolet
17000 Lakewood Blvd (90706-5523)
PHONE..................................562 925-2500
Jeffery Estabrooks, *Pr*
Patricia Estabrooks, *
EMP: 100 **EST:** 1961
SQ FT: 56,000
SALES (est): 41.44MM **Privately Held**
Web: www.chevrolet.com
SIC: 5511 7515 7538 Automobiles, new and used; Passenger car leasing; General automotive repair shops

(P-13773)
GPI CA-NIII INC
Also Called: Performance Nissan
1434 Buena Vista St (91010-2402)
PHONE..................................626 305-3000
John C Rickel, *CEO*
Frank Grese Junior, *Prin*
EMP: 87 **EST:** 1991
SALES (est): 6.71MM **Publicly Held**
Web: www.perfnissan.com
SIC: 5511 7538 7515 5531 Automobiles, new and used; General automotive repair shops; Passenger car leasing; Auto and home supply stores
PA: Group 1 Automotive, Inc.
      800 Gessner Rd Ste 500
      Houston TX

(P-13774)
GREGORY CONSULTING INC (PA)
6350 Leland St (93003-8585)
PHONE..................................805 642-0111
TOLL FREE: 888
Robert Gregory, *Pr*
Nancy Gregory, *
EMP: 135 **EST:** 1986
SQ FT: 54,000
SALES (est): 42.99MM

SALES (corp-wide): 42.99MM **Privately Held**
Web: www.paradisechevrolet.com
SIC: 5511 7538 5521 Automobiles, new and used; General automotive repair shops; Used car dealers

(P-13775)
H W HUNTER INC (PA)
Also Called: Hunter Dodge Chrysler Jeep Ram
1130 Auto Mall Dr (93534-6302)
P.O. Box 4324 (93539-4324)
PHONE..................................661 948-8411
Timothy H Fuller, *CEO*
EMP: 80 **EST:** 1956
SQ FT: 5,000
SALES (est): 23.73MM
SALES (corp-wide): 23.73MM **Privately Held**
Web: www.hunterdodgechryslerjeep.net
SIC: 5511 7538 Automobiles, new and used; General automotive repair shops

(P-13776)
HABERFELDE FORD (PA)
Also Called: Jim Burke Ford
2001 Oak St (93301-3010)
P.O. Box 2088 (93303-2088)
PHONE..................................661 328-3600
Daniel George Hay, *Pr*
Michelle Hay, *
Beverly Burke, *
Joe Hay, *
EMP: 236 **EST:** 1913
SQ FT: 102,000
SALES (est): 49.31MM
SALES (corp-wide): 49.31MM **Privately Held**
Web: www.jimburkeford.com
SIC: 5511 7538 Automobiles, new and used; General automotive repair shops

(P-13777)
HARBILL INC
Also Called: Crest Chevrolet
909 W 21st St (92405-3201)
P.O. Box 501 (92402-0501)
PHONE..................................909 883-8833
D William Bader, *CEO*
Robert Bader, *
Douglas Bader, *
Patty Bader, *
EMP: 93 **EST:** 1958
SQ FT: 20,000
SALES (est): 26.56MM **Privately Held**
Web: www.daliaauto.com
SIC: 5511 5012 5531 5521 Automobiles, new and used; Automobiles and other motor vehicles; Auto and home supply stores; Used car dealers

(P-13778)
HOEHN COMPANY INC
Also Called: Hoehn Honda
5454 Paseo Del Norte (92008-4426)
P.O. Box 789 (92018-0789)
PHONE..................................760 438-1818
TOLL FREE: 888
EMP: 80 **EST:** 1993
SQ FT: 3,000
SALES (est): 22.4MM **Privately Held**
Web: www.hoehnhonda.com
SIC: 5511 7538 Automobiles, new and used; General automotive repair shops

(P-13779)
HONDA WORLD WESTMINSTER
13600 Beach Blvd (92683-3202)
PHONE..................................714 890-8900

Jim Kitzmiller, *Pr*
Tom Chadwell, *
EMP: 175 **EST:** 1989
SQ FT: 6,000
SALES (est): 62.1MM
SALES (corp-wide): 102.66MM **Privately Held**
Web: www.honda.com
SIC: 5511 7539 5015 5012 Automobiles, new and used; Automotive repair shops, nec; Motor vehicle parts, used; Automobiles and other motor vehicles
PA: Piercey Management Services, Inc.
16901 Millikan Ave
Irvine CA
949 379-3701

(P-13780)
IDEALAB (HQ)
130 W Union St (91103-3628)
PHONE...............626 356-3654
▲ **EMP:** 82 **EST:** 1996
SQ FT: 30,000
SALES (est): 138.99MM
SALES (corp-wide): 146.11MM **Privately Held**
Web: www.idealab.com
SIC: 5511 6726 New and used car dealers; Investment offices, nec
PA: Idealab Holdings, L.L.C.
130 W Union St
Pasadena CA
626 585-6900

(P-13781)
ISUZU NORTH AMERICA CORP (HQ)
1400 S Douglass Rd Ste 100 (92806-6901)
PHONE...............714 935-9300
Masanori Katayama, *Pr*
Shinichi Takahashi, *
Masatoshi Ito, *
◆ **EMP:** 150 **EST:** 1975
SQ FT: 64,000
SALES (est): 535.14MM **Privately Held**
Web: www.isuzu.com
SIC: 5511 5084 5013 5015 Automobiles, new and used; Engines and parts, diesel; Automotive supplies and parts; Motor vehicle parts, used
PA: Isuzu Motors Limited
1-2-5, Takashima, Nishi-Ku
Yokohama KNG

(P-13782)
JACK GOSCH FORD INC
150 Carriage Cir (92545-9610)
PHONE...............951 658-3181
TOLL FREE: 800
Jack E Gosch, *Pr*
Mark E Gosch, *
Eric Gosch, *
Marc Gosch, *
Richard Rodgers, *
EMP: 100 **EST:** 1964
SQ FT: 35,000
SALES (est): 23.72MM **Privately Held**
Web: www.goschauto.com
SIC: 5511 7538 Automobiles, new and used; General automotive repair shops

(P-13783)
JACK PWELL CHRYSLER - DDGE INC
Also Called: Jack Pwell Chrysler Ddge Jeep
1625 Auto Park Way (92029-2008)
PHONE...............760 745-2880
Jack Powell Junior, *Pr*
Jack Powell Junior, *Pr*

Judith Powell, *
EMP: 85 **EST:** 1958
SQ FT: 28,000
SALES (est): 31.67MM **Privately Held**
Web: www.jeep.com
SIC: 5511 7538 5531 Automobiles, new and used; General automotive repair shops; Auto and home supply stores

(P-13784)
JEEP CHRYSLER OF ONTARIO
Also Called: Jeep Chrysler Ddge Ram Ontario
1202 Auto Center Dr (91761-2208)
PHONE...............909 390-9898
Richard D Romero, *Ch Bd*
R J Romero, *
Kathy Brown, *
Valerie Romero, *
J B Butterwick, *
EMP: 95 **EST:** 1993
SQ FT: 30,000
SALES (est): 18.52MM **Privately Held**
Web: www.jcofontario.com
SIC: 5511 7538 5531 Automobiles, new and used; General automotive repair shops; Auto and home supply stores

(P-13785)
JOHNSON FORD (PA)
Also Called: Antelope Valley Lincoln
1155 Auto Mall Dr (93534-5867)
PHONE...............888 483-0454
Michael H Johnson, *Pr*
Doug Killebrew, *
Brooke Powell, *
Bob Heninger, *
EMP: 120 **EST:** 1957
SQ FT: 70,000
SALES (est): 57.3MM
SALES (corp-wide): 57.3MM **Privately Held**
Web: www.diamondfordav.com
SIC: 5511 7538 5561 Automobiles, new and used; General automotive repair shops; Camper and travel trailer dealers

(P-13786)
KEN GRODY REDLANDS LLC
Also Called: Ken Grody Ford - Redlands
1121 W Colton Ave (92374-2935)
PHONE...............909 793-3211
William Raymond, *
Brandi Desherlia, *
EMP: 85 **EST:** 2019
SALES (est): 16.84MM **Privately Held**
Web: www.kengrodyfordredlands.com
SIC: 5511 7538 New and used car dealers; General automotive repair shops

(P-13787)
KEYES MOTORS INC (PA)
Also Called: Keyes Toyota
5855 Van Nuys Blvd (91401-4219)
PHONE...............818 782-0122
Howard Keyes, *Pr*
Lawrence Abramson, *
EMP: 80 **EST:** 1968
SQ FT: 20,000
SALES (est): 97.87MM
SALES (corp-wide): 97.87MM **Privately Held**
Web: www.keyestoyota.com
SIC: 5511 7538 7515 5012 Automobiles, new and used; General automotive repair shops; Passenger car leasing; Automobiles and other motor vehicles

(P-13788)
KEYLEX INC (PA)
Also Called: Keyes Lexus

5905 Van Nuys Blvd (91401-3624)
PHONE...............818 379-4000
Howard Keyes, *Pr*
EMP: 87 **EST:** 1989
SQ FT: 32,376
SALES (est): 39.62MM **Privately Held**
Web: www.keyeslexus.com
SIC: 5511 7538 7515 5531 Automobiles, new and used; General automotive repair shops; Passenger car leasing; Auto and home supply stores

(P-13789)
KEYSTONE FORD INC (PA)
12000 Firestone Blvd (90650-2907)
PHONE...............562 868-0825
TOLL FREE: 800
Norman P Stutzke, *Pr*
Lamberto Colon, *
Paul Stutzke, *
EMP: 130 **EST:** 1968
SQ FT: 14,000
SALES (est): 22.51MM
SALES (corp-wide): 22.51MM **Privately Held**
Web: www.ford.com
SIC: 5511 5531 7514 Automobiles, new and used; Automotive parts; Rent-a-car service

(P-13790)
LAKE CHEVROLET
31201 Auto Center Dr (92530-4424)
P.O. Box 4000 (92531-4000)
PHONE...............951 674-3116
EMP: 133
Web: www.andersonchevroletca.com
SIC: 5511 7515 5521 Automobiles, new and used; Passenger car leasing; Used car dealers

(P-13791)
LOS FELIZ FORD INC (PA)
Also Called: Star Ford Lincoln Mercury
1101 S Brand Blvd (91204-2313)
PHONE...............818 502-1901
Steve Bussjaeger, *Pr*
Tad Okumoto, *
Agnes Gurida, *
EMP: 80 **EST:** 1970
SQ FT: 75,000
SALES (est): 31.57MM
SALES (corp-wide): 31.57MM **Privately Held**
Web: www.starford.com
SIC: 5511 7515 Automobiles, new and used; Passenger car leasing

(P-13792)
M K SMITH CHEVROLET
12845 Central Ave (91710-4120)
P.O. Box 455 (91708-0455)
PHONE...............909 628-8961
Marc Smith, *CEO*
Carolyn Coble, *
Cheryl Smith, *
Marc Smith, *Ex VP*
EMP: 120 **EST:** 1941
SALES (est): 42.49MM **Privately Held**
Web: www.mksmithchevrolet.com
SIC: 5511 7549 5531 Automobiles, new and used; Automotive maintenance services; Automotive parts

(P-13793)
MAGIC ACQUISITION CORP
Also Called: Autonation Ford Valencia
23920 Creekside Rd (91355-1701)
PHONE...............661 382-4700
EMP: 350 **EST:** 1996
SALES (est): 44.93MM

SALES (corp-wide): 26.98B **Publicly Held**
Web: www.autonationford.valencia.com
SIC: 5511 7538 5531 New and used car dealers; General automotive repair shops; Auto and home supply stores
HQ: Magic Acquisition Holding, Llc
200 Sw 1st Ave
Fort Lauderdale FL
954 769-7000

(P-13794)
MARK CHRISTOPHER CHEVROLET INC (PA)
Also Called: Mark Christopher Hummer
2131 E Convention Center Way (91764-4452)
PHONE...............909 321-5860
Chris Leggio, *CEO*
Shirley Leggid, *
Loretta Holtz, *
EMP: 132 **EST:** 1986
SQ FT: 15,000
SALES (est): 82.18MM
SALES (corp-wide): 82.18MM **Privately Held**
Web: www.markchristopher.com
SIC: 5511 5521 3714 Automobiles, new and used; Used car dealers; Motor vehicle parts and accessories

(P-13795)
MARTIN CHEVROLET
23505 Hawthorne Blvd (90505-4739)
P.O. Box 2895 (90509-2895)
PHONE...............323 772-6494
TOLL FREE: 888
Joe Giacomin, *Pr*
Fran Williams, *
EMP: 100 **EST:** 1947
SQ FT: 10,000
SALES (est): 28.99MM **Privately Held**
Web: www.martinchevrolet.com
SIC: 5511 7538 Automobiles, new and used; General automotive repair shops

(P-13796)
MILLER AUTOMOTIVE GROUP INC (HQ)
Also Called: Miller Nissan
5425 Van Nuys Blvd (91401-5628)
PHONE...............818 787-8400
Fred Miller, *Ch Bd*
Michael Miller, *
Mark Miller, *
Doug Stewart, *
▲ **EMP:** 350 **EST:** 1989
SQ FT: 40,000
SALES (est): 138.97MM **Publicly Held**
Web: www.nissanofvannuys.com
SIC: 5511 7538 5521 Automobiles, new and used; General automotive repair shops; Automobiles, used cars only
PA: Group 1 Automotive, Inc.
800 Gessner Rd Ste 500
Houston TX

(P-13797)
MISSION VOLKSWAGEN INC
Also Called: Capistrano Volkswagen
32922 Valle Rd (92675-4802)
PHONE...............949 493-4511
Miles Braden, *Pr*
Miles Brandon, *
EMP: 80 **EST:** 1993
SQ FT: 3,997
SALES (est): 26.6MM **Privately Held**
Web: www.capovw.com
SIC: 5511 7538 Automobiles, new and used; General automotive repair shops

PRODUCTS & SVCS

(P-13798)
MOSSY AUTOMOTIVE GROUP INC (PA)
Also Called: Mossy Toyota
4555 Mission Bay Dr (92109-4920)
PHONE.................................858 581-4000
Philip Mossy, *Pr*
Peter Mossy, *
EMP: 100 **EST:** 2002
SALES (est): 68.2MM **Privately Held**
Web: www.mossytoyota.com
SIC: 5511 7538 Automobiles, new and used;
General automotive repair shops

(P-13799)
MOSSY FORD INC
Also Called: Quick Lane
4570 Mission Bay Dr (92109-4985)
PHONE.................................858 273-7500
Phillip Mossy, *Pr*
John Epps, *
▼ **EMP:** 200 **EST:** 1988
SQ FT: 10,000
SALES (est): 42.99MM **Privately Held**
Web: www.mossyford.com
SIC: 5511 7538 7532 7515 Automobiles,
new and used; General automotive repair
shops; Top and body repair and paint shops
; Passenger car leasing

(P-13800)
MOSSY NISSAN INC
Also Called: Mossy Nissan Kearny Mesa
8118 Clairemont Mesa Blvd (92111-1998)
PHONE.................................858 565-6608
Mike Obeso, *Mgr*
EMP: 100
Web: www.mossynissan.com
SIC: 5511 5521 7515 Automobiles, new and
used; Used car dealers; Passenger car
leasing
HQ: Nissan Mossy Inc
2700 National City Blvd
National City CA
619 474-7011

(P-13801)
MOTOR CITY SALES & SERVICE (PA)
Also Called: Motor City GMC Buick Pontiac
3101 Pacheco Rd (93313-3214)
P.O. Box 40340 (93384-0340)
PHONE.................................661 836-9000
EMP: 218 **EST:** 1945
SALES (est): 48.62MM
SALES (corp-wide): 48.62MM **Privately Held**
Web: www.motorcitywest.com
SIC: 5511 7538 Pickups, new and used;
General automotive repair shops

(P-13802)
NGP MOTORS INC
Also Called: Sunrise Ford
5500 Lankershim Blvd (91601-2724)
P.O. Box 908 (92334-0908)
PHONE.................................818 980-9800
Robert Burncati, *Pr*
Maureen Burncati, *
EMP: 131 **EST:** 1979
SQ FT: 75,000
SALES (est): 42.33MM **Privately Held**
Web: www.quicklane.com
SIC: 5511 7539 7538 Automobiles, new and
used; Automotive repair shops, nec;
General automotive repair shops

(P-13803)
NICK ALEXANDER IMPORTS
6333 S Alameda St (90001-1812)
PHONE.................................800 800-6425
TOLL FREE: 800
Elizabeth Alexander, *CEO*
Mary Alexander, *
EMP: 110 **EST:** 1978
SQ FT: 32,500
SALES (est): 57.56MM **Privately Held**
Web: www.bmwdtla.com
SIC: 5511 7549 Automobiles, new and used;
Automotive maintenance services

(P-13804)
NISSAN OF TUSTIN
Also Called: Tustin Saab
30 Auto Center Dr (92782-8401)
PHONE.................................714 669-8282
James H Parkinson, *Pr*
Mark Parkinson, *
EMP: 149 **EST:** 1972
SQ FT: 30,000
SALES (est): 45.07MM **Privately Held**
Web: www.nissanoftustin.com
SIC: 5511 6159 Automobiles, new and used;
Automobile finance leasing

(P-13805)
NOARUS INVESTMENTS INC
Also Called: Airport Honda
5850 W Centinela Ave (90045-1504)
PHONE.................................310 649-2440
Norris J Bishton, *Pr*
EMP: 100 **EST:** 1998
SALES (est): 27.63MM **Privately Held**
Web: www.honda.com
SIC: 5511 5521 5531 7538 Automobiles,
new and used; Automobiles, used cars only
; Automotive parts; General automotive
repair shops

(P-13806)
NOARUS TGG
Also Called: Toyota Scion Place
9444 Trask Ave (92844-2824)
PHONE.................................714 895-5595
Norris J Bishton, *Pr*
Gary Alwood, *
William Hurst, *General Vice President**
EMP: 97 **EST:** 1979
SQ FT: 30,000
SALES (est): 37.16MM **Privately Held**
Web: www.toyota.com
SIC: 5511 5531 7538 Automobiles, new and
used; Automotive parts; General
automotive repair shops

(P-13807)
OCEANSIDE AUTO COUNTRY INC (PA)
Also Called: Toyota Carlsbad
6030 Avenida Encinas Ste 200
(92011-1001)
PHONE.................................760 438-2000
Judith Jones-cone, *CEO*
Olen Woods, *
Michael W Wear, *
EMP: 116 **EST:** 1972
SQ FT: 3,500
SALES (est): 48.21MM
SALES (corp-wide): 48.21MM **Privately Held**
Web: www.toyota.com
SIC: 5511 7538 7532 Automobiles, new and
used; General automotive repair shops; Top
and body repair and paint shops

(P-13808)
ONTARIO AUTOMOTIVE LLC
Also Called: Penske Honda Ontario
1401 Auto Center Dr (91761-2221)
PHONE.................................909 974-3800
Roger Penske, *Ch Bd*
Greg Penske, *
Brian Kobus, *
EMP: 125 **EST:** 1990
SALES (est): 23.81MM
SALES (corp-wide): 5.16B **Privately Held**
Web: www.penskehondaontario.com
SIC: 5511 5521 5012 Automobiles, new and
used; Used car dealers; Automobiles and
other motor vehicles
PA: Penske Corporation
2555 S Telegraph Rd
Bloomfield Hills MI
248 648-2000

(P-13809)
P A MOTORCARS LLC
Also Called: Penske Motorcars
2016 E Garvey Ave S (91791-1911)
PHONE.................................877 433-3517
Greg Penske, *Pr*
Dave Summers, *
EMP: 1385 **EST:** 1995
SQ FT: 23,909
SALES (est): 4.22MM
SALES (corp-wide): 5.16B **Privately Held**
SIC: 5511 5521 7539 7538 Automobiles,
new and used; Used car dealers;
Automotive repair shops, nec; General
automotive repair shops
PA: Penske Corporation
2555 S Telegraph Rd
Bloomfield Hills MI
248 648-2000

(P-13810)
PALM SPRINGS MOTORS INC
Also Called: Palm Sprng Ford Lncoln Mercury
69-200a Highway 111 (92234)
PHONE.................................760 699-6695
Paul J Thiel, *CEO*
William S Torrance, *
Joseph A Gibbs, *
EMP: 200 **EST:** 1950
SALES (est): 51.31MM **Privately Held**
Web: www.quicklane.com
SIC: 5511 7538 Automobiles, new and used;
General automotive repair shops

(P-13811)
PARK PLACE FORD LLC
Also Called: Ford
555 W Foothill Blvd (91786-3853)
PHONE.................................909 946-5555
EMP: 83 **EST:** 2012
SQ FT: 15,000
SALES (est): 21.46MM **Privately Held**
Web: www.ford.com
SIC: 5511 7532 7549 5561 Automobiles,
new and used; Collision shops, automotive;
Emissions testing without repairs,
automotive; Travel trailers: automobile, new
and used

(P-13812)
PEARSON FORD CO (PA)
5900 Sycamore Canyon Blvd (92507-0719)
PHONE.................................877 743-0421
John Mccallan, *Pr*
EMP: 180 **EST:** 1940
SQ FT: 275,000
SALES (est): 38.09MM
SALES (corp-wide): 38.09MM **Privately Held**
Web: www.ford.com

SIC: 5511 7539 7538 5521 Automobiles,
new and used; Automotive repair shops,
nec; General automotive repair shops;
Used car dealers

(P-13813)
PERRY FORD OF POWAY LLC
Also Called: Perry Ford
12740 Poway Rd (92064-4404)
PHONE.................................858 748-1400
Perry Falk, *Managing Member*
EMP: 100 **EST:** 1995
SQ FT: 50,000
SALES (est): 26.44MM **Privately Held**
Web: www.aaronfordofpoway.com
SIC: 5511 7538 5531 5521 Automobiles,
new and used; General automotive repair
shops; Auto and home supply stores; Used
car dealers

(P-13814)
PMB MOTORCARS LLC
1829 E Garvey Ave N (91791-1403)
PHONE.................................626 384-3600
EMP: 2319
SALES (corp-wide): 5.16B **Privately Held**
Web: www.mbusa.com
SIC: 5511 7538 Automobiles, new and used;
General automotive repair shops
HQ: Pmb Motorcars, Llc
2010 E Garvey Ave S
West Covina CA
626 859-1200

(P-13815)
POWAY TOYOTA SCION INC
Also Called: Poway Toyota
13631 Poway Rd (92064-4703)
PHONE.................................858 486-2900
TOLL FREE: 800
Tim Moran, *Genl Mgr*
EMP: 129 **EST:** 1996
SQ FT: 10,000
SALES (est): 18.79MM **Privately Held**
Web: www.toyotaofpoway.com
SIC: 5511 7538 7516 Automobiles, new and
used; General automotive repair shops;
Passenger car leasing

(P-13816)
R E BARBER-FORD
Also Called: Barber Volkeswagen
3440 E Main St (93003-5012)
P.O. Box 1628 (93002-1628)
PHONE.................................805 656-4259
EMP: 135
SIC: 5511 7538 7532 5521 New and used
car dealers; General automotive repair
shops; Top and body repair and paint shops
; Used car dealers

(P-13817)
RACEWAY FORD INC
Also Called: Quick Lane
5900 Sycamore Canyon Blvd (92507-0719)
PHONE.................................951 571-9300
John Barry Mccallan Junior, *Pr*
EMP: 145 **EST:** 1956
SALES (est): 52.88MM **Privately Held**
Web: www.racewayford.com
SIC: 5511 7538 Automobiles, new and used;
General automotive repair shops

(P-13818)
RANCHO FORD INC
Also Called: Rancho
26895 Ynez Rd (92591-4695)
PHONE.................................951 699-1302
Eric Gosch, *Pr*
Marc L Gosch, *

Issac Lizarrago, *
EMP: 124 **EST:** 1984
SQ FT: 40,000
SALES (est): 48.47MM **Privately Held**
Web: www.goschfordtemecula.com
SIC: 5511 7532 7515 5521 Automobiles, new and used; Top and body repair and paint shops; Passenger car leasing; Used car dealers

(P-13819)
RHI INC (PA)
Also Called: Robertson Honda
5841 Lankershim Blvd (91601-1035)
PHONE..............................818 508-3800
TOLL FREE: 800
Robert Robertson, *Pr*
▼ **EMP:** 97 **EST:** 1970
SQ FT: 130,000
SALES (est): 46.72MM
SALES (corp-wide): 46.72MM **Privately Held**
Web: www.victoryautomotivegroup.com
SIC: 5511 7538 7532 5531 Automobiles, new and used; General automotive repair shops; Body shop, automotive; Automotive parts

(P-13820)
ROTOLO CHEVROLET INC
16666 S Highland Ave (92336-1213)
P.O. Box 457 (92334-0457)
PHONE..............................866 756-9776
Marie Waddingham, *Pr*
Nina Rotolo, *
Darinda Madeiros, *
EMP: 137 **EST:** 1971
SQ FT: 51,000
SALES (est): 197.8MM **Privately Held**
Web: www.rotolochevy.com
SIC: 5511 5521 7538 Automobiles, new and used; Used car dealers; General automotive repair shops

(P-13821)
SAN DIEGO V INC (PA)
Also Called: San Diego Volvo
5350 Kearny Mesa Rd (92111-1802)
PHONE..............................888 308-2260
TOLL FREE: 800
Stephen Hinkle, *CEO*
Wesley G Hinkle, *
Robin Seal, *
EMP: 85 **EST:** 1956
SQ FT: 9,200
SALES (est): 34.3MM
SALES (corp-wide): 34.3MM **Privately Held**
Web: www.volvocarssandiego.com
SIC: 5511 7532 Automobiles, new and used; Top and body repair and paint shops

(P-13822)
SAN FERNANDO VALLEY AUTO LLC
Also Called: Rydell Chevrolet-Northridge
18600 Devonshire St (91324-1309)
PHONE..............................818 832-1600
Kelly Cashman, *Dir*
EMP: 189
SALES (corp-wide): 98.64MM **Privately Held**
Web: www.rydells.com
SIC: 5511 7538 7532 Automobiles, new and used; General automotive repair shops; Body shop, automotive
PA: San Fernando Valley Automotive, Llc
6001 Van Nuys Blvd
Van Nuys CA
818 817-4600

(P-13823)
SEIDNER-MILLER INC
Also Called: Toyota of Glendora
1949 Auto Centre Dr (91740-6714)
PHONE..............................909 305-2000
Murrey Seidner, *Pr*
Peter Miller, *
EMP: 180 **EST:** 1993
SQ FT: 65,000
SALES (est): 44.48MM **Privately Held**
Web: www.toyotaofglendora.com
SIC: 5511 7532 7515 5521 Automobiles, new and used; Top and body repair and paint shops; Passenger car leasing; Used car dealers

(P-13824)
SELMAN CHEVROLET COMPANY
1800 E Chapman Ave (92867-7797)
P.O. Box 31 (92856-9031)
PHONE..............................714 633-3521
TOLL FREE: 800
William H Selman Junior, *CEO*
William H Selman Iii, *VP*
Daisy Kan, *
EMP: 107 **EST:** 1951
SQ FT: 4,000
SALES (est): 46.67MM **Privately Held**
Web: www.selmanchevy.com
SIC: 5511 7515 Automobiles, new and used; Passenger car leasing

(P-13825)
SIMPSON AUTOMOTIVE INC
Also Called: Simpson Buick Pontiac GMC
6600 Auto Center Dr (90621-2927)
PHONE..............................714 690-6200
David A Simpson, *Pr*
Dianna Ramsey, *
EMP: 91 **EST:** 1951
SQ FT: 46,000
SALES (est): 49.17MM **Privately Held**
Web: www.simpsonbuickgmcbuenapark.com
SIC: 5511 5531 7539 Automobiles, new and used; Auto and truck equipment and parts; Automotive repair, nec

(P-13826)
SOUTH BAY FORD INC (PA)
Also Called: Quick Lane
5100 W Rosecrans Ave (90250-6620)
P.O. Box 1550 (90251-1550)
PHONE..............................310 644-0211
TOLL FREE: 800
Gary Premeaux, *CEO*
Steve Wood, *
▼ **EMP:** 150 **EST:** 1993
SALES (est): 77.08MM
SALES (corp-wide): 77.08MM **Privately Held**
Web: www.southbayford.com
SIC: 5511 5531 7538 5521 Automobiles, new and used; Automotive parts; General automotive repair shops; Used car dealers

(P-13827)
SOUTH BAY TOYOTA
18416 S Western Ave (90248-3823)
PHONE..............................310 323-7800
David Wilson, *Pr*
David Ortiz, *General Vice President*
EMP: 141 **EST:** 1989
SQ FT: 33,000
SALES (est): 48.98MM **Privately Held**
Web: www.southbaytoyota.com
SIC: 5511 7538 7515 Automobiles, new and used; General automotive repair shops; Passenger car leasing

(P-13828)
SOUTH CNTY LXUS AT MSSION VEJO
28242 Marguerite Pkwy (92692-3704)
PHONE..............................949 347-3400
Patrick Lustin, *Genl Mgr*
EMP: 200 **EST:** 2013
SALES (est): 37.3MM **Privately Held**
Web: www.southcountylexus.com
SIC: 5511 7549 Automobiles, new and used; Automotive maintenance services

(P-13829)
SOUTHBAY EUROPEAN INC
Also Called: Southbay BMW
18800 Hawthorne Blvd (90504-5507)
PHONE..............................310 939-7300
Fritz Hitchcock, *Pr*
Peter Boesen, *
EMP: 100 **EST:** 1968
SQ FT: 150,000
SALES (est): 36.36MM **Privately Held**
Web: www.southbaybmw.com
SIC: 5511 5531 7539 Automobiles, new and used; Automotive parts; Automotive repair shops, nec

(P-13830)
SOUTHWEST MATERIAL HDLG INC (PA)
Also Called: Southwest Toyota Lift
3725 Nobel Ct (91752-3267)
P.O. Box 1070 (91752-8070)
PHONE..............................951 727-0477
Kirt Little, *CEO*
Joseph G Little, *
▲ **EMP:** 115 **EST:** 1962
SQ FT: 10,000
SALES (est): 91.04MM
SALES (corp-wide): 91.04MM **Privately Held**
Web: www.swwarehousesolutions.com
SIC: 5511 7389 7699 7359 Automobiles, new and used; Design, commercial and industrial; Industrial machinery and equipment repair; Equipment rental and leasing, nec

(P-13831)
STERLING MOTORS LTD
Also Called: Sterling BMW
3000 W Coast Hwy (92663-4004)
PHONE..............................949 645-5900
Wayne Minor, *CEO*
John Belanger, *
Steve Army, *
Jim Hutton, *
Doug Janco, *
EMP: 80 **EST:** 1955
SQ FT: 27,000
SALES (est): 32.25MM **Privately Held**
Web: www.sterlingbmw.com
SIC: 5511 7515 Automobiles, new and used; Passenger car leasing

(P-13832)
SUNLAND FORD INC
Also Called: Sunland Ford-Lincoln-Mercury
15300 Palmdale Rd (92392-2498)
PHONE..............................760 241-7751
Ken Chambers, *Pr*
EMP: 90 **EST:** 1969
SQ FT: 10,000
SALES (est): 22.82MM **Privately Held**
Web: www.sunlandfordinc.com
SIC: 5511 7538 5531 5521 Automobiles, new and used; General automotive repair shops; Auto and home supply stores; Used car dealers

(P-13833)
SUNRISE FORD
Also Called: Quick Lane
16005 Valley Blvd (92335-6419)
P.O. Box 2469 (92334-2469)
PHONE..............................909 822-4401
Robert Bruncati, *CEO*
Maureen Bruncati, *
EMP: 200 **EST:** 1944
SQ FT: 100,000
SALES (est): 59.69MM **Privately Held**
Web: www.quicklane.com
SIC: 5511 5012 7538 Automobiles, new and used; Automobiles and other motor vehicles ; General automotive repair shops

(P-13834)
SUZUKI MOTOR OF AMERICA INC (HQ)
Also Called: Suzuki USA
3251 E Imperial Hwy (92821-6795)
P.O. Box 1100 (92822-1100)
PHONE..............................714 996-7040
Takeshi Hayasaki, *Pr*
Takuya Sato, *
◆ **EMP:** 250 **EST:** 2012
SALES (est): 173.06MM **Privately Held**
Web: www.suzuki.com
SIC: 5511 3519 3799 Automobiles, new and used; Outboard motors; Recreational vehicles
PA: Suzuki Motor Corporation
300, Takatsukacho, Minami-Ku
Hamamatsu SZO

(P-13835)
TED FORD JONES INC
Also Called: Ken Grody Ford
5555 Paseo Del Norte (92008-4429)
P.O. Box 1576 (92018-1576)
PHONE..............................760 438-9171
Kurt Maletych, *Brnch Mgr*
EMP: 150
SALES (corp-wide): 45.03MM **Privately Held**
Web: www.ford.com
SIC: 5511 7538 5521 5012 Automobiles, new and used; General automotive repair shops; Used car dealers; Automobiles and other motor vehicles
PA: Ted Jones Ford, Inc.
6211 Beach Blvd
Buena Park CA
714 521-3110

(P-13836)
THREE-WAY CHEVROLET CO (PA)
4501 Wible Rd (93313-2639)
P.O. Box 9609 (93389-9609)
PHONE..............................661 847-6400
EMP: 180 **EST:** 1947
SALES (est): 157.35MM
SALES (corp-wide): 157.35MM **Privately Held**
Web: www.3waychevrolet.com
SIC: 5511 5531 7538 7515 Automobiles, new and used; Automotive parts; General automotive repair shops; Passenger car leasing

(P-13837)
TOMS TRUCK CENTER INC
Also Called: Isuzu Truck Services
1008 E 4th St (92701-4779)
P.O. Box 88 (92702-0088)
PHONE..............................714 835-1978
TOLL FREE: 800
EMP: 177
SALES (corp-wide): 76.55MM **Privately Held**

P R O D U C T S & S V C S

Web: www.ttruck.com
SIC: **5511** 5012 Automobiles, new and used;
Automobiles and other motor vehicles
PA: Tom's Truck Center, Inc.
909 N Grand Ave
Santa Ana CA
800 238-9308

(P-13838)
TOYOTA LOGISTICS SERVICES INC (DH)
19001 S Western Ave (90501-1106)
PHONE...........................310 468-4000
Randy Pflughaupt, *CEO*
Allen Decarr, *
Donald Esmond, *
◆ **EMP:** 176 **EST:** 1981
SQ FT: 600
SALES (est): 201.85MM **Privately Held**
Web: www.toyota.com
SIC: **5511** 3711 Automobiles, new and used;
Motor vehicles and car bodies
HQ: Toyota Motor Sales Usa Inc
6565 Hdqtr Dr Apt W1 3c
Plano TX
310 468-4000

(P-13839)
TOYOTA OF ORANGE INC
1400 N Tustin St (92867-3995)
PHONE...........................714 639-6750
David Wilson, *Pr*
EMP: 135 **EST:** 1972
SQ FT: 38,000
SALES (est): 60.86MM
SALES (corp-wide): 60.86MM **Privately Held**
Web: www.toyotaoforange.com
SIC: **5511** 5521 5012 Automobiles, new and used; Used car dealers; Automobiles and other motor vehicles
PA: D W W Co., Inc.
1400 N Tustin St
Orange CA
714 516-3111

(P-13840)
TOYOTA OF RIVERSIDE INC
7870 Indiana Ave (92504-4109)
PHONE...........................951 687-1622
David Wilson, *Pr*
EMP: 109 **EST:** 1969
SQ FT: 100,000
SALES (est): 52.1MM **Privately Held**
Web: www.toyotaofriverside.com
SIC: **5511** 5531 7538 5521 Automobiles, new and used; Automotive parts; General automotive repair shops; Used car dealers

(P-13841)
TUTTLE-CLICK FORD INC
Also Called: Tuttle Click Ford
43 Auto Center Dr (92618-2898)
PHONE...........................949 855-1704
Bob Tuttle, *Pr*
James H Click, *
Chris Cotter, *
Elvia Morales, *
EMP: 225 **EST:** 1980
SQ FT: 50,000
SALES (est): 49.04MM **Privately Held**
Web: www.quicklane.com
SIC: **5511** 5521 7538 Automobiles, new and used; Used car dealers; General automotive repair shops

(P-13842)
VAHI TOYOTA INC (PA)
Also Called: Valley-HI Toyota Honda
14612 Valley Center Dr (92395-4205)

P.O. Box 1508 (92393-1508)
PHONE...........................760 241-6484
Kent Browning, *Pr*
EMP: 120 **EST:** 1971
SQ FT: 17,000
SALES (est): 26.35MM
SALES (corp-wide): 26.35MM **Privately Held**
Web: www.valleyhitoyota.com
SIC: **5511** 7538 5561 5531 Automobiles, new and used; General automotive repair shops; Recreational vehicle dealers; Auto and home supply stores

(P-13843)
VILLA FORD INC
Also Called: David Wilson's Villa Ford
2550 N Tustin St (92865-3099)
PHONE...........................714 637-8222
TOLL FREE: 888
Peggy Baldwin-butler, *Pr*
Brian Butler, *
Peggy Butler, *
Karen Baldwin, *
EMP: 132 **EST:** 1970
SQ FT: 38,745
SALES (est): 47.31MM **Privately Held**
Web: www.villaford.com
SIC: **5511** 7532 7549 Automobiles, new and used; Body shop, automotive; Automotive maintenance services

(P-13844)
VOLKSWAGEN OF VAN NUYS INC
300 Hitchcock Way (93105-4002)
PHONE...........................323 873-3311
Ludwig Pflock, *Pr*
EMP: 100 **EST:** 1991
SALES (est): 25.38MM **Privately Held**
Web: www.vw.com
SIC: **5511** 7538 Automobiles, new and used; General automotive repair shops

(P-13845)
VOLKSWAGEN SANTA MONICA INC (PA)
Also Called: Lexus Santa Monica
2440 Santa Monica Blvd (90404-2039)
PHONE...........................310 829-1888
TOLL FREE: 888
Michael Sullivan, *Pr*
Kerry Sullivan, *
Hazel R Sullivan, *
EMP: 170 **EST:** 1964
SQ FT: 10,000
SALES (est): 97.95MM
SALES (corp-wide): 97.95MM **Privately Held**
Web: www.volkswagensantamonica.com
SIC: **5511** 7532 7538 Automobiles, new and used; Body shop, automotive; General automotive repair shops

(P-13846)
WALTERS AUTO SALES AND SVC INC
Also Called: Mercedes Benz of Riverside
3213 Adams St (92504-4002)
PHONE...........................888 316-4097
Steve Kienle, *Genl Mgr*
Helga Kienle, *
Lothar Wacker, *
EMP: 248 **EST:** 1964
SQ FT: 14,000
SALES (est): 53.09MM **Privately Held**
Web: walters.mercedesdealer.com
SIC: **5511** 5012 Automobiles, new and used; Automobiles and other motor vehicles

(P-13847)
WAYNE GOSSETT FORD INC
Also Called: Encinitas Ford
1424 Encinitas Blvd (92024-2930)
P.O. Box 230945 (92023-0945)
PHONE...........................760 753-6286
TOLL FREE: 800
Mark S Wheeler, *Pr*
EMP: 95 **EST:** 1960
SALES (est): 36.68MM **Privately Held**
Web: www.encinitasford.com
SIC: **5511** 7549 Automobiles, new and used; Do-it-yourself garages

(P-13848)
WILSON CYCLES SPORTS CORP
Also Called: CJ Wilson BMW Mtcyc Murrieta
26145 Jefferson Ave Ste 205 (92562-9500)
PHONE...........................951 894-5545
George Berta, *Genl Mgr*
Sarah Galin, *Prin*
EMP: 21 **EST:** 2015
SALES (est): 2.39MM **Privately Held**
Web: www.bmwgroup.com
SIC: **5511** 3751 7699 Automobiles, new and used; Motorcycle accessories; Motorcycle repair service

(P-13849)
YORK ENTERPRISES SOUTH INC
Also Called: Huntington Beach Ford
18255 Beach Blvd (92648-1351)
PHONE...........................714 842-6611
Oscar Bakhtiari, *CEO*
Donna Graham, *
EMP: 100 **EST:** 1989
SALES (est): 24.02MM **Privately Held**
Web: www.huntingtonbeachford.com
SIC: **5511** 7538 Automobiles, new and used; General automotive repair shops

5521 Used Car Dealers

(P-13850)
CARMAX INC
25560 Madison Ave (92562-9095)
PHONE...........................951 387-3887
EMP: 122
SALES (corp-wide): 29.68B **Publicly Held**
Web: www.carmax.com
SIC: **5521** 7539 Automobiles, used cars only ; Automotive repair shops, nec
PA: Carmax, Inc.
12800 Tuckahoe Creek Pkwy
Richmond VA
804 747-0422

(P-13851)
K MOTORS INC
Also Called: Toyota of El Cajon
965 Arnele Ave (92020-3001)
PHONE...........................619 270-3000
Robert Kaminsky, *Pr*
Gary Kaminsky, *
Greg Kaminsky, *
Kim Kaminsky, *
Gregory Kaminsky, *
EMP: 186 **EST:** 1956
SQ FT: 29,497
SALES (est): 53.04MM **Privately Held**
Web: www.toyota.com
SIC: **5521** 5013 5511 Automobiles, used cars only; Automotive supplies and parts; Automobiles, new and used

5531 Auto And Home Supply Stores

(P-13852)
AKH COMPANY INC
Also Called: Discount Tire Center 038
1647 W Redlands Blvd Ste C (92373)
PHONE...........................909 748-5016
Marc Fortin, *Mgr*
EMP: 88
SALES (corp-wide): 31.08MM **Privately Held**
Web: www.discounttires.com
SIC: **5531** 7539 5014 Automotive tires; Wheel alignment, automotive; Automobile tires and tubes
PA: Akh Company, Inc.
1160 N Anaheim Blvd
Anaheim CA
800 999-2878

(P-13853)
AKH COMPANY INC
Also Called: Discount Tire Center 077
23316 Sunnymead Blvd (92553-5227)
PHONE...........................951 924-5356
Juan Valdes, *Mgr*
EMP: 110
SALES (corp-wide): 31.08MM **Privately Held**
Web: www.discounttires.com
SIC: **5531** 5014 7539 Automotive tires; Automobile tires and tubes; Wheel alignment, automotive
PA: Akh Company, Inc.
1160 N Anaheim Blvd
Anaheim CA
800 999-2878

(P-13854)
ALLIED WHEEL COMPONENTS INC
Also Called: Raceline Wheels
12300 Edison Way (92841-2810)
P.O. Box 5667 (92846-0667)
PHONE...........................714 893-4160
◆ **EMP:** 38 **EST:** 1996
SQ FT: 91,000
SALES (est): 15.44MM **Privately Held**
Web: www.alliedwheel.com
SIC: **5531** 3714 Automotive tires; Wheels, motor vehicle

(P-13855)
CERTIFIED TIRE & SVC CTRS INC
Also Called: Goodyear
23920 Alessandro Blvd Ste A (92553)
PHONE...........................951 656-6466
EMP: 26
SALES (corp-wide): 24.35MM **Privately Held**
Web: www.goodyear.com
SIC: **5531** 7534 Automotive tires; Tire retreading and repair shops
PA: Certified Tire & Service Centers, Inc.
1875 Iowa Ave
Riverside CA
951 369-0025

(P-13856)
CHAMPION MOTOSPORTS INC (PA)
Also Called: Champion Cooling Systems
32373 Corydon St (92530-9604)
PHONE...........................951 245-9464
Robert Cloke, *CEO*
Cid Martin, *Pr*

▲ **EMP:** 20 **EST:** 2008
SQ FT: 48,000
SALES (est): 4.54MM **Privately Held**
Web: www.championcooling.com
SIC: 5531 5013 3714 Automotive parts;
Automotive supplies and parts; Radiators
and radiator shells and cores, motor vehicle

(P-13857)
CLASSIC CAMARO INC
Also Called: Classic Firebird
18460 Gothard St (92648-1229)
PHONE..............................714 847-6887
Jeffrey M Leonard, *CEO*
▲ **EMP:** 115 **EST:** 1977
SQ FT: 30,000
SALES (est): 24.4MM **Privately Held**
Web: www.classicindustries.com
SIC: 5531 5013 Automotive accessories;
Automotive supplies and parts

(P-13858)
DNA MOTOR INC
Also Called: Dna Motoring
801 Sentous Ave (91744-2543)
PHONE..............................626 965-8898
Jia Jie Chen, *CEO*
◆ **EMP:** 40 **EST:** 2009
SALES (est): 7.14MM **Privately Held**
Web: www.dnamotoring.com
SIC: 5531 3714 Automotive parts; Motor
vehicle parts and accessories

(P-13859)
FORNACA INC (PA)
Also Called: Frank Toyata & Scion
2400 National City Blvd (91950-6628)
P.O. Box 540 (91951-0540)
PHONE..............................866 308-9461
James Fornaca, *CEO*
Gary Fenelli, *
Ronald Fornaca, *
EMP: 140 **EST:** 1978
SQ FT: 150,000
SALES (est): 50.28MM **Privately Held**
Web: www.frankmotors.com
SIC: 5531 5511 7532 Auto and home supply
stores; Automobiles, new and used; Top
and body repair and paint shops

(P-13860)
**FRED M BOERNER MOTOR CO
(PA)**
Also Called: Boerner Truck Center
3620 E Florence Ave (90255-5905)
PHONE..............................323 560-3882
▼ **EMP:** 86 **EST:** 1926
SALES (est): 9.87MM
SALES (corp-wide): 9.87MM **Privately
Held**
SIC: 5531 7538 5012 Truck equipment and
parts; General truck repair; Truck bodies

(P-13861)
**FREEDOM PRFMCE EXHAUST
INC**
1255 Railroad St (92882-1838)
PHONE..............................951 898-4733
Flora Arteaga, *CEO*
Martin Arteaga, *
EMP: 47 **EST:** 2006
SALES (est): 6.59MM **Privately Held**
Web: www.freedomperformexhaust.com
SIC: 5531 3714 Speed shops, including race
car supplies; Mufflers (exhaust), motor
vehicle

(P-13862)
GLOBAL TRADE ALLIANCE INC
Also Called: Action Crash Parts
13642 Orden Dr (90670-6353)
PHONE..............................562 944-6422
Todd Hanson, *Mgr*
EMP: 114
SALES (corp-wide): 12.79B **Publicly Held**
SIC: 5531 5013 Automotive parts;
Automotive supplies and parts
HQ: Global Trade Alliance, Inc.
2040 S Hamilton Rd
Columbus OH
614 751-3100

(P-13863)
**GRAND PRIX ROAD TRENDS
INC (PA)**
Also Called: Grand Prix Performance
1718 Newport Blvd (92627-3010)
PHONE..............................323 962-8600
Jerry Palanjian, *Pr*
EMP: 17 **EST:** 1972
SQ FT: 2,500
SALES (est): 4.93MM
SALES (corp-wide): 4.93MM **Privately
Held**
Web: www.grandprixperformance.com
SIC: 5531 3312 Automotive tires; Wheels

(P-13864)
KRACO ENTERPRISES LLC
505 E Euclid Ave (90222-2890)
PHONE..............................310 639-0666
◆ **EMP:** 164
Web: www.kraco.com
SIC: 5531 3069 5013 Automotive
accessories; Hard rubber and molded
rubber products; Motor vehicle supplies and
new parts

(P-13865)
MOSS MOTORS LTD (PA)
400 Rutherford St (93117-3702)
PHONE..............................805 967-4546
◆ **EMP:** 130 **EST:** 1948
SALES (est): 24.14MM
SALES (corp-wide): 24.14MM **Privately
Held**
Web: www.mossmotors.com
SIC: 5531 5013 Automotive parts;
Automotive supplies and parts

(P-13866)
**ORIGINAL PARTS GROUP INC
(PA)**
Also Called: Chevelle Classics Parts & ACC
1770 Saturn Way (90740-5618)
PHONE..............................562 594-1000
David Harry Leonard, *Pr*
Anthony M Genty, *
▲ **EMP:** 84 **EST:** 1984
SQ FT: 100,000
SALES (est): 33.83MM
SALES (corp-wide): 33.83MM **Privately
Held**
Web: www.opgi.com
SIC: 5531 3465 Automotive parts; Body
parts, automobile: stamped metal

(P-13867)
PARKHOUSE TIRE SERVICE INC
Also Called: Parkhouse Tire
4660 Ruffner St (92111-2220)
PHONE..............................858 565-8473
Janette Fox, *Mgr*
EMP: 30
SALES (corp-wide): 140.36MM **Privately
Held**

Web: www.parkhousetire.com
SIC: 5531 5014 7534 Automotive tires; Tires
and tubes; Tire retreading and repair shops
PA: Parkhouse Tire Service, Inc.
6006 Shull St
Bell Gardens CA
562 928-0421

(P-13868)
**PARKHOUSE TIRE SERVICE INC
(PA)**
Also Called: Parkhouse Tire
6006 Shull St (90201-6237)
P.O. Box 2430 (90202-2430)
PHONE..............................562 928-0421
◆ **EMP:** 75 **EST:** 1971
SALES (est): 140.36MM
SALES (corp-wide): 140.36MM **Privately
Held**
Web: www.parkhousetire.com
SIC: 5531 5014 7534 Automotive tires;
Automobile tires and tubes; Rebuilding and
retreading tires

(P-13869)
**PLASTICOLOR MOLDED PDTS
INC (PA)**
Also Called: Plasticolor
801 S Acacia Ave (92831-5398)
P.O. Box 6985 (92834-6985)
PHONE..............................714 525-3880
Matthew Bagne, *CEO*
Shawn Diamond, *
Gayle Deflin, *
◆ **EMP:** 250 **EST:** 1971
SALES (est): 48.61MM
SALES (corp-wide): 48.61MM **Privately
Held**
Web: www.plasticolorinc.com
SIC: 5531 3083 Automotive accessories;
Plastics finished products, laminated

(P-13870)
SANTA MARIA TIRE INC (PA)
Also Called: SM Tire
2170 Hutton Rd Bldg A (93444-9717)
P.O. Box 6007 (93456-6007)
PHONE..............................805 347-4793
Craig Stephens, *Pr*
Brenee Stephens, *
C Kent Stephens, *
Cameron Stephens, *
Conrad Stephens Attorney, *Prin*
EMP: 75 **EST:** 1946
SALES (est): 20.64MM
SALES (corp-wide): 20.64MM **Privately
Held**
Web: www.smtire.com
SIC: 5531 7534 Automotive tires; Rebuilding
and retreading tires

(P-13871)
**SOUTHERN CAL DISC TIRE CO
INC**
Also Called: Discount Tire
4640 Telephone Rd (93003-5630)
PHONE..............................805 639-0166
Thomas Gensen, *Mgr*
EMP: 95
SQ FT: 4,500
SALES (corp-wide): 3.69B **Privately Held**
Web: www.discounttire.com
SIC: 5531 7538 Automotive tires; General
automotive repair shops
HQ: Southern California Discount Tire Co.,
Inc.
16100 N Grnway Hyden Loop
Scottsdale AZ
602 996-0201

(P-13872)
**SOUTHERN CAL DISC TIRE CO
INC**
Also Called: Discount Tire
550 N Broadway (92025-2720)
PHONE..............................760 741-9805
David Benibedez, *Mgr*
EMP: 122
SALES (corp-wide): 3.69B **Privately Held**
Web: www.discounttire.com
SIC: 5531 5014 5013 Automotive tires;
Automobile tires and tubes; Wheels, motor
vehicle
HQ: Southern California Discount Tire Co.,
Inc.
16100 N Grnway Hyden Loop
Scottsdale AZ
602 996-0201

(P-13873)
**SOUTHERN CAL DISC TIRE CO
INC**
Also Called: Discount Tire
780 Grand Ave (92078-1249)
PHONE..............................760 744-3526
Brett Harris, *Mgr*
EMP: 95
SALES (corp-wide): 3.69B **Privately Held**
Web: www.discounttire.com
SIC: 5531 5014 Automotive tires;
Automobile tires and tubes
HQ: Southern California Discount Tire Co.,
Inc.
16100 N Grnway Hyden Loop
Scottsdale AZ
602 996-0201

(P-13874)
**SOUTHERN CAL DISC TIRE CO
INC**
Also Called: Discount Tire
209 S Escondido Blvd (92025-4116)
PHONE..............................760 741-3801
Pat Fuller, *Mgr*
EMP: 122
SALES (corp-wide): 3.69B **Privately Held**
Web: www.discounttire.com
SIC: 5531 5014 5013 Automotive tires;
Automobile tires and tubes; Wheels, motor
vehicle
HQ: Southern California Discount Tire Co.,
Inc.
16100 N Grnway Hyden Loop
Scottsdale AZ
602 996-0201

(P-13875)
**SOUTHERN CAL DISC TIRE CO
INC**
Also Called: Discount Tire
685 San Rodolfo Dr (92075-2001)
PHONE..............................858 481-6387
Bruce Hopple, *Brnch Mgr*
EMP: 122
SALES (corp-wide): 3.69B **Privately Held**
Web: www.discounttire.com
SIC: 5531 5014 Automotive tires;
Automobile tires and tubes
HQ: Southern California Discount Tire Co.,
Inc.
16100 N Grnway Hyden Loop
Scottsdale AZ
602 996-0201

(P-13876)
**SOUTHERN CAL DISC TIRE CO
INC**
Also Called: Discount Tire
12651 Poway Rd (92064-4415)

PHONE....................858 486-3600
Alan Birse, *Brnch Mgr*
EMP: 122
SALES (corp-wide): 3.69B **Privately Held**
Web: www.discounttire.com
SIC: **5531** 5014 5013 Automotive tires;
Automobile tires and tubes; Wheels, motor
vehicle
HQ: Southern California Discount Tire Co.,
Inc.
16100 N Grnway Hyden Loop
Scottsdale AZ
602 996-0201

(P-13877)
SOUTHERN CAL DISC TIRE CO INC
Also Called: Discount Tire
1037 S Coast Hwy (92054-5004)
PHONE....................760 439-8539
John Toonds, *Mgr*
EMP: 122
SALES (corp-wide): 3.69B **Privately Held**
Web: www.discounttire.com
SIC: **5531** 5014 Automotive tires;
Automobile tires and tubes
HQ: Southern California Discount Tire Co.,
Inc.
16100 N Grnway Hyden Loop
Scottsdale AZ
602 996-0201

(P-13878)
SOUTHERN CAL DISC TIRE CO INC
Also Called: Discount Tire
107 N El Camino Real (92024-2802)
PHONE....................760 634-2202
Alan Brise, *Brnch Mgr*
EMP: 122
SALES (corp-wide): 3.69B **Privately Held**
Web: www.discounttire.com
SIC: **5531** 7534 Automotive tires; Tire repair
shop
HQ: Southern California Discount Tire Co.,
Inc.
16100 N Grnway Hyden Loop
Scottsdale AZ
602 996-0201

(P-13879)
SOUTHERN CAL DISC TIRE CO INC
Also Called: Discount Tire
3935 Convoy St (92111-3723)
PHONE....................858 278-0661
EMP: 122
SALES (corp-wide): 3.69B **Privately Held**
Web: www.discounttire.com
SIC: **5531** 5014 Automotive tires;
Automobile tires and tubes; Wheels, motor
vehicle
HQ: Southern California Discount Tire Co.,
Inc.
16100 N Grnway Hyden Loop
Scottsdale AZ
602 996-0201

(P-13880)
SOUTHERN CAL DISC TIRE CO INC
Also Called: Discount Tire
20741 Avalon Blvd (90746-3313)
PHONE....................310 324-2569
EMP: 122
SALES (corp-wide): 3.69B **Privately Held**
Web: www.discounttire.com
SIC: **5531** 5014 5013 Automotive tires;
Automobile tires and tubes; Wheels, motor
vehicle

HQ: Southern California Discount Tire Co.,
Inc.
16100 N Grnway Hyden Loop
Scottsdale AZ
602 996-0201

(P-13881)
SOUTHERN CAL DISC TIRE CO INC
Also Called: Discount Tire
705 S Grand Ave (91740-4141)
PHONE....................626 335-2883
Abel Ariola, *Mgr*
EMP: 95
SALES (corp-wide): 3.69B **Privately Held**
Web: www.discounttire.com
SIC: **5531** 5013 Automotive tires; Wheels,
motor vehicle
HQ: Southern California Discount Tire Co.,
Inc.
16100 N Grnway Hyden Loop
Scottsdale AZ
602 996-0201

(P-13882)
SOUTHERN CAL DISC TIRE CO INC
Also Called: Discount Tire
600 W Florida Ave (92543-4009)
PHONE....................951 929-2130
Josh Mccartner, *Mgr*
EMP: 122
SALES (corp-wide): 3.69B **Privately Held**
Web: www.discounttire.com
SIC: **5531** 5013 Automotive tires; Wheels,
motor vehicle
HQ: Southern California Discount Tire Co.,
Inc.
16100 N Grnway Hyden Loop
Scottsdale AZ
602 996-0201

(P-13883)
SOUTHERN CAL DISC TIRE CO INC
Also Called: Discount Tire
15672 Springdale St (92649-1315)
PHONE....................714 901-8226
Joe Ortiz, *Mgr*
EMP: 108
SALES (corp-wide): 3.69B **Privately Held**
Web: www.discounttire.com
SIC: **5531** 5013 Automotive tires; Wheels,
motor vehicle
HQ: Southern California Discount Tire Co.,
Inc.
16100 N Grnway Hyden Loop
Scottsdale AZ
602 996-0201

(P-13884)
TIRES WAREHOUSE LLC
18203 Mount Baldy Cir (92708-6117)
PHONE....................714 432-8851
Terry Ahlstrom, *Brnch Mgr*
EMP: 261
SALES (corp-wide): 1.56B **Privately Held**
Web: www.usautoforce.com
SIC: **5531** 5014 Automotive tires; Tires and
tubes
HQ: Tire's Warehouse, Llc
1820 Fullerton Ave # 300
Corona CA
951 808-0111

(P-13885)
TOYOTA DOWNTOWN LA
Also Called: Toyota of Downtown L.A.
714 W Olympic Blvd Ste 1131
(90015-1425)

PHONE....................213 342-3646
EMP: 154 **EST:** 1970
SALES (est): 19.82MM **Privately Held**
SIC: **5531** 7538 5511 5521 Batteries,
automotive and truck; General automotive
repair shops; Automobiles, new and used;
Used car dealers

(P-13886)
TRANSAMERICAN DISSOLUTION LLC (HQ)
Also Called: Four Wheel Parts Wholesalers
400 W Artesia Blvd (90220-5501)
PHONE....................310 900-5500
Greg Adler, *Managing Member*
◆ **EMP:** 200 **EST:** 1959
SQ FT: 120,000
SALES (est): 479.89MM
SALES (corp-wide): 8.59B **Publicly Held**
Web: www.4wheelparts.com
SIC: **5531** 5013 Automotive parts;
Automotive supplies and parts
PA: Polaris Inc.
2100 Highway 55
Medina MN
763 542-0500

(P-13887)
UNITED SYATT AMERICA CORP (PA)
Also Called: Broadway Auto Parts
920 E 1st St (92701-5365)
PHONE....................714 568-1938
Ron Hanson, *Pr*
Donna Hanson, *Sec*
EMP: 105 **EST:** 1955
SQ FT: 27,000
SALES (est): 5.88MM
SALES (corp-wide): 5.88MM **Privately Held**
SIC: **5531** 5013 Automotive parts;
Automotive supplies and parts

(P-13888)
XRP INC (PA)
5630 Imperial Hwy (90280-7420)
PHONE....................562 861-4765
David Barker, *CEO*
Debbie Singer, *Pr*
EMP: 19 **EST:** 1989
SQ FT: 25,000
SALES (est): 3.61MM **Privately Held**
Web: www.xrp.com
SIC: **5531** 3714 Automotive parts; Fuel
systems and parts, motor vehicle

5541 Gasoline Service Stations

(P-13889)
ATLANTIC RICHFIELD COMPANY (DH)
Also Called: A R C O
4 Centerpointe Dr (90623-1074)
PHONE....................800 333-3991
Robert A Malone, *Pr*
Ian Springett, *
▲ **EMP:** 2200 **EST:** 1870
SALES (est): 559.71MM
SALES (corp-wide): 241.39B **Privately Held**
Web: www.arco.com
SIC: **5541** 1321 2911 Filling stations,
gasoline; Natural gas liquids; Petroleum
refining
HQ: Bp America Inc
4101 Winfield Rd Ste 200
Warrenville IL
214 210-4835

(P-13890)
CHEVRON CORPORATION
Also Called: Chevron
324 W El Segundo Blvd (90245-3635)
PHONE....................310 615-5000
William Simok, *Ex Dir*
EMP: 812
SALES (corp-wide): 246.25B **Publicly Held**
Web: www.chevron.com
SIC: **5541** 1311 1382 1321 Filling stations,
gasoline; Crude petroleum production; Oil
and gas exploration services; Natural gas
liquids
PA: Chevron Corporation
6001 Bollinger Canyon Rd
San Ramon CA
925 326-2189

(P-13891)
EVGO SERVICES LLC
Also Called: Evgo Montgomery Co
11835 W Olympic Blvd Ste 900e
(90064-5001)
P.O. Box 642830 (90064-8287)
PHONE....................310 954-2900
Cathy Zoi, *CEO*
Olga Shevorenkova, *
Ivo Steklac, *
EMP: 298 **EST:** 2010
SQ FT: 10,000
SALES (est): 55.14MM **Publicly Held**
Web: www.evgo.com
SIC: **5541** 3694 Gasoline service stations;
Automotive electrical equipment, nec
HQ: Evgo Inc.
11835 W Olympic Blvd 900e
Los Angeles CA
877 494-3833

(P-13892)
EXXON MOBIL CORPORATION
Also Called: Exxon
12000 Calle Real (93117)
PHONE....................805 961-4093
Bob Barnes, *Brnch Mgr*
EMP: 24
SALES (corp-wide): 413.68B **Publicly Held**
Web: corporate.exxonmobil.com
SIC: **5541** 3533 Filling stations, gasoline; Oil
and gas field machinery
PA: Exxon Mobil Corporation
5959 Las Colinas Blvd
Irving TX
972 940-6000

(P-13893)
PAQ INC
Also Called: Food 4 Less
1465 Creston Rd (93446-3218)
PHONE....................805 227-1660
EMP: 96
SALES (corp-wide): 148.26B **Publicly Held**
Web: www.myfood4less.com
SIC: **5541** 5411 5141 Gasoline service
stations; Grocery stores, chain; Groceries,
general line
HQ: Paq, Inc
3021 Reynolds Ranch Pkwy # 230
Lodi CA

5551 Boat Dealers

(P-13894)
TOLLER ENTERPRISES INC (PA)
Also Called: Electra Craft
2251 Townsgate Rd (91361-2404)

658   2024 Southern California
Business Directory and Buyers Guide   ▲ = Import ▼ = Export
◆ = Import/Export

PHONE..................805 374-9455
Alex Toller, *Pr*
Cheryl Toller, *Sec*
EMP: 25 **EST:** 1979
SALES (est): 5.22MM
SALES (corp-wide): 5.22MM **Privately Held**
Web: www.electracraft.com
SIC: 5551 3732 Motor boat dealers; Boatbuilding and repairing

5561 Recreational Vehicle Dealers

(P-13895)
GIANT INLAND EMPIRE RV CTR INC (PA)
Also Called: Giant Rv
9150 Benson Ave (91763-1688)
PHONE..................909 981-0444
TOLL FREE: 800
Behzad Barouti, *CEO*
Nasser Etebar, *
EMP: 125 **EST:** 1986
SQ FT: 50,000
SALES (est): 49.87MM
SALES (corp-wide): 49.87MM **Privately Held**
Web: www.giantrv.com
SIC: 5561 7538 Recreational vehicle parts and accessories; Recreational vehicle repairs

(P-13896)
KENDON INDUSTRIES LLC
2990 E Miraloma Ave (92806-1807)
PHONE..................714 630-7144
Frank Esposito, *Managing Member*
EMP: 17 **EST:** 2014
SALES (est): 15.54MM **Privately Held**
Web: www.kendonusa.com
SIC: 5561 3792 Travel trailers: automobile, new and used; Travel trailers and campers

(P-13897)
LA MESA R V CENTER INC (PA)
Also Called: Rec Van
7430 Copley Park Pl (92111-1122)
PHONE..................858 874-8000
James R Kimbrell, *CEO*
James Walters, *
EMP: 130 **EST:** 1972
SALES (est): 209.29MM
SALES (corp-wide): 209.29MM **Privately Held**
Web: www.lamesarv.com
SIC: 5561 7538 Motor homes; Recreational vehicle repairs

5571 Motorcycle Dealers

(P-13898)
ARCH MOTORCYCLE COMPANY INC
3216 W El Segundo Blvd (90250-4823)
PHONE..................970 443-1380
Gard Hollinger, *Prin*
EMP: 35 **EST:** 2012
SALES (est): 1.31MM **Privately Held**
Web: www.archmotorcycle.com
SIC: 5571 3751 Motorcycles; Bicycles and related parts

(P-13899)
BESTOP BAJA LLC
Also Called: Baja Designs
2950 Norman Strasse Rd (92069-5946)

PHONE..................760 560-2252
John Larson, *Managing Member*
▲ **EMP:** 115 **EST:** 1992
SQ FT: 14,000
SALES (est): 24.57MM
SALES (corp-wide): 95.76MM **Privately Held**
Web: www.bajadesigns.com
SIC: 5571 3714 5013 Motorcycle parts and accessories; Motor vehicle electrical equipment; Motorcycle parts
PA: Bestop, Inc.
333 Centennial Pkwy Ste B
Louisville CO
303 464-2548

(P-13900)
JIM ONEAL DISTRIBUTING INC
Also Called: O'Neal U S A
799 Camarillo Springs Rd (93012-9468)
PHONE..................805 426-3300
Frank Kashare, *Pr*
▲ **EMP:** 40 **EST:** 1970
SALES (est): 8.08MM **Privately Held**
Web: www.oneal.com
SIC: 5571 3751 Motorcycle dealers; Motorcycles, bicycles and parts

(P-13901)
KAWASAKI MOTORS CORP USA (HQ)
26972 Burbank (92610-2506)
P.O. Box 25252 (92799-5252)
PHONE..................949 837-4683
Eigo Konya, *Pr*
Terunori Kitajima, *
Richard N Beattie, *Chief Marketing*
◆ **EMP:** 400 **EST:** 1967
SQ FT: 40,000
SALES (est): 267.77MM **Privately Held**
Web: www.kawasaki.com
SIC: 5571 5013 5084 5091 Motorcycle dealers; Motorcycle parts; Engines, gasoline ; Boats, canoes, watercrafts, and equipment
PA: Kawasaki Heavy Industries, Ltd.
1-1-3, Higashikawasakicho, Chuo-Ku
Kobe HYO

(P-13902)
OCELOT ENGINEERING INC
Also Called: Chaparral Motorsports
555 S H St (92410-3415)
PHONE..................800 841-2960
David S Damron, *Pr*
James E Damron, *
Linda J Damron, *
◆ **EMP:** 160 **EST:** 1973
SALES (est): 44.2MM **Privately Held**
Web: www.chapmoto.com
SIC: 5571 5551 5013 3751 Motorcycles; Jet skis; Motorcycle parts; Motorcycle accessories

(P-13903)
PRO CIRCUIT PRODUCTS INC (PA)
Also Called: Pro Circuit Products & Racing
2771 Wardlow Rd (92882-2869)
PHONE..................951 738-8050
Mitchell C Payton, *Prin*
◆ **EMP:** 20 **EST:** 1978
SALES (est): 9.17MM
SALES (corp-wide): 9.17MM **Privately Held**
Web: www.procircuit.com
SIC: 5571 3751 Motorcycle parts and accessories; Motorcycles and related parts

(P-13904)
YAMAHA MOTOR CORPORATION USA (HQ)
6555 Katella Ave (90630-5101)
PHONE..................714 761-7300
Mike Chrzanowski, *Pr*
Takuwy Watanabe, *
Jeff Young, *
◆ **EMP:** 400 **EST:** 1955
SQ FT: 200,000
SALES (est): 1.47B **Privately Held**
Web: www.yamaha-motor.com
SIC: 5571 5013 5091 5012 Motorcycle dealers; Motor vehicle supplies and new parts; Boats, canoes, watercrafts, and equipment; Motorcycles
PA: Yamaha Motor Co., Ltd.
2500, Shingai
Iwata SZO

5599 Automotive Dealers, Nec

(P-13905)
CARSON TRAILER INC (PA)
Also Called: Carson Trailer Sales
14831 S Maple Ave (90248-1935)
PHONE..................310 835-0876
William Modisette, *Pr*
EMP: 100 **EST:** 1991
SALES (est): 33MM **Privately Held**
Web: www.carsontrailer.com
SIC: 5599 3792 Utility trailers; Travel trailers and campers

(P-13906)
IRWIN INTERNATIONAL INC (PA)
Also Called: Aircraft Spruce Speciality Co
225 Airport Cir (92878-5027)
P.O. Box 4000 (92878-4000)
PHONE..................951 372-9555
James J Irwin, *Pr*
Elizabeth Irwin, *
▼ **EMP:** 95 **EST:** 1965
SQ FT: 5,000
SALES (est): 146.72MM
SALES (corp-wide): 146.72MM **Privately Held**
Web: www.aircraftspruce.com
SIC: 5599 5088 Aircraft instruments, equipment or parts; Aircraft and parts, nec

(P-13907)
PACIFIC BOAT TRAILERS INC (PA)
Also Called: Pacific Boat Trailers
2855 Sampson Ave (92879-6126)
PHONE..................909 902-0094
Roger Treichler, *Pr*
Vicky Treichler, *VP*
EMP: 18 **EST:** 1986
SALES (est): 4.97MM
SALES (corp-wide): 4.97MM **Privately Held**
Web: www.pacifictrailers.com
SIC: 5599 3792 Utility trailers; Travel trailers and campers

5611 Men's And Boys' Clothing Stores

(P-13908)
GURU DENIM LLC (DH)
Also Called: True Religion Apparel
500 W 190th St Ste 300 (90248-4269)
PHONE..................323 266-3072
Michael Buckley, *Managing Member*
▲ **EMP:** 150 **EST:** 2002

SALES (est): 150.48MM
SALES (corp-wide): 350MM **Privately Held**
Web: www.truereligion.com
SIC: 5611 5137 Clothing accessories: men's and boys'; Women's and children's clothing
HQ: True Religion Apparel, Inc.
500 W 190th St Ste 300
Gardena CA
323 266-3072

(P-13909)
HUB DISTRIBUTING INC (HQ)
Also Called: Anchor Blue
1260 Corona Pointe Ct (92879-5013)
PHONE..................951 340-3149
Thomas Sands, *CEO*
Elaine Gregg, *
Thomas Shaw, *
▲ **EMP:** 300 **EST:** 1947
SQ FT: 500,000
SALES (est): 37.53MM
SALES (corp-wide): 3.46B **Privately Held**
SIC: 5611 5621 5632 5137 Men's and boys' clothing stores; Women's clothing stores; Apparel accessories; Women's and children's clothing
PA: Sun Capital Partners, Inc.
5200 Town Center Cir # 450
Boca Raton FL
561 394-0550

(P-13910)
MEUNDIES INC
3650 Holdrege Ave (90016-4304)
PHONE..................888 552-6775
Jonathan Shokrian, *CEO*
EMP: 251 **EST:** 2011
SQ FT: 2,500
SALES (est): 33.9MM **Privately Held**
Web: www.meundies.com
SIC: 5611 5621 2254 Men's and boys' clothing stores; Women's clothing stores; Nightwear (nightgowns, negligees, pajamas), knit

5621 Women's Clothing Stores

(P-13911)
AMERICAN RAG COMPAGNIE
150 S La Brea Ave (90036-2910)
PHONE..................323 935-3154
Mark Werts Senior, *CEO*
Mark Werts Junior, *CFO*
▲ **EMP:** 100 **EST:** 1984
SQ FT: 15,000
SALES (est): 4.67MM **Privately Held**
Web: www.americanrag.com
SIC: 5621 5932 5137 5611 Ready-to-wear apparel, women's; Clothing, secondhand; Women's and children's clothing; Clothing, male: everyday, except suits and sportswear

(P-13912)
COUNTRY CLUB FASHIONS INC
Also Called: Theodore
6083 W Pico Blvd (90035-2648)
PHONE..................323 965-2707
EMP: 45
Web: www.theodorebh.com
SIC: 5621 5611 2337 2331 Ready-to-wear apparel, women's; Clothing, sportswear, men's and boys'; Skirts, separate: women's, misses', and juniors'; Blouses, women's and juniors': made from purchased material

P R O D U C T S & S V C S

(P-13913)
LIVING DOLL LLC
Also Called: Heart N Soul
13071 Temple Ave (91746-1418)
PHONE....................213 222-1010
▲ EMP: 19 EST: 2011
SALES (est): 2.66MM Privately Held
SIC: 5621 2335 Women's clothing stores;
    Women's, junior's, and misses' dresses

(P-13914)
LOLA BELLE BRANDS LLC
631 S Palm Ave (91803-1424)
PHONE....................855 226-3526
EMP: 17 EST: 2017
SALES (est): 579.42K Privately Held
SIC: 5621 3999 Boutiques; Candles

(P-13915)
NASTY GAL INC (HQ)
2049 Century Park E Ste 3400
(90067-3101)
PHONE....................213 542-3436
Sheree Waterson, CEO
Bob Ross, *
◆ EMP: 23 EST: 2008
SALES (est): 17.12MM
SALES (corp-wide): 2.18B Privately Held
Web: www.nastygal.com
SIC: 5621 5139 2389 Ready-to-wear
    apparel, women's; Shoes; Academic
    vestments (caps and gowns)
PA: Boohoo Group Plc
    49-51 Dale Street
    Manchester
    161 237-7700

(P-13916)
**SANCTUARY CLOTHING LLC
(PA)**
Also Called: Sanctuary Clothing
3611 N San Fernando Blvd (91505-1043)
PHONE....................818 505-0018
Kenneth Polanco, Managing Member
Debra Polanco, Chief Creative Officer
Elizabeth Fernando, Contrlr
EMP: 41 EST: 2008
SALES (est): 15.42MM
SALES (corp-wide): 15.42MM Privately
Held
Web: www.sanctuaryclothing.com
SIC: 5621 5137 2389 Ready-to-wear
    apparel, women's; Women's and children's
    dresses, suits, skirts, and blouses; Apparel
    and outerwear fabrics, cotton

(P-13917)
**TOPSON DOWNS CALIFORNIA
INC (PA)**
Also Called: Topson Downs
3840 Watseka Ave (90232-2633)
PHONE....................310 558-0300
John Poyer, Pr
Joe Wirht, *
Daniel Abramovitch, *
▲ EMP: 250 EST: 1971
SQ FT: 42,000
SALES (est): 62.4MM
SALES (corp-wide): 62.4MM Privately
Held
Web: www.topsondowns.com
SIC: 5621 5136 2211 2221 Women's
    clothing stores; Shirts, men's and boys';
    Apparel and outerwear fabrics, cotton;
    Apparel and outerwear fabric, manmade
    fiber or silk

(P-13918)
**VENTURA FEED AND PET SUPS
INC**
Also Called: Wharf, The
980 E Front St (93001-3017)
P.O. Box 1806 (93002-1806)
PHONE....................805 648-5035
Todd Butterbaugh, CEO
Darren Borgstedte, *
EMP: 42 EST: 1953
SQ FT: 13,000
SALES (est): 2.87MM Privately Held
Web: store.thewharfonline.com
SIC: 5621 5661 3999 2048 Women's
    clothing stores; Shoe stores; Pet supplies;
    Prepared feeds, nec

5632 Women's Accessory
And Specialty Stores

(P-13919)
IHEARTRAVES LLC
250 S Glendora Ave (91790-3039)
PHONE....................626 628-6482
Brian Lim, CEO
Scott Elliott, Pr
EMP: 19 EST: 2012
SALES (est): 2.37MM Privately Held
Web: www.iheartraves.com
SIC: 5632 2331 Apparel accessories;
    Women's and misses' blouses and shirts

(P-13920)
VERA BRADLEY INC
4525 La Jolla Village Dr (92122-1215)
PHONE....................858 320-9020
EMP: 27
SALES (corp-wide): 499.96MM Publicly
Held
Web: www.verabradley.com
SIC: 5632 5137 3171 Handbags; Purses;
    Handbags, women's
PA: Vera Bradley, Inc.
    12420 Stonebridge Rd
    Roanoke IN
    877 708-8372

5651 Family Clothing Stores

(P-13921)
**BURLINGTON COAT FCTRY
WHSE OF**
Also Called: Burlington Coat Factory
1201 S Baldwin Ave (91007-7582)
PHONE....................626 447-8784
Kathy Stewart, Mgr
EMP: 196 EST: 1996
SALES (est): 1.86MM
SALES (corp-wide): 8.7B Publicly Held
Web: www.burlington.com
SIC: 5651 5632 5661 5719 Family clothing
    stores; Women's accessory and specialty
    stores; Shoe stores; Miscellaneous
    homefurnishings
HQ: Burlington Coat Factory Warehouse
    Corporation
    1830 N Route 130
    Burlington NJ
    609 387-7800

(P-13922)
J & M SALES INC
Also Called: Fallas Discount Stores
15001 S Figueroa St (90248-1721)
PHONE....................310 324-9962
▲ EMP: 2500

SIC: 5651 6531 Unisex clothing stores; Real
    estate listing services

(P-13923)
MADEWELL INC
7007 Friars Rd Ste 820 (92108-1145)
PHONE....................619 491-0549
EMP: 20
SALES (corp-wide): 2.48B Privately Held
Web: stores.madewell.com
SIC: 5651 5621 2389 Family clothing stores;
    Women's clothing stores; Apparel for
    handicapped
HQ: Madewell Inc.
    225 Liberty St
    New York NY
    434 385-5792

(P-13924)
**WALKING COMPANY
HOLDINGS INC (PA)**
Also Called: Big Dog Sportswear
1800 Avenue Of The Stars Ste 300
(90067-4204)
PHONE....................805 963-8727
Andrew D Feshbach, CEO
Fred Kayne, *
Roberta J Morris, *
Anthony J Wall, Executive Business Affairs
Vice President*
Lee M Cox Senior, Retail Operations Vice
President
▲ EMP: 160 EST: 1993
SQ FT: 24,000
SALES (est): 307.79MM Privately Held
Web: www.thewalkingcompany.com
SIC: 5651 5961 5136 5137 Family clothing
    stores; Clothing, mail order (except
    women's); Sportswear, men's and boys';
    Sportswear, women's and children's

5661 Shoe Stores

(P-13925)
SKECHERS USA INC II
228 Manhattan Beach Blvd Ste 200
(90266-5356)
PHONE....................800 746-3411
Robert Greenberg, CEO
David Weinberg, CFO
◆ EMP: 4000 EST: 1994
SALES (est): 168.18MM Publicly Held
Web: www.skechers.com
SIC: 5661 3021 Shoe stores; Shoes, rubber
    or plastic molded to fabric
PA: Skechers U.S.A., Inc.
    228 Manhattan Beach Blvd # 200
    Manhattan Beach CA

(P-13926)
T AND B BOOTS INC
Also Called: Takken's Comfort Shoes
72 S Main St B (93465-9787)
PHONE....................805 434-9904
EMP: 80
SIC: 5661 7251 Men's boots; Shoe repair
    shop

5699 Miscellaneous Apparel
And Accessories

(P-13927)
511 INC (DH)
Also Called: 5.11 Tactical Series
3150 Bristol St Ste 300 (92626-3088)
PHONE....................949 800-1511
Francisco Morales, CEO
Dan Costa, Pr

John Wicks, Sec
James Mcginty, CFO
◆ EMP: 26 EST: 2003
SQ FT: 93,000
SALES (est): 151.27MM Publicly Held
Web: www.511tactical.com
SIC: 5699 2231 5139 2393 Uniforms;
    Apparel and outerwear broadwoven fabrics;
    Boots; Canvas bags
HQ: 5.11 Ta, Inc.
    4300 Spyres Way
    Modesto CA
    209 527-4511

(P-13928)
ADRENALINE LACROSSE INC
24 21st St (92102-3802)
PHONE....................888 768-8479
Alex Cade, CEO
Steve Sepeta, *
Parker Anger, *
Rory Doucette, *
Xander Ritz, *
EMP: 29 EST: 2012
SALES (est): 4.08MM Privately Held
Web: www.adrln.com
SIC: 5699 2389 Sports apparel; Men's
    miscellaneous accessories

(P-13929)
**AMERICAN SOCCER COMPANY
INC (PA)**
Also Called: Score Sports
726 E Anaheim St (90744-3635)
P.O. Box 1219 (90748-1219)
PHONE....................310 830-6161
Kevin Mahoney, Pr
◆ EMP: 172 EST: 1975
SQ FT: 30,000
SALES (est): 44.48MM
SALES (corp-wide): 44.48MM Privately
Held
Web: www.scoresports.com
SIC: 5699 2329 2339 3949 Uniforms; Men's
    and boys' athletic uniforms; Uniforms,
    athletic: women's, misses', and juniors';
    Sporting and athletic goods, nec

(P-13930)
AURELIO FELIX BARRETO III
Also Called: C-28
169 Radio Rd (92879-1724)
PHONE....................951 354-9528
▲ EMP: 125
Web: www.c28.com
SIC: 5699 5136 5137 Customized clothing
    and apparel; Men's and boy's clothing;
    Women's and children's clothing

(P-13931)
CINTAS CORPORATION
Also Called: Cintas Fire
4320 E Miraloma Ave (92807-1886)
P.O. Box 636525 (45263-6525)
PHONE....................714 646-2550
Winter Barry, Genl Mgr
EMP: 80
SALES (corp-wide): 8.82B Publicly Held
Web: www.cintas.com
SIC: 5699 7389 8711 Uniforms; Fire
    protection service other than forestry or
    public; Fire protection engineering
PA: Cintas Corporation
    6800 Cintas Blvd
    Cincinnati OH
    513 459-1200

(P-13932)
CINTAS CORPORATION NO 3
Also Called: Cintas

2829 Workman Mill Rd (90601-1549)
PHONE..................562 692-8741
Bryce Littlejohn, *Genl Mgr*
EMP: 88
SALES (corp-wide): 8.82B **Publicly Held**
Web: www.cintas.com
SIC: 5699 7218 Uniforms; Industrial
launderers
HQ: Cintas Corporation No. 3
6800 Cintas Blvd
Mason OH

(P-13933)
CINTAS CORPORATION NO 3
Also Called: Cintas
675 32nd St (92102-3301)
PHONE..................619 239-1001
Kevin Nolan, *Brnch Mgr*
EMP: 92
SQ FT: 7,000
SALES (corp-wide): 8.82B **Publicly Held**
Web: www.cintas.com
SIC: 5699 7213 Uniforms; Uniform supply
HQ: Cintas Corporation No. 3
6800 Cintas Blvd
Mason OH

(P-13934)
HOT TOPIC INC (DH)
Also Called: Shockhound
18305 San Jose Ave (91748-1237)
PHONE..................626 839-4681
Steve Vranes, *CEO*
Ash Walia, *
Tiffany Smith, *
◆ **EMP:** 800 **EST:** 1988
SQ FT: 250,000
SALES (est): 770.2MM **Publicly Held**
Web: www.hottopic.com
SIC: 5699 5632 2326 Designers, apparel;
Apparel accessories; Men's and boy's work
clothing
HQ: 212f Holdings Llc
120 Orange St
Wilmington DE

(P-13935)
PATAGONIA WORKS (PA)
259 W Santa Clara St (93001-2545)
P.O. Box 150 (93002-0150)
PHONE..................805 643-8616
◆ **EMP:** 340 **EST:** 1966
SALES (est): 415.44MM
SALES (corp-wide): 415.44MM **Privately
Held**
Web: www.patagonia.com
SIC: 5699 2339 2329 5961 Uniforms and
work clothing; Sportswear, women's; Men's
and boys' sportswear and athletic clothing;
Catalog and mail-order houses

(P-13936)
SAN DIEGO LEATHER INC
Also Called: Leather.com
340 National City Blvd (91950-1111)
PHONE..................619 477-2900
Mario P Estolano, *CEO*
Nancy Estolano, *CFO*
Tony Estolano, *Mgr*
EMP: 19 **EST:** 1969
SQ FT: 20,000
SALES (est): 2.62MM **Privately Held**
Web: www.leather.com
SIC: 5699 2386 Leather garments; Pants,
leather

5712 Furniture Stores

(P-13937)
ABC HOME FURNISHINGS INC (PA)
Also Called: A.B.C. Carpet & Home
11111 Santa Monica Blvd (90025-0437)
PHONE..................212 473-3000
Aaron Rose, *CEO*
Paulette Cole, *
▲ **EMP:** 525 **EST:** 1985
SALES (est): 55.6MM
SALES (corp-wide): 55.6MM **Privately
Held**
Web: www.abchome.com
SIC: 5712 5719 5023 Furniture stores;
Beddings and linens; Homefurnishings

(P-13938)
AMES CONSTRUCTION INC
391 N Main St Ste 302 (92878-4006)
PHONE..................951 356-1275
EMP: 300
SALES (corp-wide): 1.31B **Privately Held**
Web: www.amesconstruction.com
SIC: 5712 1751 1522 1521 Customized
furniture and cabinets; Cabinet building and
installation; Residential construction, nec;
Single-family housing construction
PA: Ames Construction, Inc.
2500 County Road 42 W
Burnsville MN
952 435-7106

(P-13939)
BKM OFFICE ENVIRONMENTS INC (PA)
Also Called: Steelcase Authorized Dealer
816 Via Alondra (93012-8045)
PHONE..................805 339-6388
Peter Sloan, *CEO*
Brenda Sloan, *Pr*
EMP: 18 **EST:** 2003
SQ FT: 10,000
SALES (est): 11.37MM
SALES (corp-wide): 11.37MM **Privately
Held**
Web: www.bkmoe.com
SIC: 5712 1799 1761 2522 Office furniture;
Office furniture installation; Roofing, siding,
and sheetmetal work; Office furniture,
except wood

(P-13940)
BOYD FLOTATION INC
Also Called: Boyd Specialty Sleep
7551 Cherry Ave (92336-4276)
PHONE..................314 997-5222
Alfred Mayen, *Mgr*
EMP: 33
Web: www.boydsleep.com
SIC: 5712 2515 Mattresses; Mattresses and
bedsprings
PA: Boyd Flotation, Inc.
2440 Adie Rd
Maryland Heights MO

(P-13941)
DIAMOND MATTRESS COMPANY INC (PA)
Also Called: Diamond Mattress Nf
3112 E Las Hermanas St (90221-5513)
PHONE..................310 638-0363
Shaun Pennington, *Pr*
Breana Pennington, *
Brian Arnold, *
▲ **EMP:** 38 **EST:** 1955
SQ FT: 31,000
SALES (est): 33.46MM

SALES (corp-wide): 33.46MM **Privately
Held**
Web: diamondmattress.myshopify.com
SIC: 5712 2515 Mattresses; Bedsprings,
assembled

(P-13942)
KAISER FOUNDATION HOSPITALS
Also Called: Kaiser Prmnnte Nat Fclties Svc
3355 E 26th St (90058-4169)
PHONE..................323 264-4310
Jose Montero, *Prin*
EMP: 124
SALES (corp-wide): 68.1B **Privately Held**
Web: www.kaisercenter.com
SIC: 5712 2434 Cabinet work, custom;
Vanities, bathroom: wood
HQ: Kaiser Foundation Hospitals Inc
1 Kaiser Plz
Oakland CA
510 271-6611

(P-13943)
LIVING SPACES FURNITURE LLC
1900 University Dr (92083-7773)
PHONE..................760 945-6805
EMP: 154
SALES (corp-wide): 774.22MM **Privately
Held**
Web: www.livingspaces.com
SIC: 5712 5021 Mattresses; Furniture
PA: Living Spaces Furniture, Llc
14501 Artesia Blvd
La Mirada CA
877 266-7300

(P-13944)
LIVING SPACES FURNITURE LLC (PA)
14501 Artesia Blvd (90638-5805)
P.O. Box 2309 (90621-0809)
PHONE..................877 266-7300
Grover Geiselman, *CEO*
▲ **EMP:** 234 **EST:** 2003
SQ FT: 136,000
SALES (est): 774.22MM
SALES (corp-wide): 774.22MM **Privately
Held**
Web: www.livingspaces.com
SIC: 5712 5021 Mattresses; Furniture

(P-13945)
MODERNICA INC (PA)
Also Called: Modernica
2901 Saco St (90058-1433)
PHONE..................323 826-1600
▲ **EMP:** 50 **EST:** 1990
SALES (est): 9.96MM **Privately Held**
Web: www.modernica.net
SIC: 5712 5021 2511 2512 Furniture stores;
Furniture; Wood household furniture;
Upholstered household furniture

(P-13946)
PBK INTERNATIONAL LLC
Also Called: Phatboykustomz
717 E Compton Blvd (90220-1103)
P.O. Box 40344 (90239-1344)
PHONE..................866 727-7195
Andrew Santana, *Mgr*
EMP: 20 **EST:** 2006
SQ FT: 20,000
SALES (est): 1.39MM **Privately Held**
Web: www.pbkdecor.com
SIC: 5712 2519 Furniture stores; Furniture,
household: glass, fiberglass, and plastic

(P-13947)
ROYAL-PEDIC MATTRESS MFG LLC (PA)
341 N Robertson Blvd (90211-1705)
PHONE..................310 278-9594
Martin E Kelemen, *Managing Member*
▲ **EMP:** 22 **EST:** 1946
SQ FT: 3,200
SALES (est): 2.59MM
SALES (corp-wide): 2.59MM **Privately
Held**
Web: www.royalpedic.com
SIC: 5712 2515 Mattresses; Mattresses and
bedsprings

5713 Floor Covering Stores

(P-13948)
B & W TILE CO INC (PA)
Also Called: B & W Tile Manufacturing
14600 S Western Ave (90249-3399)
PHONE..................310 538-9579
Joe Logan, *VP*
Joseph Logan, *
Ralph Logan, *
▲ **EMP:** 35 **EST:** 1948
SQ FT: 32,000
SALES (est): 2.37MM
SALES (corp-wide): 2.37MM **Privately
Held**
Web: www.bwtile.com
SIC: 5713 3253 Floor tile; Floor tile, ceramic

(P-13949)
BLUE RIBBON DRAPERIES INC
Also Called: Drapery Affair
7341 Adams St Ste A (90723-4007)
PHONE..................562 425-4637
Roy Donald, *CEO*
Gene Donald, *Pr*
Delrose Donald, *Sec*
EMP: 27 **EST:** 1982
SQ FT: 9,000
SALES (est): 3.63MM **Privately Held**
Web:
www.draperyaffairandfloorstore.com
SIC: 5713 2391 Floor covering stores;
Cottage sets (curtains), made from
purchased materials

(P-13950)
CHRISTIAN BROS FLRG INTRORS IN
Also Called: Christian Bros Flrg Interiors
12086 Woodside Ave (92040-2916)
PHONE..................619 443-9500
Yvonne Castelli, *CEO*
Michael Castelli, *
Mike Sally, *
EMP: 80 **EST:** 1987
SQ FT: 2,800
SALES (est): 22.52MM **Privately Held**
Web: www.cbfloorsinc.com
SIC: 5713 1752 Carpets; Carpet laying

(P-13951)
FAIRPRICE ENTERPRISES INC
Also Called: Fair Price Carpets
1070 Center St (92507-1016)
PHONE..................951 684-8578
Kurt Ritz, *CEO*
Donovan Ritz, *
Marlene Ritz, *
EMP: 60 **EST:** 1957
SQ FT: 28,000
SALES (est): 4.68MM **Privately Held**
Web: www.fairpricecarpets.com

PRODUCTS & SVCS

SIC: 5713 3281 2426 5032 Carpets; Granite, cut and shaped; Flooring, hardwood; Ceramic wall and floor tile, nec

(P-13952)
NEW IMAGE COMMERCIAL FLRG INC
Also Called: New Image Flooring
10444 Corporate Dr Ste B (92374-4531)
P.O. Box 10536 (92423-0536)
PHONE..............................909 796-3400
Sergio Delgado Senior, *Pr*
Richard Delgado, *VP*
Judy Delgado, *Sec*
▲ **EMP:** 20 **EST:** 1999
SQ FT: 8,697
SALES (est): 2.44MM **Privately Held**
SIC: 5713 3996 Floor covering stores; Asphalted-felt-base floor coverings: linoleum, carpet

(P-13953)
RM PARTNERS INC
Also Called: Sterling Carpets & Flooring
1439 S State College Blvd (92806-5718)
PHONE..............................714 765-5725
Richard Mandel, *Pr*
John Ernst, *
EMP: 40 **EST:** 1962
SQ FT: 16,000
SALES (est): 4.09MM **Privately Held**
Web: www.sterlingflooring.com
SIC: 5713 1752 2273 Carpets; Carpet laying ; Dyeing and finishing of tufted rugs and carpets

5714 Drapery And Upholstery Stores

(P-13954)
SMITHS SHADE & LINOLEUM CO INC
6588 Federal Blvd (91945-1311)
P.O. Box 1488 (91946-1488)
PHONE..............................619 299-2228
Krista Neville, *VP*
Kristie Smith, *Sec*
Ralph Smith, *Stockholder*
EMP: 20 **EST:** 1934
SQ FT: 5,000
SALES (est): 2.22MM **Privately Held**
Web: www.smithshade.com
SIC: 5714 5023 2591 Curtains; Window furnishings; Shade, curtain, and drapery hardware

5719 Miscellaneous Homefurnishings

(P-13955)
AERO SHADE CO INC (PA)
Also Called: A-Z Industries Div
8404 W 3rd St (90048-4112)
PHONE..............................323 938-2314
Jack Pitson, *Pr*
Mario Soulema, *
Shelly Soulema, *
EMP: 25 **EST:** 1942
SQ FT: 2,400
SALES (est): 2.34MM
SALES (corp-wide): 2.34MM **Privately Held**
Web: www.aeroshadeco.com
SIC: 5719 2591 5023 Window furnishings; Window shades; Window shades

(P-13956)
ANNAS LINENS INC
Also Called: Annas Linens
3550 Hyland Ave (92626-1438)
PHONE..............................714 850-0504
◆ **EMP:** 2500
Web: www.annaslinens.com
SIC: 5719 5714 5023 Linens; Drapery and upholstery stores; Window covering parts and accessories

(P-13957)
BEBE STUDIO INC
Also Called: B E B E
10250 Santa Monica Blvd Ste 6 (90067-6404)
PHONE..............................213 362-2323
Manny Mashouf, *Pr*
Gary Bosch, *
Marc So, *
▲ **EMP:** 150 **EST:** 2002
SQ FT: 46,685
SALES (est): 8.54MM
SALES (corp-wide): 24.33MM **Publicly Held**
SIC: 5719 5621 5661 2339 Linens; Women's clothing stores; Women's shoes; Women's and misses' accessories
PA: Bebe Stores, Inc.
400 Valley Dr
Brisbane CA
415 715-3900

(P-13958)
COOKINGCOM INC
1960 E Grand Ave Ste 60 (90245-5099)
PHONE..............................310 664-1283
Tracy Randall, *Pr*
Bryan Handlen, *
Larry Sales, *
Laura Shaff, *
Sarah Cohen, *Content Vice President*
EMP: 150 **EST:** 1998
SQ FT: 8,000
SALES (est): 22.26MM **Privately Held**
Web: www.cooking.com
SIC: 5719 5046 Cookware, except aluminum ; Commercial cooking and food service equipment

(P-13959)
DACOR (DH)
14425 Clark Ave (91745-1235)
P.O. Box 90070 (91715-0070)
PHONE..............................626 799-1000
Stanley Michael Joseph, *Ch Bd*
Charles J Huebner, *
Steve Joseph, *
Anthony B Joseph Iii, *Prin*
◆ **EMP:** 100 **EST:** 1965
SQ FT: 40,000
SALES (est): 86.5MM **Privately Held**
Web: www.dacor.com
SIC: 5719 3631 Kitchenware; Convection ovens, including portable: household
HQ: Samsung Electronics America, Inc.
85 Challenger Rd
Ridgefield Park NJ
201 229-4000

(P-13960)
GOOD FELLAS INDUSTRIES INC
Also Called: G F I
4400 Bandini Blvd (90058-4310)
P.O. Box 861657 (90086-1657)
PHONE..............................323 924-9495
Judd A Shipper, *CEO*
◆ **EMP:** 85 **EST:** 1997
SQ FT: 40,000
SALES (est): 15.25MM **Privately Held**

Web: www.gfi-inc.net
SIC: 5719 1799 2591 Bedding (sheets, blankets, spreads, and pillows); Drapery track installation; Shade, curtain, and drapery hardware

(P-13961)
IMPRESSIONS VANITY COMPANY (PA)
17353 Derian Ave (92614-5801)
PHONE..............................844 881-0790
Dong Kevin Choi, *CEO*
EMP: 29 **EST:** 2015
SALES (est): 8.65MM
SALES (corp-wide): 8.65MM **Privately Held**
Web: www.impressionsvanity.com
SIC: 5719 5063 2531 Mirrors; Lighting fixtures; Chairs, table and arm

(P-13962)
LA LINEN INC
1760 E 15th St (90021-2716)
PHONE..............................213 745-4004
Danny Levy, *CEO*
EMP: 30 **EST:** 2010
SQ FT: 16,500
SALES (est): 2.4MM **Privately Held**
Web: www.lalinen.com
SIC: 5719 2392 2391 Linens; Tablecloths and table settings; Curtains and draperies

(P-13963)
LINEN SALVAGE ET CIE LLC
1073 Stearns Dr (90035-2638)
PHONE..............................323 904-3100
Andrea Bernstein, *Prin*
EMP: 36 **EST:** 2018
SALES (est): 1.21MM **Privately Held**
Web: www.linensalvageetcie.com
SIC: 5719 2269 Linens; Linen fabrics: dyeing, finishing, and printing

(P-13964)
NORTH RANCH MANAGEMENT CORP
9754 Deering Ave (91311-4301)
PHONE..............................800 410-2153
Richard Goldman, *CEO*
▲ **EMP:** 70 **EST:** 2000
SALES (est): 9.88MM **Privately Held**
Web: www.dreamproducts.com
SIC: 5719 3171 3172 4813 Housewares, nec ; Women's handbags and purses; Wallets; Online service providers

(P-13965)
PRIORITY LIGHTING INC
77551 El Duna Ct Ste H (92211-4147)
PHONE..............................800 709-1119
EMP: 18 **EST:** 2009
SALES (est): 2.25MM **Privately Held**
Web: www.prioritylighting.com
SIC: 5719 3648 5063 Lighting fixtures; Lighting equipment, nec; Lighting fittings and accessories

(P-13966)
PROTEIN KITCHEN
13448 Manhasset Rd Ste 3 (92308-5799)
PHONE..............................888 899-2956
Jose Villalobos, *Pr*
EMP: 25 **EST:** 2018
SALES (est): 1.43MM **Privately Held**
Web: www.biodefensor.com
SIC: 5719 5075 3564 3569 Kitchenware; Air filters; Filters, air: furnaces, air conditioning equipment, etc.; Filters

(P-13967)
SKYCO SHADING SYSTEMS INC
3411 W Fordham Ave (92704-4422)
PHONE..............................714 708-3038
Sandra Young, *Pr*
▲ **EMP:** 28 **EST:** 1994
SQ FT: 16,000
SALES (est): 5.87MM **Privately Held**
Web: www.skycoshade.com
SIC: 5719 2431 Window furnishings; Millwork

5722 Household Appliance Stores

(P-13968)
JOHNSTONE SUPPLY INC
Also Called: Johnson Contrls Authorized Dlr
8040 Slauson Ave (90640-6620)
PHONE..............................323 722-2859
William J Salpaka, *Pr*
EMP: 92
SALES (corp-wide): 1.18B **Privately Held**
Web: www.johnsoncontrols.com
SIC: 5722 3585 5075 Gas household appliances; Parts for heating, cooling, and refrigerating equipment; Warm air heating and air conditioning
HQ: Johnstone Supply, Llc
11632 Ne Ainsworth Cir
Portland OR
503 256-3663

(P-13969)
PORTABLE CLERS SLS RENTALS INC
1250 Pacific Oaks Pl Ste 101 (92029-2908)
P.O. Box 460822 (92046-0822)
PHONE..............................760 747-9591
Mary Tennison, *Pr*
Don Tennison, *VP*
EMP: 18 **EST:** 1995
SALES (est): 2.03MM **Privately Held**
Web: www.portablecoolers.com
SIC: 5722 3585 1711 Air conditioning room units, self-contained; Parts for heating, cooling, and refrigerating equipment; Heating and air conditioning contractors

5734 Computer And Software Stores

(P-13970)
COAST TO COAST CMPT PDTS INC
4277 Valley Fair St (93063-2940)
PHONE..............................805 244-9500
Rick Roussin, *Pr*
Wendy Roussin, *
Stacy Schulman, *
▼ **EMP:** 110 **EST:** 1985
SQ FT: 8,800
SALES (est): 49.36MM **Privately Held**
Web: www.coastcoast.com
SIC: 5734 7373 7371 5112 Magnetic disks; Computer systems analysis and design; Computer software systems analysis and design, custom; Stationery and office supplies

(P-13971)
GOSECURE INC (PA)
13220 Evening Creek Dr S Ste 107 (92128-4103)
PHONE..............................301 442-3432
Neal Creighton, *CEO*
Neal Creighton, *Pr*
Robert J Mccullen, *Ofcr*

Richard Miller, *COO*
Thalia Gietzen, *CFO*
EMP: 178 **EST:** 2004
SALES (est): 22.51MM **Privately Held**
Web: www.gosecure.net
SIC: 5734 7382 7372 7373 Computer software and accessories; Protective devices, security; Publisher's computer software; Computer systems analysis and design

(P-13972)
GURUCUL SOLUTIONS LLC
222 N Pacific Coast Hwy Ste 1322 (90245)
PHONE.....................213 291-6888
Saryu Nayyar, *
Jasen Meece, *
Nilesh Dherange, *
EMP: 48 **EST:** 2010
SQ FT: 4,360
SALES (est): 5.05MM **Privately Held**
Web: www.gurucul.com
SIC: 5734 7372 Software, business and non-game; Publisher's computer software

(P-13973)
JAM CITY INC (PA)
Also Called: Social Gaming Network
3562 Eastham Dr (90232-2409)
PHONE.....................310 205-4800
EMP: 20 **EST:** 2007
SQ FT: 5,000
SALES (est): 59.07MM
SALES (corp-wide): 59.07MM **Privately Held**
Web: www.jamcity.com
SIC: 5734 3944 Software, computer games; Games, toys, and children's vehicles

(P-13974)
PCFS SOLUTIONS
Also Called: Pcfs 2000
6353 El Cajon Blvd Ste 124 (92115-2655)
PHONE.....................714 674-0009
Robert Cota, *Pr*
EMP: 21 **EST:** 1998
SALES (est): 2.47MM **Privately Held**
Web: www.pcfssolutions.com
SIC: 5734 2731 Computer software and accessories; Book publishing

(P-13975)
VELARO INCORPORATED
1234 N La Brea Ave (90038-1179)
PHONE.....................800 983-5276
Alex Bloom, *CEO*
Jasen Fici, *
Alex Bloom, *VP*
EMP: 95 **EST:** 2000
SALES (est): 4.42MM **Privately Held**
Web: www.velaro.com
SIC: 5734 7371 Software, business and non-game; Computer software development and applications

5736 Musical Instrument Stores

(P-13976)
AQUARIAN ACCESSORIES CORP
Also Called: Aquarian Drumheads
600 N Batavia St (92868-1221)
PHONE.....................714 632-0230
Ronald Marquez, *Pr*
Ray Burns, *VP Mktg*
Dave Donahue, *Treas*
Rose Marquez, *Sec*
EMP: 19 **EST:** 1980

SALES (est): 2.44MM **Privately Held**
Web: www.aquariandrumheads.com
SIC: 5736 3931 Musical instrument stores; Accordions and parts

(P-13977)
CARVIN CORP
Also Called: Carvin Guitars & Pro Sound
16262 W Bernardo Dr (92127-1879)
PHONE.....................858 487-1600
Carson Kiesel, *CEO*
Carson L Kiesel, *
Jon Kiesel, *
Paul Kiesel, *
Mark Kiesel, *
◆ **EMP:** 179 **EST:** 1946
SQ FT: 82,000
SALES (est): 8.85MM **Privately Held**
Web: www.carvinaudio.com
SIC: 5736 3931 Musical instrument stores; Guitars and parts, electric and nonelectric

(P-13978)
DEERING BANJO COMPANY INC
3733 Kenora Dr (91977-1206)
PHONE.....................619 464-8252
Charles Greg Deering, *Pr*
Janet Deering, *Sec*
▲ **EMP:** 40 **EST:** 1975
SQ FT: 18,000
SALES (est): 8.19MM **Privately Held**
Web: www.deeringbanjos.com
SIC: 5736 3548 Musical instrument stores; Welding and cutting apparatus and accessories, nec

5812 Eating Places

(P-13979)
ACCOR CORP
Also Called: Sofitel Los Angeles
8555 Beverly Blvd (90048-3303)
PHONE.....................310 278-5444
Gunter Zweimuller, *Pr*
EMP: 200 **EST:** 1986
SQ FT: 380,000
SALES (est): 24.41MM
SALES (corp-wide): 713.02MM **Privately Held**
Web: www.sofitel-los-angeles.com
SIC: 5812 7011 Eating places; Hotels
PA: Accor
82 Rue Henry Farman
Issy Les Moulineaux
146429193

(P-13980)
AIR FAYRE USA INC
1720 W 135th St (90249-2508)
PHONE.....................310 808-1061
Stephen Yapp, *CEO*
Joe Golio, *
EMP: 200 **EST:** 2008
SALES (est): 24.56MM **Privately Held**
Web: www.airfayre.com
SIC: 5812 2099 Caterers; Box lunches, for sale off premises
HQ: Journey Group Limited
One Bartholomew Close
London

(P-13981)
APPLE FARM COLLECTIONS-SLO INC (PA)
2015 Monterey St (93401-2617)
PHONE.....................805 544-2040
John E King, *Pr*
Carole D King, *
▼ **EMP:** 290 **EST:** 1977

SQ FT: 51,000
SALES (est): 11.74MM
SALES (corp-wide): 11.74MM **Privately Held**
Web: www.applefarm.com
SIC: 5812 7011 5947 Restaurant, family; independent; Motor inn; Gift shop

(P-13982)
BELMONT BREWING COMPANY INC
Also Called: B B C
25 39th Pl (90803-2806)
PHONE.....................562 433-3891
David Hansen, *Pr*
David Lott, *
Jessica Bellows, *
EMP: 21 **EST:** 1989
SQ FT: 7,000
SALES (est): 1.17MM **Privately Held**
Web: www.belmontbrewing.com
SIC: 5812 2082 American restaurant; Malt beverages

(P-13983)
BENIHANA INC
Also Called: Benihana 24
16226 Ventura Blvd (91436-2271)
PHONE.....................818 788-7121
Shugo Kanai, *Genl Mgr*
EMP: 96
SALES (corp-wide): 2.14B **Privately Held**
Web: www.benihana.com
SIC: 5812 7299 5813 Japanese restaurant; Banquet hall facilities; Cocktail lounge
HQ: Benihana Inc.
21500 Biscayne Blvd # 100
Miami FL
305 593-0770

(P-13984)
BEYOND FRANCHISE GROUP INC
Also Called: Pokeworks
220 Technology Dr Ste 120 (92618-2456)
PHONE.....................949 398-7338
EMP: 190 **EST:** 2017
SALES (est): 1.77MM **Privately Held**
Web: www.pokeworks.com
SIC: 5812 6794 Ethnic food restaurants; Franchises, selling or licensing

(P-13985)
BOILING CRAB OPERATIONS LLC
Also Called: Boiling Crab, The
5811 Mcfadden Ave (92649-1323)
PHONE.....................714 636-4885
Dada Ngo, *Managing Member*
Sinh Nguyen, *
Angela Nguyen, *
Hai Nguyen, *
EMP: 270 **EST:** 2013
SALES (est): 12.39MM **Privately Held**
Web: www.theboilingcrab.com
SIC: 5812 6794 Cajun restaurant; Franchises, selling or licensing

(P-13986)
BONAVENTURE BREWING CO INC
Also Called: Bonaventure Brewing Co
404 S Figueroa St Ste 418a (90071-1797)
PHONE.....................213 236-0802
Loren Zimmerman, *Pt*
EMP: 25 **EST:** 1997
SQ FT: 10,000
SALES (est): 974.43K **Privately Held**
Web: www.bonaventurebrewing.com

SIC: 5812 5813 2082 Chicken restaurant; Bars and lounges; Beer (alcoholic beverage)

(P-13987)
BW HOTEL LLC
Also Called: Buffalo Wild Wings
9500 Wilshire Blvd (90212-2405)
PHONE.....................310 275-5200
Kathleen Taylor, *CEO*
▲ **EMP:** 820 **EST:** 1928
SALES (est): 53.98MM **Privately Held**
Web: www.buffalowildwings.com
SIC: 5812 7011 Grills (eating places); Hotels and motels

(P-13988)
CAFE 21 GASLAMP INC
Also Called: Cafe 21
2736 Adams Ave (92116-1312)
PHONE.....................619 795-0721
Emran Javadov, *CEO*
EMP: 20 **EST:** 2011
SALES (est): 1.97MM **Privately Held**
Web: www.cafe-21.com
SIC: 5812 2099 Cafe; Food preparations, nec

(P-13989)
CALIFORNIA GARLIC COMPANY INC
Also Called: Garlic King
7651 Saint Andrews Ave (92154-8209)
PHONE.....................951 506-8883
John Rosingana, *Pr*
Peter Tarantino, *
EMP: 44 **EST:** 1999
SALES (est): 1.34MM **Privately Held**
Web: www.garlicking.net
SIC: 5812 2099 Eating places; Food preparations, nec

(P-13990)
CALIMEX DELI
711 1/2 S Kern Ave (90022-2574)
PHONE.....................323 261-7271
EMP: 20 **EST:** 1994
SQ FT: 50,000
SALES (est): 981.46K **Privately Held**
Web: www.ordercalimexdeli.com
SIC: 5812 2051 Delicatessen (eating places); ; Bakery: wholesale or wholesale/retail combined

(P-13991)
CARPENTERS SOUTHWEST ADM CORP
Also Called: Pea Soup Andersen's Restaurant
376 Avenue Of The Flags (93427-9704)
P.O. Box 195 (93427-0195)
PHONE.....................805 688-5581
Ed Sarbinie, *Mgr*
EMP: 239
SALES (corp-wide): 45.94MM **Privately Held**
Web: www.peasoupandersens.net
SIC: 5812 7299 Eating places; Banquet hall facilities
PA: Carpenters Southwest Administrative Corporation
533 S Fremont Ave
Los Angeles CA
213 386-8590

(P-13992)
CASTLE IMPORTING INC
14550 Miller Ave (92336-1696)
PHONE.....................909 428-9200
Rosangela Borruso, *CEO*
Marc Zadra, *

Richard White, *
▲ **EMP:** 45 **EST:** 1989
SALES (est): 7.28MM **Privately Held**
Web: www.castleimporting.com
SIC: 5812 2022 Eating places; Processed cheese

(P-13993)
CCF CHINA OPERATING CORP
26901 Malibu Hills Rd (91301-5354)
PHONE..............................818 871-3000
David Overton, *CEO*
EMP: 25 **EST:** 2014
SALES (est): 600.55K **Publicly Held**
SIC: 5812 2051 American restaurant; Cakes, bakery: except frozen
PA: The Cheesecake Factory Incorporated
26901 Malibu Hills Rd
Calabasas Hills CA

(P-13994)
CHEESECAKE FACTORY BAKERY INC
26950 Agoura Rd (91301-5335)
PHONE..............................818 871-3000
Keith T Carango, *CEO*
David Overton, *
Max Byfuglin, *
▲ **EMP:** 500 **EST:** 1972
SQ FT: 60,000
SALES (est): 49.85MM **Publicly Held**
Web:
www.thecheesecakefactorybakery.com
SIC: 5812 2051 Eating places; Cakes, bakery: except frozen
PA: The Cheesecake Factory Incorporated
26901 Malibu Hills Rd
Calabasas Hills CA

(P-13995)
CHEESECAKE FACTORY INC (PA)
Also Called: Cheesecake Factory, The
26901 Malibu Hills Rd (91301-5354)
PHONE..............................818 871-3000
David Overton, *Ch Bd*
David M Gordon, *Pr*
Matthew E Clark, *Ex VP*
Scarlett May, *Ex VP*
▲ **EMP:** 350 **EST:** 1972
SQ FT: 88,000
SALES (est): 3.3B **Publicly Held**
Web: www.thecheesecakefactory.com
SIC: 5812 2051 American restaurant; Cakes, bakery: except frozen

(P-13996)
CHOP STOP INC
601 N Glendale Ave (91206-2408)
PHONE..............................818 369-7350
Mark Kulkis, *CEO*
EMP: 97 **EST:** 2010
SALES (est): 5.36MM **Privately Held**
Web: www.chopstop.com
SIC: 5812 6794 Fast food restaurants and stands; Franchises, selling or licensing

(P-13997)
CITADEL PANDA EXPRESS INC
Also Called: Panda Express
899 El Centro St Ste 201 (91030-3101)
PHONE..............................626 799-9898
EMP: 118 **EST:** 1990
SQ FT: 10,000
SALES (est): 2.06MM
SALES (corp-wide): 1.64B **Privately Held**
Web: www.pandaexpress.com
SIC: 5812 6794 Chinese restaurant; Franchises, selling or licensing
HQ: Panda Express, Inc.
1683 Walnut Grove Ave

Rosemead CA

(P-13998)
CITRUS RESTAURANT LLC
8110 Aero Dr (92123-1715)
PHONE..............................858 277-8888
Kate Mendez, *Genl Mgr*
EMP: 145 **EST:** 2010
SALES (est): 4.38MM **Privately Held**
SIC: 5812 7011 American restaurant; Hotels

(P-13999)
DAD INVESTMENTS
Also Called: Cater Tots Too
2929 Halladay St (92705-5622)
PHONE..............................714 751-8500
Nadia Tayob, *Pr*
EMP: 22 **EST:** 2016
SALES (est): 1.79MM **Privately Held**
SIC: 5812 2099 Caterers; Food preparations, nec

(P-14000)
DEL TACO RESTAURANTS INC (PA)
Also Called: Del Taco
25521 Commercentre Dr Ste 200 (92630-8872)
PHONE..............................949 462-9300
Lawrence F Levy, *Ch Bd*
Chad Gretzema, *Pr*
Steven L Brake, *Ex VP*
David A Pear, *VP Opers*
M Barry Westrum, *CMO*
EMP: 169 **EST:** 1964
SQ FT: 37,500
SALES (est): 527.36MM
SALES (corp-wide): 527.36MM **Privately Held**
Web: www.deltaco.com
SIC: 5812 6794 Fast-food restaurant, chain; Franchises, selling or licensing

(P-14001)
DICKEYS BARBECUE REST INC
Also Called: Dickeys Barbecue Pit
17245 17th St (92780-1974)
PHONE..............................714 602-3874
Roland Dickey, *Brnch Mgr*
EMP: 30
SALES (corp-wide): 97.59MM **Privately Held**
Web: www.dickeys.com
SIC: 5812 2033 Barbecue restaurant; Tomato products, packaged in cans, jars, etc.
HQ: Dickey's Barbecue Restaurants, Inc.
850 Central Pkwy E # 140
Plano TX
972 248-9899

(P-14002)
DINE BRANDS GLOBAL INC (PA)
Also Called: Dine Brands Global
10 W Walnut St Fl 5 (91103-3633)
PHONE..............................818 240-6055
Stephen P Joyce, *CEO*
Richard J Dahl, *
Thomas H Song, *CFO*
Bryan R Adel, *Senior Vice President Legal*
Justin Skelton, *CIO*
EMP: 500 **EST:** 1958
SALES (est): 909.4MM
SALES (corp-wide): 909.4MM **Publicly Held**
Web: www.dinebrands.com
SIC: 5812 6794 Restaurant, family: chain; Franchises, selling or licensing

(P-14003)
DON WHITTEMORE CORP
Also Called: Dandy Don's Gourmet Ice Cream
501 Library St (91340-2523)
PHONE..............................818 994-0111
Linda Whittemore, *Pr*
Don Whittemore, *VP*
EMP: 23 **EST:** 1975
SALES (est): 656.92K **Privately Held**
Web: www.dandydons.com
SIC: 5812 2024 8743 5947 Caterers; Ice cream and ice milk; Public relations services ; Gifts and novelties

(P-14004)
EL POLLO LOCO HOLDINGS INC (PA)
3535 Harbor Blvd Ste 100 (92626-1494)
PHONE..............................714 599-5000
Laurance Roberts, *Pr*
Laurance Roberts, *Pr*
Michael G Maselli, *
Ira Fils, *Ex VP*
Maria Hollandsworth, *COO*
EMP: 156 **EST:** 1980
SQ FT: 29,880
SALES (est): 469.96MM **Publicly Held**
Web: www.elpolloloco.com
SIC: 5812 6794 Eating places; Franchises, selling or licensing

(P-14005)
FAHETAS LLC (PA)
Also Called: Green Tomato Grill
1419 N Tustin St Ste A (92867-3922)
PHONE..............................949 280-1983
Kyle Markt, *Managing Member*
Chris Stern, *
Michael Moore, *
Bruce Whistnant, *
Nicole Piscetelli, *
EMP: 100 **EST:** 2012
SALES (est): 4MM
SALES (corp-wide): 4MM **Privately Held**
Web: www.greentomatogrill.com
SIC: 5812 7371 Fast-food restaurant, chain; Computer software development and applications

(P-14006)
FAT BRANDS INC (PA)
9720 Wilshire Blvd Ste 500 (90212-2021)
PHONE..............................310 319-1850
Andrew A Wiederhorn, *Ch Bd*
James C Neuhauser, *Ex Ch Bd*
Edward H Rensi, *V Ch Bd*
EMP: 332 **EST:** 2017
SQ FT: 9,052
SALES (est): 407.22MM
SALES (corp-wide): 407.22MM **Publicly Held**
Web: www.fatbrands.com
SIC: 5812 6794 Restaurant, family: chain; Franchises, selling or licensing

(P-14007)
FGR 1 LLC
Also Called: Fresh Griller
3191 Red Hill Ave Ste 100 (92626-3451)
PHONE..............................800 653-3517
Anand Gala, *Managing Member*
EMP: 40 **EST:** 2011
SALES (est): 1.15MM **Privately Held**
SIC: 5812 7372 American restaurant; Application computer software

(P-14008)
FISH HOUSE PARTNERS ONE LLC

Also Called: Restaurants Bars & Food Svcs
5955 Melrose Ave (90038-3623)
PHONE..............................323 460-4170
Michael Cimarusti, *Managing Member*
Cristina Echiverri, *
EMP: 96 **EST:** 2015
SALES (est): 1.53MM **Privately Held**
SIC: 5812 6799 Seafood restaurants; Investors, nec

(P-14009)
FLORENCE MEAT PACKING CO INC
Also Called: F M P
9840 Everest St (90242-3114)
PHONE..............................562 401-0760
EMP: 35
SIC: 5812 2011 Eating places; Meat packing plants

(P-14010)
GAMEWORKS ENTERTAINMENT LLC (PA)
9737 Lurline Ave (91311-4404)
PHONE..............................206 521-0952
EMP: 620
SALES (est): 16.39MM
SALES (corp-wide): 16.39MM **Privately Held**
SIC: 5812 7993 Eating places; Video game arcade

(P-14011)
HANDELS HOMEMADE ICE CREAM
Also Called: Handel's Ice Cream
6403 Haven Ave (91737-3861)
PHONE..............................909 989-7065
EMP: 22 **EST:** 2012
SALES (est): 167.66K **Privately Held**
Web: www.handelsicecream.com
SIC: 5812 5149 2052 Ice cream stands or dairy bars; Bakery products; Cones, ice cream

(P-14012)
HIDEAWAY
80440 Hideaway Club Ct (92253-7867)
PHONE..............................760 777-7400
Shawn Ygnatowiz, *Genl Mgr*
Mike Finnell, *Prin*
EMP: 150 **EST:** 2006
SALES (est): 2.37MM **Privately Held**
Web: www.hideawaygolfclub.com
SIC: 5812 7041 Grills (eating places); Residence club, organization

(P-14013)
HOUSTON CHEESECAKE FCTRY CORP
26901 Malibu Hills Rd (91301-5354)
PHONE..............................818 871-3000
Michael Alan Rivero, *Pr*
EMP: 64 **EST:** 1995
SALES (est): 906.41K **Publicly Held**
Web: www.thecheesecakefactory.com
SIC: 5812 2051 American restaurant; Cakes, bakery: except frozen
PA: The Cheesecake Factory Incorporated
26901 Malibu Hills Rd
Calabasas Hills CA

(P-14014)
HUXTABLES KITCHEN INC
Also Called: Huxtable's
2100 E 49th St (90058-2825)
P.O. Box 2847 (90058)
PHONE..............................323 923-2900
▲ **EMP:** 100

Web: www.huxtables.com
SIC: 5812 2099 2015 2013 Eating places; Ready-to-eat meals, salads, and sandwiches; Poultry slaughtering and processing; Sausages and other prepared meats

(P-14015)

IL FORNAIO (AMERICA) LLC

16932 Valley View Ave Ste A (90638-5826)
PHONE....................714 752-7052
Luis Espinoza, *Brnch Mgr*
EMP: 142
SALES (corp-wide): 8.04B **Privately Held**
Web: www.ilfornaio.com
SIC: 5812 5813 5149 2051 Italian restaurant ; Drinking places; Bakery products; Bread, cake, and related products
HQ: Il Fornaio (America) Llc
770 Tamalpais Dr Ste 208
Corte Madera CA
415 945-0500

(P-14016)

JACK IN BOX INC (PA)

Also Called: Jack In The Box
9357 Spectrum Center Blvd (92123-1524)
P.O. Box 23447 (92193-3447)
PHONE....................858 571-2121
Darin S Harris, *CEO*
David L Goebel, *Non-Executive Chairman of the Board**
Dawn E Hooper, *Interim Chief Financial Officer*
Ryan Ostrom, *CMO*
Tony Darden, *Sr VP*
▲ **EMP:** 546 **EST:** 1951
SQ FT: 70,000
SALES (est): 1.69B
SALES (corp-wide): 1.69B **Publicly Held**
Web: www.jackinthebox.com
SIC: 5812 6794 Fast-food restaurant, chain; Franchises, selling or licensing

(P-14017)

JMJ ENTERPRISES INC

Also Called: Someone's In The Kitchen
5973 Reseda Blvd (91356-1505)
PHONE....................818 343-5151
Joann Roth Oseary, *Pr*
Jason Perel, ***
EMP: 120 **EST:** 1981
SQ FT: 6,000
SALES (est): 4.2MM **Privately Held**
Web: www.sitk.com
SIC: 5812 7299 7359 Caterers; Party planning service; Sound and lighting equipment rental

(P-14018)

KING EXPRESS INC

Also Called: King Ex Chinese Fd & Donut
12053 Vanowen St (91605-5962)
PHONE....................818 503-2772
Joel Lim, *Mgr*
EMP: 18 **EST:** 1993
SALES (est): 220.81K **Privately Held**
SIC: 5812 2051 Chinese restaurant; Doughnuts, except frozen

(P-14019)

KINGS HAWAIIAN BAKERY W INC (HQ)

Also Called: Kings Hawaiian Bakery
1411 W 190th St (90248-4324)
PHONE....................310 533-3250
Mark Taira, *Pr*
Curtis Taira, ***
Leatrice Taira, ***
Vaughn Taira, ***

Stella Taira, ***
▲ **EMP:** 25 **EST:** 1950
SALES (est): 142.54MM
SALES (corp-wide): 153.92MM **Privately Held**
Web: www.kingshawaiian.com
SIC: 5812 5142 2051 Restaurant, family: independent; Bakery products, frozen; Bread, cake, and related products
PA: King's Hawaiian Holding Company, Inc.
19161 Harborgate Way
Torrance CA
310 533-3250

(P-14020)

KLATCH COFFEE INC (PA)

Also Called: Coffee Klatch
8767 Onyx Ave (91730-4533)
PHONE....................909 981-4031
Mike Perry, *CEO*
Heather Perry, *VP*
Cindy Perry, *Sec*
EMP: 20 **EST:** 1993
SQ FT: 2,400
SALES (est): 4.36MM **Privately Held**
Web: shop.klatchcoffee.com
SIC: 5812 2095 Coffee shop; Coffee extracts

(P-14021)

LAS GLONDRINAS MEXICAN FD PDTS (PA)

27124 Paseo Espada Ste 803 (92675-6787)
PHONE....................949 240-3440
Arturo Galindo Junior, *Pr*
Maria Galindo, *Sec*
EMP: 18 **EST:** 1984
SQ FT: 3,000
SALES (est): 1.88MM
SALES (corp-wide): 1.88MM **Privately Held**
Web: www.lasgolondrinas.biz
SIC: 5812 2099 Mexican restaurant; Tortillas, fresh or refrigerated

(P-14022)

LAWRYS RESTAURANTS II INC

Also Called: Tam O'Shanter Inn
2980 Los Feliz Blvd (90039-1524)
PHONE....................323 664-0228
Bryan Lytle, *Mgr*
EMP: 177
SALES (corp-wide): 25.93MM **Privately Held**
Web: www.lawrysonline.com
SIC: 5812 7299 Steak restaurant; Banquet hall facilities
PA: Lawry's Restaurants Ii, Inc.
100 N La Cienega Blvd
Beverly Hills CA
626 440-5234

(P-14023)

LOFTY COFFEE INC

97 N Coast Highway 101 Ste 101 (92024-3282)
PHONE....................760 230-6747
Eric Myers, *CEO*
EMP: 100 **EST:** 2011
SALES (est): 4.26MM **Privately Held**
Web: www.loftycoffee.com
SIC: 5812 2095 Coffee shop; Coffee roasting (except by wholesale grocers)

(P-14024)

LOS ALAMITOS RACE COURSE

Also Called: Vessels Club Restaurant
4961 Katella Ave (90720-2721)
PHONE....................714 820-2800
Edward Allred, *Pt*

EMP: 200 **EST:** 1943
SQ FT: 2,000
SALES (est): 9.23MM **Privately Held**
Web: www.losalamitos.com
SIC: 5812 7948 5813 5963 Eating places; Horses, racing; Bar (drinking places); Direct selling establishments

(P-14025)

MAGIC CASTLES INC

7001 Franklin Ave (90028-8600)
PHONE....................323 851-3313
Milton P Larsen, *CEO*
Ron Wilson, ***
Bruce Cervon, ***
EMP: 100 **EST:** 1962
SQ FT: 20,000
SALES (est): 7.93MM **Privately Held**
Web: www.magiccastle.com
SIC: 5812 7997 7991 Eating places; Membership sports and recreation clubs; Physical fitness facilities

(P-14026)

MEXICALI INC

Also Called: Mexicali Restaurant
631 18th St (93301-4934)
PHONE....................661 327-3861
Sunny Crews, *Mgr*
EMP: 115
SALES (corp-wide): 4.39MM **Privately Held**
Web: www.mexicalirestaurants.com
SIC: 5812 5813 7299 Mexican restaurant; Bar (drinking places); Banquet hall facilities
PA: Mexicali, Inc.
419 Baker St
Bakersfield CA
661 327-4218

(P-14027)

MSR DESERT RESORT LP

Also Called: Hotel Associates Palm Springs
49499 Eisenhower Dr (92253-2722)
P.O. Box 659 (92247-0659)
PHONE....................760 564-5730
Michael Shannon, *Pt*
John Saer, *VP*
Nola Dyal, *VP*
Stephen Elliott, *VP*
Larry Scheerer, *VP*
▲ **EMP:** 1500 **EST:** 1926
SALES (est): 55.18MM **Privately Held**
Web: www.laquintavilla.com
SIC: 5812 7011 7997 5813 Eating places; Motel, franchised; Tennis club, membership ; Drinking places

(P-14028)

OGGIS PIZZA & BREWING COMPANY

305 Encinitas Blvd (92024-3724)
PHONE....................760 944-8170
Cherock Alcaser, *Pr*
EMP: 25 **EST:** 1998
SQ FT: 6,500
SALES (est): 397.6K **Privately Held**
Web: www.oggis.com
SIC: 5812 2082 Pizzeria, chain; Beer (alcoholic beverage)

(P-14029)

PANDA SYSTEMS INC

Also Called: Panda Express
1683 Walnut Grove Ave (91770-3711)
P.O. Box 1159 (91770-1011)
PHONE....................626 799-9898
Andrew J Cherng, *Ch Bd*
Peggy T Cherng, ***
EMP: 130 **EST:** 1988

SQ FT: 10,000
SALES (est): 9.44MM
SALES (corp-wide): 1.64B **Privately Held**
Web: www.pandaexpress.com
SIC: 5812 6794 Chinese restaurant; Franchises, selling or licensing
PA: Panda Restaurant Group, Inc.
1683 Walnut Grove Ave
Rosemead CA
626 799-9898

(P-14030)

PBF & E LLC

Also Called: Guelaguetza
3014 W Olympic Blvd (90006-2516)
PHONE....................213 427-0340
Bricia Lopez, *Managing Member*
EMP: 50 **EST:** 2000
SALES (est): 4.42MM **Privately Held**
Web: www.ilovemole.com
SIC: 5812 2087 Mexican restaurant; Cocktail mixes, nonalcoholic

(P-14031)

PIE RISE LTD

Also Called: Marie Callender's Pie Shops
29051 S Western Ave (90275-0806)
PHONE....................310 832-4559
Jim Louder, *Pt*
John Turner, *Pt*
EMP: 50 **EST:** 1971
SQ FT: 5,000
SALES (est): 977.87K **Privately Held**
Web: www.mariecallenders.com
SIC: 5812 2051 5461 Restaurant, family: chain; Pies, bakery: except frozen; Retail bakeries

(P-14032)

QDOBA RESTAURANT CORPORATION (HQ)

Also Called: Qdoba Mexican Grill
350 Camino De La Reina Fl 4 (92108)
PHONE....................858 766-4900
Susan Daggett, *CFO*
EMP: 125 **EST:** 1995
SALES (est): 128.18MM
SALES (corp-wide): 407.13MM **Privately Held**
Web: www.qdoba.com
SIC: 5812 6794 Mexican restaurant; Franchises, selling or licensing
PA: Modern Restaurant Concepts Holdings, Llc
3001 Brighton Blvd
Denver CO
917 667-7972

(P-14033)

REDONDO BEACH BREWING CO INC

1814 S Catalina Ave (90277-5505)
PHONE....................310 316-8477
John Waters, *CFO*
David Zislis, *Pr*
EMP: 21 **EST:** 1993
SQ FT: 4,500
SALES (est): 406.21K **Privately Held**
Web: www.redondobeachbrewco.com
SIC: 5812 2082 5813 Chicken restaurant; Beer (alcoholic beverage); Drinking places

(P-14034)

SANTA BARBARA COFFEE & TEA INC

Also Called: Santa Barbarba Roasting
321 Motor Way (93101-3436)
PHONE....................805 898-3700
Corey Russell, *CEO*

PRODUCTS & SVCS

EMP: 36 **EST:** 1988
SQ FT: 4,700
SALES (est): 977.06K **Privately Held**
Web: www.sbcoffee.com
SIC: 5812 2095 Coffee shop; Coffee roasting (except by wholesale grocers)

(P-14035)
SEVERSON GROUP LLC
Also Called: Severson Group, The
950 Boardwalk Ste 202 (92078-2600)
PHONE....................760 550-9976
Robert Severson, *Managing Member*
EMP: 200 **EST:** 2006
SQ FT: 10,000
SALES (est): 9.41MM **Privately Held**
Web: www.theseversongroup.com
SIC: 5812 8741 8742 8748 Contract food services; Management services; Management consulting services; Systems engineering consultant, ex. computer or professional

(P-14036)
SKYLAR CREATIONS INC
Also Called: Gelato Love
5661 Palmer Way Ste C (92010-7255)
PHONE....................760 814-8260
Paola Richard, *Pr*
EMP: 17 **EST:** 2017
SALES (est): 464.23K **Privately Held**
Web: www.gelato.love
SIC: 5812 2024 Ice cream stands or dairy bars; Ice cream and frozen deserts

(P-14037)
SPECIALTY RESTAURANTS CORP
Also Called: Castaway Restaurant, The
1250 E Harvard Rd (91501-1002)
PHONE....................818 843-5013
Saeed Fazeli, *Genl Mgr*
EMP: 241
SALES (corp-wide): 201.1MM **Privately Held**
Web: www.castawayburbank.com
SIC: 5812 7299 American restaurant; Banquet hall facilities
PA: Specialty Restaurants Corporation
150 Paularino Ave Bldg C
Costa Mesa CA
714 279-6100

(P-14038)
SYCUAN TRIBAL DEVELOPMENT
Also Called: Sycuan Resort
1530 Hilton Head Rd Ste 210 (92019-4655)
PHONE....................619 442-3425
Daniel Tucker, *Ch Bd*
Glen Quiroga, *
Codey Martinez, *
EMP: 250 **EST:** 2001
SALES (est): 8.77MM **Privately Held**
SIC: 5812 7992 7011 Eating places; Public golf courses; Hotels and motels
PA: Sycuan Band Of Kumeyaay Nation
3007 Dehesa Rd
El Cajon CA
619 445-6002

(P-14039)
TACO BELL CORP (HQ)
Also Called: Taco Bell
1 Glen Bell Way (92618-3344)
PHONE....................949 863-4500
Mark King, *CEO*
Nikki Lawson Global, *Chief Brand Officer*
▲ **EMP:** 1025 **EST:** 1962
SQ FT: 278,000
SALES (est): 508.54MM
SALES (corp-wide): 6.84B **Publicly Held**
Web: www.tacobell.com
SIC: 5812 6794 Fast-food restaurant, chain; Franchises, selling or licensing
PA: Yum Brands, Inc.
1441 Gardiner Ln
Louisville KY
502 874-8300

(P-14040)
TS ENTERPRISES INC
Also Called: La Quinta Cliff House
78250 Highway 111 (92253-2074)
PHONE....................760 360-5991
David Potesta, *Brnch Mgr*
EMP: 33
SALES (corp-wide): 23.29MM **Privately Held**
Web: www.laquintacliffhouse.com
SIC: 5812 5699 5261 2791 American restaurant; Custom tailor; Lawn and garden supplies; Typesetting
PA: T.S. Enterprises, Inc
225 W Plaza St Ste 300
Solana Beach CA
858 720-2380

(P-14041)
UNIFIED NUTRIMEALS
5469 Ferguson Dr (90022-5118)
PHONE....................323 923-9335
Shabir Kashyap, *Pr*
Hugo Meza, *
Phil Chavez, *
EMP: 85 **EST:** 2005
SALES (est): 2.49MM **Privately Held**
Web: www.unifiednm.com
SIC: 5812 2099 Contract food services; Ready-to-eat meals, salads, and sandwiches

(P-14042)
US DONUTS & YOGURT
11719 Whittier Blvd (90601-3939)
PHONE....................562 695-8867
EMP: 19 **EST:** 1996
SALES (est): 496.97K **Privately Held**
SIC: 5812 2051 Ice cream stands or dairy bars; Doughnuts, except frozen

(P-14043)
VIE DE FRANCE YAMAZAKI INC
Also Called: Vie De France 108
3046 E 50th St (90058-2918)
PHONE....................323 582-1241
Driss Goulhiane, *Brnch Mgr*
EMP: 779
Web: www.viedefrance.com
SIC: 5812 2051 Restaurant, family; chain; Breads, rolls, and buns
HQ: Vie De France Yamazaki, Inc.
2070 Chain Bridge Rd # 500
Vienna VA

(P-14044)
WARNER FOOD MANAGEMENT CO INC
4917 Genesta Ave (91316-3438)
PHONE....................818 285-2160
Sudesh Sood, *Pr*
Terry O'herrick, *Sec*
EMP: 125 **EST:** 1989
SQ FT: 2,000
SALES (est): 4.33MM **Privately Held**
SIC: 5812 8742 Fast-food restaurant, chain; Restaurant and food services consultants

(P-14045)
WKS RESTAURANT CORPORATION (PA)
Also Called: El Pollo Loco
5856 Corporate Ave Ste 200 (90630)
P.O. Box 39 (90714-0039)
PHONE....................562 425-1402
Roland Spongberg, *Pr*
Paul Tanner, *CFO*
EMP: 243 **EST:** 1987
SQ FT: 1,200
SALES (est): 200.55MM
SALES (corp-wide): 200.55MM **Privately Held**
Web: www.wksusa.com
SIC: 5812 6794 Mexican restaurant; Franchises, selling or licensing

5813 Drinking Places

(P-14046)
BELCHING BEAVER BREWERY
Also Called: Rocky Point RTD
1334 Rocky Point Dr (92056-5864)
PHONE....................760 599-5832
Tom Vogel, *CEO*
▲ **EMP:** 145 **EST:** 2012
SALES (est): 17MM **Privately Held**
Web: www.belchingbeaver.com
SIC: 5813 2082 Bars and lounges; Malt beverages

(P-14047)
CORONADO BREWING COMPANY INC (PA)
170 Orange Ave (92118-1409)
PHONE....................619 437-4452
EMP: 50 **EST:** 1996
SQ FT: 6,000
SALES (est): 10.5MM **Privately Held**
Web: www.coronadobrewing.com
SIC: 5813 2082 Bars and lounges; Malt beverages

(P-14048)
HARLAND BREWING CO LLC
10115 Carroll Canyon Rd (92131-1109)
PHONE....................858 800-4566
Jeffrey Hansson, *Managing Member*
EMP: 34 **EST:** 2018
SALES (est): 1.18MM **Privately Held**
Web: www.harlandbeer.com
SIC: 5813 2082 Bars and lounges; Beer (alcoholic beverage)

(P-14049)
LEVITY OF BREA LLC
180 S Brea Blvd (92821-4989)
PHONE....................714 482-0700
Alireza Ghaemian, *Prin*
EMP: 92 **EST:** 2015
SALES (est): 2.23MM **Privately Held**
Web: www.improv.com
SIC: 5813 7997 5812 Bars and lounges; Membership sports and recreation clubs; Buffet (eating places)

(P-14050)
MISSION BREWERY INC
1441 L St (92101-8967)
PHONE....................619 818-7147
Daniel R Selis, *Pr*
▲ **EMP:** 34 **EST:** 2010
SALES (est): 3.88MM **Privately Held**
Web: www.missionbrewery.com
SIC: 5813 5812 2082 Bars and lounges; Grills (eating places); Malt beverages

(P-14051)
PALOS VERDES GOLF CLUB
Also Called: Palos Verdes Golf & Cntry CLB
3301 Via Campesina (90274-1468)
PHONE....................310 375-2759
Gerald Kouzmanoff, *CEO*
EMP: 100 **EST:** 1967
SQ FT: 55,000
SALES (est): 9.96MM **Privately Held**
Web: www.pvgc.com
SIC: 5813 5941 7997 5812 Bar (drinking places); Golf goods and equipment; Golf club, membership; Eating places

(P-14052)
PORT BREWING
571 Carlsbad Village Dr (92008-2304)
PHONE....................760 720-7012
Gina Marsaglia, *Prin*
EMP: 19 **EST:** 2008
SALES (est): 251.49K **Privately Held**
Web: www.pizzaport.com
SIC: 5813 2082 Tavern (drinking places); Malt beverages

(P-14053)
STONE BREWING CO LLC
Also Called: Stone Brewing Co.
1999 Citracado Pkwy (92029-4158)
PHONE....................760 471-4999
▲ **EMP:** 1120 **EST:** 1996
SALES (est): 69.26MM **Privately Held**
Web: www.stonebrewing.com
SIC: 5813 2082 Bars and lounges; Ale (alcoholic beverage)

(P-14054)
TAVISTOCK RESTAURANTS LLC
Also Called: Alcatraz Brewing Company
20 City Blvd W Ste R1 (92868-3116)
PHONE....................714 939-8686
Jarred Creagan, *Mgr*
EMP: 150
SALES (corp-wide): 195.01MM **Privately Held**
Web: www.tavistockrestaurantcollection.com
SIC: 5813 5812 2082 Bars and lounges; American restaurant; Malt beverages
PA: Tavistock Restaurants Llc
6900 Tvstock Lkes Blvd St
Orlando FL
407 909-7101

5912 Drug Stores And Proprietary Stores

(P-14055)
KERN VALLEY HOSP FOUNDATION (PA)
Also Called: KERN VALLEY HOSPITAL
6412 Laurel Ave (93240-9529)
P.O. Box 1628 (93240-1628)
PHONE....................760 379-2681
Clarence Semonious, *Pr*
Anne Litz, *
Sally Partin, *
Kay Knight, *
Mary Completo, *
EMP: 300 **EST:** 1964
SQ FT: 65,000
SALES (est): 49.64K
SALES (corp-wide): 49.64K **Privately Held**
Web: www.kvhd.org
SIC: 5912 8051 Drug stores; Extended care facility

(P-14056)
SANSUM CLINIC
Also Called: Santa Brbara Med Fndtion Clnic
215 Pesetas Ln (93110-1416)
P.O. Box 1200 (93102-1200)
PHONE....................805 681-7500
Kut Ransolhoff, *CEO*
EMP: 87
SALES (corp-wide): 357.93MM **Privately Held**
Web: www.sansumclinic.org
SIC: **5912** 8011 Drug stores and proprietary stores; Offices and clinics of medical doctors
PA: Sansum Clinic
470 S Patterson Ave
Santa Barbara CA
805 681-7700

(P-14057)
SHARP HEALTHCARE (PA)
8695 Spectrum Center Blvd (92123-1489)
PHONE....................858 499-4000
Christopher Howard, *Managing Member*
Michael Murphy, *Managing Member**
Ann Pumpian, *Managing Member**
Daniel L Gross, *Managing Member**
Alison J Fleury, *Managing Member**
EMP: 760 EST: 1946
SQ FT: 15,700
SALES (est): 2.37B
SALES (corp-wide): 2.37B **Privately Held**
Web: www.sharp.com
SIC: **5912** 8741 6324 8011 Drug stores; Hospital management; Hospital and medical service plans; Offices and clinics of medical doctors

5921 Liquor Stores

(P-14058)
BEVERAGES & MORE INC
2000 N Tustin St (92865-3902)
PHONE....................714 279-8131
Lisa Young, *Mgr*
EMP: 113
SALES (corp-wide): 1.61B **Privately Held**
Web: www.bevmo.com
SIC: **5921** 5149 Hard liquor; Soft drinks
HQ: Beverages & More, Inc.
1401 Willow Pass Rd # 90
Concord CA

(P-14059)
BEVERAGES & MORE INC
875 E Birch St Ste A (92821-5769)
PHONE....................714 990-2060
Kerry Christopher, *Mgr*
EMP: 113
SALES (corp-wide): 1.61B **Privately Held**
Web: www.bevmo.com
SIC: **5921** 5149 Wine; Soft drinks
HQ: Beverages & More, Inc.
1401 Willow Pass Rd # 90
Concord CA

5932 Used Merchandise Stores

(P-14060)
DESERT AREA RESOURCES TRAINING (PA)
Also Called: DART
201 E Ridgecrest Blvd (93555-3919)
PHONE....................760 375-9787
Jinny Deangelis, *CEO*
Robert Beecroft, ***
Jeannie Luke, ***

Chris Bridges Cof Clieants, *Prin*
EMP: 100 EST: 1961
SQ FT: 10,800
SALES (est): 3.07MM
SALES (corp-wide): 3.07MM **Privately Held**
Web: www.dartontarget.org
SIC: **5932** 7349 8322 Clothing and shoes, secondhand; Janitorial service, contract basis; Association for the handicapped

(P-14061)
GOODWILL CENTRAL COAST
Also Called: Goodwill Inds San Luis Obispo
880 Industrial Way (93401-7666)
PHONE....................805 544-0542
James Burke, *Brnch Mgr*
EMP: 244
SALES (corp-wide): 46.96MM **Privately Held**
Web: www.ccgoodwill.org
SIC: **5932** 8322 Used merchandise stores; Rehabilitation services
PA: Goodwill Central Coast
1566 Moffett St
Salinas CA
831 423-8611

(P-14062)
LABELS-R-US INC
Also Called: Label Shoppe, The
1121 Fullerton Rd (91748-1232)
PHONE....................626 333-4001
Rudolph Gaytan, *CEO*
EMP: 25 EST: 1991
SQ FT: 65,000
SALES (est): 2.27MM **Privately Held**
Web: www.labelsrus.com
SIC: **5932** 2759 Used merchandise stores; Commercial printing, nec

5941 Sporting Goods And Bicycle Shops

(P-14063)
ECI WATER SKI PRODUCTS INC
Also Called: Skylon
224 Malbert St (92570-6279)
PHONE....................951 940-9999
Tom Hellwig, *Pr*
Ronna Hellwig, ***
EMP: 35 EST: 1984
SALES (est): 2.19MM **Privately Held**
Web: www.paradisesocal.com
SIC: **5941** 3949 Water sport equipment; Water skiing equipment and supplies, except skis

(P-14064)
PEDEGO LLC (PA)
Also Called: Pedego Electric Bikes
11310 Slater Ave (92708-5441)
PHONE....................800 646-8604
Brian Stech, *CEO*
◆ EMP: 23 EST: 2008
SQ FT: 39,000
SALES (est): 8.42MM **Privately Held**
Web: www.pedegoelectricbikes.com
SIC: **5941** 3751 Bicycle and bicycle parts; Bicycles and related parts

5942 Book Stores

(P-14065)
BNI PUBLICATIONS INC
Also Called: Building News
990 Park Center Dr Ste E (92081-8352)
PHONE....................760 734-1113

William Mahoney, *Pr*
William Dennis Mahoney, ***
Norman Peterson, ***
Vincent Wilhelm, ***
EMP: 38 EST: 1946
SQ FT: 2,000
SALES (est): 4.81MM **Privately Held**
Web: www.bnibooks.com
SIC: **5942** 2731 8999 Book stores; Book publishing; Lecturing services

(P-14066)
FORTY-NINER SHOPS INC
Also Called: UNIVERSITY BOOKSTORE
6049 E 7th St (90840-0007)
PHONE....................562 985-5093
Don Penrod, *CEO*
Doctor Mary Ann Takemoto, *Ch*
Ms. Mary Stephens, *Treas*
EMP: 550 EST: 1949
SQ FT: 36,000
SALES (est): 19.38MM **Privately Held**
Web: www.fortyninershops.net
SIC: **5942** 5943 5812 7021 College book stores; School supplies; Cafeteria; Dormitory, commercially operated

(P-14067)
KETAB CORPORATION
Also Called: Persian Bks Englsh-Prsian Bks
12701 Van Nuys Blvd Ste H (91331-7289)
PHONE....................310 477-7477
Bijan Khalili, *CEO*
◆ EMP: 20 EST: 1981
SQ FT: 5,000
SALES (est): 589.04K **Privately Held**
Web: www.ketab.com
SIC: **5942** 2741 Books, foreign; Directories, nec: publishing only, not printed on site

(P-14068)
NORTH ORNGE CNTY CMMTY CLLEGE
Also Called: Fullerton College Bookstore
330 E Chapman Ave (92832-2087)
PHONE....................714 992-7008
Nick Karvia, *Brnch Mgr*
EMP: 343
SALES (corp-wide): 103.05MM **Privately Held**
Web: www.nocccd.edu
SIC: **5942** 5045 College book stores; Computers, peripherals, and software
PA: North Orange County Community College District
1830 W Romneya Dr
Anaheim CA
714 808-4500

(P-14069)
PSYCHIC EYE BOOK SHOPS INC (PA)
13435 Ventura Blvd (91423-3812)
PHONE....................818 906-8263
Robert Leysen, *CEO*
Mary Karahalios, ***
EMP: 80 EST: 1984
SQ FT: 5,000
SALES (est): 9.92MM
SALES (corp-wide): 9.92MM **Privately Held**
Web: www.pebooksandgifts.com
SIC: **5942** 5947 7999 Book stores; Gift shop; Fortune tellers

5943 Stationery Stores

(P-14070)
EC DESIGN LLC
Also Called: Erin Condren
4860 W 147th St (90250-6706)
PHONE....................310 220-2362
Eric Howard, *Pr*
EMP: 26
SALES (corp-wide): 40.62MM **Privately Held**
Web: www.erincondren.com
SIC: **5943** 5049 5632 5331 Stationery stores ; School supplies; Apparel accessories; Variety stores
PA: Ec Design Llc
201 W Howard Ln
Austin TX
512 676-4200

(P-14071)
RUSH BUSINESS FORMS INC
Also Called: Informs
3860 E Eagle Dr Ste A (92807-1706)
PHONE....................714 630-5661
Louis John Katzman, *CEO*
David Flucht, *Pr*
John Katzman, *VP*
EMP: 22 EST: 1976
SQ FT: 10,000
SALES (est): 2.38MM **Privately Held**
Web: rush-business-forms-inc-in-anaheim-ca.cityfos.com
SIC: **5943** 3993 Office forms and supplies; Signs and advertising specialties

(P-14072)
W B MASON CO INC
5911 E Washington Blvd (90040-2412)
PHONE....................888 926-2766
EMP: 33
SALES (corp-wide): 1.01B **Privately Held**
Web: www.wbmason.com
SIC: **5943** 5712 2752 Office forms and supplies; Office furniture; Commercial printing, lithographic
PA: W. B. Mason Co., Inc.
59 Centre Street
Brockton MA
508 586-3434

(P-14073)
YEBO GROUP LLC
Also Called: Yebo Printing
2652 Dow Ave (92780-7208)
PHONE....................949 502-3317
Andrew Tosh, *Managing Member*
▲ EMP: 125 EST: 2008
SALES (est): 12.42MM **Privately Held**
Web: www.customboxesandpackaging.com
SIC: **5943** 2652 3086 2752 Stationery stores ; Boxes, newsboard, metal edged: made from purchased materials; Packaging and shipping materials, foamed plastics; Commercial printing, lithographic

5944 Jewelry Stores

(P-14074)
DIAMOND GOLDENWEST CORPORATION (PA)
Also Called: Jewelry Exchange, The
15732 Tustin Village Way (92780-4924)
PHONE....................714 542-9000
William S Doddridge, *Pr*
Sylvia Trujillo, ***

PRODUCTS & SVCS

EMP: 150 **EST:** 1977
SQ FT: 25,000
SALES (est): 32.72MM
SALES (corp-wide): 32.72MM **Privately Held**
Web: www.jewelryexchange.com
SIC: 5944 5094 Jewelry, precious stones and precious metals; Jewelry

(P-14075)
ENO BRANDS INC
Also Called: Alamo Rings
6481 Global Dr (90630-5227)
PHONE..................................714 220-1318
Guey Miaw Tsao, *CEO*
Chun Tsao, *CFO*
Kevin Tsao, *Sec*
EMP: 24 **EST:** 2005
SQ FT: 5,000
SALES (est): 4.87MM **Privately Held**
Web: www.enobrands.com
SIC: 5944 5094 7389 5632 Jewelry stores; Jewelry; Design services; Costume jewelry

(P-14076)
JEWELERS TOUCH
2535 E Imperial Hwy (92821-6131)
PHONE..................................714 579-1616
Ken Rutz, *Pt*
Jana Rutz, *Pt*
EMP: 20 **EST:** 1992
SALES (est): 2.24MM **Privately Held**
Web: www.jewelerstouch.com
SIC: 5944 3915 Jewelry, precious stones and precious metals; Lapidary work and diamond cutting and polishing

(P-14077)
L & L DIAMOND CO
Also Called: Bony Levy
1801 Beverly Blvd (90057-2501)
PHONE..................................213 622-5752
Bony Levy, *CEO*
EMP: 17 **EST:** 1986
SALES (est): 2.26MM **Privately Held**
SIC: 5944 3479 Jewelry stores; Engraving jewelry, silverware, or metal

(P-14078)
M & G JEWELERS INC
10823 Edison Ct (91730-3868)
PHONE..................................909 989-2929
Juan Guevara, *Pr*
Michael Insalago, *
EMP: 68 **EST:** 1991
SQ FT: 8,432
SALES (est): 11.28MM **Privately Held**
Web: www.mandgjewelers.com
SIC: 5944 3911 7631 Jewelry, precious stones and precious metals; Jewelry, precious metal; Watch repair

(P-14079)
MONEX DEPOSIT A CAL LTD PARTNR
Also Called: Monex
4910 Birch St (92660-8100)
PHONE..................................800 444-8317
Mike Carabini, *Ltd Pt*
Louis E Carabini, *Pt*
EMP: 100 **EST:** 1987
SALES (est): 8.32MM **Privately Held**
SIC: 5944 6722 3324 Jewelry, precious stones and precious metals; Management investment, open-end; Steel investment foundries

(P-14080)
S A TOP-U CORPORATION
1794 Illinois Ave (92571-9371)
PHONE..................................951 916-4025
Hans Werner Wendel, *Ch*
Pia Wendel, *
◆ **EMP:** 27 **EST:** 1984
SQ FT: 20,000
SALES (est): 1.79MM **Privately Held**
Web: www.topusa.com
SIC: 5944 3993 Clock and watch stores; Signs and advertising specialties

5945 Hobby, Toy, And Game Shops

(P-14081)
SAILING INNOVATION (US) INC
17870 Castleton St # 220 (91748-1755)
PHONE..................................626 965-6665
Steven Goldsmith, *CEO*
Valen Tong, *CFO*
Kiran Smith, *CMO*
EMP: 3187 **EST:** 2014
SALES (est): 27.7MM **Privately Held**
SIC: 5945 3651 Toys and games; Audio electronic systems

5946 Camera And Photographic Supply Stores

(P-14082)
FILMTOOLS INC (PA)
Also Called: Moviola Digital
1015 N Hollywood Way (91505-2526)
PHONE..................................323 467-1116
Joseph Paskal, *Pr*
Randy Paskal, *
Carl Nelson, *
Dana Newman, *
EMP: 50 **EST:** 1923
SQ FT: 30,000
SALES (est): 48MM
SALES (corp-wide): 48MM **Privately Held**
Web: www.filmtools.com
SIC: 5946 5043 7819 3861 Photographic supplies; Motion picture equipment; Editing services, motion picture production; Photographic equipment and supplies

(P-14083)
FREESTYLE SALES CO LTD PARTNR
Also Called: Freestyle
12231 Florence Ave (90670-3805)
P.O. Box 27924 (90027-0924)
PHONE..................................323 660-3460
Ronald M Resch, *Pt*
Leonore King, *Pt*
▲ **EMP:** 90 **EST:** 1946
SALES (est): 9.55MM **Privately Held**
Web: www.freestylephoto.com
SIC: 5946 5043 Photographic supplies; Photographic equipment and supplies

(P-14084)
SAMYS CAMERA INC (PA)
Also Called: Samy's Digital Imaging
12636 Beatrice St (90066-7312)
P.O. Box 48126 (90048-0126)
PHONE..................................310 591-2100
▲ **EMP:** 109 **EST:** 1976
SALES (est): 58.23MM
SALES (corp-wide): 58.23MM **Privately Held**
Web: www.samys.com

SIC: 5946 5731 7699 Cameras; Video recorders, players, disc players, and accessories; Camera repair shop

5947 Gift, Novelty, And Souvenir Shop

(P-14085)
ALIN PARTY SUPPLY CO
6493 Magnolia Ave (92506-2409)
PHONE..................................951 682-7441
EMP: 30
Web: www.alinpartysupply.com
SIC: 5947 7389 2759 Party favors; Balloons, novelty and toy; Invitation and stationery printing and engraving
PA: Alin Party Supply Co.
4139 Woodruff Ave
Lakewood CA

(P-14086)
HALLMARK LABS LLC
3130 Wilshire Blvd Ste 400 (90403-2300)
PHONE..................................424 210-3600
Steven Hawn, *Pr*
Jeff Mcmillen, *VP*
Dwight C Arn, *, *
Jill Marchant, *
Albert P Mauro Junior, *VP*
EMP: 117 **EST:** 2017
SQ FT: 22,831
SALES (est): 13.32MM
SALES (corp-wide): 2.72B **Privately Held**
Web: www.hallmarklabs.com
SIC: 5947 2741 8999 Greeting cards; Internet publishing and broadcasting; Personal services
PA: Hallmark Cards, Incorporated
2501 Mcgee St
Kansas City MO
816 274-5111

(P-14087)
PIECEMAKERS LLC
Also Called: Piecemaker's Country Store
1720 Adams Ave (92626-4890)
PHONE..................................714 641-3112
Doug Follette, *Managing Member*
Marie Kolasinski, *
▲ **EMP:** 21 **EST:** 1978
SQ FT: 11,467
SALES (est): 898.06K **Privately Held**
Web: www.piecemakers.com
SIC: 5947 8299 5131 5949 Gift shop; Arts and crafts schools; Piece goods and other fabrics; Quilting materials and supplies

(P-14088)
VESUKI INC
Also Called: V R Gifts
1350 W Lambert Rd Ste A (92821-2886)
PHONE..................................562 245-4000
Suru Manek, *Pr*
Kishorlal Manek, *VP*
▲ **EMP:** 18 **EST:** 1987
SALES (est): 2.38MM **Privately Held**
Web: www.vesuki.com
SIC: 5947 3499 5199 5088 Greeting cards; Magnets, permanent: metallic; Gifts and novelties; Aeronautical equipment and supplies

5949 Sewing, Needlework, And Piece Goods

(P-14089)
ROBERT KAUFMAN CO INC (PA)
Also Called: Robert Kaufman Fabrics

129 W 132nd St (90061-1619)
P.O. Box 59266 (90059-0266)
PHONE..................................310 538-3482
Kenneth Kaufman, *CEO*
Harvey Kaufman, *
Alvin Kaufman, *
Joseph Kaufman, *
◆ **EMP:** 114 **EST:** 1942
SQ FT: 24,000
SALES (est): 59.89MM
SALES (corp-wide): 59.89MM **Privately Held**
Web: www.robertkaufman.com
SIC: 5949 2299 Fabric stores piece goods; Linen fabrics

5961 Catalog And Mail-order Houses

(P-14090)
ADAPTIVE TECH GROUP INC
Also Called: Atm Fly-Ware
1635 E Burnett St (90755-3603)
PHONE..................................562 424-1100
Paul W Allen, *Pr*
▲ **EMP:** 20 **EST:** 1985
SALES (est): 4.64MM **Privately Held**
Web:
www.adaptivetechnologiesgroup.com
SIC: 5961 3651 Electronic kits and parts, mail order; Household audio equipment

(P-14091)
AL GLOBAL CORPORATION (HQ)
Also Called: Youngvity Essntial Lf Sciences
2400 Boswell Rd (91914-3553)
PHONE..................................619 934-3980
◆ **EMP:** 43 **EST:** 1996
SQ FT: 70,000
SALES (est): 32.5MM
SALES (corp-wide): 147.44MM **Publicly Held**
Web: www.youngevity.com
SIC: 5961 2043 Catalog and mail-order houses; Cereal breakfast foods
PA: Youngevity International, Inc.
2400 Boswell Rd
Chula Vista CA
619 934-3980

(P-14092)
BU RU LLC
Also Called: Shop Buru
826 E 3rd St (90013-1820)
PHONE..................................424 316-2878
Morgan Hutchinson, *Managing Member*
Brutt Hutchinson, *Managing Member*
EMP: 17 **EST:** 2013
SALES (est): 1.45MM **Privately Held**
SIC: 5961 5621 2339 Electronic shopping; Women's clothing stores; Women's and misses' athletic clothing and sportswear

(P-14093)
COLD STEEL INC (PA)
6060 Nicolle St (93003-7600)
P.O. Box 535189 (75053-5189)
PHONE..................................805 650-8481
Lynn C Thompson, *Pr*
◆ **EMP:** 18 **EST:** 1980
SQ FT: 7,000
SALES (est): 6.6MM
SALES (corp-wide): 6.6MM **Privately Held**
SIC: 5961 3421 Catalog sales; Knives: butchers', hunting, pocket, etc.

(P-14094)
HADLEY FRUIT ORCHARDS INC (PA)

48980 Seminole Dr (92230-2167)
P.O. Box 495 (92230-0495)
PHONE..............................951 849-5255
Gerald Bench, *Pr*
John Taylor, *
Dennis Flint, *
James Taylor, *
Fred Bond, *
EMP: 35 **EST:** 1931
SALES (est): 1.5MM
SALES (corp-wide): 1.5MM **Privately Held**
Web: www.hadleyfruitorchards.com
SIC: 5961 2034 5499 5441 Food, mail order;
Fruits, dried or dehydrated, except freeze-
dried; Dried fruit; Nuts

(P-14095)
MELTON INTL TACKLE INC
1375 S State College Blvd (92806-5728)
PHONE..............................714 978-9192
Tracy M Melton, *Pr*
◆ **EMP:** 28 **EST:** 1993
SALES (est): 5.44MM **Privately Held**
Web: www.meltontackle.com
SIC: 5961 5199 3949 5091 Fishing, hunting
and camping equipment and supplies: by
mail; Advertising specialties; Lures, fishing:
artificial; Boat accessories and parts

(P-14096)
MERQBIZ LLC
300 Continental Blvd Ste 640 (90245)
PHONE..............................855 637-7249
John Fox, *
EMP: 35 **EST:** 2016
SALES (est): 2.29MM **Privately Held**
Web: www.voith.com
SIC: 5961 3554 Electronic shopping; Paper
industries machinery

(P-14097)
PASSWORD ENTERPRISE INC
3200 E 29th St (90806-2321)
P.O. Box 90729 (90809-0729)
PHONE..............................562 988-8889
Sophead Naing, *CEO*
Adam Chu, *
EMP: 25 **EST:** 2013
SQ FT: 32,000
SALES (est): 2.45MM **Privately Held**
Web: www.passwordmm.com
SIC: 5961 3369 Automotive supplies and
equipment, mail order; Aerospace castings,
nonferrous: except aluminum

(P-14098)
PCM INC (HQ)
200 N Pacific Coast Hwy Ste 1050
(90245-5605)
PHONE..............................310 354-5600
Glynis A Bryan, *CFO*
EMP: 812 **EST:** 1987
SALES (est): 2.16B **Publicly Held**
Web: www.insight.com
SIC: 5961 5731 5045 5734 Computer
equipment and electronics, mail order;
Radio, television, and electronic stores;
Computers, peripherals, and software;
Personal computers
PA: Insight Enterprises, Inc.
2701 E Insight Way Ste 1
Chandler AZ

(P-14099)
**PERFORMANCE AUTOMOTIVE
WHL INC (PA)**
Also Called: Paw
20235 Nordhoff St (91311-6213)
P.O. Box 829 (91319-0829)
PHONE..............................805 499-8973

Keith E Harvie, *CEO*
Brian Mcelroy, *Pr*
EMP: 100 **EST:** 1978
SALES (est): 5.21MM
SALES (corp-wide): 5.21MM **Privately
Held**
Web: www.pawinc.com
SIC: 5961 5013 Automotive supplies and
equipment, mail order; Automotive supplies
and parts

(P-14100)
QUANTUM NETWORKS LLC
3412 Garfield Ave (90040-3104)
PHONE..............................212 993-5899
Jonathan Goldman, *Pr*
Eytan Wiener, *
EMP: 30 **EST:** 2008
SALES (est): 4.93MM
SALES (corp-wide): 4.71B **Publicly Held**
Web: www.quantumnetworks.com
SIC: 5961 5731 5065 3651 Computer
equipment and electronics, mail order;
Consumer electronic equipment, nec; Video
equipment, electronic; Household audio
and video equipment
HQ: Advantage Sales & Marketing Inc.
15310 Barranca Pkwy # 100
Irvine CA
949 797-2900

(P-14101)
QUILT IN A DAY INC
1955 Diamond St (92078-5122)
PHONE..............................760 591-0929
TOLL FREE: 800
Eleanor A Burns, *CEO*
▲ **EMP:** 37 **EST:** 1979
SQ FT: 9,000
SALES (est): 4.45MM **Privately Held**
Web: www.quiltinaday.com
SIC: 5961 5949 5192 2731 Books, mail
order (except book clubs); Quilting
materials and supplies; Books; Book
publishing

(P-14102)
RNBS CORPORATION
Also Called: Rugged Notebooks
725 S Paseo Prado (92807-4949)
PHONE..............................714 998-1828
Alan Shad, *Pr*
EMP: 20 **EST:** 2000
SALES (est): 4.47MM **Privately Held**
Web: www.tuffbooks4less.com
SIC: 5961 3571 Computers and peripheral
equipment, mail order; Electronic computers

(P-14103)
**ROAD RUNNER SPORTS INC
(PA)**
Also Called: Roadrunner Sports
5549 Copley Dr (92111-7904)
PHONE..............................858 974-4200
Michael Gotfredson, *Pr*
Scott Campbell, *
▲ **EMP:** 72 **EST:** 1987
SQ FT: 88,000
SALES (est): 136.68MM
SALES (corp-wide): 136.68MM **Privately
Held**
Web: www.roadrunnersports.com
SIC: 5961 3949 5661 Mail order house, nec;
Sporting and athletic goods, nec; Footwear,
athletic

(P-14104)
RUGGABLE LLC
17809 S Broadway (90248-3541)
PHONE..............................310 295-0098

Nathan Baldwin, *CEO*
EMP: 378 **EST:** 2017
SALES (est): 62.89MM **Privately Held**
Web: www.ruggable.com
SIC: 5961 2273 Electronic shopping; Rugs,
hand and machine made

(P-14105)
SPENCER FORREST INC
Also Called: Toppik
11777 San Vicente Blvd Ste 650
(90049-5011)
▲ **EMP:** 25 **EST:** 1981
SQ FT: 3,000
SALES (est): 2.63MM **Privately Held**
Web: www.toppik.com
SIC: 5961 3999 Cosmetics and perfumes,
mail order; Hair and hair-based products

(P-14106)
WESTATES INC
Also Called: Westates Automotive Promotions
6800 Orangethorpe Ave Ste H
(90620-1366)
PHONE..............................714 523-7600
Dale W Becker, *Pr*
Doug Pohl, *
Natalie Pohl, *
EMP: 18 **EST:** 1978
SQ FT: 12,900
SALES (est): 4.91MM **Privately Held**
Web: www.westates.net
SIC: 5961 2752 Mail order house, nec;
Offset printing

(P-14107)
WORD FOR TODAY
3232 W Macarthur Blvd # A (92704-6802)
PHONE..............................714 825-9673
Charles W Smith, *Pr*
Jeff Smith, *
EMP: 37 **EST:** 1978
SQ FT: 19,000
SALES (est): 165.95K
SALES (corp-wide): 31.18MM **Privately
Held**
Web: shop.twft.com
SIC: 5961 2731 3652 Record and/or tape
(music or video) club, mail order; Books,
publishing only; Prerecorded records and
tapes
PA: Calvary Chapel Of Costa Mesa
3800 S Fairview St
Santa Ana CA
714 979-4422

5963 Direct Selling
Establishments

(P-14108)
AVERY GROUP INC
8941 Dalton Ave (90047-3631)
PHONE..............................310 217-1070
Leatora Jefferson, *Pr*
EMP: 300 **EST:** 2006
SALES (est): 9.86MM **Privately Held**
Web: www.averygroup-inc.com
SIC: 5963 7349 Food services, direct sales;
Janitorial service, contract basis

(P-14109)
BTG TEXTILES INC
710 Union St (90640-6521)
PHONE..............................323 586-9488
▲ **EMP:** 29 **EST:** 2011
SALES (est): 1.5MM **Privately Held**
Web: www.btgtextiles.com

SIC: 5963 2299 Direct selling establishments
; Towels and towelings, linen and linen-and-
cotton mixtures

(P-14110)
ENAGIC USA INC (PA)
4115 Spencer St (90503-2419)
PHONE..............................310 542-7700
Hironari Oshiro, *Pr*
◆ **EMP:** 66 **EST:** 2003
SALES (est): 34.53MM
SALES (corp-wide): 34.53MM **Privately
Held**
Web: www.enagic.com
SIC: 5963 2086 Bottled water delivery;
Mineral water, carbonated: packaged in
cans, bottles, etc.

(P-14111)
**PERFORMANCE WATER
PRODUCTS INC**
6902 Aragon Cir (90620-1118)
PHONE..............................714 736-0137
Kristopher Mecca, *Pr*
Kari Mecca, *Sec*
John Mecca, *VP*
Mike Mecca, *Dir*
Mat Mecca, *VP*
EMP: 17 **EST:** 1992
SQ FT: 51,000
SALES (est): 8.34MM **Privately Held**
Web: www.performancewater.com
SIC: 5963 3589 Bottled water delivery;
Water purification equipment, household
type

(P-14112)
STRATA USA LLC
333 City Blvd W Fl 17 (92868-5905)
PHONE..............................888 878-7282
EMP: 25 **EST:** 2014
SALES (est): 1.33MM **Privately Held**
Web: www.strata-usa.com
SIC: 5963 0175 5122 5047 Direct sales,
telemarketing; Deciduous tree fruits;
Medical rubber goods; Hospital equipment
and furniture

5992 Florists

(P-14113)
**FOREST LAWN MEMORIAL-
PARK ASSN (PA)**
Also Called: Forest Lawn Mem Parks
Mortuary
1712 S Glendale Ave (91205-3320)
PHONE..............................323 254-3131
TOLL FREE: 800
Darin B Drabing, *CEO*
Darin B Drabing, *Pr*
Thomas Mckernan, *Ch Bd*
John Llewellyn, *
R Scott Jenkins, *
▲ **EMP:** 300 **EST:** 1906
SQ FT: 450,000
SALES (est): 214.25MM
SALES (corp-wide): 214.25MM **Privately
Held**
Web: www.forestlawn.com
SIC: 5992 6553 7261 Flowers, fresh;
Cemetery association; Funeral service and
crematories

(P-14114)
SAFEWAY INC
200 N Puente St (92821-3824)
PHONE..............................714 990-8357
EMP: 968
SALES (corp-wide): 77.65B **Publicly Held**

Web: www.safeway.com
SIC: 5992 4225 Florists; General warehousing and storage
HQ: Safeway Inc.
5918 Stoneridge Mall Rd
Pleasanton CA
925 226-5000

5993 Tobacco Stores And Stands

(P-14115)
IKRUSHER INC
11818 Clark St (91006-6000)
PHONE..............................626 256-3449
David Bo Chen, *CEO*
EMP: 84 **EST:** 2017
SALES (est): 4.26MM **Privately Held**
Web: www.ikrusher.com
SIC: 5993 3999 Tobacco stores and stands; Cigarette and cigar products and accessories

(P-14116)
VAPE CRAFT LLC
2100 Palomar Airport Rd Ste 210 (92011-4402)
PHONE..............................760 295-7484
Ben Osmanson, *Managing Member*
EMP: 20 **EST:** 2019
SALES (est): 2.23MM **Privately Held**
Web: www.vapecraftinc.com
SIC: 5993 3999 5194 ; Cigarette and cigar products and accessories; Cigars

5994 News Dealers And Newsstands

(P-14117)
HI-DESERT PUBLISHING COMPANY
Also Called: Big Bear Grizzly & Big Bear Lf
42007 Fox Farm Rd Ste 3b (92315-2192)
PHONE..............................909 866-3456
EMP: 41
SALES (corp-wide): 151.22MM **Privately Held**
SIC: 5994 2711 News dealers and newsstands; Newspapers
HQ: Hi-Desert Publishing Company
56445 29 Palms Hwy
Yucca Valley CA

5995 Optical Goods Stores

(P-14118)
GUNNAR OPTIKS LLC
2236 Rutherford Rd Ste 123 (92008-8836)
PHONE..............................858 769-2500
Joe Croft, *CEO*
◆ **EMP:** 20 **EST:** 2006
SALES (est): 4.13MM **Privately Held**
Web: www.gunnar.com
SIC: 5995 3851 Optical goods stores; Ophthalmic goods

5999 Miscellaneous Retail Stores, Nec

(P-14119)
AAA FLAG & BANNER MFG CO INC (PA)
Also Called: AAA Flag & Banner
8937 National Blvd (90034-3307)

PHONE..............................310 836-3200
Howard S Furst, *Pr*
Susan Furst, *
▲ **EMP:** 150 **EST:** 1971
SQ FT: 4,000
SALES (est): 52.94MM
SALES (corp-wide): 52.94MM **Privately Held**
Web: www.a3visual.com
SIC: 5999 2399 Flags; Banners, pennants, and flags

(P-14120)
ALIGNMED INC
Also Called: Alignmed
1936 E Deere Ave Ste 115 (92705-5733)
PHONE..............................866 987-5433
William Schultz, *Pr*
Eliana Schultz, *CFO*
▲ **EMP:** 18 **EST:** 2001
SALES (est): 5.21MM **Privately Held**
Web: www.alignmed.com
SIC: 5999 3842 Orthopedic and prosthesis applications; Braces, orthopedic

(P-14121)
ARBONNE INTERNATIONAL LLC (DH)
9400 Jeronimo Rd (92618-1907)
PHONE..............................949 770-2610
Tyler Whitehead, *CEO*
Bernadette Chala, *
Amy Humfleet, *
Astrid Van-ruymbeke, *CFO*
Jen Orlando, *GROWTH Innovation*
▲ **EMP:** 25 **EST:** 1984
SQ FT: 37,000
SALES (est): 370.87MM **Privately Held**
Web: www.arbonne.com
SIC: 5999 5961 5499 2834 Cosmetics; Cosmetics and perfumes, mail order; Vitamin food stores; Vitamin preparations
HQ: Groupe Rocher Operations
Lecc Laboratoire Europeen De Creation
La Gacilly
299297474

(P-14122)
ARBONNE INTERNATIONAL DIST INC
9400 Jeronimo Rd (92618-1907)
PHONE..............................800 272-6663
Tyler Whitehead, *CEO*
EMP: 63 **EST:** 2006
SALES (est): 2.27MM **Privately Held**
SIC: 5999 5961 5499 2834 Cosmetics; Cosmetics and perfumes, mail order; Vitamin food stores; Vitamin preparations
HQ: Arbonne International, Llc
9400 Jeronimo Rd
Irvine CA
949 770-2610

(P-14123)
AT BATTERY COMPANY INC
Also Called: Atbatt.com
28381 Constellation Rd Unit A (91355-5048)
PHONE..............................661 775-2020
Young Lee, *CEO*
◆ **EMP:** 20 **EST:** 2000
SALES (est): 2.43MM **Privately Held**
Web: www.atbatt.com
SIC: 5999 5063 3691 Electronic parts and equipment; Batteries; Alkaline cell storage batteries

(P-14124)
CALDESSO LLC
Also Called: Therm Core Products
439 S Stoddard Ave (92401-2025)
PHONE..............................909 888-2882
▲ **EMP:** 65 **EST:** 2010
SQ FT: 23,500
SALES (est): 5.64MM **Privately Held**
SIC: 5999 3567 Hot tub and spa chemicals, equipment, and supplies; Heating units and devices, industrial: electric

(P-14125)
CINEMA SECRETS INC
6639 Odessa Ave (91406-5746)
PHONE..............................818 846-0579
Barbara Stein, *Pr*
Maurice Stein, *
Michael Stein, *
Daniel Stein, *
▲ **EMP:** 60 **EST:** 1985
SALES (est): 9.4MM **Privately Held**
Web: www.cinemasecrets.com
SIC: 5999 5699 2389 5122 Cosmetics; Costumes, masquerade or theatrical; Costumes; Cosmetics

(P-14126)
CMC RESCUE INC
Also Called: CMC
6740 Cortona Dr (93117-5574)
PHONE..............................805 562-9120
James A Frank, *Ch*
Richard M Phillips, *
Elizabeth Henry, *
▲ **EMP:** 65 **EST:** 1978
SQ FT: 23,000
SALES (est): 16.6MM **Privately Held**
Web: www.cmcpro.com
SIC: 5999 5099 3842 8299 Safety supplies and equipment; Safety equipment and supplies; Personal safety equipment; Educational services

(P-14127)
COSMETIC LABORATORIES OF AMERICA LLC
Also Called: Cosmetic Laboratories America
20245 Sunburst St (91311-6219)
PHONE..............................818 717-6140
▲ **EMP:** 400
SIC: 5999 5122 2844 2833 Cosmetics; Cosmetics; Perfumes, cosmetics and other toilet preparations; Medicinals and botanicals

(P-14128)
COSMETIX WEST (PA)
2305 Utah Ave (90245-4818)
PHONE..............................310 726-3080
Ronald P Chavers, *Pr*
▲ **EMP:** 20 **EST:** 1993
SQ FT: 10,000
SALES (est): 15.91MM
SALES (corp-wide): 15.91MM **Privately Held**
Web: www.cosmetixwest.com
SIC: 5999 2844 Cosmetics; Bath salts

(P-14129)
COWAY USA INC
Also Called: Woongjin Coway USA Inc.
4221 Wilshire Blvd Ste 210 (90010-3501)
PHONE..............................213 486-1600
Hong Rae Gim, *Pr*
Hosuk Yoon, *
▲ **EMP:** 39 **EST:** 2006
SQ FT: 4,200
SALES (est): 8.9MM **Privately Held**
Web: www.coway-usa.com

SIC: 5999 3564 Water purification equipment ; Air purification equipment
PA: Coway Co., Ltd.
136-23 Yugumagoksa-Ro, Yugu-Eup Gongju

(P-14130)
DHARMA VENTURES GROUP INC (PA)
24700 Avenue Rockefeller (91355-3465)
PHONE..............................661 294-4200
Jim Snell, *Pr*
Cheryl Horn Berger, *
EMP: 280 **EST:** 2006
SQ FT: 75,000
SALES (est): 43.74MM **Privately Held**
SIC: 5999 6719 Medical apparatus and supplies; Personal holding companies, except banks

(P-14131)
DOCUSOURCE INC
Also Called: Equipment Brokers Unlimited
13100 Alondra Blvd Ste 108 (90703-2278)
PHONE..............................562 447-2600
▼ **EMP:** 80
SIC: 5999 7699 5943 Photocopy machines; Photocopy machine repair; Office forms and supplies

(P-14132)
EVOQUA WATER TECHNOLOGIES LLC
1441 E Washington Blvd (90021-3039)
PHONE..............................213 748-8511
Gary Cappeline, *Interim Chief Executive Officer*
EMP: 27
Web: www.evoqua.com
SIC: 5999 2899 Water purification equipment ; Chemical preparations, nec
HQ: Evoqua Water Technologies Llc
210 6th Ave Ste 3300
Pittsburgh PA
724 772-0044

(P-14133)
GEORGIA-PACIFIC LLC
Also Called: Georgia-Pacific
15500 Valley View Ave (90638-5230)
P.O. Box 981953 (79998-1953)
PHONE..............................562 926-8888
Sam Shah, *Prin*
EMP: 28
SALES (corp-wide): 36.93B **Privately Held**
Web: www.gp.com
SIC: 5999 5113 2653 3275 Alcoholic beverage making equipment and supplies; Corrugated and solid fiber boxes; Corrugated and solid fiber boxes; Gypsum products
HQ: Georgia-Pacific Llc
133 Peachtree St Nw
Atlanta GA
404 652-4000

(P-14134)
GRANDMA LUCYS LLC
30432 Esperanza (92688-2144)
PHONE..............................949 206-8547
Eric Shook, *Pt*
Eric Shook, *Managing Member*
EMP: 19 **EST:** 1999
SALES (est): 2.58MM **Privately Held**
Web: www.grandmalucys.com
SIC: 5999 2047 Pets and pet supplies; Dog and cat food

(P-14135)
GREATCALL INC
Also Called: Jitterbug
10945 Vista Sorrento Pkwy Ste 120
(92130-8649)
P.O. Box 4428 (92018-4428)
PHONE....................................800 733-6632
David Inns, *CEO*
Bill Yates, *CMO**
Lynn Herrick, *CLO**
Bryan Adams, *CCO**
Anne Murphy, *CIO**
EMP: 501 **EST:** 2005
SQ FT: 29,000
SALES (est): 98.39MM
SALES (corp-wide): 46.3B **Publicly Held**
Web: www.lively.com
SIC: 5999 4812 Mobile telephones and
equipment; Cellular telephone services
PA: Best Buy Co., Inc.
7601 Penn Ave S
Richfield MN
612 291-1000

(P-14136)
**INNOVATIVE DIALYSIS
PARTNERS INC**
1 World Trade Ctr Ste 2500 (90831-0002)
PHONE....................................562 495-8075
EMP: 350
SIC: 5999 8092 Medical apparatus and
supplies; Kidney dialysis centers

(P-14137)
INTELLIGENT BEAUTY LLC
Also Called: Iq Cosmetics
2301 Rosecrans Ave Ste 5000
(90245-4966)
PHONE....................................310 683-0940
▲ **EMP:** 550
Web: www.ibinc.com
SIC: 5999 2844 Cosmetics; Cosmetic
preparations

(P-14138)
**JAFRA COSMETICS INTL INC
(DH)**
Also Called: Jafra Cosmetics
1 Baxter Way Ste 150 (91362-3819)
PHONE....................................805 449-3000
Karalee Mora, *CEO*
Mauro Schnaidman, *
Stacy Wolf, *
Mark Funaki, *
James Christl, *
◆ **EMP:** 52 **EST:** 1956
SALES (est): 79.51MM **Privately Held**
Web: www.jafra.com
SIC: 5999 2844 Cosmetics; Perfumes,
cosmetics and other toilet preparations
HQ: Betterware De Mexico, S.A.P.I. De C.V.
Cruce Carretera Gdl-Ameca-Huaxtla
Km. 5
El Arenal JAL

(P-14139)
JON DAVLER INC
9440 Gidley St (91780-4211)
PHONE....................................626 941-6558
David J Sheen, *Pr*
Christina Yang, *
◆ **EMP:** 24 **EST:** 2001
SQ FT: 12,000
SALES (est): 3.04MM **Privately Held**
Web: www.jondavler.com
SIC: 5999 2844 Cosmetics; Perfumes,
cosmetics and other toilet preparations

(P-14140)
**NAPOLEON PERDIS
COSMETICS INC**
16825 Saticoy St (91406-2728)
PHONE....................................323 817-3611
Napoleon Perdis, *Pr*
Soula-marie Perdis, *Sec*
◆ **EMP:** 93 **EST:** 2005
SALES (est): 13.7MM **Privately Held**
Web: www.napoleonperdis.com
SIC: 5999 5122 Cosmetics; Cosmetics

(P-14141)
**NATIONAL ADVANCED
ENDOSCOPY DE**
22134 Sherman Way (91303-1136)
PHONE....................................818 227-2720
Fawzia Dabiri, *CEO*
John Dawoodjee, *
EMP: 25 **EST:** 1994
SQ FT: 16,000
SALES (est): 2.33MM **Privately Held**
Web: www.aed.md
SIC: 5999 3841 5047 7629 Medical
apparatus and supplies; Surgical and
medical instruments; Medical and hospital
equipment; Electrical repair shops

(P-14142)
NICE NORTH AMERICA LLC (DH)
5919 Sea Otter Pl Ste 100 (92010-6750)
P.O. Box 9003 (92018-9003)
PHONE....................................760 438-7000
Emanuel Bertolini, *CEO*
Darren Learmonth, *
◆ **EMP:** 200 **EST:** 1961
SQ FT: 32,000
SALES (est): 95.41MM
SALES (corp-wide): 865.12MM **Privately
Held**
Web: na.niceforyou.com
SIC: 5999 3699 Alarm and safety equipment
stores; Security control equipment and
systems
HQ: Nice Spa
Via Callalta 1
Oderzo TV

(P-14143)
OFFICIA IMAGING INC (PA)
5636 Ruffin Rd (92123-1317)
PHONE....................................858 348-0831
Todd Rogers, *Pr*
Cary Carlton, *
EMP: 24 **EST:** 1963
SALES (est): 9.97MM
SALES (corp-wide): 9.97MM **Privately
Held**
Web: www.office1.com
SIC: 5999 5044 3861 Photocopy machines;
Photocopy machines; Printing equipment,
photographic

(P-14144)
**PETCO HEALTH & WELLNESS
CO INC**
10850 Via Frontera (92127-1705)
PHONE....................................858 453-7845
Ronald Coughlin Junior, *Ch Bd*
Brian Larose, *CFO*
Ilene Eskenazi, *CLO Chief Human
Resources Officer*
John Zavada, *Chief*
EMP: 29000 **EST:** 2015
SQ FT: 257,000
SALES (est): 6.04B **Privately Held**
Web: corporate.petco.com
SIC: 5999 0752 Pets and pet supplies;
Animal specialty services

(P-14145)
PNK ENTERPRISES INC
Also Called: Anderson Trophy Company
12901 Saticoy St (91605-3508)
PHONE....................................818 765-3770
Wesley Starnes, *Pr*
EMP: 21 **EST:** 1965
SALES (est): 1.73MM **Privately Held**
Web: www.andersontrophy.com
SIC: 5999 3499 Trophies and plaques;
Trophies, metal, except silver

(P-14146)
RELIEF-MART INC
Also Called: Selectabed
28505 Canwood St Ste C (91301-3207)
PHONE....................................805 379-4300
Rick T Swartzburg, *CEO*
Jim Swartzburg, *
▲ **EMP:** 42 **EST:** 2001
SQ FT: 36,000
SALES (est): 500K **Privately Held**
Web: www.selectabed.com
SIC: 5999 2515 2392 Medical apparatus and
supplies; Mattresses and foundations;
Cushions and pillows

(P-14147)
**SCOPE ORTHTICS
PROSTHETICS INC (DH)**
Also Called: Scope
7720 Cardinal Ct (92123-3333)
PHONE....................................858 292-7448
Loren Saxton, *Pr*
Tony Di Santo, *
Kel Bergmann, *
EMP: 30 **EST:** 1982
SQ FT: 7,400
SALES (est): 9.35MM
SALES (corp-wide): 1.12B **Privately Held**
Web: www.hangerclinic.com
SIC: 5999 3842 Orthopedic and prosthesis
applications; Prosthetic appliances
HQ: Hanger Prosthetics & Orthotics, Inc.
10910 Domain Dr Ste 300
Austin TX
512 777-3800

(P-14148)
SEXY HAIR CONCEPTS LLC
21551 Prairie St (91311-5831)
PHONE....................................818 435-0800
◆ **EMP:** 20 **EST:** 2001
SALES (est): 10.54MM
SALES (corp-wide): 23.26B **Privately Held**
Web: www.sexyhair.com
SIC: 5999 8331 3999 Hair care products;
Skill training center; Hair and hair-based
products
PA: Henkel Ag & Co. Kgaa
Henkelstr. 67
Dusseldorf NW
2117970

(P-14149)
SMARTLABS INC
Also Called: Smarthomepro
1621 Alton Pkwy Ste 100 (92606-4846)
PHONE....................................800 762-7846
Rob Lilleness, *Ch*
◆ **EMP:** 85 **EST:** 1993
SQ FT: 59,230
SALES (est): 17.34MM **Privately Held**
Web: www.smartlabsinc.com
SIC: 5999 3822 Electronic parts and
equipment; Environmental controls

(P-14150)
**SOUTHWEST BOULDER &
STONE INC (PA)**
5002 2nd St (92028-9790)
PHONE....................................760 451-3333
TOLL FREE: 800
Michelle S Mcleod, *Pr*
Michael O Mcleod, *Sec*
▲ **EMP:** 45 **EST:** 1996
SQ FT: 4,500
SALES (est): 19.44MM **Privately Held**
Web: www.southwestboulder.com
SIC: 5999 1422 Rock and stone specimens;
Crushed and broken limestone

(P-14151)
TANGERINE EXPRESS INC
Also Called: Tangerine Office Systems
4870 Adohr Ln A (93012-8508)
PHONE....................................702 260-6650
▲ **EMP:** 20
SIC: 5999 2865 Photocopy machines; Color
lakes or toners

(P-14152)
VCA INC (DH)
Also Called: VCA
12401 W Olympic Blvd (90064-1022)
PHONE....................................310 571-6500
Doug Drew, *CEO*
Arthur J Antin, *
EMP: 102 **EST:** 1987
SQ FT: 81,000
SALES (est): 2.21B
SALES (corp-wide): 42.84B **Privately Held**
Web: www.vcahospitals.com
SIC: 5999 5047 0742 Pets and pet supplies;
Veterinarians' equipment and supplies;
Animal hospital services, pets and other
animal specialties
HQ: Mmi Holdings, Inc.
18101 Se 6th Way
Vancouver WA
360 784-5422

(P-14153)
WAXIES ENTERPRISES LLC
Also Called: Waxie Sanitary Supply
3220 S Fairview St (92704-6509)
PHONE....................................714 545-8441
TOLL FREE: 800
Laura Maloney, *Brnch Mgr*
EMP: 88
SQ FT: 78,582
Web: info.waxie.com
SIC: 5999 5191 5169 5087 Cleaning
equipment and supplies; Farm supplies;
Chemicals and allied products, nec; Service
establishment equipment
HQ: Waxie's Enterprises, Llc
9353 Waxie Way
San Diego CA
800 995-4466

6011 Federal Reserve Banks

(P-14154)
**FEDERAL RSRVE BNK SAN
FRNCISCO**
Also Called: Los Angeles Branch
950 S Grand Ave Fl 1 (90015-4202)
P.O. Box 512077 (90051-0077)
PHONE....................................213 683-2300
Mark Mullinix, *Mgr*
EMP: 640
Web: www.frbsf.org
SIC: 6011 Federal Reserve branches

HQ: Federal Reserve Bank Of San
Francisco
101 Market St
San Francisco CA
415 974-2000

6021 National Commercial Banks

(P-14155)
BANA HOME LOAN SERVICING
31303 Agoura Rd (91361-4635)
PHONE..................................213 345-7975
Rachel Fiorillo, *Sr VP*
EMP: 900 EST: 2016
SALES (est): 44.33MM Privately Held
SIC: 6021 National commercial banks

(P-14156)
BANC CALIFORNIA NATIONAL ASSN (HQ)
3 Macarthur Pl Ste 100 (92707-6067)
PHONE..................................877 770-2262
Robert Franko, *Pr*
Sean Casey, *
Lynn Sullivan, *CRCRO*
Joseph Kauder, *
Debora Vrana, *Chief Communication Officer*
EMP: 89 EST: 1941
SALES (est): 309.46MM
SALES (corp-wide): 390.12MM Publicly Held
Web: www.bancofcal.com
SIC: 6021 National commercial banks
PA: Banc Of California, Inc.
3 Macarthur Pl Ste 100
Santa Ana CA
855 361-2262

(P-14157)
BANC OF CALIFORNIA INC (PA)
3 Macarthur Pl Ste 100 (92707-6068)
P.O. Box 61452 (92602-6048)
PHONE..................................855 361-2262
Jared M Wolff, *Pr*
Robert D Sznewajs, *
Ido Dotan, *Corporate Secretary*
Robert G Dyck, *CCO*
Diana Hanson, *CAO*
EMP: 120 EST: 2002
SALES (est): 390.12MM
SALES (corp-wide): 390.12MM Publicly Held
Web: www.bancofcal.com
SIC: 6021 National commercial banks

(P-14158)
BANK OF HOPE (HQ)
3200 Wilshire Blvd Ste 1400 (90010-1325)
PHONE..................................213 639-1700
Kevin S Kim, *CEO*
Min J Kim, *Pr*
Scott Yoon-suk Whang, *Ch Bd*
Julianna Balicka, *Ex VP*
▲ EMP: 108 EST: 1985
SALES (est): 769.88MM
SALES (corp-wide): 767.51MM Publicly Held
Web: www.bankofhope.com
SIC: 6021 National commercial banks
PA: Hope Bancorp, Inc.
3200 Wilshire Blvd # 1400
Los Angeles CA
213 639-1700

(P-14159)
BBCN BANK
Also Called: California Center Bank
3731 Wilshire Blvd (90010-2828)
PHONE..................................213 251-2222
▲ EMP: 704
SIC: 6021 National commercial banks

(P-14160)
BNY MELLON NATIONAL ASSN
Also Called: Mellon
10250 Constellation Blvd Ste 2100 (90067-6200)
PHONE..................................310 551-7600
Tiffany L Barbara, *Dir*
EMP: 605
SALES (corp-wide): 19.99B Publicly Held
Web: www.bnymellon.com
SIC: 6021 National commercial banks
HQ: Bny Mellon, National Association
500 Grant St
Pittsburgh PA
412 234-5000

(P-14161)
CITIBANK FSB
Also Called: Citibank
1 World Trade Ctr Ste 100 (90831-0100)
PHONE..................................562 999-3453
Jim Drake, *Brnch Mgr*
EMP: 134
SALES (corp-wide): 101.08B Publicly Held
Web: www.citigroup.com
SIC: 6021 National commercial banks
HQ: Citibank, F.S.B.
1 Sansome St
San Francisco CA
415 627-6000

(P-14162)
CITY NATIONAL BANK
Also Called: C N B Real Estate Group
555 S Flower St Ste 2500 (90071-2326)
P.O. Box 5581 (90209-5581)
PHONE..................................310 888-6500
EMP: 161
SALES (corp-wide): 41.52B Privately Held
Web: www.cnb.com
SIC: 6021 National commercial banks
HQ: City National Bank
555 S Flower St Ste 2500
Los Angeles CA
310 888-6000

(P-14163)
CITY NATIONAL BANK (DH)
555 S Flower St Ste 2500 (90071-2326)
PHONE..................................310 888-6000
Kelly Coffey, *CEO*
Christopher J Warmuth, *
Christopher J Carey, *
Cary Walker, *Corporate Manager*
Richard Shier, *
▲ EMP: 300 EST: 1968
SQ FT: 80,000
SALES (est): 3.3B
SALES (corp-wide): 41.52B Privately Held
Web: www.cnb.com
SIC: 6021 6022 National commercial banks; State commercial banks
HQ: Rbc Usa Holdco Corporation
3 World Financial Ctr
New York NY
212 858-7200

(P-14164)
CITY NATIONAL CORPORATION
555 S Flower St (90071-2326)
▲ EMP: 3566

SIC: 6021 National commercial banks

(P-14165)
CITY NATIONAL SECURITIES INC
400 N Roxbury Dr Ste 400 (90210-5021)
PHONE..................................310 888-6393
Michael Nunnelee, *Pr*
EMP: 164 EST: 2005
SALES (est): 10.24MM
SALES (corp-wide): 41.52B Privately Held
Web: www.cnb.com
SIC: 6021 National commercial banks
HQ: City National Bank
555 S Flower St Ste 2500
Los Angeles CA
310 888-6000

(P-14166)
FIRST COMMUNITY BANCORP
5900 La Place Ct Ste 200 (92008-8832)
PHONE..................................858 756-3023
Andrew Colker, *Prin*
EMP: 99 EST: 2018
SALES (est): 13.68MM
SALES (corp-wide): 1.63B Privately Held
SIC: 6021 National commercial banks
PA: Pacwest Bancorp
9701 Wilshire Blvd # 700
Beverly Hills CA
310 887-8500

(P-14167)
FIRST NATIONAL BANK
Also Called: First National Bank
6110 El Tordo (92067)
P.O. Box 2388 (92067-2388)
PHONE..................................858 756-3023
Matthew P Wagner, *CEO*
Robert Borgman, *
Lynn M Hopkins, *
Sali Tice, *
EMP: 262 EST: 1982
SQ FT: 7,000
SALES (est): 37.07MM
SALES (corp-wide): 1.63B Privately Held
Web: www.pacwest.com
SIC: 6021 6153 National commercial banks; Purchasers of accounts receivable and commercial paper
PA: Pacwest Bancorp
9701 Wilshire Blvd # 700
Beverly Hills CA
310 887-8500

(P-14168)
HOPE BANCORP INC (PA)
3200 Wilshire Blvd Ste 1400 (90010-1333)
PHONE..................................213 639-1700
Kevin S Kim, *Ch Bd*
Julianna Balicka, *Ex VP*
EMP: 83 EST: 2000
SALES (est): 767.51MM
SALES (corp-wide): 767.51MM Publicly Held
Web: www.ir-hopebancorp.com
SIC: 6021 National commercial banks

(P-14169)
MANHATTAN BANCORP
2141 Rosecrans Ave # 1100 (90245-4747)
PHONE..................................310 606-8000
EMP: 187
SIC: 6021 National commercial banks

(P-14170)
MISSION COMMUNITY BANCORP
3380 S Higuera St (93401-6926)
PHONE..................................805 782-5000
EMP: 111

SIC: 6021 National commercial banks

(P-14171)
MUFG UNION BANK FOUNDATION
445 S Figueroa St (90071-1630)
PHONE..................................213 236-5000
Masashi Oka, *Pr*
John F Harrigan, *
W H Wofford, *
David Anderson, *
Charles D Kenny, *
EMP: 4200 EST: 1967
SALES (est): 8.3MM Privately Held
SIC: 6021 National commercial banks

(P-14172)
NORTHERN TRUST OF CALIFORNIA (INC)
Also Called: Northern Trust
201 S Lake Ave Ste 600 (91101-3016)
EMP: 285
SIC: 6021 National commercial banks

(P-14173)
PACIFIC WESTERN BANK
Also Called: Rancho Santa Fe
6110 El Tordo (92067)
PHONE..................................858 756-3023
EMP: 262
SALES (corp-wide): 1.63B Privately Held
Web: www.pacwest.com
SIC: 6021 6153 National commercial banks; Purchasers of accounts receivable and commercial paper
HQ: Pacific Western Bank
9701 Wilshire Blvd # 700
Beverly Hills CA
310 887-8500

(P-14174)
PACWEST BANCORP (PA)
9701 Wilshire Blvd Ste 700 (90212-2007)
PHONE..................................310 887-8500
Matthew P Wagner, *Pr*
John M Eggemeyer Iii, *Ch Bd*
James J Pieczynski, *V Ch Bd*
Bart R Olson, *Ex VP*
Mark T Yung, *Ex VP*
EMP: 133 EST: 1999
SALES (est): 1.63B
SALES (corp-wide): 1.63B Privately Held
Web: www.pacwestbancorp.com
SIC: 6021 National commercial banks

(P-14175)
WELLS FARGO INVESTMENTS LLC
401 B St Ste 101 (92101-4270)
PHONE..................................619 702-6949
EMP: 88
SALES (corp-wide): 82.86B Publicly Held
Web: www.wellsfargoadvisors.com
SIC: 6021 National commercial banks
HQ: Wells Fargo Investments, Llc
420 Montgomery St Frnt
San Francisco CA

(P-14176)
WELLS FARGO INVESTMENTS LLC
603 14th St (90266-4838)
PHONE..................................310 546-4235
John H Busby, *Prin*
EMP: 88
SALES (corp-wide): 82.86B Publicly Held
Web: www.wellsfargoadvisors.com
SIC: 6021 National commercial banks
HQ: Wells Fargo Investments, Llc
420 Montgomery St Frnt

San Francisco CA

6022 State Commercial Banks

(P-14177)
AMERICAN BUSINESS BANK
970 W 190th St Ste 850 (90502-1059)
PHONE...................310 808-1200
Debbie Dm, *Mgr*
EMP: 89
SALES (corp-wide): 134.55MM **Publicly Held**
Web: www.cbbank.com
SIC: 6022 State trust companies accepting deposits, commercial
PA: American Business Bank
400 S Hope St Ste 300
Los Angeles CA
213 430-4000

(P-14178)
AMERICAN BUSINESS BANK
3633 Inland Empire Blvd Ste 720 (91764-4922)
PHONE...................909 919-2040
Elaine Lopez, *Brnch Mgr*
EMP: 88
SALES (corp-wide): 134.55MM **Publicly Held**
Web: www.americanbb.bank
SIC: 6022 State commercial banks
PA: American Business Bank
400 S Hope St Ste 300
Los Angeles CA
213 430-4000

(P-14179)
AMERICAN SECURITY BANK
1401 Dove St Ste 100 (92660-2425)
PHONE...................949 440-5200
EMP: 90
SIC: 6022 State commercial banks

(P-14180)
BNY MELLON NATIONAL ASSN
Also Called: Mellon
1600 Newport Center Dr Ste 200 (92660)
PHONE...................877 420-6377
Carrie Gibson, *Prin*
EMP: 605
SALES (corp-wide): 19.99B **Publicly Held**
Web: www.bnymellon.com
SIC: 6022 State commercial banks
HQ: Bny Mellon, National Association
500 Grant St
Pittsburgh PA
412 234-5000

(P-14181)
BUSA SERVICING INC (PA)
787 W 5th St (90071-2003)
PHONE...................310 203-3400
Manuel Sanchez Lugo, *Ch Bd*
Rebecca Macieira-kaufmann, *CEO*
Thomas Levine, *Senior Vice President Legal*
Roger Johnston, *
Francisco Moreno, *
▲ **EMP:** 200 **EST:** 1963
SALES (est): 46.34MM
SALES (corp-wide): 46.34MM **Privately Held**
Web: www.citigroup.com
SIC: 6022 State commercial banks

(P-14182)
CALIFORNIA BANK & TRUST
11622 El Camino Real (92130-2051)
PHONE...................801 844-7637

David Blackford, *CEO*
Gene Louie, *
Steven Borg, *
Frank Lee, *
◆ **EMP:** 1910 **EST:** 1952
SALES (est): 157.72MM
SALES (corp-wide): 3.34B **Publicly Held**
SIC: 6022 State trust companies accepting deposits, commercial
HQ: Zions Bancorporation
1 S Main St Fl 15
Salt Lake City UT
801 844-7637

(P-14183)
CALIFORNIA REPUBLIC BANK
18400 Von Karman Ave # 630 (92612-0544)
P.O. Box 25085 (92799-5085)
PHONE...................949 270-9700
EMP: 270
SIC: 6022 State commercial banks

(P-14184)
CAPITALSOURCE BANK
130 S State College Blvd (92821-5807)
P.O. Box 2485 (92822-2485)
PHONE...................714 989-4600
EMP: 250
SIC: 6022 State commercial banks

(P-14185)
CATHAY BANK (HQ)
777 N Broadway (90012-2819)
PHONE...................626 279-3698
Dunson K Cheng, *Ch Bd*
Perry P Oei, *
James R Brewer, *
Heng W Chen, *
Irwin Wong, *
▲ **EMP:** 125 **EST:** 1962
SALES (est): 908.87MM **Publicly Held**
Web: www.cathaybank.com
SIC: 6022 State trust companies accepting deposits, commercial
PA: Cathay General Bancorp
777 N Broadway
Los Angeles CA

(P-14186)
CATHAY CAPITAL TRUST II
9650 Flair Dr (91731-3005)
PHONE...................213 625-4700
EMP: 84 **EST:** 2013
SALES (est): 1.59MM **Publicly Held**
Web: www.cathaybank.com
SIC: 6022 State commercial banks
PA: Cathay General Bancorp
777 N Broadway
Los Angeles CA

(P-14187)
CATHAY GENERAL BANCORP (PA)
777 N Broadway (90012-2819)
PHONE...................213 625-4700
Chang M Liu, *Pr*
Dunson K Cheng, *Ex Ch Bd*
Peter Wu, *V Ch Bd*
Anthony M Tang, *V Ch Bd*
Heng W Chen, *Ex VP*
EMP: 139 **EST:** 1990
SALES (est): 908.1MM **Publicly Held**
Web: www.cathaybank.com
SIC: 6022 State commercial banks

(P-14188)
CITIZENS BUSINESS BANK (HQ)
701 N Haven Ave Ste 280 (91764-4920)
P.O. Box 51000 (91761-1087)

PHONE...................909 980-4030
TOLL FREE: 877
Christopher D Myers, *Pr*
Hal W Oswalt, *
E Allen Nicholson, *
David C Harvey, *
David F Farnsworth, *CCO*
▲ **EMP:** 150 **EST:** 1973
SQ FT: 23,000
SALES (est): 566.96MM **Publicly Held**
Web: www.cbbank.com
SIC: 6022 State trust companies accepting deposits, commercial
PA: Cvb Financial Corp.
701 N Haven Ave Ste 350
Ontario CA

(P-14189)
COMMUNITY BANK
460 Sierra Madre Villa Ave (91107-2967)
PHONE...................626 577-1700
▲ **EMP:** 300
SIC: 6022 6029 State trust companies accepting deposits, commercial; Commercial banks, nec

(P-14190)
CVB FINANCIAL CORP (PA)
701 N Haven Ave Ste 350 (91764-4920)
PHONE...................909 980-4030
David A Brager, *CEO*
Hal W Oswalt, *Ch Bd*
George A Borba Junior, *V Ch Bd*
E Allen Nicholson, *CFO*
Richard H Wohl, *Ex VP*
EMP: 104 **EST:** 1981
SALES (est): 564.66MM **Publicly Held**
Web: www.cbbank.com
SIC: 6022 State commercial banks

(P-14191)
EAST WEST BANCORP INC (PA)
Also Called: East West
135 N Los Robles Ave Fl 7 (91101-4525)
PHONE...................626 768-6000
Dominic Ng, *Ch Bd*
Douglas P Krause, *Vice Chairman*
Irene H Oh, *CRO*
Parker Shi, *Ex VP*
Lisa L Kim, *Corporate Secretary*
◆ **EMP:** 270 **EST:** 1998
SALES (est): 2.62B
SALES (corp-wide): 2.62B **Publicly Held**
Web: www.eastwestbank.com
SIC: 6022 State commercial banks

(P-14192)
EAST WEST BANK (HQ)
Also Called: EAST WEST
135 N Los Robles Ave Ste 100 (91101-4526)
PHONE...................626 768-6000
Dominic Ng, *CEO*
Donald S Chow, *Ex VP*
Douglas P Krause, *Ex VP*
Thomas J Tolda, *CFO*
Irene Oh, *Sr VP*
◆ **EMP:** 300 **EST:** 1973
SQ FT: 18,000
SALES (est): 2.62B
SALES (corp-wide): 2.62B **Publicly Held**
Web: www.eastwestbank.com
SIC: 6022 State commercial banks
PA: East West Bancorp, Inc.
135 N Los Robles Ave Fl 7
Pasadena CA
626 768-6000

(P-14193)
ENTERPRISE BANK & TRUST
11939 Rancho Bernardo Rd Ste 200 (92128)
PHONE...................858 432-7000
Stephen Marsh, *Brnch Mgr*
EMP: 118
Web: www.enterprisebank.com
SIC: 6022 State trust companies accepting deposits, commercial
HQ: Enterprise Bank & Trust
150 N Meramec Ave Ste 300
Saint Louis MO
314 725-5500

(P-14194)
ENTERPRISE BANK & TRUST
17785 Center Court Dr N # 750 (90703-9310)
PHONE...................562 345-9092
EMP: 184
SIC: 6022 State trust companies accepting deposits, commercial
HQ: Enterprise Bank & Trust
150 N Meramec Ave Ste 300
Saint Louis MO
314 725-5500

(P-14195)
FARMERS MERCHANTS BNK LONG BCH (HQ)
Also Called: F&M Bank
302 Pine Ave (90802-2326)
P.O. Box 1370 (90801-1370)
PHONE...................562 437-0011
W Henry Walker, *CEO*
Kenneth G Walker, *
John Hinrichs, *
Danile K Walker, *
Michael Hess, *
▲ **EMP:** 130 **EST:** 1907
SQ FT: 150,000
SALES (est): 325.95MM **Privately Held**
Web: www.fmb.com
SIC: 6022 6029 State trust companies accepting deposits, commercial; Commercial banks, nec
PA: Palomar Enterprises, Llc
302 Pine Ave
Long Beach CA

(P-14196)
FB CORPORATION
1211 E Valley Blvd (91801-5235)
PHONE...................626 300-0880
Tim Wang, *Mgr*
EMP: 377
SALES (corp-wide): 551.63MM **Privately Held**
Web: www.first.bank
SIC: 6022 State commercial banks
PA: Fb Corporation
135 N Meramec Ave
Saint Louis MO
314 854-4600

(P-14197)
FIRST FOUNDATION INC (PA)
Also Called: FFI
18101 Von Karman Ave Ste 700 (92612-1012)
PHONE...................949 202-4160
Scott F Kavanaugh, *V Ch Bd*
Ulrich E Keller Junior, *Ex Ch Bd*
Amy Djou, *Interim Chief Financial Officer*
Kelly Rentzel, *Ex VP*
EMP: 160 **EST:** 2006
SALES (est): 452.11MM **Publicly Held**
Web: www.firstfoundationinc.com

SIC: **6022** State commercial banks

(P-14198)
HERITAGE OAKS BANCORP
1222 Vine St (93446-2332)
PHONE......................805 369-5200
EMP: 283
SIC: **6022** State commercial banks

(P-14199)
HERITAGE OAKS BANK
1222 Vine St (93446-2268)
PHONE......................805 239-5200
EMP: 220
SIC: **6022** State commercial banks

(P-14200)
MORGAN STNLEY SMITH BARNEY LLC
74199 El Paseo Ste 201 (92260-4151)
PHONE......................760 568-3500
Anthony Maddlina, *Mgr*
EMP: 125
SALES (corp-wide): 53.67B **Publicly Held**
Web: www.morganstanley.com
SIC: **6022** State commercial banks
HQ: Morgan Stanley Smith Barney, Llc
1585 Broadway
New York NY

(P-14201)
OP BANCORP (PA)
1000 Wilshire Blvd Ste 500 (90017-2457)
PHONE......................213 892-9999
Min J Kim, *Pr*
Brian Choi, *Ch Bd*
Christine Y Oh, *Ex VP*
EMP: 105 **EST:** 2016
SQ FT: 15,239
SALES (est): 105.83MM
SALES (corp-wide): 105.83MM **Publicly Held**
SIC: **6022** State commercial banks

(P-14202)
PACIFIC PREMIER BANCORP INC
3403 10th St Ste 100 (92501-3661)
PHONE......................951 274-2400
Joe Servi, *Brnch Mgr*
EMP: 87
Web: www.ppbi.com
SIC: **6022** State commercial banks
PA: Pacific Premier Bancorp, Inc.
17901 Von Karman Ave # 1
Irvine CA

(P-14203)
PACIFIC PREMIER BANCORP INC (PA)
17901 Von Karman Ave Ste 1200 (92614-6297)
PHONE......................949 864-8000
EMP: 123 **EST:** 1996
SALES (est): 857.33MM **Publicly Held**
Web: www.ppbi.com
SIC: **6022** State commercial banks

(P-14204)
PCB BANCORP (PA)
3701 Wilshire Blvd Ste 100 (90010-2804)
PHONE......................213 210-2000
Henry Kim, *Pr*
Sang Young Lee, *Ch Bd*
Timothy Chang, *Corporate Secretary*
EMP: 245 **EST:** 2007
SALES (est): 116.25MM
SALES (corp-wide): 116.25MM **Publicly Held**

Web: www.mypcbbank.com
SIC: **6022** State commercial banks

(P-14205)
PCB BANK (HQ)
3701 Wilshire Blvd Ste 900 (90010-2804)
PHONE......................213 210-2000
Hae Young Cho, *CEO*
Henry Kim, *
Heo Young Cho, *
Andrew Chung, *
Mike Kim, *Chief Lending Officer*
▲ **EMP:** 152 **EST:** 2003
SALES (est): 116.25MM
SALES (corp-wide): 116.25MM **Publicly Held**
Web: www.mypcbbank.com
SIC: **6022** State commercial banks
PA: Pcb Bancorp
3701 Wilshire Blvd # 100
Los Angeles CA
213 210-2000

(P-14206)
SEACOAST CMMERCE BANC HOLDINGS
11939 Rancho Bernardo Rd (92128-2072)
PHONE......................858 432-7000
Richard Sanborn, *CEO*
Scott R Andrews, *CAO*
S Alan Rosen, *Admn*
EMP: 200 **EST:** 2014
SALES (est): 1.66MM **Publicly Held**
Web: www.scbholdings.com
SIC: **6022** State commercial banks
PA: Enterprise Financial Services Corp
150 N Meramec Ave Ste 350
Saint Louis MO

(P-14207)
SMBC MANUBANK (DH)
Also Called: Manufacturers Bank
515 S Figueroa St 4th Fl (90071-3301)
PHONE......................213 489-6200
Mitsugu Serizawa, *CEO*
Naresh Sheth, *
Adrian Danescu, *
Ted Mergenthaler, *
Leslie A Lyons, *
▲ **EMP:** 164 **EST:** 1962
SQ FT: 69,206
SALES (est): 161.15MM **Privately Held**
Web: www.manufacturersbank.com
SIC: **6022** State commercial banks
HQ: Sumitomo Mitsui Banking Corporation
1-1-2, Marunouchi
Chiyoda-Ku TKY

(P-14208)
STANDARD CHARTERED BANK
601 S Figueroa St Ste 2775 (90017-5877)
PHONE......................626 639-8000
Jim Mc Cabe, *CEO*
EMP: 84
SALES (corp-wide): 24.84B **Privately Held**
Web: www.sc.com
SIC: **6022** **6282** **6029** State trust companies accepting deposits, commercial; Investment advisory service; Commercial banks, nec
HQ: Standard Chartered Bank
1 Basinghall Avenue
London
207 885-8888

(P-14209)
WILSHIRE BANCORP INC
3200 Wilshire Blvd (90010-1333)
PHONE......................213 387-3200
EMP: 547

SIC: **6022** State commercial banks

(P-14210)
WILSHIRE BANK
Also Called: Wilshire State Bank
3200 Wilshire Blvd Fl 10 (90010-1311)
PHONE......................213 427-1000
▲ **EMP:** 349
SIC: **6022** State commercial banks

6029 Commercial Banks, Nec

(P-14211)
BANK OF MANHATTAN
2141 Rosecrans Ave Ste 1100 (90245-4747)
PHONE......................310 606-8000
EMP: 187
SIC: **6029** Commercial banks, nec

(P-14212)
FIRST FOUNDATION INC
301 N Lake Ave Ste 100 (91101-4108)
PHONE......................626 993-1300
Carol Golbranson, *Brnch Mgr*
EMP: 231
Web: www.firstfoundationinc.com
SIC: **6029** Commercial banks, nec
PA: First Foundation Inc.
18101 Von Karman Ave # 7
Irvine CA

(P-14213)
OPUS BANK
19900 Macarthur Blvd Ste 1200 (92612-8427)
PHONE......................949 250-9800
TOLL FREE: 800
▲ **EMP:** 607
Web: www.ppbi.com
SIC: **6029** Commercial banks, nec

(P-14214)
SUMITOMO MITSUI BANKING CORP
601 S Figueroa St Ste 1800 (90017-5723)
PHONE......................213 452-7800
EMP: 115
Web: www.smbcgroup.com
SIC: **6029** Commercial banks, nec
HQ: Sumitomo Mitsui Banking Corporation
1-1-2, Marunouchi
Chiyoda-Ku TKY

6035 Federal Savings Institutions

(P-14215)
GREENBOX LOANS INC
Also Called: Greenbox
3250 Wilshire Blvd Ste 1900 (90010-1605)
PHONE......................800 919-1086
Raymond Eshaghian, *CEO*
EMP: 88 **EST:** 2000
SALES (est): 48.78MM **Privately Held**
Web: www.greenboxloans.com
SIC: **6035** **6162** Federal savings and loan associations; Loan correspondents

(P-14216)
ONEWEST BANK GROUP LLC
888 E Walnut St (91101-1895)
P.O. Box 7056 (91109-7056)
PHONE......................626 535-4870
EMP: 850
SIC: **6035** Federal savings banks

(P-14217)
PACIFIC TRUST BANK
18500 Von Karman Ave Ste 1100 (92612-0504)
P.O. Box 61452 (92602-6048)
PHONE......................949 236-5211
Robert M Franko, *CEO*
Al Majors, *
Hans Ganz, *
James P Sheehy, *
Marangal Domingo, *
EMP: 107 **EST:** 1941
SQ FT: 12,100
SALES (est): 83.94MM
SALES (corp-wide): 390.12MM **Publicly Held**
SIC: **6035** Federal savings banks
PA: Banc Of California, Inc.
3 Macarthur Pl Ste 100
Santa Ana CA
855 361-2262

(P-14218)
PAN AMERICAN BANK FSB
18191 Von Karman Ave Ste 300 (92612-7106)
PHONE......................949 224-1917
Jim Vagim, *Pr*
EMP: 350 **EST:** 1994
SQ FT: 20,000
SALES (est): 96.49MM
SALES (corp-wide): 1.95B **Publicly Held**
SIC: **6035** Federal savings and loan associations
HQ: Vroom Automotive Finance Corporation
1071 Camelback St Ste 100
Newport Beach CA
949 224-1226

(P-14219)
PFF BANCORP INC (PA)
2058 N Mills Ave Ste 139 (91711-2812)
PHONE......................213 683-6393
EMP: 852 **EST:** 1995
SALES (est): 46.19MM **Privately Held**
SIC: **6035** Federal savings and loan associations

6036 Savings Institutions, Except Federal

(P-14220)
MIZUHO BANK LTD
Also Called: MIZUHO BANK LTD
350 S Grand Ave Ste 1500 (90071-3471)
PHONE......................213 243-4500
Geoffrey Matsunaga, *Admn*
EMP: 136
Web: www.mizuhogroup.com
SIC: **6036** Savings institutions, except federal
HQ: Mizuho Bank, Ltd.
1271 Ave Of The Americas
New York NY
212 282-3000

6061 Federal Credit Unions

(P-14221)
ALTAONE FEDERAL CREDIT UNION (PA)
Also Called: Alta One Fcu
701 S China Lake Blvd (93555-5027)
P.O. Box 1209 (93556-1209)
PHONE......................760 371-7000
Stephanie Sievers, *Pr*
Denise Mattice, *
EMP: 114 **EST:** 1947
SQ FT: 33,000

SALES (est): 19.98MM
SALES (corp-wide): 19.98MM **Privately Held**
Web: www.altaone.org
SIC: 6061 Federal credit unions

(P-14222)
AMERICAN FIRST CREDIT UNION (PA)
6 Pointe Dr Ste 400 (92821-6322)
PHONE..............................562 691-1112
TOLL FREE: 800
Jon Shigematsu, *Prin*
Jon Shigematsu, *CEO*
Julie Glance, *
Brian Thompson, *CAO**
EMP: 96 **EST:** 1956
SALES (est): 38.33MM
SALES (corp-wide): 38.33MM **Privately Held**
Web: www.amerfirst.org
SIC: 6061 Federal credit unions

(P-14223)
ARROWHEAD CENTRAL CREDIT UNION (PA)
8686 Haven Ave (91730-9109)
P.O. Box 4100 (91729-4100)
PHONE..............................866 212-4333
Darin Woinarowicz, *CEO*
Marie A Alonzo, *Ch*
Susan Conjurski, *Ex VP*
Doug Hallen, *Treas*
Raymond Mesler, *CFO*
EMP: 301 **EST:** 1949
SQ FT: 40,000
SALES (est): 102.2MM
SALES (corp-wide): 102.2MM **Privately Held**
Web: www.arrowheadcu.org
SIC: 6061 Federal credit unions

(P-14224)
FIREFIGHTERS FIRST CREDIT UN (PA)
1520 W Colorado Blvd (91105-1413)
PHONE..............................323 254-1700
Dixie Abramian, *CEO*
EMP: 138 **EST:** 1935
SALES (est): 81.32MM
SALES (corp-wide): 81.32MM **Privately Held**
Web: www.firefightersfirstcu.org
SIC: 6061 Federal credit unions

(P-14225)
FIRST ENTERTAINMENT CREDIT UN (PA)
6735 Forest Lawn Dr Ste 100 (90068-1055)
P.O. Box 100 (90078-0100)
PHONE..............................323 851-3673
Charles A Bruen, *Pr*
Lucy Wander-perna, *Ch*
Dennis Tange, *
Michael Edwards, *Vice Chairman**
Irwin Jacobson, *
EMP: 80 **EST:** 1998
SQ FT: 57,000
SALES (est): 79.21MM
SALES (corp-wide): 79.21MM **Privately Held**
Web: www.firstent.org
SIC: 6061 Federal credit unions

(P-14226)
FIRST FINANCIAL FEDERAL CR UN
650 Sierra Madre Villa Ave Ste 300 (91107-2013)

PHONE..............................800 537-8491
Dietmar Huesch, *CFO*
EMP: 140 **EST:** 1974
SALES (est): 10.94MM **Privately Held**
SIC: 6061 Federal credit unions

(P-14227)
FRONTWAVE CREDIT UNION (PA)
1278 Rocky Point Dr (92056-5867)
PHONE..............................760 430-7511
Bill Birnie, *Pr*
Shilpa Edlabadkar, *
Paul Leonhardt, *CLO**
Jennifer Williams, *
EMP: 107 **EST:** 1953
SQ FT: 22,000
SALES (est): 31.72MM
SALES (corp-wide): 31.72MM **Privately Held**
Web: www.frontwavecu.com
SIC: 6061 Federal credit unions

(P-14228)
KERN FEDERAL CREDIT UNION
1717 Truxtun Ave (93301-5102)
PHONE..............................661 327-9461
Brandon Ivie, *CEO*
EMP: 87 **EST:** 1949
SQ FT: 17,000
SALES (est): 10.46MM **Privately Held**
Web: www.stratacu.org
SIC: 6061 6163 Federal credit unions; Loan brokers

(P-14229)
KINECTA FEDERAL CREDIT UNION (PA)
Also Called: KINECTA
1440 Rosecrans Ave (90266-3702)
P.O. Box 10003 (90267-7503)
PHONE..............................310 643-5400
Keith Sultemeier, *CEO*
Teresa Freeborn, *
Joseph E Whitaker, *
Steven J Glouberman, *
Sharon Moseley, *
EMP: 250 **EST:** 1940
SQ FT: 80,000
SALES (est): 261.92MM
SALES (corp-wide): 261.92MM **Privately Held**
Web: www.kinecta.org
SIC: 6061 Federal credit unions

(P-14230)
LOGIX FEDERAL CREDIT UNION (PA)
2340 N Hollywood Way (91505-1124)
P.O. Box 4130 (91310-4130)
PHONE..............................888 718-5328
Ana Fonseca, *CEO*
Jan Franklin, *
Tim Boland, *
Dave Styler, *
Ana Fonseca, *CFO*
EMP: 210 **EST:** 1937
SQ FT: 75,000
SALES (est): 230.72MM
SALES (corp-wide): 230.72MM **Privately Held**
Web: www.logixbanking.com
SIC: 6061 Federal credit unions

(P-14231)
LOS ANGELES FEDERAL CREDIT UN (PA)
Also Called: Los Angeles Federal Credit Un
300 S Glendale Ave Ste 100 (91205-1752)

PHONE..............................818 242-8640
John T Dea, *CEO*
Richard Lie, *
Leta Cook, *
Anthony Cuevas, *
EMP: 100 **EST:** 1936
SQ FT: 40,000
SALES (est): 35.44MM
SALES (corp-wide): 35.44MM **Privately Held**
Web: www.lafcu.org
SIC: 6061 Federal credit unions

(P-14232)
MISSION FEDERAL CREDIT UNION
4250 Clairemont Mesa Blvd Ste B (92117-2747)
P.O. Box 910557 (92191-0557)
PHONE..............................858 531-5106
EMP: 218
SALES (corp-wide): 119.62MM **Privately Held**
Web: www.missionfed.com
SIC: 6061 Federal credit unions
PA: Mission Federal Credit Union
5785 Oberlin Dr Ste 312
San Diego CA
858 546-2184

(P-14233)
MISSION FEDERAL SERVICES LLC (PA)
10325 Meanley Dr (92131-3011)
P.O. Box 919023 (92191-9023)
PHONE..............................858 524-2850
Debra Schwartz, *CEO*
Rose Hartley, *
Richard Hartley, *
Gary M Devan Senior, *Vice-President Information Systems*
Elaine Ziegler, *Senior Vice President Human Resources**
EMP: 150 **EST:** 1961
SQ FT: 55,000
SALES (est): 109.72MM
SALES (corp-wide): 109.72MM **Privately Held**
Web: www.missionfed.com
SIC: 6061 Federal credit unions

(P-14234)
NUVISION FINCL FEDERAL CR UN (PA)
7812 Edinger Ave Ste 100 (92647-3727)
P.O. Box 1220 (92647-1220)
PHONE..............................714 375-8000
Roger Ballard, *CEO*
John Afdem, *CFO*
Robert Geraci, *Treas*
EMP: 137 **EST:** 1935
SALES (est): 98.79MM
SALES (corp-wide): 98.79MM **Privately Held**
Web: www.nuvisionfederal.com
SIC: 6061 Federal credit unions

(P-14235)
ORANGE COUNTYS CREDIT UNION (PA)
1721 E Saint Andrew Pl (92705-4934)
P.O. Box 11777 (92711-1777)
PHONE..............................714 755-5900
Lucy Ito, *Interim Chief Executive Officer*
Dan Dillon, *
EMP: 157 **EST:** 1938
SALES (est): 94.25MM
SALES (corp-wide): 94.25MM **Privately Held**
Web: www.orangecountyscu.org

SIC: 6061 Federal credit unions

(P-14236)
SAN DIEGO COUNTY CREDIT UNION (PA)
Also Called: SDCCU
6545 Sequence Dr (92121-4363)
PHONE..............................877 732-2848
Irene Oberbauer, *Pr*
Robert Marchand, *
Heather Moshier, *
Theresa Halleck, *
Tracey Curran, *
▲ **EMP:** 239 **EST:** 1938
SQ FT: 50,000
SALES (est): 329.48MM
SALES (corp-wide): 329.48MM **Privately Held**
Web: www.sdccu.com
SIC: 6061 Federal credit unions

(P-14237)
SCE FEDERAL CREDIT UNION (PA)
Also Called: SCE FCU
12701 Schabarum Ave (91706-6807)
P.O. Box 8017 (91734-2317)
PHONE..............................626 960-6888
Dennis Huber, *CEO*
George Poitou, *
Daniel Rader, *
EMP: 90 **EST:** 1952
SQ FT: 30,000
SALES (est): 46.61MM
SALES (corp-wide): 46.61MM **Privately Held**
Web: www.scefcu.org
SIC: 6061 Federal credit unions

(P-14238)
SCHOOLSFIRST FEDERAL CREDIT UN (PA)
2115 N Broadway (92706-2613)
P.O. Box 11547 (92711-1547)
PHONE..............................714 258-4000
Bill Cheney, *CEO*
Jose Lara, *
Jim Phillips, *
Jill Meznarich, *Chief Auditor**
EMP: 270 **EST:** 1934
SALES (est): 335.16MM
SALES (corp-wide): 335.16MM **Privately Held**
Web: www.schoolsfirstfcu.org
SIC: 6061 Federal credit unions

(P-14239)
TELESIS COMMUNITY CREDIT UNION (PA)
9301 Winnetka Ave (91311-6069)
PHONE..............................818 885-1226
Grace Mayo, *Pr*
Jean Faenza, *
EMP: 90 **EST:** 1993
SQ FT: 17,000
SALES (est): 8.96MM **Privately Held**
Web: www.telesiscu.com
SIC: 6061 6163 Federal credit unions; Loan brokers

(P-14240)
UNIFY FINCL CR UN PROF CORP (PA)
2305b W 190th St (90504-6003)
P.O. Box 10018 (90267-7518)
PHONE..............................877 254-9328
Gordon M Howe, *CEO*
EMP: 80 **EST:** 1958
SALES (est): 118.97MM

SALES (corp-wide): 118.97MM **Privately Held**
Web: www.unifyfcu.com
SIC: 6061 Federal credit unions

(P-14241)
UNITED SVCS AMER FEDERAL CR UN (PA)
Also Called: USA Federal Credit Union
9999 Willow Creek Rd (92131-1117)
PHONE..............................858 831-8100
TOLL FREE: 800
Martin Cassell, *Pr*
Ron Davis, *
Jim Bedinger, *
EMP: 90 **EST:** 1953
SQ FT: 42,000
SALES (est): 19.03MM
SALES (corp-wide): 19.03MM **Privately Held**
Web: www.navyfederal.org
SIC: 6061 Federal credit unions

(P-14242)
UNIVERSITY CREDIT UNION
1500 S Sepulveda Blvd (90025-3312)
PHONE..............................310 477-6628
Charles Bumbarger, *Pr*
Tristan Dion Chen, *CMO*
EMP: 104 **EST:** 1945
SALES (est): 44.78MM **Privately Held**
Web: www.ucu.org
SIC: 6061 Federal credit unions

(P-14243)
VENTURA COUNTY CREDIT UNION (PA)
2575 Vista Del Mar Dr Ste 100 (93001-3900)
PHONE..............................805 477-4000
Joseph Schroeder, *Pr*
Linda Rossi, *
Gavin Bradley, *
Linda Sim, *
EMP: 84 **EST:** 1950
SQ FT: 22,500
SALES (est): 50.31MM
SALES (corp-wide): 50.31MM **Privately Held**
Web: www.vccuonline.net
SIC: 6061 Federal credit unions

6062 State Credit Unions

(P-14244)
ADELFI CREDIT UNION
Also Called: ECCU
955 W Imperial Hwy Ste 100 (92821-3812)
P.O. Box 2400 (92822-2400)
PHONE..............................714 671-5700
Abel Pomar, *CEO*
Gregory Talbott, *
Susan Rushing, *
Patty Staples, *
Tom Honan, *
EMP: 147 **EST:** 1964
SQ FT: 125,000
SALES (est): 55.93MM **Privately Held**
Web: www.adelfibanking.com
SIC: 6062 State credit unions, not federally chartered

(P-14245)
CALIFORNIA CREDIT UNION (PA)
701 N Brand Blvd Fl 7 (91203-1218)
P.O. Box 29100 (91209-9100)
PHONE..............................818 291-6700
Steve O'connell, *CEO*
Rebecca Collier, *

Hudson Lee, *
EMP: 120 **EST:** 1933
SALES (est): 152.71MM
SALES (corp-wide): 152.71MM **Privately Held**
Web: www.ccu.com
SIC: 6062 6061 State credit unions, not federally chartered; Federal credit unions

(P-14246)
COASTHILLS CREDIT UNION (PA)
Also Called: CSCU
1075 E Betteravia Rd (93454-7023)
P.O. Box 8000 (93456-8000)
PHONE..............................805 733-7600
Jeff York, *Pr*
Dave Upham, *
Scott Coe, *
Marty Chatham, *
Dal Widick, *
EMP: 80 **EST:** 1958
SQ FT: 30,000
SALES (est): 77.72MM
SALES (corp-wide): 77.72MM **Privately Held**
Web: www.coasthills.coop
SIC: 6062 State credit unions, not federally chartered

(P-14247)
CU COOPERATIVE SYSTEMS INC (PA)
Also Called: Co-Op Solutions
9692 Haven Ave (91730-0101)
PHONE..............................909 948-2500
Dean Michaels, *Pr*
Grace Mayo, *Vice Chairman*
Tom Sargent, *Ch Bd*
John Bommarito, *Treas*
James Hanisch, *Ex VP*
▲ **EMP:** 285 **EST:** 1981
SALES (est): 185.31MM
SALES (corp-wide): 185.31MM **Privately Held**
Web: www.co-opfs.org
SIC: 6062 State credit unions, not federally chartered

(P-14248)
LBS FINANCIAL CREDIT UNION (PA)
5505 Garden Grove Blvd Ste 500 (92683-1894)
PHONE..............................562 598-9007
Sean Hardeman, *CEO*
Sean M Hardeman, *
Gene Allen, *
Dug Woog, *
EMP: 120 **EST:** 1935
SQ FT: 63,000
SALES (est): 64.22MM
SALES (corp-wide): 64.22MM **Privately Held**
Web: www.lbsfcu.org
SIC: 6062 State credit unions, not federally chartered

(P-14249)
LOS ANGELES POLICE CREDIT UN (PA)
Also Called: L A P F C U
16150 Sherman Way (91406-3938)
P.O. Box 10188 (91410-0188)
PHONE..............................818 787-6520
Tyler E Izen, *Ch Bd*
G Michael Padgett, *
Warren D Spayth, *
Angelino Cayanan, *
EMP: 100 **EST:** 1936

SQ FT: 30,000
SALES (est): 58.55MM
SALES (corp-wide): 58.55MM **Privately Held**
Web: www.lapfcu.org
SIC: 6062 6061 State credit unions, not federally chartered; Federal credit unions

(P-14250)
NORTH ISLAND FINANCIAL CREDIT UNION
Also Called: North Island Credit Union
5898 Copley Dr Ste 100 (92111-7917)
P.O. Box 85833 (92186-5833)
PHONE..............................619 656-6525
EMP: 353
SIC: 6062 State credit unions

(P-14251)
PREMIER AMERICA CREDIT UNION (PA)
Also Called: Premier Amer Wealth MGT Group
19867 Prairie St Lbby (91311-6532)
P.O. Box 2178 (91313-2178)
PHONE..............................818 772-4000
John M Merlo, *Pr*
James Anderson, *
Nancy Wheeler-chandler, *Vice Chairman*
Liz Condercuri, *
Marge Mcnaught, *Sr VP*
EMP: 135 **EST:** 1957
SQ FT: 80,000
SALES (est): 107.51MM
SALES (corp-wide): 107.51MM **Privately Held**
Web: www.premieramerica.com
SIC: 6062 6163 State credit unions, not federally chartered; Loan brokers

(P-14252)
VISTERRA CREDIT UNION
23520 Cactus Ave (92553-8906)
P.O. Box 9500 (92552-9500)
PHONE..............................951 656-4411
EMP: 107
Web: www.visterracu.org
SIC: 6062 State credit unions

(P-14253)
WESCOM CENTRAL CREDIT UNION (PA)
123 S Marengo Ave (91101-2428)
P.O. Box 7058 (91109-7058)
PHONE..............................888 493-7266
TOLL FREE: 888
Darren Williams, *Prin*
Jane P Wood, *Prin*
Keith Pipes, *Prin*
Jonathon Bauman, *Prin*
Jeanne Brown, *Prin*
EMP: 425 **EST:** 1934
SQ FT: 90,000
SALES (est): 279.21MM
SALES (corp-wide): 279.21MM **Privately Held**
Web: www.wescom.org
SIC: 6062 State credit unions, not federally chartered

6091 Nondeposit Trust Facilities

(P-14254)
SUNAMERICA INC (HQ)
Also Called: SunAmerica
1 Sun America Ctr Fl 38 (90067-6121)
PHONE..............................310 772-6000

Eli Broad, *Ch*
Jay S Wintrob, *CEO*
James R Belardi, *Ex VP*
Michael J Akers, *Sr VP*
Mary L Cavanaugh, *Sr VP*
▲ **EMP:** 1000 **EST:** 1957
SQ FT: 95,845
SALES (est): 459.86MM
SALES (corp-wide): 56.44B **Publicly Held**
Web: www.liveatwestfield.com
SIC: 6091 6311 6211 6282 Nondeposit trust facilities; Life insurance carriers; Mutual funds, selling by independent salesperson; Manager of mutual funds, contract or fee basis
PA: American International Group, Inc.
1271 Ave Of The Americas
New York NY
212 770-7000

6099 Functions Related To Depository Banking

(P-14255)
ASSOCTED FGN EXCH HOLDINGS INC (HQ)
21045 Califa St (91367-5104)
PHONE..............................818 386-2702
Irving Barr, *Ch*
Jan Vliestra, *
Fred Kunik, *
EMP: 89 **EST:** 2006
SALES (est): 112.61MM **Publicly Held**
SIC: 6099 Foreign currency exchange
PA: Fleetcor Technologies, Inc.
3280 Peachtree Rd Ne # 2400
Atlanta GA

(P-14256)
CONTINENTAL CURRENCY SVCS INC (PA)
Also Called: Cash It Here
1108 E 17th St (92701-2600)
P.O. Box 10970 (92711-0970)
PHONE..............................714 667-6699
Fred Kunik, *Pr*
Irving Barr, *
David Wilder, *
EMP: 80 **EST:** 1977
SQ FT: 12,500
SALES (est): 98.91MM
SALES (corp-wide): 98.91MM **Privately Held**
Web: www.continentalcurrencyservices.com
SIC: 6099 Check cashing agencies

(P-14257)
CONTINENTAL EXCH SOLUTIONS INC (HQ)
Also Called: Ria Financial Service
6565 Knott Ave (90620-1139)
PHONE..............................714 522-7044
Juan C Bianchi, *CEO*
Timothy A Fanning, *
Shawn D Fielder, *
EMP: 94 **EST:** 1987
SALES (est): 377.87MM **Publicly Held**
Web: us.riafinancial.com
SIC: 6099 Electronic funds transfer network, including switching
PA: Euronet Worldwide, Inc.
11400 Tomahwk Crk Pkwy # 300
Leawood KS

(P-14258)
DEBISYS INC (PA)
Also Called: Emida Technologies
27442 Portola Pkwy Ste 150 (92610-2823)

PHONE..............................949 699-1401
Dennis Andrews, *CEO*
Jim Wodach, *
EMP: 80 **EST:** 1977
SQ FT: 10,000
SALES (est): 53.23MM
SALES (corp-wide): 53.23MM **Privately Held**
Web: www.emida.com
SIC: 6099 Automated teller machine (ATM) network

(P-14259)
E Z SERVICES
Also Called: Super Services
1101 W Lincoln Ave Ste 145 (92805-3590)
PHONE..............................714 635-7599
Rosalva Sepulveda, *Brnch Mgr*
EMP: 95
SIC: 6099 Check cashing agencies
PA: E Z Services
    1221 E 17th St
    Santa Ana CA

(P-14260)
FCTI INC (PA)
11766 Wilshire Blvd Ste 300 (90025-6538)
PHONE..............................310 405-0022
EMP: 86 **EST:** 1993
SALES (est): 36.76MM **Privately Held**
Web: www.fcti.com
SIC: 6099 Automated teller machine (ATM) network

(P-14261)
HAPPY MONEY INC
Also Called: Payoff
21515 Hawthorne Blvd Ste 200 (90503-6512)
PHONE..............................949 430-0630
EMP: 351 **EST:** 2009
SALES (est): 11.97MM **Privately Held**
Web: www.happymoney.com
SIC: 6099 Functions related to deposit banking

(P-14262)
POPULUS FINANCIAL GROUP INC
Also Called: Ace Cash Express
6302 Van Buren Blvd (92503-2051)
PHONE..............................951 509-3506
Michael Mc Knight, *Brnch Mgr*
EMP: 105
Web: www.acecashexpress.com
SIC: 6099 Check cashing agencies
HQ: Populus Financial Group, Inc.
    300 E John Carpenter Fwy # 900
    Irving TX
    972 550-5000

(P-14263)
SAN MNUEL BAND MISSION INDIANS
101 Pure Water Ln (92346-6711)
PHONE..............................909 425-4682
EMP: 118
Web: www.sanmanuel-nsn.gov
SIC: 6099 Check clearing services
PA: San Manuel Band Of Mission Indians
    26569 Community Center Dr
    Highland CA
    909 864-8933

(P-14264)
SERFIN FUNDS TRANSFER (PA)
1000 S Fremont Ave Bldg A-O (91803-8800)
PHONE..............................626 457-3070

EMP: 100 **EST:** 1994
SALES (est): 9.74MM **Privately Held**
SIC: 6099 Electronic funds transfer network, including switching

---

6111 Federal And Federally Sponsored Credit

(P-14265)
DEUTSCHE BANK NATIONAL TR CO
1999 Avenue Of The Stars Ste 3750 (90067-6022)
PHONE..............................310 788-6200
EMP: 100 **EST:** 1983
SALES (est): 161.96MM
SALES (corp-wide): 23B **Privately Held**
SIC: 6111 National Consumer Cooperative Bank
HQ: Deutsche Bank Trust Company Americas
    60 Wall St
    New York NY
    212 250-2500

(P-14266)
LAW SCHOOL FINANCIAL INC
Also Called: Law School Loans
175 S Lake Ave Unit 200 (91101-2629)
PHONE..............................626 243-1800
EMP: 190
SQ FT: 25,000
SALES (est): 15.5MM **Privately Held**
Web: www.lawschoolloans.com
SIC: 6111 Student Loan Marketing Association

6141 Personal Credit Institutions

(P-14267)
AMERICAN HONDA FINANCE CORP (DH)
Also Called: AMERICAN HONDA
1919 Torrance Blvd (90501-2722)
P.O. Box 2200 (90509-2200)
PHONE..............................310 972-2239
Hideo Tamaka, *CEO*
John Weisickle, *
Stephan Smith, *
EMP: 200 **EST:** 1980
SALES (est): 2.5B **Privately Held**
Web: www.honda.com
SIC: 6141 Financing: automobiles, furniture, etc., not a deposit bank
HQ: American Honda Motor Co., Inc.
    1919 Torrance Blvd
    Torrance CA
    310 783-2000

(P-14268)
CASHCALL INC
Also Called: Chapter Seven Lending
1 City Blvd W Ste 102 (92868-3621)
P.O. Box 66007 (92816-6007)
PHONE..............................949 752-4600
John Paul Reddam, *CEO*
Ethan Taub, *CMO* *
EMP: 1400 **EST:** 2000
SALES (est): 323.43MM **Privately Held**
Web: www.cashcall.com
SIC: 6141 Personal finance licensed loan companies, small

(P-14269)
CIG FINANCIAL LLC
Also Called: Autonation Finance

6 Executive Cir Ste 100 (92614-6732)
P.O. Box 19795 (92623-9795)
PHONE..............................877 244-4442
Greg Skjonsby, *Pr*
EMP: 102 **EST:** 2011
SALES (est): 60.2MM
SALES (corp-wide): 26.98B **Publicly Held**
Web: www.cigfinancial.com
SIC: 6141 7389 Consumer finance companies; Financial services
PA: Autonation, Inc.
    200 Sw 1st Ave Ste 1700
    Fort Lauderdale FL
    954 769-6000

(P-14270)
CITIFINANCIAL CREDIT COMPANY
Also Called: Citifinancial
2655 Del Vista Dr (91745-5244)
PHONE..............................626 712-8780
EMP: 97
SALES (corp-wide): 101.08B **Publicly Held**
SIC: 6141 Consumer finance companies
HQ: Citifinancial Credit Company
    300 Saint Paul Pl Fl 3
    Baltimore MD
    410 332-3000

(P-14271)
HYUNDAI PROTECTION PLAN INC
3161 Michelson Dr Ste 1900 (92612-4400)
PHONE..............................949 468-4000
Jwa Jin Cho, *Prin*
EMP: 297 **EST:** 2015
SALES (est): 4.51MM **Privately Held**
SIC: 6141 Automobile loans, including insurance
HQ: Hyundai Capital America
    3161 Michelson Dr # 1900
    Irvine CA

(P-14272)
MITSUBISHI MOTORS CR AMER INC (DH)
Also Called: Mmca
6400 Katella Ave (90630-5208)
P.O. Box 689040 (37068-9040)
PHONE..............................714 799-4730
Dan Booth, *Pr*
Charles Tredway, *
Ellen Gleberman, *
Hideyuki Kitamura, *
EMP: 394 **EST:** 1990
SQ FT: 32,256
SALES (est): 151.85MM **Privately Held**
Web: www.mitsubishicars.com
SIC: 6141 6159 Automobile loans, including insurance; Truck finance leasing
HQ: Mitsubishi Motors North America, Inc.
    4031 Aspen Grove Dr
    Franklin TN
    714 799-4730

(P-14273)
MONTEREY FINANCIAL SVCS INC (PA)
Also Called: Monterey Collection Services
4095 Avenida De La Plata (92056-5802)
P.O. Box 5199 (92052-5199)
PHONE..............................760 639-3500
Robert Steinke, *Pr*
Mike Gray, *
Kathi Steinke, *
EMP: 110 **EST:** 1989
SQ FT: 27,000
SALES (est): 21.84MM **Privately Held**
Web: www.montereyfinancial.com

SIC: 6141 8721 7322 8742 Consumer finance companies; Billing and bookkeeping service; Collection agency, except real estate; Financial consultant

(P-14274)
NATIONAL PLANNING CORPORATION
100 N Pacific Coast Hwy Ste 1800 (90245-5612)
PHONE..............................800 881-7174
John C Johnson, *Pr*
Sarah Corce, *
Jim Dafalco, *
Patricia Mccallop, *CCO*
EMP: 150 **EST:** 1998
SALES (est): 21.42MM **Privately Held**
Web: www.nationalplanningholdings.com
SIC: 6141 Automobile and consumer finance companies

(P-14275)
NEW AMERICAN FUNDING LLC (PA)
Also Called: Naf
14511 Myford Rd Ste 100 (92780-7057)
PHONE..............................949 430-7029
Rick Arvielo, *CEO*
Patricia Arvielo, *
Christy Bunce, *
Scott Frommert, *
EMP: 650 **EST:** 2002
SALES (est): 408.95MM **Privately Held**
Web: www.newamericanfunding.com
SIC: 6141 7371 Licensed loan companies, small; Computer software development and applications

(P-14276)
NORTH AMERICAN ACCEPTANCE CORP
Also Called: An Open Check
3191 Red Hill Ave Ste 100 (92626-3451)
PHONE..............................714 868-3195
Marco J Rasic, *CEO*
Mary Clancey Rasic, *
EMP: 123 **EST:** 2002
SQ FT: 24,000
SALES (est): 11.18MM **Privately Held**
SIC: 6141 6719 Automobile and consumer finance companies; Personal holding companies, except banks

(P-14277)
PAYOFF INC
Also Called: Happy Money
3200 Park Center Dr Ste 800 (92626-7163)
PHONE..............................949 430-0630
Scott Saunders, *CEO*
Christopher Hilliard, *CCO* *
Adam Zarlengo, *CPO* *
EMP: 89 **EST:** 2012
SQ FT: 19,500
SALES (est): 24.89MM **Privately Held**
Web: www.happymoney.com
SIC: 6141 Personal credit institutions

(P-14278)
PROFESSIONAL CR REPORTING INC
3560 Hyland Ave (92626-1438)
PHONE..............................714 556-1570
Tim Nguyen, *Admn*
EMP: 187 **EST:** 2016
SALES (est): 1.88MM
SALES (corp-wide): 288.05MM **Publicly Held**
Web: www.profcredit.com

PRODUCTS & SVCS

SIC: 6141 Personal credit institutions
PA: Meridianlink, Inc.
3560 Hyland Ave Ste 200
Costa Mesa CA
714 708-6950

6153 Short-term Business Credit

(P-14279)
AMWEST FUNDING CORP
6 Pointe Dr Ste 300 (92821-6323)
PHONE..............................714 831-3333
Ryan Kim, *Pr*
EMP: 112 **EST:** 2017
SALES (est): 17.23MM **Privately Held**
Web: www.amwestfunding.com
SIC: 6153 Working capital financing

(P-14280)
BALBOA CAPITAL CORPORATION (DH)
575 Anton Blvd Ste 1200 (92626-7685)
PHONE..............................949 756-0800
H Palmer Proctor Junior, *CEO*
EMP: 200 **EST:** 1988
SQ FT: 24,000
SALES (est): 144.3MM
SALES (corp-wide): 1.18B **Publicly Held**
Web: www.balboacapital.com
SIC: 6153 Working capital financing
HQ: Ameris Bank
305 S Main St
Moultrie GA
800 845-5219

(P-14281)
ENCORE CAPITAL GROUP INC (PA)
Also Called: Encore
350 Camino De La Reina Ste 100 (92108)
PHONE..............................877 445-4581
Ashish Masih, *Pr*
Michael P Monaco, *Non-Executive Chairman of the Board*
Jonathan C Clark, *Ex VP*
Gregory L Call, *Corporate Secretary*
Monique Dumais, *CIO*
EMP: 528 **EST:** 1990
SQ FT: 118,000
SALES (est): 1.4B
SALES (corp-wide): 1.4B **Publicly Held**
Web: www.encorecapital.com
SIC: 6153 Purchasers of accounts receivable and commercial paper

(P-14282)
HANA COMMERCIAL FINANCE LLC
1000 Wilshire Blvd Ste 570 (90017-2462)
PHONE..............................213 240-1234
Sunnie Kim, *Managing Member*
EMP: 85 **EST:** 2016
SALES (est): 6.9MM **Privately Held**
Web: www.hanafinancial.com
SIC: 6153 Factoring services

(P-14283)
INPUT 1 LLC
6200 Canoga Ave Ste 400 (91367-2459)
PHONE..............................818 340-0030
Todd Greenbaum, *Managing Member*
Jeffrey S Greenbaum, *
EMP: 110 **EST:** 1984
SQ FT: 24,000
SALES (est): 18.93MM **Privately Held**
Web: www.input1.com

SIC: 6153 7371 Short-term business credit institutions, except agricultural; Computer software development and applications

(P-14284)
MIDLAND CREDIT MANAGEMENT INC
Also Called: Midland Credit Management
350 Camino De La Reina Ste 100 (92108)
P.O. Box 939069 (92193-9069)
PHONE..............................877 240-2377
Kenneth A Vecchione, *CEO*
Carl Gregory, *
Robin Pruitt, *
Monique Dumais, *CIO*
EMP: 1800 **EST:** 1953
SALES (est): 454.67MM
SALES (corp-wide): 1.4B **Publicly Held**
Web: www.midlandcredit.com
SIC: 6153 Short-term business credit institutions, except agricultural
PA: Encore Capital Group, Inc.
350 Cmino De La Rina Ste Reina
San Diego CA
877 445-4581

(P-14285)
NATIONAL FUNDING INC (PA)
Also Called: Moneyjet
9530 Towne Centre Dr Ste 120 (92121-1972)
PHONE..............................888 733-2383
EMP: 120 **EST:** 1999
SALES (est): 14.65MM
SALES (corp-wide): 14.65MM **Privately Held**
Web: www.nationalfunding.com
SIC: 6153 6159 7389 Working capital financing; Machinery and equipment finance leasing; Financial services

(P-14286)
RELIANT SERVICES GROUP LLC
Also Called: Reliant Funding Group
9540 Towne Centre Dr Ste 100 (92121)
PHONE..............................877 850-0998
Steve Kietz, *CEO*
Adam Stettner, *
Paul Norman, *
EMP: 180 **EST:** 2000
SALES (est): 46.65MM **Privately Held**
Web: www.reliantfunding.com
SIC: 6153 Working capital financing

(P-14287)
RIVIERA FINANCE OF TEXAS INC
10430 Pioneer Blvd Ste 1 (90670-8245)
PHONE..............................562 777-1300
Sandy Newman, *Brnch Mgr*
EMP: 87
Web: www.rivierafinance.com
SIC: 6153 Factors of commercial paper
PA: Riviera Finance Of Texas, Inc
220 Avenue I
Redondo Beach CA

(P-14288)
SKYVIEW CAPITAL LLC
2000 Avenue Of The Stars Ste 810 (90067-4702)
PHONE..............................310 273-6000
Alex Soltani, *CEO*
EMP: 99 **EST:** 2002
SALES (est): 16.32MM **Privately Held**
Web: www.skyviewcapital.com
SIC: 6153 Direct working capital financing

6159 Miscellaneous Business Credit

(P-14289)
CAPITALSOURCE INC
633 W 5th St 33rd Fl (90071-2005)
PHONE..............................213 443-7700
EMP: 515
SIC: 6159 General and industrial loan institutions

(P-14290)
CAPNET FINANCIAL SERVICES INC (PA)
Also Called: Capital Network Funding Svcs
11901 Santa Monica Blvd (90025-2767)
PHONE..............................877 980-0558
John Armstron, *CEO*
Blake Johnson, *
Michael Kromnick, *
Armita Dalal, *Head*
EMP: 90 **EST:** 2001
SQ FT: 23,000
SALES (est): 12.09MM
SALES (corp-wide): 12.09MM **Privately Held**
SIC: 6159 Equipment and vehicle finance leasing companies

(P-14291)
ELECTRONIC COMMERCE LLC
Also Called: Electronic Commerce
4100 Newport Place Dr Ste 500 (92660)
PHONE..............................800 770-5520
Darnell Ponder, *Mng Pt*
Khaazra Maaranu, *
EMP: 85 **EST:** 2013
SALES (est): 8.6MM **Privately Held**
SIC: 6159 Intermediate investment banks

(P-14292)
WELLS FARGO CAPITAL FIN LLC (DH)
2450 Colorado Ave Ste 3000w (90404)
PHONE..............................310 453-7300
Sean Spring, *
EMP: 99 **EST:** 2002
SALES (est): 129.33MM
SALES (corp-wide): 82.86B **Publicly Held**
Web: www.wellsfargocapitalfinance.com
SIC: 6159 General and industrial loan institutions
HQ: Wells Fargo Bank, National Association
420 Montgomery St San
San Francisco CA
605 575-6900

(P-14293)
WESTLAKE SERVICES LLC (HQ)
Also Called: Westlake Financial Services
4751 Wilshire Blvd Ste 100 (90010-3847)
P.O. Box 76809 (90076-0809)
PHONE..............................323 692-8800
Don Hankey, *Ch Bd*
James Vagim, *Pr*
Kent Hagan, *VP*
Ian Anderson, *Pr*
Paul Kerwin, *CFO*
EMP: 123 **EST:** 1988
SQ FT: 22,000
SALES (est): 286.86MM
SALES (corp-wide): 352.68MM **Privately Held**
Web: www.westlakefinancial.com
SIC: 6159 6141 Automobile finance leasing; Personal credit institutions
PA: Hankey Investment Company, Lp
4751 Wilshire Blvd # 110

Los Angeles CA
323 692-4008

6162 Mortgage Bankers And Correspondents

(P-14294)
AMERICAN FINANCIAL NETWORK INC (PA)
Also Called: Gateway Home Realty
10 Pointe Dr Ste 330 (92821-7620)
PHONE..............................714 831-4000
John B Sherman, *Pr*
John R Sherman, *
▲ **EMP:** 200 **EST:** 2001
SQ FT: 8,000
SALES (est): 201.91MM
SALES (corp-wide): 201.91MM **Privately Held**
Web: www.afncorp.com
SIC: 6162 Mortgage bankers

(P-14295)
AMERICAN INTERNET MORTGAGE INC
Also Called: Aimloan.com, A Direct Lender
4121 Camino Del Rio S Ste 200 (92108-4103)
PHONE..............................888 411-4246
Vincent J Kasperick, *Pr*
EMP: 106 **EST:** 1998
SQ FT: 4,500
SALES (est): 22.56MM **Privately Held**
Web: www.aimloan.com
SIC: 6162 Mortgage bankers

(P-14296)
AMERIHOME INC
1 Baxter Way Ste 300 (91362-3888)
PHONE..............................888 469-0810
James S Furash, *Ch*
John Hedlund, *
Garrett Galati, *
Josh Adler, *
Mark Miller, *CRO*
EMP: 738 **EST:** 2020
SALES (est): 215.13MM
SALES (corp-wide): 215.13MM **Privately Held**
Web: www.amerihome.com
SIC: 6162 Mortgage bankers and loan correspondents
PA: A-A Mortgage Opportunities, L.P.
1 Baxter Way
Thousand Oaks CA
888 469-0810

(P-14297)
AMNET ESOP CORPORATION
Also Called: American Mortgage Network
347 Third Ave Fl 2 (91910-3929)
PHONE..............................877 354-1110
Joseph Sal Restivo, *CEO*
Shawn Stougard, *
EMP: 144 **EST:** 2019
SALES (est): 12MM **Privately Held**
Web: www.amnetmtg.com
SIC: 6162 Mortgage bankers

(P-14298)
AMNET MORTGAGE LLC
10421 Wateridge Cir Ste 250 (92121)
PHONE..............................858 909-1200
John M Robbins, *CEO*
Jay M Fuller, *Parts Vice President*
Lisa Falk, *
EMP: 759 **EST:** 1997
SQ FT: 40,400

SALES (est): 187.13MM
SALES (corp-wide): 82.86B **Publicly Held**
SIC: 6162 Mortgage bankers and loan correspondents
HQ: Wells Fargo Bank, National Association
420 Montgomery St San
San Francisco CA
605 575-6900

(P-14299)
ANCHOR LOANS LP
Also Called: Anchor Nationwide Loans
1 Baxter Way # 220 (91362-3817)
PHONE..............................310 395-0010
Stephen Pollack, *CEO*
Bryan Thompson, *CFO*
EMP: 200 **EST:** 2015
SALES (est): 41.48MM **Privately Held**
Web: www.anchorloans.com
SIC: 6162 Mortgage bankers and loan correspondents

(P-14300)
ARCS COMMERCIAL MORTGAGE CO LP (DH)
Also Called: Arcs Commercial Mortgage
26901 Agoura Rd Ste 200 (91301-5109)
PHONE..............................818 676-3274
▲ **EMP:** 110 **EST:** 1995
SQ FT: 15,000
SALES (est): 21.62MM
SALES (corp-wide): 23.54B **Publicly Held**
SIC: 6162 Mortgage bankers
HQ: Pnc Bank, National Association
300 5th Ave
Pittsburgh PA
877 762-2000

(P-14301)
ATHAS CAPITAL GROUP INC
27001 Agoura Rd Ste 200 (91301-5357)
PHONE..............................877 877-1477
Brian O'shaughnessy, *CEO*
EMP: 126 **EST:** 2007
SALES (est): 15.35MM **Privately Held**
Web: www.athascapital.com
SIC: 6162 Mortgage bankers and loan correspondents

(P-14302)
BERKSHIRE HTHWAY HM SVCS CAL P
2365 Northside Dr Ste 200 (92108-2720)
PHONE..............................619 302-8082
EMP: 111
SALES (corp-wide): 302.09B **Publicly Held**
Web: www.bhhscalifornia.com
SIC: 6162 Mortgage bankers and loan correspondents
HQ: Berkshire Hathaway Home Services California Properties
12770 El Cmino Real Ste 1
San Diego CA
858 792-6085

(P-14303)
BLUFI LENDING CORPORATION
9909 Mira Mesa Blvd # 160 (92131-3002)
EMP: 120
SIC: 6162 Loan correspondents

(P-14304)
CAL MUTUAL INC
34077 Temecula Creek Rd (92592-5646)
PHONE..............................888 700-4650
Dennis Shane Dailey, *Pr*
EMP: 87 **EST:** 2013
SALES (est): 5.54MM **Privately Held**

Web: www.calmutualmortgage.com
SIC: 6162 6531 Mortgage bankers and loan correspondents; Real estate agent, residential

(P-14305)
CARRINGTON MRTG HOLDINGS LLC
1600 S Douglass Rd Ste 110 (92806-5948)
PHONE..............................888 267-0584
EMP: 123 **EST:** 2001
SQ FT: 192,000
SALES (est): 46.47MM
SALES (corp-wide): 94.57MM **Privately Held**
SIC: 6162 Mortgage bankers and loan correspondents
PA: Carrington Capital Management Llc
1700 E Putnam Ave Ste 501
Old Greenwich CT
203 661-6186

(P-14306)
CHANGE LENDING LLC
32 Discovery Ste 160 (92618-3156)
PHONE..............................949 769-3526
EMP: 92
Web: www.changemtg.com
SIC: 6162 Mortgage bankers and loan correspondents
PA: Change Lending, Llc
175 N Riverview Dr
Anaheim CA

(P-14307)
CLEAREDGE LENDING
65 Enterprise (92656-2705)
PHONE..............................562 708-7706
EMP: 94 **EST:** 2019
SALES (est): 7.16MM **Privately Held**
Web: www.clearedgelending.com
SIC: 6162 Mortgage bankers and loan correspondents

(P-14308)
COUNTRYWIDE HOME LOANS INC (HQ)
Also Called: Countrywide
225 W Hillcrest Dr (91360-7883)
EMP: 700 **EST:** 1969
SQ FT: 220,000
SALES (est): 457.11MM
SALES (corp-wide): 94.95B **Publicly Held**
Web: www.bankofamerica.com
SIC: 6162 Mortgage bankers
PA: Bank Of America Corporation
100 N Tryon St Ste 2650
Charlotte NC
704 386-5681

(P-14309)
COUNTRYWIDE HOME LOANS INC
Also Called: Countrywide
801 N Brand Blvd Ste 750 (91203-3218)
PHONE..............................818 550-8700
Lynda Martinlawley, *Mgr*
EMP: 1567
SALES (corp-wide): 94.95B **Publicly Held**
Web: www.bankofamerica.com
SIC: 6162 Mortgage bankers
HQ: Countrywide Home Loans, Inc.
225 W Hillcrest Dr
Thousand Oaks CA

(P-14310)
DECISION READY SOLUTIONS INC
Also Called: Decision Ready

400 Spectrum Center Dr Ste 2050 (92618-5024)
PHONE..............................949 400-1126
Ravi Ramanathan, *Pr*
Dan Mahler, *CSO**
Claudia Sanchez, *
Tom Schmidt, *
EMP: 50 **EST:** 2011
SALES (est): 6MM **Privately Held**
Web: www.decisionreadysolutions.com
SIC: 6162 7371 7372 Mortgage bankers; Computer software systems analysis and design, custom; Business oriented computer software

(P-14311)
EC CLOSING CORP
Also Called: Cal Western Foreclosure Svcs
525 E Main St (92020-4007)
P.O. Box 22004 (92022-9004)
PHONE..............................800 546-1531
EMP: 80
Web: www.rickpatterson.com
SIC: 6162 Loan correspondents

(P-14312)
EMET LENDING GROUP INC
Also Called: Dream Mortgage Group
2601 Saturn St Ste 200 (92821-6702)
PHONE..............................714 933-9800
Julie Ahn, *CEO*
EMP: 80 **EST:** 2015
SALES (est): 6.39MM **Privately Held**
Web: www.emetlending.com
SIC: 6162 Mortgage bankers

(P-14313)
EQUITY SMART HOME LOANS INC
1499 Huntington Dr Ste 500 (91030-5473)
PHONE..............................626 864-8774
Pablo Martinez, *CEO*
EMP: 87 **EST:** 2016
SALES (est): 13.16MM **Privately Held**
Web: www.equitysmartloans.com
SIC: 6162 Mortgage bankers

(P-14314)
FEDERAL HOME LOAN MRTG CORP
Also Called: Freddie Mac
444 S Flower St Fl 44 (90071-2944)
PHONE..............................213 337-4200
Steve Griffin, *Mgr*
EMP: 596
SALES (corp-wide): 86.72B **Publicly Held**
Web: www.freddiemac.com
SIC: 6162 Mortgage bankers and loan correspondents
PA: Federal Home Loan Mortgage Corporation
8200 Jones Branch Dr
Mc Lean VA
703 903-2000

(P-14315)
FIN-WEST GROUP
5740 Ralston St Ste 130 (93003-6038)
PHONE..............................805 658-7435
Bob Davis, *Brnch Mgr*
EMP: 305
SALES (corp-wide): 11.57MM **Privately Held**
SIC: 6162 Mortgage bankers and loan correspondents
PA: Fin-West Group
1131 W 6th St Ste 250
Ontario CA
909 595-1996

(P-14316)
FIRST MORTGAGE CORPORATION
1131 W 6th St Ste 300 (91762-1118)
PHONE..............................909 595-1996
EMP: 430
SIC: 6162 Mortgage bankers

(P-14317)
GFS CAPITAL HOLDINGS
6499 Havenwood Cir Ste 720 (92648-6621)
PHONE..............................714 720-3918
EMP: 280
SIC: 6162 Mortgage brokers, using own money

(P-14318)
GOAL FINANCIAL LLC
401 W A St Ste 1300 (92101-7906)
PHONE..............................619 684-7600
EMP: 250 **EST:** 2004
SALES (est): 36.02MM **Privately Held**
Web: www.goalfinancial.net
SIC: 6162 Loan correspondents

(P-14319)
GOLDEN EMPIRE MORTGAGE INC
Also Called: Gem
41331 12th St W Ste 102 (93551-1423)
PHONE..............................661 949-3388
Jane Lawrence, *Brnch Mgr*
EMP: 254
Web: bcontreras.gemcorp.com
SIC: 6162 Mortgage bankers
PA: Golden Empire Mortgage, Inc.
2130 Chester Ave
Bakersfield CA

(P-14320)
GOLDEN EMPIRE MORTGAGE INC (PA)
2130 Chester Ave (93301-4471)
PHONE..............................661 328-1600
Howard Kootstra, *CEO*
EMP: 100 **EST:** 1987
SQ FT: 25,000
SALES (est): 56.06MM **Privately Held**
Web: www.gemcorp.com
SIC: 6162 Mortgage bankers

(P-14321)
GOLDEN EMPIRE MORTGAGE INC (PA)
Also Called: Gem Mortgage
1200 Discovery Dr Ste 300 (93309-7036)
PHONE..............................661 328-1600
John Copeland, *Prin*
EMP: 80 **EST:** 2006
SALES (est): 91.08MM **Privately Held**
Web: www.gemcorp.com
SIC: 6162 7371 Mortgage bankers; Computer software development

(P-14322)
GOODLEAP LLC
Also Called: Goodleap
22 Executive Park Ste 100 (92614-2700)
PHONE..............................916 290-9999
Hayes Barnard, *Pr*
EMP: 100
SALES (corp-wide): 150.56MM **Privately Held**
Web: www.goodleap.com
SIC: 6162 Mortgage bankers
PA: Goodleap, Llc
8781 Sierra College Blvd
Roseville CA
916 290-9999

(P-14323)
GUARANTEED RATE INC
230 Commerce (92602-1337)
PHONE..............................424 354-5344
EMP: 152
Web: www.rate.com
SIC: 6162 Mortgage bankers and loan correspondents
PA: Guaranteed Rate, Inc.
3940 N Ravenswood Ave
Chicago IL

(P-14324)
GUARANTEED RATE INC
1455 Frazee Rd Ste 500 (92108-4350)
PHONE..............................760 310-6008
Trent Annicharico, *Bmch Mgr*
EMP: 147
Web: www.rate.com
SIC: 6162 Mortgage bankers
PA: Guaranteed Rate, Inc.
3940 N Ravenswood Ave
Chicago IL

(P-14325)
GUARANTEED RATE INC
1065 Higuera St Ste 100 (93401-3786)
PHONE..............................805 550-6933
EMP: 150
Web: www.rate.com
SIC: 6162 Mortgage bankers and loan correspondents
PA: Guaranteed Rate, Inc.
3940 N Ravenswood Ave
Chicago IL

(P-14326)
GUILD HOLDINGS COMPANY (PA)
Also Called: Guild Mortgage
5887 Copley Dr (92111-7906)
PHONE..............................858 560-6330
Mary Ann Mcgarry, *CEO*
Patrick J Duffy, *Ch Bd*
Terry L Schmidt, *Pr*
David M Neylan, *Ex VP*
Barry H Horn, *Ex VP*
EMP: 401 **EST:** 2020
SALES (est): 1.16B
SALES (corp-wide): 1.16B **Publicly Held**
Web: ir.guildmortgage.com
SIC: 6162 Mortgage bankers and loan correspondents

(P-14327)
HOME MRTG ALIANCE CORP HMAC (PA)
Also Called: Scion Lending
4 Hutton Centre Dr Ste 500 (92707-8710)
PHONE..............................800 900-7040
Hanan Hanna, *CEO*
EMP: 408 **EST:** 2013
SALES (est): 48.27MM
SALES (corp-wide): 48.27MM **Privately Held**
Web: www.homemac.com
SIC: 6162 Mortgage bankers and loan correspondents

(P-14328)
IMPAC MORTGAGE CORP
Also Called: Impac Mortgage
19500 Jamboree Rd Ste 100 (92612-2426)
PHONE..............................949 475-3600
EMP: 298 **EST:** 2008
SALES (est): 7.86MM **Privately Held**
Web: www.cashcallmortgage.com
SIC: 6162 Mortgage bankers
PA: Impac Mortgage Holdings, Inc.
19500 Jamboree Rd Ste 100

Irvine CA

(P-14329)
INTEGRITY MORTGAGE GROUP
Also Called: Champion Mortgage
9747 Businesspark Ave (92131-1653)
PHONE..............................858 225-5000
Alexander Vari, *Pr*
EMP: 100 **EST:** 2001
SALES (est): 2.96MM **Privately Held**
Web: www.integrity-loans.com
SIC: 6162 Mortgage bankers and loan correspondents

(P-14330)
ISERVE RESIDENTIAL LENDING LLC
Also Called: Idirect Home Loans
10920 Via Frontera Ste 520 (92127-1733)
PHONE..............................858 486-4169
EMP: 100 **EST:** 2011
SALES (est): 30.86MM **Privately Held**
Web: www.iservelending.com
SIC: 6162 Bond and mortgage companies

(P-14331)
LENDERS INVESTMENT CORP
18101 Von Karman Ave Ste 400 (92612-1012)
PHONE..............................714 540-4747
Kerry M Smith, *Pr*
Bill Ammerman, *
EMP: 86 **EST:** 2003
SQ FT: 14,000
SALES (est): 5.33MM **Privately Held**
SIC: 6162 Mortgage bankers

(P-14332)
LENDSURE MORTGAGE CORP
Also Called: Talis Lending
12230 World Trade Dr (92128-3799)
PHONE..............................888 707-7811
Joseph John Lydon, *Prin*
EMP: 224 **EST:** 2016
SALES (est): 3.1MM **Privately Held**
Web: www.lendsure.com
SIC: 6162 Mortgage bankers and loan correspondents

(P-14333)
LENOX FINANCIAL MORTGAGE CORP
Also Called: Weslend Financial
200 Sandpointe Ave Ste 800 (92707-5751)
PHONE..............................949 428-5100
Wesley C Hoaglund, *CEO*
EMP: 251 **EST:** 1999
SALES (est): 77.01MM **Privately Held**
Web: www.lenoxhomeloans.com
SIC: 6162 Mortgage bankers

(P-14334)
LOANDEPOT INC (PA)
Also Called: Loandepot
6561 Irvine Center Dr (92618-2118)
PHONE..............................888 337-6888
Frank Martell, *Pr*
Anthony Hsieh, *Ofcr*
David Hayes, *CFO*
Joseph Grassi, *CRO*
Jeff Dergurahian, *Executive Capital Markets Vice President*
EMP: 492 **EST:** 2010
SQ FT: 144,398
SALES (est): 1.26B
SALES (corp-wide): 1.26B **Publicly Held**
Web: www.loandepot.com
SIC: 6162 Mortgage bankers and loan correspondents

(P-14335)
LOANDEPOT INC
25500 Commercentre Dr (92630-8855)
PHONE..............................949 470-6263
EMP: 454
SALES (corp-wide): 1.26B **Publicly Held**
Web: www.loandepot.com
SIC: 6162 Mortgage bankers and loan correspondents
PA: Loandepot, Inc.
6561 Irvine Center Dr
Irvine CA
888 337-6888

(P-14336)
LOANDEPOT INC
2080 Otay Lakes Rd # 101 (91913-1362)
PHONE..............................619 245-0115
EMP: 303
SALES (corp-wide): 1.26B **Publicly Held**
Web: www.loandepot.com
SIC: 6162 Mortgage bankers and loan correspondents
PA: Loandepot, Inc.
6561 Irvine Center Dr
Irvine CA
888 337-6888

(P-14337)
LOANDEPOTCOM LLC
42455 10th St W Ste 109 (93534-7060)
PHONE..............................661 202-1700
EMP: 851
SALES (corp-wide): 1.26B **Publicly Held**
Web: www.franklinloancenter.com
SIC: 6162 Loan correspondents
HQ: Loandepot.Com, Llc
26642 Towne Centre Dr
Foothill Ranch CA

(P-14338)
LOANDEPOTCOM LLC
901 N Palm Canyon Dr Ste 107 (92262-4449)
PHONE..............................760 797-6000
EMP: 681
SALES (corp-wide): 1.26B **Publicly Held**
Web: www.franklinloancenter.com
SIC: 6162 Mortgage bankers
HQ: Loandepot.Com, Llc
26642 Towne Centre Dr
Foothill Ranch CA

(P-14339)
LOANDEPOTCOM LLC (DH)
Also Called: Customer Loan Depot
26642 Towne Centre Dr (92610-2808)
PHONE..............................888 337-6888
Andrew Dodson, *Pr*
David Norris, *Pr*
Bryan Sullivan, *Ex VP*
Peter Macdonald, *Ex VP*
Harold Gonzalez, *Sr VP*
EMP: 963 **EST:** 2009
SALES (est): 986.92MM
SALES (corp-wide): 1.26B **Publicly Held**
Web: www.movement.com
SIC: 6162 Mortgage bankers
HQ: Ld Holdings Group Llc
26642 Towne Centre Dr
Foothill Ranch CA
888 337-6888

(P-14340)
METROPOLITAN HOME MORTGAGE INC
Also Called: Intelliloan
3090 Bristol St Ste 600 (92626-7318)
PHONE..............................949 428-0161
Daryl Preedge, *Pr*

EMP: 100 **EST:** 1993
SQ FT: 5,000
SALES (est): 20.7MM **Privately Held**
Web: www.metrohmc.com
SIC: 6162 Mortgage bankers and loan correspondents

(P-14341)
MISSION HILLS MORTGAGE CORP (HQ)
Also Called: Mission Hills Mortgage Bankers
18500 Von Karman Ave Ste 1100 (92612-0546)
PHONE..............................714 972-3832
Jay Ledbetter, *Pr*
EMP: 140 **EST:** 1969
SQ FT: 27,000
SALES (est): 86.13MM
SALES (corp-wide): 145.44MM **Privately Held**
Web: www.mhmb.com
SIC: 6162 Mortgage bankers and loan correspondents
PA: Tarbell Financial Corporation
1403 N Tustin Ave Ste 380
Santa Ana CA
714 972-0988

(P-14342)
MISSION LOANS LLC ✪
Also Called: Intention Financial Group
5 Park Plz Ste 900 (92614-8589)
PHONE..............................855 959-4500
EMP: 102 **EST:** 2022
SALES (est): 5.32MM **Privately Held**
Web: www.missionloans.com
SIC: 6162 Mortgage bankers

(P-14343)
MOUNTAIN WEST FINANCIAL INC (PA)
Also Called: Mortgage Works Financial
31 W Stuart Ave (92374-3244)
PHONE..............................909 793-1500
Gary H Martell Junior, *Pr*
Michael W Douglas, *
EMP: 391 **EST:** 1990
SALES (est): 102.05MM **Privately Held**
Web: www.mwfinc.com
SIC: 6162 Mortgage bankers

(P-14344)
NETWORK CAPITAL FUNDING CORP (PA)
Also Called: Network Capital
7700 Irvine Center Dr Fl 3 (92618-2923)
PHONE..............................949 442-0060
Tri Nguyen, *Pr*
▲ **EMP:** 345 **EST:** 2002
SALES (est): 52.59MM
SALES (corp-wide): 52.59MM **Privately Held**
Web: www.networkcapital.com
SIC: 6162 Mortgage bankers

(P-14345)
NEW CENTURY MORTGAGE CORP
Also Called: New Century Mortgage
18400 Von Karman Ave Ste 1000 (92612-1514)
PHONE..............................949 440-7030
EMP: 3261 **EST:** 1995
SALES (est): 109.24MM **Privately Held**
SIC: 6162 Mortgage bankers and loan correspondents

▲ = Import ▼ = Export
◆ = Import/Export

(P-14346)
OCMBC INC
Also Called: Ocmban
19000 Macarthur Blvd Ste 200
(92612-1420)
PHONE.....................949 679-7400
Rabi H Aziz, *CEO*
Madelina L Colon, *
EMP: 301 **EST:** 2001
SQ FT: 12,500
SALES (est): 61.94MM **Privately Held**
Web: www.lsmortgage.com
SIC: 6162 Mortgage bankers

(P-14347)
PRIVATE NAT MRTG
ACCPTANCE LLC (DH)
Also Called: Pennymac
6101 Condor Dr (91301)
PHONE.....................818 224-7401
Jeff Grogin, *CLO*
Steve Bailey, *CSO*
Doug Jones Cclo, *Prin*
EMP: 800 **EST:** 2008
SALES (est): 575.74MM
SALES (corp-wide): 1.99B **Publicly Held**
Web: www.pennymac.com
SIC: 6162 Mortgage bankers
HQ: Pnmac Holdings, Inc.
    3043 Townsgate Rd
    Westlake Village CA
    818 224-7442

(P-14348)
RUSHMORE LOAN MGT SVCS
LLC (PA)
Also Called: Rushmore Crrspndent Lnding
Svc
15480 Laguna Canyon Rd Ste 100
(92618-2132)
P.O. Box 619079 (75261-9079)
PHONE.....................949 727-4798
Terry Smith, *Managing Member*
EMP: 839 **EST:** 2008
SQ FT: 3,000
SALES (est): 165.78MM **Privately Held**
Web: www.rushmorelm.com
SIC: 6162 Mortgage bankers and loan
correspondents

(P-14349)
SEA BREEZE FINANCIAL SVCS
INC
Also Called: Sea Breeze Mortgage Services
18191 Von Karman Ave Ste 150
(92612-7102)
P.O. Box 19079 (92817-9079)
PHONE.....................949 223-9700
Leonard Hamilton, *Pr*
Curtis Green, *
EMP: 150 **EST:** 1985
SQ FT: 50,000
SALES (est): 17.62MM **Privately Held**
SIC: 6162 Mortgage bankers

(P-14350)
SUN WEST MORTGAGE
COMPANY INC (PA)
Also Called: Lowratscom 1st Lbrty Cal State
18303 Gridley Rd (90703-5400)
PHONE.....................562 326-5732
Pavan Agarwal, *CEO*
Hari S Agarwal, *
Sharda Agarwal, *
Jim Trapinski, *
Anita Agarwal, *
EMP: 141 **EST:** 1980
SQ FT: 9,800
SALES (est): 120.77MM

SALES (corp-wide): 120.77MM **Privately Held**
Web: www.swmc.com
SIC: 6162 6163 Mortgage bankers; Loan brokers

(P-14351)
SYNERGY ONE LENDING INC
Also Called: Morelends.com
3131 Camino Del Rio N Ste 150 (92108)
PHONE.....................385 273-5250
EMP: 93 **EST:** 2018
SALES (est): 7.13MM **Privately Held**
Web: www.s1l.com
SIC: 6162 Mortgage bankers and loan correspondents

(P-14352)
THRIVE MORTGAGE LLC
Also Called: Georgetown Mortgage
9587 Foothill Blvd (91730-3506)
PHONE.....................909 527-3736
EMP: 80
Web: www.thrivemortgage.com
SIC: 6162 Mortgage bankers and loan correspondents
PA: Thrive Mortgage, Llc
    4819 Williams Dr
    Georgetown TX

(P-14353)
TURNKEY FOUNDATION INC
Also Called: Nationwide
1805 E Garry Ave Ste 130 (92705-5851)
PHONE.....................949 557-6203
Ryan O'kane, *Pr*
David Arvidson, *CEO*
EMP: 88 **EST:** 2004
SALES (est): 11.87MM **Privately Held**
Web: www.arborfinancialgroup.net
SIC: 6162 6531 6411 Mortgage bankers and loan correspondents; Real estate agents and managers; Insurance agents, brokers, and service

---

6163 Loan Brokers

(P-14354)
5 ARCHES LLC
19800 Macarthur Blvd (92612-2421)
PHONE.....................949 387-8092
Shawn Miller, *CEO*
Gene Clark, *
Steven Davis, *
EMP: 95 **EST:** 2012
SALES (est): 24.66MM **Publicly Held**
SIC: 6163 Mortgage brokers arranging for loans, using money of others
PA: Redwood Trust, Inc.
    1 Belvedere Pl Ste 300
    Mill Valley CA

(P-14355)
CARNEGIE MORTGAGE LLC
Also Called: Ovation Home Loans
15480 Laguna Canyon Rd Ste 100
(92618-2132)
PHONE.....................949 379-7000
EMP: 300
Web: www.carnegiemtg.com
SIC: 6163 Mortgage brokers arranging for loans, using money of others
PA: Carnegie Mortgage Llc
    2297 Highway 33
    Trenton NJ

(P-14356)
CHANGE LENDING LLC
6265 Greenwich Dr Ste 215 (92122-5917)

PHONE.....................858 500-3060
EMP: 91
Web: www.changemtg.com
SIC: 6163 Mortgage brokers arranging for loans, using money of others
PA: Change Lending, Llc
    175 N Riverview Dr
    Anaheim CA

(P-14357)
CLEARPATH LENDING
Also Called: Clearpath Lending
15635 Alton Pkwy Ste 300 (92618-7332)
PHONE.....................949 502-3577
Amir Ali Omid, *CEO*
EMP: 130 **EST:** 2012
SALES (est): 24.26MM **Privately Held**
Web: www.clearpathlending.com
SIC: 6163 Mortgage brokers arranging for loans, using money of others

(P-14358)
DIGNIFIED HOME LOANS LLC
1 Baxter Way Ste 120 (91362-3809)
PHONE.....................818 421-7753
Preston James, *Prin*
EMP: 80 **EST:** 2013
SALES (est): 4.89MM **Privately Held**
Web: www.dignifiedhomeloans.com
SIC: 6163 Mortgage brokers arranging for loans, using money of others

(P-14359)
HOMEBRIDGE FINANCIAL SVCS
INC
15301 Ventura Blvd Ste D300
(91403-6665)
PHONE.....................818 981-0606
Douglas Rotella, *Pr*
EMP: 1700
Web: www.homebridge.com
SIC: 6163 Mortgage brokers arranging for loans, using money of others
PA: Homebridge Financial Services, Inc.
    194 Wood Ave S Fl 9
    Iselin NJ

(P-14360)
LMB OPCO LLC
Also Called: Lowermybills.com
12181 Bluff Creek Dr Ste 250 (90094-2992)
PHONE.....................310 348-6800
Jeff Hughes, *CEO*
EMP: 320 **EST:** 2016
SALES (est): 65.16MM **Privately Held**
Web: www.quickencompare.com
SIC: 6163 7389 Mortgage brokers arranging for loans, using money of others; Financial services

(P-14361)
PACIFIC BAY LENDING GROUP
Also Called: Bay Valley Mortgage
15020 La Mirada Blvd (90638-4743)
PHONE.....................714 367-5125
John Nelson, *CEO*
Christine Kim, *
EMP: 100 **EST:** 2011
SALES (est): 13.83MM **Privately Held**
Web: www.valleyviewhomeloans.com
SIC: 6163 Mortgage brokers arranging for loans, using money of others

(P-14362)
PENNYMAC CORP
27001 Agoura Rd (91301-5339)
PHONE.....................818 878-8416
EMP: 363 **EST:** 2010
SALES (est): 4.45MM **Publicly Held**
Web: www.pennymac.com

SIC: 6163 Loan brokers
PA: Pennymac Mortgage Investment Trust
    6101 Condor Dr
    Moorpark CA

(P-14363)
RMR FINANCIAL LLC (DH)
Also Called: Online Capital
610 Newport Center Dr (92660-6419)
PHONE.....................408 355-2000
EMP: 84 **EST:** 2000
SQ FT: 11,300
SALES (est): 28.4MM
SALES (corp-wide): 953.9MM **Publicly Held**
SIC: 6163 6162 Mortgage brokers arranging for loans, using money of others; Mortgage bankers
HQ: Phh Corporation
    3000 Leadenhall Rd
    Mount Laurel NJ
    856 917-1744

(P-14364)
SAND CANYON CORPORATION
(HQ)
7595 Irvine Center Dr Ste 120
(92618-2957)
P.O. Box 57080 (92619-7080)
PHONE.....................949 727-9425
Robert Dubrish, *Pr*
William O'neill, *CFO*
Steve Nadon, *
Dale M Sugimoto, *
EMP: 100 **EST:** 1992
SALES (est): 116.72MM
SALES (corp-wide): 3.47B **Publicly Held**
Web: www.sandcanyondentistry.com
SIC: 6163 6162 Loan brokers; Mortgage bankers and loan correspondents
PA: H & R Block, Inc.
    1 H And R Block Way
    Kansas City MO
    816 854-3000

(P-14365)
SECURED FUNDING
CORPORATION
2955 Red Hill Ave (92626-5907)
PHONE.....................714 689-6749
Lorne Lahodny, *Pr*
John R Lynch Junior, *VP*
Phil Dandrige, *
Joe Lindsay, *CIO**
EMP: 800 **EST:** 1993
SQ FT: 60,000
SALES (est): 46.83MM **Privately Held**
SIC: 6163 Mortgage brokers arranging for loans, using money of others

(P-14366)
STRATUS REAL ESTATE INC
Also Called: Stratus Realestate
435 Garfield Ave (91030-2249)
PHONE.....................626 441-5549
Steve Heighmler, *Pr*
EMP: 99
SALES (corp-wide): 678.49MM **Privately Held**
Web: www.stratusrealestate.com
SIC: 6163 Loan brokers
HQ: Stratus Real Estate, Inc.
    5311 Topanga Canyon Blvd # 3
    Woodland Hills CA

(P-14367)
STRATUS REAL ESTATE INC
Banning Villa Apartments
1100 N Banning Blvd Apt 111 (90744-3530)
PHONE.....................310 549-7028

Bernadette Saunder, *Mgr*
EMP: 99
SALES (corp-wide): 678.49MM **Privately Held**
Web: www.stratusrealestate.com
SIC: 6163 6513 Loan brokers; Apartment building operators
HQ: Stratus Real Estate, Inc.
5311 Topanga Canyon Blvd # 3
Woodland Hills CA

(P-14368)
TARBELL FINANCIAL CORPORATION (PA)
1403 N Tustin Ave Ste 380 (92705-8691)
PHONE...............................714 972-0988
Donald Tarbell, *CEO*
Tina Jimov, *
Elizabeth Tarbell, *
Ronald Tarbell, *
Jin Lee, *
EMP: 100 **EST:** 1982
SQ FT: 60,000
SALES (est): 145.44MM
SALES (corp-wide): 145.44MM **Privately Held**
Web: www.tarbellcareers.com
SIC: 6163 6531 6099 Mortgage brokers arranging for loans, using money of others; Real estate brokers and agents; Escrow institutions other than real estate

(P-14369)
TRANSGLOBAL HOLDING COMPANY
1045 W Huntington Dr Ste 200 (91007-8840)
PHONE...............................626 447-7888
Philip C K Hu, *Admn*
EMP: 96 **EST:** 2016
SALES (est): 1.38MM **Privately Held**
Web: www.transglobalus.com
SIC: 6163 Loan brokers

(P-14370)
UNITED VISION FINANCIAL INC
16027 Ventura Blvd # 200 (91436-2728)
PHONE...............................818 285-0211
Dan Michaels, *Pr*
EMP: 180 **EST:** 2003
SQ FT: 3,000
SALES (est): 13.08MM **Privately Held**
SIC: 6163 Mortgage brokers arranging for loans, using money of others

(P-14371)
VILLA VENETIA
2775 Mesa Verde Dr E (92626-4957)
PHONE...............................714 540-1800
United Dominion, *Pr*
EMP: 278 **EST:** 2001
SALES (est): 3.06MM
SALES (corp-wide): 678.49MM **Privately Held**
SIC: 6163 Loan brokers
HQ: Stratus Real Estate, Inc.
5311 Topanga Canyon Blvd # 3
Woodland Hills CA

6211 Security Brokers And Dealers

(P-14372)
AMERIHOME MORTGAGE COMPANY LLC
Also Called: Amerihome Mortgage
1 Baxter Way Ste 300 (91362-3811)
PHONE...............................888 469-0810

James Furash, *CEO*
Thomas Smith, *
Todd Taylor, *
EMP: 704 **EST:** 2014
SALES (est): 168.88MM
SALES (corp-wide): 3.02B **Publicly Held**
Web: www.amerihome.com
SIC: 6211 Mortgages, buying and selling
PA: Western Alliance Bancorporation
1 E Wshington St Ste 1400
Phoenix AZ
602 389-3500

(P-14373)
CARRINGTON MORTGAGE SVCS LLC
10370 Commerce Center Dr Ste 140 (91730-5806)
PHONE...............................909 226-7963
Jaleh Jenkins, *Brnch Mgr*
EMP: 152
Web: www.carringtonwholesale.com
SIC: 6211 6163 Mortgages, buying and selling; Loan brokers
PA: Carrington Mortgage Services, Llc
1600 S Douglass Rd 200a
Anaheim CA

(P-14374)
CENTURION GROUP INC (PA)
Also Called: Coast Group Financial
365 S Rancho Santa Fe Rd (92078-2338)
PHONE...............................760 471-8536
Jack Heilbron, *Pr*
Mary Lamoges, *
EMP: 125 **EST:** 1982
SQ FT: 9,000
SALES (est): 13.27MM
SALES (corp-wide): 13.27MM **Privately Held**
SIC: 6211 8111 Brokers, security; Legal services

(P-14375)
CHARGER INVESTMENT PARTNERS LP
880 Apollo St Ste 347 (90245-4752)
PHONE...............................310 372-5525
Aaron Perlmutter, *Pt*
Chris Boyle, *Pt*
Kimberly Pollack, *Pt*
EMP: 93 **EST:** 2019
SALES (est): 7.91MM **Privately Held**
Web: www.chargerinv.com
SIC: 6211 Investment bankers

(P-14376)
CHARLES SCHWAB CORPORATION
Also Called: Charles Schwab
7510 Hazard Center Dr Ste 407 (92108-4525)
PHONE...............................800 435-4000
Jim Croutch, *Prin*
EMP: 86
SALES (corp-wide): 20.76B **Publicly Held**
Web: www.schwab.com
SIC: 6211 Brokers, security
PA: The Charles Schwab Corporation
3000 Schwab Way
Westlake TX
817 859-5000

(P-14377)
CHARLES SCHWAB CORPORATION
Also Called: Charles Schwab
27580 Ynez Rd Ste A (92591-4667)
PHONE...............................800 435-4000

Mark Morgan, *Mgr*
EMP: 144
SALES (corp-wide): 20.76B **Publicly Held**
Web: www.schwab.com
SIC: 6211 6282 Brokers, security; Investment advice
PA: The Charles Schwab Corporation
3000 Schwab Way
Westlake TX
817 859-5000

(P-14378)
GOLD PARENT LP
11111 Santa Monica Blvd (90025-3333)
PHONE...............................310 954-0444
Jonathan D Sokoloff, *Prin*
EMP: 3400 **EST:** 2016
SALES (est): 68.41MM **Privately Held**
SIC: 6211 Investment bankers

(P-14379)
GOLDMAN SACHS & CO LLC
Also Called: Goldman Sachs
2121 Avenue Of The Stars Ste 2600 (90067-5050)
PHONE...............................310 407-5700
John Mallory, *Brnch Mgr*
EMP: 120
SALES (corp-wide): 68.71B **Publicly Held**
Web: www.goldmansachs.com
SIC: 6211 Investment bankers
HQ: Goldman Sachs & Co. Llc
200 West St
New York NY
212 902-1000

(P-14380)
GORES GROUP LLC (PA)
9800 Wilshire Blvd (90212-1804)
PHONE...............................310 209-3010
Alec Gores, *CEO*
Vance Diggens, *
Frank Stefanik, *
Catherine Scanlon, *
Joseph Page, *
EMP: 60 **EST:** 2003
SALES (est): 1.81B
SALES (corp-wide): 1.81B **Privately Held**
Web: www.gores.com
SIC: 6211 7372 5734 Investment firm, general brokerage; Prepackaged software; Computer software and accessories

(P-14381)
HYUNDAI ABS FUNDING LLC
3161 Michelson Dr (92612-4400)
PHONE...............................949 732-2697
EMP: 157 **EST:** 2016
SALES (est): 8.55MM **Privately Held**
SIC: 6211 Security brokers and dealers
HQ: Hyundai Capital America
3161 Michelson Dr # 1900
Irvine CA

(P-14382)
IMPERIAL CAPITAL LLC (PA)
10100 Santa Monica Blvd Ste 2400 (90067-4136)
PHONE...............................310 246-3700
Randall Wooster, *CEO*
Jason W Reese, *Ch*
Randall E Wooster, *CEO*
Timothy Sullivan, *Pr*
Mark Martis, *COO*
EMP: 85 **EST:** 1997
SALES (est): 49.63MM
SALES (corp-wide): 49.63MM **Privately Held**
Web: www.imperialcapital.com

SIC: 6211 Investment bankers

(P-14383)
INTERLINK SECURITIES CORP
20750 Ventura Blvd Ste 300 (91364-2338)
P.O. Box 4323 (91365-4323)
PHONE...............................818 992-6700
Barry Wolfe, *Pr*
EMP: 100 **EST:** 1992
SALES (est): 8.98MM **Privately Held**
SIC: 6211 6722 Security brokers and dealers ; Management investment, open-end

(P-14384)
LEONARD GREEN & PARTNERS LP (PA)
11111 Santa Monica Blvd Ste 2000 (90025-3353)
PHONE...............................310 954-0444
Jonathan Sokoloff, *Pt*
John Danhakl, *
Peter Nolan, *
Jonathan Seiffer, *
John Baumer, *
▲ **EMP:** 93 **EST:** 1989
SQ FT: 15,000
SALES (est): 3.41B **Privately Held**
Web: www.leonardgreen.com
SIC: 6211 Investment firm, general brokerage

(P-14385)
LERETA LLC (PA)
901 Corporate Center Dr (91768-2642)
PHONE...............................626 543-1765
John Walsh, *CEO*
Tyler Page, *
James V Micali, *
Cody Tillack, *
Chris Masten, *
EMP: 350 **EST:** 2009
SALES (est): 272.05MM **Privately Held**
Web: www.lereta.com
SIC: 6211 6541 6361 Tax certificate dealers; Title search companies; Real estate title insurance

(P-14386)
LPL FINANCIAL HOLDINGS INC (PA)
Also Called: Lplfh
4707 Executive Dr (92121-3091)
PHONE...............................800 877-7210
Dan H Arnold, *Pr*
James S Putnam, *Non-Executive Chairman of the Board*
Matthew J Audette, *CFO*
Greg Gates, *Technology*
Michelle Oroschakoff, *CLO*
EMP: 476 **EST:** 1989
SQ FT: 420,000
SALES (est): 8.6B **Publicly Held**
Web: www.lpl.com
SIC: 6211 6282 6091 Brokers, security; Investment advisory service; Nondeposit trust facilities

(P-14387)
M L STERN & CO LLC (DH)
8350 Wilshire Blvd Ste 300 (90211-2327)
PHONE...............................323 658-4400
Stephen F Kempa, *
EMP: 117 **EST:** 1980
SQ FT: 8,100
SALES (est): 40.29MM
SALES (corp-wide): 1.42B **Publicly Held**
Web: www.mlstern.com
SIC: 6211 Brokers, security
HQ: Hilltop Securities Holdings Llc
200 Crescent Ct Ste 1330
Dallas TX
214 855-2177

▲ = Import ▼ = Export
◆ = Import/Export

(P-14388)
MERRILL LYNCH PRCE FNNER SMITH
Also Called: Merrill Lynch
650 Town Center Dr # 500 (92626-1989)
PHONE....................714 429-2800
EMP: 88
SALES (corp-wide): 93.85B **Publicly Held**
Web: www.ml.com
SIC: **6211** 8742 Security brokers and dealers ; Financial consultant
HQ: Merrill Lynch, Pierce, Fenner & Smith Incorporated
   111 8th Ave
   New York NY
   800 637-7455

(P-14389)
MERRILL LYNCH PRCE FNNER SMITH
Also Called: Merrill Lynch Carlsbad Office
1000 Aviara Dr Ste 200 (92011-4218)
PHONE....................760 930-3100
Nick Givogri, *Mgr*
EMP: 80
SALES (corp-wide): 94.95B **Publicly Held**
Web: www.ml.com
SIC: **6211** Security brokers and dealers
HQ: Merrill Lynch, Pierce, Fenner & Smith Incorporated
   111 8th Ave
   New York NY
   800 637-7455

(P-14390)
MERRILL LYNCH PRCE FNNER SMITH
Also Called: Merrill Lynch
800 E Colorado Blvd Ste 400 (91101)
PHONE....................800 637-7455
Mark Mixon, *Mgr*
EMP: 201
SALES (corp-wide): 94.95B **Publicly Held**
Web: www.ml.com
SIC: **6211** Security brokers and dealers
HQ: Merrill Lynch, Pierce, Fenner & Smith Incorporated
   111 8th Ave
   New York NY
   800 637-7455

(P-14391)
MORGAN STNLEY SMITH BARNEY LLC
21650 Oxnard St Ste 1800 (91367-4944)
PHONE....................818 715-1800
Fred Rucker Esq, *Brnch Mgr*
EMP: 104
SALES (corp-wide): 53.67B **Publicly Held**
Web: www.morganstanley.com
SIC: **6211** Stock brokers and dealers
HQ: Morgan Stanley Smith Barney, Llc
   1585 Broadway
   New York NY

(P-14392)
MORGAN STNLEY SMITH BARNEY LLC
444 S Flower St Ste 2700 (90071-2971)
PHONE....................213 891-3200
Bruce Brereton, *Brnch Mgr*
EMP: 120
SALES (corp-wide): 53.67B **Publicly Held**
Web: www.morganstanley.com
SIC: **6211** Security brokers and dealers
HQ: Morgan Stanley Smith Barney, Llc
   1585 Broadway
   New York NY

(P-14393)
MORGAN STNLEY SMITH BARNEY LLC
Also Called: Morgan Stanley Smith Barney
101 W Broadway Ste 1800 (92101-8298)
PHONE....................619 238-1226
Nozomi Ward, *Sr VP*
EMP: 119
SALES (corp-wide): 53.67B **Publicly Held**
Web: www.morganstanley.com
SIC: **6211** Security brokers and dealers
HQ: Morgan Stanley Smith Barney, Llc
   1585 Broadway
   New York NY

(P-14394)
MORGAN STNLEY SMITH BARNEY LLC
1014 Santa Barbara St (93101-2126)
PHONE....................805 963-3381
Walter Harris, *Pr*
EMP: 104
SALES (corp-wide): 53.67B **Publicly Held**
Web: www.morganstanley.com
SIC: **6211** Stock brokers and dealers
HQ: Morgan Stanley Smith Barney, Llc
   1585 Broadway
   New York NY

(P-14395)
MORGAN STNLEY SMITH BARNEY LLC
5796 Armada Dr Ste 200 (92008-4694)
PHONE....................760 438-5100
John Condos, *Prin*
EMP: 130
SALES (corp-wide): 53.67B **Publicly Held**
Web: www.morganstanley.com
SIC: **6211** Stock brokers and dealers
HQ: Morgan Stanley Smith Barney, Llc
   1585 Broadway
   New York NY

(P-14396)
MORGAN STNLEY SMITH BARNEY LLC
1225 Prospect St Ste 202 (92037-3687)
PHONE....................212 761-4000
Emily Temporal, *Brnch Mgr*
EMP: 109
SALES (corp-wide): 53.67B **Publicly Held**
Web: www.morganstanley.com
SIC: **6211** Security brokers and dealers
HQ: Morgan Stanley Smith Barney, Llc
   1585 Broadway
   New York NY

(P-14397)
MORGAN STNLEY SMITH BARNEY LLC
10 Pointe Dr Ste 400 (92821-7620)
PHONE....................714 674-4100
Vincent Daigneault, *Prin*
EMP: 104
SALES (corp-wide): 53.67B **Publicly Held**
Web: www.morganstanley.com
SIC: **6211** Stock brokers and dealers
HQ: Morgan Stanley Smith Barney, Llc
   1585 Broadway
   New York NY

(P-14398)
MORGAN STNLEY SMITH BARNEY LLC
3750 University Ave Ste 600 (92501-3323)
PHONE....................951 682-1181
James Gibson, *Mgr*
EMP: 109

SALES (corp-wide): 53.67B **Publicly Held**
Web: www.morganstanley.com
SIC: **6211** Security brokers and dealers
HQ: Morgan Stanley Smith Barney, Llc
   1585 Broadway
   New York NY

(P-14399)
MURIEL SIEBERT & CO INC
9378 Wilshire Blvd Ste 300 (90212-3168)
PHONE....................800 993-2015
Joseph M Ramos, *Ex VP*
EMP: 100
SALES (corp-wide): 67.51MM **Publicly Held**
Web: www.siebert.com
SIC: **6211** Brokers, security
HQ: Muriel Siebert & Co., Inc.
   15 Exchange Pl Ste 615
   Jersey City NJ
   212 644-2400

(P-14400)
NATIONAL FINANCIAL SVCS LLC
19200 Von Karman Ave Ste 400 (92612-8553)
PHONE....................949 476-0157
Lawrence Goodkind, *Brnch Mgr*
EMP: 871
SALES (corp-wide): 4.35B **Privately Held**
Web: www.mybrokerageinfo.com
SIC: **6211** Investment firm, general brokerage
HQ: National Financial Services Llc
   200 Seaport Blvd Ste 630
   Boston MA
   800 471-0382

(P-14401)
PACIFIC SELECT DISTRS INC
700 Newport Center Dr Fl 4 (92660-6307)
PHONE....................949 219-3011
Gerald W Robinson, *Pr*
Audrey L Milfs, *
Edward R Byrd, *
Kathy R Gough, *Assistant Vice President Compliance**
Thomas C Sutton, *
EMP: 96 EST: 1969
SQ FT: 300,000
SALES (est): 10.67MM
SALES (corp-wide): 12.84B **Privately Held**
Web: www.pacificlife.com
SIC: **6211** Brokers, security
HQ: Pacific Life Insurance Company
   700 Newport Center Dr
   Newport Beach CA
   949 219-3011

(P-14402)
PALISADES GROUP LLC
11755 Wilshire Blvd Ste 1700 (90025-1500)
PHONE....................424 280-7560
Stephen Kirch, *CEO*
Jack Macdowell Junior, *CIO*
Justin Bodiya, *COO*
Sally Kawana, *CFO*
EMP: 143 EST: 2012
SALES (est): 4.87MM
SALES (corp-wide): 4.87MM **Privately Held**
Web: palisades.us.com
SIC: **6211** Investment firm, general brokerage
PA: The Palisades Holdings I Llc
   11755 Wilshire Blvd # 17
   Los Angeles CA
   424 280-7560

(P-14403)
PLAZA HOME MORTGAGE INC
9808 Scranton Rd (92121-3704)

PHONE....................858 346-1208
Kevin Parra, *Pr*
EMP: 108
SALES (corp-wide): 117.8MM **Privately Held**
Web: www.plazahomemortgage.com
SIC: **6211** 6162 Mortgages, buying and selling; Loan correspondents
PA: Plaza Home Mortgage, Inc.
   4820 Eastgate Mall # 100
   San Diego CA
   858 346-1200

(P-14404)
ROTH CAPITAL PARTNERS LLC (PA)
Also Called: Roth Mkm
888 San Clemente Dr (92660-6369)
PHONE....................800 678-9147
Byron Roth, *Ch*
Byron Roth, *CEO*
Gordon Roth, *COO*
Warren Dunnavant Ii, *VP*
EMP: 100 EST: 1984
SQ FT: 52,000
SALES (est): 52.8MM
SALES (corp-wide): 52.8MM **Privately Held**
Web: www.roth.com
SIC: **6211** Investment bankers

(P-14405)
SUTTER SECURITIES INC
6 Venture Ste 395 (92618-7315)
PHONE....................415 352-6300
Robert Muh, *CEO*
Frank Soriano, *Pr*
Joseph M Ducote, *Dir*
Ashford D Wood, *Dir*
Frederick Selinger, *Dir*
EMP: 87 EST: 1992
SALES (est): 4.49MM
SALES (corp-wide): 4.49MM **Privately Held**
Web: www.suttersecurities.com
SIC: **6211** Investment bankers
PA: Sutter Securities Group, Inc.
   6 Venture Ste 395
   Irvine CA
   310 504-3706

(P-14406)
TRUST COMPANY OF WEST
865 S Figueroa St Ste 1800 (90017-2543)
PHONE....................213 244-0000
EMP: 515
SIC: **6211** Bond dealers and brokers

(P-14407)
UBS AMERICAS INC
600 W Broadway Ste 2800 (92101-0906)
PHONE....................619 557-2400
EMP: 160
Web: www.ubs.com
SIC: **6211** Security brokers and dealers
HQ: Ubs Americas Inc.
   600 Washington Blvd
   Stamford CT
   203 719-3000

(P-14408)
WEDBUSH SECURITIES INC (HQ)
1000 Wilshire Blvd Ste 900 (90017-1774)
P.O. Box 30014 (90030-0014)
PHONE....................213 688-8000
Edward W Wedbush, *Pr*
Thomas Ringer, *
Peter Allman-ward, *CFO*
Earl I Feldhorn, *
V Thomas Hale, *

PRODUCTS & SVCS

EMP: 300 **EST:** 1955
SQ FT: 100,000
SALES (est): 224.6MM
SALES (corp-wide): 254.49MM **Privately Held**
Web: www.wedbush.com
SIC: 6211 Brokers, security
PA: Wedbush Capital
1000 Wilshire Blvd
Los Angeles CA
213 688-8080

(P-14409)
WELLS FARGO SECURITIES LLC
Also Called: Barrington Associates
1800 Century Park E Ste 1100
(90067-1501)
PHONE......................310 479-3500
Jim Freedman, *Brnch Mgr*
EMP: 1104
SALES (corp-wide): 82.86B **Publicly Held**
Web: www.wellsfargoadvisors.com
SIC: 6211 Security brokers and dealers
HQ: Wells Fargo Securities, Llc
550 S Tryon St
Charlotte NC

6221 Commodity Contracts Brokers, Dealers

(P-14410)
CABALLERO & SONS INC
Also Called: Beyond Meat and Company
5753 E Santa Ana Canyon Rd Ste G-380
(92807-3230)
PHONE......................562 368-1644
Perpetua Duque-hata, *Pr*
Nathaniel Caballero, *
Marivet Caballero, *
EMP: 25 **EST:** 2017
SQ FT: 500
SALES (est): 7MM **Privately Held**
SIC: 6221 2392 5141 5149 Commodity traders, contracts; Cushions and pillows; Food brokers; Beverages, except coffee and tea

(P-14411)
INVAPHARM INC
1320 W Mission Blvd (91762-4786)
PHONE......................909 757-1818
Manu Patolia, *Pr*
Kalpesh Bodar, *
Nirmala Patolia, *
EMP: 40 **EST:** 2015
SQ FT: 60,000
SALES (est): 10.52MM **Privately Held**
Web: www.invapharm.com
SIC: 6221 2023 Commodity brokers, contracts; Dietary supplements, dairy and non-dairy based

6282 Investment Advice

(P-14412)
ADVICEPERIOD
2121 Avenue Of The Stars Ste 2400
(90067-5010)
PHONE......................424 281-3600
Allison Schaengold, *Prin*
EMP: 83 **EST:** 2014
SALES (est): 4.84MM **Privately Held**
Web: www.adviceperiod.com
SIC: 6282 Investment advisory service

(P-14413)
AL HEWITT INC
4009 Mission Oaks Blvd (93012-5156)
PHONE......................661 945-7050
Alan Hewitt, *CEO*
EMP: 124 **EST:** 2005
SALES (est): 2.36MM
SALES (corp-wide): 164.45MM **Privately Held**
Web: www.merceradvisors.com
SIC: 6282 Investment advisory service
PA: Mercer Global Advisors, Inc.
1200 17th St Ste 500
Denver CO
888 885-8101

(P-14414)
ALLIANZ GLOBAL INVESTORS OF AMERICA LP
680 Newport Center Dr Ste 250 (92660)
PHONE......................949 219-2200
EMP: 1800
SIC: 6282 Investment advisory service

(P-14415)
ANDERSON KAYNE CAPITAL
1800 Avenue Of The Stars Ste 200 # 3rd
(90067)
PHONE......................800 231-7414
Richard Kayne, *Ch*
Robert Sinnott, *CEO*
Edward Cerny, *Mng Pt*
EMP: 300 **EST:** 1994
SALES (est): 24.32MM **Privately Held**
Web: www.kaynecapitalfoundation.org
SIC: 6282 Investment advisory service

(P-14416)
ATLAS CAPITAL GROUP LLC
1318 E 7th St Ste 200 (90021-1123)
PHONE......................213 988-8890
EMP: 80
Web: www.atlas-cap.com
SIC: 6282 Investment advisory service
PA: Atlas Capital Group, Llc
450 Park Ave Fl 4
New York NY

(P-14417)
BEATING WALL STREET INC (PA)
20121 Ventura Blvd Ste 305 (91364-2559)
PHONE......................818 332-9696
Hamed Khorsand, *Pr*
EMP: 230 **EST:** 2000
SALES (est): 24.71MM
SALES (corp-wide): 24.71MM **Privately Held**
Web: www.bwsfinancial.com
SIC: 6282 Investment advisory service

(P-14418)
BRANDES INV PARTNERS INC (PA)
11988 El Camino Real Ste 300
(92131-6123)
P.O. Box 919048 (92191-9048)
PHONE......................858 755-0239
Charles H Brandes, *Ch Bd*
Brent V Woods, *
Glenn R Carlson, *
Jeffrey A Busby, *
Gary Iwamura, *
EMP: 212 **EST:** 1974
SQ FT: 27,000
SALES (est): 100.4MM
SALES (corp-wide): 100.4MM **Privately Held**
Web: www.brandes.com

SIC: 6282 Investment advisory service

(P-14419)
C2 FINANCIAL CORPORATION
703 Sunset Ct (92109-7024)
PHONE......................858 220-2112
EMP: 162
SALES (corp-wide): 94.73MM **Privately Held**
Web: www.c2financial.com
SIC: 6282 Investment advice
PA: C2 Financial Corporation
10509 Vista Sorrento Pkwy # 400
San Diego CA
858 312-4900

(P-14420)
CAPITAL GROUP COMPANIES INC (PA)
Also Called: Capital Group, The
333 S Hope St Fl 55 (90071-3061)
PHONE......................213 486-9200
Tim Armour, *Ch*
Jody Jonsson, *Vice Chairman*
Rob Klausner, *
Matt O'connor, *Distributor*
EMP: 800 **EST:** 1931
SQ FT: 106,000
SALES (est): 5.43B
SALES (corp-wide): 5.43B **Privately Held**
Web: www.capitalgroup.com
SIC: 6282 6091 6722 8741 Investment advice; Nondeposit trust facilities; Mutual fund sales, on own account; Management services

(P-14421)
CAPITAL RESEARCH AND MGT CO (HQ)
333 S Hope St Fl 55 (90071-3061)
PHONE......................213 486-9200
R Michael Shanahan, *Ch Bd*
James F Rothenberg, *Ch Bd*
Timothy Armour, *CEO*
Gordon Crawford, *Sr VP*
Gina Despres, *Sr VP*
EMP: 500 **EST:** 1944
SALES (est): 597.41MM
SALES (corp-wide): 5.43B **Privately Held**
SIC: 6282 Investment research
PA: The Capital Group Companies Inc
333 S Hope St Fl 55
Los Angeles CA
213 486-9200

(P-14422)
HOULIHAN LOKEY INC (PA)
10250 Constellation Blvd Fl 5 (90067-6260)
PHONE......................310 788-5200
Scott L Beiser, *CEO*
Irwin N Gold, *
Scott J Adelson, *
David A Preiser, *
J Lindsey Alley, *CFO*
EMP: 300 **EST:** 1972
SALES (est): 1.81B
SALES (corp-wide): 1.81B **Publicly Held**
Web: www.hl.com
SIC: 6282 6211 Investment advice; Security brokers and dealers

(P-14423)
MARLIN EQUITY PARTNERS LLC (PA)
1301 Manhattan Ave (90254-3654)
PHONE......................310 364-0100
David Mcgovern, *Managing Member*
Nick Kaiser, *
Peter Spasov, *

George Kase, *
Steve Johnson, *
EMP: 80 **EST:** 2005
SALES (est): 2.15B **Privately Held**
Web: www.marlinequity.com
SIC: 6282 3661 Investment advisory service; Telephones and telephone apparatus

(P-14424)
OAKTREE CAPITAL MANAGEMENT LP (DH)
333 S Grand Ave Fl 28 (90071-1530)
PHONE......................213 830-6300
Jay Wintrob, *CEO*
Todd Molz, *COO*
EMP: 120 **EST:** 2007
SALES (est): 4.86B
SALES (corp-wide): 69.06B **Privately Held**
Web: www.oaktreecapital.com
SIC: 6282 6722 6211 Investment advisory service; Management investment, open-end ; Security brokers and dealers
HQ: Brookfield Asset Management Llc
250 Vesey St Fl 15
New York NY

(P-14425)
PACIFIC ALTRNTIVE ASSET MGT LL (HQ)
Also Called: Paamco
660 Newport Center Dr Ste 930 (92660)
PHONE......................949 261-4900
Jane Buchan, *CEO*
EMP: 94 **EST:** 2000
SALES (est): 31.66MM
SALES (corp-wide): 59.99MM **Privately Held**
Web: www.paamcoprisma.com
SIC: 6282 Investment advisory service
PA: Paamco Prisma Holdings, Llc
660 Nwport Ctr Dr Ste 930
Newport Beach CA
949 261-4900

(P-14426)
PAYDEN & RYGEL (PA)
333 S Grand Ave Ste 4000 (90071-1507)
PHONE......................213 625-1900
Joan Payden, *CEO*
Scott J Weiner, *Managing Principal GLOBAL*
Brian Matthews, *Managing Principal GLOBAL*
Brad Hersh, *
EMP: 140 **EST:** 1983
SALES (est): 60.97MM
SALES (corp-wide): 60.97MM **Privately Held**
Web: www.payden.com
SIC: 6282 6211 Investment counselors; Security brokers and dealers

(P-14427)
PLAN MEMBER FINANCIAL CORP
Also Called: Planmember Services
6187 Carpinteria Ave (93013-2805)
PHONE......................800 874-6910
Jon Ziehl, *CEO*
Terry Janeway, *
Bill Kemble, *
Trish Stone-damon, *Sec*
EMP: 100 **EST:** 1990
SQ FT: 6,000
SALES (est): 34.06MM **Privately Held**
Web: www.planmember.com
SIC: 6282 Investment counselors

(P-14428)
RESEARCH AFFILIATES CAPITAL LP
Also Called: Research Affiliates
620 Newport Center Dr Ste 900 (92660)
PHONE..............................949 325-8700
EMP: 82 **EST:** 2002
SALES (est): 21.79MM **Privately Held**
Web: www.researchaffiliates.com
SIC: 6282 Investment advisory service

(P-14429)
RESEARCH AFFILIATES MGT LLC
Also Called: Research Affiliates
620 Newport Center Dr Ste 900 (92660)
PHONE..............................949 325-8700
Rob Arnott, *CEO*
Jason Hsu, *CIO*
Katrina Sherrerd, *COO*
EMP: 80 **EST:** 2002
SALES (est): 8.23MM **Privately Held**
Web: www.researchaffiliates.com
SIC: 6282 Investment counselors

(P-14430)
TCW GROUP INC (PA)
865 S Figueroa St Ste 1800 (90017-2543)
PHONE..............................213 244-0000
David Lippman, *Pr*
Richard M Villa, *
Meredith S Jackson, *
David S Devito, *
Jeffrey Engelsman Global, *Chief Compliance Officer*
EMP: 450 **EST:** 1971
SALES (est): 232.19MM **Privately Held**
SIC: 6282 6211 Investment advisory service; Security brokers and dealers

(P-14431)
THOMAS JAMES CAPITAL INC
26940 Aliso Viejo Pkwy Ste 100 (92656-2650)
PHONE..............................949 481-7026
Thomas L Beadel, *Pr*
James Quandt, *
EMP: 150 **EST:** 2006
SQ FT: 1,400
SALES (est): 21.25MM **Privately Held**
Web: www.tjh.com
SIC: 6282 6798 Investment advisory service; Real estate investment trusts

(P-14432)
U S TRUST COMPANY NA
Also Called: US Trust
515 S Flower St Ste 2700 (90071-2216)
PHONE..............................213 861-5000
Tim Leach, *CEO*
EMP: 350 **EST:** 1982
SQ FT: 65,000
SALES (est): 49.71MM
SALES (corp-wide): 94.95B **Publicly Held**
SIC: 6282 6022 Investment advice; State commercial banks
HQ: Bank Of America Pvt Wealth Management
114 W 47th St Ste C-1
New York NY
800 878-7878

6289 Security And Commodity Service

(P-14433)
AMERICAN FUNDS SERVICE COMPANY (DH)
Also Called: Capital Group
6455 Irvine Center Dr (92618-4518)
PHONE..............................949 975-5000
EMP: 300 **EST:** 1968
SALES (est): 318.47MM
SALES (corp-wide): 5.43B **Privately Held**
Web: www.capitalgroup.com
SIC: 6289 6211 Security transfer agents; Security brokers and dealers
HQ: Capital Research And Management Company
333 S Hope St Fl 55
Los Angeles CA
213 486-9200

(P-14434)
COMPUTERSHARE INC
2335 Alaska Ave (90245-4808)
PHONE..............................800 522-6645
EMP: 360
Web: www.computershare.com
SIC: 6289 Stock transfer agents
HQ: Computershare Inc.
150 Royall St Ste 205
Canton MA

6311 Life Insurance

(P-14435)
GOLDEN STATE MUTL LF INSUR CO (PA)
1999 W Adams Blvd (90018-3514)
P.O. Box 26894 (94126-6894)
PHONE..............................713 526-4361
Larkin Teasley, *Pr*
EMP: 100 **EST:** 1925
SQ FT: 57,000
SALES (est): 20.42MM
SALES (corp-wide): 20.42MM **Privately Held**
SIC: 6311 Mutual association life insurance

(P-14436)
JOHN ALDEN LIFE INSURANCE CO
20950 Warner Center Ln Ste A (91367-6560)
PHONE..............................818 595-7600
Thomas Christenson, *Brnch Mgr*
EMP: 104
SALES (corp-wide): 10.19B **Publicly Held**
SIC: 6311 Life insurance
HQ: Alden John Life Insurance Company
501 W Michigan St
Milwaukee WI
414 271-3011

(P-14437)
JOHN HANCOCK LIFE INSUR CO USA
5000 Birch St Ste 120 (92660-8117)
PHONE..............................949 254-1440
EMP: 90
SALES (corp-wide): 32.83B **Privately Held**
Web: www.johnhancock.com
SIC: 6311 Life insurance
HQ: John Hancock Life Insurance Company (U.S.A.)
865 S Figueroa St # 3320
Los Angeles CA
213 689-0813

(P-14438)
NEW FIRST FINCL RESOURCES LLC
100 Spectrum Center Dr Ste 400 (92618-4962)
PHONE..............................949 223-2160
EMP: 212 **EST:** 1987
SALES (est): 23.6MM **Privately Held**
Web: www.ffrmembers.com
SIC: 6311 Life insurance

(P-14439)
NORTHWESTERN MUTL FINCL NETWRK (PA)
4225 Executive Sq Ste 1250 (92037-9122)
PHONE..............................619 234-3111
Garrett J Bleakley, *Owner*
EMP: 100 **EST:** 1952
SALES (est): 43.25MM **Privately Held**
Web: www.northwesternmutual.com
SIC: 6311 Life insurance

(P-14440)
PACIFIC ASSET HOLDING LLC
700 Newport Center Dr (92660-6307)
PHONE..............................949 219-3011
EMP: 189 **EST:** 1997
SALES (est): 8.48MM
SALES (corp-wide): 12.84B **Privately Held**
SIC: 6311 6371 6321 Life insurance carriers; Pension funds; Accident insurance carriers
HQ: Pacific Life Insurance Company
700 Newport Center Dr
Newport Beach CA
949 219-3011

(P-14441)
PACIFIC LIFE & ANNUITY COMPANY
700 Newport Center Dr (92660-6307)
P.O. Box 9000 (92658-9030)
PHONE..............................949 219-3011
James Morris, *Pr*
Khanh T Tran, *
Audrey L Milfs, *
Brian Klemens, *
EMP: 650 **EST:** 1982
SQ FT: 125,000
SALES (est): 203.9MM
SALES (corp-wide): 12.84B **Privately Held**
Web: www.pacificlife.com
SIC: 6311 6411 Life insurance carriers; Insurance agents, brokers, and service
HQ: Pacific Life Insurance Company
700 Newport Center Dr
Newport Beach CA
949 219-3011

(P-14442)
SUNAMERICA LIFE INSURANCE COMPANY
Also Called: SunAmerica
1 Sun America Ctr Fl 36 (90067-6100)
PHONE..............................310 772-6000
EMP: 225
SIC: 6311 Life insurance

(P-14443)
TRANSAMERICA OCCIDENTAL LIFE INSURANCE COMPANY
1150 S Olive St Fl 23 (90015-2477)
P.O. Box 2101 (90078-2101)
PHONE..............................213 742-2111
EMP: 3700
SIC: 6311 6371 6321 6324 Life insurance carriers; Pension funds; Health insurance carriers; Group hospitalization plans

---

(P-14444)
TRUCK UNDERWRITERS ASSOCIATION
Farmers Insurance
6303 Owensmouth Ave Fl 1 (91367-2200)
PHONE..............................323 932-3200
Jane Franklin, *VP*
EMP: 1078
SQ FT: 275,000
Web: www.farmers.com
SIC: 6311 6331 6321 Life insurance; Fire, marine, and casualty insurance; Accident and health insurance
HQ: Truck Underwriters Association
4680 Wilshire Blvd
Los Angeles CA
323 932-3200

6321 Accident And Health Insurance

(P-14445)
21ST CENTURY LF & HLTH CO INC (PA)
Also Called: Lifecare Assurance Company
21600 Oxnard St Ste 1500 (91367-4972)
P.O. Box 4243 (91365-4243)
PHONE..............................818 887-4436
James M Glickman, *Pr*
Alan S Hughes, *
Daniel J Di Sipio, *
Jay R Peters Fsa, *Ex VP*
Pete Diffley, *
▲ **EMP:** 241 **EST:** 1980
SQ FT: 50,000
SALES (est): 326.99MM **Privately Held**
Web: www.lifecareassurance.com
SIC: 6321 Health insurance carriers

(P-14446)
AGENT FRANCHISE LLC
9518 9th St Ste C2 (91730-4546)
PHONE..............................949 930-5025
EMP: 101 **EST:** 2014
SQ FT: 14,980
SALES (est): 22.4MM **Privately Held**
Web: www.agentfranchise.com
SIC: 6321 Accident and health insurance

(P-14447)
AUTO CLUB ENTERPRISES (PA)
3333 Fairview Rd Ms A451 (92626-1610)
P.O. Box 25001 (92799-5001)
PHONE..............................714 850-5111
Robert T Bouttier, *CEO*
Thomas Mc Kernon, *
Henry Reza Toofanian, *
John F Boyle, *
Avery Brown, *
EMP: 1200 **EST:** 1912
SQ FT: 700,000
SALES (est): 1.37B
SALES (corp-wide): 1.37B **Privately Held**
SIC: 6321 Accident and health insurance

(P-14448)
AUTO CLUB ENTERPRISES
8761 Santa Monica Blvd (90069-4538)
PHONE..............................310 914-8500
Bob Szhwab, *Mgr*
EMP: 500
SALES (corp-wide): 1.37B **Privately Held**
SIC: 6321 Accident and health insurance
PA: Auto Club Enterprises
3333 Fairview Rd Msa451
Costa Mesa CA
714 850-5111

(P-14449)
CARE 1ST HEALTH PLAN (PA)
601 Potrero Grande Dr Fl 2 (91755-7430)
PHONE....................323 889-6638
Maureen Tyson, *Pr*
Anna Tran, *
Janet Jan, *
Michael Rowan, *
Jamie Ueoka, *
EMP: 165 **EST:** 1994
SALES (est): 169.66MM **Privately Held**
Web: www.blueshieldca.com
SIC: 6321 Health insurance carriers

(P-14450)
CARELON MED BENEFITS MGT INC
505 N Brand Blvd (91203-1906)
PHONE....................847 310-0366
EMP: 586
SALES (corp-wide): 156.59B **Publicly Held**
Web: www.careloninsights.com
SIC: 6321 Health insurance carriers
HQ: Carelon Medical Benefits
    Management, Inc.
    8600 W Bryn Mawr Ave Tw
    Chicago IL

(P-14451)
CAREMORE HEALTH PLAN (HQ)
Also Called: Caremore Insurance Services
12900 Park Plaza Dr Ste 150 (90703-9329)
PHONE....................562 622-2950
TOLL FREE: 888
Leeba R Lessin, *Sup Chief Executive Officer*
Allan Hoops, *CEO*
Sergio Zaldivar, *Senior Vice President Corporate Development*
John Kao, *OF MANAGEMENT SERVICES ORGANIZATION*
Doctor Ken Kin Md, *Chief Medical Officer*
EMP: 148 **EST:** 1996
SALES (est): 111.92MM
SALES (corp-wide): 156.59B **Publicly Held**
Web: www.caremore.com
SIC: 6321 Health insurance carriers
PA: Elevance Health, Inc.
    220 Virginia Ave
    Indianapolis IN
    800 331-1476

(P-14452)
INLAND EMPIRE HEALTH PLAN (PA)
Also Called: Iehp
10801 6th St Ste 120 (91730-5987)
P.O. Box 1400 (91729-1400)
PHONE....................909 890-2000
EMP: 850 **EST:** 1994
SQ FT: 72,000
SALES (est): 715.81MM **Privately Held**
Web: www.iehp.org
SIC: 6321 6324 Health insurance carriers; Health Maintenance Organization (HMO), insurance only

(P-14453)
LIFECARE ASSURANCE COMPANY
21600 Oxnard St Fl 16 (91367-4976)
PHONE....................818 887-4436
James Glickman, *Pr*
Alan S Hughes, *
Daniel J Disipio, *
Peter Diffley, *
Dick Sato, *

EMP: 246 **EST:** 1988
SQ FT: 35,000
SALES (est): 326.99MM **Privately Held**
Web: www.lifecareassurance.com
SIC: 6321 6411 6311 Accident and health insurance; Insurance agents, brokers, and service; Life insurance
PA: 21st Century Life And Health
    Company, Inc.
    21600 Oxnard St Ste 1500
    Woodland Hills CA

(P-14454)
MOLINA HLTHCARE CAL PRTNER PLA
200 Oceangate Ste 100 (90802-4317)
PHONE....................562 435-3666
Richard Chambers, *CEO*
J Mario Molina, *
John Kotal, *
Doctor James Howatt, *Chief Medical Officer*
Terry Bayer, *
EMP: 314 **EST:** 1980
SALES (corp-wide): 4.31MM
SALES (corp-wide): 31.97B **Publicly Held**
Web: www.molinahealthcare.com
SIC: 6321 8011 Health insurance carriers; Clinic, operated by physicians
PA: Molina Healthcare, Inc.
    200 Oceangate Ste 100
    Long Beach CA
    562 435-3666

(P-14455)
SANTA BRBARA SAN LUIS OBSPO RG
Also Called: Cencal Health
4050 Calle Real (93110-3413)
PHONE....................800 421-2560
Robert Freeman, *CEO*
Kashina Bishop, *
EMP: 140 **EST:** 2009
SALES (est): 66.19MM **Privately Held**
Web: www.cencalhealth.org
SIC: 6321 Accident and health insurance

(P-14456)
STATE COMPENSATION INSUR FUND
2901 N Ventura Rd Ste 100 (93036-1126)
PHONE....................888 782-8338
Martin Goldman, *Mgr*
EMP: 90
SALES (corp-wide): 2.76B **Privately Held**
Web: www.statefundca.com
SIC: 6321 9651 Disability health insurance; Insurance commission, government
PA: State Compensation Insurance Fund
    333 Bush St Ste 800
    San Francisco CA
    888 782-8338

6324 Hospital And Medical Service Plans

(P-14457)
ADMAR CORPORATION
1551 N Tustin Ave Ste 300 (92705-8638)
P.O. Box 1049 (92702-1049)
PHONE....................714 953-9600
Kraig Boysen, *Pr*
Virginia Pascual, *
Ed Evans, *
EMP: 160 **EST:** 1973
SQ FT: 37,000
SALES (est): 62.76MM
SALES (corp-wide): 1.08B **Publicly Held**

SIC: 6324 Hospital and medical service plans
PA: Multiplan Corporation
    640 5th Ave Fl 12
    New York NY
    212 380-7500

(P-14458)
ALIGNMENT HEALTH PLAN
Also Called: Citizens Choice Health Plan
1100 W Town And Country Rd Ste 1600 (92868-4600)
PHONE....................323 728-7232
Chuck Weber, *Pr*
Elizabeth Tejada, *
Charlotte Leblanc, *CAO*
EMP: 90 **EST:** 2003
SALES (est): 23.16MM
SALES (corp-wide): 1.43B **Publicly Held**
Web: www.alignmenthealthplan.com
SIC: 6324 Health Maintenance Organization (HMO), insurance only
PA: Alignment Healthcare, Inc.
    1100 W Twn Cntry Rd # 1600
    Orange CA
    844 310-2247

(P-14459)
ALIGNMENT HEALTHCARE INC (PA)
Also Called: Alignment Health
1100 W Town And Country Rd Ste 1600 (92868-4698)
PHONE....................844 310-2247
John Kao, *CEO*
Joseph Konowiecki, *Ch Bd*
Thomas Freeman, *CFO*
Dinesh Kumar, *CMO*
Richard Cross, *Sr VP*
EMP: 52 **EST:** 2013
SQ FT: 89,000
SALES (est): 1.43B
SALES (corp-wide): 1.43B **Publicly Held**
Web: www.alignmenthealth.com
SIC: 6324 7372 Hospital and medical service plans; Prepackaged software

(P-14460)
AMERICAN SPCLTY HLTH GROUP INC
10221 Wateridge Cir Ste 201 (92121-2702)
PHONE....................858 754-2000
George T Devries, *CEO*
Robert White, *COO*
Kevin E Kujawa, *CIO*
Marcel Danko, *CFO*
▲ **EMP:** 500 **EST:** 1987
SQ FT: 148,000
SALES (est): 105.93MM **Privately Held**
Web: www.ashcompanies.com
SIC: 6324 Hospital and medical service plans
PA: American Specialty Health
    Incorporated
    12800 N Meridian St # 190
    Carmel IN

(P-14461)
BLUE CROSS OF CALIFORNIA (HQ)
Also Called: Blue Cross
21215 Burbank Blvd Ste 630 (91367-7091)
PHONE....................805 557-6050
Mark Morgan, *Pr*
Thomas C Geiser, *
Kenneth C Zurek, *
EMP: 118 **EST:** 1992
SQ FT: 427,104
SALES (est): 84.43MM
SALES (corp-wide): 156.59B **Publicly Held**

SIC: 6324 6411 Health Maintenance Organization (HMO), insurance only; Insurance agents, brokers, and service
PA: Elevance Health, Inc.
    220 Virginia Ave
    Indianapolis IN
    800 331-1476

(P-14462)
BLUE SHIELD CAL LF HLTH INSUR
2275 Rio Bonito Way Ste 250 (92108-1685)
PHONE....................619 686-4200
Matthew Leming, *Prin*
EMP: 1324
SALES (corp-wide): 8.08B **Privately Held**
Web: www.blueshieldca.com
SIC: 6324 Hospital and medical service plans
HQ: Blue Shield Of California Life & Health
    Insurance Co
    50 Beale St Ste 2000
    San Francisco CA
    415 229-5000

(P-14463)
CALIFORNIA PHYSICIANS SERVICE
Also Called: Blue Shield of California
3840 Kilroy Airport Way (90806-2452)
PHONE....................310 744-2668
Aubrey Chernick, *Brnch Mgr*
EMP: 94
SALES (corp-wide): 8.08B **Privately Held**
Web: www.blueshieldca.com
SIC: 6324 Hospital and medical service plans
PA: California Physicians' Service
    601 12th St
    Oakland CA
    510 607-2000

(P-14464)
CALIFORNIA PHYSICIANS SERVICE
Also Called: Blue Shield of California
6300 Canoga Ave Ste A (91367-8000)
PHONE....................818 598-8000
John Headberg, *Brnch Mgr*
EMP: 225
SALES (corp-wide): 8.08B **Privately Held**
Web: www.blueshieldca.com
SIC: 6324 Hospital and medical service plans
PA: California Physicians' Service
    601 12th St
    Oakland CA
    510 607-2000

(P-14465)
CIGNA BEHAVIORAL HEALTH OF CAL
Also Called: Cigna
450 N Brand Blvd Ste 500 (91203-4414)
PHONE....................800 753-0540
EMP: 308 **EST:** 2014
SALES (est): 1.32MM
SALES (corp-wide): 180.52B **Publicly Held**
SIC: 6324 Health Maintenance Organization (HMO), insurance only
HQ: Evernorth Behavioral Health, Inc
    11095 Viking Dr Ste 350
    Eden Prairie MN

(P-14466)
CIGNA HEALTHCARE CAL INC (DH)
Also Called: Cigna
400 N Brand Blvd Ste 400 (91203-2306)
P.O. Box 188045 (37422-8045)
PHONE....................818 500-6262

TOLL FREE: 800
Leroy Volberding, *Pr*
David Yeager, *Contrlr*
EMP: 400 **EST:** 1968
SQ FT: 110,000
SALES (est): 259.02MM
SALES (corp-wide): 180.52B **Publicly Held**
Web: www.cigna.com
SIC: 6324 Health Maintenance Organization (HMO), insurance only
HQ: Healthsource, Inc.
1750 Elm St Ste 800
Manchester NH
603 268-7000

(P-14467)
COUNTY OF LOS ANGELES
Also Called: Community Hlth Plan Off MGT Ca
1000 S Fremont Ave Unit 4 (91803-8859)
PHONE....................626 299-5300
Dave Beck, *Dir*
EMP: 84
Web: www.lacounty.gov
SIC: 6324 9431 Hospital and medical service plans; Mental health agency administration, government
PA: County Of Los Angeles
500 W Temple St Ste 437
Los Angeles CA
213 974-1101

(P-14468)
HEALTH NET LLC
6013 Niles St (93306-4696)
PHONE....................661 321-3904
EMP: 176
Web: www.healthnet.com
SIC: 6324 Hospital and medical service plans
HQ: Health Net, Llc
21650 Oxnard St Fl 25
Woodland Hills CA
818 676-6000

(P-14469)
HEALTH NET LLC (HQ)
21650 Oxnard St (91367-7829)
PHONE....................818 676-6000
Jay M Gellert, *Pr*
James E Woys, *Interim Treasurer**
Juanell Hefner, *
Angelee F Bouchard, *
Rich Hall, *ACTURIAL**
EMP: 250 **EST:** 2015
SQ FT: 115,488
SALES (est): 1.52B **Publicly Held**
Web: www.healthnet.com
SIC: 6324 6311 Hospital and medical service plans; Life insurance carriers
PA: Centene Corporation
7700 Forsyth Blvd Ste 800
Saint Louis MO

(P-14470)
HEALTH NET INC
21650 Oxnard St Fl 25 (91367-7829)
PHONE....................818 676-6000
EMP: 8014
SIC: 6324 6311 Hospital and medical service plans; Life insurance carriers

(P-14471)
INLAND EMPIRE HEALTH PLAN
805 W 2nd St Ste C (92410-3255)
P.O. Box 1800 (91729-1800)
PHONE....................866 228-4347
EMP: 1945
Web: www.iehp.org

SIC: 6324 8742 Health Maintenance Organization (HMO), insurance only; Hospital and health services consultant
PA: Inland Empire Health Plan
10801 6th St Ste 120
Rancho Cucamonga CA

(P-14472)
KAISER FNDTION HLTH PLAN GA IN
1850 California Ave (92881-3378)
PHONE....................951 270-1200
Anita Ward, *Mgr*
EMP: 379
SALES (corp-wide): 68.1B **Privately Held**
Web: www.kaiserpermanente.org
SIC: 6324 Hospital and medical service plans
HQ: Kaiser Foundation Health Plan Of Georgia, Inc.
3495 Piedmont Rd Ne # 9
Atlanta GA
404 364-7000

(P-14473)
KAISER FNDTION HOSP GIFT SHPPE
Also Called: Dept of Cardiologist
6041 Cadillac Ave (90034-1702)
PHONE....................323 857-3290
Ron Golden, *Mgr*
EMP: 171
SALES (corp-wide): 2.75MM **Privately Held**
Web: www.kaiserpermanentelocations.net
SIC: 6324 Hospital and medical service plans
PA: Kaiser Foundation Hospital Gift Shoppe
200 Muir Rd
Martinez CA
925 372-1000

(P-14474)
KAISER FOUNDATION HOSPITALS
Also Called: Kaiser Permanente
1011 Baldwin Park Blvd (91706-5806)
PHONE....................626 851-1011
Linda Margarita Gutierrez, *Prin*
EMP: 793
SALES (corp-wide): 68.1B **Privately Held**
Web: www.starbucks.com
SIC: 6324 Hospital and medical service plans
HQ: Kaiser Foundation Hospitals Inc
1 Kaiser Plz
Oakland CA
510 271-6611

(P-14475)
KAISER FOUNDATION HOSPITALS
Also Called: Kaiser Prmnente Downey Med Ctr
9333 Imperial Hwy (90242-2812)
PHONE....................562 657-9000
Gemma Abad, *Brnch Mgr*
EMP: 410
SALES (corp-wide): 68.1B **Privately Held**
Web: www.kaisercenter.com
SIC: 6324 Hospital and medical service plans
HQ: Kaiser Foundation Hospitals Inc
1 Kaiser Plz
Oakland CA
510 271-6611

(P-14476)
KAISER FOUNDATION HOSPITALS
Also Called: Kaiser Permanente
12470 Whittier Blvd (90602-1017)

PHONE....................866 340-5974
Beth Lopez, *Prin*
EMP: 139
SALES (corp-wide): 68.1B **Privately Held**
Web: www.kaisercenter.com
SIC: 6324 Hospital and medical service plans
HQ: Kaiser Foundation Hospitals Inc
1 Kaiser Plz
Oakland CA
510 271-6611

(P-14477)
KAISER FOUNDATION HOSPITALS
Also Called: Kaiser Foundation Health Plan
1539 W Garvey Ave N (91790-2139)
PHONE....................626 856-3045
Kwame Okoreeh, *Mgr*
EMP: 81
SQ FT: 10,403
SALES (corp-wide): 68.1B **Privately Held**
Web: www.kaiserpermanente.org
SIC: 6324 Hospital and medical service plans
HQ: Kaiser Foundation Hospitals Inc
1 Kaiser Plz
Oakland CA
510 271-6611

(P-14478)
KAISER FOUNDATION HOSPITALS
Also Called: Kaiser Foundation Health Plan
12200 Bellflower Blvd (90242-2804)
PHONE....................562 622-4190
Jim Harrington, *Brnch Mgr*
EMP: 144
SALES (corp-wide): 68.1B **Privately Held**
Web: www.kaiserpermanente.org
SIC: 6324 Hospital and medical service plans
HQ: Kaiser Foundation Hospitals Inc
1 Kaiser Plz
Oakland CA
510 271-6611

(P-14479)
KAISER FOUNDATION HOSPITALS
Also Called: Kaiser Foundation Health Plan
11666 Sherman Way (91605-5831)
PHONE....................818 503-7082
Charles Ford, *Mgr*
EMP: 162
SALES (corp-wide): 68.1B **Privately Held**
Web: www.kaiserpermanente.org
SIC: 6324 Hospital and medical service plans
HQ: Kaiser Foundation Hospitals Inc
1 Kaiser Plz
Oakland CA
510 271-6611

(P-14480)
KAISER FOUNDATION HOSPITALS
Also Called: Kaiser Permanente
3750 Grand Ave (91710-5478)
PHONE....................888 750-0036
Jonathan Rothchild, *Mgr*
EMP: 121
SALES (corp-wide): 68.1B **Privately Held**
Web: www.kaisercenter.com
SIC: 6324 Hospital and medical service plans
HQ: Kaiser Foundation Hospitals Inc
1 Kaiser Plz
Oakland CA
510 271-6611

(P-14481)
KAISER FOUNDATION HOSPITALS

Also Called: Kaiser Foundation Health Plan
9961 Sierra Ave (92335-6720)
P.O. Box None (92335)
PHONE....................909 427-3910
Gerald Mc Call, *Brnch Mgr*
EMP: 317
SALES (corp-wide): 68.1B **Privately Held**
Web: www.kaiserpermanente.org
SIC: 6324 Hospital and medical service plans
HQ: Kaiser Foundation Hospitals Inc
1 Kaiser Plz
Oakland CA
510 271-6611

(P-14482)
KAISER FOUNDATION HOSPITALS
Also Called: La Mesa Medical Offices
8080 Parkway Dr (91942-2104)
PHONE....................619 528-5000
Caroline Wu, *Prin*
EMP: 107
SALES (corp-wide): 68.1B **Privately Held**
Web: www.kaisercenter.com
SIC: 6324 Hospital and medical service plans
HQ: Kaiser Foundation Hospitals Inc
1 Kaiser Plz
Oakland CA
510 271-6611

(P-14483)
KAISER PERMANENTE
9985 Sierra Ave (92335-6720)
PHONE....................909 427-3910
Terry Bellmonte, *Prin*
EMP: 157 **EST:** 2002
SALES (est): 7.98MM **Privately Held**
SIC: 6324 Hospital and medical service plans

(P-14484)
LIBERTY DENTAL PLAN CAL INC
340 Commerce Ste 100 (92602-1358)
PHONE....................949 223-0007
Amir Hossein Neshat, *Prin*
Maja Kapic, *
EMP: 300 **EST:** 2001
SALES (est): 64.64MM **Privately Held**
Web: www.libertydentalplan.com
SIC: 6324 Dental insurance

(P-14485)
LIBERTY DENTAL PLAN CORP (PA)
340 Commerce Ste 100 (92602-1358)
PHONE....................888 703-6999
Marti Lolli, *Pr*
Rohan C Reid, *
Amir Neshat, *
Rosa Roldan, *Chief Dental Officer**
EMP: 99 **EST:** 2007
SALES (est): 98.23MM
SALES (corp-wide): 98.23MM **Privately Held**
Web: www.libertydentalplan.com
SIC: 6324 Dental insurance

(P-14486)
LOCAL INTTIVE HLTH AUTH FOR LO (PA)
Also Called: L.A. Care Health Plan
1055 W 7th St Fl 10 (90017-2750)
PHONE....................213 694-1250
EMP: 894 **EST:** 1995
SALES (est): 701.73MM **Privately Held**
Web: www.lacare.org
SIC: 6324 Health Maintenance Organization (HMO), insurance only

PRODUCTS & SVCS

(P-14487)
MANAGED DENTAL CARE
Also Called: Managed Dental Care California
6200 Canoga Ave Ste 100 (91367-2426)
PHONE..................................818 598-6599
Michael Gould, *Pr*
EMP: 172 **EST:** 1990
SALES (est): 1.71MM
SALES (corp-wide): 3.42B **Privately Held**
Web: www.manageddentalcare.net
SIC: 6324 Dental insurance
PA: Guardian Life Insurance Company Of
America
10 Hudson Yards Fl 22
New York NY
212 598-8000

(P-14488)
MANAGED HEALTH NETWORK
Also Called: Managed Health
7755 Center Ave Ste 700 (92647-9126)
PHONE..................................714 934-5519
Carol Mclean, *Brnch Mgr*
EMP: 260
Web: www.mhn.com
SIC: 6324 Hospital and medical service plans
HQ: Managed Health Network
2370 Kerner Blvd
San Rafael CA

(P-14489)
OPTUMRX INC (DH)
Also Called: Optumrx PBM Administrator Cal
2300 Main St (92614-6223)
P.O. Box 509075 (92150-9075)
PHONE..................................714 825-3600
John Michael Prince, *CEO*
Timothy Wicks, *Pr*
Jeff Park, *COO*
Jeffrey Grosklags, *CFO*
EMP: 300 **EST:** 1990
SALES (est): 23.01B
SALES (corp-wide): 324.16B **Publicly
Held**
Web: www.optumrx.com
SIC: 6324 6321 Hospital and medical
service plans; Accident and health
insurance
HQ: Optum, Inc.
11000 Optum Cir
Eden Prairie MN
952 936-1300

(P-14490)
OPTUMRX INC
Also Called: Prescription Solutions
2858 Loker Ave E Ste 100 (92010-6673)
P.O. Box 2975 (66201-1375)
PHONE..................................760 804-2399
Sean O'rourke, *Mgr*
EMP: 400
SALES (corp-wide): 324.16B **Publicly
Held**
Web: www.optumrx.com
SIC: 6324 Hospital and medical service plans
HQ: Optumrx, Inc.
2300 Main St
Irvine CA

(P-14491)
PACIFCARE HLTH PLAN
ADMNSTRTOR (DH)
Also Called: Pacificare
3120 W Lake Center Dr (92704-6917)
P.O. Box 25186 (92799-5186)
PHONE..................................714 825-5200
David Reed, *Ch Bd*
Coy F Baugh, *Treas*
EMP: 400 **EST:** 1975
SQ FT: 220,000

SALES (est): 1.02B
SALES (corp-wide): 324.16B **Publicly
Held**
SIC: 6324 Group hospitalization plans
HQ: Pacificare Health Systems, Llc
5995 Plaza Dr
Cypress CA

(P-14492)
PRIVATE MEDICAL-CARE INC
12898 Towne Center Dr (90703-8546)
PHONE..................................562 924-8311
Robert Elliott, *Pr*
EMP: 1679 **EST:** 1970
SALES (est): 4.62MM
SALES (corp-wide): 5.41B **Privately Held**
SIC: 6324 Dental insurance
PA: Delta Dental Of California
560 Mission St Ste 1300
San Francisco CA
415 972-8300

(P-14493)
SAFEGUARD HEALTH ENTPS
INC (HQ)
95 Enterprise Ste 100 (92656-2605)
PHONE..................................800 880-1800
Steven J Baileys D.d.s., *Ch Bd*
James E Buncher, *Pr*
Stephen J Baker, *Ex VP*
Ronald I Brendzel, *Sr VP*
Dennis L Gates, *Sr VP*
EMP: 355 **EST:** 1974
SQ FT: 68,000
SALES (est): 92.41MM
SALES (corp-wide): 69.9B **Publicly Held**
Web: www.metlife.com
SIC: 6324 Dental insurance
PA: Metlife, Inc.
200 Park Ave Fl 1200
New York NY
212 578-9500

(P-14494)
SCAN GROUP (PA)
3800 Kilroy Airport Way Ste 100
(90806-2494)
PHONE..................................562 308-2733
Sachin H Jain, *Pr*
Linda Rosenstock, *
Janet Kornblatt, *
Michael Plumb, *
Deepa Sheth, *Chief Corporate
Development Officer*
EMP: 306 **EST:** 1983
SALES (est): 6.11MM
SALES (corp-wide): 6.11MM **Privately
Held**
Web: www.scanhealthplan.com
SIC: 6324 Health Maintenance Organization
(HMO), insurance only

(P-14495)
SENIOR CARE (PA)
Also Called: Scan Health Plan
3800 Kilroy Airport Way (90806-2494)
P.O. Box 22616 (90801-5616)
PHONE..................................562 989-5100
David Schmidt, *CEO*
Dennis Eder, *
EMP: 650 **EST:** 1978
SQ FT: 119,219
SALES (est): 113.83MM
SALES (corp-wide): 113.83MM **Privately
Held**
Web: www.scanhealthplan.com
SIC: 6324 Health Maintenance Organization
(HMO), insurance only

(P-14496)
SHARP HEALTH PLAN
8520 Tech Way Ste 200 (92123-1450)
PHONE..................................858 499-8300
Melissa Hayden-cook, *Pr*
Rita Datko, *
Leslie Pels-beck, *VP*
Michael Byrd, *Chief Business Development
Officer*
Doctor Cary Shames, *Chief Medical Officer*
EMP: 98 **EST:** 1992
SALES (est): 918.72MM
SALES (corp-wide): 2.37B **Privately Held**
Web: www.sharphealthplan.com
SIC: 6324 Health Maintenance Organization
(HMO), insurance only
PA: Sharp Healthcare
8695 Spectrum Center Blvd
San Diego CA
858 499-4000

(P-14497)
SOUTHERN CAL PRMNNTE MED
GROUP
Also Called: Kaiser Foundation Health Plan
5855 Copley Dr Ste 250 (92111-7908)
PHONE..................................858 974-1000
Tom Cooper, *Mgr*
EMP: 371
SQ FT: 89,984
SALES (corp-wide): 68.1B **Privately Held**
Web: www.kaiserpermanente.org
SIC: 6324 Health Maintenance Organization
(HMO), insurance only
HQ: Southern California Permanente
Medical Group
393 Walnut Dr
Pasadena CA
626 405-5704

(P-14498)
SOUTHERN CAL PRMNNTE MED
GROUP
Also Called: SOUTHERN CALIFORNIA
PERMANENTE MEDICAL GROUP
6860 Avenida Encinas (92011-3201)
PHONE..................................619 528-5000
Walter Borschel, *Admn*
EMP: 175
SALES (corp-wide): 68.1B **Privately Held**
Web: www.permanente.org
SIC: 6324 Hospital and medical service plans
HQ: Southern California Permanente
Medical Group
393 Walnut Dr
Pasadena CA
626 405-5704

(P-14499)
SOUTHERN CAL PRMNNTE MED
GROUP
13652 Cantara St (91402-5423)
PHONE..................................800 272-3500
Arthur Phelps, *Brnch Mgr*
EMP: 466
SALES (corp-wide): 68.1B **Privately Held**
Web: www.permanente.org
SIC: 6324 Hospital and medical service plans
HQ: Southern California Permanente
Medical Group
393 Walnut Dr
Pasadena CA
626 405-5704

(P-14500)
SOUTHERN CAL PRMNNTE MED
GROUP
Also Called: S C P M G
1255 W Arrow Hwy (91773-2340)

PHONE..................................909 394-2505
EMP: 182
SALES (corp-wide): 68.1B **Privately Held**
SIC: 6324 Hospital and medical service plans
HQ: Southern California Permanente
Medical Group
393 Walnut Dr
Pasadena CA
626 405-5704

(P-14501)
SOUTHERN CAL PRMNNTE MED
GROUP
1511 W Garvey Ave N (91790-2138)
PHONE..................................626 960-4844
EMP: 284
SALES (corp-wide): 68.1B **Privately Held**
Web: www.permanente.org
SIC: 6324 Hospital and medical service plans
HQ: Southern California Permanente
Medical Group
393 Walnut Dr
Pasadena CA
626 405-5704

(P-14502)
SOUTHERN CAL PRMNNTE MED
GROUP
Also Called: Southern California Permanente
Medical Group
10800 Magnolia Ave (92505-3043)
PHONE..................................866 984-7483
Jeffrey A Weisz, *Prin*
EMP: 153
SALES (corp-wide): 68.1B **Privately Held**
Web: www.permanente.org
SIC: 6324 Hospital and medical service plans
HQ: Southern California Permanente
Medical Group
393 Walnut Dr
Pasadena CA
626 405-5704

(P-14503)
SOUTHERN CAL PRMNNTE MED
GROUP
Also Called: Tustin Executive Center
17542 17th St Ste 300 (92780-1960)
PHONE..................................714 734-4500
Adamma Agufoh, *Dir*
EMP: 226
SALES (corp-wide): 68.1B **Privately Held**
Web: www.permanente.org
SIC: 6324 Hospital and medical service plans
HQ: Southern California Permanente
Medical Group
393 Walnut Dr
Pasadena CA
626 405-5704

(P-14504)
UHC OF CALIFORNIA (DH)
Also Called: Pacificare Health Systems
5995 Plaza Dr (90630-5028)
PHONE..................................952 936-6615
Brad A Bowlus, *Principal Health Plan*
Joseph S Konowiecki, *
Michael Montevideo, *
EMP: 800 **EST:** 1975
SALES (est): 478.68MM
SALES (corp-wide): 324.16B **Publicly
Held**
SIC: 6324 8732 Health Maintenance
Organization (HMO), insurance only;
Commercial nonphysical research
HQ: Pacificare Health Systems, Llc
5995 Plaza Dr
Cypress CA

6331 Fire, Marine, And Casualty Insurance

(P-14505)
ALLIANZ GLOBL RISKS US INSUR (DH)
Also Called: Allianz Insurance Company
2350 W Empire Ave Ste 200 (91504-3350)
P.O. Box 970 (63366-0970)
EMP: 175 **EST:** 1938
SQ FT: 20,000
SALES (est): 243.05MM
SALES (corp-wide): 27.99B **Privately Held**
Web: commercial.allianz.com
SIC: 6331 Property damage insurance
HQ: Fireman's Fund Insurance Company
1 Progress Point Pkwy # 200
O Fallon MO
415 899-2000

(P-14506)
ARROWHEAD GEN INSUR AGCY INC (HQ)
701 B St Ste 2100 (92101-8197)
PHONE.................619 881-8600
Chris L Walker, *CEO*
Steve Boydm, *Prin*
Steve Boyd, *
Scott Marshall, *
Stephen M Lesieur, *
EMP: 240 **EST:** 1983
SQ FT: 74,000
SALES (est): 145.88MM
SALES (corp-wide): 3.57B **Publicly Held**
Web: www.arrowheadgrp.com
SIC: 6331 6411 Automobile insurance;
Insurance agents, brokers, and service
PA: Brown & Brown, Inc.
300 N Beach St
Daytona Beach FL
386 252-9601

(P-14507)
BERKSHIRE HATHAWAY HOME SERVIC
11409 Carson St (90715-2512)
PHONE.................562 809-1331
EMP: 82
SALES (corp-wide): 2.56MM **Privately Held**
Web: www.brucemulhearn.com
SIC: 6331 Property damage insurance
PA: Berkshire Hathaway Home Services
Ca Roperties
18000 Studebaker Rd # 600
Cerritos CA
562 860-2625

(P-14508)
GOLDEN EAGLE INSURANCE CORP (DH)
Also Called: Golden Eagle
525 B St Ste 1300 (92101-4421)
P.O. Box 85826 (92186-5826)
PHONE.................619 744-6000
J Paul Condrin Iii, *CEO*
Frank J Kotarba, *
EMP: 250 **EST:** 1997
SALES (est): 206.53MM
SALES (corp-wide): 20.63B **Privately Held**
SIC: 6331 Property damage insurance
HQ: Liberty Mutual Insurance Company
175 Berkeley St
Boston MA
617 357-9500

(P-14509)
HMC ASSETS LLC
2015 Manhattan Beach Blvd Ste 200 (90278-1226)
PHONE.................310 535-9293
EMP: 92 **EST:** 2010
SALES (est): 9.84MM
SALES (corp-wide): 147.22MM **Privately Held**
Web: www.wedgewoodloanassets.com
SIC: 6331 Property damage insurance
PA: Wedgewood Inc.
2015 Manhattan Beach Blvd # 102
Redondo Beach CA
310 640-3070

(P-14510)
ICW GROUP HOLDINGS INC (PA)
15025 Innovation Dr (92128-3456)
P.O. Box 509039 (92150-9039)
PHONE.................858 350-2400
Kevin M Prior, *CEO*
Ernest Rady, *
Sariborz Rostamian, *
EMP: 234 **EST:** 1974
SQ FT: 160,000
SALES (est): 610.35MM
SALES (corp-wide): 610.35MM **Privately Held**
Web: www.icwgroup.com
SIC: 6331 6411 Fire, marine and casualty
insurance and carriers; Insurance brokers,
nec

(P-14511)
KRAMER-WILSON COMPANY INC (PA)
Also Called: Century National
340 N Westlake Blvd Ste 210 (91362-7034)
P.O. Box 3999 (91609-0599)
PHONE.................818 760-0880
Weldon Wilson, *CEO*
Kevin Wilson, *
Daniel Sherrin, *
Mary Ann Wagner, *
◆ **EMP:** 240 **EST:** 1969
SALES (est): 49.1MM
SALES (corp-wide): 49.1MM **Privately Held**
SIC: 6331 Fire, marine and casualty
insurance and carriers

(P-14512)
MERCURY CASUALTY COMPANY (HQ)
Also Called: M C C
555 W Imperial Hwy (92821-4802)
P.O. Box 54600 (90054-0600)
PHONE.................323 937-1060
Gabriel Tirador, *CEO*
George Joseph, *
EMP: 600 **EST:** 1962
SALES (est): 765.86MM
SALES (corp-wide): 3.64B **Publicly Held**
Web: www.mercuryinsurance.com
SIC: 6331 6351 Automobile insurance;
Warranty insurance, home
PA: Mercury General Corporation
4484 Wilshire Blvd
Los Angeles CA
323 937-1060

(P-14513)
MERCURY GENERAL CORPORATION (PA)
Also Called: Mercury General
4484 Wilshire Blvd (90010-3710)
P.O. Box 36662 (90036-0662)
PHONE.................323 937-1060

Gabriel Tirador, *Pr*
George Joseph, *
Theodore R Stalick, *Sr VP*
Christopher Graves, *VP*
Abby Hosseini, *VP*
EMP: 634 **EST:** 1961
SQ FT: 41,000
SALES (est): 3.64B
SALES (corp-wide): 3.64B **Publicly Held**
Web: www.mercuryinsurance.com
SIC: 6331 6411 Automobile insurance;
Insurance agents, brokers, and service

(P-14514)
MERCURY INSURANCE COMPANY (HQ)
4484 Wilshire Blvd (90010-3710)
P.O. Box 54600 (90054-0600)
PHONE.................323 937-1060
Gabe Tirador, *CEO*
George Joseph, *
Ted Stalick, *
Judith Walters, *
EMP: 160 **EST:** 1972
SQ FT: 40,809
SALES (est): 1.21B
SALES (corp-wide): 3.64B **Publicly Held**
Web: www.mercuryinsurance.com
SIC: 6331 Fire, marine, and casualty
insurance
PA: Mercury General Corporation
4484 Wilshire Blvd
Los Angeles CA
323 937-1060

(P-14515)
MERCURY INSURANCE COMPANY
Also Called: Mercury Insurance Group
555 W Imperial Hwy (92821-4839)
P.O. Box 1150 (92822-1150)
PHONE.................714 671-6700
Gave Tirador, *Pr*
EMP: 89
SALES (corp-wide): 3.64B **Publicly Held**
Web: www.mercuryinsurance.com
SIC: 6331 6411 Fire, marine, and casualty
insurance; Insurance agents, brokers, and
service
HQ: Mercury Insurance Company
4484 Wilshire Blvd
Los Angeles CA
323 937-1060

(P-14516)
MERCURY INSURANCE COMPANY
1700 Greenbriar Ln (92821-5971)
PHONE.................714 255-5000
Ken Kitzmiller, *Brnch Mgr*
EMP: 1033
SALES (corp-wide): 3.64B **Publicly Held**
Web: www.mercuryinsurance.com
SIC: 6331 Fire, marine, and casualty
insurance
HQ: Mercury Insurance Company
4484 Wilshire Blvd
Los Angeles CA
323 937-1060

(P-14517)
MERCURY INSURANCE COMPANY
9635 Granite Ridge Dr Ste 200 (92123)
P.O. Box 10730 (92711-0730)
PHONE.................858 694-4100
Randy Petro, *Mgr*
EMP: 557
SALES (corp-wide): 3.64B **Publicly Held**
Web: www.mercuryinsurance.com

SIC: 6331 6399 Fire, marine, and casualty
insurance; Warranty insurance, automobile
HQ: Mercury Insurance Company
4484 Wilshire Blvd
Los Angeles CA
323 937-1060

(P-14518)
MERCURY INSURANCE COMPANY
27200 Tourney Rd Ste 400 (91355-4997)
P.O. Box 10730 (92711-0730)
PHONE.................661 291-6470
David Levy, *Mgr*
EMP: 580
SALES (corp-wide): 3.64B **Publicly Held**
Web: www.mercuryinsurance.com
SIC: 6331 Fire, marine, and casualty
insurance
HQ: Mercury Insurance Company
4484 Wilshire Blvd
Los Angeles CA
323 937-1060

(P-14519)
MERCURY INSURANCE COMPANY
Also Called: Mercury Insurance Broker
1433 Santa Monica Blvd (90404-1709)
PHONE.................310 451-4943
Ken Donaldson, *Owner*
EMP: 290
SALES (corp-wide): 3.64B **Publicly Held**
Web: www.mercuryinsurance.com
SIC: 6331 6411 Fire, marine, and casualty
insurance; Insurance agents, brokers, and
service
HQ: Mercury Insurance Company
4484 Wilshire Blvd
Los Angeles CA
323 937-1060

(P-14520)
MERCURY INSURANCE SERVICES LLC
4484 Wilshire Blvd (90010-3710)
PHONE.................323 937-1060
Gabriel Tirador, *CEO*
EMP: 2977 **EST:** 2000
SALES (est): 31.86MM
SALES (corp-wide): 3.64B **Publicly Held**
Web: www.mercuryinsurance.com
SIC: 6331 Property damage insurance
HQ: Mercury Casualty Company
555 W Imperial Hwy
Brea CA
323 937-1060

(P-14521)
MID-CENTURY INSURANCE COMPANY
6303 Owensmouth Ave Fl 1 (91367-2200)
PHONE.................323 932-7116
Ron Coble, *Sr VP*
Bob Woudstra, *
EMP: 250 **EST:** 1953
SALES (est): 95.59MM
SALES (corp-wide): 71.15B **Privately Held**
Web: www.farmers.com
SIC: 6331 6351 Automobile insurance;
Fidelity insurance
HQ: Farmers Insurance Exchange
6301 Owensmouth Ave # 750
Woodland Hills CA
888 327-6335

(P-14522)
ORION INDEMNITY COMPANY
714 W Olympic Blvd Ste 800 (90015-1425)

PHONE..................213 742-8700
Jeanette Shammas, *Ch Bd*
Nicholas J Lannotti, *
Denise M Tyson, *
EMP: 100 **EST:** 1949
SALES (est): 53.17MM
SALES (corp-wide): 3.64B **Publicly Held**
Web: www.orionindemnity.com
SIC: 6331 Fire, marine, and casualty insurance
PA: Mercury General Corporation
4484 Wilshire Blvd
Los Angeles CA
323 937-1060

(P-14523)
REPUBLIC INDEMNITY CO AMER (DH)
Also Called: Rica
4500 Park Granada Ste 300 (91302-1667)
P.O. Box 20036 (91416-0036)
PHONE..................818 990-9860
Dwayne Marioni, *CEO*
Marion Chappel, *
EMP: 129 **EST:** 1973
SQ FT: 70,000
SALES (est): 703.47MM **Publicly Held**
Web: www.republicindemnity.com
SIC: 6331 Workers' compensation insurance
HQ: Pennsylvania Company Inc
1 E 4th St
Cincinnati OH
513 579-2121

(P-14524)
REPUBLIC INDEMNITY COMPANY CAL
15821 Ventura Blvd Ste 370 (91436-2909)
P.O. Box 4275 (91365-4275)
PHONE..................818 990-9860
Dwayne T Marioni, *Pr*
Shila Euper, *
EMP: 127 **EST:** 1982
SALES (est): 22.4MM **Publicly Held**
Web: www.republicindemnity.com
SIC: 6331 Fire, marine, and casualty insurance
HQ: Republic Indemnity Company Of America
4500 Park Granada Ste 300
Calabasas CA
818 990-9860

(P-14525)
ROYAL SPECIALTY UNDWRT INC
Also Called: Rsui Group
15303 Ventura Blvd Ste 500 (91403-6619)
PHONE..................818 922-6700
Christine Chinen, *Admn*
EMP: 103
SALES (corp-wide): 302.09B **Publicly Held**
Web: www.rsui.com
SIC: 6331 6411 Fire, marine, and casualty insurance; Insurance agents, brokers, and service
HQ: Royal Specialty Underwriting, Inc.
945 E Paces Ferry Rd Ne
Atlanta GA

(P-14526)
STATE COMPENSATION INSUR FUND
21300 Victory Blvd Ste 600 (91367-2525)
P.O. Box 1950 (91365)
PHONE..................818 888-4750
Mary Powers, *Brnch Mgr*
EMP: 510
SALES (corp-wide): 2.76B **Privately Held**
Web: www.statefundca.com

SIC: 6331 9651 Workers' compensation insurance; Insurance commission, government
PA: State Compensation Insurance Fund
333 Bush St Ste 800
San Francisco CA
888 782-8338

(P-14527)
STATE COMPENSATION INSUR FUND
Also Called: Los Angles Dst Off Policy Svcs
900 Corporate Center Dr (91754-7620)
P.O. Box 65005 (93650-5005)
PHONE..................323 266-5000
Joe Codron, *Brnch Mgr*
EMP: 224
SALES (corp-wide): 2.76B **Privately Held**
Web: www.statefundca.com
SIC: 6331 9651 Workers' compensation insurance; Insurance commission, government
PA: State Compensation Insurance Fund
333 Bush St Ste 800
San Francisco CA
888 782-8338

(P-14528)
STATE COMPENSATION INSUR FUND
Also Called: Bakersfield District Office
9801 Camino Media Ste 101 (93311-1312)
P.O. Box 21810 (93390-1810)
PHONE..................661 664-4000
Robert Kean, *Mgr*
EMP: 91
SALES (corp-wide): 2.76B **Privately Held**
Web: www.statefundca.com
SIC: 6331 9651 Workers' compensation insurance; Insurance commission, government
PA: State Compensation Insurance Fund
333 Bush St Ste 800
San Francisco CA
888 782-8338

(P-14529)
STATE COMPENSATION INSUR FUND
Also Called: Santa Ana District Office
1750 E 4th St Fl 3 (92705-3929)
PHONE..................714 565-5000
Liz Glidden, *Mgr*
EMP: 241
SALES (corp-wide): 2.76B **Privately Held**
Web: www.statefundca.com
SIC: 6331 9651 Workers' compensation insurance; Insurance commission, government
PA: State Compensation Insurance Fund
333 Bush St Ste 800
San Francisco CA
888 782-8338

(P-14530)
STATE COMPENSATION INSUR FUND
Also Called: Riverside District Office
6301 Day St (92507-0902)
PHONE..................888 782-8338
Barbara Katzka, *Mgr*
EMP: 208
SALES (corp-wide): 2.76B **Privately Held**
Web: www.statefundca.com
SIC: 6331 9651 Workers' compensation insurance; Insurance commission, government
PA: State Compensation Insurance Fund
333 Bush St Ste 800
San Francisco CA
888 782-8338

(P-14531)
STATE COMPENSATION INSUR FUND
Also Called: San Diego District Office
10105 Pacific Heights Blvd Ste 120 (92121)
PHONE..................888 782-8338
Lisa Middleton, *Mgr*
EMP: 235
SALES (corp-wide): 2.76B **Privately Held**
Web: www.statefundca.com
SIC: 6331 9651 Workers' compensation insurance; Insurance commission, government
PA: State Compensation Insurance Fund
333 Bush St Ste 800
San Francisco CA
888 782-8338

(P-14532)
TRISTAR INSURANCE GROUP INC (PA)
Also Called: Tristar Risk Management
100 Oceangate Ste 700 (90802-4368)
PHONE..................562 495-6600
Thomas J Veale, *Pr*
Russ O'donnell, *Sec*
Joseph Mclaughlin, *Sr VP*
Denise J Cotter, *CFO*
EMP: 700 **EST:** 1982
SQ FT: 9,000
SALES (est): 502.12MM
SALES (corp-wide): 502.12MM **Privately Held**
Web: www.tristargroup.net
SIC: 6331 8741 Workers' compensation insurance; Management services

(P-14533)
ZENITH INSURANCE COMPANY (DH)
Also Called: Zenith A Fairfax Company, The
21255 Califa St (91367-5021)
P.O. Box 9055 (91409-9055)
PHONE..................818 713-1000
Stanley R Zax, *Ch Bd*
Jack D Miller, *Pr*
Paul Ramont, *Chief Underwriting Officer*
EMP: 400 **EST:** 1950
SQ FT: 120,000
SALES (est): 1.01B
SALES (corp-wide): 19.79B **Privately Held**
Web: www.thezenith.com
SIC: 6331 Workers' compensation insurance
HQ: Zenith National Insurance Corp.
21255 Califa St
Woodland Hills CA
818 713-1000

6351 Surety Insurance

(P-14534)
AMERICAN CONTRS INDEMNITY CO (DH)
Also Called: HCC Surety Group
801 S Figueroa St Ste 700 (90017-2523)
PHONE..................213 330-1309
Adam S Pessin, *Pr*
Michael Budnitsky, *
EMP: 150 **EST:** 1990
SALES (est): 104.02MM **Privately Held**
Web: www.tmhcc.com
SIC: 6351 Surety insurance bonding
HQ: Hcc Insurance Holdings, Inc.
13403 Northwest Fwy
Houston TX

(P-14535)
CAP-MPT (PA)
333 S Hope St Fl 8 (90071-3001)
PHONE..................213 473-8600
Jim Weidner, *CEO*
Michael Wormley Md, *Ch Bd*
Thomas Andre, *
Cindy Belcher, *
Nancy Brusegaard Johnson, *
EMP: 140 **EST:** 1977
SALES (est): 23.03MM
SALES (corp-wide): 23.03MM **Privately Held**
Web: www.capphysicians.com
SIC: 6351 Liability insurance

(P-14536)
FAR WEST BOND SERVICES CAL INC (PA)
5230 Las Virgenes Rd (91302-3448)
P.O. Box 4500 (91365-4500)
PHONE..................818 704-1111
John Savage, *Pr*
Neal Pomp, *
Steve Kay, *
▼ **EMP:** 300 **EST:** 1974
SALES (est): 86.45MM
SALES (corp-wide): 86.45MM **Privately Held**
SIC: 6351 6331 Surety insurance; Fire, marine, and casualty insurance

(P-14537)
SELECT HOME WARRANTY CA INC
222 W 6th St Ste 400 (90731-3345)
PHONE..................732 835-0110
Joseph Shrem, *CEO*
EMP: 325 **EST:** 2019
SALES (est): 25MM **Privately Held**
SIC: 6351 Warranty insurance, home

6361 Title Insurance

(P-14538)
CHICAGO TITLE INSURANCE CO (HQ)
Also Called: Chicago Title
4050 Calle Real (93110-3413)
PHONE..................805 565-6900
William Halvorsen Junior, *Pr*
A Larry Sisk, *
Peter G Leemputte, *
EMP: 150 **EST:** 1984
SQ FT: 44,637
SALES (est): 1.02B **Publicly Held**
SIC: 6361 Real estate title insurance
PA: Fidelity National Financial, Inc.
601 Riverside Ave Fl 4
Jacksonville FL

(P-14539)
FIRST AMERICAN FINANCIAL CORP (PA)
1 First American Way (92707-5913)
PHONE..................714 250-3000
EMP: 656 **EST:** 1889
SQ FT: 490,000
SALES (est): 7.61B **Publicly Held**
Web: www.firstam.com
SIC: 6361 6351 Title insurance; Surety insurance

(P-14540)
FIRST AMERICAN MORTGAGE SVCS
3 First American Way (92707-5913)

PHONE..................714 250-4210
EMP: 350 **EST:** 2009
SALES (est): 28.1MM **Privately Held**
Web: www.firstam.com
SIC: 6361 Title insurance

(P-14541)
FIRST AMERICAN TITLE INSUR CO (HQ)
Also Called: First American Mortgage Svcs
1 First American Way (92707-5913)
P.O. Box 267 (92702-0267)
PHONE..................800 854-3643
Curt G Johnson, *V Ch Bd*
Curt Caspersen, *
Mark R Amesen, *
Max Weldex, *
Kurt Pfotenhauer, *Vice Chairman*
EMP: 485 **EST:** 1889
SALES (est): 3.64B **Publicly Held**
Web: www.firstam.com
SIC: 6361 7371 Real estate title insurance;
Computer software development
PA: First American Financial Corporation
1 First American Way
Santa Ana CA

(P-14542)
LAWYERS TITLE INSURANCE CORP
Also Called: Lawyers Title Escrow
5000 Birch St (92660-2138)
PHONE..................949 223-5575
Dan Williams, *Owner*
EMP: 139
Web: www.ltic.com
SIC: 6361 Real estate title insurance
HQ: Lawyers Title Insurance Corporation
601 Riverside Ave
Jacksonville FL
888 866-3684

(P-14543)
LAWYERS TITLE INSURANCE CORP
18551 Von Karman Ave Ste 100
(92612-1552)
PHONE..................949 223-5575
EMP: 104
Web: www.ltic.com
SIC: 6361 6541 Real estate title insurance;
Title and trust companies
HQ: Lawyers Title Insurance Corporation
601 Riverside Ave
Jacksonville FL
888 866-3684

(P-14544)
LAWYERS TITLE INSURANCE CORP
2751 Park View Ct (93036-5452)
PHONE..................805 484-2701
John Arnold, *Mgr*
EMP: 521
Web: www.ltic.com
SIC: 6361 Guarantee of titles
HQ: Lawyers Title Insurance Corporation
601 Riverside Ave
Jacksonville FL
888 866-3684

(P-14545)
STEWART TITLE CALIFORNIA INC (DH)
7676 Hazard Center Dr Ste 1400
(92108-4501)
PHONE..................619 692-1600
Shari Schneider, *Pr*
Brian Glaze, *VP*

Gregg Unrath, *VP*
Linda Mundy, *Sec*
EMP: 140 **EST:** 1996
SQ FT: 44,000
SALES (est): 127.18MM
SALES (corp-wide): 3.07B **Publicly Held**
Web: www.stewart.com
SIC: 6361 Guarantee of titles
HQ: Stewart Title Company
1360 Post Oak Blvd Ste 10
Houston TX
713 625-8100

6371 Pension, Health, And Welfare Funds

(P-14546)
ASSOCIATED THIRD PARTY ADMINISTRATORS INC
Also Called: Atpa
222 N Pacific Coast Hwy # 2000
(90245-5648)
EMP: 390
SIC: 6371 6411 Union welfare, benefit, and
health funds; Insurance agents, brokers,
and service

(P-14547)
CAL SOUTHERN UNITED FOOD
Also Called: U F C Pension Trust Fund
6425 Katella Ave Ste 100 (90630-5246)
P.O. Box 6010 (90630-0010)
PHONE..................714 220-2297
P Thompson, *Admn*
EMP: 240 **EST:** 1957
SQ FT: 36,000
SALES (est): 42.82MM **Privately Held**
Web: www.scufcwfunds.com
SIC: 6371 Pension funds

(P-14548)
LOS ANGLES CNTY EMPLYEES RTRME (PA)
Also Called: Lacera
300 N Lake Ave Ste 720 (91101-5674)
P.O. Box 7060 (91109-7060)
PHONE..................626 564-6000
Gregg Rademather, *CEO*
EMP: 200 **EST:** 1938
SQ FT: 85,000
SALES (est): 2.06B
SALES (corp-wide): 2.06B **Privately Held**
Web: www.lacera.com
SIC: 6371 Pension funds

(P-14549)
MOTION PCTURE INDUST PNSION HL
11365 Ventura Blvd Ste 300 (91604-3148)
PHONE..................818 769-0007
David Wescoe, *CEO*
Chuck Killian, *
EMP: 150 **EST:** 1954
SQ FT: 12,500
SALES (est): 48.89MM **Privately Held**
SIC: 6371 Pension, health, and welfare funds

(P-14550)
SCREEN ACTORS GUILD - AMERICAN
Also Called: Screen Actors Guild-Producers
3601 W Olive Ave Fl 2 (91505-4662)
P.O. Box 7830 (91510-7830)
PHONE..................818 954-9400
EMP: 100
SALES (corp-wide): 79.3MM **Privately Held**
Web: www.sagaftraplans.org

SIC: 6371 6411 Pensions; Pension and
retirement plan consultants
PA: Screen Actors Guild - American
Federation Of Television And Radio
Artists
5757 Wilshire Blvd Fl 7
Los Angeles CA
415 391-7510

(P-14551)
SOUTHWEST ADMINISTRATORS INC
466 Foothill Blvd (91011-3503)
EMP: 300
SIC: 6371 Pension funds

6411 Insurance Agents, Brokers, And Service

(P-14552)
21ST CENTURY LIFE INSURANCE CO (DH)
Also Called: 21st Century Insurance
6301 Owensmouth Ave Ste 700
(91367-2208)
PHONE..................877 310-5687
Glenn A Pfeil, *CEO*
Michael J Cassanego, *
Dean E Stark, *
Richard R Andre, *
Kathy Doyle, *
EMP: 1800 **EST:** 1955
SQ FT: 412,000
SALES (est): 415.03MM **Privately Held**
Web: www.21st.com
SIC: 6411 Insurance agents, brokers, and
service
HQ: 21st Century North America Insurance
Company
3 Beaver Valley Rd
Wilmington DE
877 310-5687

(P-14553)
ADMINSURE INC
3380 Shelby St (91764-5567)
PHONE..................909 718-1200
Alithia Vargas-flores, *Pr*
EMP: 130 **EST:** 1982
SQ FT: 30,000
SALES (est): 19.66MM **Privately Held**
Web: www.adminsure.com
SIC: 6411 Insurance agents, nec

(P-14554)
AGIA INC (PA)
Also Called: Agia Affinity
1155 Eugenia Pl (93013-2062)
PHONE..................805 566-9191
J Christopher Burke, *Pr*
Julie L Capritto, *Sr VP*
Andrew Dowen, *Sr VP*
Susan Roe, *VP Mktg*
Carl A Adamek, *Senior Vice President
Accounting*
EMP: 231 **EST:** 1965
SQ FT: 18,000
SALES (est): 97.42MM **Privately Held**
Web: www.agia.com
SIC: 6411 Medical insurance claim
processing, contract or fee basis

(P-14555)
AIG DIRECT INSURANCE SVCS INC
Also Called: Matrix Direct Insurance Svcs
9640 Granite Ridge Dr Ste 200 (92123)
PHONE..................858 309-3000

EMP: 275 **EST:** 1995
SQ FT: 24,000
SALES (est): 105.94MM
SALES (corp-wide): 56.44B **Publicly Held**
Web: www.aigdirect.com
SIC: 6411 Insurance agents, nec
HQ: American General Life Insurance
Company
2727 Allen Pkwy Ste A
Houston TX
713 522-1111

(P-14556)
ALLSTATE FINANCIAL SVCS LLC
Also Called: Allstate
5161 Pomona Blvd Ste 212 (90022-1749)
PHONE..................323 981-8520
Carlos Godinez, *Prin*
EMP: 96
Web: www.allstate.com
SIC: 6411 Insurance agents, brokers, and
service
HQ: Allstate Financial Services, Llc
151 N 8th St
Lincoln NE
402 328-6700

(P-14557)
ALLSTATE FLORAL INC
15928 Commerce Way (90703-2319)
PHONE..................562 926-2989
EMP: 223
SALES (corp-wide): 53.44MM **Privately
Held**
Web: www.allstatefloral.com
SIC: 6411 Insurance agents and brokers
PA: Allstate Floral, Inc.
14101 Park Pl
Cerritos CA
562 926-2302

(P-14558)
AMERICAN SPCLTY HLTH PLANS CAL
10221 Wateridge Cir (92121-2702)
PHONE..................619 297-8100
George Devries, *Pr*
Robert White, *
Marcel Danko, *CFO*
EMP: 500 **EST:** 1999
SALES (est): 50.46MM **Privately Held**
Web: www.ashcompanies.com
SIC: 6411 Insurance information and
consulting services
PA: American Specialty Health
Incorporated
12800 N Meridian St # 190
Carmel IN

(P-14559)
ANCHOR GENERAL INSUR AGCY INC
10256 Meanley Dr (92131-3009)
P.O. Box 509020 (92150-9020)
PHONE..................858 527-3600
EMP: 203 **EST:** 1995
SALES (est): 44.65MM **Privately Held**
Web: www.anchorgeneral.com
SIC: 6411 Insurance agents, nec

(P-14560)
ARTHUR J GALLAGHER RISK MGMT
Also Called: Nationwide
500 N Brand Blvd Ste 100 (91203-3931)
PHONE..................818 539-2300
Gregory S Chapman, *Pr*
Gerald S Chapman, *
Paulette Chapman, *

PRODUCTS & SVCS

EMP: 80 **EST:** 1973
SALES (est): 9.47MM
SALES (corp-wide): 8.55B **Publicly Held**
Web: www.ajg.com
SIC: 6411 Insurance brokers, nec
PA: Arthur J. Gallagher & Co.
2850 Golf Rd Ste 600
Rolling Meadows IL
630 773-3800

(P-14561)
ATLAS GENERAL INSUR SVCS LLC
Also Called: Nationwide
6165 Greenwich Dr Ste 200 (92122-5911)
PHONE..............................858 529-6700
EMP: 153 **EST:** 2008
SALES (est): 32.88MM
SALES (corp-wide): 8.55B **Publicly Held**
Web: atlas.us.com
SIC: 6411 Insurance agents, nec
PA: Arthur J. Gallagher & Co.
2850 Golf Rd Ste 600
Rolling Meadows IL
630 773-3800

(P-14562)
AUTO INSURANCE SPECIALISTS LLC (DH)
Also Called: Nationwide
17785 Center Court Dr N Ste 110
(90703-8573)
PHONE..............................562 345-6247
EMP: 210 **EST:** 1968
SQ FT: 45,000
SALES (est): 59.77MM
SALES (corp-wide): 3.64B **Publicly Held**
Web: www.aisinsurance.com
SIC: 6411 Insurance brokers, nec
HQ: Ais Management, Llc
17785 Center Court Dr N # 250
Cerritos CA

(P-14563)
AUTOMOBILE CLUB SOUTHERN CAL
Also Called: AAA Auto Club
3333 Fairview Rd (92626-1698)
PHONE..............................714 885-1343
Becky Martinez, *Brnch Mgr*
EMP: 200
SALES (corp-wide): 1.08B **Privately Held**
Web: ace.aaa.com
SIC: 6411 Insurance agents, brokers, and
service
PA: Automobile Club Of Southern California
2601 S Figueroa St
Los Angeles CA
213 741-3686

(P-14564)
AUTOMOBILE CLUB SOUTHERN CAL (PA)
Also Called: A A A Automobile Club So Cal
2601 S Figueroa St (90007-3254)
P.O. Box 25001 (92799-5001)
PHONE..............................213 741-3686
John F Boyle, *CEO*
Zoo Babies, *
Peter R Mcdonald, *Sr VP*
Robert T Bouttier, *
EMP: 150 **EST:** 1900
SQ FT: 425,000
SALES (est): 1.08B
SALES (corp-wide): 1.08B **Privately Held**
Web: ace.aaa.com
SIC: 6411 8699 Insurance agents, nec;
Automobile owners' association

(P-14565)
AUTOMOBILE CLUB SOUTHERN CAL
Also Called: A A A Automobile Club So Cal
13331 Jamboree Rd (92602)
P.O. Box 11763 (92711-1763)
PHONE..............................714 973-1211
Sid Munger, *Mgr*
EMP: 172
SALES (corp-wide): 1.08B **Privately Held**
Web: ace.aaa.com
SIC: 6411 Insurance agents, brokers, and
service
PA: Automobile Club Of Southern California
2601 S Figueroa St
Los Angeles CA
213 741-3686

(P-14566)
B&C LIQUIDATING CORP (HQ)
Also Called: Nationwide
3475 E Foothill Blvd Ste 100 (91107)
P.O. Box 6030 (91102-6030)
PHONE..............................626 799-7000
EMP: 123 **EST:** 1931
SALES (est): 23.58MM
SALES (corp-wide): 474.73MM **Privately
Held**
Web: www.boltonco.com
SIC: 6411 Insurance agents, nec
PA: The Ima Financial Group Inc
1705 17th St Ste 100
Denver CO
316 267-9221

(P-14567)
BARNEY & BARNEY INC
Also Called: Loss and Risk Advisors
9171 Twne Cntre Dr 500 (92122)
P.O. Box 85638 (92186-5638)
PHONE..............................800 321-4696
EMP: 200
SIC: 6411 Property and casualty insurance
agent

(P-14568)
BITCO CNSTR INSUR AGCY INC
Also Called: Old Republic
225 S Lake Ave Ste 1050 (91101-4820)
PHONE..............................626 683-5200
Joan Miles, *CEO*
EMP: 90 **EST:** 2006
SALES (est): 18.06MM
SALES (corp-wide): 8.08B **Publicly Held**
Web: www.orcig.com
SIC: 6411 Insurance agents, brokers, and
service
HQ: Old Republic General Insurance
Group, Inc.
307 N Michigan Ave # 1418
Chicago IL

(P-14569)
CALIFORNIA FAIR PLAN ASSN
725 S Figueroa St Ste 3900 (90017-5439)
PHONE..............................213 487-0111
Stuart M Wilkinson, *Pr*
EMP: 80 **EST:** 1968
SALES (est): 16.69MM **Privately Held**
Web: www.cfpnet.com
SIC: 6411 Insurance agents, nec

(P-14570)
CALIFRNIA INSUR GUARANTEE ASSN
Also Called: C I G A
330 N Brand Blvd Ste 500 (91203-2304)
P.O. Box 29066 (91209-9066)
PHONE..............................818 844-4300

Lawrence E Mulryan, *Dir*
Wayne Wilson, *
EMP: 110 **EST:** 1969
SALES (est): 25.42MM **Privately Held**
Web: www.ciga.org
SIC: 6411 Insurance agents, brokers, and
service

(P-14571)
CARELON BHAVIORAL HLTH CAL INC
Also Called: Valueoptions of California Inc
12898 Towne Center Dr (90703-8546)
PHONE..............................800 228-1286
Juan Molina, *VP Opers*
Jolene Myrter, *
Steve Rockowitz, *
EMP: 637 **EST:** 1989
SALES (est): 2.18MM
SALES (corp-wide): 156.59B **Publicly
Held**
Web:
www.carelonbehavioralhealthca.com
SIC: 6411 6321 Insurance agents, nec;
Accident and health insurance
HQ: Fhc Health Systems, Inc
240 Corporate Blvd # 212
Norfolk VA
757 459-5100

(P-14572)
CARTEL MARKETING INC
Also Called: Insure Express Insurance Svc
5230 Las Virgenes Rd Ste 250
(91302-3448)
PHONE..............................818 483-1130
Robert M Humphreys, *Ch Bd*
Jack Edelstein, *
William Russell, *
EMP: 101 **EST:** 1984
SQ FT: 14,000
SALES (est): 9.02MM
SALES (corp-wide): 54.49MM **Privately
Held**
Web: www.cartel.net
SIC: 6411 Insurance agents, nec
HQ: Expresslink, Inc.
16501 Ventura Blvd # 300
Encino CA
818 788-5555

(P-14573)
CBIZ LIFE INSUR SOLUTIONS INC
13500 Evening Creek Dr N Ste 450
(92128-8111)
PHONE..............................858 444-3100
Timothy Moynihan, *Pr*
EMP: 126 **EST:** 1974
SALES (est): 26.17MM **Publicly Held**
Web: lifeinsurance.cbiz.com
SIC: 6411 Insurance brokers, nec
PA: Cbiz, Inc.
5959 Rockside Woods Blvd
Cleveland OH

(P-14574)
CENTURY-NATIONAL INSURANCE CO (DH)
16650 Sherman Way Ste 200 (91406-3782)
PHONE..............................818 760-0880
Weldon Wilson, *CEO*
Marie Balicki, *
Judy Osborn, *
EMP: 260 **EST:** 1955
SQ FT: 41,000
SALES (est): 91.53MM **Publicly Held**
Web: www.cnico.com
SIC: 6411 Insurance agents, nec
HQ: National General Holdings Corp.
59 Maiden Ln Fl 38

New York NY

(P-14575)
CHIVAROLI & ASSOC INC
200 N Westlake Blvd Ste 101 (91362-3784)
PHONE..............................208 338-6640
Roger Jones, *Brnch Mgr*
EMP: 97
SALES (corp-wide): 948.52K **Privately
Held**
Web: www.chivaroli.com
SIC: 6411 Insurance agents, nec
PA: Chivaroli & Assoc Inc
4500 Kruse Way Ste 100
Lake Oswego OR
503 675-0255

(P-14576)
CHOIC ADMINI INSUR SERVI
Also Called: California Choice
721 S Parker St Ste 200 (92868-4772)
PHONE..............................714 542-4200
Michael Close, *Pr*
John M Word, *
Raymond D Godeke, *
Brenda Scott, *
EMP: 500 **EST:** 1984
SALES (est): 50.26MM **Privately Held**
Web: www.choicebuilder.com
SIC: 6411 Insurance agents, nec

(P-14577)
COMMERCIAL CRRERS INSUR AGCY I
4 Centerpointe Dr Ste 300 (90623-1074)
PHONE..............................562 404-4900
Charles J Escalante, *Pr*
Henry H Escalante, *
Shannon S Walker, *
Helen M Escalante, *
EMP: 91 **EST:** 1979
SQ FT: 16,000
SALES (est): 2.69MM
SALES (corp-wide): 8.55B **Publicly Held**
Web: www.cciainsurance.com
SIC: 6411 Insurance agents, nec
HQ: Meadowbrook, Inc.
26255 American Dr
Southfield MI
248 358-1100

(P-14578)
CONEXIS BNFITS ADMNSTRATORS LP (HQ)
721 S Parker St Ste 300 (92868-4732)
PHONE..............................714 835-5006
EMP: 120 **EST:** 1988
SQ FT: 57,000
SALES (est): 53.17MM
SALES (corp-wide): 105.94MM **Privately
Held**
Web: www.cleanandpure.net
SIC: 6411 Insurance information and
consulting services
PA: Word & Brown, Insurance
Administrators, Inc.
721 S Parker St Ste 300
Orange CA
714 835-5006

(P-14579)
CONFIE HOLDING II CO (PA)
Also Called: Confie
7711 Center Ave Ste 200 (92647-9124)
PHONE..............................714 252-2500
Cesar Soriano, *CEO*
Michael Kaplan, *
Darrin Silveria, *CSO**
Tim Clark, *Chief Human Resource Officer**
Joshua Marder, *CMO**

EMP: 160 EST: 2007
SALES (est): 98.2MM
SALES (corp-wide): 98.2MM Privately Held
Web: www.nationwide.com
SIC: 6411 Insurance agents, nec

(P-14580)
COVERANCE INSUR SOLUTIONS INC
1343 6th St (90266-6041)
PHONE...............................310 856-9925
EMP: 190
SALES (corp-wide): 15.49MM Privately Held
Web: www.coveranceis.com
SIC: 6411 Insurance agents, brokers, and service
PA: Coverance Insurance Solutions, Inc.
100 W Broadway Ste 3000
Long Beach CA
231 218-6100

(P-14581)
CUSTOMZED SVCS ADMNSTRTORS INC
Also Called: Global Care Travel
9797 Aero Dr Ste 300 (92123-1891)
P.O. Box 939057 (92193-9057)
PHONE...............................858 810-2004
Christopher Carnicelli, CEO
John Martini, *
EMP: 140 EST: 1991
SALES (est): 50.22MM
SALES (corp-wide): 4.18B Privately Held
Web: www.generalitravelinsurance.com
SIC: 6411 4724 Insurance agents, nec;
Travel agencies
HQ: Generali Global Assistance, Inc.
4330 East West Hwy # 1000
Bethesda MD
240 330-1000

(P-14582)
CYBERPOLICY INC
19584 Pine Valley Ave (91326-1408)
PHONE...............................877 626-9991
Keith Moore, CEO
EMP: 103 EST: 2016
SALES (est): 4.49MM Privately Held
Web: www.cyberpolicy.com
SIC: 6411 Insurance agents, brokers, and service

(P-14583)
DEDICTED DFNED BENEFT SVCS LLC
550 N Brand Blvd Ste 1610 (91203-1964)
P.O. Box 219800 (64121-9800)
PHONE...............................415 931-1990
Karen Shapiro, CEO
EMP: 122 EST: 2006
SALES (est): 2.04MM
SALES (corp-wide): 947.08MM Privately Held
Web: www.dedicated-db.com
SIC: 6411 Pension and retirement plan consultants
PA: Ascensus, Llc
200 Dryden Rd E Ste 1000
Dresher PA
215 648-8000

(P-14584)
DEWITT STERN GROUP INC
5990 Sepulveda Blvd Ste 550 (91411-2536)
PHONE...............................818 933-2700
Jolyon F Stern, Brnch Mgr
EMP: 137

SALES (corp-wide): 87.66K Privately Held
Web: www.dewittstern.com
SIC: 6411 Insurance brokers, nec
HQ: Dewitt Stern Group, Inc.
420 Lexington Ave Rm 2700
New York NY
212 867-3550

(P-14585)
EDGEWOOD PARTNERS INSUR CTR
Also Called: Nationwide
4675 Macarthur Ct (92660-1875)
PHONE...............................949 263-0606
Dan Ryan, Brnch Mgr
EMP: 247
Web: www.epicbrokers.com
SIC: 6411 Insurance brokers, nec
PA: Edgewood Partners Insurance Center
1 California St Ste 400
San Francisco CA

(P-14586)
EPISOURCE LLC
500 W 190th St Ste 400 (90248-4290)
PHONE...............................714 452-1961
Sishir Reddy, Prin
Erik Simonsen, *
EMP: 6600 EST: 2006
SALES (est): 612.89MM Privately Held
Web: www.episource.com
SIC: 6411 Medical insurance claim processing, contract or fee basis

(P-14587)
FARMERS GROUP INC (HQ)
Also Called: Farmers Insurance
6301 Owensmouth Ave (91367-2268)
P.O. Box 2450 (49501-2450)
PHONE...............................323 932-3200
Raul Vargas, Pr
Giles Harrison, *
Melissa Joye, CMO*
▲ EMP: 2100 EST: 1927
SALES (est): 4.96B Privately Held
Web: www.farmers.com
SIC: 6411 Insurance agents, brokers, and service
PA: Zurich Insurance Group Ag
C/O Zurich Versicherungs-Gesellschaft Ag
ZUrich ZH

(P-14588)
FARMERS INSURANCE
3600 Lime St Ste 122 (92501-0911)
PHONE...............................951 681-1068
Lucinda Metcalfe, Brnch Mgr
EMP: 179
Web: agents.farmers.com
SIC: 6411 Insurance agents, brokers, and service
HQ: Farmers Insurance
6600 Sw Hampton St
Portland OR
503 372-2000

(P-14589)
FARMERS INSURANCE
113 Avondale Ave (91754-1797)
PHONE...............................626 288-0870
Yvone Ti, Brnch Mgr
EMP: 179
Web: www.farmers.com
SIC: 6411 Insurance agents and brokers
HQ: Farmers Insurance
6600 Sw Hampton St
Portland OR
503 372-2000

(P-14590)
FARMERS INSURANCE
Also Called: Farmers Insurance
6303 Owensmouth Ave Fl 1 (91367-2200)
PHONE...............................818 876-3400
Steve Wampler, Mgr
EMP: 313 EST: 2011
SALES (est): 3.14MM Privately Held
Web: www.farmers.com
SIC: 6411 Insurance agents, brokers, and service

(P-14591)
FARMERS INSURANCE
27433 Tourney Rd Ste 170 (91355-5399)
PHONE...............................661 257-0844
Corrine Mirone, Prin
EMP: 179
Web: www.farmers.com
SIC: 6411 Insurance agents, brokers, and service
HQ: Farmers Insurance
6600 Sw Hampton St
Portland OR
503 372-2000

(P-14592)
FARMERS INSURANCE EXCHANGE (DH)
Also Called: Farmers Insurance
6301 Owensmouth Ave (91367-2212)
PHONE...............................888 327-6335
Jeff Pailey, CEO
Thomas Noh, *
Eric Kappler, CPO*
EMP: 3000 EST: 1928
SQ FT: 210,000
SALES (est): 1.71B Privately Held
Web: www.farmers.com
SIC: 6411 Insurance agents and brokers
HQ: Farmers Group, Inc.
6301 Owensmouth Ave # 300
Woodland Hills CA
323 932-3200

(P-14593)
FINANCIAL GROUP INC
Also Called: Finan Group
12432 Oxnard St (91606-4510)
PHONE...............................818 308-8527
Andres Saavedra, Prin
EMP: 122
SALES (corp-wide): 1.47B Publicly Held
SIC: 6411 Insurance agents, brokers, and service
HQ: The Financial Group Inc
2555 Severn Ave Ste 100
Metairie LA
504 456-0101

(P-14594)
FIRE INSURANCE EXCHANGE (PA)
6301 Owensmouth Ave (91367-2216)
PHONE...............................323 932-3200
Martin Feinstein, Pr
John Harrington, *
Doren Hohl, *
Ron Myhan, *
EMP: 2300 EST: 1942
SALES (est): 941.33MM
SALES (corp-wide): 941.33MM Privately Held
Web: www.farmers.com
SIC: 6411 Insurance agents, brokers, and service

(P-14595)
FIRST AMRCN PRPRTY INSUR CSLTY
114 E 5th St (92701-4642)
PHONE...............................949 474-7500
Dirk Mcnamee, Pr
EMP: 138 EST: 1930
SALES (est): 1.74M Publicly Held
SIC: 6411 Insurance agents, nec
HQ: First American Specialty Insurance Company
4 First American Way
Santa Ana CA
949 474-7500

(P-14596)
FREEWAY INSURANCE (PA)
Also Called: South Coast Auto Insurance
7711 Center Ave Ste 200 (92647-9124)
P.O. Box 669 (90630-0669)
PHONE...............................714 252-2500
Elias Assaf, Pr
John Klaeb, *
Norm Hudson, *
EMP: 120 EST: 1988
SQ FT: 20,000
SALES (est): 51.45MM
SALES (corp-wide): 51.45MM Privately Held
Web: www.freeway.com
SIC: 6411 Insurance agents, nec

(P-14597)
GEICO GENERAL INSURANCE CO
Also Called: Geico
14111 Danielson St (92064-6886)
PHONE...............................858 848-8200
Elizabeth Shew, Prin
EMP: 2323
SALES (corp-wide): 302.09B Publicly Held
Web: www.geico.com
SIC: 6411 Insurance agents, nec
HQ: Geico General Insurance Company
1 Geico Plz
Washington DC

(P-14598)
GNET AGENCY
5455 Wilshire Blvd Ste 2200 (90036-4272)
PHONE...............................323 951-9399
Johnathan Rosenberg, Pr
EMP: 86 EST: 2017
SALES (est): 2.61MM Privately Held
Web: www.gnet.agency
SIC: 6411 Insurance agents, brokers, and service

(P-14599)
GROSVENOR INV MGT US INC
2308 Chelsea Rd (90274-2606)
PHONE...............................310 265-0297
Stephen Waddell, Brnch Mgr
EMP: 80
SALES (corp-wide): 7.85B Publicly Held
SIC: 6411 Pension and retirement plan consultants
HQ: Grosvenor Investment Management Us Inc.
10 New King St Ste 214
White Plains NY
914 683-3710

(P-14600)
H & H AGENCY INC (PA)
1403 N Tustin Ave Ste 280 (92705-8691)
PHONE...............................949 260-8840
Michael Weinstein, CEO

PRODUCTS & SVCS

EMP: 88 **EST:** 1969
SQ FT: 25,000
SALES (est): 9.48MM
SALES (corp-wide): 9.48MM **Privately Held**
Web: www.hhagency.com
SIC: 6411 Insurance agents, nec

(P-14601)
HEALTHSMART MANAGEMENT SERVICE
10855 Business Center Dr Ste C (90630)
P.O. Box 6300 (90630-0063)
PHONE................................714 947-8600
Carol Houchins, *Pr*
EMP: 90 **EST:** 1996
SALES (est): 9.51MM **Privately Held**
Web: www.healthsmartmso.com
SIC: 6411 8741 8721 Medical insurance claim processing, contract or fee basis; Hospital management; Billing and bookkeeping service

(P-14602)
INSURANCE COMPANY OF WEST (HQ)
Also Called: I C W
15025 Innovation Dr (92128-3455)
P.O. Box 509039 (92150-9039)
PHONE................................858 350-2400
Kevin Prior, *Pr*
Ernest Rady, *
H Michael Freet, *
EMP: 92 **EST:** 1972
SQ FT: 150,000
SALES (est): 216.83MM
SALES (corp-wide): 610.35MM **Privately Held**
Web: www.icwgroup.com
SIC: 6411 Insurance agents, nec
PA: Icw Group Holdings, Inc.
15025 Innovation Dr # 200
San Diego CA
858 350-2400

(P-14603)
INSURANCE INC SOUTHERN CAL
Also Called: Nationwide
3400 Central Ave Ste 220 (92506-2180)
PHONE................................951 300-9333
Timothy Dean, *Pr*
Nowel Milik, *VP*
◆ **EMP:** 93 **EST:** 1958
SALES (est): 4.88MM **Privately Held**
Web: www.insuranceinc.com
SIC: 6411 Insurance agents, nec

(P-14604)
JOHN HANCOCK LIFE INSUR CO USA (DH)
Also Called: John Hancock
865 S Figueroa St Ste 3320 (90017-2507)
PHONE................................213 689-0813
Emeritus D'alessandro, *CEO*
David F D'alessandro, *Pr*
Robert R Reitano, *
Gregory P Winn, *
▲ **EMP:** 2000 **EST:** 1862
SQ FT: 3,600,000
SALES (est): 653.33MM
SALES (corp-wide): 32.83B **Privately Held**
Web: www.manulife.com
SIC: 6411 6351 6371 6321 Insurance agents and brokers; Mortgage guarantee insurance ; Pensions; Accident insurance carriers
HQ: John Hancock Financial Services, Inc.
200 Clarendon St
Boston MA
617 572-6000

(P-14605)
JOHN HANCOCK LIFE INSUR CO USA
Also Called: John Hancock
10180 Telesis Ct (92121-2705)
PHONE................................858 292-1667
EMP: 120
SALES (corp-wide): 32.83B **Privately Held**
Web: www.johnhancock.com
SIC: 6411 Insurance agents and brokers
HQ: John Hancock Life Insurance Company (U.S.A.).
865 S Figueroa St # 3320
Los Angeles CA
213 689-0813

(P-14606)
KEENAN & ASSOCIATES (HQ)
2355 Crenshaw Blvd Ste 200 (90501-3325)
P.O. Box 4328 (90510-4328)
PHONE................................310 212-3344
John Keenan, *Ch Bd*
Sean Smith, *
Henry Loubet, *Senior Vice President Strategic Planning*
Keith Pippard, *
Davis Seres, *
EMP: 339 **EST:** 1972
SQ FT: 80,000
SALES (est): 389.29MM **Privately Held**
Web: www.keenan.com
SIC: 6411 Insurance brokers, nec
PA: Assuredpartners, Inc.
450 S Orange Ave Fl 4
Orlando FL

(P-14607)
LEXISNEXIS RISK ASSETS INC
Also Called: Choicepoint
2112 Business Center Dr Ste 150 (92614)
PHONE................................949 222-0028
Tim Coon, *Owner*
EMP: 108
SALES (corp-wide): 10.3B **Privately Held**
Web: risk.lexisnexis.com
SIC: 6411 Information bureaus, insurance
HQ: Lexisnexis Risk Assets Inc.
1105 N Market St Ste 501
Wilmington DE
800 458-9410

(P-14608)
LOCKTON CMPNIES LLC - PCF SRIE (HQ)
Also Called: Lockton Insurance Brokers
777 S Figueroa St Ste 5200 (90017-5800)
PHONE................................213 689-0500
Timothy J Noonan, *Pr*
Nate Mundy, *
Leonard G Fodemski, *
EMP: 294 **EST:** 2016
SQ FT: 72,300
SALES (est): 213.82MM
SALES (corp-wide): 1.61B **Privately Held**
Web: global.lockton.com
SIC: 6411 Insurance brokers, nec
PA: Lockton, Inc.
444 W 47th St Ste 900
Kansas City MO
816 960-9000

(P-14609)
MARKEL CORP
Also Called: Associated Intl Insur Co
21600 Oxnard St Ste 900 (91367-7834)
PHONE................................818 595-0600
Anthony Markel, *Pr*
Alan Kirshner, *
Steven Markel, *
EMP: 277 **EST:** 1972

SQ FT: 32,000
SALES (est): 4.73MM
SALES (corp-wide): 11.68B **Publicly Held**
Web: www.markel.com
SIC: 6411 Insurance agents, brokers, and service
HQ: Markel North America, Inc.
4521 Highwoods Pkwy
Glen Allen VA
804 747-0136

(P-14610)
MARSH & MCLENNAN AGENCY LLC
Also Called: Marsh
9171 Towne Centre Dr Ste 500 (92122-1234)
PHONE................................858 457-3414
Paul Hering, *Brnch Mgr*
EMP: 200
SALES (corp-wide): 20.72B **Publicly Held**
Web: www.marshmma.com
SIC: 6411 Insurance brokers, nec
HQ: Marsh & Mclennan Agency Llc
9850 Nw 41st St Ste 100
Doral FL

(P-14611)
MARSH RISK & INSURANCE SVCS
Also Called: MMC
633 W 5th St Ste 1200 (90071-2095)
PHONE................................213 624-5555
Melody Schwartz, *Sr VP*
EMP: 687 **EST:** 1883
SALES (est): 93.35MM
SALES (corp-wide): 20.72B **Publicly Held**
SIC: 6411 Insurance brokers, nec
PA: Marsh & Mclennan Companies, Inc.
1166 Ave Of The Americas
New York NY
212 345-5000

(P-14612)
MEDICAL EYE SERVICES INC
Also Called: Mesvision
345 Baker St (92626-4518)
P.O. Box 25209 (92799-5209)
PHONE................................714 619-4660
Aspasia Shappet, *Pr*
EMP: 91 **EST:** 1976
SQ FT: 12,000
SALES (est): 23.26MM
SALES (corp-wide): 23.26MM **Privately Held**
Web: www.mesvision.com
SIC: 6411 Insurance claim processing, except medical
PA: The Eye Care Network Of California Inc
345 Baker St
Costa Mesa CA
714 619-4660

(P-14613)
MESA INSURANCE SOLUTIONS INC
50 Castilian Dr (93117-3080)
PHONE................................805 308-6308
EMP: 210 **EST:** 2017
SALES (est): 456.47K
SALES (corp-wide): 471.88MM **Publicly Held**
SIC: 6411 Insurance agents, nec
PA: Appfolio, Inc.
70 Castilian Dr
Santa Barbara CA
805 364-6093

(P-14614)
MORRIS GRRITANO INSUR AGCY INC
Also Called: Nationwide
1122 Laurel Ln (93401-5895)
P.O. Box 1189 (93406-1189)
PHONE................................805 543-6887
Brendan Morris, *CEO*
Gene Garritano, *
Gabe Garcia, *
David Morgan, *Stockholder**
Kelly Morgan, *Stockholder**
EMP: 85 **EST:** 1916
SQ FT: 14,000
SALES (est): 22.71MM **Privately Held**
Web: www.morrisgarritano.com
SIC: 6411 Insurance agents, nec

(P-14615)
MULLIN TBG INSUR AGCY SVCS LLC (DH)
Also Called: Mullintbg
3333 Michelson Dr Ste 820 (92612-0655)
EMP: 185 **EST:** 1987
SALES (est): 96.87MM
SALES (corp-wide): 60.05B **Publicly Held**
SIC: 6411 Insurance information and consulting services
HQ: The Prudential Insurance Company Of America
751 Broad St Fl 21
Newark NJ
973 802-6000

(P-14616)
NATIONAL INSURANCE CRIME BUR
15545 Devonshire St Ste 309 (91345-2655)
PHONE................................818 895-2867
Bob Jones, *Dir*
EMP: 82
SALES (corp-wide): 59.53MM **Privately Held**
Web: www.nicb.org
SIC: 6411 Insurance agents, brokers, and service
PA: National Insurance Crime Bureau, Inc
1111 E Touhy Ave Ste 400
Des Plaines IL
847 544-7000

(P-14617)
NNA INSURANCE SERVICES LLC
9350 De Soto Ave (91311-4926)
P.O. Box 2402 (91313-2402)
PHONE................................818 739-4071
Milton G Valera, *Ch Bd*
Deborah M Thaw, *
Thomas A Heymann, *
Robert A Clarke, *
▲ **EMP:** 204 **EST:** 1957
SQ FT: 55,000
SALES (est): 24.4MM **Privately Held**
Web: www.nationalnotary.org
SIC: 6411 Insurance agents, brokers, and service

(P-14618)
NORTHWESTERN MUTL INV MGT LLC
Also Called: Northwestern Mutual Investment
610 Newport Center Dr Ste 850 (92660)
PHONE................................949 759-5555
Gary Farmer, *Ex Dir*
EMP: 162
SALES (corp-wide): 16.13B **Privately Held**
Web: www.northwesternmutual.com

SIC: 6411 6282 Insurance agents, brokers, and service; Investment advice
HQ: Northwestern Mutual Investment Management Company, Llc
720 E Wisconsin Ave
Milwaukee WI
414 271-1444

(P-14619)
PACIFIC COMPENSATION INSUR CO
3011 Townsgate Rd Ste 120 (91361-5876)
P.O. Box 5034 (91359-5034)
PHONE.............................818 575-8500
Marc E Schmittlein, *Pr*
EMP: 150 EST: 2002
SALES (est): 58.09MM
SALES (corp-wide): 808.75MM **Privately Held**
Web: www.copperpoint.com
SIC: 6411 Insurance agents, nec
HQ: Pacific Compensation Corporation
3011 Townsgate Rd Ste 120
Westlake Village CA

(P-14620)
PACIFIC INDEMNITY COMPANY
Also Called: Chubb
555 S Flower St Ste 300 (90071-2427)
PHONE.............................213 622-2334
John Fennigan, *Pr*
EMP: 300 EST: 1926
SALES (est): 92.59MM **Privately Held**
Web: www.chubb.com
SIC: 6411 6331 6351 Property and casualty insurance agent; Fire, marine, and casualty insurance: mutual; Surety insurance
HQ: Ina Chubb Holdings Inc
436 Walnut St
Philadelphia PA
215 640-1000

(P-14621)
PACIFIC PIONEER INSUR GROUP (PA)
Also Called: Nationwide
6363 Katella Ave (90630-5205)
PHONE.............................714 228-7888
EMP: 80 EST: 1989
SQ FT: 32,000
SALES (est): 13.74MM **Privately Held**
Web: www.ucageneral.com
SIC: 6411 Insurance agents, nec

(P-14622)
POLISEEK AIS INSUR SLTIONS INC
Also Called: Nationwide
17785 Center Court Dr N Ste 250 (90703-8573)
PHONE.............................866 480-7335
Mark Ribisi, *Pr*
Chris Bremer, *CAO**
Romayne Levee, *
Lani Elkin, *
Mark Casas, *
EMP: 85 EST: 2008
SALES (est): 2MM
SALES (corp-wide): 3.64B **Publicly Held**
Web: www.nationwide.com
SIC: 6411 Insurance agents, nec
HQ: Ais Management, Llc
17785 Center Court Dr N # 250
Cerritos CA

(P-14623)
PRECEPT ADVISORY GROUP LLC (DH)
Also Called: Precept Group The

130 Theory Ste 200 (92617-3065)
PHONE.............................949 955-1430
Wade R Olson, *Pr*
Alex Wasilewski, *Ex VP*
Steve Zarate, *COO*
Christopher H Coulter, *CMO*
Mercedes Meseck, *VP*
EMP: 90 EST: 1987
SQ FT: 32,000
SALES (est): 28.16MM
SALES (corp-wide): 25.36B **Publicly Held**
Web: www.bbt.com
SIC: 6411 Insurance brokers, nec
HQ: Mcgriff Insurance Services, Inc.
3201 Beechleaf Ct Ste 200
Raleigh NC
919 716-9907

(P-14624)
PREFERRED EMPLOYERS INSUR CO
9797 Aero Dr Ste 200 (92123-1898)
P.O. Box 85478 (92186-5478)
PHONE.............................619 688-3900
Linda R Smith, *CEO*
Steven A Gallacher, *
Dennis J Levesque, *Pr*
EMP: 86 EST: 1997
SALES (est): 23.91MM
SALES (corp-wide): 11.17B **Publicly Held**
Web: www.peiwc.com
SIC: 6411 Insurance information and consulting services
PA: W. R. Berkley Corporation
475 Steamboat Rd Fl 1
Greenwich CT
203 629-3000

(P-14625)
PREMIER DEALER SERVICES INC
9449 Balboa Ave Ste 300 (92123-4395)
PHONE.............................858 810-1700
John R Topits, *Pr*
Kurt Wolery, *
A Kurt Wolery, *
EMP: 100 EST: 1998
SALES (est): 9.31MM **Privately Held**
Web: www.pdsadm.com
SIC: 6411 Insurance agents, brokers, and service

(P-14626)
R MC CLOSKEY INSURANCE AGENCY
Also Called: Tax and Financial Group
4001 Macarthur Blvd Ste 300 (92660-2505)
PHONE.............................949 223-8100
Richard Mc Closkey, *Pr*
EMP: 120 EST: 1969
SQ FT: 15,000
SALES (est): 20.39MM **Privately Held**
Web: www.tfgroup.com
SIC: 6411 Insurance agents, nec

(P-14627)
ROBERT MORENO INSURANCE SVCS
3110 E Guasti Rd Ste 500 (91761-1228)
PHONE.............................714 578-3318
Robert B Moreno, *Owner*
EMP: 140 EST: 1978
SALES (est): 20.49MM **Privately Held**
Web: rmis.informins.com
SIC: 6411 Insurance agents, nec

(P-14628)
SAFECO INSURANCE COMPANY AMER

Safeco
330 N Brand Blvd Ste 680 (91203-2385)
PHONE.............................818 956-4250
Don Chambers, *Mgr*
EMP: 146
SALES (corp-wide): 20.63B **Privately Held**
Web: www.safeco.com
SIC: 6411 Insurance agents, nec
HQ: Safeco Insurance Company Of America
1001 4th Ave Ste 800
Seattle WA
206 545-5000

(P-14629)
SEDGWICK CMS HOLDINGS INC
Also Called: Sedgwick
3633 Inland Empire Blvd (91764-4922)
PHONE.............................909 477-5500
Kim Pech, *Brnch Mgr*
EMP: 147
Web: www.sedgwick.com
SIC: 6411 Insurance claim adjusters, not employed by insurance company
PA: Sedgwick Cms Holdings, Inc.
1100 Ridgeway Loop Rd # 2
Memphis TN

(P-14630)
SENECA FAMILY OF AGENCIES
Also Called: Cys Knship Sneca Tstin Wrprund
1801 Park Court Pl Bldg H (92701-5028)
PHONE.............................714 881-8600
EMP: 108
SALES (corp-wide): 150.1MM **Privately Held**
Web: www.senecafoa.org
SIC: 6411 Insurance agents, brokers, and service
PA: Seneca Family Of Agencies
8945 Golf Links Rd
Oakland CA
510 317-1444

(P-14631)
SENTRY LIFE INSURANCE COMPANY
4720 Aliso Way (92057-6821)
PHONE.............................661 274-4018
Jay Ottersen, *Mgr*
EMP: 191
SALES (corp-wide): 3.62B **Privately Held**
Web: www.sentry.com
SIC: 6411 Insurance agents, brokers, and service
HQ: Sentry Life Insurance Company
1800 N Point Dr
Stevens Point WI
715 346-6000

(P-14632)
STATE FARM GENERAL INSUR CO
Also Called: State Farm Insurance
945 Otay Lakes Rd Ste K (91913-3055)
PHONE.............................619 227-5777
Mark Witcher, *Owner*
EMP: 99
SALES (corp-wide): 27.88B **Privately Held**
Web: www.statefarm.com
SIC: 6411 Insurance agents and brokers
HQ: State Farm General Insurance Co Inc
1 State Farm Plz
Bloomington IL
309 766-2311

(P-14633)
THI HOLDINGS (DELAWARE) INC

2140 E Palmdale Blvd Ste O (93550-1202)
PHONE.............................661 266-7423
Lewis Pelser, *Mgr*
EMP: 401
SALES (corp-wide): 18.35B **Privately Held**
SIC: 6411 Insurance agents, nec
HQ: Thi Holdings (Delaware), Inc.
5915 Landerbrook Dr
Cleveland OH

(P-14634)
TM CLAIMS SERVICE INC
Also Called: Tokio Marine Michido
800 E Colorado Blvd (91101-2103)
P.O. Box 7216 (91109-7316)
PHONE.............................626 568-7800
Tommy Hasegawa, *Mgr*
EMP: 96
Web: www.tmamerica.com
SIC: 6411 Insurance brokers, nec
HQ: Tm Claims Service, Inc.
499 Wshngton Blvd Ste 150
Jersey City NJ

(P-14635)
TOKIO MARINE HIGHLAND INSURANCE SERVICES INC (DH)
Also Called: Tm Highland Insurance Services
899 El Centro St (91030-3101)
PHONE.............................626 463-6486
EMP: 100 EST: 1962
SALES (est): 84.01MM **Privately Held**
Web: www.tokiomarinehighland.com
SIC: 6411 Insurance agents, nec
HQ: Tokio Marine Kiln Insurance Limited
20 Fenchurch Street
London
207 886-9000

(P-14636)
TRG INSURANCE SERVICES
Also Called: The Rule Group
4675 Macarthur Ct (92660-8891)
PHONE.............................949 474-1550
EMP: 221 EST: 1983
SALES (est): 1.76MM **Privately Held**
SIC: 6411 Insurance brokers, nec
HQ: Integro Usa Inc.
1 State St Fl 9
New York NY
212 295-8000

(P-14637)
TRI-AD
221 W Crest St Ste 300 (92025-1737)
PHONE.............................760 743-7555
EMP: 108 EST: 2019
SALES (est): 6.42MM **Privately Held**
Web: www.tri-ad.com
SIC: 6411 Pension and retirement plan consultants

(P-14638)
TRISTAR SERVICE COMPANY INC (HQ)
100 Oceangate Ste 700 (90802-4368)
PHONE.............................562 495-6600
Thomas J Veale, *Pr*
Denise Cotter, *
Joseph Mclaughlin, *SLS*
Craig Evans, *CIO**
Shana Barrowclough, *Claims Operations Vice President**
EMP: 375 EST: 2002
SQ FT: 9,000
SALES (est): 289.94MM
SALES (corp-wide): 502.12MM **Privately Held**

SIC: **6411** 8742 Inspection and investigation services, insurance; Management consulting services
PA: Tristar Insurance Group, Inc.
100 Oceangate Ste 700
Long Beach CA
562 495-6600

(P-14639)
VALLEY INSURANCE SERVICE INC
Also Called: Brower Hale
23181 Verdugo Dr Ste 100b (92653-1313)
PHONE..................................949 707-4080
Debbie Hale, *Mgr*
EMP: 571
SALES (corp-wide): 306.15MM **Privately Held**
SIC: **6411** Insurance agents, brokers, and service
HQ: Valley Insurance Service, Inc.
4695 Macarthur Ct Ste 600
Newport Beach CA
626 966-3664

(P-14640)
VETERINARY PET INSURANCE SERVICES INC
Also Called: Dvm Insurance Agency
1800 E Imperial Hwy Ste 145 (92821)
P.O. Box 2344 (92822-2344)
PHONE..................................714 989-0555
EMP: 420
Web: www.petinsurance.com
SIC: **6411** Insurance agents, brokers, and service

(P-14641)
VETERINARY PET SERVICES INC
3060 Saturn St (92821-1732)
PHONE..................................714 989-0555
EMP: 116 EST: 2014
SALES (est): 2.66MM **Privately Held**
SIC: **6411** Insurance agents, brokers, and service

(P-14642)
WELLS FRGO INSUR SVCS MINN INC
4141 Inland Empire Blvd (91764-5004)
PHONE..................................909 481-3802
EMP: 103
SALES (corp-wide): 94.18B **Publicly Held**
SIC: **6411** Insurance agents, brokers, and service
HQ: Wells Fargo Insurance Services Of Minnesota, Inc.
400 Highway 169 S Ste 800
Minneapolis MN
952 563-0600

(P-14643)
WESTERN GENERAL INSURANCE CO
5230 Las Virgenes Rd Ste 100 (91302-3447)
P.O. Box 26894 (94126-6894)
PHONE..................................818 880-9070
Robert M Ehrlich, *Pr*
Daniel Mallut, *
John Albanese, *
Denise M Tyson, *
Marleen Kushner, *
EMP: 165 EST: 1971
SQ FT: 51,000
SALES (est): 38.35MM **Privately Held**
Web: www.westerngeneral.com

SIC: **6411** Insurance agents, nec

(P-14644)
WESTERN PENN AAA INSUR AGCY
3712 State St (93105-3104)
PHONE..................................805 682-5811
EMP: 369
SALES (corp-wide): 1.08B **Privately Held**
SIC: **6411** Insurance agents, nec
HQ: Western Penn Aaa Insurance Agency Inc
5900 Baum Blvd Ste 2
Pittsburgh PA
412 362-3300

(P-14645)
WESTWOOD INSURANCE AGENCY LLC (HQ)
6320 Canoga Ave (91367-7799)
PHONE..................................818 990-9715
John Flynn, *Pr*
Mark Nettleton, *
EMP: 89 EST: 1952
SALES (est): 17.7MM
SALES (corp-wide): 980.72MM **Publicly Held**
Web: www.westwoodinsurance.com
SIC: **6411** Insurance agents, nec
PA: Brp Group, Inc.
4211 W Boy Scout Blvd
Tampa FL
866 279-0698

(P-14646)
WOOD GUTMANN BOGART INSUR BRKG
Also Called: Nationwide
15901 Red Hill Ave Ste 100 (92780-7317)
PHONE..................................714 505-7000
Kevin S Bogart, *CEO*
EMP: 93 EST: 1984
SALES (est): 23.83MM **Privately Held**
Web: www.burnhamwgb.com
SIC: **6411** Insurance agents, nec

(P-14647)
WOOD GUTMANN BOGART INSUR BRKS
Also Called: Burnham Wgb Insur Solutions
15901 Red Hill Ave Ste 100 (92780-7318)
PHONE..................................714 505-7000
EMP: 130 EST: 1985
SQ FT: 5,500
SALES (est): 10.46MM
SALES (corp-wide): 99.6MM **Privately Held**
Web: www.burnhamwgb.com
SIC: **6411** Insurance brokers, nec
PA: Burnham Benefits Insurance Services, Llc
2211 Michelson Dr # 1200
Irvine CA
805 772-7965

(P-14648)
WORD & BROWN INSURANCE ADMINISTRATORS INC (PA)
Also Called: Cobrapro
721 S Parker St Ste 300 (92868-4732)
PHONE..................................714 835-5006
EMP: 430 EST: 1977
SALES (est): 105.94MM
SALES (corp-wide): 105.94MM **Privately Held**
Web: www.wordandbrown.com
SIC: **6411** Insurance brokers, nec

(P-14649)
WORLDWIDE HOLDINGS INC (PA)
725 S Figueroa St Ste 1900 (90017-5496)
PHONE..................................213 236-4500
Donald R Davis, *Ch*
Davis D Moore, *
Daniel Colacurcio, *
EMP: 85 EST: 1970
SQ FT: 23,000
SALES (est): 45.29MM
SALES (corp-wide): 45.29MM **Privately Held**
SIC: **6411** Insurance brokers, nec

6512 Nonresidential Building Operators

(P-14650)
6500 HLLISTER AVE PARTNERS LLC
6500 Hollister Ave (93117-3011)
PHONE..................................805 722-1362
EMP: 100 EST: 2014
SALES (est): 4MM **Privately Held**
SIC: **6512** Commercial and industrial building operation

(P-14651)
ALPINE VILLAGE
Also Called: Alpine Inn Restaurant
23670 Hawthorne Blvd (90505-5904)
PHONE..................................310 327-4384
Ursula Wilson, *CEO*
EMP: 250 EST: 1968
SALES (est): 9.92MM **Privately Held**
SIC: **6512** Commercial and industrial building operation

(P-14652)
AMERICARE HLTH RETIREMENT INC
Also Called: Silvergate San Marcos
1550 Security Pl Ofc (92078-4063)
PHONE..................................760 744-4484
Melba Dunn, *Admn*
EMP: 150
SQ FT: 51,071
SALES (corp-wide): 8.84MM **Privately Held**
Web: www.silvergaterr.com
SIC: **6512** 8051 Nonresidential building operators; Skilled nursing care facilities
PA: Americare Health & Retirement, Inc.
140 Lomas Santa Fe Dr # 1
Solana Beach CA
858 792-0696

(P-14653)
ARDEN REALTY INC
11601 Wilshire Blvd Fl 5 (90025-0509)
PHONE..................................310 966-2600
EMP: 300
Web: www.ardenrealty.com
SIC: **6512** Commercial and industrial building operation

(P-14654)
C & D WAX INC
9353 Waxie Way (92123-1036)
P.O. Box 23506 (92193-3506)
PHONE..................................858 292-5954
David Wax, *Ex VP*
Charles Wax, *
EMP: 160 EST: 1987
SALES (est): 4.76MM **Privately Held**

SIC: **6512** Nonresidential building operators

(P-14655)
CB RICHARD ELLIS STRGC PRTNERS
515 S Flower St Ste 3100 (90071-2201)
PHONE..................................213 683-4200
EMP: 100 EST: 2000
SALES (est): 7.4MM **Publicly Held**
SIC: **6512** Nonresidential building operators
PA: Cbre Group, Inc.
2100 Mckinney Ave # 1250
Dallas TX

(P-14656)
CDCF III PCF LNDMARK SCRMNTO L
Also Called: Colony Dstrssed Cr Spcial Stto
515 S Flower St 44th Fl (90071-2201)
PHONE..................................310 552-7211
EMP: 95 EST: 2016
SALES (est): 4.52MM **Privately Held**
SIC: **6512** Commercial and industrial building operation

(P-14657)
CRMLS LLC
15325 Fairfield Ranch Rd Ste 200 (91709)
PHONE..................................909 859-2040
Art Carter, *CEO*
Edward Zorn, *VP*
Adrese Roundree, *COO*
Ray Ewing, *Chief*
EMP: 106 EST: 2019
SALES (est): 4.73MM **Privately Held**
Web: go.crmls.org
SIC: **6512** Nonresidential building operators

(P-14658)
DESERT HOT SPRNG REAL PRPTS IN
Also Called: Desert Hot Springs Spa Hotel
10805 Palm Dr (92240-2511)
PHONE..................................760 329-6000
Lynn Byrnes, *CEO*
EMP: 85 EST: 1988
SQ FT: 44,070
SALES (est): 2.44MM **Privately Held**
Web: www.dhsspa.com
SIC: **6512** Nonresidential building operators

(P-14659)
DONAHUE SCHRIBER RLTY GROUP LP (PA)
Also Called: Ds Lakeshore
200 Baker St Ste 100 (92626-4551)
PHONE..................................714 545-1400
Patrick S Donahue, *CEO*
Lisa L Hirose, *Ex VP*
Lawrence P Casey, *Pr*
Mark L Whitfield, *Ex VP*
EMP: 100 EST: 1969
SQ FT: 44,805
SALES (est): 22.01MM
SALES (corp-wide): 22.01MM **Privately Held**
SIC: **6512** Shopping center, property operation only

(P-14660)
ENTREPRENEURIAL CAPITAL CORP
4100 Newport Place Dr Ste 400 (92660)
PHONE..................................949 809-3900
John K Abel, *Prin*
EMP: 240
SALES (corp-wide): 33.22MM **Privately Held**

SIC: **6512** Commercial and industrial building operation
PA: Entrepreneurial Capital Corporation
4100 Newport Place Dr # 400
Newport Beach CA
949 809-3900

(P-14661)
FORD MOTOR LAND DEV CORP
Also Called: Ford
3 Glen Bell Way Ste 100 (92618-3390)
PHONE..............................949 242-6606
Dan Werbin, *Ex Dir*
EMP: 213
SALES (corp-wide): 158.06B **Publicly Held**
Web: www.fordland.com
SIC: **6512** Commercial and industrial building operation
HQ: Ford Motor Land Development Corporation
17000 Rotunda Dr Fl 1
Dearborn MI
248 200-8804

(P-14662)
FREEDOM PROPERTIES-HEMET LLC
Also Called: Village The
27122b Paseo Espada Ste 1024 (92675-5706)
PHONE..............................949 489-0430
Cheryl L Roskamp, *Managing Member*
Ms. Cheryl L Roskamp, *Managing Member*
EMP: 250 EST: 1999
SALES (est): 6.95MM **Privately Held**
SIC: **6512** Nonresidential building operators

(P-14663)
GLENDALE ASSOCIATES LTD
Also Called: Apple Store Glendale Galleria
100 W Broadway Ste 100 (91210-1230)
PHONE..............................818 246-6737
EMP: 100 EST: 1976
SALES (est): 5.33MM **Privately Held**
Web: www.glendalegalleria.com
SIC: **6512** Shopping center, property operation only

(P-14664)
GUMBINER SAVETT INC
Also Called: Gumbiner Svett Fnkel Fnglson R
1723 Cloverfield Blvd (90404-4017)
PHONE..............................310 828-9798
Louis Savett, *Ch Bd*
Charles Gumbiner, *
Gary Finkel, *
David Rose, *
Rodney Fingleson, *
EMP: 90 EST: 1950
SQ FT: 25,000
SALES (est): 10.49MM **Privately Held**
Web: www.gscpa.com
SIC: **6512** Nonresidential building operators

(P-14665)
ICW VALENCIA LLC
11455 El Camino Real Ste 200 (92130)
PHONE..............................858 350-2600
John Chamberlain, *Prin*
EMP: 224 EST: 2013
SALES (est): 727.07K
SALES (corp-wide): 88.5MM **Privately Held**
SIC: **6512** Nonresidential building operators
PA: American Assets, Inc.
11455 El Cmno Rl Ste 140
San Diego CA
858 350-2600

(P-14666)
INSIGNIA/ESG HT PARTNERS INC (DH)
11150 Santa Monica Blvd Ste 220 (90025-3380)
PHONE..............................310 765-2600
Mary Ann Tighe, *CEO*
John Powers, *Pr*
EMP: 325 EST: 1993
SALES (est): 211.51MM **Publicly Held**
SIC: **6512** Property operation, retail establishment
HQ: Cb Richard Ellis Real Estate Services, Llc
200 Park Ave Fl 19
New York NY
212 984-8000

(P-14667)
INTEX RECREATION CORP
Also Called: INTEX RECREATION CORP
1665 Hughes Way (90810-1835)
PHONE..............................310 549-5400
EMP: 163
SALES (corp-wide): 91.03MM **Privately Held**
Web: www.intexcorp.com
SIC: **6512** Nonresidential building operators
PA: Intex Properties South Bay Corp.
4001 Via Oro Ave Ste 210
Long Beach CA
310 549-5400

(P-14668)
KATELLA PROPERTIES
10140 Grayling Ave (90603-2607)
PHONE..............................562 704-8695
Paige Harrison, *Brnch Mgr*
EMP: 85
SALES (corp-wide): 8.82MM **Privately Held**
Web: www.katellaseniorliving.com
SIC: **6512** Nonresidential building operators
PA: Katella Properties
3952 Katella Ave
Los Alamitos CA
562 596-2773

(P-14669)
LA COUNTY
5530 W 83rd St (90045-3309)
PHONE..............................310 417-5184
EMP: 84 EST: 2017
SALES (est): 1.13MM **Privately Held**
Web: www.musiccenter.org
SIC: **6512** Commercial and industrial building operation

(P-14670)
LERETA LLC
10760 4th St (91730-0975)
PHONE..............................626 332-1942
EMP: 186
Web: www.lereta.com
SIC: **6512** Commercial and industrial building operation
PA: Lereta, Llc
901 Corporate Center Dr
Pomona CA

(P-14671)
LOS ANGELES CONVEN AND EXH
Also Called: Los Angeles Dept Convetion Tou
1201 S Figueroa St (90015-1308)
PHONE..............................213 741-1151
Brad Gessner, *Genl Mgr*
EMP: 288 EST: 1968
SQ FT: 867,000

SALES (est): 23.19MM **Privately Held**
Web: www.lacclink.com
SIC: **6512** Commercial and industrial building operation

(P-14672)
MALIBU CONFERENCE CENTER INC
327 Latigo Canyon Rd (90265-2708)
PHONE..............................818 889-6440
Glen Gerson, *Pr*
EMP: 500 EST: 1985
SALES (est): 22.71MM **Privately Held**
Web: www.calamigos.com
SIC: **6512** Commercial and industrial building operation

(P-14673)
MILLS CORPORATION
Also Called: Ontario Mills Shopping Center
1 Mills Cir Ste 1 (91764-5215)
PHONE..............................909 484-8300
Laurence Siegel, *Brnch Mgr*
EMP: 91
Web: www.thefixsolutions.com
SIC: **6512** Shopping center, property operation only
HQ: The Mills Corporation
5425 Wisconsin Ave # 300
Chevy Chase MD
301 968-6000

(P-14674)
MILWOOD HEALTHCARE INC
Also Called: MAYWOOD ACRES HEALTHCARE
2641 S C St (93033-4502)
PHONE..............................626 274-4345
Alger Brion, *CEO*
EMP: 97 EST: 2007
SQ FT: 10,000
SALES (est): 2.46MM **Privately Held**
Web: www.maywoodacres.com
SIC: **6512** Nonresidential building operators

(P-14675)
NEVINS/ADAMS PROPERTIES INC (PA)
Also Called: Nevins Adams Properties
920 Garden St Ste A (93101-7465)
PHONE..............................805 963-2884
Henry Nevins, *Pr*
David Adams, *
EMP: 250 EST: 1992
SALES (est): 9.2MM
SALES (corp-wide): 9.2MM **Privately Held**
SIC: **6512** Commercial and industrial building operation

(P-14676)
OLEN COMMERCIAL REALTY CORP
Also Called: Olen Residential Realty
7 Corporate Plaza Dr (92660-7904)
PHONE..............................949 644-6536
Igor M Olenicoff, *Pr*
Andrei Olenicoff, *
EMP: 400 EST: 1974
SQ FT: 44,000
SALES (est): 23.36MM **Privately Held**
SIC: **6512** Commercial and industrial building operation

(P-14677)
ORANGE BAKERY INC
75 Parker (92618-1605)
PHONE..............................949 454-1247
EMP: 139
Web: www.orangebakery.com

SIC: **6512** Commercial and industrial building operation
HQ: Orange Bakery, Inc.
17751 Cowan
Irvine CA
949 863-1377

(P-14678)
ORMOND BEACH LP
1259 E Thousand Oaks Blvd (91362-2818)
PHONE..............................805 496-4948
Derrick Wada, *Pt*
Rick Schroeder, *Pt*
EMP: 80 EST: 2016
SALES (est): 4.15MM **Privately Held**
SIC: **6512** Nonresidential building operators

(P-14679)
PM REALTY GROUP LP
3 Park Plz Ste 450 (92614-2572)
PHONE..............................949 390-5500
Jim Proehl, *VP*
EMP: 90
Web: www.madisonmarquette.com
SIC: **6512** 7349 Nonresidential building operators; Building maintenance services, nec
HQ: Pm Realty Group, L.P.
1000 Main St Ste 2400
Houston TX
713 209-5800

(P-14680)
PREMIUM OUTLET PARTNERS LP
Desert Hills Premium Outlets
48400 Seminole Dr (92230-2125)
PHONE..............................951 849-6641
EMP: 95
SQ FT: 430,000
Web: www.simon.com
SIC: **6512** Shopping center, property operation only
HQ: Premium Outlet Partners, L.P.
225 W Washington St
Indianapolis IN

(P-14681)
PREMIUM OUTLET PARTNERS LP
Camarillo Premium Outlets
740 Ventura Blvd (93010-5842)
PHONE..............................805 445-8520
Brian Hassett, *Genl Mgr*
EMP: 95
Web: www.simon.com
SIC: **6512** Shopping center, property operation only
HQ: Premium Outlet Partners, L.P.
225 W Washington St
Indianapolis IN

(P-14682)
PREMIUM OUTLET PARTNERS LP
Also Called: Carlsbad Premium Outlets
5620 Paseo Del Norte Ste 100 (92008)
PHONE..............................760 804-9045
Caren Buksbaum, *Mgr*
EMP: 95
Web: www.simon.com
SIC: **6512** Shopping center, property operation only
HQ: Premium Outlet Partners, L.P.
225 W Washington St
Indianapolis IN

PRODUCTS & SVCS

(P-14683)
SAN DIEGO THEATRES INC
Also Called: CIVIC THEATRE
233 A St Ste 900 (92101-4003)
P.O. Box 124920 (92112-4920)
PHONE..................................619 615-4007
Carol Wallace, *CEO*
Donald M Telford, *
EMP: 200 **EST:** 2003
SALES (est): 3.53MM **Privately Held**
Web: www.sandiegotheatres.org
SIC: 6512 Theater building, ownership and operation

(P-14684)
SHEA PROPERTIES MGT CO INC
Also Called: Shea Properties
130 Vantis Dr Ste 200 (92656-2691)
P.O. Box 62814 (92602-6093)
PHONE..................................949 389-7000
Colm Macken, *CEO*
EMP: 347 **EST:** 2003
SQ FT: 48,000
SALES (est): 24.36MM
SALES (corp-wide): 2.1B **Privately Held**
Web: www.sheaproperties.com
SIC: 6512 Nonresidential building operators
PA: J. F. Shea Co., Inc.
655 Brea Canyon Rd
Walnut CA
909 594-9500

(P-14685)
SOLARI ENTERPRISES INC
1507 W Yale Ave (92867-3447)
PHONE..................................714 282-2520
Johrita Solari, *Pr*
Bruce Solari, *
EMP: 140 **EST:** 1986
SQ FT: 8,400
SALES (est): 23.89MM **Privately Held**
Web: www.solari-ent.com
SIC: 6512 Property operation, retail establishment

(P-14686)
SOUTH COAST PLAZA LLC
Also Called: South Coast Plaza Mall
3333 Bristol St Ofc (92626-1811)
PHONE..................................714 435-2000
EMP: 112
SALES (corp-wide): 44.46MM **Privately Held**
Web: www.southcoastplaza.com
SIC: 6512 Shopping center, property operation only
PA: South Coast Plaza, Llc
3333 Bristol St Ofc
Costa Mesa CA
714 546-0110

(P-14687)
STRATEGIC ASSET SERVICES LLC
27422 Portola Pkwy Ste 150 (92610-2831)
PHONE..................................949 713-0053
Young Hong, *Prin*
EMP: 92 **EST:** 2012
SALES (est): 2.51MM **Privately Held**
Web: www.strategicproperty.com
SIC: 6512 Nonresidential building operators

(P-14688)
THRIFTY OIL CO (PA)
13116 Imperial Hwy (90670-4817)
PHONE..................................562 921-3581
Ted Orden, *Pr*
Dori Barber, *
Perry Freidrich, *
EMP: 18 **EST:** 1959

SQ FT: 1,624
SALES (est): 9.39MM
SALES (corp-wide): 9.39MM **Privately Held**
SIC: 6512 2911 6552 Nonresidential building operators; Petroleum refining; Subdividers and developers, nec

(P-14689)
TITAN LED
11959 Discovery Ct (93021-7120)
PHONE..................................805 523-7500
Patrick Neff, *Pr*
EMP: 86 **EST:** 2017
SALES (est): 1.01MM **Privately Held**
Web: www.titanledus.com
SIC: 6512 Commercial and industrial building operation

(P-14690)
TOPA PROPERTY GROUP INC (HQ)
1800 Avenue Of The Stars Ste 1400 (90067-4200)
PHONE..................................310 203-9199
James Brooks, *CEO*
Jim Brooks, *
Paul Gienger, *
Carol Shane, *
Darren Bell, *
EMP: 158 **EST:** 1981
SALES (est): 47.17MM
SALES (corp-wide): 251.02MM **Privately Held**
Web: www.andersonrealestate.com
SIC: 6512 Commercial and industrial building operation
PA: Topa Equities, Ltd.
1900 Avenue Of The Stars # 1050
Los Angeles CA
310 203-9199

(P-14691)
UNIBAL-RODAMCO-WESTFIELD GROUP
2049 Century Park E 41st Fl (90067-3101)
PHONE..................................310 478-4456
EMP: 187 **EST:** 2019
SALES (est): 10.67MM **Privately Held**
Web: www.urw.com
SIC: 6512 Shopping center, property operation only

(P-14692)
UNIVERSAL SHOPPING PLAZA A CA
6281 Regio Ave (90620-1023)
PHONE..................................714 521-8899
Ho Yuan Chen, *Genl Pt*
EMP: 200 **EST:** 1987
SALES (est): 9.62MM **Privately Held**
SIC: 6512 Shopping center, property operation only

(P-14693)
UNIVERSITY BUSINESS CTR ASSOC
5383 Hollister Ave Ste 120 (93111-2304)
PHONE..................................601 354-3555
David H Hoster Ii, *CEO*
EMP: 80 **EST:** 1996
SALES (est): 4.37MM
SALES (corp-wide): 487.02MM **Publicly Held**
SIC: 6512 Commercial and industrial building operation
PA: Eastgroup Properties, Inc.
400 W Parkway Pl Ste 100
Ridgeland MS
601 354-3555

(P-14694)
WELLNEST
3787 S Vermont Ave (90007-4203)
PHONE..................................323 766-2345
EMP: 98 **EST:** 2020
SALES (est): 809.77K **Privately Held**
Web: www.wellnestla.org
SIC: 6512 Commercial and industrial building operation

(P-14695)
WELLTOWER OM GROUP LLC
301 W Huntington Dr Ste 5 (91007-3462)
PHONE..................................626 254-0552
Heidy Giron, *Brnch Mgr*
EMP: 138
SALES (corp-wide): 5.86B **Publicly Held**
Web: www.welltower.com
SIC: 6512 Commercial and industrial building operation
HQ: Welltower Om Group Llc
4500 Dorr St
Toledo OH
419 247-2800

(P-14696)
WEST SIDE REHAB CORPORATION
1755 E Martin Luther King Jr Blvd (90069-1512)
PHONE..................................323 231-4174
Dean Foley, *Pr*
EMP: 200 **EST:** 1973
SQ FT: 1,500
SALES (est): 5.83MM **Privately Held**
SIC: 6512 Commercial and industrial building operation

(P-14697)
WESTFIELD LLC (DH)
2049 Century Park E 41st Fl (90067-3101)
PHONE..................................310 478-4456
EMP: 400 **EST:** 1978
SQ FT: 120,000
SALES (est): 535.37MM
SALES (corp-wide): 206.9MM **Privately Held**
Web: www.westfield.com
SIC: 6512 Shopping center, property operation only
HQ: Westfield America, Inc.
2049 Century Park E Fl 41
Los Angeles CA
310 478-4456

(P-14698)
WESTFIELD AMERICA INC (HQ)
2049 Century Park E 41st Fl (90067-3101)
PHONE..................................310 478-4456
Peter S Lowy, *CEO*
Jean Marie Tritant, *
Peter R Schwartz, *
Elizabeth Westman, *
Mark A Stefanek, *
EMP: 200 **EST:** 1924
SALES (est): 549.55MM
SALES (corp-wide): 206.9MM **Privately Held**
Web: www.urw.com
SIC: 6512 Shopping center, property operation only
PA: Unibail-Rodamco-Westfield Se
Unibail Rodamco
Paris
145051082

(P-14699)
WESTFIELD AMERICA LTD PARTNR

2049 Century Park E Ste 4100 (90067-3101)
PHONE..................................310 277-3898
EMP: 500 **EST:** 1998
SALES (est): 97.48MM
SALES (corp-wide): 206.9MM **Privately Held**
Web: www.westfield.com
SIC: 6512 Shopping center, property operation only
HQ: Westfield, Llc
2049 Century Park E Fl 41
Los Angeles CA

(P-14700)
WILSHIRE KINGSLEY INC
Also Called: Bcd Tofu House
3575 Wilshire Blvd (90010-2303)
PHONE..................................213 382-6677
Edward S Lee, *Pr*
Hee Sook Lee, *
EMP: 100 **EST:** 2001
SALES (est): 4.42MM **Privately Held**
Web: www.bcdtofuhouse.com
SIC: 6512 Commercial and industrial building operation

(P-14701)
YAMAMOTO OF ORIENT INC (HQ)
Also Called: Yamamotoyama of America
122 Voyager St (91768-3252)
PHONE..................................909 594-7356
Nami Yamamoto, *CEO*
Kahei Yamamoto, *Ch Bd*
Hisayuki Nakagawa, *Pr*
Kaichiro Yamamoto, *Sec*
Kazuya Aburano, *Sec*
◆ **EMP:** 130 **EST:** 1975
SQ FT: 60,000
SALES (est): 62.64MM **Privately Held**
Web: www.yamamotoyama.com
SIC: 6512 5812 5149 Shopping center, property operation only; Eating places; Tea
PA: Yamamotoyama Co., Ltd.
2-5-1, Nihombashi
Chuo-Ku TKY

6513 Apartment Building Operators

(P-14702)
ADVENTIST HEALTH SYSTEM/ WEST
Also Called: ADVENTIST HEALTH SYSTEM/ WEST
2700 E 4th St (91950-3006)
PHONE..................................619 475-5040
EMP: 84
SALES (corp-wide): 789.42MM **Privately Held**
Web: www.generationsllc.com
SIC: 6513 Retirement hotel operation
PA: Adventist Health System/West, Corporation
1 Adventist Health Way
Roseville CA
844 574-5686

(P-14703)
APERTO PROPERTY MANAGEMENT INC
17351 Main St (91744-5155)
PHONE..................................626 965-1961
EMP: 353
SALES (corp-wide): 15.89MM **Privately Held**
Web: www.apertoliving.com

SIC: **6513** Apartment building operators
PA: Aperto Property Management, Inc.
2 Venture Ste 525
Irvine CA
949 873-4200

(P-14704)
BAY VISTA SENIOR HOUSING
Also Called: HUMANGOOD
1900 Huntington Dr (91010-2694)
PHONE...............................925 924-7100
Grace Chrisostomo, *Governor*
Linda Coleman, *
Andrew Mcdonald, *Governor*
Susan Tolentino, *
EMP: 278 **EST:** 2012
SALES (est): 492.48K
SALES (corp-wide): 27.02MM **Privately Held**
SIC: **6513** Retirement hotel operation
HQ: Humangood Affordable Housing
1900 Huntington Dr
Duarte CA
925 924-7163

(P-14705)
CHARLES & CYNTHIA EBERLY INC
Also Called: The Eberly Company
8383 Wilshire Blvd Ste 906 (90211-2425)
PHONE...............................323 937-6468
Charles Eberly, *Pr*
Cynthia Eberly, *
EMP: 90 **EST:** 1986
SALES (est): 8.16MM **Privately Held**
Web: www.eberlyco.com
SIC: **6513** Apartment building operators

(P-14706)
EMERITUS CORPORATION
Also Called: Villa Del Rey Retirement Inn
1351 E Washington Ave (92027-1934)
PHONE...............................760 741-3055
Pam Judkins, *Brnch Mgr*
EMP: 110
SQ FT: 60,000
SALES (corp-wide): 2.83B **Publicly Held**
Web: www.brookdaleliving.com
SIC: **6513** Retirement hotel operation
HQ: Emeritus Corporation
6737 W Wa St Ste 2300
Milwaukee WI

(P-14707)
EMERITUS CORPORATION
Also Called: Creston Village
1919 Creston Rd Ofc (93446-4475)
PHONE...............................805 239-1313
Tonya Hogue, *Dir*
EMP: 210
SALES (corp-wide): 2.83B **Publicly Held**
Web: www.brookdaleliving.com
SIC: **6513** Retirement hotel operation
HQ: Emeritus Corporation
6737 W Wa St Ste 2300
Milwaukee WI

(P-14708)
FFRT RESIDENTIAL LLC
Also Called: Fairfield Properties
5510 Morehouse Dr Ste 200 (92121-3722)
PHONE...............................858 457-2123
EMP: 135
SIC: **6513** 6552 6531 1522 Apartment building operators; Subdividers and developers, nec; Real estate agents and managers; Residential construction, nec

(P-14709)
FRONT PORCH COMMUNITIES & SVCS
Also Called: Casa De Manana
849 Coast Blvd (92037-4223)
PHONE...............................858 454-2151
Justin Weber, *Brnch Mgr*
EMP: 145
Web: www.casademanana.org
SIC: **6513** 8052 8361 Retirement hotel operation; Intermediate care facilities; Residential care
PA: Front Porch Communities And Services
800 N Brand Blvd Fl 19
Glendale CA

(P-14710)
FRONT PORCH COMMUNITIES & SVCS
Also Called: Carlsbad By The Sea
2855 Carlsbad Blvd (92008-2902)
PHONE...............................760 729-4983
Tim Wetzel, *Brnch Mgr*
EMP: 200
Web: www.frontporch.net
SIC: **6513** Retirement hotel operation
PA: Front Porch Communities And Services
800 N Brand Blvd Fl 19
Glendale CA

(P-14711)
HARVEST MANAGEMENT SUB LLC
Also Called: Las Brisas
1299 Briarwood Dr (93401-5965)
PHONE...............................805 543-0187
EMP: 3127
SALES (corp-wide): 389.7MM **Privately Held**
Web: www.holidayseniorliving.com
SIC: **6513** Retirement hotel operation
PA: Harvest Management Sub Llc
300 E Market St Ste 100
Louisville KY
503 370-7070

(P-14712)
HG FENTON COMPANY
7577 Mission Valley Rd Ste 200 (92108-4432)
PHONE...............................619 400-0120
Mike Neal, *
Robert Gottlieb, *
Henry Hunte, *
EMP: 232 **EST:** 2008
SALES (est): 25.52MM **Privately Held**
Web: www.hgfenton.com
SIC: **6513** 6519 Apartment building operators ; Real property lessors, nec

(P-14713)
HUMANGOOD SOCAL
Also Called: Windsor Manor
1230 E Windsor Rd Ofc (91205-2674)
PHONE...............................818 244-7219
Marc Herrera, *Brnch Mgr*
EMP: 105
SQ FT: 139,840
SALES (corp-wide): 27.02MM **Privately Held**
Web: www.humangood.org
SIC: **6513** Retirement hotel operation
HQ: Humangood Socal
1900 Huntington Dr
Duarte CA
925 924-7138

(P-14714)
HUMANGOOD SOCAL
Also Called: Royal Oaks
1763 Royal Oaks Dr Ofc (91010-1989)
PHONE...............................626 357-1632
Tina Heaney, *Mgr*
EMP: 87
SALES (corp-wide): 27.02MM **Privately Held**
Web: www.humangood.org
SIC: **6513** Retirement hotel operation
HQ: Humangood Socal
1900 Huntington Dr
Duarte CA
925 924-7138

(P-14715)
HUMANGOOD SOCAL
Also Called: Regents Point
19191 Harvard Ave Ofc (92612-8624)
PHONE...............................949 854-9500
Melinda Forney, *Mgr*
EMP: 122
SALES (corp-wide): 27.02MM **Privately Held**
Web: www.humangood.org
SIC: **6513** 8052 8051 Retirement hotel operation; Intermediate care facilities; Skilled nursing care facilities
HQ: Humangood Socal
1900 Huntington Dr
Duarte CA
925 924-7138

(P-14716)
HUNTINGTON BCH SENIOR HSING LP
Also Called: Huntington Gardens
18765 Florida St (92648-1999)
PHONE...............................714 842-4006
Don Jones, *Pt*
EMP: 165 **EST:** 2008
SALES (est): 235.43K
SALES (corp-wide): 8.57MM **Privately Held**
SIC: **6513** Apartment building operators
PA: Living Opportunities Management Company, Llc
3787 Worsham Ave
Long Beach CA
562 595-7567

(P-14717)
INTEGRAL SENIOR LIVING LLC (PA)
2333 State St Ste 300 (92008-1621)
PHONE...............................760 547-2863
Tracee Degrande, *
Collette Valentine, *
Suzanne Foley, *
Vince Limburg, *
EMP: 148 **EST:** 2000
SALES (est): 77.15MM
SALES (corp-wide): 77.15MM **Privately Held**
Web: www.islllc.com
SIC: **6513** Retirement hotel operation

(P-14718)
IRVINE APT COMMUNITIES LP
13212 Magnolia St Ofc (92844-1368)
PHONE...............................714 537-8500
Mike Conway, *Brnch Mgr*
EMP: 200
SALES (corp-wide): 579.21MM **Privately Held**
Web: www.irvinecompanyapartments.com
SIC: **6513** Apartment building operators
HQ: Irvine Apartment Communities, Lp
110 Innovation Dr

Irvine CA

(P-14719)
IRVINE APT COMMUNITIES LP
Also Called: Rancho Monterey Apartments
100 Robinson Dr (92782-1095)
PHONE...............................714 505-7181
EMP: 267
SALES (corp-wide): 579.21MM **Privately Held**
Web: www.irvinecompanyapartments.com
SIC: **6513** Apartment building operators
HQ: Irvine Apartment Communities, Lp
110 Innovation Dr
Irvine CA

(P-14720)
IRVINE APT COMMUNITIES LP
299 N State College Blvd (92868-1703)
PHONE...............................714 937-8900
EMP: 201
SALES (corp-wide): 579.21MM **Privately Held**
Web: www.irvinecompanyapartments.com
SIC: **6513** Apartment building operators
HQ: Irvine Apartment Communities, Lp
110 Innovation Dr
Irvine CA

(P-14721)
IRVINE APT COMMUNITIES LP
146 Berkeley (92612-4618)
PHONE...............................949 854-4942
Kevin Baldridge, *Brnch Mgr*
EMP: 200
SALES (corp-wide): 579.21MM **Privately Held**
Web: www.irvinecompany.com
SIC: **6513** Apartment building operators
HQ: Irvine Apartment Communities, Lp
110 Innovation Dr
Irvine CA

(P-14722)
IRVINE APT COMMUNITIES LP (HQ)
Also Called: I A C
110 Innovation Dr (92617-3040)
PHONE...............................949 720-5600
Raymond Watson, *Vice Chairman*
Mike Ellis, *Ex VP*
EMP: 200 **EST:** 1993
SQ FT: 8,316
SALES (est): 103.05MM
SALES (corp-wide): 579.21MM **Privately Held**
Web: www.irvinecompanyapartments.com
SIC: **6513** 6552 6798 Apartment building operators; Subdividers and developers, nec ; Real estate investment trusts
PA: The Irvine Company Llc
550 Newport Center Dr
Newport Beach CA
949 720-2000

(P-14723)
IRVINE APT COMMUNITIES LP
Also Called: 1221 Ocean Ave Apartments
1221 Ocean Ave (90401-1034)
PHONE...............................310 255-1221
Stephanie Van Dermotter, *Mgr*
EMP: 200
SALES (corp-wide): 579.21MM **Privately Held**
Web: www.1221oceanavenue.com
SIC: **6513** 6531 Apartment building operators ; Rental agent, real estate

PRODUCTS & SVCS

HQ: Irvine Apartment Communities, Lp
110 Innovation Dr
Irvine CA

(P-14724)
JOHN COLLINS CO INC
5155 Cedarwood Rd (91902-1942)
PHONE...............................818 227-2190
EMP: 97
SALES (corp-wide): 2.18MM **Privately Held**
Web: www.palmtowers.com
SIC: 6513 Apartment building operators
PA: The John Collins Co Inc
5135 N Harbor Dr
San Diego CA

(P-14725)
KISCO SENIOR LIVING LLC
Also Called: KRC Orange
620 S Glassell St (92866-3000)
PHONE...............................714 997-5355
Bruce Hoggan, *Ex Dir*
EMP: 122
SALES (corp-wide): 138.27MM **Privately Held**
Web: www.kiscoseniorliving.com
SIC: 6513 Retirement hotel operation
PA: Senior Kisco Living Llc
5790 Fleet St Ste 300
Carlsbad CA
760 804-5900

(P-14726)
MARINA CITY CLUB LP A CALI
4333 Admiralty Way (90292-5469)
PHONE...............................310 822-0611
J H Snyder, *Pt*
Lewis Geyser, *Pt*
Milton Swimmer, *Pt*
Lon Snyder, *Pt*
EMP: 125 **EST:** 1969
SQ FT: 10,000
SALES (est): 4.6MM **Privately Held**
Web: www.marinacityclub.net
SIC: 6513 7997 4493 Apartment building operators; Membership sports and recreation clubs; Marinas

(P-14727)
MONARK LP
2804 W El Segundo Blvd (90249-1551)
PHONE...............................310 769-6669
EMP: 99
SALES (est): 1.91MM **Privately Held**
SIC: 6513 Apartment building operators

(P-14728)
NATIONAL COMMUNITY RENAISSANCE
Also Called: Heritage Pointe
8590 Malven Ave (91730-4669)
PHONE...............................909 948-7579
EMP: 108
SALES (corp-wide): 330 **Privately Held**
Web: www.nationalcore.org
SIC: 6513 Apartment building operators
PA: National Community Renaissance
9692 Haven Ave Ste 100
Rancho Cucamonga CA
909 483-2444

(P-14729)
RANCE KING PROPERTIES INC (PA)
Also Called: R K Properties
3737 E Broadway (90803-6104)
PHONE...............................562 240-1000
William Rance King Junior, *Pr*

Steven King, *
EMP: 104 **EST:** 1978
SQ FT: 5,000
SALES (est): 17.97MM
SALES (corp-wide): 17.97MM **Privately Held**
Web: www.rkprop.com
SIC: 6513 Apartment building operators

(P-14730)
SENIOR RESOURCE GROUP LLC
Also Called: La Vida Del Mar Associates
850 Del Mar Downs Rd Apt 338 (92075-2725)
PHONE...............................858 519-0890
Terry Oquest, *Mgr*
EMP: 131
SALES (corp-wide): 189.7MM **Privately Held**
Web: www.srgseniorliving.com
SIC: 6513 Retirement hotel operation
PA: Senior Resource Group, Llc
500 Stevens Ave Ste 100
Solana Beach CA
858 792-9300

(P-14731)
THE PINES LTD
1423 E Washington Ave (92019-2559)
PHONE...............................619 447-1880
EMP: 111
SALES (est): 4.1MM **Privately Held**
SIC: 6513 Apartment building operators

(P-14732)
WAMC COMPANY INC
Also Called: Cal West Enterprises
7420 Clairemont Mesa Blvd (92111-1546)
PHONE...............................858 454-2753
EMP: 94 **EST:** 1995
SALES (est): 2.33MM **Privately Held**
SIC: 6513 Apartment building operators

(P-14733)
WILLIAM WARREN PROPERTIES INC
Also Called: Access Self Storage SE
201 Wilshire Blvd Ste 102 (90401-1201)
PHONE...............................310 454-1500
William Hobin, *Pr*
EMP: 100 **EST:** 2000
SALES (est): 9.56MM
SALES (corp-wide): 84.59MM **Privately Held**
Web: www.williamwarren.com
SIC: 6513 Apartment building operators
PA: The William Warren Group Inc
100 Wilshire Blvd Ste 400
Santa Monica CA
310 451-2130

6514 Dwelling Operators, Except Apartments

(P-14734)
ACTION PROPERTY MANAGEMENT INC (PA)
Also Called: Action Property Management
2603 Main St Ste 500 (92614-4261)
PHONE...............................949 450-0202
Matthew Holbrook, *CEO*
Marianne Simek, *
EMP: 90 **EST:** 1980
SQ FT: 18,000
SALES (est): 90.39MM
SALES (corp-wide): 90.39MM **Privately Held**

Web: www.actionlife.com
SIC: 6514 8641 Residential building, four or fewer units: operation; Homeowners' association

(P-14735)
DAYTON DMH INC
121 Spinnaker Ct (92014-3218)
PHONE...............................858 350-4400
Donald Ambrose, *Pr*
EMP: 172 **EST:** 1995
SALES (est): 3.11MM **Privately Held**
SIC: 6514 Dwelling operators, except apartments

6515 Mobile Home Site Operators

(P-14736)
CAREFREE COMMUNITIES INC
Also Called: Carefree Communities
1251 Old Conejo Rd (91320-1031)
PHONE...............................805 498-2612
EMP: 125
SALES (corp-wide): 2.97B **Publicly Held**
Web: www.carefreervresorts.com
SIC: 6515 Mobile home site operators
HQ: Carefree Communities Inc.
6991 E Camelback Rd B310
Scottsdale AZ
480 423-5700

6519 Real Property Lessors, Nec

(P-14737)
HG FENTON PROPERTY COMPANY (PA)
Also Called: Silverton Business Center
7577 Mission Valley Rd Ste 200 (92108)
PHONE...............................619 400-0120
Mike Neal, *Pr*
Jennifer Tokatyan, *
Geoffrey Swortwood, *
Allen Jones, *
Kevin Hill, *
EMP: 200 **EST:** 1920
SALES (est): 28.99MM
SALES (corp-wide): 28.99MM **Privately Held**
Web: www.hgfenton.com
SIC: 6519 Real property lessors, nec

(P-14738)
LAACO LTD (HQ)
Also Called: Storage West
4469 Admiralty Way (90292-5415)
PHONE...............................213 622-1254
Karen L Hathaway, *Pr*
John K Hathaway, *
Steven K Hathaway, *
Bryan J Cusworth, *
EMP: 125 **EST:** 1986
SALES (est): 6.3MM **Publicly Held**
Web: www.laac.com
SIC: 6519 7997 7011 5812 Real property lessors, nec; Yacht club, membership; Hotels; Eating places
PA: Cubesmart
5 Old Lancaster Rd
Malvern PA

(P-14739)
OLYMPUS PROPERTY
3411 State Rd (93308-4537)
PHONE...............................661 393-1700
Chandler Wonderly, *Owner*

EMP: 266
SALES (corp-wide): 27.19MM **Privately Held**
Web: www.olympusproperty.com
SIC: 6519 1741 Real property lessors, nec; Foundation building
PA: Olympus Property
500 Throckmorton St # 300
Fort Worth TX
817 795-4900

6531 Real Estate Agents And Managers

(P-14740)
1370 REALTY CORP
14545 Friar St (91411-2397)
PHONE...............................818 817-0092
EMP: 17 **EST:** 1995
SQ FT: 16,400
SALES (est): 858.44K **Privately Held**
Web: www.1370realty.com
SIC: 6531 2451 Real estate agents and managers; Mobile buildings: for commercial use

(P-14741)
ABODE COMMUNITIES LLC
1149 S Hill St Fl 7 (90015-2207)
PHONE...............................213 629-2702
Robin Hughes, *Pr*
Rick Saperstein, *
Kenneth Krug, *
Sandra Kulli, *Vice Chairman*
Holly Benson, *
▲ **EMP:** 150 **EST:** 1968
SQ FT: 10,094
SALES (est): 18.1MM **Privately Held**
Web: www.abodecommunities.org
SIC: 6531 8712 8711 Housing authority operator; Architectural services; Engineering services

(P-14742)
ABSOLUTELY ZERO CORPORATION
1 City Blvd W Ste 1000 (92868-3611)
PHONE...............................949 269-3300
Ronald Radziminsky, *Pr*
EMP: 275 **EST:** 2018
SALES (est): 24.92MM **Privately Held**
Web: www.owning.com
SIC: 6531 Real estate brokers and agents
PA: Guaranteed Rate, Inc.
3940 N Ravenswood Ave
Chicago IL

(P-14743)
ALLIANT ASSET MGT CO LLC (HQ)
26050 Mureau Rd (91302-3174)
PHONE...............................818 668-2805
Shawn Horwitz, *Managing Member*
Scott Koticks, *
Brian Goldberg, *Managing Member*
EMP: 81 **EST:** 1997
SALES (est): 27.96MM **Publicly Held**
SIC: 6531 Real estate managers
PA: Walker & Dunlop, Inc.
7272 Wscnsin Ave Ste 1300
Bethesda MD

(P-14744)
AMERICAN DEVELOPMENT CORP (PA)
3605 Long Beach Blvd Ste 410 (90807-4013)
PHONE...............................562 989-3730

Marco Gomez, *Pr*
EMP: 87 **EST:** 1994
SQ FT: 8,000
SALES (est): 3.27MM **Privately Held**
SIC: 6531 Real estate agents and managers

(P-14745)
ATLAS HOSPITALITY GROUP
1901 Main St Ste 175 (92614-0517)
PHONE.............................949 622-3400
Alan Reay, *Pr*
S Shah, *VP*
EMP: 90 **EST:** 1991
SALES (est): 5.53MM **Privately Held**
Web: www.atlashospitality.com
SIC: 6531 Real estate agent, commercial

(P-14746)
AUCTIONCOM INC
Also Called: Auction.com
1 Mauchly Ste 27 (92618-2305)
PHONE.............................800 499-6199
Jeffrey Frieden, *CEO*
James Corum, *
Virginia Pierce, *
Annamarie Giagunto, *
Joseph Joffrion, *
EMP: 200 **EST:** 1990
SQ FT: 18,000
SALES (est): 4.87MM **Privately Held**
SIC: 6531 Auction, real estate

(P-14747)
AUCTIONCOM LLC (PA)
Also Called: Auction.com
1 Mauchly (92618-2305)
PHONE.............................949 859-2777
Jeffrey Frieden, *
Keith Mclane, *Pr*
Eva Tapia, *
Eric Andrew, *
EMP: 142 **EST:** 2008
SALES (est): 162.88MM **Privately Held**
Web: www.auction.com
SIC: 6531 Real estate agents and managers

(P-14748)
BAKERSFIELD WESTWIND CORP
Also Called: Coldwell Banker
1810 Westwind Dr (93301-3027)
PHONE.............................661 327-2121
John Garone, *Pr*
EMP: 145 **EST:** 1972
SALES (est): 9.46MM **Privately Held**
Web: www.coldwellbanker.com
SIC: 6531 Real estate agent, residential

(P-14749)
BENNION DEVILLE FINE HOMES INC
Also Called: Windermere RE Coachella Vly
74850 Us Highway 111 (92210-7116)
PHONE.............................760 674-3452
Rick Fisk, *Brnch Mgr*
EMP: 378
SALES (corp-wide): 24.87MM **Privately Held**
Web: www.bdhomes.com
SIC: 6531 Real estate brokers and agents
PA: Bennion & Deville Fine Homes, Inc.
71691 Highway 111
Rancho Mirage CA
760 770-6801

(P-14750)
BERKSHIRE HTHWAY HM SVCS CA RP
9836 Atlantic Ave (90280-5219)

PHONE.............................562 307-5636
EMP: 82
SALES (corp-wide): 2.56MM **Privately Held**
Web: www.brucemulhearn.com
SIC: 6531 Real estate agent, residential
PA: Berkshire Hathaway Home Services
Ca Roperties
18000 Studebaker Rd # 600
Cerritos CA
562 860-2625

(P-14751)
BEVERLY AND COMPANY INC
15301 Ventura Blvd B305 (91403-3102)
PHONE.............................323 422-3253
Max Edward Mcdermott, *CEO*
EMP: 100 **EST:** 2018
SALES (est): 515.15K **Privately Held**
Web: www.beverlycompany.com
SIC: 6531 Real estate brokers and agents

(P-14752)
BKM DIABLO 227 LLC
1701 Quail St Ste 100 (92660-2796)
PHONE.............................602 688-6409
Brian K Malliet, *Prin*
Rene Velasquez, *
EMP: 85 **EST:** 2018
SALES (est): 3.49MM **Privately Held**
Web: www.bkmmanagementco.com
SIC: 6531 Real estate managers

(P-14753)
BUCHANAN STREET PARTNERS LP
3501 Jamboree Rd Ste 4200 (92660-2958)
PHONE.............................949 721-1414
Robert Brunswick, *CEO*
Timothy Ballard, *
James Gill, *
EMP: 85 **EST:** 2000
SALES (est): 10.16MM **Privately Held**
Web: www.buchananstreet.com
SIC: 6531 Real estate agents and managers

(P-14754)
BURLEIGH POINT LLC
Also Called: Burleigh Point, Ltd.
5600 Argosy Ave Ste 100 (92649-1063)
PHONE.............................949 428-3200
◆ **EMP:** 200
SIC: 6531 6513 Real estate agent, residential
; Residential hotel operation

(P-14755)
C B COAST NEWPORT PROPERTIES
Also Called: Coldwell Bnkr Rsdntial Rfrral
840 Newport Center Dr Ste 100 (92660)
PHONE.............................949 644-1600
Daniel F Bibb, *Pr*
Tom Queen, *
Gary Legrand, *
EMP: 2129 **EST:** 1990
SQ FT: 7,300
SALES (est): 4.77MM **Publicly Held**
Web: www.coldwellbanker.com
SIC: 6531 Real estate agent, residential
HQ: Coldwell Banker Residential Referral
Network
27271 Las Ramblas
Mission Viejo CA
949 367-1800

(P-14756)
CAMDEN DEVELOPMENT INC
27261 Las Ramblas (92691-6441)
PHONE.............................949 427-4674

EMP: 142
Web: www.camdenliving.com
SIC: 6531 Real estate agent, commercial
HQ: Camden Development, Inc.
11 Greenway Plz Ste 2400
Houston TX

(P-14757)
CARLYLE GROUP INC (PA)
9073 Nemo St Ste 100 (90069-5511)
PHONE.............................310 550-8656
Ronald Singer, *CEO*
Karen Burcombe-vogogel, *VP*
Charles Moore, *Prin*
David Lam, *VP*
▲ **EMP:** 86 **EST:** 1975
SQ FT: 3,000
SALES (est): 42.14MM
SALES (corp-wide): 42.14MM **Privately Held**
Web: www.carlyle.com
SIC: 6531 6799 Buying agent, real estate; Investors, nec

(P-14758)
CARUSO MGT LTD A CAL LTD PRTNR (PA)
Also Called: Commons At Calabasas, The
101 The Grove Dr (90036-6221)
PHONE.............................323 900-8100
Rick Caruso, *CEO*
EMP: 99 **EST:** 1991
SALES (est): 24.62MM
SALES (corp-wide): 24.62MM **Privately Held**
Web: www.caruso.com
SIC: 6531 Rental agent, real estate

(P-14759)
CBRE INC
4301 La Jolla Village Dr # 3000
(92122-1484)
PHONE.............................858 546-4600
EMP: 160
Web: www.cbre.us
SIC: 6531 Real estate agent, commercial
HQ: Cbre, Inc.
400 S Hope St Ste 25
Los Angeles CA
213 613-3333

(P-14760)
CBRE GLOBL VALUE INVESTORS LLC (DH)
Also Called: Global Innovation Partner
601 S Figueroa St Ste 49 (90017-5253)
PHONE.............................213 683-4200
Ritson Ferguson, *CEO*
Gil Borok, *
Maurice Voskuilen, *
EMP: 150 **EST:** 1972
SALES (est): 100.76MM **Publicly Held**
Web: www.cbreim.com
SIC: 6531 Real estate agent, commercial
HQ: Cbre, Inc.
2100 Mckinney Ave # 1250
Dallas TX
866 225-3099

(P-14761)
CBRE GLOBL VALUE INVESTORS LLC
Also Called: Cbre
3501 Jamboree Rd Ste 100 (92660-2940)
PHONE.............................949 725-8500
Steven Swerdlow, *Prin*
EMP: 169
Web: www.cbreim.com

SIC: 6531 Real estate agent, commercial
HQ: Cbre Global Value Investors, Llc
601 S Figueroa St Ste 49
Los Angeles CA
213 683-4200

(P-14762)
CENTURY 21 A BETTER SVC RLTY
Also Called: Century 21
5831 Firestone Blvd Ste J (90280-3718)
PHONE.............................562 806-1000
EMP: 97
SQ FT: 4,000
SALES (est): 3.76MM **Privately Held**
Web: www.c21abetterservice.com
SIC: 6531 Real estate agents and managers

(P-14763)
CHARLES DUNN RE SVCS INC (PA)
800 W 6th St Ste 600 (90017-2702)
PHONE.............................213 270-6200
Walter Conn, *CEO*
Patrick Conn, *
EMP: 86 **EST:** 1995
SQ FT: 30,000
SALES (est): 10.55MM
SALES (corp-wide): 10.55MM **Privately Held**
Web: www.charlesdunn.com
SIC: 6531 Real estate brokers and agents

(P-14764)
CHILD DEVELOPMENT INCORPORATED
17341 Jacquelyn Ln (92647-5713)
PHONE.............................714 842-4064
EMP: 362
SALES (corp-wide): 49.76MM **Privately Held**
Web: www.catalystkids.org
SIC: 6531 Real estate agents and managers
PA: Child Development Incorporated
350 Woodview Ave
Morgan Hill CA
408 556-7300

(P-14765)
CITIVEST INC
Also Called: Hydrotech Construction Group
4350 Von Karman Ave Ste 200
(92660-2041)
PHONE.............................949 705-0420
Dana Haynes, *Pr*
EMP: 90 **EST:** 1987
SALES (est): 9.57MM **Privately Held**
Web: www.citivestinc.com
SIC: 6531 Real estate managers

(P-14766)
COASTAL ALLIANCE HOLDINGS INC
Also Called: Coldwell Banker Coastl Aliance
1650 Ximeno Ave Ste 120 (90804-2179)
PHONE.............................562 370-1000
Jack Irvin, *Pr*
EMP: 140 **EST:** 2003
SALES (est): 6.58MM **Privately Held**
Web: www.cbcoastalalliance.com
SIC: 6531 Real estate agent, residential

(P-14767)
COLDWELL BANKER RESIDENTIAL RE
Also Called: Coldwell Banker
15 E Foothill Blvd (91006-2399)
PHONE.............................626 445-5500

Jack Cooley, *Prin*
EMP: 179 **EST:** 2003
SALES (est): 2.3MM **Privately Held**
Web: www.coldwellbanker.com
SIC: 6531 Real estate agent, residential

(P-14768)
COLDWELL BNKR RSDNTIAL RFRRAL (DH)
Also Called: Coldwell Banker
27271 Las Ramblas (92691-8041)
PHONE...............................949 367-1800
Robert Becker, *Pr*
Dan Happer, *CFO*
EMP: 410 **EST:** 1984
SQ FT: 6,000
SALES (est): 61.96MM **Publicly Held**
Web: www.coldwellbanker.com
SIC: 6531 Real estate agent, residential
HQ: Nrt Commercial Utah Llc
        175 Park Ave
        Madison NJ

(P-14769)
COLDWELL BNKR RSDNTIAL RFRRAL
Also Called: Coldwell Banker
201 Marine Ave (92662-1203)
P.O. Box 68 (92662-0068)
PHONE...............................949 673-8700
Steve Sutherland, *Mgr*
EMP: 1146
Web: www.coldwellbanker.com
SIC: 6531 Real estate agent, residential
HQ: Coldwell Banker Residential Referral
        Network
        27271 Las Ramblas
        Mission Viejo CA
        949 367-1800

(P-14770)
COLLEGE PARK REALTY INC (PA)
Also Called: Re/Max
10791 Los Alamitos Blvd (90720-2309)
PHONE...............................562 594-6753
Barry Binder, *Pr*
Carol Treadway, *
Betty Binder, *
EMP: 80 **EST:** 1974
SQ FT: 5,000
SALES (est): 11.93MM
SALES (corp-wide): 11.93MM **Privately Held**
Web: www.remaxcollegepark.com
SIC: 6531 Real estate agent, residential

(P-14771)
COMMON GROUNDS HOLDINGS LLC
6790 Embarcadero Ln Ste 100
(92011-3277)
PHONE...............................760 206-7861
Jacob Bates, *Prin*
EMP: 90 **EST:** 2017
SALES (est): 2.21MM **Privately Held**
Web: www.cgworkplace.com
SIC: 6531 8742 Real estate leasing and
        rentals; Real estate consultant

(P-14772)
CONAM MANAGEMENT CORPORATION (PA)
3990 Ruffin Rd Ste 100 (92123-4805)
PHONE...............................858 614-7200
J Bradley Forrester, *CEO*
Daniel Epstein, *
Frazier Crawford, *
Rob Singh, *

E Scott Dupree, *
EMP: 142 **EST:** 1975
SQ FT: 45,634
SALES (est): 96.15MM **Privately Held**
Web: www.conam.com
SIC: 6531 Real estate managers

(P-14773)
CORE REALTY HOLDINGS MGT INC
Also Called: Crh Management
1600 Dove St Ste 450 (92660-2447)
PHONE...............................949 863-1031
EMP: 99 **EST:** 2010
SALES (est): 7.22MM **Privately Held**
Web: www.crhmi.com
SIC: 6531 Real estate managers

(P-14774)
CUBEWORKCOM INC
Also Called: Cubework
900 Turnbull Canyon Rd (91745-1404)
PHONE...............................909 991-6669
James Chang, *CEO*
Christine Wei, *CCO*
EMP: 200 **EST:** 2018
SALES (est): 9.65MM **Privately Held**
Web: www.cubework.com
SIC: 6531 Real estate leasing and rentals

(P-14775)
CUSHMAN & WAKEFIELD CAL INC
10250 Constellation Blvd Ste 2200
(90067-6255)
PHONE...............................310 556-1805
Eric Olosson, *Mgr*
EMP: 405
SALES (corp-wide): 10.11B **Privately Held**
Web: www.cushmanwakefield.com
SIC: 6531 Real estate agent, commercial
HQ: Cushman & Wakefield Of California,
        Inc.
        1 Maritime Plz Ste 900
        San Francisco CA
        408 275-6730

(P-14776)
CUSHMAN & WAKEFIELD CAL INC
3760 Kilroy Airport Way (90806-2443)
PHONE...............................562 276-1400
Joe Vargus, *Mgr*
EMP: 495
SALES (corp-wide): 10.11B **Privately Held**
Web: www.cushmanwakefield.com
SIC: 6531 Real estate agent, commercial
HQ: Cushman & Wakefield Of California,
        Inc.
        1 Maritime Plz Ste 900
        San Francisco CA
        408 275-6730

(P-14777)
CUSHMAN & WAKEFIELD CAL INC
Also Called: Cushman & Wakefield California
7281 Garden Grove Blvd Ste G
(92841-4212)
PHONE...............................714 591-0451
EMP: 325
SALES (corp-wide): 10.11B **Privately Held**
Web: www.cushmanwakefield.com
SIC: 6531 Real estate agent, commercial
HQ: Cushman & Wakefield Of California,
        Inc.
        1 Maritime Plz Ste 900
        San Francisco CA
        408 275-6730

(P-14778)
CUSHMAN & WAKEFIELD CAL INC
18111 Von Karman Ave Ste 1000
(92612-7101)
PHONE...............................949 474-4004
Dee Shipley, *Mgr*
EMP: 883
SALES (corp-wide): 10.11B **Privately Held**
Web: www.cushmanwakefield.com
SIC: 6531 Real estate agent, commercial
HQ: Cushman & Wakefield Of California,
        Inc.
        1 Maritime Plz Ste 900
        San Francisco CA
        408 275-6730

(P-14779)
CUSHMAN & WAKEFIELD CAL INC
Also Called: Corporate Real Estate Advisors
12830 El Camino Real Ste 100 (92130)
PHONE...............................858 452-6500
Steve Rosetta, *Mgr*
EMP: 697
SALES (corp-wide): 10.11B **Privately Held**
Web: www.cushmanwakefield.com
SIC: 6531 8742 8732 Real estate agent,
commercial; Real estate consultant; Market
analysis, business, and economic research
HQ: Cushman & Wakefield Of California,
        Inc.
        1 Maritime Plz Ste 900
        San Francisco CA
        408 275-6730

(P-14780)
CUSHMAN & WAKEFIELD CAL INC
3011 Townsgate Rd (91361-5820)
PHONE...............................805 418-5811
EMP: 372
SALES (corp-wide): 10.11B **Privately Held**
Web: www.cushmanwakefield.com
SIC: 6531 Real estate agent, commercial
HQ: Cushman & Wakefield Of California,
        Inc.
        1 Maritime Plz Ste 900
        San Francisco CA
        408 275-6730

(P-14781)
CUSHMAN & WAKEFIELD CAL INC
770 Paseo Camarillo 315 (93010-6064)
PHONE...............................805 322-7244
EMP: 372
SALES (corp-wide): 10.11B **Privately Held**
Web: www.cushmanwakefield.com
SIC: 6531 Real estate agent, commercial
HQ: Cushman & Wakefield Of California,
        Inc.
        1 Maritime Plz Ste 900
        San Francisco CA
        408 275-6730

(P-14782)
CUSHMAN & WAKEFIELD CAL INC
Also Called: Cushman & Wakefield
3800 Concours Ste 300 (91764-5907)
PHONE...............................909 483-0077
EMP: 372
SALES (corp-wide): 10.11B **Privately Held**
Web: www.cushmanwakefield.com
SIC: 6531 Real estate agent, commercial

HQ: Cushman & Wakefield Of California,
        Inc.
        1 Maritime Plz Ste 900
        San Francisco CA
        408 275-6730

(P-14783)
CUSHMAN & WAKEFIELD CAL INC
901 Via Piemonte Ste 200 (91764-6597)
PHONE...............................909 980-3781
Luanne Alleman, *Mgr*
EMP: 465
SALES (corp-wide): 10.11B **Privately Held**
Web: www.cushmanwakefield.com
SIC: 6531 Real estate agent, commercial
HQ: Cushman & Wakefield Of California,
        Inc.
        1 Maritime Plz Ste 900
        San Francisco CA
        408 275-6730

(P-14784)
CUSHMAN REALTY CORPORATION
601 S Figueroa St Ste 4700 (90017-5752)
PHONE...............................213 627-4700
EMP: 200
SIC: 6531 Real estate brokers and agents

(P-14785)
DAYMARK REALTY ADVISORS INC
Also Called: Daymark Properties Realty
750 B St Ste 2620 (92101-8172)
PHONE...............................714 975-2999
Todd A Mikles, *CEO*
EMP: 400 **EST:** 2010
SALES (est): 10.72MM **Privately Held**
SIC: 6531 Real estate brokers and agents

(P-14786)
DEASY PENNER PODLEY
Also Called: Dpp Real Estate
30 N Baldwin Ave (91024-1956)
PHONE...............................626 408-1280
Mike Deasy, *Ch Bd*
George Penner, *
EMP: 223 **EST:** 2019
SALES (est): 4.91MM **Privately Held**
Web: www.margaretgaremore.com
SIC: 6531 Real estate brokers and agents

(P-14787)
DG REAL ESTATE INC
4766 Park Granada Ste 214 (91302-3334)
PHONE...............................818 591-8800
EMP: 94
SIC: 6531 Real estate agent, commercial
PA: Dg Real Estate Inc.
        1030 Foothill Blvd Fl 1
        La Canada CA

(P-14788)
DIAMOND RIDGE CORPORATION
Also Called: Re/Max
121 S Mountain Ave (91786-6257)
PHONE...............................909 949-0605
Jennifer Lynn Puglisi, *CEO*
EMP: 165 **EST:** 2001
SALES (est): 9.53MM **Privately Held**
Web: www.remax.com
SIC: 6531 Real estate agent, residential

(P-14789)
DONAHUE SCHRBER RLTY GROUP INC (PA)
200 Baker St Ste 100 (92626-4551)

PHONE............................714 545-1400
Thomas Schriber, *Ch Bd*
Patrick S Donahue, *
Larry Casey, *
EMP: 80 **EST:** 1954
SQ FT: 20,000
SALES (est): 27.92MM
SALES (corp-wide): 27.92MM **Privately Held**
SIC: 6531 Real estate agent, commercial

(P-14790)
DOROTHY SARKOZY
Also Called: Coldwell Banker Residential BR
3810 Valley Centre Dr Ste 906
(92130-3308)
PHONE............................858 259-0555
Dorothy Sarkozy, *Prin*
EMP: 94 **EST:** 2003
SALES (est): 994.13K **Privately Held**
Web: www.coldwellbanker.com
SIC: 6531 Real estate agent, residential

(P-14791)
EAM ENTERPRISES INC (PA)
Also Called: Crest R E O & Relocation
4005 Foothill Blvd (91214-1623)
PHONE............................818 248-9100
Razmik Mirzakhanian, *CEO*
EMP: 100 **EST:** 1991
SQ FT: 5,000
SALES (est): 9.5MM **Privately Held**
Web: www.century21.com
SIC: 6531 Real estate agent, residential

(P-14792)
EVOQ PROPERTIES INC
1318 E 7th St Ste 200 (90021-1128)
PHONE............................213 988-8890
Martin Caveroy, *CEO*
John Charles Maddux, *
Lynn Beckemeyer, *Executive Development Vice President*
Todd Nielsen, *Corporate Secretary*
Andrew Murray, *
EMP: 82 **EST:** 2006
SALES (est): 4.3MM **Privately Held**
Web: www.evoqproperties.com
SIC: 6531 Real estate agent, commercial

(P-14793)
F M TARBELL CO (HQ)
Also Called: Tarbell Realtors
1403 N Tustin Ave Ste 380 (92705-8691)
PHONE............................714 972-0988
TOLL FREE: 800
Tina Jimov, *Pr*
Donald M Tarbell, *
EMP: 110 **EST:** 1956
SQ FT: 60,000
SALES (est): 53.8MM
SALES (corp-wide): 145.44MM **Privately Held**
Web: www.jen4homes.com
SIC: 6531 Real estate agent, residential
PA: Tarbell Financial Corporation
1403 N Tustin Ave Ste 380
Santa Ana CA
714 972-0988

(P-14794)
FIRST AMERCN PROF RE SVCS INC (HQ)
200 Commerce (92602-5000)
PHONE............................714 250-1400
Larry Davidson, *Pr*
EMP: 240 **EST:** 1997
SQ FT: 28,000
SALES (est): 26.13MM **Publicly Held**
Web: www.smscorp.com

SIC: 6531 Real estate agents and managers
PA: First American Financial Corporation
1 First American Way
Santa Ana CA

(P-14795)
FIRST AMERICAN TEAM REALTY INC (PA)
Also Called: Best Financial, The
2501 Cherry Ave Ste 100 (90755-2039)
PHONE............................562 427-7765
Steve S Vong, *Pr*
EMP: 150 **EST:** 1995
SQ FT: 3,300
SALES (est): 9.59MM **Privately Held**
Web: www.firstamericanteam.com
SIC: 6531 Real estate agent, residential

(P-14796)
FIRST TEAM RE - ORANGE CNTY
32451 Golden Lantern Ste 210
(92677-5344)
PHONE............................949 240-7979
Mark Kojac, *Genl Mgr*
EMP: 335
SALES (corp-wide): 486 **Privately Held**
Web: www.firstteam.com
SIC: 6531 Real estate agent, residential
PA: First Team Real Estate - Orange
County
108 Pacifica Ste 300
Irvine CA
949 988-3000

(P-14797)
FIRST TEAM RE - ORANGE CNTY
Also Called: 1st Team Real Estate
17240 17th St (92780-1945)
PHONE............................714 544-5456
Michael Hampton, *Mgr*
EMP: 261
SALES (corp-wide): 486 **Privately Held**
Web: www.firstteam.com
SIC: 6531 Real estate agent, residential
PA: First Team Real Estate - Orange
County
108 Pacifica Ste 300
Irvine CA
949 988-3000

(P-14798)
FIRST TEAM RE - ORANGE CNTY
Also Called: First Team Real Estate
8028 E Santa Ana Canyon Rd
(92808-1108)
PHONE............................714 974-9191
EMP: 112
SALES (corp-wide): 486 **Privately Held**
Web: www.firstteam.com
SIC: 6531 Real estate brokers and agents
PA: First Team Real Estate - Orange
County
108 Pacifica Ste 300
Irvine CA
949 988-3000

(P-14799)
FIRST TEAM RE - ORANGE CNTY
Also Called: First Team Real Estate
26711 Aliso Creek Rd Ste 200a
(92656-4820)
PHONE............................949 389-0004
EMP: 150
SALES (corp-wide): 486 **Privately Held**
Web: www.firstteam.com
SIC: 6531 Real estate brokers and agents

(P-14800)
FIRST TEAM RE - ORANGE CNTY (PA)
Also Called: First Team Walk-In Realty
108 Pacifica Ste 300 (92618-7435)
PHONE............................949 988-3000
Cameron Merage, *CEO*
Michele Harrington, *
EMP: 160 **EST:** 1976
SQ FT: 8,000
SALES (est): 486
SALES (corp-wide): 486 **Privately Held**
Web: www.firstteam.com
SIC: 6531 Real estate agent, residential

(P-14801)
FIRST TEAM RE - ORANGE CNTY
12501 Seal Beach Blvd Ste 100
(90740-2763)
PHONE............................562 596-9911
Judy Sharp, *Mgr*
EMP: 224
SALES (corp-wide): 486 **Privately Held**
Web: www.firstteam.com
SIC: 6531 Real estate agent, residential
PA: First Team Real Estate - Orange
County
108 Pacifica Ste 300
Irvine CA
949 988-3000

(P-14802)
FIRSTSRVICE RSIDENTIAL CAL LLC (HQ)
Also Called: Merit Companies The
15241 Laguna Canyon Rd (92618-3146)
PHONE............................949 448-6000
Bob Cardoza, *Pr*
Katie Ward, *Prin*
EMP: 200 **EST:** 1980
SQ FT: 21,000
SALES (est): 2.89MM
SALES (corp-wide): 3.75B **Privately Held**
Web: www.fsresidential.com
SIC: 6531 Real estate managers
PA: Firstservice Corporation
1255 Bay St Suite 600
Toronto ON
416 960-9566

(P-14803)
GEMMM CORPORATION (PA)
Also Called: Prudential
2860 E Thousand Oaks Blvd (91362-3201)
PHONE............................805 496-0555
TOLL FREE: 800
Robert L Majorino, *Pr*
Robert Hamilton, *
Anthony Principe, *
Lynn Gilbert, *
EMP: 100 **EST:** 1990
SQ FT: 12,500
SALES (est): 20.67MM
SALES (corp-wide): 20.67MM **Privately Held**
Web: www.bhhscalhomes.com
SIC: 6531 Real estate agent, residential

(P-14804)
GK MANAGEMENT CO INC (PA)
5150 Overland Ave (90230-4914)
PHONE............................310 204-2050
Carole Glodney, *CEO*
Jona Goldrich, *

EMP: 150 **EST:** 1972
SALES (est): 64.47MM
SALES (corp-wide): 64.47MM **Privately Held**
Web: www.goldrichkest.com
SIC: 6531 Real estate managers

(P-14805)
GRAND PACIFIC RESORTS INC (PA)
5900 Pasteur Ct Ste 200 (92008-7336)
P.O. Box 4068 (92018-4068)
PHONE............................760 431-8500
Timothy J Stripe, *CEO*
David Brown, *
EMP: 250 **EST:** 1993
SQ FT: 22,000
SALES (est): 101.28MM **Privately Held**
Web: www.grandpacificresorts.com
SIC: 6531 7011 Time-sharing real estate
sales, leasing and rentals; Hotels and
motels

(P-14806)
GREYSTAR MANAGEMENT SVCS LP
Also Called: Greystar
620 Newport Center Dr 15th Fl (92660)
PHONE............................949 705-0010
Kevin Kaverna, *Dir*
EMP: 809
Web: www.greystar.com
SIC: 6531 Real estate managers
PA: Greystar Management Services, L.P.
750 Bering Dr Ste 300
Houston TX

(P-14807)
GREYSTAR MANAGEMENT SVCS LP
6320 Canoga Ave Ste 1512 (91367-2526)
PHONE............................818 596-2180
Grace White, *Owner*
EMP: 138
Web: www.greystar.com
SIC: 6531 Real estate brokers and agents
PA: Greystar Management Services, L.P.
750 Bering Dr Ste 300
Houston TX

(P-14808)
GRUBB & ELLIS COMPANY
1551 N Tustin Ave Ste 300 (92705-8621)
PHONE............................714 667-8252
◆ **EMP:** 4500
SIC: 6531 8742 6162 Real estate agent,
commercial; Real estate consultant;
Mortgage brokers, using own money

(P-14809)
GRUBB & ELLIS MANAGEMENT SERVICES INC
1551 N Tustin Ave Ste 300 (92705-8638)
PHONE............................412 201-8200
EMP: 1800
SIC: 6531 Real estate agents and managers

(P-14810)
HANKEN CONO ASSAD & CO INC
Also Called: Wintergreen Apts
1504 Oro Vista Rd Apt 145 (92154-4069)
PHONE............................619 575-3100
Martha Alonso, *Mgr*
EMP: 113
SALES (corp-wide): 16.83MM **Privately Held**
Web: www.sdrenting.com

SIC: **6531** 6513 Condominium manager; Apartment building operators
PA: Hanken Cono Assad & Co., Inc.
5550 Baltimore Dr Ste 200
La Mesa CA
619 698-4770

(P-14811)
HOUSE SEVEN GABLES RE INC
Also Called: Cole, Norman Anne
5753 E Santa Ana Canyon Rd Ste P
(92807-3230)
PHONE..................714 282-0306
EMP: 95
SALES (corp-wide): 22.27MM **Privately Held**
Web: www.sevengables.com
SIC: 6531 Real estate brokers and agents
PA: House Of Seven Gables Real Estate, Inc.
12651 Newport Ave
Tustin CA
714 731-3777

(P-14812)
HSF AFFILIATES LLC (PA)
Also Called: Prudential
18500 Von Karman Ave Ste 400
(92612-1511)
PHONE..................949 794-7900
Chris Stuart, *CEO*
Allan Dalton, *CFO*
Gino Blefari, *Ch*
EMP: 93 **EST:** 2012
SALES (est): 36.37MM
SALES (corp-wide): 36.37MM **Privately Held**
Web: www.hsfaffiliates.com
SIC: 6531 Real estate agent, residential

(P-14813)
I D PROPERTY CORPORATION
Also Called: Property I D
1001 Wilshire Blvd Ste 100 (90017-2415)
PHONE..................213 625-0100
Carlos Siderman, *Pr*
▲ **EMP:** 120 **EST:** 1983
SALES (est): 9.85MM **Privately Held**
Web: www.propertyid.com
SIC: 6531 8742 Real estate listing services; Real estate consultant

(P-14814)
INVESERVE CORPORATION
812 W Las Tunas Dr (91776-1021)
PHONE..................626 458-3435
Norman Chang, *Pr*
Amy Chang, *
Michael Fang, *
EMP: 80 **EST:** 1987
SALES (est): 2.77MM **Privately Held**
Web: www.inveserve.com
SIC: 6531 Real estate agent, commercial

(P-14815)
INVITATION HOMES INC
680 E Colorado Blvd (91101-6143)
PHONE..................805 372-2900
Luke Kochniuk, *Brnch Mgr*
EMP: 80
SALES (corp-wide): 2.24B **Publicly Held**
Web: www.invitationhomes.com
SIC: 6531 Real estate agents and managers
PA: Invitation Homes Inc.
1717 Main St Ste 2000
Dallas TX
972 421-3600

(P-14816)
J & M REALTY COMPANY (PA)
41 Corporate Park Ste 240 (92606-3125)
PHONE..................949 261-2727
John Woolley, *Pr*
Michael Aimola, *Genl Mgr*
EMP: 120 **EST:** 1988
SQ FT: 4,000
SALES (est): 2.44MM **Privately Held**
SIC: 6531 8641 6798 6519 Real estate managers; Homeowners' association; Real estate investment trusts; Real property lessors, nec

(P-14817)
JAMBOREE REALTY CORP (PA)
Also Called: Jamboree Management
22982 Mill Creek Dr (92653-1214)
PHONE..................949 380-0300
Fred G Sparks, *Pr*
Richard M Tucker, *
Kathleen Tucker, *
EMP: 120 **EST:** 1982
SALES (est): 8.3MM
SALES (corp-wide): 8.3MM **Privately Held**
Web: www.jamboreemanagement.com
SIC: 6531 Real estate managers

(P-14818)
KELLER WILLIAMS
Also Called: Keller Williams Realtors
2150 Hillhurst Ave (90027-2012)
PHONE..................323 300-1700
Candace Kentopian, *Prin*
EMP: 87 **EST:** 2016
SALES (est): 225.79K **Privately Held**
Web: www.themorenogroupla.com
SIC: 6531 Real estate agent, residential

(P-14819)
KELLER WLLAMS RLTY BVRLY HILLS
Also Called: Keller Williams Realtors
439 N Canon Dr Ste 300 (90210-3909)
PHONE..................310 432-6400
Paul Morris, *Prin*
EMP: 90 **EST:** 2005
SALES (est): 8.1MM **Privately Held**
Web: www.kwbeverlyhills.com
SIC: 6531 Real estate agent, residential

(P-14820)
KENNEDY-WILSON INC (PA)
151 El Camino Dr (90212-2704)
PHONE..................310 887-6400
William Mcmorrow, *Ch Bd*
Justin Enbody, *CFO*
Matt Windisch, *Pr*
John Pradhu, *VP*
EMP: 103 **EST:** 1977
SALES (est): 109.72MM **Privately Held**
Web: www.kennedywilson.com
SIC: 6531 6799 Auction, real estate; Real estate investors, except property operators

(P-14821)
KOR REALTY GROUP LLC (PA)
1212 S Flower St Fl 5 (90015-2123)
PHONE..................323 930-3700
EMP: 86 **EST:** 2001
SQ FT: 6,500
SALES (est): 2.49MM
SALES (corp-wide): 2.49MM **Privately Held**
Web: www.thekorgroup.com
SIC: 6531 Real estate managers

(P-14822)
LAGUNA WOODS VILLAGE
24351 El Toro Rd (92637-4901)
P.O. Box 2220 (92654-2220)
PHONE..................949 597-4267
Milton John, *Dir*
Russ Disbro, *Dir*
EMP: 1000 **EST:** 1964
SALES (est): 18.77K **Privately Held**
Web: www.lagunawoodsvillage.com
SIC: 6531 Real estate agents and managers

(P-14823)
LOIS LAUER REALTY (PA)
Also Called: Century 21
1998 Orange Tree Ln (92374-2841)
P.O. Box 524 (92373-0161)
PHONE..................909 748-7000
TOLL FREE: 800
David Coy, *Pr*
Shirley Harrington, *VP*
Ann Bryan, *Sec*
James H Lauer, *Dir*
EMP: 220 **EST:** 1976
SQ FT: 17,000
SALES (est): 20.49MM
SALES (corp-wide): 20.49MM **Privately Held**
Web: www.loislauer.com
SIC: 6531 Real estate agent, residential

(P-14824)
LOWE ENTERPRISES RLTY SVCS INC
Also Called: Encino Financial Center
16133 Ventura Blvd Ste 535 (91436-2403)
PHONE..................818 990-9555
Karla Akins, *Brnch Mgr*
EMP: 2383
SALES (corp-wide): 367.25MM **Privately Held**
Web: www.lowe-re.com
SIC: 6531 Real estate managers
HQ: Lowe Enterprises Realty Services, Inc.
11777 San Vicente Blvd
Los Angeles CA
310 820-6661

(P-14825)
LRES CORPORATION (PA)
Also Called: Guardian Solutions
765 The City Dr S (92868-4942)
PHONE..................714 520-5737
Roger Beane, *Pr*
Don Mask, *CAO*
Alice Sorenson, *Ex VP*
Paul Abbamonto, *COO*
Richard Cimino, *Sr VP*
EMP: 91 **EST:** 2001
SALES (est): 19.15MM
SALES (corp-wide): 19.15MM **Privately Held**
Web: www.lres.com
SIC: 6531 Real estate managers

(P-14826)
LYON STAHL INVESTMENT RE INC
239 Oregon St (90245-4215)
PHONE..................310 425-9838
EMP: 88 **EST:** 2017
SALES (est): 2.2MM **Privately Held**
Web: www.lyonstahl.com
SIC: 6531 Real estate agent, commercial

(P-14827)
M & S ACQUISITION CORPORATION (PA)
707 Wilshire Blvd Ste 5200 (90017-3501)

PHONE..................213 385-1515
Mark Santarsiero, *CFO*
Mark Santarsiero, *CEO*
Robert Kerslake, *
Merle Atkins, *
Fred Thomas, *
EMP: 115 **EST:** 1993
SALES (est): 12.92MM
SALES (corp-wide): 12.92MM **Privately Held**
SIC: 6531 8742 Appraiser, real estate; Management consulting services

(P-14828)
MAJESTIC REALTY CO (PA)
Also Called: Majestic Management Co.
13191 Crossroads Pkwy N Ste 600 (91746)
PHONE..................562 692-9581
EMP: 150 **EST:** 1948
SALES (est): 640.33K
SALES (corp-wide): 640.33K **Privately Held**
Web: www.majesticrealty.com
SIC: 6531 6552 Real estate agent, commercial; Subdividers and developers, nec

(P-14829)
MARCUS & MILLICHAP INC (PA)
Also Called: Marcus & Millichap
23975 Park Sorrento Ste 400 (91302-4014)
PHONE..................818 212-2250
Hessam Nadji, *Pr*
Mitchell R Labar, *
Steve Degennaro, *
Christopher J Zorbas, *
Andrew Strockis, *CMO*
EMP: 106 **EST:** 1971
SQ FT: 24,028
SALES (est): 1.3B
SALES (corp-wide): 1.3B **Publicly Held**
Web: www.marcusmillichap.com
SIC: 6531 Real estate agent, commercial

(P-14830)
MARSHALL REDDICK REALTY INC
Also Called: Marshall Reddick RE Netwrk
4299 Macarthur Blvd Ste 102 (92660-2019)
P.O. Box 10311 (92711-0311)
PHONE..................949 885-8180
Marshall Reddick, *CEO*
EMP: 142 **EST:** 2005
SQ FT: 3,800
SALES (est): 2.7MM **Privately Held**
Web: www.marshallreddick.com
SIC: 6531 Real estate brokers and agents

(P-14831)
MEMCO HOLDINGS INC
10390 Santa Monica Blvd # 210 (90025-5058)
PHONE..................310 277-0057
Mitchell Stein, *Pr*
EMP: 130 **EST:** 1987
SALES (est): 5.04MM **Privately Held**
SIC: 6531 Real estate managers

(P-14832)
MOONSTONE MANAGEMENT CORP (PA)
Also Called: Moonstone Hotel Properties
2905 Burton Dr (93428-4001)
PHONE..................805 927-4200
EMP: 175 **EST:** 1995
SQ FT: 5,000
SALES (est): 12.72MM **Privately Held**
Web: www.moonstonehotels.com
SIC: 6531 Real estate managers

▲ = Import ▼ = Export
◆ = Import/Export

(P-14833)
MOSS MANAGEMENT SERVICES INC
15300 Ventura Blvd Ste 405 (91403-3103)
PHONE..............................818 990-5999
Cindy Gray, *Pr*
Chris Gray, *Ex VP*
Henriette Saffron, *CFO*
EMP: 124 **EST:** 2006
SALES (est): 5.48MM **Privately Held**
SIC: 6531 Real estate managers

(P-14834)
MSE ENTERPRISES INC (PA)
Also Called: Marshall S Ezralow & Assoc
23622 Calabasas Rd Ste 200 (91302-1549)
PHONE..............................818 223-3500
Marshall S Ezralow, *Pr*
EMP: 90 **EST:** 1974
SALES (est): 4.85MM
SALES (corp-wide): 4.85MM **Privately Held**
SIC: 6531 Real estate managers

(P-14835)
MURCOR INC
Also Called: Pcv Murcor Real Estate Svcs
740 Corporate Center Dr Ste 100 (91768)
PHONE..............................909 623-4001
Keith D Murray, *Pr*
Jon D Van Deuren, *
Richard J Barkley, *
Tim Scherf, *
Cindy Nasser, *
EMP: 225 **EST:** 1981
SALES (est): 26.2MM **Privately Held**
Web: www.pcvmurcor.com
SIC: 6531 Appraiser, real estate

(P-14836)
NMS PROPERTIES INC
10960 Wilshire Blvd (90024-3711)
PHONE..............................310 656-2700
Naum Shekhter, *CEO*
Margot Shekhter, *
Kurt Lietz, *
Scott Walter, *
Dino Ciarmoli, *
EMP: 95 **EST:** 1997
SALES (est): 11.27MM **Privately Held**
Web: www.nmsproperties.com
SIC: 6531 Real estate managers

(P-14837)
ON CENTRAL REALTY INC
1648 Colorado Blvd (90041-1403)
PHONE..............................323 543-8500
Vazrik Bonyadi, *Brnch Mgr*
EMP: 314
Web: www.coldwellbanker.com
SIC: 6531 6519 Real estate brokers and agents; Real property lessors, nec
PA: On Central Realty, Inc.
1625 W Glenoaks Blvd
Glendale CA

(P-14838)
PACIFIC MONARCH RESORTS INC (PA)
Also Called: Vacation Interval Realty
4000 Macarthur Blvd Ste 600 (92660-2558)
PHONE..............................949 609-2400
Mark D Post, *CEO*
Carlton Post, *
Nick Baldwin, *
EMP: 100 **EST:** 1987
SQ FT: 20,000
SALES (est): 79.14MM
SALES (corp-wide): 79.14MM **Privately Held**

Web: www.pacificmonarchresorts.com
SIC: 6531 7011 Time-sharing real estate sales, leasing and rentals; Vacation lodges

(P-14839)
PALANGING INTERNATIONAL INC
Also Called: Coldwell Banker Royal Realty
861 Anchorage Pl (91914-4535)
PHONE..............................619 948-2459
EMP: 82 **EST:** 1986
SQ FT: 2,568
SALES (est): 8.59MM **Privately Held**
Web: www.coldwellbanker.com
SIC: 6531 Real estate agent, residential

(P-14840)
PALM REALTY BOUTIQUE INC
401 Manhattan Beach Blvd Ste B (90266-5342)
PHONE..............................310 545-2490
Cary Brett Zebrowski, *Prin*
EMP: 89 **EST:** 2007
SALES (est): 3.08MM **Privately Held**
Web: www.prbhomes.com
SIC: 6531 Real estate brokers and agents

(P-14841)
PATHSTONE FAMILY OFFICE LLC
Also Called: Pathstone Federal Street
1900 Avenue Of The Stars Ste 970 (90067-4661)
PHONE..............................888 750-7284
Steve Braverman, *Prin*
EMP: 84
SALES (corp-wide): 4.91MM **Privately Held**
Web: www.pathstone.com
SIC: 6531 Appraiser, real estate
PA: Pathstone Family Office, Llc
50 Park Row W Ste 113
Providence RI
888 750-7284

(P-14842)
PCS PROPERTY MANAGMENT LLC
11859 Wilshire Blvd Ste 600 (90025-6616)
PHONE..............................310 231-1000
Michael Ross, *Brnch Mgr*
EMP: 141
Web: www.pcsnorthvalley.com
SIC: 6531 Real estate managers
PA: Pcs Property Managment Llc
4500 Woodman Ave Ofc
Sherman Oaks CA

(P-14843)
PHASE TEN STRATEGIC CORP
Also Called: Marketing Design Group
2445 5th Ave Ste 450 (92101-1670)
PHONE..............................619 298-1445
EMP: 83 **EST:** 2014
SALES (est): 4.74MM **Privately Held**
Web: www.mdg.agency
SIC: 6531 7311 Real estate agents and managers; Advertising agencies

(P-14844)
PINNACLE ESTATE PROPERTIES (PA)
Also Called: Pinnacle Escrow Company
9137 Reseda Blvd (91324-3039)
PHONE..............................818 993-4707
Dana Potter, *Pr*
Jeff Black, *
EMP: 120 **EST:** 1985
SQ FT: 13,000

SALES (est): 20.31MM
SALES (corp-wide): 20.31MM **Privately Held**
Web: www.pinnacleestate.com
SIC: 6531 Real estate agent, residential

(P-14845)
PRO GROUP INC
Also Called: Keller Williams Realtors
4160 Temescal Canyon Rd Ste 500 (92883-4625)
PHONE..............................951 271-3000
James Brown, *Pr*
Jim Brown, *
David Clark, *
Joseph Regan, *
EMP: 195 **EST:** 2003
SQ FT: 18,000
SALES (est): 9.71MM **Privately Held**
Web: www.pgescrow.com
SIC: 6531 Real estate agent, residential

(P-14846)
PROFESSIONAL CMNTY MGT CAL INC
11860 Pierce St Ste 100 (92505-5178)
PHONE..............................951 359-2840
EMP: 85
SALES (corp-wide): 49.19MM **Privately Held**
Web: www.associaonline.com
SIC: 6531 6514 Real estate managers; Dwelling operators, except apartments
PA: Professional Community Management Of California, Inc.
27051 Twne Cntre Dr Ste 2
Foothill Ranch CA
800 369-7260

(P-14847)
PROFESSIONAL CMNTY MGT CAL INC
Also Called: P C M
850 Country Club Dr (92220-5306)
PHONE..............................951 845-2191
Mike Bennett, *Mgr*
EMP: 322
SALES (corp-wide): 49.19MM **Privately Held**
Web: www.pcminternet.com
SIC: 6531 Real estate managers
PA: Professional Community Management Of California, Inc.
27051 Twne Cntre Dr Ste 2
Foothill Ranch CA
800 369-7260

(P-14848)
PROFESSIONAL CMNTY MGT CAL INC
Also Called: Pcm
24351 El Toro Rd (92637-4901)
PHONE..............................949 206-0580
Milt Johns, *Mgr*
EMP: 186
SALES (corp-wide): 49.19MM **Privately Held**
Web: www.lagunawoodsvillage.com
SIC: 6531 Real estate managers
PA: Professional Community Management Of California, Inc.
27051 Twne Cntre Dr Ste 2
Foothill Ranch CA
800 369-7260

(P-14849)
PROFESSIONAL CMNTY MGT CAL INC
Also Called: Leisure World Resales

23522 Paseo De Valencia (92653)
P.O. Box 2220 (92654-2220)
PHONE..............................949 597-4200
EMP: 148
SALES (corp-wide): 49.19MM **Privately Held**
Web: www.pcminternet.com
SIC: 6531 Real estate managers
PA: Professional Community Management Of California, Inc.
27051 Twne Cntre Dr Ste 2
Foothill Ranch CA
800 369-7260

(P-14850)
PROFESSIONAL CMNTY MGT CAL INC
Also Called: Professional Community MGT
906 Sycamore Ave Ste 210 (92081-7851)
P.O. Box 201 (92085-0201)
PHONE..............................760 918-8040
Jim Fraker, *VP*
EMP: 99
SALES (corp-wide): 49.19MM **Privately Held**
Web: www.pcminternet.com
SIC: 6531 Real estate managers
PA: Professional Community Management Of California, Inc.
27051 Twne Cntre Dr Ste 2
Foothill Ranch CA
800 369-7260

(P-14851)
PROLAND PROPERTY MANAGMENT LLC (PA)
Also Called: Hollingshead Management
2510 W 7th St 2nd Fl (90057-3802)
PHONE..............................213 738-8175
EMP: 80 **EST:** 1998
SQ FT: 5,000
SALES (est): 2.41MM
SALES (corp-wide): 2.41MM **Privately Held**
SIC: 6531 Real estate managers

(P-14852)
PROPERTY MANAGEMENT ASSOC INC (PA)
Also Called: Capital Commercial Property
6011 Bristol Pkwy (90230-6601)
PHONE..............................323 295-2000
Thomas Spear, *Pr*
Joshua Fein, *
Patrick Lacey, *
EMP: 130 **EST:** 1991
SQ FT: 6,500
SALES (est): 12.12MM **Privately Held**
Web: www.wemanageproperties.com
SIC: 6531 Real estate managers

(P-14853)
RA SNYDER PROPERTIES INC (PA)
2399 Camino Del Rio S Ste 200 (92108)
PHONE..............................619 297-0274
Richard Snyder, *Pr*
Marietta Robinson, *
EMP: 210 **EST:** 1987
SQ FT: 2,400
SALES (est): 16.76MM
SALES (corp-wide): 16.76MM **Privately Held**
Web: www.rasnyder.com
SIC: 6531 Real estate managers

(P-14854)
RAD DIVERSIFIED REIT INC
3110 E Guasti Rd Ste 300 (91761-1262)

PRODUCTS & SVCS

PHONE.................813 723-7348
Dutch Mendenhall, *CEO*
Taylor Green, *Prin*
EMP: 80 **EST:** 2017
SALES (est): 1.3MM **Privately Held**
SIC: 6531 Real estate agents and managers

(P-14855)
RE/MAX OF VALENCIA INC (PA)
Also Called: Re/Max
25101 The Old Rd (91381-2206)
PHONE.................661 255-2650
John O'hare, *Pr*
John Ohare, *Pr*
Alice O'hare, *VP*
EMP: 123 **EST:** 1985
SQ FT: 10,000
SALES (est): 7.32MM
SALES (corp-wide): 7.32MM **Privately Held**
Web: www.remax-valencia-ca.com
SIC: 6531 8742 Real estate agent, residential
; Real estate consultant

(P-14856)
REALSELECT INC
3063 W Chapman Ave Apt 6207
(92868-1738)
PHONE.................661 803-5188
Ashley Ivey, *Brnch Mgr*
EMP: 151
SALES (corp-wide): 9.88B **Publicly Held**
Web: www.realtor.com
SIC: 6531 Real estate brokers and agents
HQ: Realselect, Inc.
30700 Russell Ranch Rd
Westlake Village CA

(P-14857)
REMAX EXEC KING HARBOR
Also Called: Re/Max
23740 Hawthorne Blvd (90505-8206)
PHONE.................310 378-9889
Sandra Sanders, *Owner*
EMP: 95 **EST:** 2001
SALES (est): 2.45MM **Privately Held**
Web: www.cmiyukihomes.com
SIC: 6531 Real estate agent, residential

(P-14858)
REMAX OLSON & ASSOCIATES INC
Also Called: Re/Max
11141 Tampa Ave (91326-2254)
PHONE.................818 366-3300
Todd C Olson, *CEO*
Keith Myers, *Ex VP*
EMP: 193 **EST:** 1987
SQ FT: 30,000
SALES (est): 5.55MM **Privately Held**
Web: www.olsonmax.com
SIC: 6531 Real estate agent, residential

(P-14859)
REMN INC
3400 Central Ave Ste 330 (92506-2164)
PHONE.................951 697-8135
EMP: 94
Web: www.homebridge.com
SIC: 6531 6211 Real estate agents and
managers; Mortgages, buying and selling
PA: Remn , Inc
194 Wood Ave S Fl 9
Iselin NJ

(P-14860)
RGC SERVICES INC
Also Called: Re/Max
601 E Daily Dr Ste 102 (93010-5838)
PHONE.................805 484-1600

EMP: 89
Web: www.remax.com
SIC: 6531 Real estate agent, residential
PA: Rgc Services, Inc.
5720 Ralston St Ste 100
Ventura CA

(P-14861)
RGC SERVICES INC (PA)
Also Called: Re/Max
5720 Ralston St Ste 100 (93003-7845)
PHONE.................805 644-1242
Glenn Sipes, *Pr*
Michael Sipes, *
Jerry Beebe, *
EMP: 110 **EST:** 1994
SQ FT: 35,000
SALES (est): 24.56MM **Privately Held**
Web: www.remax.com
SIC: 6531 Real estate agent, residential

(P-14862)
ROMAN CTHLIC BSHP OF SAN DIEGO
Also Called: Holy Cross Cemetary
4470 Hilltop Dr (92102-3651)
PHONE.................619 264-3127
Mario Deblasio, *Brnch Mgr*
EMP: 102
SALES (corp-wide): 48.57MM **Privately Held**
Web: www.holycrosssd.com
SIC: 6531 Cemetery management service
PA: The Roman Catholic Bishop Of San Diego
3888 Paducah Dr
San Diego CA
858 490-8200

(P-14863)
ROW MANAGEMENT LTD INC
499 N Canon Dr (90210-4887)
PHONE.................310 887-3671
Kevin Shahin, *Brnch Mgr*
EMP: 305
SALES (corp-wide): 38.02MM **Privately Held**
Web: www.aboardtheworld.com
SIC: 6531 Real estate agents and managers
PA: Row Management Ltd. Inc.
1551 Sawgrs Corp Pkwy
Sunrise FL
954 538-8400

(P-14864)
SATELLITE MANAGEMENT CO (PA)
Also Called: Ccts
1010 E Chestnut Ave (92701-6497)
PHONE.................714 558-2411
Ronald Jensen, *CEO*
Mary E Conzelman, *
Helen M Jensen, *
EMP: 121 **EST:** 1963
SQ FT: 800
SALES (est): 21.42MM
SALES (corp-wide): 21.42MM **Privately Held**
Web: www.satellitemanagement.com
SIC: 6531 Real estate managers

(P-14865)
SOUTHERN CAL PIPE TRADES ADM
Also Called: Marina Village
1936 Quivira Way Bldg G (92109-8315)
PHONE.................619 224-3125
Gerald Pharest, *Genl Mgr*
EMP: 92

SALES (corp-wide): 24.6MM **Privately Held**
Web: www.scptac.org
SIC: 6531 Real estate agents and managers
PA: Southern California Pipe Trades
Administrative Corp
501 Shatto Pl Ste 500
Los Angeles CA
213 385-6161

(P-14866)
SPUS7 125 CAMBRIDGEPARK LP
515 S Flower St Ste 3100 (90071-2233)
PHONE.................213 683-4200
EMP: 113 **EST:** 2014
SALES (est): 1.88MM **Publicly Held**
SIC: 6531 Real estate agent, commercial
HQ: Cbre Global Value Investors, Llc
601 S Figueroa St Ste 49
Los Angeles CA
213 683-4200

(P-14867)
SPUS7 150 CAMBRIDGEPARK LP
515 S Flower St Ste 3100 (90071-2233)
PHONE.................213 683-4200
EMP: 141 **EST:** 2014
SALES (est): 4.27MM **Publicly Held**
SIC: 6531 Real estate agent, commercial
HQ: Cbre Global Value Investors, Llc
601 S Figueroa St Ste 49
Los Angeles CA
213 683-4200

(P-14868)
SRHT PROPERTY HOLDING LLC
Also Called: Skid Row Housing Trust
1317 E 7th St (90021-1101)
PHONE.................213 683-0522
Jerrick Holloway, *Dir*
EMP: 150 **EST:** 2005
SALES (est): 3.91MM **Privately Held**
Web: tpv.72e.myftpupload.com
SIC: 6531 Real estate managers

(P-14869)
STARPINT 1031 PROPERTY MGT LLC
Also Called: Vision Realty Managements
450 N Roxbury Dr Ste 1050 (90210-4235)
PHONE.................310 247-0550
EMP: 110 **EST:** 1997
SALES (est): 12.1MM **Privately Held**
Web: www.starpointproperties.com
SIC: 6531 Real estate agent, commercial

(P-14870)
STEADFAST MANAGEMENT CO INC (PA)
Also Called: Steadfast Companies
18100 Von Karman Ave Ste 500
(92612-0162)
PHONE.................949 748-3000
Rodney F Emery, *CEO*
Dinesh K Davar, *
Michael Brown, *
EMP: 82 **EST:** 2000
SALES (est): 67.86MM
SALES (corp-wide): 67.86MM **Privately Held**
Web: www.irtliving.com
SIC: 6531 Real estate managers

(P-14871)
TEAM BRDA RE SVCS - CLDWELL BN

16787 Bernardo Center Dr Ste 6
(92128-2504)
PHONE.................858 621-5284
EMP: 81 **EST:** 2019
SALES (est): 509.05K **Privately Held**
Web: www.teambourda.com
SIC: 6531 Real estate agent, residential

(P-14872)
TEN-X FINANCE INC
Also Called: Ten-X
15295 Alton Pkwy (92618-2315)
PHONE.................949 465-8523
Steve Jacobs, *CEO*
EMP: 111 **EST:** 2013
SALES (est): 529.03K
SALES (corp-wide): 2.18B **Publicly Held**
SIC: 6531 Real estate agents and managers
HQ: Ten-X, Inc.
15295 Alton Pkwy
Irvine CA
949 465-8523

(P-14873)
TERRA VISTA MANAGEMENT INC
Also Called: Terra Vista Management
2211 Pacific Beach Dr (92109-5626)
PHONE.................858 581-4200
Micheal Gelfand, *Brnch Mgr*
EMP: 459
SALES (corp-wide): 20.52MM **Privately Held**
Web: www.campland.com
SIC: 6531 7033 4225 4226 Real estate
managers; Trailer parks and campsites;
General warehousing and storage; Special
warehousing and storage, nec
PA: Vista Terra Management Inc
445 Marine View Ave # 110
Del Mar CA
323 954-5900

(P-14874)
THOMAS JAMES HOMES INC
26880 Aliso Viejo Pkwy Ste 100
(92656-2619)
PHONE.................949 424-2356
EMP: 135 **EST:** 2019
SALES (est): 9.66MM **Privately Held**
Web: www.tjh.com
SIC: 6531 Real estate brokers and agents

(P-14875)
THOMAS PROPERTIES GROUP INC
515 S Flower St Fl 6 (90071-2241)
PHONE.................213 613-1900
▲ **EMP:** 141
SIC: 6531 Real estate brokers and agents

(P-14876)
TRG INC
Also Called: Rosenthal Group, The
1350 Abbot Kinney Blvd # 101
(90291-3893)
P.O. Box 837 (90294-0837)
PHONE.................310 396-6750
EMP: 100
SALES (est): 3.32MM **Privately Held**
Web: www.trgnational.com
SIC: 6531 Real estate agents and managers

(P-14877)
TRIYAR SV LLC (PA)
10850 Wilshire Blvd Ste 1050 (90024-4305)
PHONE.................310 234-2888
EMP: 370 **EST:** 2012
SALES (est): 23.77MM **Privately Held**

Web: www.triyar.com
SIC: 6531 Buying agent, real estate

(P-14878)
TROOP REAL ESTATE INC
4165 E Thousand Oaks Blvd Ste 100
(91362)
PHONE..............................805 402-3028
Jeff Rosenblum, *Brnch Mgr*
EMP: 123
SALES (corp-wide): 25.09MM **Privately Held**
Web: www.suzankozman.com
SIC: 6531 Real estate agent, residential
PA: Troop Real Estate, Inc.
1308 Madera Rd Ste 8
Simi Valley CA
805 581-3200

(P-14879)
TROOP REAL ESTATE INC
586 W Main St (93060-3209)
PHONE..............................805 921-0030
Brian Troop, *Owner*
EMP: 101
SALES (corp-wide): 23.18MM **Privately Held**
Web: www.karentroop.com
SIC: 6531 Real estate agent, residential
PA: Troop Real Estate, Inc.
1308 Madera Rd Ste 8
Simi Valley CA
805 581-3200

(P-14880)
TROOP REAL ESTATE INC
236 W Ojai Ave Ste 100 (93023-3274)
PHONE..............................805 640-1440
Barry Snyder, *Brnch Mgr*
EMP: 117
SALES (corp-wide): 25.09MM **Privately Held**
Web: www.karentroop.com
SIC: 6531 Real estate agent, residential
PA: Troop Real Estate, Inc.
1308 Madera Rd Ste 8
Simi Valley CA
805 581-3200

(P-14881)
TROOP REAL ESTATE INC (PA)
1308 Madera Rd Ste 8 (93065-4044)
PHONE..............................805 581-3200
Brian C Troop, *CEO*
Laura Lee Anthony, *
Deborah Mccarthy, *COO*
EMP: 95 EST: 1987
SALES (est): 23.18MM
SALES (corp-wide): 23.18MM **Privately Held**
Web: www.joebarkey.net
SIC: 6531 Real estate agent, residential

(P-14882)
US REAL ESTATE SERVICES INC
Also Called: Res.net
27442 Portola Pkwy Ste 300 (92610-2823)
PHONE..............................949 598-9920
EMP: 90 EST: 1994
SQ FT: 37,000
SALES (est): 22.15MM **Privately Held**
Web: www.usres.com
SIC: 6531 Real estate brokers and agents

(P-14883)
WEST EDGE INC
Also Called: West Edge
1061 Tierra Del Rey (91910-7821)
PHONE..............................619 475-4095
EMP: 88

Web: www.coldwellbankerwesthomes.com
SIC: 6531 Real estate agent, residential
PA: West Edge, Inc.
4538 Bonita Rd
Bonita CA

(P-14884)
WESTERN NATIONAL SECURITIES (PA)
Also Called: Ramada By Wyndham
8 Executive Cir (92614-6746)
P.O. Box 19528 (92623-9528)
PHONE..............................949 862-6200
Michael K Hayde, *CEO*
David Stone, *Ch*
Jeff Scott, *CFO*
James Gilly, *
Jerry Lapointe, *
EMP: 120 EST: 1981
SQ FT: 35,000
SALES (est): 223.07MM
SALES (corp-wide): 223.07MM **Privately Held**
Web: www.wyndhamhotels.com
SIC: 6531 7011 Real estate managers; Hotels and motels

(P-14885)
WHV RESORT GROUP INC (HQ)
Also Called: Welk Resort Center
300 Rancheros Dr Ste 310 (92069-2969)
PHONE..............................760 652-4913
Larry Welk, *CEO*
EMP: 242 EST: 1999
SALES (est): 158.46MM **Publicly Held**
Web: www.kwgoldcoast.com
SIC: 6531 6552 7992 7011 Time-sharing real estate sales, leasing and rentals; Subdividers and developers, nec; Public golf courses; Hotels and motels
PA: Marriott Vacations Worldwide Corporation
7812 Palm Pkwy
Orlando FL

(P-14886)
WOODMAN REALTY INC
Also Called: Sierra Springs Apartments
26030 Base Line St Apt 97 (92410-7066)
PHONE..............................909 425-5324
Kelly Fox, *Mgr*
EMP: 241
SIC: 6531 Real estate agent, commercial
HQ: Woodman Realty Inc.
2016 Riverside Dr
Los Angeles CA

(P-14887)
YLOPO LLC
4712 Admiralty Way 548 (90292-6905)
PHONE..............................818 915-9150
Howard Tager, *CEO*
EMP: 147 EST: 2014
SALES (est): 14.31MM **Privately Held**
Web: www.ylopo.com
SIC: 6531 Real estate agents and managers

6541 Title Abstract Offices

(P-14888)
EQUITY TITLE COMPANY (DH)
801 N Brand Blvd Ste 400 (91203-3261)
PHONE..............................818 291-4400
TOLL FREE: 800
Jim Cossell, *Pr*
EMP: 80 EST: 1979
SALES (est): 8.73MM **Publicly Held**
Web: www.equitytitle.com

SIC: 6541 Title and trust companies
HQ: Anywhere Integrated Services Llc
1000 Bishops Gate Blvd # 100
Mount Laurel NJ

(P-14889)
FIDELITY NAT TITLE INSUR CO NY
Also Called: Fidelity National
950 Hampshire Rd (91361-2805)
PHONE..............................805 370-1400
EMP: 1406
Web: newyork.fntic.com
SIC: 6541 Title and trust companies
HQ: Fidelity National Title Insurance Co Of New York
1 Pak Ave Ste 1402
New York NY
904 854-8100

(P-14890)
FIRST AMERCN HM WARRANTY CORP
8511 Fallbrook Ave (91304-3244)
P.O. Box 8030 (91309-8030)
PHONE..............................818 781-5050
Jeff Powell, *COO*
EMP: 382 EST: 2009
SALES (est): 389.22MM **Publicly Held**
Web: www.firstam.com
SIC: 6541 Title and trust companies
HQ: First American Home Buyers Protection Corporation
8521 Fallbrook Ave
West Hills CA
818 781-5050

(P-14891)
FIRST AMERICAN TITLE COMPANY
1 First American Way (92707-5913)
PHONE..............................714 250-3109
EMP: 6000 EST: 1964
SALES (est): 167.12MM **Privately Held**
Web: www.firstam.com
SIC: 6541 Title and trust companies

(P-14892)
GREENHEDGE ESCROW
2015 Manhattan Beach Blvd (90278-1226)
PHONE..............................310 640-3040
David Wehrly, *Prin*
EMP: 239 EST: 2016
SALES (est): 2.38MM
SALES (corp-wide): 147.22MM **Privately Held**
Web: www.greenhedgeescrow.com
SIC: 6541 Title and trust companies
PA: Wedgewood Inc.
2015 Manhattan Beach Blvd # 102
Redondo Beach CA
310 640-3070

(P-14893)
GUARDIAN TITLE COMPANY
300 Commerce (92602-1308)
PHONE..............................949 495-9306
E Neil Gulley, *CEO*
James Kozel, *
Gregory Blackburn, *
EMP: 100 EST: 1975
SALES (est): 21.17K **Publicly Held**
SIC: 6541 Title and trust companies
HQ: Nrt Commercial Utah Llc
175 Park Ave
Madison NJ

(P-14894)
PROPERTY INSIGHT LLC
2510 Redhill Ave (92705-5542)
PHONE..............................877 747-2537
John Walsh, *Managing Member*
Ron Sree, *
EMP: 4197 EST: 2004
SALES (est): 1.14MM
SALES (corp-wide): 7.29B **Publicly Held**
Web: www.propertyinsight.biz
SIC: 6541 Title search companies
HQ: Black Knight Real Estate Data Solutions, Llc
121 Theory Ste 100
Irvine CA
626 808-9000

(P-14895)
STEWART TITLE CALIFORNIA INC
525 N Brand Blvd Ste 200 (91203-3993)
PHONE..............................818 502-2700
Steve Lessack, *Group President*
EMP: 125
SALES (corp-wide): 3.07B **Publicly Held**
Web: www.stewart.com
SIC: 6541 Title and trust companies
HQ: Stewart Title Of California, Inc.
7676 Hazard Center Dr # 1400
San Diego CA
619 692-1600

(P-14896)
TITLE RESOURCE GROUP LLC
Also Called: TITLE RESOURCE GROUP LLC
801 N Brand Blvd (91203-1237)
PHONE..............................818 291-4400
EMP: 85
Web: www.anywhereis.re
SIC: 6541 Title and trust companies
HQ: Anywhere Integrated Services Llc
1000 Bishops Gate Blvd # 100
Mount Laurel NJ

6552 Subdividers And Developers, Nec

(P-14897)
ARCHIPELAGO DEVELOPMENT INC
P.O. Box 7050 (92067-7050)
PHONE..............................858 699-6272
Mark Edward Benjamin, *CEO*
EMP: 100 EST: 2008
SALES (est): 4.94MM **Privately Held**
SIC: 6552 Subdividers and developers, nec

(P-14898)
CENTURY PACIFIC REALTY CORP
9401 Wilshire Blvd Ste 1250 (90212-2926)
PHONE..............................310 729-9922
Irwin J Deutch, *Pr*
Charles L Schwennessen, *
Eric Maman, *
EMP: 250 EST: 1987
SQ FT: 3,500
SALES (est): 5.28MM **Privately Held**
SIC: 6552 Subdividers and developers, nec

(P-14899)
GOLDRICH & KEST INDUSTRIES LLC (PA)
5150 Overland Ave (90230-4914)
P.O. Box 3623 (90231-3623)
PHONE..............................310 204-2050
EMP: 750 EST: 1957

PRODUCTS & SVCS

SQ FT: 5,000
SALES (est): 46.55MM
SALES (corp-wide): 46.55MM **Privately Held**
Web: www.goldrichkest.com
SIC: 6552 Subdividers and developers, nec

(P-14900)
GOLDRICH KEST HIRSCH STERN LLC (PA)
5150 Overland Ave (90230-4914)
P.O. Box 3623 (90231-3623)
PHONE.................................310 204-2050
Jona Goldrich, *Pr*
Sol Kest, *
EMP: 250 **EST:** 1963
SQ FT: 5,000
SALES (est): 34.88MM
SALES (corp-wide): 34.88MM **Privately Held**
Web: www.goldrichkest.com
SIC: 6552 Land subdividers and developers, commercial

(P-14901)
KING VENTURES
285 Bridge St (93401-5510)
PHONE.................................805 544-4444
John E King, *Owner*
EMP: 126 **EST:** 1977
SQ FT: 10,000
SALES (est): 7.22MM **Privately Held**
Web: www.kingventures.net
SIC: 6552 6512 Land subdividers and developers, commercial; Commercial and industrial building operation

(P-14902)
L AND W DEVELOPERS LLC
Also Called: Contractor
1635 Centinela Ave (90302-1056)
PHONE.................................310 654-8428
Terry Williams, *Managing Member*
EMP: 25 **EST:** 2017
SALES (est): 1.06MM **Privately Held**
SIC: 6552 0782 1389 Subdividers and developers, nec; Landscape contractors; Construction, repair, and dismantling services

(P-14903)
LINCOLN PRPRTY NO 2087 LTD PRT
7777 Center Ave Ste 150 (92647-3096)
PHONE.................................214 740-3300
Mack Pogue, *Ch Bd*
EMP: 211 **EST:** 2003
SALES (est): 442.68K
SALES (corp-wide): 1.32B **Privately Held**
SIC: 6552 6531 Land subdividers and developers, commercial; Real estate managers
PA: Lincoln Property Company
2000 Mckinney Ave # 1000
Dallas TX
214 740-3300

(P-14904)
LOWE ENTERPRISES RE GROUP
Also Called: Lowe Enterprises
11777 San Vicente Blvd Ste 900 (90049-5084)
PHONE.................................310 820-6661
Bob Lowe, *Pr*
EMP: 219 **EST:** 1994
SQ FT: 10,000
SALES (est): 4.51MM
SALES (corp-wide): 367.25MM **Privately Held**
Web: www.lowe-re.com

SIC: 6552 6531 Land subdividers and developers, commercial; Real estate managers
PA: Lowe Enterprises, Inc.
11777 San Vicente Blvd # 900
Los Angeles CA
310 820-6661

(P-14905)
LPC COMMERCIAL SERVICES INC
Also Called: LPC COMMERCIAL SERVICES, INC.
915 Wilshire Blvd Ste 250 (90017-3409)
PHONE.................................213 362-9080
David Binswangar, *Brnch Mgr*
EMP: 191
SALES (corp-wide): 1.32B **Privately Held**
Web: www.lpc.com
SIC: 6552 6531 Land subdividers and developers, commercial; Real estate brokers and agents
HQ: Lpc Commercial Services Llc
2000 Mckinney Ave # 1000
Dallas TX

(P-14906)
NATIONAL CMNTY RENAISSANCE CAL (PA)
9692 Haven Ave Ste 100 (91730-0101)
PHONE.................................909 483-2444
Steven J Pontell, *CEO*
Sebastiano Sterpa, *
Orlando Cabrera, *
Tracy Thomas, *
Doretta Bryan, *
EMP: 100 **EST:** 1992
SALES (est): 47.76MM **Privately Held**
Web: www.nationalcore.org
SIC: 6552 Subdividers and developers, nec

(P-14907)
NATIONAL CMNTY RENAISSANCE CAL
8265 Aspen St Ste 100 (91730-3291)
PHONE.................................619 223-9222
Rebecca Clark, *Mgr*
EMP: 231
Web: www.nationalcore.org
SIC: 6552 Subdividers and developers, nec
PA: National Community Renaissance Of California
9692 Haven Ave Ste 100
Rancho Cucamonga CA

(P-14908)
OLSON COMPANY LLC (PA)
Also Called: Olson Homes
3010 Old Ranch Pkwy Ste 100 (90740-2750)
PHONE.................................562 596-4770
EMP: 99 **EST:** 2014
SALES (est): 24.12MM
SALES (corp-wide): 24.12MM **Privately Held**
Web: www.olsonhomes.com
SIC: 6552 Subdividers and developers, nec

(P-14909)
PANATTONI DEVELOPMENT CO INC (PA)
2442 Dupont Dr (92612-1523)
PHONE.................................916 381-1561
Carl Panattoni, *Ch*
Dudley Mitchell, *
Jacklyn Shelby, *
Greg Thurman, *
Adon Panattoni, *
EMP: 90 **EST:** 1986

SALES (est): 36.08MM
SALES (corp-wide): 36.08MM **Privately Held**
Web: www.panattoni.com
SIC: 6552 Subdividers and developers, nec

(P-14910)
SHAPELL INDUSTRIES LLC (HQ)
Also Called: S & S Construction Co
8383 Wilshire Blvd Ste 700 (90211-2425)
PHONE.................................323 655-7330
EMP: 100 **EST:** 1955
SQ FT: 25,000
SALES (est): 43.64MM
SALES (corp-wide): 10.28B **Publicly Held**
SIC: 6552 6514 1522 Land subdividers and developers, residential; Residential building, four or fewer units: operation; Residential construction, nec
PA: Toll Brothers, Inc.
1140 Virginia Dr
Fort Washington PA
215 938-8000

(P-14911)
SILVER SADDLE RANCH & CLUB INC
Also Called: McQ
7635 N San Fernando Rd (91505-1073)
PHONE.................................818 768-8808
Thomas Maney, *Pr*
Justin Child, *
Terry Hansen, *Stockholder*
EMP: 100 **EST:** 1986
SQ FT: 5,500
SALES (est): 4.74MM **Privately Held**
SIC: 6552 7041 Land subdividers and developers, residential; Residence club, organization

(P-14912)
STEELWAVE LLC
4553 Glencoe Ave Ste 300 (90292-7914)
PHONE.................................310 821-1111
EMP: 578
SALES (corp-wide): 24.17MM **Privately Held**
Web: www.steelwavellc.com
SIC: 6552 Land subdividers and developers, commercial
PA: Steelwave, Llc
999 Baker Way Ste 200
San Mateo CA
650 571-2200

(P-14913)
VOIT REAL ESTATE SERVICES LLC
2020 Main St (92614-8200)
PHONE.................................949 851-5100
Robert D Voit, *Managing Member*
Robert Voit, *Pt*
EMP: 223 **EST:** 2007
SALES (est): 13.07MM **Privately Held**
Web: www.voitco.com
SIC: 6552 6519 6531 Subdividers and developers, nec; Real property lessors, nec ; Real estate agents and managers

(P-14914)
WEBB DEL CALIFORNIA CORP (DH)
39755 Berkey Dr (92211-1106)
PHONE.................................760 772-5300
Nancy E Abbott, *Prin*
EMP: 300 **EST:** 1965
SQ FT: 14,000
SALES (est): 46.74MM
SALES (corp-wide): 16.23B **Publicly Held**

SIC: 6552 Subdividers and developers, nec
HQ: Pulte Home Company, Llc
3350 Peachtree Rd Ne # 15
Atlanta GA
248 647-2750

6553 Cemetery Subdividers And Developers

(P-14915)
FOREST LAWN CO
1712 S Glendale Ave (91205-3320)
PHONE.................................818 241-4151
John Llewellyn, *Pr*
EMP: 150 **EST:** 1906
SQ FT: 50,000
SALES (est): 17.35MM **Privately Held**
Web: www.forestlawn.com
SIC: 6553 Real property subdividers and developers, cemetery lots only

(P-14916)
INGLEWOOD PARK CEMETERY (PA)
720 E Florence Ave (90301-1482)
P.O. Box 6042 (90312-6042)
PHONE.................................310 412-6500
Daniel Villa, *Pr*
Cheryl Lewis, *
David Wharmby, *
Kevin Brown, *
Chris Winners, *
EMP: 152 **EST:** 1905
SQ FT: 14,000
SALES (est): 19.11MM
SALES (corp-wide): 19.11MM **Privately Held**
Web: www.inglewoodparkcemetery.com
SIC: 6553 Cemeteries, real estate operation

(P-14917)
ROMAN CTHLIC DIOCESE OF ORANGE
Also Called: Holy Sepulcher Cemetery
7845 E Santiago Canyon Rd (92869-1830)
PHONE.................................714 532-6551
Mike Wessner, *Dir*
EMP: 125
SALES (corp-wide): 92.62MM **Privately Held**
Web: www.occem.org
SIC: 6553 Cemeteries, real estate operation
PA: The Roman Catholic Diocese Of Orange
13280 Chapman Ave
Garden Grove CA
714 282-3000

(P-14918)
ROSE HILLS COMPANY (DH)
Also Called: Rose Hills Mem Pk & Mortuary
3888 Workman Mill Rd (90601-1626)
PHONE.................................562 699-0921
TOLL FREE: 800
Dennis Poulsen, *Ch Bd*
Kenton Woods, *
Mary Guzman, *
EMP: 595 **EST:** 1996
SQ FT: 143,950
SALES (est): 77.92MM
SALES (corp-wide): 4.11B **Publicly Held**
Web: www.rosehills.com
SIC: 6553 Real property subdividers and developers, cemetery lots only
HQ: Rose Hills Holdings Corp.
3888 Workman Mill Rd
Whittier CA
562 699-0921

(P-14919)
ROSE HILLS HOLDINGS CORP
(HQ)
Also Called: Rose Hills Mem Pk & Mortuary
3888 Workman Mill Rd (90601-1626)
PHONE...................................562 699-0921
Pat Monroe, *CEO*
EMP: 500 EST: 1996
SQ FT: 143,950
SALES (est): 87.18MM
SALES (corp-wide): 4.11B Publicly Held
Web: www.rosehills.com
SIC: 6553 Cemeteries, real estate operation
PA: Service Corporation International
   1929 Allen Pkwy
   Houston TX
   713 522-5141

6712 Bank Holding Companies

(P-14920)
BANAMEX USA BANCORP (DH)
787 W 5th St (90071-2003)
PHONE...................................310 203-3440
Salvador Villar Junior, *Pr*
Francisco Moreno Senior, *VP*
▲ **EMP: 210 EST: 1977**
SALES (est): 96.96MM
SALES (corp-wide): 101.08B Publicly Held
Web: www.citigroup.com
SIC: 6712 6029 6022 Bank holding companies; Commercial banks, nec; State commercial banks
HQ: Banco Nacional De Mexico, S.A., Integrante Del Grupo Financiero Banamex
   Isabel La Catolica No. 44
   Mexico CMX

6719 Holding Companies, Nec

(P-14921)
AME-GYU CO LTD
20000 Mariner Ave Ste 500 (90503-1670)
PHONE...................................310 214-9572
Ryo Tozu, *CEO*
Hidekazu Seo, *
Hiratsugu Aiba, *
EMP: 1100 EST: 2016
SIC: 6719 5812 Investment holding companies, except banks; Japanese restaurant

(P-14922)
AMERICAN ACADEMIC HLTH SYS LLC
222 N Pacific Coast Hwy Ste 900 (90245-5648)
PHONE...................................310 414-7200
EMP: 2850 EST: 2017
SALES (est): 60.53MM Privately Held
Web: www.americanacademic.com
SIC: 6719 8062 Investment holding companies, except banks; General medical and surgical hospitals

(P-14923)
ASP HENRY HOLDINGS INC
999 N Pacific Coast Hwy Ste 800 (90245)
PHONE...................................310 955-9200
Frank Ready, *CEO*
EMP: 600 EST: 2016
SALES (corp-wide): 6.59B Publicly Held

SIC: 6719 2952 Investment holding companies, except banks; Roof cement: asphalt, fibrous, or plastic
PA: Carlisle Companies Incorporated
   16430 N Scottsdale Rd
   Scottsdale AZ
   480 781-5000

(P-14924)
BETHAR CORPORATION
17625 Railroad St (91748-1110)
P.O. Box 8445 (91748-0445)
▲ **EMP: 180 EST: 1945**
SQ FT: 80,000
SIC: 6719 Investment holding companies, except banks

(P-14925)
BRIDGE GROUP HH INC
3636 Nobel Dr Ste 450 (92122-1062)
PHONE...................................858 455-5000
Jason Murray, *CEO*
EMP: 126 EST: 2016
SIC: 6719 Investment holding companies, except banks

(P-14926)
CCC PROPERTY HOLDINGS LLC
Also Called: Contractors Cargo Company
7223 Alondra Blvd (90723-3901)
P.O. Box 5290 (90224-5290)
PHONE...................................310 609-1957
Gerald Wheeler, *Ch Bd*
Kim Dorio, *
Carla Ann Wheeler, *
Jerry Wheeler, *
EMP: 121 EST: 2009
SIC: 6719 Investment holding companies, except banks

(P-14927)
DESSER HOLDING COMPANY LLC (HQ)
Also Called: Desser Tire & Rubber Co.
6900 W Acco St (90640-5435)
P.O. Box 1028 (90640-1028)
PHONE...................................323 721-4900
Christopher Lawler, *Ch*
Steven D Chlavin, *
Joseph Heinmiller, *
EMP: 30 EST: 2014
SALES (est): 110.7MM
SALES (corp-wide): 949.76MM Publicly Held
Web: www.desser.com
SIC: 6719 3011 3691 Investment holding companies, except banks; Airplane tires, pneumatic; Batteries, rechargeable
PA: Vse Corporation
   6348 Walker Ln
   Alexandria VA
   703 960-4600

(P-14928)
DMS UE ACQSITION HOLDINGS INC
225 Broadway Ste 2200 (92101-5011)
PHONE...................................800 466-4178
Joe Marinucci, *CEO*
EMP: 100 EST: 2019
SIC: 6719 7311 7371 Investment holding companies, except banks; Advertising consultant; Computer software development

(P-14929)
FORTRESS HOLDING GROUP LLC
5500 E Santa Ana Canyon Rd Ste 220 (92807-3154)

PHONE...................................714 202-8710
Luis Perez, *Ch*
Adam Forbs, *Pr*
EMP: 90 EST: 2009
SIC: 6719 Investment holding companies, except banks

(P-14930)
GATEWAY FRESH LLC
Also Called: Baja Fresh
3660 Grand Ave Ste A (91709-1477)
P.O. Box 1456 (91709-0049)
PHONE...................................951 378-5439
FAX: 909 548-6602
EMP: 190
SQ FT: 5,000
SIC: 6719 Investment holding companies, except banks

(P-14931)
GH GROUP INC
Also Called: Glass House Group
3645 Long Beach Blvd (90807-4018)
PHONE...................................562 264-5078
Kyle Kazan, *CEO*
Graham Farrar, *
Daryl Kato, *
Derrek Higgins, *
EMP: 250 EST: 2006
Web: www.gh-group.com
SIC: 6719 Investment holding companies, except banks

(P-14932)
HCO HOLDING I CORPORATION (HQ)
999 N Pacific Coast Hwy Ste 800 (90245-2715)
PHONE...................................323 583-5000
Mike Kenny, *
Brian C Strauss, *Parent Chief Executive Officer*
Dori M Reap, *
James F Barry, *
Robert D Armstrong, *Senior Vice President Human Resources*
◆ **EMP: 100 EST: 2005**
SALES (est): 249.72MM
SALES (corp-wide): 254.17MM Privately Held
SIC: 6719 Investment holding companies, except banks
PA: Hnc Parent, Inc.
   999 N Pacific Coast Hwy # 80
   El Segundo CA
   310 955-9200

(P-14933)
HIRSCH3667 CORP
5700 Hannum Ave Ste 250 (90230-6548)
PHONE...................................310 641-6690
EMP: 140
SIC: 6719 Investment holding companies, except banks

(P-14934)
KELLY TOYS HOLDINGS LLC
Also Called: Kelly Toys
4811 S Alameda St (90058-2805)
PHONE...................................323 923-1300
Jonathan Kelly, *Pr*
Matthew Siesel, *
David Neustein, *
EMP: 100 EST: 2020
SQ FT: 150,000
SALES (corp-wide): 302.09B Publicly Held
Web: www.squishmallows.com

SIC: 6719 5092 Investment holding companies, except banks; Toys and hobby goods and supplies
HQ: Jazwares, Llc
   1067 Shotgun Rd
   Sunrise FL

(P-14935)
MLIM HOLDINGS LLC
350 Camino De La Reina (92108-3003)
PHONE...................................619 299-3131
Douglas Manchester, *Ch*
John Lynch, *Vice Chairman*
EMP: 768 EST: 2011
SIC: 6719 Investment holding companies, except banks

(P-14936)
N2 ACQUISITION COMPANY INC
Also Called: N2 Imaging Systems
14440 Myford Rd (92606-1001)
PHONE...................................714 942-3563
Tony Bacarella, *Ch*
Timothy Boyle, *CFO*
EMP: 92 EST: 2019
SIC: 6719 Investment holding companies, except banks

(P-14937)
NRP HOLDING CO INC (PA)
1 Mauchly (92618-2305)
PHONE...................................949 583-1000
Jeffrey P Frieden, *Pr*
Robert Friedman, *
EMP: 200 EST: 2003
SQ FT: 40,000
SALES (est): 44.87MM Privately Held
Web: www.auction.com
SIC: 6719 Investment holding companies, except banks

(P-14938)
PLATINUM GROUP COMPANIES INC (PA)
Also Called: Top Finance Company
22560 La Quilla Dr (91311-1221)
P.O. Box 280518 (91328-0518)
PHONE...................................818 721-3800
David Mandel, *CEO*
Sandy To, *
EMP: 125 EST: 2005
SQ FT: 20,000
SALES (est): 39.69MM Privately Held
SIC: 6719 Personal holding companies, except banks

(P-14939)
PROJECT SKYLINE INTERMEDIATE H
360 N Crescent Dr Bldg S (90210-2529)
PHONE...................................310 712-1850
Tom Gores, *Pr*
EMP: 2020 EST: 2009
SIC: 6719 Investment holding companies, except banks

(P-14940)
PROSPECT MORTGAGE LLC
EMP: 1700 EST: 1999
SIC: 6719 Investment holding companies, except banks

(P-14941)
R AND I HOLDINGS INC
2145 Dashwood St (90712)
PHONE...................................562 483-0577
Susan Gerros, *Pr*
Jason Gerros, *
EMP: 47 EST: 2016

PRODUCTS & SVCS

SIC: 6719 5084 3799 Investment holding companies, except banks; Pneumatic tools and equipment; Trailers and trailer equipment

(P-14942)
RON RICK HOLDINGS MONTANA LLC
80795 Vista Bonita Trl (92253-7525)
PHONE...............................406 493-5606
Rick Kerscher, *Pr*
Rick Kerscherm, *Pr*
EMP: 100 **EST:** 2007
SQ FT: 7,000
SIC: 6719 Personal holding companies, except banks

(P-14943)
RSG GROUP USA INC
Also Called: Gold's Gym
7007 Romaine St Ste 101 (90038-2439)
PHONE...............................214 574-4653
Sebastian Schoepe, *CEO*
EMP: 2000 **EST:** 2020
SALES (corp-wide): 242.12K **Privately Held**
Web: www.goldsgym.com
SIC: 6719 7991 Investment holding companies, except banks; Physical fitness facilities
HQ: Rsg Group Gmbh
Tannenberg 4
Schlusselfeld BY
308 379-5500

(P-14944)
SHRYNE GROUP INC
728 E Commercial St (90012-3412)
PHONE...............................323 614-4558
Jon Avidor, *CEO*
Tak Sato, *
Elisabeth Baron, *CMO**
John Malone, *
Cary Berger, *CLO**
EMP: 2500 **EST:** 2019
Web: www.shrynegroup.com
SIC: 6719 Holding companies, nec

(P-14945)
SKEFFINGTON ENTERPRISES INC
2200 S Yale St (92704-4427)
PHONE...............................714 540-1700
William J Skeffington, *Pr*
John Skeffington, *
EMP: 100 **EST:** 1951
SQ FT: 180,000
Web: www.bensasphalt.com
SIC: 6719 Personal holding companies, except banks

(P-14946)
SOLARIANT CAPITAL LLC
301 N Lake Ave Ste 950 (91101-5105)
PHONE...............................626 544-0279
Daniel Kim, *Managing Member*
EMP: 180 **EST:** 2012
Web: www.solariantcapital.com
SIC: 6719 1629 6722 Investment holding companies, except banks; Power plant construction; Management investment, open-end

(P-14947)
STANTEC HOLDINGS DEL III INC
Also Called: Stantec Oil and Gas
5500 Ming Ave Ste 300 (93309-4683)
PHONE...............................661 396-3770
Robert Gomes, *Pr*

EMP: 460 **EST:** 2005
SALES (corp-wide): 4.23B **Privately Held**
SIC: 6719 Investment holding companies, except banks
PA: Stantec Inc
10220 103 Ave Nw Ste 300
Edmonton AB
866 782-6832

(P-14948)
SWDS HOLDINGS INC
Also Called: Swds
8659 Research Dr (92618-4204)
PHONE...............................800 395-5277
Vernon Leake, *CEO*
Michael Okada, *
Aaron Lodge, *
Jill Zack, *
EMP: 317 **EST:** 1987
Web: www.acrisurepg.com
SIC: 6719 Holding companies, nec

(P-14949)
TRANSOM POST MIDCO LLC ✪
100 N Pacific Coast Hwy # 17 (90245-4359)
PHONE...............................312 254-3300
Russell Roenick, *Managing Member*
EMP: 200 **EST:** 2022
SIC: 6719 Personal holding companies, except banks

(P-14950)
TYDG ENTERPRISES INC
10232 Palm Dr (90670-3368)
PHONE...............................562 903-9030
Michael Rashtchi, *CEO*
George Abi-aad, *Pr*
Marianne Abi-aad, *Ex VP*
Johnathan Soon, *VP Opers*
▲ **EMP:** 95 **EST:** 1985
SQ FT: 65,000
Web: www.royalcorporation.com
SIC: 6719 Investment holding companies, except banks

(P-14951)
WILBUR CURTIS CO INC
6913 W Acco St (90640-5403)
PHONE...............................800 421-6150
Ray Peden, *CEO*
Michael A Curtis, *Ex VP*
Norman Fujitaki, *CFO*
Joe Laws, *COO*
Shubham Kumar, *Finance*
◆ **EMP:** 280 **EST:** 1941
SQ FT: 175,000
SALES (corp-wide): 2.67MM **Privately Held**
Web: www.wilburcurtis.com
SIC: 6719 3589 Investment holding companies, except banks; Coffee brewing equipment
HQ: Groupe Seb Retailing
112 Chemin Du Moulin Carron
Ecully

(P-14952)
YF ART HOLDINGS GP LLC
9130 W Sunset Blvd (90069-3110)
PHONE...............................678 441-1400
Fred Boehler, *Pr*
EMP: 10600 **EST:** 2014
SIC: 6719 Investment holding companies, except banks

6722 Management Investment, Open-ended

(P-14953)
ABSOLUTE RETURN PORTFOLIO
700 Newport Center Dr (92660-6307)
P.O. Box 9000 (92658-9030)
PHONE...............................800 800-7646
EMP: 1582 **EST:** 2015
SALES (est): 2.41MM
SIC: 6722 Money market mutual funds
HQ: Pacific Life Fund Advisors Llc
700 Newport Center Dr
Newport Beach CA

(P-14954)
ALLIANCEBERNSTEIN LP
Also Called: Bernstein
1999 Avenue Of The Stars Ste 2150 (90067-6022)
PHONE...............................310 286-6000
Alan D Croll, *Brnch Mgr*
EMP: 123
SALES (corp-wide): 14.02B **Publicly Held**
Web: www.alliancebernstein.com
SIC: 6722 Money market mutual funds
HQ: Alliancebernstein L.P.
501 Commerce St
Nashville TN
212 969-1000

(P-14955)
ALTURA HOLDINGS LLC
1335 S Acacia Ave (92831-5315)
PHONE...............................714 948-8400
EMP: 300 **EST:** 2011
SALES (est): 26.57MM **Privately Held**
SIC: 6722 Management investment, open-end
PA: Silver Oak Services Partners, Llc
1560 Sherman Ave Ste 1200
Evanston IL

(P-14956)
AMERICAN FUNDS DISTRS INC (DH)
333 S Hope St Ste Levb (90071-3003)
PHONE...............................213 486-9200
Michael Johnston, *Ch Bd*
Larry Clemmensen, *
J Kelly Webb, *
Dorine Darnell, *
EMP: 116 **EST:** 1972
SQ FT: 6,000
SALES (est): 111.21MM
SALES (corp-wide): 5.43B **Privately Held**
Web: www.capitalgroup.com
SIC: 6722 Mutual fund sales, on own account
HQ: Capital Research And Management Company
333 S Hope St Fl 55
Los Angeles CA
213 486-9200

(P-14957)
AMERICAN MUTUAL FUND
333 S Hope St Fl 51 (90071-1420)
PHONE...............................213 486-9200
Jonathan B Lovelace Junior, *Ch Bd*
James K Dunton, *
James W Ratzlaff, *
Robert G O'donnell, *Pr*
Joyce Gordon, *
EMP: 200 **EST:** 1949
SQ FT: 5,000
SALES (est): 2.09B **Privately Held**

SIC: 6722 Money market mutual funds

(P-14958)
ARES MANAGEMENT CORPORATION (PA)
Also Called: Ares
2000 Avenue Of The Stars Fl 12 (90067-4733)
PHONE...............................310 201-4100
Michael J Arougheti, *Pr*
Antony P Ressler, *Ex Ch Bd*
Jarrod Phillips, *CFO*
Ryan Berry, *Chief Marketing*
Naseem Sagati Aghili, *Corporate Secretary*
EMP: 102 **EST:** 1997
SALES (est): 3.06B
SALES (corp-wide): 3.06B **Publicly Held**
Web: www.aresmgmt.com
SIC: 6722 6282 Management investment, open-end; Investment advice

(P-14959)
BELLOTA US CORP
22440 Temescal Canyon Rd (92883-4200)
PHONE...............................951 737-6515
▲ **EMP:** 150
SIC: 6722 Money market mutual funds

(P-14960)
CARMEL PARTNERS LLC
530 Wilshire Blvd Ste 203 (90401-1427)
PHONE...............................916 479-5286
EMP: 108
SALES (corp-wide): 71.55MM **Privately Held**
Web: www.carmelpartners.com
SIC: 6722 Management investment, open-end
HQ: Carmel Partners, Llc
1000 Sansome St Fl 1
San Francisco CA
415 273-2900

(P-14961)
CAUSEWAY CAPITAL MGT LLC
11111 Santa Monica Blvd Fl 15 (90025-3349)
PHONE...............................310 231-6100
Gracie Fermelia, *Managing Member*
Sarah Ketterer, *
Harry Hartford, *
EMP: 109 **EST:** 2001
SALES (est): 34.35MM **Privately Held**
Web: www.causewaycap.com
SIC: 6722 Money market mutual funds

(P-14962)
CLEARLAKE CAPITAL GROUP LP (PA)
233 Wilshire Blvd Ste 800 (90401-1207)
PHONE...............................310 400-8800
EMP: 258 **EST:** 2006
SALES (est): 3.89B **Privately Held**
Web: www.clearlake.com
SIC: 6722 Management investment, open-end

(P-14963)
GUGGENHEIM PRTNERS INV MGT LLC
100 Wilshire Blvd 5th Fl (90401-1110)
PHONE...............................310 576-1270
Robert Daviduk, *Dir*
EMP: 111
SALES (est): 27.56MM
SALES (corp-wide): 1.8B **Privately Held**
Web: www.guggenheimpartners.com
SIC: 6722 Money market mutual funds
PA: Guggenheim Partners, Llc
330 Madison Ave Rm 201

New York NY
212 739-0700

(P-14964)
LOS ANGELES CAPITAL MGT LLC (PA)
Also Called: La Capital
11150 Santa Monica Blvd Ste 200
(90025-0418)
PHONE..............................310 479-9998
Thomas Stevens, *Ch Bd*
Thomas D Stevens, *
Hal Reynolds, *
David Borger, *
Stuart Matsuda, *
EMP: 80 **EST:** 2002
SQ FT: 10,192
SALES (est): 105.64K
SALES (corp-wide): 105.64K **Privately Held**
Web: www.lacapm.com
SIC: 6722 8741 8211 6282 Management investment, open-end; Management services; Elementary and secondary schools; Investment advice

(P-14965)
MALK PARTNERS
7911 Herschel Ave Ste 400 (92037-4412)
PHONE..............................858 914-1125
Max Hong, *CEO*
EMP: 95 **EST:** 2017
SALES (est): 2.31MM **Privately Held**
Web: www.malk.com
SIC: 6722 Management investment, open-end

(P-14966)
OAKTREE HOLDINGS INC
333 S Grand Ave Fl 28 (90071)
PHONE..............................213 830-6300
EMP: 993 **EST:** 2014
SALES (est): 2.14MM **Privately Held**
SIC: 6722 Management investment, open-end
PA: Oaktree Capital Group Holdings, L.P.
333 S Grand Ave Fl 28
Los Angeles CA

(P-14967)
OAKTREE REAL ESTATE OPPRTNTIES
333 S Grand Ave Fl 28 (90071-1530)
PHONE..............................213 830-6300
EMP: 745 **EST:** 2014
SALES (est): 9.2MM **Privately Held**
Web: www.oaktreecapital.com
SIC: 6722 Money market mutual funds
PA: Oaktree Capital Group Holdings, L.P.
333 S Grand Ave Fl 28
Los Angeles CA

(P-14968)
OAKTREE STRATEGIC INCOME LLC
333 S Grand Ave Fl 28 (90071-1530)
PHONE..............................213 830-6300
EMP: 1076 **EST:** 2015
SALES (est): 9.37MM **Privately Held**
Web: www.oaktreespecialtylending.com
SIC: 6722 Money market mutual funds
PA: Oaktree Capital Group Holdings, L.P.
333 S Grand Ave Fl 28
Los Angeles CA

(P-14969)
OCM REAL ESTATE OPPRTNTIES FUN
333 S Grand Ave Fl 28 (90071-1504)

PHONE..............................213 830-6300
EMP: 414 **EST:** 2014
SALES (est): 919.41K **Privately Held**
SIC: 6722 Money market mutual funds
PA: Oaktree Capital Group Holdings, L.P.
333 S Grand Ave Fl 28
Los Angeles CA

(P-14970)
PACIFIC INVESTMENT MGT CO LLC (DH)
Also Called: Pimco
650 Newport Center Dr (92660-6392)
P.O. Box 6430 (92658-6430)
PHONE..............................949 720-6000
Emmanuel Roman, *CEO*
Jeremie Banet, *
Sai S Devabhaktuni, *Head OF CORP DISTRESSED PORTFOLIO MGMNT*
Mohamed A El-erian, *Managing Member*
Jay Jacobs, *
EMP: 240 **EST:** 1969
SQ FT: 25,000
SALES (est): 503.48MM
SALES (corp-wide): 27.99B **Privately Held**
Web: www.pimco.com
SIC: 6722 Money market mutual funds
HQ: Allianz Asset Management Of America Llc
650 Newport Center Dr
Newport Beach CA
949 219-2200

(P-14971)
PIMCO CYMAN TRST PMCO CYMAN GL
650 Newport Center Dr (92660-6424)
PHONE..............................949 720-6000
EMP: 191 **EST:** 2005
SALES (est): 1.82MM **Privately Held**
Web: www.pimco.com
SIC: 6722 Money market mutual funds

(P-14972)
SHAMROCK CAPITAL ADVISORS LLC
1100 Glendon Ave Ste 1600 (90024-3567)
PHONE..............................310 974-6600
EMP: 400 **EST:** 2010
SALES (est): 70.01MM **Privately Held**
Web: www.shamrockcap.com
SIC: 6722 Management investment, open-end

(P-14973)
WESTERN ASSET CORE PLUS BOND P
385 E Colorado Blvd (91101-1923)
PHONE..............................626 844-9400
Larry Clark, *Prin*
EMP: 139 **EST:** 2012
SALES (est): 33.54K
SALES (corp-wide): 7.85B **Publicly Held**
Web: www.westernasset.com
SIC: 6722 Money market mutual funds
HQ: Western Asset Management Company
385 E Colorado Blvd # 100
Pasadena CA
626 844-9265

(P-14974)
WILSHIRE 2015 FUND
1299 Ocean Ave Ste 700 (90401-1061)
PHONE..............................310 451-3051
EMP: 83
SALES (est): 1.15MM **Privately Held**
Web: www.wilshire.com
SIC: 6722 Money market mutual funds

6726 Investment Offices, Nec

(P-14975)
ACORNS GROW INCORPORATED (PA)
Also Called: Acorns
5300 California Ave (92617-3038)
PHONE..............................949 251-0095
Noah Kerner, *CEO*
David Hijirida, *Pr*
Seth Wunder, *CIO*
Kennedy Reynolds, *EDUCATION CONTENT*
EMP: 384 **EST:** 2012
SQ FT: 2,500
SALES (est): 99.18MM
SALES (corp-wide): 99.18MM **Privately Held**
Web: www.acorns.com
SIC: 6726 Investment offices, nec

(P-14976)
BRIDGEWEST VENTURES LLC (PA)
Also Called: Bridgewest Group, The
7310 Miramar Rd Ste 500 (92126-4222)
P.O. Box 928769 (92192-8769)
PHONE..............................858 529-6600
Masood Tayebi, *CEO*
Massih Tayebi, *Ch*
Kevin M Russell, *Chief Legal Counsel*
Saum Vahdat, *CFO*
EMP: 624 **EST:** 2014
SALES (est): 23.17MM
SALES (corp-wide): 23.17MM **Privately Held**
Web: www.bridgewestgroup.com
SIC: 6726 Management investment funds, closed-end

(P-14977)
CENTURY PK CAPITL PARTNERS LLC (PA)
2101 Rosecrans Ave Ste 4275
(90245-4749)
PHONE..............................310 867-2210
Paul J Wolf, *Mng Pt*
Charles W Roellig, *Mng Pt*
Guy Zaczepinski, *Pt*
Gina Yang, *Contrlr*
EMP: 160 **EST:** 2005
SALES (est): 98.49MM **Privately Held**
Web: www.centuryparkcapital.com
SIC: 6726 3569 3086 3448 Management investment funds, closed-end; Firefighting and related equipment; Carpet and rug cushions, foamed plastics; Ramps, prefabricated metal

(P-14978)
CHARLES SCHWAB CORPORATION
Also Called: Charles Schwab
10920 Via Frontera Ste 100 (92127-1730)
PHONE..............................800 435-4000
EMP: 86
SALES (corp-wide): 20.76B **Publicly Held**
Web: www.schwab.com
SIC: 6726 6211 Investment offices, nec; Brokers, security
PA: The Charles Schwab Corporation
3000 Schwab Way
Westlake TX
817 859-5000

(P-14979)
KINGSWOOD CAPITAL MGT LP
11111 Santa Monica Blvd Ste 1700
(90025-3333)

PHONE..............................424 744-8238
Alexander Wolf, *Pt*
EMP: 200 **EST:** 2019
SALES (est): 18.7MM **Privately Held**
Web: www.kingswood-capital.com
SIC: 6726 Investment offices, nec

(P-14980)
OASIS WEST REALTY LLC
1800 Century Park E Ste 500 (90067-1508)
PHONE..............................310 274-8066
Samuel Surloff, *
EMP: 502 **EST:** 2003
SALES (est): 47.9MM **Privately Held**
Web: www.alagemcapital.com
SIC: 6726 5947 5813 5812 Investment offices, nec; Gift shop; Drinking places; Eating places

(P-14981)
PACIFIC AVE CPITL PARTNERS LLC (PA)
2447 Pacific Coast Hwy Ste 101 (90254)
PHONE..............................424 524-9774
Christopher R Sznewajs, *Managing Member*
Joseph Villanueva, *CFO*
EMP: 418 **EST:** 2018
SALES (est): 97.68MM
SALES (corp-wide): 97.68MM **Privately Held**
Web: www.pacificavenuecapital.com
SIC: 6726 Investment offices, nec

(P-14982)
SCHAUMBOND GROUP INC (PA)
225 S Lake Ave Ste 300 (91101-3001)
PHONE..............................626 215-4998
Baohua Zheng, *Pr*
EMP: 450 **EST:** 1996
SQ FT: 8,000
SALES (est): 72.5MM **Privately Held**
SIC: 6726 Investment offices, nec

6732 Trusts: Educational, Religious, Etc.

(P-14983)
EMPOWER OUR YOUTH
Also Called: Eoy
6767 W Sunset Blvd 8-188 (90028-7177)
PHONE..............................323 203-5436
Ihkisha Levell, *Prin*
EMP: 99 **EST:** 2008
SALES (est): 1.27MM **Privately Held**
SIC: 6732 Trusts: educational, religious, etc.

(P-14984)
GREATER LOS ANGLES VTRANS RES
11301 Wilshire Blvd Bldg 114 (90073-1003)
PHONE..............................310 312-1554
Jane Cheung, *Ex Dir*
Thoyd Ellis, *
Bonita Krall, *CPO**
Ron Waldorf, *
Leila Ghayouri, *
EMP: 90 **EST:** 2018
SALES (est): 7.08MM **Privately Held**
SIC: 6732 Trusts: educational, religious, etc.

(P-14985)
UCLA FOUNDATION
10889 Wilshire Blvd Ste 1100 (90024-4200)
PHONE..............................310 794-3193
Craig Ehrlich, *Ch*
Peter Hayashida, *
Neal Axelrod, *
Jocelyn Smith, *

PRODUCTS & SVCS

EMP: 317 **EST:** 1945
SALES (est): 636.37MM **Privately Held**
Web: www.uclafoundation.org
SIC: 6732 Educational trust management

6733 Trusts, Nec

(P-14986)
2100 TRUST LLC (PA)
625 N Grand Ave (92701-4347)
PHONE..............................877 469-7344
Erek J Delorenzi, *Prin*
EMP: 200 **EST:** 2010
SALES (est): 1.04B
SALES (corp-wide): 1.04B **Privately Held**
Web: www.socalnewsgroup.com
SIC: 6733 Trusts, nec

(P-14987)
ADVENTIST HEALTH DELANO
Also Called: Wasco Medical Plaza
2300 7th St (93280-1585)
PHONE..............................661 758-4184
Bahram Ghaffari, *Brnch Mgr*
EMP: 98
SALES (corp-wide): 789.42MM **Privately Held**
Web: www.adventisthealth.org
SIC: 6733 8011 Trusts, nec; Clinic, operated by physicians
HQ: Adventist Health Delano
1401 Garces Hwy Bldg A
Delano CA
661 725-4800

(P-14988)
BENEFITS PRGRAM ADMINSITRATION
Also Called: Gciu Employer Retirement Fund
13191 Concords Pkwy N Ste 205 (91746)
PHONE..............................562 463-5000
Mathew Wenner, *Admn*
EMP: 95 **EST:** 1955
SALES (est): 469.56K
SALES (corp-wide): 9.95MM **Privately Held**
SIC: 6733 Trusts, except educational, religious, charity: management
PA: Management Applied Programming, Inc.
13191 Crssrads Pkwy N Ste
City Of Industry CA
562 463-5000

(P-14989)
CAPITAL GUARDIAN TRUST COMPANY (HQ)
333 S Hope St Fl 52 (90071-3061)
PHONE..............................213 486-9200
Richard C Barker, *Ch Bd*
Robert Ronus, *
EMP: 100 **EST:** 1968
SQ FT: 6,000
SALES (est): 49.92MM
SALES (corp-wide): 5.43B **Privately Held**
SIC: 6733 Trusts, except educational, religious, charity: management
PA: The Capital Group Companies Inc
333 S Hope St Fl 55
Los Angeles CA
213 486-9200

(P-14990)
EPIDAURUS
Also Called: Amity Foundation
3745 S Grand Ave (90007-4332)
PHONE..............................213 743-9075
Mark Schettenger, *Pr*
EMP: 272

SIC: 6733 Trusts, nec
PA: Epidaurus
721 N 4th Ave
Tucson AZ

(P-14991)
GUILD MORTGAGE COMPANY LLC (HQ)
Also Called: Guild Mortgage
5887 Copley Dr (92111-7906)
P.O. Box 85304 (92186-5304)
PHONE..............................800 365-4441
EMP: 200 **EST:** 1960
SALES (est): 901.22MM
SALES (corp-wide): 1.16B **Publicly Held**
Web: www.guildmortgage.com
SIC: 6733 6162 Trusts, except educational, religious, charity: management; Mortgage bankers
PA: Guild Holdings Company
5887 Copley Dr
San Diego CA
858 560-6330

(P-14992)
IMPAC SECURED ASSETS CORP
19500 Jamboree Rd (92612-2411)
PHONE..............................949 475-3600
Ronald Martin Morrison, *Admn*
EMP: 99 **EST:** 2008
SALES (est): 2.39MM **Privately Held**
SIC: 6733 Trusts, nec
HQ: Impac Funding Corporation
19500 Jamboree Rd
Irvine CA

(P-14993)
KAISER FOUNDATION HOSPITALS
Also Called: Orange County-Irvine Med Ctr
6640 Alton Pkwy (92618-3734)
PHONE..............................949 932-5000
EMP: 320
SALES (corp-wide): 68.1B **Privately Held**
Web: www.kaisercenter.com
SIC: 6733 Trusts, nec
HQ: Kaiser Foundation Hospitals Inc
1 Kaiser Plz
Oakland CA
510 271-6611

(P-14994)
KAISER FOUNDATION HOSPITALS
Also Called: Moreno Valley Heacock Med Offs
12815 Heacock St (92553-2836)
PHONE..............................951 601-6174
Mark Ituah, *Prin*
EMP: 84
SALES (corp-wide): 68.1B **Privately Held**
Web: www.kaisercenter.com
SIC: 6733 Trusts, nec
HQ: Kaiser Foundation Hospitals Inc
1 Kaiser Plz
Oakland CA
510 271-6611

(P-14995)
KAISER FOUNDATION HOSPITALS
Also Called: Kaiser Permanente
4647 Zion Ave (92120-2507)
PHONE..............................619 528-5888
Kathy Roper, *Mgr*
EMP: 990
SALES (corp-wide): 68.1B **Privately Held**
Web: www.kaisercenter.com
SIC: 6733 8062 Trusts, nec; General medical and surgical hospitals

HQ: Kaiser Foundation Hospitals Inc
1 Kaiser Plz
Oakland CA
510 271-6611

(P-14996)
KAISER FOUNDATION HOSPITALS
Also Called: Kaiser Permanente
5119 Pomona Blvd (90022-1711)
PHONE..............................323 881-5516
Judy Nantes, *Mgr*
EMP: 95
SALES (corp-wide): 68.1B **Privately Held**
Web: www.kaisercenter.com
SIC: 6733 Trusts, nec
HQ: Kaiser Foundation Hospitals Inc
1 Kaiser Plz
Oakland CA
510 271-6611

(P-14997)
LOMA LINDA UNIV CHLD HOSP
Also Called: LLUCH
11234 Anderson St (92354-2804)
P.O. Box 2000 (92354-0200)
PHONE..............................909 558-8000
EMP: 219 **EST:** 2011
SALES (est): 584.94MM **Privately Held**
Web: www.lluch.org
SIC: 6733 Trusts, nec

(P-14998)
MOELIS & COMPANY LLC
1999 Avenue Of The Stars Ste 1900 (90067-6022)
PHONE..............................310 443-2300
Stella Hoe, *Brnch Mgr*
EMP: 114
SALES (corp-wide): 985.3MM **Publicly Held**
Web: www.moelis.com
SIC: 6733 6282 Private estate, personal investment and vacation fund trusts; Investment advisory service
HQ: Moelis & Company Llc
399 Park Ave Fl 5
New York NY

(P-14999)
OPERATING ENGINEERS FUNDS INC (PA)
100 Corson St (91103-3892)
P.O. Box 7063 (91109-7063)
PHONE..............................866 400-5200
Mike Roddy, *CEO*
Matt Erieg, *
Chuck Killian, *
EMP: 135 **EST:** 1971
SQ FT: 84,600
SALES (est): 314.23K
SALES (corp-wide): 314.23K **Privately Held**
Web: www.oefi.org
SIC: 6733 Trusts, except educational, religious, charity: management

(P-15000)
PMT CRDIT RISK TRNSF TR 2015-1
3043 Townsgate Rd (91361-3027)
PHONE..............................818 224-7028
EMP: 88 **EST:** 2017
SALES (est): 462.97K **Publicly Held**
SIC: 6733 Trusts, nec
PA: Pennymac Mortgage Investment Trust
6101 Condor Dr
Moorpark CA

(P-15001)
PMT CRDIT RISK TRNSF TR 2015-2
3043 Townsgate Rd (91361-3027)
PHONE..............................818 224-7442
EMP: 196 **EST:** 2017
SALES (est): 968.86K **Publicly Held**
Web: www.pennymac.com
SIC: 6733 Trusts, nec
PA: Pennymac Mortgage Investment Trust
6101 Condor Dr
Moorpark CA

(P-15002)
PMT CRDIT RISK TRNSF TR 2019-2
3043 Townsgate Rd (91361-3027)
PHONE..............................818 224-7028
EMP: 88 **EST:** 2019
SALES (est): 416.95K **Publicly Held**
Web: pmt.pennymac.com
SIC: 6733 Trusts, nec
PA: Pennymac Mortgage Investment Trust
6101 Condor Dr
Moorpark CA

(P-15003)
PMT CRDIT RISK TRNSF TR 2020-1
3043 Townsgate Rd (91361-3027)
PHONE..............................818 224-7028
EMP: 118 **EST:** 2020
SALES (est): 987.58K **Publicly Held**
SIC: 6733 Trusts, nec
PA: Pennymac Mortgage Investment Trust
6101 Condor Dr
Moorpark CA

(P-15004)
PNMAC GMSR ISSUER TRUST
3043 Townsgate Rd (91361-3027)
PHONE..............................818 746-2271
EMP: 2259 **EST:** 2017
SALES (est): 7.1MM
SALES (corp-wide): 1.99B **Publicly Held**
SIC: 6733 Trusts, nec
HQ: Pnmac Holdings, Inc.
3043 Townsgate Rd
Westlake Village CA
818 224-7442

(P-15005)
QUALITY LOAN SERVICE CORP
2763 Camino Del Rio S (92108-3708)
PHONE..............................619 645-7711
Kevin R Mccarthy, *CEO*
Thomas J Holthus, *
John R Valkus, *
Dave Owen, *
Victoria Logan, *
EMP: 384 **EST:** 1988
SALES (est): 83.78MM **Privately Held**
Web: www.qualityloan.com
SIC: 6733 Trusts, except educational, religious, charity: management

(P-15006)
VARNER FAMILY LTD PARTNERSHIP (PA)
5900 E Lerdo Hwy (93263-4023)
PHONE..............................661 399-1163
James Varner, *Genl Pt*
EMP: 80 **EST:** 2000
SALES (est): 55.84MM
SALES (corp-wide): 55.84MM **Privately Held**
SIC: 6733 Private estate, personal investment and vacation fund trusts

6794 Patent Owners And Lessors

(P-15007)
ADVANCED FRESH CONCEPTS CORP (PA)
Also Called: A F C
19205 S Laurel Park Rd (90220-6032)
PHONE..............................310 604-3630
Jeffery Seiler, *CEO*
◆ EMP: 47 EST: 1986
SQ FT: 60,000
SALES (est): 48.2MM
SALES (corp-wide): 48.2MM **Privately Held**
Web: www.afcsushi.com
SIC: 6794 2032 2092 5141 Patent owners and lessors; Chinese foods, nec: packaged in cans, jars, etc.; Fresh or frozen packaged fish; Food brokers

(P-15008)
BRER AFFILIATES LLC (DH)
Also Called: Prudential
18500 Von Karman Ave Ste 400 (92612-0504)
PHONE..............................949 794-7900
John Vanderwall, *Pr*
Patti Ray, *
EMP: 208 EST: 2004
SQ FT: 55,500
SALES (est): 116.65MM
SALES (corp-wide): 60.05B **Publicly Held**
SIC: 6794 6531 Franchises, selling or licensing; Real estate agents and managers
HQ: The Prudential Insurance Company Of America
751 Broad St Fl 21
Newark NJ
973 802-6000

(P-15009)
QUALCOMM INTERNATIONAL INC (HQ)
Also Called: Qualcomm
5775 Morehouse Dr (92121-1714)
PHONE..............................858 587-1121
Steve Altman, *Pr*
Derek Aberle, *
EMP: 4000 EST: 1993
SALES (est): 253.04MM
SALES (corp-wide): 35.82B **Publicly Held**
SIC: 6794 Patent buying, licensing, leasing
PA: Qualcomm Incorporated
5775 Morehouse Dr
San Diego CA
858 587-1121

(P-15010)
UNIVERSAL STDIOS LICENSING LLC
100 Universal City Plz (91608-1002)
PHONE..............................818 695-1273
Sheetal Madadi, *Mgr*
Gabriela Kornzweig, *Sec*
EMP: 150 EST: 2010
SALES (est): 60.27MM
SALES (corp-wide): 121.43B **Publicly Held**
SIC: 6794 Copyright buying and licensing
HQ: Nbcuniversal Media, Llc
30 Rockefeller Plz Fl 2
New York NY

(P-15011)
WSM INVESTMENTS LLC
Also Called: Topco Sales
3990b Heritage Oak Ct (93063-6716)
PHONE..............................818 332-4600
Scott Tucker, *CEO*
Martin Tucker, *
Michael Siegel, *
▲ EMP: 145 EST: 2009
SQ FT: 150,000
SALES (est): 39.75MM **Privately Held**
SIC: 6794 5122 5099 4731 Performance rights, publishing and licensing; Cosmetics; Novelties, durable; Freight forwarding
PA: Lover Health Science And Technology Incorporated Co., Ltd
No.1208, Taihu Ave., Changxing Economic Development Zone, Changx Huzhou ZJ

6798 Real Estate Investment Trusts

(P-15012)
BIOMED REALTY TRUST INC (PA)
Also Called: Biomed Realty
4570 Executive Dr Ste 400 (92121-3074)
PHONE..............................858 207-2513
Alan D Gold, *Ch Bd*
R Kent Griffin Junior, *Pr*
Greg N Lubushkin, *CFO*
Gary A Kreitzer, *Ex VP*
Charlie Piscitello, *CPO*
EMP: 375 EST: 2004
SQ FT: 61,286
SALES (est): 264.45MM
SALES (corp-wide): 264.45MM **Privately Held**
Web: www.biomedrealty.com
SIC: 6798 Real estate investment trusts

(P-15013)
CORESITE LLC
624 S Grand Ave Ste 1800 (90023-1629)
PHONE..............................213 327-1231
Thomas Ray, *Brnch Mgr*
EMP: 323
Web: www.coresite.com
SIC: 6798 Real estate investment trusts
HQ: Coresite, L.L.C.
1001 17th St Ste 500
Denver CO
866 777-2673

(P-15014)
IRVINE EASTGATE OFFICE II LLC
Also Called: Irvine Company Office Property
550 Newport Center Dr (92660-7010)
P.O. Box 2460 (92658-8960)
PHONE..............................949 720-2000
Pam Van Nort, *VP*
EMP: 3000 EST: 2013
SQ FT: 3,000
SALES (est): 302.84MM **Privately Held**
Web: www.irvinecompany.com
SIC: 6798 Real estate investment trusts

(P-15015)
MACERICH COMPANY (PA)
Also Called: MACERICH
401 Wilshire Blvd Ste 700 (90401-1452)
PHONE..............................310 394-6000
Thomas E O'hern, *CEO*
Edward C Coppola, *
Scott W Kingsmore, *Ex VP*
Ann C Menard, *CLO*
Douglas J Healey, *Head OF Leasing*
EMP: 80 EST: 1965
SALES (est): 859.16MM
SALES (corp-wide): 859.16MM **Publicly Held**
Web: www.macerich.com

SIC: 6798 Real estate investment trusts

(P-15016)
PRIME ADMINISTRATION LLC
Also Called: Prime Group
357 S Curson Ave (90036-5201)
P.O. Box 360859 (90036-1359)
PHONE..............................323 549-7155
Daniel H James, *Ch*
John C Atwater, *CEO*
EMP: 522 EST: 2004
SALES (est): 96.75MM **Privately Held**
Web: www.primegrp.com
SIC: 6798 Real estate investment trusts

(P-15017)
PUBLIC STORAGE (PA)
701 Western Ave (91201-2349)
PHONE..............................818 244-8080
Joseph D Russell Junior, *Pr*
Ronald L Havner Junior, *Ch Bd*
H Thomas Boyle, *CIO*
Natalia N Johnson, *Chief*
Nathaniel A Vitan, *CLO*
EMP: 430 EST: 1980
SALES (est): 4.18B
SALES (corp-wide): 4.18B **Publicly Held**
Web: www.publicstorage.com
SIC: 6798 Real estate investment trusts

(P-15018)
WESTERN ASSET MRTG CAPITL CORP
385 E Colorado Blvd (91101-1923)
PHONE..............................626 844-9400
EMP: 804 EST: 2012
SALES (est): 74.25MM **Privately Held**
Web: www.westernassetmcc.com
SIC: 6798 Real estate investment trusts

6799 Investors, Nec

(P-15019)
7TH & C INVESTMENTS LLC
404 14th St (92101-7508)
PHONE..............................619 233-7327
James W Brennan, *Prin*
EMP: 140 EST: 2010
SALES (est): 4.64MM
SALES (corp-wide): 573.83MM **Publicly Held**
Web: www.taogroup.com
SIC: 6799 Investors, nec
PA: Sphere Entertainment Co.
2 Penn Plz
New York NY
725 258-0001

(P-15020)
ARE/CAL-SD REGION NO 62 LLC
26 N Euclid Ave (91101-1961)
PHONE..............................626 578-0777
Mark Butcher, *
EMP: 99 EST: 2019
SALES (est): 5.13MM **Privately Held**
SIC: 6799 Investors, nec

(P-15021)
BACKBONE CAPITAL ADVISORS LLC
4084 Camellia Ave (91604-3006)
PHONE..............................818 769-8016
Britt Terrell, *Prin*
EMP: 127 EST: 2011
SALES (est): 412.15K
SALES (corp-wide): 9.21MM **Privately Held**
Web: www.backbonecap.com
SIC: 6799 Investors, nec
PA: Palm Tree Llc
11755 Wilshire Blvd
Los Angeles CA
424 220-6800

(P-15022)
BROADREACH CAPITL PARTNERS LLC
6430 W Sunset Blvd Ste 504 (90028-7901)
PHONE..............................310 691-5760
Andre Ramillon, *Brnch Mgr*
EMP: 789
SALES (corp-wide): 47.1MM **Privately Held**
Web: www.broadreachcp.com
SIC: 6799 Investors, nec
PA: Broadreach Capital Partners Llc
885 Oak Grove Ave Ste 206
Menlo Park CA
650 331-2500

(P-15023)
CALL TO ACTION PARTNERS LLC (PA)
11601 Wilshire Blvd Fl 23 (90025-0509)
PHONE..............................310 996-7200
Colin Sapire, *Managing Member*
Lenny Sands, *
Richard Kam, *
▲ EMP: 100 EST: 2009
SQ FT: 9,500
SALES (est): 33MM
SALES (corp-wide): 33MM **Privately Held**
SIC: 6799 Investors, nec

(P-15024)
CENTERLINE MORTGAGE CAPITL INC
18300 Von Karman Ave Ste 600 (92612-1057)
PHONE..............................949 221-6685
Andy Mackay, *Brnch Mgr*
EMP: 392
SALES (corp-wide): 661.26MM **Privately Held**
Web: www.lument.com
SIC: 6799 Investors, nec
HQ: Centerline Mortgage Capital, Inc.
100 Church St Fl 15
New York NY
212 317-5700

(P-15025)
CLEARVIEW CAPITAL LLC
12100 Wilshire Blvd Ste 800 (90025-7140)
PHONE..............................310 806-9555
Larry Simon, *Brnch Mgr*
EMP: 916
SALES (corp-wide): 244.66MM **Privately Held**
Web: www.clearviewcap.com
SIC: 6799 Venture capital companies
PA: Clearview Capital, Llc
1010 Washington Blvd 2-9
Stamford CT
203 698-2777

(P-15026)
CORRIDOR CAPITAL LLC (PA)
12400 Wilshire Blvd Ste 645 (90025-1260)
PHONE..............................310 442-7000
Craig L Enenstein, *CEO*
Edward A Monnier, *
Cameron Reilly, *
Jessamyn Davis, *
EMP: 126 EST: 2005
SALES (est): 97.56MM **Privately Held**

PRODUCTS & SVCS

Web: www.corridor-capital.com
SIC: **6799** Venture capital companies

(P-15027)
CRESTMONT CAPITAL LLC
1422 Edinger Ave Ste 210 (92780-6298)
PHONE.....................................949 537-3882
EMP: **250** EST: **2015**
SALES (est): 22.59MM **Privately Held**
Web: www.crestmontcapital.com
SIC: **6799** Investors, nec

(P-15028)
EMP III INC
Also Called: Duarte Manor
1755 Mrtn Lthr Kng Jr Blv (90058-1522)
PHONE.....................................323 231-4174
EMP: **80** EST: **2010**
SALES (est): 2.47MM **Privately Held**
SIC: **6799** Real estate investors, except
property operators

(P-15029)
GOLDEN INTERNATIONAL
424 S Los Angeles St Ste 2 (90013-1470)
PHONE.....................................213 628-1388
Gi Hanbae, *Brnch Mgr*
EMP: **2968**
SALES (corp-wide): 20.03MM **Privately
Held**
SIC: **6799** Investors, nec
PA: Golden International
36720 Palmdale Rd
Rancho Mirage CA
760 568-1912

(P-15030)
GROVES CAPITAL INC
4025 Stonebridge Ln (92091-4602)
PHONE.....................................619 519-4453
EMP: **202** EST: **2019**
SALES (est): 5.73MM **Privately Held**
Web: www.grovescapital.com
SIC: **6799** Investors, nec

(P-15031)
IDEALAB HOLDINGS LLC (PA)
130 W Union St (91103-3628)
PHONE.....................................626 585-6900
Brent Novak, *
Marcia Goodstein, *
Craig Chrisney, *
Kristen Ding, *
EMP: **626** EST: **1996**
SALES (est): 146.11MM
SALES (corp-wide): 146.11MM **Privately
Held**
Web: www.idealab.com
SIC: **6799** 5045 5734 Venture capital
companies; Computer software; Computer
software and accessories

(P-15032)
INTREPID INV BANKERS LLC
11755 Wilshire Blvd Ste 2200 (90025-1567)
PHONE.....................................310 478-9000
Ed Bagdasarian, *CEO*
EMP: **5079** EST: **2010**
SALES (est): 8.43MM **Privately Held**
Web: www.intrepidib.com
SIC: **6799** Investors, nec
HQ: Mufg Americas Holdings Corporation
1251 Ave Of The Americas
New York NY
212 782-6800

(P-15033)
INVENTURE CAPITAL
CORPORATION (PA)

Also Called: Tala
429 Santa Monica Blvd Ste 450
(90401-3455)
PHONE.....................................213 262-6903
Shivani B Siroya, *CEO*
EMP: **542** EST: **2014**
SALES (est): 70.33MM
SALES (corp-wide): 70.33MM **Privately
Held**
Web: www.tala.co
SIC: **6799** Venture capital companies

(P-15034)
LD ACQUISITION COMPANY 16
LLC
400 Continental Blvd Ste 500 (90245-5076)
PHONE.....................................310 294-8160
Tim Brazy, *CEO*
George Doyle, *
Dan Parsons, *
Josef Bobek, *
EMP: **99** EST: **2017**
SALES (est): 3.79MM **Privately Held**
SIC: **6799** Investors, nec

(P-15035)
MATSUSHITA INTERNATIONAL
CORP (PA)
1141 Via Callejon (92673-6230)
PHONE.....................................949 498-1000
Hiroyuki Matsushita, *Pr*
EMP: **80** EST: **1990**
SALES (est): 21.11MM **Privately Held**
SIC: **6799** 3711 3714 Real estate investors,
except property operators; Automobile
assembly, including specialty automobiles;
Motor vehicle parts and accessories

(P-15036)
MCMILLIN COMPANIES LLC (PA)
Also Called: McMillin Homes
2750 Womble Rd Ste 102 (92106-6114)
P.O. Box 21010 (92021-0980)
PHONE.....................................619 477-4117
EMP: **80** EST: **1998**
SALES (est): 33.68MM
SALES (corp-wide): 33.68MM **Privately
Held**
Web: www.mcmillin.com
SIC: **6799** Real estate investors, except
property operators

(P-15037)
MEDIMPACT HOLDINGS INC
(PA)
10181 Scripps Gateway Ct (92131-5152)
PHONE.....................................858 566-2727
EMP: **817** EST: **2010**
SALES (est): 473.33MM **Privately Held**
Web: www.medimpact.com
SIC: **6799** Investors, nec

(P-15038)
MIRAMAR ACQUISITION CO LLC
Also Called: Rosewood Miramar Bch
Montecito
1759 S Jameson Ln (93108-2925)
PHONE.....................................805 900-8338
Rick J Caruso, *Prin*
EMP: **157** EST: **2015**
SALES (est): 25.91MM **Privately Held**
Web: www.rosewoodhotels.com
SIC: **6799** Investors, nec

(P-15039)
MSR HOTELS & RESORTS INC
Also Called: Sheraton Inn Bakersfield
5101 California Ave Ste 204 (93309-1623)
PHONE.....................................661 325-9700

Kole Siefken, *Mgr*
EMP: **120**
SALES (corp-wide): 53.67B **Publicly Held**
Web: www.cnl.com
SIC: **6799** Investors, nec
HQ: Msr Hotels & Resorts, Inc.
450 S Orange Ave
Orlando FL
407 650-1000

(P-15040)
NAVITAS SEMICONDUCTOR
CORP (PA)
3520 Challenger St (90503-1640)
PHONE.....................................901 685-2865
Gene Sheridan, *Ch Bd*
Ron Shelton, *Sr VP*
Ranbir Singh, *Ex VP*
EMP: **165** EST: **2020**
SALES (est): 37.94MM
SALES (corp-wide): 37.94MM **Privately
Held**
Web: www.navitassemi.com
SIC: **6799** Investors, nec

(P-15041)
NEXUS CAPITAL MANAGEMENT
LP
11100 Santa Monica Blvd (90025-3384)
PHONE.....................................424 330-8820
EMP: **925** EST: **2016**
SALES (est): 71MM **Privately Held**
Web: www.nexuslp.com
SIC: **6799** Investors, nec

(P-15042)
NNN REALTY INVESTORS LLC
19700 Fairchild Ste 300 (92612-2515)
PHONE.....................................714 667-8252
Jeffrey T Hanson, *CIO*
Todd A Mikles, *
EMP: **458** EST: **1998**
SQ FT: **18,800**
SALES (est): 13.35MM **Privately Held**
SIC: **6799** 6531 Investors, nec; Real estate
managers

(P-15043)
NOGALES INVESTORS LLC
9229 W Sunset Blvd Ste 900 (90069-3410)
PHONE.....................................310 276-7439
Luis Nogales, *Managing Member*
EMP: **275** EST: **2001**
SQ FT: **2,500**
SALES (est): 368.87K **Privately Held**
SIC: **6799** Investors, nec
PA: Nogales Investors Management, Llc
9229 W Sunset Blvd # 900
Los Angeles CA

(P-15044)
NRLL LLC
Also Called: Land Disposition Company
1 Mauchly (92618-2305)
P.O. Box 15534 (92623-5534)
PHONE.....................................949 768-7777
EMP: **360** EST: **1995**
SQ FT: **18,000**
SALES (est): 978.11K **Privately Held**
Web: www.landauction.com
SIC: **6799** Real estate investors, except
property operators
PA: Nrp Holding Co., Inc.
1 Mauchly
Irvine CA

(P-15045)
OTTS ASIA MOORER DEVON
Also Called: Newshire Investment

10015 Baring Cross St (90044-4511)
PHONE.....................................323 603-6959
Asia Otts, *Owner*
Devon Moorer, *Owner*
EMP: **105** EST: **2016**
SALES (est): 2.11MM **Privately Held**
SIC: **6799** Investors, nec

(P-15046)
PMC CAPITAL PARTNERS LLC
12243 Branford St (91352-1010)
PHONE.....................................818 896-1101
Michel Tamer, *Mng Pt*
EMP: **1000** EST: **2019**
SALES (est): 34.54MM **Privately Held**
Web: www.pmcsg.com
SIC: **6799** Venture capital companies

(P-15047)
PROVIDENCE REST PARTNERS
LLC
Also Called: Restaurant Investment
5955 Melrose Ave (90038-3623)
PHONE.....................................323 460-4170
EMP: **88** EST: **2004**
SALES (est): 3.45MM **Privately Held**
Web: www.providencela.com
SIC: **6799** 5963 Investors, nec; Food
services, direct sales

(P-15048)
REGENT LP (PA)
9720 Wilshire Blvd Fl 6 (90212-2025)
PHONE.....................................310 299-4100
Michael A Reinstein, *CEO*
Roxanna Sassanian, *CFO*
EMP: **85** EST: **2017**
SALES (est): 2.19B
SALES (corp-wide): 2.19B **Privately Held**
Web: www.regentlp.com
SIC: **6799** Investors, nec

(P-15049)
ROLL PROPERTIES INTL INC
Also Called: Paramout Farms
13646 Highway 33 (93249-9719)
PHONE.....................................661 797-6500
Bill Bowers, *Mgr*
EMP: **121**
SALES (corp-wide): 27.25MM **Privately
Held**
Web: www.rolllawgroup.com
SIC: **6799** Real estate investors, except
property operators
PA: Roll Properties International, Inc.
11444 W Olympic Blvd # 10
Los Angeles CA
310 966-5700

(P-15050)
SABAL CAPITAL PARTNERS LLC
680 E Colorado Blvd Ste 350 (91101)
PHONE.....................................949 255-1007
Pat Jackson, *CEO*
EMP: **130** EST: **2015**
SALES (est): 61.08MM
SALES (corp-wide): 7.53B **Publicly Held**
Web: www.regions.com
SIC: **6799** Investors, nec
HQ: Regions Bank
1900 5th Ave N Ste 2264
Birmingham AL
205 264-5523

(P-15051)
SOLIS CAPITAL PARTNERS LLC
3371 Calle Tres Vistas Ste 100
(92024-6679)
PHONE.....................................760 309-9436
Daniel J Lubeck, *Brnch Mgr*

▲ = Import ▼ = Export
◆ = Import/Export

EMP: 86
SALES (corp-wide): 9.68MM **Privately Held**
Web: www.soliscapital.com
SIC: 6799 Venture capital companies
PA: Solis Capital Partners, Llc
23 Corporate Plaza Dr # 215
Newport Beach CA
949 296-2440

(P-15052)
STONECALIBRE LLC (PA)
2049 Century Park E Ste 2550 (90067-3110)
PHONE..................310 774-0014
EMP: 100 **EST:** 2012
SALES (est): 61.82MM **Privately Held**
Web: www.stonecalibre.com
SIC: 6799 Investors, nec

(P-15053)
TAPETECH TOOL COMPANY
Also Called: Tapetech Tool Company
7360 Convoy Ct (92111-1110)
PHONE..................858 268-0656
EMP: 633
SALES (corp-wide): 5.33B **Publicly Held**
Web: www.amestools.com
SIC: 6799 Investors, nec
HQ: Ames Tools Corporation
1327 Northbrook Pkwy # 400
Suwanee GA

(P-15054)
TCG CAPITAL MANAGEMENT LP
12180 Millennium Ste 500 (90094-2948)
PHONE..................310 633-2900
Peter Chernin, *CEO*
EMP: 135 **EST:** 2018
SALES (est): 9.74MM **Privately Held**
SIC: 6799 Investors, nec

(P-15055)
TRANSOM CAPITAL GROUP LLC (PA)
10990 Wilshire Blvd Ste 440 (90024-3927)
PHONE..................424 293-2818
Ken Firtel, *Managing Member*
Justin Gilson, *VP*
Nathan Dastic, *CFO*
EMP: 64 **EST:** 2007
SALES (est): 1.32B
SALES (corp-wide): 1.32B **Privately Held**
Web: www.transomcap.com
SIC: 6799 5112 5943 3951 Investors, nec;
Pens and/or pencils; Writing supplies;
Fountain pens and fountain pen desk sets

(P-15056)
TRUE INVESTMENTS LLC (PA)
2260 University Dr (92660-3319)
PHONE..................949 258-9720
Alan True, *CEO*
EMP: 24 **EST:** 2012
SALES (est): 4.94MM
SALES (corp-wide): 4.94MM **Privately Held**
Web: www.truefamilyenterprises.com
SIC: 6799 7372 Investors, nec; Application computer software

(P-15057)
TRUE INVESTMENTS LLC
Also Called: True Investments LLC
6535 Caballero Blvd Unit B (90620-8106)
PHONE..................949 258-9720
EMP: 26
SALES (corp-wide): 4.94MM **Privately Held**

SIC: 6799 7372 Investors, nec; Application computer software
PA: True Investments, Llc
2260 University Dr
Newport Beach CA
949 258-9720

(P-15058)
USA ENTERPRISE INC
9777 Wilshire Blvd Ste 400 (90212-1910)
PHONE..................310 750-4246
Ahmed Sharif, *CEO*
EMP: 350 **EST:** 1999
SALES (est): 24.01MM **Privately Held**
Web: www.usaenterpriseinc.com
SIC: 6799 Real estate investors, except property operators

(P-15059)
WEDGEWOOD INC (PA)
2015 Manhattan Beach Blvd Ste 100 (90278-1230)
PHONE..................310 640-3070
Gregory L Geiser, *CEO*
David Wehrly, *
Michele Tasker, *
EMP: 88 **EST:** 1985
SQ FT: 3,200
SALES (est): 147.22MM
SALES (corp-wide): 147.22MM **Privately Held**
Web: www.wedgewood-inc.com
SIC: 6799 Real estate investors, except property operators

(P-15060)
WINDJMMER CPITL INVSTORS III L
Also Called: Westwind Equity Investors
610 Newport Center Dr Ste 1100 (92660)
PHONE..................949 706-9989
J Derek Watson, *
Mike Wattles, *
Jeff Miehe, *
Matt Anderson, *
EMP: 724 **EST:** 1990
SALES (est): 25.65MM **Privately Held**
Web: www.windjammercapital.com
SIC: 6799 Investors, nec

(P-15061)
WINDJMMER CPITL INVSTORS IV LP
610 Newport Center Dr Ste 1100 (92660)
PHONE..................919 706-9989
Bill Herkamp, *Pt*
EMP: 450 **EST:** 2011
SALES (est): 16.68MM **Privately Held**
Web: www.windjammercapital.com
SIC: 6799 Investors, nec

7011 Hotels And Motels

(P-15062)
1260 BB PROPERTY LLC
Also Called: Four Ssons Rsort Santa Barbara
1260 Channel Dr (93108-2805)
PHONE..................805 969-2261
H Ty Warner, *CEO*
▲ **EMP:** 500 **EST:** 1986
SALES (est): 58.51MM
SALES (corp-wide): 140.91MM **Privately Held**
SIC: 7011 Resort hotel
HQ: Fsb Cal Corp.
280 Chestnut Ave
Westmont IL
630 920-1515

(P-15063)
1835 COLUMBIA STREET LP
Also Called: Porto Vista Hotel
1835 Columbia St (92101-2505)
PHONE..................619 564-3993
Moe Siry, *Pt*
EMP: 80 **EST:** 1992
SALES (est): 5MM **Privately Held**
Web: www.portovistasd.com
SIC: 7011 Hotels

(P-15064)
1855 S HBR BLVD DRV HLDNGS LLC
Also Called: Sheraton Pk Ht At Anheim Rsort
1855 S Harbor Blvd (92802-3509)
PHONE..................714 750-1811
Kunthea Hang, *Prin*
Tony Bruno, *
Ian Gee, *
EMP: 250 **EST:** 2012
SALES (est): 4.68MM **Privately Held**
Web: four-points.marriott.com
SIC: 7011 Hotels

(P-15065)
51ST ST & 8TH AVE CORP
Also Called: Loews Coronado Bay Resort
4000 Coronado Bay Rd (92118-3290)
PHONE..................619 424-4000
▲ **EMP:** 206 **EST:** 1994
SALES (est): 25.08MM **Privately Held**
Web: www.loewshotels.com
SIC: 7011 Hotels

(P-15066)
6417 SELMA HOTEL LLC
Also Called: Dream Hollywood
6417 Selma Ave (90028-7310)
PHONE..................323 844-6417
Richard Heyman, *Managing Member*
EMP: 250 **EST:** 2017
SALES (est): 15.12MM **Privately Held**
Web: www.dreamhotels.com
SIC: 7011 Hotels

(P-15067)
8110 AERO HOLDING LLC
Also Called: Sheraton
8110 Aero Dr (92123-1715)
PHONE..................858 277-8888
Lucy Burni, *Managing Member*
Nabih Geha, *
EMP: 210 **EST:** 2019
SALES (est): 7.99MM **Privately Held**
Web: www.fourpointssandiegohotel.com
SIC: 7011 5813 5812 Hotels and motels;
Drinking places; Eating places

(P-15068)
901 WEST OLYMPIC BLVD LTD PRTN
Also Called: Residence Inn By Marriott
901 W Olympic Blvd (90015-1327)
PHONE..................347 992-5707
Greg Steinhauer, *Pt*
Homer Williams, *Pt*
EMP: 110 **EST:** 2011
SQ FT: 286,000
SALES (est): 4.87MM **Privately Held**
Web: residence-inn.marriott.com
SIC: 7011 Hotels and motels

(P-15069)
AGUA CLNTE BAND CHILLA INDIANS
Also Called: Agua Caliente Casino & Resort
32250 Bob Hope Dr (92270-2704)

PHONE..................760 321-2000
Ken Kettler, *Brnch Mgr*
EMP: 1000
SALES (corp-wide): 83.82MM **Privately Held**
Web: www.aguacalientecasinos.com
SIC: 7011 Casino hotel
PA: Agua Caliente Band Of Cahuilla Indians
5401 Dinah Shore Dr
Palm Springs CA
760 699-6800

(P-15070)
AGUA CLNTE BAND CHILLA INDIANS
Also Called: Spa Resort Casino
401 E Amado Rd (92262-6403)
PHONE..................800 854-1279
EMP: 453
SALES (corp-wide): 83.82MM **Privately Held**
Web: www.aguacalientecasinos.com
SIC: 7011 7991 Casino hotel; Spas
PA: Agua Caliente Band Of Cahuilla Indians
5401 Dinah Shore Dr
Palm Springs CA
760 699-6800

(P-15071)
AMENITIES DEVELOPMENT CO
Also Called: Ramada Inn
1089 Santa Anita Ave (91733-3864)
PHONE..................626 350-9588
Judy Shieh, *Prin*
EMP: 112
SALES (corp-wide): 946.93K **Privately Held**
Web: www.wyndhamhotels.com
SIC: 7011 Hotels and motels
PA: Amenities Development Co.
401 E Valley Blvd Ste 200
San Gabriel CA
626 571-6843

(P-15072)
AMERICAN KOYU CORPORATION
1733 S Anaheim Blvd (92805-6518)
P.O. Box 1145 (92878-1145)
PHONE..................626 793-0669
Yoichi Erikawa, *Pr*
EMP: 150 **EST:** 2002
SALES (est): 19.24MM **Privately Held**
Web: koyucorp.jimdofree.com
SIC: 7011 Hotels

(P-15073)
AMERICAN PRPRTY-MNAGEMENT CORP
Also Called: U. S. Grant Hotel
326 Broadway (92101-4812)
PHONE..................619 232-3121
John Gallegon, *Mgr*
EMP: 1545
SALES (corp-wide): 74.7MM **Privately Held**
Web: www.wyndhamhotels.com
SIC: 7011 Hotels
PA: American Property-Management Corporation
8910 University Center Ln # 100
San Diego CA
858 964-5500

(P-15074)
ANAHEIM - 1855 S HBR BLVD OWNE

PRODUCTS & SVCS

Also Called: Sheraton
1855 S Harbor Blvd (92802-3509)
PHONE...................714 750-1811
Ian Gee, *Prin*
EMP: 99 **EST:** 2019
SALES (est): 2.57MM **Privately Held**
Web: four-points.marriott.com
SIC: 7011 Hotels

(P-15075)
ANAHEIM PARK HOTEL
Also Called: Wyndham Hotels & Resorts
222 W Houston Ave (92832-3453)
PHONE...................714 992-1700
Fred Menoufi, *Pt*
EMP: 197 **EST:** 1989
SQ FT: 174,123
SALES (est): 1.53MM **Privately Held**
Web: www.wyndhamhotels.com
SIC: 7011 YWCA/YWHA hotel

(P-15076)
ANAHEIM PLAZA HOTEL INC
Also Called: Anaheim Hotel, The
1700 S Harbor Blvd (92802-2316)
PHONE...................714 772-5900
Saroj Patel, *CEO*
Saroj Patel, *Pr*
Rajni Patel, *VP*
EMP: 96 **EST:** 1961
SQ FT: 5,600
SALES (est): 8.99MM **Privately Held**
Web: www.theanaheimhotel.com
SIC: 7011 5812 5813 Motels; Eating places;
   Drinking places

(P-15077)
ANDAZ WEST HOLLYWOOD
8401 W Sunset Blvd (90069-1909)
PHONE...................323 656-1234
Sulynn Jew, *Prin*
EMP: 87 **EST:** 2010
SALES (est): 19.21MM **Publicly Held**
Web: westhollywood.andaz.hyatt.com
SIC: 7011 Resort hotel
HQ: Hyatt Corporation
   250 Vesey St Fl 15
   New York NY
   312 750-1234

(P-15078)
ASCOT HOTEL LP
Also Called: Hotel Angeleno
170 N Church Ln (90049-2044)
PHONE...................310 476-6411
Mark Beccaria, *Pt*
EMP: 125 **EST:** 2008
SALES (est): 16.58MM **Privately Held**
Web: www.hotelangeleno.com
SIC: 7011 Hotels

(P-15079)
ASHFORD TRS SEVEN LLC
Also Called: Residence Inn By Marriott
38305 Cook St (92211-1794)
PHONE...................760 776-0050
EMP: 91
SQ FT: 80,290
SALES (corp-wide): 445.85K **Privately
Held**
Web: courtyard.marriott.com
SIC: 7011 Hotels and motels
PA: Ashford Trs Seven Llc
   74895 Frank Sinatra Dr
   Palm Desert CA
   760 776-4150

(P-15080)
ATLAS HOTELS INC
Also Called: Town and Country

500 Hotel Cir N (92108-3005)
PHONE...................619 291-2232
EMP: 1023
SIC: 7011 5812 5813 Hotels; Eating places;
   Cocktail lounge

(P-15081)
**AVIARA FSRC ASSOCIATES
LIMITED**
7100 Aviara Resort Dr (92011-4908)
PHONE...................760 603-6800
Robert Cima, *Genl Mgr*
Aviara Resort Club, *
EMP: 1200 **EST:** 1995
SALES (est): 21.49MM **Publicly Held**
SIC: 7011 Resort hotel
HQ: Aviara Resort Associates Limited
   Partnership, A California Limited
   Partnership
   7100 Aviara Resort Dr
   Carlsbad CA

(P-15082)
AYRES - PASO ROBLES LP
Also Called: Allegretto Vineyard Resort
2700 Buena Vista Dr (93446-9530)
PHONE...................714 850-0409
EMP: 120 **EST:** 2015
SALES (est): 6.88MM **Privately Held**
Web: www.allegrettovineyardresort.com
SIC: 7011 Hotels

(P-15083)
AYRES GROUP
Also Called: Ayres Hotel Manhattan Beach
14400 Hindry Ave (90250-6740)
PHONE...................310 220-6447
Ann Williams, *Mgr*
EMP: 93
SQ FT: 85,082
Web: www.ayreshotels.com
SIC: 7011 Hotels
PA: Ayres Group
   355 Bristol St
   Costa Mesa CA

(P-15084)
**BAKERSFIELD HOSPITALITY
LLC**
6141 Knudsen Dr (93308-2904)
PHONE...................661 393-1277
Mahendra Patel, *Brnch Mgr*
EMP: 80
SALES (corp-wide): 317.13K **Privately
Held**
SIC: 7011 Hotels and motels
PA: Bakersfield Hospitality Llc
   16609 Honeybee Dr
   Tustin CA

(P-15085)
BALDWIN HOSPITALITY LLC
Also Called: Courtyard By Marriott
14635 Baldwin Park Towne Ctr
(91706-5548)
PHONE...................626 446-2988
Lina Mita, *Managing Member*
EMP: 80 **EST:** 1997
SALES (est): 2.53MM **Privately Held**
Web: courtyard.marriott.com
SIC: 7011 Hotels and motels

(P-15086)
BARONA RESORT & CASINO
1932 Wildcat Canyon Rd (92040-1553)
PHONE...................619 443-2300
Dean Allen, *Sr VP*
Linda Jordan, *Sr VP*
Nick Dillon, *Ex VP*

Troy Simpson, *Ex VP*
Rick Salinas, *Genl Mgr*
EMP: 3500 **EST:** 2005
SALES (est): 171.97MM **Privately Held**
Web: www.barona.com
SIC: 7011 Resort hotel

(P-15087)
BARTELL HOTELS
Also Called: Hilton San Diego Airport/Hrbr
1960 Harbor Island Dr (92101-1013)
PHONE...................619 291-6700
Luis Barrios, *Genl Mgr*
EMP: 100
SALES (corp-wide): 41.61MM **Privately
Held**
Web: www.bartellhotels.com
SIC: 7011 Hotels
PA: Bartell Hotels, A California Limited
   Partnership
   4875 N Harbor Dr
   San Diego CA
   619 224-1556

(P-15088)
BCRA RESORT SERVICES INC
Also Called: Bacara Resorts and Spa
8301 Hollister Ave (93117-2474)
PHONE...................805 571-3176
EMP: 150
SIC: 7011 Hotels

(P-15089)
**BEHRINGER HARVARD
WILSHIRE BLV**
Also Called: Hotel Palomar
10740 Wilshire Blvd (90024-4493)
PHONE...................310 475-8711
Ravi Sikand, *Pt*
EMP: 99 **EST:** 2006
SALES (est): 4.92MM **Privately Held**
Web:
www.hotelpalomar-beverlyhills.com
SIC: 7011 6531 Hotels; Real estate agents
   and managers

(P-15090)
**BELVEDERE HOTEL
PARTNERSHIP**
Also Called: Peninsula Beverly Hill's
9882 Santa Monica Blvd (90212-1605)
PHONE...................310 551-2888
Ali Kasikci, *Mgr*
EMP: 442
SIC: 7011 6512 5813 5812 Hotels;
   Nonresidential building operators; Drinking
   places; Eating places
PA: The Belvedere Hotel Partnership
   421 N Beverly Dr Ste 350
   Beverly Hills CA

(P-15091)
BELVEDERE PARTNERSHIP
Also Called: Peninsula Beverly Hills, The
9882 Santa Monica Blvd (90212-1605)
PHONE...................310 551-2888
Robert Zarnegan, *Pr*
▲ **EMP:** 400 **EST:** 2005
SALES (est): 25.24MM **Privately Held**
SIC: 7011 Bed and breakfast inn

(P-15092)
**BEST WESTERN STOVALLS INN
(PA)**
Also Called: Anaheim Inn
1110 W Katella Ave (92802-2805)
PHONE...................714 956-4430
James Stovall, *Pt*
Robert Stovall, *Pt*

Minta Pettis-stovall, *Pt*
Bill O'connell, *Pt*
EMP: 90 **EST:** 1966
SQ FT: 4,800
SALES (est): 22.46MM
SALES (corp-wide): 22.46MM **Privately
Held**
Web: www.bestwestern.com
SIC: 7011 Hotels and motels

(P-15093)
**BEVERLY HILLS LUXURY
HOTEL LLC**
1801 Century Park E Ste 1200
(90067-2301)
PHONE...................310 274-9999
Kenneth Bordewick, *Managing Member*
EMP: 450 **EST:** 2002
SALES (est): 33.02MM **Privately Held**
SIC: 7011 Resort hotel

(P-15094)
BH PARTNERSHIP LP (PA)
Also Called: Bahia Resort Hotels
998 W Mission Bay Dr (92109-7803)
PHONE...................858 539-7635
Anne L Evans, *Genl Pt*
William L Evans, *Pt*
Anthony Belefm, *Chief Human Resources
Officer*
EMP: 300 **EST:** 1945
SALES (est): 58.24MM
SALES (corp-wide): 58.24MM **Privately
Held**
Web: www.bahiahotel.com
SIC: 7011 6531 5812 Resort hotel; Real
   estate managers; Eating places

(P-15095)
BHR OPERATIONS LLC
Also Called: Wyndham San Diego Bayside
1355 N Harbor Dr (92101-3321)
PHONE...................619 232-3861
Joe Eustice, *Genl Mgr*
EMP: 139
SALES (corp-wide): 1.19B **Privately Held**
Web: www.wyndhamhotels.com
SIC: 7011 Hotels
HQ: Bhr Operations, L.L.C.
   125 E John Carpenter Fwy
   Irving TX
   972 444-4900

(P-15096)
BRAEMAR PARTNERSHIP
Also Called: Catamaran Resort Hotel
3999 Mission Blvd (92109-6959)
PHONE...................858 488-1081
Robert Gleason, *CFO*
Anne L Evans, *Mgr*
EMP: 350 **EST:** 1959
SALES (est): 17.99MM **Privately Held**
Web: www.catamaranresort.com
SIC: 7011 5812 5813 Resort hotel; American
   restaurant; Cocktail lounge

(P-15097)
BRISAM LAX (DE) LLC
Also Called: Holiday Inn
9901 S La Cienega Blvd (90045-5915)
PHONE...................310 649-5151
Steve Hostetter, *Genl Mgr*
EMP: 95 **EST:** 2007
SALES (est): 5.17MM **Privately Held**
Web: www.holidayinn.com
SIC: 7011 Hotels and motels

(P-15098)
BURBANK PARTNERS LLC
Also Called: Courtyard By Marriott
15433 Ventura Blvd (91403-3003)
PHONE.....................818 263-8704
EMP: 90 **EST:** 1968
SALES (est): 5.94MM **Privately Held**
Web: www.marriott.com
SIC: 7011 5813 5812 7299 Hotels and motels
; Cocktail lounge; Eating places; Banquet
hall facilities

(P-15099)
BURTON WAY HOTELS LLC
Also Called: Four Seasons Hotels Limited
300 S Doheny Dr (90048-3704)
PHONE.....................310 273-2222
Isadore Sharp, *Ch*
EMP: 92 **EST:** 2015
SALES (est): 16.56MM **Privately Held**
SIC: 7011 Hotels

(P-15100)
**BURTON WAY HTELS LTD A CAL
LTD**
Also Called: Four Seasons Ht Westlake Vlg
2 Dole Dr (91362-7300)
PHONE.....................818 575-3000
Robert Cima, *Brnch Mgr*
EMP: 215
SALES (corp-wide): 24.05MM **Privately
Held**
SIC: 7011 Hotels
PA: Burton Way Hotels, Ltd., A California
Limited Partnership
2029 Century Park E # 2200
Los Angeles CA
310 552-6623

(P-15101)
BURTON-WAY HOUSE LTD A CA
Also Called: Four Seasons Hotel
300 S Doheny Dr (90048-3704)
PHONE.....................310 273-2222
Mehdi Efpekari, *Genl Mgr*
EMP: 215
SALES (corp-wide): 24.05MM **Privately
Held**
SIC: 7011 5812 Hotels; Eating places
PA: Burton Way Hotels, Ltd., A California
Limited Partnership
2029 Century Park E # 2200
Los Angeles CA
310 552-6623

(P-15102)
BY THE BLUE SEA LLC
Also Called: Shutters On The Beach
1 Pico Blvd (90405-1063)
PHONE.....................310 458-0030
Tim Dubois, *Pr*
Klaus Mennekes, *
EMP: 350 **EST:** 2001
SALES (est): 23.88MM **Privately Held**
Web: www.shuttersonthebeach.com
SIC: 7011 Hotels

(P-15103)
C N L HOTEL DEL PARTNERS LP
1500 Orange Ave (92118-2918)
PHONE.....................619 522-8299
Todd Shallan, *Pt*
EMP: 81 **EST:** 2004
SALES (est): 912.91K **Privately Held**
Web: www.hoteldel.com
SIC: 7011 Resort hotel

(P-15104)
C W HOTELS LTD
Also Called: JW Marriott Le Merigot
1740 Ocean Ave (90401-3214)
PHONE.....................310 395-9700
Damien Hirsch, *Genl Mgr*
EMP: 150
SALES (corp-wide): 23.2MM **Privately
Held**
Web: jw-marriott.marriott.com
SIC: 7011 Hotels
PA: C W Hotels Ltd
740 Centre View Blvd
Crestview Hills KY
859 578-1100

(P-15105)
**CABAZON BAND MISSION
INDIANS**
Fantasy Spring Resort Casino
84245 Indio Springs Dr (92203-3405)
PHONE.....................760 342-5000
Jim Mccannon, *Mgr*
EMP: 520
Web: www.fantasyspringsresort.com
SIC: 7011 Casino hotel
PA: Cabazon Band Of Cahuilla Indians
84245 Indio Springs Dr
Indio CA

(P-15106)
CALHOT ILLINIOS LLC
Also Called: Ramada Inn
5250 W El Segundo Blvd (90250-4142)
PHONE.....................310 536-9800
Fred Groth, *Genl Mgr*
Kairey Choi, *Asst Mgr*
EMP: 92 **EST:** 1990
SALES (est): 319.99K **Privately Held**
Web: www.wyndhamhotels.com
SIC: 7011 5812 Hotels and motels; Eating
places

(P-15107)
**CALIFORNIA COMMERCE CLUB
INC**
Also Called: Commerce Casino
6131 Telegraph Rd (90040-2501)
PHONE.....................323 721-2100
Haig Papaian, *CEO*
Ralph Wong, *CAO**
Dante Oliveto, *
Harvey Ross, *
Deborah Payne, *
▲ **EMP:** 2600 **EST:** 1982
SQ FT: 350,000
SALES (est): 126.32MM **Privately Held**
Web: www.commercecasino.com
SIC: 7011 5812 Casino hotel; Eating places

(P-15108)
**CARSON OPERATING
COMPANY LLC**
Also Called: Doubletree By Hilton Carson
2 Civic Plaza Dr (90745-2231)
PHONE.....................310 830-9200
Greg Guthrie, *Genl Mgr*
Leroy Russell, *
EMP: 90 **EST:** 2015
SALES (est): 2.79MM **Privately Held**
Web: www.hilton.com
SIC: 7011 Hotels

(P-15109)
CAVALIER INN INC
Also Called: Cavalier Oceanfront Resort
9415 Hearst Dr (93452-9724)
PHONE.....................805 927-4688
Mona Rigdon, *Prin*

Michael Hanchett, *
EMP: 80 **EST:** 2016
SALES (est): 2.09MM **Privately Held**
Web: www.cavalierresort.com
SIC: 7011 Motels

(P-15110)
CELEBRITY CASINOS INC
Also Called: Crystal Casino & Hotel
123 E Artesia Blvd (90220-4921)
PHONE.....................310 631-3838
Mark A Kelegian, *Pr*
Haig Kelegian Junior, *CFO*
Haig Kelegian Senior, *CEO*
EMP: 400 **EST:** 2005
SQ FT: 190,000
SALES (est): 23.37MM **Privately Held**
Web: www.thecrystalcasino.com
SIC: 7011 Casino hotel

(P-15111)
**CENTURY GAMING
MANAGEMENT INC**
Also Called: Hollywood Park Casino
3883 W Century Blvd (90303-1003)
PHONE.....................310 330-2800
▲ **EMP:** 710
SIC: 7011 5813 5812 Casino hotel; Drinking
places; Eating places

(P-15112)
CHA LA MIRADA LLC
Also Called: Holiday Inn La Mirada
14299 Firestone Blvd (90638-5523)
PHONE.....................714 739-8500
EMP: 120 **EST:** 1984
SALES (est): 9.24MM **Privately Held**
Web: www.holidayinn.com
SIC: 7011 Hotels and motels

(P-15113)
CHAMPION INVESTMENT CORP
12809 Oakfield Way (92064-1520)
PHONE.....................917 712-7807
Chia-sheng Hou, *Pr*
Pi-lien Hou, *VP*
EMP: 100 **EST:** 1993
SALES (est): 2.06MM **Privately Held**
Web: www.hilton.com
SIC: 7011 Resort hotel

(P-15114)
CHEN & HUANG PARTNERS LP
Also Called: Travelodge
1400 S Bristol St (92704-3426)
PHONE.....................714 557-8700
James Chen, *Pt*
Yi-ho Huang, *Pt*
EMP: 81 **EST:** 1978
SQ FT: 50,000
SALES (est): 927.41K **Privately Held**
Web: www.wyndhamhotels.com
SIC: 7011 Hotels and motels

(P-15115)
CIM GROUP LP (PA)
Also Called: Commercial Inv MGT Group
4700 Wilshire Blvd Ste 1 (90010-3831)
PHONE.....................323 860-4900
Avraham Shemesch, *Pt*
Eric P Rubenfeld, *Pt*
EMP: 223 **EST:** 2000
SALES (est): 217.89MM
SALES (corp-wide): 217.89MM **Privately
Held**
Web: www.cimgroup.com
SIC: 7011 6798 6552 Hotels and motels;
Real estate investment trusts; Land
subdividers and developers, commercial

(P-15116)
CIM/H & H HOTEL LP
Also Called: Renaissance Hollywood Ht &
Spa
1755 N Highland Ave (90028-4403)
PHONE.....................323 856-1200
EMP: 350
Web: www.renaissancehollywood.com
SIC: 7011 Hotels

(P-15117)
CINDERELLA MOTEL
Also Called: Candy Cane Inn
1747 S Harbor Blvd (92802-2315)
PHONE.....................559 432-0118
Ralph Kazarian, *Pr*
EMP: 81
SQ FT: 65,542
SALES (corp-wide): 6.06MM **Privately
Held**
Web: www.candycaneinn.net
SIC: 7011 Motels
PA: Cinderella Motel
2416 W Shaw Ave Ste 109
Fresno CA
559 432-0118

(P-15118)
CITRUS NORTH VENTURE LLC
6591 Collins Dr Ste E11 (93021-1493)
PHONE.....................256 428-2000
Marc Pierguidi, *Sec*
EMP: 99 **EST:** 2017
SALES (est): 1.52MM **Privately Held**
SIC: 7011 Hotel, franchised

(P-15119)
CLEAR GROUP INC
Also Called: The Clear Group Inc
408 N Avalon Blvd (90074-0001)
PHONE.....................603 325-5600
Chris Barone, *Brnch Mgr*
EMP: 121
SALES (corp-wide): 249.45K **Privately
Held**
SIC: 7011 Resort hotel
PA: The Clear Group Inc
1069 E Wardlow Rd
Long Beach CA

(P-15120)
CNI THL PROPCO FE LLC
Also Called: Four Points Bakersfield
5101 California Ave (93309-1623)
PHONE.....................661 325-9700
EMP: 80 **EST:** 2017
SALES (est): 2.42MM **Privately Held**
Web: www.fourpointsbakersfield.com
SIC: 7011 Hotels and motels

(P-15121)
COMFORT CALIFORNIA INC
Also Called: Clarion Hotel
616 W Convention Way (92802-3401)
PHONE.....................714 750-3131
Mike Thomas, *Brnch Mgr*
EMP: 149
SALES (corp-wide): 96.75MM **Privately
Held**
Web: www.choicehotels.com
SIC: 7011 Hotels and motels
HQ: Comfort California, Inc.
8171 Maple Lawn Blvd # 380
Fulton MD

(P-15122)
COURTYARD OXNARD
600 E Esplanade Dr (93036-2480)
PHONE.....................805 988-3600

Patricia Tewes, *Genl Mgr*
EMP: 80 **EST:** 2009
SALES (est): 2.36MM **Privately Held**
SIC: 7011 Hotels and motels

(P-15123)
CPH MONARCH HOTEL LLC
Also Called: Waldorf Astria Mnrc Bch Rsort
1 Monarch Beach Resort (92629-4085)
PHONE..................949 234-3200
Paul Makarechian, *Pr*
▲ **EMP:** 1100 **EST:** 2001
SQ FT: 300,000
SALES (est): 52.37MM
SALES (corp-wide): 97.93MM **Privately Held**
Web:
www.waldorfastoriamonarchbeach.com
SIC: 7011 Resort hotel
PA: Waldorf Astoria Management Llc
7930 Jones Branch Dr # 1100
Mc Lean VA
703 883-1000

(P-15124)
CRESTLINE HOTELS & RESORTS INC (HQ)
Also Called: Kyoto Grand Hotel and Gardens
120 S Los Angeles St 11 (90012-3724)
PHONE..................213 629-1200
Richard Gaines, *Genl Mgr*
EMP: 130 **EST:** 1974
SALES (est): 4.22MM
SALES (corp-wide): 370.56MM **Privately Held**
Web: www.kyotograndhotel.com
SIC: 7011 5812 5813 Hotels; Restaurant, family: independent; Drinking places
PA: Crestline Hotels & Resorts, Llc
3950 University Dr # 301
Fairfax VA
571 529-6100

(P-15125)
CTC GROUP INC (DH)
Also Called: Doubletree Hotel
21333 Hawthorne Blvd (90503-5602)
PHONE..................310 540-0500
John Huang, *CEO*
EMP: 145 **EST:** 1989
SALES (est): 33.28MM
SALES (corp-wide): 2.5B **Publicly Held**
Web: www.hilton.com
SIC: 7011 Hotels and motels
HQ: Gringteam Inc
21725 Gateway Center Dr
Diamond Bar CA

(P-15126)
CUSTOM HOTEL LLC
Also Called: Hotel June, The
8639 Lincoln Blvd (90045-3503)
PHONE..................310 645-0400
Alisa Matthews, *
EMP: 398 **EST:** 2005
SALES (est): 13.14MM
SALES (corp-wide): 83.61MM **Privately Held**
Web: www.thehoteljune.com
SIC: 7011 Hotels
PA: Joie De Vivre Hospitality, Llc
1750 Geary Blvd
San Francisco CA
415 922-6000

(P-15127)
DAVIDSON HOTEL PARTNERS LP
Also Called: Agoura Hills Renaissance Hotel
30100 Agoura Rd (91301-2004)

PHONE..................818 707-1220
Larry Mills, *Pt*
EMP: 1477
Web: www.davidsonhospitality.com
SIC: 7011 Hotels and motels
PA: Davidson Hotel Partners, L.P
1 Ravinia Dr Ste 1600
Atlanta GA

(P-15128)
DESTINATION RESIDENCES LLC
Also Called: Shadow Mtn Rsort Rcquet CLB Tn
45750 San Luis Rey Ave (92260-4728)
PHONE..................760 346-4647
Sindy Calhoun, *Mgr*
EMP: 340
SALES (corp-wide): 367.25MM **Privately Held**
Web: www.destinationhotels.com
SIC: 7011 5699 6531 Resort hotel; Sports apparel; Condominium manager
HQ: Destination Residences Llc
10333 E Dry Creek Rd
Englewood CO
303 799-3830

(P-15129)
DIAMOND RESORTS LLC
Also Called: Palm Canyon Resort & Spa
2800 S Palm Canyon Dr (92264-9337)
PHONE..................760 866-1800
Allison Wickerham, *Managing Member*
Carl Ellis, *
EMP: 100 **EST:** 2004
SALES (est): 300K **Privately Held**
Web: www.tophotelreservations.com
SIC: 7011 5812 7991 Resort hotel; American restaurant; Spas

(P-15130)
DIAMONDROCK SAN DEGO TNANT LLC
Also Called: Westin San Diego
400 W Broadway (92101-3504)
PHONE..................619 239-4500
EMP: 300 **EST:** 2012
SQ FT: 337,717
SALES (est): 25.58MM
SALES (corp-wide): 1B **Publicly Held**
Web: www.westinsandiego.com
SIC: 7011 Hotels
HQ: Diamondrock Hospitality Limited Partnership
3 Bethesda Metro Ctr
Bethesda MD

(P-15131)
DISNEY ENTERPRISES INC
Also Called: Disney
1150 W Magic Way (92802-2247)
PHONE..................714 778-6600
Michael D Eisner, *Pr*
EMP: 3500
SALES (corp-wide): 88.9B **Publicly Held**
Web: www.disney.com
SIC: 7011 Resort hotel
HQ: Disney Enterprises, Inc.
500 S Buena Vista St
Burbank CA
818 560-1000

(P-15132)
DISNEYLAND INTERNATIONAL
Also Called: Disneyland
1580 S Disneyland Dr (92802-2294)
PHONE..................714 956-6746
EMP: 5000
SALES (corp-wide): 88.9B **Publicly Held**
Web: disneyland.disney.go.com

SIC: 7011 Resort hotel
HQ: Disneyland International
1313 S Harbor Blvd
Anaheim CA
714 781-4565

(P-15133)
DJONT OPERATIONS LLC
Also Called: Embassy Suites - Lax Airport S
1440 E Imperial Ave (90245-2623)
PHONE..................310 640-3600
Shar Franklin, *Genl Mgr*
EMP: 120
SALES (corp-wide): 1.19B **Privately Held**
Web: www.hilton.com
SIC: 7011 Hotels and motels
HQ: Djont Operations, L.L.C.
125 E Houston St
San Antonio TX

(P-15134)
DJONT/JPM HSPTLITY LSG SPE LLC
Also Called: Embassy Stes - Mndlay Bch Rsor
2101 Mandalay Beach Rd (93035-3638)
PHONE..................805 984-2500
Colleen Huther, *Genl Mgr*
EMP: 104
SALES (corp-wide): 1.19B **Privately Held**
Web: www.hilton.com
SIC: 7011 Hotels
HQ: Djont/Jpm Hospitality Leasing (Spe), L.L.C.
400 Arch St
Philadelphia PA

(P-15135)
DKN HOTEL LLC (PA)
42 Corporate Park Ste 200 (92606-5105)
PHONE..................714 427-4320
Nilesh Patel, *
John Jorgensen, *
Dahya Lal, *
EMP: 290 **EST:** 2002
SQ FT: 4,000
SALES (est): 38.6MM
SALES (corp-wide): 38.6MM **Privately Held**
Web: www.dknhotels.com
SIC: 7011 Hotels and motels

(P-15136)
DOLPHIN BAY HT & RESIDENCE INC
Also Called: Dolphin Bay Hotel & Residences
2727 Shell Beach Rd (93449-1602)
PHONE..................805 773-4300
Richard J Loughead Junior, *CEO*
EMP: 90 **EST:** 2005
SALES (est): 9.07MM **Privately Held**
Web: www.thedolphinbay.com
SIC: 7011 Resort hotel

(P-15137)
DONALD T STERLING CORPORATION
Also Called: Beverly Hills Plaza Hotel
10300 Wilshire Blvd (90024-4772)
PHONE..................310 275-5575
EMP: 80
SALES (corp-wide): 2.1MM **Privately Held**
Web: www.beverlyhillsplazahotel.com
SIC: 7011 Hotels
PA: Donald T. Sterling Corporation
9441 Wlshire Blvd Pnthuse Penthouse
Beverly Hills CA
310 278-8000

(P-15138)
DOUBLTREE BY HLTON HT MONROVIA
Also Called: Doubletree By Hilton
924 W Huntington Dr (91016-3112)
PHONE..................626 357-1900
Jessi Willis, *Prin*
EMP: 123 **EST:** 2010
SALES (est): 12.42MM **Privately Held**
Web: www.hilton.com
SIC: 7011 Hotels

(P-15139)
DTRS SANTA MONICA LLC
Also Called: Loews Santa Monica Beach Hotel
1700 Ocean Ave (90401-3214)
PHONE..................310 458-6700
Younes Atolah, *Genl Mgr*
Andrei Zotoff, *Managing Member*
EMP: 300 **EST:** 1989
SQ FT: 300,000
SALES (est): 15MM **Privately Held**
Web: www.loewshotels.com
SIC: 7011 Resort hotel

(P-15140)
EDWARD THOMAS COMPANIES
Also Called: Jolly Roger Inn
640 W Katella Ave (92802-3411)
PHONE..................714 782-7500
Fred Kokash, *Brnch Mgr*
EMP: 110
SALES (corp-wide): 4.63MM **Privately Held**
Web: www.edwardthomasco.com
SIC: 7011 5812 Motels; Eating places
PA: The Edward Thomas Companies
9950 Santa Monica Blvd
Beverly Hills CA
310 859-9366

(P-15141)
EDWARD THOMAS HOSPITALITY CORP
Also Called: Shutters On The Beach
1 Pico Blvd (90405-1063)
PHONE..................310 458-0030
Klaus Mennekes, *Brnch Mgr*
EMP: 349
SALES (corp-wide): 9.7MM **Privately Held**
Web: www.shuttersonthebeach.com
SIC: 7011 5812 7991 5813 Hotels; Eating places; Physical fitness facilities; Drinking places
PA: The Edward Thomas Hospitality Corp
9950 Santa Monica Blvd
Beverly Hills CA
310 859-9366

(P-15142)
EL CENTRO HOSPITALITY LLC
Also Called: Fairfield Inn
503 E Danenberg Dr (92243-8507)
PHONE..................760 353-2600
Clarissa Clark, *Prin*
EMP: 223
SALES (corp-wide): 590.12K **Privately Held**
Web: fairfield.marriott.com
SIC: 7011 Hotels and motels
PA: El Centro Hospitality, L.L.C.
2300 Tower Dr
Monroe LA
318 325-5561

(P-15143)
EL CENTRO HOSPITALITY 2 LLC
Also Called: TownePlace Suites El Centro

3003 S Dogwood Rd (92243-9160)
PHONE..............................760 370-3800
Dewey F Weaver Junior, *Brnch Mgr*
EMP: 216
SALES (corp-wide): 1.14MM **Privately Held**
Web: www.marriott.com
SIC: 7011 Hotel, franchised
PA: El Centro Hospitality 2, L.L.C.
2390 Tower Dr
Monroe LA
318 325-5561

(P-15144)
EL DORADO ENTERPRISES INC
Also Called: Hustler Casino
1000 W Redondo Beach Blvd (90247-4192)
PHONE..............................310 719-9800
Larry C Flynt, *CEO*
EMP: 760 **EST:** 2000
SALES (est): 48.29MM **Privately Held**
Web: www.hustlercasino.com
SIC: 7011 Casino hotel

(P-15145)
EMBASSY SUITES & HOTEL
Also Called: Embassy Suites
11767 Harbor Blvd (92840-2701)
PHONE..............................714 539-3300
Charlene Garcia, *OF ROOMS*
Tracy Stephens, *OF ROOMS*
Dominic Acolino, *Genl Mgr*
Charlene Garcia French, *Div Mgr*
EMP: 155 **EST:** 2002
SALES (est): 8.29MM
SALES (corp-wide): 2.5B **Publicly Held**
Web: www.hilton.com
SIC: 7011 Hotels and motels
PA: Park Hotels & Resorts Inc.
1775 Tysons Blvd Fl 7
Tysons VA
571 302-5757

(P-15146)
EMERIK HOTEL CORP
Also Called: Luxe City Center
1020 S Figueroa St (90015-1305)
PHONE..............................213 748-1291
Emerson Glazer, *Pr*
James Jones, *
Art Malmgren, *
John Kelly, *
EMP: 96 **EST:** 1987
SALES (est): 1.48MM **Privately Held**
SIC: 7011 5813 5812 Hotels; Bar (drinking places); American restaurant

(P-15147)
ENCINA PEPPER TREE JOINT VENTR
Also Called: Best Western
2220 Bath St (93105-4322)
PHONE..............................805 682-7277
EMP: 80
SALES (corp-wide): 4.89MM **Privately Held**
Web: www.bestwestern.com
SIC: 7011 Motels
PA: Pepper Encina Tree Joint Venture
3850 State St
Santa Barbara CA
805 687-5511

(P-15148)
ESTANCIA HOTEL LLC
Also Called: Estancia La Jolla Hotel & Spa
9700 N Torrey Pines Rd (92037-1102)
PHONE..............................949 474-7368
Timothy Busch, *CEO*
Brittany Enos, *Prin*

EMP: 111 **EST:** 2012
SALES (est): 13.74MM **Privately Held**
Web: www.estancialajolla.com
SIC: 7011 Resort hotel

(P-15149)
ET WHITEHALL SEASCAPE LLC
Also Called: Hotel Casa Del Mar
1910 Ocean Way (90405-1083)
PHONE..............................310 581-5533
◆ **EMP:** 202 **EST:** 1998
SQ FT: 200,000
SALES (est): 11.89MM **Privately Held**
Web: www.hotelcasadelmar.com
SIC: 7011 5812 Hotels; Eating places

(P-15150)
EUROPEAN HT INVSTORS I I A CAL
Also Called: O H I
2532 Dupont Dr (92612-1524)
PHONE..............................949 474-7368
Timothy R Busch, *Genl Pt*
EMP: 80 **EST:** 1987
SQ FT: 9,000
SALES (est): 5.69MM **Privately Held**
Web: www.thebuschfirm.com
SIC: 7011 Hotels

(P-15151)
FAIRFIELD INN BY MRROTT LTD PRT
Also Called: Marriott
1460 S Harbor Blvd (92802-2311)
PHONE..............................714 772-6777
Helen Forbs, *Mgr*
EMP: 117 **EST:** 1989
SALES (est): 9.43MM **Privately Held**
Web: www.marriott.com
SIC: 7011 Hotels and motels

(P-15152)
FESS PRKER-RED LION GEN PARTNR
Also Called: Doubletree Hotel
633 E Cabrillo Blvd (93103-3611)
PHONE..............................805 564-4333
Fess Parker, *Pt*
EMP: 138 **EST:** 1981
SALES (est): 2.72MM **Privately Held**
Web: www.hilton.com
SIC: 7011 Hotels and motels

(P-15153)
FJS INC
Also Called: Anabella Hotel The
888 S Disneyland Dr Ste 400 (92802-1847)
PHONE..............................714 905-1050
EMP: 118 **EST:** 1989
SALES (est): 8.38MM **Privately Held**
SIC: 7011 Resort hotel

(P-15154)
FORTUNA ENTERPRISES LP
Also Called: Hilton
5711 W Century Blvd (90045-5672)
PHONE..............................310 410-4000
Henry H Hsu, *Pt*
David Hsu, *Pt*
Christine Hsu, *Pt*
EMP: 450 **EST:** 1992
SQ FT: 2,700
SALES (est): 45.04MM **Privately Held**
Web: www.hilton.com
SIC: 7011 5812 5813 Hotels and motels; Eating places; Bar (drinking places)
HQ: Universal Fortuna Investment, Inc.
5711 W Century Blvd # 16
Los Angeles CA

(P-15155)
GOLDEN DOOR PROPERTIES LLC
Also Called: Golden Door
777 Deer Springs Rd (92069-9757)
PHONE..............................760 744-5777
Joanne Conway, *Managing Member*
Kathy Van Ness, *COO*
▲ **EMP:** 173 **EST:** 1958
SQ FT: 50,000
SALES (est): 21.93MM **Privately Held**
Web: www.goldendoor.com
SIC: 7011 Hotels and motels

(P-15156)
GOLDEN HOTELS LTD PARTNERSHIP
Also Called: Atrium Hotel
18700 Macarthur Blvd (92612-1409)
PHONE..............................949 833-2770
Mike Wang, *Pt*
John Wang, *
EMP: 140 **EST:** 1960
SQ FT: 120,000
SALES (est): 9.03MM **Privately Held**
Web: www.atriumhotel.com
SIC: 7011 Resort hotel

(P-15157)
GOLDEN WEST PARTNERS INC
Also Called: Golden West Casino
1001 S Union Ave (93307-3641)
PHONE..............................661 324-6936
Jaussauds Maison, *Brnch Mgr*
EMP: 218
Web: www.goldenwestcasino.com
SIC: 7011 Casino hotel
PA: Golden West Partners, Inc.
200 Spectrum Center Dr # 1250
Irvine CA

(P-15158)
GRAND DEL MAR RESORT LP
Also Called: Grand Del Mar
5300 Grand Del Mar Ct (92130-4901)
PHONE..............................858 314-2000
Tom Voss, *Pt*
EMP: 570 **EST:** 2005
SALES (est): 49.06MM **Privately Held**
Web: www.thegranddelmar.com
SIC: 7011 Resort hotel

(P-15159)
GRAND PACIFIC CARLSBAD HT LP
Also Called: Sheraton Carlsbad Resort & Spa
5480 Grand Pacific Dr (92008-4723)
PHONE..............................760 827-2400
Tim Shinkle, *CFO*
Janina Kershaw, *Contrlr*
EMP: 272 **EST:** 2008
SALES (est): 23.86MM **Privately Held**
Web: www.sheratoncarlsbad.com
SIC: 7011 Resort hotel

(P-15160)
GRAND PACIFIC RESORTS INC
Also Called: Resortime.com
5900 Pasteur Ct Ste 200 (92008-7336)
PHONE..............................760 431-8500
Sherri Weks, *Mgr*
EMP: 513
Web: www.grandpacificresorts.com
SIC: 7011 Resort hotel
PA: Grand Pacific Resorts, Inc.
5900 Pasteur Ct Ste 200
Carlsbad CA

(P-15161)
GRAND PACIFIC RESORTS SVCS LP
5900 Pasteur Ct Ste 200 (92008-7336)
PHONE..............................760 431-8500
Timothy Stripe, *Pt*
David Brown, *Pt*
EMP: 120 **EST:** 1992
SQ FT: 22,000
SALES (est): 4.55MM **Privately Held**
Web: www.grandpacificresorts.com
SIC: 7011 Resort hotel

(P-15162)
GREENS GROUP INC
16530 Bake Pkwy Ste 200 (92618-4685)
PHONE..............................949 829-4902
Ashutosh Kadakia, *CFO*
EMP: 145 **EST:** 2004
SALES (est): 6.48MM **Privately Held**
SIC: 7011 Resort hotel, franchised

(P-15163)
GRINGTEAM INC
Also Called: Doubletree By Hilton
7450 Hazard Center Dr (92108-4539)
PHONE..............................619 297-5466
Karima Zaki, *Mgr*
EMP: 300
SALES (corp-wide): 2.5B **Publicly Held**
Web: www.hilton.com
SIC: 7011 5812 Hotels and motels; Eating places
HQ: Gringteam Inc
21725 Gateway Center Dr
Diamond Bar CA

(P-15164)
GRINGTEAM INC
Also Called: Doubletree Golf Resort
800 W Ivy St Ste D (92101-1771)
PHONE..............................858 485-4145
Russ Tanakaya, *Genl Mgr*
EMP: 80
SALES (corp-wide): 2.5B **Publicly Held**
Web: www.hilton.com
SIC: 7011 Hotels and motels
HQ: Gringteam Inc
21725 Gateway Center Dr
Diamond Bar CA

(P-15165)
H & H LLC (PA)
1131 S Russell Ave (93458-6821)
PHONE..............................805 925-2036
Blanche Hollingsead, *Managing Member*
EMP: 89 **EST:** 2011
SALES (est): 2.34MM
SALES (corp-wide): 2.34MM **Privately Held**
Web: www.radissonhotels.com
SIC: 7011 Hotels and motels

(P-15166)
H D G ASSOCIATES
Also Called: Hotel Marmonte
1111 E Cabrillo Blvd (93103-3701)
PHONE..............................805 963-0744
Ruth Grande, *Pr*
EMP: 242 **EST:** 1979
SQ FT: 150,000
SALES (est): 5.48MM **Publicly Held**
Web: www.marmontehotel.com
SIC: 7011 Hotels
HQ: Hyatt Corporation
250 Vesey St Fl 15
New York NY
312 750-1234

(P-15167)
HAMPSTEAD LAFAYETTE HOTEL LLC
Also Called: Insuites Hotels
2223 El Cajon Blvd (92104-1103)
PHONE..............................619 296-2101
James Green, *Mgr*
EMP: 217
SALES (corp-wide): 1.93MM **Privately Held**
Web: www.lafayettehotelsd.com
SIC: 7011 Resort hotel
PA: Lafayette Hampstead Hotel Llc
2223 El Cajon Blvd
San Diego CA
619 296-2101

(P-15168)
HANDLERY HOTELS INC
Also Called: Handlery Hotels
950 Hotel Cir N (92108-2995)
PHONE..............................415 781-4550
John Martin, *Mgr*
EMP: 150
SALES (corp-wide): 18.71MM **Privately Held**
Web: sd.handlery.com
SIC: 7011 5941 5812 5947 Resort hotel; Golf goods and equipment; Eating places; Gift, novelty, and souvenir shop
PA: Handlery Hotels, Inc.
180 Geary St Ste 700
San Francisco CA
415 781-4550

(P-15169)
HANFORD HOTELS INC
Also Called: Hotel Hanford, The
3131 Bristol St (92626-3037)
PHONE..............................714 557-3000
Tony Eccher, *Ex Dir*
EMP: 239
SQ FT: 65,311
Web: www.hanfordhotels.com
SIC: 7011 Hotels
PA: Hanford Hotels, Inc.
17542 17th St Ste 450
Tustin CA

(P-15170)
HARBOR VIEW HOTEL VENTURES LLC
Also Called: Doubletree Ht San Diego Dwntwn
1646 Front St (92101-2920)
PHONE..............................619 239-6800
Michael Gallegos, *Managing Member*
EMP: 100 **EST:** 1997
SALES (est): 4.07MM **Privately Held**
Web: www.hilton.com
SIC: 7011 Hotels

(P-15171)
HAWAIIAN GARDENS CASINO
11871 Carson St (90716-1127)
PHONE..............................562 860-5887
David Moskowitz, *CEO*
Irving Moskowitz, *
▲ **EMP:** 1000 **EST:** 1998
SALES (est): 47.26MM **Privately Held**
Web: www.thegardenscasino.com
SIC: 7011 Casino hotel

(P-15172)
HAWAIIAN HOTELS & RESORTS INC
2830 Borchard Rd (91320-3810)
PHONE..............................805 480-0052
Edward J Hogan, *Pr*

Glenn Hogan, *
EMP: 231 **EST:** 2001
SALES (est): 2.77MM
SALES (corp-wide): 1.08B **Privately Held**
Web: www.hawaiihotels.com
SIC: 7011 Resort hotel
HQ: Pleasant Holidays, Llc
2404 Townsgate Rd
Westlake Village CA

(P-15173)
HAZENS INVESTMENT LLC
Also Called: Sheraton
6101 W Century Blvd (90045-5310)
PHONE..............................310 642-1111
Henry Pekun, *Contrlr*
EMP: 395 **EST:** 2002
SALES (est): 44.17MM **Privately Held**
Web: four-points.marriott.com
SIC: 7011 Hotels

(P-15174)
HCAL LLC
Also Called: Harrahs Resort Southern Cal
777 S Resort Dr (92082)
PHONE..............................760 751-3100
EMP: 371 **EST:** 2005
SALES (est): 10.73MM
SALES (corp-wide): 10.82B **Publicly Held**
SIC: 7011 Casino hotel
HQ: Caesars Holdings, Inc.
1 Caesars Palace Dr
Las Vegas NV

(P-15175)
HEI HOSPITALITY LLC
Also Called: Marriott
21850 Oxnard St (91367-3631)
PHONE..............................818 887-4800
Clay Andrews, *Mgr*
EMP: 167
SALES (corp-wide): 447.39MM **Privately Held**
Web: www.heihotels.com
SIC: 7011 Hotels and motels
PA: Hei Hospitality, Llc
101 Merritt 7
Norwalk CT
203 849-8844

(P-15176)
HEI LONG BEACH LLC
Also Called: Hilton Hotels
701 W Ocean Blvd (90831-3100)
PHONE..............................562 983-3400
Clark Christopher, *Prin*
EMP: 125 **EST:** 2004
SALES (est): 10.6MM
SALES (corp-wide): 447.39MM **Privately Held**
Web: www.hilton.com
SIC: 7011 Hotels
PA: Hei Hospitality, Llc
101 Merritt 7
Norwalk CT
203 849-8844

(P-15177)
HILTON GARDEN INNS MGT LLC
Also Called: Hilton
6450 Carlsbad Blvd (92011-1058)
PHONE..............................760 476-0800
Robert Moore, *Genl Mgr*
EMP: 545
SALES (corp-wide): 8.77B **Publicly Held**
Web: www.hiltongrandvacations.com
SIC: 7011 Resort hotel
HQ: Hilton Garden Inns Management Llc
7930 Jones Branch Dr
Mc Lean VA
703 883-1000

(P-15178)
HILTON LOS ANGLES UNIVERSAL CY
555 Universal Hollywood Dr (91608-1001)
PHONE..............................818 506-2500
Juan Aquinde, *Managing Member*
Matthew La Vine, *
▲ **EMP:** 184 **EST:** 2003
SALES (est): 9.04MM **Privately Held**
Web: www.hiltonuniversal.com
SIC: 7011 Hotels

(P-15179)
HILTON WOODLAND HILLS & TOWERS
6360 Canoga Ave (91367-2501)
PHONE..............................818 595-1000
Ed Debries, *Genl Mgr*
▲ **EMP:** 95 **EST:** 1989
SALES (est): 2.48MM **Privately Held**
Web: www.woodlandhillshotel.com
SIC: 7011 5813 5812 Hotels and motels; Drinking places; Eating places

(P-15180)
HISTORIC MISSION INN CORP
Also Called: Mission Inn Hotel and Spa, The
3649 Mission Inn Ave (92501-3364)
P.O. Box 1433 (92502-1433)
PHONE..............................951 784-0300
Duane R Roberts, *Pr*
Diana Rosure, *General Vice President*
Richard Shippee, *
Cliff Day, *
EMP: 460 **EST:** 1992
SALES (est): 33.22MM
SALES (corp-wide): 33.22MM **Privately Held**
Web: www.missioninn.com
SIC: 7011 7991 Resort hotel; Spas
PA: Entrepreneurial Capital Corporation
4100 Newport Place Dr # 400
Newport Beach CA
949 809-3900

(P-15181)
HISTORICAL PROPERTIES INC (PA)
Also Called: Horton Grand Hotel
311 Island Ave (92101-6923)
PHONE..............................619 230-8417
Doris J Rose, *Pr*
Santiago Ojeda, *
EMP: 96 **EST:** 1995
SQ FT: 60,000
SALES (est): 4.79MM **Privately Held**
Web: www.hortongrand.com
SIC: 7011 Hotels

(P-15182)
HOLIDAY INN EXPRESS
Also Called: Holiday Inn
2550 Erringer Rd (93065-2353)
PHONE..............................805 584-6006
Ashok Israni, *Pr*
EMP: 166 **EST:** 1987
SALES (est): 952.46K
SALES (corp-wide): 96.92MM **Privately Held**
Web: www.hiexpress.com
SIC: 7011 Hotels and motels
PA: Pacifica Hosts, Inc.
1775 Hancock St Ste 200
San Diego CA
619 296-9000

(P-15183)
HOLLYWOOD PARK CASINO CO INC

3883 W Century Blvd (90303-1003)
PHONE..............................310 330-2800
Terrence E Fancher, *Pr*
EMP: 179 **EST:** 2007
SALES (est): 25.31MM **Privately Held**
Web: www.playhpc.com
SIC: 7011 Casino hotel

(P-15184)
HONEYMOON REAL ESTATE LP
Also Called: Avalon Hotel
9400 W Olympic Blvd (90212-4552)
PHONE..............................310 277-5221
Brad Korzen, *Pt*
EMP: 90 **EST:** 1997
SQ FT: 400,000
SALES (est): 8.09MM **Privately Held**
Web: www.avalon-hotel.com
SIC: 7011 Resort hotel

(P-15185)
HOTEL BEL-AIR
701 Stone Canyon Rd (90077-2909)
PHONE..............................310 472-1211
EMP: 265 **EST:** 1994
SQ FT: 30,000
SALES (est): 9.58MM **Privately Held**
Web: www.dorchestercollection.com
SIC: 7011 Hotels
HQ: Kava Holdings, Inc.
701 Stone Canyon Rd
Los Angeles CA
310 472-1211

(P-15186)
HOTEL CIRCLE PROPERTY LLC
Also Called: Town and Country Hotel
500 Hotel Cir N (92108-3005)
PHONE..............................619 291-7131
April Shute, *Managing Member*
EMP: 500 **EST:** 2014
SQ FT: 1,132,560
SALES (est): 38.03MM **Privately Held**
Web: www.towncountry.com
SIC: 7011 Resort hotel

(P-15187)
HP LQ INVESTMENT LP
Also Called: La Quinta Resort & Club
49499 Eisenhower Dr (92253-2722)
PHONE..............................760 564-4111
EMP: 230 **EST:** 2021
SALES (est): 15.64MM
SALES (corp-wide): 8.77B **Publicly Held**
Web: www.laquintaresort.com
SIC: 7011 Resort hotel
PA: Hilton Worldwide Holdings Inc.
7930 Jones Branch Dr # 100
Mc Lean VA
703 883-1000

(P-15188)
HST LESSEE MISSION HILLS LP
Also Called: Westin Rncho Mrage Golf Rsort
71333 Dinah Shore Dr (92270-1501)
PHONE..............................760 328-5955
Hst Gp Mission Hills, *Genl Pt*
EMP: 100 **EST:** 2006
SALES (est): 15.4MM **Privately Held**
Web: www.westinmissionhills.com
SIC: 7011 Resort hotel

(P-15189)
HUMNIT HOTEL AT LAX LLC
Also Called: Concorse Ht At Los Angles Arpr
6225 W Century Blvd (90045-5311)
PHONE..............................424 702-1234
Jina Luman, *Prin*
Jina Luman, *Asst Tr*
EMP: 99 **EST:** 2013

▲ = Import ▼ = Export
◆ = Import/Export

SQ FT: 49,500
SALES (est): 7.7MM
SALES (corp-wide): 500.9MM **Publicly Held**
SIC: 7011 Hotels
PA: Amalgamated Financial Corp.
275 7th Ave
New York NY
212 255-6200

(P-15190)
HUNTINGTON HOTEL COMPANY
5951 Linea Del Cielo (92067)
PHONE.....................858 756-1131
Scott Jenkins, *CEO*
EMP: 88 **EST:** 1921
SQ FT: 5,000
SALES (est): 4.53MM **Privately Held**
Web: www.theinnatrsf.com
SIC: 7011 5812 Resort hotel; Eating places

(P-15191)
HUOYEN INTERNATIONAL INC
Also Called: Hotel Fullerton Anaheim, The
1500 S Raymond Ave (92831-5236)
P.O. Box 1071 (92822-1071)
PHONE.....................714 635-9000
EMP: 90 **EST:** 1995
SQ FT: 144,698
SALES (est): 2.21MM **Privately Held**
SIC: 7011 Hotel, franchised

(P-15192)
HYATT CORP AS AGT BRCP HEF HT
Also Called: Hyatt Hotel
7100 Aviara Resort Dr (92011-4908)
PHONE.....................760 603-6851
EMP: 90 **EST:** 2010
SALES (est): 8.1MM **Privately Held**
Web: www.parkhyattaviara.com
SIC: 7011 Resort hotel

(P-15193)
HYATT CORPORATION
Also Called: Hyatt Regency Lajolla
3777 La Jolla Village Dr (92122-1080)
PHONE.....................858 453-0018
Benjie Barin, *Owner*
EMP: 122 **EST:** 2000
SALES (est): 21.8MM **Privately Held**
Web: www.hyatt.com
SIC: 7011 Hotels

(P-15194)
HYATT CORPORATION
Also Called: Manchster Grnd Hyatt San Diego
1 Market Pl (92101-7714)
PHONE.....................619 232-1234
Ted Kanatas, *Mgr*
EMP: 222
Web: www.hosthotels.com
SIC: 7011 Hotels
HQ: Hyatt Corporation
250 Vesey St Fl 15
New York NY
312 750-1234

(P-15195)
HYATT CORPORATION
Also Called: Andaz Sandiego
600 F St (92101-6310)
PHONE.....................619 849-1234
Rusty Middleton, *Brnch Mgr*
EMP: 105
Web: www.hyattdevelopment.com
SIC: 7011 Resort hotel
HQ: Hyatt Corporation
250 Vesey St Fl 15
New York NY
312 750-1234

(P-15196)
HYATT CORPORATION
Also Called: Hyatt Los Angeles Airport
6225 W Century Blvd (90045-5311)
PHONE.....................312 750-1234
Donald J Henderson, *Mgr*
EMP: 500
Web: www.hyattdevelopment.com
SIC: 7011 5812 5813 Hotels; Restaurant, family: chain; Bar (drinking places)
HQ: Hyatt Corporation
250 Vesey St Fl 15
New York NY
312 750-1234

(P-15197)
HYATT CORPORATION
Also Called: Hyatt Hotel
8401 W Sunset Blvd (90069-1909)
PHONE.....................323 656-1234
Tim Flodin, *Mgr*
EMP: 233
Web: www.hyatt.com
SIC: 7011 5812 5813 Hotels and motels; Restaurant, family: independent; Bar (drinking places)
HQ: Hyatt Corporation
250 Vesey St Fl 15
New York NY
312 750-1234

(P-15198)
HYATT CORPORATION
Also Called: Hyatt Hotel
200 S Pine Ave (90802-4537)
PHONE.....................562 432-0161
Steve Smith, *Mgr*
EMP: 463
Web: www.hyatt.com
SIC: 7011 7299 Hotels and motels; Banquet hall facilities
HQ: Hyatt Corporation
250 Vesey St Fl 15
New York NY
312 750-1234

(P-15199)
HYATT CORPORATION
Also Called: Hyatt Hotel
17900 Jamboree Rd (92614-6211)
PHONE.....................949 975-1234
Rod T Schinnerer, *Genl Mgr*
EMP: 83
Web: www.hyatt.com
SIC: 7011 7992 7991 5813 Hotels and motels; Public golf courses; Physical fitness facilities; Drinking places
HQ: Hyatt Corporation
250 Vesey St Fl 15
New York NY
312 750-1234

(P-15200)
HYATT CORPORATION
Also Called: Hyatt Hotel
1107 Jamboree Rd (92660-6219)
PHONE.....................949 729-1234
Ruth Benjamin, *Genl Mgr*
EMP: 300
Web: www.hyatt.com
SIC: 7011 5813 5812 Hotels and motels; Drinking places; Eating places
HQ: Hyatt Corporation
250 Vesey St Fl 15
New York NY
312 750-1234

(P-15201)
HYATT CORPORATION
Also Called: Hyatt Grand Champion Resort
44600 Indian Wells Ln (92210-8707)
PHONE.....................760 341-1000
Allan Farwell, *Mgr*
EMP: 579
Web: www.hyatt.com
SIC: 7011 5813 5812 Hotels; Drinking places ; Eating places
HQ: Hyatt Corporation
250 Vesey St Fl 15
New York NY
312 750-1234

(P-15202)
HYATT REGENCY CENTURY PLAZA
2025 Avenue Of The Stars (90067-4741)
PHONE.....................310 228-1234
Rakesh Sarna, *CEO*
Ken Cruse, *
EMP: 650 **EST:** 2005
SALES (est): 9.39MM **Privately Held**
Web: centuryplaza.hyatt.com
SIC: 7011 Hotels

(P-15203)
IHG MANAGEMENT (MARYLAND) LLC
Also Called: Crown Plaza Los Angeles
5985 W Century Blvd (90045-5477)
PHONE.....................310 642-7500
William Block, *Dir Fin*
EMP: 86 **EST:** 2004
SQ FT: 14,000
SALES (est): 2.65MM **Privately Held**
Web: www.crowneplaza.com
SIC: 7011 Hotels

(P-15204)
IHG MANAGEMENT (MARYLAND) LLC
Also Called: Intercntnntal Los Angles Dwntw
900 Wilshire Blvd (90017-4701)
PHONE.....................213 688-7777
EMP: 87 **EST:** 2017
SALES (est): 4.79MM **Privately Held**
Web: dtla.intercontinental.com
SIC: 7011 Hotels

(P-15205)
IRP LAX HOTEL LLC
Also Called: Four Pnts By Shrton La Intl Ar
9750 Airport Blvd (90045-5404)
PHONE.....................310 645-4600
EMP: 240 **EST:** 1994
SQ FT: 337,720
SALES (est): 8.32MM
SALES (corp-wide): 14.38B **Publicly Held**
Web: four-points.marriott.com
SIC: 7011 Resort hotel
HQ: Tishman Hotel Corporation
100 Park Ave Fl 18
New York NY

(P-15206)
KANG FAMILY PARTNERS LLC
Also Called: Santa Ynez Valley Marriott
555 Mcmurray Rd (93427-9559)
PHONE.....................805 688-1000
Daphne Kang, *Managing Member*
EMP: 110 **EST:** 1995
SALES (est): 9.54MM **Privately Held**
Web: www.syvmarriott.com
SIC: 7011 Hotel, franchised

(P-15207)
KAVA HOLDINGS INC (DH)
Also Called: Hotel Bel-Air
701 Stone Canyon Rd (90077-2909)
PHONE.....................310 472-1211
Hj Suharafadzil, *Pr*
Christopher Cowdary, *
Helen Smith, *
Eugenio Pirri, *
Franois Delahaye, *
EMP: 200 **EST:** 1994
SQ FT: 30,000
SALES (est): 62.94MM **Privately Held**
Web: www.dorchestercollection.com
SIC: 7011 Resort hotel
HQ: Dorchester Group Limited
3 Tilney Street
London
207 629-4848

(P-15208)
KEN REAL ESTATE LEASE LTD
Also Called: Anaheim Majestic Garden Hotel
900 S Disneyland Dr (92802-1844)
PHONE.....................714 778-1700
Shigeru Sato, *Pr*
EMP: 99 **EST:** 2005
SALES (est): 9.58MM **Privately Held**
Web: www.ken-realestate.jp
SIC: 7011 Resort hotel

(P-15209)
KIMPTON HOTEL & REST GROUP LLC
6317 Wilshire Blvd (90048-5600)
PHONE.....................323 852-6000
Ashley Gochnauer, *Mgr*
EMP: 217
Web: www.kimptonhotels.com
SIC: 7011 Hotels
HQ: Kimpton Hotel & Restaurant Group Llc
222 Kearny St Ste 200
San Francisco CA
415 397-5572

(P-15210)
KINTETSU ENTERPRISES CO AMER (HQ)
Also Called: Kintetsu Enterprises Co Amer
21241 S Western Ave Ste 100 (90501)
PHONE.....................310 782-9300
Hisao Hiro, *Pr*
EMP: 200 **EST:** 1961
SALES (est): 22.87MM **Privately Held**
Web: www.miyakohybridhotel.com
SIC: 7011 6512 Hotel, franchised; Nonresidential building operators
PA: Kintetsu Group Holdings Co.,Ltd.
6-1-55, Uehonmachi, Tennoji-Ku
Osaka OSK

(P-15211)
KNOTTS BERRY FARM LLC
Also Called: Knott's Berry Farm Hotel
7675 Crescent Ave (90620-3947)
PHONE.....................714 995-1111
Stan Dlander, *Mgr*
EMP: 99
SALES (corp-wide): 1.82B **Publicly Held**
Web: www.knotts.com
SIC: 7011 Resort hotel
HQ: Berry Knott's Farm Llc
8039 Beach Blvd
Buena Park CA
714 827-1776

(P-15212)
KSL RANCHO MIRAGE OPERATING CO INC
Also Called: Rancho Las Palmas Resort & Spa
41000 Bob Hope Dr (92270-4416)
PHONE.....................760 568-2727
EMP: 500

P R O D U C T S & S V C S

Web: www.omnihotels.com
SIC: 7011 Hotels and motels

(P-15213)
KSL RESORTS HOTEL DEL CORONADO
Also Called: Hotel Del Coronado
1500 Orange Ave (92118-2918)
PHONE..................................619 435-6611
Bob Antes, *Prin*
EMP: 212 EST: 1888
SALES (est): 4.96MM
SALES (corp-wide): 8.77B **Publicly Held**
Web: www.hoteldel.com
SIC: 7011 Resort hotel
HQ: Hilton Supply Management Llc
7926 Jones Branch Dr Fl 4
Mc Lean VA
703 883-1000

(P-15214)
KT HOTELS LLC
Also Called: Pendry, The
3 Ada Ste 100 (92618-2322)
PHONE..................................949 715-5000
EMP: 136 EST: 2017
SALES (est): 3.06MM **Privately Held**
SIC: 7011 Hotels

(P-15215)
L & O ALISO VIEJO LLC
Also Called: Renaissance Hotel Clubsport
50 Enterprise (92656-6026)
PHONE..................................949 643-6700
Ed Tomlin, *Genl Mgr*
EMP: 91 EST: 2008
SALES (est): 16.5MM **Privately Held**
Web: www.evolutionswim.com
SIC: 7011 Hotels and motels

(P-15216)
L-O BEDFORD OPERATING LLC
Also Called: Doubletree Hotel Boston
11755 Wilshire Blvd Ste 1350 (90025-1506)
PHONE..................................781 275-5500
EMP: 200 EST: 2011
SALES (est): 4.8MM **Privately Held**
Web: www.hilton.com
SIC: 7011 Hotels and motels

(P-15217)
LA JOLLA BCH & TENNIS CLB INC
Also Called: Shores Restaurant
8110 Camino Del Oro (92037-3108)
PHONE..................................858 459-8271
John Cambel, *Mgr*
EMP: 285
SALES (corp-wide): 47.87MM **Privately Held**
Web: www.theshoresrestaurant.com
SIC: 7011 5812 5813 7299 Resort hotel; Restaurant, family: independent; Cocktail lounge; Banquet hall facilities
PA: La Jolla Beach & Tennis Club, Inc.
2000 Spindrift Dr
La Jolla CA
858 454-7126

(P-15218)
LAKE ARRWHEAD RSORT OPRTOR INC (HQ)
Also Called: Marriott
27984 Hwy 189 (92352)
PHONE..................................909 336-1511
TOLL FREE: 800
Carmen Rodriguez, *CEO*
Veronique Williams, *
EMP: 115 EST: 1982

SALES (est): 13.59MM
SALES (corp-wide): 20.77B **Publicly Held**
Web: www.lakearrowheadresort.com
SIC: 7011 5813 5812 Resort hotel; Drinking places; Eating places
PA: Marriott International, Inc.
7750 Wisconsin Ave
Bethesda MD
301 380-3000

(P-15219)
LANGHAM HOTELS PACIFIC CORP
Also Called: Langham Hotels International
1401 S Oak Knoll Ave (91106-4508)
PHONE..................................617 451-1900
Ka Shui Lo, *Pr*
Brett Butcher, *
EMP: 117 EST: 2007
SALES (est): 11.49MM **Privately Held**
SIC: 7011 Hotels

(P-15220)
LAV HOTEL CORP
Also Called: Whaling Bar & Grill
1132 Prospect St (92037-4533)
PHONE..................................858 454-0771
Harry Collins, *Pr*
W M Allen Senior, *Bd of Dir*
W M Allen Junior, *VP*
EMP: 250 EST: 1928
SQ FT: 1,000
SALES (est): 17.75MM **Privately Held**
Web: www.lavalencia.com
SIC: 7011 Hotels

(P-15221)
LC TRS INC
Also Called: La Costa Resort & Spa
2100 Costa Del Mar Rd (92009-6823)
PHONE..................................760 438-9111
EMP: 872
SIC: 7011 5812 Resort hotel; Eating places

(P-15222)
LFS DEVELOPMENT LLC
Also Called: Intercontinental San Diego
901 Bayfront Ct Ste 1 (92101-3050)
PHONE..................................619 501-5400
EMP: 200 EST: 1946
SALES (est): 8.37MM **Privately Held**
SIC: 7011 Hotels

(P-15223)
LH INDIAN WELLS OPERATING LLC
4500 Indian Wells Ln (92210)
PHONE..................................760 341-2200
Bob Low, *Prin*
EMP: 220 EST: 2004
SALES (est): 399.11K **Privately Held**
SIC: 7011 7991 Resort hotel; Spas
PA: Lh Indian Wells Holding, Llc
11777 San Vicente Blvd
Los Angeles CA

(P-15224)
LH UNIVERSAL OPERATING LLC
Also Called: Sheraton
333 Universal Hollywood Dr (91608-1001)
PHONE..................................818 980-1212
EMP: 280 EST: 1969
SALES (est): 24.75MM **Privately Held**
Web: www.marriott.com
SIC: 7011 Hotels

(P-15225)
LHO MSSION BAY RSIE LESSEE INC
Also Called: Hilton
1775 E Mission Bay Dr (92109-6801)
PHONE..................................619 276-4010
Greg Fracassa, *Managing Member*
EMP: 360 EST: 2005
SALES (est): 23.79MM **Privately Held**
Web: www.hilton.com
SIC: 7011 5812 5947 Resort hotel; Eating places; Gift, novelty, and souvenir shop

(P-15226)
LHOBERGE LESSEE INC
Also Called: L'Auberge Del Mar
1540 Camino Del Mar (92014-2411)
PHONE..................................858 259-1515
Jamie Sabatier, *CEO*
Charles Peck, *
Dennis Fischer, *
EMP: 250 EST: 1989
SQ FT: 84,312
SALES (est): 18.25MM **Privately Held**
Web: www.laubergedelmar.com
SIC: 7011 Resort hotel

(P-15227)
LIBOR MANAGEMENT LLC
Also Called: Country Suites By Carlson
5975 Lusk Blvd (92121-2781)
PHONE..................................858 450-7175
Rick Kroner, *Mgr*
EMP: 115
SALES (corp-wide): 1.4B **Publicly Held**
Web: www.radissonhotels.com
SIC: 7011 Hotels and motels
HQ: Libor Management Llc
701 Carlson Pkwy
Minnetonka MN

(P-15228)
LIGHTSTONE DT LA LLC ⊙
Also Called: Moxy AC Ht Dwntwn Los Angeles
1260 S Figueron St (90015)
PHONE..................................310 669-9252
EMP: 300 EST: 2022
SALES (est): 9.64MM **Privately Held**
SIC: 7011 7389 Hotels; Business services, nec

(P-15229)
LOEWS HOLLYWOOD HOTEL LLC
1755 N Highland Ave (90028-4403)
PHONE..................................323 450-2235
Jonathan Tisch, *Ch Bd*
Reggie Dominique, *
EMP: 375 EST: 2012
SALES (est): 67.38MM
SALES (corp-wide): 14.04B **Publicly Held**
Web: www.loewshotels.com
SIC: 7011 Hotels
PA: Loews Corporation
667 Madison Ave Fl 7
New York NY
212 521-2000

(P-15230)
LONG BEACH GOLDEN SAILS INC
Also Called: Best Western Golden Sails Ht
23545 Crenshaw Blvd Ste 100 (90505-5218)
PHONE..................................562 596-1631
TOLL FREE: 800
Luis Vasquez, *Pr*
Ruben Garza, *

Vicki Arreguin, *
▲ EMP: 100 EST: 1964
SQ FT: 150,000
SALES (est): 9.28MM
SALES (corp-wide): 9.28MM **Privately Held**
Web: www.goldensailshotel.com
SIC: 7011 5812 5813 Hotels and motels; Restaurant, family: independent; Bar (drinking places)
PA: Abp Hotel, Llc
2200 W Valley Blvd
Alhambra CA
562 596-1631

(P-15231)
LONG POINT DEVELOPMENT LLC
Also Called: Terranea Resort
100 Terranea Way (90275-1013)
PHONE..................................310 265-2800
Terri Haack, *Managing Member*
Jennifer Yang, *
EMP: 1000 EST: 2004
SALES (est): 138.42MM **Privately Held**
Web: www.terranea.com
SIC: 7011 Resort hotel

(P-15232)
LOWE ENTERPRISES INC (PA)
Also Called: Lei AG Seattle
11777 San Vicente Blvd Ste 900 (90049-5084)
PHONE..................................310 820-6661
Robert J Lowe Senior, *Ch*
Robert M Weekley, *Sr VP*
Peter O'keeffe, *Ex VP*
Linda Leonard, *Corporate Secretary*
EMP: 125 EST: 1972
SQ FT: 20,000
SALES (est): 367.25MM
SALES (corp-wide): 367.25MM **Privately Held**
Web: www.lowe-re.com
SIC: 7011 6552 Hotels and motels; Subdividers and developers, nec

(P-15233)
LQR PROPERTY LLC
Also Called: La Quinta Resort & Club
49499 Eisenhower Dr (92253-2722)
PHONE..................................760 564-4111
EMP: 121 EST: 2012
SALES (est): 21.67MM **Privately Held**
Web: www.lq.com
SIC: 7011 7999 Resort hotel; Golf driving range

(P-15234)
M&C HOTEL INTERESTS INC
530 Pico Blvd (90405-1223)
PHONE..................................310 399-9344
Lisa Nagahori, *Brnch Mgr*
EMP: 263
Web: www.richfield.com
SIC: 7011 Hotels
HQ: M&C Hotel Interests, Inc.
6560 Greenwood Plaza Blvd
Greenwood Village CO

(P-15235)
M4DEV LLC
Also Called: Hilton Grdn Inn San Diego Dwntw
2137 Pacific Hwy Ste A (92101-8472)
PHONE..................................619 696-6300
EMP: 100 EST: 2016
SALES (est): 2.35MM **Privately Held**
Web: www.hilton.com
SIC: 7011 Resort hotel

(P-15236)
MAJESTIC INDUSTRY HILLS LLC
Also Called: Pacific Plms Conference Resort
1 Industry Hills Pkwy (91744-5160)
PHONE...................626 810-4455
Scott Huntsman, *Brnch Mgr*
EMP: 547
SALES (corp-wide): 42.1MM **Privately Held**
Web: www.pacificpalmsresort.com
SIC: 7011 7999 7389 7299 Resort hotel;
Tennis courts, outdoor/indoor: non-membership; Convention and show services
; Banquet hall facilities
PA: Majestic Industry Hills, Llc
1 Industry Hills Pkwy
City Of Industry CA
562 692-9581

(P-15237)
MAKAR ANAHEIM LLC
Also Called: Hilton
777 W Convention Way (92802-3425)
PHONE...................714 740-4431
EMP: 1200 **EST:** 1984
SQ FT: 1,000,000
SALES (est): 44.85MM **Privately Held**
Web: www.hilton.com
SIC: 7011 Resort hotel

(P-15238)
MANCHESTER GRAND RESORTS LP
Also Called: Manchster Grnd Hyatt San Diego
1 Market Pl Fl 33 (92101-7714)
PHONE...................619 232-1234
Mark S Hoplamazian, *CEO*
Douglas F Manchester, *Pt*
Richard V Gibbons, *Pt*
H Charles Floyd, *Ex VP*
Peter Fulton, *Ex VP*
EMP: 245 **EST:** 1984
SALES (est): 44.38MM
SALES (corp-wide): 4.91B **Publicly Held**
Web: www.manchestergrandhyattsandiego.com
SIC: 7011 Hotel, franchised
PA: Host Hotels & Resorts, Inc.
4747 Bethesda Ave # 1300
Bethesda MD
240 744-1000

(P-15239)
MARCUS HOTELS INC
Also Called: Holiday Inn
4222 Vineland Ave (91602-3318)
PHONE...................818 980-8000
Kroy Walter, *Dir*
EMP: 160
SALES (corp-wide): 677.39MM **Publicly Held**
Web: www.holidayinn.com
SIC: 7011 Hotels and motels
HQ: Marcus Hotels Inc
100 E Wscnsin Ave Ste 190
Milwaukee WI

(P-15240)
MARGARTVLLE RSORT ORLNDO RSORT
Also Called: Margartville Resort Palm Sprng
1600 N Indian Canyon Dr (92262-4602)
PHONE...................760 327-8311
EMP: 235
SALES (corp-wide): 13.3MM **Privately Held**
Web: www.margaritavilleresorts.com
SIC: 7011 Resort hotel

PA: Margaritaville Resort Orlando Resort
Services, Llc
8000 Fins Up Cir
Kissimmee FL
855 995-9099

(P-15241)
MARRIOTT INTERNATIONAL INC
Also Called: Inn At Mssion San Juan Cpstran
31692 El Camino Real (92675-3221)
PHONE...................949 503-5700
Arne Sorenson, *CEO*
Kristi Kaib, *
EMP: 90 **EST:** 1997
SALES (est): 2.39MM **Privately Held**
Web: www.marriott.com
SIC: 7011 Hotels and motels

(P-15242)
MARRIOTT INTERNATIONAL INC
Also Called: Marriott
18000 Von Karman Ave (92612-1004)
PHONE...................949 724-3606
Satinder Palpa, *Brnch Mgr*
EMP: 258
SALES (corp-wide): 20.77B **Publicly Held**
Web: www.marriott.com
SIC: 7011 7389 Hotels and motels; Office facilities and secretarial service rental
PA: Marriott International, Inc.
7750 Wisconsin Ave
Bethesda MD
301 380-3000

(P-15243)
MARRIOTT INTERNATIONAL INC
Also Called: Marriott
5855 W Century Blvd (90045-5614)
PHONE...................310 641-5700
Jim Burns, *Genl Mgr*
EMP: 900
SALES (corp-wide): 20.77B **Publicly Held**
Web: www.marriott.com
SIC: 7011 7389 6513 Hotels and motels;
Office facilities and secretarial service rental
; Residential hotel operation
PA: Marriott International, Inc.
7750 Wisconsin Ave
Bethesda MD
301 380-3000

(P-15244)
MARRIOTT INTERNATIONAL INC
Also Called: Marriott
4240 La Jolla Village Dr (92037-1407)
PHONE...................858 587-1414
Paul Corsinita, *Mgr*
EMP: 337
SALES (corp-wide): 20.77B **Publicly Held**
Web: www.marriott.com
SIC: 7011 Hotels and motels
PA: Marriott International, Inc.
7750 Wisconsin Ave
Bethesda MD
301 380-3000

(P-15245)
MBP LAND LLC
Also Called: Courtyard Marriott Mission Vly
595 Hotel Cir S (92108-3403)
PHONE...................619 291-5720
John Blem, *Managing Member*
EMP: 2495 **EST:** 2000
SALES (est): 1.09MM
SALES (corp-wide): 819.71MM **Privately Held**
Web: courtyard.marriott.com
SIC: 7011 Hotels
HQ: Evolution Hospitality, Llc
1211 Puerta Del Sol # 170

San Clemente CA
949 325-1350

(P-15246)
MERISTAR SAN PEDRO HILTON LLC
Also Called: Hilton Port Los Angls-San Pdro
2800 Via Cabrillo Marina (90731-7223)
PHONE...................310 514-3344
Paul Whetsell, *Managing Member*
John Emery, *
Jeff Milnes, *
EMP: 97 **EST:** 1986
SALES (est): 2.14MM **Privately Held**
SIC: 7011 Hotels and motels
HQ: Interstate Hotels & Resorts, Inc.
5301 Headquarters Dr
Plano TX
703 387-3100

(P-15247)
MERRITT HOSPITALITY LLC
Also Called: Hilton
701 W Ocean Blvd (90831-3100)
PHONE...................562 983-3400
Grace Sun, *Sls Mgr*
EMP: 123
SALES (corp-wide): 447.39MM **Privately Held**
Web: www.hilton.com
SIC: 7011 7991 5813 5812 Resort hotel;
Physical fitness facilities; Drinking places;
Eating places
HQ: Merritt Hospitality, Llc
101 Merritt 7 Ste 14
Norwalk CT
203 849-8844

(P-15248)
MERRITT HOSPITALITY LLC
Also Called: Marriott
2701 Nutwood Ave (92831-5400)
PHONE...................714 738-7800
Tom Beebon, *Mgr*
EMP: 177
SALES (corp-wide): 447.39MM **Privately Held**
Web: www.marriott.com
SIC: 7011 7991 5813 5812 Resort hotel;
Physical fitness facilities; Drinking places;
Eating places
HQ: Merritt Hospitality, Llc
101 Merritt 7 Ste 14
Norwalk CT
203 849-8844

(P-15249)
METROPOLIS HOTEL MGT LLC
Also Called: Hotel Indigo Los Angles Dwntwn
899 Francisco St (90017-2534)
PHONE...................213 683-4855
Raymond Vermolen, *Genl Mgr*
EMP: 120 **EST:** 2016
SALES (est): 21.73MM **Privately Held**
Web: www.hotelindigo.com
SIC: 7011 Hotels
HQ: Inter-Continental Hotels Corporation
35016 Avenue D
Yucaipa CA
770 604-5000

(P-15250)
MHF MV OPERATING VI LLC
Also Called: Courtyard San Dego Mssion Vlly
595 Hotel Cir S (92108-3403)
PHONE...................619 481-5881
Robert A Indeglia Junior, *Pr*
EMP: 100 **EST:** 2019
SALES (est): 3.6MM **Privately Held**
SIC: 7011 Hotels

(P-15251)
MHRP RESORT INC
Also Called: Mountain High Ski Resort
24510 Highway 2 (92397)
P.O. Box 3010 (92397-3010)
PHONE...................760 249-5808
Russel S Bernard, *Pr*
Kenneth Liang, *
Marc Porosoff, *
W Gregory Geiger, *
EMP: 100 **EST:** 1997
SALES (est): 5.54MM **Privately Held**
Web: www.mthigh.com
SIC: 7011 Resort hotel

(P-15252)
MONDRIAN HOLDINGS LLC
8440 W Sunset Blvd (90069-1912)
PHONE...................323 848-6004
Steve Del Rosario, *
EMP: 400 **EST:** 1999
SQ FT: 500,000
SALES (est): 4.91MM **Privately Held**
Web: book.ennismore.com
SIC: 7011 Hotels

(P-15253)
MONTAGE HOTELS & RESORTS LLC (PA)
Also Called: Montage Laguna Beach
3 Ada Ste 100 (92618-2322)
P.O. Box 52031 (85072-2031)
PHONE...................949 715-5002
Alan Fuerstman, *Managing Member*
Jason Herthel, *
Iqbal Bashir, *
James D Bermingham, *
Bill Claypool, *
EMP: 640 **EST:** 2002
SQ FT: 586,000
SALES (est): 110.64MM
SALES (corp-wide): 110.64MM **Privately Held**
Web: www.montage.com
SIC: 7011 Resort hotel

(P-15254)
MOONSTONE BCH INNVSTORS A CAL
Also Called: Best Wstn Fireside Inn By Sea
6700 Moonstone Beach Dr (93428-1814)
PHONE...................805 927-8661
Karen Fyse, *Mgr*
EMP: 199
Web: www.firesideinncambria.com
SIC: 7011 Hotels
PA: Moonstone Beach Innvestors, A
California Limited Partnership
170 Nwport Ctr Dr Ste 245
Newport Beach CA

(P-15255)
MORGANS HOTEL GROUP MGT LLC
Also Called: Miramar Hotel
1555 S Jameson Ln (93108-2918)
PHONE...................805 969-2203
Philip Dailey, *Genl Mgr*
EMP: 133
SALES (corp-wide): 1.22B **Privately Held**
Web: www.sbe.com
SIC: 7011 Hotels
HQ: Morgans Hotel Group Management Llc
475 10th Ave Fl 11
New York NY

(P-15256)
MORGANS HOTEL GROUP MGT LLC

PRODUCTS & SVCS

Also Called: Mondrian Hotel
8440 W Sunset Blvd (90069-1912)
PHONE.............................323 650-8999
David Weidlich, *Genl Mgr*
EMP: 200
SALES (corp-wide): 1.22B **Privately Held**
Web: www.sbe.com
SIC: 7011 5813 5812 Hotels; Drinking places
; Eating places
HQ: Morgans Hotel Group Management Llc
475 10th Ave Fl 11
New York NY

(P-15257)
MSR HOTELS & RESORTS INC
Also Called: Residence Inn By Marriott
3701 Torrance Blvd (90503-4805)
PHONE.............................310 543-4566
David Zimmerman, *Mgr*
EMP: 120
SALES (corp-wide): 53.67B **Publicly Held**
Web: residence-inn.marriott.com
SIC: 7011 Hotels and motels
HQ: Msr Hotels & Resorts, Inc.
450 S Orange Ave
Orlando FL
407 650-1000

(P-15258)
MSR RESORT LODGING TENANT LLC
Also Called: Pga West By Wldorf Astoria MGT
49499 Eisenhower Dr (92253-2722)
P.O. Box 659 (92247-0659)
PHONE.............................760 564-4111
▲ **EMP:** 900
SIC: 7011 Hotels and motels

(P-15259)
NEW ASTER ENTERPRISES INC
Also Called: Silverlake Motel
2901 S Flower St (90007-3713)
PHONE.............................213 747-7566
Sam Tsutsumi, *Mgr*
EMP: 110
SALES (corp-wide): 156.85K **Privately Held**
SIC: 7011 Motels
PA: New Aster Enterprises, Inc.
1549 Feliz St
Monterey Park CA
626 281-8714

(P-15260)
NEWPORT HOSPITALITY GROUP INC
Also Called: Holiday Inn
801 Truxtun Ave (93301-4726)
PHONE.............................661 323-1900
Eric Iokal, *Mgr*
EMP: 100
SALES (corp-wide): 9.58MM **Privately Held**
Web: www.holidayinn.com
SIC: 7011 Hotels and motels
PA: Newport Hospitality Group Inc
1048 Irvine Ave Ste 365
Newport Beach CA
949 706-7002

(P-15261)
NHCA INC
Also Called: Crowne Plz Los Angeles Hbr Ht
2330 Grand Ave (90815-1761)
PHONE.............................310 519-8200
EMP: 151 **EST:** 1997
SALES (est): 4.84MM **Privately Held**
SIC: 7011 Hotels

(P-15262)
NOBLE INVESTMENT GROUP LLC
Also Called: Westin Long Beach Hotel, The
333 E Ocean Blvd (90802-4827)
PHONE.............................562 436-3000
Bharat Shah, *Managing Member*
EMP: 117 **EST:** 2003
SQ FT: 60,000
SALES (est): 976.12K **Privately Held**
Web: westin.marriott.com
SIC: 7011 Hotels

(P-15263)
NOBLE/UTAH LONG BEACH LLC
Also Called: Westin Long Beach Hotel, The
333 E Ocean Blvd (90802-4827)
PHONE.............................562 436-3000
Mitesh B Shah, *Managing Member*
EMP: 250 **EST:** 2005
SQ FT: 51,000
SALES (est): 21.7MM **Privately Held**
Web: westin.marriott.com
SIC: 7011 Hotels and motels
PA: Noble Investment Group, Llc
3424 Peachtree Rd Ne
Atlanta GA

(P-15264)
NORTHWEST HOTEL CORPORATION (PA)
Also Called: Howard Johnson
1380 S Harbor Blvd (92802-2310)
PHONE.............................714 776-6120
James P Edmondson, *Pr*
EMP: 108 **EST:** 1965
SQ FT: 50,000
SALES (est): 4.6MM
SALES (corp-wide): 4.6MM **Privately Held**
Web: www.wyndhamhotels.com
SIC: 7011 Hotels and motels

(P-15265)
NREA-TRC 711 LLC
Also Called: Sheraton
711 S Hope St (90017-3803)
PHONE.............................213 488-3500
EMP: 200 **EST:** 2013
SQ FT: 470,000
SALES (est): 8.57MM **Privately Held**
Web: four-points.marriott.com
SIC: 7011 Hotels

(P-15266)
OAK VALLEY HOTEL LLC
2270 Hotel Cir N (92108-2810)
PHONE.............................619 297-1101
EMP: 99 **EST:** 2016
SALES (est): 1.45MM **Privately Held**
SIC: 7011 Hotels

(P-15267)
OASIS WEST REALTY LLC
Also Called: Waldorf Astoria Beverly Hills
9850 Wilshire Blvd (90210-3115)
PHONE.............................310 860-6666
Damian Cabotaje, *Managing Member*
EMP: 161 **EST:** 2017
SALES (est): 5.11MM **Privately Held**
Web: waldorfastoria3.hilton.com
SIC: 7011 Hotels

(P-15268)
OCEAN AVENUE LLC
Also Called: Fairmont Miramar Hotel
101 Wilshire Blvd (90401-1106)
PHONE.............................310 576-7777
Ellis O'connor, *Managing Member*
EMP: 275 **EST:** 1973

SQ FT: 209,000
SALES (est): 25.87MM
SALES (corp-wide): 1.22B **Privately Held**
Web: www.fairmont.com
SIC: 7011 Hotels
HQ: Accor Services Us Llc
950 Mason St
San Francisco CA
415 772-5000

(P-15269)
OCEANS ELEVEN CASINO
Also Called: Ocean's Eleven
121 Brooks St (92054-3424)
PHONE.............................760 439-6988
Mark Kelegian, *Mng Pt*
EMP: 367 **EST:** 1996
SQ FT: 30,000
SALES (est): 22.62MM **Privately Held**
Web: www.oceans11.com
SIC: 7011 Casino hotel

(P-15270)
OH SO ORIGINAL INC
150 E Angeleno Ave (91502-1911)
PHONE.............................818 841-4770
Mark Crigler, *Pr*
Rich Reid, *
EMP: 300 **EST:** 2015
SQ FT: 100,000
SALES (est): 11.31MM **Privately Held**
Web: www.jpallenapartments.com
SIC: 7011 6513 8741 Hotel, franchised;
Apartment building operators; Hotel or
motel management

(P-15271)
OHI RESORT HOTELS LLC
Also Called: Wyndham Anaheim Garden Grove
12021 Harbor Blvd (92840-4001)
PHONE.............................714 867-5555
Jeremy Yujuico, *Prin*
EMP: 98 **EST:** 1998
SALES (est): 6.26MM **Privately Held**
Web: anaheim.crowneplaza.com
SIC: 7011 Hotels

(P-15272)
OKA & OKA HAWAII LLC
Also Called: Kona Bay Hotel
1756 Ruhland Ave (90266-7132)
PHONE.............................808 329-1393
Tracey Kimi, *Mgr*
EMP: 196
SALES (corp-wide): 2.69MM **Privately Held**
SIC: 7011 Hotels
PA: Oka & Oka Hawaii, Llc
75 5744 Alii Dr
Hilo HI
808 329-1393

(P-15273)
OLD TOWN FMLY HOSPITALITY CORP
Also Called: Fiesta De Reyes
2754 Calhoun St (92110-2706)
PHONE.............................619 246-8010
Chuck Ross, *Pr*
EMP: 240 **EST:** 2009
SQ FT: 1,600
SALES (est): 16MM **Privately Held**
Web: www.fiestadereyes.com
SIC: 7011 5812 Hotels; Eating places

(P-15274)
OLS HOTELS & RESORTS LLC
Also Called: Marriott
14635 Baldwin Park Towne Ctr
(91706-5548)

PHONE.............................626 962-6000
Peter Ehienberg, *Mgr*
EMP: 509
SALES (corp-wide): 87.68MM **Privately Held**
Web: www.springboardhospitality.com
SIC: 7011 Hotels and motels
PA: Ols Hotels & Resorts, Llc
16000 Ventura Blvd # 101
Encino CA
818 905-8280

(P-15275)
OLS HOTELS & RESORTS LLC
Also Called: Le Parc Suite Hotel
733 N West Knoll Dr (90069-5207)
PHONE.............................310 855-1115
Sam Ebeid, *CEO*
EMP: 508
SALES (corp-wide): 87.68MM **Privately Held**
Web: www.leparcsuites.com
SIC: 7011 8741 Hotels; Hotel or motel
management
PA: Ols Hotels & Resorts, Llc
16000 Ventura Blvd # 101
Encino CA
818 905-8280

(P-15276)
OMNI HOTELS CORPORATION
Also Called: Omni Hotels
41000 Bob Hope Dr (92270-4416)
PHONE.............................760 568-2727
EMP: 461
Web: www.omnihotels.com
SIC: 7011 Hotels and motels
HQ: Omni Hotels Corporation
4001 Maple Ave Ste 500
Dallas TX
972 871-5600

(P-15277)
OMNI LA COSTA RESORT & SPA LLC (DH)
2100 Costa Del Mar Rd (92009-6823)
PHONE.............................760 438-9111
Randy Zupanski, *
EMP: 104 **EST:** 2013
SALES (est): 24.47MM **Privately Held**
Web: www.omnihotels.com
SIC: 7011 Resort hotel
HQ: Omni Hotels Corporation
4001 Maple Ave Ste 500
Dallas TX
972 871-5600

(P-15278)
ORANGEWOOD LLC
Also Called: Doubltree Stes By Hlton Anheim
2085 S Harbor Blvd (92802-3513)
PHONE.............................714 750-3000
Shirish H Patel, *
EMP: 175 **EST:** 2000
SALES (est): 8.88MM **Privately Held**
Web: www.doubletreeanaheim.com
SIC: 7011 5812 Hotels and motels;
American restaurant

(P-15279)
ORLANDO WILSHIRE INVESTMENTS
Also Called: Orlando, The
8384 W 3rd St (90048-4311)
PHONE.............................323 658-6600
Kenneth Pressberg, *Pt*
Sidney Pressberg, *
EMP: 88 **EST:** 1981
SQ FT: 45,000
SALES (est): 863.38K **Privately Held**

724   2024 Southern California
Business Directory and Buyers Guide   ▲ = Import ▼ = Export
◆ = Import/Export

SIC: 7011 Hotels

(P-15280)
OTAY HOSPITALITY INC
Also Called: Holiday Inn
4450 Main St (91911-6508)
PHONE.............................619 422-2600
Suresh Patel, *Pr*
Ashok Israni, *Sec*
EMP: 96 EST: 1994
SALES (est): 824.82K **Privately Held**
Web: www.holidayinn.com
SIC: 7011 Hotels and motels

(P-15281)
OTB ACQUISITION LLC
Also Called: Sierra Vista Extended Stay
770 S Brea Blvd Ste 227 (92821-5399)
PHONE.............................520 458-0540
EMP: 151
Web: www.ontheborder.com
SIC: 7011 Hotels and motels
PA: Otb Acquisition Llc
    2201 W Royal Ln Ste 170
    Irving TX

(P-15282)
OVIS LLC
Also Called: Ojai Valley Inn & Spa
905 Country Club Rd (93023-3734)
PHONE.............................805 646-5511
TOLL FREE: 888
Stephen Crown, *Managing Member*
EMP: 600 EST: 1923
SALES (est): 49.55MM **Privately Held**
Web: www.ojaivalleyinn.com
SIC: 7011 5813 5812 Resort hotel; Drinking
    places; Eating places

(P-15283)
OXFORD PALACE HOTEL LLC
745 S Oxford Ave (90005-2909)
PHONE.............................213 382-7756
Bowhan Kim, *Prin*
Don W Chang, *
EMP: 96 EST: 1992
SALES (est): 4.75MM **Privately Held**
Web: www.oxfordhotel.com
SIC: 7011 5812 Resort hotel; Korean
    restaurant

(P-15284)
PACIFIC CAMBRIA INC
Also Called: Cambria Pines Lodge
2905 Burton Dr (93428-4001)
PHONE.............................805 927-6114
Dirk Winter, *Pr*
EMP: 90 EST: 1975
SQ FT: 70,000
SALES (est): 9.74MM **Privately Held**
Web: www.cambriapineslodge.com
SIC: 7011 5812 5813 Hotels; Restaurant,
    family: independent; Bar (drinking places)

(P-15285)
PACIFIC CATALINA HOTEL INC
Also Called: Catalina Canyon Resort
888 Country Club Dr (90704-2956)
P.O. Box 736 (90704-0736)
PHONE.............................310 510-9255
Gonzalo Rodriguez, *Genl Mgr*
EMP: 313 EST: 1977
SALES (est): 1.16MM
SALES (corp-wide): 96.92MM **Privately
Held**
Web: www.bestwestern.com
SIC: 7011 7389 Hotels; Hotel and motel
    reservation service
PA: Pacifica Hosts, Inc.
    1775 Hancock St Ste 200

San Diego CA
619 296-9000

(P-15286)
PACIFIC CITY HOTEL LLC
Also Called: Pasea Hotel & Spa
21080 Pacific Coast Hwy (92648-5305)
PHONE.............................714 698-6100
EMP: 300 EST: 2015
SALES (est): 2.8MM **Privately Held**
Web: www.meritagecollection.com
SIC: 7011 Resort hotel

(P-15287)
**PACIFIC HOTEL MANAGEMENT
INC**
Also Called: Radison Hotel Newport Beach
4545 Macarthur Blvd (92660-2022)
PHONE.............................949 608-1091
EMP: 140 EST: 2003
SALES (est): 4.55MM **Privately Held**
Web: www.radissonhotels.com
SIC: 7011 Hotels

(P-15288)
**PACIFIC HUNTINGTON HOTEL
CORP**
Also Called: Langham Huntington Hotel & Spa
1401 S Oak Knoll Ave (91106-4508)
PHONE.............................626 568-3900
Ying Shek Lo, *Pr*
EMP: 600 EST: 2000
SQ FT: 21,193
SALES (est): 49.28MM **Privately Held**
Web: www.langhamhotels.com
SIC: 7011 Resort hotel
HQ: Langham Hotels International Limited
    33/F Great Eagle Ctr
    Wan Chai HK

(P-15289)
**PACIFIC MONARCH RESORTS
INC**
Also Called: Riviera Shores
34630 Pacific Coast Hwy (92624-1301)
PHONE.............................949 248-2944
EMP: 91
SALES (corp-wide): 79.14MM **Privately
Held**
Web: www.pacificmonarchresorts.com
SIC: 7011 6531 Resort hotel; Time-sharing
    real estate sales, leasing and rentals
PA: Pacific Monarch Resorts, Inc.
    4000 Macarthur Blvd # 600
    Newport Beach CA
    949 609-2400

(P-15290)
PACIFICA HOSTS INC
Also Called: Hotel Indigo Del Mar
710 Camino Del Mar (92014-3008)
PHONE.............................858 755-1501
Susan Knapp, *Mgr*
EMP: 121
SALES (corp-wide): 96.92MM **Privately
Held**
Web: www.hotelindigo.com
SIC: 7011 Hotels
PA: Pacifica Hosts, Inc.
    1775 Hancock St Ste 200
    San Diego CA
    619 296-9000

(P-15291)
PACIFICA HOSTS INC
717 S Highway 101 (92075-2606)
PHONE.............................858 792-8200
Julio Ongpin, *Genl Mgr*
EMP: 98

SALES (corp-wide): 96.92MM **Privately
Held**
Web: www.pacificacompanies.com
SIC: 7011 Hotels
PA: Pacifica Hosts, Inc.
    1775 Hancock St Ste 200
    San Diego CA
    619 296-9000

(P-15292)
PALA CASINO SPA & RESORT
Also Called: Pala Casino
11154 Highway 76 (92059-2904)
PHONE.............................760 510-5100
TOLL FREE: 877
Robert Smith, *Ch Bd*
Bill Bembenek, *
Shauna Anton, *
Stacy Hoover, *
EMP: 1800 EST: 2000
SQ FT: 140,000
SALES (est): 206.9MM **Privately Held**
Web: www.palacasino.com
SIC: 7011 Casino hotel

(P-15293)
**PALA MESA LIMITED
PARTNERSHIP**
Also Called: Pala Mesa Resort
2001 Old Highway 395 (92028-9771)
PHONE.............................760 728-5881
Kevin Poorbaugh, *Mng Pt*
Bob Emch, *Contrlr*
Tray Crayton, *Pr*
Anil Y, *CEO*
EMP: 199 EST: 1983
SALES (est): 15.43MM **Privately Held**
Web: www.palamesa.com
SIC: 7011 7992 Resort hotel; Public golf
    courses

(P-15294)
**PALM DESERT HOSPITALITY
LLC**
Also Called: Homewood Suites
36999 Cook St (92211-6066)
PHONE.............................760 568-1600
Maria Banning, *Brnch Mgr*
EMP: 309
SALES (corp-wide): 1.94MM **Privately
Held**
Web: www.hospitalitydental.com
SIC: 7011 Hotels and motels
PA: Palm Desert Hospitality, L.L.C.
    2390 Tower Dr
    Monroe LA
    760 568-1600

(P-15295)
**PAN PCFIC HTELS RSRTS
AMER INC**
Also Called: Pan Pacific San Diego
400 W Broadway (92101-3504)
PHONE.............................619 239-4500
Jim Hollister, *Genl Mgr*
EMP: 238
SALES (corp-wide): 22.68MM **Privately
Held**
Web: www.wyndhamhotels.com
SIC: 7011 5812 Hotels; Eating places*
PA: Pan Pacific Hotels And Resorts
    America Inc.
    500 Post St Ste 800
    San Francisco CA
    415 732-7747

(P-15296)
PARADISE LESSEE INC
Also Called: Paradise Point Resort & Spa

1404 Vacation Rd (92109-7905)
PHONE.............................858 274-4630
Alfred L Young, *CEO*
EMP: 328 EST: 1962
SALES (est): 24.8MM **Publicly Held**
Web: www.paradisepoint.com
SIC: 7011 Resort hotel
PA: Pebblebrook Hotel Trust
    4747 Bethesda Ave # 1100
    Bethesda MD

(P-15297)
PARK HOTELS & RESORTS INC
Also Called: Hilton
9876 Wilshire Blvd (90210-3115)
PHONE.............................310 415-3340
Beverly Hilton, *Prin*
EMP: 113
SALES (corp-wide): 2.5B **Publicly Held**
Web: www.hilton.com
SIC: 7011 Resort hotel
PA: Park Hotels & Resorts Inc.
    1775 Tysons Blvd Fl 7
    Tysons VA
    571 302-5757

(P-15298)
**PARK MANAGEMENT GROUP
LLC**
Also Called: Jameson Inn
1825 Gillespie Wy Ste 101 (91601)
PHONE.............................404 350-9990
▲ EMP: 3500
SIC: 7011 Hotels and motels

(P-15299)
PARKER PALM SPRINGS LLC
4200 E Palm Canyon Dr (92264-5230)
PHONE.............................760 770-5000
Adam Glick, *Prin*
EMP: 95 EST: 2003
SALES (est): 8.08MM **Privately Held**
Web: www.parkerpalmsprings.com
SIC: 7011 Resort hotel

(P-15300)
**PASADENA HOTEL DEV VENTR
LP**
Also Called: Sheraton Pasadena
303 Cordova St (91101-2426)
PHONE.............................626 449-4000
Ray Serafin, *Prin*
EMP: 99 EST: 2008
SALES (est): 3.57MM **Privately Held**
Web: www.sheratonpasadena.com
SIC: 7011 Resort hotel

(P-15301)
**PAUMA BAND OF MISSION
INDIANS**
Casino Pauma
777 Pauma Reservation Rd (92061)
P.O. Box 1067 (92061-1067)
PHONE.............................760 742-2177
Richard Darder, *CEO*
EMP: 500
Web: www.casinopauma.com
SIC: 7011 Casino hotel
PA: Pauma Band Of Mission Indians
    1010 Pauma Reservation Rd
    Pauma Valley CA

(P-15302)
**PECHANGA DEVELOPMENT
CORP**
Also Called: Pechanga Resort & Casino
45000 Pechanga Pkwy (92592-5810)
P.O. Box 9041 (92589-9041)
PHONE.............................951 695-4655

◆ **EMP:** 4000 **EST:** 1995
SALES (est): 206.14MM **Privately Held**
Web: www.pechanga.com
SIC: 7011 7929 7999 Casino hotel;
    Entertainment service; Gambling
    establishment

(P-15303)
PHF II BURBANK LLC
Also Called: Burbank Airport Mariott Hotel
2500 N Hollywood Way (91505-1019)
PHONE..............................818 843-6000
Linda Davey, *Managing Member*
EMP: 220 **EST:** 2006
SALES (est): 4.61MM **Privately Held**
SIC: 7011 Hotels and motels

(P-15304)
PINNACLE HOTELS USA INC
8369 Vickers St Ste 101 (92111-2113)
PHONE..............................858 974-8201
Bharat Lall, *CEO*
Hema Lall, *
EMP: 84 **EST:** 1999
SALES (est): 7.33MM **Privately Held**
Web: www.pinnacleholdings.com
SIC: 7011 Resort hotel

(P-15305)
PINNACLE RVRSIDE HSPITALITY LP
Also Called: Riverside Marriott
3400 Market St (92501-2826)
PHONE..............................951 784-8000
Doctor Bharat Lall, *Genl Pt*
EMP: 190 **EST:** 2007
SALES (est): 9.67MM **Privately Held**
Web: www.marriott.com
SIC: 7011 Hotels

(P-15306)
PLAYA PROPER JV LLC
Also Called: Custom Hotel
8639 Lincoln Blvd (90045-3503)
PHONE..............................310 645-0400
Brad Korzen, *CEO*
Bryan De Lowe, *
Jeffrey Cruz, *
EMP: 80 **EST:** 2017
SALES (est): 2.45MM **Privately Held**
Web: www.thehoteljune.com
SIC: 7011 Hotels

(P-15307)
PORTOFINO HOTEL PARTNERS LP
Also Called: Hotel Portofino
260 Portofino Way (90277-2033)
PHONE..............................310 379-8481
Glenn Bishop, *Prin*
EMP: 151 **EST:** 1980
SALES (est): 10.06MM **Privately Held**
Web: www.hotelportofino.com
SIC: 7011 Resort hotel

(P-15308)
PORTOFINO INN & SUITES ANAHEIM
1831 S Harbor Blvd (92802-3509)
PHONE..............................714 782-7600
Jennifer Reihl, *Dir*
EMP: 291 **EST:** 2008
SALES (est): 869.27K
SALES (corp-wide): 369.62MM **Privately Held**
Web: www.portofinoinnanaheim.com
SIC: 7011 Inns
HQ: Tarsadia Hotels
    620 Nwport Ctr Dr Ste 140

Newport Beach CA

(P-15309)
PRIME HOSPITALITY LLC
Also Called: Radisson Inn
2200 E Holt Blvd (91761-7671)
PHONE..............................909 975-5000
EMP: 90
Web: www.radissonhotels.com
SIC: 7011 Hotels and motels
PA: Prime Hospitality, Llc
    2155 E Convention Ctr Way
    Ontario CA

(P-15310)
PROPER HOSPITALITY LLC
73 Market St (90291-3603)
PHONE..............................310 277-5221
EMP: 229 **EST:** 2019
SALES (est): 12.08MM **Privately Held**
Web: www.properhotel.com
SIC: 7011 Hotels

(P-15311)
PRUTEL JOINT VENTURE
Also Called: Ritz-Carlton Laguna Niguel
1 Ritz Carlton Dr (92629-4205)
PHONE..............................949 240-5064
W B Johnson, *Pt*
Prudential Realty San Francisc o Ca, *Pt*
Paul Patterson, *CFO*
Kelly Steward, *Genl Mgr*
EMP: 700 **EST:** 1984
SALES (est): 31.03MM **Privately Held**
Web: www.ritzcarlton.com
SIC: 7011 Hotels

(P-15312)
PT GAMING LLC
235 Oregon St (90245-4215)
PHONE..............................323 260-5060
Patrick Tierney, *Managing Member*
EMP: 700 **EST:** 2012
SQ FT: 7,000
SALES (est): 35.86MM **Privately Held**
Web: www.ptgaming.com
SIC: 7011 Casino hotel

(P-15313)
QUEENSBAY HOTEL LLC
Also Called: Hotel Maya
700 Queensway Dr (90802-6343)
PHONE..............................562 481-3910
Cherie Davis, *Mgr*
EMP: 100
SALES (corp-wide): 8.77MM **Privately Held**
Web: www.hotelmayalongbeach.com
SIC: 7011 Hotels
PA: Queensbay Hotel, Llc
    444 W Ocean Blvd
    Long Beach CA
    562 628-0625

(P-15314)
R P S RESORT CORP
1600 N Indian Canyon Dr (92262-4602)
PHONE..............................760 327-8311
Douglas Mccarron, *Pr*
EMP: 448 **EST:** 1990
SALES (est): 967.61K
SALES (corp-wide): 45.94MM **Privately Held**
SIC: 7011 Resort hotel
HQ: The San Bernardino Hilton
    285 E Hospitality Ln
    San Bernardino CA

(P-15315)
RADLAX GATEWAY HOTEL LLC
Also Called: Radisson Inn
6225 W Century Blvd (90045-5311)
PHONE..............................310 670-9000
Peter Dumon, *Managing Member*
EMP: 1474 **EST:** 2007
SALES (est): 2.04MM **Privately Held**
Web: www.radissonhotels.com
SIC: 7011 Hotels and motels
PA: Portfolio Hotels & Resorts, Llc
    1211 W 22nd St Ste 1002
    Oak Brook IL

(P-15316)
RAFFLES LRMITAGE BEVERLY HILLS
Also Called: L'Ermitage Hotel
9291 Burton Way (90210-3709)
PHONE..............................310 278-3344
Jack Naderkhani, *Genl Mgr*
▲ **EMP:** 249 **EST:** 1993
SALES (est): 11.74MM
SALES (corp-wide): 1.22B **Privately Held**
Web: www.viceroyhotelsandresorts.com
SIC: 7011 5813 5812 Hotels; Drinking places
    ; Eating places
HQ: Raffles International Limited
    1 Wallich Street
    Singapore

(P-15317)
RALEIGH ENTERPRISES INC (PA)
Also Called: Raleigh Holdings
5300 Melrose Ave (90038-5114)
PHONE..............................310 899-8900
Kristen J Raleigh, *CEO*
George I Rosenthal, *Ch Bd*
Mark Rosenthal, *Pr*
EMP: 130 **EST:** 1955
SQ FT: 20,000
SALES (est): 36.91MM
SALES (corp-wide): 36.91MM **Privately Held**
Web: www.raleighenterprises.com
SIC: 7011 Hotels

(P-15318)
RANCHO VLNCIA RSORT PRTNERS LL
5921 Valencia Cir (92067-9520)
P.O. Box 9126 (92067-4126)
PHONE..............................858 756-1123
Jeffrey Essakow, *Managing Member*
Hal Jacobs, *
EMP: 300 **EST:** 1989
SALES (est): 21.98MM **Privately Held**
Web: www.ranchovalencia.com
SIC: 7011 Resort hotel

(P-15319)
RED EARTH CASINO
3089 Norm Niver Rd (92274-6550)
PHONE..............................760 395-1200
Larry Drouse, *Genl Mgr*
EMP: 150 **EST:** 2007
SQ FT: 15,000
SALES (est): 16.26MM **Privately Held**
Web: www.redearthcasino.com
SIC: 7011 7993 Casino hotel; Gambling
    establishments operating coin-operated
    machines

(P-15320)
REH COMPANY
Also Called: Westgate Hotel
1055 2nd Ave (92101-4811)
PHONE..............................619 238-1818

Richard Cox, *Brnch Mgr*
EMP: 186
SALES (corp-wide): 4.43B **Privately Held**
Web: www.westgatehotel.com
SIC: 7011 Hotels
PA: Reh Company
    550 E South Temple
    Salt Lake City UT
    801 524-2700

(P-15321)
RENAISSANCE HOTEL OPERATING CO
Also Called: Marriott
9620 Airport Blvd (90045-5402)
PHONE..............................310 337-2800
Gregory Lehman, *Mgr*
EMP: 300
SALES (corp-wide): 20.77B **Publicly Held**
Web: www.marriott.com
SIC: 7011 5813 5812 7389 Hotels and motels
    ; Drinking places; Eating places; Office
    facilities and secretarial service rental
HQ: Renaissance Hotel Operating
    Company
    10400 Fernwood Rd
    Bethesda MD

(P-15322)
RENAISSANCE HOTEL OPERATING CO
Also Called: Renaissance Indian Wells
44400 Indian Wells Ln (92210-8708)
PHONE..............................760 773-4444
Tom Tabler, *Prin*
EMP: 600
SALES (corp-wide): 20.77B **Publicly Held**
Web: renaissance-hotels.marriott.com
SIC: 7011 Hotels and motels
HQ: Renaissance Hotel Operating
    Company
    10400 Fernwood Rd
    Bethesda MD

(P-15323)
RENAISSNCE ESMRALDA RESORT SPA
Also Called: Renaissance
44400 Indian Wells Ln (92210-8708)
PHONE..............................760 773-4444
John Kalinski, *Prin*
EMP: 93 **EST:** 2011
SALES (est): 8.94MM **Privately Held**
Web: www.marriott.com
SIC: 7011 Resort hotel

(P-15324)
RESORT AT PELICAN HILL LLC
22701 Pelican Hill Rd S (92657-2008)
PHONE..............................949 467-6800
Elia Gutierrez, *Dir*
EMP: 439 **EST:** 2006
SALES (est): 14.08MM **Privately Held**
Web: www.pelicanhill.com
SIC: 7011 Resort hotel

(P-15325)
RGC GASLAMP LLC
Also Called: Pendry San Diego
550 J St (92101-7020)
PHONE..............................619 738-7000
Michael Odonohue, *Prin*
EMP: 104 **EST:** 2016
SALES (est): 13.53MM **Privately Held**
Web: www.pendry.com
SIC: 7011 Resort hotel

(P-15326)
RIO VISTA DEVELOPMENT CO INC (PA)
Also Called: Holiday Inn
4222 Vineland Ave (91602-3318)
PHONE.....................818 980-8000
Scott A Mills, *Prin*
Scott Mills, *
EMP: 133 EST: 1971
SQ FT: 100,000
SALES (est): 12.33MM
SALES (corp-wide): 12.33MM **Privately Held**
Web: www.thegarland.com
SIC: 7011 Hotels and motels

(P-15327)
RITZ-CARLTON HOTEL COMPANY LLC
Also Called: Ritz Carlton Rancho Mirage
68900 Frank Sinatra Dr (92270-5300)
PHONE.....................760 321-8282
James H Palllin Junior, *Mgr*
EMP: 313
SALES (corp-wide): 20.77B **Publicly Held**
Web: www.ritzcarlton.com
SIC: 7011 Hotels
HQ: The Ritz-Carlton Hotel Company Llc
7750 Wisconsin Ave
Bethesda MD
301 380-3000

(P-15328)
RITZ-CARLTON HOTEL COMPANY LLC
Also Called: Ritz-Carlton
1 Ritz Carlton Dr (92629-4206)
PHONE.....................949 240-5020
Janinie Vanderoy, *Brnch Mgr*
EMP: 348
SALES (corp-wide): 20.77B **Publicly Held**
Web: www.ritzcarlton.com
SIC: 7011 Hotels
HQ: The Ritz-Carlton Hotel Company Llc
7750 Wisconsin Ave
Bethesda MD
301 380-3000

(P-15329)
RITZ-CARLTON HOTEL COMPANY LLC
Also Called: Ritz-Carlton
8301 Hollister Ave (93117-2474)
PHONE.....................805 968-0100
EMP: 650
SALES (corp-wide): 20.77B **Publicly Held**
Web: www.ritzcarlton.com
SIC: 7011 Resort hotel
HQ: The Ritz-Carlton Hotel Company Llc
7750 Wisconsin Ave
Bethesda MD
301 380-3000

(P-15330)
RIVIERA PALM SPRNG A TRBUTE PR
Also Called: Tribute Portfolio Hotels
1600 N Indian Canyon Dr (92262-4602)
PHONE.....................760 327-8311
EMP: 149 EST: 2015
SALES (est): 569.39K
SALES (corp-wide): 569.39K **Privately Held**
Web: www.margaritavilleresorts.com
SIC: 7011 Resort hotel
PA: Agre Dcp Palm Springs Tenant Llc
1600 N Palm Spgs
Palm Springs CA
760 327-8311

(P-15331)
RMS FOUNDATION INC
Also Called: Queen Mary Hotel
1126 Queens Hwy (90802-6331)
PHONE.....................562 435-3511
Joseph F Prevratil, *Pr*
EMP: 650 EST: 1993
SQ FT: 750,000
SALES (est): 51.05MM **Privately Held**
Web: www.queenmary.com
SIC: 7011 Hotels and motels
PA: City Of Long Beach
1800 E Wardlow Rd
Long Beach CA
562 570-6450

(P-15332)
ROOSEVELT HOTEL LLC
Also Called: Hollywood Roosevelt Hotel
7000 Hollywood Blvd (90028-6003)
PHONE.....................323 466-7000
EMP: 200 EST: 1995
SALES (est): 34.06MM **Privately Held**
Web: www.thehollywoodroosevelt.com
SIC: 7011 5813 5812 Hotels; Drinking places ; Eating places

(P-15333)
ROSANNA INC
Also Called: Avenue of Arts Wyndham Hotel
3350 Avenue Of The Arts (92626-1913)
PHONE.....................714 751-5100
Nick Price, *Genl Mgr*
Paul Sanford, *
Rachael Moorhead, *
Rosanna Chan, *
Robin Reid, *OF AUDIT*
EMP: 151 EST: 2009
SALES (est): 19.08MM **Privately Held**
Web: www.wyndhamhotels.com
SIC: 7011 5812 Hotels; Food bars

(P-15334)
RPD HOTELS 18 LLC (PA)
Also Called: Vagabond Inns
1801 S La Cienega Blvd Ste 301 (90035-4641)
PHONE.....................213 746-1531
Juan Sanchez Llaca, *Pr*
Don Johnson, *
Stewart Rubin, *
EMP: 800 EST: 1998
SALES (est): 23.05MM
SALES (corp-wide): 23.05MM **Privately Held**
Web: www.vagabondinn.com
SIC: 7011 Motels

(P-15335)
RUFFIN HOTEL CORP OF CAL
Also Called: Long Beach Marriott
4700 Airport Plaza Dr (90815-1252)
PHONE.....................562 425-5210
Phillip G Ruffin, *Pr*
EMP: 260 EST: 1993
SALES (est): 16.03MM **Privately Held**
Web: www.marriott.com
SIC: 7011 5812 5813 Hotels; Eating places; Drinking places

(P-15336)
S B H HOTEL CORPORATION
285 E Hospitality Ln (92408-3411)
PHONE.....................909 889-0133
Douglas Mccarron, *Brnch Mgr*
EMP: 547
SALES (corp-wide): 45.94MM **Privately Held**
SIC: 7011 Hotels
HQ: S B H Hotel Corporation
520 S Virgil Ave Fl 4
Los Angeles CA

(P-15337)
S W K PROPERTIES LLC
Also Called: Holiday Inn
2726 S Grand Ave Lbby (92705-5404)
PHONE.....................714 481-6300
Rod Hurt, *Mgr*
EMP: 129
SALES (corp-wide): 2.19MM **Privately Held**
Web: www.holidayinn.com
SIC: 7011 Hotels and motels
PA: S W K Properties Llc
3807 Wilshire Blvd # 122
Los Angeles CA
213 383-9204

(P-15338)
SAGE HOSPITALITY RESOURCES LLC
Also Called: Courtyard By Mrrott Los Angles
700 W Huntington Dr (91016-3104)
PHONE.....................626 357-5211
Dennis Hollingdrake, *Mgr*
EMP: 237
SALES (corp-wide): 286.23MM **Privately Held**
Web: courtyard.marriott.com
SIC: 7011 Hotels and motels
PA: Sage Hospitality Resources L.L.C.
1575 Welton St Ste 300
Denver CO
303 595-7200

(P-15339)
SAI MANAGEMENT CO INC
Also Called: Desert Inn & Suites
1600 S Harbor Blvd (92802-2314)
PHONE.....................714 772-5050
Priti Hansji, *Mgr*
EMP: 80
SALES (corp-wide): 4.91MM **Privately Held**
Web: www.anaheimdesertinn.com
SIC: 7011 Resort hotel
PA: Sai Management Co., Inc.
631 W Katella Ave
Anaheim CA
714 776-8604

(P-15340)
SAJAHTERA INC
Also Called: Beverly Hills Hotel
9641 Sunset Blvd (90210-2938)
PHONE.....................310 276-2251
Junaidi Masri, *Pr*
Edward Mady, *OF WEST COAST USA*
EMP: 600 EST: 1912
SQ FT: 10,758
SALES (est): 57.56MM **Privately Held**
Web: www.dorchestercollection.com
SIC: 7011 Resort hotel
HQ: Dorchester Group Limited
3 Tilney Street
London
207 629-4848

(P-15341)
SAN BERNARDINO HILTON (HQ)
Also Called: Hilton
285 E Hospitality Ln (92408-3411)
PHONE.....................909 889-0133
Douglas Mccarron, *Pr*
Morgan Mcpherson, *Ex Dir*
Ronald Schoen, *
EMP: 152 EST: 1984
SALES (est): 24.63MM
SALES (corp-wide): 45.94MM **Privately Held**

Web: www.hiltongrandvacations.com
SIC: 7011 6512 5812 Hotels and motels; Commercial and industrial building operation; Eating places
PA: Carpenters Southwest Administrative Corporation
533 S Fremont Ave
Los Angeles CA
213 386-8590

(P-15342)
SAN DIEGO HOTEL COMPANY LLC
Also Called: Marriott San Dego Gslamp Qrter
660 K St (92101-7036)
PHONE.....................619 696-0234
James Evans, *CFO*
▲ EMP: 135 EST: 1999
SALES (est): 6.85MM **Privately Held**
Web: www.westerninn.com
SIC: 7011 Hotels

(P-15343)
SAN DIEGO LESSEE LLC
Also Called: Doubletree By Hilton
7450 Hazard Center Dr (92108-4539)
PHONE.....................619 297-5466
Owen Wilcox, *Sec*
Deanne Brand, *
Justin Ray Healey, *
Alexandra Neely, *
Joseph Berger, *
EMP: 100 EST: 2013
SALES (est): 7.66MM
SALES (corp-wide): 2.5B **Publicly Held**
Web: www.hilton.com
SIC: 7011 Hotels and motels
PA: Park Hotels & Resorts Inc.
1775 Tysons Blvd Fl 7
Tysons VA
571 302-5757

(P-15344)
SAN DIEGO MISSION BAY RESORTS ✪
1775 E Mission Bay Dr (92109-6801)
PHONE.....................619 677-1161
EMP: 88 EST: 2022
SALES (est): 4.48MM **Privately Held**
Web: www.missionbayresort.com
SIC: 7011 Resort hotel

(P-15345)
SAN DIEGO SHERATON CORPORATION
Also Called: Starwood Hotels & Resorts
1590 Harbor Island Dr (92101-1009)
PHONE.....................619 291-6400
Robert Cartwright, *Genl Mgr*
EMP: 146 EST: 1998
SALES (est): 7.94MM
SALES (corp-wide): 20.77B **Publicly Held**
Web: sheraton.marriott.com
SIC: 7011 5813 5812 4493 Hotels; Drinking places; Eating places; Marinas
HQ: Starwood Hotels & Resorts Worldwide, Llc
7750 Wisconsin Ave
Bethesda MD
203 964-6000

(P-15346)
SAN PSQUAL BAND MSSION INDIANS
Also Called: Valley View Casino
16300 Nyemii Pass Rd (92082-6769)
P.O. Box 2379 (92082-2379)
PHONE.....................760 291-5500
TOLL FREE: 866

PRODUCTS & SVCS

Bruce Howards, *Genl Mgr*
EMP: 245
Web: www.valleyviewcasino.com
SIC: 7011 Casino hotel
PA: San Pasqual Band Of Mission Indians
16400 Kumeyaay Way
Valley Center CA

(P-15347)
SAN YSIDRO BB PROPERTY LLC
Also Called: Stonehouse Restaurant
900 San Ysidro Ln (93108-1325)
PHONE...............................805 368-6788
Seamus Mcmanus, *Managing Member*
EMP: 140 **EST:** 2000
SQ FT: 4,415
SALES (est): 13.76MM **Privately Held**
Web: www.sanysidroranch.com
SIC: 7011 5812 Hotels; Eating places

(P-15348)
SANCI MARRIOTT HOTELS
Also Called: Marriott International
2000 2nd St (92118-1551)
PHONE...............................619 435-3000
EMP: 96 **EST:** 2012
SALES (est): 1.06MM **Privately Held**
Web: www.marriott.com
SIC: 7011 Hotels and motels

(P-15349)
SANDM SAN DEGO MRRIOTT DEL MAR
11966 El Camino Real (92130-2592)
PHONE...............................858 523-1700
Jenessa Schaniel, *Prin*
EMP: 1000 **EST:** 2009
SALES (est): 18.97MM **Privately Held**
Web: www.marriott.com
SIC: 7011 Hotels

(P-15350)
SANTA MONICA HOTEL OWNER LLC
Also Called: Doubltree Stes By Hlton Snta M
1707 4th St (90401-3301)
PHONE...............................310 395-3332
EMP: 135 **EST:** 2005
SALES (est): 3.88MM **Privately Held**
SIC: 7011 Hotels

(P-15351)
SANTA MONICA PROPER JV LLC
Also Called: Santa Monica Proper Hotel
700 Wilshire Blvd (90401-1708)
PHONE...............................310 620-9990
Brad Korzen, *CEO*
EMP: 250 **EST:** 2016
SALES (est): 36.5MM **Privately Held**
Web: www.properhotel.com
SIC: 7011 Hotels

(P-15352)
SEATTLE ARPRT HOSPITALITY LLC
Also Called: Holiday Inn
170 N Church Ln (90049-2044)
PHONE...............................310 476-6411
Robert Buescher, *Genl Mgr*
EMP: 99
Web: www.holidayinn.com
SIC: 7011 5813 5812 Hotels and motels;
Drinking places; Eating places
PA: Seattle Airport Hospitality, Llc
5847 San Felipe St # 4650
Houston TX

(P-15353)
SECOND STREET CORPORATION
Also Called: Huntley Hotel Santa Monica Bch
1111 2nd St (90403-5003)
PHONE...............................310 394-5454
Sohrab Sassounian, *Pr*
Dora Levy, *Stockholder**
Helal M El-sherif, *CFO*
Shiva Aghaipour, ***
EMP: 250 **EST:** 1964
SQ FT: 185,000
SALES (est): 21.66MM **Privately Held**
Web: www.thehuntleyhotel.com
SIC: 7011 5812 Hotels; Eating places

(P-15354)
SHEN ZHEN NEW WORLD II LLC
Also Called: Sheraton
333 Universal Hollywood Dr (91608-1001)
PHONE...............................818 980-1212
EMP: 99 **EST:** 2011
SALES (est): 3.67MM **Privately Held**
Web: sheraton.marriott.com
SIC: 7011 Hotels

(P-15355)
SHERATON HT SAN DEGO MSSION VL
Also Called: Sheraton San Diego Mission Vly
1433 Camino Del Rio S (92108-3521)
PHONE...............................619 321-4602
Admiral Cynthia Adams Carlin, *Prin*
Cynthia Adams Carlin, *Admn*
Brooke Vandenbrink, *Contrlr*
EMP: 100 **EST:** 2007
SALES (est): 2.32MM **Privately Held**
Web: www.marriott.com
SIC: 7011 Hotels

(P-15356)
SHIVAY HOSPITALITY INC
1738 N Las Palmas Ave (90028-4805)
PHONE...............................323 702-7103
Pankaj Naik, *Brnch Mgr*
EMP: 94
SALES (corp-wide): 412.88K **Privately Held**
SIC: 7011 Hotels and motels
PA: Shivay Hospitality Inc
1427 Wilcox Ave
Hollywood CA

(P-15357)
SIMI WEST INC
Also Called: Grand Vista Hotel
999 Enchanted Way (93065-1998)
PHONE...............................760 346-5502
Leo Cook, *Ch Bd*
EMP: 120 **EST:** 1993
SALES (est): 9.18MM **Privately Held**
Web: www.grandvistasimi.com
SIC: 7011 Hotels and motels

(P-15358)
SIX CONTINENTS HOTELS INC
Also Called: Holiday Inn
612 Wainwight Ct (93243)
PHONE...............................661 343-3316
EMP: 122
Web: www.holidayinn.com
SIC: 7011 Hotels and motels
HQ: Six Continents Hotels, Inc
35016 Avenue D
Yucaipa CA
770 604-5000

(P-15359)
SKY COURT USA INC
Also Called: Hyatt Hotel
880 S Westlake Blvd (91361-2905)
PHONE...............................805 497-9991
Tetsuo Nishida, *Pr*
EMP: 144 **EST:** 1990
SALES (est): 710.52K **Privately Held**
Web: www.hyatt.com
SIC: 7011 Hotels and motels

(P-15360)
SLS HOTEL AT BEVERLY HILLS
465 S La Cienega Blvd (90048-4001)
PHONE...............................310 247-0400
Robert Leck, *Genl Mgr*
EMP: 101 **EST:** 2015
SALES (est): 10.41MM
SALES (corp-wide): 67.98MM **Privately Held**
Web: book.ennismore.com
SIC: 7011 Hotels
PA: The Sunrider Corporation
1625 Abalone Ave
Torrance CA
310 781-3808

(P-15361)
SMOKE TREE INC
Also Called: Smoke Tree Ranch
1850 Smoke Tree Ln (92264-1602)
PHONE...............................760 327-1221
Lisa Bell, *Mgr*
Brad Poncher, ***
EMP: 85 **EST:** 1945
SALES (est): 4.66MM **Privately Held**
Web: www.smoketreeranch.com
SIC: 7011 Resort hotel

(P-15362)
SNOW SUMMIT SKI CORPORATION (PA)
Also Called: Snow Summit
880 Summit Blvd (92315)
P.O. Box 77 (92315-0077)
PHONE...............................909 866-5766
Richard C Kun, *Pr*
Robert Law, ***
Alan Macquoid, ***
Paula Lowery, ***
Robert Tarras, ***
EMP: 150 **EST:** 1960
SQ FT: 10,000
SALES (est): 59.84MM
SALES (corp-wide): 59.84MM **Privately Held**
Web: www.bigbearmountainresort.com
SIC: 7011 5812 Ski lodge; American restaurant

(P-15363)
SOULDRIVER LESSEE INC
Also Called: Hotel Solamar
435 6th Ave (92101-7007)
PHONE...............................619 819-9500
Maria Streedy, *Pr*
EMP: 80 **EST:** 2006
SALES (est): 10.19MM **Privately Held**
Web: www.margaritavilleresorts.com
SIC: 7011 Hotels

(P-15364)
SOUTH COAST WESTIN HOTEL CO
Also Called: Starwood Hotels & Resorts
686 Anton Blvd (92626-1920)
PHONE...............................714 540-2500
Steve Heyer, *CEO*
Mike Hall, ***

Bob Jenness, ***
EMP: 99 **EST:** 1970
SALES (est): 8.44MM
SALES (corp-wide): 20.77B **Publicly Held**
Web: www.marriott.com
SIC: 7011 5812 Hotels; Eating places
HQ: Starwood Hotels & Resorts Worldwide, Llc
7750 Wisconsin Ave
Bethesda MD
203 964-6000

(P-15365)
SPA RESORT CASINO
100 N Indian Canyon Dr (92262-6414)
PHONE...............................760 883-1034
Max Ross, *CFO*
EMP: 926
SALES (corp-wide): 23.57MM **Privately Held**
Web: www.aguacalientecasinos.com
SIC: 7011 Casino hotel
PA: Spa Resort Casino
401 E Amado Rd
Palm Springs CA
888 999-1995

(P-15366)
SPECTRUM HOTEL GROUP LLC
Also Called: Doubletree Hotel
90 Pacifica (92618-3312)
PHONE...............................949 471-8888
Timothy R Busch, *General Member*
EMP: 100 **EST:** 1997
SALES (est): 1.98MM **Privately Held**
Web: www.hilton.com
SIC: 7011 7991 5812 Hotels and motels;
Physical fitness facilities; Eating places

(P-15367)
SPF CAPITAL REAL ESTATE LLC
Also Called: Crown Plaza La Harbor Hotel
601 S Palos Verdes St (90731-3329)
PHONE...............................310 519-8200
Tiegang Yin, *Prin*
Tim Yin, *Prin*
EMP: 99 **EST:** 2017
SALES (est): 5.32MM **Privately Held**
Web: www.ihg.com
SIC: 7011 Hotels

(P-15368)
SPORTSMENS LODGE HOTEL LLC
12825 Ventura Blvd (91604-2397)
PHONE...............................818 769-4700
EMP: 87 **EST:** 1962
SQ FT: 100,000
SALES (est): 1.33MM **Privately Held**
Web: www.shopsatsportsmenslodge.com
SIC: 7011 5812 5813 Hotels; American restaurant; Cocktail lounge

(P-15369)
SS HERITAGE INN ONTARIO LLC
3595 E Guasti Rd (91761-3705)
PHONE...............................909 937-5000
Aimee Fyke, *Managing Member*
EMP: 99 **EST:** 2018
SALES (est): 2.23MM **Privately Held**
SIC: 7011 Inns

(P-15370)
STARWOOD INC
402 W Broadway Ste 400 (92101-3554)
PHONE...............................888 559-1749
Deborah Pippins, *Prin*

Mark Litz, *Prin*
▲ **EMP:** 156 **EST:** 1993
SQ FT: 1,800
SALES (est): 7.16MM **Privately Held**
SIC: 7011 4731 4729 4724 Hotels and motels
; Freight forwarding; Airline ticket offices;
Travel agencies
PA: Peake & Company Limited, Thomas
177 Western Main Road Cocorite
Port-Of-Spain

(P-15371)
STARWOOD HOTEL
Also Called: Starwood Hotels & Resorts
5990 Green Valley Cir (90230-6907)
PHONE.............................310 641-7740
Ian Gee, *Managing Member*
EMP: 156 **EST:** 1999
SALES (est): 3.86MM
SALES (corp-wide): 20.77B **Publicly Held**
Web: sheraton.marriott.com
SIC: 7011 Hotels and motels
HQ: Starwood Hotels & Resorts Worldwide,
Llc
7750 Wisconsin Ave
Bethesda MD
203 964-6000

(P-15372)
STARWOOD HTELS RSRTS WRLDWIDE
Also Called: Sheraton
601 W Mckinley Ave (91768-1635)
PHONE.............................909 622-2220
John Gilbert, *Genl Mgr*
EMP: 195
SALES (corp-wide): 20.77B **Publicly Held**
Web: www.starwoodhotels.com
SIC: 7011 Hotels and motels
HQ: Starwood Hotels & Resorts Worldwide,
Llc
7750 Wisconsin Ave
Bethesda MD
203 964-6000

(P-15373)
STARWOOD HTELS RSRTS WRLDWIDE
Also Called: Starwood Hotels & Resorts
910 Broadway Cir (92101-6114)
PHONE.............................619 239-2200
Doug Korn, *Genl Mgr*
EMP: 250
SALES (corp-wide): 20.77B **Publicly Held**
Web: westin.marriott.com
SIC: 7011 7991 6512 5812 Hotels and motels
; Physical fitness facilities; Nonresidential
building operators; Eating places
HQ: Starwood Hotels & Resorts Worldwide,
Llc
7750 Wisconsin Ave
Bethesda MD
203 964-6000

(P-15374)
STOCKBRIDGE/SBE HOLDINGS LLC
Also Called: SBE
5900 Wilshire Blvd Ste 3100 (90036-5013)
PHONE.............................323 655-8000
EMP: 3000 **EST:** 2007
SALES (est): 125.29MM **Privately Held**
SIC: 7011 Hotels

(P-15375)
STONEBRIDGE RLTY ADVISORS INC
Also Called: Hampton Inn
27102 Towne Centre Dr (92610-2801)

PHONE.............................949 597-8700
John Matthews, *Mgr*
EMP: 586
Web: www.hilton.com
SIC: 7011 Hotels and motels
PA: Stonebridge Realty Advisors, Inc.
9100 E Panorama Dr # 300
Englewood CO

(P-15376)
SUMMERWOOD WINERY & INN INC
2175 Arbor Rd (93446-8620)
PHONE.............................805 227-1365
Mark Uhalley, *Pr*
▲ **EMP:** 37 **EST:** 2002
SALES (est): 2.11MM **Privately Held**
Web: www.summerwoodwine.com
SIC: 7011 2084 Bed and breakfast inn;
Wines

(P-15377)
SUN HILL PROPERTIES INC
Also Called: Hilton Los Angls/Nversal Cy Ht
555 Universal Hollywood Dr (91608-1001)
PHONE.............................818 506-2500
Denn Hu, *Ch Bd*
▲ **EMP:** 350 **EST:** 1989
SALES (est): 26.29MM **Privately Held**
Web: www.sunhillprop.com
SIC: 7011 Hotels and motels
PA: Universal Paragon Corporation
150 Executive Park Blvd # 4
San Francisco CA

(P-15378)
SUNSTONE DURANTE LLC
Also Called: Hilton San Diego/Del Mar
15575 Jimmy Durante Blvd (92014-1901)
PHONE.............................858 792-5200
Scott Sloan, *Managing Member*
Damien Proctor, *Prin*
EMP: 250 **EST:** 2005
SALES (est): 9.79MM **Privately Held**
SIC: 7011 Hotels and motels

(P-15379)
SUNSTONE HOTEL PROPERTIES INC
Also Called: Residence Inn By Marriott
1177 S Beverly Dr (90035-1119)
PHONE.............................310 228-4100
Tom Beedon, *Genl Mgr*
EMP: 149
Web: residence-inn.marriott.com
SIC: 7011 Hotels and motels
HQ: Sunstone Hotel Properties Inc
120 Vantis Dr Ste 350
Aliso Viejo CA

(P-15380)
SUNSTONE HOTEL PROPERTIES INC
Also Called: Residence Inn By Marriott
1700 N Sepulveda Blvd (90266-5015)
PHONE.............................310 546-7627
Sandi Rae Kraft, *Brnch Mgr*
EMP: 202
Web: residence-inn.marriott.com
SIC: 7011 Hotels and motels
HQ: Sunstone Hotel Properties Inc
120 Vantis Dr Ste 350
Aliso Viejo CA

(P-15381)
SUNSTONE HOTEL PROPERTIES INC (DH)
Also Called: Residence Inn By Marriott
120 Vantis Dr Ste 350 (92656-2686)

PHONE.............................949 330-4000
EMP: 120 **EST:** 1994
SALES (est): 62.7MM **Privately Held**
Web: www.hilton.com
SIC: 7011 Hotels and motels
HQ: Interstate Hotels & Resorts, Inc.
5301 Headquarters Dr
Plano TX
703 387-3100

(P-15382)
SUNSTONE TOP GUN LESSEE INC
Also Called: Embassy Suites
4550 La Jolla Village Dr (92122-1248)
PHONE.............................949 330-4000
Kenneth E Cruse, *CEO*
John V Arabia, *
Lindsay Monge, *
EMP: 150 **EST:** 2006
SALES (est): 9.27MM **Publicly Held**
Web: www.hilton.com
SIC: 7011 Hotels and motels
HQ: Sunstone Hotel Trs Lessee, Inc.
15 Enterprise Ste 200
Aliso Viejo CA

(P-15383)
SWVP DEL MAR HOTEL LLC
Also Called: Doubletree San Diego Del Mar
11915 El Camino Real (92130-2539)
PHONE.............................858 481-5900
Tom Donahue, *Mgr*
EMP: 84 **EST:** 2015
SALES (est): 1.6MM **Privately Held**
SIC: 7011 Hotel, franchised

(P-15384)
SWVP WESTLAKE LLC
Also Called: Hyatt Westlake
880 S Westlake Blvd (91361-2905)
PHONE.............................805 557-1234
David Coonan, *Genl Mgr*
EMP: 250
SALES (corp-wide): 2.29MM **Privately Held**
Web: www.swvp.com
SIC: 7011 Motels
PA: Swvp Westlake Llc
12790 El Camino Real
San Diego CA
858 480-2900

(P-15385)
SYCUAN CASINO
5469 Casino Way (92019-1823)
PHONE.............................619 445-6002
EMP: 1844
SALES (corp-wide): 93.96MM **Privately Held**
Web: www.sycuan.com
SIC: 7011 Casino hotel
PA: Sycuan Casino
5459 Casino Way
El Cajon CA
619 445-6002

(P-15386)
SYDELL HOTELS LLC
Also Called: Line Hotel, The
3515 Wilshire Blvd (90010-2301)
PHONE.............................213 381-7411
Gary J Thomas, *
EMP: 130 **EST:** 2011
SALES (est): 29.01MM
SALES (corp-wide): 29.01MM **Privately Held**
Web: www.thelinehotel.com
SIC: 7011 Resort hotel
PA: Sydell Group Llc
276 5th Ave Rm 704

New York NY
646 810-0208

(P-15387)
T-12 THREE LLC
Also Called: Hard Rock Hotel
207 5th Ave (92101-6908)
PHONE.............................619 702-3000
EMP: 356 **EST:** 2007
SALES (est): 40.92MM **Privately Held**
Web: www.hardrockhotels.com
SIC: 7011 Hotels

(P-15388)
TEMECULA HHG HOTEL DEV LP
Also Called: Home2 Sites By Hilton Temecula
28400 Rancho California Rd (92590-3617)
PHONE.............................951 331-3622
EMP: 96
SALES (corp-wide): 1.79MM **Privately Held**
Web: home2suites3.hilton.com
SIC: 7011 Hotels
PA: Temecula Hhg Hotel Development, Lp
105 Decker Ct Ste 500
Irving TX
972 510-1200

(P-15389)
THE LODGE AT TORREY PINES PARTNERSHIP L P
998 W Mission Bay Dr (92109-7803)
EMP: 275 **EST:** 1961
SALES (est): 17.04MM **Privately Held**
Web: www.lodgetorreypines.com
SIC: 7011 5812 Resort hotel; Coffee shop

(P-15390)
TIBURON HOSPITALITY LLC
Also Called: Super 8 Motel
901 Real Rd (93309-1003)
PHONE.............................661 322-1012
Mark Grotewohl, *Pt*
▲ **EMP:** 150 **EST:** 1980
SQ FT: 1,600
SALES (est): 4.32MM **Privately Held**
Web: www.wyndhamhotels.com
SIC: 7011 Hotels and motels

(P-15391)
TODAYS IV
Also Called: Westin Bonaventure Ht & Suites
404 S Figueroa St Ste 516 (90071-1798)
PHONE.............................213 835-4016
EMP: 713 **EST:** 1989
SQ FT: 1,200,000
SALES (est): 40.79MM **Privately Held**
Web: westin.marriott.com
SIC: 7011 5813 5812 Hotels; Drinking places
; Eating places
PA: Today's Hotel Corporation
1500 Van Ness Ave
San Francisco CA

(P-15392)
TORREY SUITES LP
3939 Ocean Bluff Ave (92130-8654)
PHONE.............................858 720-9500
Robert Rauch, *Genl Pt*
EMP: 84 **EST:** 2008
SALES (est): 3.85MM **Privately Held**
SIC: 7011 Hotels

(P-15393)
TRAVELODGE HOTELS INC
3327 Del Mar Ave (91770-2329)
PHONE.............................800 257-2297
EMP: 124
SALES (corp-wide): 1.5B **Publicly Held**

Web: www.wyndhamhotels.com
SIC: 7011 Hotels and motels
HQ: Travelodge Hotels, Inc.
1 Sylvan Way
Parsippany NJ
973 567-3708

(P-15394)
TRIGILD INTERNATIONAL INC
Also Called: Ramada Inn
1680 Superior Ave (92627-3652)
PHONE...................949 645-2221
Vince Andres, *Brnch Mgr*
EMP: 105
SALES (corp-wide): 20.67MM **Privately Held**
Web: www.wyndhamhotels.com
SIC: 7011 Hotels and motels
PA: Trigild International, Inc.
3323 Carmel Mountain Rd # 2
San Diego CA
858 720-6700

(P-15395)
UHG LAX PROP LLC
Also Called: Hotel Company
1985 E Grand Ave (90245-5015)
PHONE...................310 322-0999
Charu Goyal, *Managing Member*
Jordan Austin, *
Mark Lewis, *
EMP: 125 **EST:** 2017
SALES (est): 3.9MM **Privately Held**
SIC: 7011 5812 Hotels; Restaurant, family: independent

(P-15396)
UKA LLC
Also Called: Tarsadia Hotels
620 Newport Center Dr Ste 1400 (92660)
PHONE...................949 610-8000
B U Patel, *Mgr*
EMP: 495 **EST:** 1997
SQ FT: 12,000
SALES (est): 532.58K
SALES (corp-wide): 369.62MM **Privately Held**
SIC: 7011 Hotels
HQ: Tarsadia Investments, Llc
520 Newport Center Dr # 2100
Newport Beach CA
949 610-8000

(P-15397)
UNIWELL CORPORATION
Also Called: Holiday Inn
7000 Beach Blvd (90620-1832)
PHONE...................714 522-7000
Tracy Myer, *Brnch Mgr*
EMP: 150
SALES (corp-wide): 17.64MM **Privately Held**
Web: www.hibuenapark.com
SIC: 7011 5813 5812 Hotels and motels; Drinking places; Eating places
PA: Uniwell Corporation
21172 Figueroa St
Carson CA
310 782-8888

(P-15398)
URBAN COMMONS QUEENSWAY LLC
Also Called: Queen Mary, The
1126 Queens Hwy (90802-6331)
PHONE...................562 499-1611
EMP: 900 **EST:** 2016
SALES (est): 24.24MM **Privately Held**
SIC: 7011 Hotels

(P-15399)
US GRANT HOTEL VENTURES LLC
326 Broadway (92101-4800)
PHONE...................619 744-2007
EMP: 80 **EST:** 2003
SQ FT: 99,999
SALES (est): 2.66MM **Privately Held**
Web: www.grantgrill.com
SIC: 7011 Resort hotel

(P-15400)
US HOTEL AND RESORT MGT INC
Also Called: Regency Inn
2544 Newport Blvd (92627-1331)
PHONE...................949 650-2988
EMP: 227
SALES (corp-wide): 17.94MM **Privately Held**
Web: www.ramkotacompanies.com
SIC: 7011 Resort hotel
HQ: U.S. Hotel And Resort Management, Inc.
3211 W Sencore Dr
Sioux Falls SD
605 334-2371

(P-15401)
V TODAYS INC
Also Called: Holiday Inn
19800 S Vermont Ave (90502-1126)
PHONE...................310 781-9100
Belinda Zen, *CEO*
David Britton, *
EMP: 110 **EST:** 1986
SQ FT: 95,000
SALES (est): 9.05MM **Privately Held**
Web: www.holidayinn.com
SIC: 7011 Hotels and motels

(P-15402)
VALADON HOTEL LLC
Also Called: Petit Ermitage
8822 Cynthia St (90069-4502)
PHONE...................310 854-1114
Adrian Ashkenazy, *
EMP: 80 **EST:** 1997
SQ FT: 40,000
SALES (est): 15.16MM **Privately Held**
Web: www.petitermitage.com
SIC: 7011 Hotels

(P-15403)
VALENCIA GROUP LLC
94 Mayfair (92620-2149)
PHONE...................949 379-6489
EMP: 109
SALES (corp-wide): 59.42K **Privately Held**
Web: www.valenciahotelgroup.com
SIC: 7011 Hotels
PA: Valencia Group Llc
3495 Cabrillo Ave
Santa Clara CA

(P-15404)
VENTURA HSPTALITY PARTNERS LLC
Also Called: Crowne Plaza Ventura Beach
450 Harbor Blvd (93001-2708)
PHONE...................805 648-2100
EMP: 140 **EST:** 2006
SQ FT: 143,000
SALES (est): 9.07MM **Privately Held**
Web: www.ihg.com
SIC: 7011 Hotels

(P-15405)
VPB OPERATING CO LLC
147 Stimson Ave (93449-2643)
PHONE...................805 773-1011
EMP: 84
SALES (est): 1.66MM **Privately Held**
SIC: 7011 Resort hotel, franchised

(P-15406)
W LODGING INC
Also Called: Ramada Inn
1825 Gillespie Way Ste 10 (92020-0501)
PHONE...................619 258-6565
EMP: 800
SIC: 7011 5812 8741 Hotels and motels; Eating places; Hotel or motel management

(P-15407)
W LOS ANGELES
Also Called: Westwood Marquis Hotel & Grdns
930 Hilgard Ave (90024-3009)
P.O. Box 14029 (85267-4029)
PHONE...................310 208-8765
George I Rosenthal, *Pr*
Anil Sharma, *
Mark Rosenthal, *
Damien Hirsch, *
EMP: 330 **EST:** 1977
SALES (est): 21.51MM
SALES (corp-wide): 36.91MM **Privately Held**
Web: www.wlosangeles.com
SIC: 7011 Resort hotel
PA: Raleigh Enterprises, Inc.
5300 Melrose Ave Fl 4
Los Angeles CA
310 899-8900

(P-15408)
W&J BUSINESS VENTURES LLC
Also Called: Holiday Inn
8620 Airport Blvd (90045-4246)
PHONE...................310 645-7700
Hsiu Lan Lee, *
EMP: 95 **EST:** 1960
SQ FT: 700,000
SALES (est): 1.35MM **Privately Held**
Web: www.holidayinn.com
SIC: 7011 Hotels and motels

(P-15409)
WALTERS FAMILY PARTNERSHIP
Also Called: Hilton Resort In Palm Spring
400 E Tahquitz Canyon Way (92262-6605)
PHONE...................760 320-6868
Lance Walters, *Pt*
EMP: 150 **EST:** 1981
SQ FT: 200,000
SALES (est): 4.92MM **Privately Held**
SIC: 7011 5813 5812 Hotels and motels; Drinking places; Eating places

(P-15410)
WATERFRONT HOTEL LLC
Also Called: Hilton
21100 Pacific Coast Hwy (92648-5307)
PHONE...................714 845-8000
John Gilbert, *Mgr*
EMP: 298
Web: www.hilton.com
SIC: 7011 5813 5812 7299 Hotels and motels; Drinking places; Eating places; Banquet hall facilities
PA: The Waterfront Hotel Llc
660 Nwport Ctr Dr Ste 105
Newport Beach CA

(P-15411)
WCO HOTELS INC
Also Called: Disneys Grnd Clifornian Ht Spa
1600 S Disneyland Dr (92802-2317)
PHONE...................714 635-2300
Dorothy Stratton, *Brnch Mgr*
EMP: 824
SALES (corp-wide): 88.9B **Publicly Held**
SIC: 7011 Resort hotel
HQ: Wco Hotels, Inc.
1150 W Magic Way
Anaheim CA
323 636-3251

(P-15412)
WELK GROUP INC (PA)
Also Called: Welk Music Group
11400 W Olympic Blvd Ste 760 (90064-1649)
PHONE...................760 749-3000
Jon Fredricks, *Pr*
Marc L Luzzatto, *
EMP: 345 **EST:** 1955
SQ FT: 6,200
SALES (est): 47.43MM
SALES (corp-wide): 47.43MM **Privately Held**
Web: www.kwgoldcoast.com
SIC: 7011 5099 Resort hotel; Compact discs

(P-15413)
WELK GROUP INC
Also Called: Welk Resort Center
8860 Lawrence Welk Dr (92026-6403)
PHONE...................760 749-3000
Mario Trejo, *Mgr*
EMP: 400
SALES (corp-wide): 47.43MM **Privately Held**
Web: www.kwgoldcoast.com
SIC: 7011 5812 Motels; Eating places
PA: The Welk Group Inc
11400 W Olympic Blvd # 1450
Los Angeles CA
760 749-3000

(P-15414)
WEST HOLLYWOOD EDITION
9040 W Sunset Blvd (90069-1851)
PHONE...................310 795-7103
EMP: 89 **EST:** 2018
SALES (est): 9.18MM **Privately Held**
Web: www.editionhotels.com
SIC: 7011 Hotels

(P-15415)
WESTGROUP SAN DIEGO ASSOCIATES
Also Called: Paradise Point Resort
1404 Vacation Rd (92109-7905)
PHONE...................858 274-4630
David Feeney, *Pt*
EMP: 232 **EST:** 1998
SALES (est): 12.47MM **Privately Held**
Web: www.paradisepoint.com
SIC: 7011 Resort hotel

(P-15416)
WESTLAKE PROPERTIES INC
Also Called: Westlake Village Inn
31943 Agoura Rd (91361-4427)
PHONE...................818 889-0230
John Notter, *Prin*
EMP: 150 **EST:** 1974
SALES (est): 14.22MM **Privately Held**
Web: www.westlakevillageinn.com
SIC: 7011 Resort hotel

(P-15417)
WHB CORPORATION
Also Called: Millennium Biltmore Hotel
506 S Grand Ave (90071-2602)
PHONE..............................213 624-1011
John Demola, *Brnch Mgr*
EMP: 630
SIC: 7011 5812 5813 Hotels; Eating places;
Drinking places
HQ: Whb Corporation
7600 E Orchard Rd 230s
Greenwood Village CO
303 779-2000

(P-15418)
WHV RESORT GROUP INC
Also Called: Lawrence Welk Desert Oasis
34567 Cathedral Canyon Dr (92234-6637)
PHONE..............................760 770-9755
Bill Palmer, *Mgr*
EMP: 902
Web: www.kwgoldcoast.com
SIC: 7011 Resort hotel
HQ: Whv Resort Group, Inc.
300 Rancheros Dr Ste 310
San Marcos CA
760 652-4913

(P-15419)
WIN TIME LTD (PA)
Also Called: Holiday Inn Express
9335 Kearny Mesa Rd (92126-4502)
PHONE..............................858 695-2300
Herman Lin, *Genl Pt*
Chue-huang Chiu, *Pt*
Yi-ho Huang, *Pt*
EMP: 166 **EST:** 1982
SQ FT: 100,000
SALES (est): 9.44MM
SALES (corp-wide): 9.44MM **Privately
Held**
Web: www.holidayinn.com
SIC: 7011 Hotels and motels

(P-15420)
WINDSOR CAPITAL GROUP INC
Also Called: Embassy Suites
1117 N H St (93436-8115)
PHONE..............................805 735-8311
Toby Simmons, *Mgr*
EMP: 145
SALES (corp-wide): 149.18MM **Privately
Held**
Web: www.hilton.com
SIC: 7011 Hotels and motels
PA: Windsor Capital Group, Inc.
2800 28th St Ste 385
Santa Monica CA
310 566-1100

(P-15421)
WINDSOR CAPITAL GROUP INC
Also Called: Embassy Suites
29345 Rancho California Rd (92591-5201)
PHONE..............................951 676-5656
Tom Demott, *Genl Mgr*
EMP: 612
SALES (corp-wide): 149.18MM **Privately
Held**
Web: www.hilton.com
SIC: 7011 Hotels and motels
PA: Windsor Capital Group, Inc.
2800 28th St Ste 385
Santa Monica CA
310 566-1100

(P-15422)
WINDSOR CAPITAL GROUP INC
Also Called: Embassy Suites
900 E Birch St (92821-5812)

PHONE..............................714 990-6000
Regina Samy, *Mgr*
EMP: 108
SQ FT: 48,164
SALES (corp-wide): 149.18MM **Privately
Held**
Web: www.hilton.com
SIC: 7011 Hotels and motels
PA: Windsor Capital Group, Inc.
2800 28th St Ste 385
Santa Monica CA
310 566-1100

(P-15423)
WINDSOR CAPITAL GROUP INC
Also Called: Embassy Suites
1325 E Dyer Rd (92705-5615)
PHONE..............................714 241-3800
EMP: 170
SALES (corp-wide): 149.18MM **Privately
Held**
Web: www.hilton.com
SIC: 7011 5813 5812 Hotels and motels;
Drinking places; Eating places
PA: Windsor Capital Group, Inc.
2800 28th St Ste 385
Santa Monica CA
310 566-1100

(P-15424)
WINDSOR CAPITAL GROUP INC
Also Called: Pacific Suites Hotel
2800 28th St Ste 385 (90405-6211)
PHONE..............................310 566-1100
Michael D Cryan, *Mgr*
EMP: 108
SALES (corp-wide): 149.18MM **Privately
Held**
Web: www.windsorhospitality.com
SIC: 7011 Hotels
PA: Windsor Capital Group, Inc.
2800 28th St Ste 385
Santa Monica CA
310 566-1100

(P-15425)
WJ NEWPORT LLC
Also Called: Marriott
4500 Macarthur Blvd (92660-2010)
PHONE..............................949 476-2001
EMP: 190 **EST:** 2016
SALES (est): 21.45MM **Privately Held**
Web: www.marriott.com
SIC: 7011 5812 Resort hotel; Family
restaurants

(P-15426)
**WORLD TRADE CTR HT ASSOC
LTD**
Also Called: Long Beach Hilton, The
701 W Ocean Blvd (90831-3100)
PHONE..............................562 983-3400
Steve Holloway, *Corporate Controller*
Greater Los Angeles Trade Cent er, *Genl Pt*
EMP: 82 **EST:** 1990
SALES (est): 1.18MM **Privately Held**
SIC: 7011 7991 5813 5812 Hotels and motels
; Physical fitness facilities; Drinking places;
Eating places

(P-15427)
WS MMV HOTEL LLC
Also Called: San Diego Marriott Mission Vly
8757 Rio San Diego Dr (92108-1620)
PHONE..............................619 692-3800
EMP: 99 **EST:** 2016
SALES (est): 2.9MM **Privately Held**
Web: www.marriott.com
SIC: 7011 Hotels

(P-15428)
**WW SAN DIEGO HARBOR
ISLAND LLC**
Also Called: Hilton
1960 Harbor Island Dr (92101-1013)
PHONE..............................619 291-6700
Shahid Kayani, *Genl Mgr*
EMP: 120 **EST:** 1980
SALES (est): 9.7MM
SALES (corp-wide): 50.61MM **Privately
Held**
Web: www.hilton.com
SIC: 7011 Resort hotel
PA: Ww Lbv Inc.
2000 Hotel Plaza Blvd
Lake Buena Vista FL
407 828-2424

(P-15429)
YHB LONG BEACH LLC
Also Called: Holiday Inn
2640 N Lakewood Blvd (90815-1715)
PHONE..............................562 597-4401
Traycee Mayer, *Prin*
EMP: 90 **EST:** 2003
SALES (est): 6.65MM **Privately Held**
Web: www.holidayinn.com
SIC: 7011 Hotels and motels

7021 Rooming And Boarding Houses

(P-15430)
**M-AURORA WORLDWIDE (US)
LP (PA)**
2222 Corinth Ave (90064-1602)
PHONE..............................800 888-0808
▲ **EMP:** 200 **EST:** 1960
SALES (est): 74MM
SALES (corp-wide): 74MM **Privately Held**
SIC: 7021 6531 Furnished room rental; Real
estate brokers and agents

(P-15431)
**OAKWOOD CORPORATE
HOUSING INC**
7922 Day Creek Blvd (91739-8584)
PHONE..............................909 922-8272
EMP: 119
SIC: 7021 Furnished room rental
PA: Oakwood Corporate Housing, Inc.
1 World Trade Ctr # 2400
Long Beach CA

(P-15432)
**WORLDWIDE CORPORATE
HOUSING LP**
Also Called: Oakwood Temporary Housing
1 World Trade Ctr Ste 2400 (90831-2400)
PHONE..............................972 392-4747
Howard Ruby, *Pt*
EMP: 493
SALES (corp-wide): 74MM **Privately Held**
Web: www.discoverasr.com
SIC: 7021 Furnished room rental
HQ: Worldwide Corporate Housing, Lp
1 World Trade Ctr # 2400
Long Beach CA
562 473-7371

7032 Sporting And Recreational Camps

(P-15433)
ALISAL PROPERTIES (PA)
Also Called: Alisal Guest Ranch

1054 Alisal Rd (93463-3033)
PHONE..............................805 688-6411
Palmer Jackson, *Pr*
Joan Y Jackson, *VP*
Susanne Powell, *Sec*
EMP: 243 **EST:** 1946
SQ FT: 10,000
SALES (est): 26.51MM
SALES (corp-wide): 26.51MM **Privately
Held**
Web: www.alisalranch.com
SIC: 7032 7997 Sporting camps; Golf club,
membership

(P-15434)
**BIG LGUE DREAMS
CONSULTING LLC**
33700 Date Palm Dr (92234-4731)
PHONE..............................760 324-5600
Steve Navarro, *VP*
EMP: 107
SALES (corp-wide): 49.84MM **Privately
Held**
Web: www.bigleaguedreams.com
SIC: 7032 Recreational camps
PA: Big League Dreams Consulting, Llc
16333 Fairfield Ranch Rd
Chino Hills CA
909 287-1700

(P-15435)
FOREST HOME INC
Also Called: Forest Home Ministries
40000 Valley Of The Falls Dr (92339-9674)
PHONE..............................909 389-2300
EMP: 250 **EST:** 1938
SALES (est): 22.64MM **Privately Held**
Web: www.foresthome.org
SIC: 7032 Cabin camp

(P-15436)
**INTERVRSITY CHRSTN
FLLWSHP/USA**
Also Called: Campus By The Sea
Gallager&Apos;S Cove (90704)
P.O. Box 466 (90704-0466)
PHONE..............................310 510-0015
Susan Veon, *Dir*
EMP: 617
SALES (corp-wide): 119.41MM **Privately
Held**
Web: www.intervarsity.org
SIC: 7032 5942 Bible camp; Book stores
PA: Intervarsity Christian Fellowship/Usa
635 Science Dr
Madison WI
608 274-9001

(P-15437)
LLC WOODWARD WEST
28400 Stallion Springs Dr (93561-5266)
PHONE..............................661 822-7900
EMP: 143 **EST:** 2002
SALES (est): 9.64MM **Privately Held**
Web: www.woodwardwest.com
SIC: 7032 Sporting and recreational camps

(P-15438)
PALI CAMP
Also Called: Pali Adventures
30778 Hwy 18 (92382)
PHONE..............................909 867-5743
Andrew Wexler, *CEO*
EMP: 150 **EST:** 1990
SALES (est): 1.83MM **Privately Held**
Web: www.paliadventures.com
SIC: 7032 Summer camp, except day and
sports instructional

PRODUCTS & SVCS

(P-15439)
SNOW VALLEY MTN RESORT LLC
Also Called: Snow Valley Mountain Sports Pk
Hwy 18 (92382)
P.O. Box 2337 (92382-2337)
PHONE..................909 867-2751
Kevin Somes, *Genl Mgr*
EMP: 80 **EST:** 1948
SQ FT: 81,000
SALES (est): 4.72MM
SALES (corp-wide): 1.3B **Privately Held**
Web: www.bigbearmountainresort.com
SIC: 7032 7999 5812 Sporting and
recreational camps; Ski rental concession;
Eating places
HQ: Alterra Mountain Company
3501 Wazee St Ste 400
Denver CO
303 749-8200

7033 Trailer Parks And Campsites

(P-15440)
BURLINGAME INDUSTRIES INC
Also Called: Resort Campground Intl
277 Lytle Creek Rd (92358-9751)
PHONE..................909 887-7038
Bob Boyter, *Mgr*
EMP: 108
SALES (corp-wide): 95.73MM **Privately Held**
Web: www.mountainlakesca.com
SIC: 7033 Campgrounds
PA: Burlingame Industries, Incorporated
3546 N Riverside Ave
Rialto, CA
909 355-7000

(P-15441)
BURLINGAME INDUSTRIES INC (PA)
Also Called: Eagle Roofing Products
3546 N Riverside Ave (92377-3878)
PHONE..................909 355-7000
Robert C Burlingame, *Ch Bd*
Roger D Thompson, *Vice Chairman**
Kevin C Burlingame, *
Seamus P Burlingame, *
William L Robinson, *
▲ **EMP:** 100 **EST:** 1969
SQ FT: 100,000
SALES (est): 95.73MM
SALES (corp-wide): 95.73MM **Privately Held**
Web: www.eagleroofing.com
SIC: 7033 0971 3559 3259 Campgrounds;
Hunting preserve; Tile making machines;
Roofing tile, clay

(P-15442)
COLORADO RIVER ADVENTURES INC (PA)
Also Called: Yuma Lakes Resort
2715 Parker Dam Rd (92242-9712)
P.O. Box 1088 (85344-1088)
PHONE..................760 663-3737
Phil Younis, *Pr*
EMP: 112 **EST:** 1982
SQ FT: 6,500
SALES (est): 4.99MM
SALES (corp-wide): 4.99MM **Privately Held**
Web: www.coloradoriveradventures.com
SIC: 7033 8641 7032 Campgrounds; Social
club, membership; Recreational camps

7041 Membership-basis Organization Hotels

(P-15443)
MEDIEVAL TIMES ENTRMT INC (HQ)
7662 Beach Blvd (90620-1838)
PHONE..................714 523-1100
Kenneth H Kim, *Pr*
EMP: 1754 **EST:** 2001
SALES (est): 23.25MM **Privately Held**
Web: www.medievaltimes.com
SIC: 7041 7996 Membership-basis
organization hotels; Theme park,
amusement
PA: Medieval Times Entertainment, Inc.
5020 Riverside Dr Bldg 3
Irving TX

7211 Power Laundries, Family And Commercial

(P-15444)
ANITSA INC
Also Called: Valet Services
6032 Shull St (90201-6237)
PHONE..................213 237-0533
EMP: 135 **EST:** 1988
SQ FT: 65,000
SALES (est): 9.32MM **Privately Held**
SIC: 7211 8742 Power laundries, family and
commercial; Industry specialist consultants

(P-15445)
RADIANT SERVICES CORP (PA)
651 W Knox St (90248-4409)
PHONE..................310 327-6300
EMP: 235 **EST:** 1994
SALES (est): 8.8MM **Privately Held**
Web: www.radiantservices.com
SIC: 7211 7216 Power laundries, family and
commercial; Drycleaning plants, except rugs

7213 Linen Supply

(P-15446)
AMERICAN TEXTILE MAINT CO
Also Called: Medico Professional Linen Svc
1705 Hooper Ave (90021-3111)
P.O. Box 516564 (90051-0596)
PHONE..................213 749-4433
Kenny Immazumi, *Mgr*
EMP: 89
SALES (corp-wide): 88.21MM **Privately Held**
Web: www.republicmasterchefs.com
SIC: 7213 Uniform supply
PA: American Textile Maintenance
Company
1667 W Washington Blvd
Los Angeles CA
323 731-3132

(P-15447)
AMERICAN TEXTILE MAINT CO
Also Called: Master-Chef's Linen Rental
1664 W Washington Blvd (90007-1115)
PHONE..................323 735-1661
Bob Brill, *Brnch Mgr*
EMP: 155
SALES (corp-wide): 88.21MM **Privately Held**
Web: www.republicmasterchefs.com
SIC: 7213 Towel supply

PA: American Textile Maintenance
Company
1667 W Washington Blvd
Los Angeles CA
323 731-3132

(P-15448)
AMERIPRIDE SERVICES INC
Also Called: AMERIPRIDE SERVICES, INC.
5950 Alcoa Ave (90058-3925)
PHONE..................323 587-3941
TOLL FREE: 800
Ampett Easemero, *Brnch Mgr*
EMP: 111
SALES (corp-wide): 1.45B **Publicly Held**
Web: www.ameripride.com
SIC: 7213 Uniform supply
HQ: Ameripride Services, Llc
10801 Wayzata Blvd # 100
Minnetonka MN
800 750-4628

(P-15449)
BRAUN LINEN SERVICE (PA)
Also Called: A-1 Pomona Linen
16514 Garfield Ave (90723-5304)
P.O. Box 348 (90723-0348)
PHONE..................909 623-2678
Richard A Cornwell, *CEO*
William S Cornwell, *
▲ **EMP:** 125 **EST:** 1985
SQ FT: 28,000
SALES (est): 10.61MM
SALES (corp-wide): 10.61MM **Privately Held**
Web: www.braunlinen.com
SIC: 7213 Towel supply

(P-15450)
CINTAS SALES CORPORATION
Also Called: Cintas
2618 Oak St (92707-3720)
PHONE..................714 957-2852
EMP: 100
SALES (corp-wide): 8.82B **Publicly Held**
SIC: 7213 5999 5912 5699 Uniform supply;
Alarm and safety equipment stores; Drug
stores and proprietary stores; Uniforms and
work clothing
HQ: Cintas Sales Corporation
6800 Cintas Blvd
Cincinnati OH

(P-15451)
GBS LINENS INC (PA)
Also Called: GBS Party Linens
305 N Muller St (92801-5445)
PHONE..................714 778-6448
Pravin Mody, *Pr*
Sujata Mody, *
Ameer P Mody, *
Sudha Mody, *
▲ **EMP:** 100 **EST:** 1962
SQ FT: 57,000
SALES (est): 10.6MM
SALES (corp-wide): 10.6MM **Privately Held**
Web: www.gbslinens.com
SIC: 7213 2392 7211 5023 Linen supply;
Household furnishings, nec; Power
laundries, family and commercial;
Homefurnishings

(P-15452)
MISSION LINEN SUPPLY
Also Called: Mission Linen & Uniform Svc
619 W Avenue I (93534-2585)
PHONE..................661 948-5052
Dick Grever, *Mgr*
EMP: 92

SALES (corp-wide): 99.93MM **Privately Held**
Web: www.missionlinen.com
SIC: 7213 Uniform supply
PA: Mission Linen Supply
717 E Yanonali St
Santa Barbara CA
805 730-3620

(P-15453)
MISSION LINEN SUPPLY
Also Called: Mission Linen & Uniform Svc
5400 Alton Way (91710-7601)
PHONE..................909 393-6857
Louis Filveria, *Mgr*
EMP: 107
SALES (corp-wide): 99.93MM **Privately Held**
Web: www.missionlinen.com
SIC: 7213 Uniform supply
PA: Mission Linen Supply
717 E Yanonali St
Santa Barbara CA
805 730-3620

(P-15454)
MISSION LINEN SUPPLY
Also Called: Mission Linen & Uniform Svc
2727 Industry St (92054-4810)
PHONE..................760 757-9099
Graig Rogers, *Prin*
EMP: 142
SALES (corp-wide): 99.93MM **Privately Held**
Web: www.missionlinen.com
SIC: 7213 7218 Uniform supply; Industrial
launderers
PA: Mission Linen Supply
717 E Yanonali St
Santa Barbara CA
805 730-3620

(P-15455)
MISSION LINEN SUPPLY
Also Called: Mission Linen & Uniform Svc
505 Maulhardt Ave (93030-7925)
PHONE..................805 485-6794
Matthew Aguelli, *Mgr*
EMP: 82
SALES (corp-wide): 99.93MM **Privately Held**
Web: www.missionlinen.com
SIC: 7213 Uniform supply
PA: Mission Linen Supply
717 E Yanonali St
Santa Barbara CA
805 730-3620

(P-15456)
MISSION LINEN SUPPLY
Also Called: Mission Linen & Uniform Svc
712 E Montecito St (93103-3295)
PHONE..................805 962-7687
Curtos Lopez, *Mgr*
EMP: 133
SALES (corp-wide): 99.93MM **Privately Held**
Web: www.missionlinen.com
SIC: 7213 Uniform supply
PA: Mission Linen Supply
717 E Yanonali St
Santa Barbara CA
805 730-3620

(P-15457)
MISSION LINEN SUPPLY
Also Called: Mission Linen & Uniform Svc
602 S Western Ave (93458-5496)
PHONE..................805 922-3579
Bill Bently, *Genl Mgr*

EMP: 91
SALES (corp-wide): 99.93MM **Privately Held**
Web: www.missionlinen.com
SIC: 7213　Uniform supply
PA: Mission Linen Supply
　717 E Yanonali St
　Santa Barbara CA
　805 730-3620

(P-15458)
MORGAN SERVICES INC
Also Called: Morgan Linen Service
905 Yale St (90012-1724)
PHONE...............................213 485-9666
Mark Smith, *Brnch Mgr*
EMP: 95
SQ FT: 51,339
SALES (corp-wide): 72.96MM **Privately Held**
Web: www.morganservices.com
SIC: 7213 7218　Linen supply; Industrial launderers
PA: Morgan Services, Inc.
　323 N Michigan Ave
　Chicago IL
　312 346-3181

(P-15459)
SOCAL AUTO SUPPLY INC
21418 Osborne St (91304-1520)
PHONE...............................302 360-8373
EMP: 46
SIC: 7213 2676　Towel supply; Towels, napkins, and tissue paper products
PA: Socal Auto Supply Inc
　16192 Postal Hwy
　Lewes DE

(P-15460)
SPS HOLDINGS INC
1702 W 134th St (90249-2016)
P.O. Box 1368 (90249-0368)
PHONE...............................310 532-7550
Saul Shrager, *Pr*
Nelson Shrager, *
Stephen Shrager, *
EMP: 80 **EST:** 1957
SQ FT: 40,000
SALES (est): 9.45MM **Privately Held**
Web: www.unifirst.com
SIC: 7213　Uniform supply

(P-15461)
YEE YUEN LAUNDRY AND CLRS INC
Also Called: Yee Yuen Linen Service
2575 S Normandie Ave (90007-1598)
PHONE...............................323 734-7205
Deborah Morikawa, *Pr*
Cynthia Louie, *
Luis Lee, *
EMP: 80 **EST:** 1928
SQ FT: 20,000
SALES (est): 2.02MM **Privately Held**
Web: www.yeeyuenlinen.com
SIC: 7213　Linen supply

7215 Coin-operated Laundries And Cleaning

(P-15462)
WASH MLTFMILY LDRY SYSTEMS LLC (PA)
2200 195th St (90501-1120)
PHONE...............................800 421-6897
TOLL FREE: 800
Jim Gimeson, *CEO*

Arthur J Long, *
Andres De Armas, *CRO*
EMP: 150 **EST:** 2007
SQ FT: 130,000
SALES (est): 84.49MM
SALES (corp-wide): 84.49MM **Privately Held**
Web: www.wash.com
SIC: 7215　Laundry, coin-operated

7216 Drycleaning Plants, Except Rugs

(P-15463)
AMERICAN WINDOW COVERING INC
825 Williamson Ave (92832-2133)
P.O. Box 3518 (92834-3518)
PHONE...............................714 879-3880
Leland B Daniels, *Pr*
EMP: 18 **EST:** 1963
SQ FT: 2,400
SALES (est): 938.7K **Privately Held**
Web: www.awc-cwc.com
SIC: 7216 2391 5023　Drapery, curtain drycleaning; Draperies, plastic and textile: from purchased materials; Draperies

(P-15464)
PICO CLEANERS INC (PA)
9150 W Pico Blvd (90035-1320)
PHONE...............................310 274-2431
Sharam Jahanbani, *CEO*
Simon Djahanbani, *
EMP: 80 **EST:** 1963
SQ FT: 10,000
SALES (est): 4.47MM
SALES (corp-wide): 4.47MM **Privately Held**
Web: www.picocleaners.com
SIC: 7216　Cleaning and dyeing, except rugs

(P-15465)
STAR LAUNDRY SERVICES INC
Also Called: Star Services
3410 Main St (92113-3803)
PHONE...............................619 572-1009
Abraham Yang, *Pr*
EMP: 80 **EST:** 2006
SALES (est): 2.21MM **Privately Held**
Web: www.starls.com
SIC: 7216　Cleaning and dyeing, except rugs

7217 Carpet And Upholstery Cleaning

(P-15466)
BONDED INC (PA)
Also Called: Bonded Carpet
7590 Carroll Rd (92121-2415)
P.O. Box 23910 (92193-3910)
PHONE...............................858 576-8400
Mitch Adler, *Pr*
Sherri Adler, *
EMP: 80 **EST:** 1975
SALES (est): 10MM
SALES (corp-wide): 10MM **Privately Held**
Web: www.bondedinc.com
SIC: 7217 5023　Carpet and furniture cleaning on location; Homefurnishings

(P-15467)
COLT SERVICES INC
Also Called: Stanley Steemer Carpet Cleaner
9655 Via Excelencia (92126-4555)
PHONE...............................858 271-9910
TOLL FREE: 888

Steven R Thompson, *Pr*
EMP: 100 **EST:** 1979
SQ FT: 33,000
SALES (est): 7.68MM **Privately Held**
Web: www.stanleysteemer.com
SIC: 7217　Carpet and furniture cleaning on location

(P-15468)
EXPRESS CONTRACTORS INC
3810 Wacker Dr (91752-1142)
P.O. Box 310279 (92331-0279)
PHONE...............................951 360-6500
Amaer Alhamwi, *CEO*
EMP: 100 **EST:** 1992
SQ FT: 10,000
SALES (est): 10.67MM **Privately Held**
Web: www.expresscontractorsinc.com
SIC: 7217 1752 1721 1743　Carpet and rug cleaning and repairing plant; Carpet laying; Painting and paper hanging; Terrazzo, tile, marble and mosaic work

7218 Industrial Launderers

(P-15469)
MAJOR GLOVES & SAFETY INC
250 Turnbull Canyon Rd (91745-1007)
PHONE...............................626 330-8022
Shu Wen Cheng, *CEO*
Kun Shan Ho, *CFO*
Kai Wen Cheng, *Sec*
Ken Ho, *Prin*
Flora Cheng, *Prin*
▲ **EMP:** 21 **EST:** 2005
SQ FT: 38,000
SALES (est): 2.45MM **Privately Held**
Web: www.mggloves.com
SIC: 7218 5099 5999 3842　Safety glove supply; Safety equipment and supplies; Safety supplies and equipment; Gloves, safety

(P-15470)
PRUDENTIAL OVERALL SUPPLY (PA)
Also Called: Prudential Cleanroom Services
1661 Alton Pkwy (92606-4801)
P.O. Box 11210 (92711-1210)
PHONE...............................949 250-4855
Dan Clark, *CEO*
Thomas C Watts, *
Donald C Lahn, *
▲ **EMP:** 95 **EST:** 1947
SQ FT: 20,000
SALES (est): 158.2MM
SALES (corp-wide): 158.2MM **Privately Held**
Web: www.prudentialuniforms.com
SIC: 7218　Wiping towel supply

(P-15471)
UNIFIRST CORPORATION
Also Called: Unifirst
700 Etiwanda Ave Ste C (91761-8608)
PHONE...............................909 390-8670
Jeff Martin, *Mgr*
EMP: 130
SALES (corp-wide): 2.23B **Publicly Held**
Web: www.unifirst.com
SIC: 7218 7213　Industrial uniform supply; Uniform supply
PA: Unifirst Corporation
　68 Jonspin Rd
　Wilmington MA
　978 658-8888

(P-15472)
VESTIS SERVICES LLC
Also Called: Aramark Unf & Career AP LLC
115 N First St Ste 203 (91502-1857)
P.O. Box 101179 (91189-0005)
PHONE...............................818 973-3700
John Zillmer, *CEO*
Brad Drummond, *
Robert N Deitz, *
EMP: 4180 **EST:** 1976
SQ FT: 63,000
SALES (est): 375MM
SALES (corp-wide): 1.45B **Publicly Held**
Web: www.vestis.com
SIC: 7218　Industrial uniform supply
HQ: Aramark Uniform & Career Apparel Group, Inc.
　1101 Market St Ste 45
　Philadelphia PA
　215 238-3000

(P-15473)
WORKRITE UNIFORM COMPANY INC (DH)
1701 Lombard St Ste 200 (93030-8235)
PHONE...............................805 483-0175
Philip C Williamson, *CEO*
Keith Suddaby, *
Mark Adler, *
EMP: 385 **EST:** 1968
SALES (est): 23.07MM
SALES (corp-wide): 11.61B **Publicly Held**
SIC: 7218　Flame and heat resistant clothing supply
HQ: Vf Outdoor, Llc
　1551 Wewatta St
　Denver CO
　855 500-8639

7219 Laundry And Garment Services, Nec

(P-15474)
CM LAUNDRY LLC
14919 S Figueroa St (90248-1720)
PHONE...............................310 436-6170
Ernesto Munoz, *Managing Member*
EMP: 100 **EST:** 2007
SQ FT: 26,500
SALES (est): 2.27MM **Privately Held**
Web: www.cmlaundry.com
SIC: 7219　Laundry, except power and coin-operated

(P-15475)
JOB OPTIONS INCORPORATED
1110 S Washington Ave (92408-2244)
PHONE...............................909 890-4612
EMP: 820
SQ FT: 35,800
Web: www.joboptionsinc.org
SIC: 7219　Fur garment cleaning, repairing, and storage
PA: Job Options, Incorporated
　3465 Cmino Del Rio S Ste
　San Diego CA

7221 Photographic Studios, Portrait

(P-15476)
CORBIS IMAGES LLC (PA)
Also Called: Corbis
6060 Center Dr Ste 1000 (90045-8842)
PHONE...............................323 602-5700
EMP: 17 **EST:** 2005
SALES (est): 6.44MM

PRODUCTS & SVCS

SALES (corp-wide): 6.44MM **Privately Held**
Web: www.corbisentertainment.com
SIC: 7221 7372 Photographic studios, portrait; Prepackaged software

7231 Beauty Shops

(P-15477)
BEAUTY BARRAGE LLC
4340 Von Karman Ave Ste 240 (92660-2084)
PHONE..................................949 771-3399
Sonia Summers, *CEO*
Brady Heyborne, *
Alissa Spencer, *
EMP: 220 **EST:** 2015
SALES (est): 14.41MM **Privately Held**
Web: www.beautybarrage.com
SIC: 7231 8742 Beauty shops; Marketing consulting services

(P-15478)
BEAUTY BOUTIQUE INC
Also Called: Bellus Academy
1073 E Main St (92021-6247)
PHONE..................................619 442-3407
William Lynch, *Pr*
Lynelli Lynch, *VP*
EMP: 183 **EST:** 1960
SQ FT: 6,500
SALES (est): 5.32MM **Privately Held**
Web: www.bellusacademy.edu
SIC: 7231 Beauty culture school

(P-15479)
BELLAMI HAIR LLC
Also Called: Bellami Hair
21123 Nordhoff St (91311-5816)
PHONE..................................844 235-5264
Julius Salerno, *Managing Member*
EMP: 100 **EST:** 2013
SALES (est): 24.76MM
SALES (corp-wide): 26.4MM **Privately Held**
Web: www.bellamihair.com
SIC: 7231 Hairdressers
PA: Beauty Industry Group Opco Llc
1250 N Flyer Way Ste 100
Salt Lake City UT
801 206-4781

(P-15480)
ESALONCOM LLC
1910 E Maple Ave (90245-3411)
PHONE..................................866 550-2424
EMP: 100 **EST:** 2008
SALES (est): 43.07MM **Privately Held**
Web: www.esalon.com
SIC: 7231 Hairdressers

(P-15481)
MINILUXE INC
Also Called: Miniluxe
11965 San Vicente Blvd (90049-5003)
PHONE..................................424 442-1630
EMP: 93
SALES (corp-wide): 15MM **Privately Held**
Web: www.miniluxe.com
SIC: 7231 Manicurist, pedicurist
PA: Miniluxe, Inc.
1 Faneuil Hall Sq Fl 7
Boston MA
617 684-2731

(P-15482)
MURAD LLC
Also Called: Murad Spa
2141 Rosecrans Ave Ste 1151 (90245-4709)

PHONE..................................310 726-0470
Howard Murad, *Brnch Mgr*
▲ **EMP:** 118
SALES (corp-wide): 62.39B **Privately Held**
Web: www.murad.com
SIC: 7231 Facial salons
HQ: Murad, Llc
2121 Park Pl Fl 1
El Segundo CA

(P-15483)
NAIL ALLIANCE - NORTH AMER INC
4100 Bonita Pl (92835-1066)
PHONE..................................714 449-1568
EMP: 100
Web: www.gelish.com
SIC: 7231 Manicurist, pedicurist
PA: Nail Alliance - North America, Inc.
1545 Moonstone
Brea CA

(P-15484)
OGLEBY SISTERS SOAP
1804 Garnet Ave (92109-3352)
PHONE..................................212 518-1172
Linda Moncrief, *CEO*
EMP: 21 **EST:** 1985
SALES (est): 465.81K **Privately Held**
Web: www.oglebysisterssoap.com
SIC: 7231 2844 Beauty shops; Cosmetic preparations

(P-15485)
PETROSIAN ESTHETIC ENTPS LLC
Also Called: Sev Lasers
2919 W Burbank Blvd (91505-2310)
PHONE..................................818 391-8231
Angineh Petrosian, *COO*
EMP: 180 **EST:** 2013
SALES (est): 2.11MM **Privately Held**
SIC: 7231 7371 Beauty shops; Computer software development and applications

(P-15486)
SPORT CLIPS INC
Also Called: Sport Clips
4839 Clairemont Dr Ste E (92117-2727)
PHONE..................................858 273-9993
Milan Lidia, *Mgr*
EMP: 590
Web: www.sportclips.com
SIC: 7231 Beauty shops
PA: Sport Clips, Inc.
110 Sport Clips Way
Georgetown TX

7261 Funeral Service And Crematories

(P-15487)
FOREST LAWN MORTUARY
66272 Pierson Blvd (92240-3658)
PHONE..................................760 329-8737
David Wenzil, *Genl Mgr*
EMP: 482
SALES (corp-wide): 214.25MM **Privately Held**
Web: www.forestlawn.com
SIC: 7261 Funeral home
HQ: Forest Lawn Mortuary
1712 S Glendale Ave
Glendale CA

(P-15488)
NORTHSTAR MEMORIAL GROUP LLC

2562 State St (92008-1663)
P.O. Box 616 (90660-0616)
PHONE..................................800 323-1342
EMP: 103
Web: www.nsmg.com
SIC: 7261 Funeral home
PA: Northstar Memorial Group, Llc
1900 Saint James Pl # 300
Houston TX

(P-15489)
PIERCE BROTHERS (DH)
Also Called: SCI
10621 Victory Blvd (91606-3918)
PHONE..................................818 763-9121
Oliver Yeo, *Mgr*
R L Waltrip, *
David Anderson, *
Ray Gipson, *
Curtis Briggs, *
EMP: 80 **EST:** 1902
SQ FT: 10,000
SALES (est): 9.53MM
SALES (corp-wide): 4.11B **Publicly Held**
Web: www.portalofthefoldedwings.net
SIC: 7261 6553 Crematory; Cemeteries, real estate operation
HQ: Sci Funeral Services Of New York, Inc.
1929 Allen Pkwy
Houston TX

(P-15490)
SINAI TEMPLE
Also Called: Mt Sinai Mem Pk & Mortuary
5950 Forest Lawn Dr (90068-1010)
PHONE..................................323 469-6000
TOLL FREE: 800
Len Lawrence, *Mgr*
EMP: 125
SQ FT: 22,633
SALES (corp-wide): 53.77MM **Privately Held**
Web: www.mountsinaiparks.org
SIC: 7261 6553 Funeral home; Cemeteries, real estate operation
PA: Temple Sinai
10400 Wilshire Blvd
Los Angeles CA
310 474-1518

(P-15491)
TEMPLE ISRAEL OF HOLLYWOOD (PA)
Also Called: Jewish Synagogue
7300 Hollywood Blvd (90046-2904)
PHONE..................................323 876-8330
Steve Sloan, *Pr*
Jane Zuckerman, *
Renee Mochkatel, *
David Cremin, *
Nancy Ortenberg, *
EMP: 83 **EST:** 1926
SQ FT: 15,000
SALES (est): 24.87MM
SALES (corp-wide): 24.87MM **Privately Held**
Web: www.tioh.org
SIC: 7261 8299 8661 Funeral service and crematories; Religious school; Synagogue

7291 Tax Return Preparation Services

(P-15492)
AHG INC
340 S Lemon Ave 6633 (91789-2706)
PHONE..................................703 596-0111
Sanzar Kakar, *Ofcr*
EMP: 300 **EST:** 2018

SALES (est): 461.69K **Privately Held**
SIC: 7291 8721 Tax return preparation services; Accounting, auditing, and bookkeeping

(P-15493)
ANDERSEN TAX LLC
400 S Hope St Ste 2000 (90071)
PHONE..................................213 593-2300
EMP: 127
SALES (corp-wide): 112.31MM **Privately Held**
Web: www.andersen.com
SIC: 7291 Tax return preparation services
PA: Andersen Tax Llc
333 Bush St Ste 1700
San Francisco CA
415 764-2700

(P-15494)
CERIDIAN TAX SERVICE INC
Also Called: Ceridian
17390 Brookhurst St (92708-3720)
P.O. Box 20805 (92728-0805)
PHONE..................................714 963-1311
Webster Hill, *Genl Mgr*
EMP: 300 **EST:** 1998
SQ FT: 130,000
SALES (est): 24.68MM
SALES (corp-wide): 1.25B **Publicly Held**
Web: www.ceridian.com
SIC: 7291 Tax return preparation services
PA: Ceridian Hcm Holding Inc.
3311 E Old Shakopee Rd
Minneapolis MN
952 853-8100

(P-15495)
H G GROUP INC
4225 Saviers Rd (93033-7158)
PHONE..................................805 486-6463
EMP: 382
SALES (corp-wide): 185.25MM **Privately Held**
Web: www.hyatt.com
SIC: 7291 Tax return preparation services
HQ: H G Group Inc
71 S Wacker Dr Ste 1000
Chicago IL

(P-15496)
OPTIMA TAX RELIEF LLC
Also Called: Optima Protection Plan
3100 S Harbor Blvd Ste 250 (92704-6823)
PHONE..................................714 361-4636
EMP: 180 **EST:** 2010
SQ FT: 30,000
SALES (est): 26.2MM **Privately Held**
Web: www.optimataxrelief.com
SIC: 7291 Tax return preparation services

7299 Miscellaneous Personal Services

(P-15497)
AMERICAN FRUITS & FLAVORS LLC ✪
510 Park Ave (91340-2527)
PHONE..................................818 899-9574
William Haddad, *Pr*
EMP: 300 **EST:** 2023
SALES (est): 3.07MM
SALES (corp-wide): 6.31B **Publicly Held**
SIC: 7299 House sitting
PA: Monster Beverage Corporation
1 Monster Way
Corona CA
951 739-6200

(P-15498)
AMERICOR FUNDING INC
18200 Von Karman Ave Ste 600
(92612-1023)
PHONE................................866 333-8686
Banir Ganatra, *CEO*
EMP: 170 **EST:** 2008
SALES (est): 11MM **Privately Held**
Web: www.americor.com
SIC: 7299 Debt counseling or adjustment
service, individuals

(P-15499)
BEYOND FINANCE LLC
Also Called: Accredited Debt Relief
9525 Towne Centre Dr Ste 100
(92121-1995)
PHONE................................800 282-7186
Tim Ho, *CEO*
EMP: 558
SALES (corp-wide): 36.73MM **Privately
Held**
Web: www.beyondfinance.com
SIC: 7299 Debt counseling or adjustment
service, individuals
PA: Beyond Finance, Llc
7322 Southwest Fwy # 1200
Houston TX
800 282-7186

(P-15500)
CHOURA VENUE SERVICES
Also Called: Choura Vnue Svcs At Carson Ctr
4101 E Willow St (90815-1740)
PHONE................................562 426-0555
James Choura, *CEO*
EMP: 99 **EST:** 2012
SALES (est): 3.63MM **Privately Held**
Web: www.thegrandlb.com
SIC: 7299 5812 Information services,
consumer; Caterers

(P-15501)
CIRI - STROUP INC
Also Called: Mile High Valet
25135 Park Lantern (92629-2878)
PHONE................................949 488-3104
Rob Stroup, *Owner*
EMP: 103
SIC: 7299 7521 Valet parking; Automobile
parking
PA: Ciri - Stroup, Inc.
1 Park Pl Ste 200
Annapolis MD

(P-15502)
CLOUDSTAFF LLC
26895 Aliso Creek Rd # B-209
(92656-5301)
PHONE................................888 551-5339
EMP: 471
SALES (corp-wide): 12.5MM **Privately
Held**
Web: www.cloudstaffllc.com
SIC: 7299 Personal appearance services
PA: Cloudstaff Llc
1165 E San Antonio Dr
Long Beach CA
888 551-5339

(P-15503)
CLUTTER INC (PA)
3526 Hayden Ave (90232-2413)
PHONE................................800 805-4023
Ari Mir, *CEO*
EMP: 120 **EST:** 2013
SALES (est): 44.73MM
SALES (corp-wide): 44.73MM **Privately
Held**
Web: www.clutter.com

SIC: 7299 4212 Personal item care and
storage services; Moving services

(P-15504)
**CONDUIT LNGAGE
SPECIALISTS INC**
22720 Ventura Blvd Ste 100 (91364-1305)
PHONE................................859 299-3178
Art Mathews, *Brnch Mgr*
EMP: 93
SALES (corp-wide): 4.11MM **Privately
Held**
Web: www.conduitlanguage.com
SIC: 7299 Personal appearance services
PA: Conduit Language Specialists, Inc.
110 Augusta Way
Paris KY
818 389-4333

(P-15505)
DEL MAR FAIRGROUNDS
2260 Jimmy Durante Blvd (92014-2216)
PHONE................................858 792-4288
EMP: 95 **EST:** 2007
SALES (est): 8.26MM **Privately Held**
Web: www.delmarfairgrounds.com
SIC: 7299 Banquet hall facilities

(P-15506)
DESTINATION RESIDENCES LLC
Also Called: Tesancia La Jlla Ht Spa Resort
9700 N Torrey Pines Rd (92037-1102)
PHONE................................858 550-1000
Charlie Peck, *Pr*
EMP: 483
SALES (corp-wide): 367.25MM **Privately
Held**
Web: www.destinationhotels.com
SIC: 7299 7389 7991 7011 Banquet hall
facilities; Convention and show services;
Spas; Hotels
HQ: Destination Residences Llc
10333 E Dry Creek Rd
Englewood CO
303 799-3830

(P-15507)
EHARMONY INC (HQ)
Also Called: Eharmony.com
10900 Wilshire Blvd Fl 17 (90024-6522)
P.O. Box 241810 (90024-9610)
PHONE................................424 258-1199
EMP: 119 **EST:** 2000
SQ FT: 6,000
SALES (est): 38.97MM
SALES (corp-wide): 4.32B **Privately Held**
Web: www.eharmony.com
SIC: 7299 Dating service
PA: Prosiebensat.1 Media Se
Medienallee 7
Unterfohring BY
89950710

(P-15508)
GLEN IVY HOT SPRINGS
1001 Brea Mall (92821-5721)
PHONE................................714 990-2090
Jen Breakey, *Mgr*
EMP: 190
SALES (corp-wide): 12.11MM **Privately
Held**
Web: www.glenivy.com
SIC: 7299 7991 5812 5699 Massage parlor;
Spas; Cafe; Bathing suits
PA: Glen Ivy Hot Springs
25000 Glen Ivy Rd
Temescal Valley CA
951 277-3529

(P-15509)
HIGH MOON STUDIOS LLC
2051 Palomar Airport Rd Ste 250
(92011-1461)
PHONE................................760 448-3000
Peter Della Penna, *Prin*
EMP: 209 **EST:** 2006
SALES (est): 8.64MM **Privately Held**
Web: www.highmoonstudios.com
SIC: 7299 Apartment locating service

(P-15510)
**INFORMTION RFRRAL FDRTION
OF L**
Also Called: 211 La County
526 W Las Tunas Dr (91776-1111)
P.O. Box 726 (91778-0726)
PHONE................................626 350-1841
Maribel Marin, *Ex Dir*
Amy Latzer, *
EMP: 100 **EST:** 1980
SQ FT: 23,000
SALES (est): 15.52MM **Privately Held**
Web: www.211la.org
SIC: 7299 Information services, consumer

(P-15511)
INSTANT CHECKMATE LLC
Also Called: Instant Checkmate
375 Camino De La Reina Ste 400
(92108-3083)
PHONE................................800 222-8985
Steven Gray, *CEO*
EMP: 205
SALES (est): 740.91K
SALES (corp-wide): 30.74MM **Privately
Held**
Web: www.peopleconnect.us
SIC: 7299 Information services, consumer
HQ: Pubrec Llc
375 Camino De La Reina # 400
San Diego CA

(P-15512)
INTELICARE DIRECT LLC
8885 Rio San Diego Dr (92108-1626)
PHONE................................858 299-3636
Steven Gray, *CEO*
EMP: 94 **EST:** 2014
SALES (est): 9.07MM
SALES (corp-wide): 30.74MM **Privately
Held**
Web: www.desertcallconnection.com
SIC: 7299 Information services, consumer
HQ: Pubrec Llc
375 Camino De La Reina # 400
San Diego CA

(P-15513)
INTELIUS LLC
Also Called: Intelius
375 Camino De La Reina (92108-3083)
PHONE................................888 245-1655
Steven Gray, *CEO*
EMP: 180
SALES (est): 288.08K
SALES (corp-wide): 30.74MM **Privately
Held**
SIC: 7299 Information services, consumer
HQ: Pubrec Llc
375 Camino De La Reina # 400
San Diego CA

(P-15514)
**JC WEIGHT LOSS CENTRES
INC (PA)**
Also Called: Jenny Craig
5770 Fleet St (92008-4700)
PHONE................................760 696-4000

Kent Kreh, *Ch Bd*
Jenny Craig, *
Dana Fiser, *
Patti Larchet, *
Jenice Lara, *
EMP: 130 **EST:** 1985
SQ FT: 50,000
SALES (est): 25.64MM **Privately Held**
Web: www.jennycraig.com
SIC: 7299 7991 6794 Diet center, without
medical staff; Weight reducing clubs;
Franchises, selling or licensing

(P-15515)
**JET FLEET INTERNATIONAL
CORP**
Also Called: J F I
2370 Westwood Blvd Ste K (90064-2150)
PHONE................................310 440-3820
Finn Moller, *Pr*
Arcy Lariz, *
EMP: 28 **EST:** 2003
SALES (est): 1.93MM **Privately Held**
Web: www.jetfleetinternational.com
SIC: 7299 7363 2911 6361 Buyers' club;
Pilot service, aviation; Jet fuels; Title
insurance

(P-15516)
JON RENAU COLLECTION INC
2842 Whiptail Loop (92010-6760)
PHONE................................760 598-0067
John Reynolds, *CEO*
EMP: 54 **EST:** 1987
SALES (est): 1.9MM **Privately Held**
Web: www.jonrenau.com
SIC: 7299 3999 Hair weaving or replacement
; Wigs, including doll wigs, toupees, or
wiglets

(P-15517)
**MASTROIANNI FAMILY ENTPS
LTD**
Also Called: Jay's Catering
10581 Garden Grove Blvd (92843-1128)
PHONE................................310 952-1700
EMP: 360
SALES (corp-wide): 23.04MM **Privately
Held**
Web: www.jayscatering.com
SIC: 7299 Banquet hall facilities
PA: Mastroianni Family Enterprises Ltd.
10581 Garden Grove Blvd
Garden Grove CA
714 636-6045

(P-15518)
ONE CALL PLUMBER GOLETA
140 Nectarine Ave Apt 4 (93117-3359)
PHONE................................805 284-0441
One Call Plumber Goleta, *Owner*
EMP: 99 **EST:** 2001
SALES (est): 236.06K **Privately Held**
Web: www.plumbersgoleta.com
SIC: 7299 Handyman service

(P-15519)
ONE EVENTS INC
8581 Santa Monica Blvd (90069-4120)
PHONE................................310 498-5471
Nickolas William Potocic, *CEO*
EMP: 90 **EST:** 2012
SALES (est): 734.94K **Privately Held**
Web: www.oneevents.biz
SIC: 7299 Banquet hall facilities

(P-15520)
**PACIFIC EVENT PRODUCTIONS
INC (PA)**

Also Called: Pep Creations
6989 Corte Santa Fe (92121-3260)
PHONE..........................858 458-9908
Lawrence J Toll, *CEO*
George Duff, *
Joanne Mera, *
EMP: 247 **EST:** 1990
SQ FT: 30,000
SALES (est): 12.57MM **Privately Held**
Web: www.pacificevents.com
SIC: 7299 Party planning service

(P-15521)
PPS PARKING INC
1800 E Garry Ave Ste 107 (92705-5803)
P.O. Box 16635 (92623-6635)
PHONE..........................949 223-8707
Steve Paliska, *Pr*
EMP: 506 **EST:** 1982
SQ FT: 5,000
SALES (est): 14.12MM **Privately Held**
Web: www.ppsparkinginc.com
SIC: 7299 8748 Valet parking; Business
   consulting, nec

(P-15522)
SIGNATURE PARKING LLC
924 Chapala St Ste B (93101-8220)
PHONE..........................805 969-7275
EMP: 100 **EST:** 2000
SQ FT: 900
SALES (est): 2.36MM **Privately Held**
Web: www.signatureparking.com
SIC: 7299 Valet parking

(P-15523)
VIBIANA EVENTS LLC
Also Called: Vibiana
214 S Main St (90012-3708)
PHONE..........................213 626-1507
Amy Knoll Fraser, *Managing Member*
EMP: 88 **EST:** 2011
SALES (est): 2.36MM **Privately Held**
Web: www.vibiana.com
SIC: 7299 Facility rental and party planning
   services

(P-15524)
WESTERN COSTUME CO (HQ)
11041 Vanowen St (91605-6314)
PHONE..........................818 760-0900
Eddie Marks, *Pr*
EMP: 48 **EST:** 1912
SQ FT: 150,000
SALES (est): 8.49MM **Privately Held**
Web: www.westerncostume.com
SIC: 7299 2389 Costume rental; Costumes
PA: Ahs Trinity Group, Inc.
   11041 Vanowen St
   North Hollywood CA

7311 Advertising Agencies

(P-15525)
180LA LLC
12555 W Jefferson Blvd Ste 200
(90066-7032)
PHONE..........................310 382-1400
Michael Allen, *Managing Member*
Michael Alllen, *Managing Member*
EMP: 110 **EST:** 2006
SQ FT: 13,000
SALES (est): 9.66MM
SALES (corp-wide): 14.29B **Publicly Held**
Web: www.180la.com
SIC: 7311 Advertising consultant
HQ: Tbwa Worldwide Inc.
   220 E 42nd St Fl 14
   New York NY

(P-15526)
AD POPULUM LLC (PA)
1234 6th St Apt 410 (90401-1602)
P.O. Box 212 (90406-0212)
PHONE..........................619 818-7644
EMP: 90 **EST:** 2016
SALES (est): 480.06MM
SALES (corp-wide): 480.06MM **Privately
Held**
SIC: 7311 Advertising agencies

(P-15527)
ADCONION MEDIA INC (PA)
Also Called: Adconion Media Group
3301 Exposition Blvd Fl 1 (90404-5082)
PHONE..........................310 382-5521
Kristian Wilson, *Pr*
Scott Sullivan, *Global Chief Technology
Officer*
EMP: 119 **EST:** 2007
SALES (est): 10.47MM
SALES (corp-wide): 10.47MM **Privately
Held**
SIC: 7311 Advertising consultant

(P-15528)
ADVERTISE PURPLE
1431 7th St Ste 302 (90401-2751)
PHONE..........................424 272-7400
EMP: 85 **EST:** 2018
SALES (est): 870.91K **Privately Held**
Web: www.advertisepurple.com
SIC: 7311 Advertising agencies

(P-15529)
**ALCONE MARKETING GROUP
INC (HQ)**
Also Called: Jeep Gear
4 Studebaker (92618-2012)
PHONE..........................949 595-5322
William Hahn, *CEO*
Bill Hahn, *
Sean Conciatore, *CCO**
▲ **EMP:** 100 **EST:** 1983
SQ FT: 90,000
SALES (est): 29.72MM
SALES (corp-wide): 14.29B **Publicly Held**
Web: www.alcone.com
SIC: 7311 Advertising consultant
PA: Omnicom Group Inc.
   280 Park Ave Fl 31w
   New York NY
   212 415-3600

(P-15530)
CAMPBELL-EWALD COMPANY
Also Called: Campbell-Ewald-West
1840 Century Park E Ste 1600
(90067-2116)
PHONE..........................310 358-4800
Jeffrey Fisher, *Mgr*
EMP: 149
SALES (corp-wide): 10.93B **Publicly Held**
Web: www.c-e.com
SIC: 7311 Advertising consultant
HQ: Campbell-Ewald Company
   2000 Brush St Ste 601
   Detroit MI
   586 574-3400

(P-15531)
**CIMARRON PARTNER
ASSOCIATES LLC**
Also Called: Cimarron Group, The
6855 Santa Monica Blvd (90038-1119)
PHONE..........................323 337-0300
EMP: 150
Web: www.perfectdomain.com

SIC: 7311 Advertising agencies

(P-15532)
COLOR AD INC
18601 S Santa Fe Ave (90221-5901)
PHONE..........................310 632-5500
EMP: 20 **EST:** 1994
SQ FT: 33,000
SALES (est): 4.93MM **Privately Held**
Web: www.gocolorad.com
SIC: 7311 2752 Advertising agencies;
   Commercial printing, lithographic

(P-15533)
**CONTROL GROUP MEDIA CO
LLC**
Also Called: People Connect
375 Camino De La Reina Ste 400 (92101)
PHONE..........................858 242-1350
Steven Gray, *CEO*
Rick Sutton, *CFO*
Shiem Edelbrock, *Prin*
EMP: 80 **EST:** 2012
SALES (est): 5.34MM **Privately Held**
Web: www.peopleconnect.us
SIC: 7311 8743 Advertising agencies; Public
   relations services

(P-15534)
DAILEY & ASSOCIATES
8687 Melrose Ave Ste G300 (90069-5076)
P.O. Box 931629 (90093-1629)
PHONE..........................323 490-3847
Jean Grabow, *CEO*
Michelle Wong, *
Bridget Johnson, *
Bradley Johnson, *
Steven Mitchell, *
EMP: 82 **EST:** 1964
SALES (est): 10.23MM **Privately Held**
Web: www.daileyla.com
SIC: 7311 Advertising consultant

(P-15535)
DAVID & GOLIATH LLC
909 N Pacific Coast Hwy Ste 700
(90245-2724)
PHONE..........................310 445-5200
Yumi Prentice, *Pr*
Wells Davis, *Chief Strategy Officer**
Bobby Pearce, *Chief Creative Officer**
EMP: 200 **EST:** 1999
SQ FT: 1,000
SALES (est): 33.55MM **Privately Held**
Web: www.dng.com
SIC: 7311 Advertising consultant
PA: Innocean Worldwide Inc.
   308 Gangnam-Daero, Gangnam-Gu
   Seoul

(P-15536)
**DAVISELEN ADVERTISING INC
(PA)**
865 S Figueroa St Ste 1200 (90017-2543)
PHONE..........................213 688-7000
Mark Davis, *CEO*
Robert Elen, *
Thomas Saltarelli, *
Terry Sullivan, *
EMP: 172 **EST:** 1915
SQ FT: 32,000
SALES (est): 42.44MM
SALES (corp-wide): 42.44MM **Privately
Held**
Web: www.daviselen.com
SIC: 7311 Advertising consultant

(P-15537)
DEUTSCH LA INC
Also Called: Steelhead
12901 W Jefferson Blvd (90066-7023)
PHONE..........................310 862-3000
Mike Sheldon, *CEO*
EMP: 100 **EST:** 1995
SALES (est): 23.89MM
SALES (corp-wide): 10.93B **Publicly Held**
Web: www.deutschla.com
SIC: 7311 Advertising agencies
PA: The Interpublic Group Of Companies
   Inc
   909 3rd Ave
   New York NY
   212 704-1200

(P-15538)
DG2 WORLDWIDE GROUP LLC
Also Called: Dg2
12655 W Jefferson Blvd 4th Fl
(90066-7008)
PHONE..........................310 809-0899
Michael Lay, *Managing Member*
EMP: 22 **EST:** 2017
SQ FT: 10,000
SALES (est): 1.52MM **Privately Held**
SIC: 7311 3577 8748 Advertising consultant;
   Data conversion equipment, media-to-
   media: computer; Agricultural consultant

(P-15539)
DIGITAS INC
Also Called: Digitaslbi
13031 W Jefferson Blvd Ste 800
(90094-7002)
PHONE..........................617 867-1000
EMP: 105
SALES (corp-wide): 25.29MM **Privately
Held**
Web: www.digitas.com
SIC: 7311 Advertising agencies
HQ: Digitas, Inc.
   40 Water St
   Boston MA
   617 369-8000

(P-15540)
GL NEMIROW INC
Also Called: Terry Hines & Assoc
2550 N Hollywood Way Ste 502
(91505-5023)
PHONE..........................818 562-9433
Grant W Nemirow, *Pr*
Ralph Terraciano, *
EMP: 97 **EST:** 1989
SALES (est): 9.5MM **Privately Held**
SIC: 7311 Advertising agencies

(P-15541)
GRUPO GALLEGOS
Also Called: Gallegos United
300 Pacific Coast Hwy Ste 200
(92648-5109)
PHONE..........................562 256-3600
John Gallegos, *CEO*
Jennifer Mull, *
EMP: 90 **EST:** 2004
SALES (est): 14MM **Privately Held**
Web: www.gallegosunited.com
SIC: 7311 Advertising consultant

(P-15542)
HAVAS EDGE LLC (DH)
1525 Faraday Ave Ste 250 (92008-7373)
PHONE..........................760 929-0041
Steve Netzley, *CEO*
Jennifer Peabody, *
Greg Johnson, *
Eric Bush, *

EMP: 98 EST: 1988
SALES (est): 50.97MM Privately Held
Web: www.havasedge.com
SIC: 7311 Advertising agencies
HQ: Havas
29 30
Puteaux
158478000

(P-15543)
HAYES COMPANY INC
Also Called: Craftsmen Construction
5663 Balboa Ave (92111-2705)
PHONE..............................949 375-3113
Dan Hayes, Prin
EMP: 23 EST: 2007
SALES (est): 746.67K Privately Held
Web: www.hayesgc.com
SIC: 7311 1522 1389 1521 Advertising
agencies; Residential construction, nec;
Construction, repair, and dismantling
services; New construction, single-family
houses

(P-15544)
HOMES MEDIA SOLUTIONS LLC
5510 Morehouse Dr Ste 100 (92121-3721)
PHONE..............................888 510-8795
EMP: 80
Web: www.agentadvantage.com
SIC: 7311 8742 Advertising consultant;
Marketing consulting services
HQ: Homes Media Solutions, Llc
325 John Knox Rd Bldg 200
Tallahassee FL
850 350-7800

(P-15545)
HORIZON MEDIA INC
Also Called: HORIZON MEDIA, INC.
1888 Century Park E Ste 700 (90067-1702)
PHONE..............................310 282-0909
Zach Rosenberg, Brnch Mgr
EMP: 300
Web: www.horizonmedia.com
SIC: 7311 Advertising agencies
PA: Horizon Media, Llc
75 Varick St Ste 1404
New York NY

(P-15546)
ICON MEDIA DIRECT INC (PA)
5910 Lemona Ave (91411-3006)
P.O. Box 55818 (91413-0818)
PHONE..............................818 995-6400
Nancy Lazkani, CEO
Seth Klein, *
EMP: 81 EST: 1999
SQ FT: 16,445
SALES (est): 22.03MM
SALES (corp-wide): 22.03MM Privately
Held
Web: www.iconmediadirect.com
SIC: 7311 Advertising consultant

(P-15547)
IGNITE HEALTH LLC (PA)
7535 Irvine Center Dr Ste 200
(92618-2962)
PHONE..............................949 861-3200
Matt Brown, Pr
Richard E Fair, *
Timothy J Riley, *
Fabio Gratton, *
Brian Lefkowitz, Chief Creative Officer*
EMP: 99 EST: 2000
SQ FT: 15,000
SALES (est): 9.32MM
SALES (corp-wide): 9.32MM Privately
Held

Web: www.ignitehealth.com
SIC: 7311 Advertising consultant

(P-15548)
IGNITED LLC (PA)
111 Penn St (90245-3908)
PHONE..............................310 773-3100
William Rosenthal, *
Eric Springer, Chief Creative Officer*
EMP: 115 EST: 1999
SQ FT: 55,000
SALES (est): 180MM
SALES (corp-wide): 180MM Privately
Held
Web: www.ignitedusa.com
SIC: 7311 Advertising consultant

(P-15549)
**INNOCEAN WRLDWIDE
AMERICAS LLC (HQ)**
Also Called: Innocean USA
180 5th St Ste 200 (92648-7107)
PHONE..............................714 861-5200
Ilsoo Jun, Prin
Tim Murphy, COO
EMP: 216 EST: 2002
SALES (est): 78.34MM Privately Held
Web: www.innoceanusa.com
SIC: 7311 Advertising consultant
PA: Innocean Worldwide Inc.
308 Gangnam-Daero, Gangnam-Gu
Seoul

(P-15550)
**INTERACTIVE MEDIA HOLDINGS
INC**
Also Called: Viant
2722 Michelson Dr Ste 100 (92612-8905)
PHONE..............................949 861-8888
Timothy C Vanderhook, Pr
Roy E Luna, *
Chris Vanderhook, *
Larry Madden, *
EMP: 110 EST: 2004
SALES (est): 20.53MM
SALES (corp-wide): 197.17MM Publicly
Held
SIC: 7311 7313 Advertising consultant;
Newspaper advertising representative
HQ: Viant Technology Llc
2722 Michelson Dr Ste 100
Irvine CA
949 861-8888

(P-15551)
KERN ORGANIZATION INC
Also Called: Kern Direct Marketing
20955 Warner Center Ln (91367-6511)
PHONE..............................818 703-8775
Russell Kern, Pr
David Azulay, *
Tom Mackendrick, *
Zeke Ibarbia, *
Steven Orenstein, *
EMP: 80 EST: 2008
SQ FT: 11,350
SALES (est): 25.43MM
SALES (corp-wide): 14.29B Publicly Held
Web: www.thekernorg.com
SIC: 7311 Advertising consultant
PA: Omnicom Group Inc.
280 Park Ave Fl 31w
New York NY
212 415-3600

(P-15552)
KLIENTBOOST LLC
2787 Bristol St Ste 100 (92626-5956)
PHONE..............................657 203-7866
J Dane Schuesler, Managing Member

Johnathan Dane Schuesler, Managing
Member
EMP: 122 EST: 2015
SALES (est): 2.67MM Privately Held
Web: www.klientboost.com
SIC: 7311 Advertising consultant

(P-15553)
**LEGENDARY PICTURES FILMS
LLC**
2900 W Alameda Ave (91505-4220)
PHONE..............................818 688-7003
Thomas Tull, CEO
Marlon Prager, CFO
EMP: 102 EST: 2006
SALES (est): 23.08MM Privately Held
Web: www.legendary.com
SIC: 7311 Advertising agencies
PA: Legend Pictures, Llc
2900 W Alameda Ave Fl 15
Burbank CA

(P-15554)
LIQUID ADVERTISING INC
138 Eucalyptus Dr (90245-3819)
PHONE..............................310 450-2653
William Akerlof, CEO
Marlo Huang, *
Alison Hamon, *
Alison Binetti, *
Shuly Millstein, *
EMP: 91 EST: 2000
SQ FT: 2,000
SALES (est): 14.09MM Privately Held
Web: www.liquidadvertising.com
SIC: 7311 Advertising consultant

(P-15555)
LOCAL CORPORATION (PA)
Also Called: Local.com
7555 Irvine Center Dr (92618-2912)
P.O. Box 50700 (92619-0700)
PHONE..............................949 784-0800
Frederick G Thiel, CEO
Kenneth S Cragun, CFO
Erick Herring, Senior Vice President
Technology
EMP: 80 EST: 1999
SQ FT: 34,612
SALES (est): 12.93MM
SALES (corp-wide): 12.93MM Publicly
Held
Web: www.localcorporation.com
SIC: 7311 Advertising agencies

(P-15556)
**MARSHALL ADVERTISING AND
DESIGN INC**
2729 Bristol St Ste 100 (92626-7930)
PHONE..............................714 545-5757
EMP: 25
Web: www.marshallad.com
SIC: 7311 7336 2752 Advertising agencies;
Commercial art and graphic design;
Catalogs, lithographed

(P-15557)
**MEDIABRANDS WORLDWIDE
INC**
Also Called: Initiative Media North America
1840 Century Park E (90067-2101)
PHONE..............................323 370-8000
EMP: 300
SALES (corp-wide): 10.93B Publicly Held
Web: www.ipgmediabrands.com
SIC: 7311 Advertising consultant
HQ: Mediabrands Worldwide, Inc.
100 W 33rd St Fl 3
New York NY

(P-15558)
MH SUB I LLC (PA)
Also Called: Internet Brands
909 N Pacific Coast Hwy Fl 11
(90245-2724)
PHONE..............................310 280-4000
EMP: 218 EST: 2013
SALES (est): 995.07MM
SALES (corp-wide): 995.07MM Privately
Held
Web: www.edoctors.com
SIC: 7311 Advertising agencies

(P-15559)
MINDGRUVE HOLDINGS INC
627 8th Ave Ste 300 (92101-6453)
PHONE..............................619 757-1325
Chad Robley, CEO
Dan Helleusch, *
EMP: 102 EST: 2017
SALES (est): 55.36MM Privately Held
Web: www.mindgruve.com
SIC: 7311 Advertising agencies

(P-15560)
MOB SCENE LLC (PA)
Also Called: Mob Scene Creative Productions
8447 Wilshire Blvd Ste 100 (90211-3228)
PHONE..............................323 648-7200
EMP: 121 EST: 2005
SALES (est): 14.24MM Privately Held
Web: www.mobscene.com
SIC: 7311 7929 3993 7812 Advertising
consultant; Entertainment service;
Advertising artwork; Television film
production

(P-15561)
MOVERS AND SHAKERS LLC
1217 Wilshire Blvd (90403-5466)
P.O. Box 3327 (90408-3327)
PHONE..............................310 893-7051
EMP: 100 EST: 2016
SALES (est): 5.22MM Privately Held
Web: www.moversshakers.co
SIC: 7311 Advertising agencies

(P-15562)
MULLENLOWE US INC
2121 Park Pl Ste 150 (90245-4843)
PHONE..............................424 738-6500
Jennifer Diodonet, Prin
EMP: 106
SALES (corp-wide): 10.93B Publicly Held
Web: us.mullenlowe.com
SIC: 7311 8743 8742 8732 Advertising
agencies; Public relations and publicity;
Marketing consulting services; Commercial
nonphysical research
HQ: Mullenlowe U.S., Inc.
2 Drydock Ave Fl 8
Boston MA
617 226-9000

(P-15563)
MULLENLOWE US INC
12130 Millennium (90094-2945)
PHONE..............................424 738-6600
EMP: 106
SALES (corp-wide): 10.93B Publicly Held
Web: us.mullenlowe.com
SIC: 7311 Advertising consultant
HQ: Mullenlowe U.S., Inc.
2 Drydock Ave Fl 8
Boston MA
617 226-9000

(P-15564)
MUTESIX GROUP INC
Also Called: Mutesix, An Iprospect Company
5800 Bristol Pkwy Ste 500 (90230-6899)
PHONE..............................800 935-6856
Steve Weiss, *CEO*
Daniel Rutberg, *
EMP: 120 **EST:** 2018
SALES (est): 7.67MM **Privately Held**
SIC: 7311 Advertising agencies
HQ: Dentsu Uk Limited
    10 Triton Street
    London
    207 070-7700

(P-15565)
NATIONAL PROMOTIONS & ADVG INC
Also Called: N P A
3434 Overland Ave (90034-5406)
PHONE..............................310 558-8555
Peter Zackery, *Pr*
Gary Shafner, *
EMP: 37 **EST:** 1981
SQ FT: 15,000
SALES (est): 836.32K **Privately Held**
Web: www.alchemymedia.net
SIC: 7311 2752 Advertising agencies; Offset
    printing

(P-15566)
NEXSTAR DIGITAL LLC
12777 W Jefferson Blvd Ste B100
(90066-7048)
PHONE..............................310 971-9300
Morgan Harris, *Brnch Mgr*
EMP: 100
SALES (corp-wide): 5.21MM **Publicly
Held**
Web: www.nexstardigital.com
SIC: 7311 Advertising agencies
HQ: Nexstar Digital, Llc
    545 E John Carpenter Fwy
    Irving TX
    972 373-8800

(P-15567)
ONE & ALL INC (HQ)
Also Called: Regency Group
2 N Lake Ave Ste 600 (91101-1868)
EMP: 215 **EST:** 1966
SALES (est): 45.57MM
SALES (corp-wide): 14.29B **Publicly Held**
Web: www.truesense.com
SIC: 7311 Advertising agencies
PA: Omnicom Group Inc.
    280 Park Ave Fl 31w
    New York NY
    212 415-3600

(P-15568)
POSTAER RUBIN AND ASSOCIATES
2525 Colorado Ave Ste 100 (90404-5576)
PHONE..............................312 644-3636
Bill Marks, *Owner*
EMP: 216
SALES (corp-wide): 91.73MM **Privately
Held**
SIC: 7311 Advertising consultant
PA: Rubin Postaer And Associates
    2525 Colorado Ave Ste 100
    Santa Monica CA
    310 394-4000

(P-15569)
PROMOVEO HEALTH LLC
701 Palomar Airport Rd (92011-1027)
PHONE..............................760 931-4794

Rolando Collado, *
EMP: 700 **EST:** 2014
SALES (est): 24.14MM **Privately Held**
Web: www.promoveohealth.com
SIC: 7311 Advertising agencies

(P-15570)
QUIGLY-SIMPSON HEPPELWHITE INC
Also Called: Quigley-Simpson & Hepplewhite
11601 Wilshire Blvd Ste 710 (90025-0509)
PHONE..............................310 996-5800
Kathryn Browne, *CFO*
Gerald Bagg, *
Renee Hill Young, *
Alissa Stakgold, *
Duryea Ruffins, *
EMP: 150 **EST:** 2002
SQ FT: 10,500
SALES (est): 41.13MM **Privately Held**
Web: www.quigleysimpson.com
SIC: 7311 7319 Advertising agencies; Media
    buying service

(P-15571)
RAPP WORLDWIDE INC
Also Called: Rapp
12777 W Jefferson Blvd Bldg C
(90066-7048)
PHONE..............................310 563-7200
Collins Rapp, *Brnch Mgr*
EMP: 110
SALES (corp-wide): 14.29B **Publicly Held**
Web: www.rapp.com
SIC: 7311 Advertising consultant
HQ: Rapp Worldwide Inc.
    220 E 42nd St Fl 12
    New York NY

(P-15572)
REACHLOCAL INC (DH)
Also Called: Reachlocal
21700 Oxnard St Ste 1600 (91367-7586)
PHONE..............................818 274-0260
Sharon T Rowlands, *CEO*
Ross G Landsbaum, *
Kris Barton, *CPO*
Paras Maniar, *CSO*
EMP: 142 **EST:** 2004
SQ FT: 38,592
SALES (est): 276.78MM
SALES (corp-wide): 2.95B **Publicly Held**
Web: www.localiq.com
SIC: 7311 7375 Advertising consultant; On-
    line data base information retrieval
HQ: Gannett Media Corp.
    7950 Jones Branch Dr Fl 8
    Mc Lean VA
    703 854-6000

(P-15573)
RUBIN POSTAER AND ASSOCIATES (PA)
Also Called: R P Direct
2525 Colorado Ave Ste 100 (90404-5576)
PHONE..............................310 394-4000
Willam C Hagelstein, *CEO*
Gerrold R Rubin, *
Vincent Mancuso, *
Larry Postaer, *
Tom Kirk, *
EMP: 201 **EST:** 1986
SQ FT: 130,000
SALES (est): 91.73MM
SALES (corp-wide): 91.73MM **Privately
Held**
Web: www.rpa.com
SIC: 7311 Advertising consultant

(P-15574)
SAATCHI & SAATCHI N AMER LLC
Team One
3501 Sepulveda Blvd (90505-2540)
PHONE..............................310 437-2500
EMP: 250
SALES (corp-wide): 25.29MM **Privately
Held**
Web: www.teamone-usa.com
SIC: 7311 Advertising agencies
HQ: Saatchi & Saatchi North America, Llc.
    375 Hudson St
    New York NY
    212 463-2000

(P-15575)
STN DIGITAL LLC
Also Called: Digital Marketing
3033 Bunker Hill St (92109-5705)
PHONE..............................619 292-8683
David Brickley, *Managing Member*
EMP: 81 **EST:** 2013
SALES (est): 15MM **Privately Held**
Web: www.stndigital.com
SIC: 7311 Advertising agencies

(P-15576)
SUISSA MILLER ADVERTISING LLC
8687 Melrose Ave (90069-5701)
PHONE..............................310 392-9666
EMP: 100 **EST:** 1985
SQ FT: 40,000
SALES (est): 3.57MM **Privately Held**
SIC: 7311 Advertising agencies

(P-15577)
TRAILER PARK INC (PA)
6922 Hollywood Blvd Fl 12 (90028-6104)
P.O. Box 2950 (90078-2950)
PHONE..............................310 845-3000
Rick Eiserman, *Pr*
Tim Nett, *Executive Creative Director*
Benedict Coulter, *
James Hale, *Stockholder*
EMP: 100 **EST:** 2005
SQ FT: 8,000
SALES (est): 46.39MM **Privately Held**
Web: www.trailerpark.com
SIC: 7311 Advertising agencies

(P-15578)
UE AUTHORITY CO
Also Called: DMS Insurance
225 Broadway Ste 2200 (92101-5011)
PHONE..............................800 466-4178
Joe Marinucci, *CEO*
EMP: 100 **EST:** 2008
SALES (est): 22.51MM
SALES (corp-wide): 391.15MM **Publicly
Held**
SIC: 7311 7371 Advertising consultant;
    Computer software development
HQ: Digital Media Solutions, Llc
    4800 140th Ave N Ste 101
    Clearwater FL
    877 236-8632

(P-15579)
VITROROBERTSON LLC
Also Called: Vitro
225 Broadway (92101-5005)
PHONE..............................619 234-0408
Tom Sullivan, *
Alan Bonine, *
EMP: 89 **EST:** 2004
SALES (est): 38.95MM
SALES (corp-wide): 2.69B **Publicly Held**

Web: www.vitroagency.com
SIC: 7311 Advertising consultant
HQ: A + N Real Estate & Business
    Management Corporation
    1 World Trade Ctr
    New York NY

(P-15580)
WONDERFUL AGENCY
11444 W Olympic Blvd Ste 210
(90064-1559)
PHONE..............................310 966-8600
Stewart A Resnick, *CEO*
Margaret Keene, *Chief Creative Officer*
EMP: 1727 **EST:** 2016
SALES (est): 3.66MM
SALES (corp-wide): 2.04B **Privately Held**
Web: www.wonderful.com
SIC: 7311 Advertising consultant
PA: The Wonderful Company Llc
    11444 W Olympic Blvd # 210
    Los Angeles CA
    310 966-5700

(P-15581)
YOUNG & RUBICAM LLC
Wunderman Cato Jhnsn-Los Angle
4751 Wilshire Blvd Ste 201 (90010-3827)
PHONE..............................213 930-5000
EMP: 135
SALES (corp-wide): 17.37B **Privately Held**
Web: www.vmlyr.com
SIC: 7311 Advertising consultant
HQ: Young & Rubicam Llc
    3 Columbus Cir Fl 3 # 3
    New York NY
    212 210-3017

(P-15582)
YOUNG & RUBICAM LLC
Also Called: Y&R-Wcj Spectrum
7535 Irvine Center Dr (92618-2962)
PHONE..............................949 754-2000
David Murphy, *Pr*
EMP: 300
SALES (corp-wide): 17.37B **Privately Held**
Web: www.vmlyr.com
SIC: 7311 Advertising consultant
HQ: Young & Rubicam Llc
    3 Columbus Cir Fl 3 # 3
    New York NY
    212 210-3017

(P-15583)
YOUNG & RUBICAM LLC
Also Called: Landor Associates
7535 Irvine Center Dr (92618-2962)
PHONE..............................949 754-2100
Rick Eisermas, *Mgr*
EMP: 250
SALES (corp-wide): 17.37B **Privately Held**
Web: www.vmlyr.com
SIC: 7311 Advertising agencies
HQ: Young & Rubicam Llc
    3 Columbus Cir Fl 3 # 3
    New York NY
    212 210-3017

7312 Outdoor Advertising Services

(P-15584)
BAMKO INC
Also Called: Bamko
11620 Wilshire Blvd Ste 610 (90025-1706)
PHONE..............................310 470-5859
EMP: 150
Web: www.bamko.net

SIC: **7312** 7311 Outdoor advertising services
; Advertising agencies

(P-15585)
BRIMAD ENTERPRISES INC
Also Called: Creative Outdoor Advertising
2900 Adams St Ste B16 (92504-4396)
PHONE..................................951 354-8187
Eric Glaub, *Pr*
EMP: 23 **EST:** 1984
SQ FT: 10,000
SALES (est): 1.84MM **Privately Held**
Web: www.coasigns.com
SIC: **7312** 3993 Billboard advertising; Signs
and advertising specialties

(P-15586)
OUTFRONT MEDIA LLC
1731 Workman St (90031-3334)
PHONE..................................323 222-7171
EMP: 27
SALES (corp-wide): 1.77B **Publicly Held**
Web: www.outfront.com
SIC: **7312** 3993 Outdoor advertising services
; Signs and advertising specialties
HQ: Outfront Media Llc
· 405 Lexington Ave Fl 14
New York NY
212 297-6400

7313 Radio, Television, Publisher Representatives

(P-15587)
ATTN INC
5700 Wilshire Blvd Ste 375 (90036-7212)
PHONE..................................323 413-2878
Jarrett Moreno, *CEO*
Matthew Segel, *
EMP: 200 **EST:** 2014
SQ FT: 100,000
SALES (est): 11.86MM **Privately Held**
Web: www.attn.com
SIC: **7313** Electronic media advertising
representatives

(P-15588)
BEACHBODY LLC (HQ)
Also Called: Beachbody
400 Continental Blvd Ste 400 (90245-5089)
P.O. Box 1227 (90660-1227)
PHONE..................................310 883-9000
Carl Daikeler, *Ch*
Jon Congdon, *CMO**
Brad Ramberg, *
Sue Collyns, *
Bryan Muehlberger, *CIO**
▲ **EMP:** 500 **EST:** 1998
SALES (est): 663.54MM
SALES (corp-wide): 692.2MM **Publicly
Held**
Web: www.beachbody.com
SIC: **7313** 7999 Electronic media advertising
representatives; Physical fitness instruction
PA: The Beachbody Company Inc
3301 Exposition Blvd
Santa Monica CA
310 883-9000

(P-15589)
BEACHBODY COMPANY INC (PA)
3301 Exposition Blvd (90404-5045)
PHONE..................................310 883-9000
Carl Daikeler, *Ch Bd*
Carl Daikeler, *CEO*
Mark R Goldston, *Ex Ch Bd*
Robert Gifford, *Pr*
Jonathan Gelfand, *Senior Vice President
Business Development*

EMP: 208 **EST:** 2020
SQ FT: 133,000
SALES (est): 692.2MM
SALES (corp-wide): 692.2MM **Publicly
Held**
SIC: **7313** 7999 Electronic media advertising
representatives; Physical fitness instruction

(P-15590)
BLT CMMNCTIONS LLC A LTD LBLTY
6430 W Sunset Blvd Ste 800 (90028-7901)
PHONE..................................323 860-4000
EMP: 182 **EST:** 2007
SALES (est): 4.62MM **Privately Held**
Web: www.bltomato.com
SIC: **7313** Electronic media advertising
representatives

(P-15591)
CANVAS WORLDWIDE LLC
12015 Bluff Creek Dr (90094-2930)
PHONE..................................424 303-4300
Paul Woolmington, *CEO*
Madhavi Tadikonda, *CIO*
EMP: 250 **EST:** 2015
SALES (est): 79.91MM **Privately Held**
Web: www.canvasworldwide.com
SIC: **7313** Electronic media advertising
representatives
PA: Innocean Worldwide Inc.
308 Gangnam-Daero, Gangnam-Gu
Seoul

(P-15592)
EDMUNDSCOM INC (HQ)
2401 Colorado Ave Ste P1 (90404-3175)
PHONE..................................310 309-6300
Seth Berkowitz, *Pr*
Scott Fanelli, *VP*
Katti Fields, *VP*
Xiao Sun, *VP*
▲ **EMP:** 550 **EST:** 1966
SALES (est): 156.39MM **Privately Held**
Web: www.edmunds.com
SIC: **7313** Electronic media advertising
representatives
PA: Edmunds Holding Company
2401 Colorado Ave
Santa Monica CA

(P-15593)
GHOST MANAGEMENT GROUP LLC
41 Discovery (92618-3150)
PHONE..................................949 870-1400
Doug Francis, *
Albert Lopez, *
Chris Beals, *
Hendrik Davel, *Senior Controller**
EMP: 175 **EST:** 2012
SQ FT: 44,820
SALES (est): 20.79MM **Privately Held**
SIC: **7313** 7371 Electronic media advertising
representatives; Computer software
development and applications

(P-15594)
GRABIT INTERACTIVE INC
Also Called: Kerv Interactive
14724 Ventura Blvd (91403-3501)
PHONE..................................844 472-2488
Gary Mittman, *CEO*
EMP: 34 **EST:** 2016
SALES (est): 1.18MM **Privately Held**
Web: www.grabit.media
SIC: **7313** 7372 Printed media advertising
representatives; Application computer
software

(P-15595)
KARGO GLOBAL INC
1437 4th St Ste 200 (90401-2377)
PHONE..................................212 979-9000
Natalie Nelson, *Brnch Mgr*
EMP: 139
Web: www.kargo.com
SIC: **7313** 7372 7374 Electronic media
advertising representatives; Application
computer software; Computer graphics
service
PA: Kargo Global, Inc.
826 Broadway Fl 4
New York NY

(P-15596)
MEDIAALPHA INC (PA)
700 S Flower St Ste 640 (90017-4122)
PHONE..................................213 316-6256
Steven Yi, *Pr*
Tigran Sinanyan, *CFO*
EMP: 81 **EST:** 2020
SALES (est): 459.07MM
SALES (corp-wide): 459.07MM **Publicly
Held**
Web: www.mediaalpha.com
SIC: **7313** Electronic media advertising
representatives

(P-15597)
SHED MEDIA US INC
3800 Barham Blvd Ste 410 (90068-1042)
PHONE..................................323 904-4680
Nick Emmerson, *Pr*
Josh Mills, *
EMP: 106 **EST:** 2009
SALES (est): 5.55MM **Privately Held**
Web: www.shedmedia.com
SIC: **7313** Electronic media advertising
representatives

(P-15598)
STUDIO 71 LP
Also Called: Collective Digital Studio, LLC
8383 Wilshire Blvd Ste 1050 (90211-2425)
PHONE..................................323 370-1500
Michael Green, *
Dan Weinstein, *
Scott Weller, *
Jordan Toplitzky, *
EMP: 150 **EST:** 2011
SQ FT: 15,000
SALES (est): 42.61MM
SALES (corp-wide): 4.32B **Privately Held**
Web: www.studio71.com
SIC: **7313** Electronic media advertising
representatives
PA: Prosiebensat.1 Media Se
Medienallee 7
Unterfohring BY
89950710

(P-15599)
WALDBERG INC
Also Called: Refinery, The
15301 Ventura Blvd Ste 300 (91403-5813)
PHONE..................................818 843-0004
Adam Waldman, *CEO*
Brad Hochberg, *
EMP: 100 **EST:** 2006
SALES (est): 12.25MM **Privately Held**
Web: www.therefinerycreative.com
SIC: **7313** Electronic media advertising
representatives

7319 Advertising, Nec

(P-15600)
CARAT N AMER DNTSU AGEIS NTWRK
5800 Bristol Pkwy 5th Fl (90230-6696)
PHONE..................................310 255-1000
John Barnes, *Brnch Mgr*
EMP: 82
SIC: **7319** 7313 Media buying service;
Printed media advertising representatives
HQ: Carat North America Dentsu Aegeis
Network
150 E 42nd St Fl 14
New York NY
212 591-9100

(P-15601)
FASTCLICK INC
Also Called: Fastclick.com
530 E Montecito St (93103-3245)
PHONE..................................805 689-9839
EMP: 522 **EST:** 2000
SQ FT: 14,900
SALES (est): 7.48MM
SALES (corp-wide): 29.15MM **Privately
Held**
Web: www.epsilon.com
SIC: **7319** Circular and handbill distribution
HQ: Conversant, Llc
101 N Wacker Dr
Chicago IL

(P-15602)
GILS DISTRIBUTING SERVICE
Also Called: Great Western Distributing Svc
718 E 8th St (90021-1802)
PHONE..................................213 627-0539
Feleciano Gil, *Pr*
Fidel Gil, *
Gloria Gil, *
EMP: 112 **EST:** 1967
SQ FT: 5,000
SALES (est): 1.98MM **Privately Held**
SIC: **7319** 4215 Circular and handbill
distribution; Courier services, except by air

(P-15603)
IMAGE OPTIONS (PA)
Also Called: Image Options Painting & Dctg
80 Icon (92610-3000)
PHONE..................................949 586-7665
Tim Bennett, *Ch Bd*
Dave Bales, *CEO*
Brian Hite, *Pr*
Dave Brewer, *VP*
Barry Polan, *CRO**
EMP: 63 **EST:** 1999
SQ FT: 22,000
SALES (est): 24.71MM
SALES (corp-wide): 24.71MM **Privately
Held**
Web: www.imageoptions.net
SIC: **7319** 7336 2759 Display advertising
service; Commercial art and graphic design
; Commercial printing, nec

(P-15604)
WEST COAST COUPON INC
9400 Oso Ave (91311-6020)
PHONE..................................818 341-2400
Mark Fischer, *Pr*
Doug Rewers, *
EMP: 27 **EST:** 2004
SQ FT: 30,000
SALES (est): 1.38MM **Privately Held**
Web: www.westcoastcoupon.com

SIC: 7319 2731 5961 Coupon distribution; Books, publishing and printing; Computer software, mail order

(P-15605)

WILLIAMS SCOTSMAN INC

14015 Kirkham Way (92064-7146)
PHONE...............................619 710-8468
EMP: 107
SALES (corp-wide): 2.14B **Publicly Held**
Web: www.willscot.com
SIC: 7319 Poster advertising service, except outdoor
HQ: Williams Scotsman, Inc.
4646 E Van Buren St # 40
Phoenix AZ
480 894-6311

7322 Adjustment And Collection Services

(P-15606)

AMERICAN RECOVERY SERVICE INC (DH)

Also Called: Arsi of California
555 Saint Charles Dr Ste 100 (91360)
P.O. Box 1025 (91358-0025)
PHONE...............................805 379-8500
EMP: 200 **EST:** 1986
SALES (est): 24.24MM **Privately Held**
Web: www.arsigroup.com
SIC: 7322 Collection agency, except real estate
HQ: Firstsource Solutions Limited
5th Floor, Paradigm, B Wing,
Mindspace
Mumbai MH

(P-15607)

ARS NATIONAL SERVICES INC (PA)

201 W Grand Ave (92025-2603)
P.O. Box 463023 (92046-3023)
PHONE...............................800 456-5053
Jason Howerton, *Pr*
John Howerton, *
Kathy Howerton, *
John Watson, *
Jim Beck, *
EMP: 150 **EST:** 1987
SQ FT: 33,000
SALES (est): 29.52MM **Privately Held**
Web: www.arsnational.com
SIC: 7322 Collection agency, except real estate

(P-15608)

CAINE & WEINER COMPANY INC (PA)

Also Called: Caine & Weiner
5805 Sepulveda Blvd Fl 4 (91411-2508)
P.O. Box 55848 (91413-0848)
PHONE...............................818 226-6000
Greg A Cohen, *Pr*
Rick Luther, *
Brad Schaffer, *Senior Vice President Client Services*
Tony Albanesi, *CA*
Steve Simon, *SERVICES*
EMP: 90 **EST:** 1930
SQ FT: 14,400
SALES (est): 22.44MM
SALES (corp-wide): 22.44MM **Privately Held**
Web: www.caine-weiner.com
SIC: 7322 Collection agency, except real estate

(P-15609)

CMRE FINANCIAL SERVICES INC

3075 E Imperial Hwy Ste 200 (92821-6753)
PHONE...............................714 528-3200
Jeffrey Nieman, *Pr*
EMP: 450 **EST:** 2000
SQ FT: 35,000
SALES (est): 27.08MM **Privately Held**
Web: www.cmrefsi.com
SIC: 7322 Collection agency, except real estate

(P-15610)

COLLECTION TECHNOLOGY INC

Also Called: C T I
10801 6th St Ste 200 (91730-5904)
P.O. Box 2200 (91729-2200)
PHONE...............................800 743-4284
Chris Van Dellen, *CEO*
Paul Van Dellen, *
EMP: 100 **EST:** 1953
SALES (est): 10.88MM **Privately Held**
Web: www.collectiontechnology.com
SIC: 7322 Collection agency, except real estate

(P-15611)

EGS FINANCIAL CARE INC (DH)

Also Called: Total Debt Management
5 Park Plz Ste 1100 (92614-8502)
PHONE...............................877 217-4423
Jay King, *Pr*
Steven Winokur, *
Joshua Gindin, *
John R Schwab Treeas, *Prin*
▲ **EMP:** 300 **EST:** 1966
SALES (est): 138.11MM
SALES (corp-wide): 845.12MM **Privately Held**
SIC: 7322 Collection agency, except real estate
HQ: Alorica Global Solutions, Inc.
6652 Pinecrest Dr Ste 300
Plano TX

(P-15612)

FCI LENDER SERVICES INC

Also Called: F C I
8180 E Kaiser Blvd (92808-2277)
PHONE...............................800 931-2424
Michael W Griffith, *Pr*
EMP: 190 **EST:** 1982
SQ FT: 19,000
SALES (est): 33.31MM **Privately Held**
Web: www.trustfci.com
SIC: 7322 Adjustment and collection services

(P-15613)

GRANT & WEBER (PA)

Also Called: Grant & Weber Travel
26610 Agoura Rd Ste 209 (91302-2975)
P.O. Box 8669 (91372-8669)
PHONE...............................818 878-7700
Jimi Bingham, *CEO*
Ron Grossblatt, *CDO*
Spencer Weinerman, *
David Weinerman, *
Mary Kempski, *CIO*
▲ **EMP:** 85 **EST:** 1976
SQ FT: 30,000
SALES (est): 24.38MM
SALES (corp-wide): 24.38MM **Privately Held**
Web: www.grantweber.com
SIC: 7322 Collection agency, except real estate

(P-15614)

JJ MAC INTYRE CO INC (PA)

4160 Temescal Canyon Rd Ste 601 (92883-4625)
P.O. Box 78150 (92877-0138)
PHONE...............................951 898-4300
Scott M Hall, *CEO*
Kenneth A Lee, *
EMP: 115 **EST:** 1959
SQ FT: 28,254
SALES (est): 2.15MM
SALES (corp-wide): 2.15MM **Privately Held**
SIC: 7322 Collection agency, except real estate

(P-15615)

RM GALICIA INC

Also Called: Progressive Management Systems
1521 W Cameron Ave Ste 100 (91790-2738)
P.O. Box 2220 (91793-2220)
PHONE...............................626 813-6200
Timothy Chase Banta, *CEO*
William Gutierrez, *Sr VP*
EMP: 125 **EST:** 1978
SQ FT: 20,000
SALES (est): 9.12MM **Privately Held**
Web: www.pmscollects.com
SIC: 7322 Collection agency, except real estate

(P-15616)

USCB INC (PA)

Also Called: Uscb America
355 S Grand Ave Ste 3200 (90071-1591)
PHONE...............................213 985-2111
Albert Cadena, *CEO*
Melvin F Shaw, *
Thomas Isgrigg, *
Albert Cadena, *Prin*
Pat Esquivel, *
EMP: 213 **EST:** 1915
SQ FT: 34,000
SALES (est): 41.54MM
SALES (corp-wide): 41.54MM **Privately Held**
Web: www.uscbamerica.com
SIC: 7322 8741 Collection agency, except real estate; Management services

(P-15617)

VENGROFF WILLIAMS & ASSOC INC

2099 S State College Blvd Ste 600 (92806-6149)
PHONE...............................714 889-6200
Robert Sherman, *Brnch Mgr*
EMP: 102
SALES (corp-wide): 43.72MM **Privately Held**
Web: www.vengroffwilliams.com
SIC: 7322 Collection agency, except real estate
PA: Vengroff, Williams & Associates, Inc.
2211 Fruitville Rd
Sarasota FL
941 363-5200

7323 Credit Reporting Services

(P-15618)

A-CHECK AMERICA LLC (HQ)

Also Called: A-Check America, Member Act 1
1501 Research Park Dr (92507-2114)
P.O. Box 29048 (91209-9048)
PHONE...............................951 750-1501

Michael Hoyal, *Pr*
Gregg Hassler, *
▲ **EMP:** 170 **EST:** 1978
SQ FT: 30,000
SALES (est): 48.3MM
SALES (corp-wide): 766.78MM **Publicly Held**
Web: www.acheckglobal.com
SIC: 7323 7375 Credit reporting services; Information retrieval services
PA: Sterling Check Corp.
6150 Oak Tree Blvd Ste 49
Independence OH
212 736-5100

(P-15619)

BASEPOINT ANALYTICS LLC

703 Palomar Airport Rd Ste 350 (92011-1040)
PHONE...............................760 602-4971
EMP: 408 **EST:** 2004
SALES (est): 230.63K
SALES (corp-wide): 1.64B **Privately Held**
SIC: 7323 Credit reporting services
HQ: Corelogic Systems, Inc.
40 Pacifica Ste 900
Irvine CA
714 250-6400

(P-15620)

CORELOGIC CREDCO LLC

9645 Granite Ridge Dr Ste 300 (92123)
PHONE...............................619 938-7028
Kathleen Manzione, *Brnch Mgr*
EMP: 280
SALES (corp-wide): 1.64B **Privately Held**
Web: www.corelogic.com
SIC: 7323 Consumer credit reporting bureau
HQ: Corelogic Credco, Llc
40 Pacifica Ste 900
Irvine CA
800 255-0792

(P-15621)

CORELOGIC CREDCO LLC (DH)

Also Called: Corelogic Credco
40 Pacifica Ste 900 (92618-3375)
PHONE...............................800 255-0792
Jim Balas, *CFO*
EMP: 220 **EST:** 2005
SALES (est): 54.06MM
SALES (corp-wide): 1.64B **Privately Held**
Web: www.corelogic.com
SIC: 7323 8748 Consumer credit reporting bureau; Business consulting, nec
HQ: Corelogic, Inc.
40 Pacifica Ste 900
Irvine CA
866 873-3651

(P-15622)

EXPERIAN INFO SOLUTIONS INC (DH)

Also Called: Experian
475 Anton Blvd (92626-7037)
P.O. Box 5001 (92628-5001)
PHONE...............................714 830-7000
Chris Callero, *CEO*
Stephen Burnside, *Sr VP*
EMP: 3700 **EST:** 1996
SQ FT: 323,000
SALES (est): 973.87MM
SALES (corp-wide): 6.62B **Privately Held**
Web: www.experian.com
SIC: 7323 Consumer credit reporting bureau
HQ: Experian Holdings, Inc.
475 Anton Blvd
Costa Mesa CA
714 830-7000

▲ = Import ▼ = Export
◆ = Import/Export

(P-15623)
EXPERIAN MKTG SOLUTIONS LLC
Also Called: Experian Marketing
475 Anton Blvd (92626-7037)
PHONE..................714 830-7000
Kevin Dean, *Pr*
EMP: 501 **EST:** 2016
SQ FT: 4,000
SALES (est): 47.63MM
SALES (corp-wide): 912.58MM **Privately Held**
Web: www.experian.com
SIC: 7323 Consumer credit reporting bureau
PA: Vector Capital Management, L.P.
1 Market St Ste 2300
San Francisco CA
415 293-5000

(P-15624)
THE TAX CREDIT COMPANY
Also Called: Tax Credit Co, The
6464 W Sunset Blvd # 1150 (90028-8021)
PHONE..................323 927-0750
EMP: 100
SIC: 7323 8721 7291 Credit reporting services; Auditing services; Tax return preparation services

7331 Direct Mail Advertising Services

(P-15625)
AARON THOMAS & ASSOCIATES INC
Also Called: Aaron Group, The
21344 Superior St (91311-4312)
PHONE..................818 727-9040
Fred Thomas, *Pr*
Gary Thomas, *Sec*
EMP: 25 **EST:** 1980
SQ FT: 18,500
SALES (est): 997.24K **Privately Held**
Web: www.atacampaigns.com
SIC: 7331 2759 Mailing service; Commercial printing, nec

(P-15626)
ADVANCED IMAGE DIRECT LLC
Also Called: Fht Printing
1415 S Acacia Ave (92831-5317)
PHONE..................714 502-3900
Hugo Solorio, *
▲ **EMP:** 50 **EST:** 2008
SALES (est): 5.69MM
SALES (corp-wide): 29MM **Privately Held**
Web: www.advancedimagedirect.com
SIC: 7331 2752 Mailing service; Commercial printing, lithographic
PA: Real Estate Image, Inc.
1415 S Acacia Ave
Fullerton CA
714 502-3900

(P-15627)
ADVANTAGE MAILING LLC (PA)
Also Called: Advantage Mailing Service
1600 N Kraemer Blvd (92806-1410)
P.O. Box 66013 (92816-6013)
PHONE..................714 538-3881
Tom Ling, *Pr*
Brett Noss, *CFO*
EMP: 125 **EST:** 1994
SQ FT: 60,000
SALES (est): 91.39MM
SALES (corp-wide): 91.39MM **Privately Held**
Web: www.advantageinc.com

SIC: 7331 Mailing service

(P-15628)
AST SPORTSWEAR INC
P.O. Box 17219 (92817-7219)
PHONE..................714 223-2030
EMP: 395
Web: www.astsportswear.com
SIC: 7331 Mailing service
PA: Ast Sportswear, Inc.
2701 E Imperial Hwy
Brea CA

(P-15629)
BUS-LET INC
Also Called: Adcraft Business Mail
2555 Jason Ct (92056-3592)
PHONE..................323 728-6245
Mario A Morales, *Prin*
Myron Crespin, *Pr*
Alan Bailey, *VP*
Lawrence Crespin, *VP*
Regina Crespin, *Stockholder*
EMP: 21 **EST:** 1956
SQ FT: 20,000
SALES (est): 654.28K **Privately Held**
SIC: 7331 7374 2759 Mailing service; Data processing and preparation; Commercial printing, nec

(P-15630)
DIVERSIFIED MAILING INCORPORATED
Also Called: Diversified Direct
14407 Alondra Blvd (90638-5504)
P.O. Box 2270777 (75222)
PHONE..................714 994-6245
TOLL FREE: 800
EMP: 157
SIC: 7331 Direct mail advertising services

(P-15631)
FINANCIAL STATEMENT SVCS INC (PA)
Also Called: Fssi
3300 S Fairview St (92704-7004)
PHONE..................714 436-3326
Jennifer Dietz, *CEO*
Jon Dietz, *
Karen Elsbury, *
Henry Perez, *
Dan Palmquist, *
EMP: 144 **EST:** 1984
SQ FT: 167,000
SALES (est): 31.62MM
SALES (corp-wide): 31.62MM **Privately Held**
Web: www.fssi-ca.com
SIC: 7331 7374 2759 Mailing service; Data processing and preparation; Laser printing

(P-15632)
FULL/TECH SYSTEMS INC
5525 Market St (92114-2218)
PHONE..................619 297-0454
EMP: 20 **EST:** 1996
SQ FT: 20,000
SALES (est): 2.27MM **Privately Held**
Web: www.fulltech.net
SIC: 7331 7374 2752 Mailing service; Data processing and preparation; Commercial printing, lithographic

(P-15633)
LOMITA LOGISTICS LLC
Also Called: Xpo
3541 Lomita Blvd (90505-5016)
PHONE..................310 784-8485
EMP: 100

Web: internationalservices.rrd.com
SIC: 7331 Mailing service

(P-15634)
ORANGE COUNTY DIRECT MAIL INC
Also Called: Ocdm
2672 Dow Ave (92780-7208)
PHONE..................714 444-4412
Mark Cretz, *CEO*
EMP: 45 **EST:** 1990
SQ FT: 35,000
SALES (est): 9.46MM **Privately Held**
Web: www.ocdm.com
SIC: 7331 2752 Mailing service; Printed media advertising representatives; Printers' services: folding, collating, etc.; Commercial printing, lithographic

(P-15635)
REAL ESTATE IMAGE INC (PA)
Also Called: Advanced Image Direct
1415 S Acacia Ave (92831-5317)
PHONE..................714 502-3900
Ty Mcmillin, *Pr*
Perry Wilson, *
Hugo Solorio, *Product Vice President*
EMP: 150 **EST:** 1981
SQ FT: 136,000
SALES (est): 29MM
SALES (corp-wide): 29MM **Privately Held**
Web: www.advancedimagedirect.com
SIC: 7331 2752 Mailing service; Commercial printing, lithographic

(P-15636)
STAMPSCOM INC (PA)
Also Called: Stamps.com
1990 E Grand Ave (90245-5013)
PHONE..................310 482-5800
Nathan Jones, *CEO*
Kyle Huebner, *Pr*
Jeff Carberry, *CFO*
Sebastian Buerba, *CMO*
EMP: 145 **EST:** 1996
SQ FT: 99,600
SALES (est): 757.98MM
SALES (corp-wide): 757.98MM **Privately Held**
Web: www.auctane.com
SIC: 7331 5961 4813 Mailing service; Catalog and mail-order houses; Online service providers

(P-15637)
TOWNE INC
Also Called: Towne Allpoints
3441 W Macarthur Blvd (92704-6805)
PHONE..................714 540-3095
▲ **EMP:** 105
SALES (est): 10.2MM **Privately Held**
SIC: 7331 7389 Mailing service; Brokers' services

(P-15638)
TRANSAMERICAN DIRECT INC
Also Called: Transamerican
355 State Pl (92029-1359)
PHONE..................760 745-5343
Paul Barron, *CEO*
Eleanor Monica, *
▲ **EMP:** 100 **EST:** 1987
SALES (est): 9.45MM **Privately Held**
Web: www.transdirect.com
SIC: 7331 Mailing service

(P-15639)
UNIVERSAL MAIL DELIVERY SVC (PA)

Also Called: Universal Custom Courier
501 S Brand Blvd # 104 (91340-4000)
PHONE..................818 365-3144
Robert M Reznick, *CEO*
Bernard Reznick, *
Barbara Reznick, *Stockholder*
Saddie Reznick, *Stockholder*
EMP: 95 **EST:** 1953
SQ FT: 1,000
SALES (est): 2.24MM
SALES (corp-wide): 2.24MM **Privately Held**
SIC: 7331 Mailing service

7334 Photocopying And Duplicating Services

(P-15640)
ABI ATTORNEYS SERVICE INC (PA)
Also Called: ABI VIP Attorney Service
2015 W Park Ave (92373-6271)
P.O. Box 9240 (92375-2440)
PHONE..................909 793-0613
Alice J Benge, *Pr*
Chuck Benge, *Sec*
EMP: 80 **EST:** 1985
SQ FT: 7,500
SALES (est): 4.69MM
SALES (corp-wide): 4.69MM **Privately Held**
SIC: 7334 Photocopying and duplicating services

(P-15641)
AMERICAN LEGAL COPY - OC LLC
655 W Broadway Ste 200 (92101-8476)
PHONE..................415 777-4449
Joe Motz, *Prin*
EMP: 94 **EST:** 2003
SALES (est): 311.64K **Privately Held**
SIC: 7334 Photocopying and duplicating services
PA: American Legal Copy-Or, Llc
1001 4th Ave Ste 300
Seattle WA

(P-15642)
ARC DOCUMENT SOLUTIONS LLC
41521 Date St Apt 101 (92562-7088)
PHONE..................951 445-4480
EMP: 689
SALES (corp-wide): 42.08MM **Privately Held**
Web: www.e-arc.com
SIC: 7334 Blueprinting service
PA: Arc Document Solutions, Llc
12657 Alcosta Blvd # 200
San Ramon CA
925 949-5100

(P-15643)
CONCORD DOCUMENT SERVICES INC (PA)
1407 W 11th St (90015-1227)
PHONE..................213 745-3175
Fernando B Flores, *CEO*
Hector Flores, *
EMP: 27 **EST:** 1996
SALES (est): 2.48MM
SALES (corp-wide): 2.48MM **Privately Held**
Web: www.concorddt.com
SIC: 7334 3577 Photocopying and duplicating services; Optical scanning devices

PRODUCTS & SVCS

(P-15644)
CP DOCUMENT TECHNOLOGIES LLC
11835 W Olympic Blvd Ste 145 (90064-5001)
PHONE..............................310 575-6640
EMP: 50
SIC: 7334 2754 2759 Photocopying and duplicating services; Commercial printing, gravure; Commercial printing, nec
PA: Cp Document Technologies, Llc
800 W 6th St Ste 1400
Los Angeles CA

(P-15645)
CYBERCOPY INC (PA)
2766 S La Cienega Blvd (90034-2642)
P.O. Box 507 (90232-0507)
PHONE..............................310 736-1001
Paul Fridrich, CEO
EMP: 18 EST: 1997
SALES (est): 4.07MM Privately Held
Web: www.cybercopyusa.com
SIC: 7334 2754 2741 2732 Blueprinting service; Commercial printing, gravure; Art copy and poster publishing; Book printing

(P-15646)
DEL MAR BLUE PRINT CO INC
2201 San Dieguito Dr Ste E (92014-2257)
PHONE..............................858 755-5134
Michael Kraus, Pr
Kelly Kraus, VP
EMP: 24 EST: 1978
SQ FT: 4,000
SALES (est): 1.58MM Privately Held
Web: www.delmarblue.com
SIC: 7334 2752 Blueprinting service; Offset printing

(P-15647)
DVS MEDIA SERVICES (PA)
Also Called: D V S Mdia Srvces/Intelestream
2625 W Olive Ave (91505-4526)
PHONE..............................818 841-6750
Rick Appell, Managing Member
EMP: 46 EST: 2020
SALES (est): 4.96MM
SALES (corp-wide): 4.96MM Privately Held
SIC: 7334 2759 Photocopying and duplicating services; Commercial printing, nec

(P-15648)
KNOX ATTORNEY SERVICE INC (PA)
Also Called: Knox Services
1550 Hotel Cir N Ste 440 (92108-2904)
PHONE..............................619 233-9700
Stephen Knox, Pr
Steve Knox, *
Robert Porambo, *
James Nemec, *
EMP: 165 EST: 1972
SQ FT: 165,929
SALES (est): 20.55MM
SALES (corp-wide): 20.55MM Privately Held
Web: www.knoxservices.com
SIC: 7334 7389 7381 Photocopying and duplicating services; Process serving service; Private investigator

(P-15649)
LASR INC
Also Called: First Reprographic
1517 Beverly Blvd (90026-5704)
P.O. Box 749469 (90074-9469)

PHONE..............................877 591-9979
Martin Kayondo, Pr
Rick Matsumoto, *
EMP: 120 EST: 2002
SALES (est): 2.42MM Privately Held
SIC: 7334 Photocopying and duplicating services

(P-15650)
OFFICEMAX NORTH AMERICA INC
Also Called: OfficeMax
7075 Firestone Blvd (90241-4102)
PHONE..............................562 927-6444
Earl Dadis, Brnch Mgr
EMP: 121
SALES (corp-wide): 8.49B Publicly Held
SIC: 7334 Photocopying and duplicating services
HQ: Officemax North America, Inc.
263 Shuman Blvd Ste 145
Naperville IL
630 717-0791

(P-15651)
RIOT CREATIVE IMAGING
934 Venice Blvd (90015-3230)
PHONE..............................213 516-3160
EMP: 86 EST: 2010
SALES (est): 1.71MM Privately Held
Web: www.riotcolor.com
SIC: 7334 Blueprinting service

(P-15652)
SECOND IMAGE NATIONAL LLC (PA)
170 E Arrow Hwy (91773-3336)
P.O. Box 52969 (77052-2969)
PHONE..............................800 229-7477
Norman Fogwell, CEO
EMP: 145 EST: 1982
SQ FT: 25,500
SALES (est): 23.74MM
SALES (corp-wide): 23.74MM Privately Held
Web: www.ontellus.com
SIC: 7334 Photocopying and duplicating services

(P-15653)
THE ALTERNATIVE COPY SHOP INC
3887 State St Ste 12 (93105-3180)
PHONE..............................805 569-2116
EMP: 52
SIC: 7334 2759 Photocopying and duplicating services; Commercial printing, nec

7335 Commercial Photography

(P-15654)
BRANDED ENTRMT NETWRK INC (PA)
14724 Ventura Blvd Ste 1200 (91403-3501)
PHONE..............................310 342-1500
Richard R Butler, Pr
Gary Shenk, CEO
Joe Schick, CFO
Jim Mitchell, Senior Vice President Corporate Development
EMP: 233 EST: 1989
SALES (est): 96.36MM Privately Held
Web: www.bengroup.com
SIC: 7335 Photographic studio, commercial

(P-15655)
ULTRAGRAPHICS INC
2800 N Naomi St (91504-2023)
PHONE..............................818 295-3994
E Alexander Kilgo, CEO
Jon E Crossley, *
Nancy E Pasch Erlandsen, *
John T Crossley, *
EMP: 44 EST: 1980
SQ FT: 19,000
SALES (est): 4.33MM Privately Held
Web: www.ultragraphicsla.com
SIC: 7335 2752 Photographic studio, commercial; Offset printing

7336 Commercial Art And Graphic Design

(P-15656)
BLACK ANCHOR SUPPLY CO LLC
27636 Avenue Scott Ste A (91355-3973)
PHONE..............................661 309-1193
EMP: 18 EST: 2009
SALES (est): 1.02MM Privately Held
Web: www.blackanchorsupply.com
SIC: 7336 2759 Commercial art and graphic design; Screen printing

(P-15657)
BLT & ASSOCIATES INC
Also Called: BLT
6430 W Sunset Blvd Ste 800 (90028-7901)
PHONE..............................323 860-4000
Clive Baillie, Pr
Rick Lynch, *
Dawn Baillie, *
EMP: 170 EST: 1992
SQ FT: 15,000
SALES (est): 39.04MM Privately Held
SIC: 7336 Graphic arts and related design

(P-15658)
CINNABAR
4571 Electronics Pl (90039-1007)
PHONE..............................818 842-8190
EMP: 200 EST: 1982
SQ FT: 60,000
SALES (est): 21.6MM Privately Held
Web: www.cinnabar.com
SIC: 7336 3999 7819 Graphic arts and related design; Theatrical scenery; Sound effects and music production, motion picture

(P-15659)
CONSOLIDATED DESIGN WEST INC
Also Called: Cdw
1345 S Lewis St (92805-6431)
PHONE..............................714 999-1476
Victor John Perrillo, CEO
▲ EMP: 50 EST: 1990
SQ FT: 7,500
SALES (est): 15.87MM Privately Held
Web: www.consolidateddesignwest.com
SIC: 7336 2754 Package design; Commercial printing, gravure

(P-15660)
CONTINENTAL GRAPHICS CORP (HQ)
Also Called: Continental Data Graphics
4060 N Lakewood Blvd Bldg 801 (90808-1700)
PHONE..............................714 503-4200
David Malmo, CEO
Michael Parven, *
James Mills, *

EMP: 200 EST: 1986
SQ FT: 45,000
SALES (est): 92.01MM
SALES (corp-wide): 66.61B Publicly Held
Web: services.boeing.com
SIC: 7336 8741 8711 8999 Commercial art and graphic design; Management services; Engineering services; Technical writing
PA: The Boeing Company
929 Long Bridge Dr
Arlington VA
703 414-6338

(P-15661)
COUNTY OF LOS ANGELES
Also Called: Gateway
1 Gateway Plz (90012-3745)
P.O. Box 90012 (90009-0012)
PHONE..............................213 922-6210
Roger Snoball, Owner
EMP: 237
Web: www.lacounty.gov
SIC: 7336 9621 Commercial art and graphic design; Transportation department: government, nonoperating
PA: County Of Los Angeles
500 W Temple St Ste 437
Los Angeles CA
213 974-1101

(P-15662)
DANDREA GRAPHIC CORPORTION
Also Called: D'Andrea Graphics
6100 Gateway Dr (90630-4840)
PHONE..............................310 642-0260
David D'andrea, CEO
▲ EMP: 80 EST: 2005
SQ FT: 25,000
SALES (est): 17.81MM Privately Held
Web: www.dandreavisual.com
SIC: 7336 Graphic arts and related design

(P-15663)
DESIGNORY INC (HQ)
Also Called: Designory
211 E Ocean Blvd Ste 100 (90802-4808)
PHONE..............................562 624-0200
Paul Hosea, CEO
Janet M Thompson, *
Joel Fuller, *
Christine Ferguson, *
Matt Radigan, *
EMP: 115 EST: 1970
SALES (est): 26.4MM
SALES (corp-wide): 14.29B Publicly Held
Web: www.designory.com
SIC: 7336 Graphic arts and related design
PA: Omnicom Group Inc.
280 Park Ave Fl 31w
New York NY
212 415-3600

(P-15664)
DIGITAL DOMAIN MEDIA GROUP INC
Also Called: Wyndcrest Dd Florida
12641 Beatrice St (90066-7003)
EMP: 813
SIC: 7336 7812 7371 7372 Commercial art and graphic design; Non-theatrical motion picture production; Custom computer programming services; Business oriented computer software

(P-15665)
ELLENS SILK SCREENING INC
1500 Mission St (91030-3216)
PHONE..............................626 441-4415
Ellen Daigle, Pr

Joe Daigle, *Sec*
EMP: 21 **EST:** 1975
SQ FT: 2,200
SALES (est): 1.63MM **Privately Held**
Web: www.ellenssilkscreening.com
SIC: 7336 3552 Silk screen design; Silk screens for textile industry

(P-15666)
GRAPHIC INK CORP
Also Called: Graphic Ink and Graphic Ink
5382 Industrial Dr (92649-1517)
PHONE..................714 901-2805
Vincent De La Torre, *Pr*
Jenny Lynn Quilico, *
EMP: 45 **EST:** 2005
SQ FT: 6,000
SALES (est): 2.39MM **Privately Held**
Web: www.graphicink.org
SIC: 7336 2262 Commercial art and graphic design; Finishing plants, manmade

(P-15667)
IDENTIGRAPHIX INC
19866 Quiroz Ct (91789-2828)
PHONE..................909 468-4741
A Fred Mendoza, *Pr*
EMP: 25 **EST:** 1982
SQ FT: 17,000
SALES (est): 2.72MM **Privately Held**
Web: www.identigraphix.com
SIC: 7336 2396 Silk screen design; Automotive and apparel trimmings

(P-15668)
MIRUM INC
Also Called: Digitaria
350 10th Ave Ste 1200 (92101-7433)
PHONE..................619 237-5552
Daniel Khabie, *CEO*
Doug Hecht, *
Gary Correia, *
EMP: 200 **EST:** 1997
SQ FT: 4,000
SALES (est): 26.78MM
SALES (corp-wide): 17.37B **Privately Held**
SIC: 7336 Graphic arts and related design
HQ: Wunderman Thompson Llc
175 Greenwich St Fl 16
New York NY
212 210-7000

(P-15669)
MOTION THEORY INC
Also Called: Mirada
444 W Ocean Blvd Ste 1400 (90802-4522)
PHONE..................310 396-9433
Andrew Merkin, *Dir*
Matthew Cullen, *
Janell Perez, *
EMP: 110 **EST:** 2000
SQ FT: 25,000
SALES (est): 4.81MM **Privately Held**
Web: www.motiontheory.com
SIC: 7336 7371 7812 Graphic arts and related design; Computer software development and applications; Motion picture production

(P-15670)
MOTIVATIONAL SYSTEMS INC (PA)
2200 Cleveland Ave (91950-6412)
PHONE..................619 474-8246
Robert D Yound, *CEO*
David Cowan, *
Joe Jordan, *
Anthony Young, *
EMP: 100 **EST:** 1975
SQ FT: 50,000

SALES (est): 31.24MM
SALES (corp-wide): 31.24MM **Privately Held**
Web: www.motivational.com
SIC: 7336 3993 Graphic arts and related design; Signs and advertising specialties

(P-15671)
P5 GRAPHICS AND DISPLAYS INC
625 Fee Ana St (92870-6704)
PHONE..................714 808-1645
Amit Patel, *Pr*
Kirit Ramani, *VP*
EMP: 21 **EST:** 2015
SALES (est): 2.28MM **Privately Held**
Web: www.p5graphics.net
SIC: 7336 2782 Graphic arts and related design; Account books

(P-15672)
PULP STUDIO INCORPORATED
Also Called: CGB
2100 W 139th St (90249-2412)
P.O. Box 16231 (90209-2231)
PHONE..................310 815-4999
Bernard Lax, *CEO*
Lynda N Lax, *
▲ **EMP:** 60 **EST:** 1940
SQ FT: 36,000
SALES (est): 12MM **Privately Held**
Web: www.pulpstudio.com
SIC: 7336 3229 Commercial art and graphic design; Glass furnishings and accessories

(P-15673)
SCREENWORKS LLC
Also Called: Screenworks Nep
1900 Compton Ave Ste 101 (92881-7261)
PHONE..................951 279-8877
Kevin Rabbitt, *CEO*
▲ **EMP:** 1306 **EST:** 2012
SALES (est): 9.68MM
SALES (corp-wide): 421.16MM **Privately Held**
Web: www.screenworksnep.com
SIC: 7336 Graphic arts and related design
HQ: Nep Supershooters, Lp
2 Beta Dr
Pittsburgh PA
412 826-1414

(P-15674)
SESA INC (PA)
Also Called: Signco
20391 Via Guadalupe (92887-3133)
PHONE..................714 779-9700
Elaine M Roach, *CEO*
EMP: 23 **EST:** 1986
SQ FT: 18,000
SALES (est): 4.76MM
SALES (corp-wide): 4.76MM **Privately Held**
SIC: 7336 2759 3993 2396 Silk screen design; Screen printing; Signs and advertising specialties; Automotive and apparel trimmings

(P-15675)
THINKBASIC INC
Also Called: Basic Agency
350 10th Ave (92101-7433)
PHONE..................858 755-6922
Matthew Faulk, *CEO*
Ashley Reichel, *
Alisa Kuno, *
EMP: 120 **EST:** 2011
SALES (est): 6.31MM **Privately Held**
Web: www.basicagency.com

SIC: 7336 Graphic arts and related design

(P-15676)
TREND DESIGN INC
Also Called: Trend Graphics Screenprinting
1200 Lawrence Dr Ste 465 (91320-1342)
PHONE..................805 498-0457
Steve Dilallo, *Pr*
Kim Di Lallo, *Sec*
Chris Kaul, *VP*
EMP: 17 **EST:** 1987
SQ FT: 3,000
SALES (est): 1.44MM **Privately Held**
SIC: 7336 2759 Silk screen design; Screen printing

(P-15677)
TWENTIETH CNTURY FOX JAPAN INC
Also Called: News Corp - Fox
10201 W Pico Blvd (90064-2606)
PHONE..................310 369-4636
Robert B Cohen, *CEO*
EMP: 4000 **EST:** 1981
SALES (est): 38.11MM
SALES (corp-wide): 88.9B **Publicly Held**
SIC: 7336 Film strip and slide producer
HQ: Tfcf Corporation
1211 Ave Of The Americas
New York NY
212 852-7000

(P-15678)
UNIVERSITY CAL SAN DIEGO
Also Called: Graphics Department
9500 Gilman Dr Dept 908 (92093-0908)
PHONE..................858 534-2377
Larry Fox, *Dir*
EMP: 539
SALES (corp-wide): 534.4MM **Privately Held**
Web: www.ucsd.edu
SIC: 7336 8221 9411 Commercial art and graphic design; University; Administration of educational programs
HQ: University Of California, San Diego
9500 Gilman Dr
La Jolla CA
858 534-2230

7338 Secretarial And Court Reporting

(P-15679)
ASAB INC (DH)
500 N Brand Blvd Fl 3 (91203-4725)
P.O. Box 29054 (91209-9054)
PHONE..................818 551-7300
Alan Atkinson Baker, *CEO*
Sheila Atkinson-baker, *Pr*
EMP: 150 **EST:** 1987
SQ FT: 23,000
SALES (est): 36.07MM
SALES (corp-wide): 192.17MM **Privately Held**
Web: www.depo.com
SIC: 7338 Court reporting service
HQ: Veritext, Llc
290 W Mount Pleasant Ave # 3
Livingston NJ
973 410-4040

(P-15680)
INFOSEND INC (PA)
4240 E La Palma Ave (92807-1816)
PHONE..................714 993-2690
Mahmood Rezai, *CEO*
Mahmood Rezai, *Pr*
Rusteen Rezai, *COO*

EMP: 49 **EST:** 1997
SALES (est): 18.28MM
SALES (corp-wide): 18.28MM **Privately Held**
Web: www.infosend.com
SIC: 7338 2732 2741 7389 Stenographic services; Pamphlets: printing only, not published on site; Business service newsletters: publishing and printing; Presorted mail service

(P-15681)
SOFTSCRIPT INC
2215 Campus Dr (90245-0001)
PHONE..................310 451-2110
Howard Wisnicki, *CEO*
Yuriy Kotlyar, *
EMP: 1200 **EST:** 1996
SALES (est): 25.39MM **Privately Held**
Web: www.softscript.com
SIC: 7338 Court reporting service

7342 Disinfecting And Pest Control Services

(P-15682)
BANKS PEST CONTROL
7440 District Blvd Ste A (93313-4821)
P.O. Box 113 (93302-0113)
PHONE..................661 323-7858
Don Banks, *Pr*
Orland Banks, *
Janet Banks, *
EMP: 371 **EST:** 1969
SALES (est): 3.29MM
SALES (corp-wide): 2.7B **Publicly Held**
Web: www.bankspest.com
SIC: 7342 Pest control in structures
PA: Rollins, Inc.
2170 Piedmont Rd Ne
Atlanta GA
404 888-2000

(P-15683)
BUSY BEE LLC
36798 Pictor Ave (92563-4202)
PHONE..................951 404-9900
EMP: 80
SALES (corp-wide): 185.07K **Privately Held**
SIC: 7342 Disinfecting and pest control services
PA: Busy Bee Llc
27100 Sunnyridge Rd
Pls Vrds Pnsl CA

(P-15684)
CARTWRIGHT TRMT PEST CTRL INC
1376 Broadway (92021-5812)
P.O. Box 2398 (92021-0398)
PHONE..................619 442-9613
Michael Cartwright Ii, *CEO*
Michael Cartwright Senior, *VP*
Ben Cartwright, *
Willard Cartwright, *
EMP: 33 **EST:** 1962
SQ FT: 2,000
SALES (est): 2.49MM **Privately Held**
Web: www.cartwrightpest.com
SIC: 7342 2879 Exterminating and fumigating ; Insecticides and pesticides

(P-15685)
CATS USA INC
Also Called: Cats U S A Pest Control
5683 Whitnall Hwy (91601-2213)
P.O. Box 151 (91603-0151)
PHONE..................818 506-1000

Hirotaka Otomo, *Ch Bd*
EMP: 100 **EST:** 1971
SQ FT: 3,900
SALES (est): 9.76MM **Privately Held**
Web: www.catspestcontrol.com
SIC: 7342 Pest control in structures
HQ: Cats, Inc.
   15-13, Nampeidaicho
   Shibuya-Ku TKY

(P-15686)
CORKYS PEST CONTROL INC
909 Rancheros Dr (92069-3028)
PHONE.................760 432-8801
Corky Mizer, *Pr*
▲ **EMP:** 60 **EST:** 1967
SQ FT: 5,000
SALES (est): 9.84MM **Privately Held**
Web: www.corkyspest.com
SIC: 7342 0782 2879 5211 Pest control in
   structures; Lawn and garden services;
   Insecticides and pesticides; Insulation
   material, building
HQ: Anticimex Inc.
   106 Allen Rd Ste 310
   Basking Ridge NJ
   800 618-2847

(P-15687)
RENTOKIL NORTH AMERICA INC
Also Called: Target Specialty Products
15415 Marquardt Ave (90670-5711)
P.O. Box 3408 (90670-1408)
PHONE.................562 802-2238
Rich Records, *Mgr*
EMP: 100
SALES (corp-wide): 4.47B **Privately Held**
SIC: 7342 Pest control in structures
HQ: Rentokil North America, Inc.
   1125 Berkshire Blvd # 15
   Wyomissing PA
   470 643-3300

(P-15688)
YOUR WAY FUMIGATION INC
1660 Chicago Ave Ste N9 (92507-2053)
PHONE.................951 699-9116
Jose Manuel Aguilar, *Pr*
EMP: 90 **EST:** 2006
SALES (est): 2.36MM **Privately Held**
Web: www.ywfumigation.com
SIC: 7342 Pest control in structures

7349 Building Maintenance Services, Nec

(P-15689)
911 RESTORATION ENTPS INC
6932 Gross Ave (91307-2432)
PHONE.................832 887-2582
Ofer Kedem, *Brnch Mgr*
EMP: 283
SALES (corp-wide): 19.32MM **Privately Held**
Web: www.911restorationlosangeles.com
SIC: 7349 Building maintenance services,
   nec
PA: 911 Restoration Enterprises, Inc.
   7721 Densmore Ave
   Van Nuys CA
   818 373-4880

(P-15690)
ADVANCED CLNROOM MCRCLEAN CORP
Also Called: A C M
3250 S Susan St Ste A (92704-6807)

PHONE.................714 751-1152
Janet Ford, *CEO*
▲ **EMP:** 200 **EST:** 1982
SQ FT: 3,500
SALES (est): 19.65MM **Privately Held**
Web: www.advancedcleanroom.com
SIC: 7349 8734 Cleaning service, industrial
   or commercial; Testing laboratories

(P-15691)
ALL-RITE LEASING COMPANY INC
950 S Coast Dr Ste 110 (92626-1778)
PHONE.................714 957-1822
Chris Schran, *Pr*
Pauline Rosenberg, *
EMP: 269 **EST:** 1991
SALES (est): 2.44MM **Privately Held**
SIC: 7349 Building maintenance services,
   nec

(P-15692)
AMERI-KLEEN
Also Called: Ameri-Kleen Building Services
1023 E Grand Ave (93420-2504)
PHONE.................805 546-0706
Dan Erpenbach, *Brnch Mgr*
EMP: 220
Web: www.ameri-kleen.com
SIC: 7349 Janitorial service, contract basis
PA: Ameri-Kleen
   119 W Beach St
   Watsonville CA

(P-15693)
ARAMARK FACILITY SERVICES LLC
Also Called: Aramark
941 W 35th St (90007-4002)
PHONE.................213 740-8968
Ron Cote, *Mgr*
EMP: 105
Web: www.aramark.es
SIC: 7349 Janitorial service, contract basis
HQ: Aramark Facility Services, Llc
   2400 Market St Ste 209
   Philadelphia PA
   215 238-3000

(P-15694)
AVALON BUILDING MAINT INC
1832 Commercenter Cir (92408-3430)
PHONE.................714 693-2407
EMP: 400 **EST:** 1988
SQ FT: 5,000
SALES (est): 4.5MM **Privately Held**
Web:
www.avalonbuildingmaintenance-ie.com
SIC: 7349 Janitorial service, contract basis

(P-15695)
BERGENSONS PROPERTY SVCS INC
Also Called: Solve All Facility Services
3605 Ocean Ranch Blvd Ste 200
(92056-2695)
PHONE.................760 631-5111
Mark M Minasian, *CEO*
Aram Minasian, *
EMP: 2000 **EST:** 1984
SQ FT: 2,000
SALES (est): 15.03MM **Privately Held**
Web: www.kbs-services.com
SIC: 7349 Building maintenance, except
   repairs

(P-15696)
BZYA CORPORATION
100 Spectrum Center Dr Ste 900
(92618-4962)

PHONE.................949 656-3220
Susan Luo, *CEO*
EMP: 325 **EST:** 2017
SALES (est): 7.22MM **Privately Held**
SIC: 7349 Janitorial service, contract basis

(P-15697)
C&W FACILITY SERVICES INC
Also Called: Dtz
3011 Townsgate Rd Ste 410 (91361-5882)
PHONE.................805 267-7123
EMP: 1966
SALES (corp-wide): 10.11B **Privately Held**
Web: www.cwservices.com
SIC: 7349 Janitorial service, contract basis
HQ: C&W Facility Services Inc.
   117 Kendrick St Ste 250
   Needham MA
   888 751-9100

(P-15698)
CALICO BUILDING SERVICES INC
Also Called: Calico
15550 Rockfield Blvd Ste C (92618-2712)
PHONE.................949 380-8707
Ron Strand, *Pr*
Christopher Guidry, *
Thomas Miquelon, *
Orlando Fernandez, *
EMP: 185 **EST:** 1986
SQ FT: 1,700
SALES (est): 18.18MM **Privately Held**
Web: www.calicoweb.com
SIC: 7349 Janitorial service, contract basis

(P-15699)
CERTIFIED WTR DMAGE RSTRTION E
Also Called: Cwdre
5319 University Dr (92612-2965)
PHONE.................800 417-1776
Cyrus Fatoure, *Pr*
EMP: 48 **EST:** 2016
SALES (est): 2.24MM **Privately Held**
SIC: 7349 1389 6331 1521 Building
   maintenance services, nec; Construction,
   repair, and dismantling services; Property
   damage insurance; Repairing fire damage,
   single-family houses

(P-15700)
COASTAL BUILDING SERVICES INC
1433 W Central Park Ave N (92802-1417)
PHONE.................714 775-2855
Hipolito G Arias, *CEO*
Brett Dunstan, *
EMP: 300 **EST:** 1998
SALES (est): 9.27MM **Privately Held**
Web: www.cbsinc.us
SIC: 7349 Janitorial service, contract basis

(P-15701)
COME LAND MAINT SVC CO INC
1419 N San Fernando Blvd Ste 250
(91504-4185)
PHONE.................818 567-2455
Grace H Lee, *Pr*
William Lee, *
EMP: 513 **EST:** 1992
SQ FT: 12,750
SALES (est): 5.34MM **Privately Held**
SIC: 7349 Janitorial service, contract basis
PA: Come Land, Inc.
   1419 N San Fernando Blvd # 250
   Burbank CA

(P-15702)
CONTRACT SERVICES GROUP INC
Also Called: Celex Solutions
480 Capricorn St (92821-3203)
P.O. Box 8815 (92822-5815)
PHONE.................714 582-1800
John Pearce, *CEO*
Casey Pearce, *
EMP: 250 **EST:** 2003
SALES (est): 24.57MM **Privately Held**
Web: www.csgcares.com
SIC: 7349 Janitorial service, contract basis

(P-15703)
CREATIVE MAINTENANCE SYSTEMS
1340 Reynolds Ave Ste 111 (92614-5503)
PHONE.................949 852-2871
Bill Koop, *Pr*
Christina Alexander, *
EMP: 100 **EST:** 2000
SQ FT: 2,000
SALES (est): 2.13MM **Privately Held**
SIC: 7349 Janitorial service, contract basis

(P-15704)
CROWN BUILDING MAINTENANCE CO
Also Called: Able Building Maintenance
14201 Franklin Ave (92780-7008)
PHONE.................714 434-9494
Robert Hughes, *CEO*
EMP: 373
SALES (corp-wide): 7.81B **Publicly Held**
SIC: 7349 Janitorial service, contract basis
HQ: Crown Building Maintenance Co.
   600 Harrison St Ste 600 # 600
   San Francisco CA
   415 981-8070

(P-15705)
CROWN BUILDING MAINTENANCE CO
5482 Complex St Ste 108 (92123-1125)
PHONE.................858 560-5785
EMP: 280
SALES (corp-wide): 7.81B **Publicly Held**
SIC: 7349 8711 Janitorial service, contract
   basis; Engineering services
HQ: Crown Building Maintenance Co.
   600 Harrison St Ste 600 # 600
   San Francisco CA
   415 981-8070

(P-15706)
CROWN ENERGY SERVICES INC
Also Called: Able Engineering Services
2601 S Figueroa St Bldg 1 (90007)
PHONE.................213 765-7800
Ed Figueroa, *Mgr*
EMP: 1017
SALES (corp-wide): 7.81B **Publicly Held**
SIC: 7349 Janitorial service, contract basis
HQ: Crown Energy Services, Inc.
   600 Harrison St Ste 600 # 600
   San Francisco CA

(P-15707)
DIAMOND CONTRACT SERVICES INC
11432 Vanowen St (91605-6220)
PHONE.................818 565-3554
EMP: 350
Web: www.diamondcontract.com
SIC: 7349 8748 Building maintenance,
   except repairs; Business consulting, nec

(P-15708)

DIMAR ENTERPRISES INC
Also Called: Drymaster
26021 Pala Ste 150 (92691-2718)
PHONE..............................949 492-1100
Diane Combs, *CEO*
EMP: 182 EST: 2014
SALES (est): 9.44MM **Privately Held**
Web: www.drymaster.com
SIC: 7349 Building maintenance services, nec

(P-15709)

DMS FACILITY SERVICES INC
Also Called: DMS
2861 E Coronado St (92806-2504)
PHONE..............................949 975-1366
Douglas Gregory, *Prin*
EMP: 1325
SALES (corp-wide): 42.01MM **Privately Held**
Web: www.dmsfacilityservices.com
SIC: 7349 Janitorial service, contract basis
PA: Dms Facility Services, Inc.
1040 Arroyo Dr
South Pasadena CA
626 305-8500

(P-15710)

ELITE CRAFTSMAN (PA)
Also Called: Stockmar Industrial
2763 Saint Louis Ave (90755-2025)
P.O. Box 90458 (90809-0458)
PHONE..............................562 989-3511
William C Stockmar, *Pr*
Linda Pierson, *Sec*
George N Negrete, *VP*
EMP: 130 EST: 1972
SQ FT: 10,000
SALES (est): 7.89MM
SALES (corp-wide): 7.89MM **Privately Held**
SIC: 7349 Janitorial service, contract basis

(P-15711)

GMI BUILDING SERVICES INC
8001 Vickers St (92111-1917)
PHONE..............................858 279-6262
Larry Abrams, *Pr*
EMP: 225 EST: 1966
SQ FT: 15,000
SALES (est): 9.75MM **Privately Held**
SIC: 7349 5087 Janitorial service, contract basis; Janitors' supplies

(P-15712)

HAYNES BUILDING SERVICE LLC
16027 Arrow Hwy Ste I (91706-2064)
PHONE..............................626 359-6100
TOLL FREE: 800
John P Scharler, *Pr*
Michael Franco, *
EMP: 175 EST: 1982
SQ FT: 20,000
SALES (est): 2.39MM **Privately Held**
Web: www.haynesservices.com
SIC: 7349 Janitorial service, contract basis

(P-15713)

HUNTER EASTERDAY CORPORATION
1475 N Hundley St (92806-1323)
PHONE..............................714 238-3400
Sam Easterday, *CEO*
Manny Jones, *
Gilbert Anzaldua, *
Joanne Easterday, *
EMP: 135 EST: 1976

SQ FT: 4,400
SALES (est): 6.18MM **Privately Held**
Web: www.ebmcorp.com
SIC: 7349 5087 Janitorial service, contract basis; Janitors' supplies

(P-15714)

INDUSTRIAL JANITOR SERVICE
Also Called: I J S
221 N San Dimas Ave Ste 217 (91773-2649)
PHONE..............................818 782-5658
Darla Drendel, *CEO*
Darla Arturo, *
EMP: 100 EST: 1965
SQ FT: 7,500
SALES (est): 891.41K **Privately Held**
Web: www.ijsclean.com
SIC: 7349 Janitorial service, contract basis

(P-15715)

INNOVATIONS BUILDING SVCS LLC
402 S Orange Ave Apt D (91755-7554)
PHONE..............................323 787-6068
Helbert Daniel Torres, *Prin*
EMP: 100 EST: 2016
SALES (est): 2.09MM **Privately Held**
Web:
www.innovationsbuildingservices.com
SIC: 7349 Janitorial service, contract basis

(P-15716)

INNOVATIVE CLEANING SVCS LLC
44 Waterworks Way (92618-3107)
PHONE..............................949 251-9188
Jennifer Corbett-shramo, *CEO*
John Gambino, *
Jaime Aburto, *
EMP: 500 EST: 2000
SALES (est): 8.73MM **Privately Held**
Web: www.ics-oc.com
SIC: 7349 Cleaning service, industrial or commercial

(P-15717)

K & P JANITORIAL SERVICES
412 S Pacific Coast Hwy Ste 200 (90277)
PHONE..............................310 540-8878
EMP: 100 EST: 1991
SALES (est): 4.82MM **Privately Held**
Web: www.kandpjanitorial.com
SIC: 7349 Janitorial service, contract basis

(P-15718)

KBM FCLITY SLTONS HOLDINGS LLC
Also Called: Kbm Building Services
7976 Engineer Rd Ste 200 (92111-1935)
PHONE..............................858 467-0202
Brian Snow, *CEO*
Rene Tuthscher, *
Susan Cologna, *
Shaun Gordon, *
Robert Kennedy Iii, *Dir*
EMP: 500 EST: 1981
SQ FT: 10,000
SALES (est): 27.13MM
SALES (corp-wide): 51.04MM **Privately Held**
Web: www.expiredwixdomain.com
SIC: 7349 Janitorial service, contract basis
PA: Pristine Environments Inc
3605 Ocean Ranch Blvd # 200
Oceanside CA
703 245-4751

(P-15719)

LEES MAINTENANCE SERVICE INC
14740 Keswick St (91405-1205)
PHONE..............................818 988-6644
Tyrone P Ingram, *Pr*
EMP: 275 EST: 1961
SQ FT: 3,000
SALES (est): 2.79MM **Privately Held**
Web: www.leesmaint.com
SIC: 7349 5087 Janitorial service, contract basis; Laundry and dry cleaning equipment and supplies

(P-15720)

LIFE CYCLE ENGINEERING INC
7510 Airway Rd Ste 2 (92154-8303)
PHONE..............................619 785-5990
John Spencer, *Mgr*
EMP: 209
SALES (corp-wide): 73.8MM **Privately Held**
Web: www.lce.com
SIC: 7349 Building maintenance, except repairs
PA: Life Cycle Engineering, Inc.
4360 Corporate Rd Ste 100
North Charleston SC
843 744-7110

(P-15721)

LOS ANGELES UNIFIED SCHOOL DST
Also Called: Maintenance Dept
17729 S Figueroa St (90248-4237)
PHONE..............................310 808-1500
Roger Finstad, *Dir*
EMP: 88
SALES (corp-wide): 9.38B **Privately Held**
Web: www.laallcityband.com
SIC: 7349 School custodian, contract basis
PA: Los Angeles Unified School District
333 S Beaudry Ave Ste 209
Los Angeles CA
213 241-1000

(P-15722)

M-N-Z JANITORIAL SERVICES INC
2109 W Burbank Blvd (91506-1231)
PHONE..............................323 851-4115
Marc De Mauregne, *Ex VP*
Zorina Russell Kroop, *
Dennis Krebs, *Stockholder*
EMP: 110 EST: 1979
SQ FT: 1,000
SALES (est): 2.83MM **Privately Held**
Web: www.mnz.com
SIC: 7349 1799 Building maintenance, except repairs; Construction site cleanup

(P-15723)

MC-40 (PA)
Also Called: Mintie Technologies
777 N Georgia Ave (91702-2207)
PHONE..............................323 225-4111
Kevin J Mintie, *CEO*
James M Mintie, *
EMP: 122 EST: 1940
SALES (est): 12.68MM
SALES (corp-wide): 12.68MM **Privately Held**
Web: www.alliance-enviro.com
SIC: 7349 Building cleaning service

(P-15724)

MERCHANTS BUILDING MAINT CO
Also Called: Merchants Building Maintenance

1995 W Holt Ave (91768-3352)
PHONE..............................909 622-8260
Angel Meza, *Brnch Mgr*
EMP: 551
SALES (corp-wide): 90.51MM **Privately Held**
Web: www.mbmonline.com
SIC: 7349 7381 Janitorial service, contract basis; Security guard service
PA: Merchants Building Maintenance Company
1190 Monterey Pass Rd
Monterey Park CA
323 881-6701

(P-15725)

MERCHANTS BUILDING MAINT CO
606 Monterey Pass Rd Ste 202 (91754)
PHONE..............................323 881-8902
Michael Anthony Palma, *Bd of Dir*
EMP: 130
SALES (corp-wide): 90.51MM **Privately Held**
Web: www.mbmonline.com
SIC: 7349 7381 Janitorial service, contract basis; Detective and armored car services
PA: Merchants Building Maintenance Company
1190 Monterey Pass Rd
Monterey Park CA
323 881-6701

(P-15726)

MERCHANTS BUILDING MAINT CO
9555 Distribution Ave Ste 102 (92121)
PHONE..............................858 455-0163
Eric Ruiz, *Mgr*
EMP: 354
SALES (corp-wide): 90.51MM **Privately Held**
Web: www.mbmonline.com
SIC: 7349 Janitorial service, contract basis
PA: Merchants Building Maintenance Company
1190 Monterey Pass Rd
Monterey Park CA
323 881-6701

(P-15727)

MERCHANTS BUILDING MAINT CO
Also Called: Merchants Building Maintenance
1639 E Edinger Ave Ste C (92705-5013)
PHONE..............................714 973-9272
George Rodriguez, *Brnch Mgr*
EMP: 433
SALES (corp-wide): 90.51MM **Privately Held**
Web: www.mbmonline.com
SIC: 7349 Janitorial service, contract basis
PA: Merchants Building Maintenance Company
1190 Monterey Pass Rd
Monterey Park CA
323 881-6701

(P-15728)

MIDA INDUSTRIES INC
6101 Obispo Ave (90805-3799)
PHONE..............................562 616-1020
Michael T Drake, *Pr*
John Valencia, *
Dawit Kidane, *
EMP: 250 EST: 1989
SQ FT: 10,000
SALES (est): 8.84MM **Privately Held**
Web: www.midaindustries.com

PRODUCTS & SVCS

SIC: **7349** 1799 Janitorial service, contract basis; Asbestos removal and encapsulation

(P-15729)
MONTEBELLO UNIFIED SCHOOL DST
Also Called: Maintenance & Operation Dept
500 Hendricks St 2nd Fl (90640-1566)
PHONE..................................323 887-2140
Virgil Downs, *Prin*
EMP: 90
SALES (corp-wide): 539.05MM **Privately Held**
Web: www.montebello.k12.ca.us
SIC: 7349 Building maintenance services, nec
PA: Montebello Unified School District
123 S Montebello Blvd
Montebello CA
323 887-7900

(P-15730)
ONE SILVER SERVE LLC
Also Called: SERVPRO Encino/Sherman Oaks
16601 Ventura Blvd Fl 4 (91436-1921)
PHONE..................................818 995-6444
Alan Reed, *CEO*
EMP: 80 **EST:** 2005
SALES (est): 9.53MM **Privately Held**
Web:
www.servproencinoshermanoaks.com
SIC: 7349 Building maintenance services, nec

(P-15731)
OPEN AMERICA INC
Also Called: Openworks
4300 Long Beach Blvd Ste 450
(90807-2011)
PHONE..................................562 428-9210
John Palmer, *Brnch Mgr*
EMP: 188
SALES (corp-wide): 28.74MM **Privately Held**
Web: www.openworksweb.com
SIC: 7349 Janitorial service, contract basis
PA: O.P.E.N. America, Inc.
4742 N 24th St Ste 450
Phoenix AZ
602 224-0440

(P-15732)
PACIFIC BUILDING CARE INC (HQ)
3001 Red Hill Ave Bldg 6 (92626)
PHONE..................................949 261-1234
Ian Bress, *CEO*
Ted Geissler, *Pr*
Jennifer Corbett, *VP*
Robin Geissler, *Sec*
Holly Papa, *Treas*
EMP: 117 **EST:** 1970
SQ FT: 5,200
SALES (est): 21.89MM
SALES (corp-wide): 241MM **Privately Held**
SIC: 7349 Building cleaning service
PA: Commercial Cleaning Systems, Inc.
990 S Broadway Ste 200
Denver CO
303 733-8997

(P-15733)
PE FACILITY SOLUTIONS LLC (PA)
4217 Ponderosa Ave Ste A (92123-1536)
PHONE..................................858 467-0202
Shaun Gordon, *CEO*
EMP: 95 **EST:** 2017

SQ FT: 18,000
SALES (est): 2.09MM
SALES (corp-wide): 2.09MM **Privately Held**
SIC: 7349 Janitorial service, contract basis

(P-15734)
PEERLESS MAINTENANCE SVC INC
1100 S Euclid St (90631-6807)
P.O. Box 3900 (90632-3900)
PHONE..................................714 871-3380
Linda Gabriel, *Pr*
David Gabriel, *
EMP: 300 **EST:** 1979
SQ FT: 2,000
SALES (est): 8.88MM **Privately Held**
Web: www.peerlesssvc.com
SIC: 7349 Janitorial service, contract basis

(P-15735)
PEGASUS BUILDING SVCS CO INC
7966 Arjons Dr Ste A (92126-6361)
PHONE..................................858 444-2290
Judith Becker, *Pr*
Mark Tarin, *VP Opers*
Barry Becker, *Dir*
EMP: 350 **EST:** 1983
SQ FT: 12,800
SALES (est): 24.33MM **Privately Held**
Web: www.pegasusclean.com
SIC: 7349 Janitorial service, contract basis

(P-15736)
PERFORMANCE BUILDING SERVICES
Also Called: Performance Cleanroom Services
22642 Lambert St Ste 409 (92630-1645)
PHONE..................................949 364-4364
James Chriss, *Pr*
Ron Matthews, *
Robert Lynch, *
EMP: 104 **EST:** 2001
SALES (est): 4.43MM **Privately Held**
Web: www.performance-now.com
SIC: 7349 7699 Janitorial service, contract basis; Cleaning services

(P-15737)
PLATINUM CLG INDIANAPOLIS LLC
1522 2nd St (90401-2303)
PHONE..................................310 584-8000
EMP: 460 **EST:** 2008
SALES (est): 4.99MM **Privately Held**
SIC: 7349 Building and office cleaning services

(P-15738)
PRIORITY BUILDING SERVICES LLC
7313 Carroll Rd Ste G (92121-2319)
PHONE..................................858 695-1326
Simon Rocha, *Brnch Mgr*
EMP: 304
Web: www.priorityservices.net
SIC: 7349 Janitorial service, contract basis
PA: Priority Building Services Llc
1524 W Mable St
Anaheim CA

(P-15739)
PRO BUILDING MAINTENANCE INC (PA)
149 N Maple St Ste H (92878-3273)
PHONE..................................951 279-3386

EMP: 120 **EST:** 2006
SQ FT: 1,600
SALES (est): 1.73MM **Privately Held**
Web: www.probuildingmaintenance.com
SIC: 7349 Janitorial service, contract basis

(P-15740)
PROFESSIONAL MAINT SYSTEMS INC
Also Called: Professional Maint Systems
4912 Naples St (92110-3820)
P.O. Box 80038 (92138-0038)
PHONE..................................619 276-1150
Karen Berry, *CEO*
EMP: 925 **EST:** 1983
SQ FT: 9,000
SALES (est): 34.04MM **Privately Held**
Web: www.pmsjanitorial.com
SIC: 7349 Janitorial service, contract basis

(P-15741)
PRONTO JANITORIAL SVCS INC
12561 Persing Dr (90606-2713)
PHONE..................................562 273-5997
Edgar Rodas, *Pr*
EMP: 80 **EST:** 2019
SALES (est): 1.01MM **Privately Held**
SIC: 7349 Janitorial service, contract basis

(P-15742)
PROPERTY CARE BUILDING SVC LLC
126 La Porte St Ste F (91006-7190)
P.O. Box 661690 (91066-1690)
PHONE..................................626 623-6420
Everardo Amezcua, *
Victoria Amezcua, *VP*
EMP: 26 **EST:** 2013
SALES (est): 1.01MM **Privately Held**
Web:
www.propertycarebuildingservice.com
SIC: 7349 2842 7342 Janitorial service, contract basis; Sanitation preparations, disinfectants and deodorants; Disinfecting services

(P-15743)
PROTEC ASSOCIATION SERVICES (PA)
Also Called: Protec Building Services
10180 Willow Creek Rd (92131-1636)
PHONE..................................858 569-1080
EMP: 140 **EST:** 1996
SQ FT: 12,500
SALES (est): 32.38MM **Privately Held**
Web: www.protec.com
SIC: 7349 Building maintenance services, nec

(P-15744)
RESOURCE COLLECTION INC
Also Called: Command Guard Services
3771 W 242nd St Ste 205 (90505-6566)
PHONE..................................310 219-3272
Martin Benom, *Ch Bd*
Paula Benom, *
Marilyn Jacobson, *
Steven Jacobson, *
EMP: 46 **EST:** 1962
SQ FT: 15,000
SALES (est): 878.72K **Privately Held**
Web: www.resourcecollection.com
SIC: 7349 7381 0782 3564 Air duct cleaning; Guard services; Lawn and garden services; Air cleaning systems

(P-15745)
RHINO BUILDING SERVICES INC
6650 Flanders Dr Ste K (92121-3908)

PHONE..................................858 455-1440
Cody Sears, *Pr*
EMP: 120 **EST:** 1985
SQ FT: 110
SALES (est): 2.37MM **Privately Held**
Web: www.rhinoinc.com
SIC: 7349 Janitorial service, contract basis

(P-15746)
RNA ANN ARBOR INCORPORATED
508 S Smith Ave Ste A202 (92882-7605)
PHONE..................................877 762-7511
EMP: 107
SALES (corp-wide): 8.85MM **Privately Held**
Web: www.rnafacilitiesmanagement.com
SIC: 7349 Janitorial service, contract basis
PA: R.N.A. Of Ann Arbor, Incorporated
717 W Ellsworth Rd
Ann Arbor MI
877 762-7511

(P-15747)
SERVI-TEK INC
Also Called: Servi-Tek Janitorial Services
8765 Sparren Way (92129-4437)
PHONE..................................858 638-7735
Kurt G Lester, *
Eric S Friz, *
EMP: 300 **EST:** 2006
SALES (est): 14.26MM **Privately Held**
Web: www.servi-tek.net
SIC: 7349 Janitorial service, contract basis

(P-15748)
SERVICEMASTER BY BEST PROS INC
6474 Western Ave (92505-2130)
PHONE..................................951 515-9051
Filip Busuioc, *CEO*
EMP: 99 **EST:** 2018
SALES (est): 1.28MM **Privately Held**
Web: www.servicemaster.com
SIC: 7349 1799 Building maintenance services, nec; Construction site cleanup

(P-15749)
SITE CREW INC
3185 Airway Ave Ste G (92626-4601)
PHONE..................................714 668-0100
Tina Manavi, *CEO*
EMP: 300 **EST:** 2005
SQ FT: 2,160
SALES (est): 8.3MM **Privately Held**
Web: www.sitecrewinc.com
SIC: 7349 Janitorial service, contract basis

(P-15750)
SOUTHERN MANAGEMENT CORP
808 S Olive St (90014-3006)
PHONE..................................213 312-2268
EMP: 83
SALES (corp-wide): 7.81B **Publicly Held**
SIC: 7349 Building maintenance services, nec
HQ: Southern Management Corp.
6478e Highway 90
Milton FL

(P-15751)
TUTTLE FAMILY ENTERPRISES INC
Also Called: Peerless Building Maint Co
9510 Topanga Canyon Blvd (91311-4011)
PHONE..................................818 534-2566
Tim Tuttle, *CEO*
EMP: 350 **EST:** 1948

SALES (est): 3.95MM Privately Held
SIC: 7349 Building maintenance, except repairs

(P-15752)
UNISERVE FACILITIES SVCS CORP
1200 Getty Center Dr (90049-1657)
PHONE.....................310 440-6747
F Jackson, *Operations Staff*
EMP: 325
SALES (corp-wide): 16.38MM Privately Held
Web: www.uniservecorp.com
SIC: 7349 Janitorial service, contract basis
PA: Uniserve Facilities Services
Corporation
2363 S Atlantic Blvd
Commerce CA
213 533-1000

(P-15753)
UNISERVE FACILITIES SVCS CORP (PA)
Also Called: Union Building Maintenance
2363 S Atlantic Blvd (90040-1256)
PHONE.....................213 533-1000
Sam M Hwang, *Ch Bd*
EMP: 500 EST: 1966
SQ FT: 5,000
SALES (est): 16.38MM
SALES (corp-wide): 16.38MM Privately Held
Web: www.uniservecorp.com
SIC: 7349 Janitorial service, contract basis

(P-15754)
UNIVERSAL SERVICES AMERICA LP
1815 E Wilshire Ave Ste 912 (92705-4646)
PHONE.....................714 923-3700
Mark Olivas, *Brnch Mgr*
EMP: 2733
SALES (corp-wide): 12.86B Privately Held
Web: www.aus.com
SIC: 7349 Janitorial service, contract basis
HQ: Universal Services Of America, Lp
450 Exchange
Irvine CA
866 877-1965

(P-15755)
VARSITY CONTRACTORS INC
24155 Laguna Hills Mall (92653-3667)
PHONE.....................949 586-8283
EMP: 127
SALES (corp-wide): 620.83MM Privately Held
Web: www.kbs-services.com
SIC: 7349 Janitorial service, contract basis
HQ: Varsity Contractors, Inc.
1055 S 3600 W Ste 101
Salt Lake City UT
208 232-8598

(P-15756)
WURMS JANITORIAL SERVICE INC
601 S Milliken Ave (91761-7898)
PHONE.....................951 582-0003
Larry Stewart, *Pr*
Pam Costa, *
EMP: 80 EST: 1986
SALES (est): 2.17MM Privately Held
Web: www.ultrashine.com
SIC: 7349 Janitorial service, contract basis

7352 Medical Equipment Rental

(P-15757)
DIGIRAD IMAGING SOLUTIONS INC
13100 Gregg St Ste A (92064-7150)
PHONE.....................800 947-6134
EMP: 159
SALES (corp-wide): 112.15MM Publicly Held
Web: www.digirad.com
SIC: 7352 Medical equipment rental
HQ: Digirad Imaging Solutions Inc
1048 Industrial Ct Ste E
Poway CA
800 947-6134

7353 Heavy Construction Equipment Rental

(P-15758)
BIGGE GROUP
14511 Industry Cir (90638-5814)
PHONE.....................714 523-4092
EMP: 172
Web: www.bigge.com
SIC: 7353 Cranes and aerial lift equipment, rental or leasing
PA: Bigge Group
10700 Bigge St
San Leandro CA

(P-15759)
BRAGG INVESTMENT COMPANY INC (PA)
Also Called: Bragg Crane & Rigging
6251 N Paramount Blvd (90805-3713)
P.O. Box 727 (90801-0727)
PHONE.....................562 984-2400
TOLL FREE: 800
M Scott Bragg, *Pr*
Mike Roy, *
Marilynn Bragg, *VP*
Dennis Ferguson, *
Kathleen Pool-ferrin, *Sec*
◆ **EMP: 300 EST: 1946**
SQ FT: 50,000
SALES (est): 489.53MM
SALES (corp-wide): 489.53MM Privately Held
Web: www.braggcompanies.com
SIC: 7353 4213 7389 1791 Cranes and aerial lift equipment, rental or leasing; Heavy hauling, nec; Crane and aerial lift service; Structural steel erection

(P-15760)
COUNTY OF ORANGE
Also Called: All Access Rental
1631 E Wilshire Ave (92705-4504)
PHONE.....................714 647-1552
Kevin Aylesworth, *CEO*
EMP: 80
SALES (corp-wide): 5.2B Privately Held
Web: www.ocgov.com
SIC: 7353 5599 Cranes and aerial lift equipment, rental or leasing; Aircraft instruments, equipment or parts
PA: County Of Orange
400 W Civic Center Dr G36
Santa Ana CA
714 834-6200

(P-15761)
GLOBAL RENTAL CO INC
1253 Price Ave (91767-5839)

PHONE.....................909 469-5160
James Dixon, *Brnch Mgr*
EMP: 120
SALES (corp-wide): 1.21B Privately Held
Web: www.altec.com
SIC: 7353 5082 Heavy construction equipment rental; Contractor's materials
HQ: Global Rental Co., Inc.
33 Inverness Center Pkwy # 250
Hoover AL

(P-15762)
HARBOR INDUSTRIAL SVCS CORP
Also Called: Harbor Industrial
211 N Marine Ave (90744-5724)
P.O. Box 1487 (90733-1487)
PHONE.....................310 522-1193
W Michael Hawk, *Pr*
Maria Gray, *
▲ **EMP: 80 EST: 1993**
SALES (est): 10.74MM Privately Held
Web: www.harborindustrial.com
SIC: 7353 Cranes and aerial lift equipment, rental or leasing

(P-15763)
HAWTHORNE MACHINERY CO (PA)
Also Called: Hawthorne Cat
16945 Camino San Bernardo (92127-2499)
PHONE.....................858 674-7000
TOLL FREE: 800
Tee K Ness, *Pr*
David Ness, *
◆ **EMP: 200 EST: 1941**
SQ FT: 130,000
SALES (est): 176.69MM
SALES (corp-wide): 176.69MM Privately Held
Web: www.hawthornecat.com
SIC: 7353 7699 5082 7359 Heavy construction equipment rental; Construction equipment repair; Construction and mining machinery; Equipment rental and leasing, nec

(P-15764)
HAWTHORNE RENT-IT SERVICE (HQ)
Also Called: Caterpillar Authorized Dealer
16945 Camino San Bernardo (92127-2405)
PHONE.....................858 674-7000
Tee K Ness, *CEO*
Bob Price, *
Paul Hawthorne, *
Mike Johnson, *Product Vice President*
Steve Sager, *
EMP: 100 EST: 1974
SQ FT: 130,000
SALES (est): 33.17MM
SALES (corp-wide): 176.69MM Privately Held
Web: www.hawthornecat.com .
SIC: 7353 5084 Heavy construction equipment rental; Industrial machinery and equipment
PA: Hawthorne Machinery Co.
16945 Camino San Bernardo
San Diego CA
858 674-7000

(P-15765)
KINGS OIL TOOLS INC (PA)
2235 Spring St (93446-1404)
PHONE.....................805 238-9311
EMP: 30 EST: 1982
SALES (est): 11.13MM
SALES (corp-wide): 11.13MM Privately Held

Web: www.kingsoiltools.com
SIC: 7353 1389 Oil field equipment, rental or leasing; Oil and gas wells: building, repairing and dismantling

(P-15766)
THE NATIONAL BUS GROUP INC (PA)
Also Called: National Tube & Steel
15319 Chatsworth St (91345-2040)
PHONE.....................818 221-6000
James Mooneyham, *Pr*
◆ **EMP: 85 EST: 1985**
SQ FT: 24,000
SALES (est): 123.15MM
SALES (corp-wide): 123.15MM Privately Held
Web: www.rentnational.com
SIC: 7353 5039 7359 3496 Earth moving equipment, rental or leasing; Wire fence, gates, and accessories; Garage facility and tool rental; Fencing, made from purchased wire

(P-15767)
WESTERN ENERGY SERVICES CORP
3430 Getty St (93308-5248)
PHONE.....................403 984-5916
Alex R N Macausland, *CEO*
Jeffrey K Bowers, *VP*
EMP: 200 EST: 2005
SALES (est): 6.01MM Privately Held
SIC: 7353 Oil well drilling equipment, rental or leasing

7359 Equipment Rental And Leasing, Nec

(P-15768)
AERCAP GLOBAL AVIATION TRUST (HQ)
10250 Constellation Blvd Ste 3400 (90067-6200)
PHONE.....................310 788-1999
Sean Sullivan, *Pr*
Keith Helming, *
EMP: 109 EST: 2014
SALES (est): 2.25MM
SALES (corp-wide): 1.01B Privately Held
Web: www.aercap.com
SIC: 7359 6159 Aircraft rental; Equipment and vehicle finance leasing companies
PA: Aercap Holdings N.V.
Onbekend Nederlands Adres
Onbekend
35316360650

(P-15769)
AFTER-PARTY2 INC (DH)
Also Called: Classic Party Rentals
901 W Hillcrest Blvd (90301-2100)
PHONE.....................310 202-0011
Jeff Black, *Pr*
▲ **EMP: 200 EST: 1996**
SALES (est): 65.61MM
SALES (corp-wide): 10.97B Publicly Held
SIC: 7359 Party supplies rental services
HQ: Apollo Asset Management, Inc.
9 W 57th St Fl 42
New York NY

(P-15770)
AFTER-PARTY6 INC
Also Called: Classic Party Rentals
901 W Hillcrest Blvd (90301-2100)
PHONE.....................310 966-4900
EMP: 130

PRODUCTS & SVCS

SIC: 7359 Party supplies rental services

(P-15771)
AIR LEASE CORPORATION (PA)
2000 Avenue Of The Stars Ste 1000n
(90067-4734)
PHONE.................................310 553-0555
EMP: 82 EST: 2010
SALES (est): 2.32B **Publicly Held**
Web: www.airleasecorp.com
SIC: 7359 7389 Aircraft rental; Financial services

(P-15772)
BRIGHT EVENT RENTALS LLC (PA)
Also Called: Wine Country Party & Events
1640 W 190th St Ste A (90501-1122)
PHONE.................................310 202-0011
Michael Bjornstad, *Managing Member*
▲ EMP: 240 EST: 2013
SALES (est): 49.33MM
SALES (corp-wide): 49.33MM **Privately Held**
Web: www.bright.com
SIC: 7359 Party supplies rental services

(P-15773)
CELTIC LEASING CORP
Also Called: Celtic Commercial Finance
4 Park Plz Ste 300 (92614-8511)
PHONE.................................949 263-3880
EMP: 80
SIC: 7359 Equipment rental and leasing, nec

(P-15774)
CHOURA EVENTS
540 Hawaii Ave (90503-5148)
PHONE.................................310 320-6200
James Ryan Choura, *CEO*
EMP: 80 EST: 2014
SALES (est): 10.57MM **Privately Held**
Web: www.choura.co
SIC: 7359 Party supplies rental services

(P-15775)
CLASSIC PARTY RENTALS INC
Also Called: Classic Party Rentals
901 W Hillcrest Blvd A (90301-2101)
PHONE.................................310 966-4900
▲ EMP: 2500
SIC: 7359 Party supplies rental services

(P-15776)
CLASSIC/PRIME INC
Also Called: Classic Tents
540 Hawaii Ave (90503-5148)
PHONE.................................310 328-5060
EMP: 100
SIC: 7359 Tent and tarpaulin rental

(P-15777)
COMPASS GROUP USA INC
Also Called: Canteen Vending
12640 Knott St (92841-3902)
PHONE.................................714 899-2520
Ron Wanamaker, *VP*
EMP: 125
SALES (corp-wide): 29.97B **Privately Held**
Web: www.canteen.com
SIC: 7359 7699 5962 Vending machine rental
; Vending machine repair; Merchandising machine operators
HQ: Compass Group Usa, Inc.
2400 Yorkmont Rd
Charlotte NC

(P-15778)
DIAMOND ENVIRONMENTAL SVCS LP
Also Called: Diamond Environmental Services
807 E Mission Rd (92069-3002)
PHONE.................................760 744-7191
EMP: 100 EST: 1997
SQ FT: 2,000
SALES (est): 19.45MM **Privately Held**
Web: www.diamondprovides.com
SIC: 7359 Portable toilet rental

(P-15779)
DIRECT CHASSISLINK INC
Also Called: Dcli
7777 Center Ave Ste 325 (92647-9132)
PHONE.................................657 216-5846
Don Peltier, *Mgr*
EMP: 586
SALES (corp-wide): 116.43MM **Privately Held**
Web: www.dcli.com
SIC: 7359 Equipment rental and leasing, nec
PA: Direct Chassislink, Inc.
3525 Whthall Pk Dr Ste 40
Charlotte NC
704 594-3800

(P-15780)
GUZMAN GRADING AND PAVING CORP
14030 Rose Ave (92337-7047)
PHONE.................................909 428-5960
Jesus Guzman, *CEO*
EMP: 95 EST: 2003
SQ FT: 76,000
SALES (est): 4.7MM **Privately Held**
SIC: 7359 1771 1611 Equipment rental and leasing, nec; Blacktop (asphalt) work; Highway and street construction

(P-15781)
HANA FINANCIAL INC (PA)
1000 Wilshire Blvd Ste 2000 (90017-2457)
PHONE.................................213 240-1234
Sunnie S Kim, *CEO*
Young Shim, *
▲ EMP: 85 EST: 1994
SQ FT: 24,000
SALES (est): 13.65MM **Privately Held**
Web: www.hanafinancial.com
SIC: 7359 6153 6159 Equipment rental and leasing, nec; Factoring services; Small business investment companies

(P-15782)
J L FISHER INC
1000 W Isabel St (91506-1404)
PHONE.................................818 846-8366
James L Fisher, *Pr*
Cary Clayton, *
▲ EMP: 60 EST: 1951
SALES (est): 5.28MM **Privately Held**
Web: www.jlfisher.com
SIC: 7359 3861 3663 Equipment rental and leasing, nec; Motion picture apparatus and equipment; Radio and t.v. communications equipment

(P-15783)
L A PARTY RENTS INC
13520 Saticoy St (91402-6428)
PHONE.................................818 989-4300
Gerome Nehus, *Pr*
EMP: 100 EST: 1987
SALES (est): 3.83MM **Privately Held**
Web: www.lapartyrents.com
SIC: 7359 Party supplies rental services

(P-15784)
MAGIC JUMP INC
9165 Glenoaks Blvd (91352-2612)
PHONE.................................818 847-1313
TOLL FREE: 800
Andranik Bagumyan, *Pr*
Sam Bagumyan, *VP*
◆ EMP: 20 EST: 1996
SQ FT: 20,000
SALES (est): 3.43MM **Privately Held**
Web: www.magicjump.com
SIC: 7359 3069 Party supplies rental services; Balloons, advertising and toy: rubber

(P-15785)
MEETING SERVICES INC
Also Called: MSI Production Services
1125 Joshua Way (92081-7840)
PHONE.................................858 348-0100
EMP: 90
Web: www.msiprod.com
SIC: 7359 7629 5049 Audio-visual equipment and supply rental; Electrical equipment repair, high voltage; Theatrical equipment and supplies

(P-15786)
MICROFINANCIAL INCORPORATED
2801 Townsgate Rd (91361-3003)
PHONE.................................805 367-8900
Richard Latour, *CEO*
EMP: 106
SALES (corp-wide): 99.27MM **Privately Held**
Web: www.timepayment.com
SIC: 7359 Business machine and electronic equipment rental services
HQ: Microfinancial Incorporated
200 Summit Dr Ste 100
Burlington MA
781 994-4800

(P-15787)
MICROLEASE INC (DH)
6060 Sepulveda Blvd (91411-2501)
PHONE.................................866 520-0200
Gordon Curwen, *VP*
EMP: 85 EST: 2001
SQ FT: 20,000
SALES (est): 45.48MM
SALES (corp-wide): 254.4MM **Privately Held**
SIC: 7359 Rental store, general
HQ: Electro Rent Uk Limited
Unit 1
Harrow MIDDX
208 420-0200

(P-15788)
MUFG AMERICAS LEASING CORP (DH)
445 S Figueroa St Ste 2700 (90071-1602)
PHONE.................................213 488-3700
Hideya Takaishi, *CEO*
Mark Helman, *General*
Paul Nolan, *
Rory Laughna, *
David A Meehan, *
EMP: 100 EST: 1973
SALES (est): 52.41MM **Privately Held**
Web: www.mufgamericas.com
SIC: 7359 Equipment rental and leasing, nec
HQ: Mufg Americas Holdings Corporation
1251 Ave Of The Americas
New York NY
212 782-6800

(P-15789)
NATIONAL CNSTR RENTALS INC (HQ)
Also Called: National Rent A Fence Co.
15319 Chatsworth St (91345-2040)
PHONE.................................818 221-6000
James R Mooneyham, *Pr*
W Robert Mooneyham, *Executive President*
◆ EMP: 85 EST: 1961
SQ FT: 23,000
SALES (est): 89.73MM
SALES (corp-wide): 123.15MM **Privately Held**
Web: www.rentnational.com
SIC: 7359 Equipment rental and leasing, nec
PA: The National Business Group, Inc.
15319 Chatsworth St
Mission Hills CA
818 221-6000

(P-15790)
NATIONAL TRENCH SAFETY LLC
Also Called: Trench Plate Rental
13217 Laureldale Ave (90242-5140)
PHONE.................................562 602-1642
Dexter Poston, *Brnch Mgr*
EMP: 185
SALES (corp-wide): 104.07MM **Privately Held**
Web: www.ntsafety.com
SIC: 7359 Equipment rental and leasing, nec
PA: National Trench Safety, Llc
260 N Sam Houston Pkwy E
Houston TX
832 200-0988

(P-15791)
P J J ENTERPRISES INC
1250 Delevan Dr (92102-2437)
PHONE.................................619 232-6136
John Lenore, *Pr*
Roger Carey, *
Dorothy Lenore, *
EMP: 150 EST: 1966
SQ FT: 20,000
SALES (est): 904.01K
SALES (corp-wide): 45.4MM **Privately Held**
SIC: 7359 Rental store, general
PA: Lenore John & Co
1250 Delevan Dr
San Diego CA
619 232-6136

(P-15792)
PANAVISION INC (PA)
Also Called: Panavision Group
6101 Variel Ave (91367-3722)
PHONE.................................818 316-1000
▲ EMP: 550 EST: 1990
SQ FT: 150,000
SALES (est): 160.24MM **Privately Held**
Web: www.panavision.com
SIC: 7359 3861 3648 5063 Equipment rental and leasing, nec; Cameras and related equipment; Stage lighting equipment; Lighting fixtures

(P-15793)
PORTER HIRE LTD
Also Called: Heavy Equipment Rentals
13013 Temescal Canyon Rd (92883-8454)
PHONE.................................951 674-9999
◆ EMP: 46 EST: 1999
SALES (est): 16.95MM **Privately Held**

SIC: **7359** 5082 3523 Equipment rental and leasing, nec; Construction and mining machinery; Farm machinery and equipment
HQ: Porter Hire Limited
1 Mark Porter Way, Burbush
Hamilton WKO

(P-15794)
PSAV HOLDINGS LLC (PA)
111 W Ocean Blvd Ste 1110 (90802-4688)
PHONE...................562 366-0138
J Michael Mcilwain, *CEO*
Ben Erwin, *
Michael Leone, *CCO**
Cathie Kozik, *CIO**
Charlie Young, *Chief Human Resource Officer**
EMP: 122 **EST:** 2013
SALES (est): 460.08MM
SALES (corp-wide): 460.08MM **Privately Held**
Web: www.encoreglobal.com
SIC: **7359** Audio-visual equipment and supply rental

(P-15795)
RAPHAELS PARTY RENTALS INC (PA)
8606 Miramar Rd (92126-4326)
PHONE...................858 444-1692
Raphael Silverman, *Pr*
Phillip Silverman, *
Kitty Silverman, *
▲ **EMP:** 175 **EST:** 1981
SQ FT: 60,000
SALES (est): 13.6MM
SALES (corp-wide): 13.6MM **Privately Held**
Web: www.raphaels.com
SIC: **7359** Party supplies rental services

(P-15796)
RENTACENTER
183 Niblick Rd (93446-4805)
PHONE...................805 769-9030
EMP: 86 **EST:** 2015
SALES (est): 64.69K **Privately Held**
Web: www.rentacenter.com
SIC: **7359** Appliance rental

(P-15797)
RSI LEASING LLC
1314 E Puente Ave (91790-1361)
PHONE...................626 966-6129
Ronadl Chaplen, *Prin*
EMP: 95 **EST:** 2010
SALES (est): 207.25K
SALES (corp-wide): 1B **Publicly Held**
SIC: **7359** Equipment rental and leasing, nec
PA: Sotera Health Company
9100 S Hills Blvd Ste 300
Broadview Heights OH
440 262-1410

(P-15798)
SHOWROOM INTERIORS LLC
Also Called: Vesta Luxury Home Staging
8905 Rex Rd (90660-3799)
PHONE...................323 348-1551
Julianne Buckner, *Managing Member*
EMP: 105 **EST:** 2016
SALES (est): 5MM
SALES (corp-wide): 5MM **Privately Held**
SIC: **7359** Furniture rental
PA: Showroom, Inc
8905 Rex Rd
Pico Rivera CA
323 348-1551

(P-15799)
SRG HOLDINGS LLC (HQ)
500 Stevens Ave Ste 100 (92075-2055)
PHONE...................858 792-9300
J Wickliffe Peterson, *CFO*
Michael Grust, *Pr*
EMP: 411 **EST:** 1998
SQ FT: 12,300
SALES (est): 27.34MM
SALES (corp-wide): 189.7MM **Privately Held**
SIC: **7359** Business machine and electronic equipment rental services
PA: Senior Resource Group, Llc
500 Stevens Ave Ste 100
Solana Beach CA
858 792-9300

(P-15800)
SUNN AMERICA INC
Also Called: Classe Party Rentals
10280 Indiana Ct (91730-5332)
PHONE...................909 944-5756
Vishnu Reddy, *Pr*
Saritha Reddy, *
Vishnu Reddy, *CEO*
Ronald Francis, *
EMP: 30 **EST:** 1999
SALES (est): 2.15MM **Privately Held**
Web: www.classeparty.com
SIC: **7359** 7299 3999 Party supplies rental services; Party planning service; Stage hardware and equipment, except lighting

(P-15801)
TOWN & CNTRY EVENT RENTALS INC
1 N Calle Cesar Chavez (93103-3662)
PHONE...................805 770-5729
EMP: 398
SALES (corp-wide): 64.1MM **Privately Held**
Web: www.tacer.biz
SIC: **7359** Party supplies rental services
PA: Town & Country Event Rentals, Inc.
7725 Airport Bus Pkwy
Van Nuys CA
818 908-4211

(P-15802)
TOWN & CNTRY EVENT RENTALS INC (PA)
Also Called: Tacer
7725 Airport Business Pkwy (91406)
PHONE...................818 908-4211
Richard Loguercio, *CEO*
Chris Mackey, *
Christopher Keesler, *
Wayne Tay, *
▲ **EMP:** 400 **EST:** 1998
SQ FT: 1,100
SALES (est): 64.1MM
SALES (corp-wide): 64.1MM **Privately Held**
Web: www.tacer.biz
SIC: **7359** Party supplies rental services

(P-15803)
TRAFFIC CONTROL SERVICE INC
Also Called: Allied Trench Shoring Service
4695 Macarthur Ct Ste 1100 (92660-1866)
TOLL FREE: 800
EMP: 207
SIC: **7359** 5099 1799 Sign rental; Signs, except electric; Flag pole erection

(P-15804)
VARCO DE MEXICO HOLDINGS INC
Also Called: Varco Systems
743 N Eckhoff St (92868-1005)
PHONE...................714 978-1900
Richard Kertson, *VP Fin*
▲ **EMP:** 42 **EST:** 1983
SALES (est): 9.41MM
SALES (corp-wide): 7.24B **Publicly Held**
SIC: **7359** 3533 Equipment rental and leasing, nec; Oil and gas field machinery
PA: Nov Inc.
10353 Richmond Ave
Houston TX
346 223-3000

(P-15805)
VCI EVENT TECHNOLOGY INC
Also Called: Videocam
25172 Arctic Ocean Dr Ste 102 (92630-8851)
PHONE...................714 772-2002
TOLL FREE: 888
Kirk Rhinehart, *CEO*
Evan H Goldschlag, *
Kirk Rhinehart, *VP*
▲ **EMP:** 166 **EST:** 1993
SALES (est): 18.39MM **Privately Held**
Web: www.vcievents.com
SIC: **7359** Audio-visual equipment and supply rental

(P-15806)
WESTERN OILFIELDS SUPPLY CO (PA)
Also Called: Rain For Rent
3404 State Rd (93308-4538)
P.O. Box 2248 (93303-2248)
PHONE...................661 399-9124
Robert Lake, *CEO*
Maston Cunningham, *CFO*
▲ **EMP:** 150 **EST:** 1934
SQ FT: 57,000
SALES (est): 250.88MM
SALES (corp-wide): 250.88MM **Privately Held**
Web: www.rainforrent.com
SIC: **7359** 3523 5083 Equipment rental and leasing, nec; Farm machinery and equipment; Irrigation equipment

7361 Employment Agencies

(P-15807)
24-HOUR MED STAFFING SVCS LLC
1370 Valley Vista Dr Ste 280 (91765-3911)
PHONE...................909 895-8960
EMP: 110 **EST:** 2000
SALES (est): 8.71MM **Privately Held**
Web: www.24-hrmed.com
SIC: **7361** Employment agencies

(P-15808)
ACCESS NURSES INC
5935 Cornerstone Ct W Ste 300 (92121-3737)
PHONE...................858 458-4400
Alan Braynin, *CEO*
EMP: 91 **EST:** 2001
SQ FT: 20,000
SALES (est): 7.99MM **Privately Held**
Web: www.accessnurses.com
SIC: **7361** Nurses' registry

(P-15809)
ACT 1 GROUP INC (PA)
Also Called: Agileone
1999 W 190th St (90504-6202)
P.O. Box 2886 (90509-2886)
PHONE...................310 750-3400
Janice B Howroyd, *CEO*
Bernard Howroyd, *
Michael Hoyal, *
Carlton Bryant, *
Tina B Robinson, *
EMP: 90 **EST:** 1978
SQ FT: 18,026
SALES (est): 508.88MM **Privately Held**
Web: www.actonegroup.com
SIC: **7361** 8741 Employment agencies; Administrative management

(P-15810)
ADECCO EMPLOYMENT SERVICES
25301 Cabot Rd Ste 214 (92653-5505)
PHONE...................949 586-2342
Tina Robinson, *Brnch Mgr*
EMP: 150
Web: www.adeccona.com
SIC: **7361** Employment agencies
HQ: Adecco Employment Services, Inc
4800 Deerwood Campus Pkwy # 800
Jacksonville FL
631 844-7100

(P-15811)
ADVANCED MED PRSONNEL SVCS INC
12400 High Bluff Dr Ste 100 (92130-3077)
PHONE...................386 756-4395
Jennfier Fuicelli, *CEO*
EMP: 100 **EST:** 1989
SALES (est): 9.01MM
SALES (corp-wide): 5.24B **Publicly Held**
Web: www.amnhealthcare.com
SIC: **7361** 7363 Nurses' registry; Medical help service
HQ: Amn Healthcare, Inc.
12400 High Bluff Dr # 100
San Diego CA

(P-15812)
AMN HEALTHCARE INC
Also Called: American Mobile Healthcare
12235 El Camino Real Ste 200 (92130)
PHONE...................800 282-0300
EMP: 92 **EST:** 2017
SALES (est): 2MM **Privately Held**
Web: www.amnhealthcare.com
SIC: **7361** Employment agencies

(P-15813)
APPLEONE INC
Also Called: Appleone Employment Services
325 W Broadway (91204-1301)
PHONE...................818 240-8688
Marie Rounsavell, *Mgr*
EMP: 120
Web: www.appleone.com
SIC: **7361** Labor contractors (employment agency)
HQ: Appleone, Inc.
327 W Broadway
Glendale CA
818 240-8688

(P-15814)
APPLEONE INC (HQ)
Also Called: Appleone Employment Services
327 W Broadway (91204-1301)
PHONE...................818 240-8688
Janice Bryant Howroyd, *CEO*

PRODUCTS & SVCS

Bernard Howroyd, *
Michael Hoyal, *
Brett Howroyd, *
◆ EMP: 175 EST: 1964
SQ FT: 27,000
SALES (est): 145.38MM Privately Held
Web: www.appleone.com
SIC: 7361 Labor contractors (employment agency)
PA: The Act 1 Group Inc
1999 W 190th St
Torrance CA

(P-15815)
ASSISTED HOME RECOVERY INC (PA)
Also Called: Assisted Home Care
8550 Balboa Blvd Lbby (91325-5808)
PHONE..................................818 894-8117
Elaine S Donley, Adm/Dir
Bill Donley, *
EMP: 110 EST: 1979
SQ FT: 4,000
SALES (est): 11.42MM
SALES (corp-wide): 11.42MM Privately Held
SIC: 7361 Nurses' registry

(P-15816)
ATTORNEY NETWORK SERVICES INC
Also Called: Attorney Network Services
725 S Figueroa St Ste 3065 (90017-5524)
PHONE..................................213 430-0440
Nick Karapetian, Pr
Gavin Rubin, VP
EMP: 84 EST: 1997
SQ FT: 4,000
SALES (est): 2.39MM Privately Held
Web: www.karapetianrubin.com
SIC: 7361 Executive placement

(P-15817)
B2 SERVICES LLC
Also Called: At Work
17291 Irvine Blvd Ste 258 (92780-2949)
PHONE..................................714 363-3481
Lori Brower, Pr
EMP: 100 EST: 2017
SALES (est): 2.25MM Privately Held
Web: www.atwork.com
SIC: 7361 Employment agencies

(P-15818)
BARONHR LLC
13085 Central Ave Ste 4 (91710-4184)
PHONE..................................909 517-3800
EMP: 92
SALES (corp-wide): 49.76MM Privately Held
Web: www.baronhr.com
SIC: 7361 Employment agencies
PA: Baronhr, Llc
8101 E Kaiser Blvd
Anaheim CA
714 860-7800

(P-15819)
BARRETT BUSINESS SERVICES INC
862 E Hospitality Ln (92408-3530)
PHONE..................................909 890-3633
EMP: 2916
SALES (corp-wide): 1.05B Publicly Held
Web: www.bbsi.com
SIC: 7361 Employment agencies
PA: Barrett Business Services Inc
8100 Ne Parkway Dr # 200
Vancouver WA
360 828-0700

(P-15820)
BARRETT BUSINESS SERVICES INC
Also Called: B B S I
8880 Rio San Diego Dr Ste 800 (92108-1634)
PHONE..................................858 314-1100
Milan Todorovic, Brnch Mgr
EMP: 2916
SALES (corp-wide): 1.05B Publicly Held
Web: www.bbsi.com
SIC: 7361 Employment agencies
PA: Barrett Business Services Inc
8100 Ne Parkway Dr # 200
Vancouver WA
360 828-0700

(P-15821)
BARRETT BUSINESS SERVICES INC
Also Called: Bbsi Camarillo
815 Camarillo Springs Rd Ste C (93012-9457)
PHONE..................................805 987-0331
Dee Levy, Brnch Mgr
EMP: 4374
SALES (corp-wide): 1.05B Publicly Held
Web: www.bbsi.com
SIC: 7361 8742 Employment agencies; Human resource consulting services
PA: Barrett Business Services Inc
8100 Ne Parkway Dr # 200
Vancouver WA
360 828-0700

(P-15822)
BOILING POINT REST S CA INC
13668 Valley Blvd Unit C2 (91746-2572)
PHONE..................................626 551-5181
Chi How Chou, Ch
Michael Lin, *
EMP: 300 EST: 2012
SALES (est): 21.31MM Privately Held
SIC: 7361 5812 Employment agencies; Chinese restaurant

(P-15823)
BUTLER AMERICA HOLDINGS INC
12625 Frederick St Ste E2 (92553-5253)
PHONE..................................951 563-0020
EMP: 293
SALES (corp-wide): 79.52MM Privately Held
SIC: 7361 Employment agencies
PA: Butler America Holdings, Inc.
3820 State St Ste B
Santa Barbara CA
805 880-1978

(P-15824)
BUTLER AMERICA HOLDINGS INC
8647 Haven Ave Ste 100 (91730-4887)
PHONE..................................909 417-3660
Cecilia La Tour, Brnch Mgr
EMP: 293
SALES (corp-wide): 79.52MM Privately Held
SIC: 7361 Employment agencies
PA: Butler America Holdings, Inc.
3820 State St Ste B
Santa Barbara CA
805 880-1978

(P-15825)
BUTLER INTERNATIONAL INC (PA)

3820 State St Ste A (93105-3182)
PHONE..................................805 882-2200
Edward M Kopko, Ch Bd
Edward M Kopko, Ch Bd
James J Beckley, *
Mark Koscinski, *
EMP: 200 EST: 1985
SALES (est): 242.14MM
SALES (corp-wide): 242.14MM Privately Held
Web: www.butleritresources.com
SIC: 7361 8742 Employment agencies; Management consulting services

(P-15826)
CAREER GROUP INC (PA)
Also Called: Fourthfloor Fashion Talent
10100 Santa Monica Blvd Ste 900 (90067-4002)
PHONE..................................310 277-8188
Michael B Levine, CEO
Susan Levine, *
Scott H Pick, *
▲ EMP: 2100 EST: 1980
SQ FT: 11,986
SALES (est): 55.71MM
SALES (corp-wide): 55.71MM Privately Held
Web: www.careergroupcompanies.com
SIC: 7361 Executive placement

(P-15827)
CAREER STRATEGIES TMPRY INC
575 Anton Blvd Ste 630 (92626-1948)
PHONE..................................714 824-6840
Mat Mcgowen, Mgr
EMP: 104
Web: www.csi4jobs.com
SIC: 7361 Executive placement
PA: Career Strategies Temporary, Inc.
1 Chisholm Trail Rd # 210
Round Rock TX

(P-15828)
CAREER STRATEGIES TMPRY INC
78060 Calle Estado (92253-2960)
PHONE..................................760 564-5959
EMP: 104
Web: www.csi4jobs.com
SIC: 7361 Executive placement
PA: Career Strategies Temporary, Inc.
1 Chisholm Trail Rd # 210
Round Rock TX

(P-15829)
CAREER STRATEGIES TMPRY INC
21031 Ventura Blvd Ste 1005 (91364-2255)
PHONE..................................818 883-0440
EMP: 104
Web: www.csi4jobs.com
SIC: 7361 Placement agencies
PA: Career Strategies Temporary, Inc.
1 Chisholm Trail Rd # 210
Round Rock TX

(P-15830)
CAREER STRATEGIES TMPRY INC
9267 Haven Ave Ste 225 (91730-5458)
PHONE..................................909 230-4504
Darin Rado, Prin
EMP: 104
Web: www.csi4jobs.com
SIC: 7361 Placement agencies
PA: Career Strategies Temporary, Inc.
1 Chisholm Trail Rd # 210

Round Rock TX

(P-15831)
CARTER ASTON INC
9635 Granite Ridge Dr (92123-2678)
PHONE..................................858 609-2062
EMP: 112
SALES (corp-wide): 15.88B Privately Held
Web: www.astoncarter.com
SIC: 7361 Executive placement
HQ: Aston Carter, Inc.
7317 Parkway Dr
Hanover MD

(P-15832)
CENTURY HLTH STAFFING SVCS INC
1701 Westwind Dr Ste 101 (93301-3045)
PHONE..................................661 322-0606
Richard Ochieng, Pr
Lissa Harris-soto, VP
EMP: 213 EST: 2006
SQ FT: 2,000
SALES (est): 4.56MM Privately Held
Web: www.centurynurse.com
SIC: 7361 Nurses' registry

(P-15833)
CONTINUING LF COMMUNITIES LLC (PA)
Also Called: La Costa Glen
1940 Levante St (92009-5174)
PHONE..................................760 704-6400
Richard D Aschenbrenner, Managing Member
Richard D Aschenbrenner, Mgr
E Justin Wilson Iii, CEO
Warren E Spieker Junior, Mgr
EMP: 97 EST: 1991
SALES (est): 47.09MM
SALES (corp-wide): 47.09MM Privately Held
Web: www.continuinglife.com
SIC: 7361 Employment agencies

(P-15834)
CREATIVE SOLUTIONS SVCS LLC
Also Called: Higher Talent
1745 N Vista St (90046-2234)
PHONE..................................646 495-1558
Ashish Kaushal, Managing Member
EMP: 212 EST: 2016
SALES (est): 7.67MM Privately Held
Web: www.css-llc.net
SIC: 7361 Executive placement

(P-15835)
CULVER PERSONNEL AGENCIES INC
Also Called: Culver Personnel Services
445 Marine View Ave Ste 101 (92014-3969)
P.O. Box 910569 (92191-0569)
PHONE..................................888 600-5733
Timothy J Culver, Pr
John Weaver, *
EMP: 120 EST: 1979
SQ FT: 7,500
SALES (est): 4.9MM Privately Held
SIC: 7361 Executive placement

(P-15836)
CYBERCODERS INC
Also Called: Cyberscientific
6591 Irvine Center Dr Ste 200 (92618-2118)
PHONE..................................949 885-5151
Heidi Golledge, CEO

▲ = Import ▼ = Export
◆ = Import/Export

Matt Miller, *
EMP: 140 **EST:** 1999
SALES (est): 41.06MM
SALES (corp-wide): 4.58B **Publicly Held**
Web: www.cybercoders.com
SIC: 7361 Executive placement
PA: Asgn Incorporated
  4400 Cox Rd Ste 110
  Glen Allen VA
  888 482-8068

(P-15837)
DIAMOND PEO LLC
27442 Calle Arroyo Ste A (92675-6753)
PHONE.............................714 728-5186
EMP: 180 **EST:** 2016
SALES (est): 9.1MM **Privately Held**
Web: www.diamondpeo.com
SIC: 7361 Employment agencies

(P-15838)
DIVERSITY BUS SOLUTIONS INC
3532 Old Archibald Ranch Rd
(91761-9160)
PHONE.............................909 395-0243
Sandy Tribby, *CEO*
EMP: 200 **EST:** 2011
SALES (est): 4.93MM **Privately Held**
Web: www.dbsinc.org
SIC: 7361 Employment agencies

(P-15839)
E Z STAFFING INC (PA)
200 N Maryland Ave Ste 303 (91206-4276)
PHONE.............................818 845-2500
Abraham F Abirafeh, *Pr*
EMP: 298 **EST:** 1994
SALES (est): 9.99MM **Privately Held**
Web: www.ezstaffing.com
SIC: 7361 Nurses' registry

(P-15840)
EASTERN STAFFING LLC
Also Called: Select Staffing
301 Mentor Dr # 210 (93111-3339)
PHONE.............................805 882-2200
Stephen Sorensen, *Managing Member*
EMP: 542 **EST:** 2004
SALES (est): 1.82MM
SALES (corp-wide): 242.14MM **Privately Held**
Web: www.select.com
SIC: 7361 Employment agencies
PA: Butler International, Inc.
  3820 State St Ste A
  Santa Barbara CA
  805 882-2200

(P-15841)
EMPLOYNET INC
123 E 9th St Ste 103 (91786-6033)
PHONE.............................909 458-0961
EMP: 1327
SALES (corp-wide): 104.23MM **Privately Held**
Web: www.employnet.com
SIC: 7361 Employment agencies
PA: Employnet, Inc.
  2555 Garden Rd Ste H
  Monterey CA
  866 527-4473

(P-15842)
EPLICA INC
17785 Center Court Dr N (90703-8573)
PHONE.............................562 977-4300
Jade Jenkins, *Brnch Mgr*
EMP: 117
SALES (corp-wide): 139MM **Privately Held**

Web: www.eplicaservices.com
SIC: 7361 Employment agencies
PA: Eplica, Inc.
  2385 Northside Dr Ste 250
  San Diego CA
  619 260-2000

(P-15843)
EPLICA CORPORATE SERVICES INC
Also Called: Eastridge Workforce Solutions
2385 Northside Dr Ste 250 (92108-2716)
PHONE.............................619 282-1400
Seth Stein, *CEO*
EMP: 1506 **EST:** 2010
SALES (est): 3.9MM
SALES (corp-wide): 139MM **Privately Held**
SIC: 7361 Employment agencies
PA: Eplica, Inc.
  2385 Northside Dr Ste 250
  San Diego CA
  619 260-2000

(P-15844)
ESPARZA ENTERPRISES INC
51335 Cesar Chavez St Ste 112
(92236-1528)
PHONE.............................760 398-0349
Manuel Padilla, *Mgr*
EMP: 792
SALES (corp-wide): 135MM **Privately Held**
Web: www.esparzainc.com
SIC: 7361 Labor contractors (employment agency)
PA: Esparza Enterprises, Inc.
  3851 Fruitvale Ave
  Bakersfield CA
  661 831-0002

(P-15845)
ESPARZA ENTERPRISES INC
222 S Union Ave (93307-3325)
PHONE.............................661 631-0347
EMP: 792
SALES (corp-wide): 135MM **Privately Held**
Web: www.esparzainc.com
SIC: 7361 Labor contractors (employment agency)
PA: Esparza Enterprises, Inc.
  3851 Fruitvale Ave
  Bakersfield CA
  661 831-0002

(P-15846)
EXECUTIVE PERSONNEL SERVICES
1526 Brookhollow Dr Ste 83 (92705-5421)
PHONE.............................714 310-9506
Mario Mendoza, *Pr*
Alinne Espinoza, *
EMP: 300 **EST:** 2013
SALES (est): 6.68MM **Privately Held**
SIC: 7361 Executive placement

(P-15847)
GARICH INC (PA)
Also Called: The Tristaff Group
6050 Santo Rd Ste 200 (92124-1194)
PHONE.............................858 453-1331
Gary O Van Eik, *Pr*
Richard N Papike, *
EMP: 295 **EST:** 1971
SALES (est): 23.07MM
SALES (corp-wide): 23.07MM **Privately Held**
Web: www.tristaff.com

SIC: 7361 8742 Executive placement; Management consulting services

(P-15848)
GARICH INC
Also Called: Tristaff Group
504 E Alvarado St Ste 201 (92028-2364)
PHONE.............................951 302-4750
EMP: 365
SALES (corp-wide): 23.07MM **Privately Held**
Web: www.tristaff.com
SIC: 7361 Employment agencies
PA: Garich, Inc.
  6050 Santo Rd Ste 200
  San Diego CA
  858 453-1331

(P-15849)
GO-STAFF INC
9878 Complex Dr (92054)
PHONE.............................760 730-8520
EMP: 1234
SALES (corp-wide): 27.11MM **Privately Held**
Web: www.go-staff.com
SIC: 7361 Executive placement
PA: Go-Staff, Inc.
  8798 Complex Dr
  San Diego CA
  858 292-8562

(P-15850)
GO-STAFF INC
240 W Lincoln Ave (92805-2903)
PHONE.............................657 242-9350
EMP: 1234
SALES (corp-wide): 27.11MM **Privately Held**
Web: www.go-staff.com
SIC: 7361 Executive placement
PA: Go-Staff, Inc.
  8798 Complex Dr
  San Diego CA
  858 292-8562

(P-15851)
HRN SERVICES INC
520 N Brand Blvd Ste 200 (91203-4734)
PHONE.............................323 951-1450
EMP: 95
Web: www.hrnservices.com
SIC: 7361 Nurses' registry

(P-15852)
HUNTINGTON BEACH UNION HIGH
7180 Yorktown Ave (92648-2680)
P.O. Box 787 (92648-0787)
PHONE.............................714 478-7684
EMP: 103
SALES (corp-wide): 301.2MM **Privately Held**
Web: www.hbuhsd.edu
SIC: 7361 Placement agencies
PA: Huntington Beach Union High School District
  5832 Bolsa Ave
  Huntington Beach CA
  714 903-7000

(P-15853)
IBFTECH INC
Also Called: Image Business Forms
343 Main St (90245-3814)
PHONE.............................424 217-8010
John Koch, *Pr*
EMP: 100 **EST:** 1979
SQ FT: 4,000
SALES (est): 5.6MM **Privately Held**

Web: www.chiptonross.com
SIC: 7361 Executive placement

(P-15854)
INNOVATIVE PLACEMENTS INC
Also Called: Ipi Travel
12400 High Bluff Dr Ste 100 (92130-3077)
PHONE.............................800 322-9796
Letha Engelman, *Pr*
Retha Clark, *
John Engelman, *
EMP: 150 **EST:** 1999
SALES (est): 5.87MM **Privately Held**
SIC: 7361 Placement agencies

(P-15855)
INTEGRATED ASSOCIATES INC
4010 Morena Blvd Ste 222 (92117-4547)
P.O. Box 420818 (92142-0818)
PHONE.............................858 412-6189
Anthony Moser, *Prin*
Ethan Gillespie, *Stockholder*
EMP: 231 **EST:** 2012
SALES (est): 4.8MM **Privately Held**
Web: www.integratedassociatesinc.com
SIC: 7361 8748 Executive placement; Business consulting, nec

(P-15856)
JT RESOURCES INC
26372 Ruether Ave (91350-2990)
PHONE.............................661 367-6827
Darren Jackson, *Prin*
EMP: 110 **EST:** 2015
SALES (est): 9MM **Privately Held**
Web: www.jtresources.com
SIC: 7361 Labor contractors (employment agency)

(P-15857)
JWILLIAMS STAFFING INC
18022 Cowan Ste 105 (92614-6864)
PHONE.............................949 250-1923
EMP: 171 **EST:** 2019
SALES (est): 5.56MM **Privately Held**
Web: www.jwilliamsstaffing.com
SIC: 7361 Employment agencies

(P-15858)
KIMCO STAFFING SERVICES INC
Also Called: Kimco Staffing Solutions
1770 Iowa Ave Ste 160 (92507-7400)
P.O. Box 25190 (92799-5190)
PHONE.............................951 686-3800
EMP: 1039
SALES (corp-wide): 96.64MM **Privately Held**
Web: www.kimco.com
SIC: 7361 Employment agencies
PA: Kimco Staffing Services, Inc.
  17872 Cowan
  Irvine CA
  949 331-1199

(P-15859)
KIMCO STAFFING SERVICES INC
Also Called: Kimco Services
4295 Jurupa St Ste 107 (91761-1429)
PHONE.............................909 390-9881
Pammy Burton, *Mgr*
EMP: 1039
SALES (corp-wide): 96.64MM **Privately Held**
Web: www.kimco.com
SIC: 7361 Labor contractors (employment agency)
PA: Kimco Staffing Services, Inc.
  17872 Cowan

PRODUCTS & SVCS

Irvine CA
949 331-1199

(P-15860)
KIMCO STAFFING SERVICES
INC
3415 S Sepulveda Blvd Ste 1100
(90034-7090)
PHONE..............................310 622-1616
EMP: 520
SALES (corp-wide): 96.64MM **Privately
Held**
Web: www.kimco.com
SIC: 7361 Placement agencies
PA: Kimco Staffing Services, Inc.
17872 Cowan
Irvine CA
949 331-1199

(P-15861)
KINETICOM INC (PA)
333 H St (91910-5561)
PHONE..............................619 330-3100
Michael Wager, *CEO*
William Coyman, *
Casey Marquand, *
Blair Bode, *
Michael Steadman, *
EMP: 80 **EST:** 1999
SALES (est): 25.83MM
SALES (corp-wide): 25.83MM **Privately
Held**
Web: www.kineticom.com
SIC: 7361 Executive placement

(P-15862)
KORE1 LLC
530 Technology Dr Ste 150 (92618-1368)
PHONE..............................949 706-6990
Steven Quarles, *Managing Member*
EMP: 153 **EST:** 2017
SALES (est): 35.75MM **Privately Held**
Web: www.kore1.com
SIC: 7361 Executive placement

(P-15863)
KORN FERRY (PA)
Also Called: Korn Ferry
1900 Avenue Of The Stars Ste 1500
(90067-4507)
PHONE..............................310 552-1834
Gary D Burnison, *Pr*
Robert P Rozek, *CCO*
EMP: 209 **EST:** 1969
SALES (est): 2.86B
SALES (corp-wide): 2.86B **Publicly Held**
Web: www.kornferry.com
SIC: 7361 8742 Employment agencies;
Management consulting services

(P-15864)
L&T STAFFING INC
Also Called: Staffing Solutions
2122 W Whittier Blvd (90640-4013)
PHONE..............................323 727-9056
Fortino Rivera, *Brnch Mgr*
EMP: 313
SALES (corp-wide): 17.43MM **Privately
Held**
Web: www.staffingsolutions.us
SIC: 7361 Employment agencies
PA: L&T Staffing, Inc.
950 W 17th St Ste E
Santa Ana CA
714 558-1821

(P-15865)
LOAN ADMINISTRATION
NETWRK INC

Also Called: Lani
2082 Business Center Dr Ste 250 (92612)
PHONE..............................949 752-5246
Charlene Nichols, *Pr*
EMP: 100 **EST:** 1992
SALES (est): 5.76MM **Privately Held**
Web: www.lani.com
SIC: 7361 8742 Employment agencies;
Financial consultant

(P-15866)
MCM HARVESTERS INC
1585 Lirio Ave (93004-3227)
P.O. Box 4731 (93007-0731)
PHONE..............................805 659-6833
EMP: 300
SQ FT: 4,000
SALES (est): 11.48MM **Privately Held**
SIC: 7361 Labor contractors (employment
agency)

(P-15867)
MEDISCAN DIAGNOSTIC SVCS
LLC
Also Called: Mediscan Staffing Services
21050 Califa St Ste 100 (91367-5103)
PHONE..............................818 758-4224
Val Serebryany, *Pr*
EMP: 100 **EST:** 1995
SALES (est): 19.69MM
SALES (corp-wide): 2.81B **Publicly Held**
Web: www.crosscountry.com
SIC: 7361 Employment agencies
HQ: Mediscan Nursing Staffing, Llc
21050 Califa St Ste 100
Woodland Hills CA
818 758-8680

(P-15868)
MERRITT HAWKINS & ASSOC
LLC (HQ)
12400 High Bluff Dr Ste 100 (92130-3077)
PHONE..............................858 792-0711
Susan Salka Fka Nowakowski, *CEO*
Brian Scott, *
Denise Jackson, *
John Dillon, *
Maria Creps, *
EMP: 120 **EST:** 1987
SQ FT: 96,000
SALES (est): 23.57MM
SALES (corp-wide): 5.24B **Publicly Held**
Web: www.merritthawkins.com
SIC: 7361 Executive placement
PA: Amn Healthcare Services, Inc.
2999 Olympus Blvd Ste 500
Coppell TX
866 871-8519

(P-15869)
NURSECHOICE
12400 High Bluff Dr (92130-3077)
PHONE..............................866 557-6050
EMP: 94 **EST:** 2019
SALES (est): 964.34K **Privately Held**
Web: www.nursechoice.com
SIC: 7361 Employment agencies

(P-15870)
NURSEFINDERS INC
Also Called: Nursefinders
5120 W Goldleaf Cir Ste 100 (90056-1292)
PHONE..............................925 660-1153
EMP: 82
SALES (corp-wide): 995.64K **Privately
Held**
Web: www.nursefinders.com
SIC: 7361 Employment agencies
PA: Nursefinders, Inc.
12400 High Bluff Dr

San Diego CA
800 445-0459

(P-15871)
NURSEFINDERS LLC
Also Called: Nursefinders
1832 Commercenter Cir B (92408-3430)
PHONE..............................909 890-2286
TOLL FREE: 877
FAX: 909 890-2346
EMP: 150
SALES (corp-wide): 1.9B **Publicly Held**
SIC: 7361 7363 Employment agencies;
Temporary help service
HQ: Nursefinders, Llc
12400 High Bluff Dr
San Diego CA
858 314-7427

(P-15872)
NURSEFINDERS LLC (HQ)
Also Called: Nursefinders
12400 High Bluff Dr (92130-3077)
P.O. Box 919024 (92191-9024)
PHONE..............................858 314-7427
Susan Salka, *CEO*
Ralph S Henderson, *Pr*
Denise L Jackson, *Sr VP*
Chad W, *Reg Dir*
Meredith M, *Brnch Mgr*
EMP: 110 **EST:** 1975
SQ FT: 22,000
SALES (est): 91.25MM
SALES (corp-wide): 5.24B **Publicly Held**
Web: www.nursefinders.com
SIC: 7361 8082 7363 8049 Placement
agencies; Home health care services; Help
supply services; Nurses, registered and
practical
PA: Amn Healthcare Services, Inc.
2999 Olympus Blvd Ste 500
Coppell TX
866 871-8519

(P-15873)
OFFICEWORKS INC
11801 Pierce St Fl 2 (92505-4400)
PHONE..............................951 784-2534
EMP: 85
SALES (corp-wide): 22.84MM **Privately
Held**
Web: www.officeworksrx.com
SIC: 7361 Employment agencies
PA: Officeworks, Inc.
3200 E Guasti Rd Ste 100
Ontario CA
909 606-4100

(P-15874)
OS4LABOR LLC
120 N Fairway Ln Ste A (91791-1729)
PHONE..............................626 838-6745
EMP: 117 **EST:** 2008
SALES (est): 9.68MM **Privately Held**
Web: www.os4labor.com
SIC: 7361 Employment agencies

(P-15875)
OSI STAFFING INC
10913 La Reina Ave Ste B (90241-3654)
PHONE..............................562 261-5753
Jose Vazquez, *CEO*
Sid Dakoria, *
EMP: 100 **EST:** 2018
SALES (est): 4MM **Privately Held**
Web: www.osistaff.net
SIC: 7361 Placement agencies

(P-15876)
PARTNERS PRSNNEL - MGT
SVCS LL
Also Called: Nexem Staffing
3820 State St Ste B (93105-3182)
PHONE..............................805 689-8191
EMP: 16932 **EST:** 2017
SALES (est): 184.95MM
SALES (corp-wide): 184.95MM **Privately
Held**
Web: www.partnerspersonnel.com
SIC: 7361 Employment agencies
PA: Staffing Partners Holdings Inc.
3820 State St Ste B
Santa Barbara CA
805 880-1900

(P-15877)
PARTNERSHIP STAFFING SVCS
INC
Also Called: Partnership Staffing Solutions
19431 Soledad Canyon Rd A3
(91351-2632)
PHONE..............................661 542-7074
Judith Robledo, *CEO*
Richard Schonfeld, *CFO*
EMP: 710 **EST:** 2020
SALES (est): 38MM **Privately Held**
Web: www.partnershipstaffing.net
SIC: 7361 Employment agencies

(P-15878)
PDS DEFENSE INC
3100 S Harbor Blvd Ste 135 (92704-6823)
PHONE..............................214 647-9600
Dj Englert, *Mgr*
EMP: 222
Web: www.pdstech.com
SIC: 7361 Employment agencies
HQ: Pds Defense, Inc.
300 E John Carpenter Fwy
Irving TX
214 647-9600

(P-15879)
PIONEER HEALTHCARE SVCS
LLC
6255 Ferris Sq # F (92121-3232)
PHONE..............................800 683-1209
Daniel Rietti, *CEO*
Daniel Rietti, *Managing Member*
EMP: 300 **EST:** 2012
SALES (est): 20.14MM **Privately Held**
Web: www.pioneer-healthcare.com
SIC: 7361 8049 8099 Employment agencies;
Physical therapist; Blood related health
services

(P-15880)
PRECISE FIT LIMITED ONE LLC
Also Called: Pfitech
17011 Beach Blvd Ste 900 (92647-5998)
PHONE..............................310 824-1800
EMP: 380 **EST:** 2001
SQ FT: 10,000
SALES (est): 37.54MM **Privately Held**
SIC: 7361 Employment agencies

(P-15881)
PREFERRED HLTHCARE
RGISTRY INC
4909 Murphy Canyon Rd Ste 310
(92123-4349)
P.O. Box 17860 (92177-7860)
PHONE..............................800 787-6787
Melanie Reiten, *Pr*
Rebecca Edwards Diata, *
EMP: 170 **EST:** 1994
SQ FT: 2,100

▲ = Import ▼ = Export
◆ = Import/Export

SALES (est): 22.04MM **Privately Held**
Web: www.mypreferred.com
SIC: **7361** 7363 Employment agencies;
Temporary help service

(P-15882)
PRIME ONE INC
22410 Hawthorne Blvd Ste 4 (90505-2539)
PHONE..................310 378-1944
Elvira Musell, *Pr*
EMP: 156 EST: 2001
SQ FT: 1,000
SALES (est): 5.83MM **Privately Held**
SIC: **7361** Employment agencies

(P-15883)
PTS ADVANCE
Also Called: Pts
1775 Flight Way Ste 100 (92782-1845)
PHONE..................949 268-4000
EMP: 220 EST: 1995
SALES (est): 10.54MM **Privately Held**
Web: www.ptsadvance.com
SIC: **7361** Employment agencies

(P-15884)
QUANTUM WORLD
TECHNOLOGIES INC
4281 Katella Ave Ste 102 (90720-3592)
PHONE..................805 834-0532
Rakesh Srivastava, *CFO*
EMP: 450 EST: 2016
SALES (est): 50MM **Privately Held**
Web: www.quantumworldit.com
SIC: **7361** Placement agencies

(P-15885)
R&D CONSULTING GROUP INC
Also Called: R & D Partners
8910 University Center Ln Ste 400
(92122-1025)
PHONE..................415 697-2585
Nancy Baltzer, *CEO*
EMP: 125 EST: 2012
SALES (est): 12.01MM **Privately Held**
Web: www.r-dpartners.com
SIC: **7361** Labor contractors (employment
agency)

(P-15886)
RAMCO ENTERPRISES LP
325 Plaza Dr Ste 1 (93454-6929)
PHONE..................805 922-9888
EMP: 371
SALES (corp-wide): 125.53MM **Privately**
Held
Web: www.ramcoenterpriseslp.com
SIC: **7361** Executive placement
PA: Ramco Enterprises, L.P.
710 La Guardia St
Salinas CA
831 758-5272

(P-15887)
READYLINK INC
72030 Metroplex Dr (92276)
PHONE..................760 343-7000
Daniel Caliendo, *Prin*
EMP: 99 EST: 2017
SALES (est): 9.85MM **Privately Held**
Web: www.readylinkstaffing.com
SIC: **7361** Employment agencies

(P-15888)
READYLINK HEALTHCARE
72030 Metroplex Dr (92276)
P.O. Box 1047 (92276-1047)
PHONE..................760 343-7000
Barry L Treash, *Pr*

EMP: 85 EST: 2002
SALES (est): 17.62MM **Privately Held**
Web: www.readylinkstaffing.com
SIC: **7361** Nurses' registry

(P-15889)
RECRUIT 360
457 Ogle St (92627-3243)
PHONE..................949 250-4420
Greg Kennedy, *Pr*
EMP: 115 EST: 2007
SALES (est): 3.32MM **Privately Held**
Web: www.recruit360.net
SIC: **7361** Executive placement

(P-15890)
REDLANDS EMPLOYMENT
SERVICES
Also Called: Redlands Staffing Services
4295 Jurupa St Ste 110 (91761-1429)
PHONE..................951 688-0083
Matt Tahlmeyer, *Pr*
EMP: 344
Web: www.arrowstaffing.com
SIC: **7361** Placement agencies
PA: Redlands Employment Services Inc
499 W State St
Redlands CA

(P-15891)
REHABABILITIES INC
Also Called: Social Service Professionals
11835 W Olympic Blvd Ste 1090e
(90064-5001)
PHONE..................310 473-4448
Ms. Meryl Stern, *Brnch Mgr*
EMP: 235
SALES (corp-wide): 8.82MM **Privately**
Held
Web: www.rehababilities.com
SIC: **7361** Registries
PA: Rehababilities, Inc.
3401 Centre Lake Dr # 480
Ontario CA
909 989-5699

(P-15892)
SE SCHER CORPORATION
Also Called: Acrobat Staffing
2525 Camino Del Rio S Ste 200
(92108-3717)
PHONE..................858 546-8300
EMP: 663
SALES (corp-wide): 61.69MM **Privately**
Held
SIC: **7361** Executive placement
PA: S.E. Scher Corporation
303 Hegenberger Rd # 300
Oakland CA
415 431-8826

(P-15893)
SELECT TEMPORARIES LLC
(DH)
Also Called: Select Personnel Services
3820 State St (93105-3112)
PHONE..................805 882-2200
Thomas A Bickes, *Pr*
Paul Galleberg, *
Shawn W Poole, *
▲ **EMP: 90 EST:** 1985
SQ FT: 30,000
SALES (est): 19.66MM
SALES (corp-wide): 10.97B **Publicly Held**
Web: www.select.com
SIC: **7361** Employment agencies
HQ: Employment Solutions Management,
Inc.
1845 Satellite Blvd # 300
Duluth GA
770 671-1900

(P-15894)
SIGNATURE SELECT
PERSONNEL LLC
138 W Bonita Ave Ste 207 (91773-3083)
PHONE..................626 940-3351
Kenji Morinaga, *Managing Member*
Robert Morinaga, *
EMP: 500 EST: 2019
SALES (est): 14.18MM **Privately Held**
SIC: **7361** Employment agencies

(P-15895)
SOURCE ONE STAFFING LLC
5312 Irwindale Ave Ste 1h (91706-2076)
PHONE..................626 337-0560
EMP: 9500
Web: www.s1staffing.com
SIC: **7361** Employment agencies

(P-15896)
STAFF ASSISTANCE INC
Also Called: Assisted Home Care
72 Moody Ct Ste 100 (91360-7426)
PHONE..................805 371-9980
Elaine Thinney, *Brnch Mgr*
EMP: 300
SIC: **7361** 8082 Nurses' registry; Home
health care services
PA: Staff Assistance, Inc.
72 Moody Ct Ste 100
Thousand Oaks CA

(P-15897)
TEAM-ONE STAFFING
SERVICES INC
Also Called: Teamone Employment
16030 Ventura Blvd Ste 430 (91436-4457)
PHONE..................951 616-3515
EMP: 1753
Web: www.teamone.com
SIC: **7361** Placement agencies
PA: Team-One Staffing Services, Inc.
24318 Hemlock Ave Ste C1
Moreno Valley CA

(P-15898)
TEG STAFFING INC
Also Called: Eastridge Workforce Solutions
2385 Northside Dr Ste 250 (92108-2716)
PHONE..................800 918-1678
Seth Stein, *CEO*
Brandon Stanford, *
Erin Medina, *CLO*
Kasey Hadjis, *CAO*
Jairo Carrion, *
EMP: 1600 **EST:** 1971
SALES (est): 61.11MM
SALES (corp-wide): 139MM **Privately**
Held
SIC: **7361** Employment agencies
PA: Eplica, Inc.
2385 Northside Dr Ste 250
San Diego CA
619 260-2000

(P-15899)
TEMPS PLUS INC
Also Called: Sales Advantage Group
268 N Lincoln Ave Ste 12 (92882-7103)
PHONE..................951 549-8309
EMP: 234 **EST:** 1996
SALES (est): 9MM **Privately Held**
Web: www.s3staffing.com
SIC: **7361** Executive placement

(P-15900)
TETRA TECH EXECUTIVE SVCS
INC

3475 E Foothill Blvd (91107-6024)
PHONE..................626 470-2400
Sam Box, *Prin*
EMP: 162 **EST:** 2013
SALES (est): 25.82MM
SALES (corp-wide): 3.5B **Publicly Held**
Web: www.tetratech.com
SIC: **7361** Employment agencies
PA: Tetra Tech, Inc.
3475 E Foothill Blvd
Pasadena CA
626 351-4664

(P-15901)
TWOMAGNETS INC
Also Called: Clipboard Health
440 N Barranca Ave Ste 5028
(91723-1722)
PHONE..................408 837-0116
Wei Deng, *CEO*
EMP: 650 **EST:** 2016
SALES (est): 51.12MM **Privately Held**
Web: www.clipboardhealth.com
SIC: **7361** Employment agencies

(P-15902)
VISH CONSULTING SERVICES
INC
9655 Granite Ridge Dr Ste 200 (92123)
PHONE..................916 800-3762
Dhruv Bindra, *Pr*
EMP: 80 **EST:** 2011
SALES (est): 40.57MM **Privately Held**
Web: www.vishusa.com
SIC: **7361** 7363 Employment agencies;
Temporary help service

(P-15903)
WILLIAM MRRIS ENDVOR
ENTRMT LL (DH)
Also Called: Wme
9601 Wilshire Blvd (90210-5213)
PHONE..................212 586-5100
Walter Zifkin, *CEO*
Norman Brokaw, *
Jerry Katzman, *
Leonard Hirshan, *
Owen Laster, *
EMP: 200 **EST:** 1898
SQ FT: 46,000
SALES (est): 471.07MM
SALES (corp-wide): 5.27B **Publicly Held**
Web: www.wmeagency.com
SIC: **7361** Employment agencies
HQ: Endeavor Operating Company, Llc
11 Madison Ave
New York NY
212 586-5100

(P-15904)
WMBE PAYROLLING INC
Also Called: Tcwglobal
3545 Aero Ct (92123-5700)
PHONE..................858 810-3000
Samer Khouli, *CEO*
EMP: 130 **EST:** 2009
SALES (est): 349.34MM **Privately Held**
Web: www.tcwglobal.com
SIC: **7361** Placement agencies

(P-15905)
WORKWAY INC
3111 Camino Del Rio N Ste 400 (92108)
PHONE..................619 278-0012
Bea Ogle, *Mgr*
EMP: 226
Web: www.workway.com
SIC: **7361** Executive placement
PA: Workway, Inc.
5151 Belt Line Rd

Dallas TX

(P-15906)
WORKWAY INC
19742 Macarthur Blvd Ste 235
(92612-2446)
PHONE..........................949 553-8700
Jill Burdock, *Brnch Mgr*
EMP: 227
Web: www.workway.com
SIC: 7361 Labor contractors (employment agency)
PA: Workway, Inc.
    5151 Belt Line Rd
    Dallas TX

(P-15907)
WORLDBRIDGE PARTNERS
25000 Avenue Stanford Ste 250 (91355)
PHONE..........................661 775-9999
John Broderick, *Brnch Mgr*
EMP: 152
Web: www.worldbridgepartners.com
SIC: 7361 Executive placement
PA: Worldbridge Partners
    3721 Douglas Blvd
    Roseville CA

(P-15908)
XL STAFFING INC
Also Called: Excell Staffing & SEC Svcs
826 Jackman St (92020-3053)
PHONE..........................619 579-0442
EMP: 200 EST: 1996
SALES (est): 9.87MM **Privately Held**
Web: www.xlstaffing.com
SIC: 7361 7381 Executive placement; Security guard service

(P-15909)
ZIONS BANCORPORATION
Also Called: Zions Bank
200 N Pacific Coast Hwy Ste 1850 (90245)
PHONE..........................424 290-5123
EMP: 5174
SALES (corp-wide): 3.34B **Publicly Held**
Web: careers.zionsbancorp.com
SIC: 7361 Employment agencies
HQ: Zions Bancorporation
    1 S Main St Fl 15
    Salt Lake City UT
    801 844-7637

7363 Help Supply Services

(P-15910)
A P R INC
Also Called: Alpha Professional Resources
100 E Thousand Oaks Blvd Ste 240 (91360)
PHONE..........................805 379-3400
Salvador Ramirez, *Pr*
Cliff Goodwin, *
EMP: 125 EST: 1993
SQ FT: 1,100
SALES (est): 9.86MM **Privately Held**
Web: www.alphaprotemps.com
SIC: 7363 7361 Temporary help service; Employment agencies

(P-15911)
ADO STAFFING INC
Also Called: Adecco Staffing
850 Lagoon Dr Bldg 99a (91910-2001)
PHONE..........................619 691-3659
Susannah Wright, *Mgr*
EMP: 200
Web: www.olsten.com

SIC: 7363 Temporary help service
HQ: Ado Staffing, Inc.
    4800 Deerwood Campus Pkwy # 800
    Jacksonville FL
    631 844-7800

(P-15912)
ALTECH SERVICES INC
400 Continental Blvd Fl 6 (90245-5074)
PHONE..........................888 725-8324
EMP: 296
Web: www.altechts.com
SIC: 7363 7361 Help supply services; Labor contractors (employment agency)
PA: Altech Services, Inc.
    695 Us Highway 46 Ste 115
    Fairfield NJ

(P-15913)
ANDERSON ASSOC STAFFING CORP (PA)
8200 Wilshire Blvd Ste 200 (90211-2328)
PHONE..........................323 930-3170
Tom Anderson, *Pr*
EMP: 200 EST: 1997
SALES (est): 11.82MM
SALES (corp-wide): 11.82MM **Privately Held**
SIC: 7363 Temporary help service

(P-15914)
AYA HEALTHCARE INC (PA)
5930 Cornerstone Ct W Ste 300 (92121-3741)
PHONE..........................858 458-4410
Alan Braynin, *Pr*
EMP: 392 EST: 2009
SQ FT: 20,000
SALES (est): 6B **Privately Held**
Web: www.ayahealthcare.com
SIC: 7363 8049 Temporary help service; Nurses, registered and practical

(P-15915)
B2B STAFFING SERVICES INC
Also Called: B2b Payroll Services
4501 Cerritos Ave Ste 201 (90630-4215)
PHONE..........................714 243-4104
Brian Wigdor, *Pr*
Bruce Underwood, *
EMP: 350 EST: 2006
SALES (est): 12MM **Privately Held**
Web: www.b2bstaffingservices.com
SIC: 7363 Temporary help service

(P-15916)
BUTLER SERVICE GROUP INC (HQ)
3820 State St Ste A (93105-3182)
PHONE..........................201 891-5312
EMP: 100 EST: 1965
SQ FT: 82,000
SALES (est): 146.12MM
SALES (corp-wide): 242.14MM **Privately Held**
SIC: 7363 8711 8748 3661 Engineering help service; Engineering services; Communications consulting; Telephone and telegraph apparatus
PA: Butler International, Inc.
    3820 State St Ste A
    Santa Barbara CA
    805 882-2200

(P-15917)
CANON RECRUITING GROUP LLC
27651 Lincoln Pl Ste 250 (91387-8818)
PHONE..........................661 252-7400

Laurie Grayem, *CEO*
Laurie Grayem, *Managing Member*
Tim Grayem, *
EMP: 500 EST: 1980
SQ FT: 7,500
SALES (est): 23.82MM **Privately Held**
Web: www.canonrecruiting.com
SIC: 7363 7361 Office help supply service; Executive placement

(P-15918)
CARDINAL POINT CAPTAINS INC
Also Called: Cardinal Point Captains
5005 Texas St Ste 104 (92108-3722)
PHONE..........................760 438-7361
Jordan E Cousino, *CEO*
Bill Green, *CDO*
Heather Jenkins, *ACCT AND CONTRACTS*
EMP: 56 EST: 2008
SQ FT: 2,633
SALES (est): 5.39MM **Privately Held**
Web: www.cpcperforms.com
SIC: 7363 3812 Boat crew service; Search and navigation equipment

(P-15919)
CARE STFFING PROFESSIONALS INC
2151 E Convention Center Way Ste 204 (91764-5429)
PHONE..........................909 906-2060
D'andre Lampkin, *CEO*
EMP: 80 EST: 2016
SALES (est): 4.65MM **Privately Held**
Web: www.carestaffingprofessionals.com
SIC: 7363 7361 8049 8082 Medical help service; Nurses' registry; Nurses and other medical assistants; Visiting nurse service

(P-15920)
EMERGNCY MDCINE SPCLIST ORNGE
Also Called: Emsoc
1310 W Stewart Dr Ste 212 (92868-3837)
PHONE..........................714 543-8911
Matthey Mallarky, *Managing Member*
Mark Falcone Parnter, *Prin*
Jonathen Blair, *Pt*
Courtney Aldama, *Mgr*
EMP: 96 EST: 1976
SALES (est): 3.41MM **Privately Held**
Web: www.emsoc.net
SIC: 7363 Medical help service

(P-15921)
EPLICA INC (PA)
Also Called: Eastridge Workforce Solutions
2385 Northside Dr Ste 250 (92108-2703)
PHONE..........................619 260-2000
Robert Svet, *Pr*
EMP: 175 EST: 1971
SQ FT: 15,000
SALES (est): 139MM
SALES (corp-wide): 139MM **Privately Held**
Web: www.eplicaservices.com
SIC: 7363 7361 Temporary help service; Employment agencies

(P-15922)
HEALTHCARE RESOURCE GROUP
6571 Altura Blvd Ste 200 (90620-1020)
PHONE..........................562 945-7224
EMP: 192
SALES (corp-wide): 326.65MM **Publicly Held**

Web: www.hrgpros.com
SIC: 7363 Medical help service
HQ: Healthcare Resource Group, Inc
    12610 E Mirabeau Pkwy # 900
    Spokane Valley WA

(P-15923)
HOST HEALTHCARE INC
4225 Executive Sq Ste 1500 (92037-1466)
P.O. Box 927190 (92192-7190)
PHONE..........................858 999-3579
Adam Francis, *CEO*
William Bulger, *
EMP: 525 EST: 2012
SQ FT: 1,400
SALES (est): 37.09MM **Privately Held**
Web: www.hosthealthcare.com
SIC: 7363 Help supply services

(P-15924)
I N C BUILDERS INC
Also Called: Acme Staffing
1560 Ocotillo Dr Ste L (92243-4237)
PHONE..........................760 352-4200
EMP: 350
SALES (corp-wide): 11.06MM **Privately Held**
Web: www.acmestaffing.com
SIC: 7363 Temporary help service
PA: I N C Builders, Inc.
    550 E 32nd St Ste 5a
    Yuma AZ
    928 344-8367

(P-15925)
JUNE GROUP LLC
Also Called: Qualstaff Resources
9909 Mira Mesa Blvd Ste 240 (92131-3003)
PHONE..........................858 450-4290
R Scott Silver-hill, *Managing Member*
EMP: 100 EST: 2003
SALES (est): 8.4MM **Privately Held**
SIC: 7363 Temporary help service

(P-15926)
LLOYD STAFFING INC
18000 Studebaker Rd Ste 700 (90703-2679)
PHONE..........................631 777-7600
Luly Santana, *Pr*
EMP: 562
SALES (corp-wide): 48.53MM **Privately Held**
Web: www.lloydstaffing.com
SIC: 7363 Temporary help service
PA: Lloyd Staffing, Inc.
    445 Broadhollow Rd # 119
    Melville NY
    631 777-7600

(P-15927)
MAXIM HEALTHCARE SERVICES INC
1515 W 190th St (90248-4319)
PHONE..........................310 329-9115
EMP: 122
Web: www.maximhealthcare.com
SIC: 7363 Medical help service
PA: Maxim Healthcare Services, Inc.
    7227 Lee Deforest Dr
    Columbia MD

(P-15928)
MAXIM HEALTHCARE SERVICES INC
Also Called: Bakersfield Respite Homecare
5201 California Ave Ste 200 (93309-1674)
PHONE..........................661 322-3039
Reyes Robles, *Brnch Mgr*

EMP: 85
Web: www.maximhealthcare.com
SIC: 7363 Medical help service
PA: Maxim Healthcare Services, Inc.
7227 Lee Deforest Dr
Columbia MD

(P-15929)
MAXIM HEALTHCARE SERVICES INC
28470 Avenue Stanford Ste 250 (91355)
PHONE.................................661 964-6350
Kowalczyk David, *Mgr*
EMP: 86
Web: www.maximhealthcare.com
SIC: 7363 8099 8748 Medical help service;
Blood related health services; Testing
services
PA: Maxim Healthcare Services, Inc.
7227 Lee Deforest Dr
Columbia MD

(P-15930)
MAXIM HEALTHCARE SERVICES INC
801 Corporate Center Dr Ste 210
(91768-2627)
PHONE.................................626 962-6453
EMP: 85
Web: www.maximhealthcare.com
SIC: 7363 7361 Medical help service;
Nurses' registry
PA: Maxim Healthcare Services, Inc.
7227 Lee Deforest Dr
Columbia MD

(P-15931)
MAXIM HEALTHCARE SERVICES INC
Also Called: Riverside Companion Services
1845 Business Center Dr Ste 112 (92408)
PHONE.................................951 684-4148
Elijah Hall, *Mgr*
EMP: 85
Web: www.maximhealthcare.com
SIC: 7363 Medical help service
PA: Maxim Healthcare Services, Inc.
7227 Lee Deforest Dr
Columbia MD

(P-15932)
MAXIM HEALTHCARE SERVICES INC
Also Called: Temecula Homecare
27555 Ynez Rd (92591-4678)
PHONE.................................951 694-0100
Jeff Abbott, *Mgr*
EMP: 140
Web: www.maximhealthcare.com
SIC: 7363 Medical help service
PA: Maxim Healthcare Services, Inc.
7227 Lee Deforest Dr
Columbia MD

(P-15933)
MEK INDUSTRIES INC
3517 Camino Del Rio S Ste 215 (92108)
PHONE.................................858 610-9601
Marc Kranz, *CEO*
EMP: 200 EST: 2019
SALES (est): 11.65MM **Privately Held**
SIC: 7363 Manpower pools

(P-15934)
PERSONNEL PLUS INC
12052 Imperial Hwy Ste 200 (90650-3090)
P.O. Box 817 (90651-0817)
PHONE.................................562 712-5490
EMP: 155

Web: www.ppitemps.com
SIC: 7363 7361 Temporary help service;
Employment agencies

(P-15935)
PHOENIX ENGINEERING CO INC
Also Called: Phoenix Personnel
2480 Armacost Ave (90064-2714)
P.O. Box 66395 (90066-0395)
PHONE.................................310 532-1134
Silvia Maron, *Pr*
Silvia Lugo, *
EMP: 100 EST: 1974
SQ FT: 1,700
SALES (est): 4.86MM **Privately Held**
Web: www.artschangeleaders.org
SIC: 7363 7361 Office help supply service;
Employment agencies

(P-15936)
PLATINUM EMPIRE GROUP INC
Also Called: Platinum Healthcare Staffing
2430 Amsler St Ste B (90505-5302)
P.O. Box 10338 (90505-1238)
PHONE.................................310 821-5888
Arun Mahtani, *Pr*
Maluh Silvano, *
Aaron Quiboloy, *
EMP: 120 EST: 2005
SALES (est): 11.17MM **Privately Held**
Web:
www.platinumhealthcarestaffing.com
SIC: 7363 Temporary help service

(P-15937)
REMEDYTEMP INC (DH)
Also Called: Remedy Intelligent Staffing
101 Enterprise Ste 100 (92656-2604)
PHONE.................................949 425-7600
David Stephen Sorensen, *CEO*
Richard Hulme, *Ex VP*
Jeff R Mitchell, *CFO*
EMP: 143 EST: 1974
SQ FT: 51,000
SALES (est): 42.08MM
SALES (corp-wide): 10.97B **Publicly Held**
Web: www.remedystaffing.com
SIC: 7363 7361 Temporary help service;
Employment agencies
HQ: Employbridge, Llc
301 Mentor Dr Ste 210
Santa Barbara CA

(P-15938)
ROTH STAFFING COMPANIES LP (PA)
Also Called: Ultimate Staffing Services
450 N State College Blvd (92868-1708)
PHONE.................................714 939-8600
Adam Roth, *CEO*
Ben Roth, *
Pam Sexauer, *
◆ EMP: 80 EST: 1994
SALES (est): 88.3MM **Privately Held**
Web: www.rothstaffing.com
SIC: 7363 Help supply services

(P-15939)
RX PRO HEALTH LLC
12400 High Bluff Dr Ste 100 (92130-3077)
PHONE.................................858 369-4050
Susan R Salka, *CEO*
EMP: 1800 EST: 2003
SQ FT: 175,000
SALES (est): 41.9MM
SALES (corp-wide): 5.24B **Publicly Held**
SIC: 7363 Medical help service
PA: Amn Healthcare Services, Inc.
2999 Olympus Blvd Ste 500
Coppell TX
866 871-8519

(P-15940)
SAGE STAFFING CONSULTANTS INC (PA)
Also Called: Sage Staffing
27441 Tourney Rd Ste 150 (91355-5312)
PHONE.................................661 254-4026
Laura Kincaid, *CEO*
Greg Kincaid, *Pr*
EMP: 190 EST: 1987
SQ FT: 5,000
SALES (est): 4.82MM **Privately Held**
Web: www.sagestaffing.com
SIC: 7363 Temporary help service

(P-15941)
SFN GROUP INC
114 Pacifica Ste 210 (92618-3320)
PHONE.................................949 727-8500
Tammy Hawkins, *Mgr*
EMP: 716
SALES (corp-wide): 24.5B **Privately Held**
Web: www.spherion.com
SIC: 7363 Temporary help service
HQ: Sfn Group, Inc.
2050 Spectrum Blvd
Fort Lauderdale FL
954 308-7600

(P-15942)
SFN GROUP INC
Also Called: Spherion Prof Recruiting Group
4660 La Jolla Village Dr Ste 910
(92122-4601)
PHONE.................................858 458-9200
Bobby Nerini, *Mgr*
EMP: 955
SALES (corp-wide): 24.5B **Privately Held**
Web: www.spherion.com
SIC: 7363 Temporary help service
HQ: Sfn Group, Inc.
2050 Spectrum Blvd
Fort Lauderdale FL
954 308-7600

(P-15943)
SOUTHERN HOME CARE SVCS INC
Also Called: Kelly Services
2900 Bristol St Ste D107 (92626-5914)
PHONE.................................714 979-7413
Vicki Demirozu, *Dir*
EMP: 85
SALES (corp-wide): 5.27B **Privately Held**
Web: www.kellyservices.com
SIC: 7363 8082 Temporary help service;
Home health care services
HQ: Southern Home Care Services, Inc.
805 N Whittington Pkwy
Louisville KY

(P-15944)
TAD PGS INC
12062 Valley View St Ste 108 (92845-1773)
PHONE.................................800 261-3779
Latonya Walker, *Dir*
EMP: 797
Web: www.tadpgs.com
SIC: 7363 Temporary help service
HQ: Tad Pgs, Inc.
1001 3rd Ave W Ste 460
Bradenton FL
941 746-4434

(P-15945)
TAD PGS INC
10805 Holder St Ste 250 (90630-5142)
PHONE.................................571 451-2428
EMP: 797
Web: www.tadpgs.com

SIC: 7363 Temporary help service
HQ: Tad Pgs, Inc.
1001 3rd Ave W Ste 460
Bradenton FL
941 746-4434

(P-15946)
VAYA WORKFORCE SOLUTIONS LLC
5930 Cornerstone Ct W Ste 300
(92121-3741)
PHONE.................................866 687-7390
Alan Braynin, *Pr*
EMP: 150 EST: 2021
SALES (est): 11.09MM **Privately Held**
Web: www.vayaworkforce.com
SIC: 7363 Temporary help service
PA: Aya Healthcare, Inc.
5930 Cornerstone Ct W # 3
San Diego CA

(P-15947)
VOLT MANAGEMENT CORP
Also Called: Volt Workforce Solutions
7676 Hazard Center Dr Ste 1000
(92108-4503)
PHONE.................................858 576-3140
Rhona Driggs, *Brnch Mgr*
EMP: 89
SALES (corp-wide): 885.39MM **Privately Held**
Web: www.volt.ccm
SIC: 7363 Temporary help service
HQ: Volt Management Corp.
2400 Meadowbrook Pkwy
Duluth GA

(P-15948)
VOLT MANAGEMENT CORP
Also Called: Volt Temporary Services
2411 N Glassell St (92865-2717)
PHONE.................................800 654-2624
Rhona Driggs, *Brnch Mgr*
EMP: 300
SALES (corp-wide): 885.39MM **Privately Held**
Web: www.volt.com
SIC: 7363 7373 Temporary help service;
Computer integrated systems design
HQ: Volt Management Corp.
2400 Meadowbrook Pkwy
Duluth GA

(P-15949)
WORK FORCE SERVICES INC
Also Called: Work Force Staffing
1811 Oak St (93301-3062)
PHONE.................................661 327-5019
Brooks Whitehead, *Pr*
EMP: 250 EST: 1981
SALES (est): 9.86MM **Privately Held**
Web: www.wfskern.com
SIC: 7363 Temporary help service

7371 Custom Computer Programming Services

(P-15950)
3DNA CORP (PA)
Also Called: Nationbuilder
750 W 7th St Ste 201 (90017-3710)
P.O. Box 811428 (90081-0008)
PHONE.................................213 992-4809
Lea Endres, *CEO*
EMP: 127 EST: 2007
SALES (est): 21.72MM
SALES (corp-wide): 21.72MM **Privately Held**
Web: www.nationbuilder.com

PRODUCTS & SVCS

SIC: 7371 Computer software development

(P-15951)
3I INFOTECH INC
Also Called: 3I INFOTECH INC
555 Chorro St Ste B (93405-2398)
PHONE..............................805 544-8327
Mathew Philip, *CFO*
EMP: 24
Web: www.3i-infotech.com
SIC: 7371 7372 7373 7379 Computer
software development; Prepackaged
software; Computer integrated systems
design; Computer related consulting
services
HQ: 3i Infotech Inc.
110 Fieldcrest Ave Ste 25
Edison NJ

(P-15952)
A R SANTEX LLC (PA)
Also Called: Santex Group
6790 Embarcadero Ln Ste 100
(92011-3277)
PHONE..............................888 622-7098
Juan Santiago, *CEO*
Gabriela Fernandez, *CFO*
EMP: 39 EST: 1999
SALES (est): 9.65MM
SALES (corp-wide): 9.65MM **Privately
Held**
Web: www.santexgroup.com
SIC: 7371 7372 7373 Computer software
systems analysis and design, custom;
Business oriented computer software;
Systems software development services

(P-15953)
**ABACUS DATA SYSTEMS INC
(PA)**
Also Called: Abacusnext
9171 Towne Centre Dr Ste 200 (92122)
PHONE..............................858 452-4280
Keri Gohman, *CEO*
Jerome Fodor, *
Eric Cutler, *Chief Sales & Marketing Officer**
Tomas Suros, *SOLN'S**
Chris Cardinal, *OF Software ENG'G**
EMP: 158 EST: 1983
SQ FT: 10,000
SALES (est): 67.08MM
SALES (corp-wide): 67.08MM **Privately
Held**
Web: www.getcaret.com
SIC: 7371 7374 Computer software systems
analysis and design, custom; Data
processing and preparation

(P-15954)
ABACUS DATA SYSTEMS INC
Also Called: Abacusnext
3262 Holiday Ct Ste 101 (92037-1804)
PHONE..............................858 529-0020
EMP: 87 EST: 2018
SALES (est): 6.11MM **Privately Held**
Web: www.getcaret.com
SIC: 7371 Computer software development

(P-15955)
ADAPTAMED LLC
6699 Alvarado Rd Ste 2301 (92120-5241)
PHONE..............................877 478-7773
EMP: 120 EST: 2011
SALES (est): 4.74MM **Privately Held**
Web: www.ehryourway.com
SIC: 7371 Computer software development

(P-15956)
ADCOLONY INC
11400 W Olympic Blvd # 1200
(90064-1583)
PHONE..............................650 625-1262
EMP: 100 EST: 2008
SALES (est): 20.51MM **Publicly Held**
Web: www.digitalturbine.com
SIC: 7371 Computer software development
HQ: Adcolony Holdings Us, Inc.
901 Mariners Blvd Ste 250
San Mateo CA
650 625-1262

(P-15957)
ADVENT RESOURCES INC
235 W 7th St (90731-3321)
PHONE..............................310 241-1500
Ysidro Salinas, *Ch Bd*
Timothy Gill, *
EMP: 80 EST: 1984
SQ FT: 22,000
SALES (est): 13.68MM **Privately Held**
Web: www.adventresources.com
SIC: 7371 Computer software development

(P-15958)
AGENT IMAGE INC
1700 E Walnut Ave (90245-2629)
PHONE..............................310 577-9222
EMP: 400 EST: 1998
SALES (est): 23.52MM **Privately Held**
Web: www.agentimage.com
SIC: 7371 Computer software systems
analysis and design, custom

(P-15959)
AKKODIS INC
Also Called: Modis
801 N Brand Blvd Ste 250 (91203-3251)
PHONE..............................818 546-2848
Lisa Bertram, *Brnch Mgr*
EMP: 108
Web: www.modis.com
SIC: 7371 Computer software systems
analysis and design, custom
HQ: Akkodis, Inc.
4800 Deerwood Campus Pkwy
Jacksonville FL
904 360-2300

(P-15960)
**ALGORITHMIC OBJECTIVE
CORP**
Also Called: Algotive
8910 University Center Ln Ste 400
(92122-1029)
PHONE..............................858 249-9580
Pablo Castillon, *CEO*
Pablo Antonio Castillon, *
EMP: 32 EST: 2019
SALES (est): 1.03MM **Privately Held**
Web: www.algotive.ai
SIC: 7371 7372 Computer software
development; Prepackaged software

(P-15961)
ALOGENT HOLDINGS INC
Also Called: Alogent
5868 Owens Ave Ste 200 (92008-6541)
PHONE..............................760 410-9000
EMP: 80
SALES (corp-wide): 26.1MM **Privately
Held**
Web: www.alogent.com
SIC: 7371 Computer software development
PA: Alogent Holdings, Inc.
35 Technology Pkwy S # 200
Peachtree Corners GA
770 752-6400

(P-15962)
AMAZON STUDIOS LLC
9336 Washington Blvd (90232-2628)
PHONE..............................818 804-0884
Jen Salke, *CEO*
EMP: 132
Web: press.amazonstudios.com
SIC: 7371 Computer software development
and applications
HQ: Amazon Studios Llc
410 Terry Ave N
Seattle WA
310 573-2305

(P-15963)
ANAMEX CORPORATION (PA)
250 S Peralta Way (92807-3618)
PHONE..............................714 779-7055
Cung Phan, *Pr*
EMP: 47 EST: 1986
SQ FT: 10,000
SALES (est): 2.29MM **Privately Held**
SIC: 7371 7372 8711 Computer software
development; Prepackaged software;
Electrical or electronic engineering

(P-15964)
ANRE TECHNOLOGIES INC
Also Called: Anre Tech
741 W Woodbury Rd (91001-5310)
PHONE..............................818 627-5433
EMP: 150 EST: 2010
SQ FT: 600
SALES (est): 9.95MM **Privately Held**
Web: www.anretech.com
SIC: 7371 7376 7379 Computer software
development and applications; Computer
facilities management; Computer related
maintenance services

(P-15965)
**APPLIED ENGINEERING MGT
CORP**
Also Called: Aem Corporation
760 Paseo Camarillo Ste 101 (93010-6000)
P.O. Box 1263 (93011-1263)
PHONE..............................805 484-1909
Anne Morgan, *Brnch Mgr*
EMP: 250
SALES (corp-wide): 35.31MM **Privately
Held**
Web: www.aemcorp.com
SIC: 7371 Computer software development
PA: Applied Enterprise Management
Corporation
13880 Dulles Corner Ln # 300
Herndon VA
703 464-7030

(P-15966)
**APPLIED SPECTRAL IMAGING
INC**
Also Called: A S I
5315 Avenida Encinas Ste 150
(92008-4379)
PHONE..............................760 929-2840
EMP: 18 EST: 1994
SQ FT: 3,000
SALES (est): 9.03MM **Privately Held**
Web: www.spectral-imaging.com
SIC: 7371 3571 Computer software
development and applications; Electronic
computers
PA: Applied Spectral Imaging Ltd.
2 Hacarmel
Yokneam Illit

(P-15967)
ARTIC SENTINEL INC
1700 E Walnut Ave Ste 200 (90245-2648)
PHONE..............................310 227-8230
EMP: 85
SIC: 7371 7379 Computer software
development and applications; Online
services technology consultants

(P-15968)
ASHUNYA INC
642 N Eckhoff St (92868-1004)
PHONE..............................714 385-1900
Melanie Merchant, *Prin*
EMP: 88 EST: 2001
SALES (est): 10.14MM **Privately Held**
Web: www.ashunya.com
SIC: 7371 7372 7373 Computer software
development and applications; Application
computer software; Office computer
automation systems integration

(P-15969)
ASPIREZ INC
Also Called: Pegasus One
1440 N Harbor Blvd Ste 900 (92835-4127)
PHONE..............................714 485-8104
Tushar Puri, *CEO*
EMP: 87 EST: 2010
SALES (est): 1.99MM **Privately Held**
SIC: 7371 7373 7379 7372 Custom
computer programming services; Computer
integrated systems design; Computer
related maintenance services;
Prepackaged software

(P-15970)
AUDITBOARD INC (PA)
12900 Park Plaza Dr Ste 200 (90703-8564)
PHONE..............................877 769-5444
Scott Arnold, *CEO*
EMP: 100 EST: 2014
SQ FT: 10,000
SALES (est): 26.54MM
SALES (corp-wide): 26.54MM **Privately
Held**
Web: www.auditboard.com
SIC: 7371 Computer software development

(P-15971)
AUGUSTINE GAMING MGT CORP
Also Called: Augustine Casino
84001 Avenue 54 (92236-9780)
PHONE..............................760 391-9500
Jeff Bauer, *Genl Mgr*
John Corrigan, *Finance*
EMP: 99
SALES (est): 7.4MM **Privately Held**
Web: www.augustinecasino.com
SIC: 7371 Computer software development
and applications

(P-15972)
AUTOMOTUS INC
612 S Broadway Ste 409 (90014-1807)
PHONE..............................805 504-5750
Jordan Justus, *CEO*
EMP: 90 EST: 2017
SALES (est): 4.85MM **Privately Held**
Web: www.automotus.co
SIC: 7371 Computer software development
and applications

(P-15973)
AVAMAR TECHNOLOGIES INC
135 Technology Dr (92618-2402)
PHONE..............................949 743-5100
EMP: 100

SIC: **7371** Computer software development

(P-15974)
AVANQUEST NORTH AMERICA LLC (HQ)
Also Called: Nova Development
23801 Calabasas Rd Ste 2005
(91302-1547)
PHONE.................................818 591-9600
Roger Bloxberg, *CEO*
Todd Helfstein, *
Sharon Chiu, *
▲ **EMP:** 80 **EST:** 1984
SQ FT: 12,000
SALES (est): 83.58MM
SALES (corp-wide): 4.02MM **Privately Held**
Web: www.avanquest.com
SIC: **7371** Computer software development
PA: Claranova S.E.
     Avanquest Blue Squad Bvrp Software
     Cs8 Immeuble Adamas
     Courbevoie

(P-15975)
AVEVA SOFTWARE LLC
5850 El Camino Real (92008-8816)
PHONE.................................760 268-7700
Chris Porter, *Brnch Mgr*
EMP: 194
SALES (corp-wide): 82.05K **Privately Held**
Web: www.aveva.com
SIC: **7371** 5045 Computer software development; Computer software
HQ: Aveva Software, Llc
     26561 Rancho Pkwy S
     Lake Forest CA

(P-15976)
AXON NETWORKS INC (PA)
15420 Laguna Canyon Rd Ste 150
(92618-2119)
PHONE.................................949 310-4429
Martin Manniche, *CEO*
EMP: 97 **EST:** 2020
SALES (est): 3.99MM
SALES (corp-wide): 3.99MM **Privately Held**
Web: www.axon-networks.com
SIC: **7371** 8742 Custom computer programming services; General management consultant

(P-15977)
BAHARE
11769 W Sunset Blvd (90049-6903)
PHONE.................................516 472-1457
Bahareh Saleh Nia, *CEO*
EMP: 105 **EST:** 2021
SALES (est): 2.12MM **Privately Held**
SIC: **7371** 7389 Computer software development and applications; Business Activities at Non-Commercial Site

(P-15978)
BELLROCK MEDIA INC (PA)
11500 W Olympic Blvd Ste 400
(90064-1525)
PHONE.................................310 315-2727
Peter Levin, *Pr*
EMP: 26 **EST:** 2005
SALES (est): 4.77MM **Privately Held**
SIC: **7371** 3661 Software programming applications; Headsets, telephone

(P-15979)
BEN GROUP INC
14724 Ventura Blvd Ste 1200 (91403-3512)
PHONE.................................310 342-1500
Richard Ray Butler, *CEO*

Keith Moffatt, *
Ted Sheffield, *
EMP: 420 **EST:** 2017
SALES (est): 100MM **Privately Held**
SIC: **7371** 7311 Custom computer programming services; Advertising agencies

(P-15980)
BIG CART CORPORATION
16682 Millikan Ave (92606-5008)
PHONE.................................949 250-7064
Chang Ho Lee, *CEO*
EMP: 19 **EST:** 2012
SALES (est): 1.18MM **Privately Held**
Web: www.bigcartcorp.com
SIC: **7371** 3699 Computer software development and applications; Security devices

(P-15981)
BIOSERO (PA)
4770 Ruffner St (92111-1520)
PHONE.................................858 880-7376
Thomas Gilman, *Pr*
Andrea Salazar, *
Tony Morand, *
Ryan Bernhardt, *CCO**
▲ **EMP:** 33 **EST:** 2003
SQ FT: 6,000
SALES (est): 10.57MM
SALES (corp-wide): 10.57MM **Privately Held**
Web: www.biosero.com
SIC: **7371** 3569 Computer software development and applications; Assembly machines, non-metalworking

(P-15982)
BIRD RIDES INC
2501 Colorado Ave (90404-3500)
PHONE.................................866 205-2442
Evan Conroy, *Mgr*
EMP: 100
SALES (corp-wide): 244.66MM **Publicly Held**
Web: www.bird.co
SIC: **7371** Computer software development and applications
HQ: Bird Rides, Inc.
     8605 Santa Monica Blvd # 203
     West Hollywood CA
     866 205-2442

(P-15983)
BIRD RIDES INC (HQ)
Also Called: Bird
8605 Santa Monica Blvd # 20388
(90069-4109)
PHONE.................................866 205-2442
Travis Vanderzanden, *CEO*
EMP: 17 **EST:** 2017
SALES (est): 127.11MM
SALES (corp-wide): 244.66MM **Publicly Held**
Web: www.bird.co
SIC: **7371** 3751 Computer software development and applications; Bicycles and related parts
PA: Bird Global, Inc.
     392 Ne 191st St 20388
     Miami FL
     866 205-2442

(P-15984)
BIS COMPUTER SOLUTIONS INC (PA)
Also Called: Business Information Systems
5500 Alta Canyada Rd (91011-1610)
PHONE.................................818 248-4282
Miro J Macho, *Pr*

EMP: 25 **EST:** 1971
SALES (est): 3.84MM
SALES (corp-wide): 3.84MM **Privately Held**
Web: www.biscomputer.com
SIC: **7371** 7379 5045 7372 Computer software development; Computer related consulting services; Computers, peripherals, and software; Prepackaged software

(P-15985)
BLU DIGITAL GROUP INC (PA)
Also Called: Blufocus
2233 N Ontario St # 130 (91504-4503)
PHONE.................................818 527-2763
Paulette E Pantoja, *CEO*
EMP: 162 **EST:** 2007
SQ FT: 7,000
SALES (est): 12.28MM **Privately Held**
Web: www.bludigitalgroup.com
SIC: **7371** 8748 7379 Software programming applications; Systems analysis and engineering consulting services; Computer related consulting services

(P-15986)
BLUEBEAM INC (PA)
443 S Raymond Ave (91105-2630)
PHONE.................................626 788-4100
Usman Shuja, *CEO*
Richard Lee, *
Jim Atkinson, *
Miekie Liebenberg, *
EMP: 200 **EST:** 2002
SALES (est): 47.98MM
SALES (corp-wide): 47.98MM **Privately Held**
Web: www.bluebeam.com
SIC: **7371** Computer software development

(P-15987)
BOULEVARD LABS INC
626 Wilshire Blvd Ste 410 (90005-3983)
PHONE.................................323 310-2093
Matthew Danna, *CEO*
EMP: 54 **EST:** 2016
SALES (est): 6.78MM **Privately Held**
Web: www.joinblvd.com
SIC: **7371** 7389 7372 Computer software development and applications; Business Activities at Non-Commercial Site; Prepackaged software

(P-15988)
BRAIN CORPORATION
10182 Telesis Ct Ste 100 (92121-4777)
PHONE.................................858 689-7600
Eugene Izhikevich, *CEO*
David Pinn, *CFO*
EMP: 220 **EST:** 2009
SALES (est): 40MM **Privately Held**
Web: www.braincorp.com
SIC: **7371** Computer software development

(P-15989)
BUDDY GROUP INC
7 Studebaker (92618-2013)
P.O. Box 1021 (92609-1021)
PHONE.................................949 468-0042
Peter R Deutschman, *Pr*
EMP: 99 **EST:** 2007
SALES (est): 3.41MM **Privately Held**
Web: www.thebuddygroup.com
SIC: **7371** Computer software development and applications

(P-15990)
C SQUARED SOCIAL
5963 La Place Ct Ste 105 (92008-8822)

PHONE.................................858 386-7400
EMP: 97 **EST:** 2017
SALES (est): 745.31K **Privately Held**
Web: www.csquaredsocial.com
SIC: **7371** Computer software development and applications

(P-15991)
CHEQUE GUARD INC
512 S Verdugo Dr (91502-2344)
PHONE.................................818 563-9335
Emil Ramzy, *Pr*
Alfred Ramzi, *
Louris Khalaf, *
EMP: 54 **EST:** 2002
SQ FT: 6,000
SALES (est): 1.91MM **Privately Held**
Web: www.cheque-guard.com
SIC: **7371** 2893 Computer software development; Printing ink

(P-15992)
CHROMACODE INC
2330 Faraday Ave Ste 100 (92008-7216)
PHONE.................................442 244-4369
Alex Dickinson, *Bd of Dir*
Gregory Gosch, *
Lynne Rollins, *
EMP: 27 **EST:** 2014
SALES (est): 4.01MM **Privately Held**
Web: www.chromacode.com
SIC: **7371** 3841 8731 Computer software development; Diagnostic apparatus, medical ; Biological research

(P-15993)
CITRIX ONLINE LLC
Also Called: Citrix Online Group
7414 Hollister Ave (93117-2583)
PHONE.................................805 690-6400
EMP: 500
SIC: **7371** Computer software development

(P-15994)
CITRUSBYTE LLC
Also Called: Theorem LLC
21550 Oxnard St Ste 300 # 11
(91367-7109)
PHONE.................................888 969-2983
William Jessup, *Managing Member*
EMP: 30 **EST:** 2007
SALES (est): 5.51MM **Privately Held**
Web: www.theoremone.co
SIC: **7371** 7372 7373 Computer software development and applications; Business oriented computer software; Computer integrated systems design

(P-15995)
COALITION TECHNOLOGIES LLC
445 S Figueroa St Ste 3100 (90071-1635)
PHONE.................................310 905-8268
EMP: 21 **EST:** 2011
SALES (est): 2.28MM **Privately Held**
Web: www.coalitiontechnologies.com
SIC: **7371** 8743 8243 7372 Computer software writers, freelance; Public relations services; Software training, computer; Business oriented computer software

(P-15996)
CODAZEN INC
Also Called: Codazen
60 Bunsen (92618-4210)
PHONE.................................949 916-6266
Michael Merchant, *Pr*
Michael H Merchant, *
Angela Merchant, *
EMP: 85 **EST:** 2007

SALES (est): 5.2MM **Privately Held**
Web: www.codazen.com
SIC: **7371** Computer software development

(P-15997)
COMMERCIAL RE EXCH INC
Also Called: Crexi
5510 Lincoln Blvd (90094-2034)
PHONE.................................888 273-0423
Michael Degiorgio, *CEO*
Erek Benz, *
Ben Widhelm, *
Hans Ku, *CPO*
Courtney Ettus, *CMO*
EMP: **250 EST: 2015**
SQ FT: 2,000
SALES (est): 23.31MM **Privately Held**
Web: www.crexi.com
SIC: **7371** Computer software development and applications

(P-15998)
COMPULINK MANAGEMENT CTR INC (PA)
Also Called: Laserfiche Document Imaging
3443 Long Beach Blvd (90807-4432)
PHONE.................................562 988-1688
Nien-ling Wacker, *Pr*
Christopher Wacker, *
Jim Haney, *
▲ EMP: **197 EST: 1976**
SALES (est): 45.38MM
SALES (corp-wide): 45.38MM **Privately Held**
Web: www.laserfiche.com
SIC: **7371** Computer software development

(P-15999)
COMPUTER PROC UNLIMITED INC
Also Called: Cpu Medical Management Systems
9235 Activity Rd Ste 104 (92126-4440)
PHONE.................................858 530-0875
Michael Stringer, *Pr*
Douglas C Pence, *
Brian Castle, *
Jean Campbell, *
Duane Findling, *
EMP: **128 EST: 1982**
SQ FT: 11,250
SALES (est): 10.18MM
SALES (corp-wide): 276.71B **Publicly Held**
SIC: **7371** 5045 Computer software systems analysis and design, custom; Computer peripheral equipment
PA: Mckesson Corporation
6555 State Highway 161
Irving TX
972 446-4800

(P-16000)
COMPUTRITION INC (HQ)
Also Called: Dfm Dietary Food Management
8521 Fallbrook Ave Ste 100 (91304)
PHONE.................................818 961-3999
Scott Saklad, *Pr*
Kim C Goldberg, *Marketing*
EMP: **60 EST: 1981**
SQ FT: 16,763
SALES (est): 13.33MM
SALES (corp-wide): 6.62B **Privately Held**
Web: www.computrition.com
SIC: **7371** 7372 Computer software development; Prepackaged software
PA: Constellation Software Inc
20 Adelaide St E Suite 1200
Toronto ON
416 861-9677

(P-16001)
CORELATION INC
2305 Historic Decatur Rd Ste 300 (92106-6052)
PHONE.................................619 876-5074
John F Landis, *CEO*
Theresa Benavidez, *
Harold Barnabas, *
Lori Paige, *
Dwayne Jacobs, *
EMP: **200 EST: 2007**
SALES (est): 24.28MM **Privately Held**
Web: www.corelationinc.com
SIC: **7371** Computer software development

(P-16002)
CORPTAX LLC
21550 Oxnard St Ste 700 (91367-7170)
PHONE.................................818 316-2400
EMP: **133**
Web: www.corptax.com
SIC: **7371** Computer software development
PA: Corptax, Llc
2100 E Lake Cook Rd # 800
Buffalo Grove IL

(P-16003)
COUNTY OF LOS ANGELES
Also Called: Internal Services
1100 N Eastern Ave (90063-3200)
PHONE.................................562 940-4324
David Wesolik, *Genl Mgr*
EMP: **2000**
Web: www.lacounty.gov
SIC: **7371** Computer software development and applications
PA: County Of Los Angeles
500 W Temple St Ste 437
Los Angeles CA
213 974-1101

(P-16004)
CRESCENTONE INC (HQ)
Also Called: Fujitsu Glovia, Inc.
200 Continental Blvd Fl 3 (90245-4526)
PHONE.................................310 563-7000
Chikara Ono, *CEO*
Jim Errington, *Ex VP*
Masahiro Cho, *CFO*
EMP: **150 EST: 1970**
SQ FT: 53,000
SALES (est): 46.73MM **Privately Held**
Web: www.crescentone.com
SIC: **7371** 7372 Computer software development; Prepackaged software
PA: Fujitsu Limited
1-5-2, Higashishimbashi
Minato-Ku TKY

(P-16005)
CU DIRECT CORPORATION (PA)
Also Called: Cudc
2855 E Guasti Rd Ste 500 (91761-1253)
P.O. Box 51482 (91761-0082)
PHONE.................................833 908-0121
Antony Boutelle, *Pr*
Keith Sultemeier, *
Jim Laffoon, *Vice Chairman*
Jerry Neemann, *
Craig S Montesanti, *
EMP: **175 EST: 1994**
SQ FT: 30,000
SALES (est): 88.92MM
SALES (corp-wide): 88.92MM **Privately Held**
Web: www.cudirect.com
SIC: **7371** Computer software development

(P-16006)
CUBIC TRNSP SYSTEMS INC (DH)
Also Called: Cubic
9233 Balboa Ave (92123-1513)
P.O. Box 85587 (92186-5587)
PHONE.................................858 268-3100
Stephen O Shewmaker, *CEO*
Walter C Zable, *
Raymond De Kozan, *
Steve Purcell, *
◆ EMP: **550 EST: 1950**
SALES (est): 244.67MM
SALES (corp-wide): 1.48B **Privately Held**
Web: www.cubic.com
SIC: **7371** 1731 3829 Custom computer programming services; Telephone and telephone equipment installation; Fare registers, for street cars, buses, etc.
HQ: Cubic Corporation
9233 Balboa Ave
San Diego CA
858 277-6780

(P-16007)
CYBERDEFENDER CORPORATION
617 W 7th St Fl 10 (90017-3879)
PHONE.................................323 449-0774
Kevin Harris, *Interim Chief Executive Officer*
Igor Barash, *COO*
EMP: **19 EST: 2003**
SALES (est): 4.22MM **Privately Held**
Web: www.cyberdefender.com
SIC: **7371** 7372 Custom computer programming services; Prepackaged software

(P-16008)
DATA PROCESSING DESIGN INC
Also Called: Goldfax
1409 Glenneyre St Ste B (92651-3171)
PHONE.................................714 695-1000
Brendan Nolan, *CEO*
Tom Politowski, *Pr*
EMP: **21 EST: 1976**
SALES (est): 3.61MM **Privately Held**
SIC: **7371** 7372 Computer software development; Prepackaged software

(P-16009)
DATADIRECT NETWORKS INC (PA)
Also Called: D D N
9351 Deering Ave (91311-5858)
PHONE.................................818 700-7600
Alex Bouzari, *CEO*
Paul Bloch, *
Ian Angelo, *
Robert Triendl, *
Bret Weber, *
▲ EMP: **120 EST: 1988**
SQ FT: 50,000
SALES (est): 149.51MM
SALES (corp-wide): 149.51MM **Privately Held**
Web: www.ddn.com
SIC: **7371** 7374 Custom computer programming services; Data processing service

(P-16010)
DAYBREAK GAME COMPANY LLC
Also Called: Daybreak
13500 Evening Creek Dr N Ste 300 (92128-8125)
PHONE.................................858 239-0500
▲ EMP: **450 EST: 2006**

SALES (est): 49.21MM
SALES (corp-wide): 533.82K **Privately Held**
Web: maintenance.daybreakgames.com
SIC: **7371** Computer software development
PA: Enad Global 7 Ab (Publ)
Sveavagen 17, Plan 5
Stockholm
738204439

(P-16011)
DAZ SYSTEMS LLC
Also Called: Daz
1003 E 4th Pl Ste 800 (90013-2775)
PHONE.................................310 640-1300
EMP: **375 EST: 1995**
SALES (est): 38.43MM **Privately Held**
SIC: **7371** 7372 Computer software development; Prepackaged software
HQ: Accenture Llp
500 W Madison St
Chicago IL
312 693-0161

(P-16012)
DESIGN SCIENCE INC
444 W Ocean Blvd Ste 800 (90802-4529)
PHONE.................................562 442-4779
Paul Topping, *Pr*
EMP: **30 EST: 1986**
SALES (est): 5.69MM **Privately Held**
Web: www.wiris.com
SIC: **7371** 7379 7372 5045 Computer software development; Computer related consulting services; Prepackaged software; Computers, peripherals, and software

(P-16013)
DEVIATION GAMES LLC
12100 Wilshire Blvd Ste 1150 (90025-7120)
PHONE.................................310 873-5225
EMP: **98 EST: 2020**
SALES (est): 1.58MM **Privately Held**
Web: www.deviationgames.com
SIC: **7371** Computer software development and applications

(P-16014)
DISNEY CNSMR PDTS INTRCTIVE MD
Also Called: Dcpi
1201 Flower St (91201-2417)
PHONE.................................818 263-1374
James Pitaro, *Ch*
Michael White, *Sr VP*
EMP: **100 EST: 2016**
SALES (est): 3.99MM
SALES (corp-wide): 88.9B **Publicly Held**
Web: www.disneyconnect.com
SIC: **7371** Software programming applications
PA: The Walt Disney Company
500 S Buena Vista St
Burbank CA
818 560-1000

(P-16015)
DISNEY INTERACTIVE STUDIOS INC
Also Called: Disney Interactive Studios
681 W Buena Vista St (91521-0001)
PHONE.................................818 553-5000
EMP: **270**
SALES (corp-wide): 88.9B **Publicly Held**
Web: www.thewaltdisneycompany.com
SIC: **7371** Computer software development
HQ: Disney Interactive Studios, Inc.
500 S Buena Vista St
Burbank CA
818 560-1000

(P-16016)
DISNEY INTERACTIVE STUDIOS INC
601 Circle Seven Dr (91201-2332)
PHONE..............................818 560-1000
Peter Casciani, *Mgr*
EMP: 270
SALES (corp-wide): 88.9B **Publicly Held**
Web: www.thewaltdisneycompany.com
SIC: 7371 Computer software development
HQ: Disney Interactive Studios, Inc.
    500 S Buena Vista St
    Burbank CA
    818 560-1000

(P-16017)
DISTILLERY TECH INC
Also Called: Distillery
1500 Rosecrans Ave Ste 500 (90266-3707)
PHONE..............................310 776-6234
Andrey Kudievskiy, *Pr*
EMP: 220 **EST:** 2012
SALES (est): 13.7MM **Privately Held**
Web: www.distillery.com
SIC: 7371 7372 7373 Computer software
    development; Application computer software
    ; Computer systems analysis and design

(P-16018)
DOCUPACE TECHNOLOGIES LLC (PA)
400 Corporate Pointe Ste 300 (90230)
P.O. Box 92117 (89193-2117)
PHONE..............................310 445-7722
Michael Pinsker, *Managing Member*
John Cunningham, *CIO**
James Caulkins, *CRO**
EMP: 200 **EST:** 2002
SQ FT: 1,500
SALES (est): 18.78MM
SALES (corp-wide): 18.78MM **Privately Held**
Web: www.docupace.com
SIC: 7371 Computer software development

(P-16019)
DYNASTY MARKETPLACE INC
716 Hampton Dr (90291-3019)
PHONE..............................804 837-0119
Elliot Burris, *CEO*
EMP: 336 **EST:** 2016
SALES (est): 213.52K
SALES (corp-wide): 471.88MM **Publicly Held**
SIC: 7371 Computer software development
    and applications
PA: Appfolio, Inc.
    70 Castilian Dr
    Santa Barbara CA
    805 364-6093

(P-16020)
EDUCATION SYSTEMS INC
1111 Torrey Pines Rd (92037-4550)
PHONE..............................858 454-9765
Andrew Nassir, *Pr*
Andrew Nassir, *CEO*
Andrei Sergeev, *Sr VP*
EMP: 22 **EST:** 1996
SQ FT: 4,500
SALES (est): 2.01MM **Privately Held**
Web: www.emaspro.com
SIC: 7371 7372 Computer software
    development; Prepackaged software

(P-16021)
EIGHTEENTH MERIDIAN INC
Also Called: Secure-Dmz
200 Spectrum Center Ste 300
(92618-5003)

PHONE..............................714 706-3643
Erol Karabeg, *Pr*
Dino Beslic, *
EMP: 500 **EST:** 1998
SALES (est): 18.56MM **Privately Held**
SIC: 7371 Custom computer programming
    services

(P-16022)
EINFOCHIPS INC
2361 Campus Dr Ste 105 (92612-1465)
PHONE..............................949 527-6459
Pratul Shroff, *Brnch Mgr*
EMP: 86
SALES (corp-wide): 37.12B **Publicly Held**
Web: www.einfochips.com
SIC: 7371 Computer software development
HQ: Einfochips Inc.
    2025 Gateway Pl Ste 238
    San Jose CA
    408 496-1882

(P-16023)
EINSTEIN INDUSTRIES INC
Also Called: Einstein Dental
6825 Flanders Dr (92121-2905)
P.O. Box 27149 (92198-1149)
PHONE..............................858 459-1182
EMP: 180 **EST:** 1995
SALES (est): 27.09MM **Privately Held**
Web: www.einsteinlaw.com
SIC: 7371 8742 8322 Computer software
    development; Marketing consulting services
    ; Referral service for personal and social
    problems

(P-16024)
ELLIE MAE INC
Also Called: ELLIE MAE, INC.
24025 Park Sorrento Ste 210 (91302-4018)
PHONE..............................818 223-2000
EMP: 382
SALES (corp-wide): 7.29B **Publicly Held**
Web: www.icemortgagetechnology.com
SIC: 7371 Computer software systems
    analysis and design, custom
HQ: Ice Mortgage Technology, Inc.
    4420 Rosewood Dr Ste 500
    Pleasanton CA
    855 224-8572

(P-16025)
EMIDS TECH PRIVATE LTD CORP
6320 Canoga Ave (91367-2526)
PHONE..............................805 304-5986
EMP: 2157
Web: www.emids.com
SIC: 7371 Computer software development
PA: Emids Technologies Private Limited
    Corp.
    318 Seaboard Ln Ste 110
    Franklin TN

(P-16026)
EPITEC INC
515 Olive Ave (92083-3439)
PHONE..............................760 650-2515
William Grivas, *Pr*
EMP: 900
SALES (corp-wide): 79.55MM **Privately Held**
Web: www.epitec.com
SIC: 7371 Computer software systems
    analysis and design, custom
PA: Epitec, Inc.
    26555 Evergreen Rd # 1700
    Southfield MI
    248 353-6800

(P-16027)
EQUATOR LLC (HQ)
Also Called: Equator Business Solutions
6060 Center Dr Ste 500 (90045-8857)
PHONE..............................310 469-9500
EMP: 200 **EST:** 2003
SALES (est): 41.28MM
SALES (corp-wide): 2.67MM **Privately Held**
Web: www.equator.com
SIC: 7371 Computer software development
    and applications
PA: Altisource Portfolio Solutions S.A.
    Boulevard Prince Henri 33
    Luxembourg

(P-16028)
ERP INTEGRATED SOLUTIONS LLC
Also Called: Shiperp
5000 Airport Plaza Dr Ste 230 (90815)
PHONE..............................562 425-7800
Joseph Cabrera, *Pr*
Doug Cole, *
Anthony Raimo, *
EMP: 100 **EST:** 2008
SALES (est): 9.86MM **Privately Held**
Web: www.shiperp.com
SIC: 7371 Computer software development

(P-16029)
EVERNOTE CORPORATION (PA)
12671 High Bluff Dr (92130-2014)
PHONE..............................650 216-7700
Chris O'neill, *CEO*
Phil Libin, *
Stepan Pachikov Fundr, *Prin*
Jeff Shotts, *
Dave Engberg, *
▲ **EMP:** 308 **EST:** 2004
SALES (est): 97.23MM
SALES (corp-wide): 97.23MM **Privately Held**
Web: www.evernote.com
SIC: 7371 Computer software development

(P-16030)
FAIR FINANCIAL CORP (PA)
1540 2nd St Ste 200 (90401-3513)
P.O. Box 409 (10523-0409)
PHONE..............................800 584-5000
Bradley Stewart, *CEO*
Georg Bauer, *
Craig Nehamen, *
EMP: 322 **EST:** 2015
SALES (est): 23.37MM
SALES (corp-wide): 23.37MM **Privately Held**
SIC: 7371 Computer software development
    and applications

(P-16031)
FATTAIL INC (PA)
23258 Calabasas Rd Ste 102 (91302-1322)
PHONE..............................818 615-0380
Douglas Huntington, *CEO*
Stephen Pelletier, *
EMP: 28 **EST:** 2001
SALES (est): 8.35MM
SALES (corp-wide): 8.35MM **Privately Held**
Web: www.fattail.com
SIC: 7371 7372 Computer software
    development; Business oriented computer
    software

(P-16032)
FICTO HOLDINGS LLC
Also Called: Ficto
1049 Havenhurst Dr Ste 236 (90046-6002)

PHONE..............................424 250-2400
EMP: 17 **EST:** 2018
SALES (est): 3.33MM **Privately Held**
Web: www.ficto.tv
SIC: 7371 2741 Computer software
    development and applications; Internet
    publishing and broadcasting

(P-16033)
FINANCIAL INFO NETWRK INC
Also Called: F I N
11164 Bertrand Ave (91344-4005)
P.O. Box 7954 (91409-7954)
PHONE..............................818 782-0331
Jerry Sears, *Pr*
EMP: 30 **EST:** 1969
SQ FT: 6,000
SALES (est): 2.82MM **Privately Held**
Web: www.fingps.com
SIC: 7371 7372 Custom computer
    programming services; Prepackaged
    software

(P-16034)
FOREMAY INC (PA)
225 S Lake Ave Ste 300 (91101-3009)
PHONE..............................408 228-3468
Haining Fan, *CEO*
Tiffany Fan, *Pr*
EMP: 46 **EST:** 2002
SALES (est): 4.66MM **Privately Held**
Web: www.foremay.net
SIC: 7371 7373 3572 Computer software
    systems analysis and design, custom;
    Computer systems analysis and design;
    Computer storage devices

(P-16035)
FRONTECH N FUJITSU AMER INC (DH)
Also Called: Ffna
36 Technology Dr Ste 150 (92618-5308)
PHONE..............................877 766-7545
Shuhei Oyake, *Pr*
▲ **EMP:** 219 **EST:** 1990
SALES (est): 67.55MM **Privately Held**
Web: www.fujitsufrontechna.com
SIC: 7371 Computer software development
    and applications
HQ: Fujitsu Frontech Limited
    1776, Yanokuchi
    Inagi TKY

(P-16036)
G2 SOFTWARE SYSTEMS INC
4025 Hancock St Ste 105 (92110-5167)
PHONE..............................619 222-8025
EMP: 140 **EST:** 1898
SQ FT: 4,000
SALES (est): 12.56MM **Privately Held**
Web: www.g2ss.com
SIC: 7371 Computer software development

(P-16037)
GAN LIMITED
400 Spectrum Center Dr Ste 1900
(92618-5025)
PHONE..............................702 964-5777
Seamus Mcgill, *Interim Chief Executive Officer*
Simon Knock, *CIO*
Sylvia Tiscareno, *CLO*
Brian Chang, *Interim Chief Financial Officer*
EMP: 288 **EST:** 2002
SALES (est): 141.53MM **Privately Held**
Web: www.gan.com
SIC: 7371 7374 Custom computer
    programming services; Data processing
    and preparation

PRODUCTS & SVCS

(P-16038)
GEHRY TECHNOLOGIES INC
12181 Bluff Creek Dr (90094-2992)
PHONE.....................310 862-1200
Meaghan Lloyd, *CEO*
Michael Lin, *CFO*
Dhruba Kalita, *CIO*
EMP: 95 **EST:** 2002
SQ FT: 2,000
SALES (est): 14.36MM
SALES (corp-wide): 3.68B **Publicly Held**
Web: www.gehrytechnologies.com
SIC: 7371 Computer software development
and applications
PA: Trimble Inc.
10368 Westmoor Dr
Westminster CO
720 887-6100

(P-16039)
GENEX (DH)
800 Corporate Pointe Ste 100
(90230-7667)
PHONE.....................424 672-9500
EMP: 130 **EST:** 1995
SQ FT: 12,000
SALES (est): 11.15MM
SALES (corp-wide): 3.68B **Publicly Held**
Web: www.genex.com
SIC: 7371 7379 4813 Computer software
development and applications; Computer
related consulting services; Online service
providers
HQ: Hawkeye Acquisition, Inc.
1716 Locust St
Des Moines IA
515 284-3000

(P-16040)
GLOBAL SERVICE RESOURCES INC
Also Called: Computerworks Technologies
711 S Victory Blvd (91502-2426)
P.O. Box 4057 (91503-4057)
PHONE.....................800 679-7658
Nick Sefayan, *Pr*
▲ **EMP:** 80 **EST:** 1991
SQ FT: 7,000
SALES (est): 5.9MM **Privately Held**
Web: www.globalserviceresources.com
SIC: 7371 7363 Computer software
development; Labor resource services

(P-16041)
GOOD SPORTS PLUS LTD
Also Called: ARC
370 Amapola Ave Ste 208 (90501-7241)
PHONE.....................310 671-4400
Gary Lipsky, *
Kitty Cohen, *
EMP: 300 **EST:** 2002
SQ FT: 3,500
SALES (est): 30.47MM **Privately Held**
Web: www.arc-experience.com
SIC: 7371 7997 Computer software
development and applications; Outdoor
field clubs

(P-16042)
GRINDR LLC
750 N San Vicente Blvd (90069-5788)
P.O. Box 69176 (90069-0176)
PHONE.....................310 776-6680
George Arison, *CEO*
EMP: 206 **EST:** 2010
SALES (est): 31.61MM
SALES (corp-wide): 195.01MM **Publicly Held**
Web: www.grindr.com

SIC: 7371 Computer software development
PA: Grindr Inc.
750 N San Vicnte Blvd
West Hollywood CA

(P-16043)
H & R ACCOUNTS INC
Also Called: Avadyne Health
3131 Camino Del Rio N Ste 1500 (92108)
PHONE.....................619 819-8844
Linda Hevern, *Brnch Mgr*
EMP: 150
SALES (corp-wide): 50.81MM **Privately Held**
Web: www.avadynehealth.com
SIC: 7371 Computer software development
HQ: H & R Accounts, Inc.
5320 22nd Ave
Moline IL
309 736-2255

(P-16044)
HAPPYCO INC (PA)
5857 Owens Ave Ste 300 (92008-5507)
PHONE.....................415 230-9832
Jindou Lee, *CEO*
EMP: 195 **EST:** 2011
SALES (est): 18.03MM
SALES (corp-wide): 18.03MM **Privately Held**
Web: www.happy.co
SIC: 7371 Computer software development

(P-16045)
HEAT WAVES LLC
Also Called: Heat Software
4201 Jamboree Rd Unit 518 (92660-3066)
PHONE.....................719 651-4942
EMP: 135 **EST:** 2018
SALES (est): 1.25MM **Privately Held**
Web: www.heatwaves.co
SIC: 7371 Computer software development
and applications

(P-16046)
HOME JUNCTION INC
1 Venture Ste 300 (92618-7416)
PHONE.....................858 777-9533
John Perkins, *CEO*
EMP: 88 **EST:** 2013
SALES (est): 10.6MM
SALES (corp-wide): 17.24MM **Privately Held**
Web: www.homejunction.com
SIC: 7371 Computer software development
PA: Attom Data Solutions, Llc
530 Technology Dr Ste 100
Irvine CA
949 502-8300

(P-16047)
HONEY SCIENCE LLC
Also Called: Honey
963 E 4th St Ste 100 (90013-2645)
PHONE.....................949 795-1695
George Ruan, *Managing Member*
Ryan Hudson, *
EMP: 112 **EST:** 2012
SALES (est): 11.83MM
SALES (corp-wide): 27.52B **Publicly Held**
Web: www.joinhoney.com
SIC: 7371 Software programming
applications
PA: Paypal Holdings, Inc.
2211 N 1st St
San Jose CA
408 967-1000

(P-16048)
HVANTAGE TECHNOLOGIES INC (PA)
22048 Sherman Way Ste 306 (91303-3011)
PHONE.....................818 661-6301
Krishna Baderia, *CEO*
EMP: 79 **EST:** 2011
SALES (est): 4.62MM
SALES (corp-wide): 4.62MM **Privately Held**
Web: www.hvantagetechnologies.com
SIC: 7371 8748 7372 7373 Computer
software development; Systems
engineering consultant, ex. computer or
professional; Application computer software
; Systems engineering, computer related

(P-16049)
ID ANALYTICS LLC
10089 Willow Creek Rd Ste 120
(92131-1698)
PHONE.....................858 312-6200
Rick Trainor, *CEO*
EMP: 140 **EST:** 2002
SALES (est): 23.72MM
SALES (corp-wide): 10.3B **Privately Held**
Web: risk.lexisnexis.com
SIC: 7371 Computer software development
HQ: Lexisnexis Risk Solutions Inc.
1000 Alderman Dr
Alpharetta GA
678 694-6000

(P-16050)
IMAGE-X ENTERPRISES INC
Also Called: Image X
6464 Hollister Ave Ste 7g (93117-3110)
PHONE.....................805 964-3535
Mohammed Shaikh, *Ch Bd*
EMP: 17 **EST:** 1989
SQ FT: 4,000
SALES (est): 1.29MM **Privately Held**
Web: www.imagexusa.com
SIC: 7371 3577 Computer software
development; Computer peripheral
equipment, nec

(P-16051)
INDIZEN OPTICAL TECH AMER LLC
Also Called: Iot Photochromics
2925 California St Ste 201 (90503-3914)
PHONE.....................310 783-1533
Daniel Crespo, *Managing Member*
EMP: 18 **EST:** 2012
SALES (est): 1.97MM **Privately Held**
SIC: 7371 3827 Computer software systems
analysis and design, custom; Optical
instruments and lenses
HQ: Indizen Optical Technologies Sl
Calle Suero De Quilones, 34 - 36 3 Plt
Madrid M

(P-16052)
INFINITE TECHNOLOGIES LLC
1667 N Batavia St (92867-3508)
PHONE.....................786 408-7995
EMP: 147 **EST:** 2017
SALES (est): 2.54MM **Privately Held**
Web: www.infinitetechs.com
SIC: 7371 Computer software development
and applications

(P-16053)
INFOMAGNUS LLC
5882 Bolsa Ave Ste 210 (92649-5700)
PHONE.....................714 810-3430
Sal Manzo, *Managing Member*
Kaveh Mahjoob, *

EMP: 90 **EST:** 2013
SALES (est): 5.96MM **Privately Held**
Web: www.infomagnus.com
SIC: 7371 7379 Software programming
applications; Computer related consulting
services

(P-16054)
INNOVASYSTEMS INTL LLC
850 Beech St Unit 1006 (92101-2895)
PHONE.....................619 955-5890
EMP: 198
SALES (corp-wide): 46.49MM **Privately Held**
Web: www.innovasi.com
SIC: 7371 Computer software development
HQ: Innovasystems International Llc
2385 Northside Dr Ste 300
San Diego CA
619 955-5800

(P-16055)
INTELEX SYSTEMS INC
21900 Burbank Blvd Ste 3087
(91367-6469)
PHONE.....................818 992-2969
Saritha Myadam, *CEO*
Sarith Myadam, *CFO*
EMP: 84 **EST:** 2009
SALES (est): 4.38MM **Privately Held**
Web: www.intelexsystemsinc.com
SIC: 7371 Computer software development

(P-16056)
INTERNATIONAL LOTTERY & TOTALIZATOR SYSTEMS INC
Also Called: Ilts California
2310 Cousteau Ct (92081-8346)
PHONE.....................760 598-1655
EMP: 33
Web: www.ilts.com
SIC: 7371 7372 3572 Custom computer
programming services; Prepackaged
software; Computer storage devices

(P-16057)
INTERNTNAL LTTERY TTLZTOR SYST
Also Called: Ilts Delaware
2310 Cousteau Ct (92081-8346)
PHONE.....................760 598-1655
Theodore A Johnson, *
▲ **EMP:** 33 **EST:** 1999
SALES (est): 10.03MM **Privately Held**
Web: www.ilts.com
SIC: 7371 7372 3572 Custom computer
programming services; Prepackaged
software; Computer storage devices
HQ: Berjaya Lottery Management (Hk)
Limited
54/F Hopewell Ctr
Wan Chai HK

(P-16058)
IRISE (PA)
2381 Rosecrans Ave Ste 100 (90245-4920)
PHONE.....................800 556-0399
Emmet B Keeffe Iii, *CEO*
Maurice Martin, *
Jacques Marine, *
Stephen Brickley, *
Dean Terry, *
▲ **EMP:** 94 **EST:** 1997
SALES (est): 21.52MM
SALES (corp-wide): 21.52MM **Privately Held**
Web: www.irise.com
SIC: 7371 Computer software development

(P-16059)
ISAAC FAIR CORPORATION
Also Called: Mindwave Software
3661 Valley Centre Dr (92130-3321)
PHONE..........................858 369-8000
Steve Gutschow, *Prin*
EMP: 88
SALES (corp-wide): 1.51B **Publicly Held**
Web: www.fico.com
SIC: 7371 Computer software development
PA: Fair Isaac Corporation
　　5 W Mendenhall St Ste 105
　　Bozeman MT
　　406 982-7276

(P-16060)
ITREX GROUP USA CORPORATION
120 Vantis Dr Ste 545 (92656-2679)
PHONE..........................213 436-7785
EMP: 275
SALES (corp-wide): 12.84MM **Privately Held**
Web: www.itrexgroup.com
SIC: 7371 Computer software development
PA: Itrex Group Usa Corporation
　　1120 Vantis Dr Ste 545
　　Aliso Viejo CA
　　213 436-7785

(P-16061)
JAVANAN INC
Also Called: Javanan Magazine
24629 Calvert St (91367-1018)
PHONE..........................310 741-0011
Mehdi Zokaei, *CEO*
EMP: 20 **EST:** 1991
SALES (est): 1.02MM **Privately Held**
Web: www.javanan.com
SIC: 7371 2721 Computer software development and applications; Magazines: publishing only, not printed on site

(P-16062)
KOFAX INC (PA)
15211 Laguna Canyon Rd (92618-3146)
PHONE..........................949 783-1000
Reynolds Bish, *CEO*
Cort Townsend, *
Howard Dratler, *
Anthony Macciola, *
Grant Johnson, *
▼ **EMP:** 500 **EST:** 1985
SQ FT: 100,000
SALES (est): 538.26MM
SALES (corp-wide): 538.26MM **Privately Held**
Web: www.kofax.com
SIC: 7371 3577 Computer software development; Input/output equipment, computer

(P-16063)
KRG TECHNOLOGIES INC (PA)
25000 Avenue Stanford Ste 243 (91355)
PHONE..........................661 257-9967
Balamurugan Subbiah, *Pr*
Hemalatha Rajagopala, *CEO*
EMP: 490 **EST:** 2003
SQ FT: 780
SALES (est): 42.74MM
SALES (corp-wide): 42.74MM **Privately Held**
Web: www.krgtech.com
SIC: 7371 Computer software development and applications

(P-16064)
KTB SOFTWARE LLC ✪
11101 W Olympic Blvd (90064-1805)
PHONE..........................213 935-0902
Diop Mckenzie, *Managing Member*
EMP: 84 **EST:** 2023
SALES (est): 2.24MM **Privately Held**
SIC: 7371 Computer software development and applications

(P-16065)
LIMINEX INC (PA)
Also Called: Goguardian
2030 E Maple Ave Ste 100 (90245-5008)
PHONE..........................888 310-0410
Advait Shinde, *CEO*
Michael Jonas, *CFO*
Dionna Smith, *DIVERSITY*
EMP: 219 **EST:** 2014
SQ FT: 30,000
SALES (est): 58.73MM
SALES (corp-wide): 58.73MM **Privately Held**
Web: www.goguardian.com
SIC: 7371 7389 Computer software development; Business services, nec

(P-16066)
LOGILITY INC
4885 Greencraig Ln 200 (92123-1664)
PHONE..........................858 565-4238
EMP: 55
SALES (corp-wide): 123.66MM **Publicly Held**
Web: www.logility.com
SIC: 7371 7372 Computer software development; Prepackaged software
HQ: Logility, Inc.
　　470 E Paces Ferry Rd Ne
　　Atlanta GA
　　800 762-5207

(P-16067)
LUMIRADX INC
444 S Cedros Ave Ste 101 (92075-1966)
PHONE..........................951 201-9384
Jarrod Provins, *Prin*
EMP: 137
SALES (corp-wide): 421.43MM **Privately Held**
Web: www.lumiradx.com
SIC: 7371 Custom computer programming services
HQ: Lumiradx, Inc.
　　221 Crescent St Ste 502
　　Waltham MA
　　617 621-9775

(P-16068)
MAINTECH INCORPORATED
2401 N Glassell St (92865-2705)
P.O. Box 13500 (92857-8500)
PHONE..........................714 921-8000
Tony Donato, *VP*
EMP: 200
SQ FT: 1,200
SALES (corp-wide): 23.92MM **Privately Held**
Web: www.maintech.com
SIC: 7371 3577 Computer software systems analysis and design, custom; Computer peripheral equipment, nec
PA: Maintech, Incorporated
　　14 Commerce Dr Ste 200
　　Cranford NJ
　　973 330-3200

(P-16069)
MANGO TECHNOLOGIES INC (PA)

Also Called: Clickup
350 10th Ave Ste 500 (92101-7497)
PHONE..........................888 625-4258
Brian Evans, *CEO*
EMP: 694 **EST:** 2016
SALES (est): 99.03MM
SALES (corp-wide): 99.03MM **Privately Held**
Web: www.clickup.com
SIC: 7371 Computer software development and applications

(P-16070)
MARIGOLD USA INC
Also Called: Experian Qas
475 Anton Blvd (92626-7037)
PHONE..........................617 385-6786
Thomas Schutz, *Genl Mgr*
EMP: 173
SALES (corp-wide): 74.21MM **Privately Held**
Web: www.cheetahdigital.com
SIC: 7371 Computer software development
HQ: Marigold Usa, Inc.
　　72 W Adams St Fl 8
　　Chicago IL

(P-16071)
MARKET SCAN INFO SYSTEMS INC
Also Called: Market Scan
815 Camarillo Springs Rd (93012-9457)
PHONE..........................800 658-7226
Russell West, *Pr*
Carsten Preisz, *Chief Business Officer**
Mathew Hermann, *
EMP: 85 **EST:** 1987
SQ FT: 10,500
SALES (est): 10.84MM
SALES (corp-wide): 11.18B **Publicly Held**
Web: www.marketscan.com
SIC: 7371 Computer software development
PA: S&P Global Inc.
　　55 Water St
　　New York NY
　　212 438-1000

(P-16072)
MEDIMIZER SOFTWARE
Also Called: Medimizer
9920 Pacific Heights Blvd Ste 150 (92121)
PHONE..........................760 642-2000
Mark Woodruff, *Pr*
EMP: 20 **EST:** 2011
SALES (est): 1.58MM **Privately Held**
Web: www.medimizer.com
SIC: 7371 7372 Computer software development; Prepackaged software

(P-16073)
MELISSA DATA CORPORATION (PA)
Also Called: Mailers Software
22382 Avenida Empresa (92688-2112)
PHONE..........................949 858-3000
EMP: 90 **EST:** 1985
SALES (est): 7.57MM
SALES (corp-wide): 7.57MM **Privately Held**
Web: www.melissa.com
SIC: 7371 Computer software development

(P-16074)
MELLMO INC
Also Called: Roambi
131 Aberdeen Dr (92007-1821)
PHONE..........................858 847-3272
EMP: 140
SIC: 7371 Custom computer programming services

(P-16075)
MIR3 INC
3398 Carmel Mountain Rd # 100 (92121-1044)
PHONE..........................858 724-1200
EMP: 90
SIC: 7371 Computer software development and applications

(P-16076)
MITCHELL INTERNATIONAL INC (PA)
Also Called: Enlyte
9771 Clairemont Mesa Blvd Ste A (92124-1300)
P.O. Box 229001 (92192-9001)
PHONE..........................858 368-7000
Alex Sun, *CEO*
Nina Smith, *
Debbie Day, *
Dave Torrence, *
Erez Nir, *
EMP: 229 **EST:** 1977
SQ FT: 141,000
SALES (est): 3.1B
SALES (corp-wide): 3.1B **Privately Held**
Web: www.mitchell.com
SIC: 7371 Computer software development

(P-16077)
MODERN CAMPUS USA INC (PA)
1320 Flynn Rd Ste 100 (93012-8745)
PHONE..........................805 484-9400
Brian Kibby, *CEO*
Tom Nalevanko, *
EMP: 60 **EST:** 1982
SQ FT: 6,600
SALES (est): 12.37MM
SALES (corp-wide): 12.37MM **Privately Held**
Web: www.moderncampus.com
SIC: 7371 7372 Computer software development; Prepackaged software

(P-16078)
MYEVALUATIONSCOM INC
11111 W Olympic Blvd Ste 401 (90064-1842)
PHONE..........................646 422-0554
David Melamed, *Ex Dir*
EMP: 25 **EST:** 2005
SALES (est): 1.69MM **Privately Held**
Web: www.myevaluations.com
SIC: 7371 7372 Computer software systems analysis and design, custom; Educational computer software

(P-16079)
NC AMERICA LLC ✪
400 Spectrum Center Dr Fl 18 (92618-5025)
PHONE..........................949 447-6287
Taekhun Kim, *CEO*
Taekhun Kim, *Managing Member*
Eunjung Kim, *
EMP: 26 **EST:** 2023
SALES (est): 1.12MM **Privately Held**
SIC: 7371 7372 Computer software development and applications; Prepackaged software

(P-16080)
NEONROOTS LLC
8560 W Sunset Blvd Ste 500 (90069-2311)
PHONE..........................310 907-9210
Benjamin C Lee, *CEO*
EMP: 125 **EST:** 2012
SALES (est): 4.27MM **Privately Held**
Web: www.neonroots.com

P R O D U C T S   &   S V C S

SIC: **7371** Computer software development and applications

(P-16081)
NEUDESIC LLC (HQ)
Also Called: IBM
200 Spectrum Center Dr Ste 2000
(92618-5013)
PHONE..................949 754-4500
Parsa Rohani, *CEO*
Tim Marshall, *
EMP: 125 **EST:** 2001
SQ FT: 15,150
SALES (est): 25.72K
SALES (corp-wide): 60.53B **Publicly Held**
Web: www.neudesic.com
SIC: **7371** Computer software development
PA: International Business Machines
Corporation
1 New Orchard Rd Ste 1 # 1
Armonk NY
914 499-1900

(P-16082)
NEUINTEL LLC (PA)
Also Called: Pricespider
20 Pacifica Ste 1000 (92618-3307)
PHONE..................949 625-6117
Anthony Ferry, *CEO*
Jon Pfortmiller, *Pr*
Lucas Baerg, *CFO*
EMP: 80 **EST:** 2004
SQ FT: 17,000
SALES (est): 26.97MM
SALES (corp-wide): 26.97MM **Privately Held**
Web: www.pricespider.com
SIC: **7371** Computer software development

(P-16083)
NEVERSOFT ENTERTAINMENT INC
Also Called: Neversoft Entertainment
21255 Burbank Blvd Ste 600 (91367-6610)
PHONE..................818 610-4100
EMP: 37 **EST:** 1994
SALES (est): 2.47MM
SALES (corp-wide): 211.91B **Publicly Held**
SIC: **7371** 7372 Computer code authors; Prepackaged software
HQ: Activision Blizzard, Inc.
2701 Olympic Blvd Bldg B
Santa Monica CA
310 255-2000

(P-16084)
NEXGENIX INC (PA)
2 Peters Canyon Rd # 200 (92606-1798)
PHONE..................714 665-6240
Rick Dutta, *CEO*
Don Ganguly, *Ch Bd*
Mark Iwanowski, *COO*
Ravi Renduchintala, *VP*
EMP: 258 **EST:** 1990
SQ FT: 14,264
SALES (est): 19.94MM **Privately Held**
SIC: **7371** 8748 4813 Computer software development; Systems analysis or design; Online service providers

(P-16085)
NGA 911 LLC
Also Called: Telecommunication
8383 Wilshire Blvd Ste 800 (90211-2425)
PHONE..................877 899-8337
Don Ferguson, *CEO*
Jackie Barnes, *
EMP: 120 **EST:** 2016
SALES (est): 23.38MM **Privately Held**

Web: www.nga911.com
SIC: **7371** Computer software development and applications

(P-16086)
NKSFB LLC
10960 Wilshire Blvd Fl 5 (90024-3708)
PHONE..................310 277-4657
Mickey Segal, *Managing Member*
EMP: 248 **EST:** 2018
SALES (est): 8.58MM **Privately Held**
Web: www.nksfb.com
SIC: **7371** 7372 Computer software systems analysis and design, custom; Business oriented computer software

(P-16087)
NLYTE SOFTWARE AMERICAS LTD
1380 El Cajon Blvd Ste 220 (92020-5703)
PHONE..................866 386-5983
Bernard Liautaud, *Ch*
EMP: 85
SALES (corp-wide): 20.42B **Publicly Held**
Web: www.nlyte.com
SIC: **7371** Computer software development
HQ: Nlyte Software Americas Limited
275 Raritan Center Pkwy
Edison NJ

(P-16088)
NOVALOGIC INC (PA)
27489 Agoura Rd Ste 300 (91301-2419)
PHONE..................818 880-1997
John Garcia, *CEO*
David Seeholzer, *VP*
John Butrovich, *VP*
Kyle Freeman, *VP*
EMP: 95 **EST:** 1985
SALES (est): 7.14MM
SALES (corp-wide): 7.14MM **Privately Held**
Web: www.novalogic.com
SIC: **7371** 5734 7372 Computer software development; Software, business and non-game; Prepackaged software

(P-16089)
NUCLEUSHEALTH LLC
Also Called: Statrad - Radconnect
13280 Evening Creek Dr S Ste 110
(92128-4101)
PHONE..................858 251-3400
EMP: 98 **EST:** 2008
SQ FT: 8,413
SALES (est): 20.19MM
SALES (corp-wide): 324.16B **Publicly Held**
Web: www.statrad.com
SIC: **7371** 8748 Computer software development; Business consulting, nec
HQ: Change Healthcare Inc.
424 Church St Ste 1400
Nashville TN
615 932-3000

(P-16090)
OPERATION TECHNOLOGY INC
Also Called: Etap
17 Goodyear Ste 100 (92618-1812)
PHONE..................949 462-0100
Farrokh Shokooh, *Pr*
Nikta Nikzad Shokooh, *Corporate Secretary*
EMP: 90 **EST:** 1986
SQ FT: 32,000
SALES (est): 20.14MM **Privately Held**
Web: www.etap.com

SIC: **7371** 8732 8249 Computer software development; Research services, except laboratory; Business training services

(P-16091)
PACIFIC TECH SOLUTIONS LLC
15530 Rockfield Blvd Ste B4 (92618)
PHONE..................949 830-1623
Frederick Minturn, *Managing Member*
EMP: 108 **EST:** 1987
SQ FT: 3,000
SALES (est): 4.97MM **Privately Held**
Web: www.pts1.com
SIC: **7371** Computer software development
HQ: Msx International Rns Llc
26555 Evergreen Rd # 1300
Southfield MI
248 829-6300

(P-16092)
PANDEMIC STUDIOS LLC
5510 Lincoln Blvd (90094-2034)
PHONE..................310 450-5199
Joshua Resnick, *VP*
Andrew Goldman, *
Greg Borrud, *
EMP: 260 **EST:** 1998
SQ FT: 50,000
SALES (est): 22.19MM
SALES (corp-wide): 7.43B **Publicly Held**
SIC: **7371** Computer software development
HQ: Electronic Arts Redwood Llc
209 Redwood Shores Pkwy
Redwood City CA
650 628-1500

(P-16093)
PARALLEL 6 INC (PA)
1455 Frazee Rd Ste 900 (92108-4310)
PHONE..................619 452-1750
Allan Camaisa, *CEO*
Adam Halbridge, *
EMP: 30 **EST:** 2009
SQ FT: 28,000
SALES (est): 3.19MM
SALES (corp-wide): 3.19MM **Privately Held**
Web: www.parallel6.com
SIC: **7371** 7372 Computer software development; Business oriented computer software

(P-16094)
PETDESK
2044 1st Ave Ste 200 (92101-2089)
PHONE..................202 431-3045
Abraham Hanono, *Prin*
EMP: 98 **EST:** 2017
SALES (est): 5.03MM **Privately Held**
Web: www.petdesk.com
SIC: **7371** Computer software development and applications

(P-16095)
PHONE CHECK SOLUTIONS LLC
Also Called: Software
16027 Ventura Blvd Ste 605 (91436)
PHONE..................310 365-1855
Chris Sabeti, *CEO*
EMP: 358 **EST:** 2016
SALES (est): 10.75MM **Privately Held**
Web: www.phonecheck.com
SIC: **7371** Software programming applications

(P-16096)
PLATFORM SCIENCE INC
9560 Towne Centre Dr # 200 (92121-1972)
PHONE..................844 475-8724

John C Kennedy Iii, *CEO*
Chris Sultemeier, *
Greg Ivancich, *
Gerald Choung, *CRO*
EMP: 140 **EST:** 2015
SALES (est): 18.46MM **Privately Held**
Web: www.platformscience.com
SIC: **7371** 7372 Custom computer programming services; Business oriented computer software

(P-16097)
PLAYHAVEN LLC
1447 2nd St Ste 200 (90401-2301)
PHONE..................310 308-9668
Mike Jones, *Pr*
Greg Gilman, *
Tom Dare, *
EMP: 115 **EST:** 2014
SQ FT: 15,000
SALES (est): 426.1K **Privately Held**
SIC: **7371** 7311 Computer software development and applications; Advertising agencies
PA: Rockyou, Inc.
3305 Jerusalem Ave # 201
Wantagh NY

(P-16098)
PROCORE TECHNOLOGIES INC (PA)
6309 Carpinteria Ave (93013-2924)
PHONE..................866 477-6267
Craig F Courtemanche Junior, *Pr*
Craig F Courtemanche Junior, *Ch Bd*
Howard Fu, *CFO*
Benjamin C Singer, *CLO*
Joy D Durling, *CDO*
EMP: 3304 **EST:** 2002
SQ FT: 200,000
SALES (est): 720.2MM
SALES (corp-wide): 720.2MM **Publicly Held**
Web: www.procore.com
SIC: **7371** Computer software development

(P-16099)
PROLIFICS TESTING INC
24025 Park Sorrento Ste 405 (91302-4018)
PHONE..................925 485-9535
Danis Yadegar, *Pr*
Dale Lampson, *VP*
Rutesh Shah, *VP*
Armen Tekerian, *VP*
Claude Fenner, *VP*
EMP: 22 **EST:** 1988
SQ FT: 6,500
SALES (est): 4.4MM **Privately Held**
Web: www.prolifics.com
SIC: **7371** 7372 Computer software development; Prepackaged software
HQ: Prolifics Application Services, Inc.
24025 Park Sorrento # 405
Calabasas CA
646 201-4967

(P-16100)
PSYONIX LLC
Also Called: Rocket League
401 W A St Ste 2400 (92101-3524)
PHONE..................619 622-8772
David F Hagewood, *CEO*
Jessica Hagewood, *Sec*
EMP: 83 **EST:** 2012
SQ FT: 40,000
SALES (est): 11.26MM **Privately Held**
Web: www.psyonix.com
SIC: **7371** Computer software development
PA: Epic Games, Inc.
620 Crossroads Blvd

Cary NC

(P-16101)
RAINTREE SYSTEMS INC
30650 Rancho California Rd Ste 406
(92591-3279)
PHONE................................951 252-9400
Richard V Welty, *CEO*
Vu Nguyen, *CPO**
Scott Rongo, ***
EMP: 190 **EST:** 1982
SALES (est): 25.24MM **Privately Held**
Web: www.raintreeinc.com
SIC: 7371 5045 5734 Computer software development; Computer software; Computer and software stores

(P-16102)
REAPPLICATIONS INC
8910 University Center Ln Ste 300 (92122-1029)
PHONE................................619 230-0209
Richard Boyle, *CEO*
EMP: 164 **EST:** 1996
SALES (est): 962K
SALES (corp-wide): 2.18B **Publicly Held**
Web: www.reapplications.com
SIC: 7371 Computer software development
HQ: Loopnet, Inc.
101 California St # 4300
San Francisco CA

(P-16103)
RISA TECH INC
27442 Portola Pkwy Ste 200 (92610-2822)
PHONE................................949 951-5815
Amber Freund, *CEO*
EMP: 22 **EST:** 2017
SALES (est): 5.25MM
SALES (corp-wide): 771.28MM **Privately Held**
Web: www.risa.com
SIC: 7371 7372 Computer software development; Prepackaged software
PA: Nemetschek Se
Konrad-Zuse-Platz 1
Munchen BY
895404590

(P-16104)
ROGUE GAMES INC
Also Called: Rogue Games
4056 Ventura Canyon Ave (91423-4715)
PHONE................................650 483-8008
Michael Delaet, *Prin*
Michael C Delaet, *Mgr*
EMP: 20 **EST:** 2017
SALES (est): 1.27MM **Privately Held**
Web: www.rogueco.com
SIC: 7371 2741 Computer software development and applications; Miscellaneous publishing

(P-16105)
ROOTSTRAP INC
8306 Wilshire Blvd Ste 249 (90211-2304)
PHONE................................310 907-9210
David Jarrett, *CEO*
Fernando Colman, ***
Anthony Figueroa, ***
EMP: 134 **EST:** 2015
SALES (est): 4.31MM **Privately Held**
Web: www.rootstrap.com
SIC: 7371 Computer software development

(P-16106)
SAALEX CORP
27525 Enterprise Cir W Ste 101a (92590)
PHONE................................951 543-9259
EMP: 567

SALES (corp-wide): 96.07MM **Privately Held**
Web: www.saalex.com
SIC: 7371 Custom computer programming services
PA: Saalex Corp.
811 Camarillo Springs Rd A
Camarillo CA
805 482-1070

(P-16107)
SAMEDAY TECHNOLOGIES INC
Also Called: Sameday Health
523 Victoria Ave (90291-4832)
PHONE................................310 697-8126
Felix Huettenbach, *Pr*
EMP: 238 **EST:** 2021
SALES (est): 4.64MM **Privately Held**
Web: www.samedayhealth.com
SIC: 7371 Computer software development and applications

(P-16108)
SCHOOL-LINK TECHNOLOGIES INC
1437 6th St (90401-2509)
P.O. Box 2410 (90407-2410)
PHONE................................310 434-2700
EMP: 90
Web: www.heartlandschoolsolutions.com
SIC: 7371 Computer software development

(P-16109)
SCIFORMA CORPORATION
600 B St Ste 300 (92101-4505)
P.O. Box 9502 (95157-0502)
PHONE................................408 899-0398
Yann Lebihan, *CEO*
Roger Meade, ***
Charles Meade, ***
Dan Karleskint, ***
EMP: 28 **EST:** 2002
SALES (est): 9.86MM
SALES (corp-wide): 3.36MM **Privately Held**
Web: www.sciforma.com
SIC: 7371 7372 Computer software development; Prepackaged software
PA: Sciforma Holdco
9 Rue Ybry
Neuilly Sur Seine
178945570

(P-16110)
SECOND SPECTRUM INC
312 E 1st St (90012-3902)
PHONE................................213 995-6860
Yu-han Chang, *Owner*
EMP: 122 **EST:** 2013
SALES (est): 6.54MM **Privately Held**
Web: www.secondspectrum.com
SIC: 7371 Software programming applications

(P-16111)
SECUREAUTH CORPORATION (PA)
49 Discovery (92618-6713)
PHONE................................949 777-6959
Paul Trulove, *CEO*
Jeff Lo, ***
Darin Pendergraft, ***
Nick Mansour, *Executive Worldwide Sales Vice-President**
Keith Graham, ***
EMP: 186 **EST:** 2005
SALES (est): 33.75MM **Privately Held**
Web: www.secureauth.com
SIC: 7371 Computer software development

(P-16112)
SELECT DATA INC
Also Called: Select Data
4175 E La Palma Ave Ste 205 (92807-1842)
PHONE................................714 577-1000
Edward A Buckley, *CEO*
Pam Hernandez, ***
Tawny Nichols, ***
Ted A Schulte, ***
Pete Poulis, ***
EMP: 151 **EST:** 1991
SALES (est): 25.6MM **Privately Held**
Web: www.selectdata.com
SIC: 7371 7372 Computer code authors; Prepackaged software

(P-16113)
SETSCHEDULE LLC
100 Spectrum Center Dr Fl 9 (92618-4972)
PHONE................................888 222-0011
Udi Dorner, *Managing Member*
EMP: 117 **EST:** 2014
SALES (est): 10.73MM **Privately Held**
Web: www.setschedule.com
SIC: 7371 Computer software development

(P-16114)
SMART ENERGY SYSTEMS INC
Michelson Dr Ste 3370 (92612)
PHONE................................909 703-9609
EMP: 119
SALES (corp-wide): 10.19MM **Privately Held**
Web: www.sew.ai
SIC: 7371 Computer software development
PA: Smart Energy Systems, Inc.
15495 Sand Canyon Ave # 100
Irvine CA
909 703-9609

(P-16115)
SMART UTILITY SYSTEMS INC
Also Called: Smart Energy Water
19900 Macarthur Blvd Ste 370 (92612-2445)
PHONE................................909 217-3344
Kurt Sweetser, *Prin*
EMP: 100 **EST:** 2014
SALES (est): 10.54MM **Privately Held**
SIC: 7371 7373 8741 Computer software development; Systems software development services; Management services

(P-16116)
SMARTDRIVE SYSTEMS INC (PA)
9515 Towne Centre Dr (92121-1973)
PHONE................................858 225-5550
Steve Mitgang, *CEO*
Jason Palmer, ***
Michael J Baker, ***
Dan Lehman, *CORP Development**
▲ **EMP:** 97 **EST:** 2005
SALES (est): 47.27MM **Privately Held**
Web: www.smartdrive.net
SIC: 7371 Computer software development and applications

(P-16117)
SNAP INC (PA)
Also Called: Snapchat
3000 31st St Ste C (90405-3059)
PHONE................................310 399-3339
Evan Spiegel, *CEO*
Michael Lynton, ***
Derek Andersen, *CFO*
Jerry Hunter, *COO*
Robert Murphy, ***

EMP: 545 **EST:** 2010
SQ FT: 720,000
SALES (est): 4.6B
SALES (corp-wide): 4.6B **Publicly Held**
Web: www.snap.com
SIC: 7371 7372 Computer software development and applications; Application computer software

(P-16118)
SNAPCOMMS INC
155 N Lake Ave Fl 9 (91101-1849)
PHONE................................805 715-0300
Chris Leonard, *CEO*
EMP: 80 **EST:** 2012
SALES (est): 4.59MM
SALES (corp-wide): 431.89MM **Publicly Held**
Web: www.snapcomms.com
SIC: 7371 Computer software development
PA: Everbridge, Inc.
155 N Lake Ave Ste 100
Pasadena CA
818 230-9700

(P-16119)
SOFTWARE MANAGEMENT CONS LLC
Also Called: Smci
959 S Coast Dr Ste 415 (92626-7839)
PHONE................................714 662-1841
Cesar Sanchez, *Prin*
EMP: 142
SALES (corp-wide): 253.48MM **Privately Held**
Web: www.milestone.tech
SIC: 7371 Computer software development
HQ: Software Management Consultants, Llc
500 N Brand Blvd
Glendale CA
818 240-3177

(P-16120)
SOLARTIS LLC
Also Called: Solartis
1601 N Sepulveda Blvd Ste 606 (90266-5111)
PHONE................................310 251-4861
Siby Nidhiry, ***
EMP: 30 **EST:** 2000
SALES (est): 6.9MM **Privately Held**
Web: www.solartis.com
SIC: 7371 7374 7372 Computer software development; Data processing and preparation; Business oriented computer software

(P-16121)
SPIREON INC (PA)
Also Called: Goldstar
18881 Von Karman Ave Ste 1500 (92612-1582)
PHONE................................800 557-1449
Kevin Weiss, *CEO*
Brian Skutta, ***
Tim Welch, ***
Rita Parvaneh, ***
Carla Fitzgerald, *CMO**
EMP: 175 **EST:** 2002
SALES (est): 172.39MM
SALES (corp-wide): 172.39MM **Privately Held**
Web: www.spireon.com
SIC: 7371 8741 Computer software development; Business management

(P-16122)
STARTEL CORPORATION (PA)
16 Goodyear B-125 (92618-3743)
PHONE................................949 863-8700

PRODUCTS & SVCS

William Lane, *Pr*
EMP: 60 **EST:** 1980
SQ FT: 27,000
SALES (est): 11.28MM
SALES (corp-wide): 11.28MM **Privately Held**
Web: www.startel.com
SIC: 7371 3661 Computer software development; Communication headgear, telephone

(P-16123)
STONERIVER INC
770 The City Dr S Ste 5000 (92868)
PHONE..............................714 705-8227
John Grundman, *Prin*
EMP: 100
Web: www.sapiens.com
SIC: 7371 Computer software development
HQ: Stoneriver, Inc.
20 Horseneck Ln Ste 1
Greenwich CT
303 729-7500

(P-16124)
STRATACARE LLC
Also Called: Stratacare
17838 Gillette Ave Ste D (92614-6502)
P.O. Box 19600 (92623-9600)
PHONE..............................949 743-1200
Scott R Green, *CEO*
John Zavoli, *Chief Compliance Officer*
Dave Perbix, *
Michael Josephs, *
Robert Mccaffrey, *SALES*
▲ **EMP:** 250 **EST:** 1998
SALES (est): 52.43MM
SALES (corp-wide): 3.86B **Publicly Held**
Web: www.conduent.com
SIC: 7371 Computer software development
HQ: Conduent Workers Compensation Holdings, Inc.
17838 Gillette Ave
Irvine CA

(P-16125)
STRATCOM SYSTEMS INC
Also Called: Sims Software
2701 Loker Ave W Ste 130 (92010-6637)
P.O. Box 607 (92075-0607)
PHONE..............................858 481-9292
Michael Struttmann, *Pr*
EMP: 24 **EST:** 1983
SQ FT: 2,500
SALES (est): 3.15MM **Privately Held**
Web: www.simssoftware.com
SIC: 7371 7372 Computer software development; Prepackaged software

(P-16126)
STRATGIC HLTHCARE PROGRAMS LLC
6500 Hollister Ave Ste 210 (93117-3011)
PHONE..............................805 963-9446
Barbara Rosenblum, *CEO*
EMP: 94 **EST:** 2012
SALES (est): 5.85MM
SALES (corp-wide): 5.37B **Publicly Held**
Web: www.shpdata.com
SIC: 7371 Computer software development
PA: Roper Technologies, Inc.
6901 Prof Pkwy E Ste 200
Sarasota FL
941 556-2601

(P-16127)
SYMITAR SYSTEMS INC
8985 Balboa Ave (92123-1507)
PHONE..............................619 542-6700
EMP: 220 **EST:** 1984

SALES (est): 36.66MM
SALES (corp-wide): 2.08B **Publicly Held**
Web: www.jackhenry.com
SIC: 7371 Computer software development
PA: Jack Henry & Associates, Inc.
663 W Highway 60
Monett MO
417 235-6652

(P-16128)
SYSTECH SOLUTIONS INC (PA)
500 N Brand Blvd Ste 1900 (91203-3308)
PHONE..............................818 550-9690
Arun Gollapudi, *Pr*
Srinivasan Ramaswamy, *
Ashish Parikh, *
EMP: 81 **EST:** 1993
SQ FT: 1,500
SALES (est): 23.82MM
SALES (corp-wide): 23.82MM **Privately Held**
Web: www.systechusa.com
SIC: 7371 Computer software systems analysis and design, custom

(P-16129)
TADPOLE CARTESIA INC
Also Called: Tc Technology
2237 Faraday Ave Ste 120 (92008-7240)
PHONE..............................760 929-8345
Jason Linley, *Pr*
EMP: 19 **EST:** 2000
SALES (est): 2.45MM
SALES (corp-wide): 9.44MM **Privately Held**
Web: www.sspinnovations.com
SIC: 7371 7372 Computer software development; Application computer software
PA: Ssp Innovations, Llc
6766 S Revere Pkwy # 100
Centennial CO
720 279-9894

(P-16130)
TALENT & ACQUISITION LLC
Also Called: Stand 8 Technology Services
3020 Old Ranch Pkwy Ste 300 (90740-2751)
PHONE..............................888 970-9575
Quinn Fillmon, *Managing Member*
EMP: 150 **EST:** 2009
SALES (est): 10.43MM **Privately Held**
Web: www.stand8.io
SIC: 7371 7379 7363 7361 Computer software development and applications; Computer related consulting services; Help supply services; Employment agencies

(P-16131)
TAPESTRY SOLUTIONS INC (HQ)
6910 Carroll Rd (92121-2211)
PHONE..............................858 503-1990
Geoff Evans, *Pr*
Vince Monteparpe, *
Mark Young, *
Mary Ann Wagner, *
EMP: 125 **EST:** 1993
SQ FT: 36,073
SALES (est): 48.95MM
SALES (corp-wide): 66.61B **Publicly Held**
Web: www.tapestrysolutions.com
SIC: 7371 5045 Custom computer programming services; Computer software
PA: The Boeing Company
929 Long Bridge Dr
Arlington VA
703 414-6338

(P-16132)
TCG SOFTWARE SERVICES INC
320 Commerce Ste 200 (92602-1363)
PHONE..............................714 665-6200
Greg Blevins, *Brnch Mgr*
EMP: 278
SIC: 7371 Custom computer programming services
PA: Tcg Software Services, Inc.
265 Davidson Ave Ste 220
Somerset NJ

(P-16133)
TEBRA TECHNOLOGIES INC (PA)
Also Called: Kareo PM
1111 Bayside Dr Ste 150 (92625-1762)
P.O. Box 1922 (92616)
PHONE..............................888 775-2736
Daniel Rodrigues, *CEO*
Tom Giannulli, *CMO*
Tom Patterson, *
James Armijo, *
Jason Leu, *
EMP: 234 **EST:** 2004
SALES (est): 95.22MM **Privately Held**
Web: www.kareo.com
SIC: 7371 Computer software development

(P-16134)
TOMITRIBE CORPORATION
1519 6th St Apt 503 (90401-2607)
PHONE..............................310 526-7676
David Blevins, *CEO*
Amelia Eiras, *COO*
EMP: 20 **EST:** 2012
SALES (est): 1.38MM **Privately Held**
Web: www.tomitribe.com
SIC: 7371 7372 8742 Computer software development; Prepackaged software; Programmed instruction service

(P-16135)
TOUCHTONE CORPORATION
3151 Airway Ave Ste I3 (92626-4624)
P.O. Box 5719 (92616-5719)
PHONE..............................714 755-2810
Reza H Saraf, *Pr*
EMP: 20 **EST:** 1991
SQ FT: 5,000
SALES (est): 2.35MM **Privately Held**
Web: www.touchtonecorp.com
SIC: 7371 7372 Computer software writing services; Prepackaged software

(P-16136)
TRACKR INC
7410 Hollister Ave (93117-2583)
PHONE..............................855 981-1690
Christopher G Herbert, *CEO*
Christian J Smith, *
Nathan Kelly, *
Matthew Pigeon, *
EMP: 100 **EST:** 2009
SQ FT: 40,000
SALES (est): 8.78MM **Privately Held**
Web: www.thetrackr.com
SIC: 7371 Computer software development

(P-16137)
TRADE DESK INC (PA)
Also Called: Thetradedesk
42 N Chestnut St (93001-2662)
PHONE..............................805 585-3434
Jeff T Green, *Ch Bd*
Blake J Grayson, *CFO*
David R Pickles, *
Jay R Grant, *CLO*
EMP: 271 **EST:** 2009
SALES (est): 1.58B

SALES (corp-wide): 1.58B **Publicly Held**
Web: www.thetradedesk.com
SIC: 7371 7372 Software programming applications; Prepackaged software

(P-16138)
TRI-TECH SYSTEMS INC (PA)
Also Called: Triad Systems International
23801 Calabasas Rd Ste 2022 (91302-1547)
PHONE..............................818 222-6811
Cyril Cianflone, *Pr*
John Gerber, *VP*
Thomas Pickett, *Sec*
EMP: 395 **EST:** 1992
SQ FT: 3,500
SALES (est): 9.8MM
SALES (corp-wide): 9.8MM **Privately Held**
Web: www.triadsystems.com
SIC: 7371 7373 Custom computer programming services; Computer integrated systems design

(P-16139)
TRIBRIDGE HOLDINGS LLC
523 W 6th St Ste 830 (90014-1243)
PHONE..............................813 287-8887
Criatritinia Valentin, *Brnch Mgr*
EMP: 512
SALES (corp-wide): 14.43B **Publicly Held**
Web: www.dxc.com
SIC: 7371 Computer software development
HQ: Tribridge Holdings, Llc
20408 Bashan Dr Ste 231
Ashburn VA

(P-16140)
TRINUS CORPORATION
35 N Lake Ave Ste 710 (91101-4185)
PHONE..............................818 246-1143
EMP: 150 **EST:** 1995
SALES (est): 10.92MM **Privately Held**
Web: www.trinus.com
SIC: 7371 Custom computer programming services

(P-16141)
TROVATA INC (PA)
Also Called: Trovata
312 S Cedros Ave Ste 312 (92075-1943)
PHONE..............................312 914-8106
Brett Turner, *CEO*
Scott Harrington, *
Joseph Drambarean, *
EMP: 88 **EST:** 2016
SALES (est): 9.19MM
SALES (corp-wide): 9.19MM **Privately Held**
Web: www.trovata.io
SIC: 7371 Computer software development

(P-16142)
UNISYS CORPORATION
9701 Jeronimo Rd Ste 100 (92618-2076)
PHONE..............................949 380-5000
Carmen Lynch, *Mgr*
EMP: 142
SALES (corp-wide): 1.98B **Publicly Held**
Web: www.unisys.com
SIC: 7371 Computer software development
PA: Unisys Corporation
801 Lakeview Dr Ste 100
Blue Bell PA
215 986-4011

(P-16143)
UNITED SUPPORT SERVICES INC
3252 Holiday Ct Ste 110 (92037-1807)
PHONE..............................858 373-9500

Michael Fernandez, *Pr*
EMP: 190 **EST:** 2003
SQ FT: 2,600
SALES (est): 15MM **Privately Held**
Web: www.usscompany.com
SIC: 7371 8711 Custom computer
programming services; Consulting engineer

(P-16144)
UST GLOBAL INC (HQ)
Also Called: UST
5 Polaris Way (92656-5374)
PHONE.................................949 716-8757
Krishna Sudheendra, *CEO*
Paras Chandaria, *
Arun Narayanan, *
Sunil Kanchi, *CIO**
Murali Gopalan, *CCO**
EMP: 100 **EST:** 2007
SQ FT: 20,000
SALES (est): 511.43MM **Privately Held**
SIC: 7371 Computer software development
PA: Ust Holdings Ltd
C/O R&H Services Limited
Hamilton

(P-16145)
VENDOR DIRECT SOLUTIONS LLC (PA)
515 S Figueroa St Ste 1900 (90071-3336)
PHONE.................................213 362-5622
Jules Buenabenta, *Managing Member*
Jim Young, *
Ron Mcelhaney, *Dir Opers*
Angel E Nevarez, *
Stephanie Simmons, *
EMP: 247 **EST:** 2006
SQ FT: 1,200
SALES (est): 25.02MM **Privately Held**
Web: www.teamvds.com
SIC: 7371 Computer software development

(P-16146)
VERITAS TECHNOLOGIES LLC
16501 Ventura Blvd Ste 400 (91436-2007)
PHONE.................................310 202-0757
EMP: 200
SALES (corp-wide): 4.44B **Publicly Held**
Web: www.veritas.com
SIC: 7371 7375 Computer software
development and applications; Data base
information retrieval
HQ: Veritas Technologies Llc
2625 Augustine Dr
Santa Clara CA
866 837-4827

(P-16147)
VERSEIO INC
Also Called: Short Sale Agent Finder
550 W B St Fl 4 (92101-3581)
PHONE.................................888 373-9942
Tal David, *CEO*
EMP: 90 **EST:** 2012
SALES (est): 8.44MM **Privately Held**
Web: www.verse.io
SIC: 7371 Software programming
applications

(P-16148)
VISION SOLUTIONS INC (HQ)
15300 Barranca Pkwy (92618-2200)
PHONE.................................949 253-6500
Nicolaas Vlok, *Pr*
Alan Arnold, *
Don Scott, *
Robert Johnson, *
Wm Edward Vesely, *CMO**
▲ **EMP:** 90 **EST:** 1989
SQ FT: 25,000

SALES (est): 51.14MM
SALES (corp-wide): 446.91MM **Privately Held**
SIC: 7371 7373 Computer software
development; Systems integration services
PA: Precisely Software Incorporated
1700 District Ave Ste 300
Burlington MA
978 436-8900

(P-16149)
WITH INC
7 Studebaker 1 (92618-2013)
PHONE.................................714 617-1991
EMP: 26 **EST:** 2008
SALES (est): 1.78MM **Privately Held**
Web: www.medlmobile.com
SIC: 7371 7372 Software programming
applications; Application computer software

(P-16150)
X1 DISCOVERY INC
617 W 7th St Ste 604 (90017-3817)
PHONE.................................877 999-1347
John Patzakis, *CEO*
EMP: 36 **EST:** 2011
SQ FT: 2,000
SALES (est): 3.07MM **Privately Held**
Web: www.x1.com
SIC: 7371 7372 Computer software
development; Prepackaged software

(P-16151)
XBP INC
Also Called: Voipment
333 El Camino Real Ste 201 (92780)
PHONE.................................888 895-7116
John Lloyd Davis, *CEO*
Moe Navid, *
Kevin Moshayedi, *CMO**
EMP: 91 **EST:** 2015
SQ FT: 2,500
SALES (est): 360.69K
SALES (corp-wide): 41.22MM **Privately Held**
Web: www.broadvoice.com
SIC: 7371 Computer software development
PA: Quality Speaks Llc
9221 Corbin Ave Ste 260
Northridge CA
818 264-4400

(P-16152)
YARDI SYSTEMS INC (PA)
430 S Fairview Ave (93117-3637)
PHONE.................................805 699-2040
Anant Yardi, *CEO*
Gordon Morrell, *
Fritz Schindelbeck, *
John Pendergast, *
Robert Teel, *
EMP: 380 **EST:** 1982
SQ FT: 160,000
SALES (est): 856.64MM
SALES (corp-wide): 856.64MM **Privately Held**
Web: www.yardi.com
SIC: 7371 Computer software development

(P-16153)
ZESTFINANCE INC
Also Called: Zest.ai
3900 W Alameda Ave Ste 1600 (91505-4333)
PHONE.................................323 450-3000
Mike De Vere, *CEO*
Douglas Merrill, *
EMP: 85 **EST:** 2012
SALES (est): 9.65MM **Privately Held**
Web: www.zest.ai

SIC: 7371 Computer software development

7372 Prepackaged Software

(P-16154)
1ON1 LLC
8730 Wilshire Blvd Ste 350 (90211-2716)
PHONE.................................310 998-7473
Susan Josephson, *Managing Member*
EMP: 50 **EST:** 2016
SALES (est): 2.44MM **Privately Held**
SIC: 7372 Application computer software

(P-16155)
2B ADVICE LLC
6790 Embarcadero Ln (92011-3278)
PHONE.................................858 366-9750
Marcus Belke, *Admn*
EMP: 21 **EST:** 2015
SALES (est): 2.8MM
SALES (corp-wide): 2.2MM **Privately Held**
Web: www.2b-advice.com
SIC: 7372 7379 Prepackaged software;
Computer related services, nec
PA: 2b Advice Gmbh
Joseph-Schumpeter-Allee 25
Bonn NW
228926165100

(P-16156)
ACTIVISION BLIZZARD INC
Blizzard Entertainment
3 Blizzard (92618-3628)
P.O. Box 18979 (92623-8979)
PHONE.................................949 955-1380
EMP: 85
SALES (corp-wide): 211.91B **Publicly Held**
Web: www.activisionblizzard.com
SIC: 7372 Prepackaged software
HQ: Activision Blizzard, Inc.
2701 Olympic Blvd Bldg B
Santa Monica CA
310 255-2000

(P-16157)
ACTIVISION BLIZZARD INC (HQ)
Also Called: Activision Blizzard
2701 Olympic Blvd Bldg B (90404-4183)
PHONE.................................310 255-2000
Robert A Kotick, *CEO*
Brian G Kelly, *Ch Bd*
Armin Zerza, *CFO*
Brian Bulatao, *Chief*
Julie Hodges, *CPO*
EMP: 333 **EST:** 1979
SALES (est): 7.53B
SALES (corp-wide): 211.91B **Publicly Held**
Web: www.activisionblizzard.com
SIC: 7372 Prepackaged software
PA: Microsoft Corporation
1 Microsoft Way
Redmond WA
425 882-8080

(P-16158)
ADEXA INC (PA)
5777 W Century Blvd Ste 1100 (90045-5643)
PHONE.................................310 642-2100
EMP: 50 **EST:** 1994
SQ FT: 31,000
SALES (est): 17.54MM **Privately Held**
Web: www.adexa.com
SIC: 7372 Business oriented computer
software

(P-16159)
ADVISYS INC
3 Corporate Park Ste 240 (92606-5163)
PHONE.................................949 250-0794
Kenneth Kerr, *CEO*
Richard M Kettley, *
Dane Parker, *
Gregg Janes, *
Sherelyn Kettley, *
EMP: 28 **EST:** 1979
SALES (est): 4.51MM **Privately Held**
Web: www.advisys.com
SIC: 7372 Application computer software

(P-16160)
AGENCYCOM LLC
5353 Grosvenor Blvd (90066-6913)
PHONE.................................415 817-3800
Chan Suh, *CEO*
Rob Elliott, *CFO*
EMP: 400 **EST:** 1995
SQ FT: 130,000
SALES (est): 49.16MM
SALES (corp-wide): 14.29B **Publicly Held**
SIC: 7372 Application computer software
PA: Omnicom Group Inc.
280 Park Ave Fl 31w
New York NY
212 415-3600

(P-16161)
AIRA TECH CORP
Also Called: Aira Tech
3451 Via Montebello Ste 192 Pmb 214 (92009-8492)
PHONE.................................800 835-1934
Troy Otilio, *CEO*
EMP: 65 **EST:** 2015
SALES (est): 10.18MM **Privately Held**
Web: www.aira.io
SIC: 7372 Application computer software

(P-16162)
ALPHASTAR TECH SOLUTIONS LLC
2601 Main St Ste 660 (92614-4257)
PHONE.................................562 961-7827
Frank Abdi, *CEO*
Frank Abdi, *Ch Bd*
Kay Matin, *Pr*
EMP: 18 **EST:** 1989
SQ FT: 3,800
SALES (est): 4.31MM **Privately Held**
Web: www.alphastarcorp.com
SIC: 7372 7371 3724 Prepackaged software
; Computer software development;
Research and development on aircraft
engines and parts

(P-16163)
ALTUMIND INC
10620 Treena St Ste 230 (92131-1140)
PHONE.................................858 382-3956
Ali Naderi, *Managing Member*
EMP: 50 **EST:** 2021
SALES (est): 1.22MM **Privately Held**
SIC: 7372 Application computer software

(P-16164)
AMBER HOLDING INC
1601 Cloverfield Blvd (90404-4087)
PHONE.................................603 324-3000
Charles E Moran, *Pr*
Tom Mcdonald, *CFO*
Jerry Nine, *
EMP: 96 **EST:** 2009
SALES (est): 5.88MM
SALES (corp-wide): 555.12MM **Publicly Held**

PRODUCTS & SVCS

SIC: 7372 Prepackaged software'
HQ: Skillsoft (Us) Llc
300 Innovative Way # 201
Nashua NH
603 324-3000

(P-16165)
AMS
102 E Pico Blvd (90015-2506)
PHONE..................714 376-2464
EMP: 24 EST: 1983
SALES (est): 220.3K Privately Held
Web: www.amsfulfillment.com
SIC: 7372 Publisher's computer software

(P-16166)
ANCORA SOFTWARE INC (PA)
402 W Broadway Ste 400 (92101-3554)
PHONE..................888 476-4839
Noel Flynn, CEO
Jane Christie, COO
David Pintsov, COO
Nick Bova, VP
EMP: 27 EST: 2015
SALES (est): 4.92MM
SALES (corp-wide): 4.92MM Privately
Held
Web: www.ancorasoftware.com
SIC: 7372 Prepackaged software

(P-16167)
ANNEX PRO INC
4100 W Alameda Ave Fl 3 (91505-4191)
PHONE..................800 682-6639
Kerry Corlett, CEO
Kalinka Corlett, Dir
EMP: 20 EST: 2017
SALES (est): 12MM Privately Held
Web: www.annexpro.com
SIC: 7372 5734 8731 5946 Application
computer software; Computer peripheral
equipment; Computer (hardware)
development; Camera and photographic
supply stores

(P-16168)
APOTHEKA SYSTEMS INC
14040 Panay Way (90292-6697)
P.O. Box 1251 (90213-1251)
PHONE..................844 777-4455
Dennis Maliani, CEO
EMP: 30 EST: 2018
SALES (est): 1.81MM Privately Held
Web: www.apotheka.co
SIC: 7372 Application computer software

(P-16169)
APP LLC
2998 James M Wood Blvd # 4
(90006-1621)
PHONE..................213 703-7294
Daniel Cho, Prin
EMP: 26 EST: 2015
SALES (est): 82.07K Privately Held
SIC: 7372 Prepackaged software

(P-16170)
APPFOLIO INC (PA)
Also Called: Appfolio
70 Castilian Dr (93117-3027)
PHONE..................805 364-6093
Jason Randall, Pr
Andreas Von Blottnitz, *
Jonathan Walker, *
Fay Sien Goon, *
Matt Mazza, CLO*
EMP: 340 EST: 2006
SALES (est): 471.88MM
SALES (corp-wide): 471.88MM Publicly
Held

Web: www.appfolio.com
SIC: 7372 Business oriented computer
software

(P-16171)
APPFOLIO INC
Also Called: Mycase
9201 Spectrum Center Blvd Ste 100
(92123-1407)
PHONE..................866 648-1536
Troy Alford, Eng/Dir
EMP: 84
SALES (corp-wide): 471.88MM Publicly
Held
Web: www.appfolio.com
SIC: 7372 Prepackaged software
PA: Appfolio, Inc.
70 Castilian Dr
Santa Barbara CA
805 364-6093

(P-16172)
**APPLIED BIOSYSTEMS LLC
(DH)**
Also Called: Applied Biosystems
5791 Van Allen Way (92008-7321)
▲ EMP: 120 EST: 1937
SQ FT: 51,000
SALES (est): 485.64MM
SALES (corp-wide): 44.91B Publicly Held
Web: www.thermofisher.com
SIC: 7372 3826 Prepackaged software; Gas
chromatographic instruments
HQ: Life Technologies Corporation
5781 Van Allen Way
Carlsbad CA
760 603-7200

(P-16173)
**APPLIED BUSINESS SOFTWARE
INC**
Also Called: A B S
2847 Gundry Ave (90755-1812)
PHONE..................562 426-2188
Jerry Delgado, Pr
Edimia Delgado, Sec
Gerardo Delgado, VP
Eddy Delgado, VP
Nelson Noahk, Contrlr
EMP: 41 EST: 1979
SQ FT: 7,200
SALES (est): 9.04MM Privately Held
Web: www.themortgageoffice.com
SIC: 7372 5045 5734 Prepackaged software
; Computers, peripherals, and software;
Computer and software stores

(P-16174)
APPLIED STATISTICS & MGT INC
Also Called: Md-Staff
32848 Wolf Store Rd Ste A (92592-8277)
P.O. Box 2738 (92593-2738)
PHONE..................951 699-4600
Trung Phan, Pr
Nickolaus Phan, VP
EMP: 95 EST: 1982
SQ FT: 4,000
SALES (est): 12.05MM Privately Held
Web: www.mdstaff.com
SIC: 7372 7371 Prepackaged software;
Computer software systems analysis and
design, custom

(P-16175)
ARTKIVE
16225 Huston St (91436-1323)
PHONE..................310 975-9809
EMP: 24 EST: 2012
SALES (est): 380.44K Privately Held
Web: www.artkiveapp.com

SIC: 7372 Prepackaged software

(P-16176)
ARXIS TECHNOLOGY INC
2468 Tapo Canyon Rd (93063-2361)
PHONE..................805 306-7890
Christopher L Hamilton, CEO
EMP: 24 EST: 1994
SALES (est): 4.25MM Privately Held
Web: www.rklesolutions.com
SIC: 7372 Prepackaged software

(P-16177)
ASCENDER SOFTWARE INC
8885 Rio San Diego Dr Ste 270
(92108-1624)
PHONE..................877 561-7501
Theodore Kye, Prin
EMP: 251 EST: 2006
SALES (est): 875.69K
SALES (corp-wide): 309.28MM Privately
Held
Web: www.matrixmedicalnetwork.com
SIC: 7372 Prepackaged software
PA: Community Care Health Network, Llc
9201 E Mtn Vw Rd Ste 22
Scottsdale AZ
877 564-3627

(P-16178)
ASTEA INTERNATIONAL INC
8 Hughes (92618-2072)
PHONE..................949 784-5000
Carl Smith, Brnch Mgr
EMP: 23
SALES (corp-wide): 474.74K Privately
Held
Web: www.ifs.com
SIC: 7372 Business oriented computer
software
HQ: Astea International Inc.
300 Park Blvd Ste 350
Itasca IL
888 437-4968

(P-16179)
ATELIERE CREATIVE TECH INC
315 S Beverly Dr Ste 315 (90212-4309)
PHONE..................800 921-4252
EMP: 25 EST: 2020
SALES (est): 753.43K Privately Held
Web: www.ateliere.com
SIC: 7372 Application computer software

(P-16180)
ATLANTIS COMPUTING INC
900 Glenneyre St (92651-2707)
PHONE..................650 917-9471
Jason Donahue, Pr
EMP: 35 EST: 2006
SQ FT: 5,000
SALES (est): 8.86MM Privately Held
Web: www.hiveio.com
SIC: 7372 Business oriented computer
software

(P-16181)
AXIA TECHNOLOGIES INC
Also Called: Axiamed
4183 State St (93110-1817)
PHONE..................855 376-2942
Randal Clark, Pr
EMP: 21 EST: 2016
SALES (est): 4.64MM
SALES (corp-wide): 94.95B Publicly Held
Web: business.bofa.com
SIC: 7372 Prepackaged software
HQ: Bank Of America, National Association
100 N Tryon St
Charlotte NC
704 386-5681

(P-16182)
BITMAX
6600 W Sunset Blvd (90028-7160)
PHONE..................323 978-7878
EMP: 33 EST: 2019
SALES (est): 2.24MM Privately Held
Web: www.bitmax.net
SIC: 7372 Prepackaged software

(P-16183)
BLACKLINE INC (PA)
Also Called: Blackline
21300 Victory Blvd Fl 12 (91367-7734)
PHONE..................818 223-9008
Owen Ryan, Ch Bd
Mark Partin, CFO
Karole Morgan-prager, Legal
EMP: 135 EST: 2001
SQ FT: 89,000
SALES (est): 522.94MM
SALES (corp-wide): 522.94MM Publicly
Held
Web: www.blackline.com
SIC: 7372 Business oriented computer
software

(P-16184)
BLIND SQUIRREL GAMES INC
7545 Irvine Center Dr Ste 150
(92618-2930)
PHONE..................714 460-0860
Bradford Hendricks, CEO
EMP: 23 EST: 2010
SALES (est): 5.14MM Privately Held
Web: www.blindsquirrelgames.com
SIC: 7372 Home entertainment computer
software

(P-16185)
BLITZ ROCKS INC
750 B St Ste 3300 (92101-4605)
PHONE..................310 883-5183
Mauricio Duran, CEO
EMP: 18 EST: 2016
SALES (est): 911.75K
SALES (corp-wide): 5.06MM Privately
Held
Web: www.blitzrocks.com
SIC: 7372 Business oriented computer
software
PA: Sieena, Inc.
600 B St Ste 300
San Diego CA
310 455-6188

(P-16186)
**BLIZZARD ENTERTAINMENT
INC (DH)**
1 Blizzard (92618-3628)
P.O. Box 18979 (92623-8979)
PHONE..................949 955-1380
Mike Morhaime, CEO
J Allen Brack, Pr
Paul Sams, Pr
Chris Metzen, Sr VP
Todd Pawlowski, VP
▲ EMP: 85 EST: 2004
SALES (est): 155.37MM
SALES (corp-wide): 211.91B Publicly
Held
Web: careers.blizzard.com
SIC: 7372 5734 7819 Prepackaged software
; Software, computer games; Reproduction
services, motion picture production
HQ: Activision Blizzard, Inc.
2701 Olympic Blvd Bldg B
Santa Monica CA
310 255-2000

(P-16187)
BMC
300 Continental Blvd Ste 570 (90245-5072)
PHONE..............................310 321-5555
Sean Allen, *CEO*
EMP: 39 **EST:** 2009
SALES (est): 190.6K **Privately Held**
Web: www.bmc.com
SIC: 7372 Prepackaged software

(P-16188)
BPOMS/HRO INC (HQ)
8175 E Kaiser Blvd # 100 (92808-2214)
PHONE..............................714 974-2670
Patrick Dolan, *Ch Bd*
James Cortens, *COO*
Don Rutherford, *CFO*
EMP: 62 **EST:** 2008
SQ FT: 3,500
SALES (est): 6.74MM
SALES (corp-wide): 36.61MM **Privately Held**
SIC: 7372 7371 Prepackaged software;
Custom computer programming services
PA: Bpo Management Services, Inc.
8175 E Kaiser Blvd 100
Anaheim CA
714 972-2670

(P-16189)
BQE SOFTWARE INC
3825 Del Amo Blvd (90503)
PHONE..............................310 602-4020
EMP: 95 **EST:** 1995
SQ FT: 20,000
SALES (est): 12.55MM **Privately Held**
Web: www.bqe.com
SIC: 7372 5734 Application computer
software; Software, business and non-game

(P-16190)
BRENDAN TECHNOLOGIES INC
1947 Camino Vida Roble Ste 215 (92008)
PHONE..............................760 929-7500
John R Dunn Ii, *CEO*
George Dunn, *Sec*
Lowell W Giffhorn, *CFO*
▲ **EMP:** 21 **EST:** 1988
SQ FT: 3,988
SALES (est): 1.95MM **Privately Held**
Web: www.brendan.com
SIC: 7372 Business oriented computer
software

(P-16191)
BTRADE LLC
701 N Brand Blvd Ste 205 (91203-3212)
PHONE..............................818 334-4433
Steve Zapata, *Managing Member*
EMP: 25 **EST:** 2008
SALES (est): 2.52MM **Privately Held**
Web: www.btrade.com
SIC: 7372 Business oriented computer
software

(P-16192)
CALAMP CORP (PA)
Also Called: CALAMP
15635 Alton Pkwy Ste 250 (92618-7328)
PHONE..............................949 600-5600
Jason Cohenour, *Interim Chief Executive
Officer*
Henry J Maier, *
Jikun Kim, *Sr VP*
Richard Scott, *CLO*
Jeffrey Clark, *CPO*
◆ **EMP:** 96 **EST:** 1981
SQ FT: 23,000
SALES (est): 294.95MM
SALES (corp-wide): 294.95MM **Publicly Held**

Web: www.calamp.com
SIC: 7372 Application computer software

(P-16193)
CATALYST DEVELOPMENT CORP
56925 Yucca Trl (92284-7913)
PHONE..............................760 228-9653
Cary Harwin, *Pr*
Mike Stefanik, *
EMP: 22 **EST:** 1995
SALES (est): 2.04MM **Privately Held**
Web: www.catalyst.com
SIC: 7372 Business oriented computer
software

(P-16194)
CATAPULT COMMUNICATIONS CORP (DH)
26601 Agoura Rd (91302-1959)
PHONE..............................818 871-1800
Richard A Karp, *Ch Bd*
David Mayfield, *Pr*
Chris Stephenson, *VP*
Barbara J Fairhurst, *VP Opers*
Terry Eastham, *SUPPORT*
▲ **EMP:** 54 **EST:** 1985
SQ FT: 39,000
SALES (est): 3.12MM
SALES (corp-wide): 5.42B **Publicly Held**
SIC: 7372 3661 Application computer
software; Telephone and telegraph
apparatus
HQ: Ixia
26601 Agoura Rd
Calabasas CA
818 871-1800

(P-16195)
CBX SOFTWARE INC
Also Called: Tradebeyond
8910 University Center Ln Ste 400
(92122-1029)
PHONE..............................858 264-1133
Michael Hung, *CEO*
Wendy Fook, *CFO*
EMP: 39 **EST:** 1996
SALES (est): 2.02MM **Privately Held**
Web: www.tradebeyond.com
SIC: 7372 Prepackaged software

(P-16196)
CERTEMY INC
14876 Raymer St Ste 200 (91405-1219)
PHONE..............................866 907-4088
Zorik Gordon, *CEO*
Herman Berger, *CEO*
Oleg Shvarts, *Pr*
Shawn Cantor, *COO*
EMP: 18 **EST:** 2017
SALES (est): 1.06MM **Privately Held**
Web: www.certemy.com
SIC: 7372 7371 7379 Business oriented
computer software; Custom computer
programming services; Computer related
services, nec

(P-16197)
CFORIA SOFTWARE LLC
Also Called: Cforia
4333 Park Terrace Dr Ste 201
(91361-5656)
PHONE..............................818 871-9687
Karl Florida, *CEO*
Dave Mcintyre, *Pr*
Chris Caparon, *VP*
Joe Alie, *CFO*
EMP: 22 **EST:** 2001
SALES (est): 5.74MM **Privately Held**
Web: www.cforia.com

SIC: 7372 Business oriented computer
software

(P-16198)
CFS TAX SOFTWARE INC
Also Called: CFS Income Tax
1445 E Los Angeles Ave Ste 214
(93065-2828)
P.O. Box 941659 (93094-1659)
PHONE..............................805 522-1157
Ted Sullivan, *Pr*
EMP: 17 **EST:** 1982
SALES (est): 4.35MM **Privately Held**
Web: www.taxtools.com
SIC: 7372 8721 Business oriented computer
software; Accounting, auditing, and
bookkeeping

(P-16199)
CHATMETER INC
225 Broadway Ste 2200 (92101-5011)
PHONE..............................619 300-1050
EMP: 80 **EST:** 2009
SALES (est): 9.81MM **Privately Held**
Web: www.chatmeter.com
SIC: 7372 Prepackaged software

(P-16200)
CHOWNOW INC
12181 Bluff Creek Dr Ste W200
(90094-2627)
PHONE..............................888 707-2469
Eric Jaffe, *Pr*
Stuart Hathaway, *
Andre Mancl, *
EMP: 100 **EST:** 2010
SQ FT: 25,000
SALES (est): 16.12MM **Privately Held**
Web: www.chownow.com
SIC: 7372 Business oriented computer
software

(P-16201)
CHROME RIVER TECHNOLOGIES INC
5757 Wilshire Blvd Ste 270 (90036-5814)
PHONE..............................888 781-0088
Eric Friedrichsen, *CEO*
Nord Samuelson, *Pr*
Adriana Carpenter, *CFO*
Courtney Ryan, *CPO*
EMP: 158 **EST:** 2007
SALES (est): 2.51MM **Privately Held**
Web: www.chromeriver.com
SIC: 7372 Prepackaged software

(P-16202)
CLASSY INC
Also Called: Classy
350 10th Ave Ste 1300 (92101-8703)
PHONE..............................619 961-1892
Chris Himes, *CEO*
EMP: 157 **EST:** 2006
SALES (est): 22.34MM
SALES (corp-wide): 23MM **Privately Held**
Web: www.classy.org
SIC: 7372 Prepackaged software
PA: Gofundme Inc.
1010 Doyle St Ste 250
Menlo Park CA
650 260-3436

(P-16203)
CLEARLAKE CAPITAL PARTNERS
233 Wilshire Blvd Ste 800 (90401-1207)
PHONE..............................310 400-8800
John A Mckenna Junior, *Pr*
EMP: 1832 **EST:** 2012

SALES (est): 28.77MM **Privately Held**
SIC: 7372 Prepackaged software

(P-16204)
CLOUD SFTWR GROUP HOLDINGS INC
7414 Hollister Ave Goleta (90074-0001)
PHONE..............................800 424-8749
EMP: 17
SALES (corp-wide): 4.38B **Privately Held**
SIC: 7372 Prepackaged software
HQ: Cloud Software Group Holdings, Inc.
851 W Cypress Creek Rd
Fort Lauderdale FL
954 267-3000

(P-16205)
CLOUDCOVER IOT INC
Also Called: Cloudcover
14 Goodyear Ste 125b (92618-3759)
PHONE..............................888 511-2022
Jeffrey Huggins, *CEO*
EMP: 37 **EST:** 2015
SALES (est): 14.71MM **Privately Held**
Web: www.cloudcover.it
SIC: 7372 7379 7373 Prepackaged software
; Computer related maintenance services;
Systems engineering, computer related

(P-16206)
CLOUDVIRGA INC
5291 California Ave Ste 300 (92617-3221)
PHONE..............................949 799-2643
Daniel Akiva, *CEO*
Maria Moskver, *Legal*
EMP: 59 **EST:** 2015
SALES (est): 25.51MM
SALES (corp-wide): 3.07B **Publicly Held**
Web: www.cloudvirga.com
SIC: 7372 Prepackaged software
PA: Stewart Information Services
Corporation
1360 Post Oak Blvd Ste 10
Houston TX
713 625-8100

(P-16207)
CLUB SPEED LLC (PA)
300 Spectrum Center Dr (92618-4925)
PHONE..............................951 817-7073
Romir Bosu, *CEO*
Caleb Everett, *Pr*
Eric Novakovich, *Chief Strategy Officer*
EMP: 38 **EST:** 2007
SALES (est): 5.54MM
SALES (corp-wide): 5.54MM **Privately Held**
Web: www.clubspeed.com
SIC: 7372 Prepackaged software

(P-16208)
COMMERCE VELOCITY LLC
1 Technology Dr Ste J725 (92618-2353)
PHONE..............................949 756-8950
EMP: 43 **EST:** 2000
SQ FT: 5,000
SALES (est): 18.21MM **Publicly Held**
SIC: 7372 Business oriented computer
software
PA: Fidelity National Financial, Inc.
601 Riverside Ave Fl 4
Jacksonville FL

(P-16209)
COMPUGROUP MEDICAL INC
25b Technology Dr Ste 200 (92618)
PHONE..............................949 789-0500
John Tangredi, *COO*
EMP: 35
SALES (corp-wide): 1.17B **Privately Held**

PRODUCTS & SVCS

Web: www.cgm.com
SIC: 7372 Prepackaged software
HQ: Compugroup Medical, Inc.
10901 Stonelake Blvd
Austin TX
855 270-6700

(P-16210)
COMPULINK BUSINESS SYSTEMS INC (PA)
Also Called: Compulink Healthcare Solutions
1100 Business Center Cir (91320-1124)
PHONE.................................805 446-2050
Link Wilson, Pr
EMP: 117 EST: 1985
SQ FT: 15,000
SALES (est): 23.14MM
SALES (corp-wide): 23.14MM Privately Held
Web: www.compulinkadvantage.com
SIC: 7372 Business oriented computer software

(P-16211)
CONNECTPOINT INC
175 Cremona Dr Ste 160 (93117-3197)
PHONE.................................805 682-8900
Frederick A Wood, CEO
EMP: 19 EST: 2018
SALES (est): 996.27K Privately Held
Web: www.connectpointdigital.com
SIC: 7372 Prepackaged software

(P-16212)
CONSENSUS CLOUD SOLUTIONS INC (PA)
700 S Flower St Fl 15 (90017-4101)
PHONE.................................323 860-9200
Scott Turicchi, CEO
John Nebergall, COO
Steve Emberland, Contrlr
James Malone, CFO
EMP: 65 EST: 2021
SALES (est): 352.66MM
SALES (corp-wide): 352.66MM Publicly Held
Web: www.consensus.com
SIC: 7372 Prepackaged software

(P-16213)
CONSERVICE MTRING SLUTIONS INC
9950 Scripps Lake Dr Ste 101 (92131-1082)
PHONE.................................858 356-7534
Marc Conservice, CEO
EMP: 19 EST: 2012
SALES (est): 325.35K Privately Held
Web: www.conservice.com
SIC: 7372 Prepackaged software

(P-16214)
CONVERSIONPOINT HOLDINGS INC
840 Newport Center Dr Ste 450 (92660)
PHONE.................................888 706-6764
Robert Tallack, Pr
Don Walker Barrett Iii, COO
Raghu Kilambi, CFO
EMP: 85 EST: 2018
SALES (est): 2.22MM Privately Held
SIC: 7372 Prepackaged software

(P-16215)
CORNERSTONE ONDEMAND INC (HQ)
Also Called: Cornerstone
1601 Cloverfield Blvd Ste 620s (90404-4178)
PHONE.................................310 752-0200
Himanshu Palsule, CEO
Chirag Shah, *
Heidi Spirgi, CSO CGO*
Adam Weiss, CAO*
Srinivasa Ogireddy, *
EMP: 269 EST: 1999
SQ FT: 94,000
SALES (est): 740.92MM
SALES (corp-wide): 740.92MM Privately Held
Web: www.cornerstoneondemand.com
SIC: 7372 Business oriented computer software
PA: Sunshine Software Holdings, Inc.
1601 Cloverf Blvd Ste 62
Santa Monica CA

(P-16216)
CROSSROADS SOFTWARE INC
210 W Birch St Ste 207 (92821-4504)
PHONE.................................714 990-6433
Jeff Cullen, Pr
EMP: 18 EST: 1992
SQ FT: 1,000
SALES (est): 703.32K Privately Held
Web: web.crossroadssoftware.com
SIC: 7372 Prepackaged software

(P-16217)
CULTURE AMP INC (HQ)
16501 Ventura Blvd Ste 400 (91436-2007)
PHONE.................................415 326-8453
Didier Raoul Elzinga, CEO
Rodney James Hamilton, *
Douglas Mark English, *
EMP: 18 EST: 2013
SALES (est): 15.53MM Privately Held
Web: www.cultureamp.com
SIC: 7372 Prepackaged software
PA: Culture Amp Pty Ltd
L 2 29 Stewart St
Richmond VIC

(P-16218)
CUREMETRIX INC
402 W Broadway Ste 400 (92101-3554)
PHONE.................................858 333-5830
Kevin Harris, Pr
Kevin Harris, CEO
EMP: 20 EST: 2015
SALES (est): 1.27MM Privately Held
Web: www.curemetrix.com
SIC: 7372 Application computer software

(P-16219)
D3PUBLISHER OF AMERICA INC
Also Called: D3 Go
15910 Ventura Blvd Ste 800 (91436-2802)
PHONE.................................310 268-0820
Yoji Takenaka, Pr
Yuji Itoh, Non-Executive Chairman of the Board
Hidetaka Tachibana, CFO
EMP: 63 EST: 2004
SQ FT: 6,129
SALES (est): 18.5MM Privately Held
Web: www.d3go.com
SIC: 7372 Home entertainment computer software
HQ: D3 Publisher Inc.
3-5-2, Kandakajicho
Chiyoda-Ku TKY

(P-16220)
DACENSO INC
Also Called: Exemptax
2030 Main St Ste 1300 (92614-7220)
PHONE.................................888 513-9367
Thomas Weiss, CEO
EMP: 20 EST: 2019
SALES (est): 1.16MM Privately Held
Web: www.exemptax.com
SIC: 7372 Application computer software

(P-16221)
DASSAULT SYSTEMES BIOVIA CORP (DH)
Also Called: Biovia
5005 Wateridge Vista Dr (92121-5780)
PHONE.................................858 799-5000
Max Carnecchia, CEO
Michael Piraino, Ex VP
Jason Gray, Corporate Secretary
Mathew Hahn, Sr VP
Judith Ohrn Hicks, Senior Vice President Human Resources
EMP: 43 EST: 1993
SQ FT: 68,436
SALES (est): 112.23MM Privately Held
SIC: 7372 Application computer software
HQ: 3ds Acquisition Corp.
175 Wyman St
Waltham MA
781 810-5011

(P-16222)
DAVE INC (PA)
1265 S Cochran Ave (90019-2846)
PHONE.................................844 857-3283
Jason Wilk, Pr
Kyle Beilman, CFO
EMP: 219 EST: 2015
SQ FT: 36,000
SALES (est): 204.84MM
SALES (corp-wide): 204.84MM Publicly Held
Web: www.dave.com
SIC: 7372 7389 Prepackaged software; Financial services

(P-16223)
DCATALOG INC
6250 Sagebrush Bend Way (92130-6866)
PHONE.................................408 824-5648
Michael Raviv, Pr
EMP: 20 EST: 2012
SALES (est): 1.3MM Privately Held
Web: www.dcatalog.com
SIC: 7372 Application computer software

(P-16224)
DECISIONLOGIC LLC
13500 Evening Creek Dr N Ste 600 (92128-8104)
PHONE.................................858 586-0202
David Evans, Pr
EMP: 23 EST: 2011
SALES (est): 2.51MM Privately Held
Web: www.decisionlogic.com
SIC: 7372 Business oriented computer software

(P-16225)
DIGITAL ARBITRAGE DIST INC (PA)
Also Called: Cloudbeds
3033 5th Ave Ste 100 (92103-5828)
PHONE.................................888 392-9478
Adam Harris, CEO
EMP: 30 EST: 2017
SALES (est): 10.68MM
SALES (corp-wide): 10.68MM Privately Held
Web: www.cloudbeds.com
SIC: 7372 Prepackaged software

(P-16226)
DINCLOUD INC
27520 Hawthorne Blvd Ste 185 (90274-3543)
PHONE.................................310 929-1101
Mark Briggs, CEO
Ali M Dincmo, *
Mike L Chase, *
EMP: 53 EST: 2011
SQ FT: 1,500
SALES (est): 10.4MM
SALES (corp-wide): 43.76MM Privately Held
SIC: 7372 Business oriented computer software
PA: Premier Bpo, Inc.
128 N 2nd St Ste 210
Clarksville TN
931 551-8888

(P-16227)
DM SOFTWARE INC
Also Called: DM SOFTWARE INC
1842 Park Skyline Rd (92705-3120)
PHONE.................................714 953-2653
Bill Parson, Owner
EMP: 20
SALES (corp-wide): 956.82K Privately Held
SIC: 7372 Prepackaged software
PA: Dm Software
654 Jack Cir
Stateline NV
775 589-6049

(P-16228)
DORADO NETWORK SYSTEMS CORP
Also Called: Corelogic Dorado
40 Pacifica (92618-7471)
PHONE.................................650 227-7300
Dain Ehring, CEO
Karen Camp, *
EMP: 140 EST: 1998
SALES (est): 25.34MM
SALES (corp-wide): 1.64B Privately Held
Web: www.corelogic.com
SIC: 7372 Application computer software
HQ: Corelogic, Inc.
40 Pacifica Ste 900
Irvine CA
866 873-3651

(P-16229)
DOZUKI
1105 Higuera St Ste 100 (93401-3293)
P.O. Box 1465 (93406-1465)
PHONE.................................805 464-0573
EMP: 72 EST: 2015
SALES (est): 8.67MM Privately Held
Web: www.dozuki.com
SIC: 7372 Prepackaged software

(P-16230)
DREAMSTART LABS INC
2907 Shelter Island Dr Ste 105 (92106-2743)
PHONE.................................408 914-1234
Wes Wasson, CEO
EMP: 30 EST: 2016
SALES (est): 400K Privately Held
Web: www.dreamstartlabs.com
SIC: 7372 Application computer software

(P-16231)
EAGLE TOPCO LP
18200 Von Karman Ave (92612-1023)
PHONE.................................949 585-4329
EMP: 4000

SIC: **7372** Business oriented computer
software

(P-16232)
EDGATE HOLDINGS INC
4655 Cass St (92109-2813)
PHONE...............................858 712-9341
Peter Sibley, *CEO*
EMP: 32 **EST:** 2021
SALES (est): 1.45MM **Privately Held**
Web: www.edgate.com
SIC: **7372** Educational computer software

(P-16233)
EDGEWAVE INC
4225 Executive Sq Ste 1600 (92037-1487)
PHONE...............................800 782-3762
EMP: 100
SIC: **7372** Operating systems computer
software

(P-16234)
EGL HOLDCO INC
18200 Von Karman Ave # 1000
(92612-1023)
PHONE...............................800 678-7423
EMP: 4000
SALES (est): 98.44MM **Privately Held**
SIC: **7372** Prepackaged software

(P-16235)
EKNOWLEDGE GROUP INC
160 W Fthill Pkwy Ste 105 (92882)
PHONE...............................951 256-4076
Scott Hildebrandt, *Pr*
EMP: 35 **EST:** 1999
SALES (est): 1.63MM **Privately Held**
SIC: **7372** Educational computer software

(P-16236)
**ELECTRONIC CLEARING
HOUSE INC (HQ)**
730 Paseo Camarillo (93010-6064)
PHONE...............................805 419-8700
Charles J Harris, *Pr*
Alice L Cheung, *
Rick Slater, *
William Wied, *CIO**
Karl Asplund, *
EMP: 100 **EST:** 1981
SQ FT: 32,669
SALES (est): 49.29MM
SALES (corp-wide): 14.37B **Publicly Held**
Web: www.echo-inc.com
SIC: **7372** Business oriented computer
software
PA: Intuit Inc.
2700 Coast Ave
Mountain View CA
650 944-6000

(P-16237)
**ENVIRNMNTAL SYSTEMS RES
INST I**
Also Called: Esri
1411 W State St (92373-8164)
PHONE...............................909 793-2853
Laura Dangermond, *Mgr*
EMP: 46
SALES (corp-wide): 490.13MM **Privately
Held**
Web: www.esri.com
SIC: **7372** Prepackaged software
PA: Environmental Systems Research
Institute, Inc.
380 New York St
Redlands CA
909 793-2853

(P-16238)
EPIRUS INC
19145 Gramercy Pl (90501-1128)
P.O. Box 3927 (90277-1725)
PHONE...............................310 620-8678
Andy Lowery, *CEO*
Harry Marr, *
Joseph Lonsdale, *
John Tenet, *
Daniel Thompson, *
EMP: 26 **EST:** 2018
SALES (est): 1MM **Privately Held**
Web: www.epirusinc.com
SIC: **7372** 7373 0781 1771 Prepackaged
software; Computer integrated systems
design; Landscape counseling and planning
; Stucco, gunite, and grouting contractors

(P-16239)
EQUIMINE
Also Called: Propstream
26457 Rancho Pkwy S (92630-8326)
PHONE...............................877 204-9040
Brian Tepfer, *CEO*
EMP: 45 **EST:** 2006
SALES (est): 19.45MM
SALES (corp-wide): 3.07B **Publicly Held**
Web: www.propstream.com
SIC: **7372** 3429 Business oriented computer
software; Keys, locks, and related hardware
PA: Stewart Information Services
Corporation
1360 Post Oak Blvd Ste 10
Houston TX
713 625-8100

(P-16240)
ESTIFY INC
5023 Parkway Calabasas (91302-1421)
PHONE...............................801 341-1911
EMP: 33 **EST:** 2017
SALES (est): 340.33K **Privately Held**
Web: new.estify.com
SIC: **7372** Prepackaged software

(P-16241)
ETURNS INC
19700 Fairchild Ste 290 (92612-2521)
PHONE...............................949 265-2626
Richard Rockwell, *CEO*
EMP: 32 **EST:** 2010
SALES (est): 2.55MM **Privately Held**
Web: www.eturns.com
SIC: **7372** 7371 Application computer
software; Computer software development
and applications

(P-16242)
EVENTSCOM INC
Also Called: Bump.me
811 Prospect St (92037-4207)
P.O. Box 1209 (92038-1209)
PHONE...............................858 257-2300
EMP: 45 **EST:** 2009
SALES (est): 4.97MM **Privately Held**
Web: www.events.com
SIC: **7372** Publisher's computer software

(P-16243)
EVERBRIDGE INC (PA)
155 N Lake Ave Ste 900 (91101-1857)
PHONE...............................818 230-9700
David Wagner, *Pr*
Jaime Ellertson, *
David Henshall, *Vice Chairman**
Robert Hughes, *
Patrick Brickley, *
EMP: 111 **EST:** 2002
SQ FT: 45,000
SALES (est): 431.89MM

SALES (corp-wide): 431.89MM **Publicly
Held**
Web: www.everbridge.com
SIC: **7372** 4899 Prepackaged software; Data
communication services

(P-16244)
EVOCATIVE INC
600 W 7th St Ste 510 (90017-3864)
PHONE...............................888 365-2656
EMP: 75 **EST:** 1996
SQ FT: 15,000
SALES (est): 13.94MM
SALES (corp-wide): 39.94MM **Privately
Held**
Web: www.evocative.com
SIC: **7372** Application computer software
PA: Evodc, Llc
600 W 7th St Ste 510
Los Angeles CA
888 365-2656

(P-16245)
EVOLUTION ROBOTICS INC
1055 E Colorado Blvd Ste 320 (91106)
PHONE...............................626 993-3300
Paolo Pirjanian, *CEO*
Bill Gross, *
Doug Mcpherson, *Sec*
EMP: 146 **EST:** 2001
SALES (est): 11.68MM **Publicly Held**
Web: careers.evolution.com
SIC: **7372** Application computer software
PA: Irobot Corporation
8 Crosby Dr
Bedford MA

(P-16246)
FACEFIRST LLC ✪
31416 Agoura Rd Ste 250 (91361-5654)
PHONE...............................805 482-8428
EMP: 30 **EST:** 2023
SALES (est): 907.36K **Privately Held**
SIC: **7372** Prepackaged software

(P-16247)
FLASH CODE SOLUTIONS LLC
4727 Wilshire Blvd Ste 302 (90010-3806)
PHONE...............................800 633-7467
James B Davis, *Prin*
EMP: 17 **EST:** 2015
SQ FT: 2,600
SALES (est): 1.05MM **Privately Held**
Web: www.flashcodesolutions.com
SIC: **7372** Application computer software

(P-16248)
FLOOR COVERING SOFT
221 E Walnut St Ste 110 (91101-1554)
PHONE...............................626 683-9188
Steven Wang, *CEO*
▼ **EMP:** 20 **EST:** 2001
SQ FT: 2,500
SALES (est): 1.61MM **Privately Held**
Web: www.measuresquare.com
SIC: **7372** Prepackaged software

(P-16249)
**FOUNDATION 9
ENTERTAINMENT INC (PA)**
30211 Avenida De Las Bandera Ste 200
(92688)
PHONE...............................949 698-1500
James H Hearn, *CEO*
John Goldman, *
David Mann, *
EMP: 200 **EST:** 2005
SALES (est): 59.5MM **Privately Held**

SIC: **7372** Home entertainment computer
software

(P-16250)
FOUNDATION INC
Also Called: Foundation Ai
19800 Macarthur Blvd Ste 300
(92612-2421)
PHONE...............................310 294-8955
Vivek Rao, *CEO*
Vivek Rao, *Prin*
Victor Gebhardt, *
Vamsi Kasivajjala, *
EMP: 38 **EST:** 2017
SALES (est): 2.73MM **Privately Held**
Web: www.foundationai.com
SIC: **7372** 7371 Prepackaged software;
Custom computer programming services

(P-16251)
FOUNDSTONE INC
27201 Puerta Real Ste 400 (92691-8517)
PHONE...............................949 297-5600
George Kurtz, *CEO*
Stuart Mcclure, *Pr*
Gary Bahadur, *CIO**
Chris Prosise, *
William Chan, *Knowledge Management
Vice-President**
EMP: 38 **EST:** 1999
SQ FT: 15,000
SALES (est): 5.69MM
SALES (corp-wide): 1.92B **Privately Held**
Web: www.foundstone.com
SIC: **7372** Application computer software
HQ: Mcafee, Llc
6220 America Center Dr
San Jose CA

(P-16252)
FREIGHTGATE INC
Also Called: Edi Ideas
10055 Slater Ave Ste 231 (92708-4722)
PHONE...............................714 799-2833
EMP: 32 **EST:** 2000
SALES (est): 8.83MM
SALES (corp-wide): 8.83MM **Privately
Held**
Web: www.freightgate.com
SIC: **7372** 7371 Application computer
software; Computer software development
and applications
PA: Edi Ideas Inc
16051 Springdale St # 111
Huntington Beach CA
714 841-2833

(P-16253)
GAIKAI INC
65 Enterprise (92656-2705)
EMP: 51
Web: www.gaikai.com
SIC: **7372** Home entertainment computer
software

(P-16254)
GALLEY SOLUTIONS INC
712 Archer St (92109-1048)
P.O. Box 1051 (90294-1051)
PHONE...............................818 636-1538
Ian Christopher, *CEO*
Benji Koltai, *Prin*
Matthew Ferguson, *Prin*
Jason Lazarski, *Prin*
Ashley Fontana, *Prin*
EMP: 17 **EST:** 2019
SALES (est): 1.04MM **Privately Held**
Web: www.galleysolutions.com
SIC: **7372** Prepackaged software

P R O D U C T S   &   S V C S

(P-16255)
GAMEMINE LLC
439 Carroll Canal (90291-4683)
PHONE...............................310 310-3105
Flaviu Rus, *Managing Member*
Daneil Starr, *
EMP: 35 **EST:** 2017
SALES (est): 2.93MM **Privately Held**
Web: www.gamemine.com
SIC: 7372 7389 Publisher's computer
software; Business services, nec

(P-16256)
GLOBAL CASH CARD INC
3972 Barranca Pkwy Ste J610
(92606-1204)
PHONE...............................949 751-0360
EMP: 165
SIC: 7372 Business oriented computer
software

(P-16257)
GLOBAL WAVE GROUP
26970 Aliso Viejo Pkwy Ste 250
(92656-2621)
PHONE...............................949 916-9800
Zubin Mehta, *CEO*
Zubin Mehta, *Managing Member*
Rhett Rowe, *Senior Vice President
Managing*
Randy M Ruckle, *Sr VP*
EMP: 18 **EST:** 2007
SALES (est): 1.23MM **Privately Held**
Web: www.globalwavegroup.com
SIC: 7372 Prepackaged software

(P-16258)
GOVERNMENTJOBSCOM INC
Also Called: Neogov
2120 Park Pl Ste 100 (90245-4741)
PHONE...............................310 426-6304
Damir Davidovic, *CEO*
Scott Letourneau, *Pr*
EMP: 130 **EST:** 2000
SQ FT: 5,000
SALES (est): 29.72MM **Privately Held**
Web: www.neogov.com
SIC: 7372 Prepackaged software

(P-16259)
GREEN HILLS SOFTWARE LLC
(HQ)
Also Called: Green Hills Software
30 W Sola St (93101-2599)
PHONE...............................805 965-6044
Daniel O Dowd, *CEO*
Daniel O'dowd, *CEO*
Jeffrey Hazarian, *
EMP: 105 **EST:** 1986
SALES (est): 89.29MM
SALES (corp-wide): 124.94MM **Privately
Held**
Web: www.ghs.com
SIC: 7372 Prepackaged software
PA: Ghs Holding Company
30 W Sola St
Santa Barbara CA
805 965-6044

(P-16260)
GREMLIN INC
440 N Barranca Ave Ste 3101 (91789)
PHONE...............................408 214-9885
Josh Leslie, *CEO*
Kolton Andrus, *
EMP: 80 **EST:** 2016
SALES (est): 12.16MM **Privately Held**
Web: www.gremlin.com

SIC: 7372 8742 Prepackaged software;
Management consulting services

(P-16261)
GUIDANCE SOFTWARE INC
(HQ)
1055 E Colorado Blvd Ste 400 (91106)
PHONE...............................626 229-9191
Patrick Dennis, *Pr*
Barry Plaga, *
Michael Harris, *CMO**
Alfredo Gomez, *Corporate Secretary**
EMP: 215 **EST:** 2006
SQ FT: 90,000
SALES (est): 51.33MM
SALES (corp-wide): 832.31MM **Privately
Held**
Web: www.opentext.com
SIC: 7372 3572 Business oriented computer
software; Computer storage devices
PA: Open Text Corporation
275 Frank Tompa Dr
Waterloo ON
519 888-7111

(P-16262)
GUMGUM INC (PA)
1314 7th St Fl 5 (90401-1608)
PHONE...............................310 260-9666
Ophir Taz, *CEO*
Phil Schraeder, *COO*
Patrick Gildea, *CFO*
Ben Plomion, *CGO*
EMP: 20 **EST:** 2007
SALES (est): 25.96MM
SALES (corp-wide): 25.96MM **Privately
Held**
Web: www.gumgum.com
SIC: 7372 Prepackaged software

(P-16263)
HOLLYWOOD SOFTWARE INC
5000 Van Nuys Blvd Ste 300 (91403-1793)
PHONE...............................818 205-2121
Carol Dibattiste, *CEO*
Karl Anderson, *CFO*
Susan Wells, *Sr VP*
Kim Lockhart, *Sr VP*
Larry Mccourt, *Sr VP*
EMP: 20 **EST:** 1997
SALES (est): 925.59K
SALES (corp-wide): 376.42MM **Publicly
Held**
Web: www.comscore.com
SIC: 7372 Business oriented computer
software
PA: Comscore, Inc.
11950 Democracy Dr # 600
Reston VA
703 438-2000

(P-16264)
HOOKED
1524 11th St Unit C (90401-2961)
PHONE...............................805 551-4981
EMP: 31 **EST:** 2019
SALES (est): 560.35K **Privately Held**
Web: www.hookedapp.com
SIC: 7372 Prepackaged software

(P-16265)
HOYLU INC
Also Called: Hoylu La
6121 W Sunset Blvd (90028-6423)
PHONE...............................213 440-2499
EMP: 17
SALES (corp-wide): 3.98MM **Privately
Held**
Web: www.hoylu.com

SIC: 7372 Prepackaged software
PA: Hoylu, Inc.
11335 Ne 122nd Way # 105
Kirkland WA
877 554-6958

(P-16266)
HR CLOUD INC
222 N Pacific Coast Hwy Ste 2000 (90245)
PHONE...............................510 909-1993
Damir Davidovic, *CEO*
EMP: 28 **EST:** 2016
SQ FT: 10,000
SALES (est): 4.76MM **Privately Held**
Web: www.hrcloud.com
SIC: 7372 Business oriented computer
software

(P-16267)
IAMPLUS ELECTRONICS INC
(PA)
809 N Cahuenga Blvd (90038-3703)
PHONE...............................323 210-3852
Will Adams, *CEO*
Phil Molyneux, *
Chandrasekar Rathakrishnan, *
Rosemary Peschken, *
EMP: 38 **EST:** 2013
SQ FT: 6,000
SALES (est): 10.01MM
SALES (corp-wide): 10.01MM **Privately
Held**
Web: www.iamplus.services
SIC: 7372 Prepackaged software

(P-16268)
IGRAD INC
2163 Newcastle Ave Ste 100 (92007-1871)
PHONE...............................858 705-2917
Rob Labreche, *Pr*
EMP: 22 **EST:** 2009
SQ FT: 2,000
SALES (est): 2.6MM **Privately Held**
Web: www.igrad.com
SIC: 7372 Business oriented computer
software

(P-16269)
ILLUMNATE EDUCATN
HOLDINGS INC (PA)
6531 Irvine Center Dr Ste 100
(92618-2146)
PHONE...............................949 656-3133
Christine Willig, *CEO*
Shawn Mahoney, *Chief Product Officer**
Jane Snyder, *CMO**
Dick Davidson, *
EMP: 28 **EST:** 2009
SALES (est): 14.71MM
SALES (corp-wide): 14.71MM **Privately
Held**
Web: www.illuminateed.com
SIC: 7372 Educational computer software

(P-16270)
INFORM SOLUTION
INCORPORATED
201 Mentor Dr (93111-3337)
PHONE...............................805 879-6000
EMP: 20 **EST:** 1994
SALES (est): 2.12MM
SALES (corp-wide): 94.94B **Publicly Held**
SIC: 7372 Prepackaged software
HQ: Mentor Worldwide Llc
31 Technology Dr Ste 200
Irvine CA
800 636-8678

(P-16271)
INFORMTION INTGRTION
GROUP INC
457 Palm Dr Ste 200 (91202-4339)
PHONE...............................818 956-3744
Alec Baghdasaryan, *Pr*
EMP: 21 **EST:** 1995
SALES (est): 3.84MM **Privately Held**
Web: www.iigservices.com
SIC: 7372 7371 Prepackaged software;
Computer software development

(P-16272)
INTUIT INC
7535 Torrey Santa Fe Rd (92129-5704)
PHONE...............................858 780-2846
Brian Bequette, *Prin*
EMP: 182
SALES (corp-wide): 14.37B **Publicly Held**
Web: www.intuit.com
SIC: 7372 Business oriented computer
software
PA: Intuit Inc.
2700 Coast Ave
Mountain View CA
650 944-6000

(P-16273)
INTUIT INC
Also Called: Turbotax
7545 Torrey Santa Fe Rd (92129-5704)
PHONE...............................858 215-8000
Jason Jackson, *Brnch Mgr*
EMP: 300
SALES (corp-wide): 14.37B **Publicly Held**
Web: www.intuit.com
SIC: 7372 Business oriented computer
software
PA: Intuit Inc.
2700 Coast Ave
Mountain View CA
650 944-6000

(P-16274)
INTUIT INC
21650 Oxnard St Ste 2200 (91367-7824)
PHONE...............................818 436-7800
Michael Ermi, *Brnch Mgr*
EMP: 105
SALES (corp-wide): 14.37B **Publicly Held**
Web: quickbooks.intuit.com
SIC: 7372 Business oriented computer
software
PA: Intuit Inc.
2700 Coast Ave
Mountain View CA
650 944-6000

(P-16275)
INVISBLE PRTECTION
SYSTEMS INC
8847 S Halldale Ave (90047-3428)
P.O. Box 452963 (90045-8541)
PHONE...............................213 254-0463
Gregory Bryant, *CEO*
EMP: 20 **EST:** 2018
SALES (est): 724.13K **Privately Held**
Web: www.ipsitech.com
SIC: 7372 Prepackaged software

(P-16276)
IPR SOFTWARE INC
Also Called: Ipr Software
16501 Ventura Blvd Ste 424 (91436-2007)
PHONE...............................310 499-0544
J D Bowles, *Pr*
James Madden Senior, *Treas*
EMP: 22 **EST:** 2000
SQ FT: 10,000

SALES (est): 946.16K **Privately Held**
Web: www.iprsoftware.com
SIC: 7372 Application computer software

(P-16277)
IQMS LLC (DH)
2231 Wisteria Ln (93446-9820)
PHONE..............................805 227-1122
Gary Nemmers, *Pr*
Matt Ouska, *
Steve Bieszczat, *CMO*
Dan Vertachnik, *CRO*
Dan Radunz, *
EMP: 130 **EST:** 1989
SQ FT: 60,000
SALES (est): 49.15MM **Privately Held**
SIC: 7372 Prepackaged software
HQ: Dassault Systemes
10 Rue Marcel Dassault
Velizy Villacoublay
161626162

(P-16278)
ISOLUTECOM INC (PA)
9 Northam Ave (91320-3323)
PHONE..............................805 498-6259
Byron Nutley, *Interim Chief Executive Officer*
Don Hyun, *
Thomas Mangle, *
Michael Brown, *
EMP: 50 **EST:** 1999
SALES (est): 8.97MM
SALES (corp-wide): 8.97MM **Privately Held**
SIC: 7372 Business oriented computer software

(P-16279)
ITC SFTWARE SLUTIONS GROUP LLC (PA)
Also Called: Itc Solutions & Services Group
201 Sandpointe Ave Ste 305 (92707-5778)
PHONE..............................877 248-2774
Del Husain, *CEO*
Ray Jandga, *Pr*
Guru Gurumoorthy, *VP*
EMP: 49 **EST:** 2008
SQ FT: 3,000
SALES (est): 26.8MM
SALES (corp-wide): 26.8MM **Privately Held**
Web: www.itcssg.com
SIC: 7372 7371 7373 Prepackaged software; Computer software systems analysis and design, custom; Systems software development services

(P-16280)
JAM CITY INC
2255 N Ontario St (91504-3187)
PHONE..............................804 920-8760
Tiffany Van Decker, *Prin*
EMP: 76
SALES (corp-wide): 59.07MM **Privately Held**
Web: www.jamcity.com
SIC: 7372 Prepackaged software
PA: Jam City, Inc.
3562 Eastham Dr
Culver City CA
310 205-4800

(P-16281)
JURNY INC
6600 W Sunset Blvd (90028-7160)
PHONE..............................888 875-8769
Luca Zambello, *CEO*
EMP: 25 **EST:** 2018
SALES (est): 1.18MM **Privately Held**

Web: www.jurny.com
SIC: 7372 Prepackaged software

(P-16282)
JUSTENOUGH SOFTWARE CORP INC (HQ)
15440 Laguna Canyon Rd Ste 100 (92618-2139)
PHONE..............................949 706-5400
Malcolm Buxton, *Pr*
Robert Rackleff, *CFO*
EMP: 30 **EST:** 2001
SALES (est): 10.88MM
SALES (corp-wide): 28.94MM **Privately Held**
Web: www.justenoughsoftware.com
SIC: 7372 Prepackaged software
PA: Mi9 Retail Inc.
1 Financial Plz Ste 601
Fort Lauderdale FL
647 849-1101

(P-16283)
KAZUHM INC
6450 Lusk Blvd Ste E208 (92121-2756)
PHONE..............................858 771-3861
Tim O'neal, *CEO*
EMP: 20 **EST:** 2017
SALES (est): 947.17K **Privately Held**
Web: www.kazuhm.com
SIC: 7372 Business oriented computer software

(P-16284)
KINGCOM(US) LLC (DH)
3100 Ocean Park Blvd (90405-3032)
PHONE..............................424 744-5697
EMP: 44 **EST:** 2016
SALES (est): 45.9MM
SALES (corp-wide): 211.91B **Publicly Held**
SIC: 7372 Home entertainment computer software
HQ: Activision Blizzard, Inc.
2701 Olympic Blvd Bldg B
Santa Monica CA
310 255-2000

(P-16285)
KINTERA INC (HQ)
Also Called: Blackbaud Internet Solutions
9605 Scranton Rd Ste 200 (92121-1768)
PHONE..............................858 795-3000
Marc E Chardon, *CEO*
Richard Labarbera, *
Alfred R Berkeley Iii, *Ch Bd*
Richard Davidson, *CFO*
EMP: 51 **EST:** 2000
SQ FT: 38,000
SALES (corp-wide): 1.06B **Publicly Held**
SIC: 7372 Business oriented computer software
PA: Blackbaud, Inc.
65 Fairchild St
Daniel Island SC
843 216-6200

(P-16286)
KLOOMA HOLDINGS INC
113 N San Vicente Blvd (90211-2303)
PHONE..............................305 747-3315
Gary Merisier, *CEO*
EMP: 20 **EST:** 2017
SALES (est): 1.2MM **Privately Held**
SIC: 7372 Application computer software

(P-16287)
KOFAX LIMITED (PA)
15211 Laguna Canyon Rd (92618-3146)
PHONE..............................949 783-1000
Reynolds C Bish, *CEO*
Cort Townsend, *CFO*
EMP: 35 **EST:** 1985
SQ FT: 91,000
SALES (est): 94.49MM
SALES (corp-wide): 94.49MM **Privately Held**
SIC: 7372 Business oriented computer software

(P-16288)
KYRIBA CORP (PA)
4435 Eastgate Mall Ste 200 (92121)
PHONE..............................858 210-3560
Melissa Di Donato, *Ch*
Edi Poloniato, *
Catherine Moore, *
Remy Dubois, *
Fabrice Lvy, *
EMP: 50 **EST:** 2000
SALES (est): 80.82MM
SALES (corp-wide): 80.82MM **Privately Held**
Web: www.kyriba.com
SIC: 7372 Prepackaged software

(P-16289)
LAWINFOCOM INC
5901 Priestly Dr Ste 200 (92008-8825)
PHONE..............................800 397-3743
Gunter Enz, *Pr*
Cara Mae Harrison, *
EMP: 30 **EST:** 1989
SQ FT: 10,000
SALES (est): 1.95MM **Privately Held**
Web: www.lawinfo.com
SIC: 7372 8111 7375 Publisher's computer software; Legal services; Information retrieval services

(P-16290)
LCPTRACKER INC
117 E Chapman Ave (92866-1401)
P.O. Box 187 (92856-6187)
PHONE..............................714 669-0052
Mark Douglas, *Pr*
Loren Doll, *VP*
EMP: 20 **EST:** 1992
SQ FT: 1,500
SALES (est): 5.32MM **Privately Held**
Web: www.lcptracker.com
SIC: 7372 Business oriented computer software

(P-16291)
LEADCRUNCH INC (PA)
Also Called: Leadcrunch
750 B St Ste 1630 (92101-8131)
P.O. Box 712979 (92171-2979)
PHONE..............................888 708-6649
Olin Hyde, *CEO*
David Toth, *Ch Bd*
Sanjit Singh, *COO*
EMP: 27 **EST:** 2018
SALES (est): 7.5MM
SALES (corp-wide): 7.5MM **Privately Held**
Web: www.getrev.ai
SIC: 7372 Business oriented computer software

(P-16292)
LEADS360 LLC
207 Hindry Ave (90301-1519)
PHONE..............................888 843-1777
Nick Hedges, *CEO*
Charles Chase, *

Jeff Solomon, *
Christopher Adams, *
Alan Lang, *
EMP: 30 **EST:** 2005
SALES (est): 2.79MM **Privately Held**
SIC: 7372 7371 Prepackaged software; Computer software development

(P-16293)
LEARNING EXPLORER INC
924 Anacapa St Ste 4i (93101-2193)
PHONE..............................888 909-9035
Mark Rankovic, *CEO*
EMP: 17 **EST:** 2021
SALES (est): 1.01MM **Privately Held**
Web: www.learningexplorer.com
SIC: 7372 Educational computer software

(P-16294)
LIGHTSPEED SOFTWARE INC
1800 19th St (93301-4315)
PHONE..............................661 716-7600
EMP: 25 **EST:** 2017
SALES (est): 1.17MM **Privately Held**
SIC: 7372 Prepackaged software

(P-16295)
LIVEOFFICE LLC
Also Called: Advisorsquare
900 Corporate Pointe (90230-7609)
PHONE..............................877 253-2793
Matt Smith, *
Nikhil Menta, *
Jeffrey W Hausman, *
Matt Hardy, *
EMP: 73 **EST:** 2007
SQ FT: 15,000
SALES (est): 10MM
SALES (corp-wide): 3.34B **Publicly Held**
Web: www.liveoffice.com
SIC: 7372 Prepackaged software
PA: Gen Digital Inc.
60 E Rio Salado Pkwy # 1
Tempe AZ
650 527-8000

(P-16296)
LUNA IMAGING INC
2702 Media Center Dr (90065-1733)
PHONE..............................323 908-1400
Marlo Lee, *Pr*
James Lytras, *Mktg Dir*
Drake Zabriskie, *Eng/Dir*
David Larson, *S&M/Dir*
Lori Richmeier, *Genl Mgr*
EMP: 21 **EST:** 1993
SQ FT: 6,000
SALES (est): 1.34MM **Privately Held**
Web: www.lunaimaging.com
SIC: 7372 7373 Publisher's computer software; Computer integrated systems design

(P-16297)
M NEXON INC
Also Called: Nexon America
222 N Pacific Coast Hwy Ste 300 (90245-5614)
PHONE..............................213 858-5930
John Robinson, *CEO*
EMP: 49 **EST:** 2011
SALES (est): 3.25MM **Privately Held**
Web: www.nexon.com
SIC: 7372 5092 Application computer software; Video games
PA: Nexon Co., Ltd.
1-4-5, Roppongi
Minato-Ku TKY

PRODUCTS & SVCS

(P-16298)
MAGIC SOFTWARE ENTERPRISES INC
530 Technology Dr Ste 100 (92618-1350)
P.O. Box 52020 (92619-2020)
PHONE...............................949 250-1718
Eyal Karny, *CEO*
Glenn Johnson, *VP Mktg*
Fred Esquillo, *VP Fin*
Shimon Adimor, *Dir*
EMP: 20 **EST:** 1991
SALES (est): 6.59MM **Privately Held**
Web: www.magicsoftware.com
SIC: 7372 7379 7371 Prepackaged software
; Computer related consulting services;
Custom computer programming services
PA: Magic Software Enterprises Ltd.
1 Yahadut Canada
Or Yehuda

(P-16299)
MAGIC TOUCH SOFTWARE INTL
950 Boardwalk Ste 200 (92078-2600)
P.O. Box 142 (92079-0142)
PHONE...............................800 714-6490
Gary Bagheri, *CEO*
Gary Bagheri, *Pr*
George Peiov, *
EMP: 25 **EST:** 2007
SQ FT: 1,500
SALES (est): 1.22MM **Privately Held**
Web: www.magictouchsoftware.com
SIC: 7372 Business oriented computer
software

(P-16300)
MANGOMINT INC
10401 Venice Blvd 497 (90034-6491)
PHONE...............................310 496-8677
Daniel Lang, *CEO*
EMP: 40 **EST:** 2016
SALES (est): 4.84MM **Privately Held**
Web: www.mangomint.com
SIC: 7372 7371 Prepackaged software;
Software programming applications

(P-16301)
MAXXESS SYSTEMS INC (PA)
135 S State College Blvd Ste 200
(92821-5805)
PHONE...............................714 772-1000
EMP: 18 **EST:** 2003
SALES (est): 5.44MM **Privately Held**
Web: www.maxxess-systems.com
SIC: 7372 Business oriented computer
software

(P-16302)
MEDATA INC (PA)
5 Peters Canyon Rd Ste 250 (92606-1791)
PHONE...............................714 918-1310
Cy King, *CEO*
Bryan Lowe, *
Thomas Herndon, *
T Don Theis, *
Elizabeth King, *
EMP: 51 **EST:** 1975
SQ FT: 17,192
SALES (est): 136.9MM
SALES (corp-wide): 136.9MM **Privately
Held**
Web: www.medata.com
SIC: 7372 6411 Business oriented computer
software; Medical insurance claim
processing, contract or fee basis

(P-16303)
MEDIA GOBBLER INC
Also Called: Gobbler
6427 W Sunset Blvd (90028-7314)

PHONE...............................323 203-3222
Chris Kantrowitz, *CEO*
EMP: 18 **EST:** 2010
SALES (est): 707.18K **Privately Held**
Web: www.gobbler.com
SIC: 7372 Application computer software

(P-16304)
MEDIAMORPH INC (HQ)
Also Called: Whip Media Group
1841 Centinela Ave (90404-4203)
PHONE...............................212 643-0762
Rob Gardos, *CEO*
Kent Jarvi, *
Michael Sid, *Chief Strategy Officer**
Paul Giordano, *Chief Client Officer**
Jerry Inman, *
EMP: 28 **EST:** 2007
SALES (est): 9.09MM
SALES (corp-wide): 9.09MM **Privately
Held**
Web: www.whipmedia.com
SIC: 7372 Prepackaged software
PA: Whip Networks, Inc.
1841 Centinela Ave
Santa Monica CA
310 998-1976

(P-16305)
MICROVISION DEVELOPMENT INC
1734 Oriole Ct (92011-4052)
PHONE...............................760 438-7781
James Harley Mayall, *CEO*
John Gaby, *VP*
EMP: 20 **EST:** 1992
SALES (est): 1.19MM **Privately Held**
Web: www.mvd.com
SIC: 7372 Business oriented computer
software

(P-16306)
MINDSHOW
811 W 7th St Ste 400 (90017-3415)
PHONE...............................213 531-0277
EMP: 40 **EST:** 2017
SALES (est): 1.68MM **Privately Held**
Web: www.mindshow.com
SIC: 7372 Prepackaged software

(P-16307)
MINTLE ENTERPRISES INC
41571 Date St (92562-7086)
P.O. Box 3033 (92088-3033)
PHONE...............................951 506-4005
Ronald G Mintle, *CEO*
Beverly Mintle, *Sec*
James Snyder, *VP*
EMP: 18 **EST:** 1984
SALES (est): 2.84MM **Privately Held**
Web: www.yellowmagic.com
SIC: 7372 7389 Home entertainment
computer software; Business Activities at
Non-Commercial Site

(P-16308)
MIRTH CORPORATION
611 Anton Blvd Ste 500 (92626-1934)
PHONE...............................714 389-1200
Jon Teichrow, *Pr*
Gary Teichrow, *
Andrew Thorson, *
Samuel Sippl, *
EMP: 55 **EST:** 1993
SQ FT: 10,000
SALES (est): 2.8MM
SALES (corp-wide): 653.17MM **Privately
Held**
Web: www.nextgen.com

SIC: 7372 Business oriented computer
software
PA: Nextgen Healthcare, Inc.
18111 Von Karman Ave # 6
Irvine CA
949 255-2600

(P-16309)
MITRATECH HOLDINGS INC
5900 Wilshire Blvd Ste 1500 (90036-5031)
PHONE...............................323 964-0000
Jason Parkman, *CEO*
EMP: 125
SALES (corp-wide): 98.42MM **Privately
Held**
Web: www.mitratech.com
SIC: 7372 Business oriented computer
software
PA: Mitratech Holdings, Inc.
5001 Plz On The Lk Ste 11
Austin TX
512 382-7322

(P-16310)
MIXMODE INC
111 W Micheltorena St Ste 300-A
(93101-3095)
P.O. Box 92041 (93190-2041)
PHONE...............................858 225-2352
John Keister, *CEO*
John Keister, *Pr*
Fred Wilmot, *
Mark Rotolo, *CRO**
Karen Buffo, *CMO**
EMP: 40 **EST:** 2012
SALES (est): 4.79MM **Privately Held**
Web: www.mixmode.ai
SIC: 7372 Business oriented computer
software

(P-16311)
MOD2 INC
Also Called: Mod 2
3317 S Broadway (90007-4114)
PHONE...............................213 747-8424
EMP: 19 **EST:** 1992
SQ FT: 12,000
SALES (est): 810.08K **Privately Held**
Web: www.mod2.com
SIC: 7372 7371 Business oriented computer
software; Computer software systems
analysis and design, custom

(P-16312)
MODEL MATCH INC
209 Avenida Fabricante Ste 150 (92672)
PHONE...............................949 525-9405
Kirk Waldfogel, *Prin*
Drew Waterhouse, *Prin*
Steve Rennie, *Prin*
Eric Levin, *Prin*
Eric Petersen, *Prin*
EMP: 18 **EST:** 2014
SQ FT: 3,400
SALES (est): 1.11MM **Privately Held**
Web: www.modelmatch.com
SIC: 7372 Application computer software

(P-16313)
MOMCO APP INC
5598 Elgin Ave (92120-1839)
PHONE...............................619 450-6340
Jillian Darlington, *Prin*
EMP: 23 **EST:** 2016
SALES (est): 75.25K **Privately Held**
Web: www.momcoapp.com
SIC: 7372 Application computer software

(P-16314)
MSCSOFTWARE CORPORATION (HQ)
5161 California Ave Ste 200 (92617-8002)
PHONE...............................714 540-8900
Roger Assaker, *CEO*
Alex Montgomery, *
EMP: 245 **EST:** 1963
SALES (est): 125.34MM
SALES (corp-wide): 491.93K **Privately
Held**
Web: www.hexagon.com
SIC: 7372 Business oriented computer
software
PA: Hexagon Ab
Lilla Bantorget 15
Stockholm
86012620

(P-16315)
MUSICMATCH INC
16935 W Bernardo Dr Ste 270
(92127-1634)
PHONE...............................858 485-4300
Dennis Mudd, *CEO*
Peter Csathy, *
Gary Acord, *
Don Leigh, *
Chris Allen Senior Vp Mkting S tragic
Planning, *Prin*
EMP: 140 **EST:** 1997
SQ FT: 20,000
SALES (est): 22.01MM **Privately Held**
SIC: 7372 5734 Prepackaged software;
Software, business and non-game
PA: Altaba Inc.
140 E 45th St Fl 15
New York NY

(P-16316)
MY EYE MEDIA LLC
2211 N Hollywood Way (91505-1113)
PHONE...............................818 559-7200
Michael Kadenacy, *Pr*
Rodd Feingold, *CFO*
EMP: 80 **EST:** 2004
SQ FT: 20,000
SALES (est): 10.27MM
SALES (corp-wide): 20.42MM **Privately
Held**
Web: www.resillion.com
SIC: 7372 Business oriented computer
software
HQ: Eurofins Product Testing Us Holdings,
Inc.
11720 N Creek Pkwy N
Bothell WA
800 383-0085

(P-16317)
NATIONWIDE TECHNOLOGIES INC
3684 W Uva Ln (92407-1968)
PHONE...............................909 340-2770
Ajaydev Singh, *CEO*
Rares Sfetcu, *
EMP: 25 **EST:** 2019
SALES (est): 1.08MM **Privately Held**
SIC: 7372 7389 Business oriented computer
software; Business services, nec

(P-16318)
NAZCA SOLUTIONS INC
4 First American Way (92707-5913)
PHONE...............................612 279-6100
Robert Karraa, *Pr*
Ted Mondale, *General Vice President*
EMP: 45 **EST:** 2003
SQ FT: 45,000
SALES (est): 3.5MM **Publicly Held**

SIC: 7372 Application computer software
PA: First American Financial Corporation
1 First American Way
Santa Ana CA

(P-16319)
NC4 SOLTRA LLC
21515 Hawthorne Blvd # 52 (90503-6501)
PHONE...............408 489-5579
Tommy Mcdowell, *Managing Member*
EMP: 67 EST: 2016
SALES (est): 4.6MM
SALES (corp-wide): 9.82MM **Privately Held**
SIC: 7372 Prepackaged software
PA: Celerium Inc.
21515 Hawthorne Blvd # 520
Torrance CA
408 489-5579

(P-16320)
NETAPHOR SOFTWARE INC
15510 Rockfield Blvd Ste C100 (92618)
PHONE...............949 470-7955
Rakesh Mahajan, *CEO*
Shripathi Kamath, *Sec*
▼ EMP: 22 EST: 1997
SQ FT: 2,700
SALES (est): 2.36MM **Privately Held**
Web: www.netaphor.com
SIC: 7372 Business oriented computer software

(P-16321)
NETSOL TECHNOLOGIES INC (PA)
Also Called: Netsol
16000 Ventura Blvd Ste 770 (91436-2758)
PHONE...............818 222-9197
Najeeb Ghauri, *Ch Bd*
Naeem Ghauri, *Pr*
Roger Almond, *CFO*
Malea Farsai, *Corporate Counsel*
Patti L W Mcglasson, *Sr VP*
EMP: 60 EST: 1997
SQ FT: 5,000
SALES (est): 52.39MM
SALES (corp-wide): 52.39MM **Publicly Held**
Web: www.netsoltech.com
SIC: 7372 7373 7299 Business oriented computer software; Computer integrated systems design; Personal document and information services

(P-16322)
NETWORK AUTOMATION INC
3530 Wilshire Blvd Ste 1800 (90010-2335)
PHONE...............213 738-1700
Dustin Snell, *CEO*
Graham Taylor, *
EMP: 50 EST: 2004
SQ FT: 9,000
SALES (est): 11.23MM
SALES (corp-wide): 609.02MM **Privately Held**
SIC: 7372 Business oriented computer software
HQ: Fortra, Llc
11095 Viking Dr Ste 100
Eden Prairie MN
952 933-0609

(P-16323)
NETWORKFLEET
4510 Executive Dr Ste 315 (92121-3029)
PHONE...............904 233-6844
EMP: 29 EST: 2019
SALES (est): 245.01K **Privately Held**
Web: www.verizonconnect.com

SIC: 7372 Prepackaged software

(P-16324)
NETWRIX CORPORATION
300 Spectrum Center Dr Ste 200 (92618-4987)
PHONE...............888 638-9749
Steve Dickson, *Brnch Mgr*
EMP: 27
Web: www.netwrix.com
SIC: 7372 Prepackaged software
HQ: Netwrix Corporation
6160 Warren Pkwy Ste 100
Frisco TX

(P-16325)
NEW BI US GAMING LLC
10920 Via Frontera Ste 420 (92127-1729)
PHONE...............858 592-2472
Ian Bonner, *CEO*
Russell Schechter, *
Kimberly Armstrong, *
EMP: 92 EST: 2012
SALES (est): 4.97MM **Privately Held**
Web: www.vizexplorer.com
SIC: 7372 Prepackaged software

(P-16326)
NEXTGEN HEALTHCARE INC (PA)
18111 Von Karman Ave Ste 600 (92612-0199)
PHONE...............949 255-2600
David Sides, *Pr*
Jeffrey H Margolis, *
James R Arnold Junior, *Ex VP*
Srinivas S Velamoor, *Chief Growth Vice President*
Mitchell L Waters, *Executive Commercial Vice President*
EMP: 252 EST: 1974
SALES (est): 653.17MM
SALES (corp-wide): 653.17MM **Privately Held**
Web: www.nextgen.com
SIC: 7372 7373 Prepackaged software; Computer integrated systems design

(P-16327)
NILE AI INC
15260 Ventura Blvd Ste 1410 (91403-5348)
PHONE...............818 689-9107
Artin Davidian, *Admn*
EMP: 25 EST: 2020
SALES (est): 2.48MM
SALES (corp-wide): 1.04B **Privately Held**
SIC: 7372 Application computer software
HQ: Ucb Holdings, Inc.
1950 Lake Park Dr Se
Smyrna GA
770 970-7500

(P-16328)
NIS AMERICA INC
4 Hutton Centre Dr Ste 650 (92707)
PHONE...............714 540-1199
Souhei Niikawa, *CEO*
Harusato Akenaga, *
Mitsuharu Hiraoka, *
Johanna Hirota, *
▲ EMP: 40 EST: 2003
SQ FT: 1,000
SALES (est): 8.83MM **Privately Held**
Web: www.nisamerica.com
SIC: 7372 Publisher's computer software

(P-16329)
NOVASTOR CORPORATION (PA)
29209 Canwood St Ste 200 (91301-1908)
PHONE...............805 579-6700

Peter Means, *Pr*
Martin Albert, *
EMP: 30 EST: 1987
SQ FT: 7,800
SALES (est): 4.94MM
SALES (corp-wide): 4.94MM **Privately Held**
Web: www.novastor.com
SIC: 7372 7371 5734 Business oriented computer software; Custom computer programming services; Software, business and non-game

(P-16330)
NTRUST INFOTECH INC
230 Commerce Ste 180 (92602-1336)
PHONE...............562 207-1600
Srikanth Ramachandran, *CEO*
EMP: 65 EST: 2003
SALES (est): 5.59MM **Privately Held**
Web: www.ntrustinfotech.com
SIC: 7372 7371 Business oriented computer software; Computer software development and applications

(P-16331)
NUMECENT INC
530 Technology Dr Ste 375 (92618-3505)
PHONE...............949 833-2800
Tom Lagatta, *CEO*
Osman Kent, *
Ed Corrente, *
Hildy Shandell, *
EMP: 30 EST: 2012
SALES (est): 2.93MM **Privately Held**
Web: www.numecent.com
SIC: 7372 Application computer software

(P-16332)
NWP SERVICES CORPORATION (DH)
535 Anton Blvd Ste 1100 (92626-7699)
P.O. Box 19661 (92623-9661)
PHONE...............949 253-2500
EMP: 141 EST: 1995
SQ FT: 21,171
SALES (est): 48.94MM **Privately Held**
Web: www.mynwpsc.com
SIC: 7372 8721 Utility computer software; Billing and bookkeeping service
HQ: Realpage, Inc.
2201 Lakeside Blvd
Richardson TX
972 820-3000

(P-16333)
NXGN MANAGEMENT LLC
18111 Von Karman Ave Ste 600 (92612-0199)
PHONE...............949 255-2600
EMP: 25 EST: 2021
SALES (est): 5.99MM
SALES (corp-wide): 653.17MM **Privately Held**
Web: www.nextgen.com
SIC: 7372 Prepackaged software
PA: Nextgen Healthcare, Inc.
18111 Von Karman Ave # 6
Irvine CA
949 255-2600

(P-16334)
OMNITRACS MIDCO LLC
9276 Scranton Rd Ste 200 (92121-7703)
PHONE...............858 651-5812
EMP: 34 EST: 2013
SALES (est): 998.16K **Privately Held**
Web: www.omnitracs.com
SIC: 7372 Business oriented computer software

(P-16335)
ONCEHUB INC
Also Called: Reschedge
340 S Lemon Ave Ste 5585 (91789-2706)
PHONE...............650 225-5585
Rami Goraly, *CEO*
EMP: 30 EST: 2013
SALES (est): 493.46K **Privately Held**
Web: www.oncehub.com
SIC: 7372 Operating systems computer software

(P-16336)
OPEN SYSTEMS INC
5250 Lankershim Blvd Ste 620 (91601-3186)
PHONE...............317 566-6662
EMP: 41
SALES (corp-wide): 957.93MM **Privately Held**
Web: www.aptean.com
SIC: 7372 Business oriented computer software
HQ: Open Systems, Inc.
4325 Alexander Dr Ste 100
Alpharetta GA
952 403-5700

(P-16337)
OPTIMISCORP
200 Mantua Rd (90272-3349)
PHONE...............310 230-2780
EMP: 32 EST: 2006
SALES (est): 1.77MM **Privately Held**
Web: www.optimiscorp.com
SIC: 7372 Business oriented computer software

(P-16338)
ORACLE CORPORATION
Also Called: Oracle
1 Bolero (92692-5164)
PHONE...............626 315-7513
Hemesh Surana, *Brnch Mgr*
EMP: 302
SALES (corp-wide): 49.95B **Publicly Held**
Web: www.oracle.com
SIC: 7372 Prepackaged software
PA: Oracle Corporation
2300 Oracle Way
Austin TX
737 867-1000

(P-16339)
OSR ENTERPRISES INC
1910 E Stowell Rd (93454-8002)
PHONE...............805 925-1831
James O Rice, *CEO*
Owen S Rice, *
Betty E Rice, *
EMP: 45 EST: 1937
SQ FT: 1,500
SALES (est): 9.46MM **Privately Held**
Web: www.osrenterprises.com
SIC: 7372 Publisher's computer software

(P-16340)
OUTPUT INC
3014 Worthen Ave (90039-2830)
PHONE...............888 803-3175
Gregg Lehrmann, *CEO*
Gregg Lehrmann, *Pr*
Justin Calpito, *Asstg*
EMP: 18 EST: 2013
SALES (est): 5.24MM **Privately Held**
Web: www.output.com
SIC: 7372 Application computer software

(P-16341)
PAKEDGE DEVICE &
SOFTWARE INC
17011 Beach Blvd Ste 600 (92647-5962)
PHONE..............................714 880-4511
Dusan Jankov, *Brnch Mgr*
EMP: 144
SALES (corp-wide): 1.12B **Publicly Held**
Web: www.pakedge.com
SIC: 7372 Application computer software
HQ: Pakedge Device & Software Inc.
    11734 S Election Rd
    Draper UT
    650 385-8700

(P-16342)
PANORAMIC SOFTWARE
CORPORATION
Also Called: Panosoft
9650 Research Dr (92618-4666)
PHONE..............................877 558-8526
Jeff Von Waldburg, *Pr*
EMP: 17 EST: 1990
SQ FT: 1,500
SALES (est): 1.55MM **Privately Held**
Web: www.panosoft.com
SIC: 7372 7371 Prepackaged software;
    Custom computer programming services

(P-16343)
PAPAYA
14140 Ventura Blvd Ste 209 (91423-2774)
PHONE..............................310 740-6774
Dan Mintz, *Prin*
EMP: 33 EST: 2019
SALES (est): 583.86K **Privately Held**
Web: www.papayaclothing.com
SIC: 7372 Prepackaged software

(P-16344)
PARENTSQUARE INC
6144 Calle Real Ste 200a (93117-2012)
PHONE..............................888 496-3168
Sohit Wadhwa, *CEO*
Anupama Vaid, *Prin*
EMP: 65 EST: 2011
SALES (est): 5.71MM **Privately Held**
Web: www.parentsquare.com
SIC: 7372 Educational computer software

(P-16345)
PATIENTPOP INC
214 Wilshire Blvd (90401-1202)
PHONE..............................844 487-8399
Travis Schneider, *CEO*
Luke Kervin, *
David Mcneil, *Pr*
Jason Gardner, *
Taylor Timmer, *
EMP: 51 EST: 2015
SALES (est): 5.59MM **Privately Held**
Web: www.patientpop.com
SIC: 7372 Business oriented computer
    software

(P-16346)
PATRON SOLUTIONS LLC
5171 California Ave Ste 200 (92617-3066)
PHONE..............................949 823-1700
Steve Shaw, *Owner*
EMP: 245 EST: 2015
SALES (est): 6.04MM **Privately Held**
SIC: 7372 Application computer software

(P-16347)
PHOENIX TECHNOLOGIES LTD
(HQ)
150 S Los Robles Ave Ste 500
(91101-2441)

PHONE..............................408 570-1000
Rich Geruson, *Pr*
Robb Warwick, *Prin*
Nick Kaiser, *Prin*
Vladimir Jacimovic, *Prin*
George Huang, *Prin*
◆ EMP: 20 EST: 1979
SQ FT: 47,000
SALES (est): 36.29MM **Privately Held**
Web: www.phoenix.com
SIC: 7372 6794 Prepackaged software;
    Patent owners and lessors
PA: Marlin Equity Partners, Llc
    1301 Manhattan Ave
    Hermosa Beach CA

(P-16348)
PIPELINER CRM
15243 La Cruz Dr Unit 492 (90272-5328)
PHONE..............................424 280-6445
Nikoluas Kimla, *CEO*
Gerald Toumayan, *COO*
EMP: 41 EST: 2014
SALES (est): 479.32K **Privately Held**
Web: www.pipelinersales.com
SIC: 7372 Business oriented computer
    software

(P-16349)
PLANET DDS INC (PA)
Also Called: Planet DDS
3990 Westerly Pl Ste 200 (92660-2312)
PHONE..............................800 861-5098
Eric Giesecke, *CEO*
Stephen Fong, *CFO*
EMP: 33 EST: 2004
SALES (est): 14.22MM
SALES (corp-wide): 14.22MM **Privately
Held**
Web: www.planetdds.com
SIC: 7372 Application computer software

(P-16350)
PLUGG ME LNC
18100 Von Karman Ave # 850
(92612-0169)
PHONE..............................949 705-4472
Clarissa Watkins, *CEO*
EMP: 25 EST: 2019
SALES (est): 920.85K **Privately Held**
SIC: 7372 Application computer software

(P-16351)
PRATA INC
202 Bicknell Ave (90405-2317)
PHONE..............................512 823-1002
Rajat Jain, *CEO*
EMP: 20 EST: 2020
SALES (est): 714.27K **Privately Held**
SIC: 7372 Application computer software

(P-16352)
PRECISION INFORMATION LLC
Also Called: Financial Fitness Group
501 W Broadway Ste A158 (92101-3536)
PHONE..............................888 345-1285
Patrick Quirk, *Managing Member*
EMP: 17 EST: 1998
SALES (est): 1.43MM **Privately Held**
Web: www.educatedinvestor.com
SIC: 7372 Educational computer software

(P-16353)
PRISM SOFTWARE
CORPORATION
184 Technology Dr Ste 201 (92618-2401)
PHONE..............................949 855-3100
Carl S Von Bibra, *Ch*
David Ayres, *
Conrad Von Bibra, *

Michael Cheever, *
EMP: 25 EST: 1970
SALES (est): 4.36MM **Privately Held**
Web: www.prismsoftware.com
SIC: 7372 Publisher's computer software

(P-16354)
PROCEDE SOFTWARE LP
6815 Flanders Dr Ste 200 (92121-3914)
PHONE..............................858 450-4800
Peter Kneale, *Genl Pt*
Phillip Mossy, *Pt*
EMP: 20 EST: 2003
SALES (est): 4.99MM **Privately Held**
Web: www.procedesoftware.com
SIC: 7372 Business oriented computer
    software

(P-16355)
PRODUCTPLAN LLC
10 E Yanonali St Ste 2a (93101-1878)
P.O. Box 944 (93102-0944)
PHONE..............................805 618-2975
EMP: 20 EST: 2013
SALES (est): 2.11MM **Privately Held**
Web: www.productplan.com
SIC: 7372 Business oriented computer
    software

(P-16356)
PROMENADE SOFTWARE INC
16 Technology Dr Ste 100 (92618-2323)
PHONE..............................949 333-4634
Frances Cohen, *CEO*
Daniel Beard, *Dir*
Jeff Gable, *Dir*
EMP: 20 EST: 2013
SALES (est): 4.11MM **Privately Held**
Web: www.promenadesoftware.com
SIC: 7372 Prepackaged software

(P-16357)
QAD INC
6450 Via Real (93013-2903)
PHONE..............................805 684-6614
Mark Rasmussen, *Brnch Mgr*
EMP: 17
SALES (corp-wide): 471.55MM **Privately
Held**
Web: www.qad.com
SIC: 7372 Business oriented computer
    software
HQ: Qad Inc.
    101 Innovation Pl
    Santa Barbara CA
    805 566-6000

(P-16358)
QAD INC (HQ)
Also Called: Qad
101 Innovation Pl (93108-2268)
PHONE..............................805 566-6000
Anton Chilton, *CEO*
Peter R Van Cuylenburg, *
Pamela M Lopker, *
Daniel Lender, *Ex VP*
Kara Bellamy, *CAO*
EMP: 219 EST: 1979
SALES (est): 307.87MM
SALES (corp-wide): 471.55MM **Privately
Held**
Web: www.qad.com
SIC: 7372 Prepackaged software
PA: Qad Parent, Llc
    101 Innovation Pl
    Santa Barbara CA
    805 566-6000

(P-16359)
QDOS INC
Also Called: Desksite
200 Spectrum Center Dr Ste 300
(92618-5003)
PHONE..............................949 362-8888
Richard Gillam, *CEO*
Patricia Bender, *
EMP: 26 EST: 2003
SQ FT: 6,000
SALES (est): 2.24MM **Privately Held**
Web: www.desksite.com
SIC: 7372 7812 7313 7922 Home
    entertainment computer software; Motion
    picture and video production; Radio,
    television, publisher representatives;
    Television program, including commercial
    producers

(P-16360)
QED SOFTWARE LLC
Also Called: Trinium Technologies
211 E Ocean Blvd (90802-4809)
PHONE..............................310 214-3118
Michael Thomas, *CEO*
Barry Assadi, *
▲ EMP: 27 EST: 2001
SALES (est): 8.93MM **Privately Held**
Web: www.triniumtech.com
SIC: 7372 Business oriented computer
    software
PA: Wisetech Global Limited
    U 3 72 O'riordan St
    Alexandria NSW

(P-16361)
QUADROTECH SOLUTIONS INC
(PA)
Also Called: Quest
20 Enterprise (92656-7104)
PHONE..............................949 754-8000
Thomas Madsen, *CEO*
EMP: 25 EST: 2013
SALES (est): 9.1MM
SALES (corp-wide): 9.1MM **Privately Held**
SIC: 7372 Application computer software

(P-16362)
QUALER INC
10360 Sorrento Valley Rd (92121-1600)
PHONE..............................858 224-9516
Alex Spector, *CEO*
Darren Crochet, *
Ruslan Auvad, *
Michael Morozov Ce, *Prin*
EMP: 30 EST: 2018
SALES (est): 1.01MM **Privately Held**
Web: www.qualer.com
SIC: 7372 Prepackaged software

(P-16363)
QUEST SOFTWARE INC
Also Called: Cloud Automation Division
20 Enterprise (92656-7104)
PHONE..............................949 754-8000
EMP: 80
SALES (corp-wide): 647.68MM **Privately
Held**
Web: www.quest.com
SIC: 7372 Prepackaged software
PA: Quest Software Inc.
    20 Enterprise Ste 100
    Aliso Viejo CA
    949 754-8000

(P-16364)
RAILSTECH INC
730 Arizona Ave (90401-1702)
PHONE..............................267 315-2998
Dov Marmor Coe, *Prin*

Dov Marmor, *CEO*
EMP: 23 **EST:** 2020
SALES (est): 2.43MM
SALES (corp-wide): 6.76MM **Privately Held**
SIC: 7372 Business oriented computer software
PA: Railsbank Technology Limited
1, Snowden Street
London
239 431-1850

(P-16365)
REAL SOFTWARE SYSTEMS LLC (PA)
21255 Burbank Blvd Ste 220 (91367-6681)
P.O. Box 7046 (91365-7046)
PHONE...............................818 313-8000
Kent Sahin, *Managing Member*
EMP: 50 **EST:** 1993
SALES (est): 10.36MM **Privately Held**
Web: www.rightsline.com
SIC: 7372 Business oriented computer software

(P-16366)
RED GATE SOFTWARE INC
144 W Colorado Blvd Ste 200 (91105)
PHONE...............................626 993-3949
Tom Curtis, *Pr*
EMP: 23 **EST:** 2011
SQ FT: 5,500
SALES (est): 3.94MM
SALES (corp-wide): 66.95MM **Privately Held**
Web: www.red-gate.com
SIC: 7372 Business oriented computer software
HQ: Red Gate Software Limited
Cavendish House
Cambridge CAMBS
122 342-0397

(P-16367)
RELATIONAL CENTER
2717 S Robertson Blvd Apt 1 (90034-2442)
PHONE...............................323 935-1807
Traci Bivens Davis, *Prin*
EMP: 40 **EST:** 2008
SALES (est): 1.14MM **Privately Held**
Web: www.relationalcenter.org
SIC: 7372 Prepackaged software

(P-16368)
REVCO PRODUCTS
7221 Acacia Ave (92841-3908)
PHONE...............................714 891-6688
▲ **EMP:** 51 **EST:** 1977
SALES (est): 10.16MM **Privately Held**
Web: www.revcoproducts.com
SIC: 7372 Operating systems computer software

(P-16369)
RIOT GAMES INC (DH)
Also Called: Riot Games
12333 W Olympic Blvd (90064-1021)
PHONE...............................310 207-1444
Nicolas Laurent, *CEO*
Marc Merrill, *
Dylan Jadeja, *
Mark Sottosanti, *
Daniel Chang, *
▲ **EMP:** 36 **EST:** 2006
SALES (est): 798.36MM **Privately Held**
Web: www.riotgames.com
SIC: 7372 5734 Prepackaged software; Software, computer games
HQ: Tencent Holdings Limited
29/F Three Pacific Place
Wan Chai HK

(P-16370)
SAGE SOFTWARE HOLDINGS INC (HQ)
6561 Irvine Center Dr (92618-2118)
PHONE...............................866 530-7243
Stev Swenson, *CEO*
Doug Meyer, *
Mack Lout, *
Stephen Kelly, *Prin*
Steve Hare, *Prin*
EMP: 400 **EST:** 2000
SALES (est): 870.22MM
SALES (corp-wide): 2.29B **Privately Held**
SIC: 7372 7371 Business oriented computer software; Custom computer programming services
PA: The Sage Group Plc.
C23 - 5 & 6 Cobalt Park Way
Newcastle-Upon-Tyne
800 923-0344

(P-16371)
SALESCATCHER LLC
Also Called: Salescatcher
1570 N Batavia St (92867-3507)
PHONE...............................714 376-6700
Augustin Gohil, *Managing Member*
EMP: 50 **EST:** 2009
SALES (est): 3.16MM **Privately Held**
Web: www.salescatcher.io
SIC: 7372 Application computer software

(P-16372)
SALESFORCECOM INC
Also Called: SALESFORCE.COM, INC.
1442 2nd St (90401-2302)
PHONE...............................310 752-7000
Andy Demari, *Mgr*
EMP: 40
SALES (corp-wide): 31.35B **Publicly Held**
Web: www.salesforce.com
SIC: 7372 Business oriented computer software
PA: Salesforce, Inc.
415 Mission St Fl 3
San Francisco CA
415 901-7000

(P-16373)
SAVEDAILY INC
1503 S Coast Dr Ste 330 (92626-1509)
PHONE...............................562 795-7500
EMP: 19
SIC: 7372 Prepackaged software

(P-16374)
SAVIYNT INC (PA)
1301 E El Segundo Blvd Ste D (90245-4303)
PHONE...............................310 641-1664
Sachin Nayyar, *CEO*
Paul Zolfaghari, *Pr*
Amit Saha, *CGO*
Shankar Ganapathy, *COO*
Jim Jackson, *CFO*
EMP: 122 **EST:** 2011
SQ FT: 10,000
SALES (est): 83.13MM
SALES (corp-wide): 83.13MM **Privately Held**
Web: www.saviynt.com
SIC: 7372 Prepackaged software

(P-16375)
SCOPELY INC (DH)
3530 Hayden Ave Ste A (90232-2413)
PHONE...............................323 400-6618
EMP: 200 **EST:** 2011
SALES (est): 128.36MM **Privately Held**
Web: www.scopely.com
SIC: 7372 Home entertainment computer software
HQ: Savvy Games Group
Office 2.14 B, 6th Floor, Kafd, King Fahad Road
Riyadh

(P-16376)
SCORELATE INC
91301 Fairview Pl Ste 2 (91301)
PHONE...............................818 602-9176
Sean Bar, *CEO*
EMP: 25
SALES (est): 975.05K **Privately Held**
SIC: 7372 Business oriented computer software

(P-16377)
SEISMIC SOFTWARE INC (HQ)
12390 El Camino Real Ste 300 (92130)
PHONE...............................714 404-7069
John Douglas Winter, *CEO*
EMP: 59 **EST:** 2010
SALES (est): 106.78MM
SALES (corp-wide): 151.4MM **Privately Held**
Web: www.seismic.com
SIC: 7372 Prepackaged software
PA: Seismic Software Holdings, Inc.
12390 El Cmino Real Ste 3
San Diego CA

(P-16378)
SHORTCUTS SOFTWARE INC
7711 Center Ave Ste 550 (92647-3075)
PHONE...............................714 622-6600
Rebecca Randall, *CEO*
Paul Tate, *
Malcom Raward, *
EMP: 30 **EST:** 2005
SALES (est): 6.96MM
SALES (corp-wide): 6.62B **Privately Held**
Web: www.shortcuts.net
SIC: 7372 Business oriented computer software
HQ: Shortcuts Software Pty Ltd
L 2 South Tower 10 Browning St
South Brisbane QLD

(P-16379)
SHRED LABS LLC
8033 W Sunset Blvd # 1112 (90046-2401)
PHONE...............................781 285-8622
EMP: 23 **EST:** 2018
SALES (est): 100K **Privately Held**
Web: www.shred.app
SIC: 7372 7389 Application computer software; Business Activities at Non-Commercial Site

(P-16380)
SLABS INC ✪
12555 W Jefferson Blvd (90066-7032)
PHONE...............................424 289-0275
Iddris Sandu, *CEO*
EMP: 20 **EST:** 2022
SALES (est): 1.27MM **Privately Held**
SIC: 7372 Business oriented computer software

(P-16381)
SMART ACTION COMPANY LLC
300 Continental Blvd Ste 350 (90245-5042)
PHONE...............................310 776-9200
Tom Lewis, *CEO*
Peter E Voss, *Prin*
Michael Vanca, *Sr VP*
Louise Gold, *VP*
Brian Morin, *CMO*
EMP: 26 **EST:** 2008
SALES (est): 3.73MM **Privately Held**
Web: www.smartaction.ai
SIC: 7372 Prepackaged software

(P-16382)
SMART-TEK SERVICES INC (HQ)
11838 Bernardo Plaza Ct Ste 250 (92128-2434)
PHONE...............................858 798-1644
Kelly Mowrey, *COO*
Bryan Bonar, *Interim Chief Executive Officer*
EMP: 17 **EST:** 2009
SQ FT: 2,000
SALES (est): 343.27MM
SALES (corp-wide): 345.32MM **Privately Held**
Web: www.smart-tekservices.com
SIC: 7372 Business oriented computer software
PA: Trucept, Inc.
600 La Terraza Blvd
Escondido CA
866 798-1620

(P-16383)
SO CAL SOFT-PAK INCORPORATED
Also Called: Soft Pak
8525 Gibbs Dr Ste 300 (92123-1700)
PHONE...............................619 283-2338
Brian Porter, *CEO*
EMP: 31 **EST:** 1975
SQ FT: 5,000
SALES (est): 5.33MM
SALES (corp-wide): 8.51B **Publicly Held**
Web: www.soft-pak.com
SIC: 7372 8742 Business oriented computer software; Management consulting services
PA: Dover Corporation
3005 Highland Pkwy # 200
Downers Grove IL
630 541-1540

(P-16384)
SOLV ENERGY LLC
Also Called: Swinerton Builders
16798 W Bernardo Dr (92128-2850)
PHONE...............................858 622-4040
Danielle Hammersmith, *Mgr*
EMP: 446
Web: www.solvenergy.com
SIC: 7372 Prepackaged software
HQ: Solv Energy, Llc
16680 W Bernardo Dr
San Diego CA
858 251-4888

(P-16385)
SONIC VR LLC
Also Called: Sonic Vr
225 Broadway Ste 650 (92101-5039)
PHONE...............................206 227-8585
Jason Riggs, *CEO*
Joy Lyons, *Engr*
David Carr, *Engr*
Jose Arjol Acebal, *COO*
EMP: 17 **EST:** 2015
SQ FT: 6,000
SALES (est): 626.21K **Privately Held**
SIC: 7372 8731 Application computer software; Commercial physical research

(P-16386)
SPECIALISTS IN CSTM SFTWR INC
2574 Wellesley Ave (90064-2738)
PHONE...............................310 315-9660
Helen Russell, *Pr*

PRODUCTS & SVCS

Melissa Vance, *
EMP: 34 **EST:** 1979
SQ FT: 2,400
SALES (est): 3.47MM **Privately Held**
Web: www.scs-mbs.com
SIC: 7372 Prepackaged software

(P-16387)
SPRING TECHNOLOGIES CORP ✪

10170 Culver Blvd (90232-3152)
PHONE....................310 230-4000
Jonathan Finestone, *CEO*
EMP: 30 **EST:** 2022
SALES (est): 1.33MM **Privately Held**
SIC: 7372 Business oriented computer software

(P-16388)
SPRINGCOIN INC

4551 Glencoe Ave Ste 100 (90292-7902)
PHONE....................847 322-6349
Katie Fegen, *Prin*
EMP: 56
SALES (corp-wide): 704.39K **Privately Held**
Web: www.springlabs.com
SIC: 7372 Prepackaged software
PA: Springcoin, Inc.
20 W Kinzie St Ste 1700
Chicago IL
323 577-9322

(P-16389)
SRAX INC (PA)

1014 S Westlake Blvd # 14-299 (91361-3108)
PHONE....................323 205-6109
Christopher Miglino, *Ch Bd*
EMP: 54 **EST:** 2009
SALES (est): 26.71MM
SALES (corp-wide): 26.71MM **Publicly Held**
SIC: 7372 Prepackaged software

(P-16390)
STRATEGY COMPANION CORP

100 Pacifica Ste 220 (92618-7441)
PHONE....................714 460-8398
Robert Sterling, *Pr*
EMP: 70 **EST:** 2006
SALES (est): 10.99MM **Privately Held**
Web: www.strategycompanion.com
SIC: 7372 Prepackaged software
PA: Strategy Companion Corp.
Scotia Centre 4th Floor
George Town GR CAYMAN

(P-16391)
STREET SMART LLC

Also Called: Street Smart 247
100 N Pacific Coast Hwy (90245-4359)
PHONE....................866 924-4644
Cicero Lucas, *CEO*
EMP: 27 **EST:** 2019
SALES (est): 921.56K
SALES (corp-wide): 14.18MM **Privately Held**
Web: www.streetsmartrental.com
SIC: 7372 Prepackaged software
HQ: Fivepoint Payments Llc
204 Caughman Farm Ln # 201
Lexington SC
803 951-2094

(P-16392)
STROMASYS INC

871 Marlborough Ave (92507-2133)
PHONE....................919 239-8450
George Koukis, *Ch Bd*

John Prot, *
Chris Pavlou, *
Serge Pavoncello, *
EMP: 78 **EST:** 2008
SALES (est): 9.9MM
SALES (corp-wide): 600K **Privately Held**
Web: www.stromasys.com
SIC: 7372 5734 Operating systems computer software; Software, business and non-game
HQ: Stromasys Sa
Avenue Louis-Casai 84
Cointrin GE

(P-16393)
SUBJECT TECHNOLOGIES INC

345 N Maple Dr (90210-3869)
PHONE....................310 243-6484
Felix Ruano, *Prin*
EMP: 50 **EST:** 2020
SALES (est): 6.1MM **Privately Held**
Web: www.subject.com
SIC: 7372 Educational computer software

(P-16394)
SUGARSYNC INC

Also Called: Sharpcast
6922 Hollywood Blvd Ste 500 (90028-6117)
PHONE....................650 571-5105
Laura Yecies, *Pr*
Peter Chantel, *
EMP: 30 **EST:** 2004
SQ FT: 11,000
SALES (est): 8.45MM **Privately Held**
Web: www.sugarsync.com
SIC: 7372 Business oriented computer software

(P-16395)
SUNGARD TREASURY SYSTEMS INC

Also Called: Sungard
23975 Park Sorrento Ste 100 (91302-4010)
PHONE....................818 223-2300
EMP: 250
SIC: 7372 Prepackaged software

(P-16396)
SYMANTEC

Also Called: Symantec
1200 W 7th St (90017-2349)
PHONE....................213 489-3262
EMP: 67 **EST:** 2019
SALES (est): 1.53MM **Privately Held**
SIC: 7372 Prepackaged software

(P-16397)
SYSTEM1 INC (PA)

4235 Redwood Ave (90066-5605)
PHONE....................310 924-6037
Michael Blend, *Ch Bd*
Paul Filsinger, *Pr*
Tridivesh Kidambi, *CFO*
Brian Coppola, *Chief Product Officer*
EMP: 288 **EST:** 2020
SALES (est): 773.94MM
SALES (corp-wide): 773.94MM **Publicly Held**
Web: www.couponfollow.com
SIC: 7372 Business oriented computer software

(P-16398)
TDO SOFTWARE INC

6235 Lusk Blvd (92121-2731)
PHONE....................858 558-3696
Luiz Motta, *Genl Mgr*
EMP: 25 **EST:** 2004
SQ FT: 3,600
SALES (est): 6.62MM **Publicly Held**

Web: www.tdo4endo.com
SIC: 7372 Prepackaged software
PA: Sonendo, Inc.
26061 Merit Cir Ste 102
Laguna Hills CA

(P-16399)
TELESIGN HOLDINGS INC (DH)

13274 Fiji Way Ste 600 (90292-7119)
PHONE....................310 740-9700
Ryan Disraeli, *CEO*
Philipp Gast, *CFO*
Tom Powledge, *Chief Product Officer*
EMP: 30 **EST:** 2016
SALES (est): 36.59MM **Privately Held**
Web: www.telesign.com
SIC: 7372 Prepackaged software
HQ: Belgacom International Carrier Services
Boulevard Du Roi Albert Ii 27
Bruxelles

(P-16400)
TERADATA CORPORATION (PA)

Also Called: Teradata
17095 Via Del Campo (92127-1711)
PHONE....................866 548-8348
Stephen Mcmillan, *Pr*
Claire Bramley, *CFO*
Suzanne Zoumaras, *Chief Human Resources Officer*
Kathy Cullen-cote, *Chief Human Resource Officer*
EMP: 1081 **EST:** 1979
SALES (est): 1.79B **Publicly Held**
Web: www.teradata.com
SIC: 7372 3572 7371 3571 Prepackaged software; Computer storage devices; Software programming applications; Mainframe computers

(P-16401)
TESSITURA NETWORK INC

2295 Fletcher Pkwy Ste 101 (92020-2145)
PHONE....................888 643-5778
Jack B Rubin, *Pr*
Jack B Rubin, *CEO*
Andrew Recinos, *
Laura Bowden, *
Ivan Medanic, *OF*
EMP: 198 **EST:** 2002
SALES (est): 29.16MM **Privately Held**
Web: www.tessituranetwork.com
SIC: 7372 Prepackaged software

(P-16402)
TEXICAN INC

21031 Ventura Blvd Ste 1000 (91364-2227)
PHONE....................310 384-7000
Tony Reyna, *CEO*
EMP: 24 **EST:** 2013
SALES (est): 992.27K **Privately Held**
Web: www.texicaninc.com
SIC: 7372 Prepackaged software

(P-16403)
THQ INC

Also Called: Thq San Diego
21900 Burbank Blvd (91367-6469)
PHONE....................818 591-1310
EMP: 1088
Web: www.thqnordic.com
SIC: 7372 Prepackaged software

(P-16404)
THRIO INC

5230 Las Virgenes Rd Ste 210 (91302-3448)
PHONE....................858 299-7191
Edwin K Margulies, *CEO*

Rose M Sinicrope, *COO*
EMP: 25 **EST:** 2017
SALES (est): 2.16MM **Privately Held**
Web: www.thrio.com
SIC: 7372 Prepackaged software

(P-16405)
THURSBY SOFTWARE SYSTEMS LLC

1900 Carnegie Ave (92705-5520)
PHONE....................817 478-5070
William Thursby, *CEO*
EMP: 28 **EST:** 1986
SALES (est): 2.46MM **Publicly Held**
Web: shop.thursby.com
SIC: 7372 Prepackaged software
PA: Identiv, Inc.
2201 Walnut Ave Ste 100
Fremont CA

(P-16406)
TI LIMITED LLC (PA)

20335 Ventura Blvd Ste 231-239 (91364-2444)
PHONE....................323 877-5991
Alberto Gamez, *
EMP: 52 **EST:** 2016
SQ FT: 9,000
SALES (est): 9MM
SALES (corp-wide): 9MM **Privately Held**
SIC: 7372 8748 Business oriented computer software; Business consulting, nec

(P-16407)
TICKETSOCKET INC

6150 Lusk Blvd Ste 201 (92121-2739)
PHONE....................888 633-7105
EMP: 35
SALES (corp-wide): 502.14K **Privately Held**
Web: www.ticketsocket.com
SIC: 7372 Application computer software
PA: Ticketsocket, Inc.
3424 Via Oporto
Newport Beach CA
517 410-2760

(P-16408)
TIMEVALUE SOFTWARE

22 Mauchly (92618-2306)
P.O. Box 50250 (92619-0250)
PHONE....................949 727-1800
Michael Applegate, *Pr*
Charles Miller, *
EMP: 25 **EST:** 1983
SQ FT: 18,000
SALES (est): 4.77MM **Privately Held**
Web: www.timevalue.com
SIC: 7372 7371 Prepackaged software; Computer software development

(P-16409)
TOTAL CMMNICATOR SOLUTIONS INC

Also Called: Spark Compass
11150 Sta Monica Ste 600 (90025-3314)
PHONE....................619 277-1488
Brent Erik Bjojegard, *CEO*
EMP: 95 **EST:** 2012
SALES (est): 5MM **Privately Held**
Web: www.sparkcompass.com
SIC: 7372 Application computer software

(P-16410)
TRAFFIC MANAGEMENT PDTS INC

Also Called: Fivesixtwo Inc
4900 Airport Plaza Dr Ste 300 (90815)
PHONE....................800 763-3999

▲ = Import ▼ = Export
◆ = Import/Export

Jonathan E Spano, *CEO*
Ed Barrera, *
Christopher H Spano, *
EMP: 1340 **EST:** 2015
SALES (est): 1.19MM **Privately Held**
SIC: 7372 Prepackaged software
PA: Traffic Management, Inc.
    4900 Arprt Plz Dr Ste 300
    Long Beach CA

(P-16411)
TRAXERO NORTH AMERICA LLC
1730 E Holly Ave Ste 740 (90245-4404)
PHONE..............................423 497-1164
Mark Sedgley, *Managing Member*
EMP: 90 **EST:** 2020
SALES (est): 4.77MM **Privately Held**
SIC: 7372 Business oriented computer
    software

(P-16412)
UNBROKEN STUDIOS LLC
2120 Park Pl Ste 110 (90245-4741)
PHONE..............................310 741-2670
Paul Ohanian, *CEO*
Anthony Scott, *
EMP: 80 **EST:** 2018
SALES (est): 8.99MM
SALES (corp-wide): 13.85MM **Privately
Held**
Web: www.unbrokenstudios.com
SIC: 7372 Prepackaged software
PA: Pound Sand, Llc
    2120 Park Pl Ste 110
    El Segundo CA
    310 741-2670

(P-16413)
UNEEKOR INC
15770 Laguna Canyon Rd Ste 100
(92618-3187)
PHONE..............................949 328-7790
EMP: 21 **EST:** 2018
SALES (est): 1.28MM **Privately Held**
Web: www.uneekor.com
SIC: 7372 Prepackaged software

(P-16414)
UNLIMITED INNOVATIONS INC
Also Called: Cerecons
180 N Rverview Dr Ste 320 (92808)
PHONE..............................714 998-0866
FAX: 714 998-5641
EMP: 30
SQ FT: 5,000
SALES (est): 2.35MM
SALES (corp-wide): 12.81B **Privately Held**
Web: www.cerecons.com
SIC: 7372 Prepackaged software
HQ: Medecision, Inc.
    550 E Swedesford Rd # 220
    Wayne PA
    484 588-0102

(P-16415)
UPSTANDING LLC
Also Called: Mobilityware
440 Exchange Ste 100 (92602-1390)
PHONE..............................949 788-9900
John Libby, *
EMP: 180 **EST:** 1990
SQ FT: 48,000
SALES (est): 8.96MM **Privately Held**
Web: www.mobilityware.com
SIC: 7372 Business oriented computer
    software

(P-16416)
VIDEOAMP INC (PA)
2229 S Carmelina Ave (90064-1001)

PHONE..............................424 272-7774
Ross Mccray, *CEO*
EMP: 86 **EST:** 2014
SALES (est): 10.46MM
SALES (corp-wide): 10.46MM **Privately
Held**
Web: www.videoamp.com
SIC: 7372 Prepackaged software

(P-16417)
VISIONARY VR INC
409 N Plymouth Blvd (90004-3001)
PHONE..............................323 868-7443
Gil Baron, *Prin*
EMP: 24 **EST:** 2014
SALES (est): 261.37K **Privately Held**
Web: www.mindshow.com
SIC: 7372 Prepackaged software

(P-16418)
WEBMETRO
Also Called: Multivest
160 Via Verde Ste 1 (91773-3901)
PHONE..............................909 599-8885
EMP: 85
SIC: 7372 7311 Prepackaged software;
    Advertising agencies

(P-16419)
WEST COAST CONSULTING LLC
9233 Research Dr Ste 200 (92618-4294)
PHONE..............................949 250-4102
EMP: 125 **EST:** 1997
SALES (est): 9.17MM **Privately Held**
Web: www.westcoastllc.com
SIC: 7372 Prepackaged software

(P-16420)
WIND RIVER SYSTEMS INC
12770 High Bluff Dr Ste 300 (92130-3008)
PHONE..............................858 824-3100
Bryan Leblanc, *CEO*
EMP: 17
SALES (corp-wide): 17.49B **Privately Held**
Web: www.windriver.com
SIC: 7372 Prepackaged software
HQ: Wind River Systems, Inc.
    500 Wind River Way
    Alameda CA
    510 748-4100

(P-16421)
WM TECHNOLOGY INC
Also Called: Wm Technology
41 Discovery (92618-3150)
PHONE..............................844 933-3627
Christopher Beals, *CEO*
Scott Gordon, *
Juanjo Feijoo, *COO*
Arden Lee, *CFO*
Justin Dean, *CIO*
EMP: 434 **EST:** 2008
SALES (est): 215.53MM **Privately Held**
Web: www.weedmaps.com
SIC: 7372 Prepackaged software

(P-16422)
WME BI LLC
17075 Camino (92127)
PHONE..............................877 592-2472
EMP: 60 **EST:** 2012
SALES (est): 2.54MM **Privately Held**
SIC: 7372 Operating systems computer
    software

(P-16423)
WONDERWARE CORPORATION (DH)
26561 Rancho Pkwy S (92630-8301)

PHONE..............................949 727-3200
Rick Bullotta, *VP*
Brian Dibenedetto, *
Karen Hamilton, *
Peter Kent, *
Dave Pickett, *
EMP: 300 **EST:** 1993
SQ FT: 32,000
SALES (est): 40.76MM
SALES (corp-wide): 82.05K **Privately Held**
Web: www.aveva.com
SIC: 7372 Prepackaged software
HQ: Aveva Software, Llc
    26561 Rancho Pkwy S
    Lake Forest CA

(P-16424)
WORDSMART CORPORATION
10025 Mesa Rim Rd (92121-2913)
P.O. Box 366 (92038-0366)
EMP: 70 **EST:** 1990
SQ FT: 12,375
SALES (est): 2.12MM **Privately Held**
SIC: 7372 Educational computer software

(P-16425)
XPDEL INC
2625 Townsgate Rd Ste 330 (91361-5749)
PHONE..............................805 267-1214
Manish Kapoor, *CEO*
EMP: 51 **EST:** 2018
SALES (est): 7.61MM **Privately Held**
Web: www.xpdel.com
SIC: 7372 Prepackaged software

(P-16426)
YARDI KUBE INC
Also Called: Wun
430 S Fairview Ave (93117-3637)
PHONE..............................805 699-2040
EMP: 61 **EST:** 2018
SALES (est): 4.54MM **Privately Held**
Web: www.yardi.com
SIC: 7372 Prepackaged software

(P-16427)
ZWIFT INC (PA)
111 W Ocean Blvd Ste 1800 (90802-7936)
PHONE..............................855 469-9438
Eric Min, *CEO*
Kurt Beilder, *
EMP: 280 **EST:** 2014
SALES (est): 26.57MM
SALES (corp-wide): 26.57MM **Privately
Held**
Web: us.zwift.com
SIC: 7372 5961 Publisher's computer
    software; Fitness and sporting goods, mail
    order

7373 Computer Integrated Systems Design

(P-16428)
ALTERYX INC (PA)
Also Called: Alteryx
17200 Laguna Canyon Rd (92618-5403)
PHONE..............................888 836-4274
Mark Anderson, *CEO*
Dean A Stoecker, *
Robert S Jones, *Pr*
Kevin Rubin, *CFO*
Scott Davidson, *COO*
EMP: 25 **EST:** 1997
SQ FT: 180,000
SALES (est): 855.35MM
SALES (corp-wide): 855.35MM **Publicly
Held**
Web: www.alteryx.com

SIC: 7373 7372 Systems software
    development services; Prepackaged
    software

(P-16429)
AUTOMATION HOLDCO INC
10815 Rancho Bernardo Rd Ste 102
(92127)
PHONE..............................858 967-8650
Leo Castaneda, *Pr*
EMP: 80 **EST:** 2013
SALES (est): 4.55MM **Privately Held**
SIC: 7373 Systems integration services

(P-16430)
AVEVA SOFTWARE LLC (DH)
Also Called: Wonderware
26561 Rancho Pkwy S (92630-8301)
PHONE..............................949 727-3200
EMP: 350 **EST:** 2014
SALES (est): 220.34MM
SALES (corp-wide): 82.05K **Privately Held**
Web: www.aveva.com
SIC: 7373 Computer integrated systems
    design
HQ: Aveva Inc.
    11044 Res Blvd Ste A100
    Austin TX
    713 977-1225

(P-16431)
CACI ENTERPRISE SOLUTIONS LLC
1455 Frazee Rd Ste 700 (92108-4308)
PHONE..............................619 881-6000
J P London, *CEO*
EMP: 254
SALES (corp-wide): 6.7B **Publicly Held**
Web: www.caci.com
SIC: 7373 Computer integrated systems
    design
HQ: Caci Enterprise Solutions, Llc
    1100 N Glebe Rd Ste 200
    Arlington VA
    703 841-7800

(P-16432)
CAPTIVA SOFTWARE CORPORATION (DH)
10145 Pacific Heights Blvd (92121-4234)
PHONE..............................858 320-1000
Reynolds C Bish, *Pr*
Patrick L Edsell, *
Rick E Russo, *CFO*
Jim Nicol, *Executive Product Development
Vice President*
Howard Dratler, *OK Vice President*
EMP: 80 **EST:** 1986
SQ FT: 25,000
SALES (est): 25.91MM **Publicly Held**
SIC: 7373 7372 Office computer automation
    systems integration; Prepackaged software
HQ: Emc Corporation
    176 South St
    Hopkinton MA
    508 435-1000

(P-16433)
CLARITY DESIGN INC
16885 Via Del Campo Ct Ste 200
(92127-1707)
PHONE..............................858 746-3500
Thomas H Lupfer, *Pr*
Robert Melucci, *VP*
▲ **EMP:** 17 **EST:** 1991
SQ FT: 6,000
SALES (est): 4.98MM **Privately Held**
Web: www.claritydesign.com

PRODUCTS & SVCS

SIC: 7373 3672 Computer integrated systems design; Circuit boards, television and radio printed

(P-16434)
CLINICOMP INTERNATIONAL INC (PA)
9655 Towne Centre Dr (92121-1964)
PHONE.............................858 546-8202
Chris Haudenschild, *CEO*
Eloisa Haudenschild, *CFO*
William Mcdonald, *Contrlr*
Jiao Fan Ph.d., *VP*
Kelley Malott, *VP*
EMP: 99 **EST:** 1983
SQ FT: 42,000
SALES (est): 28.97MM
SALES (corp-wide): 28.97MM **Privately Held**
Web: www.clinicomp.com
SIC: 7373 7371 3571 Systems software development services; Custom computer programming services; Electronic computers

(P-16435)
COGNIZANT TRZTTO SFTWR GROUP I
3631 S Harbor Blvd Ste 200 (92704-6951)
PHONE.............................714 481-0396
Kathy Kantocello, *Contrlr*
EMP: 221
SIC: 7373 4813 Systems software development services; Internet connectivity services
HQ: Cognizant Trizetto Software Group, Inc.
9655 Maroon Cir
Englewood CO

(P-16436)
COMPUTER TECH RESOURCES INC
16 Technology Dr Ste 202 (92618-2329)
PHONE.............................714 665-6507
Alok Mundra, *Brnch Mgr*
EMP: 192
SALES (corp-wide): 95.63MM **Privately Held**
Web: www.astcorporation.com
SIC: 7373 Computer integrated systems design
HQ: Computer Technology Resources, Inc.
8333 Clairemont Mesa Blvd
San Diego CA
858 492-1400

(P-16437)
CORDOBA CORPORATION
1401 N Broadway (90012-1410)
PHONE.............................213 895-0224
George Pla, *Pr*
Maria Mehranian, *COO*
EMP: 93 **EST:** 1993
SALES (est): 1.4MM **Privately Held**
Web: www.cordobacorp.com
SIC: 7373 Computer integrated systems design

(P-16438)
CORE BTS INC
5250 Lankershim Blvd Ste 620 (91601-3112)
PHONE.............................818 766-2400
EMP: 106
Web: www.corebts.com
SIC: 7373 Systems integration services
HQ: Core Bts, Inc.
5875 Castle Creek Parkway
Indianapolis IN
317 566-6200

(P-16439)
CUBIC CORPORATION
Also Called: Cubic Defense Systems
9233 Balboa Ave (92123-1513)
PHONE.............................858 277-6780
Brigitte Jen, *Brnch Mgr*
EMP: 2000
SALES (corp-wide): 1.48B **Privately Held**
Web: www.cubic.com
SIC: 7373 Computer integrated systems design
HQ: Cubic Corporation
9233 Balboa Ave
San Diego CA
858 277-6780

(P-16440)
DISCO PRINT WHL 46 A LTD LBLTY
Also Called: Wholesale 46
1891 Alton Pkwy Ste A (92606-4985)
P.O. Box 19337 (92623-9337)
PHONE.............................949 261-8457
Elias G Khamis, *Pt*
Isa G Khamis, *Pt*
Ibrahim G Khamis, *Pt*
Juliette Khamis, *Pt*
Violette Khamis, *Pt*
EMP: 20 **EST:** 1972
SQ FT: 70,500
SALES (est): 760.19K **Privately Held**
SIC: 7373 5734 5712 5943 Systems software development services; Computer and software stores; Office furniture; Office forms and supplies

(P-16441)
ELECTRONIC ONLINE SYSTEMS INTERNATIONAL
Also Called: E O S International
2292 Faraday Ave Frnt (92008-7237)
PHONE.............................760 431-8400
EMP: 64 **EST:** 1981
SALES (est): 4.99MM **Privately Held**
SIC: 7373 7371 7372 Turnkey vendors, computer systems; Computer software development; Prepackaged software

(P-16442)
FILENET CORPORATION
3565 Harbor Blvd (92626-1405)
PHONE.............................800 345-3638
EMP: 1695
SIC: 7373 7372 Computer integrated systems design; Business oriented computer software

(P-16443)
GBL SYSTEMS CORPORATION
760 Paseo Camarillo Ste 401 (93010-6002)
PHONE.............................805 987-4345
James Buscemi, *Pr*
EMP: 35 **EST:** 1990
SQ FT: 8,228
SALES (est): 7.46MM **Privately Held**
Web: www.gblsys.com
SIC: 7373 3559 Computer integrated systems design; Electronic component making machinery

(P-16444)
GEMALTO COGENT INC (HQ)
2964 Bradley St (91107-1560)
PHONE.............................626 325-9600
Alan Pelligrini, *Pr*
Antonio Lo Brutto, *
Daniel Asraf, *
Ramsey Billups, *
Alex Woods, *

▲ **EMP:** 95 **EST:** 2004
SQ FT: 151,000
SALES (est): 47.81MM
SALES (corp-wide): 277.29MM **Privately Held**
SIC: 7373 Computer-aided system services
PA: Thales
4 Rue De La Verrerie
Meudon

(P-16445)
GENEA ENERGY PARTNERS INC
19100 Von Karman Ave Ste 550 (92612-6571)
PHONE.............................714 694-0536
Michal Pasula, *Admn*
Jon Haahr, *
Keith Voysey, *
David Balkin, *
EMP: 120 **EST:** 2006
SQ FT: 10,000
SALES (est): 10.4MM **Privately Held**
Web: www.getgenea.com
SIC: 7373 Systems software development services

(P-16446)
GREENWAVE REALITY INC
Also Called: Greenwave Systems
15420 Laguna Canyon Rd Ste 150 (92618-2119)
PHONE.............................714 805-9283
Martin Manniche, *CEO*
Peter Wilmar Christensen, *CFO*
Nate Williams, *Ex Dir*
Sharon Wang, *Ex VP*
Troy Pliska, *Sr VP*
▲ **EMP:** 20 **EST:** 2008
SALES (est): 4.66MM **Privately Held**
Web: www.greenwavesystems.com
SIC: 7373 7372 Systems software development services; Prepackaged software

(P-16447)
I3DNET LLC
7 N Fair Oaks Ave (91103-3608)
PHONE.............................800 482-6910
Yves Guillemot, *Managing Member*
EMP: 731 **EST:** 2011
SALES (est): 1.02MM
SALES (corp-wide): 2.22B **Privately Held**
Web: www.i3d.net
SIC: 7373 Local area network (LAN) systems integrator
HQ: Ubisoft, Inc.
625 3rd St
San Francisco CA
415 547-4000

(P-16448)
ICL SYSTEMS INC
19782 Macarthur Blvd Ste 260 (92612-2486)
PHONE.............................877 425-8725
Thomas Swennes, *Prin*
Thomas Swennes, *VP*
Brian Hook, *
Pat Donahoe, *
EMP: 98 **EST:** 2000
SALES (est): 9.39MM **Privately Held**
Web: www.iclsystems.com
SIC: 7373 Systems integration services

(P-16449)
INFORMATION MGT RESOURCES INC (PA)
Also Called: Imri
85 Argonaut Ste 215 (92656-4105)
PHONE.............................949 215-8889

Martha Daniel, *CEO*
EMP: 132 **EST:** 1986
SQ FT: 5,000
SALES (est): 16.61MM **Privately Held**
Web: www.imri.com
SIC: 7373 8742 7371 Computer integrated systems design; Management consulting services; Computer software systems analysis and design, custom

(P-16450)
INTERNET CORP FOR ASSGNED NMES (PA)
Also Called: Icann
12025 Waterfront Dr Ste 300 (90094-2536)
PHONE.............................310 823-9358
Cherine Chalaby, *Ch*
Chris Disspain, *Vice Chairman**
EMP: 146 **EST:** 1998
SALES (est): 84.27MM
SALES (corp-wide): 84.27MM **Privately Held**
Web: www.icann.org
SIC: 7373 Systems software development services

(P-16451)
INTERNTNAL COMMUNICATIONS CORP
Also Called: ICC Networking
11801 Pierce St Fl 2 (92505-4400)
PHONE.............................951 934-0531
▲ **EMP:** 25 **EST:** 2011
SALES (est): 2.46MM **Privately Held**
Web: www.iccnetworking.com
SIC: 7373 4812 7389 3663 Local area network (LAN) systems integrator; Radiotelephone communication; Mobile communication equipment

(P-16452)
KOAM ENGINEERING SYSTEMS INC
Also Called: K E S
7807 Convoy Ct Ste 200 (92111-1213)
PHONE.............................858 292-0922
John S Yi, *Pr*
Richard Comber, *
Erica Tofson, *
John Schiltz, *
Jim Meadows, *
EMP: 105 **EST:** 1994
SQ FT: 5,700
SALES (est): 22.05MM **Privately Held**
Web: www.kes.com
SIC: 7373 Computer integrated systems design

(P-16453)
LEADINGWAY CORPORATION (PA)
Also Called: Leadingway Knowledge Systems
4199 Campus Dr Ste 550 (92612-4694)
PHONE.............................949 509-6589
James Li, *Pr*
Wei-wei Fang, *CFO*
EMP: 18 **EST:** 1991
SQ FT: 6,600
SALES (est): 1.45MM **Privately Held**
SIC: 7373 7379 8742 7375 Systems software development services; Computer related consulting services; Management consulting services; Information retrieval services

(P-16454)
LIFERAY INC (PA)
Also Called: Liferay
1400 Montefino Ave Ste 100 (91765-5501)

PHONE..............877 543-3729
Brian Chan, *CEO*
Bryan Cheung, *CMO**
Jc Choi, *CFO*
Caris Chan, *CAO*
Michael Han, *Dir*
EMP: 1207 **EST:** 2006
SALES (est): 120K
SALES (corp-wide): 120K **Privately Held**
Web: www.liferay.com
SIC: 7373 Systems software development services

(P-16455)
LOCKHEED MARTIN UNMANNED
125 Venture Dr Ste 110 (93401-9103)
PHONE..............805 503-4340
Jesse May, *CEO*
EMP: 80
Web: www.gyrocamsystems.com
SIC: 7373 Computer systems analysis and design
HQ: Lockheed Martin Unmanned Integrated Systems, Inc.
133 W Park Loop Nw
Huntsville AL

(P-16456)
LUXURY PRESENCE INC
2805 W 233rd St (90505-3113)
PHONE..............310 955-1077
Malte Kramer, *Managing Member*
EMP: 156 **EST:** 2015
SALES (est): 3.66MM **Privately Held**
Web: www.luxurypresence.com
SIC: 7373 7371 Computer integrated systems design; Computer software systems analysis and design, custom

(P-16457)
MESFIN ENTERPRISES
Also Called: Transnational Computer Tech
222 N Pacific Coast Hwy Ste 1570 (90245)
PHONE..............310 615-0881
Wond Wossen Mesfin, *Pr*
EMP: 376 **EST:** 1978
SQ FT: 11,250
SALES (est): 35.33MM **Privately Held**
SIC: 7373 7376 5734 Systems integration services; Computer facilities management; Software, business and non-game

(P-16458)
MIRO TECHNOLOGIES INC
5643 Copley Dr (92111-7903)
P.O. Box 3707 (98124-2207)
PHONE..............858 677-2100
EMP: 150
SIC: 7373 Turnkey vendors, computer systems

(P-16459)
MIVA INC
Also Called: Miva Merchant
16870 W Bernardo Dr Ste 100 (92127-1604)
PHONE..............858 490-2570
Rick Wilson, *CEO*
Nathan Osborne, *
David Hubbard, *
EMP: 120 **EST:** 2007
SALES (est): 17.84MM **Privately Held**
Web: www.miva.com
SIC: 7373 5961 Systems software development services; Catalog and mail-order houses

(P-16460)
MOBISYSTEMS INC
4501 Mission Bay Dr Ste 3a (92109)

PHONE..............858 350-0315
Stanislav Minchev, *CEO*
Stoyan Gogov, *
EMP: 150 **EST:** 2001
SQ FT: 1,200
SALES (est): 11.33MM **Privately Held**
Web: www.mobisystems.com
SIC: 7373 Systems software development services

(P-16461)
MORPHOTRAK LLC (DH)
Also Called: Safran
5515 E La Palma Ave Ste 100 (92807-2127)
PHONE..............714 238-2000
Celeste Thomasson, *Managing Member*
Clark Nelson, *VP*
Katie Murphy, *Sec*
Florian Hebras, *CFO*
EMP: 175 **EST:** 1985
SQ FT: 32,000
SALES (est): 58.76MM
SALES (corp-wide): 2.44B **Privately Held**
Web: www.morphotrak.com
SIC: 7373 Computer integrated systems design
HQ: Idemia Identity & Security France
2 Place Samuel De Champlain
Courbevoie

(P-16462)
NETAPP INC
6320 Canoga Ave Ste 1500 (91367-2517)
PHONE..............818 227-5025
James Mccormick Iii, *Mgr*
EMP: 209
Web: www.netapp.com
SIC: 7373 Computer integrated systems design
PA: Netapp, Inc.
3060 Olsen Dr
San Jose CA

(P-16463)
NETWORK INTGRTION PARTNERS INC
Also Called: Nic Partners
11981 Jack Benny Dr Ste 103 (91739-9232)
PHONE..............909 919-2800
Franklin P Spaeth, *Pr*
EMP: 80 **EST:** 2007
SQ FT: 6,000
SALES (est): 21.82MM **Privately Held**
Web: nic.clients.zebrakick.com
SIC: 7373 Local area network (LAN) systems integrator

(P-16464)
OBERMAN TIVOLI & PICKERT INC
Also Called: Media Services
500 S Sepulveda Blvd Ste 500 (90049-3551)
PHONE..............310 440-9600
Robert Oberman, *Pr*
Barry Oberman, *
Alan Tivoli, *VP*
Sanaa Wadsworth, *
EMP: 230 **EST:** 1989
SALES (est): 23.63MM **Privately Held**
Web: www.mediaservices.com
SIC: 7373 8721 8741 Systems software development services; Payroll accounting service; Business management

(P-16465)
QUEST SOFTWARE INC (PA)
20 Enterprise Ste 100 (92656-7104)
PHONE..............949 754-8000
Patrick Nichols, *CEO*
Carolyn Mccarthy, *CFO*
EMP: 600 **EST:** 1987
SQ FT: 170,000
SALES (est): 647.68MM
SALES (corp-wide): 647.68MM **Privately Held**
Web: www.quest.com
SIC: 7373 7379 7372 Computer integrated systems design; Computer related consulting services; Business oriented computer software

(P-16466)
QUOTIT CORPORATION
721 S Parker St Ste 330 (92868-4739)
PHONE..............714 564-5000
Chad Hogan, *Sr VP*
EMP: 96 **EST:** 1999
SQ FT: 2,400
SALES (est): 4.77MM **Publicly Held**
Web: www.quotit.com
SIC: 7373 Systems software development services
HQ: National General Holdings Corp.
59 Maiden Ln Fl 38
New York NY

(P-16467)
RESULT GROUP INC
2603 Main St Ste 710 (92614-4263)
PHONE..............480 777-7130
William Derick Robson, *Pr*
David Griffiths, *
EMP: 83 **EST:** 2003
SALES (est): 389.73K
SALES (corp-wide): 6.62B **Privately Held**
SIC: 7373 7372 Systems software development services; Business oriented computer software
HQ: Wynne Systems, Inc.
2601 Main St Ste 270
Irvine CA

(P-16468)
SCIENCE APPLICATIONS INTL CORP
Also Called: Saic
4015 Hancock St (92110-5121)
PHONE..............858 826-3061
Gordon Saakamodo, *Mgr*
EMP: 600
SALES (corp-wide): 7.7B **Publicly Held**
Web: www.saic.com
SIC: 7373 Systems engineering, computer related
PA: Science Applications International Corporation
12010 Sunset Hills Rd
Reston VA
703 676-4300

(P-16469)
SECOM INTERNATIONAL (PA)
Also Called: Secom
15905 S Broadway (90248-2405)
PHONE..............310 641-1290
Ted Burton, *Pr*
Terry Bixler, *
Linda Vose, *
EMP: 52 **EST:** 1978
SALES (est): 8.27MM
SALES (corp-wide): 8.27MM **Privately Held**
Web: www.spdprk.com

SIC: 7373 3446 3559 7371 Turnkey vendors, computer systems; Architectural metalwork; Parking facility equipment and supplies; Computer software systems analysis and design, custom

(P-16470)
SOLUGENIX CORPORATION (PA)
Also Called: Solugenix
601 Valencia Ave Ste 260 (92823-6357)
PHONE..............866 749-7658
Shashi Jasthi, *CEO*
Damola Akinola, *
EMP: 138 **EST:** 2004
SQ FT: 1,600
SALES (est): 35.59MM
SALES (corp-wide): 35.59MM **Privately Held**
Web: www.solugenix.com
SIC: 7373 Computer integrated systems design

(P-16471)
SOURCE IT USA INC
1150 S Olive St (90015-2211)
PHONE..............714 318-4428
Peter Deralals, *CEO*
Peter Deralals, *Pr*
Fatana Deralals, *VP*
EMP: 22 **EST:** 2005
SALES (est): 1.8MM **Privately Held**
Web: www.sourceitusa.com
SIC: 7373 3577 Value-added resellers, computer systems; Computer peripheral equipment, nec

(P-16472)
SURVIOS INC
4501 Glencoe Ave (90292-6372)
PHONE..............310 736-1503
Nathan Burba, *CEO*
EMP: 24 **EST:** 2013
SALES (est): 2.53MM **Privately Held**
Web: www.survios.com
SIC: 7373 7372 Computer integrated systems design; Prepackaged software

(P-16473)
TRACE3 LLC (HQ)
Also Called: Trace3
7505 Irvine Center Dr Ste 100 (92618-3078)
PHONE..............949 333-2300
Rich Fennessy, *CEO*
Tyler Beecher, *
Kevin Manzo, *
EMP: 113 **EST:** 2001
SALES (est): 583.64MM
SALES (corp-wide): 583.64MM **Privately Held**
Web: www.trace3.com
SIC: 7373 Computer systems analysis and design
PA: Escape Velocity Holdings, Inc.
7505 Irvine Center Dr # 10
Irvine CA
949 333-2381

(P-16474)
TRANSCENTRA INC
20500 Belshaw Ave (90746-3506)
PHONE..............310 603-0105
Dwayne Moore, *Brnch Mgr*
EMP: 440
SALES (corp-wide): 1.08B **Publicly Held**
Web: www.exelatech.com
SIC: 7373 Systems software development services
HQ: Transcentra, Inc.
4145 Shackleford Rd # 330

Norcross GA
678 728-2500

(P-16475)
TUSIMPLE HOLDINGS INC (PA)
Also Called: Tusimple
9191 Towne Centre Dr Ste 600 (92122)
PHONE......................619 916-3144
Cheng Lu, *CEO*
Eric Tapia, *CAO*
Susan Marsch, *Interim General Counsel*
EMP: 486 **EST:** 2015
SQ FT: 80,000
SALES (est): 9.37MM
SALES (corp-wide): 9.37MM **Publicly Held**
Web: www.tusimple.com
SIC: 7373 Computer integrated systems design

(P-16476)
ULTISAT INC
Also Called: A Speedcast Co
11839 Sorrento Valley Rd (92121-1040)
PHONE......................240 243-5107
EMP: 1238
SALES (corp-wide): 423MM **Privately Held**
Web: www.ultisat.com
SIC: 7373 Systems integration services
PA: Ultisat, Inc.
14399 Penrose Pl Ste 410
Chantilly VA
240 243-5100

(P-16477)
URBAN INSIGHT INC
3530 Wilshire Blvd Ste 1285 (90010-2328)
PHONE......................213 792-2000
Chris Steins, *CEO*
Abhijeet Chavan, *COO*
EMP: 35 **EST:** 1997
SQ FT: 4,000
SALES (est): 3.99MM **Privately Held**
Web: www.urbaninsight.com
SIC: 7373 7372 7371 8748 Computer integrated systems design; Business oriented computer software; Custom computer programming services; Systems engineering consultant, ex. computer or professional

(P-16478)
WEST PUBLISHING CORPORATION
Also Called: Elite
800 Corporate Pointe Ste 150 (90230)
P.O. Box 51606 (90051-5906)
PHONE......................424 243-2100
Salim Sunderji, *VP*
EMP: 604
SALES (corp-wide): 10.66B **Publicly Held**
Web: home.westacademic.com
SIC: 7373 7371 Computer integrated systems design; Custom computer programming services
HQ: West Publishing Corporation
610 Opperman Dr
Eagan MN
651 687-7000

(P-16479)
YANG-MING INTERNATIONAL CORP
Also Called: Rackmountpro.com
595 Yorbita Rd (91744-5956)
PHONE......................626 956-0100
Betty B Shou, *Pr*
Stephen Shou, *
◆ **EMP:** 25 **EST:** 1994

SQ FT: 10,000
SALES (est): 10.83MM **Privately Held**
Web: www.rackmountpro.com
SIC: 7373 3571 Systems integration services ; Electronic computers

(P-16480)
ZMICRO INC (PA)
Also Called: Z Microsystems
9820 Summers Ridge Rd (92121-3083)
PHONE......................858 831-7000
Jack Wade, *CEO*
John Howell, *COO*
Jason Wade, *Pr*
Rick Elliott, *VP*
Angi Smart, *Contrlr*
EMP: 57 **EST:** 1986
SQ FT: 36,800
SALES (est): 22.14MM
SALES (corp-wide): 22.14MM **Privately Held**
Web: www.zmicro.com
SIC: 7373 3577 3572 Computer integrated systems design; Computer peripheral equipment, nec; Computer storage devices

---

7374 Data Processing And Preparation

(P-16481)
AMAZON PROCESSING LLC
Also Called: Appstar Financial
4619 Viewridge Ave Ste C (92123-5611)
PHONE......................858 565-1135
EMP: 195 **EST:** 2002
SALES (est): 12.08MM **Privately Held**
Web: www.appstar.net
SIC: 7374 Data processing service

(P-16482)
AUTOMATIC DATA PROCESSING INC
Also Called: ADP
3972 Barranca Pkwy Ste J610 (92606-1204)
PHONE......................949 751-0360
EMP: 165
SALES (corp-wide): 18.01B **Publicly Held**
Web: www.adp.com
SIC: 7374 Data processing service
PA: Automatic Data Processing, Inc.
1 Adp Blvd Ste 1 # 1
Roseland NJ
973 974-5000

(P-16483)
AUTOMATIC DATA PROCESSING INC
Also Called: ADP
400 W Covina Blvd (91773-2954)
PHONE......................800 225-5237
Rodney Hroblak, *Prin*
EMP: 117
SALES (corp-wide): 18.01B **Publicly Held**
Web: www.adp.com
SIC: 7374 8721 Data processing service; Accounting, auditing, and bookkeeping
PA: Automatic Data Processing, Inc.
1 Adp Blvd Ste 1 # 1
Roseland NJ
973 974-5000

(P-16484)
BLACK KNIGHT INFOSERV LLC
2500 Redhill Ave Ste 100 (92705-5518)
PHONE......................904 854-5100
Miriam Moore, *Brnch Mgr*
EMP: 171

SALES (corp-wide): 7.29B **Publicly Held**
Web: www.blackknightinc.com
SIC: 7374 Data processing and preparation
HQ: Black Knight Infoserv, Llc
601 Riverside Ave
Jacksonville FL

(P-16485)
CCH INCORPORATED
2050 W 190th St (90504-6228)
PHONE......................310 800-9800
EMP: 1221
SQ FT: 280,000
SALES (corp-wide): 5.4B **Privately Held**
Web: www.wolterskluwer.com
SIC: 7374 7372 7371 Data processing and preparation; Prepackaged software; Custom computer programming services
HQ: Cch Incorporated
2700 Lake Cook Rd
Riverwoods IL
847 267-7000

(P-16486)
CELESTIAL-SATURN PARENT INC (PA)
40 Pacifica (92618-7471)
PHONE......................949 214-1000
EMP: 139 **EST:** 2021
SALES (est): 1.64B
SALES (corp-wide): 1.64B **Privately Held**
Web: www.corelogic.com
SIC: 7374 Data processing and preparation

(P-16487)
COFA MEDIA GROUP LLC
5650 El Camino Real Ste 100a (92008)
PHONE......................877 293-2007
EMP: 87 **EST:** 2009
SALES (est): 2.35MM
SALES (corp-wide): 44.98MM **Privately Held**
Web: www.cofamedia.com
SIC: 7374 Computer graphics service
PA: Geary Lsf Group, Inc.
332 Pine St Fl 6
San Francisco CA
877 616-8226

(P-16488)
COMPUSHARE INC
3 Hutton Centre Dr Ste 700 (92707)
PHONE......................714 427-1000
EMP: 141
Web: www.compushare.com
SIC: 7374 Data processing and preparation

(P-16489)
CYBER-PRO SYSTEMS INC
Also Called: Medical Data Exchange
2121 S Towne Centre Pl Ste 200 (92806)
PHONE......................562 256-3800
Gerry Ibanez, *CEO*
Scott H Kramer, *
EMP: 162 **EST:** 1985
SALES (est): 8.88MM
SALES (corp-wide): 2.71B **Publicly Held**
Web: www.mdxnet.com
SIC: 7374 Data processing service
PA: Agilon Health, Inc.
6210 E Hwy 290 Ste 450
Austin TX
562 256-3800

(P-16490)
DESIGN PEOPLE INC
1700 E Walnut Ave Ste 400 (90245-2609)
PHONE......................800 969-5799
Jon Krabbe, *Pr*
Tiger Bitanga, *

Jon Krabbe, *CFO*
Luigi Amante, *
EMP: 160 **EST:** 1998
SQ FT: 9,200
SALES (est): 9.69MM **Privately Held**
Web: www.thedesignpeople.com
SIC: 7374 Computer graphics service

(P-16491)
ELEVATED RESOURCES INC (PA)
3990 Westerly Pl Ste 270 (92660-2348)
PHONE......................949 419-6632
EMP: 225 **EST:** 2007
SQ FT: 1,900
SALES (est): 18.22MM **Privately Held**
Web: www.elevatedresources.com
SIC: 7374 Data processing and preparation

(P-16492)
EMERALD CONNECT LLC (HQ)
15050 Avenue Of Science Ste 200 (92128-3419)
PHONE......................800 233-2834
Adam D Amsterdam, *Managing Member*
Sharon Greener, *
Heather Hinkle, *
Heidi Saucier, *OF DIGITAL STRAT*
EMP: 100 **EST:** 1986
SQ FT: 35,000
SALES (est): 17.26MM **Publicly Held**
Web: www.broadridge.com
SIC: 7374 7331 Data processing service; Mailing service
PA: Broadridge Financial Solutions, Inc.
5 Dakota Dr Ste 300
New Hyde Park NY

(P-16493)
ENCLARITY INC
16815 Von Karman Ave Ste 125 (92606-2404)
PHONE......................949 797-7160
Sean Downs, *CEO*
Thomas Suk, *
Warren Gouk Andrea, *
Paul Perleberg, *
Scott Marber, *
EMP: 363 **EST:** 2005
SQ FT: 3,500
SALES (est): 5.39MM
SALES (corp-wide): 10.3B **Privately Held**
Web: risk.lexisnexis.com
SIC: 7374 Data processing service
HQ: Lexisnexis Risk Solutions Inc.
1000 Alderman Dr
Alpharetta GA
678 694-6000

(P-16494)
ENERVEE CORPORATION
11845 W Olympic Blvd Ste 1100w (90064-1149)
PHONE......................844 363-7833
Matthias Kurwig, *CEO*
Donald Epperson, *
EMP: 102 **EST:** 2009
SALES (est): 11.28MM **Privately Held**
Web: www.enervee.com
SIC: 7374 Computer processing services

(P-16495)
EPOCHCOM LLC
Also Called: Epoch.com
3110 Main St Ste 220 (90405-5353)
PHONE......................310 664-5700
Joel Hall, *Managing Member*
Esther Martinez, *
EMP: 150 **EST:** 2004
SQ FT: 22,000

SALES (est): 14.69MM **Privately Held**
Web: www.epoch.com
SIC: 7374 Data processing service

(P-16496)
EXECUPRINT INC
24963 Avenue Tibbitts (91355-3427)
PHONE..................................818 993-8184
Amin Farag, *Pr*
Esther Farag, *Prin*
Bassem Farag, *Prin*
Michael Farag, *Prin*
EMP: 18 EST: 1975
SQ FT: 6,000
SALES (est): 2.48MM **Privately Held**
Web: www.execuprint.com
SIC: 7374 2752 2759 Computer graphics service; Offset printing; Commercial printing, nec

(P-16497)
GOODRX HOLDINGS INC (PA)
Also Called: Goodrx
2701 Olympic Blvd (90404-4183)
PHONE..................................855 268-2822
Scott Wagner, *Interim Chief Executive Officer*
Trevor Bezdek, *
Douglas Hirsch, *CMO*
Karsten Voermann, *CFO*
Raj Beri, *COO*
EMP: 300 EST: 2011
SQ FT: 132,000
SALES (est): 766.55MM
SALES (corp-wide): 766.55MM **Publicly Held**
Web: www.goodrx.com
SIC: 7374 Computer processing services

(P-16498)
GREENSOFT TECHNOLOGY INC
155 S El Molino Ave Ste 100 (91101-2563)
PHONE..................................323 254-5961
Larry Yen, *Pr*
Jon Wu, *
EMP: 121 EST: 2002
SALES (est): 5.94MM **Privately Held**
Web: www.greensofttech.com
SIC: 7374 Data processing service

(P-16499)
HONK TECHNOLOGIES INC
2251 Barry Ave (90064-1401)
P.O. Box 910 (90078-0910)
PHONE..................................800 979-3162
Corey Brundage, *CEO*
Dan Rosenthal, *
EMP: 151 EST: 2014
SQ FT: 8,000
SALES (est): 75MM **Privately Held**
Web: www.honkforhelp.com
SIC: 7374 7372 7372 Data processing and preparation; Business oriented computer software; Custom computer programming services

(P-16500)
IKANO COMMUNICATIONS INC (PA)
Also Called: A & S Technologies
9221 Corbin Ave Ste 260 (91324-1625)
PHONE..................................801 924-0900
EMP: 91 EST: 1991
SQ FT: 50,000
SALES (est): 17.46MM **Privately Held**
Web: www.ikano.com
SIC: 7374 Data processing and preparation

(P-16501)
LEAF GROUP LTD (HQ)
Also Called: Leaf Group
1655 26th St (90404-4016)
PHONE..................................310 394-6400
EMP: 133 EST: 2006
SALES (est): 62.96MM
SALES (corp-wide): 3.92B **Publicly Held**
Web: www.leafgroup.com
SIC: 7374 Data processing and preparation
PA: Graham Holdings Company
1300 17th St N Fl 17
Arlington VA
703 345-6362

(P-16502)
LEGALZOOMCOM INC (PA)
Also Called: LEGALZOOM
101 N Brand Blvd Fl 11 (91203-2638)
PHONE..................................323 962-8600
EMP: 300 EST: 2000
SQ FT: 56,000
SALES (est): 619.98MM **Publicly Held**
Web: www.legalzoom.com
SIC: 7374 8111 Data processing and preparation; Legal services

(P-16503)
MANAGEMENT APPLIED PRGRM INC (PA)
Also Called: Benefit Programs ADM
13191 Crossroads Pkwy N Ste 205 (91746)
PHONE..................................562 463-5000
Phiroze Dalal, *CEO*
Hormazd Dalal, *
EMP: 95 EST: 1964
SALES (est): 9.95MM
SALES (corp-wide): 9.95MM **Privately Held**
Web: www.mapinc.com
SIC: 7374 Data processing service

(P-16504)
MERCURY DEFENSE SYSTEMS INC
Also Called: Mercury Systems
10855 Business Center Dr Ste A (90630)
PHONE..................................714 898-8200
EMP: 85
Web: www.mrcy.com
SIC: 7374 Data processing service

(P-16505)
MERCURY SYSTEMS INC
10855 Business Center Dr Ste A (90630)
PHONE..................................714 898-8200
EMP: 85
SALES (corp-wide): 973.88MM **Publicly Held**
Web: www.mrcy.com
SIC: 7374 Data processing service
PA: Mercury Systems, Inc.
50 Minuteman Rd
Andover MA
978 256-1300

(P-16506)
MINDBODY INC (PA)
Also Called: Mindbody
651 Tank Farm Rd (93401-7062)
PHONE..................................877 755-4279
Richard Stollmeyer, *Ch Bd*
Josh Mccarter, *Pr*
Michael Mansbach, *
Brett White, *
Kimberly Lytikainen, *CLO*
EMP: 109 EST: 2001
SALES (est): 456.62MM **Privately Held**
Web: www.mindbodyonline.com

SIC: 7374 7372 8741 Data processing and preparation; Business oriented computer software; Business management

(P-16507)
MOCEAN LLC
Also Called: Mocean
2440 S Sepulveda Blvd Ste 150 (90064-1786)
PHONE..................................310 481-0808
Craig R Murray, *Managing Member*
Michael Mcintyre, *Pr*
EMP: 200 EST: 2000
SALES (est): 24.18MM **Privately Held**
Web: www.moceanla.com
SIC: 7374 7822 Computer graphics service; Motion picture distribution

(P-16508)
NEAR INTELLIGENCE INC
100 W Walnut St Ste A-4 (91124-0001)
PHONE..................................628 889-7680
John Faieta, *CFO*
Anil Mathews, *Ch Bd*
Shobhit Shukla, *Pr*
Rahul Agarwal, *CFO*
Gladys Kong, *COO*
EMP: 261 EST: 2012
SQ FT: 26,752
SALES (est): 12.49MM **Privately Held**
SIC: 7374 Data processing and preparation

(P-16509)
ORDERMARK INC
12045 Waterfront Dr Ste 400 # 3 (90094-3226)
P.O. Box 260206 (91426-0206)
PHONE..................................833 673-3762
Alex Canter, *CEO*
Mike Jacobs, *COO*
Paul Allen, *Ofcr*
EMP: 105 EST: 2017
SALES (est): 5.64MM **Privately Held**
Web: www.ordermark.com
SIC: 7374 Data processing and preparation

(P-16510)
PAYMENT CLOUD LLC
Also Called: Paymentcloud
16501 Ventura Blvd Ste 300 (91436-2007)
PHONE..................................800 988-2215
Shawn Silver, *CEO*
Shawn Silver, *CEO*
EMP: 81 EST: 2017
SALES (est): 4.61MM **Privately Held**
Web: www.paymentcloudinc.com
SIC: 7374 Data processing and preparation

(P-16511)
ROCKSTAR SAN DIEGO INC
2200 Faraday Ave Ste 200 (92008-7233)
PHONE..................................760 929-0700
Allan Wasserman, *Pr*
EMP: 70 EST: 1984
SQ FT: 24,000
SALES (est): 9.43MM **Publicly Held**
SIC: 7374 7372 Computer graphics service; Prepackaged software
PA: Take-Two Interactive Software, Inc.
110 W 44th St
New York NY

(P-16512)
RUITENG INTERNET TECHNOLOGY CO
1344 W Foothill Blvd D (91702-2846)
PHONE..................................302 597-7438
Canzhi Zhen, *Prin*
Chris Zhang, *
Wendy Huang, *

◆ EMP: 220 EST: 2018
SQ FT: 500
SALES (est): 3.53MM **Privately Held**
SIC: 7374 Computer graphics service

(P-16513)
S E O P INC
1621 Alton Pkwy Ste 150 (92606-4875)
PHONE..................................949 682-7906
Gary Hagins, *CEO*
Rhonda Spears, *
EMP: 150 EST: 2001
SALES (est): 13.88MM **Privately Held**
Web: www.seop.com
SIC: 7374 Computer graphics service

(P-16514)
SAN DIEGO DATA PROCESSING CORPORATION INC
202 C St 3rd Fl (92101-4806)
PHONE..................................858 581-9600
EMP: 11130
Web: www.sddpc.org
SIC: 7374 Data processing service

(P-16515)
SECURE ONE DATA SOLUTIONS LLC
11090 Artesia Blvd Ste D (90703-2545)
PHONE..................................562 924-7056
David Sandobal, *Pr*
EMP: 90
Web: www.secure1outsource.com
SIC: 7374 Keypunch service
PA: Secure One Data Solutions, Llc
2801 N 33rd Ave Ste 1
Phoenix AZ

(P-16516)
SONY PICTURES IMAGEWORKS INC
9050 Washington Blvd (90232-2518)
PHONE..................................310 840-8000
Michelle Grady, *Pr*
Ken Ralston, *
EMP: 1000 EST: 1992
SALES (est): 56.2MM **Privately Held**
Web: www.imageworks.com
SIC: 7374 Computer graphics service
HQ: Sony Pictures Entertainment, Inc.
10202 Washington Blvd
Culver City CA
310 244-4000

(P-16517)
SPOUTABLE LLC
4150 Mission Blvd Ste 220 (92109-5054)
PHONE..................................609 743-7491
EMP: 165 EST: 2015
SALES (est): 355.89K
SALES (corp-wide): 87.06MM **Privately Held**
Web: www.sovrn.com
SIC: 7374 Computer graphics service
PA: Proper Media, Llc
4150 Mission Blvd Ste 220
San Diego CA
702 427-7949

(P-16518)
TEALIUM INC (PA)
11095 Torreyana Rd Fl 2 (92121-1104)
PHONE..................................858 779-1344
Jeffrey W Lunsford, *CEO*
Ali Behnam, *
Doug Lindroth, *
Peter Ching, *
Ted Purcell, *CRO*
EMP: 558 EST: 2008

PRODUCTS & SVCS

SQ FT: 40,864
SALES (est): 69.06MM **Privately Held**
Web: www.tealium.com
SIC: 7374 7371 Computer graphics service; Computer software development

(P-16519)
TEGRA118 WEALTH SOLUTIONS INC (HQ)
700 N San Vicente Blvd Ste G605 (90069-5060)
PHONE................................888 800-0188
Cheryl Nash, *Pr*
Andrew Schwartz, *
EMP: 139 **EST:** 2011
SALES (est): 24.06MM
SALES (corp-wide): 95.29MM **Privately Held**
SIC: 7374 7371 Data processing service; Computer software development and applications
PA: Investcloud, Inc.
700 N San Vincte Blvd
West Hollywood CA
310 385-7394

(P-16520)
UNIVERSITY CAL SAN DIEGO
Also Called: San Diego Supercomputer Center
10100 Hopkins Dr (92093-0001)
P.O. Box 85608 (92186-5608)
PHONE................................858 534-5000
Michael Norman, *Dir*
EMP: 286
SALES (corp-wide): 534.4MM **Privately Held**
Web: www.sdsc.edu
SIC: 7374 8731 8221 9411 Data processing and preparation; Commercial physical research; University; Administration of educational programs
HQ: University Of California, San Diego
9500 Gilman Dr
La Jolla CA
858 534-2230

(P-16521)
VERIZON CONNECT TELO INC (DH)
15505 Sand Canyon Ave (92618-3114)
PHONE................................844 617-1100
Ralph Mason, *CEO*
A Newth Morris Iv, *TELOGIS ROUTE & TELOGIS NAV*
Jason Koch, *TELOGIS FLEET*
Susan Heystee, *
Ted Serentelos, *
▼ **EMP:** 150 **EST:** 2001
SALES (est): 64.88MM
SALES (corp-wide): 136.84B **Publicly Held**
Web: www.verizonconnect.com
SIC: 7374 Data processing and preparation
HQ: Verizon Connect Inc.
5055 N Point Pkwy
Alpharetta GA
404 573-5800

(P-16522)
YAHOO CV LLC
11985 Bluff Creek Dr (90094-2929)
PHONE................................408 349-3300
EMP: 188
SIC: 7374 Data processing and preparation
HQ: Yahoo Cv, Llc
701 First Ave
Sunnyvale CA

(P-16523)
Z57 INC
2443 Impala Dr Ste B (92010-7227)
PHONE................................858 623-5577
EMP: 105
SALES (corp-wide): 6.62B **Privately Held**
Web: www.z57.com
SIC: 7374 Computer graphics service
HQ: Z57, Inc.
11350 Mccormick Ep 3 Rd # 200
Hunt Valley MD
858 623-5577

7375 Information Retrieval Services

(P-16524)
ACCURATE BACKGROUND LLC (PA)
Also Called: Selectforce
200 Spectrum Center Dr Ste 1100 (92618-5003)
PHONE................................800 784-3911
Tim Dowd, *CEO*
David C Dickerson, *
Brian Fujioka, *
Rashid Ismail, *
Aaron Hayes, *
EMP: 315 **EST:** 1998
SQ FT: 98,024
SALES (est): 117.65MM
SALES (corp-wide): 117.65MM **Privately Held**
Web: www.accurate.com
SIC: 7375 Information retrieval services

(P-16525)
COUNTY OF LOS ANGELES
Also Called: Department of Mental Health
320 W Temple St Fl 9 (90012-3217)
PHONE................................213 974-0515
Jacqueline Criddell, *Mgr*
EMP: 150
Web: www.lacounty.gov
SIC: 7375 9131 Information retrieval services; Executive and legislative combined, level of government
PA: County Of Los Angeles
500 W Temple St Ste 437
Los Angeles CA
213 974-1101

(P-16526)
E-TIMES CORPORATION (PA)
601 S Figueroa St Ste 5000 (90017-3883)
PHONE................................213 452-6720
Chiharu Nakahara, *Pr*
EMP: 300 **EST:** 2003
SALES (est): 9.6MM
SALES (corp-wide): 9.6MM **Privately Held**
Web: www.etimesltd.com
SIC: 7375 7374 8742 Information retrieval services; Computer graphics service; Administrative services consultant

(P-16527)
EDMUNDS HOLDING COMPANY (PA)
Also Called: Edmunds.com
2401 Colorado Ave (90404-3585)
PHONE................................310 309-6300
Avi Steinlauf, *CEO*
Seth Berkowitz, *Pr*
Charles Farrell, *CFO*
EMP: 650 **EST:** 1962
SALES (est): 156.39MM **Privately Held**
Web: www.edmunds.com

SIC: 7375 Information retrieval services

(P-16528)
ELAVON INC
700 S Western Ave (90005-5113)
PHONE................................865 403-7000
John Macht, *Brnch Mgr*
EMP: 400
SALES (corp-wide): 27.4B **Publicly Held**
Web: www.elavon.com
SIC: 7375 Information retrieval services
HQ: Elavon, Inc.
2 Concourse Pkwy Ste 800
Atlanta GA

(P-16529)
GROUNDWORK OPEN SOURCE INC
23332 Mill Creek Dr Ste 155 (92653-7911)
PHONE................................415 992-4500
Dave Lilly, *CEO*
EMP: 100 **EST:** 2004
SALES (est): 9.31MM
SALES (corp-wide): 609.02MM **Privately Held**
Web: www.gwos.com
SIC: 7375 7371 On-line data base information retrieval; Custom computer programming services
HQ: Fox Technologies, Inc.
6455 City West Pkwy
Eden Prairie MN
800 328-1000

(P-16530)
LIFESCRIPT INC
Also Called: Lifescript
4000 Macarthur Blvd Ste 800 (92660-2544)
PHONE................................949 454-0422
EMP: 110
Web: www.everydayhealth.com
SIC: 7375 Information retrieval services

(P-16531)
LOGICMONITOR INC (PA)
820 State St Fl 5 (93101-3271)
PHONE................................805 394-8632
Christina Kosmowski, *CEO*
Kevin Mcgibben, *Ofcr*
Steven Francis, *CPO*
Jie Song, *
Andrew Arrastia, *
EMP: 152 **EST:** 2007
SALES (est): 86.84MM **Privately Held**
Web: www.logicmonitor.com
SIC: 7375 Information retrieval services

(P-16532)
LOWERMYBILLS INC
Also Called: Lowermybills.com
12181 Bluff Creek Dr Ste 250 (90094-2992)
PHONE................................310 348-6800
EMP: 200
SIC: 7375 Information retrieval services

(P-16533)
RELATIONEDGE LLC
10120 Pacific Heights Blvd Ste 110 (92121-4205)
PHONE................................858 451-4665
Matthew Stoyka, *CEO*
EMP: 125 **EST:** 2013
SALES (est): 23.43MM
SALES (corp-wide): 3.12B **Publicly Held**
SIC: 7375 On-line data base information retrieval
HQ: Rackspace Us, Inc.
1 Fanatical Pl
Windcrest TX
210 728-4549

(P-16534)
REPRINTS DESK INC
15821 Ventura Blvd Ste 165 (91436-2915)
PHONE................................310 477-0354
Alan Urban, *CFO*
EMP: 92 **EST:** 2006
SQ FT: 2,500
SALES (est): 10.41MM **Publicly Held**
Web: www.researchsolutions.com
SIC: 7375 Information retrieval services
PA: Research Solutions, Inc.
16350 Ventura Blvd Ste D
Encino CA

(P-16535)
SAGE SOFTWARE INC
Sage
7595 Irvine Center Dr Ste 200 (92618-2957)
PHONE................................949 753-1222
John Kang, *Brnch Mgr*
EMP: 50
SALES (corp-wide): 2.29B **Privately Held**
Web: na.sage.com
SIC: 7375 7374 7372 3089 Information retrieval services; Data processing and preparation; Prepackaged software; Plastics processing
HQ: Sage Software, Inc.
271 17th St Nw Ste 1100
Atlanta GA
866 996-7243

(P-16536)
TROJAN PROFESSIONAL SVCS INC
11075 Knott Ave Ste A (90630-5135)
P.O. Box 1270 (90720-1270)
PHONE................................714 816-7169
Mark Dunn, *CEO*
Ingrid M Kidd, *
Chris Iseri, *
EMP: 99 **EST:** 1976
SALES (est): 10.12MM **Privately Held**
Web: www.trojanonline.com
SIC: 7375 Data base information retrieval

(P-16537)
WESTERN FELD INVSTIGATIONS INC (PA)
Also Called: Releasepoint
405 W Foothill Blvd Ste 204 (91711-2786)
P.O. Box 246 (91740-0246)
PHONE................................800 999-9589
Gerard F Halvey, *Pr*
Clair Halvey, *VP*
Derrick Halvey, *VP*
EMP: 94 **EST:** 1972
SALES (est): 8.1MM
SALES (corp-wide): 8.1MM **Privately Held**
Web: www.wfi-inc.com
SIC: 7375 Information retrieval services

(P-16538)
ZOOMINFO TECHNOLOGIES LLC
Dept La 24789 (91185-0001)
PHONE................................360 783-6924
Henry Schuck, *Managing Member*
EMP: 592
SALES (corp-wide): 1.1B **Publicly Held**
Web: www.zoominfo.com
SIC: 7375 Information retrieval services
HQ: Zoominfo Technologies Llc
805 Broadway St Ste 900
Vancouver WA
360 783-6800

7376 Computer Facilities Management

(P-16539)
ALLIED DIGITAL SERVICES LLC
1075 Mt Vernon Ave (92507-1828)
PHONE..............................310 431-2361
Paresh Shah, *CEO*
EMP: 115
Web: www.allieddigital.net
SIC: 7376 Computer facilities management
HQ: Allied Digital Services, Llc
     680 Knox St Ste 200
     Torrance CA

(P-16540)
TPUSA - FHCS INC (DH)
Also Called: Teleperformance
215 N Marengo Ave Ste 160 (91101-1525)
PHONE..............................213 873-5100
Jeff Balagna, *Pr*
Dean Duncan, *
Peter Phan, *
EMP: 200 **EST:** 1998
SQ FT: 1,029,146
SALES (est): 22.42MM
SALES (corp-wide): 226.27MM **Privately Held**
Web: www.teleperformance.com
SIC: 7376 7373 Computer facilities management; Systems integration services
HQ: Tpusa, Inc.
     5295 S Commerce Dr # 600
     Murray UT
     801 257-5800

7378 Computer Maintenance And Repair

(P-16541)
BCP SYSTEMS INC
1560 S Sinclair St (92806-5933)
PHONE..............................714 202-3900
Carlos P Torres, *CEO*
William W Price, *
EMP: 60 **EST:** 1994
SALES (est): 10.09MM **Privately Held**
Web: www.bcpsystems.com
SIC: 7378 3571 5063 Computer and data processing equipment repair/maintenance; Electronic computers; Electrical apparatus and equipment

(P-16542)
HYUNDAI AUTOEVER AMERICA LLC
Also Called: Haea
10550 Talbert Ave 3rd Fl (92708-6032)
PHONE..............................714 965-3000
EMP: 284 **EST:** 2004
SQ FT: 20,000
SALES (est): 60.01MM **Privately Held**
Web: www.haeaus.com
SIC: 7378 Computer and data processing equipment repair/maintenance
HQ: Hyundai Motor America
     10550 Talbert Ave
     Fountain Valley CA
     714 965-3000

(P-16543)
QUEST INTL MONITOR SVC INC (PA)
Also Called: Quest International
60 Parker 65 (92618)
PHONE..............................949 581-9900
Shahnam Arshadi, *Pr*

Kamyar Katouzian, *
▲ **EMP:** 60 **EST:** 1985
SALES (est): 31.55MM
SALES (corp-wide): 31.55MM **Privately Held**
Web: www.questinc.com
SIC: 7378 7379 7371 7373 Computer maintenance and repair; Computer related maintenance services; Custom computer programming services; Systems integration services

(P-16544)
RAKWORX INC
1 Mason (92618-2514)
PHONE..............................949 215-1362
Yue Cong, *VP*
Zhiyong Ding, *
EMP: 150 **EST:** 2016
SALES (est): 4.09MM **Privately Held**
Web: www.rakworx.com
SIC: 7378 3577 Computer and data processing equipment repair/maintenance; Data conversion equipment, media-to-media: computer

(P-16545)
VALTRON TECHNOLOGIES INC
28309 Avenue Crocker (91355-1251)
PHONE..............................805 257-0333
Andrew Hart, *Pr*
Steve Nober, *
EMP: 95 **EST:** 1988
SQ FT: 48,000
SALES (est): 1.7MM **Privately Held**
SIC: 7378 5734 Computer and data processing equipment repair/maintenance; Modems, monitors, terminals, and disk drives: computers

7379 Computer Related Services, Nec

(P-16546)
A P R CONSULTING INC
17852 17th St Ste 206 (92780-2143)
PHONE..............................714 544-3696
Darryl Stone, *Brnch Mgr*
EMP: 787
Web: www.aprconsulting.com
SIC: 7379 7371 Computer related maintenance services; Custom computer programming services
PA: A P R Consulting, Inc.
     1370 Valley Vista Dr # 280
     Diamond Bar CA

(P-16547)
ADAMS COMM & ENGRG TECH INC
1875 Century Park E Ste 1130 (90067-2253)
PHONE..............................301 861-5000
Charles Adams, *Pr*
EMP: 125
SALES (corp-wide): 27.37MM **Privately Held**
Web: www.adamscomm.com
SIC: 7379 Online services technology consultants
PA: Adams Communication & Engineering Technology, Inc.
     10740 Parkridge Blvd # 700
     Reston VA
     443 345-5285

(P-16548)
ADCOM INTERACTIVE MEDIA INC
Also Called: Admedia
21200 Oxnard St # 429 (91367-5014)
PHONE..............................800 296-7104
EMP: 100 **EST:** 2009
SALES (est): 6.9MM **Privately Held**
Web: www.admedia.com
SIC: 7379 Online services technology consultants

(P-16549)
AIMINSIGHT SOLUTIONS INC
Also Called: A.I.M. Services
4127 Berryman Ave (90066-5425)
PHONE..............................310 313-0047
Amjad Khanmohamed, *Pr*
Imtiaz Khanmohamed, *VP*
EMP: 17 **EST:** 2011
SALES (est): 453.11K **Privately Held**
Web: www.aiminsight.com
SIC: 7379 7371 8742 7372 Computer related consulting services; Computer software systems analysis and design, custom; Management consulting services; Business oriented computer software

(P-16550)
AJILON LLC
4590 Macarthur Blvd (92660-2030)
PHONE..............................949 955-0100
EMP: 201
Web: www.lhh.com
SIC: 7379 Diskette duplicating service
HQ: Ajilon Llc
     4800 Deerwood Campus Pkwy # 800
     Jacksonville FL
     631 844-7800

(P-16551)
ALPHABOLD
2011 Palomar Airport Rd Ste 305 (92011-1432)
PHONE..............................949 637-7148
EMP: 84 **EST:** 2017
SALES (est): 2.38MM **Privately Held**
Web: www.alphabold.com
SIC: 7379 Computer related consulting services

(P-16552)
ASSIGN CORPORATION
200 N Maryland Ave Ste 204 (91206-4262)
PHONE..............................818 247-7100
Umesh Lalwani, *CEO*
EMP: 120 **EST:** 1997
SQ FT: 1,300
SALES (est): 2.36MM **Privately Held**
SIC: 7379 Online services technology consultants

(P-16553)
AVIDEX INDUSTRIES LLC
20382 Hermana Cir (92630-8701)
PHONE..............................949 428-6333
Mike Stammire, *Brnch Mgr*
EMP: 100
Web: www.avidex.com
SIC: 7379 1731 Computer related services; Electrical work
HQ: Avidex Industries, L.L.C.
     1100 Crescent Green # 200
     Cary NC
     919 772-8604

(P-16554)
BERNARDO TECHNICAL SERVICES

Also Called: Btsi
16885 W Bernardo Dr # 210 (92127-1618)
PHONE..............................858 779-9276
EMP: 18 **EST:** 2006
SQ FT: 2,300
SALES (est): 2.28MM **Privately Held**
Web: www.btsihq.com
SIC: 7379 3399 Computer related consulting services; Laminating steel

(P-16555)
BITSCOPIC INC
10866 Wilshire Blvd Ste 400 (90024)
PHONE..............................650 503-3120
Payam Etminani, *CEO*
EMP: 20 **EST:** 2012
SALES (est): 1.22MM **Privately Held**
Web: www.bitscopic.com
SIC: 7379 7371 7372 7373 Computer related consulting services; Computer software writing services; Prepackaged software; Systems software development services

(P-16556)
BLYTHECO INC (PA)
530 Technology Dr Ste 100 (92618-1350)
PHONE..............................949 583-9500
Stephen P Blythe, *CEO*
Lori Seal, *
EMP: 45 **EST:** 1980
SALES (est): 24.25MM
SALES (corp-wide): 24.25MM **Privately Held**
Web: www.blytheco.com
SIC: 7379 7372 7371 Computer related consulting services; Prepackaged software; Computer software systems analysis and design, custom

(P-16557)
BOUGHTS INC
5927 Balfour Ct (92008-7375)
PHONE..............................619 895-7246
Amir Tafreshi, *Pr*
EMP: 30 **EST:** 2011
SALES (est): 1.13MM **Privately Held**
SIC: 7379 3842 Online services technology consultants; Respirators

(P-16558)
CAYLENT INC
4521 Campus Dr Ste 344 (92612-2621)
PHONE..............................800 215-9124
Lori Williams, *CEO*
Valerie Henderson, *Pr*
Jacob Hill, *CFO*
Ginger Siedschlag, *COO*
EMP: 176 **EST:** 2015
SQ FT: 450
SALES (est): 10.79MM **Privately Held**
Web: www.caylent.com
SIC: 7379 Computer related consulting services

(P-16559)
CPUTER INC
Also Called: Ground Force One
2110 Artesia Blvd (90278-3073)
PHONE..............................844 394-1538
Nikolai Nedovodin, *CEO*
EMP: 84 **EST:** 2013
SALES (est): 2.83MM **Privately Held**
Web: www.cputer.com
SIC: 7379 4119 Computer related consulting services; Limousine rental, with driver

(P-16560)
CROWDSTRIKE INC
400 Continental Blvd Ste 275 (90245-5076)

PRODUCTS & SVCS

PHONE................888 512-8906
EMP: 104
SALES (corp-wide): 2.24B **Publicly Held**
Web: www.crowdstrikeracing.com
SIC: 7379 Computer related maintenance services
HQ: Crowdstrike, Inc.
206 E 9th St Ste 1400
Austin TX

(P-16561)
CROWDSTRIKE INC
15440 Laguna Canyon Rd Ste 250 (92618-2138)
PHONE................888 512-8906
EMP: 104
SALES (corp-wide): 2.24B **Publicly Held**
Web: www.crowdstrikeracing.com
SIC: 7379 Computer related maintenance services
HQ: Crowdstrike, Inc.
206 E 9th St Ste 1400
Austin TX

(P-16562)
CROWDSTRIKE INC
15441 Laguna Canyon Rd, Ste 260 (92618)
PHONE................888 512-8906
EMP: 104
SALES (corp-wide): 2.24B **Publicly Held**
Web: www.crowdstrikeracing.com
SIC: 7379 Computer related maintenance services
HQ: Crowdstrike, Inc.
206 E 9th St Ste 1400
Austin TX

(P-16563)
DEFENSEWEB TECHNOLOGIES INC
Also Called: Nliven
10188 Telesis Ct Ste 300 (92121-4779)
P.O. Box 14601 (40214-0601)
PHONE................858 272-8505
EMP: 90
Web: www.transcendinsights.com
SIC: 7379 7371 Computer related consulting services; Computer software development

(P-16564)
DELTA COMPUTER CONSULTING
25550 Hawthorne Blvd Ste 106 (90505-6831)
PHONE................310 541-9440
Marzieh Daneshvar, *Pr*
Masih Hakimpour, *
EMP: 180 **EST:** 1987
SQ FT: 2,000
SALES (est): 10.86MM **Privately Held**
Web: www.deltacci.com
SIC: 7379 Computer related consulting services

(P-16565)
DYNTEK INC (PA)
5241 California Ave Ste 150 (92617-3215)
PHONE................949 271-6700
Ron Ben-yishay, *Dir*
Michael Gullard, *Ch*
Karen S Rosenberger, *CFO*
EMP: 105 **EST:** 1989
SQ FT: 10,250
SALES (est): 108.89MM **Privately Held**
Web: www.dyntek.com
SIC: 7379 Online services technology consultants

(P-16566)
ETHERWAN SYSTEMS INC
2301 E Winston Rd (92806-5542)
P.O. Box 1048 (92781-1048)
PHONE................714 779-3800
Mitch Yang, *Pr*
▲ **EMP:** 100 **EST:** 1996
SQ FT: 5,000
SALES (est): 18.46MM
SALES (corp-wide): 3.37B **Privately Held**
Web: www.etherwan.com
SIC: 7379 3577 Computer related maintenance services; Computer peripheral equipment, nec
HQ: Etherwan Systems, Inc.
8f, No. 2, Alley 6, Lane 235, Baoqiao Rd.
New Taipei City TAP

(P-16567)
EXOIS INC
Also Called: Datadivider
2567 Ingleton Ave (92009-3060)
PHONE................408 777-6630
Jonathan Clark, *CEO*
John D Clark, *
EMP: 249 **EST:** 2004
SQ FT: 2,000
SALES (est): 794.3K
SALES (corp-wide): 44.89MM **Privately Held**
Web: www.exois.com
SIC: 7379 Computer related consulting services
PA: Sharedlabs, Inc.
6 E Bay St Fl 4
Jacksonville FL
800 960-0149

(P-16568)
GEEK SQUAD INC
Also Called: Geek Squad
12989 Park Plaza Dr (90703-8565)
PHONE................562 402-1555
EMP: 88
SALES (corp-wide): 46.3B **Publicly Held**
Web: www.bestbuy.com
SIC: 7379 Computer related consulting services
HQ: Geek Squad, Inc.
1213 Washington Ave N
Minneapolis MN

(P-16569)
GENERAL NETWORKS CORPORATION
3524 Ocean View Blvd (91208-1212)
PHONE................818 249-1962
Robert Todd Withers, *Pr*
Todd Withers, *
David Horwatt, *
Randall C Wise, *
Cort Baker, *
EMP: 60 **EST:** 1986
SQ FT: 3,600
SALES (est): 12.57MM **Privately Held**
Web: www.gennet.com
SIC: 7379 5045 7372 Computer related consulting services; Terminals, computer; Prepackaged software

(P-16570)
INTEGRATED INTERMODAL SVCS INC
8600 Banana Ave (92335-3033)
PHONE................909 355-4100
Greg Philip Stefflre, *Pr*
EMP: 100 **EST:** 1991
SALES (est): 2.23MM **Privately Held**

SIC: 7379 Computer related maintenance services

(P-16571)
INTEGRATED MEDIA TECH INC (PA)
Also Called: I M T
832 N Victory Blvd (91502-1630)
PHONE................818 761-9770
Bruce Lyon, *CEO*
Jackson Fluor, *CFO*
Mike Braico, *Ex VP*
EMP: 91 **EST:** 2007
SALES (est): 21.34MM **Privately Held**
Web: www.imtglobalinc.com
SIC: 7379 Online services technology consultants

(P-16572)
INVISION NETWORKING LLC
333 City Blvd W Ste 1700 (92868-5905)
PHONE................949 309-3441
Justin Johnson, *CEO*
EMP: 135 **EST:** 2006
SALES (est): 3.71MM **Privately Held**
Web: www.invisionnetworking.com
SIC: 7379 Computer related consulting services

(P-16573)
ISPACE INC
840 Apollo St Ste 100 (90245-4641)
PHONE................310 563-3800
Suresh Kothapalli, *CEO*
EMP: 139 **EST:** 2000
SALES (est): 38.96MM **Privately Held**
Web: www.ispace.com
SIC: 7379 Online services technology consultants

(P-16574)
ITEK SERVICES INC
25501 Arctic Ocean Dr (92630-8827)
PHONE................949 770-4835
Donald W Rowley, *CEO*
John Curl, *
EMP: 100 **EST:** 2004
SQ FT: 12,000
SALES (est): 12.39MM **Privately Held**
Web: www.itekservices.com
SIC: 7379 Computer related maintenance services

(P-16575)
KAIZEN SYNDICATE LLC
10413 Magical Waters Ct (91978-2037)
PHONE................858 309-2028
EMP: 103 **EST:** 2019
SALES (est): 1.52MM **Privately Held**
Web: www.kaizensecurity.life
SIC: 7379 5047 Online services technology consultants; Medical equipment and supplies

(P-16576)
KODELLA LLC
17922 Fitch Ste 200 (92614-1611)
PHONE................844 563-3552
Chris Heath, *CEO*
EMP: 104 **EST:** 2016
SALES (est): 10.3MM **Privately Held**
Web: www.kodella.com
SIC: 7379 8243 Computer related consulting services; Software training, computer

(P-16577)
KORE1 INC
530 Technology Dr Ste 150 (92618-1368)
PHONE................949 706-6990

Brian Hunt, *CEO*
Steven Quarles, *
EMP: 100 **EST:** 2005
SALES (est): 35.75MM **Privately Held**
Web: www.kore1.com
SIC: 7379 Online services technology consultants

(P-16578)
LEIDOS GOVERNMENT SERVICES INC
500 N Via Val Verde (90640-2358)
PHONE................323 721-6979
Nate Sadorian, *Brnch Mgr*
EMP: 158
SIC: 7379 7372 Computer related consulting services; Prepackaged software
HQ: Leidos Government Services, Inc.
9737 Washingtonian Blvd
Gaithersburg MD
856 486-5156

(P-16579)
MCLAREN STRATEGIC SOLUTIONS
1 Park Plz Ste 600 (92614-5987)
PHONE................310 564-6754
John Vilina, *CFO*
EMP: 100 **EST:** 2020
SALES (est): 25MM **Privately Held**
Web: www.mclarensv.com
SIC: 7379 Online services technology consultants

(P-16580)
MISSION CLOUD SERVICES INC (PA)
9350 Wilshire Blvd Ste 203 (90212-3214)
PHONE................855 647-7466
Simon Anderson, *CEO*
EMP: 104 **EST:** 2017
SALES (est): 15.52MM
SALES (corp-wide): 15.52MM **Privately Held**
Web: www.missioncloud.com
SIC: 7379 Computer related consulting services

(P-16581)
NC INTERACTIVE LLC
Also Called: Ncsoft
660 Newport Center Dr Ste 800 (92660)
PHONE................512 623-8700
Songyee Yoon, *Prin*
EMP: 100
SIC: 7379 Computer related consulting services
HQ: Nc Interactive Llc
3180 139th Ave Se Ste 500
Bellevue WA
206 588-7200

(P-16582)
NOWCOM LLC
Also Called: Hankey Group
4751 Wilshire Blvd Ste 205 (90010-3860)
PHONE................323 746-6888
EMP: 165 **EST:** 1996
SQ FT: 4,800
SALES (est): 20.29MM
SALES (corp-wide): 352.68MM **Privately Held**
Web: www.nowcom.com
SIC: 7379 Online services technology consultants
PA: Hankey Investment Company, Lp
4751 Wilshire Blvd # 110
Los Angeles CA
323 692-4008

(P-16583)

NZXT INC (PA)
15736 E Valley Blvd (91744-3927)
PHONE..............................800 228-9395
Johnny Chun Ju Hou, *CEO*
▲ EMP: 326 EST: 2015
SALES (est): 80.55MM
SALES (corp-wide): 80.55MM **Privately Held**
Web: www.nzxt.com
SIC: 7379 3571 5045 Computer hardware requirements analysis; Computers, digital, analog or hybrid; Computers, peripherals, and software

(P-16584)

ONEHEALTH SOLUTIONS INC
420 Stevens Ave Ste 200 (92075-2078)
PHONE..............................858 947-6333
Bruce Springer, *Pr*
John Shade, *
Jeff Goe, *
Chuck Mitchell, *
EMP: 133 EST: 2011
SALES (est): 911.58K **Privately Held**
SIC: 7379 Online services technology consultants
HQ: Simplywell, Inc.
10670 N Cntl Expy Ste 700
Dallas TX
214 827-4400

(P-16585)

OSI DIGITAL INC (PA)
26745 Malibu Hills Rd (91301-5355)
PHONE..............................818 992-2700
EMP: 40 EST: 1995
SALES (est): 24.49MM **Privately Held**
Web: www.osidigital.com
SIC: 7379 7372 7371 8741 Online services technology consultants; Application computer software; Computer software development; Management services

(P-16586)

OUTLOOK AMUSEMENTS INC
3746 Foothill Blvd (91214-1740)
PHONE..............................818 433-3800
Jason Freeland, *CEO*
Tim Youd, *
Thomas Wszalek, *
Tom Wszalek, *
EMP: 150 EST: 2003
SALES (est): 24.84MM **Privately Held**
Web: www.outlookamusements.com
SIC: 7379 Online services technology consultants

(P-16587)

OVATION TECH INC
Also Called: L M S
17551 Von Karman Ave (92614-6207)
PHONE..............................949 271-0054
Stacey Powell, *CEO*
Jon Schmidt, *
Jeff Greene, *
Steve Youngblood, *
Minh Vu, *
EMP: 110 EST: 2000
SQ FT: 20,000
SALES (est): 15.52MM **Privately Held**
Web: www.lmsservice.com
SIC: 7379 Computer related consulting services

(P-16588)

PARTNERS INFORMATION TECH (HQ)
Also Called: Calance
888 S Disneyland Dr Ste 500 (92802-1847)

PHONE..............................714 736-4487
Amit Govil, *Ch*
Bill Darden, *
Asit Govil, *
EMP: 100 EST: 2011
SALES (est): 48.96MM **Privately Held**
SIC: 7379 Online services technology consultants
PA: Calance Software Private Limited
Suite No. 201, Greenwood Plaza
Gurugram HR

(P-16589)

PEGASUS SQUIRE INC
12021 Wilshire Blvd Ste 770 (90025-1206)
PHONE..............................866 208-6837
Scott Cooper, *CEO*
EMP: 100 EST: 2002
SALES (est): 3.47MM **Privately Held**
Web: www.pegasussquire.com
SIC: 7379 Computer related consulting services

(P-16590)

PRAMIRA INC
404 N Berry St (92821-3104)
PHONE..............................800 678-1169
Omar Houari, *CEO*
EMP: 125 EST: 2014
SALES (est): 15.53MM **Privately Held**
Web: www.pramira.com
SIC: 7379 8711 Computer related consulting services; Engineering services

(P-16591)

PRECISEQ INC
11601 Wilshire Blvd Ste 500 (90025-0509)
PHONE..............................310 709-6094
Mark Dorner, *Mng Pt*
Guy Livneh, *
EMP: 80 EST: 2015
SQ FT: 1,200
SALES (est): 2.46MM **Privately Held**
SIC: 7379 Computer related consulting services

(P-16592)

PRO-TEK CONSULTING (PA)
21300 Victory Blvd Ste 240 (91367-2525)
PHONE..............................805 807-5571
Raj Kessireddy, *CEO*
Divya Reddy Pyreddy, *
EMP: 110 EST: 2010
SQ FT: 2,400
SALES (est): 9.49MM
SALES (corp-wide): 9.49MM **Privately Held**
Web: www.pro-tekconsulting.com
SIC: 7379 Online services technology consultants

(P-16593)

PROSITES INC
38977 Sky Canyon Dr Ste 200 (92563-2682)
PHONE..............................888 932-3644
Jeffry Tobin, *Pr*
EMP: 139 EST: 2003
SALES (est): 15.59MM **Privately Held**
Web: www.prosites.com
SIC: 7379 Computer related maintenance services

(P-16594)

ROBERT POOL
Also Called: Laser Image Plus
14751 Franklin Ave Ste B (92780-7272)
PHONE..............................714 556-5277
Robert Pool, *Owner*
EMP: 20 EST: 1986

SALES (est): 958.49K **Privately Held**
Web: www.laserimageplus.com
SIC: 7379 3955 Computer related maintenance services; Print cartridges for laser and other computer printers

(P-16595)

SADA SYSTEMS INC (PA)
Also Called: Sada
5250 Lankershim Blvd Ste 720 (91601-3188)
PHONE..............................818 766-2400
Tony Safoian, *CEO*
Annie Safoian, *
Hovig Safoian, *
Matt Lawrence, *
Dana Berg, *
EMP: 106 EST: 2000
SQ FT: 10,503
SALES (est): 42.54MM
SALES (corp-wide): 42.54MM **Privately Held**
Web: www.sada.com
SIC: 7379 Computer related consulting services

(P-16596)

SCIENCE APPLICATIONS INTL CORP
Also Called: Saic Government Solutions
4065 Hancock St (92110-5151)
PHONE..............................703 676-4300
EMP: 99
SALES (corp-wide): 7.7B **Publicly Held**
Web: www.saic.com
SIC: 7379 Computer related consulting services
PA: Science Applications International Corporation
12010 Sunset Hills Rd
Reston VA
703 676-4300

(P-16597)

SENSATA TECHNOLOGIES INC
Also Called: BEI Industrial Encoders
1461 Lawrence Dr (91320-1303)
PHONE..............................805 716-0322
Glenn Avolio, *Division Head*
EMP: 70
SALES (corp-wide): 4.03B **Privately Held**
Web: www.sensata.com
SIC: 7379 3827 3663 Computer related maintenance services; Optical instruments and lenses; Radio and t.v. communications equipment
HQ: Sensata Technologies, Inc.
529 Pleasant St
Attleboro MA

(P-16598)

SENTEK CONSULTING INC
Also Called: Sentek Global
2811 Nimitz Blvd Ste G (92106-4311)
PHONE..............................619 543-9550
Eric Basu, *CEO*
Jason Galetti, *
Peter Kuebler, *
EMP: 129 EST: 2001
SALES (est): 25.33MM
SALES (corp-wide): 696.23K **Privately Held**
Web: www.sentekglobal.com
SIC: 7379 Online services technology consultants
HQ: Deloitte Consulting Llp
30 Rockefeller Plz
New York NY
212 492-4000

(P-16599)

SIMULSTAT INCORPORATED
440 Stevens Ave Ste 200 (92075-2059)
PHONE..............................858 546-4337
C Adam Sharp, *Pr*
EMP: 86 EST: 2001
SALES (est): 5.6MM **Privately Held**
Web: www.simulstat.com
SIC: 7379 Computer related consulting services

(P-16600)

SOCAL TECHNOLOGIES LLC
1305 Oakdale Ave (92021-8540)
PHONE..............................619 635-1128
Marwa Hasan Farhan, *CEO*
Saif Farhan, *Managing Member*
EMP: 23 EST: 2019
SALES (est): 597.68K **Privately Held**
Web: www.socal-technologies.com
SIC: 7379 1389 1799 1442 Computer related consulting services; Construction, repair, and dismantling services; Construction site cleanup; Construction sand mining

(P-16601)

SOFTWARE MANAGEMENT CONS LLC (HQ)
Also Called: Smci
500 N Brand Blvd (91203-1923)
PHONE..............................818 240-3177
Spencer L Karpf, *CEO*
EMP: 320 EST: 1976
SALES (est): 54.97MM
SALES (corp-wide): 253.48MM **Privately Held**
Web: www.milestone.tech
SIC: 7379 7361 Computer related consulting services; Placement agencies
PA: Milestone Technologies Inc.
2201 Walnut Ave Ste 290
Fremont CA
510 651-2454

(P-16602)

STEMCONNECTOR LLC
Also Called: STEMCONNECTOR LLC
1500 Rosecrans Ave Ste 500 (90266-3763)
PHONE..............................424 543-4074
Joanne Webber, *Prin*
EMP: 93
SALES (corp-wide): 662.32K **Privately Held**
Web: www.stemconnector.com
SIC: 7379 Computer related consulting services
PA: Stemconnector, Llc
2005 Market St Ste 3300
Philadelphia PA
215 656-3552

(P-16603)

STRATA INFORMATION GROUP INC
3935 Harney St Ste 203 (92110-2849)
PHONE..............................619 296-0170
Henry A Eimstad, *Pr*
Frank Vaskelis, *
Tiffany Palacz, *
Jon Poole, *
EMP: 93 EST: 1988
SQ FT: 2,000
SALES (est): 11.81MM **Privately Held**
Web: www.sigcorp.com
SIC: 7379 Online services technology consultants

(P-16604)
TACTICAL ENGRG & ANALIS INC (PA)
6050 Santo Rd Ste 250 (92124-6104)
P.O. Box 421425 (92142-1425)
PHONE....................................858 573-9869
Lawrence Massaro, *Pr*
Lawrence Massaro, *VP*
Robert Rosado, *
EMP: 82 **EST:** 1998
SQ FT: 14,000
SALES (est): 35.23MM
SALES (corp-wide): 35.23MM **Privately Held**
Web: www.tac-eng.com
SIC: 7379 8711 Computer related consulting services; Engineering services

(P-16605)
TAHEEM JOHNSON INC
1237 S Victoria Ave (93035-1292)
PHONE....................................818 835-3785
Taheem M Johnson, *CEO*
EMP: 80 **EST:** 2021
SALES (est): 1.48MM **Privately Held**
Web: corp.taheemjohnson.com
SIC: 7379 Online services technology consultants

(P-16606)
TENSORIOT INC
625 The City Dr S Ste 485 (92868-4924)
PHONE....................................909 342-2459
Ravikumar Raghunathan, *CEO*
EMP: 87 **EST:** 2017
SALES (est): 2.89MM **Privately Held**
Web: www.tensoriot.com
SIC: 7379 7371 Computer related consulting services; Computer software development and applications

(P-16607)
TIGERCONNECT INC (PA)
2054 Broadway (90404-2910)
PHONE....................................310 401-1820
Jeffrey Evans, *CEO*
Sean Whiteley, *COO*
John Friedman, *Dir*
Herbert Madan, *Dir*
EMP: 61 **EST:** 2010
SALES (est): 20.92MM
SALES (corp-wide): 20.92MM **Privately Held**
Web: www.tigerconnect.com
SIC: 7379 7372 7373 Computer related maintenance services; Publisher's computer software; Computer systems analysis and design

(P-16608)
UNITED STATES TECHNICAL SVCS
Also Called: Usts
16541 Gothard St Ste 214 (92647-4436)
PHONE....................................714 374-6300
Bob Polk, *Pr*
John Courtney, *
Cynthia Dugger, *
EMP: 122 **EST:** 1998
SQ FT: 2,500
SALES (est): 10.81MM **Privately Held**
Web: www.usts.com
SIC: 7379 Online services technology consultants

(P-16609)
US DATA MANAGEMENT LLC (PA)
Also Called: Usdm Life Science

535 Chapala St (93101-3411)
PHONE....................................888 231-0816
Kevin Brown, *CEO*
Kevin Brown, *Managing Member*
Vega Finucan, *
EMP: 100 **EST:** 2000
SQ FT: 4,000
SALES (est): 17.75MM
SALES (corp-wide): 17.75MM **Privately Held**
Web: www.akanewmedia.com
SIC: 7379 Computer related consulting services

(P-16610)
VERYS LLC
Also Called: Verys
1251 E Dyer Rd Ste 210 (92705-5660)
PHONE....................................949 423-3295
Christopher B Antonius, *CEO*
Mike Alan Zerkel, *Pr*
EMP: 125 **EST:** 2012
SQ FT: 15,500
SALES (est): 13.48MM
SALES (corp-wide): 332.34MM **Privately Held**
Web: www.verys.com
SIC: 7379 7371 7372 Online services technology consultants; Computer software development and applications; Application computer software
PA: West Monroe Partners, Llc
　　311 W Monroe St Ste 1400
　　Chicago IL
　　312 602-4000

(P-16611)
WE SEE DRAGONS LLC
1100 Glendon Ave Ste 1700 (90024-3588)
PHONE....................................310 361-5700
Zack Zalon, *Mng Pt*
EMP: 105 **EST:** 2014
SALES (est): 3.74MM **Privately Held**
Web: www.weseedragons.com
SIC: 7379 Computer related maintenance services

7381 Detective And Armored Car Services

(P-16612)
ABM ONSITE SERVICES INC
3337 Michelson Dr Ste Cn7 (92612-1699)
PHONE....................................949 863-9100
EMP: 931
SALES (corp-wide): 7.81B **Publicly Held**
Web: www.abm.com
SIC: 7381 7521 8711 7349 Security guard service; Automobile parking; Engineering services; Janitorial service, contract basis
HQ: Abm Onsite Services, Inc.
　　1 Liberty Plz Fl 7
　　New York NY

(P-16613)
AEGIS SEC & INVESTIGATIONS INC
10866 Washington Blvd Ste 308 (90232-3610)
PHONE....................................310 838-2787
Jeffrey Nathaniel Zisner, *CEO*
EMP: 102 **EST:** 2010
SALES (est): 9.3MM **Privately Held**
Web: www.aegis.com
SIC: 7381 Security guard service

(P-16614)
ALLIED PROTECTION SERVICES INC
Also Called: Armed/Xctive Prtction Armed Un
24303 Berendo Ave (90710-1839)
PHONE....................................310 330-8314
Leon Brooks, *Pr*
EMP: 178 **EST:** 1999
SALES (est): 7.13MM **Privately Held**
Web: www.alliedprotection.com
SIC: 7381 Security guard service

(P-16615)
AMERICAN EGLE PRTCTIVE SVCS IN
Also Called: American Eagle Protective Svcs
425 W Kelso St (90301-2539)
PHONE....................................310 412-0019
Joelle Fopoussi Epoh, *CEO*
Alma Serrano, *
EMP: 90 **EST:** 2011
SALES (est): 2.33MM **Privately Held**
Web: www.aeprotectiveservices.com
SIC: 7381 Security guard service

(P-16616)
AMERICAN GUARD SERVICES INC (PA)
1125 W 190th St (90248-4303)
PHONE....................................310 645-6200
Sherine Assal, *Pr*
EMP: 400 **EST:** 1997
SQ FT: 28,000
SALES (est): 97.91MM
SALES (corp-wide): 97.91MM **Privately Held**
Web: www.americanguardservices.com
SIC: 7381 Security guard service

(P-16617)
AMERICAN POWER SEC SVC INC
1451 Rimpau Ave Ste 207 (92879-7522)
PHONE....................................866 974-9994
Mohamed Faty, *Pr*
EMP: 85 **EST:** 2015
SALES (est): 550K **Privately Held**
Web: www.americanpowersecurity.com
SIC: 7381 Security guard service

(P-16618)
AMERICAN PROTECTION GROUP INC (PA)
Also Called: Apg
8741 Van Nuys Blvd Ste 202 (91402-2440)
PHONE....................................818 279-2433
Anthony Brown, *Pr*
EMP: 107 **EST:** 2012
SALES (est): 5.4MM
SALES (corp-wide): 5.4MM **Privately Held**
Web: www.apg-svcs.com
SIC: 7381 5063 7382 Security guard service; Alarm systems, nec; Burglar alarm maintenance and monitoring

(P-16619)
AMERICAN PRTCTIVE SVCS INVSTGT
12471 Balsam Rd (92395-9474)
P.O. Box 4640 (91765-0640)
PHONE....................................626 705-8600
Allan Bailey, *Pr*
EMP: 225 **EST:** 1998
SALES (est): 2.71MM **Privately Held**
SIC: 7381 Security guard service

(P-16620)
ANDREWS INTERNATIONAL INC (DH)
455 N Moss St (91502-1727)
PHONE....................................818 487-4060
Randy Andrews, *Pr*
Roger Andrews, *VP*
Michael Topf, *CFO*
Ty Richmond, *COO*
James Wood, *COO*
EMP: 1700 **EST:** 1986
SQ FT: 5,000
SALES (est): 108.53MM
SALES (corp-wide): 251B **Privately Held**
Web: www.andrewsinternational.com
SIC: 7381 Security guard service
HQ: Allied Security Holdings Llc
　　161 Washington St Ste 600
　　Conshohocken PA
　　484 351-1300

(P-16621)
ANDREWS INTERNATIONAL INC
Also Called: Vance Executive Protection
11601 Wilshire Blvd Ste 500 (90025-0509)
PHONE....................................310 575-4844
Rocco Barnes, *Dir*
EMP: 371
SALES (corp-wide): 251B **Privately Held**
SIC: 7381 Security guard service
HQ: Andrews International, Inc.
　　5870 Trinity Pkwy Ste 300
　　Centreville VA
　　703 592-1400

(P-16622)
ATI SYSTEMS INTERNATIONAL INC
8807 Complex Dr (92123-1403)
PHONE....................................858 715-8484
Tony Vasquez, *Brnch Mgr*
EMP: 5038
SALES (corp-wide): 175.11MM **Privately Held**
Web: www.garda.com
SIC: 7381 Detective and armored car services
HQ: Ati Systems International, Inc.
　　2000 Nw Corp Blvd Ste 101
　　Boca Raton FL
　　561 939-7000

(P-16623)
BABYLON SECURITY SERVICES INC
6032 One Half Vineland Ave (91606)
PHONE....................................818 766-8122
Arvin Younan, *Prin*
EMP: 85 **EST:** 1997
SALES (est): 2MM **Privately Held**
SIC: 7381 Security guard service

(P-16624)
BARRYS SECURITY SERVICES INC (PA)
16739 Van Buren Blvd (92504-5744)
PHONE....................................951 789-7575
Michelle Barry, *CEO*
Martin Morales, *
EMP: 188 **EST:** 1999
SQ FT: 5,000
SALES (est): 4.16MM
SALES (corp-wide): 4.16MM **Privately Held**
Web: www.weguard.biz
SIC: 7381 Security guard service

(P-16625)
BOYD AND ASSOCIATES
445 E Esplanade Dr Ste 210 (93036-2126)
PHONE..................................805 988-8298
Kathy Correll, *Mgr*
EMP: 80
SALES (corp-wide): 14.27MM **Privately Held**
Web: www.boydsecurity.com
SIC: 7381 Security guard service
PA: Boyd And Associates
2191 E Thompson Blvd
Ventura CA
818 752-1888

(P-16626)
BOYD AND ASSOCIATES (PA)
2191 E Thompson Blvd (93001-3538)
PHONE..................................818 752-1888
Raymond G Boyd Senior, *Ch Bd*
Barbara K Boyd, *
Daniel Boyd, *
EMP: 160 **EST:** 1967
SQ FT: 8,000
SALES (est): 14.27MM
SALES (corp-wide): 14.27MM **Privately Held**
Web: www.boydsecurity.com
SIC: 7381 7382 Security guard service;
Security systems services

(P-16627)
BRINKS INCORPORATED
Also Called: Brink's
7191 Patterson Dr (92841-1415)
PHONE..................................714 903-9272
Al Kent, *Mgr*
EMP: 120
SALES (corp-wide): 4.54B **Publicly Held**
Web: us.brinks.com
SIC: 7381 Armored car services
HQ: Brink's, Incorporated
1801 Bayberry Ct Ste 400
Richmond VA
804 289-9600

(P-16628)
CALIFRNIA SUTHLAND PRIVATE SEC
1818 S State College Blvd (92806-6053)
PHONE..................................714 367-4005
Alessandro Hickey, *CEO*
Alessandro Hickey, *Managing Member*
Juan Arevalo, *
Joesph Fasano, *
EMP: 200 **EST:** 2019
SALES (est): 3.45MM **Privately Held**
Web: www.californiasouthlandinc.com
SIC: 7381 Security guard service

(P-16629)
CITIGUARD INC
22736 Vanowen St Ste 300 (91307-2656)
PHONE..................................800 613-5903
Sammy Nomir, *Pr*
EMP: 475 **EST:** 2015
SALES (est): 18.32MM **Privately Held**
Web: www.mysecurityguards.com
SIC: 7381 Security guard service

(P-16630)
COMMERCIAL PROTECTIVE SVCS INC
Also Called: CPS Security
17215 Studebaker Rd Ste 205
(90703-2523)
PHONE..................................310 515-5290
Christopher Coffey, *Pr*
William R Babcock, *

EMP: 1800 **EST:** 1997
SALES (est): 46.16MM **Privately Held**
SIC: 7381 Security guard service

(P-16631)
COMMUNITY PATROL INC
1420 E Edinger Ave Ste 213 (92705-4816)
PHONE..................................657 247-4744
Alicia Ledesma, *Owner*
EMP: 90 **EST:** 2019
SALES (est): 2.29MM **Privately Held**
SIC: 7381 Security guard service

(P-16632)
CONSTRUCTION PROTECTIVE SERVICES INC (PA)
Also Called: Commercial Protective Services
436 W Walnut St (90248-3137)
PHONE..................................800 257-5512
EMP: 700 **EST:** 1992
SALES (est): 51.88MM **Privately Held**
Web: www.garda.com
SIC: 7381 7382 Security guard service;
Confinement surveillance systems
maintenance and monitoring

(P-16633)
CONTEMPORARY SERVICES CORP (PA)
Also Called: C S C
17101 Superior St (91325-1961)
PHONE..................................818 885-5150
Damon Zumwalt, *CEO*
Jim Granger, *
▲ **EMP:** 517 **EST:** 1972
SQ FT: 20,000
SALES (est): 297.45MM
SALES (corp-wide): 297.45MM **Privately Held**
Web: www.csc-usa.com
SIC: 7381 Security guard service

(P-16634)
CORNERSTONE PROTECTIVE SVCS
400 Continental Blvd Ste 6056
(90245-5076)
PHONE..................................888 848-4791
Maxwell Okoh, *CEO*
EMP: 200 **EST:** 2020
SALES (est): 2.49MM **Privately Held**
SIC: 7381 Detective and armored car
services

(P-16635)
COTTRELL PAUL ENTERPRISES LLC (PA)
Also Called: Unique Protective Services
16654 Soledad Canyon Rd Ste 233
(91387-3217)
PHONE..................................661 212-2357
Paul Cottrell, *Managing Member*
EMP: 120 **EST:** 1997
SQ FT: 400
SALES (est): 3.02MM **Privately Held**
SIC: 7381 Security guard service

(P-16636)
CROSSING GUARD COMPANY
10440 Pioneer Blvd Ste 5 (90670-8238)
PHONE..................................310 202-8284
EMP: 1762 **EST:** 2011
SALES (est): 170.58K
SALES (corp-wide): 50.15MM **Privately Held**
Web:
www.thecrossingguardcompany.com
SIC: 7381 Guard services
PA: All-City Management Services, Inc.
10440 Pioneer Blvd Ste 5

Santa Fe Springs CA
310 202-8284

(P-16637)
DAVID SHIELD SECURITY INC
Also Called: Dss
23945 Calabasas Rd Ste 102 (91302-1503)
PHONE..................................310 849-4950
Athan Bazaz, *Pr*
Snir Warshaziak, *
EMP: 100 **EST:** 2015
SALES (est): 5MM **Privately Held**
Web: www.davidshieldsecurity.com
SIC: 7381 Security guard service

(P-16638)
DIPLOMATIC SECURITY SVCS LLC
7581 Etiwanda Ave (91739)
PHONE..................................909 463-8409
EMP: 99 **EST:** 2014
SQ FT: 1,500
SALES (est): 784.5K **Privately Held**
SIC: 7381 Security guard service

(P-16639)
EAGLE SECURITY SERVICES INC
12903 S Normandie Ave (90249-2123)
PHONE..................................310 642-0656
Mohsen Kamel, *Pr*
EMP: 150 **EST:** 2003
SQ FT: 5,000
SALES (est): 6.22MM **Privately Held**
Web: www.eagless.com
SIC: 7381 Security guard service

(P-16640)
ELITE ENFRCMENT SEC SLTONS INC
29970 Technology Dr Ste 117d
(92563-2645)
PHONE..................................866 354-8308
Kevin Roncevich, *Brnch Mgr*
EMP: 112
SALES (corp-wide): 4.62MM **Privately Held**
SIC: 7381 Security guard service
PA: Elite Enforcement Security Solutions,
Inc.
1290 N Hancock St Ste 101
Anaheim CA
866 354-8308

(P-16641)
ELITE SHOW SERVICES INC
2878 Camino Del Rio S Ste 260 (92108)
PHONE..................................619 574-1589
John Kontopuls, *CEO*
John Kontopuls, *Pr*
Gus Kontopuls, *
EMP: 3123 **EST:** 1995
SALES (est): 91.02MM **Privately Held**
Web: www.elitesecuritystaffing.com
SIC: 7381 Security guard service

(P-16642)
FPK SECURITY INC
Also Called: Fpk Investigaions
28348 Constellation Rd Ste 880
(91355-5097)
P.O. Box 55597 (91385-0597)
PHONE..................................661 702-9091
Mark David, *CEO*
Robert Esquivel, *
EMP: 365 **EST:** 2005
SQ FT: 1,200
SALES (est): 10.87MM **Privately Held**
Web: www.fpksecurity.com

SIC: 7381 Security guard service

(P-16643)
GARDA CL WEST INC (HQ)
Also Called: Gcl W
1612 W Pico Blvd (90015-2410)
PHONE..................................213 383-3611
Stephan Cretier, *Pr*
Chris W Jamroz, *
▲ **EMP:** 375 **EST:** 2015
SQ FT: 25,000
SALES (est): 290.58MM
SALES (corp-wide): 726.35MM **Privately Held**
SIC: 7381 Security guard service
PA: Gardaworld Cash Services, Inc.
2000 Nw Corporate Blvd
Boca Raton FL
561 939-7000

(P-16644)
GOLDEN WEST SECURITY
Also Called: Golden West K-9
12502 Van Nuys Blvd Ste 215
(91331-1321)
PHONE..................................818 897-5965
Chris Monica, *CEO*
Ralf Santarelli, *Pr*
EMP: 120 **EST:** 1971
SALES (est): 2.49MM **Privately Held**
Web: www.goldenwestsecurityinc.com
SIC: 7381 Security guard service

(P-16645)
GSG PROTECTIVE SERVICES CA INC
15901 Hawthorne Blvd Ste 324 (90278)
PHONE..................................310 371-5300
Marks Victor, *Prin*
EMP: 182 **EST:** 2014
SALES (est): 870.61K **Privately Held**
SIC: 7381 Security guard service

(P-16646)
GUARD MANAGEMENT INC
Also Called: G M I
8001 Vickers St (92111-1917)
PHONE..................................858 279-8282
Larry Abrams, *Pr*
EMP: 154 **EST:** 1992
SALES (est): 8.38MM **Privately Held**
Web: www.aus.com
SIC: 7381 Security guard service

(P-16647)
GUARD-SYSTEMS INC
1910 S Archibald Ave Ste M2 (91761-8502)
PHONE..................................909 947-5400
Patrick Crawford, *Mgr*
EMP: 567
SALES (corp-wide): 15.51MM **Privately Held**
Web: www.guardsystemsinc.com
SIC: 7381 Protective services, guard
PA: Guard-Systems, Inc.
1190 Monterey Pass Rd
Monterey Park CA
626 443-0031

(P-16648)
GUARD-SYSTEMS INC
Also Called: Guard Systems District 1
1190 Monterey Pass Rd (91754-3615)
PHONE..................................323 881-6715
Theodore Haas, *Owner*
EMP: 568
SALES (corp-wide): 15.51MM **Privately Held**
Web: www.guardsystemsinc.com

SIC: **7381** Security guard service
PA: Guard-Systems, Inc.
1190 Monterey Pass Rd
Monterey Park CA
626 443-0031

(P-16649)
GUARDIAN INTL SOLUTIONS
Also Called: Patrol and Security Services
3415 S Sepulveda Blvd Ste 1100
(90034-6060)
PHONE..............................323 528-6555
Rodney Finnell, *CEO*
EMP: 95 **EST:** 2017
SALES (est): 2.7MM **Privately Held**
SIC: **7381** Security guard service

(P-16650)
GUARDSMARK LLC (DH)
1551 N Tustin Ave Ste 650 (92705-8664)
PHONE..............................714 619-9700
Steven S Jones, *CEO*
EMP: 102 **EST:** 2002
SQ FT: 32,107
SALES (est): 195.15MM
SALES (corp-wide): 12.86B **Privately Held**
SIC: **7381** 8742 2721 Security guard service;
Industry specialist consultants; Periodicals,
publishing only
HQ: Universal Protection Service, Lp
450 Exchange Ste 100
Irvine CA
866 877-1965

(P-16651)
**HAYES PROTECTIVE SERVICES
INC**
2930 W Imperial Hwy 200b (90303-3143)
P.O. Box 4684 (90749-4684)
PHONE..............................323 755-2282
Berlin Hayes, *Pr*
EMP: 210 **EST:** 1986
SALES (est): 4.09MM **Privately Held**
SIC: **7381** Security guard service

(P-16652)
HORSEMEN INC
16911 Algonquin St (92649-3812)
PHONE..............................714 847-4243
Patrick Carroll, *Pr*
EMP: 100 **EST:** 1995
SALES (est): 7.16MM **Privately Held**
Web: www.horsemeninc.com
SIC: **7381** Private investigator

(P-16653)
**INTER-CON SECURITY
SYSTEMS INC (PA)**
210 S De Lacey Ave (91105-2048)
PHONE..............................626 535-2200
Enrique Hernandez Junior, *Ch Bd*
Roland A Hernandez, *
EMP: 19885 **EST:** 1973
SQ FT: 17,000
SALES (est): 362.19MM
SALES (corp-wide): 362.19MM **Privately
Held**
Web: www.icsecurity.com
SIC: **7381** Security guard service

(P-16654)
LANDMARK EVENT STAFFING
4790 Irvine Blvd Ste 105 (92620-1998)
PHONE..............................714 293-4248
Peter Kranske, *Pr*
EMP: 1259
Web: www.aus.com
SIC: **7381** Security guard service
PA: Landmark Event Staffing Services, Inc.
4131 Harbor Walk Dr

Fort Collins CO

(P-16655)
LANTZ SECURITY SYSTEMS INC
101 N Westlake Blvd Ste 200 (91362-3753)
PHONE..............................805 496-5775
Terry Oestreich, *Mgr*
EMP: 147
Web: www.lantzsecurity.com
SIC: **7381** 7382 Security guard service;
Security systems services
PA: Lantz Security Systems, Inc.
43440 Sahuayo St
Lancaster CA

(P-16656)
**LAO-HMONG SECURITY
AGENCY INC**
10682 Trask Ave (92843-2407)
PHONE..............................714 533-6776
Mouasu Bliaya, *Pr*
George Moua, *
EMP: 100 **EST:** 1981
SALES (est): 2.41MM **Privately Held**
Web: www.l-hsa.com
SIC: **7381** Security guard service

(P-16657)
LOCATOR SERVICES INC
Also Called: Able Patrol & Guard
4616 Mission Gorge Pl (92120-4133)
PHONE..............................619 229-6100
George Grauer, *Pr*
Diane G Edwards, *
George Grauer Junior, *VP*
Deborah L Kopki, *
EMP: 120 **EST:** 1964
SQ FT: 4,500
SALES (est): 7.92MM **Privately Held**
Web: www.ablepatrolandguard.com
SIC: **7381** Security guard service

(P-16658)
M & S SECURITY SERVICES INC
Also Called: Westside Security Patrol
2900 L St (93301-2351)
PHONE..............................661 397-9616
Marvin Fuller Senior, *CEO*
Steve Fuller, *
Darlene Fuller, *
EMP: 100 **EST:** 1972
SQ FT: 3,000
SALES (est): 5MM **Privately Held**
Web: www.mssecurityservices.com
SIC: **7381** 7382 1731 Protective services,
guard; Security systems services; Fire
detection and burglar alarm systems
specialization

(P-16659)
**MULHOLLAND SEC & PATROL
INC**
Also Called: Centurion Group, The
11454 San Vicente Blvd (90049-6208)
PHONE..............................818 755-0202
David Rosenberg, *Pr*
Steven Lemmer, *
Daniel Campbell, *
EMP: 350 **EST:** 1992
SQ FT: 2,500
SALES (est): 15.72MM **Privately Held**
Web: www.centuriongroup.com
SIC: **7381** Protective services, guard

(P-16660)
NAFEES MEMON
Also Called: Nafees Mmon Cmmand Intl SEC
Sv
6819 Sepulveda Blvd Ste 312
(91405-4463)

PHONE..............................818 997-1666
Nafees Memon, *Owner*
EMP: 90 **EST:** 2008
SQ FT: 700
SALES (est): 3MM **Privately Held**
Web: www.commandinternational.com
SIC: **7381** Security guard service

(P-16661)
NASTEC INTERNATIONAL INC
23875 Ventura Blvd Ste 204 (91302-1420)
PHONE..............................818 222-0355
▼ **EMP:** 100 **EST:** 1994
SQ FT: 3,109
SALES (est): 5.99MM **Privately Held**
Web: www.nastec.com
SIC: **7381** 1731 6411 Detective services;
Safety and security specialization;
Inspection and investigation services,
insurance

(P-16662)
**NATIONWIDE GUARD SERVICES
INC**
9327 Fairway View Pl Ste 200 (91730)
PHONE..............................909 608-1112
EMP: 325 **EST:** 1984
SALES (est): 10.54MM **Privately Held**
Web: www.nwguards.com
SIC: **7381** Security guard service

(P-16663)
**NORTH AMRCN SEC
INVESTIGATIONS**
550 E Carson Plaza Dr Ste 222
(90746-3229)
PHONE..............................323 634-1911
Kenny Hillman, *Pr*
Arthur Lopez, *
EMP: 100 **EST:** 2004
SQ FT: 6,000
SALES (est): 2.26MM **Privately Held**
Web: www.nasi-pi.com
SIC: **7381** Security guard service

(P-16664)
OFF DUTY OFFICERS INC
2365 La Mirada Dr (92081-7863)
PHONE..............................888 408-5900
EMP: 1300 **EST:** 1993
SQ FT: 4,000
SALES (est): 38.84MM **Privately Held**
Web: www.offdutyofficers.com
SIC: **7381** 8742 Security guard service;
Management consulting services

(P-16665)
**OLINN SECURITY
INCORPORATED**
1027 S Palm Canyon Dr (92264-8378)
PHONE..............................760 320-5303
Kimberly Olinn, *CEO*
Kimberly S Olinn, *
EMP: 130 **EST:** 1985
SALES (est): 4.1MM **Privately Held**
Web: www.olinnsecurityinc.com
SIC: **7381** Security guard service

(P-16666)
**OPSEC SPECIALIZED
PROTECTION**
44262 Division St Ste A (93535-3548)
PHONE..............................661 942-3999
Fred Porras, *Owner*
Jeannie Groff, *
EMP: 99 **EST:** 2001
SALES (est): 2.43MM **Privately Held**
Web: www.opsecpro.com

SIC: **7381** Security guard service

(P-16667)
**PACIFIC NATIONAL SECURITY
INC**
3719 Robertson Blvd (90232-2304)
PHONE..............................310 842-7073
EMP: 225
Web: www.pacificnationalsecurity.com
SIC: **7381** Security guard service

(P-16668)
PACWEST SECURITY SERVICES
Also Called: PACWEST SECURITY
SERVICES
1545 Wilshire Blvd Ste 302 (90017-4501)
PHONE..............................213 413-3500
Salvador Crespo, *Brnch Mgr*
EMP: 155
Web: www.pacwestsecurity.com
SIC: **7381** Security guard service
PA: Silvino Nieto
3303 Harbor Blvd Ste A103
Costa Mesa CA

(P-16669)
PACWEST SECURITY SERVICES
Also Called: PACWEST SECURITY
SERVICES
2990 Inland Empire Blvd (91764-4899)
PHONE..............................909 948-0279
Jery Winkfield, *Brnch Mgr*
EMP: 104
Web: www.pacwestsecurity.com
SIC: **7381** Security guard service
PA: Silvino Nieto
3303 Harbor Blvd Ste A103
Costa Mesa CA

(P-16670)
**PICORE BRISTAIN INITIATIVE
INC**
Also Called: Pbi
23679 Calabasas Rd # 215 (91302-1502)
PHONE..............................818 888-3659
EMP: 100 **EST:** 2010
SQ FT: 3,000
SALES (est): 1.96MM **Privately Held**
SIC: **7381** Security guard service

(P-16671)
**PROFESSIONAL SECURITY
CONS (PA)**
Also Called: Professional Security Cons
11454 San Vicente Blvd 2nd Fl
(90049-6208)
PHONE..............................310 207-7729
Moshe Alon, *Pr*
Ilene Alon, *
EMP: 100 **EST:** 1985
SALES (est): 59.1MM **Privately Held**
Web: www.pscsite.com
SIC: **7381** 7382 Security guard service;
Security systems services

(P-16672)
PROTECT-US
3505 Cadillac Ave (92626-1448)
PHONE..............................714 721-8127
Nadiya Aziz, *Prin*
EMP: 180 **EST:** 2018
SALES (est): 1.96MM **Privately Held**
Web: www.protect.us
SIC: **7381** Security guard service

(P-16673)
**REEL SECURITY CALIFORNIA
INC**

15303 Ventura Blvd Ste 1080 (91403-3110)
PHONE..........................818 928-4737
Mario Inez Ramirez, *CEO*
Bradley Bush, *
EMP: 99 **EST:** 2017
SALES (est): 1.54MM **Privately Held**
Web: www.reelsecurity.com
SIC: 7381 Security guard service

(P-16674)
RICHMAN MANAGEMENT CORPORATION
35400 Bob Hope Dr Ste 107 (92270-1772)
PHONE..........................760 832-8520
EMP: 358
SALES (corp-wide): 168.49K **Privately Held**
Web: www.therichmangroup.com
SIC: 7381 Security guard service
HQ: Richman Management Corporation
   7840 Mssion Ctr Ct Ste 10
   San Diego CA
   619 275-7007

(P-16675)
RICHMAN MANAGEMENT CORPORATION
Also Called: Heritage Security Services
41743 Entp Cir N Ste 209 (92590)
PHONE..........................909 296-6189
EMP: 287
SALES (corp-wide): 168.49K **Privately Held**
Web: www.therichmangroup.com
SIC: 7381 Security guard service
HQ: Richman Management Corporation
   7840 Mssion Ctr Ct Ste 10
   San Diego CA
   619 275-7007

(P-16676)
RJN INVESTIGATIONS INC
360 E 1st St Ste 696 (92780-3211)
P.O. Box 55451 (92517-0451)
PHONE..........................951 686-7638
Robert Nagle, *Pr*
Fred Martino, *
EMP: 80 **EST:** 1992
SALES (est): 4.48MM **Privately Held**
Web: www.rjninv.com
SIC: 7381 Detective agency

(P-16677)
SAFEGUARD ON DEMAND INC
Also Called: Security and Patrol Services
11037 Warner Ave # 297 (92708-4007)
PHONE..........................800 640-2327
Ahmad B Nawabi, *CEO*
Ahmad Nawabi, *
EMP: 125 **EST:** 2015
SALES (est): 2.43MM **Privately Held**
Web: www.safeguardondemand.com
SIC: 7381 Security guard service

(P-16678)
SECTRAN SECURITY INCORPORATED (PA)
Also Called: Sectran Armored Truck Service
7633 Industry Ave (90660-4301)
P.O. Box 7267 (90022-0967)
PHONE..........................562 948-1446
Fred Kunik, *Pr*
Irving Barr, *
EMP: 141 **EST:** 1982
SQ FT: 19,736
SALES (est): 17.38MM
SALES (corp-wide): 17.38MM **Privately Held**
Web: www.sectransecurity.com

SIC: 7381 Armored car services

(P-16679)
SECURE NET ALLIANCE
Also Called: Security Company
601 S Glenoaks Blvd Ste 409 (91502-1474)
PHONE..........................818 848-4900
Jonathan Kraut, *CEO*
Jonathan Kraut, *Pt*
Levi Quintana, *CEO*
EMP: 85 **EST:** 2007
SALES (est): 3.16MM **Privately Held**
Web: www.securenetprotect.com
SIC: 7381 Security guard service

(P-16680)
SECURITAS SEC SVCS USA INC
Also Called: Western Operations Center
4330 Park Terrace Dr (91361-4630)
PHONE..........................818 706-6800
Edie Stafford, *Mgr*
EMP: 350
SALES (corp-wide): 12.7B **Privately Held**
Web: www.securitasinc.com
SIC: 7381 Security guard service
HQ: Securitas Security Services Usa, Inc.
   9 Campus Dr Ste 25
   Parsippany NJ
   973 267-5300

(P-16681)
SECURITECH SECURITY SVCS INC
2733 N San Fernando Rd (90065-1318)
P.O. Box 65097 (90065-0097)
PHONE..........................213 387-5050
Serge Tachdjian, *Pr*
Adriana Alvarez, *
EMP: 110 **EST:** 1999
SALES (est): 4.87MM **Privately Held**
Web: www.securitechguards.com
SIC: 7381 Security guard service

(P-16682)
SECURITY INDUST SPCIALISTS INC
477 N Oak St (90302-3314)
PHONE..........................323 924-9147
EMP: 978
SALES (corp-wide): 143.82MM **Privately Held**
Web: www.sis.us
SIC: 7381 Detective services
PA: Security Industry Specialists, Inc.
   6071 Bristol Pkwy
   Culver City CA
   310 215-5100

(P-16683)
SECURITY INDUST SPCIALISTS INC (PA)
Also Called: SIS
6071 Bristol Pkwy (90230-6601)
PHONE..........................310 215-5100
John Spesak, *CEO*
Tom Seltz, *
Kit Knudsen, *
EMP: 132 **EST:** 1999
SQ FT: 9,000
SALES (est): 143.82MM
SALES (corp-wide): 143.82MM **Privately Held**
Web: www.sis.us
SIC: 7381 5065 Security guard service;
   Security control equipment and systems

(P-16684)
SERVEXO
Also Called: Servexo Protective Service

1411 W 190th St Ste 475 (90248-432?)
P.O. Box 9017 (90734-9017)
PHONE..........................323 527-9994
John Palmer, *CEO*
EMP: 500 **EST:** 2012
SALES (est): 5.33MM **Privately Held**
Web: www.servexousa.com
SIC: 7381 Protective services, guard

(P-16685)
SHIELD SECURITY INC
21110 Vanowen St (91303-2821)
PHONE..........................818 239-5800
Kenneth Klosterman, *Brnch Mgr*
EMP: 220
SALES (corp-wide): 12.86B **Privately Held**
Web: www.clementshieldsecurity.com
SIC: 7381 Security guard service
HQ: Shield Security, Inc.
   1551 N Tustin Ave Ste 650
   Santa Ana CA
   714 210-1501

(P-16686)
SHIELD SECURITY INC
150 E Wardlow Rd (90807-4417)
PHONE..........................562 283-1100
Leo Green, *Mgr*
EMP: 457
SALES (corp-wide): 12.86B **Privately Held**
Web: www.clementshieldsecurity.com
SIC: 7381 Security guard service
HQ: Shield Security, Inc.
   1551 N Tustin Ave Ste 650
   Santa Ana CA
   714 210-1501

(P-16687)
SHIELD SECURITY INC (DH)
1551 N Tustin Ave Ste 650 (92705-8664)
PHONE..........................714 210-1501
Ed Klosterman Junior, *Pr*
Kenneth Klosterman, *
EMP: 300 **EST:** 1964
SQ FT: 5,500
SALES (est): 44.08MM
SALES (corp-wide): 12.86B **Privately Held**
Web: www.clementshieldsecurity.com
SIC: 7381 Security guard service
HQ: Universal Protection Service, Lp
   450 Exchange Ste 100
   Irvine CA
   866 877-1965

(P-16688)
SHIELD SECURITY INC
265 N Euclid Ave (91786-6038)
PHONE..........................909 920-1173
Paul Srankowski, *Mgr*
EMP: 324
SALES (corp-wide): 12.86B **Privately Held**
Web: www.clementshieldsecurity.com
SIC: 7381 Security guard service
HQ: Shield Security, Inc.
   1551 N Tustin Ave Ste 650
   Santa Ana CA
   714 210-1501

(P-16689)
SIGNAL 88 LLC
Also Called: Signal 88
821 S Rockefeller Ave (91761-8119)
PHONE..........................714 713-5306
Mark Anderson, *Brnch Mgr*
EMP: 874
SALES (corp-wide): 30.1MM **Privately Held**
Web: www.teamsignal.com
SIC: 7381 Guard services
PA: Signal 88, Llc
   3880 S 149th St Ste 102

Omaha NE
877 498-8494

(P-16690)
SOS SECURITY INCORPORATED
3000 S Robertson Blvd Ste 100 (90034-3145)
PHONE..........................310 392-9600
Doug Hamilton, *Mgr*
EMP: 122
SALES (corp-wide): 51.62MM **Privately Held**
Web: www.sossecurity.com
SIC: 7381 Security guard service
PA: Sos Security Incorporated
   1915 Us Highway 46 Ste 1
   Parsippany NJ
   973 402-6600

(P-16691)
SOUTHWEST PATROL INC
1800 E Lambert Rd Ste 155 (92821-4396)
PHONE..........................909 861-1884
TOLL FREE: 800
EMP: 86 **EST:** 1992
SALES (est): 4.27MM **Privately Held**
Web: www.southwestpatrol.com
SIC: 7381 Security guard service

(P-16692)
SOUTHWEST PROTECTIVE SVCS INC
Also Called: Southwest Security
404 W Heil Ave (92243-3328)
P.O. Box 2915 (92244-2915)
PHONE..........................760 996-1285
Jason Jackson, *CEO*
EMP: 250 **EST:** 2015
SALES (est): 4.35MM **Privately Held**
Web: www.southwestsecurity.net
SIC: 7381 Guard services

(P-16693)
SPECTRUM SECURITY SERVICES INC (PA)
13967 Campo Rd Ste 101 (91935-3232)
P.O. Box 744 (91935-0744)
PHONE..........................619 669-6660
Sam Ersan, *Pr*
Porter Erent, *
EMP: 212 **EST:** 1989
SQ FT: 1,200
SALES (est): 14.29MM **Privately Held**
Web:
www.spectrumdetentionservices.com
SIC: 7381 Security guard service

(P-16694)
STAFF PRO INC
675 Convention Way (92101-7805)
PHONE..........................619 544-1774
Mike Hernandez, *Mgr*
EMP: 1498
Web: www.staffpro.com
SIC: 7381 Security guard service
PA: Staff Pro Inc.
   5455 Garden Grove Blvd
   Westminster CA

(P-16695)
STAR PRO SECURITY PATROL INC
3303 Harbor Blvd Ste B3 (92626-1517)
PHONE..........................714 617-5056
Sally Covington, *Pr*
EMP: 124 **EST:** 2016
SALES (est): 2.29MM **Privately Held**
Web: www.starprosecurity.com

PRODUCTS & SVCS

SIC: 7381 Security guard service

(P-16696)
TRANS-WEST SERVICES INC
8503 Crippen St (93311-8993)
PHONE....................661 381-2900
Brooke L Antonioni, *Pr*
Duane Williams, *
Katy Williams, *
EMP: 300 EST: 1973
SQ FT: 8,500
SALES (est): 22.58MM **Privately Held**
Web: www.trans-west.net
SIC: 7381 Security guard service

(P-16697)
UNITED FACILITY SOLUTIONS INC
Also Called: Command Gard Srvces Wsa Srvces
19208 S Vermont Ave Ste 200
(90248-4414)
PHONE....................310 743-3000
Martin Benom, *CEO*
Mark Myers, *Pr*
EMP: 400 EST: 2015
SALES (est): 4.63MM **Privately Held**
Web: www.commandguards.com
SIC: 7381 7349 Security guard service;
Janitorial service, contract basis

(P-16698)
UNITED GUARD SECURITY INC
1100 W Town And Country Rd Ste 1250
(92868-4633)
PHONE....................714 242-4051
Ismael Zita, *CEO*
EMP: 128
SALES (corp-wide): 9.5MM **Privately Held**
Web: www.unitedguardsecurity.net
SIC: 7381 Security guard service
PA: United Guard Security Inc.
879 W 190th St Ste 280
Gardena CA
800 228-2505

(P-16699)
UNITED GUARD SECURITY INC
473 E Carnegie Dr Ste 200 (92408)
PHONE....................909 402-0754
Ismael Zita, *CEO*
EMP: 128
SALES (corp-wide): 9.5MM **Privately Held**
Web: www.unitedguardsecurity.net
SIC: 7381 Security guard service
PA: United Guard Security Inc.
879 W 190th St Ste 280
Gardena CA
800 228-2505

(P-16700)
UNIVERSAL PROTECTION SVC LP (HQ)
Also Called: Allied Universal Security Svcs
450 Exchange Ste 100 (92602-5002)
PHONE....................866 877-1965
Brian Cescolini, *Pt*
Steve Jones, *Pt*
EMP: 88 EST: 2009
SALES (est): 695.68MM
SALES (corp-wide): 12.86B **Privately Held**
Web: www.aus.com
SIC: 7381 Security guard service
PA: Atlas Ontario Lp
199 Bay St Suite 4000
Toronto ON
484 351-1586

(P-16701)
UNIVERSAL PRTCTION SEC SYSTEMS (DH)
1815 E Wilshire Ave Ste 910 (92705-4646)
PHONE....................714 923-3700
EMP: 100 EST: 2009
SALES (est): 13.91MM
SALES (corp-wide): 12.86B **Privately Held**
SIC: 7381 Security guard service
HQ: Universal Services Of America, Lp
450 Exchange
Irvine CA
866 877-1965

(P-16702)
UNIVERSAL SERVICES AMERICA LP
77725 Enfield Ln (92211-0468)
PHONE....................760 200-2865
EMP: 5044
SALES (corp-wide): 12.86B **Privately Held**
Web: www.aus.com
SIC: 7381 Security guard service
HQ: Universal Services Of America, Lp
450 Exchange
Irvine CA
866 877-1965

(P-16703)
UNIVERSAL SERVICES AMERICA LP (HQ)
Also Called: Allied Universal
450 Exchange (92602-5002)
PHONE....................866 877-1965
Steve Jones, *CEO*
EMP: 100 EST: 2001
SALES (est): 1.22B
SALES (corp-wide): 12.86B **Privately Held**
Web: www.aus.com
SIC: 7381 7349 Security guard service;
Janitorial service, contract basis
PA: Atlas Ontario Lp
199 Bay St Suite 4000
Toronto ON
484 351-1586

(P-16704)
US SECURITY ASSOCIATES INC
Also Called: US Security Associates
455 N Moss St (91502-1727)
PHONE....................818 697-1809
EMP: 298
SALES (corp-wide): 251B **Privately Held**
Web: www.ussecurityassociates.com
SIC: 7381 Security guard service
HQ: U.S. Security Associates, Inc.
200 Mansell Ct E Fl 5
Roswell GA

(P-16705)
US SECURITY ASSOCIATES INC
2275 W 190th St Ste 100 (90504-6007)
PHONE....................714 352-0773
Richard L Wyckoff, *Brnch Mgr*
EMP: 426
SALES (corp-wide): 251B **Privately Held**
Web: www.ussecurityassociates.com
SIC: 7381 Security guard service
HQ: U.S. Security Associates, Inc.
200 Mansell Ct E Fl 5
Roswell GA

(P-16706)
VENUE MANAGEMENT SYSTEMS INC
Also Called: V M S
2041 E Gladstone St Ste A (91740-5385)
P.O. Box 25 (91773-0025)
PHONE....................626 445-6000

Charles E Mcintyre, *Pr*
EMP: 6000 EST: 2001
SQ FT: 35,000
SALES (est): 10.95MM **Privately Held**
Web: www.venueservices.com
SIC: 7381 7363 8742 Detective and armored
car services; Employee leasing service;
Human resource consulting services

(P-16707)
VESCOM CORPORATION (PA)
1125 W 190th St (90248-4303)
PHONE....................207 945-5051
Sherif Assal, *Pr*
Pamela J Treadwell, *
EMP: 622 EST: 1986
SALES (est): 9.08MM **Privately Held**
Web: www.vescom.com
SIC: 7381 Security guard service

(P-16708)
VETS SECURING AMERICA INC
1125 W 190th St (90248-4303)
PHONE....................310 645-6200
Gerald A Gregory, *Pr*
EMP: 4000 EST: 2008
SALES (est): 17.51MM **Privately Held**
Web: www.vetssecuringamerica.com
SIC: 7381 Security guard service

(P-16709)
WHELAN SECURITY CO
400 Continental Blvd (90245-5033)
PHONE....................310 343-8628
Gregory Twardowski, *Brnch Mgr*
EMP: 196
SALES (corp-wide): 175.11MM **Privately Held**
Web: www.garda.com
SIC: 7381 Security guard service
HQ: Whelan Security Co.
1699 S Hanley Rd Ste 350
Saint Louis MO
314 644-3227

(P-16710)
WORLD PRIVATE SECURITY INC
16921 Parthenia St Ste 201 (91343-4568)
PHONE....................818 894-1800
Fred Youssif, *Pr*
Jeannette Youssif, *
EMP: 200 EST: 1997
SALES (est): 2.11MM **Privately Held**
Web: www.worldsecurityinc.com
SIC: 7381 Security guard service

(P-16711)
WORLDWIDE SECURITY ASSOC INC (HQ)
10311 S La Cienega Blvd (90045-6109)
PHONE....................310 743-3000
EMP: 300 EST: 1991
SQ FT: 5,000
SALES (est): 55.12MM **Privately Held**
SIC: 7381 Security guard service
PA: Wsa Group Inc
19208 S Vermont Ave 200
Gardena CA

(P-16712)
WSA GROUP INC
19208 S Vermont Ave # 200 (90248-4414)
PHONE....................310 743-3000
Andres Martinez, *Pr*
James E Bush, *
EMP: 2000 EST: 1991
SQ FT: 10,000
SALES (est): 13.23MM **Privately Held**

SIC: 7381 7349 Security guard service;
Janitorial service, contract basis

7382 Security Systems Services

(P-16713)
313 ACQUISITION LLC
1111 Citrus St Ste 1 (92507-1735)
PHONE....................801 234-6374
Jakob Imig, *Brnch Mgr*
EMP: 4888
SALES (corp-wide): 493.76MM **Privately Held**
SIC: 7382 Security systems services
PA: 313 Acquisition Llc
4931 N 300 W
Provo UT
877 404-4129

(P-16714)
ACCURATE SECURITY PROS INC
9919 Hibert St Ste D (92131-1076)
PHONE....................858 271-1155
Gregory Parks, *CEO*
Gregory A Parks, *Pr*
EMP: 22 EST: 1983
SQ FT: 3,800
SALES (est): 2.34MM **Privately Held**
Web: www.accuratesecuritypros.com
SIC: 7382 3429 5065 5099 Security systems
services; Door opening and closing
devices, except electrical; Security control
equipment and systems; Locks and lock
sets

(P-16715)
ADT LLC
Also Called: Protection One
1120 Palmyrita Ave Ste 280 (92507-1709)
PHONE....................951 782-6900
EMP: 209
SALES (corp-wide): 6.4B **Publicly Held**
Web: www.adt.com
SIC: 7382 5999 5063 1731 Burglar alarm
maintenance and monitoring; Alarm signal
systems; Burglar alarm systems; Safety
and security specialization
HQ: Adt Llc
1501 W Yamato Rd
Boca Raton FL
561 988-3600

(P-16716)
ADT LLC
731 E Ball Rd (92805-5950)
PHONE....................714 450-6461
EMP: 110
SALES (corp-wide): 6.4B **Publicly Held**
Web: www.adt.com
SIC: 7382 Security systems services
HQ: Adt Llc
1501 W Yamato Rd
Boca Raton FL
561 988-3600

(P-16717)
ADT LLC
Also Called: Home Security and HM Ctrl Svcs
475 N Muller St (92801-5452)
PHONE....................626 593-1020
EMP: 122
SALES (corp-wide): 6.4B **Publicly Held**
Web: www.adt.com
SIC: 7382 Burglar alarm maintenance and
monitoring
HQ: Adt Llc
1501 W Yamato Rd

Boca Raton FL
561 988-3600

(P-16718)
ADT LLC
9201 Oakdale Ave Ste 100 (91311-6543)
PHONE.................................818 464-5001
EMP: 110
SALES (corp-wide): 6.4B **Publicly Held**
Web: www.adt.com
SIC: 7382 Security systems services
HQ: Adt Llc
     1501 W Yamato Rd
     Boca Raton FL
     561 988-3600

(P-16719)
ADT LLC
26074 Avenue Hall Ste 1 (91355-3444)
PHONE.................................818 373-6200
Ron Bogen, *Brnch Mgr*
EMP: 113
SALES (corp-wide): 6.4B **Publicly Held**
Web: www.adt.com
SIC: 7382 5999 Burglar alarm maintenance
     and monitoring; Alarm and safety
     equipment stores
HQ: Adt Llc
     1501 W Yamato Rd
     Boca Raton FL
     561 988-3600

(P-16720)
ADT LLC
Also Called: ADT Security Services
1808 Commercenter W Ste E (92408-3302)
PHONE.................................951 824-7205
EMP: 104
SALES (corp-wide): 6.4B **Publicly Held**
Web: www.adt.com
SIC: 7382 Burglar alarm maintenance and
     monitoring
HQ: Adt Llc
     1501 W Yamato Rd
     Boca Raton FL
     561 988-3600

(P-16721)
ADVANCED PROTECTION INDS LLC
Also Called: National Monitoring Center
25341 Commercentre Dr (92630-8856)
PHONE.................................800 662-1711
Woodie Andrawos, *Pr*
Todd Shuff, *
Frank Farag, *
EMP: 99 **EST:** 2018
SALES (est): 18.46MM **Privately Held**
Web: www.nmccentral.com
SIC: 7382 Burglar alarm maintenance and
     monitoring

(P-16722)
AERO PORT SERVICES INC (PA)
216 W Florence Ave (90301-1213)
PHONE.................................310 623-8230
Chris Paik, *Pr*
Robert Yim, *
Julie Hong, *
Stephan Park, *
▲ **EMP:** 848 **EST:** 2002
SALES (est): 51.25MM
SALES (corp-wide): 51.25MM **Privately Held**
Web: www.aeroportservices.com
SIC: 7382 Security systems services

(P-16723)
AMERICAN SECURITY FORCE INC
Also Called: Security Services
5430 E Olympic Blvd (90022-5113)
PHONE.................................323 722-8585
Albert Williams, *CEO*
Albert Williams, *Pr*
EMP: 100 **EST:** 1993
SQ FT: 3,700
SALES (est): 10.86MM **Privately Held**
Web: www.americansecurityforce.com
SIC: 7382 7381 Burglar alarm maintenance
     and monitoring; Protective services, guard

(P-16724)
BRIGHTCLOUD INC
4370 La Jolla Village Dr Ste 820
(92122-1277)
PHONE.................................858 652-4803
Quinn Curtis, *Pr*
EMP: 280 **EST:** 2005
SALES (est): 445.92K
SALES (corp-wide): 832.31MM **Privately Held**
Web: www.brightcloud.com
SIC: 7382 Security systems services
HQ: Webroot Inc.
     385 Interlocken Blvd # 800
     Broomfield CO
     303 442-3813

(P-16725)
CODE RED FIRE INC
544 Montebello Way (90640-5118)
P.O. Box 1552 (90640-7552)
PHONE.................................323 726-0982
Matthew Mccarrick, *CEO*
EMP: 23 **EST:** 2012
SALES (est): 995.47K **Privately Held**
Web: www.crfireinc.com
SIC: 7382 1711 3999 2813 Fire alarm
     maintenance and monitoring; Fire sprinkler
     system installation; Grenades, hand (fire
     extinguishers); Dry ice, carbon dioxide
     (solid)

(P-16726)
CONTEMPORARY SERVICES CORP
369 Van Ness Way Ste 702 (90501-6245)
PHONE.................................310 320-8418
Roy Sukimoto, *Brnch Mgr*
EMP: 124
SALES (corp-wide): 297.45MM **Privately Held**
Web: www.csc-usa.com
SIC: 7382 7381 7299 Security systems
     services; Guard services; Party planning
     service
PA: Contemporary Services Corporation
     17101 Superior St
     Northridge CA
     818 885-5150

(P-16727)
CORPORATE ALNCE STRATEGIES INC
3410 La Sierra Ave Ste F244 (92503-5270)
PHONE.................................877 777-7487
Leah L Pinto, *Dir*
Leah Pinto, *
EMP: 115 **EST:** 2015
SALES (est): 3.6MM **Privately Held**
Web:
www.corporatealliancestrategies.com
SIC: 7382 Security systems services

(P-16728)
DELTA SCIENTIFIC CORPORATION (PA)
40355 Delta Ln (93551-3616)
PHONE.................................661 575-1100
Harry D Dickinson, *CEO*
David Dickinson, *
Richard I Winger, *
Keith Bobrosky, *
◆ **EMP:** 188 **EST:** 1974
SQ FT: 200,000
SALES (est): 24.6MM
SALES (corp-wide): 24.6MM **Privately Held**
Web: www.deltascientific.com
SIC: 7382 Security systems services

(P-16729)
DIAL SECURITY INC (PA)
Also Called: Dial Communications
760 W Ventura Blvd (93010-8382)
P.O. Box 34781 (20827-0781)
PHONE.................................805 389-6700
William H Dundas, *Pr*
EMP: 250 **EST:** 1974
SQ FT: 12,000
SALES (est): 17.39MM
SALES (corp-wide): 17.39MM **Privately Held**
Web: www.dialcomm.com
SIC: 7382 7381 Protective devices, security;
     Detective and armored car services

(P-16730)
DTIQ HOLDINGS INC
Also Called: Dtt
1755 N Main St (90031-2516)
PHONE.................................323 576-1400
Sam Naficy, *CEO*
Jeffrey Moran, *
Thomas M Moran, *
Michael Sutton, *
Adam Watson, *
EMP: 119 **EST:** 2009
SALES (est): 1.11MM **Privately Held**
Web: www.dtiq.com
SIC: 7382 Confinement surveillance systems
     maintenance and monitoring

(P-16731)
EASTERNCCTV (USA) LLC
Also Called: Ens Security
525 Parriott Pl W (91745-1033)
PHONE.................................626 961-8999
Xianjie Xiong, *Pr*
EMP: 171
SALES (corp-wide): 23.24MM **Privately Held**
Web: www.enssecurity.com
SIC: 7382 Security systems services
PA: Easterncctv (Usa), Llc
     50 Commercial St
     Plainview NY
     516 870-3779

(P-16732)
EDGEWORTH INTEGRATION LLC
2360 Shasta Way Ste F (93065-1800)
PHONE.................................805 915-0211
EMP: 85
SALES (corp-wide): 2.09MM **Privately Held**
Web: www.edgeworthsecurity.com
SIC: 7382 Security systems services
PA: Edgeworth Integration, Llc
     1000 Commerce Dr Fl 2
     Pittsburgh PA
     800 421-9130

(P-16733)
ELITE INTRACTIVE SOLUTIONS INC
1200 W 7th St Ste L1-180 (90017-6411)
PHONE.................................310 740-5426
Aria Kozak, *Pr*
Jordan Lippel, *Chief Business Development Officer*
John Valdez, *Chief Business Development Officer*
Michael Zatulov, *
EMP: 32 **EST:** 2001
SQ FT: 8,000
SALES (est): 4.94MM **Privately Held**
Web: www.eliteisi.com
SIC: 7382 1731 3629 3669 Burglar alarm
     maintenance and monitoring; Electrical work
     ; Electronic generation equipment; Visual
     communication systems

(P-16734)
ENTERPRISE SECURITY INC (PA)
Also Called: Enterprise Security Solutions
22860 Savi Ranch Pkwy (92887-4610)
PHONE.................................714 630-9100
Samuel Troy Laughlin, *CEO*
Troy Laughlin, *
Daniel Steiner, *
Joseph Emens, *
EMP: 74 **EST:** 2000
SALES (est): 10.73MM **Privately Held**
Web: www.entersecurity.com
SIC: 7382 3699 3429 6211 Protective
     devices, security; Security devices; Security
     cable locking systems; Dealers, security

(P-16735)
EVENT INTELLIGENCE GROUP
4140 Jackson Ave (90232-3234)
PHONE.................................310 237-5375
Allen Cook, *CEO*
EMP: 96 **EST:** 2014
SALES (est): 384.3K **Privately Held**
SIC: 7382 Security systems services
PA: Tourtechsupport, Inc.
     1723 Round Rock Dr
     Raleigh NC

(P-16736)
EZVIZ INC
18639 Railroad St (91748-1317)
PHONE.................................855 693-9849
Shengyang Jin, *CEO*
Jeffrey He, *
Hsin Lin, *
Yuying Wang, *
EMP: 200 **EST:** 2015
SQ FT: 32,000
SALES (est): 6.13MM **Privately Held**
Web: www.ezviz.com
SIC: 7382 Confinement surveillance systems
     maintenance and monitoring
HQ: Hikvision Usa Inc.
     18639 Railroad St
     City Of Industry CA
     909 895-0400

(P-16737)
G4S JUSTICE SERVICES LLC
Also Called: G4s Government Services
1290 N Hancock St Ste 103 (92807-1925)
PHONE.................................800 589-6003
EMP: 56 **EST:** 1995
SALES (est): 7.05MM
SALES (corp-wide): 94.13MM **Privately Held**
SIC: 7382 3669 Fire alarm maintenance and
     monitoring; Emergency alarms
PA: Sentinel Offender Services Llc
     1290 N Hancock St Ste 103

Anaheim CA
949 453-1550

(P-16738)
GLARE TECHNOLOGY USA INC
30898 Wealth St (92563-2534)
PHONE.............................909 437-6999
Laith Salih, *CEO*
EMP: 120 **EST:** 2015
SALES (est): 1.71MM **Privately Held**
Web: www.rideglarewheel.com
SIC: 7382 Security systems services

(P-16739)
GUARDIAN INTEGRATED SEC INC (PA)
21828 Lassen St Ste A (91311-3603)
PHONE.............................800 400-3167
Abraham Ramzan, *CEO*
EMP: 120 **EST:** 2014
SALES (est): 6.58MM
SALES (corp-wide): 6.58MM **Privately Held**
Web:
www.guardianintegratedsecurity.com
SIC: 7382 Security systems services

(P-16740)
HARRISON IYKE
Also Called: Diplomatic Security Services
7611 Etiwanda Ave (91739-9715)
PHONE.............................909 463-8409
EMP: 99
SALES (est): 4.7MM **Privately Held**
SIC: 7382 Security systems services

(P-16741)
HIKVISION USA INC (HQ)
18639 Railroad St (91748-1317)
PHONE.............................909 895-0400
Jeffrey He, *CEO*
Ning Tang, *
Tony Yang, *
▲ **EMP:** 120 **EST:** 2007
SALES (est): 44.12MM **Privately Held**
Web: www.hikvision.com
SIC: 7382 Confinement surveillance systems maintenance and monitoring
PA: Hangzhou Hikvision Digital Technology Co., Ltd.
No.518, Wulianwang Street, Binjiang District
Hangzhou ZJ

(P-16742)
IDENTITY INTLLIGENCE GROUP LLC
Also Called: Idiq
43454 Business Park Dr (92590-5530)
PHONE.............................626 522-7993
Scott Hermann, *Managing Member*
EMP: 232 **EST:** 2010
SALES (est): 12.55MM **Privately Held**
Web: www.idiq.com
SIC: 7382 Security systems services

(P-16743)
JOHNSON CONTROLS
12728 Shoemaker Ave (90670-6345)
PHONE.............................562 405-3817
Andy Bernot, *Mgr*
EMP: 150
SIC: 7382 1731 1711 Security systems services; Fire detection and burglar alarm systems specialization; Plumbing, heating, air-conditioning
HQ: Johnson Controls Fire Protection Lp
6600 Congress Ave
Boca Raton FL
561 988-7200

(P-16744)
KESA INCORPORATED
Also Called: Constrction Instlltion Mint Gr
960 E Discovery Ln (92801-1149)
PHONE.............................714 956-2827
Nancy L Rojo, *Pr*
William B Morrill, *
EMP: 40 **EST:** 2003
SALES (est): 9.77MM **Privately Held**
Web: www.kesacorp.com
SIC: 7382 3577 Burglar alarm maintenance and monitoring; Computer peripheral equipment, nec

(P-16745)
KRATOS PUBLIC SAFETY & SECURITY SOLUTIONS INC
4820 Eastgate Mall Ste 200 (92121)
PHONE.............................858 812-7300
EMP: 99
SIC: 7382 Security systems services

(P-16746)
LIFE ALERT EMRGNCY RSPONSE INC (PA)
Also Called: Life Alert
16027 Ventura Blvd Ste 400 (91436-2728)
PHONE.............................800 247-0000
Isaac Shepher, *Pr*
Miriam Shepher, *
Felix Leung, *
▲ **EMP:** 175 **EST:** 1987
SQ FT: 29,489
SALES (est): 51.34MM
SALES (corp-wide): 51.34MM **Privately Held**
Web: www.lifealert.com
SIC: 7382 5731 Confinement surveillance systems maintenance and monitoring; Consumer electronic equipment, nec

(P-16747)
LOUROE ELECTRONICS INC
6955 Valjean Ave (91406-4716)
PHONE.............................818 994-6498
Louis Weiss, *Pr*
Richard S Brent, *
Donald Schiffer, *
Pilar Frickey, *
Cameron Javdani, *
▼ **EMP:** 28 **EST:** 1979
SQ FT: 17,000
SALES (est): 5.21MM **Privately Held**
Web: www.louroe.com
SIC: 7382 3651 Burglar alarm maintenance and monitoring; Audio electronic systems

(P-16748)
NAVTRAK LLC
20 Enterprise Ste 100 (92656-7104)
PHONE.............................410 548-2337
EMP: 97
SIC: 7382 Security systems services

(P-16749)
POST ALARM SYSTEMS (PA)
Also Called: Post Alarm Systems Patrol Svcs
47 E Saint Joseph St (91006-2861)
PHONE.............................626 446-7159
William Post, *Pr*
Bill Post, *
Lois Post, *
EMP: 98 **EST:** 1956
SQ FT: 10,500
SALES (est): 12.46MM
SALES (corp-wide): 12.46MM **Privately Held**
Web: www.postalarm.com

SIC: 7382 1731 5063 Burglar alarm maintenance and monitoring; Fire detection and burglar alarm systems specialization; Electrical apparatus and equipment

(P-16750)
REALDEFENSE LLC (PA)
Also Called: PC Cleaner
150 S Los Robles Ave Ste 400 (91101-2441)
PHONE.............................801 895-7907
Gary Guseinov, *CEO*
Sean Whiteley, *Pr*
EMP: 30 **EST:** 2017
SALES (est): 74.63MM
SALES (corp-wide): 74.63MM **Privately Held**
Web: www.realdefen.se
SIC: 7382 7372 Security systems services; Prepackaged software

(P-16751)
SAFESMART ACCESS INC
13238 Florence Ave (90670-4510)
PHONE.............................310 410-1525
EMP: 22 **EST:** 2017
SALES (est): 669.2K **Privately Held**
Web: www.safesmartaccess.com
SIC: 7382 3446 Security systems services; Ornamental metalwork

(P-16752)
SECURITAS TECHNOLOGY CORP
7002 Convoy Ct (92111-1017)
PHONE.............................858 812-7349
EMP: 99
SALES (corp-wide): 12.7B **Privately Held**
Web: www.securitases.com
SIC: 7382 Security systems services
HQ: Securitas Technology Corporation
3800 Tabs Dr
Uniontown OH
800 548-4478

(P-16753)
SENTINEL MONITORING CORP (HQ)
220 Technology Dr Ste 200 (92618-2424)
PHONE.............................949 453-1550
Robert Contestabile, *Pr*
EMP: 100 **EST:** 1993
SALES (est): 10.3MM
SALES (corp-wide): 94.13MM **Privately Held**
Web: www.sentineladvantage.com
SIC: 7382 Confinement surveillance systems maintenance and monitoring
PA: Sentinel Offender Services Llc
1290 N Hancock St Ste 103
Anaheim CA
949 453-1550

(P-16754)
SENTINEL OFFENDER SERVICES LLC (PA)
1290 N Hancock St Ste 103 (92807-1925)
PHONE.............................949 453-1550
EMP: 85 **EST:** 1993
SALES (est): 94.13MM
SALES (corp-wide): 94.13MM **Privately Held**
Web: www.sentineladvantage.com
SIC: 7382 Confinement surveillance systems maintenance and monitoring

(P-16755)
STAFF PRO INC (PA)
Also Called: Allied Universal Event Svcs

5455 Garden Grove Blvd (92683-1891)
PHONE.............................714 230-7200
Cory Meredith, *CEO*
EMP: 700 **EST:** 1987
SALES (est): 96.94MM **Privately Held**
Web: www.staffpro.com
SIC: 7382 8741 Security systems services; Management services

(P-16756)
SYMONS FIRE PROTECTION INC
Also Called: Fire Sprnklr Fire Alarm Dsign
9475 Chesapeake Dr Ste A (92123-1337)
PHONE.............................619 588-6364
Jamil Shamoon, *Pr*
David Symons, *
EMP: 110 **EST:** 1993
SALES (est): 8.39MM **Privately Held**
Web: www.symonsfp.com
SIC: 7382 1731 8711 7389 Fire alarm maintenance and monitoring; Fire detection and burglar alarm systems specialization; Building construction consultant; Inspection and testing services

(P-16757)
TAD GROUP LLC
5000 Birch St Ste 3000 (92660-2140)
PHONE.............................949 476-3601
EMP: 150 **EST:** 2007
SALES (est): 2.87MM **Privately Held**
Web: www.sunsnow.com
SIC: 7382 7373 Security systems services; Computer integrated systems design

7383 News Syndicates

(P-16758)
BUENA VISTA TELEVISION (DH)
Also Called: Buena Vista TV Advg Sls
500 S Buena Vista St (91521-0001)
PHONE.............................818 560-1878
Janice Marinelli, *CEO*
Mort Marcus, *
Marsha Reed, *
Jed Cohen, *
Anne L Buettner, *
▲ **EMP:** 129 **EST:** 1985
SALES (est): 20.81MM
SALES (corp-wide): 88.9B **Publicly Held**
Web: www.thewaltdisneycompany.com
SIC: 7383 News feature syndicate
HQ: Disney Enterprises, Inc.
500 S Buena Vista St
Burbank CA
818 560-1000

(P-16759)
THE COPLEY PRESS INC
Also Called: Copley Newspapers
7776 Ivanhoe Ave (92037-4572)
P.O. Box 1530 (92038-1530)
PHONE.............................858 454-0411
EMP: 4170
SIC: 7383 2711 7011 News syndicates; Newspapers, publishing and printing; Resort hotel

7384 Photofinish Laboratories

(P-16760)
COLOREDGE
3520 W Valhalla Dr (91505-1126)
PHONE.............................818 842-1121
Mike Lannin, *CEO*
EMP: 204 **EST:** 1957
SQ FT: 60,000

▲ = Import ▼ = Export
◆ = Import/Export

SALES (est): 3.68MM **Privately Held**
Web: www.coloredge.com
SIC: 7384 Photofinish laboratories
HQ: Coloredge, Inc.
190 Jony Dr
Carlstadt NJ
212 594-4800

(P-16761)
JAKE HEY INCORPORATED
Also Called: A & I Color Laboratory
257 S Lake St (91502-2111)
PHONE.....................323 856-5280
David Alexander, *Pr*
James Ishihara, *
EMP: 144 **EST:** 1978
SQ FT: 16,000
SALES (est): 4.01MM **Privately Held**
Web: www.aandibooks.com
SIC: 7384 Photofinishing laboratory

(P-16762)
TECHNICOLOR INC
Also Called: Technicolor Lab
2255 N Ontario St Ste 180 (91504-4509)
PHONE.....................818 260-4577
Joe Berchtold, *Pr*
EMP: 400 **EST:** 1966
SALES (est): 39.42MM **Privately Held**
SIC: 7384 Photofinish laboratories

7389 Business Services, Nec

(P-16763)
A J PARENT COMPANY INC (PA)
Also Called: Americas Printer.com
6910 Aragon Cir Ste 6 (90620-8103)
PHONE.....................714 521-1100
Arthur Parent, *CEO*
EMP: 88 **EST:** 1997
SALES (est): 18.16MM
SALES (corp-wide): 18.16MM **Privately Held**
Web: www.americasprinter.com
SIC: 7389 2752 Printers' services: folding, collating, etc.; Commercial printing, lithographic

(P-16764)
A THREAD AHEAD INC
1925 1st St (91340-2609)
P.O. Box 889 (91341-0889)
PHONE.....................818 837-1984
EMP: 20 **EST:** 2010
SALES (est): 3MM **Privately Held**
Web: www.athreadahead.com
SIC: 7389 2759 Advertising, promotional, and trade show services; Screen printing

(P-16765)
AARON THOMAS COMPANY INC (PA)
Also Called: Aaron Thomas
7421 Chapman Ave (92841-2115)
PHONE.....................714 894-4468
Aerick Bacon, *Pr*
James T Chang, *
Thomas Bacon, *
Jean Chang, *
Linda Bacon, *
▲ **EMP:** 125 **EST:** 1973
SQ FT: 207,000
SALES (est): 44.17MM
SALES (corp-wide): 44.17MM **Privately Held**
Web: www.packaging.com
SIC: 7389 Packaging and labeling services

(P-16766)
ABI DOCUMENT SUPPORT SVCS LLC
Also Called: ABI Document Support Services
10459 Mountain View Ave Ste E (92354-2033)
PHONE.....................909 793-0613
David Benge, *Brnch Mgr*
EMP: 86
Web: www.abidss.com
SIC: 7389 5044 Microfilm recording and developing service; Office equipment
HQ: Abi Document Support Services, Llc
3534 E Sunshine St Ste L
Springfield MO

(P-16767)
ADVANSTAR COMMUNICATIONS INC
2901 28th St Ste 100 (90405-2975)
PHONE.....................310 857-7500
Danny Phillips, *Mgr*
EMP: 22
SALES (corp-wide): 2.72B **Privately Held**
Web: epay.advanstar.com
SIC: 7389 2721 7331 Trade show arrangement; Magazines: publishing only, not printed on site; Direct mail advertising services
HQ: Advanstar Communications Inc.
2501 Colorado Ave Ste 280
Santa Monica CA
310 857-7500

(P-16768)
ADVANSTAR COMMUNICATIONS INC (DH)
Also Called: Advanstar Global
2501 Colorado Ave Ste 280 (90404-3754)
PHONE.....................310 857-7500
◆ **EMP:** 177 **EST:** 1987
SALES (est): 40.29MM
SALES (corp-wide): 2.72B **Privately Held**
Web: epay.advanstar.com
SIC: 7389 2721 7331 Trade show arrangement; Magazines: publishing only, not printed on site; Direct mail advertising services
HQ: Ubm Limited
240 Blackfriars Road
London
207 921-5000

(P-16769)
AFFINITY AUTO PROGRAMS INC
Also Called: Costco Auto Program
10251 Vista Sorrento Pkwy Ste 300 (92121)
PHONE.....................858 643-9324
Jeff Skeen, *Pr*
Gary Drean, *
EMP: 266 **EST:** 1988
SQ FT: 34,000
SALES (est): 90.16MM **Privately Held**
Web: www.costcoauto.com
SIC: 7389 Advertising, promotional, and trade show services

(P-16770)
ALL-PRO BAIL BONDS INC
530 Hacienda Dr Ste 104d (92081-6640)
PHONE.....................760 512-1969
Steffan Gibbs, *Brnch Mgr*
EMP: 100
SALES (corp-wide): 8.75MM **Privately Held**
Web: www.allprobailbond.com
SIC: 7389 Bail bonding

PA: All-Pro Bail Bonds Inc.
512 Via De La Vlle Ste 30 Valle
Solana Beach CA
858 481-1200

(P-16771)
ALORICA CUSTOMER CARE INC
8885 Rio San Diego Dr Ste 107 (92108-1624)
PHONE.....................619 298-7103
EMP: 100
SALES (corp-wide): 845.12MM **Privately Held**
SIC: 7389 Telemarketing services
HQ: Alorica Customer Care, Inc.
5085 W Park Blvd Ste 300
Plano TX

(P-16772)
ALORICA CUSTOMER CARE INC
5161 California Ave Ste 100 (92617-8002)
PHONE.....................941 906-9000
EMP: 175
SALES (corp-wide): 845.12MM **Privately Held**
Web: www.alorica.com
SIC: 7389 Telemarketing services
HQ: Alorica Customer Care, Inc.
5085 W Park Blvd Ste 300
Plano TX

(P-16773)
ALORICA INC (PA)
5161 California Ave Ste 100 (92617-8002)
PHONE.....................866 256-7422
Greg Haller, *CEO*
Chris Crowley, *Chief Commercial Officer*
Steve Phillips, *CIO*
Max Schwendner, *CFO*
▲ **EMP:** 100 **EST:** 1999
SALES (est): 845.12MM
SALES (corp-wide): 845.12MM **Privately Held**
Web: www.alorica.com
SIC: 7389 Telephone answering service

(P-16774)
ALTERNATIVE IRA SERVICES LLC
Also Called: Bitcoin Ira
15303 Ventura Blvd Ste 1060 (91403-3110)
PHONE.....................877 936-7175
EMP: 201 **EST:** 2016
SALES (est): 2.53MM **Privately Held**
Web: www.bitcoinira.com
SIC: 7389 Financial services

(P-16775)
AMERICAN COPAK CORPORATION
9175 Eton Ave (91311-5806)
PHONE.....................818 576-1000
Steven A Brooker, *Pr*
EMP: 150 **EST:** 1987
SQ FT: 150,000
SALES (est): 4.28MM **Privately Held**
Web: www.americancopak.com
SIC: 7389 Packaging and labeling services

(P-16776)
AMERICAN HEALTH CONNECTION
8484 Wilshire Blvd Ste 501 (90211-3243)
PHONE.....................424 226-0420
Yuriy Koltyar, *CEO*
Azabeh Williamson, *
EMP: 850 **EST:** 2011
SQ FT: 3,500
SALES (est): 30.14MM **Privately Held**

Web:
www.americanhealthconnection.com
SIC: 7389 Telemarketing services

(P-16777)
AMKOM DESIGN GROUP INC
2598 Fortune Way Ste J (92081-8442)
PHONE.....................760 295-1957
Ernest Kasparov, *CEO*
Shlaen Gregory, *
Greg Shlaen, *
Henry Belkin, *
EMP: 25 **EST:** 2016
SALES (est): 1.08MM **Privately Held**
Web: www.amkominc.com
SIC: 7389 3663 Design services; Radio and t.v. communications equipment

(P-16778)
ANDREW LAUREN COMPANY INC
15225 Alton Pkwy Unit 300 (92618-2345)
PHONE.....................949 861-4222
Mark Noonan, *Prin*
EMP: 117
Web: int.andrewlauren.com
SIC: 7389 5713 Interior design services; Carpets
PA: The Andrew Lauren Company Inc
8909 Kenamar Dr Ste 101
San Diego CA

(P-16779)
ANHEUSER-BUSCH LLC
Also Called: Anheuser-Busch
15800 Roscoe Blvd (91406-1350)
PHONE.....................805 381-4700
Charles Cindric, *Mgr*
EMP: 255
SALES (corp-wide): 1.31B **Privately Held**
Web: www.budweisertours.com
SIC: 7389 Office facilities and secretarial service rental
HQ: Anheuser-Busch, Llc
1 Busch Pl
Saint Louis MO
800 342-5283

(P-16780)
ANOVIA PAYMENTS LLC
1 Macarthur Pl (92707-5944)
PHONE.....................469 621-0166
Kevin Jones, *Pr*
Steven Neel, *CFO*
Tom Bannon, *VP Opers*
Gary Grubbs, *Executive Technology Vice President*
EMP: 84 **EST:** 2013
SALES (est): 2.84MM **Privately Held**
Web: www.spherecommerce.com
SIC: 7389 Credit card service

(P-16781)
ANSWER FINANCIAL INC (HQ)
15910 Ventura Blvd Fl 6 (91436-2803)
PHONE.....................818 644-4000
Robert J Slingerland, *CEO*
Daniel John Bryce, *
Peter Foley, *
John E Galaviz, *
Craig Lozofsky, *
EMP: 200 **EST:** 2006
SQ FT: 45,000
SALES (est): 66.55MM **Publicly Held**
Web: www.answerfinancial.com
SIC: 7389 6411 Brokers, business: buying and selling business enterprises; Property and casualty insurance agent
PA: The Allstate Corporation
3100 Sanders Rd

Northbrook IL

(P-16782)
ARVATO USA LLC
2053 E Jay St (91764-1847)
PHONE.................................502 356-8063
Dominik Dittrich, *Brnch Mgr*
EMP: 106
SALES (corp-wide): 54.57MM **Privately Held**
SIC: 7389 Telephone answering service
HQ: Arvato Usa Llc
    51 Sawyer Rd Ste 620
    Waltham MA
    661 702-2700

(P-16783)
ASSOCTED LDSCP DSPLAY GROUP IN
Also Called: Associated Group
1005 Mateo St (90021-1715)
PHONE.................................714 558-6100
Laurie Resnick, *Pr*
Greg Salmeri, *
Angelica Arreola Seasonal Disp lay, *Dir*
Angela Hicks, *
EMP: 90 **EST:** 1986
SALES (est): 9MM **Privately Held**
Web: www.ag-ca.com
SIC: 7389 0781 Plant care service;
    Landscape services

(P-16784)
AUTOCRIB INC
2882 Dow Ave (92780-7258)
PHONE.................................714 274-0400
Stephen Pixley, *CEO*
▲ **EMP:** 150 **EST:** 1999
SQ FT: 58,000
SALES (est): 43.82MM
SALES (corp-wide): 4.49B **Publicly Held**
Web: www.autocrib.com
SIC: 7389 3581 Inventory computing service
    ; Automatic vending machines
PA: Snap-On Incorporated
    2801 80th St
    Kenosha WI
    262 656-5200

(P-16785)
AZTECS TELECOM INC
1353 Walker Ln (92879-1775)
PHONE.................................714 373-1560
Robert Lopez, *CEO*
EMP: 80 **EST:** 2000
SALES (est): 5.17MM **Privately Held**
Web: www.aztecs.net
SIC: 7389 1731 Telephone services;
    Communications specialization

(P-16786)
B RILEY SECURITIES INC
11100 Santa Monica Blvd (90025-3384)
PHONE.................................310 966-1444
Bryant Riley, *CEO*
EMP: 126 **EST:** 1989
SALES (est): 15.96MM **Publicly Held**
Web: www.brileyfin.com
SIC: 7389 Financial services
PA: B. Riley Financial, Inc.
    11100 Santa Monica Blvd
    Los Angeles CA

(P-16787)
BANCOLMBIA PR INTRNACIONAL INC
2625 E Florence Ave Ste E (90255-4756)
PHONE.................................323 582-2255
Julio Melara Junior, *Mgr*

EMP: 95
Web: www.bancolombiamiami.com
SIC: 7389 Financial services
HQ: Bancolombia Puerto Rico Internacional Inc.
    270 Munoz Rivera Ste 502
    San Juan PR

(P-16788)
BANKCARD SERVICES (PA)
21281 S Western Ave (90501-2958)
PHONE.................................213 365-1122
EMP: 110 **EST:** 2012
SALES (est): 24.85MM
SALES (corp-wide): 24.85MM **Privately Held**
Web: www.navyz.com
SIC: 7389 Credit card service

(P-16789)
BANKCARD USA MERCHANT SRVC
5701 Lindero Canyon Rd (91362-4060)
PHONE.................................818 597-7000
EMP: 85 **EST:** 1993
SQ FT: 20,000
SALES (est): 146.14K **Privately Held**
Web: www.bankcardusa.com
SIC: 7389 Credit card service

(P-16790)
BAXALTA US INC
17511 Armstrong Ave (92614-5725)
PHONE.................................949 474-6301
EMP: 192
SIC: 7389 Personal service agents, brokers, and bureaus
HQ: Baxalta Us Inc.
    1200 Lakeside Dr
    Bannockburn IL
    224 948-2000

(P-16791)
BEAUMONT NIELSEN MARINE INC
2420 Shelter Island Dr (92106-3112)
P.O. Box 6633 (92166-0633)
PHONE.................................619 223-2628
Don Beaumont, *Pr*
Thomas A Nielsen, *
EMP: 29 **EST:** 1979
SALES (est): 3.76MM **Privately Held**
Web: www.nielsenbeaumont.com
SIC: 7389 3732 Repossession service;
    Yachts, building and repairing

(P-16792)
BENRICH SERVICE COMPANY INC (PA)
3190 Airport Loop Dr Ste G (92626)
PHONE.................................714 241-0284
Peter W Bendheim, *Pr*
Redge Henn, *
EMP: 27 **EST:** 1958
SALES (est): 9.79MM
SALES (corp-wide): 9.79MM **Privately Held**
Web: www.benrichservice.com
SIC: 7389 3433 Water softener service;
    Heating equipment, except electric

(P-16793)
BEST SIGNS INC (PA)
1550 S Gene Autry Trl (92264-3505)
PHONE.................................760 320-3042
Jesse Cross, *VP*
Jim Cross, *
EMP: 26 **EST:** 1960
SQ FT: 6,000

SALES (est): 5.26MM
SALES (corp-wide): 5.26MM **Privately Held**
Web: www.bestsignsinc.com
SIC: 7389 3993 1799 Sign painting and
    lettering shop; Signs and advertising
    specialties; Sign installation and
    maintenance

(P-16794)
BIU INC
9268 1/2 Hall Rd (90241-5308)
PHONE.................................909 556-1311
EMP: 91
SALES (corp-wide): 295.56K **Privately Held**
Web: www.xgirlusa.com
SIC: 7389 Personal service agents, brokers, and bureaus
PA: Biu Inc.
    3100 Airway Ave
    Costa Mesa CA
    714 785-4751

(P-16795)
BOOST MOBILE LLC
6316 Irvine Blvd (92620-2102)
PHONE.................................949 451-1563
EMP: 1290
SIC: 7389 Telephone services

(P-16796)
CALIFRNIA CLNIC PLSTIC SURGERY
73180 El Paseo (92260-4218)
PHONE.................................760 346-0611
EMP: 184
SALES (corp-wide): 3.97MM **Privately Held**
SIC: 7389 Personal service agents, brokers, and bureaus
PA: California Clinic Plastic Surgery
    100 E California Blvd
    Pasadena CA
    626 817-0818

(P-16797)
CARDSERVICE INTERNATIONAL INC (DH)
5898 Condor Dr # 220 (93021-2603)
EMP: 450 **EST:** 2002
SQ FT: 34,000
SALES (est): 49.55MM
SALES (corp-wide): 17.74B **Publicly Held**
SIC: 7389 6153 Credit card service; Short-term business credit institutions, except agricultural
HQ: First Data Corporation
    255 Fiserv Dr
    Brookfield WI

(P-16798)
CARECREDIT LLC
555 Anton Blvd Ste 700 (92626-7659)
PHONE.................................800 300-3046
EMP: 120 **EST:** 1996
SALES (est): 12.63MM
SALES (corp-wide): 17.53B **Publicly Held**
Web: www.carecredit.com
SIC: 7389 8742 Financial services; Banking and finance consultant
PA: Synchrony Financial
    777 Long Ridge Rd Ste 2
    Stamford CT
    203 585-2400

(P-16799)
CAW COWIE INC (PA)
Also Called: Colin Cowie Lifestyle

7 Ginger Root Ln (90275-5907)
PHONE.................................212 396-9007
Colin Cowie, *CEO*
Stuart Brownstein, *
David Berke, *
EMP: 25 **EST:** 1994
SALES (est): 4.9MM
SALES (corp-wide): 4.9MM **Privately Held**
Web: www.rsclarkenergy.com
SIC: 7389 7299 5023 2731 Interior design
    services; Party planning service; Decorative
    home furnishings and supplies; Book
    publishing

(P-16800)
CERAMIC DECORATING COMPANY INC
4651 Sheila St (90040-1003)
PHONE.................................323 268-5135
Chad A Johnson, *CEO*
Burnell D Johnson, *
W Allan Johnson, *
Allan Johnson, *
EMP: 50 **EST:** 1934
SQ FT: 30,290
SALES (est): 4.1MM **Privately Held**
Web: www.ceramicdecoratingco.com
SIC: 7389 2396 Labeling bottles, cans,
    cartons, etc.; Automotive and apparel
    trimmings

(P-16801)
CETERA FINANCIAL GROUP INC (PA)
655 W Broadway Ste 1680 (92101-8495)
PHONE.................................866 489-3100
EMP: 443 **EST:** 2009
SQ FT: 70,000
SALES (est): 315.75K **Privately Held**
Web: www.cetera.com
SIC: 7389 6282 Financial services;
    Investment advisory service

(P-16802)
CIRTECH INC
Also Called: Apct Anaheim
250 E Emerson Ave (92865-3317)
PHONE.................................714 921-0860
Brad Reese, *Pr*
Frank E Reese, *
EMP: 50 **EST:** 1965
SQ FT: 30,000
SALES (est): 729.17K
SALES (corp-wide): 7MM **Privately Held**
Web: www.apct.com
SIC: 7389 3672 Printed circuitry graphic
    layout; Printed circuit boards
PA: Apct Holdings, Llc
    3495 De La Cruz Blvd
    Santa Clara CA
    408 727-6442

(P-16803)
COASTAL INTL HOLDINGS LLC
Also Called: Coastal International
2832 Walnut Ave Ste B (92780-7002)
PHONE.................................714 635-1200
EMP: 285
SALES (corp-wide): 33.79MM **Privately Held**
Web: www.coastalintl.com
SIC: 7389 Trade show arrangement
PA: Coastal International Holdings, Llc
    3 Harbor Dr
    Sausalito CA
    415 339-1700

(P-16804)
CONSOLDTED FIRE PROTECTION LLC (HQ)
153 Technology Dr Ste 200 (92618-2402)
PHONE..............................949 727-3277
Keith Fielding, *
Steve Shaffer, *
EMP: 800 **EST:** 1999
SALES (est): 52.85MM **Privately Held**
Web: www.cfpfire.com
SIC: 7389 Fire protection service other than forestry or public
PA: Mx Holdings Us, Inc.
153 Technology Dr Ste 200
Irvine CA

(P-16805)
CONTRACT LABELING SERVICE INC
13885 Ramona Ave (91710-5426)
PHONE..............................909 937-0344
Trevor Metcalf, CEO
Alexander Riff, *
Carolyn Johnson, *
▲ **EMP:** 48 **EST:** 1992
SALES (est): 4.64MM **Privately Held**
Web: www.contractlabel.com
SIC: 7389 3552 Packaging and labeling services; Silk screens for textile industry

(P-16806)
COUNTRY VILLA SERVICE CORP
39950 Vista Del Sol (92270-3206)
PHONE..............................760 340-0053
Georgeanne Slapper, Brnch Mgr
EMP: 102
SALES (corp-wide): 88.5MM **Privately Held**
Web: www.evictionlawyer.com
SIC: 7389 Personal service agents, brokers, and bureaus
PA: Country Villa Service Corp.
2400 E Katella Ave # 800
Anaheim CA
310 574-3733

(P-16807)
COUNTY OF LOS ANGELES
Also Called: Internal Services Dept
1100 N Eastern Ave (90063-3200)
PHONE..............................323 267-2771
Linnette Bookman, Superintnt
EMP: 85
Web: www.lacounty.gov
SIC: 7389 9631 Telephone services; Communications commission, government
PA: County Of Los Angeles
500 W Temple St Ste 437
Los Angeles CA
213 974-1101

(P-16808)
COUNTY OF SAN DIEGO
Also Called: Public Works
5510 Overland Ave Ste 410 (92123-1239)
PHONE..............................858 694-2960
Wayne Williams, Mgr
EMP: 187
Web: www.sdcda.org
SIC: 7389 Personal service agents, brokers, and bureaus
PA: County Of San Diego
1600 Pacific Hwy Ste 209
San Diego CA
619 531-5880

(P-16809)
CPPG INC
3905 E Miraloma Ave (92806-6201)

PHONE..............................714 572-3662
Louis Torres, Pr
Justino Cantu, VP
EMP: 18 **EST:** 1987
SQ FT: 15,000
SALES (est): 453.78K **Privately Held**
Web: www.cppginc.com
SIC: 7389 3471 Grinding, precision: commercial or industrial; Chromium plating of metals or formed products

(P-16810)
CREATIVE DESIGN CONSULTANTS (PA)
Also Called: C D C
2915 Red Hill Ave Ste G201 (92626-5923)
PHONE..............................714 641-4868
Dana Eggerts, Prin
Christie Pettus, Prin
Julie Ann Stark, Prin
Lisa Kells, Prin
Cassie Nguyen, Prin
EMP: 95 **EST:** 1994
SQ FT: 9,988
SALES (est): 11.24MM
SALES (corp-wide): 11.24MM **Privately Held**
Web: www.cdcdesigns.com
SIC: 7389 Interior designer

(P-16811)
CREDIBILITY CORP
22761 Pacific Coast Hwy (90265-5064)
PHONE..............................310 456-8271
EMP: 732
Web: www.credibility.com
SIC: 7389 Financial services

(P-16812)
CREDIT CARD SERVICES INC (PA)
Also Called: Bankcard Services
21281 S Western Ave (90501-2958)
PHONE..............................213 365-1122
Patrick S Hong, CEO
EMP: 95 **EST:** 1996
SQ FT: 17,000
SALES (est): 20.26MM **Privately Held**
Web: www.navyz.com
SIC: 7389 Credit card service

(P-16813)
DA VINCI SCHOOLS FUND
201 N Douglas St (90245-4637)
PHONE..............................310 725-5800
Matthew Wunder, Admn
EMP: 204 **EST:** 2017
SALES (est): 35.36MM **Privately Held**
Web: www.davincischools.org
SIC: 7389 Design services

(P-16814)
DATA COUNCIL LLC
Also Called: Logix3
15310 Barranca Pkwy Ste 100 (92618-2215)
PHONE..............................904 512-3200
John Kocher, Pr
Lloyd Kammerer, Prin
EMP: 100 **EST:** 2014
SALES (est): 9.86MM
SALES (corp-wide): 4.71B **Publicly Held**
Web: www.thedatacouncil.com
SIC: 7389 Commodity inspection
HQ: Advantage Sales & Marketing Llc
15310 Barranca Pkwy # 100
Irvine CA
949 797-2900

(P-16815)
DECOR INTERIOR DESIGN INC
21530 Sherman Way (91303-1536)
PHONE..............................818 962-4800
Ronda Jackson, CEO
EMP: 21 **EST:** 2005
SALES (est): 4.52MM **Privately Held**
Web: www.designsbydecor.com
SIC: 7389 7349 1799 2521 Interior designer; Building and office cleaning services; Office furniture installation; Wood office furniture

(P-16816)
DEKRA-LITE INDUSTRIES INC
Also Called: DI Imaging
3102 W Alton Ave (92704-6817)
PHONE..............................714 436-0705
Jeffrey Lopez, CEO
▲ **EMP:** 80 **EST:** 1987
SQ FT: 30,000
SALES (est): 12.82MM **Privately Held**
Web: www.dekra-lite.com
SIC: 7389 5999 3999 Decoration service for special events; Art, picture frames, and decorations; Advertising curtains

(P-16817)
DF ONE OPERATOR LLC
11 Via Santanella (92270-5817)
PHONE..............................310 961-9739
EMP: 84
SALES (corp-wide): 2.61MM **Privately Held**
SIC: 7389 Personal service agents, brokers, and bureaus
PA: Df One Operator Llc
65441 Two Bunch Palms Trl
Desert Hot Springs CA
605 472-5422

(P-16818)
DIBA FASHIONS INC
472 N Bowling Green Way (90049-2820)
PHONE..............................323 232-3775
John Gir Daneshrad, Pr
Shahin Daneshrad, *
EMP: 70 **EST:** 1980
SQ FT: 22,400
SALES (est): 1.75MM **Privately Held**
SIC: 7389 2339 Sewing contractor; Women's and misses' outerwear, nec

(P-16819)
DYNOVAS INC
Also Called: Dynovas
12250 Iavelli Way (92064-6818)
PHONE..............................508 717-7494
Quinn Mcallister, Pr
Robert Kolozs, Prin
EMP: 18 **EST:** 2020
SALES (est): 1.24MM **Privately Held**
Web: www.dynovas.com
SIC: 7389 3429 3769 3731 Business Activities at Non-Commercial Site; Aircraft hardware; Space vehicle equipment, nec; Dredges, building and repairing

(P-16820)
E & C FASHION INC
Also Called: Pacific Concept Laundry
1420 Esperanza St (90023-3914)
PHONE..............................323 262-0099
William Moo Han Bae, CEO
Maria Bae, *
Elizabeth Bae, *
Claudia Kye, *
▲ **EMP:** 300 **EST:** 1989
SALES (est): 9.96MM **Privately Held**
Web: www.atomicdenim.com

SIC: 7389 Sewing contractor

(P-16821)
EAGLE MED PCKG STRLIZATION INC
Also Called: Eagle Med Packg Sterilization
2921 Union Rd Ste A (93446-7316)
P.O. Box 1228 (93447-1228)
PHONE..............................805 238-7401
Doyle Timmons, Pr
EMP: 35 **EST:** 1992
SQ FT: 10,000
SALES (est): 4.99MM **Privately Held**
Web: www.eaglemed.com
SIC: 7389 3841 Packaging and labeling services; Surgical and medical instruments

(P-16822)
EDISON ENERGY LLC
2 Park Plz Ste 200 (92614-8569)
PHONE..............................949 491-1633
EMP: 189 **EST:** 2012
SALES (est): 5.57MM **Privately Held**
SIC: 7389 Business services, nec

(P-16823)
FACTER DIRECT LTD
4751 Wilshire Blvd Ste 140 (90010-3827)
PHONE..............................323 634-1999
Larry Keefer, Contrlr
EMP: 252
SALES (corp-wide): 9.8MM **Privately Held**
SIC: 7389 8742 Telemarketing services; Marketing consulting services
PA: Facter Direct Ltd
11500 W Olympic Blvd
Los Angeles CA
310 788-9000

(P-16824)
FEDEX SERVICES
5391 Rickenbacker Rd (90201-6439)
PHONE..............................323 881-3400
EMP: 80 **EST:** 2014
SALES (est): 162.97K **Privately Held**
SIC: 7389 4215 Courier or messenger service; Courier services, except by air

(P-16825)
FINANCIAL SVC CTRS COOP INC
924 Overland Ct (91773-1742)
PHONE..............................909 753-1213
EMP: 101
SALES (corp-wide): 1.38MM **Privately Held**
Web: www.fscc.com
SIC: 7389 Financial services
PA: Financial Service Centers Cooperative, Inc.
2855 E Guasti Rd Ste 202
Ontario CA
888 372-2669

(P-16826)
FLAGSHIP CREDIT ACCEPTANCE LLC
7525 Irvine Center Dr (92618-3066)
PHONE..............................949 748-7172
EMP: 113
Web: www.flagshipcredit.com
SIC: 7389 Financial services
PA: Flagship Credit Acceptance Llc
3 Christy Dr Ste 203
Chadds Ford PA

(P-16827)
FNTECH
3000 W Segerstrom Ave (92704-6526)
PHONE..............................714 429-7833

Jeremy Muir, *CEO*
EMP: 91 **EST:** 2010
SALES (est): 9.56MM **Privately Held**
Web: www.fntech.com
SIC: 7389 Decoration service for special
events

(P-16828)
FOREVER 21 LOGISTICS LLC
110 E 9th St Ste C910 (90079-5804)
PHONE...............................888 494-3837
◆ **EMP:** 399 **EST:** 2002
SALES (est): 9.35MM
SALES (corp-wide): 100.19K **Privately
Held**
SIC: 7389 Purchasing service
HQ: Forever 21 Retail, Inc.
110 E 9th St Ste C500
Los Angeles CA
323 343-9368

(P-16829)
FREEMAN EXPOSITIONS LLC
Also Called: Freeman
2170 S Towne Centre Pl Ste 100
(92806-6127)
PHONE...............................714 254-3400
Pattie Balding, *Mgr*
EMP: 200
SALES (corp-wide): 1.56B **Privately Held**
Web: www.freeman.com
SIC: 7389 Trade show arrangement
HQ: Freeman Expositions, Llc
1600 Viceroy Dr Ste 100
Dallas TX
214 445-1000

(P-16830)
FRESH GRILL LLC
111 E Garry Ave (92707-4201)
PHONE...............................714 444-2126
▲ **EMP:** 200 **EST:** 1996
SQ FT: 27,000
SALES (est): 22.45MM **Privately Held**
Web: www.freshgrillfoods.com
SIC: 7389 Packaging and labeling services

(P-16831)
GELFAND RENNERT &
FELDMAN LLP (PA)
1880 Century Park E Ste 1600
(90067-1661)
PHONE...............................310 553-1707
Marshall M Gelfand, *Mng Pt*
Tyson Beem, *Pt*
Todd Gelfand, *Pt*
EMP: 200 **EST:** 1967
SALES (est): 67.85K
SALES (corp-wide): 67.85K **Privately Held**
Web: www.grfllp.com
SIC: 7389 8721 8741 Legal and tax services
; Accounting, auditing, and bookkeeping;
Business management

(P-16832)
GENERAL WATER SYSTEMS
1525 E 6th St (92879-1716)
PHONE...............................951 278-8992
Tim Boylen, *Pr*
Tim Boylen, *CEO*
EMP: 17 **EST:** 2020
SALES (est): 1.25MM **Privately Held**
Web: www.gwslp.com
SIC: 7389 3585 3532 3589 Water softener
service; Air conditioning equipment,
complete; Feeders, ore and aggregate;
Water treatment equipment, industrial

(P-16833)
GLOBAL CUSTOMER
SERVICES INC
17373 Lilac St (92345-5162)
PHONE...............................760 995-7949
David Syfrig, *CEO*
Kevin Senart, *
Ernie Bernard, *
Alejandro Joffroy, *
EMP: 100 **EST:** 2021
SALES (est): 15MM
SALES (corp-wide): 214.75MM **Privately
Held**
Web: www.go-gcs.com
SIC: 7389 Flagging service (traffic control)
PA: Arizona Pipeline Company
17372 Lilac St
Hesperia CA
760 244-8212

(P-16834)
GLOBAL EXPRNCE
SPECIALISTS INC
Also Called: Ges
18504 Beach Blvd Unit 511 (92648-0915)
PHONE...............................619 498-6300
Tom Robins, *Mgr*
EMP: 166
Web: www.ges.com
SIC: 7389 Convention and show services
HQ: Global Experience Specialists, Inc.
7000 Lindell Rd
Las Vegas NV
702 515-5500

(P-16835)
GLOBAL LANGUAGE
SOLUTIONS LLC
19800 Macarthur Blvd (92612-2402)
PHONE...............................949 798-1400
EMP: 100 **EST:** 1994
SQ FT: 7,500
SALES (est): 7.74MM **Privately Held**
SIC: 7389 Translation services
PA: Welocalize, Inc.
15 W 37th St Fl 4
New York NY

(P-16836)
GOODWILL SRVING THE PPLE
STHER (PA)
Also Called: Links Sign Lngage Intrprting S
800 W Pacific Coast Hwy (90806-5243)
PHONE...............................562 435-3411
Janet Mccarthy, *CEO*
EMP: 100 **EST:** 1939
SQ FT: 80,000
SALES (est): 32.29MM
SALES (corp-wide): 32.29MM **Privately
Held**
Web: www.linksinterpreting.com
SIC: 7389 8331 5932 Translation services;
Job training and related services; Used
merchandise stores

(P-16837)
GRANDALL DISTRIBUTING CO
INC
321 El Bonito Ave (91204-2707)
PHONE...............................818 242-6640
Jose M Granda, *Pr*
Melisa J Granda, *
Joseph J Granda, *
Jessica J Granda, *
EMP: 30 **EST:** 1966
SQ FT: 18,000
SALES (est): 2.01MM **Privately Held**
Web: www.grandall.com

SIC: 7389 2844 Cosmetic kits, assembling
and packaging; Cosmetic preparations

(P-16838)
HCT PACKAGING INC (PA)
Also Called: Hct Group
2800 28th St Ste 240 (90405-6214)
PHONE...............................310 260-7680
Tim Thorpe, *Pr*
◆ **EMP:** 125 **EST:** 1996
SQ FT: 1,500
SALES (est): 17.17MM
SALES (corp-wide): 17.17MM **Privately
Held**
Web: www.hctgroup.com
SIC: 7389 Packaging and labeling services

(P-16839)
HERITAGE AUCTIONS INC
9478 W Olympic Blvd (90212-4246)
PHONE...............................310 300-8390
Greg Rohan, *Pr*
EMP: 100 **EST:** 2010
SALES (est): 4.57MM **Privately Held**
SIC: 7389 Auctioneers, fee basis

(P-16840)
HIGH TIMES PRODUCTIONS INC
10990 Wilshire Blvd (90024-3913)
PHONE...............................844 933-3287
EMP: 204 **EST:** 1991
SALES (est): 1.02MM **Privately Held**
Web: ir.hightimes.com
SIC: 7389 Advertising, promotional, and
trade show services

(P-16841)
HOLLYWOOD SPORTS PARK
LLC
Also Called: Giant Sportz Paintball Park
9030 Somerset Blvd (90706-3402)
PHONE...............................562 867-9600
Dennis Bukowski, *Managing Member*
▲ **EMP:** 100 **EST:** 1999
SQ FT: 20,000
SALES (est): 7.28MM **Privately Held**
Web: www.hollywoodsports.com
SIC: 7389 Personal service agents, brokers,
and bureaus

(P-16842)
HYDROPROCESSING
ASSOCIATES LLC
Also Called: Hpa-USA
19122 S Santa Fe Ave (90221-5910)
PHONE...............................310 667-6456
Kees Ooms, *Brnch Mgr*
EMP: 81
SALES (corp-wide): 94.66MM **Privately
Held**
Web: www.swatservice.com
SIC: 7389 Petroleum refinery inspection
service
HQ: Hydroprocessing Associates, Llc
40492 Cannon Rd
Gonzales LA

(P-16843)
HYPER-TECH LLC
2993 Yucca Dr (93012-9252)
PHONE...............................805 988-2000
Mark Grant, *Pt*
Gaston M Grant, *Pt*
EMP: 18 **EST:** 2008
SALES (est): 1.18MM **Privately Held**
SIC: 7389 3499 Design, commercial and
industrial; Machine bases, metal

(P-16844)
INCIRCLE LLC
44000 Winchester Rd (92590-2578)
PHONE...............................800 843-7477
EMP: 597 **EST:** 2018
SALES (est): 468.79K
SALES (corp-wide): 539.81MM **Privately
Held**
SIC: 7389 Business Activities at Non-
Commercial Site
PA: Fff Enterprises, Inc.
44000 Winchester Rd
Temecula CA
951 296-2500

(P-16845)
INDUSTRIAL STITCHTECH INC
520 Library St (91340-2524)
PHONE...............................818 361-6319
Ed Perez, *Pr*
EMP: 150 **EST:** 1996
SQ FT: 35,000
SALES (est): 3.52MM **Privately Held**
Web: www.industrialstitchtech.com
SIC: 7389 Sewing contractor

(P-16846)
INGENUITY STUDIOS INTL INC
941 N Highland Ave 2nd Fl (90038-2412)
PHONE...............................323 460-6096
David Lebensfeld, *CEO*
EMP: 165 **EST:** 2004
SALES (est): 6.9MM **Privately Held**
Web: www.ingenuitystudios.com
SIC: 7389 Recording studio, noncommercial
records

(P-16847)
INNOVATION SPECIALTIES
Also Called: Clockparts
11869 Teale St Ste 302 (90230-7701)
PHONE...............................888 827-2387
EMP: 198
SALES (corp-wide): 28.37MM **Privately
Held**
Web: www.clockparts.com
SIC: 7389 Product endorsement service
PA: Innovation Specialties
11869 Teale St
Culver City CA
310 398-8116

(P-16848)
INSPECTORATE AMERICA CORP
Also Called: INSPECTORATE AMERICA
CORPORATION
3401 Jack Northrop Ave (90250-4428)
PHONE...............................800 424-0099
EMP: 148
SALES (corp-wide): 247.19MM **Privately
Held**
Web: www.bvna.com
SIC: 7389 Petroleum refinery inspection
service
HQ: Bureau Veritas Commodities And
Trade, Inc.
1300 Hercules Ave Ste 105
Houston TX
713 944-2000

(P-16849)
INTERIOR SPECIALISTS INC
15822 Bernardo Center Dr Ste 1
(92127-2362)
PHONE...............................909 983-5386
EMP: 300
SALES (corp-wide): 499.75MM **Privately
Held**
Web: www.interiorlogicgroup.com
SIC: 7389 Interior designer

▲ = Import ▼ = Export
◆ = Import/Export

HQ: Interior Specialists, Inc.
1630 Faraday Ave
Carlsbad CA
760 929-6700

(P-16850)
IPAYMENT INC
3325 Wilshire Blvd Ste 535 (90010-1703)
PHONE..............................213 387-1353
Guillermo Ramirez, *Brnch Mgr*
EMP: 285
SALES (corp-wide): 239.18MM **Privately Held**
Web: www.paysafe.com
SIC: 7389 Credit card service
HQ: Ipayment, Inc.
30721 Russell Ranch Rd # 200
Westlake Village CA
212 802-7200

(P-16851)
ISOVAC ENGINEERING INC
614 Justin Ave (91201-2327)
PHONE..............................818 552-6200
George R Neff, *Pr*
EMP: 25 EST: 1957
SALES (est): 2.44MM **Privately Held**
Web: www.isovac.com
SIC: 7389 3825 3829 3826 Inspection and testing services; Semiconductor test equipment; Measuring and controlling devices, nec; Analytical instruments

(P-16852)
JENCO PRODUCTIONS INC (PA)
401 S J St (92410-2605)
PHONE..............................909 381-9453
Jennifer Imbriani, *Pr*
◆ EMP: 160 EST: 1995
SQ FT: 50,000
SALES (est): 24.82MM
SALES (corp-wide): 24.82MM **Privately Held**
Web: www.jencoproductions.com
SIC: 7389 2789 2653 7331 Packaging and labeling services; Bookbinding and related work; Boxes, corrugated: made from purchased materials; Mailing service

(P-16853)
KIM CHONG
Also Called: Union 76
2105 E 25th St (90058-1125)
PHONE..............................323 581-4700
Chong Kim, *Owner*
EMP: 20 EST: 1987
SQ FT: 10,300
SALES (est): 737.77K **Privately Held**
SIC: 7389 2395 Embroidery advertising; Embroidery products, except Schiffli machine

(P-16854)
KIRSCHENMAN ENTERPRISES SLS LP
12826 Edison Hwy (93220)
P.O. Box 27 (93220-0027)
PHONE..............................661 366-5736
EMP: 120 EST: 2009
SQ FT: 5,000
SALES (est): 100MM **Privately Held**
Web: www.kirschenman.com
SIC: 7389 Brokers, business: buying and selling business enterprises

(P-16855)
KOOS MANUFACTURING INC
Also Called: Big Star
2741 Seminole Ave (90280-5550)
PHONE..............................323 249-1000

U Yul Ku, *CEO*
John Hur, *
Nathan Aroonprapun, *
▲ EMP: 639 EST: 1985
SQ FT: 180,000
SALES (est): 39.61MM **Privately Held**
Web: www.koos.com
SIC: 7389 2325 2339 2369 Sewing contractor; Jeans: men's, youths', and boys' ; Jeans: women's, misses', and juniors'; Jeans: girls', children's, and infants'

(P-16856)
KPWR RADIO LLC
9550 Firestone Blvd Ste 105 (90241-5560)
PHONE..............................562 745-2300
Alex Meruelo, *Managing Member*
EMP: 150 EST: 2017
SALES (est): 9.51MM
SALES (corp-wide): 10.68MM **Privately Held**
SIC: 7389 Music and broadcasting services
PA: Meruelo Group Llc
9550 Firestone Blvd # 105
Downey CA
562 745-2300

(P-16857)
KUKDONG APPAREL AMERICA INC
17100 Pioneer Blvd Ste 230 (90701-2776)
PHONE..............................562 403-0044
Sang Ki Pyon, *CEO*
Caz Eyun, *CFO*
▲ EMP: 20 EST: 1999
SQ FT: 5,000
SALES (est): 9.06MM **Privately Held**
Web: www.kd.co.kr
SIC: 7389 2386 Apparel designers, commercial; Garments, leather
PA: Kukdong Corporation
6, 7/F
Seoul

(P-16858)
LA JOLLA GROUP INC (PA)
Also Called: Ljg
14350 Myford Rd (92606-1002)
PHONE..............................949 428-2800
Michael Pratt, *CEO*
▲ EMP: 426 EST: 2007
SALES (est): 50.18MM
SALES (corp-wide): 50.18MM **Privately Held**
Web: www.lajollagroup.com
SIC: 7389 6794 2326 Apparel designers, commercial; Copyright buying and licensing ; Men's and boy's work clothing

(P-16859)
LAKEWOOD PARK HEALTH CTR INC (PA)
12023 Lakewood Blvd (90242-2699)
PHONE..............................562 869-0978
Daniel Zilafro, *Pr*
EMP: 285 EST: 1985
SALES (est): 4.94MM **Privately Held**
Web: www.lwhealthcare.com
SIC: 7389 Personal service agents, brokers, and bureaus

(P-16860)
LARK INDUSTRIES INC (DH)
Also Called: Residential Design Services
18565 Jamboree Rd Ste 125 (92612-2543)
PHONE..............................714 701-4200
Kendall Hoyd, *Pr*
Kip Cruze, *
EMP: 61 EST: 1988
SALES (est): 98.53MM

SALES (corp-wide): 499.77MM **Privately Held**
Web: www.interiorlogicgroup.com
SIC: 7389 3281 Interior design services; Cut stone and stone products
HQ: Interior Logic Group, Inc.
18565 Jamboree Rd Ste 125
Irvine CA
800 959-8333

(P-16861)
LAUNDRY DESIGN LLC
4079 Redwood Ave Ste A (90066-5143)
PHONE..............................323 933-2800
Troy Moore, *Managing Member*
EMP: 145 EST: 2005
SALES (est): 988.21K **Privately Held**
Web: www.laundry.studio
SIC: 7389 Design, commercial and industrial

(P-16862)
LINDSEY & SONS
Also Called: Flo-CHI
1226 E 76th St (90001-2416)
PHONE..............................657 306-5369
Andre Lindsey Senior, *Pr*
EMP: 100 EST: 2021
SALES (est): 1.11MM **Privately Held**
SIC: 7389 Business Activities at Non-Commercial Site

(P-16863)
LIVE NATION ENTERTAINMENT INC (PA)
Also Called: Live Nation
9348 Civic Center Dr Lbby (90210-3642)
PHONE..............................310 867-7000
Michael Rapino, *Pr*
Greg Maffei, *Non-Executive Chairman of the Board*
Joe Berchtold, *Pr*
Brian Capo, *CAO*
▲ EMP: 200 EST: 2005
SALES (est): 16.68B **Publicly Held**
Web: www.livenationentertainment.com
SIC: 7389 7922 7941 Promoters of shows and exhibitions; Entertainment promotion; Sports clubs, managers, and promoters

(P-16864)
LOS ANGELES UNIFIED SCHOOL DST
Also Called: L A U S D
8525 Rex Rd (90660-6702)
PHONE..............................562 654-9007
Marc Monforte, *Brnch Mgr*
EMP: 105
SALES (corp-wide): 9.38B **Privately Held**
Web: www.laallcityband.com
SIC: 7389 Purchasing service
PA: Los Angeles Unified School District
333 S Beaudry Ave Ste 209
Los Angeles CA
213 241-1000

(P-16865)
MABIE MARKETING GROUP INC
Also Called: California Marketing
8352 Clairemont Mesa Blvd (92111-1302)
P.O. Box 33708 (92163-3708)
PHONE..............................858 279-5585
John Mabie, *Pr*
Ramyar Ravansari, *
EMP: 200 EST: 1984
SALES (est): 15.5MM **Privately Held**
Web: www.calmarketinggroup.com
SIC: 7389 Telemarketing services

(P-16866)
MACRO-PRO INC (PA)
Also Called: Micro-Pro Microfilming Svcs
2400 Grand Ave (90815-1762)
P.O. Box 90459 (90809-0459)
PHONE..............................562 595-0900
Patty Waldeck, *Pr*
EMP: 140 EST: 1988
SQ FT: 24,000
SALES (est): 8.35MM
SALES (corp-wide): 8.35MM **Privately Held**
Web: www.macropro.com
SIC: 7389 7334 Legal and tax services; Photocopying and duplicating services

(P-16867)
MARINER SYSTEMS INC (PA)
114 C Ave (92118-1435)
PHONE..............................305 266-7255
Carlos M Collazo, *Pr*
Carlos M Collazo, *Ch Bd*
Neil Park, *
EMP: 50 EST: 1982
SALES (est): 2.37MM
SALES (corp-wide): 2.37MM **Privately Held**
Web: www.carlocksmithcoronado.com
SIC: 7389 7374 7372 7371 Telephone services; Data processing service; Prepackaged software; Custom computer programming services

(P-16868)
MATH HOLDINGS INC (PA)
Also Called: Motivtnal Flfilment Lgstics Sv
15820 Euclid Ave (91708-9162)
PHONE..............................909 517-2200
▲ EMP: 229 EST: 1977
SQ FT: 300,000
SALES (est): 47.01MM **Privately Held**
Web: www.mfals.com
SIC: 7389 8748 4225 Telemarketing services ; Business consulting, nec; General warehousing and storage

(P-16869)
MB COATINGS INC
1540 S Lewis St (92805-6423)
PHONE..............................714 625-2118
Michael Bartle, *Pr*
Amanda Bartle, *
EMP: 80 EST: 1996
SALES (est): 4.85MM **Privately Held**
Web: www.mbcoatings.com
SIC: 7389 Hand painting, textile

(P-16870)
MEDHOLDINGS OF NEWNAN LLC
Also Called: Capitol Records
1750 Vine St (90028-5209)
PHONE..............................213 462-6252
EMP: 1500
SIC: 7389 8999 Music and broadcasting services; Music arranging and composing

(P-16871)
MEDUSIND SOLUTIONS INC (PA)
31103 Rancho Viejo Rd Ste 2150 (92675-1759)
PHONE..............................949 240-8895
Rajiv Sahney, *Ch*
Vipul Bansal, *
Robert Beck, *
Dhiren Kapadia, *
Kranti Munje, *
EMP: 80 EST: 2002
SALES (est): 7.26MM
SALES (corp-wide): 7.26MM **Privately Held**

Web: www.medusind.com
SIC: **7389** Personal service agents, brokers, and bureaus

(P-16872)
MEGA APPRAISERS INC
14724 Ventura Blvd Ste 800 (91403-3501)
PHONE...............................818 246-7370
Levon Hairapetian, *Pr*
EMP: 600 **EST:** 2003
SALES (est): 7.68MM **Privately Held**
Web: www.megaappraisers.com
SIC: **7389** Appraisers, except real estate

(P-16873)
MERCHANT OF TENNIS INC
1625 Proforma Ave (91761-7607)
PHONE...............................909 923-3388
Larry Khemlani, *Prin*
EMP: 663
SALES (corp-wide): 491.1MM **Privately Held**
Web: www.merchantoftennis.com
SIC: **7389** Packaging and labeling services
HQ: The Merchant Of Tennis Inc
8737 Wilshire Blvd
Beverly Hills CA
310 228-4000

(P-16874)
MERIBEAR PRODUCTIONS INC
Also Called: Meredith Baer & Associates
4100 Ardmore Ave (90280-3246)
PHONE...............................310 204-5353
Meridith Baer, *Pr*
▲ **EMP:** 90 **EST:** 1980
SQ FT: 55,000
SALES (est): 14.97MM **Privately Held**
Web: www.meridithbaer.com
SIC: **7389** Interior design services

(P-16875)
MERICAL LLC
447 W Freedom Ave (92865-2644)
PHONE...............................714 685-0977
Jeffrey Stallings, *Brnch Mgr*
EMP: 130
SALES (corp-wide): 200.29MM **Privately Held**
Web: www.merical.com
SIC: **7389** Packaging and labeling services
HQ: Merical, Llc
2995 E Miraloma Ave
Anaheim CA
714 238-7225

(P-16876)
MERICAL LLC
Also Called: Merical/Vita-Pak
233 E Bristol Ln (92865-2715)
PHONE...............................714 283-9551
EMP: 335
SALES (corp-wide): 200.29MM **Privately Held**
Web: www.merical.com
SIC: **7389** Packaging and labeling services
HQ: Merical, Llc
2995 E Miraloma Ave
Anaheim CA
714 238-7225

(P-16877)
MERICAL LLC
445 W Freedom Ave (92865-2644)
PHONE...............................714 238-7225
Roshni Patel, *Mgr*
EMP: 117
SALES (corp-wide): 200.29MM **Privately Held**
Web: www.merical.com

SIC: **7389** Packaging and labeling services
HQ: Merical, Llc
2995 E Miraloma Ave
Anaheim CA
714 238-7225

(P-16878)
METROPOLITAN IMPORTS LLC
16311 Ventura Blvd (91436-2124)
PHONE...............................646 980-5343
Starr King Williams Iii, *Managing Member*
EMP: 144 **EST:** 2014
SALES (est): 52MM **Privately Held**
Web: www.metropolitanimports.com
SIC: **7389 7999** Yacht brokers; Pleasure boat rental

(P-16879)
MKTG INC
Also Called: MKTG, INC.
5800 Bristol Pkwy Ste 500 (90230-6899)
PHONE...............................310 972-7900
Patty Hubbard, *Brnch Mgr*
EMP: 438
Web: www.mktg.com
SIC: **7389** Advertising, promotional, and trade show services
HQ: 'mktg, Inc.'
32 Avenue Of The Americas # 1
New York NY

(P-16880)
MODERN DEV CO A LTD PARTNR
Also Called: Paramount Swap Meet
7900 All America City Way (90723-3400)
PHONE...............................949 646-6400
Darren Kurkowski, *Brnch Mgr*
EMP: 84
SALES (corp-wide): 9.58MM **Privately Held**
Web: www.paramountswap.com
SIC: **7389** Flea market
PA: Modern Development Co, A Limited Partnership
496 N Coast Hwy Ste A
Laguna Beach CA
949 646-6400

(P-16881)
MONTEBELLO UNIFIED SCHOOL DST
831 Perry Ave (90640-2429)
PHONE...............................323 440-2899
EMP: 90
SALES (corp-wide): 539.05MM **Privately Held**
Web: www.montebello.k12.ca.us
SIC: **7389** Business Activities at Non-Commercial Site
PA: Montebello Unified School District
123 S Montebello Blvd
Montebello CA
323 887-7900

(P-16882)
MVENTIX INC (PA)
Also Called: Mventix
21600 Oxnard St Ste 1700 (91367-4972)
PHONE...............................818 337-3747
Kristian Beloff, *CEO*
Vesselin Kavrakov, *Research & Development*
Pavel Monev, *
EMP: 70 **EST:** 2004
SQ FT: 6,606
SALES (est): 8.91MM
SALES (corp-wide): 8.91MM **Privately Held**
Web: www.mventix.com

SIC: **7389 8732 7372** Advertising, promotional, and trade show services; Survey service: marketing, location, etc.; Business oriented computer software

(P-16883)
N PHILANTHROPY LLC
1132 E 12th St (90021-2206)
PHONE...............................213 278-0754
Yvonne Niami, *Managing Member*
EMP: 18 **EST:** 2013
SALES (est): 1.75MM **Privately Held**
SIC: **7389 2339** Textile and apparel services; Athletic clothing: women's, misses', and juniors'

(P-16884)
NETWORK TELEPHONE SERVICES INC (PA)
Also Called: N T S
21135 Erwin St (91367-3713)
PHONE...............................800 742-5687
Joseph Preston, *CEO*
Daniel Coleman, *
EMP: 87 **EST:** 1988
SQ FT: 70,000
SALES (est): 21.82MM
SALES (corp-wide): 21.82MM **Privately Held**
Web: www.nts.net
SIC: **7389 4813 7374** Telephone services; Internet connectivity services; Data processing and preparation

(P-16885)
NEW CREW PRODUCTION CORP
1100 W 135th St (90247-1919)
PHONE...............................323 234-8880
Kris Park, *Pr*
Joseph Park, *
▲ **EMP:** 110 **EST:** 2002
SALES (est): 2.01MM **Privately Held**
Web: www.newcrewproductioncorp.com
SIC: **7389** Sewing contractor

(P-16886)
NEWPORT DIVERSIFIED INC
Santa Fe Springs Swap Meet
13963 Alondra Blvd (90670-5814)
PHONE...............................562 921-4359
EMP: 101
SQ FT: 10,846
SALES (corp-wide): 14.72MM **Privately Held**
Web: www.sfsswapmeet.com
SIC: **7389 5932** Flea market; Used merchandise stores
PA: Newport Diversified, Inc.
4695 Macarthur Ct # 1420
Newport Beach CA
949 851-1355

(P-16887)
NEWPORT DIVERSIFIED INC
Also Called: Parkway Bowl
1286 Fletcher Pkwy (92020-1826)
PHONE...............................619 448-4111
Tony Casarrubia, *Mgr*
EMP: 101
SALES (corp-wide): 14.72MM **Privately Held**
Web: www.nd-inc.com
SIC: **7389 7933 7996** Flea market; Bowling centers; Amusement parks
PA: Newport Diversified, Inc.
4695 Macarthur Ct # 1420
Newport Beach CA
949 851-1355

(P-16888)
NOR-CAL BEVERAGE CO INC
Also Called: Norcal Beverage Co
1226 N Olive St (92801-2543)
PHONE...............................714 526-8600
William Mcfarland, *Mgr*
EMP: 69
SALES (corp-wide): 231.77MM **Privately Held**
Web: www.ncbev.com
SIC: **7389 2033** Packaging and labeling services; Canned fruits and specialties
PA: Nor-Cal Beverage Co., Inc.
2150 Stone Blvd
West Sacramento CA
916 372-0600

(P-16889)
NSI GROUP LLC (PA)
Also Called: Nsi - Natural Sourcing Intl
17031 Ventura Blvd (91316-4128)
PHONE...............................818 639-8335
EMP: 19 **EST:** 2013
SQ FT: 7,000
SALES (est): 6.64MM
SALES (corp-wide): 6.64MM **Privately Held**
Web: www.nsifood.com
SIC: **7389 2034** Packaging and labeling services; Dried and dehydrated fruits

(P-16890)
OCEANX LLC (PA)
100 N Pacific Coast Hwy Ste 1500 (90245)
PHONE...............................310 774-4088
Steve Adams, *Managing Member*
EMP: 98 **EST:** 2015
SALES (est): 39.85MM
SALES (corp-wide): 39.85MM **Privately Held**
Web: www.oceanx.com
SIC: **7389 4731** Subscription fulfillment services: magazine, newspaper, etc.; Freight transportation arrangement

(P-16891)
OCS AMERICA INC (DH)
Also Called: Ocs Bookstore
22912 Lockness Ave (90501-5117)
PHONE...............................310 417-0650
Yutaka Otake, *Ch Bd*
Susan Onuman, *
Takuya Hiraiwa, *
▲ **EMP:** 39 **EST:** 1972
SALES (est): 11.29MM **Privately Held**
Web: www.ocs-india.com
SIC: **7389 5192 2711 5942** Courier or messenger service; Newspapers; Newspapers: publishing only, not printed on site; Books, foreign
HQ: Overseas Courier Service Co., Ltd.
3-9-27, Tatsumi
Koto-Ku TKY

(P-16892)
OEOE CORP
927 S Grand View St # 10 (90006-2176)
PHONE...............................213 387-0933
Young Hawk Oh, *Brnch Mgr*
EMP: 122
SALES (corp-wide): 342.2K **Privately Held**
SIC: **7389** Personal service agents, brokers, and bureaus
PA: Oeoe Corp
1740 S Los Angeles St
Los Angeles CA

(P-16893)
ONEIL DIGITAL SOLUTIONS LLC
12655 Beatrice St (90066-7300)

PHONE..............................310 448-6407
David Woodley, Contrlr
EMP: 201
SALES (corp-wide): 335.64MM **Privately Held**
Web: www.oneildigitalsolutions.com
SIC: 7389 2752 5045 Mailbox rental and related service; Commercial printing, lithographic; Computer software
HQ: O'neil Digital Solutions, Llc
3100 E Plano Pkwy
Plano TX
972 881-1282

(P-16894)
ONTARIO CONVENTION CENTER CORP
Also Called: Smg Management Facility
2000 E Convention Center Way (91764-5633)
PHONE..............................909 937-3000
Dick Walsh, Mayor
Michael K Krouse, CEO
EMP: 328 **EST:** 1995
SQ FT: 225,000
SALES (est): 3.3MM
SALES (corp-wide): 461.59MM **Privately Held**
Web: www.gocvb.org
SIC: 7389 Convention and show services
PA: City Of Ontario
303 E B St
Ontario CA
909 395-2012

(P-16895)
ORANGE COAST TITLE COMPANY (PA)
1551 N Tustin Ave Ste 300 (92705-8638)
P.O. Box 11825 (92711-1825)
PHONE..............................714 558-2836
Mike Kaluger, Pr
EMP: 100 **EST:** 1973
SQ FT: 24,000
SALES (est): 106.01MM **Privately Held**
Web: www.octitle.com
SIC: 7389 6361 6541 Personal service agents, brokers, and bureaus; Title insurance; Title and trust companies

(P-16896)
ORANGE COURIER INC
Also Called: Asbury
15300 Desman Rd (90638-5762)
P.O. Box 5308 (92704-0308)
PHONE..............................714 384-3600
Evell T Stanley, Pr
▲ **EMP:** 300 **EST:** 1992
SALES (est): 28.43MM **Privately Held**
Web: www.orangecourier.com
SIC: 7389 4213 4225 Courier or messenger service; Trucking, except local; General warehousing and storage

(P-16897)
PACIFIC ASIAN ENTERPRISES INC (PA)
Also Called: Nordhavn Yachts
25001 Dana Dr (92629-3005)
P.O. Box 874 (92629-0874)
PHONE..............................949 496-4848
Dan Streech, Pr
Jeffrey Leishman, Sec
James Leishman, CFO
◆ **EMP:** 30 **EST:** 1978
SQ FT: 3,500
SALES (est): 8.01MM
SALES (corp-wide): 8.01MM **Privately Held**
Web: www.nordhavn.com

SIC: 7389 3732 Yacht brokers; Yachts, building and repairing

(P-16898)
PAR WESTERN LINE CONTRS LLC
11276 5th St Ste 100 (91730-0922)
PHONE..............................760 737-0925
Jim Stapp, Pr
Irene Anderson, CTRL*
Travis Walser, *
Kody Kilshaw, *
EMP: 550 **EST:** 2000
SQ FT: 800
SALES (est): 41.48MM
SALES (corp-wide): 17.07B **Publicly Held**
Web: www.parwlc.com
SIC: 7389 8711 1731 1623 Mapmaking services; Engineering services; General electrical contractor; Oil and gas line and compressor station construction
PA: Quanta Services, Inc.
2727 North Loop W Ste 100
Houston TX
713 629-7600

(P-16899)
PARADIGM INDUSTRIES INC
2522 E 37th St (90058-1725)
PHONE..............................310 965-1900
William Jun, CEO
Chu Kim, *
▲ **EMP:** 80 **EST:** 2000
SALES (est): 2.49MM **Privately Held**
Web: www.paradigmindustries.net
SIC: 7389 Textile and apparel services

(P-16900)
PARTNERS CAPITAL GROUP INC (PA)
Also Called: Partners Capital Group
201 Sandpointe Ave Ste 500 (92707-5778)
PHONE..............................949 916-3900
Mark Davin, CEO
EMP: 80 **EST:** 2005
SQ FT: 25,000
SALES (est): 29.42MM **Privately Held**
Web: www.partnerscapitalgrp.com
SIC: 7389 Financial services

(P-16901)
PASADENA CENTER OPERATING CO
Also Called: Pasadena Convention Center
300 E Green St (91101-2399)
PHONE..............................626 795-9311
Michael Ross, CEO
EMP: 116 **EST:** 1973
SQ FT: 32,000
SALES (est): 24.24MM **Privately Held**
Web: www.visitpasadena.com
SIC: 7389 Convention and show services

(P-16902)
PERFECT IMPRESSION INC
Also Called: Perfect Banner, The
27111 Aliso Creek Rd Ste 145 (92656-3367)
PHONE..............................949 305-0797
Suzie Abrahams, Pr
EMP: 28 **EST:** 2008
SALES (est): 2.28MM **Privately Held**
Web: www.theperfectimpression.com
SIC: 7389 2395 Embroidery advertising; Embroidery and art needlework

(P-16903)
PHONE WARE INC
8902 Activity Rd Ste A (92126-4471)

PHONE..............................858 530-8550
William J Nassir, Pr
Hazel Nassir, *
EMP: 366 **EST:** 1974
SQ FT: 20,000
SALES (est): 23.72MM **Privately Held**
Web: www.phonewareinc.com
SIC: 7389 8742 Telemarketing services; Marketing consulting services

(P-16904)
PIONEER THEATRES INC
Also Called: Roadium Open Air Market
2500 Redondo Beach Blvd (90504-1529)
PHONE..............................310 532-8183
William Fleischman, Pr
William Warnick, *
EMP: 110 **EST:** 1949
SQ FT: 3,000
SALES (est): 4.58MM **Privately Held**
Web: www.roadium.com
SIC: 7389 5431 Flea market; Fruit and vegetable markets

(P-16905)
PIXAR
500 N Buena Vista St (91505-3209)
PHONE..............................510 922-4075
Jody B Silverman, Brnch Mgr
EMP: 208
SALES (corp-wide): 88.9B **Publicly Held**
Web: www.pixar.com
SIC: 7389 Business Activities at Non-Commercial Site
HQ: Pixar
1200 Park Ave
Emeryville CA
510 922-3000

(P-16906)
PML INC
Also Called: Precision Measurement Labs
201 W Beach Ave (90302-2902)
PHONE..............................310 671-4345
David Tolin, Pr
EMP: 22 **EST:** 1986
SQ FT: 3,900
SALES (est): 556.13K **Privately Held**
Web: www.yourcovers.com
SIC: 7389 3543 Inspection and testing services; Industrial patterns

(P-16907)
PRODUCTIVE PLAYHOUSE INC (PA)
25231 Paseo De Alicia Ste 205 (92653-4645)
PHONE..............................323 250-3445
Harry Ralston, CEO
EMP: 268 **EST:** 2009
SALES (est): 9.62MM
SALES (corp-wide): 9.62MM **Privately Held**
Web: www.productiveplayhouse.com
SIC: 7389 Translation services

(P-16908)
PROLOGIC RDMPTION SLUTIONS INC (PA)
2121 Rosecrans Ave (90245-4743)
PHONE..............................310 322-7774
William Atkinson, CEO
Paul Cooley, Pr
John Mccurry, Ex VP
Robb Warwick, CFO
Kelly Fuller, CCO
EMP: 700 **EST:** 2008
SALES (est): 36.8MM
SALES (corp-wide): 36.8MM **Privately Held**

SIC: 7389 Coupon redemption service

(P-16909)
PROMPT DELIVERY INC
Also Called: Southern California Messenger
5757 Wilshire Blvd Ph 3 (90036-3681)
PHONE..............................858 549-8000
Mike Dysland, Mgr
EMP: 100
SIC: 7389 4212 Courier or messenger service; Delivery service, vehicular
PA: Prompt Delivery, Inc.
5757 Wilshire Blvd # 210
Los Angeles CA

(P-16910)
PUFF GLOBAL INC
Also Called: Puff Candy,
402 W Broadway Ste 400 (92101-3554)
PHONE..............................619 520-3499
David Soria, CEO
▲ **EMP:** 80 **EST:** 2013
SALES (est): 2.72MM **Privately Held**
SIC: 7389 Business Activities at Non-Commercial Site

(P-16911)
QOLOGY DIRECT LLC
Also Called: Centerfield Media
12130 Millennium Ste 600 (90094-2819)
PHONE..............................310 341-4420
Brett Cravatt, Pr
Jason Cohen, Pr
EMP: 170 **EST:** 2012
SQ FT: 90,000
SALES (est): 10.08MM
SALES (corp-wide): 60.59MM **Privately Held**
Web: www.centerfield.com
SIC: 7389 Telephone services
HQ: Qology Direct Holdings, Inc.
12130 Millennium Ste 600
Los Angeles CA

(P-16912)
R G CANNING ENTERPRISES INC
4515 E 59th Pl (90270-3201)
PHONE..............................323 560-7469
Richard G Canning, Pr
Charles R Canning, *
EMP: 215 **EST:** 1955
SQ FT: 50,000
SALES (est): 4.96MM **Privately Held**
Web: www.rgcshows.com
SIC: 7389 Promoters of shows and exhibitions

(P-16913)
REASON FOUNDATION
5737 Mesmer Ave (90230-6316)
PHONE..............................310 391-2245
David Nott, Pr
Mike Alissi, *
EMP: 35 **EST:** 1968
SQ FT: 6,300
SALES (est): 15.23MM **Privately Held**
Web: www.reason.org
SIC: 7389 2741 2721 Speakers' bureau; Newsletter publishing; Magazines: publishing and printing

(P-16914)
REGUS BUSINESS CENTRE LLC
Also Called: Plaza Tower 1
600 Anton Blvd Ste 1100 (92626-7100)
PHONE..............................714 371-4000
Karen Barbeau, Mgr
EMP: 212
SALES (corp-wide): 3.31B **Privately Held**

PRODUCTS & SVCS

Web: www.regus.com
SIC: 7389 Office facilities and secretarial service rental
HQ: Regus Business Centre Llc
15455 Dallas Pkwy Ste 600
Addison TX
972 361-8100

(P-16915)
RGIS LLC
Also Called: Rgis, Llc
1937 W Chapman Ave (92868-2632)
PHONE..................................714 938-0663
EMP: 133
SALES (corp-wide): 156.24MM **Privately Held**
Web: www.rgis.com
SIC: 7389 Inventory computing service
PA: Wis Ivs, Llc
2000 Taylor Rd
Auburn Hills MI
248 221-4000

(P-16916)
RGIS LLC
Also Called: Rgis, Llc
365 S Rancho Santa Fe Rd Ste 103
(92078-2338)
PHONE..................................760 736-9241
EMP: 165
SALES (corp-wide): 156.24MM **Privately Held**
Web: www.rgis.com
SIC: 7389 Inventory computing service
PA: Wis Ivs, Llc
2000 Taylor Rd
Auburn Hills MI
248 221-4000

(P-16917)
RGN-SAN DIEGO I LLC
350 10th Ave Ste 1000 (92101-8705)
PHONE..................................619 344-2500
EMP: 207
SALES (corp-wide): 3.31B **Privately Held**
SIC: 7389 Office facilities and secretarial service rental
HQ: Diego I Rgn-San Llc
15305 Dallas Pkwy Ste 400
Addison TX
972 361-8100

(P-16918)
ROBERTS CONTAINER CORPORATION
Also Called: Roberts Cosmetics and Cntrs
9131 Oakdale Ave Ste 110 (91311-6503)
PHONE..................................818 727-1700
Jacquelyn Irene Medina, *CEO*
◆ EMP: 22 EST: 1986
SQ FT: 28,000
SALES (est): 2.56MM **Privately Held**
Web: www.robertsbeauty.com
SIC: 7389 2844 Cosmetic kits, assembling and packaging; Bath salts

(P-16919)
ROSE & SHORE INC
5151 Alcoa Ave (90058-3715)
P.O. Box 58225 (90058-0225)
PHONE..................................323 826-2144
Irwin Miller, *Pr*
Carol Miller, *
EMP: 320 EST: 1968
SQ FT: 60,000
SALES (est): 25.22MM **Privately Held**
Web: www.roseandshore.com
SIC: 7389 5147 Packaging and labeling services; Meats, cured or smoked

(P-16920)
RVL PACKAGING INC
31330 Oak Crest Dr (91361-4632)
PHONE..................................818 735-5000
▼ EMP: 200
SIC: 7389 2396 2241 Packaging and labeling services; Automotive and apparel trimmings; Narrow fabric mills

(P-16921)
SAN DEGO CNVNTION CTR CORP INC (PA)
Also Called: Convention Center
111 W Harbor Dr (92101-7822)
PHONE..................................619 782-4388
Clifford R Rippetoe, *CEO*
Mardeen Mattix, *
▲ EMP: 281 EST: 1984
SALES (est): 50.5MM
SALES (corp-wide): 50.5MM **Privately Held**
Web: www.visitsandiego.com
SIC: 7389 Convention and show services

(P-16922)
SAN MNUEL BAND MISSION INDIANS
Also Called: San Manuel Fire Dept
26540 Indian Service Rd (92346-1714)
PHONE..................................909 864-6928
EMP: 118
Web: www.sanmanuel-nsn.gov
SIC: 7389 Fire protection service other than forestry or public
PA: San Manuel Band Of Mission Indians
26569 Community Center Dr
Highland CA
909 864-8933

(P-16923)
SCILEX PHARMACEUTICALS INC (HQ)
4955 Directors Pl Ste 100 (92121-3836)
PHONE..................................949 441-2270
Anthony P Mack, *Pr*
Jiong Shao, *Ex VP*
EMP: 19 EST: 2012
SQ FT: 3,000
SALES (est): 2.02MM
SALES (corp-wide): 62.84MM **Publicly Held**
Web: www.scilexholding.com
SIC: 7389 5122 2834 Packaging and labeling services; Pharmaceuticals; Pharmaceutical preparations
PA: Sorrento Therapeutics, Inc.
4955 Directors Pl Ste 100
San Diego CA
858 203-4100

(P-16924)
SD&A TELESERVICES INC (HQ)
5757 W Century Blvd Ste 300 (90045-6432)
EMP: 300 EST: 2004
SALES (est): 22.02MM
SALES (corp-wide): 71.07MM **Privately Held**
Web: www.sdats.com
SIC: 7389 Telemarketing services
PA: Robert W. Woodruff Arts Center, Inc.
1280 Peachtree St Ne
Atlanta GA
404 733-4200

(P-16925)
SEVEN ONE INC (PA)
Also Called: Professonal Tele Answering Svc
21540 Prairie St Ste E (91311-5814)

PHONE..................................818 904-3435
James Thompson, *Pr*
EMP: 83 EST: 1983
SQ FT: 4,000
SALES (est): 2.43MM **Privately Held**
Web: www.answer24live.com
SIC: 7389 Telephone answering service

(P-16926)
SHERYL LOWE DESIGNS LLC
1187 Coast Village Rd Ste 156 (93108-2737)
PHONE..................................805 969-1742
Sheryl Lowe, *CEO*
Jaden Levit, *CFO*
Jane Davis, *Dir*
EMP: 20 EST: 2010
SQ FT: 1,500
SALES (est): 1.38MM **Privately Held**
Web: www.sheryllowejewelry.com
SIC: 7389 3911 Design services; Jewelry apparel

(P-16927)
SHINWOO P&C USA INC (HQ)
2177 Britannia Blvd Ste 203 (92154-8307)
PHONE..................................619 407-7164
Il Kim, *CEO*
▲ EMP: 348 EST: 2007
SQ FT: 300
SALES (est): 26.35MM **Privately Held**
SIC: 7389 Packaging and labeling services
PA: Shinan Packaging Co.,Ltd.
19b-5l, Banwol Industrial Complex
Ansan

(P-16928)
SIGUE CORPORATION (PA)
Also Called: Sigue
13190 Telfair Ave (91342-3573)
PHONE..................................818 837-5939
Guillermo Dela Vina, *CEO*
Christina M Pappas, *
Alfredo Dela Vina, *
EMP: 100 EST: 1996
SQ FT: 3,000
SALES (est): 109.03MM
SALES (corp-wide): 109.03MM **Privately Held**
Web: www.sigue.com
SIC: 7389 4822 Financial services; Telegraph and other communications

(P-16929)
SIMPLE SCIENCE INC
1626 Ohms Way (92627-4329)
PHONE..................................949 335-1099
Christian Henderson, *Pr*
EMP: 40 EST: 2009
SALES (est): 5.07MM **Privately Held**
Web: www.simple.science
SIC: 7389 7812 7371 7311 Design services; Video production; Software programming applications; Advertising agencies

(P-16930)
SINECERA INC
Also Called: Crown Vly Precision Machining
5397 3rd St (91706-2085)
PHONE..................................626 962-1087
Donald Brown, *CEO*
Dale B Mikus, *CFO*
EMP: 80 EST: 1984
SQ FT: 10,500
SALES (est): 24.79MM
SALES (corp-wide): 101.1MM **Privately Held**
Web: www.crownprecision.com

SIC: 7389 3492 Grinding, precision: commercial or industrial; Control valves, aircraft: hydraulic and pneumatic
PA: H-D Advanced Manufacturing Company
2418 Greens Rd
Houston TX
346 219-0320

(P-16931)
SKDY OF SAN DIEGO INC
Also Called: Skyline Displays of San Diego
6455 Weathers Pl (92121-2958)
PHONE..................................858 552-9033
John Lethert, *Pr*
Joseph Lethert, *VP*
EMP: 21 EST: 1986
SQ FT: 14,850
SALES (est): 2.46MM **Privately Held**
Web: www.skylinesandiego.com
SIC: 7389 3993 Trade show arrangement; Signs and advertising specialties

(P-16932)
SOBOBA BAND LUISENO INDIANS
Also Called: Soboba Casino
22777 Soboba Rd (92583-2935)
PHONE..................................951 665-1000
TOLL FREE: 888
EMP: 900
Web: www.soboba.com
SIC: 7389 7011 Personal service agents, brokers, and bureaus; Casino hotel
PA: Soboba Band Of Luiseno Indians
23906 Soboba Rd
San Jacinto CA
951 654-2765

(P-16933)
SOCIAL JUNKY INC
7874 Palmetto Ave (92336-2744)
PHONE..................................213 999-1275
Shannon Bryant, *CEO*
EMP: 43 EST: 2021
SALES (est): 1.12MM **Privately Held**
SIC: 7389 2836 7929 Business Activities at Non-Commercial Site; Culture media; Entertainers and entertainment groups

(P-16934)
STANTEC ARCHITECTURE INC
Also Called: Rnl Design
801 S Figueroa St Ste 300 (90017-3007)
PHONE..................................213 955-9775
Patrick Mckelvey, *Brnch Mgr*
EMP: 355
SALES (corp-wide): 4.23B **Privately Held**
Web: www.stantec.com
SIC: 7389 8712 Interior designer; Architectural engineering
HQ: Stantec Architecture Inc.
224 S Michigan Ave # 1400
Chicago IL
336 714-7413

(P-16935)
STRATEGIC OPERATIONS INC
4705 Ruffin Rd (92123-1611)
PHONE..................................858 244-0559
Stuart Segall, *CEO*
EMP: 250 EST: 2002
SQ FT: 12,000
SALES (est): 24.34MM **Privately Held**
Web: www.strategic-operations.com
SIC: 7389 Personal service agents, brokers, and bureaus

(P-16936)
SUGAR FOODS LLC
Also Called: Sygma Network, The
9500 El Dorado Ave (91352-1339)
PHONE..............................818 768-7900
Stephen Odell, *Pt*
EMP: 200
SALES (corp-wide): 286.33MM Privately
Held
Web: www.sugarfoods.com
SIC: 7389 2099 2062 Packaging and
labeling services; Food preparations, nec;
Cane sugar refining
PA: Sugar Foods Llc
3059 Townsgate Rd Ste 101
Westlake Village CA
805 396-5000

(P-16937)
SUPER CENTER CONCEPTS INC
Also Called: Superior Grocers
133 W Avenue 45 (90065-3022)
PHONE..............................323 223-3878
Chris Gonzalez, *Dist Mgr*
EMP: 157
Web: www.superiorgrocers.com
SIC: 7389 Design services
PA: Super Center Concepts, Inc.
15510 Carmenita Rd
Santa Fe Springs CA

(P-16938)
SWISSTEX CALIFORNIA INC
(PA)
13660 S Figueroa St (90061-1023)
PHONE..............................310 516-6800
▲ EMP: 104 EST: 1995
SALES (est): 21.72MM Privately Held
Web: www.swisstex-ca.com
SIC: 7389 Textile and apparel services

(P-16939)
SYNC BROKERAGE INC
22020 Clarendon St Ste 200 (91367-6335)
PHONE..............................818 770-3663
Wael Khalafawi, *Prin*
EMP: 88 EST: 2017
SALES (est): 5.2MM Privately Held
Web: www.syncbrokerage.com
SIC: 7389 Brokers' services

(P-16940)
TBWA CHIAT/DAY INC
5353 Grosvenor Blvd (90066-6913)
PHONE..............................310 305-5000
Lee Clow, *Mgr*
EMP: 374
SALES (corp-wide): 14.29B Publicly Held
Web: www.tbwachiatdayla.com
SIC: 7389 Interior design services
HQ: Tbwa Chiat/Day Inc.
220 E 42nd St
New York NY
212 804-1000

(P-16941)
TECHNICON DESIGN
CORPORATION
30011 Ivy Glenn Dr Ste 115 (92677-5016)
PHONE..............................949 218-1300
Frank Goodchild, *Pr*
Danton Fitch, *
Helen Carstens, *
EMP: 120 EST: 1989
SALES (est): 20.36MM
SALES (corp-wide): 1.17MM Privately
Held
Web: www.technicondesign.com
SIC: 7389 Design services

PA: Technicon Design Limited
Technicon House
Luton BEDS
158 250-6600

(P-16942)
TECMA GROUP LLC
6020 Progressive Ave (92154-6633)
PHONE..............................619 918-7371
EMP: 968
Web: www.tecma.com
SIC: 7389 Brokers' services
PA: The Tecma Group L L C
2000 Wyoming Ave Ste A
El Paso TX

(P-16943)
THOUSAND OAKS PRTG & SPC
INC
Also Called: T/O Printing
5334 Sterling Center Dr (91361-4612)
PHONE..............................818 706-8330
Steve Mahr, *Pr*
▲ EMP: 140 EST: 1981
SQ FT: 60,000
SALES (est): 21.05MM
SALES (corp-wide): 15B Privately Held
Web: www.rrd.com
SIC: 7389 2752 Printing broker; Offset
printing
HQ: Consolidated Graphics, Inc.
5858 Westheimer Rd # 200
Houston TX

(P-16944)
THYDE INC (PA)
300 El Sobrante Rd (92879-5757)
PHONE..............................951 817-2300
Tim Hyde, *Pr*
EMP: 200 EST: 1984
SQ FT: 70,000
SALES (est): 19.61MM
SALES (corp-wide): 19.61MM Privately
Held
SIC: 7389 Packaging and labeling services

(P-16945)
TRAFFIC MANAGEMENT INC
(PA)
4900 Airport Plaza Dr Ste 300 (90815)
PHONE..............................562 595-4278
▲ EMP: 144 EST: 1992
SALES (est): 105.24MM Privately Held
Web: www.trafficmanagement.com
SIC: 7389 8741 Flagging service (traffic
control); Business management

(P-16946)
TRANS-PAK INCORPORATED
Also Called: Transpak Los Angeles
2601 S Garnsey St (92707-3338)
PHONE..............................310 618-6937
EMP: 108
SALES (corp-wide): 130.93MM Privately
Held
Web: www.transpak.com
SIC: 7389 Packaging and labeling services
PA: Transpak, Inc.
520 Marburg Way
San Jose CA
408 254-0500

(P-16947)
TRANSPRTTION OPRTION MGT
SLTON ✪
1917 Palomar Oaks Way Ste 110
(92008-5512)
PHONE..............................858 391-0260
Lee Wilcox, *Pr*

Steve Haddix, *
Brad White, *
Cindy Adamos, *
EMP: 250 EST: 2023
SALES (est): 45MM Privately Held
SIC: 7389 Personal service agents, brokers,
and bureaus

(P-16948)
UNITED TALENT AGENCY LLC
Also Called: United Talent Agency, LLC
9336 Civic Center Dr (90210-3604)
PHONE..............................310 776-8160
EMP: 102
SALES (corp-wide): 231.9MM Privately
Held
Web: www.unitedtalent.com
SIC: 7389 Personal service agents, brokers,
and bureaus
PA: United Talent Agency Holdings, Inc.
888 7th Ave Ste 922
New York NY
310 273-6700

(P-16949)
UNIVERSAL CARD INC
Also Called: Merchant Services
9012 Research Dr Ste 200 (92618-4254)
PHONE..............................949 861-4000
Jason Moore, *Pr*
Jason W Moore, *
Robert Parisi, *
EMP: 400 EST: 2000
SQ FT: 40,000
SALES (est): 22.95MM Privately Held
Web: www.merchantsvcs.com
SIC: 7389 Credit card service

(P-16950)
UNIVERSAL MUS GROUP DIST
CORP
111 Universal Hollywood Dr Ste 1420
(91608-1054)
PHONE..............................818 508-9550
Clarence Mcdonald, *Brnch Mgr*
EMP: 93
Web: www.universalmusic.com
SIC: 7389 Music recording producer
HQ: Universal Music Group Distribution,
Corp.
2220 Colorado Ave
Santa Monica CA
310 235-4700

(P-16951)
UNIVERSAL MUS INVESTMENTS
INC (HQ)
2220 Colorado Ave (90404-3506)
PHONE..............................888 583-7176
Lucian C Grainge, *CEO*
Joe Arambula, *
▲ EMP: 80 EST: 1996
SALES (est): 100.67MM Privately Held
Web: www.universalmusic.com
SIC: 7389 7929 Music recording producer;
Musical entertainers
PA: Vivendi Se
42 Avenue De Friedland
Paris

(P-16952)
UNIVERSAL MUSIC GROUP INC
(HQ)
2220 Colorado Ave (90404-3506)
PHONE..............................310 865-0770
Lucian Grainge, *CEO*
Jeffrey Harleston, *
Philippe Flageul, *
Boyd Muir, *

▲ EMP: 100 EST: 1998
SALES (est): 509.22MM Privately Held
Web: www.universalmusic.com
SIC: 7389 2741 Music recording producer;
Miscellaneous publishing
PA: Universal Music Group N.V.
's-Gravelandseweg 80
Hilversum NH

(P-16953)
UNIVERSITY CALIFORNIA
IRVINE
1001 Health Sciences Rd (92617-3054)
PHONE..............................949 824-6483
EMP: 125
SALES (corp-wide): 534.4MM Privately
Held
Web: www.uci.edu
SIC: 7389 Automobile recovery service
HQ: University Of California, Irvine
510 Aldrich Hall
Irvine CA
949 824-5011

(P-16954)
UNSPOKEN LANGUAGE
SERVICES INC
1370 Valley Vista Dr Ste 200 (91765-3911)
PHONE..............................626 532-8096
Amanda Martin, *
EMP: 498 EST: 2019
SALES (est): 9.3MM Privately Held
Web: www.unspokenasl.com
SIC: 7389 Translation services

(P-16955)
UPS STORE INC (HQ)
Also Called: Mail Boxes Etc
6060 Cornerstone Ct W (92121-3712)
PHONE..............................858 455-8800
Walter T Davis, *CEO*
Michelle Van Slyke, *
EMP: 313 EST: 1980
SQ FT: 66,000
SALES (est): 154.51MM
SALES (corp-wide): 100.34B Publicly
Held
Web: www.theupsstore.com
SIC: 7389 8742 4783 Mailbox rental and
related service; Business management
consultant; Packing goods for shipping
PA: United Parcel Service, Inc.
55 Glenlake Pkwy
Atlanta GA
404 828-6000

(P-16956)
VASTEK INC
1230 Columbia St Ste 1180 (92101-8520)
PHONE..............................925 948-5701
Vikash Mishra, *CEO*
EMP: 171 EST: 2015
SQ FT: 1,600
SALES (est): 17.73MM Privately Held
Web: www.vastekgroup.com
SIC: 7389 7371 Air pollution measuring
service; Custom computer programming
services

(P-16957)
VINTAGE DESIGN LLC
8310 Juniper Creek Ln (92126-1072)
PHONE..............................858 695-9544
Elizabeth Casey, *Brnch Mgr*
EMP: 94
SALES (corp-wide): 321MM Privately
Held
Web: www.vintagedesigninc.com
SIC: 7389 Interior decorating
HQ: Vintage Design, Llc
25200 Commercentre Dr

PRODUCTS & SVCS

Lake Forest CA
949 900-5400

(P-16958)
VISUAL PAK SAN DIEGO LLC
2320 Paseo De Las Americas Ste 201
(92154)
PHONE..............................847 689-1000
David Waldron, *Managing Member*
▲ EMP: 250 EST: 2012
SALES (est): 5.11MM Privately Held
Web: www.visualpak.com
SIC: 7389 Packaging and labeling services

(P-16959)
VOLCOM LLC (HQ)
Also Called: Stone Entertainment
1740 Monrovia Ave (92627-4407)
PHONE..............................949 646-2175
Todd Hymel, *CEO*
Jason Steris, *
John W Fearnley, *
Tom D Ruiz, *
Ryan Immegart, *
EMP: 200 EST: 1991
SQ FT: 104,000
SALES (est): 103.81MM Privately Held
Web: www.volcom.com
SIC: 7389 2253 7822 5136 Design services;
Bathing suits and swimwear, knit; Motion
picture and tape distribution; Men's and
boy's clothing
PA: Authentic Brands Group Llc
1411 Broadway Fl 4
New York NY

(P-16960)
VOLTEGE INC
10571 Los Alamitos Blvd (90720-2113)
PHONE..............................714 369-8068
EMP: 24
SALES (corp-wide): 906.49K Privately
Held
Web: www.voltege.com
SIC: 7389 3441 3444 Personal service
agents, brokers, and bureaus; Fabricated
structural metal; Sheet metalwork
PA: Voltege, Inc
11 Pastora
Foothill Ranch CA
949 273-3822

(P-16961)
VXI GLOBAL SOLUTIONS LLC
(PA)
Also Called: Vxi Global Solutions
220 W 1st St Fl 3 (90012-4105)
PHONE..............................213 739-4720
Eva Yi Hui Wang, *Pr*
Kit Wan, *VP*
Steven Wang, *CFO*
David Zhou, *COO*
Jared Morrison, *COO*
EMP: 1200 EST: 1998
SALES (est): 342.05MM
SALES (corp-wide): 342.05MM Privately
Held
Web: www.vxi.com
SIC: 7389 Telemarketing services

(P-16962)
WARNER BROS RECORDS INC
(DH)
777 S Santa Fe Ave (90021-1750)
PHONE..............................818 846-9090
Livia Tortella, *
Rob Cavallo, *
Lenny Warnoker, *
Murray Gitlin, *
EMP: 460 EST: 1958

SALES (est): 198.94MM Publicly Held
Web: www.warnerrecords.com
SIC: 7389 Music recording producer
HQ: Warner Music Inc.
1633 Broadway
New York NY

(P-16963)
WASHINGTON INVENTORY
SERVICE
Also Called: Wis
9265 Sky Park Ct Ste 100 (92123-4303)
PHONE..............................858 565-8111
Jim Rose, *CEO*
Howard L Madden, *
Tom Compogiannis, *
EMP: 1000 EST: 1960
SQ FT: 30,000
SALES (est): 64.08MM Publicly Held
SIC: 7389 Inventory computing service
HQ: Western Inventory Service Ltd.
335 Britannia Rd E Suite 102
Mississauga ON
905 677-1947

(P-16964)
WE PACK IT ALL LLC
2745 Huntington Dr (91010-2302)
PHONE..............................626 301-9214
George Gellert, *
Robert Gellert, *
Sharon Bershtel, *
Mark Lebovitz, *
EMP: 155 EST: 1972
SQ FT: 50,000
SALES (est): 28.15MM Privately Held
Web: www.wepackitall.com
SIC: 7389 Packaging and labeling services

(P-16965)
WELLS FARGO CAPITAL
FINANCE INC
Also Called: Wfcf Technology E2040-030
2450 Colo Ave 3000w 3rd Fl (90404)
PHONE..............................310 453-7300
▲ EMP: 195
SIC: 7389 Financial services

(P-16966)
WET (PA)
Also Called: Wet Design
10847 Sherman Way (91352-4829)
PHONE..............................818 769-6200
Mark W Fuller, *CEO*
Shemi Hart, *
Tania Avedissian, *
Helen Park, *
Maria Villamil, *
▲ EMP: 184 EST: 1983
SQ FT: 112,000
SALES (est): 47.15MM
SALES (corp-wide): 47.15MM Privately
Held
Web: www.wetdesign.com
SIC: 7389 8711 3443 Design services;
Engineering services; Metal parts

(P-16967)
WHEAT GROUP INC
9950 Summers Ridge Rd Ste 160
(92121-3099)
P.O. Box 502416 (92150-2416)
PHONE..............................858 673-2070
Chad Grismer, *CEO*
Kelly Grismer, *
Rafael Asaria, *
◆ EMP: 47 EST: 1998
SQ FT: 26,000
SALES (est): 1.01MM Privately Held

SIC: 7389 2389 Styling of fashions, apparel,
furniture, textiles, etc.; Men's miscellaneous
accessories
PA: United Legwear Company, Llc
48 W 38th St Fl 3
New York NY

(P-16968)
YELLOWPAGESCOM LLC (DH)
Also Called: Dexyp
611 N Brand Blvd Ste 500 (91203-3293)
PHONE..............................818 937-5500
Williams Clenney, *
Brad Mohs, *
EMP: 260 EST: 2004
SALES (est): 62.72MM
SALES (corp-wide): 1.2B Publicly Held
SIC: 7389 Telephone directory distribution,
contract or fee basis
HQ: Thryv, Inc.
2200 W Airfield Dr
Dfw Airport TX
972 453-7000

7513 Truck Rental And
Leasing, Without Drivers

(P-16969)
EL CAMINO RENTAL
5701 El Camino Real (92008-7202)
PHONE..............................760 438-7368
Mike Taylor, *Mgr*
EMP: 50 EST: 2004
SALES (est): 872.13K Privately Held
SIC: 7513 7519 7359 5261 Truck rental and
leasing, no drivers; Trailer rental; Tool rental
; Retail nurseries and garden stores

(P-16970)
PENSKE CORPORATION
6551 Ventura Blvd (93003-7229)
PHONE..............................805 983-3788
Owen Donahue, *Prin*
EMP: 160
SALES (corp-wide): 5.16B Privately Held
Web: www.pensketruckrental.com
SIC: 7513 Truck rental and leasing, no
drivers
PA: Penske Corporation
2555 S Telegraph Rd
Bloomfield Hills MI
248 648-2000

(P-16971)
PENSKE MOTOR GROUP LLC
Also Called: Penske
2010 E Garvey Ave S (91791-1911)
PHONE..............................626 859-1200
Glen Hightman, *Brnch Mgr*
EMP: 277
SALES (corp-wide): 5.16B Privately Held
Web: www.pensketruckrental.com
SIC: 7513 7538 Truck rental and leasing, no
drivers; General automotive repair shops
HQ: Penske Motor Group, Llc
3534 Peck Rd
El Monte CA

(P-16972)
PENSKE TRANSPORTATION
MGT LLC
2280 Wardlow Cir (92878-9078)
PHONE..............................844 847-9518
EMP: 82
SALES (corp-wide): 2.11B Privately Held
Web: www.penskelogistics.com
SIC: 7513 Truck rental and leasing, no
drivers

HQ: Penske Transportation Management
Llc
2675 Morgantown Rd
Reading PA
800 529-6531

(P-16973)
ROLLINS LEASING LLC
Also Called: Rollins Truck Rental-Leasing
18305 Arenth Ave (91748-1226)
PHONE..............................626 913-7186
Dave Bettson, *Mgr*
EMP: 88
SQ FT: 10,370
SALES (corp-wide): 2.11B Privately Held
Web: www.pensketruckrental.com
SIC: 7513 Truck rental and leasing, no
drivers
HQ: Rollins Leasing Llc
2200 Concord Pike
Wilmington DE
302 426-2700

(P-16974)
RP AUTOMOTIVE II INC
Also Called: Penske Ford Chula Vista
560 Auto Park Dr (91911-6026)
PHONE..............................619 656-2500
Roger S Penske Junior, *Brnch Mgr*
EMP: 90
SALES (corp-wide): 48.07MM Privately
Held
Web: www.pensketruckrental.com
SIC: 7513 Truck rental and leasing, no
drivers
PA: Rp Automotive Ii, Inc.
9136 Firestone Blvd
Downey CA
626 430-9011

(P-16975)
U-HAUL BUSINESS
CONSULTANTS
Also Called: U-Haul
314 E 6th St (92879-1520)
PHONE..............................951 736-7811
EMP: 249
SALES (corp-wide): 5.86B Publicly Held
Web: www.uhaul.com
SIC: 7513 Truck rental and leasing, no
drivers
HQ: U-Haul Business Consultants, Inc
2727 N Central Ave
Phoenix AZ
602 263-6011

(P-16976)
U-HAUL LEASING & SALES CO
Also Called: U-Haul
23730 Sunnymead Blvd (92553-3022)
PHONE..............................951 485-2003
Timothy Faust, *Mgr*
EMP: 371
SALES (corp-wide): 5.86B Publicly Held
Web: www.uhaul.com
SIC: 7513 7519 5984 5531 Truck rental and
leasing, no drivers; Trailer rental; Propane
gas, bottled; Trailer hitches, automotive
HQ: U-Haul Leasing & Sales Co.
2727 N Central Ave
Phoenix AZ
602 263-6011

7514 Passenger Car Rental

(P-16977)
ALAMO RENTAL (US) INC
Also Called: Alamo Rent A Car
3400 E Tahquitz Canyon Way Ste 5
(92262-6966)

PHONE..............................760 778-6271
EMP: 91
SALES (corp-wide): 7.04B Privately Held
Web: www.alamo.com
SIC: 7514 Rent-a-car service
HQ: Alamo Rental (Us) Inc.
   600 Corporate Park Dr
   Saint Louis MO

(P-16978)
ALAMO RENTAL (US) INC
Also Called: Alamo Rent A Car
711 W Katella Ave (92802-3412)
PHONE..............................714 748-7368
William R Smith, *S*
EMP: 82
SALES (corp-wide): 7.04B Privately Held
Web: www.alamo.com
SIC: 7514 Rent-a-car service
HQ: Alamo Rental (Us) Inc.
   600 Corporate Park Dr
   Saint Louis MO

(P-16979)
ALAMO RENTAL (US) INC
Also Called: Alamo Rent A Car
3450 E Airport Dr Ste 300 (91761-7669)
PHONE..............................888 826-6893
Michael Stephens, *Mgr*
EMP: 100
SALES (corp-wide): 7.04B Privately Held
Web: www.alamo.com
SIC: 7514 Rent-a-car service
HQ: Alamo Rental (Us) Inc.
   600 Corporate Park Dr
   Saint Louis MO

(P-16980)
ALAMO RENTAL (US) INC
Also Called: Alamo Rent A Car
9020 Aviation Blvd (90301-2907)
PHONE..............................310 649-2242
Cesar Saurez, *Mgr*
EMP: 109
SALES (corp-wide): 7.04B Privately Held
Web: www.alamo.com
SIC: 7514 Rent-a-car service
HQ: Alamo Rental (Us) Inc.
   600 Corporate Park Dr
   Saint Louis MO

(P-16981)
ENTERPRISE RNT--CAR LOS ANGLES (DH)
Also Called: Enterprise Rent-A-Car
333 City Blvd W Ste 1000 (92868-2921)
PHONE..............................657 221-4400
Andrew C Taylor, *
Pamela Nicholson, *
Greg Stubblefield, *
William W Snyder, *
▲ **EMP:** 90 **EST:** 1957
SQ FT: 30,000
SALES (est): 755.11MM
SALES (corp-wide): 7.04B Privately Held
Web: www.enterprise.com
SIC: 7514 7513 5511 Rent-a-car service;
   Truck rental and leasing, no drivers; Trucks,
   tractors, and trailers: new and used
HQ: Enterprise Holdings, Inc.
   600 Corporate Park Dr
   Saint Louis MO
   314 512-5000

(P-16982)
FOX RENT A CAR INC
Also Called: Europcar
5500 W Century Blvd (90045-5914)
PHONE..............................310 342-5155
Allen Rezapour, *Pr*

EMP: 104
SALES (corp-wide): 290.01B Privately Held
Web: www.foxrentcar.com
SIC: 7514 Passenger car rental
HQ: Fox Rent A Car, Inc.
   4135 S 100th East Ave
   Tulsa OK

(P-16983)
FOX RENT A CAR INC
1776 E Holt Blvd (91761-2110)
PHONE..............................909 635-6390
Syed Mahdi, *Brnch Mgr*
EMP: 90
SALES (corp-wide): 290.01B Privately Held
Web: www.foxrentcar.com
SIC: 7514 Rent-a-car service
HQ: Fox Rent A Car, Inc.
   4135 S 100th East Ave
   Tulsa OK

7515 Passenger Car Leasing

(P-16984)
EL CAJON MOTORS (PA)
Also Called: El Cajon Ford
1595 E Main St (92021-5902)
P.O. Box 1236 (92022-1236)
PHONE..............................619 579-8888
Paul F Leader, *Pr*
Andrew Breech, *
John Blake, *
▲ **EMP:** 100 **EST:** 1946
SQ FT: 311,226
SALES (est): 9.23MM
SALES (corp-wide): 9.23MM Privately Held
Web: www.quicklane.com
SIC: 7515 5511 7538 Passenger car leasing;
   Automobiles, new and used; General
   automotive repair shops

(P-16985)
EXECUTIVE CAR LEASING COMPANY (PA)
Also Called: Newco Auto Leasing
7807 Santa Monica Blvd (90046-5398)
P.O. Box 933009 (90093-3009)
PHONE..............................800 800-3932
EMP: 100 **EST:** 1953
SALES (est): 9.26MM
SALES (corp-wide): 9.26MM Privately Held
Web: www.executivecarleasing.com
SIC: 7515 7513 Passenger car leasing;
   Truck leasing, without drivers

7519 Utility Trailer Rental

(P-16986)
EL MONTE RENTS INC (HQ)
Also Called: El Monte Rv
12818 Firestone Blvd (90670-5404)
PHONE..............................562 404-9300
Kenneth Schork, *CEO*
EMP: 110 **EST:** 1970
SALES (est): 48.03MM **Privately Held**
Web: www.elmonterv.com
SIC: 7519 5561 Motor home rental; Motor
   homes
PA: Tourism Holdings Limited
   L 1, 83 Beach Road
   Auckland AUK

7521 Automobile Parking

(P-16987)
ABM PARKING SERVICES INC
Also Called: Ampco Airport Parking
1150 S Olive St Fl 19 (90015-2479)
PHONE..............................213 284-7600
▲ **EMP:** 9469
SIC: 7521 7349 Parking lots; Janitorial
   service, contract basis

(P-16988)
ALL STAR PARKING
Also Called: Wally Parking
9700 Bellanca Ave (90045-5510)
PHONE..............................310 337-1944
Sohal Islam, *Genl Mgr*
Charles Bassett, *Genl Mgr*
Carl Calhoun, *Mgr*
EMP: 102 **EST:** 2001
SALES (est): 3.87MM **Privately Held**
Web: www.wallypark.com
SIC: 7521 Parking lots

(P-16989)
AMERIPARK LLC
17165 Von Karman Ave Ste 110
(92614-0905)
PHONE..............................949 279-7525
Josh Hess, *Brnch Mgr*
EMP: 300
SALES (corp-wide): 1.71B Privately Held
Web: www.ameripark.com
SIC: 7521 Parking lots
HQ: Ameripark, Llc
   233 Peachtree St Ne # 2600
   Atlanta GA

(P-16990)
EVERPARK INC
3470 Wilshire Blvd Ste 940 (90010-2207)
PHONE..............................310 987-6922
Alazar Asmamaw, *CEO*
Abiy Wouldgerema, *
Abbi Abebe, *
EMP: 200 **EST:** 2007
SALES (est): 2.89MM **Privately Held**
Web: www.everpark.com
SIC: 7521 Automobile parking

(P-16991)
L AND R AUTO PARKS INC
Also Called: Joe's Auto Parks
707 Wilshire Blvd Ste 4300 (90017-3601)
PHONE..............................213 784-3018
Charles Bassett, *Pr*
Mark Funk, *
Jeff Matsuno, *
Gabriel Rubin, *
Stuart Rubin Board, *Prin*
EMP: 250 **EST:** 1951
SQ FT: 5,000
SALES (est): 19.79MM **Privately Held**
Web: www.joesautoparks.com
SIC: 7521 7542 7371 Parking lots;
   Carwashes; Computer software
   development and applications

(P-16992)
LAZ KARP ASSOCIATES LLC
1400 Ivar Ave (90028-8122)
PHONE..............................323 464-4190
EMP: 164
Web: www.lazparking.com
SIC: 7521 Parking lots
PA: Laz Karp Associates, Llc
   1 Financial Plz
   Hartford CT

(P-16993)
MODERN PARKING INC
415 N Bedford Dr (90210-4302)
PHONE..............................310 271-1125
EMP: 167
Web: www.modernparking.com
SIC: 7521 Parking garage
PA: Modern Parking, Inc.
   303 S Union Ave Fl 1
   Los Angeles CA

(P-16994)
MODERN PARKING INC
14110 Palawan Way (90292-6231)
PHONE..............................310 821-1081
Arisur Rahnan, *Prin*
EMP: 167
Web: www.modernparking.com
SIC: 7521 Parking garage
PA: Modern Parking, Inc.
   303 S Union Ave Fl 1
   Los Angeles CA

(P-16995)
MODERN PARKING INC
4955 Van Nuys Blvd Frnt (91403-1813)
PHONE..............................818 783-3143
EMP: 167
Web: www.modernparking.com
SIC: 7521 Parking garage
PA: Modern Parking, Inc.
   303 S Union Ave Fl 1
   Los Angeles CA

(P-16996)
MODERN PARKING INC
1025 W Laurel St Ste 105 (92101-1254)
PHONE..............................619 233-0412
Richard Viera, *Brnch Mgr*
EMP: 167
Web: www.modernparking.com
SIC: 7521 Parking garage
PA: Modern Parking, Inc.
   303 S Union Ave Fl 1
   Los Angeles CA

(P-16997)
PARKING COMPANY OF AMERICA
Also Called: Pcamp
3165 Garfield Ave (90040-3217)
PHONE..............................562 862-2118
Alex Martin Chaves Junior, *Pr*
Eric Chaves, *
EMP: 100 **EST:** 1990
SALES (est): 9.34MM **Privately Held**
Web: www.parkpca.com
SIC: 7521 Parking lots

(P-16998)
PARKING CONCEPTS INC
33 E Green St (91105-2022)
PHONE..............................626 577-8963
EMP: 96
SALES (corp-wide): 51.57MM Privately Held
Web: www.parkingconcepts.com
SIC: 7521 Parking lots
PA: Parking Concepts, Inc.
   12 Mauchly Ste I
   Irvine CA
   949 753-7525

(P-16999)
PARKING CONCEPTS INC
12001 Vista Del Mar (90293-8518)
PHONE..............................310 322-5008
Zahid Hossian, *Brnch Mgr*
EMP: 97

PRODUCTS & SVCS

SALES (corp-wide): 51.57MM **Privately Held**
Web: www.parkingconcepts.com
SIC: 7521 Parking lots
PA: Parking Concepts, Inc.
12 Mauchly Ste I
Irvine CA
949 753-7525

(P-17000)
PARKING CONCEPTS INC
1036 Broxton Ave (90024-2824)
PHONE..................................310 208-1611
Jorge Lopez, *Mgr*
EMP: 97
SALES (corp-wide): 51.57MM **Privately Held**
Web: www.parkingconcepts.com
SIC: 7521 Parking lots
PA: Parking Concepts, Inc.
12 Mauchly Ste I
Irvine CA
949 753-7525

(P-17001)
PARKING CONCEPTS INC
1801 Georgia St (90015-3477)
PHONE..................................213 746-5764
Bob Hindle, *Mgr*
EMP: 242
SALES (corp-wide): 51.57MM **Privately Held**
Web: www.parkingconcepts.com
SIC: 7521 8748 Parking lots; Traffic consultant
PA: Parking Concepts, Inc.
12 Mauchly Ste I
Irvine CA
949 753-7525

(P-17002)
PARKING CONCEPTS INC
14110 Palawan Way (90292-6231)
PHONE..................................310 821-1081
Frank Vargas, *Genl Mgr*
EMP: 97
SALES (corp-wide): 51.57MM **Privately Held**
Web: www.parkingconcepts.com
SIC: 7521 8741 Parking lots; Management services
PA: Parking Concepts, Inc.
12 Mauchly Ste I
Irvine CA
949 753-7525

(P-17003)
PARKING CONCEPTS INC
800 Wilshire Blvd (90017-2604)
PHONE..................................213 623-2661
Juan Cortes, *Brnch Mgr*
EMP: 97
SALES (corp-wide): 51.57MM **Privately Held**
Web: www.parkingconcepts.com
SIC: 7521 Parking lots
PA: Parking Concepts, Inc.
12 Mauchly Ste I
Irvine CA
949 753-7525

(P-17004)
PARKING CONCEPTS INC
1020 W Civic Center Dr (92703-2303)
PHONE..................................714 543-5725
Gilbert Bernick, *Brnch Mgr*
EMP: 96
SALES (corp-wide): 51.57MM **Privately Held**
Web: www.parkingconcepts.com

SIC: 7521 Parking lots
PA: Parking Concepts, Inc.
12 Mauchly Ste I
Irvine CA
949 753-7525

(P-17005)
PCAM LLC
3165 Garfield Ave (90040-3217)
PHONE..................................562 862-2118
EMP: 80 EST: 2011
SALES (est): 12.77MM **Privately Held**
Web: www.parkpca.com
SIC: 7521 Parking lots

(P-17006)
PROFESSIONAL PARKING
309 Palm St (92661-1200)
PHONE..................................949 723-4027
Ralph Caldin, *Brnch Mgr*
EMP: 114
SIC: 7521 Parking garage
HQ: Professional Parking
2799 E 21st St
Signal Hill CA

(P-17007)
RESORT PARKING SERVICES INC
39755 Berkey Dr # B (92211-1106)
PHONE..................................760 328-4041
Mario Gardner, *Pr*
EMP: 120 EST: 1973
SQ FT: 1,100
SALES (est): 4.84MM **Privately Held**
Web: www.resortparkingservices.com
SIC: 7521 7299 Parking lots; Personal item care and storage services

(P-17008)
VALET PARKING SVC A CAL PARTNR (PA)
Also Called: Valet Parking Service
6933 Hollywood Blvd (90028-6146)
PHONE..................................323 465-5873
Anthony Policella, *CEO*
EMP: 1268 EST: 1946
SQ FT: 10,000
SALES (est): 24.42MM
SALES (corp-wide): 24.42MM **Privately Held**
Web: www.lazparking.com
SIC: 7521 7299 Parking lots; Valet parking

7532 Top And Body Repair And Paint Shops

(P-17009)
CALIBER BODYWORKS TEXAS INC
Also Called: Caliber Collision Centers
5 Auto Center Dr (92782-8402)
PHONE..................................714 665-3905
David Adams, *Brnch Mgr*
EMP: 100
SALES (corp-wide): 1.07MM **Privately Held**
Web: www.caliber.com
SIC: 7532 Body shop, automotive
PA: Caliber Bodyworks Of Texas Llc
2941 Lake Vista Dr
Lewisville TX
469 794-5653

(P-17010)
HOLMES BODY SHOP-ALHAMBRA

1130 E Main St (91801-4111)
PHONE..................................626 282-6173
EMP: 111 EST: 1992
SALES (est): 238.23K
SALES (corp-wide): 4.84MM **Privately Held**
SIC: 7532 Body shop, automotive
PA: Holmes Body Shop-Alhambra, Inc.
466 Foothill Blvd
La Canada Flintridge CA
626 795-6447

(P-17011)
M2 AUTOMOTIVE
1100 Colorado Ave 2nd Fl (90401-3010)
PHONE..................................310 399-3887
D Hunt Ramsbottom Junior, *CEO*
EMP: 750 EST: 1996
SALES (est): 3.94MM **Privately Held**
SIC: 7532 Collision shops, automotive

(P-17012)
MAIMONE LIQUIDATING CORP (PA)
Also Called: Marco's Auto Body
1390 E Palm St (91001-2042)
PHONE..................................626 286-5691
Marco G Maimone, *Pr*
Carl Canzano, *
Lillian Maimone, *
EMP: 100 EST: 1974
SQ FT: 14,000
SALES (est): 2.69MM
SALES (corp-wide): 2.69MM **Privately Held**
Web: www.caliber.com
SIC: 7532 7539 Body shop, automotive; Frame and front end repair services

(P-17013)
METRO TRUCK BODY INC
240 Citation Cir (92878-5022)
PHONE..................................310 532-5570
Vincent Xavier Rigali, *CEO*
▲ EMP: 47 EST: 1968
SQ FT: 20,000
SALES (est): 2.36MM **Privately Held**
Web: www.metrotruckbody.com
SIC: 7532 3713 5012 5531 Body shop, automotive; Truck bodies (motor vehicles); Truck bodies; Truck equipment and parts

(P-17014)
PLATINUM PERFORMANCE INC
760 Mcmurray Rd (93427-2510)
PHONE..................................800 553-2400
Kristin Peck, *CEO*
Kate Russo, *
EMP: 80 EST: 1997
SALES (est): 590.6K **Privately Held**
Web: www.platinumperformance.com
SIC: 7532 Body shop, automotive

(P-17015)
REDLANDS FORD INC
1121 W Colton Ave (92374-2935)
PHONE..................................909 793-3211
Steve Rojas, *CEO*
Steve Rojas, *Pr*
Tracey Hooper, *
EMP: 85 EST: 2002
SALES (est): 10.56MM **Privately Held**
Web: www.redlandsford.com
SIC: 7532 5511 Body shop, automotive; Automobiles, new and used

(P-17016)
SAN DIEGO SATURN RETAILERS INC

Miramar Collision Center
9985 Huennekens St (92121-2918)
PHONE..................................858 373-3001
Gary Leger, *Mgr*
EMP: 94
SQ FT: 24,766
Web: www.teamkiaofelcajon.com
SIC: 7532 Collision shops, automotive
PA: San Diego Saturn Retailers, Inc.
541 N Johnson Ave
El Cajon CA

(P-17017)
SHOWTIME CUSTOM COACH INC
2461 Deep Creek Dr (92382)
P.O. Box 2409 (92382-2409)
PHONE..................................909 867-7025
Armando Nava, *Pr*
Martha Nava, *VP*
Lisa Makeig, *Sec*
EMP: 17 EST: 1986
SQ FT: 7,000
SALES (est): 809.25K **Privately Held**
Web: www.showtimecustomcoach.com
SIC: 7532 3711 Collision shops, automotive; Automobile assembly, including specialty automobiles

(P-17018)
UNIVERSAL METAL PLATING (PA)
626 1/2 S Gerhart Ave (90022-3488)
PHONE..................................626 969-7931
Jesus Martinez, *Pt*
EMP: 18 EST: 1978
SALES (est): 999.54K
SALES (corp-wide): 999.54K **Privately Held**
Web: www.universalplating.com
SIC: 7532 3471 Bump shops, automotive repair; Plating of metals or formed products

(P-17019)
WAND TOPCO INC
4774 W Adams Blvd (90016-2949)
PHONE..................................323 734-3333
EMP: 3253
SALES (corp-wide): 517.67MM **Privately Held**
SIC: 7532 Body shop, automotive
PA: Wand Topco Inc
2941 Lake Vista Dr
Lewisville TX
469 948-9500

7534 Tire Retreading And Repair Shops

(P-17020)
BRIDGESTONE AMERICAS
Also Called: GCR Tires & Service 185
14521 Hawthorne Ave (92335-2508)
PHONE..................................909 770-8523
EMP: 21
Web: www.bridgestonetire.com
SIC: 7534 5531 Tire repair shop; Automotive tires
HQ: Bridgestone Americas Tire Operations, Llc
200 4th Ave S Ste 100
Nashville TN
615 937-1000

(P-17021)
FREMONT & PURDON INC
Also Called: Fremont
836 E Orange Grove Blvd (91104-4553)

PHONE..............................626 795-6282
Steve Jabourian, *Pr*
Eric Gorzynski, *VP*
EMP: 21 **EST:** 1928
SQ FT: 3,000
SALES (est): 968.29K **Privately Held**
Web: www.fremontandpurdon.com
SIC: 7534 7533 7538 7532 Tire repair shop;
Muffler shop, sale or repair and installation;
General automotive repair shops; Body
shop, automotive

(P-17022)
JIMS TIRE CENTER SIMI VLY INC
Also Called: Jim's Tire Center Simi Valley
1525 E Los Angeles Ave (93065-2017)
PHONE..............................805 581-1104
James Farpelha, *Pr*
Barbara Farpelha, *
EMP: 18 **EST:** 1992
SQ FT: 8,000
SALES (est): 2.17MM **Privately Held**
Web: www.jimstirecenter.com
SIC: 7534 7539 Tire retreading and repair
shops; Brake services

(P-17023)
NEW PRIDE TIRE LLC
1511 E Orangethorpe Ave Ste D
(92831-5204)
PHONE..............................310 631-7000
Edward Eunjong Kim, *Pr*
EMP: 50
Web: www.newpridetire.com
SIC: 7534 1799 Rebuilding and retreading
tires; Antenna installation
HQ: New Pride Tire, Llc
2900 Main St Bldg 137
Alameda CA
510 567-8800

(P-17024)
SCHER TIRE INC (PA)
3863 Tyler St (92503-3430)
PHONE..............................951 343-3100
EMP: 20 **EST:** 1981
SALES (est): 12.51MM
SALES (corp-wide): 12.51MM **Privately
Held**
Web: www.schertire.com
SIC: 7534 Tire retreading and repair shops

7537 Automotive
Transmission Repair Shops

(P-17025)
H & A TRANSMISSIONS INC
8727 Rochester Ave (91730-4908)
PHONE..............................909 941-9020
Gilbert H Dickason, *CEO*
Corina Dickason, *
▲ **EMP:** 26 **EST:** 1992
SQ FT: 3,500
SALES (est): 6.05MM **Privately Held**
Web: www.handatrans.com
SIC: 7537 3714 Automotive transmission
repair shops; Axle housings and shafts,
motor vehicle

7538 General Automotive
Repair Shops

(P-17026)
ADVANCED INNOVATIVE TECH
CORP
1675 W Park Ave (92373-8072)
PHONE..............................417 831-9444

EMP: 87
Web: www.trakmotive.com
SIC: 7538 General automotive repair shops
PA: Advanced Innovative Technology
Corporation
350 Nevada St
Redlands CA

(P-17027)
ALLIED LUBE INC
Also Called: Jiffy Lube
3087 Edinger Ave (92780-7240)
PHONE..............................949 651-8814
EMP: 84
Web: www.jiffylube.com
SIC: 7538 7549 General automotive repair
shops; Lubrication service, automotive
PA: Allied Lube, Inc.
27240 La Paz Rd
Mission Viejo CA

(P-17028)
ALTEC INDUSTRIES INC
Also Called: Pomona Service Center
2882 Pomona Blvd (91768-3224)
PHONE..............................909 444-0444
Rick Thompson, *Mgr*
EMP: 21
SQ FT: 13,240
SALES (corp-wide): 1.21B **Privately Held**
Web: www.altec.com
SIC: 7538 3713 3711 3531 General truck
repair; Truck bodies and parts; Motor
vehicles and car bodies; Construction
machinery
HQ: Altec Industries, Inc.
210 Inverness Center Dr
Birmingham AL
205 991-7733

(P-17029)
BRAKE DEPOT SYSTEMS INC
1205 E 1st St (92701-6324)
PHONE..............................714 623-9030
EMP: 258
Web: www.tiredepotcompany.com
SIC: 7538 General automotive repair shops
PA: Brake Depot Systems Inc
8901 Sw Canyon Rd
Portland OR

(P-17030)
CENTRAL CALIFORNIA POWER
19487 Broken Ct (93263-3146)
P.O. Box 1934 (93303-1934)
PHONE..............................661 589-2870
Rhoderick E Headley, *CEO*
Rhoderick E Headley, *Pr*
Blake Headley, *
EMP: 25 **EST:** 1982
SQ FT: 15,000
SALES (est): 8.8MM **Privately Held**
Web: www.gensets.com
SIC: 7538 7359 3569 Truck engine repair,
except industrial; Equipment rental and
leasing, nec; Gas generators

(P-17031)
CITY CHEVROLET OF SAN
DIEGO
Also Called: City Chevrolet of Volkswagen
2111 Morena Blvd (92110-3440)
P.O. Box 85345 (92186-5345)
PHONE..............................619 276-6171
EMP: 148 **EST:** 2016
SALES (est): 14.57MM **Privately Held**

SIC: 7538 5511 7515 5015 General
automotive repair shops; Automobiles, new
and used; Passenger car leasing;
Automotive supplies, used: wholesale and
retail

(P-17032)
IRONMAN RENEWAL LLC
2535 Anselmo Dr (92879-8092)
PHONE..............................951 735-3710
EMP: 87
SIC: 7538 Truck engine repair, except
industrial

(P-17033)
LANCASTER CMNTY SVCS
FNDTION I
Also Called: Development Services
46008 7th St W (93534-7602)
PHONE..............................661 723-6230
Randy Williams, *Mgr*
EMP: 200
Web: www.cityoflancasterca.org
SIC: 7538 9111 General automotive repair
shops; Mayors' office
PA: The Lancaster Community Services
Foundation I
44933 Fern Ave
Lancaster CA
661 723-6000

(P-17034)
LOS ANGELES TRUCK
CENTERS LLC (PA)
Also Called: Velocity Vehicle Group
2429 Peck Rd (90601-1605)
P.O. Box 101284 (91189-0005)
PHONE..............................562 447-1200
EMP: 90 **EST:** 1998
SALES (est): 233.56MM
SALES (corp-wide): 233.56MM **Privately
Held**
Web: www.velocityvehiclegroup.com
SIC: 7538 5012 5013 7532 Truck engine
repair, except industrial; Trucks, commercial
; Truck parts and accessories; Body shop,
trucks

(P-17035)
MISSION SERVICE INC
1800 Avenue Of The Stars Ste 1400
(90067-4216)
PHONE..............................323 266-2593
John E Anderson, *Pr*
John E Anderson Junior, *Treas*
EMP: 1160 **EST:** 1976
SALES (est): 996.26K
SALES (corp-wide): 251.02MM **Privately
Held**
SIC: 7538 Truck engine repair, except
industrial
PA: Topa Equities, Ltd.
1900 Avenue Of The Stars # 1050
Los Angeles CA
310 203-9199

(P-17036)
QUALIS AUTOMOTIVE LLC
21046 Figueroa St (90745-1906)
PHONE..............................859 689-7772
EMP: 100
SALES (corp-wide): 70.48MM **Privately
Held**
Web: www.centricparts.com
SIC: 7538 General automotive repair shops
PA: Qualis Automotive, L.L.C.
14528 Bonelli St
City Of Industry CA
310 218-1082

(P-17037)
R&C MOTOR CORPORATION
Also Called: Claremont Toyota
601 Auto Center Dr (91711-5470)
PHONE..............................909 625-1500
EMP: 200 **EST:** 1992
SALES (est): 19.24MM **Privately Held**
Web: www.claremonttoyota.com
SIC: 7538 5511 General automotive repair
shops; Automobiles, new and used

(P-17038)
SANGERA BUICK INC
Also Called: Mercedes Benz of Bakersfield
5600 Gasoline Alley Dr (93313-3737)
PHONE..............................661 833-5200
Damon Culbertson, *Pr*
Mehnga Sangera, *
Hardev Sangera, *
EMP: 85 **EST:** 1969
SQ FT: 20,000
SALES (est): 10.63MM **Privately Held**
Web: www.sangera.com
SIC: 7538 5531 5511 General automotive
repair shops; Automotive parts;
Automobiles, new and used

(P-17039)
TED FORD JONES INC (PA)
Also Called: Ken Grody Ford
6211 Beach Blvd (90621-2307)
P.O. Box 2154 (90621-0654)
PHONE..............................714 521-3110
Kenneth B Grody, *Pr*
Ken Grody, *
Curt Maletych, *
▼ **EMP:** 110 **EST:** 1995
SQ FT: 4,500
SALES (est): 45.03MM
SALES (corp-wide): 45.03MM **Privately
Held**
Web: www.quicklane.com
SIC: 7538 5511 General automotive repair
shops; Automobiles, new and used

(P-17040)
VROOM AUTOMOTIVE FINANCE
CORP (HQ)
1071 Camelback St Ste 100 (92660-3046)
PHONE..............................949 224-1226
James Vagim, *Pr*
Guillermo Bron, *Ch Bd*
Ravi R Gandhi, *Credit RISK*
Steve Singh, *COO*
EMP: 382 **EST:** 1998
SQ FT: 31,214
SALES (est): 96.49MM
SALES (corp-wide): 1.95B **Publicly Held**
SIC: 7538 General automotive repair shops
PA: Vroom, Inc.
1375 Broadway Fl 11
New York NY
855 524-1300

7539 Automotive Repair
Shops, Nec

(P-17041)
AIRDRAULICS INC
13261 Saticoy St (91605-3401)
PHONE..............................818 982-1400
Dan Tracey, *CEO*
Devin Tracey, *
EMP: 25 **EST:** 1986
SQ FT: 5,000
SALES (est): 7.77MM **Privately Held**
Web: www.airdraulicsinc.com

SIC: **7539** 3599 5013 5084 Automotive repair shops, nec; Machine and other job shop work; Automotive servicing equipment ; Industrial machinery and equipment

(P-17042)
EIGHT POINT TRAILER CORP
14770 Slover Ave (92337-7234)
PHONE...............................909 357-9227
Gregory Anderson, *Pr*
EMP: 19 **EST:** 1948
SQ FT: 28,000
SALES (est): 1.36MM **Privately Held**
Web: www.eightpointtrailer.com
SIC: 7539 3715 5013 Trailer repair; Truck trailers; Truck parts and accessories

(P-17043)
JAMES MAGNA LTD
Also Called: Northstar Engineering
8782 Lanyard Ct (91730-0804)
PHONE...............................909 391-2025
Mike Maedel, *CEO*
Gene Gregory, *VP*
◆ **EMP:** 17 **EST:** 1991
SQ FT: 19,696
SALES (est): 4MM **Privately Held**
Web: www.nsecal.com
SIC: 7539 3599 Fuel system repair, motor vehicle; Machine shop, jobbing and repair

(P-17044)
ST GEORGE AUTO CENTER INC
Also Called: Stg Auto Group
13861 Harbor Blvd (92843-4043)
P.O. Box 2129 (91763-0629)
PHONE...............................657 212-5042
EMP: 85
SALES (corp-wide): 8.3MM **Privately Held**
SIC: 7539 Automotive repair shops, nec
PA: St. George Auto Center, Inc.
10325 Central Ave
Montclair CA
909 341-1189

7542 Carwashes

(P-17045)
BLUE BEACON USA LP
Also Called: Blue Beacon of Wheeler Ridge
5831 Santa Elena Dr (93203-9705)
PHONE...............................661 858-2090
Jose Gonzalez, *Mgr*
EMP: 107
SALES (corp-wide): 38MM **Privately Held**
Web: www.bluebeacon.com
SIC: 7542 Truck wash
PA: Blue Beacon U.S.A., L.P.
500 Graves Blvd
Salina KS
785 825-2221

(P-17046)
CAR WASH PARTNERS INC
Also Called: CAR WASH PARTNERS, INC.
2619 Mount Vernon Ave (93306-2900)
PHONE...............................661 377-1020
EMP: 131
SALES (corp-wide): 876.51MM **Publicly Held**
Web: www.mistercarwash.com
SIC: 7542 Washing and polishing, automotive
HQ: Car Wash Partners, Llc
222 E 5th St
Tucson AZ
520 615-4000

(P-17047)
DYNAMIC AUTO IMAGES INC
Also Called: Dynamic Detail
2860 Michelle Ste 140 (92606-1007)
PHONE...............................714 771-3400
Tom Miller, *Pr*
EMP: 300 **EST:** 2004
SALES (est): 8.95MM **Privately Held**
Web: www.dynamicautoimages.com
SIC: 7542 7532 Washing and polishing, automotive; Collision shops, automotive

(P-17048)
EXECUTIVE AUTO RECONDITIONING
Also Called: Dealership Auto Dtail Rstrtons
522 E Duarte Rd (91016-4604)
PHONE...............................626 416-3322
Miguel Alvarado, *CEO*
EMP: 45 **EST:** 2017
SALES (est): 1.77MM **Privately Held**
SIC: 7542 7532 3842 Carwashes; Body shop, automotive; Cosmetic restorations

(P-17049)
VICTORVILLE SPEEDWASH INC
13311 Main St (92345-9132)
PHONE...............................760 998-2482
EMP: 80
SALES (corp-wide): 876.51MM **Publicly Held**
Web: www.mistercarwash.com
SIC: 7542 Washing and polishing, automotive
HQ: Victorville Speedwash Inc.
12147 Industrial Blvd
Victorville CA
760 962-9700

(P-17050)
VICTORVILLE SPEEDWASH INC
15200 Palmdale Rd (92392-2502)
PHONE...............................760 388-0112
EMP: 80
SALES (corp-wide): 876.51MM **Publicly Held**
Web: www.mistercarwash.com
SIC: 7542 Washing and polishing, automotive
HQ: Victorville Speedwash Inc.
12147 Industrial Blvd
Victorville CA
760 962-9700

(P-17051)
VICTORVILLE SPEEDWASH INC
12875 Bear Valley Rd (92392-9786)
PHONE...............................760 388-0113
EMP: 80
SALES (corp-wide): 876.51MM **Publicly Held**
Web: www.mistercarwash.com
SIC: 7542 Washing and polishing, automotive
HQ: Victorville Speedwash Inc.
12147 Industrial Blvd
Victorville CA
760 962-9700

7549 Automotive Services, Nec

(P-17052)
AMERIT FLEET SOLUTIONS INC
15325 Manila St (92337-7261)
PHONE...............................909 357-0100
David Kristy, *Mgr*
EMP: 665

Web: www.ameritfleetsolutions.com
SIC: 7549 Inspection and diagnostic service, automotive
HQ: Amerit Fleet Solutions Inc.
1333 N California Blvd # 345
Walnut Creek CA
877 512-6374

(P-17053)
AUTOMOTIVE TSTG & DEV SVCS INC (PA)
400 Etiwanda Ave (91761-8637)
PHONE...............................909 390-1100
Devon Larry Smith, *CEO*
Kay Smith, *
▲ **EMP:** 185 **EST:** 1989
SQ FT: 24,000
SALES (est): 16.41MM **Privately Held**
Web: www.automotivetesting.com
SIC: 7549 8734 8711 Emissions testing without repairs, automotive; Testing laboratories; Engineering services

(P-17054)
COMPLETE COACH WORKS
42882 Ivy St (92562-7218)
PHONE...............................800 300-3751
EMP: 227
SALES (corp-wide): 54.62MM **Privately Held**
Web: www.completecoach.com
SIC: 7549 Trailer maintenance
HQ: Complete Coach Works
1863 Service Ct
Riverside CA

(P-17055)
EZ LUBE LLC
Also Called: Valvoline Instant Oil Change
3599 Harbor Blvd (92626-1405)
PHONE...............................714 966-1647
EMP: 126
SALES (corp-wide): 21.83MM **Privately Held**
Web: www.expresscare.com
SIC: 7549 Lubrication service, automotive
PA: Ez Lube, Llc
3540 Howard Way Ste 200
Costa Mesa CA

(P-17056)
EZ LUBE LLC
Also Called: EZ Lube- Costco
13421 Washington Blvd (90292-5658)
PHONE...............................310 821-2517
Doug Paysse, *Mgr*
EMP: 130
SALES (corp-wide): 21.83MM **Privately Held**
Web: www.ezlube.com
SIC: 7549 Lubrication service, automotive
PA: Ez Lube, Llc
3540 Howard Way Ste 200
Costa Mesa CA

(P-17057)
JANS TOWING INC
134 N Valencia Ave (91741-2477)
PHONE...............................909 596-9060
Jan Qualkenbush, *Brnch Mgr*
EMP: 157
Web: www.janstowing.com
SIC: 7549 Towing service, automotive
PA: Jan's Towing Inc.
1045 W Kirkwall Rd
Azusa CA

(P-17058)
METROPRO ROAD SERVICES INC
Also Called: A & P Towing-Metropro Rd Svcs
957 W 17th St (92627-4402)
PHONE...............................714 556-7600
TOLL FREE: 800
Bradley T Humphreys, *CEO*
Jody Campbell, *
EMP: 100 **EST:** 1998
SALES (est): 1.92MM **Privately Held**
Web: www.metro-pro.com
SIC: 7549 Towing service, automotive

(P-17059)
SINGER VEHICLE DESIGN LLC (PA)
19500 S Vermont Ave (90502-1120)
PHONE...............................213 592-2728
Mazen Fawaz, *CEO*
Robert Peter Dickinson, *CPO*
Jason Grant, *CFO*
Jason Franklin, *COO*
EMP: 250 **EST:** 2009
SALES (est): 25.24MM
SALES (corp-wide): 25.24MM **Privately Held**
Web: www.singervehicledesign.com
SIC: 7549 3714 Automotive customizing services, nonfactory basis; Acceleration equipment, motor vehicle

7622 Radio And Television Repair

(P-17060)
DISH FOR ALL INC
148 S Escondido Blvd (92025-4115)
PHONE...............................760 690-3869
Ahed Ihmud, *Pr*
Rania Abedel Whab, *
Mike Arfat, *
EMP: 30 **EST:** 2007
SQ FT: 4,000
SALES (est): 410.16K **Privately Held**
Web: www.dishforall.com
SIC: 7622 5731 3679 Radio and television receiver installation; Radio, television, and electronic stores; Antennas, satellite: household use

7623 Refrigeration Service And Repair

(P-17061)
ARCTICOM GROUP RFRGN LLC
Also Called: PMC Southwest LLC
3675 De Forest Cir (91752-1139)
PHONE...............................916 484-3190
Sean Patrick, *Pr*
EMP: 406 **EST:** 2017
SALES (est): 9.67MM
SALES (corp-wide): 71.46MM **Privately Held**
Web: www.pmc-southwest.com
SIC: 7623 Refrigeration service and repair
PA: The Arcticom Group Llc
1676 N California Blvd # 420
Walnut Creek CA
925 334-7222

(P-17062)
CLIMA-TECH INC
1820 Town And Country Dr (92860-3616)
PHONE...............................909 613-5513
William C Valenzuela, *CEO*
Husein Aziz, *

Ada Roberts, *
EMP: 89 **EST:** 2004
SALES (est): 9.96MM **Privately Held**
Web: www.climatechref.com
SIC: 7623 1711 Refrigeration service and repair; Refrigeration contractor

(P-17063)
CONTROL AIR ENTERPRISES LLC
1390 Armorlite Dr (92069-1342)
PHONE..............................760 744-2727
Mike Eepn, *Brnch Mgr*
EMP: 475
SALES (corp-wide): 277.7MM **Privately Held**
Web: www.controlac.com
SIC: 7623 1711 Refrigeration service and repair; Heating systems repair and maintenance
PA: Control Air Enterprises Llc
5200 E La Palma Ave
Anaheim CA
714 777-8600

(P-17064)
MERCY AIR TRI-COUNTY LLC
1670 Miro Way (92376-8629)
P.O. Box 2532 (92334-2532)
PHONE..............................909 829-1051
David Dolstein, *Managing Member*
EMP: 250 **EST:** 1989
SQ FT: 11,288
SALES (est): 3.39MM
SALES (corp-wide): 1.71B **Privately Held**
SIC: 7623 4119 3721 7359 Air conditioning repair; Local passenger transportation, nec; Helicopters; Aircraft and industrial truck rental services
HQ: Air Methods Corporation
5500 S Quebec St Ste 300
Greenwood Village CO
855 896-9067

(P-17065)
MRV SERVICE AIR INC
Also Called: Mrv Crane
937 High St (93215-1704)
P.O. Box 535 (93216-0535)
PHONE..............................661 725-3400
EMP: 18 **EST:** 2007
SQ FT: 7,200
SALES (est): 959K **Privately Held**
Web: www.mrvserviceair.com
SIC: 7623 3444 Air conditioning repair; Sheet metalwork

7629 Electrical Repair Shops

(P-17066)
5 STAR SERVICE INC
18723 Via Princessa (91387-4954)
PHONE..............................323 647-7777
Sardor Umrdinov, *CEO*
EMP: 50 **EST:** 2018
SALES (est): 603.76K **Privately Held**
SIC: 7629 1389 Electrical household appliance repair; Construction, repair, and dismantling services

(P-17067)
ABLE CABLE INC (PA)
Also Called: A C I Communications
5115 Douglas Fir Rd Ste A (91302-2588)
PHONE..............................818 223-3600
Russell Ramas, *Pr*
Russell Ramas, *CEO*
Michael Collette, *
David Gardner, *

EMP: 175 **EST:** 1983
SQ FT: 3,500
SALES (est): 9.72MM
SALES (corp-wide): 9.72MM **Privately Held**
Web: www.acicommunications.com
SIC: 7629 1731 4813 Telephone set repair; Telephone and telephone equipment installation; Telephone communication, except radio

(P-17068)
AUTHORIZED CELLULAR SERVICE
Also Called: ACS
8808 S Sepulveda Blvd (90045-4810)
PHONE..............................310 466-4144
EMP: 100 **EST:** 1993
SQ FT: 10,000
SALES (est): 1.71MM **Privately Held**
SIC: 7629 5999 Telephone set repair; Telephone equipment and systems

(P-17069)
BSH HOME APPLIANCES CORP (DH)
1901 Main St Ste 600 (92614-0521)
PHONE..............................949 440-7100
TOLL FREE: 800
◆ **EMP:** 220 **EST:** 1996
SQ FT: 52,000
SALES (est): 529.92MM
SALES (corp-wide): 230.19MM **Privately Held**
Web: www.bsh-group.com
SIC: 7629 Electrical household appliance repair
HQ: Bsh Hausgerate Gmbh
Carl-Wery-Str. 34
Munchen BY
89459001

(P-17070)
PRO CIRCUITS MANUFACTURING INC ✪
16464 Via Esprillo (92127-1702)
PHONE..............................858 899-4747
Jay Madhani, *CEO*
Jay G Madhani, *CEO*
Daljit K Dhindsa, *Pr*
EMP: 21 **EST:** 2023
SALES (est): 405.64K **Privately Held**
Web: www.pcmi-usa.com
SIC: 7629 3672 5961 3315 Electronic equipment repair; Printed circuit boards; Computer equipment and electronics, mail order; Wire and fabricated wire products

(P-17071)
RUBEN & LEON INC
Also Called: Takyo Tyco
5002 Venice Blvd (90019-5308)
PHONE..............................323 937-4445
TOLL FREE: 800
Ruben Cielak, *Pr*
Leon Cielak, *VP*
EMP: 20 **EST:** 1983
SQ FT: 8,000
SALES (est): 2.22MM **Privately Held**
Web: www.tykosigns.com
SIC: 7629 5063 5719 3993 Electrical equipment repair services; Light bulbs and related supplies; Lighting, lamps, and accessories; Advertising artwork

(P-17072)
SCHROFF INC
Also Called: Pentair Equipment Protection
7328 Trade St (92121-3435)

PHONE..............................858 740-2400
Robert Bradley, *Brnch Mgr*
EMP: 120
Web: schroff.nvent.com
SIC: 7629 3469 Telecommunication equipment repair (except telephones); Electronic enclosures, stamped or pressed metal
HQ: Schroff, Inc.
170 Commerce Dr
Warwick RI
763 204-7700

(P-17073)
SCOTTEL VOICE & DATA INC
Also Called: Black Box Network Services
6100 Center Dr Ste 720 (90045-9228)
PHONE..............................310 737-7300
George Robertson, *Genl Mgr*
EMP: 130 **EST:** 1984
SQ FT: 5,200
SALES (est): 4.5MM **Privately Held**
SIC: 7629 1731 Telecommunication equipment repair (except telephones); Telephone and telephone equipment installation
HQ: Black Box Corporation
1000 Park Dr
Lawrence PA
724 746-5500

(P-17074)
TELENET VOIP INC
Also Called: Telenet
850 N Park View Dr (90245-4914)
PHONE..............................310 253-9000
TOLL FREE: 800
Asghar Ghassemy, *Pr*
Nicol Payab, *
EMP: 65 **EST:** 1977
SQ FT: 11,000
SALES (est): 11.94MM **Privately Held**
Web: www.telenetvoip.com
SIC: 7629 7379 7382 3612 Telephone set repair; Computer related consulting services ; Security systems services; Transmission and distribution voltage regulators

(P-17075)
TESTEQUITY LLC (PA)
Also Called: Techni-Tools
6100 Condor Dr (93021-2608)
PHONE..............................805 498-9933
Ruzz Frazee, *Pr*
Nick Hawtrey, *
▲ **EMP:** 166 **EST:** 1971
SQ FT: 75,000
SALES (est): 163.89MM **Privately Held**
Web: www.testequity.com
SIC: 7629 3825 Electrical equipment repair services; Test equipment for electronic and electrical circuits

(P-17076)
WILLIS ELECTRIC INC
Also Called: Willis Electric Company
4465 Buck Owens Blvd (93308-4939)
P.O. Box 81085 (93380-1085)
PHONE..............................661 324-2781
William A Willis, *Pr*
EMP: 29 **EST:** 1987
SQ FT: 8,500
SALES (est): 1.88MM **Privately Held**
Web:
www.williselectricmotorcompany.com
SIC: 7629 5999 7694 Electrical repair shops; Motors, electric; Electric motor repair

---

7641 Reupholstery And Furniture Repair

(P-17077)
GUYS PATIO INC
Also Called: Patio Guys
2907 Oak St (92707-3722)
PHONE..............................844 968-7485
Jan Vanderlinden, *Pr*
EMP: 25 **EST:** 1978
SALES (est): 1.42MM **Privately Held**
Web: www.patioguys.com
SIC: 7641 5712 5021 2514 Furniture repair and maintenance; Furniture stores; Outdoor and lawn furniture, nec; Metal household furniture

(P-17078)
MOYES CUSTOM FURNITURE INC
1884 Pomona Rd (92878-3278)
PHONE..............................714 729-0234
Brian Moyes, *Pr*
Jane Moyes, *
David Moyes Secratry, *Prin*
EMP: 50 **EST:** 1961
SQ FT: 59,000
SALES (est): 1.72MM **Privately Held**
Web: www.moyesfurniture.com
SIC: 7641 2512 Reupholstery; Upholstered household furniture

7692 Welding Repair

(P-17079)
AG-WELD INC
1236 G St (93280-2359)
P.O. Box 637 (93280-0637)
PHONE..............................661 758-3061
Jeff Mehlberg, *CEO*
Bedi Mehlberg, *VP*
Patty Mehlberg, *Contrlr*
▲ **EMP:** 17 **EST:** 1980
SQ FT: 20,000
SALES (est): 880K **Privately Held**
Web: www.ag-weld.com
SIC: 7692 Welding repair

(P-17080)
CAMERON WELDING SUPPLY (PA)
Also Called: Cameron Welding
11061 Dale Ave (90680-3206)
P.O. Box 266 (90680-0266)
PHONE..............................714 530-9353
Elizabeth Perry, *CEO*
Joseph Churilla, *
▲ **EMP:** 36 **EST:** 1963
SQ FT: 4,500
SALES (est): 11.48MM
SALES (corp-wide): 11.48MM **Privately Held**
Web: www.cameronwelding.com
SIC: 7692 5999 Welding repair; Welding supplies

(P-17081)
CLP INC (PA)
Also Called: Rick's Hitches & Welding
1546 E Main St (92021-5901)
PHONE..............................619 444-3105
Richard Preston, *Pr*
Betty Preston, *
EMP: 30 **EST:** 1974
SQ FT: 23,500
SALES: 994.42K
SALES (corp-wide): 994.42K **Privately Held**

Web: www.ricksrvcenters.com
SIC: 7692 7533 7699 Welding repair; Muffler shop, sale or repair and installation; Recreational vehicle repair services

(P-17082)
CW INDUSTRIES INC (PA)
1735 Santa Fe Ave (90813-1242)
PHONE..................562 432-5421
EMP: 49 **EST:** 1979
SQ FT: 22,000
SALES (est): 7.8MM **Privately Held**
Web: www.cwindustries.us
SIC: 7692 Welding repair

(P-17083)
DIP BRAZE INC
9131 De Garmo Ave (91352-2696)
PHONE..................818 768-1555
Gail Brown, *Pr*
Robert Gebo, *
EMP: 25 **EST:** 1956
SQ FT: 10,500
SALES (est): 2.13MM **Privately Held**
Web: www.dipbraze.com
SIC: 7692 3398 Brazing; Metal heat treating

(P-17084)
HANSENS WELDING INC
358 W 168th St (90248-2733)
PHONE..................310 329-6888
Gary D Hansen, *CEO*
Robert Hansen, *
Shauna Hansen, *
EMP: 25 **EST:** 1949
SQ FT: 26,000
SALES (est): 3.72MM **Privately Held**
Web: www.hansenswelding.com
SIC: 7692 Welding repair

(P-17085)
HAYES WELDING INC (PA)
Also Called: Valew Welding & Fabrication
12522 Violet Rd (92301-2704)
P.O. Box 310 (92301-0310)
PHONE..................760 246-4878
Roger L Hayes, *CEO*
Velma D Hayes, *Pr*
Vernon L Hayes, *VP*
▲ **EMP:** 91 **EST:** 1954
SQ FT: 45,000
SALES (est): 14.27MM
SALES (corp-wide): 14.27MM **Privately Held**
Web: www.valew.com
SIC: 7692 3465 3714 3713 Welding repair; Automotive stampings; Fuel systems and parts, motor vehicle; Truck and bus bodies

(P-17086)
HL WELDING INC
2434 Southport Way Ste L (91950-8796)
PHONE..................619 336-9231
Charles Eva, *COO*
Hoa Vu, *VP*
Henry Le, *Pr*
EMP: 24 **EST:** 2016
SALES (est): 2.78MM **Privately Held**
Web: www.hlweldinginc.com
SIC: 7692 Welding repair

(P-17087)
IRONMAN INC
20555 Superior St (91311-4418)
PHONE..................818 341-0980
Joe Salem, *CEO*
Ziva Salem, *
Ben Salem, *
Tish Byrne, *
EMP: 25 **EST:** 1987

SALES (est): 4.74MM **Privately Held**
Web: www.ironmaninc.net
SIC: 7692 Welding repair

(P-17088)
J AND D STL FBRICATION REPR LP
2360 Westgate Rd (93455-1046)
P.O. Box 5487 (93456-5487)
PHONE..................805 928-9674
Joe Trevino, *Pt*
David Cox, *Pt*
EMP: 17 **EST:** 2018
SALES (est): 185.31K **Privately Held**
Web: www.jdfabandweld.com
SIC: 7692 Welding repair

(P-17089)
JETI INC
Also Called: Jet I
14578 Hawthorne Ave (92335-2507)
PHONE..................909 357-2966
John Lowery, *Pr*
Jose Gradilla, *VP*
EMP: 17 **EST:** 1983
SQ FT: 10,000
SALES (est): 935.88K **Privately Held**
Web: www.jeti.com
SIC: 7692 Welding repair

(P-17090)
JOBSITE STUD WELDING
9445 Washburn Rd (90242-2912)
PHONE..................855 885-7883
EMP: 24 **EST:** 2018
SALES (est): 1.18MM **Privately Held**
Web: www.jobsitestud.com
SIC: 7692 Welding repair

(P-17091)
JON STEEL ERECTORS INC
1431 S Gage St (92408-2835)
PHONE..................909 799-0005
Octavio Arellano, *Pr*
EMP: 22 **EST:** 2005
SALES (est): 2.21MM **Privately Held**
Web: www.jonsteelinc.com
SIC: 7692 5082 1791 Welding repair; General construction machinery and equipment; Structural steel erection

(P-17092)
KATHLEEN BRUGGER
Also Called: J&K Welding
6815 Foxtail Ct (91739-1577)
PHONE..................,909 226-1372
Kathleen Brugger, *Owner*
EMP: 20 **EST:** 1982
SALES (est): 247.78K **Privately Held**
SIC: 7692 Welding repair

(P-17093)
MARLEON INC
Also Called: Southern Cal Pebblestone
3202 W Rosecrans Ave (90250-8225)
PHONE..................310 679-1242
Leon Hanley, *Pr*
EMP: 18 **EST:** 1960
SQ FT: 3,000
SALES (est): 467.24K **Privately Held**
SIC: 7692 2431 Welding repair; Staircases, stairs and railings

(P-17094)
RETTIG MACHINE INC
301 Kansas St (92373-8153)
P.O. Box 7460 (92375-0460)
PHONE..................909 793-7811
Franz A Rettig Senior, *Pr*

Robert A Rettig, *
Franz A Rettig Junior, *VP*
Susan L Rettig, *
EMP: 25 **EST:** 1952
SQ FT: 37,000
SALES (est): 2.19MM **Privately Held**
Web: www.rettigmachine.com
SIC: 7692 3599 Welding repair; Machine shop, jobbing and repair

(P-17095)
SOUTHCOAST WELDING & MFG LLC
2591 Faivre St Ste 1 (91911-7146)
PHONE..................619 429-1337
Patrick Shoup, *Pr*
Jay Parast, *
Leo Mathieu, *
EMP: 270 **EST:** 2004
SQ FT: 82,000
SALES (est): 44.01MM **Privately Held**
Web: www.southcoastwelding.net
SIC: 7692 Welding repair

(P-17096)
T L FABRICATIONS LP
2921 E Coronado St (92806-2502)
PHONE..................562 802-3980
Ryan Kerrigan, *Pr*
Michael Hsu, *
▲ **EMP:** 60 **EST:** 1980
SQ FT: 30,000
SALES (est): 6.5MM **Privately Held**
SIC: 7692 Welding repair

(P-17097)
TIKOS TANKS INC
Also Called: Rte Welding
14561 Hawthorne Ave (92335-2508)
PHONE..................951 757-8014
EMP: 24 **EST:** 2007
SALES (est): 2.01MM **Privately Held**
Web: www.rtewelding.com
SIC: 7692 Welding repair

(P-17098)
WELDLOGIC INC
Also Called: Weldlogic Gas & Supply
2651 Lavery Ct (91320-1502)
PHONE..................805 375-1670
Robert Elizarraz, *Pr*
Jack Froschauer, *
▲ **EMP:** 65 **EST:** 1980
SQ FT: 25,000
SALES (est): 9.44MM **Privately Held**
Web: www.weldlogic.com
SIC: 7692 Welding repair

(P-17099)
WEST COAST WLDG & PIPING INC
Also Called: Pipline
750 W Hueneme Rd (93033-9013)
PHONE..................805 246-5841
Gabriel Nunez, *Managing Member*
Jose Vargas, *
Mike Barbey, *
EMP: 80 **EST:** 2018
SALES (est): 1.21MM **Privately Held**
Web: www.wcwpiping.com
SIC: 7692 Welding repair

(P-17100)
WYMORE INC
697 S Dogwood Rd (92243-4604)
P.O. Box 2618 (92244-2618)
PHONE..................760 352-2045
Marla Wymore Stilwell, *Pr*
Michael Mouser, *

Richard C Wymore, *
Thomas A Wymore, *
EMP: 30 **EST:** 1947
SQ FT: 25,200
SALES (est): 2.27MM **Privately Held**
Web: www.wymoreinc.com
SIC: 7692 3599 5251 5085 Welding repair; Machine shop, jobbing and repair; Tools; Tools, nec

7694 Armature Rewinding Shops

(P-17101)
BAKERSFIELD ELC MTR REPR INC
Also Called: B E M R
121 W Sumner St (93301-4137)
PHONE..................661 327-3583
Michael Wayne Langston, *Pr*
Jerry Endicott, *Pr*
Nina Endicott, *VP*
EMP: 26 **EST:** 1949
SQ FT: 12,350
SALES (est): 1.33MM **Privately Held**
Web: www.electricmotorworks.com
SIC: 7694 5063 Rewinding services; Motors, electric

(P-17102)
BAY CITY ELECTRIC WORKS INC
15515 Markar Rd (92064-2314)
PHONE..................858 486-1054
Thomas D Claycomb, *Prin*
EMP: 17 **EST:** 2008
SALES (est): 418.83K **Privately Held**
Web: www.bcew.com
SIC: 7694 Electric motor repair

(P-17103)
E & L ELECTRIC
12322 Los Nietos Rd (90670-2912)
PHONE..................562 903-9272
Mike Fitch, *Pr*
EMP: 17 **EST:** 1959
SQ FT: 10,000
SALES (est): 2.14MM **Privately Held**
Web: www.eandlelectric.com
SIC: 7694 5063 Electric motor repair; Motors, electric

(P-17104)
ELECTRIC MOTOR WORKS INC
803 Inyo Street At 21st St (93305-5127)
P.O. Box 3349 (93385-3349)
PHONE..................661 327-4271
L B Thomasl B Thomas, *CEO*
L B Thomasl B Thomas, *Pr*
Chuck Thomas, *VP*
EMP: 20 **EST:** 1939
SQ FT: 7,600
SALES (est): 2.29MM **Privately Held**
Web: www.electricmotorworks.com
SIC: 7694 5063 Electric motor repair; Motors, electric

(P-17105)
EURTON ELECTRIC COMPANY INC
9920 Painter Ave (90605-2759)
P.O. Box 2113 (90670-0113)
PHONE..................562 946-4477
John Buchanan, *
Heather Buchanan, *
▲ **EMP:** 25 **EST:** 1973
SQ FT: 10,000
SALES (est): 3.8MM **Privately Held**

Web: www.eurtonelectric.com
SIC: **7694** 5063 Rewinding services;
  Electrical supplies, nec

(P-17106)
GRECH MOTORS LLC (PA)
6915 Arlington Ave (92504-1905)
PHONE..................951 688-8347
Edward P Grech, *Managing Member*
EMP: 25 EST: 2012
SALES (est): 24.57MM
SALES (corp-wide): 24.57MM **Privately
Held**
Web: www.grechmotors.com
SIC: **7694** Electric motor repair

(P-17107)
**R A REED ELECTRIC COMPANY
(PA)**
Also Called: Reed Electric & Field Service
5503 S Boyle Ave (90058-3932)
PHONE..................323 587-2284
John A Richard Junior, *Pr*
Dorothy J Richard, *
Alex Wong, *
EMP: 29 EST: 1929
SQ FT: 55,000
SALES (est): 6.22MM
SALES (corp-wide): 6.22MM **Privately
Held**
SIC: **7694** 5063 Electric motor repair;
  Motors, electric

(P-17108)
**SULZER ELCTR-MCHNCAL
SVCS US I**
620 S Rancho Ave (92324-3243)
PHONE..................909 825-7971
Gary Patton, *Brnch Mgr*
EMP: 50
SIC: **7694** 5063 Electric motor repair;
  Motors, electric
HQ: Sulzer Electro-Mechanical Services
  (Us) Inc.
  1910 Jasmine Dr
  Pasadena TX
  713 473-3231

(P-17109)
**SUPERIOR ELECTRIC MTR SVC
INC**
4622 Alcoa Ave (90058-2416)
PHONE..................323 583-1040
Vicky Marachelian, *Pr*
Art Marachelian, *VP*
EMP: 18 EST: 1963
SQ FT: 12,000
SALES (est): 4.76MM **Privately Held**
Web: www.superiorelectricmotors.com
SIC: **7694** 5063 Electric motor repair;
  Motors, electric

(P-17110)
WRIGHTS SUPPLY INC
Also Called: Foothill Electric Motors
25888 Springbrook Ave (91350-2565)
PHONE..................661 254-8400
Steve Dalton, *Genl Mgr*
EMP: 97
SALES (corp-wide): 9.97MM **Privately
Held**
Web: www.wrightssupply.com
SIC: **7694** 7699 5999 5084 Electric motor
  repair; Pumps and pumping equipment
  repair; Engine and motor equipment and
  supplies; Water pumps (industrial)
PA: Wright's Supply, Inc.
  640 Allen Ave
  Glendale CA
  818 242-1418

7699 Repair Services, Nec

(P-17111)
**ACTION CLEANING
CORPORATION**
1668 Newton Ave (92113-1013)
PHONE..................619 233-1881
Roberto Victoria, *Pr*
EMP: 40 EST: 1982
SALES (est): 8.85MM **Privately Held**
Web: www.action-cleaning.com
SIC: **7699** 4212 3732 Tank and boiler
  cleaning service; Hazardous waste transport
  ; Boatbuilding and repairing

(P-17112)
AER TECHNOLOGIES INC
Also Called: Aer Logistics
650 Columbia St (92821-2912)
PHONE..................714 871-7357
Kim Quick, *CEO*
Michael Mcgroarty, *Pr*
Ingrid Osborne, *
EMP: 320 EST: 1953
SQ FT: 50,000
SALES (est): 24.98MM **Privately Held**
Web: www.aertech.com
SIC: **7699** Precision instrument repair

(P-17113)
AEROWORX INC
Also Called: Aero Worx
2565 W 237th St (90505-5216)
PHONE..................310 891-0300
Gary E Furlong, *Pr*
Carol Furlong, *
▼ **EMP: 30 EST:** 1999
SQ FT: 38,800
SALES (est): 7.61MM **Privately Held**
Web: www.aero-worx.com
SIC: **7699** 3569 3492 3724 Industrial
  equipment services; Industrial shock
  absorbers; Control valves, aircraft:
  hydraulic and pneumatic; Pumps, aircraft
  engine

(P-17114)
ALPHATECH GENERAL INC
Also Called: Ametek-Ameron
4750 Littlejohn St (91706-2274)
PHONE..................626 337-4640
EMP: 90
SIC: **7699** 3812 Aircraft and heavy
  equipment repair services; Aircraft/
  aerospace flight instruments and guidance
  systems

(P-17115)
**AMERICAN COOLING TOWER
INC (PA)**
Also Called: American Cooling Tower
3130 W Harvard St (92704-3937)
PHONE..................714 898-2436
Erik Johnson, *Pr*
EMP: 19 EST: 1990
SQ FT: 3,500
SALES (est): 4.73MM **Privately Held**
Web: www.americancoolingtower.com
SIC: **7699** 3444 Tank repair and cleaning
  services; Cooling towers, sheet metal

(P-17116)
**AMERICAN VISION WINDOWS
INC**
Also Called: American Vision Baths
2125 N Madera Rd Ste A (93065-7709)
PHONE..................805 582-1833
William Herren, *CEO*

Monica Estrada, *
Al Alfieri, *
EMP: 215 EST: 1999
SALES (est): 24.92MM **Privately Held**
Web: www.americanvisionwindows.com
SIC: **7699** 1799 5031 Door and window
  repair; Home/office interiors finishing,
  furnishing and remodeling; Metal doors,
  sash and trim

(P-17117)
BRIDPORT ERIE AVIATION INC
Also Called: Amsafe Bridport
6900 Orangethorpe Ave (90620-1390)
PHONE..................714 634-8801
Sal Valle, *Genl Mgr*
Keith Mcconnell, *Pr*
Dennis Gilbert, *VP*
Harold Handelsman, *Sec*
Habib Enayetullah, *Treas*
EMP: 48 EST: 2000
SALES (est): 947.88K **Privately Held**
Web: www.amsafebridport.com
SIC: **7699** 7363 3728 Aircraft and heavy
  equipment repair services; Pilot service,
  aviation; Aircraft body and wing assemblies
  and parts

(P-17118)
CALI FRAMING SUPPLIES LLC
Also Called: Cali Framing
20450 Plummer St (91311-5372)
PHONE..................818 899-7777
▲ **EMP: 20 EST:** 2009
SALES (est): 2.28MM **Privately Held**
Web: www.califraming.com
SIC: **7699** 3999 Picture framing, custom;
  Framed artwork

(P-17119)
**CHROMALLOY SAN DIEGO
CORP**
7007 Consolidated Way (92121-2604)
PHONE..................858 877-2800
Armand F Lauzon Junior, *CEO*
Carlo Luzzatto, *
David G Albert, *
Michael Beffel, *
John Mckirdy, *VP*
EMP: 120 EST: 1986
SQ FT: 120,000
SALES (est): 16.69MM
SALES (corp-wide): 1.2B **Privately Held**
Web: www.chromalloy.com
SIC: **7699** 3724 Aircraft and heavy
  equipment repair services; Aircraft engines
  and engine parts
HQ: Chromalloy American Llc
  330 Blaisdell Rd
  Orangeburg NY
  845 230-7355

(P-17120)
**COLLECTORS UNIVERSE INC
(PA)**
Also Called: Collectors Universe
1610 E Saint Andrew Pl (92705-4931)
P.O. Box 6280 (92658-6280)
PHONE..................949 567-1234
Joseph J Orlando, *CEO*
Bruce A Stevens, *
Joseph J Wallace, *CFO*
EMP: 233 EST: 1986
SQ FT: 62,755
SALES (est): 78.89MM
SALES (corp-wide): 78.89MM **Privately
Held**
Web: www.collectors.com
SIC: **7699** Hobby and collectors services

(P-17121)
CROTHALL SERVICES GROUP
14710 Northam St (90638-5620)
PHONE..................714 562-9275
Frank Arcos, *Brnch Mgr*
EMP: 1208
SALES (corp-wide): 29.97B **Privately Held**
Web: www.crothall.com
SIC: **7699** Hospital equipment repair services
HQ: Crothall Services Group
  1500 Liberty Ridge Dr # 210
  Chesterbrook PA

(P-17122)
**CURTISS-WRIGHT
CORPORATION**
Also Called: Sgt Dresser-Rand
1675 Brandywine Ave Ste E (91911-6064)
PHONE..................619 656-4740
Joshua Guedsse, *Service Center Manager*
EMP: 44
SALES (corp-wide): 2.56B **Publicly Held**
Web: www.curtisswright.com
SIC: **7699** 3731 Industrial machinery and
  equipment repair; Shipbuilding and repairing
PA: Curtiss-Wright Corporation
  130 Harbour Place Dr # 300
  Davidson NC
  704 869-4600

(P-17123)
DK VALVE & SUPPLY INC
Also Called: DK Amans Valve & Supply
2385 E Artesia Blvd (90805-1707)
PHONE..................562 529-8400
David Kinzler, *CEO*
Eddie Kinzler, *Dir*
EMP: 31 EST: 1987
SALES (est): 3.49MM **Privately Held**
Web: www.dkamans.com
SIC: **7699** 3491 Valve repair, industrial;
  Industrial valves

(P-17124)
DUCLOS LENSES INC
Also Called: Duclos Lenses
20222 Bahama St (91311-6203)
PHONE..................818 773-0600
Paul Duclos, *Pr*
Michelle Duclos, *CFO*
EMP: 17 EST: 2013
SALES (est): 2.22MM **Privately Held**
Web: www.ducloslenses.com
SIC: **7699** 5731 3861 Camera repair shop;
  Video cameras and accessories; Lens
  shades, camera

(P-17125)
EDN AVIATION INC
6720 Valjean Ave (91406-5818)
PHONE..................818 988-8826
Motti Kurzweil, *Pr*
EMP: 45 EST: 1987
SQ FT: 15,000
SALES (est): 9.21MM
SALES (corp-wide): 168.68MM **Privately
Held**
Web: www.ednaviation.com
SIC: **7699** 3728 Aircraft and heavy
  equipment repair services; R and D by
  manuf., aircraft parts and auxiliary
  equipment
HQ: Velocity Aerospace Group, Inc.
  495 Lake Mirror Rd
  Atlanta GA
  214 988-9898

PRODUCTS & SVCS

(P-17126)
EVANS HYDRO INC
Also Called: Evans Hydro
18128 S Santa Fe Ave (90221-5517)
PHONE.............................310 608-5801
James R Byrom, *Pr*
EMP: 28 **EST:** 1929
SQ FT: 16,000
SALES (est): 8.08MM
SALES (corp-wide): 90.2MM **Privately Held**
Web: www.hydroinc.com
SIC: 7699 7694 5084 Pumps and pumping equipment repair; Armature rewinding shops; Pumps and pumping equipment, nec
PA: Hydro, Inc.
834 W Madison St
Chicago IL
312 738-3000

(P-17127)
EXCEL PICTURE FRAMES INC
647 E 59th St (90001-1001)
PHONE.............................323 231-0244
Rafael Delgado, *CEO*
Antonio Delgado Senior, *Pr*
EMP: 50 **EST:** 1992
SALES (est): 2.37MM **Privately Held**
Web: www.excelimagegroup.com
SIC: 7699 2791 Picture framing, custom; Photocomposition, for the printing trade

(P-17128)
FLEETWOOD MOTOR HOMES-CALIF INC
Also Called: Fleetwood Homes
2350 Fleetwood Dr (92509-2409)
PHONE.............................951 274-2000
David Lewis, *Brnch Mgr*
EMP: 185
SIC: 7699 5271 Mobile home repair; Mobile home dealers
HQ: Fleetwood Motor Homes-Calif.Inc
3125 Myers St
Riverside CA
951 354-3000

(P-17129)
GENERAL CONVEYOR INC
Also Called: Cleveland Tramrail So Calif
13385 Estelle St (92879-1881)
PHONE.............................951 734-3460
▼ **EMP:** 35
Web: www.himado.com
SIC: 7699 1796 3531 3536 Industrial machinery and equipment repair; Machinery installation; Backhoes, tractors, cranes, plows, and similar equipment; Hoists, cranes, and monorails

(P-17130)
GENESIS TECH PARTNERS LLC
21540 Plummer St Ste A (91311-4143)
PHONE.............................800 950-2647
EMP: 240 **EST:** 1998
SQ FT: 3,000
SALES (est): 319K
SALES (corp-wide): 3.7B **Privately Held**
SIC: 7699 Medical equipment repair, non-electric
HQ: Cohr, Inc.
10510 Twin Lakes Pkwy
Charlotte NC
704 948-5700

(P-17131)
HAWKER PACIFIC AEROSPACE
11240 Sherman Way (91352-4942)
PHONE.............................818 765-6201
Bernd Riggers, *CEO*

Brian Carr, *
Troy Trower, *
◆ **EMP:** 355 **EST:** 1980
SQ FT: 193,000
SALES (est): 49.57MM
SALES (corp-wide): 34.03B **Privately Held**
Web: www.lufthansa-technik.com
SIC: 7699 5088 3728 Hydraulic equipment repair; Aircraft and parts, nec; Aircraft parts and equipment, nec
HQ: Lufthansa Technik Ag
Weg Beim Jager 193
Hamburg HH
4050700

(P-17132)
HRD AERO SYSTEMS INC (PA)
25555 Avenue Stanford (91355-1101)
PHONE.............................661 295-0670
Tom Salamone, *Pr*
Tim Mcbride, *CFO*
◆ **EMP:** 101 **EST:** 1986
SQ FT: 70,000
SALES (est): 12.22MM **Privately Held**
Web: www.hrd-aerosystems.com
SIC: 7699 8711 Aircraft and heavy equipment repair services; Aviation and/or aeronautical engineering

(P-17133)
HYDRALIC SYSTEMS CMPONENTS INC
Also Called: Rupe's Hydraulics Sales & Svc
725 N Twin Oaks Valley Rd (92069-1713)
PHONE.............................760 744-9350
Patrick John Maluso, *CEO*
Stephanie Jennison, *
▲ **EMP:** 29 **EST:** 1977
SQ FT: 36,000
SALES (est): 5.08MM **Privately Held**
Web: www.rupeshydraulics.com
SIC: 7699 5084 3559 Hydraulic equipment repair; Hydraulic systems equipment and supplies; Ammunition and explosives, loading machinery

(P-17134)
INNOVATIVE EMERGENCY EQUIPMENT
1616 Marlborough Ave (92507-2041)
PHONE.............................951 222-2270
Sheri Kelley, *Prin*
EMP: 22 **EST:** 2016
SALES (est): 1.06MM **Privately Held**
Web: www.idsmp.com
SIC: 7699 3669 Repair services, nec; Sirens, electric: vehicle, marine, industrial, and air raid

(P-17135)
INTERFACE WELDING
20722 Belshaw Ave (90746-3510)
PHONE.............................310 323-4944
A S Wadleigh, *Pr*
EMP: 20 **EST:** 1967
SQ FT: 12,000
SALES (est): 2.43MM **Privately Held**
Web: www.interfacewelding.com
SIC: 7699 7692 3769 3728 Welding equipment repair; Welding repair; Space vehicle equipment, nec; Aircraft parts and equipment, nec

(P-17136)
KONE INC
1540 Scenic Ave # 100 (92626-1408)
PHONE.............................714 890-7080
Jeff Schultz, *Mgr*
EMP: 35
Web: www.kone.us

SIC: 7699 3534 1796 Elevators: inspection, service, and repair; Elevators and moving stairways; Installing building equipment
HQ: Kone Inc.
3333 Warrenville Rd
Lisle IL
630 577-1650

(P-17137)
MARINE GROUP BOAT WORKS LLC
Also Called: Marine Group Boat Works
997 G St (91910-3414)
PHONE.............................619 427-6767
Herb Engel, *Managing Member*
Arthur E Engel, *
Todd Roberts, *
▲ **EMP:** 115 **EST:** 2008
SALES (est): 32.96MM **Privately Held**
Web: www.marinegroupbw.com
SIC: 7699 Boat repair

(P-17138)
MCKENNA BOILER WORKS INC
2601 Industry St (92054-4808)
PHONE.............................323 221-1171
Howard Smith, *Pr*
Richard R Smith, *
James F Smith, *
EMP: 35 **EST:** 1921
SALES (est): 4.24MM **Privately Held**
Web: www.mckennaboiler.com
SIC: 7699 3823 Boiler repair shop; Boiler controls: industrial, power, and marine type

(P-17139)
MELAN INC
13700 Alton Pkwy Ste 154-2 (92618-1628)
PHONE.............................818 489-1745
Mickaiel H Kamran, *Brnch Mgr*
EMP: 85
SALES (corp-wide): 504.69K **Privately Held**
SIC: 7699 Industrial machinery and equipment repair
PA: Melan, Inc.
23151 Verdugo Dr Ste 103
Laguna Hills CA
818 489-1745

(P-17140)
NAVY UNITED STATES DEPARTMENT
Also Called: Maintenance Dept
311 Navy Base Ventura County (93042-0001)
PHONE.............................805 989-1328
Art Baulyut, *Mgr*
EMP: 250
Web: www.navy.mil
SIC: 7699 9711 Aircraft and heavy equipment repair services; Navy
HQ: United States Department Of The Navy
1200 Navy Pentagon
Washington DC

(P-17141)
OMNI OPTICAL PRODUCTS INC
22605 La Palma Ave Ste 505 (92887-6713)
PHONE.............................714 692-1400
Jeffrey Frank, *Brnch Mgr*
EMP: 31
SALES (corp-wide): 5.02MM **Privately Held**
SIC: 7699 5048 3827 Photographic and optical goods equipment repair services; Optometric equipment and supplies; Optical instruments and lenses
PA: Omni Optical Products, Inc.
17282 Eastman

Irvine CA
714 634-5700

(P-17142)
OXYHEAL HEALTH GROUP INC
3224 Hoover Ave (91950-7224)
PHONE.............................619 336-2022
EMP: 250
SIC: 7699 Industrial equipment services

(P-17143)
PACIFIC COAST ELEVATOR CORP
Also Called: Amtech Elevator Services
3041 Roswell St (90065-2213)
PHONE.............................323 345-2550
Tom Bertsch, *Brnch Mgr*
EMP: 85
SALES (corp-wide): 13.69B **Publicly Held**
Web: www.amtechelevator.com
SIC: 7699 1796 Elevators: inspection, service, and repair; Elevator installation and conversion
HQ: Pacific Coast Elevator Corporation
1 Farm Springs Rd
Farmington CT
860 676-6000

(P-17144)
PASSPORT TECHNOLOGY USA INC
Also Called: Asai
400 N Brand Blvd Ste 800 (91203-2366)
PHONE.............................818 957-5471
Cleve Tzung, *CEO*
Scott Dowty, *
John Steely, *Chief Operations*
Paul Nielsen, *
Jason H King, *CRO*
EMP: 33 **EST:** 1997
SQ FT: 1,200
SALES (est): 8.43MM **Privately Held**
Web: www.passporttechnology.com
SIC: 7699 3578 6099 Automated teller machine (ATM) repair; Automatic teller machines (ATM); Automated teller machine (ATM) network

(P-17145)
PEGGS COMPANY INC (PA)
4851 Felspar St (92509-3024)
P.O. Box 907 (91752-0907)
PHONE.............................253 584-9548
Brett Nelson, *Pr*
Chresten Revelle Nelson, *
John L Peggs, *
◆ **EMP:** 100 **EST:** 1964
SQ FT: 80,000
SALES (est): 32.15MM
SALES (corp-wide): 32.15MM **Privately Held**
Web: www.thepeggscompany.com
SIC: 7699 3496 5046 7359 Shopping cart repair; Miscellaneous fabricated wire products; Commercial equipment, nec; Equipment rental and leasing, nec

(P-17146)
PKL SERVICES INC
14265 Danielson St (92064-8818)
PHONE.............................858 679-1755
Samuel Flores Junior, *Pr*
Linda Young, *
David K Howell, *
Michael Nisley, *
Paul Callan, *
EMP: 160 **EST:** 2003
SQ FT: 6,000
SALES (est): 29.42MM **Privately Held**
Web: www.pklservices.com

SIC: **7699** Aircraft and heavy equipment repair services

(P-17147)
PORTER BOILER SERVICE INC
1166 E 23rd St (90755-3447)
PHONE...................................562 426-2528
George Hrebien, *Pr*
Nooshin Singhal, *
EMP: 25 **EST:** 1958
SQ FT: 5,000
SALES (est): 2.42MM **Privately Held**
Web: www.porterboiler.com
SIC: **7699** 1711 3443 Boiler repair shop; Boiler maintenance contractor; Fabricated plate work (boiler shop)

(P-17148)
REDMAN EQUIPMENT & MFG CO
19800 Normandie Ave (90502-1112)
PHONE...................................310 329-1134
Gerald E Redman, *
Janelle Redman, *
▲ **EMP:** 48 **EST:** 1962
SQ FT: 8,000
SALES (est): 4.99MM
SALES (corp-wide): 11.08B **Publicly Held**
Web: www.redmaneq.com
SIC: **7699** 3443 Boiler and heating repair services; Heat exchangers, condensers, and components
HQ: Ohmstede Ltd.
   895 N Main St
   Beaumont TX
   409 833-6375

(P-17149)
RUSSELL-WARNER INC
Also Called: Roto-Rooter
24971 Avenue Stanford (91355-1278)
P.O. Box 74 (89411-0074)
PHONE...................................661 257-9200
EMP: 240
SIC: **7699** 6794 1711 Sewer cleaning and rodding; Patent owners and lessors; Plumbing, heating, air-conditioning

(P-17150)
SA CAMP PUMP COMPANY
Also Called: SA Camp Pump and Drilling Co
17876 Zerker Rd (93308-9221)
P.O. Box 82575 (93380-2575)
PHONE...................................661 399-2976
James S Camp, *Pr*
EMP: 60 **EST:** 1952
SQ FT: 10,000
SALES (est): 18.46MM
SALES (corp-wide): 22.14MM **Privately Held**
Web: www.sacampcompanies.com
SIC: **7699** 3561 Agricultural equipment repair services; Pumps and pumping equipment
PA: S A Camp Companies
   17876 Zerker Rd
   Bakersfield CA
   661 399-4451

(P-17151)
SAM SCHAFFER INC
Also Called: Weld-It Co
3015 E Echo Hill Way (92867-1905)
PHONE...................................323 263-7524
Stephen Schaffer, *VP*
EMP: 43 **EST:** 1946
SALES (est): 2.5MM **Privately Held**
Web: www.welditco.com
SIC: **7699** 3559 Industrial machinery and equipment repair; Petroleum refinery equipment

(P-17152)
SCHINDLER ELEVATOR CORPORATION
16450 Foothill Blvd Ste 200 (91342)
PHONE...................................818 336-3000
Lance Howard, *Mgr*
EMP: 240
Web: us.schindler.com
SIC: **7699** Elevators: inspection, service, and repair
HQ: Schindler Elevator Corporation
   20 Whippany Rd
   Morristown NJ
   973 397-6500

(P-17153)
SOUTH BAY SAND BLSTG TANK CLG
Also Called: Sbsbtc
326 W 30th St (91950-7206)
P.O. Box 13009 (92170-3009)
PHONE...................................619 238-8338
Canuto Lopez, *CEO*
EMP: 100 **EST:** 1991
SQ FT: 60,000
SALES (est): 11.96MM **Privately Held**
Web: www.sobaysandblast.com
SIC: **7699** 4212 Ship boiler and tank cleaning and repair, contractors; Hazardous waste transport

(P-17154)
STAVROS ENTERPRISES INC
Also Called: Facilitec West
681 Arrow Grand Cir (91722-2146)
PHONE...................................888 463-2293
Anthony Emanuel Stavros, *CEO*
EMP: 30 **EST:** 2006
SALES (est): 2.17MM **Privately Held**
Web: www.facilitecwest.com
SIC: **7699** 3272 Cleaning services; Grease traps, concrete

(P-17155)
SUNVAIR AEROSPACE GROUP INC (PA)
29145 The Old Rd (91355-1015)
PHONE...................................661 294-3777
Udo Reider, *CEO*
Glenn Miller, *
EMP: 80 **EST:** 2014
SQ FT: 77,000
SALES (est): 30.27MM
SALES (corp-wide): 30.27MM **Privately Held**
Web: www.sunvair.com
SIC: **7699** Aircraft and heavy equipment repair services

(P-17156)
SURVIVAL SYSTEMS INTL INC (PA)
Also Called: Ssi
34140 Valley Center Rd (92082-6017)
P.O. Box 1855 (92082-1855)
PHONE...................................760 749-6800
George Beatty, *CEO*
Mark Beatty, *
Colin Hooper, *
▲ **EMP:** 95 **EST:** 1968
SQ FT: 100,000
SALES (est): 20.08MM
SALES (corp-wide): 20.08MM **Privately Held**
Web:
www.survivalsystemsinternational.com
SIC: **7699** 3531 3086 Industrial equipment services; Winches; Plastics foam products

(P-17157)
TARSCO HOLDINGS LLC
11905 Regentview Ave (90241-5515)
PHONE...................................562 869-0200
Terry S Warren, *Managing Member*
EMP: 121 **EST:** 2007
SALES (est): 1.84MM
SALES (corp-wide): 164.48MM **Privately Held**
Web: www.tfwarren.com
SIC: **7699** Tank repair
PA: T.F. Warren Group Inc
   57 Old Onondaga Rd W
   Brantford ON
   519 756-8222

(P-17158)
TEAGUE CUSTOM MARINE INC
28115 Avenue Stanford (91355-1106)
PHONE...................................661 295-7000
Robert Teague, *Pr*
EMP: 19 **EST:** 1992
SQ FT: 30,000
SALES (est): 912.43K **Privately Held**
Web: www.teaguecustommarine.com
SIC: **7699** 5088 3732 7948 Boat repair; Marine crafts and supplies; Motorboats, inboard or outboard: building and repairing; Boat racing

(P-17159)
TECH KNOWLEDGE ASSOCIATES LLC
Also Called: Tka
1 Centerpointe Dr Ste 200 (90623-1050)
PHONE...................................714 735-3810
Joe Randolph, *CEO*
Ed Wong, *
Steve Gilbert, *
EMP: 80 **EST:** 2011
SALES (est): 24.98MM
SALES (corp-wide): 32.76MM **Privately Held**
Web: www.ii-techknow.com
SIC: **7699** Medical equipment repair, non-electric
HQ: St. Joseph Health System
   3345 Michelson Dr Ste 100
   Irvine CA
   949 381-4000

(P-17160)
TED LEVINE DRUM CO (PA)
1817 Chico Ave (91733-2943)
P.O. Box 3246 (91733-0246)
PHONE...................................626 579-1084
TOLL FREE: 800
Ozzie Levine, *Pr*
EMP: 80 **EST:** 1983
SQ FT: 200,000
SALES (est): 9.41MM
SALES (corp-wide): 9.41MM **Privately Held**
Web: www.tldrumco.com
SIC: **7699** 4959 3412 Industrial equipment services; Sanitary services, nec; Metal barrels, drums, and pails

(P-17161)
UPWIND BLADE SOLUTIONS INC
2869 Historic Decatur Rd Ste 100 (92106-6176)
PHONE...................................866 927-3142
Marty Crotty, *CEO*
Bo Thisted, *Pr*
Bryan Coggins, *CFO*
EMP: 288 **EST:** 2011
SALES (est): 4.58MM
SALES (corp-wide): 15.08B **Privately Held**

SIC: **7699** Pumps and pumping equipment repair
HQ: Upwind Solutions, Inc.
   1417 Nw Everett St
   Portland OR

(P-17162)
WARDLOW 2 LP (PA)
333 S Grand Ave Ste 4070 (90071-1544)
PHONE...................................562 432-8066
Steven B Mcleod, *Pt*
Joe Gregorio, *Pt*
EMP: 99 **EST:** 2007
SALES (est): 20.38MM **Privately Held**
SIC: **7699** Construction equipment repair

(P-17163)
WESTERN PUMP INC (PA)
Also Called: Competrol A Western Pump Co
3235 F St (92102-3315)
PHONE...................................619 239-9988
Dennis Rethmeier, *CEO*
Ryan Rethmeier, *
Janice C Rethmeier, *
▲ **EMP:** 55 **EST:** 1988
SQ FT: 10,000
SALES (est): 28.96MM
SALES (corp-wide): 28.96MM **Privately Held**
Web: www.westernpump.com
SIC: **7699** 5084 1799 3728 Tank repair and cleaning services; Petroleum industry machinery; Petroleum storage tanks, pumping and draining; Aircraft parts and equipment, nec

(P-17164)
WHITING DOOR MFG CORP
301 S Milliken Ave (91761-7800)
PHONE...................................909 877-0120
Abdullah Eren, *Brnch Mgr*
EMP: 92
SQ FT: 5,400
SALES (corp-wide): 101.87MM **Privately Held**
Web: www.whitingdoor.com
SIC: **7699** 3713 5531 5211 Door and window repair; Truck and bus bodies; Truck equipment and parts; Garage doors, sale and installation
PA: Whiting Door Mfg Corp
   113 Cedar St
   Akron NY
   716 542-5427

7812 Motion Picture And Video Production

(P-17165)
ABC FAMILY WORLDWIDE INC (HQ)
Also Called: ABC Family
500 S Buena Vista St (91521-0001)
PHONE...................................818 560-1000
EMP: 500 **EST:** 1996
SALES (est): 268.48MM
SALES (corp-wide): 82.72B **Publicly Held**
Web: www.thewaltdisneycompany.com
SIC: **7812** 4841 Cartoon production, television; Cable and other pay television services
PA: The Walt Disney Company
   500 S Buena Vista St
   Burbank CA
   818 560-1000

PRODUCTS & SVCS

(P-17166)
ADVANCED DIGITAL SERVICES INC (PA)
Also Called: A D S
948 N Cahuenga Blvd (90038-2615)
PHONE....................323 962-8585
Thomas Engdahl, *Pr*
Andrew Mcintyre, *Ch Bd*
Brad Weyl, *
▲ **EMP:** 87 **EST:** 1989
SQ FT: 33,000
SALES (est): 9.51MM **Privately Held**
Web: www.adshollywood.com
SIC: 7812 7819 Video tape production; Film processing, editing, and titling: motion picture

(P-17167)
AFRICAJUN LLC
Also Called: Matrix
39874 Golfers Dr (93551-2982)
PHONE....................310 403-1673
Charit Selico, *CEO*
EMP: 20 **EST:** 2017
SALES (est): 430.48K **Privately Held**
Web: www.africajun.com
SIC: 7812 8099 2099 8399 Television film production; Medical services organization; Seasonings and spices; Community development groups

(P-17168)
ALLIED ENTERTAINMENT GROUP INC (PA)
Also Called: Allied Artists International
273 W Allen Ave (91746)
PHONE....................626 330-0600
Greg Hammond, *Pr*
John Mason, *
Ashley D Posner, *
Kim Richards, *
Robert Fitzpatrick, *
◆ **EMP:** 325 **EST:** 1999
SQ FT: 60,000
SALES (est): 7.53MM
SALES (corp-wide): 7.53MM **Privately Held**
Web: www.alliedentertainment.com
SIC: 7812 Video production

(P-17169)
ARTISAN ENTERTAINMENT INC
2700 Colorado Ave Ste 200 (90404-5502)
PHONE....................310 449-9200
Wayne Levin, *Pr*
James W Barge, *
Brian James Gladstone, *
Kristine Klimczak, *
EMP: 1000 **EST:** 1988
SALES (est): 21.01MM
SALES (corp-wide): 3.85B **Privately Held**
SIC: 7812 Motion picture production
HQ: Lions Gate Entertainment Inc.
2700 Colorado Ave Ste 200
Santa Monica CA
310 449-9200

(P-17170)
BARNSTORM VFX INC
2860 N Naomi St (91504-2023)
PHONE....................818 792-1899
Bharti Sattar, *Managing Member*
EMP: 91 **EST:** 2015
SALES (est): 9.8MM **Privately Held**
Web: www.barnstormvfx.com
SIC: 7812 Video production

(P-17171)
BENTO BOX ENTERTAINMENT LLC
5161 Lankershim Blvd Ste 120 (91601-3718)
PHONE....................818 333-7700
Scott Greenberg, *CEO*
Brett Coker, *COO*
EMP: 300 **EST:** 2009
SALES (est): 40.55MM
SALES (corp-wide): 14.91B **Publicly Held**
Web: www.bentoboxent.com
SIC: 7812 Motion picture production and distribution
HQ: Fox Television Stations, Inc.
1999 S Bundy Dr
Los Angeles CA
310 584-2000

(P-17172)
BRILLSTEIN ENTRMT PARTNERS LLC (HQ)
Also Called: Brillstein Grey Entertainment
9150 Wilshire Blvd Ste 350 (90212-3427)
PHONE....................310 205-5100
Brad Grey, *Pr*
EMP: 90 **EST:** 1980
SALES (est): 16.29MM
SALES (corp-wide): 116.26MM **Privately Held**
Web: www.bepmedia.com
SIC: 7812 Television film production
PA: Wasserman Media Group, Llc
10900 Wilshire Blvd Fl 12
Los Angeles CA
310 407-0200

(P-17173)
BUENA VISTA INTERNATIONAL INC
350 S Buena Vista St (91521-0004)
PHONE....................818 295-5200
EMP: 115
SALES (corp-wide): 82.72B **Publicly Held**
SIC: 7812 7822 3695 Video tape production; Video tapes, recorded: wholesale; Video recording tape, blank
HQ: Buena Vista International Inc
500 S Buena Vista St
Burbank CA
818 560-1000

(P-17174)
BUNIM-MURRAY PRODUCTIONS
Also Called: Bmp
1015 Grandview Ave (91201-2205)
PHONE....................818 756-5100
Jon Murray, *
Gil Goldschein, *
Mark Lebowitz, *
Julie Pizzi, *
▲ **EMP:** 150 **EST:** 1989
SQ FT: 20,000
SALES (est): 31.14MM
SALES (corp-wide): 12.61MM **Privately Held**
Web: www.bunim-murray.com
SIC: 7812 Television film production
HQ: Banijay Entertainment
5 Rue Francois 1er
Paris
143189191

(P-17175)
CBS STUDIOS INC
4024 Radford Ave (91604-2190)
PHONE....................818 655-5160
David Stapf, *CEO*
Eris Gray, *CFO*

Christa A D'alimonte, *Sec*
EMP: 150 **EST:** 2005
SALES (est): 12.4MM **Privately Held**
Web: www.radfordsc.com
SIC: 7812 Motion picture and video production

(P-17176)
COLUMBIA PICTURES INDS INC
4024 Radford Ave (91604-2101)
PHONE....................818 655-5820
Cynthia Phillips, *Prin*
EMP: 85
SIC: 7812 Motion picture and video production
HQ: Columbia Pictures Industries, Inc.
10202 Washington Blvd
Culver City CA
310 244-4000

(P-17177)
COLUMBIA PICTURES INDS INC (DH)
Also Called: Columbia Pictures
10202 Washington Blvd (90232-3119)
PHONE....................310 244-4000
Michael Lynton, *CEO*
Ronald Jacobi, *Ex VP*
Doug Belgrad, *Pr*
Edgar Howells, *CFO*
EMP: 200 **EST:** 1987
SALES (est): 69.43MM **Privately Held**
SIC: 7812 Motion picture production and distribution
HQ: Sony Pictures Entertainment, Inc.
10202 Washington Blvd
Culver City CA
310 244-4000

(P-17178)
CRAFTY APES LLC (PA)
127 Lomita St (90245-4114)
PHONE....................310 837-3900
EMP: 542 **EST:** 2011
SALES (est): 18.63MM
SALES (corp-wide): 18.63MM **Privately Held**
Web: www.craftyapes.com
SIC: 7812 Video production

(P-17179)
CREATIVE PARK PRODUCTIONS LLC
Also Called: Universal Studios
100 Universal City Plz (91608-1002)
PHONE....................818 622-3702
EMP: 157 **EST:** 2002
SALES (est): 19.77MM **Privately Held**
SIC: 7812 Motion picture and video production

(P-17180)
CRUNCHYROLL LLC (DH)
Also Called: Funimation Entertainment
10202 Washington Blvd (90232-3119)
PHONE....................972 355-7300
General Fukunaga, *Pr*
Greg Stevenson, *CFO*
▲ **EMP:** 82 **EST:** 1994
SALES (est): 23.78MM **Privately Held**
Web: www.funimation.com
SIC: 7812 4813 7822 Cartoon production, television; Internet host services; Video tapes, recorded: wholesale
HQ: Sony Pictures Entertainment, Inc.
10202 Washington Blvd
Culver City CA
310 244-4000

(P-17181)
DIGITAL DOMAIN 30 INC (PA)
12641 Beatrice St (90066-7003)
PHONE....................213 797-3100
Daniel Seah, *CEO*
Od Welch, *
Amit Chopra, *
Rich Flier Md, *Prin*
John Lagerling, *
EMP: 300 **EST:** 2012
SALES (est): 72.99MM
SALES (corp-wide): 72.99MM **Privately Held**
Web: www.digitaldomain.com
SIC: 7812 Video production

(P-17182)
DISNEY ENTERPRISES INC
Also Called: Disney
1313 S Harbor Blvd (92802-2309)
PHONE....................407 397-6000
Marlene Madrid, *Mgr*
EMP: 100
SALES (corp-wide): 88.9B **Publicly Held**
Web: www.thewaltdisneycompany.com
SIC: 7812 Motion picture production and distribution, television
HQ: Disney Enterprises, Inc.
500 S Buena Vista St
Burbank CA
818 560-1000

(P-17183)
DISNEY ENTERPRISES INC
Also Called: Disney
700 W Ball Rd (92802-1843)
P.O. Box 3232 (92803-3232)
PHONE....................714 781-1651
Matt Ouimet, *Brnch Mgr*
EMP: 213
SALES (corp-wide): 88.9B **Publicly Held**
Web: www.disney.com
SIC: 7812 Motion picture production and distribution
HQ: Disney Enterprises, Inc.
500 S Buena Vista St
Burbank CA
818 560-1000

(P-17184)
DISNEY ENTERPRISES INC
Also Called: Disney
1101 Flower St (91201-2415)
PHONE....................818 553-4103
EMP: 80
SALES (corp-wide): 88.9B **Publicly Held**
Web: www.disney.com
SIC: 7812 Motion picture production and distribution, television
HQ: Disney Enterprises, Inc.
500 S Buena Vista St
Burbank CA
818 560-1000

(P-17185)
DISNEY INCORPORATED (DH)
Also Called: Disney
500 S Buena Vista St (91521-0001)
PHONE....................818 560-1000
Matthew L Mcginnis, *CEO*
Sanford M Litvack, *
▲ **EMP:** 150 **EST:** 1952
SALES (est): 411.73MM
SALES (corp-wide): 88.9B **Publicly Held**
Web: www.disney.com
SIC: 7812 Motion picture production and distribution
HQ: Disney Enterprises, Inc.
500 S Buena Vista St
Burbank CA
818 560-1000

(P-17186)
DREAMWORKS ANIMATION PUBG LLC
1000 Flower St (91201-3007)
PHONE................................818 695-5000
EMP: 1019 **EST:** 2014
SALES (est): 948.34K
SALES (corp-wide): 121.43B **Publicly Held**
SIC: 7812 Motion picture and video production
HQ: Dwa Holdings, Llc
1000 Flower St
Glendale CA
818 695-5000

(P-17187)
DWA HOLDINGS LLC (DH)
1000 Flower St (91201-3007)
PHONE................................818 695-5000
Mellody Hobson, *Prin*
Jeffrey Katzenberg, *
Ann Daly, *
Fazal Merchant, *
Steven A Adams, *CAO**
EMP: 97 **EST:** 1994
SQ FT: 500,000
SALES (est): 501.05MM
SALES (corp-wide): 121.43B **Publicly Held**
Web: research.dreamworks.com
SIC: 7812 Cartoon motion picture production
HQ: Nbcuniversal Media, Llc
30 Rockefeller Plz Fl 2
New York NY

(P-17188)
EFILM LLC
Also Called: E Film Digital Labratories
1144 N Las Palmas Ave (90038-1209)
PHONE................................323 463-7041
Dominik J Schmidt, *
EMP: 150 **EST:** 2002
SALES (est): 22.96MM **Privately Held**
Web: www.company3.com
SIC: 7812 Video production

(P-17189)
ENDEMOL SHINE NORTH AMERICA
5161 Lankershim Blvd Ste 400 (91601-4962)
PHONE................................747 529-8000
Sharon Levy, *CEO*
EMP: 82 **EST:** 2015
SALES (est): 1.76MM **Privately Held**
Web: www.endemolshine.us
SIC: 7812 Motion picture production

(P-17190)
FANCY LIFE ENTERPRISES LLC (PA) ✪
Also Called: Fancy Life Studios
8030 La Mesa Blvd Pmb 3039 (91942-0335)
PHONE................................619 560-9890
Seana Earls, *Managing Member*
EMP: 125 **EST:** 2022
SALES (est): 12MM
SALES (corp-wide): 12MM **Privately Held**
Web: fancy-life-studios.business.site
SIC: 7812 Television film production

(P-17191)
FILM ROMAN LLC
6320 Canoga Ave Ste 450 (91367-2526)
PHONE................................818 748-4000
Dana Booton, *Mgr*
EMP: 214

SQ FT: 87,000
SALES (corp-wide): 3.85B **Privately Held**
Web: www.filmroman.com
SIC: 7812 Cartoon motion picture production
HQ: Film Roman, Llc.
8900 Liberty Cir
Englewood CO
720 852-6327

(P-17192)
FOCUS FEATURES LLC (DH)
1540 2nd St Ste 200 (90401-3513)
EMP: 89 **EST:** 1999
SQ FT: 30,000
SALES (est): 25.11MM
SALES (corp-wide): 121.43B **Publicly Held**
Web: www.focusfeatures.com
SIC: 7812 Motion picture production and distribution
HQ: Nbcuniversal Media, Llc
30 Rockefeller Plz Fl 2
New York NY

(P-17193)
FONCO CREATIVE SERVICES
Also Called: Fonco Studios
1310 N San Fernando Rd (90065-1237)
PHONE................................415 254-5460
Phuong Davis, *Owner*
EMP: 19 **EST:** 1997
SALES (est): 1.15MM **Privately Held**
Web: www.foncostudios.com
SIC: 7812 7819 7336 3999 Video production ; Equipment and prop rental, motion picture production; Commercial art and graphic design; Miniatures

(P-17194)
FOX NET INC
Also Called: 20th Century Fox Studio
10201 W Pico Blvd (90064-2606)
PHONE................................310 369-1000
Chase Carey, *Pr*
EMP: 1219 **EST:** 1992
SALES (est): 30.76MM
SALES (corp-wide): 88.9B **Publicly Held**
SIC: 7812 Motion picture and video production
HQ: Twentieth Television, Inc.
10201 W Pico Blvd
Los Angeles CA

(P-17195)
HARPO PRODUCTIONS INC
Also Called: Harpo Entertainment Group
7619 N Patriot Way (91405-5648)
PHONE................................312 633-1000
Oprah Winfrey, *Ch Bd*
Tim Bennett, *
Doug Pattison, *
Bill Becker, *General Vice President**
EMP: 200 **EST:** 1988
SALES (est): 9.09MM **Privately Held**
SIC: 7812 Television film production

(P-17196)
HUNGRY HEART MEDIA INC
Also Called: Wondros
5450 W Washington Blvd (90016-1135)
PHONE................................323 951-0010
Jesse Dylan, *CEO*
EMP: 140 **EST:** 2011
SALES (est): 21.16MM **Privately Held**
Web: www.wondros.com
SIC: 7812 8742 Motion picture and video production; Marketing consulting services

(P-17197)
IGNITION CREATIVE LLC
1201 W 5th St Ste T1100 (90017-5158)
PHONE................................310 315-6300
EMP: 82 **EST:** 2003
SALES (est): 10.13MM **Privately Held**
Web: www.ignitioncreative.com
SIC: 7812 Video production

(P-17198)
LIONS GATE FILMS INC
2700 Colorado Ave (90404-3553)
PHONE................................310 449-9200
Jon Feltheimer, *Pr*
James Keegan, *
Steve Beeks, *
EMP: 147 **EST:** 1998
SQ FT: 30,000
SALES (est): 43.79MM
SALES (corp-wide): 3.85B **Privately Held**
Web: www.lionsgate.com
SIC: 7812 Motion picture production
HQ: Lions Gate Entertainment Inc.
2700 Colorado Ave Ste 200
Santa Monica CA
310 449-9200

(P-17199)
LUMA PICTURES INC
1453 3rd Street Promenade Ste 400 (90401-3428)
PHONE................................310 888-8738
Payam Shohadai, *Pr*
John Betdul, *
EMP: 171 **EST:** 2002
SALES (est): 14.74MM **Privately Held**
Web: www.luma.inc
SIC: 7812 Motion picture and video production

(P-17200)
MERLOT FILM PRODUCTIONS INC
Also Called: CBS Network News
7800 Beverly Blvd (90036-2112)
PHONE................................323 575-2906
EMP: 93 **EST:** 1996
SALES (est): 14.15MM
SALES (corp-wide): 30.15B **Publicly Held**
SIC: 7812 4833 Motion picture and video production; Television broadcasting stations
HQ: Cbs Broadcasting Inc.
524 W 57th St
New York NY
212 975-4321

(P-17201)
METRO-GOLDWYN-MAYER INC (DH)
Also Called: MGM
245 N Beverly Dr (90210-5319)
PHONE................................310 449-3000
EMP: 300 **EST:** 1996
SQ FT: 131,400
SALES (est): 1.04B **Publicly Held**
Web: www.mgm.com
SIC: 7812 Motion picture production and distribution
HQ: Mgm Holdings Ii, Inc.
245 N Beverly Dr
Beverly Hills CA
310 449-3000

(P-17202)
NBC UNIVERSAL INC
100 Universal City Plz (91608-1002)
◆ **EMP:** 532
SIC: 7812 Motion picture production and distribution

(P-17203)
NW ENTERTAINMENT INC (PA)
Also Called: New Wave Entertainment
2660 W Olive Ave (91505-4525)
PHONE................................818 295-5000
Paul Apel, *CEO*
Alan Duke, *
Greg Woertz, *
Brian Volk-weiss, *Pr*
Matt Sample, *
▲ **EMP:** 110 **EST:** 1986
SQ FT: 40,000
SALES (est): 37.24MM
SALES (corp-wide): 37.24MM **Privately Held**
SIC: 7812 Motion picture production

(P-17204)
ORION PICTURES CORPORATION
245 N Beverly Dr (90210-5319)
PHONE................................310 449-3000
Alex Yemenidjian, *Ch Bd*
Daniel J Taylor, *
EMP: 1000 **EST:** 1995
SALES (est): 20.77MM **Publicly Held**
SIC: 7812 Motion picture production and distribution
HQ: Metro-Goldwyn-Mayer, Inc.
245 N Beverly Dr
Beverly Hills CA

(P-17205)
PARAMOUNT PICTURES CORPORATION (HQ)
Also Called: Paramount Studios
5555 Melrose Ave (90038-3197)
PHONE................................323 956-5000
Brian Robbins, *Pr*
Jim Gianopulos, *Ch Bd*
Rob Moore, *V Ch Bd*
Frederick Huntsberry, *COO*
Mark Badagliacca, *Ex VP*
◆ **EMP:** 1700 **EST:** 1912
SALES (est): 648.72MM
SALES (corp-wide): 30.15B **Publicly Held**
Web: www.paramountstudiotour.com
SIC: 7812 4833 7829 5099 Motion picture production and distribution, television; Television broadcasting stations; Motion picture distribution services; Video cassettes, accessories and supplies
PA: Paramount Global
1515 Broadway
New York NY
212 258-6000

(P-17206)
PARAMUNT OVRSEAS PRDCTIONS INC
5515 Melrose Ave (90038-3149)
PHONE................................323 956-5225
▲ **EMP:** 734 **EST:** 1980
SALES (est): 7.87MM
SALES (corp-wide): 30.15B **Publicly Held**
Web: www.paramount.com
SIC: 7812 Motion picture and video production
PA: Paramount Global
1515 Broadway
New York NY
212 258-6000

(P-17207)
PIE TOWN PRODUCTIONS INC
5433 Laurel Canyon Blvd (91607-2114)
PHONE................................818 255-9300
EMP: 160 **EST:** 1994
SALES (est): 5.04MM **Privately Held**

PRODUCTS & SVCS

Web: www.pietown.tv
SIC: 7812 Video production

(P-17208)
PILGRIM STUDIOS INC
12020 Chandler Blvd Ste 200 (91607)
PHONE.....................818 728-8800
Craig M Piligian, *CEO*
EMP: 86 EST: 2013
SALES (est): 3.23MM Privately Held
Web: www.pilgrimmediagroup.com
SIC: 7812 Video production

(P-17209)
PLAYBOY ENTRMT GROUP INC (DH)
2300 W Empire Ave (91504-3341)
PHONE.....................323 276-4000
Brinda Viloa, *Dir*
James Griffiths, *
EMP: 139 EST: 1984
SALES (est): 22.09MM
SALES (corp-wide): 266.93MM Publicly Held
Web: www.criticalcontent.com
SIC: 7812 Video tape production
HQ: Playboy Enterprises, Inc.
10960 Wilshire Blvd Fl 22
Los Angeles CA
310 424-1800

(P-17210)
POINT360
1133 N Hollywood Way (91505-2528)
PHONE.....................818 556-5700
Brian Ehrlich, *Mgr*
EMP: 96
Web: www.point360.com
SIC: 7812 Video production
PA: Point.360
2701 Media Center Dr
Los Angeles CA

(P-17211)
POWER STUDIOS INC
Also Called: Digital Domain
300 Rose Ave (90291-2628)
PHONE.....................310 314-2800
EMP: 200
SIC: 7812 7819 Motion picture production;
Services allied to motion pictures

(P-17212)
PRAGER UNIVERSITY FOUNDATION
15021 Ventura Blvd Ste 552 (91403-2442)
PHONE.....................833 772-4378
Marissa Streit, *CEO*
EMP: 92 EST: 2011
SALES (est): 56.63MM Privately Held
Web: www.prageru.com
SIC: 7812 Motion picture and video
production

(P-17213)
RESPAWN ENTERTAINMENT LLC
20131 Prairie St (91311-6106)
PHONE.....................818 960-4400
Jason West, *Managing Member*
▲ EMP: 160 EST: 2010
SALES (est): 15.23MM
SALES (corp-wide): 7.43B Publicly Held
Web: www.respawn.com
SIC: 7812 Video production
PA: Electronic Arts Inc.
209 Redwood Shores Pkwy
Redwood City CA
650 628-1500

(P-17214)
RHYTHM AND HUES INC (PA)
Also Called: Rhythm & Hues Studios
2100 E Grand Ave Ste A (90245-5055)
PHONE.....................310 448-7500
John Hughes, *Pr*
Pauline Tso, *Sec*
Keith Goldfarb, *Stockholder**
EMP: 207 EST: 1987
SALES (est): 13.58MM
SALES (corp-wide): 13.58MM Privately Held
SIC: 7812 Cartoon production, television

(P-17215)
ROUNDABOUT ENTERTAINMENT INC
Also Called: Secuto Music
217 S Lake St (91502-2111)
PHONE.....................818 842-9300
Craig S Clark, *CEO*
EMP: 84 EST: 1992
SQ FT: 6,000
SALES (est): 10.8MM Privately Held
Web: www.roundabout.com
SIC: 7812 Video production

(P-17216)
SAINT JSEPH COMMUNICATIONS INC (PA)
Also Called: Catholic Resource Center
1243 E Shamwood St (91790-2348)
P.O. Box 720 (91793-0720)
PHONE.....................626 331-3549
Terry Barber, *Pr*
EMP: 25 EST: 1988
SALES (est): 2.46MM
SALES (corp-wide): 2.46MM Privately Held
Web: www.cedarhouse.co
SIC: 7812 2741 7822 Motion picture and
video production; Miscellaneous publishing;
Motion picture and tape distribution

(P-17217)
SCANLINE VFX INC
6087 W Sunset Blvd (90028-6434)
PHONE.....................310 827-1555
EMP: 1200 EST: 2019
SALES (est): 37.44MM Privately Held
Web: www.scanlinevfx.com
SIC: 7812 Video production

(P-17218)
SCANLINEVFX LA LLC
Also Called: Eyeline Studios
6087 W Sunset Blvd (90028-6434)
PHONE.....................310 827-1555
EMP: 179 EST: 2007
SALES (est): 12.94MM Publicly Held
Web: www.scanlinevfx.com
SIC: 7812 Video production
PA: Netflix, Inc.
121 Albright Way
Los Gatos CA

(P-17219)
SDI MEDIA USA INC (HQ)
Also Called: Iyuno-Sdi Group
6060 Center Dr Ste 100 (90045-1574)
PHONE.....................310 388-8800
Mark Howorth, *Pr*
EMP: 95 EST: 1974
SQ FT: 13,000
SALES (est): 48.85MM
SALES (corp-wide): 48.85MM Privately Held
Web: www.iyuno.com

SIC: 7812 Video production
PA: Iyuno Media Group
3601 W Olive Ave Ste 650
Burbank CA
818 812-1213

(P-17220)
SONY MEDIA CLOUD SERVICES LLC
10202 Washington Blvd (90232-3119)
PHONE.....................877 683-9124
EMP: 50 EST: 2013
SALES (est): 1.09MM Privately Held
Web: www.cimediacloud.com
SIC: 7812 7372 Video production; Business
oriented computer software
PA: Sony Group Corporation
1-7-1, Konan
Minato-Ku TKY

(P-17221)
SONY PCTRES WRLDWIDE ACQSTONS
10202 Washington Blvd (90232-3119)
PHONE.....................310 244-4000
Rory Bruer, *Pr*
EMP: 101 EST: 1988
SALES (est): 2.37MM Privately Held
Web: www.sonypictures.com
SIC: 7812 Video production
PA: Sony Group Corporation
1-7-1, Konan
Minato-Ku TKY

(P-17222)
SONY PICTURES ENTRMT INC (DH)
Also Called: Sony Pictures Studios
10202 Washington Blvd (90232-3119)
PHONE.....................310 244-4000
Tony Vinciquerra, *Ch*
Robert Lawson, *Ex VP*
George Rose, *WORLDWIDE PEOPLE & ORGANIZATION*
▲ EMP: 3000 EST: 1982
SALES (est): 1.55B Privately Held
Web: www.sonypictures.com
SIC: 7812 7822 7832 Motion picture
production and distribution; Distribution,
exclusive of production: motion picture;
Motion picture theaters, except drive-in
HQ: Sony Corporation Of America
25 Madison Ave Fl 27
New York NY

(P-17223)
SONY PICTURES STUDIOS INC
10202 Washington Blvd (90232-3195)
PHONE.....................310 244-4000
Jack Kindberg, *Pr*
Jared Jussim, *
EMP: 228 EST: 1989
SALES (est): 5.92MM Privately Held
Web: www.sonypicturesstudios.com
SIC: 7812 Motion picture production
HQ: Sony Pictures Entertainment, Inc.
10202 Washington Blvd
Culver City CA
310 244-4000

(P-17224)
SONY PICTURES TELEVISION INC (DH)
10202 Washington Blvd (90232-3119)
PHONE.....................310 244-7625
Ravi Ahuja, *Ch*
Keith Le Goy, *
Jeff Frost, *
Jason Clodfelter, *

Wayne Garvie, *
▲ EMP: 300 EST: 1982
SALES (est): 22.16MM Privately Held
Web: www.sonypictures.com
SIC: 7812 Motion picture production and
distribution, television
HQ: Sony Pictures Entertainment, Inc.
10202 Washington Blvd
Culver City CA
310 244-4000

(P-17225)
STUDIO CITY
5161 Lankershim Blvd # 200 (91601-4962)
PHONE.....................818 557-7777
Stuart Weiss, *Prin*
EMP: 95 EST: 2008
SALES (est): 5.24MM Privately Held
Web: www.scpxl.com
SIC: 7812 5049 Motion picture and video
production; Professional equipment, nec

(P-17226)
STUDIO DISTRIBUTION SVCS LLC
4000 Warner Blvd (91522-0001)
PHONE.....................818 954-6000
Eddie Cunningham, *Managing Member*
EMP: 140 EST: 2020
SALES (est): 3.99MM Privately Held
SIC: 7812 Motion picture production and
distribution

(P-17227)
STX FINANCING LLC
Also Called: Stx Entertainment
3900 W Alameda Ave Fl 32 (91505-4316)
PHONE.....................310 742-2300
Robert Simonds, *Ch*
Noah Fogelson, *CEO*
Andrew Warren, *CFO*
EMP: 107 EST: 2014
SALES (est): 29.98MM Privately Held
Web: www.erosstx.com
SIC: 7812 Motion picture production and
distribution, television
PA: Najafi Companies, Llc
2525 E Camelback Rd Ste 8
Phoenix AZ

(P-17228)
TWENTETH CNTURY FOX HM ENTRMT (PA)
10201 W Pico Blvd (90064-2606)
PHONE.....................310 369-1000
EMP: 1000 EST: 1953
SQ FT: 25,000
SALES (est): 43.19MM Privately Held
SIC: 7812 Television film production

(P-17229)
UNIVERSAL CITY STUDIOS LLLP
Also Called: Universal Studios
100 Universal City Plz (91608-1085)
PHONE.....................818 622-8477
▲ EMP: 7400
SIC: 7812 7996 Motion picture production
and distribution; Theme park, amusement

(P-17230)
UNIVERSAL CY STDIOS PRDCTONS L (DH)
Also Called: Nbcuniversal Television Dist
100 Universal City Plz (91608-1002)
PHONE.....................818 777-1000
Ron Meyer, *Pr*
Maren Christensen, *Ex VP*
Kenneth L Kahrs, *Ex VP*
Lynn A Calpeter, *Ex VP*

Rick Finkelstein, *Ex VP*
▲ **EMP:** 25 **EST:** 2002
SALES (est): 190.23MM
SALES (corp-wide): 121.43B **Publicly Held**
SIC: 7812 3652 2741 5947 Motion picture production and distribution; Phonograph records, prerecorded; Music, sheet: publishing and printing; Gift shop
HQ: Vivendi Universal Entertainment Lllp
30 Rockefeller Plz
New York NY
212 664-4444

(P-17231)
UNIVERSAL STUDIOS COMPANY LLC (DH)
100 Universal City Plz (91608-1002)
PHONE....................818 777-1000
Adam Fogelson, *Ch*
Donna Langley, *
Ron Meyer, *
Sean Gamble, *
▲ **EMP:** 605 **EST:** 1958
SQ FT: 100,000
SALES (est): 986.31MM
SALES (corp-wide): 121.43B **Publicly Held**
Web:
www.universalstudioshollywood.com
SIC: 7812 3652 2741 5947 Motion picture production and distribution; Phonograph records, prerecorded; Music, sheet: publishing and printing; Gift shop
HQ: Nbcuniversal Media, Llc
30 Rockefeller Plz Fl 2
New York NY

(P-17232)
WALT DISNEY MUSIC COMPANY (DH)
Also Called: Disney
500 S Buena Vista St (91521-0007)
P.O. Box 3232 (92803-3232)
PHONE....................818 560-1000
Tom Macdougall, *Pr*
Robert Cavallo, *Ch Bd*
Cathleen Tass, *Treas*
Cathleen M Taff, *CEO*
▲ **EMP:** 148 **EST:** 1947
SALES (est): 51.25MM
SALES (corp-wide): 88.9B **Publicly Held**
Web: www.thewaltdisneycompany.com
SIC: 7812 Motion picture and video production
HQ: Disney Enterprises, Inc.
500 S Buena Vista St
Burbank CA
818 560-1000

(P-17233)
WALT DISNEY PICTURES
Also Called: Disney
811 Sonora Ave (91201-2433)
PHONE....................818 409-2200
Meredith Roberts, *Sr VP*
EMP: 300 **EST:** 1983
SQ FT: 461,000
SALES (est): 43.33MM
SALES (corp-wide): 88.9B **Publicly Held**
Web: movies.disney.com
SIC: 7812 Motion picture and video production
PA: The Walt Disney Company
500 S Buena Vista St
Burbank CA
818 560-1000

(P-17234)
WALT DISNEY RECORDS DIRECT (DH)
Also Called: Disney
500 S Buena Vista St (91521-0007)
PHONE....................818 560-1000
Alan H Bergman, *Sr VP*
Rob Moore, *
Nick Franklin, *
Marsha Reed, *
◆ **EMP:** 2990 **EST:** 1996
SQ FT: 600,000
SALES (est): 112.36MM
SALES (corp-wide): 82.72B **Publicly Held**
Web: www.thewaltdisneycompany.com
SIC: 7812 Motion picture production and distribution
HQ: Disney Enterprises, Inc.
500 S Buena Vista St
Burbank CA
818 560-1000

(P-17235)
WARNER BROS ENTERTAINMENT INC (DH)
Also Called: Victory Studio
4000 Warner Blvd (91522-0002)
P.O. Box 29113 (71903-9113)
PHONE....................818 954-6000
Ann Sarnoff, *CEO*
Alan Horn, *
John Schulman, *
Barry M Meyer, *
◆ **EMP:** 132 **EST:** 2001
SALES (est): 542.49MM **Publicly Held**
Web: www.warnerbros.com
SIC: 7812 Television film production
HQ: Warner Media, Llc
30 Hudson Yards
New York NY

(P-17236)
WARNER BROS ENTERTAINMENT INC
Also Called: Warner Bros Studio Facilities
3500 W Olive Ave Ste 200 (91505-4644)
PHONE....................818 954-2209
Steven Singer, *Brnch Mgr*
EMP: 168
Web: www.warnerbros.com
SIC: 7812 Television film production
HQ: Warner Bros. Entertainment Inc.
4000 Warner Blvd
Burbank CA
818 954-6000

(P-17237)
WARNER BROS HOME ENTRMT INC (DH)
4000 Warner Blvd Bldg 160 (91522-0002)
P.O. Box 9153 (02021-9153)
PHONE....................818 954-6000
James Cardwell, *Pr*
Edward Byrnes, *
Frank Walsh, *
Timmy Treu, *
Ronald J Sanders, *
▲ **EMP:** 80 **EST:** 1978
SQ FT: 12,000
SALES (est): 52.95MM **Publicly Held**
SIC: 7812 Television film production
HQ: Warner Bros. Entertainment Inc.
4000 Warner Blvd
Burbank CA
818 954-6000

(P-17238)
WARNER BROS INTL TV DIST INC

4000 Warner Blvd (91522-0002)
PHONE....................818 954-6000
Robert Blair, *Pr*
Margee Schubert, *
EMP: 99 **EST:** 2003
SALES (est): 5.39MM **Publicly Held**
SIC: 7812 Television film production
HQ: Warner Bros. Entertainment Inc.
4000 Warner Blvd
Burbank CA
818 954-6000

(P-17239)
YOBS TECHNOLOGIES INC
Also Called: Yobs
615 Childs Way Tro 370 (90089-0024)
PHONE....................213 713-3825
Raphael Danilo, *Pr*
Federico Dubini, *
EMP: 50 **EST:** 2016
SALES (est): 821.27K **Privately Held**
Web: www.yobstech.com
SIC: 7812 8742 7389 3652 Educational motion picture production; Programmed instruction service; Business services, nec; Prerecorded records and tapes

(P-17240)
ZOIC INC
Also Called: Zoic Studios
3582 Eastham Dr (90232-2409)
PHONE....................310 838-0770
Loni Peristere, *CEO*
Chris Jones, *
Tim Mcbride, *Treas*
EMP: 125 **EST:** 2002
SQ FT: 15,000
SALES (est): 12.94MM **Privately Held**
Web: www.zoicstudios.com
SIC: 7812 Video production

(P-17241)
ZOO DIGITAL PRODUCTION LLC
Also Called: Zoo
2201 Park Pl Ste 100 (90245-4909)
PHONE....................310 220-3939
Laura Herbers, *Adm/Asst*
EMP: 169 **EST:** 2010
SALES (est): 23.18MM **Privately Held**
Web: www.zoodigital.com
SIC: 7812 Video production

7819 Services Allied To Motion Pictures

(P-17242)
A FILML INC
Also Called: Filml.a
737 N Western Ave # 101 (90029-3725)
PHONE....................213 977-8600
Paul Audley, *Pr*
Paul Audley, *Pr*
Denise Gutches, *
EMP: 95 **EST:** 1995
SALES (est): 12.36MM **Privately Held**
Web: www.filmla.com
SIC: 7819 Services allied to motion pictures

(P-17243)
ALAN GORDON ENTERPRISES INC
5625 Melrose Ave (90038-3909)
PHONE....................323 466-3561
Grant Loucks, *Pr*
Don Sahlein, *
◆ **EMP:** 24 **EST:** 1945
SQ FT: 15,000
SALES (est): 2.41MM **Privately Held**
Web: www.alangordon.com

SIC: 7819 3861 Equipment rental, motion picture; Photographic equipment and supplies

(P-17244)
ANNAPURNA PICTURES LLC
817 Hilldale Ave (90069-4906)
PHONE....................310 385-7701
EMP: 88 **EST:** 2017
SALES (est): 3.61MM **Privately Held**
Web: www.annapurna.com
SIC: 7819 Film processing, editing, and titling: motion picture

(P-17245)
CHAPMN/LNARD STDIO EQP CNADA I (PA)
12950 Raymer St (91605-4211)
PHONE....................323 877-5309
Leonard Chapman, *Pr*
Michael Chapman, *
▲ **EMP:** 145 **EST:** 1945
SQ FT: 300,000
SALES (est): 20.97MM
SALES (corp-wide): 20.97MM **Privately Held**
Web: www.chapman-leonard.com
SIC: 7819 Studio property rental, motion picture

(P-17246)
CONDOR PRODUCTIONS LLC
245 N Beverly Dr (90210-5319)
PHONE....................310 449-3000
EMP: 99 **EST:** 2016
SQ FT: 5,000
SALES (est): 293.23K **Privately Held**
SIC: 7819 TV tape services: editing, transfers, etc.

(P-17247)
DE LA MARE ENGINEERING INC
1908 1st St (91340-2691)
PHONE....................818 365-9208
George Jackman, *Pr*
EMP: 21 **EST:** 1952
SALES (est): 435.42K **Privately Held**
SIC: 7819 3679 Services allied to motion pictures; Electronic circuits

(P-17248)
DIRECTORS GUILD AMERICA INC (PA)
Also Called: D G A
7920 W Sunset Blvd (90046-3300)
PHONE....................310 289-2000
Jay D Roth, *Ex Dir*
Lesli Linka Glatter, *
Ed Sherin, *
Martha Coolidge, *
Max Schindler, *
EMP: 110 **EST:** 1936
SQ FT: 100,000
SALES (est): 40.88MM
SALES (corp-wide): 40.88MM **Privately Held**
Web: www.dga.org
SIC: 7819 8631 Directors, independent: motion picture; Labor organizations

(P-17249)
DNEG NORTH AMERICA INC (PA)
Also Called: Prime Focus World
5750 Hannum Ave Ste 100 (90230-6666)
PHONE....................323 461-7887
Namit Malhotra, *CEO*
Robert Hummel, *
Sue Murphree, *

Oliver Welch, *
Anshul Doshi, *Prin*
EMP: 85 **EST:** 1985
SQ FT: 50,000
SALES (est): 12.83MM
SALES (corp-wide): 12.83MM **Privately Held**
SIC: 7819 Sound effects and music production, motion picture

(P-17250)
DTS INC (DH)
5220 Las Virgenes Rd (91302-1064)
PHONE......................818 436-1000
Jon E Kirchner, *CEO*
Melvin L Flanigan, *
Blake A Welcher, *
Kevin Doohan, *CMO**
Kris M Graves, *
▲ **EMP:** 150 **EST:** 1990
SQ FT: 89,000
SALES (est): 52.35MM
SALES (corp-wide): 438.93MM **Publicly Held**
Web: www.dts.com
SIC: 7819 3651 Services allied to motion pictures; Household audio and video equipment
HQ: Adeia Holdings Inc.
3025 Orchard Pkwy
San Jose CA
408 473-2500

(P-17251)
F J & J CORPORATION
Also Called: Leonetti Company
6938 Shadygrove St (91042-3144)
PHONE......................505 452-1700
Frank Leonetti, *Pr*
Matthew Leonetti, *VP*
EMP: 19 **EST:** 1955
SQ FT: 28,250
SALES (est): 1.28MM **Privately Held**
SIC: 7819 3861 Equipment rental, motion picture; Motion picture apparatus and equipment

(P-17252)
FOR CALI PRODUCTIONS LLC
5555 Melrose Ave Bldg 213 (90038-3996)
PHONE......................323 956-9500
EMP: 287
SIC: 7819 Services allied to motion pictures
HQ: For Cali Productions, Llc
5808 W Sunset Blvd
Los Angeles CA
323 956-9508

(P-17253)
FOTO-KEM INDUSTRIES INC (PA)
Also Called: Foto Kem Film & Video
2801 W Alameda Ave (91505-4405)
P.O. Box 7755 (91510-7755)
PHONE......................818 846-3102
William F Brodersen, *CEO*
Christine M Burdick, *
Gerald D Brodersen Junior, *VP*
▲ **EMP:** 249 **EST:** 1963
SQ FT: 43,000
SALES (est): 44.05MM
SALES (corp-wide): 44.05MM **Privately Held**
Web: www.fotokem.com
SIC: 7819 Laboratory service, motion picture

(P-17254)
FUSEFX LLC
Also Called: Fusefx
14823 Califa St (91411-3108)

PHONE......................818 237-5052
David Altenau, *CEO*
Tim Jacobsen, *Chief Development Officer*
EMP: 300 **EST:** 2006
SQ FT: 12,500
SALES (est): 23.37MM **Privately Held**
Web: www.fusefx.com
SIC: 7819 Visual effects production

(P-17255)
HOLLYWOOD RNTALS PROD SVCS LLC (PA)
5300 Melrose Ave (90038-5111)
PHONE......................818 407-7800
Mark A Rosenthal, *Managing Member*
▲ **EMP:** 100 **EST:** 2000
SQ FT: 100,000
SALES (est): 9.55MM
SALES (corp-wide): 9.55MM **Privately Held**
Web: www.the-mbsgroup.com
SIC: 7819 Equipment rental, motion picture

(P-17256)
LEGEND FILMS
2200 Faraday Ave Ste 100 (92008-7233)
PHONE......................858 793-4420
EMP: 350 **EST:** 2013
SALES (est): 997.36K **Privately Held**
Web: www.legendfilms.com
SIC: 7819 Services allied to motion pictures

(P-17257)
NEP BEXEL INC (HQ)
Also Called: Bexel
7850 Ruffner Ave Ste B (91406-1619)
PHONE......................818 565-4399
EMP: 80 **EST:** 1980
SALES (est): 24.93MM
SALES (corp-wide): 421.16MM **Privately Held**
Web: www.bexel.com
SIC: 7819 5731 5065 Equipment rental, motion picture; Video cameras and accessories; Electronic parts and equipment, nec
PA: Nep Group, Inc.
2 Beta Dr
Pittsburgh PA
412 826-1414

(P-17258)
OLIVE AVENUE PRODUCTIONS LLC
4000 Warner Blvd (91522-0001)
PHONE......................770 214-7052
EMP: 500 **EST:** 2018
SALES (est): 5.39MM **Privately Held**
SIC: 7819 Developing and laboratory services, motion picture

(P-17259)
OMEGA/CINEMA PROPS INC
1515 E 15th St (90021-2711)
PHONE......................323 466-8201
E Jay Krause, *Pr*
Cheryl Jordan, *
▲ **EMP:** 90 **EST:** 1967
SQ FT: 300,000
SALES (est): 9.39MM **Privately Held**
Web: www.omegacinemaprops.com
SIC: 7819 Equipment rental, motion picture

(P-17260)
PIXOMONDO LLC
2055 S Barrington Ave (90025-1276)
PHONE......................310 394-0555
Jonny Slow, *CEO*
EMP: 662 **EST:** 2008

SALES (est): 79.07MM **Privately Held**
Web: www.pixomondo.com
SIC: 7819 Visual effects production
HQ: Sony Pictures Entertainment, Inc.
10202 Washington Blvd
Culver City CA
310 244-4000

(P-17261)
POINT360 (PA)
Also Called: Digital Film Labs
2701 Media Center Dr (90065-1700)
PHONE......................818 565-1400
Haig S Bagerdjian, *Ch Bd*
Alan R Steel, *Executive Vice President Finance & Administration*
EMP: 82 **EST:** 1997
SQ FT: 64,600
SALES (est): 20.63MM **Privately Held**
Web: www.point360.com
SIC: 7819 7822 7829 Video tape or disk reproduction; Motion picture and tape distribution; Motion picture distribution services

(P-17262)
POST GROUP INC (PA)
1415 N Cahuenga Blvd (90028-8125)
P.O. Box 3870 (91617-3870)
PHONE......................323 462-2300
Frederic Rheinstein, *Ch*
Vincent Lyons, *
Duke Gallagher, *
EMP: 110 **EST:** 1974
SQ FT: 40,000
SALES (est): 9.26MM
SALES (corp-wide): 9.26MM **Privately Held**
Web: www.postgroup.com
SIC: 7819 7812 Editing services, motion picture production; Motion picture and video production

(P-17263)
RUNWAY INC
1330 Vine St (90028-8140)
P.O. Box 1536 (90078-1536)
PHONE......................310 636-2000
Roberta Margolis, *Pr*
EMP: 80 **EST:** 1974
SQ FT: 17,500
SALES (est): 4.48MM **Privately Held**
Web: www.runway.com
SIC: 7819 Video tape or disk reproduction

(P-17264)
STAR WAGGONS LLC
13334 Ralston Ave (91342-7608)
PHONE......................818 367-5946
EMP: 87 **EST:** 1979
SALES (est): 8.25MM **Publicly Held**
Web: www.ziostudioservices.com
SIC: 7819 Studio property rental, motion picture
PA: Hudson Pacific Properties, Inc.
11601 Wilshire Blvd # 16
Los Angeles CA

(P-17265)
STEREO D LLC
Also Called: Stereod
3355 W Empire Ave 1st Fl (91504-3160)
P.O. Box 892164 (92589-2164)
PHONE......................818 861-3100
William Sherak, *Pr*
Milton Adamou, *
Prafull Gade, *
Aaron Parry, *
EMP: 88 **EST:** 2009
SQ FT: 55,000

SALES (est): 2.1MM **Privately Held**
Web: www.sdfxstudios.com
SIC: 7819 Editing services, motion picture production

(P-17266)
TECHNCLOR CRATIVE SVCS USA INC
Also Called: Technicolor Creative Studios
8921 Lindblade St (90232-2438)
PHONE......................818 260-1214
Timothy Sarnoff, *CEO*
Richard Andrews, *
John Hancock, *
Claude Gagnon, *
EMP: 450 **EST:** 1980
SQ FT: 25,000
SALES (est): 43.9MM **Privately Held**
Web: www.technicolor.com
SIC: 7819 Video tape or disk reproduction
PA: Vantiva
10 Boulevard De Grenelle
Paris

(P-17267)
TECHNCLOR VDOCASSETTE MICH INC (DH)
Also Called: Technicolor Video Service
3601 Calle Tecate Ste 120 (93012-5057)
PHONE......................805 445-1122
Lanni Ormonvo, *Pr*
John H Oliphant, *
▲ **EMP:** 500 **EST:** 1987
SALES (est): 93.72MM **Privately Held**
SIC: 7819 Video tape or disk reproduction
HQ: Technicolor Thomson Group, Inc
2233 N Ontario St Ste 300
Burbank CA

(P-17268)
TECHNICOLOR THOMSON GROUP INC (HQ)
Also Called: Technicolor Entertainment Svcs
2233 N Ontario St Ste 300 (91504-4500)
◆ **EMP:** 291 **EST:** 1922
SALES (est): 118.56MM **Privately Held**
SIC: 7819 7384 Video tape or disk reproduction; Photofinish laboratories
PA: Vantiva
10 Boulevard De Grenelle
Paris

(P-17269)
TEN PUBLISHING MEDIA LLC (PA)
831 S Douglas St (90245-4956)
PHONE......................310 531-9900
Scott P Dickey, *CEO*
Peter H Englehart, *Ch Bd*
Chris Argentieri, *Pr*
John B Bode, *Ex VP*
Stephanie S Justice, *Ex VP*
EMP: 230 **EST:** 1991
SALES (est): 24.68MM **Privately Held**
SIC: 7819 Visual effects production

(P-17270)
TESTRONIC INC
Also Called: Testronic Labs
111 N First St Ste 204 (91502-1851)
PHONE......................818 845-3223
Dominic Wheatley, *CEO*
▲ **EMP:** 135 **EST:** 1996
SALES (est): 9.33MM **Privately Held**
Web: www.testroniclabs.com
SIC: 7819 Video tape or disk reproduction

(P-17271)
VANTIVA SUP CHAIN SLUTIONS INC (HQ)
Also Called: Technicolor Video Services
3601 Calle Tecate Ste 120 (93012-5057)
PHONE....................805 445-1122
Lanny Raimondo, *CEO*
Orlando F Raimondo, *
Patricia Dave, *
◆ **EMP: 500 EST:** 1983
SALES (est): 480.55MM **Privately Held**
SIC: 7819 Video tape or disk reproduction
PA: Vantiva
10 Boulevard De Grenelle
Paris

(P-17272)
VANTIVA SUP CHAIN SLUTIONS INC
Also Called: Accounts Payable Department
5491 E Philadelphia St (91761-2807)
P.O. Box 2459 (91729-2459)
PHONE....................909 974-2016
EMP: 106
SIC: 7819 Video tape or disk reproduction
HQ: Vantiva Supply Chain Solutions, Inc.
3601 Calle Tecate Ste 120
Camarillo CA

(P-17273)
WALT DSNEY IMGNRING RES DEV IN (DH)
Also Called: Disney
1401 Flower St (91201-2421)
P.O. Box 25020 (91221-5020)
PHONE....................818 544-6500
Thomas O Staggs, *CEO*
Craig Russell, *DESIGN DELIVERY**
Bruce Vaughn, *CREATIVE**
Martin A Sklar, *
Jessica Hodgins, *
◆ **EMP: 1011 EST:** 1986
SQ FT: 100,000
SALES (est): 88.5MM
SALES (corp-wide): 82.72B **Publicly Held**
Web: www.disneyimaginations.com
SIC: 7819 8712 1542 8741 Visual effects
production; Architectural services; Custom
builders, non-residential; Management
services
HQ: Disney Enterprises, Inc.
500 S Buena Vista St
Burbank CA
818 560-1000

7822 Motion Picture And Tape Distribution

(P-17274)
BRAT INC
913 N Highland Ave (90038-2412)
PHONE....................619 410-3403
EMP: 82 **EST:** 2019
SALES (est): 2.41MM **Privately Held**
Web: www.brat.tv
SIC: 7822 Motion picture and tape
distribution

(P-17275)
CHP
11338 Walnut St (92374-7611)
PHONE....................909 213-3788
Glen Brian Copeland, *Prin*
EMP: 97 **EST:** 2011
SALES (est): 450.42K **Privately Held**
Web: chp.ca.gov
SIC: 7822 Motion picture and tape
distribution

(P-17276)
DELUXE NMS INC
4499 Glencoe Ave (90292-6357)
PHONE....................310 760-8500
Cyril Drabinsky, *CEO*
EMP: 200 **EST:** 2010
SQ FT: 20,000
SALES (est): 17.2MM
SALES (corp-wide): 2.24B **Publicly Held**
Web: www.dadcdigital.com
SIC: 7822 7374 Motion picture and tape
distribution; Data processing and
preparation
PA: Deluxe Corporation
801 Marquette Ave
Minneapolis MN
651 483-7111

(P-17277)
GRAMERCY PRODUCTIONS LLC
100 Universal City Plz Bldg 2150 (91608)
PHONE....................818 777-1677
John Alfred, *Ofcr*
EMP: 86 **EST:** 2010
SALES (est): 522.12K
SALES (corp-wide): 121.43B **Publicly Held**
SIC: 7822 Motion picture and tape
distribution
HQ: Focus Features Productions Llc
100 Unvrsal Cy Plz Bldg 2
Universal City CA
818 777-1677

(P-17278)
LIONSGATE PRODUCTIONS INC
2700 Colorado Ave Ste 200 (90404-5502)
PHONE....................310 255-3937
Jon Feltheimer, *CEO*
Steve Beeks, *
Wayne Levin, *
Michael Burns, *Vice Chairman*
Wayne Levin, *Chief Strategic Officer**
EMP: 283 **EST:** 2010
SALES (est): 55.62MM
SALES (corp-wide): 3.85B **Privately Held**
SIC: 7822 Motion picture and tape
distribution
HQ: Lions Gate Entertainment Inc.
2700 Colorado Ave Ste 200
Santa Monica CA
310 449-9200

(P-17279)
SONAR ENTERTAINMENT INC (PA)
2834 Colorado Ave Ste 300 (90404-3644)
PHONE....................424 230-7140
Thomas F Lesinski, *CEO*
Henry S Hoberman, *
William J Aliber, *
Joel E Denton, *Distributor**
EMP: 80 **EST:** 2007
SALES (est): 53.07MM
SALES (corp-wide): 53.07MM **Privately Held**
Web: www.halcyonstudios.tv
SIC: 7822 Motion picture and tape
distribution

(P-17280)
TWENTIETH CNTURY FOX INTL CORP (HQ)
Also Called: Fox
10201 W Pico Blvd Bldg 1 (90064-2606)
Rural Route 900 (90213)
PHONE....................310 369-1000
Robert A Iger, *CEO*
◆ **EMP:** 233 **EST:** 1972
SQ FT: 115,000

SALES (est): 1.31MM
SALES (corp-wide): 82.72B **Publicly Held**
Web: www.fox.com
SIC: 7822 7922 Motion picture distribution;
Television program, including commercial
producers
PA: The Walt Disney Company
500 S Buena Vista St
Burbank CA
818 560-1000

(P-17281)
UNITED ARTISTS CORPORATION
10250 Constellation Blvd Fl 19
(90067-6200)
PHONE....................310 449-3000
Danny Rosett, *Pr*
EMP: 108 **EST:** 1986
SALES (est): 4.15MM **Publicly Held**
SIC: 7822 Distribution, exclusive of
production: motion picture
HQ: Metro-Goldwyn-Mayer Studios Inc.
245 N Beverly Dr
Beverly Hills CA
310 449-3000

(P-17282)
UNITED ARTISTS FILMS COMPANY (DH)
Also Called: United Artist Releasing
245 N Beverly Dr (90210-5319)
PHONE....................310 449-3000
Alex Yemenidjian, *Pr*
EMP: 195 **EST:** 1987
SALES (est): 4.49MM **Publicly Held**
SIC: 7822 Distribution, exclusive of
production: motion picture
HQ: Mgm Holdings Ii, Inc.
245 N Beverly Dr
Beverly Hills CA
310 449-3000

(P-17283)
UNITED ARTISTS PRODUCTIONS INC
10250 Constellation Blvd Fl 19
(90067-6200)
PHONE....................310 449-3000
Christopher Mcgurk, *Pr*
EMP: 222 **EST:** 1995
SALES (est): 1.45MM **Publicly Held**
SIC: 7822 Distribution, exclusive of
production: motion picture
HQ: United Artists Pictures Inc.
10250 Constellation Blvd
Los Angeles CA

(P-17284)
UNITED ARTISTS TELEVISION CORP
10250 Constellation Blvd Fl 27
(90067-6200)
PHONE....................310 449-3000
EMP: 267 **EST:** 1931
SALES (est): 802.07K **Publicly Held**
SIC: 7822 Distribution, exclusive of
production: motion picture
HQ: United Artists Pictures Inc.
10250 Constellation Blvd
Los Angeles CA

(P-17285)
WARNER BROS TRANSATLANTIC INC
Also Called: Warner Bros
3300 W Olive Ave Ste 200 (91505-4658)
PHONE....................818 977-6384
EMP: 256
Web: www.cwtv.com

SIC: 7822 Distribution, exclusive of
production: motion picture
HQ: Warner Bros. (Transatlantic), Inc.
4000 Warner Blvd
Burbank CA

(P-17286)
WARNER BROS TRANSATLANTIC INC
Warner Bros
4001 W Olive Ave (91505-4272)
PHONE....................818 954-5990
Dan Romanelli, *Brnch Mgr*
EMP: 322
Web: property.warnerbros.com
SIC: 7822 Distribution, exclusive of
production: motion picture
HQ: Warner Bros. (Transatlantic), Inc.
4000 Warner Blvd
Burbank CA

7829 Motion Picture Distribution Services

(P-17287)
OUR ALCHEMY LLC
Also Called: Alchemy
5900 Wilshire Blvd Fl 18 (90036-5013)
PHONE....................310 893-6289
EMP: 80 **EST:** 2010
SQ FT: 30,000
SALES (est): 5.6MM **Privately Held**
Web: www.ouralchemy.com
SIC: 7829 Motion picture distribution services

7832 Motion Picture Theaters, Except Drive-in

(P-17288)
CARMIKE CINEMAS LLC
Also Called: Carmike Cinemas
166 W Hillcrest Dr (91360-4209)
PHONE....................805 494-4702
EMP: 87
Web: www.amctheatres.com
SIC: 7832 Exhibitors, itinerant: motion picture
HQ: Carmike Cinemas, Llc
11500 Ash St
Leawood KS
913 213-2000

(P-17289)
CENTURY THEATRES INC
7777 Edinger Ave Ste 170 (92647-8690)
PHONE....................714 373-4573
EMP: 174
Web: www.cinemark.com
SIC: 7832 Motion picture theaters, except
drive-in
HQ: Century Theatres, Inc
3900 Dallas Pkwy Ste 500
Plano TX
972 665-1000

(P-17290)
DECURION CORPORATION (PA)
120 N Robertson Blvd Fl 3 (90048-3115)
PHONE....................310 659-9432
Michael R Forman, *Pr*
Jerome Forman, *
James Cotter, *
EMP: 100 **EST:** 1966
SQ FT: 31,000
SALES (est): 175.87MM
SALES (corp-wide): 175.87MM **Privately Held**
Web: www.decurion.com

SIC: 7832 7833 Motion picture theaters, except drive-in; Drive-in motion picture theaters

(P-17291)
EDWARDS THEATRES INC
Also Called: Kaleidioscope Stadium Cinema
27741 Crown Valley Pkwy Ste 301 (92691-6532)
PHONE..................949 582-4078
EMP: 156
SIC: 7832 Motion picture theaters, except drive-in
HQ: Edwards Theatres, Inc.
　　300 Newport Center Dr
　　Newport Beach CA
　　949 640-4600

(P-17292)
EDWARDS THEATRES INC (DH)
Also Called: Edwards Theatres Circuit, Inc.
300 Newport Center Dr (92660-7529)
PHONE..................949 640-4600
James Edwards Iii, Ch Bd
Steve Coffey, *
Joan Randolph, *
Marcella Sheldon, *
EMP: 118 EST: 1930
SQ FT: 30,000
SALES (est): 82.16MM Privately Held
SIC: 7832 Motion picture theaters, except drive-in
HQ: Regal Cinemas, Inc.
　　101 E Blount Ave
　　Knoxville TN

(P-17293)
EDWARDS THEATRES INC
Also Called: La Verne Cinema 12
1950 Foothill Blvd (91750-3557)
PHONE..................844 462-7342
EMP: 175
SIC: 7832 Motion picture theaters, except drive-in
HQ: Edwards Theatres, Inc.
　　300 Newport Center Dr
　　Newport Beach CA
　　949 640-4600

(P-17294)
EDWARDS THEATRES CIRCUIT INC
Also Called: Rancho San Diego Cinema 16
2951 Jamacha Rd (92019-4342)
PHONE..................619 660-3460
EMP: 161
SIC: 7832 Motion picture theaters, except drive-in
HQ: Edwards Theatres, Inc.
　　300 Newport Center Dr
　　Newport Beach CA
　　949 640-4600

(P-17295)
EDWARDS THEATRES CIRCUIT INC
Also Called: Mira Mesa Stadium 18
10733 Westview Pkwy (92126-2963)
PHONE..................858 635-7716
Peter Brandon Pt, Brnch Mgr
EMP: 161
SIC: 7832 Motion picture theaters, except drive-in
HQ: Edwards Theatres, Inc.
　　300 Newport Center Dr
　　Newport Beach CA
　　949 640-4600

(P-17296)
EDWARDS THEATRES CIRCUIT INC
Also Called: Mesa Pointe Stadium 12
901 S Coast Dr (92626-1747)
PHONE..................714 428-0962
Minh Duong, Brnch Mgr
EMP: 179
SIC: 7832 Motion picture theaters, except drive-in
HQ: Edwards Theatres, Inc.
　　300 Newport Center Dr
　　Newport Beach CA
　　949 640-4600

(P-17297)
EDWARDS THEATRES CIRCUIT INC
Also Called: Edwards Cinemas University
4245 Campus Dr (92612-2752)
PHONE..................949 854-8811
Mike Peterson, Brnch Mgr
EMP: 170
SIC: 7832 Motion picture theaters, except drive-in
HQ: Edwards Theatres, Inc.
　　300 Newport Center Dr
　　Newport Beach CA
　　949 640-4600

(P-17298)
EDWARDS THEATRES CIRCUIT INC
Also Called: Temecula Stadium Cinemas 15
40750 Winchester Rd (92591-5524)
PHONE..................951 296-0144
EMP: 169
SIC: 7832 Motion picture theaters, except drive-in
HQ: Edwards Theatres, Inc.
　　300 Newport Center Dr
　　Newport Beach CA
　　949 640-4600

(P-17299)
HARKINS THEATRES INC
3100 Chino Ave (91709-3518)
PHONE..................909 627-8010
Sarah Yeats, Prin
EMP: 99
Web: www.harkins.com
SIC: 7832 Motion picture theaters, except drive-in
PA: Harkins Theatres, Inc.
　　8901 E Mcdonald Dr
　　Scottsdale AZ

(P-17300)
HARKINS THEATRES INC
27481 San Bernardino Ave (92374-5032)
PHONE..................909 793-7993
EMP: 86
Web: www.harkins.com
SIC: 7832 Motion picture theaters, except drive-in
PA: Harkins Theatres, Inc.
　　8901 E Mcdonald Dr
　　Scottsdale AZ

(P-17301)
KRIKORIAN PREMIERE THEATRE LLC
25 Main St (92083-5800)
PHONE..................760 945-7469
EMP: 93
SALES (corp-wide): 25.61MM Privately Held
SIC: 7832 Motion picture theaters, except drive-in

PA: Krikorian Premiere Theatre Llc
　　2275 W 190th St
　　Torrance CA
　　310 856-1270

(P-17302)
KRIKORIAN PREMIERE THEATRE LLC
8540 Whittier Blvd (90660-2520)
PHONE..................562 205-3456
EMP: 93
SALES (corp-wide): 25.61MM Privately Held
SIC: 7832 Motion picture theaters, except drive-in
PA: Krikorian Premiere Theatre Llc
　　2275 W 190th St
　　Torrance CA
　　310 856-1270

(P-17303)
KRIKORIAN PREMIERE THEATRE LLC
8290 La Palma Ave (90620)
PHONE..................714 826-7469
Ted Goldbeck, Brnch Mgr
EMP: 94
SALES (corp-wide): 25.61MM Privately Held
SIC: 7832 Motion picture theaters, except drive-in
PA: Krikorian Premiere Theatre Llc
　　2275 W 190th St
　　Torrance CA
　　310 856-1270

(P-17304)
WESTSTAR CINEMAS INC
Also Called: Man Theateres
180 Promenade Way Ste R (91362-3826)
PHONE..................805 379-8966
Joseph Leptore, Mgr
EMP: 109
SALES (corp-wide): 22.59MM Privately Held
SIC: 7832 Motion picture theaters, except drive-in
PA: Weststar Cinemas, Inc.
　　16530 Ventura Blvd # 500
　　Encino CA
　　818 784-6266

7833 Drive-in Motion Picture Theaters

(P-17305)
CENTURY THEATRES INC
Also Called: Century Downtown 10
555 E Main St (93001-2628)
PHONE..................805 641-6555
EMP: 251
Web: www.cinemark.com
SIC: 7833 7832 Drive-in motion picture theaters; Motion picture theaters, except drive-in
HQ: Century Theatres, Inc
　　3900 Dallas Pkwy Ste 500
　　Plano TX
　　972 665-1000

(P-17306)
CENTURY THEATRES INC
Also Called: Century 8
12827 Victory Blvd (91606-3012)
PHONE..................818 508-1943
Terrell Hammack, Brnch Mgr
EMP: 251
Web: www.cinemark.com

SIC: 7833 7832 Drive-in motion picture theaters; Motion picture theaters, except drive-in
HQ: Century Theatres, Inc
　　3900 Dallas Pkwy Ste 500
　　Plano TX
　　972 665-1000

7841 Video Tape Rental

(P-17307)
EROS STX GLOBAL CORPORATION
3900 W Alameda Ave Fl 32 (91505-4316)
PHONE..................818 524-7000
Kishore Lulla, C Executive*
Rishika Lulla Singh, *
Andrew Warren, CFO
EMP: 502 EST: 1977
SALES (est): 434.26MM Privately Held
Web: www.erosmediaworld.com
SIC: 7841 Video disk/tape rental to the general public

7911 Dance Studios, Schools, And Halls

(P-17308)
I2K LLC
748 N Mckeever Ave (91702-2349)
PHONE..................626 969-7780
EMP: 20 EST: 2015
SALES (est): 515.01K Privately Held
Web: www.i2kairpad.com
SIC: 7911 3061 Dance hall services; Medical and surgical rubber tubing (extruded and lathe-cut)

7922 Theatrical Producers And Services

(P-17309)
ADVENTIST MEDIA CENTER INC (PA)
Also Called: It Is Written
11291 Pierce St (92505-2705)
P.O. Box 101 (93062-0101)
PHONE..................805 955-7777
Daniel R Jackson, CEO
Marshall Chase, *
Warren Judd, *
Daniel Jackson, *
▲ EMP: 183 EST: 1972
SQ FT: 76,000
SALES (est): 566.81K
SALES (corp-wide): 566.81K Privately Held
Web: www.adventistmediaministries.com
SIC: 7922 Television program, including commercial producers

(P-17310)
AEG PRESENTS LLC (DH)
Also Called: AEG Presents
425 W 11th St (90015-3459)
PHONE..................323 930-5700
Jay Marciano, Ch
Jorge Melendez, *
John Meglen, *
Paul Gongaware, *
Shawn A Trell, *
▲ EMP: 140 EST: 2002
SQ FT: 16,400
SALES (est): 21.64MM Privately Held
Web: www.aegpresents.com

SIC: 7922 Entertainment promotion
HQ: Anschutz Entertainment Group, Inc.
800 W Olympic Blvd # 305
Los Angeles CA
213 763-7700

(P-17311)
AGENCY FOR PERFORMING ARTS INC (PA)
405 S Beverly Dr Ste 500 (90212-4401)
PHONE..............................310 557-9049
James Gosnell, *Pr*
EMP: 100 EST: 1962
SALES (est): 39.99MM
SALES (corp-wide): 39.99MM **Privately Held**
Web: www.apa-agency.com
SIC: 7922 Theatrical producers and services

(P-17312)
CENTER THTRE GROUP LOS ANGELES (PA)
601 W Temple St (90012-2621)
PHONE..............................213 972-7344
Meghan Pressman, *CEO*
Stephen Rountree, *
William Ahmanson, *
Kiki Gindler, *
Brindell Gottlieb, *
▲ EMP: 130 EST: 1966
SQ FT: 20,000
SALES (est): 15.78MM
SALES (corp-wide): 15.78MM **Privately Held**
Web: www.centertheatregroup.org
SIC: 7922 Theatrical companies

(P-17313)
CITY OF DOWNEY
Also Called: Downey Civic Theatre
8435 Firestone Blvd (90241-3843)
P.O. Box 607 (90241-0607)
PHONE..............................562 861-8211
Gerald Caton, *Mgr*
EMP: 108
SALES (corp-wide): 148.39MM **Privately Held**
Web: www.downeyca.org
SIC: 7922 Legitimate live theater producers
PA: City Of Downey
11111 Brookshire Ave
Downey CA
562 869-7331

(P-17314)
CREATIVE ARTSTS AGCY HLDNGS LL (PA)
Also Called: C A A
2000 Avenue Of The Stars Ste 100 (90067-4700)
PHONE..............................424 288-2000
Steve Hasker, *CEO*
Rick Nicita, *Ch*
Lee Gabler, *VP*
Richard Lovett, *VP*
Bruce King, *Finance*
EMP: 800 EST: 1975
SALES (est): 524.81MM
SALES (corp-wide): 524.81MM **Privately Held**
Web: www.caa.com
SIC: 7922 Agent or manager for entertainers

(P-17315)
FRIENDS OF CULTURAL CENTER INC
Also Called: McCallum Theatre
73000 Fred Waring Dr (92260-2800)
PHONE..............................760 346-6505

Jamie Grant, *Pr*
William Towers, *
Harold Matzner, *Vice Chairman*
Ron Gregroire, *
Robert Mcconnaughey, *CFO*
EMP: 100 EST: 1973
SQ FT: 66,000
SALES (est): 20.41MM **Privately Held**
Web: www.mccallumtheatre.com
SIC: 7922 Legitimate live theater producers

(P-17316)
J C ENTERTAINMENT LTG SVCS INC
Also Called: E L S
5435 W San Fernando Rd (90039-1014)
PHONE..............................818 252-7481
John Allen Chuck, *CEO*
Kevin Dowling, *
Derek Smith, *
Todd Richards, *
EMP: 106 EST: 1991
SQ FT: 69,000
SALES (est): 4.74MM **Privately Held**
Web: www.4wall.com
SIC: 7922 5719 Equipment rental, theatrical; Lighting, lamps, and accessories

(P-17317)
LAGUNA PLAYHOUSE (PA)
606 Laguna Canyon Rd (92651-1837)
P.O. Box 1747 (92652-1747)
PHONE..............................949 497-2787
Karen Wood, *CEO*
Richard Stein, *
Bob Crowson, *
EMP: 225 EST: 1920
SQ FT: 19,000
SALES (est): 2.83MM
SALES (corp-wide): 2.83MM **Privately Held**
Web: www.lagunaplayhouse.com
SIC: 7922 Legitimate live theater producers

(P-17318)
LOS ANGELES OPERA COMPANY
135 N Grand Ave Ste 327 (90012-3018)
PHONE..............................213 972-7219
▲ EMP: 500 EST: 1966
SALES (est): 46.17MM **Privately Held**
Web: www.laopera.org
SIC: 7922 Theatrical producers and services

(P-17319)
MAGIC MOUNTAIN LLC
Also Called: Six Flags Magic Mountain
26101 Magic Mountain Pkwy (91355-1052)
P.O. Box 5500 (91380-5500)
PHONE..............................661 255-4100
▲ EMP: 216 EST: 2006
SALES (est): 8.89MM
SALES (corp-wide): 1.36B **Publicly Held**
Web: www.sixflags.com
SIC: 7922 7996 Entertainment promotion; Theme park, amusement
PA: Six Flags Entertainment Corp
1000 Ballpark Way Ste 400
Arlington TX
972 595-5000

(P-17320)
MANAGEMENT 360
9111 Wilshire Blvd (90210-5508)
P.O. Box A (90213-3087)
PHONE..............................310 272-7000
Evelyn O Neill, *Prin*
EMP: 94 EST: 1992
SALES (est): 5.45MM **Privately Held**
Web: www.management360.com

SIC: 7922 Agent or manager for entertainers

(P-17321)
NBC STUDIOS INC
Also Called: NBC
100 Universal City Plz Fl 3 (91608-1002)
PHONE..............................818 777-1000
EMP: 1000
SIC: 7922 Television program, including commercial producers

(P-17322)
OLD GLOBE THEATRE
Also Called: OLD GLOBE
1363 Old Globe Way (92101-1696)
P.O. Box 122171 (92112-2171)
PHONE..............................619 234-5623
Michael G Murphy, *CEO*
Louis Spisto, *
Mark Somers, *
▲ EMP: 500 EST: 1937
SALES (est): 34.22MM **Privately Held**
Web: www.theoldglobe.org
SIC: 7922 Performing arts center production

(P-17323)
PERFORMING ARTS CTR LOS ANGLES
Also Called: Music Center
135 N Grand Ave Ste 314 (90012-3018)
PHONE..............................213 972-7512
John Emerson, *Ch Bd*
Stephen Rountree, *
William Taylor, *
Lisa Whitney, *Prin*
Lisa Specht, *
▲ EMP: 250 EST: 1961
SQ FT: 24,000
SALES (est): 37.37MM
SALES (corp-wide): 37.37MM **Privately Held**
Web: www.musiccenter.org
SIC: 7922 Theatrical production services
PA: The Music Center Of Los Angeles County Inc
135 N Grand Ave Ste 201
Los Angeles CA
213 972-8007

(P-17324)
PRDCTIONS N FREMANTLE AMER INC (DH)
Also Called: Fremantle Media
2900 W Alameda Ave Unit 800 (91505-4216)
PHONE..............................818 748-1100
Thom Beers, *CEO*
Dan Goldberg, *
Donna Redier Linsk, *
Ellen Goldstein, *
EMP: 100 EST: 1995
SALES (est): 39.03MM
SALES (corp-wide): 54.57MM **Privately Held**
Web: www.fremantle.com
SIC: 7922 Television program, including commercial producers
HQ: Fremantlemedia Group Limited
1 Stephen Street
London
207 691-6000

(P-17325)
PREMIERE RADIO NETWORK INC (DH)
Also Called: Prn Radio Networks
15260 Ventura Blvd Ste 400 (91403-5349)
PHONE..............................818 377-5300
Stephen C Lehman, *CEO*

Kraig T Kitchin, *
Timothy M Kelly, *
EMP: 200 EST: 1987
SQ FT: 15,000
SALES (est): 21.93MM **Publicly Held**
Web: www.premierenetworks.com
SIC: 7922 7389 4832 Radio producers; Advertising, promotional, and trade show services; Radio broadcasting stations
HQ: Jacor Communications Company
200 E Basse Rd
San Antonio TX
210 822-2828

(P-17326)
RADFORD STUDIO CENTER LLC
Also Called: CBS Studio Center
4024 Radford Ave (91604-2101)
PHONE..............................818 655-5000
Michael Klausman, *Pr*
Nina Tassler, *
EMP: 300 EST: 1927
SALES (est): 49.7MM
SALES (corp-wide): 30.15B **Publicly Held**
Web: www.radfordsc.com
SIC: 7922 6512 7999 Television program, including commercial producers; Nonresidential building operators; Martial arts school, nec
HQ: Cbs Broadcasting Inc.
524 W 57th St
New York NY
212 975-4321

(P-17327)
SAN DEGO REPERTORY THEATRE INC
79 Horton Plz (92101-6144)
PHONE..............................619 231-3586
Samuel Woodhouse, *Dir*
EMP: 99 EST: 1976
SQ FT: 40,000
SALES (est): 6.02MM **Privately Held**
Web: www.sdrep.org
SIC: 7922 Legitimate live theater producers

(P-17328)
SAN DIEGO OPERA ASSOCIATION
3074 Commercial St (92113-1413)
PHONE..............................619 232-5911
EMP: 225
SALES (corp-wide): 9.59MM **Privately Held**
Web: www.sdopera.org
SIC: 7922 Opera company
PA: San Diego Opera Association Inc
233 A St Ste 500
San Diego CA
619 232-7636

(P-17329)
SAN DIEGO OPERA ASSOCIATION
Also Called: Scenic Studio
3064 Commercial St (92113-1413)
PHONE..............................619 232-5911
Ron Allen, *Mgr*
EMP: 225
SQ FT: 35,000
SALES (corp-wide): 9.59MM **Privately Held**
Web: www.sdopera.org
SIC: 7922 Legitimate live theater producers
PA: San Diego Opera Association Inc
233 A St Ste 500
San Diego CA
619 232-7636

(P-17330)
THE GERSH AGENCY LLC (PA)
9465 Wilshire Blvd Fl 6 (90212-2605)
PHONE...................................310 274-6611
Robert Gersh, *Pr*
David Gersh, *VP*
Beatrice Gersh, *VP*
EMP: 100 **EST:** 1949
SQ FT: 15,000
SALES (est): 20.5MM
SALES (corp-wide): 20.5MM **Privately Held**
Web: www.gersh.com
SIC: 7922 Talent agent, theatrical

(P-17331)
TICKETSCOM LLC (DH)
Also Called: Tickets.com, Inc.
535 Anton Blvd Ste 250 (92626-7694)
PHONE...................................714 327-5400
Joe Choti, *Pr*
Cristine Hurley, *
Curt Clausen, *
Larry D Witherspoon, *
John Walker, *
EMP: 28 **EST:** 1995
SALES (est): 40.57MM
SALES (corp-wide): 4.71MM **Privately Held**
Web: provenue.tickets.com
SIC: 7922 7372 Ticket agency, theatrical; Application computer software
HQ: Mlb Advanced Media, L.P.
1271 Ave Of The Americas
New York NY
212 485-3444

(P-17332)
WESTSTAR CINEMAS INC
742 W Lancaster Blvd (93534-3130)
PHONE...................................661 723-9392
EMP: 219
SALES (corp-wide): 22.59MM **Privately Held**
SIC: 7922 Theatrical companies
PA: Weststar Cinemas, Inc.
16530 Ventura Blvd # 500
Encino CA
818 784-6266

(P-17333)
WILLIAM MRRIS ENDVOR ENTRMT FN (DH)
9601 Wilshire Blvd Fl 3 (90210-5219)
PHONE...................................310 285-9000
Tom Strickler, *Pr*
Richard Rosen, *
Adam Venit, *
Phillip Raskind, *
EMP: 180 **EST:** 2000
SALES (est): 47.24MM
SALES (corp-wide): 5.27B **Publicly Held**
Web: www.wmeagency.com
SIC: 7922 7829 Talent agent, theatrical; Motion picture distribution services
HQ: William Morris Endeavor
Entertainment, Llc
9601 Wilshire Blvd
Beverly Hills CA
212 586-5100

(P-17334)
WILLIAM MRRIS ENDVOR ENTRMT LL
Also Called: William Morris Consulting
9601 Wilshire Blvd Fl 3 (90210-5219)
PHONE...................................310 285-9000
Chris Newman, *Brnch Mgr*
EMP: 393
SALES (corp-wide): 5.27B **Publicly Held**

Web: www.wmeagency.com
SIC: 7922 Talent agent, theatrical
HQ: William Morris Endeavor
Entertainment, Llc
9601 Wilshire Blvd
Beverly Hills CA
212 586-5100

7929 Entertainers And Entertainment Groups

(P-17335)
ANSCHUTZ ENTRMT GROUP INC (HQ)
Also Called: AEG Worldwide
800 W Olympic Blvd Ste 305 (90015-1366)
PHONE...................................213 763-7700
Tim Leiweke, *Pr*
Dan Beckerman, *
Tracy Hartman, *
Dennis Dennehy, *CCO*
EMP: 154 **EST:** 1994
SALES (est): 431.33K **Privately Held**
Web: www.aegworldwide.com
SIC: 7929 Entertainment service
PA: The Anschutz Corporation
555 17th St Ste 2400
Denver CO

(P-17336)
ESL GAMING AMERICA INC
Also Called: Esl
1212 Chestnut St (91506-1627)
PHONE...................................818 861-7315
Ralf Reichert, *CEO*
EMP: 99 **EST:** 2014
SALES (est): 8.57MM **Privately Held**
Web: www.esl.com
SIC: 7929 Entertainment service
HQ: Savvy Games Group
Office 2.14 B, 6th Floor, Kafd, King
Fahad Road
Riyadh

(P-17337)
HOB ENTERTAINMENT LLC
Also Called: House of Blues Anaheim
400 W Disney Way Ste 337 (92802-2912)
PHONE...................................714 520-2310
Darryl Taketa, *Brnch Mgr*
EMP: 181
Web: www.houseofblues.com
SIC: 7929 Entertainment service
HQ: Hob Entertainment, Llc
7060 Hollywood Blvd
Los Angeles CA

(P-17338)
HOB ENTERTAINMENT LLC (DH)
Also Called: House of Blues
7060 Hollywood Blvd (90028-6014)
PHONE...................................323 769-4600
Michael Rapino, *CEO*
Joseph C Kaczorowski, *
Peter Cyffka, *
EMP: 172 **EST:** 1993
SQ FT: 53,000
SALES (est): 305.78MM **Publicly Held**
Web: www.houseofblues.com
SIC: 7929 Entertainment service
HQ: Live Nation Worldwide, Inc.
430 W 15th St
New York NY
917 421-5100

(P-17339)
HOUSE OF BLUES CONCERTS INC (DH)

6255 W Sunset Blvd Fl 16 (90028-7403)
PHONE...................................323 769-4977
Joe Kazoworski, *Pr*
EMP: 150 **EST:** 1978
SALES (est): 19.21MM **Publicly Held**
Web: www.houseofblues.com
SIC: 7929 Entertainment service
HQ: Hob Entertainment, Llc
7060 Hollywood Blvd
Los Angeles CA

(P-17340)
ILLUMINATION ENTERTAINMENT
2043 Colorado Ave (90404-3415)
PHONE...................................626 298-1879
Chris Meledandri, *CEO*
EMP: 141 **EST:** 2007
SALES (est): 31.1MM
SALES (corp-wide): 121.43B **Publicly Held**
Web:
www.illuminationentertainment.com
SIC: 7929 Entertainment service
HQ: Universal Studios Limited
1 Central St. Giles
London
203 618-8000

(P-17341)
INMOTION ENTRMT GROUP LLC
3225 N Harbor Dr (92101-1024)
PHONE...................................904 332-0459
EMP: 106
Web: www.inmotionstores.com
SIC: 7929 Entertainers
HQ: Inmotion Entertainment Group, Llc
3755 W Sunset Rd Ste A
Las Vegas NV
904 332-0450

(P-17342)
INSOMNIAC INC
Also Called: Insomniac
5023 Parkway Calabasas (91302-1421)
PHONE...................................323 874-7020
Pasquale Rotella, *CEO*
Simon Rust Lamb, *
John Boyle, *Interim Chief Financial Officer*
▲ **EMP:** 195 **EST:** 1998
SALES (est): 48.35MM **Privately Held**
Web: www.insomniac.com
SIC: 7929 Entertainment service

(P-17343)
LIVE NATION WORLDWIDE INC (HQ)
Also Called: Observatory, The
9348 Civic Center Dr Lbby (90210-3642)
PHONE...................................310 867-7000
Kathy Willard, *CEO*
EMP: 8800 **EST:** 1997
SALES (est): 116.81MM **Publicly Held**
Web: www.livenationentertainment.com
SIC: 7929 Entertainers and entertainment groups
PA: Live Nation Entertainment, Inc.
9348 Civic Center Dr Lbby
Beverly Hills CA

(P-17344)
LOS ANGELES PHILHARMONIC ASSN (PA)
Also Called: L A PHILHARMONIC
151 S Grand Ave (90012-3034)
P.O. Box 1951 (90078-1951)
PHONE...................................213 972-7300
Chad Smith, *CEO*
Thomas L Beckmen, *
Alan Wayte, *
Ben Cadwallader, *

Gail Samuel, *HOLLYWOOD BOWL*
EMP: 200 **EST:** 1934
SQ FT: 13,467
SALES (est): 158.2MM
SALES (corp-wide): 158.2MM **Privately Held**
Web: www.laphil.com
SIC: 7929 Symphony orchestra

(P-17345)
LOS ANGELES PHILHARMONIC ASSN
Also Called: Hollywood Bowl
2301 N Highland Ave (90068-2742)
PHONE...................................323 850-2060
Ed Tom, *Dir*
EMP: 899
SALES (corp-wide): 158.2MM **Privately Held**
Web: www.laphil.com
SIC: 7929 Entertainment group
PA: Los Angeles Philharmonic Association
151 S Grand Ave
Los Angeles CA
213 972-7300

(P-17346)
MAKER STUDIOS LLC (DH)
3515 Eastham Dr (90232-2440)
PHONE...................................310 606-2182
Courtney Holt, *CEO*
Lisa Donovan, *
EMP: 250 **EST:** 2009
SQ FT: 20,000
SALES (est): 49.51MM
SALES (corp-wide): 88.9B **Publicly Held**
SIC: 7929 Entertainment service
HQ: Twdc Enterprises 18 Corp.
500 S Buena Vista St
Burbank CA

(P-17347)
NOW CASTING INC
211 N Victory Blvd (91502-1839)
PHONE...................................818 588-3732
Robert Stewart, *CEO*
Melody Stewart, *Sec*
Richard La Fond, *COO*
EMP: 110 **EST:** 1997
SALES (est): 975.91K **Privately Held**
Web: www.nowcasting.com
SIC: 7929 Entertainment service

(P-17348)
RED BULL NORTH AMERICA INC (HQ)
Also Called: Red Bull TV
1630 Stewart St (90404-4020)
PHONE...................................310 460-5356
▲ **EMP:** 100 **EST:** 1995
SALES (est): 412.82MM
SALES (corp-wide): 10.06B **Privately Held**
Web: www.redbull.com
SIC: 7929 Entertainment service
PA: Red Bull Gmbh
Am Brunnen 1
Fuschl Am See
66265820

(P-17349)
SAN DEGO SYMPHONY ORCHSTRA ASS
1245 7th Ave (92101-4302)
PHONE...................................619 235-0800
Edward B Gill, *Ex Dir*
EMP: 110 **EST:** 1928
SALES (est): 89.36MM **Privately Held**
Web: www.sandiegosymphony.org

SIC: 7929 Symphony orchestra

(P-17350)
SAN DIEGO SYMPHONY FOUNDATION
1245 7th Ave (92101-4398)
PHONE..............................619 235-0800
EMP: 135 **EST:** 2011
SALES (est): 925.95K **Privately Held**
Web: www.sandiegosymphony.org
SIC: 7929 Symphony orchestra

(P-17351)
SPECIAL EVENT AUDIO SVCS INC
35889 Shetland Hls E (92028-6519)
PHONE..............................800 518-9144
Mitchell J Grant, *CEO*
EMP: 31 **EST:** 2014
SALES (est): 6.46MM **Privately Held**
Web: www.seaspro.com
SIC: 7929 5099 3651 Orchestras or bands, nec; Video and audio equipment; Audio electronic systems

(P-17352)
SPSV ENTERTAINMENT LLC
Also Called: Skypark At Santa's Village
28950 State Highway 18 (92385-0460)
P.O. Box 369 (92385-0369)
PHONE..............................909 744-9373
William Johnson, *Managing Member*
EMP: 99 **EST:** 2016
SALES (est): 5.21MM **Privately Held**
Web: www.skyparksantasvillage.com
SIC: 7929 Entertainers and entertainment groups

(P-17353)
TWENTY MILE PRODUCTIONS LLC
11833 Mississippi Ave Ste 101 (90025-6135)
PHONE..............................412 251-0767
Margaret Ellison, *
EMP: 150 **EST:** 2013
SALES (est): 1.13MM **Privately Held**
SIC: 7929 Entertainment group

(P-17354)
TWO BIT CIRCUS DTLA LLC
Also Called: Two Bit Circus
634 Mateo St (90021-1312)
PHONE..............................323 438-9808
Brent Bushnell, *Prin*
Eric Co Gradam, *Prin*
Kimberly Schaefer, *
Christopher Ogilvie, *
EMP: 80 **EST:** 2018
SALES (est): 1.4MM **Privately Held**
Web: www.twobitcircus.com
SIC: 7929 Entertainment service

(P-17355)
YOU ME AND SCIENCES INC ✪
202 W Manchester Ave (90293-7710)
P.O. Box 90307 (90009-0307)
PHONE..............................310 406-7350
Jessica Lesley, *CEO*
EMP: 85 **EST:** 2022
SALES (est): 1.61MM **Privately Held**
Web: www.youmeandsciences.com
SIC: 7929 Entertainment service

7933 Bowling Centers

(P-17356)
GABLE HOUSE INC
Also Called: Gable House Bowl
1611 S Pacific Coast Hwy (90277-5605)
PHONE..............................310 378-2265
Michael Mickey Cogan, *Pr*
EMP: 100 **EST:** 1959
SALES (est): 5.14MM **Privately Held**
Web: www.gablehousebowl.com
SIC: 7933 5813 5812 Ten pin center; Bar (drinking places); Snack bar

(P-17357)
LUCKY STRIKE ENTERTAINMENT INC
800 W Olympic Blvd Ste 250 (90015-1366)
PHONE..............................213 542-4880
Bobby Braydoy, *Brnch Mgr*
EMP: 297
Web: www.luckystrikeent.com
SIC: 7933 5813 5812 Ten pin center; Tavern (drinking places); American restaurant
PA: Lucky Strike Entertainment, Inc.
15260 Ventura Blvd # 1110
Sherman Oaks CA

(P-17358)
LUCKY STRIKE ENTERTAINMENT LLC
Also Called: Lucky Strike Novi
15260 Ventura Blvd Ste 1110 (91403-5346)
PHONE..............................248 374-3420
Eddie Bourque, *Brnch Mgr*
EMP: 84
SALES (corp-wide): 1.06B **Publicly Held**
Web: www.luckystrikeent.com
SIC: 7933 Ten pin center
HQ: Lucky Strike Entertainment, Llc
16350 Ventura Blvd Ste D
Encino CA
818 933-3752

(P-17359)
LUCKY STRIKE ENTERTAINMENT LLC
20 City Blvd W Ste G2 (92868-3131)
PHONE..............................248 374-3420
Ismail Saleem, *Brnch Mgr*
EMP: 99
SALES (corp-wide): 1.06B **Publicly Held**
Web: www.luckystrikeent.com
SIC: 7933 Ten pin center
HQ: Lucky Strike Entertainment, Llc
16350 Ventura Blvd Ste D
Encino CA
818 933-3752

(P-17360)
NATIONWIDE THEATRES CORP
Also Called: Cal Coffee Shop
2500 Carson St (90712-4107)
PHONE..............................562 421-8448
Tom Moeller, *Mgr*
EMP: 2720
SALES (corp-wide): 175.87MM **Privately Held**
Web: www.calbowl.com
SIC: 7933 5813 5812 Ten pin center; Cocktail lounge; Coffee shop
HQ: Nationwide Theatres Corp.
120 N Robertson Blvd Fl 3
Los Angeles CA
310 657-8420

7941 Sports Clubs, Managers, And Promoters

(P-17361)
ANAHEIM ARENA MANAGEMENT LLC
Also Called: AAM
2695 E Katella Ave (92806-5904)
PHONE..............................714 704-2400
Michael Schulman, *
Angela Wergechik, *
James Pearson, *
EMP: 600 **EST:** 2001
SQ FT: 106,000
SALES (est): 81.4MM **Privately Held**
Web: www.hondacenter.com
SIC: 7941 Sports field or stadium operator, promoting sports events

(P-17362)
ANAHEIM DUCKS HOCKEY CLUB LLC (PA)
2695 E Katella Ave (92806-5904)
PHONE..............................714 940-2900
Michel Schulman, *Managing Member*
Doug Heller, *
Bob Murray, *
Tim Ryan, *
David Mcnab, *Sr VP*
EMP: 81 **EST:** 2005
SALES (est): 30.81MM **Privately Held**
Web: www.anaheimteamstore.com
SIC: 7941 Sports clubs, managers, and promoters

(P-17363)
ANGELS BASEBALL LP (PA)
Also Called: Los Angeles Angels of Anaheim
2000 E Gene Autry Way (92806-6143)
PHONE..............................714 940-2000
Dennis Kuhl, *Genl Pt*
Bill Beverage, *Pt*
Molly Jolly, *Pt*
Tim Mead, *Pt*
Richard Mcclemmy, *Pt*
EMP: 790 **EST:** 1996
SALES (est): 113.58MM
SALES (corp-wide): 113.58MM **Privately Held**
Web: www.mlb.com
SIC: 7941 Baseball club, professional and semi-professional

(P-17364)
BIG LGUE DREAMS CONSULTING LLC
2155 Trumble Rd (92571-9211)
PHONE..............................619 846-8855
EMP: 107
SALES (corp-wide): 49.84MM **Privately Held**
Web: www.bigleaguedreams.com
SIC: 7941 Sports field or stadium operator, promoting sports events
PA: Big League Dreams Consulting, Llc
16333 Fairfield Ranch Rd
Chino Hills CA
909 287-1700

(P-17365)
BIG LGUE DREAMS CONSULTING LLC
2100 S Azusa Ave (91792-1507)
PHONE..............................626 839-1100
Jeffrey Odekirk, *Prin*
EMP: 107
SALES (corp-wide): 49.84MM **Privately Held**

Web: www.bigleaguedreams.com
SIC: 7941 Sports field or stadium operator, promoting sports events
PA: Big League Dreams Consulting, Llc
16333 Fairfield Ranch Rd
Chino Hills CA
909 287-1700

(P-17366)
CALIFORNIA SPORTSERVICE INC
Also Called: San Diego Padres
100 Park Blvd (92101-7405)
PHONE..............................619 795-5000
Jeremy M Jacobs, *Pr*
EMP: 362 **EST:** 1940
SALES (est): 24.28MM
SALES (corp-wide): 2.9B **Privately Held**
Web: www.mlb.com
SIC: 7941 Baseball club, professional and semi-professional
HQ: Delaware North Companies Sportservice, Inc.
250 Delaware Ave
Buffalo NY
716 858-5000

(P-17367)
CITY OF SAN DIEGO
Also Called: Petco Park
100 Park Blvd (92101-7405)
PHONE..............................619 795-5000
John Morris, *Pr*
EMP: 263
SALES (corp-wide): 2.67B **Privately Held**
Web: www.petcoparkinsider.com
SIC: 7941 Sports field or stadium operator, promoting sports events
PA: City Of San Diego
202 C St
San Diego CA
619 236-6330

(P-17368)
ENDEAVOR GROUP HOLDINGS INC (PA)
9601 Wilshire Blvd Fl 3 (90210-5219)
PHONE..............................310 285-9000
Ariel Emanuel, *CEO*
Patrick Whitesell, *Ex Ch Bd*
Egon Durban, *Ch Bd*
Mark Shapiro, *Pr*
Jason Lublin, *CFO*
EMP: 90 **EST:** 2019
SALES (est): 5.27B
SALES (corp-wide): 5.27B **Publicly Held**
Web: www.mainconcept.com
SIC: 7941 Sports field or stadium operator, promoting sports events

(P-17369)
FOX BASEBALL HOLDINGS INC
1000 Vin Scully Ave (90012-2112)
PHONE..............................323 224-1500
Frank Mccourt, *Pr*
EMP: 233 **EST:** 2000
SALES (est): 2.31MM
SALES (corp-wide): 88.9B **Publicly Held**
SIC: 7941 Baseball club, professional and semi-professional
HQ: Fox Entertainment Group, Llc
1211 Ave Of The Americas
New York NY
212 852-7000

(P-17370)
FOX BSB HOLDCO INC (HQ)
Also Called: Dodger Stadium
1000 Vin Scully Ave (90012-2112)
PHONE..............................323 224-1500

PRODUCTS & SVCS

Steve Soboroff, *Vice Chairman*
Ron Wheeler, *
Santiago Fernandez, *
Dannis Mannion, *
Peter Wilhelm, *CFO*
EMP: 367 **EST:** 1971
SQ FT: 20,000
SALES (est): 5.17MM
SALES (corp-wide): 1.8B **Privately Held**
Web: www.mlb.com
SIC: 7941 Baseball club, professional and semi-professional
PA: Guggenheim Partners, Llc
330 Madison Ave Rm 201
New York NY
212 739-0700

(P-17371)
GEMINI BASKETBALL LLC
Also Called: Los Angeles Sparks
9100 Wilshire Blvd Ste 700e (90212-3415)
PHONE.................................213 929-1300
Paula Williams Madison, *CEO*
EMP: 83 **EST:** 2006
SALES (est): 2.33MM **Privately Held**
Web: sparks.wnba.com
SIC: 7941 Basketball club

(P-17372)
IMMORTALS LLC
11460 W Washington Blvd (90066-6030)
P.O. Box 641729 (90064-6729)
PHONE.................................310 554-8267
Noah Whinston, *CEO*
Ari Segal, *COO*
Jonathan Stein, *VP*
EMP: 85 **EST:** 2015
SQ FT: 30,000
SALES (est): 1.55MM **Privately Held**
Web: www.cityofimmortals.com
SIC: 7941 Professional and semi-professional sports clubs

(P-17373)
INLAND EMPIRE 66ERS BSBAL CLB
280 Se St (92401-2009)
PHONE.................................909 888-9922
David Elmore, *Ch*
Donna Tuttle, *
Jhon Fonsaker, *
EMP: 110 **EST:** 1993
SQ FT: 600
SALES (est): 37.76K
SALES (corp-wide): 34.1MM **Privately Held**
Web: inlandempire.66ers.milb.com
SIC: 7941 Baseball club, professional and semi-professional
PA: The Elmore Group Ltd
19 N Grant St Ste 2
Hinsdale IL
630 325-6228

(P-17374)
LA CLIPPERS LLC
1212 S Flower St Fl 5 (90015-2117)
PHONE.................................213 742-7500
Steven A Ballmer, *Managing Member*
EMP: 221 **EST:** 2014
SALES (est): 12.13MM **Privately Held**
Web: www.clippers.com
SIC: 7941 Basketball club

(P-17375)
LA SPORTS PROPERTIES INC
Also Called: Los Angeles Clippers
1212 S Flower St Fl 5 (90015-2123)
PHONE.................................213 742-7500
Dick Parsons, *Interim Chief Executive Officer*

Andrew Roeser, *Ex VP*
EMP: 195 **EST:** 1946
SQ FT: 5,000
SALES (est): 24.44MM **Privately Held**
SIC: 7941 Basketball club

(P-17376)
LIVE NATION WORLDWIDE INC
Also Called: Clear Channel Entertainment
325 N Maple Dr (90210-3429)
PHONE.................................310 867-7000
Jennifer Scott, *Mgr*
EMP: 300
SIC: 7941 Sports clubs, managers, and promoters
HQ: Live Nation Worldwide, Inc.
430 W 15th St
New York NY
917 421-5100

(P-17377)
LOS ANGELES RAMS LLC (PA)
Also Called: ST LOUIS RAMS
29899 Agoura Rd (91301-2511)
PHONE.................................314 982-7267
E Stanley Kroenke, *Managing Member*
Kevin Demoff, *Managing Member*
Les Snead, *Managing Member*
Tony Pastoors, *Managing Member*
EMP: 100 **EST:** 1939
SALES (est): 1.23MM
SALES (corp-wide): 1.23MM **Privately Held**
Web: www.therams.com
SIC: 7941 Football club

(P-17378)
NFL PROPERTIES LLC
Also Called: Nfl Network
10950 Washington Blvd Ste 100 (90232-4032)
PHONE.................................310 840-4635
Steve Bernstein, *Prin*
EMP: 100
SALES (corp-wide): 603.28MM **Privately Held**
Web: www.nfl.com
SIC: 7941 Football club
PA: Nfl Properties Llc
345 Park Ave
New York NY
212 450-2000

(P-17379)
NIKE USA INC
222 E Redondo Beach Blvd Ste C (90248-2302)
PHONE.................................310 670-6770
EMP: 4981
SALES (corp-wide): 51.22B **Publicly Held**
SIC: 7941 Sports clubs, managers, and promoters
HQ: Nike Usa, Inc.
1 Sw Bowerman Dr
Beaverton OR

(P-17380)
PADRES LP
Also Called: San Diego Padres
100 Park Blvd Petco Park (92101)
P.O. Box 122000 (92112-2000)
PHONE.................................619 795-5000
EMP: 1100 **EST:** 1969
SQ FT: 3,000
SALES (est): 265.26MM **Privately Held**
Web: www.mlb.com
SIC: 7941 Baseball club, professional and semi-professional

(P-17381)
PSE HOLDING LLC (DH)
Also Called: The Palace of Auburn Hills
360 N Crescent Dr (90210-4874)
PHONE.................................248 377-0165
EMP: 300 **EST:** 1985
SALES (est): 115.27MM **Privately Held**
SIC: 7941 7922 Stadium event operator services; Summer theater
HQ: Pistons Palace Holdings, Llc
360 N Crescent Dr
Beverly Hills CA
310 228-9521

(P-17382)
SOCAL SPORTSNET LLC
100 Park Blvd (92101-7405)
PHONE.................................619 795-5000
EMP: 588 **EST:** 2012
SALES (est): 591.9K
SALES (corp-wide): 12.1MM **Privately Held**
Web: www.mlb.com
SIC: 7941 Baseball club, professional and semi-professional
PA: Padre Time, Llc
100 Park Blvd
San Diego CA
619 795-5000

(P-17383)
ULTIMATE FGHTING PRDCTONS INTL ☺
9601 Wilshire Blvd (90210-5213)
PHONE.................................310 285-9000
EMP: 144 **EST:** 2023
SALES (est): 124.58K
SALES (corp-wide): 5.27B **Publicly Held**
SIC: 7941 Sports field or stadium operator, promoting sports events
PA: Endeavor Group Holdings, Inc.
9601 Wilshire Blvd Fl 3
Beverly Hills CA
310 285-9000

(P-17384)
WME IMG LLC (DH)
Also Called: International Merchandising
9601 Wilshire Blvd (90210-5213)
PHONE.................................212 586-5100
Ari Emanuel, *CEO*
Patrick Whitesell, *
Richard Miao, *
Neil Graff, *
Jason Lublin, *
EMP: 202 **EST:** 1961
SALES (est): 113.75MM
SALES (corp-wide): 5.27B **Publicly Held**
Web: www.endeavorco.com
SIC: 7941 8742 Sports promotion; Business planning and organizing services
HQ: William Morris Endeavor Entertainment, Llc
9601 Wilshire Blvd
Beverly Hills CA
212 586-5100

7948 Racing, Including Track Operation

(P-17385)
DEL MAR THOROUGHBRED CLUB
Also Called: SURFSIDE RACE PLACE AT DEL MAR
2260 Jimmy Durante Blvd (92014-2216)
P.O. Box 700 (92014-0700)
PHONE.................................858 755-1141

Joe Harper, *Pr*
Craig Fravel, *
Mike Ernst, *
Tom Robbins, *
Craig Dado, *
▲ **EMP:** 400 **EST:** 1970
SALES (est): 40.31MM **Privately Held**
Web: www.dmtc.com
SIC: 7948 Thoroughbred horse racing

(P-17386)
LOS ANGELES TURF CLUB INC (DH)
Also Called: Santa Anita Park
285 W Huntington Dr (91007-3439)
P.O. Box 60014 (91066-6014)
PHONE.................................626 574-6330
Gregory C Avioli, *CEO*
Frank Stronach, *Ch Bd*
George Haines Ii, *Pr*
Frank Demarco Junior, *VP*
▲ **EMP:** 109 **EST:** 1964
SALES (est): 71.29MM
SALES (corp-wide): 37.84B **Privately Held**
Web: www.santaanita.com
SIC: 7948 Horse race track operation
HQ: Magna Car Top Systems Of America, Inc.
456 Wimpole Dr
Rochester Hills MI
248 836-4500

(P-17387)
NATIONAL HOT ROD ASSOCIATION (PA)
Also Called: Nhra
140 Via Verde Ste 100 (91773-5117)
P.O. Box 5555 (91740-0950)
PHONE.................................626 914-4761
Wally Parks, *Dir*
Richard Wells, *
EMP: 200 **EST:** 1951
SQ FT: 30,000
SALES (corp-wide): 84.07MM **Privately Held**
Web: www.nhra.com
SIC: 7948 2711 2741 Auto race track operation; Newspapers: publishing only, not printed on site; Miscellaneous publishing

(P-17388)
YOUBETCOM INC (HQ)
2600 W Olive Ave Fl 5 (91505-4572)
PHONE.................................818 668-2100
EMP: 105 **EST:** 1995
SQ FT: 3,000
SALES (est): 2.8MM
SALES (corp-wide): 1.81B **Publicly Held**
SIC: 7948 Race track operation
PA: Churchill Downs Incorporated
600 N Hurstbourne Pkwy # 400
Louisville KY
502 636-4400

7991 Physical Fitness Facilities

(P-17389)
24 HOUR FITNESS USA LLC (HQ)
Also Called: 24 Hour Fitness
1265 Laurel Tree Ln Ste 200 (92011-4221)
PHONE.................................925 543-3100
Karl Sanft, *CEO*
Tony Ueber, *
Frank Napolitano, *
Patrick Flanagan, *
▲ **EMP:** 183 **EST:** 1983

SALES (est): 815.88MM
SALES (corp-wide): 815.88MM **Privately Held**
Web: www.24hourfitness.com
SIC: 7991 Health club
PA: All Day Holdings Llc
1265 Laurel Tree Ln # 200
Carlsbad CA
925 543-3100

(P-17390)
24 HOUR FITNESS WORLDWIDE INC
1265 Laurel Tree Ln Ste 200 (92011-4221)
PHONE.................................925 543-3100
EMP: 7184
Web: www.24hourfit.com
SIC: 7991 Health club

(P-17391)
ASPYR HOLDINGS LLC
Also Called: Aspyr
270 Baker St Ste 300 (92626-4584)
PHONE.................................714 651-1840
Marc Thomas, *CEO*
Peter Felner, *
Ryan Kersten, *
EMP: 450 **EST:** 2019
SIC: 7991 6794 Physical fitness facilities;
Patent owners and lessors

(P-17392)
BA SPORTS NUTRITION LLC
630 Clinton Pl (90210-1917)
PHONE.................................718 357-7402
EMP: 80 **EST:** 2019
SALES (est): 1.38MM **Privately Held**
Web: www.drinkbodyarmor.com
SIC: 7991 Physical fitness facilities

(P-17393)
BALLY TOTAL FITNESS CORPORATION
Also Called: Bally Total Fitness
12440 Imperial Hwy # 300 (90650-3178)
P.O. Box 739 (60039-0739)
PHONE.................................562 484-2000
▲ **EMP:** 12340
SIC: 7991 Health club

(P-17394)
BAY CLUBS COMPANY LLC
Also Called: Spectrum Club Thousand Oaks
19867 Prairie St Ste 200 (91311-6533)
PHONE.................................805 778-0888
Adam Kinaan, *Mgr*
EMP: 294
SALES (corp-wide): 5.09MM **Privately Held**
Web: www.bayclubs.com
SIC: 7991 8049 Health club; Physical therapist
HQ: The Bay Clubs Company Llc
1 Lombard St
San Francisco CA
415 781-1874

(P-17395)
BAY CLUBS COMPANY LLC
Also Called: Spectrum Club
6833 Park Ter (90045-1539)
PHONE.................................310 216-3060
Thomas Broks, *Genl Mgr*
EMP: 294
SALES (corp-wide): 5.09MM **Privately Held**
Web: www.bayclubs.com
SIC: 7991 Health club
HQ: The Bay Clubs Company Llc
1 Lombard St

San Francisco CA
415 781-1874

(P-17396)
ENCINO LIVING LLC
16710 Magnolia Blvd (91436-1012)
PHONE.................................818 907-1343
Danny Petrasek, *Brnch Mgr*
EMP: 120
SALES (corp-wide): 790.77K **Privately Held**
Web: www.encinoseniorliving.com
SIC: 7991 Health club
PA: Encino Living Llc
7515 Woodley Ave
Van Nuys CA
818 781-9119

(P-17397)
EQUINOX-76TH STREET INC
1835 S Sepulveda Blvd (90025-6941)
PHONE.................................310 479-5200
Tonya Jacobs, *Mgr*
EMP: 97
SALES (corp-wide): 2.05B **Privately Held**
SIC: 7991 Health club
HQ: Equinox-76th Street, Inc.
895 Broadway Fl 3
New York NY

(P-17398)
EQUINOX-76TH STREET INC
Also Called: Equinox Fitness Club
10250 Santa Monica Blvd (90067-6404)
PHONE.................................310 552-0420
Mathew Herbert, *Brnch Mgr*
EMP: 87
SALES (corp-wide): 2.05B **Privately Held**
SIC: 7991 Health club
HQ: Equinox-76th Street, Inc.
895 Broadway Fl 3
New York NY

(P-17399)
EQUINOX-76TH STREET INC
Also Called: Equinox Fitness Club
19540 Jamboree Rd (92612-8448)
PHONE.................................949 296-1700
Herb Umphreyville, *Genl Mgr*
EMP: 90
SALES (corp-wide): 2.05B **Privately Held**
SIC: 7991 Health club
HQ: Equinox-76th Street, Inc.
895 Broadway Fl 3
New York NY

(P-17400)
HEATWAVE LLC
Also Called: Perspire Sauna Studio
1308 Bison Ave (92660-9070)
PHONE.................................949 717-7588
EMP: 85 **EST:** 2018
SALES (est): 389.56K **Privately Held**
Web: www.perspiresaunastudio.com
SIC: 7991 Spas

(P-17401)
JAZZERCISE INC (PA)
Also Called: Jazzercise
2460 Impala Dr (92010-7226)
PHONE.................................760 476-1750
Judi Sheppard Missett, *CEO*
Sally Baldridge, *
Shanna Missett Nelson, *
EMP: 100 **EST:** 1972
SQ FT: 24,228
SALES (est): 12.2MM
SALES (corp-wide): 12.2MM **Privately Held**
Web: www.jazzercise.com

SIC: 7991 6794 5961 Aerobic dance and exercise classes; Franchises, selling or licensing; Fitness and sporting goods, mail order

(P-17402)
LA BONNE VIE INC
2723 Shell Beach Rd (93449-1629)
PHONE.................................805 773-5003
Maureen Raynaud-loughead, *Pr*
EMP: 100 **EST:** 2005
SALES (est): 225.48K **Privately Held**
SIC: 7991 Spas

(P-17403)
LA BOXING FRANCHISE CORP
1241 E Dyer Rd Ste 100 (92705-5611)
PHONE.................................714 668-0911
Anthony Geisler, *Pr*
▲ **EMP:** 348 **EST:** 1992
SALES (est): 3.85MM
SALES (corp-wide): 89.52MM **Privately Held**
SIC: 7991 Physical fitness facilities
PA: U Gym, Llc
1501 Quail St Ste 100
Newport Beach CA
714 668-0911

(P-17404)
LA WORKOUT INC
Also Called: La Workout Camarillo West
500 Paseo Camarillo (93010-5900)
PHONE.................................805 482-8884
Steve Rivera, *Brnch Mgr*
EMP: 115
Web: www.perfectdomain.com
SIC: 7991 Health club
PA: La Workout, Inc.
2510g Las Posas Rd Ste 44
Camarillo CA

(P-17405)
LIFE TIME INC
1055 Wall St (92037-4400)
PHONE.................................858 459-0281
EMP: 91
SALES (corp-wide): 1.82B **Publicly Held**
Web: www.lifetime.life
SIC: 7991 Health club
HQ: Life Time, Inc.
2902 Corporate Pl
Chanhassen MN

(P-17406)
LIFE TIME INC
Also Called: Life Time Fitness
111 Avenida Vista Montana (92672-6094)
PHONE.................................949 492-1515
Steve Johnson, *Pr*
EMP: 91
SALES (corp-wide): 1.82B **Publicly Held**
Web: www.lifetime.life
SIC: 7991 Health club
HQ: Life Time, Inc.
2902 Corporate Pl
Chanhassen MN

(P-17407)
LOS ANGELES ATHLETIC CLUB INC
431 W 7th St (90014-1691)
PHONE.................................213 625-2211
Karen Hathaway, *Pr*
Bryan Cusworth, *
EMP: 182 **EST:** 1986
SALES (est): 6.3MM **Publicly Held**
Web: www.laac.com

SIC: 7991 Athletic club and gymnasiums, membership
HQ: Laaco, Ltd.
4469 Admiralty Way
Marina Del Rey CA
213 622-1254

(P-17408)
MUSCLEBOUND INC
Also Called: Golds Gym
19835 Nordhoff St (91324-3331)
PHONE.................................818 349-0123
EMP: 350 **EST:** 1990
SQ FT: 8,625
SALES (est): 16.26MM **Privately Held**
Web: www.goldsgym.com
SIC: 7991 Physical fitness facilities

(P-17409)
NUZUNA CORPORATION
Also Called: Nuzuna Fitness
1451 Quail St Ste 104 (92660-2747)
P.O. Box 8807 (92658-8807)
PHONE.................................949 335-7790
Charlie Laverty, *CEO*
Aileen Pham, *
Raymond Godeke, *
EMP: 90 **EST:** 2019
SALES (est): 3.63MM **Privately Held**
Web: www.nuzunafit.com
SIC: 7991 Physical fitness facilities

(P-17410)
OLYMPIX FITNESS LLC
4101 E Olympic Plz (90803-2807)
PHONE.................................562 366-4600
EMP: 91 **EST:** 2016
SALES (est): 212K **Privately Held**
SIC: 7991 Physical fitness facilities

(P-17411)
ROW HOUSE FRANCHISE LLC
Also Called: Row House
17877 Von Karman Ave Ste 100 (92614-4201)
PHONE.................................949 341-5585
Eric Von Frohlich, *CEO*
EMP: 151 **EST:** 2017
SALES (est): 9.96MM
SALES (corp-wide): 244.95MM **Publicly Held**
Web: www.therowhouse.com
SIC: 7991 6794 Physical fitness clubs with training equipment; Franchises, selling or licensing
HQ: Xponential Fitness Llc
17877 Von Karman Ave # 1
Irvine CA
949 346-3000

(P-17412)
RSG GROUP NORTH AMERICA LP
7007 Romaine St Ste 101 (90038-2439)
PHONE.................................714 609-0572
Sebastian Schoepe, *CEO*
EMP: 220 **EST:** 2016
SALES (est): 4.04MM **Privately Held**
SIC: 7991 Physical fitness facilities

(P-17413)
SALVATION ARMY RAY & JOAN
Also Called: Salvation Army
6845 University Ave (92115-5829)
PHONE.................................619 287-5762
James Knaggs, *Pr*
David Hudson, *
EMP: 300 **EST:** 1998
SALES (est): 22.58MM
SALES (corp-wide): 2.41B **Privately Held**

Web: sd.kroccenter.org
SIC: **7991** 8661 7032 7922 Physical fitness clubs with training equipment; Miscellaneous denomination church; Sporting and recreational camps; Community theater production
PA: The Salvation Army National Corporation
615 Slaters Ln
Alexandria VA
703 684-5500

(P-17414)
SPA HAVENS LP
Also Called: Cal-A-Vie
29402 Spa Haven Way (92084-2234)
PHONE..........................760 945-2055
John Havens, *Owner*
▲ **EMP:** 105 **EST:** 1984
SALES (est): 12.49MM **Privately Held**
Web: www.cal-a-vie.com
SIC: **7991** Spas

(P-17415)
SPECTRUM CLUBS INC
840 Apollo St Ste 100 (90245-4701)
PHONE..........................310 727-9300
EMP: 1600
SIC: **7991** Health club

(P-17416)
THINK TOGETHER
12016 Telegraph Rd (90670-3784)
PHONE..........................562 236-3835
EMP: 344
SALES (corp-wide): 75.71MM **Privately Held**
Web: www.thinktogether.org
SIC: **7991** Physical fitness facilities
PA: Think Together
2101 E 4th St Ste 200b
Santa Ana CA
714 543-3807

(P-17417)
TRI-CITY HOSPITAL DISTRICT
Also Called: Tri-City Wellness Center
6250 El Camino Real (92009-1608)
PHONE..........................760 931-3171
EMP: 374
SALES (corp-wide): 319.28MM **Privately Held**
Web: www.tricitywellness.com
SIC: **7991** Health club
PA: Tri-City Hospital District (Inc)
4002 Vista Way
Oceanside CA
760 724-8411

(P-17418)
TW HOLDINGS INC
10805 Rancho Bernardo Rd Ste 120 (92127)
PHONE..........................858 217-8750
Gene Lamott, *CEO*
Karen Wischmann, *
Rob Zielinski, *
EMP: 600 **EST:** 2007
SALES (est): 8.57MM **Privately Held**
SIC: **7991** Physical fitness clubs with training equipment

(P-17419)
WORLD GYM INTERNATIONAL LLC
Also Called: World Gym Fitness Centers
1901 Avenue Of The Stars Ste 1100 (90067-6001)
PHONE..........................310 557-8804
EMP: 108 **EST:** 2008

SALES (est): 2.33MM **Privately Held**
Web: www.worldgym.com
SIC: **7991** 6794 Health club; Franchises, selling or licensing

(P-17420)
XPONENTIAL FITNESS INC (PA)
17877 Von Karman Ave Ste 100 (92614-4201)
PHONE..........................949 346-3000
Anthony Geisler, *CEO*
Mark Grabowski, *Non-Executive Chairman of the Board*
Sarah Luna, *Pr*
Ryan Junk, *COO*
John Meloun, *CFO*
EMP: 270 **EST:** 2017
SALES (est): 244.95MM
SALES (corp-wide): 244.95MM **Publicly Held**
Web: www.xponential.com
SIC: **7991** Athletic club and gymnasiums, membership

7992 Public Golf Courses

(P-17421)
CHAPMAN GOLF DEVELOPMENT LLC
Also Called: Tradition Golf Club
78505 Avenue 52 (92253-2802)
PHONE..........................760 564-8723
David Chapman, *Managing Member*
EMP: 100 **EST:** 1999
SALES (est): 1.9MM **Privately Held**
SIC: **7992** Public golf courses

(P-17422)
COUNTY OF LOS ANGELES
Also Called: Parks and Recreation Dept
1875 Fairplex Dr (91768-1240)
PHONE..........................909 231-0549
Chad Hackman, *Genl Mgr*
EMP: 180
Web: www.mountainmeadowsgc.com
SIC: **7992** 9512 7299 Public golf courses; Recreational program administration, government; Wedding chapel, privately operated
PA: County Of Los Angeles
500 W Temple St Ste 437
Los Angeles CA
213 974-1101

(P-17423)
CROCKETT & COINC (PA)
Also Called: Bonita Golf Club
5120 Robinwood Rd Ste A22 (91902-1930)
P.O. Box 445 (91908-0445)
PHONE..........................619 267-6410
Phillip Crockett, *Pr*
James Crockett, *
Maryann Daly, *
EMP: 20 **EST:** 1961
SQ FT: 30,000
SALES (est): 4.72MM
SALES (corp-wide): 4.72MM **Privately Held**
Web: new.bonitagolf.net
SIC: **7992** 5813 5812 3111 Public golf courses; Bar (drinking places); Eating places; Leather tanning and finishing

(P-17424)
CROCKETT & COINC
Also Called: Bonita Golf Club
5540 Sweetwater Rd (91902-2137)
PHONE..........................619 267-1103
Clayton Crockett, *Prin*

EMP: 80
SALES (corp-wide): 4.72MM **Privately Held**
Web: new.bonitagolf.net
SIC: **7992** 5812 Public golf courses; Eating places
PA: Crockett & Co.Inc.
5120 Robinwood Rd Ste A22
Bonita CA
619 267-6410

(P-17425)
DESERT WILLOW GOLF RESORT INC
Also Called: Desert Willow Golf Course
38995 Desert Willow Dr (92260-1674)
PHONE..........................760 346-0015
Richard Mogensen, *Genl Mgr*
EMP: 150 **EST:** 1997
SQ FT: 33,000
SALES (est): 2.51MM **Privately Held**
Web: www.desertwillow.com
SIC: **7992** Public golf courses

(P-17426)
EL PRADO GOLF COURSE LP
6555 Pine Ave (91708-9192)
PHONE..........................909 597-1751
Bruce Jenke, *Genl Pt*
G Barton Heuler, *Pt*
Anthony Foo, *Pt*
Walter Heuler, *Pt*
EMP: 80 **EST:** 1975
SQ FT: 5,000
SALES (est): 4.67MM **Privately Held**
Web: www.elpradogolfcourses.com
SIC: **7992** Public golf courses

(P-17427)
ESTATES AT TRUMP NAT GOLF CLB
Also Called: Trump Nat Golf CLB Los Angeles
1 Trump National Dr (90275-6173)
PHONE..........................310 265-5000
Jill Martin, *CEO*
Mike Vandergles, *Prin*
EMP: 203 **EST:** 2002
SALES (est): 10.88MM
SALES (corp-wide): 2.37MM **Privately Held**
Web: www.trumpnationallosangeles.com
SIC: **7992** Public golf courses
HQ: Trump Golf Management Llc
725 5th Ave Bsmt A
New York NY
212 832-2000

(P-17428)
GLEN ANNIE GOLF CLUB
Also Called: Annie Golf Club
405 Glen Annie Rd (93117-1427)
PHONE..........................805 968-6400
Richard Nahas, *Genl Mgr*
EMP: 80 **EST:** 1997
SALES (est): 2.47MM **Privately Held**
Web: www.glenanniegolf.com
SIC: **7992** Public golf courses

(P-17429)
GOLF MANAGEMENT OPERATING LLC ✪
50200 Avnida Vista Bonita (92253)
PHONE..........................760 777-4839
Jim Hinckley, *Pr*
Doug Howe, *
Greg Adair, *
Jack Marquardt, *
Melissa Mckibben, *Prin*
EMP: 2800 **EST:** 2022

SALES (est): 4.42MM **Privately Held**
SIC: **7992** Public golf courses

(P-17430)
GREEN RIVER GOLF CORPORATION
Also Called: Green River Golf Course
5215 Green River Rd (92878-9404)
PHONE..........................714 970-8411
Judy Saguchi, *Pr*
EMP: 100 **EST:** 1977
SQ FT: 30,000
SALES (est): 9.56MM **Privately Held**
Web: weddings.playgreenriver.com
SIC: **7992** 5941 5813 5812 Public golf courses; Sporting goods and bicycle shops; Drinking places; Eating places
PA: Courseco, Inc.
5341 Old Redwood Hwy # 202
Petaluma CA

(P-17431)
HERITAGE GOLF GROUP LLC
Also Called: Talega Golf Club
990 Avenida Talega (92673-6849)
PHONE..........................949 369-6226
David Foster, *Brnch Mgr*
EMP: 89
SALES (corp-wide): 97.99MM **Privately Held**
SIC: **7992** Public golf courses
PA: Heritage Golf Group, Llc
12750 High Bluff Dr Fl 4
San Diego CA
858 720-0694

(P-17432)
HERITAGE GOLF GROUP LLC
Also Called: Valencia Country Club
27330 Tourney Rd (91355-1806)
PHONE..........................661 254-4401
Jim Fitzsimmons, *Mgr*
EMP: 115
SALES (corp-wide): 97.99MM **Privately Held**
SIC: **7992** Public golf courses
PA: Heritage Golf Group, Llc
12750 High Bluff Dr Fl 4
San Diego CA
858 720-0694

(P-17433)
KSL RECREATION MANAGEMENT OPERATIONS LLC
50905 Avenida Bermudas (92253-8910)
PHONE..........................760 564-8000
EMP: 8000
SIC: **7992** 7011 Public golf courses; Hotels and motels

(P-17434)
LAKESIDE GOLF CLUB
4500 W Lakeside Dr (91505-4088)
P.O. Box 2386 (91610-0386)
PHONE..........................818 984-0601
Jerry Fard, *Mgr*
Michael E Henry, *CEO*
EMP: 98 **EST:** 1924
SQ FT: 25,000
SALES (est): 11.57MM **Privately Held**
Web: www.lakesidegolfclub.com
SIC: **7992** Public golf courses

(P-17435)
LOS SERRANOS GOLF CLUB
Also Called: Los Serranos Golf & Cntry CLB
15656 Yorba Ave (91709-3129)
PHONE..........................909 597-1769

John A Kramer Junior, *CEO*
John A Kramer Senior, *Pr*
Ronald Kramer, *
Gloria Kramer, *Stockholder**
Kevin Sullivan, *
EMP: 135 **EST:** 1953
SQ FT: 41,896
SALES (est): 6.66MM **Privately Held**
Web: www.losserranoscountryclub.com
SIC: 7992 5812 5813 Public golf courses;
American restaurant; Cocktail lounge

(P-17436)
MADISON CLUB OWNERS ASSN
Also Called: Madison Club, The
53035 Meriwether Way (92253-5535)
P.O. Box 1558 (92247-1558)
PHONE..............................760 777-9320
Douglas Siebold, *CEO*
Brian Ellis, *
EMP: 125 **EST:** 2006
SQ FT: 70,000
SALES (est): 10.61MM
SALES (corp-wide): 435.04MM **Privately Held**
Web: www.madisonclubca.com
SIC: 7992 Public golf courses
PA: Discovery Land Company, Llc
14605 N 73rd St
Scottsdale AZ
480 624-5200

(P-17437)
MCMILLIN COMMUNITIES INC
Also Called: Temeku Hills
41687 Temeku Dr (92591-3909)
PHONE..............................951 506-3303
Sonia Howard, *Brnch Mgr*
EMP: 940
SALES (corp-wide): 46.31MM **Privately Held**
Web: www.mcmillin.com
SIC: 7992 Public golf courses
PA: Mcmillin Communities, Inc.
2750 Womble Rd Ste 102
San Diego CA
619 477-4117

(P-17438)
MESA VERDE PARTNERS
Also Called: Costa Mesa Country Club
1701 Golf Course Dr (92626-5049)
PHONE..............................714 540-7500
Scott Henderson, *Pt*
EMP: 120 **EST:** 1992
SQ FT: 12,000
SALES (est): 5.65MM
SALES (corp-wide): 8.81MM **Privately Held**
Web: www.costamesacountryclub.com
SIC: 7992 7997 5813 5812 Public golf courses; Membership sports and recreation clubs; Drinking places; Eating places
PA: Santa Anita Associates
405 S Santa Anita Ave
Arcadia CA
626 447-2764

(P-17439)
MILE SQUARE GOLF COURSE
10401 Warner Ave (92708-1604)
PHONE..............................714 962-5541
David A Rainville, *Pt*
EMP: 109 **EST:** 1969
SQ FT: 12,000
SALES (est): 4.45MM **Privately Held**
Web: www.milesquaregolfcourse.com
SIC: 7992 7999 5812 Public golf courses; Golf driving range; American restaurant

(P-17440)
MONARCH BEACH GOLF LINKS (HQ)
50 Monarch Beach Resort N (92629-4084)
PHONE..............................949 240-8247
Hale Kelly, *Dir*
EMP: 80 **EST:** 1983
SALES (est): 9.95MM **Privately Held**
Web: www.monarchbeachgolf.com
SIC: 7992 Public golf courses
PA: Troon Golf, L.L.C.
15044 N Scottsdale Rd # 300
Scottsdale AZ

(P-17441)
SILVER ROCK RESORT GOLF CLUB
79179 Ahmanson Ln (92253-5715)
PHONE..............................760 777-8884
EMP: 100 **EST:** 2005
SALES (est): 4.6MM
SALES (corp-wide): 91.88MM **Privately Held**
Web: www.silverrock.org
SIC: 7992 Public golf courses
PA: City Of La Quinta
78495 Calle Tampico
La Quinta CA
760 777-7000

(P-17442)
TRILOGY GOLF AT LA QUINTA
60151 Trilogy Pkwy (92253-7640)
PHONE..............................760 771-0707
Tom Williams Pga, *Genl Mgr*
Marge Deschaak, *
Ralph Bernhisel, *
EMP: 306 **EST:** 2004
SALES (est): 2.36MM
SALES (corp-wide): 2.1B **Privately Held**
Web: www.thegolfclubatlaquinta.com
SIC: 7992 Public golf courses
HQ: J.F. Shea Construction, Inc.
655 Brea Canyon Rd
Walnut CA
909 594-9500

(P-17443)
WELK GROUP INC
Also Called: Foutains Executive Course
8860 Lawrence Welk Dr (92026-6403)
PHONE..............................760 749-3225
EMP: 147
SALES (corp-wide): 47.43MM **Privately Held**
Web: www.kwgoldcoast.com
SIC: 7992 7011 Public golf courses; Resort hotel
PA: The Welk Group Inc
11400 W Olympic Blvd # 1450
Los Angeles CA
760 749-3000

7993 Coin-operated Amusement Devices

(P-17444)
CAMPO BAND MISSIONS INDIANS
Also Called: Golden Acorn Casino & Trvl Ctr
1800 Golden Acorn Way (91906-2301)
P.O. Box 310 (91906-0310)
PHONE..............................619 938-6000
Don Trimble, *Mgr*
EMP: 330
Web: www.goldenacorncasino.com

SIC: 7993 5812 Gambling establishments operating coin-operated machines; American restaurant
PA: Campo Band Of Missions Indians
36190 Church Rd
Campo CA

(P-17445)
PLAYERS WEST AMUSEMENTS INC (PA)
Also Called: Toy Barn
2360 Sturgis Rd Ste A (93030-8956)
PHONE..............................805 983-1400
Jack G Mann, *Pr*
▲ **EMP:** 38 **EST:** 1991
SALES (est): 2.29MM **Privately Held**
Web: www.toybarn.com
SIC: 7993 5092 3942 Amusement machine rental, coin-operated; Toys and hobby goods and supplies; Dolls and stuffed toys

(P-17446)
SEGA ENTERTAINMENT USA INC
600 N Brand Blvd 5th Fl (91203-4207)
PHONE..............................310 217-9500
▲ **EMP:** 1550
SIC: 7993 Coin-operated amusement devices

7996 Amusement Parks

(P-17447)
CITY OF LANCASTER
Also Called: Big Eight
43011 N 10th St W (93534-6012)
PHONE..............................661 723-6071
Jeff Campbell, *Brnch Mgr*
EMP: 153
Web: www.cityoflancasterca.org
SIC: 7996 Amusement parks
PA: City Of Lancaster
44933 Fern Ave
Lancaster CA

(P-17448)
DISNEYLAND INTERNATIONAL (DH)
Also Called: Disneyland
1313 S Harbor Blvd (92802-2309)
PHONE..............................714 781-4565
James Thomas, *Pr*
James Cora, *Ch Bd*
Michael Eisner, *Dir*
Richard Nunis, *Dir*
Doris Smith, *Sec*
EMP: 200 **EST:** 1961
SALES (est): 260.45MM
SALES (corp-wide): 88.9B **Publicly Held**
Web: disneyland.disney.go.com
SIC: 7996 Theme park, amusement
HQ: Disney Enterprises, Inc.
500 S Buena Vista St
Burbank CA
818 560-1000

(P-17449)
KNOTTS BERRY FARM LLC (HQ)
Also Called: Knott's Berry Farm
8039 Beach Blvd (90620-3200)
P.O. Box 5002 (90622-5002)
PHONE..............................714 827-1776
Jack Falfas, *Pt*
▲ **EMP:** 500 **EST:** 1920
SQ FT: 5,000
SALES (est): 170.68MM
SALES (corp-wide): 1.82B **Publicly Held**
Web: www.knotts.com
SIC: 7996 Theme park, amusement
PA: Cedar Fair, L.P.
1 Cedar Point Dr

Sandusky OH
419 627-2344

(P-17450)
LEGOLAND CALIFORNIA LLC
Also Called: Legoland California Resort
1 Legoland Dr (92008-4610)
PHONE..............................760 450-3661
▲ **EMP:** 400 **EST:** 1994
SALES (est): 89.5MM
SALES (corp-wide): 2.42B **Privately Held**
Web: www.legoland.com
SIC: 7996 Theme park, amusement
HQ: Merlin Entertainments Group Limited
Link House
Poole

(P-17451)
RAGING WATERS GROUP INC
Also Called: Raging Waters
111 Raging Waters Dr (91773-3998)
PHONE..............................909 802-2200
EMP: 1092 **EST:** 2000
SALES (est): 9.97MM
SALES (corp-wide): 53.97MM **Privately Held**
Web: www.ragingwaters.com
SIC: 7996 Theme park, amusement
PA: Alfa Smartparks, Inc
1 W Adams St Ste 200
Jacksonville FL
904 358-1027

(P-17452)
RAVINE WATERPARK LLC
Also Called: Ravine Waterpark, The
2301 Airport Rd (93446-8549)
PHONE..............................805 237-8500
James Walsh, *Prin*
EMP: 205 **EST:** 2004
SALES (est): 4.94MM **Privately Held**
Web: www.ravinewaterpark.com
SIC: 7996 Theme park, amusement

(P-17453)
SANTA MONICA AMUSEMENTS LLC
Also Called: Pacific Park
380 Santa Monica Pier (90401-3128)
PHONE..............................310 451-9641
Mary Ann Powell, *CEO*
Jeff Klocke, *
David Gillam, *
Dana Wyatt, *
EMP: 325 **EST:** 1992
SQ FT: 70,000
SALES (est): 24.91MM **Privately Held**
Web: www.pacpark.com
SIC: 7996 Theme park, amusement

(P-17454)
SEAWORLD PARKS & ENTRMT LLC
1660 S Shores Rd (92109-7906)
PHONE..............................619 226-3910
Sam Munoz, *Brnch Mgr*
EMP: 82
Web: www.seaworld.com
SIC: 7996 Theme park, amusement
PA: Seaworld Parks & Entertainment Llc
500 Sea World Dr
San Diego CA

(P-17455)
SIX FLAGS MAGIC MOUNTAIN INC
26101 Magic Mountain Pkwy (91355-1095)
P.O. Box 5500 (91380-5500)
PHONE..............................661 255-4100

Larry B Cochran, *CEO*
EMP: 85 **EST:** 1979
SALES (est): 26.27MM
SALES (corp-wide): 1.36B **Publicly Held**
Web: www.sixflags.com
SIC: 7996 Theme park, amusement
PA: Six Flags Entertainment Corp
1000 Ballpark Way Ste 400
Arlington TX
972 595-5000

(P-17456)
WALT DISNEY COMPANY (PA)
Also Called: Disney
500 S Buena Vista St (91521-0007)
PHONE..............................818 560-1000
Robert A Iger, *CEO*
EMP: 1381 **EST:** 1923
SALES (est): 88.9B
SALES (corp-wide): 88.9B **Publicly Held**
Web: www.thewaltdisneycompany.com
SIC: 7996 4841 Amusement parks; Cable
television services

7997 Membership Sports And Recreation Clubs

(P-17457)
1334 PARTNERS LP
Also Called: Manhattan Country Club
1330 Park View Ave (90266-3704)
PHONE..............................310 546-5656
Keith Brackpool, *Pt*
EMP: 100 **EST:** 1982
SQ FT: 80,000
SALES (est): 8.22MM **Privately Held**
SIC: 7997 6512 7991 5813 Country club,
membership; Commercial and industrial
building operation; Physical fitness facilities
; Drinking places

(P-17458)
AGI HOLDING CORP (PA)
Also Called: Affinity Group
2575 Vista Del Mar Dr (93001-3900)
P.O. Box 6888 (80155-6888)
PHONE..............................805 667-4100
Stephen Adams, *CEO*
Joe Mcadams, *Pr*
Mark Boggess, *
Michael Schneider, *
Mister Stephen Adams, *Prin*
◆ **EMP:** 49 **EST:** 1988
SQ FT: 74,000
SALES (est): 80.18MM
SALES (corp-wide): 80.18MM **Privately
Held**
Web: www.goodsam.com
SIC: 7997 2741 Membership sports and
recreation clubs; Directories, nec:
publishing and printing

(P-17459)
ALTADENA TOWN AND COUNTRY CLUB
2290 Country Club Dr (91001-3202)
PHONE..............................626 345-9088
David Edens, *Pr*
EMP: 80 **EST:** 1946
SQ FT: 50,000
SALES (est): 5.98MM **Privately Held**
Web: www.altaclub.com
SIC: 7997 Country club, membership

(P-17460)
AMERICAN GOLF CORPORATION (HQ)
909 N Pacific Coast Hwy Ste 650
(90245-2715)

PHONE..............................310 664-4000
Meng Lai, *CFO*
Kim Wong, *
Keith Brown, *
Jim Allison, *
Craig Kniffen, *
EMP: 150 **EST:** 1973
SALES (est): 281.77MM **Privately Held**
Web: www.americangolf.com
SIC: 7997 7999 5812 5941 Golf club,
membership; Golf services and
professionals; Eating places; Golf goods
and equipment
PA: Drive Shack Inc.
10670 N Cntl Expy Ste 700
Dallas TX

(P-17461)
ANNANDALE GOLF CLUB
1 N San Rafael Ave (91105-1299)
PHONE..............................626 796-6125
Christoff Granger, *Genl Mgr*
EMP: 125 **EST:** 1905
SQ FT: 10,000
SALES (est): 11.75MM **Privately Held**
Web: www.annandalegolf.com
SIC: 7997 Golf club, membership

(P-17462)
ANTELOPE VLY CNTRY CLB IMPRV
39800 Country Club Dr (93551-2970)
PHONE..............................661 947-3142
Mark Range, *
EMP: 150 **EST:** 1952
SQ FT: 22,000
SALES (est): 3.76MM **Privately Held**
Web:
www.antelopevalleycountryclub.com
SIC: 7997 Country club, membership

(P-17463)
BALBOA BAY CLUB INC (HQ)
1221 W Coast Hwy (92663-5092)
PHONE..............................949 645-5000
David Wooten, *Pr*
W D Ray, *
EMP: 260 **EST:** 1948
SALES (est): 24.76MM
SALES (corp-wide): 46.07MM **Privately
Held**
Web: www.balboabayclub.com
SIC: 7997 7011 Country club, membership;
Resort hotel
PA: International Bay Clubs, Llc
1221 W Coast Hwy Ste 145
Newport Beach CA
949 645-5000

(P-17464)
BAY CLUBS COMPANY LLC
Also Called: Sanctuary Spa
12000 Carmel Country Rd (92130-6101)
PHONE..............................858 509-9933
EMP: 294
SALES (corp-wide): 5.09MM **Privately
Held**
Web: www.bayclubs.com
SIC: 7997 Membership sports and recreation
clubs
HQ: The Bay Clubs Company Llc
1 Lombard St
San Francisco CA
415 781-1874

(P-17465)
BAY CLUBS COMPANY LLC
6144 Calle Real (93117-2012)
PHONE..............................805 964-0556
Jody Moon, *Brnch Mgr*

EMP: 294
SALES (corp-wide): 5.09MM **Privately
Held**
Web: www.bayclubs.com
SIC: 7997 Membership sports and recreation
clubs
HQ: The Bay Clubs Company Llc
1 Lombard St
San Francisco CA
415 781-1874

(P-17466)
BAY CLUBS COMPANY LLC
21 W Carrillo St (93101-3212)
PHONE..............................805 965-0999
Ramone Adams, *Mgr*
EMP: 294
SALES (corp-wide): 5.09MM **Privately
Held**
Web: www.bayclubs.com
SIC: 7997 Membership sports and recreation
clubs
HQ: The Bay Clubs Company Llc
1 Lombard St
San Francisco CA
415 781-1874

(P-17467)
BAY CLUBS COMPANY LLC
3908 State St (93105-3114)
PHONE..............................805 563-8700
Cindy Capra, *Mgr*
EMP: 294
SALES (corp-wide): 5.09MM **Privately
Held**
Web: www.bayclubs.com
SIC: 7997 Membership sports and recreation
clubs
HQ: The Bay Clubs Company Llc
1 Lombard St
San Francisco CA
415 781-1874

(P-17468)
BAY CLUBS COMPANY LLC
2250 Park Pl (91362-1717)
PHONE..............................310 643-6878
Alyce Jones, *Brnch Mgr*
EMP: 294
SALES (corp-wide): 5.09MM **Privately
Held**
Web: www.bayclubs.com
SIC: 7997 Membership sports and recreation
clubs
HQ: The Bay Clubs Company Llc
1 Lombard St
San Francisco CA
415 781-1874

(P-17469)
BAY CLUBS COMPANY LLC
51 Peninsula Ctr Ste 51d (90275)
PHONE..............................310 541-2582
Eric Rogers, *Genl Mgr*
EMP: 294
SALES (corp-wide): 5.09MM **Privately
Held**
Web: www.bayclubs.com
SIC: 7997 Membership sports and recreation
clubs
HQ: The Bay Clubs Company Llc
1 Lombard St
San Francisco CA
415 781-1874

(P-17470)
BAY CLUBS COMPANY LLC
2425 Olympic Blvd Ste 100 (90404-4030)
PHONE..............................310 829-4995
Andy Gillen, *COO*

EMP: 294
SALES (corp-wide): 5.09MM **Privately
Held**
Web: www.bayclubs.com
SIC: 7997 Membership sports and recreation
clubs
HQ: The Bay Clubs Company Llc
1 Lombard St
San Francisco CA
415 781-1874

(P-17471)
BEL-AIR BAY CLUB LTD
16801 Pacific Coast Hwy (90272-3350)
PHONE..............................310 230-4700
William Howard, *CEO*
EMP: 200 **EST:** 1927
SQ FT: 7,500
SALES (est): 12.04MM **Privately Held**
Web: www.belairbayclub.com
SIC: 7997 Membership sports and recreation
clubs

(P-17472)
BEL-AIR COUNTRY CLUB
10768 Bellagio Rd (90077-3799)
PHONE..............................310 472-9563
Joseph Wagner, *Genl Mgr*
Peter Best, *
EMP: 140 **EST:** 1924
SQ FT: 10,000
SALES (est): 14.61MM **Privately Held**
Web: www.bel-aircc.golf
SIC: 7997 5941 Country club, membership;
Golf goods and equipment

(P-17473)
BELLA COLLINA SAN CLEMENTE
200 Avenida La Pata (92673-6301)
PHONE..............................949 498-6604
EMP: 80 **EST:** 2009
SALES (est): 2.27MM **Privately Held**
Web: www.bellacollinasanclemente.com
SIC: 7997 Country club, membership

(P-17474)
BIG CANYON COUNTRY CLUB
1 Big Canyon Dr (92660-5299)
PHONE..............................949 644-5404
Donald Tippett, *CEO*
William Stamply, *
EMP: 180 **EST:** 1971
SQ FT: 50,000
SALES (est): 24.83MM **Privately Held**
Web: www.bigcanyoncc.org
SIC: 7997 Country club, membership

(P-17475)
BIGHORN GOLF CLUB CHARITIES
255 Palowet Dr (92260-7311)
PHONE..............................760 773-2468
Carl T Cardinalli, *Pr*
Joe Curtis, *
EMP: 190 **EST:** 1990
SALES (est): 1.66MM **Privately Held**
Web: www.bighorngolf.com
SIC: 7997 7992 Country club, membership;
Public golf courses

(P-17476)
BRAEMAR COUNTRY CLUB INC
Also Called: Braemar Country Club
4001 Reseda Blvd (91356-5330)
P.O. Box 570217 (91357-0217)
PHONE..............................323 873-6880
Steven Held, *Mgr*
EMP: 199 **EST:** 1959

SQ FT: 20,000
SALES (est): 9.13MM
SALES (corp-wide): 2.44B **Privately Held**
Web: www.invitedclubs.com
SIC: 7997 Country club, membership
HQ: Clubcorp Usa, Inc.
  5215 N O Connor Blvd # 2
  Irving TX
  972 243-6191

(P-17477)
BRENTWOOD COUNTRY CLUB
LOS ANGELES
Also Called: BRENTWOOD COUNTRY CLUB
590 S Burlingame Ave (90049-4826)
PHONE...........................310 451-8011
EMP: 100 EST: 1948
SALES (est): 17.68MM **Privately Held**
Web: www.brentwoodcc.net
SIC: 7997 Country club, membership

(P-17478)
CLAREMONT TENNIS CLUB
Also Called: Claremont Club, The
1777 Monte Vista Ave (91711-2916)
P.O. Box 157 (91785-0157)
PHONE...........................909 625-9515
Michael G Alpert, *Pr*
Geoffrey Clark, *
EMP: 200 EST: 1973
SQ FT: 40,000
SALES (est): 21.08MM **Privately Held**
Web: www.claremontclub.com
SIC: 7997 7991 5812 Membership sports
  and recreation clubs; Health club; Eating
  places

(P-17479)
COMEDY CLUB OXNARD LLC
Also Called: Levity Live
591 Collection Blvd (93036-5454)
PHONE...........................805 535-5400
Alireza Ghaemian, *Prin*
EMP: 88 EST: 2015
SALES (est): 991.77K **Privately Held**
SIC: 7997 Membership sports and recreation
  clubs

(P-17480)
DEL MAR COUNTRY CLUB INC
6001 Clubhouse Dr (92067-9589)
P.O. Box 9866 (92067-4866)
PHONE...........................858 759-5500
Madeleine Pickens, *Pr*
EMP: 90 EST: 1993
SQ FT: 18,000
SALES (est): 10.12MM **Privately Held**
Web: www.delmarcountryclub.com
SIC: 7997 Country club, membership

(P-17481)
DHCCNP
Also Called: DESERT HORIZONS
COUNTRY CLUB
44900 Desert Horizons Dr (92210-7401)
PHONE...........................760 340-4646
Jurgen Gross, *Mgr*
EMP: 86 EST: 1979
SQ FT: 30,000
SALES (est): 5.47MM **Privately Held**
Web: www.deserthorizons.org
SIC: 7997 7992 5812 Country club,
  membership; Public golf courses; Eating
  places

(P-17482)
EL CABALLERO COUNTRY
CLUB
18300 Tarzana Dr (91356-4216)

PHONE...........................818 654-3000
Bary West, *Pr*
Gary Diamond, *
Peter Jimenez, *
EMP: 125 EST: 1956
SQ FT: 20,000
SALES (est): 11.28MM **Privately Held**
Web: www.elcaballerocc.com
SIC: 7997 7992 5812 Country club,
  membership; Public golf courses; Eating
  places

(P-17483)
ELDORADO COUNTRY CLUB
46000 E Eldorado Dr (92210-8631)
PHONE...........................760 346-8081
Geoff Hasley, *Pr*
EMP: 200 EST: 1959
SQ FT: 50,000
SALES (est): 18.17MM **Privately Held**
Web: www.eldoradocc.org
SIC: 7997 5812 Golf club, membership;
  Eating places

(P-17484)
FAIRBANKS RANCH CNTRY
CLB INC
15150 San Dieguito Rd (92067)
P.O. Box 8586 (92067-8586)
PHONE...........................858 259-8811
Mike Kendall, *CEO*
Brad Forrester, *
Stan Kinsey, *
Robert Macier, *
EMP: 180 EST: 1983
SQ FT: 35,000
SALES (est): 13.41MM **Privately Held**
Web: www.bayclubs.com
SIC: 7997 Country club, membership

(P-17485)
FRIENDLY HLLS CNTRY CLB
FNDTIO
8500 Villaverde Dr (90605-1342)
PHONE...........................562 698-0331
Dave Goodrich, *COO*
Chris Banner, *
EMP: 110 EST: 1969
SQ FT: 42,000
SALES (est): 5.4MM **Privately Held**
Web: www.friendlyhillscc.com
SIC: 7997 Country club, membership

(P-17486)
GLENDORA COUNTRY CLUB
2400 Country Club Drive (91741)
PHONE...........................626 335-4051
Jack Stoughton, *CEO*
Jim Leahy, *
Mike Kerstetter, *
Bill Mckinley, *Treas*
Susan Taylor, *
EMP: 90 EST: 1954
SQ FT: 10,000
SALES (est): 5.98MM **Privately Held**
Web: www.glendoracountryclub.com
SIC: 7997 5812 5813 Country club,
  membership; Eating places; Drinking places

(P-17487)
HACIENDA GOLF CLUB
718 East Rd (90631-8155)
PHONE...........................562 694-1081
Frank Cordeiro, *Genl Mgr*
EMP: 95 EST: 1919
SQ FT: 30,000
SALES (est): 7.73MM **Privately Held**
Web: www.haciendagolfclub.com

SIC: 7997 5812 5813 Golf club, membership
  ; American restaurant; Bar (drinking places)

(P-17488)
HIDEAWAY CLUB
Also Called: Hideaway
80440 Hideaway Club Ct (92253-7867)
P.O. Box 1540 (92247-1540)
PHONE...........................760 777-7400
Brian J Ellis, *CEO*
EMP: 466 EST: 2015
SALES (est): 8.91MM
SALES (corp-wide): 435.04MM **Privately
Held**
Web: www.hideawaygolfclub.com
SIC: 7997 6531 Membership sports and
  recreation clubs; Real estate agents and
  managers
PA: Discovery Land Company, Llc
  14605 N 73rd St
  Scottsdale AZ
  480 624-5200

(P-17489)
HILLCREST COUNTRY CLUB
10000 W Pico Blvd (90064-3417)
PHONE...........................310 553-8911
John Jameson, *Pr*
John Goldsmith, *CEO*
Tom Driefus, *CFO*
Richard Powell, *Prin*
Leonard Fisher, *Prin*
EMP: 180 EST: 1920
SQ FT: 69,081
SALES (est): 25.59MM **Privately Held**
Web: www.hcc-la.com
SIC: 7997 Country club, membership

(P-17490)
INTERNATIONAL BAY CLUBS
LLC (PA)
Also Called: Balboa Bay Club and Resort
1221 W Coast Hwy Ste 145 (92663-5001)
PHONE...........................949 645-5000
Todd M Pickup, *CEO*
David Wooten, *Pr*
EMP: 105 EST: 1948
SQ FT: 330,000
SALES (est): 46.07MM
SALES (corp-wide): 46.07MM **Privately
Held**
Web: www.balboabayclub.com
SIC: 7997 4493 6552 7011 Country club,
  membership; Marinas; Land subdividers
  and developers, residential; Hotels and
  motels

(P-17491)
JONATHAN CLUB
Also Called: Jonathan Beach Club
850 Palisades Beach Rd (90403-1008)
PHONE...........................310 393-9245
Ernie Dunn, *Mgr*
EMP: 100
SQ FT: 12,784
SALES (corp-wide): 30.26MM **Privately
Held**
Web: www.jc.org
SIC: 7997 5812 8641 Beach club,
  membership; Grills (eating places); Civic
  and social associations
PA: Jonathan Club
  545 S Figueroa St
  Los Angeles CA
  213 624-0881

(P-17492)
LA CANADA FLINTRIDGE
CNTRY CLB
5500 Godbey Dr (91011-1836)

PHONE...........................818 790-0611
Gilbert Dreyfus, *Pr*
Evelyn Dreyfus, *
EMP: 80 EST: 1977
SQ FT: 24,000
SALES (est): 6.01MM **Privately Held**
Web: www.lcfcountryclub.com
SIC: 7997 Country club, membership

(P-17493)
LA CUMBRE COUNTRY CLUB
4015 Via Laguna (93110-2298)
PHONE...........................805 687-2421
Brian Bahman, *Genl Mgr*
EMP: 100 EST: 1956
SQ FT: 8,000
SALES (est): 13.16MM **Privately Held**
Web: www.lacumbrecc.org
SIC: 7997 Country club, membership

(P-17494)
LA JOLLA BCH & TENNIS CLB
INC (PA)
Also Called: Marine Room Restaurant
2000 Spindrift Dr (92037-3237)
PHONE...........................858 454-7126
William J Kellogg, *CEO*
Jeannie Porter, *
▲ EMP: 165 EST: 1940
SQ FT: 3,500
SALES (est): 47.87MM
SALES (corp-wide): 47.87MM **Privately
Held**
Web: www.ljbtc.com
SIC: 7997 8742 Membership sports and
  recreation clubs; Food and beverage
  consultant

(P-17495)
LA JOLLA COUNTRY CLUB INC
7301 High Ave (92037-5210)
PHONE...........................858 454-9601
Andrew Gorton, *Genl Mgr*
EMP: 91 EST: 1928
SQ FT: 39,000
SALES (est): 14.02MM **Privately Held**
Web: www.lajollacountryclub.com
SIC: 7997 5812 5941 5813 Golf club,
  membership; Eating places; Golf goods and
  equipment; Bar (drinking places)

(P-17496)
LAFC PARTNERS LLLP
818 W 7th St Ste 1200 (90017-3435)
PHONE...........................213 334-4239
EMP: 260
SALES (corp-wide): 10.95MM **Privately
Held**
Web: www.lafc.com
SIC: 7997 Membership sports and recreation
  clubs
PA: Lafc Partners, Lllp
  4751 Wilshire Blvd
  Los Angeles CA
  323 648-6000

(P-17497)
LAKES COUNTRY CLUB ASSN
INC (PA)
Also Called: Lakes Country Club, The
161 Old Ranch Rd (92211-3211)
PHONE...........................760 568-4321
Gerald Lee Hagood, *Pr*
Ron Phipps, *
Sandy Seddon, *
Frank Melon, *
EMP: 125 EST: 1982
SQ FT: 3,600
SALES (est): 14.35MM
SALES (corp-wide): 14.35MM **Privately
Held**

Web: www.thelakescc.com
SIC: **7997** 5941 5812 Country club, membership; Sporting goods and bicycle shops; Eating places

(P-17498)

LAS POSAS COUNTRY CLUB INC

Also Called: Lpcc
955 Fairway Dr (93010-8499)
PHONE..................805 482-4518
Todd Keefer, *Genl Mgr*
EMP: 146 **EST:** 1957
SALES (est): 2.29MM
SALES (corp-wide): 45.8MM **Privately Held**
Web: www.lasposascc.com
SIC: **7997** 7992 5812 0781 Country club, membership; Public golf courses; Eating places; Landscape counseling and planning
PA: Century Golf Partners Management Lp
5430 Lyndon B Johnson Fwy
Dallas TX
972 419-1400

(P-17499)

LOS ANGELES COUNTRY CLUB

10101 Wilshire Blvd (90024-4703)
PHONE..................310 276-6104
Kirk O Reese, *Prin*
EMP: 250 **EST:** 1898
SQ FT: 75,000
SALES (est): 24.95MM **Privately Held**
Web: www.thelacc.org
SIC: **7997** Country club, membership

(P-17500)

MESA VERDE COUNTRY CLUB

3000 Club House Rd (92626-3599)
PHONE..................714 549-0377
John Hayhoe, *CEO*
Robert Heflin, *
Diane Burnes, *
EMP: 125 **EST:** 1959
SQ FT: 34,000
SALES (est): 11.86MM **Privately Held**
Web: www.mesaverdecc.com
SIC: **7997** Country club, membership

(P-17501)

MISSION HILLS COUNTRY CLUB INC

34600 Mission Hills Dr (92270-1300)
PHONE..................760 324-9400
Josh Tanner, *Genl Mgr*
Doug Howe, *
EMP: 130 **EST:** 1983
SQ FT: 75,000
SALES (est): 9.9MM
SALES (corp-wide): 2.44B **Privately Held**
Web: www.invitedclubs.com
SIC: **7997** 7992 5812 Country club, membership; Public golf courses; Eating places
HQ: Clubcorp Usa, Inc.
5215 N O Connor Blvd # 2
Irving TX
972 243-6191

(P-17502)

MISSION VIEJO COUNTRY CLUB

26200 Country Club Dr (92691-5905)
PHONE..................949 582-1550
Michael Lance Kennedy, *Managing Member*
Chad Pettit, *
Enrique Martinez, *
Scot Dey, *
Veronica Alva Roman, *
EMP: 103 **EST:** 1969
SALES (est): 9.05MM **Privately Held**
Web: www.missionviejocc.com

SIC: **7997** 7991 5812 7299 Country club, membership; Physical fitness facilities; Eating places; Banquet hall facilities

(P-17503)

MONTECITO COUNTRY CLUB INC

920 Summit Rd (93108-2326)
PHONE..................805 969-0800
Tai Warner, *Pr*
Hiro Suzuki, *
EMP: 100 **EST:** 1921
SQ FT: 10,000
SALES (est): 10.49MM **Privately Held**
Web: www.montecitoclub1918.com
SIC: **7997** 5812 5813 Country club, membership; Eating places; Bar (drinking places)
PA: Tsukamoto Corporation Co., Ltd.
1-6-5, Nihombashihoncho
Chuo-Ku TKY

(P-17504)

NEWPORT BEACH COUNTRY CLUB INC

Also Called: Newport Beach Country Club
1 Clubhouse Dr (92660-7107)
PHONE..................949 644-9550
David Wooten, *Pr*
Jerry Anderson, *General Vice President**
Gerald Johnson, *
EMP: 90 **EST:** 1985
SALES (est): 6.55MM
SALES (corp-wide): 46.07MM **Privately Held**
Web: www.newportbeachcc.com
SIC: **7997** 7991 5941 5813 Country club, membership; Physical fitness facilities; Sporting goods and bicycle shops; Drinking places
PA: International Bay Clubs, Llc
1221 W Coast Hwy Ste 145
Newport Beach CA
949 645-5000

(P-17505)

NORTH RANCH COUNTRY CLUB

4761 Valley Spring Dr (91362-4399)
PHONE..................818 889-3531
Mark Bagaaso, *CEO*
Scott London, *
EMP: 160 **EST:** 1976
SQ FT: 53,000
SALES (est): 14.71MM **Privately Held**
Web: www.northranchcc.org
SIC: **7997** 5812 5941 Country club, membership; Eating places; Sporting goods and bicycle shops

(P-17506)

OAKMONT COUNTRY CLUB

3100 Country Club Dr (91208-1799)
PHONE..................818 542-4260
Pat Dahlson, *CEO*
John Schiller, *
Michael Hyler, *
EMP: 125 **EST:** 1955
SQ FT: 37,000
SALES (est): 13.7MM **Privately Held**
Web: www.oakmontcc.com
SIC: **7997** Country club, membership

(P-17507)

PORTER VALLEY COUNTRY CLUB INC

Also Called: Porter Valley Catering
19216 Singing Hills Dr (91326-1799)
PHONE..................818 360-1071
Robert H Dedman, *Ch Bd*

John Beckett, *
Doug Howe, *
EMP: 110 **EST:** 1966
SQ FT: 18,000
SALES (est): 8.28MM
SALES (corp-wide): 2.44B **Privately Held**
Web: www.invitedclubs.com
SIC: **7997** 5812 5941 Golf club, membership; Steak restaurant; Sporting goods and bicycle shops
HQ: Clubcorp Usa, Inc.
5215 N O Connor Blvd # 2
Irving TX
972 243-6191

(P-17508)

RANCHO SANTA FE ASSOCIATION

Also Called: Rancho Sante Fe Golf Club
5827 Viadelacumere (92067)
P.O. Box A (92067-0359)
PHONE..................858 756-1182
Stephen Nordstrom, *Mgr*
EMP: 100
SALES (corp-wide): 26.07MM **Privately Held**
Web: www.rsfgolfclub.com
SIC: **7997** Golf club, membership
PA: Rancho Santa Fe Association
17022 Avenida De Acacias
Rancho Santa Fe CA
858 756-1174

(P-17509)

RED HILL COUNTRY CLUB

8358 Red Hill Country Club Dr (91730-1899)
PHONE..................909 982-1358
Rob Mocskley, *Pr*
EMP: 92 **EST:** 1921
SQ FT: 20,000
SALES (est): 7.19MM **Privately Held**
Web: www.redhillcc.com
SIC: **7997** 5812 Country club, membership; Eating places

(P-17510)

REDLANDS COUNTRY CLUB

1749 Garden St (92373-7248)
PHONE..................909 793-2661
Scott Reding, *Pr*
Jason Murphy, *
EMP: 80 **EST:** 1946
SQ FT: 22,000
SALES (est): 6.67MM **Privately Held**
Web: www.redlandscountryclub.com
SIC: **7997** 5812 5813 Country club, membership; Snack shop; Bar (drinking places)

(P-17511)

RESERVE CLUB

49400 Desert Butte Trl (92210-7075)
PHONE..................760 674-2222
Kenneth Novack, *Pr*
C Ted Mccarter, *Treas*
EMP: 80 **EST:** 1998
SQ FT: 10,000
SALES (est): 8.82MM **Privately Held**
Web: www.thereserveclub.com
SIC: **7997** Country club, membership

(P-17512)

ROLLING HILLS COUNTRY CLUB

Also Called: Rolling Hlls Cntry CLB Golf Sp
1 Chandler Ranch Rd (90274-3301)
PHONE..................424 903-0000
EMP: 82 **EST:** 1965
SALES (est): 16.91MM **Privately Held**
Web: www.rollinghillscc.com

SIC: **7997** 5941 Country club, membership; Golf goods and equipment

(P-17513)

ROSE BOWL AQUATICS CENTER

360 N Arroyo Blvd (91103-3201)
PHONE..................626 564-0330
Judy Biggs, *Ex Dir*
Kurt Knop, *
Robert Kamins, *
Alison Laster, *
Lyn Beckett Cacciatore, *
EMP: 80 **EST:** 1992
SALES (est): 7.85MM **Privately Held**
Web: www.rosebowlaquatics.org
SIC: **7997** Swimming club, membership

(P-17514)

SADDLEBACK VLY

25631 Peter A Hartman Way (92691-3142)
PHONE..................949 586-1234
Don Cuzick, *Prin*
EMP: 82 **EST:** 2008
SALES (est): 7.24MM **Privately Held**
Web: www.svusd.org
SIC: **7997** Membership sports and recreation clubs

(P-17515)

SAN DIEGO COUNTRY CLUB INC

88 L St (91911-1499)
PHONE..................619 422-8895
David Morris, *Genl Mgr*
EMP: 125 **EST:** 1896
SQ FT: 36,140
SALES (est): 7.76MM **Privately Held**
Web: www.sandiegocountryclub.org
SIC: **7997** Country club, membership

(P-17516)

SAN DIEGO STATE UNIVERSITY

Also Called: San Diego State Aztecs
5302 55th St (92182-0001)
PHONE..................619 594-4263
John Jentz, *CEO*
EMP: 200
SALES (corp-wide): 534.4MM **Privately Held**
Web: www.sdsu.edu
SIC: **7997** 7922 4832 Membership sports and recreation clubs; Theatrical producers and services; Sports
HQ: San Diego State University
5500 Campanile Dr
San Diego CA

(P-17517)

SAN GABRIEL COUNTRY CLUB

350 E Hermosa Dr (91775-2346)
PHONE..................626 287-9671
Tom Dukes, *Pr*
EMP: 80 **EST:** 1904
SQ FT: 48,000
SALES (est): 8.76MM **Privately Held**
Web: www.sangabrielcc.com
SIC: **7997** Country club, membership

(P-17518)

SAN LUIS OBISPO GOLF CNTRY CLB

Also Called: Slogcc
255 Country Club Dr (93401-8939)
PHONE..................805 543-3400
David Cole, *Pr*
Carol Kerwin, *
Christopher Simpson, *
EMP: 110 **EST:** 1958
SQ FT: 10,000

SALES (est): 11.82MM **Privately Held**
Web: www.slocountryclub.com
SIC: **7997** Country club, membership

(P-17519)
SANTA ANA COUNTRY CLUB
20382 Newport Blvd (92707-5396)
PHONE..............................714 556-3000
Joseph Jj Wagner, *Prin*
Joseph J Wagner, *CEO*
EMP: 100 EST: 1914
SALES (est): 12.21MM **Privately Held**
Web: www.santaanacc.org
SIC: **7997** Country club, membership

(P-17520)
SANTALUZ CLUB INC
8170 Caminito Santaluz E (92127-2577)
PHONE..............................858 759-3120
Steve Cowell, *CEO*
James Hoselton, *
Michael Forsum, *
Timothy A Kaehr, *
Terry D Randall, *
EMP: 120 EST: 2000
SQ FT: 19,000
SALES (est): 16.77MM **Privately Held**
Web: www.thesantaluzclub.com
SIC: **7997** Country club, membership

(P-17521)
SATICOY COUNTRY CLUB
4450 Clubhouse Dr (93066-9798)
PHONE..............................805 647-1153
Douglas Taxton, *Pr*
Kathy Sube, *
James R Van Wyck, *
EMP: 80 EST: 1921
SALES (est): 34.18K **Privately Held**
Web: www.thesaticoyclub.com
SIC: **7997** Country club, membership

(P-17522)
SEVEN OAKS COUNTRY CLUB
2000 Grand Lakes Ave (93311-2931)
P.O. Box 11165 (93389-1165)
PHONE..............................661 664-6404
David H Murdock, *CEO*
Bruce Freeman, *
Don Ciota, *
EMP: 125 EST: 1991
SQ FT: 39,000
SALES (est): 14.72MM **Privately Held**
Web: www.sevenoakscountryclub.com
SIC: **7997** Country club, membership

(P-17523)
SHADY CANYON GOLF CLUB INC
100 Shady Canyon Dr (92603-0301)
PHONE..............................949 856-7000
James T Wood, *CEO*
Thomas Heggi, *
Robert Leenhouts, *
EMP: 157 EST: 2003
SALES (est): 269.42K **Privately Held**
Web: www.shadycanyongolfclub.com
SIC: **7997** Country club, membership

(P-17524)
SHERWOOD COUNTRY CLUB
320 W Stafford Rd (91361-5000)
PHONE..............................805 496-3036
Lance Fisher, *Genl Mgr*
EMP: 133 EST: 1989
SALES (est): 14.91MM **Privately Held**
Web: www.sherwoodcc.com
SIC: **7997** Country club, membership

(P-17525)
SPANISH HILLS CLUB LLC
999 Crestview Ave (93010-7429)
PHONE..............................805 388-5000
Alain O'connor, *Managing Member*
EMP: 99 EST: 2019
SALES (est): 835.84K **Privately Held**
Web: www.thespanishillsclub.com
SIC: **7997** Country club, membership

(P-17526)
SPANISH HILLS COUNTRY CLUB (PA)
999 Crestview Ave (93010-8493)
PHONE..............................805 389-1644
Joe Topper, *Pr*
Steve Thomas, *
EMP: 150 EST: 1989
SQ FT: 42,000
SALES (est): 11.46MM **Privately Held**
Web: www.thespanishillsclub.com
SIC: **7997** Country club, membership

(P-17527)
STOCKDALE COUNTRY CLUB
7001 Stockdale Hwy (93309-1313)
P.O. Box 9727 (93389-9727)
PHONE..............................661 832-0310
Sam Monroe, *Pr*
Linda Voiland, *
Michael Davis, *
EMP: 100 EST: 1925
SQ FT: 12,000
SALES (est): 7.24MM **Privately Held**
Web: www.stockdalecc.com
SIC: **7997** Country club, membership

(P-17528)
TEAM SO-CAL INC
1811 Knoll Dr Ste A (93003-7321)
PHONE..............................805 650-9946
Essam Hishmeh, *CEO*
EMP: 400 EST: 2009
SALES (est): 4.79MM **Privately Held**
SIC: **7997** Membership sports and recreation clubs

(P-17529)
TGA FRANCHISE SPT HOLDINGS LLC
Also Called: Tga Premier Sports
1960 E Grand Ave Ste 811 (90245-5156)
PHONE..............................310 333-0622
EMP: 81 EST: 2019
SALES (est): 1.11MM **Privately Held**
Web: www.playtga.com
SIC: **7997 6794** Membership sports and recreation clubs; Franchises, selling or licensing

(P-17530)
THE SAN DIEGO YACHT CLUB
1011 Anchorage Ln (92106-3005)
PHONE..............................619 221-8400
EMP: 120 EST: 1886
SALES (est): 9.55MM **Privately Held**
Web: www.sdyc.org
SIC: **7997** Yacht club, membership

(P-17531)
TOSCANA COUNTRY CLUB INC
76009 Via Club Villa (92210-7851)
PHONE..............................760 404-1444
Paul K Levy, *CEO*
EMP: 150 EST: 2004
SALES (est): 15.74MM **Privately Held**
Web: www.toscanacc.com
SIC: **7997** Country club, membership

(P-17532)
VICTORIA CLUB
2521 Arroyo Dr (92506-1598)
PHONE..............................951 683-5323
EMP: 105 EST: 1903
SALES (est): 4.98MM **Privately Held**
Web: www.victoriaclub.com
SIC: **7997** Country club, membership

(P-17533)
VINTAGE CLUB
75001 Vintage Dr W (92210-7304)
PHONE..............................760 340-0500
John Buttemiller Broker Sales E, *Prin*
Marc D Ray, *
John Buttemiller Broker, *Sls Dir*
Carmen Wolfe, *Marketing TRANSACTION**
Jamie Shelton, *PGA Professional**
EMP: 90 EST: 1979
SQ FT: 86,000
SALES (est): 22.42MM **Privately Held**
Web: www.thevintageclub.com
SIC: **7997 5813 5812 5941** Country club, membership; Bar (drinking places); American restaurant; Golf goods and equipment

(P-17534)
VIRGINIA CNTRY CLB OF LONG BCH
4602 N Virginia Rd (90807-1916)
PHONE..............................562 427-0924
Jamie Mulligan, *CEO*
EMP: 110 EST: 1909
SQ FT: 15,000
SALES (est): 9.12MM **Privately Held**
Web: www.vcc1909.org
SIC: **7997** Country club, membership

(P-17535)
WELK GROUP INC
Also Called: Meadow Lake Country Club
10333 Meadow Glen Way E (92026-6918)
PHONE..............................760 749-0983
Brad Van Horn, *Mgr*
EMP: 216
SQ FT: 5,000
SALES (corp-wide): 47.43MM **Privately Held**
Web: www.kwgoldcoast.com
SIC: **7997** Country club, membership
PA: The Welk Group Inc
    11400 W Olympic Blvd # 1450
    Los Angeles CA
    760 749-3000

(P-17536)
WESTGROUP KONA KAI LLC
Also Called: Kona Kai Resort Hotel
1551 Shelter Island Dr (92106-3102)
PHONE..............................619 221-8000
EMP: 99 EST: 2011
SALES (est): 9.21MM **Privately Held**
Web: www.resortkonakai.com
SIC: **7997 7011** Membership sports and recreation clubs; Resort hotel

(P-17537)
WILSHIRE COUNTRY CLUB
301 N Rossmore Ave (90004-2499)
PHONE..............................323 934-6050
Jeffrey Ornstein, *CEO*
Norman Branchflower, *
Doctor Mirion Bowers Md, *VP*
EMP: 94 EST: 1919
SQ FT: 50,000
SALES (est): 12.18MM **Privately Held**
Web: www.wilshirecountryclub.com

SIC: **7997 5941 5812** Country club, membership; Sporting goods and bicycle shops; Eating places

7999 Amusement And Recreation, Nec

(P-17538)
29 PALMS ENTERPRISES CORP
Also Called: Spotlight 29 Casino
46200 Harrison Pl (92236-2087)
PHONE..............................760 775-5566
Darrel Mike, *Pr*
EMP: 600 EST: 1995
SQ FT: 70,000
SALES (est): 71.39MM **Privately Held**
Web: www.spotlight29.com
SIC: **7999 5812** Gambling establishment; Eating places

(P-17539)
ADVENTURE CITY INC
1238 S Beach Blvd (92804-4828)
PHONE..............................714 821-3311
Allan Ansdell Junior, *Pr*
Yvonne Ansdell, *
EMP: 100 EST: 1992
SALES (est): 5.97MM **Privately Held**
Web: www.adventurecity.com
SIC: **7999 7996** Tourist attractions, amusement park concessions and rides; Amusement parks

(P-17540)
ANSCHUTZ STHERN CAL SPT CMPLX
Also Called: Stop Hop Center
18400 Avalon Blvd Ste 100 (90746-2180)
PHONE..............................310 630-2000
Katherine Pandolfo, *Genl Mgr*
Anschutz Grp, *
Kedie Pendolfo, *
EMP: 160 EST: 2000
SALES (est): 346.8K **Privately Held**
SIC: **7999 7941** Exhibition and carnival operation services; Sports field or stadium operator, promoting sports events
HQ: Anschutz Entertainment Group, Inc.
    800 W Olympic Blvd # 305
    Los Angeles CA
    213 763-7700

(P-17541)
BELL GARDENS BICYCLE CLUB INC
Also Called: Bicycle Club Casino
888 Bicycle Casino Dr (90201-7617)
PHONE..............................562 806-4646
George Hardie, *Pr*
George G Hardie, *
EMP: 1300 EST: 1984
SQ FT: 110,000
SALES (est): 42.37MM **Privately Held**
Web: www.thebike.com
SIC: **7999 5812** Card rooms; Coffee shop

(P-17542)
CAESARS ENTRTNMENT OPRTING INC
Also Called: Harrah's
777 Harrahs Rincon Way (92082-5343)
PHONE..............................760 751-3100
Janet Deronio, *Brnch Mgr*
EMP: 1400
SALES (corp-wide): 10.82B **Publicly Held**
Web: www.harrahssocal.com
SIC: **7999 7011** Gambling establishment; Casino hotel

HQ: Caesars Entertainment Operating
Company, Inc.
1 Caesars Palace Dr
Las Vegas NV
702 407-6000

(P-17543)
CAHUILLA CREEK REST & CASINO
Also Called: Cahuilla Creek Casino
52702 Us Highway 371 (92539-8707)
PHONE..............................951 763-1200
Leonardo Pasquarelli, Genl Mgr
Jon Gregory, *
EMP: 103 EST: 1996
SQ FT: 14,000
SALES (est): 18.88MM Privately Held
Web: www.cahuillacasinohotel.com
SIC: 7999 5812 5813 Gambling
establishment; American restaurant; Bar
(drinking places)

(P-17544)
CTOUR HOLIDAY LLC
222 E Huntington Dr Ste 105 (91016-8014)
PHONE..............................323 261-8811
Charlie Lu, Managing Member
EMP: 300 EST: 2016
SALES (est): 4.17MM Privately Held
Web: www.seagullholiday.com.cn
SIC: 7999 Tour and guide services

(P-17545)
DISNEY REGIONAL ENTRMT INC (DH)
Also Called: Disney
500 S Buena Vista St (91521-0001)
PHONE..............................818 560-1000
EMP: 200 EST: 1996
SALES (est): 80.4MM
SALES (corp-wide): 88.9B Publicly Held
Web: www.thewaltdisneycompany.com
SIC: 7999 5812 5813 Recreation center;
Eating places; Drinking places
HQ: Twdc Enterprises 18 Corp.
500 S Buena Vista St
Burbank CA

(P-17546)
DROPZONE WATERPARK
2165 Trumble Rd (92571-9211)
PHONE..............................951 210-1600
Erica Bice, Dir
EMP: 150 EST: 2014
SALES (est): 443.58K Privately Held
Web: www.dropzonewaterpark.com
SIC: 7999 Recreation services

(P-17547)
EAST VALLEY TOURIST DEV AUTH
Also Called: Fantasy Springs Resort Casino
84245 Indio Springs Dr (92203-3405)
PHONE..............................760 342-5000
John James, Ch Bd
Mark Benitez, *
Brenda Soulliere, *
Angela Roosevelt, *
EMP: 1200 EST: 1983
SQ FT: 94,000
SALES (est): 79.1MM Privately Held
Web: www.starbucks.com
SIC: 7999 Gambling establishment

(P-17548)
EASTBIZ CORPORATION
3501 Jack Northrop Ave (90250-4444)
PHONE..............................310 212-7134
EMP: 114

SIC: 7999 5091 Sporting goods rental, nec;
Sporting and recreation goods

(P-17549)
FAIRPLEX ENTERPRISES INC
1101 W Mckinley Ave (91768-1650)
PHONE..............................909 623-3111
James Henwood, Pr
▲ EMP: 125 EST: 2011
SALES (est): 25.06MM
SALES (corp-wide): 57.69MM Privately
Held
Web: www.fairplex.com
SIC: 7999 Fair, nsk
PA: Los Angeles County Fair Association
1101 W Mckinley Ave
Pomona CA
909 623-3111

(P-17550)
FAZE CLAN INC
720 N Cahuenga Blvd (90038-3702)
PHONE..............................818 688-6373
Lee Trink, CEO
Erik Anderson, *
EMP: 496 EST: 2016
SALES (est): 45.5MM
SALES (corp-wide): 70.02MM Publicly
Held
Web: www.fazeclan.com
SIC: 7999 5961 Games, instruction;
Electronic shopping
PA: Faze Holdings Inc.
720 N Cahuenga Blvd
Los Angeles CA
818 688-6373

(P-17551)
FAZE HOLDINGS INC (PA)
720 N Cahuenga Blvd (90038-3702)
PHONE..............................818 688-6373
Lee Trink, Ch Bd
Zach Katz, Pr
Tamara Brandt, CLO
Kainoa Henry, CLO
Christoph Pachler, CFO
EMP: 106 EST: 2010
SALES (est): 70.02MM
SALES (corp-wide): 70.02MM Publicly
Held
SIC: 7999 5961 Games, instruction;
Electronic shopping

(P-17552)
FIT ATHLETIC CLUB
12171 World Trade Dr (92128-3709)
PHONE..............................858 592-2440
Robin Brumley, Dir
EMP: 82 EST: 2016
SALES (est): 5.13MM Privately Held
Web: www.fitathletic.com
SIC: 7999 7991 Yoga instruction; Physical
fitness clubs with training equipment

(P-17553)
FORTISS LLC
1100 S Flower St Ste 3100 (90015-2127)
PHONE..............................323 415-4900
John Park, Managing Member
Michael Vasey, *
EMP: 80 EST: 2004
SALES (est): 11.87MM Privately Held
Web: www.fortiss.com
SIC: 7999 Card and game services

(P-17554)
HAWAIIAN GARDENS CASINO
11871 Carson St (90716-1127)
PHONE..............................562 860-5887
FAX: 562 860-5823

EMP: 840
SALES (corp-wide): 63.26MM Privately
Held
SIC: 7999 Card and game services
PA: Hawaiian Gardens Casino
21520 Pioneer Blvd # 305
Hawaiian Gardens CA
562 860-5887

(P-17555)
KIDS EMPIRE USA LLC
Also Called: Kids Empire
8605 Santa Monica Blvd (90069-4109)
PHONE..............................424 527-1039
Haim Elbaz, CEO
EMP: 93 EST: 2017
SALES (est): 1.28MM Privately Held
SIC: 7999 6794 Recreation services;
Franchises, selling or licensing

(P-17556)
LOS ANGELES COUNTY FAIR ASSN (PA)
Also Called: Fairplex Rv Park
1101 W Mckinley Ave (91768-1639)
PHONE..............................909 623-3111
Ronald Bolding, Dir
Micheal Seder, *
EMP: 100 EST: 1922
SALES (est): 57.69MM
SALES (corp-wide): 57.69MM Privately
Held
Web: www.fairplex.com
SIC: 7999 8412 Fair, nsk; Museums and art
galleries

(P-17557)
MARINE CORPS COMMUNITY SVCS
Also Called: Moral Welfare and Recreation
Acs Mccs Attn Semper Fi Box 555020
Marine Corp Base (92055)
PHONE..............................760 725-6195
Mike Wilkinson, Department Director
EMP: 182
SQ FT: 1,152
Web: www.marines.mil
SIC: 7999 9711 Recreation services; Marine
Corps
HQ: Marine Corps Community Services
3044 Catlin Ave
Quantico VA
703 432-0109

(P-17558)
MARINE CORPS COMMUNITY SVCS
Also Called: Marine Corps Cmnty Svcs Dept
2273 Elrod Ave (92145-0001)
P.O. Box 452008 (92145-2008)
PHONE..............................858 577-1061
Mary Bradford, Dir
EMP: 262
Web: www.marines.mil
SIC: 7999 9711 Recreation center; Marine
Corps
HQ: Marine Corps Community Services
3044 Catlin Ave
Quantico VA
703 432-0109

(P-17559)
MORONGO BAND MISSION INDIANS
Also Called: Morongo Casino Resort Spa
49500 Seminole Dr (92230-2202)
P.O. Box 366 (92230-0366)
PHONE..............................951 849-3080
Dual Cooper, Brnch Mgr

EMP: 150
Web: www.morongocasinoresort.com
SIC: 7999 9131 Gambling establishment;
Indian Reservation
PA: Morongo Band Of Mission Indians
12700 Pumarra Rd
Banning CA
951 849-4697

(P-17560)
MOUNTAIN VISTA GOLF COURSE AT
38180 Del Webb Blvd (92211-1256)
PHONE..............................760 200-2200
Andrea Goodwin, Pr
John Celli, *
Ron Delgado, *
Bill Wirian, *
Chuck Carpenter, *
EMP: 85 EST: 1992
SQ FT: 300
SALES (est): 30MM Privately Held
Web: www.mountainvistagolfclub.com
SIC: 7999 Golf services and professionals

(P-17561)
QUECHAN INDIAN TRIBE
Also Called: Quechan Gaming Commission
450 Quechan Rd (92283-9676)
P.O. Box 2737 (85366-2573)
PHONE..............................760 572-2413
EMP: 106
Web: www.paradise-casinos.com
SIC: 7999 5812 Gambling establishment;
Eating places
PA: Quechan Indian Tribe
350 Picacho Rd
Winterhaven CA
760 572-0213

(P-17562)
RIVIERA COUNTRY CLUB INC
Also Called: Grand Slam Tennis Program
1250 Capri Dr (90272-4001)
PHONE..............................310 454-6591
Noboru Watanabe, CEO
EMP: 118 EST: 1989
SALES (est): 13.29MM Privately Held
Web: www.therivieracountryclub.com
SIC: 7999 7997 Tennis club, non-
membership; Membership sports and
recreation clubs

(P-17563)
ROCKIN JUMP HOLDINGS LLC
Also Called: Rockin' Jump Trampoline
1301 W Rancho Vista Blvd Ste B
(93551-3101)
PHONE..............................661 233-9907
EMP: 301
SALES (corp-wide): 51.07MM Privately
Held
Web: www.rockinjump.com
SIC: 7999 Trampoline operation
HQ: Rockin' Jump Holdings, Llc
18 Crow Canyon Ct Ste 350
San Ramon CA
925 401-7200

(P-17564)
S J S ENTERPRISE INC
Also Called: S C Village
9030 Somerset Blvd (90706-3402)
PHONE..............................949 489-9000
EMP: 150 EST: 1987
SALES (est): 2.46MM Privately Held
Web: www.hollywoodsports.com
SIC: 7999 Indoor court clubs

(P-17565)
SAN BRNRDINO CNTY RGONAL PARKS
777 E Rialto Ave (92415-1005)
PHONE.............................909 387-2583
EMP: 99 EST: 2020
SALES (est): 522.95K Privately Held
Web: parks.sbcounty.gov
SIC: 7999 Recreation center

(P-17566)
SAN MANUEL ENTERTAINMENT AUTH (PA)
Also Called: Yaamava Rsort Csino At San Mnu
777 San Manuel Blvd (92346-6713)
PHONE.............................909 864-5050
TOLL FREE: 800
James Ramos, Ch
Rebecca Spalding, CFO
Jimmy Starcher, Ex Dir
Steve Lengeo, Ex Dir
Rikki Tanenbaum, COO
▲ EMP: 2950 EST: 1987
SALES (est): 154.97MM
SALES (corp-wide): 154.97MM Privately Held
Web: www.yaamava.com
SIC: 7999 Bingo hall

(P-17567)
SYCUAN CASINO (PA)
Also Called: Sycuan Resort and Casino
5459 Casino Way (92019)
PHONE.............................619 445-6002
John Denius, Genl Mgr
Angela Scantling, *
EMP: 156 EST: 1983
SQ FT: 236,000
SALES (est): 93.96MM
SALES (corp-wide): 93.96MM Privately Held
Web: www.sycuan.com
SIC: 7999 7997 Gambling establishment; Membership sports and recreation clubs

(P-17568)
T ALLANCE ONE - PALM SPRNG LLC
Also Called: Doubltree Palm Sprng Golf Rsor
67967 Vista Chino (92234-7408)
PHONE.............................760 322-7000
EMP: 99 EST: 2013
SALES (est): 2.46MM Privately Held
Web: www.doubletreepalmsprings.com
SIC: 7999 Golf professionals

(P-17569)
TICKETMASTER CORPORATION
Also Called: Ticketmaster
7060 Hollywood Blvd Ste 2 (90028-6030)
PHONE.............................323 769-4600
EMP: 4390
SIC: 7999 7922 Ticket sales office for sporting events, contract; Theatrical producers and services

(P-17570)
TICKETMASTER ENTERTAINMENT LLC
8800 W Sunset Blvd (90069-2105)
PHONE.............................800 653-8000
EMP: 4390 EST: 2010
SALES (est): 103.99MM Publicly Held
SIC: 7999 Ticket sales office for sporting events, contract
PA: Live Nation Entertainment, Inc.
9348 Civic Center Dr Lbby
Beverly Hills CA

(P-17571)
TICKETMASTER GROUP INC
Also Called: Ticketmaster
3701 Wilshire Blvd Fl 9 (90010-2804)
PHONE.............................800 745-3000
EMP: 4390
SIC: 7999 Ticket sales office for sporting events, contract

(P-17572)
TICKETMSTER NEW VNTRES HLDNGS (HQ)
Also Called: Ticketmaster
325 N Maple Dr (90210-3428)
PHONE.............................800 653-8000
Irving Azoff, CEO
EMP: 104 EST: 1996
SALES (est): 59.47MM Publicly Held
SIC: 7999 Ticket sales office for sporting events, contract
PA: Live Nation Entertainment, Inc.
9348 Civic Center Dr Lbby
Beverly Hills CA

(P-17573)
TIERRA DEL SOL FOUNDATION
Also Called: Tierra Del Soul
250 W 1st St Ste 120 (91711-4741)
PHONE.............................909 626-8301
Rebecca Hamm, Brnch Mgr
EMP: 85
SALES (corp-wide): 21.23MM Privately Held
Web: www.tierradelsol.org
SIC: 7999 5999 Art gallery, commercial; Art dealers
PA: Tierra Del Sol Foundation
9919 Sunland Blvd
Sunland CA
818 352-1419

(P-17574)
TOYOTA ARENA
4000 E Ontario Center Pkwy (91764-7966)
PHONE.............................909 244-5500
EMP: 92 EST: 2019
SALES (est): 5.82MM Privately Held
Web: www.toyota-arena.com
SIC: 7999 Ice skating rink operation

(P-17575)
TUMBLEWEED EDUCTL ENTPS INC
Also Called: Tumbleweed Day Camp
1024 Hanley Ave (90049-1306)
P.O. Box 49291 (90049-0291)
PHONE.............................310 444-3232
Erin Benfield, Pr
EMP: 160 EST: 1954
SQ FT: 6,500
SALES (est): 12.04MM Privately Held
Web: www.tumbleweedtransportation.com
SIC: 7999 4151 Day camp; School buses

(P-17576)
UNITED STUDIOS SELF DEF INC
28251 Marguerite Pkwy Ste J (92692-3721)
PHONE.............................949 293-1391
EMP: 99
Web: www.ussd.com
SIC: 7999 Martial arts school, nec
PA: United Studios Of Self Defense, Inc.
23402 S Pointe Dr
Laguna Hills CA

(P-17577)
UNITED STUDIOS SELF DEF INC
13331 Poway Rd (92064-4625)

PHONE.............................858 486-8773
Zachary Cummings Smith, Pr
EMP: 99
Web: www.ussd.com
SIC: 7999 Martial arts school, nec
PA: United Studios Of Self Defense, Inc.
23402 S Pointe Dr
Laguna Hills CA

(P-17578)
VOLUME SERVICES INC
111 W Harbor Dr (92101-7822)
PHONE.............................619 525-5800
EMP: 261
SALES (corp-wide): 206.19MM Privately Held
Web: us.sodexo.com
SIC: 7999 Concession operator
HQ: Volume Services, Inc.
2187 Atlantic St Ste 6
Stamford CT

(P-17579)
VOLUME SERVICES INC
5333 Zoo Dr (90027-1451)
PHONE.............................323 644-6038
Greg Edgar, Mgr
EMP: 261
SALES (corp-wide): 206.19MM Privately Held
Web: us.sodexo.com
SIC: 7999 Concession operator
HQ: Volume Services, Inc.
2187 Atlantic St Ste 6
Stamford CT

(P-17580)
YOGA BOX LLC
909 Grand Ave (92109-4051)
PHONE.............................619 994-1915
EMP: 24 EST: 2019
SALES (est): 375.52K Privately Held
Web: www.yogabox.com
SIC: 7999 7372 Yoga instruction; Application computer software

(P-17581)
ZUFFA MEXICO LLC ✪
9601 Wilshire Blvd Fl 3 (90210-5219)
PHONE.............................310 285-9000
EMP: 144 EST: 2023
SALES (est): 124.58K
SALES (corp-wide): 5.27B Publicly Held
SIC: 7999 Amusement and recreation, nec
PA: Endeavor Group Holdings, Inc.
9601 Wilshire Blvd Fl 3
Beverly Hills CA
310 285-9000

8011 Offices And Clinics Of Medical Doctors

(P-17582)
ADVANCED PROF IMGING MED GROUP
Also Called: Seven California Med Diagnstc
1109 S Central Ave (91204-2212)
PHONE.............................818 244-4646
EMP: 133
SALES (corp-wide): 2.31MM Privately Held
SIC: 8011 Radiologist
PA: Advanced Professional Imaging Medical Group
6905 Oslo Cir Ste F
Buena Park CA
714 995-5400

(P-17583)
AGILE OCCUPATIONAL MEDICINE PC
710 N Euclid St Ste 107 (92801-4132)
PHONE.............................949 464-4036
EMP: 83
SALES (corp-wide): 12.24MM Privately Held
Web: www.agileoccmed.com
SIC: 8011 Pediatrician
PA: Agile Occupational Medicine, Pc
3200 Bristol St Ste 600
Costa Mesa CA
407 413-5350

(P-17584)
ALL CARE MEDICAL GROUP INC
Also Called: Professional Svcs Med Group
31 Crescent Street (90255)
PHONE.............................408 278-3550
Samuel Rotenberg Md, Dir
EMP: 85 EST: 1946
SQ FT: 33,000
SALES (est): 9.15MM Privately Held
Web: www.allcaremg.com
SIC: 8011 Physicians' office, including specialists

(P-17585)
ALTAMED HEALTH SERVICES CORP
6330 Rugby Ave Ste 200 (90255-6938)
PHONE.............................323 277-7678
Yorka Rodriguez, Mgr
EMP: 81
SALES (corp-wide): 1.05B Privately Held
Web: www.altamed.org
SIC: 8011 8322 Gynecologist; Individual and family services
PA: Altamed Health Services Corporation
2040 Camfield Ave
Commerce CA
323 725-8751

(P-17586)
ALTAMED HEALTH SERVICES CORP
Also Called: Ultimate
1500 Hughes Way Ste A150 (90810-1883)
PHONE.............................562 923-9414
Chikita Emel, Dir
EMP: 150
SALES (corp-wide): 1.05B Privately Held
Web: www.altamed.org
SIC: 8011 Gynecologist
PA: Altamed Health Services Corporation
2040 Camfield Ave
Commerce CA
323 725-8751

(P-17587)
ALTAMED HEALTH SERVICES CORP
Also Called: Altamed Adhc Golden Age
3820 Martin Luther King Jr Blvd (90262-3625)
PHONE.............................310 632-0415
Peter M Feldman, Prin
EMP: 134
SALES (corp-wide): 1.05B Privately Held
Web: www.altamed.org
SIC: 8011 8099 Gynecologist; Medical services organization
PA: Altamed Health Services Corporation
2040 Camfield Ave
Commerce CA
323 725-8751

PRODUCTS & SVCS

(P-17588)

ALTAMED HEALTH SERVICES CORP

5427 Whittier Blvd (90022-4101)
PHONE..................................323 980-4466
Irene Avilar, *Prin*
EMP: 128
SALES (corp-wide): 1.05B **Privately Held**
Web: www.altamedfoundation.org
SIC: 8011 Clinic, operated by physicians
PA: Altamed Health Services Corporation
2040 Camfield Ave
Commerce CA
323 725-8751

(P-17589)

ALTAMED HEALTH SERVICES CORP

2219 E 1st St (90033-3901)
PHONE..................................323 269-0421
Shi Y Wong, *Brnch Mgr*
EMP: 137
SALES (corp-wide): 1.05B **Privately Held**
Web: www.altamedfoundation.org
SIC: 8011 8099 Gynecologist; Medical services organization
PA: Altamed Health Services Corporation
2040 Camfield Ave
Commerce CA
323 725-8751

(P-17590)

ALTAMED HEALTH SERVICES CORP

Also Called: Senior Health and Activity Ctr
5425 Pomona Blvd (90022-1716)
PHONE..................................323 728-0411
Mariela Bauer, *Brnch Mgr*
EMP: 178
SQ FT: 24,369
SALES (corp-wide): 1.05B **Privately Held**
Web: www.altamedfoundation.org
SIC: 8011 8099 Gynecologist; Medical services organization
PA: Altamed Health Services Corporation
2040 Camfield Ave
Commerce CA
323 725-8751

(P-17591)

ALTAMED HEALTH SERVICES CORP (PA)

2040 Camfield Ave (90040-1574)
PHONE..................................323 725-8751
Castulo De La Rocha, *CEO*
Zoila D Escobar, *
Marie S Torres, *
Jose U Esparza, *
EMP: 135 EST: 1970
SQ FT: 27,345
SALES (est): 1.05B
SALES (corp-wide): 1.05B **Privately Held**
Web: www.altamed.org
SIC: 8011 8099 Gynecologist; Medical services organization

(P-17592)

AMN HEALTHCARE INC (HQ)

12400 High Bluff Dr Ste 100 (92130-3077)
PHONE..................................858 792-0711
Susan R Nowakowski, *CEO*
Susan R Salka, *Pr*
Julie Fletcher, *VP*
Marcia Faller, *VP*
Denise L Jackson, *VP*
EMP: 253 EST: 1985
SALES (est): 643.21MM
SALES (corp-wide): 5.24B **Publicly Held**
Web: www.amnhealthcare.com

SIC: 8011 Primary care medical clinic
PA: Amn Healthcare Services, Inc.
2999 Olympus Blvd Ste 500
Coppell TX
866 871-8519

(P-17593)

ANESTHSIA MED GROUP SNTA BRBAR

Also Called: Anesthsia Med Group Snta Brbar
514 W Pueblo St Fl 2 (93105-6219)
PHONE..................................805 682-7751
Eric Amador, *Dir*
Douglas Etsel, *
John King, *
Clinton Lagrange, *
Derrick Willsey, *
EMP: 89 EST: 1970
SALES (est): 9.91MM **Privately Held**
Web: www.amgsb.com
SIC: 8011 Anesthesiologist

(P-17594)

ANTELOPE VALLEY HOSPITAL INC

Ob Clinic
1600 W Avenue J (93534-2894)
PHONE..................................661 726-6180
Vikki Haley, *Prin*
EMP: 341
SALES (corp-wide): 494.78MM **Privately Held**
Web: www.avmc.org
SIC: 8011 Offices and clinics of medical doctors
PA: Antelope Valley Health Care District
1600 W Avenue J
Lancaster CA
661 949-5000

(P-17595)

ARROYO VSTA FMLY HLTH FNDATION

Also Called: Arroyo Vista Family Health Ctr
2411 N Broadway (90031-2218)
PHONE..................................323 224-2188
Line Fernandez, *Mgr*
EMP: 100
SQ FT: 13,435
Web: www.arroyovista.org
SIC: 8011 Clinic, operated by physicians
PA: Arroyo Vista Family Health Foundation
6000 N Figueroa St
Los Angeles CA

(P-17596)

ASSOCIATED STUDENTS UCLA

Also Called: Ucla Mdcn SC Phrmclgy
650 Charles Young Dr S Rm 23120 (90095-0001)
PHONE..................................310 825-9451
Michael Phelps, *Prin*
EMP: 82
SALES (corp-wide): 47.49MM **Privately Held**
Web: asucla.ucla.edu
SIC: 8011 General and family practice, physician/surgeon
PA: Associated Students U.C.L.A.
308 Westwood Plz
Los Angeles CA
310 794-8836

(P-17597)

BAKERSFIELD FAMILY MEDICAL GROUP INC (PA)

Also Called: Bakersfield Family Medical Ctr
4580 California Ave (93309-7013)
P.O. Box 12022 (93389-2022)

PHONE..................................661 327-4411
EMP: 94 EST: 1984
SALES (est): 26.9MM
SALES (corp-wide): 26.9MM **Privately Held**
Web: www.bfmc.com
SIC: 8011 Medical centers

(P-17598)

BALBOA NPHROLOGY MED GROUP INC

4225 Executive Sq Ste 450 (92037-8411)
PHONE..................................858 810-8000
EMP: 222
SALES (est): 11.24MM **Privately Held**
Web: www.balboacare.com
SIC: 8011 Nephrologist

(P-17599)

BEAVER MEDICAL CLINIC INC (PA)

1615 Orange Tree Ln (92374-2804)
P.O. Box 10069 (92423-0069)
PHONE..................................909 793-3311
Robert Klein, *Pr*
EMP: 190 EST: 1945
SQ FT: 79,212
SALES (est): 342.5K
SALES (corp-wide): 342.5K **Privately Held**
Web: bmg.optum.com
SIC: 8011 Clinic, operated by physicians

(P-17600)

BEAVER MEDICAL GROUP LP (HQ)

Also Called: Beaver Medical Clinic
7000 Boulder Ave (92346-3348)
PHONE..................................909 425-3321
John Goodman, *CEO*
Robert Rentschler, *
James Watson Md, *Ltd Pt*
Robert Bourne Md, *Ltd Pt*
EMP: 155 EST: 1995
SALES (est): 34.46MM **Privately Held**
Web: bmg.optum.com
SIC: 8011 General and family practice, physician/surgeon
PA: Epic Management, L.P.
1615 Orange Tree Ln
Redlands CA

(P-17601)

BECKMAN RES INST OF THE CY HOP

1500 Duarte Rd (91010-3012)
PHONE..................................626 359-8111
Michael A Friedman, *CEO*
Harlan Levine, *
Robert Stone, *
Terry Blackwood, *
Ric Magnuson, *
EMP: 250 EST: 1979
SALES (est): 288.28MM
SALES (corp-wide): 334.97MM **Privately Held**
Web: www.cityofhope.org
SIC: 8011 Offices and clinics of medical doctors
PA: City Of Hope
1500 Duarte Rd
Duarte CA
626 256-4673

(P-17602)

BORREGO CMNTY HLTH FOUNDATION

Also Called: Borrego Health
651 N State St Ste 5 (92583-6574)
PHONE..................................951 487-8506

Michael D Dew, *Brnch Mgr*
EMP: 140
SALES (corp-wide): 235.82MM **Privately Held**
Web: www.borregohealth.org
SIC: 8011 Clinic, operated by physicians
PA: Borrego Community Health Foundation
587 Palm Canyon Dr # 208
Borrego Springs CA
855 436-1234

(P-17603)

BORREGO CMNTY HLTH FOUNDATION

11750 Cholla Dr Ste B (92240-3066)
PHONE..................................760 251-0044
EMP: 140
SALES (corp-wide): 235.82MM **Privately Held**
Web: www.borregohealth.org
SIC: 8011 Clinic, operated by physicians
PA: Borrego Community Health Foundation
587 Palm Canyon Dr # 208
Borrego Springs CA
855 436-1234

(P-17604)

BORREGO CMNTY HLTH FOUNDATION

1121 E Washington Ave (92025-2214)
PHONE..................................760 466-1080
EMP: 139
SALES (corp-wide): 235.82MM **Privately Held**
Web: www.borregohealth.org
SIC: 8011 Clinic, operated by physicians
PA: Borrego Community Health Foundation
587 Palm Canyon Dr # 208
Borrego Springs CA
855 436-1234

(P-17605)

BORREGO CMNTY HLTH FOUNDATION (PA)

Also Called: Borrego Medical Center
587 Palm Canyon Dr Ste 208 (92004-4000)
P.O. Box 2369 (92004-2369)
PHONE..................................855 436-1234
Isaac Lee, *CRO*
Bruce E Smith, *
Dianna Troncoso, *
EMP: 140 EST: 1990
SQ FT: 8,054
SALES (est): 235.82MM
SALES (corp-wide): 235.82MM **Privately Held**
Web: www.borregohealth.org
SIC: 8011 Offices and clinics of medical doctors

(P-17606)

BRIGHT HEALTH PHYSICIANS (PA)

15725 Whittier Blvd Ste 500 (90603-2350)
PHONE..................................562 947-8478
William H Stimmler Md, *Ch Bd*
Keith Miyamoto Md, *VP*
Berent Gray Md, *Sec*
EMP: 140 EST: 1991
SQ FT: 50,000
SALES (est): 38.79MM **Privately Held**
Web: www.pihhealth.org
SIC: 8011 Physicians' office, including specialists

(P-17607)

CABRILLO CRDOLGY MED GROUP INC

2241 Wankel Way Ste C (93030-0191)

PHONE..................805 983-0922
David Schmidt Md, *Pr*
David E Schmidt, *
Richard Rothchild Md, *Treas*
Scott Zager, *
Esam Obed, *
EMP: 81 **EST:** 1971
SALES (est): 9.22MM **Privately Held**
SIC: 8011 Cardiologist and cardio-vascular specialist

(P-17608)
CARBON HEALTH TECHNOLOGIES INC
500 First St (93446-3742)
PHONE..................805 226-4222
EMP: 102
SALES (corp-wide): 104.49MM **Privately Held**
Web: www.carbonhealth.com
SIC: 8011 Freestanding emergency medical center
PA: Carbon Health Technologies, Inc.
2100 Franklin St Ste 355
Oakland CA
415 223-2858

(P-17609)
CARBON HEALTH TECHNOLOGIES INC
1421 W Macarthur Blvd Ste E (92704-7318)
PHONE..................714 710-3030
Tom Long Le, *Prin*
EMP: 102
SALES (corp-wide): 104.49MM **Privately Held**
Web: www.carbonhealth.com
SIC: 8011 Physicians' office, including specialists
PA: Carbon Health Technologies, Inc.
2100 Franklin St Ste 355
Oakland CA
415 223-2858

(P-17610)
CARDIONET INC
Also Called: CARDIONET, INC.
750 B St Ste 1400 (92101-8190)
PHONE..................619 243-7500
Jim Sweeney, *Prin*
EMP: 83
SALES (corp-wide): 133.64MM **Privately Held**
Web: www.cardionet.com
SIC: 8011 Cardiologist and cardio-vascular specialist
HQ: Cardionet, Llc
1000 Cedar Hollow Rd # 10
Malvern PA
610 729-7000

(P-17611)
CB TANG MD INCORPORATED
Also Called: Long Beach Medical Clinic
1250 Pacific Ave (90813-3026)
PHONE..................562 437-0831
EMP: 96
Web: www.tangandcompany.com
SIC: 8011 Occupational and industrial specialist, physician/surgeon

(P-17612)
CEDARS-SINAI MEDICAL CENTER
Also Called: Cardiac Noninvasive Laboratory
127 S San Vicente Blvd Rm 3417 (90048-3311)
PHONE..................310 423-3849

Timothy Henry, *Dir*
EMP: 329
SALES (corp-wide): 4.7B **Privately Held**
Web: www.cedars-sinai.org
SIC: 8011 Cardiologist and cardio-vascular specialist
PA: Cedars-Sinai Medical Center
8700 Beverly Blvd
West Hollywood CA
310 423-3277

(P-17613)
CEDARS-SINAI MEDICAL CENTER
Also Called: Radiation Onclogy - Cdrs-Snai
8720 Beverly Blvd Lower Level Ste Ac1010 (90048)
PHONE..................310 423-4208
Palmer Burnison Hakami, *Prin*
EMP: 89
SALES (corp-wide): 4.7B **Privately Held**
Web: www.cedars-sinai.org
SIC: 8011 Physicians' office, including specialists
PA: Cedars-Sinai Medical Center
8700 Beverly Blvd
West Hollywood CA
310 423-3277

(P-17614)
CENTRAL CARDIOLOGY MED CLINIC
2901 Sillect Ave Ste 100 (93308-6370)
P.O. Box 1139 (93302-1139)
PHONE..................661 395-0000
Brijesh Bahmbi, *Pt*
William Nyitray Md, *Pt*
Peter Nalos Md, *Pt*
EMP: 120 **EST:** 1974
SALES (est): 21.49MM **Privately Held**
Web: www.heart24.com
SIC: 8011 Cardiologist and cardio-vascular specialist

(P-17615)
CHA HEALTH SYSTEMS INC (PA)
Also Called: Cha Renetative Medicine
3731 Wilshire Blvd Ste 850 (90010-2851)
PHONE..................213 487-3211
Doctor K Cha, *CEO*
Jean Yi, *COO*
Thomas J May, *CAO*
EMP: 1250 **EST:** 2004
SALES (est): 81.88MM **Privately Held**
Web: www.hollywoodpresbyterian.com
SIC: 8011 Clinic, operated by physicians

(P-17616)
CHILDRENS CLNIC SRVING CHLDREN
701 E 28th St Ste 200 (90806-2784)
PHONE..................562 264-4638
Elisa A Nicholas, *Ex Dir*
Maria Y Chandler, *
Jina Lee Lawler, *
Knut P Thune, *
Albert P Ocampo, *
EMP: 320 **EST:** 1939
SQ FT: 24,000
SALES (est): 50.37MM **Privately Held**
Web: www.thechildrensclinic.org
SIC: 8011 Clinic, operated by physicians

(P-17617)
CHILDRENS HEALTHCARE CAL
Also Called: Pediatric Cancer Research
455 S Main St (92868-3835)
P.O. Box 5700 (92863-5700)
PHONE..................714 997-3000

Kimberly Crite, *CEO*
EMP: 300
Web: www.choc.org
SIC: 8011 Pediatrician
PA: Children's Healthcare Of California
1201 W La Veta Ave
Orange CA

(P-17618)
CHILDRENS ONCOLOGY GROUP
1333 S Mayflower Ave Ste 260 (91016-4066)
PHONE..................626 241-1500
Joseph Woelkers, *CEO*
EMP: 119 **EST:** 2013
SALES (est): 2.96MM **Privately Held**
Web: www.childrensoncologygroup.org
SIC: 8011 Oncologist

(P-17619)
CHILDRENS SPCLSTS OF SAN DEGO (PA)
Also Called: Childrens Associated Med Group
3020 Childrens Way (92123-4223)
PHONE..................858 576-1700
Michael Segall Md, *Pr*
Robin Steinhorn, *
EMP: 350 **EST:** 1978
SALES (est): 17.87MM
SALES (corp-wide): 17.87MM **Privately Held**
Web: www.rchsd.org
SIC: 8011 Physicians' office, including specialists

(P-17620)
CHINO MEDICAL GROUP INC
5475 Walnut Ave (91710-2699)
PHONE..................909 591-6446
J Alex Lira Md, *Pr*
Fidel F Pinzon Md, *VP*
Jeffrey R Unger Md, *VP*
Steven Pulverman, *
EMP: 100 **EST:** 1977
SQ FT: 36,000
SALES (est): 9.87MM **Privately Held**
Web: www.myfamilymg.com
SIC: 8011 8031 Clinic, operated by physicians; Offices and clinics of osteopathic physicians

(P-17621)
CIRRUS HEALTH II LP
Also Called: Laguna Hills Surgery Center
24331 El Toro Rd Ste 150 (92637-8818)
PHONE..................949 855-0562
Kim Wood, *Prin*
EMP: 113
SALES (corp-wide): 22.62MM **Privately Held**
SIC: 8011 Clinic, operated by physicians
PA: Cirrus Health Ii, L.P.
2800 E Highway 114 # 300
Trophy Club TX
214 217-0100

(P-17622)
CITY OF HOPE
Also Called: City of Hope Medical Group
209 Fair Oaks Ave (91030-1814)
PHONE..................626 396-2900
Melinda Lane, *Dir*
EMP: 106
SALES (corp-wide): 334.97MM **Privately Held**
Web: www.cityofhope.org
SIC: 8011 Medical centers
PA: City Of Hope
1500 Duarte Rd
Duarte CA
626 256-4673

(P-17623)
CLINIC INC
Also Called: TO HELP EVERYONE HEALTH AND WE
3834 S Western Ave (90062-1104)
PHONE..................323 730-1920
Jamesina E Henderson, *Ex Dir*
EMP: 85 **EST:** 1974
SQ FT: 26,000
SALES (est): 18.5MM **Privately Held**
Web: www.tohelpeveryone.org
SIC: 8011 Clinic, operated by physicians

(P-17624)
CLINICA SIERRA VISTA
Also Called: Clinica Srra Vsta Adult Mntal
8787 Hall Rd (93241-1953)
P.O. Box 457 (93241-0457)
PHONE..................661 845-3717
Mercedes Macias, *Brnch Mgr*
EMP: 86
SALES (corp-wide): 165.74MM **Privately Held**
Web: www.clinicasierravista.org
SIC: 8011 Clinic, operated by physicians
PA: Clinica Sierra Vista
1430 Truxtun Ave Ste 400
Bakersfield CA
661 635-3050

(P-17625)
CLINICA SIERRA VISTA (PA)
Also Called: KERN RIVER HEALTH CENTER
1430 Truxtun Ave Ste 400 (93301-5216)
P.O. Box 1559 (93302-1559)
PHONE..................661 635-3050
Stacy Ferreira, *CEO*
Stacy Ferreira, *Chief Human Resource Officer*
Matthew Clark, *
EMP: 90 **EST:** 1971
SQ FT: 14,599
SALES (est): 165.74MM
SALES (corp-wide): 165.74MM **Privately Held**
Web: www.clinicasierravista.org
SIC: 8011 Clinic, operated by physicians

(P-17626)
CNS INC
5215 Ashe Rd (93313-2069)
PHONE..................661 872-3408
Dennis R Hays, *Prin*
EMP: 92 **EST:** 2009
SALES (est): 4.72MM **Privately Held**
Web: www.neuroskills.com
SIC: 8011 Internal medicine, physician/surgeon

(P-17627)
COASTAL RDTION ONCLOGY MED GRO
1240 S Westlake Blvd Ste 103 (91361-1929)
PHONE..................805 494-4483
Kimberly Commins, *Dir*
Lauren Lovett, *Dir*
EMP: 99 **EST:** 2018
SALES (est): 2.15MM **Privately Held**
SIC: 8011 Oncologist

(P-17628)
COMMUNITY HEALTH GROUP
2420 Fenton St Ste 100 (91914-3516)
PHONE..................800 224-7766
Norma A Diaz, *CEO*
William Rice, *
EMP: 140 **EST:** 1982
SQ FT: 26,000
SALES (est): 59.17MM **Privately Held**

Web: www.chgsd.com
SIC: 8011 Health maintenance organization

(P-17629)
COMMUNITY HEALTH SYSTEMS INC
Also Called: MORENO VALLEY FAMILY HEALTH CE
21801 Alessandro Blvd (92553-8202)
PHONE..............................951 571-2300
Lori Holeman, *CEO*
Yolanda Gomez, *
EMP: 130 **EST:** 1984
SALES (est): 32.27MM **Privately Held**
Web: www.chsica.org
SIC: 8011 Primary care medical clinic

(P-17630)
COMMUNITY HLTHCARE PARTNER INC
Also Called: COLORADO RIVER MEDICAL CENTER
1401 Bailey Ave (92363-3103)
PHONE..............................760 326-4531
Bing Lum, *Ex VP*
Knaya Tabora, *Prin*
EMP: 100 **EST:** 1999
SQ FT: 46,000
SALES (est): 10.4MM **Privately Held**
Web: www.crmccares.com
SIC: 8011 8062 Clinic, operated by physicians; General medical and surgical hospitals

(P-17631)
COR MEDICA TECHNOLOGY (PA)
Also Called: Cor Medica
188 Technology Dr Ste F (92618-2459)
PHONE..............................949 353-4554
Fouad Ghaly, *CEO*
David Sestini, *Pr*
Rachel Everett, *Sr VP*
Robert Prestwood, *VP*
Katalina Csoka, *Dir*
EMP: 22 **EST:** 2015
SQ FT: 2,200
SALES (est): 2.76MM
SALES (corp-wide): 2.76MM **Privately Held**
SIC: 8011 3841 Cardiologist and cardio-vascular specialist; Diagnostic apparatus, medical

(P-17632)
CORONA REGIONAL MED CTR LLC
800 S Main St (92882-3420)
PHONE..............................951 737-4343
EMP: 219 **EST:** 2009
SALES (est): 10.7MM **Privately Held**
SIC: 8011 Medical centers

(P-17633)
COUNTY OF LOS ANGELES
Also Called: Health Services, Dept of
1900 Zonal Ave (90033-1033)
P.O. Box 866001 (90086-6001)
PHONE..............................323 226-7131
Linda Guerra, *Mgr*
EMP: 521
Web: www.lacounty.gov
SIC: 8011 9431 Offices and clinics of medical doctors; Administration of public health programs
PA: County Of Los Angeles
500 W Temple St Ste 437
Los Angeles CA
213 974-1101

(P-17634)
COUNTY OF LOS ANGELES
Also Called: Hudson H Clude Cmplete Hlth Ct
2829 S Grand Ave (90007-3304)
PHONE..............................213 744-3919
Michael Mills, *Admn*
EMP: 85
Web: www.lacounty.gov
SIC: 8011 9431 8093 Medical centers; Administration of public health programs; Specialty outpatient clinics, nec
PA: County Of Los Angeles
500 W Temple St Ste 437
Los Angeles CA
213 974-1101

(P-17635)
COUNTY OF RIVERSIDE
Also Called: Rubidoux Family Care Center
5256 Mission Blvd (92509-4624)
PHONE..............................951 955-0840
Koen Brown, *Ex Dir*
EMP: 156
SALES (corp-wide): 4.58B **Privately Held**
Web: www.ruhealth.org
SIC: 8011 Clinic, operated by physicians
PA: County Of Riverside
4080 Lemon St Fl 11
Riverside CA
951 955-1110

(P-17636)
COUNTY OF RIVERSIDE
Also Called: Public Social Services
26520 Cactus Ave (92555-3927)
PHONE..............................951 486-4000
Donna Matney, *Admn*
EMP: 547
SALES (corp-wide): 4.58B **Privately Held**
Web: www.countyofriverside.us
SIC: 8011 9431 Medical centers; Mental health agency administration, government
PA: County Of Riverside
4080 Lemon St Fl 11
Riverside CA
951 955-1110

(P-17637)
COUNTY OF RIVERSIDE
Also Called: Community Health Agency
26520 Cactus Ave (92555-3927)
PHONE..............................951 486-4000
TOLL FREE: 800
Jim Watkins, *Prin*
EMP: 411
SALES (corp-wide): 4.58B **Privately Held**
Web: www.countyofriverside.us
SIC: 8011 9431 Medical centers; Public health agency administration, government
PA: County Of Riverside
4080 Lemon St Fl 11
Riverside CA
951 955-1110

(P-17638)
COVID CLINIC INC
16541 Gothard St (92647-4473)
PHONE..............................877 219-8378
Matthew Collins, *CEO*
Matthew Abinante, *CFO*
EMP: 340 **EST:** 2020
SALES (est): 198.82MM **Privately Held**
Web: www.covidclinic.org
SIC: 8011 Offices and clinics of medical doctors

(P-17639)
CUROLOGY INC
5717 Pacific Center Blvd Ste 200 (92121)
PHONE..............................617 959-2480

EMP: 436
SALES (corp-wide): 49.59MM **Privately Held**
Web: www.curology.com
SIC: 8011 Dermatologist
PA: Curology, Inc
353 Sacramento St # 2000
San Francisco CA
858 859-1188

(P-17640)
DAVITA MAGAN MANAGEMENT INC (DH)
Also Called: M M C
420 W Rowland St (91723-2943)
PHONE..............................626 331-6411
Bradley J Rosenberg, *Prin*
Howard Ort Md, *Ex VP*
EMP: 250 **EST:** 1975
SQ FT: 66,000
SALES (est): 54.95MM **Publicly Held**
Web: www.optum.com
SIC: 8011 Clinic, operated by physicians
HQ: Optumcare Management, Llc
2175 Park Pl
El Segundo CA

(P-17641)
DEPARTMENT OF PUBLIC HEALTH
Also Called: Radiologic Health Branch
1500 Capitol Ave 5 Fl Ms 7610 (92101)
P.O. Box 997414 (92101)
PHONE..............................619 338-2493
Michael Dorsey, *Mgr*
EMP: 239
SALES (corp-wide): 534.4MM **Privately Held**
Web: main.sbcounty.gov
SIC: 8011 Radiologist
HQ: Department Of Public Health
1615 Capitol Ave
Sacramento CA
916 449-5560

(P-17642)
DESERT CRDLGY CONS MED GROUP I
Also Called: Desert Cardiology Cons Med G
39000 Bob Hope Dr (92270-3221)
PHONE..............................760 346-0642
Keenan F Barber Md, *VP*
Charles W Shaeffer Junior, *Sec*
Merle R Bolton, *
Barry Hackshaw, *
EMP: 141 **EST:** 1974
SALES (est): 11.35MM **Privately Held**
Web: www.desertcard.com
SIC: 8011 Cardiologist and cardio-vascular specialist

(P-17643)
DESERT MEDICAL GROUP INC (PA)
Also Called: Desert Oasis Healthcare
275 N El Cielo Rd Ste D-402 (92262-6972)
PHONE..............................760 320-8814
Richard E Merkin Md, *Pr*
EMP: 240 **EST:** 1981
SQ FT: 13,000
SALES (est): 49.93MM
SALES (corp-wide): 49.93MM **Privately Held**
SIC: 8011 General and family practice, physician/surgeon

(P-17644)
DESERT VALLEY MED GROUP INC (PA)

Also Called: Desert Valley Medical Group
16850 Bear Valley Rd (92395-5794)
PHONE..............................760 241-8000
Prem Reddy Md, *CEO*
Lex Reddy, *
M Mansukhani, *
EMP: 300 **EST:** 1981
SQ FT: 15,000
SALES (est): 49.04MM
SALES (corp-wide): 49.04MM **Privately Held**
Web:
www.desertvalleymedicalgroup.com
SIC: 8011 Physicians' office, including specialists

(P-17645)
DIAGNSTIC INTRVNTNAL SRGCAL CT
13160 Mindanao Way Ste 150 (90292-6358)
PHONE..............................310 574-0400
Robert S Bray Junior, *Pr*
Keren Reiter, *
EMP: 100 **EST:** 2006
SALES (est): 8MM **Privately Held**
SIC: 8011 Orthopedic physician

(P-17646)
EISENHOWER MEDICAL CENTER
Also Called: Dessert Cancer Care
57475 29 Palms Hwy Ste 104 (92284-2906)
PHONE..............................760 228-9900
EMP: 83
SALES (corp-wide): 3.81MM **Privately Held**
Web: www.eisenhowerhealth.org
SIC: 8011 Medical centers
PA: Eisenhower Medical Center
39000 Bob Hope Dr
Rancho Mirage CA
760 340-3911

(P-17647)
EISENHOWER MEDICAL CENTER
Also Called: Eisenhower-Memory-Care-center
34450 Gateway Dr (92211-0843)
PHONE..............................760 836-0232
EMP: 206
SALES (corp-wide): 3.81MM **Privately Held**
Web: www.eisenhowerhealth.org
SIC: 8011 Medical centers
PA: Eisenhower Medical Center
39000 Bob Hope Dr
Rancho Mirage GA
760 340-3911

(P-17648)
EMANATE HEALTH
Also Called: Emanate Health
1722 Desire Ave Ste 206 (91748-2970)
PHONE..............................626 912-5282
EMP: 160
SALES (corp-wide): 515.46MM **Privately Held**
Web: www.emanatehealth.org
SIC: 8011 Physicians' office, including specialists
PA: Emanate Health Medical Center
1115 S Sunset Ave
West Covina CA
626 962-4011

(P-17649)
EMERGENT MEDICAL ASSOCIATES
Also Called: Pacifica Emergency Med Assoc
16237 Ventura Blvd (91436-2201)
PHONE..................818 995-5350
Irv E Edwards, *Prin*
EMP: 97
SALES (corp-wide): 5.59MM **Privately Held**
Web: www.ema.us
SIC: **8011** Medical centers
PA: Emergent Medical Associates
111 N Sepulveda Blvd # 210
Manhattan Beach CA
310 379-2134

(P-17650)
ENKI HEALTH AND RES SYSTEMS
Also Called: Enki Health Care
160 S 7th Ave (91746-3211)
PHONE..................626 961-8971
Maria M Carmichael, *Dir*
EMP: 88
SALES (corp-wide): 22.76MM **Privately Held**
Web: www.enkihealth.org
SIC: **8011** 8733 Psychiatric clinic; Medical research
PA: Enki Health And Research Systems
150 E Olive Ave Ste 203
Burbank CA
818 973-4899

(P-17651)
EXER HOLDING COMPANY LLC
15503 Ventura Blvd (91436-3114)
PHONE..................818 287-0894
EMP: 195 EST: 2014
SALES (est): 24.45MM **Privately Held**
Web: www.exerurgentcare.com
SIC: **8011** Clinic, operated by physicians

(P-17652)
FAMILY HLTH CTRS SAN DIEGO INC
1845 Logan Ave (92113-2111)
PHONE..................619 515-2526
Gracie Duram, *Brnch Mgr*
EMP: 347
SALES (corp-wide): 147.12MM **Privately Held**
Web: www.fhcsd.org
SIC: **8011** Clinic, operated by physicians
PA: Family Health Centers Of San Diego, Inc.
823 Gateway Center Way
San Diego CA
619 515-2303

(P-17653)
FAMILY HLTH CTRS SAN DIEGO INC
2391 Island Ave (92102-2941)
PHONE..................619 515-2435
Martha Barba, *Mgr*
EMP: 348
SALES (corp-wide): 147.12MM **Privately Held**
Web: www.fhcsd.org
SIC: **8011** Clinic, operated by physicians
PA: Family Health Centers Of San Diego, Inc.
823 Gateway Center Way
San Diego CA
619 515-2303

(P-17654)
FAMILY HLTH CTRS SAN DIEGO INC
5379 El Cajon Blvd (92115-4730)
PHONE..................619 515-2400
Tom Murray, *Owner*
EMP: 348
SALES (corp-wide): 147.12MM **Privately Held**
Web: www.fhcsd.org
SIC: **8011** Clinic, operated by physicians
PA: Family Health Centers Of San Diego, Inc.
823 Gateway Center Way
San Diego CA
619 515-2303

(P-17655)
FAMILY HLTH CTRS SAN DIEGO INC
Also Called: Family Health Center San Diego
8788 Jamacha Rd (91977-4035)
PHONE..................619 515-2555
EMP: 348
SQ FT: 10,970
SALES (corp-wide): 147.12MM **Privately Held**
Web: www.fhcsd.org
SIC: **8011** Clinic, operated by physicians
PA: Family Health Centers Of San Diego, Inc.
823 Gateway Center Way
San Diego CA
619 515-2303

(P-17656)
FAMILY HLTH CTRS SAN DIEGO INC
Also Called: Beach Area Family Health Ctr
3705 Mission Blvd (92109-7104)
PHONE..................619 515-2444
Gracie Duram, *Dir*
EMP: 348
SALES (corp-wide): 147.12MM **Privately Held**
Web: www.fhcsd.org
SIC: **8011** Clinic, operated by physicians
PA: Family Health Centers Of San Diego, Inc.
823 Gateway Center Way
San Diego CA
619 515-2303

(P-17657)
FLORENCE WSTN MED CLINIC INC
13500 Van Nuys Blvd (91331-3028)
PHONE..................818 896-2999
EMP: 115
SALES (corp-wide): 914.05K **Privately Held**
Web: www.florencewesternmc.com
SIC: **8011** Clinic, operated by physicians
PA: Florence Western Medical Clinic, Inc.
7301 S Western Ave
Los Angeles CA
323 778-2131

(P-17658)
GARDEN GROVE ADVANCED IMAGING
1510 Cotner Ave (90025-3303)
PHONE..................310 445-2800
EMP: 144 EST: 2015
SALES (est): 9.83MM **Publicly Held**
Web: www.radnet.com
SIC: **8011** Radiologist
HQ: Radnet Management Iii, Inc.
1510 Cotner Ave
Los Angeles CA
310 445-2800

(P-17659)
GARFIELD IMAGING CENTER INC
555 N Garfield Ave (91754-1202)
PHONE..................626 572-0912
Clark Gardner Md, *Pr*
EMP: 102 EST: 1980
SQ FT: 3,000
SALES (est): 2.54MM
SALES (corp-wide): 359.96MM **Privately Held**
Web: www.garfieldimaging.com
SIC: **8011** Radiologist
HQ: Insight Health Services Corp.
5775 Wayzata Blvd Ste 400
Minneapolis MN

(P-17660)
GOOD SAMARITAN HOSPITAL AUX
1225 Wilshire Blvd (90017-1901)
PHONE..................213 977-2121
Andrew Leeka, *CEO*
EMP: 284 EST: 2001
SALES (est): 44.66K **Privately Held**
SIC: **8011** Medical centers

(P-17661)
GRAYBILL MEDICAL GROUP INC (PA)
225 E 2nd Ave (92025-4249)
PHONE..................866 228-2236
Floyd Farley, *CEO*
David Borecky, *
Marvin V Beddoe, *
George A Pleitez, *
EMP: 180 EST: 1932
SALES (est): 50MM
SALES (corp-wide): 50MM **Privately Held**
Web: www.graybill.org
SIC: **8011** General and family practice, physician/surgeon

(P-17662)
GROVE DIAGNSTC IMAGING CTR INC
8805 Haven Ave Ste 120 (91730-5149)
PHONE..................909 982-8638
Broc Larouche, *Genl Mgr*
EMP: 455
Web: www.radnet.com
SIC: **8011** Radiologist
HQ: Grove Diagnostic Imaging Center, Inc.
8283 Grove Ave Ste 101
Rancho Cucamonga CA

(P-17663)
HEALTHSMART PACIFIC INC
Also Called: Health Smart Clinic
2683 Pacific Ave (90806-2610)
PHONE..................562 595-1911
Mike Drobot, *CEO*
EMP: 294
SALES (corp-wide): 42.31MM **Privately Held**
SIC: **8011** Clinic, operated by physicians
PA: Healthsmart Pacific, Inc.
5150 E Pacific Cst Hwy # 200
Long Beach CA
562 595-1911

(P-17664)
HERALD CHRISTIAN HEALTH CENTER (PA)
3401 Aero Jet Ave (91731-2801)
PHONE..................626 286-8700
David Lee, *CEO*
Emily Szeto, *
Carolin Eng, *
EMP: 80 EST: 2005
SALES (est): 15.14MM **Privately Held**
Web: www.hchcla.org
SIC: **8011** 8021 Primary care medical clinic; Dental clinics and offices

(P-17665)
HIGH DSERT MED CORP A MED GROU (PA)
Also Called: Heritage Health Care
43839 15th St W (93534-4756)
P.O. Box 7007 (93539-7007)
PHONE..................661 945-5984
Richard N Merkin, *CEO*
Charles M Lim, *Dir*
Rafael Gonzalez, *Admn*
Don V Parazo, *Dir*
Anthony J Dulgeroff, *Dir*
EMP: 120 EST: 1984
SQ FT: 25,000
SALES (est): 43.89MM
SALES (corp-wide): 43.89MM **Privately Held**
Web: www.hdmg.net
SIC: **8011** Clinic, operated by physicians

(P-17666)
HOUSE EAR CLINIC INC (PA)
Also Called: House Ear
1245 Wilshire Blvd Ste 812 (90017-4808)
P.O. Box 52001 (85072-2001)
PHONE..................213 483-9930
Derald E Brackmann Md, *Pr*
John W House Md, *Treas*
Antonio De La Cruz Md, *Sec*
EMP: 87 EST: 1969
SALES (est): 11.02MM
SALES (corp-wide): 11.02MM **Privately Held**
Web: www.houseinstitute.com
SIC: **8011** 5999 Ears, nose, and throat specialist: physician/surgeon; Hearing aids

(P-17667)
HUNTINGTON MEDICAL FOUNDATION
10 Congress St Ste 208 (91105-3027)
PHONE..................626 795-4210
Donna Ellis, *Mgr*
EMP: 91
Web: www.huntingtonhealth.org
SIC: **8011** Internal medicine, physician/surgeon
PA: The Huntington Medical Foundation
100 W California Blvd
Pasadena CA

(P-17668)
HUTCHINS HEALTHCARE INC
27101 Puerta Real Ste 450 (92691-8566)
PHONE..................949 487-9500
Kevin Reese, *Pr*
Beverly Wittekind, *Sec*
EMP: 83 EST: 2016
SALES (est): 2.49MM
SALES (corp-wide): 3.03B **Publicly Held**
SIC: **8011** Offices and clinics of medical doctors
PA: The Ensign Group Inc
29222 Rncho Vejo Rd Ste 1
San Juan Capistrano CA
949 487-9500

PRODUCTS & SVCS

(P-17669)
IMAGING HLTHCARE
SPCALISTS LLC
6386 Alvarado Ct (92120-4905)
PHONE..................619 229-2299
EMP: 108
Web: www.imaginghealthcare.com
SIC: 8011 Radiologist
PA: Imaging Healthcare Specialists, Llc
150 W Washington St
San Diego CA

(P-17670)
INDIAN HEALTH COUNCIL INC
(PA)
50100 Golsh Rd (92082-5338)
P.O. Box 406 (92061-0406)
PHONE..................760 749-1410
EMP: 96 **EST:** 1970
SALES (est): 18.68MM **Privately Held**
Web: www.indianhealth.com
SIC: 8011 Clinic, operated by physicians

(P-17671)
INSITE DIGESTIVE HEALTH
CARE
225 W Broadway Ste 350 (91204-1303)
PHONE..................626 817-2900
Alaa Abousaif, *Brnch Mgr*
EMP: 42
SALES (corp-wide): 22.36MM **Privately Held**
Web: www.insitedigestive.com
SIC: 8011 2834 General and family practice, physician/surgeon; Chlorination tablets and kits (water purification)
PA: Insite Digestive Health Care
5525 Etiwanda Ave Ste 110
Tarzana CA
818 437-8105

(P-17672)
IPC HEALTHCARE INC (DH)
4605 Lankershim Blvd Ste 617
(91602-1856)
PHONE..................888 447-2362
Adam D Singer, *CEO*
R Jeffrey Taylor, *Pr*
Richard H Kline Iii, *CFO*
Kerry E Weiner, *CMO*
Richard G Russell, *CDO*
EMP: 173 **EST:** 1995
SALES (est): 408.74MM
SALES (corp-wide): 3.6B **Privately Held**
SIC: 8011 Physicians' office, including specialists
HQ: Team Health Holdings, Inc.
265 Brkview Cntre Way Ste
Knoxville TN
865 693-1000

(P-17673)
JAMES M LALLY DO
5451 Walnut Ave (91710-2609)
PHONE..................909 464-8600
Dan Galles, *CFO*
EMP: 93 **EST:** 2017
SALES (est): 457.9K **Privately Held**
Web: www.cvmc.com
SIC: 8011 Offices and clinics of medical doctors

(P-17674)
KAISER FOUNDATION
HOSPITALS
Also Called: Kaiser Permanente
1301 California St (92374-2910)
PHONE..................888 750-0036
Cindy Wong, *Dir*

EMP: 121
SALES (corp-wide): 68.1B **Privately Held**
Web: www.kaisercenter.com
SIC: 8011 Medical centers
HQ: Kaiser Foundation Hospitals Inc
1 Kaiser Plz
Oakland CA
510 271-6611

(P-17675)
KAISER FOUNDATION
HOSPITALS
Also Called: Ontario Vineyard Medical Offs
2295 S Vineyard Ave (91761-7925)
PHONE..................909 724-5000
EMP: 104
SALES (corp-wide): 68.1B **Privately Held**
Web: www.kaisercenter.com
SIC: 8011 Medical centers
HQ: Kaiser Foundation Hospitals Inc
1 Kaiser Plz
Oakland CA
510 271-6611

(P-17676)
KAISER FOUNDATION
HOSPITALS
Also Called: Kaiser Permanente
9961 Sierra Ave (92335-6720)
PHONE..................909 427-5000
William Meyer, *Prin*
EMP: 1535
SALES (corp-wide): 68.1B **Privately Held**
Web: www.kaisercenter.com
SIC: 8011 Medical centers
HQ: Kaiser Foundation Hospitals Inc
1 Kaiser Plz
Oakland CA
510 271-6611

(P-17677)
KAISER FOUNDATION
HOSPITALS
Also Called: Kaiser Permanente
780 Shadowridge Dr (92083-7986)
PHONE..................619 528-5000
TOLL FREE: 800
Leslei Oliver, *Mgr*
EMP: 92
SALES (corp-wide): 68.1B **Privately Held**
Web: www.kaisercenter.com
SIC: 8011 Medical centers
HQ: Kaiser Foundation Hospitals Inc
1 Kaiser Plz
Oakland CA
510 271-6611

(P-17678)
KAISER FOUNDATION
HOSPITALS
Also Called: El Cajon Medical Offices
250 Travelodge Dr (92020-4126)
PHONE..................619 528-5000
Carolyn Bonner, *Admn*
EMP: 81
SQ FT: 47,486
SALES (corp-wide): 68.1B **Privately Held**
Web: www.kaisercenter.com
SIC: 8011 Medical centers
HQ: Kaiser Foundation Hospitals Inc
1 Kaiser Plz
Oakland CA
510 271-6611

(P-17679)
KAISER FOUNDATION
HOSPITALS
Also Called: Escondido Medical Offices
732 N Broadway (92025-1897)

PHONE..................619 528-5000
Han Kim, *Mgr*
EMP: 104
SALES (corp-wide): 68.1B **Privately Held**
Web: www.kaisercenter.com
SIC: 8011 Medical centers
HQ: Kaiser Foundation Hospitals Inc
1 Kaiser Plz
Oakland CA
510 271-6611

(P-17680)
KAISER FOUNDATION
HOSPITALS
10800 Magnolia Ave (92505-3000)
PHONE..................951 353-3790
Laura Estrada, *Brnch Mgr*
EMP: 89
SALES (corp-wide): 68.1B **Privately Held**
Web: www.kaisercenter.com
SIC: 8011 Offices and clinics of medical doctors
HQ: Kaiser Foundation Hospitals Inc
1 Kaiser Plz
Oakland CA
510 271-6611

(P-17681)
KAISER FOUNDATION
HOSPITALS
Also Called: Riverside Medical Center
10800 Magnolia Ave (92505-3000)
PHONE..................951 353-2000
Vita Willett, *Dir*
EMP: 678
SALES (corp-wide): 68.1B **Privately Held**
Web: www.kaisercenter.com
SIC: 8011 8062 Medical centers; General medical and surgical hospitals
HQ: Kaiser Foundation Hospitals Inc
1 Kaiser Plz
Oakland CA
510 271-6611

(P-17682)
KAISER FOUNDATION
HOSPITALS
Also Called: Kaiser Prmnnte Mreno Vly Med C
27300 Iris Ave (92555-4802)
PHONE..................951 243-0811
Tom Mc Ciltock, *Mgr*
EMP: 1451
SALES (corp-wide): 68.1B **Privately Held**
Web: www.kaisercenter.com
SIC: 8011 Medical centers
HQ: Kaiser Foundation Hospitals Inc
1 Kaiser Plz
Oakland CA
510 271-6611

(P-17683)
KAISER FOUNDATION
HOSPITALS
Also Called: Lakeview Medical Offices
411 N Lakeview Ave (92807-3028)
PHONE..................714 279-4675
Suzie Characky, *Mgr*
EMP: 107
SALES (corp-wide): 68.1B **Privately Held**
Web: www.kaisercenter.com
SIC: 8011 Medical centers
HQ: Kaiser Foundation Hospitals Inc
1 Kaiser Plz
Oakland CA
510 271-6611

(P-17684)
KAISER FOUNDATION
HOSPITALS

Also Called: Kaiser Permanente
12100 Euclid St (92840-3304)
PHONE..................714 741-3448
Betty Bohner, *Admn*
EMP: 121
SALES (corp-wide): 68.1B **Privately Held**
Web: www.kaisercenter.com
SIC: 8011 Medical centers
HQ: Kaiser Foundation Hospitals Inc
1 Kaiser Plz
Oakland CA
510 271-6611

(P-17685)
KAISER FOUNDATION
HOSPITALS
Also Called: La Palma Medical Offices
5 Centerpointe Dr (90623-1050)
PHONE..................714 562-3420
Josefina Guzman-inouye, *Mgr*
EMP: 118
SALES (corp-wide): 68.1B **Privately Held**
Web: www.kaisercenter.com
SIC: 8011 Offices and clinics of medical doctors
HQ: Kaiser Foundation Hospitals Inc
1 Kaiser Plz
Oakland CA
510 271-6611

(P-17686)
KAISER FOUNDATION
HOSPITALS
Also Called: Kaiser Permanente
1900 E 4th St (92705-3910)
PHONE..................714 967-4700
EMP: 178
SALES (corp-wide): 68.1B **Privately Held**
Web: www.kaisercenter.com
SIC: 8011 Medical centers
HQ: Kaiser Foundation Hospitals Inc
1 Kaiser Plz
Oakland CA
510 271-6611

(P-17687)
KAISER FOUNDATION
HOSPITALS
13652 Cantara St (91402-5423)
PHONE..................818 375-4023
Andrea D Mason O T R, *Brnch Mgr*
EMP: 141
SALES (corp-wide): 68.1B **Privately Held**
Web: www.kaisercenter.com
SIC: 8011 Internal medicine practitioners
HQ: Kaiser Foundation Hospitals Inc
1 Kaiser Plz
Oakland CA
510 271-6611

(P-17688)
KAISER FOUNDATION
HOSPITALS
6041 Cadillac Ave (90034-1700)
PHONE..................323 857-2000
Kenneth Nudelman, *Brnch Mgr*
EMP: 127
SALES (corp-wide): 68.1B **Privately Held**
Web: www.kaisercenter.com
SIC: 8011 Physicians' office, including specialists
HQ: Kaiser Foundation Hospitals Inc
1 Kaiser Plz
Oakland CA
510 271-6611

(P-17689)
KAISER FOUNDATION
HOSPITALS

Also Called: Kaiser Prmnnte W Los Angles Me
6041 Cadillac Ave (90034-1700)
PHONE..................................323 857-2000
Howard Fullman, *Dir*
EMP: 1518
SALES (corp-wide): 68.1B Privately Held
Web: www.kaisercenter.com
SIC: 8011 Medical centers
HQ: Kaiser Foundation Hospitals Inc
   1 Kaiser Plz
   Oakland CA
   510 271-6611

(P-17690)
KAISER FOUNDATION HOSPITALS
Also Called: Kaiser Permanente
13651 Willard St (91402)
PHONE..................................818 375-2000
Dev Mahadevan, *Prin*
EMP: 2490
SALES (corp-wide): 68.1B Privately Held
Web: www.kaisercenter.com
SIC: 8011 Medical centers
HQ: Kaiser Foundation Hospitals Inc
   1 Kaiser Plz
   Oakland CA
   510 271-6611

(P-17691)
KAISER FOUNDATION HOSPITALS
Also Called: Kaiser Permanente
25825 Vermont Ave (90710-3518)
PHONE..................................310 325-5111
Mary Ann Barnes, *Brnch Mgr*
EMP: 912
SALES (corp-wide): 68.1B Privately Held
Web: www.kaisercenter.com
SIC: 8011 Medical centers
HQ: Kaiser Foundation Hospitals Inc
   1 Kaiser Plz
   Oakland CA
   510 271-6611

(P-17692)
KAISER FOUNDATION HOSPITALS
1550 N Edgemont St (90027-5210)
PHONE..................................323 783-7955
EMP: 92
SALES (corp-wide): 68.1B Privately Held
Web: www.kaisercenter.com
SIC: 8011 Offices and clinics of medical doctors
HQ: Kaiser Foundation Hospitals Inc
   1 Kaiser Plz
   Oakland CA
   510 271-6611

(P-17693)
KAISER FOUNDATION HOSPITALS
Also Called: Glendale Medical Offices
444 W Glenoaks Blvd (91202-2917)
PHONE..................................818 552-3000
Avetis Tashyan, *Brnch Mgr*
EMP: 139
SALES (corp-wide): 68.1B Privately Held
Web: www.kaisercenter.com
SIC: 8011 Medical centers
HQ: Kaiser Foundation Hospitals Inc
   1 Kaiser Plz
   Oakland CA
   510 271-6611

(P-17694)
KAISER FOUNDATION HOSPITALS
Also Called: Kaiser Prmnnte Psadena Med Off
3280 E Foothill Blvd (91107-3148)
P.O. Box 7005 (91109-7005)
PHONE..................................626 440-5639
EMP: 144
SALES (corp-wide): 68.1B Privately Held
Web: www.kaisercenter.com
SIC: 8011 Medical centers
HQ: Kaiser Foundation Hospitals Inc
   1 Kaiser Plz
   Oakland CA
   510 271-6611

(P-17695)
KAISER FOUNDATION HOSPITALS
Also Called: Kaiser Permanente
1515 N Vermont Ave Fl 3 (90027-5337)
PHONE..................................323 783-8306
Cecilia Militante, *Prin*
EMP: 234
SALES (corp-wide): 68.1B Privately Held
Web: www.kaisercenter.com
SIC: 8011 Dermatologist
HQ: Kaiser Foundation Hospitals Inc
   1 Kaiser Plz
   Oakland CA
   510 271-6611

(P-17696)
KAISER FOUNDATION HOSPITALS
Also Called: Kaiser Permanente
110 N La Brea Ave (90301-1708)
PHONE..................................310 419-3303
Victor Ahaiwe, *Pr*
EMP: 81
SALES (corp-wide): 68.1B Privately Held
Web: www.kaisercenter.com
SIC: 8011 Medical centers
HQ: Kaiser Foundation Hospitals Inc
   1 Kaiser Plz
   Oakland CA
   510 271-6611

(P-17697)
KAISER FOUNDATION HOSPITALS
Also Called: Stockdale Medical Offices
3501 Stockdale Hwy (93309-2150)
PHONE..................................661 398-5011
Ky P Ho, *Prin*
EMP: 141
SALES (corp-wide): 68.1B Privately Held
Web: www.kaisercenter.com
SIC: 8011 Medical centers
HQ: Kaiser Foundation Hospitals Inc
   1 Kaiser Plz
   Oakland CA
   510 271-6611

(P-17698)
KAISER FOUNDATION HOSPITALS
Also Called: Kaiser Permanente
5055 California Ave Ste 110 (93309-0701)
P.O. Box 12099 (93389-2099)
PHONE..................................661 334-2020
EMP: 87
SALES (corp-wide): 68.1B Privately Held
Web: www.kaisercenter.com
SIC: 8011 Medical centers
HQ: Kaiser Foundation Hospitals Inc
   1 Kaiser Plz
   Oakland CA
   510 271-6611

(P-17699)
KAISER PRMNNTE SCHL ANESTHESIA
100 S Los Robles Ste 501 (91101-2453)
PHONE..................................626 564-3016
Kaiser Permanente, *Owner*
EMP: 134 EST: 2009
SALES (est): 29.65MM Privately Held
Web: www.kpsan.org
SIC: 8011 Anesthesiologist

(P-17700)
KECK MEDICAL CENTER OF USC
1520 San Pablo St (90033-5310)
PHONE..................................323 371-9535
Melina Thaxton, *Mgr*
EMP: 91
SALES (corp-wide): 861.65MM Privately Held
Web: www.keckmedicine.org
SIC: 8011 General and family practice, physician/surgeon
PA: Keck Medical Center Of Usc
   1510 San Pablo St
   Los Angeles CA
   800 872-2273

(P-17701)
KERN HEALTH SYSTEMS INC
Also Called: Kern Family Helathcare
2900 Buck Owens Blvd (93308-6316)
P.O. Box 85000 (93380-5000)
PHONE..................................661 664-5000
Carol L Sorrell, *CEO*
EMP: 98 EST: 1995
SQ FT: 16,000
SALES (est): 26.74MM Privately Held
Web: www.kernfamilyhealthcare.com
SIC: 8011 Clinic, operated by physicians

(P-17702)
LA JOLLA ORTHPDIC SRGERY CTR L
4120 La Jolla Village Dr (92037-1406)
PHONE..................................858 657-0055
Scott Leggett, *Managing Member*
EMP: 98 EST: 2000
SALES (est): 11.11MM Privately Held
Web: www.osclajolla.com
SIC: 8011 Orthopedic physician

(P-17703)
LA MAESTRA FAMILY CLINIC INC (PA)
Also Called: LA MAESTRA COMMUNITY HEALTH CE
4060 Fairmount Ave (92105-1608)
PHONE..................................619 584-1612
Zara Marselian, *CEO*
Samuel Mirelles, *
Carlos Hanessian, *
Alex Pantoja, *
Alejandrina Areizaga, *
EMP: 197 EST: 1991
SQ FT: 5,000
SALES (est): 78.1MM Privately Held
Web: www.lamaestra.org
SIC: 8011 Clinic, operated by physicians

(P-17704)
LAC & USC MEDICAL CENTER
2051 Marengo St (90033-1352)
P.O. Box 861749 (90086-1749)
PHONE..................................323 409-2345
Marisa Danbee, *Prin*
EMP: 85 EST: 2009
SALES (est): 40.23MM Privately Held
Web: dhs.lacounty.gov

SIC: 8011 Primary care medical clinic

(P-17705)
LANCASTER CRDLGY MED GROUP INC (PA)
Also Called: Physicians Referral Service
43847 Heaton Ave Ste B (93534-4922)
PHONE..................................661 726-3058
Shun K Sunder Md, *Pr*
E Ekong Md, *VP*
Kanagaratham Sivalingam Md, *Sec*
EMP: 80 EST: 1976
SQ FT: 30,000
SALES (est): 4.5MM
SALES (corp-wide): 4.5MM Privately Held
SIC: 8011 Cardiologist and cardio-vascular specialist

(P-17706)
LINDA LOMA UNIV HLTH CARE (PA)
11175 Campus St A-1108 (92350-1700)
PHONE..................................909 558-4729
Trevor Wright, *CEO*
Roger Hadley, *Pr*
David B Hinshaw Junior Md, *V Ch Bd*
Brian Bull Md, *Sec*
EMP: 850 EST: 1989
SQ FT: 70,000
SALES (est): 208.25MM Privately Held
Web: home.llu.edu
SIC: 8011 Clinic, operated by physicians

(P-17707)
LOMA LNDA UNIV FMLY MED GROUP
25455 Barton Rd Ste 204b (92354-3130)
PHONE..................................909 558-6600
John Testerman, *Pr*
EMP: 83 EST: 1980
SALES (est): 3.08MM Privately Held
Web: www.lluh.org
SIC: 8011 Clinic, operated by physicians

(P-17708)
LOS ANGELES FREE CLINIC
5205 Melrose Ave (90038-3144)
PHONE..................................323 653-1990
EMP: 110
SALES (corp-wide): 39.22MM Privately Held
Web: www.sabancommunityclinic.org
SIC: 8011 Clinic, operated by physicians
PA: The Los Angeles Free Clinic
   8405 Beverly Blvd
   Los Angeles CA
   323 653-8622

(P-17709)
LOS ROBLES REGIONAL MED CTR
150 Via Merida (91362-3816)
PHONE..................................805 370-4531
Simin Shandiz, *Prin*
EMP: 261
Web: www.losrobleshospital.com
SIC: 8011 Medical centers
HQ: Los Robles Regional Medical Center
   215 W Janss Rd
   Thousand Oaks CA

(P-17710)
LOS ROBLES REGIONAL MED CTR
Also Called: Neuroscience Gamma Knife Ctr
2200 Lynn Rd (91360-2071)
PHONE..................................805 494-0880
Cherrie De La La Cruz, *Prin*

EMP: 261
Web: www.californiagammaknife.com
SIC: 8011 Neurologist
HQ: Los Robles Regional Medical Center
215 W Janss Rd
Thousand Oaks CA

(P-17711)
MAINSTAY MEDICAL LIMITED
2159 India St Ste 200 (92101-1766)
PHONE......................619 261-9144
Jason Hannon, *CEO*
EMP: 80 **EST:** 2008
SALES (est): 516.01K **Privately Held**
SIC: 8011 Primary care medical clinic

(P-17712)
MICHA-RETTENMAIER PARTNERSHIP
Also Called: Gynecologic Oncology Assoc
351 Hospital Rd Ste 507 (92663-3500)
PHONE......................714 280-1645
John Paul Micha Md, *Pt*
Mark A Rettenmaier Md, *Pt*
EMP: 88 **EST:** 1989
SQ FT: 3,500
SALES (est): 9.77MM **Privately Held**
Web: www.hoag.org
SIC: 8011 Gynecologist

(P-17713)
MISSION INTERNAL MED GROUP INC
Also Called: West Coast Physical Therapy
27882 Forbes Rd Ste 110 (92677-1267)
PHONE......................949 364-3605
Joan Shrum-brown, *Prin*
EMP: 91
SALES (corp-wide): 19.19MM **Privately Held**
SIC: 8011 8049 Cardiologist and cardio-vascular specialist; Physical therapist
PA: Mission Internal Medical Group, Inc.
26732 Crown Valley Pkwy # 351
Mission Viejo CA
949 282-1600

(P-17714)
MISSION INTERNAL MED GROUP INC
Also Called: Arthur Loussararian MD
26800 Crown Valley Ste 103 (92691-6389)
PHONE......................949 364-3570
Arthur Loussararian, *Prin*
EMP: 90
SALES (corp-wide): 19.19MM **Privately Held**
SIC: 8011 Primary care medical clinic
PA: Mission Internal Medical Group, Inc.
26732 Crown Valley Pkwy # 351
Mission Viejo CA
949 282-1600

(P-17715)
MOHAWK MEDICAL GROUP INC
9500 Stockdale Hwy Ste 200 (93311-3621)
PHONE......................661 324-4747
Jorge Deltoro, *Pr*
Luis Cousin, *
EMP: 80 **EST:** 1985
SQ FT: 18,500
SALES (est): 5.63MM **Privately Held**
SIC: 8011 General and family practice, physician/surgeon

(P-17716)
MOLINA HEALTHCARE INC (PA)
Also Called: Molina Healthcare

200 Oceangate Ste 100 (90802-4317)
P.O. Box 22813 (90801-5813)
PHONE......................562 435-3666
Joseph M Zubretsky, *Pr*
Dale B Wolf, *Non-Executive Chairman of the Board*
Ronna E Romney, *
EMP: 2800 **EST:** 1980
SALES (est): 31.97B
SALES (corp-wide): 31.97B **Publicly Held**
Web: www.molinahealthcare.com
SIC: 8011 6324 Health maintenance organization; Hospital and medical service plans

(P-17717)
MOLINA HEALTHCARE CALIFORNIA
200 Oceangate Ste 100 (90802-4303)
PHONE......................800 526-8196
EMP: 2115 **EST:** 2016
SALES (est): 2.02MM
SALES (corp-wide): 31.97B **Publicly Held**
Web: www.molinahealthcare.com
SIC: 8011 Offices and clinics of medical doctors
PA: Molina Healthcare, Inc.
200 Oceangate Ste 100
Long Beach CA
562 435-3666

(P-17718)
MOLINA PATHWAYS LLC
200 Oceangate Ste 100 (90802-4317)
PHONE......................562 491-5773
Craig Bass, *CEO*
EMP: 498 **EST:** 2011
SALES (est): 2.36MM
SALES (corp-wide): 31.97B **Publicly Held**
SIC: 8011 Health maintenance organization
PA: Molina Healthcare, Inc.
200 Oceangate Ste 100
Long Beach CA
562 435-3666

(P-17719)
MONARCH HEALTHCARE A MEDICAL
675 Camino De Los Mares Ste 300 (92673)
PHONE......................949 489-1960
Adam Crawford D.o.s., *Brnch Mgr*
EMP: 159
SALES (corp-wide): 324.16B **Publicly Held**
Web: www.monarchhealthcare.com
SIC: 8011 Group health association
HQ: Monarch Healthcare, A Medical Group, Inc.
11 Technology Dr
Irvine CA

(P-17720)
MONARCH HEALTHCARE A MEDICAL (HQ)
11 Technology Dr (92618-2302)
PHONE......................949 923-3200
Bartley Asner, *CEO*
Jay J Cohen Md, *VP*
Steven Rudy Md, *VP*
James Selevan Md, *Mgr*
Marvin Gordon Md, *CFO*
EMP: 98 **EST:** 1986
SQ FT: 75,000
SALES (est): 95.06MM
SALES (corp-wide): 324.16B **Publicly Held**
Web: www.monarchhealthcare.com
SIC: 8011 Group health association
PA: Unitedhealth Group Incorporated
9900 Bren Rd E Ste 300w

Minnetonka MN
952 936-1300

(P-17721)
N S C CHANNEL ISLANDS INC
Also Called: HealthSouth
2300 Wankel Way (93030-2665)
PHONE......................805 485-1908
Susan Clark, *Admn*
EMP: 485 **EST:** 1995
SQ FT: 14,000
SALES (est): 18.71MM
SALES (corp-wide): 4.35B **Publicly Held**
SIC: 8011 Surgeon
HQ: Healthsouth Rehabilitation Hospital Of Cypress, Llc
9001 Liberty Pkwy
Birmingham AL

(P-17722)
NAVY UNITED STATES DEPARTMENT
Also Called: Branch Medical Center
19871 Mitscher Way (92145-5103)
P.O. Box 452002 (92145-2002)
PHONE......................858 577-9849
EMP: 300
Web: www.navy.mil
SIC: 8011 9711 Medical centers; Navy
HQ: United States Department Of The Navy
1200 Navy Pentagon
Washington DC

(P-17723)
NEIGHBORHOOD HEALTHCARE
460 N Elm St (92025-3002)
PHONE......................760 737-2000
EMP: 136
SQ FT: 9,288
SALES (corp-wide): 184.76MM **Privately Held**
Web: www.nhcare.org
SIC: 8011 Clinic, operated by physicians
PA: Neighborhood Healthcare
425 N Date St
Escondido CA
760 737-6934

(P-17724)
NEW SPIRIT NATURALS INC (PA)
615 W Allen Ave (91773-1447)
PHONE......................909 592-4445
Larry Milam, *Pr*
◆ **EMP:** 20 **EST:** 1982
SQ FT: 25,000
SALES (est): 6.78MM
SALES (corp-wide): 6.78MM **Privately Held**
Web: www.newspirit.com
SIC: 8011 5122 2032 2844 Offices and clinics of medical doctors; Drugs, proprietaries, and sundries; Canned specialties; Shampoos, rinses, conditioners: hair

(P-17725)
NEWPORT BEACH SURGERY CTR LLC
361 Hospital Rd Ste 124 (92663-3521)
PHONE......................949 631-0988
Perter Broekelschen, *Managing Member*
Harvey Heinrichs, *Managing Member*
Bruce Albert, *
Robert Anderson, *
EMP: 120 **EST:** 1992
SQ FT: 10,000
SALES (est): 15.69MM **Privately Held**

Web:
www.newportbeachsurgerycenter.com
SIC: 8011 Surgeon

(P-17726)
NORTH COUNTY HEALTH PRJ INC
1130 2nd St (92024-5008)
PHONE......................760 736-6767
Patricia Cheu, *Prin*
EMP: 125
SQ FT: 7,513
SALES (corp-wide): 97.36MM **Privately Held**
Web: www.nchs-health.org
SIC: 8011 Clinic, operated by physicians
PA: North County Health Project Incorporated
150 Valpreda Rd Frnt
San Marcos CA
760 736-6755

(P-17727)
NORTH COUNTY HEALTH PRJ INC (PA)
Also Called: NORTH COUNTY SERVICES
150 Valpreda Rd Frnt (92069-2944)
PHONE......................760 736-6755
Irma Cota, *CEO*
Kathy Martinez, *
EMP: 221 **EST:** 1973
SQ FT: 69,880
SALES (est): 97.36MM
SALES (corp-wide): 97.36MM **Privately Held**
Web: www.nchs-health.org
SIC: 8011 Clinic, operated by physicians

(P-17728)
OAK GROVE INST FOUNDATION INC (PA)
Also Called: Oak Grove Center
24275 Jefferson Ave (92562-7285)
PHONE......................951 677-5599
Tamara L Wilson, *CEO*
Barry Soper, *
Fe Santiago, *
EMP: 148 **EST:** 1986
SQ FT: 39,000
SALES (est): 23.08MM **Privately Held**
Web: www.oakgrovecenter.org
SIC: 8011 8211 8361 Psychiatric clinic; Specialty education; Residential care

(P-17729)
OLIVE VIEW-UCLA MEDICAL CENTER (PA)
Also Called: Valley Care Olive View Med Ctr
14445 Olive View Dr (91342-1437)
PHONE......................818 364-1555
Carolyn Rhee, *CEO*
EMP: 85 **EST:** 2001
SALES (est): 80.94MM
SALES (corp-wide): 80.94MM **Privately Held**
Web: www.uclaoliveview.org
SIC: 8011 Medical centers

(P-17730)
OMNI FAMILY HEALTH (PA)
Also Called: COMMUNITY HEALTH CENTER
4900 California Ave Ste 400b (93309-7081)
P.O. Box 1060 (93263-1060)
PHONE......................661 459-1900
Francisco L Castillon, *CEO*
Novira Irawan, *
Petrus Tjandra, *
Aurora Cooper, *
EMP: 80 **EST:** 1978

SQ FT: 14,000
SALES (est): 129.62MM
SALES (corp-wide): 129.62MM **Privately Held**
Web: www.omnifamilyhealth.org
SIC: **8011** Clinic, operated by physicians

(P-17731)
OPERATION SAMAHAN INC
Also Called: Camino Ruiz Suite 235
10737 Camino Ruiz Ste 235138 (92126-2375)
PHONE..............................619 477-4451
Dirk Virbel, *CEO*
EMP: 128
SALES (corp-wide): 15.49MM **Privately Held**
Web: www.operationsamahan.org
SIC: **8011** 8021 Clinic, operated by physicians; Offices and clinics of dentists
PA: Operation Samahan, Inc.
1428 Highland Ave
National City CA
619 477-4451

(P-17732)
OPTUMCARE MANAGEMENT LLC (HQ)
Also Called: Healthcare Partners Med Group
2175 Park Pl (90245-4705)
PHONE..............................310 354-4200
EMP: 600 **EST:** 1994
SQ FT: 38,000
SALES (est): 596.22MM **Publicly Held**
SIC: **8011** Group health association
PA: Davita Inc.
2000 16th St
Denver CO

(P-17733)
OPTUMCARE MANAGEMENT LLC
Harriman Jones Medical
2600 Redondo Ave Ste 405 (90806-2330)
PHONE..............................562 988-7000
Jill R Cortese, *Prin*
EMP: 146
SIC: **8011** Clinic, operated by physicians
HQ: Optumcare Management, Llc
2175 Park Pl
El Segundo CA

(P-17734)
ORANGE COAST WNS MED GROUP INC
1031 Avenida Pico Ste 204 (92673-6352)
PHONE..............................949 829-5522
EMP: 85
SALES (corp-wide): 16.1MM **Privately Held**
Web: www.ocwmg.com
SIC: **8011** Gynecologist
PA: Orange Coast Women's Medical Group, Inc.
24411 Health Center Dr # 200
Laguna Hills CA
949 829-5500

(P-17735)
PEDIATRIC & FAMILY MEDICAL CTR
Also Called: EISNER PEDIATRIC & FAMILY MEDI
1530 S Olive St (90015-3023)
PHONE..............................213 342-3325
Carl Coan, *CEO*
Kevin Rossi, *
Edward Matthews Iii, *V Ch*
Irma Avila, *

Carl Edward Coan, *
EMP: 160 **EST:** 1920
SQ FT: 21,000
SALES (est): 61.7MM **Privately Held**
Web: www.eisnerhealth.org
SIC: **8011** Clinic, operated by physicians

(P-17736)
PEDIATRIC NROLOGY THERAPEUTICS
7090 Miratech Dr (92121-3109)
PHONE..............................858 304-6440
Melissa D Knopp, *Dir*
EMP: 82 **EST:** 2017
SALES (est): 237.28K **Privately Held**
Web: www.corticacare.com
SIC: **8011** Neurologist

(P-17737)
PEOPLE CREATING SUCCESS INC
380 Arneill Rd (93010-6406)
PHONE..............................805 644-9480
Marie Mcmanus, *Brnch Mgr*
EMP: 99
SALES (corp-wide): 14.09MM **Privately Held**
Web: www.pcs-services.org
SIC: **8011** Offices and clinics of medical doctors
PA: People Creating Success, Inc.
2585 Teller Rd
Newbury Park CA
805 375-9222

(P-17738)
PERMANENTE MEDICAL GROUP INC
Also Called: S C P M G
25825 Vermont Ave (90710-3518)
PHONE..............................310 325-5111
TOLL FREE: 800
Leroy Foster, *Mgr*
EMP: 522
SALES (corp-wide): 68.1B **Privately Held**
Web: www.permanente.org
SIC: **8011** Medical centers
HQ: The Permanente Medical Group Inc
1950 Franklin St Fl 7th
Oakland CA
866 858-2226

(P-17739)
PREMIER OTPTENT SRGERY CTR INC
Also Called: Amsurg
900 E Washington St Ste 155 (92324-7111)
PHONE..............................909 370-2190
David Wood, *Pr*
EMP: 103 **EST:** 2000
SQ FT: 70,000
SALES (est): 2.47MM **Privately Held**
Web: www.premierosc.com
SIC: **8011** Surgeon

(P-17740)
PROGRESSIVE HEALTH CARE SYSTEM
Also Called: P H S
8510 Balboa Blvd Ste 150 (91325-5810)
PHONE..............................818 707-9603
EMP: 100 **EST:** 1999
SQ FT: 10,000
SALES (est): 4.49MM **Privately Held**
Web: www.msophs.com
SIC: **8011** Offices and clinics of medical doctors

(P-17741)
PROSPECT MEDICAL HOLDINGS INC (PA)
3415 S Sepulveda Blvd Fl 9 (90034-6060)
PHONE..............................310 943-4500
Samuel Lee, *Ch Bd*
Mike Heather, *
Donna Vigil, *
Linda Hodges, *
EMP: 211 **EST:** 1993
SQ FT: 7,154
SALES (est): 3.91B
SALES (corp-wide): 3.91B **Privately Held**
Web: www.pmh.com
SIC: **8011** Health maintenance organization

(P-17742)
PROVIDNCE FACEY MED FOUNDATION (PA)
15451 San Fernando Mission Blvd (91345-1301)
PHONE..............................818 365-9531
Bill Gill, *CEO*
Jim Corwin, *
EMP: 170 **EST:** 1991
SQ FT: 306,000
SALES (est): 91.37MM
SALES (corp-wide): 91.37MM **Privately Held**
Web: www.facey.com
SIC: **8011** Physicians' office, including specialists

(P-17743)
PROVIDNCE FACEY MED FOUNDATION
27924 Seco Canyon Rd (91350-3870)
PHONE..............................661 513-2100
Joan Rhee, *Mgr*
EMP: 91
SALES (corp-wide): 91.37MM **Privately Held**
Web: www.facey.com
SIC: **8011** Physicians' office, including specialists
PA: Providence Facey Medical Foundation
15451 San Frnndo Mssion B
Mission Hills CA
818 365-9531

(P-17744)
PROVIDNCE FACEY MED FOUNDATION
11165 Sepulveda Blvd (91345-1113)
PHONE..............................818 365-9531
Judy Breen, *Brnch Mgr*
EMP: 122
SALES (corp-wide): 91.37MM **Privately Held**
Web: www.facey.com
SIC: **8011** Physicians' office, including specialists
PA: Providence Facey Medical Foundation
15451 San Frnndo Mssion B
Mission Hills CA
818 365-9531

(P-17745)
QUEENSCARE HEALTH CENTERS
4618 Fountain Ave (90029-1830)
PHONE..............................323 644-6180
Guillermo Diaz, *Brnch Mgr*
EMP: 83
SALES (corp-wide): 36.05MM **Privately Held**
Web: www.queenscarehealthcenters.org
SIC: **8011** Clinic, operated by physicians
PA: Queenscare Health Centers
950 Suth Grnd Ave Fl 2
Los Angeles CA
323 669-4301

(P-17746)
QUEENSCARE HEALTH CENTERS
Also Called: Queenscare Fmly Clnics - Estsi
4816 E 3rd St (90022-1602)
PHONE..............................323 780-4510
Evelyn Moody, *Mgr*
EMP: 82
SALES (corp-wide): 36.05MM **Privately Held**
Web: www.queenscarehealthcenters.org
SIC: **8011** Clinic, operated by physicians
PA: Queenscare Health Centers
950 Suth Grnd Ave Fl 2
Los Angeles CA
323 669-4301

(P-17747)
RADIOLOGY PARTNERS INC (HQ)
Also Called: Cirpa Radiology Management
2101 E El Segundo Blvd Ste 401 (90245-4518)
PHONE..............................424 290-8004
Richard Whitney, *CEO*
EMP: 500 **EST:** 2012
SALES (est): 126.78MM
SALES (corp-wide): 137.27MM **Privately Held**
Web: www.radpartners.com
SIC: **8011** Radiologist
PA: Radiology Partners Holdings, Llc
2330 Utah Ave Ste 200
El Segundo CA
424 290-8004

(P-17748)
RADIOLOGY PRTNERS HOLDINGS LLC (PA)
2330 Utah Ave Ste 200 (90245-4817)
PHONE..............................424 290-8004
Rich Whitney, *CEO*
Jay Bronner, *Pr*
Steve Tumbarello, *CFO*
Anthony Gabriel, *COO*
Krishna Nallamshetty, *CMO*
EMP: 118 **EST:** 2013
SALES (est): 137.27MM
SALES (corp-wide): 137.27MM **Privately Held**
SIC: **8011** Radiologist

(P-17749)
RAVI PATEL MD INC
Also Called: Comprehensive Blood Cancer Ctr
6501 Truxtun Ave (93309-0633)
PHONE..............................661 862-7113
EMP: 250 **EST:** 1987
SALES (est): 30.27MM **Privately Held**
Web: www.cbccusa.com
SIC: **8011** Medical centers

(P-17750)
REDWOOD FAMILY CARE NETWRK INC
13920 City Center Dr (91709-5432)
PHONE..............................909 942-0218
David Catrell, *Pr*
EMP: 2300 **EST:** 2021
SALES (est): 70.95MM **Privately Held**
Web: www.redwoodfcn.com
SIC: **8011** Medical centers

PRODUCTS & SVCS

(P-17751)
RENEW MEDICAL GROUP INC
1125 S Beverly Dr Ste 720 (90035-1180)
PHONE..................310 929-9790
EMP: 84
SALES (corp-wide): 899.19K **Privately Held**
SIC: 8011 Medical centers
PA: Renew Medical Group, Inc.
3142 Vista Way Ste 206
Oceanside CA
760 721-4000

(P-17752)
RIVERSD-SAN BRNRDINO CNTY INDI
Also Called: Soboba Indian Health Clinic
607 Donna Way (92583-5517)
PHONE..................951 654-0803
Maria Adams, *Mgr*
EMP: 135
SALES (corp-wide): 63.44MM **Privately Held**
Web: www.rsbcihi.org
SIC: 8011 Clinic, operated by physicians
PA: Riverside-San Bernardino County Indian Health, Inc.
11980 Mount Vernon Ave
Grand Terrace CA
909 864-1097

(P-17753)
RIVERSD-SAN BRNRDINO CNTY INDI (PA)
11980 Mount Vernon Ave (92313-5172)
PHONE..................909 864-1097
Jackie Wisespirit, *Pr*
Charles Castello, *
Faith Morreo, *
Brandie Miranda, *
Bill Thomsen, *
EMP: 113 **EST:** 1974
SQ FT: 38,000
SALES (est): 63.44MM
SALES (corp-wide): 63.44MM **Privately Held**
Web: www.rsbcihi.org
SIC: 8011 8093 Clinic, operated by physicians; Specialty outpatient clinics, nec

(P-17754)
RIVERSIDE MEDICAL CLINIC INC (PA)
Also Called: Riverside Med Clnic Ptient Ctr
3660 Arlington Ave (92506-3912)
PHONE..................951 683-6370
Steven E Larson, *Pr*
Judy Carpenter, *
Steven E Larson, *Pr*
EMP: 89 **EST:** 1993
SQ FT: 65,000
SALES (est): 102.29MM
SALES (corp-wide): 102.29MM **Privately Held**
Web: www.riversidemedicalclinic.com
SIC: 8011 Clinic, operated by physicians

(P-17755)
SAINT JHNS HLTH CTR FOUNDATION
Wayne, John Cancer Institute
2200 Santa Monica Blvd (90404-2312)
PHONE..................310 315-6111
Donald Mortan, *Dir*
EMP: 125
SQ FT: 7,100
SALES (corp-wide): 10.75B **Privately Held**
Web: www.pacificneuroscienceinstitute.org

SIC: 8011 8731 Primary care medical clinic; Commercial physical research
HQ: Saint John's Health Center Foundation.
2121 Santa Monica Blvd
Santa Monica CA
310 829-5511

(P-17756)
SAN DEGO PTHLGSTS MED GROUP IN
7592 Metropolitan Dr Ste 406 (92108)
PHONE..................619 297-4012
Carla Stayboldt Md, *Pr*
Bruce Robbins Md, *Ex VP*
Ralph Shishido Md, *Sec*
Slavek Niewiadomski Md, *Treas*
David Francis Md, *VP*
EMP: 120 **EST:** 1969
SQ FT: 3,500
SALES (est): 8.06MM **Privately Held**
Web: www.sdpath.com
SIC: 8011 Pathologist

(P-17757)
SAN DIEGO FAMILY CARE (PA)
Also Called: LINDA VISTA HEALTH CARE CENTER
6973 Linda Vista Rd (92111-6342)
PHONE..................858 279-0925
Roberta L Feinberg, *CEO*
Manuel Quintanar, *
EMP: 93 **EST:** 1972
SALES (est): 31.6MM
SALES (corp-wide): 31.6MM **Privately Held**
Web: www.sdfamilycare.org
SIC: 8011 Clinic, operated by physicians

(P-17758)
SAN GBRIEL AMBLTORY SRGERY CTR
207 S Santa Anita St Ste G16 (91776-1146)
PHONE..................626 300-5300
Brenda Durgin, *Mgr*
EMP: 156 **EST:** 2003
SALES (est): 31.57MM
SALES (corp-wide): 19.58B **Publicly Held**
SIC: 8011 Opthalmologist
HQ: United Surgical Partners International, Inc.
14201 Dallas Pkwy
Dallas TX
972 713-3500

(P-17759)
SANTA MONICA BAY PHYSICIANS HE (PA)
Also Called: Bay Area Community Med Group
5767 W Century Blvd (90045-5631)
PHONE..................310 417-5900
Eileen Mcgrath, *Pr*
Doctor Steven Seizer, *VP*
Doctor David Cutler, *Sec*
Doctor Richard Zachrich, *Treas*
EMP: 85 **EST:** 1985
SALES (est): 21.28MM
SALES (corp-wide): 21.28MM **Privately Held**
Web: www.uclahealth.org
SIC: 8011 Clinic, operated by physicians

(P-17760)
SB WATERMAN HOLDINGS INC (PA)
1700 N Waterman Ave (92404-5115)
PHONE..................909 883-8611
James Malin, *CEO*
James W Malin, *

Paul G Godfrey Md, *VP*
Thomas Hellwig, *
Louis Francisco Md, *Treas*
EMP: 150 **EST:** 1954
SQ FT: 55,000
SALES (est): 21.33MM
SALES (corp-wide): 21.33MM **Privately Held**
Web: www.sbmed.com
SIC: 8011 Clinic, operated by physicians

(P-17761)
SCRIBEMD LLC
1310 W Stewart Dr Ste 212 (92868-3837)
PHONE..................714 543-8911
Coutney Aldama, *CEO*
Matthew Mullarky, *
EMP: 90 **EST:** 2009
SALES (est): 1.23MM **Privately Held**
Web: www.scribemd.com
SIC: 8011 Offices and clinics of medical doctors

(P-17762)
SENTE INC
2310 Camino Vida Roble Ste 101 (92011)
PHONE..................800 205-6774
Laurent Combredet, *Pr*
▲ **EMP:** 45 **EST:** 2007
SALES (est): 9.16MM **Privately Held**
Web: www.sentelabs.com
SIC: 8011 2834 Dermatologist; Dermatologicals

(P-17763)
SERRA COMMUNITY MED CLINIC INC
Also Called: Serra Community Medical Clinic
9375 San Fernando Rd (91352-1428)
PHONE..................818 768-3000
Sadayappa K Durairaj, *CEO*
Doctor Arnold Jacobs, *Treas*
Doctor Carlos Jimenez, *Sec*
Dan Bumgarner, *
Kumar Soundar, *
EMP: 163 **EST:** 1975
SQ FT: 60,000
SALES (est): 23.5MM **Privately Held**
Web: www.serramedicalgroup.com
SIC: 8011 Clinic, operated by physicians

(P-17764)
SHARP HEALTHCARE
8860 Center Dr Ste 450 (91942-7001)
PHONE..................619 460-6200
Scott Musicant, *Brnch Mgr*
EMP: 86
SALES (corp-wide): 2.37B **Privately Held**
Web: www.vascularsandiego.com
SIC: 8011 General and family practice, physician/surgeon
PA: Sharp Healthcare
8695 Spectrum Center Blvd
San Diego CA
858 499-4000

(P-17765)
SHARP RES-STEALY MED GROUP INC
7862 El Cajon Blvd Ste C (91942-6712)
PHONE..................619 644-6405
Behrooz Akbarnia, *Prin*
EMP: 176
Web: www.sharp.com
SIC: 8011 Internal medicine practitioners
PA: Sharp Rees-Stealy Medical Group, Inc.
300 Fir St
San Diego CA

(P-17766)
SHARP RES-STEALY MED GROUP INC
3555 Kenyon St Ste 200 (92110-5341)
PHONE..................619 221-9547
Betty Thompson, *Mgr*
EMP: 177
Web: www.sharp.com
SIC: 8011 Physicians' office, including specialists
PA: Sharp Rees-Stealy Medical Group, Inc.
300 Fir St
San Diego CA

(P-17767)
SLEEP DATA SERVICES LLC
5471 Kearny Villa Rd Ste 200 (92123)
PHONE..................619 299-6299
Gaston Sanchez, *Prin*
EMP: 90 **EST:** 2017
SALES (est): 9.62MM **Privately Held**
Web: www.sleepdata.com
SIC: 8011 Offices and clinics of medical doctors

(P-17768)
SOUTH CENTRAL FAMILY HLTH CTR
4425 S Central Ave (90011-3629)
PHONE..................323 908-4200
Richard Veloz, *Pr*
Paul Ramos, *
Ruby Raya Morones, *CMO*
Sandra Tatum Green, *
EMP: 92 **EST:** 1983
SQ FT: 13,000
SALES (est): 39.21MM **Privately Held**
Web: www.scfhc.org
SIC: 8011 Clinic, operated by physicians

(P-17769)
SOUTH CNTY ORTHPD SPCLSTS A ME
Also Called: Orthowest
24331 El Toro Rd Ste 200 (92637-3116)
PHONE..................949 586-3200
James Mullen, *Pr*
Lance J Wrobel, *
Larry M Gursten, *
Lonnie J Moskow, *
Kyle W Coker, *
EMP: 91 **EST:** 1994
SALES (est): 23.94MM **Privately Held**
Web: www.scosortho.com
SIC: 8011 Orthopedic physician

(P-17770)
SOUTHERN CA GASTROENTEROLOGY
50 Alessandro Pl Ste A30 (91105-3141)
PHONE..................818 425-9761
Mary Yebremian, *Prin*
EMP: 92 **EST:** 2016
SALES (est): 1.06MM **Privately Held**
Web: www.insitedigestive.com
SIC: 8011 Gastronomist

(P-17771)
SOUTHERN CA HLTH & RHBLTN PRG
2610 Industry Way Ste A (90262-4028)
PHONE..................310 631-8004
Doctor Jack M Barbour, *CFO*
Rita Floyd, *
EMP: 165 **EST:** 1993
SQ FT: 6,000
SALES (est): 10.42MM **Privately Held**
Web: www.scharpca.com

SIC: 8011 Psychiatric clinic

(P-17772)
SOUTHERN CAL ORTHPD INST LP (PA)
6815 Noble Ave (91405-6516)
PHONE....................818 901-6600
Marc J Friedman, *Pt*
EMP: 135 **EST:** 1992
SALES (est): 171.1K **Privately Held**
Web: www.scoi.com
SIC: 8011 8249 Orthopedic physician; Medical training services

(P-17773)
SOUTHERN CAL PRMNNTE MED GROUP
Also Called: S C P M G
5620 Mesmer Ave (90230-6315)
PHONE....................310 737-4900
Olive Goldsmith, *Mgr*
EMP: 175
SALES (corp-wide): 68.1B **Privately Held**
Web: www.permanente.org
SIC: 8011 Medical centers
HQ: Southern California Permanente
Medical Group
393 Walnut Dr
Pasadena CA
626 405-5704

(P-17774)
SOUTHERN CAL PRMNNTE MED GROUP
Also Called: S C P M G
110 N La Brea Ave (90301-1708)
PHONE....................310 419-3306
Helen Jones, *Mgr*
EMP: 160
SALES (corp-wide): 68.1B **Privately Held**
Web: www.permanente.org
SIC: 8011 Medical centers
HQ: Southern California Permanente
Medical Group
393 Walnut Dr
Pasadena CA
626 405-5704

(P-17775)
SOUTHERN CAL PRMNNTE MED GROUP
Also Called: S C P M G
7825 Atlantic Ave (90201-5022)
PHONE....................323 562-6459
Maria Gonzalez, *Prin*
EMP: 175
SALES (corp-wide): 68.1B **Privately Held**
Web: www.permanente.org
SIC: 8011 Medical centers
HQ: Southern California Permanente
Medical Group
393 Walnut Dr
Pasadena CA
626 405-5704

(P-17776)
SOUTHERN CAL PRMNNTE MED GROUP
Also Called: S C P M G
21263 Erwin St (91367-3715)
PHONE....................818 592-3038
Cary Glass, *Brnch Mgr*
EMP: 189
SALES (corp-wide): 68.1B **Privately Held**
Web: www.permanente.org
SIC: 8011 Medical centers

HQ: Southern California Permanente
Medical Group
393 Walnut Dr
Pasadena CA
626 405-5704

(P-17777)
SOUTHERN CAL PRMNNTE MED GROUP
Also Called: S C P M G
27107 Tourney Rd (91355-1860)
PHONE....................661 222-2150
EMP: 182
SALES (corp-wide): 68.1B **Privately Held**
Web: www.permanente.org
SIC: 8011 Medical centers
HQ: Southern California Permanente
Medical Group
393 Walnut Dr
Pasadena CA
626 405-5704

(P-17778)
SOUTHERN CAL PRMNNTE MED GROUP
3501 Stockdale Hwy (93309-2150)
PHONE....................661 398-5085
EMP: 153
SALES (corp-wide): 68.1B **Privately Held**
Web: www.permanente.org
SIC: 8011 Medical centers
HQ: Southern California Permanente
Medical Group
393 Walnut Dr
Pasadena CA
626 405-5704

(P-17779)
SOUTHERN CAL PRMNNTE MED GROUP
5055 California Ave (93309-0701)
PHONE....................661 334-2020
EMP: 189
SALES (corp-wide): 68.1B **Privately Held**
Web: www.permanente.org
SIC: 8011 Medical centers
HQ: Southern California Permanente
Medical Group
393 Walnut Dr
Pasadena CA
626 405-5704

(P-17780)
SOUTHERN CAL PRMNNTE MED GROUP
3830 Martin Luther King Jr Blvd (90262-3625)
PHONE....................310 604-5700
EMP: 211
SALES (corp-wide): 68.1B **Privately Held**
Web: www.permanente.org
SIC: 8011 Medical centers
HQ: Southern California Permanente
Medical Group
393 Walnut Dr
Pasadena CA
626 405-5704

(P-17781)
SOUTHERN CAL PRMNNTE MED GROUP
6041 Cadillac Ave (90034-1702)
PHONE....................323 857-2000
Larry Poston, *Dir*
EMP: 211
SALES (corp-wide): 68.1B **Privately Held**
Web: www.permanente.org
SIC: 8011 Radiologist

(P-17782)
SOUTHERN CAL PRMNNTE MED GROUP
25825 Vermont Ave (90710-3518)
PHONE....................800 780-1230
EMP: 182
SALES (corp-wide): 68.1B **Privately Held**
Web: www.permanente.org
SIC: 8011 Medical centers
HQ: Southern California Permanente
Medical Group
393 Walnut Dr
Pasadena CA
626 405-5704

(P-17783)
SOUTHERN CAL PRMNNTE MED GROUP
4841 Hollywood Blvd (90027-5301)
PHONE....................323 783-5455
EMP: 233
SALES (corp-wide): 68.1B **Privately Held**
Web: www.permanente.org
SIC: 8011 Medical centers
HQ: Southern California Permanente
Medical Group
393 Walnut Dr
Pasadena CA
626 405-5704

(P-17784)
SOUTHERN CAL PRMNNTE MED GROUP
Also Called: Orthopedics Department
4760 W Sunset Blvd (90027-6063)
PHONE....................323 783-4893
Dolores Cobbarrubias, *Off Mgr*
EMP: 182
SALES (corp-wide): 68.1B **Privately Held**
Web: www.permanente.org
SIC: 8011 Orthopedic physician
HQ: Southern California Permanente
Medical Group
393 Walnut Dr
Pasadena CA
626 405-5704

(P-17785)
SOUTHERN CAL PRMNNTE MED GROUP
Also Called: Kaiser Permanente
4647 Zion Ave (92120-2507)
PHONE....................619 528-5000
Terry Belmont, *Prin*
EMP: 371
SALES (corp-wide): 68.1B **Privately Held**
Web: www.permanente.org
SIC: 8011 Medical centers
HQ: Southern California Permanente
Medical Group
393 Walnut Dr
Pasadena CA
626 405-5704

(P-17786)
SOUTHERN CAL PRMNNTE MED GROUP
Also Called: S C P M G
1630 E Main St (92021-5204)
PHONE....................619 528-5000
Brenda Scott-mead, *Mgr*
EMP: 182
SALES (corp-wide): 68.1B **Privately Held**

Web: www.permanente.org
SIC: 8011 Medical centers
HQ: Southern California Permanente
Medical Group
393 Walnut Dr
Pasadena CA
626 405-5704

(P-17787)
SOUTHERN CAL PRMNNTE MED GROUP
Also Called: S C P M G
4405 Vandever Ave (92120-3315)
PHONE....................619 516-6000
Thomas Volle, *Mgr*
EMP: 197
SALES (corp-wide): 68.1B **Privately Held**
Web: www.permanente.org
SIC: 8011 Medical centers
HQ: Southern California Permanente
Medical Group
393 Walnut Dr
Pasadena CA
626 405-5704

(P-17788)
SOUTHERN CAL PRMNNTE MED GROUP
Also Called: S C P M G
732 N Broadway (92025-1870)
PHONE....................760 839-7200
Alex Anderson, *Mgr*
EMP: 153
SALES (corp-wide): 68.1B **Privately Held**
Web: www.permanente.org
SIC: 8011 Medical centers
HQ: Southern California Permanente
Medical Group
393 Walnut Dr
Pasadena CA
626 405-5704

(P-17789)
SOUTHERN CAL PRMNNTE MED GROUP
Also Called: S C P M G
789 E Cooley Dr (92324-4007)
PHONE....................909 370-2501
EMP: 160
SALES (corp-wide): 68.1B **Privately Held**
Web: www.permanente.org
SIC: 8011 Medical centers
HQ: Southern California Permanente
Medical Group
393 Walnut Dr
Pasadena CA
626 405-5704

(P-17790)
SOUTHERN CAL PRMNNTE MED GROUP
6 Willard (92604-4694)
PHONE....................949 262-5780
Debra Dannemeyer, *Admn*
EMP: 182
SALES (corp-wide): 68.1B **Privately Held**
Web: www.permanente.org
SIC: 8011 Clinic, operated by physicians
HQ: Southern California Permanente
Medical Group
393 Walnut Dr
Pasadena CA
626 405-5704

(P-17791)
SOUTHERN CAL PRMNNTE MED GROUP
18081 Beach Blvd (92648-1304)
PHONE....................714 841-7293

P R O D U C T S & S V C S

EMP: 153
SALES (corp-wide): 68.1B **Privately Held**
Web: www.permanente.org
SIC: 8011 Medical centers
HQ: Southern California Permanente
   Medical Group
   393 Walnut Dr
   Pasadena CA
   626 405-5704

(P-17792)
SOUTHERN CAL PRMNNTE MED GROUP
Also Called: S C P M G
411 N Lakeview Ave (92807-3028)
PHONE..............................714 279-4675
Ryan Williams, *Mgr*
EMP: 160
SALES (corp-wide): 68.1B **Privately Held**
Web: www.permanente.org
SIC: 8011 Offices and clinics of medical
   doctors
HQ: Southern California Permanente
   Medical Group
   393 Walnut Dr
   Pasadena CA
   626 405-5704

(P-17793)
SOUTHERN CAL PRMNNTE MED GROUP
Also Called: S C P M G
30400 Camino Capistrano (92675-1300)
PHONE..............................949 234-2139
EMP: 160
SALES (corp-wide): 68.1B **Privately Held**
Web: www.permanente.org
SIC: 8011 Medical centers
HQ: Southern California Permanente
   Medical Group
   393 Walnut Dr
   Pasadena CA
   626 405-5704

(P-17794)
SOUTHERN CAL PRMNNTE MED GROUP
Also Called: S C P M G
1900 E 4th St (92705-3910)
PHONE..............................714 967-4760
Julie White-dahlgren, *Brnch Mgr*
EMP: 153
SALES (corp-wide): 68.1B **Privately Held**
Web: www.permanente.org
SIC: 8011 8049 Obstetrician; Psychiatric
   social worker
HQ: Southern California Permanente
   Medical Group
   393 Walnut Dr
   Pasadena CA
   626 405-5704

(P-17795)
ST JSEPH HERITG MED GROUP LLC (PA)
Also Called: Yorba Park Medical Group
2212 E 4th St Ste 201 (92705-3872)
PHONE..............................714 633-1011
Charles Foster, *Pr*
Benjamin Harper Md, *Prin*
C R Burke, *
Ivan Nichols Md, *Prin*
Dennis Long Md, *Treas*
▲ **EMP:** 134 **EST:** 1964
SQ FT: 58,000
SALES (est): 24.53MM
SALES (corp-wide): 24.53MM **Privately
Held**
Web: www.sjhmg.org

SIC: 8011 General and family practice,
   physician/surgeon

(P-17796)
SUCCESS HEALTHCARE 1 LLC
Also Called: Acute Psychiatric Hospital
7500 Hellman Ave (91770-2216)
PHONE..............................626 288-1160
EMP: 633
SALES (corp-wide): 87.5MM **Privately
Held**
Web: www.silverlakemc.com
SIC: 8011 Offices and clinics of medical
   doctors
PA: Success Healthcare 1, Llc
   1711 W Temple St
   Los Angeles CA
   213 989-6100

(P-17797)
SULPIZIO CARDIOVASCULAR CENTER
9434 Medical Center Dr (92037-1337)
PHONE..............................858 657-7000
EMP: 110 **EST:** 2015
SALES (est): 2.34MM
SALES (corp-wide): 534.4MM **Privately
Held**
Web: health.ucsd.edu
SIC: 8011 Cardiologist and cardio-vascular
   specialist
HQ: University Of California, San Diego
   9500 Gilman Dr
   La Jolla CA
   858 534-2230

(P-17798)
SUN HEALTHCARE GROUP INC (DH)
27442 Portola Pkwy Ste 200 (92610-2822)
▲ **EMP:** 300 **EST:** 1993
SALES (est): 2.28B
SALES (corp-wide): 5.86B **Publicly Held**
Web: www.sunh.com
SIC: 8011 8322 Medical insurance plan;
   Referral service for personal and social
   problems
HQ: Genesis Hc Llc
   101 E State St
   Kennett Square PA
   610 444-6350

(P-17799)
SYMBION INC
Also Called: Specialty Surgical of Westlake
696 Hampshire Rd Ste 100 (91361-4456)
PHONE..............................805 413-7920
Kelly Kapp, *Brnch Mgr*
EMP: 127
Web: www.surgerypartners.com
SIC: 8011 Surgeon
HQ: Symbion, Inc.
   340 Seven Springs Way
   Brentwood TN
   615 234-5900

(P-17800)
SYMBION INC
Also Called: Specialty Sugical Ctr Encino
16501 Ventura Blvd Ste 103 (91436-2007)
PHONE..............................818 501-1080
Michael Roub, *Brnch Mgr*
EMP: 119
Web: www.surgerypartners.com
SIC: 8011 Surgeon
HQ: Symbion, Inc.
   340 Seven Springs Way
   Brentwood TN
   615 234-5900

(P-17801)
TENET HEALTHSYSTEM MEDICAL INC
Also Called: Lakewood Regional Medical Ctr
3700 South St (90712-1419)
PHONE..............................562 531-2550
Carol Mammolite, *Brnch Mgr*
EMP: 474
SALES (corp-wide): 19.58B **Publicly Held**
Web: validate.perfdrive.com
SIC: 8011 8062 Medical centers; General
   medical and surgical hospitals
HQ: Tenet Healthsystem Medical, Inc.
   14201 Dallas Pkwy
   Dallas TX
   469 893-2000

(P-17802)
TENET HEALTHSYSTEM MEDICAL INC
Los Alamitos Med Ctr
3751 Katella Ave (90720-3113)
PHONE..............................805 546-7698
Michelle Finney, *Prin*
EMP: 263
SALES (corp-wide): 19.58B **Publicly Held**
Web: validate.perfdrive.com
SIC: 8011 8062 Offices and clinics of
   medical doctors; General medical and
   surgical hospitals
HQ: Tenet Healthsystem Medical, Inc.
   14201 Dallas Pkwy
   Dallas TX
   469 893-2000

(P-17803)
TENET HEALTHSYSTEM MEDICAL INC
Also Called: Leisure World Pharmacy
1661 Golden Rain Rd (90740-4907)
P.O. Box 2685 (90740-1685)
PHONE..............................562 493-9581
Diana Doyle, *Mgr*
EMP: 148
SALES (corp-wide): 19.58B **Publicly Held**
Web: www.mygnp.com
SIC: 8011 5912 Offices and clinics of
   medical doctors; Drug stores
HQ: Tenet Healthsystem Medical, Inc.
   14201 Dallas Pkwy
   Dallas TX
   469 893-2000

(P-17804)
THE ORTHOPEDIC INSTITUTE OF
616 Witmer St (90017-2308)
PHONE..............................213 977-2010
EMP: 5027 **EST:** 1990
SALES (est): 840.73K
SALES (corp-wide): 923.01K **Privately
Held**
SIC: 8011 Orthopedic physician
HQ: Pih Health Good Samaritan Hospital
   1225 Wilshire Blvd
   Los Angeles CA
   213 977-2121

(P-17805)
TOWER HMTLOGY ONCLOGY MED GROU
9090 Wilshire Blvd Ste 200 (90211-1848)
P.O. Box 5624 (90209-5605)
PHONE..............................310 888-8680
Robert W Decker Md, *Pt*
Leland M Green Md, *Pt*
EMP: 94 **EST:** 1992
SQ FT: 13,000
SALES (est): 9.61MM **Privately Held**

Web: www.cedars-sinai.org
SIC: 8011 Hematologist

(P-17806)
TRANSLTNAL PLMNARY IMMNLOGY RE
Also Called: Southern Cal Fd Allergy Inst
701 E 28th St Ste 419 (90806-2775)
PHONE..............................562 490-9900
Doctor Inderpal Randhawa, *Prin*
EMP: 90 **EST:** 2016
SALES (est): 10.32MM **Privately Held**
Web: www.foodallergyinstitute.com
SIC: 8011 Allergist

(P-17807)
TRUECARE ✪
150 Valpreda Rd (92069-2973)
PHONE..............................760 736-6767
Michelle D Gonzalez, *Pr*
EMP: 158 **EST:** 2022
SALES (est): 12.72MM **Privately Held**
Web: www.truecare.org
SIC: 8011 Primary care medical clinic

(P-17808)
TRUXTUN RADIOLOGY MED GROUP LP
20960 Sage Ln Ste B (93561-6408)
PHONE..............................661 822-6619
EMP: 141
Web: www.radnet.com
SIC: 8011 Radiology
HQ: Truxtun Radiology Medical Group, Lp
   1817 Truxtun Ave
   Bakersfield CA

(P-17809)
TRUXTUN RADIOLOGY MED GROUP LP
3940 San Dimas St (93301-1458)
PHONE..............................661 325-6200
Girish Patel, *Brnch Mgr*
EMP: 141
Web: www.radnet.com
SIC: 8011 Radiology
HQ: Truxtun Radiology Medical Group, Lp
   1817 Truxtun Ave
   Bakersfield CA

(P-17810)
TRUXTUN RADIOLOGY MED GROUP LP
1917 Truxtun Ave (93301-5010)
PHONE..............................661 616-1201
EMP: 141
Web: www.radnet.com
SIC: 8011 Radiologist
HQ: Truxtun Radiology Medical Group, Lp
   1817 Truxtun Ave
   Bakersfield CA

(P-17811)
TRUXTUN RADIOLOGY MED GROUP LP
11622 Harrington St (93311-9273)
PHONE..............................661 205-6567
EMP: 141
Web: www.radnet.com
SIC: 8011 Radiologist
HQ: Truxtun Radiology Medical Group, Lp
   1817 Truxtun Ave
   Bakersfield CA

(P-17812)
TWIN CITIES COMMUNITY HOSP INC
1100 Las Tablas Rd (93465-9704)

PHONE...............................805 434-3500
Mark P Lisa, *CEO*
Paul Posmosga, *
EMP: 450 **EST:** 1977
SQ FT: 120,000
SALES (est): 17.75K
SALES (corp-wide): 19.58B **Publicly Held**
SIC: 8011 8062 Medical centers; General medical and surgical hospitals
PA: Tenet Healthcare Corporation
14201 Dallas Pkwy
Dallas TX
469 893-2200

(P-17813)
UCSD NEUROSCIENCE CENTER
6645 Alvarado Rd (92120-5208)
PHONE...............................619 287-7661
David D Barba, *Prin*
EMP: 100 **EST:** 2010
SALES (est): 223.47K **Privately Held**
SIC: 8011 Primary care medical clinic

(P-17814)
UNITED FMLY CARE INC A MED COR
8110 Mango Ave Ste 104 (92335-3603)
PHONE...............................909 874-1679
Keith Schauermann, *Pr*
EMP: 120 **EST:** 1999
SALES (est): 10.69MM **Privately Held**
Web: pmg.optum.com
SIC: 8011 General and family practice, physician/surgeon

(P-17815)
UNIVERSITY CALIFORNIA IRVINE
Also Called: Barr, Ronald J MD /UCI Med Gro
101 The City Dr S (92868-3201)
PHONE...............................714 456-7890
EMP: 114
SALES (corp-wide): 534.4MM **Privately Held**
Web: www.uci.edu
SIC: 8011 8221 9411 Dermatologist; University; Administration of educational programs
HQ: University Of California, Irvine
510 Aldrich Hall
Irvine CA
949 824-5011

(P-17816)
UNIVERSITY CALIFORNIA IRVINE
Also Called: UIC
101 The City Dr S Ste 313 (92868-3201)
PHONE...............................714 456-6966
Sharon Mccarthy, *Mgr*
EMP: 80
SALES (corp-wide): 534.4MM **Privately Held**
Web: www.uci.edu
SIC: 8011 8221 9411 Surgeon; University; Administration of educational programs
HQ: University Of California, Irvine
510 Aldrich Hall
Irvine CA
949 824-5011

(P-17817)
UNIVERSITY CALIFORNIA IRVINE
Also Called: Uc Irvine Hlth Rgonal Burn Ctr
101 The City Dr S Bldg 1a (92868-3201)
PHONE...............................714 456-6170
EMP: 1757
SALES (corp-wide): 534.4MM **Privately Held**

Web: www.uci.edu
SIC: 8011 8221 9411 Medical centers; University; Administration of educational programs
HQ: University Of California, Irvine
510 Aldrich Hall
Irvine CA
949 824-5011

(P-17818)
UNIVERSITY CALIFORNIA IRVINE
Also Called: UCI Family Health Center
800 N Main St (92701-3576)
PHONE...............................714 480-2443
Nancy Downey Hurtado, *Mgr*
EMP: 262
SQ FT: 49,361
SALES (corp-wide): 534.4MM **Privately Held**
Web: www.uci.edu
SIC: 8011 8221 9411 Medical centers; University; Administration of educational programs
HQ: University Of California, Irvine
510 Aldrich Hall
Irvine CA
949 824-5011

(P-17819)
UPLIFT FAMILY SERVICES
Also Called: Asian Pacific Family Center
9353 Valley Blvd Ste C (91770-1923)
PHONE...............................626 287-2988
Terry Gock, *Dir*
EMP: 95
SALES (corp-wide): 147.1MM **Privately Held**
Web: www.pacificclinics.org
SIC: 8011 8322 8093 Clinic, operated by physicians; Individual and family services; Mental health clinic, outpatient
PA: Uplift Family Services
251 Llewellyn Ave
Campbell CA
408 379-3790

(P-17820)
US DERMATOLOGY MEDICAL MANAGEMENT INC
1401 N Batavia St Ste 204 (92867-3500)
P.O. Box 7587 (78683-7587)
PHONE...............................817 962-2157
EMP: 92
SIC: 8011 Dermatologist

(P-17821)
VALLEY COMMUNITY HEALTHCARE
6801 Coldwater Canyon Ave Ste 1b (91605-5164)
PHONE...............................818 763-8836
Paula Wilson, *CEO*
Lee Huey, *
EMP: 300 **EST:** 1970
SQ FT: 15,000
SALES (est): 32.36MM **Privately Held**
Web: www.valleycommunityhealthcare.org
SIC: 8011 Clinic, operated by physicians

(P-17822)
VANGUARD HEALTH SYSTEMS INC
Also Called: North Anaheim Surgery Center
1154 N Euclid St (92801-1955)
PHONE...............................714 635-6272
J Rasmussen, *Admn*
Jeanette Rasmussen, *Admn*

EMP: 387 **EST:** 1991
SQ FT: 12,000
SALES (est): 7.99MM
SALES (corp-wide): 19.58B **Publicly Held**
SIC: 8011 5999 Ambulatory surgical center; Medical apparatus and supplies
HQ: Vanguard Health Systems, Inc.
20 Burton Hills Blvd # 100
Nashville TN
615 665-6000

(P-17823)
VENICE FMLY CLINIC FOUNDATION (PA)
604 Rose Ave (90291-2767)
PHONE...............................310 664-7703
Mitesh Popat, *CEO*
Lee Rosenberg, *
Karl Keener, *
Gordon Lee, *
William Flumenbaum, *Ch*
EMP: 84 **EST:** 2010
SALES (est): 84.76MM
SALES (corp-wide): 84.76MM **Privately Held**
Web: www.venicefamilyclinic.org
SIC: 8011 Clinic, operated by physicians

(P-17824)
VENTURA CNTY OBSTET GYNCLGIC M
2795 Loma Vista Rd (93003-1544)
PHONE...............................805 643-8695
Richard Reisman, *Pr*
Steven Coyle, *VP*
John C Gustafson, *Sec*
EMP: 92 **EST:** 1977
SALES (est): 5.72MM **Privately Held**
Web: www.vtaobgyn.com
SIC: 8011 Gynecologist

(P-17825)
VENTURA COUNTY MEDICAL CENTER
Also Called: Santa Paula Hospital
845 N 10th St Ste 3 (93060-1348)
PHONE...............................805 933-8600
EMP: 121
SALES (corp-wide): 77.09MM **Privately Held**
Web: www.vchca.org
SIC: 8011 Medical centers
PA: Ventura County Medical Center
3291 Loma Vista Rd
Ventura CA
805 652-6000

(P-17826)
VENTURA COUNTY MEDICAL CENTER
Also Called: Ana Nacapa Surgical Associates
3291 Loma Vista Rd Bldg 343 (93003-3099)
PHONE...............................805 652-6201
Scott Arnold, *Prin*
EMP: 114
SALES (corp-wide): 77.09MM **Privately Held**
Web: www.anacapasurgical.com
SIC: 8011 Medical centers
PA: Ventura County Medical Center
3291 Loma Vista Rd
Ventura CA
805 652-6000

(P-17827)
VERDUGO HLLS PSYCHTHRAPY CTR A (PA)
Also Called: Pacific Child and Family Assoc

410 Arden Ave Ste 201 (91203-4006)
PHONE...............................818 241-6780
Ira Heilveil, *Pr*
EMP: 115 **EST:** 1988
SALES (est): 13.31MM **Privately Held**
SIC: 8011 Psychoanalyst

(P-17828)
VETERANS HEALTH ADMINISTRATION
Also Called: West Los Angeles V A Med Ctr
11301 Wilshire Blvd (90073-1003)
PHONE...............................310 478-3711
Donna Beiter, *Dir*
EMP: 1403
Web: benefits.va.gov
SIC: 8011 9451 Clinic, operated by physicians; Administration of veterans' affairs, Federal government
HQ: Veterans Health Administration
810 Vermont Ave Nw
Washington DC

(P-17829)
VETERANS HEALTH ADMINISTRATION
Also Called: Loma Linda Healthcare Sys 605
11201 Benton St (92357-1000)
PHONE...............................909 825-7084
Debbie Romero, *Brnch Mgr*
EMP: 1409
Web: benefits.va.gov
SIC: 8011 9451 Medical centers; Administration of veterans' affairs, Federal government
HQ: Veterans Health Administration
810 Vermont Ave Nw
Washington DC

(P-17830)
WATTS HEALTHCARE CORPORATION (PA)
Also Called: WATTS HEALTH
10300 Compton Ave (90002-3628)
PHONE...............................323 564-4331
Roderick Seamster, *Pr*
Roderick Seamster, *Pr*
Carroll J Mcneely, *CFO*
EMP: 180 **EST:** 2002
SALES (est): 39.95MM
SALES (corp-wide): 39.95MM **Privately Held**
Web: www.wattshealth.org
SIC: 8011 Clinic, operated by physicians

(P-17831)
WEST COVINA MEDICAL CLINIC INC (PA)
1500 W West Covina Pkwy Ste 100 (91790-2708)
PHONE...............................626 960-8614
Ziad Dabuni, *Pr*
Doctor Ziad Dabuni, *Pr*
Doctor Shivani Shah, *Ex VP*
Doctor Lucio Sanchez, *Sec*
Doctor Suntheetha Ali, *Treas*
EMP: 222 **EST:** 1950
SQ FT: 50,000
SALES (est): 9.18MM
SALES (corp-wide): 9.18MM **Privately Held**
SIC: 8011 Clinic, operated by physicians

(P-17832)
WEST DERMATOLOGY MED MGT INC (PA)
Also Called: West Dermatology
680 Newport Center Dr Ste 150 (92660)
PHONE...............................909 793-3000

P R O D U C T S & S V C S

J Robert West, *Pr*
EMP: 532 **EST:** 2004
SALES (est): 47.44MM
SALES (corp-wide): 47.44MM **Privately Held**
Web: www.westdermatology.com
SIC: 8011 Dermatologist

(P-17833)
WESTSIDE CRDVSCLAR MED GROUP I
99 N La Cienega Blvd Ste 203 (90211-2222)
PHONE...................310 289-9955
Norman E Lepor, *Prin*
EMP: 162
SALES (corp-wide): 8.57MM **Privately Held**
SIC: 8011 Radiologist
PA: Westside Cardiovascular Medical Group, Inc.
99 N La Cienega Blvd # 10
Beverly Hills CA
310 623-1150

(P-17834)
WHITE MEMORIAL MEDICAL CENTER
1720 E Cesar E Chavez Ave (90033-2414)
PHONE...................323 260-5739
Beth D Zachary, *Brnch Mgr*
EMP: 800
SALES (corp-wide): 789.42MM **Privately Held**
Web: www.adventisthealth.org
SIC: 8011 Medical centers
HQ: White Memorial Medical Center Inc
1720 E Cesar E Chavez Ave
Los Angeles CA
323 268-5000

8021 Offices And Clinics Of Dentists

(P-17835)
BOYD DENTAL CORPORATION
362 E Vanderbilt Way (92408-3593)
PHONE...................909 890-0421
EMP: 91
SALES (corp-wide): 1.02MM **Privately Held**
Web: www.idcsanbernardino.com
SIC: 8021 Dentists' office
PA: Boyd Dental Corporation
599 Inland Center Dr # 110
San Bernardino CA
909 384-1111

(P-17836)
CHROMIUM DENTAL II LLC
Also Called: Labs.dental
1524 Brookhollow Dr (92705-5426)
PHONE...................949 733-3111
Charbel Louis Karam, *Managing Member*
EMP: 220 **EST:** 2018
SALES (est): 9.56MM **Privately Held**
SIC: 8021 Dentists' office

(P-17837)
FAMILY HLTH CTRS SAN DIEGO INC
1809 National Ave (92113-2113)
PHONE...................619 515-2300
Brian Woolford Md, *Dir*
EMP: 348
SALES (corp-wide): 147.12MM **Privately Held**
Web: www.fhcsd.org

SIC: 8021 Offices and clinics of dentists
PA: Family Health Centers Of San Diego, Inc.
823 Gateway Center Way
San Diego CA
619 515-2303

(P-17838)
LANCE RYGG DENTAL CORP
10405 Tierrasanta Blvd (92124-2603)
PHONE...................858 492-9300
EMP: 162
SIC: 8021 Dentists' office
PA: Lance Rygg Dental Corp
2860 Michelle Fl 2
Irvine CA

(P-17839)
LEONID M GLSMAN DDS A DNTL COR
Also Called: Dentalville
5021 Florence Ave (90201-3802)
PHONE...................323 560-4514
EMP: 130
SALES (corp-wide): 4.66MM **Privately Held**
Web: www.panoramacitydentistca.com
SIC: 8021 Dentists' office
PA: Leonid M. Glosman, D.D.S., A Dental Corporation
7864 Van Nuys Blvd
Panorama City CA
323 266-1000

(P-17840)
LOUIS F MASCOLA DDS
Also Called: MASCOLA, LOUIS F DDS
3660 Lomita Blvd (90505-3938)
PHONE...................310 986-2930
Bartok Garcia, *Brnch Mgr*
EMP: 142
SALES (corp-wide): 874.34K **Privately Held**
Web: www.mascoladds.com
SIC: 8021 Dentists' office
PA: Louis F. Mascola, D.D.S., Inc.
770 W 9th St
San Pedro CA
310 831-2377

(P-17841)
MARINE CORPS COMMUNITY SVCS
Camp Pendleton Marine Corps Base (92055)
P.O. Box 555221 (92055-5221)
PHONE...................760 725-5187
EMP: 161
Web: www.marines.mil
SIC: 8021 9711 Offices and clinics of dentists ; Marine Corps
HQ: Marine Corps Community Services
3044 Catlin Ave
Quantico VA
703 432-0109

(P-17842)
MY KIDS DENTIST
24635 Madison Ave Ste E (92562-7556)
PHONE...................951 600-1062
Theresa Gomez, *Brnch Mgr*
EMP: 400
SALES (corp-wide): 13.98MM **Privately Held**
Web: www.mkdmurrieta.com
SIC: 8021 Dentists' office
PA: My Kid's Dentist
17000 Red Hill Ave
Irvine CA
909 854-1437

(P-17843)
PACIFIC DENTAL SERVICES LLC (PA)
Also Called: Pds
17000 Red Hill Ave (92614-5626)
P.O. Box 19723 (92623-9723)
PHONE...................714 845-8500
▲ **EMP:** 300 **EST:** 1991
SQ FT: 40,000
SALES (est): 1.77MM **Privately Held**
Web: www.pacificdentalservices.com
SIC: 8021 6794 Dental clinic; Franchises, selling or licensing

(P-17844)
PACIFIC DNTL SVCS HOLDG CO INC
17000 Red Hill Ave (92614-5626)
PHONE...................714 845-8500
Stephen E Thorne Iv, *CEO*
EMP: 114 **EST:** 2013
SALES (est): 9.05MM **Privately Held**
Web: www.pacificdentalservices.com
SIC: 8021 6794 Dental clinic; Franchises, selling or licensing

(P-17845)
PETER WYLAN DDS
Also Called: Bellflower Dental Group
10318 Rosecrans Ave (90706-2702)
PHONE...................562 925-3765
Peter Wylan D.d.s., *Owner*
EMP: 100 **EST:** 1955
SQ FT: 2,000
SALES (est): 4.64MM **Privately Held**
Web: www.bellflowerdentalgroup.com
SIC: 8021 8072 Dentists' office; Dental laboratories

(P-17846)
PREMIER DENTAL HOLDINGS INC (PA)
Also Called: Sonrava
530 S Main St Ste 600 (92868-4544)
P.O. Box 14227 (92863-1227)
PHONE...................714 480-3000
Daniel Crowley, *CEO*
EMP: 264 **EST:** 2010
SALES (est): 734.01MM
SALES (corp-wide): 734.01MM **Privately Held**
Web: www.westerndental.com
SIC: 8021 Dental clinic

(P-17847)
SETAREHSHENAS DENTAL CORP
1197 E Los Angeles Ave Ste E (93065-2868)
PHONE...................805 583-5700
Katayoun Setarehshenas, *Brnch Mgr*
EMP: 161
SIC: 8021 Dentists' office
PA: Setarehshenas Dental Corp
2860 Michelle Fl 2
Irvine CA

(P-17848)
TOAN D NGUYEN DDS INC
Also Called: TOAN D NGUYEN DDS INC
213 N San Dimas Ave (91773-2649)
PHONE...................909 599-3398
EMP: 87
SALES (corp-wide): 280.72K **Privately Held**
Web: www.sandimasdentistry.com
SIC: 8021 Dentists' office
PA: Toan D. Nguyen, D.D.S., Inc.
511 E 1st St Ste C

Tustin CA
562 926-3354

(P-17849)
WESTERN DENTAL SERVICES INC (HQ)
Also Called: Western Dental & Orthodontics
530 S Main St Ste 600 (92868-4544)
P.O. Box 14227 (92863-1227)
PHONE...................714 480-3000
TOLL FREE: 800
Daniel D Crowley, *CEO*
Jeffrey Miller, *CLO**
John Luther, *Chief Dental Officer**
Preet M Takkar, *
William Dembereckyj, *
EMP: 350 **EST:** 1984
SALES (est): 733.77MM
SALES (corp-wide): 734.01MM **Privately Held**
Web: www.westerndental.com
SIC: 8021 Dentists' office
PA: Premier Dental Holdings, Inc.
530 S Main St Ste 600
Orange CA
714 480-3000

8031 Offices And Clinics Of Osteopathic Physicians

(P-17850)
CARBON HEALTH TECHNOLOGIES INC
Also Called: La Costa Urgent Care
6971 El Camino Real Ste 101 (92009)
P.O. Box 355 (92067-0355)
PHONE...................760 603-3221
EMP: 136
SALES (corp-wide): 104.49MM **Privately Held**
Web: www.carbonhealth.com
SIC: 8031 8011 Offices and clinics of osteopathic physicians; Freestanding emergency medical center
PA: Carbon Health Technologies, Inc.
2100 Franklin St Ste 355
Oakland CA
415 223-2858

(P-17851)
PROVIDNCE FACEY MED FOUNDATION
Also Called: Exer
2655 1st St (93065-1547)
PHONE...................805 206-2000
EMP: 91
SALES (corp-wide): 91.37MM **Privately Held**
Web: www.facey.com
SIC: 8031 8011 Offices and clinics of osteopathic physicians; Offices and clinics of medical doctors
PA: Providence Facey Medical Foundation
15451 San Frnndo Mssion B
Mission Hills CA
818 365-9531

(P-17852)
PROVIDNCE FACEY MED FOUNDATION
191 S Buena Vista St (91505-4554)
PHONE...................818 861-7831
Jennifer Sung Md, *Brnch Mgr*
EMP: 91
SALES (corp-wide): 91.37MM **Privately Held**
Web: www.facey.com

SIC: **8031** 8011 Offices and clinics of osteopathic physicians; Offices and clinics of medical doctors
PA: Providence Facey Medical Foundation
15451 San Frnndo Mssion B
Mission Hills CA
818 365-9531

(P-17853)
VISTA COMMUNITY CLINIC (PA)
1000 Vale Terrace Dr (92084-5218)
PHONE..............................760 631-5000
Fernando Sanudo, *CEO*
Michele Lambert, *
EMP: **280** EST: 1972
SQ FT: 60,000
SALES (est): 83.58MM
SALES (corp-wide): 83.58MM **Privately Held**
Web: www.vistacommunityclinic.org
SIC: **8031** 8011 Offices and clinics of osteopathic physicians; Medical centers

8041 Offices And Clinics Of Chiropractors

(P-17854)
CHIROTECH INC
Also Called: Chirotouch
9265 Sky Park Ct Ste 200 (92123-4312)
PHONE..............................619 528-0040
Ron Nielle, *Owner*
EMP: **217** EST: 2007
SALES (est): 11.79MM **Privately Held**
Web: www.chirotouch.com
SIC: **8041** Offices and clinics of chiropractors

8042 Offices And Clinics Of Optometrists

(P-17855)
JAMES G MEYERS & ASSOCIATES
Also Called: Eye Exam of California
4353 La Jolla Village Dr Ste 180 (92122-1259)
PHONE..............................858 622-2165
Elliott Shapiro, *Owner*
EMP: **30**
SALES (corp-wide): 5.21MM **Privately Held**
Web: www.shapirofamilyoptometry.com
SIC: **8042** 3851 Offices and clinics of optometrists; Contact lenses
PA: James G Meyers & Associates
11700 Princeton Pike
Cincinnati OH
513 671-0111

(P-17856)
TOTAL VISION LLC
27271 Las Ramblas Ste 200a (92691-8041)
PHONE..............................949 652-7242
Scott Strachan, *Pr*
Doug Lattime, *VP Fin*
Broke Jakovich, *VP Opers*
EMP: **194** EST: 2014
SQ FT: 3,000
SALES (est): 19MM
SALES (corp-wide): 19MM **Privately Held**
Web: www.yourtotalvision.com
SIC: **8042** Group and corporate practice, optometrist
PA: Total Vision Holdings, Llc
277 Park Ave Fl 27
New York NY
212 704-5364

8049 Offices Of Health Practitioner

(P-17857)
BUTTERFLY IMPRINTS LLC
5545 Woodruff Ave # 35 (90713-1534)
PHONE..............................657 464-5188
EMP: **21**
SALES (corp-wide): 50.4K **Privately Held**
Web: www.imprinteducationconsulting.com
SIC: **8049** 7372 Psychologist, psychotherapist and hypnotist; Business oriented computer software
PA: Butterfly Imprints, Llc
5318 Knoxville Ave
Lakewood CA
657 464-5188

(P-17858)
CASA CLINA HOSP CTRS FOR HLTHC
910 E Alosta Ave (91702-2709)
PHONE..............................626 334-8735
EMP: **149**
SALES (corp-wide): 136.57MM **Privately Held**
Web: www.casacolina.org
SIC: **8049** Physical therapist
HQ: Casa Colina Hospital And Centers For Healthcare
255 E Bonita Ave
Pomona CA
909 596-7733

(P-17859)
CHE SNIOR PSYCHLOGICAL SVCS PC
4929 Wilshire Blvd Ste 510 (90010-3808)
PHONE..............................888 307-0893
Joe Tritel, *Brnch Mgr*
EMP: **110**
SALES (corp-wide): 22.32MM **Privately Held**
Web: www.cheservices.com
SIC: **8049** Clinical psychologist
PA: Che Senior Psychological Services, P.C.
3512 Quentin Rd
Brooklyn NY
718 854-8370

(P-17860)
IN STEPPS INC
Also Called: SUPPORT, TREATMENT, & EDUCATIO
10 Skypark Circle, Suite 110 (92614)
PHONE..............................949 474-1493
Y E M Bruinsma, *Ex Dir*
Yvonne E M Bruinsma, *Ex Dir*
Lindsey Lewis, *Reg Dir*
EMP: **99** EST: 2010
SALES (est): 202.24K **Privately Held**
Web: www.instepps.com
SIC: **8049** Occupational therapist

(P-17861)
INLAND VALLEY PARTNERS LLC
Also Called: Inland Valley Care & Rehab Ctr
250 W Artesia St (91768-1807)
PHONE..............................909 623-7100
EMP: **250** EST: 1998
SALES (est): 31.86MM **Privately Held**
Web: www.inlandvalleyhopepartners.org
SIC: **8049** Nurses and other medical assistants

(P-17862)
INSTITUTE FOR APPLIED BHVIOR A (PA)
Also Called: Iaba
5601 W Slauson Ave (90230-6589)
PHONE..............................310 649-0499
Gary W Lavigna Ph.d., *Pr*
▲ EMP: **140** EST: 1982
SALES (est): 25.84MM
SALES (corp-wide): 25.84MM **Privately Held**
Web: www.iaba.com
SIC: **8049** 8741 8093 Clinical psychologist; Management services; Specialty outpatient clinics, nec

(P-17863)
INSTITUTE FOR APPLIED BHVIOR A
9221 Corbin Ave (91324-2483)
PHONE..............................818 341-1933
EMP: **83**
SALES (corp-wide): 25.84MM **Privately Held**
Web: www.iaba.com
SIC: **8049** Nutrition specialist
PA: Institute For Applied Behavior Analysis, A Psychological Corporation
5601 W Slauson Ave # 290
Culver City CA
310 649-0499

(P-17864)
INSTITUTE FOR APPLIED BHVIOR A
Also Called: Iaba
2310 E Ponderosa Dr Ste 1 (93010-4747)
PHONE..............................805 987-5886
Gary Lavigna, *Dir*
EMP: **84**
SALES (corp-wide): 25.84MM **Privately Held**
Web: www.iaba.com
SIC: **8049** 8399 Clinical psychologist; Community development groups
PA: Institute For Applied Behavior Analysis, A Psychological Corporation
5601 W Slauson Ave # 290
Culver City CA
310 649-0499

(P-17865)
INTERCARE THERAPY INC
4221 Wilshire Blvd Ste 300a (90010-3537)
PHONE..............................323 866-1880
Naomi Heller, *Pr*
Eri Heller, *
EMP: **130** EST: 1979
SALES (est): 16.26MM **Privately Held**
Web: www.intercaretherapy.com
SIC: **8049** Psychologist, psychotherapist and hypnotist

(P-17866)
INTERFACE REHAB INC
774 S Placentia Ave Ste 200 (92870-6838)
PHONE..............................714 646-8300
EMP: **1000** EST: 1995
SQ FT: 10,000
SALES (est): 98.26MM **Privately Held**
Web: www.interfacerehab.com
SIC: **8049** Physical therapist

(P-17867)
INTERGRO REHAB SERVICE
13211 Foothill Blvd (92705-6203)
PHONE..............................714 901-4200
Sherrilyn Tong, *Pr*
EMP: **80** EST: 1990
SALES (est): 9.95MM **Privately Held**
Web: www.intergrorehab.com
SIC: **8049** Physical therapist

(P-17868)
LOCUMS UNLIMITED LLC
4141 Jutland Dr Ste 305 (92117-3657)
PHONE..............................619 550-3763
EMP: **979** EST: 2015
SALES (est): 1.75MM **Privately Held**
SIC: **8049** Nurses and other medical assistants
PA: Aya Healthcare, Inc.
5930 Cornerstone Ct W # 3
San Diego CA

(P-17869)
MICHAEL G FRTNSCE PHYSCL THRAP
Also Called: Fortanasce & Associates
24630 Washington Ave Ste 200 (92562-6131)
P.O. Box 661150 (91066-1150)
PHONE..............................626 446-7027
Michael Fortanasce, *Pr*
EMP: **120** EST: 1981
SALES (est): 3.72MM **Privately Held**
SIC: **8049** Physiotherapist

(P-17870)
RANCHO PHYSICAL THERAPY INC
Also Called: Rancho Physical Therapy
277 Rancheros Dr (92069-2976)
PHONE..............................760 752-1011
James Lin, *Brnch Mgr*
EMP: **166**
SALES (corp-wide): 9.79MM **Privately Held**
Web: www.ranchopt.com
SIC: **8049** 8011 Physical therapist; Offices and clinics of medical doctors
PA: Rancho Physical Therapy, Inc.
24630 Washington Ave # 200
Murrieta CA
951 696-9353

(P-17871)
ROBERT BALLARD REHAB HOSPITAL (HQ)
Also Called: Ballard Rehabilitation Hosp
1760 W 16th St (92411-1160)
PHONE..............................909 473-1200
Edward Palacios, *CEO*
Mary Hunt, *COO*
▲ EMP: **93** EST: 1993
SALES (est): 21.56MM
SALES (corp-wide): 690.44MM **Privately Held**
Web: www.ballardrehab.com
SIC: **8049** 8051 8069 Physical therapist; Skilled nursing care facilities; Specialty hospitals, except psychiatric
PA: Vibra Healthcare, Llc
4600 Lena Dr
Mechanicsburg PA
717 591-5700

(P-17872)
TAO OF WLLNESS SNTA MNICA A PR
171 S Los Robles Ave (91101-2417)
PHONE..............................626 397-1000
Emm Wang, *Brnch Mgr*
EMP: **87**
SALES (corp-wide): 4.51MM **Privately Held**
Web: www.taoofwellness.com
SIC: **8049** Acupuncturist

PRODUCTS & SVCS

PA: Tao Of Wellness Santa Monica, A
Professional Acupuncture Corporation
1240 6th St
Santa Monica CA
310 917-2200

(P-17873)
VENTURA COUNTY MEDICAL CENTER
300 Hillmont Ave (93003-1651)
PHONE..............................805 652-6729
Myung Ryang, *Prin*
EMP: 207
SALES (corp-wide): 77.09MM **Privately Held**
Web: www.vchca.org
SIC: 8049 Clinical psychologist
PA: Ventura County Medical Center
3291 Loma Vista Rd
Ventura CA
805 652-6000

(P-17874)
VISTA JV PARTNERS LLC ✪
2035 Corte Del Nogal Ste 200
(92011-1459)
PHONE..............................214 738-2771
Ajay Gupta, *CEO*
Herschel Sharp, *Sr VP*
EMP: 300 EST: 2023
SALES (est): 4.84MM **Privately Held**
SIC: 8049 Physical therapist

8051 Skilled Nursing Care Facilities

(P-17875)
ACCREDITED NURSING SERVICES
Also Called: Accredited Nursing Care
80 S Lake Ave Ste 630 (91101-4971)
PHONE..............................626 573-1234
Teresa Salvino, *Mgr*
EMP: 235
SALES (corp-wide): 32.94MM **Privately Held**
SIC: 8051 Skilled nursing care facilities
PA: Accredited Nursing Services
17141 Ventura Blvd # 201
Encino CA
818 986-6017

(P-17876)
AHMC GARFIELD MEDICAL CTR LP
Also Called: Garfield Medical Center
525 N Garfield Ave (91754-1202)
PHONE..............................626 573-2222
Patrick Petre, *CEO*
Steve Maekewa, *Pt*
EMP: 150 EST: 1997
SALES (est): 87.61MM
SALES (corp-wide): 476.02MM **Privately Held**
Web: www.ahmchealth.com
SIC: 8051 8062 Skilled nursing care facilities
; General medical and surgical hospitals
PA: Ahmc Healthcare Inc.
506 W Valley Blvd Ste 300
San Gabriel CA
626 943-7526

(P-17877)
AIR FORCE VILLAGE WEST INC
Also Called: Village West Health Center
17050 Arnold Dr (92518-2806)
PHONE..............................951 697-2000
Mary Carruthers, *CEO*

James L Melin, *Prin*
Charles Dalton, *
Ervin Reed, *
EMP: 350 EST: 1985
SQ FT: 494,000
SALES (est): 5.76MM **Privately Held**
Web: www.westmontliving.com
SIC: 8051 8052 Convalescent home with continuous nursing care; Intermediate care facilities

(P-17878)
ALAMITOS-BELMONT REHAB INC
Also Called: Alamitos Blmont Rhblttion Hosp
3901 E 4th St (90814-1632)
PHONE..............................562 434-8421
Shaun Dahl, *Admn*
Darian Dahl, *
EMP: 150 EST: 1969
SQ FT: 30,000
SALES (est): 11.7MM **Privately Held**
Web: www.alamitosbelmont.com
SIC: 8051 Skilled nursing care facilities

(P-17879)
AMADA ENTERPRISES INC
Also Called: View Heights Convalescent Hosp
12619 Avalon Blvd (90061-2727)
PHONE..............................323 757-1881
Shedrick D Jones, *CEO*
John Jones, *
EMP: 135 EST: 1968
SQ FT: 36,600
SALES (est): 13.61MM **Privately Held**
Web: www.viewheights.com
SIC: 8051 Convalescent home with continuous nursing care

(P-17880)
AMERICAN RETIREMENT CORP
2107 Ocean Ave (90405-2299)
PHONE..............................310 399-3227
EMP: 104
SALES (corp-wide): 2.83B **Publicly Held**
Web: www.brookdale.com
SIC: 8051 Skilled nursing care facilities
HQ: American Retirement Corporation
111 Westwood Pl Ste 200
Brentwood TN
615 221-2250

(P-17881)
ANTELOPE VLY RETIREMENT HM INC
Also Called: Antelope Vly Retirement Manor
44523 15th St W (93534-2847)
PHONE..............................661 949-5584
Mark Aronoss, *Brnch Mgr*
EMP: 179
SALES (corp-wide): 11.41MM **Privately Held**
SIC: 8051 8361 Skilled nursing care facilities ; Residential care
PA: Antelope Valley Retirement Home, Inc.
44523 15th St W
Lancaster CA
661 949-5584

(P-17882)
ASH HOLDINGS LLC
Also Called: Redlands Healthcare Center
1620 W Fern Ave (92373-4918)
PHONE..............................909 793-2609
Novie Sitanggang, *Managing Member*
EMP: 85 EST: 1999
SALES (est): 9.03MM
SALES (corp-wide): 1.53B **Privately Held**
Web: www.redlandshealthcarecenter.com

SIC: 8051 Skilled nursing care facilities
HQ: California Opco, Llc
100 E San Marcos Blvd
San Marcos CA

(P-17883)
ASMB LLC
Also Called: Berkley East Healthcare Center
2021 Arizona Ave (90404-1335)
PHONE..............................949 347-7100
Ryan Case, *CEO*
Jeffrey Bradshaw, *
EMP: 99 EST: 2019
SALES (est): 5.02MM **Privately Held**
Web: www.berkleyeast.com
SIC: 8051 Convalescent home with continuous nursing care

(P-17884)
ATHERTON BAPTIST HOMES
214 S Atlantic Blvd (91801-3298)
PHONE..............................626 863-1710
Craig Statton, *Pr*
Dennis E Mcfadden, *Pr*
Jackie Pascual, *
Angela Paniagua, *
Dale Torry, *
EMP: 200 EST: 1914
SQ FT: 42,000
SALES (est): 24.63MM **Privately Held**
Web: www.abh.org
SIC: 8051 Convalescent home with continuous nursing care

(P-17885)
B-SPRING VALLEY LLC
Also Called: Brighton Place Spring Valley
9009 Campo Rd (91977-1112)
PHONE..............................619 797-3991
EMP: 91 EST: 2006
SALES (est): 9.5MM **Privately Held**
Web: www.brightonplacesv.com
SIC: 8051 Convalescent home with continuous nursing care

(P-17886)
BAKERSFIELD HLTHCARE WLLNESS CN
Also Called: Rehabilitation Ctr Bakersfield
2211 Mount Vernon Ave (93306-3309)
PHONE..............................661 872-2121
EMP: 99 EST: 2009
SALES (est): 8.75MM **Privately Held**
Web: www.bakersfieldrehabilitation.com
SIC: 8051 Convalescent home with continuous nursing care

(P-17887)
BAKERSFIELDIDENCE OPCO LLC
Also Called: Kern River Transitional Care
5151 Knudsen Dr (93308-7199)
PHONE..............................661 399-2472
Jason Murray, *Prin*
Mark Hancock, *
EMP: 182 EST: 2016
SALES (est): 11.48MM
SALES (corp-wide): 1.53B **Privately Held**
Web: www.kernrivertc.com
SIC: 8051 Convalescent home with continuous nursing care
HQ: Providence Group North, Llc
262 N University Ave
Farmington UT
801 447-9829

(P-17888)
BAYSHORE HEALTHCARE INC
Also Called: Bella Vsta Trnstional Care Ctr

3033 Augusta St (93401-5820)
PHONE..............................805 544-5100
Benjamin Flinders, *CEO*
Johannah Tamba, *
Paul Mclean, *Sec*
EMP: 160 EST: 1975
SQ FT: 43,000
SALES (est): 8.59MM **Privately Held**
Web: www.compass-health.com
SIC: 8051 Convalescent home with continuous nursing care

(P-17889)
BAYSIDE HEALTHCARE INC
Also Called: South Bay Post Acute Care
553 F St (91910-3515)
PHONE..............................619 426-8611
Glenn Matthews, *Prin*
Perris Bennett, *
EMP: 176 EST: 2014
SALES (est): 4.8MM **Privately Held**
SIC: 8051 Skilled nursing care facilities

(P-17890)
BEAVER DAM HEALTH CARE CENTER
Also Called: Beverly Healthcare
340 Victoria St (92627-1914)
P.O. Box 1933 (92079-1933)
PHONE..............................949 642-0387
David Sedgwick, *Ex Dir*
EMP: 83
SALES (corp-wide): 825.28MM **Privately Held**
Web: www.victoriacares.com
SIC: 8051 Convalescent home with continuous nursing care
PA: Golden Living Llc
5220 Tennyson Pkwy # 400
Plano TX
972 372-6300

(P-17891)
BELL VILLA CARE ASSOCIATES LLC
Also Called: Rose Villa Healthcare Center
9028 Rose St (90706-6418)
PHONE..............................562 925-4252
David Howell, *Ex Dir*
EMP: 95 EST: 2003
SALES (est): 1.72MM **Privately Held**
Web: www.rosevillahealthcare.com
SIC: 8051 Convalescent home with continuous nursing care

(P-17892)
BEVERLY WEST HEALTH CARE INC
1020 S Fairfax Ave (90019-4401)
PHONE..............................323 938-2451
Louise Koss, *Pr*
Lydia Cruz, *
EMP: 85 EST: 1981
SQ FT: 23,848
SALES (est): 8.77MM **Privately Held**
SIC: 8051 Convalescent home with continuous nursing care

(P-17893)
BRIDGESTONE LIVING LLC
27101 Puerta Real Ste 450 (92691-8566)
PHONE..............................949 487-9500
John Gurrieri, *Pr*
EMP: 87 EST: 2014
SALES (est): 7.44MM
SALES (corp-wide): 3.03B **Publicly Held**
SIC: 8051 Skilled nursing care facilities
PA: The Ensign Group Inc
29222 Rncho Vejo Rd Ste 1

▲ = Import ▼ = Export
◆ = Import/Export

San Juan Capistrano CA
949 487-9500

(P-17894)
BURLINGTON CONVALESCENT HOSP (PA)
Also Called: View Park Convalescent Center
845 S Burlington Ave (90057-4296)
PHONE..............................213 381-5585
Jacob Friedman, *Pr*
Ervin Friedman, *
Kathleen Becker, *
EMP: 100 **EST:** 1967
SQ FT: 5,000
SALES (est): 11.13MM
SALES (corp-wide): 11.13MM Privately Held
Web: www.alternativesforseniors.com
SIC: 8051 8059 8052 Convalescent home with continuous nursing care; Convalescent home; Intermediate care facilities

(P-17895)
BURLINGTON CONVALESCENT HOSP
Also Called: View Park Convalescent Center
3737 Don Felipe Dr (90008-4210)
PHONE..............................323 295-7737
Joe Voltes, *Mgr*
EMP: 179
SQ FT: 40,000
SALES (corp-wide): 9.61MM Privately Held
Web: www.alternativesforseniors.com
SIC: 8051 Convalescent home with continuous nursing care
PA: Burlington Convalescent Hospital
845 S Burlington Ave
Los Angeles CA
213 381-5585

(P-17896)
CALIMESA OPERATIONS LLC
Also Called: CALIMESA POST ACUTE
13542 2nd St (92399-5396)
PHONE..............................909 795-2421
Covey Christensen, *
EMP: 105 **EST:** 2015
SALES (est): 9.66MM Privately Held
SIC: 8051 Skilled nursing care facilities

(P-17897)
CAMBRIDGE SIERRA HOLDINGS LLC
Also Called: RECHE CANYON REGIONAL REHAB CE
1350 Reche Canyon Rd (92324-9528)
PHONE..............................909 370-4411
Rb Bridges, *CEO*
EMP: 350 **EST:** 1991
SALES (est): 26.56MM Privately Held
SIC: 8051 Convalescent home with continuous nursing care

(P-17898)
CEDAR HOLDINGS LLC
Also Called: Highland Palms Healthcare Ctr
7534 Palm Ave (92346-3736)
PHONE..............................909 862-0611
Ryan Mccook, *Managing Member*
EMP: 99 **EST:** 2001
SALES (est): 9.45MM
SALES (corp-wide): 1.53B Privately Held
Web: www.highlandpalmshc.com
SIC: 8051 Convalescent home with continuous nursing care
HQ: California Opco, Llc
100 E San Marcos Blvd
San Marcos CA

(P-17899)
CEDAR OPERATIONS LLC
Also Called: Cedar Mountain Post Acute
11970 4th St (92399-2720)
PHONE..............................909 790-2273
EMP: 140 **EST:** 2001
SALES (est): 13.56MM
SALES (corp-wide): 28.4MM Privately Held
SIC: 8051 Skilled nursing care facilities
PA: Madison Creek Partners, Llc
26522 La Alameda Ste 300
Mission Viejo CA
949 449-2500

(P-17900)
CENTINELA SKLLED NRSING WLLNES
950 S Flower St (90301-4111)
PHONE..............................310 674-3216
Nichole Tons, *VP*
EMP: 99 **EST:** 2008
SQ FT: 6,000
SALES (est): 8.81MM Privately Held
Web: www.centinelanursingwest.com
SIC: 8051 Skilled nursing care facilities

(P-17901)
CHA HOLLYWOOD MEDICAL CTR LP
4636 Fountain Ave (90029-1830)
PHONE..............................213 413-3000
Annette Brunin, *Brnch Mgr*
EMP: 1487
Web: www.hollywoodpresbyterian.com
SIC: 8051 Skilled nursing care facilities
HQ: Cha Hollywood Medical Center Lp
1300 N Vermont Ave
Los Angeles CA
213 413-3000

(P-17902)
COASTAL VIEW HALTHCARE CTR LLC
Also Called: Coastal View Healthcare Center
4904 Telegraph Rd (93003-4109)
PHONE..............................805 642-4101
EMP: 96 **EST:** 2012
SALES (est): 10.96MM Privately Held
Web: www.coastalviewhcc.com
SIC: 8051 Convalescent home with continuous nursing care

(P-17903)
COLDWATER CARE CENTER LLC
Also Called: Sherman Village Hlth Care Ctr
12750 Riverside Dr (91607-3319)
PHONE..............................818 766-6105
EMP: 170 **EST:** 2010
SALES (est): 14.62MM Privately Held
Web: www.shermanvillagehc.com
SIC: 8051 Convalescent home with continuous nursing care

(P-17904)
COMMUNITY CARE CENTER
8665 La Mesa Blvd (91942-9503)
PHONE..............................619 465-0702
EMP: 85 **EST:** 2019
SALES (est): 19.44MM Privately Held
Web: www.communitycarectr.com
SIC: 8051 Convalescent home with continuous nursing care

(P-17905)
COMMUNITY CARE ON PALM RVRSIDE

4768 Palm Ave (92501-4012)
PHONE..............................951 686-9001
Ezequiel Bercovich, *Prin*
EMP: 85 **EST:** 2020
SALES (est): 1.1MM Privately Held
Web: www.cconpalm.com
SIC: 8051 Skilled nursing care facilities

(P-17906)
COMPASS HEALTH INC
Also Called: Compas Health
290 Heather Ct (93465-9738)
PHONE..............................805 434-3035
Mark Woolpert, *Pr*
EMP: 155
Web: www.compass-health.com
SIC: 8051 Convalescent home with continuous nursing care
PA: Compass Health, Inc.
200 S 13th St Ste 208
Grover Beach CA

(P-17907)
COMPASS HEALTH INC
Also Called: Mission View Health Center
1425 Woodside Dr (93401-5936)
PHONE..............................805 543-0210
Linda Lindsey, *Mgr*
EMP: 155
Web: www.compass-health.com
SIC: 8051 Skilled nursing care facilities
PA: Compass Health, Inc.
200 S 13th St Ste 208
Grover Beach CA

(P-17908)
COMPASS HEALTH INC
Also Called: Bayside Care Center
1405 Teresa Dr (93442-2457)
PHONE..............................805 772-7372
Harold Carder, *Mgr*
EMP: 155
Web: www.compass-health.com
SIC: 8051 Skilled nursing care facilities
PA: Compass Health, Inc.
200 S 13th St Ste 208
Grover Beach CA

(P-17909)
COMPASS HEALTH INC
Also Called: Arroyo Grande Care Center
1212 Farroll Ave (93420-3718)
PHONE..............................805 489-8137
Harold Carder, *Admn*
EMP: 155
Web: www.compass-health.com
SIC: 8051 Skilled nursing care facilities
PA: Compass Health, Inc.
200 S 13th St Ste 208
Grover Beach CA

(P-17910)
COMPASS HEALTH INC
Also Called: Danish Care Center
10805 El Camino Real (93422-8868)
PHONE..............................805 466-9254
Mark Woolpert, *Pr*
EMP: 155
Web: www.compass-health.com
SIC: 8051 Skilled nursing care facilities
PA: Compass Health, Inc.
200 S 13th St Ste 208
Grover Beach CA

(P-17911)
COMPASS HEALTH INC
Also Called: Alto Lucero Transitional Care
3880 Via Lucero (93110-1605)
PHONE..............................805 687-6651
Kirk Klotthor, *Admn*

EMP: 155
Web: www.compass-health.com
SIC: 8051 Convalescent home with continuous nursing care
PA: Compass Health, Inc.
200 S 13th St Ste 208
Grover Beach CA

(P-17912)
COUNTRY HILLS HEALTH CARE INC
Also Called: Country Hills Post Acute
1580 Broadway (92021-5124)
PHONE..............................619 441-8745
Glen Larson, *Pr*
EMP: 247 **EST:** 1991
SALES (est): 34.85MM Privately Held
Web: www.countryhills.com
SIC: 8051 Convalescent home with continuous nursing care

(P-17913)
COUNTRY VILLA NURSING CTR INC
Also Called: COUNTRY VILLA NURSING & REHABI
340 S Alvarado St (90057-2915)
PHONE..............................213 484-9730
Stephen Reissman, *CEO*
Steven Reissman, *CEO*
Diane Reissman, *Sr VP*
Eddie Rowles, *VP*
EMP: 125 **EST:** 1990
SQ FT: 18,000
SALES (est): 22.3MM Privately Held
Web: www.losangelesrehabwc.com
SIC: 8051 Convalescent home with continuous nursing care

(P-17914)
COUNTRY VILLA SERVICE CORP
1208 S Central Ave (91204-2504)
PHONE..............................818 246-5516
Adam Mitchel, *Admn*
EMP: 102
SALES (corp-wide): 88.5MM Privately Held
Web: www.evictionlawyer.com
SIC: 8051 Skilled nursing care facilities
PA: Country Villa Service Corp.
2400 E Katella Ave # 800
Anaheim CA
310 574-3733

(P-17915)
COUNTRY VILLA SERVICE CORP
3611 E Imperial Hwy (90262-2608)
PHONE..............................310 537-2500
EMP: 102
SALES (corp-wide): 88.5MM Privately Held
Web: www.evictionlawyer.com
SIC: 8051 Convalescent home with continuous nursing care
PA: Country Villa Service Corp.
2400 E Katella Ave # 800
Anaheim CA
310 574-3733

(P-17916)
COUNTRY VILLA SERVICE CORP
400 W Huntington Dr (91007-3470)
PHONE..............................626 445-2421
Shelly Andresen, *Prin*
EMP: 102
SALES (corp-wide): 88.5MM Privately Held
Web: www.huntingtondrivehcc.com
SIC: 8051 Skilled nursing care facilities
PA: Country Villa Service Corp.
2400 E Katella Ave # 800

Anaheim CA
310 574-3733

(P-17917)
COVENANT CARE CALIFORNIA LLC
Also Called: Buena Vista Care Center
160 S Patterson Ave (93111-2006)
PHONE..............................805 964-4871
David Hibarger, *Brnch Mgr*
EMP: 99
Web: www.covenantcare.com
SIC: 8051 Convalescent home with continuous nursing care
HQ: Covenant Care California, Llc
120 Vantis Dr Ste 200
Aliso Viejo CA

(P-17918)
COVENANT CARE LA JOLLA LLC
Also Called: La Jolla Nrsing Rhbltation Ctr
2552 Torrey Pines Rd Ste 1 (92037-3432)
PHONE..............................858 453-5810
Lisa Parker, *Admn*
Carol Tiaadwai, *Admn*
EMP: 200 **EST:** 2005
SALES (est): 30.77MM **Privately Held**
SIC: 8051 Convalescent home with continuous nursing care
HQ: Covenant Care California, Llc
120 Vantis Dr Ste 200
Aliso Viejo CA

(P-17919)
COVENANT CARE LLC (PA)
120 Vantis Dr Ste 200 (92656-2677)
PHONE..............................949 349-1200
EMP: 413 **EST:** 1994
SALES (est): 561.46MM **Privately Held**
SIC: 8051 Skilled nursing care facilities

(P-17920)
COVENANT RTIREMENT COMMUNITIES
Also Called: COVENANT RETIREMENT COMMUNITIES
2550 Treasure Dr (93105-4148)
PHONE..............................805 687-0701
EMP: 80
Web: www.covliving.org
SIC: 8051 Skilled nursing care facilities
HQ: Covenant Living West
5700 Old Orchard Rd # 10
Skokie IL

(P-17921)
COVENTRY COURT HEALTH CENTER
2040 S Euclid St (92802-3111)
PHONE..............................714 636-2800
Saun Dohl, *CEO*
EMP: 200 **EST:** 2000
SALES (est): 9.31MM **Privately Held**
Web: www.coventrycourt.org
SIC: 8051 Skilled nursing care facilities

(P-17922)
COVINA REHABILITATION CENTER
Also Called: REGENCY HEALTH SERVICES
261 W Badillo St (91723-1907)
PHONE..............................626 967-3874
Teresa Dearmond, *Dir*
Agnes Maron, *
EMP: 110 **EST:** 1971
SQ FT: 27,800
SALES (est): 11.96MM **Privately Held**

SIC: 8051 Skilled nursing care facilities

(P-17923)
CULVER WEST HEALTH CENTER LLC
4035 Grand View Blvd (90066-5211)
PHONE..............................310 390-9506
EMP: 90 **EST:** 1996
SQ FT: 25,000
SALES (est): 9.4MM **Privately Held**
Web: www.culverwest.com
SIC: 8051 Convalescent home with continuous nursing care

(P-17924)
DEL RIO SANITARIUM INC
Also Called: Del Rio Convalescent
7002 Gage Ave (90201-2014)
PHONE..............................562 927-6586
Joy Thune, *Pr*
EMP: 150 **EST:** 1963
SALES (est): 11.37MM **Privately Held**
SIC: 8051 Skilled nursing care facilities

(P-17925)
DEL ROSA VILLA INC
2018 Del Rosa Ave (92404-5642)
PHONE..............................909 885-3261
Carol Wagner Nha, *Admn*
Thomas S Plott, *
Elizabeth Plott, *
EMP: 85 **EST:** 1965
SQ FT: 20,000
SALES (est): 4.66MM **Privately Held**
Web: www.delrosavillapostacute.com
SIC: 8051 Convalescent home with continuous nursing care

(P-17926)
DELANO DST SKLLED NRSING FCLTY
1509 Tokay St (93215-3603)
PHONE..............................661 720-2100
Dennis Karnowski, *Admn*
EMP: 113 **EST:** 1991
SQ FT: 30,000
SALES (est): 23.48MM **Privately Held**
Web: www.nksthd.org
SIC: 8051 Convalescent home with continuous nursing care

(P-17927)
DOUGLAS FIR HOLDINGS LLC
Also Called: Huntington Vly Healthcare Ctr
8382 Newman Ave (92647-7038)
PHONE..............................714 842-5551
Brad Truhar, *Admn*
EMP: 145 **EST:** 2000
SALES (est): 18.28MM
SALES (corp-wide): 1.53B **Privately Held**
Web: www.hvhcc.com
SIC: 8051 Convalescent home with continuous nursing care
HQ: California Opco, Llc
100 E San Marcos Blvd
San Marcos CA

(P-17928)
DOWNEY COMMUNITY HEALTH CENTER
8425 Iowa St (90241-4929)
P.O. Box 340 (90241-0340)
PHONE..............................562 862-6506
Rich Coberly, *Admn*
Stanley Diller, *
EMP: 175 **EST:** 1980
SQ FT: 60,000
SALES (est): 21.79MM **Privately Held**

Web: www.downeycommunityhealthcenter.com
SIC: 8051 Convalescent home with continuous nursing care

(P-17929)
EISENBERG VLG OF THE LOS ANGLE
18855 Victory Blvd (91335-6445)
PHONE..............................818 774-3372
EMP: 83 **EST:** 2011
SALES (est): 32.73MM **Privately Held**
Web: www.lajhealth.org
SIC: 8051 Skilled nursing care facilities

(P-17930)
ELDORADO CARE CENTER LP
Also Called: Avocado Post Acute
510 E Washington Ave (92020-5324)
PHONE..............................619 440-1211
Jacob Graff, *Owner*
EMP: 298 **EST:** 2008
SALES (est): 39.22MM **Privately Held**
Web: www.avocadopostacute.com
SIC: 8051 8322 Convalescent home with continuous nursing care; Adult day care center

(P-17931)
EMERITUS CORPORATION
Also Called: Terrace, The
22325 Barton Rd (92313-5006)
PHONE..............................909 420-0153
Larry Smith, *Dir*
EMP: 150
SALES (corp-wide): 2.83B **Publicly Held**
Web: www.brookdaleliving.com
SIC: 8051 Skilled nursing care facilities
HQ: Emeritus Corporation
6737 W Wa St Ste 2300
Milwaukee WI

(P-17932)
EMERITUS CORPORATION
Also Called: Brookdale Clairemont
5219 Clairemont Mesa Blvd (92117-2206)
PHONE..............................858 292-8044
S Wheeler, *Ex Dir*
EMP: 170
SALES (corp-wide): 2.83B **Publicly Held**
Web: www.brookdaleliving.com
SIC: 8051 Skilled nursing care facilities
HQ: Emeritus Corporation
6737 W Wa St Ste 2300
Milwaukee WI

(P-17933)
EMERITUS CORPORATION
142 S Prospect St (92869-3842)
PHONE..............................714 639-3590
Bernice Holmes, *Ex Dir*
EMP: 140
SALES (corp-wide): 2.83B **Publicly Held**
Web: www.brookdaleliving.com
SIC: 8051 Skilled nursing care facilities
HQ: Emeritus Corporation
6737 W Wa St Ste 2300
Milwaukee WI

(P-17934)
EMERITUS CORPORATION
Also Called: Rosewood Court
411 E Commonwealth Ave (92832-2018)
PHONE..............................714 441-0644
Jane Kim, *Off Mgr*
EMP: 160
SALES (corp-wide): 2.83B **Publicly Held**
Web: www.emeritus.com
SIC: 8051 Skilled nursing care facilities
HQ: Emeritus Corporation
6737 W Wa St Ste 2300

Milwaukee WI

(P-17935)
EMERITUS CORPORATION
1001 N Lyon Ave (92545-1753)
PHONE..............................951 744-9861
EMP: 110
SALES (corp-wide): 2.83B **Publicly Held**
Web: www.brookdaleliving.com
SIC: 8051 Skilled nursing care facilities
HQ: Emeritus Corporation
6737 W Wa St Ste 2300
Milwaukee WI

(P-17936)
EMERITUS CORPORATION
Also Called: Emeritus At San Dimas
1740 S San Dimas Ave (91773-5108)
PHONE..............................909 394-0304
George Dualan, *Brnch Mgr*
EMP: 140
SALES (corp-wide): 2.83B **Publicly Held**
Web: www.brookdaleliving.com
SIC: 8051 Skilled nursing care facilities
HQ: Emeritus Corporation
6737 W Wa St Ste 2300
Milwaukee WI

(P-17937)
EMERITUS CORPORATION
Also Called: Emeritus At Casa Glendale
426 Piedmont Ave (91206-3448)
PHONE..............................818 246-7457
David Wilkens, *Brnch Mgr*
EMP: 150
SALES (corp-wide): 2.83B **Publicly Held**
Web: www.emeritus.com
SIC: 8051 Skilled nursing care facilities
HQ: Emeritus Corporation
6737 W Wa St Ste 2300
Milwaukee WI

(P-17938)
EMERITUS CORPORATION
Also Called: Emeritus At Villa Colima
19850 Colima Rd (91789-3411)
PHONE..............................909 595-5030
Wanda Reynolds, *Brnch Mgr*
EMP: 110
SALES (corp-wide): 2.83B **Publicly Held**
Web: www.brookdaleliving.com
SIC: 8051 Skilled nursing care facilities
HQ: Emeritus Corporation
6737 W Wa St Ste 2300
Milwaukee WI

(P-17939)
ENDURA HEALTHCARE INC
29222 Rancho Viejo Rd Ste 127 (92675)
PHONE..............................949 487-9500
EMP: 110 **EST:** 2014
SALES (est): 6.37MM
SALES (corp-wide): 3.03B **Publicly Held**
SIC: 8051 Skilled nursing care facilities
PA: The Ensign Group Inc
29222 Rncho Vejo Rd Ste 1
San Juan Capistrano CA
949 487-9500

(P-17940)
ENSIGN GROUP INC
Also Called: Panaroma Gardens
9541 Van Nuys Blvd (91402-1315)
PHONE..............................818 893-6385
Alicia Gamero, *Admn*
EMP: 202
SALES (corp-wide): 3.03B **Publicly Held**
Web: www.ensigngroup.net
SIC: 8051 Convalescent home with continuous nursing care

PA: The Ensign Group Inc
29222 Rncho Vejo Rd Ste 1
San Juan Capistrano CA
949 487-9500

(P-17941)
ENSIGN GROUP INC
Also Called: Whittier Hills Health Care Ctr
10426 Bogardus Ave (90603-2642)
PHONE..............................562 947-7817
Lisa Matarazzo, *Admn*
EMP: 198
SQ FT: 36,316
SALES (corp-wide): 3.03B **Publicly Held**
Web: www.ensigngroup.net
SIC: 8051 8059 Convalescent home with
continuous nursing care; Rest home, with
health care
PA: The Ensign Group Inc
29222 Rncho Vejo Rd Ste 1
San Juan Capistrano CA
949 487-9500

(P-17942)
ENSIGN GROUP INC
Also Called: Downey Care Center
13007 Paramount Blvd (90242-4329)
PHONE..............................562 923-9301
Marc Brian, *Prin*
EMP: 202
SALES (corp-wide): 3.03B **Publicly Held**
Web: www.ensigngroup.net
SIC: 8051 Convalescent home with
continuous nursing care
PA: The Ensign Group Inc
29222 Rncho Vejo Rd Ste 1
San Juan Capistrano CA
949 487-9500

(P-17943)
ENSIGN GROUP INC
Also Called: Mission Care Center
4800 Delta Ave (91770-1127)
PHONE..............................626 607-2400
Tin Nelson, *Dir*
EMP: 87
SALES (corp-wide): 3.03B **Publicly Held**
Web: www.missioncareandrehab.com
SIC: 8051 Convalescent home with
continuous nursing care
PA: The Ensign Group Inc
29222 Rncho Vejo Rd Ste 1
San Juan Capistrano CA
949 487-9500

(P-17944)
ENSIGN PALM I LLC
Also Called: ENSIGN
2990 E Ramon Rd (92264-7931)
PHONE..............................760 323-2638
Soon Burnam, *Treas*
Leeron Hever, *Admn*
EMP: 133 **EST:** 2001
SALES (est): 10.26MM
SALES (corp-wide): 3.03B **Publicly Held**
Web: www.premiercarecenter.net
SIC: 8051 Convalescent home with
continuous nursing care
PA: The Ensign Group Inc
29222 Rncho Vejo Rd Ste 1
San Juan Capistrano CA
949 487-9500

(P-17945)
ENSIGN SERVICES INC
29222 Rancho Viejo Rd Ste 127 (92675)
PHONE..............................949 487-9500
EMP: 90 **EST:** 2002
SALES (est): 51.62MM
SALES (corp-wide): 3.03B **Publicly Held**

Web: www.ensigngroup.net
SIC: 8051 Convalescent home with
continuous nursing care
PA: The Ensign Group Inc
29222 Rncho Vejo Rd Ste 1
San Juan Capistrano CA
949 487-9500

(P-17946)
ENSIGN SOUTHLAND LLC
Also Called: Southland Care
29222 Rancho Viejo Rd Ste 127 (92675)
PHONE..............................949 487-9500
EMP: 239 **EST:** 2000
SALES (est): 9.43MM
SALES (corp-wide): 3.03B **Publicly Held**
SIC: 8051 Extended care facility
PA: The Ensign Group Inc
29222 Rncho Vejo Rd Ste 1
San Juan Capistrano CA
949 487-9500

(P-17947)
ENSIGN WHITTIER EAST LLC
Also Called: ENSIGN
10426 Bogardus Ave (90603-2642)
PHONE..............................562 947-7817
EMP: 124 **EST:** 2001
SALES (est): 19.32MM
SALES (corp-wide): 3.03B **Publicly Held**
Web: www.whittierhillshealthcare.com
SIC: 8051 Convalescent home with
continuous nursing care
PA: The Ensign Group Inc
29222 Rncho Vejo Rd Ste 1
San Juan Capistrano CA
949 487-9500

(P-17948)
EPISCOPAL COMMUNITIES & SERVIC
Also Called: Canterbury, The
5801 Crestridge Rd (90275-4961)
PHONE..............................310 544-2204
Consuelo Haire, *Brnch Mgr*
EMP: 100
SALES (corp-wide): 86.44MM **Privately Held**
Web: www.ecsforseniors.org
SIC: 8051 8361 8059 Extended care facility;
Aged home; Personal care home, with
health care
PA: Episcopal Communities & Services For
Seniors
605 E Huntington Dr # 207
Monrovia CA
626 403-5880

(P-17949)
ESTRELLA INC
Also Called: Woodruff Convalescent Center
1340 Highland Ave # 12 (91010-2520)
PHONE..............................562 925-6418
Liberation De Leon Md, *Pr*
EMP: 110 **EST:** 1969
SALES (est): 6.25MM **Privately Held**
Web: www.estrella.com
SIC: 8051 Convalescent home with
continuous nursing care

(P-17950)
EVERGREEN AT LAKEPORT LLC
Also Called: Evergreen Healthcare Center
6212 Tudor Way (93306-7067)
PHONE..............................661 871-3133
Gloria Melliti, *Mgr*
EMP: 100
SALES (corp-wide): 9.75MM **Privately Held**

SIC: 8051 Convalescent home with
continuous nursing care
PA: Evergreen At Lakeport, L.L.C.
1291 Craig Ave
Lakeport CA
707 263-6382

(P-17951)
EVERGREEN HEALTH CARE LLC
323 Campus Dr (93203-1047)
PHONE..............................661 854-4475
Cody Rasmussen, *Ex Dir*
Rush Melliti, *
EMP: 1450 **EST:** 1985
SALES (est): 22.93MM
SALES (corp-wide): 900.43MM **Privately Held**
SIC: 8051 Convalescent home with
continuous nursing care
HQ: Evergreen At Chico, L.L.C.
4601 Ne 77th Ave Ste 300
Vancouver WA
530 342-4885

(P-17952)
FIVE STAR SENIOR LIVING INC
Also Called: Remington Club I & II
16925 Hierba Dr (92128-2688)
PHONE..............................858 673-6300
Kristen Crinigan, *Ex Dir*
EMP: 149
SALES (corp-wide): 934.59MM **Privately Held**
Web: www.theremingtonclub.com
SIC: 8051 Skilled nursing care facilities
HQ: Alerislife Inc.
255 Washington St Ste 300
Newton MA

(P-17953)
FREEDOM VILLAGE HEALTHCARE CTR
Also Called: REHABWORKS AT FREEDOM
VILLAGE
23442 El Toro Rd Bldg 2 (92630-6992)
PHONE..............................949 472-4733
EMP: 109 **EST:** 1977
SALES (est): 23.54MM **Privately Held**
Web: www.freedomvillage.org
SIC: 8051 8052 Convalescent home with
continuous nursing care; Intermediate care
facilities

(P-17954)
FRONT PORCH COMMUNITIES & SVCS
Also Called: Kingsley Manor
1055 N Kingsley Dr (90029-1207)
PHONE..............................323 661-1128
Cindy Gonzales, *Prin*
EMP: 174
SQ FT: 106,521
Web: www.frontporch.net
SIC: 8051 Skilled nursing care facilities
PA: Front Porch Communities And Services
800 N Brand Blvd Fl 19
Glendale CA

(P-17955)
FRONT PORCH COMMUNITIES & SVCS
Also Called: Fredericka Manor Care Center
111 Third Ave (91910-1822)
PHONE..............................619 427-2777
Loraine Wiencek, *Brnch Mgr*
EMP: 113
Web: www.frederickamanor.org
SIC: 8051 Convalescent home with
continuous nursing care

PA: Front Porch Communities And Services
800 N Brand Blvd Fl 19
Glendale CA

(P-17956)
FULLERTON HLTHCARE WLLNESS CNT
Also Called: Evergreen Fullerton Healthcare
2222 N Harbor Blvd (92835-2605)
PHONE..............................714 992-5701
Shlomo Rechnitz, *Pt*
Sharrod Brooks, *Pt*
EMP: 125 **EST:** 2013
SALES (est): 22.73MM **Privately Held**
Web: www.sunnyhillshc.com
SIC: 8051 Convalescent home with
continuous nursing care

(P-17957)
GARDEN CREST CNVLSCENT HOSP IN
Also Called: GARDEN CREST
RETIREMENT RESIDE
909 Lucile Ave (90026-1598)
PHONE..............................323 663-8281
Paul Barron, *CEO*
Vera Barron, *
EMP: 90 **EST:** 1954
SQ FT: 30,000
SALES (est): 6.95MM **Privately Held**
Web: www.gardencrestweb.com
SIC: 8051 8059 8322 Convalescent home
with continuous nursing care; Convalescent
home; Old age assistance

(P-17958)
GARDEN GROVE MEDICAL INVESTORS (HQ)
Also Called: Garden Grove Rehabilitation
12332 Garden Grove Blvd (92843-1804)
PHONE..............................714 534-1041
Nelia Yonzen, *Ex Dir*
EMP: 93 **EST:** 1976
SQ FT: 10,000
SALES (est): 130.3K
SALES (corp-wide): 139.21MM **Privately Held**
SIC: 8051 8069 Convalescent home with
continuous nursing care; Specialty
hospitals, except psychiatric
PA: Life Care Centers Of America, Inc.
3570 Keith St Nw
Cleveland TN
423 472-9585

(P-17959)
GARDENA RETIREMENT CENTER INC
14741 S Vermont Ave (90247-3098)
PHONE..............................310 327-4091
EMP: 104
SALES (corp-wide): 3.55MM **Privately Held**
Web: www.gardenaretirement.com
SIC: 8051 Skilled nursing care facilities
PA: Gardena Retirement-Center, Inc.
11627 Telg Rd Ste 200
Santa Fe Springs CA
310 327-4091

(P-17960)
GATE THREE HEALTHCARE LLC
Also Called: Palm Ter Hlthcare Rhbltition Ct
24962 Calle Aragon (92637-3883)
PHONE..............................949 587-9000
EMP: 172 **EST:** 2004
SALES (est): 14.43MM
SALES (corp-wide): 3.03B **Publicly Held**
Web: www.palmterracecares.com

SIC: 8051 Convalescent home with continuous nursing care
PA: The Ensign Group Inc
29222 Rncho Vejo Rd Ste 1
San Juan Capistrano CA
949 487-9500

(P-17961)
GENESIS HEALTHCARE LLC
425 Barcellus Ave (93454-6901)
PHONE.................805 922-3558
EMP: 757
Web: www.villamariapostacute.com
SIC: 8051 Convalescent home with continuous nursing care
HQ: Genesis Healthcare Llc
101 E State St
Kennett Square PA

(P-17962)
GENESIS HEALTHCARE LLC
Also Called: Spring Senior Assisted Living
20900 Earl St Ste 100 (90503-4309)
PHONE.................310 370-3594
EMP: 234
Web: www.genesishcc.com
SIC: 8051 Skilled nursing care facilities
HQ: Genesis Healthcare Llc
101 E State St
Kennett Square PA

(P-17963)
GEORGIA ATKISON SNF LLC
Also Called: Alliance Nrsing Rhbltation Ctr
3825 Durfee Ave (91732-2505)
PHONE.................626 444-2535
Eli Quinones, Managing Member
EMP: 81 EST: 1996
SQ FT: 30,000
SALES (est): 10.12MM Privately Held
SIC: 8051 Convalescent home with continuous nursing care

(P-17964)
GERI-CARE INC
Also Called: Harbor Post Accute Care Center
21521 S Vermont Ave (90502-1939)
PHONE.................310 320-0961
Emmanuel David, Pr
EMP: 100 EST: 1975
SQ FT: 30,000
SALES (est): 10.81MM Privately Held
Web: www.harborpostacute.com
SIC: 8051 Convalescent home with continuous nursing care

(P-17965)
GOLDEN STATE HABILITATION CONV (PA)
Also Called: Golden State Care Center
1758 Big Dalton Ave (91706-5910)
PHONE.................626 962-3274
Eden Salceda, Pr
Emmanual David, *
Claudio Hernandez, *
EMP: 175 EST: 1971
SALES (est): 9.1MM Privately Held
Web: www.gsccdd.com
SIC: 8051 8361 8052 Convalescent home with continuous nursing care; Residential care; Intermediate care facilities

(P-17966)
GPH MEDICAL & LEGAL SERVICES (PA)
Also Called: G P H Medical Services
468 N Camden Dr (90210-4507)
PHONE.................213 207-2700
▲ EMP: 187 EST: 1986

SQ FT: 4,000
SALES (est): 12.12MM Privately Held
Web: www.nulegal.com
SIC: 8051 8059 7361 7812 Skilled nursing care facilities; Convalescent home; Nurses' registry; Television film production

(P-17967)
GRAND AVENUE HLTH HOLDINGS LLC
29222 Rancho Viejo Rd Ste 127 (92675)
PHONE.................949 487-9500
EMP: 92 EST: 2018
SALES (est): 2.93MM
SALES (corp-wide): 3.03B Publicly Held
SIC: 8051 Convalescent home with continuous nursing care
PA: The Ensign Group Inc
29222 Rncho Vejo Rd Ste 1
San Juan Capistrano CA
949 487-9500

(P-17968)
HARBOR GLEN CARE CENTER
Also Called: Arbor Glen Care Center
1033 E Arrow Hwy (91740-6110)
PHONE.................626 963-7531
Kevin Thomas, Owner
EMP: 161 EST: 2000
SALES (est): 23.2MM
SALES (corp-wide): 3.03B Publicly Held
Web: www.arborglencare.com
SIC: 8051 Convalescent home with continuous nursing care
PA: The Ensign Group Inc
29222 Rncho Vejo Rd Ste 1
San Juan Capistrano CA
949 487-9500

(P-17969)
HCR MANORCARE MED SVCS FLA LLC
Also Called: Manorcare Health Services
24962 Calle Aragon (92653)
PHONE.................949 587-9000
EMP: 150
SALES (corp-wide): 2.27B Publicly Held
SIC: 8051 Skilled nursing care facilities
HQ: Hcr Manorcare Medical Services Of Florida, Llc
333 N Summit St Ste 100
Toledo OH
419 252-5500

(P-17970)
HEALTHCARE CTR OF DOWNEY LLC
Also Called: Lakewood Healthcare Center
12023 Lakewood Blvd (90242-2635)
PHONE.................562 869-0978
Vince Hambright, CEO
EMP: 250 EST: 2011
SQ FT: 1,076,391
SALES (est): 19.44MM Privately Held
Web: www.lwhealthcare.com
SIC: 8051 Mental retardation hospital

(P-17971)
HEALTHCARE INVESTMENTS INC (PA)
Also Called: Rosecrans Care Center
1140 W Rosecrans Ave (90247-2664)
PHONE.................310 323-3194
Pompeyo Rosales, Pr
Gonzalo Delrosario, *
EMP: 91 EST: 1991
SALES (est): 12.64MM Privately Held
SIC: 8051 Convalescent home with continuous nursing care

(P-17972)
HEALTHCARE MANAGEMENT SYSTEMS INC
Also Called: Bradley Court
900 Lane Ave Ste 190 (91914-3502)
PHONE.................619 521-9641
EMP: 120
SIC: 8051 Skilled nursing care facilities

(P-17973)
HERITAGE HEALTH CARE INC
Also Called: Heritage Gardens Hlth Care Ctr
25271 Barton Rd (92354-3013)
PHONE.................909 796-0216
Stephen Flood, CEO
Stephen Flood, Dir
Gregory S Goings, *
Jim Kilian, *
EMP: 150 EST: 1963
SALES (est): 10.93MM Privately Held
Web: www.progressivecarecenters.com
SIC: 8051 8059 Skilled nursing care facilities; Rest home, with health care

(P-17974)
HIGHLAND HLTHCARE CMLLIA GRDNS
Also Called: Camellia Gardens Care Center
1920 N Fair Oaks Ave (91103-1623)
PHONE.................626 798-6777
Samuel Chazanow, CEO
Bernard Friedman, *
EMP: 130 EST: 2019
SALES (est): 9.34MM Privately Held
Web: www.camelliagardenscc.com
SIC: 8051 Convalescent home with continuous nursing care

(P-17975)
HYDE PK REHABILITATION CTR LLC
6520 West Blvd (90043-4311)
PHONE.................323 753-1354
EMP: 90
SALES (est): 1.01MM Privately Held
SIC: 8051 Skilled nursing care facilities

(P-17976)
IMAGINATIVE HORIZONS INC
Also Called: Hillcrest Manor Sanitarium
1889 National City Blvd (91950-5517)
PHONE.................619 477-1176
Gary Byrnes, Pr
Rosella Byrnes, *
EMP: 84 EST: 1930
SQ FT: 30,000
SALES (est): 4.29MM Privately Held
Web: www.specialized-care.com
SIC: 8051 Skilled nursing care facilities

(P-17977)
INLAND CHRSTN HM FUNDATION INC
1950 S Mountain Ave Ofc (91762-6709)
PHONE.................909 395-9322
David Stienstra, Pr
Karen Miedema, *
EMP: 114 EST: 1973
SQ FT: 100,000
SALES (est): 86.27K Privately Held
Web: www.ichome.org
SIC: 8051 8052 6513 8361 Skilled nursing care facilities; Intermediate care facilities; Retirement hotel operation; Residential care

(P-17978)
INTERCOMMUNITY CARE CTRS INC

Also Called: Intercommunity Care Center
2626 Grand Ave (90815-1707)
PHONE.................562 427-8915
Russel Boydston, Brnch Mgr
EMP: 141
SQ FT: 32,159
SALES (corp-wide): 8.8MM Privately Held
Web: www.iccare.org
SIC: 8051 Convalescent home with continuous nursing care
PA: Intercommunity Care Centers, Inc.
2660 Grand Ave
Long Beach CA
562 426-1368

(P-17979)
J P H CONSULTING INC
4515 Huntington Dr S (90032-1940)
PHONE.................323 934-5660
EMP: 138
SALES (corp-wide): 52.03MM Privately Held
SIC: 8051 Skilled nursing care facilities
PA: J P H Consulting, Inc.
1101 Crenshaw Blvd
Los Angeles CA
323 934-5660

(P-17980)
JEWISH HM FOR THE AGING ORNGE
Also Called: HERITAGE POINTE
27356 Bellogente (92691-6341)
PHONE.................949 364-9685
David Zarnow, VP
Rena Loveless, *
EMP: 120 EST: 1969
SQ FT: 88,928
SALES (est): 12.33MM Privately Held
Web: www.heritagepointe.org
SIC: 8051 Skilled nursing care facilities

(P-17981)
KATELLA PROPERTIES
Also Called: Alamitos W Convalescent Hosp
3902 Katella Ave (90720-3304)
PHONE.................562 596-5561
Marilyn Gelgincolin, Dir
EMP: 85
SALES (corp-wide): 8.82MM Privately Held
Web: www.alamitoswest.com
SIC: 8051 Convalescent home with continuous nursing care
PA: Katella Properties
3952 Katella Ave
Los Alamitos CA
562 596-2773

(P-17982)
KNOLLS CONVALESCENT HOSP INC (PA)
Also Called: Desert Knlls Convalescent Hosp
16890 Green Tree Blvd (92395-5618)
PHONE.................760 245-5361
Gary L Bechtold, Pr
Larry Bechtold, *
Fred Bechtold, *
EMP: 130 EST: 1971
SQ FT: 5,421
SALES (est): 14.35MM
SALES (corp-wide): 14.35MM Privately Held
Web: www.knollswestpostacute.com
SIC: 8051 8052 Convalescent home with continuous nursing care; Intermediate care facilities

(P-17983)

KNOLLS WEST ENTERPRISE

Also Called: Knolls West Residential Care
16890 Green Tree Blvd (92395-5618)
PHONE.................................760 245-0107
Larry Bechtold, *Pt*
Gary Bechtold, *Pt*
Fred Bechtold, *Pt*
EMP: 161 **EST:** 1979
SQ FT: 44,000
SALES (est): 9.4MM
SALES (corp-wide): 14.35MM **Privately Held**
Web: www.knollswestpostacute.com
SIC: 8051 Convalescent home with continuous nursing care
PA: Knolls Convalescent Hospital, Inc.
16890 Green Tree Blvd
Victorville CA
760 245-5361

(P-17984)

LA JOLLA SKILLED INC

Also Called: ENSIGN
3884 Nobel Dr (92122-5700)
PHONE.................................858 625-8700
Glenn Matthews, *CEO*
Craig Fitch, *
Soon Burnam, *
EMP: 124 **EST:** 2014
SALES (est): 9.59MM
SALES (corp-wide): 3.03B **Publicly Held**
Web: www.sprlj.com
SIC: 8051 Convalescent home with continuous nursing care
PA: The Ensign Group Inc
29222 Rncho Vejo Rd Ste 1
San Juan Capistrano CA
949 487-9500

(P-17985)

LEMON GROVE HEALTH ASSOC LLC

Also Called: Lemon Grove Care Rhbltttion Ctr
8351 Broadway (91945-2009)
PHONE.................................619 463-0294
Preet Kambo, *Ex Dir*
Mason Hunter, *
EMP: 298 **EST:** 2004
SALES (est): 23.25MM
SALES (corp-wide): 3.03B **Publicly Held**
Web: www.lemongrovecare.com
SIC: 8051 Convalescent home with continuous nursing care
PA: The Ensign Group Inc
29222 Rncho Vejo Rd Ste 1
San Juan Capistrano CA
949 487-9500

(P-17986)

LIFE CARE CENTERS AMERICA INC

27555 Rimrock Rd (92311-4230)
PHONE.................................760 252-2515
EMP: 188
SALES (corp-wide): 139.21MM **Privately Held**
Web: www.lcca.com
SIC: 8051 Convalescent home with continuous nursing care
PA: Life Care Centers Of America, Inc.
3570 Keith St Nw
Cleveland TN
423 472-9585

(P-17987)

LIFE CARE CENTERS AMERICA INC

Also Called: Life Care Centers of Escondido

1980 Felicita Rd (92025-5922)
PHONE.................................760 741-6109
Trent Weaver, *Admn*
EMP: 198
SALES (corp-wide): 139.21MM **Privately Held**
Web: www.lcca.com
SIC: 8051 Convalescent home with continuous nursing care
PA: Life Care Centers Of America, Inc.
3570 Keith St Nw
Cleveland TN
423 472-9585

(P-17988)

LIFE CARE CENTERS AMERICA INC

Also Called: Mirada Hlls Rehb Cnvlscent Hos
12200 La Mirada Blvd (90638-1306)
PHONE.................................562 947-8691
Selina Stewart, *Ex Dir*
EMP: 181
SALES (corp-wide): 139.21MM **Privately Held**
Web: www.lcca.com
SIC: 8051 Convalescent home with continuous nursing care
PA: Life Care Centers Of America, Inc.
3570 Keith St Nw
Cleveland TN
423 472-9585

(P-17989)

LIFE CARE CENTERS AMERICA INC

Also Called: Life Care Center of Norwalk
12350 Rosecrans Ave (90650-5064)
PHONE.................................562 921-6624
Steve Ramsdel, *VP*
EMP: 80
SALES (corp-wide): 139.21MM **Privately Held**
Web: www.lcca.com
SIC: 8051 Convalescent home with continuous nursing care
PA: Life Care Centers Of America, Inc.
3570 Keith St Nw
Cleveland TN
423 472-9585

(P-17990)

LIFE CARE CENTERS AMERICA INC

Also Called: Imperial Convalescent
11926 La Mirada Blvd (90638-1303)
PHONE.................................562 943-7156
Ted Stultz, *Mgr*
EMP: 139
SALES (corp-wide): 139.21MM **Privately Held**
Web: www.lcca.com
SIC: 8051 8741 Convalescent home with continuous nursing care; Management services
PA: Life Care Centers Of America, Inc.
3570 Keith St Nw
Cleveland TN
423 472-9585

(P-17991)

LIFE CARE CENTERS AMERICA INC

Also Called: Bel Tren Vlla Cnvalescent Hosp
16910 Woodruff Ave (90706-6036)
PHONE.................................562 867-1761
Tooren Bel, *Mgr*
EMP: 132
SALES (corp-wide): 139.21MM **Privately Held**
Web: www.lcca.com

SIC: 8051 Convalescent home with continuous nursing care
PA: Life Care Centers Of America, Inc.
3570 Keith St Nw
Cleveland TN
423 472-9585

(P-17992)

LIFE CARE CENTERS AMERICA INC

Also Called: Life Care Center of La Habra
1233 W La Habra Blvd (90631-5226)
PHONE.................................562 690-0852
Daniel Husband, *Admn*
EMP: 240
SALES (corp-wide): 139.21MM **Privately Held**
Web: www.lcca.com
SIC: 8051 Convalescent home with continuous nursing care
PA: Life Care Centers Of America, Inc.
3570 Keith St Nw
Cleveland TN
423 472-9585

(P-17993)

LIFE CARE RESIDENCES INC

Also Called: OAK HILL RESIDENTIAL CARE
612 Tranquility Gln (92027-3984)
P.O. Box 463094 (92046-3094)
PHONE.................................760 743-8843
John Gamble, *Dir*
Fie Gamble, *
Mary G Mcvickar, *Dir*
EMP: 23 **EST:** 1988
SQ FT: 36,000
SALES (est): 26.52K **Privately Held**
Web: www.hiddenglenn.org
SIC: 8051 1542 3732 Extended care facility; Commercial and office building contractors; Yachts, building and repairing

(P-17994)

LIGHTHOUSE HEALTHCARE CTR LLC

2222 Santa Ana S (90059-1350)
PHONE.................................323 564-4461
EMP: 99 **EST:** 2007
SALES (est): 16.01MM **Privately Held**
SIC: 8051 Skilled nursing care facilities

(P-17995)

LITTLE SSTERS OF THE POOR LOS

Also Called: Jeanne Jugan, A Residence
2100 S Western Ave (90732-4331)
PHONE.................................310 548-0625
Margaret Mcarthy, *Pr*
Michael Mugan, *
Clotilde Jardim, *
EMP: 100 **EST:** 1905
SQ FT: 145,530
SALES (est): 8.34MM **Privately Held**
Web: www.littlesistersofthepoorsanpedro.org
SIC: 8051 8361 8052 Extended care facility; Residential care; Intermediate care facilities

(P-17996)

LONG BEACH CARE CENTER INC

2615 Grand Ave (90815-1708)
PHONE.................................562 426-6141
William A Nelson, *Pr*
EMP: 108 **EST:** 2003
SQ FT: 43,962
SALES (est): 18.54MM **Privately Held**
Web: www.longbeach.gov

SIC: 8051 Convalescent home with continuous nursing care
PA: Life Care Centers Of America, Inc.
3570 Keith St Nw
Cleveland TN
423 472-9585

(P-17997)

LONGWOOD MANAGEMENT CORP

Also Called: Imperial Crest Healthcare Ctr
11834 Inglewood Ave (90250-2731)
PHONE.................................310 679-1461
Robert Villalub, *Admn*
EMP: 125
SALES (corp-wide): 79.33MM **Privately Held**
Web: www.longwoodmgmt.com
SIC: 8051 Convalescent home with continuous nursing care
PA: Longwood Management Corp.
4032 Wilshire Blvd Fl 6
Los Angeles CA
213 389-6900

(P-17998)

LONGWOOD MANAGEMENT CORP

Also Called: Magnolia Grdns Convalescent HM
17922 San Fernando Mission Blvd (91344-4043)
PHONE.................................818 360-1864
Ojijoji Gervacio, *Prin*
EMP: 99
SALES (corp-wide): 79.33MM **Privately Held**
Web: www.longwoodmgmt.com
SIC: 8051 Convalescent home with continuous nursing care
PA: Longwood Management Corp.
4032 Wilshire Blvd Fl 6
Los Angeles CA
213 389-6900

(P-17999)

LONGWOOD MANAGEMENT CORP

Also Called: Green Acres Lodge
8101 Hill Dr (91770-4169)
PHONE.................................626 280-2293
Karen Fugate, *Admn*
EMP: 110
SALES (corp-wide): 79.33MM **Privately Held**
Web: www.longwoodmgmt.com
SIC: 8051 Convalescent home with continuous nursing care
PA: Longwood Management Corp.
4032 Wilshire Blvd Fl 6
Los Angeles CA
213 389-6900

(P-18000)

LONGWOOD MANAGEMENT CORP

Also Called: San Gabriel Convalescent Ctr
8035 Hill Dr (91770-4116)
PHONE.................................626 280-4820
Gigi Garcia, *Brnch Mgr*
EMP: 122
SALES (corp-wide): 79.33MM **Privately Held**
Web: www.longwoodmgmt.com
SIC: 8051 Convalescent home with continuous nursing care
PA: Longwood Management Corp.
4032 Wilshire Blvd Fl 6
Los Angeles CA
213 389-6900

PRODUCTS & SVCS

(P-18001)
LONGWOOD MANAGEMENT CORP
Also Called: Crenshaw Nursing
1900 S Longwood Ave (90016-1408)
PHONE..................323 933-1560
Gilbert Fimbres, *Mgr*
EMP: 119
SALES (corp-wide): 79.33MM **Privately Held**
Web: www.longwoodmgmt.com
SIC: 8051 8052 Convalescent home with continuous nursing care; Intermediate care facilities
PA: Longwood Management Corp.
　4032 Wilshire Blvd Fl 6
　Los Angeles CA
　213 389-6900

(P-18002)
LOS ANGLES JEWISH HM FOR AGING
Also Called: Eisenberg Village
18855 Victory Blvd (91335-6445)
PHONE..................818 774-3000
Kathleen Glass, *Mgr*
EMP: 500
SALES (corp-wide): 32.41MM **Privately Held**
Web: www.lajhealth.org
SIC: 8051 Convalescent home with continuous nursing care
PA: Los Angeles Jewish Home For The Aging
　7150 Tampa Ave
　Reseda CA
　818 774-3000

(P-18003)
LOS ANGLES JEWISH HM FOR AGING (PA)
Also Called: Grancell Village
7150 Tampa Ave (91335-3700)
PHONE..................818 774-3000
Andrew Berman, *Ch Bd*
Jeffrey Glassman, *
Molly Forrest, *
Sherri B Cunningham, *
Shelly J Ryan, *
EMP: 400 **EST:** 1912
SQ FT: 35,000
SALES (est): 32.41MM
SALES (corp-wide): 32.41MM **Privately Held**
Web: www.lajhealth.org
SIC: 8051 8361 Skilled nursing care facilities ; Residential care

(P-18004)
MARINER HEALTH CARE INC
Also Called: Autumn Hills Convalescent Home
430 N Glendale Ave (91206-3309)
PHONE..................818 246-5677
Jenik Akopian, *Prin*
EMP: 95
SALES (corp-wide): 1.02B **Privately Held**
Web: www.marinerhealthcare.com
SIC: 8051 Extended care facility
PA: Mariner Health Care, Inc.
　3060 Mercer University Dr # 200
　Atlanta GA
　678 443-7000

(P-18005)
MARINER HEALTH CARE INC
Also Called: El Rancho Vista Hlth Care Ctr
8925 Mines Ave (90660-3006)
PHONE..................562 942-7019
Richard Widerynski, *Mgr*

EMP: 99
SALES (corp-wide): 1.02B **Privately Held**
Web: www.elranchovista.com
SIC: 8051 Convalescent home with continuous nursing care
PA: Mariner Health Care, Inc.
　3060 Mercer University Dr # 200
　Atlanta GA
　678 443-7000

(P-18006)
MARINER HEALTH CARE INC
Also Called: Verdugo Vista Healthcare Ctr
3050 Montrose Ave (91214-3619)
PHONE..................818 957-0850
Jeri-enn Shelton, *Admn*
EMP: 97
SALES (corp-wide): 1.02B **Privately Held**
Web: www.marinerhealthcare.com
SIC: 8051 Extended care facility
PA: Mariner Health Care, Inc.
　3060 Mercer University Dr # 200
　Atlanta GA
　678 443-7000

(P-18007)
MARINER HEALTH CARE INC
Also Called: Driftwood Health Care Ctr
4109 Emerald St (90503-3105)
PHONE..................310 371-4628
Jennifer Torgrude, *Mgr*
EMP: 125
SALES (corp-wide): 1.02B **Privately Held**
Web: www.driftwoodhc.com
SIC: 8051 Convalescent home with continuous nursing care
PA: Mariner Health Care, Inc.
　3060 Mercer University Dr # 200
　Atlanta GA
　678 443-7000

(P-18008)
MARINER HEALTH CARE INC
Also Called: Monterey Palms Health Care Ctr
44610 Monterey Ave (92260-3326)
PHONE..................760 776-7700
J Simanjunt, *Admn*
EMP: 157
SALES (corp-wide): 1.02B **Privately Held**
Web: www.marinerhealthcare.com
SIC: 8051 Extended care facility
PA: Mariner Health Care, Inc.
　3060 Mercer University Dr # 200
　Atlanta GA
　678 443-7000

(P-18009)
MARK & FRED ENTERPRISES
Also Called: West Anaheim Care Center
645 S Beach Blvd (92804-3102)
PHONE..................714 821-1993
Mark Landry, *Mng Pt*
Connie Black, *Pt*
EMP: 125 **EST:** 1989
SQ FT: 39,000
SALES (est): 14.2MM **Privately Held**
Web: www.beachcreekpostacute.com
SIC: 8051 Convalescent home with continuous nursing care

(P-18010)
MARLORA INVESTMENTS LLC
Also Called: Marlora Post Accute Rhblttion
3801 E Anaheim St (90804-4004)
PHONE..................562 494-3311
EMP: 100 **EST:** 1998
SQ FT: 22,118
SALES (est): 8.57MM **Privately Held**
Web: www.marlora.com

SIC: 8051 Convalescent home with continuous nursing care

(P-18011)
MARY HLTH OF SICK CNVLSCENT NR
2929 Theresa Dr (91320-3136)
PHONE..................805 498-3644
Jody Rupp, *Admn*
Sister Purificaion Fererro, *
Diane Zimanski, *
EMP: 92 **EST:** 1964
SQ FT: 5,000
SALES (est): 7.42MM **Privately Held**
Web: www.maryhealth.com
SIC: 8051 Convalescent home with continuous nursing care

(P-18012)
MEK ESCONDIDO LLC
Also Called: Escondido Post Acute Rehab
421 E Mission Ave (92025-1909)
PHONE..................760 747-0430
EMP: 180 **EST:** 2000
SALES (est): 13.94MM **Privately Held**
SIC: 8051 Convalescent home with continuous nursing care

(P-18013)
MESA VRDE CNVALESCENT HOSP INC
Also Called: Mesa Verde Prosecute Care
661 Center St (92627-2708)
PHONE..................949 548-5584
Rita Simms, *Admn*
Joseph Munoz, *
Joye Tsuchiyama, *
EMP: 200 **EST:** 1972
SALES (est): 22.73MM **Privately Held**
Web: www.mesaverdehealthcare.com
SIC: 8051 Convalescent home with continuous nursing care

(P-18014)
MIRAMONTE ENTERPRISES LLC
Also Called: San Jacinto Healthcare
275 N San Jacinto St (92543-4453)
PHONE..................951 658-9441
Emmanuel B David, *Pr*
EMP: 134 **EST:** 2005
SQ FT: 22,968
SALES (est): 8.3MM **Privately Held**
Web: www.sjsnf.com
SIC: 8051 Convalescent home with continuous nursing care

(P-18015)
MISSION HILLS HEALTH CARE INC
Also Called: Mission Hills Healthcare Ctr
726 Torrance St (92103-3813)
PHONE..................619 297-4086
Patrick Higgins, *Admn*
Leah Higgins, *
EMP: 92 **EST:** 1990
SALES (est): 10.56MM **Privately Held**
Web: www.missionhillshealthcare.com
SIC: 8051 Convalescent home with continuous nursing care

(P-18016)
MONTECITO RETIREMENT ASSN
Also Called: Casa Dorinda
300 Hot Springs Rd (93108-2037)
PHONE..................805 969-8011
Robin Drew, *CFO*
EMP: 265 **EST:** 1973
SQ FT: 350,000

SALES (est): 24.99MM **Privately Held**
Web: www.casadorinda.org
SIC: 8051 8052 8361 Skilled nursing care facilities; Personal care facility; Rest home, with health care incidental

(P-18017)
MT MIQUEL COVENANT VILLAGE
325 Kempton St (91977-5810)
PHONE..................619 479-4790
Rich Miller, *Dir*
EMP: 151 **EST:** 1993
SQ FT: 316,465
SALES (est): 21.89MM **Privately Held**
Web: www.covlivingmountmiguel.org
SIC: 8051 Skilled nursing care facilities
PA: Covenant Living Communities And Services
　5700 Old Orchard Rd
　Skokie IL

(P-18018)
MT RUBIDOUXIDENCE OPCO LLC
Also Called: Jurupa Hills Post Acute
6401 33rd St (92509-1404)
PHONE..................951 681-2200
Jason Murray, *Prin*
Mark Hancock, *
Debra Gogerty, *
EMP: 199 **EST:** 2015
SALES (est): 31.59MM
SALES (corp-wide): 1.53B **Privately Held**
SIC: 8051 Skilled nursing care facilities
HQ: Providence Group Of Southern California, Llc
　262 N University Ave
　Farmington UT
　801 447-9829

(P-18019)
NAVIGAGE FOUNDATION (PA)
849 Foothill Blvd Ste 8 (91011-3368)
PHONE..................818 790-2522
Judy Vallas, *CEO*
EMP: 100 **EST:** 1932
SQ FT: 90,000
SALES (est): 570.33K
SALES (corp-wide): 570.33K **Privately Held**
SIC: 8051 8059 8052 Skilled nursing care facilities; Rest home, with health care; Intermediate care facilities

(P-18020)
OCEANSIDE HARBOR HOLDINGS LLC ✪
Also Called: Beach Creek Post-Acute
645 S Beach Blvd (92804-3102)
PHONE..................760 331-3177
Curt Rodriguez, *
EMP: 200 **EST:** 2022
SALES (est): 9.19MM **Privately Held**
SIC: 8051 Skilled nursing care facilities

(P-18021)
ORANGE HLTHCARE WLLNESS CNTRE
920 W La Veta Ave (92868-4302)
PHONE..................714 633-3568
EMP: 110 **EST:** 2009
SALES (est): 9.39MM **Privately Held**
Web: www.orangerehabilitation.com
SIC: 8051 Convalescent home with continuous nursing care

(P-18022)
ORCHARD - POST ACUTE CARE CTR
12385 Washington Blvd (90606-2502)
PHONE..............................562 693-7701
Rich Jorgensen, *Prin*
EMP: 110 **EST:** 2011
SALES (est): 26.99MM
SALES (corp-wide): 3.03B **Publicly Held**
Web: www.theorchardpostacute.com
SIC: 8051 Convalescent home with continuous nursing care
PA: The Ensign Group Inc
29222 Rncho Vejo Rd Ste 1
San Juan Capistrano CA
949 487-9500

(P-18023)
PACIFIC PALMS HEALTHCARE LLC
Empress Rehabilitation Center
1020 Termino Ave (90804-4123)
PHONE..............................562 433-6791
EMP: 88
SALES (corp-wide): 9.04MM **Privately Held**
Web: www.ppsnf.com
SIC: 8051 Convalescent home with continuous nursing care
PA: Pacific Palms Healthcare, Llc
1020 Termino Ave
Long Beach CA
562 433-6791

(P-18024)
PALMCREST GRAND CARE CTR INC
3501 Cedar Ave (90807-3809)
PHONE..............................562 595-4551
William Nelson, *Pr*
EMP: 99 **EST:** 2004
SALES (est): 4.05MM **Privately Held**
Web:
www.palmcrestgrandretirement.com
SIC: 8051 Skilled nursing care facilities

(P-18025)
PALMCREST MEDALLION CONVALESC
3355 Pacific Pl (90806-1239)
PHONE..............................562 595-4336
FAX: 562 424-6499
EMP: 85
SQ FT: 30,000
SALES (est): 1.71MM **Privately Held**
SIC: 8051 Skilled nursing care facilities

(P-18026)
PARKVIEW JLIAN CNVLESCENT HOSP
1801 Julian Ave (93304-6419)
PHONE..............................661 831-9150
Ligia Denham, *VP*
Douglas Rice, *
EMP: 130 **EST:** 1971
SQ FT: 8,000
SALES (est): 8.35MM **Privately Held**
Web: www.parkviewjulian-snf.com
SIC: 8051 Convalescent home with continuous nursing care

(P-18027)
PARKVIEW JULIAN LLC
Also Called: Parkview Julian Healthcare Ctr
1801 Julian Ave (93304-6419)
PHONE..............................661 831-9150
David Levy, *Managing Member*
Moshe Frankel, *Managing Member*
EMP: 150 **EST:** 2017

SALES (est): 7.29MM **Privately Held**
SIC: 8051 Convalescent home with continuous nursing care

(P-18028)
PASADENA HOSPITAL ASSN LTD
Also Called: Huntington Extended Care Ctr
716 S Fair Oaks Ave (91105-2618)
PHONE..............................626 397-3322
Ken Hoff, *Mgr*
EMP: 386
SALES (corp-wide): 688.61MM **Privately Held**
Web: www.huntingtonhealth.org
SIC: 8051 Skilled nursing care facilities
PA: Pasadena Hospital Association, Ltd.
100 W California Blvd
Pasadena CA
626 397-5000

(P-18029)
PASADENA MADOWS NURSING CTR LP
150 Bellefontaine St (91105-3102)
PHONE..............................626 796-1103
Pnina Graff, *Pt*
EMP: 99 **EST:** 2012
SALES (est): 5.08MM **Privately Held**
Web: www.pasadenameadows.com
SIC: 8051 Skilled nursing care facilities

(P-18030)
PENNANT GROUP INC
Also Called: Mainplace Senior Living
1800 W Culver Ave (92868-4127)
PHONE..............................714 978-2534
EMP: 303
SALES (corp-wide): 473.24MM **Publicly Held**
Web: www.pennantgroup.com
SIC: 8051 Convalescent home with continuous nursing care
PA: The Pennant Group Inc
1675 E Riverside Dr # 150
Eagle ID
208 506-6100

(P-18031)
PLUM HEALTHCARE GROUP LLC
100 E San Marcos Blvd Ste 200 (92069-2986)
PHONE..............................760 471-0388
EMP: 223 **EST:** 1999
SALES (est): 45.68MM
SALES (corp-wide): 1.53B **Privately Held**
Web: www.plumhealthcaregroup.com
SIC: 8051 Skilled nursing care facilities
HQ: Bay Bridge Capital Partners, Llc
262 N University Ave
Farmington UT
801 447-9829

(P-18032)
POINT LOMA RHBLITATION CTR LLC
Also Called: Pavilion At Ocean Point, The
3202 Duke St (92110-5401)
PHONE..............................619 308-3200
EMP: 130 **EST:** 2006
SQ FT: 30,895
SALES (est): 10.02MM **Privately Held**
Web: www.pointlomarehab.com
SIC: 8051 Convalescent home with continuous nursing care

(P-18033)
POMERADO OPERATIONS LLC
Also Called: BOULDER CREEK POST ACUTE

12696 Monte Vista Rd (92064-2500)
PHONE..............................858 487-6242
Covey Christensen, *CEO*
Travis Greenwood, *
Leland Bruce, *
James Gamett, *
EMP: 99 **EST:** 2014
SALES (est): 18.52MM **Privately Held**
Web: www.bouldercreekpa.care
SIC: 8051 Convalescent home with continuous nursing care

(P-18034)
POWERS PARK HEALTHCARE INC
Also Called: Channel Islands Post Acute
3880 Via Lucero (93110-1605)
PHONE..............................805 687-6651
Cory Monette, *Ex Dir*
EMP: 99 **EST:** 2019
SALES (est): 17.3MM **Privately Held**
Web: www.channelislandspa.com
SIC: 8051 Convalescent home with continuous nursing care

(P-18035)
RAMONA CARE INC
Also Called: Ramona Nrsing Rhbilitation Ctr
11900 Ramona Blvd (91732-2314)
PHONE..............................626 442-5721
Michael Hyer, *Pr*
Victor Lundquist, *
Jeffrey Daly, *
EMP: 140 **EST:** 1990
SQ FT: 35,000
SALES (est): 9.14MM **Privately Held**
Web: www.ramonarehab.com
SIC: 8051 Convalescent home with continuous nursing care

(P-18036)
REHABLTION CNTRE OF BVRLY HLLS
580 S San Vicente Blvd (90048-4621)
PHONE..............................323 782-1500
Eldon Teper, *Pr*
EMP: 200 **EST:** 1998
SALES (est): 16.62MM **Privately Held**
Web: www.rehabcentre.com
SIC: 8051 Convalescent home with continuous nursing care

(P-18037)
REHABLTTION CTR OF ORNGE CNTY
9021 Knott Ave (90620-4138)
PHONE..............................714 826-2330
Peter Madigan, *Pr*
Robert Nelson, *
EMP: 125 **EST:** 1967
SALES (est): 11.8MM **Privately Held**
SIC: 8051 8059 Convalescent home with continuous nursing care; Rest home, with health care

(P-18038)
RIDGECREST HEALTHCARE INC
5808 Monterey Rd (90042-4926)
PHONE..............................760 446-3591
Kristine Parel, *Prin*
EMP: 82
Web: www.windsorridgecrest.com
SIC: 8051 Convalescent home with continuous nursing care
PA: Ridgecrest Healthcare, Inc.
1131 N China Lake Blvd
Ridgecrest CA

(P-18039)
RIVERA SANATARIUM INC
Also Called: Colonial Gardens Nursing Home
7246 Rosemead Blvd (90660-4010)
P.O. Box 2098 (90662-2098)
PHONE..............................562 949-2591
Elizabeth Stephens, *Pr*
Kent Stephens, *
EMP: 86 **EST:** 1959
SQ FT: 30,000
SALES (est): 8.72MM **Privately Held**
SIC: 8051 Convalescent home with continuous nursing care

(P-18040)
RIVERSIDE CARE INC
Also Called: Valencia Gardens Health Care Center
4301 Caroline Ct (92506-2902)
PHONE..............................951 683-7111
Ted Holt, *Pr*
Jenny Ortiz, *
Spencer E Olsen, *
EMP: 130 **EST:** 1971
SALES (est): 10.92MM **Privately Held**
Web: www.valenciagardenshealth.com
SIC: 8051 Convalescent home with continuous nursing care
PA: North American Client Services, Inc.
25910 Acero Ste 350
Mission Viejo CA

(P-18041)
RIVERSIDE EQUITIES LLC
Also Called: SUN MAR HEALTH CARE
8487 Magnolia Ave (92504-3222)
PHONE..............................951 688-2222
Frank Johnson, *CEO*
Irving Bauman, *
EMP: 372 **EST:** 2008
SALES (est): 8.75MM **Privately Held**
Web: www.missioncarecenter.com
SIC: 8051 Convalescent home with continuous nursing care
PA: Sun Mar Management Services
3050 Saturn St Ste 201
Brea CA

(P-18042)
RIVIERA NURSING & CONVA
Also Called: Riviera Health Care Center
8203 Telegraph Rd (90660-4905)
PHONE..............................562 806-2576
Morris Weiss, *Pr*
Bessie Weiss, *
EMP: 118 **EST:** 1966
SQ FT: 60,000
SALES (est): 9.14MM **Privately Held**
Web: www.rivierahealthcare.com
SIC: 8051 8059 Convalescent home with continuous nursing care; Convalescent home

(P-18043)
ROWLAND CONVALESCENT HOSP INC
Also Called: ROWLAND, THE
330 W Rowland St (91723-2941)
PHONE..............................626 967-2741
Anthony Kalomas, *Pr*
EMP: 100 **EST:** 1979
SQ FT: 30,000
SALES (est): 6.92MM **Privately Held**
Web: www.rowlandconvalescent.com
SIC: 8051 Convalescent home with continuous nursing care

PRODUCTS & SVCS

(P-18044)
RRT ENTERPRISES LP
Also Called: RRT ENTERPRISES LP
855 N Fairfax Ave (90046-7207)
PHONE.................................323 653-1521
Stephen Reissman, *Brnch Mgr*
EMP: 225
SALES (corp-wide): 16.4MM **Privately Held**
SIC: 8051 Skilled nursing care facilities
PA: Rrt Enterprises L.P.
3966 Marcasel Ave
Los Angeles CA
310 397-2372

(P-18045)
RRT ENTERPRISES LP (PA)
Also Called: Country Vlla Mar Vsta Nrsing C
3966 Marcasel Ave (90066-4616)
PHONE.................................310 397-2372
Stephen Reissman, *Genl Pt*
Diane Reissman, *Genl Pt*
EMP: 125 EST: 1972
SQ FT: 18,000
SALES (est): 16.4MM
SALES (corp-wide): 16.4MM **Privately Held**
SIC: 8051 Skilled nursing care facilities

(P-18046)
SAN DIEGO HEBREW HOMES (PA)
Also Called: LEICHTAG ASSISTED LIVING
211 Saxony Rd (92024-2721)
PHONE.................................760 942-2695
Yehudi Gaffen, *Ch*
Betty Byrnes, *Vice Chairman**
Mitchell Berner, *Vice Chairman**
Pam Ferris, *
Robin P Israel, *
EMP: 180 EST: 1944
SQ FT: 219,000
SALES (est): 21.03MM
SALES (corp-wide): 21.03MM **Privately Held**
Web: www.seacrestvillage.org
SIC: 8051 8059 6513 Skilled nursing care facilities; Rest home, with health care; Retirement hotel operation

(P-18047)
SAN PEDRO CONVALESCENT HM INC
Also Called: Los Palos Convalescent Hosp
1430 W 6th St (90732-3503)
PHONE.................................310 832-6431
Celia Valdomar, *Pr*
EMP: 90 EST: 1963
SQ FT: 10,000
SALES (est): 8.28MM **Privately Held**
Web: www.lpconv.com
SIC: 8051 Convalescent home with continuous nursing care

(P-18048)
SANTA ANITA CNVLSCENT HOSP RTR
5522 Gracewood Ave (91780)
PHONE.................................626 579-0310
Martin J Weiss, *Pr*
Jacob Kasirer, *
Ronni J Mayer, *
EMP: 150 EST: 1968
SQ FT: 88,615
SALES (est): 24.63MM
SALES (corp-wide): 74.01MM **Privately Held**
Web: www.santaanita-convalescent.com

SIC: 8051 Convalescent home with continuous nursing care
PA: Golden State Health Centers, Inc.
13347 Ventura Blvd
Sherman Oaks CA
818 385-3200

(P-18049)
SEA BREEZE HEALTH CARE INC
7781 Garfield Ave (92648-2026)
PHONE.................................714 847-9671
Seth Braithwaite, *Pr*
Victor Lundquist, *
Jeffrey Daly, *
EMP: 132 EST: 2003
SQ FT: 14,895
SALES (est): 4.92MM **Privately Held**
Web: www.beachsidenursing.com
SIC: 8051 Convalescent home with continuous nursing care

(P-18050)
SELA HEALTHCARE INC
Also Called: Holiday Manor Care Center
20554 Roscoe Blvd (91306-1746)
PHONE.................................818 341-9800
Victorio Ocbena Sosing, *Prin*
EMP: 310
SALES (corp-wide): 13.3MM **Privately Held**
SIC: 8051 Convalescent home with continuous nursing care
PA: Sela Healthcare, Inc.
867 E 11th St
Upland CA
909 985-1981

(P-18051)
SELA HEALTHCARE INC (PA)
Also Called: Holiday Manor Care Center
867 E 11th St (91786-4867)
PHONE.................................909 985-1981
Philip Weinberger, *CEO*
Marylnynn Mahan, *
EMP: 140 EST: 2002
SQ FT: 60,000
SALES (est): 13.3MM
SALES (corp-wide): 13.3MM **Privately Held**
SIC: 8051 Skilled nursing care facilities

(P-18052)
SHARON CARE CENTER LLC
Also Called: GENESIS HEALTHCARE CORPORATION
8167 W 3rd St (90048-4314)
PHONE.................................323 655-2023
Isaac Shabat, *Ex Dir*
EMP: 97 EST: 2003
SALES (est): 12.06MM
SALES (corp-wide): 5.86B **Publicly Held**
Web: www.sharoncarecenter.com
SIC: 8051 8059 Skilled nursing care facilities; Convalescent home
HQ: Genesis Hc Llc
101 E State St
Kennett Square PA
610 444-6350

(P-18053)
SILVERADO SENIOR LIVING INC
Also Called: Huntington Memory Care Cmnty
1118 N Stoneman Ave (91801-1007)
PHONE.................................626 872-3941
Vida Gwin, *Admn*
EMP: 90
SALES (corp-wide): 130.57K **Privately Held**
Web: www.silverado.com

SIC: 8051 Skilled nursing care facilities
PA: Senior Silverado Living Inc
6400 Oak Cyn Ste 200
Irvine CA
949 240-7200

(P-18054)
SKILLED HEALTHCARE LLC (DH)
27442 Portola Pkwy Ste 200 (92610-2822)
PHONE.................................949 282-5800
Richard Edwards, *
EMP: 131 EST: 1963
SQ FT: 22,000
SALES (est): 639.73MM **Privately Held**
Web: www.skilledhealthcare.com
SIC: 8051 6513 5122 Convalescent home with continuous nursing care; Retirement hotel operation; Drugs, proprietaries, and sundries
HQ: Genesis Healthcare Llc
101 E State St
Kennett Square PA

(P-18055)
SKYLINE HLTHCARE WLLNESS CTR L
Also Called: SKYLINE HEALTHCARE CENTER
3032 Rowena Ave (90039-2005)
PHONE.................................323 665-1185
Bernon Aguilar, *Admn*
Sharrod Brooks, *
EMP: 99 EST: 2010
SALES (est): 7.69MM **Privately Held**
Web: www.skylinehc.com
SIC: 8051 Convalescent home with continuous nursing care

(P-18056)
SOLVANG LUTHERAN HOME INC
Also Called: Atterdag Village of Solvang
636 Atterdag Rd (93463-2687)
PHONE.................................805 688-3263
EMP: 120 EST: 1951
SALES (est): 14.12MM **Privately Held**
Web: www.peoplewhocare.com
SIC: 8051 8052 6513 Skilled nursing care facilities; Intermediate care facilities; Apartment building operators

(P-18057)
SPRING VALLEY POST ACUTE LLC
14973 Hesperia Rd (92395-3923)
PHONE.................................760 245-6477
David Johnson, *Managing Member*
Thomas Chambers, *Managing Member**
Matheson Chambers, *Managing Member**
EMP: 200 EST: 2013
SALES (est): 20.09MM **Privately Held**
Web: www.springvalleypostacute.com
SIC: 8051 Convalescent home with continuous nursing care

(P-18058)
STERLING CARE INC
Also Called: Paradise Valley Manor
2575 E 8th St (91950-2913)
PHONE.................................619 470-6700
Kenneth M Funk, *Prin*
EMP: 117
SALES (est): 1.53MM
SALES (corp-wide): 1.53B **Privately Held**
SIC: 8051 Convalescent home with continuous nursing care
PA: Providence Group, Inc.
262 N University Ave
Farmington UT
801 447-9829

(P-18059)
STJOHN GOD RTIREMENT CARE CTR
2468 S St Andrews Pl (90018-2042)
PHONE.................................323 731-0641
Admiral Michael Bessimer, *Prin*
Michael Bessimer, *Admn*
EMP: 200 EST: 1942
SQ FT: 99,392
SALES (est): 25.81MM **Privately Held**
Web: www.stjogrcc.org
SIC: 8051 8052 Skilled nursing care facilities; Intermediate care facilities

(P-18060)
SUNRISE SENIOR LIVING MGT INC
3140 El Camino Real (92008-2108)
PHONE.................................760 720-9898
Sylvia Segi, *Prin*
EMP: 147
SALES (corp-wide): 2.92B **Privately Held**
Web: www.sunriseseniorliving.com
SIC: 8051 Skilled nursing care facilities
HQ: Sunrise Senior Living Management, Inc.
7902 Westpark Dr
Mc Lean VA
703 273-7500

(P-18061)
TORRANCE CARE CENTER WEST INC
4333 Torrance Blvd (90503-4401)
PHONE.................................310 370-4561
EMP: 180 EST: 1999
SALES (est): 21.96MM **Privately Held**
Web: www.torranceca.gov
SIC: 8051 Convalescent home with continuous nursing care

(P-18062)
TOWN CNTRY MNOR OF CHRSTN MSSN
555 E Memory Ln Side (92706-1753)
PHONE.................................714 547-7581
Dirk De Wolfe, *Admn*
EMP: 210 EST: 1975
SQ FT: 208,000
SALES (est): 24.69MM **Privately Held**
SIC: 8051 8052 Skilled nursing care facilities; Nursing home, except skilled and intermediate care facility; Intermediate care facilities

(P-18063)
TRINITY HEALTH SYSTEMS (PA)
Also Called: Villa Maria Care Center
14318 Ohio St (91706-2553)
PHONE.................................626 960-1971
Randal Kleis, *Pr*
EMP: 80 EST: 1989
SQ FT: 35,000
SALES (est): 11.47MM
SALES (corp-wide): 11.47MM **Privately Held**
Web: www.sierraviewcarecenter.com
SIC: 8051 Convalescent home with continuous nursing care

(P-18064)
UPLAND COMMUNITY CARE INC
Also Called: ENSIGN
1221 E Arrow Hwy (91786-4911)
PHONE.................................909 985-1903
Owen Hammond, *CEO*
EMP: 152 EST: 2008
SALES (est): 28.05MM
SALES (corp-wide): 3.03B **Publicly Held**

Web: www.uplandcare.com
SIC: 8051 Convalescent home with continuous nursing care
PA: The Ensign Group Inc
29222 Rncho Vejo Rd Ste 1
San Juan Capistrano CA
949 487-9500

(P-18065)
US SKILLSERVE INC
Also Called: Community Cnvlscent Hosp Mntcl
9620 Fremont Ave (91763-2320)
PHONE..........................909 621-4751
Johannes Simanjuntak, *Brnch Mgr*
EMP: 987
SALES (corp-wide): 23.84MM **Privately Held**
Web: www.communityech.com
SIC: 8051 Convalescent home with continuous nursing care
PA: U.S. Skillserve Inc
4115 E Broadway Ste A
Long Beach CA
562 930-0777

(P-18066)
VALLEY VSTA NRSING TRNSTNAL CA
Also Called: Valley Vsta Nrsing Trnstnal Ca
6120 Vineland Ave (91606-4914)
PHONE..........................818 763-6275
EMP: 170 **EST:** 2017
SALES (est): 7.48MM **Privately Held**
SIC: 8051 Convalescent home with continuous nursing care

(P-18067)
VICTORIA CARE CENTER
5445 Everglades St (93003-6523)
PHONE..........................805 642-1736
Scott Porter, *Ex Dir*
Jay Brady, *
EMP: 100 **EST:** 1987
SQ FT: 85,000
SALES (est): 18.73MM **Privately Held**
Web: www.victoriacarecenter.com
SIC: 8051 Convalescent home with continuous nursing care
PA: Beverly Health Care Corporation
5445 Everglades St
Ventura CA

(P-18068)
VICTORIA VNTURA ASSSTED LVING
27101 Puerta Real Ste 450 (92691-8566)
PHONE..........................805 642-1736
EMP: 87 **EST:** 2014
SALES (est): 24.74MM
SALES (corp-wide): 3.03B **Publicly Held**
SIC: 8051 Convalescent home with continuous nursing care
PA: The Ensign Group Inc
29222 Rncho Vejo Rd Ste 1
San Juan Capistrano CA
949 487-9500

(P-18069)
VICTORIA VNTURA HEALTHCARE LLC
Also Called: Victoria Care Center
5445 Everglades St (93003-6523)
PHONE..........................805 642-1736
Tim Cooley, *Ex Dir*
EMP: 262 **EST:** 2003
SALES (est): 13.41MM **Privately Held**
Web: www.victoriacarecenter.com

SIC: 8051 Convalescent home with continuous nursing care

(P-18070)
VILLA CONVALESCENT HOSP INC
Also Called: VILLA CONVALESCENT HOSPITAL
8965 Magnolia Ave (92503-4432)
PHONE..........................951 689-5788
Admiral Jacob Paulson, *Prin*
EMP: 90 **EST:** 1971
SQ FT: 25,000
SALES (est): 9.4MM **Privately Held**
Web: www.villahealthcare.com
SIC: 8051 Convalescent home with continuous nursing care

(P-18071)
VISTA PACIFICA ENTERPRISES INC (PA)
Also Called: Vista Pacifica Center
3674 Pacific Ave (92509-1948)
PHONE..........................951 682-4833
Cheryl Jumonville, *CEO*
A L Braswell Junior, *Pr*
Ruth Braswell, *Stockholder**
James Braswell, *Stockholder**
EMP: 180 **EST:** 1988
SALES (est): 19.68MM **Privately Held**
Web: www.vistapacificaent.com
SIC: 8051 8059 Convalescent home with continuous nursing care; Domiciliary care

(P-18072)
VISTA WOODS HEALTH ASSOC LLC
Also Called: Vista Knoll Spclzed Care Fclty
2000 Westwood Rd (92083-5123)
PHONE..........................760 630-2273
Ron Cook, *Managing Member*
EMP: 162 **EST:** 2003
SALES (est): 28.3MM
SALES (corp-wide): 3.03B **Publicly Held**
Web: www.vistaknoll.com
SIC: 8051 Convalescent home with continuous nursing care
PA: The Ensign Group Inc
29222 Rncho Vejo Rd Ste 1
San Juan Capistrano CA
949 487-9500

(P-18073)
WATERMAN CONVALESCENT HOSP INC (PA)
Also Called: Mt Rubidoux Convalescent Hosp
1850 N Waterman Ave (92404-4895)
PHONE..........................909 882-1215
Thomas Plott, *Pr*
Mister Terry Steege, *Acct Ex*
Elizabeth Plott, *
EMP: 109 **EST:** 1964
SQ FT: 13,000
SALES (est): 9.92MM
SALES (corp-wide): 9.92MM **Privately Held**
SIC: 8051 Convalescent home with continuous nursing care

(P-18074)
WATERMARK RTRMENT CMMNTIES INC
Also Called: Fountains At The Carlotta, The
41505 Carlotta Dr (92211-3279)
PHONE..........................760 346-5420
EMP: 98
Web: www.watermarkcommunities.com
SIC: 8051 8052 Skilled nursing care facilities ; Intermediate care facilities

HQ: Watermark Retirement Communities, Inc.
2020 W Rudasill Rd
Tucson AZ

(P-18075)
WEST CNTINELA VLY CARE CTR INC
Also Called: Centinela Skld Nrng Wlns Cntr
950 S Flower St (90301-4186)
PHONE..........................310 674-3216
EMP: 99
SALES (est): 5.7MM **Privately Held**
SIC: 8051 Skilled nursing care facilities

(P-18076)
WESTLAKE HEALTH CARE CENTER
1101 Crenshaw Blvd (90019-3112)
PHONE..........................805 494-1233
Jeoung Lee, *Pr*
EMP: 318 **EST:** 2001
SALES (est): 16.79MM
SALES (corp-wide): 52.03MM **Privately Held**
SIC: 8051 Skilled nursing care facilities
PA: J P H Consulting, Inc.
1101 Crenshaw Blvd
Los Angeles CA
323 934-5660

(P-18077)
WESTWOOD HEALTHCARE CENTER LP
Also Called: COUNTRY VILLA WESTWOOD NURSING
12121 Santa Monica Blvd (90025-2515)
PHONE..........................310 826-0821
Stephen Reissman, *Genl Pt*
Hillard Torgan, *Pt*
EMP: 81 **EST:** 1970
SQ FT: 18,000
SALES (est): 10.96MM **Privately Held**
SIC: 8051 Skilled nursing care facilities

(P-18078)
WINDSOR ANAHEIM HEALTHCARE (PA)
Also Called: Windsor Grdns Cnvlescent Ctr A
3415 W Ball Rd (92804-3708)
PHONE..........................714 826-8950
Lee Samson, *Pr*
EMP: 164 **EST:** 1996
SQ FT: 37,245
SALES (est): 23.85MM **Privately Held**
Web: www.anaheimhealthcare.com
SIC: 8051 Convalescent home with continuous nursing care

(P-18079)
WINDSOR TWIN PLMS HLTHCARE CTR
Also Called: Windsor Palms Care Ctr Artesia
11900 Artesia Blvd (90701-4039)
PHONE..........................562 865-0271
EMP: 133 **EST:** 2005
SALES (est): 28.44MM **Privately Held**
Web: www.windsorartesia.com
SIC: 8051 Convalescent home with continuous nursing care
PA: Lexington Group International, Inc
9200 W Sunset Blvd # 950
West Hollywood CA

8052 Intermediate Care Facilities

(P-18080)
ARCADIA GARDENS MGT CORP
Also Called: Independnt Asstd Lvng & Memory
720 W Camino Real Ave (91007-7839)
PHONE..........................626 574-8571
Julie Chirikian, *Pr*
David Chirikian, *
EMP: 100 **EST:** 2004
SQ FT: 120,320
SALES (est): 9.11MM **Privately Held**
Web:
www.arcadiagardensretirement.com
SIC: 8052 Intermediate care facilities

(P-18081)
BLYTH/WNDSOR CNTRY PK HLTHCARE
3232 E Artesia Blvd (90805-2811)
PHONE..........................310 385-1090
Jon Peralez, *Prin*
EMP: 99 **EST:** 2013
SALES (est): 8.04MM **Privately Held**
SIC: 8052 Intermediate care facilities

(P-18082)
CHARTER HOSPICE COLTON LLC
1007 E Cooley Dr Ste 100 (92324-3901)
PHONE..........................909 825-2969
Fred Frank, *Pr*
EMP: 120 **EST:** 2008
SALES (est): 17.04MM **Privately Held**
Web: www.charterhcg.com
SIC: 8052 Personal care facility

(P-18083)
DEL ROSA VILLAIDENCE OPCO LLC
Also Called: Del Rosa Villa
2018 Del Rosa Ave (92404-5642)
PHONE..........................909 885-3261
Jason Murray, *Prin*
Mark Hancock, *
EMP: 330 **EST:** 2014
SALES (est): 3.92MM
SALES (corp-wide): 1.53B **Privately Held**
Web: www.delrosavillapostacute.com
SIC: 8052 Intermediate care facilities
HQ: Providence Group Of Southern California, Llc
262 N University Ave
Farmington UT
801 447-9829

(P-18084)
HILLSIDE HOUSE
1235 Veronica Springs Rd (93105-4522)
PHONE..........................805 687-0788
Michael Rassler, *Ex Dir*
Pam Flynt, *
Craig Olson, *
Peter Troesch, *
Chuck Klein, *
EMP: 98 **EST:** 1945
SQ FT: 24,000
SALES (est): 7.45MM **Privately Held**
Web: www.hillsidesb.org
SIC: 8052 Home for the mentally retarded, with health care

(P-18085)
HOME STREET OPERATIONS LLC
114 Pacifica Ste 230 (92618-3317)

PHONE..............949 449-2500
EMP: 82
SALES (corp-wide): 1.86MM **Privately Held**
SIC: 8052 Intermediate care facilities
PA: Home Street Operations, Llc
　4001 Home St
　Castle Rock CO
　303 688-3174

(P-18086)
INLAND VALLEY HOSPICE CO
19167 Us Highway 18 Ste 6 (92307-2561)
PHONE..............760 243-2501
EMP: 84
Web: www.inlandvalleyhospice.com
SIC: 8052 Personal care facility
PA: Inland Valley Hospice Co
　3770 Myers St
　Riverside CA

(P-18087)
KERN VALLEYIDENCE OPCO LLC
Also Called: San Jquin Nrsing Rhblttion Ctr
3601 San Dimas St (93301-1405)
PHONE..............661 323-2894
Jason Murray, *CEO*
Mark Hancock, *CFO*
EMP: 131 **EST:** 2017
SALES (est): 11.57MM
SALES (corp-wide): 1.53B **Privately Held**
SIC: 8052 Intermediate care facilities
HQ: Providence Group Wine Country, Llc
　262 N University Ave
　Farmington UT
　801 447-9829

(P-18088)
L & A CARE CORPORATION
Also Called: Roze Room Hospice
5000 Overland Ave Ste 101 (90230-4969)
PHONE..............310 202-7693
Lena M Beker, *Brnch Mgr*
EMP: 112
SALES (corp-wide): 3.22MM **Privately Held**
Web: www.rozeroom.org
SIC: 8052 Personal care facility
PA: L & A Care Corporation
　18107 Sherman Way Ste 100
　Reseda CA
　323 938-1155

(P-18089)
LEISURE CARE LLC
Also Called: Fairwinds-West Hills
8138 Woodlake Ave (91304-3500)
PHONE..............818 713-0900
Pat Luc, *Genl Mgr*
EMP: 115
SALES (corp-wide): 106.71MM **Privately Held**
Web: www.leisurecare.com
SIC: 8052 Intermediate care facilities
HQ: Leisure Care, Llc
　999 3rd Ave Ste 4550
　Seattle WA
　206 436-7827

(P-18090)
LOS ANGLES CNTY RNCHO LOS AMGO
7601 Imperial Hwy (90242-3456)
PHONE..............562 385-7111
Jorge Orozco, *CEO*
EMP: 1400 **EST:** 2009
SALES (est): 108.38MM **Privately Held**
Web: dhs.lacounty.gov

SIC: 8052 Personal care facility
PA: Rancho Los Amigos National
　Rehabiliatation Center
　7601 Imperial Hwy
　Downey CA

(P-18091)
NEW VISTA BEHAVIORAL HLTH LLC
3 Park Plz Ste 550 (92614-2537)
PHONE..............949 284-0095
Jennifer Hale, *Brnch Mgr*
EMP: 99
SALES (corp-wide): 13.46MM **Privately Held**
Web: www.pristenhealth.com
SIC: 8052 Home for the mentally retarded, with health care
PA: New Vista Behavioral Health, Llc
　1901 Newport Blvd Ste 204
　Costa Mesa CA
　888 316-3665

(P-18092)
OJAI HEALTHIDENCE OPCO LLC
Also Called: Ojai Health & Rehabilitation
601 N Montgomery St (93023-2751)
PHONE..............805 646-8124
EMP: 192 **EST:** 2014
SALES (est): 2.28MM
SALES (corp-wide): 1.53B **Privately Held**
SIC: 8052 Intermediate care facilities
HQ: Providence Group North, Llc
　262 N University Ave
　Farmington UT
　801 447-9829

(P-18093)
ONTARIOIDENCE OPCO LLC
Also Called: Las Colinas Post Acute
800 E 5th St (91764-2432)
PHONE..............909 984-8629
Jason Murray, *Prin*
Mark Hancock, *"*
EMP: 439 **EST:** 2014
SALES (est): 7.97MM
SALES (corp-wide): 1.53B **Privately Held**
SIC: 8052 Intermediate care facilities
HQ: Providence Group Of Southern California, Llc
　262 N University Ave
　Farmington UT
　801 447-9829

(P-18094)
ORANGE TREEIDENCE OPCO LLC
Also Called: Riverwalk Post Acute
4000 Harrison St (92503-3514)
PHONE..............951 785-6060
Jason Murray, *Prin*
Mark Hancock, *"*
EMP: 351 **EST:** 2014
SALES (est): 3.02MM
SALES (corp-wide): 1.53B **Privately Held**
SIC: 8052 Intermediate care facilities
HQ: Providence Group Of Southern California, Llc
　262 N University Ave
　Farmington UT
　801 447-9829

(P-18095)
PARKSIDE HEALTHCARE INC
Also Called: Parkside Health & Wellness Ctr
444 W Lexington Ave (92020-4416)
PHONE..............619 442-7744
Matthew Oldroyd, *Prin*

EMP: 85 **EST:** 2014
SALES (est): 3.1MM **Privately Held**
Web: www.parksidehealth.net
SIC: 8052 Intermediate care facilities

(P-18096)
RANCHO VISTA HEALTH CENTER
Also Called: Rancho Vista
200 Grapevine Rd Apt 15 (92083-4042)
PHONE..............760 941-1480
Alan Shigley, *Ex Dir*
EMP: 178 **EST:** 1983
SALES (est): 11.27MM
SALES (corp-wide): 40.58MM **Privately Held**
SIC: 8052 8051 8361 Intermediate care facilities; Skilled nursing care facilities; Residential care
PA: Activcare Living, Inc.
　10603 Rancho Bernardo Rd
　San Diego CA
　858 565-4424

(P-18097)
RES-CARE INC
22635 Alessandro Blvd (92553-8550)
PHONE..............951 653-1311
EMP: 83
SALES (corp-wide): 5.27B **Privately Held**
Web: www.rescare.com
SIC: 8052 Home for the mentally retarded, with health care
HQ: Res-Care, Inc.
　805 N Whittington Pkwy
　Louisville KY
　502 394-2100

(P-18098)
RES-CARE INC
2120 Foothill Blvd Ste 205 (91750-2941)
PHONE..............909 596-5360
Jill Crowell, *Mgr*
EMP: 83
SALES (corp-wide): 5.27B **Privately Held**
Web: www.rescare.com
SIC: 8052 Home for the mentally retarded, with health care
HQ: Res-Care, Inc.
　805 N Whittington Pkwy
　Louisville KY
　502 394-2100

(P-18099)
VALLEY VILLAGE
8727 Fenwick St (91040-1952)
PHONE..............818 446-0366
EMP: 113
SALES (corp-wide): 21.42MM **Privately Held**
Web: www.valleyvillage.org
SIC: 8052 Intermediate care facilities
PA: Valley Village
　20830 Sherman Way
　Winnetka CA
　818 587-9450

(P-18100)
VITAS HEALTHCARE CORPORATION
9106 Pulsar Ct Ste D (92883-4632)
PHONE..............858 805-6254
EMP: 97
SALES (corp-wide): 2.13B **Publicly Held**
Web: www.vitas.com
SIC: 8052 Personal care facility
HQ: Vitas Healthcare Corporation
　201 S Biscayne Blvd # 400
　Miami FL
　305 374-4143

(P-18101)
VITAS HEALTHCARE CORPORATION
333 N Lantana St Ste 124 (93010-9007)
PHONE..............805 437-2100
Rita Peddycoart, *Mgr*
EMP: 97
SALES (corp-wide): 2.13B **Publicly Held**
Web: www.vitas.com
SIC: 8052 Personal care facility
HQ: Vitas Healthcare Corporation
　201 S Biscayne Blvd # 400
　Miami FL
　305 374-4143

(P-18102)
WATERMANIDENCE OPCO LLC
Also Called: Waterman Canyon Post Acute
1850 N Waterman Ave (92404-4831)
PHONE..............909 882-1215
Jason Murray, *Prin*
Mark Hancock, *"*
EMP: 330 **EST:** 2014
SALES (est): 4.79MM
SALES (corp-wide): 1.53B **Privately Held**
SIC: 8052 Intermediate care facilities
HQ: Providence Group Of Southern California, Llc
　262 N University Ave
　Farmington UT
　801 447-9829

(P-18103)
WATTS HEALTH FOUNDATION INC (HQ)
Also Called: Uhp Healthcare
3405 W Imperial Hwy Ste 304 (90303-2219)
PHONE..............310 424-2220
Doctor Clyde W Oden, *Pr*
Jennifer Stapalding, *CEO*
Ron Bolding V Press, *Business Operations*
EMP: 400 **EST:** 1967
SALES (est): 69.59MM
SALES (corp-wide): 70.19MM **Privately Held**
Web: www.wattshealth.org
SIC: 8052 8011 8741 Intermediate care facilities; Health maintenance organization; Management services
PA: Watts Health Systems, Inc.
　3405 W Imperial Hwy
　Inglewood CA
　310 424-2220

(P-18104)
WEST VALLEYIDENCE OPCO LLC
Also Called: West Valley Post Acute
7057 Shoup Ave (91307-2335)
PHONE..............818 348-8422
Jason Murray, *Prin*
Mark Hancock, *Prin*
EMP: 152 **EST:** 2015
SALES (est): 4.26MM
SALES (corp-wide): 1.53B **Privately Held**
SIC: 8052 Intermediate care facilities
HQ: Providence Group North, Llc
　262 N University Ave
　Farmington UT
　801 447-9829

8059 Nursing And Personal Care, Nec

(P-18105)
AMBERWOOD CONVALESCENT HOSP
6071 York Blvd (90042-3503)
PHONE.....................323 254-3407
Jeanie Barrett, *Admn*
Ben Garrett, *
EMP: 100 EST: 1967
SALES (est): 4.09MM
SALES (corp-wide): 4.51MM Privately Held
Web: www.yorkhealthcareandwellness.com
SIC: 8059 Convalescent home
PA: Casner Consolidated, Llc.
1020 Huntington Dr
San Marino CA
626 282-8443

(P-18106)
ANTELOPE VLY RETIREMENT HM INC
Also Called: A V Nursing Care Center
44567 15th St W (93534-2803)
PHONE.....................661 949-5524
Alfred Jones, *Mgr*
EMP: 178
SALES (corp-wide): 11.41MM Privately Held
Web: www.yolocare2.com
SIC: 8059 8051 Convalescent home; Skilled nursing care facilities
PA: Antelope Valley Retirement Home, Inc.
44523 15th St W
Lancaster CA
661 949-5584

(P-18107)
ANTELOPE VLY RETIREMENT HM INC
Also Called: Antelope Vly Convalecent Hosp
44445 15th St W (93534-2801)
PHONE.....................661 948-7501
Marsha Weldon, *Dir*
EMP: 178
SALES (corp-wide): 11.41MM Privately Held
SIC: 8059 8051 Convalescent home; Skilled nursing care facilities
PA: Antelope Valley Retirement Home, Inc.
44523 15th St W
Lancaster CA
661 949-5584

(P-18108)
ARARAT HOME LOS ANGELES INC
Also Called: Ararat Convalescent Hospital
2373 Colorado Blvd (90041-1157)
PHONE.....................323 256-8012
Violette Alahaidoyan, *Brnch Mgr*
EMP: 131
SQ FT: 9,104
SALES (corp-wide): 37.97MM Privately Held
Web: www.ararathome.org
SIC: 8059 8051 Convalescent home; Skilled nursing care facilities
PA: Ararat Home Of Los Angeles, Inc.
15105 Mission Hills Rd
Mission Hills CA
818 365-3000

(P-18109)
ARARAT HOME LOS ANGELES INC
Also Called: Ararat Nursing Facility
15099 Mission Hills Rd (91345-1102)
PHONE.....................818 837-1800
M Kebhichien, *Admn*
EMP: 109
SALES (corp-wide): 37.97MM Privately Held
Web: www.ararathome.org
SIC: 8059 8051 Nursing home, except skilled and intermediate care facility; Skilled nursing care facilities
PA: Ararat Home of Los Angeles, Inc.
15105 Mission Hills Rd
Mission Hills CA
818 365-3000

(P-18110)
ARCADIA CONVALESCENT HOSP INC (PA)
Also Called: Arcadia Health Care Center
1601 S Baldwin Ave (91007-7930)
PHONE.....................626 445-2170
Orlando Clarizio Junior, *CEO*
EMP: 117 EST: 1962
SQ FT: 21,342
SALES (est): 18.4MM
SALES (corp-wide): 18.4MM Privately Held
Web: www.arcadiahcc.com
SIC: 8059 8051 Convalescent home; Skilled nursing care facilities

(P-18111)
ARTESIA CHRISTIAN HOME INC
11614 183rd St (90701-5506)
PHONE.....................562 865-5218
Elroy Van Derley, *Ex Dir*
EMP: 140 EST: 1947
SQ FT: 43,223
SALES (est): 11.87MM Privately Held
Web: www.achome.org
SIC: 8059 8052 8051 Convalescent home; Intermediate care facilities; Skilled nursing care facilities

(P-18112)
BERKELEY E CONVALESCENT HOSP
Also Called: Berkeley E Convalescent Hosp
2021 Arizona Ave (90404-1335)
PHONE.....................310 829-5377
Paul Bartolucce, *Adm/Dir*
Saul Galper, *
EMP: 150 EST: 1965
SQ FT: 10,000
SALES (est): 10.72MM Privately Held
SIC: 8059 Convalescent home

(P-18113)
BERNARDO HTS HEALTHCARE INC
Also Called: Carmel Mtn Rhab Healthcare Ctr
11895 Avenue Of Industry (92128-3423)
PHONE.....................858 673-0101
Christopher R Christensen, *CEO*
Covey C Christensen, *
Matt Rutter, *
EMP: 188 EST: 2005
SALES (est): 21.34MM
SALES (corp-wide): 3.03B Publicly Held
Web: www.carmelmountain.net
SIC: 8059 8051 8011 Nursing home, except skilled and intermediate care facility; Skilled nursing care facilities; Clinic, operated by physicians
PA: The Ensign Group Inc
29222 Rncho Vejo Rd Ste 1
San Juan Capistrano CA
949 487-9500

(P-18114)
BRIGHTON CONVALESCENT CENTER
1836 N Fair Oaks Ave (91103-1619)
PHONE.....................626 798-9124
Alex Makabuhay, *Admn*
Pat Capello, *
Rose Wilson, *Management Company* *
EMP: 100 EST: 1992
SALES (est): 10.71MM Privately Held
Web: www.brighton1836.com
SIC: 8059 8051 Convalescent home; Skilled nursing care facilities

(P-18115)
BUENA VENTURA CARE CENTER INC
Also Called: Leisure Glen Convalescent Ctr
1505 Colby Dr (91205-3307)
PHONE.....................818 247-4476
Yolanda Wise, *Admn*
EMP: 80
SALES (corp-wide): 8.37MM Privately Held
SIC: 8059 8051 Convalescent home; Skilled nursing care facilities
PA: East Los Angeles Healthcare, Llc
1016 S Record Ave
Los Angeles CA
323 268-0106

(P-18116)
CARE CHOICE HEALTH SYSTEMS INC
Also Called: Care Choice Home Care
1151 S Santa Fe Ave (92083-7228)
PHONE.....................760 798-4508
Tara Pardo, *CEO*
EMP: 120 EST: 2015
SALES (est): 6.34MM Privately Held
Web: www.carechoicehomecare.com
SIC: 8059 8082 Personal care home, with health care; Home health care services

(P-18117)
CLEAR VIEW SANITARIUM INC
Also Called: Clear View Sanitarium
15823 S Western Ave (90247-3703)
PHONE.....................310 538-2323
Mark D Towns, *CEO*
Jeffrey B Towns, *
EMP: 175 EST: 1937
SQ FT: 40,000
SALES (est): 7.08MM Privately Held
Web: www.clearviewcare.com
SIC: 8059 Home for the mentally retarded, ex. skilled or intermediate

(P-18118)
COUNTRY VILLA SERVICE CORP
112 E Broadway (91776-1805)
PHONE.....................626 285-2165
J Caballero, *Admn*
EMP: 102
SALES (corp-wide): 88.5MM Privately Held
Web: www.evictionlawyer.com
SIC: 8059 Nursing home, except skilled and intermediate care facility
PA: Country Villa Service Corp.
2400 E Katella Ave # 800
Anaheim CA
310 574-3733

(P-18119)
CPCC INC
Also Called: CHATSWORTH PARK HEALTH CARE CE
10610 Owensmouth Ave (91311-2151)
PHONE.....................818 882-3200
John Sorensen, *Pr*
Greg Ethington, *
EMP: 99 EST: 1982
SALES (est): 15.05MM Privately Held
Web: www.chatsworthparkcare.com
SIC: 8059 8051 Convalescent home; Skilled nursing care facilities

(P-18120)
CRESTWOOD BEHAVIORAL HLTH INC
Also Called: 1115 Bakersfield Mhrc
6700 Eucalyptus Dr Ste A (93306-6076)
PHONE.....................661 363-8127
Sukhdeep Kaur, *Prin*
EMP: 82
SALES (corp-wide): 278.96MM Privately Held
Web: www.crestwoodbehavioralhealth.com
SIC: 8059 Home for the mentally retarded, ex. skilled or intermediate
PA: Crestwood Behavioral Health, Inc.
520 Capitol Mall Ste 800
Sacramento CA
209 955-2326

(P-18121)
CRESTWOOD BEHAVIORAL HLTH INC
Also Called: 1154 San Diego Mhrc
5550 University Ave Ste A (92105-2307)
PHONE.....................619 481-6790
Robyn Ramsey, *Admn*
EMP: 155
SALES (corp-wide): 278.96MM Privately Held
Web: www.crestwoodbehavioralhealth.com
SIC: 8059 Home for the mentally retarded, ex. skilled or intermediate
PA: Crestwood Behavioral Health, Inc.
520 Capitol Mall Ste 800
Sacramento CA
209 955-2326

(P-18122)
CRESTWOOD BEHAVIORAL HLTH INC
Also Called: 1167 Fallbrook Mhrc
624 E Elder St (92028-3004)
PHONE.....................760 451-4165
Corey Hise, *Admn*
EMP: 132
SALES (corp-wide): 278.96MM Privately Held
Web: www.crestwoodbehavioralhealth.com
SIC: 8059 Home for the mentally retarded, ex. skilled or intermediate
PA: Crestwood Behavioral Health, Inc.
520 Capitol Mall Ste 800
Sacramento CA
209 955-2326

(P-18123)
ENSIGN SAN DIMAS LLC
Also Called: Arbor Glen Care Center
1033 E Arrow Hwy (91740-6110)
PHONE.....................626 963-7531
Steve Powell, *Operations*
Don R Bybee, *Prin*
EMP: 106 EST: 2010
SALES (est): 10.65MM

PRODUCTS & SVCS

SALES (corp-wide): 3.03B **Publicly Held**
Web: www.arborglencare.com
SIC: 8059 Convalescent home
PA: The Ensign Group Inc
29222 Rncho Vejo Rd Ste 1
San Juan Capistrano CA
949 487-9500

(P-18124)
FRONT PORCH COMMUNITIES & SVCS
3775 Modoc Rd (93105-4474)
PHONE......................805 687-0793
Roberta Jacobsen, *Brnch Mgr*
EMP: 84
SQ FT: 68,000
Web: www.frontporch.net
SIC: 8059 8051 Rest home, with health care; Skilled nursing care facilities
PA: Front Porch Communities And Services
800 N Brand Blvd Fl 19
Glendale CA

(P-18125)
FRONT PRCH CMMNTIES OPRTING GR
Also Called: FREDERICKA MANOR CARE CENTER
800 N Brand Blvd Fl 19 (91203-1231)
PHONE.....................,.........800 233-3709
John Woodward, *CEO*
EMP: 190 **EST:** 2013
SALES (est): 80.38MM **Privately Held**
Web: www.frontporch.net
SIC: 8059 Nursing and personal care, nec

(P-18126)
GENESIS HEALTHCARE LLC
Also Called: Fountain View Cnvalescent Hosp
5310 Fountain Ave (90029-1005)
PHONE......................323 461-9961
EMP: 633
Web: www.genesishcc.com
SIC: 8059 8051 8069 Convalescent home; Skilled nursing care facilities; Specialty hospitals, except psychiatric
HQ: Genesis Healthcare Llc
101 E State St
Kennett Square PA

(P-18127)
GERI-CARE II INC
Also Called: Vermont Care Center
22035 S Vermont Ave (90502-2120)
P.O. Box 6069 (90504-0069)
PHONE......................310 328-0812
Emmanuel David, *Pr*
Engelica Vivillanueva, *
EMP: 250 **EST:** 1989
SQ FT: 40,000
SALES (est): 13.17MM **Privately Held**
Web: www.vermonthc.com
SIC: 8059 8051 Convalescent home; Skilled nursing care facilities

(P-18128)
GIBRALTAR CNVALESCENT HOSP INC
Also Called: Sunset Manor Convalescent Hosp
2720 Nevada Ave (91733-2318)
PHONE......................626 443-9425
Marcel Morales, *Mgr*
EMP: 100
SALES (corp-wide): 9.31MM **Privately Held**
Web: www.sunsetmanorcare.com
SIC: 8059 8051 Convalescent home; Skilled nursing care facilities

PA: Gibraltar Convalescent Hospital, Inc.
3050 Saturn St Ste 201
Brea CA
714 577-3880

(P-18129)
GOLDEN CARE INC
Also Called: Valley Manor Convalescent Hosp
6120 Vineland Ave (91606-4914)
PHONE......................818 763-6275
Evelyn Del Rosario, *Pr*
Gonzalo Del Rosario, *
EMP: 80 **EST:** 1963
SQ FT: 32,000
SALES (est): 4.56MM **Privately Held**
SIC: 8059 8361 Convalescent home; Residential care

(P-18130)
GOLDEN STATE HEALTH CTRS INC
Also Called: Ocean View Convelesent Hosp
1340 15th St (90404-1802)
PHONE......................310 451-9706
Dina Closas R.n., *Dir*
EMP: 200
SALES (corp-wide): 74.01MM **Privately Held**
Web: www.goldenstatehealth.com
SIC: 8059 8051 Convalescent home; Skilled nursing care facilities
PA: Golden State Health Centers, Inc.
13347 Ventura Blvd
Sherman Oaks CA
818 385-3200

(P-18131)
HILLSDALE GROUP LP
Also Called: Sherman Village Hlth Care Ctr
12750 Riverside Dr (91607-3319)
PHONE......................818 623-2170
Rich Terrell, *Prin*
EMP: 249
SALES (corp-wide): 24.71MM **Privately Held**
SIC: 8059 8051 8093 8011 Convalescent home; Skilled nursing care facilities; Rehabilitation center, outpatient treatment; Clinic, operated by physicians
PA: The Hillsdale Group L P
1199 Howard Ave Ste 200
Burlingame CA

(P-18132)
HUMANGOOD (PA)
Also Called: Terraces At Squaw Peak
1900 Huntington Dr (91010-2694)
PHONE......................602 906-4024
John Cochran, *CEO*
EMP: 110 **EST:** 1959
SALES (est): 27.02MM
SALES (corp-wide): 27.02MM **Privately Held**
Web: www.humangood.org
SIC: 8059 8051 8322 Rest home, with health care; Skilled nursing care facilities; Old age assistance

(P-18133)
HUMANGOOD NORCAL
Also Called: Rosewood Retirement Community
1401 New Stine Rd (93309-3530)
PHONE......................661 834-0620
Ellen Renner, *Brnch Mgr*
EMP: 121
SALES (corp-wide): 27.02MM **Privately Held**
Web: www.humangood.org

SIC: 8059 8052 8051 Rest home, with health care; Intermediate care facilities; Skilled nursing care facilities
HQ: Humangood Norcal
1900 Huntington Dr
Duarte CA
925 924-7100

(P-18134)
HUMANGOOD NORCAL
Also Called: Plymouth Village
900 Salem Dr (92373-6147)
PHONE......................909 793-1233
Keith Kasin, *Brnch Mgr*
EMP: 170
SQ FT: 8,000
SALES (corp-wide): 27.02MM **Privately Held**
Web: www.humangood.org
SIC: 8059 8051 Rest home, with health care; Skilled nursing care facilities
HQ: Humangood Norcal
1900 Huntington Dr
Duarte CA
925 924-7100

(P-18135)
LEXINGTON GROUP INTERNATIONAL
260 E Market St (90805-5910)
PHONE......................562 428-4681
EMP: 180
SIC: 8059 Convalescent home
PA: Lexington Group International, Inc
9200 W Sunset Blvd # 950
West Hollywood CA

(P-18136)
LIFE CARE CENTERS AMERICA INC
Also Called: Vista Del Mar Health Centers
304 N Melrose Dr (92083-4814)
PHONE......................760 724-8222
Michael Ramstead, *Brnch Mgr*
EMP: 229
SALES (corp-wide): 139.21MM **Privately Held**
Web: www.lcca.com
SIC: 8059 8051 Convalescent home; Skilled nursing care facilities
PA: Life Care Centers Of America, Inc.
3570 Keith St Nw
Cleveland TN
423 472-9585

(P-18137)
LONGWOOD MANAGEMENT CORP
Also Called: Sunny View Care Center
2000 W Washington Blvd (90018-1637)
PHONE......................323 735-5146
Amber Gooden, *Admn*
EMP: 100
SALES (corp-wide): 79.33MM **Privately Held**
Web: www.longwoodmgmt.com
SIC: 8059 Convalescent home
PA: Longwood Management Corp.
4032 Wilshire Blvd Fl 6
Los Angeles CA
213 389-6900

(P-18138)
LONGWOOD MANAGEMENT CORP
Also Called: Broadway Manor Care Center
605 W Broadway (91204-1007)
PHONE......................818 246-7174
Dolly Piper, *Mgr*

EMP: 96
SQ FT: 7,000
SALES (corp-wide): 79.33MM **Privately Held**
Web: www.broadwaymanorhc.com
SIC: 8059 8051 Convalescent home; Skilled nursing care facilities
PA: Longwood Management Corp.
4032 Wilshire Blvd Fl 6
Los Angeles CA
213 389-6900

(P-18139)
LONGWOOD MANAGEMENT CORP
Also Called: Aldon Ter Convalsent Hosptial
1240 S Hoover St (90006-3606)
PHONE......................213 382-8461
John Sicat, *Prin*
EMP: 155
SALES (corp-wide): 79.33MM **Privately Held**
Web: www.longwoodmgmt.com
SIC: 8059 8051 Convalescent home; Skilled nursing care facilities
PA: Longwood Management Corp.
4032 Wilshire Blvd Fl 6
Los Angeles CA
213 389-6900

(P-18140)
LONGWOOD MANAGEMENT CORP
Also Called: Imperial Care Center
11429 Ventura Blvd (91604-3143)
PHONE......................818 980-8200
Emma Dellanuoni, *Mgr*
EMP: 150
SQ FT: 29,525
SALES (corp-wide): 79.33MM **Privately Held**
Web: www.studiocityrehab.com
SIC: 8059 8051 Convalescent home; Skilled nursing care facilities
PA: Longwood Management Corp.
4032 Wilshire Blvd Fl 6
Los Angeles CA
213 389-6900

(P-18141)
LONGWOOD MANAGEMENT CORP
Also Called: Live Oak Rehab
537 W Live Oak St (91776-1149)
PHONE......................626 289-3763
Ranita Phan, *Mgr*
EMP: 130
SALES (corp-wide): 79.33MM **Privately Held**
Web: www.liveoakrehab.com
SIC: 8059 8051 Convalescent home; Skilled nursing care facilities
PA: Longwood Management Corp.
4032 Wilshire Blvd Fl 6
Los Angeles CA
213 389-6900

(P-18142)
LONGWOOD MANAGEMENT CORP
Also Called: Colonial Care Center
1913 E 5th St (90802-2024)
PHONE......................562 432-5751
EMP: 128
SALES (corp-wide): 79.33MM **Privately Held**
Web: www.longwoodmgmt.com
SIC: 8059 8051 Convalescent home; Skilled nursing care facilities
PA: Longwood Management Corp.
4032 Wilshire Blvd Fl 6

Los Angeles CA
213 389-6900

(P-18143)
MAGNOLIA RHBLTTION NURSING CTR
Also Called: Magnolia Convalescent Hospital
8133 Magnolia Ave (92504-3409)
PHONE.....................951 688-4321
Larry Mays, *Pr*
Bennie J Mays, *
Bobbie N Mays, *
Grant Edgeson, *
EMP: 140 EST: 1971
SQ FT: 25,000
SALES (est): 9.51MM **Privately Held**
Web: www.magnolia-rehab.com
SIC: **8059** 8051 Convalescent home; Skilled nursing care facilities

(P-18144)
MARLINDA MANAGEMENT INC (PA)
Also Called: Sherwood Guest Home
3351 E Imperial Hwy (90262-3305)
PHONE.....................310 631-6122
Martha Lang, *Pr*
Linda Gassoumis, *
EMP: 120 EST: 1961
SALES (est): 4.17MM
SALES (corp-wide): 4.17MM **Privately Held**
SIC: **8059** Convalescent home

(P-18145)
MARYCREST MANOR
10664 Saint James Dr (90230-5498)
PHONE.....................310 838-2778
Sister V Del Carmen, *Admn*
Sister Veronica Del Carmen, *Admn*
EMP: 94 EST: 1961
SQ FT: 43,449
SALES (est): 7.79MM **Privately Held**
Web: www.marycrestculvercity.com
SIC: **8059** 8051 Convalescent home; Skilled nursing care facilities

(P-18146)
NEW VISTA HEALTH SERVICES
Also Called: New Vsta Post Acute Care Ctr W
1516 Sawtelle Blvd (90025-3207)
PHONE.....................310 477-5501
Eugene Tipo, *Admn*
EMP: 224
SALES (corp-wide): 11.41MM **Privately Held**
Web: www.newvista.us
SIC: **8059** 8051 Nursing home, except skilled and intermediate care facility; Skilled nursing care facilities
PA: New Vista Health Services, Inc
1987 Vartikian Ave
Clovis CA
559 298-3236

(P-18147)
NEW VISTA HEALTH SERVICES
Also Called: New Vsta Nrsing Rhbltation Ctr
8647 Fenwick St (91040-1957)
PHONE.....................818 352-1421
Robert Craig, *Pr*
EMP: 224
SALES (corp-wide): 11.41MM **Privately Held**
Web: www.newvista.us
SIC: **8059** 8361 Nursing home, except skilled and intermediate care facility; Rehabilitation center, residential: health care incidental
PA: New Vista Health Services, Inc
1987 Vartikian Ave

Clovis CA
559 298-3236

(P-18148)
OLYMPIA CONVALESCENT HOSPITAL
1100 S Alvarado St (90006-4110)
PHONE.....................213 487-3000
Otto Schwartz, *Admn*
Sam Lidell, *
Andre Pollak, *
EMP: 115 EST: 1971
SQ FT: 25,000
SALES (est): 12.59MM **Privately Held**
Web: www.olympia.com
SIC: **8059** 8051 Convalescent home; Skilled nursing care facilities

(P-18149)
ORANGE CNTY RYALE CNVLSCENT HO (PA)
Also Called: Royale Convalescent Hospital
1030 W Warner Ave (92707-3147)
PHONE.....................714 546-6450
Mitchell Kantor, *Pr*
Donald Connelly Admtr, *Prin*
EMP: 330 EST: 1965
SQ FT: 87,000
SALES (est): 17.01MM
SALES (corp-wide): 17.01MM **Privately Held**
Web: www.royalehealth.com
SIC: **8059** 8051 Convalescent home; Skilled nursing care facilities

(P-18150)
PACIFIC HAVEN CONVALESCENT HM
12072 Trask Ave (92843-3881)
PHONE.....................714 534-1942
Mike Uranga, *Admn*
EMP: 100 EST: 1978
SALES (est): 11.36MM **Privately Held**
Web: www.pachaven.com
SIC: **8059** 8051 Convalescent home; Skilled nursing care facilities

(P-18151)
PARK MARINO CONVALESCENT CTR
2585 E Washington Blvd (91107-1446)
PHONE.....................626 463-4105
Admiral William Kite, *Prin*
EMP: 181 EST: 1966
SALES (est): 5.01MM
SALES (corp-wide): 9.98MM **Privately Held**
Web: www.parkmarino.com
SIC: **8059** 8051 Convalescent home; Skilled nursing care facilities
PA: Diversified Health Services (Del)
136 Washington Ave
Richmond CA
510 231-6200

(P-18152)
PILGRIM PLACE IN CLAREMONT (PA)
625 Mayflower Rd (91711-4240)
PHONE.....................909 399-5500
William R Cunitz, *Pr*
Joyce Yarborough, *
Sue Fairley, *
Bernard Valek, *
Mary Ann Macias, *
EMP: 175 EST: 1914
SQ FT: 2,000
SALES (est): 22.23MM
SALES (corp-wide): 22.23MM **Privately Held**

Web: www.pilgrimplace.org
SIC: **8059** 8051 8052 Rest home, with health care; Skilled nursing care facilities; Intermediate care facilities

(P-18153)
SAN BERNARDINO CARE COMPANY
467 E Gilbert St (92404-5318)
PHONE.....................909 884-4781
Jenq Chen, *Pr*
EMP: 110 EST: 2004
SALES (est): 5.22MM **Privately Held**
SIC: **8059** Convalescent home

(P-18154)
SAN DEGO CTR FOR CHLDREN FNDTI (PA)
3002 Armstrong St (92111-5702)
PHONE.....................858 277-9550
Moises Baron, *CEO*
EMP: 90 EST: 1887
SQ FT: 38,000
SALES (est): 24.56MM
SALES (corp-wide): 24.56MM **Privately Held**
Web: www.centerforchildren.org
SIC: **8059** 8361 Personal care home, with health care; Residential care

(P-18155)
TWO PALMS NURSING CENTER INC
Also Called: Marlinda Imperial Hospital
150 Bellefontaine St (91105-3102)
PHONE.....................626 796-1103
EMP: 185
SQ FT: 28,955
SALES (corp-wide): 3.22MM **Privately Held**
Web: www.pasadenameadows.com
SIC: **8059** 8051 Convalescent home; Skilled nursing care facilities
PA: Two Palms Nursing Center, Inc.
2637 E Washington Blvd
Pasadena CA
626 798-8991

(P-18156)
UNITED CONVALESCENT FACILITIES
Also Called: University Park Healthcare Ctr
230 E Adams Blvd (90011-1426)
PHONE.....................213 748-0491
Doug Easton, *Owner*
EMP: 80 EST: 1998
SQ FT: 1,300
SALES (est): 8.1MM **Privately Held**
SIC: **8059** Nursing home, except skilled and intermediate care facility

(P-18157)
UNITED MEDICAL MANAGEMENT INC
Also Called: Valley Healthcare
1680 N Waterman Ave (92404-5113)
PHONE.....................909 886-5291
Alan Hull, *Admn*
EMP: 125 EST: 1982
SQ FT: 30,000
SALES (est): 7.24MM **Privately Held**
Web: www.progressivecarecenters.com
SIC: **8059** 8051 8322 Convalescent home; Skilled nursing care facilities; Rehabilitation services

(P-18158)
VALLE VSTA CNVLESCENT HOSP INC
1025 W 2nd Ave (92025-3839)
PHONE.....................760 745-1288
Kristina Kuivon, *CEO*
EMP: 85 EST: 1961
SQ FT: 19,000
SALES (est): 4.45MM **Privately Held**
SIC: **8059** Convalescent home
PA: Covenant Care, Llc
120 Vantis Dr Ste 200
Aliso Viejo CA

(P-18159)
VILLA DE LA MAR INC
Also Called: Bel Vista Healthcare Center
5001 E Anaheim St (90804-3214)
PHONE.....................562 494-5001
Alan Anderson, *Pr*
Dorothy Erickson, *
EMP: 160 EST: 1983
SALES (est): 10.37MM
SALES (corp-wide): 1.53B **Privately Held**
Web: www.belvista.com
SIC: **8059** Convalescent home
PA: Providence Group, Inc.
262 N University Ave
Farmington UT
801 447-9829

(P-18160)
WINDSOR CYPRESS GRDNS HLTHCARE
Also Called: Windsor Cypress Garden
9025 Colorado Ave (92503-2157)
PHONE.....................951 688-3643
Lee Samson, *CEO*
Stanley Angermeir, *
Edward Erzen, *
EMP: 2963 EST: 1972
SALES (est): 28.39MM **Privately Held**
SIC: **8059** 8051 Convalescent home; Skilled nursing care facilities
PA: S&F Management Company, Llc
1901 Avenue Of The Stars # 1060
Los Angeles CA

8062 General Medical And Surgical Hospitals

(P-18161)
ADVENTIST HEALTH DELANO
Also Called: Delano Regional Medical Center
1205 Garces Hwy Ste 208 (93215-3658)
PHONE.....................661 721-5337
Ester Bumabod, *Mgr*
EMP: 131
SALES (corp-wide): 789.42MM **Privately Held**
Web: www.adventisthealth.org
SIC: **8062** 5047 General medical and surgical hospitals; Therapy equipment
HQ: Adventist Health Delano
1401 Garces Hwy Bldg A
Delano CA
661 725-4800

(P-18162)
ADVENTIST HEALTH DELANO (HQ)
Also Called: Delano Regional Medical Center
1401 Garces Hwy (93215-3699)
P.O. Box 460 (93216-0460)
PHONE.....................661 725-4800
EMP: 523 EST: 1973
SALES (est): 98.9MM
SALES (corp-wide): 789.42MM **Privately Held**

PRODUCTS & SVCS

Web: www.adventisthealth.org
SIC: **8062** General medical and surgical hospitals
PA: Adventist Health System/West, Corporation
1 Adventist Health Way
Roseville CA
844 574-5686

(P-18163)
ADVENTIST HEALTH MED TEHACHAPI (PA)
305 S Robinson St (93561-1726)
P.O. Box 669 (93581-0669)
PHONE...............................661 750-4848
Eugene Suksi, *CEO*
Allen Burgess, *
EMP: 108 EST: 1949
SQ FT: 18,000
SALES (est): 2.95MM
SALES (corp-wide): 2.95MM **Privately Held**
Web: www.tvhd.org
SIC: **8062** General medical and surgical hospitals

(P-18164)
ADVENTIST HLTH SYSTM/WEST CORP
Also Called: Bakersfield Heart Hospital
3001 Sillect Ave (93308-6337)
PHONE...............................661 316-6000
Kerry Heinrich, *Brnch Mgr*
EMP: 336
SALES (corp-wide): 789.42MM **Privately Held**
Web: www.adventisthealth.org
SIC: **8062** General medical and surgical hospitals
PA: Adventist Health System/West, Corporation
1 Adventist Health Way
Roseville CA
844 574-5686

(P-18165)
AHM GEMCH INC
Also Called: Greater El Monte Cmnty Hosp
1701 Santa Anita Ave (91733-3411)
PHONE...............................626 579-7777
Jeffrey Flocken, *CEO*
Patrick Steinhauser, *COO*
Gary Louis, *CFO*
EMP: 180 EST: 1973
SQ FT: 71,500
SALES (est): 40.24MM
SALES (corp-wide): 476.02MM **Privately Held**
Web: www.ahmchealth.com
SIC: **8062** General medical and surgical hospitals
PA: Ahmc Healthcare Inc.
506 W Valley Blvd Ste 300
San Gabriel CA
626 943-7526

(P-18166)
AHMC ANHEIM RGIONAL MED CTR LP
1111 W La Palma Ave (92801-2804)
PHONE...............................714 774-1450
Barry Arbuckle, *Prin*
Jane Cutler, *
Donald Lorack, *
Kathy Doi, *
▲ EMP: 4203 EST: 1959
SQ FT: 500
SALES (est): 23.89MM
SALES (corp-wide): 476.02MM **Privately Held**

Web: www.ahmchealth.com
SIC: **8062** General medical and surgical hospitals
PA: Ahmc Healthcare Inc.
506 W Valley Blvd Ste 300
San Gabriel CA
626 943-7526

(P-18167)
AHMC ANHEIM RGIONAL MED CTR LP (PA)
Also Called: Anaheim Regional Medical Ctr
1111 W La Palma Ave (92801-2804)
PHONE...............................714 774-1450
Patrick Petre, *CEO*
Deborah Webber, *
Kathy Doi, *
Marie Trembath, *
EMP: 976 EST: 1958
SALES (est): 137.25MM
SALES (corp-wide): 137.25MM **Privately Held**
Web: www.ahmchealth.com
SIC: **8062** 8069 General medical and surgical hospitals; Childrens' hospital

(P-18168)
AHMC HEALTHCARE INC (PA)
506 W Valley Blvd Ste 300 (91776-5716)
PHONE...............................626 943-7526
Jonathan Wu Md, *CEO*
EMP: 150 EST: 2004
SALES (est): 476.02MM
SALES (corp-wide): 476.02MM **Privately Held**
Web: www.ahmchealth.com
SIC: **8062** 8641 General medical and surgical hospitals; Civic and social associations

(P-18169)
AHMC HEALTHCARE INC
1701 Santa Anita Ave (91733-3411)
PHONE...............................626 579-7777
EMP: 94
SALES (corp-wide): 476.02MM **Privately Held**
Web: www.ahmchealth.com
SIC: **8062** General medical and surgical hospitals
PA: Ahmc Healthcare Inc.
506 W Valley Blvd Ste 300
San Gabriel CA
626 943-7526

(P-18170)
AHMC WHITTIER HOSP MED CTR LP
9080 Colima Rd (90605-1600)
PHONE...............................562 945-3561
Richard Castro, *CEO*
EMP: 850 EST: 2001
SQ FT: 16,782
SALES (est): 96.67MM
SALES (corp-wide): 476.02MM **Privately Held**
Web: www.ahmchealth.com
SIC: **8062** General medical and surgical hospitals
PA: Ahmc Healthcare Inc.
506 W Valley Blvd Ste 300
San Gabriel CA
626 943-7526

(P-18171)
ALAKOR HEALTHCARE LLC
Also Called: MONROVIA MEMORIAL HOSPITAL
323 S Heliotrope Ave (91016-2914)
PHONE...............................626 408-9800

Jon Woods, *
Ron Kupferstein, *
EMP: 126 EST: 2004
SQ FT: 10,000
SALES (est): 15.69MM **Privately Held**
Web: www.monroviamemorial.com
SIC: **8062** General medical and surgical hospitals

(P-18172)
ALHAMBRA HOSPITAL MED CTR LP
Also Called: Alhambra Hospital Medical Ctr
100 S Raymond Ave (91801-3166)
PHONE...............................626 570-1606
Iris Lai, *Managing Member*
EMP: 160 EST: 1920
SQ FT: 200,000
SALES (est): 79.79MM
SALES (corp-wide): 476.02MM **Privately Held**
Web: www.alhambrahospital.com
SIC: **8062** General medical and surgical hospitals
PA: Ahmc Healthcare Inc.
506 W Valley Blvd Ste 300
San Gabriel CA
626 943-7526

(P-18173)
ALTA HEALTHCARE SYSTEM LLC (HQ)
4081 E Olympic Blvd (90023-3330)
PHONE...............................323 267-0477
David Topper, *Managing Member*
Sam Lee, *
EMP: 250 EST: 1998
SALES (est): 108.98MM
SALES (corp-wide): 3.91B **Privately Held**
Web: www.schculver.city
SIC: **8062** General medical and surgical hospitals
PA: Prospect Medical Holdings, Inc.
3415 S Sepulveda Blvd # 9
Los Angeles CA
310 943-4500

(P-18174)
ALTA HOSPITALS SYSTEM LLC
Also Called: Foothill Regional Medical Ctr
14662 Newport Ave (92780-6064)
PHONE...............................714 619-7700
EMP: 575
SALES (corp-wide): 3.91B **Privately Held**
Web: www.pmh.com
SIC: **8062** General medical and surgical hospitals
HQ: Alta Hospitals System, Llc
3415 S Sepulveda Blvd # 9
Los Angeles CA

(P-18175)
ALVARADO HOSPITAL LLC (DH)
6655 Alvarado Rd (92120-5208)
PHONE...............................619 287-3270
Darlene Wetton, *
Gudrun Moll, *
EMP: 232 EST: 1989
SALES (est): 71.09MM
SALES (corp-wide): 534.4MM **Privately Held**
Web: www.alvaradohospital.com
SIC: **8062** General medical and surgical hospitals
HQ: University Of California, San Diego
9500 Gilman Dr
La Jolla CA
858 534-2230

(P-18176)
ALVARADO HOSPITAL MED CTR INC
6655 Alvarado Rd (92120-5208)
PHONE...............................619 287-3270
Sharilee Smith, *Pr*
EMP: 791 EST: 2000
SALES (est): 122.61MM
SALES (corp-wide): 19.58B **Publicly Held**
Web: health.ucsd.edu
SIC: **8062** General medical and surgical hospitals
PA: Tenet Healthcare Corporation
14201 Dallas Pkwy
Dallas TX
469 893-2200

(P-18177)
AMERICAN HLTHCARE SYSTEMS CORP (PA)
505 N Brand Blvd Ste 1110 (91203-3932)
PHONE...............................818 646-9933
Michael Sarian, *Dir*
Aimee Gill, *VP*
Aramais Paronyan, *CMO*
Jonathan Burket, *CCO*
EMP: 293 EST: 2021
SALES (est): 143.23MM
SALES (corp-wide): 143.23MM **Privately Held**
SIC: **8062** General medical and surgical hospitals

(P-18178)
AMISUB OF CALIFORNIA INC (DH)
Also Called: Amisub
18321 Clark St (91356-3501)
PHONE...............................818 881-0800
Dale Surowitz, *CEO*
Don Kreitz, *
Nick Lymberopolous, *
EMP: 900 EST: 1979
SQ FT: 180,000
SALES (est): 98.79MM
SALES (corp-wide): 19.58B **Publicly Held**
SIC: **8062** General medical and surgical hospitals
HQ: Tenet Healthsystem Medical, Inc.
14201 Dallas Pkwy
Dallas TX
469 893-2000

(P-18179)
ANAHEIM GLOBAL MEDICAL CENTER
1025 S Anaheim Blvd (92805-5806)
PHONE...............................714 533-6220
Jamie You, *CEO*
Marven E Howard, *
Jason Liu, *
EMP: 975 EST: 1981
SALES (est): 108.46MM **Privately Held**
Web: www.anaheimglobalmedicalcenter.com
SIC: **8062** General medical and surgical hospitals
HQ: Kpc Healthcare, Inc.
1301 N Tustin Ave
Santa Ana CA
714 953-3652

(P-18180)
ANAHEIM REGIONAL MEDICAL CTR
Also Called: Cardiac Unit
1111 W La Palma Ave (92801-2804)
PHONE...............................714 774-1450
EMP: 112

▲ = Import ▼ = Export
◆ = Import/Export

SALES (corp-wide): 137.25MM **Privately Held**
Web: www.ahmchealth.com
SIC: 8062 General medical and surgical hospitals
PA: Ahmc Anaheim Regional Medical Center Lp
1111 W La Palma Ave
Anaheim CA
714 774-1450

(P-18181)
ANAHEIM REGIONAL MEDICAL CTR
Also Called: Ahmc
1211 W La Palma Ave (92801-2815)
PHONE...............714 999-3847
Patrick Petre, *Brnch Mgr*
EMP: 112
SALES (corp-wide): 137.25MM **Privately Held**
Web: www.ahmchealth.com
SIC: 8062 General medical and surgical hospitals
PA: Ahmc Anaheim Regional Medical Center Lp
1111 W La Palma Ave
Anaheim CA
714 774-1450

(P-18182)
ANTELOPE VALLEY HEALTH CARE DI (PA)
Also Called: Avmc
1600 W Avenue J (93534-2814)
P.O. Box 7001 (93539-7001)
PHONE...............661 949-5000
Edward Mirzabegian, *CEO*
Abdallah Farrukh, *
Dennis Empey, *
Slavka Rehacek, *
EMP: 1660 **EST:** 1955
SQ FT: 300,000
SALES (est): 494.78MM
SALES (corp-wide): 494.78MM **Privately Held**
Web: www.avmc.com
SIC: 8062 General medical and surgical hospitals

(P-18183)
ANTELOPE VALLEY HOSPITAL INC
Also Called: Antelope Valley Hlth Care Dst
44335 Lowtree Ave (93534-4167)
PHONE...............661 949-5000
Cheryl Akerly, *Brnch Mgr*
EMP: 221
SALES (corp-wide): 494.78MM **Privately Held**
Web: www.avmc.org
SIC: 8062 General medical and surgical hospitals
PA: Antelope Valley Health Care District
1600 W Avenue J
Lancaster CA
661 949-5000

(P-18184)
ANTELOPE VALLEY HOSPITAL INC
Antelope Otpatient Imaging Ctr
44105 15th St W Ste 100 (93534-4090)
PHONE...............661 726-6050
Veronica Munoz-rivera, *Brnch Mgr*
EMP: 172
SALES (corp-wide): 494.78MM **Privately Held**
Web: www.avmc.org

SIC: 8062 8099 General medical and surgical hospitals; Medical services organization
PA: Antelope Valley Health Care District
1600 W Avenue J
Lancaster CA
661 949-5000

(P-18185)
ANTELOPE VALLEY HOSPITAL INC
Also Called: Antelope Valley Home Care
44335 Lowtree Ave (93534-4167)
PHONE...............661 949-5936
Patti Sheldon, *Mgr*
EMP: 149
SALES (corp-wide): 494.78MM **Privately Held**
Web: www.avmc.org
SIC: 8062 8082 General medical and surgical hospitals; Home health care services
PA: Antelope Valley Health Care District
1600 W Avenue J
Lancaster CA
661 949-5000

(P-18186)
ARROWHEAD REGIONAL MEDICAL CTR
Also Called: Armc
400 N Pepper Ave (92324-1801)
PHONE...............909 580-1000
Patrick Petre, *Dir*
Sam Hessami, *CMO*
EMP: 2500 **EST:** 1952
SQ FT: 950,000
SALES (est): 595.65MM
SALES (corp-wide): 4.01B **Privately Held**
Web: www.arrowheadregional.org
SIC: 8062 General medical and surgical hospitals
PA: San Bernardino County
385 N Arrowhead Ave
San Bernardino CA
909 387-3841

(P-18187)
ARROYO GRANDE COMMUNITY HOSPITAL
Also Called: Emergency Dept Dignity Hlth
345 S Halcyon Rd (93420-3817)
PHONE...............805 473-7626
EMP: 400
SIC: 8062 General medical and surgical hospitals

(P-18188)
AUXILARY OF MSSION HOSP MSSION
Also Called: Mission Hospital
27700 Medical Center Rd (92691-6426)
PHONE...............949 364-1400
Eduardo Jordan, *Ch Bd*
Kenn Mcfarland, *Pr*
Vicki J Veal, *
EMP: 1242 **EST:** 2011
SALES (est): 156.11K
SALES (corp-wide): 765.86MM **Privately Held**
Web: www.mission4health.com
SIC: 8062 General medical and surgical hospitals
PA: Mission Hospital Regional Medical Center Inc
27700 Medical Center Rd
Mission Viejo CA
949 364-1400

(P-18189)
BAKERSFIELD MEMORIAL HOSPITAL
Also Called: Memorial Center
420 34th St (93301-2237)
P.O. Box 2400 (85002-2400)
PHONE...............661 327-1792
Jon Van Boening, *CEO*
Gordon K Foster, *
EMP: 1100 **EST:** 1953
SQ FT: 364,000
SALES (est): 566.75MM **Privately Held**
Web: www.dignityhealth.org
SIC: 8062 Hospital, affiliated with AMA residency
HQ: Dignity Health
185 Berry St Ste 200
San Francisco CA
415 438-5500

(P-18190)
BEAR VLY CMNTY HEALTHCARE DST (PA)
41870 Garstin Dr (92315-2088)
PHONE...............909 866-6501
Raymond Hino, *CEO*
Donna Nicely, *
Barbara Espinoza, *
Christopher Fagan, *
EMP: 150 **EST:** 1985
SQ FT: 25,000
SALES (est): 341.35K
SALES (corp-wide): 341.35K **Privately Held**
Web:
www.bearvalleycommunityhospital.com
SIC: 8062 General medical and surgical hospitals

(P-18191)
BEVERLY COMMUNITY HOSP ASSN (PA)
Also Called: Beverly Hospital
309 W Beverly Blvd (90640-4308)
PHONE...............323 726-1222
Alice Cheng, *CEO*
Gary Kiff, *
Renee D Martinez, *
David I Chambers, *
Mohammad A, *
EMP: 937 **EST:** 1949
SQ FT: 274,000
SALES (est): 145.51MM
SALES (corp-wide): 145.51MM **Privately Held**
Web: www.beverly.org
SIC: 8062 General medical and surgical hospitals

(P-18192)
BIO-MED SERVICES INC
Also Called: Prime Healthcare Services
3300 E Guasti Rd (91761-8655)
PHONE...............909 235-4400
Prem Reddy, *CEO*
EMP: 85 **EST:** 2006
SALES (est): 29.17MM
SALES (corp-wide): 1.03B **Privately Held**
SIC: 8062 General medical and surgical hospitals
HQ: Prime Healthcare Services Inc
3480 E Guasti Rd
Ontario CA

(P-18193)
BROTMAN MEDICAL CENTER INC
Also Called: Southern Cal Hosp At Culver Cy
3828 Delmas Ter (90232-6806)

PHONE...............310 836-7000
TOLL FREE: 800
Michael Klepin, *CEO*
EMP: 300 **EST:** 1961
SQ FT: 183,000
SALES (est): 61.07MM
SALES (corp-wide): 3.91B **Privately Held**
Web: www.sch-culvercity.com
SIC: 8062 General medical and surgical hospitals
PA: Prospect Medical Holdings, Inc.
3415 S Sepulveda Blvd # 9
Los Angeles CA
310 943-4500

(P-18194)
CALIFRNIA HOSP MED CTR FNDTION
1401 S Grand Ave (90015-3010)
PHONE...............213 742-5867
Phillip C Hill, *Ch Bd*
Nathan R Nusbaum, *
Clark Underwood, *
David Milovich, *
Linda Bolor, *
▲ **EMP:** 1500 **EST:** 1926
SQ FT: 800,000
SALES (est): 249.47MM **Privately Held**
Web: www.supportcaliforniahospital.org
SIC: 8062 Hospital, med school affiliated with nursing and residency
HQ: Dignity Health
185 Berry St Ste 200
San Francisco CA
415 438-5500

(P-18195)
CASA CLINA HOSP CTRS FOR HLTHC (HQ)
Also Called: CASA COLINA HOSPITAL AND CENTE
255 E Bonita Ave (91767-1923)
P.O. Box 6001 (91769-6001)
PHONE...............909 596-7733
Kelly Linden, *Pr*
Steve Norin, *
Randy Blackman, *Vice Chairman*
Mary Lou Jensen, *
Stephen Graeber, *
▲ **EMP:** 500 **EST:** 1936
SQ FT: 90,000
SALES (est): 92.94MM
SALES (corp-wide): 136.57MM **Privately Held**
Web: www.casacolina.org
SIC: 8062 General medical and surgical hospitals
PA: Casa Colina, Inc.
255 E Bonita Ave
Pomona CA
909 596-7733

(P-18196)
CATHOLIC HLTHCARE W STHERN CAL (HQ)
1050 Linden Ave (90813-3321)
PHONE...............562 491-9000
EMP: 125
SALES (est): 43.27MM
SALES (corp-wide): 7.06B **Privately Held**
SIC: 8062 General medical and surgical hospitals
PA: Dignity Health
185 Berry St Ste 300
San Francisco CA
415 438-5500

(P-18197)
CEDARS-SINAI MEDICAL CENTER

Also Called: Nephrology
8635 W 3rd St Ste 1195 (90048-6146)
P.O. Box 48956 (90048-0956)
PHONE...................................310 824-3664
Larry Froch, *Prin*
EMP: 438
SALES (corp-wide): 4.7B **Privately Held**
Web: www.cedars-sinai.org
SIC: 8062 General medical and surgical
　　hospitals
PA: Cedars-Sinai Medical Center
　　8700 Beverly Blvd
　　West Hollywood CA
　　310 423-3277

(P-18198)
CEDARS-SINAI MEDICAL CENTER
Also Called: Cedars Surgical Research Ctr
8700 Beverly Blvd # 4018 (90048-1804)
PHONE...................................310 855-7701
Linda Protcor, *Div Mgr*
EMP: 308
SALES (corp-wide): 4.7B **Privately Held**
Web: www.cedars-sinai.org
SIC: 8062 8733 General medical and
　　surgical hospitals; Medical research
PA: Cedars-Sinai Medical Center
　　8700 Beverly Blvd
　　West Hollywood CA
　　310 423-3277

(P-18199)
CEDARS-SINAI MEDICAL CENTER
8797 Beverly Blvd Ste 220 (90048-1892)
PHONE...................................310 423-5468
EMP: 89
SALES (corp-wide): 4.7B **Privately Held**
Web: www.cedars-sinai.org
SIC: 8062 General medical and surgical
　　hospitals
PA: Cedars-Sinai Medical Center
　　8700 Beverly Blvd
　　West Hollywood CA
　　310 423-3277

(P-18200)
CEDARS-SINAI MEDICAL CENTER
8727 W 3rd St (90048-3843)
PHONE...................................310 423-6451
Eric Fee, *Genl Mgr*
EMP: 113
SALES (corp-wide): 4.7B **Privately Held**
Web: www.cedars-sinai.org
SIC: 8062 General medical and surgical
　　hospitals
PA: Cedars-Sinai Medical Center
　　8700 Beverly Blvd
　　West Hollywood CA
　　310 423-3277

(P-18201)
CEDARS-SINAI MEDICAL CENTER
8730 Alden Dr West 220 (90048-3690)
PHONE...................................310 423-2587
EMP: 177
SALES (corp-wide): 4.7B **Privately Held**
Web: www.cedars-sinai.org
SIC: 8062 General medical and surgical
　　hospitals
PA: Cedars-Sinai Medical Center
　　8700 Beverly Blvd
　　West Hollywood CA
　　310 423-3277

(P-18202)
CEDARS-SINAI MEDICAL CENTER
Also Called: Clinical Translational RES Ctr
8723 Alden Dr (90048-3692)
PHONE...................................310 423-8965
EMP: 286
SALES (corp-wide): 4.7B **Privately Held**
Web: www.cedars-sinai.org
SIC: 8062 General medical and surgical
　　hospitals
PA: Cedars-Sinai Medical Center
　　8700 Beverly Blvd
　　West Hollywood CA
　　310 423-3277

(P-18203)
CEDARS-SINAI MEDICAL CENTER
Anesthesiology Department
8700 Beverly Blvd Ste 8211 (90048-1804)
PHONE...................................310 423-5841
Tom Pirscelac, *Admn*
EMP: 156
SALES (corp-wide): 4.7B **Privately Held**
Web: www.cedars-sinai.org
SIC: 8062 3841 General medical and
　　surgical hospitals; Anesthesia apparatus
PA: Cedars-Sinai Medical Center
　　8700 Beverly Blvd
　　West Hollywood CA
　　310 423-3277

(P-18204)
CEDARS-SINAI MEDICAL CENTER
8700 Beverly Blvd Ste 2216 (90048-1804)
PHONE...................................310 423-5147
Thomas Priselac, *Pr*
EMP: 89
SALES (corp-wide): 4.7B **Privately Held**
Web: www.cedars-sinai.org
SIC: 8062 General medical and surgical
　　hospitals
PA: Cedars-Sinai Medical Center
　　8700 Beverly Blvd
　　West Hollywood CA
　　310 423-3277

(P-18205)
CEDARS-SINAI MEDICAL CENTER
310 N San Vicente Blvd (90048-1810)
PHONE...................................310 423-9310
Sylvia Salgado Estrada, *Prin*
EMP: 112
SALES (corp-wide): 4.7B **Privately Held**
Web: www.cedars-sinai.org
SIC: 8062 General medical and surgical
　　hospitals
PA: Cedars-Sinai Medical Center
　　8700 Beverly Blvd
　　West Hollywood CA
　　310 423-3277

(P-18206)
CEDARS-SINAI MEDICAL CENTER
99 N La Cienega Blvd Ste Mezz
(90211-2222)
PHONE...................................310 967-1884
Lloyd Greig, *Brnch Mgr*
EMP: 110
SALES (corp-wide): 4.7B **Privately Held**
Web: www.cedars-sinai.org
SIC: 8062 General medical and surgical
　　hospitals
PA: Cedars-Sinai Medical Center
　　8700 Beverly Blvd

West Hollywood CA
310 423-3277

(P-18207)
CEDARS-SINAI MEDICAL CENTER
Also Called: Cedars-Sinai Home Care
8635 W 3rd St Ste 1165w (90048-6134)
PHONE...................................310 423-3277
Sheldon King, *Pr*
EMP: 481
SALES (corp-wide): 4.7B **Privately Held**
Web: www.cedars-sinai.org
SIC: 8062 General medical and surgical
　　hospitals
PA: Cedars-Sinai Medical Center
　　8700 Beverly Blvd
　　West Hollywood CA
　　310 423-3277

(P-18208)
CEDARS-SINAI MEDICAL CENTER
Also Called: Medical Genetics
444 S San Vicente Blvd Ste 1001
(90048-4170)
PHONE...................................310 423-9520
David Rimoin, *Mgr*
EMP: 459
SALES (corp-wide): 4.7B **Privately Held**
Web: www.cedars-sinai.org
SIC: 8062 8099 General medical and
　　surgical hospitals; Health screening service
PA: Cedars-Sinai Medical Center
　　8700 Beverly Blvd
　　West Hollywood CA
　　310 423-3277

(P-18209)
CEDARS-SINAI MEDICAL CENTER
4100 W 190th St (90504-5513)
PHONE...................................310 967-1900
Clyde Goldman, *Prin*
EMP: 640
SALES (corp-wide): 4.7B **Privately Held**
Web: www.cedars-sinai.org
SIC: 8062 8011 General medical and
　　surgical hospitals; Medical centers
PA: Cedars-Sinai Medical Center
　　8700 Beverly Blvd
　　West Hollywood CA
　　310 423-3277

(P-18210)
CEDARS-SINAI MEDICAL CENTER
Also Called: Health System Medical Network
250 N Robertson Blvd # 101 (90211-1788)
PHONE...................................310 385-3400
EMP: 634
SALES (corp-wide): 4.7B **Privately Held**
Web: www.cedars-sinai.org
SIC: 8062 8011 General medical and
　　surgical hospitals; Offices and clinics of
　　medical doctors
PA: Cedars-Sinai Medical Center
　　8700 Beverly Blvd
　　West Hollywood CA
　　310 423-3277

(P-18211)
CEDARS-SINAI MEDICAL CENTER
Emergency Services
8700 Beverly Blvd Ste 1103 (90048-1804)
PHONE...................................310 423-8780
EMP: 155
SALES (corp-wide): 4.7B **Privately Held**

Web: www.cedars-sinai.org
SIC: 8062 General medical and surgical
　　hospitals
PA: Cedars-Sinai Medical Center
　　8700 Beverly Blvd
　　West Hollywood CA
　　310 423-3277

(P-18212)
CFHS HOLDINGS INC
Also Called: Centinela Frman Rgonal Med Ctr
555 E Hardy St (90301-4011)
PHONE...................................310 673-4660
Michael Rembis, *Brnch Mgr*
EMP: 777
SALES (corp-wide): 4.7B **Privately Held**
Web: www.marinahospital.com
SIC: 8062 General medical and surgical
　　hospitals
HQ: Cfhs Holdings, Inc.
　　4650 Lincoln Blvd
　　Marina Del Rey CA

(P-18213)
CFHS HOLDINGS INC
Also Called: Centinela Frman Rgonal Med Ctr
4650 Lincoln Blvd (90292-6306)
PHONE...................................310 823-8911
EMP: 906
SQ FT: 150,000
SALES (corp-wide): 4.7B **Privately Held**
Web: www.marinahospital.com
SIC: 8062 General medical and surgical
　　hospitals
HQ: Cfhs Holdings, Inc.
　　4650 Lincoln Blvd
　　Marina Del Rey CA

(P-18214)
CFHS HOLDINGS INC
Also Called: Centinela Frman Rgonal Med Ctr
4640 Admiralty Way Ste 650 (90292-6667)
PHONE...................................310 448-7800
Bob Bokern, *Prin*
EMP: 1036
SALES (corp-wide): 4.7B **Privately Held**
Web: www.marinahospital.com
SIC: 8062 General medical and surgical
　　hospitals
HQ: Cfhs Holdings, Inc.
　　4650 Lincoln Blvd
　　Marina Del Rey CA

(P-18215)
CHAPMAN GLOBAL MEDICAL CTR INC
Also Called: Chapman Family Health
2601 E Chapman Ave (92869-3206)
PHONE...................................714 633-0011
TOLL FREE: 800
Matt Whaley, *CEO*
Robert Heinemeier, *
EMP: 425 **EST:** 1968
SQ FT: 96,000
SALES (est): 98.36K **Privately Held**
Web:
www.chapmanglobalmedicalcenter.com
SIC: 8062 General medical and surgical
　　hospitals
HQ: Kpc Healthcare, Inc.
　　1301 N Tustin Ave
　　Santa Ana CA
　　714 953-3652

(P-18216)
CHILDRENS HOSPITAL LOS ANGELES
Also Called: Saban Research Institute, The
4661 W Sunset Blvd (90027-6042)
PHONE...................................323 361-2751

Cheryl Saban, *Brnch Mgr*
EMP: 450
SALES (corp-wide): 1.58B **Privately Held**
Web: www.chla.org
SIC: 8062 General medical and surgical hospitals
PA: The Childrens Hospital Los Angeles
4650 W Sunset Blvd
Los Angeles CA
323 660-2450

(P-18217)
CHILDRENS HOSPITAL ORANGE CNTY
Also Called: Choc Mission
455 S Main St (92868-3835)
PHONE..............................949 365-2416
Kerri Ruppert Schiller, *Prin*
EMP: 410
SALES (corp-wide): 1.11B **Privately Held**
Web: www.choc.org
SIC: 8062 General medical and surgical hospitals
PA: Children's Hospital Of Orange County
1201 W La Veta Ave
Orange CA
714 509-8300

(P-18218)
CHILDRENS HOSPITAL ORANGE CNTY
980 Roosevelt (92620-3672)
PHONE..............................949 387-2586
EMP: 128
SALES (corp-wide): 1.11B **Privately Held**
Web: www.choc.org
SIC: 8062 8099 8082 6321 General medical and surgical hospitals; Childbirth preparation clinic; Home health care services; Accident and health insurance
PA: Children's Hospital Of Orange County
1201 W La Veta Ave
Orange CA
714 509-8300

(P-18219)
CHILDRENS HOSPITAL ORANGE CNTY (PA)
Also Called: Choc
1201 W La Veta Ave (92868-4203)
PHONE..............................714 509-8300
Kimberly Cripe, *Pr*
L Kenneth Heuler D.d.s., *Ch Bd*
Jessica L Miley, *CDO**
Kim Milstien, *
EMP: 2040 **EST:** 1950
SQ FT: 328,200
SALES (est): 1.11B
SALES (corp-wide): 1.11B **Privately Held**
Web: www.choc.org
SIC: 8062 General medical and surgical hospitals

(P-18220)
CHILDRENS HOSPITAL ORANGE CNTY
Also Called: Choc Childern's
10602 Chapman Ave Ste 200 (92840-3147)
PHONE..............................714 638-5990
Gina Sue Cadogan, *Brnch Mgr*
EMP: 256
SALES (corp-wide): 1.11B **Privately Held**
Web: www.choc.org
SIC: 8062 General medical and surgical hospitals
PA: Children's Hospital Of Orange County
1201 W La Veta Ave
Orange CA
714 509-8300

(P-18221)
CITRUS VLY HLTH PARTNERS INC
Also Called: Queen of The Valley Campus
1115 S Sunset Ave (91790-3940)
PHONE..............................626 962-4011
Debbie Segaram, *Brnch Mgr*
EMP: 954
Web: www.emanatehealth.org
SIC: 8062 General medical and surgical hospitals
PA: Emanate Health Medical Group
210 W San Bernardino Rd
Covina CA

(P-18222)
CITY HOPE NATIONAL MEDICAL CTR (HQ)
Also Called: City of Hope Corona
1500 Duarte Rd (91010-3012)
PHONE..............................626 256-4673
Michael A Friedman, *CEO*
Robert Stone, *
EMP: 549 **EST:** 1948
SALES (est): 1.99B
SALES (corp-wide): 334.97MM **Privately Held**
Web: www.cityofhope.org
SIC: 8062 General medical and surgical hospitals
PA: City Of Hope
1500 Duarte Rd
Duarte CA
626 256-4673

(P-18223)
COLLEGE HOSPITAL COSTA MESA MSO INC (HQ)
Also Called: COLLEGE HOSPITAL CERRITOS
301 Victoria St (92627-1995)
PHONE..............................949 642-2734
EMP: 100 **EST:** 1968
SALES (est): 39.57MM
SALES (corp-wide): 72.33MM **Privately Held**
Web: www.chc.la
SIC: 8062 General medical and surgical hospitals
PA: College Hospital, Inc.
10802 College Pl
Cerritos CA
562 924-9581

(P-18224)
COMMUNITY HOSP SAN BERNARDINO (DH)
1805 Medical Center Dr (92411-1217)
PHONE..............................909 887-6333
June Collisone, *Pr*
Ed Sorenson, *
Darryl Vanzenbosch, *CFO*
EMP: 350 **EST:** 1938
SALES (est): 266.28MM **Privately Held**
Web: www.dignityhealth.org
SIC: 8062 Hospital, affiliated with AMA residency
HQ: Dignity Health
185 Berry St Ste 200
San Francisco CA
415 438-5500

(P-18225)
COMMUNITY HOSPITAL LONG BEACH
Also Called: Community Hospital
1760 Termino Ave Ste 105 (90804-2104)
P.O. Box 92456 (90809-2456)
PHONE..............................562 494-0600

John Bishop, *CEO*
Krikor Jansian, *
Julie Shepard Resources, *Coordtr*
Kevin Peterson, *
EMP: 570 **EST:** 2000
SALES (est): 80.11MM **Privately Held**
Web: www.chlbfoundation.org
SIC: 8062 Hospital, affiliated with AMA residency
PA: Memorial Health Services
17360 Brookhurst St # 160
Fountain Valley CA

(P-18226)
COMMUNITY MEM HOSP SAN BNVNTUR
Also Called: Purchasing Department
147 N Brent St (93003-2809)
PHONE..............................805 652-5072
▲ **EMP:** 96 **EST:** 1927
SALES (est): 16.18MM **Privately Held**
Web: www.mycmh.org
SIC: 8062 General medical and surgical hospitals

(P-18227)
COMMUNITY MEMORIAL HEALTH SYS
Also Called: Ojai Valley Community Hospital
1306 Maricopa Hwy (93023-3131)
PHONE..............................805 646-1401
Gary Wilde, *Pr*
EMP: 120
SALES (corp-wide): 526.61MM **Privately Held**
Web: www.mycmh.org
SIC: 8062 General medical and surgical hospitals
PA: Community Memorial Health System
147 N Brent St
Ventura CA
805 652-5011

(P-18228)
COMMUNITY MEMORIAL HEALTH SYS (PA)
Also Called: Community Memorial Hospital
147 N Brent St (93003-2809)
PHONE..............................805 652-5011
Gary Wilde, *Pr*
Adam Thunell, *
David Glyar, *
▲ **EMP:** 1881 **EST:** 1933
SQ FT: 174,000
SALES (est): 526.61MM
SALES (corp-wide): 526.61MM **Privately Held**
Web: www.mycmh.org
SIC: 8062 General medical and surgical hospitals

(P-18229)
COTTAGE HEALTH
2050 Viborg Rd (93463-2220)
PHONE..............................805 688-6432
EMP: 85
SALES (corp-wide): 152.81MM **Privately Held**
SIC: 8062 General medical and surgical hospitals
PA: Cottage Health
400 W Pueblo St
Santa Barbara CA
805 682-7111

(P-18230)
COUNTY OF KERN
Public Health Dept
1700 Mount Vernon Ave (93306-4018)

P.O. Box 3519 (93385-3519)
PHONE..............................661 326-2054
Peter Bryan, *CEO*
EMP: 800
Web: www.kerncounty.com
SIC: 8062 9431 General medical and surgical hospitals; Administration of public health programs
PA: County Of Kern
1115 Truxtun Ave Rm 505
Bakersfield CA
661 868-3690

(P-18231)
COUNTY OF LOS ANGELES
Also Called: Health Services Dept
1000 W Carson St 8th Fl (90274)
PHONE..............................310 222-2401
Miguel Ortiz Marroquin, *CEO*
EMP: 124
Web: www.lacounty.gov
SIC: 8062 9431 General medical and surgical hospitals; Administration of public health programs
PA: County Of Los Angeles
500 W Temple St Ste 437
Los Angeles CA
213 974-1101

(P-18232)
COUNTY OF LOS ANGELES
Also Called: Health Services, Dept of
12025 Wilmington Ave (90059-3019)
PHONE..............................310 668-4545
Willie T May, *Ex Dir*
EMP: 256
Web: www.lacounty.gov
SIC: 8062 9431 General medical and surgical hospitals; Administration of public health programs
PA: County Of Los Angeles
500 W Temple St Ste 437
Los Angeles CA
213 974-1101

(P-18233)
COUNTY OF LOS ANGELES
Also Called: Health Services Dept
1100 N Mission Rd Rm 236 (90033-1017)
PHONE..............................323 226-6021
Scott Drewgan, *Dir*
EMP: 123
Web: www.lacounty.gov
SIC: 8062 9431 General medical and surgical hospitals; Administration of public health programs
PA: County Of Los Angeles
500 W Temple St Ste 437
Los Angeles CA
213 974-1101

(P-18234)
COUNTY OF LOS ANGELES
Also Called: Los Angles Cnty Cntl Jail Hosp
450 Bauchet St (90012-2907)
PHONE..............................213 473-6100
Don Knable, *Ch Bd*
EMP: 123
Web: www.lacounty.gov
SIC: 8062 9431 General medical and surgical hospitals; Administration of public health programs, County government
PA: County Of Los Angeles
500 W Temple St Ste 437
Los Angeles CA
213 974-1101

(P-18235)
COUNTY OF SAN LUIS OBISPO
Also Called: County General Hospital

PRODUCTS & SVCS

2180 Johnson Ave (93401-4558)
PHONE.........................805 781-4753
Nancy Rosen, *Mgr*
EMP: 105
SQ FT: 4,500
Web: slocounty.ca.gov
SIC: 8062 8721 General medical and surgical hospitals; Accounting, auditing, and bookkeeping
PA: County Of San Luis Obispo Government Center Rm 300 San Luis Obispo CA 805 781-5040

(P-18236)
DEANCO HEALTHCARE LLC
Also Called: MISSION COMMUNITY HOSPITAL
14850 Roscoe Blvd (91402-4618)
PHONE.........................818 787-2222
EMP: 700 EST: 2010
SALES (est): 156.97MM **Privately Held**
Web: www.mchonline.org
SIC: 8062 General medical and surgical hospitals

(P-18237)
DESERT REGIONAL MED CTR INC (HQ)
Also Called: Tenet
1150 N Indian Canyon Dr (92262-4872)
P.O. Box 2739 (92263-2739)
PHONE.........................760 323-6511
TOLL FREE: 888
Michele Finney, *Pr*
Frank Ercoli, *
Ralph M Steiger, *
EMP: 1200 EST: 1948
SQ FT: 400,000
SALES (est): 217MM
SALES (corp-wide): 19.58B **Publicly Held**
Web: www.desertfamilymed.com
SIC: 8062 General medical and surgical hospitals
PA: Tenet Healthcare Corporation 14201 Dallas Pkwy Dallas TX 469 893-2200

(P-18238)
DESERT VALLEY HOSPITAL INC (DH)
16850 Bear Valley Rd (92395-5794)
PHONE.........................760 241-8000
Margaret R Peterson, *CEO*
Roger Krissman, *
▲ **EMP:** 181 EST: 1985
SQ FT: 63,000
SALES (est): 208.51MM
SALES (corp-wide): 1.03B **Privately Held**
Web: www.dvmc.com
SIC: 8062 General medical and surgical hospitals
HQ: Prime Healthcare Services Inc 3480 E Guasti Rd Ontario CA

(P-18239)
DIGNITY HEALTH
Also Called: St. Johns Pleasant Valley Hosp
2309 Antonio Ave (93010-1414)
PHONE.........................805 389-5800
Daniel Herlinger, *Brnch Mgr*
EMP: 250
Web: www.dignityhealth.org
SIC: 8062 General medical and surgical hospitals
HQ: Dignity Health 185 Berry St Ste 200 San Francisco CA 415 438-5500

(P-18240)
DIGNITY HEALTH
Also Called: St Johns Regional Medical Ctr
1600 N Rose Ave (93030-3722)
PHONE.........................805 988-2500
George West, *Brnch Mgr*
EMP: 1900
Web: www.dignityhealth.org
SIC: 8062 General medical and surgical hospitals
HQ: Dignity Health 185 Berry St Ste 200 San Francisco CA 415 438-5500

(P-18241)
DIGNITY HEALTH
Also Called: Marian Regional Medical Center
1400 E Church St (93454-5906)
PHONE.........................805 739-3000
Charles Cova, *Pr*
EMP: 400
Web: www.dignityhealth.org
SIC: 8062 8011 General medical and surgical hospitals; Offices and clinics of medical doctors
HQ: Dignity Health 185 Berry St Ste 200 San Francisco CA 415 438-5500

(P-18242)
DIGNITY HEALTH
Also Called: Pedi Center
400 Old River Rd (93311-9781)
P.O. Box 119 (93302-0119)
PHONE.........................661 663-6000
Kirk Douglas, *Brnch Mgr*
EMP: 255
Web: www.dignityhealth.org
SIC: 8062 8099 8011 General medical and surgical hospitals; Childbirth preparation clinic; Offices and clinics of medical doctors
HQ: Dignity Health 185 Berry St Ste 200 San Francisco CA 415 438-5500

(P-18243)
DIGNITY HEALTH
Also Called: Saint John's Hospital X Ray
200 Oceangate (90802-4302)
PHONE.........................805 988-2868
Steve Higgs Managing, *Brnch Mgr*
EMP: 474
Web: www.dignityhealth.org
SIC: 8062 General medical and surgical hospitals
HQ: Dignity Health 185 Berry St Ste 200 San Francisco CA 415 438-5500

(P-18244)
DIGNITY HEALTH
Also Called: Northridge Hospital Med Ctr
18300 Roscoe Blvd (91325-4105)
PHONE.........................818 885-8500
Paul Watkins, *Pr*
EMP: 1750
Web: www.dignityhealth.org
SIC: 8062 General medical and surgical hospitals
HQ: Dignity Health 185 Berry St Ste 200 San Francisco CA 415 438-5500

(P-18245)
DIGNITY HEALTH
Also Called: Saint Mary Medical Center
1050 Linden Ave (90813-3321)
PHONE.........................562 491-9000
Chris Diccio, *Prin*
EMP: 179
Web: www.dignityhealth.org
SIC: 8062 General medical and surgical hospitals
HQ: Dignity Health 185 Berry St Ste 200 San Francisco CA 415 438-5500

(P-18246)
DOCTORS HOSPITAL W COVINA INC
Also Called: WEST COVINA PHYSICAL THERAPY
725 S Orange Ave (91790-2614)
PHONE.........................626 338-8481
Pareed Mohamed, *CEO*
Akbar Omar Md, *VP*
Jong Kim Md, *Treas*
Pareed Aliyar Md, *Sec*
EMP: 155 EST: 1958
SQ FT: 50,000
SALES (est): 25MM **Privately Held**
SIC: 8062 8049 General medical and surgical hospitals; Physical therapist

(P-18247)
EAST LOS ANGLES DCTORS HOSP IN
4060 Whittier Blvd (90023-2526)
EMP: 350 EST: 1978
SALES (est): 74.22MM
SALES (corp-wide): 218.29MM **Privately Held**
Web: www.eladoctorshospital.com
SIC: 8062 Hospital, affiliated with AMA residency
PA: Pipeline Health, Llc 898 N Pcf Cast Hwy Ste 70 El Segundo CA 310 379-2134

(P-18248)
EAST VALLEY GLENDORA HOSP LLC
Also Called: Glendora Oaks Bhvral Hlth Hosp
150 W Route 66 (91740-6207)
PHONE.........................626 852-5000
Robert Gordon, *
EMP: 448 EST: 1957
SQ FT: 60,592
SALES (est): 48.12MM **Privately Held**
Web: www.glendorahospital.com
SIC: 8062 General medical and surgical hospitals
PA: College Health Enterprises, Llc 11627 Telg Rd Ste 200 Santa Fe Springs CA

(P-18249)
EISENHOWER MEDICAL CENTER
45280 Seeley Dr (92253-6834)
PHONE.........................760 610-7200
EMP: 248
SALES (corp-wide): 3.81MM **Privately Held**
Web: www.eisenhowerhealth.org
SIC: 8062 General medical and surgical hospitals
PA: Eisenhower Medical Center 39000 Bob Hope Dr Rancho Mirage CA 760 340-3911

(P-18250)
EISENHOWER MEDICAL CENTER
555 E Tachevah Dr (92262-5750)
PHONE.........................760 325-6621
EMP: 124
SALES (corp-wide): 3.81MM **Privately Held**
Web: www.eisenhowerhealth.org
SIC: 8062 General medical and surgical hospitals
PA: Eisenhower Medical Center 39000 Bob Hope Dr Rancho Mirage CA 760 340-3911

(P-18251)
EISENHOWER MEDICAL CENTER (PA)
Also Called: Eisenhower Health
39000 Bob Hope Dr (92270-3221)
PHONE.........................760 340-3911
G Aubrey Serfling, *CEO*
Martin Massiello, *
Kimberly Osborne, *
Liz Guignier, *
Joseph Scherger, *
▲ **EMP:** 2000 EST: 1971
SQ FT: 240,000
SALES (est): 3.81MM
SALES (corp-wide): 3.81MM **Privately Held**
Web: www.eisenhowerhealth.org
SIC: 8062 8082 General medical and surgical hospitals; Home health care services

(P-18252)
EL CENTRO RGNAL MED CTR FNDTIO (PA)
Also Called: E C R M C
1415 Ross Ave (92243-4306)
PHONE.........................760 339-7100
Pablo Velez, *CEO*
Robert R Frantz, *
David Momberg, *
Barbara Blevins, *
Debra Drifkill, *
EMP: 603 EST: 2005
SQ FT: 187,044
SALES (est): 212.33K **Privately Held**
Web: www.ecrmc.org
SIC: 8062 General medical and surgical hospitals

(P-18253)
EMANATE HEALTH
Also Called: Citrus Vly Hlth Care Partners
427 W Carroll Ave (91741-4214)
PHONE.........................626 857-3477
Sue Benson, *Dir*
EMP: 495
SALES (corp-wide): 515.46MM **Privately Held**
Web: www.emanatehealth.org
SIC: 8062 General medical and surgical hospitals
PA: Emanate Health Medical Center 1115 S Sunset Ave West Covina CA 626 962-4011

(P-18254)
EMANATE HEALTH MEDICAL CENTER
Also Called: Human Resources Department
140 W College St (91723-2007)
PHONE.........................626 858-8515
Robert H Curry, *Admn*

EMP: 413
SALES (corp-wide): 515.46MM **Privately Held**
Web: www.emanatehealth.org
SIC: 8062 General medical and surgical hospitals
PA: Emanate Health Medical Center
1115 S Sunset Ave
West Covina CA
626 962-4011

(P-18255)
EMANATE HEALTH MEDICAL CENTER
Also Called: Queen of The Valley Hospital
1115 S Sunset Ave (91790-3940)
PHONE..............................626 963-8411
Robert Curry, *Pr*
EMP: 329
SALES (corp-wide): 515.46MM **Privately Held**
Web: www.emanatehealth.org
SIC: 8062 General medical and surgical hospitals
PA: Emanate Health Medical Center
1115 S Sunset Ave
West Covina CA
626 962-4011

(P-18256)
EMANATE HEALTH MEDICAL CENTER
Also Called: Inter Community Hospital
210 W San Bernardino Rd (91723-1515)
PHONE..............................626 331-7331
TOLL FREE: 877
Jim Yoshioka, *Pr*
EMP: 863
SALES (corp-wide): 515.46MM **Privately Held**
Web: www.emanatehealth.org
SIC: 8062 General medical and surgical hospitals
PA: Emanate Health Medical Center
1115 S Sunset Ave
West Covina CA
626 962-4011

(P-18257)
EMANATE HEALTH MEDICAL CENTER (PA)
Also Called: Emanate Health
1115 S Sunset Ave (91790-3940)
P.O. Box 6108 (91722-5108)
PHONE..............................626 962-4011
Robert Curry, *Pr*
Elvia Foulke, *
Roger Sharma, *
EMP: 1229 **EST:** 1959
SQ FT: 285,000
SALES (est): 515.46MM
SALES (corp-wide): 515.46MM **Privately Held**
Web: www.emanatehealth.org
SIC: 8062 General medical and surgical hospitals

(P-18258)
EMANATE HEALTH MEDICAL GROUP (PA)
Also Called: Emanate Hlth Intr-Cmmnity Hosp
210 W San Bernardino Rd (91723-1515)
P.O. Box 6108 (91722-5108)
PHONE..............................626 331-7331
Robert Curry, *CEO*
James Yoshioka, *Pr*
Alvia Polk, *Ex VP*
Lois Conyers, *Sr VP*
Paveljit Bindra, *CMO*
EMP: 1200 **EST:** 1983

SQ FT: 237,000
SALES (est): 75.42MM **Privately Held**
Web: www.emanatehealth.org
SIC: 8062 General medical and surgical hospitals

(P-18259)
EMANATE HLTH FTHILL PRSBT HOSP (PA)
Also Called: Foothill Presbyterian Hospital
250 S Grand Ave (91741-4218)
PHONE..............................626 857-3145
Robert Curry, *Pr*
Earl Washington Cmh, *Prin*
Admiral Diana Zenner, *Prin*
Ed Tronez, *
Melissa Howard, *Chief Nurse*
EMP: 97 **EST:** 1973
SQ FT: 104,371
SALES (est): 122MM
SALES (corp-wide): 122MM **Privately Held**
SIC: 8062 Hospital, affiliated with AMA residency

(P-18260)
FOOTHILL REGIONAL MEDICAL CTR
Also Called: NEWPORT SPECIALTY HOSPITAL
14662 Newport Ave (92780-6064)
PHONE..............................310 943-4500
EMP: 115 **EST:** 2014
SALES (est): 78.64MM **Privately Held**
Web:
www.foothillregionalmedicalcenter.com
SIC: 8062 General medical and surgical hospitals

(P-18261)
FOUNTAIN VLY RGNAL HOSP MED CT
17100 Euclid St (92708-4004)
P.O. Box 8010 (92728-8010)
PHONE..............................714 966-7200
Clay Farell, *CEO*
Edward F Littlejohn, *COO*
Ken Jordan, *CFO*
C J Lee, *Chief Strategy Officer*
EMP: 1200 **EST:** 1969
SALES (est): 239.53MM
SALES (corp-wide): 19.58B **Publicly Held**
Web: validate.perfdrive.com
SIC: 8062 Hospital, affiliated with AMA residency
HQ: Tenet Healthsystem Medical, Inc.
14201 Dallas Pkwy
Dallas TX
469 893-2000

(P-18262)
FRENCH HOSPITAL MEDICAL CENTER (DH)
1911 Johnson Ave (93401-4197)
PHONE..............................805 543-5353
Jim Copeland, *Ch*
Allan Iftiniuk, *
Sue Anderson, *
EMP: 480 **EST:** 1946
SQ FT: 80,000
SALES (est): 196.54MM **Privately Held**
Web: www.dignityhealth.org
SIC: 8062 Hospital, affiliated with AMA residency
HQ: Dignity Health
185 Berry St Ste 200
San Francisco CA
415 438-5500

(P-18263)
GARDENA HOSPITAL LP
Also Called: Memorial Hospital of Gardena
1145 W Redondo Beach Blvd (90247-3511)
PHONE..............................310 532-4200
Kathy Wojno, *CEO*
John N Loizeaux-witte, *Pt*
David Lee, *CFO*
EMP: 760 **EST:** 1999
SALES (est): 141.92MM
SALES (corp-wide): 218.29MM **Privately Held**
Web:
www.memorialhospitalgardena.com
SIC: 8062 General medical and surgical hospitals
PA: Pipeline Health, Llc
898 N Pcf Cast Hwy Ste 70
El Segundo CA
310 379-2134

(P-18264)
GARDENS REGIONAL HOSPITAL AND MEDICAL CENTER INCORPORATED
Also Called: Gardens Regional Hosp Med Ctr
21530 Pioneer Blvd (90716-2608)
PHONE..............................877 877-1104
EMP: 350
Web: www.tcrmc.org
SIC: 8062 General medical and surgical hospitals

(P-18265)
GLENDALE ADVENTIST MEDICAL CTR (HQ)
1509 Wilson Ter (91206-4007)
PHONE..............................818 409-8000
Kevin A Roberts, *Pr*
Irene Bourdon, *
Warren Tetz, *
Kelly Turner, *
Judy Blair, *
EMP: 2550 **EST:** 1905
SQ FT: 700,000
SALES (est): 486.07MM
SALES (corp-wide): 789.42MM **Privately Held**
Web: www.adventisthealth.org
SIC: 8062 8093 8011 General medical and surgical hospitals; Mental health clinic, outpatient; Freestanding emergency medical center
PA: Adventist Health System/West, Corporation
1 Adventist Health Way
Roseville CA
844 574-5686

(P-18266)
GLENDALE MEM HLTH FOUNDATION
1420 S Central Ave (91204-2508)
PHONE..............................818 502-2375
EMP: 248 **EST:** 1981
SALES (est): 213.36MM **Privately Held**
Web: www.supportglendale.org
SIC: 8062 General medical and surgical hospitals
HQ: Dignity Health
185 Berry St Ste 200
San Francisco CA
415 438-5500

(P-18267)
GLENDALE MEMORIAL HEALTH CORP
Also Called: Glendale Memorial Breast Ctr
222 W Eulalia St (91204-2849)

PHONE..............................818 502-2323
FAX: 818 502-4747
EMP: 1000
SALES (corp-wide): 7.06B **Privately Held**
SIC: 8062 8099 General medical and surgical hospitals; Medical services organization
HQ: Glendale Memorial Health Corporation
1420 S Central Ave
Glendale CA
818 502-1900

(P-18268)
GLENDALE MEMORIAL HEALTH CORPORATION
Also Called: Glendale Memorial Center
1420 S Central Ave (91204-2508)
PHONE..............................818 502-1900
EMP: 1245
Web: www.supportglendale.org
SIC: 8062 General medical and surgical hospitals

(P-18269)
GLENOAKS CONVALESCENT HOSPITAL
409 W Glenoaks Blvd (91202-2916)
PHONE..............................818 240-4300
Elaine Levine, *Pt*
EMP: 85 **EST:** 1984
SQ FT: 22,306
SALES (est): 8.62MM **Privately Held**
Web: www.gshci.com
SIC: 8062 General medical and surgical hospitals

(P-18270)
GOLETA VALLEY COTTAGE HOSP AUX
Also Called: Cottage Health System
351 S Patterson Ave (93111-2403)
P.O. Box 689 (93102-0689)
PHONE..............................805 681-6468
Ronald C Werft, *Pr*
Robert Knight, *
Diane Wisby, *
Joan Bricher, *
Joanne Rapp, *
EMP: 300 **EST:** 1966
SQ FT: 92,273
SALES (est): 104.45MM
SALES (corp-wide): 152.81MM **Privately Held**
SIC: 8062 General medical and surgical hospitals
PA: Cottage Health
400 W Pueblo St
Santa Barbara CA
805 682-7111

(P-18271)
GOOD SMRTAN HOSP A CAL LTD PRT
901 Olive Dr (93308-4137)
P.O. Box 85002 (93380-5002)
PHONE..............................661 903-9555
Amandeep Basra, *Pr*
Andrew B Leeka, *
Anand Manohara, *
Sakrepatna Manohara, *
David Huff, *
EMP: 400 **EST:** 1965
SQ FT: 49,001
SALES (est): 23.75MM **Privately Held**
Web: www.goodsamhospital.com
SIC: 8062 8063 8069 General medical and surgical hospitals; Psychiatric hospitals; Specialty hospitals, except psychiatric

(P-18272)
GROSSMONT HOSPITAL
CORPORATION (HQ)
5555 Grossmont Center Dr (91942-3077)
PHONE.............................619 740-6000
Dan Gross, *CEO*
EMP: 1740 EST: 1953
SQ FT: 494,000
SALES (est): 959.59MM
SALES (corp-wide): 2.37B **Privately Held**
Web: www.sharp.com
SIC: 8062 General medical and surgical
   hospitals
PA: Sharp Healthcare
   8695 Spectrum Center Blvd
   San Diego CA
   858 499-4000

(P-18273)
GROSSMONT HOSPITAL
CORPORATION
Also Called: Grossmont Home Hlth & Hospice
8881 Fletcher Pkwy Ste 105 (91942-3134)
PHONE..............................619 667-1900
Jean Cruise, *Mgr*
EMP: 353
SALES (corp-wide): 2.37B **Privately Held**
Web: www.sharp.com
SIC: 8062 8082 General medical and
   surgical hospitals; Home health care
   services
HQ: Grossmont Hospital Corporation
   5555 Grossmont Center Dr
   La Mesa CA
   619 740-6000

(P-18274)
HDMC HOLDINGS LLC
Also Called: Hi-Desert Medical Center
6601 White Feather Rd (92252-6607)
PHONE..............................760 366-3711
Jeffrey Koury, *CEO*
EMP: 132 EST: 2015
SALES (est): 20.46MM
SALES (corp-wide): 19.58B **Publicly Held**
SIC: 8062 General medical and surgical
   hospitals
PA: Tenet Healthcare Corporation
   14201 Dallas Pkwy
   Dallas TX
   469 893-2200

(P-18275)
HEALTH INVESTMENT
CORPORATION
14642 Newport Ave Ste 388 (92780-6059)
PHONE..............................714 669-2085
EMP: 1700
SIC: 8062 General medical and surgical
   hospitals

(P-18276)
HEALTH RESOURCES CORP
Also Called: Coastal Community Hospital
2701 S Bristol St (92704-6201)
PHONE..............................714 754-5454
Trevor Fetter, *Pr*
EMP: 400 EST: 1984
SALES (est): 51.08MM **Privately Held**
SIC: 8062 General medical and surgical
   hospitals
HQ: Kpc Healthcare, Inc.
   1301 N Tustin Ave
   Santa Ana CA
   714 953-3652

(P-18277)
HEALTHSMART PACIFIC INC
(PA)

Also Called: Long Beach Pain Center
5150 E Pacific Coast Hwy Ste 200
(90804-3312)
PHONE.............................562 595-1911
TOLL FREE: 800
Michael D Drobot, *
G William Hammer, *Prin*
EMP: 610 EST: 1932
SALES (est): 42.31MM
SALES (corp-wide): 42.31MM **Privately Held**
SIC: 8062 General medical and surgical
   hospitals

(P-18278)
HEMET VALLEY MEDICAL
CENTER-EDUCATION
Also Called: Hemet Valley Medical Center
1117 E Devonshire Ave (92543-3083)
PHONE..............................951 652-2811
EMP: 1200
Web: www.hemetglobalmedcenter.com
SIC: 8062 General medical and surgical
   hospitals

(P-18279)
HENRY MAYO NEWHALL MEM
HOSP (PA)
23845 Mcbean Pkwy (91355-2001)
PHONE..............................661 253-8000
Roger E Seaver, *Pr*
Elizabeth Hopp, *Ch Bd*
Robert Pretzlaff, *CMO*
EMP: 1314 EST: 1972
SQ FT: 210,000
SALES (est): 458.62MM
SALES (corp-wide): 458.62MM **Privately
Held**
Web: www.henrymayo.com
SIC: 8062 General medical and surgical
   hospitals

(P-18280)
HENRY MAYO NWHALL MEM
HLTH FND
Also Called: Henrymayo Newhall Mem Hosp
23845 Mcbean Pkwy (91355-2001)
P.O. Box 55279 (91385-0279)
PHONE..............................661 253-8000
Roger Seaver, *Pr*
EMP: 1500 EST: 1972
SALES (est): 411.3MM **Privately Held**
SIC: 8062 General medical and surgical
   hospitals

(P-18281)
HOAG CLINIC
Also Called: HOAG CORPORATE HEALTH
1 Hoag Dr (92663-4162)
P.O. Box 6100 (92658-6100)
PHONE..............................949 764-1888
EMP: 342 EST: 1995
SALES (est): 211.63MM **Privately Held**
Web: www.hoag.org
SIC: 8062 General medical and surgical
   hospitals

(P-18282)
HOAG FAMILY CANCER
INSTITUTE
1190 Baker St (92626-4108)
PHONE..............................949 764-7777
Inga Barillas, *Brnch Mgr*
EMP: 195
Web: www.hoag.org
SIC: 8062 General medical and surgical
   hospitals
PA: Hoag Family Cancer Institute
   1 Hoag Dr Bldg 41

Newport Beach CA

(P-18283)
HOAG HOSPITAL IRVINE
16200 Sand Canyon Ave (92618-3714)
PHONE..............................949 764-4624
EMP: 91 EST: 2009
SALES (est): 26.16MM **Privately Held**
Web: www.hoag.org
SIC: 8062 General medical and surgical
   hospitals

(P-18284)
HOAG MEMORIAL HOSPITAL
PRESBT (PA)
1 Hoag Dr (92663-4162)
P.O. Box 6100 (92658-6100)
PHONE..............................949 764-4624
Robert Braithwaite, *Pr*
Flynn A Andrizzi, *
Kathy Azeez-narain, *Chief Digital Officer*
EMP: 3600 EST: 1944
SALES (est): 1.28B **Privately Held**
Web: www.hoag.org
SIC: 8062 General medical and surgical
   hospitals

(P-18285)
HOAG ORTHOPEDIC INSTITUTE
LLC
Also Called: Hoag Orthpd Inst Srgery Ctr -
22 Corporate Plaza Dr Ste 150
(92660-7999)
PHONE..............................949 515-0708
James Caillouette, *Ch Bd*
EMP: 346
SALES (corp-wide): 143.89MM **Privately
Held**
Web: www.hoagorthopedicinstitute.com
SIC: 8062 General medical and surgical
   hospitals
PA: Hoag Orthopedic Institute, Llc
   16250 Sand Canyon Ave
   Irvine CA
   949 764-8690

(P-18286)
HOLLYWOOD CMNTY HOSP
MED CTR I
Also Called: Hollywood Cmnty Hosp
Hollywood
6245 De Longpre Ave (90028-8253)
PHONE..............................323 462-2271
Robert Starling, *CEO*
Ron Messenger, *
Manfred Krukemeyer, *
EMP: 220 EST: 1982
SQ FT: 100,000
SALES (est): 26.98MM
SALES (corp-wide): 3.91B **Privately Held**
Web: www.sch-hollywood.com
SIC: 8062 Hospital, affiliated with AMA
   residency
HQ: Southern California Healthcare
   System, Inc.
   3415 S Sepulveda Blvd 9thf
   Los Angeles CA

(P-18287)
HOLLYWOOD MEDICAL
CENTER LP
Also Called: Hollywood Presbyterian Med Ctr
1300 N Vermont Ave (90027-6098)
PHONE..............................213 413-3000
Jeff Nelson, *Pt*
EMP: 1250 EST: 1928
SALES (est): 81.88MM **Privately Held**
Web: www.hollywoodpresbyterian.com

SIC: 8062 General medical and surgical
   hospitals
PA: Cha Health Systems, Inc
   3731 Wilshire Blvd # 850
   Los Angeles CA

(P-18288)
HOSPITAL OF BARSTOW INC
(DH)
Also Called: Barstow Community Hospital
820 E Mountain View St (92311-3004)
PHONE..............................760 256-1761
Justin Sheridan, *CEO*
Shawn Curtis, *
EMP: 91 EST: 1958
SQ FT: 54,000
SALES (est): 66.23MM
SALES (corp-wide): 1.69B **Privately Held**
Web: www.barstowhospital.com
SIC: 8062 Hospital, affiliated with AMA
   residency
HQ: Qhc California Holdings, Llc
   1573 Mallory Ln
   Brentwood TN

(P-18289)
HUNTINGTON MEDICAL
FOUNDATION
65 N Madison Ave Ste 800 (91101-2038)
PHONE..............................626 792-3141
Laura Hernandez, *Mgr*
EMP: 121
Web: www.huntingtonhealth.org
SIC: 8062 General medical and surgical
   hospitals
PA: The Huntington Medical Foundation
   100 W California Blvd
   Pasadena CA

(P-18290)
INLAND VLY RGIONAL MED CTR
INC
36485 Inland Valley Dr (92595-9681)
PHONE..............................951 677-1111
Alan B Miller, *CEO*
Barry Thorfinnson, *
EMP: 500 EST: 1983
SQ FT: 77,000
SALES (est): 98.03MM
SALES (corp-wide): 13.4B **Publicly Held**
Web: www.inlandvalleymedcenter.com
SIC: 8062 8011 General medical and
   surgical hospitals; Clinic, operated by
   physicians
PA: Universal Health Services, Inc.
   367 S Gulph Rd
   King Of Prussia PA
   610 768-3300

(P-18291)
JFK MEMORIAL HOSPITAL INC
47111 Monroe St (92201-6739)
PHONE..............................760 347-6191
Gary Honts, *Pr*
EMP: 189 EST: 2001
SALES (est): 29.3MM
SALES (corp-wide): 19.58B **Publicly Held**
SIC: 8062 General medical and surgical
   hospitals
PA: Tenet Healthcare Corporation
   14201 Dallas Pkwy
   Dallas TX
   469 893-2200

(P-18292)
JOHN F KENNEDY MEM HOSP
AUX
Also Called: DES PERES HOSPITAL, INC.
47111 Monroe St (92201-6799)

PHONE...............................760 347-6191
TOLL FREE: 800
Gary Honts, *CEO*
EMP: 650 EST: 1986
SALES (est): 1.01MM
SALES (corp-wide): 72.97MM **Privately Held**
SIC: 8062 Hospital, affiliated with AMA residency
HQ: St. Luke's Des Peres Episcopal-Presbyterian Hospital
2345 Dougherty Ferry Rd
Saint Louis MO
314 966-9100

(P-18293)
JUPITER BELLFLOWER DOCTORS HOSPITAL
Also Called: Bellflower Medical Center
3699 Wilshire Blvd Ste 540 (90010-2718)
EMP: 500
SIC: 8062 General medical and surgical hospitals

(P-18294)
KAISER FOUNDATION HOSPITALS
400 S Sepulveda Blvd (90266-6814)
PHONE...............................310 937-4311
EMP: 139
SALES (corp-wide): 68.1B **Privately Held**
Web: www.kaisercenter.com
SIC: 8062 General medical and surgical hospitals
HQ: Kaiser Foundation Hospitals Inc
1 Kaiser Plz
Oakland CA
510 271-6611

(P-18295)
KAISER FOUNDATION HOSPITALS
4733 W Sunset Blvd Fl 2 (90027-6021)
PHONE...............................323 783-4011
EMP: 167
SALES (corp-wide): 68.1B **Privately Held**
Web: www.kaisercenter.com
SIC: 8062 General medical and surgical hospitals
HQ: Kaiser Foundation Hospitals Inc
1 Kaiser Plz
Oakland CA
510 271-6611

(P-18296)
KAISER FOUNDATION HOSPITALS
Also Called: Kaiser Permanente
1255 W Arrow Hwy (91773-2340)
PHONE...............................909 394-2530
Will Tatum, *Mgr*
EMP: 167
SQ FT: 23,801
SALES (corp-wide): 68.1B **Privately Held**
Web: www.kaisercenter.com
SIC: 8062 8011 General medical and surgical hospitals; General and family practice, physician/surgeon
HQ: Kaiser Foundation Hospitals Inc
1 Kaiser Plz
Oakland CA
510 271-6611

(P-18297)
KAISER FOUNDATION HOSPITALS
Also Called: Cudahy Medical Offices
7825 Atlantic Ave (90201-5022)
PHONE...............................323 562-6400

Karen Warren, *Mgr*
EMP: 101
SALES (corp-wide): 68.1B **Privately Held**
Web: www.kaisercenter.com
SIC: 8062 General medical and surgical hospitals
HQ: Kaiser Foundation Hospitals Inc
1 Kaiser Plz
Oakland CA
510 271-6611

(P-18298)
KAISER FOUNDATION HOSPITALS
Also Called: Gardena Medical Offices
15446 S Western Ave (90249-4319)
PHONE...............................310 517-2956
Mary Mauch, *Mgr*
EMP: 173
SQ FT: 114,575
SALES (corp-wide): 68.1B **Privately Held**
Web: www.kaisercenter.com
SIC: 8062 General medical and surgical hospitals
HQ: Kaiser Foundation Hospitals Inc
1 Kaiser Plz
Oakland CA
510 271-6611

(P-18299)
KAISER FOUNDATION HOSPITALS
20000 Rinaldi St (91326-4900)
PHONE...............................833 574-2273
EMP: 87
SALES (corp-wide): 68.1B **Privately Held**
Web: www.kaisercenter.com
SIC: 8062 General medical and surgical hospitals
HQ: Kaiser Foundation Hospitals Inc
1 Kaiser Plz
Oakland CA
510 271-6611

(P-18300)
KAISER FOUNDATION HOSPITALS
Also Called: Kaiser Permanente
1055 E Colorado Blvd Ste 100 (91106)
PHONE...............................626 440-5659
Jeanine Boudakian, *Brnch Mgr*
EMP: 500
SALES (corp-wide): 68.1B **Privately Held**
Web: www.kaisercenter.com
SIC: 8062 General medical and surgical hospitals
HQ: Kaiser Foundation Hospitals Inc
1 Kaiser Plz
Oakland CA
510 271-6611

(P-18301)
KAISER FOUNDATION HOSPITALS
Also Called: Kaiser Permanente
8800 Ming Ave (93311-1308)
PHONE...............................661 412-6777
EMP: 208
SALES (corp-wide): 68.1B **Privately Held**
Web: www.kaisercenter.com
SIC: 8062 General medical and surgical hospitals
HQ: Kaiser Foundation Hospitals Inc
1 Kaiser Plz
Oakland CA
510 271-6611

(P-18302)
KAISER FOUNDATION HOSPITALS
Also Called: Kaiser Permanente
5601 De Soto Ave (91367-6701)
PHONE...............................818 719-2000
Cathy Casas, *Admn*
EMP: 1200
SALES (corp-wide): 68.1B **Privately Held**
Web: www.kaisercenter.com
SIC: 8062 General medical and surgical hospitals
HQ: Kaiser Foundation Hospitals Inc
1 Kaiser Plz
Oakland CA
510 271-6611

(P-18303)
KAISER FOUNDATION HOSPITALS
Also Called: Kaiser Permanente
43112 15th St W (93534-6219)
PHONE...............................661 726-2500
Barbara Fordice, *Genl Mgr*
EMP: 508
SALES (corp-wide): 68.1B **Privately Held**
Web: www.kaisercenter.com
SIC: 8062 Hospital, affiliated with AMA residency
HQ: Kaiser Foundation Hospitals Inc
1 Kaiser Plz
Oakland CA
510 271-6611

(P-18304)
KAISER FOUNDATION HOSPITALS
Also Called: Wildomar Medical Offices
36450 Inland Valley Dr Ste 204 (92595-9583)
PHONE...............................951 353-2000
Geoffrey Gomez, *Prin*
EMP: 222
SALES (corp-wide): 68.1B **Privately Held**
Web: www.kaisercenter.com
SIC: 8062 General medical and surgical hospitals
HQ: Kaiser Foundation Hospitals Inc
1 Kaiser Plz
Oakland CA
510 271-6611

(P-18305)
KAISER FOUNDATION HOSPITALS
Also Called: Barranca Medical Offices
6 Willard (92604-4694)
PHONE...............................949 262-5780
George Disalvo, *Owner*
EMP: 219
SQ FT: 51,080
SALES (corp-wide): 68.1B **Privately Held**
Web: www.kaisercenter.com
SIC: 8062 General medical and surgical hospitals
HQ: Kaiser Foundation Hospitals Inc
1 Kaiser Plz
Oakland CA
510 271-6611

(P-18306)
KAISER FOUNDATION HOSPITALS
Also Called: Kaiser Permanente
12620 Prescott Ave (92782-1066)
PHONE...............................951 353-4000
Danh V Le, *Dir*
EMP: 127
SALES (corp-wide): 68.1B **Privately Held**

Web: www.kaisercenter.com
SIC: 8062 General medical and surgical hospitals
HQ: Kaiser Foundation Hospitals Inc
1 Kaiser Plz
Oakland CA
510 271-6611

(P-18307)
KAISER FOUNDATION HOSPITALS
Also Called: Kaiser Prmnnte Ornge Cnty-Nhei
3440 E La Palma Ave (92806-2020)
PHONE...............................714 644-2000
Patrick Steinhauser, *Brnch Mgr*
EMP: 3893
SQ FT: 125,000
SALES (corp-wide): 68.1B **Privately Held**
Web: www.kaisercenter.com
SIC: 8062 8011 General medical and surgical hospitals; General and family practice, physician/surgeon
HQ: Kaiser Foundation Hospitals Inc
1 Kaiser Plz
Oakland CA
510 271-6611

(P-18308)
KAISER FOUNDATION HOSPITALS
Also Called: Kaiser Permanente
4405 Vandever Ave Fl 5 (92120-3315)
PHONE...............................619 528-2583
David Mandler, *Mgr*
EMP: 185
SALES (corp-wide): 68.1B **Privately Held**
Web: www.kaisercenter.com
SIC: 8062 General medical and surgical hospitals
HQ: Kaiser Foundation Hospitals Inc
1 Kaiser Plz
Oakland CA
510 271-6611

(P-18309)
KAISER FOUNDATION HOSPITALS
Also Called: Kaiser Permanente
9455 Clairemont Mesa Blvd (92123-1297)
PHONE...............................858 573-1504
EMP: 136
SALES (corp-wide): 68.1B **Privately Held**
Web: www.kaisercenter.com
SIC: 8062 8011 General medical and surgical hospitals; Medical centers
HQ: Kaiser Foundation Hospitals Inc
1 Kaiser Plz
Oakland CA
510 271-6611

(P-18310)
KAISER FOUNDATION HOSPITALS
Also Called: Bostonia Medical Offices
1630 E Main St (92021-5204)
PHONE...............................619 528-5000
EMP: 150
SALES (corp-wide): 68.1B **Privately Held**
Web: www.kaisercenter.com
SIC: 8062 General medical and surgical hospitals
HQ: Kaiser Foundation Hospitals Inc
1 Kaiser Plz
Oakland CA
510 271-6611

(P-18311)
KAISER PERMANENTE WATTS C
1465 E 103rd St (90002-3306)

PRODUCTS & SVCS

PHONE...................323 564-7911
Vikki Franklin, *Dir*
EMP: 96 **EST:** 2013
SALES (est): 8.23MM **Privately Held**
Web: community.kp.org
SIC: 8062 General medical and surgical
hospitals

(P-18312)
KECK HOSPITAL OF USC
1500 San Pablo St (90033-5313)
PHONE...................800 872-2273
Thomas E Jackiewicz, *CEO*
James J Uli Junior, *CFO*
▲ **EMP:** 898 **EST:** 2009
SALES (est): 1.13B **Privately Held**
Web: www.keckmedicine.org
SIC: 8062 General medical and surgical
hospitals

(P-18313)
KECK SCHOOL
Also Called: Hoffman Medical Research Ctr
2011 Zonal Ave (90089-0110)
PHONE...................323 442-1179
Michael E Selsted, *Ch*
Fernando Zambrano, *CFO*
EMP: 82 **EST:** 2014
SALES (est): 7.22MM **Privately Held**
Web: www.keckmedicine.org
SIC: 8062 Hospital, med school affiliated
with nursing and residency

(P-18314)
KENNETH CORP
Also Called: Garden Grove Hospital
12601 Garden Grove Blvd (92843-1908)
PHONE...................714 537-5160
Edward Mirzabegian, *CEO*
Hassan Alkhouli, *
EMP: 615 **EST:** 1951
SQ FT: 133,083
SALES (est): 76.84MM **Privately Held**
Web: www.gardengrovehospital.com
SIC: 8062 General medical and surgical
hospitals

(P-18315)
KERN COUNTY HOSPITAL
AUTHORITY (PA)
1700 Mount Vernon Ave (93306-4018)
PHONE...................661 326-2102
Russell Judd, *CEO*
Tyler Whitezell, *Admn Execs*
Andrew Cantu, *CFO*
EMP: 499 **EST:** 1865
SQ FT: 29,800
SALES (est): 52.71MM
SALES (corp-wide): 52.71MM **Privately
Held**
Web: www.kernmedical.com
SIC: 8062 General medical and surgical
hospitals

(P-18316)
KND DEVELOPMENT 55 LLC
Also Called: Kindred Hospital - Rancho
10841 White Oak Ave (91730-3817)
PHONE...................909 581-6400
Miller Debroah, *Dir*
EMP: 108 **EST:** 2007
SALES (est): 35.86MM **Privately Held**
SIC: 8062 General medical and surgical
hospitals

(P-18317)
KPC GLOBAL MEDICAL
CENTERS INC (DH)
Also Called: PHH

1117 E Devonshire Ave (92543-3083)
PHONE...................714 953-3500
Kali Chaudhuri, *Ch*
Sreenivasa Nakka, *
Ashok Agarwal, *
Kali Priyo Chaudhuri, *
Rakesh Gupta, *
EMP: 125 **EST:** 2009
SALES (est): 169.46MM **Privately Held**
Web: www.hemetglobalmedcenter.com
SIC: 8062 General medical and surgical
hospitals
HQ: Kpc Healthcare, Inc.
1301 N Tustin Ave
Santa Ana CA
714 953-3652

(P-18318)
LA METROPOLITAN MEDICAL
CENTER
2231 Southwest Dr (90043-4523)
PHONE...................323 730-7300
TOLL FREE: 800
EMP: 600
Web: www.lammc.com
SIC: 8062 General medical and surgical
hospitals

(P-18319)
LA PALMA HOSPITAL MEDICAL
CENTER
Also Called: La Palma Intercommunity Hosp
7901 Walker St (90623-1764)
PHONE...................714 670-7400
TOLL FREE: 800
EMP: 400
Web:
www.lapalmaintercommunityhospital.com
SIC: 8062 General medical and surgical
hospitals

(P-18320)
LAC USC COUNTY HOSPITAL
2051 Marengo St (90033-1352)
PHONE...................323 226-2622
EMP: 92
SALES (est): 522.17K **Privately Held**
SIC: 8062 General medical and surgical
hospitals

(P-18321)
LAC USC MEDICAL CENTER
Also Called: Los Angeles County Hospital
1200 N State St Rm 5250 (90089-1001)
P.O. Box 63 (90078-0063)
EMP: 143 **EST:** 1992
SALES (est): 54.37MM **Privately Held**
Web: www.usc.edu
SIC: 8062 6324 General medical and
surgical hospitals; Hospital and medical
service plans

(P-18322)
LAKEWOOD REGIONAL MED
CTR INC
Also Called: Lakewood Regional Medical Ctr
3700 South St (90712-1419)
P.O. Box 6070 (90714-6070)
PHONE...................562 531-2550
John Grah, *CEO*
Ronald Galonsky, *
Mark Korth, *
Lani Dickinson, *
Michael Paul Amos, *
EMP: 900 **EST:** 2001
SALES (est): 139.5MM
SALES (corp-wide): 19.58B **Publicly Held**
SIC: 8062 Hospital, affiliated with AMA
residency
PA: Tenet Healthcare Corporation
14201 Dallas Pkwy

Dallas TX
469 893-2200

(P-18323)
LINDA LOMA UNIV HLTH CARE
(HQ)
11370 Anderson St Ste 3900 (92354-3450)
P.O. Box 2000 (92354-0200)
PHONE...................909 558-2806
Richard Hart, *Pr*
Rosita Fike, *
EMP: 125 **EST:** 1967
SALES (est): 171.21MM
SALES (corp-wide): 388.6MM **Privately
Held**
Web: www.lomalindafertility.com
SIC: 8062 8011 8051 5999 Hospital, medical
school affiliated with residency; Medical
centers; Extended care facility;
Convalescent equipment and supplies
PA: Loma Linda University
11060 Anderson St Mga
Loma Linda CA
909 558-4540

(P-18324)
LITTLE COMPANY MARY
HOSPITAL
Also Called: Leader Drug Store
4101 Torrance Blvd (90503-4664)
PHONE...................310 540-7676
Joseph Zanetta, *CEO*
Elizabeth Zuanich, *
▲ **EMP:** 1200 **EST:** 1957
SQ FT: 300,000
SALES (est): 18.03MM
SALES (corp-wide): 32.76MM **Privately
Held**
SIC: 8062 8051 General medical and
surgical hospitals; Skilled nursing care
facilities
HQ: Providence Health System-Southern
California
1801 Lind Ave Sw
Renton WA
425 525-3355

(P-18325)
LITTLE COMPANY OF MARY
HEALTH SERVICES
Also Called: Little Company Mary Svc Area
4101 Torrance Blvd (90503-4607)
PHONE...................310 540-7676
EMP: 2946
SIC: 8062 8741 General medical and
surgical hospitals; Hospital management

(P-18326)
LOMA LINDA UNIVERSITY MED
CTR (DH)
Also Called: LLUMC
11234 Anderson St (92354-2871)
P.O. Box 2000 (92354-0200)
PHONE...................909 558-4000
TOLL FREE: 800
Richard H Hart, *CEO*
James Jesse, *
Richard Catalano, *
Noni Patchett, *
EMP: 4600 **EST:** 1967
SQ FT: 630,000
SALES (est): 1.59B
SALES (corp-wide): 388.6MM **Privately
Held**
Web: www.lluh.org
SIC: 8062 8011 8051 5999 Hospital, medical
school affiliated with residency; Medical
centers; Extended care facility; Medical
apparatus and supplies
HQ: Loma Linda University Health Care
11370 Anderson St # 3900

Loma Linda CA
909 558-2806

(P-18327)
LOMA LINDA UNIVERSITY MED
CTR
26780 Barton Rd (92373-4308)
PHONE...................909 558-4000
EMP: 84
SALES (corp-wide): 388.6MM **Privately
Held**
Web: www.lluh.org
SIC: 8062 General medical and surgical
hospitals
HQ: Loma Linda University Medical Center
11234 Anderson St
Loma Linda CA
909 558-4000

(P-18328)
LOMA LINDA UNIVERSITY MED
CTR
Also Called: Behavioral Medicine Center
1710 Barton Rd (92373-5304)
PHONE...................909 558-9275
Ruthita Fike, *Mgr*
EMP: 90
SQ FT: 62,476
SALES (corp-wide): 388.6MM **Privately
Held**
Web: www.lluh.org
SIC: 8062 8221 Hospital, medical school
affiliation; University
HQ: Loma Linda University Medical Center
11234 Anderson St
Loma Linda CA
909 558-4000

(P-18329)
LOMA LINDA UNIVERSITY MED
CTR
11370 Anderson St (92354-3450)
P.O. Box 728 (92354-0728)
PHONE...................909 558-4385
EMP: 107
SALES (corp-wide): 388.6MM **Privately
Held**
Web: www.lluh.org
SIC: 8062 General medical and surgical
hospitals
HQ: Loma Linda University Medical Center
11234 Anderson St
Loma Linda CA
909 558-4000

(P-18330)
LOMA LNDA - INLAND EMPIRE
CNSR
Also Called: Loma Linda University Med Ctr
11234 Anderson St (92354-2804)
PHONE...................909 558-4000
Daniel Giang, *Pr*
EMP: 141 **EST:** 2013
SALES (est): 6.03MM **Privately Held**
SIC: 8062 Hospital, medical school affiliated
with residency

(P-18331)
LOMPOC VALLEY MEDICAL
CENTER
Also Called: Mammography Center
1111 E Ocean Ave Ste 2 (93436-2500)
PHONE...................805 735-9229
Jim Raggio, *Brnch Mgr*
EMP: 173
SALES (est): 137.58MM **Privately
Held**
Web: www.lompocvmc.com

SIC: 8062 General medical and surgical hospitals
PA: Lompoc Valley Medical Center
1515 E Ocean Ave
Lompoc CA
805 737-3300

(P-18332)
LOMPOC VALLEY MEDICAL CENTER (PA)
Also Called: Lompoc Skilled Care Center
1515 E Ocean Ave (93436-7092)
P.O. Box 1058 (93438-1058)
PHONE..............................805 737-3300
Jim Raggio, CEO
Naishadh Buch, *
Jayne Scalise, *
EMP: 325 EST: 1947
SQ FT: 150,000
SALES (est): 137.58MM
SALES (corp-wide): 137.58MM **Privately Held**
Web: www.lompocvmc.com
SIC: 8062 8051 Hospital, affiliated with AMA residency; Skilled nursing care facilities

(P-18333)
LONG BEACH MEDICAL CENTER
1720 Termino Ave (90804-2104)
PHONE..............................562 933-0085
EMP: 128
Web: www.memorialcare.org
SIC: 8062 General medical and surgical hospitals
HQ: Long Beach Medical Center
2801 Atlantic Ave Fl 2
Long Beach CA
562 933-2000

(P-18334)
LONG BEACH MEDICAL CENTER
Also Called: Infusion Care
450 E Spring St Ste 11 (90806-1608)
PHONE..............................562 933-7701
Gerald Nichrossan, Brnch Mgr
EMP: 118
Web: www.memorialcare.org
SIC: 8062 General medical and surgical hospitals
HQ: Long Beach Medical Center
2801 Atlantic Ave Fl 2
Long Beach CA
562 933-2000

(P-18335)
LONG BEACH MEDICAL CENTER (HQ)
Also Called: Miller Children's Hospital
2801 Atlantic Ave Fl 2 (90806-1701)
PHONE..............................562 933-2000
John Bishop, CEO
Barry Arbuckle Ph.d., Pr
Judy Fix, *
Scott Joslyn, CIO*
Thomas Poole, *
EMP: 2000 EST: 1907
SQ FT: 1,100,000
SALES (est): 633.63MM **Privately Held**
Web: www.memorialcare.org
SIC: 8062 General medical and surgical hospitals
PA: Memorial Health Services
17360 Brookhurst St # 160
Fountain Valley CA

(P-18336)
LONG BEACH MEMORIAL MED CTR
Also Called: LONG BEACH MEMORIAL MEDICAL CENTER

1057 Pine Ave (90813-3118)
PHONE..............................562 933-0432
Renee May, Brnch Mgr
EMP: 118
Web: www.thechildrensclinic.org
SIC: 8062 General medical and surgical hospitals
HQ: Long Beach Medical Center
2801 Atlantic Ave Fl 2
Long Beach CA
562 933-2000

(P-18337)
LONGWOOD MANAGEMENT CORP
Also Called: Shea Convalescent Hospital
7716 Pickering Ave (90602-2001)
PHONE..............................562 693-5240
Richard Esconrias, Mgr
EMP: 96
SALES (corp-wide): 79.33MM **Privately Held**
Web: www.longwoodmgmt.com
SIC: 8062 8051 8011 General medical and surgical hospitals; Skilled nursing care facilities; Offices and clinics of medical doctors
PA: Longwood Management Corp.
4032 Wilshire Blvd Fl 6
Los Angeles CA
213 389-6900

(P-18338)
LOS ALAMITOS MEDICAL CTR INC (HQ)
3751 Katella Ave (90720-3113)
P.O. Box 533 (90720-0533)
PHONE..............................714 826-6400
TOLL FREE: 800
Kent Clayton, CEO
Margaret Watkins, *
Alice Livingood Co, President Elect
EMP: 1100 EST: 1970
SQ FT: 900
SALES (est): 171.28MM
SALES (corp-wide): 19.58B **Publicly Held**
Web: www.losalamitosmri.com
SIC: 8062 General medical and surgical hospitals
PA: Tenet Healthcare Corporation
14201 Dallas Pkwy
Dallas TX
469 893-2200

(P-18339)
LOS ROBLES REGIONAL MED CTR (DH)
Also Called: Los Robles Hospital & Med Ctr
215 W Janss Rd (91360-1847)
PHONE..............................805 497-2727
Natalie Mussi, CEO
◆ EMP: 917 EST: 1978
SQ FT: 475
SALES (est): 334.05K **Publicly Held**
Web: www.losrobleshospital.com
SIC: 8062 General medical and surgical hospitals
HQ: Hca Inc.
1 Park Plz
Nashville TN
615 344-9551

(P-18340)
MARIAN COMMUNITY CLINIC
117 W Bunny Ave (93458-2805)
P.O. Box 2400 (85002-2400)
PHONE..............................805 739-3867
Eugen Alarco, CEO
Lupe Terrones, Dir
EMP: 83 EST: 1997

SALES (est): 120.17MM **Privately Held**
Web: www.dignityhealth.org
SIC: 8062 General medical and surgical hospitals
HQ: Dignity Health
185 Berry St Ste 200
San Francisco CA
415 438-5500

(P-18341)
MARIAN MEDICAL CENTER
Also Called: Marian Regional Medical Center
1400 E Church St (93454-5906)
PHONE..............................805 739-3000
EMP: 1000
Web: www.supportmarianmedical.org
SIC: 8062 General medical and surgical hospitals

(P-18342)
MEMORIAL HEALTH SERVICES (PA)
Also Called: Memorial Care Medical Centers
17360 Brookhurst St Ste 160 (92708-3720)
P.O. Box 20894 (92728-0894)
PHONE..............................714 377-2900
Barry Arbuckle, Pr
Diane Laird, *
Rick Graniere, CIO*
Karen Testman, *
Terri Cammarano, *
EMP: 460 EST: 1937
SALES (est): 2.69B **Privately Held**
Web: www.memorialcare.org
SIC: 8062 General medical and surgical hospitals

(P-18343)
MEMORIAL HLTH SVCS - UNIV CAL (PA)
2801 Atlantic Ave (90806-1701)
PHONE..............................562 933-2000
Edward Quilligan, CEO
Diana Hendel, *
Darrel Brownell, *
EMP: 1138 EST: 1907
SQ FT: 1,000,000
SALES (est): 411.78MM
SALES (corp-wide): 411.78MM **Privately Held**
Web: www.memorialcare.org
SIC: 8062 8741 General medical and surgical hospitals; Management services

(P-18344)
MEMORIAL HOSPITAL OF GARDENA
4060 Woody Blvd (90023)
PHONE..............................323 268-5514
EMP: 400
SIC: 8062 Hospital, affiliated with AMA residency

(P-18345)
MISSION HOSP REGIONAL MED CTR (PA)
Also Called: Mission Hospital
27700 Medical Center Rd (92691-6426)
PHONE..............................949 364-1400
Seth Peigen, CEO
EMP: 1349 EST: 1941
SQ FT: 750,000
SALES (est): 765.86MM
SALES (corp-wide): 765.86MM **Privately Held**
Web: www.mission4health.com
SIC: 8062 General medical and surgical hospitals

(P-18346)
MONTEREY PARK HOSPITAL
Also Called: Monterey Park Hospital
900 S Atlantic Blvd (91754-4780)
PHONE..............................626 570-9000
Philip A Cohen, CEO
Robert M Dubbs, *
Robert W Fleming Junior, Sr VP
EMP: 150 EST: 1972
SQ FT: 90,575
SALES (est): 34.31MM
SALES (corp-wide): 476.02MM **Privately Held**
Web: www.ahmchealth.com
SIC: 8062 General medical and surgical hospitals
PA: Ahmc Healthcare Inc.
506 W Valley Blvd Ste 300
San Gabriel CA
626 943-7526

(P-18347)
MOTION PICTURE AND TV FUND (PA)
Also Called: Bob Hope Health Center
23388 Mulholland Dr Ste 200 (91364-2733)
P.O. Box 51151 (90051-5451)
PHONE..............................818 876-1777
Robert Beitcher, CEO
Bob Pisano, *
Joseph Fischer, *
Jay Roth, *
EMP: 688 EST: 1924
SQ FT: 50,000
SALES (est): 29.84MM
SALES (corp-wide): 29.84MM **Privately Held**
Web: www.mptf.com
SIC: 8062 8051 8011 8351 General medical and surgical hospitals; Convalescent home with continuous nursing care; Medical centers; Child day care services

(P-18348)
MOUNTAIN VIEW CHILD CARE INC (PA)
Also Called: Totally Kids Rhbilitation Hosp
1720 Mountain View Ave (92354-1799)
PHONE..............................909 796-6915
Doug Pagett, CEO
Cynthia Capetillo, *
Donald Nydam, *
Hal Karlin, *
Loma Linda, *
EMP: 275 EST: 1972
SALES (est): 48.34MM **Privately Held**
Web: www.totallykids.com
SIC: 8062 8052 8051 General medical and surgical hospitals; Intermediate care facilities; Skilled nursing care facilities

(P-18349)
MOUNTAINS COMMUNITY HOSP FNDTN
Also Called: Mountains Community Hospital
29101 Hospital Rd (92352-9706)
P.O. Box 70 (92352-0070)
PHONE..............................909 336-3651
Don Willerth, CEO
EMP: 180 EST: 1957
SQ FT: 18,500
SALES (est): 24.11MM **Privately Held**
Web: www.mchcares.com
SIC: 8062 8051 General medical and surgical hospitals; Skilled nursing care facilities

(P-18350)
NAVY UNITED STATES DEPARTMENT
Also Called: Naval Medical Center
34800 Bob Wilson Dr (92134-1098)
PHONE..................................619 532-6400
Esther Lynn, *Brnch Mgr*
EMP: 4250
Web: www.navy.mil
SIC: 8062 9711 General medical and surgical hospitals; Navy
HQ: United States Department Of The Navy
1200 Navy Pentagon
Washington DC

(P-18351)
NIX HOSPITALS SYSTEM LLC (HQ)
Also Called: Nix Healthcare System
3415 S Sepulveda Blvd Ste 900 (90034-6981)
PHONE..................................210 271-1800
John F Strieby, *Pr*
Rob Elders, *
EMP: 108 **EST:** 2011
SALES (est): 113.34MM
SALES (corp-wide): 3.91B **Privately Held**
SIC: 8062 General medical and surgical hospitals
PA: Prospect Medical Holdings, Inc.
3415 S Sepulveda Blvd # 9
Los Angeles CA
310 943-4500

(P-18352)
NORTH KERN S TULARE HOSP DST
Also Called: Delano Dst Sklled Nrsing Fclty
1509 Tokay St (93215-3603)
PHONE..................................661 720-2126
Silva Soto, *Pr*
Dio Telmo, *Admn*
Elson De Guzman, *Contrlr*
Jaime Mendoza, *Prin*
Femme Adebayo, *Prin*
EMP: 230 **EST:** 1966
SALES (est): 14.4MM **Privately Held**
Web: www.nksthd.org
SIC: 8062 General medical and surgical hospitals

(P-18353)
OLYMPIA HEALTH CARE LLC
Also Called: Olympia Medical Center
5900 W Olympic Blvd (90036-4671)
P.O. Box 351209 (90035-9609)
PHONE..................................323 938-3161
Karen Knueven, *
Babur Ozkan, *
EMP: 875 **EST:** 2004
SQ FT: 500,000
SALES (est): 185.86MM **Privately Held**
Web: www.olympiamc.com
SIC: 8062 Hospital, affiliated with AMA residency
PA: Alecto Healthcare Services Llc
101 N Brand Blvd Ste 1920
Glendale CA

(P-18354)
ORANGE CNTY GLOBL MED CTR AUX (DH)
Also Called: Western Medical Center Aux
1301 N Tustin Ave (92705-8619)
PHONE..................................714 835-3555
Dan Brothman, *CEO*
Patricia Stites, *
EMP: 200 **EST:** 1998
SALES (est): 105.84MM **Privately Held**

Web: www.orangecountyglobalmedicalcenter.com
SIC: 8062 General medical and surgical hospitals
HQ: Kpc Healthcare, Inc.
1301 N Tustin Ave
Santa Ana CA
714 953-3652

(P-18355)
ORANGE COAST MEMORIAL MED CTR (HQ)
9920 Talbert Ave (92708-5153)
PHONE..................................714 378-7000
TOLL FREE: 888
EMP: 522 **EST:** 1995
SQ FT: 40,361
SALES (est): 377.3MM **Privately Held**
Web: www.memorialcare.org
SIC: 8062 General medical and surgical hospitals
PA: Memorial Health Services
17360 Brookhurst St # 160
Fountain Valley CA

(P-18356)
ORANGTREE CNVALESCENT HOSP INC
Also Called: Plott Family Care Centers
4000 Harrison St (92503-3514)
PHONE..................................951 785-6060
Elizabeth Plott, *Pr*
EMP: 120 **EST:** 1983
SALES (est): 7.67MM **Privately Held**
SIC: 8062 8051 General medical and surgical hospitals; Skilled nursing care facilities

(P-18357)
ORTHOPAEDIC HOSPITAL (PA)
Also Called: Orthopaedic Inst For Children
403 W Adams Blvd (90007-2664)
P.O. Box 60132 (90060-0132)
PHONE..................................213 742-1000
Anthony A Scaduto, *Pr*
Diane Moon, *
EMP: 168 **EST:** 1923
SQ FT: 105,000
SALES (est): 13.5MM
SALES (corp-wide): 13.5MM **Privately Held**
Web: www.luskinoic.org
SIC: 8062 8011 General medical and surgical hospitals; Primary care medical clinic

(P-18358)
PACIFIC HEALTH CORPORATION
Also Called: Tustin Hospital
14642 Newport Ave (92780-6057)
PHONE..................................714 838-9600
EMP: 1700
Web: www.pacifichealthcorp.com
SIC: 8062 General medical and surgical hospitals

(P-18359)
PACIFICA OF VALLEY CORPORATION
Also Called: PACIFICA HOSPITAL OF THE VALLE
9449 San Fernando Rd (91352-1421)
PHONE..................................818 767-3310
Paul Tuft, *Ch Bd*
Ayman Mousa, *
EMP: 607 **EST:** 1996
SQ FT: 148,020
SALES (est): 97.12MM **Privately Held**
Web: www.pacificahospital.com

SIC: 8062 Hospital, affiliated with AMA residency

(P-18360)
PALO VERDE HEALTH CARE DST
Also Called: Palo Verde Hospital
250 N 1st St (92225-1702)
PHONE..................................760 922-4115
Sandra J Anaya, *CEO*
Dennis Rutherford, *
EMP: 180 **EST:** 1938
SALES (est): 23.8MM **Privately Held**
Web: www.paloverdehospital.org
SIC: 8062 8069 General medical and surgical hospitals; Specialty hospitals, except psychiatric

(P-18361)
PALO VERDE HOSPITAL ASSN
250 N 1st St (92225-1702)
PHONE..................................760 922-4115
Sandra J Anaya, *CEO*
Larry Blitz, *
Jim Carney, *
David Conejo, *
Beatrice Pinon, *
EMP: 135 **EST:** 1948
SQ FT: 44,000
SALES (est): 26.72MM **Privately Held**
Web: www.paloverdehospital.org
SIC: 8062 General medical and surgical hospitals

(P-18362)
PALOMAR HEALTH
Also Called: Patient Business Services
152255 Innovation Dr (92128)
PHONE..................................858 675-5218
Laurie Rose, *Mgr*
EMP: 300
SALES (corp-wide): 679.43K **Privately Held**
Web: www.palomarhealth.org
SIC: 8062 General medical and surgical hospitals
PA: Palomar Health
2125 Citracado Pkwy # 300
Escondido CA
442 281-5000

(P-18363)
PALOMAR HEALTH
Also Called: Palomar Medical Center
15615 Pomerado Rd (92064-2405)
PHONE..................................760 739-3000
Michael Covert, *CEO*
EMP: 1200
SALES (corp-wide): 679.43K **Privately Held**
Web: www.palomarhealth.org
SIC: 8062 General medical and surgical hospitals
PA: Palomar Health
2125 Citracado Pkwy # 300
Escondido CA
442 281-5000

(P-18364)
PALOMAR HEALTH
Also Called: Pomerado Hospital
15615 Pomerado Rd (92064-2405)
PHONE..................................858 613-4000
TOLL FREE: 800
Jim Flinn, *Admn*
EMP: 182
SALES (corp-wide): 679.43K **Privately Held**
Web: www.palomarhealth.org

SIC: 8062 General medical and surgical hospitals
PA: Palomar Health
2125 Citracado Pkwy # 300
Escondido CA
442 281-5000

(P-18365)
PALOMAR HEALTH (PA)
Also Called: Palomar Medical Center
2125 Citracado Pkwy Ste 300 (92029-4159)
PHONE..................................442 281-5000
Doug Moir, *Pr*
Tanya Howell, *
EMP: 180 **EST:** 1950
SALES (est): 679.43K
SALES (corp-wide): 679.43K **Privately Held**
Web: www.palomarhealth.org
SIC: 8062 8059 General medical and surgical hospitals; Convalescent home

(P-18366)
PALOMAR HEALTH MEDICAL GROUP (HQ)
Also Called: Arch Health Partners
15611 Pomerado Rd Ste 575 (92064-2440)
PHONE..................................858 675-3100
Deanna Kyrimis, *CEO*
Hugh King, *
Matt Niedzwiecki, *
EMP: 168 **EST:** 2009
SALES (est): 163.61MM
SALES (corp-wide): 679.43K **Privately Held**
Web: www.palomarhealthmedicalgroup.org
SIC: 8062 General medical and surgical hospitals
PA: Palomar Health
2125 Citracado Pkwy # 300
Escondido CA
442 281-5000

(P-18367)
PALOMAR HEALTH TECHNOLOGY INC
2140 Enterprise St (92029-2000)
PHONE..................................442 281-5000
Diane Hansen, *CEO*
EMP: 134 **EST:** 2011
SALES (est): 59.99MM
SALES (corp-wide): 679.43K **Privately Held**
Web: www.palomarhealth.org
SIC: 8062 General medical and surgical hospitals
PA: Palomar Health
2125 Citracado Pkwy # 300
Escondido CA
442 281-5000

(P-18368)
PALOMAR MEDICAL CENTER
Also Called: Pomerado Hospital
15615 Pomerado Rd (92064-2405)
PHONE..................................858 613-4000
Dianne Hansen, *CEO*
EMP: 368 **EST:** 2013
SALES (est): 218.46K
SALES (corp-wide): 679.43K **Privately Held**
Web: www.palomarhealth.org
SIC: 8062 General medical and surgical hospitals
PA: Palomar Health
2125 Citracado Pkwy # 300
Escondido CA
442 281-5000

(P-18369)
PAMC LTD (PA)
Also Called: Pamc Health Foundation
531 W College St (90012-2315)
PHONE..............................213 624-8411
John Edwards, *CEO*
EMP: 530 **EST:** 1989
SQ FT: 75,600
SALES (est): 19.13MM **Privately Held**
Web: www.pamc.net
SIC: 8062 General medical and surgical
hospitals

(P-18370)
**PARACLSUS LOS ANGLES
CMNTY HOS**
Also Called: LOS ANGELES COMMUNITY
HOSPITAL
4081 E Olympic Blvd (90023-3330)
PHONE..............................323 267-0477
EMP: 250 **EST:** 1983
SALES (est): 194.63MM **Privately Held**
Web: www.lach-la.com
SIC: 8062 General medical and surgical
hospitals

(P-18371)
PARADISE VALLEY HOSPITAL
Also Called: West Health Care
180 Otay Lakes Rd Ste 100 (91902-2464)
PHONE..............................619 472-7474
Connie Mayo, *Dir*
EMP: 251
SALES (corp-wide): 140.77MM **Privately
Held**
Web: www.paradisevalleyhospital.net
SIC: 8062 General medical and surgical
hospitals
PA: Paradise Valley Hospital
2400 E 4th St
National City CA
619 470-4100

(P-18372)
**PARADISE VALLEY HOSPITAL
(PA)**
2400 E 4th St (91950-2098)
PHONE..............................619 470-4100
Alan Soderblom, *CEO*
Luin Leon, *
Robert Carmen, *
Prem Reddy, *
Neerav Jadeja, *
EMP: 925 **EST:** 1904
SQ FT: 230,000
SALES (est): 140.77MM
SALES (corp-wide): 140.77MM **Privately
Held**
Web: www.paradisevalleyhospital.net
SIC: 8062 General medical and surgical
hospitals

(P-18373)
**PARKVIEW CMNTY HOSP MED
CTR**
3865 Jackson St (92503-3919)
PHONE..............................951 354-7404
Norm Martin, *Pr*
Doug Drumwright, *
EMP: 1149 **EST:** 1966
SQ FT: 132,651
SALES (est): 162.74MM
SALES (corp-wide): 162.74MM **Privately
Held**
Web: www.ahmchealth.com
SIC: 8062 8011 General medical and
surgical hospitals; Offices and clinics of
medical doctors
PA: Doctors Hospital Of Riverside Llc
3865 Jackson St

Riverside CA
951 354-7404

(P-18374)
**PASADENA HOSPITAL ASSN
LTD (PA)**
Also Called: Huntington Memorial Hospital
100 W California Blvd (91105-3010)
P.O. Box 440746 (77244-0746)
PHONE..............................626 397-5000
Lori J Morgan, *CEO*
Lois Matthews, *
Stephen A Ralph, *
Jim Noble, *
Jane Haderlein, *
EMP: 2100 **EST:** 1892
SQ FT: 928,000
SALES (est): 688.61MM
SALES (corp-wide): 688.61MM **Privately
Held**
Web: www.huntingtonhealth.org
SIC: 8062 General medical and surgical
hospitals

(P-18375)
**PERRIS VALLEY CMNTY HOSP
LLC**
Also Called: Vista Hospital Riverside
10841 White Oak Ave (91730-3817)
PHONE..............................909 581-6400
EMP: 227
SIC: 8062 General medical and surgical
hospitals
PA: Perris Valley Community Hospital, Llc
2224 Medical Center Dr
Perris CA

(P-18376)
PIH HEALTH INC (PA)
Also Called: Integrted Healthcare Dlvry Sys
12401 Washington Blvd (90602-1006)
PHONE..............................562 698-0811
Jane Dicus, *Ch*
Richard Atwood, *Vice Chairman*
Efrain Aceves, *
Kenton Woods, *
Ronald Yoshihara, *
EMP: 1100 **EST:** 1981
SQ FT: 500,000
SALES (est): 923.01K
SALES (corp-wide): 923.01K **Privately
Held**
SIC: 8062 8011 General medical and
surgical hospitals; Offices and clinics of
medical doctors

(P-18377)
**PIH HEALTH DOWNEY
HOSPITAL (HQ)**
Also Called: General Acute Care Hospital
11500 Brookshire Ave (90241-4917)
PHONE..............................562 698-0811
James R West, *Pr*
Bryan Smolskis, *
Efrain Aceves, *
Kenton Woods, *
Peggy Chulack, *CAO*
EMP: 254 **EST:** 1956
SQ FT: 225,000
SALES (est): 203.49MM
SALES (corp-wide): 923.01K **Privately
Held**
SIC: 8062 General medical and surgical
hospitals
PA: Pih Health, Inc.
12401 Washington Blvd
Whittier CA
562 698-0811

(P-18378)
**PIH HEALTH GOOD SAMARITAN
HOSP (HQ)**
Also Called: INTEGRATED HEALTHCARE
DELIVERY
1225 Wilshire Blvd (90017-1901)
PHONE..............................213 977-2121
James West, *CEO*
Charles Munger, *
Alan Ino, *
▲ **EMP:** 1610 **EST:** 1885
SQ FT: 10,000
SALES (est): 435.92MM
SALES (corp-wide): 923.01K **Privately
Held**
SIC: 8062 Hospital, affiliated with AMA
residency
PA: Pih Health, Inc.
12401 Washington Blvd
Whittier CA
562 698-0811

(P-18379)
PIH HEALTH HOSPITAL - WHITTI
Also Called: Downey Regional Medical Center
11500 Brookshire Ave (90241-4917)
PHONE..............................562 904-5482
James R West, *CEO*
EMP: 1150
SALES (corp-wide): 923.01K **Privately
Held**
SIC: 8062 8071 General medical and
surgical hospitals; Medical laboratories
HQ: Pih Health Whittier Hospital
12401 Washington Blvd
Whittier CA
562 698-0811

(P-18380)
**PIH HEALTH WHITTIER
HOSPITAL (HQ)**
Also Called: General Acute Care Hospital
12401 Washington Blvd (90602-1006)
PHONE..............................562 698-0811
James R West, *CEO*
Anita Chou, *
Ramona Pratt, *
EMP: 1900 **EST:** 1954
SQ FT: 500,000
SALES (est): 861.97MM
SALES (corp-wide): 923.01K **Privately
Held**
SIC: 8062 General medical and surgical
hospitals
PA: Pih Health, Inc.
12401 Washington Blvd
Whittier CA
562 698-0811

(P-18381)
**PIONEERS MEM HEALTHCARE
DST (PA)**
Also Called: PIONEERS MEMORIAL
HOSPITAL
207 W Legion Rd (92227-7780)
PHONE..............................760 351-3333
Christopher R Bjornberg, *CEO*
Daniel Heckathorne, *
Justina Aguirre, *
EMP: 571 **EST:** 1947
SQ FT: 171,445
SALES (est): 133.71MM
SALES (corp-wide): 133.71MM **Privately
Held**
Web: www.pmhd.org
SIC: 8062 Hospital, affiliated with AMA
residency

(P-18382)
PIPELINE HEALTH LLC (PA)
898 N Pacific Coast Hwy Ste 700 (90245)
PHONE..............................310 379-2134
EMP: 94 **EST:** 2014
SALES (est): 218.29MM
SALES (corp-wide): 218.29MM **Privately
Held**
Web: www.pipelinehealth.us
SIC: 8062 General medical and surgical
hospitals

(P-18383)
**POMONA VALLEY HOSPITAL
MED CTR (PA)**
Also Called: Pvhmc
1798 N Garey Ave (91767-2918)
PHONE..............................909 865-9500
Richard E Yochum, *CEO*
Alan Smith, *
Michael Nelson, *
Kurt Weinmeister, *
EMP: 2121 **EST:** 1903
SQ FT: 362,000
SALES (est): 701.76MM
SALES (corp-wide): 701.76MM **Privately
Held**
Web: www.pvhmc.org
SIC: 8062 Hospital, medical school affiliated
with residency

(P-18384)
**PRIME HALTHCARE
FOUNDATION INC (PA)**
3480 E Guasti Rd (91761-7684)
PHONE..............................909 235-4400
Prem Reddy, *CEO*
EMP: 107 **EST:** 2006
SALES (est): 1.03B
SALES (corp-wide): 1.03B **Privately Held**
Web: www.primehealthcare.com
SIC: 8062 General medical and surgical
hospitals

(P-18385)
**PRIME HEALTHCARE ANAHEIM
LLC**
Also Called: West Anaheim Medical Center
3033 W Orange Ave (92804-3156)
PHONE..............................714 827-3000
Virg Narbutas, *CEO*
Kora Guoyavatin, *
EMP: 800 **EST:** 1963
SQ FT: 180,000
SALES (est): 139.44MM
SALES (corp-wide): 1.03B **Privately Held**
Web: www.westanaheimmedctr.com
SIC: 8062 Hospital, affiliated with AMA
residency
HQ: Prime Healthcare Services Inc
3480 E Guasti Rd
Ontario CA

(P-18386)
**PRIME HEALTHCARE
CENTINELA LLC**
Also Called: Centinela Hospital Medical
Center
555 E Hardy St (90301-4011)
PHONE..............................310 673-4660
Linda Bradley, *CEO*
Barbara Kokolowski, *SVS*
EMP: 1000 **EST:** 1952
SALES (est): 262.74MM
SALES (corp-wide): 1.03B **Privately Held**
Web: www.centinelamed.com
SIC: 8062 General medical and surgical
hospitals
HQ: Prime Healthcare Services Inc
3480 E Guasti Rd

PRODUCTS & SVCS

Ontario CA

(P-18387)

PRIME HEALTHCARE SERVICES-MONT

5000 San Bernardino St (91763-2326)
PHONE...............................909 625-5411
EMP: 1384
SALES (est): 107.71MM
SALES (corp-wide): 1.03B **Privately Held**
Web: www.montclair-hospital.org
SIC: 8062 General medical and surgical hospitals
PA: Prime Healthcare Foundation, Inc.
3480 E Guasti Rd
Ontario CA
909 235-4400

(P-18388)

PRIME HLTHCARE HNTNGTON BCH LL

Also Called: Huntington Beach Hospital
17772 Beach Blvd (92647-6819)
PHONE...............................714 843-5000
EMP: 480 **EST:** 1957
SQ FT: 100,000
SALES (est): 61.25MM
SALES (corp-wide): 1.03B **Privately Held**
Web: www.hbhospital.org
SIC: 8062 General medical and surgical hospitals
HQ: Prime Healthcare Services Inc
3480 E Guasti Rd
Ontario CA

(P-18389)

PRIME HLTHCARE SRVCS-MNTCLAIR (DH)

Also Called: Montclair Hospital Medical Center
5000 San Bernardino St (91763-2326)
PHONE...............................909 625-5411
Jennifer Ramirez, *Ex Sec*
Prem Reddy, *
EMP: 234 **EST:** 1999
SALES (est): 62.26MM
SALES (corp-wide): 1.03B **Privately Held**
Web: www.montclair-hospital.org
SIC: 8062 General medical and surgical hospitals
HQ: Prime Healthcare Services Inc
3480 E Guasti Rd
Ontario CA

(P-18390)

PRIME HLTHCARE SRVCS-MNTCLAIR

Also Called: Urgent Care Center
5000 San Bernardino St (91763-2326)
PHONE...............................909 625-5411
David Chu, *Mgr*
EMP: 216
SALES (corp-wide): 1.03B **Privately Held**
Web: www.montclair-hospital.org
SIC: 8062 General medical and surgical hospitals
HQ: Prime Healthcare Services-Montclair, Llc
5000 San Bernardino St
Montclair CA
909 625-5411

(P-18391)

PRIME HLTHCARE SVCS - ENCINO H

16237 Ventura Blvd (91436-2201)
PHONE...............................818 995-5000
Bockhi Park, *CEO*
Bockhi Park, *Prin*

Prem Reddy, *
EMP: 400 **EST:** 2008
SALES (est): 100.85MM
SALES (corp-wide): 1.03B **Privately Held**
Web: www.encinomed.org
SIC: 8062 General medical and surgical hospitals
HQ: Prime Healthcare Services Inc
3480 E Guasti Rd
Ontario CA

(P-18392)

PRIME HLTHCARE SVCS - PMPA LLC (DH)

Also Called: Pampa Regional Medical Center
3300 E Guasti Rd Ste 300 (91761-8657)
PHONE...............................909 235-4400
Brad Morse, *CEO*
Steven Smith, *
Harsha Upadhyay, *
EMP: 149 **EST:** 1960
SQ FT: 150,000
SALES (est): 41.36MM
SALES (corp-wide): 1.03B **Privately Held**
Web: www.primehealthcare.com
SIC: 8062 General medical and surgical hospitals
HQ: Prime Healthcare Services Inc
3480 E Guasti Rd
Ontario CA

(P-18393)

PRIME HLTHCARE SVCS - SAN DMAS

Also Called: San Dimas Community Hospital
1350 W Covina Blvd (91773-3245)
PHONE...............................909 599-6811
TOLL FREE: 800
Gregory Brentano, *CEO*
Harold Way, *
EMP: 350 **EST:** 1982
SQ FT: 90,000
SALES (est): 58.27MM
SALES (corp-wide): 1.03B **Privately Held**
Web: www.sandimashospital.com
SIC: 8062 General medical and surgical hospitals
HQ: Prime Healthcare Services Inc
3480 E Guasti Rd
Ontario CA

(P-18394)

PRIME HLTHCARE SVCS - SHRMAN O

Also Called: Sherman Oaks Hospital
4929 Van Nuys Blvd (91403-1702)
PHONE...............................818 981-7111
Prem Reddy, *CEO*
John Deady, *CFO*
EMP: 500 **EST:** 2004
SQ FT: 36,000
SALES (est): 97.87MM
SALES (corp-wide): 1.03B **Privately Held**
Web: www.shermanoakshospital.org
SIC: 8062 General medical and surgical hospitals
HQ: Prime Healthcare Services Inc
3480 E Guasti Rd
Ontario CA

(P-18395)

PRIME HLTHCARE SVCS - ST JOHN (DH)

3500 S 4th St (91761)
PHONE...............................913 680-6000
TOLL FREE: 800
Randall G Nyp, *CEO*
EMP: 97 **EST:** 1864
SQ FT: 96,000
SALES (est): 44.62MM

SALES (corp-wide): 1.03B **Privately Held**
Web: www.prime-healthcare.com
SIC: 8062 General medical and surgical hospitals
HQ: Prime Healthcare Services Inc
3480 E Guasti Rd
Ontario CA

(P-18396)

PROVIDENCE HEALTH & SVCS - ORE

Also Called: Providence Holy Cross Med Ctr
15031 Rinaldi St (91345-1207)
PHONE...............................818 365-8051
David Mast, *Brnch Mgr*
EMP: 3898
SALES (corp-wide): 32.76MM **Privately Held**
Web: www.providence.org
SIC: 8062 General medical and surgical hospitals
HQ: Providence Health & Services - Oregon
1801 Lind Ave Sw
Renton WA
425 525-3355

(P-18397)

PROVIDENCE HEALTH SYSTEM

Providence St Joseph Med Ctr
501 S Buena Vista St (91505-4809)
PHONE...............................818 843-5111
Georgianne Johnson, *COO*
EMP: 2000
SALES (corp-wide): 32.76MM **Privately Held**
Web: www.providence.org
SIC: 8062 General medical and surgical hospitals
HQ: Providence Health System-Southern California
1801 Lind Ave Sw
Renton WA
425 525-3355

(P-18398)

PROVIDENCE HOLY CROSS MEDICAL (PA)

Also Called: Providence
15031 Rinaldi St (91345-1207)
PHONE...............................818 365-8051
Lee Kanon Alpert, *Ch*
June E Drake, *
Jodi Hein, *
▲ **EMP:** 439 **EST:** 1960
SALES (est): 557.56MM
SALES (corp-wide): 557.56MM **Privately Held**
SIC: 8062 General medical and surgical hospitals

(P-18399)

PROVIDENCE MEDICAL FOUNDATION (DH)

Also Called: PROVIDENCE HOME HEALTH ORANGE
200 W Center Street Promenade Ste 800 (92805-3960)
PHONE...............................714 712-3308
EMP: 150 **EST:** 1961
SALES (est): 1.09B
SALES (corp-wide): 32.76MM **Privately Held**
Web: www.psjhmedgroups.org
SIC: 8062 General medical and surgical hospitals
HQ: St. Joseph Health System
3345 Michelson Dr Ste 100
Irvine CA
949 381-4000

(P-18400)

PROVIDENCE ST JOHNS HLTH CTR

Also Called: St. John's Health Center
2121 Santa Monica Blvd (90404-2303)
PHONE...............................971 268-7643
Marcel Loh, *CEO*
Donald Larsen Junior, *Chief Medical Officer*
Brian Anderson, *Contracts Director**
Guadalupe Martinez, *Finance**
EMP: 350 **EST:** 1940
SQ FT: 60,000
SALES (est): 401MM **Privately Held**
SIC: 8062 General medical and surgical hospitals

(P-18401)

PROVIDENCE TARZANA MEDICAL CTR

18321 Clark St (91356-3501)
PHONE...............................818 881-0800
Dale Surowitz, *CEO*
Nick Lymberopoulos, *
EMP: 1300 **EST:** 1973
SALES (est): 291.91MM **Privately Held**
Web: www.tarzanacme.com
SIC: 8062 General medical and surgical hospitals

(P-18402)

PROVIDNCE HLTH SVCS FNDTN/SAN

Also Called: Providnce Holy Cross Fundation
501 S Buena Vista St (91505-4809)
PHONE...............................818 843-5111
Patricia Modrzejewski, *CEO*
Lee Kanon Alpert, *
Thomas Mcdevitt, *Contrlr*
EMP: 2000 **EST:** 1980
SALES (est): 63.69MM **Privately Held**
SIC: 8062 General medical and surgical hospitals

(P-18403)

RADY CHILDRENS HOSP & HLTH CTR (PA)

Also Called: Children's Hospital
3020 Childrens Way (92123-4223)
PHONE...............................858 576-1700
TOLL FREE: 800
EMP: 1700 **EST:** 1980
SALES (est): 2.01B **Privately Held**
Web: www.rchsd.org
SIC: 8062 General medical and surgical hospitals

(P-18404)

RADY CHLD HOSPITAL-SAN DIEGO (HQ)

Also Called: CHILDREN'S HOSPITAL
3020 Childrens Way (92123-4223)
PHONE...............................858 576-1700
Donald Kearns, *CEO*
Jill Strickland, *CAO**
EMP: 2000 **EST:** 1952
SQ FT: 276,000
SALES (est): 1.91B **Privately Held**
Web: www.rchsd.org
SIC: 8062 General medical and surgical hospitals
PA: Rady Children's Hospital And Health Center
3020 Childrens Way
San Diego CA

(P-18405)

RAMONA RHBLTTION POST ACUTE CA

Also Called: Ramona Rhblttion Post Acute Ca
485 W Johnston Ave (92543-7012)
PHONE..................................951 652-0011
Stan Leland, *Pr*
Heidi Vickers, *
EMP: 120 EST: 1995
SQ FT: 30,000
SALES (est): 9.68MM **Privately Held**
Web: www.ramona-rehab.com
SIC: 8062 8051 General medical and
surgical hospitals; Convalescent home with
continuous nursing care

(P-18406)
REDLANDS COMMUNITY HOSPITAL (PA)
350 Terracina Blvd (92373-4897)
PHONE..................................909 335-5500
EMP: 97 EST: 1927
SALES (est): 213.73MM **Privately Held**
Web: www.redlandshospital.org
SIC: 8062 General medical and surgical
hospitals

(P-18407)
RIDGECREST REGIONAL HOSPITAL (PA)
Also Called: Southern Sierra Medical Clinic
1081 N China Lake Blvd (93555-3130)
PHONE..................................760 446-3551
James A Suver, *CEO*
Donna Kiser, *
EMP: 470 EST: 1962
SQ FT: 80,000
SALES (est): 156.64MM
SALES (corp-wide): 156.64MM **Privately Held**
Web: www.rrh.org
SIC: 8062 General medical and surgical
hospitals

(P-18408)
RIVERSIDE CMNTY HLTH SYSTEMS (DH)
Also Called: Riverside Community Hospital
4445 Magnolia Ave 6th Fl (92501-4135)
PHONE..................................951 788-3000
Partrick Brilliant, *Pr*
Tracey Fernandez, *
Doug Long, *
EMP: 1195 EST: 1901
SQ FT: 386,100
SALES (est): 162.72MM **Publicly Held**
Web:
www.riversidecommunityhospital.com
SIC: 8062 8011 General medical and
surgical hospitals; Offices and clinics of
medical doctors
HQ: Hca Inc.
1 Park Plz
Nashville TN
615 344-9551

(P-18409)
RIVERSIDE UNIV HLTH SYS FNDTIO (PA)
Also Called: Riverside Cnty Rgional Med Ctr
4065 County Circle Dr (92503-3410)
PHONE..................................951 358-5000
Douglas D Bagley, *CEO*
David Runke, *
Ellie Bennett, *
EMP: 459 EST: 1989
SALES (est): 4.17MM **Privately Held**
Web: www.ruhealth.org
SIC: 8062 General medical and surgical
hospitals

(P-18410)
RIVERSIDE UNIVERSITY HEALTH
Also Called: Ruhs-Emergency Department
26520 Cactus Ave (92555-3927)
PHONE..................................951 486-4000
EMP: 341
Web: www.ruhealth.org
SIC: 8062 General medical and surgical
hospitals
PA: Riverside University Health System
Foundation
4065 County Circle Dr
Riverside CA

(P-18411)
SADDLEBACK MEMORIAL MED CTR (HQ)
Also Called: Memorlcare Heart Vascular Inst
24451 Health Center Dr Fl 1 (92653-3689)
PHONE..................................949 837-4500
Steve Geidt, *CEO*
Barry Arbuckle, *
Karen Testman, *
Rick Graniere, *
Adolfo Chanez, *
EMP: 1020 EST: 1969
SQ FT: 195,000
SALES (est): 349.15MM **Privately Held**
Web: www.memorialcare.org
SIC: 8062 8011 8093 8099 General medical
and surgical hospitals; Medical centers;
Rehabilitation center, outpatient treatment;
Blood related health services
PA: Memorial Health Services
17360 Brookhurst St # 160
Fountain Valley CA

(P-18412)
SAINT JOHNS HEALTH CENTER FOUNDATION (DH)
Also Called: Saint John's Health Center
2121 Santa Monica Blvd (90404-2303)
PHONE..................................310 829-5511
TOLL FREE: 888
EMP: 1100 EST: 1942
SALES (est): 69.62MM
SALES (corp-wide): 10.75B **Privately Held**
Web: www.saintjohnsfoundation.org
SIC: 8062 General medical and surgical
hospitals
HQ: Sisters Of Charity Of Leavenworth
Health System, Inc.
500 Eldorado Blvd # 6300
Broomfield CO
303 813-5000

(P-18413)
SAN ANTONIO REGIONAL HOSPITAL (PA)
999 San Bernardino Rd (91786-4920)
PHONE..................................909 985-2811
John Chapman, *CEO*
Jim Milhiser, *
Wah-chung Hsu, *CFO*
▲ EMP: 1900 EST: 1920
SQ FT: 349,000
SALES (est): 424.66MM
SALES (corp-wide): 424.66MM **Privately Held**
Web: www.sarh.org
SIC: 8062 5912 General medical and
surgical hospitals; Drug stores and
proprietary stores

(P-18414)
SAN GABRIEL VALLEY MEDICAL CTR
438 W Las Tunas Dr (91776-1216)
PHONE..................................626 289-5454

Thomas Mone, *CEO*
Edward Shuey, *
Richard Polver, *
Harold Way, *
EMP: 850 EST: 1964
SQ FT: 42,000
SALES (est): 106.77MM **Privately Held**
Web: www.ahmchealth.com
SIC: 8062 General medical and surgical
hospitals
HQ: Dignity Health
185 Berry St Ste 200
San Francisco CA
415 438-5500

(P-18415)
SAN GORGONIO MEMORIAL HOSPITAL
600 N Highland Springs Ave (92220-3046)
PHONE..................................951 845-1121
Steve Barron, *CEO*
EMP: 819 EST: 1990
SALES (est): 57.5MM **Privately Held**
Web: www.sgmh.org
SIC: 8062 General medical and surgical
hospitals

(P-18416)
SAN GRGNIO MEM HOSP FOUNDATION (PA)
600 N Highland Springs Ave (92220-3046)
PHONE..................................951 845-1121
Steven Barron, *CEO*
Jerilynn Kaibel, *
Denae Reagins, *
Olivia Hershey, *
Dorothy Ellis, *
EMP: 244 EST: 1990
SQ FT: 76,000
SALES (est): 88.29MM
SALES (corp-wide): 88.29MM **Privately Held**
Web: www.sgmh.org
SIC: 8062 Hospital, affiliated with AMA
residency

(P-18417)
SAN JOAQUIN COMMUNITY HOSPITAL (PA)
Also Called: Adventist Health Bakersfield
2615 Chester Ave (93301-2014)
PHONE..................................661 395-3000
Sharlet Briggs, *Pr*
EMP: 850 EST: 1910
SQ FT: 137,000
SALES (est): 477.16MM
SALES (corp-wide): 477.16MM **Privately Held**
Web: www.adventisthealth.org
SIC: 8062 8011 General medical and
surgical hospitals; Offices and clinics of
medical doctors

(P-18418)
SAN PEDRO PENINSULA HOSPITAL
Also Called: Little Co Mary- San Pedro Hosp
1300 W 7th St (90732-3593)
PHONE..................................310 832-3311
EMP: 880
SIC: 8062 8051 5912 General medical and
surgical hospitals; Skilled nursing care
facilities; Drug stores

(P-18419)
SANTA BARBARA COTTAGE HOSPITAL
Pathology Department
400 W Pueblo St (93105-4353)

P.O. Box 689 (93102-0689)
PHONE..................................805 569-7367
Ron Werdt, *Pr*
EMP: 290
SALES (corp-wide): 152.81MM **Privately Held**
SIC: 8062 General medical and surgical
hospitals
HQ: Santa Barbara Cottage Hospital
Foundation
400 W Pueblo St
Santa Barbara CA
805 682-7111

(P-18420)
SANTA BRBARA CTTAGE HOSP FNDTI
Respiratory Care
400 W Pueblo St (93105-4353)
PHONE..................................805 569-7224
Doctor Phillip Michael, *Dir*
EMP: 340
SALES (corp-wide): 152.81MM **Privately Held**
SIC: 8062 General medical and surgical
hospitals
HQ: Santa Barbara Cottage Hospital
Foundation
400 W Pueblo St
Santa Barbara CA
805 682-7111

(P-18421)
SANTA BRBARA CTTAGE HOSP FNDTI
Also Called: Santa Barbara Cnty Social Svcs
2125 Centerpointe Pkwy (93455-1337)
PHONE..................................805 346-7135
Charlene Chase, *Dir*
EMP: 271
SALES (corp-wide): 152.81MM **Privately Held**
SIC: 8062 General medical and surgical
hospitals
HQ: Santa Barbara Cottage Hospital
Foundation
400 W Pueblo St
Santa Barbara CA
805 682-7111

(P-18422)
SANTA BRBARA CTTAGE HOSP FNDTI (HQ)
Also Called: Cottage Childrens Medical Ctr
400 W Pueblo St (93105-4353)
P.O. Box 689 (93102-0689)
PHONE..................................805 682-7111
Ronald C Werft, *CEO*
Steven Fellows, *
Brett Tande, *
EMP: 149 EST: 1982
SQ FT: 485,874
SALES (est): 772.02MM
SALES (corp-wide): 152.81MM **Privately Held**
SIC: 8062 Hospital, AMA approved residency
PA: Cottage Health
400 W Pueblo St
Santa Barbara CA
805 682-7111

(P-18423)
SANTA TERESITA INC (PA)
Also Called: MANOR AT SANTA TERESITA HOSPIT
819 Buena Vista St (91010-1703)
PHONE..................................626 359-3243
Sister Mary Clare Mancini, *CEO*
EMP: 276 EST: 1955
SQ FT: 232,165

SALES (est): 11.19MM
SALES (corp-wide): 11.19MM **Privately Held**
Web: www.santa-teresita.org
SIC: **8062** 8051 General medical and surgical hospitals; Skilled nursing care facilities

(P-18424)
SCRIPPS CLINIC
12395 El Camino Real Ste 112 (92130-3082)
P.O. Box 2469 (92038-2469)
PHONE...............................858 794-1250
Chris Van Gorder, *CEO*
Doctor Hubert Greenway, *CEO*
James Collins, *Pr*
EMP: 162 EST: 1999
SALES (est): 111.83MM **Privately Held**
Web: www.scripps.org
SIC: **8062** General medical and surgical hospitals

(P-18425)
SCRIPPS HEALTH (PA)
10140 Campus Point Dr (92121-1520)
PHONE...............................800 727-4777
Chris D Van Gorder, *Pr*
Brett Tande, *
Richard Sheridan, *
A Brent Eastman Md, *Chief Medical Officer*
John B Engle, *Chief Development Officer*
EMP: 2514 EST: 1924
SQ FT: 95,000
SALES (est): 4.06B
SALES (corp-wide): 4.06B **Privately Held**
Web: www.scripps.org
SIC: **8062** 8049 8042 8043 General medical and surgical hospitals; Physical therapist; Offices and clinics of optometrists; Offices and clinics of podiatrists

(P-18426)
SCRIPPS HEALTH
Also Called: Scripps Mercy Hospital
4077 5th Ave (92103-2105)
PHONE...............................619 294-8111
Jacqueline Saucier, *Dir*
EMP: 140
SALES (corp-wide): 4.06B **Privately Held**
Web: www.scripps.org
SIC: **8062** General medical and surgical hospitals
PA: Scripps Health
10140 Campus Point Dr # 415
San Diego CA
800 727-4777

(P-18427)
SCRIPPS HEALTH
Also Called: Scripps Rancho Bernardo
15004 Innovation Dr (92128-3491)
PHONE...............................858 271-9770
Melody Stewart, *Admn*
EMP: 113
SALES (corp-wide): 4.06B **Privately Held**
Web: www.scripps.org
SIC: **8062** General medical and surgical hospitals
PA: Scripps Health
10140 Campus Point Dr # 415
San Diego CA
800 727-4777

(P-18428)
SCRIPPS HEALTH
Also Called: Scripps Mem Hosp - Encinatas
354 Santa Fe Dr (92024-5142)
P.O. Box 230817 (92023-0817)
PHONE...............................760 753-6501

Rebecca Ropchan, *Brnch Mgr*
EMP: 250
SALES (corp-wide): 4.06B **Privately Held**
Web: www.scripps.org
SIC: **8062** 5912 General medical and surgical hospitals; Drug stores
PA: Scripps Health
10140 Campus Point Dr # 415
San Diego CA
800 727-4777

(P-18429)
SCRIPPS HEALTH
Also Called: Scripps Mercy Hospitals
435 H St (91910-4307)
PHONE...............................619 691-7000
Pott Hoff, *COO*
EMP: 97
SALES (corp-wide): 4.06B **Privately Held**
Web: www.scripps.org
SIC: **8062** General medical and surgical hospitals
PA: Scripps Health
10140 Campus Point Dr # 415
San Diego CA
800 727-4777

(P-18430)
SCRIPPS HEALTH
Also Called: Scripps Green Hospital
10666 N Torrey Pines Rd (92037-1027)
PHONE...............................858 455-9100
Robin Brown, *Brnch Mgr*
EMP: 326
SALES (corp-wide): 4.06B **Privately Held**
Web: www.scripps.org
SIC: **8062** General medical and surgical hospitals
PA: Scripps Health
10140 Campus Point Dr # 415
San Diego CA
800 727-4777

(P-18431)
SCRIPPS HEALTH
Also Called: Scripps Mercy Hospital
4077 5th Ave (92103-2105)
PHONE...............................619 294-8111
EMP: 99
SQ FT: 3,062
SALES (corp-wide): 4.06B **Privately Held**
Web: www.scripps.org
SIC: **8062** General medical and surgical hospitals
PA: Scripps Health
10140 Campus Point Dr # 415
San Diego CA
800 727-4777

(P-18432)
SCRIPPS HEALTH
Also Called: Scripps Mem Hospital-La Jolla
9888 Genesee Ave (92037-1205)
PHONE...............................858 626-6150
James Bruffey, *Brnch Mgr*
EMP: 326
SALES (corp-wide): 4.06B **Privately Held**
Web: www.scripps.org
SIC: **8062** General medical and surgical hospitals
PA: Scripps Health
10140 Campus Point Dr # 415
San Diego CA
800 727-4777

(P-18433)
SCRIPPS MERCY HOSPITAL
4077 5th Ave # Mer35 (92103-2105)
PHONE...............................619 294-8111
Andrew C Ping, *Prin*

EMP: 93 EST: 2004
SALES (est): 708.46MM **Privately Held**
Web: www.scripps.org
SIC: **8062** General medical and surgical hospitals

(P-18434)
SCRIPPS MMRAL-XIMED MED CTR LP
Also Called: Scripps Health
9850 Genesee Ave Ste 900 (92037-1220)
PHONE...............................858 882-8350
Brian Huizar, *Prin*
EMP: 88 EST: 1991
SALES (est): 17.9MM **Privately Held**
SIC: **8062** 8049 General medical and surgical hospitals; Physical therapist

(P-18435)
SHARP CHULA VISTA MEDICAL CTR
Also Called: Sharp Chula Vista Medical Ctr
751 Medical Center Ct (91911-6617)
PHONE...............................619 502-5800
Chris Boyd, *CEO*
Michael Murphy, *
Rick King, *
EMP: 1600 EST: 1944
SQ FT: 270,205
SALES (est): 503.43MM
SALES (corp-wide): 2.37B **Privately Held**
Web: www.sharp.com
SIC: **8062** General medical and surgical hospitals
PA: Sharp Healthcare
8695 Spectrum Center Blvd
San Diego CA
858 499-4000

(P-18436)
SHARP CHULA VISTA MEDICAL CTR
8695 Spectrum Center Blvd (92123-1489)
PHONE...............................858 499-5150
Chris Boyd, *CEO*
EMP: 99 EST: 2007
SALES (est): 4.69MM **Privately Held**
Web: www.sharp.com
SIC: **8062** General medical and surgical hospitals

(P-18437)
SHARP CORONADO HOSPITAL & HEALTHCARE CENTER
Also Called: Coronado Hospital
250 Prospect Pl (92118-1943)
PHONE...............................619 522-3600
EMP: 550 EST: 1938
SALES (est): 155.84MM
SALES (corp-wide): 2.37B **Privately Held**
SIC: **8062** General medical and surgical hospitals
PA: Sharp Healthcare
8695 Spectrum Center Blvd
San Diego CA
858 499-4000

(P-18438)
SHARP HEALTHCARE
Also Called: Birch Ptrick Convalescent Cntr
751 Medical Center Ct (91911-6617)
PHONE...............................858 499-2000
Lily Reyes, *Dir*
EMP: 145
SALES (corp-wide): 2.37B **Privately Held**
Web: www.sharp.com
SIC: **8062** General medical and surgical hospitals
PA: Sharp Healthcare
8695 Spectrum Center Blvd

San Diego CA
858 499-4000

(P-18439)
SHARP HEALTHCARE
Also Called: Sharp Rees-Stealy
8008 Frost St Ste 106 (92123-4229)
PHONE...............................858 939-5434
EMP: 151
SALES (corp-wide): 2.37B **Privately Held**
Web: www.sharp.com
SIC: **8062** General medical and surgical hospitals
PA: Sharp Healthcare
8695 Spectrum Center Blvd
San Diego CA
858 499-4000

(P-18440)
SHARP HEALTHCARE ACO LLC
Also Called: SHARP HEALTHCARE ACO, LLC
7910 Frost St Ste 280 (92123-2752)
PHONE...............................619 398-2988
EMP: 94
SALES (corp-wide): 2.37B **Privately Held**
Web: www.sharp.com
SIC: **8062** General medical and surgical hospitals
PA: Sharp Healthcare
8695 Spectrum Center Blvd
San Diego CA
858 499-4000

(P-18441)
SHARP HEALTHCARE ACO LLC
Also Called: Sharp Rees-Stealy Div
300 Fir St (92101-2327)
PHONE...............................619 446-1575
Donna Mills, *Admn*
EMP: 219
SQ FT: 61,608
SALES (corp-wide): 2.37B **Privately Held**
Web: www.sharp.com
SIC: **8062** General medical and surgical hospitals
PA: Sharp Healthcare
8695 Spectrum Center Blvd
San Diego CA
858 499-4000

(P-18442)
SHARP HEALTHCARE ACO LLC
Also Called: Sharp Health Care
3554 Ruffin Rd Ste Soca (92123-2596)
PHONE...............................858 627-5152
Alison Fleury, *Brnch Mgr*
EMP: 672
SALES (corp-wide): 2.37B **Privately Held**
Web: www.sharp.com
SIC: **8062** General medical and surgical hospitals
PA: Sharp Healthcare
8695 Spectrum Center Blvd
San Diego CA
858 499-4000

(P-18443)
SHARP MEMORIAL HOSPITAL (HQ)
7901 Frost St (92123-2701)
PHONE...............................858 939-3636
Tim Smith, *CEO*
▲ EMP: 3000 EST: 1957
SALES (est): 1.44B
SALES (corp-wide): 2.37B **Privately Held**
Web: www.sharp.com
SIC: **8062** General medical and surgical hospitals
PA: Sharp Healthcare
8695 Spectrum Center Blvd

San Diego CA
858 499-4000

(P-18444)
SIERRA VISTA HOSPITAL INC (HQ)
Also Called: Sierra Vista Regional Med Ctr
1010 Murray Ave (93405-8801)
P.O. Box 1367 (93406-1367)
PHONE..............................805 546-7600
Joseph Deschryver, *CEO*
Candace Markwith, *
Richard Phillips, *
Rollie Pirkl, *
Michael Keleman, *
EMP: 575 **EST:** 1968
SQ FT: 138,690
SALES (est): 150.01MM
SALES (corp-wide): 19.58B **Publicly Held**
SIC: 8062 General medical and surgical hospitals
PA: Tenet Healthcare Corporation
14201 Dallas Pkwy
Dallas TX
469 893-2200

(P-18445)
SIMI VLY HOSP & HLTH CARE SVCS
Also Called: Aspen Surgery Center
2750 Sycamore Dr (93065-1502)
PHONE..............................805 955-6000
EMP: 562
SALES (corp-wide): 789.42MM **Privately Held**
Web: www.adventisthealth.org
SIC: 8062 General medical and surgical hospitals
HQ: Simi Valley Hospital And Health Care Services
2975 Sycamore Dr
Simi Valley CA

(P-18446)
SIMI VLY HOSP & HLTH CARE SVCS (HQ)
Also Called: Simi Vly Hosp & Hlth Care Svcs
2975 Sycamore Dr (93065-1201)
PHONE..............................805 955-6000
Margaret Peterson, *Pr*
Caroline Esparza, *
Clif Patten, *
EMP: 228 **EST:** 1960
SALES (est): 199.33MM
SALES (corp-wide): 789.42MM **Privately Held**
Web: www.adventisthealth.org
SIC: 8062 General medical and surgical hospitals
PA: Adventist Health System/West, Corporation
1 Adventist Health Way
Roseville CA
844 574-5686

(P-18447)
SOUTH COAST GLOBAL MED CTR INC
2701 S Bristol St (92704-6201)
PHONE..............................714 754-5454
Jamie Yoo, *CEO*
EMP: 93 **EST:** 2004
SALES (est): 10.68MM **Privately Held**
Web: www.southcoastglobalmedicalcenter.com
SIC: 8062 General medical and surgical hospitals

(P-18448)
SOUTHERN CAL HALTHCARE SYS INC (HQ)
3415 S Sepulveda Blvd 9th Fl (90034-6060)
PHONE..............................310 943-4500
David R Topper, *CEO*
EMP: 189 **EST:** 1998
SALES (est): 102.52MM
SALES (corp-wide): 3.91B **Privately Held**
SIC: 8062 General medical and surgical hospitals
PA: Prospect Medical Holdings, Inc.
3415 S Sepulveda Blvd # 9
Los Angeles CA
310 943-4500

(P-18449)
SOUTHERN CAL HALTHCARE SYS INC
Also Called: Southern Cal Hosp At Culver Cy
3828 Delmas Ter (90232-2713)
PHONE..............................310 836-7000
EMP: 492
SALES (corp-wide): 3.91B **Privately Held**
SIC: 8062 General medical and surgical hospitals
HQ: Southern California Healthcare System, Inc.
3415 S Sepulveda Blvd 9thf
Los Angeles CA

(P-18450)
SOUTHERN CAL PRMNNTE MED GROUP
26415 Carl Boyer Dr (91350-5824)
PHONE..............................661 290-3100
EMP: 255
SALES (corp-wide): 68.1B **Privately Held**
Web: www.permanente.org
SIC: 8062 General medical and surgical hospitals
HQ: Southern California Permanente Medical Group
393 Walnut Dr
Pasadena CA
626 405-5704

(P-18451)
SOUTHERN CAL PRMNNTE MED GROUP
Also Called: Kaiser Permanente
9353 Imperial Hwy Garden Medical Bldg Flr 3 (90242-2812)
PHONE..............................562 657-2200
EMP: 480
SALES (corp-wide): 68.1B **Privately Held**
Web: www.permanente.org
SIC: 8062 General medical and surgical hospitals
HQ: Southern California Permanente Medical Group
393 Walnut Dr
Pasadena CA
626 405-5704

(P-18452)
SOUTHERN CAL PRMNNTE MED GROUP
Also Called: S C P M G
9961 Sierra Ave (92335-6720)
PHONE..............................909 427-5000
Gerald Mccall, *Brnch Mgr*
EMP: 459
SALES (corp-wide): 68.1B **Privately Held**
Web: www.permanente.org
SIC: 8062 General medical and surgical hospitals

HQ: Southern California Permanente Medical Group
393 Walnut Dr
Pasadena CA
626 405-5704

(P-18453)
SOUTHERN CAL SPCIALTY CARE INC
Also Called: Kindred Hospital La Mirata
845 N Lark Ellen Ave (91791-1069)
PHONE..............................626 339-5451
Nenda Estudillo, *Dir*
EMP: 250
SQ FT: 34,082
SALES (corp-wide): 13.68B **Privately Held**
SIC: 8062 General medical and surgical hospitals
HQ: Southern California Specialty Care, Llc
14900 Imperial Hwy
La Mirada CA

(P-18454)
SOUTHERN CAL SPCIALTY CARE INC
Also Called: Kindred Hospital Santa Ana
1901 College Ave (92706-2334)
PHONE..............................714 564-7800
Rich Mccarthy, *Prin*
EMP: 250
SALES (corp-wide): 13.68B **Privately Held**
Web: www.kindredhospitals.com
SIC: 8062 General medical and surgical hospitals
HQ: Southern California Specialty Care, Llc
14900 Imperial Hwy
La Mirada CA

(P-18455)
SOUTHERN CAL SPCIALTY CARE LLC (DH)
Also Called: Southern Cal Spcialty Care Inc
14900 Imperial Hwy (90638-2172)
PHONE..............................562 944-1900
Ty Richardson, *Pr*
Robin Rapp, *Admn*
Judie Sheldon, *CCO*
George Burkley, *COO*
EMP: 100 **EST:** 1994
SQ FT: 74,074
SALES (est): 60.81MM
SALES (corp-wide): 13.68B **Privately Held**
SIC: 8062 General medical and surgical hospitals
HQ: Specialty Healthcare Services, Inc
680 S 4th St
Louisville KY
502 596-7300

(P-18456)
SOUTHWEST HEALTHCARE SYS AUX
Also Called: Business Department
38977 Sky Canyon Dr Ste 200 (92563-2681)
PHONE..............................800 404-6627
Paula Dalbeck, *Contrlr*
EMP: 712
SALES (corp-wide): 13.4B **Publicly Held**
Web: www.southwesthealthcare.com
SIC: 8062 General medical and surgical hospitals
HQ: Southwest Healthcare System Auxiliary
25500 Medical Center Dr
Murrieta CA

(P-18457)
SOUTHWEST HEALTHCARE SYS AUX (HQ)

HQ: Southern California Permanente Medical Group
393 Walnut Dr
Pasadena CA
626 405-5704

Also Called: Rancho Springs Medical Center
25500 Medical Center Dr (92562-5965)
PHONE..............................951 696-6000
Brad Neet, *CEO*
Diane Moon, *
Barry Thorfenson, *
▲ **EMP:** 450 **EST:** 1989
SALES (est): 72.54K
SALES (corp-wide): 13.4B **Publicly Held**
Web: www.swranchosprings.com
SIC: 8062 8051 8059 4119 General medical and surgical hospitals; Skilled nursing care facilities; Convalescent home; Ambulance service
PA: Universal Health Services, Inc.
367 S Gulph Rd
King Of Prussia PA
610 768-3300

(P-18458)
ST BERNARDINE MED CTR AUX INC
Also Called: Inland Empire Heart Institute
2101 N Waterman Ave (92404-4836)
PHONE..............................909 881-4320
TOLL FREE: 877
Ed Langden, *Dir*
EMP: 107
Web: www.dignityhealth.org
SIC: 8062 General medical and surgical hospitals
HQ: St. Bernardine Medical Center Auxiliary, Inc.
2101 N Waterman Ave
San Bernardino CA
909 883-8711

(P-18459)
ST BERNARDINE MEDICAL CENTER
2101 N Waterman Ave (92404-4836)
PHONE..............................909 883-8711
Darryl Vandenbosch, *Pr*
Paul Steinke, *CFO*
Charlie Abraham, *CMO*
EMP: 127 **EST:** 1931
SQ FT: 433,484
SALES (est): 19.9MM **Privately Held**
Web: www.dignityhealth.org
SIC: 8062 General medical and surgical hospitals
HQ: Dignity Health
185 Berry St Ste 200
San Francisco CA
415 438-5500

(P-18460)
ST FRANCIS MEDICAL CENTER (DH)
Also Called: SFMC
3630 E Imperial Hwy (90262-2609)
P.O. Box 1387 (94070-7387)
PHONE..............................310 900-8900
Clay Farell, *CEO*
EMP: 182 **EST:** 2001
SALES (est): 532.13MM
SALES (corp-wide): 1.03B **Privately Held**
Web: www.stfrancismedicalcenter.com
SIC: 8062 General medical and surgical hospitals
HQ: Prime Healthcare Services Inc
3480 E Guasti Rd
Ontario CA

(P-18461)
ST JOSEPH HOSPITAL OF ORANGE
Also Called: St Josephs Physical Rehab Svcs
1310 W Stewart Dr Ste 203 (92868-3837)
PHONE..............................714 771-8222

Paul Pursell, *Ex Dir*
EMP: 101
SALES (corp-wide): 32.76MM **Privately Held**
Web: www.sjo.org
SIC: 8062 8322 General medical and surgical hospitals; Rehabilitation services
HQ: St. Joseph Hospital Of Orange
1100 W Stewart Dr
Orange CA
714 633-9111

(P-18462)
ST JOSEPH HOSPITAL OF ORANGE
Also Called: Information Systems
363 S Main St Ste 211 (92868-3825)
PHONE...............................714 771-8006
Dennise Masiello, *Dir*
EMP: 101
SQ FT: 15,605
SALES (corp-wide): 32.76MM **Privately Held**
Web: www.sjo.org
SIC: 8062 General medical and surgical hospitals
HQ: St. Joseph Hospital Of Orange
1100 W Stewart Dr
Orange CA
714 633-9111

(P-18463)
ST JOSEPH HOSPITAL OF ORANGE
Also Called: Business Office
3345 Michelson Dr Ste 100 (92612-0693)
PHONE...............................714 568-5500
EMP: 132
SALES (corp-wide): 32.76MM **Privately Held**
Web: www.sjo.org
SIC: 8062 General medical and surgical hospitals
HQ: St. Joseph Hospital Of Orange
1100 W Stewart Dr
Orange CA
714 633-9111

(P-18464)
ST JOSEPH HOSPITAL OF ORANGE
Also Called: Renal Center
1100 W Stewart Dr (92868-3891)
P.O. Box 5600 (92863-5600)
PHONE...............................714 771-8037
EMP: 91
SALES (corp-wide): 32.76MM **Privately Held**
Web: www.sjo.org
SIC: 8062 General medical and surgical hospitals
HQ: St. Joseph Hospital Of Orange
1100 W Stewart Dr
Orange CA
714 633-9111

(P-18465)
ST JOSEPH HOSPITAL OF ORANGE (DH)
1100 W Stewart Dr (92868-3891)
P.O. Box 5600 (92863-5600)
PHONE...............................714 633-9111
Larry K Ainsworth, *Pr*
Jim Cora, *
Warren D Johnson, *
Tina Nycroft, *
Martin J Feldman, *Chief of Staff*
EMP: 2100 **EST:** 1929
SQ FT: 448,000
SALES (est): 627.27MM

SALES (corp-wide): 32.76MM **Privately Held**
Web: www.sjo.org
SIC: 8062 General medical and surgical hospitals
HQ: St. Joseph Health System
3345 Michelson Dr Ste 100
Irvine CA
949 381-4000

(P-18466)
ST JUDE HOSPITAL (DH)
Also Called: St Jude Medical Center
101 E Valencia Mesa Dr (92835-3875)
PHONE...............................714 871-3280
TOLL FREE: 800
Robert Fraschetti, *Pr*
Lee Penrose, *
Doreen Dann, *
▲ **EMP:** 2582 **EST:** 1942
SQ FT: 190,000
SALES (est): 791.38MM
SALES (corp-wide): 32.76MM **Privately Held**
Web: www.stjudemedicalcenter.org
SIC: 8062 General medical and surgical hospitals
HQ: St. Joseph Health System
3345 Michelson Dr Ste 100
Irvine CA
949 381-4000

(P-18467)
ST MARY MEDICAL CENTER (DH)
Also Called: St Mary's School of Nursing
1050 Linden Ave (90813-3321)
P.O. Box 887 (90801-0887)
PHONE...............................562 491-9000
Trammie Mcmann, *CEO*
Tammie Mcmann, *CEO*
Ed S Engessers, *
Alan Garrett, *
Tiffany Caster, *
EMP: 1929 **EST:** 1924
SQ FT: 700,000
SALES (est): 254.75MM **Privately Held**
Web: www.stmarymed.com
SIC: 8062 Hospital, med school affiliated with nursing and residency
HQ: Dignity Health
185 Berry St Ste 200
San Francisco CA
415 438-5500

(P-18468)
ST MARY MEDICAL CENTER LLC (PA)
18300 Us Highway 18 (92307-2206)
PHONE...............................760 242-2311
David Klein, *Pr*
Marilyn Drone, *
Tracey Fernandez, *
Kelly Linden, *
Judy Wagner, *
EMP: 542 **EST:** 1956
SQ FT: 92,000
SALES (est): 377.15MM
SALES (corp-wide): 377.15MM **Privately Held**
Web: www.stmaryapplevalley.com
SIC: 8062 General medical and surgical hospitals

(P-18469)
ST MARY MEDICAL CENTER LLC
Also Called: Materals MGT At St Mary Med Ct
16000 Kasota Rd (92307)
P.O. Box 7025 (92307-0731)

PHONE...............................760 946-8767
Leland Glisson, *Mgr*
EMP: 808
SALES (corp-wide): 377.15MM **Privately Held**
Web: www.stmaryapplevalley.com
SIC: 8062 General medical and surgical hospitals
PA: St. Mary Medical Center, Llc
18300 Us Highway 18
Apple Valley CA
760 242-2311

(P-18470)
TEAM HEALTH HOLDINGS INC
Also Called: Sharp Grssmont Hosp Emrgncy Ca
5555 Grossmont Center Dr (91942-3019)
PHONE...............................619 740-4401
EMP: 406
SALES (corp-wide): 3.6B **Privately Held**
Web: www.sharp.com
SIC: 8062 General medical and surgical hospitals
HQ: Team Health Holdings, Inc.
265 Brkview Cntre Way Ste
Knoxville TN
865 693-1000

(P-18471)
TEMPLE HOSPITAL CORPORATION
Also Called: Temple Community Hospital
242 N Hoover St (90004-3628)
PHONE...............................213 355-3200
EMP: 350
Web: www.templecommunityhospital.com
SIC: 8062 General medical and surgical hospitals

(P-18472)
TENET HEALTH SYSTEMS NORRIS
Also Called: KENNETH NORRIS CANCER HOSPITAL
1441 Eastlake Ave (90089-1019)
PHONE...............................323 865-3000
Scott Evans, *CEO*
Strawn Steele, *
EMP: 352 **EST:** 1982
SQ FT: 175,000
SALES (est): 280.59MM **Privately Held**
Web: www.keckmedicine.org
SIC: 8062 General medical and surgical hospitals

(P-18473)
TENET HEALTHSYSTEM MEDICAL INC
Also Called: Irvine Regional Hospital
1400 S Douglass Rd Ste 250 (92806)
PHONE...............................714 428-6800
Donald Lorack, *CEO*
EMP: 241
SALES (corp-wide): 19.58B **Publicly Held**
Web: validate.perfdrive.com
SIC: 8062 General medical and surgical hospitals
HQ: Tenet Healthsystem Medical, Inc.
14201 Dallas Pkwy
Dallas TX
469 893-2000

(P-18474)
THOUSAND OAKS SURGICAL HOSP LP
401 Rolling Oaks Dr (91361-1050)
PHONE...............................805 777-7750
Micheal Bass, *Pt*

EMP: 100 **EST:** 1999
SQ FT: 50,000
SALES (est): 13.98MM **Privately Held**
Web: www.losrobleshospital.com
SIC: 8062 General medical and surgical hospitals

(P-18475)
TORRANCE HEALTH ASSN INC (PA)
Also Called: Physician Office Support Svcs
3330 Lomita Blvd (90505-5002)
P.O. Box 13717 (90503-0717)
PHONE...............................310 325-9110
John Mcnamara, *Sr VP*
Bill Larson, *
Sally Eberhard, *
Bernadette Reid, *
EMP: 3000 **EST:** 1985
SQ FT: 180,000
SALES (est): 913.85MM **Privately Held**
Web: www.torrancememorialipa.org
SIC: 8062 General medical and surgical hospitals

(P-18476)
TORRANCE MEMORIAL MEDICAL CTR (HQ)
3330 Lomita Blvd (90505-5002)
PHONE...............................310 325-9110
Keith Hobbs, *Pr*
EMP: 1500 **EST:** 1925
SALES (est): 838.38MM **Privately Held**
Web: www.torrancememorial.org
SIC: 8062 Hospital, affiliated with AMA residency
PA: Torrance Health Association, Inc.
3330 Lomita Blvd
Torrance CA

(P-18477)
TORRANCE MEMORIAL MEDICAL CTR
Also Called: Torrance Memorial Breast Diagn
855 Manhattan Beach Blvd Ste 208 (90266-4965)
PHONE...............................310 939-7847
EMP: 408
Web: www.torrancememorial.org
SIC: 8062 General medical and surgical hospitals
HQ: Torrance Memorial Medical Center
3330 Lomita Blvd
Torrance CA
310 325-9110

(P-18478)
TORRANCE MEMORIAL MEDICAL CTR
3333 Skypark Dr Ste 200 (90505-5035)
PHONE...............................310 784-6316
EMP: 408
Web: www.torrancememorial.org
SIC: 8062 General medical and surgical hospitals
HQ: Torrance Memorial Medical Center
3330 Lomita Blvd
Torrance CA
310 325-9110

(P-18479)
TORRANCE MEMORIAL MEDICAL CTR
22411 Hawthorne Blvd (90505-2507)
PHONE...............................310 784-3740
EMP: 340
Web: www.torrancememorial.org
SIC: 8062 Hospital, affiliated with AMA residency

▲ = Import ▼ = Export
◆ = Import/Export

HQ: Torrance Memorial Medical Center
3330 Lomita Blvd
Torrance CA
310 325-9110

(P-18480)
TRI-CITY HOSPITAL DISTRICT (PA)
Also Called: Tri-City Medical Center
4002 Vista Way (92056-4506)
PHONE..............................760 724-8411
Steve Dietlin, *CEO*
Ray Rivas, *CFO*
EMP: 2100 EST: 1957
SQ FT: 50,000
SALES (est): 319.28MM
SALES (corp-wide): 319.28MM **Privately Held**
Web: www.tricitymed.org
SIC: **8062** General medical and surgical hospitals

(P-18481)
TUSTIN HOSPITAL AND MEDICAL CENTER
Also Called: Newport Specialty Hospital
3699 Wilshire Blvd # 540 (90010-2723)
PHONE..............................714 619-7700
EMP: 360
SIC: **8062** General medical and surgical hospitals

(P-18482)
UHS-CORONA INC (HQ)
Also Called: Corona Regional Med Ctr Hosp
800 S Main St (92882-3420)
PHONE..............................951 737-4343
Marvin Pember, *CEO*
Ken Rivers, *
Alan B Miller, *
Kevan Metcalf, *
▲ EMP: 900 EST: 1978
SALES (est): 220.6MM
SALES (corp-wide): 13.4B **Publicly Held**
Web: www.swhcoronaregional.com
SIC: **8062** General medical and surgical hospitals
PA: Universal Health Services, Inc.
367 S Gulph Rd
King Of Prussia PA
610 768-3300

(P-18483)
UNIVERSITY CAL LOS ANGELES
Also Called: Ronald Reagan Ucla Medical Ctr
757 Westwood Plz (90095-8358)
PHONE..............................310 825-9111
EMP: 2056
SALES (corp-wide): 534.4MM **Privately Held**
Web: www.ucla.edu
SIC: **8062** 8221 9411 General medical and surgical hospitals; University; Administration of educational programs
HQ: University Of California, Los Angeles
405 Hilgard Ave
Los Angeles CA

(P-18484)
UNIVERSITY CAL SAN DIEGO
Also Called: Ucsd Thornton Hospital
9300 Campus Point Dr (92037-1300)
P.O. Box 409 (92075-0409)
PHONE..............................858 657-7000
Paul Hensler, *Dir*
EMP: 1364
SALES (corp-wide): 534.4MM **Privately Held**
Web: www.ucsd.edu

SIC: **8062** 8221 9411 General medical and surgical hospitals; University; Administration of educational programs
HQ: University Of California, San Diego
9500 Gilman Dr
La Jolla CA
858 534-2230

(P-18485)
UNIVERSITY CAL SAN DIEGO
Also Called: U C S D Medical Center
402 Dickinson St Ste 380 (92103-6902)
PHONE..............................619 543-6170
Doctor Kenneth Kaushkay, *Ch*
EMP: 154
SALES (corp-wide): 534.4MM **Privately Held**
Web: www.ucsd.edu
SIC: **8062** 8221 9411 General medical and surgical hospitals; University; Administration of educational programs
HQ: University Of California, San Diego
9500 Gilman Dr
La Jolla CA
858 534-2230

(P-18486)
UNIVERSITY CAL SAN DIEGO
Also Called: Medical Center
200 W Arbor Dr Frnt (92103-9000)
PHONE..............................619 543-6654
Richard Likeweg, *Mgr*
EMP: 4000
SALES (corp-wide): 534.4MM **Privately Held**
Web: www.ucsd.edu
SIC: **8062** 8221 9411 General medical and surgical hospitals; University; Administration of educational programs
HQ: University Of California, San Diego
9500 Gilman Dr
La Jolla CA
858 534-2230

(P-18487)
UNIVERSITY CALIFORNIA IRVINE
Also Called: UCI Cancer Center
101 The City Dr S (92868-3201)
PHONE..............................714 456-8000
Michael Lekawa, *Pr*
EMP: 478
SALES (corp-wide): 534.4MM **Privately Held**
Web: www.ucihealth.org
SIC: **8062** General medical and surgical hospitals
HQ: University Of California, Irvine
510 Aldrich Hall
Irvine CA
949 824-5011

(P-18488)
UNIVERSITY CALIFORNIA IRVINE
Also Called: Uc Irvine Medical Center
101 The City Dr S (92868-3201)
PHONE..............................714 456-6011
Mary Piccione, *Ex Dir*
EMP: 3000
SALES (corp-wide): 534.4MM **Privately Held**
Web: www.ucihealth.org
SIC: **8062** 8221 9411 General medical and surgical hospitals; University; Administration of educational programs, State government
HQ: University Of California, Irvine
510 Aldrich Hall
Irvine CA
949 824-5011

(P-18489)
UNIVERSITY CALIFORNIA IRVINE
Also Called: Irvine Medical Center
200 S Manchester Ave Ste 400 (92868-3220)
PHONE..............................714 456-5558
Joy Grosse, *Dir*
EMP: 114
SALES (corp-wide): 534.4MM **Privately Held**
Web: www.ucihealth.org
SIC: **8062** 8221 9411 General medical and surgical hospitals; University; Administration of educational programs
HQ: University Of California, Irvine
510 Aldrich Hall
Irvine CA
949 824-5011

(P-18490)
UNIVERSITY CALIFORNIA IRVINE
Also Called: UCI Westminster Medical Center
15355 Brookhurst St Ste 102 (92683-7077)
PHONE..............................714 775-3066
TOLL FREE: 888
EMP: 114
SALES (corp-wide): 534.4MM **Privately Held**
Web: www.uci.edu
SIC: **8062** 8221 9411 General medical and surgical hospitals; University; Administration of educational programs
HQ: University Of California, Irvine
510 Aldrich Hall
Irvine CA
949 824-5011

(P-18491)
UNIVERSITY SOUTHERN CALIFORNIA
Also Called: Usc University Hospital
1500 San Pablo St (90033-5313)
PHONE..............................323 442-8500
Paul Vivano, *Dir*
EMP: 875
SALES (corp-wide): 5.57B **Privately Held**
Web: www.usc.edu
SIC: **8062** 8011 General medical and surgical hospitals; Offices and clinics of medical doctors
PA: University Of Southern California
3720 S Flower St Fl 3
Los Angeles CA
213 740-7762

(P-18492)
USC ARCADIA HOSPITAL (PA)
Also Called: Methodist Hospital
300 W Huntington Dr (91007-3402)
PHONE..............................626 898-8000
TOLL FREE: 800
Ikenna Mmeje, *Pr*
Steven A Sisto, *
William E Grigg, *
Clifford R Daniels, *
EMP: 933 EST: 1903
SQ FT: 100,000
SALES (est): 267.48MM
SALES (corp-wide): 267.48MM **Privately Held**
Web: www.uscarcadiahospital.org
SIC: **8062** General medical and surgical hospitals

(P-18493)
USC VERDUGO HILLS HOSPITAL LLC
1812 Verdugo Blvd (91208-1407)
PHONE..............................818 790-7100
Armand Dorian, *CEO*
Debbie Walsh, *
Cynthia Trousdale, *
Thomas Jackiewicz, *
Hack Lash, *
EMP: 750 EST: 2013
SQ FT: 45,000
SALES (est): 223.31MM
SALES (corp-wide): 5.57B **Privately Held**
Web: www.uscvhh.org
SIC: **8062** Hospital, affiliated with AMA residency
PA: University Of Southern California
3720 S Flower St Fl 3
Los Angeles CA
213 740-7762

(P-18494)
USC VRDUGO HLLS HOSP FUNDATION (HQ)
Also Called: U S C
1812 Verdugo Blvd (91208-1407)
PHONE..............................800 872-2273
TOLL FREE: 800
Paul Craig, *CEO*
Debbie L Walsh, *Pr*
EMP: 446 EST: 1947
SQ FT: 225,000
SALES (est): 891.27K
SALES (corp-wide): 5.57B **Privately Held**
Web: www.uscvhh.org
SIC: **8062** General medical and surgical hospitals
PA: University Of Southern California
3720 S Flower St Fl 3
Los Angeles CA
213 740-7762

(P-18495)
VALLEY HOSPITAL MEDICAL CENTER FOUNDATION
Also Called: Calex
18300 Roscoe Blvd (91325-4105)
PHONE..............................818 885-8500
EMP: 1000
Web: www.pvhmc.org
SIC: **8062** General medical and surgical hospitals

(P-18496)
VALLEY PRESBYTERIAN HOSPITAL
Also Called: V P H
15107 Vanowen St (91405-4597)
PHONE..............................818 782-6600
Gustavo Valdespino, *CEO*
Ray Moss, *CIO*
Michelle Quigley, *VP*
Jean Rico, *Sr VP*
Norma Resneder, *Sr VP*
EMP: 1600 EST: 1948
SQ FT: 400,000
SALES (est): 475.76MM **Privately Held**
Web: www.valleypres.org
SIC: **8062** General medical and surgical hospitals

(P-18497)
VERDUGO HILLS HOSPITAL INC
1812 Verdugo Blvd (91208-1409)
PHONE..............................818 790-7100
Leonard Labella, *Pr*
EMP: 216 EST: 1947
SALES (est): 49.42MM **Privately Held**
Web: www.uscvhh.org
SIC: **8062** Hospital, affiliated with AMA residency

PRODUCTS & SVCS

(P-18498)
VERITAS HEALTH SERVICES INC
Also Called: Chino Valley Medical Center
5451 Walnut Ave (91710-2609)
PHONE..................................909 464-8600
Parrish Scarboro, *CEO*
Irv E Edwards, *
EMP: 600 EST: 2000
SALES (est): 106.21MM
SALES (corp-wide): 1.03B **Privately Held**
Web: www.cvmc.com
SIC: 8062 General medical and surgical hospitals
HQ: Prime Healthcare Services Inc
3480 E Guasti Rd
Ontario CA

(P-18499)
VIBRA HEALTHCARE LLC
Also Called: Vibra Hospital of San Diego
555 Washington St (92103-2289)
PHONE..................................619 260-8300
TOLL FREE: 800
Meeta Jones, *CEO*
EMP: 221
SALES (corp-wide): 690.44MM **Privately Held**
Web: www.vibrahealthcare.com
SIC: 8062 8069 8322 General medical and surgical hospitals; Specialty hospitals, except psychiatric; Rehabilitation services
PA: Vibra Healthcare, Llc
4600 Lena Dr
Mechanicsburg PA
717 591-5700

(P-18500)
VISTA SPCLTY HOSP STHERN CAL L
Also Called: Vista Hospital San Gabriel Vly
14148 Francisquito Ave (91706-6120)
PHONE..................................626 388-2700
Marc C Ferrell, *Pt*
EMP: 88 EST: 2003
SQ FT: 44,400
SALES (est): 18.72MM **Privately Held**
SIC: 8062 General medical and surgical hospitals

(P-18501)
WHITE MEMORIAL MEDICAL CENTER (HQ)
Also Called: CECILLA GONZALEZ DE AL HOYA CA
1720 E Cesar E Chavez Ave (90033-2414)
PHONE..................................323 268-5000
Beth D Zachary, *CEO*
Terri Day, *
John G Raffoul, *
Roland Fargo, *
Mary Anne Chern, *
EMP: 1200 EST: 1913
SQ FT: 454,000
SALES (est): 412.24MM
SALES (corp-wide): 789.42MM **Privately Held**
Web: www.adventisthealth.org
SIC: 8062 General medical and surgical hospitals
PA: Adventist Health System/West, Corporation
1 Adventist Health Way
Roseville CA
844 574-5686

(P-18502)
WHITTIER HOSPITAL MED CTR INC
9080 Colima Rd (90605-1600)
PHONE..................................562 945-3561
Richard Castro, *CEO*
EMP: 180 EST: 1962
SQ FT: 144,000
SALES (est): 27.14MM
SALES (corp-wide): 476.02MM **Privately Held**
Web: www.ahmchealth.com
SIC: 8062 General medical and surgical hospitals
PA: Ahmc Healthcare Inc.
506 W Valley Blvd Ste 300
San Gabriel CA
626 943-7526

8063 Psychiatric Hospitals

(P-18503)
ALTA HLLYWOOD CMNTY HOSP VAN N
14433 Emelita St (91401-4213)
PHONE..................................818 787-1511
Irving Loube, *Pr*
Claude Lowen, *
EMP: 99 EST: 1969
SQ FT: 34,192
SALES (est): 6.5MM
SALES (corp-wide): 3.91B **Privately Held**
Web: www.sch-vannuys.com
SIC: 8063 Psychiatric hospitals
HQ: Southern California Healthcare System, Inc.
3415 S Sepulveda Blvd 9thf
Los Angeles CA

(P-18504)
AURORA LAS ENCINAS LLC
Also Called: Aurora Las Encinas Hospital
2900 E Del Mar Blvd (91107-4375)
PHONE..................................626 795-9901
EMP: 236 EST: 1903
SQ FT: 132,000
SALES (est): 31.46MM **Publicly Held**
Web: www.lasencinashospital.com
SIC: 8063 8069 Mental hospital, except for the mentally retarded; Alcoholism rehabilitation hospital
HQ: Hca Inc.
1 Park Plz
Nashville TN
615 344-9551

(P-18505)
BAKERSFELD BHVRAL HLTHCARE HOS
5201 White Ln (93309-6200)
PHONE..................................661 398-1800
Jeff Chinn, *CEO*
EMP: 235 EST: 2015
SALES (est): 18.72MM **Privately Held**
Web: www.bakersfieldbehavioral.com
SIC: 8063 8011 Psychiatric hospitals; Medical centers

(P-18506)
CALIFRNIA DEPT STATE HOSPITALS
Also Called: Fairview Developmental Center
2501 Harbor Blvd (92626-6143)
PHONE..................................714 957-5000
Michael Hatton, *Prin*
EMP: 1724
SALES (corp-wide): 534.4MM **Privately Held**
Web: www.ca.gov
SIC: 8063 9431 Mental hospital, except for the mentally retarded; Mental health agency administration, government

HQ: California Department Of State Hospitals
1600 9th St Ste 350
Sacramento CA

(P-18507)
CALIFRNIA DEPT STATE HOSPITALS
Also Called: Patton State Hospital
3102 E Highland Ave (92369-7813)
PHONE..................................909 425-7000
Bruce Parks, *Dir*
EMP: 953
SALES (corp-wide): 534.4MM **Privately Held**
Web: dsh.ca.gov
SIC: 8063 9431 Mental hospital, except for the mentally retarded; Mental health agency administration, government
HQ: California Department Of State Hospitals
1600 9th St Ste 350
Sacramento CA

(P-18508)
CALIFRNIA DEPT STATE HOSPITALS
Also Called: Atascadero State Hospital
10333 El Camino Real (93422-5808)
P.O. Box 7001 (93423-7001)
PHONE..................................805 468-2000
John De Morales, *Brnch Mgr*
EMP: 1156
SALES (corp-wide): 534.4MM **Privately Held**
Web: dsh.ca.gov
SIC: 8063 9431 8062 Mental hospital, except for the mentally retarded; Mental health agency administration, government; General medical and surgical hospitals
HQ: California Department Of State Hospitals
1600 9th St Ste 350
Sacramento CA

(P-18509)
CANYON RIDGE HOSPITAL INC
Also Called: UHS
5353 G St (91710-5250)
PHONE..................................909 590-3700
Peggy Minnick, *CEO*
EMP: 408 EST: 1990
SALES (est): 46.67MM
SALES (corp-wide): 13.4B **Publicly Held**
Web: www.canyonridgehospital.com
SIC: 8063 8093 Mental hospital, except for the mentally retarded; Mental health clinic, outpatient
HQ: Willow Springs, Llc
6640 Carothers Pkwy # 400
Franklin TN
615 312-5700

(P-18510)
CHARTER BHVRAL HLTH SYS S C/CH
Also Called: Charter Oak Hospital
1161 E Covina Blvd (91724-1523)
PHONE..................................626 966-1632
Todd Smith, *CEO*
EMP: 104 EST: 1997
SALES (est): 18.68MM **Privately Held**
Web: www.charteroakhospital.com
SIC: 8063 Psychiatric hospitals

(P-18511)
COLLEGE HOSPITAL INC (PA)
Also Called: College Hospital Cerritos
10802 College Pl (90703-1579)
PHONE..................................562 924-9581
TOLL FREE: 800
Stephen A Witt, *Pr*
Bessie Weiss, *
EMP: 300 EST: 1973
SQ FT: 60,000
SALES (est): 72.33MM
SALES (corp-wide): 72.33MM **Privately Held**
Web: www.chc.la
SIC: 8063 Mental hospital, except for the mentally retarded

(P-18512)
COUNTY OF SAN DIEGO
Also Called: Health & Human Services
3853 Rosecrans St (92110-3115)
PHONE..................................619 692-8200
Karen Hogan, *CEO*
EMP: 250
Web: www.sandiegocounty.gov
SIC: 8063 9431 Psychiatric hospitals; Administration of public health programs
PA: County Of San Diego
1600 Pacific Hwy Ste 209
San Diego CA
619 531-5880

(P-18513)
GATEWAYS HOSP MENTAL HLTH CTR (PA)
1891 Effie St (90026-1711)
PHONE..................................323 644-2000
Mara Pelsman, *CEO*
Jeff Emery, *
EMP: 150 EST: 1953
SQ FT: 40,000
SALES (est): 37.02MM
SALES (corp-wide): 37.02MM **Privately Held**
Web: www.gatewayshospital.org
SIC: 8063 8093 Mental hospital, except for the mentally retarded; Mental health clinic, outpatient

(P-18514)
KAISER FOUNDATION HOSPITALS
Also Called: Kaiser Mental Health Center
765 W College St (90012-1181)
PHONE..................................213 580-7200
Kurt Hastings, *Mgr*
EMP: 170
SQ FT: 66,697
SALES (corp-wide): 68.1B **Privately Held**
Web: www.kaisercenter.com
SIC: 8063 Psychiatric hospitals
HQ: Kaiser Foundation Hospitals Inc
1 Kaiser Plz
Oakland CA
510 271-6611

(P-18515)
KEDREN COMMUNITY HLTH CTR INC (PA)
Also Called: Kedren Acute Psychtric Hosp Cm
4211 Avalon Blvd (90011-5622)
PHONE..................................323 233-0425
John Griffith, *Pr*
John Griffith Ph.d., *Pr*
Lupe Ross, *
Robert Lawson, *
EMP: 400 EST: 1965
SQ FT: 144,000
SALES (est): 42.85MM
SALES (corp-wide): 42.85MM **Privately Held**
Web: www.kedren.org

SIC: 8063 8093 Mental hospital, except for the mentally retarded; Specialty outpatient clinics, nec

(P-18516)
LANDMARK MEDICAL SERVICES INC
Also Called: Landmark Medical Center
2030 N Garey Ave (91767-2722)
PHONE..............................909 593-2585
Rose Horsman, *Pr*
EMP: 100 **EST:** 1971
SQ FT: 27,500
SALES (est): 9.82MM **Privately Held**
Web: www.landmarkmedicalcenter.net
SIC: 8063 Mental hospital, except for the mentally retarded

(P-18517)
PINE GROVE HOSPITAL CORP
9449 San Fernando Rd (91352-1421)
PHONE..............................818 348-0500
Paul R Tuft, *Pr*
EMP: 180 **EST:** 1998
SALES (est): 2.55MM **Privately Held**
SIC: 8063 Psychiatric hospitals

(P-18518)
SHARP MEMORIAL HOSPITAL
Also Called: Sharp Mesa Vista Hospital
7850 Vista Hill Ave (92123-2717)
PHONE..............................858 278-4110
Carolyn Mason, *Dir*
EMP: 250
SALES (corp-wide): 2.37B **Privately Held**
Web: www.sharp.com
SIC: 8063 8069 8093 Psychiatric hospitals; Substance abuse hospitals; Specialty outpatient clinics, nec
HQ: Sharp Memorial Hospital
7901 Frost St
San Diego CA
858 939-3636

8069 Specialty Hospitals, Except Psychiatric

(P-18519)
AKUA BEHAVIORAL HEALTH INC (PA)
Also Called: Akua Mind & Body
20271 Sw Birch St Ste 200 (92660-1752)
PHONE..............................949 777-2283
Stephen Mercurio, *CEO*
EMP: 111 **EST:** 2014
SALES (est): 15.66MM
SALES (corp-wide): 15.66MM **Privately Held**
Web: www.akuamindbody.com
SIC: 8069 8322 Drug addiction rehabilitation hospital; Rehabilitation services

(P-18520)
BARLOW GROUP (PA)
Also Called: Barlow Respitory Hospital
2000 Stadium Way (90026-2606)
PHONE..............................213 250-4200
Margaret W Crane, *CEO*
EMP: 250 **EST:** 1994
SALES (est): 21.07MM
SALES (corp-wide): 21.07MM **Privately Held**
Web: www.barlowhospital.org
SIC: 8069 7389 8733 Specialty hospitals, except psychiatric; Fund raising organizations; Medical research

(P-18521)
BARLOW RESPIRATORY HOSPITAL
12401 Washington Blvd (90602-1006)
PHONE..............................562 698-0811
Priscilla Jahangiri, *Brnch Mgr*
EMP: 1650
SALES (corp-wide): 68.31MM **Privately Held**
Web: www.barlowhospital.org
SIC: 8069 Respiratory hospital
PA: Barlow Respiratory Hospital
2000 Stadium Way
Los Angeles CA
213 250-4200

(P-18522)
BARLOW RESPIRATORY HOSPITAL (PA)
2000 Stadium Way (90026-2606)
PHONE..............................213 250-4200
Margaret W Crane, *CEO*
Edward Engesser, *
EMP: 250 **EST:** 1902
SQ FT: 80,000
SALES (est): 68.31MM
SALES (corp-wide): 68.31MM **Privately Held**
Web: www.barlowhospital.org
SIC: 8069 Specialty hospitals, except psychiatric

(P-18523)
CHILDRENS HEALTHCARE CAL (PA)
Also Called: Choc Children's
1201 W La Veta Ave (92868-4203)
PHONE..............................714 997-3000
Kimberly C Cripe, *Pr*
Maria Minon Md, *VP*
Kerri Ruppert, *
Thomas Brotherton, *
EMP: 1500 **EST:** 1986
SALES (est): 30.63MM **Privately Held**
Web: www.choc.org
SIC: 8069 Childrens' hospital

(P-18524)
CHILDRENS HOSPITAL LOS ANGELES (PA)
4650 W Sunset Blvd (90027-6062)
PHONE..............................323 660-2450
Richard Cordova, *Pr*
Lannie Tonnu, *
Alexandra Carter, *CDO*
Lara Khouri, *
Conrad Band, *CIO*
▲ **EMP:** 2212 **EST:** 1901
SQ FT: 750,000
SALES (est): 1.58B
SALES (corp-wide): 1.58B **Privately Held**
Web: www.chla.us
SIC: 8069 8062 Childrens' hospital; General medical and surgical hospitals

(P-18525)
COUNTY OF LOS ANGELES
Also Called: Department of Health Services
1240 N Mission Rd (90033-1019)
PHONE..............................323 226-3468
Barbara Oliver, *Ex Dir*
EMP: 114
Web: www.lacounty.gov
SIC: 8069 9431 8062 Specialty hospitals, except psychiatric; Administration of public health programs; General medical and surgical hospitals
PA: County Of Los Angeles
500 W Temple St Ste 437
Los Angeles CA
213 974-1101

(P-18526)
COUNTY OF LOS ANGELES
Also Called: Health Services, Dept of
38200 Lake Hughes Rd (91384-4100)
PHONE..............................661 223-8700
Lynne Dahl, *Admn*
EMP: 95
Web: www.lacounty.gov
SIC: 8069 9431 Drug addiction rehabilitation hospital; Administration of public health programs
PA: County Of Los Angeles
500 W Temple St Ste 437
Los Angeles CA
213 974-1101

(P-18527)
COUNTY OF LOS ANGELES
Also Called: Health Services, Dept of
30500 Arrastre Canyon Rd (93510-2160)
P.O. Box 25 (93510-0025)
PHONE..............................661 223-8700
Suzanna Kassinger, *Admn*
EMP: 103
Web: www.lacounty.gov
SIC: 8069 9431 8361 Alcoholism rehabilitation hospital; Administration of public health programs; Residential care
PA: County Of Los Angeles
500 W Temple St Ste 437
Los Angeles CA
213 974-1101

(P-18528)
GOODEN CENTER
191 N El Molino Ave (91101-1804)
PHONE..............................626 356-0078
Thomas Mcnulty, *Prin*
Budd Williams, *
EMP: 85 **EST:** 1962
SALES (est): 7.04MM **Privately Held**
Web: www.goodencenter.org
SIC: 8069 8361 8093 Alcoholism rehabilitation hospital; Rehabilitation center, residential: health care incidental; Mental health clinic, outpatient

(P-18529)
KOREAN COMMUNITY SERVICES INC
Also Called: Kc Services
451 W Lincoln Ave Ste 100 (92805-2912)
PHONE..............................714 527-6561
Ellen Ahn, *CEO*
Ellen Ahn, *Ex Dir*
Kay Ahn, *
EMP: 120 **EST:** 1977
SALES (est): 8.12MM **Privately Held**
Web: www.kcsinc.org
SIC: 8069 8322 8011 Drug addiction rehabilitation hospital; Social service center ; Offices and clinics of medical doctors

(P-18530)
MARINE CORPS UNITED STATES
Also Called: Camp Pendleton Hospital
Camp Pendleton (92055)
P.O. Box 555191 (92055-5191)
PHONE..............................760 725-1304
Richard R Jeffries, *Mgr*
EMP: 1000
Web: www.marines.mil
SIC: 8069 9711 Specialty hospitals, except psychiatric; Marine Corps
HQ: United States Marine Corps
Branch Hlth Clnic Bldg 5
Beaufort SC

(P-18531)
PALOMAR HEALTH
800 W Valley Pkwy Ste 201 (92025-2557)
PHONE..............................760 740-6311
Bob Henker, *CEO*
EMP: 207
SALES (corp-wide): 679.43K **Privately Held**
Web: www.palomarhealth.org
SIC: 8069 Specialty hospitals, except psychiatric
PA: Palomar Health
2125 Citracado Pkwy # 300
Escondido CA
442 281-5000

(P-18532)
SHARP MCDONALD CENTER
7989 Linda Vista Rd (92111-5106)
PHONE..............................858 637-6920
Daniel L Gross, *Ex VP*
EMP: 800 **EST:** 2001
SALES (est): 22.24MM
SALES (corp-wide): 2.37B **Privately Held**
Web: www.sharp.com
SIC: 8069 Drug addiction rehabilitation hospital
PA: Sharp Healthcare
8695 Spectrum Center Blvd
San Diego CA
858 499-4000

(P-18533)
SHIELDS FOR FAMILIES (PA)
Also Called: SHIELDS
11601 S Western Ave (90047-5006)
P.O. Box 59129 (90059-0129)
PHONE..............................323 242-5000
Kathryn S Icenhower, *CEO*
Xylina Bean Md, *Pr*
Norma Mtume, *
Charlene K Smith, *
Gerald Phillips, *
EMP: 82 **EST:** 1991
SALES (est): 26.21MM
SALES (corp-wide): 26.21MM **Privately Held**
Web: www.shieldsforfamilies.org
SIC: 8069 Drug addiction rehabilitation hospital

(P-18534)
SHRINERS HSPITALS FOR CHILDREN
Also Called: Shriner's Hospital
909 S Fair Oaks Ave (91105-2625)
PHONE..............................626 389-9300
Wendy Hill, *Brnch Mgr*
EMP: 276
Web: www.shrinerschildrens.org
SIC: 8069 8062 Childrens' hospital; General medical and surgical hospitals
PA: Shriners Hospitals For Children
2900 N Rocky Point Dr
Tampa FL

(P-18535)
SHRINERS HSPITALS FOR CHILDREN
3160 Genieva St (91020)
PHONE..............................213 368-3302
Frank Labonte, *Dir*
EMP: 287
Web: www.shrinerschildrens.org
SIC: 8069 8062 Childrens' hospital; General medical and surgical hospitals
PA: Shriners Hospitals For Children
2900 N Rocky Point Dr

PRODUCTS & SVCS

Tampa FL

(P-18536)
SOCIAL SCIENCE SERVICE CENTER
Also Called: CEDAR HOUSE REHABILITATION CEN
18612 Santa Ana Ave (92316-2636)
PHONE.................................909 421-7120
Daniel Gakgolla, *CEO*
Allen Eisenman, *
EMP: 89 **EST:** 1973
SQ FT: 29,000
SALES (est): 8.12MM **Privately Held**
Web: www.cedarhouse.org
SIC: 8069 8322 Alcoholism rehabilitation hospital; Individual and family services

(P-18537)
TENET HEALTHSYSTEM MEDICAL INC
Also Called: Placentia Linda Hospital
1301 N Rose Dr (92870-3802)
PHONE.................................714 993-2000
Kent Clayton, *CEO*
EMP: 409
SALES (corp-wide): 19.58B **Publicly Held**
Web: validate.perfdrive.com
SIC: 8069 8011 8062 Specialty hospitals, except psychiatric; Offices and clinics of medical doctors; General medical and surgical hospitals
HQ: Tenet Healthsystem Medical, Inc.
14201 Dallas Pkwy
Dallas TX
469 893-2000

8071 Medical Laboratories

(P-18538)
ALLIANCE HEALTHCARE SVCS INC (DH)
Also Called: Alliance
18201 Von Karman Ave Ste 600 (92612-1000)
P.O. Box 19532 (92623-9532)
PHONE.................................800 544-3215
Rhonda Longmore Grund, *CEO*
Percy C Tomlinson, *
Laurie R Miller, *
Richard W Johns, *
EMP: 250 **EST:** 1983
SALES (est): 550.72MM
SALES (corp-wide): 825.97MM **Privately Held**
Web: www.alliancehealthcareservices-us.com
SIC: 8071 Ultrasound laboratory
HQ: Akumin Operating Corp.
8300 W Sunrise Blvd
Plantation FL
855 332-2390

(P-18539)
BIORA THERAPEUTICS INC (PA)
4330 La Jolla Village Dr Ste 300 (92122-6201)
P.O. Box 674425 (48267-4425)
PHONE.................................855 293-2639
Adi Mohanty, *CEO*
Jeffrey D Alter, *
Eric D'esparbes, *CFO*
Ariella Kelman, *Chief Medical Officer*
EMP: 86 **EST:** 2010
SQ FT: 25,800
SALES (est): 305K
SALES (corp-wide): 305K **Publicly Held**
Web: www.bioratherapeutics.com

SIC: 8071 8731 Medical laboratories; Biotechnical research, commercial

(P-18540)
BIOTHERANOSTICS INC (HQ)
9640 Towne Centre Dr Ste 200 (92121-1986)
P.O. Box 749249 (90074-9249)
PHONE.................................877 886-6739
EMP: 40 **EST:** 1996
SALES (est): 24.64MM
SALES (corp-wide): 3.91B **Publicly Held**
Web: www.biotheranostics.com
SIC: 8071 2835 Medical laboratories; In vitro diagnostics
PA: Hologic, Inc.
250 Campus Dr
Marlborough MA
508 263-2900

(P-18541)
CAP DIAGNOSTICS LLC
Also Called: Pathnostics
15545 Sand Canyon Ave (92618-3114)
PHONE.................................714 966-1221
Matt Tate, *
EMP: 170 **EST:** 2014
SALES (est): 25.57MM **Privately Held**
Web: www.pathnostics.com
SIC: 8071 Medical laboratories

(P-18542)
CLARIENT INC
Also Called: Chromavision Medical Systems
33171 Paseo Cerveza (92675-4870)
PHONE.................................949 445-7300
FAX: 949 443-3366
EMP: 201
SALES (est): 808.69K
SALES (corp-wide): 244.08MM **Publicly Held**
SIC: 8071 Biological laboratory
HQ: Clarient Diagnostic Services Inc
31 Columbia
Aliso Viejo CA
949 445-7300

(P-18543)
CONSOLDTED MED BO- ANALYSIS INC (PA)
Also Called: Cmb Laboratory
10700 Walker St (90630-4703)
P.O. Box 2369 (90630-1869)
PHONE.................................714 657-7369
Chin Kuo Fan, *Pr*
Cam Chinh Fan, *Sr VP*
Michelle Fan, *
Gloria Fan, *Stockholder*
EMP: 100 **EST:** 1979
SQ FT: 11,000
SALES (est): 9.55MM
SALES (corp-wide): 9.55MM **Privately Held**
Web: www.cmblabs.com
SIC: 8071 Testing laboratories

(P-18544)
CURATIVE-KORVA LLC
605 E Huntington Dr (91016-6352)
PHONE.................................424 645-7575
Jonathan Martin, *Managing Member*
EMP: 85 **EST:** 2020
SALES (est): 8.88MM **Privately Held**
SIC: 8071 Medical laboratories

(P-18545)
DECIPHER CORP
6925 Lusk Blvd Ste 200 (92121-2789)
PHONE.................................888 975-4540
Tina Nova, *CEO*

Doug Dolginow, *Prin*
Brent Vetter, *CFO*
Elai Davicioni, *Pr*
EMP: 100 **EST:** 2012
SQ FT: 15,000
SALES (est): 23.62MM
SALES (corp-wide): 5.41MM **Privately Held**
Web: www.decipherbio.com
SIC: 8071 Biological laboratory
PA: Genomedx Biosciences Inc
430-1152 Mainland St
Vancouver BC
888 975-4540

(P-18546)
DR SYSTEMS INC
Also Called: Dominator Radiology Systems
10140 Mesa Rim Rd (92121-2914)
PHONE.................................858 625-3344
EMP: 205
SIC: 8071 Testing laboratories

(P-18547)
EISENHOWER MEDICAL CENTER
Also Called: Clinical Research
39000 Bob Hope Dr Frnt (92270-3230)
PHONE.................................760 773-1364
Lile Matthews, *Dir*
EMP: 124
SALES (corp-wide): 3.81MM **Privately Held**
Web: www.eisenhowerhealth.org
SIC: 8071 Medical laboratories
PA: Eisenhower Medical Center
39000 Bob Hope Dr
Rancho Mirage CA
760 340-3911

(P-18548)
EPIC SCIENCES INC
9381 Judicial Dr Ste 200 (92121-3832)
PHONE.................................858 356-6610
Lloyd Sanders, *Pr*
Michael Rodriguez, *
Mike Coward, *
Michael Giske, *CIO*
Chockalingam Palaniappan, *CIO*
EMP: 80 **EST:** 2008
SALES (est): 27.57MM **Privately Held**
Web: www.epicsciences.com
SIC: 8071 Blood analysis laboratory

(P-18549)
EXAGEN INC
1261 Liberty Way Ste C (92081-8356)
PHONE.................................505 272-7966
Robert Mignatti, *Pr*
EMP: 134
SALES (corp-wide): 45.56MM **Publicly Held**
Web: www.exagen.com
SIC: 8071 Medical laboratories
PA: Exagen Inc.
1221 Liberty Way Ste C
Vista CA
760 560-1501

(P-18550)
FOCUS DIAGNOSTICS INC
Also Called: Focus Diagnostics
11331 Valley View St Ste 150 (90630-5300)
PHONE.................................714 220-1900
John Hurrell Ph.d., *Pr*
EMP: 400 **EST:** 1978
SQ FT: 36,000
SALES (est): 48.61MM
SALES (corp-wide): 9.88B **Publicly Held**
Web: int.diasorin.com

SIC: 8071 Testing laboratories
PA: Quest Diagnostics Incorporated
500 Plaza Dr Ste G
Secaucus NJ
973 520-2700

(P-18551)
FULGENT GENETICS INC (PA)
4399 Santa Anita Ave (91731-1648)
PHONE.................................626 350-0537
Ming Hsieh, *Ch Bd*
Jian Xie, *Pr*
Paul Kim, *CFO*
Han Lin Gao, *CSO*
EMP: 893 **EST:** 2012
SQ FT: 12,000
SALES (est): 618.97MM
SALES (corp-wide): 618.97MM **Publicly Held**
Web: www.fulgentgenetics.com
SIC: 8071 Testing laboratories

(P-18552)
HEALTHQUEST CLINICAL LAB INC
9805 Research Dr (92618-4304)
PHONE.................................909 445-9727
Thomas Giancursio, *Brnch Mgr*
EMP: 93
SALES (corp-wide): 4.32MM **Privately Held**
Web: www.hqesoterics.com
SIC: 8071 Testing laboratories
PA: Healthquest Clinical Laboratory, Inc.
1800 Carnegie Ave
Santa Ana CA
714 418-5867

(P-18553)
IMMUNALYSIS CORPORATION
829 Towne Center Dr (91767-5901)
PHONE.................................909 482-0840
Kahi Luu, *Prin*
EMP: 80 **EST:** 1975
SALES (est): 5.61MM **Privately Held**
Web: www.immunalysis.com
SIC: 8071 Testing laboratories

(P-18554)
KAN-DI-KI LLC (HQ)
Also Called: Diagnostic Labs & Rdlgy
2820 N Ontario St (91504-2015)
PHONE.................................818 549-1880
David F Smith Iii, *Managing Member*
EMP: 95 **EST:** 2008
SQ FT: 7,000
SALES (est): 108.56MM **Privately Held**
Web: www.tridentcare.com
SIC: 8071 Testing laboratories
PA: Trident Usa Health Services, Llc
930 Ridgebrook Rd Fl 3
Sparks Glencoe MD

(P-18555)
LATARA ENTERPRISE INC (PA)
Also Called: Foundation Laboratory
1716 W Holt Ave (91768-3333)
PHONE.................................909 623-9301
Stepan Vartanian, *CEO*
Linda Vartanian, *Prin*
Taleen Vartanian, *Prin*
Lala Vartanian, *Prin*
Ara Vartanian, *Treas*
EMP: 120 **EST:** 1966
SQ FT: 19,000
SALES (est): 25.34MM
SALES (corp-wide): 25.34MM **Privately Held**
Web: www.foundationlaboratory.com

SIC: 8071 Pathological laboratory

(P-18556)
LOTUS CLINICAL RESEARCH LLC
100 W California Blvd (91105-3010)
PHONE.....................626 381-9830
Neil Singla, *CSO*
Sonia Kaur D.o.s., *Dir*
Anne Arriaga, *
EMP: 100 EST: 2008
SALES (est): 11.47MM Privately Held
Web: www.lotuscr.com
SIC: 8071 Medical laboratories

(P-18557)
NICHOLS INST REFERENCE LABS (DH)
33608 Ortega Hwy (92675-2042)
PHONE.....................949 728-4000
Douglas Harrington, *Pr*
Charles Olson, *
Murugan R Pandian, *Senior Science Director*
Chuck Miller, *
Michael O'gorman, *Supply Vice President*
EMP: 525 EST: 1971
SQ FT: 240,000
SALES (est): 43.15MM
SALES (corp-wide): 9.88B Publicly Held
Web: www.questdiagnostics.com
SIC: 8071 Testing laboratories
HQ: Quest Diagnostics Nichols Institute
33608 Ortega Hwy
San Juan Capistrano CA
949 728-4000

(P-18558)
POLYPEPTIDE LABORATORIES INC (HQ)
365 Maple Ave (90503-2602)
PHONE.....................310 782-3569
▲ EMP: 53 EST: 1996
SQ FT: 19,200
SALES (est): 53.49MM Privately Held
Web: www.polypeptide.com
SIC: 8071 2836 8731 2834 Medical laboratories; Biological products, except diagnostic; Biotechnical research, commercial; Pharmaceutical preparations
PA: Polypeptide Laboratories Holding (Ppl) Ab
Soldattorpsv 5
Limhamn

(P-18559)
PRIMEX CLINICAL LABS INC (PA)
16742 Stagg St Ste 120 (91406-1641)
EMP: 80 EST: 1996
SQ FT: 3,000
SALES (est): 24.69MM Privately Held
Web: www.primexlab.com
SIC: 8071 Blood analysis laboratory

(P-18560)
PRODUCTION ENGINEERING & MCH
14955 Hilton Dr (92336-2082)
PHONE.....................909 721-2455
Thomas Kearns, *Prin*
EMP: 21 EST: 2012
SALES (est): 1.27MM Privately Held
Web: www.pemmachining.com
SIC: 8071 3599 Medical laboratories; Machine shop, jobbing and repair

(P-18561)
PROFORM INC
Also Called: Proform Labs
1140 S Rockefeller Ave (91761-2201)
PHONE.....................707 752-9010
Sean Phillip Thomas, *CEO*
EMP: 100 EST: 2016
SALES (est): 3.11MM Privately Held
SIC: 8071 Biological laboratory

(P-18562)
RADNET INC (PA)
1510 Cotner Ave (90025-3303)
PHONE.....................310 478-7808
Howard G Berger, *Ch Bd*
Mark D Stolper, *Ex VP*
Mital Patel, *Ex VP*
David J Katz, *CLO*
Ranjan Jayanathan, *CIO*
EMP: 520 EST: 1985
SQ FT: 21,500
SALES (est): 1.43B Publicly Held
Web: www.radnet.com
SIC: 8071 Ultrasound laboratory

(P-18563)
SAMARITAN IMAGING CENTER
1245 Wilshire Blvd Ste 205 (90017-1901)
PHONE.....................213 977-2140
Andrew B Leeka, *CEO*
EMP: 5019 EST: 2010
SALES (est): 661.09K
SALES (corp-wide): 923.01K Privately Held
Web: www.samaritanimagingcenter.com
SIC: 8071 Medical laboratories
HQ: Pih Health Good Samaritan Hospital
1225 Wilshire Blvd
Los Angeles CA
213 977-2121

(P-18564)
SEQUENOM CTR FOR MLCLAR MDCINE
Also Called: Sequenom Laboratories
3595 John Hopkins Ct (92121-1121)
PHONE.....................858 202-9051
Jeffrey D Linton, *Sec*
Carolyn D Beaver, *
Kelly L Perez, *
Daniel Grosu, *
◆ EMP: 350 EST: 2008
SALES (est): 8.63MM Publicly Held
Web: womenshealth.labcorp.com
SIC: 8071 Medical laboratories
HQ: Sequenom, Inc.
3595 John Hopkins Ct
San Diego CA

(P-18565)
SPECIALTY LABORATORIES INC (DH)
Also Called: Quest Dgnstics Nchols Inst Vln
27027 Tourney Rd (91355-5386)
PHONE.....................661 799-6543
R Keith Laughman, *Pr*
Vicki Difrancesco, *
▲ EMP: 633 EST: 1975
SALES (est): 71.32MM
SALES (corp-wide): 9.88B Publicly Held
Web: www.questdiagnostics.com
SIC: 8071 Testing laboratories
HQ: Ameripath, Inc.
7108 Fairway Dr Ste 335
Palm Beach Gardens FL
561 712-6200

(P-18566)
THAIHOT INVESTMENT CO US LTD
18201 Von Karman Ave Ste 600 (92612-1000)
PHONE.....................949 242-5300
EMP: 2450 EST: 2017
SALES (est): 24.35MM Privately Held
SIC: 8071 Medical laboratories
PA: Tahoe Investment Group Co., Ltd.
No.333, Wusi North Road
Fuzhou FJ

(P-18567)
UNILAB CORPORATION (HQ)
Also Called: Quest Diagnostics
8401 Fallbrook Ave (91304-3226)
PHONE.....................818 737-6000
Surya Mohapatra, *CEO*
Robert Moverley, *
EMP: 400 EST: 1992
SALES (est): 118.21MM
SALES (corp-wide): 9.88B Publicly Held
Web: www.questdiagnostics.com
SIC: 8071 Testing laboratories
PA: Quest Diagnostics Incorporated
500 Plaza Dr Ste G
Secaucus NJ
973 520-2700

(P-18568)
UNITED LAB SERVICES INC
2479 S Vicentia Ave (92882-5934)
PHONE.....................951 444-0467
Anabelle Myers, *CEO*
EMP: 80 EST: 2015
SALES (est): 1.81MM Privately Held
SIC: 8071 Medical laboratories

8072 Dental Laboratories

(P-18569)
BURBANK DENTAL LABORATORY INC
2101 Floyd St (91504-3411)
PHONE.....................818 841-2256
Anatony Sedler, *CEO*
Tony Sedler, *
Robert Vartanian, *
David French, *
▲ EMP: 175 EST: 1980
SALES (est): 22.59MM Privately Held
Web: www.burbankdental.com
SIC: 8072 Dental laboratories

(P-18570)
JAMES R GLDWELL DNTL CRMICS IN (PA)
Also Called: Glidewell Laboratories
4141 Macarthur Blvd (92660-2015)
PHONE.....................949 440-2600
James R Glidewell, *CEO*
Jim Shuck, *
Glenn Sasaki, *
Greg Minzenmayer, *
Gary M Pritchard, *
▲ EMP: 1100 EST: 1969
SQ FT: 72,000
SALES (est): 460.81MM
SALES (corp-wide): 460.81MM Privately Held
Web: www.glidewelldental.com
SIC: 8072 Crown and bridge production

(P-18571)
KEATING DENTAL ARTS INC
Also Called: Keating Dental Lab
16881 Hale Ave Ste A (92606-5068)

PHONE.....................949 955-2100
Shaun Keating, *Pr*
EMP: 105 EST: 2002
SQ FT: 26,000
SALES (est): 12.26MM Privately Held
Web: www.keatingdentallab.com
SIC: 8072 Crown and bridge production

(P-18572)
NOBEL BIOCARE USA LLC
22715 Savi Ranch Pkwy (92887-4609)
PHONE.....................714 282-4800
Thomas Olsen, *Pr*
Frederick Walther, *Treas*
▲ EMP: 500 EST: 2004
SQ FT: 150,000
SALES (est): 101.09MM
SALES (corp-wide): 31.47B Publicly Held
Web: www.nobelbiocare.com
SIC: 8072 Dental laboratories
PA: Danaher Corporation
2200 Penn Ave Nw Ste 800w
Washington DC
202 828-0850

(P-18573)
POSCA BROTHERS DENTAL LAB INC
641 W Willow St (90806-2832)
PHONE.....................562 427-1811
Alex Posca, *Pr*
Angel Jorge Posca, *
Yanette Posca, *
▲ EMP: 55 EST: 1965
SQ FT: 5,000
SALES (est): 2.33MM Privately Held
Web: www.poscabrothers.com
SIC: 8072 3843 Dental laboratories; Teeth, artificial (not made in dental laboratories)

(P-18574)
PRISMATIK DENTALCRAFT INC
4141 Macarthur Blvd (92660-2015)
PHONE.....................949 399-1930
James R Glidewell, *CEO*
▲ EMP: 93 EST: 2005
SALES (est): 16.77MM
SALES (corp-wide): 460.81MM Privately Held
Web: www.glidewelldental.com
SIC: 8072 Dental laboratories
PA: James R. Glidewell, Dental Ceramics, Inc.
4141 Macarthur Blvd
Newport Beach CA
949 440-2600

(P-18575)
TRIDENT LABS LLC
Also Called: Trident Dental Labratories
12000 Aviation Blvd (90250-3438)
PHONE.....................310 915-9121
Laurence K Fishman, *Pr*
Richard B Mc Donald, *
▲ EMP: 125 EST: 1988
SQ FT: 16,000
SALES (est): 21.52MM
SALES (corp-wide): 165.17MM Privately Held
Web: www.tridentlab.com
SIC: 8072 Crown and bridge production
PA: Gdc Holdings, Inc.
1701 Military Trl
Jupiter FL
763 398-0654

(P-18576)
WEST COAST DENTAL LABS LLC
12002 Aviation Blvd (90250-3438)

PRODUCTS & SVCS

PHONE..............................855 220-5600
Chuck Stapleton, *Genl Mgr*
EMP: 322 **EST:** 2017
SALES (est): 761.18K
SALES (corp-wide): 339.71MM **Privately Held**
Web: www.wcdlabs.com
SIC: 8072 Crown and bridge production
PA: National Dentex Labs Llc
1701 Military Trl
Jupiter FL
561 537-8300

8082 Home Health Care Services

(P-18577)
365 HOME CARE
10225 Austin Dr Ste 208 (91978-1522)
PHONE..............................310 908-5179
Ebele Enunwa, *Ex Dir*
EMP: 80 **EST:** 2020
SALES (est): 2.72MM **Privately Held**
SIC: 8082 Home health care services

(P-18578)
ABC HOME HEALTH CARE LLC
5090 Shoreham Pl Ste 209 (92122-5935)
PHONE..............................858 455-5000
Joseph Monteforte, *Ex Dir*
Hamideh F Panabi, *Managing Member*
Hamid Alebrahim, *Managing Member*
EMP: 125 **EST:** 1993
SALES (est): 1.11MM **Privately Held**
Web: www.bridgehh.com
SIC: 8082 7371 Home health care services;
Computer software development and
applications

(P-18579)
ACCENTCARE INC
5050 Murphy Canyon Rd Ste 200 (92123)
PHONE..............................858 576-7410
EMP: 413
SALES (corp-wide): 2.44B **Privately Held**
Web: www.accentcare.com
SIC: 8082 7389 Home health care services;
Business services, nec
HQ: Accentcare, Inc.
17855 Dallas Pkwy
Dallas TX
800 834-3059

(P-18580)
ACCENTCARE HM HLTH EL CNTRO IN
2344 S 2nd St Ste A (92243-5606)
PHONE..............................760 352-4022
Melanie Ihler, *CEO*
EMP: 294 **EST:** 1994
SALES (est): 2.44MM
SALES (corp-wide): 2.44B **Privately Held**
Web: www.accentcare.com
SIC: 8082 Home health care services
HQ: Accentcare Home Health, Inc.
135 Technology Dr Ste 150
Irvine CA

(P-18581)
ACCENTCARE HOME HLTH YUMA INC
1455 Auto Center Dr Ste 125 (91761-2254)
PHONE..............................909 605-7000
Connie Morris, *Pr*
Melanie Ihler, *
Anna Trappett, *
EMP: 594 **EST:** 1992
SALES (est): 9.3MM

SALES (corp-wide): 2.44B **Privately Held**
Web: www.accentcare.com
SIC: 8082 Home health care services
HQ: Accentcare Home Health, Inc.
135 Technology Dr Ste 150
Irvine CA

(P-18582)
ACCREDITED FMS INC
5955 De Soto Ave Ste 136 (91367-5122)
PHONE..............................818 435-4200
EMP: 660 **EST:** 2012
SALES (est): 815.53K
SALES (corp-wide): 1.79B **Publicly Held**
SIC: 8082 Home health care services
PA: Aveanna Healthcare Holdings Inc.
400 Intrstate N Pkwy Se S
Atlanta GA
770 441-1580

(P-18583)
ACCREDITED NURSING SERVICES
Also Called: Accredited Nursing Care
3570 Camino Del Rio N Ste 108 (92108)
PHONE..............................818 986-1234
Carol Speakman, *Mgr*
EMP: 150
SALES (corp-wide): 32.94MM **Privately Held**
Web: www.aveanna.com
SIC: 8082 Home health care services
PA: Accredited Nursing Services
17141 Ventura Blvd # 201
Encino CA
818 986-6017

(P-18584)
ACCREDITED NURSING SERVICES
Also Called: Accredited Nursing Care
950 S Coast Dr Ste 215 (92626-1751)
PHONE..............................714 973-1234
Meryll Jones, *Mgr*
EMP: 232
SALES (corp-wide): 32.94MM **Privately Held**
SIC: 8082 Home health care services
PA: Accredited Nursing Services
17141 Ventura Blvd # 201
Encino CA
818 986-6017

(P-18585)
ACTION HLTH CARE PRSNNEL SVCS
3020 Old Ranch Pkwy Ste 300 (90740-2765)
PHONE..............................562 799-5523
Renee Steele, *CEO*
EMP: 150 **EST:** 1977
SALES (est): 2.07MM **Privately Held**
SIC: 8082 Home health care services

(P-18586)
AEGIS SENIOR COMMUNITIES LLC
Also Called: Aegis of Granada Hills
10801 Lindley Ave (91344-4441)
PHONE..............................818 363-3373
Bill Phelps, *Brnch Mgr*
EMP: 130
SALES (corp-wide): 137.21MM **Privately Held**
Web: www.aegisliving.com
SIC: 8082 8052 8051 8361 Home health care services; Intermediate care facilities; Skilled nursing care facilities; Residential care

PA: Senior Aegis Communities Llc
415 118th Ave Se
Bellevue WA
866 688-5829

(P-18587)
AEGIS SENIOR COMMUNITIES LLC
Also Called: Aegis of Ventura
4964 Telegraph Rd (93003-8181)
PHONE..............................805 650-1114
Hugh Carter, *Mgr*
EMP: 91
SALES (corp-wide): 137.21MM **Privately Held**
Web: www.aegisliving.com
SIC: 8082 8051 Home health care services; Skilled nursing care facilities
PA: Senior Aegis Communities Llc
415 118th Ave Se
Bellevue WA
866 688-5829

(P-18588)
ALL VALLEY HOME HLTH CARE INC
Also Called: All Valley Home Care
3665 Ruffin Rd Ste 103 (92123-1871)
PHONE..............................619 276-8001
EMP: 100 **EST:** 2013
SQ FT: 2,500
SALES (est): 3.71MM **Privately Held**
SIC: 8082 Home health care services

(P-18589)
AMERICAN PRIVATE DUTY INC
Also Called: American Untd HM Care Crp-Priv
13111 Ventura Blvd Ste 100 (91604-2218)
PHONE..............................818 386-6358
Ann Koshy, *Pr*
EMP: 80 **EST:** 1999
SALES (est): 4.29MM **Privately Held**
SIC: 8082 Visiting nurse service

(P-18590)
AMERICARE HOME HEALTH INC
16501 Sherman Way Ste 225 (91406-3787)
PHONE..............................818 881-0005
Karo Yepremian, *CEO*
EMP: 99 **EST:** 2012
SALES (est): 2.63MM **Privately Held**
Web: www.americarehhinc.com
SIC: 8082 Home health care services

(P-18591)
AXELACARE HOLDINGS INC
12604 Hiddencreek Way Ste C (90703-2137)
PHONE..............................714 522-8802
EMP: 182
SIC: 8082 Home health care services
PA: Axelacare Holdings, Inc.
15529 College Blvd
Lenexa KS

(P-18592)
BARRY & TAFFY INC
Also Called: Accredited Home Care
5955 De Soto Ave Ste 160 (91367-5101)
PHONE..............................818 986-1234
Millette Arrendondo, *Pr*
EMP: 2113 **EST:** 2010
SALES (est): 3.84MM
SALES (corp-wide): 1.79B **Publicly Held**
SIC: 8082 Home health care services
PA: Aveanna Healthcare Holdings Inc.
400 Intrstate N Pkwy Se S
Atlanta GA
770 441-1580

(P-18593)
BERGER INC
Also Called: Accredited Home Care
5955 De Soto Ave Ste 160 (91367-5101)
PHONE..............................818 986-1234
EMP: 5137 **EST:** 1980
SALES (est): 12.3MM
SALES (corp-wide): 1.79B **Publicly Held**
Web: www.aveanna.com
SIC: 8082 Home health care services
PA: Aveanna Healthcare Holdings Inc.
400 Intrstate N Pkwy Se S
Atlanta GA
770 441-1580

(P-18594)
BJZ LLC
Also Called: Always Best Care Desert Cities
45150 Club Dr (92210-8806)
PHONE..............................760 851-0740
Neil Zwack, *Admn*
Neil Zwack, *Managing Member*
Bonnie Zwack, *Managing Member**
EMP: 140 **EST:** 2013
SALES (est): 3.16MM **Privately Held**
Web: www.alwaysbestcare.com
SIC: 8082 Home health care services

(P-18595)
BRANLYN PROMINENCE INC
Also Called: Home Instead Senior Care
13334 Amargosa Rd (92392-8504)
PHONE..............................760 843-5655
Chris Parmelee, *Genl Mgr*
EMP: 130
SQ FT: 1,800
Web: www.homeinstead.com
SIC: 8082 Home health care services
PA: Branlyn Prominence, Inc.
9213 Archibald Ave
Rancho Cucamonga CA

(P-18596)
BRANLYN PROMINENCE INC (PA)
Also Called: Home Instead Senior Care
9213 Archibald Ave (91730-5207)
PHONE..............................909 476-9030
Brandi Johnson, *CEO*
Lynda Patriquin, *
EMP: 100 **EST:** 2000
SALES (est): 8.72MM **Privately Held**
Web: www.homeinstead.com
SIC: 8082 Home health care services

(P-18597)
BRIDGE HOME HEALTH LLC
5090 Shoreham Pl Ste 109 (92122-5934)
PHONE..............................858 277-5200
EMP: 88 **EST:** 2017
SALES (est): 5.91MM **Privately Held**
Web: www.bridgehh.com
SIC: 8082 Home health care services

(P-18598)
BRIGHTSTAR CARE LAKE FOREST
26023 Acero Ste 100 (92691-7942)
PHONE..............................949 837-7000
Mark Woodsum, *CEO*
Mark Woodsum, *Prin*
EMP: 275 **EST:** 2014
SALES (est): 8.34MM **Privately Held**
SIC: 8082 Home health care services

(P-18599)
BUENA VISTA MGT SVCS LLC
Also Called: Windward Life Care
2045 1st Ave (92101-2011)

P.O. Box 87371 (92138-7371)
PHONE..............................619 450-4300
Norman Hannay, *Owner*
Norman J Hannay, *Owner*
EMP: 130 **EST:** 2004
SQ FT: 2,000
SALES (est): 9.85MM **Privately Held**
Web: www.windwardlifecare.com
SIC: 8082 Home health care services

(P-18600)
CARE UNLIMITED HEALTH SVCS INC
1025 W Arrow Hwy Ste 103 (91740-5407)
PHONE..............................626 332-3767
Carol Wedderburn, *CEO*
EMP: 90 **EST:** 1995
SALES (est): 5.99MM **Privately Held**
Web: www.careunltd.com
SIC: 8082 Home health care services

(P-18601)
CENTRAL HEALTH PLAN CAL INC
1540 Bridgegate Dr (91765-3912)
PHONE..............................626 938-7120
Sam Kam, *Pr*
EMP: 175 **EST:** 2001
SQ FT: 16,144
SALES (est): 48.71MM
SALES (corp-wide): 2.41B **Publicly Held**
Web: www.centralhealthplan.com
SIC: 8082 Home health care services
PA: Bright Health Group, Inc.
      8000 Norman Center Dr # 120
      Minneapolis MN
      612 238-1321

(P-18602)
CLINICS ON DEMAND INC
11000 Wilshire Blvd (90024-3601)
PHONE..............................310 709-7355
Shahrouz Ghodsian, *CEO*
EMP: 81 **EST:** 2015
SALES (est): 8.5MM **Privately Held**
SIC: 8082 Home health care services

(P-18603)
COASTAL CMNTY SENIOR CARE LLC
Also Called: Home Instead Senior Care
5500 E Atherton St Ste 216 (90815-4016)
PHONE..............................562 596-4884
Donald Pierce, *Managing Member*
EMP: 140 **EST:** 2015
SQ FT: 2,300
SALES (est): 4.24MM **Privately Held**
Web: www.homeinstead.com
SIC: 8082 Home health care services

(P-18604)
CONFIDO LLC
Also Called: 123 Home Care
1055 E Colorado Blvd (91106-2341)
PHONE..............................310 361-8558
Graeme Freeman, *CEO*
Ryan Baxter, *
Mark Schellinger, *
EMP: 1900 **EST:** 2018
SALES (est): 59.97MM **Privately Held**
Web: www.thekey.com
SIC: 8082 Home health care services

(P-18605)
CORE HOLDINGS INC
Also Called: Maxin
17291 Irvine Blvd Ste 404 (92780-2932)
PHONE..............................714 969-2342
Ryan Dammieir, *CEO*

EMP: 250 **EST:** 1992
SQ FT: 1,200
SALES (est): 2.95MM **Privately Held**
SIC: 8082 Home health care services

(P-18606)
COX ENTERPRISES LLC
Also Called: Home Helpers of North County
325 W 3rd Ave Ste 101 (92025-4140)
PHONE..............................858 822-8587
Christopher Cox, *Managing Member*
EMP: 80 **EST:** 2018
SALES (est): 2.25MM **Privately Held**
Web: www.homehelpershomecare.com
SIC: 8082 Home health care services

(P-18607)
CRESCENT HEALTHCARE INC (DH)
11980 Telegraph Rd Ste 100 (90670)
PHONE..............................714 520-6300
Paul Mastrapa, *CEO*
William P Forster, *
Pamela Bowen, *CIO*
EMP: 150 **EST:** 1992
SQ FT: 26,000
SALES (est): 58.88MM
SALES (corp-wide): 139.08B **Publicly Held**
Web: www.crescenthealthcare.com
SIC: 8082 Home health care services
HQ: Walgreen Co.
      200 Wilmot Rd
      Deerfield IL
      800 925-4733

(P-18608)
CTSH LLC
640 N Tustin Ave Ste 201 (92705-3783)
PHONE..............................949 916-6705
EMP: 87 **EST:** 2014
SALES (est): 1.47MM **Privately Held**
Web: www.caretostayhome.com
SIC: 8082 Home health care services

(P-18609)
DUNN & BERGER INC
Also Called: Accredited Nursing Care
5955 De Soto Ave Ste 160 (91367-5101)
PHONE..............................818 986-1234
Barry Berger, *Pr*
EMP: 500 **EST:** 1980
SALES (est): 24.01MM
SALES (corp-wide): 1.79B **Publicly Held**
SIC: 8082 Home health care services
PA: Aveanna Healthcare Holdings Inc.
      400 Intrstate N Pkwy Se S
      Atlanta GA
      770 441-1580

(P-18610)
DYNAMIC HOME CARE SERVICE INC (PA)
Also Called: Dynamic Home Care
14260 Ventura Blvd Ste 301 (91423-2734)
PHONE..............................818 981-4446
Nissan Pardo, *CEO*
Carol Silver, *
EMP: 100 **EST:** 1987
SALES (est): 12.56MM **Privately Held**
Web: www.dynamicnursing.com
SIC: 8082 Visiting nurse service

(P-18611)
EISENHOWER MEDICAL CENTER
Also Called: Eisenhower Health Services
39000 Bob Hope Dr Ste 102 (92270-3221)
PHONE..............................760 773-1888

EMP: 206
SALES (corp-wide): 3.81MM **Privately Held**
Web: www.eisenhowerhealth.org
SIC: 8082 8062 Home health care services; General medical and surgical hospitals
PA: Eisenhower Medical Center
      39000 Bob Hope Dr
      Rancho Mirage CA
      760 340-3911

(P-18612)
ELIZABETH HOSPICE INC (PA)
800 W Valley Pkwy (92025-2557)
PHONE..............................760 737-2050
Sarah Mcspadden, *CEO*
Laura Miller, *
Kiprian Skavinski, *
Jan Jones, *
Andrea Goodwin, *
EMP: 200 **EST:** 1978
SALES (est): 41.15MM
SALES (corp-wide): 41.15MM **Privately Held**
Web: www.elizabethhospice.org
SIC: 8082 Home health care services

(P-18613)
FAITH JONES & ASSOCIATES INC (PA)
Also Called: Aall Care In Home Services
7801 Mission Center Ct Ste 106 (92108)
PHONE..............................619 297-9601
Faith Jones, *Pr*
Norman Jones, *
EMP: 90 **EST:** 1995
SQ FT: 1,200
SALES (est): 9.69MM
SALES (corp-wide): 9.69MM **Privately Held**
Web: www.aallcare.com
SIC: 8082 Home health care services

(P-18614)
FIRSTAT NURSING SERVICES INC
411 Camino Del Rio S Ste 100 (92108)
PHONE..............................619 220-7600
Linnea Goodrich, *Owner*
Kathleen Tickle, *
EMP: 105 **EST:** 1997
SQ FT: 1,800
SALES (est): 5.87MM **Privately Held**
Web: www.firstatofsandiego.com
SIC: 8082 Visiting nurse service

(P-18615)
GRANDCARE HEALTH SERVICES LLC (PA)
3452 E Foothill Blvd Ste 700 (91107)
PHONE..............................866 554-2447
David Bell, *Managing Member*
EMP: 150 **EST:** 2014
SALES (est): 19.05MM
SALES (corp-wide): 19.05MM **Privately Held**
Web: www.grandcarehealth.com
SIC: 8082 Home health care services

(P-18616)
HELP UNLMTED PERSONNEL SVC INC
Also Called: Help Unlimited
3202 E Ojai Ave (93023-9320)
PHONE..............................805 962-4646
Leanna Mcnealy, *Mgr*
EMP: 675
Web: www.arosacare.com

SIC: 8082 7363 Visiting nurse service; Medical help service
PA: Help Unlimited Personnel Service, Inc.
      1957 Eastman Ave
      Ventura CA

(P-18617)
HUNTINGTON CARE LLC
Also Called: Huntington Home Care
3452 E Foothill Blvd Ste 760 (91107)
PHONE..............................877 405-6990
EMP: 185 **EST:** 2007
SALES (est): 1.73MM
SALES (corp-wide): 19.05MM **Privately Held**
Web: www.24hrcares.com
SIC: 8082 Home health care services
PA: Grandcare Health Services Llc
      3452 E Fthill Blvd Ste 70
      Pasadena CA
      866 554-2447

(P-18618)
INTERHEALTH SERVICES INC (HQ)
Also Called: Presbyterian Inter Cmnty Hosp
12401 Washington Blvd (90602-1006)
PHONE..............................562 698-0811
Daniel F Adams, *Pr*
Gary Koger, *
Peggy Chulack, *
Jim West, *
EMP: 143 **EST:** 1983
SQ FT: 1,000
SALES (est): 42.38MM
SALES (corp-wide): 923.01K **Privately Held**
SIC: 8082 8062 Home health care services; General medical and surgical hospitals
PA: Pih Health, Inc.
      12401 Washington Blvd
      Whittier CA
      562 698-0811

(P-18619)
INTERIM HEALTHCARE INC
Also Called: Interim Services
7000 Indiana Ave Ste 107 (92506-4153)
PHONE..............................951 684-6111
Marianne Thompson, *Mgr*
EMP: 105
SQ FT: 2,000
Web: www.interimhealthcare.com
SIC: 8082 Home health care services
PA: Interim Healthcare Inc.
      1551 Sawgrs Corp Pkwy # 230
      Sunrise FL

(P-18620)
INTERIM HLTHCARE SAN DIEGO LLC
5625 Ruffin Rd Ste 225 (92123-6396)
PHONE..............................858 576-9501
EMP: 305 **EST:** 2020
SALES (est): 1.08MM **Privately Held**
SIC: 8082 Home health care services
PA: Interim Healthcare Inc.
      1551 Sawgrs Corp Pkwy # 230
      Sunrise FL

(P-18621)
JAMES REBECCA PROUTY ENTPS INC
Also Called: Always Best Care Temecula Vly
43980 Margarita Rd Ste 102 (92592-2782)
PHONE..............................951 292-9777
Rebecca Prouty, *Pr*
Rebecca Prouty, *Prin*
James Prouty, *

PRODUCTS & SVCS

EMP: 80 **EST:** 2013
SALES (est): 1.38MM **Privately Held**
Web: www.alwaysbestcare.com
SIC: 8082 Home health care services

(P-18622)
LAGUNA HOME HEALTH SVCS LLC
25411 Cabot Rd Ste 205 (92653-5525)
PHONE..............................949 707-5023
Michael Lovell, *Pr*
EMP: 133 **EST:** 2008
SALES (est): 2.22MM **Privately Held**
SIC: 8082 Home health care services

(P-18623)
LANDMARK HEALTH LLC
7755 Center Ave Ste 630 (92647-9152)
PHONE..............................657 237-2450
Nick Loporcaro, *CEO*
Carol Devol, *COO*
Brandon Kerns, *CFO*
Michael Le, *CMO*
Eric Van Horn, *Chief Business Officer*
EMP: 300 **EST:** 2013
SALES (est): 50.13MM
SALES (corp-wide): 324.16B **Publicly Held**
Web: www.landmarkhealth.org
SIC: 8082 Home health care services
PA: Unitedhealth Group Incorporated
9900 Bren Rd E Ste 300w
Minnetonka MN
952 936-1300

(P-18624)
LIBERTY RESIDENTIAL SVCS INC
12700 Stowe Dr Ste 110 (92064-8875)
PHONE..............................858 500-0852
Herbert T Caskey, *Pr*
EMP: 100 **EST:** 2007
SALES (est): 8.64MM
SALES (corp-wide): 28.73MM **Privately Held**
SIC: 8082 Home health care services
PA: Liberty Healthcare Corporation
401 E City Ave Ste 820
Bala Cynwyd PA
610 668-8800

(P-18625)
LIVHOME INC (PA)
Also Called: Arosa
5670 Wilshire Blvd Ste 500 (90036-5679)
PHONE..............................800 807-5854
TOLL FREE: 877
Mike Nicholson, *Ch Bd*
Cody D Legler, *Chief Clinical Officer*
EMP: 1299 **EST:** 1999
SQ FT: 7,454
SALES (est): 95.64MM
SALES (corp-wide): 95.64MM **Privately Held**
Web: www.arosacare.com
SIC: 8082 Home health care services

(P-18626)
MAXIM HEALTHCARE SERVICES INC
3580 Wilshire Blvd Ste 1000 (90010-2501)
PHONE..............................866 465-5678
EMP: 300
Web: www.maximhealthcare.com
SIC: 8082 Home health care services
PA: Maxim Healthcare Services, Inc.
7227 Lee Deforest Dr
Columbia MD

(P-18627)
MAXIM HEALTHCARE SERVICES INC
Also Called: Poway Homecare
3111 Camino Del Rio N Ste 1200 (92108)
PHONE..............................619 299-9350
Jeremy Vanleeuwen, *Mgr*
EMP: 309
Web: www.maximhealthcare.com
SIC: 8082 Home health care services
PA: Maxim Healthcare Services, Inc.
7227 Lee Deforest Dr
Columbia MD

(P-18628)
MAXIM HEALTHCARE SERVICES INC
Also Called: Victorville Homecare
560 E Hospitality Ln Ste 400 (92408-3545)
PHONE..............................760 243-3377
Angie R Wiechert, *Mgr*
EMP: 169
Web: www.maximhealthcare.com
SIC: 8082 Home health care services
PA: Maxim Healthcare Services, Inc.
7227 Lee Deforest Dr
Columbia MD

(P-18629)
MISSION HM HLTH SAN DIEGO LLC
Also Called: Mission Healthcare
2365 Northside Dr Ste 200 (92108-2703)
PHONE..............................619 757-2700
Kerry E Pawl, *CEO*
Brad Parrish, *
Todd Fontenot, *
Mag Vanoosten, *COO*
EMP: 85 **EST:** 2009
SALES (est): 10.37MM **Privately Held**
Web: www.homewithmission.com
SIC: 8082 Home health care services

(P-18630)
NO ORDINARY MOMENTS INC
16742 Gothard St Ste 115 (92647-4564)
PHONE..............................714 848-3800
Luis Pena, *Pr*
EMP: 86 **EST:** 1996
SALES (est): 9.52MM **Privately Held**
Web: www.noordinarymoments.com
SIC: 8082 8322 Home health care services; Emergency social services

(P-18631)
NORTH COAST HOME CARE INC
Also Called: Homewatch Caregivers
5927 Balfour Ct Ste 111 (92008-7376)
PHONE..............................760 260-8700
Tanya Finnerty, *Pr*
Michael Finnerty, *
EMP: 80 **EST:** 2011
SQ FT: 1,000
SALES (est): 4.31MM **Privately Held**
Web: www.homewatchcaregivers.com
SIC: 8082 Home health care services

(P-18632)
PACIFICARE HEALTH SYSTEMS LLC (HQ)
Also Called: Pacificare Health Systems
5995 Plaza Dr (90630-5028)
PHONE..............................714 952-1121
EMP: 550 **EST:** 1996
SQ FT: 104,000
SALES (est): 1.98B
SALES (corp-wide): 324.16B **Publicly Held**

Web: www.unitedhealthgroup.com
SIC: 8082 6321 Home health care services; Accident and health insurance carriers
PA: Unitedhealth Group Incorporated
9900 Bren Rd E Ste 300w
Minnetonka MN
952 936-1300

(P-18633)
PEGASUS HM HLTH CARE A CAL COR
Also Called: Pegasus Home Health Services
505 N Brand Blvd Ste 1000 (91203-3924)
PHONE..............................818 551-1932
Pamela Spiszman, *Pr*
▼ **EMP:** 80 **EST:** 1994
SALES (est): 9.91MM **Privately Held**
Web: www.pegasushomecare.com
SIC: 8082 Visiting nurse service

(P-18634)
PEOPLES CARE INC
Also Called: PEOPLE'S CARE INC.
13901 Amargosa Rd Ste 101 (92392-2409)
PHONE..............................760 962-1900
Stacey Minwalla, *Owner*
EMP: 183
SALES (corp-wide): 62.27MM **Privately Held**
Web: www.peoplescare.com
SIC: 8082 Home health care services
PA: Peoples Care Inc.
13920 City Center Dr # 290
Chino Hills CA
855 773-6753

(P-18635)
PREMIER HEALTHCARE SVCS LLC (DH)
Also Called: Phs Staffing
3030 Old Ranch Pkwy Ste 100 (90740-2766)
PHONE..............................626 204-7930
Anthony H Strange, *CEO*
EMP: 200 **EST:** 2005
SALES (est): 52.45MM
SALES (corp-wide): 1.79B **Publicly Held**
Web: www.aveanna.com
SIC: 8082 Home health care services
HQ: Aveanna Healthcare Llc
400 Intrstate N Pkwy Se S
Atlanta GA
770 441-1580

(P-18636)
PREMIER INFSION HLTHCARE SVCS
Also Called: Premier Infusion Care
19500 Normandie Ave (90502-1108)
PHONE..............................310 328-3897
Saman Refua, *CEO*
EMP: 99 **EST:** 2004
SALES (est): 14.91MM **Privately Held**
Web: www.premierinfusion.com
SIC: 8082 Home health care services

(P-18637)
RAMONA COMMUNITY SERVICES CORP (HQ)
Also Called: Ramona Vna & Hospice
890 W Stetson Ave Ste A (92543-7311)
PHONE..............................951 658-9288
Patricia Mcbe, *Brnch Mgr*
Carol Wood, *
Patrick Searl, *
Mark Fredrickson, *
John Brudin, *
EMP: 150 **EST:** 1987
SQ FT: 14,000

SALES (est): 22.83MM **Privately Held**
SIC: 8082 Visiting nurse service
PA: Kpc Group Inc.
9 Kpc Pkwy 301
Corona CA

(P-18638)
ROCK CANYON HEALTHCARE INC
Also Called: Riverwalk PST-Cute Rhblitation
27101 Puerta Real Ste 450 (92691-8566)
PHONE..............................719 404-1000
Dave Jorgensen, *Pr*
Beverly Wittekind, *
Soon Burnam, *
Ron Cook, *
EMP: 250 **EST:** 2014
SALES (est): 19.22MM
SALES (corp-wide): 3.03B **Publicly Held**
Web: www.rockcanyonrehab.com
SIC: 8082 Home health care services
PA: The Ensign Group Inc
29222 Rncho Vejo Rd Ste 1
San Juan Capistrano CA
949 487-9500

(P-18639)
SAILS WASHINGTON INC
13920 City Center Dr Ste 290 (91709-5432)
P.O. Box 1026 (98014-1026)
PHONE..............................425 333-4114
Michael Kaiser, *CEO*
Anthony Keuter, *
Matthew Cottrell, *
EMP: 500 **EST:** 2004
SALES (est): 22.29MM **Privately Held**
Web: www.sailswashington.com
SIC: 8082 Home health care services

(P-18640)
SAN DIEGO HOSPICE & PALLIATIVE CARE CORPORATION
Also Called: San Diego Hospice & Palliative
4311 3rd Ave (92103-1407)
P.O. Box 3008 (91944-3008)
PHONE..............................619 688-1600
TOLL FREE: 866
EMP: 600
Web: www.tibbiaromatik2018.org
SIC: 8082 Home health care services

(P-18641)
SELECT HOME CARE
2393 Townsgate Rd Ste 100 (91361-2513)
PHONE..............................805 777-3855
EMP: 100 **EST:** 2007
SALES (est): 9.7MM **Privately Held**
Web: www.selecthomecare.com
SIC: 8082 Home health care services

(P-18642)
ST JOSEPH HEALTH PER CARE SVCS
1315 Corona Pointe Ct Ste 201 (92879-1785)
PHONE..............................800 365-1110
Greg Henderson, *Prin*
EMP: 99
SALES (corp-wide): 7.78MM **Privately Held**
Web: www.nursenextdoor.com
SIC: 8082 Home health care services
PA: St Joseph Health Personal Care Services
200 W Center St Promenade
Anaheim CA
714 712-7100

(P-18643)
ST JSEPH HLTH SYS HM CARE SVC
200 W Center Street Promenade (92805-3960)
PHONE..................714 712-9500
Jeffrey Hammond, *Managing Member*
Susan Harvey, *
EMP: 800 **EST:** 2015
SALES (est): 71.9MM
SALES (corp-wide): 32.76MM **Privately Held**
SIC: 8082 Home health care services
HQ: St. Joseph Health System
3345 Michelson Dr Ste 100
Irvine CA
949 381-4000

(P-18644)
STAFF ASSISTANCE INC (PA)
Also Called: Staff Assistance
72 Moody Ct Ste 100 (91360-7426)
PHONE..................818 894-7879
Bill Donley, *Ch Bd*
Elaine S Donley, *
EMP: 300 **EST:** 1992
SQ FT: 800
SALES (est): 24.72MM **Privately Held**
SIC: 8082 Home health care services

(P-18645)
TEXAS HOME HEALTH AMERICA LP (PA)
Also Called: Texas Home Health of America
1455 Auto Center Dr Ste 200 (91761-2254)
PHONE..................972 201-3800
Steve Abshire, *Pt*
Judy Bishop, *Pt*
Duff Whitaker, *Pt*
Mark Lamp, *Pt*
EMP: 100 **EST:** 1969
SQ FT: 18,000
SALES (est): 1.15MM
SALES (corp-wide): 1.15MM **Privately Held**
Web: www.accentcare.com
SIC: 8082 Home health care services

(P-18646)
TIFFANY HOMECARE INC (PA)
Also Called: Always Right Home Care
9700 Reseda Blvd Ste 105 (91324-5516)
PHONE..................818 886-1602
Larry S Spaeter, *CEO*
EMP: 497 **EST:** 2003
SQ FT: 1,200
SALES (est): 8.14MM
SALES (corp-wide): 8.14MM **Privately Held**
SIC: 8082 Home health care services

(P-18647)
UCLA HEALTH AUXILIARY
10920 Wilshire Blvd Ste 400 (90024-6502)
PHONE..................310 267-4327
David T Feinberg, *Pr*
Patricia Kapur, *
Patty Cuen, *
EMP: 504 **EST:** 1981
SALES (est): 103.63MM **Privately Held**
Web: www.uclahealth.org
SIC: 8082 Home health care services

(P-18648)
ULTRACARE SERVICES LLC
1117 W Manchester Blvd Ste B (90301-1500)
PHONE..................818 266-9668
EMP: 94 **EST:** 2014

SALES (est): 2.28MM **Privately Held**
SIC: 8082 Home health care services

(P-18649)
UNIVERSAL HOME CARE INC
151 N San Vicente Blvd Ste 200 (90211-2323)
PHONE..................323 653-9222
EMP: 200 **EST:** 1995
SALES (est): 3.55MM **Privately Held**
Web: www.universalhomecare.org
SIC: 8082 Home health care services

(P-18650)
US CARENET SERVICES LLC
42225 10th St W Ste 2b (93534-7080)
PHONE..................661 945-7350
Michelle Shah, *Dir*
EMP: 102
SALES (corp-wide): 106.24MM **Privately Held**
SIC: 8082 Visiting nurse service
HQ: Us Carenet Services, Llc
699 Broad St Ste 1001
Augusta GA

(P-18651)
VISITING NRSE ASSN OF INLAND C (PA)
Also Called: Vnaic
600 W Santa Ana Blvd Ste 114 (92701-4558)
P.O. Box 1649 (92502-1649)
PHONE..................951 413-1200
Mike A Rusnak, *Pr*
EMP: 720 **EST:** 1960
SALES (est): 35.35MM
SALES (corp-wide): 35.35MM **Privately Held**
Web: www.vnacalifornia.org
SIC: 8082 Visiting nurse service

(P-18652)
VISITING NURSE & HOSPICE
512 E Gutierrez St (93103-5220)
PHONE..................805 965-5555
Karen M Wallace, *CFO*
EMP: 150 **EST:** 2017
SALES (est): 5.16MM **Privately Held**
Web: www.vna.health
SIC: 8082 Home health care services

(P-18653)
VISITING NURSE & HOSPICE CARE (PA)
Also Called: VISITING NURSE & HOSPICE CARE
509 E Montecito St Ste 200 (93103-3216)
PHONE..................805 965-5555
Lynda Tanner, *CEO*
Michelle Martinich, *
Rick Keith, *
Neil Levinson, *
Mary Pritchard, *
EMP: 122 **EST:** 1910
SQ FT: 13,765
SALES (est): 32.91MM
SALES (corp-wide): 32.91MM **Privately Held**
Web: www.vna.health
SIC: 8082 Home health care services

(P-18654)
VNA OF GREATER LOS ANGELES INC
17682 Mitchell N Ste 100 (92614-6037)
PHONE..................951 252-5314
Rajnit Walia, *CEO*
EMP: 99 **EST:** 2005

SALES (est): 1.2MM **Privately Held**
SIC: 8082 Home health care services

(P-18655)
VNACARE (PA)
Also Called: VNA PRIVATE DUTY CARE
412 E Vanderbilt Way Ste 100 (92408-3552)
P.O. Box 908 (91711-0908)
PHONE..................909 624-3574
Marsha Fox, *Pr*
EMP: 93 **EST:** 1952
SALES (est): 22.48MM
SALES (corp-wide): 22.48MM **Privately Held**
Web: www.vnacare.com
SIC: 8082 Visiting nurse service

8092 Kidney Dialysis Centers

(P-18656)
APHERESIS CARE GROUP INC
570 N 2nd St (92021-6448)
PHONE..................619 440-4612
Mats Wahlstrom, *Prin*
EMP: 85
SALES (corp-wide): 20.15B **Privately Held**
Web: www.renalcaregroup.com
SIC: 8092 Kidney dialysis centers
HQ: Apheresis Care Group, Inc.
920 Winter St
Waltham MA
781 699-9000

(P-18657)
DAVITA INC
Also Called: Davita Hesperia Dialysis Ctr
14135 Main St Ste 501 (92345-8090)
PHONE..................310 536-2406
Javier J Rodriguez, *CEO*
EMP: 104 **EST:** 1994
SALES (est): 16.54MM **Privately Held**
Web: www.davita.com
SIC: 8092 Kidney dialysis centers

(P-18658)
DAVITA INC
15271 Laguna Canyon Rd (92618-3146)
PHONE..................949 930-4400
Viki Anderson, *Brnch Mgr*
EMP: 270
Web: www.davita.com
SIC: 8092 Kidney dialysis centers
PA: Davita Inc.
2000 16th St
Denver CO

(P-18659)
HARBOR-UCLA MED FOUNDATION INC
Also Called: Ucla Hbr Dlysis Ctr Med Fndtio
21602 S Vermont Ave (90502-1940)
PHONE..................310 533-0413
Patricia Hall, *Mgr*
EMP: 300
Web: www.harbor-ucla.org
SIC: 8092 Kidney dialysis centers
PA: Harbor-Ucla Medical Foundation, Inc.
21840 Normandie Ave Ste 1
Torrance CA

(P-18660)
RAI CARE CENTERS COLTON LLC
Also Called: Rai West C Colton
1275 W C St (92324-1916)
PHONE..................909 430-0930
Monique Hartell, *Brnch Mgr*

EMP: 225
SALES (corp-wide): 20.15B **Privately Held**
Web: www.freseniuskidneycare.com
SIC: 8092 Kidney dialysis centers
HQ: Rai Care Centers Of Colton, Llc
920 Winter St
Waltham MA
781 699-9000

(P-18661)
RAI CARE CENTERS LYNWOOD LLC
Also Called: Fresenius Kidney Care Lynwood
7700 Imperial Hwy Ste R (90242-3466)
PHONE..................562 401-0155
EMP: 91
SALES (corp-wide): 20.15B **Privately Held**
Web: www.fmcna.com
SIC: 8092 Kidney dialysis centers
HQ: Rai Care Centers Of Lynwood, Llc
920 Winter St
Waltham MA
781 699-9000

(P-18662)
RAI CARE CTRS STHERN CAL II LL
Also Called: Rai Centinela Inglewood
1416 Centinela Ave (90302-1142)
PHONE..................310 673-6865
Monique Hartell, *Brnch Mgr*
EMP: 128
SALES (corp-wide): 20.15B **Privately Held**
SIC: 8092 Kidney dialysis centers
HQ: Rai Care Centers Of Southern California Ii, Llc
920 Winter St
Waltham MA
781 699-9000

(P-18663)
RAI CARE CTRS STHERN CAL II LL
Also Called: Rai-Fletcher Parkway-El Cajon
858 Fletcher Pkwy (92020-1818)
PHONE..................619 442-4122
Aida Smith, *Managing Member*
EMP: 128
SALES (corp-wide): 20.15B **Privately Held**
SIC: 8092 Kidney dialysis centers
HQ: Rai Care Centers Of Southern California Ii, Llc
920 Winter St
Waltham MA
781 699-9000

(P-18664)
RAI CARE CTRS STHERN CAL II LL
Rai Mission Gorge San Diego
7007 Mission Gorge Rd 1st Fl (92120-2422)
PHONE..................619 229-1070
Monique Hartell, *Brnch Mgr*
EMP: 128
SALES (corp-wide): 20.15B **Privately Held**
SIC: 8092 Kidney dialysis centers
HQ: Rai Care Centers Of Southern California Ii, Llc
920 Winter St
Waltham MA
781 699-9000

(P-18665)
RAI CARE CTRS STHERN CAL II LL
Also Called: Rai Corporate Way Palm Desert
41501 Corporate Way (92260-1974)
PHONE..................760 346-7588

Monique Hartell, *Brnch Mgr*
EMP: 171
SALES (corp-wide): 20.15B **Privately Held**
SIC: 8092 Kidney dialysis centers
HQ: Rai Care Centers Of Southern
California Ii, Llc
920 Winter St
Waltham MA
781 699-9000

(P-18666)
SANTA BRBARA ARTFL KDNEY CTR L
1704 State St (93101-2522)
PHONE..............................805 682-9942
Thomas Allen Md, *Pt*
Michael Fisher Md, *Pt*
EMP: 89 **EST:** 1987
SALES (est): 8.79MM **Privately Held**
SIC: 8092 Kidney dialysis centers

8093 Specialty Outpatient Clinics, Nec

(P-18667)
ALPINE CONVALESCENT CENTER INC
Also Called: Alpine Special Treatment Ctr
2120 Alpine Blvd (91901-2113)
PHONE..............................619 659-3120
Michael E Doyle, *CEO*
EMP: 100 **EST:** 1972
SQ FT: 15,000
SALES (est): 22.67MM **Privately Held**
Web: www.astci.com
SIC: 8093 Rehabilitation center, outpatient
treatment

(P-18668)
AMANECER CMNTY CNSLING SVC A N
1200 Wilshire Blvd Ste 200 (90017-1908)
PHONE..............................213 481-7464
Tim Ryder, *Ex Dir*
Frank Chargualaf, *
EMP: 100 **EST:** 1975
SALES (est): 11.26MM **Privately Held**
Web: www.amanecerla.org
SIC: 8093 Mental health clinic, outpatient

(P-18669)
ARC - IMPERIAL VALLEY
340 E 1st St (92231-2732)
PHONE..............................760 768-1944
Alex King, *Prin*
EMP: 42
SALES (corp-wide): 14.1MM **Privately Held**
Web: www.arciv.org
SIC: 8093 4783 2051 5812 Rehabilitation
center, outpatient treatment; Packing goods
for shipping; Bakery: wholesale or
wholesale/retail combined; Delicatessen
(eating places)
PA: Arc - Imperial Valley
298 E Ross Ave
El Centro CA
760 352-0180

(P-18670)
BEHAVIORAL HEALTH WORKS INC
1301 E Orangewood Ave (92805-6807)
PHONE..............................800 249-1266
Robert Douk, *CEO*
EMP: 99 **EST:** 2011
SALES (est): 17.11MM **Privately Held**
Web: www.bhwcares.com

SIC: 8093 Mental health clinic, outpatient

(P-18671)
BEHAVIORAL LEARNING NETWRK LLC
10700 Santa Monica Blvd Ste 100
(90025-4768)
PHONE..............................310 871-6800
Gregory Elsky, *Prin*
EMP: 92 **EST:** 2013
SALES (est): 2.34MM **Privately Held**
Web: www.blnautism.com
SIC: 8093 Mental health clinic, outpatient

(P-18672)
BETTY FORD CENTER (HQ)
39000 Bob Hope Dr (92270-3297)
P.O. Box 1560 (92270-1056)
PHONE..............................760 773-4100
TOLL FREE: 800
Mark Mishek, *Pr*
James Blaha, *
Jim Steinhagen, *
EMP: 250 **EST:** 1983
SALES (est): 38.29MM
SALES (corp-wide): 236.83MM **Privately Held**
Web: www.hazeldenbettyford.org
SIC: 8093 Substance abuse clinics
(outpatient)
PA: Hazelden Betty Ford Foundation
15251 Pleasant Valley Rd
Center City MN
651 213-4000

(P-18673)
BH-SD OPCO LLC (PA)
Also Called: ALVARADO PARKWAY
INSTITUTE
7050 Parkway Dr (91942-1535)
PHONE..............................619 465-4411
Patrick Ziemer, *CEO*
Chad Engbrecht, *
James Adamson, *
EMP: 94 **EST:** 2014
SALES (est): 30.95MM
SALES (corp-wide): 30.95MM **Privately Held**
Web: www.apibhs.com
SIC: 8093 Mental health clinic, outpatient

(P-18674)
BRAND THERAPY LLC
7376 W 88th St (90045-3466)
PHONE..............................415 336-6411
Lisa Welch, *Prin*
EMP: 84 **EST:** 2018
SALES (est): 270.42K **Privately Held**
SIC: 8093 Rehabilitation center, outpatient
treatment

(P-18675)
CENTER FOR ATISM RES EVLTION S
Also Called: Cares
8787 Complex Dr Ste 300 (92123-1453)
PHONE..............................858 444-8823
Olanderia Brown, *Mgr*
EMP: 107 **EST:** 2007
SALES (est): 2.34MM
SALES (corp-wide): 33.56MM **Privately Held**
SIC: 8093 Mental health clinic, outpatient
PA: Fred Finch Youth Center
3800 Coolidge Ave
Oakland CA
510 773-6669

(P-18676)
CENTER FOR DSCOVERY ADOLOSCENT
4136 Ann Arbor Rd (90712-3817)
PHONE..............................562 425-6404
Craig Brown, *Dir*
EMP: 92 **EST:** 1997
SALES (est): 1.02MM **Privately Held**
Web: www.centerfordiscovery.com
SIC: 8093 Mental health clinic, outpatient

(P-18677)
CENTRE FOR NEURO SKILLS (PA)
5215 Ashe Rd (93313-2069)
PHONE..............................661 872-3408
Mark J Ashley, *
Ken Chief Strategy Diashyn, *Development Officer*
EMP: 450 **EST:** 1980
SQ FT: 14,000
SALES (est): 80.36MM
SALES (corp-wide): 80.36MM **Privately Held**
Web: www.neuroskills.com
SIC: 8093 Rehabilitation center, outpatient
treatment

(P-18678)
CENTRO DE SALUD DE LA COMUNI (PA)
Also Called: San Ysidro Health
1601 Precision Park Ln (92173-1345)
PHONE..............................619 428-4463
Kevin Mattson, *CEO*
Ed Martinez, *
M Gutierrez, *
EMP: 80 **EST:** 1969
SQ FT: 2,000
SALES (est): 69.69MM
SALES (corp-wide): 69.69MM **Privately Held**
Web: www.syhc.org
SIC: 8093 8011 Specialty outpatient clinics,
nec; Offices and clinics of medical doctors

(P-18679)
CHILD AND FAMILY GUIDANCE CTR (PA)
Also Called: NORTHPOINT DAY
TREATMENT SCH
9650 Zelzah Ave (91325-2003)
PHONE..............................818 739-5140
Roy Marshall, *Ex Dir*
Russell Jones, *
Robert Garcia, *
Stephen J Howard Ph.d., *VP*
Bonnie Weissman, *
EMP: 200 **EST:** 1961
SQ FT: 35,000
SALES (est): 29.83MM
SALES (corp-wide): 29.83MM **Privately Held**
Web: www.childguidance.org
SIC: 8093 Mental health clinic, outpatient

(P-18680)
CHILD GUIDANCE CENTER INC
525 Cabrillo Park Dr Ste 300 (92701-5017)
PHONE..............................714 953-4455
Lori Pack, *Ex Dir*
Christine Kiehl, *
EMP: 106 **EST:** 2008
SALES (est): 9.75MM **Privately Held**
Web: www.childguidancecenteroc.org
SIC: 8093 Mental health clinic, outpatient

(P-18681)
COMMUNITY ACTION PRTNR SAN LUI
Also Called: E O C Health Services
705 Grand Ave (93401-2639)
PHONE..............................805 544-2478
Janice Wolf, *Mgr*
EMP: 127
SALES (corp-wide): 99.11MM **Privately Held**
Web: www.capslo.org
SIC: 8093 Family planning clinic
PA: Community Action Partnership Of San
Luis Obispo County, Inc.
1030 Southwood Dr
San Luis Obispo CA
805 544-4355

(P-18682)
COMPREHENSIVE CANCER CENTERS INC
8201 Beverly Blvd (90048-4505)
PHONE..............................323 966-3400
EMP: 120
SIC: 8093 Specialty outpatient clinics, nec

(P-18683)
COUNTY OF LOS ANGELES
Also Called: Health Services, Dept of
7601 Imperial Hwy (90242-3456)
PHONE..............................562 401-7088
Valeria Orange, *Dir*
EMP: 616
Web: www.lacounty.gov
SIC: 8093 9431 Rehabilitation center,
outpatient treatment; Administration of
public health programs, County government
PA: County Of Los Angeles
500 W Temple St Ste 437
Los Angeles CA
213 974-1101

(P-18684)
COUNTY OF LOS ANGELES
Also Called: Health Dept
5850 S Main St (90003-1215)
PHONE..............................323 897-6187
Floretta Taylor, *Dir*
EMP: 426
Web: www.lacounty.gov
SIC: 8093 9431 8011 Specialty outpatient
clinics, nec; Administration of public health
programs; Offices and clinics of medical
doctors
PA: County Of Los Angeles
500 W Temple St Ste 437
Los Angeles CA
213 974-1101

(P-18685)
CRC HEALTH CORPORATE
Also Called: Recovery Solutions Santa Ana
2101 E 1st St (92705-4007)
PHONE..............................714 542-3581
Tfu Bach Tran, *Mgr*
EMP: 1318
Web: www.ctcprograms.com
SIC: 8093 Drug clinic, outpatient
HQ: Crc Health Corporate
20400 Stevns Crk Blvd
Cupertino CA
408 367-0044

(P-18686)
CRC HEALTH GROUP INC
1021 W La Cadena Dr (92501-1413)
PHONE..............................951 784-8010
Tammy Elkins, *Brnch Mgr*
EMP: 143

Web: www.acadiahealthcare.com
SIC: 8093 Mental health clinic, outpatient
HQ: Crc Health Group, Inc.
6100 Tower Cir Ste 1000
Franklin TN

(P-18687)
DEL AMO HOSPITAL INC
Also Called: Del AMO Hospital
23700 Camino Del Sol (90505-5000)
PHONE.................................310 530-1151
TOLL FREE: 800
Lisa Moncen, *CEO*
Alan B Miller, *
Kirk E Gorman, *
Sidney Miller, *
EMP: 300 EST: 1991
SQ FT: 88,000
SALES (est): 45.01MM
SALES (corp-wide): 13.4B Publicly Held
Web: www.delamobehavioralhealth.com
SIC: 8093 Mental health clinic, outpatient
PA: Universal Health Services, Inc.
367 S Gulph Rd
King Of Prussia PA
610 768-3300

(P-18688)
DESTINATIONS FOR TEENS
20951 Burbank Blvd Ste D (91367-6696)
PHONE.................................818 737-2221
EMP: 84 EST: 2019
SALES (est): 1.01MM Privately Held
Web: www.destinationsforteens.com
SIC: 8093 Substance abuse clinics
(outpatient)

(P-18689)
DEVEREUX FOUNDATION
Also Called: Devereux California Center
7055 Seaway Dr (93117-4358)
P.O. Box 6784 (93160-6784)
PHONE.................................805 968-2525
Amy Evans, *Prin*
EMP: 275
SALES (corp-wide): 516.85MM Privately
Held
Web: www.devereux.org
SIC: 8093 Mental health clinic, outpatient
PA: Devereux Foundation
444 Devereux Dr
Villanova PA
610 542-3057

(P-18690)
DISCOVERY PRACTICE MGT INC
Also Called: Center For Discovery
18401 Von Karman Ave Ste 500
(92612-1542)
PHONE.................................714 828-1800
Craig Brown, *CEO*
Mark Hobbins, *Pr*
Robert Weitzman, *CFO*
Jennifer Gorman, *Dir Opers*
EMP: 432 EST: 2007
SALES (est): 40.52MM Privately Held
Web: www.centerfordiscovery.com
SIC: 8093 Mental health clinic, outpatient

(P-18691)
DUAL DIAGNOSIS TRTMNT CTR INC (PA)
Also Called: Sovereign Health of California
1211 Puerta Del Sol # 200 (92673-6306)
PHONE.................................949 276-5553
Tonmoy Sharma, *CEO*
Rishi Barkataki, *
EMP: 178 EST: 1983
SALES (est): 49.58MM
SALES (corp-wide): 49.58MM Privately
Held

Web: www.alphabet-soup.net
SIC: 8093 Mental health clinic, outpatient

(P-18692)
EVOLVE TREATMENT CENTERS
600 N Sepulveda Blvd (90049-2108)
PHONE.................................310 622-1420
Michelle Gross, *CEO*
EMP: 90 EST: 2014
SALES (est): 814.05K Privately Held
Web: www.evolvetreatment.com
SIC: 8093 Mental health clinic, outpatient

(P-18693)
GREATER VALLEY MEDICAL GROUP
Also Called: Healthcare Partners
14600 Sherman Way Ste 300 (91405-2272)
PHONE.................................818 781-7097
EMP: 147
SALES (corp-wide): 9.39MM Privately
Held
SIC: 8093 8011 Specialty outpatient clinics,
nec; Offices and clinics of medical doctors
PA: Greater Valley Medical Group
Incorporated
11600 Indian Hills Rd # 300
Mission Hills CA
818 838-4500

(P-18694)
HELIX HEALTHCARE INC
Also Called: Alvarado Parkway Institute
7050 Parkway Dr (91942-1535)
PHONE.................................619 465-4411
Roy Rodriguez, *CEO*
Mohammed Bari, *
Saleem Ishaque, *
Robert Sanders, *Stockholder*
EMP: 310 EST: 2003
SQ FT: 37,354
SALES (est): 26.76MM Privately Held
Web: www.apibhs.com
SIC: 8093 Mental health clinic, outpatient

(P-18695)
HELP GROUP WEST (PA)
13130 Burbank Blvd (91401-6037)
PHONE.................................818 781-0360
Barbara Firestone, *Pr*
Susan Berman Ph, *Ex VP*
Michael Love, *
EMP: 200 EST: 1999
SQ FT: 100,000
SALES (est): 17.88MM
SALES (corp-wide): 17.88MM Privately
Held
Web: www.thehelpgroup.org
SIC: 8093 Speech defect clinic

(P-18696)
HILLVIEW MENTAL HEALTH CTR INC
12450 Van Nuys Blvd Ste 200
(91331-1352)
PHONE.................................818 896-1161
Eva S Mccraven, *Pr*
Beth K Meltzer, *
Julie E Jones, *
Jack L Avila, *
Konstantinos N Tripodis, *
EMP: 80 EST: 1984
SQ FT: 17,600
SALES (est): 10.27MM Privately Held
Web: www.hillviewmhc.org
SIC: 8093 Mental health clinic, outpatient

(P-18697)
INSTITUTE FOR BHVORAL HLTH INC
1905 Business Center Dr Ste 100 (92408)
PHONE.................................909 289-1041
Azadeh K Jebelli, *Pr*
EMP: 265 EST: 2013
SALES (est): 13.01MM Privately Held
Web: www.ibhcare.com
SIC: 8093 Mental health clinic, outpatient

(P-18698)
INTERSTATE RHBLTATION SVCS LLC
333 E Glenoaks Blvd Ste 204 (91207-2074)
PHONE.................................818 244-5656
Sandy Pietsch, *
EMP: 120 EST: 1986
SALES (est): 21.74MM Privately Held
Web: www.interstaterehab.com
SIC: 8093 Rehabilitation center, outpatient
treatment

(P-18699)
KAISER FOUNDATION HOSPITALS
Also Called: Kaiser Permanente
23621 Main St (90745-5743)
PHONE.................................310 513-6707
EMP: 113
SALES (corp-wide): 68.1B Privately Held
Web: www.kaisercenter.com
SIC: 8093 8062 Specialty outpatient clinics,
nec; General medical and surgical hospitals
HQ: Kaiser Foundation Hospitals Inc
1 Kaiser Plz
Oakland CA
510 271-6611

(P-18700)
KERN COUNTY HOSPITAL AUTHORITY
1902 B St (93301-3526)
P.O. Box 3519 (93385-3519)
PHONE.................................661 843-7380
EMP: 501
SALES (corp-wide): 52.71MM Privately
Held
Web: www.kernmedical.com
SIC: 8093 Mental health clinic, outpatient
PA: Kern County Hospital Authority
1700 Mount Vernon Ave
Bakersfield CA
661 326-2102

(P-18701)
LA VENTANA TREATMENT PROGRAMS
1408 E Thousand Oaks Blvd (91362-2889)
PHONE.................................805 644-5745
Steve Zamarripa, *Owner*
EMP: 82 EST: 2019
SALES (est): 2.43MM Privately Held
Web: www.laventanatreatment.com
SIC: 8093 Mental health clinic, outpatient

(P-18702)
MHM SERVICES INC
230 Station Way (93420-3358)
PHONE.................................805 904-6678
EMP: 160
Web: www.centurionmanagedcare.com
SIC: 8093 Mental health clinic, outpatient
HQ: Mhm Services, Inc.
1593 Spring Hill Rd # 600
Vienna VA
703 749-4600

(P-18703)
NATIONAL THERAPEUTIC SVCS INC (PA)
Also Called: Northbound Treatment Services
3822 Campus Dr Ste 100 (92660-2607)
PHONE.................................866 311-0003
Michael Neatherton, *Pr*
Paul Alexander, *
Ray Pacini, *
David Allen Gates, *
Devon Wayt, *
EMP: 98 EST: 1995
SALES (est): 22.39MM
SALES (corp-wide): 22.39MM Privately
Held
Web: www.northboundtreatment.com
SIC: 8093 Alcohol clinic, outpatient

(P-18704)
PACIFIC CLNICS PSDENA CALWORKS
2550 E Foothill Blvd (91107-3406)
PHONE.................................626 419-3228
Miriam Shenfeld, *Prin*
EMP: 128 EST: 2003
SALES (est): 711.53K Privately Held
Web: www.pacificclinics.org
SIC: 8093 Mental health clinic, outpatient

(P-18705)
PASSAGES MALIBU
Also Called: Passages Mlibu DRG Rhab
Alchol
6428 Meadows Ct (90265-4492)
P.O. Box 6302 (90264-6302)
PHONE.................................888 777-8525
✿ EMP: 81 EST: 2010
SALES (est): 4.45MM Privately Held
Web: www.passagesmalibu.com
SIC: 8093 Substance abuse clinics
(outpatient)

(P-18706)
PEDIATRIC THERAPY NETWORK
1815 W 213th St Ste 100 (90501-7803)
PHONE.................................310 328-0276
Zoe Mailloux, *Ex Dir*
EMP: 119 EST: 1996
SQ FT: 20,000
SALES (est): 10.21MM Privately Held
Web: www.pediatrictherapynetwork.org
SIC: 8093 Rehabilitation center, outpatient
treatment

(P-18707)
PLANNED PARENTHOOD LOS ANGELES (PA)
400 W 30th St (90007-3320)
PHONE.................................213 284-3200
Sue Dunlap, *Pr*
Mark Kimura, *
Adrianne Black, *
Linda Pahl, *
EMP: 80 EST: 1965
SQ FT: 30,000
SALES (est): 99.98MM
SALES (corp-wide): 99.98MM Privately
Held
Web: www.plannedparenthood.org
SIC: 8093 Family planning clinic

(P-18708)
PLANNED PRNTHOOD OF PCF STHWES (PA)
1075 Camino Del Rio S Ste 100
(92108-3516)
PHONE.................................619 881-4500
Darrah Johnson, *CEO*
Len Dodson, *CFO*

EMP: 100 EST: 1964
SQ FT: 24,000
SALES (est): 146.19MM
SALES (corp-wide): 146.19MM **Privately
Held**
Web: www.plannedparenthood.org
SIC: **8093** Family planning clinic

(P-18709)
**PLANNED PRNTHOOD OF PCF
STHWES**
1964 Via Ctr (92081-6056)
PHONE...........................619 881-4500
Darrah D Johnson, *Mgr*
EMP: 100
SALES (corp-wide): 146.19MM **Privately
Held**
Web: www.plannedparenthood.org
SIC: **8093** Family planning clinic
PA: Planned Parenthood Of The Pacific
Southwest
1075 Camino Del Rio S
San Diego CA
619 881-4500

(P-18710)
**PLANNED PRNTHOOD OF PCF
STHWES**
4501 Mission Bay Dr Ste 1c (92109)
PHONE...........................619 881-4652
Darrah D Johnson, *Mgr*
EMP: 100
SALES (corp-wide): 146.19MM **Privately
Held**
Web: www.plannedparenthood.org
SIC: **8093** Family planning clinic
PA: Planned Parenthood Of The Pacific
Southwest
1075 Camino Del Rio S
San Diego CA
619 881-4500

(P-18711)
REHAB ALLIANCE
22995 Mill Creek Dr Ste A (92653-1271)
PHONE...........................949 707-5555
Betsy Gazda, *Prin*
EMP: 97 EST: 2003
SALES (est): 6.47MM **Privately Held**
Web: www.rehaballiance.com
SIC: **8093** Rehabilitation center, outpatient
treatment

(P-18712)
REIMAGINE NETWORK (PA)
Also Called: REHABILITATION INSTITUTE
OF OR
1601 E Saint Andrew Pl (92705-4932)
PHONE...........................714 633-7400
Praim S Singh, *Dir*
EMP: 130 EST: 1950
SALES (est): 12.18MM
SALES (corp-wide): 12.18MM **Privately
Held**
Web: www.riorehab.org
SIC: **8093** Rehabilitation center, outpatient
treatment

(P-18713)
RIO
Also Called: Rehabltition Inst Sthern Cal Ri
1601 E Saint Andrew Pl (92705-4940)
PHONE...........................714 633-7400
Glenn Motola, *Ex Dir*
Parim Singh, *
John Berry, *
EMP: 233 EST: 1964
SALES (est): 9.58MM **Privately Held**
Web: www.reimagineoc.org

SIC: **8093** 8351 Rehabilitation center,
outpatient treatment; Child day care
services

(P-18714)
RIVERSIDE-SAN BERNARDINO
11555 1/2 Potrero Rd (92220-6946)
PHONE...........................951 849-4761
EMP: 102
SALES (corp-wide): 63.44MM **Privately
Held**
Web: www.rsbcihi.org
SIC: **8093** 8011 Specialty outpatient clinics,
nec; Offices and clinics of medical doctors
PA: Riverside-San Bernardino County
Indian Health, Inc.
11980 Mount Vernon Ave
Grand Terrace CA
909 864-1097

(P-18715)
SAFE REFUGE
Also Called: SOBRIETY HOUSE
1041 Redondo Ave (90804-3928)
PHONE...........................562 987-5722
Kathryn Romo, *Ex Dir*
EMP: 80 EST: 1988
SQ FT: 2,300
SALES (est): 8.7MM **Privately Held**
Web: www.saferefuge.info
SIC: **8093** Substance abuse clinics
(outpatient)

(P-18716)
SAN FERNANDO CITY OF INC
10605 Balboa Blvd Ste 100 (91344-6367)
PHONE...........................818 832-2400
Wendi Tovey, *Brnch Mgr*
EMP: 97
SALES (corp-wide): 40.97MM **Privately
Held**
Web: www.ci.san-fernando.ca.us
SIC: **8093** 9111 Mental health clinic,
outpatient; County supervisors' and
executives' office
PA: San Fernando, City Of Inc
117 N Macneil St
San Fernando CA
818 898-1201

(P-18717)
SOUTH BAYLO UNIVERSITY
Also Called: South Baylo Acupuncture Clinic
2727 W 6th St (90057-3111)
PHONE...........................213 999-0297
David J Park, *Pr*
EMP: 136
SALES (corp-wide): 4.43MM **Privately
Held**
Web: www.southbaylo.edu
SIC: **8093** 8221 8049 Specialty outpatient
clinics, nec; University; Acupuncturist
PA: South Baylo University
1126 N Brookhurst St
Anaheim CA
714 533-1495

(P-18718)
**SOUTH CNTL HLTH RHBLTTION
PRGR**
Also Called: Barbour & Floyd Medical Assoc
2620 Industry Way (90262-4024)
PHONE...........................310 667-4070
Jack M Barbour, *Prin*
EMP: 97
Web: www.barbourandfloydla.org
SIC: **8093** Rehabilitation center, outpatient
treatment

PA: South Central Health & Rehabilitation
Program
2610 Industry Way Ste A
Lynwood CA

(P-18719)
**SOUTH COAST CHILDRENS
SOC INC**
24950 Redlands Blvd (92354-4032)
PHONE...........................909 478-3377
EMP: 186
SALES (corp-wide): 36.84MM **Privately
Held**
Web: www.sccs4kids.org
SIC: **8093** Mental health clinic, outpatient
PA: South Coast Children's Society, Inc.
25910 Acero Ste 160
Mission Viejo CA
714 966-8650

(P-18720)
**SOUTHERN INDIAN HEALTH
COUNCIL (PA)**
4058 Willows Rd (91901-1668)
P.O. Box 2128 (91903-2128)
PHONE...........................619 445-1188
Laura Caswell, *CEO*
Carolina Monsano, *
Donna James, *
EMP: 100 EST: 1980
SQ FT: 11,000
SALES (est): 26.82MM
SALES (corp-wide): 26.82MM **Privately
Held**
Web: www.sihc.org
SIC: **8093** Specialty outpatient clinics, nec

(P-18721)
**TARZANA TREATMENT
CENTERS INC (PA)**
18646 Oxnard St (91356-1411)
PHONE...........................818 996-1051
TOLL FREE: 800
Albert Senella, *Pr*
Sylvia Cadena, *
Bobbi Sloan, *
EMP: 160 EST: 1972
SQ FT: 14,000
SALES (est): 110.26MM
SALES (corp-wide): 110.26MM **Privately
Held**
Web: www.tarzanatc.org
SIC: **8093** 8322 8063 Mental health clinic,
outpatient; Individual and family services;
Psychiatric hospitals

(P-18722)
**TARZANA TREATMENT
CENTERS INC**
2101 Magnolia Ave (90806-4521)
PHONE...........................562 218-1868
Angela Knox, *Brnch Mgr*
EMP: 107
SQ FT: 11,482
SALES (corp-wide): 110.26MM **Privately
Held**
Web: www.tarzanatc.org
SIC: **8093** Substance abuse clinics
(outpatient)
PA: Tarzana Treatment Centers, Inc.
18646 Oxnard St
Tarzana CA
818 996-1051

(P-18723)
**TARZANA TREATMENT
CENTERS INC**
Also Called: Tarzana Treatment Ctr
44447 10th St W (93534-3324)

PHONE...........................661 726-2630
Theresa Scott, *Dir*
EMP: 107
SALES (corp-wide): 110.26MM **Privately
Held**
Web: www.tarzanatc.org
SIC: **8093** 8069 8011 Drug clinic, outpatient;
Drug addiction rehabilitation hospital; Clinic,
operated by physicians
PA: Tarzana Treatment Centers, Inc.
18646 Oxnard St
Tarzana CA
818 996-1051

(P-18724)
**TARZANA TREATMENT
CENTERS INC**
Also Called: Tarzana Trtmnt Ctrs LNG Bch O
5190 Atlantic Ave (90805-6510)
PHONE...........................562 428-4111
EMP: 80
SALES (corp-wide): 110.26MM **Privately
Held**
Web: www.tarzanatc.org
SIC: **8093** 8299 Substance abuse clinics
(outpatient); Airline training
PA: Tarzana Treatment Centers, Inc.
18646 Oxnard St
Tarzana CA
818 996-1051

(P-18725)
TELECARE CORPORATION
Also Called: La Casa Mhrc
6060 N Paramount Blvd (90805-3711)
PHONE...........................562 630-8672
Anne Bakar, *CEO*
EMP: 197 EST: 1965
SALES (est): 28.28MM
SALES (corp-wide): 440.9MM **Privately
Held**
Web: www.telecarecorp.com
SIC: **8093** Mental health clinic, outpatient
PA: Telecare Corporation
1080 Marina Village Pkwy # 100
Alameda CA
510 337-7950

(P-18726)
**TRI-CITY MENTAL HEALTH
AUTH (PA)**
Also Called: Tri City Mental Health Center
2008 N Garey Ave (91767-2722)
PHONE...........................909 623-6131
TOLL FREE: 866
Antonette Navarro, *Ex Dir*
Diana Acosta, *
EMP: 85 EST: 1960
SQ FT: 12,000
SALES (est): 10.29MM
SALES (corp-wide): 10.29MM **Privately
Held**
Web: www.tricitymhs.org
SIC: **8093** 8322 Mental health clinic,
outpatient; Individual and family services

(P-18727)
UHS-CORONA INC
Also Called: Corona Rgnal Med Ctr Rhbltion
730 Magnolia Ave (92879-3117)
PHONE...........................951 736-7200
EMP: 200
SALES (corp-wide): 13.4B **Publicly Held**
Web: www.swhcoronaregional.com
SIC: **8093** 8062 8069 8051 Rehabilitation
center, outpatient treatment; General
medical and surgical hospitals; Specialty
hospitals, except psychiatric; Skilled
nursing care facilities
HQ: Uhs-Corona, Inc.
800 S Main St

888   2024 Southern California
Business Directory and Buyers Guide   ▲ = Import ▼ = Export
◆ = Import/Export

Corona CA
951 737-4343

(P-18728)

UNITED AMRCN INDIAN INVLVMENT (PA)
1125 W 6th St Ste 103 (90017-1896)
PHONE..............................213 202-3970
Joseph Quintana, *Dir*
Carrie Johnson Ph.d., *Dir*
David L Rambeau, *
EMP: 122 EST: 1974
SQ FT: 26,000
SALES (est): 10.38MM
SALES (corp-wide): 10.38MM **Privately Held**
Web: www.uaii.org
SIC: 8093 Rehabilitation center, outpatient treatment

(P-18729)

UNIVERSAL CARE INC (HQ)
Also Called: Smile Wide Dental
19762 Macarthur Blvd Ste 100 (92612-2424)
PHONE..............................562 424-6200
Howard E Davis, *CEO*
Jay Davis, *
Jeffrey Davis, *
Mark Gunter, *
EMP: 350 EST: 1983
SQ FT: 73,000
SALES (est): 54.72MM
SALES (corp-wide): 2.41B **Publicly Held**
Web: www.bndhmo.com
SIC: 8093 Specialty outpatient clinics, nec
PA: Bright Health Group, Inc.
8000 Norman Center Dr # 120
Minneapolis MN
612 238-1321

(P-18730)

VICTOR CMNTY SUPPORT SVCS INC
1105 E Florida Ave (92543-4512)
PHONE..............................951 212-1770
EMP: 127
SALES (corp-wide): 69.1MM **Privately Held**
Web: www.victor.org
SIC: 8093 Mental health clinic, outpatient
PA: Victor Community Support Services, Inc.
1360 E Lassen Ave
Chico CA
530 893-0758

(P-18731)

VICTOR CMNTY SUPPORT SVCS INC
15095 Amargosa Rd Ste 201 (92394-1875)
PHONE..............................760 987-8225
Angie R Wiechert, *Mgr*
EMP: 196
SALES (corp-wide): 69.1MM **Privately Held**
Web: www.victor.org
SIC: 8093 Mental health clinic, outpatient
PA: Victor Community Support Services, Inc.
1360 E Lassen Ave
Chico CA
530 893-0758

(P-18732)

VICTOR CMNTY SUPPORT SVCS INC
Also Called: Desert Mountain Fics
14360 St Andrews Dr Ste 11 (92395-4341)

PHONE..............................760 245-4695
Alan Mann, *Brnch Mgr*
EMP: 114
SALES (corp-wide): 69.1MM **Privately Held**
SIC: 8093 Mental health clinic, outpatient
PA: Victor Community Support Services, Inc.
1360 E Lassen Ave
Chico CA
530 893-0758

(P-18733)

VICTOR CMNTY SUPPORT SVCS INC
Also Called: San Bernardino Fics
1908 Business Center Dr Ste 109 (92408)
PHONE..............................909 890-5930
Paula Quijano, *Brnch Mgr*
EMP: 107
SALES (corp-wide): 69.1MM **Privately Held**
Web: www.victor.org
SIC: 8093 Mental health clinic, outpatient
PA: Victor Community Support Services, Inc.
1360 E Lassen Ave
Chico CA
530 893-0758

(P-18734)

WORKING WITH AUTISM INC
14724 Ventura Blvd Ste 1110 (91403-3511)
PHONE..............................818 501-4240
Jennifer Sabin, *Dir*
EMP: 100 EST: 1997
SALES (est): 5.2MM **Privately Held**
Web: www.workingwithautism.com
SIC: 8093 Mental health clinic, outpatient

8099 Health And Allied Services, Nec

(P-18735)

ABLE HEALTH GROUP LLC
41990 Cook St Ste 2004 (92211-6105)
PHONE..............................760 610-2093
Gilbert Mwansa, *Admn*
EMP: 80 EST: 2017
SALES (est): 1.68MM **Privately Held**
SIC: 8099 Health and allied services, nec

(P-18736)

ACCOUNTBLE HLTH CRE IPA A PROF
2525 Cherry Ave Ste 225 (90755-2057)
PHONE..............................562 435-3333
Thomas Lam, *CEO*
EMP: 111 EST: 1993
SALES (est): 985.73K **Publicly Held**
SIC: 8099 Physical examination and testing services
HQ: Apc-Lsma Designated Shareholder Medical Corporation
1668 S Garfield Ave Fl 2
Alhambra CA
626 282-0288

(P-18737)

AHMC HEALTHCARE INC
506 W Valley Blvd Ste 300 (91776-5716)
PHONE..............................626 248-3452
EMP: 257
SALES (corp-wide): 476.02MM **Privately Held**
Web: www.ahmchealth.com

SIC: 8099 8062 Blood bank; General medical and surgical hospitals
PA: Ahmc Healthcare Inc.
506 W Valley Blvd Ste 300
San Gabriel CA
626 943-7526

(P-18738)

ALTAMED HEALTH SERVICES CORP
Also Called: Altamed Med & Dntl Group Bell
8627 Atlantic Ave (90280-3501)
PHONE..............................323 562-6700
Erika Sockaci, *Brnch Mgr*
EMP: 144
SALES (corp-wide): 1.05B **Privately Held**
Web: www.altamed.org
SIC: 8099 8011 Medical services organization; Gynecologist
PA: Altamed Health Services Corporation
2040 Camfield Ave
Commerce CA
323 725-8751

(P-18739)

ALTAMED HEALTH SERVICES CORP
Also Called: Altamed Med Dntl Grp Whttier W
3945 Whittier Blvd (90023-2440)
PHONE..............................323 307-0400
Angela Arredondo, *Brnch Mgr*
EMP: 160
SALES (corp-wide): 1.05B **Privately Held**
Web: www.altamedfoundation.org
SIC: 8099 8011 Medical services organization; Gynecologist
PA: Altamed Health Services Corporation
2040 Camfield Ave
Commerce CA
323 725-8751

(P-18740)

ALTAMED HEALTH SERVICES CORP
Also Called: Slauson Plaza Med Group
9436 Slauson Ave (90660-4748)
PHONE..............................562 949-8717
Alfredo Nunez, *Brnch Mgr*
EMP: 129
SALES (corp-wide): 1.05B **Privately Held**
Web: www.altamed.org
SIC: 8099 8011 Medical services organization; Clinic, operated by physicians
PA: Altamed Health Services Corporation
2040 Camfield Ave
Commerce CA
323 725-8751

(P-18741)

ALTAMED HEALTH SERVICES CORP
Also Called: Alta Med Health Services
10418 Valley Blvd Ste B (91731-3600)
PHONE..............................626 453-8466
EMP: 137
SALES (corp-wide): 1.05B **Privately Held**
Web: www.altamed.org
SIC: 8099 8011 Medical services organization; Gynecologist
PA: Altamed Health Services Corporation
2040 Camfield Ave
Commerce CA
323 725-8751

(P-18742)

ARBORMED INC (PA)
725 W Town And Country Rd (92868-4703)
PHONE..............................714 689-1500
EMP: 123 EST: 1995

SQ FT: 11,000
SALES (est): 14.55MM **Privately Held**
SIC: 8099 8742 Medical services organization; Management consulting services

(P-18743)

AYA LOCUMS SERVICES INC
5930 Cornerstone Ct W Ste 300 (92121-3772)
PHONE..............................866 687-7390
Alan Braynin, *Pr*
EMP: 538 EST: 2018
SALES (est): 288.11K **Privately Held**
SIC: 8099 Medical services organization
PA: Aya Healthcare, Inc.
5930 Cornerstone Ct W # 3
San Diego CA

(P-18744)

BAYMARK HEALTH SERVICES LA INC
11682 Atlantic Ave (90262-3832)
PHONE..............................310 761-4762
EMP: 203
SALES (corp-wide): 106.29MM **Privately Held**
Web: www.baymark.com
SIC: 8099 Childbirth preparation clinic
PA: Baymark Health Services Of Louisiana, Inc.
1720 Lakepointe Dr # 117
Lewisville TX
214 379-3300

(P-18745)

BHC ALHAMBRA HOSPITAL INC
Also Called: Bhc Alhambra Hospital
4619 Rosemead Blvd (91770-1478)
PHONE..............................626 286-1191
EMP: 350
SALES (est): 21.89MM **Privately Held**
Web: www.bhcalhambra.com
SIC: 8099 Blood related health services

(P-18746)

BIO-MEDICS INC
371 W Highland Ave (92405-4011)
PHONE..............................909 883-9501
Gary Crandall, *Mgr*
EMP: 121
SIC: 8099 Blood bank
PA: Bio-Medics, Inc.
2187 Monitor Dr
Park City UT

(P-18747)

BLOOD BNK SAN BRNRDINO RVRSIDE (HQ)
Also Called: Lifestream
384 W Orange Show Rd (92408-2028)
P.O. Box 1429 (92402-1429)
PHONE..............................909 885-6503
Frederick B Axelrod, *CEO*
Joseph Dunn, *
Susan Marquez, *
EMP: 240 EST: 1951
SQ FT: 50,000
SALES (est): 63.6MM
SALES (corp-wide): 526.62MM **Privately Held**
Web: www.lstream.org
SIC: 8099 2836 Blood bank; Blood derivatives
PA: Vitalant
9305 E Via De Ventura
Scottsdale AZ
800 288-2199

(P-18748)
BMS HEALTHCARE INC
8925 Mines Ave (90660-3006)
PHONE..............................562 942-7019
Mordechai Stock, *Prin*
EMP: 130 **EST:** 2010
SALES (est): 4.33MM **Privately Held**
SIC: 8099 Health and allied services, nec

(P-18749)
CALIFRNIA DEPT DVLPMENTAL SVCS
Also Called: CA Department Development Svc
696 Ramon (92234)
PHONE..............................760 770-6248
Kathleen Waegner, *Dir*
EMP: 453
SALES (corp-wide): 534.4MM **Privately Held**
SIC: 8099 Physical examination and testing services
HQ: California Department Of Developmental Services
1215 O St
Sacramento CA

(P-18750)
CALIFRNIA FRNSIC MED GROUP INC
800 S Victoria Ave (93009-0001)
PHONE..............................805 654-3343
Elaine Hustedt, *VP*
EMP: 186
SALES (corp-wide): 8.65MM **Privately Held**
SIC: 8099 Medical services organization
PA: California Forensic Medical Group, Incorporated
1283 Murfreesboro Pike # 500
Nashville TN
831 649-8994

(P-18751)
CAMDEN CENTER INC
10780 Santa Monica Blvd Ste 105 (90025-4749)
PHONE..............................310 526-3807
Jason Schiffman, *Prin*
EMP: 90 **EST:** 2011
SALES (est): 5.21MM **Privately Held**
Web: www.camdencenter.com
SIC: 8099 Health and allied services, nec

(P-18752)
CHARLES RVER LABS CELL SLTONS (HQ)
Also Called: Hemacare Corporation
8500 Balboa Blvd Ste 130 (91325-3503)
PHONE..............................877 310-0717
James C Foster, *Pr*
EMP: 93 **EST:** 1978
SQ FT: 19,600
SALES (est): 43.43MM
SALES (corp-wide): 3.98B **Publicly Held**
Web: www.hemacaredonorcenter.com
SIC: 8099 5122 Blood related health services; Blood plasma
PA: Charles River Laboratories International, Inc.
251 Ballardvale St
Wilmington MA
781 222-6000

(P-18753)
CHE BEHAVIORAL HEALTH SERVICES
5838 Edison Pl Ste 100 (92008-5520)
PHONE..............................760 300-3664

Lucy Janoyan, *COO*
EMP: 175 **EST:** 2018
SALES (est): 11.72MM **Privately Held**
Web: www.cheservices.com
SIC: 8099 Health and allied services, nec

(P-18754)
CITRUS VLY HLTH PARTNERS INC
Also Called: CITRUS VALLEY HEALTH PARTNERS, INC.
1325 N Grand Ave Ste 300 (91724-4046)
PHONE..............................626 732-3100
Carol Eaton, *Prin*
EMP: 382
Web: www.emanatehealth.org
SIC: 8099 Blood related health services
PA: Emanate Health Medical Group
210 W San Bernardino Rd
Covina CA

(P-18755)
COMPRHNSIVE INDUS DSBLITY MGT
Also Called: Cid Management
2555 Townsgate Rd Ste 125 (91361-2605)
P.O. Box 4379 (91359-1379)
PHONE..............................866 301-6568
Steven Cardinale, *CEO*
Andy Smith, *
EMP: 90 **EST:** 2002
SQ FT: 5,500
SALES (est): 8.35MM
SALES (corp-wide): 3.1B **Privately Held**
Web: www.genexservices.com
SIC: 8099 8741 Medical services organization; Nursing and personal care facility management
HQ: Genex Services, Llc
440 E Swedesford Rd Ste 1
Wayne PA
610 964-5100

(P-18756)
CORTICA HEALTHCARE INC
7090 Miratech Dr (92121-3109)
PHONE..............................858 304-6440
EMP: 309 **EST:** 2017
SALES (est): 11.78MM **Privately Held**
Web: www.corticacare.com
SIC: 8099 Health and allied services, nec

(P-18757)
DAVID-KLEIS II LLC
Also Called: PALM GROVE HEALTHCARE
1665 E Eighth St (92223-2512)
PHONE..............................951 845-3125
EMP: 86 **EST:** 2013
SALES (est): 6.72MM **Privately Held**
Web: www.pghsnf.com
SIC: 8099 Health and allied services, nec

(P-18758)
DISCOVERY HEALTH SERVICES
Also Called: Discovery Medical Staffing
5726 La Jolla Blvd Ste 104 (92037-7344)
PHONE..............................858 459-0785
Jeffrey Sternberg, *CEO*
Preston A Moreno, *
Lisa Hargrove, *
EMP: 286 **EST:** 2012
SALES (est): 17.18MM **Privately Held**
Web: www.discoveryhealthus.com
SIC: 8099 Blood related health services

(P-18759)
DRIP HYDRATION
11948 Gorham Ave Apt 3 (90049-5394)
PHONE..............................323 333-9634

EMP: 89 **EST:** 2018
SALES (est): 4.99MM **Privately Held**
Web: www.driphydration.com
SIC: 8099 Health and allied services, nec

(P-18760)
DUAL DIAGNOSIS TRTMNT CTR INC
Also Called: Sovereign Health
69640 Highway 111 (92270-2868)
PHONE..............................949 324-4531
Tonmoy Sharma, *Brnch Mgr*
EMP: 194
SALES (corp-wide): 54.63MM **Privately Held**
Web: www.omacl.co.uk
SIC: 8099 Childbirth preparation clinic
PA: Dual Diagnosis Treatment Center, Inc.
1211 Puerta Del Sol # 200
San Clemente CA
949 276-5553

(P-18761)
EASY CARE MSO LLC
3780 Kilroy Airport Way Ste 530 (90806-2459)
PHONE..............................562 676-9600
Michelle Bui, *Pr*
EMP: 103 **EST:** 2014
SALES (est): 3.9MM
SALES (corp-wide): 31.97B **Publicly Held**
Web: www.easycaremso.com
SIC: 8099 Medical services organization
PA: Molina Healthcare, Inc.
200 Oceangate Ste 100
Long Beach CA
562 435-3666

(P-18762)
ELIZABETH GLASER PEDIA
16130 Ventura Blvd Ste 250 (91436-2503)
PHONE..............................310 231-0400
Charles Lyons, *Brnch Mgr*
EMP: 457
SALES (corp-wide): 187.69MM **Privately Held**
Web: www.pedaids.org
SIC: 8099 Medical services organization
PA: Elizabeth Glaser Pediatric Aids Foundation
1140 Conn Ave Nw Ste 200
Washington DC
920 770-0103

(P-18763)
EXAMONE WORLD WIDE INC
Also Called: Examone
7480 Mission Valley Rd Ste 101 (92108-4433)
PHONE..............................619 299-3926
EMP: 100
SALES (corp-wide): 9.88B **Publicly Held**
Web: www.myexamone.com
SIC: 8099 Physical examination service, insurance
HQ: Examone World Wide, Inc.
10101 Renner Blvd
Lenexa KS
913 888-1770

(P-18764)
FAMILY HLTH CTRS SAN DIEGO INC
7592 Broadway (91945-1604)
PHONE..............................619 515-2550
Elizabeth A Samuels, *Pr*
EMP: 348
SALES (corp-wide): 147.12MM **Privately Held**
Web: www.fhcsd.org

SIC: 8099 Blood related health services
PA: Family Health Centers Of San Diego, Inc.
823 Gateway Center Way
San Diego CA
619 515-2303

(P-18765)
GOOD HEALTH INC
Also Called: Premier Pharmacy Service
410 Cloverleaf Dr (91706-6511)
PHONE..............................714 961-7930
Stephen Edward Samuel, *CEO*
EMP: 149 **EST:** 1971
SALES (est): 32.49MM **Privately Held**
Web: www.premierpharmacyservices.com
SIC: 8099 Blood related health services

(P-18766)
GRIFOLS BIO SUPPLIES INC
980 Park Center Dr Ste F (92081-8351)
PHONE..............................760 651-4042
Mark Viray, *Mgr*
EMP: 195
SALES (corp-wide): 92.52MM **Privately Held**
Web: www.interstatebloodbank.com
SIC: 8099 Blood bank
PA: Grifols Bio Supplies Inc.
5125 Elmore Rd Ste 6
Memphis TN
901 384-6200

(P-18767)
HARBOR HEALTH SYSTEMS LLC
3501 Jamboree Rd Ste 540 (92660-2950)
P.O. Box 1145 (60009-1145)
PHONE..............................949 273-7020
EMP: 212 **EST:** 2001
SALES (est): 2.47MM **Privately Held**
Web: www.harborhealthsytems.com
SIC: 8099 7372 Blood related health services; Business oriented computer software
PA: One Call Medical, Inc.
841 Prudential Dr Ste 204
Jacksonville FL

(P-18768)
HEALTH SERVICES ADVISORY GROUP
700 N Brand Blvd Fl 1 (91203-3236)
PHONE..............................818 409-9220
Lawrence Shapiro, *Prin*
EMP: 184 **EST:** 2011
SALES (est): 2.27MM
SALES (corp-wide): 53.02MM **Privately Held**
Web: www.belderadvanced.com
SIC: 8099 Blood related health services
PA: Health Services Holdings, Inc.
3133 E Camelback Rd # 140
Phoenix AZ
602 264-6382

(P-18769)
HEALTHCARE TALENT
26090 Towne Centre Dr (92610-3441)
PHONE..............................714 341-1197
Keith J Hollis, *Admn*
EMP: 80 **EST:** 2017
SALES (est): 1.76MM **Privately Held**
Web: www.healthcaretalent.net
SIC: 8099 Health and allied services, nec

(P-18770)
HERITAGE MEDICAL GROUP
Also Called: HERITAGE MEDICAL GROUP

12370 Hesperia Rd Ste 6 (92395-4787)
PHONE..............................760 956-1286
Stanley Wohl, *Brnch Mgr*
EMP: 261
Web: www.bfmc.com
SIC: 8099 Blood related health services
PA: Heritage Medical Group, Inc.
4580 California Ave
Bakersfield CA

(P-18771)
INDUSTRIAL MEDICAL SUPPORT INC
3320 E Airport Way (90806-2410)
PHONE..............................877 878-9185
Michael Donoghue, *CEO*
Ryan La Bounty, *
EMP: 800 EST: 2014
SALES (est): 22.16MM **Privately Held**
SIC: 8099 Medical services organization

(P-18772)
JWCH INSTITUTE INC
14371 Clark Ave (90706-2901)
PHONE..............................562 867-7999
Alvaro Ballesteros, *Brnch Mgr*
EMP: 177
SALES (corp-wide): 112.81MM **Privately Held**
Web: www.jwchinstitute.org
SIC: 8099 Blood related health services
PA: Jwch Institute, Inc.
5650 Jillson St
Commerce CA
323 477-1171

(P-18773)
JWCH INSTITUTE INC
8530 Firestone Blvd (90241-4926)
PHONE..............................562 862-1000
EMP: 178
SALES (corp-wide): 112.81MM **Privately Held**
Web: www.jwchinstitute.org
SIC: 8099 Childbirth preparation clinic
PA: Jwch Institute, Inc.
5650 Jillson St
Commerce CA
323 477-1171

(P-18774)
KELLY THOMAS MD UCSD HLTH CARE
Also Called: Ucsd
200 W Arbor Dr (92103-9000)
PHONE..............................619 543-2885
Lydia Ikeda, *Prin*
Ed Babakaian Md, *Prin*
EMP: 230 EST: 2001
SALES (est): 31.81MM **Privately Held**
Web: www.ucsd.edu
SIC: 8099 Childbirth preparation clinic

(P-18775)
LEGACY HEALTHCARE CENTER LLC
1570 N Fair Oaks Ave (91103-1822)
PHONE..............................626 798-0558
Raphael Oscherowitz, *Prin*
Dov Jacobs, *
EMP: 90 EST: 2016
SALES (est): 2.24MM **Privately Held**
SIC: 8099 Health and allied services, nec

(P-18776)
LIFE TIME FITNESS INC
Also Called: LIFE TIME FITNESS, INC.
28221 Crown Valley Pkwy (92677-1427)
PHONE..............................949 238-2700

EMP: 168
SALES (corp-wide): 1.82B **Publicly Held**
Web: www.lifetime.life
SIC: 8099 7991 7299 Nutrition services; Physical fitness clubs with training equipment; Personal appearance services
HQ: Life Time, Inc.
2902 Corporate Pl
Chanhassen MN

(P-18777)
LOS ANGLES CNTY DEPT MNTAL HLT
3205 N Lakewood Blvd (90808-1733)
PHONE..............................213 738-4431
Jonathan E Sherin, *Prin*
EMP: 89 EST: 2019
SALES (est): 1.29MM **Privately Held**
Web: dmh.lacounty.gov
SIC: 8099 Health and allied services, nec

(P-18778)
LOS ANGLES CNTY DVLPMNTAL SVCS
Also Called: FRANK D LANTERMAN REGIONAL CEN
3303 Wilshire Blvd Ste 700 (90010-1704)
PHONE..............................213 383-1300
Dianne Anand, *Ex Dir*
EMP: 180 EST: 1979
SQ FT: 80,000
SALES (est): 299.93MM **Privately Held**
Web: www.lanterman.org
SIC: 8099 8322 8093 Medical services organization; Individual and family services; Mental health clinic, outpatient

(P-18779)
MARTIN LTHER KING JR-LOS ANGLE
Also Called: Martin Lther King Jr Cmnty Hos
1680 E 120th St (90059-3026)
PHONE..............................424 338-8000
EMP: 271 EST: 2010
SALES (est): 366.59MM **Privately Held**
Web: www.mlkch.org
SIC: 8099 Childbirth preparation clinic

(P-18780)
MEDASEND BIOMEDICAL INC (PA)
1402 Daisy Ave (90813-1521)
PHONE..............................800 200-3581
Steve Grand, *CEO*
Stephanie Harrison, *VP*
EMP: 150 EST: 1999
SQ FT: 10,000
SALES (est): 6.67MM
SALES (corp-wide): 6.67MM **Privately Held**
Web: www.medasend.com
SIC: 8099 4953 Health screening service; Hazardous waste collection and disposal

(P-18781)
MOLINA HEALTHCARE INC
1 Golden Shore (90802-4202)
PHONE..............................562 435-3666
Sriram Bharadwaj, *Brnch Mgr*
EMP: 158
SALES (corp-wide): 31.97B **Publicly Held**
Web: www.molinahealthcare.com
SIC: 8099 Blood related health services
PA: Molina Healthcare, Inc.
200 Oceangate Ste 100
Long Beach CA
562 435-3666

(P-18782)
MONARCH HLTHCARE A MED GROUP I
2562 State St (92008-1663)
PHONE..............................760 730-9448
EMP: 119
SALES (corp-wide): 324.16B **Publicly Held**
Web: www.monarchhealthcare.com
SIC: 8099 Blood related health services
HQ: Monarch Healthcare, A Medical Group, Inc.
11 Technology Dr
Irvine CA

(P-18783)
NALU MEDICAL INC
2320 Faraday Ave Ste 100 (92008-7241)
PHONE..............................760 603-8466
Earl R Fender, *Pr*
Keegan Harper, *Ch Bd*
EMP: 133 EST: 2015
SALES (est): 10.68MM **Privately Held**
Web: www.nalumed.com
SIC: 8099 Childbirth preparation clinic

(P-18784)
NAVY UNITED STATES DEPARTMENT
Also Called: Naval Hosp Twntynine Plms Gfeb
1145 Sturgis Rd (92278)
PHONE..............................760 830-2124
Eugene Dearstine, *CFO*
EMP: 99
Web: www.navy.mil
SIC: 8099 Blood related health services
HQ: United States Department Of The Navy
1200 Navy Pentagon
Washington DC

(P-18785)
NEIGHBORHOOD HEALTHCARE
401 E Valley Pkwy (92025-3317)
PHONE..............................760 737-6903
EMP: 100
SALES (corp-wide): 184.76MM **Privately Held**
Web: www.nhcare.org
SIC: 8099 Childbirth preparation clinic
PA: Neighborhood Healthcare
425 N Date St
Escondido CA
760 737-6934

(P-18786)
NOVA SKILLED HOME HEALTH INC
3300 N San Fernando Blvd Ste 201 (91504-2530)
PHONE..............................323 658-6232
Nelson Aguilar, *CEO*
Julita Fraley, *
Carol Vega, *
EMP: 136 EST: 2018
SALES (est): 4.13MM **Privately Held**
SIC: 8099 Health and allied services, nec

(P-18787)
OPTUMCARE MEDICAL GROUP
800 Corporate Dr Ste 100 (92694-1153)
PHONE..............................949 364-9112
EMP: 83 EST: 2019
SALES (est): 1.52MM **Privately Held**
Web: www.optum.com
SIC: 8099 Health and allied services, nec

(P-18788)
PERFORMANCE HEALTH MED GROUP
13252 Garden Grove Blvd Ste 112 (92843-2270)
PHONE..............................714 740-1778
Lanett Bell, *Mgr*
EMP: 91
SALES (corp-wide): 951.3K **Privately Held**
SIC: 8099 Blood related health services
PA: Performance Health Medical Group
21707 Hawthorne Blvd # 20
Torrance CA
310 540-9699

(P-18789)
PPONEXT WEST INC
1501 Hughes Way Ste 400 (90810-1865)
PHONE..............................888 446-6098
Barbara E Rodin Ph.d., *Pr*
EMP: 385 EST: 1999
SALES (est): 745.21K
SALES (corp-wide): 1.08B **Publicly Held**
SIC: 8099 Medical services organization
HQ: Beech Street Corporation
25550 Cmmrcntre Dr Ste 20
Lake Forest CA
949 672-1000

(P-18790)
PROVIDNCE FACEY MED FOUNDATION
11211 Sepulveda Blvd (91345-1115)
PHONE..............................818 837-5677
Cathy Hawes, *Brnch Mgr*
EMP: 152
SALES (corp-wide): 91.37MM **Privately Held**
Web: www.facey.com
SIC: 8099 8042 8011 Medical services organization; Offices and clinics of optometrists; Offices and clinics of medical doctors
PA: Providence Facey Medical Foundation
15451 San Frnndo Mssion B
Mission Hills CA
818 365-9531

(P-18791)
PROVIDNCE FACEY MED FOUNDATION
Also Called: Facey Medical Group
17909 Soledad Canyon Rd (91387-3210)
PHONE..............................661 250-5225
Leslie Holland, *Brnch Mgr*
EMP: 122
SALES (corp-wide): 91.37MM **Privately Held**
Web: www.facey.com
SIC: 8099 8011 Medical services organization; Offices and clinics of medical doctors
PA: Providence Facey Medical Foundation
15451 San Frnndo Mssion B
Mission Hills CA
818 365-9531

(P-18792)
PROVISIO MEDICAL INC
10815 Rancho Bernardo Rd Ste 110 (92127)
PHONE..............................508 740-9940
Stephen Eric Ryan, *CEO*
EMP: 19 EST: 2014
SALES (est): 4.98MM **Privately Held**
Web: www.provisiomedical.com
SIC: 8099 3841 Medical services organization; Surgical and medical instruments

PRODUCTS & SVCS

(P-18793)
PUBLIC HLTH FNDATION ENTPS INC
125 E Anaheim St (90744-4590)
PHONE..............................310 518-2835
EMP: 140
SALES (corp-wide): 92.05MM **Privately Held**
Web: www.phfewic.org
SIC: 8099 Blood related health services
PA: Public Health Foundation Enterprises, Inc.
13300 Crssrds Pkwy N
City Of Industry CA
800 201-7320

(P-18794)
PUBLIC HLTH FNDATION ENTPS INC
Also Called: Wic
12781 Shama Rd (91732)
PHONE..............................626 856-6618
Juan Chong, *Brnch Mgr*
EMP: 140
SALES (corp-wide): 92.05MM **Privately Held**
Web: www.phfewic.org
SIC: 8099 Blood related health services
PA: Public Health Foundation Enterprises, Inc.
13300 Crssrds Pkwy N
City Of Industry CA
800 201-7320

(P-18795)
PUBLIC HLTH FNDATION ENTPS INC
3648 E Olympic Blvd (90023-3129)
PHONE..............................323 261-6388
EMP: 140
SALES (corp-wide): 92.05MM **Privately Held**
Web: www.helunahealth.org
SIC: 8099 Blood related health services
PA: Public Health Foundation Enterprises, Inc.
13300 Crssrds Pkwy N
City Of Industry CA
800 201-7320

(P-18796)
PUBLIC HLTH FNDATION ENTPS INC
8666 Whittier Blvd (90660-2655)
PHONE..............................562 801-2323
Nicolle Fevere, *Prin*
EMP: 140
SALES (corp-wide): 92.05MM **Privately Held**
Web: www.helunahealth.org
SIC: 8099 Blood related health services
PA: Public Health Foundation Enterprises, Inc.
13300 Crssrds Pkwy N
City Of Industry CA
800 201-7320

(P-18797)
PUBLIC HLTH FNDATION ENTPS INC
1649 W Washington Blvd (90007-1116)
PHONE..............................323 733-9381
Eloise Jenks, *Pr*
EMP: 140
SALES (corp-wide): 92.05MM **Privately Held**
Web: www.helunahealth.org
SIC: 8099 Blood related health services

PA: Public Health Foundation Enterprises, Inc.
13300 Crssrds Pkwy N
City Of Industry CA
800 201-7320

(P-18798)
QTC MANAGEMENT INC (DH)
924 Overland Ct (91773-1742)
PHONE..............................800 682-9701
Elizabeth Porter, *CEO*
▼ EMP: 99 EST: 1981
SQ FT: 20,000
SALES (est): 61.61MM **Publicly Held**
Web: www.qtcm.com
SIC: 8099 Medical services organization
HQ: Qtc Holdings Inc.
9737 Washingtonian Blvd
Gaithersburg MD
909 859-2100

(P-18799)
QTC MDCAL GROUP INC A MED CORP
Also Called: Qtc Medical Group
924 Overland Ct (91773-1742)
PHONE..............................800 260-1515
Brant Kim, *CEO*
EMP: 1000 EST: 1984
SALES (est): 51.09MM **Privately Held**
Web: www.qtcm.com
SIC: 8099 Medical services organization

(P-18800)
REGENTS OF THE UNIVERSITY CAL
Also Called: Santa Monica Ucla Medical Ctr
1250 16th St (90404-1249)
PHONE..............................310 267-9308
Johnese Spisso, *Prin*
Felicia Rue, *
Paul Staton, *
EMP: 99 EST: 1996
SALES (est): 9.74MM **Privately Held**
SIC: 8099 Health and allied services, nec

(P-18801)
SAN BRNRDINO CY UNFIED SCHL DS
Also Called: Nutrition Services
1257 Northpark Blvd (92407-2946)
PHONE..............................909 881-8000
EMP: 83
SALES (corp-wide): 952.38MM **Privately Held**
Web: www.sbcusd.com
SIC: 8099 8211 Nutrition services; Elementary school, nec
PA: San Bernardino City Unified School District
777 N F St
San Bernardino CA
909 381-1100

(P-18802)
SAN DIEGO BLOOD BANK (PA)
Also Called: San Diego Blood Bnk Foundation
3636 Gateway Center Ave Ste 100
(92102-4508)
PHONE..............................619 400-8132
TOLL FREE: 800
Ramona Walker, *CEO*
▲ EMP: 155 EST: 1950
SQ FT: 132,000
SALES (est): 41.12MM
SALES (corp-wide): 41.12MM **Privately Held**
Web: www.sandiegobloodbank.org

SIC: 8099 8071 Blood bank; Medical laboratories

(P-18803)
SCRIBEAMERICA LLC
840 Apollo St Ste 231 (90245-4762)
PHONE..............................877 819-5900
Michael Murphy, *Brnch Mgr*
EMP: 365
Web: www.scribeamerica.com
SIC: 8099 Blood related health services
HQ: Scribeamerica, Llc
1200 E Las Olas Blvd # 201
Fort Lauderdale FL

(P-18804)
SENSEI WELLNESS HOLDINGS INC
1119 Colorado Ave Ste 18 (90401-3009)
PHONE..............................602 499-9862
Kevin Kelly, *CEO*
EMP: 92 EST: 2020
SALES (est): 11.33MM **Privately Held**
Web: www.sensei.com
SIC: 8099 Health screening service

(P-18805)
SOUTHERN CAL PRMNNTE MED GROUP
Also Called: SOUTHERN CALIFORNIA PERMANENTE MEDICAL GROUP
23781 Maquina (92691-2716)
PHONE..............................949 376-8619
EMP: 189
SALES (corp-wide): 68.1B **Privately Held**
Web: www.permanente.org
SIC: 8099 Blood related health services
HQ: Southern California Permanente Medical Group
393 Walnut Dr
Pasadena CA
626 405-5704

(P-18806)
STAR OF CA LLC
501 Marin St (91360-4266)
PHONE..............................805 379-1401
Doug Moes, *Brnch Mgr*
EMP: 94
SALES (corp-wide): 165.05MM **Privately Held**
Web: www.starofca.com
SIC: 8099 Medical services organization
HQ: Star Of Ca, Llc
4880 Market St
Ventura CA

(P-18807)
STAR OF CA LLC (HQ)
4880 Market St (93003-7783)
PHONE..............................805 644-7827
Doug Moes, *Pr*
Quy Neel, *CCO*
Jennifer Johnson, *Dir Opers*
Tom Forde, *Contrlr*
EMP: 110 EST: 2006
SQ FT: 6,640
SALES (est): 53.82MM
SALES (corp-wide): 165.05MM **Privately Held**
Web: www.starofca.com
SIC: 8099 8049 8322 Medical services organization; Clinical psychologist; Individual and family services
PA: Pediatric Therapy Services, Llc
184 High St Ste 701
Boston MA
800 337-5965

(P-18808)
STAR OF CA LLC
15260 Ventura Blvd (91403-5307)
PHONE..............................818 986-7827
Alison Stanley, *Brnch Mgr*
EMP: 95
SALES (corp-wide): 165.05MM **Privately Held**
Web: www.starofca.com
SIC: 8099 Medical services organization
HQ: Star Of Ca, Llc
4880 Market St
Ventura CA

(P-18809)
STAR OF CALIFORNIA
Also Called: STAR OF CALIFORNIA, A PROFESSIONAL PSYCHOLOGICAL CORPORATION
8834 Morro Rd (93422-3953)
PHONE..............................805 466-1638
EMP: 95
SALES (corp-wide): 165.05MM **Privately Held**
Web: www.starofca.com
SIC: 8099 Medical services organization
HQ: Star Of Ca, Llc
4880 Market St
Ventura CA

(P-18810)
SYNERGY ORTHPD SPECIALISTS INC
4445 Eastgate Mall Ste 103 (92121)
PHONE..............................858 450-7118
Brent Noon, *CEO*
EMP: 83 EST: 2012
SALES (est): 5.36MM **Privately Held**
Web: www.synergysmg.com
SIC: 8099 Blood related health services

(P-18811)
TARGETED MEDICAL PHARMA INC
2980 N Beverly Glen Cir Ste 100
(90077-1735)
PHONE..............................310 474-9809
EMP: 17 EST: 2003
SALES (est): 2.05MM
SALES (corp-wide): 7.06MM **Privately Held**
SIC: 8099 5912 2023 Nutrition services; Drug stores and proprietary stores; Dietary supplements, dairy and non-dairy based
PA: Targeted Medical Pharma, Inc.
2980 N Beverly Glen Cir # 301
Los Angeles CA
310 474-9809

(P-18812)
UC IRVINE HEALTH
200 S Manchester Ave Ste 400
(92868-3220)
PHONE..............................714 456-6191
EMP: 95 EST: 2018
SALES (est): 2.48MM **Privately Held**
Web: www.ucihealth.org
SIC: 8099 Health and allied services, nec

(P-18813)
UNIVERSITY CALIFORNIA IRVINE
Also Called: UCI Health Blood Donor Center
106 B Student Ctr (92697-0001)
PHONE..............................949 824-2662
EMP: 80
SALES (corp-wide): 534.4MM **Privately Held**
Web: www.uci.edu

▲ = Import ▼ = Export
◆ = Import/Export

SIC: **8099** Blood donor station
HQ: University Of California, Irvine
510 Aldrich Hall
Irvine CA
949 824-5011

(P-18814)
UNIVERSITY CALIFORNIA
IRVINE
31865 Circle Dr (92651-6860)
PHONE...............................949 939-7106
EMP: 80
SALES (corp-wide): 534.4MM **Privately Held**
Web: www.uci.edu
SIC: **8099** Blood related health services
HQ: University Of California, Irvine
510 Aldrich Hall
Irvine CA
949 824-5011

(P-18815)
VENTURA CNTY MD-CAL
MNGED CARE
Also Called: Gold Coast Health Plan
711 E Daily Dr Ste 106 (93010-6082)
PHONE...............................888 301-1228
Michael P Engelhard, *CEO*
EMP: 87 **EST:** 2010
SALES (est): 51.41MM **Privately Held**
Web: www.goldcoasthealthplan.org
SIC: **8099** Medical services organization

(P-18816)
WESTLAKE OAKS
HEALTHCARE LLC
Also Called: Sherwood Oaks Post Acute
250 Fairview Rd (91361-2456)
PHONE...............................805 494-1233
EMP: 107 **EST:** 2020
SALES (est): 4.47MM
SALES (corp-wide): 1.53B **Privately Held**
SIC: **8099** Health and allied services, nec
PA: Providence Group, Inc.
262 N University Ave
Farmington UT
801 447-9829

8111 Legal Services

(P-18817)
A BUCHALTER PROFESSIONAL
CORP (PA)
1000 Wilshire Blvd Ste 1500 (90017-2457)
PHONE...............................213 891-0700
Adam Bass, *CEO*
EMP: 209 **EST:** 1970
SQ FT: 84,000
SALES (est): 48.43MM
SALES (corp-wide): 48.43MM **Privately Held**
Web: www.buchalter.com
SIC: **8111** General practice law office

(P-18818)
ALDRIDGE PITE LLP
4375 Jutland Dr Ste 200 (92117-3600)
P.O. Box 17935 (92177-7923)
PHONE...............................858 750-7700
EMP: 401
SALES (corp-wide): 99.58MM **Privately Held**
Web: www.aldridgepite.com
SIC: **8111** Real estate law
PA: Aldridge Pite Llp
3575 Piedmont Rd Ne 15-500
Atlanta GA
404 994-7400

(P-18819)
ALLEN MTKINS LECK GMBLE
MLLORY (PA)
Also Called: Allen Matkins
865 S Figueroa St Ste 2800 (90017-2543)
PHONE...............................213 622-5555
David L Osias, *Mng Pt*
Frederick L Allen, *Pt*
Michael L Matkins, *Pt*
John C Gamble, *Pt*
Richard C Mallory, *Pt*
EMP: 130 **EST:** 1986
SQ FT: 40,000
SALES (est): 51.83MM
SALES (corp-wide): 51.83MM **Privately Held**
Web: www.allenmatkins.com
SIC: **8111** General practice law office

(P-18820)
ARNOLD PORTER KAYE
SCHOLER LLP
Also Called: Arnold & Porter
777 S Figueroa St Ste 4400 (90017-5800)
PHONE...............................213 243-4000
Peter Blinkley, *Brnch Mgr*
EMP: 96
SALES (corp-wide): 814.71K **Privately Held**
Web: www.arnoldporter.com
SIC: **8111** General practice attorney, lawyer
PA: Arnold & Porter Kaye Scholer Llp
601 Massachusetts Ave Nw
Washington DC
202 942-5000

(P-18821)
ATKINSON ANDLSON LOYA
RUUD ROM (PA)
Also Called: Atkinson Andelson Loya
12800 Center Court Dr S Ste 300 (90703-9363)
PHONE...............................562 653-3200
James C Romo, *CEO*
Steven Atkinson, *
Steven Andelson, *
Paul Loya, *
EMP: 150 **EST:** 1979
SALES (est): 38.23MM
SALES (corp-wide): 38.23MM **Privately Held**
Web: www.aalrr.com
SIC: **8111** General practice attorney, lawyer

(P-18822)
AUSTIN SIDLEY CA LLP
555 W 5th St Ste 4000 (90013-3000)
PHONE...............................213 896-6000
Dan Clivner, *Pt*
EMP: 172 **EST:** 2001
SALES (est): 10.56MM
SALES (corp-wide): 511.15MM **Privately Held**
SIC: **8111** General practice attorney, lawyer
PA: Sidley Austin Llp
1 S Dearborn St Ste 900
Chicago IL
312 853-7000

(P-18823)
BAKER & HOSTETLER LLP
11601 Wilshire Blvd Fl 14 (90025-1744)
PHONE...............................310 820-8800
John F Cermak Junior, *Mng Pt*
EMP: 85
SALES (corp-wide): 309.55K **Privately Held**
Web: www.bakerlaw.com

SIC: **8111** General practice attorney, lawyer
PA: Baker & Hostetler Llp
127 Public Sq Ste 2000
Cleveland OH
216 621-0200

(P-18824)
BAKER & HOSTETLER LLP
600 Anton Blvd Ste 900 (92626-7193)
PHONE...............................714 754-6600
George T Mooradian, *Pt*
EMP: 85
SQ FT: 6,000
SALES (corp-wide): 309.55K **Privately Held**
Web: www.bakerlaw.com
SIC: **8111** General practice attorney, lawyer
PA: Baker & Hostetler Llp
127 Public Sq Ste 2000
Cleveland OH
216 621-0200

(P-18825)
BAKER & MCKENZIE LLP
10250 Constellation Blvd Ste 1850 (90067-6278)
PHONE...............................310 201-4728
EMP: 125
SALES (corp-wide): 782.22MM **Privately Held**
Web: www.bakermckenzie.com
SIC: **8111** General practice law office
PA: Baker & Mckenzie Llp
300 E Randolph St # 5000
Chicago IL
312 861-8000

(P-18826)
BARNES & THORNBURG LLP
2029 Century Park E Ste 300 (90067-2904)
PHONE...............................310 284-3880
EMP: 113
SALES (corp-wide): 85.65MM **Privately Held**
Web: www.btlaw.com
SIC: **8111** General practice attorney, lawyer
PA: Barnes & Thornburg Llp
240 E Jackson Blvd
Elkhart IN
317 236-1313

(P-18827)
BARNES FIRM LC
633 W 5th St Ste 1750 (90071-3547)
PHONE...............................800 800-0000
Stephen E Barnes, *CEO*
EMP: 95 **EST:** 2017
SALES (est): 2.18MM **Privately Held**
Web: www.thebarnesfirm.com
SIC: **8111** General practice attorney, lawyer

(P-18828)
BD&J PC
9701 Wilshire Blvd Ste 630 (90212-2158)
PHONE...............................855 906-3699
EMP: 84 **EST:** 2007
SALES (est): 8.28MM **Privately Held**
Web: www.bdjinjurylawyers.com
SIC: **8111** General practice law office

(P-18829)
BLAKELY SOKOLOFF TAYLOR &
ZAFMAN LLP
Also Called: Bstz
12400 Wilshire Blvd Ste 700 (90025-1019)
PHONE...............................310 207-3800
EMP: 240
Web: www.womblebonddickinson.com

SIC: **8111** Specialized law offices, attorneys

(P-18830)
BMC GROUP INC
Also Called: Bankruptcy Management Cons
300 Continental Blvd Ste 570 (90245)
PHONE...............................310 321-5555
Shawn Allen, *Pr*
EMP: 100
Web: www.bmcgroup.com
SIC: **8111** Bankruptcy referee
PA: The Bmc Group Inc
3732 W 120th St
Hawthorne CA

(P-18831)
BONNE BRDGES MLLER OKEFE
NCHOL (PA)
355 S Grand Ave Ste 1750 (90071-1562)
PHONE...............................213 480-1900
David J O'keefe, *Pr*
James D Nichols, *
George Peterson, *
EMP: 100 **EST:** 1961
SALES (est): 17.48MM
SALES (corp-wide): 17.48MM **Privately Held**
Web: www.bonnebridges.com
SIC: **8111** General practice attorney, lawyer

(P-18832)
BURKE WILLIAMS & SORENSEN
LLP (PA)
Also Called: Burke
444 S Flower St Ste 2400 (90071-2953)
PHONE...............................213 236-0600
John J Welsh, *Mng Pt*
James T Bradshaw Junior, *Pt*
Carl K Newton, *Pt*
Leland C Dolley, *Pt*
Neil F Yeager, *Pt*
EMP: 90 **EST:** 1927
SQ FT: 51,000
SALES (est): 25.16MM
SALES (corp-wide): 25.16MM **Privately Held**
Web: www.bwslaw.com
SIC: **8111** General practice attorney, lawyer

(P-18833)
CALIFORNIA CITY SAN
BERNARDINO (PA)
290 N D St (92401-1702)
PHONE...............................909 384-7272
R Carey Davis, *Mayor*
Mark Scoth, *
Gigi Hannah, *City Clerk**
David Kennedy, *City Treasurer**
Gary Saiz, *City Attorney**
EMP: 352 **EST:** 1854
SALES (est): 264.9MM
SALES (corp-wide): 264.9MM **Privately Held**
Web: www.sbcity.org
SIC: **8111** Administrative and government law

(P-18834)
CARSON KURTZMAN
CONSULTANTS (DH)
Also Called: K C C
2335 Alaska Ave (90245-4808)
PHONE...............................310 823-9000
Johnathan Carson, *
EMP: 180 **EST:** 2001
SQ FT: 46,000
SALES (est): 53.77MM **Privately Held**
Web: www.kccllc.com
SIC: **8111** Specialized legal services
HQ: Computershare Inc.
150 Royall St Ste 205

Canton MA

(P-18835)

CHILDRENS LAW CENTER CAL (PA)

101 Centre Plaza Dr (91754-2155)
PHONE...................323 980-8700
Leslie Starr Heimov, *CEO*
EMP: 88 **EST:** 1989
SALES (est): 73.27MM **Privately Held**
Web: www.clccal.org
SIC: 8111 Legal aid service

(P-18836)

CHRISTIE PARKER & HALE LLP (PA)

655 N Central Ave Ste 2300 (91203-1422)
P.O. Box 29001 (91209-9001)
PHONE...................626 795-9900
EMP: 130 **EST:** 1946
SALES (est): 18.85MM
SALES (corp-wide): 18.85MM **Privately Held**
Web: www.lewisroca.com
SIC: 8111 General practice attorney, lawyer

(P-18837)

COLLINSON LAW A PROF CORP

21515 Hawthorne Blvd Ste 800 (90503-6517)
PHONE...................424 212-7777
Lisa Collinson, *Brnch Mgr*
EMP: 185
SALES (corp-wide): 3.6MM **Privately Held**
Web: www.cdiglaw.com
SIC: 8111 General practice law office
PA: Collinson Law, A Professional Corporation
1600 Rosecrans Ave Fl 4
Manhattan Beach CA
310 321-7670

(P-18838)

COMPEX LEGAL SERVICES INC (PA)

325 Maple Ave (90503-2602)
PHONE...................310 782-1801
Paul Boroditsch, *CEO*
Nitin Mehta, *Ch*
Anthony Bazurto, *Sr VP*
Humildad Pasimio, *VP*
Rajesh Rangaswamy, *VP*
▲ **EMP:** 120 **EST:** 1974
SQ FT: 47,740
SALES (est): 55.91MM
SALES (corp-wide): 55.91MM **Privately Held**
Web: www.compexlegal.com
SIC: 8111 7338 7334 Specialized legal services; Secretarial and court reporting; Photocopying and duplicating services

(P-18839)

COOKSEY TLEN GAGE DFFY WOOG A (PA)

535 Anton Blvd Fl 10 (92626-1912)
PHONE...................714 431-1100
David Cooksey, *Pr*
Robert L Toolen, *VP*
EMP: 91 **EST:** 1970
SALES (est): 9.85MM
SALES (corp-wide): 9.85MM **Privately Held**
Web: www.cookseylaw.com
SIC: 8111 General practice attorney, lawyer

(P-18840)

COUNTY OF LOS ANGELES

Also Called: District Attorney
210 W Temple St Fl 18 (90012-3229)
PHONE...................213 974-3512
Jackie Lazey, *Mgr*
EMP: 114
SIC: 8111 9222 General practice attorney, lawyer; District attorneys' office
PA: County Of Los Angeles
500 W Temple St Ste 437
Los Angeles CA
213 974-1101

(P-18841)

COUNTY OF RIVERSIDE

Also Called: Public Defender- Main Office
4075 Main St (92501-3701)
PHONE...................951 955-6000
Gary Windom, *Admn*
EMP: 200
SALES (corp-wide): 4.58B **Privately Held**
Web: www.countyofriverside.us
SIC: 8111 9222 Legal services; Public defenders' office
PA: County Of Riverside
4080 Lemon St Fl 11
Riverside CA
951 955-1110

(P-18842)

COUNTY OF SAN DIEGO

District Attorney
330 W Broadway Ste 1020 (92101-3827)
PHONE...................619 531-4040
Steven Silva, *Sec*
EMP: 101
Web: www.sdcda.org
SIC: 8111 9222 Specialized legal services; District attorneys' office
PA: County Of San Diego
1600 Pacific Hwy Ste 209
San Diego CA
619 531-5880

(P-18843)

COVINGTON & BURLING LLP

1999 Avenue Of The Stars Ste 3500 (90067-4643)
PHONE...................424 332-4800
Michelle Liffman, *Brnch Mgr*
EMP: 102
SALES (corp-wide): 422.72MM **Privately Held**
Web: www.cov.com
SIC: 8111 General practice law office
PA: Covington & Burling Llp
1 City Ctr 850 10th St Nw
Washington DC
202 662-6000

(P-18844)

COX CASTLE & NICHOLSON LLP (PA)

Also Called: Cox Castle
2029 Century Park E Ste 2100 (90002-3076)
PHONE...................310 284-2200
Gary A Glick, *Pt*
Edward F Quigley, *Pt*
David W Wensley, *Pt*
Mathew A Wyman, *Pt*
Marlene Goodfried, *Pt*
EMP: 165 **EST:** 1968
SQ FT: 60,000
SALES (est): 41.42MM
SALES (corp-wide): 41.42MM **Privately Held**
Web: www.coxcastle.com

SIC: 8111 General practice attorney, lawyer

(P-18845)

CROWELL & MORING LLP

3 Park Plz Ste 2000 (92614-2591)
PHONE...................949 263-8400
Daniel Sasse, *Mgr*
EMP: 120
SALES (corp-wide): 400MM **Privately Held**
Web: www.crowell.com
SIC: 8111 Specialized law offices, attorneys
PA: Crowell & Moring Llp
1001 Pennsylvania Ave Nw # 10
Washington DC
202 624-2500

(P-18846)

CROWELL & MORING LLP

515 S Flower St Ste 4000 (90071-2258)
PHONE...................213 622-4750
Mark Neighbor, *Brnch Mgr*
EMP: 113
SALES (corp-wide): 400MM **Privately Held**
Web: www.crowell.com
SIC: 8111 Specialized law offices, attorneys
PA: Crowell & Moring Llp
1001 Pennsylvania Ave Nw # 10
Washington DC
202 624-2500

(P-18847)

DAVIS WRIGHT TREMAINE LLP

865 S Figueroa St Ste 2400 (90017-2566)
PHONE...................213 633-6800
Mary Haas, *Pt*
EMP: 114
SALES (corp-wide): 238.76MM **Privately Held**
Web: www.dwt.com
SIC: 8111 General practice attorney, lawyer
PA: Davis Wright Tremaine Llp
920 5th Ave Ste 3300
Seattle WA
206 622-3150

(P-18848)

DENTONS US LLP

Also Called: A Dentons Innovation Wirthlin
601 S Figueroa St Ste 2500 (90017-5704)
PHONE...................213 623-9300
Edwin Reeser, *Genl Mgr*
EMP: 150
SALES (corp-wide): 473.25MM **Privately Held**
Web: www.dentons.com
SIC: 8111 Specialized law offices, attorneys
PA: Dentons Us Llp
233 S Wacker Dr Ste 5900
Chicago IL
312 876-8000

(P-18849)

DLA PIPER LLP (US)

2000 Avenue Of The Stars Ste 400n (90067-4735)
PHONE...................310 595-3000
Ronnie Decesare, *Brnch Mgr*
EMP: 102
Web: www.dlapiper.com
SIC: 8111 Corporate, partnership and business law
HQ: Dla Piper Llp (Us)
650 S Exeter St
Baltimore MD
410 580-3000

(P-18850)

DOMINGUEZ LAW GROUP PC

Also Called: Law Offices Juan J. Dominguez
3250 Wilshire Blvd Ste 1750 (90010-1613)
PHONE...................213 388-7788
Juan J Dominguez, *Pr*
EMP: 100 **EST:** 1988
SQ FT: 5,000
SALES (est): 12.3MM **Privately Held**
Web: www.dominguezfirm.com
SIC: 8111 General practice attorney, lawyer

(P-18851)

ELKINS KALT WNTRAUB RBEN GRTSI

10345 W Olympic Blvd (90064-2524)
PHONE...................310 746-4431
EMP: 81 **EST:** 2019
SALES (est): 4.42MM **Privately Held**
Web: www.elkinskalt.com
SIC: 8111 General practice attorney, lawyer

(P-18852)

ELLIS GRGE CPLLONE OBRIEN ANNG

2121 Avenue Of The Stars Fl 30 (90067-5010)
PHONE...................310 274-7100
Eric George, *Mng Pt*
Allen Browne, *Pt*
Peter Ross, *Pt*
EMP: 100 **EST:** 1985
SALES (est): 10.95MM **Privately Held**
Web: www.egcfirm.com
SIC: 8111 General practice law office

(P-18853)

EPSTEIN BECKER & GREEN PC

1875 Century Park E Ste 500 (90067-2253)
PHONE...................310 556-8861
Sandy Siciliano, *Mgr*
EMP: 202
SALES (corp-wide): 99.62MM **Privately Held**
Web: www.ebglaw.com
SIC: 8111 General practice attorney, lawyer
PA: Epstein Becker & Green, P.C.
875 3rd Ave Fl 19
New York NY
212 351-4500

(P-18854)

FISH & RICHARDSON PC

12390 El Camino Real (92130-3162)
PHONE...................858 678-5070
EMP: 153
SALES (corp-wide): 132.63MM **Privately Held**
Web: www.fr.com
SIC: 8111 General practice law office
PA: Fish & Richardson P.C.
1 Marina Park Dr Ste 1700
Boston MA
617 542-5070

(P-18855)

FISHER & PHILLIPS LLP

2050 Main St Ste 1000 (92614-8240)
PHONE...................949 851-2424
James Mcdonald, *Pt*
EMP: 102
SALES (corp-wide): 171.23MM **Privately Held**
Web: www.fisherphillips.com
SIC: 8111 General practice attorney, lawyer
PA: Fisher & Phillips Llp
1230 Peachtree St Ne # 3300
Atlanta GA
404 231-1400

(P-18856)
FULWIDER AND PATTON LLP
111 W Ocean Blvd Ste 1510 (90802-4622)
PHONE....................310 824-5555
Richard A Bardin, *Mng Pt*
Katherine Mcdaniel, *Pt*
David Pitman, *
Scott Hansen, *
EMP: 100 **EST:** 1938
SALES (est): 13.61MM **Privately Held**
Web: www.fulpat.com
SIC: 8111 General practice law office

(P-18857)
GIBSON DUNN & CRUTCHER INC
333 S Grand Ave (90071-3197)
PHONE....................213 229-7000
Kenneth M Doran, *Pr*
EMP: 201 **EST:** 1969
SALES (est): 207.81K
SALES (corp-wide): 1.97MM **Privately Held**
Web: www.gibsondunn.com
SIC: 8111 General practice law office
PA: Gibson, Dunn & Crutcher Llp
333 S Grand Ave Ste 4600
Los Angeles CA
213 229-7000

(P-18858)
GIBSON DUNN & CRUTCHER LLP (PA)
333 S Grand Ave Ste 4600 (90071-1512)
PHONE....................213 229-7000
Kenneth M Doran, *Prin*
Dan Mummery, *Prin*
M Sean Royall, *Prin*
Frederick Brown, *Prin*
Theodore B Olson, *Prin*
EMP: 500 **EST:** 1880
SQ FT: 250,000
SALES (est): 1.97MM
SALES (corp-wide): 1.97MM **Privately Held**
Web: www.gibsondunn.com
SIC: 8111 General practice law office

(P-18859)
GIBSON DUNN & CRUTCHER LLP
2029 Century Park E Ste 4000 (90002-3076)
PHONE....................310 552-8500
Julie Denton, *Genl Mgr*
EMP: 95
SALES (corp-wide): 1.97MM **Privately Held**
Web: www.gibsondunn.com
SIC: 8111 General practice law office
PA: Gibson, Dunn & Crutcher Llp
333 S Grand Ave Ste 4600
Los Angeles CA
213 229-7000

(P-18860)
GIBSON DUNN & CRUTCHER LLP
3161 Michelson Dr Ste 1200 (92612-4400)
PHONE....................949 451-3800
Karen Kubani, *Brnch Mgr*
EMP: 93
SALES (corp-wide): 1.97MM **Privately Held**
Web: www.gibsondunn.com
SIC: 8111 General practice law office
PA: Gibson, Dunn & Crutcher Llp
333 S Grand Ave Ste 4600
Los Angeles CA
213 229-7000

(P-18861)
GIRARDI KEESE (PA)
1126 Wilshire Blvd (90017-1904)
PHONE....................213 977-0211
Thomas V Girardi, *Pt*
Robert M Keese, *Pt*
EMP: 95 **EST:** 1976
SQ FT: 5,000
SALES (est): 9.67MM
SALES (corp-wide): 9.67MM **Privately Held**
Web: www.girardikeese.com
SIC: 8111 General practice law office

(P-18862)
GLASER WEIL FINK JACOBS (PA)
10250 Constellation Blvd Fl 19 (90067-6229)
PHONE....................310 553-3000
Terry Christensen, *Mng Pt*
Barry E Fink, *
Patricia L Glaser, *
Peter Weil, *
Allen Gilbert, *
EMP: 160 **EST:** 1988
SQ FT: 76,000
SALES (est): 34.42MM
SALES (corp-wide): 34.42MM **Privately Held**
Web: www.glaserweil.com
SIC: 8111 General practice law office

(P-18863)
GORDON REES SCULLY MANSUKHANI
633 W 5th St 52nd Fl (90071-2005)
PHONE....................213 576-5000
Scott Sirlin, *Brnch Mgr*
EMP: 106
SALES (corp-wide): 271.79MM **Privately Held**
Web: www.grsm.com
SIC: 8111 Specialized law offices, attorneys
PA: Gordon Rees Scully Mansukhani, Llp.
275 Battery St Ste 2000
San Francisco CA
415 986-5900

(P-18864)
GORDON REES SCULLY MANSUKHANI
101 W Broadway Ste 1600 (92101-8217)
PHONE....................619 696-6700
Gary Zacher, *Mng Pt*
EMP: 141
SQ FT: 7,000
SALES (corp-wide): 271.79MM **Privately Held**
Web: www.grsm.com
SIC: 8111 Specialized law offices, attorneys
PA: Gordon Rees Scully Mansukhani, Llp.
275 Battery St Ste 2000
San Francisco CA
415 986-5900

(P-18865)
GREENBERG GLSKER FLDS CLMAN MC
2049 Century Park E Ste 2600 (90067-3101)
PHONE....................310 553-3610
Jonathan R Fitzgarrald, *Prin*
Arthur N Greenberg, *Pt*
Stephen Claman, *Pt*
Bert Fields, *Pt*
Ricardo P Cestero, *Pt*
EMP: 200 **EST:** 1959
SQ FT: 80,000

SALES (est): 26.18MM **Privately Held**
Web: www.greenbergglusker.com
SIC: 8111 General practice attorney, lawyer

(P-18866)
GREENBERG TRAURIG LLP
Also Called: Greenberg Traurig
18565 Jamboree Rd Ste 500 (92612-2562)
PHONE....................949 732-6500
Ray Lee, *Mng Pt*
EMP: 96
SALES (corp-wide): 495.87MM **Privately Held**
Web: www.gtlaw.com
SIC: 8111 General practice attorney, lawyer
HQ: Greenberg Traurig, Llp
1 Intl Pl Ste 2000
Boston MA

(P-18867)
HAIGHT BROWN & BONESTEEL LLP (PA)
Also Called: Haight
555 S Flower St Ste 4500 (90071)
PHONE....................213 542-8000
S Christian Stouder, *Mng Pt*
Carolyn Harper, *CFO*
EMP: 80 **EST:** 1980
SQ FT: 36,265
SALES (est): 22.77MM
SALES (corp-wide): 22.77MM **Privately Held**
Web: www.hbblaw.com
SIC: 8111 General practice law office

(P-18868)
HIGGS FLETCHER & MACK LLP
Also Called: Goproto
401 W A St Ste 2600 (92101-3524)
PHONE....................619 236-1551
John Morrell, *Genl Pt*
Anna F Roppo, *Pt*
Phillip C Samouis, *Pt*
EMP: 150 **EST:** 1939
SQ FT: 45,000
SALES (est): 25.77MM **Privately Held**
Web: www.higgslaw.com
SIC: 8111 General practice attorney, lawyer

(P-18869)
HILL FARRER & BURRILL
Also Called: One California Plaza
300 S Grand Ave Fl 37 (90071-3147)
PHONE....................213 620-0460
Scott Gilmore, *Pt*
Jack R White, *Pt*
Kyle D Brown, *Pt*
William M Bitting, *Pt*
Stanley E Tobin, *Pt*
EMP: 100 **EST:** 1923
SQ FT: 32,000
SALES (est): 13.7MM **Privately Held**
Web: www.hillfarrer.com
SIC: 8111 General practice law office

(P-18870)
HOLLAND & KNIGHT LLP
400 S Hope St Ste 800 (90071-2809)
PHONE....................213 896-2400
Maita Prout, *Mgr*
EMP: 97
SALES (corp-wide): 430.83MM **Privately Held**
Web: foundation.hklaw.com
SIC: 8111 General practice attorney, lawyer
PA: Holland & Knight Llp
524 Grand Regency Blvd
Brandon FL
813 901-4200

(P-18871)
HUESTON HENNIGAN LLP
523 W 6th St Ste 400 (90014-1208)
PHONE....................213 788-4340
Marshall A Camp, *Pt*
Douglas J Dixon, *Pt*
Alexander C D Giza, *Pt*
Brian J Hennigan, *Pt*
John C Hueston, *Pt*
EMP: 80 **EST:** 2015
SQ FT: 25,000
SALES (est): 10.7MM **Privately Held**
Web: www.hueston.com
SIC: 8111 General practice attorney, lawyer

(P-18872)
IMHOFF & ASSOCIATES PC
Also Called: Miller and Associates
12424 Wilshire Blvd Ste 770 (90025-1065)
PHONE....................310 691-2200
Jim Stefanucci, *Mgr*
EMP: 100 **EST:** 2001
SALES (est): 10.95MM **Privately Held**
Web: www.criminalattorney.com
SIC: 8111 General practice law office

(P-18873)
IMMIGRANT DEFENDERS LAW CENTER
Also Called: IMMDEF
634 S Spring St Fl 10 (90014-3912)
PHONE....................213 634-0999
Lindsay Toczylowski, *Ex Dir*
Susan Alva, *
EMP: 85 **EST:** 2015
SALES (est): 12.13MM **Privately Held**
Web: www.immdef.org
SIC: 8111 Legal services

(P-18874)
IRELL & MANELLA LLP
840 Newport Center Dr Ste 400 (92660)
PHONE....................949 760-0991
Nancy Adams, *Mgr*
EMP: 365
SALES (corp-wide): 49.86MM **Privately Held**
Web: www.irell.com
SIC: 8111 General practice attorney, lawyer
PA: Irell & Manella Llp
1800 Avenue Of The Stars # 900
Los Angeles CA
310 277-1010

(P-18875)
IRELL & MANELLA LLP (PA)
1800 Avenue Of The Stars Ste 900 (90067-4276)
PHONE....................310 277-1010
Keith Orso, *Pt*
Ben Hattenbach, *Pt*
Lisa Glasser, *Pt*
Matt Ashley, *Ofcr*
Thomas Edwards, *Ex Dir*
EMP: 185 **EST:** 1941
SQ FT: 154,000
SALES (est): 49.86MM
SALES (corp-wide): 49.86MM **Privately Held**
Web: www.irell.com
SIC: 8111 General practice law office

(P-18876)
JACKOWAY TYRMAN WRTHMER ASTEN
1925 Century Park E 2nd Fl (90067-2701)
PHONE....................310 553-0305
Barry Hirsch, *Pr*
EMP: 100 **EST:** 1976

SQ FT: 3,000
SALES (est): 9.25MM **Privately Held**
Web: www.jtwamm.com
SIC: 8111 General practice law office

(P-18877)
JACOBY & MEYERS ATTYS LLP
10900 Wilshire Blvd Ste 930 (90024-6501)
PHONE..............................310 312-3300
Mirtha Lopez, *Prin*
EMP: 87 **EST:** 2019
SALES (est): 2.08MM **Privately Held**
Web: www.jacobymeyers.com
SIC: 8111 General practice attorney, lawyer

(P-18878)
JEFFER MNGELS BTLR MTCHELL LLP (PA)
Also Called: Jmbm
1900 Avenue Of The Stars Fl 7
(90067-4301)
PHONE..............................310 203-8080
Bruce P Jeffer, *Managing Member*
Bruce P Jeffer, *Mng Pt*
Robert E Mangels, *Pt*
James R Butler Junior, *Pt*
Mark Marmaro, *Pt*
▲ **EMP:** 190 **EST:** 1981
SALES (est): 46.29MM
SALES (corp-wide): 46.29MM **Privately Held**
Web: www.jmbm.com
SIC: 8111 General practice attorney, lawyer

(P-18879)
JONES DAY LIMITED PARTNERSHIP
Also Called: Jones Day
555 S Flower St Fl 50 (90071-2452)
PHONE..............................213 489-3939
Brian A Sun, *Pt*
EMP: 106
SALES (corp-wide): 414.45MM **Privately Held**
Web: www.jonesday.com
SIC: 8111 7389 General practice attorney, lawyer; Personal service agents, brokers, and bureaus
PA: Jones Day Limited Partnership
N Point 901 Lakeside Ave
Cleveland OH
216 586-3939

(P-18880)
K&L GATES LLP
10100 Santa Monica Blvd Ste 700
(90067-4104)
PHONE..............................310 552-5000
Karen Doyle, *Mgr*
EMP: 81
SALES (corp-wide): 1.18B **Privately Held**
Web: www.klgates.com
SIC: 8111 General practice law office
PA: K&L Gates Llp
210 6th Ave Ste 1100
Pittsburgh PA
412 355-6500

(P-18881)
KEESAL YOUNG LOGAN A PROF CORP (PA)
400 Oceangate (90802-4325)
PHONE..............................562 436-2000
Samuel A Keesal Junior, *CEO*
J Stephen Young, *
EMP: 90 **EST:** 1970
SQ FT: 65,000
SALES (est): 10.57K
SALES (corp-wide): 10.57K **Privately Held**

Web: www.kyl.com
SIC: 8111 General practice law office

(P-18882)
KIRKLAND & ELLIS LLP
2049 Century Park E Ste 3700
(90067-3101)
PHONE..............................310 552-4200
EMP: 100
SALES (corp-wide): 504.86MM **Privately Held**
Web: www.kirkland.com
SIC: 8111 General practice attorney, lawyer
PA: Kirkland & Ellis Llp
300 N La Salle Dr # 2400
Chicago IL
312 862-2000

(P-18883)
KIRKLAND & ELLIS LLP
555 S Flower St Ste 3700 (90071-2432)
PHONE..............................213 680-8400
EMP: 175
SALES (corp-wide): 504.86MM **Privately Held**
Web: www.kirkland.com
SIC: 8111 General practice attorney, lawyer
PA: Kirkland & Ellis Llp
300 N La Salle Dr # 2400
Chicago IL
312 862-2000

(P-18884)
KIRKLAND & ELLIS LLP
333 S Hope St Ste 3000 (90071-3039)
PHONE..............................213 680-8400
Cynthia Barnes, *Off Mgr*
EMP: 500
SALES (corp-wide): 504.86MM **Privately Held**
Web: www.kirkland.com
SIC: 8111 General practice law office
PA: Kirkland & Ellis Llp
300 N La Salle Dr # 2400
Chicago IL
312 862-2000

(P-18885)
KNIGHT LAW GROUP LLP
10250 Constellation Blvd Ste 2500
(90067-6225)
P.O. Box 512906 (90051-0906)
PHONE..............................424 355-1155
EMP: 83 **EST:** 2018
SALES (est): 10.07MM **Privately Held**
Web: www.lemonlawhelp.com
SIC: 8111 General practice law office

(P-18886)
KNOBBE MARTENS OLSON BEAR LLP (PA)
2040 Main St Fl 14 (92614-8214)
PHONE..............................949 760-0404
Steven J Nataupsky, *Mng Pt*
Steven Nataupsky, *
James B Bear, *
William B Bunker, *
William H Nieman, *
EMP: 350 **EST:** 1962
SQ FT: 120,000
SALES (est): 66.71MM
SALES (corp-wide): 66.71MM **Privately Held**
Web: www.knobbe.com
SIC: 8111 General practice law office

(P-18887)
LA FOLETTE JOHNSON DEHASS SESL

865 S Figueroa St # 3200 (90017-2507)
PHONE..............................213 426-3600
Eva Cohen, *Dir Fin*
EMP: 88 **EST:** 2010
SALES (est): 2.82MM **Privately Held**
SIC: 8111 General practice attorney, lawyer

(P-18888)
LA FOLLTTE JHNSON DE HAAS FSLE (PA)
701 N Brand Blvd Ste 600 (91203-1213)
PHONE..............................213 426-3600
Daren T Johnson, *Pr*
Louis De Haas Junior, *VP*
Don Fesler, *
Brian Birnie, *
Alfred Gerisch Junior, *Treas*
EMP: 105 **EST:** 1953
SALES (est): 17.99MM
SALES (corp-wide): 17.99MM **Privately Held**
Web: www.ljdfa.com
SIC: 8111 General practice law office

(P-18889)
LATHAM & WATKINS LLP
555 W 5th St Ste 300 (90013-1020)
PHONE..............................213 891-7108
EMP: 265
SALES (corp-wide): 486.91MM **Privately Held**
Web: rg-www-prod-cd.azurewebsites.net
SIC: 8111 General practice attorney, lawyer
PA: Latham & Watkins Llp
555 W 5th St Ste 300
Los Angeles CA
213 485-1234

(P-18890)
LATHAM & WATKINS LLP
650 Town Center Dr Ste 2000
(92626-7135)
PHONE..............................714 540-1235
Shayne Kennedy, *Mng Pt*
EMP: 316
SALES (corp-wide): 486.91MM **Privately Held**
Web: rg-www-prod-cd.azurewebsites.net
SIC: 8111 General practice attorney, lawyer
PA: Latham & Watkins Llp
555 W 5th St Ste 300
Los Angeles CA
213 485-1234

(P-18891)
LATHAM & WATKINS LLP (PA)
555 W 5th St Ste 300 (90013-1020)
PHONE..............................213 485-1234
David Gordon, *Pt*
John Clair, *Pt*
Allen Wang, *Pt*
Philip Rossetti, *Pt*
Jean Paul Poitras, *Pt*
EMP: 570 **EST:** 1934
SALES (est): 486.91MM
SALES (corp-wide): 486.91MM **Privately Held**
Web: rg-www-prod-cd.azurewebsites.net
SIC: 8111 General practice attorney, lawyer

(P-18892)
LATHAM & WATKINS LLP
12670 High Bluff Dr Ste 100 (92130-3086)
PHONE..............................858 523-5400
Bruce Shepard, *Pt*
EMP: 334
SALES (corp-wide): 486.91MM **Privately Held**
Web: rg-www-prod-cd.azurewebsites.net

SIC: 8111 General practice attorney, lawyer
PA: Latham & Watkins Llp
555 W 5th St Ste 300
Los Angeles CA
213 485-1234

(P-18893)
LAW OFFCES LES ZEVE A PROF COR
30 Corporate Park Ste 450 (92606-3401)
PHONE..............................714 848-7920
Les Zieve, *Prin*
Mark Kayton, *
EMP: 105 **EST:** 1991
SQ FT: 1,000
SALES (est): 10.52MM **Privately Held**
SIC: 8111 General practice attorney, lawyer

(P-18894)
LEGAL SOLUTIONS HOLDINGS INC
Also Called: Getmedlegal
955 Overland Ct Ste 200 (91773-1747)
PHONE..............................800 244-3495
Greg Webber, *CEO*
Kenneth Gleockler, *
Keahi Kakugawa, *
Harren Investors Ii Lp, *Prin*
Harren Investors Ii-b Lp, *Prin*
EMP: 237 **EST:** 1986
SALES (est): 9.35MM **Privately Held**
SIC: 8111 Legal services

(P-18895)
LEWIS BRSBOIS BSGARD SMITH LLP
650 Town Center Dr Ste 1400
(92626-1989)
PHONE..............................714 545-9200
Shawn Derfer, *Mgr*
EMP: 109
SALES (corp-wide): 284.92MM **Privately Held**
Web: www.lewisbrisbois.com
SIC: 8111 General practice law office
PA: Lewis Brisbois Bisgaard & Smith Llp
633 W 5th St Ste 4000
Los Angeles CA
213 250-1800

(P-18896)
LEWIS BRSBOIS BSGARD SMITH LLP (PA)
633 W 5th St Ste 4000 (90071-2074)
PHONE..............................213 250-1800
Robert F Lewis, *Mng Pt*
Roy M Brisbois, *Pt*
Christopher P Bisgaard, *Pt*
EMP: 650 **EST:** 1979
SQ FT: 80,000
SALES (est): 284.92MM
SALES (corp-wide): 284.92MM **Privately Held**
Web: www.lewisbrisbois.com
SIC: 8111 General practice law office

(P-18897)
LEWIS BRSBOIS BSGARD SMITH LLP
701 B St Ste 1900 (92101-8198)
PHONE..............................619 233-1006
Susan O' Brien, *Mgr*
EMP: 163
SALES (corp-wide): 284.92MM **Privately Held**
Web: www.lewisbrisbois.com
SIC: 8111 General practice law office
PA: Lewis Brisbois Bisgaard & Smith Llp
633 W 5th St Ste 4000

Los Angeles CA
213 250-1800

(P-18898)
LINER LLP
Also Called: Liner Law
1100 Glendon Ave 14th (90024-3503)
PHONE.....................310 500-3500
Stuart A Liner, *Mng Pt*
EMP: 104 **EST:** 1996
SQ FT: 21,000
SALES (est): 23.43MM **Privately Held**
Web: www.linerlawgroup.com
SIC: 8111 General practice law office
HQ: Dla Piper Llp (Us)
650 S Exeter St
Baltimore MD
410 580-3000

(P-18899)
LLC BATES WHITE
322 8th St (92014-2807)
PHONE.....................858 523-2150
Dorris Ballentine, *Brnch Mgr*
EMP: 130
SALES (corp-wide): 44.11MM **Privately Held**
Web: www.bateswhite.com
SIC: 8111 General practice attorney, lawyer
PA: Bates White, Llc
2001 K St Nw Bldg Ste 5
Washington DC
202 747-1436

(P-18900)
LLP MAYER BROWN
Also Called: Mayer Brown & Platt
350 S Grand Ave Ste 2500 (90071-3486)
PHONE.....................213 229-9500
Jim Tancula, *Mgr*
EMP: 430
SALES (corp-wide): 456.54MM **Privately Held**
SIC: 8111 General practice attorney, lawyer
PA: Mayer Brown Llp
71 S Wacker Dr Ste 3300
Chicago IL
312 782-0600

(P-18901)
LOEB & LOEB LLP (PA)
Also Called: Loeb & Loeb
10100 Santa Monica Blvd Ste 2200
(90067-4120)
PHONE.....................310 282-2000
Barry I Slotnick, *Ch*
Jerry Post, *Chief*
Kenneth B Anderson, *Pt*
Stan Johnson, *Ch*
Robert A Meyer, *Ch*
EMP: 134 **EST:** 1909
SALES (est): 66.83MM
SALES (corp-wide): 66.83MM **Privately Held**
Web: www.loeb.com
SIC: 8111 General practice attorney, lawyer

(P-18902)
MALCOLM & CISNEROS A LAW CORP
Also Called: Malcolm Cisneros
2112 Business Center Dr Ste 100
(92612-7137)
PHONE.....................949 252-9400
William Malcolm, *CEO*
Arturo Cisneros, *
EMP: 110 **EST:** 1992
SALES (est): 12.31MM **Privately Held**
Web: www.malcolmcisneros.com

SIC: 8111 General practice law office

(P-18903)
MANATT PHELPS & PHILLIPS LLP (PA)
2049 Century Park E Ste 1700
(90067-3101)
PHONE.....................310 312-4000
EMP: 420 **EST:** 1965
SALES (est): 137.56MM
SALES (corp-wide): 137.56MM **Privately Held**
Web: www.manatt.com
SIC: 8111 General practice law office

(P-18904)
MANNING KASS ELLROD RMREZ TRST (PA)
801 S Figueroa St 15th Fl (90017-5504)
PHONE.....................213 624-6900
Steven D Manning, *Mng Pt*
EMP: 150 **EST:** 1994
SALES (est): 33.97MM **Privately Held**
Web: www.manningkass.com
SIC: 8111 General practice attorney, lawyer

(P-18905)
MED-LEGAL LLC
955 Overland Ct Ste 200 (91773-1747)
PHONE.....................626 653-5160
Moonesh Arora, *CEO*
Michael Salzano, *
Kenneth E Gleockler, *
EMP: 150 **EST:** 2010
SALES (est): 9.6MM **Privately Held**
SIC: 8111 Legal aid service

(P-18906)
MICHAEL SULLIVAN & ASSOC LLP
2401 E El Segundo Blvd (90245-4655)
P.O. Box 85059 (92186-5059)
PHONE.....................310 337-4480
Michael W Sullivan, *Pt*
EMP: 147 **EST:** 2012
SALES (est): 11.05MM **Privately Held**
Web: www.sullivanattorneys.com
SIC: 8111 General practice attorney, lawyer

(P-18907)
MILBANK TWEED HDLEY MCCLOY LLP
Also Called: Milbank Global Securities
2029 Century Park E (90002-3076)
PHONE.....................424 386-4000
David C Frauman, *Dir*
EMP: 120
SQ FT: 40,000
SALES (corp-wide): 133.63MM **Privately Held**
Web: www.milbank.com
SIC: 8111 Corporate, partnership and business law
PA: Milbank Llp
55 Hudson Yards
New York NY
212 530-5000

(P-18908)
MINTZ LEVIN COHN FERRIS GL
3580 Carmel Mountain Rd Ste 300
(92130-6768)
PHONE.....................858 314-1500
EMP: 100
SALES (corp-wide): 199.9MM **Privately Held**
Web: www.mintz.com

SIC: 8111 General practice law office
PA: Mintz, Levin, Cohn, Ferris, Glovsky
And Popeo, P.C.
1 Financial Ctr
Boston MA
617 348-4951

(P-18909)
MITCHELL SILBERBERG KNUPP LLP (PA)
Also Called: Mitchell Slbrberg Knupp Fndtio
2049 Century Park E Fl 18 (90067-3120)
PHONE.....................310 312-2000
Jeffrey K Eisen, *Prin*
Thomas P Lambert, *Mng Pt*
Kevin E Gaut, *COO*
Jerry Kaufman, *Ex Dir*
EMP: 198 **EST:** 1908
SALES (est): 38.88MM
SALES (corp-wide): 38.88MM **Privately Held**
Web: www.msk.com
SIC: 8111 General practice law office

(P-18910)
MORRIS POLICH & PURDY LLP (PA)
1055 W 7th St Ste 2400 (90017-2550)
PHONE.....................213 891-9100
Theodore D Levin, *Pt*
Douglas C Purdy, *Pt*
Walter Lipsman, *Pt*
Jeff Barron, *Pt*
James Chantland, *Pt*
EMP: 100 **EST:** 1969
SQ FT: 40,000
SALES (est): 18.97MM
SALES (corp-wide): 18.97MM **Privately Held**
Web: www.mpplaw.com
SIC: 8111 General practice attorney, lawyer

(P-18911)
MORRISON & FOERSTER LLP
Also Called: Morrison & Foerster
707 Wilshire Blvd Ste 6000 (90017-3501)
PHONE.....................213 892-5200
Gregory Koltun, *Mng Pt*
EMP: 250
SALES (corp-wide): 392.26MM **Privately Held**
Web: www.mofo.com
SIC: 8111 General practice attorney, lawyer
PA: Morrison & Foerster Llp
425 Market St Fl 32
San Francisco CA
415 268-7000

(P-18912)
MORRISON & FOERSTER LLP
12531 High Bluff Dr Ste 100 (92130-3014)
PHONE.....................858 720-5100
Mark Zebrowski, *Mng Pt*
EMP: 421
SALES (corp-wide): 392.26MM **Privately Held**
Web: www.mofo.com
SIC: 8111 General practice attorney, lawyer
PA: Morrison & Foerster Llp
425 Market St Fl 32
San Francisco CA
415 268-7000

(P-18913)
MUNGER TOLLES & OLSON LLP
350 S Grand Ave Fl 50 (90071-3426)
PHONE.....................213 683-9100
Sandra Seville-jones Mng Ptrn, *Prin*
EMP: 482 **EST:** 2001
SALES (est): 28.97MM **Privately Held**

Web: www.mto.com
SIC: 8111 Corporate, partnership and business law

(P-18914)
MUNGER TOLLES OLSON FOUNDATION (PA)
350 S Grand Ave Fl 50 (90071-3426)
PHONE.....................213 683-9100
O'malley M Miller, *CEO*
Robert Johnson, *
Bart Williams, *
Mark Helm, *
Steven B Weisburd, *
EMP: 420 **EST:** 1962
SQ FT: 100,000
SALES (est): 2.18MM
SALES (corp-wide): 2.18MM **Privately Held**
Web: www.mto.com
SIC: 8111 General practice attorney, lawyer

(P-18915)
MURCHISON & CUMMING LLP (PA)
Also Called: M & C
801 S Grand Ave Ste 900 (90017-4624)
PHONE.....................213 623-7400
Friedrich W Seitz, *Pt*
Michael D Mc Evoy, *Sr Pt*
Michael Lawler, *Sr Pt*
Steven L Smilay, *Sr Pt*
Kenneth Moreno, *Sr Pt*
EMP: 100 **EST:** 1952
SQ FT: 30,000
SALES (est): 26.77MM
SALES (corp-wide): 26.77MM **Privately Held**
Web: www.murchisonlaw.com
SIC: 8111 General practice law office

(P-18916)
MUSICK PEELER & GARRETT LLP (PA)
624 S Grand Ave Ste 2000 (90023-1629)
PHONE.....................213 629-7600
R Joseph De Briyn, *Mng Pt*
Wayne Littlefied, *Pt*
Gary Overstreet, *Pt*
Edward Landrey, *Pt*
Peter J Diedrich, *Pt*
EMP: 168 **EST:** 1937
SQ FT: 100,000
SALES (est): 21.28MM
SALES (corp-wide): 21.28MM **Privately Held**
Web: www.musickpeeler.com
SIC: 8111 General practice law office

(P-18917)
NATIONAL ATTNY COLLECTION SVCS
700 N Brand Blvd Fl 2 (91203-1247)
PHONE.....................818 547-9760
A Donovan, *CEO*
John Weinstein, *
EMP: 251 **EST:** 2005
SALES (est): 9.29MM **Privately Held**
SIC: 8111 Debt collection law

(P-18918)
NEWMEYER & DILLION LLP (PA)
895 Dove St Ste 500 (92660-2999)
PHONE.....................949 854-7000
Gregory L Dillion, *Pt*
Thomas F Newmeyer, *Pt*
John A O Hara, *Pt*
Michael S Cucchissi, *Pt*
Joseph A Ferrentino, *Pt*

PRODUCTS & SVCS

EMP: 115 **EST:** 1984
SQ FT: 52,000
SALES (est): 26.3MM **Privately Held**
Web: www.newmeyeranddillion.com
SIC: 8111 General practice attorney, lawyer

(P-18919)
OMELVENY & MYERS LLP (PA)
400 S Hope St 18th Fl (90071-1904)
PHONE...................213 430-6000
Arthur Culvahouse Junior, *Mng Pt*
Arthur Culvahouse Junior, *Managing Member*
Bradley Butwin, *Managing Member**
Stephen Brody, *
Chuck Diamond, *
EMP: 850 **EST:** 1885
SQ FT: 250,000
SALES (est): 208.14MM
SALES (corp-wide): 208.14MM **Privately Held**
Web: www.omm.com
SIC: 8111 General practice law office

(P-18920)
PACHULSKI STANG ZEHL JONES LLP (PA)
Also Called: Pszyjw
10100 Santa Monica Blvd Ste 1100 (90067-4114)
PHONE...................310 277-6910
Richard M Pachulski, *Pr*
Dean A Ziehl, *
James I Stang, *
EMP: 90 **EST:** 1983
SQ FT: 21,000
SALES (est): 23.09MM **Privately Held**
Web: www.pszjlaw.com
SIC: 8111 General practice law office

(P-18921)
PALMIERI TYLER WNER WLHELM WLD
1900 Main St Ste 700 (92614-7328)
P.O. Box 19712 (92623-9712)
PHONE...................949 851-9400
James E Wilhelm, *Pt*
Dennis Tyler, *
Alan Wiener, *
Mike Greene, *
Robert Ihrke, *
EMP: 100 **EST:** 1986
SQ FT: 34,000
SALES (est): 15.38MM **Privately Held**
Web: www.ptwww.com
SIC: 8111 General practice attorney, lawyer

(P-18922)
PAUL HASTINGS LLP (PA)
515 S Flower St Fl 25 (90071-2228)
PHONE...................213 683-6000
Greg Nitzkowski, *Pt*
Seth M Zachary, *
Elena R Baca, *
EMP: 1884 **EST:** 2011
SQ FT: 209,000
SALES (est): 413.45MM
SALES (corp-wide): 413.45MM **Privately Held**
Web: www.paulhastings.com
SIC: 8111 General practice law office

(P-18923)
PAUL HASTINGS LLP
4747 Executive Dr Ste 1200 (92121-3114)
PHONE...................858 458-3000
Craig Price, *Admn*
EMP: 98
SALES (corp-wide): 413.45MM **Privately Held**

Web: www.paulhastings.com
SIC: 8111 General practice law office
PA: Paul Hastings Llp
515 S Flower St Fl 25
Los Angeles CA
213 683-6000

(P-18924)
PILLSBURY WNTHROP SHAW PTTMAN
Also Called: Pillsbury
725 S Figueroa St Ste 2800 (90017-5524)
PHONE...................213 488-7100
Melissa Burton, *Admn*
EMP: 128
SALES (corp-wide): 192.22MM **Privately Held**
Web: www.pillsburylaw.com
SIC: 8111 General practice law office
PA: Pillsbury Winthrop Shaw Pittman Llp
31 W 52nd St Fl 29
New York NY
212 858-1000

(P-18925)
PIRCHER NICHOLS & MEEKS (PA)
1925 Century Park E Ste 1700 (90067-2740)
PHONE...................310 201-0132
Gary Laughlin, *Sr Pt*
Leo Pircher, *Sr Pt*
Eugene Leone, *Sr Pt*
Stevens Carey, *Sr Pt*
EMP: 95 **EST:** 1983
SQ FT: 35,000
SALES (est): 17.16MM
SALES (corp-wide): 17.16MM **Privately Held**
Web: www.hklaw.com
SIC: 8111 General practice attorney, lawyer

(P-18926)
PRICE LAW GROUP A PROF CORP (PA)
Also Called: Plg Law Group
15760 Ventura Blvd Ste 800 (91436-3044)
PHONE...................818 995-4540
Stuart M Price, *Pr*
EMP: 115 **EST:** 1991
SQ FT: 15,000
SALES (est): 11.54MM **Privately Held**
Web: www.resolvelawgroup.com
SIC: 8111 General practice law office

(P-18927)
PRINDLE DECKER & AMARO LLP (PA)
310 Golden Shore Fl 4 (90802-4232)
P.O. Box 22711 (90801-5711)
PHONE...................562 436-3946
EMP: 85 **EST:** 1990
SALES (est): 8.45MM **Privately Held**
Web: www.pdalaw.com
SIC: 8111 Specialized law offices, attorneys

(P-18928)
PROCOPIO CORY HARGREAVES & SAVITCH LLP (PA)
530 B St Ste 2200 (92101-4435)
PHONE...................619 238-1900
EMP: 215 **EST:** 1946
SALES (est): 22.06MM
SALES (corp-wide): 22.06MM **Privately Held**
Web: www.procopio.com

(P-18929)
PUBLIC COUNSEL
610 S Ardmore Ave (90005-2322)
PHONE...................213 385-2977
Margaret Morrow, *Pr*
Madaline Kleiner, *
EMP: 94 **EST:** 1970
SQ FT: 12,000
SALES (est): 17.52MM **Privately Held**
Web: www.publiccounsel.org
SIC: 8111 Specialized law offices, attorneys

(P-18930)
QUINN EMNUEL URQHART SLLVAN LL (PA)
Also Called: Quinn Emmanuel Trial Lawyers
865 S Figueroa St Fl 10 (90017-5003)
PHONE...................213 443-3000
John B Quinn, *Pt*
Christopher Tayback, *Pt*
William Burck, *Co-Managing Partner*
Michael Carlinsky, *Co-Managing Partner*
EMP: 366 **EST:** 1986
SALES (est): 131MM
SALES (corp-wide): 131MM **Privately Held**
Web: www.quinnemanuel.com
SIC: 8111 Specialized law offices, attorneys

(P-18931)
REED SMITH LLP
355 S Grand Ave Ste 2900 (90071-1514)
PHONE...................213 457-8000
Peter Kennedy, *Office Managing Partner*
EMP: 158
SALES (corp-wide): 488.93MM **Privately Held**
Web: www.reedsmith.com
SIC: 8111 General practice attorney, lawyer
PA: Reed Smith Llp
225 5th Ave Ste 1200
Pittsburgh PA
412 288-3131

(P-18932)
RICHARDS WTSON GRSHON A PROF C (PA)
Also Called: RW&g
355 S Grand Ave 40th Fl (90071-1560)
PHONE...................213 626-8484
Laurence S Wiener, *CEO*
Kayser O Sume Cmb, *Prin*
James L Markman, *
Craig A Steele, *
William L Strausz, *
▲ **EMP:** 120 **EST:** 1954
SQ FT: 45,000
SALES (est): 17.44MM
SALES (corp-wide): 17.44MM **Privately Held**
Web: www.rwglaw.com
SIC: 8111 General practice law office

(P-18933)
ROBBINS GELLER RUDMAN DOWD LLP (PA)
655 W Broadway Ste 1900 (92101-8498)
PHONE...................619 231-1058
Michael J Dowd, *
Darren J Robbins, *
Paul J Geller, *
Samuel H Rudman, *
EMP: 300 **EST:** 2004
SQ FT: 135,000
SALES (est): 50.72MM
SALES (corp-wide): 50.72MM **Privately Held**

Web: www.rgrdlaw.com
SIC: 8111 Corporate, partnership and business law

(P-18934)
ROPERS MAJESKI A PROF CORP
445 S Figueroa St Ste 3000 (90071-1602)
PHONE...................213 312-2000
Allan Anderson, *Mgr*
EMP: 217
SALES (corp-wide): 5.2MM **Privately Held**
Web: www.ropers.com
SIC: 8111 General practice law office
PA: Ropers Majeski, A Professional Corporation
535 Middlefield Rd # 245
Menlo Park CA
650 364-8200

(P-18935)
RUSS AUGUST & KABAT LLP
12424 Wilshire Blvd Ste 1200 (90025-1031)
PHONE...................310 826-7474
Larry C Russ, *Prin*
Jules L Kabat, *
Laura K Stanton, *
Richard L August, *
Even Kent, *
EMP: 97 **EST:** 1981
SALES (est): 12.8MM **Privately Held**
Web: www.raklaw.com
SIC: 8111 General practice attorney, lawyer

(P-18936)
RUTAN & TUCKER LLP (PA)
18575 Jamboree Rd Ste 900 (92612-2526)
P.O. Box 1950 (92628-1950)
PHONE...................714 641-5100
Richard Boden, *Managing Member*
Paul F Marx, *Managing Member**
Jodi Brooks, *Managing Member**
Tony Malkani, *Managing Member**
EMP: 265 **EST:** 1935
SALES (est): 48.58MM
SALES (corp-wide): 48.58MM **Privately Held**
Web: www.rutan.com
SIC: 8111 General practice attorney, lawyer

(P-18937)
SAUL EWING ARNSTEIN & LEHR LLP
Also Called: Saul Ewing Arnstein & Lehr LLP
1888 Century Park E Fl 19 (90067-1702)
PHONE...................310 398-6100
EMP: 94
SALES (corp-wide): 120.22MM **Privately Held**
Web: www.saul.com
SIC: 8111 General practice law office
PA: Saul Ewing Llp
1500 Market St Fl 38
Philadelphia PA
215 972-7777

(P-18938)
SDCDA
2125 Park Blvd (92101-4753)
PHONE...................619 459-9632
EMP: 187 **EST:** 2013
SALES (est): 625.95K **Privately Held**
Web: www.sdcda.org
SIC: 8111 Legal services

(P-18939)
SELTZER CPLAN MCMHON VTEK A LA (PA)
750 B St Ste 2100 (92101-8177)

▲ = Import ▼ = Export
◆ = Import/Export

PHONE..................619 685-3003
Robert Caplan, *Pr*
Gerald L Mc Mahon, *
John H Alspaugh, *
Neal P Panish, *
EMP: 165 **EST:** 1970
SQ FT: 78,000
SALES (est): 15.68MM
SALES (corp-wide): 15.68MM **Privately
Held**
Web: www.scmv.com
SIC: 8111 General practice attorney, lawyer

(P-18940)
SEYFARTH SHAW LLP
2029 Century Park E Ste 3300
(90002-3076)
PHONE..................310 277-7200
Sandy Abrahamian, *Brnch Mgr*
EMP: 200
SALES (corp-wide): 474.05MM **Privately
Held**
Web: www.seyfarth.com
SIC: 8111 General practice law office
PA: Seyfarth Shaw Llp
233 S Wacker Dr Ste 8000
Chicago IL
312 460-5000

(P-18941)
**SHEPPARD MLLIN RCHTER
HMPTON L**
501 W Broadway Fl 19 (92101-8541)
PHONE..................619 338-6500
Robert Sbardellati, *Brnch Mgr*
EMP: 89
SALES (corp-wide): 181.58MM **Privately
Held**
Web: www.sheppardmullin.com
SIC: 8111 General practice law office
PA: Sheppard, Mullin, Richter & Hampton,
Llp
333 S Hope St Fl 43
Los Angeles CA
213 620-1780

(P-18942)
**SHEPPARD MLLIN RCHTER
HMPTON L**
12275 El Camino Real Ste 100 (92130)
PHONE..................858 720-8900
Shannon Petersen, *Brnch Mgr*
EMP: 84
SALES (corp-wide): 181.58MM **Privately
Held**
Web: www.sheppardmullin.com
SIC: 8111 General practice law office
PA: Sheppard, Mullin, Richter & Hampton,
Llp
333 S Hope St Fl 43
Los Angeles CA
213 620-1780

(P-18943)
**SHEPPARD MLLIN RCHTER
HMPTON L (PA)**
Also Called: Sheppard Mullin
333 S Hope St Fl 43 (90071-1422)
PHONE..................213 620-1780
Guy N Halgren, *Ch Bd*
Robert Beall, *Administrative Partner*
Robert Zuber, *Ex Dir*
Lawrence Braun, *Pt*
Charles Barker, *Pt*
EMP: 370 **EST:** 1927
SQ FT: 52,820
SALES (est): 181.58MM
SALES (corp-wide): 181.58MM **Privately
Held**
Web: www.sheppardmullin.com

SIC: 8111 General practice law office

(P-18944)
**SHEPPARD MLLIN RCHTER
HMPTON L**
650 Town Center Dr Fl 10 (92626-1993)
PHONE..................714 513-5100
EMP: 80
SALES (corp-wide): 181.58MM **Privately
Held**
Web: www.sheppardmullin.com
SIC: 8111 General practice law office
PA: Sheppard, Mullin, Richter & Hampton,
Llp
333 S Hope St Fl 43
Los Angeles CA
213 620-1780

(P-18945)
SHOOK HARDY & BACON LLP
5 Park Plz Ste 1600 (92614-2546)
PHONE..................949 475-1500
Michelle Fujimoto, *Mgr*
EMP: 239
SALES (corp-wide): 147.91MM **Privately
Held**
Web: www.shb.com
SIC: 8111 General practice law office
PA: Shook, Hardy & Bacon L.L.P.
2555 Grand Blvd
Kansas City MO
816 474-6550

(P-18946)
**SKADDEN ARPS SLATE
MEAGHER & F**
300 S Grand Ave Ste 3400 (90071-3137)
PHONE..................213 687-5000
Rand S April, *Pt*
EMP: 250
Web: www.skadden.com
SIC: 8111 General practice attorney, lawyer
HQ: Skadden, Arps, Slate, Meagher &
Flom Llp
One Mnhttan W 395 9th Ave
New York NY
212 735-3000

(P-18947)
SMS TRANSPORTATION INC
18516 S Broadway (90248-4615)
PHONE..................310 527-9200
John W Harris, *Prin*
EMP: 100 **EST:** 2005
SALES (est): 4.94MM **Privately Held**
Web: www.smstransportation.net
SIC: 8111 Legal services

(P-18948)
SNELL & WILMER LLP
Also Called: Snell & Wilmer
600 Anton Blvd Ste 1400 (92626-7689)
PHONE..................714 427-7000
Andrea Bryant, *Prin*
EMP: 82
SQ FT: 3,000
SALES (corp-wide): 80.35MM **Privately
Held**
Web: www.swlaw.com
SIC: 8111 General practice attorney, lawyer
PA: Snell & Wilmer L.L.P.
1 E Washington St
Phoenix AZ
602 382-6000

(P-18949)
**STRADLING YCCA CRLSON
RUTH A P (PA)**
660 Newport Center Dr Ste 1600 (92660)

PHONE..................949 725-4000
John F Cannon, *Prin*
Nick E Yocca, *
William Rauth, *
Keith C Schaaf, *
Rick C Goodman, *
EMP: 200 **EST:** 1975
SQ FT: 64,000
SALES (est): 40.69MM
SALES (corp-wide): 40.69MM **Privately
Held**
Web: www.stradlinglaw.com
SIC: 8111 General practice law office

(P-18950)
**STROOCK & STROOCK &
LAVAN LLP**
Also Called: Stroock & Stroock & Lavan
2029 Century Park E Ste 1800
(90002-3076)
PHONE..................310 556-5800
Diane Cohen, *Brnch Mgr*
EMP: 150
SALES (corp-wide): 26.46K **Privately Held**
Web: www.stroock.com
SIC: 8111 General practice attorney, lawyer
PA: Stroock & Stroock & Lavan Llp
180 Maiden Ln Fl 26
New York NY
212 806-5400

(P-18951)
**TOBIN LUCKS A PROF CORP
(PA)**
Also Called: Tobin Lucks
8511 Fallbrook Ave Ste 400 (91304)
P.O. Box 4502 (91365-4502)
PHONE..................818 226-3400
Irvin Lucks, *Mng Pt*
Donald Tobin, *
Irvin Lucks, *Pt*
Edwin Lucks, *
EMP: 97 **EST:** 1982
SALES (est): 24.04MM
SALES (corp-wide): 24.04MM **Privately
Held**
Web: www.tobinlucks.com
SIC: 8111 General practice law office

(P-18952)
**TROUTMAN PPPER HMLTON
SNDERS L**
Also Called: Troutman Sanders
5 Park Plz Ste 1400 (92614-2545)
PHONE..................949 622-2700
David B Allen, *Pt*
EMP: 86
SALES (corp-wide): 161.17MM **Privately
Held**
Web: www.troutman.com
SIC: 8111 General practice attorney, lawyer
PA: Troutman Pepper Hamilton Sanders Llp
600 Peachtree St Ne # 300
Atlanta GA
404 885-3000

(P-18953)
TROYGOULD PC
1801 Century Park E Ste 1600
(90067-2301)
PHONE..................310 553-4441
Sanford J Hillsberg, *Prin*
Diane Gordon, *
EMP: 80 **EST:** 1970
SQ FT: 24,000
SALES (est): 12.43MM **Privately Held**
Web: www.troygould.com
SIC: 8111 General practice attorney, lawyer

(P-18954)
**WASSERMAN COMDEN &
CASSELMAN (PA)**
5567 Reseda Blvd Ste 330 (91356-2699)
P.O. Box 7033 (91357-7033)
PHONE..................323 872-0995
Steve Wasserman, *Pt*
David B Casselman, *
Clifford H Pearson, *
Leonard J Comden, *
EMP: 88 **EST:** 1976
SQ FT: 15,000
SALES (est): 8.42MM
SALES (corp-wide): 8.42MM **Privately
Held**
Web: www.wassermanlawgroup.com
SIC: 8111 General practice law office

(P-18955)
WELLS MEDIA GROUP INC (PA)
Also Called: Insurance Journal
3570 Camino Del Rio N Ste 100 (92108)
PHONE..................619 584-1100
Mark Wells, *Pr*
EMP: 19 **EST:** 1923
SQ FT: 3,600
SALES (est): 5.17MM
SALES (corp-wide): 5.17MM **Privately
Held**
Web: www.insurancejournal.com
SIC: 8111 2721 Legal services; Magazines:
publishing and printing

(P-18956)
WHITE & CASE LLP
555 S Flower St Ste 2700 (90071-2433)
PHONE..................213 620-7724
EMP: 103
SALES (corp-wide): 567.88MM **Privately
Held**
Web: www.whitecase.com
SIC: 8111 General practice law office
PA: White & Case Llp
1221 Ave Of The Amrcas St
New York NY
212 819-8200

(P-18957)
**WINGERT GRBING BRBKER
JSTKIE L**
1230 Columbia St Ste 400 (92101-8502)
PHONE..................619 232-8151
Stephen Grebing, *Pt*
Charles Grebing, *Pt*
Michael Anello, *Pt*
Alan Brubaker, *Pt*
James Goodwin, *Pt*
EMP: 100 **EST:** 1974
SALES (est): 8.62MM **Privately Held**
Web: www.wingertlaw.com
SIC: 8111 General practice attorney, lawyer

(P-18958)
WITHERS BERGMAN LLP
Also Called: Withers Bergman
12830 El Camino Real Ste 350
(92130-2977)
PHONE..................203 974-0412
EMP: 348
Web: www.withersworldwide.com
SIC: 8111 General practice attorney, lawyer
HQ: Withers Bergman Llp
157 Church St Fl 19
New Haven CT
203 789-1320

(P-18959)
**WOMBLE BOND DICKINSON
(US) LLP**

PRODUCTS & SVCS

400 Spectrum Center Dr (92618-4934)
PHONE..................310 207-3800
EMP: 240
SALES (corp-wide): 218.48MM **Privately Held**
Web: www.womblebonddickinson.com
SIC: 8111 Specialized law offices, attorneys
PA: Womble Bond Dickinson (Us) Llp
1 W 4th St
Winston Salem NC
336 721-3600

(P-18960)
ZBS LAW LLP
30 Corporate Park Ste 450 (92606-3401)
PHONE..................714 848-7920
Les Zieve, *Pt*
Paul Kim, *Prin*
EMP: 85 **EST:** 2020
SALES (est): 4.28MM **Privately Held**
Web: www.zbslaw.com
SIC: 8111 Real estate law

(P-18961)
ZIFFREN B B F G-L S&C FND
1801 Century Park W Fl 7 (90067-6401)
PHONE..................310 552-3388
Kenneth Ziffren, *Owner*
Kenneth Ziffren, *Prin*
Harry M Brittenham, *
John G Branca, *
Dennis Luderer, *
EMP: 103 **EST:** 1979
SQ FT: 33,000
SALES (est): 17.17MM **Privately Held**
Web: www.ziffrenlaw.com
SIC: 8111 General practice law office

8211 Elementary And Secondary Schools

(P-18962)
ADAT ARI EL
Also Called: Adat ARI El Day School
12020 Burbank Blvd (91607-2198)
PHONE..................818 766-4992
Joanne Klein, *Ex Dir*
EMP: 150 **EST:** 1938
SQ FT: 97,410
SALES (est): 9.16MM **Privately Held**
Web: www.aaedayschool.org
SIC: 8211 8661 8351 8299 Private elementary school; Temples; Montessori child development center; Religious school

(P-18963)
BEAUMONT UNFIED SCHL DST PUB F
Also Called: Community Day School
126 W Fifth St (92223-2142)
PHONE..................951 845-6580
Douglas Walter, *Prin*
EMP: 410
SALES (corp-wide): 205.74MM **Privately Held**
Web: www.beaumontusd.us
SIC: 8211 8351 Public elementary and secondary schools; Group day care center
PA: Beaumont Unified School District Public Facilities Corporation
350 W Brookside
Cherry Valley CA
951 845-1631

(P-18964)
BRAWLEY UNION HIGH SCHOOL DIST (PA)
480 N Imperial Ave (92227-1625)

PHONE..................760 312-6068
Hasnik Danielian, *Superintnt*
Jenifer Layaye, *
EMP: 88 **EST:** 1908
SALES (est): 39.63MM
SALES (corp-wide): 39.63MM **Privately Held**
Web: www.brawleyhigh.org
SIC: 8211 8351 High school, junior or senior, nec; Preschool center

(P-18965)
DUBNOFF CTR FOR CHILD DEV EDCT (PA)
10526 Dubnoff Way (91606-3921)
PHONE..................818 755-4950
Sandra Babcock, *Pr*
Sandra Sternig-babcock, *Pr*
EMP: 94 **EST:** 1948
SQ FT: 13,968
SALES (est): 5.59MM
SALES (corp-wide): 5.59MM **Privately Held**
SIC: 8211 8093 8361 Specialty education; Specialty outpatient clinics, nec; Residential care

(P-18966)
FIRST ASSMBLY OF GOD BKRSFIELD
Also Called: Stockdale Christian School
4901 California Ave (93309-1111)
PHONE..................661 327-2227
Reverend Steven Hunt, *Ch Bd*
Kevin Harrel, *
Rick Roper, *
EMP: 90 **EST:** 1924
SQ FT: 60,000
SALES (est): 20.78MM **Privately Held**
Web: www.stockdalechristian.com
SIC: 8211 8351 Elementary and secondary schools; Preschool center

(P-18967)
GARDEN GROVE UNIFIED SCHL DST
Also Called: Alamitos Intermediate School
12381 Dale St (92841-3219)
PHONE..................714 663-6101
Christina Pflughoft, *Prin*
EMP: 42
SALES (corp-wide): 755.47MM **Privately Held**
Web: alamitos.ggusd.us
SIC: 8211 2731 Public junior high school; Book publishing
PA: Garden Grove Unified School District
10331 Stanford Ave
Garden Grove CA
714 663-6000

(P-18968)
GUADALUPE UNION SCHOOL DST (PA)
4465 9th St (93434-1436)
P.O. Box 788 (93434-0788)
PHONE..................805 343-2114
Ed Cora, *Superintnt*
Celia Ramos, *
Jeffrey Alvarez, *
EMP: 114 **EST:** 1890
SALES (est): 36.96MM
SALES (corp-wide): 36.96MM **Privately Held**
Web: www.guadusd.org
SIC: 8211 8741 Public elementary school; Management services

(P-18969)
HEMET UNIFIED SCHOOL DISTRICT
Also Called: Nutrition Services
2075 W Acacia Ave (92545-3746)
PHONE..................951 765-5100
Kathy Anderson, *Brnch Mgr*
EMP: 80
SALES (corp-wide): 452.75MM **Privately Held**
Web: www.hemetusd.org
SIC: 8211 8734 Public elementary and secondary schools; Testing laboratories
PA: Hemet Unified School District
1791 W Acacia Ave
Hemet CA
951 765-5100

(P-18970)
HEMET UNIFIED SCHOOL DISTRICT
Also Called: Santa Fe Middle School
985 N Cawston Ave (92545-1551)
P.O. Box 881 (92546-0881)
PHONE..................951 765-6287
Todd Biggert, *Prin*
EMP: 80
SALES (corp-wide): 452.75MM **Privately Held**
Web: ranchoviejo.hemetusd.org
SIC: 8211 8699 Public elementary and secondary schools; Personal interest organization
PA: Hemet Unified School District
1791 W Acacia Ave
Hemet CA
951 765-5100

(P-18971)
INCLUSIVE EDCATN CMNTY PRTNR I
Also Called: Iecp
2323 Roosevelt Blvd Apt 3 (93035-4480)
PHONE..................805 985-4808
Rick B Clemens, *Pr*
Rick Clemens, *
EMP: 300 **EST:** 2002
SALES (est): 11.05MM **Privately Held**
Web: www.iecp.us
SIC: 8211 8351 Specialty education; Preschool center

(P-18972)
LAGUNA BLANCA SCHOOL (PA)
4125 Paloma Dr (93110-2146)
PHONE..................805 687-2461
Sue Smith, *Mgr*
EMP: 94 **EST:** 1933
SQ FT: 24,857
SALES (est): 19.66MM
SALES (corp-wide): 19.66MM **Privately Held**
Web: www.lagunablanca.org
SIC: 8211 8748 Private elementary and secondary schools; Business consulting, nec

(P-18973)
LONG BEACH UNIFIED SCHOOL DST
Also Called: Muir Elementary School
3038 Delta Ave (90810-2843)
PHONE..................562 426-5571
Sophia Griffieth, *Prin*
EMP: 94
SALES (corp-wide): 788.46MM **Privately Held**
Web: www.lbschools.net

SIC: 8211 6531 Public junior high school; Rental agent, real estate
PA: Long Beach Unified School District
1515 Hughes Way
Long Beach CA
562 997-8000

(P-18974)
LOS ANGELES UNIFIED SCHOOL DST
Also Called: West Valley Occupational Ctr
6200 Winnetka Ave (91367-3826)
PHONE..................818 346-3540
Candace Lee, *Prin*
EMP: 136
SALES (corp-wide): 9.38B **Privately Held**
Web: www.wvoc.net
SIC: 8211 8299 8331 Public elementary and secondary schools; Educational service, nondegree granting: continuing educ.; Job training and related services
PA: Los Angeles Unified School District
333 S Beaudry Ave Ste 209
Los Angeles CA
213 241-1000

(P-18975)
LYNWOOD UNIFIED SCHOOL DST
Also Called: Lindbergh Child Care Center
12120 Lindbergh Ave (90262-4701)
PHONE..................310 631-7308
Maria Noriega, *Dir*
EMP: 88
SQ FT: 3,790
SALES (corp-wide): 236.59MM **Privately Held**
Web: www.mylusd.org
SIC: 8211 8351 Public elementary and secondary schools; Child day care services
PA: Lynwood Unified School District
11321 Bullis Rd
Lynwood CA
310 886-1600

(P-18976)
NATIONAL SCHOOL DISTRICT
Also Called: Maintenace Operations Svc Ctr
1400 N Ave (91950-4825)
PHONE..................619 336-7770
Jerry O'hara, *Prin*
EMP: 202
SALES (corp-wide): 95.04MM **Privately Held**
Web: www.nsd.us
SIC: 8211 7349 Public elementary and secondary schools; School custodian, contract basis
PA: National School District
1500 N Ave
National City CA
619 336-7500

(P-18977)
OJAI VALLEY SCHOOL (PA)
Also Called: OVS
723 El Paseo Rd (93023-2498)
PHONE..................805 646-1423
EMP: 83 **EST:** 1911
SALES (est): 16.08MM
SALES (corp-wide): 16.08MM **Privately Held**
Web: www.ovs.org
SIC: 8211 8351 Private combined elementary and secondary school; Child day care services

(P-18978)
PAGE PRIVATE SCHOOL
419 S Robertson Blvd (90211-3603)
PHONE..............................323 272-3429
EMP: 81
SQ FT: 7,074
SALES (corp-wide): 3.2MM **Privately Held**
Web: www.pageacademyca.com
SIC: **8211** 8351 Private elementary school; Group day care center
PA: Page Private School
    657 Victoria St
    Costa Mesa CA
    949 515-1700

(P-18979)
POLYTECHNIC SCHOOL
1030 E California Blvd (91106-4042)
PHONE..............................626 792-2147
John W Bracker, *Head of School*
Wendy Munger, *
EMP: 331 EST: 1907
SALES (est): 47.3MM **Privately Held**
Web: www.polytechnic.org
SIC: **8211** 8351 Kindergarten; Preschool center

(P-18980)
ROMAN CTHLIC DIOCESE OF ORANGE
Also Called: St Josephs School
801 N Bradford Ave (92870-4515)
PHONE..............................714 528-1794
Joann Telles, *Prin*
EMP: 234
SALES (corp-wide): 92.62MM **Privately Held**
Web: www.rcbo.org
SIC: **8211** 8661 7389 Catholic junior high school; Catholic Church; Fund raising organizations
PA: The Roman Catholic Diocese Of Orange
    13280 Chapman Ave
    Garden Grove CA
    714 282-3000

(P-18981)
ROMAN CTHLIC DIOCESE OF ORANGE
Also Called: Saint Cecilia School
1311 Sycamore Ave (92780-6276)
PHONE..............................714 544-1533
Mary Alvarado, *Prin*
EMP: 141
SALES (corp-wide): 92.62MM **Privately Held**
Web: www.morethanschool.org
SIC: **8211** 8351 Catholic combined elementary and secondary school; Preschool center
PA: The Roman Catholic Diocese Of Orange
    13280 Chapman Ave
    Garden Grove CA
    714 282-3000

(P-18982)
ROMAN CTHLIC DIOCESE OF ORANGE
Also Called: Santa Mrgrita Cthlic High Schl
22062 Antonio Pkwy (92688-1993)
PHONE..............................949 766-6000
Mary B Dougherty, *Prin*
EMP: 200
SQ FT: 142,959
SALES (corp-wide): 92.62MM **Privately Held**
Web: www.smhs.org

SIC: **8211** 2721 Catholic senior high school; Periodicals
PA: The Roman Catholic Diocese Of Orange
    13280 Chapman Ave
    Garden Grove CA
    714 282-3000

(P-18983)
SAN DIEGO CMNTY COLLEGE DST
Also Called: Cesar Chavez Center
1960 National Ave (92113-2116)
PHONE..............................619 388-4850
Rudy Kastelic, *Brnch Mgr*
EMP: 103
SQ FT: 4,521
SALES (corp-wide): 146.65MM **Privately Held**
Web: www.sdccd.edu
SIC: **8211** 8742 Public adult education school; Management consulting services
PA: San Diego Community College District
    3375 Camino Del Rio S
    San Diego CA
    619 388-6500

(P-18984)
SIERRA CANYON INC
Also Called: Sierra Canyon Day Camp
11052 Independence Ave (91311-1562)
PHONE..............................818 882-8121
Jim Skruneis, *Pr*
Howard Wang, *
Stephen Horwitz, *
EMP: 86 EST: 1971
SQ FT: 35,000
SALES (est): 5.66MM **Privately Held**
Web: www.sierracanyondaycamp.com
SIC: **8211** 7999 Private elementary and secondary schools; Day camp

(P-18985)
TUSTIN UNIFIED SCHOOL DISTRICT
Also Called: Lestonnac Preschool
16791 E Main St (92780-4034)
PHONE..............................714 542-4271
Sharon Lamtrecht, *Prin*
EMP: 101
SALES (corp-wide): 366.56MM **Privately Held**
Web: www.sjdlschool.com
SIC: **8211** 8351 Public elementary and secondary schools; Preschool center
PA: Tustin Unified School District
    300 S C St
    Tustin CA
    714 730-7515

(P-18986)
VISTA DEL MAR CHILD FMLY SVCS (PA)
3200 Motor Ave (90034-3710)
PHONE..............................310 836-1223
Roosevelena Wilson, *CEO*
EMP: 262 EST: 1908
SQ FT: 100,000
SALES (est): 40.28MM
SALES (corp-wide): 40.28MM **Privately Held**
Web: www.vistadelmar.org
SIC: **8211** 8361 Elementary and secondary schools; Mentally handicapped home

(P-18987)
WEST ANGELES CH GOD IN CHRST
Also Called: West Angeles Christian Academy

3010 Crenshaw Blvd (90016-4263)
PHONE..............................323 731-2567
Deloris A Dumbar, *Prin*
EMP: 152
SALES (corp-wide): 21.89MM **Privately Held**
Web: www.westa.org
SIC: **8211** 6512 Private elementary school; Theater building, ownership and operation
PA: West Angeles Church Of God In Christ
    3045 Crenshaw Blvd
    Los Angeles CA
    323 733-8300

(P-18988)
WHITTIER UNION HIGH SCHL DIST
Also Called: Capc Adult Services
7200 Greenleaf Ave Ste 170 (90602-1367)
PHONE..............................562 693-8826
Dan Hulbert, *Dir*
EMP: 106
SALES (corp-wide): 206.51MM **Privately Held**
Web: www.wuhsd.org
SIC: **8211** 8322 Public elementary and secondary schools; Social services for the handicapped
PA: Whittier Union High School Dist
    9401 Painter Ave
    Whittier CA
    562 698-8121

8221 Colleges And Universities

(P-18989)
ASSOCIATED STUDENTS UCLA
Also Called: Ucla Dept of Design Media
11000 Kinross Ave Ave Ste 245 (90095-2000)
P.O. Box 951615 (90095-1615)
PHONE..............................310 206-8282
Diane Mills, *Prin*
EMP: 237
SALES (corp-wide): 47.49MM **Privately Held**
Web: asucla.ucla.edu
SIC: **8221** 7336 University; Graphic arts and related design
PA: Associated Students U.C.L.A.
    308 Westwood Plz
    Los Angeles CA
    310 794-8836

(P-18990)
LOS ANGELES UNIFIED SCHOOL DST
Also Called: Central Shop
1240 Naomi Ave (90021-2393)
PHONE..............................213 763-2900
Herman Perez, *Dir*
EMP: 80
SALES (corp-wide): 9.38B **Privately Held**
Web: www.laallcityband.com
SIC: **8221** 7349 Colleges and universities; Building maintenance services, nec
PA: Los Angeles Unified School District
    333 S Beaudry Ave Ste 209
    Los Angeles CA
    213 241-1000

(P-18991)
MARSHALL B KETCHUM UNIVERSITY (PA)
Also Called: OPTOMETRIC CENTER OF LOS ANGEL
2575 Yorba Linda Blvd (92831-1699)
PHONE..............................714 463-7567

EMP: 160 EST: 1911
SALES (est): 41.85MM
SALES (corp-wide): 41.85MM **Privately Held**
Web: www.ketchum.edu
SIC: **8221** 8042 Professional schools; Offices and clinics of optometrists

(P-18992)
SAN DIEGO STATE UNIVERSITY
Also Called: K P B S
5200 Campanile Dr (92182-1901)
PHONE..............................619 594-1515
Tom Karlo, *Mgr*
EMP: 100
SALES (corp-wide): 534.4MM **Privately Held**
Web: www.kpbs.org
SIC: **8221** 9411 4832 University; Administration of educational programs, State government; Educational
HQ: San Diego State University
    5500 Campanile Dr
    San Diego CA

(P-18993)
UNIVERSITY CAL LOS ANGELES
Tanms Engineering Research Ctr
420 Westwood Plz Rm 7702 (90095-0001)
PHONE..............................310 825-7852
EMP: 200
SALES (corp-wide): 534.4MM **Privately Held**
Web: www.ucla.edu
SIC: **8221** 8733 9411 University; Noncommercial research organizations; Administration of educational programs
HQ: University Of California, Los Angeles
    405 Hilgard Ave
    Los Angeles CA

(P-18994)
UNIVERSITY CALIFORNIA IRVINE
Also Called: Social Sciences
3151 Social Science Plz (92697-5100)
PHONE..............................949 824-7725
EMP: 171
SALES (corp-wide): 534.4MM **Privately Held**
Web: www.uci.edu
SIC: **8221** 9411 8062 University; Administration of educational programs; General medical and surgical hospitals
HQ: University Of California, Irvine
    510 Aldrich Hall
    Irvine CA
    949 824-5011

(P-18995)
VANGUARD UNIV SOUTHERN CAL
55 Fair Dr (92626-6520)
PHONE..............................714 668-6163
Michael Beals, *CEO*
EMP: 200 EST: 1921
SQ FT: 420,000
SALES (est): 100.21MM **Privately Held**
Web: www.vanguard.edu
SIC: **8221** 8699 College, except junior; Charitable organization

---

8222 Junior Colleges

(P-18996)
SAN DIEGO CMNTY COLLEGE DST
Also Called: San Diego City College
1313 Twelfth Ave (92101-4712)

PRODUCTS & SVCS

PHONE...............................619 388-3453
Terrence J Burgess, *Prin*
EMP: 81
SALES (corp-wide): 146.65MM **Privately Held**
Web: www.sdccd.edu
SIC: 8222 8641 Community college; Civic and social associations
PA: San Diego Community College District
3375 Camino Del Rio S
San Diego CA
619 388-6500

(P-18997)
SAN DIEGO CMNTY COLLEGE DST
Also Called: San Diego Mesa College
7250 Mesa College Dr (92111-4902)
PHONE...............................619 388-2600
Pamela Luster, *Pr*
EMP: 1500
SALES (corp-wide): 146.65MM **Privately Held**
Web: www.sdccd.edu
SIC: 8222 8412 Community college; Museums and art galleries
PA: San Diego Community College District
3375 Camino Del Rio S
San Diego CA
619 388-6500

(P-18998)
SANTA BRBARA CMNTY COLLEGE DST
Also Called: Academy of Cosmetology
525 Anacapa St (93101-1603)
PHONE...............................805 683-4191
Ben Partee, *Mgr*
EMP: 497
SALES (corp-wide): 82.58MM **Privately Held**
Web: www.sbcc.edu
SIC: 8222 7231 Community college; Cosmetology school
PA: Santa Barbara Community College District
721 Cliff Dr
Santa Barbara CA
805 965-0581

8231 Libraries

(P-18999)
HUNTINGTON LIB ART CLLCTONS BT
1151 Oxford Rd (91108-1218)
PHONE...............................626 405-2100
Robert F Erburu, *Ch Bd*
Robert Skotheim, *
Steve Koblik, *
Laurie Sowd, *
▲ **EMP:** 380 **EST:** 1919
SALES (est): 128.86MM **Privately Held**
Web: www.huntington.org
SIC: 8231 8412 8422 Public library; Art gallery, noncommercial; Botanical garden

---

8243 Data Processing Schools

(P-19000)
IT DIVISION INC
Also Called: Apeiro Technologies
9170 Irvine Center Dr Ste 200 (92618-4614)
PHONE...............................678 648-2709
Lavanya Nilagiri, *CEO*
Neeta Prasad, *

Shruti Nilagiri, *
Vivek Jaiswal, *
EMP: 103 **EST:** 2006
SALES (est): 2.61MM **Privately Held**
Web: www.apeiro.us
SIC: 8243 7371 7373 Software training, computer; Computer software systems analysis and design, custom; Systems software development services

(P-19001)
NEW HRZNS SRVING INDVDALS WITH (PA)
Also Called: NEW HORIZONS CENTER & WORKSHOP
15725 Parthenia St (91343-4913)
PHONE...............................818 894-9301
Cynthia Kawa, *CEO*
▲ **EMP:** 100 **EST:** 1954
SQ FT: 60,000
SALES (est): 16.98MM
SALES (corp-wide): 16.98MM **Privately Held**
Web: www.newhorizons-sfv.org
SIC: 8243 2052 Software training, computer; Cookies

8249 Vocational Schools, Nec

(P-19002)
CONCORDE CAREER COLLEGES INC
Concorde Career College
12412 Victory Blvd (91606-3134)
PHONE...............................818 766-8151
Carmen Bowen, *Dir*
EMP: 93
SQ FT: 5,500
SALES (corp-wide): 75.67MM **Privately Held**
Web: www.concorde.edu
SIC: 8249 8621 Medical and dental assistant school; Professional organizations
PA: Concorde Career Colleges, Inc
6701 W 64th St Ste 200
Mission KS
913 831-9977

(P-19003)
GEMOLOGICAL INSTITUTE AMER INC (PA)
Also Called: Gemological Institute America
5345 Armada Dr (92008-4602)
PHONE...............................760 603-4000
Susan M Jacques, *Pr*
Tom Moses, *LABORATORY Research*
David Tearle, *
EMP: 1000 **EST:** 1931
SQ FT: 300,000
SALES (est): 358.37MM
SALES (corp-wide): 358.37MM **Privately Held**
Web: www.gia.edu
SIC: 8249 8733 Trade school; Noncommercial research organizations

(P-19004)
REAL ESTATE TRAINERS INC
212 Twne Cntre Pl Ste 100 (92806)
PHONE...............................800 282-2352
Jerry Mcharg, *Pr*
EMP: 35 **EST:** 1972
SQ FT: 17,000
SALES (est): 245.27K
SALES (corp-wide): 2.16MM **Privately Held**
Web: www.retrainersca.com
SIC: 8249 2721 Real estate and insurance school; Periodicals

PA: Universal Training Corporation
2121 S Twne Cntre Pl Ste
Anaheim CA
714 972-2211

(P-19005)
THE CODING SOURCE LLC
Also Called: Altegra Health
3415 S Sepulveda Blvd Ste 900 (90034-6981)
PHONE...............................866 235-7553
EMP: 250
Web: www.thecodingsource.com
SIC: 8249 7374 8331 7361 Medical training services; Data entry service; Job training and related services; Employment agencies

(P-19006)
UNIVERSAL TECHNICAL INST INC
Also Called: Uti
9494 Haven Ave (91730-5843)
PHONE...............................909 484-1929
EMP: 130
SALES (corp-wide): 607.41MM **Publicly Held**
Web: www.uti.edu
SIC: 8249 7389 Trade school; Personal service agents, brokers, and bureaus
PA: Universal Technical Institute, Inc.
4225 E Windrose Dr # 200
Phoenix AZ
623 445-9500

8299 Schools And Educational Services

(P-19007)
AMERICAN ASSN CRTCAL CARE NRSE
Also Called: A A C N
27071 Aliso Creek Rd (92656-3399)
PHONE...............................949 362-2000
Dana Woods, *CEO*
Teri Lynn Kiss, *President Elect*
Michael Willett, *
Mary Zellinger, *
Linda Bay, *
EMP: 128 **EST:** 1969
SALES (est): 38.31MM **Privately Held**
Web: www.aacn.org
SIC: 8299 8331 8621 Educational services; Job training and related services; Professional organizations

(P-19008)
BOYS GRLS CLUBS GRDN GROVE INC (PA)
10540 Chapman Ave (92840-3101)
PHONE...............................714 530-0430
Mark Surmanian, *CEO*
EMP: 225 **EST:** 1952
SQ FT: 12,000
SALES (est): 11.91MM
SALES (corp-wide): 11.91MM **Privately Held**
Web: www.bgcgg.org
SIC: 8299 8699 Educational services; Charitable organization

(P-19009)
CROSSRADS CHRSTN SCHOLS CORONA
2380 Fullerton Ave (92881-3111)
PHONE...............................951 278-3199
Dough Husen, *Superintnt*
EMP: 145 **EST:** 2001
SQ FT: 1,088

SALES (est): 10.47MM **Privately Held**
Web: www.crossroadsschool.org
SIC: 8299 8211 8351 8699 Religious school; High school, junior or senior, nec; Preschool center; Charitable organization

(P-19010)
GREENWOOD HALL INC
6230 Wilshire Blvd Ste 136 (90048-5126)
PHONE...............................310 905-8300
John Hall, *Ch Bd*
Bill Bradfield, *
EMP: 111 **EST:** 1997
SALES (est): 14.12MM **Privately Held**
Web: www.answernet.com
SIC: 8299 8741 8742 7374 Educational services; Management services; Management consulting services; Data processing service

(P-19011)
LEARNING OVATIONS INC
16 Coltrane Ct (92617-4131)
PHONE...............................734 904-1459
Jay Connor, *CEO*
Elliot Amiel, *
Alia Gates, *
Nick Voegeli, *
EMP: 28 **EST:** 2013
SALES (est): 7.06MM
SALES (corp-wide): 1.7B **Publicly Held**
Web: www.learningovations.com
SIC: 8299 7372 Educational services; Educational computer software
PA: Scholastic Corporation
557 Broadway Lbby 1
New York NY
212 343-6100

(P-19012)
MUSIC & ARTS
650 E Parkridge Ave Ste 115 (92879-1091)
PHONE...............................951 735-5924
EMP: 25 **EST:** 2019
SALES (est): 458.3K **Privately Held**
Web: stores.musicarts.com
SIC: 8299 5736 3931 Music school; Musical instrument stores; Musical instruments

(P-19013)
NAPCA FOUNDATION
2600 W Olive Ave Ste 500 (91505-4525)
PHONE...............................800 799-4640
Aaron Smith, *Ex Dir*
EMP: 563 **EST:** 2012
SALES (est): 10.94MM **Privately Held**
Web: www.napcafoundation.org
SIC: 8299 8732 7999 8742 Educational services; Educational research; Instruction schools, camps, and services; School, college, university consultant

(P-19014)
SOUTHERN CAL PRMNNTE MED GROUP
1465 E 103rd St (90002-3306)
PHONE...............................323 564-7911
Joanne Robinson, *Dir*
EMP: 124
SALES (corp-wide): 68.1B **Privately Held**
Web: www.permanente.org
SIC: 8299 6324 8351 Educational services; Group hospitalization plans; Preschool center
HQ: Southern California Permanente Medical Group
393 Walnut Dr
Pasadena CA
626 405-5704

(P-19015)

VISTA HILL FOUNDATION
Also Called: Stein Sam & Rose Education Ctr
6145 Decena Dr (92120-3511)
PHONE..............................619 281-5511
Joan Richard, *Prin*
EMP: 90
SALES (corp-wide): 34.66MM **Privately Held**
Web: www.vistahill.org
SIC: 8299 8351 8093 Educational services; Child day care services; Mental health clinic, outpatient
PA: Vista Hill Foundation
8910 Clairemont Mesa Blvd
San Diego CA
585 514-5100

8322 Individual And Family Services

(P-19016)

ABRAZAR INC
Also Called: ABRAZAR ELDERLY ASSISTANCE
7101 Wyoming St (92683-3811)
PHONE..............................714 893-3581
Gloria Reyes, *CEO*
Mario Ortega, *
EMP: 80 **EST:** 1975
SALES (est): 9.31MM **Privately Held**
Web: www.abrazarinc.com
SIC: 8322 Social service center

(P-19017)

AIDS PROJECT LOS ANGELES (PA)
Also Called: Aids Project La
611 S Kingsley Dr (90005-2319)
PHONE..............................213 201-1600
Craig E Thompson, *CEO*
Robyn Goldman, *
EMP: 90 **EST:** 1983
SALES (est): 55.51MM
SALES (corp-wide): 55.51MM **Privately Held**
Web: www.aplahealth.org
SIC: 8322 Social service center

(P-19018)

ALPHA PROJECT FOR HOMELESS
Also Called: Casa Raphael
993 Postal Way (92083-6945)
PHONE..............................760 630-9922
EMP: 153
Web: www.alphaproject.org
SIC: 8322 8361 Community center; Halfway group home, persons with social or personal problems
PA: Alpha Project For The Homeless
3737 5th Ave Ste 203
San Diego CA

(P-19019)

AMERICAN NATIONAL RED CROSS
Also Called: American Nat Red Crss-Blood Sv
100 Red Cross Cir (91768-2580)
PHONE..............................909 859-7006
Joan Manning, *Genl Mgr*
EMP: 103
SALES (corp-wide): 3.18B **Privately Held**
Web: www.redcross.org
SIC: 8322 Social service center
PA: The American National Red Cross
431 18th St Nw
Washington DC
202 737-8300

(P-19020)

AMERICAN NATIONAL RED CROSS
Also Called: Red Cross
1450 S Central Ave (90021-2627)
PHONE..............................310 445-9900
EMP: 137
SALES (corp-wide): 3.18B **Privately Held**
Web: www.redcross.org
SIC: 8322 Social service center
PA: The American National Red Cross
431 18th St Nw
Washington DC
202 737-8300

(P-19021)

AMERICAN RED CROSS LOS ANGLES (PA)
Also Called: American Red Cross
1320 Newton St (90021-2724)
PHONE..............................310 445-9900
TOLL FREE: 800
Roger Dixon, *CEO*
Kirk Richard Hyde, *
William Niese, *
Thomas E Stephenson, *
Michelle Mccarthy, *Chief Financial*
EMP: 150 **EST:** 1916
SALES (est): 6.76MM
SALES (corp-wide): 6.76MM **Privately Held**
Web: www.redcross.org
SIC: 8322 Social service center

(P-19022)

AMERICAN RED CROSS SAN DG-MPRI (PA)
Also Called: American Red Cross
3950 Calle Fortunada (92123-1827)
PHONE..............................858 309-1200
Joe Craver, *CEO*
EMP: 90 **EST:** 1898
SALES (est): 8.76MM
SALES (corp-wide): 8.76MM **Privately Held**
Web: www.redcross.org
SIC: 8322 Social service center

(P-19023)

AMIGO BABY INC
Also Called: Healthcare
1901 N Rice Ave Ste 325 (93030-7912)
P.O. Box 6757 (91359-6757)
PHONE..............................805 901-1237
Pablo Velez, *CEO*
EMP: 80 **EST:** 2004
SALES (est): 5.82MM **Privately Held**
Web: www.amigobaby.com
SIC: 8322 8099 Social service center; Health and allied services, nec

(P-19024)

AUTISM SPCTRUM INTRVNTIONS INC
713 W Commonwealth Ave Ste A (92832)
PHONE..............................562 972-4846
Timothy M Prior, *Prin*
EMP: 116 **EST:** 2008
SALES (est): 6.38MM **Privately Held**
Web: www.asiautism.com
SIC: 8322 Individual and family services

(P-19025)

AVIVA FAMILY & CHILDRENS SVCS (PA)
1701 Camino Palmero St (90046-2902)
PHONE..............................323 876-0550
Ira J Kruskol, *Dir*

EMP: 99 **EST:** 1976
SALES (est): 8.99MM
SALES (corp-wide): 8.99MM **Privately Held**
Web: www.aviva.org
SIC: 8322 Social service center

(P-19026)

AYA LIVING INC
1450 Frazee Rd (92108-4337)
PHONE..............................619 446-6469
Matthew Williams, *Ex Dir*
EMP: 120 **EST:** 2010
SALES (est): 4MM **Privately Held**
Web: www.ayaliving.com
SIC: 8322 Individual and family services

(P-19027)

BEHAVRAL HLTHCARE SLUTIONS INC
9465 Farnham St (92123-1308)
PHONE..............................858 573-2600
Kimberly Bond, *Pr*
EMP: 131 **EST:** 2010
SALES (est): 707.72K
SALES (corp-wide): 95.19MM **Privately Held**
SIC: 8322 Rehabilitation services
PA: Mental Health Systems, Inc.
9465 Farnham St
San Diego CA
858 573-2600

(P-19028)

BERKSHIRE HATHAWAY HOME SERVIC
231 S Glendora Ave (91741-3419)
PHONE..............................626 335-6001
EMP: 82
SALES (corp-wide): 2.56MM **Privately Held**
Web: www.brucemulhearn.com
SIC: 8322 Homemakers' service
PA: Berkshire Hathaway Home Services Ca Roperties
18000 Studebaker Rd # 600
Cerritos CA
562 860-2625

(P-19029)

BLC RESIDENTIAL CARE INC
1455 W 112th St (90047-4926)
PHONE..............................310 722-7541
Brenda Chandler, *Pr*
EMP: 80 **EST:** 2004
SALES (est): 701.41K **Privately Held**
SIC: 8322 Adult day care center

(P-19030)

BRAILLE INSTITUTE AMERICA INC (PA)
Also Called: Braille Institute
741 N Vermont Ave (90029-3594)
PHONE..............................323 663-1111
Lester M Sussman, *Ch Bd*
Les Stocker, *
Peter Mindnich, *
Rezaur Rahman, *
EMP: 208 **EST:** 1919
SQ FT: 167,079
SALES (est): 37.68MM
SALES (corp-wide): 37.68MM **Privately Held**
Web: www.brailleinstitute.org
SIC: 8322 8231 2731 2759 Individual and family services; Specialized libraries; Textbooks: publishing and printing; Commercial printing, nec

(P-19031)

CAROLYN E WYLIE CTR FOR CHLDRE
4164 Brockton Ave (92501-3400)
PHONE..............................951 683-5193
Mickey Rubinson, *CEO*
Melody Amaral, *
EMP: 100 **EST:** 1976
SQ FT: 3,000
SALES (est): 3.86MM **Privately Held**
Web: www.wyliecenter.org
SIC: 8322 8093 8049 Individual and family services; Mental health clinic, outpatient; Psychotherapist, except M.D.

(P-19032)

CASA CLINA HOSP CTRS FOR HLTHC
Also Called: Rancho Pino Verdi
11981 Midway Ave (92356-7517)
P.O. Box 1760 (92356-1760)
PHONE..............................760 248-6245
Michael Stayer, *Mgr*
EMP: 149
SQ FT: 2,934
SALES (corp-wide): 136.57MM **Privately Held**
Web: www.casacolina.org
SIC: 8322 Rehabilitation services
HQ: Casa Colina Hospital And Centers For Healthcare
255 E Bonita Ave
Pomona CA
909 596-7733

(P-19033)

CASA COLINA INC (PA)
Also Called: Casa Clina Hosp Ctrs For Hlthc
255 E Bonita Ave (91767-1923)
PHONE..............................909 596-7733
EMP: 800 **EST:** 1981
SALES (est): 136.57MM
SALES (corp-wide): 136.57MM **Privately Held**
Web: www.casacolina.org
SIC: 8322 8011 Rehabilitation services; Ambulatory surgical center

(P-19034)

CASA PCFICA CTRS FOR CHLDREN F (PA)
Also Called: CASA PACIFICA
1722 S Lewis Rd (93012-8520)
PHONE..............................805 482-3260
Shawna Morris, *CEO*
Felice Ginsberg, *
Michael Redard, *
EMP: 175 **EST:** 1988
SQ FT: 63,000
SALES (est): 27.97MM **Privately Held**
Web: www.casapacifica.org
SIC: 8322 8361 8211 Child related social services; Residential care for children; Specialty education

(P-19035)

CATHOLIC CHRTIES SNTA CLARA CN
Also Called: Catholic Charities
303 N Ventura Ave Ste A (93001-1961)
PHONE..............................805 643-4694
Robert Batdazian, *Dir*
EMP: 88
SALES (corp-wide): 54.57MM **Privately Held**
Web: www.catholiccharitiessCC.org
SIC: 8322 Social service center

PA: Catholic Charities Of Santa Clara
County
2625 Zanker Rd Ste 200
San Jose CA
408 468-0100

(P-19036)
CHILD & FAMILY CENTER
21545 Centre Pointe Pkwy (91350-2947)
PHONE.....................661 259-9439
Joan Aschoff, *CEO*
Victor Chavira, *
Bert Paras, *
Evelyn Vega-aguilar, *Dir*
EMP: 120 **EST:** 1976
SQ FT: 26,581
SALES (est): 13.76MM **Privately Held**
Web: www.childfamilycenter.org
SIC: 8322 8099 8093 8049 Family
counseling services; Childbirth preparation
clinic; Mental health clinic, outpatient;
Clinical psychologist

(P-19037)
CHILD CARE RESOURCE
CENTER INC
250 Grand Cypress Ave Ste 601
(93551-3675)
PHONE.....................661 723-3246
EMP: 204
SALES (corp-wide): 404.36MM **Privately
Held**
Web: www.ccrcca.org
SIC: 8322 Child related social services
PA: Child Care Resource Center, Inc.
20001 Prairie St
Chatsworth CA
818 717-1000

(P-19038)
CHILD CARE RESOURCE
CENTER INC (PA)
20001 Prairie St (91311-6508)
PHONE.....................818 717-1000
Michael Olenick, *CEO*
Michael Olenick, *Pr*
Lorraine Schrag, *
Casey Quinn, *
Ellen Cervantes, *
EMP: 130 **EST:** 1976
SALES (est): 404.36MM
SALES (corp-wide): 404.36MM **Privately
Held**
Web: www.ccrcca.org
SIC: 8322 Child related social services

(P-19039)
CHILD DEV RSRCES OF
VNTURA CNT (PA)
Also Called: C D R
221 Ventura Blvd (93036-0277)
PHONE.....................805 485-7878
Jack Hinojosa, *CEO*
EMP: 200 **EST:** 1974
SQ FT: 67,007
SALES (est): 62.02MM
SALES (corp-wide): 62.02MM **Privately
Held**
Web: www.cdrv.org
SIC: 8322 8699 Child guidance agency;
Charitable organization

(P-19040)
CHILD DEVELOPMENT
INSTITUTE
Also Called: CDI
18050 Vanowen St (91335-5638)
PHONE.....................818 888-4559
Joan Samaltese, *Ex Dir*

Dana Kalek, *
Steve Lenhert, *
Tessa Graham, *
EMP: 93 **EST:** 1995
SALES (est): 4.45MM **Privately Held**
Web: www.cdikids.org
SIC: 8322 Child related social services

(P-19041)
CHILDNET YOUTH & FMLY
SVCS INC (PA)
Also Called: Childnet
3545 Long Beach Blvd Ste 200
(90807-3904)
P.O. Box 4550 (90804-0550)
PHONE.....................562 498-5500
Kathy L Hughes, *CEO*
EMP: 177 **EST:** 1970
SALES (est): 33.63MM
SALES (corp-wide): 33.63MM **Privately
Held**
Web: www.childnet.net
SIC: 8322 Child related social services

(P-19042)
CHILDRENS BUREAU
SOUTHERN CAL (PA)
1910 Magnolia Ave (90007-1220)
PHONE.....................213 342-0100
Alex Morales, *Pr*
Sona Chandwani, *
EMP: 107 **EST:** 1904
SQ FT: 43,000
SALES (est): 47.48MM
SALES (corp-wide): 47.48MM **Privately
Held**
Web: www.all4kids.org
SIC: 8322 Child related social services

(P-19043)
CHILDRENS INST LOS ANGELES
679 S New Hampshire Ave (90005-1355)
PHONE.....................213 383-2765
Mary Emmons, *Brnch Mgr*
EMP: 850
SALES (corp-wide): 392.05K **Privately
Held**
Web: www.childrensinstitute.org
SIC: 8322 Social service center
PA: Children's Institute Of Los Angeles
2121 W Temple St
Los Angeles CA
213 385-5100

(P-19044)
CHILDRENS INSTITUTE INC (PA)
2121 W Temple St (90026-4915)
PHONE.....................213 385-5100
Martine Singer, *CEO*
Eugene Straub, *CFOO**
Todd Sosna, *CPO**
James Colon, *
EMP: 190 **EST:** 1906
SQ FT: 18,000
SALES (est): 75.05MM
SALES (corp-wide): 75.05MM **Privately
Held**
Web: www.childrensinstitute.org
SIC: 8322 8699 Child related social services;
Charitable organization

(P-19045)
CITY OF BAKERSFIELD
Rabobank Arena Thter Cnvntion
1001 Truxtun Ave (93301-4714)
PHONE.....................661 852-7300
John Dorman, *Genl Mgr*
EMP: 123
SALES (corp-wide): 519.74MM **Privately
Held**

Web: www.mechanicsbankarena.com
SIC: 8322 9111 6512 Community center;
Mayors' office; Nonresidential building
operators
PA: City Of Bakersfield
1600 Truxtun Ave Fl 5th
Bakersfield CA
661 326-3000

(P-19046)
COMMUNITY ACTION
PARTNERSHIP
3970 Short St (93401-7567)
PHONE.....................805 541-4122
EMP: 97
SALES (corp-wide): 99.11MM **Privately
Held**
Web: www.capslo.org
SIC: 8322 Individual and family services
PA: Community Action Partnership Of San
Luis Obispo County, Inc.
1030 Southwood Dr
San Luis Obispo CA
805 544-4355

(P-19047)
COMMUNITY ACTION PRTNR
ORNGE C
Also Called: OC FOOD BANK
11870 Monarch St (92841-2113)
PHONE.....................714 897-6670
Gregory C Scott, *CEO*
Caroline Coleman, *
EMP: 105 **EST:** 1965
SQ FT: 86,300
SALES (est): 38.76MM **Privately Held**
Web: www.capoc.org
SIC: 8322 Social service center

(P-19048)
COMMUNITY FOOD
CONNECTION
14047 Twin Peaks Rd (92064-3039)
PHONE.....................858 751-4613
William Rearick, *Prin*
Kim Rearick, *
EMP: 80 **EST:** 2014
SALES (est): 529.5K **Privately Held**
Web:
www.thecommunityfoodconnection.com
SIC: 8322 Social service center

(P-19049)
COMMUNITY INTERFACE
SERVICES
981 Vale Terrace Dr (92084-5213)
PHONE.....................760 729-3866
Rose Mueller Hanson, *Pr*
EMP: 100 **EST:** 1983
SALES (est): 13.68MM **Privately Held**
Web:
www.communityinterfaceservices.org
SIC: 8322 Social service center

(P-19050)
COMMUNITY SUPPORT
OPTIONS INC
1401 Poso Dr (93280-2584)
P.O. Box 8018 (93280-8108)
PHONE.....................661 758-5331
John Stockton, *CEO*
Anna Poggi, *
Jose Hernandez, *
Ben Goosen, *
Violet Ratzlass, *
EMP: 102 **EST:** 1974
SQ FT: 9,000
SALES (est): 2.19MM **Privately Held**
Web: www.cso-svd.org

SIC: 8322 Association for the handicapped

(P-19051)
CORE CMNTY ORGNZED RLIEF
EFFOR
Also Called: Core
910 N Hill St (90012-1715)
PHONE.....................323 934-4400
EMP: 400 **EST:** 2010
SALES (est): 62.01MM **Privately Held**
Web: www.coreresponse.org
SIC: 8322 Temporary relief service

(P-19052)
COUNCIL ON AGING - STHERN
CAL
2 Executive Cir Ste 175 (92614-6773)
PHONE.....................714 479-0107
Lisa Wright Jenkins, *CEO*
EMP: 83 **EST:** 1973
SALES (est): 6.84MM **Privately Held**
Web: www.coasc.org
SIC: 8322 Senior citizens' center or
association

(P-19053)
COUNTRY VILLA SERVICE CORP
3000 N Gate Rd (90740-2535)
PHONE.....................562 598-2477
Jennifer Rose, *Brnch Mgr*
EMP: 103
SALES (corp-wide): 88.5MM **Privately
Held**
Web: www.evictionlawyer.com
SIC: 8322 8011 Rehabilitation services;
Medical centers
PA: Country Villa Service Corp.
2400 E Katella Ave # 800
Anaheim CA
310 574-3733

(P-19054)
COUNTRY VLLA RNCHO MRAGE
HLTHC
39950 Vista Del Sol (92270-3206)
PHONE.....................760 340-0053
Scott Gillis, *Admn*
EMP: 200 **EST:** 2007
SALES (est): 3.89MM **Privately Held**
Web: www.ranchomiragehcc.com
SIC: 8322 Rehabilitation services

(P-19055)
COUNTY OF LOS ANGELES
Also Called: Probation Department
5300 W Avenue I (93536-8312)
PHONE.....................661 940-4181
Willie Doyle, *Dir*
EMP: 89
Web: www.lacounty.gov
SIC: 8322 9223 Probation office;
Correctional institutions
PA: County Of Los Angeles
500 W Temple St Ste 437
Los Angeles CA
213 974-1101

(P-19056)
COUNTY OF LOS ANGELES
Also Called: Child Support Services
5770 S Eastern Ave 4th Fl (90040-2948)
PHONE.....................323 889-3405
Steven Golightly, *Mgr*
EMP: 267
Web: www.lacounty.gov
SIC: 8322 9441 Child related social services;
Administration of social and manpower
programs
PA: County Of Los Angeles
500 W Temple St Ste 437

Los Angeles CA
213 974-1101

(P-19057)

COUNTY OF LOS ANGELES

Also Called: Dept Children and Family Svcs
4060 Watson Plaza Dr (90712-4033)
PHONE..............................562 497-3500
Joy Russell, *Admn*
EMP: 95
Web: www.lacounty.gov
SIC: 8322 9111 Childrens' aid society;
Executive offices
PA: County Of Los Angeles
500 W Temple St Ste 437
Los Angeles CA
213 974-1101

(P-19058)

COUNTY OF LOS ANGELES

Also Called: Probation Dept
320 W Temple St Ste 1101 (90012-3289)
PHONE..............................213 974-9331
Mike Verilla, *Dir*
EMP: 85
Web: www.lacounty.gov
SIC: 8322 9223 8093 Probation office;
Correctional institutions; Mental health
clinic, outpatient
PA: County Of Los Angeles
500 W Temple St Ste 437
Los Angeles CA
213 974-1101

(P-19059)

COUNTY OF LOS ANGELES

Also Called: La County Probation
8240 Broadway Ave (90606-3120)
PHONE..............................562 908-3119
Donna Rose, *Mgr*
EMP: 85
Web: www.lacounty.gov
SIC: 8322 9111 Probation office; County
supervisors' and executives' office
PA: County Of Los Angeles
500 W Temple St Ste 437
Los Angeles CA
213 974-1101

(P-19060)

COUNTY OF LOS ANGELES

Also Called: Probation Department
1601 Eastlake Ave (90033-1009)
PHONE..............................323 226-8511
Taula Heath, *Dir*
EMP: 85
Web: www.lacounty.gov
SIC: 8322 Probation office
PA: County Of Los Angeles
500 W Temple St Ste 437
Los Angeles CA
213 974-1101

(P-19061)

COUNTY OF LOS ANGELES

Also Called: Probation Department
7285 Quill Dr (90242-2001)
PHONE..............................562 940-6856
Sheryl Cooke, *Superintnt*
EMP: 91
SALES (corp-wide): 31.7B **Privately Held**
Web: www.lacounty.gov
SIC: 8322 9223 Probation office;
Correctional institutions
PA: County Of Los Angeles
500 W Temple St Ste 437
Los Angeles CA
213 974-1101

(P-19062)

COUNTY OF LOS ANGELES

Also Called: Probation Dept
14414 Delano St (91401-2703)
PHONE..............................818 374-2000
Ed Johnson, *Dir*
EMP: 85
Web: www.lacounty.gov
SIC: 8322 9223 Probation office;
Correctional institutions
PA: County Of Los Angeles
500 W Temple St Ste 437
Los Angeles CA
213 974-1101

(P-19063)

COUNTY OF LOS ANGELES

Also Called: Probation Dept
4849 Civic Center Way (90022-1679)
PHONE..............................323 780-2185
Debbie Nelson, *Dir*
EMP: 142
Web: www.lacounty.gov
SIC: 8322 9223 Probation office;
Correctional institutions
PA: County Of Los Angeles
500 W Temple St Ste 437
Los Angeles CA
213 974-1101

(P-19064)

COUNTY OF LOS ANGELES

Also Called: Department Children Fmly Svcs
501 Shatto Pl Ste 301 (90020-1749)
PHONE..............................213 351-7257
Bill Browning, *Dir*
EMP: 85
Web: www.lacounty.gov
SIC: 8322 9111 Senior citizens' center or
association; Executive offices
PA: County Of Los Angeles
500 W Temple St Ste 437
Los Angeles CA
213 974-1101

(P-19065)

COUNTY OF ORANGE

Also Called: District Attorney
8141 13th St (92683-4576)
PHONE..............................714 896-7188
Gary Tackett, *Brnch Mgr*
EMP: 85
SALES (corp-wide): 5.2B **Privately Held**
Web: www.ocgov.com
SIC: 8322 9211 Substance abuse counseling
; Courts
PA: County Of Orange
400 W Civic Center Dr G36
Santa Ana CA
714 834-6200

(P-19066)

COUNTY OF RIVERSIDE

Also Called: Community Action Prtnr Rvrside
2038 Iowa Ave Ste 102 (92507-2471)
PHONE..............................951 955-4900
Maria Y Juarez, *Mgr*
EMP: 81
SALES (corp-wide): 4.58B **Privately Held**
Web: www.capriverside.org
SIC: 8322 9441 Individual and family
services; Administration of social and
manpower programs
PA: County Of Riverside
4080 Lemon St Fl 11
Riverside CA
951 955-1110

(P-19067)

COUNTY OF SAN DIEGO

Also Called: Probation Dept
330 W Broadway Ste 1100 (92101-3827)
P.O. Box 23596 (92193-3596)
PHONE..............................619 515-8202
Don Blevins, *Dir*
EMP: 920
Web: www.sandiegocounty.gov
SIC: 8322 9431 Probation office;
Administration of public health programs
PA: County Of San Diego
1600 Pacific Hwy Ste 209
San Diego CA
619 531-5880

(P-19068)

COUNTY OF VENTURA

Also Called: County Ventura Human
Resources
800 S Victoria Ave (93009-0003)
PHONE..............................805 654-2561
Jodi Lee Prior, *Brnch Mgr*
EMP: 104
SALES (corp-wide): 165.04MM **Privately
Held**
Web: www.ventura.org
SIC: 8322 9441 Individual and family
services; Administration of social and
human resources
PA: County Of Ventura
800 S Victoria Ave
Ventura CA
805 654-2644

(P-19069)

CRYSTAL STAIRS INC (PA)

5110 W Goldleaf Cir Ste 150 (90056-1287)
PHONE..............................323 299-8998
Jackie B Majors, *CEO*
Dianna Torres, *
Doctor Karen Hill-scott, *Pr*
Carolyn Moultrie, *
Javier La Fianza, *
EMP: 330 **EST:** 1980
SQ FT: 83,000
SALES (est): 252.73MM
SALES (corp-wide): 252.73MM **Privately
Held**
Web: www.crystalstairs.org
SIC: 8322 Social service center

(P-19070)

DEAN L DAVIS MD

Also Called: Mercy Hospital
2215 Truxtun Ave (93301-3602)
P.O. Box 119 (93302-0119)
PHONE..............................661 632-5000
Dean L Davis Md, *Owner*
EMP: 20 **EST:** 1996
SALES (est): 9.59MM **Privately Held**
SIC: 8322 3842 Community center;
Gynecological supplies and appliances

(P-19071)

DESERT ARC

Also Called: DESERT VALLEY INDUSTRIES
73255 Country Club Dr (92260-2309)
PHONE..............................760 346-1611
Kurt Parish, *Admn*
Ruth Goodsell, *
Robin Keagen, *
Robert Anzalone, *
Rosemary Fausel, *
EMP: 256 **EST:** 1959
SQ FT: 12,000
SALES (est): 17.11MM **Privately Held**
Web: www.desertarc.org
SIC: 8322 Association for the handicapped

(P-19072)

DIDI HIRSCH PSYCHIATRIC SVC (PA)

Also Called: Didi Hrsch Cmnty Mntal Hlth Ct
4760 Sepulveda Blvd (90230-4820)
PHONE..............................310 390-6612
Michael Wierwille, *Ch*
Kita S Curry, *
Andrew Rubin, *
John Mcgann, *VP Fin*
Martin Frank, *
EMP: 150 **EST:** 1944
SQ FT: 35,000
SALES (est): 56.18MM
SALES (corp-wide): 56.18MM **Privately
Held**
Web: www.didihirsch.org
SIC: 8322 8093 Family counseling services;
Mental health clinic, outpatient

(P-19073)

EAST LOS ANGLES RMRKBLE CTZENS

Also Called: EL ARCA
3839 Selig Pl (90031-3143)
PHONE..............................323 223-3079
Carlos Madrid, *Ex Dir*
John Menchaca, *
EMP: 100 **EST:** 1969
SQ FT: 23,360
SALES (est): 5.1MM **Privately Held**
Web: www.elarcainc.org
SIC: 8322 Social services for the
handicapped

(P-19074)

EASTERN LOS ANGLES RGNAL CTR F (PA)

1000 S Fremont Ave Unit 23 (91803-8800)
P.O. Box 7916 (91802-7916)
PHONE..............................626 299-4700
Gloria Wong, *Ex Dir*
EMP: 242 **EST:** 1969
SQ FT: 31,704
SALES (est): 196.34MM
SALES (corp-wide): 196.34MM **Privately
Held**
Web: www.elarc.org
SIC: 8322 Association for the handicapped

(P-19075)

EGGLESTON YOUTH CENTERS INC (PA)

256 W Badillo St (91723-1906)
P.O. Box 638 (91706-0638)
PHONE..............................626 480-8107
Clarence Brown, *Ex Dir*
Don Gutierrez, *
April Mitchell, *Brand President**
EMP: 90 **EST:** 1975
SQ FT: 7,616
SALES (est): 11.26MM
SALES (corp-wide): 11.26MM **Privately
Held**
Web: www.egglestonyouthcenter.org
SIC: 8322 Social service center

(P-19076)

EL NIDO FAMILY CENTERS (PA)

10200 Sepulveda Blvd Ste 350
(91345-3318)
PHONE..............................818 830-3646
Liz Herrera, *Dir*
EMP: 130 **EST:** 1957
SQ FT: 3,650
SALES (est): 14.16MM
SALES (corp-wide): 14.16MM **Privately
Held**
Web: www.elnidofamilycenters.org

PRODUCTS & SVCS

SIC: 8322 -Social service center

(P-19077)
EPISCOPAL COMMUNITY SERVICES
Also Called: Ecs-National City Head Start
2432 E 18th St (91950-5143)
PHONE..............................619 470-0720
Leanna Cobarrubias, *Dir*
EMP: 96
SALES (corp-wide): 32.67MM **Privately Held**
Web: www.ecscalifornia.org
SIC: 8322 Social service center
PA: Episcopal Community Services
401 Mile Of Cars Way
National City CA
619 228-2800

(P-19078)
ESSENCE OF AMERICA
1855 1st Ave Ste 103 (92101-2650)
P.O. Box 23682 (92193-3682)
PHONE..............................312 805-9365
EMP: 25 EST: 2011
SALES (est): 200K **Privately Held**
SIC: 8322 5812 2099 2599 Meal delivery program; Restaurant, family: independent; Syrups; Food wagons, restaurant

(P-19079)
FAMILY ASSISTANCE PROGRAM
Also Called: OUR HOUSE
15075 Seventh St (92395-3810)
PHONE..............................760 843-0701
Darryl Evey, *CEO*
Darryl Evey, *Ex Dir*
Elsa Scott, *
EMP: 92 EST: 1985
SQ FT: 4,960
SALES (est): 8.51MM **Privately Held**
Web: www.familyassist.org
SIC: 8322 Social service center

(P-19080)
FAMILY SVC AGCY SNTA BRBARA CN
123 W Gutierrez St (93101-3424)
PHONE..............................805 965-1001
Denise Cicourel, *Admn*
EMP: 100 EST: 1901
SALES (est): 15.16MM **Privately Held**
Web: www.fsacares.org
SIC: 8322 Social service center

(P-19081)
FIRST 5 LA
750 N Alameda St Ste 300 (90012-3870)
PHONE..............................213 482-5920
Kim Belsh, *Prin*
EMP: 147 EST: 2008
SALES (est): 29.41MM **Privately Held**
Web: www.first5la.org
SIC: 8322 Child guidance agency

(P-19082)
FOOTHILL FAMILY SERVICE
3629 Santa Anita Ave Ste 201 (91731-2449)
PHONE..............................626 246-1240
EMP: 113
SALES (corp-wide): 29.83MM **Privately Held**
Web: www.foothillfamily.org
SIC: 8322 Family counseling services
PA: Foothill Family Service
2500 E Fthill Blvd Ste 30
Pasadena CA
626 993-3000

(P-19083)
FOOTHILL FAMILY SERVICE
2500 E Foothill Blvd Ste 300 (91107)
PHONE..............................626 795-6907
Helen Morran-wolf, *Mgr*
EMP: 113
SALES (corp-wide): 29.83MM **Privately Held**
Web: www.foothillfamily.org
SIC: 8322 Family counseling services
PA: Foothill Family Service
2500 E Fthill Blvd Ste 30
Pasadena CA
626 993-3000

(P-19084)
G&L PENASQUITOS INC
Also Called: Arbors, The
10584 Rancho Carmel Dr (92128-3629)
PHONE..............................858 538-0802
Gary Penovich, *Ex Dir*
EMP: 934 EST: 1998
SQ FT: 48,685
SALES (est): 718.1K
SALES (corp-wide): 49.16MM **Privately Held**
SIC: 8322 Individual and family services
PA: G&L Realty Corp, Llc
439 N Bedford Dr
Beverly Hills CA
310 273-9930

(P-19085)
GRASSHOPPER HOUSE PARTNERS LLC
Also Called: Passages
6428 Meadows Ct (90265-4492)
PHONE..............................310 589-2880
Pax Prentiss, *
EMP: 105 EST: 2000
SQ FT: 16,000
SALES (est): 9.01MM **Privately Held**
Web: www.passagesmalibu.com
SIC: 8322 Rehabilitation services

(P-19086)
HATHAWY-SYCMRES CHILD FMLY SVC
Also Called: Hathaway Children and Family
12502 Van Nuys Blvd Ste 120 (91331-1321)
PHONE..............................626 395-7100
Muriel Gaudin, *Mgr*
EMP: 211
SALES (corp-wide): 64.09MM **Privately Held**
Web: www.sycamores.org
SIC: 8322 Child related social services
PA: Hathaway-Sycamores Child And Family Services
100 W Walnut St Ste 375
Pasadena CA
626 395-7100

(P-19087)
HATHAWY-SYCMRES CHILD FMLY SVC
3741 Stocker St Ste 101 (90008-5150)
PHONE..............................323 733-0322
Debbie Manners, *Brnch Mgr*
EMP: 250
SALES (corp-wide): 64.09MM **Privately Held**
Web: www.sycamores.org
SIC: 8322 Child related social services

PA: Hathaway-Sycamores Child And Family Services
100 W Walnut St Ste 375
Pasadena CA
626 395-7100

(P-19088)
HELP CHILDREN WORLD FOUNDATION
Also Called: INTERNATIONAL CHILDREN'S CHARI
26500 Agoura Rd Ste 657 (91302-1952)
PHONE..............................818 706-9848
Lev M Leznik, *Pr*
Andrew Grey, *
Veronica Duval, *
Michael Teilmann, *
EMP: 300 EST: 1991
SQ FT: 2,200
SALES (est): 10.68MM **Privately Held**
SIC: 8322 Childrens' aid society

(P-19089)
HILLSIDES
940 Avenue 64 (91105-2711)
PHONE..............................323 254-2274
Joseph M Costa, *CEO*
Ryan Herren, *
Amy Ley-sanchez, *Ex VP*
EMP: 460 EST: 1913
SQ FT: 18,217
SALES (est): 51.1MM **Privately Held**
Web: www.recruiting.com
SIC: 8322 Individual and family services

(P-19090)
HOMEBOY INDUSTRIES (PA)
Also Called: Homeboy Bakery
130 Bruno St (90012-1815)
PHONE..............................323 526-1254
Greg Boyle, *Ex Dir*
Thomas Vozzo, *Prin*
Jack Faherty, *
John Brady, *
EMP: 270 EST: 2000
SQ FT: 3,690
SALES (est): 33.03MM **Privately Held**
Web: www.homeboyindustries.org
SIC: 8322 Rehabilitation services

(P-19091)
HORRIGAN ENTERPRISES INC
Also Called: Crossrads Adult Day Hlth Care
7945 Cartilla Ave (91730-3076)
PHONE..............................909 481-9663
EMP: 153
SALES (corp-wide): 4.74MM **Privately Held**
Web: www.industry386.com
SIC: 8322 Adult day care center
PA: Horrigan Enterprises, Inc.
1636 Country Club Dr
Redlands CA
909 484-5561

(P-19092)
IN-ROADS CREATIVE PROGRAMS
9057 Arrow Rte Ste 120 (91730-4452)
PHONE..............................909 989-9944
Sharon Barton, *Brnch Mgr*
EMP: 367
Web: www.in-roads.net
SIC: 8322 Adult day care center
PA: In-Roads Creative Programs, Inc
7955 Webster St Ste 7
Highland CA

(P-19093)
IN-ROADS CREATIVE PROGRAMS
1951 E Saint Andrews Dr (91761-6447)
PHONE..............................909 947-9142
Sharon Barton, *Brnch Mgr*
EMP: 367
Web: www.in-roads.net
SIC: 8322 Childrens' aid society
PA: In-Roads Creative Programs, Inc
7955 Webster St Ste 7
Highland CA

(P-19094)
INCLUSION SERVICES LLC
Also Called: Inclusion Services
7255 Greenleaf Ave Ste 20 (90602-1340)
PHONE..............................562 945-2000
Cesar Torres, *Managing Member*
Israel Ibenez, *Managing Member*
EMP: 103 EST: 2009
SALES (est): 9.49MM **Privately Held**
Web: www.inclusionsvs.org
SIC: 8322 8331 Social services for the handicapped; Skill training center

(P-19095)
INLAND CNTIES REGIONAL CTR INC (PA)
Also Called: Inland Regional Center
1365 S Waterman Ave (92408-2804)
P.O. Box 19037 (92423-9037)
PHONE..............................909 890-3000
Carol A Fitzgibbons, *CEO*
Carol Fitzgibbons, *
EMP: 173 EST: 1971
SQ FT: 82,000
SALES (est): 744.4MM
SALES (corp-wide): 744.4MM **Privately Held**
Web: www.inlandrc.org
SIC: 8322 Social service center

(P-19096)
INTERFACE COMMUNITY (PA)
Also Called: INTERFACE CHILDREN FAMILY SERV
4001 Mission Oaks Blvd Ste I (93012-5121)
PHONE..............................805 485-6114
Charles T Watson, *Pr*
Dale Stoeber, *
Terryl Miller, *CPO*
EMP: 88 EST: 1975
SQ FT: 3,000
SALES (est): 13.2MM
SALES (corp-wide): 13.2MM **Privately Held**
Web: www.icfs.org
SIC: 8322 Social service center

(P-19097)
INTERFAITH COMMUNITY SVCS INC
Also Called: Interfaith Community Services
250 N Ash St (92027-3026)
PHONE..............................760 489-6380
Greg Anglea, *Ex Dir*
Leonard Jacobson, *
Suzanne Pohlman, *
EMP: 100 EST: 1982
SALES (est): 30.32MM **Privately Held**
Web: www.interfaithservices.org
SIC: 8322 Social service center

(P-19098)
INTERNATIONAL MEDICAL CORPS (PA)
Also Called: IMC
12400 Wilshire Blvd Ste 1500 (90025-1019)

PHONE.................................310 826-7800
Nancy Aossey, *Pr*
Ingrid Renaud, *
Ky Luu, *Ofcr*
EMP: 4500 **EST:** 1984
SALES (est): 220.72MM
SALES (corp-wide): 220.72MM **Privately Held**
Web: www.internationalmedicalcorps.org
SIC: 8322 Disaster service

(P-19099)
INTERVAL HOUSE
6615 E Pacific Coast Hwy Ste 170 (90803)
P.O. Box 3356 (90740-2356)
PHONE.................................562 594-4555
Robert Armstrong, *Pr*
Carol Williams, *
Elizabeth Lambert, *
Christine Delabre, *
Sharon Wie, *
EMP: 91 **EST:** 1979
SALES (est): 10.35MM **Privately Held**
Web: www.intervalhouse.org
SIC: 8322 Emergency shelters

(P-19100)
JEWISH COMMUNITY CTR LONG BCH
Also Called: ALPERT JEWISH COMMUNITY CENTRE
3801 E Willow St (90815-1734)
PHONE.................................562 426-7601
Gordon Lentzner, *Pr*
EMP: 150 **EST:** 1948
SQ FT: 90,000
SALES (est): 5.29MM **Privately Held**
Web: www.alpertjcc.org
SIC: 8322 Community center

(P-19101)
JEWISH FAMILY SVC LOS ANGELES
Also Called: Senior Nutrition Program
330 N Fairfax Ave (90036-2109)
PHONE.................................323 937-5900
Eileen Mccouliffe, *Dir*
EMP: 147
SALES (corp-wide): 55.36MM **Privately Held**
Web: www.jfla.org
SIC: 8322 Social service center
PA: Jewish Family Service Of Los Angeles
330 N Fairfax Ave
Los Angeles CA
323 761-8800

(P-19102)
JEWISH FAMILY SVC SAN DIEGO (PA)
Also Called: Jewish Family Service
8804 Balboa Ave (92123-1506)
PHONE.................................858 637-3000
Michael Hopkins, *CEO*
Emily Jennewein, *
Felicia Mandelbaum, *
EMP: 204 **EST:** 1936
SQ FT: 25,000
SALES (est): 81.99MM
SALES (corp-wide): 81.99MM **Privately Held**
Web: www.jfssd.org
SIC: 8322 Social service center

(P-19103)
JONI AND FRIENDS FOUNDATION (PA)
30009 Ladyface Ct (91301-2583)
PHONE.................................818 707-5664

Joni E Tada, *CEO*
Douglas Mazza, *
Billy Burnett, *
◆ **EMP:** 84 **EST:** 1979
SQ FT: 30,000
SALES (est): 9.91MM
SALES (corp-wide): 9.91MM **Privately Held**
Web: www.joniandfriends.org
SIC: 8322 Association for the handicapped

(P-19104)
JVS SOCAL
6505 Wilshire Blvd (90048-4906)
PHONE.................................323 761-8879
Alan Levey, *Prin*
EMP: 268 **EST:** 1931
SALES (est): 28.76MM **Privately Held**
Web: www.jvs-socal.org
SIC: 8322 Individual and family services

(P-19105)
JWCH INSTITUTE INC
Also Called: Jwch Medical Center
3591 E Imperial Hwy (90262-2654)
PHONE.................................310 223-1035
Al Basceros, *Mgr*
EMP: 178
SALES (corp-wide): 112.81MM **Privately Held**
Web: www.jwchinstitute.org
SIC: 8322 8093 Individual and family services; Family planning clinic
PA: Jwch Institute, Inc.
5650 Jillson St
Commerce CA
323 477-1171

(P-19106)
KEDREN COMMUNITY HLTH CTR INC
3800 S Figueroa St (90037-1206)
PHONE.................................323 524-0634
John Griffith, *Pr*
EMP: 133
SALES (corp-wide): 42.85MM **Privately Held**
Web: www.kedren.org
SIC: 8322 Community center
PA: Kedren Community Health Center, Inc.
4211 Avalon Blvd
Los Angeles CA
323 233-0425

(P-19107)
LA ASCCION NCNAL PRO PRSNAS MY
Also Called: National Assn For Hispanic
1452 W Temple St Ste 100 (90026-5649)
PHONE.................................213 202-5900
Zecia Soto, *Prin*
EMP: 703
SALES (corp-wide): 13.34MM **Privately Held**
SIC: 8322 7361 8611 Social service center; Employment agencies; Business associations
PA: La Asociacion Nacional Pro Personas Mayores
234 E Colo Blvd Ste 300
Pasadena CA
626 564-1988

(P-19108)
LAURAS HOUSE
33 Journey Ste 150 (92656-5364)
PHONE.................................949 361-3775
EMP: 92 **EST:** 1994
SALES (est): 4.04MM **Privately Held**
Web: www.laurashouse.org

SIC: 8322 Social service center

(P-19109)
LIFE STEPS FOUNDATION INC
500 E 4th St (90802-2501)
PHONE.................................562 436-0751
Kristine Engels, *Dir*
EMP: 93
Web: www.lifestepsfoundation.org
SIC: 8322 8399 Social service center; Community development groups
PA: Life Steps Foundation, Inc.
5757 W Century Blvd # 575
Los Angeles CA

(P-19110)
LOS ANGELES HOMELESS SVCS AUTH
Also Called: L A H S A
707 Wilshire Blvd Ste 1000 (90017-3729)
PHONE.................................213 683-3333
Heidi Marston, *Ex Dir*
EMP: 558 **EST:** 1993
SALES (est): 93.78MM **Privately Held**
Web: www.lahsa.org
SIC: 8322 Social service center

(P-19111)
LOS ANGELES REGIONAL FOOD BANK
1734 E 41st St (90058-1502)
PHONE.................................323 234-3030
Michael Flood, *Pr*
Michael Flood, *Pr*
Czarina Luna, *
EMP: 185 **EST:** 1977
SALES (est): 251.17MM **Privately Held**
Web: www.lafoodbank.org
SIC: 8322 8699 Meal delivery program; Charitable organization

(P-19112)
MEXICAN AMRCN OPRTNTY FNDATION (PA)
Also Called: Maof
401 N Garfield Ave (90640-2901)
P.O. Box 4602 (90640-9311)
PHONE.................................323 890-9600
Martin Vasquez Castro, *Pr*
Carlos J Viramontes, *
EMP: 100 **EST:** 1963
SQ FT: 25,000
SALES (est): 116.75MM
SALES (corp-wide): 116.75MM **Privately Held**
Web: www.maof.org
SIC: 8322 Social service center

(P-19113)
MEXICAN AMRCN OPRTNTY FNDATION
Also Called: Maof Commerce
5657 E Washington Blvd (90040-1405)
PHONE.................................323 890-1555
Martin Castro, *Pr*
EMP: 86
SALES (corp-wide): 116.75MM **Privately Held**
Web: www.maof.org
SIC: 8322 Social service center
PA: Mexican American Opportunity Foundation
401 N Garfield Ave
Montebello CA
323 890-9600

(P-19114)
MYHHBS INC
237 N Central Ave Ste A (91203-3526)
PHONE.................................888 969-4427
EMP: 85 **EST:** 2016
SALES (est): 1.19MM **Privately Held**
Web: www.myhhbs.com
SIC: 8322 General counseling services

(P-19115)
NEIGHBORHOOD HOUSE ASSOCIATION (PA)
Also Called: N H A
5660 Copley Dr (92111-7902)
PHONE.................................858 715-2642
Rudolph A Johnson Iii, *CEO*
EMP: 500 **EST:** 1914
SQ FT: 60,000
SALES (est): 106.3MM
SALES (corp-wide): 106.3MM **Privately Held**
Web: www.neighborhoodhouse.org
SIC: 8322 Neighborhood center

(P-19116)
NEW ALTERNATIVES INCORPORATED
8755 Aero Dr Ste 230 (92123-1750)
PHONE.................................619 863-5855
EMP: 581
SALES (corp-wide): 65.42MM **Privately Held**
Web: www.newalternativesfund.com
SIC: 8322 Social service center
PA: New Alternatives, Incorporated
3589 4th Ave
San Diego CA
619 543-0293

(P-19117)
NEW DIRECTIONS INC (PA)
Also Called: NEW DIRECTIONS FOR VETERANS
11303 Wilshire Blvd Bldg 116 (90025-5069)
P.O. Box 25536 (90025-0536)
PHONE.................................310 914-4045
EMP: 80 **EST:** 1989
SQ FT: 60,000
SALES (est): 8.82MM **Privately Held**
Web: www.ndvets.org
SIC: 8322 Substance abuse counseling

(P-19118)
OAK GROVE INST FOUNDATION INC
1251 N A St (92570-1911)
PHONE.................................951 238-6022
EMP: 240
Web: www.oakgrovecenter.org
SIC: 8322 Child related social services
PA: Oak Grove Institute Foundation, Inc.
24275 Jefferson Ave
Murrieta CA

(P-19119)
OPTIMA FAMILY SERVICES INC
253 N San Gabriel Blvd (91107-3429)
PHONE.................................323 300-6066
Oscar A Carvajal, *Prin*
EMP: 178 **EST:** 2008
SALES (est): 6.83MM **Privately Held**
Web: www.optimafamilyservices.com
SIC: 8322 General counseling services

(P-19120)
ORANGE CNTY ADULT ACHVMENT CTR
Also Called: MY DAY COUNTS

PRODUCTS & SVCS

225 W Carl Karcher Way (92801-2499)
PHONE.............................714 744-5301
Michael Galliano, *CEO*
Patrick Faraday, *
Richard Farmer, *
Laurie Vinkavich, *
Jack Salseda, *
▲ EMP: 135 EST: 1955
SQ FT: 57,000
SALES (est): 9.73MM **Privately Held**
Web: www.mydaycounts.org
SIC: 8322 Social service center

(P-19121)
ORANGEWOOD FOUNDATION
1575 E 17th St (92705-8506)
PHONE.............................714 619-0200
Chris Simonsen, *CEO*
John Luker, *
EMP: 85 EST: 1980
SQ FT: 22,340
SALES (est): 24.46MM **Privately Held**
Web: www.orangewoodfoundation.org
SIC: 8322 Child related social services

(P-19122)
PATH
340 N Madison Ave (90004-3504)
PHONE.............................323 644-2216
Joel John Roberts, *Pr*
Jennifer Hark Dietz, *
Sandy Oluwek, *
Sarah Kolish, *
La Keishia Childers, *
EMP: 828 EST: 1984
SALES (est): 131.55MM **Privately Held**
Web: www.epath.org
SIC: 8322 Social service center

(P-19123)
PEOPLE CONCERN
Safe Haven
1751 Cloverfield Blvd (90404-4007)
PHONE.............................310 883-1222
Andrew Schwich, *Dir*
EMP: 174
SALES (corp-wide): 85.14MM **Privately Held**
Web: www.thepeopleconcern.org
SIC: 8322 Emergency shelters
PA: The People Concern
　　2116 Arlington Ave # 100
　　Los Angeles CA
　　323 334-9000

(P-19124)
PEOPLE CONCERN
Daybreak
1751 Cloverfield Blvd (90404-4007)
PHONE.............................310 450-0650
Anya Booker, *Dir*
EMP: 174
SALES (corp-wide): 85.14MM **Privately Held**
Web: www.thepeopleconcern.org
SIC: 8322 Community center
PA: The People Concern
　　2116 Arlington Ave # 100
　　Los Angeles CA
　　323 334-9000

(P-19125)
PEOPLE CREATING SUCCESS INC
1607 E Palmdale Blvd Ste H (93550-7801)
PHONE.............................661 225-9700
Robert Donery, *Bmch Mgr*
EMP: 99
SALES (corp-wide): 14.09MM **Privately Held**

Web: www.pcs-services.org
SIC: 8322 Individual and family services
PA: People Creating Success, Inc.
　　2585 Teller Rd
　　Newbury Park CA
　　805 375-9222

(P-19126)
PEOPLE CREATING SUCCESS INC
5350 Hollister Ave Ste I (93111-2326)
PHONE.............................805 692-5290
Brian Fay, *Mgr*
EMP: 99
SALES (corp-wide): 14.09MM **Privately Held**
Web: www.pcs-services.org
SIC: 8322 Social service center
PA: People Creating Success, Inc.
　　2585 Teller Rd
　　Newbury Park CA
　　805 375-9222

(P-19127)
PRIORITY CTR ENDING THE GNRTNA
Also Called: WELCOME BABY
1940 E Deere Ave Ste 100 (92705-5718)
PHONE.............................714 543-4333
Scott Trotter, *Ex Dir*
Stephanie Enano, *
EMP: 99 EST: 1983
SALES (est): 8.84MM **Privately Held**
Web: www.theprioritycenter.org
SIC: 8322 Child related social services

(P-19128)
PROJECT CONCERN INTERNATIONAL (PA)
Also Called: PCI
5151 Murphy Canyon Rd Ste 320 (92123-4330)
PHONE.............................858 279-9690
Carrie Hessler-radelet, *Pr*
George Guimaraes, *
Kote Lomidze, *
Janine Schooley, *
Mark O Donnell, *
EMP: 124 EST: 1961
SQ FT: 12,000
SALES (est): 12.21MM
SALES (corp-wide): 12.21MM **Privately Held**
Web: www.pciglobal.org
SIC: 8322 Social service center

(P-19129)
PROTOTYPES CENTERS FOR INNOV
Also Called: Prototypes
1000 N Alameda St Ste 390 (90012-1804)
PHONE.............................213 542-3838
Cassandra Loch, *Pr*
Maryann Fraser, *
EMP: 250 EST: 1986
SQ FT: 8,400
SALES (est): 20.14MM **Privately Held**
Web: www.healthright360.org
SIC: 8322 General counseling services

(P-19130)
PUBLIC HLTH FNDATION ENTPS INC
13181 Crossroads Pkwy N (91746-3419)
PHONE.............................626 856-6600
Eliose Jenks, *Bmch Mgr*
EMP: 140
SALES (corp-wide): 92.05MM **Privately Held**

Web: www.phfewic.org
SIC: 8322 Social service center
PA: Public Health Foundation Enterprises, Inc.
　　13300 Crssrds Pkwy N
　　City Of Industry CA
　　800 201-7320

(P-19131)
SALVATION ARMY (HQ)
Also Called: Salvation Army Western Ttry
30840 Hawthorne Blvd (90275-5301)
PHONE.............................562 264-3600
James M Knaggs, *CEO*
Commissioner Carolyn R Knaggs
Territorial, *MINISTRIES*
Colonel David E Hudson, *Chief Secretary*
Susan Lawrence, *
Kenneth Hodder, *
▼ EMP: 140 EST: 1865
SALES (est): 516.57K
SALES (corp-wide): 2.41B **Privately Held**
Web: www.salvationarmy.org
SIC: 8322 Social service center
PA: The Salvation Army National Corporation
　　615 Slaters Ln
　　Alexandria VA
　　703 684-5500

(P-19132)
SAN BRNRDINO CNTY PRBTION OFFC
4370 Hallmark Pkwy Ste 105 (92407-7710)
PHONE.............................909 887-2544
Laura Pleasant, *VP*
EMP: 407 EST: 2007
SALES (est): 556.91K **Privately Held**
Web:
www.sanbernardinocountyprobation.org
SIC: 8322 Probation office

(P-19133)
SAN DEGO SECOND CHANCE PROGRAM
6145 Imperial Ave (92114-4213)
PHONE.............................619 266-2506
EMP: 35 EST: 1992
SALES (est): 2.84MM **Privately Held**
Web: www.secondchanceprogram.org
SIC: 8322 7361 3965 Social service center; Employment agencies; Fasteners, buttons, needles, and pins

(P-19134)
SAN DG-MPRIAL CNTIES DVLPMNTAL (PA)
4355 Ruffin Rd Ste 220 (92123-4308)
PHONE.............................858 576-2996
Carlos Flores, *Ex Dir*
Judy Wallace Patton, *
Edward Kenney, *
EMP: 286 EST: 1982
SQ FT: 62,000
SALES (est): 576.43MM
SALES (corp-wide): 576.43MM **Privately Held**
Web: www.sdrc.org
SIC: 8322 Social services for the handicapped

(P-19135)
SAN GBRL/PMONA VLLEYS DVLPMNTA
Also Called: SAN GABRIEL/POMONA REGIONAL CE
75 Rancho Camino Dr (91766-4728)
PHONE.............................909 620-7722
R Keith Penman, *Ex Dir*

R Keith Penman, *Ex Dir*
Carol Tomblin, *
John Hunt, *
EMP: 323 EST: 1986
SQ FT: 100,000
SALES (est): 320.15MM **Privately Held**
Web: www.sgprc.org
SIC: 8322 Social service center

(P-19136)
SANTEE SENIOR RETIREMENT COM
Also Called: Pointe At Lantern Crest, The
400 Lantern Crest Way (92071-4633)
PHONE.............................619 955-0901
Kaan Ciftci, *Ex Dir*
EMP: 104
Web:
www.lanterncrestseniorlivingsantee.com
SIC: 8322 Senior citizens' center or association
PA: Santee Senior Retirement Communities, Llc
　　8510 Railroad Ave
　　Santee CA

(P-19137)
SBCS CORPORATION
430 F St (91910-3711)
PHONE.............................619 420-3620
Kathryn Lembo, *Ex Dir*
EMP: 200 EST: 1971
SQ FT: 2,900
SALES (est): 34.79MM **Privately Held**
Web: www.case-5-19-cv-07071.info
SIC: 8322 Social service center

(P-19138)
SECOND HRVEST FD BNK ORNGE CNT
8014 Marine Way (92618-2235)
PHONE.............................949 653-2900
Claudia Bonilla Keller, *CEO*
Chrislynn Vanskiver, *
Joyce Foley, *
EMP: 80 EST: 2008
SALES (est): 91.57MM **Privately Held**
Web: www.feedoc.org
SIC: 8322 Social service center

(P-19139)
SENECA FAMILY OF AGENCIES
2130 N Ventura Rd (93036-2246)
PHONE.............................805 278-0355
EMP: 215
SALES (corp-wide): 150.1MM **Privately Held**
Web: www.senecafoa.org
SIC: 8322 Social service center
PA: Seneca Family of Agencies
　　8945 Golf Links Rd
　　Oakland CA
　　510 317-1444

(P-19140)
SEXUAL RECOVERY INSTITUTE INC
1964 Westwood Blvd Ste 400 (90025-4695)
PHONE.............................310 360-0130
David A Sack, *CEO*
Robert Weiss, *
EMP: 305 EST: 1955
SALES (est): 8.01MM
SALES (corp-wide): 78.49MM **Privately Held**
Web: www.sexualrecovery.com
SIC: 8322 General counseling services
PA: Elements Behavioral Health, Inc.
　　5000 Arprt Plz Ste 100
　　Long Beach CA
　　562 741-6470

(P-19141)
SOCIAL ADVCTES FOR YUTH SAN DE
4275 El Cajon Blvd Ste 101 (92105-1293)
PHONE..................................619 283-9624
Nancy G Hornberger, *CEO*
EMP: 177
SALES (corp-wide): 18.31MM **Privately Held**
Web: www.saysandiego.org
SIC: 8322 Social service center
PA: Social Advocates For Youth, San Diego, Inc.
4775 Viewridge Ave
San Diego CA
858 565-4148

(P-19142)
SOUTH BAY CTR FOR COUNSELING
Also Called: SOUTH BAY CENTER FOR COMMUNITY
540 N Marine Ave (90744-5528)
PHONE..................................310 414-2090
Colleen Mooney, *Ex Dir*
Maria Lomibao, *
EMP: 90 **EST:** 1974
SALES (est): 7.76MM **Privately Held**
Web: www.sbccthrivela.org
SIC: 8322 General counseling services

(P-19143)
ST JOSEPH CENTER
Also Called: SAINT JOSEPH CENTER VOLUNTEER
204 Hampton Dr (90291-8633)
PHONE..................................310 396-6468
Felecia Adams, *VP*
Va Lecia Adams Kellum, *Ex Dir*
Paul Rubenstein, *
Tifara Monroe, *
John Mcgann, *CFO*
EMP: 85 **EST:** 1976
SQ FT: 32,000
SALES (est): 51.82MM **Privately Held**
Web: www.stjosephctr.org
SIC: 8322 8331 8351 Social service center; Job training services; Child day care services

(P-19144)
ST JOSEPH HOSPICE
Also Called: Saint Joseph Hlth Sys Hospice
200 W Center Street Promenade (92805-3960)
PHONE..................................714 712-7100
Linda Glomp, *Dir*
Ron Nagano, *
Maire Blaistell, *
EMP: 246 **EST:** 1994
SQ FT: 3,000
SALES (est): 1.84MM
SALES (corp-wide): 32.76MM **Privately Held**
Web: www.hospice.io
SIC: 8322 8063 Geriatric social service; Psychiatric hospitals
HQ: St. Joseph Home Care Network
441 College Ave
Santa Rosa CA
714 712-9500

(P-19145)
STRAIGHT TALK INC
Also Called: Straight Talk Counseling Ctr
13710 La Mirada Blvd (90638-3028)
PHONE..................................562 943-0195
Meg Kalugan, *Mgr*
EMP: 90
SALES (corp-wide): 1.57MM **Privately Held**

Web: www.straighttalkcounseling.org
SIC: 8322 General counseling services
PA: Straight Talk Clinic, Incorporated
5712 Camp St
Cypress CA
714 828-2000

(P-19146)
TOWARD MAXIMUM INDEPENDENCE (PA)
Also Called: T M I
4740 Murphy Canyon Rd Ste 300 (92123-4385)
PHONE..................................858 467-0600
Kerby Wohlander, *Dir*
EMP: 125 **EST:** 1981
SQ FT: 5,700
SALES (est): 19.66MM **Privately Held**
Web: www.tmi-inc.org
SIC: 8322 Social services for the handicapped

(P-19147)
TRI-CNTIES ASSN FOR DVLPMNTLLY
Also Called: Tri-Counties Regional Center
1146 Farmhouse Ln (93401-8362)
PHONE..................................805 543-2833
Frank Bush, *Dir*
EMP: 104
SALES (corp-wide): 388.4MM **Privately Held**
Web: www.tri-counties.org
SIC: 8322 Association for the handicapped
PA: Tri-Counties Association For The Developmentally Disabled, Inc.
520 E Montecito St
Santa Barbara CA
805 962-7881

(P-19148)
TURNING POINT FOR GOD
P.O. Box 3838 (92163-1838)
PHONE..................................619 258-3600
David Jeremiah, *Prin*
EMP: 93 **EST:** 2010
SALES (est): 479.88K **Privately Held**
Web: www.davidjeremiah.ca
SIC: 8322 Individual and family services

(P-19149)
TURNING POINT MINISTRIES
Also Called: TURNING POINT COUNSELING
1370 Brea Blvd Ste 245 (92835-4173)
PHONE..................................800 998-6329
TOLL FREE: 800
EMP: 93 **EST:** 1983
SQ FT: 2,500
SALES (est): 1.15MM **Privately Held**
Web: www.turningpointcounseling.org
SIC: 8322 Family counseling services

(P-19150)
UNITED CRBRAL PLSY ASSN ORNGE
Also Called: Ucp of Orange County
1251 E Dyer Rd Ste 150 (92705-5662)
PHONE..................................949 333-6400
Ramin Baschshi, *CEO*
EMP: 400 **EST:** 1953
SQ FT: 5,000
SALES (est): 6.38MM **Privately Held**
SIC: 8322 Social service center

(P-19151)
UNITED CRBRAL PLSY ASSN SAN LU
Also Called: Ride On Transportation
3620 Sacramento Dr Ste 201 (93401-7215)

PHONE..................................805 543-2039
Mark Shaffer, *Ex Dir*
EMP: 100 **EST:** 1991
SQ FT: 1,600
SALES (est): 6.02MM **Privately Held**
Web: www.ride-on.org
SIC: 8322 Social service center

(P-19152)
UPLIFT FAMILY SERVICES
800 S Santa Anita Ave (91006-3536)
PHONE..................................626 254-5000
Kathryn Mccarthy, *Pr*
EMP: 581
SALES (corp-wide): 147.1MM **Privately Held**
Web: www.pacificclinics.org
SIC: 8322 Individual and family services
PA: Uplift Family Services
251 Llewellyn Ave
Campbell CA
408 379-3790

(P-19153)
VINTAGE SENIOR MANAGEMENT INC
Also Called: VINTAGE SENIOR MANAGEMENT, INC.
2721 W Willow St (91505-4544)
PHONE..................................818 954-9500
Brian Flornes, *Brnch Mgr*
EMP: 832
SIC: 8322 Geriatric social service
PA: Senior Vintage Management Inc
23 Corporate Plaza Dr # 190
Newport Beach CA

(P-19154)
VISTA CARE GROUP LLC (PA)
Also Called: Vista Gardens
1863 Devon Pl (92084-7624)
PHONE..................................760 295-3900
Avelen Delgado, *Admn*
Harry Crowell, *
Joe Balbas, *
EMP: 80 **EST:** 2010
SALES (est): 4.16MM
SALES (corp-wide): 4.16MM **Privately Held**
Web: www.vistagardensmemorycare.com
SIC: 8322 Senior citizens' center or association

(P-19155)
VISTA HILL FOUNDATION
4125 Alpha St (92113-4553)
PHONE..................................619 266-0166
EMP: 90
SALES (corp-wide): 34.66MM **Privately Held**
Web: www.vistahill.org
SIC: 8322 8051 Geriatric social service; Skilled nursing care facilities
PA: Vista Hill Foundation
8910 Clairemont Mesa Blvd
San Diego CA
585 514-5100

(P-19156)
VOLUNTEERS OF AMER LOS ANGELES
Also Called: Volunteers of America
2100 N Broadway Ste 300 (92706-2624)
PHONE..................................714 426-9834
EMP: 80
SALES (corp-wide): 98.98MM **Privately Held**
Web: www.voala.org

SIC: 8322 Social service center
PA: Volunteers Of America Of Los Angeles
3600 Wilshire Blvd # 1500
Los Angeles CA
213 389-1500

(P-19157)
VOLUNTEERS OF AMER LOS ANGELES
Also Called: Volunteers of America
1032 W 18th St (90015-3324)
PHONE..................................213 749-0362
Ernest Green, *Dir*
EMP: 105
SALES (corp-wide): 98.98MM **Privately Held**
Web: www.voala.org
SIC: 8322 Social service center
PA: Volunteers Of America Of Los Angeles
3600 Wilshire Blvd # 1500
Los Angeles CA
213 389-1500

(P-19158)
VOLUNTEERS OF AMER LOS ANGELES
Also Called: Volunteers of America
522 N Dangler Ave (90022-1218)
PHONE..................................323 780-3770
EMP: 106
SALES (corp-wide): 98.98MM **Privately Held**
Web: www.voala.org
SIC: 8322 Social service center
PA: Volunteers Of America Of Los Angeles
3600 Wilshire Blvd # 1500
Los Angeles CA
213 389-1500

(P-19159)
VOLUNTEERS OF AMER LOS ANGELES
Also Called: Volunteers of America
1760 W Cameron Ave Ste 104 (91790-2739)
PHONE..................................626 337-9878
EMP: 80
SALES (corp-wide): 98.98MM **Privately Held**
Web: www.voala.org
SIC: 8322 Social service center
PA: Volunteers Of America Of Los Angeles
3600 Wilshire Blvd # 1500
Los Angeles CA
213 389-1500

(P-19160)
VOLUNTEERS OF AMER LOS ANGELES
Also Called: Volunteers of America
25141 Avenida Rondel (91355-3205)
PHONE..................................661 290-2829
EMP: 80
SALES (corp-wide): 98.98MM **Privately Held**
Web: www.voala.org
SIC: 8322 Social service center
PA: Volunteers Of America Of Los Angeles
3600 Wilshire Blvd # 1500
Los Angeles CA
213 389-1500

(P-19161)
VOLUNTEERS OF AMER LOS ANGELES
Also Called: Voa Plainview Head Start
10819 Plainview Ave (91042-1633)
PHONE..................................818 352-5974
EMP: 106

SALES (corp-wide): 98.98MM **Privately Held**
Web: www.voala.org
SIC: **8322** Social service center
PA: Volunteers Of America Of Los Angeles
3600 Wilshire Blvd # 1500
Los Angeles CA
213 389-1500

(P-19162)
VOLUNTEERS OF AMER LOS ANGELES
Also Called: Volunteers of America
6724 Tujunga Ave (91606-1910)
PHONE..............................818 769-3617
EMP: 106
SALES (corp-wide): 98.98MM **Privately Held**
Web: www.voala.org
SIC: **8322** Social service center
PA: Volunteers Of America Of Los Angeles
3600 Wilshire Blvd # 1500
Los Angeles CA
213 389-1500

(P-19163)
VOLUNTEERS OF AMER LOS ANGELES
Also Called: Maud Booth Family Center
11243 Kittridge St (91606-2605)
PHONE..............................818 506-0597
Felix Cruz, *Mgr*
EMP: 133
SALES (corp-wide): 98.98MM **Privately Held**
Web: www.voala.org
SIC: **8322** Social service center
PA: Volunteers Of America Of Los Angeles
3600 Wilshire Blvd # 1500
Los Angeles CA
213 389-1500

(P-19164)
VOLUNTEERS OF AMER LOS ANGELES
Also Called: Voa
515 E 6th St Fl 9 (90021-1009)
PHONE..............................213 627-8002
Jim Howat, *Dir*
EMP: 106
SQ FT: 15,346
SALES (corp-wide): 98.98MM **Privately Held**
Web: www.voala.org
SIC: **8322** Social service center
PA: Volunteers Of America Of Los Angeles
3600 Wilshire Blvd # 1500
Los Angeles CA
213 389-1500

(P-19165)
VOLUNTEERS OF AMER LOS ANGELES
Also Called: Volunteers of America
12550 Van Nuys Blvd (91331-1354)
PHONE..............................818 834-8957
Letecia Aguirre, *Prin*
EMP: 80
SALES (corp-wide): 98.98MM **Privately Held**
Web: www.voala.org
SIC: **8322** Social service center
PA: Volunteers Of America Of Los Angeles
3600 Wilshire Blvd # 1500
Los Angeles CA
213 389-1500

(P-19166)
VOLUNTEERS OF AMER LOS ANGELES
Also Called: Volunteers of America
334 Figueroa St (90744-4804)
PHONE..............................310 830-3404
EMP: 106
SALES (corp-wide): 98.98MM **Privately Held**
Web: www.voala.org
SIC: **8322** Social service center
PA: Volunteers Of America Of Los Angeles
3600 Wilshire Blvd # 1500
Los Angeles CA
213 389-1500

(P-19167)
WATTS LABOR COMMUNITY ACTION
Also Called: Wlcac
4142 Palmwood Dr Apt 11 (90008-2355)
PHONE..............................323 563-5639
Timothy Watkins, *CEO*
EMP: 169
SALES (corp-wide): 24.79MM **Privately Held**
Web: www.wlcac.org
SIC: **8322** 7299 Social service center; Handyman service
PA: Watts Labor Community Action Committee
10950 S Central Ave
Los Angeles CA
323 563-5639

(P-19168)
WEINGART CENTER ASSOCIATION
Also Called: WEINGART CENTER FOR THE HOMELE
566 S San Pedro St (90013-2102)
PHONE..............................213 622-6359
Kevin Murray, *Pr*
Warren Loui, *
Sonny Santa Ines, *
EMP: 150 EST: 1984
SQ FT: 175,000
SALES (est): 29.86MM **Privately Held**
Web: www.weingart.org
SIC: **8322** Emergency social services

(P-19169)
WELLNEST EMTONAL HLTH WELLNESS (PA)
3031 S Vermont Ave (90007-3033)
PHONE..............................323 373-2400
Charlene Dimas-peinado, *CEO*
EMP: 110 EST: 1924
SALES (est): 30.2MM
SALES (corp-wide): 30.2MM **Privately Held**
Web: www.wellnestla.org
SIC: **8322** Child guidance agency

(P-19170)
WOMANHAVEN
Also Called: CENTER FOR FAMILY SOLUTIONS
510 W Main St Ste 106 (92243-2900)
P.O. Box 2219 (92244-2219)
PHONE..............................760 353-6922
Gina Vargas, *Ex Dir*
Yereida Soto, *
EMP: 90 EST: 1977
SALES (est): 3.29MM **Privately Held**
Web: www.womanhaven.org
SIC: **8322** Social service center

(P-19171)
WORK INC
3070 Skyway Dr Ste 104 (93455-1830)
PHONE..............................805 739-0451
Ed Hartman, *Pr*
Kathy Webb, *Ex Dir*
EMP: 81 EST: 1968
SALES (est): 459.57K **Privately Held**
Web: www.momentum4work.org
SIC: **8322** Adult day care center
HQ: The Chimes Inc
4815 Seton Dr
Baltimore MD
410 358-6400

8331 Job Training And Related Services

(P-19172)
ABILITY COUNTS INC (PA)
775 Trademark Cir Ste 101 (92879-2084)
PHONE..............................951 734-6595
Joyce Hearn, *CEO*
EMP: 99 EST: 1980
SQ FT: 28,000
SALES (est): 7.51MM
SALES (corp-wide): 7.51MM **Privately Held**
Web: www.abilitycounts.org
SIC: **8331** Sheltered workshop

(P-19173)
ADVOCACY FOR RSPECT CHICE - LO (PA)
Also Called: HILLSIDE ENTERPRISES - AR & C
4519 E Stearns St (90815-2540)
PHONE..............................562 597-7716
Marion Lieberman, *CEO*
EMP: 81 EST: 1952
SQ FT: 35,000
SALES (est): 5.9MM
SALES (corp-wide): 5.9MM **Privately Held**
Web: www.hillsideenterprises.org
SIC: **8331** Sheltered workshop

(P-19174)
APPRENTICE JRNYMEN TRNING TR F
Also Called: COMPTON TRAINING CENTER
7850 Haskell Ave (91406-1907)
PHONE..............................310 604-0892
Raymond Levangie Iii, *Ex Dir*
EMP: 222 EST: 1956
SALES (est): 30.36MM **Privately Held**
Web: www.ajtraining.org
SIC: **8331** Job training services

(P-19175)
ASIAN REHABILITATION SVC INC
Also Called: ARS
312 N Spring St Ste B30 (90012-3152)
PHONE..............................213 680-3790
EMP: 120
SALES (corp-wide): 2.14MM **Privately Held**
Web: www.asianrehab.org
SIC: **8331** Vocational rehabilitation agency
PA: Asian Rehabilitation Service, Inc.
750 E Green St Ste 301
Pasadena CA
562 632-1141

(P-19176)
BAKERSFELD ASSN FOR RTRDED CTZ

2240 S Union Ave (93307-4158)
PHONE..............................661 834-2272
Jim Baldwin, *Pr*
EMP: 98 EST: 1951
SQ FT: 30,000
SALES (est): 10.75MM **Privately Held**
SIC: **8331** Sheltered workshop

(P-19177)
BEST OPPORTUNITIES INC
Also Called: BEST OPPORTUNITIES
22450 Headquarters Ave (92307-4304)
PHONE..............................760 628-0111
Karin Etheridge, *CEO*
Richard O'brien, *Pr*
EMP: 140 EST: 1981
SQ FT: 5,000
SALES (est): 6.12MM **Privately Held**
Web: www.bestopportunities.org
SIC: **8331** Vocational rehabilitation agency

(P-19178)
BUFFINI & COMPANY (PA)
6349 Palomar Oaks Ct (92011-1428)
PHONE..............................760 827-2100
EMP: 182 EST: 1995
SALES (est): 42.9MM **Privately Held**
Web: www.buffiniandcompany.com
SIC: **8331** Job training services

(P-19179)
CALIFRNIA DEPT DVLPMENTAL SVCS
Also Called: Fairview Developmental Center
2501 Harbor Blvd (92626-6143)
PHONE..............................714 957-5151
Bill Wilson, *Ex Dir*
EMP: 754
SALES (corp-wide): 534.4MM **Privately Held**
Web: dds.ca.gov
SIC: **8331** 9431 8361 Job training and related services; Administration of public health programs; Residential care
HQ: California Department Of Developmental Services
1215 O St
Sacramento CA

(P-19180)
CHINATOWN SERVICE CENTER (PA)
767 N Hill St Ste 400 (90012-2381)
PHONE..............................213 808-1701
Peter Ng, *CEO*
Peter Ng, *Pr*
Lawrence Lue, *
Henry Kwong, *
Gloria Tang, *
EMP: 80 EST: 1975
SQ FT: 20,000
SALES (est): 14.7MM
SALES (corp-wide): 14.7MM **Privately Held**
Web: www.cscla.org
SIC: **8331** 8322 8011 Job counseling; Family (marriage) counseling; Clinic, operated by physicians

(P-19181)
CITY OF SANTA ANA
Also Called: Santa Ana Job Training Program
1000 E Santa Ana Blvd Ste 107 (92701-3900)
PHONE..............................714 647-6545
Judy Shenlee, *Mgr*
EMP: 87
SALES (corp-wide): 555.62MM **Privately Held**
Web: www.santa-ana.org

SIC: **8331** 9111 Job training services; Mayors' office
PA: City Of Santa Ana
20 Civic Center Plz Fl 8
Santa Ana CA
714 647-5400

(P-19182)
CONSERVATION CORPS LONG BEACH
340 Nieto Ave (90814-1845)
PHONE................................562 986-1249
Samara Ashley, *Prin*
Mike Bassett, *
Mario R Beas, *
EMP: 165 **EST:** 1987
SQ FT: 10,000
SALES (est): 6.78MM **Privately Held**
Web: www.cclb-corps.org
SIC: **8331** 8322 Community service employment training program; Individual and family services

(P-19183)
EXCEPTIONAL CHLD FOUNDATION
Also Called: Par Services
1430 Venice Blvd (90006-4818)
PHONE................................213 748-3556
Nanette Cruz, *Prin*
EMP: 219
SALES (corp-wide): 28.26MM **Privately Held**
Web: www.ecf.net
SIC: **8331** Job training and related services
PA: Exceptional Children's Foundation
5350 Machado Ln
Culver City CA
310 204-3300

(P-19184)
EXCEPTIONAL CHLD FOUNDATION (PA)
Also Called: PAR SERVICES
5350 Machado Ln (90230-8800)
PHONE................................310 204-3300
Veronica Arteaga, *Pr*
EMP: 120 **EST:** 1946
SQ FT: 45,000
SALES (est): 28.26MM
SALES (corp-wide): 28.26MM **Privately Held**
Web: www.ecf.net
SIC: **8331** Vocational training agency

(P-19185)
FONTANA RESOURCES AT WORK
9460 Sierra Ave (92335-2411)
P.O. Box 848 (92334-0848)
PHONE................................909 428-3833
Joseph Varela, *Ex Dir*
EMP: 44 **EST:** 1965
SQ FT: 22,600
SALES (est): 1.94MM **Privately Held**
Web: www.fontanaresources.com
SIC: **8331** 3444 Vocational rehabilitation agency; Sheet metalwork

(P-19186)
GOODWILL INDS ORANGE CNTY CAL
Also Called: Goodwill Industries
5880 Edinger Ave (92649-1705)
PHONE................................714 881-3986
EMP: 110
SALES (corp-wide): 49.48MM **Privately Held**
Web: www.ocgoodwill.org

SIC: **8331** Job training and related services
PA: Goodwill Industries Of Orange County, California
410 N Fairview St
Santa Ana CA
714 547-6308

(P-19187)
LINCOLN TRNING CTR RHBLTTION W
Also Called: LINCOLN TRAINING CENTER
2643 Loma Ave (91733-1419)
PHONE................................626 442-0621
Judith Angelo, *CEO*
Eric Brown, *
David Nelson, *Vice Chairman**
Judy Angelo, *
EMP: 85 **EST:** 1964
SQ FT: 30,000
SALES (est): 25.51MM **Privately Held**
Web: www.lincolntc.org
SIC: **8331** Vocational rehabilitation agency

(P-19188)
METROPLTAN AREA ADVSORY CMMTTE (PA)
Also Called: M A A C Project
1355 Third Ave (91911-4302)
PHONE................................619 426-3595
Arnulfo Manriquez, *CEO*
Antonio Pizano, *
Austin Foye, *
EMP: 100 **EST:** 1965
SQ FT: 820,000
SALES (est): 62.25MM
SALES (corp-wide): 62.25MM **Privately Held**
Web: www.maacproject.org
SIC: **8331** 8351 8748 Job training services; Head Start center, except in conjunction with school; Energy conservation consultant

(P-19189)
OPTIONS FOR ALL INC
5050 Murphy Canyon Rd Ste 220 (92123-4399)
PHONE................................858 565-9870
Richard Gutierrez, *CFO*
EMP: 426
SALES (corp-wide): 23.36MM **Privately Held**
Web: www.optionsforall.org
SIC: **8331** Job training and related services
PA: Options For All, Inc.
5050 Murphy Canyon Rd # 220
San Diego CA
858 565-9870

(P-19190)
OWL EDUCATION AND TRAINING INC
2465 Campus Dr (92612-1502)
PHONE................................949 797-2000
Gregory J Burden, *Pr*
Stephen Seastrom, *
EMP: 280 **EST:** 2005
SQ FT: 22,800
SALES (est): 2.46MM
SALES (corp-wide): 126.07MM **Privately Held**
Web: www.owlcompanies.com
SIC: **8331** Job training and related services
PA: Owl Companies
2465 Campus Dr
Irvine CA
949 797-2000

(P-19191)
PACIFIC ASIAN CNSRTIUM IN EMPL (PA)
Also Called: P A C E
1055 Wilshire Blvd Ste 1475 (90017-2431)
PHONE................................213 353-3982
Kerry N Doi, *Ex Dir*
EMP: 130 **EST:** 1976
SQ FT: 20,000
SALES (est): 30.46MM
SALES (corp-wide): 30.46MM **Privately Held**
Web: www.pacela.org
SIC: **8331** 8322 7361 1521 Community service employment training program; Individual and family services; Labor contractors (employment agency); New construction, single-family houses

(P-19192)
SPECIAL SERVICE FOR GROUPS INC (PA)
Also Called: Special Service For Groups Ssg
905 E 8th St (90021-1805)
PHONE................................213 368-1888
Herbert K Hatanaka, *CEO*
Donna Wong, *
Donald A Kincey, *
EMP: 100 **EST:** 1952
SALES (est): 133.16MM
SALES (corp-wide): 133.16MM **Privately Held**
Web: www.ssg.org
SIC: **8331** 8093 8399 Vocational rehabilitation agency; Mental health clinic, outpatient; Advocacy group

(P-19193)
VALLEY LGHT CTR FOR SCIAL ADVN
Also Called: VALLEY LIGHT INDUSTRIES
109 W 6th St (91702-2875)
PHONE................................626 337-6200
Sheryl Newman, *CEO*
EMP: 80 **EST:** 1970
SALES (est): 3.17MM **Privately Held**
Web: www.valleylight.org
SIC: **8331** Job training and related services

(P-19194)
VALLEY RESOURCE CENTER INC (PA)
Also Called: Valley Resource Center
1285 N Santa Fe St (92543-1823)
PHONE................................951 766-8659
Lee Trisler, *CEO*
EMP: 50 **EST:** 1979
SQ FT: 80,000
SALES (est): 8.09MM
SALES (corp-wide): 8.09MM **Privately Held**
Web: www.weexceed.org
SIC: **8331** 2389 Vocational training agency; Apparel for handicapped

(P-19195)
VOCATIONAL IMPRV PROGRAM INC (PA)
9210 Rochester Ave (91730-5521)
PHONE................................909 483-5924
Wendy A Rogina, *CEO*
Rick Rogina, *
M Stephen Cho, *
Christopher J Mcardle, *Treas*
EMP: 90 **EST:** 1986
SQ FT: 23,000
SALES (est): 19.46MM **Privately Held**
Web: www.vipsolutions.com

SIC: **8331** Vocational rehabilitation agency

(P-19196)
VOCATIONAL VISIONS
26041 Pala (92691-2705)
PHONE................................949 837-7280
Joan Mckinney, *CEO*
Kathryn Hebel, *
EMP: 170 **EST:** 1975
SQ FT: 17,000
SALES (est): 8.25MM **Privately Held**
Web: www.vocationalvisions.org
SIC: **8331** Sheltered workshop

(P-19197)
VTC ENTERPRISES (PA)
2445 A St (93455-1401)
P.O. Box 1187 (93456-1187)
PHONE................................805 928-5000
Jason Telander, *CEO*
Doctor Mark Malangko, *Pr*
Henry M Grennan, *
Lisa Walker, *
Cole Kinney, *
EMP: 96 **EST:** 1962
SQ FT: 21,093
SALES (est): 11.44MM
SALES (corp-wide): 11.44MM **Privately Held**
Web: www.vtc-sm.org
SIC: **8331** Vocational rehabilitation agency

(P-19198)
WESTVIEW SERVICES INC
Also Called: Westview Vocational Services
1655 S Euclid St Ste A (92802-2400)
PHONE................................714 635-2444
Greg Gann, *CEO*
EMP: 91
SQ FT: 5,952
SALES (corp-wide): 14.51MM **Privately Held**
Web: www.westviewservices.org
SIC: **8331** Vocational rehabilitation agency
PA: Westview Services, Inc
10522 Katella Ave
Anaheim CA
714 517-6606

(P-19199)
WESTVIEW SERVICES INC
1515 W Cameron Ave Ste 310 (91790-2726)
PHONE................................626 962-0956
Patricia Stock, *Mgr*
EMP: 80
SALES (corp-wide): 14.51MM **Privately Held**
Web: www.westviewservices.org
SIC: **8331** 5999 Job training and related services; Technical aids for the handicapped
PA: Westview Services, Inc
10522 Katella Ave
Anaheim CA
714 517-6606

8351 Child Day Care Services

(P-19200)
ALLIES FOR EVERY CHILD INC
5721 W Slauson Ave Ste 200 (90230-6554)
PHONE................................310 846-4100
Heather Carrigan, *CEO*
Richard Klein, *
EMP: 88 **EST:** 1987
SQ FT: 18,000
SALES (est): 10.82MM **Privately Held**
Web: www.alliesforeverychild.org

PRODUCTS & SVCS

SIC: 8351 8322 Child day care services;
Child related social services

(P-19201)
CALIFORNIA CHILDRENS ACADEMY
Also Called: Early Learning Center
233 N Breed St (90033-2902)
PHONE.........................323 263-3846
Monica Barahona, *Dir*
EMP: 144
Web: www.californiachildrensacademy.org
SIC: 8351 Preschool center
PA: California Children's Academy
2701 N Main St
Los Angeles CA

(P-19202)
CALVARY CHURCH SANTA ANA INC
1010 N Tustin Ave (92705-3598)
PHONE.........................714 973-4800
Pastor Michael Welles, *Prin*
Michael Welles, *Executive Pastor*
EMP: 160 EST: 1932
SQ FT: 133,000
SALES (est): 11.48MM **Privately Held**
Web: www.calvarylife.org
SIC: 8351 8661 Nursery school;
Miscellaneous denomination church

(P-19203)
CAROUSEL CHILD CARE CORP
8333 Airport Blvd (90045-4244)
PHONE.........................310 216-6641
Sandy Montano, *Brnch Mgr*
EMP: 107
SALES (corp-wide): 21.36MM **Privately Held**
Web: www.carouselschool.com
SIC: 8351 Preschool center
PA: Carousel Child Care Corporation
7899 La Tijera Blvd
Los Angeles CA
310 645-9222

(P-19204)
CHILD CARE RESOURCE CENTER INC
Also Called: Volunteers America Head Start
454 S Kalisher St (91340-3535)
PHONE.........................818 837-0097
EMP: 204
SALES (corp-wide): 404.36MM **Privately Held**
Web: www.ccrcca.org
SIC: 8351 Child day care services
PA: Child Care Resource Center, Inc.
20001 Prairie St
Chatsworth CA
818 717-1000

(P-19205)
CHILD DEVELOPMENT INCORPORATED
Also Called: Turtle Rock Cdc
5151 Amalfi Dr (92603-3443)
PHONE.........................949 854-5060
EMP: 363
SALES (corp-wide): 49.76MM **Privately Held**
Web: www.catalystkids.org
SIC: 8351 Preschool center
PA: Child Development Incorporated
350 Woodview Ave
Morgan Hill CA
408 556-7300

(P-19206)
CHILDRENS HOSPITAL ORANGE CNTY
500 Superior Ave (92663-3657)
PHONE.........................949 631-2062
EMP: 102
SALES (corp-wide): 1.11B **Privately Held**
Web: www.choc.org
SIC: 8351 Child day care services
PA: Children's Hospital Of Orange County
1201 W La Veta Ave
Orange CA
714 509-8300

(P-19207)
COMMUNITY ACTION PRTNR SAN LUI
Also Called: Day Care Center
805 Fiero Ln Ste A (93401-8700)
PHONE.........................805 541-2272
Sheri Wilson, *Dir*
EMP: 127
SALES (corp-wide): 99.11MM **Privately Held**
Web: www.capslo.org
SIC: 8351 Head Start center, except in
conjunction with school
PA: Community Action Partnership Of San
Luis Obispo County, Inc.
1030 Southwood Dr
San Luis Obispo CA
805 544-4355

(P-19208)
COMMUNITY DEV INST HEAD START
12988 Bowron Rd (92064-5790)
PHONE.........................858 668-2985
EMP: 263
SALES (corp-wide): 73.75MM **Privately Held**
Web: www.cditeam.org
SIC: 8351 Head Start center, except in
conjunction with school
PA: Community Development Institute
Head Start
10065 E Harvard Ave # 700
Denver CO
720 747-5100

(P-19209)
EBEN-EZER CHLD DAY CARE CTR
Also Called: EBEN-EZER CHILDREN'S DAY
CARE CENTER
3970 Maine Ave Bldg B (91706-4220)
PHONE.........................626 960-7100
EMP: 91
SALES (corp-wide): 2.1MM **Privately Held**
Web: www.kids1st.org
SIC: 8351 Preschool center
PA: Eben-Ezer Children's Day Care Center
13232 Kagel Canyon St
Pacoima CA
818 897-5427

(P-19210)
FSA ARLANZA CHILD DEV CTR
8172 Magnolia Ave (92504-3441)
PHONE.........................951 353-0129
Vianca Hernandez, *Brnch Mgr*
EMP: 96
Web: www.fsaca.org
SIC: 8351 8322 Child day care services;
Family counseling services
PA: Fsa Arlanza Child Dev Ctr
7801 Gramercy Pl
Riverside CA

(P-19211)
GARDEN GROVE UNIFIED SCHL DST
Also Called: Bryant Elementary School
8371 Orangewood Ave (92841-1517)
PHONE.........................714 663-6437
Sharon Hazelleaf, *Prin*
EMP: 84
SALES (corp-wide): 755.47MM **Privately Held**
Web: bryant.ggusd.us
SIC: 8351 Preschool center
PA: Garden Grove Unified School District
10331 Stanford Ave
Garden Grove CA
714 663-6000

(P-19212)
HARMONIUM INC (PA)
Also Called: EPICENTRE
5440 Morehouse Dr Ste 1000 (92121-6701)
PHONE.........................858 684-3080
Rosa Ana Lozada, *CEO*
Melinda Mallie, *
EMP: 150 EST: 1975
SALES (est): 10.15MM
SALES (corp-wide): 10.15MM **Privately Held**
Web: www.harmoniumsd.org
SIC: 8351 Preschool center

(P-19213)
KARE KLUB
9995 Carmel Mountain Rd Ste B8
(92129-2889)
PHONE.........................858 538-5437
Trudy Khodabande, *Brnch Mgr*
EMP: 88
SALES (corp-wide): 2.62MM **Privately Held**
Web: www.kidscareclub.com
SIC: 8351 Preschool center
PA: Kare Klub
10414 Craftsman Way
San Diego CA
858 675-7000

(P-19214)
LEPORT EDUCATIONAL INST INC
Also Called: Leport Schools
1 Technology Dr Bldg A (92618-2350)
PHONE.........................914 374-8860
Ramandeep S Girn, *CEO*
EMP: 255 EST: 2000
SALES (est): 24.4MM **Privately Held**
Web: www.leportschools.com
SIC: 8351 Montessori child development
center

(P-19215)
LEPORT SCHOOLS
1 Technology Dr Ste H100 (92618-5300)
PHONE.........................714 377-6035
Vanessa Stewart, *Prin*
EMP: 89 EST: 2015
SALES (est): 1.11MM **Privately Held**
Web: www.leportschools.com
SIC: 8351 Montessori child development
center

(P-19216)
MARINE CORPS COMMUNITY SVCS
Also Called: Browne Child Development Ctr
202860 San Jacinto Rd (92054)
PHONE.........................760 725-2817
Maria Langlie, *Dir*
EMP: 141

Web: www.usmc-mccs.org
SIC: 8351 9711 Child day care services;
Marine Corps
HQ: Marine Corps Community Services
3044 Catlin Ave
Quantico VA
703 432-0109

(P-19217)
MARINE CORPS COMMUNITY SVCS
Also Called: San Onofre Child Care Center
Basilone Rd Bldg 51080 (92055)
P.O. Box 555020 (92055-5020)
PHONE.........................760 725-7311
Kanoe Serguson, *Dir*
EMP: 161
Web: www.usmc-mccs.org
SIC: 8351 9711 Child day care services;
Marine Corps
HQ: Marine Corps Community Services
3044 Catlin Ave
Quantico VA
703 432-0109

(P-19218)
MARYVALE DAY CARE CENTER
Also Called: Maryvale Edcatn Fmly Rsrce Ctr
2502 Huntington Dr (91010-2221)
PHONE.........................626 357-1514
Steve Gunther, *Dir*
EMP: 122
SALES (corp-wide): 14.48MM **Privately Held**
Web: www.maryvale.org
SIC: 8351 Preschool center
PA: Maryvale Day Care Center
1050 Maryvale Dr
Cheektowaga NY
626 280-6511

(P-19219)
MCKINLEY CHILD DEVELOPMENT CTR
6822 N Paramount Blvd (90805-1937)
PHONE.........................562 531-6182
EMP: 90
SALES (corp-wide): 75.08K **Privately Held**
SIC: 8351 Child day care services
PA: Mckinley Child Development Ctr
3401 Monroe St Ne
Albuquerque NM
505 888-8134

(P-19220)
MONTE VISTA CHILD CARE CTR INC
7976 Beechwood Dr (91701-1830)
PHONE.........................909 476-6780
EMP: 85
SALES (corp-wide): 1.02MM **Privately Held**
SIC: 8351 Group day care center
PA: Monte Vista Child Care Center, Inc.
13342 Victoria St
Rancho Cucamonga CA
909 544-0040

(P-19221)
MOUNTAIN VIEW CHILD CARE INC
Also Called: Totally Kids Spcalty Hlth Care
10716 La Tuna Canyon Rd (91352-2130)
PHONE.........................818 252-5863
Michelle Nydam, *Brnch Mgr*
EMP: 150
Web: www.totallykids.com
SIC: 8351 Child day care services
PA: Mountain View Child Care, Inc.
1720 Mountain View Ave

Loma Linda CA

(P-19222)
NAVY EXCHANGE SERVICE COMMAND
Also Called: Naval Station Child Dev Ctr
2375 Recreation Way (92136-5518)
PHONE..............................619 556-7466
EMP: 97
Web: www.mynavyexchange.com
SIC: 8351 9711 Child day care services; Navy
HQ: Navy Exchange Service Command
3280 Virginia Beach Blvd
Virginia Beach VA
757 463-6200

(P-19223)
PACIFIC CLINICS HEAD START
171 N Altadena Dr (91107-7318)
PHONE..............................626 254-5000
Wassy Tesfa, *Ex Dir*
EMP: 130 **EST:** 2021
SALES (est): 919.62K **Privately Held**
Web: www.headstartprogram.us
SIC: 8351 Head Start center, except in conjunction with school

(P-19224)
PEOPLES CARE INC
Also Called: PEOPLE'S CARE INC.
12215 Telegraph Rd Ste 208 (90670)
PHONE..............................562 320-0174
Torres Cesaer, *Prin*
EMP: 138
SALES (corp-wide): 62.27MM **Privately Held**
Web: www.peoplescare.com
SIC: 8351 Child day care services
PA: Peoples Care Inc.
13920 City Center Dr # 290
Chino Hills CA
855 773-6753

(P-19225)
PREGEL AMERICA INC
116 S Brent Cir (91789-3050)
PHONE..............................909 598-8980
EMP: 115
SALES (corp-wide): 161.91MM **Privately Held**
Web: www.pregelamerica.com
SIC: 8351 5149 Child day care services; Groceries and related products, nec
HQ: Pregel America, Inc.
4450 Fortune Ave Nw
Concord NC
704 707-0300

(P-19226)
PRIME HEALTH CARE
Also Called: San Dimas Community Hospital
1350 W Covina Blvd (91773-3245)
PHONE..............................909 394-2727
Prim Reddy, *Owner*
EMP: 134 **EST:** 2010
SALES (est): 2.88MM **Privately Held**
Web: www.primehealthcare.com
SIC: 8351 8062 Child day care services; General medical and surgical hospitals

(P-19227)
RGBX INC
Also Called: Heritage Oak Prvate Elmntary S
16971 Imperial Hwy (92886-1663)
PHONE..............................714 524-1350
Phyllis Cygan, *Pr*
Gregory Cygan, *
Latrese Jackson, *
Jennifer Tafolla, *

Kimberly Ford, *
EMP: 91 **EST:** 1992
SQ FT: 22,000
SALES (est): 6.54MM **Privately Held**
Web: www.heritageoak.org
SIC: 8351 8211 Preschool center; Elementary school, nec

(P-19228)
THINK TOGETHER
22620 Goldencrest Dr Ste 104 (92553-9032)
PHONE..............................951 571-9944
EMP: 345
SALES (corp-wide): 75.71MM **Privately Held**
Web: www.thinktogether.org
SIC: 8351 Child day care services
PA: Think Together
2101 E 4th St Ste 200b
Santa Ana CA
714 543-3807

(P-19229)
THINK TOGETHER
202 E Airport Dr Ste 200 (92408-3429)
PHONE..............................909 723-1400
EMP: 344
SALES (corp-wide): 75.71MM **Privately Held**
Web: www.thinktogether.org
SIC: 8351 Child day care services
PA: Think Together
2101 E 4th St Ste 200b
Santa Ana CA
714 543-3807

(P-19230)
THINK TOGETHER
800 S Barranca Ave Ste 120 (91723-3625)
PHONE..............................626 373-2311
Tom Lopez, *Brnch Mgr*
EMP: 345
SALES (corp-wide): 75.71MM **Privately Held**
Web: www.thinktogether.org
SIC: 8351 Child day care services
PA: Think Together
2101 E 4th St Ste 200b
Santa Ana CA
714 543-3807

(P-19231)
TIGER WOODS LEARNING CENTER
1 Tiger Woods Way (92801-5039)
PHONE..............................714 765-8040
Evan Tello, *Mgr*
EMP: 95 **EST:** 2006
SALES (est): 13.22MM **Privately Held**
SIC: 8351 Child day care services

(P-19232)
TUTOR TIME LEARNING CTRS LLC
5805 Corporate Ave (90630-4730)
PHONE..............................714 484-1000
Jennifer Gardea, *Dir*
EMP: 177
Web: www.tutortime.com
SIC: 8351 Preschool center
HQ: Tutor Time Learning Centers, Llc
21333 Haggerty Rd Ste 300
Novi MI
248 697-9000

(P-19233)
TUTOR TIME LEARNING CTRS LLC

5855 De Soto Ave (91367-5202)
PHONE..............................818 710-1677
EMP: 189
Web: www.tutortime.com
SIC: 8351 Preschool center
HQ: Tutor Time Learning Centers, Llc
21333 Haggerty Rd Ste 300
Novi MI
248 697-9000

8361 Residential Care

(P-19234)
AEGIS ASSSTED LIVING PRPTS LLC
Also Called: Aegis At Shadowridge
1440 S Melrose Dr (92056-5394)
PHONE..............................760 806-3600
Gregory Case, *Mgr*
EMP: 117
SALES (corp-wide): 137.21MM **Privately Held**
Web: www.aegisliving.com
SIC: 8361 Aged home
HQ: Aegis Assisted Living Properties, Llc
220 Concourse Blvd
Santa Rosa CA
707 535-3200

(P-19235)
AEGIS SENIOR COMMUNITIES LLC
Also Called: Aegis of Laguna Niguel
32170 Niguel Rd (92677-4264)
PHONE..............................949 496-8080
Pamela Kerr, *Ex Dir*
EMP: 156
SALES (corp-wide): 137.21MM **Privately Held**
Web: www.aegisliving.com
SIC: 8361 Residential care
PA: Senior Aegis Communities Llc
415 118th Ave Se
Bellevue WA
866 688-5829

(P-19236)
ALLIANCE CHILDRENS SERVICES
Also Called: Mentor California
1001 Tower Way Ste 110 (93309-1586)
PHONE..............................661 863-0350
Andretta Stokes, *Mgr*
EMP: 114
SALES (corp-wide): 2.49MM **Privately Held**
SIC: 8361 Mentally handicapped home
PA: Alliance Children's Services Inc
313 Congress St Fl 5
Boston MA
617 790-4800

(P-19237)
ATRIA ASSISTED LIVING GROUP
Also Called: Atria Delsol
23792 Marguerite Pkwy (92692-1583)
PHONE..............................949 427-8191
Michael D Ball, *Ex Dir*
Jeannine Sackett, *
Denise Platt, *
Iris Sanchez, *
EMP: 216 **EST:** 1983
SALES (est): 4.77MM
SALES (corp-wide): 4.13B **Publicly Held**
Web: www.atriaseniorliving.com
SIC: 8361 Aged home
HQ: Atria Management Company, Llc
300 E Market St Ste 100
Louisville KY

(P-19238)
ATRIA MANAGEMENT COMPANY LLC
5308 Monroe Ave (92115-3427)
PHONE..............................619 326-0190
EMP: 135
SALES (corp-wide): 4.13B **Publicly Held**
Web: www.atriaseniorliving.com
SIC: 8361 Aged home
HQ: Atria Management Company, Llc
300 E Market St Ste 100
Louisville KY

(P-19239)
ATRIA MANAGEMENT COMPANY LLC
1342 N Escondido Blvd (92026-2508)
PHONE..............................760 480-8155
EMP: 316
SALES (corp-wide): 4.13B **Publicly Held**
Web: www.atriaseniorliving.com
SIC: 8361 Aged home
HQ: Atria Management Company, Llc
300 E Market St Ste 100
Louisville KY

(P-19240)
AVANTGARDE SENIOR LIVING
5645 Lindley Ave (91356-2557)
PHONE..............................818 881-0055
Jason Adelman, *Prin*
EMP: 102 **EST:** 2010
SALES (est): 6.2MM **Privately Held**
Web: www.avantgardeseniorliving.com
SIC: 8361 Aged home

(P-19241)
BOYS REPUBLIC (PA)
Also Called: GIRLS REPUBLIC
1907 Boys Republic Dr (91709-5447)
PHONE..............................909 902-6690
Dennis Slattery, *CEO*
Timothy J Kay, *
Robert Key, *
Jeff Seymour, *
Nadine Bosen, *
EMP: 150 **EST:** 1907
SQ FT: 173,000
SALES (est): 24.04MM
SALES (corp-wide): 24.04MM **Privately Held**
Web: www.boysrepublic.org
SIC: 8361 Group foster home

(P-19242)
BRETHREN HILLCREST HOMES
Also Called: HILLCREST
2705 Mountain View Dr Ofc (91750-4313)
PHONE..............................909 593-4917
Matthew Neeley, *Pr*
Barbara Feliciano, *
EMP: 230 **EST:** 1947
SQ FT: 34,000
SALES (est): 28.63MM **Privately Held**
Web: www.livingathillcrest.org
SIC: 8361 8059 8051 Rest home, with health care incidental; Nursing home, except skilled and intermediate care facility; Extended care facility

(P-19243)
BRITTANY HOUSE LLC
5401 E Centralia St (90808-1452)
PHONE..............................562 421-4717
Colleen Rosatti, *Ex Dir*
EMP: 129 **EST:** 1989
SQ FT: 43,018
SALES (est): 18.52MM
SALES (corp-wide): 40.58MM **Privately Held**

Web: www.activcareliving.com
SIC: 8361 Aged home
PA: Activcare Living, Inc.
10603 Rancho Bernardo Rd
San Diego CA
858 565-4424

(P-19244)
CALIFORNIA FRIENDS HOMES
Also Called: QUAKER GARDENS
12151 Dale Ave (90680-3889)
PHONE..............................714 530-9100
Randy Brown, *CEO*
Gina Kolb, *
Glenda Hementiza, *
EMP: 315 EST: 1962
SQ FT: 10,000
SALES (est): 18.84MM **Privately Held**
Web: www.rowntreegardens.org
SIC: 8361 8051 Aged home; Convalescent
home with continuous nursing care

(P-19245)
CASA DE LAS CAMPANAS INC (PA)
18655 W Bernardo Dr (92127-3099)
PHONE..............................858 451-9152
Jill Sorenson, *Ex Dir*
Robert L Reeves, *
David Johnson, *
EMP: 97 EST: 1988
SQ FT: 709,627
SALES (est): 49.52MM
SALES (corp-wide): 49.52MM **Privately Held**
Web: www.casadelascampanas.com
SIC: 8361 8052 8051 6513 Aged home;
Intermediate care facilities; Skilled nursing
care facilities; Apartment building operators

(P-19246)
CASA-PACIFICA INC
Also Called: Freedom Properties
2200 W Acacia Ave Ofc (92545-3737)
PHONE..............................951 658-3369
Mary Ann Casino, *Dir*
EMP: 251
SALES (corp-wide): 26.84MM **Privately Held**
Web: www.casapacifica.org
SIC: 8361 8059 Geriatric residential care;
Rest home, with health care
PA: Casa-Pacifica, Inc
23442 El Toro Rd
San Juan Capistrano CA
949 489-0430

(P-19247)
CASA-PACIFICA INC
Also Called: Freedom Properties Village
2400 W Acacia Ave (92545-3743)
PHONE..............................951 766-5116
EMP: 251
SALES (corp-wide): 26.84MM **Privately Held**
Web: www.casapacifica.org
SIC: 8361 8052 8051 6513 Aged home;
Intermediate care facilities; Skilled nursing
care facilities; Apartment building operators
PA: Casa-Pacifica, Inc
23442 El Toro Rd
San Juan Capistrano CA
949 489-0430

(P-19248)
CHILDHELP INC
Also Called: Child Help Head Start Center
14700 Manzanita Rd (92223-3026)
P.O. Box 247 (92223-0247)
PHONE..............................951 845-6737

Klara Pakozdi, *Mgr*
EMP: 123
SALES (corp-wide): 48.34MM **Privately Held**
Web: www.childhelp.org
SIC: 8361 Children's home
PA: Childhelp, Inc.
6730 N Scottsdale Rd # 150
Scottsdale AZ
480 922-8212

(P-19249)
CLIFF VIEW TERRACE INC
Also Called: Mission Terrace
623 W Junipero St (93105-4213)
PHONE..............................805 682-7443
Eve Murphy, *Mgr*
EMP: 83
SALES (corp-wide): 10.24MM **Privately Held**
Web: www.missionterracesb.com
SIC: 8361 8051 Aged home; Convalescent
home with continuous nursing care
PA: Cliff View Terrace, Inc.
1020 Cliff Dr
Santa Barbara CA
805 963-7556

(P-19250)
COLLWOOD TER STELLAR CARE INC
4518 54th St (92115-3527)
PHONE..............................619 287-2920
Chris Cho, *Pr*
EMP: 90 EST: 2008
SALES (est): 4.38MM **Privately Held**
Web: www.stellarcaresd.com
SIC: 8361 Aged home

(P-19251)
COMPASS HEALTH INC
Also Called: Wyndham Residence
222 S Elm St (93420-6012)
PHONE..............................805 474-7260
Mark Woolpert, *Pr*
EMP: 155
Web: www.wyndhamresidence.com
SIC: 8361 Aged home
PA: Compass Health, Inc.
200 S 13th St Ste 208
Grover Beach CA

(P-19252)
CORECARE III
Also Called: Morningside of Fullerton
800 Morningside Dr (92835-3597)
PHONE..............................714 256-8000
Carl Wilkins, *Admn*
EMP: 130 EST: 1989
SQ FT: 24,000
SALES (est): 13.7MM **Privately Held**
Web: www.morningsideoffullerton.com
SIC: 8361 8052 Aged home; Intermediate
care facilities

(P-19253)
COUNSELING AND RESEARCH ASSOC (PA)
Also Called: MASADA HOMES
108 W Victoria St (90248-3523)
P.O. Box 47001 (90247-6801)
PHONE..............................310 715-2020
George Igi, *Ex Dir*
Bernard Smith, *
EMP: 125 EST: 1966
SQ FT: 2,500
SALES (est): 16.77MM
SALES (corp-wide): 16.77MM **Privately Held**
Web: www.masadahomes.org

SIC: 8361 Children's home

(P-19254)
COUNTY OF LOS ANGELES
1605 Eastlake Ave (90033-1009)
PHONE..............................323 226-8611
Richard Shumsky, *Mgr*
EMP: 95
Web: www.lacounty.gov
SIC: 8361 9111 Juvenile correctional facilities
; Executive offices
PA: County Of Los Angeles
500 W Temple St Ste 437
Los Angeles CA
213 974-1101

(P-19255)
COVENANT HOUSE CALIFORNIA
Also Called: CHC
1325 N Western Ave (90027-5615)
PHONE..............................323 461-3131
Luz Juan, *CEO*
George Lozano, *
Patrick S Mccabe, *Ex Dir*
EMP: 150 EST: 1986
SQ FT: 16,000
SALES (est): 20.29MM **Privately Held**
Web: www.covenanthousecalifornia.org
SIC: 8361 Children's home

(P-19256)
COVENANT LIVING WEST
Also Called: Covenant Living At Samarkand
2550 Treasure Dr (93105-4148)
PHONE..............................805 687-0701
Kenneth D Noreen, *Admn*
EMP: 80
Web: www.covliving.org
SIC: 8361 8059 Aged home; Rest home,
with health care
HQ: Covenant Living West
5700 Old Orchard Rd # 10
Skokie IL

(P-19257)
COVENANT LIVING WEST
Also Called: Covenant Living At Mt Miguel
325 Kempton St (91977-5810)
PHONE..............................619 931-1114
Thad Rothrock, *Mgr*
EMP: 80
Web: www.covlivingmountmiguel.org
SIC: 8361 Aged home
HQ: Covenant Living West
5700 Old Orchard Rd # 10
Skokie IL

(P-19258)
CRESTWOOD BEHAVIORAL HLTH INC
Also Called: 1170 Lompoc Mhrc
303 S C St (93436-7305)
PHONE..............................805 308-8720
Charlotte Acosta, *Admn*
EMP: 85
SALES (corp-wide): 278.96MM **Privately Held**
Web:
www.crestwoodbehavioralhealth.com
SIC: 8361 Residential care
PA: Crestwood Behavioral Health, Inc.
520 Capitol Mall Ste 800
Sacramento CA
209 955-2326

(P-19259)
DAVID AND MARGARET HOME INC
Also Called: David Margaret Youth Fmly Svcs

1350 3rd St (91750-5299)
PHONE..............................909 596-5921
Arun Tolia, *Pr*
Cindy Walkenbach, *
Charles C Rich, *
Timothy Evans, *
Sabina Sullivan, *
EMP: 240 EST: 1910
SQ FT: 40,000
SALES (est): 16.71MM **Privately Held**
Web: www.davidandmargaret.org
SIC: 8361 8322 Emotionally disturbed home;
Individual and family services

(P-19260)
E R I T INC (PA)
Also Called: TERI COMMON GROUNDS CAFE & COF
251 Airport Rd (92058-1201)
PHONE..............................760 433-6024
Cheryl Kilmer, *Ex Dir*
William E Mara, *
EMP: 85 EST: 1980
SQ FT: 15,000
SALES (est): 26.04MM
SALES (corp-wide): 26.04MM **Privately Held**
Web: www.teriinc.org
SIC: 8361 Retarded home

(P-19261)
ENSIGN GROUP INC
1405 E Main St (93454-4801)
PHONE..............................805 925-8713
Shawn Taylor, *Brnch Mgr*
EMP: 129
SALES (corp-wide): 3.03B **Publicly Held**
Web: www.ensigngroup.net
SIC: 8361 6513 Geriatric residential care;
Retirement hotel operation
PA: The Ensign Group Inc
29222 Rncho Vejo Rd Ste 1
San Juan Capistrano CA
949 487-9500

(P-19262)
FIVE ACRES - THE BYS GRLS AID
Also Called: FIVE ACRES
760 Mountain View St (91001-4925)
PHONE..............................626 798-6793
Chanel W Boutakidis, *CEO*
Daniel Braun, *
Cathy Clement, *OF PHILANTHROPHY**
Robert A Ketch, *Executive Director Emeritus**
Kim Hutchigs, *
EMP: 419 EST: 1888
SQ FT: 70,000
SALES (est): 44.13MM **Privately Held**
SIC: 8361 8322 8211 Children's home;
Public welfare center; Public combined
elementary and secondary school

(P-19263)
FLORENCE CRTTNTON SVCS ORNGE C
Also Called: CRITTENTON SERVICES FOR CHILDR
801 E Chapman Ave Ste 203 (92831-3846)
P.O. Box 9 (92836-0009)
PHONE..............................714 680-9000
Joyce Capelle, *CEO*
EMP: 320 EST: 1966
SALES (est): 36.22MM **Privately Held**
Web: www.crittentonsocal.org
SIC: 8361 Residential care for children

(P-19264)
GOOD SHEPHERD LUTHERAN HM OF W
2949 Alamo St (93063-2185)
PHONE.................805 526-2482
Brian Dietrich, *Prin*
EMP: 163
SALES (corp-wide): 14.31MM **Privately Held**
Web: www.gsls-simi.com
SIC: **8361** 8059 Residential care for the handicapped; Personal care home, with health care
PA: Good Shepherd Lutheran Home Of The West
24800 Chrisanta Dr # 250
Mission Viejo CA
559 791-2000

(P-19265)
HAMBURGER HOME (PA)
Also Called: AVIVA CENTER
7120 Franklin Ave (90046-3002)
PHONE.................323 876-0550
Regina Bette, *Pr*
EMP: 90 EST: 1915
SQ FT: 25,000
SALES (est): 17.58MM
SALES (corp-wide): 17.58MM **Privately Held**
Web: www.aviva.org
SIC: **8361** Children's home

(P-19266)
HARBOR HEALTH CARE INC
9461 Flower St (90706-5705)
PHONE.................562 866-7054
Cheryl Hutchins, *Pr*
EMP: 200 EST: 1999
SALES (est): 10.04MM **Privately Held**
Web: www.harborhealthcare.org
SIC: **8361** Mentally handicapped home

(P-19267)
HATHAWY-SYCMRES CHILD FMLY SVC
840 N Avenue 66 (90042-1508)
PHONE.................323 257-9600
Jim Cheney, *Pr*
EMP: 92
SALES (corp-wide): 64.09MM **Privately Held**
Web: www.sycamores.org
SIC: **8361** 8093 Emotionally disturbed home; Mental health clinic, outpatient
PA: Hathaway-Sycamores Child And Family Services
100 W Walnut St Ste 375
Pasadena CA
626 395-7100

(P-19268)
HAYNES FAMILY PROGRAMS INC
Also Called: LEROY HAYNES CENTER
233 Baseline Rd (91750-2353)
P.O. Box 400 (91750-0400)
PHONE.................909 593-2581
Daniel Maydeck, *Pr*
Tony Williams, *
Frank Linebaugh, *
EMP: 125 EST: 1946
SQ FT: 72,466
SALES (est): 22.85MM **Privately Held**
Web: www.leroyhaynes.org
SIC: **8361** 8211 8099 Boys' towns; Specialty education; Medical services organization

(P-19269)
HEALTHVIEW INC (PA)
Also Called: Harbor View House
921 S Beacon St (90731-3740)
PHONE.................310 638-4113
Susan Jane Major, *CEO*
EMP: 135 EST: 1965
SQ FT: 110,000
SALES (est): 4.57MM
SALES (corp-wide): 4.57MM **Privately Held**
Web: www.hvi.com
SIC: **8361** 8052 Mentally handicapped home; Home for the mentally retarded, with health care

(P-19270)
HOLLENBECK PALMS
Also Called: HOLLENBECK HOME FOR THE AGED
24431 Lyons Ave Apt 336 (91321-2342)
PHONE.................323 263-6195
William G Heideman Junior, *Pr*
Johnny Young, *Contrlr*
Morris Shockley, *VP*
EMP: 170 EST: 1890
SALES (est): 21.48MM **Privately Held**
Web: www.hollenbeckpalms.com
SIC: **8361** Aged home

(P-19271)
HOME GUIDING HANDS CORPORATION (PA)
1908 Friendship Dr (92020-1129)
PHONE.................619 938-2850
Mark Klaus, *CEO*
Carol A Fitzgibbons, *
Jan Adams, *
EMP: 266 EST: 1961
SALES (est): 29.77MM
SALES (corp-wide): 29.77MM **Privately Held**
Web: www.guidinghands.org
SIC: **8361** 8052 Residential care for the handicapped; Intermediate care facilities

(P-19272)
HOPE HSE FOR MLTPLE HNDCPPED I (PA)
Also Called: Schmitt House
4215 Peck Rd (91732-2113)
PHONE.................626 443-1313
D Bernstein, *
David Bernstein, *
EMP: 100 EST: 1963
SQ FT: 15,000
SALES (est): 9.55MM
SALES (corp-wide): 9.55MM **Privately Held**
Web: www.hopehouse.org
SIC: **8361** Residential care for the handicapped

(P-19273)
HUMANGOOD SOCAL
Also Called: Buena Vista Manor
802 Buena Vista St (91010-1702)
PHONE.................626 359-8141
Judy Phornkein, *Mgr*
EMP: 122
SALES (corp-wide): 27.02MM **Privately Held**
Web: www.humangood.org
SIC: **8361** Aged home
HQ: Humangood Socal
1900 Huntington Dr
Duarte CA
925 924-7138

(P-19274)
HUMANGOOD SOCAL
Also Called: White Sands of La Jolla Clinic
7450 Olivetas Ave Ofc (92037-4900)
PHONE.................858 454-4201
Wendy Matalon, *Brnch Mgr*
EMP: 227
SALES (corp-wide): 27.02MM **Privately Held**
Web: www.humangood.org
SIC: **8361** 8051 Aged home; Skilled nursing care facilities
HQ: Humangood Socal
1900 Huntington Dr
Duarte CA
925 924-7138

(P-19275)
HUMANGOOD SOCAL
Also Called: Redwood Senior Homes & Svcs
710 W 13th Ave (92025-5511)
PHONE.................760 747-4306
EMP: 210
SQ FT: 8,552
SALES (corp-wide): 27.02MM **Privately Held**
Web: www.humangood.org
SIC: **8361** Aged home
HQ: Humangood Socal
1900 Huntington Dr
Duarte CA
925 924-7138

(P-19276)
INDEPENDENT OPTIONS INC
5095 Murphy Canyon Rd (92123-4348)
PHONE.................858 598-5260
EMP: 99
SALES (corp-wide): 15.69MM **Privately Held**
Web: www.independentoptions.org
SIC: **8361** Mentally handicapped home
PA: Independent Options, Inc.
391 Corporate Terrace Cir # 102
Corona CA
951 279-2585

(P-19277)
INDEPENDENT OPTIONS INC
2625 Sherwood Ave (92831-1418)
PHONE.................714 738-4991
P Dennis Mattson, *Pr*
EMP: 100
SALES (corp-wide): 15.69MM **Privately Held**
Web: www.independentoptions.org
SIC: **8361** 8059 Mentally handicapped home; Personal care home, with health care
PA: Independent Options, Inc.
391 Corporate Terrace Cir # 102
Corona CA
951 279-2585

(P-19278)
LAMP INC
Also Called: Lamp Community
2116 Arlington Ave Lbby (90018-1365)
PHONE.................213 488-9559
Donna Gallup, *CEO*
Kim Carson, *
EMP: 110 EST: 1985
SQ FT: 4,500
SALES (est): 14.53MM **Privately Held**
Web: www.lampcommunity.org
SIC: **8361** Residential care for the handicapped

(P-19279)
LAS VILLAS DEL NORTE
1325 Las Villas Way (92026-1946)

PHONE.................760 741-1047
Jolene M Farish, *Ex Dir*
EMP: 180 EST: 1989
SALES (est): 6.65MM **Privately Held**
Web: www.lasvillasdelnorteseniorliving.com
SIC: **8361** 8051 Geriatric residential care; Skilled nursing care facilities

(P-19280)
LEISURE CARE LLC
Also Called: Wellington Crt Asssted Lving C
601 Sunset Blvd (91007-6319)
PHONE.................626 447-0106
Tamara Pribble, *Mgr*
EMP: 115
SALES (corp-wide): 106.71MM **Privately Held**
Web: www.leisurecare.com
SIC: **8361** Aged home
HQ: Leisure Care, Llc
999 3rd Ave Ste 4550
Seattle WA
206 436-7827

(P-19281)
LEISURE CARE LLC
Also Called: Nohl Ranch Inn
380 S Anaheim Hills Rd Ofc (92807-4026)
PHONE.................714 974-1616
Wanda Reynolds, *Brnch Mgr*
EMP: 124
SQ FT: 82,222
SALES (corp-wide): 106.71MM **Privately Held**
Web: www.leisurecare.com
SIC: **8361** 8051 Aged home; Skilled nursing care facilities
HQ: Leisure Care, Llc
999 3rd Ave Ste 4550
Seattle WA
206 436-7827

(P-19282)
LONGWOOD MANAGEMENT CORP
Also Called: Rosecrans Villa
14110 Cordary Ave (90250-8005)
PHONE.................310 675-9163
Boris Blumkin, *Mgr*
EMP: 85
SALES (corp-wide): 79.33MM **Privately Held**
Web: www.longwoodmgmt.com
SIC: **8361** Aged home
PA: Longwood Management Corp.
4032 Wilshire Blvd Fl 6
Los Angeles CA
213 389-6900

(P-19283)
LOS ANGELES RESIDENTIAL COMM F
29890 Bouquet Canyon Rd (91390-5111)
PHONE.................661 296-8636
Kathy Sturky, *Ex Dir*
EMP: 85 EST: 1959
SQ FT: 5,000
SALES (est): 4.7MM **Privately Held**
Web: www.larcfoundation.org
SIC: **8361** 8322 8051 Mentally handicapped home; Individual and family services; Skilled nursing care facilities

(P-19284)
MARYVALE
7600 Graves Ave (91770-3414)
P.O. Box 1039 (91770-1000)
PHONE.................626 280-6510
Steve Gunter, *CEO*

EMP: 152 EST: 2011
SALES (est): 16.3MM Privately Held
Web: www.maryvale.org
SIC: 8361 8322 Residential care for children; Public welfare center

(P-19285)
MCKINLEY CHILDRENS CENTER INC (PA)
180 Via Verde Ste 200 (91773-3901)
PHONE.................................909 599-1227
Anil Vadatary, *CEO*
Michael Frazer, *
EMP: 190 EST: 1890
SALES (est): 31.38MM
SALES (corp-wide): 31.38MM **Privately Held**
Web: www.mckinleycc.org
SIC: 8361 8211 Boys' towns; Private elementary and secondary schools

(P-19286)
MEADOWBROOK VLG CHRSTN RTRMENT
100 Holland Gln (92026-1354)
PHONE.................................760 746-2500
Jacob Bronwer, *Pr*
Sarah Rogh, *
EMP: 109 EST: 2004
SALES (est): 10.74MM Privately Held
Web: www.meadowbrookvillage.org
SIC: 8361 Aged home

(P-19287)
MONTE VISTA GROVE HOMES
2889 San Pasqual St (91107-5364)
PHONE.................................626 796-6135
M Helen Baatz, *Ex Dir*
EMP: 85 EST: 1924
SQ FT: 12,000
SALES (est): 5.68MM Privately Held
Web: www.mvgh.org
SIC: 8361 Aged home

(P-19288)
MORNINGSTAR SENIOR MGT LLC
Also Called: Morningstar of Mission Viejo
28570 Marguerite Pkwy (92692-3713)
PHONE.................................949 298-3675
Dyan Summerell, *Ex Dir*
EMP: 120
SALES (corp-wide): 95.1MM Privately Held
Web: www.morningstarseniorliving.com
SIC: 8361 Residential care
PA: Morningstar Senior Management, Llc
7555 E Hampden Ave # 501
Denver CO
303 750-5522

(P-19289)
NATIONAL MENTOR HOLDINGS INC
Also Called: Horrigan Cole Enterprises
30033 Technology Dr (92563-3520)
PHONE.................................951 677-1453
EMP: 321
SALES (corp-wide): 1.67B Privately Held
Web: www.sevitahealth.com
SIC: 8361 Residential care
HQ: National Mentor Holdings, Inc.
313 Congress St Fl 5
Boston MA
617 790-4800

(P-19290)
NURSECORE MANAGEMENT SVCS LLC
1010 S Broadway Ste A (93454-6600)
PHONE.................................805 938-7660
Veronica Aburto, *Brnch Mgr*
EMP: 571
Web: www.nursecore.com
SIC: 8361 8082 8049 7361 Residential care; Home health care services; Nurses and other medical assistants; Nurses' registry
PA: Nursecore Management Services, Llc
2201 Brookhllw Plz Dr # 450
Arlington TX

(P-19291)
OLIVE CREST (PA)
Also Called: Olive Crest
2130 E 4th St Ste 200 (92705-3818)
PHONE.................................714 543-5437
Donald A Verleur, *CEO*
Lois Verleur, *
EMP: 300 EST: 1973
SQ FT: 40,000
SALES (est): 69.49MM
SALES (corp-wide): 69.49MM **Privately Held**
Web: www.olivecrest.org
SIC: 8361 8322 Emotionally disturbed home; Individual and family services

(P-19292)
OMNITRANS
Also Called: Omnitrans Access
234 S I St (92410-2408)
PHONE.................................909 383-1680
Brian Niemann, *Prin*
EMP: 219
SALES (corp-wide): 8.48MM Privately Held
Web: www.omnitrans.org
SIC: 8361 Physically handicapped home
PA: Omnitrans
1700 W 5th St
San Bernardino CA
909 379-7100

(P-19293)
PACIFIC LODGE YOUTH SVCS INC
Also Called: Pacific Lodge Boy's Home
4900 Serrania Ave (91364-3301)
P.O. Box 308 (91365-0308)
PHONE.................................818 347-1577
Leslie King, *Ch*
Lisa Alegria, *
EMP: 110 EST: 1923
SQ FT: 22,634
SALES (est): 5.01K Privately Held
Web: www.oyhfs.org
SIC: 8361 Residential care

(P-19294)
PEPPERMINT RIDGE (PA)
Also Called: Ridge
825 Magnolia Ave (92879-3129)
PHONE.................................951 273-7320
Danette Mccarnes, *Ex Dir*
EMP: 83 EST: 1965
SQ FT: 25,000
SALES (est): 8.2MM
SALES (corp-wide): 8.2MM Privately Held
Web: www.peppermintridge.org
SIC: 8361 8322 Mentally handicapped home ; Individual and family services

(P-19295)
PHOENIX HOUSES LOS ANGELES INC
Also Called: PHOENIX HOUSE
11600 Eldridge Ave (91342-6506)
PHONE.................................818 686-3000
Winifred Wechsler, *Pr*
EMP: 99 EST: 2000
SALES (est): 8.68MM
SALES (corp-wide): 16.69MM **Privately Held**
SIC: 8361 Rehabilitation center, residential: health care incidental
PA: Phoenix Houses Of California, Inc.
11600 Eldridge Ave
Sylmar CA
818 896-1121

(P-19296)
RANCHO SAN ANTONIO BOYS HM INC (PA)
21000 Plummer St (91311-4903)
PHONE.................................818 882-6400
Aubree Sweeney, *Ex Dir*
Brother John Crowe, *
Nicholas Rizzo, *Finance**
EMP: 100 EST: 1933
SALES (est): 15.32MM
SALES (corp-wide): 15.32MM **Privately Held**
Web: www.ranchosanantonio.org
SIC: 8361 Boys' towns

(P-19297)
REDWOOD ELDERLINK SCPH
Also Called: Redwood Elderlink & Homelink
710 W 13th Ave (92025-5511)
PHONE.................................760 480-1030
Kurt Norden, *Dir*
Tom Vedvick, *Ch*
Dan Johnson, *Pr*
Fran Hillebrecht, *Treas*
Doug Best, *Sec*
EMP: 437 EST: 1989
SQ FT: 200,000
SALES (est): 4.6MM
SALES (corp-wide): 27.02MM **Privately Held**
Web: www.humangood.org
SIC: 8361 8742 Aged home; Compensation and benefits planning consultant
HQ: Humangood Socal
1900 Huntington Dr
Duarte CA
925 924-7138

(P-19298)
ROSEMARY CHILDRENS SERVICES (PA)
36 S Kinneloa Ave # 200 (91107-3853)
PHONE.................................626 844-3033
Greg Wessels, *Ex Dir*
Sungo Wang, *
Lynn Lu, *
Veronica Fuentes, *
Lesley Evangelista, *
EMP: 101 EST: 1920
SQ FT: 9,000
SALES (est): 4.42MM
SALES (corp-wide): 4.42MM **Privately Held**
Web: www.rosemarychildren.org
SIC: 8361 Emotionally disturbed home

(P-19299)
SILVERADO SNIOR LVING HLDNGS
6400 Oak Cyn Ste 200 (92618-5201)
PHONE.................................949 240-7200
Loren B Shook, *CEO*
Kristina Hulsey, *Chief Compliance Officer**
EMP: 4000 EST: 2010
SALES (est): 153.97MM Privately Held
Web: www.silverado.com
SIC: 8361 Aged home

(P-19300)
SISTERS OF NZARETH LOS ANGELES
3333 Manning Ave (90064-4804)
PHONE.................................310 839-2361
Margarette Brody, *Admn*
EMP: 100 EST: 1935
SQ FT: 62,558
SALES (est): 6.65MM Privately Held
Web: www.sistersofnazareth.com
SIC: 8361 Aged home

(P-19301)
SOLHEIM LUTHERAN HOME
2236 Merton Ave (90041-1915)
PHONE.................................323 257-7518
James Graunke, *Prin*
Norma Heaton, *
Antonio Davila, *
Sherry Wait, *
EMP: 185 EST: 1923
SQ FT: 82,591
SALES (est): 15.16MM Privately Held
Web: www.solheimlutheran.org
SIC: 8361 Aged home

(P-19302)
ST ANNES FAMILY SERVICES
155 N Occidental Blvd (90026-4641)
PHONE.................................213 381-2931
Lorna Little, *Pr*
Mike Cazares, *CFO*
Janice Kanellis Cpoo, *Prin*
EMP: 158 EST: 1941
SQ FT: 100,000
SALES (est): 37.32MM Privately Held
Web: www.stannes.org
SIC: 8361 Rehabilitation center, residential: health care incidental

(P-19303)
SUNRISE SENIOR LIVING MGT INC
Also Called: Claremont Pl Assisted Living
120 W San Jose Ave (91711-5294)
PHONE.................................909 447-5259
Nancy Halleck, *Ex Dir*
EMP: 218
SQ FT: 4,900
SALES (corp-wide): 2.92B Privately Held
Web: www.sunriseseniorliving.com
SIC: 8361 8051 8082 Geriatric residential care; Skilled nursing care facilities; Home health care services
HQ: Sunrise Senior Living Management, Inc.
7902 Westpark Dr
Mc Lean VA
703 273-7500

(P-19304)
SUSAN J HARRIS INC
Also Called: Therapy Specialist
344 F St Ste 100 (91910-2645)
PHONE.................................619 498-8450
EMP: 211
SALES (corp-wide): 21.68MM Privately Held
Web: www.therapyspecialists.net
SIC: 8361 8049 Rehabilitation center, residential: health care incidental; Occupational therapist

PA: New Life Physical Therapy Services
San Diego, Inc.
344 F St Ste 202
Chula Vista CA
858 514-0375

(P-19305)
TIERRA DEL SOL FOUNDATION (PA)
9919 Sunland Blvd (91040-1529)
PHONE..................................818 352-1419
Steve Miller, *Ex Dir*
EMP: 95 **EST:** 1971
SQ FT: 20,000
SALES (est): 21.23MM
SALES (corp-wide): 21.23MM **Privately Held**
Web: www.tierradelsol.org
SIC: **8361** 8211 8322 Mentally handicapped home; Public special education school; Individual and family services

(P-19306)
VICTOR TREATMENT CENTERS INC
Also Called: Victor Treatment Centers
1053 N D St (92410-3521)
PHONE..................................951 436-5200
Jana Trew, *Brnch Mgr*
EMP: 80
SALES (corp-wide): 23.04MM **Privately Held**
Web: www.victor.org
SIC: **8361** Emotionally disturbed home
PA: Victor Treatment Centers, Inc.
1360 E Lassen Ave
Chico CA
530 893-0758

(P-19307)
VILLAGE AT NORTHRIDGE
9222 Corbin Ave (91324-2409)
PHONE..................................818 514-4497
EMP: 97 **EST:** 2008
SALES (est): 20.69MM
SALES (corp-wide): 189.7MM **Privately Held**
Web: www.srgseniorliving.com
SIC: **8361** Aged home
PA: Senior Resource Group, Llc
500 Stevens Ave Ste 100
Solana Beach CA
858 792-9300

(P-19308)
VILLAS DE CRLSBAD LTD A CAL LT
Also Called: Las Villas De Carlsbad
3500 Lake Blvd (92056-4600)
PHONE..................................760 434-7116
Jack Rowe, *Owner*
EMP: 97
SIC: **8361** Aged home
PA: Villas De Carlsbad, Ltd., A California Limited Partnership
9619 Chesapeake Dr # 103
San Diego CA

(P-19309)
VISTA DEL MAR CHILD FMLY SVCS
1533 Euclid St (90404-3306)
PHONE..................................310 836-1223
Louis Josephson, *Brnch Mgr*
EMP: 238
SALES (corp-wide): 40.28MM **Privately Held**
Web: www.vistadelmar.org

SIC: **8361** Mentally handicapped home
PA: Vista Del Mar Child And Family Services
3200 Motor Ave
Los Angeles CA
310 836-1223

(P-19310)
WALDEN HOUSE INC
845 E Arrow Hwy (91767-2535)
PHONE..................................626 258-0300
Grace Gerarto, *Mgr*
EMP: 128
SALES (corp-wide): 26.49MM **Privately Held**
Web: www.healthright360.org
SIC: **8361** Group foster home
PA: Walden House, Inc.
520 Townsend St
San Francisco CA
415 554-1100

(P-19311)
WHITE RABBIT PARTNERS INC
9000 W Sunset Blvd Ste 1500 (90069-5815)
PHONE..................................310 975-1450
Andrew W Spanswick, *CEO*
Andrew William Spanswick, *CEO*
EMP: 150 **EST:** 2009
SALES (est): 3.82MM **Privately Held**
SIC: **8361** Residential care

8399 Social Services, Nec

(P-19312)
ARC OF SAN DIEGO
Also Called: ARC - SD E Cnty Training Ctrs
1855 John Towers Ave (92020-1116)
PHONE..................................619 448-2415
Millie Oveross, *Mgr*
EMP: 348
SALES (corp-wide): 33.64MM **Privately Held**
Web: www.arc-sd.com
SIC: **8399** 8361 Advocacy group; Physically handicapped home
PA: The Arc Of San Diego
3030 Market St
San Diego CA
619 685-1175

(P-19313)
ARC OF SAN DIEGO
1336 Rancheros Dr Ste 100 (92069-3089)
PHONE..................................760 740-6800
Laura Orcutt, *Dir*
EMP: 464
SALES (corp-wide): 33.64MM **Privately Held**
Web: www.arc-sd.com
SIC: **8399** 8322 Advocacy group; Association for the handicapped
PA: The Arc Of San Diego
3030 Market St
San Diego CA
619 685-1175

(P-19314)
ARC OF SAN DIEGO (PA)
Also Called: ARC Enterprises
3030 Market St (92102-3230)
PHONE..................................619 685-1175
David W Schneider, *CEO*
Anthony J Desalis, *
Rich Coppa, *
Chad Lyle, *
Jennifer Bates Navarra, *
▲ **EMP:** 200 **EST:** 1953

SQ FT: 55,093
SALES (est): 33.64MM
SALES (corp-wide): 33.64MM **Privately Held**
Web: www.arc-sd.com
SIC: **8399** 8351 8361 8322 Advocacy group; Child day care services; Retarded home; Individual and family services

(P-19315)
ASSOCIATED STUDENTS UCLA (PA)
Also Called: Asucla
308 Westwood Plz (90095-8355)
PHONE..................................310 794-8836
Pouria Abbassi, *Ex Dir*
Donna Baker, *Finance*
EMP: 500 **EST:** 1919
SQ FT: 200,000
SALES (est): 47.49MM
SALES (corp-wide): 47.49MM **Privately Held**
Web: asucla.ucla.edu
SIC: **8399** 5942 Council for social agency; Book stores

(P-19316)
ASSOCIATED STUDENTS UCLA
924 Westwood Blvd (90024-2910)
PHONE..................................310 794-0242
Roseanna P Malone, *Brnch Mgr*
EMP: 199
SALES (corp-wide): 47.49MM **Privately Held**
Web: www.ucla.edu
SIC: **8399** Council for social agency
PA: Associated Students U.C.L.A.
308 Westwood Plz
Los Angeles CA
310 794-8836

(P-19317)
BEACH CITIES HEALTH DISTRICT
1200 Del Amo St (90277-3050)
PHONE..................................310 374-3426
Tom Bakaly, *Mgr*
Tom Bakaly, *CEO*
Monica Suua, *
EMP: 147 **EST:** 1955
SALES (est): 15.47MM **Privately Held**
Web: www.bchd.org
SIC: **8399** Health systems agency

(P-19318)
CALIFORNIA ENDOWMENT (PA)
1000 N Alameda St (90012-1804)
PHONE..................................213 928-8800
EMP: 80 **EST:** 1995
SQ FT: 110,000
SALES (est): 461.75MM **Privately Held**
Web: www.calendow.org
SIC: **8399** Fund raising organization, non-fee basis

(P-19319)
CITY OF HOPE
City Hope Development Center
1500 Duarte Rd (91010-3012)
PHONE..................................213 202-5735
Kathleen Cane, *Brnch Mgr*
EMP: 392
SALES (corp-wide): 334.97MM **Privately Held**
Web: www.cityofhope.org
SIC: **8399** 9532 Fund raising organization, non-fee basis; Urban and community development
PA: City Of Hope
1500 Duarte Rd

Duarte CA
626 256-4673

(P-19320)
COMMUNITY ACTION PARTNR KERN
315 Stine Rd (93309-3268)
PHONE..................................661 835-5405
Luz Adams, *Brnch Mgr*
EMP: 81
SALES (corp-wide): 117.9MM **Privately Held**
Web: www.capk.org
SIC: **8399** Community action agency
PA: Community Action Partnership Of Kern
5005 Business Park N
Bakersfield CA
661 336-5236

(P-19321)
COMMUNITY ACTION PARTNR KERN
814 N Norma St (93555-3509)
PHONE..................................760 371-1469
Maria Harley, *Brnch Mgr*
EMP: 85
SALES (corp-wide): 117.9MM **Privately Held**
Web: www.capk.org
SIC: **8399** 8351 Community action agency; Child day care services
PA: Community Action Partnership Of Kern
5005 Business Park N
Bakersfield CA
661 336-5236

(P-19322)
COMMUNITY ACTION PRTNR SAN BRN
Also Called: CAPSBC
696 S Tippecanoe Ave (92408-2607)
PHONE..................................909 723-1500
Patricia L Nickols, *CEO*
Richard Schmidt, *
Joanne Gilbert, *
Socorro Enriquez, *Vice Chairman*
Ammie Hines, *
EMP: 88 **EST:** 1965
SALES (est): 31.88MM **Privately Held**
Web: www.capsbc.org
SIC: **8399** 8699 Community action agency; Charitable organization

(P-19323)
COMMUNITY PARTNERS (PA)
1000 N Alameda St Ste 240 (90012-1804)
PHONE..................................213 346-3200
Paul Vandeventer, *Pr*
Gary Erickson, *
Janet Elliott, *
EMP: 198 **EST:** 1990
SALES (est): 84.73MM **Privately Held**
Web: www.communitypartners.org
SIC: **8399** Social service information exchange

(P-19324)
DVEAL CORPORATION
Also Called: D'Veal Family and Youth Svcs
2750 E Washington Blvd Ste 230 (91107-1448)
P.O. Box 40255 (91114-7255)
PHONE..................................626 296-8900
John Mccall, *Ex Dir*
EMP: 107 **EST:** 1996
SQ FT: 7,500
SALES (est): 8.62MM **Privately Held**
Web: www.dveal.com

PRODUCTS & SVCS

SIC: 8399 Community action agency

(P-19325)
ESSENTIAL ACCESS HEALTH (PA)
Also Called: Cfhc
3600 Wilshire Blvd Ste 600 (90010-2610)
PHONE...............................213 386-5614
Julie Rabinovitz, *Pr*
Nomsa Khalfani, *
Brenda Flores, *
Ron Frezieres, *
Amy Moy, *
EMP: 81 EST: 1968
SQ FT: 18,000
SALES (est): 28.71MM
SALES (corp-wide): 28.71MM **Privately Held**
Web: www.essentialaccess.org
SIC: 8399 8011 8099 Fund raising organization, non-fee basis; Primary care medical clinic; Medical services organization

(P-19326)
GREATER LOS ANGELES ZOO ASSN
Also Called: GLAZA
5333 Zoo Dr (90027-1451)
PHONE...............................323 644-4200
Connie M Morgan, *Pr*
Jeb Bonner, *
Genie Vasels, *
Eugenia Vasels, *
Phyllis Kupferstein, *
EMP: 100 EST: 1963
SQ FT: 8,200
SALES (est): 20.39MM **Privately Held**
Web: www.lazoo.org
SIC: 8399 7999 Fund raising organization, non-fee basis; Concession operator

(P-19327)
HARBOR DVLPMNTAL DSBLTIES FNDT
Also Called: HARBOR REGIONAL CENTER
21231 Hawthorne Blvd (90503-5501)
P.O. Box 2930 (90509-2930)
PHONE...............................310 540-1711
Judy Wada, *CFO*
EMP: 225 EST: 1977
SQ FT: 60,000
SALES (est): 301.25MM **Privately Held**
Web: www.harborrc.org
SIC: 8399 Council for social agency

(P-19328)
HEALTH ADVOCATES LLC
Also Called: Health Advocates
21540 Plummer St Ste B (91311-0888)
PHONE...............................818 995-9500
Al Leibovic, *Managing Member*
Aaron Leibovic, *Managing Member*
EMP: 371 EST: 1997
SQ FT: 40,900
SALES (est): 47.69MM **Privately Held**
Web: www.healthadvocates.com
SIC: 8399 Advocacy group

(P-19329)
INTERNTNAL FNDTION FOR KREA UN
3435 Wilshire Blvd Ste 480 (90010-1901)
PHONE...............................213 550-2182
Willie Wang-pyo Seung, *CEO*
EMP: 300 EST: 2016
SALES (est): 202.98K **Privately Held**
Web: www.ifku.org
SIC: 8399 Advocacy group

(P-19330)
INTOUCH TECHNOLOGIES INC (HQ)
Also Called: Intouch Health
7402 Hollister Ave (93117-2583)
PHONE...............................805 562-8686
Yulun Wang, *Ch*
Paul Evans, *
Michael Chan, *
Charles S Jordan, *
David Adornetto, *
EMP: 102 EST: 2002
SQ FT: 1,600
SALES (est): 60.31MM **Publicly Held**
Web: www.teladochealth.com
SIC: 8399 7379 Health systems agency; Computer related consulting services
PA: Teladoc Health, Inc.
2 Manhattanville Rd # 203
Purchase NY

(P-19331)
KERN REGIONAL CENTER (PA)
3200 N Sillect Ave (93308-6333)
P.O. Box 2536 (93303-2536)
PHONE...............................661 327-8531
TOLL FREE: 800
Michal Clark, *Ex Dir*
Jerry Bowman, *
Duane Law, *
EMP: 147 EST: 1971
SQ FT: 33,000
SALES (est): 231.95MM
SALES (corp-wide): 231.95MM **Privately Held**
Web: www.kernrc.org
SIC: 8399 Social service information exchange

(P-19332)
KEYSTONE NPS LLC
Also Called: Keystone Educatn & Youth Svcs
9994 County Farm Rd (92503-3518)
PHONE...............................951 785-0504
EMP: 196
SALES (corp-wide): 13.4B **Publicly Held**
SIC: 8399 8211 Advocacy group; Private elementary and secondary schools
HQ: Keystone Nps Llc
11980 Mount Vernon Ave
Grand Terrace CA
909 633-6354

(P-19333)
KEYSTONE NPS LLC (DH)
Also Called: Keystone Schools-Ramona
11980 Mount Vernon Ave (92313-5172)
PHONE...............................909 633-6354
Alfredo Alvarado, *Prin*
Martha Petrey, *
Don Whitfield, *
EMP: 100 EST: 1978
SALES (est): 22.49MM
SALES (corp-wide): 13.4B **Publicly Held**
SIC: 8399 Advocacy group
HQ: Children's Comprehensive Services, Inc.
3401 West End Ave Ste 400
Nashville TN
615 250-0000

(P-19334)
LAWRENCE FMLY JWISH CMNTY CTRS (PA)
4126 Executive Dr (92037-1348)
PHONE...............................858 362-1144
Craig Schluss, *Pr*
David Wax, *
Nancy Johnson, *
EMP: 150 EST: 1945

SALES (est): 12.11MM
SALES (corp-wide): 12.11MM **Privately Held**
Web: www.lfjcc.org
SIC: 8399 8351 Community development groups; Child day care services

(P-19335)
LOS ANGELES LGBT CENTER (PA)
Also Called: L.A. GAY & LESBIAN CENTER
1625 Schrader Blvd (90028-6213)
P.O. Box 2988 (90078-2988)
PHONE...............................323 993-7618
Lorri L Jean, *CEO*
Michael Holtzman, *
EMP: 148 EST: 1972
SQ FT: 45,000
SALES (est): 149.11MM
SALES (corp-wide): 149.11MM **Privately Held**
Web: www.lalgbtcenter.org
SIC: 8399 Advocacy group

(P-19336)
NEW ADVNCES FOR PPLE WITH DSBL
Also Called: Napd
4032 Jewett Ave (93301-1114)
PHONE...............................661 322-9735
EMP: 106
SALES (corp-wide): 6.36MM **Privately Held**
Web: www.napd-bak.org
SIC: 8399 Community development groups
PA: New Advances For People With Disabilities
3400 N Sillect Ave
Bakersfield CA
661 395-1361

(P-19337)
ORTHALLIANCE INC
Also Called: Orthalliances
21535 Hawthorne Blvd Ste 200 (90503-6604)
PHONE...............................310 792-1300
Sam Westover, *Pr*
Paul H Hayase, *
James C Wilson, *
EMP: 1700 EST: 1996
SQ FT: 4,200
SALES (est): 23.92MM **Privately Held**
Web: www.orthalliance.com
SIC: 8399 8742 8741 Advocacy group; Management consulting services; Business management
PA: Orthosynetics, Inc.
3850 N Causeway Blvd # 800
Metairie LA

(P-19338)
PENNY LANE CENTERS (PA)
15305 Rayen St (91343-5117)
P.O. Box 2548 (91393-2548)
PHONE...............................818 892-3423
Arthur Barr, *Pr*
Ivelise Markovits, *
Peter Padin, *Assistant Executive Director*
EMP: 275 EST: 1967
SQ FT: 7,000
SALES (est): 57.33MM
SALES (corp-wide): 57.33MM **Privately Held**
Web: www.pennylane.org
SIC: 8399 Social service information exchange

(P-19339)
PREMIER DISABILITY SVCS LLC
909 N Pacific Coast Hwy Fl 11 (90245-2724)
PHONE...............................310 280-4000
Robert N Brisco, *Mgr*
EMP: 99 EST: 2020
SALES (est): 1.01MM **Privately Held**
Web: www.premierdisability.com
SIC: 8399 Advocacy group

(P-19340)
SAN DIEGO RESCUE MISSION INC (PA)
Also Called: CITY RESCUE MISSION
299 17th St (92101-7665)
P.O. Box 80427 (92138-0427)
PHONE...............................619 819-1880
Herb Johnson, *CEO*
John Suderman, *
Shari Finney Houser, *
C Greg Helton, *
Cathy Christianson, *
EMP: 99 EST: 1955
SALES (est): 26.9MM
SALES (corp-wide): 26.9MM **Privately Held**
Web: www.sdrescue.org
SIC: 8399 5932 8322 Social change association; Used merchandise stores; Emergency shelters

(P-19341)
SHARP HEALTHCARE FOUNDATION
8695 Spectrum Center Blvd (92123-1489)
PHONE...............................858 499-4800
William Littlejohn, *CEO*
Marsha Lubick, *
EMP: 164 EST: 1979
SALES (est): 23.93MM
SALES (corp-wide): 2.37B **Privately Held**
Web: www.sharp.com
SIC: 8399 Fund raising organization, non-fee basis
PA: Sharp Healthcare
8695 Spectrum Center Blvd
San Diego CA
858 499-4000

(P-19342)
SOUTH CNTL LOS ANGLES RGNAL CT (PA)
Also Called: SCLARC
2500 S Western Ave (90018-2609)
PHONE...............................213 744-7000
Dexter Henderson, *CEO*
Roy Doronila, *
EMP: 104 EST: 1983
SQ FT: 110,470
SALES (est): 455.32MM
SALES (corp-wide): 455.32MM **Privately Held**
Web: www.sclarc.org
SIC: 8399 Health and welfare council

(P-19343)
SOUTH CNTL LOS ANGLES RGNAL CT
650 W Adams Blvd (90007-2580)
PHONE...............................231 744-8484
EMP: 134
SALES (corp-wide): 455.32MM **Privately Held**
Web: www.sclarc.org
SIC: 8399 Health and welfare council

PA: South Central Los Angeles Regional Center For Developmentally Disabled Persons, Inc.
2500 S Western Ave
Los Angeles CA
213 744-7000

(P-19344)
SPECIAL SERVICE FOR GROUPS INC
Also Called: Occupational Therapy Training
19401 S Vermont Ave Ste A200 (90502-4418)
PHONE..............................310 323-6887
Sarah Bream, *Brnch Mgr*
EMP: 132
SALES (corp-wide): 133.16MM **Privately Held**
Web: www.ottp.org
SIC: 8399 8322 Community action agency; Individual and family services
PA: Special Service For Groups, Inc.
905 E 8th St
Los Angeles CA
213 368-1888

(P-19345)
SPECIAL SERVICE FOR GROUPS INC
520 S La Fayette Park Pl # 30 (90057-1607)
PHONE..............................213 553-1800
Herbert Hatanaka, *Brnch Mgr*
EMP: 131
SALES (corp-wide): 133.16MM **Privately Held**
Web: www.ssg.org
SIC: 8399 Community development groups
PA: Special Service For Groups, Inc.
905 E 8th St
Los Angeles CA
213 368-1888

(P-19346)
UNITED WAY INC (PA)
Also Called: United Way Greater Los Angeles
1150 S Olive St Ste T-500 (90015-2481)
PHONE..............................213 808-6220
Caroline W Nahas, *Ch Bd*
Elise Buik, *
Les Brockhurst, *
Alicia Lara, *
Mae Tuck, *
▲ **EMP:** 95 **EST:** 1962
SQ FT: 40,000
SALES (est): 49.6MM
SALES (corp-wide): 49.6MM **Privately Held**
Web: 100.unitedwayla.org
SIC: 8399 Fund raising organization, non-fee basis

(P-19347)
WESTSIDE JEWISH CMNTY CTR INC (PA)
5870 W Olympic Blvd (90036-4657)
PHONE..............................323 938-2531
Brian Greene, *Ex Dir*
EMP: 200 **EST:** 1932
SQ FT: 150,000
SALES (est): 2.31MM
SALES (corp-wide): 2.31MM **Privately Held**
Web: www.westsidejcc.org
SIC: 8399 8641 8322 Community development groups; Civic and social associations; Individual and family services

---

8412 Museums And Art Galleries

(P-19348)
ACADEMY MUSEUM MOTION PICTURES
6067 Wilshire Blvd (90036-3604)
PHONE..............................310 247-3000
Bill Kramer, *Pr*
EMP: 212 **EST:** 2021
SALES (est): 6.1MM **Privately Held**
Web: www.academymuseum.org
SIC: 8412 Museum

(P-19349)
ARMAND HMMER MSEUM OF ART CLTR
Also Called: HAMMER MUSEUM
10899 Wilshire Blvd (90024-4343)
PHONE..............................310 443-7000
Michael Rubel, *Dir*
Steven A Olsen, *
▲ **EMP:** 101 **EST:** 1989
SQ FT: 20,000
SALES (est): 34.99MM **Privately Held**
Web: hammer.ucla.edu
SIC: 8412 Museum

(P-19350)
AUTRY MUSEUM OF AMERICAN WEST
Also Called: AUTRY MUSEUM
4700 Western Heritage Way (90027-1462)
PHONE..............................323 667-2000
Richard West, *Prin*
Richard West, *Pr*
Robert Caragher, *
Maren Dougherty, *
Susan Harlow, *
EMP: 140 **EST:** 1984
SQ FT: 144,000
SALES (est): 12.35MM **Privately Held**
Web: www.theautry.org
SIC: 8412 5947 5812 6512 Museum; Gift shop; Cafeteria; Theater building, ownership and operation

(P-19351)
CALIFRNIA CTR FOR ARTS ESCNDID
340 N Escondido Blvd (92025-2600)
PHONE..............................760 839-4138
Vicky Basehore, *Pr*
Lee Cavell Board, *Prin*
EMP: 185 **EST:** 1989
SALES (est): 5.23MM **Privately Held**
Web: www.artcenter.org
SIC: 8412 5999 Arts or science center; Art dealers

(P-19352)
CALIFRNIA SCNCE CTR FOUNDATION
700 Exposition Park Dr (90037-1210)
PHONE..............................213 744-2545
Jeffrey N Rudolph, *Pr*
Cynthia Pygin, *
EMP: 260 **EST:** 1949
SALES (est): 28.6MM
SALES (corp-wide): 534.4MM **Privately Held**
SIC: 8412 7832 5947 Museum; Motion picture theaters, except drive-in; Gifts and novelties
HQ: California Natural Resources Agency
715 P St
Sacramento CA

(P-19353)
DISCOVERY SCNCE CTR ORNGE CNTY
2500 N Main St (92705-6600)
PHONE..............................866 552-2823
Daniel Bolar, *Ch Bd*
Joseph Adams, *Pr*
▲ **EMP:** 135 **EST:** 1998
SALES (est): 12.79MM **Privately Held**
Web: www.discoverycube.org
SIC: 8412 Museum

(P-19354)
KIDSPCE A PRTICIPATORY MUSEUM
Also Called: KIDSPACE
480 N Arroyo Blvd (91103-3269)
PHONE..............................626 449-9144
EMP: 83 **EST:** 1979
SALES (est): 4.39MM **Privately Held**
Web: www.kidspacemuseum.org
SIC: 8412 Museum

(P-19355)
LOS ANGELES CNTY MSEUM OF ART
Also Called: Lacma
5905 Wilshire Blvd (90036-4504)
PHONE..............................323 857-6000
Michael Govan, *CEO*
Ann Rowland, *
John Bowsher, *
Jane Burrell, *
Fred Goldstein, *
▲ **EMP:** 430 **EST:** 2011
SALES (est): 11.58MM **Privately Held**
Web: www.lacma.org
SIC: 8412 Museum

(P-19356)
MUSEUM ASSOCIATES
Also Called: La County Museum of Art
5905 Wilshire Blvd (90036-4504)
PHONE..............................323 857-6172
Michael Gavin, *Dir*
EMP: 400 **EST:** 1938
SALES (est): 230.97MM **Privately Held**
Web: www.lacma.org
SIC: 8412 Museum

(P-19357)
MUSEUM OF CONTEMPORARY ART (PA)
250 S Grand Ave (90012-3021)
PHONE..............................213 626-6222
Charles Young, *CEO*
Michael Harrison, *
Jeffrey Deitch, *
▲ **EMP:** 150 **EST:** 1979
SQ FT: 100,000
SALES (est): 28.96MM
SALES (corp-wide): 28.96MM **Privately Held**
Web: www.moca.org
SIC: 8412 Museum

(P-19358)
NEW CHILDRENS MUSEUM
200 W Island Ave (92101-6850)
PHONE..............................619 233-8792
Judy Forrester, *Ex Dir*
Kay Wagner, *
Robert Sain, *
Rachel Teagle, *
Julianne Markow, *
EMP: 90 **EST:** 1981
SQ FT: 50,000
SALES (est): 4.09MM **Privately Held**
Web: www.thinkplaycreate.org

SIC: 8412 Museum

(P-19359)
NORTON SMON MSEUM ART AT PSDEN
411 W Colorado Blvd (91105-1825)
PHONE..............................626 449-6840
Ronald H Dykhuizen, *Prin*
Jennifer J Simon, *
Walter W Timoshuk, *
Robert Walker, *
▲ **EMP:** 100 **EST:** 1924
SQ FT: 70,000
SALES (est): 8.6MM **Privately Held**
Web: www.nortonsimon.org
SIC: 8412 Museum

(P-19360)
PALM SPRINGS ART MUSEUM INC
101 N Museum Dr (92262-5659)
P.O. Box 2310 (92263-2310)
PHONE..............................760 322-4800
Donna Macmillan, *Ch Bd*
Rochelle Steinerm, *Chief Curator*
Adam Lerner, *
▲ **EMP:** 96 **EST:** 1938
SQ FT: 75,000
SALES (est): 8.92MM **Privately Held**
Web: www.psmuseum.org
SIC: 8412 Museum

(P-19361)
REUBEN H FLEET SCIENCE CENTER
1875 El Prado (92101-1625)
P.O. Box 33303 (92163-3303)
PHONE..............................619 238-1233
Gary Thomas Phillips, *CEO*
Jeffrey Kirsch, *
Craig A Blower, *
EMP: 105 **EST:** 1957
SQ FT: 93,500
SALES (est): 7.32MM **Privately Held**
Web: www.fleetscience.org
SIC: 8412 Museum

(P-19362)
SAN DIEGO MUSEUM OF ART
1450 El Prado (92101-1618)
P.O. Box 122107 (92112-2107)
PHONE..............................619 696-1909
Philip Tom Gildred, *CEO*
Roxanna Velasquez, *
Reed Viekerman, *Asst Dir*
▲ **EMP:** 82 **EST:** 1925
SQ FT: 96,278
SALES (est): 14MM **Privately Held**
Web: www.sdmart.org
SIC: 8412 Museum

(P-19363)
SANTA BRBARA MSEUM NTRAL HSTOR
2559 Puesta Del Sol (93105-2936)
PHONE..............................805 682-4711
Luke Swetland, *CEO*
Karl Hutterer, *
Diane Wondowloski, *
Palmer Jackson Junior, *Pr*
Carolyn Chandler, *
EMP: 95 **EST:** 1916
SALES (est): 7.85MM **Privately Held**
Web: www.sbnature.org
SIC: 8412 Museum

PRODUCTS & SVCS

(P-19364)

SKIRBALL CULTURAL CENTER
Also Called: SKIRBALL CULTURAL CENTER
2701 N Sepulveda Blvd (90049-6833)
PHONE.................................310 440-4500
Uri D Herscher, *Pr*
Leslie K Johnson, *
▲ EMP: 150 EST: 1995
SQ FT: 65,000
SALES (est): 16.43MM **Privately Held**
Web: www.skirball.org
SIC: 8412 Museum

(P-19365)

THE J PAUL GETTY TRUST (PA)
Also Called: Getty Publications
1200 Getty Center Dr Ste 500
(90049-1657)
PHONE.................................310 440-7300
▲ EMP: 1431 EST: 1953
SALES (est): 149.74MM
SALES (corp-wide): 149.74MM **Privately Held**
Web: www.getty.edu
SIC: 8412 Museums and art galleries

8422 Botanical And Zoological Gardens

(P-19366)

AQUARIUM OF PACIFIC (PA)
100 Aquarium Way (90802-8126)
PHONE.................................562 590-3100
▲ EMP: 220 EST: 1997
SQ FT: 10,000
SALES (est): 55.28MM **Privately Held**
Web: www.aquariumofpacific.org
SIC: 8422 Aquarium

(P-19367)

LIVING DESERT
47900 Portola Ave (92260-6156)
PHONE.................................760 346-5694
Allen Monroe, *CEO*
Terrie Correll, *
Dwight Middendorf, *
Sarah Clapp, *
Peter Siminski, *
EMP: 124 EST: 1970
SQ FT: 1,700
SALES (est): 34.59MM **Privately Held**
Web: www.livingdesert.org
SIC: 8422 5947 Aquariums and zoological gardens; Gift shop

(P-19368)

SANTA BRBARA ZLGCAL FOUNDATION
Also Called: SANTA BARBARA ZOO
500 Ninos Dr (93103-3759)
PHONE.................................805 962-1673
Yul Vanek, *CEO*
Nancy Mctoldridge, *COO*
Carol Bedford, *
Fred Clough, *
Diane Pearson, *
▲ EMP: 130 EST: 1961
SQ FT: 1,200
SALES (est): 18.28MM **Privately Held**
Web: www.sbzoo.org
SIC: 8422 Zoological garden, noncommercial

(P-19369)

ZOOLOGICAL SOCIETY SAN DIEGO (PA)
Also Called: San Diego Zoo Wildlife Aliance
2920 Zoo Dr (92101-1646)
P.O. Box 120551 (92112-0551)

PHONE.................................619 231-1515
Paul Baribault, *CEO*
Shawn Dixon, *COO*
David Franco, *CFO*
◆ EMP: 1500 EST: 1916
SALES (est): 422.09MM
SALES (corp-wide): 422.09MM **Privately Held**
Web: www.sandiegozoowildlifealliance.org
SIC: 8422 Aquarium

(P-19370)

ZOOLOGICAL SOCIETY SAN DIEGO
Also Called: San Diego Wild Animal Park
15500 San Pasqual Valley Rd
(92027-7017)
PHONE.................................760 747-8702
Robert Mcclure, *Mgr*
EMP: 215
SALES (corp-wide): 422.09MM **Privately Held**
Web: www.sandiegozoowildlifealliance.org
SIC: 8422 7999 Animal and reptile exhibit; Tourist attraction, commercial
PA: Zoological Society Of San Diego
2920 Zoo Dr
San Diego CA
619 231-1515

(P-19371)

ZOOLOGICAL SOCIETY SAN DIEGO
Also Called: San Diego Zoo
2920 Zoo Dr (92101-1646)
P.O. Box 120551 (92112-0551)
PHONE.................................619 744-3325
Richard Farrar, *Dir*
EMP: 143
SALES (corp-wide): 422.09MM **Privately Held**
Web: www.sandiegozoowildlifealliance.org
SIC: 8422 Botanical and zoological gardens
PA: Zoological Society Of San Diego
2920 Zoo Dr
San Diego CA
619 231-1515

(P-19372)

ZOOLOGICAL SOCIETY SAN DIEGO
Also Called: San Diego Zoo
10946 Willow Ct Ste 200 (92127-2417)
PHONE.................................619 231-1515
Janet Matsuura, *Dir*
EMP: 173
SALES (corp-wide): 422.09MM **Privately Held**
Web: www.sandiegozoowildlifealliance.org
SIC: 8422 Animal and reptile exhibit
PA: Zoological Society Of San Diego
2920 Zoo Dr
San Diego CA
619 231-1515

8611 Business Associations

(P-19373)

ALL STATE ASSOCIATION INC
11487 San Fernando Rd (91340-3406)
PHONE.................................877 425-2558
Steve Avetyan, *CEO*
Alfred Megrabyan, *
Armen Karibyan, *
EMP: 250 EST: 2003

SALES (est): 9.56MM **Privately Held**
SIC: 8611 Trade associations

(P-19374)

CALIFORNIA ASSN REALTORS INC (PA)
525 S Virgil Ave (90020-1403)
PHONE.................................213 739-8200
Joel S Singer, *
Joel S Singer, *
Lefrancis Arnold, *
Don Flyn, *
Don Faught, *
EMP: 110 EST: 1907
SQ FT: 52,000
SALES (est): 51.06MM
SALES (corp-wide): 51.06MM **Privately Held**
Web: zfp.car.org
SIC: 8611 8742 Real estate board; Real estate consultant

(P-19375)

CALIFORNIA RE ASSN INC
Also Called: California Real Estate
525 S Virgil Ave (90020-1403)
PHONE.................................213 739-8200
EMP: 85 EST: 1996
SQ FT: 52,000
SALES (est): 1.9MM
SALES (corp-wide): 51.06MM **Privately Held**
SIC: 8611 Real estate board
PA: California Association Of Realtors, Inc.
525 S Virgil Ave
Los Angeles CA
213 739-8200

(P-19376)

CITY ORANGE POLICE ASSN INC
1107 N Batavia St (92867-4615)
P.O. Box 906 (92856-6906)
PHONE.................................714 457-5340
EMP: 216 EST: 1980
SALES (est): 390.11K **Privately Held**
Web: www.copa33.org
SIC: 8611 Business associations

(P-19377)

ELECTRA OWNERS ASSOC
700 W E St (92101-5984)
PHONE.................................619 236-3310
J E Martin, *Prin*
EMP: 200 EST: 2008
SALES (est): 999.58K
SALES (corp-wide): 90.39MM **Privately Held**
Web: electraownersassociation.buildinglink.com
SIC: 8611 Business associations
PA: Action Property Management, Inc.
2603 Main St Ste 500
Irvine CA
949 450-0202

(P-19378)

EPSILON SYSTEMS SOLUTIONS INC
2101 Haffley Ave # A (91950-6416)
PHONE.................................619 474-3252
Robert Duran, *Brnch Mgr*
EMP: 134
SALES (corp-wide): 110MM **Privately Held**
Web: www.epsilonsystems.com
SIC: 8611 Shipping and steamship company association
PA: Epsilon Systems Solutions, Inc.
9444 Balboa Ave Ste 100
San Diego CA
619 702-1700

(P-19379)

INSTITUTE OF ELEC ELEC ENGNERS
Also Called: Ieee Computer Society
10662 Los Vaqueros Cir (90720-2513)
P.O. Box 3014 (90720-1314)
PHONE.................................714 821-8380
Linda Ashworth, *Admn*
EMP: 85
SALES (corp-wide): 524.8MM **Privately Held**
Web: ieeeshutpages.s3-website-us-west-2.amazonaws.com
SIC: 8611 Trade associations
PA: The Institute Of Electrical And Electronics Engineers Incorporated
445 Hoes Ln
Piscataway NJ
212 419-7900

(P-19380)

LOS ANGLES AREA CHMBER CMMERCE
350 S Bixel St (90017-1418)
PHONE.................................213 580-7500
Maria S Salinas, *Pr*
Gary Toebben, *Pr*
David Eads, *COO*
Benjamin Stilp, *CFO*
Mark Louchheim, *Ch Bd*
EMP: 85 EST: 2009
SALES (est): 6.08MM **Privately Held**
Web: www.lachamber.com
SIC: 8611 Chamber of Commerce

(P-19381)

MENS APPAREL GUILD IN CAL INC
Also Called: Magic International
2901 28th St Ste 100 (90405-2975)
PHONE.................................310 857-7500
Joe Loggia, *Pr*
EMP: 98 EST: 1932
SALES (est): 2.4MM
SALES (corp-wide): 2.72B **Privately Held**
SIC: 8611 Manufacturers' institute
HQ: Advanstar Communications Inc.
2501 Colorado Ave Ste 280
Santa Monica CA
310 857-7500

(P-19382)

MERCY HOUSE LIVING CENTERS
Also Called: Mercy Hse Trnstnal Living Ctrs
807 N Garfield St (92701-3821)
P.O. Box 1905 (92702-1905)
PHONE.................................714 836-7188
Larry Haynes, *Ex Dir*
Jerome Karcher, *
Carrie Delaurie, *
EMP: 170 EST: 1988
SQ FT: 19,000
SALES (est): 19.91MM **Privately Held**
Web: www.mercyhouse.net
SIC: 8611 Community affairs and services

(P-19383)

MIDI MANUFACTURERS ASSN INC
Also Called: Midi Association, The
85 Matisse Cir (92656-3864)
PHONE.................................714 227-0068
Athan Billias, *Pr*
Lee Whitmore, *Treas*
Jean-baptiste Thiebaut, *Sec*
EMP: 98 EST: 1985
SALES (est): 629.62K **Privately Held**

SIC: 8611 Trade associations

(P-19384)
SAN DIEGO ASSN GOVERNMENTS (PA)
Also Called: Regional Transportation Comm
401 B St Ste 800 (92101-4231)
PHONE.....................619 699-1900
Jack Dale, *Ch*
Jim Janney, *
Don Higginson, *
Gary L Gallegos, *
EMP: 250 EST: 1972
SQ FT: 20,000
SALES (est): 222.55MM
SALES (corp-wide): 222.55MM **Privately Held**
Web: www.sandag.org
SIC: 8611 Business associations

(P-19385)
SATICOY LEMON ASSOCIATION
600 E 3rd St (93030-6001)
P.O. Box 46 (93061-0046)
PHONE.....................805 654-6543
EMP: 99
SALES (corp-wide): 26.61MM **Privately Held**
Web: www.saticoylemon.com
SIC: 8611 Growers' associations
PA: Saticoy Lemon Association
103 N Peck Rd
Santa Paula CA
805 654-6500

(P-19386)
WESTERN GROWERS ASSOCIATION (PA)
Also Called: W G A
6501 Irvine Center Dr (92618-2134)
P.O. Box 57089 (92619-7089)
PHONE.....................949 863-1000
Tom A Nassif, *CEO*
Steve Patricio, *
Matt Mcinerney, *Ex VP*
Ward Kennedy, *
Dave Puglia, *
EMP: 150 EST: 1926
SALES (est): 42.45MM
SALES (corp-wide): 42.45MM **Privately Held**
Web: www.wga.com
SIC: 8611 8111 Growers' associations; Legal services

(P-19387)
WONDERFUL CITRUS COOPERATIVE
5001 California Ave Ste 230 (93309-1671)
PHONE.....................661 720-2400
EMP: 520
Web: www.wonderfulcitrus.com
SIC: 8611 Growers' marketing advisory service
PA: Wonderful Citrus Cooperative
1901 S Lexington St
Delano CA

8621 Professional Organizations

(P-19388)
ACADEMY MPIC ARTS & SCIENCES (PA)
8949 Wilshire Blvd (90211-1907)
PHONE.....................310 247-3000
Dawn Hudson, *CEO*
Janet Yang, *

Bruce Davis, *
Andy Horn, *
Meredith Shea Chief Membership Impact Industry, *Ofcr*
EMP: 100 EST: 1927
SQ FT: 35,000
SALES (est): 287.95MM
SALES (corp-wide): 287.95MM **Privately Held**
Web: www.oscars.org
SIC: 8621 7819 8611 Professional organizations; Services allied to motion pictures; Business associations

(P-19389)
ASSOCTION MXCAN AMRCN EDCATORS
Also Called: Norwalk Unified School Dst
12820 Pioneer Blvd (90650-2875)
PHONE.....................562 868-0431
Hasmik Danielian, *Superintnt*
EMP: 93
Web: www.nlmusd.org
SIC: 8621 Education and teacher association
PA: Association Of Mexican American Educators
2511 W 3rd St
Los Angeles CA

(P-19390)
ATTAINMENT HOLDCO LLC
Also Called: Instride
700 S Flower St Ste 1800 (90017-4205)
PHONE.....................310 954-1578
Stephen Chu, *Managing Member*
Jonathan Lau, *COO*
Dan Bock, *CCO*
Jeff Stark, *CFO*
EMP: 151 EST: 2019
SALES (est): 11.83MM **Privately Held**
Web: www.instride.com
SIC: 8621 Education and teacher association

(P-19391)
CALIFORNIA CANCER SPECIALISTS MEDICAL GROUP INC
1333 S Mayflower Ave # 200 (91016-4032)
PHONE.....................626 775-3200
EMP: 320
SIC: 8621 7389 Medical field-related associations; Financial services

(P-19392)
CAPITAL INVSTMNTS VNTURES CORP (PA)
Also Called: Civco
30151 Tomas (92688-2125)
PHONE.....................949 858-0647
Drew Richardson, *Pr*
Gary Prenovost, *
Marjorie Kelso Int'l, *Prs Dir*
Brian Cronin, *
◆ EMP: 195 EST: 1975
SQ FT: 95,000
SALES (est): 64.57MM
SALES (corp-wide): 64.57MM **Privately Held**
Web: www.padi.com
SIC: 8621 4724 Professional organizations; Travel agencies

(P-19393)
COOPERTIVE AMRCN PHYSCIANS INC (PA)
Also Called: Cap-Mpt
333 S Hope St Fl 8 (90071-3001)
PHONE.....................213 473-8600
James Weidner, *CEO*

Thomas Andrem, *VP*
Cindy Belcher, *COO*
Nancy Brusegaard Johnson, *Sr VP*
John Donaldson, *CFO*
EMP: 100 EST: 1975
SALES (est): 21.15MM
SALES (corp-wide): 21.15MM **Privately Held**
Web: www.capphysicians.com
SIC: 8621 Medical field-related associations

(P-19394)
COUNTY OF LOS ANGELES
313 N Figueroa St 9th Fl (90012-2602)
PHONE.....................213 240-8412
Thomas L Garthwaite, *Brnch Mgr*
EMP: 114
Web: www.lacounty.gov
SIC: 8621 9431 Professional organizations; Prenatal (maternity) health program administration, govt.
PA: County Of Los Angeles
500 W Temple St Ste 437
Los Angeles CA
213 974-1101

(P-19395)
LEIGHTON GROUP INC
75450 Gerald Ford Dr Ste 301 (92211-6022)
PHONE.....................760 776-4192
EMP: 165
SALES (corp-wide): 163.8MM **Privately Held**
Web: www.leightongroup.com
SIC: 8621 Professional organizations
HQ: Leighton Group, Inc.
2600 Michelson Dr Ste 400
Irvine CA
949 250-1421

(P-19396)
LOS ANGELES COUNTY BAR ASSN (PA)
Also Called: LOS ANGELES LAWYER MAGAZINE
444 S Flower St (90071-2926)
P.O. Box 55020 (90055-2020)
PHONE.....................213 627-2727
Paul R Kiesel, *Pr*
Sally Suchil, *
▲ EMP: 85 EST: 1878
SALES (est): 8.13MM
SALES (corp-wide): 8.13MM **Privately Held**
Web: www.lacba.org
SIC: 8621 Bar association

(P-19397)
MEDIMPACT HLTHCARE SYSTEMS INC (HQ)
10181 Scripps Gateway Ct (92131-5152)
PHONE.....................858 566-2727
Frederick Howe, *Ch Bd*
James Gollaher, *CFO*
EMP: 160 EST: 1989
SQ FT: 100,000
SALES (est): 134.05MM **Privately Held**
Web: www.medimpact.com
SIC: 8621 Medical field-related associations
PA: Medimpact Holdings, Inc.
10181 Scripps Gateway Ct
San Diego CA

(P-19398)
NATIONAL NOTARY ASSOCIATION
Also Called: Nna Insurance Services
9350 De Soto Ave (91311-4926)

PHONE.....................800 876-6827
EMP: 204 EST: 1984
SALES (est): 26.08MM **Privately Held**
Web: www.nationalnotary.org
SIC: 8621 Professional organizations

(P-19399)
ORANGE CNTY HLTH AUTH A PUB AG
Also Called: Orange County Health Authority
505 City Pkwy W (92868-2924)
PHONE.....................714 246-8500
Richard Chambers, *CEO*
Michael Schrader, *
Richard Helmer, *Chief Medical Officer**
Ladan Khamseh, *
EMP: 432 EST: 1994
SQ FT: 200,000
SALES (est): 103.83MM **Privately Held**
Web: www.caloptima.org
SIC: 8621 Professional organizations

(P-19400)
ORANGE COUNTY HEALTH CARE AGCY
405 W 5th St Ste 700 (92701-4534)
PHONE.....................714 568-5683
Jenny Qian, *Prin*
EMP: 99 EST: 2014
SALES (est): 10.34MM **Privately Held**
Web: www.ochealthinfo.com
SIC: 8621 Health association

(P-19401)
PADI AMERICAS INC
Also Called: Padi
30151 Tomas (92688-2125)
P.O. Box 7005 (92688-7005)
PHONE.....................949 858-7234
Drew Richardson, *Prin*
◆ EMP: 200 EST: 1967
SQ FT: 96,000
SALES (est): 51.74MM
SALES (corp-wide): 64.57MM **Privately Held**
Web: www.padi.com
SIC: 8621 Education and teacher association
HQ: Padi Worldwide Corp.
30151 Tomas
Rcho Sta Marg CA
949 858-7234

(P-19402)
REGAL MEDICAL GROUP INC (PA)
Also Called: Heritage California Aco
8510 Balboa Blvd Ste 275 (91325-5809)
PHONE.....................818 654-3400
EMP: 111 EST: 1986
SALES (est): 66.89MM **Privately Held**
Web: www.regalmed.com
SIC: 8621 Medical field-related associations

(P-19403)
SHARP COMMUNITY MEDICAL GROUP
Also Called: SCMG
8695 Spectrum Center Blvd (92123-1489)
PHONE.....................858 499-4525
Kenneth Roth, *Pr*
EMP: 200 EST: 1989
SALES (est): 552.32MM
SALES (corp-wide): 2.37B **Privately Held**
Web: www.scmg.org
SIC: 8621 Professional organizations
PA: Sharp Healthcare
8695 Spectrum Center Blvd
San Diego CA
858 499-4000

PRODUCTS & SVCS

(P-19404)
STATE BAR OF CALIFORNIA
755 Santa Rosa St Ste 310 (93401-4805)
PHONE...............................805 544-7551
EMP: 92
SALES (corp-wide): 91.35MM Privately Held
Web: calbar.ca.gov
SIC: 8621 Bar association
PA: State Bar Of California
180 Howard St Fl Grnd
San Francisco CA
415 538-2000

(P-19405)
STATE BAR OF CALIFORNIA
845 S Figueroa St (90017-2515)
PHONE...............................213 765-1520
EMP: 93
SALES (corp-wide): 91.35MM Privately Held
Web: calbar.ca.gov
SIC: 8621 Bar association
PA: State Bar Of California
180 Howard St Fl Grnd
San Francisco CA
415 538-2000

(P-19406)
TRUCK UNDERWRITERS ASSOCIATION (DH)
4680 Wilshire Blvd (90010-3807)
PHONE...............................323 932-3200
Leonard H Gelfand, Pr
Gerald Faulwell, *
Martin Feinstein, *
John Lynch, *
Jason Katz, *
EMP: 1767 EST: 1935
SALES (est): 51MM Privately Held
SIC: 8621 Professional organizations
HQ: Farmers Group, Inc.
6301 Owensmouth Ave # 300
Woodland Hills CA
323 932-3200

8631 Labor Organizations

(P-19407)
AMERICAN FDRTION MSCANS LCAL 4
Also Called: AMERICAN FEDERATION OF MUSICIA
3220 Winona Ave (91504-2544)
PHONE...............................323 462-2161
John Acosta, Pr
Rick Baptist, *
Gary Lasley, *
EMP: 95 EST: 1897
SALES (est): 3.47MM
SALES (corp-wide): 13.67MM Privately Held
Web: www.afm47.org
SIC: 8631 Labor union
PA: American Federation Of Musicians Of
The United States & Canada (Inc)
1501 Broadway Fl 9
New York NY
212 869-1330

(P-19408)
ART DRCTORS GILD ITSE LCAL 876
11969 Ventura Blvd Ste 200 (91604-2630)
PHONE...............................818 762-9995
Mimi Gramatky, Pr
Scott Roth, Dir
Jim Wallis, VP
Cate Bangs, Treas

Judy Cosgrove, Sec
EMP: 126 EST: 1937
SQ FT: 19,040
SALES (est): 10.84MM Privately Held
Web: www.adg.org
SIC: 8631 Labor organizations

(P-19409)
IATSE AFFL PRPRTY CRFTSPRSON L
12021 Riverside Dr (91607-3726)
PHONE...............................818 769-2500
Erik Nelson, Pr
EMP: 138 EST: 1939
SQ FT: 17,947
SALES (est): 11.16MM Privately Held
Web: www.local44.org
SIC: 8631 Labor union

(P-19410)
INTERNTIONAL UN OPER ENGINEERS
Also Called: Local 12
1647 W Lugonia Ave (92374-2048)
PHONE...............................909 307-8700
Ron Sikroski, Mgr
EMP: 595
SALES (corp-wide): 70.57MM Privately Held
Web: www.oefi.org
SIC: 8631 Labor union
PA: International Union Of Operating Engineers
1121 L St Ste 401
Sacramento CA
916 444-6880

(P-19411)
INTERNTIONAL UN OPER ENGINEERS
Also Called: Local 12
3935 Normal St (92103-3585)
PHONE...............................619 295-3186
Dan Hawn, Mgr
EMP: 594
SQ FT: 4,500
SALES (corp-wide): 70.57MM Privately Held
SIC: 8631 Labor union
PA: International Union Of Operating Engineers
1121 L St Ste 401
Sacramento CA
916 444-6880

(P-19412)
SEIU LOCAL 721
1545 Wilshire Blvd Ste 100 (90017-4510)
PHONE...............................213 368-8660
Annelle Grajeda, Owner
EMP: 175 EST: 2007
SALES (est): 142.29K Privately Held
Web: www.seiu721.org
SIC: 8631 Labor union

(P-19413)
SOUTHERN CAL IBW-NECA HLTH TR
100 Corson St Ste 200 (91103-3841)
PHONE...............................323 221-5861
EMP: 89 EST: 2010
SALES (est): 139.15MM
SALES (corp-wide): 139.15MM Privately Held
Web: www.scibew-neca.org
SIC: 8631 Labor union

PA: Southern California Ibew-Neca
Administrative Corporation
100 Corson St Ste 200
Pasadena CA
323 221-5861

(P-19414)
SOUTHWEST CRPNTERS TRNING FUND
533 S Fremont Ave Ste 700 (90071-1712)
PHONE...............................213 386-8590
EMP: 81 EST: 2012
SALES (est): 36.64MM Privately Held
Web: www.swmsctf.org
SIC: 8631 Labor union

(P-19415)
SOUTHWEST RGNAL CNCIL CRPNTERS
7111 Firestone Blvd (90621-2958)
PHONE...............................714 571-0449
EMP: 92
SALES (corp-wide): 26.99MM Privately Held
Web: www.swcarpenters.org
SIC: 8631 Labor union
PA: Southwest Regional Council Of Carpenters
533 S Fremont Ave Fl 10
Los Angeles CA
213 385-1457

(P-19416)
TEMPORARY STAFFING UNION
19800 Macarthur Blvd Ste 300 (92612-2421)
PHONE...............................714 728-5186
Veronica Lake, CEO
Fe Santos, *
EMP: 4000 EST: 2018
SQ FT: 1,500
SALES (est): 7.05MM Privately Held
SIC: 8631 Labor union

(P-19417)
UNITE HAIR
2870 Whiptail Loop Ste 100 (92010-6709)
PHONE...............................760 585-1800
EMP: 94 EST: 2017
SALES (est): 527.04K Privately Held
Web: www.unitehair.com
SIC: 8631 Labor organizations

(P-19418)
UNITED FARM WORKERS AMERICA (PA)
29700 Woodford Tehachapi Rd (93531)
P.O. Box 62 (93531-0062)
PHONE...............................661 822-5571
Arturo Rodriguez, Pr
Irv Hershenbaum, *
Tanis Ybarra, *
Liz Villarino, *
EMP: 110 EST: 1966
SQ FT: 5,000
SALES (est): 9.96MM
SALES (corp-wide): 9.96MM Privately Held
Web: www.ufw.org
SIC: 8631 Labor union

(P-19419)
WRITERS GUILD AMERICA WEST INC
7000 W 3rd St (90048-4321)
PHONE...............................323 951-4000
David Young, CEO
David Weiss, Prin
Elias Davis, Sec

David Young, Ex Dir
Chris Keyser, Prin
EMP: 160 EST: 1954
SQ FT: 67,000
SALES (est): 48.31MM Privately Held
Web: www.wga.org
SIC: 8631 Labor union

8641 Civic And Social Associations

(P-19420)
21515 HAWTHORNE OWNER LLC
21535 Hawthorne Blvd Ste 100 (90503-6604)
PHONE...............................310 406-3730
Margaret Powell, *
Jenny Blanchart, *
EMP: 100 EST: 2014
SALES (est): 1.06MM Privately Held
SIC: 8641 Dwelling-related associations

(P-19421)
ACLU FNDATION SOUTHERN CAL LLC
Also Called: American Cvil Lbrties Un Sther
765 The City Dr S Ste 360 (92868-6913)
PHONE...............................213 977-9500
James Gilliam, Managing Member
Mark Rosenbaum, Managing Member*
EMP: 83 EST: 2007
SALES (est): 18.83MM Privately Held
Web: www.aclusocal.org
SIC: 8641 Civic and social associations

(P-19422)
AFRICAN WOMEN RISING
801 Cold Springs Rd (93108-1016)
PHONE...............................415 278-1784
EMP: 200 EST: 2007
SALES (est): 2.12MM Privately Held
Web: www.africanwomenrising.org
SIC: 8641 Civic and social associations

(P-19423)
ARMED SERVICES YMCA OF USA
3293 Santo Rd (92124-3340)
PHONE...............................858 751-5755
Kim Ney, Ex Dir
EMP: 122
SALES (corp-wide): 7.42MM Privately Held
Web: www.asymca.org
SIC: 8641 Youth organizations
PA: Armed Services Ymca Of The U.S.A.
14040 Central Loop B
Woodbridge VA
703 445-3986

(P-19424)
ASSOCTED STDNTS CAL STATE UNIV
Also Called: A S I
1212 N Bellflower Blvd Ste 220 (90815-4148)
PHONE...............................562 985-4994
Richard Haller, Ex Dir
EMP: 222 EST: 1956
SQ FT: 184,000
SALES (est): 16.84MM Privately Held
Web: www.asicsulb.org
SIC: 8641 University club

(P-19425)
BEAR VALLEY SPRINGS ASSN
29541 Rollingoak Dr (93561-7133)
PHONE..................................661 821-5537
Todd Lander, *Pr*
Terry Quinn, *
Larry Thompson, *
Tim Hawkins, *
EMP: 200 **EST:** 1970
SQ FT: 2,000
SALES (est): 7.45MM **Privately Held**
Web: www.bvsa.org
SIC: 8641 Homeowners' association

(P-19426)
BOYS & GIRLS CLUBS SOUTH CNTY
847 Encina Ave (91932-2135)
P.O. Box 520 (91933-0520)
PHONE..................................619 424-2266
Ken Blinsman, *Pr*
EMP: 100 **EST:** 1982
SALES (est): 4.85MM **Privately Held**
Web: www.bgcscounty.org
SIC: 8641 5812 Youth organizations; Eating places

(P-19427)
BOYS GIRLS CLUBS OF KERN CNTY
Also Called: Boy's & Girls Club Bakersfield
801 Niles St (93305-4419)
PHONE..................................661 325-3730
Zane Smith, *Dir*
Ed Kuhn, *
Bill Campbell, *
Craig Stickler, *
Tricia Ceccarill, *
EMP: 500 **EST:** 1971
SALES (est): 9.29MM **Privately Held**
Web: www.bgclubsofkerncounty.org
SIC: 8641 8322 Boy Scout organization; Individual and family services

(P-19428)
BOYS GRLS CLB BRBANK GRTER E V
300 E Angeleno Ave (91502-1311)
PHONE..................................818 842-9333
EMP: 99 **EST:** 1994
SQ FT: 6,000
SALES (est): 3.15MM **Privately Held**
Web: www.bgcburbank.org
SIC: 8641 Youth organizations

(P-19429)
BOYS GRLS CLB SNTA MONICA INC
Also Called: BOYS & GIRLS CLUBS OF SANTA MO
1220 Lincoln Blvd (90401-1704)
PHONE..................................310 361-8500
Aaron Young, *Dir*
EMP: 83 **EST:** 1943
SQ FT: 6,000
SALES (est): 3.03MM **Privately Held**
Web: www.smbgc.org
SIC: 8641 7997 Youth organizations; Membership sports and recreation clubs

(P-19430)
BOYS GRLS CLUBS HUNTINGTON VLY (PA)
Also Called: BOYS & GIRLS CLUBS OF HUNTINGT
16582 Brookhurst St (92708-2353)
PHONE..................................714 531-2582
Tanya Hoxsie, *Pr*

EMP: 89 **EST:** 1967
SALES (est): 8.67MM **Privately Held**
Web: www.bgchv.com
SIC: 8641 Youth organizations

(P-19431)
CALIFORNIA CLUB
538 S Flower St (90071-2548)
PHONE..................................213 622-1391
Robert C Baker, *CEO*
EMP: 185 **EST:** 1888
SALES (est): 11.13MM **Privately Held**
Web: www.californiaclub.org
SIC: 8641 7041 Business persons club; Residence club, organization

(P-19432)
CATHOLIC EDUCATION FOUNDA
3424 Wilshire Blvd Ste 24 (90010-2263)
PHONE..................................213 637-7475
Kathleen Ash, *Prin*
EMP: 85 **EST:** 2014
SALES (est): 912.82K **Privately Held**
Web: www.cefdn.org
SIC: 8641 Civic and social associations

(P-19433)
CHANNEL ISLNDS YUNG MNS CHRSTN
301 W Figueroa St (93101-3632)
PHONE..................................805 963-8775
Teri Bradford Rouse, *Brnch Mgr*
EMP: 87
SALES (corp-wide): 19.77MM **Privately Held**
Web: www.ciymca.org
SIC: 8641 Youth organizations
PA: Channel Islands Young Men's Christian Association
1180 Eugenia Pl
Carpinteria CA
805 569-1103

(P-19434)
CHANNEL ISLNDS YUNG MNS CHRSTN
Also Called: Lompoc Family YMCA
201 W College Ave (93436-4415)
PHONE..................................805 736-3483
Dan Powell, *Brnch Mgr*
EMP: 87
SALES (corp-wide): 19.77MM **Privately Held**
Web: www.ciymca.org
SIC: 8641 7991 8351 7032 Youth organizations; Physical fitness facilities; Child day care services; Youth camps
PA: Channel Islands Young Men's Christian Association
1180 Eugenia Pl
Carpinteria CA
805 569-1103

(P-19435)
CHANNEL ISLNDS YUNG MNS CHRSTN
Also Called: Santa Barbara Family YMCA
36 Hitchcock Way (93105-3102)
PHONE..................................805 687-7727
Tim Hardy, *Brnch Mgr*
EMP: 88
SALES (corp-wide): 19.77MM **Privately Held**
Web: www.ciymca.org
SIC: 8641 7991 8351 7032 Youth organizations; Physical fitness facilities; Child day care services; Youth camps

PA: Channel Islands Young Men's Christian Association
1180 Eugenia Pl
Carpinteria CA
805 569-1103

(P-19436)
CHANNEL ISLNDS YUNG MNS CHRSTN
Also Called: Montecito Family YMCA
591 Santa Rosa Ln (93108-2145)
PHONE..................................805 969-3288
Yvonne Rubio, *Dir*
EMP: 88
SALES (corp-wide): 19.77MM **Privately Held**
Web: www.ciymca.org
SIC: 8641 7991 8351 7032 Youth organizations; Physical fitness facilities; Child day care services; Youth camps
PA: Channel Islands Young Men's Christian Association
1180 Eugenia Pl
Carpinteria CA
805 569-1103

(P-19437)
CHANNEL ISLNDS YUNG MNS CHRSTN
Also Called: Stuart C. Gildred Family YMCA
900 N Refugio Rd (93460-9314)
PHONE..................................805 686-2037
Paula Parisotto, *Brnch Mgr*
EMP: 88
SALES (corp-wide): 19.77MM **Privately Held**
Web: www.ciymca.org
SIC: 8641 7991 8351 7032 Youth organizations; Physical fitness facilities; Child day care services; Youth camps
PA: Channel Islands Young Men's Christian Association
1180 Eugenia Pl
Carpinteria CA
805 569-1103

(P-19438)
CHANNEL ISLNDS YUNG MNS CHRSTN
Also Called: Camarillo Family YMCA
3111 Village Park Dr (93012)
PHONE..................................805 484-0423
Marge Castellano, *Dir*
EMP: 88
SALES (corp-wide): 19.77MM **Privately Held**
Web: www.ciymca.org
SIC: 8641 7991 8351 7032 Youth organizations; Physical fitness facilities; Child day care services; Youth camps
PA: Channel Islands Young Men's Christian Association
1180 Eugenia Pl
Carpinteria CA
805 569-1103

(P-19439)
CHANNEL ISLNDS YUNG MNS CHRSTN
Also Called: Ventura Family YMCA
3760 Telegraph Rd (93003-3421)
PHONE..................................805 484-0423
Sarah Abrams, *Dir*
EMP: 88
SALES (corp-wide): 19.77MM **Privately Held**
Web: www.ciymca.org
SIC: 8641 7991 8351 7032 Youth organizations; Physical fitness facilities; Child day care services; Youth camps

PA: Channel Islands Young Men's Christian Association
1180 Eugenia Pl
Carpinteria CA
805 569-1103

(P-19440)
COUNTY OF RIVERSIDE
Also Called: Riverside Crona Rsrce Cnsrvtio
4500 Glenwood Dr Ste A (92501-3066)
PHONE..................................951 683-7691
Shelli Lamb, *Dist Mgr*
EMP: 149
SALES (corp-wide): 4.58B **Privately Held**
Web: www.rcrcd.org
SIC: 8641 9512 Environmental protection organization; Land, mineral, and wildlife conservation, County government
PA: County Of Riverside
4080 Lemon St Fl 11
Riverside CA
951 955-1110

(P-19441)
CRESCENTA-CANADA YMCA (PA)
Also Called: YMCA Crescenta-Canada
1930 Foothill Blvd (91011-1933)
PHONE..................................818 790-0123
Larry Hall, *CEO*
Ken Gorvetzian, *
EMP: 150 **EST:** 1953
SALES (est): 115.62K
SALES (corp-wide): 115.62K **Privately Held**
Web: www.ymcafoothills.org
SIC: 8641 7991 8351 7032 Youth organizations; Physical fitness facilities; Child day care services; Youth camps

(P-19442)
CRESCENTA-CANADA YMCA
Also Called: Learning Tree Pre-School
6840 Foothill Blvd (91042-2711)
PHONE..................................818 352-3255
Kathi Brink, *Brnch Mgr*
EMP: 130
SALES (corp-wide): 115.62K **Privately Held**
Web: www.ymcafoothills.org
SIC: 8641 7991 8351 7032 Youth organizations; Physical fitness facilities; Child day care services; Youth camps
PA: Crescenta-Canada Ymca
1930 Foothill Blvd
La Canada CA
818 790-0123

(P-19443)
D A V INDUSTRIES
1049 Elkelton Blvd (91977-4720)
PHONE..................................619 337-9244
William D Mudd, *Pr*
Bernard Bandish, *
Clifford Caldwell, *
Donald Pouliot, *
EMP: 100 **EST:** 1967
SQ FT: 8,000
SALES (est): 11.28MM **Privately Held**
Web: www.davveteransthriftstores.com
SIC: 8641 5932 Veterans' organization; Clothing, secondhand

(P-19444)
DS LAKESHORE LP
200 Baker St Ste 100 (92626-4551)
PHONE..................................916 286-5231
Patrick S Donahue, *Pt*
Trina Perales, *Pt*
EMP: 99 **EST:** 2019

PRODUCTS & SVCS

SALES (est): 268.71K **Privately Held**
SIC: 8641 Civic and social associations

(P-19445)
ELIZABETH GLSER PDTRIC AIDS FN
2950 31st St Ste 125 (90405-3098)
PHONE....................................310 593-0047
Jeff Gaffney, *Brnch Mgr*
EMP: 457
SALES (corp-wide): 187.69MM **Privately Held**
Web: www.pedaids.org
SIC: 8641 Civic and social associations
PA: Elizabeth Glaser Pediatric Aids
    Foundation
    1140 Conn Ave Nw Ste 200
    Washington DC
    920 770-0103

(P-19446)
EXCEPTIONAL CHLD FOUNDATION
11124 Fairbanks Way (90230-4945)
PHONE....................................310 915-6606
EMP: 110
SALES (corp-wide): 28.26MM **Privately Held**
Web: www.ecf.net
SIC: 8641 Civic and social associations
PA: Exceptional Children's Foundation
    5350 Machado Ln
    Culver City CA
    310 204-3300

(P-19447)
GIRL SCUTS GREATER LOS ANGELES (PA)
423 N La Brea Ave (90302-3408)
PHONE....................................626 677-2265
Lise Luttgens, *CEO*
Sylvia Rosenberger, *
Christa Weddle, *
Emily Ausbrook Chief Mission D elivery, *Ofcr*
EMP: 114 **EST:** 1924
SALES (est): 25.32MM
SALES (corp-wide): 25.32MM **Privately Held**
Web: www.girlscoutsla.org
SIC: 8641 Girl Scout organization

(P-19448)
GIRL SCUTS SAN DG-MPRIAL CNCIL (PA)
Also Called: GIRL SCOUTS SAN DIEGO
1231 Upas St (92103-5127)
PHONE....................................619 610-0751
Jo Dee C Jacob, *CEO*
▼ **EMP:** 94 **EST:** 1917
SQ FT: 7,926
SALES (est): 9.99MM
SALES (corp-wide): 9.99MM **Privately Held**
Web: www.sdgirlscouts.org
SIC: 8641 Girl Scout organization

(P-19449)
GREATER LOS ANGLES AREA CNCIL (PA)
Also Called: BOY SCOUTS OF AMERICA
2333 Scout Way (90026-4912)
PHONE....................................213 413-4400
Cash Sutton, *Pr*
EMP: 93 **EST:** 1935
SALES (est): 7.98MM
SALES (corp-wide): 7.98MM **Privately Held**
Web: www.glaacbsa.org

SIC: 8641 Boy Scout organization

(P-19450)
JEWISH CMNTY FNDTION LOS ANGLE (PA)
6505 Wilshire Blvd Ste 1150 (90048-4906)
PHONE....................................323 761-8700
Richard V Sandler, *Ch Bd*
Leslie E Bider, *
J Sanderson, *
Arlene Freedman, *
Jack Klein, *
EMP: 150 **EST:** 1937
SQ FT: 100,000
SALES (est): 43.79MM
SALES (corp-wide): 43.79MM **Privately Held**
Web: www.jewishla.org
SIC: 8641 8661 Community membership club ; Religious organizations

(P-19451)
JONATHAN CLUB (PA)
545 S Figueroa St (90071-1704)
PHONE....................................213 624-0881
Gregory J Dumas, *Pr*
James Abbott, *
Norm Rich, *
Randolph P Sinnott, *
◆ **EMP:** 200 **EST:** 1895
SQ FT: 230,276
SALES (est): 30.26MM
SALES (corp-wide): 30.26MM **Privately Held**
Web: www.jc.org
SIC: 8641 Social club, membership

(P-19452)
LA COUNTY SHERIFF PDC NO
211 W Temple St (90012-4086)
PHONE....................................661 294-6312
EMP: 233 **EST:** 2018
SALES (est): 4.05MM **Privately Held**
Web: www.lasd.org
SIC: 8641 Civic and social associations

(P-19453)
LAKE FREST NO II MSTR HMWNERS
Also Called: SUN & SAIL CLUB
24752 Toledo Ln (92630-2318)
PHONE....................................949 586-0860
Sonny Morper, *Pr*
Ted Brackez, *
Terri Graham, *
Ken Hedge, *
EMP: 80 **EST:** 1971
SQ FT: 9,000
SALES (est): 4.71MM **Privately Held**
Web: www.liveinlakeforest.com
SIC: 8641 Homeowners' association

(P-19454)
LAKE MISSION VIEJO ASSOCIATION
22555 Olympiad Rd (92692-1118)
PHONE....................................949 770-1313
Fred Mellenbruch, *Pr*
Jane Chadburn, *
Senator Jeff Miklaus, *VP*
Wayne Dunn, *
Sid Wittenberg, *
EMP: 90 **EST:** 1978
SQ FT: 7,400
SALES (est): 9.02MM **Privately Held**
Web: www.lakemissionviejo.org
SIC: 8641 Homeowners' association

(P-19455)
MARAVILLA FOUNDATION (PA)
5729 Union Pacific Ave (90022-5134)
PHONE....................................323 721-4162
Alex M Sotomayor, *CEO*
Paul Lopez, *
Robert Lagunas, *
George Ross, *
EMP: 151 **EST:** 1967
SQ FT: 30,000
SALES (est): 13.93MM
SALES (corp-wide): 13.93MM **Privately Held**
Web: www.maravilla.org
SIC: 8641 Civic and social associations

(P-19456)
MILKEN FAMILY FOUNDATION
1250 4th St Fl 1 (90401-1418)
PHONE....................................310 570-4800
Lowell J Milken, *Pr*
Susan Fox, *
EMP: 200 **EST:** 1986
SALES (est): 8.45MM **Privately Held**
Web: www.mff.org
SIC: 8641 Civic and social associations

(P-19457)
OXNARD POLICE DEPARTMENT
251 S C St (93030-5789)
PHONE....................................805 385-8300
EMP: 350 **EST:** 1960
SALES (est): 10.02MM **Privately Held**
Web: www.oxnardpd.org
SIC: 8641 Veterans' organization

(P-19458)
PUBLIC HLTH FNDATION ENTPS INC (PA)
Also Called: Heluna Health
13300 Crossroads Pkwy N Ste 450 (91746)
PHONE....................................800 201-7320
Blain Cutler, *Pr*
Eric Ramanathan, *
Devecchio Finley, *Vice Chairman*
Robert Jenks, *
Tamara Joseph, *
EMP: 177 **EST:** 1968
SQ FT: 25,000
SALES (est): 92.05MM
SALES (corp-wide): 92.05MM **Privately Held**
Web: www.helunahealth.org
SIC: 8641 Civic and social associations

(P-19459)
PUBLIC HLTH FNDATION ENTPS INC
277 S Atlantic Blvd (90022-1734)
PHONE....................................323 263-0262
Laurie Hill, *Prin*
EMP: 140
SALES (corp-wide): 92.05MM **Privately Held**
Web: www.phfewic.org
SIC: 8641 Civic and social associations
PA: Public Health Foundation Enterprises, Inc.
    13300 Crssrds Pkwy N
    City Of Industry CA
    800 201-7320

(P-19460)
PUBLIC HLTH FNDATION ENTPS INC
Also Called: Wic
1640 W Carson St Ste G (90501-3877)
PHONE....................................310 320-5215
EMP: 140

SALES (corp-wide): 92.05MM **Privately Held**
Web: www.helunahealth.org
SIC: 8641 Civic and social associations
PA: Public Health Foundation Enterprises, Inc.
    13300 Crssrds Pkwy N
    City Of Industry CA
    800 201-7320

(P-19461)
SAN DIEGO COUNTRY ESTATES ASSN
Also Called: SAN VICENTE INN & GOLF CLUB
24157 San Vicente Rd (92065-4166)
PHONE....................................760 789-3788
Jim Piva, *Pr*
EMP: 147 **EST:** 1972
SQ FT: 14,000
SALES (est): 12.16MM **Privately Held**
Web: www.sdcea.net
SIC: 8641 7997 7992 7011 Homeowners' association; Membership sports and recreation clubs; Public golf courses; Vacation lodges

(P-19462)
SAVICE INC
30052 Tomas (92688-2127)
PHONE....................................949 888-2444
Phu Hoang, *Prin*
EMP: 98 **EST:** 2008
SALES (est): 71K **Privately Held**
SIC: 8641 Civic and social associations

(P-19463)
SHRINERS INTERNATIONAL
Also Called: Shriners Hspitals For Children
909 S Fair Oaks Ave (91105-2625)
PHONE....................................626 389-9300
EMP: 124
Web: www.shrinersinternational.org
SIC: 8641 Fraternal associations
PA: Shriners Hospitals For Children
    2900 N Rocky Point Dr
    Tampa FL

(P-19464)
SILVER LAKES ASSOCIATION
Also Called: Homeowners Association
15273 Orchard Hill Ln (92342-7824)
P.O. Box 179 (92342-0179)
PHONE....................................760 245-1606
Michael Bennett, *Genl Mgr*
EMP: 90 **EST:** 1976
SQ FT: 3,000
SALES (est): 5.02MM **Privately Held**
Web: www.silverlakesassociation.com
SIC: 8641 Homeowners' association

(P-19465)
SUN CITY PALM DSERT CMNTY ASSN (PA)
Also Called: Palm Desert Community Assn
38180 Del Webb Blvd (92211-1256)
PHONE....................................760 200-2100
EMP: 80 **EST:** 1992
SQ FT: 4,000
SALES (est): 16.7MM **Privately Held**
Web: www.scpdca.com
SIC: 8641 7992 7997 Dwelling-related associations; Public golf courses; Country club, membership

(P-19466)
THEATER ARTS FNDTION SAN DEGO
Also Called: LA JOLLA PLAYHOUSE

2910 La Jolla Village Dr (92093-5100)
P.O. Box 12039 (92039-2039)
PHONE................................858 623-3366
Jeffrey Ressler Ch Person, *Prin*
Steven Libman, *
Lynelle Lynch Ch Person, *Prin*
Tim Scott Ch Person, *Prin*
Michael Bartell, *
EMP: 250 EST: 1954
SQ FT: 1,440
SALES (est): 6.05MM Privately Held
Web: www.lajollaplayhouse.org
SIC: 8641 7922 Civic associations;
Theatrical producers and services

(P-19467)
UPLAND HIGHLANDERS HIGH PTSA
565 W 11th St (91786-4660)
PHONE................................909 949-7880
EMP: 88 EST: 2010
SALES (est): 50.15K Privately Held
Web: uhs.upland.k12.ca.us
SIC: 8641 Parent-teachers' association

(P-19468)
URBAN CORPS SAN DIEGO COUNTY
3127 Jefferson St (92110-4422)
P.O. Box 80156 (92138-0156)
PHONE................................619 235-6884
Sam Duran, *CEO*
Michael Sterns, *
EMP: 132 EST: 1989
SQ FT: 25,000
SALES (est): 14.3MM Privately Held
Web: www.urbancorpssd.org
SIC: 8641 Youth organizations

(P-19469)
VALLEY HUNT CLUB
520 S Orange Grove Blvd (91105-1799)
PHONE................................626 793-7134
David Mole, *CEO*
Donald F Crumrine, *
EMP: 85 EST: 1888
SQ FT: 40,000
SALES (est): 7.36MM Privately Held
Web: www.valleyhuntclub.com
SIC: 8641 Social club, membership

(P-19470)
VETERANS MED RES FNDTION SAN D
3350 La Jolla Village Dr Ste 151a (92161-0002)
PHONE................................858 642-3080
EMP: 250 EST: 1986
SALES (est): 16.37MM Privately Held
Web: www.vmrf.org
SIC: 8641 Civic and social associations

(P-19471)
WEST END YUNG MNS CHRISTN ASSN
Also Called: Ontario/Montclair YMCA
1257 E D St (91764-4329)
P.O. Box 3220 (91761-0922)
PHONE................................909 477-2780
Dianna Lee-mitchell, *Dir*
EMP: 115
SALES (corp-wide): 4.73MM Privately Held
Web: www.weymca.org
SIC: 8641 7991 8351 7032 Youth
organizations; Physical fitness facilities;
Child day care services; Youth camps

PA: West End Young Men's Christian
Association Inc
1150 E Foothill Blvd
Upland CA
909 481-0722

(P-19472)
WEST END YUNG MNS CHRISTN ASSN
Also Called: Chino Valley YMCA
5665 Edison Ave (91710-9051)
PHONE................................909 597-7445
EMP: 115
SALES (corp-wide): 4.73MM Privately Held
Web: www.weymca.org
SIC: 8641 7991 8351 7032 Youth
organizations; Physical fitness facilities;
Child day care services; Youth camps
PA: West End Young Men's Christian
Association Inc
1150 E Foothill Blvd
Upland CA
909 481-0722

(P-19473)
WORLD MVIE AWRDS ORGNZTION WMA
9171 Wilshire Blvd # 500a (90210-5530)
PHONE................................833 375-5857
Lily Alphonsis, *CEO*
Royal Vincent, *CFO*
EMP: 99 EST: 2018
SALES (est): 198.74K Privately Held
SIC: 8641 Civic and social associations

(P-19474)
YMCA OF EAST VALLEY
Also Called: YMCA Camp Edwards
42842 Jenks Lake Rd E (92305-9769)
P.O. Box 277 (92305-0277)
PHONE................................909 794-1702
Loren Werner, *Dir*
EMP: 121
SALES (corp-wide): 15.69MM Privately Held
Web: www.ymcaeastvalley.org
SIC: 8641 7991 8351 7032 Youth
organizations; Physical fitness facilities;
Child day care services; Youth camps
PA: Ymca Of The East Valley
500 E Citrus Ave
Redlands CA
909 798-9622

(P-19475)
YMCA OF EAST VALLEY
Also Called: San Bernardino Family YMCA
808 E 21st St (92404-4874)
PHONE................................909 881-9622
Bill Blank, *Dir*
EMP: 121
SALES (corp-wide): 15.69MM Privately Held
Web: www.ymcaeastvalley.org
SIC: 8641 7991 8351 7032 Youth
organizations; Physical fitness facilities;
Child day care services; Youth camps
PA: Ymca Of The East Valley
500 E Citrus Ave
Redlands CA
909 798-9622

(P-19476)
YMCA OF EAST VALLEY (PA)
500 E Citrus Ave (92373-5285)
PHONE................................909 798-9622
Darwin Barnett, *CEO*
Ken Stein, *
Perry Mecate, *

Doug Thorne, *
Carmen Barney, *
EMP: 125 EST: 1887
SQ FT: 100,000
SALES (est): 15.69MM
SALES (corp-wide): 15.69MM Privately Held
Web: www.ymcaeastvalley.org
SIC: 8641 Youth organizations

(P-19477)
YMCA OF SAN DIEGO COUNTY
Also Called: La Jolla YMCA
8355 Cliffridge Ave (92037-2107)
PHONE................................858 453-3483
Sam Wurtzbacher, *Dir*
EMP: 266
SALES (corp-wide): 391K Privately Held
Web: www.ymca.org
SIC: 8641 8351 7997 Youth organizations;
Child day care services; Membership sports
and recreation clubs
PA: Ymca Of San Diego County
3708 Ruffin Rd
San Diego CA
858 292-9622

(P-19478)
YMCA OF SAN DIEGO COUNTY
Also Called: Borderview Y M C A
3085 Beyer Blvd Ste 105 (92154-3479)
PHONE................................619 428-1168
Mauricio Gonzalez, *Ex Dir*
EMP: 141
SALES (corp-wide): 391K Privately Held
Web: www.ymcasd.org
SIC: 8641 7991 8351 7032 Youth
organizations; Physical fitness facilities;
Child day care services; Youth camps
PA: Ymca Of San Diego County
3708 Ruffin Rd
San Diego CA
858 292-9622

(P-19479)
YMCA OF SAN DIEGO COUNTY
Also Called: Pelomar Family YMCA
200 Saxony Rd (92024-2720)
PHONE................................760 745-7490
Alfredo Velasco, *Mgr*
EMP: 232
SALES (corp-wide): 391K Privately Held
Web: www.ymcasd.org
SIC: 8641 7991 8351 7032 Youth
organizations; Physical fitness facilities;
Child day care services; Youth camps
PA: Ymca Of San Diego County
3708 Ruffin Rd
San Diego CA
858 292-9622

(P-19480)
YMCA OF SAN DIEGO COUNTY
Also Called: Young Mens Christn Assocation
8881 Dallas St (91942-3297)
PHONE................................619 464-1323
Steve Rowe, *Ex Dir*
EMP: 232
SALES (corp-wide): 391K Privately Held
Web: www.ymcasd.org
SIC: 8641 7991 8351 7032 Youth
organizations; Physical fitness facilities;
Child day care services; Youth camps
PA: Ymca Of San Diego County
3708 Ruffin Rd
San Diego CA
858 292-9622

(P-19481)
YMCA OF SAN DIEGO COUNTY
Also Called: Copley Family YMCA
5505 Friars Rd (92110-2682)
PHONE................................619 280-9622
Kischa Hill, *Dir*
EMP: 305
SALES (corp-wide): 391K Privately Held
Web: www.ymcasd.org
SIC: 8641 7991 8351 7032 Youth
organizations; Physical fitness facilities;
Child day care services; Youth camps
PA: Ymca Of San Diego County
3708 Ruffin Rd
San Diego CA
858 292-9622

(P-19482)
YMCA OF SAN DIEGO COUNTY
Also Called: Magdalena Ecke Family YMCA
200 Saxony Rd (92024-2720)
PHONE................................858 292-4034
Susan J Cocke, *Brnch Mgr*
EMP: 373
SALES (corp-wide): 391K Privately Held
Web: www.ymca.org
SIC: 8641 8351 8322 7997 Youth
organizations; Child day care services;
Youth center; Membership sports and
recreation clubs
PA: Ymca Of San Diego County
3708 Ruffin Rd
San Diego CA
858 292-9622

(P-19483)
YMCA OF SAN DIEGO COUNTY
Also Called: YMCA Youth & Family Services
2927 Meade Ave (92116-4251)
PHONE................................619 281-8313
Cesar Marcano, *Ex Dir*
EMP: 141
SALES (corp-wide): 391K Privately Held
Web: www.ymcasd.org
SIC: 8641 7991 8351 7032 Youth
organizations; Physical fitness facilities;
Child day care services; Youth camps
PA: Ymca Of San Diego County
3708 Ruffin Rd
San Diego CA
858 292-9622

(P-19484)
YMCA OF SAN DIEGO COUNTY
Also Called: Peninsula Family YMCA
Sunshine
2150 Beryl St Ste 18 (92109-3617)
PHONE................................619 226-8888
Andrea Sanchez, *Dir*
EMP: 328
SQ FT: 3,500
SALES (corp-wide): 391K Privately Held
Web: www.ymcasd.org
SIC: 8641 8322 Youth organizations;
Individual and family services
PA: Ymca Of San Diego County
3708 Ruffin Rd
San Diego CA
858 292-9622

(P-19485)
YMCA OF SAN DIEGO COUNTY
Also Called: Jackie Robinson Family YMCA
5505 Friars Rd (92110-2682)
PHONE................................619 264-0144
Mike Brunker, *Ex Dir*
EMP: 204
SALES (corp-wide): 391K Privately Held
Web: www.ymcasd.org

SIC: **8641** 7991 8351 7032 Youth organizations; Physical fitness facilities; Child day care services; Youth camps
PA: Ymca Of San Diego County
3708 Ruffin Rd
San Diego CA
858 292-9622

(P-19486)
YMCA OF SAN DIEGO COUNTY
Also Called: YMCA Child Care Resource Svcs
3333 Camino Del Rio S Ste 400 (92108-3837)
PHONE...............................619 521-3055
Debbie Macdonald, *Dir*
EMP: 180
SALES (corp-wide): 391K **Privately Held**
Web: www.ymcasd.org
SIC: **8641** 7991 8351 7032 Youth organizations; Physical fitness facilities; Child day care services; Youth camps
PA: Ymca Of San Diego County
3708 Ruffin Rd
San Diego CA
858 292-9622

(P-19487)
YMCA OF SAN DIEGO COUNTY
Also Called: YMCA Overnight Camp
4761 Pine Hills Rd (92036)
P.O. Box 2440 (92036-2440)
PHONE...............................760 765-0642
Thomas Madeyski, *Ex Dir*
EMP: 175
SALES (corp-wide): 391K **Privately Held**
Web: www.ymcasd.org
SIC: **8641** 7991 8351 7032 Youth organizations; Physical fitness facilities; Child day care services; Youth camps
PA: Ymca Of San Diego County
3708 Ruffin Rd
San Diego CA
858 292-9622

(P-19488)
YMCA OF SAN DIEGO COUNTY
Also Called: Mission Valley YMCA
5505 Friars Rd (92110-2682)
PHONE...............................619 298-3576
Dick Webster, *Mgr*
EMP: 315
SALES (corp-wide): 391K **Privately Held**
Web: www.ymcasd.org
SIC: **8641** 7997 Youth organizations; Membership sports and recreation clubs
PA: Ymca Of San Diego County
3708 Ruffin Rd
San Diego CA
858 292-9622

(P-19489)
YMCA OF SAN DIEGO COUNTY
Also Called: Joe & Mary Mottino YMCA
200 Saxony Rd (92024-2720)
PHONE...............................760 758-0808
Jeff Guzzardo, *Brnch Mgr*
EMP: 164
SALES (corp-wide): 391K **Privately Held**
Web: www.ymcasd.org
SIC: **8641** 8322 Youth organizations; Individual and family services
PA: Ymca Of San Diego County
3708 Ruffin Rd
San Diego CA
858 292-9622

(P-19490)
YMCA OF SAN DIEGO COUNTY
Also Called: Oz North Coast Y M C A
215 Barnes St (92054-3472)

PHONE...............................760 721-8930
Kim Morgan, *Mgr*
EMP: 136
SQ FT: 3,567
SALES (corp-wide): 391K **Privately Held**
Web: www.ymcasd.org
SIC: **8641** 7991 8351 7032 Youth organizations; Physical fitness facilities; Child day care services; Youth camps
PA: Ymca Of San Diego County
3708 Ruffin Rd
San Diego CA
858 292-9622

(P-19491)
YMCA OF SAN DIEGO COUNTY (PA)
Also Called: Y, The
3708 Ruffin Rd (92123-1812)
PHONE...............................858 292-9622
Todd Tibbits, *Pr*
John Merritt, *
Charmaine Carter, *
EMP: 248 **EST:** 1882
SQ FT: 19,600
SALES (est): 391K
SALES (corp-wide): 391K **Privately Held**
Web: www.ymcasd.org
SIC: **8641** Youth organizations

(P-19492)
YOUNG MNS CHRSTN ASSN BRBANK C (PA)
321 E Magnolia Blvd (91502-1132)
PHONE...............................818 845-8551
Mary Cutone, *CEO*
Bryan Snodgrasss, *
EMP: 100 **EST:** 1924
SQ FT: 47,000
SALES (est): 5.91MM
SALES (corp-wide): 5.91MM **Privately Held**
Web: www.burbankymca.org
SIC: **8641** 7991 8351 7032 Youth organizations; Physical fitness facilities; Child day care services; Youth camps

(P-19493)
YOUNG MNS CHRSTN ASSN GLNDALE
Also Called: GLENDALE YMCA SWIM SCHOOL
140 N Louise St (91206-4226)
PHONE...............................818 484-8256
Tom Tyler, *CEO*
EMP: 86 **EST:** 1924
SQ FT: 15,000
SALES (est): 3.86MM **Privately Held**
Web: www.glendaleymca.org
SIC: **8641** Youth organizations

(P-19494)
YOUNG MNS CHRSTN ASSN MTRO LOS
Also Called: National Fitness Testing
1553 Schrader Blvd (90028)
PHONE...............................323 467-4161
Rosa Najera, *Brnch Mgr*
EMP: 134
SALES (corp-wide): 73.8MM **Privately Held**
Web: www.ymcala.org
SIC: **8641** Youth organizations
PA: Young Men's Christian Association Of Metropolitan Los Angeles
625 S New Hampshire Ave
Los Angeles CA
213 380-6448

(P-19495)
YOUNG MNS CHRSTN ASSN ORNGE CN
Also Called: YMCA
2300 University Dr (92660-3313)
PHONE...............................949 642-9990
Joy Hyde, *Genl Mgr*
EMP: 93
SQ FT: 17,976
SALES (corp-wide): 33.29MM **Privately Held**
Web: www.ymcaoc.org
SIC: **8641** 7991 Youth organizations; Physical fitness facilities
PA: Young Men's Christian Association Of Orange County
13821 Newport Ave Ste 200
Tustin CA
714 549-9622

(P-19496)
YOUNG MNS CHRSTN ASSN ORNGE CN
Also Called: Saddle Back Valley YMCA
27341 Trabuco Cir (92692-1939)
PHONE...............................949 859-9622
EMP: 92
SALES (corp-wide): 33.29MM **Privately Held**
Web: www.ymcaoc.org
SIC: **8641** 7991 8351 7032 Youth organizations; Physical fitness facilities; Child day care services; Youth camps
PA: Young Men's Christian Association Of Orange County
13821 Newport Ave Ste 200
Tustin CA
714 549-9622

(P-19497)
YOUNG WNS CHRSTN ASSN GRTER LO
Also Called: Angeles Mesa YWCA Chldren Lrng
2519 W Vernon Ave (90008-3927)
PHONE...............................323 295-4288
Hertistine Taylor, *Dir*
EMP: 132
SALES (corp-wide): 12.45MM **Privately Held**
Web: www.ywcagla.org
SIC: **8641** 8351 Youth organizations; Child day care services
PA: Young Women's Christian Association Of Greater Los Angeles, California
1020 S Olive St Fl 7
Los Angeles CA
213 365-2991

(P-19498)
YOUNG WNS CHRSTN ASSN GRTER LO
Also Called: YWCA
2501 W Vernon Ave (90008-3927)
PHONE...............................323 295-4280
EMP: 116
SALES (corp-wide): 12.45MM **Privately Held**
Web: www.ywcagla.org
SIC: **8641** Youth organizations
PA: Young Women's Christian Association Of Greater Los Angeles, California
1020 S Olive St Fl 7
Los Angeles CA
213 365-2991

8661 Religious Organizations

(P-19499)
CRENSHAW CHRSTN CTR CH LOS ANG (PA)
Also Called: Ever Increasing Faith Ministry
7901 S Vermont Ave (90044-3531)
P.O. Box 90000 (90009-9201)
PHONE...............................323 758-3777
Frederick K C Price, *CEO*
Angela Evans, *
Craig Hays, *
Cheryl Price, *
Jeanette Fant, *
▲ **EMP:** 294 **EST:** 1973
SALES (est): 14.19MM
SALES (corp-wide): 14.19MM **Privately Held**
Web: www.crenshawchristiancenter.net
SIC: **8661** 7812 Community Church; Motion picture and video production

(P-19500)
CRYSTAL CATHEDRAL MINISTRIES (PA)
12901 Lewis St (92840-6207)
P.O. Box 100 (92842-0100)
PHONE...............................714 622-2900
Robert V Schuller, *CEO*
Fred Southard, *
▲ **EMP:** 250 **EST:** 1955
SQ FT: 135,000
SALES (est): 9.95MM
SALES (corp-wide): 9.95MM **Privately Held**
Web: www.hourofpower.org
SIC: **8661** 7812 Apostolic Church; Television film production

(P-19501)
HOSPITLLER ORDER OF ST JOHN GO
2468 S St Andrews Pl (90018-2042)
PHONE...............................323 731-0641
Arlene De Guzman Hospitaller, *Prin*
EMP: 362 **EST:** 2009
SALES (est): 1.08MM **Privately Held**
SIC: **8661** 8399 Religious organizations; Health and welfare council

(P-19502)
INTERNTNAL CH OF FRSQARE GOSPL (PA)
Also Called: Foursquare International
1910 W Sunset Blvd (90026-3275)
P.O. Box 26902 (90026-0176)
PHONE...............................714 701-1818
Glenn C Burris Junior, *Pr*
Jared Roth, *
James C Scott Junior, *VP*
Sterling Brackett, *
Tammy Dunahoo, *
▲ **EMP:** 100 **EST:** 1921
SQ FT: 110,000
SALES (est): 175.95MM
SALES (corp-wide): 175.95MM **Privately Held**
Web: www.foursquare.org
SIC: **8661** 6512 7032 8211 Miscellaneous denomination church; Nonresidential building operators; Sporting and recreational camps; Elementary and secondary schools

(P-19503)
LOS ANGELES INTL CH CHRST
Also Called: Los Angeles Church of Christ
2716 Ocean Park Blvd Ste 2006 (90405-5207)

PHONE..............................213 351-2300
Brian Gold, COO
Chris Yen, *
Michael Wooten, Co-Secretary*
EMP: 160 EST: 1989
SALES (est): 13MM Privately Held
Web: www.laicc.net
SIC: 8661 7371 Miscellaneous denomination church; Computer software development and applications

(P-19504)
MORRIS CRULLO WORLD EVANGELISM (PA)
875 Hotel Cir S # 2 (92108-3406)
P.O. Box 85277 (92186-5277)
PHONE..............................858 277-2200
Reverend Morris Cerullo, Pr
Lynn Hodge, *
Teresa Cerullo, *
EMP: 77 EST: 1961
SALES (est): 24.35MM
SALES (corp-wide): 24.35MM Privately Held
Web: www.mcwe.com
SIC: 8661 2741 Churches, temples, and shrines; Miscellaneous publishing

(P-19505)
SELF-REALIZATION FELLOWSHIP CH (PA)
Also Called: Self Realization Fellowship
3880 San Rafael Ave (90065-3219)
PHONE..............................323 225-2471
Faye Wright, Pr
Mrinalini Mata, *
▲ EMP: 35 EST: 1935
SALES (est): 27.07MM
SALES (corp-wide): 27.07MM Privately Held
Web: www.yogananda.org
SIC: 8661 2741 Miscellaneous denomination church; Miscellaneous publishing

(P-19506)
SINAI TEMPLE (PA)
Also Called: Mt Sinai Mem Pk & Mortuary
10400 Wilshire Blvd (90024-4600)
PHONE..............................310 474-1518
Howard Lesner, Admn
Howard Lesner, Ex Dir
Joel Weinstein, *
EMP: 300 EST: 1908
SQ FT: 100,000
SALES (est): 53.77MM
SALES (corp-wide): 53.77MM Privately Held
Web: www.registrar-transfers.com
SIC: 8661 7261 5947 Synagogue; Funeral service and crematories; Gift shop

(P-19507)
SISTERS OF ST JOSEPH ORANGE
240 Ocean Ave (90740-6029)
PHONE..............................562 430-4638
Catherine Gray, Prin
EMP: 2767
SALES (corp-wide): 32.76MM Privately Held
Web: www.csjorange.org
SIC: 8661 8062 Convent; General medical and surgical hospitals
HQ: Sisters Of St. Joseph Of Orange
480 S Batavia St
Orange CA
714 633-8121

(P-19508)
ST JHNS LTHRAN CH BAKERSFIELD
Also Called: St Johns Lthran Schl Chldren C
4500 Buena Vista Rd (93311-9702)
PHONE..............................661 665-7815
Pastor Dennis Hilken, Prin
Eric Van Scharrel, *
Evan Anwyl, *
Mike Kinsey, *
EMP: 105 EST: 1904
SQ FT: 40,000
SALES (est): 7MM Privately Held
Web: www.sjlchurch.org
SIC: 8661 8211 7371 Lutheran Church; Private elementary school; Computer software development and applications

8699 Membership Organizations, Nec

(P-19509)
AFFINITY DEVELOPMENT GROUP INC
Also Called: A D G
10590 W Ocean Air Dr Ste 300 (92130)
PHONE..............................858 643-9324
Jeff Skeen, Pr
Gary Drean, *
Greg Siebenthal, *
Eric Campbell, CSO*
EMP: 120 EST: 1997
SALES (est): 22.94MM Privately Held
Web: www.affinitydev.com
SIC: 8699 Automobile owners' association

(P-19510)
AGUA CLNTE BAND CHILLA INDIANS (PA)
5401 Dinah Shore Dr (92264-5970)
PHONE..............................760 699-6800
Jeff L Grubbe, Ch
Larry N Olinger, Vice Chairman*
Vincent Gonzales Iii, Sec
EMP: 696 EST: 1988
SALES (est): 83.82MM
SALES (corp-wide): 83.82MM Privately Held
Web: www.dwa.org
SIC: 8699 6552 7999 Reading rooms and other cultural organizations; Subdividers and developers, nec; Tour and guide services

(P-19511)
ASSOCTED STDNTS SAN DEGO STATE (PA)
Also Called: Mission Bay Aquatic Center
5500 Campanile Dr (92182-0001)
PHONE..............................619 594-0234
Christina Brown, Ex Dir
EMP: 900 EST: 1897
SALES (est): 36.31MM
SALES (corp-wide): 36.31MM Privately Held
Web: www.mbaquaticcenter.com
SIC: 8699 Automobile owners' association

(P-19512)
ASSOCTED STDNTS SAN DEGO STATE
Also Called: Associated Students & Faculty San Diego State University (92182-0001)
PHONE..............................619 594-5200
Lana Heck, Prin
EMP: 190
SALES (corp-wide): 36.31MM Privately Held

Web: www.mbaquaticcenter.com
SIC: 8699 Automobile owners' association
PA: Associated Students, San Diego State University
5500 Campanile Dr
San Diego CA
619 594-0234

(P-19513)
AUTOMOBILE CLUB SOUTHERN CAL
Also Called: AAA
4973 Clairemont Dr Ste C (92117-2793)
P.O. Box 17527 (92177-7527)
PHONE..............................858 483-4960
Thomas Mckernan, Brnch Mgr
EMP: 153
SALES (corp-wide): 1.08B Privately Held
Web: ace.aaa.com
SIC: 8699 Automobile owners' association
PA: Automobile Club Of Southern California
2601 S Figueroa St
Los Angeles CA
213 741-3686

(P-19514)
AUTOMOBILE CLUB SOUTHERN CAL
Also Called: AAA
2440 Hotel Cir N Ste 100 (92108-2823)
PHONE..............................619 233-1000
Jill Clark, Mgr
EMP: 96
SALES (corp-wide): 1.08B Privately Held
Web: ace.aaa.com
SIC: 8699 Automobile owners' association
PA: Automobile Club Of Southern California
2601 S Figueroa St
Los Angeles CA
213 741-3686

(P-19515)
AUTOMOBILE CLUB SOUTHERN CAL
Also Called: AAA
800 La Terraza Blvd (92025-3817)
PHONE..............................760 745-2124
Theresa Tentschert, Mgr
EMP: 115
SQ FT: 49,100
SALES (corp-wide): 1.08B Privately Held
Web: ace.aaa.com
SIC: 8699 Automobile owners' association
PA: Automobile Club Of Southern California
2601 S Figueroa St
Los Angeles CA
213 741-3686

(P-19516)
AUTOMOBILE CLUB SOUTHERN CAL
Also Called: AAA
5402 Philadelphia St Ste A (91710-2488)
P.O. Box 1846 (91708-1846)
PHONE..............................909 591-9451
Tim Irwin, Mgr
EMP: 115
SALES (corp-wide): 1.08B Privately Held
Web: ace.aaa.com
SIC: 8699 Automobile owners' association
PA: Automobile Club Of Southern California
2601 S Figueroa St
Los Angeles CA
213 741-3686

(P-19517)
AUTOMOBILE CLUB SOUTHERN CAL
3712 State St (93105-3135)

Web: www.mbaquaticcenter.com

PHONE..............................805 682-5811
Nancy Alexander, Brnch Mgr
EMP: 114
SALES (corp-wide): 1.08B Privately Held
Web: ace.aaa.com
SIC: 8699 Automobile owners' association
PA: Automobile Club Of Southern California
2601 S Figueroa St
Los Angeles CA
213 741-3686

(P-19518)
AUTOMOBILE CLUB SOUTHERN CAL
3700 Central Ave (92506-2421)
P.O. Box 2217 (92516-2217)
PHONE..............................951 684-4250
Richard Meyer, Brnch Mgr
EMP: 96
SALES (corp-wide): 1.08B Privately Held
Web: ace.aaa.com
SIC: 8699 Automobile owners' association
PA: Automobile Club Of Southern California
2601 S Figueroa St
Los Angeles CA
213 741-3686

(P-19519)
AUTOMOBILE CLUB SOUTHERN CAL
Also Called: AAA
420 N Euclid St (92801-5505)
PHONE..............................714 774-2392
Conny Kuhm, Mgr
EMP: 96
SALES (corp-wide): 1.08B Privately Held
Web: ace.aaa.com
SIC: 8699 Automobile owners' association
PA: Automobile Club Of Southern California
2601 S Figueroa St
Los Angeles CA
213 741-3686

(P-19520)
AUTOMOBILE CLUB SOUTHERN CAL
2730 Santa Monica Blvd (90404-2408)
PHONE..............................310 453-1909
Vasile Dejeu, Mgr
EMP: 134
SQ FT: 10,000
SALES (corp-wide): 1.08B Privately Held
Web: ace.aaa.com
SIC: 8699 Automobile owners' association
PA: Automobile Club Of Southern California
2601 S Figueroa St
Los Angeles CA
213 741-3686

(P-19521)
AUTOMOBILE CLUB SOUTHERN CAL
Also Called: A A A Automobile Club So Cal
4800 Airport Plaza Dr Ste 100 (90815-1274)
PHONE..............................562 425-8350
Susan Dabinett, Mgr
EMP: 96
SQ FT: 7,200
SALES (corp-wide): 1.08B Privately Held
Web: ace.aaa.com
SIC: 8699 Automobile owners' association
PA: Automobile Club Of Southern California
2601 S Figueroa St
Los Angeles CA
213 741-3686

PRODUCTS & SVCS

(P-19522)
AUTOMOBILE CLUB SOUTHERN CAL
Also Called: AAA
8761 Santa Monica Blvd (90069-4538)
PHONE..................................323 525-0018
EMP: 96
SALES (corp-wide): 1.08B **Privately Held**
Web: ace.aaa.com
SIC: 8699 Automobile owners' association
PA: Automobile Club Of Southern California
2601 S Figueroa St
Los Angeles CA
213 741-3686

(P-19523)
AUTOMOBILE CLUB SOUTHERN CAL
Also Called: AAA
23001 Hawthorne Blvd (90505-3702)
P.O. Box 4298 (90510-4298)
PHONE..................................310 325-3111
Bud Hudson, *Brnch Mgr*
EMP: 135
SQ FT: 34,720
SALES (corp-wide): 1.08B **Privately Held**
Web: ace.aaa.com
SIC: 8699 Automobile owners' association
PA: Automobile Club Of Southern California
2601 S Figueroa St
Los Angeles CA
213 741-3686

(P-19524)
AUTOMOBILE CLUB SOUTHERN CAL
Also Called: AAA
8223 Firestone Blvd (90241-4809)
PHONE..................................562 904-5970
Mirtha Rodriguez, *Brnch Mgr*
EMP: 115
SALES (corp-wide): 1.08B **Privately Held**
Web: ace.aaa.com
SIC: 8699 Automobile owners' association
PA: Automobile Club Of Southern California
2601 S Figueroa St
Los Angeles CA
213 741-3686

(P-19525)
AUTOMOBILE CLUB SOUTHERN CAL
Also Called: AAA
700 S Aviation Blvd (90266-7106)
PHONE..................................310 376-0521
John Dm, *Mgr*
EMP: 115
SQ FT: 7,815
SALES (corp-wide): 1.08B **Privately Held**
Web: ace.aaa.com
SIC: 8699 Automobile owners' association
PA: Automobile Club Of Southern California
2601 S Figueroa St
Los Angeles CA
213 741-3686

(P-19526)
BEST FRIENDS ANIMAL SOCIETY
1845 Pontius Ave (90025-4305)
PHONE..................................818 643-3989
Marc Peralta, *Mgr*
EMP: 246
Web: www.bestfriends.org
SIC: 8699 Animal humane society
PA: Best Friends Animal Society
5001 Angel Canyon Rd
Kanab UT

(P-19527)
CARLSBAD FIREFIGHTERS ASSN
2560 Orion Way (92010-7240)
P.O. Box 945 (92018-0945)
PHONE..................................760 729-3730
Josh Clark, *Pr*
EMP: 80 **EST:** 1970
SALES (est): 205.96K **Privately Held**
Web: www.carlsbadfdf.org
SIC: 8699 Charitable organization

(P-19528)
CHG FOUNDATION
740 Bay Blvd (91910-5254)
PHONE..................................619 422-0422
Sheila Martz, *Dir*
EMP: 372 **EST:** 1999
SALES (est): 1.2B **Privately Held**
SIC: 8699 Charitable organization

(P-19529)
GOODWILL INDS SAN DIEGO CNTY
Also Called: Goodwill Industries
3841 Plaza Dr Ste 902 (92056-4649)
PHONE..................................760 806-7670
Tim Hurley, *Mgr*
EMP: 85
SALES (corp-wide): 70.31MM **Privately Held**
Web: www.sdgoodwill.org
SIC: 8699 8331 5932 Charitable organization
; Vocational rehabilitation agency; Used
merchandise stores
PA: Goodwill Industries Of San Diego
County
3663 Rosecrans St
San Diego CA
619 225-2200

(P-19530)
INLAND EMPIRE CHPTR-SSCTION CR
2210 E Route 66 (91740-4661)
PHONE..................................512 478-9000
EMP: 82 **EST:** 2009
SALES (est): 4.13K **Privately Held**
SIC: 8699 Membership organizations, nec

(P-19531)
LOS ANGELES MEM COLISEUM COMM
Also Called: La Sports Arena
3911 S Figueroa St (90037-1207)
PHONE..................................213 747-7111
Kevin Daly, *Admn*
Don Knabe, *
Gregory Hellmold, *
John Sandbrook, *
EMP: 500 **EST:** 1923
SQ FT: 2,000
SALES (est): 21.59MM **Privately Held**
Web: www.lacoliseum.com
SIC: 8699 Athletic organizations

(P-19532)
MEMORIAL MEDICAL CENTER FOUNDATION
Also Called: MILLER CHILDREN'S HOSPITAL
2801 Atlantic Ave (90806-1701)
P.O. Box 1428 (90801-1428)
PHONE..................................562 933-2273
EMP: 947 **EST:** 1964
SALES (est): 14.33MM **Privately Held**
Web: www.memorialcare.org

SIC: 8699 Charitable organization
HQ: Long Beach Medical Center
2801 Atlantic Ave Fl 2
Long Beach CA
562 933-2000

(P-19533)
PLAY VERSUS INC
Also Called: Playvs
2236 S Barrington Ave Ste A (90064-1231)
PHONE..................................949 636-4193
Jon Chapman, *CEO*
EMP: 95 **EST:** 2018
SALES (est): 7.56MM **Privately Held**
Web: www.playvs.com
SIC: 8699 Amateur sports promotion

(P-19534)
THINK TOGETHER
17270 Bear Valley Rd Ste 103 (92395-5881)
PHONE..................................760 269-1230
EMP: 344
SALES (corp-wide): 75.71MM **Privately Held**
Web: www.thinktogether.org
SIC: 8699 8351 Charitable organization;
Child day care services
PA: Think Together
2101 E 4th St Ste 200b
Santa Ana CA
714 543-3807

(P-19535)
U C SAN DIEGO FOUNDATION
Also Called: UC SAN DIEGO
9500 Gilman Dr (92093-5004)
PHONE..................................858 534-1032
EMP: 218 **EST:** 1972
SALES (est): 216.43MM **Privately Held**
Web: www.ucsd.edu
SIC: 8699 Charitable organization

(P-19536)
USA TRAVEL SERVICES LLC
714 Washington Blvd (90292-5543)
PHONE..................................207 899-8803
EMP: 800 **EST:** 2016
SALES (est): 1.37MM **Privately Held**
SIC: 8699 Travel club

(P-19537)
WORLD VISION INTERNATIONAL (PA)
800 W Chestnut Ave (91016-3198)
P.O. Box 9716 (98063-9716)
PHONE..................................626 303-8811
Andrew Morley, *CEO*
Kevin Jenkins, *
Valdir Steuernagel, *
Denis St Amour, *
▼ **EMP:** 196 **EST:** 1977
SQ FT: 94,000
SALES (est): 40.95MM
SALES (corp-wide): 40.95MM **Privately Held**
Web: www.wvi.org
SIC: 8699 Charitable organization

8711 Engineering Services

(P-19538)
ABM FACILITY SERVICES LLC
Also Called: A B M
152 Technology Dr (92618-2401)
PHONE..................................949 330-1555
EMP: 1391

SIC: 8711 Engineering services

(P-19539)
ABS CONSULTING INC
Also Called: ABS Group
420 Exchange Ste 200 (92602-1319)
PHONE..................................714 734-4242
Doug Frazier, *CEO*
Peter Yanev, *Pr*
Jim Johnson, *COO*
George Reitter, *CFO*
EMP: 100 **EST:** 1970
SALES (est): 9.25MM
SALES (corp-wide): 455.19MM **Privately Held**
Web: www.abs-group.com
SIC: 8711 8742 Consulting engineer;
Management consulting services
HQ: Abs Group Of Companies, Inc.
1701 City Plaza Dr
Spring TX

(P-19540)
ACCUNEX INC
Also Called: Accurate Electronics
20700 Lassen St (91311-4507)
PHONE..................................818 882-5858
Farid Jadali, *Pr*
Roxana Coronado, *
▲ **EMP:** 50 **EST:** 1998
SQ FT: 25,000
SALES (est): 8.84MM **Privately Held**
Web: www.accurate-elec.com
SIC: 8711 3679 Engineering services;
Electronic circuits

(P-19541)
ACS ENGINEERING INC
Also Called: Asce
33 Hammond Ste 209 (92618-1637)
PHONE..................................949 297-3777
Babak Kavoossi, *Pr*
Babak Kavoossi, *Prin*
EMP: 20 **EST:** 2011
SQ FT: 5,000
SALES (est): 2.54MM **Privately Held**
Web: www.acsengineering.net
SIC: 8711 1731 3613 Consulting engineer;
Electrical work; Control panels, electric

(P-19542)
AIR LIQUIDE ELECTRONICS US LP
Also Called: Air Lquide Globl E C Solutions
1831 Carnegie Ave (92705-5528)
PHONE..................................713 624-8000
EMP: 4366
SALES (corp-wide): 109.44MM **Privately Held**
Web: engineering.airliquide.com
SIC: 8711 Engineering services
HQ: Air Liquide Electronics U.S. Lp
9101 Lyndon B Johnson Fwy # 800
Dallas TX
972 301-5200

(P-19543)
ALBERT A WEBB ASSOCIATES (PA)
Also Called: Webb
3788 Mccray St (92506-2927)
PHONE..................................951 686-1070
A Hubert Webb, *Ch*
Matt Webb, *
Scott Webb, *
Roger D Prend Pe, *
Todd R Smith, *
EMP: 127 **EST:** 1949
SQ FT: 20,000
SALES (est): 32.56MM

SALES (corp-wide): 32.56MM **Privately Held**
Web: www.webbassociates.com
SIC: 8711 Civil engineering

(P-19544)
ALLEN ENGINEERING CONTRACTOR INC
1655 Riverview Dr (92408-3016)
PHONE..................909 478-5500
EMP: 165
Web: www.allenec.com
SIC: 8711 Construction and civil engineering

(P-19545)
AME UNMANNED AIR SYSTEMS INC
Also Called: Lockheed Martin Unmndd
125 Venture Dr Ste 110 (93401-9103)
PHONE..................805 541-4448
EMP: 80
Web: www.ameuas.com
SIC: 8711 Aviation and/or aeronautical engineering

(P-19546)
AMERESCO SOLAR LLC
42175 Zevo Dr (92590-2503)
PHONE..................888 967-6527
EMP: 479
Web: www.ameresco.com
SIC: 8711 Energy conservation engineering
HQ: Ameresco Solar Llc
111 Speen St Ste 410
Framingham MA
508 661-2200

(P-19547)
AMP DISPLAY INC (PA)
9856 6th St (91730-5714)
P.O. Box 1735 (91729-1735)
PHONE..................909 980-1310
Jason Young, *Pr*
EMP: 21 EST: 1999
SQ FT: 12,000
SALES (est): 2.14MM
SALES (corp-wide): 2.14MM **Privately Held**
Web: www.ampdisplay.com
SIC: 8711 3679 Engineering services; Liquid crystal displays (LCD)

(P-19548)
APPLIED COMPANIES
28020 Avenue Stanford (91355-1105)
P.O. Box 802078 (91380-2078)
PHONE..................661 257-0090
Mary Elizabeth Klinger, *CEO*
Joseph Klinger, *Development**
EMP: 50 EST: 1962
SQ FT: 58,000
SALES (est): 13.71MM **Privately Held**
Web: www.appliedcompanies.net
SIC: 8711 3585 3443 3621 Mechanical engineering; Ice making machinery; Cylinders, pressure: metal plate; Motors and generators

(P-19549)
ARUP NORTH AMERICA LIMITED
12777 W Jefferson Blvd Ste 300 (90066-7034)
PHONE..................310 578-4182
Tony Panossian, *Brnch Mgr*
EMP: 308
Web: www.arup.com
SIC: 8711 Consulting engineer
HQ: Arup North America Limited
560 Mission St Fl 7

San Francisco CA

(P-19550)
AUSGAR TECHNOLOGIES INC
10721 Treena St Ste 100 (92131-1185)
PHONE..................855 428-7427
Jonathan Dien, *Pr*
Karen Dien, *
Eric Lofgren, *
Saul Dien, *
EMP: 115 EST: 2003
SQ FT: 16,000
SALES (est): 21.88MM **Privately Held**
Web: www.ausgar.com
SIC: 8711 7371 7373 7379 Consulting engineer; Custom computer programming services; Computer integrated systems design; Computer related consulting services

(P-19551)
BAE SYSTEMS MARITIME ENGINEERING & SERVICES INC
7330 Engineer Rd Ste A (92111-1434)
P.O. Box 13308 (92170-3308)
PHONE..................619 238-1000
EMP: 370
SIC: 8711 Engineering services

(P-19552)
BAS ENGINEERING INC
11899 8th St (91730-5501)
PHONE..................909 484-2575
Ajesh Bhakta, *Prin*
EMP: 18 EST: 2012
SALES (est): 1.07MM **Privately Held**
Web: basengineering.thebluebook.com
SIC: 8711 3312 Engineering services; Blast furnaces and steel mills

(P-19553)
BINOPTICS LLC
977 S Meridian Ave (91803-1250)
PHONE..................607 257-3200
Norman Kwong, *Brnch Mgr*
EMP: 134
SIC: 8711 Engineering services
HQ: Binoptics, Llc
9 Brown Rd
Ithaca NY
607 257-3200

(P-19554)
BIT MEDTECH LLC
15870 Bernardo Center Dr (92127-2320)
PHONE..................858 613-1200
EMP: 60 EST: 1999
SALES (est): 4.65MM **Privately Held**
SIC: 8711 3841 Engineering services; Surgical and medical instruments

(P-19555)
BKF ENGINEERS/AGS
Also Called: BKF ENGINEERS/AGS
4675 Macarthur Ct Ste 400 (92660-8834)
PHONE..................949 526-8400
Isaac Kontorovsky, *Brnch Mgr*
EMP: 85
SALES (corp-wide): 100.83MM **Privately Held**
Web: www.bkf.com
SIC: 8711 Civil engineering
PA: Bkf Engineers
255 Shoreline Dr Ste 200
Redwood City CA
650 482-6300

(P-19556)
BOYLE ENGINEERING CORPORATION
999 W Town And Country Rd (92868-4713)
PHONE..................949 476-3300
EMP: 400
SIC: 8711 8712 Engineering services; Architectural engineering

(P-19557)
BRINDERSON LLC (DH)
18841 S Broadwick St (90220-6429)
PHONE..................714 466-7100
William Gary, *CEO*
EMP: 150 EST: 1993
SALES (est): 292.81MM **Privately Held**
Web: www.aegion.com
SIC: 8711 1629 Engineering services; Dams, waterways, docks, and other marine construction
HQ: Brock Holdings Iii, Llc
10343 Sam Houston Park Dr
Houston TX
281 807-8200

(P-19558)
BURNS & MCDONNELL INC
140 S State College Blvd Ste 100 (92821-5850)
PHONE..................714 256-1595
Ken Gerling, *Brnch Mgr*
EMP: 80
SALES (corp-wide): 1.26B **Privately Held**
Web: www.burnsmcd.com
SIC: 8711 Consulting engineer
PA: Burns & Mcdonnell, Inc.
9400 Ward Pkwy
Kansas City MO
816 333-9400

(P-19559)
C D LYON CONSTRUCTION INC (PA)
380 W Stanley Ave (93001-1350)
P.O. Box 1456 (93002-1456)
PHONE..................805 653-0173
Christopher D Lyon, *CEO*
Debra C Lyon, *
EMP: 80 EST: 1986
SALES (est): 21.22MM
SALES (corp-wide): 21.22MM **Privately Held**
Web: www.cdlyon.com
SIC: 8711 Petroleum engineering

(P-19560)
CALIFORNIA SEMICONDUCTOR TECH
Also Called: Calsemi
429 Santa Monica Blvd (90401-3401)
PHONE..................310 579-2939
Antonio Garcia, *CEO*
Jose Luis Lopez, *
EMP: 120 EST: 2013
SALES (est): 3.4MM **Privately Held**
Web: www.calsemi-tech.com
SIC: 8711 Engineering services

(P-19561)
CAPITAL ENGINEERING LLC
Also Called: Capital Engineering
2830 Temple Ave (90806-2213)
PHONE..................562 612-1302
EMP: 80
SALES (corp-wide): 5.62B **Privately Held**
Web: www.capital-engineering.com
SIC: 8711 Consulting engineer
HQ: Capital Engineering Llc
436 Creamery Way Ste H100

Exton PA
219 791-1984

(P-19562)
CDM CONSTRUCTORS INC
9220 Cleveland Ave Ste 100 (91730-8560)
PHONE..................909 579-3500
Joyce Jackson, *Brnch Mgr*
EMP: 90
SALES (corp-wide): 1.42B **Privately Held**
Web: www.cdmsmith.com
SIC: 8711 Consulting engineer
HQ: Cdm Constructors Inc.
75 State St Ste 701
Boston MA

(P-19563)
CITY OF GLENDALE
Also Called: Engineering Public Works
633 E Broadway Ste 205 (91206-4310)
PHONE..................818 548-3945
Lou Le Blanc, *Dir*
EMP: 111
SALES (corp-wide): 390.24MM **Privately Held**
Web: www.glendaleca.gov
SIC: 8711 9511 Engineering services; Air, water, and solid waste management
PA: City Of Glendale
141 N Glendale Ave Fl 2
Glendale CA
818 548-2085

(P-19564)
CONCEPT TECHNOLOGY INC
2941 W Macarthur Blvd Ste 136 (92704-6952)
PHONE..................949 851-6550
EMP: 430
SALES (corp-wide): 4.82MM **Privately Held**
Web: www.concepttechnologyinc.com
SIC: 8711 Consulting engineer
PA: Concept Technology, Inc.
895 Dove St Fl 3
Newport Beach CA
949 854-7047

(P-19565)
CONCEPT TECHNOLOGY INC (PA)
895 Dove St 3rd Fl (92660-2941)
PHONE..................949 854-7047
Mahesh P Badani, *Pr*
▲ EMP: 60 EST: 1981
SALES (est): 4.82MM
SALES (corp-wide): 4.82MM **Privately Held**
Web: www.concepttechnologyinc.com
SIC: 8711 3599 8742 3825 Consulting engineer; Machine shop, jobbing and repair ; Management information systems consultant; Radio frequency measuring equipment

(P-19566)
CONSTRUCTION TSTG & ENGRG INC
Also Called: CONSTRUCTION TESTING & ENGINEERING, INC.
14538 Meridian Pkwy Ste A (92518-3018)
PHONE..................951 571-4081
Vincent Patula, *Brnch Mgr*
EMP: 334
SALES (corp-wide): 462.96MM **Privately Held**
Web: www.teamues.com
SIC: 8711 Civil engineering

P R O D U C T S & S V C S

HQ: Construction Testing & Engineering, Inc.
1441 Montiel Rd Ste 115
Escondido CA

(P-19567)
COUNTY OF LOS ANGELES
Also Called: Engineering Division
44933 Fern Ave (93534-2461)
PHONE.................................661 723-6088
Bert Perry, *Brnch Mgr*
EMP: 123
Web: www.lacounty.gov
SIC: 8711 9111 Engineering services; Executive offices
PA: County Of Los Angeles
500 W Temple St Ste 437
Los Angeles CA
213 974-1101

(P-19568)
CURRENT RENEWABLES ENGRG INC
1760 Chicago Ave Ste J13 (92507-2360)
PHONE.................................951 405-1733
Methode Maniraguha, *CEO*
EMP: 18 EST: 2018
SALES (est): 1.63MM **Privately Held**
Web: www.creng.co
SIC: 8711 5045 7372 Engineering services; Computer software; Business oriented computer software

(P-19569)
CURTISS-WRGHT CNTRLS ELCTRNIC
28965 Avenue Penn (91355-4185)
PHONE.................................661 257-4430
Val Zarov, *Brnch Mgr*
EMP: 194
SALES (corp-wide): 2.56B **Publicly Held**
Web: www.curtisswright.com
SIC: 8711 Engineering services
HQ: Curtiss-Wright Controls Electronic Systems, Inc.
28965 Avenue Penn
Santa Clarita CA
661 702-1494

(P-19570)
CUSTOM BUILT MACHINERY INC
Also Called: C B M
2614 S Hickory St (92707-3714)
PHONE.................................714 424-9250
Milan Chrena, *CEO*
Victor Escobedo, *
Milan Chrena, *Pr*
Pete Marloski, *Stockholder*
EMP: 25 EST: 1995
SQ FT: 11,000
SALES (est): 2.02MM **Privately Held**
SIC: 8711 3559 Engineering services; Pharmaceutical machinery

(P-19571)
DEVELOPMENT RESOURCE CONS INC (PA)
160 S Old Springs Rd Ste 210 (92808-1260)
PHONE.................................714 685-6860
Lawrence Gates, *Pr*
EMP: 90 EST: 1997
SQ FT: 12,000
SALES (est): 12.4MM
SALES (corp-wide): 12.4MM **Privately Held**
SIC: 8711 Civil engineering

(P-19572)
DEX CORPORATION
Also Called: Data Exchange
3600 Via Pescador (93012-5051)
PHONE.................................805 388-1711
Sheldon Malchiconfqs, *CEO*
EMP: 150 EST: 2015
SQ FT: 100,000
SALES (est): 12.06MM **Privately Held**
Web: www.dex.com
SIC: 8711 5065 Engineering services; Electronic parts

(P-19573)
DIVERGENT TECHNOLOGIES INC
Also Called: Divergent 3d
19601 Hamilton Ave (90502-1309)
PHONE.................................424 542-2158
Kevin Czinger, *Pr*
Ursula Ster, *
EMP: 150 EST: 2021
SALES (est): 32.04MM **Privately Held**
Web: www.divergent3d.com
SIC: 8711 Mechanical engineering

(P-19574)
DIVERSIFIED PRJ SVCS INTL INC (PA)
5351 Olive Dr Ste 100 (93308-2926)
PHONE.................................661 371-2800
Robert Chambers, *Pr*
EMP: 80 EST: 2007
SALES (est): 15.65MM
SALES (corp-wide): 15.65MM **Privately Held**
Web: www.dpsiinc.com
SIC: 8711 Consulting engineer

(P-19575)
DMS FACILITY SERVICES LLC
2861 E Coronado St (92806-2504)
PHONE.................................949 975-1366
Richard E Dotts, *Brnch Mgr*
EMP: 659
Web: www.dmsfacilityservices.com
SIC: 8711 Engineering services
PA: Dms Facility Services, Llc
1040 Arroyo Dr
South Pasadena CA

(P-19576)
DMS FACILITY SERVICES LLC
5735 Kearny Villa Rd Ste 108 (92123)
PHONE.................................858 560-4191
John Harris, *Brnch Mgr*
EMP: 686
Web: www.dmsfacilityservices.com
SIC: 8711 7349 0781 Engineering services; Janitorial service, contract basis; Landscape services
PA: Dms Facility Services, Llc
1040 Arroyo Dr
South Pasadena CA

(P-19577)
DUDEK INC (PA)
605 3rd St (92024-3513)
PHONE.................................760 942-5147
Joseph Monaco, *CEO*
Eric Wilson, *
Christine Moore, *
Emily Hart, *
Helder Guimaraes, *
EMP: 100 EST: 1980
SQ FT: 50,000
SALES (est): 132.78MM
SALES (corp-wide): 132.78MM **Privately Held**

Web: www.dudek.com
SIC: 8711 8748 Civil engineering; Environmental consultant

(P-19578)
EDSI
700 Ammunition Rd Bldg 103 (92028-3187)
PHONE.................................760 731-3501
Rick Lengerke, *Brnch Mgr*
EMP: 94
SALES (corp-wide): 22.28MM **Privately Held**
Web: www.edsi.com
SIC: 8711 Engineering services
PA: Edsi
22835 Savi Ranch Pkwy F
Yorba Linda CA
951 272-8689

(P-19579)
EICHLEAY INC
500 N State College Blvd (92868-1637)
PHONE.................................562 256-8600
Lori M Lofstrom, *Brnch Mgr*
EMP: 149
Web: www.eichleay.com
SIC: 8711 Consulting engineer
PA: Eichleay, Inc.
1390 Willow Pass Rd # 60
Concord CA

(P-19580)
ELITE ENGINEERING CONTRS INC
16619 S Broadway (90248-2715)
PHONE.................................310 465-8333
Brian Perazzolo, *CEO*
Jason M Metoyer, *Prin*
EMP: 20 EST: 2017
SALES (est): 2.41MM **Privately Held**
Web: www.eliteengineering.net
SIC: 8711 1771 1081 Engineering services; Stucco, gunite, and grouting contractors; Metal mining exploration and development services

(P-19581)
EMBEE PROCESSING LLC
Also Called: Embee Plating
2158 S Hathaway St (92705-5249)
PHONE.................................714 546-9842
Michael Coburn, *CEO*
Scott Chrisman, *
Derek Watson, *
▲ EMP: 385 EST: 1947
SQ FT: 100,000
SALES (est): 23.51MM **Privately Held**
Web: www.embee.com
SIC: 8711 3398 3479 8734 Aviation and/or aeronautical engineering; Shot peening (treating steel to reduce fatigue); Coating of metals and formed products; Metallurgical testing laboratory

(P-19582)
ENCORE SEMI INC
7310 Miramar Rd Ste 410 (92126-4226)
PHONE.................................858 225-4993
EMP: 67 EST: 2011
SALES (est): 8.07MM **Privately Held**
Web: www.encoresemi.com
SIC: 8711 3674 Engineering services; Integrated circuits, semiconductor networks, etc.

(P-19583)
ENGINEERING PARTNERS INC
Also Called: E P I
10150 Meanley Dr Ste 200 (92131-3008)
PHONE.................................858 824-1761

Romeo Flores, *Pr*
EMP: 95 EST: 1985
SQ FT: 2,500
SALES (est): 9.45MM **Privately Held**
Web: www.engineeringpartners.com
SIC: 8711 Consulting engineer

(P-19584)
ENGINRNG SFTWR SYS SLTONS INC (PA)
Also Called: E S 3
600 B St (92101-4501)
PHONE.................................619 338-0380
Teri Sgammato, *Pr*
Chuck Dahms, *
Doug Wiser, *
Craig Edwards, *
EMP: 80 EST: 2001
SALES (est): 22.78MM
SALES (corp-wide): 22.78MM **Privately Held**
Web: www.es3inc.com
SIC: 8711 Engineering services

(P-19585)
EPSILON SYSTEMS SLTONS MSSION
9242 Lightwave Ave Ste 100 (92123-6402)
PHONE.................................619 702-1700
Alan Stewart, *CFO*
Robin Nordberg, *
EMP: 99 EST: 2011
SALES (est): 3.33MM **Privately Held**
Web: www.epsilonsystems.com
SIC: 8711 Electrical or electronic engineering

(P-19586)
EPSILON SYSTEMS SOLUTIONS INC (PA)
9444 Balboa Ave Ste 100 (92123-4351)
PHONE.................................619 702-1700
Bryan Min, *CEO*
Joe Quinn, *
EMP: 100 EST: 1990
SQ FT: 50,000
SALES (est): 110MM
SALES (corp-wide): 110MM **Privately Held**
Web: www.epsilonsystems.com
SIC: 8711 Engineering services

(P-19587)
ES ENGINEERING SERVICES LLC
4 Park Plz Ste 790 (92614-5262)
PHONE.................................949 988-3500
Vijay Menthripragada, *CEO*
EMP: 85 EST: 2015
SALES (est): 4.71MM
SALES (corp-wide): 544.42MM **Publicly Held**
SIC: 8711 8748 Engineering services; Systems analysis and engineering consulting services
PA: Montrose Environmental Group, Inc.
5120 Northshore Dr
North Little Rock AR
501 900-6400

(P-19588)
FIRE PROTECTION GROUP AMER INC
3712 W Jefferson Blvd (90016-4208)
P.O. Box 180520 (90018-9682)
PHONE.................................323 732-4200
George Saadian, *Pr*
Louise Tchaman, *
EMP: 40 EST: 1985
SQ FT: 20,000

SALES (est): 2.2MM **Privately Held**
Web: www.firesprinkler.com
SIC: **8711** 1711 3569 1731 Fire protection engineering; Fire sprinkler system installation; Firefighting and related equipment; Fire detection and burglar alarm systems specialization

(P-19589)
FLINT ENERGY SERVICES INC
1999 Avenue Of The Stars Ste 2600 (90067-6022)
PHONE..................213 593-8000
EMP: 102
SALES (corp-wide): 14.38B **Publicly Held**
Web: www.aecom.com
SIC: **8711** Engineering services
HQ: Flint Energy Services Inc.
7595 E Technology Way # 200
Denver CO
918 294-3030

(P-19590)
FLUOR CORPORATION
Also Called: Trs Staffing Solutions
3 Polaris Way (92656-5338)
PHONE..................949 349-2000
Tim Kirk, *Prin*
EMP: 99
SALES (corp-wide): 13.74B **Publicly Held**
Web: www.fluor.com
SIC: **8711** 7363 Engineering services; Help supply services
PA: Fluor Corporation
6700 Las Colinas Blvd
Irving TX
469 398-7000

(P-19591)
FLUOR DANIEL EURASIA INC (DH)
1 Fluor Daniel Dr (92698-1000)
PHONE..................949 349-2000
Alan Beckman, *CEO*
S T Hall, *Treas*
EMP: 25 EST: 1965
SALES (est): 1.3MM
SALES (corp-wide): 13.74B **Publicly Held**
SIC: **8711** 1541 1629 8742 Engineering services; Industrial buildings, new construction, nec; Industrial plant construction; Maintenance management consultant
HQ: Fluor Enterprises, Inc.
6700 Las Colinas Blvd
Irving TX
469 398-7000

(P-19592)
FLUOR PLANT SERVICES INTL INC
Also Called: Fluor Daniel
1 Enterprise (92656-2606)
PHONE..................949 349-2000
D Michael Steuert, *CFO*
EMP: 100 EST: 1900
SALES (est): 26.72MM
SALES (corp-wide): 13.74B **Publicly Held**
Web: www.microsemi.com
SIC: **8711** Engineering services
PA: Fluor Corporation
6700 Las Colinas Blvd
Irving TX
469 398-7000

(P-19593)
FORTEL TRAFFIC INC
5310 E Hunter Ave (92807-2053)
PHONE..................714 701-9800
Emery B Dyer, *Pr*

Jayne M Dyer, *Sec*
▼ EMP: 17 EST: 1995
SQ FT: 14,000
SALES (est): 2.48MM **Privately Held**
Web: www.vcalm.com
SIC: **8711** 3669 Consulting engineer; Traffic signals, electric

(P-19594)
FORWARD SLOPE INCORPORATED (PA)
Also Called: Forward Slope.
2020 Camino Del Rio N Ste 400 (92108)
PHONE..................619 299-4400
Carlos Persichetti, *Pr*
Kevin Noonan, *VP*
EMP: 127 EST: 1997
SALES (est): 26.22MM
SALES (corp-wide): 26.22MM **Privately Held**
Web: www.forwardslope.com
SIC: **8711** 7371 7389 Consulting engineer; Software programming applications; Financial services

(P-19595)
FRICTION MATERIALS LLC
2525 W 190th St (90504-6002)
PHONE..................248 362-3600
Andre Bezuszka, *Managing Member*
EMP: 132 EST: 2002
SALES (est): 10.02MM
SALES (corp-wide): 3.63B **Privately Held**
SIC: **8711** Engineering services
PA: Garrett Motion Inc.
47548 Halyard Dr
Plymouth MI
734 359-5901

(P-19596)
FTI CONSULTING INC
350 S Grand Ave Ste 3000 (90071-3424)
PHONE..................213 689-1200
Stewart Kahn, *Pr*
EMP: 80
SALES (corp-wide): 3.03B **Publicly Held**
Web: www.fticonsulting.com
SIC: **8711** 8748 8742 Consulting engineer; Business consulting, nec; Management consulting services
PA: Fti Consulting, Inc.
555 12th St Nw Ste 700
Washington DC
202 312-9100

(P-19597)
FUSCOE ENGINEERING INC (PA)
15535 Sand Canyon Ave (92618-3114)
PHONE..................949 474-1960
Patrick Fuscoe, *Pr*
EMP: 85 EST: 1992
SALES (est): 20.61MM **Privately Held**
Web: www.fuscoe.com
SIC: **8711** Civil engineering

(P-19598)
GARRETT J GENTRY GEN ENGRG INC
1297 W 9th St (91786-5706)
PHONE..................909 693-3391
Garrett J Gentry, *Pr*
Bryan Copping, *
EMP: 100 EST: 2013
SALES (est): 15.82MM **Privately Held**
Web: www.gjgentry.com
SIC: **8711** Acoustical engineering

(P-19599)
GEOCON INCORPORATED
6960 Flanders Dr (92121-3992)
PHONE..................858 558-6900
Joesph Vettel, *CEO*
Michael Chapin, *
William Lydon, *
EMP: 100 EST: 1971
SALES (est): 18.42MM **Privately Held**
Web: www.geoconinc.com
SIC: **8711** Consulting engineer

(P-19600)
GLENN A RICK ENGRG & DEV CO (PA)
Also Called: Rick Engineering Company
5620 Friars Rd (92110-2513)
PHONE..................619 291-0708
Roger Ball, *Prin*
Paul J Iezzi, *
Robert A Stockton, *
Dennis C Bowling, *
Deborah B Ragione, *
EMP: 212 EST: 1955
SQ FT: 50,000
SALES (est): 48.11MM
SALES (corp-wide): 48.11MM **Privately Held**
Web: www.rickengineering.com
SIC: **8711** Civil engineering

(P-19601)
GRADIENT ENGINEERS INC
Also Called: Leighton & Associates
17781 Cowan Ste 140 (92614-6009)
PHONE..................949 477-0555
EMP: 156 EST: 1996
SALES (est): 325.55K
SALES (corp-wide): 154.82MM **Privately Held**
SIC: **8711** 8744 Consulting engineer; Environmental remediation
HQ: Leighton Group, Inc.
2600 Michelson Dr Ste 400
Irvine CA
949 250-1421

(P-19602)
GRYPHON MARINE LLC
Also Called: Gryphon
694 Moss St (91911-1616)
PHONE..................619 407-4010
Ms. Karlovic, *CEO*
EMP: 90
SALES (corp-wide): 2.52B **Privately Held**
Web: www.mantech.com
SIC: **8711** Engineering services
HQ: Gryphon Marine, Llc
4600 Village Ave Ste 100
Norfolk VA
757 763-6666

(P-19603)
HETHERINGTON ENGINEERING (PA)
4333 Apache St (92056-2913)
PHONE..................760 931-1917
Mark Hetherington, *Pr*
EMP: 227 EST: 1986
SALES (est): 2.56MM
SALES (corp-wide): 2.56MM **Privately Held**
Web: www.hetheringtonengineering.com
SIC: **8711** Consulting engineer

(P-19604)
HII FLEET SUPPORT GROUP LLC
131 W 33rd St Ste 100a (91950-7266)
PHONE..................619 474-8820

Suliman Haidar, *Mgr*
EMP: 180
SIC: **8711** Engineering services
HQ: Hii Fleet Support Group Llc
5701 Cleveland St
Virginia Beach VA
757 463-6666

(P-19605)
HNTB CORPORATION
401 B St Ste 510 (92101-4285)
PHONE..................619 684-6586
Joanne Manthey, *Brnch Mgr*
EMP: 102
SALES (corp-wide): 1.53B **Privately Held**
Web: www.hntb.com
SIC: **8711** Consulting engineer
HQ: Hntb Corporation
715 Kirk Dr
Kansas City MO
816 472-1201

(P-19606)
HNTB CORPORATION
3633 Inland Empire Blvd (91764-4922)
PHONE..................909 727-5600
Craig Denson, *Brnch Mgr*
EMP: 82
SALES (corp-wide): 1.53B **Privately Held**
Web: www.hntb.com
SIC: **8711** Consulting engineer
HQ: Hntb Corporation
715 Kirk Dr
Kansas City MO
816 472-1201

(P-19607)
HNTB CORPORATION
6 Hutton Centre Dr Ste 500 (92707)
PHONE..................714 460-1600
Andres Ocon, *Brnch Mgr*
EMP: 115
SALES (corp-wide): 1.53B **Privately Held**
Web: www.hntb.com
SIC: **8711** Consulting engineer
HQ: Hntb Corporation
715 Kirk Dr
Kansas City MO
816 472-1201

(P-19608)
HNTB GERWICK WATER SOLUTIONS
200 Sandpointe Ave (92707-5751)
PHONE..................714 460-1600
EMP: 150
SALES (est): 3.78MM **Privately Held**
SIC: **8711** 8712 Consulting engineer; Architectural services

(P-19609)
HOLMES & NARVER INC (HQ)
999 W Town And Country Rd (92868-4713)
P.O. Box 6240 (92863-6240)
PHONE..................714 567-2400
Danny Seal, *CEO*
Raymond Landy, *
Dennis Deslatte, *
Tina Clugston, *
EMP: 250 EST: 1933
SQ FT: 100,000
SALES (est): 24.57MM
SALES (corp-wide): 14.38B **Publicly Held**
SIC: **8711** 8742 8741 1542 Engineering services; Training and development consultant; Construction management; Nonresidential construction, nec
PA: Aecom
13355 Noel Rd Ste 400
Dallas TX
972 788-1000

(P-19610)
HUNSAKER & ASSOC IRVINE INC
2900 Adams St Ste A15 (92504-4337)
PHONE.................................951 352-7200
Brad Hay, *Brnch Mgr*
EMP: 300
SALES (corp-wide): 54.08MM **Privately Held**
Web: www.hnagi.com
SIC: 8711 Civil engineering
PA: Hunsaker & Associates Irvine, Inc.
3 Hughes
Irvine CA
949 583-1010

(P-19611)
HUNSAKER & ASSOC IRVINE INC (PA)
Also Called: Hunsaker & Associates
3 Hughes (92618-2021)
PHONE.................................949 583-1010
Richard Hunsaker, *CEO*
Douglas Snyder, *
Kamal Karam, *
Doug Staley, *
EMP: 100 **EST:** 1976
SQ FT: 27,000
SALES (est): 54.08MM
SALES (corp-wide): 54.08MM **Privately Held**
Web: www.hnagi.com
SIC: 8711 8713 Civil engineering; Surveying services

(P-19612)
HYUNDAI AMER TECHNICAL CTR INC
Also Called: Kia Design Center America
101 Peters Canyon Rd (92606-1790)
PHONE.................................734 337-2500
EMP: 113
Web: www.hatci.com
SIC: 8711 8734 Designing: ship, boat, machine, and product; Automobile proving and testing ground
HQ: Hyundai America Technical Center Incorporated
6800 Geddes Rd
Ypsilanti MI
734 337-2500

(P-19613)
INDUS TECHNOLOGY INC
2243 San Diego Ave Ste 200 (92110-2069)
PHONE.................................619 299-2555
James B Lasswell, *Pr*
Will Nevilles, *
Eric Macgregor, *
Jan Perez, *
Rebecca Spane, *
EMP: 230 **EST:** 1991
SQ FT: 12,000
SALES (est): 49.51MM **Privately Held**
Web: www.industechnology.com
SIC: 8711 Engineering services

(P-19614)
INNOVATIVE ENGRG SYSTEMS INC (PA)
Also Called: Ies Engineering
8800 Crippen St (93311-9686)
P.O. Box 20610 (93390-0610)
PHONE.................................661 381-7800
David Wolfer, *Pr*
EMP: 100 **EST:** 2002
SQ FT: 20,000
SALES (est): 26.33MM **Privately Held**
Web: www.agilitechgroup.com

SIC: 8711 1731 Consulting engineer; Electrical work

(P-19615)
INTERNATIONAL ENERGY SERVICES USA INC
Also Called: International Energy Svcs Co
3445 Kashiwa St (90505-4024)
PHONE.................................310 257-8222
EMP: 200
SIC: 8711 Engineering services

(P-19616)
INTERNTONAL STRL ENGINEERS INC
Also Called: I S E
11926 S La Cienega Blvd (90250-3463)
P.O. Box 836 (90251-0836)
PHONE.................................310 643-7310
Bengt Mossberg, *Pr*
EMP: 22 **EST:** 1970
SALES (est): 395.5K **Privately Held**
Web: www.i-s-e.com
SIC: 8711 7371 7372 Consulting engineer; Computer software development; Prepackaged software

(P-19617)
JACOBS ATCS FEMA A JOINT VENTR
155 N Lake Ave Fl 5 (91101-1849)
PHONE.................................571 218-1115
Ed Pogreba, *Prin*
EMP: 99 **EST:** 2017
SALES (est): 1.53MM **Privately Held**
SIC: 8711 8712 8748 8741 Consulting engineer; Architectural services; Business consulting, nec; Management services

(P-19618)
JACOBS CIVIL INC
1500 Hughes Way Ste B400 (90810-1882)
PHONE.................................310 847-2500
EMP: 229
SALES (corp-wide): 14.92B **Publicly Held**
SIC: 8711 Consulting engineer
HQ: Jacobs Civil Inc.
501 N Broadway
Saint Louis MO

(P-19619)
JACOBS ENGINEERING COMPANY
1111 S Arroyo Pkwy (91105-3254)
P.O. Box 7084 (91109-7084)
PHONE.................................626 449-2171
EMP: 4000 **EST:** 1979
SALES (est): 42.54MM
SALES (corp-wide): 14.09B **Publicly Held**
SIC: 8711 1629 Engineering services; Chemical plant and refinery construction
HQ: Jacobs Engineering Group Inc.
1999 Bryan St Ste 1200
Dallas TX
214 583-8500

(P-19620)
JACOBS ENGINEERING GROUP INC
2600 Michelson Dr Ste 500 (92612-6506)
PHONE.................................949 224-7500
Dan Grubb, *Brnch Mgr*
EMP: 88
SALES (corp-wide): 14.92B **Publicly Held**
Web: www.jacobs.com
SIC: 8711 Consulting engineer
HQ: Jacobs Engineering Group Inc.
1999 Bryan St Ste 3500

Dallas TX
214 583-8500

(P-19621)
JACOBS ENGINEERING GROUP INC
1111 S Arroyo Pkwy (91105-3254)
P.O. Box 7084 (91109-7084)
PHONE.................................626 578-3500
EMP: 89
SALES (corp-wide): 14.92B **Publicly Held**
Web: www.jacobs.com
SIC: 8711 Consulting engineer
HQ: Jacobs Engineering Group Inc.
1999 Bryan St Ste 3500
Dallas TX
214 583-8500

(P-19622)
JACOBS ENGINEERING INC (DH)
155 N Lake Ave (91101-1849)
P.O. Box 7084 (91109-7084)
PHONE.................................626 578-3500
Craig L Martin, *CEO*
Noel G Watson, *
EMP: 161 **EST:** 1971
SALES (est): 110.24MM
SALES (corp-wide): 14.92B **Publicly Held**
Web: www.jacobs.com
SIC: 8711 Consulting engineer
HQ: Jacobs Engineering Group Inc.
1999 Bryan St Ste 3500
Dallas TX
214 583-8500

(P-19623)
JACOBS GOVERNMENT SERVICES CO
2600 Michelson Dr Ste 500 (92612-6506)
PHONE.................................949 224-7500
Issam Khalaf, *VP*
EMP: 230
SALES (corp-wide): 14.92B **Publicly Held**
Web: www.jacobs.com
SIC: 8711 Engineering services
HQ: Jacobs Government Services Company
155 N Lake Ave Ste 150
Pasadena CA

(P-19624)
JACOBS INTERNATIONAL LTD INC
155 N Lake Ave Ste 800 (91101-1857)
P.O. Box 7084 (91109-7084)
PHONE.................................626 578-3500
Craig Martin, *Pr*
Jeff Sanders, *
John W Prosser Junior, *Treas*
EMP: 300 **EST:** 2002
SQ FT: 120,000
SALES (est): 71.22MM
SALES (corp-wide): 14.92B **Publicly Held**
SIC: 8711 Consulting engineer
HQ: Jacobs Engineering Group Inc.
1999 Bryan St Ste 3500
Dallas TX
214 583-8500

(P-19625)
JACOBS PROJECT MANAGEMENT CO
2600 Michelson Dr Ste 500 (92612-6506)
PHONE.................................949 224-7695
Les Steinberger, *Mgr*
Frank Joyce, *
EMP: 99 **EST:** 2008
SALES (est): 5.19MM
SALES (corp-wide): 14.92B **Publicly Held**

SIC: 8711 Consulting engineer
HQ: Jacobs Engineering Group Inc.
1999 Bryan St Ste 3500
Dallas TX
214 583-8500

(P-19626)
JSL TECHNOLOGIES INC
1451 N Rice Ave Ste A (93030-7991)
PHONE.................................805 985-7700
Joseph T Black Iii, *Pr*
Ben Fujikawa, *
Jed Williams, *
EMP: 305 **EST:** 2008
SQ FT: 22,155
SALES (est): 28MM **Privately Held**
Web: www.jsltechinc.com
SIC: 8711 Consulting engineer

(P-19627)
JT3 LLC
190 S Wolfe Ave Bldg 1260 (93524-6501)
PHONE.................................661 277-4900
James Tedeschi, *Mgr*
EMP: 1340
SALES (corp-wide): 150MM **Privately Held**
SIC: 8711 Engineering services
PA: Jt3, L.L.C.
821 Grier Dr
Las Vegas NV
704 492-2181

(P-19628)
K&B ELECTRIC LLC
Also Called: K&B Engineering
290 Corporate Terrace Cir Ste 200 (92879-6033)
PHONE.................................951 808-9501
Sandee Gibbs, *Managing Member*
Trey Gibbs, *
EMP: 158 **EST:** 2011
SALES (est): 3.77MM **Privately Held**
Web: www.kbeng.net
SIC: 8711 Engineering services

(P-19629)
K&B ENGINEERING
290 Corporate Terrace Cir Ste 200 (92879-6033)
PHONE.................................951 808-9501
Trey Gibbs, *Owner*
EMP: 200 **EST:** 2007
SALES (est): 24.61MM **Privately Held**
Web: www.kbeng.net
SIC: 8711 Consulting engineer

(P-19630)
KINEMETRICS INC (DH)
222 Vista Ave (91107-3278)
PHONE.................................626 795-2220
Tadashi Jimbo, *CEO*
Melvin Lund, *
Ogie Kuraica, *
Ian Standley, *
Michelle Harrington, *
EMP: 59 **EST:** 1969
SQ FT: 50,000
SALES (est): 24.84MM **Privately Held**
Web: www.kinemetrics.com
SIC: 8711 3829 Engineering services; Seismographs
HQ: Oyo Corporation U.S.A.
245 N Carmelo Ave Ste 101
Pasadena CA

(P-19631)
KLEINFELDER INC (HQ)
Also Called: Kleinfelder
770 1st Ave Ste 400 (92101-6171)

P.O. Box 51958 (90051-6258)
PHONE..............................619 831-4600
John Murphy, *CFO*
Deborah Butera, *
Carl Lowman, *
Daniel Brockman, *
Lisa Millet, *Central Division**
EMP: 160 **EST:** 1962
SQ FT: 5,000
SALES (est): 249.41MM
SALES (corp-wide): 458.93MM **Privately Held**
Web: www.kleinfelder.com
SIC: 8711 8712 Consulting engineer; Architectural engineering
PA: The Kleinfelder Group Inc
770 1st Ave Ste 400
San Diego CA
619 831-4600

(P-19632)
KLEINFELDER ASSOCIATES
550 W C St Ste 1200 (92101-3532)
PHONE..............................619 831-4600
George J Pierson, *Pr*
Russ Carey, *
John Pilkington, *
Bart Patton, *
Larry Peterson, *
EMP: 104 **EST:** 1985
SALES (est): 15.66MM
SALES (corp-wide): 458.93MM **Privately Held**
Web: www.kleinfelder.com
SIC: 8711 Consulting engineer
PA: The Kleinfelder Group Inc
770 1st Ave Ste 400
San Diego CA
619 831-4600

(P-19633)
KLEINFELDER GROUP INC (PA)
770 1st Ave Ste 400 (92101-6171)
PHONE..............................619 831-4600
Louis Armstrong, *Pr*
Lisa Millet, *Ex VP*
Jeff Hill, *Dist Vice President*
Ann Masey, *Prin*
Erik Soderquist, *Ex VP*
EMP: 175 **EST:** 1985
SALES (est): 458.93MM
SALES (corp-wide): 458.93MM **Privately Held**
Web: www.kleinfelder.com
SIC: 8711 Consulting engineer

(P-19634)
KPFF INC
K P F F Consulting Engineers
18500 Von Karman Ave Ste 1000 (92612-0527)
PHONE..............................949 252-1022
Roger Young, *Prin*
EMP: 86
SALES (corp-wide): 108.51MM **Privately Held**
Web: www.kpff.com
SIC: 8711 Consulting engineer
PA: Kpff, Inc.
1601 5th Ave Ste 1300
Seattle WA
206 225-2980

(P-19635)
KRATOS TECH TRNING SLTIONS INC (HQ)
10680 Treena St Ste 600 (92131-2487)
PHONE..............................858 812-7300
Eric M Demarco, *Pr*
Deanna H Lund, *Ex VP*

Laura L Siegal, *Corporate Controller**
Deborah S Butera, *Sec*
Phil Carrai, *VP Opers*
EMP: 94 **EST:** 1966
SQ FT: 25,000
SALES (est): 121.41MM **Publicly Held**
Web: www.kratosdefense.com
SIC: 8711 Engineering services
PA: Kratos Defense & Security Solutions, Inc.
10680 Treena St Ste 600
San Diego CA

(P-19636)
L3 MARIPRO INC
1522 Cook Pl (93117-3124)
PHONE..............................805 683-3881
EMP: 90
SIC: 8711 Marine engineering

(P-19637)
LAMER STREET KREATIONS CORP
Also Called: Calwest Mfg and Lsk Suspension
13815 Arrow Blvd (92335-0255)
PHONE..............................909 305-4824
Aaron Rifkin, *Pr*
Aaron Riskin, *
Van Syverud, *
EMP: 25 **EST:** 2012
SALES (est): 1.22MM **Privately Held**
SIC: 8711 3499 3569 Sanitary engineers; Fire- or burglary-resistive products; Robots, assembly line: industrial and commercial

(P-19638)
LASH CONSTRUCTION INC
721 Carpinteria St (93103-3623)
P.O. Box 4640 (93140-4640)
PHONE..............................805 963-3553
EMP: 99 **EST:** 1978
SALES (est): 4.44MM **Privately Held**
Web: www.lashconstruction.com
SIC: 8711 1623 Engineering services; Underground utilities contractor

(P-19639)
LINQUEST CORPORATION (PA)
5140 W Goldleaf Cir Ste 400 (90056-1299)
PHONE..............................323 924-1600
Timothy Dills, *Pr*
Matthew Klein, *
Greg Young, *COO*
Douglas Manya, *
Richard Martin, *CIO**
EMP: 200 **EST:** 2003
SQ FT: 20,000
SALES (est): 116.91MM
SALES (corp-wide): 116.91MM **Privately Held**
Web: www.linquest.com
SIC: 8711 Aviation and/or aeronautical engineering

(P-19640)
LOCKHEED MARTIN SERVICES LLC
Also Called: Lockheed Martin
645 Marsat Ct Ste D (91911-7141)
PHONE..............................619 271-9831
EMP: 365
SIC: 8711 Engineering services
HQ: Lockheed Martin Services, Llc
700 N Frederick Ave
Gaithersburg MD

(P-19641)
LOS ANGELES ENGINEERING INC

633 N Barranca Ave (91723-1229)
PHONE..............................626 869-1400
Henry Angus O'brien, *Pr*
Henry Angus O'brien, *Pr*
Aaron O'brien, *VP*
Beth Ballard, *
Melody Turner, *
EMP: 110 **EST:** 1987
SQ FT: 33,000
SALES (est): 47.57MM **Privately Held**
Web: www.laeng.net
SIC: 8711 1622 Construction and civil engineering; Bridge, tunnel, and elevated highway construction

(P-19642)
MANGAN INC (PA)
3901 Via Oro Ave (90810-1800)
PHONE..............................310 835-8080
Richard D Mangan, *Ch Bd*
Richard D Mangan, *Prin*
Russell Seward, *
Amin Solehjou, *
Christopher Lopez, *
EMP: 90 **EST:** 1991
SQ FT: 15,000
SALES (est): 50.72MM **Privately Held**
Web: www.manganinc.com
SIC: 8711 Consulting engineer

(P-19643)
MARVIN ENGINEERING CO INC (PA)
Also Called: Marvin Group, The
261 W Beach Ave (90302-2904)
PHONE..............................310 674-5030
Howard Gussman, *CEO*
Ariel Lechter, *
Craig Snaguski, *
▲ **EMP:** 580 **EST:** 1963
SQ FT: 300,000
SALES (est): 149.54MM
SALES (corp-wide): 149.54MM **Privately Held**
Web: www.marvingroup.com
SIC: 8711 Consulting engineer

(P-19644)
MEEDER EQUIPMENT COMPANY
12323 6th St (91739-9224)
PHONE..............................909 463-0600
EMP: 19
SALES (corp-wide): 16.99MM **Privately Held**
Web: www.meeder.com
SIC: 8711 3433 3824 Engineering services; Heating equipment, except electric; Fluid meters and counting devices
PA: Meeder Equipment Company
3495 S Maple Ave
Fresno CA
559 485-0979

(P-19645)
MGC SYSTEMS CORP
Also Called: Marcom Eng'g System
73 Bunsen (92618-4218)
PHONE..............................714 442-2064
Otulio Gutierrez, *Brnch Mgr*
EMP: 26 **EST:** 2013
SALES (est): 365.65K **Privately Held**
Web: www.mircom.com
SIC: 8711 3669 Engineering services; Fire alarm apparatus, electric

(P-19646)
MICHAEL BAKER INTERNATIONAL INC (DH)
5 Hutton Centre Dr Ste 500 (92707)
Rural Route 57057 (92619)

PHONE..............................949 472-3505
EMP: 350 **EST:** 1944
SALES (est): 48.71MM
SALES (corp-wide): 1.03B **Privately Held**
Web: www.mbakerintl.com
SIC: 8711 8713 Civil engineering; Surveying services
HQ: Michael Baker International Holdco Corporation
100 Airside Dr
Moon Township PA
412 269-6300

(P-19647)
MICROWAVE APPLICATIONS GROUP
Also Called: M A G
3030 Industrial Pkwy (93455-1881)
PHONE..............................805 928-5711
Steven Van Dyke, *CEO*
Tom Janzen, *
Scott Mckechnie, *VP*
Robin Hopp, *
EMP: 26 **EST:** 1969
SQ FT: 22,000
SALES (est): 5.16MM **Privately Held**
Web: www.magsmx.com
SIC: 8711 3679 Engineering services; Microwave components

(P-19648)
MNS ENGINEERS INC (PA)
201 N Calle Cesar Chavez Ste 300 (93103-3256)
PHONE..............................805 692-6921
James A Salvito, *
Mark E Reinhardt, *
Gregory A Chelini, *
Jeffrey L Edwards, *
Shawn M Kowalewski, *
EMP: 94 **EST:** 1962
SQ FT: 7,000
SALES (est): 26.35MM
SALES (corp-wide): 26.35MM **Privately Held**
Web: www.mnsengineers.com
SIC: 8711 8713 Civil engineering; Surveying services

(P-19649)
MOBILENET SERVICES INC (PA)
18 Morgan Ste 200 (92618-2074)
PHONE..............................949 951-4444
Richard Grant, *Pr*
Eugene Powell, *
Edward Krol, *
Lorenzo Mills, *
Rodelio Santos, *
EMP: 180 **EST:** 2002
SQ FT: 17,500
SALES (est): 38.03MM
SALES (corp-wide): 38.03MM **Privately Held**
Web: www.mobilenet.net
SIC: 8711 4813 Engineering services; Telephone communication, except radio

(P-19650)
MODELO GROUP INC
16751 Millikan Ave (92606-5009)
PHONE..............................562 446-5091
Jose Vazquez, *CEO*
EMP: 25 **EST:** 2004
SALES (est): 1MM **Privately Held**
SIC: 8711 7373 3999 Engineering services; Computer-aided design (CAD) systems service; Barber and beauty shop equipment

PRODUCTS & SVCS

(P-19651)
MSM INDUSTRIES INC
12660 Magnolia Ave (92503-4636)
PHONE.....................................951 735-0834
Darryl Clare, *Pr*
Peter Taylor, *
Craig Sparling, *
Carl Maas, *
EMP: 31 **EST:** 2002
SALES (est): 4.89MM **Privately Held**
Web: www.msm-ind.com
SIC: 8711 2891 2515 Engineering services;
Epoxy adhesives; Mattresses, containing
felt, foam rubber, urethane, etc.

(P-19652)
NATIONAL SECURITY TECH LLC
5520 Ekwill St Ste B (93111-2335)
PHONE.....................................805 681-2432
EMP: 481
SALES (corp-wide): 497.8MM **Privately
Held**
Web: www.nstec.com
SIC: 8711 1629 Civil engineering; Industrial
plant construction
PA: National Security Technologies, Llc
2621 Losee Rd
North Las Vegas NV
702 295-1000

(P-19653)
NATIONAL TELECONSULTANTS INC
550 N Brand Blvd Fl 17 (91203-1904)
PHONE.....................................818 265-4400
Eliot P Graham, *Managing Member*
Charles C Phelan, *
Peter Adamiak, *
EMP: 108 **EST:** 1981
SQ FT: 35,400
SALES (est): 21.46MM **Privately Held**
Web: www.ntc.com
SIC: 8711 Electrical or electronic engineering

(P-19654)
NAVAL FACILITIES ENGINEER COMM
1220 Pacific Hwy (92132-5101)
PHONE.....................................619 532-1158
Shahraam Plaseied, *Prin*
Nancy Wright, *Acctnt*
Captain Darius Banaji, *COO*
EMP: 99 **EST:** 2014
SQ FT: 4,000
SALES (est): 2.46MM **Privately Held**
SIC: 8711 1623 8744 Pollution control
engineering; Underground utilities contractor
; Base maintenance (providing personnel
on continuing basis)

(P-19655)
NEST PARENT INC
2125 E Katella Ave Ste 250 (92806-6072)
PHONE.....................................310 551-0101
Gerald L Parsky, *Pr*
John T Mapes, *
EMP: 1207 **EST:** 2012
SALES (est): 23.1MM **Privately Held**
SIC: 8711 Consulting engineer

(P-19656)
NV5 INC
Also Called: Nolte, George S & Associates
15092 Avenue Of Science # 200
(92128-3404)
PHONE.....................................858 385-0500
Carmen Kasmer, *Dir*
EMP: 200
SALES (corp-wide): 786.78MM **Publicly
Held**

Web: www.nv5.com
SIC: 8711 8713 Civil engineering; Surveying
services
HQ: Nv5, Inc.
2525 Natomas Park Dr # 300
Sacramento CA
916 641-9100

(P-19657)
OASIS SYSTEMS LLC
4125 Market St Ste 12 (93003-5642)
PHONE.....................................805 644-2191
EMP: 104
SALES (corp-wide): 98.12MM **Privately
Held**
Web: www.oasissystems.com
SIC: 8711 Marine engineering
PA: Oasis Systems, Llc
200 Summit Dr Ste 510
Burlington MA
781 676-7333

(P-19658)
ONCORE MANUFACTURING LLC (HQ)
Also Called: Neo Tech
9340 Owensmouth Ave (91311-6915)
PHONE.....................................818 734-6500
Sudesh Arora, *Pr*
Laura Siegal, *CFO*
Kunal Sharma, *COO*
David Brakenwagen Csmo, *Prin*
▲ **EMP:** 700 **EST:** 2001
SALES (est): 146.23MM
SALES (corp-wide): 1.43B **Privately Held**
Web: www.neotech.com
SIC: 8711 3672 Electrical or electronic
engineering; Printed circuit boards
PA: Natel Engineering Company, Llc
9340 Owensmouth Ave
Chatsworth CA
818 495-8617

(P-19659)
ONE SUN POWER INC
3451 Via Montebello Ste 511 (92009-8492)
PHONE.....................................844 360-9600
James Joseph Holmes, *CEO*
EMP: 3231 **EST:** 2017
SALES (est): 37.94MM **Privately Held**
SIC: 8711 Energy conservation engineering

(P-19660)
P2S INC
4660 La Jolla Village Dr (92122-4605)
PHONE.....................................562 497-2999
EMP: 195
Web: www.p2sinc.com
SIC: 8711 Consulting engineer
PA: P2s Inc.
5000 E Spring St Ste 800
Long Beach CA

(P-19661)
PACIFIC HYDROTECH CORPORATION
314 E 3rd St (92570-2225)
PHONE.....................................951 943-8803
J Kirk Harns, *Pr*
Sean Finnegan, *
Bobby Owens, *
Joselito Guintu, *
Dale Mckay, *VP*
EMP: 135 **EST:** 1987
SQ FT: 1,500
SALES (est): 65.73MM **Privately Held**
Web: www.pachydro.com
SIC: 8711 Construction and civil engineering

(P-19662)
PACIFICA SERVICES INC
106 S Mentor Ave Ste 200 (91106-2931)
PHONE.....................................626 405-0131
Ernest M Camacho, *Pr*
Stephen Caropino, *
EMP: 84 **EST:** 1979
SQ FT: 15,000
SALES (est): 8.55MM **Privately Held**
Web: www.pacificaservices.com
SIC: 8711 7629 8741 Civil engineering;
Electronic equipment repair; Construction
management

(P-19663)
PANASONIC AVIONICS CORPORATION (DH)
3347 Michelson Dr Ste 100 (92612-0661)
PHONE.....................................949 672-2000
Kenneth W Sain, *CEO*
Seigo Tada, *
Jessica L Hodkinson, *
▲ **EMP:** 400 **EST:** 1990
SQ FT: 20,000
SALES (est): 925.13MM **Privately Held**
Web: www.panasonic.aero
SIC: 8711 3728 Aviation and/or aeronautical
engineering; Aircraft parts and equipment,
nec
HQ: Panasonic Corporation Of North
America
2 Riverfront Plz Ste 200
Newark NJ
201 348-7000

(P-19664)
PARSONS ENGRG SCIENCE INC (DH)
100 W Walnut St (91103-3696)
P.O. Box 88954 (60695-1954)
PHONE.....................................626 440-2000
Charles Harrington, *CEO*
Mary Ann Hopkins, *
Curtis A Bower, *
Nicholas L Presecan, *
Gary L Stone, *
EMP: 500 **EST:** 1946
SALES (est): 494.32MM
SALES (corp-wide): 4.2B **Publicly Held**
Web: www.parsons.com
SIC: 8711 Consulting engineer
HQ: Parsons Government Services Inc.
5875 Trinity Pkwy Ste 230
Centreville VA
703 988-8500

(P-19665)
PARSONS GOVERNMENT SVCS INC
525 B St Ste 1600 (92101-4401)
PHONE.....................................619 685-0085
Christopher Bush, *VP*
EMP: 301
SALES (corp-wide): 4.2B **Publicly Held**
Web: www.parsons.com
SIC: 8711 Engineering services
HQ: Parsons Government Services Inc.
5875 Trinity Pkwy Ste 230
Centreville VA
703 988-8500

(P-19666)
PARSONS INTL CAYMAN ISLANDS
100 W Walnut St (91124-0001)
PHONE.....................................626 440-6000
William E Hall, *Pr*
EMP: 2000 **EST:** 1994
SALES (est): 29.54MM

SALES (corp-wide): 4.2B **Publicly Held**
Web: www.parsons.com
SIC: 8711 8741 Engineering services;
Management services
HQ: Parsons Government Services Inc.
5875 Trinity Pkwy Ste 230
Centreville VA
703 988-8500

(P-19667)
PARSONS SERVICE CORPORATION
100 W Walnut St (91124-0001)
PHONE.....................................626 440-2000
Geoge L Ball, *Prin*
EMP: 797 **EST:** 1977
SALES (est): 10.1MM **Privately Held**
Web: www.parsons.com
SIC: 8711 Construction and civil engineering

(P-19668)
PARSONS WTR INFRASTRUCTURE INC
100 W Walnut St (91124-0001)
PHONE.....................................626 440-7000
Virginia Grebbien, *CEO*
Anthony F Leketa, *
EMP: 82 **EST:** 2003
SQ FT: 1,220,000
SALES (est): 2.45MM
SALES (corp-wide): 4.2B **Publicly Held**
Web: www.parsons.com
SIC: 8711 Consulting engineer
PA: The Parsons Corporation
5875 Trinity Pkwy Ste 300
Centreville VA
703 988-8500

(P-19669)
PENFIELD & SMITH ENGINEERS INC
Also Called: Penfield & Smith
111 E Victoria St (93101-2072)
P.O. Box 98 (93102-0098)
PHONE.....................................805 963-9532
EMP: 80
SIC: 8711 8713 Civil engineering; Surveying
services

(P-19670)
PHG ENGINEERING SERVICES LLC
27481 Ganso (92691-3646)
PHONE.....................................714 283-8288
EMP: 100 **EST:** 2017
SALES (est): 3.34MM **Privately Held**
SIC: 8711 Engineering services

(P-19671)
PHOTON RESEARCH ASSOCIATES INC
9985 Pacific Heights Blvd Ste 200 (92121)
PHONE.....................................858 455-9741
EMP: 187
SIC: 8711 5045 8733 Aviation and/or
aeronautical engineering; Computer
software; Scientific research agency

(P-19672)
PROCESSES UNLIMITED INTERNATIONAL INC
Also Called: Processes Unlimited
5500 Ming Ave Ste 400 (93309-9119)
PHONE.....................................661 396-3770
EMP: 330
SIC: 8711 Engineering services

(P-19673)
PROTOTYPE ENGINEERING AND MANUFACTURING INC
140 E 162nd St (90248-2802)
PHONE....................310 532-6305
EMP: 24
Web: www.prototypeengineering.com
SIC: 8711 3825 Electrical or electronic engineering; Test equipment for electronic and electric measurement

(P-19674)
PTSI MANAGED SERVICES INC
100 W Walnut St (91124-0001)
PHONE....................626 440-3118
Mary Ann Hopkins, *Pr*
EMP: 99 EST: 1983
SALES (est): 4.71MM
SALES (corp-wide): 4.2B **Publicly Held**
Web: www.parsons.com
SIC: 8711 Engineering services
PA: The Parsons Corporation
5875 Trinity Pkwy Ste 300
Centreville VA
703 988-8500

(P-19675)
QUARTUS ENGINEERING INC (PA)
9689 Towne Centre Dr (92121-1964)
PHONE....................858 875-6000
John Williams, *CEO*
Mark Stabb, *
Chris Flanigan, *
Doug Botos, *
Jeff Frantz, *
EMP: 159 EST: 1997
SQ FT: 3,100
SALES (est): 36.79MM
SALES (corp-wide): 36.79MM **Privately Held**
Web: www.quartus.com
SIC: 8711 Consulting engineer

(P-19676)
R AND L LOPEZ ASSOCIATES INC (PA)
Also Called: Lopez & Associates Engineers
3649 Tyler Ave (91731-2505)
PHONE....................626 330-5296
Lourdes P Lopez, *Pr*
Remberto Lopez, *
EMP: 80 EST: 1979
SQ FT: 2,700
SALES (est): 2.37MM **Privately Held**
SIC: 8711 Consulting engineer

(P-19677)
RAYTHEON SECURE INFORMATION SYSTEMS LLC
Also Called: Raytheon
2000 E El Segundo Blvd (90245-4501)
PHONE....................310 647-9438
EMP: 226
SIC: 8711 Electrical or electronic engineering

(P-19678)
REZEK EQUIPMENT
970 Reece St (92411-2346)
PHONE....................909 885-6221
Ronald Rezek Junior, *Owner*
EMP: 19 EST: 1980
SQ FT: 74,000
SALES (est): 477.73K **Privately Held**
Web: www.ronrezek.com
SIC: 8711 3648 Civil engineering; Lighting equipment, nec

(P-19679)
RIALTO BIOENERGY FACILITY LLC
5780 Fleet St Ste 310 (92008-4700)
PHONE....................760 436-8870
Arun Sharma, *Managing Member*
EMP: 250 EST: 2013
SQ FT: 12,937
SALES (est): 22.37MM
SALES (corp-wide): 121.24MM **Privately Held**
Web: www.anaergia.com
SIC: 8711 Energy conservation engineering
PA: Anaergia Inc
4210 South Service Rd
Burlington ON
905 766-3333

(P-19680)
ROCK WEST COMPOSITES INC
7625 Panasonic Way (92154-8204)
PHONE....................858 537-6260
James Gormican, *Brnch Mgr*
EMP: 25
Web: www.rockwestcomposites.com
SIC: 8711 3624 Engineering services; Carbon and graphite products
PA: Rock West Composites, Inc.
7625 Panasonic Way
San Diego CA

(P-19681)
ROVE ENGINEERING INC
398 E Aurora Dr (92243-9603)
PHONE....................760 425-0001
Steven Eugenio, *Pr*
EMP: 95 EST: 2018
SALES (est): 20.32MM **Privately Held**
SIC: 8711 1611 Engineering services; General contractor, highway and street construction

(P-19682)
SAALEX CORP (PA)
Also Called: Saalex Solutions
811 Camarillo Springs Rd Ste A (93012-9465)
PHONE....................805 482-1070
Travis Mack, *Pr*
Elaine Reese, *
Lisa Cortes, *
EMP: 245 EST: 1999
SQ FT: 7,000
SALES (est): 96.07MM
SALES (corp-wide): 96.07MM **Privately Held**
Web: www.saalex.com
SIC: 8711 7379 Consulting engineer; Computer related consulting services

(P-19683)
SABRE SYSTEMS INC
3111 Camino Del Rio N Ste 400 (92108)
PHONE....................619 528-2226
EMP: 87
Web: www.sabresystems.com
SIC: 8711 Engineering services
PA: Sabre Systems, Inc.
125 County Line Rd # 180
Warminster PA

(P-19684)
SAN DIEGO COMPOSITES INC
9220 Activity Rd Ste 100 (92126-4420)
PHONE....................858 751-0450
Marc Duvall, *CEO*
Jeff Murphy, *
EMP: 70 EST: 2003
SQ FT: 70,000
SALES (est): 18.96MM

SALES (corp-wide): 189.21MM **Privately Held**
Web: www.appliedcomposites.com
SIC: 8711 8734 3761 3764 Consulting engineer; Testing laboratories; Guided missiles and space vehicles; Space propulsion units and parts
PA: Applied Composites Holdings, Llc
25692 Atlantic Ocean Dr
Lake Forest CA
949 716-3511

(P-19685)
SAN DIEGO SERVICES LLC
Also Called: Paragon Services Engineering
5415 Oberlin Dr (92121-1716)
PHONE....................858 654-0102
Rosemary Dymek, *Prin*
Wesley S Dymek, *Prin*
EMP: 150 EST: 1999
SQ FT: 2,477
SALES (est): 17.32MM **Privately Held**
Web: paragonservices.us.com
SIC: 8711 Engineering services

(P-19686)
SC WRIGHT CONSTRUCTION INC
3838 Camino Del Rio N Ste 370 (92108)
P.O. Box 3250 (91944-3250)
PHONE....................619 698-6909
Steven C Wright, *Pr*
EMP: 400 EST: 1997
SALES (est): 27.86MM **Privately Held**
Web: www.scwright.com
SIC: 8711 Building construction consultant

(P-19687)
SCICON TECHNOLOGIES CORP (PA)
27525 Newhall Ranch Rd Ste 2 (91355-4003)
PHONE....................661 295-8630
Thomas J Bulger, *Pr*
Marie Bulger, *
▲ EMP: 50 EST: 1989
SQ FT: 25,000
SALES (est): 10.56MM **Privately Held**
Web: www.scicontech.com
SIC: 8711 3999 Mechanical engineering; Models, except toy

(P-19688)
SEP GROUP INC
11374 Turtleback Ln (92127-2009)
P.O. Box 270475 (92198-2475)
PHONE....................858 876-4621
Abtin Sepehri, *CEO*
EMP: 25 EST: 1998
SALES (est): 907.87K **Privately Held**
SIC: 8711 1611 1542 1389 Construction and civil engineering; General contractor, highway and street construction; Commercial and office building contractors; Construction, repair, and dismantling services

(P-19689)
SERCO INC
9350 Waxie Way Ste 400 (92123-1056)
PHONE....................858 569-8979
Kent Brown, *Brnch Mgr*
EMP: 132
SALES (corp-wide): 5.46B **Privately Held**
Web: www.serco.com
SIC: 8711 Engineering services
HQ: Serco Inc.
12930 Worldgate Dr # 600
Herndon VA

(P-19690)
SIA ENGINEERING (USA) INC
7001 W Imperial Hwy (90045-6313)
PHONE....................310 957-2928
Chandra Nair, *CEO*
Cheng Hian Tan, *
Chiuyen Tseng, *
EMP: 151 EST: 2008
SALES (est): 10.39MM **Privately Held**
SIC: 8711 Consulting engineer

(P-19691)
SITESOL
Also Called: Site Sltions Cnstr Integration
7372 Sycamore Canyon Blvd (92508-2335)
P.O. Box 91747 (90809-1747)
PHONE....................562 746-5884
Kristine Glaeser, *CEO*
Peter Glaeser, *
EMP: 85 EST: 2010
SALES (est): 2.46MM **Privately Held**
Web: www.sitesol.us
SIC: 8711 Construction and civil engineering

(P-19692)
SONIC INDUSTRIES INC
Also Called: Airframer R
20030 Normandie Ave (90502-1210)
PHONE....................310 532-8382
Jamie King, *CEO*
▲ EMP: 150 EST: 1966
SQ FT: 65,000
SALES (est): 23.56MM
SALES (corp-wide): 1.47B **Publicly Held**
SIC: 8711 7699 Machine tool design; Aviation propeller and blade repair
HQ: Roller Bearing Company Of America, Inc.
102 Willenbrock Rd
Oxford CT
203 267-7001

(P-19693)
SPEARMAN AEROSPACE INC
9215 Greenleaf Ave (90670-3028)
PHONE....................714 523-4751
Urio Zanetti, *Pr*
EMP: 25 EST: 2013
SALES (est): 10MM **Privately Held**
Web: www.spearmanaerospace.com
SIC: 8711 3721 Aviation and/or aeronautical engineering; Aircraft

(P-19694)
SPEC SERVICES INC
10540 Talbert Ave Ste 100e (92708-6051)
PHONE....................714 963-8077
Kim R Henry, *Pr*
Dan Letcher, *
Chuck Lake, *
EMP: 290 EST: 1981
SQ FT: 16,000
SALES (est): 49.39MM **Privately Held**
Web: www.specservices.com
SIC: 8711 Consulting engineer

(P-19695)
SSC CONSTRUCTION INC
4195 Chino Hills Pkwy (91709-2618)
PHONE....................951 278-1177
Gregory E Larkin, *CEO*
Neil Nehmens, *
EMP: 80 EST: 1999
SALES (est): 4.44MM **Privately Held**
Web: www.ssconstruction.net
SIC: 8711 Engineering services

PRODUCTS & SVCS

(P-19696)
STEARNS CONRAD AND SCHMIDT CONSULTING ENGINEERS INC (PA)
Also Called: Scs Engineers
3900 Kilroy Airport Way Ste 100 (90806-2453)
PHONE.....................562 426-9544
EMP: 100 EST: 1970
SALES (est): 438.81MM
SALES (corp-wide): 438.81MM **Privately Held**
Web: www.scsengineers.com
SIC: 8711 1541 8748 Consulting engineer; Industrial buildings, new construction, nec; Environmental consultant

(P-19697)
SYSTEMS APPLICATION & TECH INC
Also Called: Sa-Tech
1000 Town Center Dr Ste 110 (93036-1100)
P.O. Box 25 (93044-0025)
PHONE.....................805 487-7373
Geoff Dezavala, *Sr VP*
EMP: 80
Web: www.sa-techinc.com
SIC: 8711 Consulting engineer
PA: Systems Application & Technologies, Inc.
1101 Merc Ln Ste 200
Largo MD

(P-19698)
SYSTEMS ENGINEERING & MGT CO (PA)
Also Called: Semco
1430 Vantage Ct (92081-8568)
PHONE.....................760 727-7800
William M Tincup, *Pr*
Doug Ocull, *
Michael Samuels, *
▼ EMP: 35 EST: 1982
SQ FT: 42,000
SALES (est): 10MM
SALES (corp-wide): 10MM **Privately Held**
Web: www.semco.com
SIC: 8711 3812 3825 3663 Consulting engineer; Search and navigation equipment; Instruments to measure electricity; Radio and t.v. communications equipment

(P-19699)
TECHNIP USA INC
Also Called: TP USA
555 W Arrow Hwy (91711-4805)
PHONE.....................909 447-3600
Gary Keyser, *Brnch Mgr*
EMP: 400
Web: www.technipfmc.com
SIC: 8711 Petroleum engineering
PA: Technip Energies Usa, Inc.
11720 Katy Fwy
Houston TX

(P-19700)
TEN STONE WBSTER PRCESS TECH
555 W Arrow Hwy (91711-4805)
PHONE.....................909 447-3600
Gary Keyser, *Brnch Mgr*
EMP: 281
Web: www.ten.com
SIC: 8711 Chemical engineering
HQ: T.En Stone & Webster Process Technology, Inc.
11740 Katy Fwy Ste 100
Houston TX
281 870-1111

(P-19701)
TETRA TECH INC (PA)
Also Called: Tetra Tech
3475 E Foothill Blvd (91107-6024)
PHONE.....................626 351-4664
Dan L Batrack, *Ch Bd*
Jill Hudkins, *Pr*
Steven M Burdick, *Ex VP*
Leslie L Shoemaker, *SUSTAIN LEADERSHIP Development*
Preston Hopson, *CCO*
EMP: 200 EST: 1966
SALES (est): 3.5B
SALES (corp-wide): 3.5B **Publicly Held**
Web: www.tetratech.com
SIC: 8711 Engineering services

(P-19702)
TETRA TECH INC
17885 Von Karman Ave Ste 500 (92614-5227)
PHONE.....................949 263-0846
Jack Chicca, *Brnch Mgr*
EMP: 85
SALES (corp-wide): 3.5B **Publicly Held**
Web: www.tetratech.com
SIC: 8711 Consulting engineer
PA: Tetra Tech, Inc.
3475 E Foothill Blvd
Pasadena CA
626 351-4664

(P-19703)
TETRA TECH NUS INC
3475 E Foothill Blvd (91107-6024)
PHONE.....................412 921-7090
Dan L Batrack, *CEO*
Janet Mandel, *
John Trepanowski, *
Steven M Burdick, *
Ronald Chu, *
▲ EMP: 149 EST: 1960
SALES (est): 2.52MM
SALES (corp-wide): 3.5B **Publicly Held**
Web: www.tetratech.com
SIC: 8711 Consulting engineer
PA: Tetra Tech, Inc.
3475 E Foothill Blvd
Pasadena CA
626 351-4664

(P-19704)
THERMAL ENGRG INTL USA INC (HQ)
Also Called: Thermal Engineering
18000 Studebaker Rd Ste 400 (90703-2691)
PHONE.....................323 726-0641
Kenneth Murakoshi, *CEO*
Thomas Richardson, *
Micahel D Leclair, *
William J Ferguson Junior, *Law Vice President*
Kenneth Murakoshi, *Sr VP*
◆ EMP: 70 EST: 1969
SQ FT: 18,000
SALES (est): 51.01MM
SALES (corp-wide): 509.03MM **Privately Held**
Web: www.babcockpower.com
SIC: 8711 3443 Professional engineer; Air coolers, metal plate
PA: Babcock Power Inc.
222 Rosewood Dr
Danvers MA
978 646-3300

(P-19705)
THORPE TECHNOLOGIES INC (DH)
449 W Allen Ave Ste 119 (91773-1453)
PHONE.....................562 903-8230
John E Allen, *Pr*
Thomas A Carpenter, *
EMP: 25 EST: 1988
SALES (est): 9.45MM
SALES (corp-wide): 38.46MM **Privately Held**
Web: www.thorpetech.com
SIC: 8711 3567 Engineering services; Industrial furnaces and ovens
HQ: Thorpe Holding Company
9905 Painter Ave Ste D
Whittier CA

(P-19706)
TOYON RESEARCH CORPORATION (PA)
6800 Cortona Dr (93117-3139)
PHONE.....................805 968-6787
Kevin Sullivan, *
Dave Wright, *
Paul Castleberg, *
Chuck Nardo, *
EMP: 200 EST: 1980
SQ FT: 16,000
SALES (est): 49.8MM
SALES (corp-wide): 49.8MM **Privately Held**
Web: www.toyon.com
SIC: 8711 7371 Electrical or electronic engineering; Custom computer programming services

(P-19707)
TRANSTECH ENGINEERS INC (PA)
13367 Benson Ave (91710-5246)
PHONE.....................909 595-8599
Allen Cayir, *Pr*
Sybil Cayir, *
EMP: 85 EST: 1989
SQ FT: 10,000
SALES (est): 10.25MM **Privately Held**
Web: www.transtech.org
SIC: 8711 Civil engineering

(P-19708)
TRI STAR ENGINEERING INC
6774 Calle De Linea Ste 106 (92154-8020)
PHONE.....................619 710-8038
Alfred Lybred, *Mgr*
EMP: 86
Web: www.star3.com
SIC: 8711 Engineering services
PA: Tri Star Engineering, Inc.
1801 S Liberty Dr Ste 200
Bloomington IN

(P-19709)
TRUST AUTOMATION INC
125 Venture Dr Ste 110 (93401-9103)
PHONE.....................805 544-0761
Ty Safreno, *CEO*
Trudie Safreno, *
Brett Keegan, *
Chuck Kass, *
Dave Rennie, *
▲ EMP: 65 EST: 1990
SQ FT: 100,000
SALES (est): 21.38MM **Privately Held**
Web: www.trustautomation.com
SIC: 8711 3812 3731 3621 Machine tool design; Antennas, radar or communications; Submersible marine robots, manned or unmanned; Generators for gas-electric or oil-electric vehicles

(P-19710)
TTG ENGINEERS
Also Called: Mbe
300 N Lake Ave Fl 14 (91101-4164)
PHONE.....................626 463-2800
▲ EMP: 350
SIC: 8711 Consulting engineer

(P-19711)
UCI CONSTRUCTION INC
3900 Fruitvale Ave (93308-5114)
PHONE.....................661 587-0192
David Krugh, *Brnch Mgr*
EMP: 98
SALES (corp-wide): 24.78MM **Privately Held**
Web: www.uciconstruction.com
SIC: 8711 Professional engineer
PA: U.C.I. Construction, Inc.
167 Grobric Ct
Fairfield CA
925 370-9808

(P-19712)
UNITED INDUSTRIES GROUP INC
Also Called: U I G
11 Rancho Cir (92630-8324)
P.O. Box 8009 (92658-8009)
PHONE.....................949 759-3200
James P Mansour, *Pr*
John Mensell, *
EMP: 26 EST: 1969
SQ FT: 10,000
SALES (est): 5.69MM **Privately Held**
Web: www.unitedind.com
SIC: 8711 3589 Engineering services; Water treatment equipment, industrial

(P-19713)
URS GROUP INC
Also Called: URS
3995 Via Oro Ave (90810-1869)
PHONE.....................562 420-2933
Wilfrido Simbol, *Brnch Mgr*
EMP: 90
SALES (corp-wide): 14.38B **Publicly Held**
Web: www.aecom.com
SIC: 8711 8712 Structural engineering; Architectural engineering
HQ: Urs Group, Inc.
300 S Grand Ave Ste 900
Los Angeles CA
213 593-8000

(P-19714)
UTILITY TRAFFIC SERVICES LLC
2845 E Spring St (90806-2417)
PHONE.....................562 264-2355
Ed Barrera, *Managing Member*
EMP: 266 EST: 2020
SALES (est): 928.77K **Privately Held**
SIC: 8711 Consulting engineer
PA: Traffic Management, Inc.
4900 Arprt Plz Dr Ste 300
Long Beach CA

(P-19715)
VANGUARD SPACE TECH INC
Also Called: Alliance Spacesystems
4398 Corporate Center Dr (90720-2537)
PHONE.....................858 587-4210
Frank Belknap, *CEO*
Ronald Miller, *
John Richer, *
EMP: 101 EST: 1994
SQ FT: 50,000
SALES (est): 13.8MM
SALES (corp-wide): 211MM **Publicly Held**
Web: www.appliedcomposites.com

SIC: **8711** Aviation and/or aeronautical engineering
HQ: Solaero Technologies Corp.
10420 Res Rd Se Bldg 1
Albuquerque NM
505 332-5000

(P-19716)
VT MILCOM INC
1660 Logan Ave Ste 2 (92113-1044)
PHONE..................................619 424-9024
Brian Upthegrove, *Brnch Mgr*
EMP: 100
SALES (corp-wide): 1.59B **Privately Held**
Web: www.mlupino.com
SIC: **8711** Engineering services
HQ: Vt Milcom Inc.
448 Viking Dr Ste 350
Virginia Beach VA
757 463-2800

(P-19717)
W M LYLES CO
2810 Unicorn Rd (93308-6853)
PHONE..................................661 387-1600
Mike Burson, *Pr*
EMP: 113
SALES (corp-wide): 17.85MM **Privately Held**
Web: www.wmlylesco.com
SIC: **8711** 1623 Engineering services; Pipeline construction, nsk
HQ: W. M. Lyles Co.
525 W Alluvial Ave
Fresno CA
559 441-1900

(P-19718)
WESTWIND ENGINEERING INC
625 Esplanade Unit 70 (90277-4150)
PHONE..................................310 831-3454
Mary Anne Graves, *CEO*
Carl Graves, *
EMP: 150 **EST:** 1992
SQ FT: 2,400
SALES (est): 13MM **Privately Held**
Web: www.westwind111.com
SIC: **8711** 7363 Engineering services; Temporary help service

(P-19719)
WILLDAN GROUP INC (PA)
2401 E Katella Ave Ste 300 (92806-5909)
PHONE..................................800 424-9144
Thomas D Brisbin, *Ch Bd*
Michael A Bieber, *
Daniel Chow, *
Creighton Early, *
Micah Chen, *
EMP: 116 **EST:** 1964
SQ FT: 18,000
SALES (est): 429.14MM
SALES (corp-wide): 429.14MM **Publicly Held**
Web: www.willdan.com
SIC: **8711** 8748 Civil engineering; Urban planning and consulting services

(P-19720)
WSP USA INC
Also Called: Odeh Engineers
15231 Laguna Canyon Rd (92618-7714)
PHONE..................................714 973-4880
Charline Talmer, *Genl Mgr*
EMP: 100
SALES (corp-wide): 8.88B **Privately Held**
Web: www.wsp.com
SIC: **8711** Consulting engineer
HQ: Wsp Usa Inc.
250 W 34th St Fl 4

New York NY
212 465-5000

(P-19721)
XLR8 SERVICES INC
Also Called: Xlr8 Ems
1020 Calle Negocio Ste A (92673-6205)
PHONE..................................949 498-9578
Jason Powell, *Pr*
EMP: 23 **EST:** 2013
SALES (est): 7.52MM **Privately Held**
Web: www.xlr8ems.com
SIC: **8711** 3825 3829 Electrical or electronic engineering; Digital test equipment, electronic and electrical circuits; Geophysical or meteorological electronic equipment

---

8712 Architectural Services

(P-19722)
AECOM SERVICES INC (HQ)
300 S Grand Ave Ste 900 (90071-3135)
PHONE..................................213 593-8000
Michael S Burke, *CEO*
Raymond Landy, *Pr*
Kelly Olson, *VP*
Paul Steinke, *Ex VP*
Deborah Klem, *Sr VP*
EMP: 250 **EST:** 1946
SALES (est): 2.12B
SALES (corp-wide): 14.38B **Publicly Held**
Web: www.aecom.com
SIC: **8712** 8741 8711 Architectural services; Management services; Engineering services
PA: Aecom
13355 Noel Rd Ste 400
Dallas TX
972 788-1000

(P-19723)
ARCHITECTS ORANGE INC
Also Called: Ao
144 N Orange St (92866-1400)
PHONE..................................714 639-9860
Jack Selman, *Sr Pt*
Darrel Hebenstreit, *
Hugh Rose, *
Jim Dietze, *
Rc Alley Iii, *Pt*
EMP: 200 **EST:** 1973
SQ FT: 10,000
SALES (est): 37.4MM **Privately Held**
Web: www.aoarchitects.com
SIC: **8712** Architectural engineering

(P-19724)
ARCHITECTURAL MTLS USA INC
4025 Camino Del Rio S Ste 300 (92108)
PHONE..................................888 219-2126
Greg Romine, *CEO*
Serhan Emre, *
EMP: 70 **EST:** 1997
SALES (est): 2.39MM **Privately Held**
Web: www.architecturalmaterials.com
SIC: **8712** 3999 3211 5039 Architectural engineering; Barber and beauty shop equipment; Construction glass; Prefabricated structures

(P-19725)
AUSTIN VEUM RBBINS PRTNERS INC (PA)
501 W Broadway Ste A (92101-3562)
PHONE..................................619 231-1960
EMP: 83 **EST:** 1995
SQ FT: 12,500
SALES (est): 3.75MM **Privately Held**

SIC: **8712** Architectural engineering

(P-19726)
BJARKE INGELS GROUP NYC LLC
310 Wilshire Blvd (90401-1312)
PHONE..................................347 549-4141
EMP: 196
SALES (corp-wide): 101.84MM **Privately Held**
SIC: **8712** Architectural services
HQ: Bjarke Ingels Group Nyc Llc
45 Main St Fl 900
Brooklyn NY
917 287-4326

(P-19727)
DLR GROUP INC (HQ)
700 S Flower St Ste 2200 (90017)
PHONE..................................213 800-9400
Adrian O Cohen, *Pr*
Daniel A Munn, *
Jon P Anderson, *
Darrell L Stelling, *
Pamela Touschner, *
EMP: 140 **EST:** 1997
SALES (est): 24.79MM
SALES (corp-wide): 183.73MM **Privately Held**
Web: www.dlrgroup.com
SIC: **8712** 8711 Architectural engineering; Engineering services
PA: Dlr Holding Company
6457 Frances St Ste 200
Omaha NE
402 393-4100

(P-19728)
GEHRY PARTNERS LLP
12541 Beatrice St (90066-7001)
PHONE..................................310 482-3000
Frank Gehry, *Pt*
Berta Gehry, *
Brian Aamoth, *
John Bowers, *
Anand Devarajan, *
EMP: 130 **EST:** 2001
SQ FT: 12,100
SALES (est): 21.66MM **Privately Held**
Web: www.foga.com
SIC: **8712** Architectural services

(P-19729)
GKK CORPORATION (PA)
Also Called: Gkkworks
2355 Main St Ste 220 (92614-4251)
PHONE..................................949 250-1500
Praful Kulkarni, *Pr*
David Hunt, *
Mike Helton, *Prin*
Sam Porter, *Prin*
EMP: 85 **EST:** 1991
SQ FT: 11,000
SALES (est): 32.74MM **Privately Held**
SIC: **8712** 8711 Architectural engineering; Building construction consultant

(P-19730)
HAWKINS BROWN USA INC
8500 Steller Dr Ste 1 (90232-2453)
PHONE..................................310 600-2695
Matthew Ollier, *Prin*
EMP: 276 **EST:** 2017
SALES (est): 4.77MM **Privately Held**
Web: www.hawkinsbrown.com
SIC: **8712** Architectural engineering

(P-19731)
HELLMUTH OBATA & KASSABAUM INC
757 S Alameda St (90021-1679)
PHONE..................................310 838-9555
EMP: 97
SALES (corp-wide): 457.53MM **Privately Held**
Web: www.hok.com
SIC: **8712** 8711 Architectural engineering; Engineering services
HQ: Hellmuth, Obata & Kassabaum, Inc.
1 Bush St Ste 200
San Francisco CA

(P-19732)
HMC GROUP (HQ)
Also Called: HMC Architects
3546 Concours (91764-5584)
PHONE..................................909 989-9979
Brian Staton, *CEO*
▲ **EMP:** 165 **EST:** 1941
SQ FT: 58,000
SALES (est): 53.1MM
SALES (corp-wide): 93.14MM **Privately Held**
Web: www.hmcarchitects.com
SIC: **8712** Architectural engineering
PA: Hmc Holdings, Inc.
3546 Concours
Ontario CA
909 989-9979

(P-19733)
JOHNSON FAIN INC
1201 N Broadway (90012-1407)
PHONE..................................323 224-6000
R Scott Johnson, *
Sherry Miller, *
EMP: 80 **EST:** 1950
SQ FT: 26,000
SALES (est): 8.66MM **Privately Held**
Web: www.johnsonfain.com
SIC: **8712** 7389 Architectural engineering; Interior design services

(P-19734)
LAMAR JHNSON COLLABORATIVE INC
8590 National Blvd (90232-2443)
PHONE..................................424 361-3960
EMP: 209
SALES (corp-wide): 878.7MM **Privately Held**
Web: www.theljc.com
SIC: **8712** Architectural engineering
HQ: The Lamar Johnson Collaborative Inc
35 E Wacker Dr Ste 1300
Chicago IL
312 429-0400

(P-19735)
LPA INC (PA)
5301 California Ave Ste 100 (92617-3224)
PHONE..................................949 261-1001
Wendy Rogers, *CEO*
Dan Heinfeld, *
James Kelly, *
Charles Pruitt, *
◆ **EMP:** 180 **EST:** 1971
SQ FT: 33,700
SALES (est): 36.63MM
SALES (corp-wide): 36.63MM **Privately Held**
Web: www.lpadesignstudios.com
SIC: **8712** 8711 0781 Architectural engineering; Engineering services; Landscape counseling and planning

PRODUCTS & SVCS

(P-19736)

M ARTHUR GENSLER JR ASSOC INC

Also Called: Gensler
4675 Macarthur Ct Ste 100 (92660-8811)
PHONE..................949 863-9434
Kim Graham, *Brnch Mgr*
EMP: 108
SALES (corp-wide): 1.84B **Privately Held**
Web: www.gensler.com
SIC: **8712** Architectural engineering
PA: M. Arthur Gensler Jr. & Associates, Inc.
220 Montgomery St Ste 200
San Francisco CA
415 433-3700

(P-19737)

M ARTHUR GENSLER JR ASSOC INC

Also Called: Gensler and Associates
500 S Figueroa St (90071-1705)
PHONE..................213 927-3600
Rob Jernigan, *Brnch Mgr*
EMP: 249
SALES (corp-wide): 1.84B **Privately Held**
Web: www.gensler.com
SIC: **8712** 7389 Architectural engineering;
Design, commercial and industrial
PA: M. Arthur Gensler Jr. & Associates, Inc.
220 Montgomery St Ste 200
San Francisco CA
415 433-3700

(P-19738)

MARTIN AC PARTNERS INC

444 S Flower St Ste 1200 (90071-1802)
PHONE..................213 683-1900
Robert Newsom, *Pr*
Christopher C Martin, *
David C Martin, *
EMP: 116 EST: 1906
SALES (est): 12.69MM **Privately Held**
Web: www.acmartin.com
SIC: **8712** Architectural services

(P-19739)

NTD ARCHITECTS

Also Called: NTD Architecture
9665 Chesapeake Dr # 365 (92123-1367)
PHONE..................858 565-4440
EMP: 98
SIC: **8712** Architectural services

(P-19740)

RRM DESIGN GROUP (PA)

3765 S Higuera St Ste 102 (93401-7437)
PHONE..................805 439-0442
Victor Montgomery, *Ch Bd*
John Wilbanks, *
Keith Gurnee, *
EMP: 99 EST: 1973
SQ FT: 23,000
SALES (est): 17.86MM
SALES (corp-wide): 17.86MM **Privately Held**
Web: www.rrmdesign.com
SIC: **8712** Architectural engineering

(P-19741)

STANTEC ARCHITECTURE INC

38 Technology Dr Ste 200 (92618-5310)
PHONE..................949 923-6000
Eric Nielsen, *VP*
EMP: 290
SALES (corp-wide): 4.23B **Privately Held**
Web: www.stantec.com
SIC: **8712** 8711 4111 Architectural services;
Engineering services; Local and suburban
transit

HQ: Stantec Architecture Inc.
224 S Michigan Ave # 1400
Chicago IL
336 714-7413

(P-19742)

STANTEC ARCHITECTURE INC

300 N Lake Ave Ste 400 (91101-4169)
PHONE..................626 796-9141
Simon Bluestone, *Brnch Mgr*
EMP: 88
SALES (corp-wide): 4.23B **Privately Held**
Web: www.stantec.com
SIC: **8712** Architectural services
HQ: Stantec Architecture Inc.
224 S Michigan Ave # 1400
Chicago IL
336 714-7413

(P-19743)

STANTEC CONSULTING SVCS INC

38 Technology Dr Ste 100 (92618-5312)
PHONE..................949 923-6000
Bob Gomes, *Brnch Mgr*
EMP: 117
SALES (corp-wide): 4.23B **Privately Held**
Web: www.stantec.com
SIC: **8712** 8711 Architectural services;
Engineering services
HQ: Stantec Consulting Services Inc.
410 17th St Ste 1400
Denver CO
303 410-4000

(P-19744)

STV ARCHITECTS INC

1055 W 7th St Ste 3150 (90017-2556)
PHONE..................213 482-9444
Wagih Andraos, *Mgr*
EMP: 162
SALES (corp-wide): 261.09MM **Privately Held**
Web: www.stvinc.com
SIC: **8712** 8742 8711 Architectural
engineering; Transportation consultant;
Consulting engineer
HQ: Stv Architects Inc
205 W Welsh Dr
Douglassville PA
610 385-8200

(P-19745)

UNIVERSITY CAL SAN DIEGO

Also Called: Ucsd Fac & Design
10280 N Torrey Pines Rd Ste 470
(92037-1033)
PHONE..................858 534-2177
M Boone Hellmann, *Brnch Mgr*
EMP: 88
SALES (corp-wide): 534.4MM **Privately Held**
Web: www.ucsd.edu
SIC: **8712** 8221 9411 Architectural services;
University; Administration of educational
programs
HQ: University Of California, San Diego
9500 Gilman Dr
La Jolla CA
858 534-2230

(P-19746)

WARE MALCOMB (PA)

10 Edelman (92618-4312)
PHONE..................949 660-9128
Kenneth Wink, *CEO*
Lawrence R Armstrong, *
Jay Todisco, *
Matthew Brady, *
Tobin Sloane, *

▲ EMP: 137 EST: 1972
SQ FT: 22,000
SALES (est): 52.29MM
SALES (corp-wide): 52.29MM **Privately Held**
Web: www.waremalcomb.com
SIC: **8712** 7336 8711 7389 Architectural
engineering; Commercial art and graphic
design; Civil engineering; Interior design
services

(P-19747)

WIMBERLY ALLSON TONG GOO NA IN

Also Called: Watg
300 Spectrum Center Dr Ste 500
(92618-4989)
PHONE..................949 574-8500
Mike Seyle, *CEO*
Monica Cuervo, *
EMP: 98 EST: 2006
SALES (est): 6.81MM **Privately Held**
Web: www.watg.com
SIC: **8712** Architectural services

(P-19748)

ZIMMER GNSUL FRSCA ARCHTCTS LL

Also Called: Zimmer Gnsul Frsca Partnr Amer
515 S Flower St Ste 3700 (90071-2221)
PHONE..................213 617-1901
Rachel Morris, *Mgr*
EMP: 118
SALES (corp-wide): 48.63MM **Privately Held**
SIC: **8712** 7389 Architectural engineering;
Interior designer
PA: Zimmer Gunsul Frasca Architects Llp
1223 Sw Washington St # 200
Portland OR
503 224-3860

8713 Surveying Services

(P-19749)

PSOMAS

Also Called: Bonterra Psomas
5 Hutton Centre Dr Ste 300 (92707)
PHONE..................714 751-7373
Ryan Mclean, *Mgr*
EMP: 97
SALES (corp-wide): 67.87MM **Privately Held**
Web: www.psomas.com
SIC: **8713** 8711 Surveying services;
Consulting engineer
PA: Psomas
865 S Figueroa St # 3200
Los Angeles CA
213 223-1400

(P-19750)

PSOMAS (PA)

865 S Figueroa St (90017-2507)
PHONE..................213 223-1400
Ryan Mclean, *Pr*
EMP: 125 EST: 1946
SALES (est): 67.87MM
SALES (corp-wide): 67.87MM **Privately Held**
Web: www.psomas.com
SIC: **8713** 8711 Surveying services;
Engineering services

8721 Accounting, Auditing, And Bookkeeping

(P-19751)

ARMANINO LLP

11766 Wilshire Blvd Fl 9 (90025-6538)
PHONE..................310 478-4148
EMP: 309
SALES (corp-wide): 311.23MM **Privately Held**
Web: www.armanino.com
SIC: **8721** Certified public accountant
PA: Armanino Llp
2700 Camino Ramon Ste 350
San Ramon CA
925 790-2600

(P-19752)

BAKER TILLY US LLP

15760 Ventura Blvd Ste 1100 (91436-3000)
PHONE..................818 981-2600
William Wolf, *Brnch Mgr*
EMP: 434
SALES (corp-wide): 1.5B **Privately Held**
Web: www.bakertilly.com
SIC: **8721** Certified public accountant
PA: Baker Tilly Us, Llp
205 N Michigan Ave # 2800
Chicago IL
312 729-8000

(P-19753)

BAKER TILLY US LLP

11150 Santa Monica Blvd Ste 600
(90025-0479)
PHONE..................310 826-4474
Lew Thomashaw, *Brnch Mgr*
EMP: 780
SALES (corp-wide): 1.5B **Privately Held**
Web: www.bakertilly.com
SIC: **8721** Certified public accountant
PA: Baker Tilly Us, Llp
205 N Michigan Ave # 2800
Chicago IL
312 729-8000

(P-19754)

BAKER TILLY US LLP

Also Called: Baker Tilly California
18500 Von Karman Ave Fl 10 (92612-0527)
PHONE..................949 222-2999
Thomas Bennett, *Mng Pt*
EMP: 520
SALES (corp-wide): 1.5B **Privately Held**
Web: www.bakertilly.com
SIC: **8721** Certified public accountant
PA: Baker Tilly Us, Llp
205 N Michigan Ave # 2800
Chicago IL
312 729-8000

(P-19755)

BAKER TILLY US LLP

3655 Nobel Dr Ste 300 (92122-1050)
PHONE..................858 597-4100
Vanessa Liguzinski, *Brnch Mgr*
EMP: 434
SALES (corp-wide): 1.5B **Privately Held**
Web: www.bakertilly.com
SIC: **8721** Certified public accountant
PA: Baker Tilly Us, Llp
205 N Michigan Ave # 2800
Chicago IL
312 729-8000

(P-19756)

BRAULT

Also Called: Emergency Groups' Office

180 Via Verde Ste 100 (91773-3993)
PHONE..................626 447-0296
EMP: 200 EST: 2015
SALES (est): 10.21MM Privately Held
Web: www.brault.us
SIC: 8721 Billing and bookkeeping service

(P-19757)
CACHET FINANCIAL SERVICES
175 S Lake Ave Unit 200 (91101-2629)
PHONE..................626 578-9400
Aberash Asfaw, Pr
Alden Blowers, Pr
EMP: 95 EST: 2001
SALES (est): 4.51MM
SALES (corp-wide): 7.62MM Privately Held
Web: www.cachetservices.com
SIC: 8721 Payroll accounting service
PA: Financial Business Group Holdings
1932 E Deere Ave Ste 200
Santa Ana CA
949 225-3000

(P-19758)
CALIFORNIA BUSINESS BUREAU INC (PA)
Also Called: Medical Billing Services
1711 S Mountain Ave (91016-4256)
P.O. Box 5010 (91017-7110)
PHONE..................626 303-1515
Michael J Sigal, Pr
EMP: 132 EST: 1973
SQ FT: 24,000
SALES (est): 12.43MM
SALES (corp-wide): 12.43MM Privately Held
Web: www.cbbinc.com
SIC: 8721 Billing and bookkeeping service

(P-19759)
CALIFORNIA STATE UNIV LONG BCH
Also Called: Bursar's Office
1250 N Bellflower Blvd Bh155 (90840-0004)
PHONE..................562 985-1764
Randy Nielson, Supervisor
EMP: 207
SALES (corp-wide): 534.4MM Privately Held
Web: www.csulb.edu
SIC: 8721 8221 9411 Accounting, auditing, and bookkeeping; University; Administration of educational programs
HQ: California State University, Long Beach
1250 N Bellflower Blvd
Long Beach CA
562 985-4111

(P-19760)
CAST & CREW LLC (PA)
Also Called: Cast and Crew Entrmt Svcs
2300 W Empire Ave Ste 500 (91504-5399)
PHONE..................818 570-6180
Eric Belcher, Pr
Sally Knutson, *
Shardell Cavaliere, LIFE SERVCS*
Andrew Patterson, *
EMP: 195 EST: 1976
SQ FT: 12,000
SALES (est): 58.77MM
SALES (corp-wide): 58.77MM Privately Held
Web: www.castandcrew.com
SIC: 8721 Payroll accounting service

(P-19761)
CLIFTONLARSONALLEN LLP
Also Called: Nsbn
1925 Century Park E 16th Fl (90067-2701)
PHONE..................310 273-2501
Randy Wells, Brnch Mgr
EMP: 91
SALES (corp-wide): 966.83MM Privately Held
Web: www.claconnect.com
SIC: 8721 Accounting services, except auditing
PA: Cliftonlarsonallen Llp
220 S 6th St Ste 300
Minneapolis MN
612 376-4500

(P-19762)
COMPUTERIZED MGT SVCS INC
Also Called: CMS
4100 Guardian St Ste 205 (93063-6721)
P.O. Box 190 (93062-0190)
PHONE..................805 522-5940
J Daryl Favale, Pr
EMP: 100 EST: 1985
SQ FT: 7,500
SALES (est): 6.67MM
SALES (corp-wide): 49.46MM Privately Held
Web: www.xifin.com
SIC: 8721 Billing and bookkeeping service
PA: Xifin, Inc.
12225 El Camino Real
San Diego CA
858 793-5700

(P-19763)
CONSIDINE CNSDINE AN ACCNTNCY
8989 Rio San Diego Dr Ste 250 (92108-1629)
PHONE..................619 231-1977
Perry S Wright, CEO
Timothy Considine, *
Don Bonk, *
Jerry Hotz, *
Charles E Considine, *
EMP: 107 EST: 1946
SQ FT: 20,000
SALES (est): 198.03K Privately Held
Web: www.cccpa.com
SIC: 8721 Certified public accountant

(P-19764)
COUNTY OF LOS ANGELES
Also Called: Internal Services Department
1100 N Eastern Ave (90063-3200)
PHONE..................323 267-2136
Scott Minnix, Dir
EMP: 1800
Web: www.lacounty.gov
SIC: 8721 Accounting, auditing, and bookkeeping
PA: County Of Los Angeles
500 W Temple St Ste 437
Los Angeles CA
213 974-1101

(P-19765)
COUNTY OF VENTURA
Auditor /controller
800 S Victoria Ave Ste 1540 (93009-0001)
PHONE..................805 654-3152
Christine Cohens, Mgr
EMP: 87
SALES (corp-wide): 165.04MM Privately Held
Web: www.ventura.org
SIC: 8721 9311 Auditing services; Controllers' office, government

PA: County Of Ventura
800 S Victoria Ave
Ventura CA
805 654-2644

(P-19766)
DELOITTE & TOUCHE LLP
12830 El Camino Real Ste 600 (92130)
PHONE..................619 232-6500
Cathy Jennings, Mgr
EMP: 1321
SALES (corp-wide): 696.23K Privately Held
Web: www.deloitte.com
SIC: 8721 7291 Certified public accountant; Tax return preparation services
HQ: Deloitte & Touche Llp
30 Rockefeller Plz # 4350
New York NY
212 492-4000

(P-19767)
DELOITTE & TOUCHE LLP
555 W 5th St Ste 2700 (90013-1024)
PHONE..................213 688-0800
Byron David, Brnch Mgr
EMP: 1000
SALES (corp-wide): 696.23K Privately Held
Web: www.deloitte.com
SIC: 8721 Accounting services, except auditing
HQ: Deloitte & Touche Llp
30 Rockefeller Plz # 4350
New York NY
212 492-4000

(P-19768)
DELOITTE & TOUCHE LLP
695 Town Center Dr Ste 1200 (92626-7188)
PHONE..................714 436-7419
Bob Grant, Mgr
EMP: 221
SALES (corp-wide): 696.23K Privately Held
Web: www.deloitte.com
SIC: 8721 7291 Accounting services, except auditing; Tax return preparation services
HQ: Deloitte & Touche Llp
30 Rockefeller Plz # 4350
New York NY
212 492-4000

(P-19769)
DELOITTE TAX LLP
555 W 5th St Ste 2700 (90013-1024)
PHONE..................404 885-6754
EMP: 104
SALES (corp-wide): 696.23K Privately Held
Web: www.deloitte.com
SIC: 8721 Auditing services
HQ: Deloitte Tax Llp
30 Rockefeller Plz
New York NY
212 492-4000

(P-19770)
EGO INC
Also Called: Emergency Groups Office
180 Via Verde Ste 100 (91773-3993)
PHONE..................626 447-0296
Andrea Brault, Pr
Del Brault, *
Jane Brault, *
James Blakeman, *
EMP: 150 EST: 1990
SQ FT: 8,500
SALES (est): 24.04MM Privately Held

Web: www.brault.us
SIC: 8721 Billing and bookkeeping service

(P-19771)
EIDE BAILLY LLP
10681 Foothill Blvd Ste 300 (91730)
PHONE..................909 466-4410
Dave Stende, Mng Pt
EMP: 300
SALES (corp-wide): 537.56MM Privately Held
Web: www.eidebailly.com
SIC: 8721 Certified public accountant
PA: Eide Bailly Llp
4310 17th Ave S
Fargo ND
701 239-8500

(P-19772)
ENTERTAINMENT PARTNERS INC (PA)
2950 N Hollywood Way (91505-1072)
PHONE..................818 955-6000
Mark Goldstein, CEO
George Vaughan, *
EMP: 295 EST: 1992
SQ FT: 38,000
SALES (est): 55.81MM Privately Held
Web: www.ep.com
SIC: 8721 Payroll accounting service

(P-19773)
ERNST & YOUNG LLP
Also Called: Ey
18101 Von Karman Ave Ste 1700 (92612-0164)
PHONE..................949 794-2300
Linda Minx, Off Mgr
EMP: 450
SALES (corp-wide): 27.95MM Privately Held
Web: www.ey.com
SIC: 8721 8742 Certified public accountant; Business management consultant
PA: Ernst & Young Llp
1 Manhattan W Fl 6
New York NY
703 747-0049

(P-19774)
ERNST & YOUNG LLP
Also Called: Ey
725 S Figueroa St Ste 200 (90017-5403)
PHONE..................213 977-3200
Jeff Kaufman, Mgr
EMP: 1000
SALES (corp-wide): 27.95MM Privately Held
Web: www.ey.com
SIC: 8721 8742 7291 Certified public accountant; Business management consultant; Tax return preparation services
PA: Ernst & Young Llp
1 Manhattan W Fl 6
New York NY
703 747-0049

(P-19775)
ERNST & YOUNG LLP
Also Called: Ey
4365 Executive Dr Ste 1600 (92121-2101)
PHONE..................858 535-7200
Michael J Hartnett, Mgr
EMP: 111
SALES (corp-wide): 27.95MM Privately Held
Web: www.ey.com
SIC: 8721 8742 7291 Certified public accountant; Business management consultant; Tax return preparation services

PA: Ernst & Young Llp
1 Manhattan W Fl 6
New York NY
703 747-0049

(P-19776)
**FILM PAYROLL SERVICES INC
(PA)**
Also Called: Quantos Payroll
500 S Sepulveda Blvd Fl 4 (90049-3550)
PHONE..............................310 440-9600
Gregory Pickert, *CEO*
EMP: 100 **EST:** 1978
SQ FT: 5,000
SALES (est): 16.28MM **Privately Held**
Web: www.mediaservices.com
SIC: 8721 Payroll accounting service

(P-19777)
GREEN HASSON & JANKS LLP
700 S Flower St Ste 3300 (90017-3701)
PHONE..............................310 873-1600
Leon Janks, *Pt*
William Cline, *
EMP: 120 **EST:** 1953
SALES (est): 25.68MM **Privately Held**
Web: www.ghjadvisors.com
SIC: 8721 Certified public accountant

(P-19778)
**GURSEY SCHNEIDER & CO LLC
(PA)**
1888 Century Park E Ste 900 (90067-1702)
PHONE..............................310 552-0960
Donald Gursey, *
David Blumenthal, *
Robert Watts, *
Rosanna Purzycki, *
EMP: 117 **EST:** 1964
SQ FT: 12,000
SALES (est): 179.49K
SALES (corp-wide): 179.49K **Privately
Held**
Web: www.gursey.com
SIC: 8721 Certified public accountant

(P-19779)
**HAGEN STREIFF NEWTON &
OSHIRO ACCOUNTANTS PC**
4667 Macarthur Blvd Ste 400 (92660-1817)
PHONE..............................949 390-7647
EMP: 99
SIC: 8721 Calculating and statistical service

(P-19780)
**HOLTHOUSE CARLIN VAN
TRIGT LLP (PA)**
Also Called: H C V T
11444 W Olympic Blvd Fl 11 (90064-1500)
PHONE..............................310 566-1900
Philip Holthouse, *Mng Pt*
James Carlin, *
John Van Trigt, *
Zach Shuman, *
Blake Christian, *
EMP: 110 **EST:** 1991
SALES (est): 36.22MM **Privately Held**
Web: www.hcvt.com
SIC: 8721 Certified public accountant

(P-19781)
**INFINEON TECH AMERICAS
CORP**
Interntnal Rctfr/Ccunting Dept
222 Kansas St (90245-4315)
PHONE..............................310 726-8000
Michael Mcgee, *Mgr*
EMP: 699

SALES (corp-wide): 17.72B **Privately Held**
Web: www.infineon.com
SIC: 8721 3674 Accounting, auditing, and
bookkeeping; Semiconductors and related
devices
HQ: Infineon Technologies Americas Corp.
101 N Pacific Coast Hwy
El Segundo CA
310 726-8200

(P-19782)
JS HELD LLC
4667 Macarthur Blvd Ste 400 (92660-1817)
PHONE..............................949 390-7647
EMP: 99
SALES (corp-wide): 200MM **Privately
Held**
Web: www.jsheld.com
SIC: 8721 Calculating and statistical service
PA: J.S. Held Llc
50 Jericho Quadrangle # 117
Jericho NY
516 621-2900

(P-19783)
KBKG INC
225 S Lake Ave Ste 400 (91101-3010)
PHONE..............................626 449-4225
EMP: 160 **EST:** 2001
SALES (est): 12.07MM **Privately Held**
Web: www.kbkg.com
SIC: 8721 Certified public accountant

(P-19784)
KPMG LLP
4464 Jasmine Ave (90232-3429)
PHONE..............................703 286-8175
Daniel Smith, *Mgr*
EMP: 99
SALES (corp-wide): 1.34B **Privately Held**
Web: www.home.kpmg
SIC: 8721 Certified public accountant
PA: Kpmg Llp
345 Park Ave
New York NY
212 758-9700

(P-19785)
KPMG LLP
20 Pacifica Ste 700 (92618-3391)
PHONE..............................949 885-5400
EMP: 120
SALES (corp-wide): 1.34B **Privately Held**
Web: www.home.kpmg
SIC: 8721 Certified public accountant
PA: Kpmg Llp
345 Park Ave
New York NY
212 758-9700

(P-19786)
KROST (PA)
Also Called: Krost Bumgarten Kniss Guerrero
225 S Lake Ave Ste 400 (91101-3010)
PHONE..............................626 449-4225
Richard B Krost, *CEO*
Gregory Kniss, *
EMP: 170 **EST:** 1936
SALES (est): 13.73MM
SALES (corp-wide): 13.73MM **Privately
Held**
Web: www.krostcpas.com
SIC: 8721 Accounting services, except
auditing

(P-19787)
**LANCE SOLL & LUNGHARD
LLP**
203 N Brea Blvd Ste 203 (92821-4056)
PHONE..............................714 672-0022

Ronald Stumpf, *Pr*
Gregory N Lewis, *
Edward J Leiber, *
Sherry Radmore, *
Yen Nguyen, *
EMP: 100 **EST:** 1968
SQ FT: 7,000
SALES (est): 5.54MM **Privately Held**
Web: www.lslcpas.com
SIC: 8721 Certified public accountant

(P-19788)
LLP MOSS ADAMS
2040 Main St Ste 900 (92614-8213)
PHONE..............................949 221-4000
Roger Weninger, *Brnch Mgr*
EMP: 118
SALES (corp-wide): 317.2MM **Privately
Held**
Web: www.mossadams.com
SIC: 8721 Certified public accountant
PA: Moss Adams Llp
999 3rd Ave Ste 2800
Seattle WA
206 302-6800

(P-19789)
LLP MOSS ADAMS
21700 Oxnard St Ste 300 (91367-7561)
PHONE..............................310 477-0450
Rod Green, *Pt*
EMP: 150
SALES (corp-wide): 317.2MM **Privately
Held**
Web: www.mossadams.com
SIC: 8721 Certified public accountant
PA: Moss Adams Llp
999 3rd Ave Ste 2800
Seattle WA
206 302-6800

(P-19790)
LLP MOSS ADAMS
4747 Executive Dr Ste 1300 (92121-3114)
PHONE..............................858 627-1400
Laura Roos, *Pt*
EMP: 94
SALES (corp-wide): 317.2MM **Privately
Held**
Web: www.mossadams.com
SIC: 8721 Certified public accountant
PA: Moss Adams Llp
999 3rd Ave Ste 2800
Seattle WA
206 302-6800

(P-19791)
MACIAS GINI & OCONNELL LLP
700 S Flower St Ste 800 (90017-4105)
PHONE..............................213 408-8700
EMP: 105
Web: www.mgocpa.com
SIC: 8721 Certified public accountant
PA: Macias Gini & O'connell Llp
500 Capitol Mall Ste 2200
Sacramento CA

(P-19792)
MACIAS GINI & OCONNELL LLP
Also Called: Beverly Office of Mgo
2121 Avenue Of The Stars Ste 2200
(90067-5046)
PHONE..............................323 653-8300
EMP: 104
Web: www.mgocpa.com
SIC: 8721 Certified public accountant
PA: Macias Gini & O'connell Llp
500 Capitol Mall Ste 2200
Sacramento CA

(P-19793)
MACIAS GINI & OCONNELL LLP
Also Called: Mgo
2121 Avenue Of The Stars Ste 2200
(90067-5046)
PHONE..............................916 928-4600
EMP: 104
Web: www.mgocpa.com
SIC: 8721 Certified public accountant
PA: Macias Gini & O'connell Llp
500 Capitol Mall Ste 2200
Sacramento CA

(P-19794)
MARCUM LLP
600 Anton Blvd Ste 1600 (92626-7652)
PHONE..............................949 236-5600
Philip Wilson, *Mgr*
EMP: 80
SALES (corp-wide): 379.94MM **Privately
Held**
Web: www.marcumllp.com
SIC: 8721 Certified public accountant
PA: Marcum Llp
730 3rd Ave Fl 11
New York NY
212 485-5500

(P-19795)
**MILLER KAPLAN ARASE LLP
(PA)**
Also Called: Cahn, Jsph/Miller Kaplan Arase
4123 Lankershim Blvd (91602-2828)
PHONE..............................818 769-2010
EMP: 129 **EST:** 1940
SALES (est): 17.38MM
SALES (corp-wide): 17.38MM **Privately
Held**
Web: www.millerkaplan.com
SIC: 8721 Certified public accountant

(P-19796)
**MURPHY MURPHY & MURPHY
INC**
6261 Katella Ave (90630-5200)
PHONE..............................562 594-6678
Patrick G Murphy, *CEO*
EMP: 92 **EST:** 2009
SALES (est): 8.52MM **Privately Held**
Web: www.murphy3.com
SIC: 8721 Certified public accountant

(P-19797)
NEW TALCO ENTERPRISES LLC
Also Called: Caps Payroll
2300 W Empire Ave (91504-3341)
PHONE..............................310 280-0755
Doug Sylvester, *CEO*
Frank Devito, *
David Lee, *CIO**
Fran Lucci-pannozzo, *CMO*
Anne Plechner, *
EMP: 97 **EST:** 2010
SALES (est): 2.31MM
SALES (corp-wide): 58.77MM **Privately
Held**
SIC: 8721 Payroll accounting service
PA: Cast & Crew Llc
2300 W Empire Ave Ste 500
Burbank CA
818 570-6180

(P-19798)
**OMEGA ACCOUNTING
SOLUTIONS INC**
15101 Alton Pkwy Ste 450 (92618-2372)
PHONE..............................949 348-2433
Jay Woods, *Prin*
EMP: 82 **EST:** 2008

SALES (est): 3.34MM Privately Held
Web: www.omega-accounting.com
SIC: 8721 Accounting, auditing, and
bookkeeping

(P-19799)
OPTIMA OFFICE INC
5120 Shoreham Pl Ste 285 (92122-5992)
PHONE...............................858 361-0481
EMP: 83 EST: 2018
SALES (est): 2.75MM Privately Held
Web: www.optimaoffice.com
SIC: 8721 Accounting, auditing, and
bookkeeping

(P-19800)
**PHYSICIAN SUPPORT SYSTEMS
INC (DH)**
1131 W 6th St Ste 300 (91762-1118)
PHONE...............................717 653-5340
Douglas Estock, *Pr*
EMP: 400 EST: 1991
SALES (est): 16.49MM
SALES (corp-wide): 276.71B Publicly
Held
Web: www.pssbilling.com
SIC: 8721 Billing and bookkeeping service
HQ: Ndchealth Corporation
1564 Northeast Expy Ne
Brookhaven GA
404 728-2000

(P-19801)
PHYSICIANS CHOICE LLC
21860 Burbank Blvd Ste 120 (91367-6477)
P.O. Box 4419 (91365-4419)
PHONE...............................818 340-9988
EMP: 80 EST: 1999
SQ FT: 10,000
SALES (est): 4.82MM Privately Held
Web: www.physchoice.com
SIC: 8721 Billing and bookkeeping service

(P-19802)
**PRICEWATERHOUSECOOPERS
LLP**
601 S Figueroa St Ste 900 (90017-5743)
PHONE...............................213 356-6000
EMP: 122
SQ FT: 400
SALES (corp-wide): 6.79B Privately Held
Web: www.pwc.com
SIC: 8721 Certified public accountant
PA: Pricewaterhousecoopers Llp
300 Madison Ave
New York NY
646 471-4000

(P-19803)
RBZ LLP
11766 Wilshire Blvd Fl 9 (90025-6548)
PHONE...............................310 478-4148
EMP: 150
Web: www.armanino.com
SIC: 8721 Certified public accountant

(P-19804)
SIGNATURE ANALYTICS LLC
10120 Pacific Heights Blvd Ste 110 (92121)
PHONE...............................888 284-3842
EMP: 84 EST: 2016
SALES (est): 1.1MM Privately Held
Web: www.signatureanalytics.com
SIC: 8721 Accounting, auditing, and
bookkeeping

(P-19805)
SINGERLEWAK LLP (PA)
Also Called: Singerlewak

10960 Wilshire Blvd Fl 7 (90024-3710)
PHONE...............................310 477-3924
Jim Pitrat, *Mng Pt*
Jim Pitrat Mng Pttnr, *Prin*
Norman Greenbaum, *Pt*
William D Simon, *Pt*
David Free, *Pt*
◆ EMP: 120 EST: 1959
SALES (est): 48.95MM
SALES (corp-wide): 48.95MM Privately
Held
Web: www.singerlewak.com
SIC: 8721 8742 Certified public accountant;
Business management consultant

(P-19806)
TEAM COMPANIES LLC (PA)
Also Called: Team Services
2300 W Empire Ave Ste 500 (91504-3350)
PHONE...............................818 558-3261
Greg Smith, *Pr*
An De Vooght, *
Geoffrey Matus, *
EMP: 90 EST: 1992
SALES (est): 22.8MM
SALES (corp-wide): 22.8MM Privately
Held
Web: www.theteamcompanies.com
SIC: 8721 Payroll accounting service

(P-19807)
TGG ACCOUNTING
10188 Telesis Ct Ste 130 (92121-4779)
PHONE...............................760 697-1033
Andrew Ruff, *Pr*
Andrew Ruff, *Pr*
Matt Garrett, *CEO*
EMP: 98 EST: 2013
SALES (est): 2.33MM Privately Held
Web: www.tgg-accounting.com
SIC: 8721 8748 Payroll accounting service;
Business consulting, nec

(P-19808)
**UNIVERSITY CALIFORNIA
IRVINE**
Also Called: Accounting and Fiscal Services
120 Theory Ste 200 (92617-3210)
PHONE...............................949 824-6828
Griselda Duran Optns, *Mgr*
EMP: 80
SALES (corp-wide): 534.4MM Privately
Held
Web: www.uci.edu
SIC: 8721 Accounting, auditing, and
bookkeeping
HQ: University Of California, Irvine
510 Aldrich Hall
Irvine CA
949 824-5011

(P-19809)
**UNIVERSITY CALIFORNIA
IRVINE**
Also Called: UCI Division Plastic Surgery
200 S Manchester Ave Ste 650
(92868-3220)
PHONE...............................714 456-6655
EMP: 80
SALES (corp-wide): 534.4MM Privately
Held
Web: www.uciplasticsurgery.com
SIC: 8721 8221 9411 Accounting, auditing,
and bookkeeping; University;
Administration of educational programs
HQ: University Of California, Irvine
510 Aldrich Hall
Irvine CA
949 824-5011

(P-19810)
WINDES INC (PA)
3780 Kilroy Airport Way Ste 600
(90806-2451)
P.O. Box 87 (90801-0087)
PHONE...............................562 435-1191
John L Dicarlo, *CEO*
Scott J Dionne, *
EMP: 100 EST: 1926
SQ FT: 26,560
SALES (est): 21.23MM
SALES (corp-wide): 21.23MM Privately
Held
Web: www.windes.com
SIC: 8721 Certified public accountant

(P-19811)
WRIGHT FORD YOUNG & CO
16140 Sand Canyon Ave (92618-3715)
PHONE...............................949 910-2727
EMP: 85 EST: 2019
SALES (est): 3.13MM Privately Held
Web: www.cpa-wfy.com
SIC: 8721 Certified public accountant

8731 Commercial Physical Research

(P-19812)
ACEA BIOSCIENCES INC
6779 Mesa Ridge Rd Ste 100 (92121-2996)
PHONE...............................858 724-0928
Xiao Xu, *Pr*
Xiaobo Wang, *
▲ EMP: 85 EST: 2001
SALES (est): 19.76MM
SALES (corp-wide): 6.85B Publicly Held
SIC: 8731 Biotechnical research, commercial
PA: Agilent Technologies, Inc.
5301 Stevens Creek Blvd
Santa Clara CA
800 227-9770

(P-19813)
AEROSPACE CORPORATION
P.O. Box 91337 (90009-1337)
PHONE...............................310 336-7270
EMP: 89
SALES (corp-wide): 1.2B Privately Held
Web: www.aerospace.org
SIC: 8731 Commercial physical research
PA: The Aerospace Corporation
2310 E El Segundo Blvd
El Segundo CA
310 336-5000

(P-19814)
AGENDIA INC
22 Morgan (92618-2022)
PHONE...............................949 540-6300
Mark R Straley, *CEO*
Brian Dow, *CFO*
Kurt Schmidt, *CFO*
Glen Fredenberg, *CFO*
Neil M Barth, *Chief Medical Officer*
EMP: 107 EST: 2008
SALES (est): 33.18MM
SALES (corp-wide): 57.46MM Privately
Held
Web: www.agendia.com
SIC: 8731 Biotechnical research, commercial
PA: Agendia N.V.
Radarweg 60
Amsterdam NH
204621500

(P-19815)
**AGOURON
PHARMACEUTICALS INC**
3550 General Atomics Ct Bldg 9
(92121-1122)
PHONE...............................858 455-3200
Peter Johnson, *Pr*
EMP: 130
SALES (corp-wide): 100.33B Publicly
Held
Web: www.agi.org
SIC: 8731 5122 Biotechnical research,
commercial; Pharmaceuticals
HQ: Agouron Pharmaceuticals, Inc.
10777 Science Center Dr
San Diego CA
858 622-3000

(P-19816)
**AGOURON
PHARMACEUTICALS INC**
3301 N Torrey Pines Ct (92037-1022)
PHONE...............................858 622-3000
Evaristo Cruz, *Mgr*
EMP: 409
SALES (corp-wide): 100.33B Publicly
Held
Web: www.agi.org
SIC: 8731 Biotechnical research, commercial
HQ: Agouron Pharmaceuticals, Inc.
10777 Science Center Dr
San Diego CA
858 622-3000

(P-19817)
ALIMENTIV US INC
10581 Roselle St Ste 110 (92121-1521)
PHONE...............................858 356-5665
Denise Stark, *Prin*
EMP: 86 EST: 2013
SALES (est): 478.35K
SALES (corp-wide): 52.45MM Privately
Held
Web: www.alimentiv.com
SIC: 8731 8011 Biotechnical research,
commercial; General and family practice,
physician/surgeon
PA: Alimentiv Inc.
100 Dundas St Suite 200
London ON
226 270-7868

(P-19818)
**ALLELE BIO &
PHARMACEUTICALS**
6868 Nancy Ridge Dr (92121-2217)
PHONE...............................858 410-0299
Jiwu Wang, *CEO*
EMP: 237
SALES (corp-wide): 8.97MM Privately
Held
Web: www.allelebiotech.com
SIC: 8731 Biotechnical research, commercial
PA: Allele Biotechnology And
Pharmaceuticals, Inc.
6404 Nancy Ridge Dr
San Diego CA
858 587-6645

(P-19819)
AMT DATASOUTH CORP (PA)
Also Called: A M T
3222 Corte Malpaso (93012-8000)
PHONE...............................805 388-5799
Joseph E Eichberger, *Ch Bd*
James Nolan, *VP*
Chris Biggers, *VP*
◆ EMP: 20 EST: 1982
SALES (est): 9.91MM

P R O D U C T S   &   S V C S

SALES (corp-wide): 9.91MM **Privately Held**
Web: www.amtdatasouth.com
SIC: 8731 5045 7379 3577 Computer (hardware) development; Printers, computer ; Computer related maintenance services; Computer peripheral equipment, nec

(P-19820)
ANSUN BIOPHARMA INC
Also Called: Ansun
10045 Mesa Rim Rd (92121-2913)
PHONE...............................858 452-2631
Nancy Chang, *CEO*
George Wang, *
Stanley Lewis, *CMO**
EMP: 25 **EST:** 2003
SQ FT: 12,000
SALES (est): 5.8MM **Privately Held**
Web: www.ansunbiopharma.com
SIC: 8731 2834 Biotechnical research, commercial; Druggists' preparations (pharmaceuticals)

(P-19821)
APPLIED RESEARCH ASSOC INC
10833 Valley View St Ste 250 (90630-5045)
PHONE...............................505 881-8074
Robert H Sues, *Brnch Mgr*
EMP: 99
SALES (corp-wide): 418.64MM **Privately Held**
Web: www.ara.com
SIC: 8731 Commercial physical research
HQ: Applied Research Associates, Inc.
4300 San Mateo Blvd Ne
Albuquerque NM
505 883-3636

(P-19822)
ARCTURUS THERAPEUTICS INC
10628 Science Center Dr Ste 250 (92121-1150)
PHONE...............................858 900-2660
Joseph Payne, *Pr*
Andrew Sassine, *
Steve Hughes, *CDO**
Lance Kurata, *CLO**
EMP: 150 **EST:** 2013
SALES (est): 29.73MM **Privately Held**
Web: www.arcturusrx.com
SIC: 8731 Biotechnical research, commercial

(P-19823)
AVERY CORP
207 N Goode Ave Fl 6 (91203-1364)
PHONE...............................626 304-2000
Dean Scarborough, *Pr*
EMP: 200 **EST:** 1968
SALES (est): 16.14MM
SALES (corp-wide): 9.04B **Publicly Held**
Web: www.avery.com
SIC: 8731 Biological research
PA: Avery Dennison Corporation
8080 Norton Pkwy
Mentor OH
440 534-6000

(P-19824)
BIODURO LLC
72 Fairbanks (92618-1668)
PHONE...............................858 529-6600
Kent M Payne, *Brnch Mgr*
EMP: 264
Web: www.bioduro-sundia.com
SIC: 8731 Biotechnical research, commercial
PA: Bioduro Llc
11011 Torreyana Rd
San Diego CA

(P-19825)
BIODURO LLC (PA)
11011 Torreyana Rd (92121-1104)
PHONE...............................858 529-6600
Kent M Payne, *CEO*
Teo Nee Chuan, *
EMP: 40 **EST:** 2005
SALES (est): 53.39MM **Privately Held**
Web: www.bioduro-sundia.com
SIC: 8731 2834 Biotechnical research, commercial; Medicines, capsuled or ampuled

(P-19826)
BIOLEGEND INC (HQ)
8999 Biolegend Way (92121-2284)
PHONE...............................858 455-9588
Gene Lay, *Pr*
Kent Johnson, *
◆ **EMP:** 103 **EST:** 2002
SQ FT: 75,000
SALES (est): 93.5MM
SALES (corp-wide): 3.31B **Publicly Held**
Web: www.biolegend.com
SIC: 8731 Biotechnical research, commercial
PA: Revvity, Inc.
940 Winter St
Waltham MA
781 663-6900

(P-19827)
BIOLEGEND CNS INC
Also Called: Covance Antibody Services
8999 Biolegend Way (92121-2284)
PHONE...............................781 915-5200
Joseph Herring, *CEO*
Kent Johnson, *CFO*
EMP: 21 **EST:** 1983
SALES (est): 1.07MM
SALES (corp-wide): 3.31B **Publicly Held**
Web: www.biolegend.com
SIC: 8731 2819 Biotechnical research, commercial; Chemicals, reagent grade: refined from technical grade
HQ: Biolegend, Inc.
8999 Biolegend Way
San Diego CA
858 455-9588

(P-19828)
BIOQUIP PRODUCTS INC
2321 E Gladwick St (90220-6209)
PHONE...............................310 667-8800
▲ **EMP:** 30 **EST:** 1947
SALES (est): 4.9MM **Privately Held**
Web: www.bioquip.com
SIC: 8731 3821 Biological research; Laboratory apparatus and furniture

(P-19829)
BIOSPACE INC
Also Called: Inbody
13850 Cerritos Corporate Dr Ste C (90703-2467)
PHONE...............................323 932-6503
Ki Chul Cha, *Pr*
Hak Hee Yun, *
▲ **EMP:** 86 **EST:** 2000
SQ FT: 35,319
SALES (est): 18.64MM **Privately Held**
Web: www.inbody.com
SIC: 8731 3821 Energy research; Calibration tapes, for physical testing machines
PA: Shenzhen Longgang District Baolong Kangxing Fruit Firm
No.419-420, Chishi Gang Xiaoqu Tongfu Road, Longxin Community, B Shenzhen GD

(P-19830)
CIBUS GLOBAL LTD
6455 Nancy Ridge Dr (92121-2249)
PHONE...............................858 450-0008
Peter Beetham, *Pr*
Rory Riggs, *
Gerhard Prante, *
Greg Gocal, *CSO*
Jim Hinrichs, *CFO*
EMP: 134 **EST:** 2001
SQ FT: 53,000
SALES (est): 7.41MM **Privately Held**
Web: www.cibus.com
SIC: 8731 Biotechnical research, commercial

(P-19831)
COI PHARMACEUTICALS INC
11099 N Torrey Pines Rd Ste 290 (92037-1029)
PHONE...............................858 750-4700
Jay Lichter, *CEO*
EMP: 37 **EST:** 2013
SALES (est): 9.33MM **Privately Held**
Web: www.avalonbioventures.com
SIC: 8731 2834 Biological research; Pharmaceutical preparations

(P-19832)
DERMTECH OPERATIONS INC
12340 El Camino Real Ste 200 (92130)
PHONE...............................866 450-4223
EMP: 260 **EST:** 1995
SQ FT: 9,000
SALES (est): 1.72MM
SALES (corp-wide): 14.52MM **Publicly Held**
Web: www.dermtech.com
SIC: 8731 Biotechnical research, commercial
PA: Dermtech, Inc.
12340 El Camino Real
San Diego CA
866 450-4223

(P-19833)
DISNEY RESEARCH PITTSBURGH
532 Paula Ave (91201-2328)
PHONE...............................412 623-1800
EMP: 199 **EST:** 2011
SALES (est): 892.38K
SALES (corp-wide): 88.9B **Publicly Held**
SIC: 8731 Commercial research laboratory
HQ: Walt Disney Imagineering Research & Development, Inc.
1401 Flower St
Glendale CA
818 544-6500

(P-19834)
DUPONT DISPLAYS INC
600 Ward Dr Ste C (93111-2300)
PHONE...............................805 562-5400
Steve Quindlen, *Brnch Mgr*
EMP: 135
SALES (corp-wide): 17.45B **Publicly Held**
Web: www.dupont.com
SIC: 8731 Commercial physical research
HQ: Dupont Displays, Inc.
974 Centre Rd
Wilmington DE

(P-19835)
EBIOSCIENCE INC
Also Called: Affymetrix
10255 Science Center Dr (92121-1117)
PHONE...............................858 642-2058
EMP: 200
Web: www.thermofisher.com

SIC: 8731 Biotechnical research, commercial

(P-19836)
ENVIRONMENTAL SCIENCE ASSOC
Also Called: ESA
626 Wilshire Blvd Ste 1100 (90017-2934)
PHONE...............................213 599-4300
Melissa Gross, *Mgr*
EMP: 135
SALES (corp-wide): 62.52MM **Privately Held**
Web: www.esassoc.com
SIC: 8731 8748 Environmental research; Environmental consultant
PA: Environmental Science Associates
575 Market St Ste 3700
San Francisco CA
415 896-5900

(P-19837)
ESTUDYSITE
752 Medical Center Ct Ste 304 (91911-6658)
PHONE...............................619 955-5246
Tom Wardle, *CEO*
EMP: 109
SQ FT: 4,000
SALES (corp-wide): 34.11MM **Privately Held**
Web: www.velocityclinical.com
SIC: 8731 Biotechnical research, commercial
HQ: Estudysite
5565 Grossmont Center Dr
La Mesa CA
619 704-2750

(P-19838)
F6S NETWORK LIMITED
16935 Encino Hills Dr (91436-4007)
PHONE...............................619 818-4363
Sean Kane, *CEO*
EMP: 80 **EST:** 2020
SALES (est): 1.28MM **Privately Held**
SIC: 8731 Commercial physical research

(P-19839)
FLUXERGY INC (PA)
Also Called: Carter Laboratories
30 Fairbanks (92618-1623)
PHONE...............................949 305-4201
Tej Patel, *Pr*
Ryan Revilla, *
Jonathan Tu, *
EMP: 34 **EST:** 2013
SALES (est): 10.44MM
SALES (corp-wide): 10.44MM **Privately Held**
Web: www.fluxergy.com
SIC: 8731 3841 Biotechnical research, commercial; Diagnostic apparatus, medical

(P-19840)
GARRETT MOTION INC
Garrett Advancing Motion
2525 W 190th St (90504-6002)
PHONE...............................310 512-5424
Craig Balis, *Brnch Mgr*
EMP: 132
SALES (corp-wide): 3.63B **Privately Held**
Web: www.garrettmotion.com
SIC: 8731 Commercial research laboratory
PA: Garrett Motion Inc.
47548 Halyard Dr
Plymouth MI
734 359-5901

▲ = Import ▼ = Export
◆ = Import/Export

(P-19841)
GENERAL ATOMICS
Also Called: Shipping and Receiving
3483 Dunhill St (92121-1200)
P.O. Box 85608 (92186-5608)
PHONE....................858 455-4141
Jene Spence, *Mgr*
EMP: 88
Web: www.ga.com
SIC: 8731 Commercial physical research
HQ: General Atomics
3550 General Atomics Ct
San Diego CA
858 455-2810

(P-19842)
GENERAL ATOMICS
16969 Mesamint St (92127-2407)
PHONE....................858 676-7100
Anthony Navarra, *Co-Vice President*
EMP: 99
Web: www.ga.com
SIC: 8731 Commercial physical research
HQ: General Atomics
3550 General Atomics Ct
San Diego CA
858 455-2810

(P-19843)
GENERAL ATOMICS
Also Called: General Atomics Energy Pdts
4949 Greencraig Ln (92123-1675)
PHONE....................858 455-4000
Joel Ennis, *Genl Mgr*
EMP: 170
Web: www.ga.com
SIC: 8731 7371 3823 Commercial physical
research; Custom computer programming
services; Process control instruments
HQ: General Atomics
3550 General Atomics Ct
San Diego CA
858 455-2810

(P-19844)
GENTEX CORPORATION
Also Called: Western Operations
9859 7th St (91730-5244)
PHONE....................909 481-7667
Robert Mccay, *Brnch Mgr*
EMP: 90
SALES (corp-wide): 97.07MM **Privately
Held**
Web: www.gentexcorp.com
SIC: 8731 3845 3841 Commercial research
laboratory; Electromedical equipment;
Surgical and medical instruments
PA: Gentex Corporation
324 Main St
Simpson PA
570 282-3550

(P-19845)
HALOZYME INC
Also Called: Halozyme Therapeutics
12390 El Camino Real (92130-3190)
PHONE....................858 794-8889
Helen I Torley, *CEO*
Harry J Leonhardt, *Sec*
Laureen Stelzer, *CFO*
EMP: 216 **EST:** 1998
SALES (est): 24.93MM
SALES (corp-wide): 660.12MM **Publicly
Held**
Web: www.halozyme.com
SIC: 8731 Biotechnical research, commercial
PA: Halozyme Therapeutics, Inc.
12390 El Camino Real # 150
San Diego CA
858 794-8889

(P-19846)
HII FLEET SUPPORT GROUP LLC
9444 Balboa Ave Ste 400 (92123-4378)
PHONE....................858 522-6319
Michelle Wurl, *Dir*
EMP: 258
SIC: 8731 8711 Commercial physical
research; Engineering services
HQ: Hii Fleet Support Group Llc
5701 Cleveland St
Virginia Beach VA
757 463-6666

(P-19847)
INOVA DIAGNOSTICS INC (HQ)
Also Called: Werfen
9900 Old Grove Rd (92131-1638)
PHONE....................858 586-9900
Carlos Pascual, *CEO*
Javier Gomez, *
▲ **EMP:** 285 **EST:** 1987
SQ FT: 81,000
SALES (est): 93.05MM **Privately Held**
Web: www.werfen.com
SIC: 8731 2835 Medical research,
commercial; In vitro diagnostics
PA: Werfen S.A.
Plaza Europa, 21 - 23
L'hospitalet De Llobregat B

(P-19848)
INVASIX INC
Also Called: Inmode Aesthetic Solutions
17 Hughes (92618-1902)
PHONE....................855 418-5306
Moshe Mizrahy, *CEO*
Shakil Lakhani, *
Yair Malca, *
EMP: 99 **EST:** 2008
SALES (est): 9.4MM **Privately Held**
Web: www.inmodemd.com
SIC: 8731 5047 Medical research,
commercial; Electro-medical equipment

(P-19849)
ISE CORPORATION
Also Called: I S E
12302 Kerran St (92064-6884)
PHONE....................858 413-1720
▲ **EMP:** 140
SIC: 8731 3621 Commercial physical
research; Electric motor and generator parts

(P-19850)
ISOTIS ORTHOBIOLOGICS INC
2 Goodyear Ste A (92618-2052)
PHONE....................949 595-8710
Keith Valentine, *CEO*
Peter J Arduini, *
Christian S Schade, *
▲ **EMP:** 150 **EST:** 1990
SALES (est): 22.65MM **Privately Held**
Web: www.seaspine.com
SIC: 8731 5047 Biotechnical research,
commercial; Surgical equipment and
supplies
HQ: Isotis International Sarl
C/O Fidulem Sa
Lausanne VD

(P-19851)
KITE PHARMA INC (HQ)
Also Called: Kite, A Gilead Company
2400 Broadway Ste 100 (90404-3058)
PHONE....................310 824-9999
EMP: 99 **EST:** 2009
SQ FT: 20,000
SALES (est): 66.52MM
SALES (corp-wide): 27.28B **Publicly Held**
Web: www.kitepharma.com

SIC: 8731 2836 Biotechnical research,
commercial; Biological products, except
diagnostic
PA: Gilead Sciences, Inc.
333 Lakeside Dr
Foster City CA
650 574-3000

(P-19852)
LEIDOS INC
Also Called: Saic
Naval Air Station (92135)
PHONE....................858 826-6000
EMP: 66
Web: www.leidos.com
SIC: 8731 7373 8742 3679 Commercial
physical research; Systems engineering,
computer related; Training and
development consultant; Recording and
playback apparatus, including phonograph
HQ: Leidos, Inc.
1750 Presidents St
Reston VA
571 526-6000

(P-19853)
LEIDOS INC
4161 Campus Point Ct Stop Em3
(92121-1513)
PHONE....................858 826-9416
Paul Chang, *Mgr*
EMP: 109
Web: www.leidos.com
SIC: 8731 Commercial physical research
HQ: Leidos, Inc.
1750 Presidents St
Reston VA
571 526-6000

(P-19854)
LEIDOS INC
Also Called: Reveal Imaging
2985 Scott St (92081-8339)
PHONE....................858 826-9090
EMP: 130
Web: www.leidos.com
SIC: 8731 3829 3826 Commercial physical
research; Measuring and controlling
devices, nec; Analytical instruments
HQ: Leidos, Inc.
1750 Presidents St
Reston VA
571 526-6000

(P-19855)
LEIDOS INC
Also Called: Saic
10260 Campus Point Dr Bldg C
(92121-1522)
PHONE....................703 676-4300
Jere Drummond, *Dir*
EMP: 107
Web: www.leidos.com
SIC: 8731 7373 Commercial physical
research; Systems software development
services
HQ: Leidos, Inc.
1750 Presidents St
Reston VA
571 526-6000

(P-19856)
LEIDOS ENGRG & SCIENCES LLC
1330 30th St Ste A (92154-3471)
PHONE....................619 542-3130
Karen Parizeau, *Mgr*
EMP: 129
SIC: 8731 Natural resource research
HQ: Leidos Engineering & Sciences, Llc
9737 Washingtonian Blvd

Gaithersburg MD
301 240-7000

(P-19857)
M&B SCIENCES INC
4445 Eastgate Mall (92121-1979)
PHONE....................858 812-8735
Eddilisa Martin, *CEO*
EMP: 20 **EST:** 2021
SALES (est): 1.28MM **Privately Held**
Web: www.mbsciences.com
SIC: 8731 7372 Biotechnical research,
commercial; Prepackaged software

(P-19858)
MARAVAI LF SCNCES HOLDINGS LLC (HQ)
10770 Wateridge Cir Ste 100 (92121)
PHONE....................650 697-3600
Eric Tardif, *Pr*
EMP: 148 **EST:** 2014
SALES (est): 32.29MM
SALES (corp-wide): 883MM **Publicly Held**
Web: www.maravai.com
SIC: 8731 Commercial physical research
PA: Maravai Lifesciences Holdings, Inc.
10770 Wtridge Cir Ste 200
San Diego CA
858 546-0004

(P-19859)
MEMORIAL HEALTHTEC LABRATORIES
9920 Talbert Ave (92708-5153)
PHONE....................714 962-4677
Marcia Manker, *Mgr*
EMP: 2447
Web: www.memorialcare.org
SIC: 8731 Commercial physical research
HQ: Memorial Healthtec Labratories Inc
2865 Atlantic Ave Ste 203
Long Beach CA

(P-19860)
MERCURY MISSION SYSTEMS LLC
20701 Manhattan Pl (90501-1829)
PHONE....................310 320-3088
Mark Bruington, *Brnch Mgr*
EMP: 22
SALES (corp-wide): 973.88MM **Publicly
Held**
Web: www.mrcy.com
SIC: 8731 3812 7299 Commercial research
laboratory; Search and navigation
equipment; Information services, consumer
HQ: Mercury Mission Systems, Llc
50 Minuteman Rd
Andover MA
978 256-1300

(P-19861)
MOTECH AMERICAS LLC
Also Called: GE Energy
1300 Valley Vista Dr Ste 207 (91765-3940)
PHONE....................302 451-7500
▲ **EMP:** 320
Web: www.motech-americas.com
SIC: 8731 3674 Energy research; Solar cells

(P-19862)
MYST THERAPEUTICS INC
570 Westwood Plz Bldg 114 (90095-8352)
PHONE....................415 516-8450
Sammy Farah, *CEO*
EMP: 93 **EST:** 2019
SALES (est): 485.83K
SALES (corp-wide): 5.25MM **Publicly
Held**

SIC: **8731** Medical research, commercial
PA: Turnstone Biologics Corp.
9310 Athena Cir Ste 300
La Jolla CA
347 897-5988

(P-19863)
NANTCELL INC
9920 Jefferson Blvd (90232-3506)
PHONE.................................562 397-3639
Richard Adcock, *CEO*
EMP: 385 EST: 2014
SALES (est): 157.41K **Publicly Held**
Web: www.immunitybio.com
SIC: **8731** Biological research
PA: Immunitybio, Inc.
3530 John Hopkins Ct
San Diego CA

(P-19864)
NAVIGATE BIOPHARMA SVCS INC
1890 Rutherford Rd (92008-7326)
PHONE.................................866 992-4939
Kevin Zou, *CEO*
EMP: 180 EST: 2016
SALES (est): 21.16MM **Privately Held**
Web: www.navigatebp.com
SIC: **8731** Biotechnical research, commercial
HQ: Novartis Finance Corporation
1 Health Plz
East Hanover NJ

(P-19865)
NORTHROP GRMMN SPCE & MSSN SYS
Space Technology Sector
862 E Hospitality Ln (92408-3530)
PHONE.................................909 382-6800
FAX: 909 382-6249
EMP: 200
SIC: **8731** 7373 Commercial physical
research; Computer integrated systems
design
HQ: Northrop Grumman Space & Mission
Systems Corp.
6379 San Ignacio Ave
San Jose CA
703 280-2900

(P-19866)
NOVARTIS INST FOR FNCTNAL GNMI
Also Called: Nibr
10675 John J Hopkins Dr (92121-1127)
PHONE.................................858 812-1500
Hans Seidel, *Pr*
Timothy Smith, *VP*
Karl Olsen, *CFO*
Robert Downs, *Ex Dir*
Daniel Vasella Md, *Prin*
EMP: 956 EST: 1998
SALES (est): 49.86MM **Privately Held**
Web: www.gnf.org
SIC: **8731** Biotechnical research, commercial
HQ: Novartis Institutes For Biomedical
Research, Inc.
700 Main St
Cambridge MA
617 777-8276

(P-19867)
NOYMED CORP
1101 N Pacific Ave Ste 303 (91202)
PHONE.................................800 224-2090
Armen Margaryan, *CEO*
Tatevik Simonyan, *
EMP: 130 EST: 2020
SALES (est): 8MM **Privately Held**

Web: www.noymed.com
SIC: **8731** Commercial physical research

(P-19868)
ONE LAMBDA INC (HQ)
22801 Roscoe Blvd (91304-3200)
PHONE.................................747 494-1000
Seth H Hoogasian, *CEO*
George M Ayoub, *
Don Arii, *
James Keegan, *
Emiko Terasaki, *Corporate Secretary*
EMP: 82 EST: 1984
SQ FT: 53,000
SALES (est): 47.83MM
SALES (corp-wide): 44.91B **Publicly Held**
Web: www.thermofisher.com
SIC: **8731** Biotechnical research, commercial
PA: Thermo Fisher Scientific Inc.
168 3rd Ave
Waltham MA
781 622-1000

(P-19869)
OPTO-KNOWLEDGE SYSTEMS INC
Also Called: Optoknowledge
19805 Hamilton Ave (90502-1341)
PHONE.................................310 756-0520
Christopher Holmes Parker, *Prin*
Ilana Gat, *
Joel Gat, *
EMP: 29 EST: 1991
SQ FT: 14,000
SALES (est): 5.74MM **Privately Held**
Web: www.oksi.ai
SIC: **8731** 3827 Engineering laboratory,
except testing; Optical instruments and
lenses

(P-19870)
PAREXEL INTERNATIONAL CORP
Also Called: PAREXEL INTERNATIONAL
CORPORATION
1560 E Chevy Chase Dr Ste 140
(91206-4105)
PHONE.................................818 254-7076
Mollie Barrett, *Dir*
EMP: 108
SALES (corp-wide): 2.44B **Privately Held**
Web: www.parexel.com
SIC: **8731** Biotechnical research, commercial
HQ: Parexel International (Ma) Corporation
275 Grove St Ste 3101
Auburndale MA
617 454-9300

(P-19871)
PHARMARON INC
6 Venture Ste 250 (92618-7354)
PHONE.................................949 788-0586
Boliang Lou, *Owner*
EMP: 18585
Web: www.pharmaron.com
SIC: **8731** Biotechnical research, commercial
HQ: Pharmaron, Inc.
201 E Jefferson St # 304
Louisville KY
502 569-1047

(P-19872)
PROSCIENTO INC (PA)
855 Third Ave Ste 3340 (91911-1350)
PHONE.................................619 427-1300
Marcus Hompesch, *CEO*
Linda Morrow, *COO*
Markus Hofmann, *CFO*
Christian Weyer, *Chief Development Officer*
EMP: 170 EST: 2002

SQ FT: 20,000
SALES (est): 30.74MM
SALES (corp-wide): 30.74MM **Privately
Held**
Web: www.prosciento.com
SIC: **8731** Biotechnical research, commercial

(P-19873)
REVEAL BIOSCIENCES INC
6760 Top Gun St Ste 110 (92121-4152)
PHONE.................................858 274-3663
Claire Weston, *Pr*
EMP: 25 EST: 2012
SALES (est): 2.56MM **Privately Held**
Web: www.revealbio.com
SIC: **8731** 2835 Biotechnical research,
commercial; Cytology and histology
diagnostic agents

(P-19874)
SEMINIS INC (DH)
2700 Camino Del Sol (93030-7967)
PHONE.................................805 485-7317
◆ EMP: 300 EST: 1995
SALES (est): 128.3MM
SALES (corp-wide): 52.7B **Privately Held**
Web: vegetables.bayer.com
SIC: **8731** 8742 2099 Agricultural research;
Productivity improvement consultant; Food
preparations, nec
HQ: Bayer Northern Production Co., Llc
800 N Lindbergh Blvd
Saint Louis MO
314 694-1000

(P-19875)
SEQUENOM INC (HQ)
3595 John Hopkins Ct (92121-1121)
PHONE.................................858 202-9000
EMP: 80 EST: 1994
SALES (est): 43.43MM **Publicly Held**
Web: womenshealth.labcorp.com
SIC: **8731** Biological research
PA: Laboratory Corporation Of America
Holdings
358 S Main St
Burlington NC

(P-19876)
TAE TECHNOLOGIES INC (PA)
Also Called: Tae Technologies
19631 Pauling (92610-2607)
P.O. Box 7010 (92688-7010)
PHONE.................................949 830-2117
Michl Binderbauer, *CEO*
Mark J Lewis, *Pr*
EMP: 155 EST: 2002
SALES (est): 60.78MM
SALES (corp-wide): 60.78MM **Privately
Held**
Web: www.tae.com
SIC: **8731** Energy research

(P-19877)
TALON THERAPEUTICS INC
18200 Von Karman Ave Ste 700
(92612-1023)
PHONE.................................949 788-6700
Joseph W Turgeon, *CEO*
EMP: 89 EST: 2002
SQ FT: 50,000
SALES (est): 5.11MM **Privately Held**
SIC: **8731** 2834 Commercial physical
research; Pharmaceutical preparations
PA: Spectrum Pharmaceuticals, Inc.
2 Atlantic Ave Fl 6
Boston MA

(P-19878)
TANNER RESEARCH INC
1851 Huntington Dr (91010-2635)
PHONE.................................626 471-9700
EMP: 20 EST: 1988
SALES (est): 4.82MM **Privately Held**
Web: www.tanner.com
SIC: **8731** 5045 3549 7371 Computer
(hardware) development; Computer
software; Assembly machines, including
robotic; Computer software development

(P-19879)
TANVEX BIOPHARMA USA INC (PA)
Also Called: L J B
10394 Pacific Center Ct (92121-4340)
PHONE.................................858 210-4100
Allen Chao, *CEO*
Chi-chuan Chen, *Pr*
EMP: 134 EST: 1984
SALES (est): 49.54MM
SALES (corp-wide): 49.54MM **Privately
Held**
Web: www.tanvex.com
SIC: **8731** Biotechnical research, commercial

(P-19880)
TELEDYNE SCENTIFIC IMAGING LLC
Also Called: Teledyne Judson Technologies
5212 Verdugo Way (93012-8662)
PHONE.................................805 373-4979
James Beletic, *Pr*
EMP: 91
SQ FT: 54,295
SALES (corp-wide): 5.46B **Publicly Held**
Web: www.teledyne-si.com
SIC: **8731** Commercial physical research
HQ: Teledyne Scientific & Imaging, Llc
1049 Camino Dos Rios
Thousand Oaks CA

(P-19881)
TELEDYNE SCENTIFIC IMAGING LLC (HQ)
Also Called: Teledyne Scientific Company
1049 Camino Dos Rios (91360-2362)
PHONE.................................805 373-4545
EMP: 125 EST: 1962
SQ FT: 161,000
SALES (est): 97.3MM
SALES (corp-wide): 5.46B **Publicly Held**
Web: www.teledyne-si.com
SIC: **8731** 8732 8733 Commercial physical
research; Commercial nonphysical research
; Noncommercial research organizations
PA: Teledyne Technologies Inc
1049 Camino Dos Rios
Thousand Oaks CA
805 373-4545

(P-19882)
THE SALK INSTITUTE FOR BIOLOGICAL STUDIES SAN DIEGO CALIFORNIA
Also Called: SALK INSTITUTE, THE
10010 N Torrey Pines Rd (92037-1002)
P.O. Box 85800 (92186-5800)
PHONE.................................858 453-4100
EMP: 1100 EST: 1960
SALES (est): 162.33MM **Privately Held**
Web: www.salk.edu
SIC: **8731** Commercial physical research

(P-19883)
TISSUE-GROWN CORPORATION
15245 W Telegraph Rd (93060-3039)

PHONE..............................805 525-1975
Carolyn Sluis, *Pr*
◆ **EMP:** 85 **EST:** 1986
SQ FT: 10,500
SALES (est): 2MM **Privately Held**
Web: www.tissuegrown.com
SIC: 8731 Biotechnical research, commercial

(P-19884)
TNK THERAPEUTICS INC (HQ)
9380 Judicial Dr (92121-3830)
PHONE..............................858 210-3700
Henry Ji, *CEO*
EMP: 191 **EST:** 2015
SALES (est): 9.07MM
SALES (corp-wide): 62.84MM **Publicly Held**
Web: www.sorrentotherapeutics.com
SIC: 8731 Medical research, commercial
PA: Sorrento Therapeutics, Inc.
4955 Directors Pl Ste 100
San Diego CA
858 203-4100

(P-19885)
TRILINK BIOTECHNOLOGIES LLC
10770 Wateridge Cir Ste 200 (92121)
PHONE..............................800 863-6801
EMP: 159 **EST:** 1996
SQ FT: 40,000
SALES (est): 44.23MM
SALES (corp-wide): 883MM **Publicly Held**
Web: www.trilinkbiotech.com
SIC: 8731 8748 Biotechnical research, commercial; Test development and evaluation service
PA: Maravai Lifesciences Holdings, Inc.
10770 Wtridge Cir Ste 200
San Diego CA
858 546-0004

(P-19886)
TURNING POINT THERAPEUTICS INC
10300 Campus Point Dr (92121-1504)
PHONE..............................858 926-5251
Athena Countouriotis, *Pr*
Andrew Partridge, *CCO*
Annette North, *Ex VP*
Brian Baker, *VP Fin*
EMP: 87 **EST:** 2013
SALES (est): 30.83MM
SALES (corp-wide): 46.16B **Publicly Held**
Web: www.bms.com
SIC: 8731 Biotechnical research, commercial
PA: Bristol-Myers Squibb Company
430 E 29th St Fl 14
New York NY
212 546-4000

(P-19887)
UNIVERSITY CALIFORNIA IRVINE
Also Called: Henry Samueli School Engrg
2220 Engineering Gtwy (92697-0001)
PHONE..............................949 824-2819
Doctor G P Li, *Dir*
EMP: 604
SALES (corp-wide): 534.4MM **Privately Held**
Web: www.uci.edu
SIC: 8731 8221 9411 Electronic research; University; Administration of educational programs
HQ: University Of Califomia, Irvine
510 Aldrich Hall
Irvine CA
949 824-5011

(P-19888)
VIRIDOS INC
250 W Schrimpf Rd (92233-9745)
PHONE..............................858 754-2900
EMP: 99
Web: www.viridos.com
SIC: 8731 Biotechnical research, commercial
HQ: Viridos, Inc.
11149 N Torrey Pines Rd
La Jolla CA

(P-19889)
WILDCAT DISCOVERY TECH INC
6255 Ferris Sq Ste A (92121-3232)
PHONE..............................858 550-1980
Mark Gresser, *CEO*
Mark Grasser, *Pr*
Steven Kaye, *Prin*
Jon Jacobs, *VP*
Laura Marion, *CFO*
EMP: 59 **EST:** 2006
SALES (est): 10.05MM **Privately Held**
Web: www.wildcatdiscovery.com
SIC: 8731 2819 Biotechnical research, commercial; Industrial inorganic chemicals, nec

---

8732 Commercial Nonphysical Research

(P-19890)
CHASE GROUP LLC
Also Called: Simi Vly Care & Rehabilitation
5270 E Los Angeles Ave (93063-4137)
PHONE..............................805 522-9155
Phil Chase, *Mgr*
EMP: 295
Web: www.chasegroup.us
SIC: 8732 8742 Research services, except laboratory; Management consulting services
PA: The Chase Group Llc
5374 Long Shadow Ct
Westlake Village CA

(P-19891)
DAVIS RESEARCH LLC
26610 Agoura Rd Ste 240 (91302-1954)
PHONE..............................818 591-2408
William A Davis Iii, *Managing Member*
EMP: 150 **EST:** 1970
SALES (est): 14.07MM **Privately Held**
Web: www.davisresearch.com
SIC: 8732 Market analysis or research

(P-19892)
GENERAL ATOMICS (HQ)
3550 General Atomics Ct (92121-1194)
P.O. Box 85608 (92186-5608)
PHONE..............................858 455-2810
J Neal Blue, *Pr*
Linden Blue, *
Liam Kelly, *
Robert S Forney, *
Jeffrey Quintenz, *
▲ **EMP:** 2015 **EST:** 1955
SQ FT: 1,000,000
SALES (est): 1.2B **Privately Held**
Web: www.ga.com
SIC: 8732 Commercial sociological and educational research
PA: General Atomic Technologies Corporation
3550 General Atomics Ct
San Diego CA

(P-19893)
GFK ETILIZE INC
34145 Pacific Coast Hwy 636 (92629-2808)

PHONE..............................888 608-1212
Azhar Hameed, *Brnch Mgr*
EMP: 87
Web: www.etilize.com
SIC: 8732 Market analysis or research
HQ: Gfk Etilize, Inc.
18662 Macarthur Blvd # 20
Irvine CA

(P-19894)
HENKEL US OPERATIONS CORP
14000 Jamboree Rd (92606-1730)
PHONE..............................714 368-8000
Jim Heaton, *Brnch Mgr*
EMP: 104
SALES (corp-wide): 23.26B **Privately Held**
Web: www.henkel.com
SIC: 8732 Business research service
HQ: Henkel Us Operations Corporation
1 Henkel Way
Rocky Hill CT
860 571-5100

(P-19895)
HI LLC (PA)
Also Called: Kernel
10361 Jefferson Blvd (90232-3511)
PHONE..............................757 655-4113
Bryan Johnson, *Managing Member*
EMP: 90 **EST:** 2016
SQ FT: 3,500
SALES (est): 4.23MM
SALES (corp-wide): 4.23MM **Privately Held**
SIC: 8732 Business research service

(P-19896)
HIGH DSERT PRTNR IN ACDMIC EXC
Also Called: Lewis Center For Eductl RES
17500 Mana Rd (92307-2181)
PHONE..............................760 946-5414
Lisa Lamb, *CEO*
Teresa Dowd, *
EMP: 350 **EST:** 1992
SQ FT: 35,000
SALES (est): 35.41MM **Privately Held**
Web: www.lewiscenter.org
SIC: 8732 Commercial nonphysical research

(P-19897)
HONDA R&D AMERICAS LLC
Also Called: Honda
1900 Harpers Way (90501-1521)
PHONE..............................310 781-5500
▲ **EMP:** 1537
Web: www.hondaresearch.com
SIC: 8732 Market analysis or research

(P-19898)
HRL LABORATORIES LLC
Also Called: Hughes Research Laboratories
3011 Malibu Canyon Rd (90265-4797)
PHONE..............................310 317-5000
Penrose Albright, *Pr*
Roger Gronwald, *CFO*
◆ **EMP:** 647 **EST:** 1997
SQ FT: 250,000
SALES (est): 106.52MM **Privately Held**
Web: www.hrl.com
SIC: 8732 Commercial sociological and educational research

(P-19899)
INFORMA RESEARCH SERVICES INC (HQ)
26565 Agoura Rd Ste 300 (91302-1958)
PHONE..............................818 880-8877
Michael E Adler, *Pr*

Charles A Miwa, *
Lori Jomsky, *
EMP: 193 **EST:** 1993
SQ FT: 16,000
SALES (est): 50.64MM
SALES (corp-wide): 2.72B **Privately Held**
Web: financialintelligence.informa.com
SIC: 8732 Market analysis or research
PA: Informa Plc
5 Howick Place
London
208 052-0400

(P-19900)
INSTANTLY INC
Also Called: Usamp
16501 Ventura Blvd # 300 (91436-2067)
PHONE..............................866 872-4006
EMP: 200
SIC: 8732 Market analysis or research

(P-19901)
INTERVIEWING SERVICE AMER LLC (PA)
Also Called: ISA
15400 Sherman Way Ste 400 (91406-4211)
PHONE..............................818 989-1044
Michael Halberstam, *Ch*
Tony Kretzmer, *
John Fitzpatrick, *
Vicky Agalsoff, *
EMP: 250 **EST:** 1982
SQ FT: 20,000
SALES (est): 21.54MM
SALES (corp-wide): 21.54MM **Privately Held**
Web: www.isacorp.com
SIC: 8732 Market analysis or research

(P-19902)
IPSOS OTX CORPORATION (HQ)
300 Corporate Pointe Ste 500 (90230)
PHONE..............................310 736-3400
Shelley Zalis, *CEO*
Jeff Dean, *
EMP: 210 **EST:** 2003
SALES (est): 31.23MM
SALES (corp-wide): 392.59K **Privately Held**
Web: www.ipsosotx.com
SIC: 8732 Market analysis or research
PA: Ipsos
35 Rue Du Val De Marne
Paris
141989000

(P-19903)
IQVIA INC (DH)
Also Called: SK&a
2601 Main St Ste 650 (92614-4228)
PHONE..............................866 267-4479
David Escalante Junior, *Pr*
Al M Cosentino, *
Jaqueline Aguilera, *
Albert Chang, *
EMP: 87 **EST:** 1998
SQ FT: 12,000
SALES (est): 11.88MM
SALES (corp-wide): 8.5MM **Privately Held**
Web: www.onekeydata.com
SIC: 8732 Market analysis or research
HQ: Cegedim Inc.
1425 Us Highway 206
Bedminster NJ

(P-19904)
JD POWER AND ASSOCIATES INC
2625 Townsgate Rd Ste 100 (91361-5737)
PHONE..............................805 418-8000

PRODUCTS & SVCS

Dan Sullivan, *Prin*
EMP: 123 **EST:** 2018
SALES (est): 5.2MM **Privately Held**
Web: www.jdpower.com
SIC: 8732 Commercial nonphysical research

(P-19905)
LUTH RESEARCH INC (PA)
Also Called: Surveysavvy.com
404 Camino Del Rio S Ste 505 (92108)
P.O. Box 12557 (92112-3557)
PHONE..............................619 234-5884
Roseanne Luth, *Pr*
Charles Rosen, *
EMP: 305 **EST:** 1977
SALES (est): 46.58MM
SALES (corp-wide): 46.58MM **Privately Held**
Web: www.luthresearch.com
SIC: 8732 Market analysis or research

(P-19906)
MATERIAL HOLDINGS LLC (PA)
Also Called: Lrw Group
1900 Avenue Of The Stars Ste 1600
(90067-4606)
PHONE..............................310 553-0550
David Sackman, *Ch*
Arnold Fishman, *
Cathy Lindquist, *
EMP: 140 **EST:** 1973
SQ FT: 24,560
SALES (est): 65.39MM
SALES (corp-wide): 65.39MM **Privately Held**
Web: www.lrwonline.com
SIC: 8732 Market analysis or research

(P-19907)
NATIONAL RESEARCH GROUP INC
Also Called: National Research Group
12101 Bluff Creek Dr (90094-2627)
PHONE..............................323 406-6200
Jon Penn, *CEO*
Jeff Hall, *
James Mcnamara, *Ex VP*
Jenny Swisher, *
Ray Ydoyaga, *
EMP: 278 **EST:** 1977
SALES (est): 22.69MM
SALES (corp-wide): 2.69B **Publicly Held**
SIC: 8732 Market analysis or research
HQ: A + N Real Estate & Business
  Management Corporation
  1 World Trade Ctr
  New York NY

(P-19908)
NITTO DENKO TECHNICAL CORP
Also Called: Nitto
501 Via Del Monte (92058-1251)
PHONE..............................760 435-7011
Kenji Matsumoto, *Pr*
EMP: 99 **EST:** 1985
SALES (est): 16.11MM **Privately Held**
Web: www.ndtcorp.com
SIC: 8732 3089 3462 Research services,
  except laboratory; Automotive parts, plastic;
  Automotive and internal combustion engine
  forgings
PA: Nitto Denko Corporation
  4-20, Ofukacho, Kita-Ku
  Osaka OSK

(P-19909)
ORANGE CNTY NRPSYCHTRIC RES CT

Also Called: NRC Research Institute
1400 S Grand Ave Ste 611 (90015-3068)
PHONE..............................213 992-9216
EMP: 90
SALES (corp-wide): 4.63MM **Privately Held**
Web: www.nrcresearch.com
SIC: 8732 Commercial nonphysical research
PA: Orange County Neuropsychiatric
  Research Center, Llc
  1010 W Chapman Ave
  Orange CA
  714 289-1100

(P-19910)
PROSEARCH STRATEGIES LLC
3250 Wilshire Blvd Ste 301 (90010-1577)
PHONE..............................877 447-7291
Julia Kim Hasenzahl, *CEO*
EMP: 132 **EST:** 2005
SALES (est): 17.82MM **Privately Held**
Web: www.prosearchstrategies.com
SIC: 8732 Research services, except
  laboratory

(P-19911)
QUINTILES PACIFIC INCORPORATED
10201 Wateridge Cir Ste 300 (92121)
PHONE..............................858 552-3400
EMP: 371
SIC: 8732 Market analysis or research
HQ: Quintiles Pacific Incorporated
  448 E Middlefield Rd
  Mountain View CA
  650 567-2000

(P-19912)
SOLEIL COMMUNICATIONS LLC
Also Called: Prodata Research
2655 Camino Del Rio N Ste 110 (92108)
PHONE..............................619 624-2888
Michael Gehrig, *Managing Member*
EMP: 118 **EST:** 2002
SALES (est): 818.93K
SALES (corp-wide): 47.43MM **Privately Held**
SIC: 8732 Market analysis or research
PA: The Welk Group Inc
  11400 W Olympic Blvd # 1450
  Los Angeles CA
  760 749-3000

(P-19913)
STREAMELEMENTS INC
11400 W Olympic Blvd (90064-1550)
PHONE..............................323 928-7848
Udi Hoffmann, *Managing Member*
Udi Hoffmann, *CFO*
EMP: 99 **EST:** 2017
SALES (est): 1.72MM **Privately Held**
SIC: 8732 Commercial nonphysical research

(P-19914)
UNIVERSITY CAL RIVERSIDE
Also Called: Uc Riverside RES Economic Dev
1160 University Ave (92507-4545)
PHONE..............................951 827-4801
Stan Fletcher, *Dir*
EMP: 232
SALES (corp-wide): 534.4MM **Privately Held**
Web: www.ucr.edu
SIC: 8732 8221 9411 Economic research;
  University; Administration of educational
  programs
HQ: University Of California, Riverside,
  Alumni Association
  900 University Ave
  Riverside CA
  951 827-1012

(P-19915)
XDBS CORPORATION
Also Called: Xdbsb2b
3501 Jack Northrop Ave (90250-4433)
PHONE..............................844 932-7356
Julie Strong, *CEO*
Kartik Anand, *
EMP: 192 **EST:** 2012
SQ FT: 4,000
SALES (est): 1.18MM **Privately Held**
Web: www.xdbsworldwide.com
SIC: 8732 7389 5963 8742 Survey service:
  marketing, location, etc.; Telemarketing
  services; Direct sales, telemarketing; Sales
  (including sales management) consultant

(P-19916)
ZEFR INC
Also Called: Movieclips.com
4101 Redwood Ave (90066-5603)
PHONE..............................310 392-3555
Rich Raddon, *CEO*
Toby Byrne, *
EMP: 437 **EST:** 2010
SALES (est): 27.52MM **Privately Held**
Web: www.zefr.com
SIC: 8732 7371 Market analysis, business,
  and economic research; Software
  programming applications

8733 Noncommercial Research Organizations

(P-19917)
AMERICAN REGENT INC
536 Vanguard Way (92821-3932)
PHONE..............................714 989-5058
Donald F Hodgson, *Brnch Mgr*
EMP: 40
Web: www.americanregent.com
SIC: 8733 2834 Noncommercial research
  organizations; Pharmaceutical preparations
HQ: American Regent, Inc.
  5 Ramsay Rd
  Shirley NY
  631 924-4000

(P-19918)
BIOSPLICE THERAPEUTICS INC
9360 Towne Centre Dr (92121-3057)
PHONE..............................858 926-2900
Osman Kibar, *CEO*
EMP: 82 **EST:** 2007
SALES (est): 11.2MM **Privately Held**
Web: www.biosplice.com
SIC: 8733 Medical research

(P-19919)
BRENTWOOD BMDICAL RES INST INC
11301 Wilshire Blvd Bldg 114 (90073-1003)
P.O. Box 25027 (90025-0027)
PHONE..............................310 312-1554
Kenneth Hickman, *CEO*
Thoyd Ellis, *
EMP: 130 **EST:** 1988
SQ FT: 1,500
SALES (est): 4.85MM **Privately Held**
Web: www.brentwoodresearch.org
SIC: 8733 Medical research

(P-19920)
CALIFORNIA INSTITUTE FOR BIOMEDICAL RESEARCH
Also Called: California Institute For
11119 N Torrey Pines Rd (92037-1046)
PHONE..............................858 242-1000
EMP: 110

Web: www.calibr.org
SIC: 8733 Medical research

(P-19921)
CALIFORNIA INSTITUTE TECH
Also Called: Jet Propulsion Laboratory
4800 Oak Grove Dr (91109-8001)
PHONE..............................818 354-9154
Michael Watkins, *Dir*
EMP: 6000
SALES (corp-wide): 3.31B **Privately Held**
Web: www.caltech.edu
SIC: 8733 Research institute
PA: California Institute Of Technology
  1200 E California Blvd
  Pasadena CA
  626 395-6811

(P-19922)
CARNEGIE INSTITUTION WASH
Also Called: Observatories of The Carnegie
813 Santa Barbara St (91101-1232)
PHONE..............................626 577-1122
Wendy L Freedman, *Dir*
EMP: 100
SQ FT: 24,075
SALES (corp-wide): 164.74MM **Privately Held**
Web: obs.carnegiescience.edu
SIC: 8733 7999 Scientific research agency;
  Observation tower operation
PA: Carnegie Institution Of Washington
  1530 P St Nw
  Washington DC
  202 387-6400

(P-19923)
CHILDRENS INST LOS ANGELES (PA)
2121 W Temple St (90026-4915)
PHONE..............................213 385-5100
Bradley Myslinski, *Pr*
Martine Singer, *
Eugene Straub, *
EMP: 150 **EST:** 2011
SALES (est): 392.05K
SALES (corp-wide): 392.05K **Privately Held**
Web: www.childrensinstitute.org
SIC: 8733 Noncommercial research
  organizations

(P-19924)
DOHENY EYE INSTITUTE (PA)
150 N Orange Grove Blvd (91103-3534)
PHONE..............................323 342-7120
EMP: 100 **EST:** 1947
SALES (est): 20.91MM
SALES (corp-wide): 20.91MM **Privately Held**
Web: www.doheny.org
SIC: 8733 Medical research

(P-19925)
DXTERITY DIAGNOSTICS INC (PA)
19500 S Rancho Way Ste 116
(90220-6012)
PHONE..............................310 537-7857
Doctor Bob Terbrueggen, *CEO*
Bill Coty, *
Jim Healy, *
Aviva Jacobs, *
Brett Swansiger, *Chief Commercialization Officer*
EMP: 39 **EST:** 2006
SQ FT: 14,000
SALES (est): 8.45MM **Privately Held**
Web: www.dxterity.com

SIC: **8733** 8071 2835 Medical research;
Medical laboratories; Diagnostic substances

(P-19926)
HEALTHPOINT CAPITAL LLC (PA)
9920 Pacific Heights Blvd Ste 150 (92121)
PHONE...............................212 935-7780
John H Foster, *CEO*
Mike Mogul, *
EMP: 160 **EST:** 2002
SALES (est): 8.27MM
SALES (corp-wide): 8.27MM **Privately Held**
Web: www.healthpointcapital.com
SIC: 8733 Medical research

(P-19927)
HISAMITSU PHARMACEUTICAL CO INC
2730 Loker Ave W (92010-6603)
PHONE...............................760 931-1756
EMP: 626
SIC: 8733 Medical research

(P-19928)
HOUSE RESEARCH INSTITUTE
2100 W 3rd St Ste 500 (90057-1922)
PHONE...............................213 353-7012
EMP: 160
SIC: 8733 Medical research

(P-19929)
INSTITUTE FOR DEFENSE ANALYSES
Center For Communications RES
4320 Westerra Ct (92121-1969)
PHONE...............................858 622-5439
Joe Buhler, *Mgr*
EMP: 170
SALES (corp-wide): 311.3MM **Privately Held**
Web: www.ida.org
SIC: 8733 Research institute
PA: Institute For Defense Analyses Inc
730 E Glebe Rd
Alexandria VA
703 845-2000

(P-19930)
J CRAIG VENTER INSTITUTE INC (PA)
4120 Capricorn Ln (92037-3498)
PHONE...............................301 795-7000
J Craig Venter, *CEO*
Karen Nelson, *
Reid Adler, *
Kathleen L Mattis, *
Robert Friedman, *
EMP: 275 **EST:** 1993
SQ FT: 125,000
SALES (est): 25.45MM
SALES (corp-wide): 25.45MM **Privately Held**
Web: www.jcvi.org
SIC: 8733 8731 Research institute;
Biological research

(P-19931)
JWCH INSTITUTE INC
6912 Ajax Ave (90201-4057)
PHONE...............................323 562-5813
Annabel Munoz, *Mgr*
EMP: 178
SALES (corp-wide): 112.81MM **Privately Held**
Web: www.jwchinstitute.org
SIC: 8733 Noncommercial research organizations

PA: Jwch Institute, Inc.
5650 Jillson St
Commerce CA
323 477-1171

(P-19932)
JWCH INSTITUTE INC
12360 Firestone Blvd (90650-4324)
PHONE...............................562 281-0306
Oyamendan Itohan, *COO*
EMP: 178
SALES (corp-wide): 112.81MM **Privately Held**
Web: www.jwchinstitute.org
SIC: 8733 Noncommercial research organizations
PA: Jwch Institute, Inc.
5650 Jillson St
Commerce CA
323 477-1171

(P-19933)
LA JOLLA INST FOR IMMUNOLOGY
Also Called: La Jolla Inst For Allrgy Immnl
9420 Athena Cir (92037-1387)
PHONE...............................858 752-6500
Erica Ollmann Saphire, *Pr*
Stephen Wilson Ph.d., *Ex VP*
Michael Dollar, *CFO*
Eric Zwisler, *Ch Bd*
Skip Carpowich, *CFO*
EMP: 400 **EST:** 1988
SQ FT: 87,000
SALES (est): 102.02MM **Privately Held**
Web: www.lji.org
SIC: 8733 8731 Medical research;
Biotechnical research, commercial

(P-19934)
LUNDQUIST INSTITUTE FOR BIOMEDICAL INNOVATION AT HARBOR-UCLA MEDICAL CENTER
Also Called: LA BIOMED
1124 W Carson St (90502-2006)
PHONE...............................877 452-2674
EMP: 800 **EST:** 1952
SALES (est): 85.15MM **Privately Held**
Web: www.lundquist.org
SIC: 8733 Medical research

(P-19935)
MIND RESEARCH INSTITUTE
Also Called: Music Intllgnce Neuro Dev Inst
5281 California Ave Ste 300 (92617-3219)
PHONE...............................949 345-8700
Brett Woudenberg, *CEO*
Matthew Peterson Crdo, *Prin*
Josephine Garrett, *CFO*
EMP: 160 **EST:** 2000
SALES (est): 24.87MM **Privately Held**
Web: www.mindresearch.org
SIC: 8733 Medical research

(P-19936)
MITRE CORPORATION
Also Called: Washington C3 Center
2756 Locust St (92106-1447)
PHONE...............................619 758-7818
David Coomber, *Mgr*
EMP: 99
SALES (corp-wide): 990.87MM **Privately Held**
Web: www.mitre.org
SIC: 8733 Research institute
PA: The Mitre Corporation
202 Burlington Rd
Bedford MA
781 271-2000

(P-19937)
NANOCOMPOSIX LLC
4878 Ronson Ct Ste J (92111-1806)
PHONE...............................858 565-4227
Steven Oldenburg, *Pr*
EMP: 90 **EST:** 2004
SQ FT: 16,000
SALES (est): 14MM
SALES (corp-wide): 14MM **Privately Held**
Web: www.nanocomposix.com
SIC: 8733 Scientific research agency
PA: Fortis Life Sciences, Llc
222 Berkeley St Fl 18
Boston MA

(P-19938)
NANTCELL INC
2040 E Mariposa Ave (90245-5027)
PHONE...............................310 883-1300
Patrick Soon-shiong, *CEO*
EMP: 220 **EST:** 2014
SALES (est): 10.17MM
SALES (corp-wide): 158.26K **Publicly Held**
SIC: 8733 Bacteriological research
PA: Nantworks, Llc
9920 Jefferson Blvd
Culver City CA
310 883-1300

(P-19939)
PERATON TECHNOLOGY SVCS INC
2750 Womble Rd Ste 202 (92106-6111)
PHONE...............................571 313-6000
John Curtis, *CEO*
EMP: 19
SQ FT: 10,000
SALES (corp-wide): 2.28B **Privately Held**
SIC: 8733 3812 7372 8711 Economic research, noncommercial; Defense systems and equipment; Application computer software; Professional engineer
HQ: Peraton Technology Services Inc.
12975 Worldgate Dr # 100
Herndon VA
571 313-6000

(P-19940)
RANCHO RESEARCH INSTITUTE
Also Called: RRI
7601 Imperial Hwy (90242-3456)
P.O. Box 3500 (90242-3500)
PHONE...............................562 401-8111
Julia Laplount, *CEO*
Yaga Szlachcic, *
EMP: 175 **EST:** 1956
SQ FT: 15,000
SALES (est): 9.21MM **Privately Held**
Web: www.ranchoresearch.org
SIC: 8733 Educational research agency

(P-19941)
SANFORD BRNHAM PRBYS MED DSCVE (PA)
Also Called: SBP
10901 N Torrey Pines Rd (92037-1005)
PHONE...............................858 795-5000
C Randal Mills, *CEO*
Kristiina Vuori, *
Robin Ryan, *
Gary Chessum, *
EMP: 966 **EST:** 1976
SQ FT: 397,000
SALES (est): 122.95MM
SALES (corp-wide): 122.95MM **Privately Held**
Web: www.sbpdiscovery.org
SIC: 8733 Research institute

(P-19942)
SCIENCELL RESEARCH LABS INC
1610 Faraday Ave (92008-7313)
PHONE...............................760 602-8549
James Shen, *Pr*
Yong Juan Yu, *
Jim Shen, *
EMP: 40 **EST:** 1990
SQ FT: 9,000
SALES (est): 6.73MM **Privately Held**
Web: www.sciencellonline.com
SIC: 8733 8731 2836 Medical research; Commercial physical research; Biological products, except diagnostic

(P-19943)
SCRIPPS RESEARCH INSTITUTE (PA)
10550 N Torrey Pines Rd (92037-1000)
PHONE...............................858 784-1000
Peter G Schultz, *CEO*
John D Diekman, *
Steve A Kay, *
Cary E Thomas, *
Donna J Weston, *
EMP: 90 **EST:** 1990
SALES (est): 652.04MM **Privately Held**
Web: www.scripps.edu
SIC: 8733 Research institute

(P-19944)
SCRIPPS RESEARCH INSTITUTE
Also Called: Calibr A Division Scripps RES
11119 N Torrey Pines Rd Ste 100 (92037-1046)
PHONE...............................858 242-1000
EMP: 99
Web: www.scripps.edu
SIC: 8733 Medical research
PA: The Scripps Research Institute
10550 N Torrey Pines Rd
La Jolla CA

(P-19945)
SOUTHERN CAL INST FOR RES EDCA
Also Called: S C I R E
5901 E 7th St 151 (90822-5201)
P.O. Box 15298 (90815-0298)
PHONE...............................562 826-8139
Timothy R Morgan, *Pr*
Moti Kashyap Md, *Treas*
EMP: 80 **EST:** 1989
SALES (est): 3.4MM **Privately Held**
Web: www.scire-lb.org
SIC: 8733 Medical research

(P-19946)
TAKEDA DEV CTR AMERICAS INC (HQ)
Also Called: Tcal
9625 Towne Centre Dr (92121-1964)
PHONE...............................858 622-8528
Keith Wilson, *Pr*
Tetsuyuki Maruyama, *Dir*
James Morley, *Dir*
David J Weitz J.d., *Genl Mgr*
EMP: 151 **EST:** 2001
SALES (est): 41.41MM **Privately Held**
Web: www.pint.com
SIC: 8733 2834 Biotechnical research, noncommercial; Pharmaceutical preparations

PRODUCTS & SVCS

PA: Takeda Pharmaceutical Company
Limited
2-1-1, Nihombashihoncho
Chuo-Ku TKY

(P-19947)
THE AEROSPACE
CORPORATION (PA)
2310 E El Segundo Blvd (90245-4609)
P.O. Box 92957 (90009-2957)
PHONE.................................310 336-5000
EMP: 2313 **EST:** 1960
SALES (est): 1.2B
SALES (corp-wide): 1.2B **Privately Held**
Web: www.aerospace.org
SIC: 8733 8711 8731 Scientific research
agency; Engineering services; Commercial
physical research

(P-19948)
THE RAND CORPORATION (PA)
Also Called: Rand
1776 Main St (90401-3297)
P.O. Box 2138 (90407-2138)
PHONE.................................310 393-0411
EMP: 900 **EST:** 1948
SALES (est): 399.09MM
SALES (corp-wide): 399.09MM **Privately
Held**
Web: www.rand.org
SIC: 8733 8732 8742 Noncommercial
research organizations; Commercial
nonphysical research; Management
consulting services

(P-19949)
TMT INTRNTONAL
OBSERVATORY LLC
100 W Walnut St Ste 300 (91124-0001)
PHONE.................................626 395-1651
Henry Yang, *Managing Member*
Edward Stone, *Managing Member**
Dean Currie, *
Fiona Harrison, *
B Thomas Soifer, *
EMP: 80 **EST:** 2014
SALES (est): 25.56MM **Privately Held**
Web: www.tmt.org
SIC: 8733 Scientific research agency

(P-19950)
UNITED STTES DEPT ENRGY
BRKLEY
Also Called: Lawrence Berkeley National Lab
555 W Imperial Hwy (92821-4802)
PHONE.................................510 486-7089
EMP: 153
Web: www.es.net
SIC: 8733 9611 Noncommercial research
organizations; Energy development and
conservation agency, government
HQ: United States Department Of Energy
Berkeley Office
1 Cyclotron Rd
Berkeley CA
510 486-5784

(P-19951)
USC INFORMATION SCIENCES
INST
4676 Admiralty Way Ste 1001
(90292-6622)
PHONE.................................310 448-9438
Jerry R Hobbs, *Prin*
EMP: 243 **EST:** 2015
SALES (est): 3.65MM **Privately Held**
Web: www.isi.edu
SIC: 8733 Research institute

(P-19952)
VIACYTE INC
5580 Morehouse Dr Ste 100 (92121-1755)
PHONE.................................858 455-3708
Paul K Laikind, *Pr*
Allan Robins, *VP*
Howard Foyt, *VP*
Anthony Gringeri, *Chief Development
Officer*
EMP: 55 **EST:** 1999
SALES (est): 18.04MM **Privately Held**
Web: www.vrtx.com
SIC: 8733 2836 Medical research; Biological
products, except diagnostic

(P-19953)
WHITTIER INST FOR DIABETES
10140 Campus Point Dr (92121-1520)
PHONE.................................877 944-8843
Athena Tsimikas, *Ex Dir*
EMP: 91 **EST:** 1980
SALES (est): 1.17MM
SALES (corp-wide): 4.06B **Privately Held**
Web: www.scripps.org
SIC: 8733 Medical research
PA: Scripps Health
10140 Campus Point Dr # 415
San Diego CA
800 727-4777

8734 Testing Laboratories

(P-19954)
911 HEALTH INC
701 Santa Monica Blvd Ste 300
(90401-2624)
PHONE.................................310 560-8509
Steve Farzam, *COO*
EMP: 99
SALES (est): 3.27MM **Privately Held**
SIC: 8734 Testing laboratories

(P-19955)
AIRCRAFT XRAY
LABORATORIES INC
5216 Pacific Blvd (90255-2595)
PHONE.................................323 587-4141
Gary G Newton, *CEO*
James Newton, *
Sandi Spelic, *
Justin Guzman, *
EMP: 80 **EST:** 1938
SQ FT: 60,000
SALES (est): 8.29MM **Privately Held**
Web: www.aircraftxray.com
SIC: 8734 7384 3471 Testing laboratories;
Photograph developing and retouching;
Plating and polishing

(P-19956)
ALCON VISION LLC
20521 Lake Forest Dr (92630-7741)
PHONE.................................949 505-6890
EMP: 487
Web: www.alcon.com
SIC: 8734 Testing laboratories
HQ: Alcon Vision, Llc
6201 South Fwy
Fort Worth TX
817 293-0450

(P-19957)
ANALYSTS INC
Also Called: Analysts Maintenance and Labs
3401 Jack Northrop Ave (90250-4428)
P.O. Box 2955 (90509-2955)
PHONE.................................800 424-0099
EMP: 148
Web: www.oil-testing.com

SIC: 8734 Product testing laboratory, safety
or performance

(P-19958)
ANALYTICAL PACE SERVICES
LLC
4100 Atlas Ct (93308-4510)
PHONE.................................800 878-4911
Stuart Buttram, *Brnch Mgr*
EMP: 104
Web: www.bclabs.com
SIC: 8734 Water testing laboratory
HQ: Pace Analytical Services, Llc
2665 Long Lake Rd Ste 300
Saint Paul MN

(P-19959)
APTIM CORP
18100 Von Karman Ave # 450
(92612-0169)
PHONE.................................949 261-6441
EMP: 502
SALES (corp-wide): 2.2B **Privately Held**
SIC: 8734 Pollution testing
HQ: Aptim Corp.
10001 Woodloch Forest Dr # 450
The Woodlands TX
832 823-2700

(P-19960)
CALIFORNIA LAB SCIENCES
LLC
Also Called: West Pacific Medical Lab
10200 Pioneer Blvd Ste 500 (90670-6000)
PHONE.................................562 758-6900
EMP: 300 **EST:** 2009
SALES (est): 23.13MM **Privately Held**
SIC: 8734 Testing laboratories

(P-19961)
CATALENT SAN DIEGO INC
7330 Carroll Rd Ste 200 (92121-2364)
PHONE.................................858 805-6383
Timothy Scott, *Pr*
Bryan Knox, *OF PHARMACEUTICS**
Jason Everett, *
EMP: 120 **EST:** 1999
SQ FT: 6,600
SALES (est): 22.99MM **Publicly Held**
Web: www.catalent.com
SIC: 8734 8731 Testing laboratories;
Commercial research laboratory
HQ: Catalent Pharma Solutions, Inc.
14 Schoolhouse Rd
Somerset NJ

(P-19962)
CERTIFIED LABORATORIES LLC
3125 N Damon Way (91505-1016)
PHONE.................................818 845-0070
Doug Shepard, *Mgr*
EMP: 1503
SALES (corp-wide): 43.93MM **Privately
Held**
Web: www.certified-laboratories.com
SIC: 8734 Food testing service
PA: Certified Laboratories, Llc
65 Marcus Dr
Melville NY
516 576-1400

(P-19963)
CLARIENT DIAGNOSTIC SVCS
INC
31 Columbia (92656-1460)
PHONE.................................888 443-3310
Cindy Collins, *CEO*
Michael Brown, *
Mark Machulcz, *

Renika Seghal, *
EMP: 159 **EST:** 2004
SALES (est): 1.98MM
SALES (corp-wide): 509.73MM **Publicly
Held**
Web: www.neogenomics.com
SIC: 8734 Testing laboratories
HQ: Clarient, Inc.
31 Columbia
Aliso Viejo CA
949 445-7300

(P-19964)
COLOR DESIGN LABORATORY
INC (PA)
Also Called: Color Design Labs
21329 Nordhoff St (91311-5819)
PHONE.................................818 341-5100
Gilberto Amparo, *CEO*
Maria Amparo, *
Maria Gonzalez, *
▲ **EMP:** 100 **EST:** 2010
SQ FT: 9,000
SALES (est): 11MM **Privately Held**
Web: www.colordesignlaboratory.com
SIC: 8734 Testing laboratories

(P-19965)
CONSUMER SAFETY
ANALYTICS LLC
Also Called: Cannasafe
7027 Hayvenhurst Ave (91406-3802)
PHONE.................................818 922-2416
Aaron Riley, *Prin*
Antonio Frazier, *Prin*
Bosco Ramirez, *Prin*
EMP: 99 **EST:** 2017
SALES (est): 4.73MM **Privately Held**
SIC: 8734 Testing laboratories

(P-19966)
COUNTY OF LOS ANGELES
Also Called: Hertzbrg-Dvis Frnsic Scnce Ctr
1800 Paseo Rancho Castilla (90032-4210)
PHONE.................................323 267-6167
Joseph Hourigan, *Brnch Mgr*
EMP: 142
Web: www.lacounty.gov
SIC: 8734 8731 Forensic laboratory;
Commercial physical research
PA: County Of Los Angeles
500 W Temple St Ste 437
Los Angeles CA
213 974-1101

(P-19967)
DICKSON TESTING CO INC (DH)
11126 Palmer Ave (90280-7410)
PHONE.................................562 862-8378
Robert Lyddon, *Pr*
Jim Scanell, *
EMP: 80 **EST:** 1970
SQ FT: 40,000
SALES (est): 19.46MM
SALES (corp-wide): 302.09B **Publicly
Held**
Web: www.dicksontesting.com
SIC: 8734 Metallurgical testing laboratory
HQ: Precision Castparts Corp.
5885 Meadows Rd Ste 620
Lake Oswego OR
503 946-4800

(P-19968)
ELEMENT MATERIALS (DH)
15062 Bolsa Chica St (92649-1023)
PHONE.................................714 892-1961
Charles Noall, *Pr*
Pete Regan, *
Jo Wetz, *

▲ = Import ▼ = Export
◆ = Import/Export

Jeff Joyce, *
Eelco Niermeijer, *
▲ **EMP:** 80 **EST:** 1997
SQ FT: 4,500
SALES (est): 23.05MM **Privately Held**
Web: www.element.com
SIC: 8734 Metallurgical testing laboratory
HQ: Element Materials Technology Group
Us Holdings Inc.
15062 Bolsa Chica St
Huntington Beach CA
714 892-1961

(P-19969)
ELEMENT MTRLS TECH HB INC
Also Called: Element Rancho Dominguez
18100 S Wilmington Ave (90220-5909)
PHONE..............................310 632-8500
Chuck Gee, *Genl Mgr*
EMP: 86
Web: www.element.com
SIC: 8734 Metallurgical testing laboratory
HQ: Element Materials Technology
Huntington Beach Llc
15062 Bolsa Chica St
Huntington Beach CA
714 892-1961

(P-19970)
ELLISON INSTITUTE LLC (PA)
Also Called: Ellisson Institute Technology
12414 Exposition Blvd (90064-1016)
PHONE..............................310 228-6400
Paul Marinelli, *CEO*
Jason Bowman, *
EMP: 118 **EST:** 2019
SQ FT: 80,000
SALES (est): 10.43MM
SALES (corp-wide): 10.43MM **Privately Held**
Web: www.eitm.org
SIC: 8734 Testing laboratories

(P-19971)
EUROFINS EATON ANALYTICAL LLC (DH)
750 Royal Oaks Dr Ste 100 (91016-3629)
PHONE..............................626 386-1100
Wilson Hershey, *Ch*
Bosco Ramirez, *
Andrew Eaton, *
Yongtao Bruce Li, *Dir*
EMP: 93 **EST:** 2012
SALES (est): 24.27MM
SALES (corp-wide): 220.81K **Privately Held**
Web: www.eurofinsus.com
SIC: 8734 Testing laboratories
HQ: Eurofins Lancaster Laboratories, Inc.
2425 New Holland Pike
Lancaster PA
717 656-2300

(P-19972)
FORENSIC ANALYTICAL SPC INC
Also Called: Forensic Analytical
20535 Belshaw Ave (90746-3505)
PHONE..............................310 763-2374
Bruce White, *Prin*
EMP: 94
SALES (corp-wide): 9.45MM **Privately Held**
Web: www.facs.com
SIC: 8734 8748 8731 8071 Forensic laboratory; Environmental consultant; Commercial physical research; Medical laboratories

PA: Forensic Analytical Specialties Incorporated
3777 Depot Rd Ste 409
Hayward CA
510 887-8828

(P-19973)
HAMPTON TDDER TCHNCAL SVCS INC
4571 State St (91763-6129)
P.O. Box 2338 (91763-0838)
PHONE..............................909 628-1256
Matthew C Tedder Senior, *Pr*
EMP: 19 **EST:** 1972
SQ FT: 20,000
SALES (est): 2.38MM **Privately Held**
Web: www.httstesting.com
SIC: 8734 1731 1623 8711 Testing laboratories; Electrical work; Electric power line construction; Engineering services

(P-19974)
HYUNDAI AMER TECHNICAL CTR INC
Also Called: Hyundai America/Tech Center
12610 Eastend Ave (91710-3006)
PHONE..............................909 627-3525
Scott Kin, *Mgr*
EMP: 113
SQ FT: 19,620
Web: www.hatci.com
SIC: 8734 8711 Product testing laboratories; Mechanical engineering
HQ: Hyundai America Technical Center Incorporated
6800 Geddes Rd
Ypsilanti MI
734 337-2500

(P-19975)
INTERTEK USA INC
Also Called: Intertek Pharmaceutical Svcs
10420 Wateridge Cir (92121-5773)
PHONE..............................858 558-2599
Arron Xu, *Mgr*
EMP: 100
SALES (corp-wide): 3.84B **Privately Held**
Web: www.intertek.com
SIC: 8734 Testing laboratories
HQ: Intertek Usa Inc.
200 Westlake Park Blvd # 1010
Houston TX
713 543-3600

(P-19976)
MICRO PRCISION CALIBRATION INC
Also Called: Micro Precision
2165 N Glassell St (92865-3307)
PHONE..............................714 901-5659
EMP: 150
SALES (corp-wide): 66.84MM **Privately Held**
Web: www.microprecision.com
SIC: 8734 Calibration and certification
PA: Micro Precision Calibration, Inc.
22835 Industrial Pl
Grass Valley CA
530 268-1860

(P-19977)
MILLENNIUM HEALTH LLC
16981 Via Tazon Ste F (92127-1645)
PHONE..............................877 451-3534
Jennifer Strickland, *CEO*
Howard Appel, *
David Cohen, *
Martin Price, *
Janna Sipes, *Regional COMP**

EMP: 258 **EST:** 2007
SALES (est): 79.25MM **Privately Held**
Web: www.millenniumhealth.com
SIC: 8734 Testing laboratories

(P-19978)
NATIONAL GENETICS INSTITUTE
2440 S Sepulveda Blvd Ste 235 (90064-1748)
PHONE..............................310 996-6610
Mike Aicher, *CEO*
Geri Cox, *
EMP: 200 **EST:** 1991
SQ FT: 35,000
SALES (est): 10.71MM **Publicly Held**
Web: plasma.labcorp.com
SIC: 8734 Testing laboratories
PA: Laboratory Corporation Of America Holdings
358 S Main St
Burlington NC

(P-19979)
NUMERADE LABS INC
1155 Rexford Ave (91107-1712)
PHONE..............................213 536-1489
EMP: 100 **EST:** 2019
SALES (est): 143.86K **Privately Held**
Web: www.numerade.com
SIC: 8734 7371 Testing laboratories; Computer software development and applications

(P-19980)
PHAMATECH INCORPORATED
15175 Innovation Dr (92128-3401)
PHONE..............................888 635-5840
▲ **EMP:** 200 **EST:** 1991
SQ FT: 50,000
SALES (est): 22.68MM **Privately Held**
Web: www.phamatech.com
SIC: 8734 5047 Forensic laboratory; Medical laboratory equipment

(P-19981)
PIXEL LABS LLC
Also Called: Helium 10
500 Technology Dr Ste 450 (92618-1384)
PHONE..............................512 560-5961
EMP: 93 **EST:** 2016
SALES (est): 3.64MM **Privately Held**
Web: www.helium10.com
SIC: 8734 Testing laboratories

(P-19982)
SCANTIBODIES LABORATORY INC (PA)
9336 Abraham Way (92071-2861)
PHONE..............................619 258-9300
Thomas L Cantor, *CEO*
John Van Duzer, *
▲ **EMP:** 240 **EST:** 1976
SQ FT: 60,500
SALES (est): 41.96MM
SALES (corp-wide): 41.96MM **Privately Held**
Web: www.scantibodies.com
SIC: 8734 Testing laboratories

(P-19983)
SHOGUN LABS INC (PA)
340 S Lemon Ave # 1085 (91789-270*)
PHONE..............................317 676-2719
Finbarr Taylor, *CEO*
EMP: 146 **EST:** 2015
SALES (est): 12.55MM
SALES (corp-wide): 12.55MM **Privately Held**
Web: www.getshogun.com

SIC: 8734 Testing laboratories

(P-19984)
TANDEX TEST LABS INC
15849 Business Center Dr (91706-2053)
PHONE..............................626 962-7166
Brian Peale, *Pr*
Charles T Goolsby, *
EMP: 49 **EST:** 1980
SQ FT: 15,000
SALES (est): 9.37MM **Privately Held**
Web: www.tandexlabs.com
SIC: 8734 3674 Testing laboratories; Hybrid integrated circuits

(P-19985)
TWINING INC (PA)
Also Called: Twining Laboratories
2883 E Spring St Ste 300 (90806-2417)
PHONE..............................562 426-3355
Edward Butch M Twining Junior, *CEO*
Brian Kramer, *
Robert M Ryan, *
Boris Stein D Sc, *VP*
Linas Vitkus, *
EMP: 82 **EST:** 1959
SQ FT: 13,600
SALES (est): 24.71MM
SALES (corp-wide): 24.71MM **Privately Held**
Web: www.twininginc.com
SIC: 8734 Testing laboratories

(P-19986)
WESTPAC LABS INC
10200 Pioneer Blvd # 500 (90670-6000)
PHONE..............................562 906-5227
EMP: 452
SALES (est): 53MM **Privately Held**
Web: www.westpaclab.com
SIC: 8734 8071 Testing laboratories; Pathological laboratory

8741 Management Services

(P-19987)
360 HEALTH PLAN INC
Also Called: 360 Clinic
13800 Arizona St Ste 104 (92683-3951)
PHONE..............................800 446-8888
Vince Pien, *CEO*
David Ngo, *CFO*
Mike Lee, *COO*
EMP: 200 **EST:** 2020
SALES (est): 5.85MM **Privately Held**
Web: www.360clinic.md
SIC: 8741 Hospital management

(P-19988)
ACTIVCARE LIVING INC (PA)
10603 Rancho Bernardo Rd (92127-5722)
PHONE..............................858 565-4424
William Major Chance, *CEO*
D Kevin Moriarty, *VP*
Frank A Virgadamo, *
B Renee Barnard, *
Todd A Shetter, *
EMP: 180 **EST:** 1979
SQ FT: 9,000
SALES (est): 40.58MM
SALES (corp-wide): 40.58MM **Privately Held**
Web: www.activcareliving.com
SIC: 8741 Nursing and personal care facility management

(P-19989)
AEG MANAGEMENT LACC LLC
Also Called: Los Angeles Convention Center

PRODUCTS & SVCS

1201 S Figueroa St (90015-1308)
PHONE..................................213 741-1151
Brad Gessner, *Sr VP*
Greg Rosicky, *
Carisa Malanum, *
Ellen Schwartz, *
Keith Hilsgen, *
EMP: 220 **EST:** 2013
SALES (est): 44.87MM
SALES (corp-wide): 16.52K **Privately Held**
Web: www.lacclink.com
SIC: 8741 Business management
PA: Aeg Facilities, Llc
   800 W Olympic Blvd # 305
   Los Angeles CA
   213 763-7700

(P-19990)
AJIT HEALTHCARE INC
316 S Westlake Ave (90057-2906)
PHONE..................................213 484-0510
Jasvant N Modi, *Pr*
Sagar Parikh, *Prin*
EMP: 80 **EST:** 2004
SALES (est): 3.99MM **Privately Held**
Web: www.wlchospital.com
SIC: 8741 Nursing and personal care facility management

(P-19991)
ALLEGIS RESIDENTIAL SVCS INC
Also Called: Aspm-Sandiego
9340 Hazard Way Ste B2 (92123-1218)
PHONE..................................858 430-5700
Karen Martinez, *CEO*
Jorge Martinez, *
Steve Howe, *
EMP: 80 **EST:** 1971
SQ FT: 4,000
SALES (est): 13.14MM **Privately Held**
Web: www.aspm-sandiego.com
SIC: 8741 Business management
PA: S.H.E. Manages Properties, Inc.
   9340 Hazard Way Ste B2
   San Diego CA

(P-19992)
ALLZONE MANAGEMENT SVCS INC
Also Called: Allzone Management Solutions
3795 La Crescenta Ave Ste 200 (91208-1057)
PHONE..................................213 291-8879
Jonathan Rodrigues, *Pr*
EMP: 500 **EST:** 2011
SALES (est): 11.76MM **Privately Held**
Web: www.allzonems.com
SIC: 8741 Management services

(P-19993)
ALTER MANAGEMENT LLC
Also Called: Alter Health Group
34232 Pacific Coast Hwy Ste D (92629-3854)
PHONE..................................949 629-0214
Michael Castanon, *Prin*
EMP: 100 **EST:** 2018
SALES (est): 2.29MM **Privately Held**
SIC: 8741 Management services

(P-19994)
ALTURA MANAGEMENT SERVICES LLC
1401 N Montebello Blvd (90640-2584)
PHONE..................................323 768-2898
Jose Esparza, *CFO*
EMP: 375 **EST:** 2015
SALES (est): 9.77MM **Privately Held**

SIC: 8741 Management services

(P-19995)
AMERICAN INTGRTED RSOURCES INC
Also Called: Air Demolition and Envmtl
2341 N Pacific St (92865-2601)
PHONE..................................714 921-4100
Thomas C Stevens, *CEO*
EMP: 80 **EST:** 2013
SALES (est): 9.95MM **Privately Held**
Web: www.american-integrated.com
SIC: 8741 Construction management

(P-19996)
AMERICAN MANAGEMENT SVCS W LLC
1240 Bethel Ln (93458-8386)
PHONE..................................805 352-1921
EMP: 143
SALES (corp-wide): 146.69MM **Privately Held**
SIC: 8741 Management services
PA: American Management Services West Llc
   11235 Se 6th St
   Bellevue WA
   206 215-9700

(P-19997)
AMERICAN MZHOU DNGPO GROUP INC
4520 Maine Ave (91706-2671)
PHONE..................................626 820-9239
Gang Wang, *CEO*
EMP: 100 **EST:** 2012
SALES (est): 2.31MM **Privately Held**
SIC: 8741 Restaurant management

(P-19998)
APPLECARE MEDICAL MGT LLC
18 Centerpointe Dr Ste 100 (90623-1028)
P.O. Box 6014 (90702-6014)
PHONE..................................714 443-4507
EMP: 108 **EST:** 2010
SALES (est): 15.02MM
SALES (corp-wide): 324.16B **Publicly Held**
Web: www.applecaremedical.com
SIC: 8741 Nursing and personal care facility management
PA: Unitedhealth Group Incorporated
   9900 Bren Rd E Ste 300w
   Minnetonka MN
   952 936-1300

(P-19999)
AVSC INTLLCTUAL PRPRTY MGT INC
111 W Ocean Blvd Ste 1110 (90802-4688)
PHONE..................................562 366-1924
J Michael Mcilwain, *CEO*
EMP: 303 **EST:** 1998
SALES (est): 1.99MM
SALES (corp-wide): 460.08MM **Privately Held**
SIC: 8741 Business management
HQ: Audio Visual Services Co.
   5100 River Rd Ste 300
   Schiller Park IL
   847 222-9800

(P-20000)
AWI MANAGEMENT CORPORATION
1800 E Lakeshore Dr (92530-4469)
PHONE..................................951 674-8200
Angelica Chaidez, *Brnch Mgr*

EMP: 120
SALES (corp-wide): 29.21MM **Privately Held**
Web: www.awimc.com
SIC: 8741 Business management
PA: Awi Management Corporation
   120 Center St
   Auburn CA
   530 745-6170

(P-20001)
AZUL HOSPITALITY GROUP INC
800 W Ivy St Ste D (92101-1771)
PHONE..................................619 223-4200
Alvaro Fraile, *CEO*
Douglas Leiber, *
Mark Crisci, *
EMP: 166 **EST:** 2007
SALES (est): 12.66MM **Privately Held**
Web: www.azulhospitalygroup.com
SIC: 8741 Business management

(P-20002)
BEECH STREET CORPORATION (HQ)
25550 Commercentre Dr Ste 200 (92630)
PHONE..................................949 672-1000
William Fickling Junior, *Ch*
William Hale, *
Norm Werthwein, *
Rick Markus, *
Jon Bird, *
EMP: 350 **EST:** 1951
SQ FT: 60,000
SALES (est): 50.67MM
SALES (corp-wide): 1.08B **Publicly Held**
SIC: 8741 Administrative management
PA: Multiplan Corporation
   640 5th Ave Fl 12
   New York NY
   212 380-7500

(P-20003)
BJS RESTAURANT OPERATIONS CO
Also Called: BJ's Restaurant & Brewhouse
7755 Center Ave Ste 300 (92647-3084)
PHONE..................................714 500-2440
EMP: 358 **EST:** 2017
SALES (est): 2.45MM
SALES (corp-wide): 1.28B **Publicly Held**
SIC: 8741 Restaurant management
PA: Bj's Restaurants, Inc.
   7755 Center Ave Ste 300
   Huntington Beach CA
   714 500-2400

(P-20004)
BON APPETIT MANAGEMENT CO
Also Called: Getty Center
1200 Getty Center Dr Ste 100 (90049-1657)
PHONE..................................310 440-6209
Javier Ramirez, *Mgr*
EMP: 196
SALES (corp-wide): 29.97B **Privately Held**
Web: www.bamco.com
SIC: 8741 Restaurant management
HQ: Bon Appetit Management Co.
   201 Rdwood Shres Pkwy Ste
   Redwood City CA
   650 798-8000

(P-20005)
BON APPETIT MANAGEMENT CO
Also Called: Bon Appetit
1200 Getty Center Dr (90049-1657)

PHONE..................................310 440-6052
EMP: 195
SALES (corp-wide): 29.97B **Privately Held**
Web: www.bamco.com
SIC: 8741 Management services
HQ: Bon Appetit Management Co.
   201 Rdwood Shres Pkwy Ste
   Redwood City CA
   650 798-8000

(P-20006)
BON APPETIT MANAGEMENT CO
1050 N Mills Ave (91711-3908)
PHONE..................................909 607-2788
EMP: 207
SALES (corp-wide): 29.97B **Privately Held**
Web: www.bamco.com
SIC: 8741 Management services
HQ: Bon Appetit Management Co.
   201 Rdwood Shres Pkwy Ste
   Redwood City CA
   650 798-8000

(P-20007)
BUFFALO SPOT MGT GROUP LLC
7245 Garden Grove Blvd Ste E (92841-4216)
PHONE..................................949 354-0884
Ivan Flores, *Managing Member*
EMP: 110 **EST:** 2016
SALES (est): 9.01MM **Privately Held**
SIC: 8741 Restaurant management

(P-20008)
CAELUS CORPORATION
20472 Crescent Bay Dr Ste 100 (92630-8849)
P.O. Box 51865 (92619-1865)
PHONE..................................949 877-7170
Andre Afshar, *CEO*
EMP: 25 **EST:** 2017
SALES (est): 1.29MM **Privately Held**
SIC: 8741 1389 1522 1542 Construction management; Construction, repair, and dismantling services; Residential construction, nec; Custom builders, non-residential

(P-20009)
CAL STATE LA UNIV AUX SVCS INC
Also Called: UAS
5151 State University Dr (90032-4226)
PHONE..................................323 343-2531
Tariq Marji, *Ex Dir*
▲ **EMP:** 600 **EST:** 1954
SQ FT: 108,000
SALES (est): 39.05MM **Privately Held**
Web: www.calstatela.edu
SIC: 8741 5942 5651 5812 Business management; College book stores; Unisex clothing stores; Cafeteria

(P-20010)
CAMARILLO HEALTHCARE CENTER
205 Granada St (93010-7715)
PHONE..................................805 482-9805
Erica Olsen, *Admn*
Angie Chavz, *Admn*
EMP: 96 **EST:** 2007
SALES (est): 10.45MM
SALES (corp-wide): 3.03B **Publicly Held**
Web: www.camarillohealthcare.com
SIC: 8741 Nursing and personal care facility management
PA: The Ensign Group Inc
   29222 Rncho Vejo Rd Ste 1

San Juan Capistrano CA
949 487-9500

(P-20011)
CAREMORE MEDICAL MANAGEMENT COMPANY A CALIFORNIA LIMITED PARTNERSHIP
Also Called: Caremore AP
12900 Park Plaza Dr Ste 150 (90703-9329)
PHONE.................................562 741-4300
EMP: 900
SIC: 8741 5047 Business management; Medical equipment and supplies

(P-20012)
CHAN FAMILY PARTNERSHIP LP
801 S Grand Ave Apt 1811 (90017-4673)
PHONE.................................626 322-7132
Ann Chan, *Pt*
EMP: 100 EST: 2017
SALES (est): 2.4MM **Privately Held**
SIC: 8741 Restaurant management

(P-20013)
CITY OF HOPE (PA)
1500 Duarte Rd (91010-3012)
PHONE.................................626 256-4673
TOLL FREE: 800
EMP: 260 EST: 1929
SALES (est): 334.97MM
SALES (corp-wide): 334.97MM **Privately Held**
Web: www.cityofhope.org
SIC: 8741 8399 Hospital management; Fund raising organization, non-fee basis

(P-20014)
CITY OF MENIFEE
29844 Haun Rd (92586-6539)
PHONE.................................951 672-6777
Kathy Benett, *City Clerk**
EMP: 90 EST: 2008
SALES (est): 123.4MM **Privately Held**
Web: www.cityofmenifee.us
SIC: 8741 Personnel management

(P-20015)
COLLECTIVE MGT GROUP LLC
Also Called: Collective Management Group
8383 Wilshire Blvd Ste 1050 (90211-2425)
PHONE.................................323 655-8585
Reza Izad, *
Gary Binkow, *
Jordan Berliant, *
Jordan Toplitzky, *
EMP: 206 EST: 1999
SQ FT: 15,000
SALES (est): 7.41MM **Privately Held**
SIC: 8741 Management services

(P-20016)
COUNTRY VILLA SERVICE CORP
3233 W Pico Blvd (90019-3640)
PHONE.................................323 734-9122
Mike Demchuck, *Mgr*
EMP: 102
SALES (corp-wide): 88.5MM **Privately Held**
Web: www.evictionlawyer.com
SIC: 8741 8051 Nursing and personal care facility management; Skilled nursing care facilities
PA: Country Villa Service Corp.
2400 E Katella Ave # 800
Anaheim CA
310 574-3733

(P-20017)
COUNTRY VILLA SERVICE CORP
3002 Rowena Ave (90039-2005)
PHONE.................................323 666-1544
Stephen Rissman, *Pr*
EMP: 103
SALES (corp-wide): 88.5MM **Privately Held**
Web: www.evictionlawyer.com
SIC: 8741 8051 Nursing and personal care facility management; Skilled nursing care facilities
PA: Country Villa Service Corp.
2400 E Katella Ave # 800
Anaheim CA
310 574-3733

(P-20018)
COUNTRY VILLA SERVICE CORP
1730 Grand Ave (90804-2011)
PHONE.................................562 597-8817
EMP: 102
SALES (corp-wide): 88.5MM **Privately Held**
Web: www.evictionlawyer.com
SIC: 8741 Nursing and personal care facility management
PA: Country Villa Service Corp.
2400 E Katella Ave # 800
Anaheim CA
310 574-3733

(P-20019)
COUNTRY VILLA SERVICE CORP
615 W Duarte Rd (91016-4436)
PHONE.................................626 358-4547
Sam Chia, *Brnch Mgr*
EMP: 102
SALES (corp-wide): 88.5MM **Privately Held**
Web: www.evictionlawyer.com
SIC: 8741 Management services
PA: Country Villa Service Corp.
2400 E Katella Ave # 800
Anaheim CA
310 574-3733

(P-20020)
COUNTRY VILLA SERVICE CORP
Also Called: Country Villa E Convalescent
2415 S Western Ave (90018-2608)
PHONE.................................323 734-1101
Phadra Johnson, *Mgr*
EMP: 102
SALES (corp-wide): 88.5MM **Privately Held**
Web: www.evictionlawyer.com
SIC: 8741 8051 8011 8059 Nursing and personal care facility management; Skilled nursing care facilities; Clinic, operated by physicians; Convalescent home
PA: Country Villa Service Corp.
2400 E Katella Ave # 800
Anaheim CA
310 574-3733

(P-20021)
COUNTRY VILLA SERVICE CORP (PA)
Also Called: Country Villa Health Services
2400 E Katella Ave Ste 800 (92806-5945)
PHONE.................................310 574-3733
Stephen Reissman, *CEO*
Diane Reissman, *
Cheryl Petterson, *
EMP: 80 EST: 1972
SQ FT: 24,000
SALES (est): 88.5MM
SALES (corp-wide): 88.5MM **Privately Held**

Web: www.evictionlawyer.com
SIC: 8741 Nursing and personal care facility management

(P-20022)
COUNTY OF LOS ANGELES
Also Called: Internal Services Department
9150 Imperial Hwy (90242-2835)
PHONE.................................562 940-2907
Dave Chittenten, *Dir*
EMP: 104
Web: www.lacounty.gov
SIC: 8741 9199 Administrative management; General government administration
PA: County Of Los Angeles
500 W Temple St Ste 437
Los Angeles CA
213 974-1101

(P-20023)
CURATIVE INC
605 E Huntington Dr (91016-6353)
PHONE.................................650 713-8928
EMP: 802 EST: 2020
SALES (est): 24.62MM **Privately Held**
Web: www.curative.com
SIC: 8741 Management services

(P-20024)
D I F GROUP INC
Also Called: Manufacture
1942 E 46th St (90058-2004)
PHONE.................................323 231-8800
EMP: 23 EST: 2010
SALES (est): 1.58MM **Privately Held**
SIC: 8741 3161 Management services; Clothing and apparel carrying cases

(P-20025)
DAICEL AMERICA HOLDINGS INC
21515 Hawthorne Blvd Ste 600 (90503-6501)
PHONE.................................480 798-6737
Kenichi Tanaka, *Brnch Mgr*
EMP: 338
Web: www.daicelamerica.com
SIC: 8741 Administrative management
HQ: Daicel America Holdings, Inc.
1 Parker Plz
Fort Lee NJ
201 461-4466

(P-20026)
DCL MARITIME LLC
Also Called: Disney Cruise Line
500 S Buena Vista St (91521-0001)
PHONE.................................818 560-1000
EMP: 175 EST: 2016
SALES (est): 6.1MM
SALES (corp-wide): 88.9B **Publicly Held**
SIC: 8741 Management services
PA: The Walt Disney Company
500 S Buena Vista St
Burbank CA
818 560-1000

(P-20027)
DHS CONSULTING LLC
1820 E 1st St Ste 410 (92705-8311)
PHONE.................................714 276-1135
EMP: 140 EST: 2012
SQ FT: 6,000
SALES (est): 27.82MM **Privately Held**
Web: www.anseradvisory.com
SIC: 8741 Construction management
HQ: Anser Advisory, Llc
2677 N Main St Ste 400
Santa Ana CA
310 351-8907

(P-20028)
ENTEGRIS INC
4175 Santa Fe Rd (93401-8159)
PHONE.................................805 541-9299
EMP: 63
SALES (corp-wide): 3.28B **Publicly Held**
Web: www.entegris.com
SIC: 8741 3674 Management services; Semiconductors and related devices
PA: Entegris, Inc.
129 Concord Rd
Billerica MA
978 436-6500

(P-20029)
EPIC MANAGEMENT LP (PA)
1615 Orange Tree Ln (92374-2804)
P.O. Box 19020 (92423-9020)
PHONE.................................909 799-1818
EMP: 86 EST: 1995
SALES (est): 45.17MM **Privately Held**
Web: www.epicmanagementlp.com
SIC: 8741 Nursing and personal care facility management

(P-20030)
FAR EAST NATIONAL BANK
977 N Broadway Ste 306 (90012-1786)
P.O. Box Po Box 54198 (90099-0001)
PHONE.................................213 687-1300
EMP: 354
SIC: 8741 6021 Management services; National commercial banks

(P-20031)
FINANCIAL GROUP INC
1991 Country Pl (93023-4190)
PHONE.................................805 646-7974
EMP: 122
SALES (corp-wide): 1.47B **Publicly Held**
SIC: 8741 Management services
HQ: The Financial Group Inc
2555 Severn Ave Ste 100
Metairie LA
504 456-0101

(P-20032)
FIRSTSRVICE RSIDENTIAL CAL LLC
3415 S Sepulveda Blvd Ste 720 (90034-6060)
PHONE.................................213 213-0886
Gregg Evangelho, *Brnch Mgr*
EMP: 119
SALES (corp-wide): 3.75B **Privately Held**
Web: www.fsresidential.com
SIC: 8741 6531 Business management; Real estate managers
HQ: Firstservice Residential California, Llc
15241 Laguna Canyon Rd
Irvine CA
949 448-6000

(P-20033)
FUJITEC AMERICA INC
12170 Mora Dr Ste 1 (90670-7339)
PHONE.................................310 464-8270
Timothy Mooney, *Mgr*
EMP: 122
Web: www.fujitecamerica.com
SIC: 8741 1796 Business management; Elevator installation and conversion
HQ: Fujitec America Inc
7258 Innovation Way
Mason OH
513 755-6100

P R O D U C T S & S V C S

(P-20034)
GHP MANAGEMENT CORPORATION
270 N Canon Dr (90210-5323)
PHONE..............................310 432-1441
Geoffrey H Palmer, *Brnch Mgr*
EMP: 202
SALES (corp-wide): 23.93MM **Privately Held**
Web: www.ghpmgmt.com
SIC: 8741 Business management
PA: Ghp Management Corporation
1082 W 7th St
Los Angeles CA
213 213-0190

(P-20035)
GLOBAL-DINING INC CALIFORNIA
1212 3rd Street Promenade (90401-1308)
PHONE..............................310 576-9922
Kozo Hasegawa, *CEO*
EMP: 85 EST: 1990
SALES (est): 8.64MM **Privately Held**
Web: www.globaldiningca.com
SIC: 8741 Restaurant management
PA: Global-Dining, Inc.
7-1-5, Minamiaoyama
Minato-Ku TKY

(P-20036)
GRIMMWAY ENTERPRISES INC
Grimmway Fresh Processing
14141 Di Giorgio Rd (93203-9518)
P.O. Box 81498 (93380-1498)
PHONE..............................661 854-6200
Jeff Meger, *Pr*
EMP: 94
SALES (corp-wide): 1.86B **Privately Held**
Web: www.grimmway.com
SIC: 8741 2099 2037 Management services; Food preparations, nec; Frozen fruits and vegetables
PA: Grimmway Enterprises, Inc.
14141 Di Giorgio Rd
Arvin CA
800 301-3101

(P-20037)
HARBOR-UCLA MED FOUNDATION INC (PA)
Also Called: Harbor Ucla Med Foundation
21840 Normandie Ave Ste 100 (90502-2047)
PHONE..............................310 222-5015
Chester Choi, *CEO*
EMP: 100 EST: 1967
SQ FT: 45,000
SALES (est): 4.17MM **Privately Held**
Web: www.harbor-ucla.org
SIC: 8741 Hospital management

(P-20038)
HOTCHKIS WILEY CAPITL MGT LLC (PA)
725 S Figueroa St Ste 3900 (90017-5439)
PHONE..............................213 430-1000
EMP: 139 EST: 1980
SQ FT: 12,000
SALES (est): 24.1MM
SALES (corp-wide): 24.1MM **Privately Held**
Web: www.hwcm.com
SIC: 8741 6211 Financial management for business; Security brokers and dealers

(P-20039)
HOTEL MANAGERS GROUP LLC
Also Called: Hotel Managers Group
11590 W Bernardo Ct Ste 211 (92127-1622)
PHONE..............................858 673-1534
Joel Biggs, *Managing Member*
Charles W Giacomini, *Managing Member**
Michelle Demayo, *
EMP: 400 EST: 1996
SALES (est): 23.42MM **Privately Held**
Web: www.hotelmanagersgroup.com
SIC: 8741 7011 7041 Hotel or motel management; Hotels and motels; Membership-basis organization hotels

(P-20040)
IKEA PURCHASING SVCS US INC
600 N San Fernando Blvd (91502-1021)
PHONE..............................818 841-3500
Chris Maynard, *Mgr*
EMP: 104
Web: www.ikea.com
SIC: 8741 8721 5712 Administrative management; Accounting, auditing, and bookkeeping; Furniture stores
HQ: Ikea Purchasing Services (Us) Inc.
7810 Katy Fwy
Houston TX

(P-20041)
INLAND CNTIES REGIONAL CTR INC
Also Called: Inland Regional Center
1500 Iowa Ave Ste 100 (92507-2165)
PHONE..............................951 826-2600
Lavina Johnson, *Brnch Mgr*
EMP: 224
SALES (corp-wide): 744.4MM **Privately Held**
Web: www.inlandrc.org
SIC: 8741 Management services
PA: Inland Counties Regional Center, Inc.
1365 S Waterman Ave
San Bernardino CA
909 890-3000

(P-20042)
JC RESORTS LLC
Also Called: Surf Sand Hotel
1555 S Coast Hwy (92651-3226)
PHONE..............................949 376-2779
Blaise Bartell, *Brnch Mgr*
EMP: 646
Web: www.surfandsandresort.com
SIC: 8741 5813 7011 Hotel or motel management; Drinking places; Eating places; Hotels
PA: Jc Resorts Llc
533 Coast Blvd S
La Jolla CA

(P-20043)
JC RESORTS LLC
Also Called: Encinitas Ranch Golf Course
4154 Maryland St (92103-2330)
PHONE..............................760 944-1936
Rod Landville, *Mgr*
EMP: 325
Web: www.jcgolf.com
SIC: 8741 7992 Hotel or motel management; Public golf courses
PA: Jc Resorts Llc
533 Coast Blvd S
La Jolla CA

(P-20044)
JC RESORTS LLC
Also Called: Rancho Bernardo Inn
17550 Bernardo Oaks Dr (92128-2112)
PHONE..............................858 675-8500
Jhon Gates, *Brnch Mgr*
EMP: 219
Web: www.ranchobernardoinn.com
SIC: 8741 7991 5813 5812 Hotel or motel management; Physical fitness facilities; Drinking places; Eating places
PA: Jc Resorts Llc
533 Coast Blvd S
La Jolla CA

(P-20045)
JIPC MANAGEMENT INC
Also Called: John's Incredible Pizza Co
22342 Avenida Empresa Ste 220 (92688)
PHONE..............................949 916-2000
John M Parlet, *Pr*
EMP: 1000 EST: 1998
SALES (est): 36MM **Privately Held**
Web: www.johnspizza.com
SIC: 8741 Restaurant management

(P-20046)
JUVENILE JUSTICE DIVISION CAL
Also Called: Ventura Yuth Crrctional Fcilty
3100 Wright Rd (93010-8307)
PHONE..............................805 485-7951
Vivian Craford, *Superintnt*
EMP: 897
SALES (corp-wide): 534.4MM **Privately Held**
SIC: 8741 9223 Office management; House of correction, government
HQ: Juvenile Justice Division, California
1515 S St Ste 502s
Sacramento CA

(P-20047)
KA MANAGEMENT II INC
5820 Oberlin Dr Ste 201 (92121-3743)
PHONE..............................858 404-6080
Kayvon Agahnia, *CEO*
Kambiz Agahnia, *Ch*
Ken Assi, *CIO*
EMP: 90 EST: 2015
SALES (est): 8.48MM **Privately Held**
SIC: 8741 Financial management for business

(P-20048)
KEIRO SERVICES
Also Called: KEIRO SENIOR HEALTH CARE
420 E 3rd St Ste 1000 (90013-1648)
PHONE..............................213 873-5700
Shawn Miyake, *CEO*
EMP: 500 EST: 1984
SQ FT: 26,000
SALES (est): 1.59MM **Privately Held**
Web: www.keiro.org
SIC: 8741 Nursing and personal care facility management

(P-20049)
LA 1000 SANTA FE LLC
1000 S Santa Fe Ave (90021-1741)
PHONE..............................213 205-1000
EMP: 210 EST: 2019
SALES (est): 8.68MM **Privately Held**
SIC: 8741 Hotel or motel management

(P-20050)
LAKESIDE SYSTEMS INC
Also Called: Lakeside Medical Systems
8510 Balboa Blvd Ste 150 (91325-5810)
PHONE..............................866 654-3471
EMP: 700 EST: 1991
SQ FT: 20,000
SALES (est): 24.69MM
SALES (corp-wide): 58.33MM **Privately Held**
SIC: 8741 8742 6411 Management services; Management consulting services; Insurance agents, brokers, and service
PA: Heritage Provider Network Inc
8510 Balboa Blvd Ste 285
Northridge CA
818 654-3461

(P-20051)
LEGACY PRTNERS RESIDENTIAL INC
5141 California Ave Ste 100 (92617-3060)
PHONE..............................949 930-6600
Deborah Dodd, *Brnch Mgr*
EMP: 205
SALES (corp-wide): 49.67MM **Privately Held**
Web: www.legacypartners.com
SIC: 8741 Management services
PA: Legacy Partners Residential, Inc.
950 Tower Ln Ste 900
Foster City CA
650 571-2250

(P-20052)
LEWIS MANAGEMENT CORP
1154 N Mountain Ave (91786-3633)
PHONE..............................909 985-0971
John M Goodman, *CEO*
EMP: 128 EST: 2017
SALES (est): 7.43MM **Privately Held**
Web: www.lewisgroupofcompanies.com
SIC: 8741 Management services

(P-20053)
LEXXIOM INC
99 N San Antonio Ave Ste 330 (91786-4575)
PHONE..............................909 581-7313
Robert Lemelin, *Pr*
Brian Lemelin, *
Leo Lemelin, *
EMP: 360 EST: 2000
SALES (est): 13.56MM **Privately Held**
Web: www.lexxiom.com
SIC: 8741 Administrative management

(P-20054)
LFC CORPORATE SERVICES INC
17 Corporate Plaza Dr Ste 200 (92660-7902)
PHONE..............................949 640-4950
Alisha A Lange, *Pr*
EMP: 93 EST: 1994
SALES (est): 3.98MM **Privately Held**
Web: www.lfc.com
SIC: 8741 Management services

(P-20055)
LION-VALLEN LTD PARTNERSHIP
22 Area Aven A Bldg #2234 (92055)
P.O. Box 555045 (92055-5045)
PHONE..............................760 385-4885
EMP: 95
SALES (corp-wide): 13.99MM **Privately Held**
SIC: 8741 Management services
HQ: Lion-Vallen Limited Partnership
7200 Poe Ave Ste 400
Dayton OH

▲ = Import ▼ = Export
◆ = Import/Export

(P-20056)
LIVINGSTON MEM VNA HLTH CORP
Also Called: Livingston Mem Vsting Nrse Ass
1996 Eastman Ave Ste 101 (93003-5768)
PHONE..............................805 642-0239
Lanyard K Dial Md, *Pr*
Judy Hecox, *
Charles Hair Md, *Ch Bd*
Jeffrey Paul, *
EMP: 292 EST: 1947
SQ FT: 12,600
SALES (est): 16.68MM Privately Held
Web: www.lmvna.org
SIC: 8741 8082 Hospital management;
Home health care services

(P-20057)
LOS ANGELES RAMS LLC
Also Called: La Rams Football Club
10271 W Pico Blvd (90064-2606)
P.O. Box 69216 (90069-0216)
PHONE..............................310 277-4700
John Shaw, *Prin*
EMP: 104
SALES (corp-wide): 1.23MM Privately Held
Web: www.therams.com
SIC: 8741 7941 Administrative management;
Football club
PA: The Los Angeles Rams Llc
29899 Agoura Rd
Agoura Hills CA
314 982-7267

(P-20058)
MARINER HEALTH CARE INC
Also Called: Palm Springs Health Care Ctr
277 S Sunrise Way (92262-6738)
PHONE..............................760 327-8541
Darrin Tharp, *Admn*
EMP: 97
SALES (corp-wide): 1.02B Privately Held
Web: www.marinerhealthcare.com
SIC: 8741 8322 Nursing and personal care
facility management; Rehabilitation services
PA: Mariner Health Care, Inc.
3060 Mercer University Dr # 200
Atlanta GA
678 443-7000

(P-20059)
MEDICAL NETWORK INC
Also Called: MBC Systems
1809 É Dyer Rd Ste 311 (92705-5740)
PHONE..............................949 863-0022
David Conrad, *Pr*
Michael Weinstein, *Ch*
EMP: 80 EST: 1993
SQ FT: 3,500
SALES (est): 9.98MM Privately Held
Web: www.mbcsystems.com
SIC: 8741 Hospital management

(P-20060)
MENTOR MDIA USA SUP CHAIN MGT
865 S Washington Ave (92408-2237)
PHONE..............................909 930-0800
Kok Khoon Lim, *CEO*
▲ EMP: 80 EST: 2008
SALES (est): 21.15MM
SALES (corp-wide): 7.13B Privately Held
SIC: 8741 8742 Business management;
Business planning and organizing services
HQ: Mentor Media Ltd
47 Jalan Buroh
Singapore

(P-20061)
MIG MANAGEMENT SERVICES LLC
660 Newport Center Dr Ste 1300 (92660-6401)
PHONE..............................949 474-5800
EMP: 80 EST: 2010
SALES (est): 6.65MM
SALES (corp-wide): 25.45MM Privately Held
Web: www.migcap.com
SIC: 8741 Management services
PA: Mig Capital, Llc
660 Nwport Ctr Dr Ste 13
Newport Beach CA
949 474-5800

(P-20062)
MIKE ROVNER CONSTRUCTION INC
22600 Lambert St (92630-6201)
PHONE..............................949 458-1562
Mike Rovner, *Brnch Mgr*
EMP: 141
Web: www.rovnerconstruction.com
SIC: 8741 1522 1521 Construction
management; Residential construction, nec
; Single-family housing construction
PA: Mike Rovner Construction, Inc.
5400 Tech Cir
Moorpark CA

(P-20063)
MONTAGE HOTELS & RESORTS LLC
Also Called: Montage Laguna Beach
30801 Coast Hwy (92651-4221)
PHONE..............................949 715-6000
Alan Fuerstman, *CEO*
EMP: 600
SALES (corp-wide): 110.64MM Privately Held
Web: www.montage.com
SIC: 8741 7011 5813 5812 Hotel or motel
management; Hotels; Drinking places;
Eating places
PA: Montage Hotels & Resorts, Llc
3 Ada Ste 100
Irvine CA
949 715-5002

(P-20064)
MTC FINANCIAL INC
Also Called: Trustee Corps
17100 Gillette Ave (92614-5603)
PHONE..............................949 252-8300
Rande Johnsen, *CEO*
EMP: 90 EST: 1992
SALES (est): 9.47MM Privately Held
Web: www.trusteecorps.com
SIC: 8741 Management services

(P-20065)
NAVIGATORS MANAGEMENT CO INC
19100 Von Karman Ave (92612-1539)
PHONE..............................949 255-4860
EMP: 166
SIC: 8741 Management services
HQ: Navigators Management Company, Inc.
6 International Dr # 100
Port Chester NY
412 995-2255

(P-20066)
NCN MANAGEMENT LLC
5838 Edison Pl Ste 100 (92008-5520)
PHONE..............................800 275-3243
Michael Lawler, *CEO*

Vu Nguyen, *CIO*
EMP: 175 EST: 2015
SALES (est): 4.67MM Privately Held
SIC: 8741 Management services

(P-20067)
NELSON BROS PROPERTY MGT INC
Also Called: Nelson Brothers Property MGT
16b Journey Ste 200 (92656-3317)
PHONE..............................949 916-7300
Patrick Nelson, *Pr*
EMP: 134 EST: 2007
SALES (est): 4.83MM Privately Held
Web: www.nelson-brotherscm.com
SIC: 8741 Management services

(P-20068)
NETWORK MANAGEMENT GROUP INC (PA)
1100 S Flower St Ste 3110 (90015-2287)
PHONE..............................323 263-2632
John Park, *Pr*
EMP: 160 EST: 1997
SQ FT: 2,039
SALES (est): 3.17MM
SALES (corp-wide): 3.17MM Privately Held
SIC: 8741 8742 Business management;
Management consulting services

(P-20069)
NETWORK MEDICAL MANAGEMENT INC
1668 S Garfield Ave Ste 100 (91801)
PHONE..............................626 282-0288
Gary Augusta, *Pr*
Hing Ang, *COO*
Mihir Shah, *CFO*
EMP: 130 EST: 1994
SQ FT: 14,000
SALES (est): 15.03MM Publicly Held
Web:
www.networkmedicalmanagement.com
SIC: 8741 Hospital management
PA: Apollo Medical Holdings, Inc.
1668 S Garfield Ave Fl 2
Alhambra CA

(P-20070)
NORTH AMERICAN CLIENT SVCS INC (PA)
25910 Acero Ste 350 (92691-7908)
PHONE..............................949 240-2423
Darian Dahl, *Pr*
Jonathan Sloey, *
Jeffrey Daly, *
John L Sorensen, *
Timothy J Paulsen, *
▲ EMP: 175 EST: 1989
SALES (est): 48.37MM Privately Held
Web: www.nahci.com
SIC: 8741 Nursing and personal care facility
management

(P-20071)
ONNI PROPERTIES LLC
Also Called: Level Furnished Living
888 S Olive St (90014-3006)
PHONE..............................213 568-0278
Javier Sepeda, *Genl Mgr*
EMP: 206
SALES (corp-wide): 26.35MM Privately Held
Web: www.onni.com
SIC: 8741 Business management
PA: Onni Properties Llc
5055 N 32nd St
Phoenix AZ
602 595-4810

(P-20072)
ONTRAPORT INC
2040 Alameda Padre Serra Ste 220 (93103-1704)
PHONE..............................805 568-1424
Landon Ray, *CEO*
Lena Requist, *
EMP: 142 EST: 2012
SQ FT: 35,000
SALES (est): 18.85MM Privately Held
Web: www.ontraport.com
SIC: 8741 Business management

(P-20073)
OREQ CORPORATION
Also Called: Orchem Division
42306 Remington Ave (92590-2512)
PHONE..............................951 296-5076
Jess L Hetzner, *CEO*
Ron Hetzner, *
▲ EMP: 82 EST: 1999
SALES (est): 12.76MM Privately Held
Web: www.oreqcorp.com
SIC: 8741 5941 5091 Business management
; Water sport equipment; Spa equipment
and supplies

(P-20074)
PACIFIC GARDENS MED CTR LLC
21530 Pioneer Blvd (90716-2608)
PHONE..............................562 860-0401
EMP: 250 EST: 2017
SALES (est): 21.65MM Privately Held
SIC: 8741 Hospital management

(P-20075)
PACIFIC LIFE FUND ADVISORS LLC
Pacific Asset Management
700 Newport Center Dr (92660-6307)
PHONE..............................949 260-9000
Rex Olson, *Prin*
EMP: 264
SALES (corp-wide): 12.84B Privately Held
Web: www.pacificlife.com
SIC: 8741 Financial management for
business
HQ: Pacific Life Fund Advisors Llc
700 Newport Center Dr
Newport Beach CA

(P-20076)
PACIFIC VENTURES LTD
Also Called: Jacmar Companies, The
2200 W Valley Blvd (91803-1928)
PHONE..............................626 576-0737
William H Tilley, *CEO*
Jim Dalpozzo, *
Randy Hill, *
EMP: 250 EST: 1976
SQ FT: 20,000
SALES (est): 8.24MM Privately Held
SIC: 8741 6722 Restaurant management;
Management investment, open-end

(P-20077)
PARSONS CONSTRUCTORS INC
Also Called: PARSONS
100 W Walnut St (91103-3697)
PHONE..............................626 440-2000
Chuck Harrington, *CEO*
Robert Camp, *
EMP: 1682 EST: 1978
SALES (est): 6.33MM
SALES (corp-wide): 4.2B Publicly Held
Web: www.parsons.com
SIC: 8741 8711 Management services;
Engineering services

PRODUCTS & SVCS

PA: The Parsons Corporation
5875 Trinity Pkwy Ste 300
Centreville VA
703 988-8500

(P-20078)
PIPELINE GROUP LLC
2850 Redhill Ave Ste 110 (92705-5537)
PHONE..............................949 296-8375
David Sundling, *CEO*
Raju Patel, *Sec*
EMP: 151 **EST:** 2011
SALES (est): 1.9MM
SALES (corp-wide): 37.72MM **Privately Held**
Web: www.gopipeline.com
SIC: 8741 Management services
HQ: Pegasus Sub-Intermediate Corp
1 Letterman Dr Bldg C
San Francisco CA
919 378-2215

(P-20079)
PREMIER HLTHCARE SOLUTIONS INC
Also Called: Premier IMS Insurance Services
12225 El Camino Real (92130-2084)
PHONE..............................858 569-8629
Susan Devore, *Brnch Mgr*
EMP: 108
SALES (corp-wide): 1.34B **Publicly Held**
Web: www.premierinc.com
SIC: 8741 Management services
HQ: Premier Healthcare Solutions, Inc.
13034 Balntyn Corp Pl
Charlotte NC
704 357-0022

(P-20080)
PRIMARY CARE ASSOD MED GROUP I
3998 Vista Way Ste B (92056-4514)
PHONE..............................760 724-1033
Jeannette Brody, *Mgr*
EMP: 112
SALES (corp-wide): 4.52MM **Privately Held**
SIC: 8741 Administrative management
PA: Primary Care Associated Medical Group, Inc.
1635 Lake San Marcos Dr
San Marcos CA
760 471-7505

(P-20081)
PRIMARY PROVIDER MGT CO INC (HQ)
Also Called: Ppmc
2115 Compton Ave Ste 301 (92881-7272)
PHONE..............................951 280-7700
Robert Dukes Md, *CEO*
Robert Dukes, *CEO*
Maureen B Tyson, *
EMP: 90 **EST:** 1983
SQ FT: 23,500
SALES (est): 28.35MM
SALES (corp-wide): 2.71B **Publicly Held**
SIC: 8741 Business management
PA: Agilon Health, Inc.
6210 E Hwy 290 Ste 450
Austin TX
562 256-3800

(P-20082)
PROACTIVE RISK MANAGEMENT INC
22617 Hawthorne Blvd (90505-2510)
PHONE..............................213 840-8856
Benoit Grenier, *CEO*

EMP: 100 **EST:** 2014
SALES (est): 4.93MM **Privately Held**
Web: www.parminc.com
SIC: 8741 Business management

(P-20083)
PROFESSIONAL COMMUNITY MGT CAL
Also Called: Pcm
23081 Via Campo Verde (92656)
PHONE..............................949 380-0725
Richard Lee, *Brnch Mgr*
EMP: 111
SALES (corp-wide): 49.19MM **Privately Held**
Web: www.pcminternet.com
SIC: 8741 6519 Business management; Real property lessors, nec
PA: Professional Community Management Of California, Inc.
27051 Twne Cntre Dr Ste 2
Foothill Ranch CA
800 369-7260

(P-20084)
PROSPECT MEDICAL GROUP INC (HQ)
1920 E 17th St Ste 200 (92705-8626)
PHONE..............................714 796-5900
Jacob Y Terner Md, *Pr*
Mitchell Lew Md, *CEO*
Mike Heather, *
Stewart Kahn, *
EMP: 350 **EST:** 1986
SQ FT: 2,420
SALES (est): 32.89MM
SALES (corp-wide): 3.91B **Privately Held**
Web: www.prospectmedical.com
SIC: 8741 Hospital management
PA: Prospect Medical Holdings, Inc.
3415 S Sepulveda Blvd # 9
Los Angeles CA
310 943-4500

(P-20085)
PROSPECT MEDICAL SYSTEMS INC (HQ)
Also Called: Genesis Health Care
600 City Pkwy W Ste 800 (92868-2915)
PHONE..............................714 667-8156
Mitchell Lew Md, *CEO*
Brice Keyser Senior, *Dir Fin*
EMP: 127 **EST:** 1996
SALES (est): 43.01MM
SALES (corp-wide): 3.91B **Privately Held**
Web: www.prospectmedical.com
SIC: 8741 Hospital management
PA: Prospect Medical Holdings, Inc.
3415 S Sepulveda Blvd # 9
Los Angeles CA
310 943-4500

(P-20086)
PROVIDENT FINANCIAL MANAGEMENT
3130 Wilshire Blvd Ste 600 (90403-2349)
P.O. Box 4084 (90411-4084)
PHONE..............................310 282-0477
Ivan Axelrod, *Mng Pt*
Barry Siegel, *
EMP: 95 **EST:** 1981
SQ FT: 34,000
SALES (est): 2.61MM **Privately Held**
Web: www.providentfm.com
SIC: 8741 Financial management for business

(P-20087)
RAYMOND GROUP (PA)
Also Called: Orange Cnty George M Raymond N
520 W Walnut Ave (92868-2233)
PHONE..............................714 771-7670
Travis Winsor, *CEO*
James Watson, *
Mary Raymond, *
Tom Obrien, *
Michael Potter, *
EMP: 95 **EST:** 1955
SQ FT: 20,000
SALES (est): 36.98MM
SALES (corp-wide): 36.98MM **Privately Held**
Web: www.raymondgroup.com
SIC: 8741 Construction management

(P-20088)
RELOCITY INC
10250 Constellation Blvd Ste 100 (90067-6200)
PHONE..............................323 207-9160
Klaus Siegmann, *CEO*
EMP: 120 **EST:** 2016
SQ FT: 800
SALES (est): 17.43MM **Privately Held**
Web: www.relocity.com
SIC: 8741 Management services

(P-20089)
RENOVO SOLUTIONS LLC (PA)
4 Executive Cir Ste 185 (92614-6791)
PHONE..............................714 599-7969
Joseph Happ, *CIO*
Donald K Carson, *OF WEST COAST*
Haresh Saitiani, *
Fernando Castorena, *
EMP: 300 **EST:** 2009
SQ FT: 5,400
SALES (est): 73.08MM
SALES (corp-wide): 73.08MM **Privately Held**
Web: www.renovo1.com
SIC: 8741 Hospital management

(P-20090)
RHS CORP
Also Called: REDLANDS COMMUNITY HOSPITAL
350 Terracina Blvd (92373-4850)
PHONE..............................909 335-5500
James R Holmes, *Pr*
EMP: 1450 **EST:** 1985
SQ FT: 265,000
SALES (est): 550.43K **Privately Held**
Web: www.redlandshospital.org
SIC: 8741 Hospital management

(P-20091)
SCRIPPS CLINIC MED GROUP INC
12395 El Camino Real Ste 112 (92130)
PHONE..............................858 554-9000
Doctor Hugh Greenway, *CEO*
EMP: 157 **EST:** 1999
SALES (est): 17.86MM
SALES (corp-wide): 4.06B **Privately Held**
Web: www.scripps.org
SIC: 8741 Management services
PA: Scripps Health
10140 Campus Point Dr # 415
San Diego CA
800 727-4777

(P-20092)
SETHI MANAGEMENT INC
6156 Innovation Way (92009-1728)
P.O. Box 235927 (92023-5927)

PHONE..............................760 692-5288
Jeetander Sethi, *CEO*
EMP: 154 **EST:** 2009
SALES (est): 40MM **Privately Held**
Web: www.sethimanagement.com
SIC: 8741 Business management

(P-20093)
SMILE BRANDS GROUP INC (PA)
Also Called: Bright Now Dental
100 Spectrum Center Dr Ste 1500 (92618-4963)
PHONE..............................714 668-1300
Steven C Bilt, *CEO*
Stan Andrakowicz, *
Robert C Crim, *CDO*
George Suda, *CIO*
Cheryl Dore, *Chief Human Resource Officer*
EMP: 90 **EST:** 1978
SQ FT: 15,000
SALES (est): 295.09MM
SALES (corp-wide): 295.09MM **Privately Held**
Web: www.smilebrands.com
SIC: 8741 8021 Management services; Dental clinics and offices

(P-20094)
SMITH BROADCASTING GROUP INC (PA)
2315 Red Rose Way (93109-1259)
PHONE..............................805 965-0400
Debrah Egar, *Ex Sec*
David A Fitz, *
EMP: 165 **EST:** 1985
SALES (est): 6.69MM
SALES (corp-wide): 6.69MM **Privately Held**
SIC: 8741 8742 Business management; Management consulting services

(P-20095)
SNF MANAGEMENT
1901 Avenue Of The Stars (90067-4608)
PHONE..............................310 385-1090
Lee Samson, *Pr*
EMP: 94 **EST:** 2010
SALES (est): 9.87MM **Privately Held**
Web: www.windsorcares.com
SIC: 8741 Management services

(P-20096)
SOLPAC CONSTRUCTION INC
Also Called: Soltek Pacific Construction Co
2424 Congress St (92110-2819)
PHONE..............................619 296-6247
Stephen Thompson, *CEO*
Brandon Richie, *
John Myers, *
Kevin Cammall, *
Robert Thompson, *
EMP: 130 **EST:** 2005
SQ FT: 12,291
SALES (est): 177.75MM **Privately Held**
Web: www.soltekpacific.com
SIC: 8741 1542 1611 Construction management; Commercial and office building contractors; General contractor, highway and street construction

(P-20097)
SOUTH COAST PLAZA SECURITY
695 Town Center Dr Ste 50 (92626-1924)
PHONE..............................714 435-2180
Craig Farrow, *Mgr*
EMP: 120 **EST:** 1989
SALES (est): 2.3MM **Privately Held**

SIC: 8741 Management services

(P-20098)
SOUTHERN IMPLANTS INC
5 Holland Ste 209 (92618-2576)
PHONE...................949 273-8505
Michael Kehoe, *Pr*
Michael Nealon, *
EMP: 125 EST: 2007
SALES (est): 4.78MM **Privately Held**
Web: www.southernimplants.us
SIC: 8741 Management services

(P-20099)
SPEARMINT RHINO CMPNIES WRLDWI
1875 Tandem (92860-3606)
PHONE...................951 371-3788
Dyanna Gray, *CEO*
Kathy Vercher, *Pr*
Kathy Mcdonald, *VP*
Dena Hernandez, *CFO*
EMP: 88 EST: 1996
SQ FT: 5,000
SALES (est): 6.62MM **Privately Held**
Web: www.spearmintrhino.com
SIC: 8741 Business management

(P-20100)
STREAMLAND MEDIA LLC
1117 W Isabel St (91506-1405)
PHONE...................416 909-2103
EMP: 103
SALES (corp-wide): 5.51MM **Privately Held**
Web: www.streamlandmedia.com
SIC: 8741 Management services
PA: Streamland Media Llc
1132 Vine St
Los Angeles CA

(P-20101)
SUNAMERICA INVESTMENTS INC (DH)
Also Called: SunAmerica
1 Sun America Ctr Fl 37 (90067-6121)
PHONE...................310 772-6000
Eli Broad, *Pr*
EMP: 80 EST: 1978
SQ FT: 76,000
SALES (est): 21.75MM
SALES (corp-wide): 56.44B **Publicly Held**
SIC: 8741 6211 6282 7311 Administrative management; Security brokers and dealers; Investment advisory service; Advertising agencies
HQ: Sunamerica Inc.
1 Sun America Ctr Fl 38
Los Angeles CA
310 772-6000

(P-20102)
SUNROAD ASSET MANAGEMENT INC
4445 Eastgate Mall Ste 400 (92121)
PHONE...................858 362-8500
Dan Feldman, *Pr*
EMP: 119 EST: 1986
SALES (est): 2.23MM **Privately Held**
Web: www.sunroadenterprises.com
SIC: 8741 Business management
PA: Sunroad Holding Corporation
8620 Spectrum Center Blvd
San Diego CA

(P-20103)
SYLMARK INC (PA)
Also Called: Sylmark Group
7821 Orion Ave Ste 200 (91406-2032)

PHONE...................818 217-2000
Peter Spiegel, *Pr*
Steven Ober, *
Mark Funk, *
EMP: 90 EST: 1998
SALES (est): 20.39MM
SALES (corp-wide): 20.39MM **Privately Held**
Web: www.sylmark.com
SIC: 8741 Management services

(P-20104)
TCT MOBILE INC
189 Technology Dr (92618-2402)
PHONE...................949 892-2990
Xin Zhang, *Pr*
Juanjuan Feng, *
Qian Wen, *
EMP: 100 EST: 2008
SALES (est): 16.74MM
SALES (corp-wide): 4.15MM **Privately Held**
Web: us.alcatelmobile.com
SIC: 8741 8711 7389 8721 Management services; Engineering services; Financial services; Accounting, auditing, and bookkeeping
HQ: Tcl Communication Technology Holdings Limited
C/O: Conyers Trust Company (Cayman) Limited
George Town GR CAYMAN

(P-20105)
TEICHERT ENRGY UTLTIES GROUP I
3780 Kilroy Airport Way (90806-2457)
PHONE...................916 484-3011
Thomas J Griffith, *CEO*
EMP: 97 EST: 2019
SALES (est): 2.47MM **Privately Held**
Web: www.teichert.com
SIC: 8741 Construction management

(P-20106)
TRANSCOSMOS OMNICONNECT LLC
879 W 190th St Ste 1050 (90248-4224)
PHONE...................310 630-0072
EMP: 100 EST: 2019
SALES (est): 6.52MM
SALES (corp-wide): 23.83MM **Privately Held**
SIC: 8741 Management services
PA: Trans Cosmos America, Inc.
879 W 190th St Ste 410
Gardena CA
310 630-0072

(P-20107)
TRICOM MANAGEMENT INC
Also Called: United Owners Services
4025 E La Palma Ave Ste 101 (92807-1734)
PHONE...................714 630-2029
Woody Cary, *Pr*
EMP: 200 EST: 1979
SQ FT: 9,000
SALES (est): 7.95MM **Privately Held**
Web: www.tricommanagement.com
SIC: 8741 7389 Management services; Time-share condominium exchange

(P-20108)
TRILAR MANAGEMENT GROUP
1025 S Gilbert St (92543-7090)
PHONE...................951 925-2021
Susan A York, *Brnch Mgr*
EMP: 127
SALES (corp-wide): 9.37MM **Privately Held**

Web: www.ctmmanagement.com
SIC: 8741 Business management
PA: Trilar Management Group
2225 Faraday Ave Ste A
Carlsbad CA
760 603-3205

(P-20109)
TRIPALINK CORP
600 Wilshire Blvd Ste 1540 (90005-3983)
PHONE...................323 717-9139
Donghal Li, *Prin*
EMP: 133 EST: 2016
SALES (est): 5.03MM **Privately Held**
Web: www.tripalink.com
SIC: 8741 Management services

(P-20110)
TROON GOLF LLC
Also Called: Indian Wells Golf Resort
44500 Indian Wells Ln (92210-8746)
PHONE...................760 346-4653
Rich Carter, *Genl Mgr*
EMP: 130
Web: www.indianwellsgolfresort.com
SIC: 8741 7997 Management services; Country club, membership
PA: Troon Golf, L.L.C.
15044 N Scottsdale Rd # 300
Scottsdale AZ

(P-20111)
TWENTY4SEVEN HOTELS CCRP
520 Newport Center Dr Ste 520 (92660)
PHONE...................949 734-6400
David Wani, *CEO*
Drew Hardy, *
EMP: 500 EST: 2002
SQ FT: 15,000
SALES (est): 25.73MM **Privately Held**
Web: www.247hotels.com
SIC: 8741 Hotel or motel management

(P-20112)
VENTURA MEDICAL MANAGEMENT LLC
2601 E Main St (93003-2801)
PHONE...................805 477-6220
EMP: 325 EST: 2002
SALES (est): 23.13MM **Privately Held**
Web: www.ventura.org
SIC: 8741 Hospital management

(P-20113)
VILLAGE MANAGEMENT SVCS INC
24351 El Toro Rd (92637-4901)
PHONE...................949 597-4360
EMP: 100 EST: 2016
SALES (est): 2.37MM **Privately Held**
Web: www.lagunawoodsvillage.com
SIC: 8741 Management services

(P-20114)
VPM MANAGEMENT INC
2400 Main St Ste 201 (92614-6271)
PHONE...................949 863-1500
Philip H Mcnamee, *CEO*
Scott J Barker, *Managing Member*
Steve Tomlin, *
Mark Ellis, *
EMP: 150 EST: 1997
SALES (est): 9.34MM **Privately Held**
Web: www.vpmmanagement.com
SIC: 8741 Management services

(P-20115)
WARMINGTON MR 14 ASSOC LLC

Also Called: Warmington
3090 Pullman St (92626-5901)
PHONE...................714 557-5511
EMP: 87 EST: 2013
SALES (est): 5.07MM **Privately Held**
Web: www.homesbywarmington.com
SIC: 8741 Business management

(P-20116)
WARNER BROS DISTRIBUTING INC
Warner Bros. Pictures Domestic
4000 Warner Blvd Bldg 154 (91522-0002)
PHONE...................818 954-6000
Dan Fellman, *Brnch Mgr*
EMP: 418
SIC: 8741 7822 Management services; Distribution, exclusive of production: motion picture
HQ: Warner Bros. Distributing Inc.
4000 Warner Blvd
Burbank CA

(P-20117)
WESTERN NATIONAL CONTRACTORS
8 Executive Cir (92614-6746)
PHONE...................949 862-6200
Michael Hayde, *CEO*
Jeffrey R Scott, *
John Townsend, *
Randy Avery, *
Larry Johnson, *
EMP: 88 EST: 2004
SALES (est): 14.11MM **Privately Held**
Web: www.wng.com
SIC: 8741 Construction management

(P-20118)
WESTREC PROPERTIES INC
16633 Ventura Blvd Fl 6 (91436-1826)
PHONE...................818 907-0400
EMP: 477 EST: 1990
SALES (est): 1.01MM **Privately Held**
SIC: 8741 Administrative management
PA: Westrec Financial, Inc.
16633 Ventura Blvd Fl 6
Encino CA

(P-20119)
WHISKEY GIRL
702 5th Ave (92101-6918)
PHONE...................619 236-1616
Jerry Lopez, *Genl Mgr*
EMP: 152 EST: 2011
SALES (est): 1.55MM
SALES (corp-wide): 9.95MM **Privately Held**
Web: www.whiskeygirl.com
SIC: 8741 5813 Restaurant management; Night clubs
PA: Buffalo Joe's, L. P.
1620 5th Ave Ste 770
San Diego CA
619 235-6796

(P-20120)
WOLF & RAVEN LLC
206 W 4th St Ste 439 (92701-4679)
PHONE...................800 431-6471
Josue B Vazquez, *CEO*
EMP: 99 EST: 2021
SALES (est): 2.2MM **Privately Held**
SIC: 8741 8742 Business management; Business management consultant

(P-20121)
ZA MANAGEMENT
101 N Robertson Blvd (90211-2191)

PRODUCTS & SVCS

PHONE..................310 271-2200
Alexander Zaks, *CEO*
EMP: 90 **EST:** 2001
SALES (est): 2.42MM **Privately Held**
SIC: 8741 Management services

(P-20122)
ZERO GRAVITY MANAGEMENT
11110 Ohio Ave Ste 100 (90025-3329)
PHONE..................310 656-9440
EMP: 84 **EST:** 2016
SALES (est): 1.05MM **Privately Held**
Web: www.zerogravitymanagement.com
SIC: 8741 Management services

8742 Management Consulting Services

(P-20123)
AA BLOCKS LLC
9823 Pacific Heights Blvd Ste F (92121)
PHONE..................858 523-8231
Branden G Lee, *Mgr*
EMP: 92 **EST:** 2017
SALES (est): 2.5MM **Privately Held**
Web: www.aablocks.com
SIC: 8742 Business management consultant

(P-20124)
ACCENTURE FEDERAL SERVICES LLC
Also Called: Accenture National SEC Svcs
1615 Murray Canyon Rd Ste 400
(92108-4314)
PHONE..................619 574-2400
Jim Wangler, *Brnch Mgr*
EMP: 1394
Web: www.accenture.com
SIC: 8742 7361 8711 7373 Business
management consultant; Employment
agencies; Engineering services; Computer
integrated systems design
HQ: Accenture Federal Services Llc
800 N Glebe Rd Ste 300
Arlington VA
703 947-2000

(P-20125)
ADVANTAGE SALES & MKTG INC (DH)
Also Called: Advantage Solutions
15310 Barranca Pkwy Ste 100
(92618-2236)
PHONE..................949 797-2900
David Peacock, *CEO*
Robert Murray, *
Chris Growe, *
Bryce Robinson, *
Humberto Domingues, *
▲ **EMP:** 250 **EST:** 1997
SQ FT: 48,000
SALES (est): 1.56B
SALES (corp-wide): 4.71B **Publicly Held**
Web: www.advantagesolutions.net
SIC: 8742 Business management consultant
HQ: Advantage Solutions Inc.
15310 Barranca Pkwy # 100
Irvine CA
949 797-2900

(P-20126)
ADVANTAGE SALES & MKTG LLC (DH)
Also Called: Advantage Solutions
15310 Barranca Pkwy Ste 100
(92618-2236)
PHONE..................949 797-2900
Dave Peacock, *CEO*

Chris Growe, *
Bryce Robinson, *
Kelli Hammersmith, *Chief Communication Officer*
Pamela Morris-thompson, *Chief Human Resources Officer*
EMP: 250 **EST:** 1987
SALES (est): 497.31MM
SALES (corp-wide): 4.71B **Publicly Held**
Web: www.advantagesolutions.net
SIC: 8742 8743 8732 7311 Marketing
consulting services; Sales promotion;
Market analysis or research; Advertising
agencies
HQ: Advantage Solutions Inc.
15310 Barranca Pkwy # 100
Irvine CA
949 797-2900

(P-20127)
ALAN B WHITSON COMPANY INC
1507 W Alton Ave (92704-7219)
P.O. Box 9229 (92728-9229)
PHONE..................949 955-1200
Alan B Whitson, *Pr*
EMP: 750 **EST:** 1990
SQ FT: 18,000
SALES (est): 9.92MM **Privately Held**
SIC: 8742 1389 5411 Corporation organizing
consultant; Servicing oil and gas wells;
Convenience stores, chain

(P-20128)
ALTRUIST CORP
3030 La Cienega Blvd (90232-7315)
PHONE..................949 370-5096
EMP: 102 **EST:** 2008
SALES (est): 7.17MM **Privately Held**
Web: www.altruist.com
SIC: 8742 Financial consultant

(P-20129)
ALVAREZ MRSAL BUS CNSLTING LLC
Also Called: ALVAREZ & MARSAL
BUSINESS CONSULTING LLC
2029 Century Park E (90002-3076)
PHONE..................310 975-2600
Dora Alverez, *Prin*
EMP: 157
SALES (corp-wide): 1.22B **Privately Held**
Web: www.alvarezandmarsal.com
SIC: 8742 Management consulting services
PA: Alvarez & Marsal Corporate
Performance Improvement, Llc
600 Madison Ave Fl 8
New York NY
212 759-4433

(P-20130)
AMCO FOODS INC
601 E Glenoaks Blvd Ste 108 (91207-1760)
PHONE..................818 247-4716
Bobken Amirian, *Pr*
Nick Amirian, *
Brian Polthow, *
Nareg Amirian, *
EMP: 475 **EST:** 1999
SALES (est): 9.89MM **Privately Held**
SIC: 8742 Business management consultant

(P-20131)
AMTEX SUPPLY HOLDINGS INC
736 Inland Center Dr (92408-1806)
PHONE..................909 985-8918
EMP: 120
SALES (corp-wide): 17.12MM **Privately Held**

SIC: 8742 Management consulting services
PA: Amtex Supply Holdings, Inc.
544 Lakeview Pkwy Ste 300
Vernon Hills IL
800 766-6676

(P-20132)
ANTHOS GROUP INC
705 N Douglas St (90245-2830)
PHONE..................888 778-2986
Shan Umer, *Pr*
EMP: 25 **EST:** 2019
SALES (est): 2.05MM **Privately Held**
Web: www.tidl.com
SIC: 8742 5047 2834 6111 Manufacturing
management consultant; Medical
equipment and supplies; Pharmaceutical
preparations; Export/Import Bank

(P-20133)
APN BUSINESS RESOURCES INC
21418 Osborne St (91304-1520)
PHONE..................818 717-9980
Michael Noori, *CEO*
Khosrow Noori, *
EMP: 85 **EST:** 2011
SALES (est): 15MM **Privately Held**
SIC: 8742 8748 Business planning and
organizing services; Business consulting,
nec

(P-20134)
ARTEMIS CONSULTING LLC
Also Called: Artemis Consulting
1012 W Washington St (92103-1808)
PHONE..................619 573-6328
Adam Svoboda, *Managing Member*
▲ **EMP:** 81 **EST:** 2005
SALES (est): 11.71MM **Privately Held**
Web: www.consultartemis.com
SIC: 8742 8741 8748 Management
engineering; Administrative management;
Systems analysis and engineering
consulting services

(P-20135)
AUNT RUBYS LLC
1014 E Carson St (90807-3636)
PHONE..................562 326-6783
Todd Dotson, *Prin*
EMP: 50 **EST:** 2017
SALES (est): 1.11MM **Privately Held**
SIC: 8742 7381 2771 8322 Corporation
organizing consultant; Security guard
service; Greeting cards; Adult day care
center

(P-20136)
AVASANT LLC (PA)
1960 E Grand Ave Ste 1050 (90245-5096)
PHONE..................310 643-3030
Kevin Parikh, *Managing Member*
Robert Randolph, *
EMP: 80 **EST:** 2006
SQ FT: 6,000
SALES (est): 16.77MM
SALES (corp-wide): 16.77MM **Privately Held**
Web: www.avasant.com
SIC: 8742 Marketing consulting services

(P-20137)
AVETA HEALTH SOLUTION INC
3990 Concours Ste 500 (91764-7983)
PHONE..................909 605-8000
Tim O'rourke, *Pr*
Rod St Clair, *Chief Medical Officer*
Marcia Anderson, *
Carol Hairston, *Health Service Vice President*

EMP: 379 **EST:** 2010
SALES (est): 384.16K
SALES (corp-wide): 1.8MM **Privately Held**
SIC: 8742 Hospital and health services
consultant
HQ: Innovacare Services Company Llc
6900 Tavistock Lakes Blvd
Orlando FL

(P-20138)
BAIN & COMPANY INC
1901 Avenue Of The Stars Ste 2000
(90067-6021)
PHONE..................310 229-3000
Kevin Badkoubehi, *Brnch Mgr*
EMP: 85
SALES (corp-wide): 995.84MM **Privately Held**
Web: www.bain.com
SIC: 8742 Business management consultant
PA: Bain & Company, Inc.
131 Dartmouth St Ste 901
Boston MA
617 572-2000

(P-20139)
BASKETBALL MARKETING CO INC
Also Called: and 1
101 Enterprise Ste 100 (92656-2604)
PHONE..................610 249-2255
Kevin Wulff, *Pr*
▲ **EMP:** 135 **EST:** 2006
SALES (est): 2.26MM
SALES (corp-wide): 2.97B **Publicly Held**
SIC: 8742 Marketing consulting services
HQ: American Sporting Goods Corp
101 Enterprise Ste 200
Aliso Viejo CA
949 267-2800

(P-20140)
BEACON RESOURCES LLC
17300 Red Hill Ave (92614-5643)
PHONE..................949 955-1773
Mike Kelly, *
EMP: 244 **EST:** 2010
SALES (est): 16.64MM
SALES (corp-wide): 166.95MM **Privately Held**
Web: www.addisongroup.com
SIC: 8742 Business planning and organizing
services
HQ: David M. Lewis Company, Llc
20750 Ventura Blvd # 300
Woodland Hills CA

(P-20141)
BLANCHARD TRAINING AND DEV INC (PA)
Also Called: Ken Blanchard Companies, The
125 State Pl (92029-1323)
PHONE..................760 489-5005
Thomas J Mckee, *CEO*
Howard Farfel, *
Deborah K Blanchard, *
Scott Blanchard, *
▼ **EMP:** 200 **EST:** 1978
SALES (est): 61.26MM
SALES (corp-wide): 61.26MM **Privately Held**
Web: www.blanchard.com
SIC: 8742 Training and development
consultant

(P-20142)
BLUE SKY ELEARN LLC
Also Called: Bluesky Broadcast
5405 Morehouse Dr Ste 340 (92121-4725)
PHONE..................877 925-8375

Philip Forte, *CEO*
EMP: 20 **EST:** 2002
SALES (est): 4.19MM **Privately Held**
Web: www.blueskyelearn.com
SIC: 8742 7389 7372 8299 Business planning and organizing services; Teleconferencing services; Educational computer software; Educational services

(P-20143)
BON APPETIT MANAGEMENT CO
1259 E Colton Ave (92374-3755)
PHONE..............................909 748-8970
Bret Martin, *Genl Mgr*
EMP: 217
SALES (corp-wide): 29.97B **Privately Held**
Web: www.bamco.com
SIC: 8742 Administrative services consultant
HQ: Bon Appetit Management Co.
201 Rdwood Shres Pkwy Ste
Redwood City CA
650 798-8000

(P-20144)
BRANDED GROUP INC
Also Called: Facilities MGT & Coml RPS Svcs
222 S Harbor Blvd Ste 500 (92805-3702)
PHONE..............................323 940-1444
Mike Kurland, *CEO*
Kiira Esposito, *
Jerry Jonathan Thomas Iii, *Pr*
EMP: 218 **EST:** 2014
SQ FT: 13,372
SALES (est): 11.89MM **Privately Held**
Web: www.branded-group.com
SIC: 8742 8741 Maintenance management consultant; Construction management

(P-20145)
BRIDGWTER CONSULTING GROUP INC
18881 Von Karman Ave Ste 1450 (92612-8517)
PHONE..............................949 535-1755
Mark Montgomery, *CEO*
EMP: 90 **EST:** 2015
SQ FT: 1,600
SALES (est): 9.41MM **Privately Held**
Web: www.bridgewcg.com
SIC: 8742 7379 Management consulting services; Online services technology consultants

(P-20146)
BRIOTIX
515 Marin St Ste 318 (91360-4116)
PHONE..............................805 864-2711
EMP: 85 **EST:** 2016
SALES (est): 510.03K **Privately Held**
Web: www.briotix.com
SIC: 8742 Management consulting services

(P-20147)
CASHMERE AGENCY INC
5242 W Adams Blvd (90016-2628)
PHONE..............................323 928-5080
Ryan Ford, *Pr*
Eric Enjem, *CFO*
EMP: 154 **EST:** 2021
SALES (est): 3.55MM **Privately Held**
Web: www.cashmereagency.com
SIC: 8742 Marketing consulting services

(P-20148)
CATALYST SPEECH LLC
Also Called: Catalyst Spech Lngage Pthology
205 S Broadway Ste 217 (90012-3607)
PHONE..............................213 346-9945

Ji Soo Kim, *CEO*
EMP: 403 **EST:** 2015
SALES (est): 635.61K
SALES (corp-wide): 165.05MM **Privately Held**
SIC: 8742 Hospital and health services consultant
PA: Pediatric Therapy Services, Llc
184 High St Ste 701
Boston MA
800 337-5965

(P-20149)
CHASE GROUP LLC
Also Called: Center At Parkwest, The
6740 Wilbur Ave (91335-5179)
PHONE..............................818 708-3533
Phil Chase, *Brnch Mgr*
EMP: 295
Web: www.chasegroup.us
SIC: 8742 8049 Management consulting services; Nurses and other medical assistants
PA: The Chase Group Llc
5374 Long Shadow Ct
Westlake Village CA

(P-20150)
CITY OF IRVINE
Also Called: Dept of Public Works
6427 Oak Cyn (92618-5202)
P.O. Box 19575 (92623-9575)
PHONE..............................949 724-7600
Allison Hart, *Mgr*
EMP: 161
Web: www.cityofirvine.org
SIC: 8742 9111 8748 7349 Public utilities consultant; Mayors' office; Business consulting, nec; Building maintenance services, nec
PA: City Of Irvine
1 Civic Center Plz
Irvine CA
949 724-6000

(P-20151)
CITY OF OXNARD (PA)
Also Called: Oxnard City Hall
300 W 3rd St (93030-5729)
PHONE..............................805 385-7803
Doctor Thomas E Holden, *Mayor*
▲ **EMP:** 150 **EST:** 1903
SQ FT: 11,000
SALES (est): 301.04MM
SALES (corp-wide): 301.04MM **Privately Held**
Web: www.oxnard.org
SIC: 8742 Industrial and labor consulting services

(P-20152)
CLOUD9 ESPORTS INC
Also Called: London Spitfire
2720 Neilson Way Unt 5697 (90405-4060)
PHONE..............................424 256-8391
Jack Etienne, *CEO*
Tricia Sugita, *CMO*
EMP: 99 **EST:** 2016
SALES (est): 2.56MM **Privately Held**
Web: www.cloud9.gg
SIC: 8742 Business management consultant

(P-20153)
CO-PRODUCTION INTL INC
8716 Sherwood Ter (92154-7718)
PHONE..............................619 429-4344
EMP: 2300 **EST:** 1997
SALES (est): 23MM **Privately Held**
Web: www.co-production.net

SIC: 8742 Marketing consulting services
PA: Co-Production De Tijuana, S.A. De C.V.
Blvd. Carretera Libre Antiguo Camino Tijuana
Tijuana BCN

(P-20154)
COCKRAM CONSTRUCTION INC
16340 Roscoe Blvd (91406-1204)
PHONE..............................818 650-0999
David Judd, *Pr*
Malcolm W Batten, *
Robert Sirgiovanni, *
Louis E Sciuto, *
Rene Alicea, *
EMP: 315 **EST:** 2000
SALES (est): 16.79MM **Privately Held**
Web: www.cockram.com
SIC: 8742 8741 1541 Construction project management consultant; Construction management; Food products manufacturing or packing plant construction
HQ: Kajima Cockram International Pty Ltd
Level 2 6 Palmer Parade
Cremorne VIC

(P-20155)
CONCRETE WEST CONSTRUCTION INC
1235 N Tustin Ave (92807-1603)
PHONE..............................949 448-9940
Amber Zamora, *Pr*
EMP: 18 **EST:** 2017
SALES (est): 2.19MM **Privately Held**
Web: www.concretewest.com
SIC: 8742 1389 1542 5051 Construction project management consultant; Construction, repair, and dismantling services; Nonresidential construction, nec; Forms, concrete construction (steel)

(P-20156)
CONSUMER RESOURCE NETWORK LLC
Also Called: Launchpad Communications
4420 E Miraloma Ave Ste J (92807-1839)
PHONE..............................800 291-4794
EMP: 340 **EST:** 1995
SALES (est): 19.49MM **Privately Held**
SIC: 8742 Marketing consulting services

(P-20157)
CORPORATE VISIONS INC
2705 Avenida De Anita Apt 29 (92010-8355)
PHONE..............................760 458-0914
Mark Valle, *Prin*
EMP: 155
SALES (corp-wide): 28.8MM **Privately Held**
Web: www.corporatevisions.com
SIC: 8742 Marketing consulting services
PA: Corporate Visions Inc
5455 Kietzke Ln
Reno NV
415 464-4400

(P-20158)
COVARIO INC
9255 Towne Centre Dr Ste 600 (92121-3039)
PHONE..............................858 397-1500
EMP: 96
SIC: 8742 Marketing consulting services

(P-20159)
CPE HR INC
9000 W Sunset Blvd Ste 900 (90069-5801)

PHONE..............................310 270-9800
Harold Walt, *CEO*
Faith Branvold, *
Grace Drulias, *
EMP: 90 **EST:** 1982
SALES (est): 8.69MM **Privately Held**
Web: www.modernhr.com
SIC: 8742 Human resource consulting services

(P-20160)
CROWN GOLF PROPERTIES LP
Also Called: Tustin Ranch Golf Club
12442 Tustin Ranch Rd (92782-1000)
PHONE..............................714 730-1611
Steve Plummer, *Mgr*
EMP: 237
SALES (corp-wide): 92.11MM **Privately Held**
Web: www.tustinranchgolf.com
SIC: 8742 7997 7992 Business management consultant; Membership sports and recreation clubs; Public golf courses
PA: Crown Golf Properties, Lp
222 N La Salle St # 2000
Chicago IL
312 395-7701

(P-20161)
CROWNE COLD STORAGE LLC
786 Road 188 (93215-9508)
PHONE..............................661 725-6458
Cliff Woolley, *Managing Member*
EMP: 50 **EST:** 2014
SALES (est): 3.14MM **Privately Held**
SIC: 8742 2033 Business management consultant; Apple sauce: packaged in cans, jars, etc.

(P-20162)
DENKEN SOLUTIONS INC
9170 Irvine Center Dr Ste 200 (92618-4614)
PHONE..............................949 630-5263
Rajendra Maddula, *CEO*
Eddie Gallardo, *
Rajendra Maddula, *Dir*
EMP: 250 **EST:** 2010
SQ FT: 4,000
SALES (est): 16.8MM **Privately Held**
Web: www.denkensolutions.com
SIC: 8742 8748 7371 7361 Management consulting services; Systems analysis and engineering consulting services; Computer software systems analysis and design, custom; Employment agencies

(P-20163)
DIAGNOSTIC HEALTH CORPORATION
Also Called: Diagnostic Health Los Angeles
6801 Park Ter (90045-1543)
PHONE..............................310 665-7180
Janet Bateman, *Prin*
EMP: 192
SALES (corp-wide): 1.81B **Privately Held**
SIC: 8742 Hospital and health services consultant
HQ: Diagnostic Health Corporation
22 Inverness Pkwy Ste 425
Birmingham AL

(P-20164)
DOWLING ADVISORY GROUP
3579 E Foothill Blvd Ste 651 (91107-3119)
PHONE..............................626 319-1369
James Dowling, *Owner*
EMP: 100 **EST:** 2010
SALES (est): 2.78MM **Privately Held**
Web: www.dowlingadvisorygroup.com

P R O D U C T S & S V C S

SIC: 8742 Business management consultant

(P-20165)
EASTERN GOLDFIELDS INC
1660 Hotel Cir N Ste 207 (92108-2803)
PHONE.................................619 497-2555
Michael Mcchesney, *CEO*
EMP: 218 **EST:** 1998
SALES (est): 4.83MM **Privately Held**
Web: www.easterngoldfields.com
SIC: 8742 Management consulting services

(P-20166)
ECG MANAGEMENT CONSULTANT
11512 El Camino Real Ste 200 (92130)
PHONE.................................206 689-2200
EMP: 121 **EST:** 2019
SALES (est): 5.99MM **Privately Held**
Web: www.ecgmc.com
SIC: 8742 Business management consultant

(P-20167)
EGON ZEHNDER INTERNATIONAL
350 S Grand Ave Ste 3580 (90071-3456)
P.O. Box 27264 (90027-0264)
PHONE.................................213 337-1500
A Daniel Meiland, *CEO*
EMP: 342 **EST:** 1987
SQ FT: 4,300
SALES (est): 3.05MM **Privately Held**
Web: www.egonzehnder.com
SIC: 8742 7361 Personnel management
consultant; Executive placement
HQ: Egon Zehnder International Inc.
520 Madison Ave Fl 23
New York NY
212 519-6000

(P-20168)
ENBIO CORP
150 E Olive Ave Ste 114 (91502-1849)
PHONE.................................818 953-9976
Arthur Zenian, *CEO*
◆ **EMP:** 142 **EST:** 2008
SQ FT: 1,500
SALES (est): 11.77MM **Privately Held**
Web: www.enbiocorp.com
SIC: 8742 Hospital and health services
consultant

(P-20169)
EXULT INC
121 Innovation Dr Ste 200 (92617-3094)
P.O. Box 6300 (92658-6300)
PHONE.................................949 856-8800
James C Madden V, *Ch Bd*
Kevin Campbell, *
John Adams, *
Stephen M Unterberger, *Executive
Business Model Operations Vice President*
Robert E Ball, *CPO*
EMP: 2424 **EST:** 1998
SQ FT: 22,000
SALES (est): 47.29MM
SALES (corp-wide): 3.13B **Publicly Held**
Web: www.exult.net
SIC: 8742 Human resource consulting
services
HQ: Alight (Us), Llc
200 E Randolph St Ll3
Chicago IL
312 381-1000

(P-20170)
FAIRWAY TECHNOLOGIES LLC (PA)
4370 La Jolla Village Dr Ste 500
(92122-1249)

PHONE.................................858 454-4471
Brett Humphrey, *CEO*
EMP: 90 **EST:** 2002
SALES (est): 9.24MM
SALES (corp-wide): 9.24MM **Privately Held**
Web: www.accenture.com
SIC: 8742 Business management consultant

(P-20171)
FINANCIAL TECH SLTONS INTL INC
Also Called: Ftsi
406 E Huntington Dr Ste 100 (91016-3638)
PHONE.................................818 241-9571
Susan Baird Napier, *CEO*
Susan Baird Napier, *Pr*
John De La Pena, *
EMP: 140 **EST:** 2000
SALES (est): 38.98MM **Privately Held**
Web: www.ftsius.com
SIC: 8742 Banking and finance consultant

(P-20172)
FISHERIES RESOURCE VLNTR CORPS
109 Stanford Ln (90740-2533)
PHONE.................................562 596-9261
Thomas J Walsh, *Pr*
EMP: 113 **EST:** 2011
SALES (est): 2.3MM **Privately Held**
Web: www.frvc.net
SIC: 8742 Business planning and organizing
services

(P-20173)
FPG SERVICES LLC
Also Called: Ovation Fertility
15821 Ventura Blvd Ste 625 (91436-4780)
PHONE.................................818 858-1080
EMP: 140 **EST:** 2015
SALES (est): 1.85MM **Privately Held**
SIC: 8742 Management consulting services

(P-20174)
GANZ USA LLC
16525 Sherman Way Ste C5 (91406-3753)
PHONE.................................818 901-0077
Marilyn Smith, *Brnch Mgr*
EMP: 107
SIC: 8742 5199 Management consulting
services; Gifts and novelties
HQ: Ganz U.S.A., Llc
3855 Shallowford Rd # 220
Marietta GA

(P-20175)
GAVIN DE BECKER & ASSOC GP LLC
Also Called: Gavin De Becker & Associates
350 N Glendale Ave Ste 517 (91206-3794)
PHONE.................................818 505-0177
Gavin De Becker, *Managing Member*
Michael La Fever, *
EMP: 180 **EST:** 1979
SQ FT: 1,600
SALES (est): 39.15MM **Privately Held**
Web: www.gdba.com
SIC: 8742 Business management consultant

(P-20176)
GCORP CONSULTING
2831 Camino Del Rio S Ste 311 (92108)
PHONE.................................619 587-3160
Alba Graham, *CEO*
James Graham, *
EMP: 147 **EST:** 2011
SALES (est): 12.32MM **Privately Held**
Web: www.gcorpconsulting.com

SIC: 8742 8711 7379 8243 Management
consulting services; Engineering services;
Online services technology consultants;
Software training, computer

(P-20177)
GOETZMAN GROUP INC
21333 Oxnard St Ste 200 (91367-5194)
PHONE.................................818 595-1112
Greg Goetzman, *Pr*
EMP: 90 **EST:** 1998
SALES (est): 7.82MM **Privately Held**
Web: www.goetzmangroup.com
SIC: 8742 8721 Management consulting
services; Accounting, auditing, and
bookkeeping

(P-20178)
GREENHOUSE AGENCY INC
4100 Birch St Ste 500 (92660-2273)
PHONE.................................949 752-7542
Sean Roche, *Prin*
EMP: 224 **EST:** 2012
SALES (est): 6.04MM **Privately Held**
Web: www.greenhouseagency.com
SIC: 8742 Marketing consulting services

(P-20179)
HATCHBEAUTY AGENCY LLC (PA)
355 S Grand Ave (90071-3152)
PHONE.................................310 396-7070
◆ **EMP:** 30 **EST:** 2008
SALES (est): 9.89MM **Privately Held**
SIC: 8742 2844 5122 Marketing consulting
services; Perfumes, cosmetics and other
toilet preparations; Cosmetics, perfumes,
and hair products

(P-20180)
HEALTHCARE FINANCE DIRECT LLC
1707 Eye St Ste 300 (93301-5208)
PHONE.................................661 616-4400
Tyler Johnson, *CEO*
Mark Weighall, *CFO*
EMP: 84 **EST:** 2009
SALES (est): 7.15MM **Privately Held**
Web: www.gohfd.com
SIC: 8742 Financial consultant

(P-20181)
HEIDELBERG INVESTMENT GROUP IN ✪
4957 Onaknoll Ave (90043-1020)
PHONE.................................213 884-7747
Laron Heidelberg, *CEO*
Whitney Cornell, *Mgr*
Paul Heidelberg, *Admn*
EMP: 122 **EST:** 2022
SALES (est): 8.7MM **Privately Held**
SIC: 8742 7389 Real estate consultant;
Business Activities at Non-Commercial Site

(P-20182)
HUMAN RESOURCE CAPITL CONS INC
Also Called: Hrc Consultants
6236 Paseo Colina (92009-2103)
PHONE.................................760 518-8816
Anisa D Towns, *Pr*
Pierre A Towns, *
EMP: 142 **EST:** 2003
SALES (est): 424.49K **Privately Held**
Web: www.hrcconsultants.com
SIC: 8742 Training and development
consultant
PA: Onyx Global Hr Llc
110 Pine Ave Ste 920

Long Beach CA

(P-20183)
HUMETRIX HOLDINGS INC
1155 Camino Del Mar Ste 5 (92014-2605)
PHONE.................................858 259-8987
Bettina Experton, *Pr*
Claudia M Ellison, *VP*
EMP: 20 **EST:** 1988
SALES (est): 4.39MM **Privately Held**
Web: www.humetrix.com
SIC: 8742 5047 3841 Hospital and health
services consultant; Medical and hospital
equipment; Surgical and medical
instruments

(P-20184)
INDEPENDENT FINCL GROUP LLC
12671 High Bluff Dr Ste 200 (92130-3018)
PHONE.................................858 436-3180
EMP: 106 **EST:** 2003
SALES (est): 5.71MM **Privately Held**
Web: www.ifgsd.com
SIC: 8742 Financial consultant

(P-20185)
INFORMATION FORECAST INC
Also Called: Infocast
22144 Clarendon St Ste 280 (91367-6321)
PHONE.................................818 888-4445
William A Meyer, *Pr*
Bill Meyer, *
Carin Ralph, *
EMP: 30 **EST:** 1986
SALES (est): 7.62MM **Privately Held**
Web: www.infocastinc.com
SIC: 8742 2721 Public utilities consultant;
Magazines: publishing only, not printed on
site

(P-20186)
INFOSPAN
31878 Del Obispo St Ste 118 (92675-3223)
PHONE.................................949 260-9990
Farooq Bajwa, *Pr*
P Kyle Moody, *
Rizwan Uraizee, *
Dan Johnson, *
Gregory J White, *
EMP: 750 **EST:** 2003
SQ FT: 8,000
SALES (est): 12.92MM **Privately Held**
Web: www.ispaninc.com
SIC: 8742 Management consulting services

(P-20187)
KINGS GARDEN LLC
Also Called: Kings Garden Royal Deliveries
3540 N Anza Rd (92262-1606)
PHONE.................................760 275-4969
Lauri Kibby, *Managing Member*
Michael King, *Managing Member*
EMP: 180 **EST:** 2018
SALES (est): 4.53MM **Privately Held**
Web: www.kingsgarden.com
SIC: 8742 Marketing consulting services

(P-20188)
KORN FERRY (US) (HQ)
Also Called: Hay Group
1900 Avenue Of The Stars Ste 2600
(90067-4507)
PHONE.................................310 552-1834
EMP: 250 **EST:** 1963
SALES (est): 101.24MM
SALES (corp-wide): 2.86B **Publicly Held**
SIC: 8742 Human resource consulting
services
PA: Korn Ferry
1900 Avenue Of The Stars # 2600

Los Angeles CA
310 552-1834

(P-20189)
KPC GROUP INC (PA)
9 Kpc Pkwy # 301 (92879-7102)
PHONE...................................951 782-8812
Michael O'brien, *Pr*
EMP: 167 EST: 2006
SALES (est): 573.02MM **Privately Held**
Web: www.thekpcgroup.com
SIC: 8742 Financial consultant

(P-20190)
LOLLICUP FRANCHISING LLC
6185 Kimball Ave (91708-9126)
PHONE...................................626 965-8882
Alan Yu, *Prin*
EMP: 155 EST: 2009
SALES (est): 1.35MM
SALES (corp-wide): 364.24MM **Publicly Held**
Web: www.lollicupfresh.com
SIC: 8742 5149 Food and beverage consultant; Coffee and tea
PA: Karat Packaging Inc.
     6185 Kimball Ave
     Chino CA
     626 965-8882

(P-20191)
LOTUS WORKFORCE LLC
Also Called: Human Capital Select, LLC
5930 Cornerstone Ct W Ste 300
(92121-3741)
PHONE...................................480 264-0773
Martha White, *Pr*
EMP: 734 EST: 2012
SALES (est): 1.07MM **Privately Held**
Web: www.hcselect.com
SIC: 8742 Human resource consulting services
PA: Aya Healthcare, Inc.
     5930 Cornerstone Ct W # 3
     San Diego CA

(P-20192)
LPL HOLDINGS INC (HQ)
Also Called: Lpl Holdings
4707 Executive Dr (92121-3091)
PHONE...................................858 450-9606
Mark Casady, *Ch*
EMP: 90 EST: 1989
SALES (est): 619.96MM **Publicly Held**
Web: www.lpl.com
SIC: 8742 Financial consultant
PA: Lpl Financial Holdings Inc.
     4707 Executive Dr
     San Diego CA

(P-20193)
MANAGEMENT TRUST ASSN INC
12607 Hiddencreek Way Ste R
(90703-2146)
PHONE...................................562 926-3372
Christie Alviso, *Admn*
EMP: 145
Web: www.managementtrust.com
SIC: 8742 8741 Management consulting services; Business management
PA: The Management Trust Association Inc
     15661 Red Hill Ave # 201
     Tustin CA

(P-20194)
MAPP DIGITAL US LLC
4660 La Jolla Village Dr Ste 100
(92122-4625)
PHONE...................................619 342-4340
Steve Warren, *CEO*

Jonah Sulak, *
Cody Kase, *
Eric Hinkle, *
Juhan Lee, *
EMP: 308 EST: 2000
SALES (est): 50MM **Privately Held**
Web: www.mapp.com
SIC: 8742 Marketing consulting services
PA: Marlin Equity Partners, Llc
     1301 Manhattan Ave
     Hermosa Beach CA

(P-20195)
MATT CONSTRUCTION CORPORATION (PA)
9814 Norwalk Blvd Ste 100 (90670-2997)
PHONE...................................562 903-2277
Paul J Matt, *CEO*
Steve F Matt, *
Alan B Matt, *
EMP: 108 EST: 1991
SQ FT: 21,000
SALES (est): 38.53MM **Privately Held**
Web: www.mattconstruction.com
SIC: 8742 Construction project management consultant

(P-20196)
MEDICAL MANAGEMENT CONS INC
Also Called: MMC
6046 Cornerstone Ct W (92121-4758)
PHONE...................................858 587-0609
Mister Rahmani, *Mgr*
EMP: 4950
SALES (corp-wide): 39.85MM **Privately Held**
Web: www.mmchr.com
SIC: 8742 Hospital and health services consultant
PA: Medical Management Consultants, Inc.
     8150 Beverly Blvd
     Los Angeles CA
     310 659-3835

(P-20197)
MEDICAL SPC MANAGERS INC
Also Called: Medical Specialty Billing
1 City Blvd W Ste 1100 (92868-3647)
PHONE...................................714 571-5000
Matt Haberman, *CEO*
Barry Haberman, *
Uri Klugman, *
Monica Bahr, *
Randy Brooks, *
EMP: 115 EST: 1990
SQ FT: 29,000
SALES (est): 17.71MM **Privately Held**
Web: www.msmhealth.com
SIC: 8742 8721 Hospital and health services consultant; Billing and bookkeeping service

(P-20198)
METROSTUDY INC
Also Called: Zonda Intelligence
4000 Macarthur Blvd Ste 40 (92660-2543)
PHONE...................................714 619-7800
Jeff Meyers, *CEO*
Diana Stewart, *
EMP: 184 EST: 2013
SALES (est): 8.15MM **Privately Held**
Web: www.zondahome.com
SIC: 8742 7379 Real estate consultant; Computer related consulting services

(P-20199)
MGID INC
1149 3rd St Ste 210 (90403-7201)
PHONE...................................424 322-8059
Ben Artikov, *Acctnt*

EMP: 91 EST: 2011
SALES (est): 1.87MM **Privately Held**
Web: www.mgid.com
SIC: 8742 Marketing consulting services

(P-20200)
MICHAELSON CONNOR & BOUL (PA)
5312 Bolsa Ave (92649-1062)
PHONE...................................714 230-3600
EMP: 100 EST: 1994
SQ FT: 12,500
SALES (est): 12.95MM **Privately Held**
Web: www.mcbreo.com
SIC: 8742 Real estate consultant

(P-20201)
MINDLANCE INC
Also Called: MINDLANCE INC.
10679 Westview Pkwy Fl 2 (92126-2961)
PHONE...................................858 433-9298
EMP: 1735
SALES (corp-wide): 198.49MM **Privately Held**
Web: www.mindlance.com
SIC: 8742 Human resource consulting services
PA: Mindlance, Inc.
     1095 Morris Ave Ste 101
     Union NJ
     201 386-5400

(P-20202)
MODERN HR INC
7590 N Glenoaks Blvd (91504-1011)
PHONE...................................877 842-4988
Dana Holmes, *Prin*
EMP: 95 EST: 2019
SALES (est): 4.42MM **Privately Held**
Web: www.modernhr.com
SIC: 8742 Business planning and organizing services

(P-20203)
MORRIS & WILLNER PARTNERS
Also Called: Mw Partners
2151 Michelson Dr Ste 185 (92612-1371)
PHONE...................................949 705-0682
Divya Pyreddy, *CEO*
EMP: 100 EST: 2010
SALES (est): 7.18MM **Privately Held**
Web: www.mwpartners.net
SIC: 8742 Management consulting services

(P-20204)
MUTH MACHINE WORKS
4510 Rutile St (92509-2649)
PHONE...................................951 685-1521
Dwayne Gleason, *Mgr*
EMP: 80
SALES (corp-wide): 49.61MM **Privately Held**
SIC: 8742 Manufacturing management consultant
HQ: Muth Machine Works
     8042 Katella Ave
     Stanton CA

(P-20205)
NAN MCKAY AND ASSOCIATES INC
1810 Gillespie Way Ste 202 (92020-0917)
PHONE...................................619 258-1855
Nan Mckay, *Pr*
James Mckay, *VP*
John Mckay, *CEO*
Raymond Adair, *
Dorian Jenkins, *
EMP: 58 EST: 1980

SQ FT: 14,000
SALES (est): 18.73MM **Privately Held**
Web: www.nanmckay.com
SIC: 8742 7371 2731 Training and development consultant; Computer software development; Textbooks: publishing and printing

(P-20206)
NATIONAL TOUR INTGRTED RSRCES
23141 Arroyo Vis Ste 100 (92688-2613)
PHONE...................................949 215-6330
Johnny R Capels, *Pr*
EMP: 23 EST: 2009
SQ FT: 6,000
SALES (est): 2.24MM **Privately Held**
Web: www.nationaltourintegrated.com
SIC: 8742 3448 Marketing consulting services; Prefabricated metal buildings and components

(P-20207)
NATIONSBENEFITS LLC
1540 Scenic Ave (92626-1408)
PHONE...................................877 439-2665
EMP: 95
SALES (corp-wide): 125.57MM **Privately Held**
Web: www.nationsbenefits.com
SIC: 8742 6371 6411 Pension, health, and welfare consulting services; Pension, health, and welfare funds; Insurance agents, brokers, and service
PA: Nationsbenefits, Llc
     1700 N University Dr
     Plantation FL
     877 439-2665

(P-20208)
NBC CONSULTING INC
Also Called: Pacific Health and Welness
2110 Artesia Blvd Ste 323 (90278-3073)
PHONE...................................310 798-5000
Neal M Bychek, *Pr*
Robin Bychek, *
EMP: 100 EST: 2004
SALES (est): 1MM **Privately Held**
Web: www.nbc-consulting.com
SIC: 8742 Hospital and health services consultant

(P-20209)
NCOMPASS INTERNATIONAL LLC
Also Called: Ncompass International
12101 Crenshaw Blvd Ste 800
(90250-3458)
PHONE...................................323 785-1700
Donna Direnzo Graves, *Pr*
Kae Erickson, *
EMP: 138 EST: 2003
SALES (est): 24.53MM **Privately Held**
Web: www.ncompassonline.com
SIC: 8742 Marketing consulting services

(P-20210)
NORTHGATE GONZALEZ INC
425 S Soto St (90033-4315)
PHONE...................................323 262-0595
Estela Gonz Lez De Ortiz, *Prin*
EMP: 396
SALES (corp-wide): 512.69MM **Privately Held**
Web: www.northgatemarket.com
SIC: 8742 5411 Marketing consulting services; Grocery stores
PA: Northgate Gonzalez, Inc.
     1201 N Magnolia Ave
     Anaheim CA
     714 778-3784

PRODUCTS & SVCS

(P-20211)
NVE INC
912 N La Cienega Blvd 2nd Fl
(90069-4848)
PHONE......................323 512-8400
Brett Nathan Hyman, *CEO*
EMP: 100 **EST:** 2005
SALES (est): 10.71MM **Privately Held**
Web: www.experiencenve.com
SIC: 8742 Marketing consulting services

(P-20212)
OCTAGON INC
1840 Century Park E Ste 200 (90067-2101)
PHONE......................310 967-2473
EMP: 214
SALES (corp-wide): 10.93B **Publicly Held**
Web: www.octagon.com
SIC: 8742 Marketing consulting services
HQ: Octagon, Inc.
290 Harbor Dr Fl 3
Stamford CT
203 354-7400

(P-20213)
ODME SOLUTIONS LLC
1963 Christy Ln (92014-2239)
PHONE......................619 227-0059
EMP: 90 **EST:** 2012
SALES (est): 7.01MM **Privately Held**
Web: www.odmesolutions.com
SIC: 8742 8748 7389 Management
consulting services; Business consulting,
nec; Business Activities at Non-Commercial
Site

(P-20214)
ONE HEART WORLDWIDE
Also Called: One H.E.A.R.T.
8141 El Extenso Ct (92119-1134)
PHONE......................415 379-4762
David Murphy, *CEO*
Arlene Samen, *
Toshiko Dignam, *
Julie Dargis, *
Sibylle Kristensen, *
EMP: 85 **EST:** 2006
SALES (est): 2.28MM **Privately Held**
Web: www.oneheartworldwide.org
SIC: 8742 Training and development
consultant

(P-20215)
**ONLINE MARKETING GROUP
LLC**
Also Called: Zoek
530 Technology Dr Ste 100 (92618-1350)
PHONE......................888 737-9635
Samuel Riemer, *CEO*
Doug Powell, *
EMP: 106 **EST:** 2015
SALES (est): 7.7MM **Privately Held**
Web: www.gozoek.com
SIC: 8742 Marketing consulting services

(P-20216)
OPERAM INC
1041 N Formosa Ave 500 (90046-6703)
PHONE......................855 673-7261
Johnny Wong, *Prin*
EMP: 84 **EST:** 2015
SQ FT: 23,000
SALES (est): 9.44MM **Privately Held**
Web: www.operam.com
SIC: 8742 Marketing consulting services

(P-20217)
PATHOLOGY INC
19951 Mariner Ave Ste 150 (90503-1738)

PHONE......................310 769-0561
EMP: 356
Web: www.pathologyinc.com
SIC: 8742 8071 Hospital and health services
consultant; Medical laboratories

(P-20218)
**PENSINMARK RTIREMENT
GROUP LLC**
24 E Cota St Ste 200 (93101-1665)
PHONE......................805 456-6260
Troy G Hammond, *Managing Member*
EMP: 132 **EST:** 2008
SALES (est): 1.81MM **Privately Held**
Web: www.pensionmark.com
SIC: 8742 Financial consultant

(P-20219)
PHYSICIANS DATATRUST INC
17215 Studebaker Rd Ste 220
(90703-2548)
PHONE......................562 860-8771
Marla Lease, *Mgr*
EMP: 125
SALES (corp-wide): 9.24MM **Privately
Held**
Web: www.pdtrust.com
SIC: 8742 Hospital and health services
consultant
PA: Physicians Datatrust, Inc.
161 Thunder Dr Ste 212
Vista CA
760 941-7309

(P-20220)
PLUG CONNECTION LLC
3742 Blue Bird Canyon Rd (92084-7432)
PHONE......................760 631-0992
Ken Altman, *Managing Member*
EMP: 106 **EST:** 2016
SALES (est): 2.6MM **Privately Held**
Web: www.plugconnection.com
SIC: 8742 Business management consultant

(P-20221)
PMCS GROUP INC
2600 E Pacific Coast Hwy Ste 160 (90804)
PHONE......................562 498-0808
Walid Azar, *Pr*
Violene Azar, *
Walid Azar, *VP*
EMP: 100 **EST:** 2005
SALES (est): 7.97MM **Privately Held**
Web: www.pmcsgroup.net
SIC: 8742 Construction project management
consultant

(P-20222)
POSTALIO INC
75 Higuera St Ste 240 (93401-5425)
PHONE......................408 616-9284
Erik Kostelnik, *CEO*
EMP: 72 **EST:** 2019
SALES (est): 3.56MM **Privately Held**
Web: www.postal.com
SIC: 8742 5734 7372 Marketing consulting
services; Software, business and non-game
; Business oriented computer software

(P-20223)
**POWER DIGITAL MARKETING
INC (PA)**
2251 San Diego Ave Ste A250
(92110-2927)
PHONE......................619 501-1211
Grayson Lafrenz, *CEO*
Sasha Dagayev, *Ex VP*
Corey Eulas, *CSO*
EMP: 340 **EST:** 2012

SALES (est): 89.21MM
SALES (corp-wide): 89.21MM **Privately
Held**
Web: www.powerdigitalmarketing.com
SIC: 8742 Marketing consulting services

(P-20224)
POWERSOURCE TALENT LLC
12655 W Jefferson Blvd Ste 400
(90066-7008)
PHONE......................424 835-0878
Lisa Tran Mckee, *CEO*
Mike Bassignani, *
EMP: 101 **EST:** 2017
SALES (est): 3.4MM **Privately Held**
Web: www.powersourcetalent.com
SIC: 8742 Management consulting services

(P-20225)
PWC STRATEGY& (US) LLC
601 S Figueroa St Ste 900 (90017-5743)
PHONE......................213 356-6000
EMP: 113
SALES (corp-wide): 6.79B **Privately Held**
Web: www.pwc.com
SIC: 8742 Management consulting services
HQ: Pwc Strategy& (Us) Llc
101 Park Ave Fl 18
New York NY

(P-20226)
RALIS SERVICES CORP
Also Called: Ralis
1 City Blvd W Ste 600 (92868-3639)
PHONE......................844 347-2547
Delbert O Meeks, *CEO*
Mike Chiang, *
EMP: 150 **EST:** 2014
SALES (est): 6MM **Privately Held**
Web: www.ralisservices.com
SIC: 8742 7371 8721 Human resource
consulting services; Custom computer
programming services; Accounting
services, except auditing

(P-20227)
**RALPH BRENNAN REST GROUP
LLC**
Also Called: Red Fish Grill
1590 S Disneyland Dr (92802-2319)
PHONE......................714 776-5200
Kiki Lungquist, *Brnch Mgr*
EMP: 125
Web: www.neworleans-food.com
SIC: 8742 Restaurant and food services
consultants
PA: The Ralph Brennan Restaurant Group
Llc
550 Bienville St
New Orleans LA

(P-20228)
RED PEAK GROUP LLC
23975 Park Sorrento # 410 (91302-4031)
PHONE......................818 222-7762
EMP: 90 **EST:** 2009
SALES (est): 5.32MM **Privately Held**
SIC: 8742 Marketing consulting services

(P-20229)
REEL AXIS INC
1902 Wright Pl Ste 200 (92008-6583)
PHONE......................760 826-9246
Chris Lee, *CEO*
EMP: 19
SALES (corp-wide): 1.07MM **Privately
Held**
Web: www.reelaxis.com

SIC: 8742 7372 Marketing consulting
services; Application computer software
PA: Reel Axis, Inc.
1521 Hunsaker St
Oceanside CA
760 826-9246

(P-20230)
**RESOURCES CONNECTION INC
(PA)**
Also Called: Resources Global Professionals
17101 Armstrong Ave Ste 100
(92614-5742)
PHONE......................714 430-6400
Kate W Duchene, *
Donald B Murray, *
Jennifer Ryu, *Ex VP*
John D Bower, *CAO*
EMP: 198 **EST:** 1996
SQ FT: 56,200
SALES (est): 775.64MM **Publicly Held**
Web: www.rgp.com
SIC: 8742 7389 8721 Business management
consultant; Financial services; Accounting,
auditing, and bookkeeping

(P-20231)
RMD GROUP INC
2311 E South St (90805-4424)
PHONE......................562 866-9288
Ralph Holguin, *Pr*
EMP: 300 **EST:** 2008
SALES (est): 20.24MM **Privately Held**
Web: www.rmdgroupinc.com
SIC: 8742 Marketing consulting services

(P-20232)
**ROCKY POINT INVESTMENTS
LLC (HQ)**
Also Called: Creative Channel Services LLC
6601 Center Dr W Ste 400 (90045-1577)
PHONE......................310 482-6500
Andy Restivo, *CEO*
George Plumb, *
Hanoz Gandhi, *
Michael Butler, *
EMP: 105 **EST:** 1995
SALES (est): 99.11MM
SALES (corp-wide): 14.29B **Publicly Held**
SIC: 8742 Marketing consulting services
PA: Omnicom Group Inc.
280 Park Ave Fl 31w
New York NY
212 415-3600

(P-20233)
SABAN BRANDS LLC (HQ)
10100 Santa Monica Blvd Ste 500
(90067-4003)
PHONE......................310 557-5230
Elie Dekel, *Managing Member*
William Kehoe, *Managing Member*
Nina Leong, *Managing Member*
Kirk Bloomgarden, *Managing Member*
Rami Yanni, *Managing Member*
EMP: 88 **EST:** 2010
SQ FT: 605,000
SALES (est): 16.5MM
SALES (corp-wide): 54.98MM **Privately
Held**
Web: www.saban.com
SIC: 8742 General management consultant
PA: Global Reach 18, Inc.
10100 Santa Monica Blvd
Los Angeles CA
310 203-5850

(P-20234)
SCORPION DESIGN LLC (PA)
27750 Entertainment Dr (91355-1091)
PHONE..............................661 702-0100
Rustin Kretz, *CEO*
Daniel Street, *Pr*
Raj Ramanan, *COO*
EMP: 585 **EST:** 2003
SQ FT: 100,000
SALES (est): 117.78MM
SALES (corp-wide): 117.78MM **Privately Held**
Web: www.scorpion.co
SIC: 8742 Marketing consulting services

(P-20235)
SHEIN TECHNOLOGY LLC (PA)
777 S Alameda St Fl 2 (90021-1657)
PHONE..............................213 628-4008
EMP: 500 **EST:** 2021
SALES (est): 56.93MM
SALES (corp-wide): 56.93MM **Privately Held**
SIC: 8742 Management consulting services

(P-20236)
SHELL OIL COMPANY
Also Called: Shell
511 N Brookhurst St (92801-5231)
P.O. Box 4848 (92803-4848)
PHONE..............................714 991-9200
Roger Underwood, *Brnch Mgr*
EMP: 125
SALES (corp-wide): 381.31B **Privately Held**
Web: www.shell.com
SIC: 8742 Industry specialist consultants
HQ: Shell Usa, Inc.
150 N Dairy Ashford Rd
Houston TX
832 337-2000

(P-20237)
SITE HELPERS LLC
25232 Steinbeck Ave (91381-1240)
PHONE..............................877 217-5395
Danika Weber, *Managing Member*
EMP: 100 **EST:** 2021
SALES (est): 1.32MM **Privately Held**
SIC: 8742 7389 Marketing consulting services; Business services, nec

(P-20238)
SKIN LAUNDRY HOLDINGS INC
130 Lomita St (90245-4113)
PHONE..............................424 220-8826
Gregg Throgmartin, *CEO*
Christopher Carey, *COO*
Paul Pugh, *CFO*
EMP: 330 **EST:** 2015
SALES (est): 13.92MM **Privately Held**
Web: www.skinlaundry.com
SIC: 8742 7371 Business management consultant; Computer software development and applications

(P-20239)
SL BLUE GARDEN CORP
3790 Keri Way (92028-8139)
PHONE..............................626 633-2672
Susan Luo, *CEO*
EMP: 126 **EST:** 2014
SALES (est): 4.11MM **Privately Held**
SIC: 8742 Management consulting services

(P-20240)
SMART CIRCLE INTERNATIONAL LLC (PA)
Also Called: Smart Circle, The

4490 Von Karman Ave (92660-2008)
PHONE..............................949 587-9207
Michael Meryash, *CEO*
George Graffy, *
Jigna Patel, *
Paul Sunny, *
EMP: 90 **EST:** 2007
SQ FT: 10,700
SALES (est): 327.12MM **Privately Held**
Web: www.smartcircle.com
SIC: 8742 Marketing consulting services

(P-20241)
SMG HOLDINGS LLC
Also Called: Palm Springs Convention Center
277 N Avenida Caballeros (92262-6440)
PHONE..............................760 325-6611
Jim Dunn, *Brnch Mgr*
EMP: 84
SALES (corp-wide): 422MM **Privately Held**
Web: www.visitpalmsprings.com
SIC: 8742 7389 Business management consultant; Convention and show services
HQ: Smg Holdings, Llc
300 Cnshohckn State Rd # 450
Conshohocken PA

(P-20242)
SMITH-EMERY INTERNATIONAL INC (PA)
791 E Washington Blvd Fl 3 (90021-3043)
PHONE..............................213 741-8500
James E Patridge, *Pr*
Helen Choe, *
EMP: 222 **EST:** 1976
SQ FT: 32,380
SALES (est): 41.71MM **Privately Held**
Web: www.smithemeryinternational.com
SIC: 8742 Management consulting services

(P-20243)
SODEXO MANAGEMENT INC
450 World Way (90045-5812)
PHONE..............................310 646-3738
EMP: 1634
SALES (corp-wide): 206.19MM **Privately Held**
Web: www.sodexo.com
SIC: 8742 Food and beverage consultant
HQ: Sodexo Management Inc.
9801 Washingtonian Blvd
Gaithersburg MD

(P-20244)
SOLUTIONZ INC ✪
1029 Swarthmore Ave (90272-2506)
PHONE..............................888 815-0322
EMP: 227 **EST:** 2022
SALES (est): 6.04MM **Privately Held**
Web: www.solutionzinc.com
SIC: 8742 Business management consultant

(P-20245)
SPOTIFY USA INC
555 Mateo St (90013-2647)
PHONE..............................213 505-3040
EMP: 412
SALES (corp-wide): 2.67MM **Privately Held**
SIC: 8742 Management consulting services
HQ: Spotify Usa Inc.
150 Greenwich St Fl 62
New York NY

(P-20246)
SQA SERVICES INC
Also Called: Sqa Services
425 Via Corta Ste 203 (90274-1358)
P.O. Box 5220 (90274-9672)

PHONE..............................800 333-6180
EMP: 267 **EST:** 1995
SQ FT: 8,000
SALES (est): 24.08MM **Privately Held**
Web: www.sqaservices.com
SIC: 8742 Quality assurance consultant

(P-20247)
ST MARYS MEDICAL CENTER
Also Called: ST MARY'S MEDICAL CENTER
1050 Linden Ave (90813-3321)
PHONE..............................562 491-9230
EMP: 3663
SALES (corp-wide): 19.58B **Publicly Held**
Web: validate.perfdrive.com
SIC: 8742 Hospital and health services consultant
HQ: St. Mary's Medical Center, Inc.
901 45th St
Mangonia Park FL
561 844-6300

(P-20248)
STARDUST STUDIOS INC
1823 Colorado Ave (90404-3411)
PHONE..............................310 399-6047
Matthew Marquis, *Pt*
Jake Banks, *Pt*
EMP: 86 **EST:** 2003
SALES (est): 2.91MM **Privately Held**
Web: www.stardust.tv
SIC: 8742 7374 Marketing consulting services; Computer graphics service

(P-20249)
STONE CANYON INDS HOLDINGS LLC (PA)
1875 Century Park E Ste 320 (90067-2539)
PHONE..............................424 316-2061
James Fordyce, *CEO*
Michael C Salvator, *COO*
Michael Neumann, *Pr*
EMP: 56 **EST:** 2018
SALES (est): 1.22B
SALES (corp-wide): 1.22B **Privately Held**
Web: www.scihinc.com
SIC: 8742 2899 Industrial consultant; Heat treating salts

(P-20250)
SULLIVNCRTSMNROE INSUR SVCS LL (PA)
Also Called: Nationwide
1920 Main St Ste 600 (92614-7200)
P.O. Box 19763 (92623-9763)
PHONE..............................800 427-3253
John Monroe, *CEO*
David Kummer, *
Shawn Kraatz, *
Jeannine Coronado, *
William Curtis, *
EMP: 103 **EST:** 1987
SQ FT: 22,000
SALES (est): 38.34MM
SALES (corp-wide): 38.34MM **Privately Held**
Web: www.sullivancurtismonroe.com
SIC: 8742 6411 Management consulting services; Insurance brokers, nec

(P-20251)
SUN PACIFIC MARKETING COOP INC
33502 Lerdo Hwy (93308-9438)
PHONE..............................213 612-9957
Berne H Evans Iii, *Brnch Mgr*
EMP: 395
SALES (corp-wide): 92.65MM **Privately Held**

Web: www.sunpacific.com
SIC: 8742 Marketing consulting services
PA: Sun Pacific Marketing Cooperative, Inc.
1095 E Green St
Pasadena CA
213 612-9957

(P-20252)
SWINERTON RENEWABLE ENERGY
16680 W Bernardo Dr (92127-1900)
PHONE..............................858 622-4040
EMP: 179 **EST:** 2021
SALES (est): 2.37MM **Privately Held**
Web: www.swinerton.com
SIC: 8742 Business management consultant

(P-20253)
T G T ENTERPRISES INC
Also Called: Anderson
12650 Danielson Ct (92064-6822)
PHONE..............................858 413-0300
Randy Dale, *CEO*
Scott Hopkins, *Ex VP*
Todd Stoker, *COO*
EMP: 145 **EST:** 1976
SQ FT: 77,000
SALES (est): 33.92MM **Privately Held**
Web: www.andersondd.com
SIC: 8742 2759 7311 Marketing consulting services; Commercial printing, nec; Advertising agencies

(P-20254)
TACNA INTERNATIONAL CORP
Also Called: Thermalflex
9255 Customhouse Plz Ste G (92154-7636)
PHONE..............................619 661-1261
Ross Baldwin, *CEO*
▲ **EMP:** 19 **EST:** 1984
SQ FT: 18,000
SALES (est): 7MM **Privately Held**
Web: www.tacna.net
SIC: 8742 3677 3052 Management consulting services; Transformers power supply, electronic type; Rubber hose

(P-20255)
TECHNICAL MICRO CONS INC (PA)
Also Called: Technology Management Concepts
807 N Park View Dr Ste 150 (90245-4932)
PHONE..............................310 559-3982
Jennifer Harris, *Pr*
EMP: 25 **EST:** 1985
SQ FT: 3,000
SALES (est): 4.76MM
SALES (corp-wide): 4.76MM **Privately Held**
Web: www.abouttmc.com
SIC: 8742 7372 5734 Management information systems consultant; Prepackaged software; Software, business and non-game

(P-20256)
TECOLOTE RESEARCH INC
2120 E Grand Ave Ste 200 (90245-2565)
PHONE..............................310 640-4700
James Takayesu, *Pr*
EMP: 105
SALES (corp-wide): 47.38MM **Privately Held**
Web: www.tecolote.com
SIC: 8742 8731 Management consulting services; Commercial physical research
PA: Tecolote Research, Inc.
420 S Fairview Ave # 201

PRODUCTS & SVCS

Goleta CA
805 571-6366

(P-20257)
TECOLOTE RESEARCH INC
Also Called: Santa Barbara Group
5266 Hollister Ave Ste 301 (93111-2089)
PHONE..............................805 964-6963
James Suttle, *Brnch Mgr*
EMP: 142
SALES (corp-wide): 47.38MM **Privately Held**
Web: www.tecolote.com
SIC: 8742 Marketing consulting services
PA: Tecolote Research, Inc.
420 S Fairview Ave # 201
Goleta CA
805 571-6366

(P-20258)
TELESECTOR RESOURCES GROUP INC
Also Called: Verizon
5010 Azusa Canyon Rd (91706-1830)
PHONE..............................626 813-4538
Nancy Cano, *Mgr*
EMP: 393
SALES (corp-wide): 136.84B **Publicly Held**
SIC: 8742 Management consulting services
HQ: Telesector Resources Group, Inc.
140 West St
New York NY
212 395-1000

(P-20259)
TELESTAR INTERNATIONAL CORP
Also Called: Telestar Material
5536 Balboa Blvd (91316-1505)
PHONE..............................818 582-3018
Frank Liu, *Pr*
Charlie Fu, *
Karen Liu, *
EMP: 46 **EST:** 1976
SALES (est): 4.81MM **Privately Held**
SIC: 8742 3861 3663 Marketing consulting services; Photographic equipment and supplies; Antennas, transmitting and communications

(P-20260)
THOMAS ST JOHN INC
10877 Wilshire Blvd Ste 1550 (90024-4351)
PHONE..............................424 273-1172
Laura Skinner, *Prin*
EMP: 81 **EST:** 2009
SALES (est): 8.84MM **Privately Held**
Web: www.thomasstjohn.com
SIC: 8742 Quality assurance consultant

(P-20261)
TITANUM HEALTH CARE
1414 S Grand Ave (90015-3067)
PHONE..............................213 765-8123
Gray William Miller, *CEO*
EMP: 81 **EST:** 2016
SALES (est): 528.84K **Privately Held**
Web: www.tihealthcare.com
SIC: 8742 Hospital and health services consultant

(P-20262)
TOM PONTON INDUSTRIES INC
Also Called: Ponton Industries
22901 Savi Ranch Pkwy Ste B (92887-4615)
PHONE..............................714 998-9073
Martin H Ponton, *Pr*

Carl Pino, *VP*
Karen Pettifer, *Sec*
EMP: 19 **EST:** 1972
SALES (est): 2.32MM **Privately Held**
Web: www.pontonind.com
SIC: 8742 3823 Industrial consultant; Absorption analyzers: infrared, x-ray, etc.: industrial

(P-20263)
TORRID MERCHANDISING INC
18501 San Jose Ave (91748-1330)
PHONE..............................626 667-1002
Lisa Harper, *CEO*
Tim Martin, *
Chinwe Abaelu, *
Elizabeth Munoz, *Chief Creative Officer*
▲ **EMP:** 418 **EST:** 2015
SALES (est): 4.73MM **Publicly Held**
SIC: 8742 5621 Merchandising consultant; Ready-to-wear apparel, women's
HQ: Torrid Holdings Inc.
18501 San Jose Ave
City Of Industry CA
626 667-1002

(P-20264)
TOTAL RECON SOLUTIONS INC
27 Oakbrook (92679-4741)
PHONE..............................949 584-8417
EMP: 90 **EST:** 2011
SALES (est): 2.06MM **Privately Held**
SIC: 8742 Management consulting services

(P-20265)
TRI-AD ACTUARIES INC
Also Called: Tri-Ad
221 W Crest St Ste 300 (92025-1728)
PHONE..............................760 743-7555
Thad Hamilton, *CEO*
Curtis Hamilton, *
Judy Simons, *
Thad Hamilton, *VP*
Robert Krier, *
EMP: 117 **EST:** 1973
SQ FT: 17,500
SALES (est): 9.25MM **Privately Held**
Web: www.tri-ad.com
SIC: 8742 6411 Human resource consulting services; Pension and retirement plan consultants

(P-20266)
TRINAMIX INC (PA)
35 Amoret Dr (92602-0770)
PHONE..............................408 507-3583
Amit Sharma, *CEO*
Molly Chakraborty, *Pr*
Sandeep Goyal, *CFO*
EMP: 289 **EST:** 2008
SALES (est): 15.25MM
SALES (corp-wide): 15.25MM **Privately Held**
Web: www.trinamix.com
SIC: 8742 7379 7361 Management consulting services; Computer related consulting services; Labor contractors (employment agency)

(P-20267)
VENTURA COUNTY MEDICAL CENTER
825 N 10th St (93060-1309)
PHONE..............................805 677-5184
EMP: 100
SALES (corp-wide): 77.09MM **Privately Held**
Web: www.vchca.org
SIC: 8742 Business planning and organizing services

PA: Ventura County Medical Center
3291 Loma Vista Rd
Ventura CA
805 652-6000

(P-20268)
VISTAGE INTERNATIONAL INC (PA)
Also Called: Executive Committee, The
4840 Eastgate Mall (92121-1977)
PHONE..............................858 523-6800
Rafael Pastor, *CEO*
Rafael Pastor, *Ch Bd*
Leon Shapiro, *
Richard Carr, *
Ruby Randall, *
EMP: 88 **EST:** 1998
SALES (est): 42.39MM
SALES (corp-wide): 42.39MM **Privately Held**
Web: www.vistage.com
SIC: 8742 Business planning and organizing services

(P-20269)
VISTANCIA MARKETING LLC
Also Called: Shea Homes Ltd Prtnershp
655 Brea Canyon Rd (91789-3078)
PHONE..............................909 594-9500
John Francisshea, *Prin*
EMP: 166 **EST:** 2003
SALES (est): 1.6MM
SALES (corp-wide): 2.1B **Privately Held**
Web: www.jfshea.com
SIC: 8742 Marketing consulting services
HQ: Shea Homes Limited Partnership, A California Limited Partnership
655 Brea Canyon Rd
Walnut CA

(P-20270)
WASSERMAN MEDIA GROUP LLC (PA)
Also Called: Wasserman
10900 Wilshire Blvd Ste 1200 (90024-6548)
PHONE..............................310 407-0200
Casey Wasserman, *Managing Member*
Tim Chadwick, *
Dean Christopher, *
EMP: 115 **EST:** 2003
SQ FT: 40,000
SALES (est): 116.26MM
SALES (corp-wide): 116.26MM **Privately Held**
Web: www.teamwass.com
SIC: 8742 Marketing consulting services

(P-20271)
WATTS HEALTH SYSTEMS INC (PA)
3405 W Imperial Hwy (90303-2219)
PHONE..............................310 424-2220
Clyde W Oden, *Pr*
EMP: 700 **EST:** 1983
SALES (est): 70.19MM
SALES (corp-wide): 70.19MM **Privately Held**
Web: www.wattshealthsystems.com
SIC: 8742 Hospital and health services consultant

(P-20272)
WELLMADE INC
Also Called: Polagram
800 E 12th St (90021-2198)
PHONE..............................213 221-1123
Jin Kim, *Pr*
EMP: 100 **EST:** 2018
SALES (est): 3.46MM **Privately Held**

Web: www.wellmadeusa.com
SIC: 8742 Business management consultant

(P-20273)
WEST CAPITAL LENDING INC
15233 Ventura Blvd Ste 120 (91403-2201)
PHONE..............................818 501-2666
EMP: 113
SALES (corp-wide): 2.72MM **Privately Held**
Web: www.westcapitallending.com
SIC: 8742 Business management consultant
PA: West Capital Lending, Inc.
24 Executive Park Ste 250
Irvine CA
949 652-3943

(P-20274)
WILLIS NORTH AMERICA INC
Also Called: Willis Insurance Services Cal
18101 Von Karman Ave Ste 600 (92612-1012)
PHONE..............................909 476-3300
Bryan Fitzpatrick, *Prin*
EMP: 103
Web: www.wtwco.com
SIC: 8742 Management consulting services
HQ: Willis North America Inc.
200 Liberty St Fl 7
New York NY
212 915-8888

(P-20275)
WILSHIRE ADVISORS LLC (PA)
1299 Ocean Ave Ste 700 (90401-1061)
PHONE..............................310 451-3051
Dennis A Tito, *CEO*
John C Hindman, *
Michael Wauters, *
Renna Lalji, *
EMP: 210 **EST:** 1972
SQ FT: 57,530
SALES (est): 51.6MM
SALES (corp-wide): 51.6MM **Privately Held**
Web: www.wilshire.com
SIC: 8742 Financial consultant

(P-20276)
WPROMOTE LLC (PA)
101 Continental Blvd (90245-4516)
PHONE..............................310 421-4844
Michael Mothner, *Pr*
Paul Rappoport, *
Michael Block, *
Paul Dumais, *
Michael Stone, *CRO*
EMP: 98 **EST:** 2004
SALES (est): 55.47MM
SALES (corp-wide): 55.47MM **Privately Held**
Web: www.wpromote.com
SIC: 8742 Marketing consulting services

(P-20277)
YOUNG & RUBICAM LLC
1735 Irvine Center Dr (92618)
PHONE..............................949 224-6300
David Murphy, *Pr*
EMP: 300
SALES (corp-wide): 17.37B **Privately Held**
Web: www.vmlyr.com
SIC: 8742 Marketing consulting services
HQ: Young & Rubicam Llc
3 Columbus Cir Fl 3 # 3
New York NY
212 210-3017

(P-20278)
YOUR PRACTICE ONLINE LLC (PA)
4590 Macarthur Blvd Ste 500 (92660-2030)
PHONE..............................877 388-8569
Doctor Prem Lobo, *Managing Member*
EMP: 109 **EST:** 2004
SALES (est): 8.31MM **Privately Held**
Web: www.yourpracticeonline.net
SIC: 8742 Marketing consulting services

(P-20279)
ZENLEADS INC
Also Called: Apollo.io
440 N Barranca Ave # 4750 (91723-1722)
PHONE..............................415 640-9303
Tianyuan Zheng, *CEO*
Malvin Hoxhallari, *
EMP: 500 **EST:** 2016
SALES (est): 22.58MM **Privately Held**
Web: www.apollo.io
SIC: 8742 Marketing consulting services

(P-20280)
ZIPRECRUITER INC
Also Called: ZIPRECRUITER
604 Arizona Ave (90401-1610)
PHONE..............................877 252-1062
EMP: 1150 **EST:** 2010
SQ FT: 60,000
SALES (est): 904.65MM **Privately Held**
Web: www.ziprecruiter.com
SIC: 8742 7371 Human resource consulting
services; Custom computer programming
services

8743 Public Relations Services

(P-20281)
BEHR PROCESS SALES COMPANY
3000 S Main St Apt 84e (92707-4225)
P.O. Box 1287 (92702-1287)
PHONE..............................714 545-7101
Kevin Jaffe, *Pt*
John V Croul, *Pt*
EMP: 24 **EST:** 1969
SQ FT: 54,000
SALES (est): 6.1MM **Privately Held**
Web: www.behr.com
SIC: 8743 2851 5198 Sales promotion;
Varnishes, nec; Paints, varnishes, and
supplies

(P-20282)
BNI ENTERPRISES INC
Also Called: B N I
545 College Commerce Way (91786-4377)
PHONE..............................909 305-1818
Ivan Misner, *Ch*
EMP: 600 **EST:** 1985
SQ FT: 33,000
SALES (est): 23MM **Privately Held**
SIC: 8743 Promotion service

(P-20283)
CALIBRE INTERNATIONAL LLC (PA)
Also Called: High Caliber Line
6250 N Irwindale Ave (91702-3208)
PHONE..............................626 969-4660
Catherine Oas, *
◆ **EMP:** 120 **EST:** 1998
SQ FT: 100,000
SALES (est): 23.2MM
SALES (corp-wide): 23.2MM **Privately Held**

Web: www.highcaliberline.com
SIC: 8743 2759 Promotion service;
Promotional printing

(P-20284)
HAVAS FORMULA LLC
1215 Cushman Ave (92110-3904)
PHONE..............................619 234-0345
EMP: 100 **EST:** 2014
SQ FT: 2,700
SALES (est): 23.62MM **Privately Held**
Web: www.havasformula.com
SIC: 8743 Public relations and publicity
HQ: Havas
29 30
Puteaux
158478000

(P-20285)
MAGIC WORKFORCE SOLUTIONS LLC
9100 Wilshire Blvd Ste 700e (90212)
PHONE..............................310 246-6153
Earvin Johnson, *CEO*
Eric Holoman, *
Kawanna Brown, *
EMP: 515 **EST:** 2007
SALES (est): 327.89K
SALES (corp-wide): 72.76MM **Privately
Held**
SIC: 8743 Promotion service
PA: Magic Johnson Enterprises, Inc.
9100 Wilshire Blvd 700e
Beverly Hills CA
310 247-2033

8744 Facilities Support Services

(P-20286)
ACEPEX MANAGEMENT CORPORATION
2707 Saturn St (92821-6705)
PHONE..............................909 625-6900
Henry C Rhee, *CEO*
EMP: 150 **EST:** 1989
SALES (est): 22.88MM **Privately Held**
Web: www.acepex.com
SIC: 8744 Base maintenance (providing
personnel on continuing basis)

(P-20287)
ADVANCED CLEANUP TECH INC
Also Called: Acti
230 E C St (90744-6612)
PHONE..............................310 763-1423
Ruben Garcia, *CEO*
EMP: 260 **EST:** 1992
SALES (est): 15.68MM **Privately Held**
Web: www.actihazmat.com
SIC: 8744 Environmental remediation

(P-20288)
AMERITAC INC (PA)
24 Toscana Way W (92270-1978)
P.O. Box 2550 (92270-1088)
PHONE..............................925 989-2942
Isiah Harris, *Pr*
Lawrence Stevens, *
EMP: 80 **EST:** 1994
SQ FT: 2,024
SALES (est): 5.33MM **Privately Held**
Web: www.ameritac.net
SIC: 8744 Base maintenance (providing
personnel on continuing basis)

(P-20289)
ARGUS MANAGEMENT COMPANY LLC
Also Called: Argus Medical Management
5150 E Pacific Coast Hwy Ste 500 (90804)
PHONE..............................562 299-5200
EMP: 300 **EST:** 1995
SQ FT: 2,500
SALES (est): 23.01MM **Privately Held**
Web: www.argusmso.com
SIC: 8744 Facilities support services

(P-20290)
CAMSTON WRATHER LLC
2856 Whiptail Loop (92010-6708)
PHONE..............................858 525-9999
Dirk Wray, *CEO*
Mark Evans, *
Aaron Kamenash, *
EMP: 250 **EST:** 2014
SQ FT: 1,000
SALES (est): 6.64MM **Privately Held**
Web: www.camstonwrather.com
SIC: 8744 8711 1629 1041 Environmental
remediation; Mining engineer; Land
reclamation; Placer gold mining

(P-20291)
CHUGACH GOVERNMENT SVCS INC
9466 Black Mountain Rd Ste 240
(92126-4550)
PHONE..............................858 578-0276
Kevin Terry, *Mgr*
EMP: 487
SALES (corp-wide): 1.41B **Privately Held**
Web: www.chugach.com
SIC: 8744 Facilities support services
HQ: Chugach Government Services, Inc.
3800 Cntrpint Dr Ste 1200
Anchorage AK

(P-20292)
HENRY CALL INC
Bldg 861 Clark And Arguello (93437)
PHONE..............................805 734-2762
Robert Clark, *Mgr*
EMP: 153
Web: www.callhenry.com
SIC: 8744 7371 8742 Base maintenance
(providing personnel on continuing basis);
Computer software development;
Management consulting services
PA: Call Henry Inc
1425 Chaffee Dr Ste 3
Titusville FL

(P-20293)
INDYNE INC
1036 California Blvd Bldg 11013
(93437-6202)
PHONE..............................805 606-7225
Kenneth A Cinal, *Brnch Mgr*
EMP: 323
SALES (corp-wide): 97.78MM **Privately
Held**
Web: www.indyneinc.com
SIC: 8744 Base maintenance (providing
personnel on continuing basis)
PA: Indyne, Inc.
46561 Expedition Dr 100
Lexington Park MD
703 903-6900

(P-20294)
INNOVATIVE CNSTR SOLUTIONS
575 Anton Blvd Ste 850 (92626-1912)
PHONE..............................714 893-6366
Hirad Emadi, *Pr*

John R White, *
EMP: 105 **EST:** 1999
SQ FT: 2,000
SALES (est): 25.05MM **Privately Held**
Web: www.icsinc.tv
SIC: 8744 1795 Environmental remediation;
Demolition, buildings and other structures

(P-20295)
M & E TECHNICAL SERVICES L L C
Also Called: Mets//
3601 Bayview Dr (90266-3225)
PHONE..............................256 964-6486
EMP: 100
Web: www.metechservices.com
SIC: 8744 4225 4731 7539 Facilities support
services; General warehousing and storage
; Freight transportation arrangement;
Automotive repair shops, nec

(P-20296)
MILITARY CALIFORNIA DEPARTMENT
Also Called: CA Arng 115th Rsg
11300 Lexington Dr Bldg 1000
(90720-5002)
PHONE..............................562 795-2065
Chi Huynh, *Brnch Mgr*
EMP: 500
SALES (corp-wide): 534.4MM **Privately
Held**
SIC: 8744 Facilities support services
HQ: Department Of Military California
9800 Goethe Rd 10
Sacramento CA

(P-20297)
OLYMPUS BUILDING SERVICES INC
Also Called: OLYMPUS BUILDING
SERVICES INC
441 La Moree Rd (92078-5017)
PHONE..............................760 750-4629
Anthony Hipple, *Brnch Mgr*
EMP: 920
SALES (corp-wide): 620.83MM **Privately
Held**
Web: www.olympusinc.com
SIC: 8744 Facilities support services
HQ: Olympus Building Services, Llc
1430 E Missouri Ave B205
Phoenix AZ
480 284-8018

(P-20298)
PONDER ENVIRONMENTAL SVCS INC
19484 Broken Ct (93263-3146)
PHONE..............................661 589-7771
Curtis Fox, *Mgr*
EMP: 25
SALES (corp-wide): 16.11MM **Privately
Held**
Web:
www.ponderenvironmentalservices.com
SIC: 8744 4959 2899 Environmental
remediation; Environmental cleanup
services; Fuel tank or engine cleaning
chemicals
PA: Ponder Environmental Services, Inc.
4563 E 2nd St
Benicia CA
707 748-7775

(P-20299)
PRO ENERGY SERVICES GROUP LLC
2060 Aldergrove Ave (92029-1901)

PRODUCTS & SVCS

PHONE................760 789-7149
EMP: 290 **EST:** 2012
SALES (est): 21.48MM **Privately Held**
Web: www.proeservices.com
SIC: 8744 Facilities support services

(P-20300)
SWISS PORT CORP
Also Called: Swissport
11001 Aviation Blvd (90045-6123)
PHONE................310 417-0258
Armin Unternaehrer, *VP*
▲ **EMP:** 265 **EST:** 1958
SALES (est): 9.71MM **Privately Held**
Web: www.swissport.com
SIC: 8744 4581 Facilities support services; Airports, flying fields, and services

(P-20301)
TECHFLOW INC (PA)
Also Called: Techflow Scntfic A Div Tchflow
9889 Willow Creek Rd Ste 100 (92131-1119)
PHONE................858 412-8000
Robert Baum, *CEO*
Mark Carter, *
Lorie Atoe, *
EMP: 104 **EST:** 1995
SQ FT: 19,000
SALES (est): 48.08MM
SALES (corp-wide): 48.08MM **Privately Held**
Web: www.techflow.com
SIC: 8744 8711 8748 Facilities support services; Engineering services; Systems analysis and engineering consulting services

(P-20302)
ULTURA INC
Also Called: Ultura
3605 Long Beach Blvd Ste 201 (90807-4024)
PHONE................562 661-4999
EMP: 128
SIC: 8744 3399 Environmental remediation; Iron ore recovery from open hearth slag

(P-20303)
WORKCARE INC
300 S Harbor Blvd Ste 600 (92805-3718)
PHONE................714 978-7488
Doctor Peter P Greaney, *CEO*
William E Nixon, *
Paula Sandrock, *
Mason D Harrell Iii, *Chief Medical Officer*
EMP: 181 **EST:** 1997
SQ FT: 11,000
SALES (est): 25.83MM **Privately Held**
Web: www.workcare.com
SIC: 8744 8011 Facilities support services; Offices and clinics of medical doctors

8748 Business Consulting, Nec

(P-20304)
3E COMPANY ENV EC N ENG (PA)
Also Called: 3e
3207 Grey Hawk Ct (92010-6662)
PHONE................760 602-8700
Gregory Gartland, *CEO*
Justin Byron, *
Audrey Jean, *
EMP: 102 **EST:** 1985
SQ FT: 38,139
SALES (est): 118.07MM **Privately Held**
Web: www.3eco.com

SIC: 8748 8731 8711 Environmental consultant; Environmental research; Consulting engineer

(P-20305)
8020 CONSULTING LLC
6303 Owensmouth Ave Fl 10 (91367-2262)
PHONE................818 523-3201
David Lewis, *CEO*
Kelly Swartzel, *
EMP: 86 **EST:** 2013
SALES (est): 3.58MM **Privately Held**
Web: www.8020consulting.com
SIC: 8748 Business consulting, nec

(P-20306)
ADVANCED CORPORATE SVCS INC
Also Called: ACS Cloud Partners
2416 Amsler St (90505-5302)
PHONE................310 937-6848
Eric A Asquino, *Pr*
EMP: 20 **EST:** 2002
SQ FT: 1,500
SALES (est): 5MM **Privately Held**
Web: www.acscp.com
SIC: 8748 7372 Telecommunications consultant; Application computer software

(P-20307)
AECOM TECHNICAL SERVICES INC (HQ)
300 S Grand Ave Fl 9 (90071-3135)
PHONE................213 593-8100
Timothy H Keener, *CEO*
▲ **EMP:** 100 **EST:** 1970
SQ FT: 43,000
SALES (est): 1.18B
SALES (corp-wide): 14.38B **Publicly Held**
Web: www.aecom.com
SIC: 8748 4953 8742 8711 Environmental consultant; Refuse systems; Industry specialist consultants; Engineering services
PA: Aecom
13355 Noel Rd Ste 400
Dallas TX
972 788-1000

(P-20308)
AECOM USA INC
999 W Town And Country Rd (92868-4713)
PHONE................714 567-2501
Bruce Toro, *Mgr*
EMP: 105
SALES (corp-wide): 14.38B **Publicly Held**
SIC: 8748 Business consulting, nec
HQ: Aecom Usa, Inc.
605 3rd Ave
New York NY
212 973-2900

(P-20309)
AECOM USA INC
300 S Grand Ave Ste 900 (90071-3135)
PHONE................213 593-8100
Frederick Werner, *Brnch Mgr*
EMP: 95
SALES (corp-wide): 14.38B **Publicly Held**
SIC: 8748 Business consulting, nec
HQ: Aecom Usa, Inc.
605 3rd Ave
New York NY
212 973-2900

(P-20310)
AECOM USA INC
515 S Figueroa St Ste 400 (90071-3323)
PHONE................213 330-7200

EMP: 95
SALES (corp-wide): 14.38B **Publicly Held**
Web: www.aecom.com
SIC: 8748 Business consulting, nec
HQ: Aecom Usa, Inc.
605 3rd Ave
New York NY
212 973-2900

(P-20311)
AECOM USA INC
401 W A St Ste 1200 (92101-7905)
PHONE................858 947-7144
Frederick William Werner, *Brnch Mgr*
EMP: 137
SALES (corp-wide): 14.38B **Publicly Held**
SIC: 8748 8741 Business consulting, nec; Construction management
HQ: Aecom Usa, Inc.
605 3rd Ave
New York NY
212 973-2900

(P-20312)
ALIANTEL INC
1940 W Corporate Way (92801-5373)
PHONE................714 829-1650
EMP: 90 **EST:** 1996
SALES (est): 12.95MM **Privately Held**
SIC: 8748 7389 Telecommunications consultant; Telephone services

(P-20313)
ALLIANT INSURANCE SERVICES INC (PA)
Also Called: Nationwide
18100 Von Karman Ave Ste 1000 (92612-7196)
P.O. Box 6450 (92658-6450)
PHONE................949 756-0271
Thomas Corbett, *Ch Bd*
Greg Zimmer, *
Ilene Anders, *
Peter Carpenter, *
Diana Kiehl, *
EMP: 175 **EST:** 1925
SALES (est): 1.15B
SALES (corp-wide): 1.15B **Privately Held**
Web: www.alliant.com
SIC: 8748 6411 Business consulting, nec; Insurance agents, nec

(P-20314)
ANKURA CONSULTING GROUP LLC
633 W 5th St Fl 28 (90071-3502)
PHONE................213 223-2109
Shannon Nolan, *Prin*
EMP: 139
SALES (corp-wide): 110MM **Privately Held**
Web: www.ankura.com
SIC: 8748 Business consulting, nec
HQ: Ankura Consulting Group, Llc
485 Lexington Ave Fl 10
New York NY
212 818-1555

(P-20315)
APTIM CORP
1230 Columbia St Ste 1200 (92101-8517)
PHONE................619 239-1690
EMP: 260
SALES (corp-wide): 2.2B **Privately Held**
SIC: 8748 Environmental consultant
HQ: Aptim Corp.
10001 Woodloch Forest Dr # 450
The Woodlands TX
832 823-2700

(P-20316)
BE SMITH INC
12400 High Bluff Dr Ste 100 (92130-3077)
PHONE................913 341-9116
John Doug Smith, *CEO*
Lisa Carr, *
Colleen Chapp, *
Brian Christianson, *
Mark Madden, *
EMP: 271 **EST:** 1980
SALES (est): 22.81MM
SALES (corp-wide): 5.24B **Publicly Held**
Web: www.besmith.com
SIC: 8748 Business consulting, nec
PA: Amn Healthcare Services, Inc.
2999 Olympus Blvd Ste 500
Coppell TX
866 871-8519

(P-20317)
BEHAVIORAL SCIENCE TECHNOLOGY INC (PA)
Also Called: Dekra Insight
1000 Town Center Dr Ste 600 (93036-1100)
PHONE................805 646-0166
EMP: 82 **EST:** 1981
SALES (est): 22.24MM
SALES (corp-wide): 22.24MM **Privately Held**
SIC: 8748 Safety training service

(P-20318)
BEYONDSOFT CONSULTING INC
19009 S Laurel Park Rd Spc 6 (90220-6054)
PHONE................310 532-2822
EMP: 120
Web: www.beyondsoft.com
SIC: 8748 Business consulting, nec
HQ: Beyondsoft Consulting, Inc.
10700 Northup Way Ste 120
Bellevue WA
425 332-4520

(P-20319)
BON SUISSE INC
392 W Walnut Ave (92832-2351)
PHONE................714 578-0001
EMP: 30
Web: www.bonsuisse.com
SIC: 8748 5149 2052 Agricultural consultant; Bakery products; Cones, ice cream
PA: Bon Suisse Inc.
11860 Cmnty Rd Ste 100
Poway CA

(P-20320)
BROADBAND TELECOM INC
515 S Flower St Fl 36 (90071-2221)
PHONE................818 450-5714
EMP: 203
SALES (corp-wide): 34.06MM **Privately Held**
Web: www.broadbandtele.net
SIC: 8748 Telecommunications consultant
HQ: Broadband Telecom, Inc.
100 Quentin Roosevelt Blv
Garden City NY
718 713-8417

(P-20321)
BY REFERRAL ONLY INC
2035 Corte Del Nogal Ste 200 (92011-1445)
PHONE................760 707-1300
Joseph F Stumpf, *Pr*
EMP: 100 **EST:** 1991
SALES (est): 9.65MM **Privately Held**

Web: www.byreferralonly.com
SIC: 8748 Educational consultant

(P-20322)
C M E CORP
1051 S East St (92805-5749)
PHONE.....................714 632-6939
EMP: 195
SALES (corp-wide): 22.17MM **Privately Held**
Web: www.cmecorp.com
SIC: 8748 Business consulting, nec
PA: C. M. E. Corp.
1206 Jefferson Blvd
Warwick RI
800 338-2372

(P-20323)
CAL SOUTHERN ASSN GOVERNMENTS (PA)
Also Called: S C A G
900 Wilshire Blvd Ste 1700 (90017-4701)
PHONE.....................213 236-1800
Hasan Ikhrata, *Ex Dir*
Basil Panas, *
EMP: 116 EST: 1965
SQ FT: 50,000
SALES (est): 15.54MM
SALES (corp-wide): 15.54MM **Privately Held**
Web: scag.ca.gov
SIC: 8748 Urban planning and consulting services

(P-20324)
CASK NX LLC
Also Called: Cask
8910 University Center Ln Ste 400 (92122-1029)
P.O. Box 927170 (92192-7170)
PHONE.....................858 232-8900
Mark Larsen, *Pr*
Jayson Rosenfeld, *
Craig Amundsen, *
Kent Moddelmog, *
Jason Young, *
EMP: 200 EST: 2018
SALES (est): 22.4MM **Privately Held**
Web: www.casknx.com
SIC: 8748 Business consulting, nec

(P-20325)
CDSNET LLC
Also Called: Fmsinfoserv
6053 W Century Blvd (90045-6430)
PHONE.....................310 981-9500
Michael Griffus, *Pr*
Francis G Homan, *CFO*
EMP: 441 EST: 2006
SALES (est): 940.63K
SALES (corp-wide): 4.23MM **Privately Held**
SIC: 8748 Business consulting, nec
HQ: Keolis Transit America, Inc.
53 State St Fl 11
Boston MA

(P-20326)
CENTER FOR SUSTAINABLE ENERGY
3980 Sherman St Ste 170 (92110-4314)
PHONE.....................858 244-1177
Michael Akavan, *Bd*
Mary Mcgroarty, *Ch Bd*
Lawrence E Goldenhersh, *
Michael Akavan Former, *BD*
Nick Leibham, *Vice Chairman*
EMP: 87 EST: 2001
SALES (est): 246.28MM **Privately Held**
Web: www.energycenter.org

SIC: 8748 Energy conservation consultant

(P-20327)
CHAMBERS GROUP INC (PA)
5 Hutton Centre Dr Ste 750 (92707)
PHONE.....................949 261-5414
EMP: 80 EST: 1978
SALES (est): 10.2MM **Privately Held**
Web: www.chambersgroupinc.com
SIC: 8748 Environmental consultant

(P-20328)
CHANNELWAVE SOFTWARE INC
27081 Aliso Creek Rd (92656-5365)
PHONE.....................949 448-4500
Rob Hagen, *Mgr*
EMP: 83
Web: www.channelwave.com
SIC: 8748 8742 Business consulting, nec; Management consulting services
HQ: Channelwave Software, Inc.
1 Kendall Sq Bldg 200
Cambridge MA

(P-20329)
CITY OF NORCO
Also Called: Successor Agcy To Nrco Cmnty R
2870 Clark Ave (92860-1903)
PHONE.....................951 270-5617
EMP: 100
SALES (corp-wide): 49.71MM **Privately Held**
Web: www.norco.ca.us
SIC: 8748 Urban planning and consulting services
PA: City Of Norco
2870 Clark Ave
Norco CA
951 270-5617

(P-20330)
DATATRACE TITLE
200 Commerce (92602-5000)
PHONE.....................800 221-2056
EMP: 95 EST: 2019
SALES (est): 829.81K **Privately Held**
SIC: 8748 Business consulting, nec

(P-20331)
DELOITTE CONSULTING LLP
350 S Grand Ave Ste 200 (90071-3469)
PHONE.....................212 489-1600
Laura Conlin, *Brnch Mgr*
EMP: 385
SALES (corp-wide): 696.23K **Privately Held**
SIC: 8748 Business consulting, nec
HQ: Deloitte Consulting Llp
30 Rockefeller Plz
New York NY
212 492-4000

(P-20332)
EDGE MORTGAGE ADVISORY CO LLC
2125 E Katella Ave Ste 350 (92806-6072)
PHONE.....................714 564-5800
Doug Speaker, *
EMP: 88 EST: 2009
SALES (est): 9.89MM **Privately Held**
Web: www.edgemac.com
SIC: 8748 Business consulting, nec

(P-20333)
ENVENT CORPORATION (PA)
3220 E 29th St (90806-2321)
PHONE.....................562 997-9465
EMP: 93 EST: 1992

SQ FT: 6,400
SALES (est): 38.89MM **Privately Held**
Web: www.enventcorporation.com
SIC: 8748 Environmental consultant

(P-20334)
ENVIRONMENTAL RESOLUTIONS INC
Also Called: Cardno Eri
25371 Commercentre Dr Ste 250 (92630)
PHONE.....................949 457-8950
Steve M Zigan, *CEO*
Robert L Kroeger, *VP*
EMP: 300 EST: 1989
SQ FT: 14,100
SALES (est): 22.46MM **Privately Held**
Web: www.eri-us.com
SIC: 8748 8744 Environmental consultant; Environmental remediation
HQ: Cardno Usa, Inc.
8310 S Valley Hwy Ste 300
Englewood CO

(P-20335)
ENVIRONMENTAL SCIENCE ASSOC
9191 Towne Centre Dr Ste 340 (92122)
PHONE.....................858 638-0900
Ralene Cavataio, *Brnch Mgr*
EMP: 105
SALES (corp-wide): 62.52MM **Privately Held**
Web: www.esassoc.com
SIC: 8748 Environmental consultant
PA: Environmental Science Associates
575 Market St Ste 3700
San Francisco CA
415 896-5900

(P-20336)
FRYMAN MANAGEMENT INC
18 Goodyear Ste 105 (92618-3749)
PHONE.....................949 481-5211
Ross Fryman, *Pr*
EMP: 88 EST: 2014
SALES (est): 4.35MM **Privately Held**
Web: www.frymanmanagement.com
SIC: 8748 Traffic consultant

(P-20337)
GATEB CONSULTING INC
815 Hampton Dr Unit 1b (90291-5702)
PHONE.....................310 526-8323
Sarah Iskander, *CEO*
EMP: 90 EST: 2013
SALES (est): 3.82MM **Privately Held**
Web: www.gateb.com
SIC: 8748 Business consulting, nec

(P-20338)
GEOCON CONSULTANTS INC (PA)
Also Called: Geocon
6960 Flanders Dr (92121-3992)
PHONE.....................858 558-6900
Michael Chapin, *CEO*
Joe Vettel, *
John Hoobs, *
John Juhrend, *
Neal Berliner, *
EMP: 85 EST: 1987
SQ FT: 10,000
SALES (est): 27.86MM **Privately Held**
Web: www.geoconinc.com
SIC: 8748 8711 Environmental consultant; Engineering services

(P-20339)
GEOLOGICS CORPORATION
25375 Orchard Village Rd Ste 102 (91355-3000)
PHONE.....................661 259-5767
Fernando Arroyo, *Mgr*
EMP: 273
Web: www.geologics.com
SIC: 8748 8711 7379 Systems analysis and engineering consulting services; Consulting engineer; Computer related consulting services
PA: Geologics Corporation
5500 Cherokee Ave Ste 400
Alexandria VA

(P-20340)
GIBSON OVERSEAS INC
7776 Tippecanoe Ave (92410-4537)
PHONE.....................323 832-8900
EMP: 169
SALES (corp-wide): 221.89MM **Privately Held**
Web: www.gibsonhomewares.com
SIC: 8748 Business consulting, nec
PA: Gibson Overseas, Inc.
2410 Yates Ave
Commerce CA
323 832-8900

(P-20341)
GOLDMAN DATA LLC
2156 N Shaffer St (92865-3407)
PHONE.....................714 283-5889
EMP: 87
SALES (corp-wide): 5.81MM **Privately Held**
Web: www.goldmandata.com
SIC: 8748 Business consulting, nec
PA: Goldman Data, Llc
1407 N Batavia St Ste 106
Orange CA

(P-20342)
GREATER LOS ANGLES CNTY VCTOR
12545 Florence Ave (90670-3919)
PHONE.....................562 944-7976
Trucmai Nguyen-dever, *Mgr*
EMP: 132 EST: 2019
SALES (est): 12.84MM **Privately Held**
Web: www.glamosquito.org
SIC: 8748 Environmental consultant

(P-20343)
HIGHER GROUND EDUCATION INC (PA)
10 Orchard Ste 200 (92630-8309)
PHONE.....................949 836-9401
Ramandeep Grin, *CEO*
Ramandeep Girn, *
Rebecca Girn, *
Guy Barnett, *
EMP: 307 EST: 2016
SALES (est): 53.85MM
SALES (corp-wide): 53.85MM **Privately Held**
Web: www.tohigherground.com
SIC: 8748 8299 Business consulting, nec; Educational services

(P-20344)
HQE SYSTEMS INC
27419 Via Industria (92590-3752)
PHONE.....................800 967-3036
Qais Alkurdi, *CEO*
Henry Hernandez, *
EMP: 65 EST: 2013
SALES (est): 5.02MM **Privately Held**

PRODUCTS & SVCS

Web: www.hqesystems.com
SIC: 8748 7629 3669 3571 Systems analysis and engineering consulting services; Telecommunication equipment repair (except telephones); Emergency alarms; Electronic computers

(P-20345)
HUMANO LLC
4231 Balboa Ave (92117-5504)
PHONE..................844 448-6266
EMP: 87 **EST:** 2018
SALES (est): 4.22MM **Privately Held**
Web: www.humano.net
SIC: 8748 Business consulting, nec

(P-20346)
IACCESS TECHNOLOGIES INC (PA)
1251 E Dyer Rd Ste 160 (92705-5655)
P.O. Box 53545 (92619-3545)
PHONE..................714 922-9158
Hasan I Ramlaoui, *CEO*
Max Todorov, *Dir Fin*
EMP: 48 **EST:** 2003
SALES (est): 10.77MM
SALES (corp-wide): 10.77MM **Privately Held**
Web: www.iaccesstech.com
SIC: 8748 3812 3699 3728 Business consulting, nec; Aircraft/aerospace flight instruments and guidance systems; Flight simulators (training aids), electronic; Refueling equipment for use in flight, airplane

(P-20347)
IBASET INC (PA)
26812 Vista Ter (92630-8115)
PHONE..................949 598-5200
Ladeira Poonian, *Ch Bd*
Naveen Poonian, *
Daniel De Haas, *
EMP: 45 **EST:** 2015
SQ FT: 28,000
SALES (est): 11.03MM
SALES (corp-wide): 11.03MM **Privately Held**
Web: www.ibaset.com
SIC: 8748 7371 7372 Business consulting, nec; Custom computer programming services; Application computer software

(P-20348)
ICF JONES & STOKES INC
525 B St Ste 1700 (92101-4478)
PHONE..................858 578-8964
Tevon Muto, *Brnch Mgr*
EMP: 111
SALES (corp-wide): 1.78B **Publicly Held**
Web: www.icf.com
SIC: 8748 Environmental consultant
HQ: Icf Jones & Stokes, Inc
1902 Reston Metro Plz
Reston VA
703 934-3000

(P-20349)
IES COMMERCIAL INC
Also Called: Ies
9211 Irvine Blvd (92618-1645)
PHONE..................949 222-0320
EMP: 88
Web: www.ielectric.com
SIC: 8748 Business consulting, nec
HQ: Ies Commercial, Inc.
2801 S Fair Ln Ste 101
Tempe AZ
480 379-6200

(P-20350)
IN MONTROSE WTR SSTNBLITY SVCS
Also Called: Mwss
4 Park Plz Ste 790 (92614-5262)
PHONE..................949 988-3500
Vijay Manthripragada, *Pr*
Jose Revuelta, *
Nasym Afsari, *
Allan Dicks, *
EMP: 90 **EST:** 2019
SALES (est): 16.22MM
SALES (corp-wide): 544.42MM **Publicly Held**
Web: www.montrose-env.com
SIC: 8748 8744 Environmental consultant; Environmental remediation
PA: Montrose Environmental Group, Inc.
5120 Northshore Dr
North Little Rock AR
501 900-6400

(P-20351)
INDIE LLC
32 Journey Ste 100 (92656-5329)
PHONE..................949 608-0854
EMP: 170 **EST:** 2017
SALES (est): 972.08K
SALES (corp-wide): 110.8MM **Publicly Held**
Web: www.indiesemi.com
SIC: 8748 Business consulting, nec
PA: Indie Semiconductor, Inc.
32 Journey Ste 100
Aliso Viejo CA
949 608-0854

(P-20352)
INNOVATIVE VHCL SOLUTIONS LLC
5831 Research Dr (92649-1349)
PHONE..................714 896-8267
Lisa Kuhn, *Mgr*
EMP: 116
SALES (corp-wide): 11.91MM **Privately Held**
Web: www.innovativevehicle.com
SIC: 8748 Business consulting, nec
PA: Innovative Vehicle Solutions Llc
3241 Benchmark Dr
Ladson SC
843 376-3822

(P-20353)
IRVINE TECHNOLOGY CORPORATION
2850 Redhill Ave Ste 230 (92705-5550)
PHONE..................714 445-2624
Nicole Mcmackin, *Pr*
Janet Thornby, *
Michael Rose, *
Kevin Orlando, *
EMP: 160 **EST:** 2000
SALES (est): 19.05MM **Privately Held**
Web: www.irvinetechcorp.com
SIC: 8748 7363 7371 7379 Business consulting, nec; Temporary help service; Software programming applications; Computer related consulting services

(P-20354)
IVY ENTERPRISES INC
5564 E 61st St (90040-3406)
PHONE..................323 887-8661
Jane Kim, *Mgr*
EMP: 440
Web: www.myivyusa.com
SIC: 8748 Business consulting, nec
HQ: Ivy Enterprises, Inc.
25 Harbor Park Dr

Port Washington NY

(P-20355)
JAG PROFESSIONAL SERVICES INC
2008 Walnut Ave (90266-2841)
P.O. Box 3007 (90245-8107)
PHONE..................310 945-5648
Judith Hinkley, *CEO*
EMP: 126 **EST:** 2001
SQ FT: 1,000
SALES (est): 2.77MM **Privately Held**
Web: www.jagprof.com
SIC: 8748 Business consulting, nec

(P-20356)
JOHNSON JOHNSON INNOVATION LLC
Also Called: Jlabs
3210 Merryfield Row (92121-1126)
PHONE..................858 242-1504
Tom Heyman, *Pr*
EMP: 503 **EST:** 2016
SALES (est): 43.66MM
SALES (corp-wide): 94.94B **Publicly Held**
SIC: 8748 Test development and evaluation service
PA: Johnson & Johnson
1 Johnson And Johnson Plz
New Brunswick NJ
732 524-0400

(P-20357)
KINKISHARYO INTERNATIONAL
2825 E Avenue P (93550-2177)
PHONE..................661 265-1647
EMP: 116 **EST:** 2014
SALES (est): 6.51MM **Privately Held**
Web: www.kinkisharyo.com
SIC: 8748 Business consulting, nec
HQ: Kinkisharyo International, L.L.C.
1960 E Grand Ave Ste 1210
El Segundo CA
424 276-1803

(P-20358)
KROS-WISE
435 E Carmel St (92078-4362)
PHONE..................619 607-2899
Lily Aragon, *Pr*
EMP: 150 **EST:** 2004
SALES (est): 18.7MM **Privately Held**
Web: www.kros-wise.com
SIC: 8748 Business consulting, nec

(P-20359)
LANDTEC NORTH AMERICA INC
Also Called: Viasensor
850 Via Lata Ste 112 (92324-3985)
P.O. Box 935668 (31193-5668)
PHONE..................909 783-3636
Christopher Cummins, *Pr*
Wing Lau, *
EMP: 25 **EST:** 2006
SQ FT: 15,000
SALES (est): 2.47MM
SALES (corp-wide): 2.14B **Publicly Held**
Web: www.landtecna.com
SIC: 8748 3825 Environmental consultant; Digital test equipment, electronic and electrical circuits
PA: Graco Inc.
88 11th Ave Ne
Minneapolis MN
612 623-6000

(P-20360)
LSA ASSOCIATES INC (PA)
Also Called: L S A

3210 El Camino Real Ste 100 (92602-1366)
PHONE..................949 553-0666
Les Card, *CEO*
Rob Mccann, *Pr*
James Baum, *
EMP: 110 **EST:** 1974
SALES (est): 39.11MM
SALES (corp-wide): 39.11MM **Privately Held**
Web: www.lsa.net
SIC: 8748 Environmental consultant

(P-20361)
LUSIVE DECOR
Also Called: Luxe Light and Home
3400 Medford St (90063-2530)
PHONE..................323 227-9207
Jason Kai Cooper, *CEO*
EMP: 57 **EST:** 2006
SALES (est): 11.72MM **Privately Held**
Web: www.lusive.com
SIC: 8748 3646 Lighting consultant; Ceiling systems, luminous

(P-20362)
MIDNIGHT SUN ENTERPRISES INC
Also Called: Spearmint Rhino Gentlemens CLB
19900 Normandie Ave (90502-1113)
PHONE..................310 532-2427
Kathy Vercher, *Prin*
EMP: 86 **EST:** 2008
SALES (est): 2.33MM **Privately Held**
SIC: 8748 Business consulting, nec

(P-20363)
MSLA MANAGEMENT LLC
1294 E Colorado Blvd (91106-1901)
PHONE..................626 824-6020
Michael Lambert, *CEO*
Sahniah Siciarz-lambert, *Pr*
Robert Worth Oberrender, *
EMP: 612 **EST:** 2016
SALES (est): 766.87K
SALES (corp-wide): 324.16B **Publicly Held**
SIC: 8748 Business consulting, nec
HQ: Optumserve Health Services, Inc.
328 Front St S
La Crosse WI
866 284-8788

(P-20364)
NETFORTRIS ACQUISITION CO INC
11954 S La Cienega Blvd (90250-3465)
PHONE..................877 366-2548
Grant Evans, *CEO*
EMP: 80
SALES (corp-wide): 32.6MM **Privately Held**
Web: www.sangoma.com
SIC: 8748 Telecommunications consultant
PA: Netfortris Acquisition Co., Inc.
5340 Legacy Dr
Plano TX
877 366-2548

(P-20365)
NETFORTRIS ACQUISITION CO INC
200 Corporate Pointe Ste 300 (90230)
PHONE..................310 861-4300
Chris Vuillaume, *Brnch Mgr*
EMP: 80
SALES (corp-wide): 32.6MM **Privately Held**

Web: www.sangoma.com
SIC: 8748 Telecommunications consultant
PA: Netfortris Acquisition Co., Inc.
5340 Legacy Dr
Plano TX
877 366-2548

(P-20366)
NETWORK SLTONS PRVIDER USA INC
1240 Rosecrans Ave (90266-2555)
PHONE..............................213 985-2173
EMP: 33 EST: 2011
SQ FT: 8,000
SALES (est): 1.89MM **Privately Held**
Web: www.networksolutionsprovider.com
SIC: 8748 7379 3571 4813 Telecommunications consultant; Online services technology consultants; Computers, digital, analog or hybrid; Internet connectivity services

(P-20367)
NINYO MORE GTCHNCAL ENVMTL SCN (PA)
5710 Ruffin Rd (92123-1013)
PHONE..............................858 576-1000
Avram Ninyo, CEO
EMP: 80 EST: 1986
SQ FT: 24,000
SALES (est): 51.87MM
SALES (corp-wide): 51.87MM **Privately Held**
Web: www.ninyoandmoore.com
SIC: 8748 Environmental consultant

(P-20368)
NORTH LA COUNTY REGIONAL CTR (PA)
9200 Oakdale Ave Ste 100 (91311-6505)
PHONE..............................818 778-1900
George Stevens, Dir
Ellen Stein, *
EMP: 280 EST: 1974
SQ FT: 57,000
SALES (est): 645.13MM **Privately Held**
Web: www.nlacrc.org
SIC: 8748 Test development and evaluation service

(P-20369)
OCEAN PARK COMMUNITY CENTER
Turning Point
1447 16th St (90404-2715)
PHONE..............................310 828-6717
Patricia Bauman, Dir
EMP: 175
SALES (corp-wide): 85.14MM **Privately Held**
Web: www.thepeopleconcern.org
SIC: 8748 Urban planning and consulting services
PA: The People Concern
2116 Arlington Ave # 100
Los Angeles CA
323 334-9000

(P-20370)
PATRIOT WASTEWATER LLC
314 W Freedom Ave (92865-2647)
PHONE..............................714 921-4545
Richard Yukihiro, Mgr
EMP: 122 EST: 2015
SALES (est): 328.53K **Privately Held**
Web: www.patriotenvironmental.com
SIC: 8748 Environmental consultant
HQ: Patriot Environmental Services, Inc.
508 East E St Ste A

Wilmington CA
562 436-2614

(P-20371)
PCS LINK INC
Also Called: Greenwood & Hall
12424 Wilshire Blvd Ste 1030 (90025-1031)
PHONE..............................949 655-5000
EMP: 310 EST: 1997
SALES (est): 9.55MM **Privately Held**
SIC: 8748 Communications consulting

(P-20372)
PROJECT DESIGN CONSULTANTS LLC
Also Called: PDC A Bowman Company
701 B St Ste 800 (92101-8162)
PHONE..............................619 235-6471
Gregory M Shields, CEO
William R Dick, *
Debby Reece, *
EMP: 92 EST: 1976
SQ FT: 22,000
SALES (est): 10.8MM **Publicly Held**
Web: www.projectdesign.com
SIC: 8748 8711 8713 Urban planning and consulting services; Civil engineering; Surveying services
PA: Bowman Consulting Group Ltd.
12355 Sunrise Valley Dr # 5
Reston VA

(P-20373)
PSI SERVICES LLC (PA)
Also Called: PSI
611 N Brand Blvd Ste 10 (91203-3290)
PHONE..............................818 847-6180
EMP: 80 EST: 2001
SALES (est): 160.35MM
SALES (corp-wide): 160.35MM **Privately Held**
Web: www.psiexams.com
SIC: 8748 Testing services

(P-20374)
QMERIT ELECTRIFICATION LLC (PA)
2 Venture Ste 550 (92618-7406)
PHONE..............................888 272-0090
Tracy Price, Managing Member
Jon Holland, *
EMP: 116 EST: 2020
SALES (est): 5.16MM
SALES (corp-wide): 5.16MM **Privately Held**
Web: www.qmerit.com
SIC: 8748 Energy conservation consultant

(P-20375)
RECON ENVIRONMENTAL INC (PA)
Also Called: Recon
3111 Camino Del Rio N Ste 600 (92108)
PHONE..............................619 308-9333
Robert Hobbs, Pr
Michael Page, *
Lee Sherwood, *
Jennifer Campos, *
Charles Bull, *
EMP: 82 EST: 1977
SALES (est): 20.4MM
SALES (corp-wide): 20.4MM **Privately Held**
Web: www.recon-us.com
SIC: 8748 Environmental consultant

(P-20376)
RINCON CONSULTANTS INC
1530 Monterey St Ste D (93401-2969)

PHONE..............................805 547-0900
EMP: 238
Web: www.rinconconsultants.com
SIC: 8748 Environmental consultant
PA: Rincon Consultants, Inc.
180 N Ashwood Ave
Ventura CA

(P-20377)
SANYO NORTH AMERICA CORP
Also Called: Sanyo Fisher Company
2055 Sanyo Ave (92154-6234)
PHONE..............................619 661-1134
◆ EMP: 400
SIC: 8748 3632 Business consulting, nec; Household refrigerators and freezers

(P-20378)
SIERRA MONOLITHICS INC (HQ)
103 W Torrance Blvd (90277-3633)
PHONE..............................310 698-1000
Charles Harper, CEO
Javed Patel, Pr
Trevor Roots, CFO
EMP: 27 EST: 1986
SQ FT: 15,000
SALES (est): 10.86MM
SALES (corp-wide): 756.53MM **Publicly Held**
Web: www.jariettech.com
SIC: 8748 8731 3812 Communications consulting; Electronic research; Radar systems and equipment
PA: Semtech Corporation
200 Flynn Rd
Camarillo CA
805 498-2111

(P-20379)
SLALOM LLC
Also Called: SLALOM, LLC
300 Spectrum Center Dr Ste 1500 (92618-3095)
PHONE..............................949 450-1100
EMP: 218
Web: www.slalom.com
SIC: 8748 Business consulting, nec
PA: Slalom, Inc.
821 2nd Ave Ste 1900
Seattle WA

(P-20380)
SLR INTERNATIONAL CORPORATION
20 Corporate Park Ste 200 (92606-3111)
PHONE..............................949 553-8417
Rebecca Hjelm, Brnch Mgr
EMP: 621
SALES (corp-wide): 2.14MM **Privately Held**
Web: www.slrconsulting.com
SIC: 8748 Environmental consultant
HQ: Slr International Corporation
22118 20th Ave Se Ste G20
Bothell WA
425 402-8800

(P-20381)
SOURCE 44 LLC
Also Called: Source Intelligence
4660 La Jolla Village Dr Ste 100 (92122-4604)
PHONE..............................877 916-6337
Glenn Trout, CEO
Matt Thorn, *
Lina Ramos, *
Jennifer Kraus, *
Dan Dague, Chief Development Officer*
EMP: 130 EST: 2009
SALES (est): 12.18MM

SALES (corp-wide): 12.18MM **Privately Held**
Web: www.sourceintelligence.com
SIC: 8748 7371 Environmental consultant; Computer software development
PA: Pg Source Acquisition, Inc.
4660 La Jolla Village Dr # 1
San Diego CA
877 916-6337

(P-20382)
SOUTH CAST A QLTY MGT DST BLDG (PA)
Also Called: A Q M D
21865 Copley Dr (91765-4178)
P.O. Box 4940 (91765-0940)
PHONE..............................909 396-2000
Raymond E Robinson, CEO
Barry R Wallerstein, *
EMP: 720 EST: 1955
SQ FT: 350
SALES (est): 449.02MM
SALES (corp-wide): 449.02MM **Privately Held**
Web: www.aqmd.gov
SIC: 8748 Environmental consultant

(P-20383)
T-FORCE INC (PA)
Also Called: T-Force
4695 Macarthur Ct (92660-1882)
PHONE..............................949 208-1527
Raid Al-khawaldeh, Pr
EMP: 98 EST: 2004
SALES (est): 9.73MM
SALES (corp-wide): 9.73MM **Privately Held**
Web: www.tforcelogistics.com
SIC: 8748 7379 Telecommunications consultant; Online services technology consultants

(P-20384)
TANGOE-PL INC
9920 Pacific Heights Blvd Ste 200 (92121)
P.O. Box 509088 (92150-9088)
EMP: 235
SIC: 8748 Telecommunications consultant

(P-20385)
TEAM RISK MGT STRATEGIES LLC
Also Called: Trust Employee ADM & MGT
3131 Camino Del Rio N Ste 650 (92108)
PHONE..............................877 767-8728
Terence J Keating, Pr
Arthur D Candland, *
Cheryl Doss, *
EMP: 2500 EST: 2003
SALES (est): 83.61MM **Privately Held**
Web: www.teamemployer.com
SIC: 8748 Employee programs administration

(P-20386)
TRC SOLUTIONS INC (HQ)
Also Called: Alton Geoscience
9685 Research Dr Ste 100 (92618-4657)
PHONE..............................949 753-0101
Christopher P Vincze, CEO
Thomas W Bennet Junior, CFO
John Cowdery, *
Martin H Dodd, *
Ed Wiegele, *
EMP: 125 EST: 1981
SQ FT: 47,000
SALES (est): 26.35MM
SALES (corp-wide): 482.42MM **Privately Held**
SIC: 8748 8711 Environmental consultant; Engineering services

PA: Trc Companies, Inc.
21 Griffin Rd N
Windsor CT
860 298-9692

(P-20387)
VENTEGRA INC A CAL BENEFT CORP
450 N Brand Blvd Ste 600 (91203-2349)
PHONE..................................858 551-8111
Robert Taketomo, *Pr*
Mariana Ritchie, *
Don Schoenly, *
Mike Gannon, *
Michele Yoon, *
EMP: 85 EST: 2004
SALES (est): 6.07MM **Privately Held**
Web: www.ventegra.com
SIC: 8748 Business consulting, nec

(P-20388)
VETERANS EZ INFO INC
Also Called: Veterans EZ Info
1901 1st Ave Ste 192 (92101-2322)
PHONE..................................866 839-1329
James Miner, *Ch Bd*
Phonprapha Miner, *
EMP: 138 EST: 2012
SQ FT: 1,200
SALES (est): 24MM **Privately Held**
Web: www.vetsez.com
SIC: 8748 7371 7373 Business consulting, nec; Computer software development; Computer systems analysis and design

(P-20389)
VINCULUMS SERVICES LLC
Also Called: Vinculums
10 Pasteur Ste 100 (92618-3823)
PHONE..................................949 783-3552
Paul Foster, *CEO*
Lisa Di Giovanna, *
Brian Woodward, *
Norm Alexander, *
EMP: 220 EST: 2005
SQ FT: 8,000
SALES (est): 32.7MM
SALES (corp-wide): 753.86MM **Privately Held**
Web: www.qualtekservices.com
SIC: 8748 Telecommunications consultant
HQ: Qualtek Llc
475 Sentry Pkwy E # 1000
Blue Bell PA
484 804-4500

(P-20390)
VOLT TELECOM GROUP INC
Also Called: Volt Telecom Group
218 Helicopter Cir (92878-5031)
PHONE..................................951 493-8900
EMP: 260
SALES (corp-wide): 885.39MM **Privately Held**
Web: www.volt-telecom.com
SIC: 8748 Telecommunications consultant
HQ: Volt Telecommunications Group, Inc.
2400 Meadowbrook Pkwy
Duluth GA
212 704-2400

(P-20391)
WARNER BROS CONSUMER PDTS INC (DH)
4001 W Olive Ave (91505-4272)
PHONE..................................818 954-7980
Brad Globe, *Pr*
Dan Romanelli, *Pr*
Randy Blotky, *Sr VP*
John Schulman, *Sec*

▲ EMP: 112 EST: 2003
SALES (est): 26.86MM **Publicly Held**
SIC: 8748 5961 Business consulting, nec; Novelty merchandise, mail order
HQ: Warner Bros. Entertainment Inc.
4000 Warner Blvd
Burbank CA
818 954-6000

(P-20392)
YUCAIPA COMPANIES LLC (PA)
9130 W Sunset Blvd (90069-3110)
PHONE..................................310 789-7200
Ronald W Burkle, *Managing Member*
Scott Stedman, *
EMP: 150 EST: 1986
SALES (est): 247.94MM
SALES (corp-wide): 247.94MM **Privately Held**
Web: www.yucaipaco.com
SIC: 8748 6719 6726 Business consulting, nec; Investment holding companies, except banks; Investment offices, nec

(P-20393)
ZERO GRAVITY CONSULTING LLC
458 N Doheny Dr (90069-7563)
PHONE..................................310 989-7989
Jonathan Cohen, *Pr*
EMP: 713 EST: 2015
SALES (est): 25MM **Privately Held**
SIC: 8748 Business consulting, nec

8999 Services, Nec

(P-20394)
DATA TRACE INFO SVCS LLC (HQ)
4 First American Way (92707-5913)
PHONE..................................714 250-6700
EMP: 100 EST: 2000
SALES (est): 9.34MM **Publicly Held**
Web: www.datatracetitle.com
SIC: 8999 Information bureau
PA: First American Financial Corporation
1 First American Way
Santa Ana CA

(P-20395)
ESSENSE
Also Called: Maxus USA
6300 Wilshire Blvd Ste 720 (90048-5204)
PHONE..................................323 202-4650
EMP: 711 EST: 2015
SALES (est): 242.78K
SALES (corp-wide): 17.37B **Privately Held**
SIC: 8999 Communication services
HQ: Maxus Communications Llc
498 Fashion Ave
New York NY
212 297-8300

(P-20396)
HEALTHCARE SERVICES GROUP INC
5199 E Pacific Coast Hwy Ste 402 (90804-3309)
PHONE..................................562 494-7939
Mike Hammond, *Prin*
EMP: 1154
SALES (corp-wide): 1.76B **Publicly Held**
Web: www.hcsgcorp.com
SIC: 8999 Artists and artists' studios
PA: Healthcare Services Group Inc
3220 Tillman Dr Ste 300
Bensalem PA
215 639-4274

(P-20397)
MGM AND UA SERVICES COMPANY
245 N Beverly Dr (90210-5319)
PHONE..................................310 449-3000
Gary Barber, *Pr*
EMP: 560 EST: 1994
SALES (est): 3.51MM **Publicly Held**
SIC: 8999 Artists and artists' studios
HQ: Metro-Goldwyn-Mayer, Inc.
245 N Beverly Dr
Beverly Hills CA

(P-20398)
OVERSEAS SERVICE CORPORATION
Also Called: Ocean Service
8221 Arjons Dr Ste B2 (92126-6319)
PHONE..................................858 408-0751
Paul Hogan, *Pr*
EMP: 232
SALES (corp-wide): 36.64MM **Privately Held**
Web: www.oscweb.com
SIC: 8999 Actuarial consultant
PA: Overseas Service Corporation
1100 Nrthpint Pkwy Ste 20
West Palm Beach FL
561 683-4090

(P-20399)
PACE LITHOGRAPHERS INC
Also Called: Pace Marketing Communications
18030 Cortney Ct (91748-1202)
PHONE..................................626 913-2108
Robert Bennitt, *Pr*
Robert Bennitt, *Pr*
Carl Bennitt Junior, *VP Opers*
Carl Bennitt Senior Sales, *Prin*
EMP: 35 EST: 1970
SQ FT: 27,000
SALES (est): 4.97MM **Privately Held**
Web: www.engagepace.com
SIC: 8999 2752 Communication services; Commercial printing, lithographic

(P-20400)
RIVERSIDE CNTY FLOOD CTRL WTR
1995 Market St (92501-1719)
PHONE..................................951 955-1200
Jason Uhley, *Prin*
EMP: 210 EST: 1945
SALES (est): 87.05MM **Privately Held**
Web: www.rcflood.org
SIC: 8999 Natural resource preservation service

(P-20401)
RUBIO ARTS CORPORATION
1313 S Harbor Blvd (92802-2309)
PHONE..................................407 849-1643
EMP: 111
SALES (corp-wide): 2.27MM **Privately Held**
SIC: 8999 Artist
PA: Rubio Arts Corporation
8100 Chancellor Dr # 100
Orlando FL
407 849-1643

(P-20402)
WEAPON X SECURITY INC
297 Country Club Dr (93065-6632)
P.O. Box 940835 (93094-0835)
PHONE..................................818 818-9950
EMP: 80 EST: 2018
SALES (est): 962.55K **Privately Held**
Web: www.weaponxsecurity.com

SIC: 8999 1731 7381 Personal services; Safety and security specialization; Security guard service

---

9111 Executive Offices

(P-20403)
CITY OF CERRITOS
Also Called: Cerritos Ctr For Prfrmg Arts
18125 Bloomfield Ave (90703-8577)
PHONE..................................562 916-8500
TOLL FREE: 800
EMP: 150
SALES (corp-wide): 100.13MM **Privately Held**
Web: www.cerritoscenter.com
SIC: 9111 7922 Executive offices, Local government; Legitimate live theater producers
PA: City Of Cerritos
18125 Bloomfield Ave
Cerritos CA
562 860-0311

(P-20404)
CITY OF CULVER CITY
Also Called: Transportation Department
4343 Duquesne Ave (90232-2944)
PHONE..................................310 253-6525
Steven Cunningham, *Mgr*
EMP: 100
SALES (corp-wide): 147.32MM **Privately Held**
Web: www.culvercity.org
SIC: 9111 8611 Executive offices, state and local; Business associations
PA: City Of Culver City
9770 Culver Blvd
Culver City CA
310 253-5640

(P-20405)
COUNTY OF VENTURA
Also Called: Family Care Center
3291 Loma Vista Rd (93003-3099)
PHONE..................................805 652-6100
Judy Mullins, *Mgr*
EMP: 80
SALES (corp-wide): 165.04MM **Privately Held**
Web: www.ventura.org
SIC: 9111 8322 Executive offices, County government; Adult day care center
PA: County Of Ventura
800 S Victoria Ave
Ventura CA
805 654-2644

(P-20406)
LOS ANGLES CNTY MSEUM NTRAL HS (PA)
900 Exposition Blvd (90007-4057)
PHONE..................................213 763-3466
Lori Bettison-varga, *Pr*
Egbert Gutierrez, *
EMP: 210 EST: 1913
SQ FT: 450,000
SALES (est): 64.34MM
SALES (corp-wide): 64.34MM **Privately Held**
Web: www.nhm.org
SIC: 9111 8399 8412 County supervisors' and executives' office; Fund raising organization, non-fee basis; Museums and art galleries

▲ = Import ▼ = Export
◆ = Import/Export

9131 Executive And Legislative Combined

(P-20407)
SAN PSQUAL BAND MSSION INDIANS (PA)
16400 Kumeyaay Way (92082-6796)
P.O. Box 365 (92082-0365)
PHONE..............................760 749-3200
Allen Lawson, *Ch*
EMP: 99 **EST:** 1971
Web:
www.sanpasqualbandofmissionindians.org
SIC: 9131 6733 Indian Reservation; Trusts, nec

9199 General Government, Nec

(P-20408)
CALIFORNIA DEPT OF PUB HLTH
681 S Parker St Ste 200 (92868-4719)
PHONE..............................714 567-2906
Jacqueline Lincer, *Brnch Mgr*
EMP: 206
SALES (corp-wide): 534.4MM **Privately Held**
Web: cdph.ca.gov
SIC: 9199 8051 General government administration, State government; Extended care facility
HQ: The California Department Of Public Health
1615 Capitol Ave
Sacramento CA
916 558-1784

(P-20409)
COUNTY OF ORANGE
Also Called: Public Fclities Resources Dept
1300 S Grand Ave Ste B (92705-4407)
PHONE..............................714 567-7444
Manny Apodaca, *Brnch Mgr*
EMP: 40
SALES (corp-wide): 5.2B **Privately Held**
Web: www.ocgov.com
SIC: 9199 2759 General government administration; Commercial printing, nec
PA: County Of Orange
400 W Civic Center Dr G36
Santa Ana CA
714 834-6200

(P-20410)
COUNTY OF SAN DIEGO
5560 Overland Ave Ste 410 (92123-1204)
PHONE..............................858 505-6100
Danielle Enriquez, *CFO*
EMP: 87
SQ FT: 10,000
Web: www.sdcda.org
SIC: 9199 6531 General government administration; Real estate brokers and agents
PA: County Of San Diego
1600 Pacific Hwy Ste 209
San Diego CA
619 531-5880

9221 Police Protection

(P-20411)
SAN DIEGO UNIFIED PORT DST
Also Called: San Diego Unified Hbr Police
3380 N Harbor Dr (92101-1023)
PHONE..............................619 686-6585
Betty Kelepecz, *Brnch Mgr*
EMP: 107
SALES (corp-wide): 167.04MM **Privately Held**
Web: www.portofsandiego.org
SIC: 9221 4491 Police protection; Marine cargo handling
PA: San Diego Unified Port District
3165 Pacific Hwy
San Diego CA
619 686-6200

9222 Legal Counsel And Prosecution

(P-20412)
COUNTY OF LOS ANGELES
Also Called: District Attorney
42011 4th St W Ste 3530 (93534-7196)
PHONE..............................661 974-7700
Steve Cooley, *Admn*
EMP: 85
Web: www.lacounty.gov
SIC: 9222 8111 District attorneys' office; General practice attorney, lawyer
PA: County Of Los Angeles
500 W Temple St Ste 437
Los Angeles CA
213 974-1101

9431 Administration Of Public Health Programs

(P-20413)
CITY OF LONG BEACH
Also Called: Long Bch Dept Hlth & Humn Svcs
2525 Grand Ave (90815-1765)
PHONE..............................562 570-4000
Ronald Arias, *Dir*
EMP: 103
SQ FT: 56,733
Web: www.longbeach.gov
SIC: 9431 8322 Administration of public health programs, Local government; Individual and family services
PA: City Of Long Beach
1800 E Wardlow Rd
Long Beach CA
562 570-6450

(P-20414)
COUNTY OF LOS ANGELES
Also Called: Department of Mental Health
510 S Vermont Ave Fl 1 (90020-1912)
PHONE..............................213 738-4601
Richard Kushi, *Brnch Mgr*
EMP: 114
Web: www.lacounty.gov
SIC: 9431 8093 Mental health agency administration, government; Mental health clinic, outpatient
PA: County Of Los Angeles
500 W Temple St Ste 437
Los Angeles CA
213 974-1101

(P-20415)
REGIONAL CTR ORANGE CNTY INC (PA)
Also Called: DEVELOPMENT DISABILITIES CENTE
1525 N Tustin Ave (92705-8621)
P.O. Box 22010 (92702-2010)
PHONE..............................714 796-5100
William J Bowman, *Ex Dir*
EMP: 309 **EST:** 1977
SQ FT: 41,128
SALES (est): 522.74MM
SALES (corp-wide): 522.74MM **Privately Held**
Web: www.rcocdd.com
SIC: 9431 8322 Mental health agency administration, government; Individual and family services

9441 Administration Of Social And Manpower Programs

(P-20416)
COUNTY OF KERN
Also Called: Employers Training Resource
1600 E Belle Ter Ste 5 (93307-3872)
PHONE..............................661 336-6871
Verna Lewis, *Ex Dir*
EMP: 113
Web: www.kerncounty.com
SIC: 9441 8331 Administration of social and manpower programs; Job training and related services
PA: County Of Kern
1115 Truxtun Ave Rm 505
Bakersfield CA
661 868-3690

(P-20417)
COUNTY OF RIVERSIDE
Also Called: Community Health Agency
4065 County Circle Dr (92503-3410)
P.O. Box 7849 (92513-7849)
PHONE..............................951 358-5000
Gary Feldman, *Asst Dir*
EMP: 118
SALES (corp-wide): 4.58B **Privately Held**
Web: www.countyofriverside.us
SIC: 9441 8621 Public welfare administration: nonoperating, government; Health association
PA: County Of Riverside
4080 Lemon St Fl 11
Riverside CA
951 955-1110

9621 Regulation, Administration Of Transportation

(P-20418)
CITY OF LOS ANGELES
Harbor Dept- Port Los Angeles
425 S Palos Verdes St (90731-3309)
P.O. Box 151 (90733-0151)
PHONE..............................310 732-3734
EMP: 650
Web: www.lacity.org
SIC: 9621 8721 Water vessels and port regulating agencies; Accounting services, except auditing
PA: City Of Los Angeles
200 N Spring St Ste 303
Los Angeles CA
213 978-0600

9641 Regulation Of Agricultural Marketing

(P-20419)
CALIFORNIA DEPT FD AGRICULTURE
Also Called: Del Mar Fair Grounds
2260 Jimmy Durante Blvd (92014-2216)
PHONE..............................858 755-1161
Carlene Moore, *CEO*
EMP: 758
SALES (corp-wide): 534.4MM **Privately Held**
Web: www.sdfair5k.com
SIC: 9641 7948 Food inspection agency, government; Racing, including track operation
HQ: California Department Of Food And Agriculture
1220 N St Fl 4
Sacramento CA

ALPHABETIC SECTION

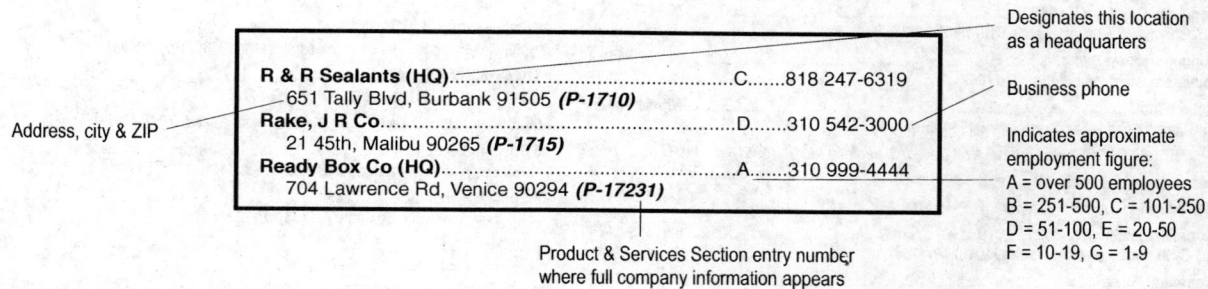

Designates this location as a headquarters

Business phone

Indicates approximate employment figure:
A = over 500 employees
B = 251-500, C = 101-250
D = 51-100, E = 20-50
F = 10-19, G = 1-9

Address, city & ZIP

R & R Sealants (HQ).................................C.......818 247-6319
651 Tally Blvd, Burbank 91505 **(P-1710)**
Rake, J R Co..D......310 542-3000
21 45th, Malibu 90265 **(P-1715)**
Ready Box Co (HQ)...............................A.......310 999-4444
704 Lawrence Rd, Venice 90294 **(P-17231)**

Product & Services Section entry number where full company information appears

See footnotes for symbols and codes identification.
- Companies listed alphabetically.
- Complete physical or mailing address.

---

10 Day Parts Inc ....E...... 951 279-4810
20109 Paseo Del Prado Walnut (91789) **(P-4923)**

1115 Bakersfield Mhrc, Bakersfield Also Called: Crestwood Behavioral Hlth Inc **(P-18120)**

1154 San Diego Mhrc, San Diego Also Called: Crestwood Behavioral Hlth Inc **(P-18121)**

1167 Fallbrook Mhrc, Fallbrook Also Called: Crestwood Behavioral Hlth Inc **(P-18122)**

1170 Lompoc Mhrc, Lompoc Also Called: Crestwood Behavioral Hlth Inc **(P-19258)**

1221 Ocean Ave Apartments, Santa Monica Also Called: Irvine APT Communities LP **(P-14723)**

123 Home Care, Pasadena Also Called: Confido LLC **(P-18604)**

1260 Bb Property LLC ....B...... 805 969-2261
1260 Channel Dr Santa Barbara (93108) **(P-15062)**

1334 Partners LP ....D...... 310 546-5656
1330 Park View Ave Manhattan Beach (90266) **(P-17457)**

1370 Realty Corp ....F...... 818 817-0092
14545 Friar St Van Nuys (91411) **(P-14740)**

180 Snacks Inc ....E...... 714 238-1192
1173 N Armando St Anaheim (92806) **(P-1532)**

180la LLC ....C...... 310 382-1400
12555 W Jefferson Blvd Ste 200 Los Angeles (90066) **(P-15525)**

1835 Columbia Street LP ....D...... 619 564-3993
1835 Columbia St San Diego (92101) **(P-15063)**

1855 S Hbr Blvd Drv Hldngs LLC ....C...... 714 750-1811
1855 S Harbor Blvd Anaheim (92802) **(P-15064)**

1859 Inc ....D...... 858 648-2470
11425 Sorrento Valley Rd Ste 2 San Diego (92121) **(P-4025)**

1928 Jewelry Company, Burbank Also Called: Mel Bernie and Company Inc **(P-12965)**

1on1 LLC ....E...... 310 998-7473
8730 Wilshire Blvd Ste 350 Beverly Hills (90211) **(P-16154)**

1perfectchoice ....F...... 909 594-8855
21908 Valley Blvd Walnut (91789) **(P-3018)**

1st Century Builders Inc ....F...... 818 254-7183
5737 Kanan Rd Agoura Hills (91301) **(P-418)**

1st Team Real Estate, Tustin Also Called: First Team RE - Orange Cnty **(P-14797)**

2.95 Guys, Poway Also Called: Smoothreads Inc **(P-2541)**

20/20 Mobile Corp ....D...... 909 587-2973
3380 La Sierra Ave Riverside (92503) **(P-11842)**

20/20 Plumbing & Heating Inc (PA)..........D...... 951 396-2020
7343 Orangewood Dr Ste B Riverside (92504) **(P-722)**

20/20 Plumbing & Heating Inc ....C...... 760 535-3101
674 Rancheros Dr San Marcos (92069) **(P-723)**

20th Century Fox Studio, Los Angeles Also Called: Fox Net Inc **(P-17194)**

2100 Freedom Inc (HQ)........................D...... 714 796-7000
625 N Grand Ave Santa Ana (92701) **(P-3253)**

2100 Trust LLC (PA)...........................C...... 877 469-7344
625 N Grand Ave Santa Ana (92701) **(P-14986)**

211 La County, San Gabriel Also Called: Informtion Rfrral Fdrtion of L **(P-15510)**

21515 Hawthorne Owner LLC ....D...... 310 406-3730
21535 Hawthorne Blvd Ste 100 Torrance (90503) **(P-19420)**

21st Century Insurance, Woodland Hills Also Called: 21st Century Life Insurance Co **(P-14552)**

21st Century Lf & Hlth Co Inc (PA)..........C...... 818 887-4436
21600 Oxnard St Ste 1500 Woodland Hills (91367) **(P-14445)**

21st Century Life Insurance Co (DH)........A...... 877 310-5687
6301 Owensmouth Ave Ste 700 Woodland Hills (91367) **(P-14552)**

24 Hour Fitness, Carlsbad Also Called: 24 Hour Fitness Usa LLC **(P-17389)**

24 Hour Fitness Usa LLC (HQ)...............C...... 925 543-3100
1265 Laurel Tree Ln Ste 200 Carlsbad (92011) **(P-17389)**

24 Hour Fitness Worldwide Inc ....A...... 925 543-3100
1265 Laurel Tree Ln Ste 200 Carlsbad (92011) **(P-17390)**

24-Hour Med Staffing Svcs LLC ....C...... 909 895-8960
1370 Valley Vista Dr Ste 280 Diamond Bar (91765) **(P-15807)**

24/7 Studio Equipment Inc ....D...... 818 840-8247
3111 N Kenwood St Burbank (91505) **(P-8487)**

29 Palms Enterprises Corp ....A...... 760 775-5566
46200 Harrison Pl Coachella (92236) **(P-17538)**

2b Advice LLC ....E...... 858 366-9750
6790 Embarcadero Ln Carlsbad (92011) **(P-16155)**

2nd Source Wire & Cable, Walnut Also Called: 2nd Source Wire & Cable Inc **(P-5575)**

2nd Source Wire & Cable Inc ....D...... 714 482-2866
20445 E Walnut Dr N Walnut (91789) **(P-5575)**

3 D CAM, Chatsworth Also Called: 3d Cam Inc **(P-4924)**

3 Point Distribution LLC ....E...... 949 266-2700
2139 Placentia Ave Costa Mesa (92627) **(P-2188)**

3-D Precision Machine Inc ....E...... 951 296-5449
42132 Remington Ave Temecula (92590) **(P-7717)**

3-V Fastener Co Inc ....D...... 949 888-7700
630 E Lambert Rd Brea (92821) **(P-6429)**

313 Acquisition LLC ....A...... 801 234-6374
1111 Citrus St Ste 1 Riverside (92507) **(P-16713)**

360 Clinic, Westminster Also Called: 360 Health Plan Inc **(P-19987)**

360 Health Plan Inc ....C...... 800 446-8888
13800 Arizona St Ste 104 Westminster (92683) **(P-19987)**

365 Delivery Inc ....D...... 818 815-5005
440 E Huntington Dr Ste 300 Arcadia (91006) **(P-11436)**

365 Home Care ....D...... 310 908-5179
10225 Austin Dr Ste 208 Spring Valley (91978) **(P-18577)**

3d Cam Inc ....E...... 818 407-0220
9801 Variel Ave Chatsworth (91311) **(P-4924)**

3d Infotech (PA)................................E...... 949 988-0200
7 Hubble Irvine (92618) **(P-10111)**

3d Instruments LLC ....D...... 714 399-9200
4990 E Hunter Ave Anaheim (92807) **(P-10112)**

3d Machine Co Inc ....E...... 714 777-8985
4790 E Wesley Dr Anaheim (92807) **(P-7718)**

3d/International Inc ....C...... 661 250-2020
20724 Centre Pointe Pkwy Unit 1 Santa Clarita (91350) **(P-4341)**

3dcam International Corp ....F...... 818 773-8777
9801 Variel Ave Chatsworth (91311) **(P-7719)**

3dna Corp (PA)..................................C...... 213 992-4809
750 W 7th St Ste 201 Los Angeles (90017) **(P-15950)**

ALPHABETIC

Employee Codes: A=Over 500 employees, B=251-500
C=101-250, D=51-100, E=20-50, F=10-19, G=1-9

2024 Southern California
Business Directory and Buyers Guide

© Mergent Inc. 1-800-342-5647
971

3e, Carlsbad *Also Called: 3E Company Env Ec n Eng (P-20304)*

3E Company Env Ec n Eng (PA) .... **C...... 760 602-8700**
3207 Grey Hawk Ct Carlsbad (92010) *(P-20304)*

3h Communication Systems Inc .... E...... 949 529-1583
3 Winterbranch Irvine (92604) *(P-11867)*

3i Infotech Inc .... E...... 805 544-8327
555 Chorro St Ste B San Luis Obispo (93405) *(P-15951)*

3I INFOTECH INC, San Luis Obispo *Also Called: 3i Infotech Inc (P-15951)*

3M, Monrovia *Also Called: 3M Company (P-4754)*

3M, Corona *Also Called: 3M Company (P-5548)*

3M Company .... E...... 626 358-0136
1601 S Shamrock Ave Monrovia (91016) *(P-4754)*

3M Company .... D...... 951 737-3441
18750 Minnesota Rd Corona (92881) *(P-5548)*

3M Company .... B...... 949 863-1360
2111 Mcgaw Ave Irvine (92614) *(P-10726)*

3M Technical Ceramics Inc (HQ) .... **D...... 949 862-9600**
1922 Barranca Pkwy Irvine (92606) *(P-5562)*

3M Technical Ceramics Inc .... E...... 949 756-0642
17466 Daimler St Irvine (92614) *(P-5563)*

3M Unitek, Monrovia *Also Called: 3M Unitek Corporation (P-10727)*

3M Unitek Corporation .... B...... 626 445-7960
2724 Peck Rd Monrovia (91016) *(P-10727)*

3s Sign Services Inc .... E...... 714 683-1120
1320 N Red Gum St Anaheim (92806) *(P-11093)*

3y Power Technology Inc .... F...... 949 450-0152
80 Bunsen Irvine (92618) *(P-8987)*

4 Earth Farms LLC (PA) .... **B...... 323 201-5800**
5555 E Olympic Blvd Commerce (90022) *(P-13311)*

4 Flight, Rancho Cucamonga *Also Called: Safran Cabin Inc (P-9789)*

4 Over, Glendale *Also Called: 4 Over LLC (P-3725)*

4 Over LLC (HQ) .... **E...... 818 246-1170**
1225 Los Angeles St Glendale (91204) *(P-3725)*

4 What Its Worth Inc (PA) .... **D...... 323 728-4503**
5815 Smithway St Commerce (90040) *(P-2189)*

4 Wheel Parts Wholesalers LLC .... B...... 310 900-7725
400 W Artesia Blvd Compton (90220) *(P-12230)*

418 Media, Los Angeles *Also Called: 418 Media LLC (P-3421)*

418 Media LLC .... E...... 614 350-3960
1875 Century Park E Ste 370 Los Angeles (90067) *(P-3421)*

4excelsior, Anaheim *Also Called: Excelsior Nutrition Inc (P-4001)*

4inkjets, Long Beach *Also Called: Ld Products Inc (P-3054)*

4I Technologies Inc .... C...... 817 538-0974
325 Weakley St Calexico (92231) *(P-7181)*

4liberty Inc .... D...... 619 400-1000
7675 Dagget St Ste 200 San Diego (92111) *(P-858)*

5 Arches LLC .... D...... 949 387-8092
19800 Macarthur Blvd Irvine (92612) *(P-14354)*

5 Star Service Inc .... E...... 323 647-7777
18723 Via Princessa Santa Clarita (91387) *(P-17066)*

5.11 Tactical Series, Costa Mesa *Also Called: 511 Inc (P-13927)*

511 Inc (DH) .... **E...... 949 800-1511**
3150 Bristol St Ste 300 Costa Mesa (92626) *(P-13927)*

51st St & 8th Ave Corp .... C...... 619 424-4000
4000 Coronado Bay Rd Coronado (92118) *(P-15065)*

5e Boron Americas LLC .... E...... 442 292-2120
27555 Hector Rd Newberry Springs (92365) *(P-413)*

5th Axis Inc (PA) .... **C...... 858 505-0432**
7140 Engineer Rd San Diego (92111) *(P-7720)*

6417 Selma Hotel LLC .... C...... 323 844-6417
6417 Selma Ave Los Angeles (90028) *(P-15066)*

6500 Hllister Ave Partners LLC .... D...... 805 722-1362
6500 Hollister Ave Goleta (93117) *(P-14650)*

6th Street Partners LLC .... F...... 213 377-5277
3950 W 6th St 201 Los Angeles (90020) *(P-3019)*

7 Up / R C Bottling Co, Vernon *Also Called: American Bottling Company (P-1679)*

75s Corp .... E...... 323 234-7708
800 E 62nd St Los Angeles (90001) *(P-12949)*

7th & C Investments LLC .... C...... 619 233-7327
404 14th St San Diego (92101) *(P-15019)*

7th Standard Ranch Company .... B...... 661 399-0416
33374 Lerdo Hwy Bakersfield (93308) *(P-26)*

8020 Consulting LLC .... D...... 818 523-3201
6303 Owensmouth Ave Fl 10 Woodland Hills (91367) *(P-20305)*

8110 Aero Holding LLC .... C...... 858 277-8888
8110 Aero Dr San Diego (92123) *(P-15067)*

860, Shameless, Hot Wire, Los Angeles *Also Called: JT Design Studio Inc (P-2338)*

88 Special Sweet Inc .... E...... 909 525-7055
2437 Lee Ave South El Monte (91733) *(P-3144)*

88 Special Sweet Inc .... D...... 909 525-7055
2437 Lee Ave South El Monte (91733) *(P-3227)*

89908 Inc .... E...... 949 221-0023
15651 Mosher Ave Tustin (92780) *(P-9338)*

901 West Olympic Blvd Ltd Prtn .... C...... 347 992-5707
901 W Olympic Blvd Los Angeles (90015) *(P-15068)*

911 Health Inc .... D...... 310 560-8509
701 Santa Monica Blvd Ste 300 Santa Monica (90401) *(P-19954)*

911 Restoration Entps Inc .... B...... 832 887-2582
6932 Gross Ave West Hills (91307) *(P-15689)*

911 Restoration of San Diego, San Diego *Also Called: Demor Enterprises Inc (P-1154)*

99 Cents Only Stores, Commerce *Also Called: 99 Cents Only Stores LLC (P-13524)*

99 Cents Only Stores LLC (HQ) .... **B...... 323 980-8145**
4000 Union Pacific Ave Commerce (90023) *(P-13524)*

99 Ranch Market, Buena Park *Also Called: Tawa Supermarket Inc (P-1404)*

A & A Feros Non Feros Met LLC .... E...... 213 622-9995
640 S Hill St Los Angeles (90014) *(P-6173)*

A & A Machine & Dev Co Inc .... F...... 310 532-7706
16625 Gramercy Pl Gardena (90247) *(P-7721)*

A & A Ready Mix Concrete, Newport Beach *Also Called: Lebata Inc (P-5485)*

A & A Ready Mixed Concrete Inc (PA) .... **E...... 949 253-2800**
4621 Teller Ave Ste 130 Newport Beach (92660) *(P-5457)*

A & B Aerospace Inc .... E...... 626 334-2976
612 S Ayon Ave Azusa (91702) *(P-7722)*

A & B Brush Mfg Corp .... F...... 626 303-8856
1150 3 Ranch Rd Duarte (91010) *(P-11083)*

A & B Equipment, Corona *Also Called: Boudreau Pipeline Corporation (P-663)*

A & D Fire Protection Inc .... D...... 619 258-7697
7130 Convoy Ct San Diego (92111) *(P-724)*

A & D Plating Inc .... F...... 760 480-4580
2265 Micro Pl Ste A Escondido (92029) *(P-6572)*

A & D Precision Mfg Inc .... E...... 714 779-2714
4751 E Hunter Ave Anaheim (92807) *(P-7723)*

A & H Communications Inc .... C...... 949 250-4555
15 Chrysler Irvine (92618) *(P-656)*

A & H Engineering & Mfg Inc .... E...... 562 623-9717
17109 Edwards Rd Cerritos (90703) *(P-7724)*

A & H Tool Engineering, Cerritos *Also Called: A & H Engineering & Mfg Inc (P-7724)*

A & I Color Laboratory, Burbank *Also Called: Jake Hey Incorporated (P-16761)*

A & J Industries Inc .... F...... 310 216-2170
1430 240th St Harbor City (90710) *(P-2707)*

A & J Manufacturing, Harbor City *Also Called: A & J Industries Inc (P-2707)*

A & J Manufacturing Company .... E...... 714 544-9570
70 Icon Foothill Ranch (92610) *(P-6490)*

A & M Electronics Inc .... E...... 661 257-3680
25018 Avenue Kearny Valencia (91355) *(P-8637)*

A & M Engineering Inc .... D...... 626 813-2020
15854 Salvatiera St Irwindale (91706) *(P-7725)*

A & M Sculpture Lighting, Los Angeles *Also Called: A & M Sculptured Metals LLC (P-6174)*

A & M Sculptured Metals LLC .... F...... 323 263-2221
1781 N Indiana St Los Angeles (90063) *(P-6174)*

A & P Towing-Metropro Rd Svcs, Costa Mesa *Also Called: Metropro Road Services Inc (P-17058)*

A & R, Carson *Also Called: A & R Engineering Co Inc (P-7726)*

A & R Engineering Co Inc .... D...... 310 603-9060
1053 E Bedmar St Carson (90746) *(P-7726)*

A & S Case Company Inc .... E...... 800 394-6181
5260 Vineland Ave North Hollywood (91601) *(P-2729)*

A & S Mold and Die Corp .... D...... 818 341-5393
9705 Eton Ave Chatsworth (91311) *(P-4925)*

A & S Technologies, Northridge *Also Called: Ikano Communications Inc (P-16500)*

Mergent email: customerrelations@mergent.com
972

2024 Southern California
Business Directory and Buyers Guide

(P-0000) Products & Services Section entry number
(PA)=Parent Co (HQ)=Headquarters (DH)=Div Headquarters

A A A Automobile Club So Cal, Los Angeles *Also Called: Automobile Club Southern Cal (P-14564)*

A A A Automobile Club So Cal, Irvine *Also Called: Automobile Club Southern Cal (P-14565)*

A A A Automobile Club So Cal, Long Beach *Also Called: Automobile Club Southern Cal (P-19521)*

A A A Partitions, Los Angeles *Also Called: King Wire Partitions Inc (P-6400)*

A A C N, Aliso Viejo *Also Called: American Assn Crtcal Care Nrse (P-19007)*

A A Cater Truck Mfg Co Inc .... E...... 323 233-2343
750 E Slauson Ave Los Angeles (90011) *(P-2824)*

A A Construction, Rialto *Also Called: Arnett Construction Inc (P-1122)*

A A E Aerospace & Coml Tech, Huntington Beach *Also Called: American Automated Engrg Inc (P-9914)*

A A Gonzalez Inc .... D...... 818 367-2242
13264 Ralston Ave Rancho Cascades (91342) *(P-965)*

A A P, Gardena *Also Called: American Aircraft Products Inc (P-6186)*

A and G Inc (HQ) .... A...... 714 765-0400
11296 Harrel St Jurupa Valley (91752) *(P-2190)*

A and M Welding Inc .... E...... 310 329-2700
16935 S Broadway Gardena (90248) *(P-5986)*

A B, Sylmar *Also Called: Advanced Bionics LLC (P-10632)*

A B C Restaurant Equipment Co, South El Monte *Also Called: Master Enterprises Inc (P-6267)*

A B M, Irvine *Also Called: ABM Facility Services LLC (P-19538)*

A B S, City Of Industry *Also Called: Magnell Associate Inc (P-12425)*

A B S, Signal Hill *Also Called: Applied Business Software Inc (P-16173)*

A Breast Pump and More, Carlsbad *Also Called: Hygeia II Medical Group Inc (P-10807)*

A Buchalter Professional Corp (PA) .... C...... 213 891-0700
1000 Wilshire Blvd Ste 1500 Los Angeles (90017) *(P-18817)*

A C I Communications, Calabasas *Also Called: Able Cable Inc (P-17067)*

A C M, Santa Ana *Also Called: Advanced Clnroom McRclean Corp (P-15690)*

A C T, Garden Grove *Also Called: Associated Components Technology Inc (P-6812)*

A C T, Fountain Valley *Also Called: Advanced Charging Tech Inc (P-8199)*

A Cdg Boeing Company .... C...... 562 608-2000
4060 N Lakewood Blvd Long Beach (90808) *(P-9584)*

A Clark/Mccarthy Joint Venture .... A...... 714 429-9779
18201 Von Karman Ave # 800 Irvine (92612) *(P-419)*

A Class Precision Inc .... F...... 951 549-9706
13395 Estelle St Corona (92879) *(P-1036)*

A Commom Thread, Los Angeles *Also Called: Dda Holdings Inc (P-2317)*

A D G, San Diego *Also Called: Affinity Development Group Inc (P-19509)*

A D S, Los Angeles *Also Called: Advanced Digital Services Inc (P-17166)*

A Deluxe Entrmt Svcs Group Co, Burbank *Also Called: Deluxe Encore Inc (P-11916)*

A Dentons Innovation Wirthlin, Los Angeles *Also Called: Dentons US LLP (P-18848)*

A Development Stage Company, Beverly Hills *Also Called: Stratos Renewables Corporation (P-4531)*

A Division Continental Can Co, Santa Ana *Also Called: Altium Packaging LP (P-4871)*

A E M, Hawthorne *Also Called: Nmsp Inc (P-9432)*

A F C, Rancho Dominguez *Also Called: Advanced Fresh Concepts Corp (P-15007)*

A Fab, Lake Forest *Also Called: American Deburring Inc (P-7757)*

A Filml Inc .... D...... 213 977-8600
737 N Western Ave # 101 Los Angeles (90029) *(P-17242)*

A G Hacienda Incorporated .... B...... 661 792-2418
32794 Sherwood Ave Mc Farland (93250) *(P-11437)*

A H Plating, Valencia *Also Called: Sunvair Overhaul Inc (P-9806)*

A J Fasteners Inc .... E...... 714 630-1556
2800 E Miraloma Ave Anaheim (92806) *(P-6430)*

A J Parent Company Inc (PA) .... D...... 714 521-1100
6910 Aragon Cir Ste 6 Buena Park (90620) *(P-16763)*

A Lighting By Design, La Habra *Also Called: Albd Electric and Cable (P-863)*

A Lot To Say Inc .... E...... 877 366-8448
1541 S Vineyard Ave Ontario (91761) *(P-2543)*

A M Cabinets Inc (PA) .... D...... 310 532-1919
239 E Gardena Blvd Gardena (90248) *(P-2876)*

A M I/Coast Magnetics Inc .... E...... 323 936-6188
5333 W Washington Blvd Los Angeles (90016) *(P-8932)*

A M Ortega Construction Inc (PA) .... C...... 619 390-1988
10125 Channel Rd Lakeside (92040) *(P-859)*

A M T, Camarillo *Also Called: Amt Datasouth Corp (P-19819)*

A Media, El Segundo *Also Called: Sabot Publishing Inc (P-3388)*

A O Reed & Co LLC .... B...... 858 565-4131
4777 Ruffner St San Diego (92111) *(P-725)*

A P R Consulting Inc .... A...... 714 544-3696
17852 17th St Ste 206 Tustin (92780) *(P-16546)*

A P R Inc .... C...... 805 379-3400
100 E Thousand Oaks Blvd Ste 240 Thousand Oaks (91360) *(P-15910)*

A P S, Santa Clarita *Also Called: Applied Polytech Systems Inc (P-2743)*

A P V Crepaco, Lake Forest *Also Called: SPX Flow Us LLC (P-6159)*

A Plus International Inc (PA) .... D...... 909 591-5168
5138 Eucalyptus Ave Chino (91710) *(P-12466)*

A Plus Label Inc .... E...... 714 229-9811
3215 W Warner Ave Santa Ana (92704) *(P-3228)*

A Q M D, Diamond Bar *Also Called: South Cast A Qlty MGT Dst Bldg (P-20382)*

A Q Pharmaceuticals Inc .... E...... 714 903-1000
11555 Monarch St Ste C Garden Grove (92841) *(P-4026)*

A R C O, La Palma *Also Called: Atlantic Richfield Company (P-13889)*

A R Electronics Inc .... E...... 760 343-1200
31290 Plantation Dr Thousand Palms (92276) *(P-8988)*

A R O Service, Anaheim *Also Called: Aircraft Repair & Overhaul Svc (P-11686)*

A R P, Santa Paula *Also Called: Automotive Racing Products Inc (P-5899)*

A R P, Ventura *Also Called: Automotive Racing Products Inc (P-5900)*

A R Santex LLC (PA) .... E...... 888 622-7098
6790 Embarcadero Ln Ste 100 Carlsbad (92011) *(P-15952)*

A Royal Wolf Portable Stor Inc .... E...... 310 719-1048
400 E Compton Blvd Gardena (90248) *(P-12843)*

A Rudin Inc (PA) .... D...... 323 589-5547
6062 Alcoa Ave Vernon (90058) *(P-2793)*

A Rudin Designs, Vernon *Also Called: A Rudin Inc (P-2793)*

A S I, Valencia *Also Called: Advanced Semiconductor Inc (P-8758)*

A S I, Valencia *Also Called: Asi Semiconductor Inc (P-8770)*

A S I, Carlsbad *Also Called: Applied Spectral Imaging Inc (P-15966)*

A S I, Long Beach *Also Called: Assocted Stdnts Cal State Univ (P-19424)*

A S I American, Corona *Also Called: Spangler Industries Inc (P-4796)*

A S P, Irvine *Also Called: Advanced Sterlization (P-10417)*

A Shoc Beverage LLC .... E...... 949 490-1612
844 Production Pl Newport Beach (92663) *(P-1437)*

A Speedcast Co, San Diego *Also Called: Ultisat Inc (P-16476)*

A Steris Company, Ontario *Also Called: Isomedix Operations Inc (P-10675)*

A T A, Paso Robles *Also Called: Applied Technologies Assoc Inc (P-10352)*

A T E, Oceanside *Also Called: Advanced Thrmlforming Entp (P-4931)*

A T Parker Inc (PA) .... E...... 818 755-1700
10866 Chandler Blvd North Hollywood (91601) *(P-9189)*

A T S, Burbank *Also Called: Accratronics Seals Corporation (P-8990)*

A T T, Orange *Also Called: Air Tube Transfer Systems Inc (P-6968)*

A Thanks Million Inc .... F...... 858 432-7744
8195 Mercury Ct Ste 140 San Diego (92111) *(P-2404)*

A Thread Ahead Inc .... E...... 818 837-1984
1925 1st St San Fernando (91340) *(P-16764)*

A Transportation, Tarzana *Also Called: Airey Enterprises LLC (P-12900)*

A V Nursing Care Center, Lancaster *Also Called: Antelope Vly Retirement HM Inc (P-18106)*

A V Poles and Lighting Inc .... E...... 661 945-2731
43827 Division St Lancaster (93535) *(P-8302)*

A W Chang Corporation (PA) .... E...... 310 764-2000
6945 Atlantic Ave Long Beach (90805) *(P-13078)*

A-1 Engraving Co Inc .... E...... 562 861-2216
1230 N Jefferson St Anaheim (92807) *(P-6681)*

A-1 Enterprises Inc .... E...... 714 630-3390
2831 E La Cresta Ave Anaheim (92806) *(P-1141)*

A-1 Fence, Anaheim *Also Called: A-1 Enterprises Inc (P-1141)*

A-1 Grit Co, Riverside *Also Called: Newman Bros California Inc (P-2620)*

A-1 Metal Products Inc .... E...... 323 721-3334
2707 Supply Ave Commerce (90040) *(P-6175)*

A-1 Pomona Linen, Paramount *Also Called: Braun Linen Service (P-15449)*

A-Aztec Rents & Sells Inc (PA) .... C...... 310 347-3010
2665 Columbia St Torrance (90503) *(P-2498)*

A-Check America LLC (HQ) .... C...... 951 750-1501
1501 Research Park Dr Riverside (92507) *(P-15618)*

Employee Codes: A=Over 500 employees, B=251-500
C=101-250, D=51-100, E=20-50, F=10-19, G=1-9

2024 Southern California
Business Directory and Buyers Guide

© Mergent Inc. 1-800-342-5647

973

ALPHABETIC

A-Check America, Member Act 1, Riverside *Also Called: A-Check America LLC (P-15618)*

A-Info Inc ....E....... 949 346-7326
60 Tesla Irvine (92618) *(P-9585)*

A-List, Vernon *Also Called: Just For Wraps Inc (P-2339)*

A-Mark, El Segundo *Also Called: A-Mark Precious Metals Inc (P-12959)*

A-Mark Precious Metals Inc (PA)...................D....... 310 587-1477
2121 Rosecrans Ave Ste 6300 El Segundo (90245) *(P-12959)*

A-Team Delivers LLC ....D....... 858 254-8401
12127 Mall Blvd Ste A322 Victorville (92392) *(P-11438)*

A-W Engineering Company Inc ....E....... 562 945-1041
8528 Dice Rd Santa Fe Springs (90670) *(P-6491)*

A-Z Bus Sales Inc (PA).................................D....... 951 781-7188
1900 S Riverside Ave Colton (92324) *(P-12217)*

A-Z Bussales, Colton *Also Called: A-Z Emissions Solutions Inc (P-9190)*

A-Z Emissions Solutions Inc ....E....... 951 781-1856
1900 S Riverside Ave Colton (92324) *(P-9190)*

A-Z Industries Div, Los Angeles *Also Called: Aero Shade Co Inc (P-13955)*

A-Z Mfg Inc ....E....... 714 444-4446
3101 W Segerstrom Ave Santa Ana (92704) *(P-7727)*

A.B.C. Carpet & Home, Los Angeles *Also Called: ABC Home Furnishings Inc (P-13937)*

A.I.M. Services, Los Angeles *Also Called: Aiminsight Solutions Inc (P-16549)*

A.J. Metal Manufacturing, Corona *Also Called: Aqua Performance Inc (P-12925)*

A&A Fulfillment Center, Vernon *Also Called: A&A Global Imports LLC (P-4926)*

A&A Global Imports LLC (PA)........................D....... 888 315-2453
1801 E 41st St Vernon (90058) *(P-4926)*

A&A Jewelry Supply, Los Angeles *Also Called: Adfa Incorporated (P-6684)*

A&R Tarpaulins Inc ....E....... 909 829-4444
16246 Valley Blvd Fontana (92335) *(P-2497)*

A2z Color Graphics, Van Nuys *Also Called: Investment Enterprises Inc (P-3772)*

AA Blocks LLC ....D....... 858 523-8231
9823 Pacific Heights Blvd Ste F San Diego (92121) *(P-20123)*

Aa Leasing, Los Angeles *Also Called: Vahe Enterprises Inc (P-9337)*

AAA, San Diego *Also Called: Automobile Club Southern Cal (P-19513)*

AAA, San Diego *Also Called: Automobile Club Southern Cal (P-19514)*

AAA, Escondido *Also Called: Automobile Club Southern Cal (P-19515)*

AAA, Chino *Also Called: Automobile Club Southern Cal (P-19516)*

AAA, Anaheim *Also Called: Automobile Club Southern Cal (P-19519)*

AAA, West Hollywood *Also Called: Automobile Club Southern Cal (P-19522)*

AAA, Torrance *Also Called: Automobile Club Southern Cal (P-19523)*

AAA, Downey *Also Called: Automobile Club Southern Cal (P-19524)*

AAA, Manhattan Beach *Also Called: Automobile Club Southern Cal (P-19525)*

AAA Auto Club, Costa Mesa *Also Called: Automobile Club Southern Cal (P-14563)*

AAA Elctrcal Cmmunications Inc (PA)..............C....... 800 892-4784
25007 Anza Dr Valencia (91355) *(P-860)*

AAA Electric Motor Sales & Svc (PA)..............F....... 213 749-2367
1346 Venice Blvd Los Angeles (90006) *(P-12581)*

AAA Facility Services, Valencia *Also Called: AAA Elctrcal Cmmunications Inc (P-860)*

AAA Flag & Banner, Los Angeles *Also Called: AAA Flag & Banner Mfg Co Inc (P-14119)*

AAA Flag & Banner Mfg Co Inc (PA)................C....... 310 836-3200
8937 National Blvd Los Angeles (90034) *(P-14119)*

AAA Imaging & Supplies Inc ....E....... 714 431-0570
2313 S Susan St Santa Ana (92704) *(P-12375)*

AAA Imaging Solutions, Santa Ana *Also Called: AAA Imaging & Supplies Inc (P-12375)*

AAA Pallet, Perris *Also Called: AAA Pallet Recycling & Mfg Inc (P-2713)*

AAA Pallet, Mentone *Also Called: Power Pt Inc (P-6996)*

AAA Pallet Recycling & Mfg Inc ....E....... 951 681-7748
23120 Oleander Ave Perris (92570) *(P-2713)*

AAA Plating & Inspection Inc ....D....... 323 979-8930
424 E Dixon St Compton (90222) *(P-6573)*

AAC, Irvine *Also Called: American Audio Component Inc (P-8995)*

Aadi, Pacific Palisades *Also Called: Aadi Bioscience Inc (P-4027)*

Aadi Bioscience Inc (PA)..............................E....... 424 744-8055
17383 W Sunset Blvd Ste A250 Pacific Palisades (90272) *(P-4027)*

AAF Steel Structural, Victorville *Also Called: Afakori Inc (P-5990)*

Aall Care In Home Services, San Diego *Also Called: Faith Jones & Associates Inc (P-18613)*

Aalto Scientific Ltd ....E....... 800 748-6674
1959 Kellogg Ave Carlsbad (92008) *(P-10408)*

AAM, Anaheim *Also Called: Anaheim Arena Management LLC (P-17361)*

Aamp of America ....E....... 805 338-6800
2500 E Francis St Ontario (91761) *(P-9191)*

Aap Division, Inglewood *Also Called: Engineered Magnetics Inc (P-8205)*

AAR Manufacturing Inc ....C....... 714 634-8807
2220 E Cerritos Ave Anaheim (92806) *(P-6129)*

Aard Industries Inc ....E....... 951 296-0844
42075 Avenida Alvarado Temecula (92590) *(P-6797)*

Aard Spring & Stamping, Temecula *Also Called: Aard Industries Inc (P-6797)*

Aardvark Clay & Supplies Inc (PA).................E....... 714 541-4157
1400 E Pomona St Santa Ana (92705) *(P-11048)*

Aaren Scientific Inc (DH)..............................D....... 909 937-1033
1040 S Vintage Ave Ste A Ontario (91761) *(P-10306)*

Aaron Corporation ....C....... 323 235-5959
2645 Industry Way Lynwood (90262) *(P-2297)*

Aaron Group, The, Chatsworth *Also Called: Aaron Thomas & Associates Inc (P-15625)*

Aaron Thomas, Garden Grove *Also Called: Aaron Thomas Company Inc (P-16765)*

Aaron Thomas & Associates Inc ....E....... 818 727-9040
21344 Superior St Chatsworth (91311) *(P-15625)*

Aaron Thomas Company Inc (PA)...................C....... 714 894-4468
7421 Chapman Ave Garden Grove (92841) *(P-16765)*

AB Cellular Holding LLC ....A....... 562 468-6846
1452 Edinger Ave Tustin (92780) *(P-11868)*

AB Mauri Food Inc ....E....... 562 483-4619
12604 Hiddencreek Way Ste A Cerritos (90703) *(P-1845)*

AB&r Inc ....E....... 323 727-0007
5849 Smithway St Commerce (90040) *(P-2298)*

Abacus Data Systems Inc (PA)......................C....... 858 452-4280
9171 Towne Centre Dr Ste 200 San Diego (92122) *(P-15953)*

Abacus Data Systems Inc ....D....... 858 529-0020
3262 Holiday Ct Ste 101 La Jolla (92037) *(P-15954)*

Abacus Powder Coating ....E....... 626 443-7556
1829 Tyler Ave South El Monte (91733) *(P-6682)*

Abacusnext, San Diego *Also Called: Abacus Data Systems Inc (P-15953)*

Abacusnext, La Jolla *Also Called: Abacus Data Systems Inc (P-15954)*

Abad Foam Inc ....E....... 714 994-2223
6560 Caballero Blvd Buena Park (90620) *(P-4868)*

Abalquiga, Los Angeles *Also Called: La Princesita Tortilleria Inc (P-1931)*

ABB Enterprise Software Inc ....D....... 213 743-4819
4600 Colorado Blvd Los Angeles (90039) *(P-8755)*

ABB ENTERPRISE SOFTWARE INC., Los Angeles *Also Called: ABB Enterprise Software Inc (P-8755)*

Abba Roller LLC (DH)...................................F....... 909 947-1244
1351 E Philadelphia St Ontario (91761) *(P-4755)*

Abbey Carpet, National City *Also Called: Sids Carpet Barn (P-12315)*

Abbott Laboratories ....E....... 818 493-2388
15900 Valley View Ct Sylmar (91342) *(P-4028)*

Abbott Rapid Diagnos, San Diego *Also Called: Abbott Rapid Dx North Amer LLC (P-10409)*

Abbott Rapid Dx North Amer LLC ....E....... 858 805-3804
5995 Pacific Center Blvd San Diego (92121) *(P-10409)*

Abbott Technologies Inc ....E....... 818 504-0644
8203 Vineland Ave Sun Valley (91352) *(P-8086)*

Abbott Vascular, Murrieta *Also Called: Abbott Vascular Inc (P-10410)*

Abbott Vascular Inc ....B....... 951 941-2400
26531 Ynez Rd Temecula (92591) *(P-4029)*

Abbott Vascular Inc ....A....... 408 845-3186
30590 Cochise Cir Murrieta (92563) *(P-10410)*

Abbott Vascular Inc ....A....... 951 914-2400
42301 Zevo Dr Ste D Temecula (92590) *(P-10411)*

Abbyson Living Corp ....C....... 805 465-5500
26500 Agoura Rd Ste 102 Calabasas (91302) *(P-12276)*

ABC, Burbank *Also Called: ABC Cable Networks Group (P-11918)*

ABC - Clio Inc (HQ).....................................C....... 805 968-1911
147 Castilian Dr Santa Barbara (93117) *(P-3397)*

ABC Bus Inc ....D....... 714 444-5888
1485 Dale Way Costa Mesa (92626) *(P-12218)*

ABC Cable Networks Group (HQ)....................C....... 818 460-7477
500 S Buena Vista St Burbank (91521) *(P-11918)*

ABC Custom Wood Shutters Inc ....E....... 949 595-0300
20561 Pascal Way Lake Forest (92630) *(P-2581)*

ABC Family, Burbank *Also Called: ABC Family Worldwide Inc (P-17165)*

Mergent email: customerrelations@mergent.com
974

2024 Southern California
Business Directory and Buyers Guide

(P-0000) Products & Services Section entry number
(PA)=Parent Co (HQ)=Headquarters (DH)=Div Headquarters

ABC Family Worldwide Inc (HQ)...................................B....... 818 560-1000
500 S Buena Vista St Burbank (91521) *(P-17165)*

ABC Home Furnishings Inc (PA)............................A....... 212 473-3000
11111 Santa Monica Blvd Los Angeles (90025) *(P-13937)*

ABC Home Health Care Llc ....C...... 858 455-5000
5090 Shoreham Pl Ste 209 San Diego (92122) *(P-18578)*

ABC Imaging, Santa Fe Springs *Also Called: ABC Imaging of Washington (P-3727)*

ABC Imaging of Washington ....F....... 949 419-3728
17240 Red Hill Ave Irvine (92614) *(P-3726)*

ABC Imaging of Washington ....F....... 562 375-7280
13573 Larwin Cir Santa Fe Springs (90670) *(P-3727)*

ABC School Equipment Inc ....D....... 951 817-2200
1451 E 6th St Corona (92879) *(P-12525)*

ABC Sheet Metal, Anaheim *Also Called: Steeldyne Industries (P-6323)*

ABC Signature Studios Inc ....D....... 818 560-1000
500 S Buena Vista St Burbank (91521) *(P-11937)*

ABC Valencia, Corona *Also Called: Amerisourcebergen Drug Corp (P-13028)*

ABC-Clio, Santa Barbara *Also Called: ABC - Clio Inc (P-3397)*

Abco Insulation, Azusa *Also Called: Oj Insulation LP (P-985)*

Abel Automatics LLC ....E....... 805 388-3721
165 N Aviador St Camarillo (93010) *(P-6407)*

Abel Reels, Camarillo *Also Called: Abel Automatics LLC (P-6407)*

Aben, Chatsworth *Also Called: Aben Machine Products Inc (P-7728)*

Aben Machine Products Inc ....F....... 818 960-4502
9550 Owensmouth Ave Chatsworth (91311) *(P-7728)*

Aberdeen, Santa Fe Springs *Also Called: Source Code LLC (P-7451)*

Abex Display Systems Inc (PA).............................C...... 800 537-0231
355 Parkside Dr San Fernando (91340) *(P-3077)*

Abex Exhibit Systems, San Fernando *Also Called: Abex Display Systems Inc (P-3077)*

ABF Prints Inc ....F....... 909 875-7163
102 N Riverside Ave Rialto (92376) *(P-3728)*

Abhe & Svoboda Inc ....D....... 619 659-1320
880 Tavern Rd Alpine (91901) *(P-527)*

ABI Attorneys Service Inc (PA).............................D....... 909 793-0613
2015 W Park Ave Redlands (92373) *(P-15640)*

ABI Document Support Services, Loma Linda *Also Called: ABI Document Support Svcs LLC (P-16766)*

ABI Document Support Svcs LLC ....D....... 909 793-0613
10459 Mountain View Ave Ste E Loma Linda (92354) *(P-16766)*

ABI VIP Attorney Service, Redlands *Also Called: ABI Attorneys Service Inc (P-15640)*

Ability, Carson *Also Called: American Fruits & Flavors LLC (P-1751)*

Ability Counts Inc (PA)..D....... 951 734-6595
775 Trademark Cir Ste 101 Corona (92879) *(P-19172)*

Abis Signs Inc ....F....... 626 818-4329
14240 Don Julian Rd Ste E City Of Industry (91746) *(P-11094)*

ABIS SIGNS INC, City Of Industry *Also Called: Abis Signs Inc (P-11094)*

Abl Space Systems Company ....D....... 424 321-5049
224 Oregon St El Segundo (90245) *(P-9890)*

Able Building Maintenance, Tustin *Also Called: Crown Building Maintenance Co (P-15704)*

Able Cable Inc (PA)..C...... 818 223-3600
5115 Douglas Fir Rd Ste A Calabasas (91302) *(P-17067)*

Able Card Corporation, Irwindale *Also Called: Million Corporation (P-3787)*

Able Design and Fabrication, Rancho Dominguez *Also Called: Adf Incorporated (P-6349)*

Able Engineering Services, Los Angeles *Also Called: Crown Energy Services Inc (P-15706)*

Able Freight Services LLC (PA)..............................D...... 310 568-8883
5340 W 104th St Los Angeles (90045) *(P-11734)*

Able Health Group LLC ....D...... 760 610-2093
41990 Cook St Ste 2004 Palm Desert (92211) *(P-18735)*

Able Industrial Products Inc (PA)...........................E...... 909 930-1585
2006 S Baker Ave Ontario (91761) *(P-4718)*

Able Iron Works ....E...... 909 397-5300
222 Hershey St Pomona (91767) *(P-5987)*

Able Patrol & Guard, San Diego *Also Called: Locator Services Inc (P-16657)*

Able Sheet Metal Inc (PA).......................................E...... 323 269-2181
614 N Ford Blvd Los Angeles (90022) *(P-6176)*

ABM Facility Services LLC ....A....... 949 330-1555
152 Technology Dr Irvine (92618) *(P-19538)*

ABM Onsite Services Inc ....A....... 949 863-9100
3337 Michelson Dr Ste Cn7 Irvine (92612) *(P-16612)*

ABM Parking Services Inc ....A....... 213 284-7600
1150 S Olive St Fl 19 Los Angeles (90015) *(P-16987)*

Abode Communities LLC ....C...... 213 629-2702
1149 S Hill St Fl 7 Los Angeles (90015) *(P-14741)*

Above & Beyond Balloons Inc ....E...... 949 586-8470
1 Wrigley Irvine (92618) *(P-11185)*

Above and Beyond, Irvine *Also Called: Above & Beyond Balloons Inc (P-11185)*

Abracon ....E...... 949 546-8000
30332 Esperanza Rcho Sta Marg (92688) *(P-8989)*

Abrasive Finishing Co ....F....... 310 323-7175
14920 S Main St Gardena (90248) *(P-5820)*

Abraxis Bioscience LLC (DH).................................C...... 800 564-0216
11755 Wilshire Blvd Fl 20 Los Angeles (90025) *(P-4030)*

Abrazar Inc ....D....... 714 893-3581
7101 Wyoming St Westminster (92683) *(P-19016)*

ABRAZAR ELDERLY ASSISTANCE, Westminster *Also Called: Abrazar Inc (P-19016)*

Abrisa Industrial Glass Inc (HQ).............................D....... 805 525-4902
200 Hallock Dr Santa Paula (93060) *(P-10307)*

Abrisa Technologies ....E...... 805 525-4902
200 Hallock Dr Santa Paula (93060) *(P-10308)*

ABS By Allen Schwartz, Encino *Also Called: Aquarius Rags LLC (P-2275)*

ABS By Allen Schwartz LLC (HQ)...........................E...... 213 895-4400
15821 Ventura Blvd Ste 270 Encino (91436) *(P-2299)*

ABS Consulting Inc ....D....... 714 734-4242
420 Exchange Ste 200 Irvine (92602) *(P-19539)*

ABS Group, Irvine *Also Called: ABS Consulting Inc (P-19539)*

Absolute Board Co Inc ....F....... 760 295-2201
4040 Calle Platino Ste 102 Oceanside (92056) *(P-10969)*

Absolute EDM, Carlsbad *Also Called: Diligent Solutions Inc (P-7818)*

Absolute Graphic Tech USA Inc ....E...... 909 597-1133
235 Jason Ct Corona (92879) *(P-8167)*

Absolute Packaging Inc ....E...... 714 630-3020
1201 N Miller St Anaheim (92806) *(P-3145)*

Absolute Pro Music, Los Angeles *Also Called: Absolute Usa Inc (P-8389)*

Absolute Return Portfolio ....A....... 800 800-7646
700 Newport Center Dr Newport Beach (92660) *(P-14953)*

Absolute Screenprint Inc ....C...... 714 529-2120
333 Cliffwood Park St Brea (92821) *(P-2525)*

Absolute Technologies, Anaheim *Also Called: D & D Gear Incorporated (P-9670)*

Absolute Usa Inc ....E...... 213 744-0044
1800 E Washington Blvd Los Angeles (90021) *(P-8389)*

Absolutely Zero Corporation ....B....... 949 269-3300
1 City Blvd W Ste 1000 Orange (92868) *(P-14742)*

Abtech Incorporated ....E...... 714 550-9961
3420 W Fordham Ave Santa Ana (92704) *(P-2971)*

AC Irrigation Holdco LLC ....C...... 661 368-3550
10000 Stockdale Hwy Ste 100 Bakersfield (93311) *(P-95)*

AC Pro Inc (PA)..C...... 951 360-7849
11700 Industry Ave Fontana (92337) *(P-12750)*

AC Products Inc ....E...... 714 630-7311
9930 Painter Ave Whittier (90605) *(P-4555)*

AC Propulsion Inc ....E...... 909 592-5399
441 Borrego Ct San Dimas (91773) *(P-8133)*

AC Tech, Garden Grove *Also Called: Advanced Chemistry & Technology Inc (P-4556)*

AC&a Enterprises LLC (HQ)....................................E...... 949 716-3511
25671 Commercentre Dr Lake Forest (92630) *(P-9559)*

ACADEMIC CAP & GOWN, Chatsworth *Also Called: Academic Ch Choir Gwns Mfg Inc (P-2437)*

Academic Ch Choir Gwns Mfg Inc ....E...... 818 886-8697
8944 Mason Ave Chatsworth (91311) *(P-2437)*

Academy Mpic Arts & Sciences (PA).......................D....... 310 247-3000
8949 Wilshire Blvd Beverly Hills (90211) *(P-19388)*

Academy Museum Motion Pictures ....C...... 310 247-3000
6067 Wilshire Blvd Los Angeles (90036) *(P-19348)*

Academy of Cosmetology, Santa Barbara *Also Called: Santa Brbara Cmnty College Dst (P-18998)*

Acadia, San Diego *Also Called: Acadia Pharmaceuticals Inc (P-4031)*

Acadia Pharmaceuticals Inc (PA)...........................A....... 858 558-2871
12830 El Camino Real Ste 400 San Diego (92130) *(P-4031)*

Accelerated Memory Prod Inc ....E...... 714 460-9800
1317 E Edinger Ave Santa Ana (92705) *(P-8756)*

Employee Codes: A=Over 500 employees, B=251-500
C=101-250, D=51-100, E=20-50, F=10-19, G=1-9

2024 Southern California
Business Directory and Buyers Guide

© Mergent Inc. 1-800-342-5647
975

Accent Awnings, Santa Ana *Also Called: Accent Industries Inc (P-6096)*

Accent Ceilings, City Of Industry *Also Called: Adams-Campbell Company Ltd (P-6177)*

Accent Industries Inc (PA) .... F....... **714 708-1389**
1600 E Saint Gertrude Pl Santa Ana (92705) *(P-6096)*

Accent Plastics, Chino *Also Called: Dacha Enterprises Inc (P-5000)*

Accentcare Inc .... B....... 858 576-7410
5050 Murphy Canyon Rd Ste 200 San Diego (92123) *(P-18579)*

Accentcare HM Hlth El Cntro In .... B....... 760 352-4022
2344 S 2nd St Ste A El Centro (92243) *(P-18580)*

Accentcare Home Hlth Yuma Inc .... A....... 909 605-7000
1455 Auto Center Dr Ste 125 Ontario (91761) *(P-18581)*

Accenture Federal Services LLC .... A....... 619 574-2400
1615 Murray Canyon Rd Ste 400 San Diego (92108) *(P-20124)*

Accenture National SEC Svcs, San Diego *Also Called: Accenture Federal Services LLC (P-20124)*

Acceptedcom LLC .... E....... 310 815-9553
2229 S Canfield Ave Los Angeles (90034) *(P-3422)*

Acces I/O Products Inc .... F....... 858 550-9559
10623 Roselle St San Diego (92121) *(P-7503)*

Access Biologicals, Vista *Also Called: Grifols Usa LLC (P-4320)*

Access Business Group LLC .... B....... 808 422-9482
12825 Leffingwell Ave Santa Fe Springs (90670) *(P-13420)*

Access Business Group LLC .... B....... 714 562-6200
5600 Beach Blvd Buena Park (90621) *(P-13421)*

Access Business Group LLC .... B....... 714 562-7914
5609 River Way Buena Park (90621) *(P-13422)*

Access Info Holdings LLC .... A....... 909 459-1417
12135 Davis St Moreno Valley (92557) *(P-11631)*

Access Logistics, Santa Fe Springs *Also Called: Access Business Group LLC (P-13420)*

Access Marketing, San Luis Obispo *Also Called: ITW Global Tire Repair Inc (P-4698)*

Access Nurses Inc .... D....... 858 458-4400
5935 Cornerstone Ct W Ste 300 San Diego (92121) *(P-15808)*

ACCESS PARATRANSIT, El Monte *Also Called: Access Services (P-11314)*

Access Professional Inc .... F....... 858 571-4444
1955 Cordell Ct Ste 104 El Cajon (92020) *(P-6347)*

Access Professional Systems, El Cajon *Also Called: Access Professional Inc (P-6347)*

Access Scientific Inc .... F....... 858 354-8761
1042 N El Camino Real Ste B-349 Encinitas (92024) *(P-10412)*

Access Self Storage SE, Santa Monica *Also Called: William Warren Properties Inc (P-14733)*

Access Services .... D....... 213 270-6000
3449 Santa Anita Ave El Monte (91731) *(P-11314)*

Acclaim Lighting LLC .... E....... 323 213-4626
6122 S Eastern Ave Commerce (90040) *(P-8303)*

Acclarent Inc .... B....... 650 687-5888
31 Technology Dr Ste 200 Irvine (92618) *(P-10413)*

Acco, Pasadena *Also Called: Acco Engineered Systems Inc (P-726)*

Acco Engineered Systems Inc .... E....... 661 631-1975
3559 Landco Dr Ste B Bakersfield (93308) *(P-7593)*

Acco Engineered Systems Inc (PA) .... A....... **818 244-6571**
888 E Walnut St Pasadena (91101) *(P-726)*

Accolade Pharma USA .... E....... 626 279-9699
13260 Temple Ave City Of Industry (91746) *(P-4032)*

Accor Corp .... C....... 310 278-5444
8555 Beverly Blvd Los Angeles (90048) *(P-13979)*

Accountble Hlth Cre IPA A Prof .... C....... 562 435-3333
2525 Cherry Ave Ste 225 Signal Hill (90755) *(P-18736)*

Accounting and Fiscal Services, Irvine *Also Called: University California Irvine (P-19808)*

Accounts Payable Department, Ontario *Also Called: Vantiva Sup Chain Slutions Inc (P-17272)*

Accratronics Seals Corporation .... D....... 818 843-1500
2211 Kenmere Ave Burbank (91504) *(P-8990)*

Accredited Debt Relief, San Diego *Also Called: Beyond Finance LLC (P-15499)*

Accredited Fms Inc .... A....... 818 435-4200
5955 De Soto Ave Ste 136 Woodland Hills (91367) *(P-18582)*

Accredited Home Care, Woodland Hills *Also Called: Barry & Taffy Inc (P-18592)*

Accredited Home Care, Woodland Hills *Also Called: Berger Inc (P-18593)*

Accredited Nursing Care, Pasadena *Also Called: Accredited Nursing Services (P-17875)*

Accredited Nursing Care, San Diego *Also Called: Accredited Nursing Services (P-18583)*

Accredited Nursing Care, Costa Mesa *Also Called: Accredited Nursing Services (P-18584)*

Accredited Nursing Care, Woodland Hills *Also Called: Dunn & Berger Inc (P-18609)*

Accredited Nursing Services .... C....... 626 573-1234
80 S Lake Ave Ste 630 Pasadena (91101) *(P-17875)*

Accredited Nursing Services .... C....... 818 986-1234
3570 Camino Del Rio N Ste 108 San Diego (92108) *(P-18583)*

Accredited Nursing Services .... C....... 714 973-1234
950 S Coast Dr Ste 215 Costa Mesa (92626) *(P-18584)*

Accriva Dgnostics Holdings Inc (DH) .... B....... **858 404-8203**
6260 Sequence Dr San Diego (92121) *(P-10414)*

Accu-Blend Corporation .... F....... 626 334-7744
364 Malbert St Perris (92570) *(P-4638)*

Accu-Seal Sencorpwhite Inc .... F....... 760 591-9800
225 Bingham Dr Ste B San Marcos (92069) *(P-7342)*

Accu-Sembly Inc .... D....... 626 357-3447
1835 Huntington Dr Duarte (91010) *(P-8638)*

Accu-Tech Laser Processing Inc .... E....... 760 744-6692
1175 Linda Vista Dr San Marcos (92078) *(P-7729)*

Accudyne Engineering & Eqp, Bell *Also Called: West Coast-Accudyne Inc (P-7042)*

Accunex Inc .... E....... 818 882-5858
20700 Lassen St Chatsworth (91311) *(P-19540)*

Accurate Air Engineering, Cerritos *Also Called: Atlas Copco Compressors LLC (P-7306)*

Accurate Background LLC (PA) .... B....... **800 784-3911**
200 Spectrum Center Dr Ste 1100 Irvine (92618) *(P-16524)*

Accurate Circuit Engrg Inc .... D....... 714 546-2162
3019 Kilson Dr Santa Ana (92707) *(P-8639)*

Accurate Electronics, Chatsworth *Also Called: Accunex Inc (P-19540)*

Accurate Engineering Inc .... E....... 818 768-3919
8710 Telfair Ave Sun Valley (91352) *(P-8640)*

Accurate Grinding and Mfg Corp .... E....... 951 479-0909
807 E Parkridge Ave Corona (92879) *(P-9560)*

Accurate Laminated Pdts Inc .... E....... 714 632-2773
1826 Dawns Way Fullerton (92831) *(P-2644)*

Accurate Manufacturing Company, Glendale *Also Called: McCoppin Enterprises (P-7923)*

Accurate Plating Company .... E....... 323 268-8567
2811 Alcazar St Los Angeles (90033) *(P-6574)*

Accurate Prfmce Machining Inc .... E....... 714 434-7811
2255 S Grand Ave Santa Ana (92705) *(P-7730)*

Accurate Security Pros Inc .... E....... 858 271-1155
9919 Hibert St Ste D San Diego (92131) *(P-16714)*

Accurate Steel Treating Inc .... E....... 562 927-6528
10008 Miller Way South Gate (90280) *(P-5821)*

Accurate Technology, Anaheim *Also Called: Gledhill/Lyons Inc (P-9701)*

Accuride International Inc (PA) .... E....... **562 903-0200**
12311 Shoemaker Ave Santa Fe Springs (90670) *(P-5894)*

Accutek Packaging Equipment Co (PA) .... E....... **760 734-4177**
2980 Scott St Vista (92081) *(P-7343)*

Accuturn Corporation .... E....... 951 656-6621
7189 Old 215 Frontage Rd Ste 101 Moreno Valley (92553) *(P-9936)*

Acd LLC (DH) .... D....... **949 261-7533**
2321 Pullman St Santa Ana (92705) *(P-6130)*

Ace, Anaheim *Also Called: Anaheim Custom Extruders Inc (P-4941)*

Ace, Santa Ana *Also Called: Accurate Circuit Engrg Inc (P-8639)*

Ace Air Manufacturing .... F....... 310 323-7246
1430 W 135th St Gardena (90249) *(P-9586)*

Ace Boiler, Santa Ana *Also Called: Ajax Boiler Inc (P-6131)*

Ace Cash Express, Riverside *Also Called: Populus Financial Group Inc (P-14262)*

Ace Clearwater Enterprises Inc .... E....... 310 538-5380
1614 Kona Dr Compton (90220) *(P-7045)*

Ace Clearwater Enterprises Inc (PA) .... D....... **310 323-2140**
19815 Magellan Dr Torrance (90502) *(P-9587)*

Ace Commercial Inc .... E....... 562 946-6664
10310 Pioneer Blvd Ste 1 Santa Fe Springs (90670) *(P-3505)*

Ace Fence Company, La Puente *Also Called: AZ Construction Inc (P-421)*

Ace Hardware, Baldwin Park *Also Called: Nichols Lumber & Hardware Co (P-12337)*

Ace Heaters LLC .... E....... 951 738-2230
130 Klug Cir Corona (92878) *(P-7594)*

Ace Hydraulic Sales & Svc Inc .... F....... 661 327-0571
2901 Gibson St Bakersfield (93308) *(P-12783)*

Ace Industries Inc .... E....... 619 482-2700
195 Mace St Chula Vista (91911) *(P-7731)*

Ace Iron Inc .... E....... 510 324-3300
929 Howard St Marina Del Rey (90292) *(P-6348)*

Ace Machine Shop Inc .... D...... 310 608-2277
11200 Wright Rd Lynwood (90262) *(P-7732)*

Ace Sushi, Torrance *Also Called: Asiana Cuisine Enterprises Inc (P-1854)*

Ace Tube Bending .... E...... 949 362-2220
14 Journey Aliso Viejo (92656) *(P-7733)*

Ace Wireless & Trading Inc .... B...... 949 748-5700
3031 Orange Ave Ste B Santa Ana (92707) *(P-12640)*

Acea Biosciences Inc .... D...... 858 724-0928
6779 Mesa Ridge Rd Ste 100 San Diego (92121) *(P-19812)*

Acepex Management Corporation .... C...... 909 625-6900
2707 Saturn St Brea (92821) *(P-20286)*

Acg Ecopack, Ontario *Also Called: Advanced Color Graphics (P-3506)*

Ach Mechanical Contractors Inc .... D...... 909 307-2850
411 Business Center Ct Redlands (92373) *(P-727)*

Achates Power Inc .... D...... 858 535-9920
4060 Sorrento Valley Blvd Ste A San Diego (92121) *(P-9339)*

Aci International (PA) .... D...... 310 889-3400
844 Moraga Dr Los Angeles (90049) *(P-13157)*

Aci Medical LLC .... E...... 760 744-4400
1857 Diamond St Ste A San Marcos (92078) *(P-10415)*

Acker Stone Industries Inc (DH) .... E...... 951 674-0047
13296 Temescal Canyon Rd Corona (92883) *(P-5397)*

Ackley Metal Products Inc .... F...... 714 979-7431
1311 E Saint Gertrude Pl Ste B Santa Ana (92705) *(P-7734)*

Aclu Fndation Southern Cal LLC .... D...... 213 977-9500
765 The City Dr S Ste 360 Orange (92868) *(P-19421)*

Acme Auto Headlining, Long Beach *Also Called: Acme Headlining Co (P-9340)*

Acme Castings Inc .... E...... 323 583-3129
6009 Santa Fe Ave Huntington Park (90255) *(P-5800)*

Acme Cryogenics Inc .... E...... 805 981-4500
531 Sandy Cir Oxnard (93036) *(P-7219)*

Acme Divac Industries, Newport Beach *Also Called: C&H Hydraulics Inc (P-9647)*

Acme Headlining Co .... D...... 562 432-0281
550 W 16th St Long Beach (90813) *(P-9340)*

Acme Portable Machines Inc .... E...... 626 610-1888
1330 Mountain View Cir Azusa (91702) *(P-7414)*

Acme Staffing, El Centro *Also Called: I N C Builders Inc (P-15924)*

Acme Tool Grinding Company, Santa Ana *Also Called: Connelly Machine Wks (P-7808)*

Acme United Corporation .... E...... 714 557-2001
630 Young St Santa Ana (92705) *(P-3039)*

Acme Vial, Paso Robles *Also Called: Acme Vial & Glass Co (P-5320)*

Acme Vial & Glass Co .... E...... 805 239-2666
1601 Commerce Way Paso Robles (93446) *(P-5320)*

Acon Laboratories Inc (PA) .... E...... 858 875-8000
10125 Mesa Rim Rd San Diego (92121) *(P-4261)*

Acorn Engineering Company (PA) .... A...... 800 488-8999
15125 Proctor Ave City Of Industry (91746) *(P-4593)*

Acorn Newspaper Inc .... E...... 818 706-0266
30423 Canwood St Ste 108 Agoura Hills (91301) *(P-3254)*

Acorn Paper Products Co., Los Angeles *Also Called: Oak Paper Products Co Inc (P-13011)*

Acorn Vac, Chino *Also Called: Acornvac Inc (P-5961)*

Acorn-Gencon Plastics LLC .... D...... 909 591-8461
13818 Oaks Ave Chino (91710) *(P-4927)*

Acorns, Irvine *Also Called: Acorns Grow Incorporated (P-14975)*

Acorns Grow Incorporated (PA) .... B...... 949 251-0095
5300 California Ave Irvine (92617) *(P-14975)*

Acornvac Inc .... E...... 909 902-1141
13818 Oaks Ave Chino (91710) *(P-5961)*

Acosta Inc .... C...... 714 988-1500
480 Apollo St Ste C Brea (92821) *(P-13167)*

Acosta Sales & Marketing, Brea *Also Called: Acosta Inc (P-13167)*

Acousticfab LLC (DH) .... D...... 661 257-2242
28150 Industry Dr Valencia (91355) *(P-6772)*

Acp Noxtat Inc .... F...... 714 547-5477
1112 E Washington Ave Santa Ana (92701) *(P-3920)*

Acpt, Huntington Beach *Also Called: Advanced Cmpsite Pdts Tech Inc (P-4928)*

Acralight International, Santa Ana *Also Called: International Skylights (P-5316)*

Acrl, Chatsworth *Also Called: Advanced Cosmetic RES Labs Inc (P-11187)*

Acrobat Staffing, San Diego *Also Called: SE Scher Corporation (P-15892)*

Acromil LLC .... D...... 951 808-9929
1168 Sherborn St Corona (92879) *(P-9588)*

Acromil LLC (HQ) .... C...... 626 964-2522
18421 Railroad St City Of Industry (91748) *(P-9589)*

Acromil Corporation (PA) .... C...... 626 964-2522
18421 Railroad St City Of Industry (91748) *(P-9590)*

Acrontos Manufacturing Inc .... E...... 714 850-9133
1641 E Saint Gertrude Pl Santa Ana (92705) *(P-6492)*

Acrylic Distribution, Sun Valley *Also Called: Acrylic Distribution Corp (P-2867)*

Acrylic Distribution Corp .... E...... 818 767-8448
8421 Lankershim Blvd Sun Valley (91352) *(P-2867)*

ACS, Los Angeles *Also Called: Authorized Cellular Service (P-17068)*

ACS Cloud Partners, Torrance *Also Called: Advanced Corporate Svcs Inc (P-20306)*

ACS Communications Inc .... D...... 310 767-2145
680 Knox St Ste 150 Torrance (90502) *(P-861)*

ACS Engineering Inc .... E...... 949 297-3777
33 Hammond Ste 209 Irvine (92618) *(P-19541)*

Acsco Products Inc .... E...... 818 953-2240
313 N Lake St Burbank (91502) *(P-9341)*

Acss, Beaumont *Also Called: Anderson Chrnesky Strl Stl Inc (P-5992)*

Act 1 Group Inc (PA) .... D...... 310 750-3400
1999 W 190th St Torrance (90504) *(P-15809)*

Act Fulfillment Inc (PA) .... C...... 909 930-9083
3155 Universe Dr Jurupa Valley (91752) *(P-11560)*

Actavis LLC .... E...... 951 493-5582
132 Business Center Dr Corona (92878) *(P-4033)*

Actavis LLC .... D...... 909 270-1400
311 Bonnie Cir Corona (92878) *(P-4034)*

Acti, Wilmington *Also Called: Advanced Cleanup Tech Inc (P-20287)*

Acti Corporation Inc .... E...... 949 753-0352
18 Technology Dr Ste 139 Irvine (92618) *(P-8390)*

Action, Ontario *Also Called: Action Embroidery Corp (P-2544)*

Action Bag & Cover Inc .... D...... 714 965-7777
18401 Mount Langley St Fountain Valley (92708) *(P-2491)*

Action Cleaning Corporation .... E...... 619 233-1881
1668 Newton Ave San Diego (92113) *(P-17111)*

Action Crash Parts, Santa Fe Springs *Also Called: Global Trade Alliance Inc (P-13862)*

Action Electronic Assembly Inc .... E...... 760 510-0003
2872 S Santa Fe Ave San Marcos (92069) *(P-8641)*

Action Embroidery Corp (PA) .... C...... 909 983-1359
1315 W Brooks St Ontario (91762) *(P-2544)*

Action Hlth Care Prsnnel Svcs .... C...... 562 799-5523
3020 Old Ranch Pkwy Ste 300 Seal Beach (90740) *(P-18585)*

Action Messenger Service, Los Angeles *Also Called: Peach Inc (P-11537)*

Action Powder Coating LLC .... F...... 858 566-2288
7949 Stromesa Ct Ste D San Diego (92126) *(P-6683)*

Action Property Management, Irvine *Also Called: Action Property Management Inc (P-14734)*

Action Property Management Inc (PA) .... D...... 949 450-0202
2603 Main St Ste 500 Irvine (92614) *(P-14734)*

Action Stamping Inc .... E...... 626 914-7466
517 S Glendora Ave Glendora (91741) *(P-6493)*

Actionpac Scales & Automation, Santa Paula *Also Called: Coastal Cnting Indus Scale Inc (P-7110)*

Activcare Living Inc (PA) .... C...... 858 565-4424
10603 Rancho Bernardo Rd San Diego (92127) *(P-19988)*

Active Window Products .... D...... 323 245-5185
5431 W San Fernando Rd Los Angeles (90039) *(P-6097)*

Activeapparel Inc (PA) .... F...... 951 361-0060
11076 Venture Dr Jurupa Valley (91752) *(P-2191)*

Activeon Inc (PA) .... E...... 858 798-3300
10905 Technology Pl San Diego (92127) *(P-8391)*

Activision .... E...... 424 320-9000
9465 Wilshire Blvd Ste 400 Beverly Hills (90212) *(P-3423)*

Activision Blizzard, Santa Monica *Also Called: Activision Blizzard Inc (P-16157)*

Activision Blizzard Inc .... D...... 949 955-1380
3 Blizzard Irvine (92618) *(P-16156)*

Activision Blizzard Inc (HQ) .... B...... 310 255-2000
2701 Olympic Blvd Bldg B Santa Monica (90404) *(P-16157)*

Actron Manufacturing Inc .... D...... 951 371-0885
1841 Railroad St Corona (92878) *(P-5895)*

Acufast Aircraft Products Inc .... E...... 818 365-7077
12445 Gladstone Ave Sylmar (91342) *(P-9591)*

A L P H A B E T I C

Acuprint, Los Angeles *Also Called: Ink & Color Inc (P-3595)*

Acushnet Company .... B....... 760 804-6500
2819 Loker Ave E Carlsbad (92010) *(P-10970)*

Acute Psychiatric Hospital, Rosemead *Also Called: Success Healthcare 1 LLC (P-17796)*

ACUTUS MEDICAL, Carlsbad *Also Called: Acutus Medical Inc (P-10416)*

Acutus Medical Inc .... B....... 442 232-6080
2210 Faraday Ave Ste 100 Carlsbad (92008) *(P-10416)*

Acx Intermodal Inc .... C....... 310 241-6229
920 E Pacific Coast Hwy Wilmington (90744) *(P-13485)*

Ad Art Company, Vernon *Also Called: RJ Acquisition Corp (P-3808)*

Ad Populum LLC (PA)..D..... 619 818-7644
1234 6th St Apt 410 Santa Monica (90401) *(P-15526)*

Ad/S Companies, Corona *Also Called: Architectural Design Signs Inc (P-11097)*

Adam Nutrition Inc .... C....... 951 361-1120
11010 Hopkins St Ste B Jurupa Valley (91752) *(P-4035)*

Adam Nutrition, A Division Ivc, Irvine *Also Called: International Vitamin Corp (P-4137)*

Adams and Brooks Inc .... C....... 909 880-2305
4345 Hallmark Pkwy San Bernardino (92407) *(P-1533)*

Adams Business Media, Palm Springs *Also Called: Adams Trade Press LP (P-3340)*

Adams Comm & Engrg Tech Inc ....C....... 301 861-5000
1875 Century Park E Ste 1130 Los Angeles (90067) *(P-16547)*

Adams Rite Aerospace Inc (DH)............................. D....... 714 278-6500
4141 N Palm St Fullerton (92835) *(P-9592)*

Adams Steel, Anaheim *Also Called: Self Serve Auto Dismantlers (P-12957)*

Adams Trade Press LP (PA)..................................... E....... 760 318-7000
420 S Palm Canyon Dr Palm Springs (92262) *(P-3340)*

Adams-Campbell Company Ltd (PA).........................D..... 626 330-3425
15343 Proctor Ave City Of Industry (91745) *(P-6177)*

Adapt Automation Inc .... E....... 714 662-4454
1661 Palm St Ste A Santa Ana (92701) *(P-7166)*

Adaptamed LLC .... C....... 877 478-7773
6699 Alvarado Rd Ste 2301 San Diego (92120) *(P-15955)*

Adaptive Aerospace Corporation .... E....... 661 300-0616
501 Bailey Ave Tehachapi (93561) *(P-9593)*

Adaptive Digital Systems Inc .... E....... 949 955-3116
20322 Sw Acacia St Ste 200 Newport Beach (92660) *(P-8488)*

Adaptive Tech Group Inc .... E....... 562 424-1100
1635 E Burnett St Signal Hill (90755) *(P-14090)*

Adat ARI El ....C....... 818 766-4992
12020 Burbank Blvd Valley Village (91607) *(P-18962)*

Adat ARI El Day School, Valley Village *Also Called: Adat ARI El (P-18962)*

ADB Industries .... B....... 310 679-9193
1400 Manhattan Ave Fullerton (92831) *(P-5822)*

ADC Aerospace, Buena Park *Also Called: Alloy Die Casting Co (P-5756)*

Adco Products Inc .... D....... 937 339-6267
23091 Mill Creek Dr Laguna Hills (92653) *(P-8991)*

Adcolony Inc .... D....... 650 625-1262
11400 W Olympic Blvd # 1200 Los Angeles (90064) *(P-15956)*

Adcom Interactive Media Inc .... D....... 800 296-7104
21200 Oxnard St # 429 Woodland Hills (91367) *(P-16548)*

Adconion Media Inc (PA)... C...... 310 382-5521
3301 Exposition Blvd Fl 1 Santa Monica (90404) *(P-15527)*

Adconion Media Group, Santa Monica *Also Called: Adconion Media Inc (P-15527)*

Adcraft Business Mail, Oceanside *Also Called: Bus-Let Inc (P-15629)*

Adcraft Labels, Anaheim *Also Called: Adcraft Products Co Inc (P-3729)*

Adcraft Products Co Inc .... E....... 714 776-1230
1230 S Sherman St Anaheim (92805) *(P-3729)*

Add-On Cmpt Peripherals Inc .... C....... 949 546-8200
15775 Gateway Cir Tustin (92780) *(P-7504)*

Add-On Cmpt Peripherals LLC .... D....... 949 546-8200
15775 Gateway Cir Tustin (92780) *(P-7459)*

Addaday Inc .... E....... 424 259-3368
12304 Santa Monica Blvd Ste 355 Los Angeles (90025) *(P-10971)*

Addition Manufacturing Technologies CA Inc .... E....... 760 597-5220
1391 Specialty Dr Ste A Vista (92081) *(P-7028)*

Addon Networks, Tustin *Also Called: Add-On Cmpt Peripherals LLC (P-7459)*

Adecco Employment Services .... C....... 949 586-2342
25301 Cabot Rd Ste 214 Aliso Viejo (92653) *(P-15810)*

Adecco Staffing, Chula Vista *Also Called: Ado Staffing Inc (P-15911)*

Adelanto Elementary School Dst .... E....... 760 530-7680
14350 Bellflower St Adelanto (92301) *(P-1846)*

Adelfi Credit Union ....C....... 714 671-5700
955 W Imperial Hwy Ste 100 Brea (92821) *(P-14244)*

Adept Fasteners Inc (PA)..C..... 661 257-6600
27949 Hancock Pkwy Valencia (91355) *(P-9594)*

Adept Process Services Inc .... E....... 619 434-3194
609 Anita St Chula Vista (91911) *(P-9852)*

Adesa Corporation LLC .... D....... 619 661-5565
2175 Cactus Rd San Diego (92154) *(P-12219)*

Adesa International LLC (PA)................................... E..... 909 321-8240
1440 S Vineyard Ave Ontario (91761) *(P-1319)*

Adesso Inc .... C....... 909 839-2929
20659 Valley Blvd Walnut (91789) *(P-12392)*

Adexa Inc (PA).. E..... 310 642-2100
5777 W Century Blvd Ste 1100 Los Angeles (90045) *(P-16158)*

Adf Incorporated .... E....... 310 669-9700
1550 W Mahalo Pl Rancho Dominguez (90220) *(P-6349)*

Adfa Incorporated .... E....... 213 627-8004
319 W 6th St Los Angeles (90014) *(P-6684)*

ADI, Compton *Also Called: American Dawn Inc (P-2134)*

ADI, Valencia *Also Called: Aerospace Dynamics Intl Inc (P-9602)*

ADI, San Bernardino *Also Called: Aviation & Defense Inc (P-11689)*

Adicio Inc .... D....... 760 602-9502
5857 Owens Ave Ste 300 Carlsbad (92008) *(P-11869)*

Adient Aerospace LLC (PA)..................................... C..... 949 514-1851
2850 Skyway Dr Santa Maria (93455) *(P-11684)*

Adj Products LLC (PA)...C..... 323 582-2650
6122 S Eastern Ave Commerce (90040) *(P-12582)*

ADM Works LLC .... E....... 714 245-0536
1343 E Wilshire Ave Santa Ana (92705) *(P-5778)*

Admar Corporation .... C....... 714 953-9600
1551 N Tustin Ave Ste 300 Santa Ana (92705) *(P-14457)*

Admedia, Woodland Hills *Also Called: Adcom Interactive Media Inc (P-16548)*

Administrative Svcs Coop Inc .... C....... 310 715-1968
1515 W 190th St Ste 200 Gardena (90249) *(P-11412)*

Adminsure Inc .... C....... 909 718-1200
3380 Shelby St Ontario (91764) *(P-14553)*

Adnet Media, Los Angeles *Also Called: Xbiz (P-3395)*

Ado Staffing Inc ....C....... 619 691-3659
850 Lagoon Dr Bldg 99a Chula Vista (91910) *(P-15911)*

Adonis Inc .... E....... 951 432-3960
475 N Sheridan St Corona (92878) *(P-4376)*

Adopt-A-Beach, Costa Mesa *Also Called: Adopt-A-Highway Maintenance (P-607)*

Adopt-A-Highway Maintenance ....C....... 800 200-0003
3158 Red Hill Ave Ste 200 Costa Mesa (92626) *(P-607)*

ADP, Irvine *Also Called: Automatic Data Processing Inc (P-16482)*

ADP, San Dimas *Also Called: Automatic Data Processing Inc (P-16483)*

Adrenaline Lacrosse Inc .... E....... 888 768-8479
24 21st St San Diego (92102) *(P-13928)*

Adriennes Gourmet Foods .... D....... 805 964-6848
849 Ward Dr Santa Barbara (93111) *(P-1501)*

ADS Techonlogy, Walnut *Also Called: Adesso Inc (P-12392)*

ADT LLC .... C....... 951 782-6900
1120 Palmyrita Ave Ste 280 Riverside (92507) *(P-16715)*

ADT LLC .... C....... 714 450-6461
731 E Ball Rd Anaheim (92805) *(P-16716)*

ADT LLC .... C....... 626 593-1020
475 N Muller St Anaheim (92801) *(P-16717)*

ADT LLC .... C....... 818 464-5001
9201 Oakdale Ave Ste 100 Chatsworth (91311) *(P-16718)*

ADT LLC .... C....... 818 373-6200
26074 Avenue Hall Ste 1 Valencia (91355) *(P-16719)*

ADT LLC .... C....... 951 824-7205
1808 Commercenter W Ste E San Bernardino (92408) *(P-16720)*

ADT Security Services, San Bernardino *Also Called: ADT LLC (P-16720)*

Adtech Optics, City Of Industry *Also Called: Adtech Photonics Inc (P-8757)*

Adtech Photonics Inc .... E....... 626 956-1000
18007 Cortney Ct City Of Industry (91748) *(P-8757)*

Adti Media LLC .... E....... 951 795-4446
1257 Simpson Way Escondido (92029) *(P-11095)*

Adult Video News, Chatsworth *Also Called: Avn Media Network Inc (P-3398)*

2024 Southern California
Business Directory and Buyers Guide

Advance Adapters Inc ....E....... 805 238-7000
4320 Aerotech Center Way Paso Robles (93446) *(P-9342)*

Advance Adapters LLC ....E....... 805 238-7000
4320 Aerotech Center Way Paso Robles (93446) *(P-9343)*

Advance Beverage Co Inc ....D....... 661 833-3783
5200 District Blvd Bakersfield (93313) *(P-13457)*

Advance Disposal Company, Hesperia *Also Called: Best Way Disposal Co Inc (P-12159)*

Advance Overhead Door Inc ....:..F....... 818 781-5590
15829 Stagg St Van Nuys (91406) *(P-6098)*

Advance Paper Box Company ....C....... 323 750-2550
6100 S Gramercy Pl Los Angeles (90047) *(P-3078)*

Advance Plastics, National City *Also Called: B and P Plastics Inc (P-4952)*

Advance Screw Products, South El Monte *Also Called: Bci Inc (P-7778)*

Advance Storage Products, Huntington Beach *Also Called: JCM Industries Inc (P-2982)*

Advance-Tech Plating Inc ....F....... 714 630-7093
1061 N Grove St Anaheim (92806) *(P-6575)*

Advanced Aerospace ....E....... 714 265-6200
10781 Forbes Ave Garden Grove (92843) *(P-7595)*

Advanced Air, Hawthorne *Also Called: Advanced Air LLC (P-11679)*

Advanced Air LLC ....C....... 310 644-3344
12101 Crenshaw Blvd Ste 100 Hawthorne (90250) *(P-11679)*

Advanced Aircraft Seal, Riverside *Also Called: Sphere Alliance Inc (P-3973)*

Advanced Arm Dynamics (PA) ....E....... 310 372-3050
123 W Torrance Blvd Ste 203 Redondo Beach (90277) *(P-10631)*

Advanced Biohealing.com, San Diego *Also Called: Shire Rgenerative Medicine Inc (P-4233)*

Advanced Bionics LLC (HQ) ....B....... 661 362-1400
12740 San Fernando Rd Sylmar (91342) *(P-10632)*

Advanced Bionics LLC ....E....... 310 819-4004
26081 Avenue Hall Valencia (91355) *(P-10787)*

Advanced Bionics Corporation (HQ) ....C....... 661 362-1400
28515 Westinghouse Pl Valencia (91355) *(P-10633)*

Advanced Building Systems Inc ....E....... 818 652-4252
11905 Regentview Ave Downey (90241) *(P-11186)*

Advanced Charging Tech Inc ....E....... 877 228-5922
17260 Newhope St Fountain Valley (92708) *(P-8199)*

Advanced Chemical Technology ....E....... 800 527-9607
3540 E 26th St Vernon (90058) *(P-3879)*

Advanced Chemical Technology, Vernon *Also Called: Advanced Chemical Technology (P-3879)*

Advanced Chemical Trnspt Inc ....C....... 951 790-7989
600 Iowa St Redlands (92373) *(P-11439)*

Advanced Chemistry & Technology Inc ....D....... 714 373-8118
7341 Anaconda Ave Garden Grove (92841) *(P-4556)*

Advanced Circuits Inc ....E....... 818 345-1993
17067 Cantara St Van Nuys (91406) *(P-8642)*

Advanced Cleanup Tech Inc ....B....... 310 763-1423
230 E C St Wilmington (90744) *(P-20287)*

Advanced Clnroom McRclean Corp ....C....... 714 751-1152
3250 S Susan St Ste A Santa Ana (92704) *(P-15690)*

Advanced Clutch Technology Inc ....E....... 661 940-7555
206 E Avenue K4 Lancaster (93535) *(P-9344)*

Advanced Cmpsite Pdts Tech Inc ....E....... 714 895-5544
15602 Chemical Ln Huntington Beach (92649) *(P-4928)*

Advanced Color Graphics ....D....... 909 930-1500
1921 S Business Pkwy Ontario (91761) *(P-3506)*

Advanced Corporate Svcs Inc ....E....... 310 937-6848
2416 Amsler St Torrance (90505) *(P-20306)*

Advanced Cosmetic RES Labs Inc ....E....... 818 709-9945
20550 Prairie St Chatsworth (91311) *(P-11187)*

Advanced Crtcal Care Emrgncy S ....C....... 310 558-6111
9599 Jefferson Blvd Culver City (90232) *(P-122)*

Advanced Cutting Tools Inc ....E....... 714 842-9376
17741 Metzler Ln Huntington Beach (92647) *(P-5871)*

Advanced Digital Mfg LLC ....E....... 714 245-0536
1343 E Wilshire Ave Santa Ana (92705) *(P-9595)*

Advanced Digital Services Inc (PA) ....D....... 323 962-8585
948 N Cahuenga Blvd Los Angeles (90038) *(P-17166)*

Advanced Digital Tech Intl, Escondido *Also Called: Adti Media LLC (P-11095)*

Advanced Electromagnetics Inc ....E....... 619 449-9492
1320 Air Wing Rd Ste 101 San Diego (92154) *(P-10113)*

Advanced Electronic Solutions, Irvine *Also Called: Patric Communications Inc (P-924)*

Advanced Engineering & EDM Inc ....F....... 858 679-6800
13007 Kirkham Way Ste A Poway (92064) *(P-7735)*

Advanced Enginering and EDM ....E....... 858 679-6800
13007 Kirkham Way Ste A Poway (92064) *(P-7736)*

Advanced Engrg Mlding Tech Inc ....E....... 888 264-0392
6510 Box Springs Blvd Ste B Riverside (92507) *(P-4929)*

Advanced Equipment Corporation (PA) ....E....... 714 635-5350
2401 W Commonwealth Ave Fullerton (92833) *(P-2972)*

Advanced Flow Engineering Inc (PA) ....E....... 951 493-7155
252 Granite St Corona (92879) *(P-9345)*

Advanced Flow Engineering Inc ....F....... 951 493-7100
1375 Sampson Ave Corona (92879) *(P-9346)*

Advanced Foam Inc ....F....... 310 515-0728
1745 W 134th St Gardena (90249) *(P-4869)*

Advanced Fresh Cncpts Frnchise ....E....... 310 604-3200
19700 Mariner Ave Torrance (90503) *(P-1798)*

Advanced Fresh Concepts Corp (PA) ....E....... 310 604-3630
19205 S Laurel Park Rd Rancho Dominguez (90220) *(P-15007)*

Advanced Grund Systems Engrg L (HQ) ....E....... 562 906-9300
10805 Painter Ave Santa Fe Springs (90670) *(P-9561)*

Advanced Hpc Inc ....F....... 858 716-8262
8228 Mercury Ct Ste 100 San Diego (92111) *(P-7460)*

Advanced Image Direct, Fullerton *Also Called: Real Estate Image Inc (P-15635)*

Advanced Image Direct LLC ....E....... 714 502-3900
1415 S Acacia Ave Fullerton (92831) *(P-15626)*

Advanced Industrial Services, Bakersfield *Also Called: CL Knox Inc (P-340)*

Advanced Industrial Svcs Cal, Paramount *Also Called: Advanced Industrial Svcs Inc (P-841)*

Advanced Industrial Svcs Inc ....D....... 562 940-8305
7831 Alondra Blvd Paramount (90723) *(P-841)*

Advanced Innovative Tech Corp ....D....... 417 831-9444
1675 W Park Ave Redlands (92373) *(P-17026)*

Advanced Innvtive Rcvery Tech ....E....... 949 273-8100
3401 Space Center Ct Ste 811b Jurupa Valley (91752) *(P-2841)*

Advanced Instruments, Pomona *Also Called: Analytical Industries Inc (P-10117)*

Advanced Joining Technologies Inc ....E....... 949 756-8091
3030 Red Hill Ave Santa Ana (92705) *(P-7737)*

Advanced Machining Tooling Inc ....E....... 858 486-9050
13535 Danielson St Poway (92064) *(P-7046)*

Advanced Materials Inc (HQ) ....E....... 310 537-5444
20211 S Susana Rd Compton (90221) *(P-4930)*

Advanced McHning Solutions Inc ....E....... 619 671-3055
3523 Main St Ste 606 Chula Vista (91911) *(P-7738)*

Advanced Med Prsonnel Svcs Inc ....D....... 386 756-4395
12400 High Bluff Dr Ste 100 San Diego (92130) *(P-15811)*

Advanced Metal Mfg Inc ....E....... 805 322-4161
49 Strathearn Pl Simi Valley (93065) *(P-6178)*

Advanced Micro Instruments Inc ....E....... 714 848-5533
225 Paularino Ave Costa Mesa (92626) *(P-10349)*

Advanced Mold Technology Inc ....F
16507 Celadon Ct Chino Hills (91709) *(P-7047)*

Advanced Motion Controls, Camarillo *Also Called: Barta - Schoenewald Inc (P-8135)*

Advanced Mp Technology LLC (DH) ....C....... 800 492-3113
27271 Las Ramblas Ste 300 Mission Viejo (92691) *(P-12641)*

Advanced Mtls Joining Corp (PA) ....E....... 626 449-2696
2858 E Walnut St Pasadena (91107) *(P-9596)*

Advanced Multimodal Dist Inc ....C....... 800 838-3058
14822 Central Ave Chino (91710) *(P-11826)*

Advanced Office, Irvine *Also Called: Integrus LLC (P-12384)*

Advanced Photonix, Camarillo *Also Called: OSI Optoelectronics Inc (P-8858)*

Advanced Phrm Svcs Inc ....F....... 714 903-1006
11555 Monarch St Ste B Garden Grove (92841) *(P-13027)*

Advanced Process Services Inc ....E....... 323 278-6530
4350 E Washington Blvd Commerce (90023) *(P-6752)*

Advanced Products, Costa Mesa *Also Called: Pro-Lite Inc (P-11146)*

Advanced Prof Imging Med Group ....C....... 818 244-4646
1109 S Central Ave Glendale (91204) *(P-17582)*

Advanced Protection Inds LLC ....D....... 800 662-1711
25341 Commercentre Dr Lake Forest (92630) *(P-16721)*

Advanced Publishing Tech Inc ....F....... 818 557-3035
1105 N Hollywood Way Burbank (91505) *(P-3424)*

Advanced Semiconductor Inc ....D....... 818 982-1200
24955 Avenue Kearny Valencia (91355) *(P-8758)*

Employee Codes: A=Over 500 employees, B=251-500
C=101-250, D=51-100, E=20-50, F=10-19, G=1-9

2024 Southern California
Business Directory and Buyers Guide

© Mergent Inc. 1-800-342-5647

979

Advanced Sterlization (HQ)...C....... 800 595-0200
33 Technology Dr Irvine (92618) *(P-10417)*

Advanced Strlztion Pdts Lgstic, Fontana *Also Called: Advanced Strlztion Pdts Svcs I*
(P-11561)

Advanced Strlztion Pdts Svcs I .... B....... 909 350-6987
13135 Napa St Fontana (92335) *(P-11561)*

Advanced Structural Tech Inc ....C....... 805 204-9133
950 Richmond Ave Oxnard (93030) *(P-6457)*

Advanced Technology Co, Pasadena *Also Called: Advanced Mtls Joining Corp (P-9596)*

Advanced Thermal Sciences Corp (DH)......................E....... 714 688-4200
3355 E La Palma Ave Anaheim (92806) *(P-8759)*

Advanced Thrmlforming Entp Inc ....E....... 760 722-4400
3750 Oceanic Way Oceanside (92056) *(P-4931)*

Advanced Uv Inc (PA).. E....... 562 407-0299
16350 Manning Way Cerritos (90703) *(P-7635)*

Advanced Vision Science Inc ....E....... 805 683-3851
5743 Thornwood Dr Goleta (93117) *(P-10831)*

Advanced Vsual Image Dsign LLC ....E....... 951 279-2138
229 N Sherman Ave Irvine (92614) *(P-3507)*

Advanced Waveguide Tech ....E....... 949 297-3564
23192 Alcalde Dr Ste E Laguna Hills (92653) *(P-8992)*

Advanced Web Offset Inc ....D....... 760 727-1700
2260 Oak Ridge Way Vista (92081) *(P-3730)*

Advanstar Communications Inc ....D....... 714 513-8400
2525 Main St Ste 300 Irvine (92614) *(P-3341)*

Advanstar Communications Inc .... E....... 310 857-7500
2901 28th St Ste 100 Santa Monica (90405) *(P-16767)*

Advanstar Communications Inc (DH)...........................C....... 310 857-7500
2501 Colorado Ave Ste 280 Santa Monica (90404) *(P-16768)*

Advanstar Global, Santa Monica *Also Called: Advanstar Communications Inc (P-16768)*

Advantage Adhesives Inc ....E....... 909 204-4990
8345 White Oak Ave Rancho Cucamonga (91730) *(P-4557)*

Advantage Backhoes, Blue Jay *Also Called: Travis Snyder (P-6944)*

Advantage Chemical LLC ....E....... 951 225-4631
27375 Via Industria Temecula (92590) *(P-13423)*

Advantage Custom Fixtures, Los Angeles *Also Called: American Furniture Systems Inc*
(P-2902)

Advantage Ford, Duarte *Also Called: Advantage Ford Lincoln Mercury (P-13735)*

Advantage Ford Lincoln Mercury ....D....... 626 305-9188
1031 Central Ave Duarte (91010) *(P-13735)*

Advantage Mailing LLC (PA).......................................C....... 714 538-3881
1600 N Kraemer Blvd Anaheim (92806) *(P-15627)*

Advantage Mailing Service, Anaheim *Also Called: Advantage Mailing LLC (P-15627)*

Advantage Manufacturing Inc ....E....... 714 505-1166
616 S Santa Fe St Santa Ana (92705) *(P-12583)*

Advantage Media Services Inc ....C....... 661 705-7588
28220 Industry Dr Valencia (91355) *(P-11562)*

Advantage Sales & Mktg Inc (DH)...............................C....... 949 797-2900
15310 Barranca Pkwy Ste 100 Irvine (92618) *(P-20125)*

Advantage Sales & Mktg LLC (DH)..............................C....... 949 797-2900
15310 Barranca Pkwy Ste 100 Irvine (92618) *(P-20126)*

Advantage Solutions, Irvine *Also Called: Advantage Sales & Mktg Inc (P-20125)*

Advantage Solutions, Irvine *Also Called: Advantage Sales & Mktg LLC (P-20126)*

Advantage-Crown Sls & Mktg LLC (DH)......................A....... 714 780-3000
1400 S Douglass Rd Ste 200 Anaheim (92806) *(P-13168)*

Advantest Test Solutions Inc ....D....... 949 523-6900
26211 Enterprise Way Lake Forest (92630) *(P-8760)*

Advent Resources Inc ....D....... 310 241-1500
235 W 7th St San Pedro (90731) *(P-15957)*

Adventist Health Bakersfield, Bakersfield *Also Called: San Joaquin Community Hospital*
(P-18417)

Adventist Health Delano ....D....... 661 758-4184
2300 7th St Wasco (93280) *(P-14987)*

Adventist Health Delano ....C....... 661 721-5337
1205 Garces Hwy Ste 208 Delano (93215) *(P-18161)*

Adventist Health Delano (HQ).....................................A....... 661 725-4800
1401 Garces Hwy Delano (93215) *(P-18162)*

Adventist Health Med Tehachapi (PA).........................C....... 661 750-4848
305 S Robinson St Tehachapi (93561) *(P-18163)*

Adventist Health System/West ....D....... 619 475-5040
2700 E 4th St National City (91950) *(P-14702)*

ADVENTIST HEALTH SYSTEM/WEST, National City *Also Called: Adventist Health System/*
West (P-14702)

Adventist Hlth Systm/West Corp ....B....... 661 316-6000
3001 Sillect Ave Bakersfield (93308) *(P-18164)*

Adventist Media Center Inc (PA).................................C....... 805 955-7777
11291 Pierce St Riverside (92505) *(P-17309)*

Adventure City Inc ....D....... 714 821-3311
1238 S Beach Blvd Anaheim (92804) *(P-17539)*

Advertise Purple ....D....... 424 272-7400
1431 7th St Ste 302 Santa Monica (90401) *(P-15528)*

Adviceperiod ....D....... 424 281-3600
2121 Avenue Of The Stars Ste 2400 Los Angeles (90067) *(P-14412)*

Advisorsquare, Culver City *Also Called: Liveoffice LLC (P-16295)*

Advisys Inc ....E....... 949 250-0794
3 Corporate Park Ste 240 Irvine (92606) *(P-16159)*

Advocacy For Rspect Chice - Lo (PA)..........................D....... 562 597-7716
4519 E Stearns St Long Beach (90815) *(P-19173)*

Adwest, Anaheim *Also Called: Adwest Technologies Inc (P-7317)*

Adwest Technologies Inc (HQ)....................................E....... 714 632-8595
4222 E La Palma Ave Anaheim (92807) *(P-7317)*

AEC - Able Engineering Company Inc ....C....... 805 685-2262
600 Pine Ave Goleta (93117) *(P-5988)*

Aecom Services Inc (HQ)...C....... 213 593-8000
300 S Grand Ave Ste 900 Los Angeles (90071) *(P-19722)*

Aecom Technical Services Inc (HQ)............................D....... 213 593-8100
300 S Grand Ave Fl 9 Los Angeles (90071) *(P-20307)*

Aecom Usa Inc ....C....... 714 567-2501
999 W Town And Country Rd Orange (92868) *(P-20308)*

Aecom Usa Inc ....D....... 213 593-8000
300 S Grand Ave Ste 900 Los Angeles (90071) *(P-20309)*

Aecom Usa Inc ....D....... 213 330-7200
515 S Figueroa St Ste 400 Los Angeles (90071) *(P-20310)*

Aecom Usa Inc ....C....... 858 947-7144
401 W A St Ste 1200 San Diego (92101) *(P-20311)*

AEG Management Lacc LLC ....C....... 213 741-1151
1201 S Figueroa St Los Angeles (90015) *(P-19989)*

AEG Presents, Los Angeles *Also Called: AEG Presents LLC (P-17310)*

AEG Presents LLC (DH)..C....... 323 930-5700
425 W 11th St Los Angeles (90015) *(P-17310)*

AEG Worldwide, Los Angeles *Also Called: Anschutz Entrmt Group Inc (P-17335)*

Aegis Asssted Living Prpts LLC ....C....... 760 806-3600
1440 S Melrose Dr Oceanside (92056) *(P-19234)*

Aegis At Shadowridge, Oceanside *Also Called: Aegis Asssted Living Prpts LLC (P-19234)*

Aegis Biodefense, San Diego *Also Called: Aegis Life Inc (P-4036)*

Aegis Life Inc ....E....... 650 666-5287
3033 Science Park Rd Ste 270 San Diego (92121) *(P-4036)*

Aegis of Granada Hills, Granada Hills *Also Called: Aegis Senior Communities LLC (P-18586)*

Aegis of Laguna Niguel, Laguna Niguel *Also Called: Aegis Senior Communities LLC*
(P-19235)

Aegis of Ventura, Ventura *Also Called: Aegis Senior Communities LLC (P-18587)*

Aegis SEC & Investigations Inc ....C....... 310 838-2787
10866 Washington Blvd Ste 308 Culver City (90232) *(P-16613)*

Aegis Senior Communities LLC ....C....... 818 363-3373
10801 Lindley Ave Granada Hills (91344) *(P-18586)*

Aegis Senior Communities LLC ....D....... 805 650-1114
4964 Telegraph Rd Ventura (93003) *(P-18587)*

Aegis Senior Communities LLC ....C....... 949 496-8080
32170 Niguel Rd Laguna Niguel (92677) *(P-19235)*

Aem Corporation, Camarillo *Also Called: Applied Engineering MGT Corp (P-15965)*

Aemi, San Diego *Also Called: Advanced Electromagnetics Inc (P-10113)*

Aemi Holdings LLC ....D....... 858 481-0210
6610 Cobra Way San Diego (92121) *(P-8116)*

Aer Logistics, Brea *Also Called: Aer Technologies Inc (P-17112)*

Aer Technologies Inc ....B....... 714 871-7357
650 Columbia St Brea (92821) *(P-17112)*

Aera Energy LLC ....D....... 661 334-3100
19590 7th Standard Rd Mc Kittrick (93251) *(P-244)*

Aera Energy LLC ....A....... 661 665-5000
10000 Ming Ave Bakersfield (93311) *(P-245)*

Aera Energy Services Company ....C....... 661 665-4400
59231 Main Camp Rd Mc Kittrick (93251) *(P-275)*

Aera Energy Services Company .... C 661 665-3200
29235 Highway 33 Maricopa (93252) *(P-276)*

Aera Energy Services Company (HQ) .... A 661 665-5000
10000 Ming Ave Bakersfield (93311) *(P-277)*

Aera Energy South Midway, Maricopa *Also Called: Aera Energy Services Company (P-276)*

Aercap Global Aviation Trust (HQ) .... C 310 788-1999
10250 Constellation Blvd Ste 3400 Los Angeles (90067) *(P-15768)*

Aero ARC .... E 310 324-3400
16634 S Figueroa St Gardena (90248) *(P-6179)*

Aero Bending Company .... D 661 948-2363
560 Auto Center Dr Ste A Palmdale (93551) *(P-6180)*

Aero Chip Inc .... E 562 404-6300
13563 Freeway Dr Santa Fe Springs (90670) *(P-7739)*

Aero Dynamic Machining Inc .... D 714 379-1073
7472 Chapman Ave Garden Grove (92841) *(P-7740)*

Aero Engineering, Valencia *Also Called: Aero Engineering & Mfg Co LLC (P-9597)*

Aero Engineering & Mfg Co LLC .... D 661 295-0875
28217 Avenue Crocker Valencia (91355) *(P-9597)*

Aero Industries LLC .... B 805 688-6734
139 Industrial Way Buellton (93427) *(P-7741)*

Aero Mechanism Precision Inc .... E 818 886-1855
21700 Marilla St Chatsworth (91311) *(P-7742)*

Aero Pacific Corporation .... C 714 961-9200
20445 E Walnut Dr N Walnut (91789) *(P-9598)*

Aero Performance, Corona *Also Called: Irwin Aviation Inc (P-9725)*

Aero Port Services Inc (PA) .... A 310 623-8230
216 W Florence Ave Inglewood (90301) *(P-16722)*

Aero Powder Coating Inc .... E 323 264-6405
710 Monterey Pass Rd Monterey Park (91754) *(P-6685)*

Aero Precision Engineering .... E 310 642-9747
11300 Hindry Ave Los Angeles (90045) *(P-6181)*

Aero Products Co., Los Angeles *Also Called: Coating Specialties Inc (P-9660)*

Aero Shade Co Inc (PA) .... E 323 938-2314
8404 W 3rd St Los Angeles (90048) *(P-13955)*

Aero Worx, Torrance *Also Called: Aeroworx Inc (P-17113)*

Aero-Craft Hydraulics Inc .... E 951 736-4690
392 N Smith Ave Corona (92878) *(P-9599)*

Aero-Electric Connector Inc (PA) .... B 310 618-3737
2280 W 208th St Torrance (90501) *(P-8253)*

Aero-k .... E 626 350-5125
2040 E Dyer Rd Santa Ana (92705) *(P-7743)*

Aeroantenna Technology Inc .... C 818 993-3842
20732 Lassen St Chatsworth (91311) *(P-9937)*

Aerocraft Heat Treating Co Inc .... D 562 674-2400
15701 Minnesota Ave Paramount (90723) *(P-5823)*

Aerodynamic Engineering Inc .... E 714 891-2651
15495 Graham St Huntington Beach (92649) *(P-7744)*

Aerodyne Prcsion Machining Inc .... E 714 891-1311
5471 Argosy Ave Huntington Beach (92649) *(P-7745)*

Aerofab Corporation .... F 714 635-0902
4001 E Leaverton Ct Anaheim (92807) *(P-5989)*

Aerofit LLC .... C 714 521-5060
1425 S Acacia Ave Fullerton (92831) *(P-6836)*

Aeroflex Incorporated .... E 800 843-1553
15375 Barranca Pkwy Ste F106 Irvine (92618) *(P-8761)*

Aeroflite Enterprises Inc .... D 714 773-4251
261 Gemini Ave Brea (92821) *(P-8959)*

Aerofoam Industries Inc .... D 951 245-4429
31855 Corydon St Lake Elsinore (92530) *(P-2920)*

Aerojet Rcketdyne Holdings Inc (HQ) .... D 310 252-8100
222 N Pacific Coast Hwy Ste 500 El Segundo (90245) *(P-9938)*

Aerojet Rocketdyne, Canoga Park *Also Called: Aerojet Rocketdyne De Inc (P-4510)*

Aerojet Rocketdyne De Inc (DH) .... C 818 586-1000
8900 De Soto Ave Canoga Park (91304) *(P-4510)*

Aerojet Rocketdyne De Inc .... B 818 586-9629
8495 Carla Ln West Hills (91304) *(P-4511)*

Aerojet Rocketdyne De Inc .... C 818 586-1000
9001 Lurline Ave Chatsworth (91311) *(P-4512)*

Aerojet Rocketdyne De Inc .... A 818 586-1000
6633 Canoga Ave Canoga Park (91303) *(P-9562)*

Aerol Co, Rancho Dominguez *Also Called: Aerol Co Inc (P-5779)*

Aerol Co Inc .... E 310 762-2660
19560 S Rancho Way Rancho Dominguez (90220) *(P-5779)*

Aeroliant Manufacturing Inc .... E 310 257-1903
1613 Lockness Pl Torrance (90501) *(P-7746)*

Aerontics Systems Arspc Strctr, San Diego *Also Called: Northrop Grumman Systems Corp (P-10032)*

Aeroshear Aviation Svcs Inc (PA) .... E 818 779-1650
7701 Woodley Ave 200 Van Nuys (91406) *(P-9600)*

Aerospace Corporation .... D 310 336-7270
Los Angeles (90009) *(P-19813)*

Aerospace Driven Tech Inc .... F 949 553-1606
2807 Catherine Way Santa Ana (92705) *(P-9601)*

Aerospace Dynamics Intl Inc (DH) .... C 661 257-3535
25540 Rye Canyon Rd Valencia (91355) *(P-9602)*

Aerospace Dynamics Intl Inc .... B 661 310-6986
25575 Rye Canyon Rd Santa Clarita (91355) *(P-9603)*

Aerospace Engineering LLC (PA) .... D 714 996-8178
2632 Saturn St Brea (92821) *(P-9604)*

Aerospace Engineering LLC .... E 714 641-5884
2141 S Standard Ave Santa Ana (92707) *(P-9605)*

Aerospace Engrg Support Corp .... E 310 297-4050
645 Hawaii St El Segundo (90245) *(P-9606)*

Aerospace Fasteners Group, Santa Ana *Also Called: SPS Technologies LLC (P-11076)*

Aerospace Parts Holdings Inc .... A 949 877-3630
3150 E Miraloma Ave Anaheim (92806) *(P-9607)*

Aerospace Systems, Redondo Beach *Also Called: Northrop Grumman Systems Corp (P-9546)*

Aerospace Tool & Grinding Inc .... E 562 802-3339
14020 Shoemaker Ave Norwalk (90650) *(P-7002)*

Aerotec Alloys Inc .... E 562 809-1378
10632 Alondra Blvd Norwalk (90650) *(P-5755)*

Aerotech News and Review Inc (PA) .... E 661 945-5634
220 E Avenue K4 Ste 4 Lancaster (93535) *(P-3342)*

Aerotek Inc .... A 805 604-3000
2751 Park View Ct Ste 221 Oxnard (93036) *(P-7747)*

Aerotransporte De Carge Union .... B 310 649-0069
5625 W Imperial Hwy Los Angeles (90045) *(P-11656)*

Aerounion, Los Angeles *Also Called: Aerotransporte De Carge Union (P-11656)*

Aerovironment Inc .... E 626 357-9983
825 S Myrtle Ave Monrovia (91016) *(P-9503)*

Aerovironment Inc .... E 805 520-8350
900 Innovators Way Simi Valley (93065) *(P-9504)*

Aerovironment Inc .... E 626 357-9983
1610 S Magnolia Ave Monrovia (91016) *(P-9505)*

Aerovironment Inc .... E 626 357-9983
222 E Huntington Dr Ste 118 Monrovia (91016) *(P-9506)*

Aeroworx Inc .... E 310 891-0300
2565 W 237th St Torrance (90505) *(P-17113)*

AES, Long Beach *Also Called: AES Alamitos LLC (P-12016)*

AES Alamitos LLC .... E 562 493-7891
690 N Studebaker Rd Long Beach (90803) *(P-12016)*

AES NDT .... E 310 947-6755
1821 W 213th St Ste L Torrance (90501) *(P-10350)*

Aethercomm Inc .... C 760 208-6002
3205 Lionshead Ave Carlsbad (92010) *(P-8489)*

Afakori Inc .... E 949 859-4277
18173 Osborne Rd Victorville (92394) *(P-5990)*

Afc Distribution Corp .... C 310 604-3630
19205 S Laurel Park Rd Rancho Dominguez (90220) *(P-13169)*

Afc Trading & Wholesale Inc .... E 323 223-7738
4738 Valley Blvd Los Angeles (90032) *(P-13170)*

Afcfc, Torrance *Also Called: Advanced Fresh Cncpts Frnchise (P-1798)*

Afco, Alhambra *Also Called: Alhambra Foundry Company Ltd (P-5643)*

Afco, Gardena *Also Called: Abrasive Finishing Co (P-5820)*

Afe Power, Corona *Also Called: Advanced Flow Engineering Inc (P-9345)*

Aferin LLC .... E 562 903-1500
9808 Alburtis Ave Santa Fe Springs (90670) *(P-7461)*

Affinity Auto Programs Inc .... B 858 643-9324
10251 Vista Sorrento Pkwy Ste 300 San Diego (92121) *(P-16769)*

Affinity Development Group Inc .... C 858 643-9324
10590 W Ocean Air Dr Ste 300 San Diego (92130) *(P-19509)*

Affinity Group, Ventura *Also Called: Agi Holding Corp (P-17458)*

Employee Codes: A=Over 500 employees, B=251-500
C=101-250, D=51-100, E=20-50, F=10-19, G=1-9

2024 Southern California
Business Directory and Buyers Guide

© Mergent Inc. 1-800-342-5647
981

ALPHABETIC

Affinity Lath & Plaster Inc ....E....... 760 207-5311
1414 Tiffany Ln Vista (92084) *(P-7003)*

Affluent Living Publication, Anaheim *Also Called: Affluent Target Marketing Inc (P-3343)*

Affluent Target Marketing Inc ....E....... 714 446-6280
3855 E La Palma Ave Ste 250 Anaheim (92807) *(P-3343)*

Affymetrix, San Diego *Also Called: Ebioscience Inc (P-19835)*

Affymetrix Inc ....E....... 858 642-2058
5893 Oberlin Dr San Diego (92121) *(P-10232)*

AFP, City Of Industry *Also Called: Alum-A-Fold Pacific Inc (P-5686)*

Afr Apparel International Inc ....D....... 818 773-5000
25365 Prado De La Felicidad Calabasas (91302) *(P-2386)*

Africajun LLC ....E....... 310 403-1673
39874 Golfers Dr Palmdale (93551) *(P-17167)*

African Women Rising ....C....... 415 278-1784
801 Cold Springs Rd Santa Barbara (93108) *(P-19422)*

After Capture, Los Angeles *Also Called: Rangefinder Publishing Co Inc (P-3385)*

After-Party2 Inc (DH) ....C....... 310 202-0011
901 W Hillcrest Blvd Inglewood (90301) *(P-15769)*

After-Party6 Inc ....C....... 310 966-4900
901 W Hillcrest Blvd Inglewood (90301) *(P-15770)*

AG Adriano Goldschmied Inc (PA) ....E....... 323 357-1111
2741 Seminole Ave South Gate (90280) *(P-2167)*

AG Global Products LLC ....F....... 323 334-2900
15408 Blackburn Ave Norwalk (90650) *(P-8229)*

AG Jeans, South Gate *Also Called: AG Adriano Goldschmied Inc (P-2167)*

AG Millworks, Ventura *Also Called: Art Glass Etc Inc (P-2585)*

AG Rx (PA) ....D....... 805 487-0696
751 S Rose Ave Oxnard (93030) *(P-13486)*

Ag-Weld Inc ....F....... 661 758-3061
1236 G St Wasco (93280) *(P-17079)*

Ag-Wise Enterprises Inc (PA) ....C....... 661 325-1567
5100 California Ave Ste 209 Bakersfield (93309) *(P-134)*

AGA Precision Systems Inc ....E....... 714 540-3163
122 E Dyer Rd Santa Ana (92707) *(P-7748)*

Age Incorporated ....E....... 562 483-7300
14831 Spring Ave Santa Fe Springs (90670) *(P-8117)*

Agency For Performing Arts Inc (PA) ....D....... 310 557-9049
405 S Beverly Dr Ste 500 Beverly Hills (90212) *(P-17311)*

Agencycom LLC ....B....... 415 817-3800
5353 Grosvenor Blvd Los Angeles (90066) *(P-16160)*

Agendia Inc ....C....... 949 540-6300
22 Morgan Irvine (92618) *(P-19814)*

Agent Franchise LLC ....C....... 949 930-5025
9518 9th St Ste C2 Rancho Cucamonga (91730) *(P-14446)*

Agent Image Inc ....B....... 310 577-9222
1700 E Walnut Ave El Segundo (90245) *(P-15958)*

Agents West Inc ....E....... 949 614-0293
6 Hughes Ste 210 Irvine (92618) *(P-9192)*

Agi Holding Corp (PA) ....E....... 805 667-4100
2575 Vista Del Mar Dr Ventura (93001) *(P-17458)*

Agia Affinity, Carpinteria *Also Called: AGIA Inc (P-14554)*

AGIA Inc (PA) ....C....... 805 566-9191
1155 Eugenia Pl Carpinteria (93013) *(P-14554)*

Agile, Corona *Also Called: Agile Sourcing Partners Inc (P-12109)*

Agile Occupational Medicine PC ....D....... 949 464-4036
710 N Euclid St Ste 107 Anaheim (92801) *(P-17583)*

Agile Rf Inc ....E....... 805 968-5159
93 Castilian Dr Santa Barbara (93117) *(P-8993)*

Agile Sourcing Partners Inc ....C....... 951 279-4154
2385 Railroad St Corona (92878) *(P-12109)*

Agile Technologies Inc ....E....... 949 454-8030
2 Orion Aliso Viejo (92656) *(P-8762)*

Agilent Technologies, Carpinteria *Also Called: Agilent Technologies Inc (P-10181)*

Agilent Technologies Inc ....E....... 805 566-6655
1170 Mark Ave Carpinteria (93013) *(P-10180)*

Agilent Technologies Inc ....D....... 805 566-1405
6392 Via Real Carpinteria (93013) *(P-10181)*

Agilent Technologies Inc ....E....... 858 373-6300
11011 N Torrey Pines Rd La Jolla (92037) *(P-10182)*

Agileone, Torrance *Also Called: Act 1 Group Inc (P-15809)*

Agilex Flavors & Fragrances, Commerce *Also Called: Key Essentials Inc (P-1779)*

Agility Fuel Systems LLC (DH) ....F....... 949 236-5520
1815 Carnegie Ave Santa Ana (92705) *(P-9347)*

Agility Holdings Inc (DH) ....D....... 714 617-6300
310 Commerce Ste 250 Irvine (92602) *(P-11735)*

Agility Logistics, Irvine *Also Called: Agility Holdings Inc (P-11735)*

Agility Logistics Corp (DH) ....D....... 714 617-6300
310 Commerce Ste 250 Irvine (92602) *(P-11736)*

Agl, Temecula *Also Called: Artificial Grass Liquidators (P-11192)*

AGM California Inc ....C....... 661 328-0118
1400 Easton Dr Ste 144 Bakersfield (93309) *(P-11919)*

Agoura Hills Renaissance Hotel, Agoura Hills *Also Called: Davidson Hotel Partners Lp (P-15127)*

Agouron Pharmaceuticals Inc (HQ) ....E....... 858 622-3000
10777 Science Center Dr San Diego (92121) *(P-4037)*

Agouron Pharmaceuticals Inc ....C....... 858 455-3200
3550 General Atomics Ct Bldg 9 San Diego (92121) *(P-19815)*

Agouron Pharmaceuticals Inc ....B....... 858 622-3000
3301 N Torrey Pines Ct La Jolla (92037) *(P-19816)*

Agri Service Inc ....E....... 760 295-6255
3720 Oceanic Way Ste 204 Oceanside (92056) *(P-12153)*

Agri-Cel Inc ....E....... 661 792-2107
401 Road 192 Delano (93215) *(P-4870)*

Agri-Empire ....C....... 951 654-7311
630 W 7th St San Jacinto (92583) *(P-13312)*

Agron Inc (PA) ....D....... 310 473-7223
2440 S Sepulveda Blvd Ste 201 Los Angeles (90064) *(P-2397)*

AGS Usa LLC ....C....... 323 588-2200
1210 Rexford Ave Pasadena (91107) *(P-2272)*

Agse, Santa Fe Springs *Also Called: Advanced Grund Systems Engrg L (P-9561)*

Agt, Corona *Also Called: Absolute Graphic Tech USA Inc (P-8167)*

Agua Caliente Casino & Resort, Rancho Mirage *Also Called: Agua Clnte Band Chilla Indians (P-15069)*

Agua Clnte Band Chilla Indians ....A....... 760 321-2000
32250 Bob Hope Dr Rancho Mirage (92270) *(P-15069)*

Agua Clnte Band Chilla Indians ....B....... 800 854-1279
401 E Amado Rd Palm Springs (92262) *(P-15070)*

Agua Clnte Band Chilla Indians (PA) ....A....... 760 699-6800
5401 Dinah Shore Dr Palm Springs (92264) *(P-19510)*

Agua Dulce Vineyards LLC ....E....... 661 268-7402
9640 Sierra Hwy Agua Dulce (91390) *(P-1610)*

Ahf-Ducommun Incorporated (HQ) ....C....... 310 380-5390
268 E Gardena Blvd Gardena (90248) *(P-9608)*

Ahg Inc ....B....... 703 596-0111
340 S Lemon Ave 6633 Walnut (91789) *(P-15492)*

Ahi Investment Inc (DH) ....E....... 818 979-0030
675 Glenoaks Blvd San Fernando (91340) *(P-13525)*

Ahm Gemch Inc ....C....... 626 579-7777
1701 Santa Anita Ave El Monte (91733) *(P-18165)*

Ahmc, Anaheim *Also Called: Anaheim Regional Medical Ctr (P-18181)*

Ahmc Anheim Rgional Med Ctr LP ....A....... 714 774-1450
1111 W La Palma Ave Anaheim (92801) *(P-18166)*

Ahmc Anheim Rgional Med Ctr LP (PA) ....A....... 714 774-1450
1111 W La Palma Ave Anaheim (92801) *(P-18167)*

Ahmc Garfield Medical Ctr LP ....C....... 626 573-2222
525 N Garfield Ave Monterey Park (91754) *(P-17876)*

Ahmc Healthcare Inc (PA) ....C....... 626 943-7526
506 W Valley Blvd Ste 300 San Gabriel (91776) *(P-18168)*

Ahmc Healthcare Inc ....D....... 626 579-7777
1701 Santa Anita Ave South El Monte (91733) *(P-18169)*

Ahmc Healthcare Inc ....B....... 626 248-3452
506 W Valley Blvd Ste 300 San Gabriel (91776) *(P-18737)*

Ahmc Whittier Hosp Med Ctr LP ....A....... 562 945-3561
9080 Colima Rd Whittier (90605) *(P-18170)*

Ahs Trinity Group Inc (PA) ....E....... 818 508-2105
11041 Vanowen St North Hollywood (91605) *(P-2438)*

Ahw, Long Beach *Also Called: Aircraft Hardware West (P-12899)*

Al Foods Corporation (PA) ....E....... 323 222-0827
1700 N Soto St Los Angeles (90033) *(P-13289)*

Aibot US Operation Inc ....E....... 562 283-3286
2883 E Spring St Ste 200 Long Beach (90806) *(P-9507)*

Mergent email: customerrelations@mergent.com
982

2024 Southern California
Business Directory and Buyers Guide

(P-0000) Products & Services Section entry number
(PA)=Parent Co (HQ)=Headquarters (DH)=Div Headquarters

Aids Project La, Los Angeles Also Called: Aids Project Los Angeles (P-19017)

Aids Project Los Angeles (PA) ....D...... 213 201-1600
611 S Kingsley Dr Los Angeles (90005) (P-19017)

AIG Direct Insurance Svcs Inc ....B...... 858 309-3000
9640 Granite Ridge Dr Ste 200 San Diego (92123) (P-14555)

Aih LLC (DH) ....E...... 760 930-4600
5810 Van Allen Way Carlsbad (92008) (P-8134)

Aii Beauty, Commerce Also Called: American Intl Inds Inc (P-4378)

Aiminsight Solutions Inc ....F...... 310 313-0047
4127 Berryman Ave Los Angeles (90066) (P-16549)

Aimloan.com, A Direct Lender, San Diego Also Called: American Internet Mortgage Inc
(P-14295)

Aio Acquisition Inc (HQ) ....D...... 800 333-3795
3200 E Guasti Rd Ste 300 Ontario (91761) (P-3425)

Air & Gas Tech Inc ....E...... 619 955-5980
11433 Woodside Ave Santee (92071) (P-9853)

Air 88 Inc ....D...... 858 277-1453
3753 John J Montgomery Dr San Diego (92123) (P-11685)

Air Cabin Engineering Inc ....E...... 714 637-4111
231 W Blueridge Ave Orange (92865) (P-9609)

Air Combat Systems, Palmdale Also Called: Northrop Grumman Systems Corp (P-9547)

Air Components Inc ....E...... 909 980-8224
10235 Indiana Ct Rancho Cucamonga (91730) (P-9610)

Air Demolition and Envmtl, Orange Also Called: American Intgrted Rsources Inc (P-19995)

Air Electro Inc (PA) ....C...... 818 407-5400
9452 De Soto Ave Chatsworth (91311) (P-12642)

Air Express Intl USA Inc ....D...... 310 297-4401
19900 S Vermont Ave Ste A Torrance (90502) (P-11737)

Air Fayre USA Inc ....C...... 310 808-1061
1720 W 135th St Gardena (90249) (P-13980)

Air Flow Research, Valencia Also Called: Air Flow Research Heads Inc (P-9348)

Air Flow Research Heads Inc ....E...... 661 257-8124
28611 Industry Dr Valencia (91355) (P-9348)

Air Force Village West Inc ....B...... 951 697-2000
17050 Arnold Dr Riverside (92518) (P-17877)

Air Frame Mfg & Supply Co Inc ....E...... 661 257-7728
26135 Technology Dr Valencia (91355) (P-12898)

Air Frame Mfg. & Supply Co., Valencia Also Called: Air Frame Mfg & Supply Co Inc (P-12898)

Air Gap International, Placentia Also Called: Altinex Inc (P-8493)

Air Group Leasing Inc ....A...... 310 684-4095
1111 E Watson Center Rd Ste C Carson (90745) (P-11738)

Air Lease Corporation (PA) ....D...... 310 553-0555
2000 Avenue Of The Stars Ste 1000n Los Angeles (90067) (P-15771)

Air Liquide Electronics US LP ....A...... 310 549-7079
1502 W Anaheim St Wilmington (90744) (P-3860)

Air Liquide Electronics US LP ....A...... 713 624-8000
1831 Carnegie Ave Santa Ana (92705) (P-19542)

Air Louvers Inc ....E...... 800 554-6077
6285 Randolph St Commerce (90040) (P-6099)

Air Lquide Globl E C Solutions, Santa Ana Also Called: Air Liquide Electronics US LP
(P-19542)

Air New Zealand Limited ....D...... 310 648-7000
222 N Pacific Coast Hwy Ste 900 El Segundo (90245) (P-11657)

Air Products, Vernon Also Called: Evonik Corporation (P-4605)

Air Products and Chemicals Inc ....B...... 760 931-9555
1969 Palomar Oaks Way Carlsbad (92011) (P-3861)

Air Source Industries Inc ....F...... 562 426-4017
3976 Cherry Ave Long Beach (90807) (P-3862)

Air Tube Transfer Systems Inc ....E...... 714 363-0700
715 N Cypress St Orange (92867) (P-6968)

Air-TEC, Carson Also Called: Clay Dunn Enterprises Inc (P-754)

Air-Trak ....E...... 858 677-9950
15090 Avenue Of Science Ste 103 San Diego (92128) (P-8490)

Air-Vol Block Inc ....E...... 805 543-1314
1 Suburban Rd San Luis Obispo (93401) (P-5387)

Aira Tech, Carlsbad Also Called: Aira Tech Corp (P-16161)

Aira Tech Corp ....D...... 800 835-1934
3451 Via Montebello Ste 192 Pmb 214 Carlsbad (92009) (P-16161)

Airborne Components, Carson Also Called: Stanford Mu Corporation (P-9921)

Airborne Systems N Amer CA Inc ....C...... 714 662-1400
3100 W Segerstrom Ave Santa Ana (92704) (P-2545)

Airborne Technologies, Camarillo Also Called: Airborne Technologies Inc (P-9611)

Airborne Technologies Inc ....C...... 805 389-3700
999 Avenida Acaso Camarillo (93012) (P-9611)

Aircarbon, Huntington Beach Also Called: Newlight Technologies Inc (P-5115)

Aircraft Hardware West ....E...... 562 961-9324
2180 Temple Ave Long Beach (90804) (P-12899)

Aircraft Hinge Inc ....E...... 661 257-3434
28338 Constellation Rd Ste 970 Santa Clarita (91355) (P-9612)

Aircraft Repair & Overhaul Svc (PA) ....E...... 714 630-9494
1186 N Grove St Anaheim (92806) (P-11686)

Aircraft Spruce Speciality Co, Corona Also Called: Irwin International Inc (P-13906)

Aircraft Stamping Company Inc ....E...... 323 283-1239
1285 Paseo Alicia San Dimas (91773) (P-6182)

Aircraft Xray Laboratories Inc ....D...... 323 587-4141
5216 Pacific Blvd Huntington Park (90255) (P-19955)

Airdraulics Inc ....E...... 818 982-1400
13261 Saticoy St North Hollywood (91605) (P-17041)

Airdyne Refrigeration, Cerritos Also Called: ARI Industries Inc (P-7600)

Airdyne Refrigeration, Cerritos Also Called: Refrigerator Manufacturers LLC (P-7622)

Aire-Rite AC & Rfrgn LLC ....D...... 714 895-2338
15122 Bolsa Chica St Huntington Beach (92649) (P-728)

Airey Enterprises LLC ....C...... 818 530-3362
5530 Corbin Ave Ste 325 Tarzana (91356) (P-12900)

Airframer R, Torrance Also Called: Sonic Industries Inc (P-19692)

AIRGAIN, San Diego Also Called: Airgain Inc (P-8491)

Airgain Inc (PA) ....E...... 760 579-0200
3611 Valley Centre Dr Ste 150 San Diego (92130) (P-8491)

Airgas, Long Beach Also Called: Airgas Inc (P-3863)

Airgas, City Of Industry Also Called: Airgas Safety Inc (P-12784)

Airgas Inc ....E...... 510 429-4216
3737 Worsham Ave Long Beach (90808) (P-3863)

Airgas Safety Inc ....E...... 562 699-5239
2355 Workman Mill Rd City Of Industry (90601) (P-12784)

Airgas Usa LLC ....D...... 562 945-1383
8832 Dice Rd Santa Fe Springs (90670) (P-3864)

Airgas Usa LLC ....E...... 562 906-8700
9756 Santa Fe Springs Rd Santa Fe Springs (90670) (P-3865)

Airgas Usa LLC ....A...... 562 497-1991
3737 Worsham Ave Long Beach (90808) (P-12785)

Airo Industries Company ....E...... 818 838-1008
429 Jessie St San Fernando (91340) (P-2921)

Airport Connection Inc ....C...... 805 389-8196
95 Dawson Dr Camarillo (93012) (P-11315)

Airport Honda, Los Angeles Also Called: Noarus Investments Inc (P-13805)

Airport Marina Ford, Los Angeles Also Called: Fox Hills Auto Inc (P-13769)

Airport Terminal MGT Inc ....B...... 310 988-1492
6851 W Imperial Hwy Los Angeles (90045) (P-11687)

Airtech Advanced Mtls Group, Huntington Beach Also Called: Airtech International Inc
(P-9613)

Airtech International Inc (PA) ....C...... 714 899-8100
5700 Skylab Rd Huntington Beach (92647) (P-9613)

Airx Utility Surveyors Inc (PA) ....D...... 760 480-2347
785 E Mission Rd # 100 San Marcos (92069) (P-657)

Ais Construction Company ....D...... 805 928-9467
7015 Vista Del Rincon Dr Ventura (93001) (P-528)

Aisling Industries, Calexico Also Called: Creation Tech Calexico Inc (P-8667)

AITA Clutch Inc ....E...... 323 585-4140
960 S Santa Fe Ave Compton (90221) (P-9349)

Aitech Defense Systems Inc ....D...... 818 700-2000
19756 Prairie St Chatsworth (91311) (P-9193)

Aitech Rugged Group (PA) ....E...... 818 700-2000
19756 Prairie St Chatsworth (91311) (P-9194)

AJ Kirkwood & Associates Inc ....B...... 714 505-1977
4300 N Harbor Blvd Fullerton (92835) (P-862)

Ajax Boiler Inc ....D...... 714 437-9050
2701 S Harbor Blvd Santa Ana (92704) (P-6131)

Ajax Forge Company (PA) ....F...... 323 582-6307
1956 E 48th St Vernon (90058) (P-6458)

Ajg Inc ....E...... 323 346-0171
7220 E Slauson Ave Commerce (90040) (P-2425)

Employee Codes: A=Over 500 employees, B=251-500
C=101-250, D=51-100, E=20-50, F=10-19, G=1-9

2024 Southern California
Business Directory and Buyers Guide

© Mergent Inc. 1-800-342-5647
983

Ajilon LLC .... C...... 949 955-0100
4590 Macarthur Blvd Newport Beach (92660) *(P-16550)*

Ajinomoto Althea Inc (HQ) .... **C...... 858 882-0123**
11040 Roselle St San Diego (92121) *(P-10418)*

Ajinomoto Bio-Pharma Services, San Diego *Also Called: Ajinomoto Althea Inc (P-10418)*

Ajinomoto Foods North Amer Inc .... C...... 909 477-4700
4200 Concours Ste 100 Ontario (91764) *(P-1382)*

Ajinomoto Foods North Amer Inc (DH) .... **D...... 909 477-4700**
4200 Concours Ste 100 Ontario (91764) *(P-1383)*

Ajit Healthcare Inc .... D...... 213 484-0510
316 S Westlake Ave Los Angeles (90057) *(P-19990)*

Ajr Trucking Inc .... D...... 310 707-1120
435 E Weber Ave Compton (90222) *(P-11440)*

AK Industries, Compton *Also Called: Allan Kidd (P-8254)*

Akcea Therapeutics, Carlsbad *Also Called: Akcea Therapeutics Inc (P-4038)*

Akcea Therapeutics Inc (HQ) .... **D...... 617 207-0202**
2850 Gazelle Ct Carlsbad (92010) *(P-4038)*

Aker International .... E...... 619 423-5182
2248 Main St Ste 4 Chula Vista (91911) *(P-5305)*

Aker Leather Products, Chula Vista *Also Called: Aker International Inc (P-5305)*

Akh Company Inc .... D...... 909 748-5016
1647 W Redlands Blvd Ste C Redlands (92373) *(P-13852)*

Akh Company Inc .... C...... 951 924-5356
23316 Sunnymead Blvd Moreno Valley (92553) *(P-13853)*

Akkodis Inc .... C...... 818 546-2848
801 N Brand Blvd Ste 250 Glendale (91203) *(P-15959)*

Akra Plastic Products Inc .... E...... 909 930-1999
1504 E Cedar St Ontario (91761) *(P-4932)*

Aks, Amy K Su, Garden Grove *Also Called: Bodywaves Inc (P-2414)*

Akua Behavioral Health Inc (PA) .... **C...... 949 777-2283**
20271 Sw Birch St Ste 200 Newport Beach (92660) *(P-18519)*

Akua Mind & Body, Newport Beach *Also Called: Akua Behavioral Health Inc (P-18519)*

Al Asher & Sons Inc .... E...... 800 896-2480
5301 Valley Blvd Los Angeles (90032) *(P-13736)*

Al Global Corporation (HQ) .... **E...... 619 934-3980**
2400 Boswell Rd Chula Vista (91914) *(P-14091)*

Al Hewitt Inc .... C...... 661 945-7050
4009 Mission Oaks Blvd Camarillo (93012) *(P-14413)*

Al Industries, Santa Ana *Also Called: Acronots Manufacturing Inc (P-6492)*

Al Johnson Company, Camarillo *Also Called: Gc International Inc (P-8460)*

Al Shellco LLC (HQ) .... **C...... 570 296-6444**
9330 Scranton Rd Ste 600 San Diego (92121) *(P-8392)*

Alabama Metal Industries Corp .... C...... 909 350-9280
11093 Beech Ave Fontana (92337) *(P-6350)*

Alabbasi, Perris *Also Called: Mamco Inc (P-632)*

Alaco Ladder Company .... E...... 909 591-7561
5167 G St Chino (91710) *(P-2750)*

Alaco Ladder Company, Chino *Also Called: B E & P Enterprises LLC (P-2751)*

Alakor Healthcare LLC .... C...... 626 408-9800
323 S Heliotrope Ave Monrovia (91016) *(P-18171)*

Alameda Construction Svcs Inc .... E...... 310 635-3277
2528 E 125th St Compton (90222) *(P-404)*

Alamitos Blmont Rhbltttion Hosp, Long Beach *Also Called: Alamitos-Belmont Rehab Inc (P-17878)*

Alamitos Intermediate School, Garden Grove *Also Called: Garden Grove Unified Schl Dst (P-18967)*

Alamitos W Convalescent Hosp, Los Alamitos *Also Called: Katella Properties (P-17981)*

Alamitos-Belmont Rehab Inc .... C...... 562 434-8421
3901 E 4th St Long Beach (90814) *(P-17878)*

Alamo Rent A Car, Palm Springs *Also Called: Alamo Rental (us) Inc (P-16977)*

Alamo Rent A Car, Anaheim *Also Called: Alamo Rental (us) Inc (P-16978)*

Alamo Rent A Car, Ontario *Also Called: Alamo Rental (us) Inc (P-16979)*

Alamo Rent A Car, Inglewood *Also Called: Alamo Rental (us) Inc (P-16980)*

Alamo Rental (us) Inc .... D...... 760 778-6271
3400 E Tahquitz Canyon Way Ste 5 Palm Springs (92262) *(P-16977)*

Alamo Rental (us) Inc .... D...... 714 748-7368
711 W Katella Ave Anaheim (92802) *(P-16978)*

Alamo Rental (us) Inc .... D...... 888 826-6893
3450 E Airport Dr Ste 300 Ontario (91761) *(P-16979)*

Alamo Rental (us) Inc .... C...... 310 649-2242
9020 Aviation Blvd Inglewood (90301) *(P-16980)*

Alamo Rings, Cypress *Also Called: Eno Brands Inc (P-14075)*

Alan B Whitson Company Inc .... A...... 949 955-1200
1507 W Alton Ave Santa Ana (92704) *(P-20127)*

Alan Gordon Enterprises Inc .... E...... 323 466-3561
5625 Melrose Ave Los Angeles (90038) *(P-17243)*

Alan Johnson Prfmce Engrg Inc .... E...... 805 922-1202
1097 Foxen Canyon Rd Santa Maria (93454) *(P-9274)*

Alanic International Corp .... E...... 855 525-2642
8730 Wilshire Blvd Ph Beverly Hills (90211) *(P-2133)*

Alard Machine Products, Gardena *Also Called: GT Precision Inc (P-6415)*

Alarin Aircraft Hinge Inc .... E...... 323 725-1666
6231 Randolph St Commerce (90040) *(P-5896)*

Alastin Skincare Inc .... C...... 844 858-7546
3129 Tiger Run Ct Ste 109 Carlsbad (92010) *(P-4377)*

Alatus Aerosystems .... C...... 909 217-9047
20415 E Walnut Dr N Walnut (91789) *(P-9614)*

Alatus Aerosystems .... D...... 626 498-7376
9301 Mason Ave Chatsworth (91311) *(P-9615)*

Alatus Aerosystems (PA) .... **E...... 610 965-1630**
9301 Mason Ave Chatsworth (91311) *(P-9616)*

Alatus Aerosystems .... D...... 714 732-0559
9301 Mason Ave Chatsworth (91311) *(P-9617)*

Albany Farms Inc (PA) .... **E...... 877 832-8269**
10680 W Pico Blvd Ste 230 Los Angeles (90064) *(P-1847)*

Albany Farms Inc .... E...... 213 330-6573
625 Fair Oaks Ave Ste 125 South Pasadena (91030) *(P-1848)*

Albd Electric and Cable .... D...... 949 440-1216
1031 S Leslie St La Habra (90631) *(P-863)*

Albers Dairy Equipment. Inc, Chino *Also Called: Albers Mfg Co Inc (P-6898)*

Albers Mfg Co Inc (PA) .... **E...... 909 597-5537**
14323 Albers Way Chino (91710) *(P-6898)*

Albert A Webb Associates (PA) .... **C...... 951 686-1070**
3788 Mccray St Riverside (92506) *(P-19543)*

Albertson's Distribution Ctr, Irvine *Also Called: Albertsons LLC (P-11563)*

Albertsons 6514, Riverside *Also Called: Albertsons LLC (P-13692)*

Albertsons 6798, Lake Elsinore *Also Called: Albertsons LLC (P-13693)*

Albertsons LLC .... D...... 949 855-2465
9300 Toledo Way Irvine (92618) *(P-11563)*

Albertsons LLC .... D...... 951 656-6603
8938 Trautwein Rd Ste A Riverside (92508) *(P-13692)*

Albertsons LLC .... E...... 951 245-4461
30901 Riverside Dr Lake Elsinore (92530) *(P-13693)*

Albireo Energy, Poway *Also Called: Electronic Control Systems LLC (P-894)*

Alcast Mfg Inc .... E...... 310 542-3581
2910 Fisk Ln Redondo Beach (90278) *(P-5770)*

Alcast Mfg Inc (PA) .... **E...... 310 542-3581**
7355 E Slauson Ave Commerce (90040) *(P-5780)*

Alcatel-Lucent, Newbury Park *Also Called: Nokia of America Corporation (P-8481)*

Alcatel-Lucent Enterprise USA, Thousand Oaks *Also Called: Ale USA Inc (P-8492)*

Alcatraz Brewing Company, Orange *Also Called: Tavistock Restaurants LLC (P-14054)*

Alchem Plastics Inc .... C...... 714 523-2260
14263 Gannet St La Mirada (90638) *(P-4831)*

Alchemi, San Luis Obispo *Also Called: Myogenix Incorporated (P-4173)*

Alchemy, Los Angeles *Also Called: Our Alchemy LLC (P-17287)*

Alco Designs, Gardena *Also Called: Vege-Mist Inc (P-7633)*

Alco Engrg & Tooling Corp .... E...... 714 556-6060
3001 Oak St Santa Ana (92707) *(P-7749)*

Alco Metal Fab, Santa Ana *Also Called: Alco Engrg & Tooling Corp (P-7749)*

Alco Plating Corp (PA) .... **E...... 213 749-7561**
1400 Long Beach Ave Los Angeles (90021) *(P-6576)*

Alcoa Fastening Systems .... E...... 909 483-2333
11711 Arrow Rte Rancho Cucamonga (91730) *(P-11068)*

Alcon, Irvine *Also Called: Alcon Lensx Inc (P-10419)*

Alcon Lensx Inc (DH) .... **D...... 949 753-1393**
15800 Alton Pkwy Irvine (92618) *(P-10419)*

Alcon Lighting Inc .... E...... 310 733-1248
2845 S Robertson Blvd Los Angeles (90034) *(P-8304)*

Alcon Research Ltd .... D...... 949 387-2142
15800 Alton Pkwy Irvine (92618) *(P-10420)*

ALCON RESEARCH, LTD., Irvine *Also Called: Alcon Research Ltd (P-10420)*

Alcon Surgical, Irvine *Also Called: Alcon Vision LLC (P-10422)*

Alcon Vision LLC .... B...... 949 753-6218
24514 Sunshine Dr Laguna Niguel (92677) *(P-10421)*

Alcon Vision LLC .... A...... 949 753-6488
15800 Alton Pkwy Irvine (92618) *(P-10422)*

Alcon Vision LLC .... B...... 949 505-6890
20521 Lake Forest Dr Lake Forest (92630) *(P-19956)*

Alcone Marketing Group Inc (HQ) .... D...... 949 595-5322
4 Studebaker Irvine (92618) *(P-15529)*

Aldila Golf Corp .... C...... 858 513-1801
13450 Stowe Dr Poway (92064) *(P-10972)*

Aldila Golf Corp (DH) .... D...... 858 513-1801
1945 Kellogg Ave Carlsbad (92008) *(P-10973)*

Aldila Materials Tech Corp (DH) .... E...... 858 486-6970
13450 Stowe Dr Poway (92064) *(P-4592)*

Aldo Fragale .... E...... 310 324-0050
17813 S Main St Ste 111 Gardena (90248) *(P-7750)*

Aldon Ter Convalsent Hosptial, Los Angeles *Also Called: Longwood Management Corp (P-18139)*

Aldridge Pite LLP .... B...... 858 750-7700
4375 Jutland Dr Ste 200 San Diego (92117) *(P-18818)*

Ale USA Inc .... A...... 818 880-3500
2000 Corporate Center Dr Thousand Oaks (91320) *(P-8492)*

Alegacy, Santa Fe Springs *Also Called: Alegacy Fdsrvice Pdts Group In (P-3020)*

Alegacy Fdsrvice Pdts Group In .... D...... 562 320-3100
12683 Corral Pl Santa Fe Springs (90670) *(P-3020)*

Aleph Group Inc .... E...... 951 213-4815
1900 E Alessandro Blvd Ste 105 Riverside (92508) *(P-9275)*

Aleratec Inc .... E...... 818 678-6900
21722 Lassen St Chatsworth (91311) *(P-7415)*

Alere Connect LLC .... E...... 888 876-3327
9975 Summers Ridge Rd San Diego (92121) *(P-10788)*

Alere Inc .... D...... 858 805-2000
9975 Summers Ridge Rd San Diego (92121) *(P-4262)*

Alere Inc ....F...... 858 805-3810
5995 Pacific Center Blvd Ste 108 San Diego (92121) *(P-4263)*

Alere of San Diego, San Diego *Also Called: Alere Inc (P-4263)*

Alere San Diego Inc (DH) .... C...... 858 455-4808
9975 Summers Ridge Rd San Diego (92121) *(P-4264)*

Alere San Diego Inc .... A...... 909 482-0840
829 Towne Center Dr Pomona (91767) *(P-4265)*

Alert Plating, Sun Valley *Also Called: Alert Plating Company (P-6577)*

Alert Plating Company .... E...... 818 771-9304
9939 Glenoaks Blvd Sun Valley (91352) *(P-6577)*

Alesmith Brewing Company, San Diego *Also Called: Jdz Inc (P-1593)*

Alex and Jane, Maywood *Also Called: KSM Garment Inc (P-2250)*

Alexander Dennis Incorporated .... A...... 951 244-9429
31566 Railroad Canyon Rd Ste 3 Canyon Lake (92587) *(P-12220)*

Alexander Henry Fabrics Inc .... E...... 818 562-8200
1550 Flower St Glendale (91201) *(P-13079)*

Alexander's Moving & Storage, Tustin *Also Called: Stanley G Alexander Inc (P-11505)*

Alexs Tile Works Inc .... E...... 805 967-5308
5920 Matthews St Goleta (93117) *(P-1003)*

Alfa Scientific Designs Inc .... D...... 858 513-3888
13200 Gregg St Poway (92064) *(P-4266)*

Alflex, Compton *Also Called: Southwire Inc (P-5691)*

Alfred Louie Incorporated ....F...... 661 831-2520
4501 Shepard St Bakersfield (93313) *(P-1849)*

Alfred Music Publishing, Van Nuys *Also Called: The Full Void 2 Inc (P-3417)*

Alg Inc .... B...... 424 258-8026
120 Broadway Ste 200 Santa Monica (90401) *(P-3426)*

Alger International, Los Angeles *Also Called: Alger-Triton Inc (P-8285)*

Alger Precision Machining LLC .... C...... 909 986-4591
724 S Bon View Ave Ontario (91761) *(P-6408)*

Alger-Triton Inc .... E...... 310 229-9500
5600 W Jefferson Blvd Los Angeles (90016) *(P-8285)*

Algorithmic Objective Corp .... E...... 858 249-9580
8910 University Center Ln Ste 400 San Diego (92122) *(P-15960)*

Algotive, San Diego *Also Called: Algorithmic Objective Corp (P-15960)*

Alhambra Foundry Company Ltd .... E...... 626 289-4294
1147 S Meridian Ave Alhambra (91803) *(P-5643)*

Alhambra Hospital Med Ctr LP .... C...... 626 570-1606
100 S Raymond Ave Alhambra (91801) *(P-18172)*

Alhambra Hospital Medical Ctr, Alhambra *Also Called: Alhambra Hospital Med Ctr LP (P-18172)*

Alhambra Motors Inc .... C...... 626 576-1114
1400 W Main St Alhambra (91801) *(P-13737)*

Aliantel Inc .... D...... 714 829-1650
1940 W Corporate Way Anaheim (92801) *(P-20312)*

Alice G Fink-Painter, Santa Fe Springs *Also Called: Spec Tool Company (P-9801)*

Align Aerospace LLC (PA) .... B...... 818 727-7800
9401 De Soto Ave Chatsworth (91311) *(P-9618)*

Align Precision - Anaheim Inc (DH) .... D...... 714 961-9200
7100 Belgrave Ave Garden Grove (92841) *(P-9619)*

Alignmed, Santa Ana *Also Called: Alignmed Inc (P-14120)*

Alignmed Inc ....F...... 866 987-5433
1936 E Deere Ave Ste 115 Santa Ana (92705) *(P-14120)*

Alignment Health, Orange *Also Called: Alignment Healthcare Inc (P-14459)*

Alignment Health Plan .... D...... 323 728-7232
1100 W Town And Country Rd Ste 1600 Orange (92868) *(P-14458)*

Alignment Healthcare Inc (PA) .... D...... 844 310-2247
1100 W Town And Country Rd Ste 1600 Orange (92868) *(P-14459)*

Alimentiv US Inc .... D...... 858 356-5665
10581 Roselle St Ste 110 San Diego (92121) *(P-19817)*

Alin Party Supply Co .... C...... 951 682-7441
6493 Magnolia Ave Riverside (92506) *(P-14085)*

Aline Systems, Cerritos *Also Called: Aline Systems Corporation (P-7344)*

Aline Systems Corporation .... E...... 562 229-9727
13844 Struikman Rd Cerritos (90703) *(P-7344)*

Aliquantum International Inc .... E...... 909 773-0880
2009 S Parco Ave Ontario (91761) *(P-10945)*

Alisal Guest Ranch, Solvang *Also Called: Alisal Properties (P-15433)*

Alisal Properties (PA) .... C...... 805 688-6411
1054 Alisal Rd Solvang (93463) *(P-15433)*

Alj, Camarillo *Also Called: Gc International Inc (P-5794)*

All 4-Pcb North America Inc ....F...... 866 734-9403
345 Mira Loma Ave Glendale (91204) *(P-7751)*

All About Printing, Canoga Park *Also Called: Barrys Printing Inc (P-3517)*

All Access Apparel Inc (PA) .... C...... 323 889-4300
1515 Gage Rd Montebello (90640) *(P-2273)*

All Access Rental, Santa Ana *Also Called: County of Orange (P-15760)*

All Access Stging Prdctons Inc (PA) .... E...... 310 784-2464
1320 Storm Pkwy Torrance (90501) *(P-8350)*

All American Asphalt .... C...... 951 736-7617
1776 All American Way Corona (92879) *(P-608)*

All American Cabinetry Inc ....F...... 818 376-0500
13901 Saticoy St Van Nuys (91402) *(P-2941)*

All American Drill Bushing, San Fernando *Also Called: All American Products Group Inc (P-4594)*

All American Pipe Bending, Santa Ana *Also Called: Saf-T-Co Supply (P-8283)*

All American Products Group Inc .... E...... 818 361-0059
1135 Aviation Pl San Fernando (91340) *(P-4594)*

All American Racers Inc .... C...... 714 540-1771
2334 S Broadway Santa Ana (92707) *(P-9871)*

All American Sterile Coat, Van Nuys *Also Called: All American Cabinetry Inc (P-2941)*

All Amrcan Injction Mlding Svc, Temecula *Also Called: TST Molding LLC (P-5236)*

All Care Medical Group Inc .... D...... 408 278-3550
31 Crescent Street Huntington Park (90255) *(P-17584)*

All Counties Courier Inc .... C...... 714 599-9300
1900 S State College Blvd Ste 450 Anaheim (92806) *(P-11525)*

All Diameter Grinding Inc .... E...... 714 744-1200
725 N Main St Orange (92868) *(P-7752)*

All Manufacturers Inc .... C...... 951 280-4200
1831 Commerce St Ste 101 Corona (92878) *(P-10423)*

All Metals Processing of San Diego Inc ....C...... 714 828-8238
8401 Standustrial St Stanton (90680) *(P-6578)*

All Mtals Proc Orange Cnty LLC .... C...... 714 828-8238
8401 Standustrial St Stanton (90680) *(P-6579)*

All New Stamping Co .... C...... 626 443-8813
10801 Lower Azusa Rd El Monte (91731) *(P-6494)*

All One God Faith Inc (PA) .... C...... 844 937-2551
1335 Park Center Dr Vista (92081) *(P-4332)*

Employee Codes: A=Over 500 employees, B=251-500
C=101-250, D=51-100, E=20-50, F=10-19, G=1-9

2024 Southern California
Business Directory and Buyers Guide

© Mergent Inc. 1-800-342-5647

985

All One God Faith Inc ....D....... 760 599-4010
1225 Park Center Dr Ste D Vista (92081) *(P-4333)*

All Power Manufacturing Co ....C....... 562 802-2640
13141 Molette St Santa Fe Springs (90670) *(P-9620)*

All Risk Shield Inc ....E....... 866 991-7190
1244 Pine St Ste 211 Paso Robles (93446) *(P-325)*

All Source Coatings Inc ....E....... 858 586-0903
10625 Scripps Ranch Blvd Ste D San Diego (92131) *(P-6686)*

All Star Parking ....C....... 310 337-1944
9700 Bellanca Ave Los Angeles (90045) *(P-16988)*

All Star Precision ....E....... 909 944-8373
8739 Lion St Rancho Cucamonga (91730) *(P-7753)*

All State Association Inc ....C....... 877 425-2558
11487 San Fernando Rd San Fernando (91340) *(P-19373)*

All Strong Industry (usa) Inc (PA) ....**E....... 909 598-6494**
326 Paseo Tesoro Walnut (91789) *(P-3000)*

All Valley Home Care, San Diego *Also Called: All Valley Home Hlth Care Inc (P-18588)*

All Valley Home Hlth Care Inc ....D....... 619 276-8001
3665 Ruffin Rd Ste 103 San Diego (92123) *(P-18588)*

All Wall Inc ....D....... 760 600-5108
46150 Commerce St Ste 102 Indio (92201) *(P-966)*

All West Plastics Inc ....E....... 714 894-9922
5451 Argosy Ave Huntington Beach (92649) *(P-4827)*

All-Power Plastcs Div Dial, Los Angeles *Also Called: Dial Industries Inc (P-5008)*

All-Pro Bail Bonds Inc ....D....... 760 512-1969
530 Hacienda Dr Ste 104d Vista (92081) *(P-16770)*

All-Rite Leasing Company Inc ....B....... 714 957-1822
950 S Coast Dr Ste 110 Costa Mesa (92626) *(P-15691)*

All-Star Lettering Inc ....E....... 562 404-5995
9419 Ann St Santa Fe Springs (90670) *(P-3731)*

All-Ways Metal Inc ....E....... 310 217-1177
401 E Alondra Blvd Gardena (90248) *(P-6183)*

Allan Aircraft Supply Co LLC ....E....... 818 765-4992
11643 Vanowen St North Hollywood (91605) *(P-6786)*

Allan Company, Baldwin Park *Also Called: Cedarwood-Young Company (P-12165)*

Allan Company, Baldwin Park *Also Called: Cedarwood-Young Company (P-12952)*

Allan Kidd ....E....... 310 762-1600
3115 E Las Hermanas St Compton (90221) *(P-8254)*

Allbirds Inc ....F....... 949 942-1233
1125 Newport Center Dr Newport Beach (92660) *(P-5264)*

Allbirds Inc ....F....... 424 502-2383
860 S Pacific Coast Hwy El Segundo (90245) *(P-5265)*

Allbirds Inc ....F....... 626 344-2622
77 West Colorado Blvd Pasadena (91105) *(P-5266)*

Allbirds Inc ....F....... 213 374-2354
10250 Santa Monica Blvd Ste 1985 Los Angeles (90067) *(P-5267)*

Allbirds Inc ....F....... 213 374-3533
12833 Ventura Blvd Studio City (91604) *(P-5268)*

Allbirds Inc ....F....... 424 295-9968
1335 Abbot Kinney Blvd Venice (90291) *(P-5269)*

Allbirds Inc ....F....... 442 273-5519
1923 Calle Barcelona Bldg 3 Carlsbad (92009) *(P-5270)*

Allbirds Inc ....F....... 858 987-9533
4301 La Jolla Village Dr Ste 2010 San Diego (92122) *(P-5271)*

Allblack Co Inc ....E....... 562 946-2955
13090 Park St Santa Fe Springs (90670) *(P-6580)*

Allclear Inc ....E....... 424 316-1596
200 N Pacific Coast Hwy Ste 1350 El Segundo (90245) *(P-9508)*

Allegion Access Tech LLC ....E....... 858 431-5940
8380 Camino Santa Fe Ste 100 San Diego (92121) *(P-5872)*

Allegion Access Tech LLC ....E....... 909 628-9272
15750 Jurupa Ave Fontana (92337) *(P-5873)*

Allegis Residential Svcs Inc ....D....... 858 430-5700
9340 Hazard Way Ste B2 San Diego (92123) *(P-19991)*

Allegra Print & Imaging, San Diego *Also Called: JA Ferrari Print Imaging LLC (P-3605)*

Allegretto Vineyard Resort, Paso Robles *Also Called: Ayres - Paso Robles LP (P-15082)*

Allele Bio & Pharmaceuticals ....C....... 858 410-0299
6868 Nancy Ridge Dr San Diego (92121) *(P-19818)*

Allen Associates, Santa Barbara *Also Called: Dennis Allen Associates (P-428)*

Allen Engineering Contractor Inc ....C...... 909 478-5500
1655 Riverview Dr San Bernardino (92408) *(P-19544)*

Allen Matkins, Los Angeles *Also Called: Allen Mtkins Leck Gmble Mllory (P-18819)*

Allen Mold Inc ....F....... 714 538-6517
1100 W Katella Ave N Orange (92867) *(P-4933)*

Allen Mtkins Leck Gmble Mllory (PA)...........**C....... 213 622-5555**
865 S Figueroa St Ste 2800 Los Angeles (90017) *(P-18819)*

Allergan, Irvine *Also Called: Allergan Spclty Thrpeutics Inc (P-4040)*

Allergan Sales LLC (DH)..**A....... 862 261-7000**
2525 Dupont Dr Irvine (92612) *(P-4039)*

Allergan Spclty Thrpeutics Inc ....A....... 714 246-4500
2525 Dupont Dr Irvine (92612) *(P-4040)*

Allergan Usa Inc ....A....... 714 427-1900
18581 Teller Ave Irvine (92612) *(P-4041)*

Allermed Laboratories Inc ....E....... 858 292-1060
7203 Convoy Ct San Diego (92111) *(P-3989)*

Allhealth ....E....... 213 538-0762
515 S Figueroa St Ste 1300 Los Angeles (90071) *(P-7416)*

Alliance, Irvine *Also Called: Alliance Healthcare Svcs Inc (P-18538)*

Alliance Air Products Llc (DH).............................**D....... 619 428-9688**
2285 Michael Faraday Dr Ste 15 San Diego (92154) *(P-7596)*

Alliance Air Products Llc ....B....... 619 664-0027
9565 Heinrich Hertz Dr Ste 1 San Diego (92154) *(P-7597)*

Alliance Apparel Inc ....E....... 323 888-8900
3422 Garfield Ave Commerce (90040) *(P-2229)*

Alliance Childrens Services ....C....... 661 863-0350
1001 Tower Way Ste 110 Bakersfield (93309) *(P-19236)*

Alliance Ground Intl LLC ....A....... 310 646-2446
6181 W Imperial Hwy Los Angeles (90045) *(P-11688)*

Alliance Healthcare Svcs Inc (DH)........................**C....... 800 544-3215**
18201 Von Karman Ave Ste 600 Irvine (92612) *(P-18538)*

Alliance Medical Products Inc ....E....... 949 664-9616
9292 Jeronimo Rd Irvine (92618) *(P-10424)*

Alliance Medical Products Inc (DH).....................**E....... 949 768-4690**
9342 Jeronimo Rd Irvine (92618) *(P-10425)*

Alliance Metal Products Inc ....C....... 818 709-1204
20844 Plummer St Chatsworth (91311) *(P-6184)*

Alliance Nrsing Rhbltation Ctr, El Monte *Also Called: Georgia Atkison Snf LLC (P-17963)*

Alliance Ready Mix Inc ....D....... 805 556-3015
310 James Way Ste 210 Pismo Beach (93449) *(P-5458)*

Alliance Spacesystems, Los Alamitos *Also Called: Vanguard Space Tech Inc (P-19715)*

Alliance Spacesystems LLC ....C....... 714 226-1400
4398 Corporate Center Dr Los Alamitos (90720) *(P-8162)*

Alliancebernstein LP ....C....... 310 286-6000
1999 Avenue Of The Stars Ste 2150 Los Angeles (90067) *(P-14954)*

Alliant Asset MGT Co LLC (HQ)...........................**D....... 818 668-2805**
26050 Mureau Rd Calabasas (91302) *(P-14743)*

Alliant Insurance Services Inc (PA).......................**C....... 949 756-0271**
18100 Von Karman Ave Ste 1000 Irvine (92612) *(P-20313)*

Alliant Tchsystems Oprtons LLC ....B....... 818 887-8195
9401 Corbin Ave Northridge (91324) *(P-9939)*

Alliant Tchsystems Oprtons LLC ....F....... 818 887-8185
21250 Califa St Woodland Hills (91367) *(P-9940)*

Alliant Tchsystems Oprtons LLC ....E....... 818 887-8195
9401 Corbin Ave Northridge (91324) *(P-9941)*

Allianz Global Investors of America LP ....A....... 949 219-2200
680 Newport Center Dr Ste 250 Newport Beach (92660) *(P-14414)*

Allianz Globl Risks US Insur (DH).........................**C**
2350 W Empire Ave Ste 200 Burbank (91504) *(P-14505)*

Allianz Insurance Company, Burbank *Also Called: Allianz Globl Risks US Insur (P-14505)*

Allianz Sweeper Company C
5405 Industrial Pkwy San Bernardino (92407) *(P-9276)*

Allied Artists International, City Of Industry *Also Called: Allied Entertainment Group Inc (P-17168)*

Allied Bio Medical, Ventura *Also Called: Implantech Associates Inc (P-10670)*

Allied Company Holdings Inc ....C....... 661 510-6533
28311 Constellation Rd Santa Clarita (91355) *(P-13458)*

Allied Company Holdings Inc (PA).........................**D....... 818 493-6400**
13235 Golden State Rd Sylmar (91342) *(P-13459)*

Allied Components Intl ....E....... 949 356-1780
19671 Descartes Foothill Ranch (92610) *(P-8933)*

Allied Digital Services LLC ....C....... 310 431-2361
1075 Mt Vernon Ave Riverside (92507) *(P-16539)*

Allied Electronic Services Inc ....E...... 714 245-2500
1342 E Borchard Ave Santa Ana (92705) *(P-8643)*

Allied Entertainment Group Inc (PA)..............B...... 626 330-0600
273 W Allen Ave City Of Industry (91746) *(P-17168)*

Allied Harbor Aerospace Fas, Corona *Also Called: All Manufacturers Inc (P-10423)*

Allied International, Valencia *Also Called: Allied International LLC (P-12712)*

Allied International LLC ....E...... 818 364-2333
28955 Avenue Sherman Valencia (91355) *(P-12712)*

Allied Lube Inc ....D...... 949 651-8814
3087 Edinger Ave Tustin (92780) *(P-17027)*

Allied Mdular Bldg Systems Inc (PA)..............E...... 714 516-1188
642 W Nicolas Ave Orange (92868) *(P-6373)*

Allied Mechanical Products, Ontario *Also Called: Tower Industries Inc (P-8050)*

Allied Mechanical Products, Ontario *Also Called: Tower Mechanical Products Inc (P-10085)*

Allied Protection Services Inc ....C...... 310 330-8314
24303 Berendo Ave Harbor City (90710) *(P-16614)*

Allied Signal Aerospace, Torrance *Also Called: Alliedsignal Arospc Svc Corp (P-5807)*

Allied Steel Co Inc ....D...... 951 241-7000
1027 Palmyrita Ave Riverside (92507) *(P-1098)*

Allied Trench Shoring Service, Newport Beach *Also Called: Traffic Control Service Inc (P-15803)*

Allied Universal ....C...... 619 444-0219
9320 Hazard Way Ste A1 San Diego (92123) *(P-864)*

Allied Universal, Irvine *Also Called: Universal Services America LP (P-16703)*

Allied Universal Event Svcs, Westminster *Also Called: Staff Pro Inc (P-16755)*

Allied Universal Security Svcs, Irvine *Also Called: Universal Protection Svc LP (P-16700)*

Allied West Paper Corp ....D...... 909 349-0710
11101 Etiwanda Ave Unit 100 Fontana (92337) *(P-3040)*

Allied Wheel Components Inc ....E...... 714 893-4160
12300 Edison Way Garden Grove (92841) *(P-13854)*

Alliedsignal Arospc Svc Corp (HQ)................D...... 310 323-9500
2525 W 190th St Torrance (90504) *(P-5807)*

Allies For Every Child Inc ....D...... 310 846-4100
5721 W Slauson Ave Ste 200 Culver City (90230) *(P-19200)*

Allison-Kaufman Co ....E...... 818 373-5100
7640 Haskell Ave Van Nuys (91406) *(P-10894)*

Alloy Die Casting Co ....C...... 714 521-9800
6550 Caballero Blvd Buena Park (90620) *(P-5756)*

Alloy Processing, Compton *Also Called: Kens Spray Equipment Inc (P-6715)*

Allstar Microelectronics Inc ....F...... 949 546-0888
30191 Avenida De Las Bandera Rancho Santa Margari (92688) *(P-7462)*

Allstarshop.com, Rancho Santa Margari *Also Called: Allstar Microelectronics Inc (P-7462)*

Allstate, Los Angeles *Also Called: Allstate Financial Svcs LLC (P-14556)*

Allstate Financial Svcs LLC ....D...... 323 981-8520
5161 Pomona Blvd Ste 212 Los Angeles (90022) *(P-14556)*

Allstate Floral Inc ....C...... 562 926-2989
15928 Commerce Way Cerritos (90703) *(P-14557)*

Allstate Imaging Inc (PA)........................D...... 818 678-4550
21621 Nordhoff St Chatsworth (91311) *(P-12381)*

Alltec Integrated Mfg Inc ....E...... 805 595-3500
2240 S Thornburg St Santa Maria (93455) *(P-4934)*

Alltech Industries Inc ....E...... 323 450-2168
301 E Pomona Blvd Monterey Park (91755) *(P-865)*

Ally Enterprises ....E...... 661 412-9933
5001 E Commercecenter Dr Ste 260 Bakersfield (93309) *(P-326)*

Allzone Management Solutions, Glendale *Also Called: Allzone Management Svcs Inc (P-19992)*

Allzone Management Svcs Inc ....B...... 213 291-8879
3795 La Crescenta Ave Ste 200 Glendale (91208) *(P-19992)*

Almack Liners Inc ....E...... 818 718-5878
9541 Cozycroft Ave Chatsworth (91311) *(P-2274)*

Almatron Electronics Inc ....E...... 714 557-6000
644 Young St Santa Ana (92705) *(P-8644)*

Alogent, Carlsbad *Also Called: Alogent Holdings Inc (P-15961)*

Alogent Holdings Inc ....D...... 760 410-9000
5868 Owens Ave Ste 200 Carlsbad (92008) *(P-15961)*

Alor International Ltd ....E...... 858 454-0011
11722 Sorrento Valley Rd San Diego (92121) *(P-10895)*

Alorica Customer Care Inc ....D...... 619 298-7103
8885 Rio San Diego Dr Ste 107 San Diego (92108) *(P-16771)*

Alorica Customer Care Inc ....C...... 941 906-9000
5161 California Ave Ste 100 Irvine (92617) *(P-16772)*

Alorica Inc (PA)..............................D...... 866 256-7422
5161 California Ave Ste 100 Irvine (92617) *(P-16773)*

Alpargatas Usa Inc ....E...... 646 277-7171
513 Boccaccio Ave Venice (90291) *(P-5274)*

Alpase, Chino *Also Called: Tst Inc (P-5685)*

Alpena Sausage Inc ....E...... 818 505-9482
5329 Craner Ave North Hollywood (91601) *(P-1210)*

ALPERT JEWISH COMMUNITY CENTRE, Long Beach *Also Called: Jewish Community Ctr Long Bch (P-19100)*

Alpha & Omega Pavers, Calimesa *Also Called: Paver Decor Masonry Inc (P-639)*

Alpha Aviation Components Inc (PA).............E...... 818 894-8801
16772 Schoenborn St North Hills (91343) *(P-7754)*

Alpha Corporation of Tennessee ....C...... 951 657-5161
19991 Seaton Ave Perris (92570) *(P-3921)*

Alpha Dental of Utah Inc ....C...... 562 467-7759
12898 Towne Center Dr Cerritos (90703) *(P-10728)*

Alpha Materials Inc ....E...... 951 788-5150
6170 20th St Riverside (92509) *(P-5459)*

Alpha Mechanical Inc ....C...... 858 278-3500
4990 Greencraig Ln Ste A San Diego (92123) *(P-729)*

Alpha Mechanical Heating & Air Conditioning Inc .....C...... 858 279-1300
4885 Greencraig Ln San Diego (92123) *(P-730)*

Alpha Omega Swiss Inc ....E...... 714 692-8009
23305 La Palma Ave Yorba Linda (92887) *(P-6409)*

Alpha Polishing Corporation (PA)..............D...... 323 263-7593
1313 Mirasol St Los Angeles (90023) *(P-6581)*

Alpha Printing & Graphics Inc ....E...... 626 851-9800
12758 Schabarum Ave Irwindale (91706) *(P-3508)*

Alpha Products Inc ....E...... 805 981-8666
351 Irving Dr Oxnard (93030) *(P-8960)*

Alpha Professional Resources, Thousand Oaks *Also Called: A P R Inc (P-15910)*

Alpha Project For Homeless ....C...... 760 630-9922
993 Postal Way Vista (92083) *(P-19018)*

Alpha Sensors Inc ....E...... 949 250-6578
24024 Humphries Rd Tecate (91980) *(P-10114)*

Alpha Technics, Tecate *Also Called: Alpha Sensors Inc (P-10114)*

Alpha Technics Inc ....C...... 949 250-6578
24024 Humphries Rd Tecate (91980) *(P-10115)*

Alpha-Owens Corning, Perris *Also Called: Alpha Corporation of Tennessee (P-3921)*

Alphabold ....D...... 949 637-7148
2011 Palomar Airport Rd Ste 305 Carlsbad (92011) *(P-16551)*

Alphacoat Finishing LLC ....E...... 949 748-7796
9350 Cabot Dr San Diego (92126) *(P-6687)*

Alphaeon Corporation ....C...... 949 284-4555
17901 Von Karman Ave Ste 150 Irvine (92614) *(P-12467)*

Alphastar Tech Solutions LLC ....F...... 562 961-7827
2601 Main St Ste 660 Irvine (92614) *(P-16162)*

Alphatec, Carlsbad *Also Called: Alphatec Holdings Inc (P-10426)*

Alphatec Holdings Inc (PA)....................C...... 760 431-9286
1950 Camino Vida Roble Carlsbad (92008) *(P-10426)*

Alphatec Spine Inc (HQ)......................C...... 760 431-9286
1950 Camino Vida Roble Carlsbad (92008) *(P-10634)*

Alphatech General Inc ....D...... 626 337-4640
4750 Littlejohn St Baldwin Park (91706) *(P-17114)*

Alpine Convalescent Center Inc ....D...... 619 659-3120
2120 Alpine Blvd Alpine (91901) *(P-18667)*

Alpine Inn Restaurant, Torrance *Also Called: Alpine Village (P-14651)*

Alpine Special Treatment Ctr, Alpine *Also Called: Alpine Convalescent Center Inc (P-18667)*

Alpine Village ....C...... 310 327-4384
23670 Hawthorne Blvd Torrance (90505) *(P-14651)*

Alpinestars USA ....D...... 310 891-0222
2780 W 237th St Torrance (90505) *(P-2230)*

Alpinestars USA, Torrance *Also Called: Alpinestars USA (P-2230)*

Als Garden Art Inc (PA)......................B...... 909 424-0221
311 W Citrus St Colton (92324) *(P-5564)*

Als Group Inc ....D...... 909 622-7555
1788 W 2nd St Pomona (91766) *(P-12786)*

Alstyle AP & Activewear MGT Co (HQ)..........A...... 714 765-0400
1501 E Cerritos Ave Anaheim (92805) *(P-13118)*

Employee Codes: A=Over 500 employees, B=251-500
C=101-250, D=51-100, E=20-50, F=10-19, G=1-9

2024 Southern California
Business Directory and Buyers Guide

© Mergent Inc. 1-800-342-5647
987

ALPHABETIC

Alstyle Apparel, Jurupa Valley *Also Called: A and G Inc (P-2190)*

Alstyle Apparel LLC .... A...... 714 765-0400
1501 E Cerritos Ave Anaheim (92805) *(P-2009)*

Alta Healthcare System LLC (HQ) .... C...... 323 267-0477
4081 E Olympic Blvd Los Angeles (90023) *(P-18173)*

Alta Hllywood Cmnty Hosp Van N .... D...... 818 787-1511
14433 Emelita St Van Nuys (91401) *(P-18503)*

Alta Hospitals System LLC .... A...... 714 619-7700
14662 Newport Ave Tustin (92780) *(P-18174)*

Alta Med Health Services, El Monte *Also Called: Altamed Health Services Corp (P-18741)*

Alta One Fcu, Ridgecrest *Also Called: Altaone Federal Credit Union (P-14221)*

Alta-Dena Certified Dairy LLC (DH) .... B...... 626 964-6401
17637 E Valley Blvd City Of Industry (91744) *(P-89)*

Altadena Town and Country Club .... D...... 626 345-9088
2290 Country Club Dr Altadena (91001) *(P-17459)*

Altair Lighting, Compton *Also Called: Jimway Inc (P-8369)*

Altamed Adhc Golden Age, Lynwood *Also Called: Altamed Health Services Corp (P-17587)*

Altamed Health Services Corp .... D...... 323 277-7678
6330 Rugby Ave Ste 200 Huntington Park (90255) *(P-17585)*

Altamed Health Services Corp .... C...... 562 923-9414
1500 Hughes Way Ste A150 Long Beach (90810) *(P-17586)*

Altamed Health Services Corp .... C...... 310 632-0415
3820 Martin Luther King Jr Blvd Lynwood (90262) *(P-17587)*

Altamed Health Services Corp .... C...... 323 980-4466
5427 Whittier Blvd Los Angeles (90022) *(P-17588)*

Altamed Health Services Corp .... C...... 323 269-0421
2219 E 1st St Los Angeles (90033) *(P-17589)*

Altamed Health Services Corp .... C...... 323 728-0411
5425 Pomona Blvd Los Angeles (90022) *(P-17590)*

Altamed Health Services Corp (PA) .... C...... 323 725-8751
2040 Camfield Ave Commerce (90040) *(P-17591)*

Altamed Health Services Corp .... C...... 323 562-6700
8627 Atlantic Ave South Gate (90280) *(P-18738)*

Altamed Health Services Corp .... C...... 323 307-0400
3945 Whittier Blvd Los Angeles (90023) *(P-18739)*

Altamed Health Services Corp .... C...... 562 949-8717
9436 Slauson Ave Pico Rivera (90660) *(P-18740)*

Altamed Health Services Corp .... C...... 626 453-8466
10418 Valley Blvd Ste B El Monte (91731) *(P-18741)*

Altamed Med & Dntl Group Bell, South Gate *Also Called: Altamed Health Services Corp (P-18738)*

Altamed Med Dntl Grp Whttier W, Los Angeles *Also Called: Altamed Health Services Corp (P-18739)*

Altametrics, Costa Mesa *Also Called: Altametrics Hosting LLC (P-12393)*

Altametrics Hosting LLC .... C...... 800 676-1281
3191 Red Hill Ave Ste 100 Costa Mesa (92626) *(P-12393)*

Altaone Federal Credit Union (PA) .... C...... 760 371-7000
701 S China Lake Blvd Ridgecrest (93555) *(P-14221)*

Altec Inc .... E...... 661 679-4177
1127 Carrier Parkway Ave Bakersfield (93308) *(P-6924)*

Altec Industries Inc .... E...... 909 444-0444
2882 Pomona Blvd Pomona (91768) *(P-17028)*

Altech Services Inc .... B...... 888 725-8324
400 Continental Blvd Fl 6 El Segundo (90245) *(P-15912)*

Altegra Health, Los Angeles *Also Called: The Coding Source LLC (P-19005)*

Alter Health Group, Dana Point *Also Called: Alter Management LLC (P-19993)*

Alter Management LLC .... D...... 949 629-0214
34232 Pacific Coast Hwy Ste D Dana Point (92629) *(P-19993)*

Alternative Ira Services LLC .... C...... 877 936-7175
15303 Ventura Blvd Ste 1060 Sherman Oaks (91403) *(P-16774)*

Alternative Press Magazine Inc .... E...... 216 631-1510
4321 W Magnolia Blvd Burbank (91505) *(P-3344)*

Alteryx, Irvine *Also Called: Alteryx Inc (P-16428)*

Alteryx Inc (PA) .... E...... 888 836-4274
17200 Laguna Canyon Rd Irvine (92618) *(P-16428)*

Altinex Inc .... E...... 714 990-0877
500 S Jefferson St Placentia (92870) *(P-8493)*

Altium Holdings LLC .... A...... 951 340-9390
12165 Madera Way Riverside (92503) *(P-4935)*

Altium Packaging .... D...... 626 856-2100
4516 Azusa Canyon Rd Irwindale (91706) *(P-4936)*

ALTIUM PACKAGING, Irwindale *Also Called: Altium Packaging (P-4936)*

Altium Packaging LLC .... D...... 310 952-8736
1500 E 223rd St Carson (90745) *(P-4856)*

Altium Packaging LLC .... D...... 888 425-7343
1070 Samuelson St City Of Industry (91748) *(P-4937)*

Altium Packaging LP .... D...... 714 241-6640
1217 E Saint Gertrude Pl Santa Ana (92707) *(P-4871)*

Altium Packaging LP .... E...... 909 590-7334
14312 Central Ave Chino (91710) *(P-4938)*

Altman Flowers, Fallbrook *Also Called: Altman Specialty Plants LLC (P-13499)*

Altman Plants, Vista *Also Called: Altman Specialty Plants LLC (P-13500)*

Altman Specialty Plants LLC .... B...... 800 348-4881
2575 Olive Hill Rd Fallbrook (92028) *(P-13499)*

Altman Specialty Plants LLC (PA) .... A...... 800 348-4881
3742 Blue Bird Canyon Rd Vista (92084) *(P-13500)*

Altmans, Beverly Hills *Also Called: Altmans Products LLC (P-5957)*

Altmans Products LLC .... E...... 310 274-5896
301 N Robertson Blvd Beverly Hills (90211) *(P-5957)*

Alto Lucero Transitional Care, Santa Barbara *Also Called: Compass Health Inc (P-17911)*

Alton Geoscience, Irvine *Also Called: TRC Solutions Inc (P-20386)*

Altour International Inc .... B...... 310 571-6000
10635 Santa Monica Blvd Ste 200 Los Angeles (90025) *(P-11711)*

Altour International Inc (PA) .... D...... 310 571-6000
12100 W Olympic Blvd Ste 300 Los Angeles (90064) *(P-11712)*

Altour Travel Master, Los Angeles *Also Called: Altour International Inc (P-11711)*

Altro Usa Inc .... D...... 562 944-8292
12648 Clark St Santa Fe Springs (90670) *(P-11183)*

Altruist Corp .... C...... 949 370-5096
3030 La Cienega Blvd Culver City (90232) *(P-20128)*

Alts Tool & Machine Inc .... D...... 619 562-6653
10926 Woodside Ave N Santee (92071) *(P-7755)*

Altumind Inc .... E...... 858 382-3956
10620 Treena St Ste 230 San Diego (92131) *(P-16163)*

Altura Holdings LLC .... B...... 714 948-8400
1335 S Acacia Ave Fullerton (92831) *(P-14955)*

Altura Management Services LLC .... B...... 323 768-2898
1401 N Montebello Blvd Montebello (90640) *(P-19994)*

Alturdyne Power Systems Inc .... E...... 619 343-3204
1405 N Johnson Ave El Cajon (92020) *(P-6877)*

Alum-A-Fold Pacific Inc .... E...... 562 699-4550
3730 Capitol Ave City Of Industry (90601) *(P-5686)*

Alum-Alloy Co Inc .... E...... 909 986-0410
603 S Hope Ave Ontario (91761) *(P-6475)*

Alumen-8, Oceanside *Also Called: Amerillum LLC (P-8353)*

Aluminum Casting Company, Ontario *Also Called: Employee Owned PCF Cast Pdts I (P-5792)*

Aluminum Die Casting Co Inc .... D...... 951 681-3900
10775 San Sevaine Way Jurupa Valley (91752) *(P-5757)*

Aluminum Precision Pdts Inc (PA) .... A...... 714 546-8125
3333 W Warner Ave Santa Ana (92704) *(P-5669)*

Aluminum Precision Pdts Inc .... E...... 805 488-4401
1001 Mcwane Blvd Oxnard (93033) *(P-12534)*

Alumistar Inc .... E...... 562 633-6673
520 S Palmetto Ave Ontario (91762) *(P-5781)*

Aluratek, Irvine *Also Called: Aluratek Inc (P-12394)*

Aluratek Inc .... E...... 866 580-1978
15241 Barranca Pkwy Irvine (92618) *(P-12394)*

Alva Manufacturing Inc .... E...... 714 237-0925
236 E Orangethorpe Ave Placentia (92870) *(P-9621)*

Alvarado Hospital LLC (DH) .... C...... 619 287-3270
6655 Alvarado Rd San Diego (92120) *(P-18175)*

Alvarado Hospital Med Ctr Inc .... A...... 619 287-3270
6655 Alvarado Rd San Diego (92120) *(P-18176)*

Alvarado Manufacturing Co Inc .... C...... 909 591-8431
12660 Colony Ct Chino (91710) *(P-10351)*

ALVARADO PARKWAY INSTITUTE, La Mesa *Also Called: Bh-SD Opco LLC (P-18673)*

Alvarado Parkway Institute, La Mesa *Also Called: Helix Healthcare Inc (P-18694)*

ALVAREZ & MARSAL BUSINESS CONSULTING LLC, Los Angeles *Also Called: Alvarez Mrsal Bus Cnsltng LLC (P-20129)*

Alvarez Mrsal Bus Cnsltng LLC .... C...... 310 975-2600
2029 Century Park E Los Angeles (90002) *(P-20129)*

Mergent email: customerrelations@mergent.com
988

2024 Southern California
Business Directory and Buyers Guide

(P-0000) Products & Services Section entry number
(PA)=Parent Co (HQ)=Headquarters (DH)=Div Headquarters

Always Best Care Desert Cities, Indian Wells Also Called: Bjz LLC **(P-18594)**

Always Best Care Temecula Vly, Temecula Also Called: James Rebecca Prouty Entps Inc **(P-18621)**

Always Right Home Care, Northridge Also Called: Tiffany Homecare Inc **(P-18646)**

Alyn Industries Inc .... D...... 818 988-7696
16028 Arminta St Van Nuys (91406) **(P-8994)**

AM Castenada Inc .... E...... 951 686-3966
1450 University Ave Ste P Riverside (92507) **(P-10916)**

AM Machining Inc .... F...... 714 367-0830
7422 Walnut Ave Buena Park (90620) **(P-12901)**

Am-PM Sewer & Drain Cleaning, San Diego Also Called: Bill Howe Plumbing Inc **(P-744)**

Am-Tek Engineering Inc .... F...... 909 673-1633
1180 E Francis St Ste C Ontario (91761) **(P-7756)**

Am-Touch Dental, Valencia Also Called: American Med & Hosp Sup Co Inc **(P-12468)**

Am/PM Mini Market, La Palma Also Called: Prestige Stations Inc **(P-13702)**

Amada America Inc .... D...... 714 739-2111
100 S Puente St Brea (92821) **(P-6688)**

Amada Enterprises Inc .... C...... 323 757-1881
12619 Avalon Blvd Los Angeles (90061) **(P-17879)**

Amada Weld Tech Inc (DH) .... E...... 626 303-5676
1820 S Myrtle Ave Monrovia (91016) **(P-7155)**

Amada Weld Tech Inc .... E...... 626 303-5676
245 E El Norte St Monrovia (91016) **(P-10427)**

Amag Technology Inc .... E...... 310 518-2380
2205 W 126th St Ste B Hawthorne (90250) **(P-7505)**

Amanecer Cmnty Cnsling Svc A N .... D...... 213 481-7464
1200 Wilshire Blvd Ste 200 Los Angeles (90017) **(P-18668)**

Amaretto Orchards LLC .... E...... 661 399-9697
32331 Famoso Woody Rd Mc Farland (93250) **(P-11188)**

Amass Brands Inc .... E...... 619 204-2560
860 E Stowell Rd Santa Maria (93454) **(P-3990)**

Amatix, Sun Valley Also Called: Marfred Industries **(P-3117)**

Amawaterways LLC (PA) .... C...... 800 626-0126
4500 Park Granada # 200 Calabasas (91302) **(P-11713)**

Amaya Curiel Corporation .... A...... 619 661-1230
9775 Marconi Dr Ste G San Diego (92154) **(P-492)**

Amaya Curiel Y CIA S.A., San Diego Also Called: Amaya Curiel Corporation **(P-492)**

Amays Bakery & Noodle Co Inc (PA) .... D...... 213 626-2713
837 E Commercial St Los Angeles (90012) **(P-1502)**

Amazing Coachella Inc .... D...... 760 398-0151
85810 Peter Rabbit Ln Coachella (92236) **(P-6)**

Amazing Steel, Montclair Also Called: Mitchell Fabrication **(P-6056)**

Amazing Steel Company .... E...... 909 590-0393
4564 Mission Blvd Montclair (91763) **(P-5991)**

Amazon Processing LLC .... C...... 858 565-1135
4619 Viewridge Ave Ste C San Diego (92123) **(P-16481)**

Amazon Studios LLC .... C...... 818 804-0884
9336 Washington Blvd Culver City (90232) **(P-15962)**

Amazon.Com, San Bernardino Also Called: Amazoncom Inc **(P-11564)**

Amazoncom Inc .... D...... 626 260-6954
1910 E Central Ave San Bernardino (92408) **(P-11564)**

Ambay Circuits Inc .... E...... 818 786-8241
16117 Leadwell St Van Nuys (91406) **(P-8645)**

Amber Chemical Inc .... E...... 661 325-2072
5201 Boylan St Bakersfield (93308) **(P-3880)**

Amber Holding Inc .... D...... 603 324-3000
1601 Cloverfield Blvd Santa Monica (90404) **(P-16164)**

Amber Steel Co., Rialto Also Called: H Wayne Lewis Inc **(P-6398)**

Amberwood Convalescent Hosp .... D...... 323 254-3407
6071 York Blvd Los Angeles (90042) **(P-18105)**

Ambiance Apparel, Los Angeles Also Called: Ambiance USA Inc **(P-2302)**

Ambiance Transportation LLC .... D...... 818 955-5757
6901 San Fernando Rd Glendale (91201) **(P-11827)**

Ambiance USA Inc .... E...... 213 765-9600
930 Towne Ave Los Angeles (90021) **(P-2300)**

Ambiance USA Inc .... E...... 323 587-0007
2465 E 23rd St Los Angeles (90058) **(P-2301)**

Ambiance USA Inc (PA) .... D...... 323 587-0007
2415 E 15th St Los Angeles (90021) **(P-2302)**

Ambit Biosciences Corporation .... D...... 858 334-2100
10201 Wateridge Cir Ste 200 San Diego (92121) **(P-4042)**

Ambit Engineering Corporation .... D...... 714 557-1074
2640 Halladay St Santa Ana (92705) **(P-7048)**

Ambrit Industries Inc .... E...... 818 243-1224
432 Magnolia Ave Glendale (91204) **(P-7029)**

Ambrx Inc (PA) .... D...... 858 875-2400
10975 N Torrey Pines Rd Ste 100 La Jolla (92037) **(P-4043)**

Ambulnz Health LLC .... B...... 877 311-5555
12531 Vanowen St North Hollywood (91605) **(P-11370)**

AMC, Stanton Also Called: All Metals Processing of San Diego Inc **(P-6578)**

AMC Machining Inc .... E...... 805 238-5452
1540 Commerce Way Paso Robles (93446) **(P-6394)**

Amco Foods Inc .... B...... 818 247-4716
601 E Glenoaks Blvd Ste 108 Glendale (91207) **(P-20130)**

Amcor Flexibles Healthcare, Commerce Also Called: Amcor Flexibles LLC **(P-3148)**

Amcor Flexibles LLC .... A...... 323 721-6777
5416 Union Pacific Ave Commerce (90022) **(P-3148)**

Amcor Industries Inc .... E...... 323 585-2852
6131 Knott Ave Buena Park (90620) **(P-9350)**

AMD International Tech LLC .... E...... 909 985-8300
1725 S Campus Ave Ontario (91761) **(P-6185)**

AME Unmanned Air Systems Inc .... D...... 805 541-4448
125 Venture Dr Ste 110 San Luis Obispo (93401) **(P-19545)**

AME-Gyu Co Ltd .... A...... 310 214-9572
20000 Mariner Ave Ste 500 Torrance (90503) **(P-14921)**

Ameditech Inc .... C...... 858 535-1968
9940 Mesa Rim Rd San Diego (92121) **(P-10428)**

Amenities Development Co .... C...... 626 350-9588
1089 Santa Anita Ave El Monte (91733) **(P-15071)**

Amerasia Furn Cmpnnts Mfg Impr .... E...... 310 638-0570
2772 Norton Ave Lynwood (90262) **(P-2794)**

Ameresco Solar LLC .... B...... 888 967-6527
42175 Zevo Dr Temecula (92590) **(P-19546)**

Amerex Company, Riverside Also Called: Nsa Holdings Inc **(P-5121)**

Amergence Technology Inc .... E...... 909 859-8400
295 Brea Canyon Rd Walnut (91789) **(P-7220)**

Ameri-Fax, Orange Also Called: Positive Concepts Inc **(P-3243)**

Ameri-Kleen .... E...... 805 546-0706
1023 E Grand Ave Arroyo Grande (93420) **(P-15692)**

Ameri-Kleen Building Services, Arroyo Grande Also Called: Ameri-Kleen **(P-15692)**

America Wood Finishes Inc .... E...... 323 232-8256
728 E 59th St Los Angeles (90001) **(P-4474)**

American & Efird LLC .... F...... 323 724-6884
6098 Rickenbacker Rd Commerce (90040) **(P-2123)**

American Academic Hlth Sys LLC .... A...... 310 414-7200
222 N Pacific Coast Hwy Ste 900 El Segundo (90245) **(P-14922)**

American Aircraft Products Inc .... D...... 310 532-7434
15411 S Broadway Gardena (90248) **(P-6186)**

American Airframe Inc .... E...... 805 240-1608
1201 Vanguard Dr Oxnard (93033) **(P-9622)**

American Airlines Inc .... B...... 310 646-4553
400 World Way Ste F Los Angeles (90045) **(P-11658)**

American Airlines/Eagle, Long Beach Also Called: Piedmont Airlines Inc **(P-11668)**

American AP Dyg & Finshg Inc .... E...... 310 644-4001
747 Warehouse St Los Angeles (90021) **(P-2045)**

American Apparel, Los Angeles Also Called: American AP Dyg & Finshg Inc **(P-2045)**

American Apparel, Los Angeles Also Called: American Apparel (usa) LLC **(P-2439)**

American Apparel, Los Angeles Also Called: App Winddown LLC **(P-2441)**

American Apparel (usa) LLC .... E...... 213 488-0226
747 Warehouse St Los Angeles (90021) **(P-2439)**

American Arium .... E...... 949 623-7090
17791 Fitch Irvine (92614) **(P-8763)**

American Assn Crtcal Care Nrse .... C...... 949 362-2000
27071 Aliso Creek Rd Aliso Viejo (92656) **(P-19007)**

American Assod Roofg Distrs, Monterey Park Also Called: Oakcroft Associates Inc **(P-12776)**

American Audio Component Inc .... E...... 909 596-3788
20 Fairbanks Ste 198 Irvine (92618) **(P-8995)**

American Automated Engrg Inc .... D...... 714 898-9951
5382 Argosy Ave Huntington Beach (92649) **(P-9914)**

American Bath Factory, Corona Also Called: Le Elegant Bath Inc **(P-4919)**

American Beef Packers Inc ....C...... 909 628-4888
13677 Yorba Ave Chino (91710) *(P-132)*

American Best Car Parts, Anaheim *Also Called: American Fabrication Corp (P-9351)*

American Bicycle Security Co, Santa Paula *Also Called: Turtle Storage Ltd (P-2997)*

American Bottling Company ....D...... 818 898-1471
1166 Arroyo St San Fernando (91340) *(P-1677)*

American Bottling Company ....D...... 951 341-7500
1188 Mt Vernon Ave Riverside (92507) *(P-1678)*

American Bottling Company ....C...... 323 268-7779
3220 E 26th St Vernon (90058) *(P-1679)*

American Bottling Company ....C...... 714 974-8560
1166 Arroyo St Orange (92865) *(P-1680)*

American Bottling Company ....D...... 661 323-7921
230 E 18th St Bakersfield (93305) *(P-1681)*

American Bottling Company ....D...... 805 928-1001
618 Hanson Way Santa Maria (93458) *(P-1682)*

American Brass & Alum Fndry Co ....E...... 800 545-9988
2060 Garfield Ave Commerce (90040) *(P-5962)*

American Building Supply, Rialto *Also Called: Jeld-Wen Inc (P-12334)*

American Business Bank ....D...... 310 808-1200
970 W 190th St Ste 850 Torrance (90502) *(P-14177)*

American Business Bank ....D...... 909 919-2040
3633 Inland Empire Blvd Ste 720 Ontario (91764) *(P-14178)*

American Cabinet Works Inc ....E...... 310 715-6815
13518 S Normandie Ave Gardena (90249) *(P-2582)*

American Capacitor Corporation ....E...... 626 814-4444
5367 3rd St Irwindale (91706) *(P-8925)*

American Circuit Tech Inc (PA) ....**E...... 714 777-2480**
5330 E Hunter Ave Anaheim (92807) *(P-8646)*

American Compaction Eqp Inc ....E...... 949 661-2921
29380 Hunco Way Lake Elsinore (92530) *(P-6925)*

American Condenser, Gardena *Also Called: American Condenser & Coil LLC (P-7598)*

American Condenser & Coil LLC ....D...... 310 327-8600
1628 W 139th St Gardena (90249) *(P-7598)*

American Consumer Products LLC ....D...... 323 289-6610
120 E 8th St Ste 908 Los Angeles (90014) *(P-4595)*

American Contrs Indemnity Co (DH) ....**C...... 213 330-1309**
801 S Figueroa St Ste 700 Los Angeles (90017) *(P-14534)*

American Cooling Tower, Santa Ana *Also Called: American Cooling Tower Inc (P-17115)*

American Cooling Tower Inc (PA) ....**F...... 714 898-2436**
3130 W Harvard St Santa Ana (92704) *(P-17115)*

American Copak Corporation ....C...... 818 576-1000
9175 Eton Ave Chatsworth (91311) *(P-16775)*

American Cover Design 26 Inc ....E...... 323 582-8666
2131 E 52nd St Vernon (90058) *(P-2108)*

American Cvil Lbrties Un Sther, Orange *Also Called: Aclu Fndation Southern Cal LLC (P-19421)*

American Dawn Inc (PA) ....**D...... 800 821-2221**
401 W Artesia Blvd Compton (90220) *(P-2134)*

American De Rosa Lamparts LLC ....D...... 800 777-4440
10650 4th St Rancho Cucamonga (91730) *(P-493)*

American Deburring Inc ....E...... 949 457-9790
20742 Linear Ln Lake Forest (92630) *(P-7757)*

American Designs, Los Angeles *Also Called: Kesmor Associates (P-10903)*

American Development Corp (PA) ....**D...... 562 989-3730**
3605 Long Beach Blvd Ste 410 Long Beach (90807) *(P-14744)*

American Die Casting Inc ....E...... 909 356-7768
14576 Fontlee Ln Fontana (92335) *(P-5771)*

American Dj Group of Companies, Commerce *Also Called: D J American Supply Inc (P-12972)*

American Eagle Mfg Co ....E...... 949 251-0722
18301 Von Karman Ave Ste 1000 Irvine (92612) *(P-9872)*

American Eagle Motorcycles, Irvine *Also Called: American Eagle Mfg Co (P-9872)*

American Eagle Protective Svcs, Inglewood *Also Called: American Egle Prtctive Svcs In (P-16615)*

American Egle Prtctive Svcs In ....D...... 310 412-0019
425 W Kelso St Inglewood (90301) *(P-16615)*

American Electronics, Carson *Also Called: Ducommun Labarge Tech Inc (P-9680)*

American Elements, Los Angeles *Also Called: Merelex Corporation (P-3899)*

American Etching & Mfg ....E...... 323 875-3910
13730 Desmond St Pacoima (91331) *(P-6689)*

American Fabrication, Bakersfield *Also Called: Russell Fabrication Corp (P-6852)*

American Fabrication Corp (PA) ....**D...... 714 632-1709**
2891 E Via Martens Anaheim (92806) *(P-9351)*

American Faucet Coatings Corp ....E...... 760 598-5895
3280 Corporate Vw Vista (92081) *(P-12295)*

American Fdrtion Mscans Lcal 4 ....D...... 323 462-2161
3220 Winona Ave Burbank (91504) *(P-19407)*

AMERICAN FEDERATION OF MUSICIA, Burbank *Also Called: American Fdrtion Mscans Lcal 4 (P-19407)*

American Financial Network Inc (PA) ....**C...... 714 831-4000**
10 Pointe Dr Ste 330 Brea (92821) *(P-14294)*

American First Credit Union (PA) ....**D...... 562 691-1112**
6 Pointe Dr Ste 400 Brea (92821) *(P-14222)*

American Fish and Seafood, Los Angeles *Also Called: Prospect Enterprises Inc (P-13283)*

American Fleet & Ret Graphics ....E...... 909 937-7570
2091 Del Rio Way Ontario (91761) *(P-11096)*

American Foam & Packaging, Gardena *Also Called: Amfoam Inc (P-4872)*

American Foam Fiber & Sups Inc (PA) ....**E...... 626 969-7268**
255 S 7th Ave Ste A City Of Industry (91746) *(P-2135)*

American Food Co, Los Angeles *Also Called: Afc Trading & Wholesale Inc (P-13170)*

American Food Ingredients Inc ....E...... 760 967-6287
4021 Avenida De La Plata Ste 501 Oceanside (92056) *(P-1354)*

American Foothill Pubg Co Inc ....E...... 818 352-7878
10009 Commerce Ave Tujunga (91042) *(P-3732)*

American Fruits & Flavors LLC ....E...... 818 899-9574
1527 Knowles Ave Los Angeles (90063) *(P-1748)*

American Fruits & Flavors LLC ....E...... 818 899-9574
1565 Knowles Ave Los Angeles (90063) *(P-1749)*

American Fruits & Flavors LLC ....D...... 213 624-1831
400 S Central Ave Los Angeles (90013) *(P-1750)*

American Fruits & Flavors LLC ....D...... 310 522-1844
22560 Lucerne St Carson (90745) *(P-1751)*

American Fruits & Flavors LLC ....D...... 323 881-8321
3001 Sierra Pine Ave Vernon (90058) *(P-1752)*

American Fruits & Flavors LLC ....E...... 562 320-2802
13530 Rosecrans Ave Santa Fe Springs (90670) *(P-1753)*

American Fruits & Flavors LLC (HQ) ....**C...... 818 899-9574**
10725 Sutter Ave Pacoima (91331) *(P-1754)*

American Fruits & Flavors LLC ....E...... 909 291-2620
9345 Santa Anita Ave Rancho Cucamonga (91730) *(P-1755)*

American Fruits & Flavors LLC ....B...... 818 899-9574
510 Park Ave San Fernando (91340) *(P-15497)*

American Funds Distrs Inc (DH) ....**C...... 213 486-9200**
333 S Hope St Ste Levb Los Angeles (90071) *(P-14956)*

American Funds Service Company (DH) ....**B...... 949 975-5000**
6455 Irvine Center Dr Irvine (92618) *(P-14433)*

American Furniture Alliance, Corona *Also Called: Widly Inc (P-2864)*

American Furniture Systems Inc ....E...... 626 457-9900
14105 Avalon Blvd Los Angeles (90061) *(P-2902)*

American Future Tech Corp ....C...... 888 462-3899
529 Baldwin Park Blvd City Of Industry (91746) *(P-12395)*

American Garment Sewing, Pasadena *Also Called: AGS Usa LLC (P-2272)*

American General Tool Group ....E...... 760 745-7993
929 Poinsettia Ave Ste 101 Vista (92081) *(P-4692)*

American Golf Construction, Canoga Park *Also Called: American Landscape Inc (P-139)*

American Golf Corporation (HQ) ....**C...... 310 664-4000**
909 N Pacific Coast Hwy Ste 650 El Segundo (90245) *(P-17460)*

American Graphic Board Inc ....D...... 323 721-0585
5880 E Slauson Ave Commerce (90040) *(P-3041)*

American Green Lights, San Diego *Also Called: American Green Lights LLC (P-12101)*

American Green Lights LLC ....E...... 858 547-8837
10755 Scripps Poway Pkwy Ste 419 San Diego (92131) *(P-12101)*

American Grip Inc ....E...... 818 768-8922
8468 Kewen Ave Sun Valley (91352) *(P-8351)*

American Guard Services Inc (PA) ....**B...... 310 645-6200**
1125 W 190th St Gardena (90248) *(P-16616)*

American Handgunner and Guns, Escondido *Also Called: Publishers Development Corp (P-3382)*

American Health Connection ....A...... 424 226-0420
8484 Wilshire Blvd Ste 501 Beverly Hills (90211) *(P-16776)*

American Hlthcare Systems Corp (PA) ....**B...... 818 646-9933**
505 N Brand Blvd Ste 1110 Glendale (91203) *(P-18177)*

Mergent email: customerrelations@mergent.com
990

2024 Southern California
Business Directory and Buyers Guide

(P-0000) Products & Services Section entry number
(PA)=Parent Co (HQ)=Headquarters (DH)=Div Headquarters

American Honda, Torrance *Also Called: American Honda Motor Co Inc (P-12221)*

AMERICAN HONDA, Torrance *Also Called: American Honda Finance Corp (P-14267)*

American Honda Finance Corp (DH)..C...... 310 972-2239
1919 Torrance Blvd Torrance (90501) *(P-14267)*

American Honda Motor Co Inc (HQ)...A...... 310 783-2000
1919 Torrance Blvd Torrance (90501) *(P-12221)*

American Household Company, Los Angeles *Also Called: Housewares International Inc (P-5054)*

American HX Auto Trade Inc ....D...... 909 484-1010
4845 Via Del Cerro Yorba Linda (92887) *(P-9277)*

American Industrial Manufacturing Services Inc ....C...... 951 698-3379
41673 Corning Pl Murrieta (92562) *(P-9162)*

American Industrial Source Inc ....D...... 800 661-0622
15759 Strathern St Ste 1 Van Nuys (91406) *(P-12844)*

American Integrity Corp ....E...... 760 247-1082
13510 Central Rd Apple Valley (92308) *(P-4939)*

American International, San Fernando *Also Called: American Intrntnl-Steel Cast D (P-5782)*

American International Inds, Commerce *Also Called: Glamour Industries Co (P-13042)*

American Internet Mortgage Inc ....C...... 888 411-4246
4121 Camino Del Rio S Ste 200 San Diego (92108) *(P-14295)*

American Intgrted Rsources Inc ....D...... 714 921-4100
2341 N Pacific St Orange (92865) *(P-19995)*

American Intl Inds Inc ....A...... 323 728-2999
2220 Gaspar Ave Commerce (90040) *(P-4378)*

American Intrntnl-Steel Cast D ....E...... 818 365-8000
860 Arroyo St San Fernando (91340) *(P-5782)*

American Kal Enterprises Inc (PA)............................D...... 626 338-7308
4265 Puente Ave Baldwin Park (91706) *(P-12713)*

American Koyu Corporation ....C...... 626 793-0669
1733 S Anaheim Blvd Anaheim (92805) *(P-15072)*

American Lab and Systems, Los Angeles *Also Called: Mjw Inc (P-7283)*

American Landscape Inc ....C...... 818 999-2041
7013 Owensmouth Ave Canoga Park (91303) *(P-139)*

American Landscape MGT Inc (PA)...........................C...... 818 999-2041
7013 Owensmouth Ave Canoga Park (91303) *(P-140)*

American Legal Copy - Oc LLC ....D...... 415 777-4449
655 W Broadway Ste 200 San Diego (92101) *(P-15641)*

American Mailing & Prtg Svc, Anaheim *Also Called: Sharon Havriluk (P-3840)*

American Management Svcs W LLC ....C...... 805 352-1921
1240 Bethel Ln Santa Maria (93458) *(P-19996)*

American Marble, Vista *Also Called: Kammerer Enterprises Inc (P-5529)*

American Marble & Onyx Coinc ....F...... 323 776-0900
10321 S La Cienega Blvd Los Angeles (90045) *(P-5524)*

American Med & Hosp Sup Co Inc ....E...... 661 294-1213
28703 Industry Dr Valencia (91355) *(P-12468)*

American Med O & P Clinic Inc ....E...... 818 281-5747
4955 Van Nuys Blvd Sherman Oaks (91403) *(P-10635)*

American Med Rspnse Inland Emp (HQ)......................D...... 951 782-5200
879 Marlborough Ave Riverside (92507) *(P-11371)*

American Medical Response, Palm Springs *Also Called: American Medical Response Inc (P-11372)*

American Medical Response Inc ....C...... 760 883-5000
1111 Montalvo Way Palm Springs (92262) *(P-11372)*

American Medical Tech Inc ....D...... 949 553-0359
17595 Cartwright Rd Irvine (92614) *(P-12469)*

American Metal, Pomona *Also Called: American Mtal Mfg Resource Inc (P-9563)*

American Metal Bearing Company ....E...... 714 892-5527
7191 Acacia Ave Garden Grove (92841) *(P-7296)*

American Metal Filter Company ....F...... 619 628-1917
611 Marsat Ct Chula Vista (91911) *(P-7318)*

American Mobile Healthcare, San Diego *Also Called: Amn Healthcare Inc (P-15812)*

American Mortgage Network, Chula Vista *Also Called: Amnet Esop Corporation (P-14297)*

American Mtal Mfg Resource Inc ....E...... 909 620-4500
1989 W Holt Ave Pomona (91768) *(P-9563)*

American Multimedia TV USA ....D...... 626 466-1038
530 S Lake Ave Unit 368 Pasadena (91101) *(P-11938)*

American Mutual Fund ....C...... 213 486-9200
333 S Hope St Fl 51 Los Angeles (90071) *(P-14957)*

American Mzhou Dngpo Group Inc ....D...... 626 820-9239
4520 Maine Ave Baldwin Park (91706) *(P-19997)*

American Nail Plate Ltg Inc ....D...... 909 982-1807
9044 Del Mar Ave Montclair (91763) *(P-8286)*

American Nat Red Crss-Blood Sv, Pomona *Also Called: American National Red Cross (P-19019)*

American National Mfg Inc ....D...... 951 273-7888
252 Mariah Cir Corona (92879) *(P-2842)*

American National Red Cross ....C...... 909 859-7006
100 Red Cross Cir Pomona (91768) *(P-19019)*

American National Red Cross ....C...... 310 445-9900
1450 S Central Ave Los Angeles (90021) *(P-19020)*

American Naturals Company LLC ....E...... 323 201-6891
3737 Longridge Ave Sherman Oaks (91423) *(P-1850)*

American Nuts LLC (HQ)..C...... 818 364-8855
12950 San Fernando Rd Sylmar (91342) *(P-13262)*

American Pacific Plastic Fabricators Inc ....E...... 714 891-3191
7130 Fenwick Ln Westminster (92683) *(P-3922)*

American Paper & Plastics LLC ....C...... 626 444-0000
550 S 7th Ave City Of Industry (91746) *(P-13526)*

American Paper & Provisions, City Of Industry *Also Called: American Paper & Plastics LLC (P-13526)*

American PCF Prtrs College Inc ....E...... 949 250-3212
675 N Main St Orange (92868) *(P-3509)*

American Peptide Company Inc ....D...... 408 733-7604
1271 Avenida Chelsea Vista (92081) *(P-4297)*

American Plant Services Inc (PA).............................E...... 562 630-1773
6242 N Paramount Blvd Long Beach (90805) *(P-5576)*

American Plastic Products Inc ....D...... 818 504-1073
9243 Glenoaks Blvd Sun Valley (91352) *(P-7049)*

American Power SEC Svc Inc ....D...... 866 974-9994
1451 Rimpau Ave Ste 207 Corona (92879) *(P-16617)*

American Power Solutions Inc ....E...... 714 626-0300
14355 Industry Cir La Mirada (90638) *(P-8352)*

American Precision Hydraulics ....E...... 714 903-8610
5601 Research Dr Huntington Beach (92649) *(P-7030)*

American Precision Sheet Metal, Chatsworth *Also Called: Keith E Archambeau Sr Inc (P-6260)*

American Printworks, Vernon *Also Called: P&Y T-Shrts Silk Screening Inc (P-7178)*

American Private Duty Inc ....D...... 818 386-6358
13111 Ventura Blvd Ste 100 Studio City (91604) *(P-18589)*

American Prof Ambulance Corp ....D...... 818 996-2200
16945 Sherman Way Van Nuys (91406) *(P-11373)*

American Protection Group Inc (PA)..........................C...... 818 279-2433
8741 Van Nuys Blvd Ste 202 Panorama City (91402) *(P-16618)*

American Prprty-Mnagement Corp ....A...... 619 232-3121
326 Broadway San Diego (92101) *(P-15073)*

American Prtctive Svcs Invstgt ....C...... 626 705-8600
12471 Balsam Rd Victorville (92395) *(P-16619)*

American Quality Tools, Riverside *Also Called: American Quality Tools Inc (P-7106)*

American Quality Tools Inc ....E...... 951 280-4700
12650 Magnolia Ave Ste B Riverside (92503) *(P-7106)*

American Quilting Company Inc ....E...... 323 233-2500
1540 Calzona St Los Angeles (90023) *(P-2513)*

American Rag Compagnie ....D...... 323 935-3154
150 S La Brea Ave Los Angeles (90036) *(P-13911)*

American Range Corporation ....C...... 818 897-0808
13592 Desmond St Pacoima (91331) *(P-6187)*

American Ready Mix, Escondido *Also Called: Superior Ready Mix Concrete LP (P-5513)*

American Recovery Service Inc (DH)........................C...... 805 379-8500
555 Saint Charles Dr Ste 100 Thousand Oaks (91360) *(P-15606)*

American Red Cross, Los Angeles *Also Called: American Red Cross Los Angles (P-19021)*

American Red Cross, San Diego *Also Called: American Red Cross San Dg-Mpri (P-19022)*

American Red Cross Los Angles (PA).......................C...... 310 445-9900
1320 Newton St Los Angeles (90021) *(P-19021)*

American Red Cross San Dg-Mpri (PA)......................D...... 858 309-1200
3950 Calle Fortunada San Diego (92123) *(P-19022)*

American Regent Inc ....E...... 714 989-5058
536 Vanguard Way Brea (92821) *(P-19917)*

American Reliance Inc ....E...... 626 443-6818
789 N Fair Oaks Ave Pasadena (91103) *(P-7417)*

American Retirement Corp ....C...... 310 399-3227
2107 Ocean Ave Santa Monica (90405) *(P-17880)*

Employee Codes: A=Over 500 employees, B=251-500
C=101-250, D=51-100, E=20-50, F=10-19, G=1-9

2024 Southern California
Business Directory and Buyers Guide

© Mergent Inc. 1-800-342-5647

991

American Rigging & Supply, San Diego *Also Called: Carpenter Group* **(P-12846)**

American Rim Supply Inc .... E....... 760 431-3666
1955 Kellogg Ave Carlsbad (92008) **(P-9352)**

American Rotary Broom Co Inc .... E....... 909 629-9117
688 New York Dr Pomona (91768) **(P-11084)**

American Scale Co Inc .... E....... 800 773-7225
21326 E Arrow Hwy Covina (91724) **(P-12396)**

American Scence Tech As T Corp .... D....... 310 773-1978
2372 Morse Ave Ste 571 Irvine (92614) **(P-9509)**

American Security Bank .... D....... 949 440-5200
1401 Dove St Ste 100 Newport Beach (92660) **(P-14179)**

American Security Force Inc .... D....... 323 722-8585
5430 E Olympic Blvd Commerce (90022) **(P-16723)**

American Security Products Co .... C....... 951 685-9680
11925 Pacific Ave Fontana (92337) **(P-6855)**

American Sheet Metal, El Cajon *Also Called: Asm Construction Inc* **(P-6194)**

American Single Sheets, Redlands *Also Called: Continental Datalabel Inc* **(P-3233)**

American Soc Cmpsers Athors Pb .... D....... 323 883-1000
7920 W Sunset Blvd Ste 300 Los Angeles (90046) **(P-3427)**

American Soccer Company Inc (PA) .... **C....... 310 830-6161**
726 E Anaheim St Wilmington (90744) **(P-13929)**

American Solar LLC .... E....... 323 250-1307
8484 Wilshire Blvd Ste 630 Beverly Hills (90211) **(P-5977)**

American Solar Advantage Inc .... E....... 877 765-2388
13348 Monte Vista Ave Chino (91710) **(P-8764)**

American Solar Direct Inc .... C....... 424 214-6700
11766 Wilshire Blvd Ste 500 Los Angeles (90025) **(P-866)**

American Spclty Hlth Group Inc .... B....... 858 754-2000
10221 Wateridge Cir Ste 201 San Diego (92121) **(P-14460)**

American Spclty Hlth Plans Cal .... B....... 619 297-8100
10221 Wateridge Cir San Diego (92121) **(P-14558)**

American States Water Company (PA) .... **A....... 909 394-3600**
630 E Foothill Blvd San Dimas (91773) **(P-12114)**

American Suzuki Motor Corporation .... B....... 714 996-7040
3251 E Imperial Hwy Brea (92821) **(P-13738)**

American Textile Maint Co .... D....... 213 749-4433
1705 Hooper Ave Los Angeles (90021) **(P-15446)**

American Textile Maint Co .... C....... 323 735-1661
1664 W Washington Blvd Los Angeles (90007) **(P-15447)**

American Tooth Industries .... D....... 805 487-9868
1200 Stellar Dr Oxnard (93033) **(P-12470)**

American Transportation Co LLC .... D....... 818 660-2343
635 W Colorado St Ste 108a Glendale (91204) **(P-11828)**

American Traveler Inc .... E....... 909 466-4000
9509 Feron Blvd Rancho Cucamonga (91730) **(P-5283)**

American Turn-Key Fabricators, Rancho Cucamonga *Also Called: Romeros Engineering Inc* **(P-8005)**

American Ultraviolet West Inc .... E....... 310 784-2930
23555 Telo Ave Torrance (90505) **(P-6969)**

American Untd HM Care Crp-Priv, Studio City *Also Called: American Private Duty Inc* **(P-18589)**

American Vanguard Corporation (PA) .... **D....... 949 260-1200**
4695 Macarthur Ct Newport Beach (92660) **(P-4545)**

American Vision Baths, Simi Valley *Also Called: American Vision Windows Inc* **(P-17116)**

American Vision Windows Inc .... C....... 805 582-1833
2125 N Madera Rd Ste A Simi Valley (93065) **(P-17116)**

American Window Covering Inc .... F....... 714 879-3880
825 Williamson Ave Fullerton (92832) **(P-15463)**

American Wire Inc .... F....... 909 884-9990
784 S Lugo Ave San Bernardino (92408) **(P-6810)**

American Wire Sales, Rancho Dominguez *Also Called: Standard Wire & Cable Co* **(P-5750)**

American Woodmark Corporation .... B....... 714 449-2200
400 E Orangethorpe Ave Anaheim (92801) **(P-2645)**

American Wrecking Inc .... D....... 626 350-8303
2459 Lee Ave South El Monte (91733) **(P-1129)**

American Yeast Corporation .... E....... 661 834-1050
5455 District Blvd Bakersfield (93313) **(P-1851)**

American Zabin Intl Inc .... E....... 213 746-3770
3933 S Hill St Los Angeles (90037) **(P-3733)**

American Zinc Enterprises, Walnut *Also Called: Sea Shield Marine Products* **(P-5768)**

Americantours Intl LLC (HQ) .... **C....... 310 641-9953**
6053 W Century Blvd Ste 700 Los Angeles (90045) **(P-11714)**

Americare Ambulance .... C....... 760 739-9723
10730 Thornmint Rd San Diego (92127) **(P-11374)**

AMERICARE AMBULANCE, San Diego *Also Called: Americare Ambulance* **(P-11374)**

Americare Hlth Retirement Inc .... C....... 760 744-4484
1550 Security Pl Ofc San Marcos (92078) **(P-14652)**

Americare Home Health Inc .... D....... 818 881-0005
16501 Sherman Way Ste 225 Van Nuys (91406) **(P-18590)**

Americas Finest Carpet Company, Chula Vista *Also Called: Home Carpet Investment Inc* **(P-1030)**

Americas Gold Inc .... E....... 213 688-4904
650 S Hill St Ste 224 Los Angeles (90014) **(P-10896)**

Americas Gold - Amrcas Damonds, Los Angeles *Also Called: Americas Gold Inc* **(P-10896)**

Americas Printer.com, Buena Park *Also Called: A J Parent Company Inc* **(P-16763)**

Americas Regional Division, San Diego *Also Called: Synergy Health Ast LLC* **(P-10612)**

Americas Styrenics LLC .... D....... 424 488-3757
305 Crenshaw Blvd Torrance (90503) **(P-3923)**

Americh Corporation (PA) .... **C....... 818 982-1711**
13222 Saticoy St North Hollywood (91605) **(P-10636)**

Americhip, Gardena *Also Called: Americhip Inc* **(P-3510)**

Americhip Inc (PA) .... **E....... 310 323-3697**
19032 S Vermont Ave Gardena (90248) **(P-3510)**

Americold Logistics LLC .... C....... 909 937-2200
5401 Santa Ana St Ontario (91761) **(P-11549)**

Americold Logistics LLC .... D....... 909 390-4950
700 Malaga St Ontario (91761) **(P-11550)**

Americold Realty, Ontario *Also Called: Americold Logistics LLC* **(P-11550)**

Americon .... F....... 805 987-0412
900 Flynn Rd Camarillo (93012) **(P-2877)**

Americor Funding Inc .... C....... 866 333-8686
18200 Von Karman Ave Ste 600 Irvine (92612) **(P-15498)**

Ameriflex Inc .... D....... 951 737-5557
2390 Railroad St Corona (92878) **(P-6837)**

Ameriflight LLC .... C....... 818 847-0000
4700 W Empire Ave Burbank (91505) **(P-11659)**

Amerihome Inc .... A....... 888 469-0810
1 Baxter Way Ste 300 Westlake Village (91362) **(P-14296)**

Amerihome Mortgage, Westlake Village *Also Called: Amerihome Mortgage Company LLC* **(P-14372)**

Amerihome Mortgage Company LLC .... A....... 888 469-0810
1 Baxter Way Ste 300 Westlake Village (91362) **(P-14372)**

Amerillum LLC .... D....... 760 727-7675
3728 Maritime Way Oceanside (92056) **(P-8353)**

Ameripark LLC .... B....... 949 279-7525
17165 Von Karman Ave Ste 110 Irvine (92614) **(P-16989)**

Ameripec Inc .... C....... 714 690-9191
6965 Aragon Cir Buena Park (90620) **(P-1683)**

Ameripharma, Orange *Also Called: Harpers Pharmacy Inc* **(P-4129)**

Ameripharma Specialty Phrm Div .... F....... 877 778-3773
132 S Anita Dr Orange (92868) **(P-4044)**

Ameripride Services Inc .... C....... 323 587-3941
5950 Alcoa Ave Vernon (90058) **(P-15448)**

AMERIPRIDE SERVICES, INC., Vernon *Also Called: Ameripride Services Inc* **(P-15448)**

Amerisourcebergen Drug Corp .... C....... 951 371-2000
1851 California Ave Corona (92881) **(P-13028)**

Amerit Fleet Solutions Inc .... A....... 909 357-0100
15325 Manila St Fontana (92337) **(P-17052)**

Ameritac Inc (PA) .... **D....... 925 989-2942**
24 Toscana Way W Rancho Mirage (92270) **(P-20288)**

Ameritex International, Los Angeles *Also Called: Amtex California Inc* **(P-2462)**

Ameritrans Express Inc .... F....... 818 201-0524
15130 Ventura Blvd # 313 Sherman Oaks (91403) **(P-11739)**

Ameron International Corp .... C....... 425 258-2616
1020 B St Fillmore (93015) **(P-5398)**

Ameron International Corp .... D....... 805 524-0223
1020 B St Fillmore (93015) **(P-5399)**

Ameron Protective Coatings, Fillmore *Also Called: Ameron International Corp* **(P-5398)**

Ames Construction Inc .... B....... 951 356-1275
391 N Main St Ste 302 Corona (92878) **(P-13938)**

Ames Industrial, Los Angeles *Also Called: Ames Rubber Mfg Co Inc* **(P-4756)**

Ames Rubber Mfg Co Inc .... E....... 818 240-9313
4516 Brazil St Los Angeles (90039) **(P-4756)**

Ametek Ameron LLC (HQ)..D...... 626 856-0101
4750 Littlejohn St Baldwin Park (91706) *(P-10116)*

Ametek HCC, Rosemead *Also Called: Hermetic Seal Corporation (P-9056)*

Ametek Intellipower, Orange *Also Called: Intellipower Inc (P-12670)*

Ametek Programmable Power, San Diego *Also Called: Ametek Programmable Power Inc (P-10183)*

Ametek Programmable Power Inc (HQ)................B...... 858 450-0085
9250 Brown Deer Rd San Diego (92121) *(P-10183)*

Ametek-Ameron, Baldwin Park *Also Called: Alphatech General Inc (P-17114)*

AMF Anaheim LLC ....C...... 714 363-9206
2100 E Orangewood Ave Anaheim (92806) *(P-6188)*

AMF Support Surfaces Inc (DH).........................C...... 951 549-6800
1691 N Delilah St Corona (92879) *(P-2843)*

Amflex Plastics Incorporated ....E...... 760 643-1756
4039 Calle Platino Ste G Oceanside (92056) *(P-4709)*

Amfoam Inc (PA)...E...... 310 327-4003
15110 S Broadway Gardena (90248) *(P-4872)*

AMG Employee Management Inc ....F...... 323 254-7448
1220 S Central Ave Ste 203 Glendale (91204) *(P-10891)*

AMG Torrance LLC (DH)...................................... E...... 310 515-2584
5401 Business Dr Huntington Beach (92649) *(P-9623)*

Amgen Inc ....C...... 805 447-1000
1840 De Havilland Dr Newbury Park (91320) *(P-4045)*

Amgen Inc (PA)..A...... 805 447-1000
1 Amgen Center Dr Thousand Oaks (91320) *(P-4298)*

Amgen Manufacturing Limited ....E...... 787 656-2000
1 Amgen Center Dr Newbury Park (91320) *(P-11189)*

Amgen USA Inc (HQ)...D...... 805 447-1000
1 Amgen Center Dr Thousand Oaks (91320) *(P-4046)*

Amgraph, Ontario *Also Called: American Fleet & Ret Graphics (P-11096)*

AMI, Costa Mesa *Also Called: Advanced Micro Instruments Inc (P-10349)*

Amiad Filtration Systems, Oxnard *Also Called: Amiad USA Inc (P-7637)*

Amiad USA Inc ....E...... 805 988-3323
1251 Maulhardt Ave Oxnard (93030) *(P-7636)*

Amiad USA Inc ....E...... 805 988-3323
1251 Maulhardt Ave Oxnard (93030) *(P-7637)*

Amico Fontana, Fontana *Also Called: Alabama Metal Industries Corp (P-6350)*

Amigo Baby Inc ....D...... 805 901-1237
1901 N Rice Ave Ste 325 Oxnard (93030) *(P-19023)*

Aminco International USA Inc ....D...... 949 457-3261
20571 Crescent Bay Dr Lake Forest (92630) *(P-10897)*

Amiri, Los Angeles *Also Called: Atelier Luxury Group LLC (P-2527)*

Amisub, Tarzana *Also Called: Amisub of California Inc (P-18178)*

Amisub of California Inc (DH).............................A...... 818 881-0800
18321 Clark St Tarzana (91356) *(P-18178)*

Amity Foundation, Los Angeles *Also Called: Epidaurus (P-14990)*

Amk Foodservices Inc ....C...... 805 544-7600
830 Capitolio Way San Luis Obispo (93401) *(P-13171)*

Amkom Design Group Inc ....E...... 760 295-1957
2598 Fortune Way Ste J Vista (92081) *(P-16777)*

Amn Healthcare Inc (HQ)...B...... 858 792-0711
12400 High Bluff Dr Ste 100 San Diego (92130) *(P-17592)*

Amn Healthcare Inc ....D...... 800 282-0300
12235 El Camino Real Ste 200 San Diego (92130) *(P-15812)*

Amnet Esop Corporation ....C...... 877 354-1110
347 Third Ave Fl 2 Chula Vista (91910) *(P-14297)*

Amnet Mortgage LLC ....A...... 858 909-1200
10421 Wateridge Cir Ste 250 San Diego (92121) *(P-14298)*

AMO Usa Inc ....C...... 714 247-8200
1700 E Saint Andrew Pl Santa Ana (92705) *(P-10429)*

Amonix Inc ....C...... 562 344-4750
1709 Apollo Ct Seal Beach (90740) *(P-8765)*

Amoretti, Oxnard *Also Called: Noushig Inc (P-1486)*

Amoseastern Apparel Inc ....E...... 323 909-1010
2684 Lacy St Apt 307 Los Angeles (90031) *(P-2526)*

AMP, Santa Ana *Also Called: Accelerated Memory Prod Inc (P-8756)*

AMP Display Inc ....E...... 909 980-1310
9856 6th St Rancho Cucamonga (91730) *(P-19547)*

AMP Plus Inc ....D...... 323 231-2600
2042 E Vernon Ave Vernon (90058) *(P-8344)*

AMP Research, Tustin *Also Called: 89908 Inc (P-9338)*

AMP Research, Brea *Also Called: Lund Motion Products Inc (P-9417)*

Ampac Usa Inc ....E...... 435 291-0961
5255 State St 5275 Montclair (91763) *(P-7638)*

Ampam Parks Mechanical Inc ....A...... 310 835-1532
17036 Avalon Blvd Carson (90746) *(P-731)*

Ampco Airport Parking, Los Angeles *Also Called: ABM Parking Services Inc (P-16987)*

Ampco Contracting Inc ....C...... 949 955-2255
17991 Cowan Irvine (92614) *(P-12207)*

Amphastar, Rancho Cucamonga *Also Called: Amphastar Pharmaceuticals Inc (P-4047)*

Amphastar Pharmaceuticals, Chino *Also Called: Amphastar Pharmaceuticals Inc (P-4048)*

Amphastar Pharmaceuticals Inc (PA)............C...... 909 980-9484
11570 6th St Rancho Cucamonga (91730) *(P-4047)*

Amphastar Pharmaceuticals Inc ....E...... 909 590-1828
13760 Magnolia Ave Chino (91710) *(P-4048)*

Amphion, Rancho Cucamonga *Also Called: Executive Safe and SEC Corp (P-6863)*

Amplifier Technologies Inc (HQ)...........................E...... 323 278-0001
7133 Telegraph Rd Montebello (90640) *(P-8494)*

AMpm Maintenance Corporation ....E...... 424 230-1300
1010 E 14th St Los Angeles (90021) *(P-2136)*

Ampronix LLC ....D...... 949 273-8000
15 Whatney Irvine (92618) *(P-10789)*

Amrapur Overseas Incorporated (PA)................E...... 714 893-8808
1560 E 6th St Ste 101 Corona (92879) *(P-2137)*

Amrel, Pasadena *Also Called: American Reliance Inc (P-7417)*

Amrep Inc ....B...... 770 422-2071
1555 S Cucamonga Ave Ontario (91761) *(P-4342)*

Amrep Manufacturing Co LLC ....B...... 877 468-9278
1555 S Cucamonga Ave Ontario (91761) *(P-7221)*

Amrex Electrotherapy Equipment, Paramount *Also Called: Amrex-Zetron Inc (P-9195)*

Amrex-Zetron Inc ....F...... 310 527-6868
7034 Jackson St Paramount (90723) *(P-9195)*

Amro Fabricating Corporation (PA).....................C...... 626 579-2200
1430 Amro Way South El Monte (91733) *(P-9624)*

Amron, Vista *Also Called: Amron International Inc (P-10974)*

Amron International Inc (PA)....................................D...... 760 208-6500
1380 Aspen Way Vista (92081) *(P-10974)*

AMS ....E...... 714 376-2464
102 E Pico Blvd Los Angeles (90015) *(P-16165)*

AMS, Anaheim *Also Called: Walnut Investment Corp (P-12344)*

AMS American Mech Svcs MD Inc ....C...... 714 888-6820
2116 E Walnut Ave Fullerton (92831) *(P-732)*

AMS Fulfillment, Valencia *Also Called: Advantage Media Services Inc (P-11562)*

AMS Plastics Inc (HQ)...D...... 619 713-2000
20109 Paseo Del Prado Walnut (91789) *(P-4940)*

Amsafe Bridport, Buena Park *Also Called: Bridport-Air Carrier Inc (P-2499)*

Amsafe Bridport, Buena Park *Also Called: Bridport Erie Aviation Inc (P-17117)*

Amscan Inc ....E...... 714 972-2626
804 W Town & Country Rd Orange (92868) *(P-3141)*

Amsco US Inc ....C...... 562 630-0333
15341 Texaco Ave Paramount (90723) *(P-8996)*

Amscope, Irvine *Also Called: United Scope LLC (P-10345)*

Amsec, Fontana *Also Called: American Security Products Co (P-6855)*

Amsurg, Colton *Also Called: Premier Otptent Srgery Ctr Inc (P-17739)*

Amt Datasouth Corp (PA)...E...... 805 388-5799
3222 Corte Malpaso Camarillo (93012) *(P-19819)*

Amtech Elevator Services, Los Angeles *Also Called: Pacific Coast Elevator Corp (P-17143)*

Amtek, Poway *Also Called: United Security Products Inc (P-9266)*

Amtex California Inc ....E...... 323 859-2200
113 S Utah St Los Angeles (90033) *(P-2462)*

Amtex Supply Holdings Inc ....C...... 909 985-8918
736 Inland Center Dr San Bernardino (92408) *(P-20131)*

Amtrend Corporation ....D...... 714 630-2070
1458 Manhattan Ave Fullerton (92831) *(P-2942)*

Amtv USA, Pasadena *Also Called: American Multimedia TV USA (P-11938)*

Amvac Chemical Corporation (HQ).......................E...... 323 264-3910
4695 Macarthur Ct Ste 1200 Newport Beach (92660) *(P-4546)*

Amwear USA Inc ....E...... 800 858-6755
250 Benjamin Dr Corona (92879) *(P-2148)*

Employee Codes: A=Over 500 employees, B=251-500
C=101-250, D=51-100, E=20-50, F=10-19, G=1-9

2024 Southern California
Business Directory and Buyers Guide

© Mergent Inc. 1-800-342-5647
993

A
L
P
H
A
B
E
T
I
C

Amwest Funding Corp ....C....... 714 831-3333
6 Pointe Dr Ste 300 Brea (92821) *(P-14279)*

Amylin Ohio LLC ....A....... 858 552-2200
9360 Towne Centre Dr San Diego (92121) *(P-4049)*

An Open Check, Costa Mesa *Also Called: North American Acceptance Corp* *(P-14276)*

Ana Global LLC (PA)..D....... 619 482-9990
2360 Marconi Ct San Diego (92154) *(P-2865)*

Ana Nacapa Surgical Associates, Ventura *Also Called: Ventura County Medical Center* *(P-17826)*

Anabella Hotel The, Anaheim *Also Called: Fjs Inc (P-15153)*

Anabolic Incorporated ....E....... 949 863-0340
17802 Gillette Ave Irvine (92614) *(P-4050)*

Anacapa Boatyard, Newport Beach *Also Called: Anacapa Marine Services (P-9854)*

Anacapa Marine Services (PA) ....F....... 805 985-1818
151 Shipyard Way Ste 5 Newport Beach (92663) *(P-9854)*

Anaco Inc ....C....... 951 372-2732
311 Corporate Terrace Cir Corona (92879) *(P-7375)*

Anacom General Corporation ....E....... 714 774-8484
1240 S Claudina St Anaheim (92805) *(P-8393)*

Anacom Medtek, Anaheim *Also Called: Anacom General Corporation (P-8393)*

Anadite Cal Restoration Tr ....C....... 562 861-2205
10647 Garfield Ave South Gate (90280) *(P-6582)*

Anaergia Services LLC ....E....... 760 436-8870
705 Palomar Airport Rd Ste 200 Carlsbad (92011) *(P-705)*

Anaheim - 1855 S Hbr Blvd Owne ....D....... 714 750-1811
1855 S Harbor Blvd Anaheim (92802) *(P-15074)*

Anaheim Arena Management LLC ....A....... 714 704-2400
2695 E Katella Ave Anaheim (92806) *(P-17361)*

Anaheim Automation Inc ....D....... 714 992-6990
4985 E Landon Dr Anaheim (92807) *(P-8168)*

Anaheim Custom Extruders Inc ....E....... 714 693-8508
1360 N Mccan St Anaheim (92806) *(P-4941)*

Anaheim Ducks Hockey Club LLC (PA)...............D....... 714 940-2900
2695 E Katella Ave Anaheim (92806) *(P-17362)*

Anaheim Extrusion Co Inc ....D....... 714 630-3111
1330 N Kraemer Blvd Anaheim (92806) *(P-5693)*

Anaheim Global Medical Center ....A....... 714 533-6220
1025 S Anaheim Blvd Anaheim (92805) *(P-18179)*

Anaheim Hotel, The, Anaheim *Also Called: Anaheim Plaza Hotel Inc (P-15076)*

Anaheim Inn, Anaheim *Also Called: Best Western Stovalls Inn (P-15092)*

Anaheim Majestic Garden Hotel, Anaheim *Also Called: Ken Real Estate Lease Ltd (P-15208)*

Anaheim Park Hotel ....C....... 714 992-1700
222 W Houston Ave Fullerton (92832) *(P-15075)*

Anaheim Plant, Anaheim *Also Called: Stepan Company (P-3975)*

Anaheim Plaza Hotel Inc ....D....... 714 772-5900
1700 S Harbor Blvd Anaheim (92802) *(P-15076)*

Anaheim Precision Mfg, Orange *Also Called: APM Manufacturing (P-9626)*

Anaheim Regional Medical Ctr ....C....... 714 774-1450
1111 W La Palma Ave Anaheim (92801) *(P-18180)*

Anaheim Regional Medical Ctr ....C....... 714 999-3847
1211 W La Palma Ave Anaheim (92801) *(P-18181)*

Anaheim Regional Medical Ctr, Anaheim *Also Called: Ahmc Anheim Rgional Med Ctr LP* *(P-18167)*

Anaheim Wire Products Inc ....E....... 714 563-8300
1009 E Vermont Ave Anaheim (92805) *(P-6811)*

Anajet LLC ....E....... 714 662-3200
1100 Valencia Ave Tustin (92780) *(P-7182)*

Analog, La Verne *Also Called: Micro Analog Inc (P-8838)*

Analysts Inc ....C....... 800 424-0099
3401 Jack Northrop Ave Hawthorne (90250) *(P-19957)*

Analysts Maintenance and Labs, Hawthorne *Also Called: Analysts Inc (P-19957)*

Analytic Endodontics, Orange *Also Called: Sybron Dental Specialties Inc (P-10772)*

Analytical Industries Inc ....E....... 909 392-6900
2855 Metropolitan Pl Pomona (91767) *(P-10117)*

Analytical Pace Services LLC ....C....... 800 878-4911
4100 Atlas Ct Bakersfield (93308) *(P-19958)*

Analytik Jena US LLC ....F....... 781 376-9899
2066 W 11th St Upland (91786) *(P-10233)*

Anamex Corporation (PA).....................................E....... 714 779-7055
250 S Peralta Way Anaheim (92807) *(P-15963)*

Anaplex Corporation ....E....... 714 522-4481
15547 Garfield Ave Paramount (90723) *(P-6583)*

Anaptysbio, San Diego *Also Called: Anaptysbio Inc (P-4051)*

Anaptysbio Inc (PA) ....D....... 858 362-6295
10770 Wateridge Cir Ste 210 San Diego (92121) *(P-4051)*

Anatase Products, Tehachapi *Also Called: Henway Inc (P-11070)*

Anatesco Inc ....F....... 661 399-6990
128 Bedford Way Bakersfield (93308) *(P-327)*

Anatex, Van Nuys *Also Called: Anatex Enterprises Inc (P-12933)*

Anatex Enterprises Inc ....E....... 818 908-1888
15911 Arminta St Van Nuys (91406) *(P-12933)*

Anatomic Global Inc ....C....... 800 874-7237
1241 Old Temescal Rd # 103 Corona (92881) *(P-2465)*

Anaya Brothers Cutting LLC ....D....... 323 582-5758
3130 Leonis Blvd Vernon (90058) *(P-2440)*

Anc Technology Inc ....D....... 805 530-3958
10195 Stockton Rd Moorpark (93021) *(P-8647)*

Ancca Corporation ....D....... 949 553-0084
7 Goddard Irvine (92618) *(P-967)*

Anchen Pharmaceuticals Inc ....C....... 949 639-8100
5 Goodyear Irvine (92618) *(P-4052)*

Anchor Audio Inc ....D....... 760 827-7100
5931 Darwin Ct Carlsbad (92008) *(P-8394)*

Anchor Blue, Corona *Also Called: Hub Distributing Inc (P-13909)*

Anchor General Insur Agcy Inc ....C....... 858 527-3600
10256 Meanley Dr San Diego (92131) *(P-14559)*

Anchor Loans LP ....C....... 310 395-0010
1 Baxter Way # 220 Westlake Village (91362) *(P-14299)*

Anchor Nationwide Loans, Westlake Village *Also Called: Anchor Loans LP (P-14299)*

Anchored Prints ....E....... 714 929-9317
1199 N Grove St Anaheim (92806) *(P-3511)*

Anco, San Bernardino *Also Called: Anco International Inc (P-6787)*

Anco International Inc ....E....... 909 887-2521
19851 Cajon Blvd San Bernardino (92407) *(P-6787)*

Ancon Marine LLC ....C....... 562 326-5900
2735 Rose Ave Signal Hill (90755) *(P-11441)*

Ancon Services, Signal Hill *Also Called: Ancon Marine LLC (P-11441)*

Ancora Software Inc (PA) ....E....... 888 476-4839
402 W Broadway Ste 400 San Diego (92101) *(P-16166)*

Ancra International LLC ....C....... 626 765-4818
601 S Vincent Ave Azusa (91702) *(P-6984)*

Ancra International LLC (HQ) ....C....... 626 765-4800
601 S Vincent Ave Azusa (91702) *(P-6985)*

and 1, Aliso Viejo *Also Called: Basketball Marketing Co Inc (P-20139)*

Andanov Music, Burbank *Also Called: Hollywood Records Inc (P-8461)*

Andari, El Monte *Also Called: Andari Fashion Inc (P-2192)*

Andari Fashion Inc ....C....... 626 575-2759
9626 Telstar Ave El Monte (91731) *(P-2192)*

Andaz Sandiego, San Diego *Also Called: Hyatt Corporation (P-15195)*

Andaz West Hollywood ....D....... 323 656-1234
8401 W Sunset Blvd Los Angeles (90069) *(P-15077)*

Anderco Inc ....E....... 714 446-9508
540 Airpark Dr Fullerton (92833) *(P-2583)*

Andersen Commercial Plbg Inc ....C....... 909 599-5950
1608 Yeager Ave La Verne (91750) *(P-733)*

Andersen Industries Inc ....E....... 760 246-8766
17079 Muskrat Ave Adelanto (92301) *(P-9489)*

Andersen Tax LLC ....C....... 213 593-2300
400 S Hope St Ste 2000 Los Angeles (90071) *(P-15493)*

Anderson, Poway *Also Called: T G T Enterprises Inc (P-20253)*

Anderson & Howard Electric Inc ....C....... 949 250-4555
15 Chrysler Irvine (92618) *(P-867)*

Anderson Assoc Staffing Corp (PA) ....C....... 323 930-3170
8200 Wilshire Blvd Ste 200 Beverly Hills (90211) *(P-15913)*

Anderson Burton Cnstr Inc (PA) ....D....... 805 481-5096
121 Nevada St Arroyo Grande (93420) *(P-529)*

Anderson Chrnesky Strl Stl Inc ....D....... 951 769-5700
353 Risco Cir Beaumont (92223) *(P-5992)*

Anderson Howard, Irvine *Also Called: Anderson & Howard Electric Inc (P-867)*

Anderson Kayne Capital ....B....... 800 231-7414
1800 Avenue Of The Stars Ste 200 # 3rd Los Angeles (90067) *(P-14415)*

Mergent email: customerrelations@mergent.com
994

2024 Southern California
Business Directory and Buyers Guide

(P-0000) Products & Services Section entry number
(PA)=Parent Co (HQ)=Headquarters (DH)=Div Headquarters

Anderson La Inc .... D...... 323 460-4115
3550 Tyburn St Los Angeles (90065) *(P-3512)*

Anderson Plbg Htg A Condition, El Cajon *Also Called: Walter Anderson Plumbing Inc (P-833)*

Anderson Printing, Los Angeles *Also Called: Anderson La Inc (P-3512)*

Anderson Trophy Company, North Hollywood *Also Called: Pnk Enterprises Inc (P-14145)*

Andrew Alexander Inc .... D...... 323 752-0066
1306 S Alameda St Compton (90221) *(P-5254)*

Andrew L Youngquist Cnstr Inc .... D...... 949 862-5611
3187 Red Hill Ave Ste 200 Costa Mesa (92626) *(P-530)*

Andrew Lauren Company Inc .... C...... 949 861-4222
15225 Alton Pkwy Unit 300 Irvine (92618) *(P-16778)*

Andrew LLC .... F...... 909 270-9356
17058 Lagos Dr Chino Hills (91709) *(P-1406)*

Andrews International Inc (DH)............................ A...... 818 487-4060
455 N Moss St Burbank (91502) *(P-16620)*

Andrews International Inc .... B...... 310 575-4844
11601 Wilshire Blvd Ste 500 Los Angeles (90025) *(P-16621)*

Androp Packaging Inc .... E...... 909 605-8842
4400 E Francis St Ontario (91761) *(P-3079)*

Anduril Industries Inc .... E...... 949 891-1607
2910 S Tech Center Dr Santa Ana (92705) *(P-9942)*

Anduril Industries Inc (PA)................................... E...... 949 891-1607
1400 Anduril Costa Mesa (92626) *(P-9943)*

Andwin Corporation (PA)....................................... D...... 818 999-2828
167 W Cochran St Simi Valley (93065) *(P-13003)*

Andwin Scientific, Simi Valley *Also Called: Andwin Corporation (P-13003)*

Andy Anand Chocolates, Chino *Also Called: Hira Paris Inc (P-1542)*

Anemostat Products, Carson *Also Called: Mestek Inc (P-7619)*

Anesthsia Med Group Snta Brbar .... D...... 805 682-7751
514 W Pueblo St Fl 2 Santa Barbara (93105) *(P-17593)*

Anesthsia Med Group Snta Brbar, Santa Barbara *Also Called: Anesthsia Med Group Snta Brbar (P-17593)*

Angel City Public Hse & Brewry .... E...... 562 983-6880
216 S Alameda St Los Angeles (90012) *(P-1576)*

Angeles Mesa YWCA Chldren Lrng, Los Angeles *Also Called: Young Wns Chrstn Assn Grter Lo (P-19497)*

Angell & Giroux Inc .... D...... 323 269-8596
2727 Alcazar St Los Angeles (90033) *(P-2903)*

Angels Baseball LP (PA).. A...... 714 940-2000
2000 E Gene Autry Way Anaheim (92806) *(P-17363)*

Angelus Block Co Inc (PA)..................................... E...... 714 637-8594
11374 Tuxford St Sun Valley (91352) *(P-5388)*

Angelus Machine Corp Intl .... D...... 323 583-2171
4900 Pacific Blvd Vernon (90058) *(P-7031)*

Anheuser-Busch, Pomona *Also Called: Anheuser-Busch LLC (P-1577)*

Anheuser-Busch, Santa Fe Springs *Also Called: Anheuser-Busch LLC (P-1578)*

Anheuser-Busch, Carson *Also Called: Anheuser-Busch LLC (P-1579)*

Anheuser-Busch, San Diego *Also Called: Anheuser-Busch LLC (P-1580)*

Anheuser-Busch, Van Nuys *Also Called: Anheuser-Busch LLC (P-16779)*

Anheuser-Busch LLC .... C...... 951 782-3935
2800 S Reservoir St Pomona (91766) *(P-1577)*

Anheuser-Busch LLC .... E...... 562 699-3424
12065 Pike St Santa Fe Springs (90670) *(P-1578)*

Anheuser-Busch LLC .... E...... 310 761-4600
20499 S Reeves Ave Carson (90810) *(P-1579)*

Anheuser-Busch LLC .... D...... 858 581-7000
5959 Santa Fe St San Diego (92109) *(P-1580)*

Anheuser-Busch LLC .... B...... 805 381-4700
15800 Roscoe Blvd Van Nuys (91406) *(P-16779)*

Aniise Skin Care, Los Angeles *Also Called: Global Sales Inc (P-4415)*

Anillo Industries, Orange *Also Called: Anillo Industries Inc (P-6431)*

Anillo Industries, Orange *Also Called: Hightower Plating & Mfg Co (P-6626)*

Anillo Industries Inc (PA)..................................... E...... 714 637-7000
2090 N Glassell St Orange (92865) *(P-6431)*

Anitas Mexican Foods Corp .... E...... 909 884-8706
3392 N Mike Daley Dr San Bernardino (92407) *(P-1823)*

Anitas Mexican Foods Corp (PA)........................... D...... 909 884-8706
3454 N Mike Daley Dr San Bernardino (92407) *(P-1824)*

Anitsa Inc .... C...... 213 237-0533
6032 Shull St Bell Gardens (90201) *(P-15444)*

Anjolee, San Diego *Also Called: Sunrise Jewelry Mfg Corp (P-10912)*

Ankura Consulting Group LLC .... C...... 213 223-2109
633 W 5th St Fl 28 Los Angeles (90071) *(P-20314)*

Anmar Precision Components Inc .... E...... 818 764-0901
7424 Greenbush Ave North Hollywood (91605) *(P-9625)*

Annandale Golf Club .... C...... 626 796-6125
1 N San Rafael Ave Pasadena (91105) *(P-17461)*

Annapurna Pictures LLC .... D...... 310 385-7701
817 Hilldale Ave West Hollywood (90069) *(P-17244)*

Annas Linens, Costa Mesa *Also Called: Annas Linens Inc (P-13956)*

Annas Linens Inc .... A...... 714 850-0504
3550 Hyland Ave Costa Mesa (92626) *(P-13956)*

Annex Pro Inc .... E...... 800 682-6639
4100 W Alameda Ave Fl 3 Burbank (91505) *(P-16167)*

Annie Golf Club, Goleta *Also Called: Glen Annie Golf Club (P-17428)*

Anns Trading Company Inc .... E...... 323 585-4702
5333 S Downey Rd Vernon (90058) *(P-13527)*

Anodizing Industries Inc .... E...... 323 227-4916
5222 Alhambra Ave Los Angeles (90032) *(P-6584)*

Anodyne Inc .... E...... 714 549-3321
2230 S Susan St Santa Ana (92704) *(P-6585)*

Anokiwave Inc (PA).. E...... 858 792-9910
5355 Mira Sorrento Pl Ste 300 San Diego (92121) *(P-8766)*

Anoroc, Compton *Also Called: Anoroc Precision Shtmtl Inc (P-6189)*

Anoroc Precision Shtmtl Inc .... E...... 310 515-6015
19122 S Santa Fe Ave Compton (90221) *(P-6189)*

Anovia Payments LLC .... D...... 469 621-0166
1 Macarthur Pl Santa Ana (92707) *(P-16780)*

Anp Lighting, Montclair *Also Called: American Nail Plate Ltg Inc (P-8286)*

Anre Tech, Altadena *Also Called: Anre Technologies Inc (P-15964)*

Anre Technologies Inc .... C...... 818 627-5433
741 W Woodbury Rd Altadena (91001) *(P-15964)*

Ansar Gallery Inc .... C...... 949 220-0000
2505 El Camino Rd Tustin (92782) *(P-13172)*

Anschutz Entrmt Group Inc (HQ)......................... C...... 213 763-7700
800 W Olympic Blvd Ste 305 Los Angeles (90015) *(P-17335)*

Anschutz Film Group LLC (HQ).............................. E...... 310 887-1000
10201 W Pico Blvd # 52 Los Angeles (90064) *(P-10858)*

Anschutz Sthern Cal Spt Cmplex .... C...... 310 630-2000
18400 Avalon Blvd Ste 100 Carson (90746) *(P-17540)*

Ansell Sndel Med Solutions LLC .... E...... 818 534-2500
9301 Oakdale Ave Ste 300 Chatsworth (91311) *(P-10637)*

Ansun, San Diego *Also Called: Ansun Biopharma Inc (P-19820)*

Ansun Biopharma Inc .... E...... 858 452-2631
10045 Mesa Rim Rd San Diego (92121) *(P-19820)*

Answer Financial Inc (HQ).................................... C...... 818 644-4000
15910 Ventura Blvd Fl 6 Encino (91436) *(P-16781)*

Antaeus Fashions Group Inc .... F...... 626 452-0797
2400 Chico Ave South El Monte (91733) *(P-2193)*

Antaky Quilting Company, Los Angeles *Also Called: American Quilting Company Inc (P-2513)*

Antcom, Torrance *Also Called: Antcom Corporation (P-8495)*

Antcom Corporation .... E...... 310 782-1076
367 Van Ness Way Ste 602 Torrance (90501) *(P-8495)*

Antelope Valley Health Care Di (PA).................... A...... 661 949-5000
1600 W Avenue J Lancaster (93534) *(P-18182)*

Antelope Valley Hlth Care Dst, Lancaster *Also Called: Antelope Valley Hospital Inc (P-18183)*

Antelope Valley Home Care, Lancaster *Also Called: Antelope Valley Hospital Inc (P-18185)*

Antelope Valley Hospital Inc .... B...... 661 726-6180
1600 W Avenue J Lancaster (93534) *(P-17594)*

Antelope Valley Hospital Inc .... C...... 661 949-5000
44335 Lowtree Ave Lancaster (93534) *(P-18183)*

Antelope Valley Hospital Inc .... C...... 661 726-6050
44105 15th St W Ste 100 Lancaster (93534) *(P-18184)*

Antelope Valley Hospital Inc .... C...... 661 949-5936
44335 Lowtree Ave Lancaster (93534) *(P-18185)*

Antelope Valley Lincoln, Lancaster *Also Called: Johnson Ford (P-13785)*

Antelope Valley Newspapers Inc .... E...... 661 940-1000
44939 10th St W Lancaster (93534) *(P-3255)*

Antelope Valley Press, Lancaster *Also Called: Antelope Valley Newspapers Inc (P-3255)*

Antelope Vly Cntry CLB Imprv .... C...... 661 947-3142
39800 Country Club Dr Palmdale (93551) *(P-17462)*

Employee Codes: A=Over 500 employees, B=251-500
C=101-250, D=51-100, E=20-50, F=10-19, G=1-9

2024 Southern California
Business Directory and Buyers Guide

© Mergent Inc. 1-800-342-5647

995

A
L
P
H
A
B
E
T
I
C

Antelope Vly Convalecent Hosp, Lancaster *Also Called: Antelope Vly Retirement HM Inc* *(P-18107)*

Antelope Vly Retirement HM Inc ....C...... 661 949-5584
   44523 15th St W Lancaster (93534) *(P-17881)*

Antelope Vly Retirement HM Inc ....C...... 661 949-5524
   44567 15th St W Lancaster (93534) *(P-18106)*

Antelope Vly Retirement HM Inc ....C...... 661 948-7501
   44445 15th St W Lancaster (93534) *(P-18107)*

Antelope Vly Retirement Manor, Lancaster *Also Called: Antelope Vly Retirement HM Inc* *(P-17881)*

Antelope Vly Schl Trnsp Agcy ....C...... 661 952-3106
   670 W Avenue L8 Lancaster (93534) *(P-11419)*

Antenna Audio Inc (PA)...A...... 203 523-0320
   555 W 5th St Ste 3725 Los Angeles (90013) *(P-11727)*

Antenna International, Los Angeles *Also Called: Antenna Audio Inc (P-11727)*

Antenna Works, Long Beach *Also Called: Metra Electronics Corporation (P-9423)*

Antex Knitting Mills, Los Angeles *Also Called: Tenenblatt Corporation (P-2080)*

Antex Knitting Mills, Los Angeles *Also Called: Matchmaster Dyg & Finshg Inc (P-2103)*

Antex Knitting Mills, Los Angeles *Also Called: Guru Knits Inc (P-2242)*

Anthony Inc ....E...... 818 365-9451
   12812 Arroyo St Sylmar (91342) *(P-5333)*

Anthony Inc (DH)..A...... 818 365-9451
   12391 Montero Ave Sylmar (91342) *(P-7599)*

Anthony California Inc (PA)..E...... 909 627-0351
   14485 Monte Vista Ave Chino (91710) *(P-8287)*

Anthony International, Sylmar *Also Called: Anthony Inc (P-5333)*

Anthony International, Sylmar *Also Called: Anthony Inc (P-7599)*

Anthony Vineyards Inc ....D...... 760 391-5488
   52301 Enterprise Way Coachella (92236) *(P-27)*

Anthony Welded Products Inc (PA)...E...... 661 721-7211
   1447 S Lexington St Delano (93215) *(P-6986)*

Anthos Group Inc ....E...... 888 778-2986
   705 N Douglas St El Segundo (90245) *(P-20132)*

Antigen Discovery, Irvine *Also Called: Immport Therapeutics Inc (P-10783)*

Antique Apparatus Company, Torrance *Also Called: Rock-Ola Manufacturing Corp (P-8431)*

Antis Roofg Waterproofing LLC ....D...... 949 461-9222
   2649 Campus Dr Irvine (92612) *(P-1142)*

Antis Roofing, Irvine *Also Called: Antis Roofg Waterproofing LLC (P-1142)*

Anura Plastic Engineerign ....E...... 626 814-9684
   5050 Rivergrade Rd Baldwin Park (91706) *(P-4942)*

Anvil Cases Inc ....C...... 626 968-4100
   1242 E Edna Pl Unit B Covina (91724) *(P-5284)*

Anvil Iron, Gardena *Also Called: Anvil Steel Corporation (P-1099)*

Anvil Steel Corporation ....D...... 310 329-5811
   134 W 168th St Gardena (90248) *(P-1099)*

Anwright Corporation ....E...... 818 896-2465
   10225 Glenoaks Blvd Pacoima (91331) *(P-6410)*

Anydata Corporation ....D...... 949 900-6040
   5405 Alton Pkwy Irvine (92604) *(P-8496)*

Anzo USA, Chino *Also Called: C G Motor Sports Inc (P-4973)*

Ao, Orange *Also Called: Architects Orange Inc (P-19723)*

Aoc LLC ....D...... 951 657-5161
   19991 Seaton Ave Perris (92570) *(P-2124)*

AOC California Plant, Perris *Also Called: Aoc LLC (P-2124)*

AOC USA, Pico Rivera *Also Called: Lubricating Specialties Company (P-4687)*

Aoclsc Inc ....C...... 813 248-1988
   8015 Paramount Blvd Pico Rivera (90660) *(P-4677)*

Aoclsc Inc ....E...... 562 776-4000
   3365 E Slauson Ave Vernon (90058) *(P-4678)*

Aocusa, Pico Rivera *Also Called: Aoclsc Inc (P-4677)*

Aocusa, Vernon *Also Called: Aoclsc Inc (P-4678)*

AOE International Inc ....E
   20611 Belshaw Ave Carson (90746) *(P-4053)*

Aos, Torrance *Also Called: Finest Hour Holdings Inc (P-10660)*

AP Parpro Inc ....E...... 619 498-9004
   2700 S Fairview St Santa Ana (92704) *(P-8169)*

AP Precision Metals Inc ....E...... 619 628-0003
   1215 30th St San Diego (92154) *(P-6190)*

Apct Anaheim, Orange *Also Called: Cirtech Inc (P-16802)*

Apct Orange County, Placentia *Also Called: Cartel Electronics LLC (P-8657)*

Apeel Sciences, Goleta *Also Called: Apeel Technology Inc (P-98)*

Apeel Technology Inc (PA)..B...... 805 203-0146
   71 S Los Carneros Rd Goleta (93117) *(P-98)*

Apeiro Technologies, Irvine *Also Called: It Division Inc (P-19000)*

Apem Inc (HQ)...E...... 978 372-1602
   970 Park Center Dr Vista (92081) *(P-7506)*

Apem Inc ....D...... 760 598-2518
   970 Park Center Dr Vista (92081) *(P-8997)*

Aperio, Vista *Also Called: Leica Biosystems Imaging Inc (P-10269)*

Aperto Property Management Inc ....B...... 626 965-1961
   17351 Main St La Puente (91744) *(P-14703)*

Apex Bulk Commodities, Adelanto *Also Called: Apex Bulk Commodities Inc (P-11442)*

Apex Bulk Commodities Inc (PA)..C...... 760 246-6077
   12531 Violet Rd Ste A Adelanto (92301) *(P-11442)*

Apex Container Services, Commerce *Also Called: Apex Drum Company Inc (P-2730)*

Apex Conveyor Corp ....F...... 951 304-7808
   40001 Via Caseta Murrieta (92562) *(P-6970)*

Apex Design Tech., Corona *Also Called: Btl Machine (P-7790)*

Apex Design Technology, Anaheim *Also Called: Apex Technology Holdings Inc (P-9944)*

Apex Drum Company Inc ....F...... 323 721-8994
   6226 Ferguson Dr Commerce (90022) *(P-2730)*

Apex Logistics Intl Inc (PA)..C...... 310 665-0288
   18554 S Susana Rd Compton (90221) *(P-11740)*

Apex Medical Technologies Inc ....E...... 858 535-0012
   10064 Mesa Ridge Ct Ste 202 San Diego (92121) *(P-10430)*

Apex Precision Technologies Inc ....E...... 317 821-1000
   23622 Calabasas Rd Ste 323 Calabasas (91302) *(P-9353)*

Apex Technology Holdings Inc ....A...... 321 270-3630
   2850 E Coronado St Anaheim (92806) *(P-9944)*

Apex USA, Compton *Also Called: Apex Logistics Intl Inc (P-11740)*

Apffels Coffee, Santa Fe Springs *Also Called: Apffels Coffee Inc (P-1814)*

Apffels Coffee Inc ....D...... 562 309-0400
   12115 Pacific St Santa Fe Springs (90670) *(P-1814)*

Apg, Panorama City *Also Called: American Protection Group Inc (P-16618)*

Apheresis Care Group Inc ....D...... 619 440-4612
   570 N 2nd St El Cajon (92021) *(P-18656)*

API Kirk Containers ....E...... 323 278-5400
   2131 Garfield Ave Commerce (90040) *(P-4943)*

Apic Corporation ....D...... 310 642-7975
   5800 Uplander Way Culver City (90230) *(P-8767)*

Apical Industries Inc ....D...... 760 724-5300
   3030 Enterprise Ct Ste A Vista (92081) *(P-12902)*

APM Manufacturing ....C...... 714 453-0100
   341 W Blueridge Ave Orange (92865) *(P-9510)*

APM Manufacturing (HQ)...E...... 714 453-0100
   1738 N Neville St Orange (92865) *(P-9626)*

APM Terminals Pacific LLC ....B...... 310 221-4000
   2500 Navy Way Pier 400 San Pedro (90731) *(P-11741)*

APn Business Resources Inc ....D...... 818 717-9980
   21418 Osborne St Canoga Park (91304) *(P-20133)*

Apogee Electronics, Santa Monica *Also Called: Apogee Electronics Corporation (P-8395)*

Apogee Electronics Corporation ....E...... 310 584-9394
   1715 Berkeley St Santa Monica (90404) *(P-8395)*

Apollo Printing & Graphics, Anaheim *Also Called: Tajen Graphics Inc (P-3693)*

Apollo.io, Covina *Also Called: Zenleads Inc (P-20279)*

Apon Industries Corp C
   10005 Marconi Dr Ste 2 San Diego (92154) *(P-4944)*

Apon Medical Molding and Assembly Inc ....D...... 619 793-4887
   10005 Marconi Dr Ste B San Diego (92154) *(P-4757)*

Apotheka Systems Inc ....E...... 844 777-4455
   14040 Panay Way Marina Del Rey (90292) *(P-16168)*

App LLC ....E...... 213 703-7294
   2998 James M Wood Blvd # 4 Los Angeles (90006) *(P-16169)*

App Wholesale LLC ....B...... 323 980-8315
   3686 E Olympic Blvd Los Angeles (90023) *(P-13350)*

App Winddown LLC (HQ)..C
   747 Warehouse St Los Angeles (90021) *(P-2441)*

Apparel House USA, Gardena *Also Called: Stanzino Inc (P-2032)*

Apparel Newsgroup, The, Los Angeles *Also Called: Mnm Corporation (P-3372)*

Mergent email: customerrelations@mergent.com
996

2024 Southern California
Business Directory and Buyers Guide

(P-0000) Products & Services Section entry number
(PA)=Parent Co (HQ)=Headquarters (DH)=Div Headquarters

Apparel Prod Svcs Globl LLC .... E...... 818 700-3700
8954 Lurline Ave Chatsworth (91311) *(P-2303)*

Apperson Inc (PA).. D...... 562 356-3333
17315 Studebaker Rd Ste 211 Cerritos (90703) *(P-3828)*

Appfolio, Santa Barbara *Also Called: Appfolio Inc (P-16170)*

Appfolio Inc (PA).. B...... 805 364-6093
70 Castilian Dr Santa Barbara (93117) *(P-16170)*

Appfolio Inc .... D...... 866 648-1536
9201 Spectrum Center Blvd Ste 100 San Diego (92123) *(P-16171)*

Apple Farm Collections-Slo Inc (PA)............................... B...... 805 544-2040
2015 Monterey St San Luis Obispo (93401) *(P-13981)*

Apple Graphics Inc .... E...... 626 301-4287
3550 Tyburn St Los Angeles (90065) *(P-3513)*

Apple Paper Converting Inc .... E...... 714 632-3195
3800 E Miraloma Ave Anaheim (92806) *(P-3229)*

Apple Store Glendale Galleria, Glendale *Also Called: Glendale Associates Ltd (P-14663)*

Apple Tree International Corp .... F...... 626 679-7025
1375 E Locust St Ste B Ontario (91761) *(P-7418)*

Applecare Medical MGT LLC .... C...... 714 443-4507
18 Centerpointe Dr Ste 100 La Palma (90623) *(P-19998)*

Appleone Employment Services, Glendale *Also Called: AppleOne Inc (P-15813)*

Appleone Employment Services, Glendale *Also Called: AppleOne Inc (P-15814)*

AppleOne Inc .... C...... 818 240-8688
325 W Broadway Glendale (91204) *(P-15813)*

AppleOne Inc (HQ).. C...... 818 240-8688
327 W Broadway Glendale (91204) *(P-15814)*

Applied Biosystems, Carlsbad *Also Called: Applied Biosystems LLC (P-16172)*

Applied Biosystems LLC (DH)... C
5791 Van Allen Way Carlsbad (92008) *(P-16172)*

Applied Business Software Inc .... E...... 562 426-2188
2847 Gundry Ave Signal Hill (90755) *(P-16173)*

Applied Cardiac Systems Inc .... D...... 949 855-9366
1 Hughes Ste A Irvine (92618) *(P-10431)*

Applied Cmpsite Structures Inc (HQ)............................. D...... 714 990-6300
1195 Columbia St Brea (92821) *(P-9627)*

Applied Coatings & Linings .... E...... 626 280-6354
3224 Rosemead Blvd El Monte (91731) *(P-6690)*

Applied Companies .... E...... 661 257-0090
28020 Avenue Stanford Santa Clarita (91355) *(P-19548)*

Applied Engineering MGT Corp .... C...... 805 484-1909
760 Paseo Camarillo Ste 101 Camarillo (93010) *(P-15965)*

Applied Instrument Tech Inc .... E...... 909 204-3700
2121 Aviation Dr Upland (91786) *(P-10234)*

Applied Manufacturing LLC .... A...... 949 713-8000
22872 Avenida Empresa Rcho Sta Marg (92688) *(P-10432)*

Applied Medical Corporation (PA)................................... C...... 949 713-8000
22872 Avenida Empresa Rcho Sta Marg (92688) *(P-10433)*

Applied Medical Corporation .... A...... 949 713-2174
30152 Aventura Rcho Sta Marg (92688) *(P-10434)*

Applied Medical Dist Corp .... A...... 949 713-8000
22872 Avenida Empresa Rcho Sta Marg (92688) *(P-10435)*

Applied Medical Distribution, Rcho Sta Marg *Also Called: Applied Medical Resources Corp*
(P-10437)

Applied Medical Resources .... E...... 949 459-1042
30152 Esperanza Rcho Sta Marg (92688) *(P-10436)*

Applied Medical Resources, Rcho Sta Marg *Also Called: Applied Medical Corporation*
(P-10433)

Applied Medical Resources Corp (HQ)........................... D...... 949 713-8000
22872 Avenida Empresa Rcho Sta Marg (92688) *(P-10437)*

Applied Membranes Inc .... C...... 760 727-3711
2450 Business Park Dr Vista (92081) *(P-7639)*

Applied Mlecular Evolution Inc (HQ)............................. E...... 858 597-4990
10300 Campus Point Dr Ste 200 San Diego (92121) *(P-4054)*

Applied Polytech Systems Inc .... E...... 818 504-9261
26000 Springbrook Ave Ste 102 Santa Clarita (91350) *(P-2743)*

Applied Powdercoat Inc .... E...... 805 981-1991
3101 Camino Del Sol Oxnard (93030) *(P-6691)*

Applied Research Assoc Inc .... D...... 505 881-8074
10833 Valley View St Ste 250 Cypress (90630) *(P-19821)*

Applied Silicone, Carpinteria *Also Called: Applied Silicone Company LLC (P-13424)*

Applied Silicone Company LLC .... D...... 805 525-5657
1050 Cindy Ln Carpinteria (93013) *(P-13424)*

Applied Spectral Imaging Inc .... F...... 760 929-2840
5315 Avenida Encinas Ste 150 Carlsbad (92008) *(P-15966)*

Applied Statistics & MGT Inc .... D...... 951 699-4600
32848 Wolf Store Rd Ste A Temecula (92592) *(P-16174)*

Applied Technologies Assoc Inc (HQ)............................ C...... 805 239-9100
3025 Buena Vista Dr Paso Robles (93446) *(P-10352)*

Apprentice Jrnymen Trning Tr F .... C...... 310 604-0892
7850 Haskell Ave Van Nuys (91406) *(P-19174)*

Approved Aeronautics LLC .... E...... 951 200-3730
9130 Pulsar Ct Corona (92883) *(P-9628)*

Appstar Financial, San Diego *Also Called: Amazon Processing LLC (P-16481)*

APR Engineering Inc .... E...... 562 983-3800
1812 W 9th St Long Beach (90813) *(P-9833)*

Apricorn LLC .... E...... 858 513-2000
12191 Kirkham Rd Poway (92064) *(P-7507)*

Apricot Designs Inc .... D...... 626 966-3299
677 Arrow Grand Cir Covina (91722) *(P-10438)*

APS Global, Chatsworth *Also Called: Apparel Prod Svcs Globl LLC (P-2303)*

APS Marine, Chula Vista *Also Called: Adept Process Services Inc (P-9852)*

APT Electronics, Anaheim *Also Called: APT Electronics Inc (P-8648)*

APT Electronics Inc .... C...... 714 687-6760
241 N Crescent Way Anaheim (92801) *(P-8648)*

APT Manufacturing LLC .... F...... 714 632-0040
2899 E Coronado St Ste E Anaheim (92806) *(P-7004)*

APT Metal Fabricators Inc .... E...... 818 896-7478
11164 Bradley Ave Pacoima (91331) *(P-6495)*

Aptco LLC (PA).. D...... 661 792-2107
31381 Pond Rd Bldg 2 Mc Farland (93250) *(P-3924)*

Aptim Corp .... A...... 949 261-6441
18100 Von Karman Ave # 450 Irvine (92612) *(P-19959)*

Aptim Corp .... B...... 619 239-1690
1230 Columbia St Ste 1200 San Diego (92101) *(P-20315)*

Aptim Federal Services LLC .... A...... 619 239-1690
1230 Columbia St Ste 1200 San Diego (92101) *(P-420)*

Aputure Imaging Industries .... E...... 626 295-6133
1715 N Gower St Los Angeles (90028) *(P-5322)*

APV Manufacturing & Engrg Co, Buena Park *Also Called: AM Machining Inc (P-12901)*

Apw Knox-Seeman Warehouse Inc (HQ).......................... D...... 310 604-4373
1073 E Artesia Blvd Carson (90746) *(P-12231)*

Aq Lighting Group, Santa Clarita *Also Called: Aq Lighting Group Texas Inc (P-12584)*

Aq Lighting Group Texas Inc .... E...... 818 534-5300
28486 Westinghouse Pl Ste 120 Santa Clarita (91355) *(P-12584)*

Aqi, Ontario *Also Called: Aliquantum International Inc (P-10945)*

Aqseptence Group Inc .... C...... 661 323-1506
1901 E Brundage Ln Ste A Bakersfield (93307) *(P-3925)*

AQSEPTENCE GROUP, INC., Bakersfield *Also Called: Aqseptence Group Inc (P-3925)*

Aqua Performance Inc .... E...... 951 340-2056
425 N Smith Ave Corona (92878) *(P-12925)*

Aqua Pro Properties Vii LP .... B...... 310 516-9911
2000 W 135th St Gardena (90249) *(P-7222)*

Aqua Products Inc (DH).. E...... 973 857-2700
2882 Whiptail Loop Ste 100 Carlsbad (92010) *(P-7640)*

Aqua-Lung America Inc (DH).. C...... 760 376-9813
2105 Rutherford Rd Carlsbad (92008) *(P-9945)*

Aquafine Corporation (HQ)... D...... 661 257-4770
29010 Avenue Paine Valencia (91355) *(P-7641)*

Aquahydrate Inc .... E...... 310 559-5058
5870 W Jefferson Blvd Ste D Los Angeles (90016) *(P-1684)*

Aqualung Group, Carlsbad *Also Called: Aqua-Lung America Inc (P-9945)*

Aquamar Inc .... C...... 909 481-4700
10888 7th St Rancho Cucamonga (91730) *(P-1791)*

Aquamor LLC (PA).. D...... 951 541-9517
42188 Rio Nedo Temecula (92590) *(P-7642)*

Aquaneering Inc .... E...... 858 578-2028
7960 Stromesa Ct San Diego (92126) *(P-6899)*

Aquarian Accessories Corp .... F...... 714 632-0230
600 N Batavia St Orange (92868) *(P-13976)*

Aquarian Drumheads, Orange *Also Called: Aquarian Accessories Corp (P-13976)*

Aquarium of Pacific (PA).. C...... 562 590-3100
100 Aquarium Way Long Beach (90802) *(P-19366)*

Employee Codes: A=Over 500 employees, B=251-500
C=101-250, D=51-100, E=20-50, F=10-19, G=1-9

2024 Southern California
Business Directory and Buyers Guide

© Mergent Inc. 1-800-342-5647
997

A
L
P
H
A
B
E
T
I
C

Aquarius Rags LLC (PA)..D...... 213 895-4400
15821 Ventura Blvd Ste 270 Encino (91436) *(P-2275)*

Aquastar Pool Productions, Ventura *Also Called: Aquastar Pool Products Inc (P-7268)*

Aquastar Pool Products Inc ....E...... 877 768-2717
2340 Palma Dr Ste 104 Ventura (93003) *(P-7268)*

Aquasyn LLC ....F...... 818 350-0423
9525 Owensmouth Ave Ste E Chatsworth (91311) *(P-6753)*

Aquatec International Inc ....D...... 949 225-2200
17422 Pullman St Irvine (92614) *(P-7269)*

Aquatec Water Systems, Irvine *Also Called: Aquatec International Inc (P-7269)*

Aquatic Co ....B...... 714 993-1220
1700 N Delilah St Corona (92879) *(P-4911)*

Aquatic Co ....C...... 714 993-1220
8101 E Kaiser Blvd Ste 200 Anaheim (92808) *(P-4912)*

Aquatic Industries Inc ....E...... 800 877-2005
8101 E Kaiser Blvd Ste 200 Anaheim (92808) *(P-4913)*

Aqueos Corporation (PA)..E...... 805 364-0570
418 Chapala St Ste E Santa Barbara (93101) *(P-6952)*

Aqueos Corporation ....C...... 805 676-4330
2550 Eastman Ave Ventura (93003) *(P-6953)*

Aqueous Technologies Corp ....E...... 909 944-7771
1678 N Maple St Corona (92878) *(P-7643)*

Aquiesse, Moorpark *Also Called: Global Uxe Inc (P-11220)*

Aquire, Norwalk *Also Called: Aquirecorps Norwalk Auto Auctn (P-12222)*

Aquirecorps Norwalk Auto Auctn ....C...... 562 864-7464
12405 Rosecrans Ave Norwalk (90650) *(P-12222)*

AR Tech Aerospace, Fontana *Also Called: A&R Tarpaulins Inc (P-2497)*

Araca Merchandise LP ....D...... 818 743-5400
459 Park Ave San Fernando (91340) *(P-3734)*

Araco Enterprises LLC ....B...... 818 767-0675
9189 De Garmo Ave Sun Valley (91352) *(P-12154)*

Arakelian Enterprises Inc ....C...... 818 768-2644
11121 Pendleton St Sun Valley (91352) *(P-11443)*

Arakelian Enterprises Inc ....B...... 626 336-3636
15045 Salt Lake Ave City Of Industry (91746) *(P-12155)*

Arakelian Enterprises Inc (PA)....................................B...... 626 336-3636
14048 Valley Blvd City Of Industry (91746) *(P-12156)*

Arakelian Enterprises Inc ....C...... 951 342-3300
687 Iowa Ave Riverside (92507) *(P-12157)*

Aram Precision Tool & Die Inc ....E...... 818 998-1000
9758 Cozycroft Ave Chatsworth (91311) *(P-7758)*

Aramark, Los Angeles *Also Called: Aramark Facility Services LLC (P-15693)*

Aramark Facility Services LLC ....C...... 213 740-8968
941 W 35th St Los Angeles (90007) *(P-15693)*

Aramark Unf & Career AP LLC, Burbank *Also Called: Vestis Services LLC (P-15472)*

Aramark Uniform Mfg Co ....E...... 800 999-8989
115 N First St Burbank (91502) *(P-11190)*

Aranda Tooling Inc ....D...... 714 379-6565
13950 Yorba Ave Chino (91710) *(P-7759)*

Ararat Convalescent Hospital, Los Angeles *Also Called: Ararat Home Los Angeles Inc (P-18108)*

Ararat Home Los Angeles Inc ....C...... 323 256-8012
2373 Colorado Blvd Los Angeles (90041) *(P-18108)*

Ararat Home Los Angeles Inc ....C...... 818 837-1800
15099 Mission Hills Rd Mission Hills (91345) *(P-18109)*

Ararat Nursing Facility, Mission Hills *Also Called: Ararat Home Los Angeles Inc (P-18109)*

ARB, Lake Forest *Also Called: Juniper Rock Corporation (P-400)*

Arb Inc (HQ)..C...... 949 598-9242
26000 Commercentre Dr Lake Forest (92630) *(P-658)*

Arbiter Systems Incorporated (PA)..............................E...... 805 237-3831
1324 Vendels Cir Ste 121 Paso Robles (93446) *(P-10184)*

Arbonne International LLC (DH).................................E...... 949 770-2610
9400 Jeronimo Rd Irvine (92618) *(P-14121)*

Arbonne International Dist Inc ....D...... 800 272-6663
9400 Jeronimo Rd Irvine (92618) *(P-14122)*

Arbor Glen Care Center, Glendora *Also Called: Harbor Glen Care Center (P-17968)*

Arbor Glen Care Center, Glendora *Also Called: Ensign San Dimas LLC (P-18123)*

Arbormed Inc (PA)...C...... 714 689-1500
725 W Town And Country Rd Orange (92868) *(P-18742)*

Arbors, The, San Diego *Also Called: G&L Penasquitos Inc (P-19084)*

ARC, Torrance *Also Called: Good Sports Plus Ltd (P-16041)*

ARC - Imperial Valley ....E...... 760 768-1944
340 E 1st St Calexico (92231) *(P-18669)*

ARC - SD E Cnty Training Ctrs, El Cajon *Also Called: ARC of San Diego (P-19312)*

ARC Document Solutions LLC ....A...... 951 445-4480
41521 Date St Apt 101 Murrieta (92562) *(P-15642)*

ARC Enterprises, San Diego *Also Called: ARC of San Diego (P-19314)*

ARC of San Diego ....B...... 619 448-2415
1855 John Towers Ave El Cajon (92020) *(P-19312)*

ARC of San Diego ....B...... 760 740-6800
1336 Rancheros Dr Ste 100 San Marcos (92069) *(P-19313)*

ARC of San Diego (PA)...C...... 619 685-1175
3030 Market St San Diego (92102) *(P-19314)*

ARC Plastics Inc ....E...... 562 802-3299
14010 Shoemaker Ave Norwalk (90650) *(P-4945)*

ARC Products, San Diego *Also Called: Ssco Manufacturing Inc (P-7162)*

ARC Vineyards LLC ....E...... 805 937-3901
5391 Presquile Dr Santa Maria (93455) *(P-1611)*

Arcadia Inc ....E...... 310 665-0490
2323 Firestone Blvd South Gate (90280) *(P-6100)*

Arcadia Cabinetry LLC ....F...... 909 550-0074
5467 Brooks St Montclair (91763) *(P-2646)*

Arcadia Convalescent Hosp Inc (PA)...........................C...... 626 445-2170
1601 S Baldwin Ave Arcadia (91007) *(P-18110)*

Arcadia Gardens MGT Corp ....D...... 626 574-8571
720 W Camino Real Ave Arcadia (91007) *(P-18080)*

Arcadia Health Care Center, Arcadia *Also Called: Arcadia Convalescent Hosp Inc (P-18110)*

Arcadia Norcal, Vernon *Also Called: Arcadia Products LLC (P-5717)*

Arcadia Products LLC (HQ)...C...... 323 771-9819
2301 E Vernon Ave Vernon (90058) *(P-5717)*

Arcadia, Inc., South Gate *Also Called: Arcadia Inc (P-6100)*

Arch Health Partners, Poway *Also Called: Palomar Health Medical Group (P-18366)*

Arch Med Sltons - Escndido LLC ....C...... 760 432-9785
950 Borra Pl Escondido (92029) *(P-10439)*

Arch Motorcycle Company Inc ....E...... 970 443-1380
3216 W El Segundo Blvd Hawthorne (90250) *(P-13898)*

Archion, Glendora *Also Called: Postvision Inc (P-7479)*

Archipelago Inc ....C...... 213 743-9200
1548 18th St Santa Monica (90404) *(P-4379)*

Archipelago Botanicals, Santa Monica *Also Called: Archipelago Inc (P-4379)*

Archipelago Development Inc ....D...... 858 699-6272
Rancho Santa Fe (92067) *(P-14897)*

Architctral Mllwk Snta Barbara ....E...... 805 965-7011
8 N Nopal St Santa Barbara (93103) *(P-2584)*

Architects Orange Inc ....C...... 714 639-9860
144 N Orange St Orange (92866) *(P-19723)*

Architectural Design Signs Inc (PA)............................D...... 951 278-0680
1160 Railroad St Corona (92882) *(P-11097)*

Architectural Enterprises Inc ....E...... 323 268-4000
5821 Randolph St Commerce (90040) *(P-6351)*

Architectural Iron Works, San Luis Obispo *Also Called: Kairos Manufacturing Inc (P-11237)*

Architectural Mtls USA Inc ....D...... 888 219-2126
4025 Camino Del Rio S Ste 300 San Diego (92108) *(P-19724)*

Architectural Shtmtl Contr, Murrieta *Also Called: Pgc Construction Inc (P-450)*

Architectural Window Shades, Pasadena *Also Called: Roberson Construction (P-3012)*

Architectural Woodworking Co ....D...... 626 570-4125
582 Monterey Pass Rd Monterey Park (91754) *(P-2943)*

Arciero Brothers Inc ....C...... 714 238-6600
5614 E La Palma Ave Anaheim (92807) *(P-1058)*

Arconic Fastening Systems, Carson *Also Called: Huck International Inc (P-6445)*

Arconic Fastening Systems, City Of Industry *Also Called: Valley-Todeco Inc (P-6456)*

Arconic Fstening Systems Rings, Sylmar *Also Called: JW Manufacturing Inc (P-6447)*

Arcs Commercial Mortgage, Calabasas *Also Called: Arcs Commercial Mortgage Co LP (P-14300)*

Arcs Commercial Mortgage Co LP (DH).......................C...... 818 676-3274
26901 Agoura Rd Ste 200 Calabasas (91301) *(P-14300)*

Arctic Glacier USA Inc ....C...... 310 638-0321
17011 Central Ave Carson (90746) *(P-1835)*

Arcticom Group Rfrgn LLC ....B...... 916 484-3190
3675 De Forest Cir Jurupa Valley (91752) *(P-17061)*

Mergent email: customerrelations@mergent.com
998

2024 Southern California
Business Directory and Buyers Guide

(P-0000) Products & Services Section entry number
(PA)=Parent Co (HQ)=Headquarters (DH)=Div Headquarters

Arcturus, San Diego Also Called: Arcturus Thrptics Holdings Inc (P-4055)

Arcturus Therapeutics Inc .... C 858 900-2660
10628 Science Center Dr Ste 250 San Diego (92121) (P-19822)

Arcturus Thrptics Holdings Inc (PA) .... C 858 900-2660
10628 Science Center Dr Ste 250 San Diego (92121) (P-4055)

ARCUTIS BIOTHERAPEUTICS, Westlake Village Also Called: Arcutis Biotherapeutics Inc (P-4056)

Arcutis Biotherapeutics Inc (PA) .... E 805 418-5006
3027 Townsgate Rd Ste 300 Westlake Village (91361) (P-4056)

Arden Engineering Inc (DH) .... E 949 877-3642
3130 E Miraloma Ave Anaheim (92806) (P-9629)

Arden Engineering Inc .... C 714 998-6410
1878 N Main St Orange (92865) (P-9630)

Arden Engineering Holdings Inc (DH) .... E 714 998-6410
1878 N Main St Orange (92865) (P-9631)

Arden Realty Inc .... B 310 966-2600
11601 Wilshire Blvd Fl 5 Los Angeles (90025) (P-14653)

Arden/Paradise Manufacturing, Victorville Also Called: Paradise Manufacturing Co Inc (P-2507)

Ardent Mills LLC .... E 951 201-1170
2020 E Steel Rd Colton (92324) (P-1407)

Ardent Mills LLC .... E 909 887-3407
19684 Cajon Blvd San Bernardino (92407) (P-1408)

Ardmore Home Design Inc (PA) .... E 626 803-7769
918 S Stimson Ave City Of Industry (91745) (P-2795)

Ardwin Freight, Burbank Also Called: Ardwin Inc (P-11471)

Ardwin Inc .... C 818 767-7777
2940 N Hollywood Way Burbank (91505) (P-11471)

Are/Cal-Sd Region No 62 LLC .... D 626 578-0777
26 N Euclid Ave Pasadena (91101) (P-15020)

Arecont Vision LLC .... C 818 937-0700
425 E Colorado St Fl 7700 Glendale (91205) (P-8200)

Aremac Associates Inc .... E 626 303-8795
2004 S Myrtle Ave Monrovia (91016) (P-7760)

Aremac Heat Treating Inc .... E 626 333-3898
330 S 9th Ave City Of Industry (91746) (P-5824)

Arena Painting Contractors Inc .... D 310 316-2446
525 E Alondra Blvd Gardena (90248) (P-842)

Ares, Los Angeles Also Called: Ares Management Corporation (P-14958)

Ares Management Corporation (PA) .... C 310 201-4100
2000 Avenue Of The Stars Fl 12 Los Angeles (90067) (P-14958)

Arete Associates (PA) .... C 818 885-2200
9301 Corbin Ave Ste 2000 Northridge (91324) (P-9946)

Arete Associates, Northridge Also Called: Arete Associates (P-9946)

Arevalo Tortilleria Inc .... E 323 888-1711
3033 Supply Ave Commerce (90040) (P-1852)

Arevalo Tortilleria Inc (PA) .... D 323 888-1711
1537 W Mines Ave Montebello (90640) (P-1853)

Arey Jones Eductl Solutions, San Diego Also Called: Broadway Typewriter Co Inc (P-12401)

Arga Cntrls A Unit Elctro Swtc, Rancho Cucamonga Also Called: Electro Switch Corp (P-9036)

Argee, Santee Also Called: Argee Mfg Co San Diego Inc (P-4946)

Argee Mfg Co San Diego Inc .... D 619 449-5050
9550 Pathway St Santee (92071) (P-4946)

Argen Corporation (PA) .... C 858 455-7900
8515 Miralani Dr San Diego (92126) (P-5673)

Argeso, Rosemead Also Called: M Argeso & Co Inc (P-4644)

Argo Spring Mfg Co Inc .... D 800 252-2740
13930 Shoemaker Ave Norwalk (90650) (P-6780)

Argon St Inc .... D 703 270-6927
6696 Mesa Ridge Rd Ste A San Diego (92121) (P-9947)

Argonaut .... E 310 822-1629
5355 Mcconnell Ave Los Angeles (90066) (P-3256)

Arguello Inc .... E 805 567-1632
17100 Calle Mariposa Reina Goleta (93117) (P-290)

Argus Management Company LLC .... B 562 299-5200
5150 E Pacific Coast Hwy Ste 500 Long Beach (90804) (P-20289)

Argus Medical Management, Long Beach Also Called: Argus Management Company LLC (P-20289)

Argyle Precision, Orange Also Called: ISI Detention Contg Group Inc (P-7877)

ARI Industries Inc .... D 714 993-3700
17018 Edwards Rd Cerritos (90703) (P-7600)

Ariana Air Freight, Orange Also Called: Wood Space Industries Inc (P-11635)

Arias Industries Inc .... E 310 532-9737
275 Roswell Ave Long Beach (90803) (P-9354)

Arias Pistons, Long Beach Also Called: Arias Industries Inc (P-9354)

Aries 33 LLC .... E 310 355-8330
3400 S Main St Los Angeles (90007) (P-2194)

Aries Beef LLC .... E 818 526-4855
17 W Magnolia Blvd Burbank (91502) (P-1211)

Aries Prepared Beef Company .... F 818 771-0181
11850 Sheldon St Sun Valley (91352) (P-1426)

Arium, Irvine Also Called: American Arium (P-8763)

Ariza Cheese Co Inc .... E 562 630-4144
7602 Jackson St Paramount (90723) (P-1251)

Ariza Global Foods Inc .... E 562 630-4144
7602 Jackson St Paramount (90723) (P-1252)

Arizeke Pharmacueticals Inc .... E 858 455-6907
6828 Nncy Rdge Dr Ste 400 San Diego (92121) (P-4057)

Arizona Pipeline Company .... C 951 270-3100
1745 Sampson Ave Corona (92879) (P-659)

Arizona Pipeline Company (PA) .... B 760 244-8212
17372 Lilac St Hesperia (92345) (P-660)

Arizona Portland Cement, Glendora Also Called: Calportland Company (P-5362)

Arjo Inc .... B 714 412-1170
17502 Fabrica Way Cerritos (90703) (P-12471)

Ark Animal Health Inc .... E 858 203-4100
4955 Directors Pl San Diego (92121) (P-4299)

Arkebauer Properties, Irvine Also Called: Western National Prpts LLC (P-480)

Arkema Coating Resins, Torrance Also Called: Arkema Inc (P-3855)

Arkema Inc .... D 310 214-5327
19206 Hawthorne Blvd Torrance (90503) (P-3855)

Arktura LLC (HQ) .... E 310 532-1050
966 Sandhill Ave Carson (90746) (P-2868)

Arlo, Carlsbad Also Called: Arlo Technologies Inc (P-8396)

Arlo Technologies Inc (PA) .... D 408 890-3900
2200 Faraday Ave Ste 150 Carlsbad (92008) (P-8396)

Arlon Graphics LLC (HQ) .... C 714 985-6300
200 Boysenberry Ln Placentia (92870) (P-4805)

Arlon LLC .... C 714 540-2811
2811 S Harbor Blvd Santa Ana (92704) (P-4947)

Arm Inc .... A 858 453-1900
5375 Mira Sorrento Pl Ste 540 San Diego (92121) (P-8768)

Armand Hmmer Mseum of Art Cltr .... C 310 443-7000
10899 Wilshire Blvd Los Angeles (90024) (P-19349)

Armanino LLP .... B 310 478-4148
11766 Wilshire Blvd Fl 9 Los Angeles (90025) (P-19751)

Armata Pharmaceuticals, Marina Del Rey Also Called: Armata Pharmaceuticals Inc (P-4300)

Armata Pharmaceuticals Inc (PA) .... E 310 665-2928
4503 Glencoe Ave Marina Del Rey (90292) (P-4300)

Armc, Colton Also Called: Arrowhead Regional Medical Ctr (P-18186)

Armed Services YMCA of USA .... C 858 751-5755
3293 Santo Rd San Diego (92124) (P-19423)

Armed/Xctive Prtction Armed Un, Harbor City Also Called: Allied Protection Services Inc (P-16614)

Armen Living, Valencia Also Called: Legacy Commercial Holdings Inc (P-2779)

Armor Dermalogics LLC .... E 714 202-6424
9151 Atlanta Ave # 5864 Huntington Beach (92615) (P-1259)

Armorcast Products Company Inc .... E 909 390-1365
500 S Dupont Ave Ontario (91761) (P-4948)

Armorcast Products Company Inc (DH) .... C 818 982-3600
9140 Lurline Ave Chatsworth (91311) (P-6191)

Armored Group Inc .... E 818 767-3030
11555 Cantara St North Hollywood (91605) (P-2708)

Armtec Countermeasures Co (DH) .... F 760 398-0143
85901 Avenue 53 Coachella (92236) (P-9948)

Armtec Defense Products Co (DH) .... B 760 398-0143
85901 Avenue 53 Coachella (92236) (P-6749)

Armtec Defense Technologies, Coachella Also Called: Armtec Defense Products Co (P-6749)

Arnaco Industrial Coatings .... E 562 222-1022
8445 Warvale St Pico Rivera (90660) (P-6692)

Arnco .... E 323 249-7500
5141 Firestone Pl South Gate (90280) (P-3984)

Employee Codes: A=Over 500 employees, B=251-500
C=101-250, D=51-100, E=20-50, F=10-19, G=1-9

2024 Southern California
Business Directory and Buyers Guide

© Mergent Inc. 1-800-342-5647
999

ALPHABETIC

Arnett Construction Inc .... E...... 909 421-7960
626 W 1st St Rialto (92376) *(P-1122)*

Arnies Supply Service Ltd (PA) .... **E... 323 263-1696**
1541 N Ditman Ave Los Angeles (90063) *(P-2714)*

Arnold & Porter, Los Angeles *Also Called: Arnold Porter Kaye Scholer LLP (P-18820)*

Arnold Magnetics, Camarillo *Also Called: Arnold Magnetics Corporation (P-8087)*

Arnold Magnetics Corporation .... D...... 805 484-4221
841 Avenida Acaso Ste A Camarillo (93012) *(P-8087)*

Arnold Porter Kaye Scholer LLP .... D...... 213 243-4000
777 S Figueroa St Ste 4400 Los Angeles (90017) *(P-18820)*

Arnold-Gonsalves Engrg Inc .... E...... 909 465-1579
5731 Chino Ave Chino (91710) *(P-7761)*

Arosa, Los Angeles *Also Called: Livhome Inc (P-18625)*

Arrietta Incorporated .... E...... 626 334-0302
429 N Azusa Ave Azusa (91702) *(P-13694)*

Arriver Holdco Inc .... A...... 858 587-1121
5775 Morehouse Dr San Diego (92121) *(P-9163)*

Arrk North America Inc .... C...... 858 552-1587
4660 La Jolla Village Dr Ste 100 San Diego (92122) *(P-6192)*

Arrow Engineering .... E...... 626 960-2806
4946 Azusa Canyon Rd Irwindale (91706) *(P-7762)*

Arrow Screw Products Inc .... E...... 805 928-2269
941 W Mccoy Ln Santa Maria (93455) *(P-7763)*

Arrow Transit Mix .... E...... 661 945-7600
507 E Avenue L12 Lancaster (93535) *(P-5460)*

Arrow Truck Bodies & Eqp Inc .... E...... 909 947-3991
1639 S Campus Ave Ontario (91761) *(P-9316)*

Arrowhead Brass & Plumbing LLC .... D...... 800 332-4267
5147 Alhambra Ave Los Angeles (90032) *(P-734)*

Arrowhead Central Credit Union (PA) .... **B... 866 212-4333**
8686 Haven Ave Rancho Cucamonga (91730) *(P-14223)*

Arrowhead Gen Insur Agcy Inc (HQ) .... **C... 619 881-8600**
701 B St Ste 2100 San Diego (92101) *(P-14506)*

Arrowhead Pharmaceuticals Inc .... E...... 626 304-3400
10102 Hoyt Park Dr San Diego (92131) *(P-4058)*

Arrowhead Products, Los Alamitos *Also Called: Arrowhead Products Corporation (P-9632)*

Arrowhead Products Corporation .... A...... 714 822-2513
4411 Katella Ave Los Alamitos (90720) *(P-9632)*

Arrowhead Regional Medical Ctr .... A...... 909 580-1000
400 N Pepper Ave Colton (92324) *(P-18186)*

Arrowhead Water, Orange *Also Called: Bluetriton Brands Inc (P-13355)*

Arroyo Grande Care Center, Arroyo Grande *Also Called: Compass Health Inc (P-17909)*

Arroyo Grande Community Hospital .... B...... 805 473-7626
345 S Halcyon Rd Arroyo Grande (93420) *(P-18187)*

Arroyo Vista Family Health Ctr, Los Angeles *Also Called: Arroyo Vsta Fmly Hlth Fndation (P-17595)*

Arroyo Vsta Fmly Hlth Fndation .... D...... 323 224-2188
2411 N Broadway Los Angeles (90031) *(P-17595)*

ARS, Burbank *Also Called: Hutchinson Arospc & Indust Inc (P-9707)*

ARS, Los Angeles *Also Called: Asian Rehabilitation Svc Inc (P-19175)*

ARS National Services Inc (PA) .... **C... 800 456-5053**
201 W Grand Ave Escondido (92025) *(P-15607)*

Arsi of California, Thousand Oaks *Also Called: American Recovery Service Inc (P-15606)* .

Art Bronze Inc .... F...... 818 897-2222
11275 San Fernando Rd San Fernando (91340) *(P-5801)*

Art Drctors Gild Itse Lcal 876 .... C...... 818 762-9995
11969 Ventura Blvd Ste 200 Studio City (91604) *(P-19408)*

Art Glass Etc Inc .... E...... 805 644-4494
3111 Golf Course Dr Ventura (93003) *(P-2585)*

Art Mold Die Casting Inc .... E...... 818 767-6464
11872 Sheldon St Sun Valley (91352) *(P-7050)*

Art Plates, Rancho Cucamonga *Also Called: Pitbull Gym Incorporated (P-5137)*

Artboxx Framing Inc .... E...... 310 604-6933
555 W Victoria St Compton (90220) *(P-11191)*

Artcraft Bedding and Draperies, Commerce *Also Called: Artcraft Bedspreads Mfg Inc (P-2010)*

Artcraft Bedspreads Mfg Inc .... E
6466 Fleet St Commerce (90040) *(P-2010)*

Artcrafters Cabinets .... E...... 818 752-8960
5446 Cleon Ave North Hollywood (91601) *(P-2647)*

Arte De Mexico, North Hollywood *Also Called: Arte De Mexico Inc (P-8305)*

Arte De Mexico Inc (PA) .... **D... 818 753-4559**
1000 Chestnut St Burbank (91506) *(P-2904)*

Arte De Mexico Inc .... D...... 818 753-4510
5506 Riverton Ave North Hollywood (91601) *(P-8305)*

Artemis Consulting, San Diego *Also Called: Artemis Consulting LLC (P-20134)*

Artemis Consulting LLC .... D...... 619 573-6328
1012 W Washington St San Diego (92103) *(P-20134)*

Artesia Christian Home Inc .... C...... 562 865-5218
11614 183rd St Artesia (90701) *(P-18111)*

Artesia Sawdust Products Inc .... E...... 909 947-5983
13434 S Ontario Ave Ontario (91761) *(P-2564)*

Artesyn Offices and Mfg Fcilty, Simi Valley *Also Called: Repligen Corporation (P-4329)*

Arthrex Inc .... C...... 805 964-8104
460 Ward Dr Ste C Santa Barbara (93111) *(P-10440)*

Arthrex California Technology, Santa Barbara *Also Called: Arthrex Inc (P-10440)*

Arthur Dogswell LLC (PA) .... **E... 888 559-8833**
11301 W Olympic Blvd Ste 520 Los Angeles (90064) *(P-1427)*

Arthur J Gallagher Risk Mgmt .... D...... 818 539-2300
500 N Brand Blvd Ste 100 Glendale (91203) *(P-14560)*

Arthur Loussararian MD, Mission Viejo *Also Called: Mission Internal Med Group Inc (P-17714)*

Arthurmade Plastics Inc .... D...... 323 721-7325
2131 Garfield Ave Commerce (90040) *(P-4949)*

Artic Sentinel Inc .... D...... 310 227-8230
1700 E Walnut Ave Ste 200 El Segundo (90245) *(P-15967)*

Artifacts International, Chula Vista *Also Called: Califrnia Furn Collections Inc (P-2869)*

Artificial Grass Liquidators .... E...... 951 677-3377
42505 Rio Nedo Temecula (92590) *(P-11192)*

Artimex Iron Inc .... C...... 619 444-3155
315 Cypress Ln El Cajon (92020) *(P-1100)*

Artisan Entertainment Inc .... A...... 310 449-9200
2700 Colorado Ave Ste 200 Santa Monica (90404) *(P-17169)*

Artisan House Inc .... E...... 818 767-7476
8238 Lankershim Blvd North Hollywood (91605) *(P-6856)*

Artisan House, Inc, North Hollywood *Also Called: Artisan House Inc (P-6856)*

Artisan Nameplate Awards Corp .... E...... 714 556-6222
2730 S Shannon St Santa Ana (92704) *(P-3735)*

Artisan Screen Printing Inc .... C...... 626 815-2700
1055 W 5th St Azusa (91702) *(P-3736)*

Artisan Vehicle Systems Inc .... D...... 805 402-6856
742 Pancho Rd Camarillo (93012) *(P-9278)*

Artissimo Designs LLC (HQ) .... **E... 310 906-3700**
2100 E Grand Ave Ste 400 El Segundo (90245) *(P-3230)*

Artistic Coverings Inc .... E...... 562 404-9343
14135 Artesia Blvd Cerritos (90703) *(P-4873)*

Artistic Pltg & Met Finshg Inc .... E...... 619 661-1691
2801 E Miraloma Ave Anaheim (92806) *(P-6586)*

Artistic Welding .... D...... 310 515-4922
505 E Gardena Blvd Gardena (90248) *(P-6193)*

Artistry In Motion Inc .... E...... 818 994-7388
19411 Londelius St Northridge (91324) *(P-3231)*

Artiva, Chino *Also Called: Artiva USA Inc (P-8288)*

Artiva, Santa Fe Springs *Also Called: Artiva USA Inc (P-8289)*

Artiva USA Inc (PA) .... **E... 909 628-1388**
13901 Magnolia Ave Chino (91710) *(P-8288)*

Artiva USA Inc .... E...... 562 298-8968
12866 Ann St Ste 1 Santa Fe Springs (90670) *(P-8289)*

Artkive .... E...... 310 975-9809
16225 Huston St Encino (91436) *(P-16175)*

Arto Brick / California Pavers .... E...... 310 768-8500
15209 S Broadway Gardena (90248) *(P-5371)*

Arto Brick and Cal Pavers, Gardena *Also Called: Arto Brick / California Pavers (P-5371)*

Arts & Crafts Press, San Diego *Also Called: Rush Press Inc (P-3681)*

Arts Elegance Inc .... E...... 626 793-4794
154 W Bellevue Dr Pasadena (91105) *(P-10898)*

Artsons Manufacturing Company .... E...... 323 773-3469
11121 Garfield Ave South Gate (90280) *(P-5577)*

Arup North America Limited .... B...... 310 578-4182
12777 W Jefferson Blvd Ste 300 Los Angeles (90066) *(P-19549)*

Arvato Services, Valencia *Also Called: Bertelsmann Inc (P-3399)*

Arvato USA LLC .... C...... 502 356-8063
2053 E Jay St Ontario (91764) *(P-16782)*

Arvinyl Laminates LP .... E...... 951 371-7800
233 N Sherman Ave Corona (92882) *(P-4806)*

Arxis Technology Inc .... E...... 805 306-7890
2468 Tapo Canyon Rd Simi Valley (93063) *(P-16176)*

Aryzta Sweet Life, Santa Ana *Also Called: The Sweet Life Enterprises Inc (P-1418)*

Asa, Oxnard *Also Called: Advanced Structural Tech Inc (P-6457)*

Asa Power BDH Engrg & Cnstr, Chino *Also Called: American Solar Advantage Inc (P-8764)*

Asab Inc (DH) .... C...... **818 551-7300**
500 N Brand Blvd Fl 3 Glendale (91203) *(P-15679)*

Asai, Glendale *Also Called: Passport Technology Usa Inc (P-17144)*

Asbury, La Mirada *Also Called: Orange Courier Inc (P-16896)*

ASC, Valencia *Also Called: ASC Process Systems Inc (P-7360)*

ASC Group Inc .... A...... 818 896-1101
12243 Branford St Sun Valley (91352) *(P-8769)*

ASC Process Systems Inc (PA) .... C...... **818 833-0088**
28402 Livingston Ave Valencia (91355) *(P-7360)*

Ascap, Los Angeles *Also Called: American Soc Cmpsers Athors Pb (P-3427)*

Asce, Irvine *Also Called: ACS Engineering Inc (P-19541)*

Ascender Software Inc .... B...... 877 561-7501
8885 Rio San Diego Dr Ste 270 San Diego (92108) *(P-16177)*

Ascent Aerospace .... D...... 586 726-0500
1395 S Lyon St Santa Ana (92705) *(P-9949)*

Ascent Manufacturing LLC .... E...... 714 540-6414
2545 W Via Palma Anaheim (92801) *(P-6496)*

Asco Sintering Co .... E...... 323 725-3550
2750 Garfield Ave Commerce (90040) *(P-5897)*

Ascot Hotel LP .... C...... 310 476-6411
170 N Church Ln Los Angeles (90049) *(P-15078)*

Asdak International .... E...... 714 449-0733
1809 1/2 N Orangethorpe Park Anaheim (92801) *(P-5382)*

Aseptic Technology, Yorba Linda *Also Called: Aseptic Technology LLC (P-1335)*

Aseptic Technology LLC .... C...... 714 694-0168
24855 Corbit Pl Yorba Linda (92887) *(P-1335)*

Ash Holdings LLC .... D...... 909 793-2609
1620 W Fern Ave Redlands (92373) *(P-17882)*

Ashford Trs Seven LLC .... D...... 760 776-0050
38305 Cook St Palm Desert (92211) *(P-15079)*

Ashley Furniture, Ridgecrest *Also Called: Mpb Furniture Corporation (P-2812)*

Ashley Furniture, Redlands *Also Called: Ashley Furniture Inds LLC (P-11565)*

Ashley Furniture Inds LLC .... B...... 909 825-4900
2250 W Lugonia Ave Redlands (92374) *(P-11565)*

Ashtel Dental, Ontario *Also Called: Ashtel Studios Inc (P-10780)*

Ashtel Studios Inc .... E...... 909 434-0911
1610 E Philadelphia St Ontario (91761) *(P-10780)*

Ashunya Inc .... D...... 714 385-1900
642 N Eckhoff St Orange (92868) *(P-15968)*

Ashworth Inc .... A...... 760 438-6610
2765 Loker Ave W Carlsbad (92010) *(P-2195)*

Ashworth Studio, Carlsbad *Also Called: Ashworth Inc (P-2195)*

ASI Hastings Inc .... C...... 619 590-9300
4870 Viewridge Ave Ste 200 San Diego (92123) *(P-735)*

Asi Heating, Air and Solar, San Diego *Also Called: ASI Hastings Inc (P-735)*

Asi Semiconductor Inc .... E...... 818 982-1200
24955 Avenue Kearny Valencia (91355) *(P-8770)*

Asia Food Inc .... E...... 626 284-1328
566 Monterey Pass Rd Monterey Park (91754) *(P-1188)*

Asia Plastics Inc .... E...... 626 448-8100
9347 Rush St South El Monte (91733) *(P-3178)*

Asia-Pacific California Inc .... E...... 626 281-8500
923 E Valley Blvd Ste 203 San Gabriel (91776) *(P-3257)*

Asian European Products Inc .... E...... 949 553-3900
18071 Fitch Fl 250 Irvine (92614) *(P-12232)*

Asian Pacific Family Center, Rosemead *Also Called: Uplift Family Services (P-17819)*

Asian Rehabilitation Svc Inc .... C...... 213 680-3790
312 N Spring St Ste B30 Los Angeles (90012) *(P-19175)*

Asiana Cuisine Enterprises Inc .... A...... 310 327-2223
22771 S Western Ave Ste 100 Torrance (90501) *(P-1854)*

Asics America Corporation (HQ) .... C...... **949 453-8888**
7755 Irvine Center Dr Ste 400 Irvine (92618) *(P-13158)*

Asics Tiger, Irvine *Also Called: Asics America Corporation (P-13158)*

Asm Construction Inc .... E...... 619 449-1966
1947 John Towers Ave El Cajon (92020) *(P-6194)*

Asmb LLC .... D...... 949 347-7100
2021 Arizona Ave Santa Monica (90404) *(P-17883)*

Asml Us Inc .... B...... 760 443-6244
1 Viper Way Ste A Vista (92081) *(P-7223)*

Asml Us LLC .... A...... 858 385-6500
17075 Thornmint Ct San Diego (92127) *(P-7224)*

ASML US, Inc., Vista *Also Called: Asml Us Inc (P-7223)*

Asp Henry Holdings Inc .... A...... 310 955-9200
999 N Pacific Coast Hwy Ste 800 El Segundo (90245) *(P-14923)*

Aspen Medical Products LLC .... D...... 949 681-0200
6481 Oak Cyn Irvine (92618) *(P-10441)*

Aspen Surgery Center, Simi Valley *Also Called: Simi Vly Hosp & Hlth Care Svcs (P-18445)*

Asphalt Dr Inc .... E...... 661 437-5995
7440 Downing Ave Bakersfield (93308) *(P-4667)*

Asphalt Fabric and Engrg Inc .... D...... 562 997-4129
2683 Lime Ave Signal Hill (90755) *(P-10975)*

Aspire Bakeries Holdco LLC (HQ) .... D...... **844 992-7747**
6701 Center Dr W Ste 850 Los Angeles (90045) *(P-1503)*

Aspire Bakeries Holdings LLC (DH) .... F...... **844 992-7747**
6701 Center Dr W Ste 850 Los Angeles (90045) *(P-1504)*

Aspire Bakeries LLC (DH) .... C...... **844 992-7747**
6701 Center Dr W Ste 850 Los Angeles (90045) *(P-1505)*

Aspire Bakeries LLC .... C...... 818 904-8230
15963 Strathern St Van Nuys (91406) *(P-1506)*

Aspire Bakeries LLC .... C...... 714 478-4656
357 W Santa Ana Ave Bloomington (92316) *(P-1507)*

Aspire Bakeries LLC .... C...... 909 472-3500
1220 S Baker Ave Ontario (91761) *(P-13351)*

Aspire Bakeries LLC .... C...... 661 832-0409
6501 District Blvd Bakersfield (93313) *(P-13352)*

Aspire Bakeries Midco LLC (DH) .... F...... **844 992-7747**
6701 Center Dr W Ste 850 Los Angeles (90045) *(P-1508)*

Aspirez Inc .... D...... 714 485-8104
1440 N Harbor Blvd Ste 900 Fullerton (92835) *(P-15969)*

Aspm-Sandiego, San Diego *Also Called: Allegis Residential Svcs Inc (P-19991)*

Aspyr, Costa Mesa *Also Called: Aspyr Holdings LLC (P-17391)*

Aspyr Holdings LLC .... B...... 714 651-1840
270 Baker St Ste 300 Costa Mesa (92626) *(P-17391)*

Asrock America Inc .... E...... 909 590-8308
13848 Magnolia Ave Chino (91710) *(P-8649)*

Assa Abloy ACC Door Cntrls Gro .... C...... 805 642-2600
4226 Transport St Ventura (93003) *(P-5898)*

Assa Abloy Rsdential Group Inc .... A...... 626 369-4718
600 Baldwin Park Blvd City Of Industry (91746) *(P-12714)*

Assa Abloy Rsdential Group Inc (HQ) .... C...... **626 961-0413**
12801 Schabarum Ave Irwindale (91706) *(P-12715)*

Assembly Automation, Duarte *Also Called: Assembly Automation Industries (P-7764)*

Assembly Automation Industries .... E...... 626 303-2777
1849 Business Center Dr Duarte (91010) *(P-7764)*

Assign Corporation .... C...... 818 247-7100
200 N Maryland Ave Ste 204 Glendale (91206) *(P-16552)*

Assisted Home Care, Northridge *Also Called: Assisted Home Recovery Inc (P-15815)*

Assisted Home Care, Thousand Oaks *Also Called: Staff Assistance Inc (P-15896)*

Assisted Home Recovery Inc (PA) .... C...... **818 894-8117**
8550 Balboa Blvd Lbby Northridge (91325) *(P-15815)*

Associate Mech Contrs Inc .... C...... 760 294-3517
622 S Vinewood St Escondido (92029) *(P-736)*

Associated Cnstr & Engrg Inc (PA) .... E...... 949 455-2682
23232 Peralta Dr Ste 206 Laguna Hills (92653) *(P-5400)*

Associated Components Technology Inc .... E...... 714 265-4800
13932 Nautilus Dr Garden Grove (92843) *(P-6812)*

Associated Desert Newspaper (DH) .... E...... **760 337-3400**
205 N 8th St El Centro (92243) *(P-3258)*

Associated Desert Shoppers Inc (DH) .... D...... 760 346-1729
73400 Highway 111 Palm Desert (92260) *(P-3428)*

Associated Electrics Inc (HQ) .... F...... **949 544-7500**
21062 Bake Pkwy 100 Lake Forest (92630) *(P-10946)*

Associated Engineering Company, Lake Forest *Also Called: Berry-Perussi Inc (P-6498)*

Employee Codes: A=Over 500 employees, B=251-500
C=101-250, D=51-100, E=20-50, F=10-19, G=1-9

2024 Southern California
Business Directory and Buyers Guide

© Mergent Inc. 1-800-342-5647
1001

A
L
P
H
A
B
E
T
I
C

Associated Group, Los Angeles *Also Called: Assocted Ldscp Dsplay Group In (P-16783)*

Associated Intl Insur Co, Woodland Hills *Also Called: Markel Corp (P-14609)*

Associated Microbreweries Inc .... D...... 858 587-2739
9675 Scranton Rd San Diego (92121) *(P-1581)*

Associated Microbreweries Inc .... D...... 619 234-2739
1157 Columbia St San Diego (92101) *(P-1582)*

Associated Microbreweries Inc (PA) .... E...... 858 273-2739
5985 Santa Fe St San Diego (92109) *(P-1583)*

Associated Microbreweries Inc .... D...... 714 546-2739
901 S Coast Dr Ste A Costa Mesa (92626) *(P-1584)*

Associated Plating Company .... E...... 562 946-5525
9636 Ann St Santa Fe Springs (90670) *(P-6587)*

Associated Ready Mix Con Inc .... D...... 818 504-3100
8946 Bradley Ave Sun Valley (91352) *(P-5461)*

Associated Ready Mix Concrete, Baldwin Park *Also Called: Standard Concrete Products Inc (P-5504)*

ASSOCIATED READY MIX CONCRETE, INC., Sun Valley *Also Called: Associated Ready Mix Con Inc (P-5461)*

Associated Ready Mixed Con Inc (PA) .... E...... 949 253-2800
4621 Teller Ave Ste 130 Newport Beach (92660) *(P-5462)*

Associated Students & Faculty, San Diego *Also Called: Assocted Stdnts San Dego State (P-19512)*

Associated Students UCLA .... C...... 310 825-2787
308 Westwood Plz Ste 118 Los Angeles (90095) *(P-3259)*

Associated Students UCLA .... D...... 310 825-9451
650 Charles Young Dr S Rm 23120 Los Angeles (90095) *(P-17596)*

Associated Students UCLA .... C...... 310 206-8282
11000 Kinross Ave Ave Ste 245 Los Angeles (90095) *(P-18989)*

Associated Students UCLA (PA) .... B...... 310 794-8836
308 Westwood Plz Los Angeles (90095) *(P-19315)*

Associated Students UCLA .... C...... 310 794-0242
924 Westwood Blvd Los Angeles (90024) *(P-19316)*

Associated Third Party Administrators Inc .... B
222 N Pacific Coast Hwy # 2000 El Segundo (90245) *(P-14546)*

Assocted Fgn Exch Holdings Inc (HQ) .... D...... 818 386-2702
21045 Califa St Woodland Hills (91367) *(P-14255)*

Assocted Ldscp Dsplay Group In .... D...... 714 558-6100
1005 Mateo St Los Angeles (90021) *(P-16783)*

Assocted McRbrwries Ltd A Cal .... F...... 858 273-2739
5985 Santa Fe St San Diego (92109) *(P-1585)*

Assocted Stdnts Cal State Univ .... C...... 562 985-4994
1212 N Bellflower Blvd Ste 220 Long Beach (90815) *(P-19424)*

Assocted Stdnts San Dego State (PA) .... A...... 619 594-0234
5500 Campanile Dr San Diego (92182) *(P-19511)*

Assocted Stdnts San Dego State .... C...... 619 594-5200
San Diego State University San Diego (92182) *(P-19512)*

Assoction Mxcan Amrcn Edcators .... D...... 562 868-0431
12820 Pioneer Blvd Norwalk (90650) *(P-19389)*

AST Sportswear Inc (PA) .... D...... 714 223-2030
2701 E Imperial Hwy Brea (92821) *(P-2405)*

AST Sportswear Inc .... B...... 714 223-2030
Anaheim (92817) *(P-15628)*

Astea International Inc .... E...... 949 784-5000
8 Hughes Irvine (92618) *(P-16178)*

Astec International Holding, Carlsbad *Also Called: Aih LLC (P-8134)*

Astella, Jurupa Valley *Also Called: March Products Inc (P-11249)*

Asteres Inc (PA) .... E...... 858 777-8600
10650 Treena St Ste 105 San Diego (92131) *(P-7583)*

Astor Manufacturing .... E...... 661 645-5585
779 Anita St Ste B Chula Vista (91911) *(P-9633)*

Astra Communications Inc .... F...... 818 859-7305
1101 Chestnut St Burbank (91506) *(P-8497)*

Astra Oil Company Inc .... C...... 714 969-6569
301 Main St Ste 201 Huntington Beach (92648) *(P-13447)*

Astro Aluminum Treating Co .... D...... 562 923-4344
11040 Palmer Ave South Gate (90280) *(P-5825)*

Astro Chrome and Polsg Corp .... E...... 818 781-1463
8136 Lankershim Blvd North Hollywood (91605) *(P-6693)*

Astro Converters Inc (PA) .... E...... 800 752-5003
2370 Oak Ridge Way Ste B Vista (92081) *(P-3210)*

Astro Display Company Inc .... E...... 909 605-2875
4247 E Airport Dr Ontario (91761) *(P-11098)*

Astro Mechanical Contractors Inc .... D...... 619 442-9686
603 S Marshall Ave El Cajon (92020) *(P-737)*

Astro News, Lancaster *Also Called: Aerotech News and Review Inc (P-3342)*

Astro Packaging, Anaheim *Also Called: Reliable Packaging Systems Inc (P-4579)*

Astro Paper & Envelopes, Vista *Also Called: Astro Converters Inc (P-3210)*

Astro Seal Inc .... E...... 951 787-6670
827 Palmyrita Ave Ste B Riverside (92507) *(P-8998)*

Astro Spar Inc .... E...... 626 839-7858
3130 E Miraloma Ave Anaheim (92806) *(P-9634)*

Astro-Tek Industries LLC .... D...... 714 238-0022
1198 N Kraemer Blvd Anaheim (92806) *(P-9635)*

Astrobotic Technology Inc .... D...... 888 488-8455
1570 Sabovich St Mojave (93501) *(P-9891)*

Astrochef LLC .... D...... 213 627-9860
1111 Mateo St Los Angeles (90021) *(P-1384)*

Astrologie California, Commerce *Also Called: Ajg Inc (P-2425)*

Astron Corporation .... E...... 949 458-7277
9 Autry Irvine (92618) *(P-8934)*

Astronic .... C...... 949 454-1180
2 Orion Aliso Viejo (92656) *(P-8650)*

Astronics Company, Pasadena *Also Called: Sabrin Corporation (P-9781)*

Astronics Test Systems Inc (HQ) .... C...... 800 722-2528
2652 Mcgaw Ave Irvine (92614) *(P-10185)*

Astrophysics Inc (PA) .... C...... 909 598-5488
21481 Ferrero City Of Industry (91789) *(P-10781)*

Asturies Manufacturing Co Inc .... E...... 951 270-1766
310 Cessna Cir Corona (92878) *(P-9636)*

Asucla, Los Angeles *Also Called: Associated Students UCLA (P-19315)*

Asucla Publications, Los Angeles *Also Called: Associated Students UCLA (P-3259)*

Asylum Research, Santa Barbara *Also Called: Oxford Instrs Asylum RES Inc (P-10279)*

At & T Wireless Service, Tustin *Also Called: AB Cellular Holding LLC (P-11868)*

At Apollo Technologies LLC .... E...... 949 888-0573
31441 Santa Margarita Pkwy Ste A219 Rcho Sta Marg (92688) *(P-4596)*

At Battery Company Inc .... E...... 661 775-2020
28381 Constellation Rd Unit A Valencia (91355) *(P-14123)*

At Work, Tustin *Also Called: B2 Services Llc (P-15817)*

AT&T, San Diego *Also Called: New Cingular Wireless Svcs Inc (P-11851)*

AT&T Corp .... B...... 714 284-2878
Rm 620 Anaheim (92805) *(P-11843)*

AT&T Corp .... D...... 303 596-8431
2260 E Imperial Hwy El Segundo (90245) *(P-11844)*

AT&T Services Inc .... E...... 213 975-4089
1010 Wilshire Blvd Los Angeles (90017) *(P-11870)*

AT&T Services Inc .... E...... 760 489-3187
950 W Washington Ave Escondido (92025) *(P-11871)*

Atara Bio, Thousand Oaks *Also Called: Atara Biotherapeutics Inc (P-4301)*

Atara Biotherapeutics Inc (PA) .... A...... 650 278-8930
2380 Conejo Spectrum St Ste 200 Thousand Oaks (91320) *(P-4301)*

Atascadero State Hospital, Atascadero *Also Called: Califrnia Dept State Hospitals (P-18508)*

Atbatt.com, Valencia *Also Called: At Battery Company Inc (P-14123)*

Atco Rubber Products Inc .... F...... 951 788-4345
3080 12th St Riverside (92507) *(P-6132)*

Atec Spine, Carlsbad *Also Called: Alphatec Spine Inc (P-10634)*

Atelier Luxury Group LLC .... E...... 310 751-2444
1330 Channing St Los Angeles (90021) *(P-2527)*

Ateliere Creative Tech Inc .... E...... 800 921-4252
315 S Beverly Dr Ste 315 Beverly Hills (90212) *(P-16179)*

Aten Technology Inc .... D...... 949 453-8782
15365 Barranca Pkwy Irvine (92618) *(P-12397)*

Atg - Designing Mobility Inc (DH) .... E...... 562 921-0258
11075 Knott Ave Ste B Cypress (90630) *(P-12472)*

Athanor Group Inc .... E...... 909 467-1205
921 E California St Ontario (91761) *(P-6411)*

Athas Capital Group Inc .... C...... 877 877-1477
27001 Agoura Rd Ste 200 Agoura Hills (91301) *(P-14301)*

Athena Pick Your Fit, Tustin *Also Called: Raj Manufacturing Inc (P-2365)*

Athens Disposal Company Inc (PA) .... B...... 626 336-3636
14048 Valley Blvd La Puente (91746) *(P-12158)*

Athens Environmental Services, Sun Valley *Also Called: Araco Enterprises LLC (P-12154)*

Mergent email: customerrelations@mergent.com
1002

2024 Southern California
Business Directory and Buyers Guide

(P-0000) Products & Services Section entry number
(PA)=Parent Co (HQ)=Headquarters (DH)=Div Headquarters

Athens Services, Sun Valley *Also Called: Arakelian Enterprises Inc (P-11443)*

Athens Services, City Of Industry *Also Called: Arakelian Enterprises Inc (P-12155)*

Athens Services, City Of Industry *Also Called: Arakelian Enterprises Inc (P-12156)*

Atherton Baptist Homes .... C...... 626 863-1710
214 S Atlantic Blvd Alhambra (91801) *(P-17884)*

ATI, Anaheim *Also Called: ATI Restoration LLC (P-1143)*

ATI Forged Products, Irvine *Also Called: Chen-Tech Industries Inc (P-10480)*

ATI Restoration LLC (PA) .... C...... 714 283-9990
3360 E La Palma Ave Anaheim (92806) *(P-1143)*

ATI Systems International Inc .... A...... 858 715-8484
8807 Complex Dr San Diego (92123) *(P-16622)*

ATI Windows, Riverside *Also Called: San Joaquin Window Inc (P-6121)*

Atk, San Diego *Also Called: Composite Optics Incorporated (P-9916)*

Atk Arspace Strctres Test Fclt, San Diego *Also Called: Atk Space Systems LLC (P-9951)*

Atk Audiotek, Valencia *Also Called: Sound River Corporation (P-936)*

Atk Launch Systems LLC .... B...... 858 592-2509
16707 Via Del Campo Ct San Diego (92127) *(P-9950)*

Atk Mission Research, Goleta *Also Called: Mission Research Corporation (P-9999)*

Atk Space Systems LLC .... D...... 858 487-0970
16707 Via Del Campo Ct San Diego (92127) *(P-9951)*

Atk Space Systems LLC .... D...... 858 621-5700
7130 Miramar Rd Ste 100b San Diego (92121) *(P-9952)*

Atk Space Systems LLC .... D...... 805 685-2262
600 Pine Ave Goleta (93117) *(P-9953)*

Atk Space Systems LLC (DH) .... E...... 323 722-0222
6033 Bandini Blvd Commerce (90040) *(P-9954)*

Atk Space Systems LLC .... D...... 310 343-3799
1960 E Grand Ave Ste 1150 El Segundo (90245) *(P-9955)*

Atk Space Systems LLC .... D...... 626 351-0205
370 N Halstead St Pasadena (91107) *(P-9956)*

Atkinson Andelson Loya, Cerritos *Also Called: Atkinson Andlson Loya Ruud Rom (P-18821)*

Atkinson Andlson Loya Ruud Rom (PA) .... C...... 562 653-3200
12800 Center Court Dr S Ste 300 Cerritos (90703) *(P-18821)*

Atkinson Construction Inc .... B...... 303 410-2540
18201 Von Karman Ave Ste 800 Irvine (92612) *(P-609)*

Atlantic Box & Carton Company, Pico Rivera *Also Called: Jkv Inc (P-3113)*

Atlantic Express of California, Long Beach *Also Called: Atlantic Express Trnsp (P-11375)*

Atlantic Express Trnsp .... C...... 562 997-6868
2450 Long Beach Blvd Long Beach (90806) *(P-11375)*

Atlantic Pacific Automotive, Jurupa Valley *Also Called: Highline Aftermarket LLC (P-12242)*

Atlantic Representations Inc .... E...... 562 903-9550
10018 Santa Fe Springs Rd Santa Fe Springs (90670) *(P-2825)*

Atlantic Richfield Company (DH) .... A...... 800 333-3991
4 Centerpointe Dr La Palma (90623) *(P-13889)*

Atlantis Computing Inc .... E...... 650 917-9471
900 Glenneyre St Laguna Beach (92651) *(P-16180)*

Atlantis Enterprises Inc .... E...... 818 712-0572
8100 Remmet Ave Ste 1 Canoga Park (91304) *(P-13528)*

Atlantis Seafood LLC .... D...... 626 626-4900
10501 Valley Blvd Ste 1820 El Monte (91731) *(P-1799)*

Atlas Capital Group LLC .... D...... 213 988-8890
1318 E 7th St Ste 200 Los Angeles (90021) *(P-14416)*

Atlas Carpet Mills Inc .... C...... 323 724-7930
3201 S Susan St Santa Ana (92704) *(P-2109)*

Atlas Construction Supply Inc .... E...... 714 441-9500
7550 Stage Rd Buena Park (90621) *(P-12347)*

Atlas Copco, Santa Maria *Also Called: Atlas Copco Mafi-Trench Co LLC (P-7319)*

Atlas Copco Compressors LLC .... E...... 562 484-6370
16207 Carmenita Rd Cerritos (90703) *(P-7306)*

Atlas Copco Mafi-Trench Co LLC (DH) .... C...... 805 928-5757
3037 Industrial Pkwy Santa Maria (93455) *(P-7319)*

Atlas Foam Products .... F...... 818 837-3626
12836 Arroyo St Sylmar (91342) *(P-4874)*

Atlas Galvanizing LLC .... E...... 323 587-6247
2639 Leonis Blvd Vernon (90058) *(P-6694)*

Atlas General Insur Svcs LLC .... C...... 858 529-6700
6165 Greenwich Dr Ste 200 San Diego (92122) *(P-14561)*

Atlas Hospitality Group .... D...... 949 622-3400
1901 Main St Ste 175 Irvine (92614) *(P-14745)*

Atlas Hotels Inc .... A...... 619 291-2232
500 Hotel Cir N San Diego (92108) *(P-15080)*

Atlas Lithium Corporation .... E...... 213 590-2500
433 N Camden Dr Ste 810 Beverly Hills (90210) *(P-415)*

Atlas Mechanical Inc (PA) .... D...... 858 554-0700
8260 Camino Santa Fe Ste B San Diego (92121) *(P-738)*

Atlas Pacific Corporation (PA) .... E...... 909 421-1200
2803 Industrial Dr Bloomington (92316) *(P-12950)*

Atlas Roofing Corporation .... E...... 626 334-5358
2335 Roll Dr Ste 4121 San Diego (92154) *(P-4875)*

Atlas Sheet Metal Inc .... F...... 949 600-8787
19 Musick Irvine (92618) *(P-6195)*

Atlas Spring Mfgcorp .... E...... 310 532-6200
10635 Santa Monica Blvd Ste 320 Los Angeles (90025) *(P-6798)*

Atlas Survival Shelters LLC .... E...... 323 727-7084
7407 Telegraph Rd Montebello (90640) *(P-2826)*

Atm Fly-Ware, Signal Hill *Also Called: Adaptive Tech Group Inc (P-14090)*

Atmospheric-Greenscreen, Los Angeles *Also Called: Greenscreen (P-163)*

Atomica Corp .... C...... 805 681-2807
75 Robin Hill Rd Goleta (93117) *(P-8771)*

Atpa, El Segundo *Also Called: Associated Third Party Administrators Inc (P-14546)*

Atr Sales Inc .... E...... 714 432-8411
110 E Garry Ave Santa Ana (92707) *(P-7376)*

Atra-Flex, Santa Ana *Also Called: Atr Sales Inc (P-7376)*

Atria Assisted Living Group .... C...... 949 427-8191
23792 Marguerite Pkwy Mission Viejo (92692) *(P-19237)*

Atria Delsol, Mission Viejo *Also Called: Atria Assisted Living Group (P-19237)*

Atria Management Company LLC .... C...... 619 326-0190
5308 Monroe Ave San Diego (92115) *(P-19238)*

Atria Management Company LLC .... B...... 760 480-8155
1342 N Escondido Blvd Escondido (92026) *(P-19239)*

Atrium Door & Win Co Ariz Inc .... C...... 714 693-0601
5455 E La Palma Ave Ste A Anaheim (92807) *(P-12324)*

Atrium Hotel, Irvine *Also Called: Golden Hotels Ltd Partnership (P-15156)*

Ats Systems, Rcho Sta Marg *Also Called: Ats Workholding Llc (P-7107)*

Ats Tool Inc .... E...... 949 888-1744
30222 Esperanza Rcho Sta Marg (92688) *(P-7051)*

Ats Workholding, Rcho Sta Marg *Also Called: Ats Tool Inc (P-7051)*

Ats Workholding Llc (PA) .... E...... 800 321-1833
30222 Esperanza Rcho Sta Marg (92688) *(P-7107)*

Attainment Holdco LLC .... C...... 310 954-1578
700 S Flower St Ste 1800 Los Angeles (90017) *(P-19390)*

Atterdag Village of Solvang, Solvang *Also Called: Solvang Lutheran Home Inc (P-18056)*

Attn Inc .... C...... 323 413-2878
5700 Wilshire Blvd Ste 375 Los Angeles (90036) *(P-15587)*

Attorney Network Services, Los Angeles *Also Called: Attorney Network Services Inc (P-15816)*

Attorney Network Services Inc .... D...... 213 430-0440
725 S Figueroa St Ste 3065 Los Angeles (90017) *(P-15816)*

Atx Networks (san Diego) Corp (DH) .... E...... 858 546-5050
8880 Rehco Rd San Diego (92121) *(P-8498)*

Atxco Inc .... E...... 650 334-2079
3030 Bunker Hill St Ste 325 San Diego (92109) *(P-4059)*

Atyr Pharma, San Diego *Also Called: Atyr Pharma Inc (P-4302)*

Atyr Pharma Inc (PA) .... E...... 858 731-8389
10240 Sorrento Valley Rd Ste 300 San Diego (92121) *(P-4302)*

Auction.com, Irvine *Also Called: Auctioncom Inc (P-14746)*

Auction.com, Irvine *Also Called: Auctioncom LLC (P-14747)*

Auctioncom Inc .... C...... 800 499-6199
1 Mauchly Ste 27 Irvine (92618) *(P-14746)*

Auctioncom LLC (PA) .... C...... 949 859-2777
1 Mauchly Irvine (92618) *(P-14747)*

Audience Inc .... E...... 323 413-2370
5670 Wilshire Blvd Ste 100 Los Angeles (90036) *(P-3429)*

Audio Images, Irvine *Also Called: Henrys Adio Vsual Slutions Inc (P-8417)*

Audio Video Color Corporation (PA) .... C...... 424 213-7500
17707 S Santa Fe Ave E Rncho Dmngz (90221) *(P-3149)*

Audiolink, Thousand Palms *Also Called: A R Electronics Inc (P-8988)*

Auditboard Inc (PA) .... D...... 877 769-5444
12900 Park Plaza Dr Ste 200 Cerritos (90703) *(P-15970)*

Auger Industries Inc .... F...... 714 577-9350
390 E Crowther Ave Placentia (92870) *(P-7765)*

Employee Codes: A=Over 500 employees, B=251-500
C=101-250, D=51-100, E=20-50, F=10-19, G=1-9

2024 Southern California
Business Directory and Buyers Guide

© Mergent Inc. 1-800-342-5647
1003

ALPHABETIC

Augerscope Inc ....E
10375 Wilshire Blvd 1b Los Angeles (90024) *(P-5874)*

August Accessories, Thousand Oaks *Also Called: August Hat Company Inc (P-2398)*

August Hat Company Inc (PA) ....**E...... 805 983-4651**
2021 Calle Yucca Thousand Oaks (91360) *(P-2398)*

Augustine Casino, Coachella *Also Called: Augustine Gaming MGT Corp (P-15971)*

Augustine Gaming MGT Corp ....D...... 760 391-9500
84001 Avenue 54 Coachella (92236) *(P-15971)*

Aunt Rubys LLC ....E...... 562 326-6783
1014 E Carson St Long Beach (90807) *(P-20135)*

Auptix and Flock Freight, Encinitas *Also Called: Flock Freight Inc (P-11761)*

Aurasound Inc ....D...... 949 829-4000
1801 E Edinger Ave Ste 190 Santa Ana (92705) *(P-8397)*

Aurelio Felix Barreto III ....C...... 951 354-9528
169 Radio Rd Corona (92879) *(P-13930)*

Aurident Incorporated ....E...... 714 870-1851
610 S State College Blvd Fullerton (92831) *(P-10729)*

Aurora, Pico Rivera *Also Called: Aurora World Inc (P-12934)*

Aurora Las Encinas LLC ....C...... 626 795-9901
2900 E Del Mar Blvd Pasadena (91107) *(P-18504)*

Aurora Las Encinas Hospital, Pasadena *Also Called: Aurora Las Encinas LLC (P-18504)*

Aurora World Inc ....C...... 562 205-1222
8820 Mercury Ln Pico Rivera (90660) *(P-12934)*

Aurum Assembly Plus Inc ....E...... 858 578-8710
8829 Production Ave San Diego (92121) *(P-8651)*

Ausgar Technologies Inc ....C...... 855 428-7427
10721 Treena St Ste 100 San Diego (92131) *(P-19550)*

Auspex Pharmaceuticals Inc ....E...... 858 558-2400
3333 N Torrey Pines Ct Ste 400 La Jolla (92037) *(P-4060)*

Austin Commercial LP ....C...... 619 446-5637
402 W Broadway Ste 400 San Diego (92101) *(P-531)*

Austin Commercial LP ....C...... 310 421-0269
5901 W Century Blvd Ste 600 Los Angeles (90045) *(P-532)*

Austin Sidley CA LLP ....C...... 213 896-6000
555 W 5th St Ste 4000 Los Angeles (90013) *(P-18822)*

Austin Veum Rbbins Prtners Inc (PA) ....**D...... 619 231-1960**
501 W Broadway Ste A San Diego (92101) *(P-19725)*

Authorized Cellular Service ....D...... 310 466-4144
8808 S Sepulveda Blvd Los Angeles (90045) *(P-17068)*

Autism Spctrum Intrvntions Inc ....C...... 562 972-4846
713 W Commonwealth Ave Ste A Fullerton (92832) *(P-19024)*

Auto Club Enterprises (PA) ....**A...... 714 850-5111**
3333 Fairview Rd Ms A451 Costa Mesa (92626) *(P-14447)*

Auto Club Enterprises ....B...... 310 914-8500
8761 Santa Monica Blvd West Hollywood (90069) *(P-14448)*

Auto Doctor, Temecula *Also Called: Thompson Magnetics Inc (P-9130)*

Auto Edge Solutions, Pacoima *Also Called: Moc Products Company Inc (P-4622)*

Auto Insurance Specialists LLC (DH) ....C...... 562 345-6247
17785 Center Court Dr N Ste 110 Cerritos (90703) *(P-14562)*

Auto Motive Power Inc ....C...... 800 894-7104
11643 Telegraph Rd Santa Fe Springs (90670) *(P-9355)*

Auto Pride, Anaheim *Also Called: Cal-State Auto Parts Inc (P-12236)*

Auto Trend Products, Vernon *Also Called: Punch Press Products Inc (P-7092)*

Auto Value, San Bernardino *Also Called: Metropolitan Automotive Warehouse (P-12248)*

Autocrib Inc ....C...... 714 274-0400
2882 Dow Ave Tustin (92780) *(P-16784)*

Autoliv Akr Fcilty -Casa Whse, San Diego *Also Called: Autoliv Asp Inc (P-2546)*

Autoliv Asp Inc ....E...... 619 662-8018
9355 Airway Rd San Diego (92154) *(P-2546)*

Autoliv Safety Technology Inc ....A...... 619 662-8000
2475 Paseo De Las Americas Ste A San Diego (92154) *(P-2547)*

Automatic Data Processing Inc ....C...... 949 751-0360
3972 Barranca Pkwy Ste J610 Irvine (92606) *(P-16482)*

Automatic Data Processing Inc ....C...... 800 225-5237
400 W Covina Blvd San Dimas (91773) *(P-16483)*

Automatic Screw Mch Pdts Co, Brea *Also Called: Nelson Stud Welding Inc (P-12867)*

Automation Electronics, Chatsworth *Also Called: RJA Industries Inc (P-9107)*

Automation Gt, Carlsbad *Also Called: Laurelwood Industries Inc (P-7907)*

Automation Holdco Inc ....D...... 858 967-8650
10815 Rancho Bernardo Rd Ste 102 San Diego (92127) *(P-16429)*

Automation Plating Corporation ....E...... 323 245-4951
927 Thompson Ave Glendale (91201) *(P-6588)*

Automation Printing Co (PA) ....**E...... 213 488-1230**
1230 Long Beach Ave Los Angeles (90021) *(P-3850)*

Automation West Inc ....E...... 714 556-7381
1605 E Saint Gertrude Pl Santa Ana (92705) *(P-7766)*

Automax Styling Inc ....E...... 951 530-1876
16833 Krameria Ave Riverside (92504) *(P-9356)*

Automobile Club Southern Cal ....C...... 714 885-1343
3333 Fairview Rd Costa Mesa (92626) *(P-14563)*

Automobile Club Southern Cal (PA) ....**C...... 213 741-3686**
2601 S Figueroa St Los Angeles (90007) *(P-14564)*

Automobile Club Southern Cal ....C...... 714 973-1211
13331 Jamboree Rd Irvine (92602) *(P-14565)*

Automobile Club Southern Cal ....C...... 858 483-4960
4973 Clairemont Dr Ste C San Diego (92117) *(P-19513)*

Automobile Club Southern Cal ....D...... 619 233-1000
2440 Hotel Cir N Ste 100 San Diego (92108) *(P-19514)*

Automobile Club Southern Cal ....C...... 760 745-2124
800 La Terraza Blvd Escondido (92025) *(P-19515)*

Automobile Club Southern Cal ....C...... 909 591-9451
5402 Philadelphia St Ste A Chino (91710) *(P-19516)*

Automobile Club Southern Cal ....C...... 805 682-5811
3712 State St Santa Barbara (93105) *(P-19517)*

Automobile Club Southern Cal ....D...... 951 684-4250
3700 Central Ave Riverside (92506) *(P-19518)*

Automobile Club Southern Cal ....C...... 714 774-2392
420 N Euclid St Anaheim (92801) *(P-19519)*

Automobile Club Southern Cal ....C...... 310 453-1909
2730 Santa Monica Blvd Santa Monica (90404) *(P-19520)*

Automobile Club Southern Cal ....D...... 562 425-8350
4800 Airport Plaza Dr Ste 100 Long Beach (90815) *(P-19521)*

Automobile Club Southern Cal ....D...... 323 525-0018
8761 Santa Monica Blvd West Hollywood (90069) *(P-19522)*

Automobile Club Southern Cal ....C...... 310 325-3111
23001 Hawthorne Blvd Torrance (90505) *(P-19523)*

Automobile Club Southern Cal ....C...... 562 904-5970
8223 Firestone Blvd Downey (90241) *(P-19524)*

Automobile Club Southern Cal ....C...... 310 376-0521
700 S Aviation Blvd Manhattan Beach (90266) *(P-19525)*

Automoco LLC ....E...... 707 544-4761
9142 Independence Ave Chatsworth (91311) *(P-9357)*

Automotive Racing Products Inc ....C...... 805 525-1497
1760 E Lemonwood Dr Santa Paula (93060) *(P-5899)*

Automotive Racing Products Inc (PA) ....**D...... 805 339-2200**
1863 Eastman Ave Ventura (93003) *(P-5900)*

Automotive Tstg & Dev Svcs Inc (PA) ....**C...... 909 390-1100**
400 Etiwanda Ave Ontario (91761) *(P-17053)*

Automotus Inc ....D...... 805 504-5750
612 S Broadway Ste 409 Los Angeles (90014) *(P-15972)*

Autonation Finance, Irvine *Also Called: Cig Financial LLC (P-14269)*

Autonation Ford Valencia, Valencia *Also Called: Magic Acquisition Corp (P-13793)*

Autonomous Inc ....E...... 844 949-3879
21800 Opportunity Way Riverside (92518) *(P-2905)*

Autonomous Medical Devices Inc ....E...... 310 641-2700
10524 S La Cienega Blvd Inglewood (90304) *(P-10235)*

Autonomous Medical Devices Inc (PA) ....**E...... 657 660-6800**
3511 W Sunflower Ave Santa Ana (92704) *(P-10236)*

Autosplice, San Diego *Also Called: Autosplice Parent Inc (P-8255)*

Autosplice Parent Inc (PA) ....**C...... 858 535-0077**
10431 Wateridge Cir Ste 110 San Diego (92121) *(P-8255)*

Autostore Integrator, Valencia *Also Called: Sdi Industries Inc (P-6977)*

AUTRY MUSEUM, Los Angeles *Also Called: Autry Museum of American West (P-19350)*

Autry Museum of American West ....C...... 323 667-2000
4700 Western Heritage Way Los Angeles (90027) *(P-19350)*

Autumn Hills Convalescent Home, Glendale *Also Called: Mariner Health Care Inc (P-18004)*

Auxilary of Mssion Hosp Mssion ....A...... 949 364-1400
27700 Medical Center Rd Mission Viejo (92691) *(P-18188)*

Ava James, Los Angeles *Also Called: C-Quest Inc (P-2234)*

Avadyne Health, San Diego *Also Called: H & R Accounts Inc (P-16043)*

Avalon Apparel LLC (PA) ....**C...... 323 581-3511**
2520 W 6th St Los Angeles (90057) *(P-2276)*

Mergent email: customerrelations@mergent.com
1004

2024 Southern California
Business Directory and Buyers Guide

(P-0000) Products & Services Section entry number
(PA)=Parent Co (HQ)=Headquarters (DH)=Div Headquarters

Avalon Building Maint Inc .... B...... 714 693-2407
  1832 Commercenter Cir San Bernardino (92408) *(P-15694)*

Avalon Communications, Hawthorne *Also Called: Technology Training Corp (P-3695)*

Avalon Glass & Mirror, Carson *Also Called: Avalon Glass & Mirror Company (P-5334)*

Avalon Glass & Mirror Company .... D...... 323 321-8806
  642 Alondra Blvd Carson (90746) *(P-5334)*

Avalon Hotel, Beverly Hills *Also Called: Honeymoon Real Estate LP (P-15184)*

Avalon Shutters Inc .... C...... 909 937-4900
  3407 N Perris Blvd Perris (92571) *(P-2586)*

Avalon Transportation Co, Culver City *Also Called: Virgin Fish Inc (P-11409)*

Avamar Technologies Inc .... D...... 949 743-5100
  135 Technology Dr Irvine (92618) *(P-15973)*

Avanir Pharmaceuticals Inc (DH).......................D...... 949 389-6700
  30 Enterprise Ste 200 Aliso Viejo (92656) *(P-4061)*

Avanquest North America LLC (HQ)....................D...... 818 591-9600
  23801 Calabasas Rd Ste 2005 Calabasas (91302) *(P-15974)*

Avante Health Solutions, San Clemente *Also Called: Pacific Medical Group Inc (P-12504)*

Avantec Manufacturing Inc ....E...... 714 532-6197
  1811 N Case St Orange (92865) *(P-8652)*

Avantgarde Senior Living .... C...... 818 881-0055
  5645 Lindley Ave Tarzana (91356) *(P-19240)*

Avantus Aerospace Inc ....E...... 562 633-6626
  14957 Gwenchris Ct Paramount (90723) *(P-5901)*

Avantus Aerospace Inc (DH)..............................C...... 661 295-8620
  29101 The Old Rd Valencia (91355) *(P-9637)*

Avanzato Technology Corp ....E...... 312 509-0506
  5335 Mcconnell Ave Los Angeles (90066) *(P-7225)*

Avasant LLC (PA)...D...... 310 643-3030
  1960 E Grand Ave Ste 1050 El Segundo (90245) *(P-20136)*

Avatar Machine LLC ....E...... 714 434-2737
  18100 Mount Washington St Fountain Valley (92708) *(P-7767)*

Avatar Technology Inc ....E...... 909 598-7696
  339 Cheryl Ln City Of Industry (91789) *(P-12398)*

Avcorp Cmpsite Fabrication Inc ....B...... 310 970-5658
  1600 W 135th St Gardena (90249) *(P-9638)*

Avd, Newport Beach *Also Called: American Vanguard Corporation (P-4545)*

Avenue Medical Equipment Inc ....E...... 949 680-7444
  38062 Encanto Rd Murrieta (92563) *(P-12473)*

Avenue of Arts Wyndham Hotel, Costa Mesa *Also Called: Rosanna Inc (P-15333)*

Aveox Inc ....E...... 805 915-0200
  2265 Ward Ave Ste A Simi Valley (93065) *(P-8201)*

Avery Corp ....C...... 626 304-2000
  207 N Goode Ave Fl 6 Glendale (91203) *(P-19823)*

Avery Dennison Corporation ....D...... 909 987-4631
  11195 Eucalyptus St Rancho Cucamonga (91730) *(P-3163)*

Avery Dennison Corporation ....B...... 714 674-8500
  50 Pointe Dr Brea (92821) *(P-3164)*

Avery Dennison Corporation ....C...... 626 304-2000
  2900 Bradley St Pasadena (91107) *(P-3165)*

Avery Dennison Foundation ....D...... 626 304-2000
  207 N Goode Ave Ste 500 Glendale (91203) *(P-3166)*

Avery Dennison Office Products Co Inc ....A
  50 Pointe Dr Brea (92821) *(P-3216)*

Avery Dnnson Ret Info Svcs LLC (HQ)................D...... 626 304-2000
  207 N Goode Ave Fl 6 Glendale (91203) *(P-3217)*

Avery Group Inc ....B...... 310 217-1070
  8941 Dalton Ave Los Angeles (90047) *(P-14108)*

Avery Products Corporation (DH)..........................C...... 714 674-8500
  50 Pointe Dr Brea (92821) *(P-3218)*

Avery Products Corporation ....C...... 619 671-1022
  6987 Calle De Linea Ste 101 San Diego (92154) *(P-3219)*

Aveta Health Solution Inc ....B...... 909 605-8000
  3990 Concours Ste 500 Ontario (91764) *(P-20137)*

Aveva Software LLC ....C...... 760 268-7700
  5850 El Camino Real Carlsbad (92008) *(P-15975)*

Aveva Software LLC (DH)....................................B...... 949 727-3200
  26561 Rancho Pkwy S Lake Forest (92630) *(P-16430)*

Aviara Fsrc Associates Limited ....A...... 760 603-6800
  7100 Aviara Resort Dr Carlsbad (92011) *(P-15081)*

Aviation & Defense Inc ....C...... 909 382-3487
  255 S Leland Norton Way San Bernardino (92408) *(P-11689)*

Aviation Equipment Processing, Costa Mesa *Also Called: Flare Group (P-9688)*

Aviation Maintenance Group Inc ....D...... 714 469-0515
  8352 Kimball Ave Hngr 3 Chino (91708) *(P-11690)*

Avibank, North Hollywood *Also Called: Avibank Mfg Inc (P-9639)*

Avibank Mfg Inc ....D...... 661 257-2329
  25323 Rye Canyon Rd Valencia (91355) *(P-5902)*

Avibank Mfg Inc (DH)..C...... 818 392-2100
  11500 Sherman Way North Hollywood (91605) *(P-9639)*

Avid, Norco *Also Called: Avid Idntification Systems Inc (P-8772)*

Avid, Burbank *Also Called: Avid Technology Inc (P-10859)*

Avid Bioservices, Tustin *Also Called: Avid Bioservices Inc (P-4062)*

Avid Bioservices, Tustin *Also Called: Pphm Inc (P-13063)*

Avid Bioservices Inc (PA)...................................C...... 714 508-6100
  14191 Myford Rd Tustin (92780) *(P-4062)*

Avid Bioservices Inc ....C...... 714 508-6000
  14272 Franklin Ave Ste 115 Tustin (92780) *(P-4063)*

Avid Idntification Systems Inc (PA)......................D...... 951 371-7505
  3185 Hamner Ave Norco (92860) *(P-8772)*

Avid Ink, Irvine *Also Called: Advanced Vsual Image Dsign LLC (P-3507)*

Avid Technology Inc ....E...... 818 557-2520
  101 S 1st St Ste 200 Burbank (91502) *(P-10859)*

Avidex Industries LLC ....D...... 949 428-6333
  20382 Hermana Cir Lake Forest (92630) *(P-16553)*

Avidity Biosciences, San Diego *Also Called: Avidity Biosciences Inc (P-4064)*

Avidity Biosciences Inc ....E...... 858 401-7900
  10578 Science Center Dr Ste 125 San Diego (92121) *(P-4064)*

Avient Colorants USA LLC ....E...... 909 606-1325
  14355 Ramona Ave Chino (91710) *(P-4513)*

Avient Corporation ....E...... 310 513-7100
  2104 E 223rd St Carson (90810) *(P-3926)*

Avilas Garden Art (PA)...D...... 909 350-4546
  14608 Merrill Ave Fontana (92335) *(P-5401)*

Avion Graphics Inc ....E...... 949 472-0438
  27192 Burbank Foothill Ranch (92610) *(P-3514)*

Avis Roto Die Co ....E...... 323 255-7070
  1560 N San Fernando Rd Los Angeles (90065) *(P-7052)*

Avista Technologies Inc ....F...... 760 744-0536
  140 Bosstick Blvd San Marcos (92069) *(P-4597)*

Avita Medical, Valencia *Also Called: Avita Medical Americas LLC (P-12474)*

Avita Medical Americas LLC ....C...... 661 367-9170
  28159 Avenue Stanford Ste 220 Valencia (91355) *(P-12474)*

Avita Therapeutics Inc ....F...... 661 367-9170
  28159 Avenue Stanford Ste 220 Valencia (91355) *(P-10442)*

Avitex Inc (PA)..C...... 818 994-6487
  20362 Plummer St Chatsworth (91311) *(P-2011)*

AVIVA CENTER, Los Angeles *Also Called: Hamburger Home (P-19265)*

Aviva Family & Childrens Svcs (PA)......................D...... 323 876-0550
  1701 Camino Palmero St Los Angeles (90046) *(P-19025)*

Avjet Corporation (DH)...D...... 818 841-6190
  4301 W Empire Ave Burbank (91505) *(P-11680)*

Avmc, Lancaster *Also Called: Antelope Valley Health Care Di (P-18182)*

Avn Media Network Inc ....E...... 818 718-5788
  9400 Penfield Ave Chatsworth (91311) *(P-3398)*

Avocado Packer & Shipper, Murrieta *Also Called: West Pak Avocado Inc (P-117)*

Avocado Post Acute, El Cajon *Also Called: Eldorado Care Center LP (P-17930)*

Avr Global Tech, Escondido *Also Called: Avr Global Technologies Inc (P-8999)*

Avr Global Technologies Inc (PA).........................C...... 949 391-1180
  500 La Terraza Blvd Ste 150 Escondido (92025) *(P-8999)*

Avsc Intllctual Prprty MGT Inc ....B...... 562 366-1924
  111 W Ocean Blvd Ste 1110 Long Beach (90802) *(P-19999)*

Avt Inc ....E...... 951 737-1057
  341 Bonnie Cir Ste 102 Corona (92880) *(P-7590)*

AVX Antenna, Inc., San Diego *Also Called: Kyocera AVX Cmpnnts San Dego I (P-8529)*

AVX Filters Corporation ....D...... 818 767-6770
  11144 Penrose St Sun Valley (91352) *(P-7382)*

AW Die Engraving Inc ....E...... 714 521-7910
  8550 Roland St Buena Park (90621) *(P-7053)*

Awake Inc ....E...... 818 365-9361
  10700 Valley View St Cypress (90630) *(P-2277)*

Award Metals, Baldwin Park *Also Called: Pacific Award Metals Inc (P-6283)*

Employee Codes: A=Over 500 employees, B=251-500
C=101-250, D=51-100, E=20-50, F=10-19, G=1-9

2024 Southern California
Business Directory and Buyers Guide

© Mergent Inc. 1-800-342-5647

1005

Award Metals, Jurupa Valley *Also Called: Pacific Award Metals Inc (P-6284)*

Award Packaging Spc Corp .... E....... 323 727-1200
12855 Midway Pl Cerritos (90703) *(P-3080)*

Aware Products Inc .... F..... 818 206-6700
9250 Mason Ave Chatsworth (91311) *(P-4380)*

Aware Products LLC .... C....... 818 206-6700
9250 Mason Ave Chatsworth (91311) *(P-4381)*

Awe, San Diego *Also Called: Herring Networks Inc (P-11954)*

Awesome Products Inc (PA)..C....... 714 562-8873
6370 Altura Blvd Buena Park (90620) *(P-4343)*

Awhap Acquisition Corp .... C....... 888 611-4328
28358 Constellation Rd Ste 698 Valencia (91355) *(P-739)*

AWI Management Corporation .... C....... 951 674-8200
1800 E Lakeshore Dr Lake Elsinore (92530) *(P-20000)*

Awo, Vista *Also Called: Advanced Web Offset Inc (P-3730)*

AWR, San Dimas *Also Called: American States Water Company (P-12114)*

Ax II Inc .... E....... 310 292-6523
13921 S Figueroa St Los Angeles (90061) *(P-2053)*

Axelacare Holdings Inc .... C....... 714 522-8802
12604 Hiddencreek Way Ste C Cerritos (90703) *(P-18591)*

Axelgaard, Fallbrook *Also Called: Axelgaard Manufacturing Co (P-10790)*

Axelgaard Manufacturing, Fallbrook *Also Called: Axelgaard Manufacturing Co (P-10791)*

Axelgaard Manufacturing Co (PA) .... D...... 760 723-7554
520 Industrial Way Fallbrook (92028) *(P-10790)*

Axelgaard Manufacturing Co .... E....... 760 723-7554
329 W Aviation Rd Fallbrook (92028) *(P-10791)*

Axeon Water Technologies .... D...... 760 723-5417
40980 County Center Dr Ste 100 Temecula (92591) *(P-7644)*

Axia Technologies Inc .... E....... 855 376-2942
4183 State St Santa Barbara (93110) *(P-16181)*

Axiamed, Santa Barbara *Also Called: Axia Technologies Inc (P-16181)*

Axiom Designs & Printing, Glendale *Also Called: Axiomprint Inc (P-3515)*

Axiom Label & Packaging, Compton *Also Called: Resource Label Group LLC (P-3723)*

Axiom Label Group, Compton *Also Called: Kmr Label LLC (P-3719)*

Axiom Materials Inc .... E....... 949 623-4400
2320 Pullman St Santa Ana (92705) *(P-4558)*

Axiom Medical Incorporated .... E....... 310 533-9020
19320 Van Ness Ave Torrance (90501) *(P-10443)*

Axiomprint Inc .... F....... 747 888-7777
4544 San Fernando Rd Ste 210 Glendale (91204) *(P-3515)*

Axium Packaging LLC .... A...... 909 969-0766
5701 Clark St Ontario (91761) *(P-4950)*

Axon Networks Inc (PA)..D...... 949 310-4429
15420 Laguna Canyon Rd Ste 150 Irvine (92618) *(P-15976)*

Axxis Corporation .... E....... 951 436-9921
1535 Nandina Ave Perris (92571) *(P-7768)*

Aya Healthcare Inc (PA)... B...... 858 458-4410
5930 Cornerstone Ct W Ste 300 San Diego (92121) *(P-15914)*

Aya Living Inc .... C....... 619 446-6469
1450 Frazee Rd San Diego (92108) *(P-19026)*

Aya Locums Services Inc .... A...... 866 687-7390
5930 Cornerstone Ct W Ste 300 San Diego (92121) *(P-18743)*

Aylesva Inc .... C....... 562 688-0592
14537 Garfield Ave Paramount (90723) *(P-13159)*

Aymar Engineering .... F....... 619 562-1121
9434 Abraham Way Santee (92071) *(P-6196)*

Ayo Food, Delano *Also Called: Ayo Foods LLC (P-1305)*

Ayo Foods LLC .... E....... 661 345-5457
927 Main St Delano (93215) *(P-1305)*

Ayres - Paso Robles LP .... C....... 714 850-0409
2700 Buena Vista Dr Paso Robles (93446) *(P-15082)*

Ayres Group .... D...... 310 220-6447
14400 Hindry Ave Hawthorne (90250) *(P-15083)*

Ayres Hotel Manhattan Beach, Hawthorne *Also Called: Ayres Group (P-15083)*

AZ Construction Inc (PA)..C...... 626 333-0727
727 Glendora Ave La Puente (91744) *(P-421)*

AZ Displays Inc .... E....... 949 831-5000
2410 Birch St Vista (92081) *(P-9000)*

AZ Manufacturing, Santa Ana *Also Called: A-Z Mfg Inc (P-7727)*

Aza Industries Inc (PA) .... E....... 760 560-0440
1410 Vantage Ct Vista (92081) *(P-10976)*

Azaa Investments Inc (PA)... E....... 858 569-8111
6602 Convoy Ct Ste 200 San Diego (92111) *(P-9279)*

Azimc Investments Inc .... C....... 818 678-1200
8901 Canoga Ave Canoga Park (91304) *(P-12233)*

Azitex Knitting Mills, Los Angeles *Also Called: Azitex Trading Corp (P-2083)*

Azitex Trading Corp .... D...... 213 745-7072
1850 E 15th St Los Angeles (90021) *(P-2083)*

Aztec Container, Vista *Also Called: Aztec Technology Corporation (P-5993)*

Aztec Landscaping Inc (PA)..C...... 619 464-3303
7980 Lemon Grove Way Lemon Grove (91945) *(P-183)*

Aztec Manufacturing Inc (PA).....................................E...... 858 513-4350
13821 Danielson St Poway (92064) *(P-6432)*

Aztec Technology Corporation (PA)............................E...... 760 727-2300
2550 S Santa Fe Ave Vista (92084) *(P-5993)*

Aztec Tents, Torrance *Also Called: A-Aztec Rents & Sells Inc (P-2498)*

Aztec Washer Company, Poway *Also Called: Aztec Manufacturing Inc (P-6432)*

Azteca Landscape .... D...... 951 369-9210
4073 Mennes Ave Riverside (92509) *(P-141)*

Aztecs Telecom Inc .... D...... 714 373-1560
1353 Walker Ln Corona (92879) *(P-16785)*

Azul Hospitality Group Inc .... C....... 619 223-4200
800 W Ivy St Ste D San Diego (92101) *(P-20001)*

Azumex Corp .... E....... 619 710-8855
2365 Michael Faraday Dr San Diego (92154) *(P-1530)*

Azure Microdynamics Inc .... D...... 949 699-3344
19652 Descartes Foothill Ranch (92610) *(P-7769)*

Azusa Engineering Inc .... F....... 626 966-4071
1542 W Industrial Park St Covina (91722) *(P-9358)*

Azusa Rock LLC .... E....... 619 440-2363
3605 Dehesa Rd El Cajon (92019) *(P-398)*

B & B Battery (usa) Inc (PA)......................................F...... 323 278-1900
6415 Randolph St Commerce (90040) *(P-9158)*

B & B Nurseries Inc .... C....... 951 352-8383
9505 Cleveland Ave Riverside (92503) *(P-13501)*

B & B Pipe and Tool Co (PA)......................................E...... 562 424-0704
3035 Walnut Ave Long Beach (90807) *(P-328)*

B & B Pipe and Tool Co .... C....... 661 323-8208
2301 Parker Ln Bakersfield (93308) *(P-7770)*

B & B Plastics Inc .... E....... 909 829-3606
1892 W Casmalia St Rialto (92377) *(P-3927)*

B & B Plastics Recyclers Inc (PA)..............................E...... 909 829-3606
3040 N Locust Ave Rialto (92377) *(P-12951)*

B & B Specialties Inc (PA)...D...... 714 985-3000
4321 E La Palma Ave Anaheim (92807) *(P-5903)*

B & B Specialties Inc .... D...... 714 985-3075
4321 E La Palma Ave Anaheim (92807) *(P-12716)*

B & C Nutritional Products Inc .... D...... 714 238-7225
2995 E Miraloma Ave Anaheim (92806) *(P-3991)*

B & E Manufacturing Co Inc .... E....... 714 898-2269
12151 Monarch St Garden Grove (92841) *(P-9640)*

B & G Electronic Assembly Inc .... F....... 909 608-2077
10350 Regis Ct Rancho Cucamonga (91730) *(P-9001)*

B & G House of Printing, Gardena *Also Called: Matsuda House Printing Inc (P-3632)*

B & I Fender, San Diego *Also Called: B & I Fender Trims Inc (P-9359)*

B & I Fender Trims Inc .... E....... 718 326-4323
1401 Air Wing Rd San Diego (92154) *(P-9359)*

B & M Racing & Prfmce Pdts, Chatsworth *Also Called: Automoco LLC (P-9357)*

B & S Plastics Inc .... C....... 805 981-0262
2200 Sturgis Rd Oxnard (93030) *(P-4951)*

B & W, Carlsbad *Also Called: Equity International Inc (P-12658)*

B & W Tile Co Inc (PA)...E...... 310 538-9579
14600 S Western Ave Gardena (90249) *(P-13948)*

B & W Tile Manufacturing, Gardena *Also Called: B & W Tile Co Inc (P-13948)*

B and P Plastics Inc .... E....... 619 477-1893
225 W 30th St National City (91950) *(P-4952)*

B and Z Printing Inc .... E....... 714 892-2000
1300 E Wakeham Ave # B Santa Ana (92705) *(P-3516)*

B B Blu, Los Angeles *Also Called: Treivush Industries Inc (P-2380)*

B B C, Long Beach *Also Called: Belmont Brewing Company Inc (P-13982)*

B B G Management Group (PA)...................................E...... 909 797-9581
12164 California St Yucaipa (92399) *(P-13263)*

Mergent email: customerrelations@mergent.com
1006

2024 Southern California
Business Directory and Buyers Guide

(P-0000) Products & Services Section entry number
(PA)=Parent Co (HQ)=Headquarters (DH)=Div Headquarters

B B S I, San Diego *Also Called: Barrett Business Services Inc (P-15820)*

B Braun Medical, Irvine *Also Called: B Braun Medical Inc (P-10445)*

B Braun Medical Inc .... A....... 610 691-5400
2525 Mcgaw Ave Irvine (92614) *(P-10444)*

B Braun Medical Inc .... E....... 949 660-3151
2206 Alton Pkwy Irvine (92606) *(P-10445)*

B Braun Medical Inc .... E....... 949 660-2581
2488 Alton Pkwy Irvine (92606) *(P-10446)*

B Braun Medical Inc .... C....... 909 906-7575
1151 Mildred St Ste B Ontario (91761) *(P-10447)*

B C I, San Diego *Also Called: Brehm Communications Inc (P-3522)*

B D L, Brea *Also Called: Belt Drives Ltd (P-9874)*

B E & P Enterprises LLC (PA).................................. E....... 909 591-7561
5167 G St Chino (91710) *(P-2751)*

B E B E, Los Angeles *Also Called: Bebe Studio Inc (P-13957)*

B E M R, Bakersfield *Also Called: Bakersfield Elc Mtr Repr Inc (P-17101)*

B F, Riverside *Also Called: Brenner-Fiedler & Assoc Inc (P-10355)*

B F I Labels, Yorba Linda *Also Called: Beckers Fabrication Inc (P-3167)*

B J Bindery Inc .... D....... 714 835-7342
833 S Grand Ave Santa Ana (92705) *(P-3844)*

B L S Limousine Service, Los Angeles *Also Called: Bls Lmsine Svc Los Angeles Inc (P-11376)*

B M S, Poway *Also Called: Broadcast Microwave Svcs LLC (P-8501)*

B M W of Riverside, Riverside *Also Called: David A Campbell Corporation (P-13753)*

B N I, Upland *Also Called: Bni Enterprises Inc (P-20282)*

B P W, Santa Fe Springs *Also Called: Brown-Pacific Inc (P-5579)*

B Riley Securities Inc .... C....... 310 966-1444
11100 Santa Monica Blvd Los Angeles (90025) *(P-16786)*

B S K T Inc .... F....... 818 349-1566
8447 Canoga Ave Canoga Park (91304) *(P-7771)*

B T I, City Of Industry *Also Called: Battery Technology Inc (P-9143)*

B T I Areospace & Electronics, Chino *Also Called: Bti Aerospace & Electronics (P-7789)*

B W Implement Co .... E....... 661 764-5254
288 W Front St Buttonwillow (93206) *(P-6900)*

B Young Enterprises Inc .... D....... 858 748-0935
12254 Iavelli Way Poway (92064) *(P-2648)*

B-Reel Films Inc .... E....... 917 388-3836
8383 Wilshire Blvd Ste 1000 Beverly Hills (90211) *(P-7419)*

B-Spring Valley LLC .... D....... 619 797-3991
9009 Campo Rd Spring Valley (91977) *(P-17885)*

B.T.i Tool Engineering, Santee *Also Called: T I B Inc (P-8042)*

B/E Aerospace Inc .... C....... 714 896-9001
7155 Fenwick Ln Westminster (92683) *(P-9641)*

B/E Aerospace Macrolink .... E....... 714 777-8800
1500 N Kellogg Dr Anaheim (92807) *(P-9642)*

B&A Health Products Co, Brea *Also Called: Lifebloom Corporation (P-4159)*

B&B Industrial Services Inc (PA)............................ B....... 909 428-3167
14549 Manzanita Dr Fontana (92335) *(P-955)*

B&B Manufacturing Co (PA).................................. C....... 661 257-2161
27940 Beale Ct Santa Clarita (91355) *(P-7772)*

B&B Spring Co, Cerritos *Also Called: Clio Inc (P-6802)*

B&C Liquidating Corp (HQ).................................. C....... 626 799-7000
3475 E Foothill Blvd Ste 100 Pasadena (91107) *(P-14566)*

B&D Investment Partners Inc (PA)......................... E....... 661 255-0955
20950 Centre Pointe Pkwy Santa Clarita (91350) *(P-4344)*

B&K Precision Corporation (PA)............................. F....... 714 921-9095
22820 Savi Ranch Pkwy Yorba Linda (92887) *(P-10186)*

B&W Custom Restaurant Eqp Inc .... E....... 714 578-0332
541 E Jamie Ave La Habra (90631) *(P-7645)*

B2 Services Llc .... D....... 714 363-3481
17291 Irvine Blvd Ste 258 Tustin (92780) *(P-15817)*

B2b Payroll Services, Cypress *Also Called: B2b Staffing Services Inc (P-15915)*

B2b Staffing Services Inc .... B....... 714 243-4104
4501 Cerritos Ave Ste 201 Cypress (90630) *(P-15915)*

Ba Holdings Inc (DH).. E....... 951 684-5110
3016 Kansas Ave Bldg 1 Riverside (92507) *(P-6133)*

Ba Sports Nutrition LLC .... D....... 718 357-7402
630 Clinton Pl Beverly Hills (90210) *(P-17392)*

Baatz Enterprises Inc .... E....... 323 660-4866
2223 W San Bernardino Rd West Covina (91790) *(P-9280)*

Bab Hydraulics, Fontana *Also Called: Bab Steering Hydraulics (P-9360)*

Bab Steering Hydraulics (PA)............................... E....... 208 573-4502
14554 Whittram Ave Fontana (92335) *(P-9360)*

Babcock Enterprises Inc .... E....... 805 736-1455
5175 E Highway 246 Lompoc (93436) *(P-28)*

Babcock Vineyards, Lompoc *Also Called: Babcock Enterprises Inc (P-28)*

Baby Guess Inc .... E....... 213 765-3100
1444 S Alameda St Los Angeles (90021) *(P-2413)*

Baby Phat, Commerce *Also Called: BP Clothing LLC (P-13119)*

Babylon Security Services Inc .... D....... 818 766-8122
6032 One Half Vineland Ave North Hollywood (91606) *(P-16623)*

Bacara Resorts and Spa, Santa Barbara *Also Called: Bcra Resort Services Inc (P-15088)*

Bace Manufacturing Inc (HQ)............................... A....... 714 630-6002
3125 E Coronado St Anaheim (92806) *(P-4953)*

Bachem, Torrance *Also Called: Bachem Bioscience Inc (P-4305)*

Bachem Americas Inc .... D....... 888 422-2436
1271 Avenida Chelsea Vista (92081) *(P-4065)*

Bachem Americas Inc (DH).................................. E....... 310 784-4440
3132 Kashiwa St Torrance (90505) *(P-4303)*

Bachem Americas Inc .... D....... 310 784-4440
3152 Kashiwa St Torrance (90505) *(P-4304)*

Bachem Bioscience Inc .... E....... 310 784-7322
3132 Kashiwa St Torrance (90505) *(P-4305)*

Bachem California, Torrance *Also Called: Bachem Americas Inc (P-4303)*

Bachem Vista BSD, Vista *Also Called: Bachem Americas Inc (P-4065)*

Back Support Systems Inc .... F....... 760 329-1472
1064 N E St San Bernardino (92410) *(P-4876)*

Backbone Capital Advisors LLC .... C....... 818 769-8016
4084 Camellia Ave Studio City (91604) *(P-15021)*

Bae Systems, San Diego *Also Called: Bae Systems Info Elctrnic Syst (P-10187)*

Bae Systems Info Elctrnic Syst .... A....... 858 592-5000
10920 Technology Pl San Diego (92127) *(P-10187)*

Bae Systems Land Armaments LP .... E....... 619 455-0213
1650 Industrial Blvd Chula Vista (91911) *(P-9957)*

Bae Systems Maritime Engineering & Services Inc ..... B....... 619 238-1000
7330 Engineer Rd Ste A San Diego (92111) *(P-19551)*

Bae Systems National Security Solutions Inc .... A....... 858 592-5000
10920 Technology Pl San Diego (92127) *(P-10188)*

Bae Systems San Dego Ship Repr .... A....... 619 238-1000
2205 Belt St San Diego (92113) *(P-9834)*

Bae Systems Tech Sltons Svcs I .... E....... 858 278-3042
9650 Chesapeake Dr San Diego (92123) *(P-9958)*

Bae Systems Tech Sol Srvc Inc .... A....... 661 816-3474
Acreage 56 & 66 Bldg 70 Mojave (93501) *(P-9959)*

Bagcraftpapercon I LLC .... D....... 626 961-6766
515 Turnbull Canyon Rd City Of Industry (91745) *(P-3197)*

Baggage Service, Los Angeles *Also Called: China Airlines Ltd (P-11661)*

Baghouse and Indus Shtmtl Svcs, Corona *Also Called: MS Industrial Shtmtl Inc (P-6276)*

Bagmasters, Corona *Also Called: CTA Manufacturing Inc (P-2493)*

Bahare .... C....... 516 472-1457
11769 W Sunset Blvd Los Angeles (90049) *(P-15977)*

Bahia Resort Hotels, San Diego *Also Called: Bh Partnership LP (P-15094)*

Baier Marine Company Inc .... E....... 800 455-3917
2920 Airway Ave Costa Mesa (92626) *(P-5904)*

Bain & Company Inc .... D....... 310 229-3000
1901 Avenue Of The Stars Ste 2000 Los Angeles (90067) *(P-20138)*

Baja Designs, San Marcos *Also Called: Bestop Baja LLC (P-13899)*

Baja Fresh, Chino Hills *Also Called: Gateway Fresh LLC (P-14930)*

Baja Fresh Supermarket .... B....... 760 843-7730
14827 Seventh St Victorville (92395) *(P-93)*

Bake R Us Inc .... C....... 310 630-5873
2632 Wilshire Blvd Ste 463 Santa Monica (90403) *(P-1451)*

Baked Bear LLC .... F....... 760 704-8140
587 S Coast Highway 101 Encinitas (92024) *(P-1292)*

Baked In The Sun .... C....... 760 591-9045
2560 Progress St Vista (92081) *(P-1452)*

Bakell LLC .... D....... 800 292-2137
24723 Redlands Blvd Ste F Loma Linda (92354) *(P-494)*

Bakemark, Pico Rivera *Also Called: Bakemark USA LLC (P-13353)*

Bakemark USA LLC (PA)...................................... D....... 562 949-1054
7351 Crider Ave Pico Rivera (90660) *(P-13353)*

Employee Codes: A=Over 500 employees, B=251-500
C=101-250, D=51-100, E=20-50, F=10-19, G=1-9

2024 Southern California
Business Directory and Buyers Guide

© Mergent Inc. 1-800-342-5647

1007

Baker & Hostetler LLP .... D...... 310 820-8800
11601 Wilshire Blvd Fl 14 Los Angeles (90025) *(P-18823)*

Baker & Hostetler LLP .... D...... 714 754-6600
600 Anton Blvd Ste 900 Costa Mesa (92626) *(P-18824)*

Baker & McKenzie LLP .... C...... 310 201-4728
10250 Constellation Blvd Ste 1850 Los Angeles (90067) *(P-18825)*

Baker & Taylor LLC .... C...... 858 457-2500
10350 Barnes Canyon Rd Ste 100 San Diego (92121) *(P-13493)*

Baker & Taylor Holdings LLC .... A...... 858 457-2500
10350 Barnes Canyon Rd San Diego (92121) *(P-12399)*

Baker & Taylor Marketing Svc, San Diego *Also Called: Baker & Taylor Holdings LLC*
(P-12399)

Baker Commodities Inc (PA) .... C...... 323 268-2801
4020 Bandini Blvd Vernon (90058) *(P-1566)*

Baker Coupling Company Inc .... E...... 323 583-3444
2929 S Santa Fe Ave Vernon (90058) *(P-6838)*

Baker Electric & Renewables LLC .... A...... 760 745-2001
1298 Pacific Oaks Pl Escondido (92029) *(P-868)*

Baker Furnace, Brea *Also Called: Baker Furnace Inc (P-7361)*

Baker Furnace Inc .... F...... 714 223-7262
2680 Orbiter St Brea (92821) *(P-7361)*

Baker Tilly California, Irvine *Also Called: Baker Tilly Us LLP (P-19754)*

Baker Tilly Us LLP .... B...... 818 981-2600
15760 Ventura Blvd Ste 1100 Encino (91436) *(P-19752)*

Baker Tilly Us LLP .... A...... 310 826-4474
11150 Santa Monica Blvd Ste 600 Los Angeles (90025) *(P-19753)*

Baker Tilly Us LLP .... A...... 949 222-2999
18500 Von Karman Ave Fl 10 Irvine (92612) *(P-19754)*

Baker Tilly Us LLP .... B...... 858 597-4100
3655 Nobel Dr Ste 300 San Diego (92122) *(P-19755)*

Bakers Kneaded LLC .... E...... 310 819-8700
148 W 132nd St Ste D Los Angeles (90061) *(P-1453)*

Bakersfield Assn For Rtrded Ctz .... D...... 661 834-2272
2240 S Union Ave Bakersfield (93307) *(P-19176)*

Bakersfield Bhvral Hlthcare Hos .... C...... 661 398-1800
5201 White Ln Bakersfield (93309) *(P-18505)*

Bakersfield Hlthcare Wllness CN .... D...... 661 872-2121
2211 Mount Vernon Ave Bakersfield (93306) *(P-17886)*

Bakersfield District Office, Bakersfield *Also Called: State Compensation Insur Fund (P-14528)*

Bakersfield Elc Mtr Repr Inc .... E...... 661 327-3583
121 W Sumner St Bakersfield (93301) *(P-17101)*

Bakersfield Family Medical Ctr, Bakersfield *Also Called: Bakersfield Family Medical Group Inc*
(P-17597)

Bakersfield Family Medical Group Inc (PA) .... D...... 661 327-4411
4580 California Ave Bakersfield (93309) *(P-17597)*

Bakersfield Heart Hospital, Bakersfield *Also Called: Adventist Hlth Systm/West Corp*
(P-18164)

Bakersfield Hospitality LLC .... D...... 661 393-1277
6141 Knudsen Dr Bakersfield (93308) *(P-15084)*

Bakersfield Machine Co Inc .... D...... 661 709-1992
5605 North Chester Ave Ext Bakersfield (93308) *(P-7773)*

Bakersfield Memorial Hospital .... A...... 661 327-1792
420 34th St Bakersfield (93301) *(P-18189)*

Bakersfield Respite Homecare, Bakersfield *Also Called: Maxim Healthcare Services Inc*
(P-15928)

Bakersfield Shingles Wholesale Inc .... D...... 661 327-3727
4 P St Bakersfield (93304) *(P-12370)*

Bakersfield Westwind Corp .... C...... 661 327-2121
1810 Westwind Dr Bakersfield (93301) *(P-14748)*

Bakersfieldidence Opco LLC .... C...... 661 399-2472
5151 Knudsen Dr Bakersfield (93308) *(P-17887)*

Bakery Ex Southern Cal LLC .... D...... 714 446-9470
1910 W Malvern Ave Fullerton (92833) *(P-13354)*

Bal Seal Engineering LLC (DH) .... C...... 949 460-2100
19650 Pauling Foothill Ranch (92610) *(P-6799)*

Balaji Trading Inc .... D...... 909 444-7999
4850 Eucalyptus Ave Chino (91710) *(P-8468)*

Balance Foods Inc .... E...... 323 838-5555
5743 Smithway St Ste 103 Commerce (90040) *(P-13264)*

Balboa Bay Club Inc (HQ) .... B...... 949 645-5000
1221 W Coast Hwy Newport Beach (92663) *(P-17463)*

Balboa Bay Club and Resort, Newport Beach *Also Called: International Bay Clubs LLC*
(P-17490)

Balboa Capital Corporation (DH) .... C...... 949 756-0800
575 Anton Blvd Ste 1200 Costa Mesa (92626) *(P-14280)*

Balboa Manufacturing Co LLC (PA) .... E...... 858 715-0060
4909 Murphy Canyon Rd Ste 310 San Diego (92123) *(P-2063)*

Balboa Nphrology Med Group Inc .... C...... 858 810-8000
4225 Executive Sq Ste 450 La Jolla (92037) *(P-17598)*

Balboa Water Group LLC (HQ) .... D...... 714 384-0384
3030 Airway Ave Ste B Costa Mesa (92626) *(P-8170)*

Balda C Brewer Inc (DH) .... D...... 714 630-6810
4501 E Wall St Ontario (91761) *(P-4954)*

Balda HK Plastics Inc .... E...... 760 757-1100
3229 Roymar Rd Oceanside (92058) *(P-6412)*

Balda Precision Inc (DH) .... D...... 760 757-1100
3233 Roymar Rd Oceanside (92058) *(P-6413)*

Baldwin Brass, Lake Forest *Also Called: Baldwin Hardware Corporation (P-5905)*

Baldwin Hardware Corporation (HQ) .... A...... 949 672-4000
19701 Da Vinci Lake Forest (92610) *(P-5905)*

Baldwin Hospitality LLC .... D...... 626 446-2988
14635 Baldwin Park Towne Ctr Baldwin Park (91706) *(P-15085)*

Balfour Beatty Cnstr LLC .... D...... 858 635-7400
13520 Evening Creek Dr N Ste 270 San Diego (92128) *(P-533)*

Bali Construction Inc .... D...... 626 442-8003
9852 Joe Vargas Way South El Monte (91733) *(P-661)*

Ball TEC, Los Angeles *Also Called: Micro Surface Engr Inc (P-5855)*

Ballard & Tighe Publishers, Brea *Also Called: Educational Ideas Incorporated (P-3443)*

Ballard Rehabilitation Hosp, San Bernardino *Also Called: Robert Ballard Rehab Hospital*
(P-17871)

Bally Total Fitness, Norwalk *Also Called: Bally Total Fitness Corporation (P-17393)*

Bally Total Fitness Corporation .... A...... 562 484-2000
12440 Imperial Hwy # 300 Norwalk (90650) *(P-17393)*

Balt Usa LLC .... D...... 949 788-1443
29 Parker Ste 100 Irvine (92618) *(P-12475)*

Baltic Ltvian Unvrsal Elec LLC .... E...... 818 879-5200
5706 Corsa Ave Westlake Village (91362) *(P-8398)*

Bambeck Systems Inc (PA) .... F...... 949 250-3100
1921 Carnegie Ave Ste 3a Santa Ana (92705) *(P-10118)*

Bamko, Los Angeles *Also Called: Bamko Inc (P-15584)*

Bamko Inc .... C...... 310 470-5859
11620 Wilshire Blvd Ste 610 Los Angeles (90025) *(P-15584)*

Bana Home Loan Servicing .... A...... 213 345-7975
31303 Agoura Rd Westlake Village (91361) *(P-14155)*

Banamex USA Bancorp (DH) .... C...... 310 203-3440
787 W 5th St Los Angeles (90071) *(P-14920)*

Banc California National Assn (HQ) .... D...... 877 770-2262
3 Macarthur Pl Ste 100 Santa Ana (92707) *(P-14156)*

Banc of California Inc (PA) .... C...... 855 361-2262
3 Macarthur Pl Ste 100 Santa Ana (92707) *(P-14157)*

Bancolmbia PR Intrnacional Inc .... D...... 323 582-2255
2625 E Florence Ave Ste E Huntington Park (90255) *(P-16787)*

Bandai Namco Entrtmt Amer Inc .... C...... 408 235-2000
23 Odyssey Irvine (92618) *(P-12935)*

Bandai Nmco Toys Cllctbles AME (DH) .... D...... 949 271-6000
23 Odyssey Irvine (92618) *(P-10947)*

Bandel Mfg Inc .... E...... 818 246-7493
4459 Alger St Los Angeles (90039) *(P-6497)*

Bandlock Corporation .... D...... 909 947-7500
1734 S Vineyard Ave Ontario (91761) *(P-4955)*

Bandy Manufacturing LLC .... D...... 818 846-9020
3420 N San Fernando Blvd Burbank (91504) *(P-9643)*

Bandy Ranch Floral Corp .... C...... 805 757-9905
2755 Dos Aarons Way Ste B Vista (92081) *(P-13502)*

Bang Printing, Palmdale *Also Called: D & J Printing Inc (P-3555)*

Bank C Plating Co, Los Angeles *Also Called: We Five-R Corporation (P-6679)*

Bank of Hope (HQ) .... C...... 213 639-1700
3200 Wilshire Blvd Ste 1400 Los Angeles (90010) *(P-14158)*

Bank of Manhattan .... C...... 310 606-8000
2141 Rosecrans Ave Ste 1100 El Segundo (90245) *(P-14211)*

Bankcard Services (PA) .... C...... 213 365-1122
21281 S Western Ave Torrance (90501) *(P-16788)*

Bankcard Services, Torrance *Also Called: Credit Card Services Inc (P-16812)*

Bankcard USA Merchant Srvc ....D...... 818 597-7000
5701 Lindero Canyon Rd Westlake Village (91362) *(P-16789)*

Bankruptcy Management Cons, El Segundo *Also Called: BMC Group Inc (P-18830)*

Banks Pest Control ....B...... 661 323-7858
7440 District Blvd Ste A Bakersfield (93313) *(P-15682)*

Banks Power Products, Azusa *Also Called: Gale Banks Engineering (P-6894)*

Banner American Products Inc ....F...... 951 296-9780
42381 Rio Nedo Temecula (92590) *(P-7774)*

Banner Mattress Inc ....D...... 909 835-4200
1501 E Cooley Dr Ste B Colton (92324) *(P-2844)*

Banner Solutions, Anaheim *Also Called: Mid-West Wholesale Hardware Co (P-5932)*

Bapko Metal Inc ....D...... 714 639-9380
721 S Parker St Ste 300 Orange (92868) *(P-1101)*

Bar Code Specialties Inc ....E...... 877 411-2633
12272 Monarch St Garden Grove (92841) *(P-7508)*

Bar None Inc ....F...... 714 259-8450
1302 Santa Fe Dr Tustin (92780) *(P-1671)*

Bar-S Foods Co ....D...... 323 589-3600
4919 Alcoa Ave Vernon (90058) *(P-1212)*

Bar-S Foods Co. Los Angeles, Vernon *Also Called: Bar-S Foods Co (P-1212)*

Barber Volkeswagen, Ventura *Also Called: R E Barber-Ford (P-13816)*

Barber Welding and Mfg Co ....E...... 562 928-2570
7171 Scout Ave Bell Gardens (90201) *(P-7775)*

Barber-Webb Company Inc (PA)...E...... 541 488-4821
12912 Lakeland Rd Santa Fe Springs (90670) *(P-4956)*

Barbour & Floyd Medical Assoc, Lynwood *Also Called: South Cntl Hlth Rhbltton Prgr (P-18718)*

Barco Uniforms Inc ....B...... 310 323-7315
350 W Rosecrans Ave Gardena (90248) *(P-2149)*

Bare Nothings Inc (PA) ....E...... 714 848-8532
17705 Sampson Ln Huntington Beach (92647) *(P-2304)*

Bargain Rent-A-Car ....C...... 562 865-7447
18800 Studebaker Rd Cerritos (90703) *(P-13739)*

Barkens Hardchrome Inc ....E...... 310 632-2000
239 E Greenleaf Blvd Compton (90220) *(P-7226)*

Barksdale Inc (DH) ....C...... 323 583-6243
3211 Fruitland Ave Vernon (90058) *(P-10353)*

Barlow Group (PA)...C...... 213 250-4200
2000 Stadium Way Los Angeles (90026) *(P-18520)*

Barlow Respiratory Hospital ....A...... 562 698-0811
12401 Washington Blvd Whittier (90602) *(P-18521)*

Barlow Respiratory Hospital (PA)..C...... 213 250-4200
2000 Stadium Way Los Angeles (90026) *(P-18522)*

Barlow Respitory Hospital, Los Angeles *Also Called: Barlow Group (P-18520)*

Barnes & Thornburg LLP ....C...... 310 284-3880
2029 Century Park E Ste 300 Los Angeles (90067) *(P-18826)*

Barnes Firm LC ....D...... 800 800-0000
633 W 5th St Ste 1750 Los Angeles (90071) *(P-18827)*

Barnes Plastics, Gardena *Also Called: Barnes Plastics Inc (P-4957)*

Barnes Plastics Inc ....E...... 310 329-6301
18903 Anelo Ave Gardena (90248) *(P-4957)*

Barnett Performance Products, Ventura *Also Called: Barnett Tool & Engineering (P-9873)*

Barnett Tool & Engineering ....D...... 805 642-9435
2238 Palma Dr Ventura (93003) *(P-9873)*

Barney & Barney Inc ....C...... 800 321-4696
9171 Twne Cntre Dr 500 San Diego (92122) *(P-14567)*

Barnhart Inc ....B...... 858 635-7400
10620 Treena St Ste 300 San Diego (92131) *(P-534)*

Barnstorm Vfx Inc ....D...... 818 792-1899
2860 N Naomi St Burbank (91504) *(P-17170)*

Baron Paper Company, Oceanside *Also Called: Triple D and DS (P-3251)*

Barona Resort & Casino ....A...... 619 443-2300
1932 Wildcat Canyon Rd Lakeside (92040) *(P-15086)*

Baronhr LLC ....D...... 909 517-3800
13085 Central Ave Ste 4 Chino (91710) *(P-15818)*

Barr Engineering Inc ....D...... 562 944-1722
19 Castano Rcho Sta Marg (92688) *(P-740)*

Barr, Ronald J MD /UCI Med Gro, Orange *Also Called: University California Irvine (P-17815)*

Barranca Diamond Products, Torrance *Also Called: Barranca Holdings Ltd (P-7108)*

Barranca Holdings Ltd ....C...... 310 523-5867
22815 Frampton Ave Torrance (90501) *(P-7108)*

Barranca Medical Offices, Irvine *Also Called: Kaiser Foundation Hospitals (P-18305)*

Barrett Business Services Inc ....A...... 909 890-3633
862 E Hospitality Ln San Bernardino (92408) *(P-15819)*

Barrett Business Services Inc ....A...... 858 314-1100
8880 Rio San Diego Dr Ste 800 San Diego (92108) *(P-15820)*

Barrett Business Services Inc ....A...... 805 987-0331
815 Camarillo Springs Rd Ste C Camarillo (93012) *(P-15821)*

Barrette Outdoor Living Inc ....F...... 800 336-2383
1151 Palmyrita Ave Riverside (92507) *(P-5610)*

Barrington Associates, Los Angeles *Also Called: Wells Fargo Securities LLC (P-14409)*

Barrot Corporation ....E...... 949 852-1640
1881 Kaiser Ave Irvine (92614) *(P-7054)*

Barry & Taffy Inc ....A...... 818 986-1234
5955 De Soto Ave Ste 160 Woodland Hills (91367) *(P-18592)*

Barry Avenue Plating Co Inc ....D...... 310 478-0078
2210 Barry Ave Los Angeles (90064) *(P-6589)*

Barry Controls Aerospace, Burbank *Also Called: Hutchinson Arospc & Indust Inc (P-4767)*

Barrys Printing Inc ....E...... 818 998-8600
9005 Eton Ave Ste D Canoga Park (91304) *(P-3517)*

Barrys Security Services Inc (PA)..C...... 951 789-7575
16739 Van Buren Blvd Riverside (92504) *(P-16624)*

Barstow Community Hospital, Barstow *Also Called: Hospital of Barstow Inc (P-18288)*

Barta - Schoenewald Inc (PA)..C...... 805 389-1935
3805 Calle Tecate Camarillo (93012) *(P-8135)*

Bartco Lighting Inc ....D...... 714 230-3200
5761 Research Dr Huntington Beach (92649) *(P-12585)*

Bartell Hotels ....D...... 619 291-6700
1960 Harbor Island Dr San Diego (92101) *(P-15087)*

Bartley Optical, Irwindale *Also Called: Essilor Laboratories Amer Inc (P-12524)*

Barton Perreira LLC ....E...... 949 305-5360
459 Wald Irvine (92618) *(P-10832)*

Barzillai Manufacturing Co Inc ....F...... 909 947-4200
1410 S Cucamonga Ave Ontario (91761) *(P-6197)*

Bas Engineering Inc ....F...... 909 484-2575
11899 8th St Rancho Cucamonga (91730) *(P-19552)*

Basaw, North Hollywood *Also Called: Basaw Manufacturing Inc (P-2709)*

Basaw Manufacturing, North Hollywood *Also Called: Basaw Manufacturing Inc (P-2710)*

Basaw Manufacturing Inc ....E...... 818 765-6650
13340 Raymer North Hollywood (91605) *(P-2709)*

Basaw Manufacturing Inc (PA)..E...... 818 765-6650
11323 Hartland St North Hollywood (91605) *(P-2710)*

Base Lite Corporation ....E...... 909 444-2776
12260 Eastend Ave Chino (91710) *(P-8290)*

Baselite, Chino *Also Called: Base Lite Corporation (P-8290)*

Basepoint Analytics LLC ....B...... 760 602-4971
703 Palomar Airport Rd Ste 350 Carlsbad (92011) *(P-15619)*

BASF Corporation ....C...... 714 921-1430
138 E Meats Ave Orange (92865) *(P-4514)*

BASF Corporation ....E...... 714 521-6085
6700 8th St Buena Park (90620) *(P-4515)*

BASF Enzymes LLC (DH) ....D...... 858 431-8520
3550 John Hopkins Ct San Diego (92121) *(P-4516)*

Basic Agency, San Diego *Also Called: Thinkbasic Inc (P-15675)*

Basic Electronics Inc ....E...... 714 530-2400
11371 Monarch St Garden Grove (92841) *(P-9002)*

Basic Energy Services Inc ....E...... 661 588-3800
6710 Stewart Way Bakersfield (93308) *(P-329)*

Basic Industries Intl Inc (PA)...C...... 951 226-1500
10850 Wilshire Blvd Los Angeles (90024) *(P-6134)*

Basin Marine Inc ....E...... 949 673-0360
829 Harbor Island Dr Ste A Newport Beach (92660) *(P-9855)*

Basin Marine Shipyard, Newport Beach *Also Called: Basin Marine Inc (P-9855)*

Basketball Marketing Co Inc ....C...... 610 249-2255
101 Enterprise Ste 100 Aliso Viejo (92656) *(P-20139)*

Basmat Inc (PA)...D...... 310 325-2063
1531 240th St Harbor City (90710) *(P-6198)*

Bassani Exhaust, Anaheim *Also Called: Bassani Manufacturing (P-6839)*

Bassani Manufacturing ....E...... 714 630-1821
2900 E La Jolla St Anaheim (92806) *(P-6839)*

Employee Codes: A=Over 500 employees, B=251-500
C=101-250, D=51-100, E=20-50, F=10-19, G=1-9

2024 Southern California
Business Directory and Buyers Guide

© Mergent Inc. 1-800-342-5647

1009

ALPHABETIC

Batchmaster Software, Irvine *Also Called: Eworkplace Manufacturing Inc (P-12412)*

Baton Lock and Hardware Co Inc ....E...... 714 265-3636
14275 Commerce Dr Garden Grove (92843) *(P-5906)*

Baton Security, Garden Grove *Also Called: Baton Lock and Hardware Co Inc (P-5906)*

Battery Systems Inc ....C...... 714 667-9320
12322 Monarch St Garden Grove (92841) *(P-12234)*

Battery Systems Inc ....D...... 818 474-1500
16725 Roscoe Blvd North Hills (91343) *(P-12586)*

Battery Systems Inc ....D...... 951 894-2960
26151 Jefferson Ave Ste A Murrieta (92562) *(P-12643)*

Battery Technology Inc (PA) ....**D...... 626 336-6878**
16651 E Johnson Dr City Of Industry (91745) *(P-9143)*

Battery-Biz Inc ....D...... 800 848-6782
1380 Flynn Rd Camarillo (93012) *(P-9164)*

Battle-Tested Strategies LLC ....D...... 661 802-6509
650 Commerce Ave Ste E Palmdale (93551) *(P-11526)*

Bau Furniture Mfg Inc ....D...... 949 643-2729
21 Kelly Ln Ladera Ranch (92694) *(P-2767)*

Baumann Engineering ....D...... 909 621-4181
212 S Cambridge Ave Claremont (91711) *(P-7776)*

Bausch & Lomb, Irvine *Also Called: Bausch & Lomb Incorporated (P-10833)*

Bausch & Lomb Incorporated ....C...... 949 788-6000
15273 Alton Pkwy Ste 100 Irvine (92618) *(P-10833)*

Bausch & Lomb Surgical Div, Irvine *Also Called: Eyeonics Inc (P-10840)*

Bausman and Company Inc (PA) ....**C...... 909 947-0139**
1500 Crafton Ave Mentone (92359) *(P-2878)*

Baxalta US Inc ....A...... 818 240-5600
4501 Colorado Blvd Los Angeles (90039) *(P-4066)*

Baxalta US Inc ....B...... 805 498-8664
1700 Rancho Conejo Blvd Thousand Oaks (91320) *(P-10448)*

Baxalta US Inc ....C...... 949 474-6301
17511 Armstrong Ave Irvine (92614) *(P-16790)*

Baxco Pharmaceutical Inc ....F...... 626 610-7088
2393 Bateman Ave Duarte (91010) *(P-4067)*

Baxstra Inc ....E...... 323 770-4171
1224 W 132nd St Gardena (90247) *(P-2568)*

Baxter Healthcare Corporation ....C...... 949 474-6301
17511 Armstrong Ave Irvine (92614) *(P-10449)*

Baxter Healthcare Corporation ....D...... 805 372-3000
1 Baxter Way Ste 100 Westlake Village (91362) *(P-13029)*

Baxter Medication Delivery, Irvine *Also Called: Baxter Healthcare Corporation (P-10449)*

Bay Area Community Med Group, Los Angeles *Also Called: Santa Monica Bay Physicians He (P-17759)*

Bay Cities Container Corp ....F...... 562 302-2552
9206 Santa Fe Springs Rd Santa Fe Springs (90670) *(P-3081)*

Bay Cities Container Corp (PA) ....**D...... 562 948-3751**
5138 Industry Ave Pico Rivera (90660) *(P-3082)*

Bay Cities Container Corp ....E...... 562 551-2946
9206 Santa Fe Springs Rd Santa Fe Springs (90670) *(P-3150)*

Bay Cities Logistics, Pico Rivera *Also Called: Bay Cities Container Corp (P-3082)*

BAY CITIES METAL PRODUCTS, Gardena *Also Called: Bay Cities Tin Shop Inc (P-6199)*

Bay Cities Tin Shop Inc ....C...... 310 660-0351
301 E Alondra Blvd Gardena (90248) *(P-6199)*

Bay City Electric Works Inc ....F...... 858 486-1054
15515 Markar Rd Poway (92064) *(P-17102)*

Bay City Equipment Inds Inc ....D...... 619 938-8200
13625 Danielson St Poway (92064) *(P-12587)*

Bay City Marine Inc (PA) ....**E...... 619 477-3991**
1625 Cleveland Ave National City (91950) *(P-5994)*

Bay City Television Inc (PA) ....**D...... 858 279-6666**
8253 Ronson Rd San Diego (92111) *(P-11939)*

Bay Clubs Company LLC ....B...... 805 778-0888
19867 Prairie St Ste 200 Chatsworth (91311) *(P-17394)*

Bay Clubs Company LLC ....B...... 310 216-3060
6833 Park Ter Los Angeles (90045) *(P-17395)*

Bay Clubs Company LLC ....B...... 858 509-9933
12000 Carmel Country Rd San Diego (92130) *(P-17464)*

Bay Clubs Company LLC ....B...... 805 964-0556
6144 Calle Real Goleta (93117) *(P-17465)*

Bay Clubs Company LLC ....B...... 805 965-0999
21 W Carrillo St Santa Barbara (93101) *(P-17466)*

Bay Clubs Company LLC ....B...... 805 563-8700
3908 State St Santa Barbara (93105) *(P-17467)*

Bay Clubs Company LLC ....B...... 310 643-6878
2250 Park Pl Thousand Oaks (91362) *(P-17468)*

Bay Clubs Company LLC ....B...... 310 541-2582
51 Peninsula Ctr Ste 51d Rancho Palos Verdes (90275) *(P-17469)*

Bay Clubs Company LLC ....B...... 310 829-4995
2425 Olympic Blvd Ste 100 Santa Monica (90404) *(P-17470)*

Bay Sheet Metal Inc ....E...... 619 401-9270
9343 Bond Ave Ste C El Cajon (92021) *(P-6200)*

Bay Valley Mortgage, La Mirada *Also Called: Pacific Bay Lending Group (P-14361)*

Bay Vista Senior Housing ....B...... 925 924-7100
1900 Huntington Dr Duarte (91010) *(P-14704)*

Bayless Manufacturing LLC ....C...... 661 257-3373
26140 Avenue Hall Valencia (91355) *(P-7777)*

Baymark Health Services La Inc ....C...... 310 761-4762
11682 Atlantic Ave Lynwood (90262) *(P-18744)*

Baymarr Constructors Inc ....C...... 661 395-1676
6950 Mcdivitt Dr Bakersfield (93313) *(P-1059)*

Bayshore Healthcare Inc ....C...... 805 544-5100
3033 Augusta St San Luis Obispo (93401) *(P-17888)*

Bayside Care Center, Morro Bay *Also Called: Compass Health Inc (P-17908)*

Bayside Healthcare Inc ....C...... 619 426-8611
553 F St Chula Vista (91910) *(P-17889)*

Baywa R.E., Irvine *Also Called: Baywa RE Operation Svcs LLC (P-741)*

Baywa R.E.renewable Energy, Irvine *Also Called: Baywa RE Solar Projects LLC (P-8774)*

Baywa RE Epc LLC ....E...... 949 398-3915
17901 Von Karman Ave Ste 1050 Irvine (92614) *(P-8773)*

Baywa RE Operation Svcs LLC ....E...... 949 398-3915
18575 Jamboree Rd Ste 850 Irvine (92612) *(P-741)*

Baywa RE Solar Projects LLC (DH) ....**C...... 949 398-3915**
18575 Jamboree Rd Ste 850 Irvine (92612) *(P-8774)*

Bazz Houston Co, Garden Grove *Also Called: Houston Bazz Co (P-6522)*

Bb Co Inc ....E...... 213 550-1158
1753 E 21st St Los Angeles (90058) *(P-2305)*

Bbcn Bank ....A...... 213 251-2222
3731 Wilshire Blvd Los Angeles (90010) *(P-14159)*

Bbe Sound Inc (PA) ....**E...... 714 897-6766**
2548 Fender Ave Ste G Fullerton (92831) *(P-10921)*

Bbeautiful LLC ....E...... 626 610-2332
1361 Mountain View Cir Azusa (91702) *(P-4382)*

Bbm Fairway Inc (PA) ....**C**
3520 Challenger St Torrance (90503) *(P-3345)*

Bbsi Camarillo, Camarillo *Also Called: Barrett Business Services Inc (P-15821)*

Bcd Food Inc ....F...... 310 323-1200
13507 S Normandie Ave Gardena (90249) *(P-1855)*

Bcd Industries Corp ....F...... 760 927-8988
24298 Via Vargas Dr Moreno Valley (92553) *(P-11193)*

Bcd Tofu House, Los Angeles *Also Called: Wilshire Kingsley Inc (P-14700)*

Bci Inc ....E...... 626 579-4234
1822 Belcroft Ave South El Monte (91733) *(P-7778)*

BCM Customer Service ....D...... 858 679-5757
12155 Kirkham Rd Poway (92064) *(P-742)*

Bcp Systems Inc ....D...... 714 202-3900
1560 S Sinclair St Anaheim (92806) *(P-16541)*

Bcra Resort Services Inc ....C...... 805 571-3176
8301 Hollister Ave Santa Barbara (93117) *(P-15088)*

Bd Carefusion, San Diego *Also Called: Carefusion Corporation (P-10795)*

BD&j PC ....D...... 855 906-3699
9701 Wilshire Blvd Ste 630 Beverly Hills (90212) *(P-18828)*

Bdc Distribution Center, Redlands *Also Called: Becton Dickinson and Company (P-10241)*

Bdc Epoxy Systems Inc ....E...... 562 944-6177
12903 Sunshine Ave Santa Fe Springs (90670) *(P-3928)*

Bdfco Inc ....D...... 714 228-2900
1926 Kauai Dr Costa Mesa (92626) *(P-8601)*

BDR Industries Inc ....E...... 818 341-2112
9700 Owensmouth Ave Lbby Chatsworth (91311) *(P-7509)*

BDR Industries Inc (PA) ....**D...... 661 940-8554**
820 E Avenue L12 Lancaster (93535) *(P-11969)*

Be Beauty, Garden Grove *Also Called: Cali Chem Inc (P-4387)*

Mergent email: customerrelations@mergent.com
1010

2024 Southern California
Business Directory and Buyers Guide

(P-0000) Products & Services Section entry number
(PA)=Parent Co (HQ)=Headquarters (DH)=Div Headquarters

Be Bop Clothing .... B....... 323 846-0121
5833 Avalon Blvd Los Angeles (90003) *(P-2306)*

Be Services Company Inc (HQ) ....**E.... 626 284-9901**
1200 Columbia Ave Riverside (92507) *(P-9003)*

Be Services Company Inc .... B....... 626 284-9901
300 Cypress Ave Alhambra (91801) *(P-9004)*

BE Smith Inc .... B....... 913 341-9116
12400 High Bluff Dr Ste 100 San Diego (92130) *(P-20316)*

Beach Area Family Health Ctr, San Diego *Also Called: Family Hlth Ctrs San Diego Inc
(P-17656)*

Beach Cities Health District .... C....... 310 374-3426
1200 Del Amo St Redondo Beach (90277) *(P-19317)*

Beach Creek Post-Acute, Anaheim *Also Called: Oceanside Harbor Holdings LLC (P-18020)*

Beach House Group, El Segundo *Also Called: Beach House Group LLC (P-11194)*

Beach House Group LLC ....D....... 310 356-6180
222 N Pacific Coast Hwy Fl 10 El Segundo (90245) *(P-11194)*

Beach News, Encinitas *Also Called: Coast News Inc (P-3266)*

Beach Paving Inc .... E....... 714 978-2414
749 N Poplar St Orange (92868) *(P-1060)*

Beach Reporter, Rlng Hls Est *Also Called: National Media Inc (P-3308)*

Beach State, Moorpark *Also Called: Picnic Time Inc (P-11269)*

Beachbody, El Segundo *Also Called: Beachbody LLC (P-15588)*

Beachbody LLC (HQ) ....**B.... 310 883-9000**
400 Continental Blvd Ste 400 El Segundo (90245) *(P-15588)*

Beachbody Company Inc (PA) ....**C.... 310 883-9000**
3301 Exposition Blvd Santa Monica (90404) *(P-15589)*

Beacon Concrete Inc .... F....... 323 889-7775
1597 S Bluff Rd Montebello (90640) *(P-5463)*

Beacon Manufacturing Inc .... E....... 714 529-0980
1000 Beacon St Brea (92821) *(P-3992)*

Beacon Pacific Inc .... C....... 714 288-1974
675 N Batavia St Orange (92868) *(P-12366)*

Beacon Resources LLC .... C....... 949 955-1773
17300 Red Hill Ave Irvine (92614) *(P-20140)*

Beador Construction Co Inc ....D....... 951 674-7352
2900 Bristol St Costa Mesa (92626) *(P-610)*

Bear Communications Inc ....D....... 619 263-2159
8290 Vickers St Ste D San Diego (92111) *(P-12644)*

Bear Communications Inc ....D....... 310 854-2327
8584 Venice Blvd Los Angeles (90034) *(P-12645)*

Bear State Kitchen, Los Angeles *Also Called: Jackson Manufacturing LLC (P-1339)*

Bear Valley Springs Assn .... C....... 661 821-5537
29541 Rollingoak Dr Tehachapi (93561) *(P-19425)*

Bear Vly Cmnty Healthcare Dst (PA) ....**C.... 909 866-6501**
41870 Garstin Dr Big Bear Lake (92315) *(P-18190)*

Bearcom Wireless Worldwide, San Diego *Also Called: Bear Communications Inc (P-12644)*

Bearcom Wireless Worldwide, Los Angeles *Also Called: Bear Communications Inc (P-12645)*

Bearsaver, Ontario *Also Called: Compumeric Engineering Inc (P-6216)*

Beating Wall Street Inc (PA) ....**C.... 818 332-9696**
20121 Ventura Blvd Ste 305 Woodland Hills (91364) *(P-14417)*

Beats By Dre, Culver City *Also Called: Beats Electronics LLC (P-8399)*

Beats Electronics LLC .... B....... 424 326-4679
8600 Hayden Pl Culver City (90232) *(P-8399)*

Beauchamp Distributing Company ....D....... 310 639-5320
1911 S Santa Fe Ave Compton (90221) *(P-13460)*

Beaumont Juice Inc ....D....... 951 769-7171
550 B St Beaumont (92223) *(P-1336)*

Beaumont Nielsen Marine Inc .... E....... 619 223-2628
2420 Shelter Island Dr San Diego (92106) *(P-16791)*

Beaumont Unfied Schl Dst Pub F .... B....... 951 845-6580
126 W Fifth St Beaumont (92223) *(P-18963)*

Beauty & Health International .... E....... 714 903-9730
7541 Anthony Ave Garden Grove (92841) *(P-4068)*

Beauty 21 Cosmetics Inc .... C....... 909 945-2220
2021 S Archibald Ave Ontario (91761) *(P-13030)*

Beauty Barrage LLC .... C....... 949 771-3399
4340 Von Karman Ave Ste 240 Newport Beach (92660) *(P-15477)*

Beauty Boutique Inc .... C....... 619 442-3407
1073 E Main St El Cajon (92021) *(P-15478)*

Beauty Health Company (PA) ....**B.... 800 603-4996**
2165 E Spring St Long Beach (90806) *(P-10450)*

Beauty Tent Inc .... E....... 323 717-7131
1131 N Kenmore Ave Apt 6 Los Angeles (90029) *(P-11195)*

Beaver Dam Health Care Center ....D....... 949 642-0387
340 Victoria St Costa Mesa (92627) *(P-17890)*

Beaver Medical Clinic, Highland *Also Called: Beaver Medical Group LP (P-17600)*

Beaver Medical Clinic Inc (PA) ....**C.... 909 793-3311**
1615 Orange Tree Ln Redlands (92374) *(P-17599)*

Beaver Medical Group LP (HQ) ....**C.... 909 425-3321**
7000 Boulder Ave Highland (92346) *(P-17600)*

Beazer, Brea *Also Called: Beazer Mortgage Corporation (P-482)*

Beazer Mortgage Corporation ....D....... 714 480-1635
1800 E Imperial Hwy Ste 200 Brea (92821) *(P-482)*

Bebe Studio Inc .... C....... 213 362-2323
10250 Santa Monica Blvd Ste 6 Los Angeles (90067) *(P-13957)*

Becca, Anaheim *Also Called: The Lunada Bay Corporation (P-2418)*

Becker Automotive Design USA, Oxnard *Also Called: Becker Automotive Designs Inc
(P-9281)*

Becker Automotive Designs Inc .... E....... 805 487-5227
1711 Ives Ave Oxnard (93033) *(P-9281)*

Becker Specialty Corporation ....D....... 909 356-1095
15310 Arrow Blvd Fontana (92335) *(P-8935)*

Beckers Fabrication Inc .... E....... 714 692-1600
22465 La Palma Ave Yorba Linda (92887) *(P-3167)*

Beckman Coulter Inc .... C....... 760 438-9151
2470 Faraday Ave Carlsbad (92010) *(P-10237)*

Beckman Coulter Inc .... C....... 818 970-2161
250 S Kraemer Blvd Brea (92821) *(P-10451)*

Beckman Coulter Inc (HQ) ....**A.... 714 993-5321**
250 S Kraemer Blvd Brea (92821) *(P-10238)*

Beckman Instruments Inc .... E....... 714 871-4848
2500 N Harbor Blvd Fullerton (92835) *(P-10239)*

Beckman Instruments Inc ....D....... 626 309-0110
8733 Scott St Rosemead (91770) *(P-10240)*

Beckman RES Inst of The Cy Hop .... C....... 626 359-8111
1500 Duarte Rd Duarte (91010) *(P-17601)*

Beckmen Vineyards .... E....... 805 688-8664
2670 Ontiveros Rd Los Olivos (93441) *(P-29)*

Becton Dickinson and Company ....D....... 909 748-7300
2200 W San Bernardino Ave Redlands (92374) *(P-10241)*

Becton Dickinson and Company ....D....... 888 876-4287
3750 Torrey View Ct San Diego (92130) *(P-10452)*

Bed Time Originals, El Segundo *Also Called: Lambs & Ivy Inc (P-2475)*

Bedrosian's Tile, Sylmar *Also Called: Paragon Industries Inc (P-1006)*

Bedrosian's Tiles & Stone, Anaheim *Also Called: Paragon Industries Inc (P-13668)*

Bee Wire & Cable Inc .... E....... 909 923-5800
2850 E Spruce St Ontario (91761) *(P-5730)*

Beech Street Corporation (HQ) ....**B.... 949 672-1000**
25550 Commercentre Dr Ste 200 Lake Forest (92630) *(P-20002)*

Beef Jerky Factory, Colton *Also Called: Hawa Corporation (P-1220)*

Beemak Plastics LLC ....D....... 800 421-4393
1515 S Harris Ct Anaheim (92806) *(P-4958)*

Beemak-Idl Display Products, Anaheim *Also Called: Beemak Plastics LLC (P-4958)*

Bega, Carpinteria *Also Called: Bega North America Inc (P-8354)*

Bega North America Inc ....D....... 805 684-0533
1000 Bega Way Carpinteria (93013) *(P-8354)*

Behavioral Health Works Inc ....D....... 800 249-1266
1301 E Orangewood Ave Anaheim (92805) *(P-18670)*

Behavioral Learning Netwrk LLC ....D....... 310 871-6800
10700 Santa Monica Blvd Ste 100 Los Angeles (90025) *(P-18671)*

Behavioral Medicine Center, Redlands *Also Called: Loma Linda University Med Ctr (P-18328)*

Behavioral Science Technology Inc (PA) ....**D.... 805 646-0166**
1000 Town Center Dr Ste 600 Oxnard (93036) *(P-20317)*

Behavral Hlthcare Slutions Inc .... C....... 858 573-2600
9465 Farnham St San Diego (92123) *(P-19027)*

Behr Holdings Corporation (HQ) ....**E.... 714 545-7101**
3400 W Segerstrom Ave Santa Ana (92704) *(P-4475)*

Behr Paint Company, Santa Ana *Also Called: Behr Process Corporation (P-4476)*

Behr Paint Corp., Santa Ana *Also Called: Behr Sales Inc (P-4481)*

Behr Process Corporation (DH) ....**A.... 714 545-7101**
1801 E Saint Andrew Pl Santa Ana (92705) *(P-4476)*

A
L
P
H
A
B
E
T
I
C

Employee Codes: A=Over 500 employees, B=251-500
C=101-250, D=51-100, E=20-50, F=10-19, G=1-9

2024 Southern California
Business Directory and Buyers Guide

© Mergent Inc. 1-800-342-5647

1011

Behr Process Corporation .... F...... 714 545-7101
1603 W Alton Ave Santa Ana (92704) *(P-4477)*

Behr Process Corporation .... F...... 714 545-7101
3400 W Garry Ave Santa Ana (92704) *(P-4478)*

Behr Process Corporation .... E...... 714 545-7101
3130 S Harbor Blvd Ste 520 Santa Ana (92704) *(P-4479)*

Behr Process Corporation .... F...... 714 545-7101
3500 W Segerstrom Ave Santa Ana (92704) *(P-4480)*

Behr Process Sales Company .... E...... 714 545-7101
3000 S Main St Apt 84e Santa Ana (92707) *(P-20281)*

Behr Sales Inc (HQ) .... C...... **714 545-7101**
3400 W Segerstrom Ave Santa Ana (92704) *(P-4481)*

Behringer Harvard Wilshire Blv .... D...... 310 475-8711
10740 Wilshire Blvd Los Angeles (90024) *(P-15089)*

BEI Industrial Encoders, Thousand Oaks *Also Called: Carros Sensors Systems Co LLC* *(P-10359)*

BEI Industrial Encoders, Thousand Oaks *Also Called: Sensata Technologies Inc (P-16597)*

BEI North America LLC (DH) .... C...... **805 716-0642**
1461 Lawrence Dr Thousand Oaks (91320) *(P-10354)*

Bel Tren Vlla Cnvalescent Hosp, Bellflower *Also Called: Life Care Centers America Inc* *(P-17991)*

Bel Vista Healthcare Center, Long Beach *Also Called: Villa De La Mar Inc (P-18159)*

Bel-Air Bay Club Ltd .... C...... 310 230-4700
16801 Pacific Coast Hwy Pacific Palisades (90272) *(P-17471)*

Bel-Air Cases, Ontario *Also Called: California Quality Plas Inc (P-4976)*

Bel-Air Country Club .... C...... 310 472-9563
10768 Bellagio Rd Los Angeles (90077) *(P-17472)*

Belagio Enterprises Inc .... E...... 323 731-6934
3737 Ross St Vernon (90058) *(P-2012)*

Belching Beaver Brewery .... C...... 760 599-5832
1334 Rocky Point Dr Oceanside (92056) *(P-14046)*

Belco Packaging Systems Inc .... E...... 626 357-9566
910 S Mountain Ave Monrovia (91016) *(P-7345)*

Belden Inc .... A...... 310 639-9473
1048 E Burgrove St Carson (90746) *(P-5731)*

Belding Golf Bag Company, The, Oxnard *Also Called: Illah Sports Inc (P-11004)*

Belinda, Vernon *Also Called: New Pride Corporation (P-13138)*

Belkin, El Segundo *Also Called: Belkin Inc (P-8400)*

Belkin Inc .... A...... 800 223-5546
555 S Aviation Blvd El Segundo (90245) *(P-8400)*

Belkin Components, El Segundo *Also Called: Belkin International Inc (P-7510)*

Belkin International Inc (DH) .... B...... 310 751-5100
555 S Aviation Blvd Ste 180 El Segundo (90245) *(P-7510)*

Bell Bros Steel Inc .... E...... 951 784-0903
1510 Palmyrita Ave Riverside (92507) *(P-5995)*

Bell Foundry Co (PA) .... D...... 323 564-5701
5310 Southern Ave South Gate (90280) *(P-10977)*

Bell Gardens Bicycle Club Inc .... A...... 562 806-4646
888 Bicycle Casino Dr Bell Gardens (90201) *(P-17541)*

Bell Villa Care Associates LLC .... D...... 562 925-4252
9028 Rose St Bellflower (90706) *(P-17891)*

Bella Collina San Clemente .... D...... 949 498-6604
200 Avenida La Pata San Clemente (92673) *(P-17473)*

Bella K .... E...... 213 559-7916
724 E 10th St Ste A Los Angeles (90021) *(P-5255)*

Bella Terra Nursery Inc .... D...... 619 585-1118
302 Hollister St San Diego (92154) *(P-13503)*

Bella Vsta Trnstional Care Ctr, San Luis Obispo *Also Called: Bayshore Healthcare Inc* *(P-17888)*

Bellami Hair, Chatsworth *Also Called: Bellami Hair LLC (P-15479)*

Bellami Hair LLC .... D...... 844 235-5264
21123 Nordhoff St Chatsworth (91311) *(P-15479)*

Belldini, Los Angeles *Also Called: Flirt Inc (P-13126)*

Bellflower Dental Group, Bellflower *Also Called: Peter Wylan DDS (P-17845)*

Bellflower Medical Center, Los Angeles *Also Called: Jupiter Bellflower Doctors Hospital* *(P-18293)*

Bellota US Corp .... C...... 951 737-6515
22440 Temescal Canyon Rd Corona (92883) *(P-14959)*

Bellows Mfg & RES Inc .... E...... 818 838-1333
864 Arroyo St San Fernando (91340) *(P-5996)*

Bellrock Media Inc (PA) .... E...... **310 315-2727**
11500 W Olympic Blvd Ste 400 Los Angeles (90064) *(P-15978)*

Bellus Academy, El Cajon *Also Called: Beauty Boutique Inc (P-15478)*

Belmont Brewing Company Inc .... E...... 562 433-3891
25 39th Pl Long Beach (90803) *(P-13982)*

Belport Company Inc (PA) .... F...... **805 484-1051**
4825 Calle Alto Camarillo (93012) *(P-10730)*

Belshire, Foothill Ranch *Also Called: Belshire Trnsp Svcs Inc (P-11444)*

Belshire Trnsp Svcs Inc .... C...... 949 460-5200
25971 Towne Centre Dr Foothill Ranch (92610) *(P-11444)*

Belt Drives Ltd .... E...... 714 693-1313
505 W Lambert Rd Brea (92821) *(P-9874)*

Belvedere Hotel Partnership .... B...... 310 551-2888
9882 Santa Monica Blvd Beverly Hills (90212) *(P-15090)*

Belvedere Partnership .... B...... 310 551-2888
9882 Santa Monica Blvd Beverly Hills (90212) *(P-15091)*

Bemco Inc (PA) .... E...... **805 583-4970**
2255 Union Pl Simi Valley (93065) *(P-10242)*

Bemus Landscape Inc .... B...... 714 557-7910
951 Calle Negocio Ste D San Clemente (92673) *(P-706)*

Ben F Smith Inc .... C...... 858 271-4320
8655 Miramar Pl Ste B San Diego (92121) *(P-1061)*

Ben Group Inc .... B...... 310 342-1500
14724 Ventura Blvd Ste 1200 Sherman Oaks (91403) *(P-15979)*

Bench 2 Bench Technologies, Fullerton *Also Called: Winonics Inc (P-8753)*

Bench Depot, Tecate *Also Called: Benchpro Inc (P-12277)*

Benchmark, Moorpark *Also Called: Benchmark Elec Mfg Sltons Mrpa (P-8653)*

Benchmark Contractors, Santa Monica *Also Called: Morley Builders Inc (P-512)*

Benchmark Elec Mfg Sltons Mrpa .... A...... 805 532-2800
200 Science Dr Moorpark (93021) *(P-8653)*

Benchmark Elec Phoenix Inc .... B...... 619 397-2402
1659 Gailes Blvd San Diego (92154) *(P-8654)*

Benchmark Landscape Svcs Inc .... C...... 858 513-7190
12575 Stowe Dr Poway (92064) *(P-142)*

Benchmark Secure Technology, Santa Ana *Also Called: Secure Comm Systems Inc (P-8577)*

Benchpro Inc .... C...... 619 478-9400
23949 Tecate Mission Rd Tecate (91980) *(P-12277)*

Bend-Tek Inc .... D...... 714 210-8966
2205 S Yale St Santa Ana (92704) *(P-6201)*

Bender Ccp Inc (PA) .... E...... **707 745-9970**
2150 E 37th St Vernon (90058) *(P-7779)*

Bender Ready Mix Inc .... E...... 714 560-0744
516 S Santa Fe St Santa Ana (92705) *(P-5464)*

Bender Ready Mix Concrete, Santa Ana *Also Called: Bender Ready Mix Inc (P-5464)*

Bender US, Vernon *Also Called: Bender Ccp Inc (P-7779)*

Bendick Precision Inc .... E...... 626 445-0217
56 La Porte St Arcadia (91006) *(P-7780)*

Bendpak Inc (PA) .... C...... **805 933-9970**
30440 Agoura Rd Agoura Hills (91301) *(P-7227)*

Benefit Programs ADM, City Of Industry *Also Called: Management Applied Prgrm Inc* *(P-16503)*

Benefits Prgram Adminsitration .... D...... 562 463-5000
13191 Concords Pkwy N Ste 205 City Of Industry (91746) *(P-14988)*

Benetrac, San Diego *Also Called: Paychex Benefit Tech Inc (P-11896)*

Benevolence Food Products LLC .... E...... 888 832-3738
2761 Saturn St Ste D Brea (92821) *(P-1856)*

Benihana 24, Encino *Also Called: Benihana Inc (P-13983)*

Benihana Inc .... D...... 818 788-7121
16226 Ventura Blvd Encino (91436) *(P-13983)*

Benjamin Moore Authorized Ret, Corona *Also Called: Ganahl Lumber Company (P-13576)*

Bennett Entps A Cal Ldscp Cntg .... D...... 310 534-3543
25889 Belle Porte Ave Harbor City (90710) *(P-143)*

Bennett Landscape, Harbor City *Also Called: Bennett Entps A Cal Ldscp Cntg (P-143)*

Bennion Deville Fine Homes Inc .... B...... 760 674-3452
74850 Us Highway 111 Indian Wells (92210) *(P-14749)*

Benny Enterprises Inc .... E...... 619 592-4455
1100 N Johnson Ave Ste 110 El Cajon (92020) *(P-13461)*

Benrich Service Company Inc (PA) .... E...... **714 241-0284**
3190 Airport Loop Dr Ste G Costa Mesa (92626) *(P-16792)*

Bens Asphalt & Maint Co Inc .... D...... 951 248-1103
2537 Rubidoux Blvd Riverside (92509) *(P-611)*

Bent Manufacturing Co Inc .... D....... 714 842-0600
17311 Nichols Ln Huntington Beach (92647) *(P-4959)*

Bent Manufacturing Company, Huntington Beach *Also Called: Bent Manufacturing Co Inc*
(P-4959)

Bentley Mills, City Of Industry *Also Called: Bentley Mills Inc (P-2110)*

Bentley Mills Inc (PA).. C....... 626 333-4585
14641 Don Julian Rd City Of Industry (91746) *(P-2110)*

Bentley-Simonson Inc ....E....... 805 650-2794
1746f S Victoria Ave Ste 382 Ventura (93003) *(P-246)*

Bento Box Entertainment LLC .... B....... 818 333-7700
5161 Lankershim Blvd Ste 120 North Hollywood (91601) *(P-17171)*

Beonca Machine Inc .... F....... 909 392-9991
1680 Curtiss Ct La Verne (91750) *(P-7781)*

Beranek LLC ....E....... 310 328-9094
2340 W 205th St Torrance (90501) *(P-7782)*

Berenice 2 AM Corp ....E....... 858 255-8693
8008 Girard Ave Ste 150 La Jolla (92037) *(P-1293)*

Berg Lacquer Co (PA).. D....... 323 261-8114
3150 E Pico Blvd Los Angeles (90023) *(P-13523)*

Bergandi Machinery Company, Ontario *Also Called: Bmci Inc (P-7167)*

Bergelectric Corp (PA).. D....... 760 638-2374
3182 Lionshead Ave Carlsbad (92010) *(P-869)*

Bergelectric Corp .... A....... 760 746-1003
3182 Lionshead Ave Carlsbad (92010) *(P-870)*

Bergelectric Corp .... D....... 760 291-8100
955 Borra Pl Escondido (92029) *(P-871)*

Bergelectric Corp .... C....... 949 250-7005
15776 Gateway Cir Tustin (92780) *(P-872)*

Bergensons Property Svcs Inc .... A....... 760 631-5111
3605 Ocean Ranch Blvd Ste 200 Oceanside (92056) *(P-15695)*

Berger Inc .... A....... 818 986-1234
5955 De Soto Ave Ste 160 Woodland Hills (91367) *(P-18593)*

Berger Bros Inc .... B....... 626 334-2699
154 N Aspan Ave Azusa (91702) *(P-968)*

Bergman Kprs LLC (PA)... C....... 714 924-7000
2850 Saturn St Ste 100 Brea (92821) *(P-535)*

Bergsen Inc ....E....... 562 236-9787
12241 Florence Ave Santa Fe Springs (90670) *(P-12535)*

Bericap, Ontario *Also Called: Bericap LLC (P-4960)*

Bericap LLC .... D....... 905 634-2248
1671 Champagne Ave Ste B Ontario (91761) *(P-4960)*

Berkeley E Convalescent Hosp .... C....... 310 829-5377
2021 Arizona Ave Santa Monica (90404) *(P-18112)*

Berkeley E Convalescent Hosp, Santa Monica *Also Called: Berkeley E Convalescent Hosp*
(P-18112)

Berkeley Farms LLC .... B....... 510 265-8600
17637 E Valley Blvd City Of Industry (91744) *(P-1306)*

Berkley East Healthcare Center, Santa Monica *Also Called: Asmb LLC (P-17883)*

Berkshire Hathaway Home Servic .... D....... 562 809-1331
11409 Carson St Lakewood (90715) *(P-14507)*

Berkshire Hathaway Home Servic .... D....... 626 335-6001
231 S Glendora Ave Glendora (91741) *(P-19028)*

Berkshire Hthway HM Svcs CA Rp .... D....... 562 307-5636
9836 Atlantic Ave South Gate (90280) *(P-14750)*

Berkshire Hthway HM Svcs Cal P .... C....... 619 302-8082
2365 Northside Dr Ste 200 San Diego (92108) *(P-14302)*

Bermingham Cntrls Inc A Cal Co (PA)...................... E....... 562 860-0463
11144 Business Cir Cerritos (90703) *(P-6754)*

Bernardo Hts Healthcare Inc .... C....... 858 673-0101
11895 Avenue Of Industry San Diego (92128) *(P-18113)*

Bernardo Technical Services .... F....... 858 779-9276
16885 W Bernardo Dr # 210 San Diego (92127) *(P-16554)*

Bernards Builders Inc .... B....... 818 898-1521
555 1st St San Fernando (91340) *(P-467)*

Bernel Inc .... C....... 714 778-6070
501 W Southern Ave Orange (92865) *(P-743)*

Bernell Hydraulics Inc (PA)..................................... E....... 909 899-1751
8821 Etiwanda Ave Rancho Cucamonga (91739) *(P-7710)*

Berney-Karp Inc .... D....... 323 260-7122
3350 E 26th St Vernon (90058) *(P-5383)*

Bernhardt and Bernhardt Inc .... E....... 714 544-0708
14771 Myford Rd Ste D Tustin (92780) *(P-7005)*

Berns Bros Inc .... F....... 562 437-0471
1250 W 17th St Long Beach (90813) *(P-7783)*

Bernstein, Los Angeles *Also Called: Alliancebernstein LP (P-14954)*

Berri Pro Inc .... F....... 781 929-8288
840 Apollo St Ste 100 El Segundo (90245) *(P-1756)*

Berry Global Inc .... C....... 909 465-9055
14000 Monte Vista Ave Chino (91710) *(P-4961)*

Berry Global Inc .... D....... 714 777-5200
4875 E Hunter Ave Anaheim (92807) *(P-4962)*

Berry Global Films LLC .... C....... 909 517-2872
14000 Monte Vista Ave Chino (91710) *(P-4807)*

Berry Petroleum Company LLC (HQ)........................ E....... 661 616-3900
11117 River Run Blvd Bakersfield (93311) *(P-247)*

Berry Petroleum Company LLC .... D....... 661 255-6066
25121 Sierra Hwy Newhall (91321) *(P-248)*

Berry Petroleum Company LLC .... D....... 661 769-8820
28700 Hovey Hills Rd Taft (93268) *(P-249)*

Berry-Perussi Inc .... E....... 949 461-7000
25131 Arctic Ocean Dr Lake Forest (92630) *(P-6498)*

Bert-Co, Ontario *Also Called: Bert-Co Industries Inc (P-3518)*

Bert-Co Industries Inc .... C....... 323 669-5700
2150 S Parco Ave Ontario (91761) *(P-3518)*

Bert-Co. of Ontario CA, Ontario *Also Called: Edelmann Usa Inc (P-11111)*

Bertelsmann Inc .... A....... 661 702-2700
29011 Commerce Center Dr Valencia (91355) *(P-3399)*

Beryl Lockhart Enterprises, Sun Valley *Also Called: Ble Inc (P-278)*

Besser Company, Compton *Also Called: Concrete Mold Corporation (P-7063)*

Best Buy Imports, Vernon *Also Called: Makabi 26 Inc (P-5090)*

Best Cheer Stone Inc (PA)...................................... E....... 714 399-1588
3190 E Miraloma Ave Anaheim (92806) *(P-12348)*

Best Contracting Services Inc (PA).......................... B....... 310 328-9176
19027 S Hamilton Ave Gardena (90248) *(P-1037)*

Best Data Products Inc .... D....... 818 534-1414
9236 Deering Ave Chatsworth (91311) *(P-7511)*

Best Financial, The, Signal Hill *Also Called: First American Team Realty Inc (P-14795)*

Best Formulations, City Of Industry *Also Called: Best Formulations LLC (P-1857)*

Best Formulations Inc .... C....... 626 912-9998
17775 Rowland St City Of Industry (91748) *(P-4069)*

BEST FORMULATIONS INC., City Of Industry *Also Called: Best Formulations Inc (P-4069)*

Best Formulations LLC (HQ).................................... E....... 626 912-9998
17758 Rowland St City Of Industry (91748) *(P-1857)*

Best Friends Animal Society .... C....... 818 643-3989
1845 Pontius Ave Los Angeles (90025) *(P-19526)*

Best Interiors Inc (PA).. C....... 714 490-7999
2100 E Via Burton Anaheim (92806) *(P-969)*

Best Interiors Inc .... E....... 858 715-3760
4395 Murphy Canyon Rd San Diego (92123) *(P-970)*

Best Label Company, Cerritos *Also Called: Resource Label Group LLC (P-3679)*

BEST OPPORTUNITIES, Apple Valley *Also Called: BEST Opportunities Inc (P-19177)*

BEST Opportunities Inc .... C....... 760 628-0111
22450 Headquarters Ave Apple Valley (92307) *(P-19177)*

Best Overnight Express, Irwindale *Also Called: Best Overnite Express Inc (P-11472)*

Best Overnite Express Inc (PA)............................... D....... 626 256-6340
406 Live Oak Ave Irwindale (91706) *(P-11472)*

Best Redwood, San Diego *Also Called: Rtmex Inc (P-2579)*

Best Roll-Up Door Inc .... E....... 562 802-2233
13202 Arctic Cir Santa Fe Springs (90670) *(P-6101)*

Best Signs Inc (PA).. E....... 760 320-3042
1550 S Gene Autry Trl Palm Springs (92264) *(P-16793)*

Best Way Disposal Co Inc .... C....... 760 244-9773
17105 Mesa St Hesperia (92345) *(P-12159)*

Best Way Marble, Los Angeles *Also Called: Best-Way Marble & Tile Co Inc (P-5525)*

Best Western, Santa Barbara *Also Called: Encina Pepper Tree Joint Ventr (P-15147)*

Best Western Golden Sails Ht, Torrance *Also Called: Long Beach Golden Sails Inc (P-15230)*

Best Western Stovalls Inn (PA)................................ D....... 714 956-4430
1110 W Katella Ave Anaheim (92802) *(P-15092)*

Best Wstn Fireside Inn By Sea, Cambria *Also Called: Moonstone Bch Innvstors A Cal*
(P-15254)

Best- In- West .... E....... 909 947-6507
2279 Eagle Glen Pkwy Ste 112 Corona (92883) *(P-2514)*

ALPHABETIC

Employee Codes: A=Over 500 employees, B=251-500
C=101-250, D=51-100, E=20-50, F=10-19, G=1-9

2024 Southern California
Business Directory and Buyers Guide

© Mergent Inc. 1-800-342-5647

1013

Best-In-West Emblem Co, Corona *Also Called: Best- In- West (P-2514)*

Best-Way Distributing Co, Sylmar *Also Called: Allied Company Holdings Inc (P-13459)*

Best-Way Marble & Tile Co Inc ....E...... 323 266-6794
5037 Telegraph Rd Los Angeles (90022) *(P-5525)*

Bestforms Inc ....E...... 805 388-0503
1135 Avenida Acaso Camarillo (93012) *(P-3829)*

Bestop Baja LLC ....C...... 760 560-2252
2950 Norman Strasse Rd San Marcos (92069) *(P-13899)*

Bestpack Packaging Systems, Ontario *Also Called: Future Commodities Intl Inc (P-7348)*

Bestsio LLC ....F...... 626 841-8543
1230 Santa Anita Ave Ste D South El Monte (91733) *(P-10899)*

Bestway Sandwiches Inc (PA)..................................**E...... 818 361-1800**
28209 Avenue Stanford Valencia (91355) *(P-1454)*,

Beta Bionics Inc ....D...... 949 297-6635
11 Hughes Irvine (92618) *(P-10792)*

Beta Offshore, Long Beach *Also Called: Beta Operating Company LLC (P-250)*

Beta Operating Company LLC ....D...... 562 628-1526
111 W Ocean Blvd Long Beach (90802) *(P-250)*

Bethar Corporation C
17625 Railroad St City Of Industry (91748) *(P-14924)*

Bethlehem Construction Inc ....D...... 661 758-1001
425 J St Wasco (93280) *(P-495)*

Better Bakery Co, Ventura *Also Called: Better Bakery LLC (P-1509)*

Better Bakery LLC ....C...... 661 294-9882
444 E Santa Clara St Ventura (93001) *(P-1509)*

Better Bar Manufacturing LLC ....E...... 951 525-3111
6975 Arlington Ave Riverside (92503) *(P-1260)*

Better Beverages Inc (PA)..................................**E...... 562 924-8321**
10624 Midway Ave Cerritos (90703) *(P-1757)*

Better Mens Clothes, Los Angeles *Also Called: Hirsh Inc (P-353)*

Better Night LLC ....D...... 619 299-6299
5471 Kearny Villa Rd Ste 200 San Diego (92123) *(P-12476)*

Better Nutritionals LLC ....D...... 310 356-9019
3380 Horseless Carriage Rd Norco (92860) *(P-1261)*

Better Nutritionals LLC ....D...... 310 356-9019
3350 Horseless Carriage Rd Norco (92860) *(P-1262)*

Better Nutritionals LLC ....E...... 310 356-9019
17120 S Figueroa St Ste B Gardena (90248) *(P-1263)*

Betts Company ....E...... 909 427-9988
10771 Almond Ave Ste B Fontana (92337) *(P-6800)*

Betts Truck Parts, Fontana *Also Called: Betts Company (P-6800)*

Betty Ford Center (HQ)..................................**C...... 760 773-4100**
39000 Bob Hope Dr Rancho Mirage (92270) *(P-18672)*

Beveragefactory.com, San Diego *Also Called: Cydea Inc (P-1620)*

Beverages & More Inc ....C...... 949 643-3020
28011 Greenfield Dr Laguna Niguel (92677) *(P-1685)*

Beverages & More Inc ....C...... 714 891-1242
6820 Katella Ave Cypress (90630) *(P-12760)*

Beverages & More Inc ....C...... 714 279-8131
2000 N Tustin St Orange (92865) *(P-14058)*

Beverages & More Inc ....C...... 714 990-2060
875 E Birch St Ste A Brea (92821) *(P-14059)*

Beverly and Company Inc ....D...... 323 422-3253
15301 Ventura Blvd B305 Sherman Oaks (91403) *(P-14751)*

Beverly Community Hosp Assn (PA)..................................**A...... 323 726-1222**
309 W Beverly Blvd Montebello (90640) *(P-18191)*

Beverly Furniture, Pomona *Also Called: Rbf Lifestyle Holdings LLC (P-2897)*

Beverly Healthcare, Costa Mesa *Also Called: Beaver Dam Health Care Center (P-17890)*

Beverway Hills BMW, Los Angeles *Also Called: FAA Beverly Hills Inc (P-13765)*

Beverly Hills Hotel, Beverly Hills *Also Called: Sajahtera Inc (P-15340)*

Beverly Hills Luxury Hotel LLC ....B...... 310 274-9999
1801 Century Park E Ste 1200 Los Angeles (90067) *(P-15093)*

Beverly Hills Plaza Hotel, Los Angeles *Also Called: Donald T Sterling Corporation (P-15137)*

Beverly Hospital, Montebello *Also Called: Beverly Community Hosp Assn (P-18191)*

Beverly Office of Mgo, Los Angeles *Also Called: Macias Gini & OConnell LLP (P-19792)*

Beverly West Health Care Inc ....D...... 323 938-2451
1020 S Fairfax Ave Los Angeles (90019) *(P-17892)*

Bevmo, Laguna Niguel *Also Called: Beverages & More Inc (P-1685)*

Bevpack, Van Nuys *Also Called: Power Brands Consulting LLC (P-1602)*

Bexel, Van Nuys *Also Called: Nep Bexel Inc (P-17257)*

Bey-Berk International (PA)..................................**E...... 818 773-7534**
9145 Deering Ave Chatsworth (91311) *(P-6857)*

Beyond Finance LLC ....A...... 800 282-7186
9525 Towne Centre Dr Ste 100 San Diego (92121) *(P-15499)*

Beyond Franchise Group Inc ....C...... 949 398-7338
220 Technology Dr Ste 120 Irvine (92618) *(P-13984)*

Beyond Meat Inc ....C...... 866 756-4112
888 N Douglas St Ste 100 El Segundo (90245) *(P-1213)*

Beyond Meat Inc (PA)..................................**E...... 866 756-4112**
119 Standard St El Segundo (90245) *(P-1385)*

Beyond Meat and Company, Anaheim *Also Called: Caballero & Sons Inc (P-14410)*

Beyondsoft Consulting Inc ....C...... 310 532-2822
19009 S Laurel Park Rd Spc 6 Compton (90220) *(P-20318)*

BF Suma Pharmaceuticals Inc ....E...... 626 285-8366
5077 Walnut Grove Ave San Gabriel (91776) *(P-4070)*

Bh Partnership LP (PA)..................................**B...... 858 539-7635**
998 W Mission Bay Dr San Diego (92109) *(P-15094)*

Bh-SD Opco LLC (PA)..................................**D...... 619 465-4411**
7050 Parkway Dr La Mesa (91942) *(P-18673)*

Bh-Tech Inc ....A...... 858 694-0900
6174 Lemonglaze Ct San Diego (92130) *(P-4963)*

Bhc Alhambra Hospital, Rosemead *Also Called: Bhc Alhambra Hospital Inc (P-18745)*

Bhc Alhambra Hospital Inc ....B...... 626 286-1191
4619 Rosemead Blvd Rosemead (91770) *(P-18745)*

Bhc Industries, Compton *Also Called: Barkens Hardchrome Inc (P-7226)*

BHC Industries Inc ....E...... 310 632-2000
239 E Greenleaf Blvd Compton (90220) *(P-6590)*

Bhr Operations LLC ....C...... 619 232-3861
1355 N Harbor Dr San Diego (92101) *(P-15095)*

Bhu Food, San Diego *Also Called: Lauras Orgnal Bston Brwnies In (P-1479)*

Bi Nutraceuticals Inc ....C...... 310 669-2100
2384 E Pacifica Pl Rancho Dominguez (90220) *(P-1758)*

Bi Technologies Corporation (HQ)..................................**B...... 714 447-2300**
120 S State College Blvd Ste 175 Brea (92821) *(P-9005)*

Bi-Search International Inc ....D...... 714 258-4500
17550 Gillette Ave Irvine (92614) *(P-9006)*

Bicara Ltd ....E...... 310 316-6222
318 Avenue I Ste 65 Redondo Beach (90277) *(P-13290)*

Bicycle Club Casino, Bell Gardens *Also Called: Bell Gardens Bicycle Club Inc (P-17541)*

Bien Air, Irvine *Also Called: Bien Air Usa Inc (P-10731)*

Bien Air Usa Inc ....D...... 949 477-6050
8861 Research Dr Ste 100 Irvine (92618) *(P-10731)*

Big 5 Electronics Inc ....E...... 562 941-4669
13452 Alondra Blvd Cerritos (90703) *(P-8401)*

Big Bear Bowling Barn Inc ....E...... 909 878-2695
40625 Big Bear Blvd Big Bear Lake (92315) *(P-1144)*

Big Bear Grizzly & Big Bear Lf, Big Bear Lake *Also Called: Hi-Desert Publishing Company (P-14117)*

Big Brand Tire & Service ....D...... 951 679-6266
26920 Newport Rd Menifee (92584) *(P-4693)*

Big Brand Tire & Svc - Menifee, Menifee *Also Called: Big Brand Tire & Service (P-4693)*

Big Canyon Country Club ....C...... 949 644-5404
1 Big Canyon Dr Newport Beach (92660) *(P-17474)*

Big Cart Corporation ....F...... 949 250-7064
16682 Millikan Ave Irvine (92606) *(P-15980)*

Big Dog Sportswear, Los Angeles *Also Called: Walking Company Holdings Inc (P-13924)*

Big Eight, Lancaster *Also Called: City of Lancaster (P-17447)*

BIG Enterprises ....E...... 626 448-1449
9702 Rush St El Monte (91733) *(P-6374)*

Big Five Electronics, Cerritos *Also Called: Big 5 Electronics Inc (P-8401)*

Big Horn Wealth Management Inc ....D...... 951 273-7900
2577 Research Dr Corona (92882) *(P-3519)*

Big League Pillows LLC ....F...... 949 422-8443
1600 Vine St Apt 1034 Los Angeles (90028) *(P-2466)*

Big Lgue Dreams Consulting LLC ....C...... 760 324-5600
33700 Date Palm Dr Cathedral City (92234) *(P-15434)*

Big Lgue Dreams Consulting LLC ....C...... 619 846-8855
2155 Trumble Rd Perris (92571) *(P-17364)*

Big Lgue Dreams Consulting LLC ....C...... 626 839-1100
2100 S Azusa Ave West Covina (91792) *(P-17365)*

Big Nickel, Palm Desert *Also Called: Daniels Inc (P-3439)*

Big Star, South Gate *Also Called: Koos Manufacturing Inc (P-16855)*

Big Strike, Los Angeles *Also Called: Tlmf Inc (P-2290)*

Big T Industries, Lake Forest *Also Called: Big Train Inc (P-1294)*

Big Train Inc ....C...... 949 340-8800
25392 Commercentre Dr Lake Forest (92630) *(P-1294)*

Big Tree Furniture & Inds Inc (PA)...........................**E...... 310 894-7500**
760 S Vail Ave Montebello (90640) *(P-2768)*

Bigfogg Inc (PA)..**F...... 951 587-2460**
30818 Wealth St Murrieta (92563) *(P-7601)*

Bigge Group ....C...... 714 523-4092
14511 Industry Cir La Mirada (90638) *(P-15758)*

Bighorn Golf Club Charities ....C...... 760 773-2468
255 Palowet Dr Palm Desert (92260) *(P-17475)*

Bijan, Beverly Hills *Also Called: Fashion World Incorporated (P-13102)*

Bikes Online Inc ....D...... 650 272-3378
2711 Loker Ave W Carlsbad (92010) *(P-12926)*

Bill & Daves Ldscp Maint Inc ....C...... 714 850-0213
1401 E Edinger Ave Santa Ana (92705) *(P-144)*

Bill Howe Plumbing Inc ....D...... 800 245-5469
9210 Sky Park Ct San Diego (92123) *(P-744)*

Billabong, Huntington Beach *Also Called: Boardriders Inc (P-2198)*

Billy Blues, Commerce *Also Called: AB&r Inc (P-2298)*

Bilt-Well Roofing & Mtl Co, Los Angeles *Also Called: Sbb Roofing Inc (P-1054)*

Bimbo Bakeries Usa Inc ....F...... 323 720-6099
480 S Vail Ave Montebello (90640) *(P-1455)*

Bimbo Bakeries USA, Inc, Montebello *Also Called: Bimbo Bakeries Usa Inc (P-1455)*

Bimeda Inc ....C...... 626 815-1680
5539 Ayon Ave Irwindale (91706) *(P-4071)*

Binder Metal Products Inc ....D...... 800 233-0896
14909 S Broadway Gardena (90248) *(P-6499)*

Bingo Publishers Incorporated ....E...... 949 581-5410
24881 Alicia Pkwy Ste E Laguna Hills (92653) *(P-3430)*

Binoptics LLC ....C...... 607 257-3200
977 S Meridian Ave Alhambra (91803) *(P-19553)*

Bio Hazard Inc ....E...... 213 625-2116
6247 Randolph St Commerce (90040) *(P-13529)*

Bio-Med Services Inc ....D...... 909 235-4400
3300 E Guasti Rd Ontario (91761) *(P-18192)*

Bio-Medical Devices Inc ....E...... 949 752-9642
17171 Daimler St Irvine (92614) *(P-10453)*

Bio-Medical Devices Intl Inc ....E...... 949 752-9642
17171 Daimler St Irvine (92614) *(P-10454)*

Bio-Medics Inc ....C...... 909 883-9501
371 W Highland Ave San Bernardino (92405) *(P-18746)*

Bio-Nutraceuticals Inc (PA)...................................**F...... 818 727-0246**
21820 Marilla St Chatsworth (91311) *(P-4072)*

Bio-Nutritional RES Group Inc ....C...... 714 427-6990
6 Morgan Ste 100 Irvine (92618) *(P-1264)*

Bio-RAD Laboratories Inc ....D...... 949 598-1200
9500 Jeronimo Rd Irvine (92618) *(P-3993)*

Bio-Reigns Inc ....D...... 949 922-2032
1451 Edinger Ave Ste D Tustin (92780) *(P-11196)*

BIOATLA, San Diego *Also Called: Bioatla Inc (P-4306)*

Bioatla Inc ....E...... 858 558-0708
11085 Torreyana Rd San Diego (92121) *(P-4306)*

Biocell Laboratories Inc ....E...... 310 537-3300
2001 E University Dr Rancho Dominguez (90220) *(P-4267)*

Biodot Inc (HQ)..**D...... 949 440-3685**
2852 Alton Pkwy Irvine (92606) *(P-10119)*

Bioduro LLC ....B...... 858 529-6600
72 Fairbanks Irvine (92618) *(P-19824)*

Bioduro LLC (PA)..**E...... 858 529-6600**
11011 Torreyana Rd San Diego (92121) *(P-19825)*

Biofilm Inc ....D...... 760 727-9030
3225 Executive Rdg Vista (92081) *(P-10455)*

Biogeneral Inc ....E...... 858 453-4451
9925 Mesa Rim Rd San Diego (92121) *(P-10456)*

Bioject Inc ....E...... 503 692-8001
6769 Mesa Ridge Rd Ste 99 San Diego (92121) *(P-10457)*

Biolase Inc ....D...... 949 361-1200
4225 Prado Rd Ste 102 Corona (92878) *(P-10732)*

Biolegend Inc (HQ)...**C...... 858 455-9588**
8999 Biolegend Way San Diego (92121) *(P-19826)*

Biolegend Cns Inc ....E...... 781 915-5200
8999 Biolegend Way San Diego (92121) *(P-19827)*

Biomed California Inc ....E...... 310 665-1121
721 S Glasgow Ave Ste C Inglewood (90301) *(P-4073)*

Biomed Realty, San Diego *Also Called: Biomed Realty Trust Inc (P-15012)*

Biomed Realty Trust Inc (PA).................................**B...... 858 207-2513**
4570 Executive Dr Ste 400 San Diego (92121) *(P-15012)*

BIOMERICA, Irvine *Also Called: Biomerica Inc (P-4268)*

Biomerica Inc (PA)...**F...... 949 645-2111**
17571 Von Karman Ave Irvine (92614) *(P-4268)*

Biomet Inc ....E...... 949 453-3200
181 Technology Dr Irvine (92618) *(P-10638)*

BIONANO GENOMICS, San Diego *Also Called: Bionano Genomics Inc (P-10243)*

Bionano Genomics Inc (PA)....................................**D...... 858 888-7600**
9540 Towne Centre Dr Ste 100 San Diego (92121) *(P-10243)*

Bioness Inc ....C...... 661 362-4850
25103 Rye Canyon Loop Valencia (91355) *(P-10793)*

Bionime USA Corporation ....E...... 909 781-6969
1450 E Spruce St Ste B Ontario (91761) *(P-12477)*

Biopac Systems Inc ....E...... 805 685-0066
42 Aero Camino Goleta (93117) *(P-10244)*

Bioplate Inc ....E...... 310 815-2100
570 S Melrose St Placentia (92870) *(P-10458)*

Bioquip Products Inc ....E...... 310 667-8800
2321 E Gladwick St Rancho Dominguez (90220) *(P-19828)*

Biora Therapeutics Inc (PA)....................................**D...... 855 293-2639**
4330 La Jolla Village Dr Ste 300 San Diego (92122) *(P-18539)*

Biorad Inc ....E...... 949 598-1200
9500 Jeronimo Rd Irvine (92618) *(P-10245)*

Biorx Laboratories, Commerce *Also Called: Biorx Pharmaceuticals Inc (P-4074)*

Biorx Pharmaceuticals Inc ....E...... 323 725-3100
6320 Chalet Dr Commerce (90040) *(P-4074)*

Bioscience Research Reagents, Temecula *Also Called: EMD Millipore Corporation (P-4313)*

Bioseal ....E...... 714 528-4695
167 W Orangethorpe Ave Placentia (92870) *(P-10459)*

Biosense Webster Inc (HQ).....................................**C...... 909 839-8500**
31 Technology Dr Ste 200 Irvine (92618) *(P-10794)*

Biosero (PA)..**E...... 858 880-7376**
4770 Ruffner St San Diego (92111) *(P-15981)*

Bioserv Corporation ....E...... 917 817-1326
5340 Eastgate Mall San Diego (92121) *(P-4269)*

Bioserve, San Diego *Also Called: Bioserv Corporation (P-4269)*

Biosite Inc ....C...... 510 683-9063
9975 Summers Ridge Rd San Diego (92121) *(P-12478)*

Biosource International Inc ....E...... 805 659-5759
5791 Van Allen Way Carlsbad (92008) *(P-4270)*

Biospace Inc ....E...... 323 932-6503
13850 Cerritos Corporate Dr Ste C Cerritos (90703) *(P-19829)*

Biospherical Instruments Inc ....E...... 619 686-1888
5340 Riley St San Diego (92110) *(P-9960)*

Biosplice Therapeutics Inc ....D...... 858 926-2900
9360 Towne Centre Dr San Diego (92121) *(P-19918)*

Biosys Healthcare, Yorba Linda *Also Called: Viasys Respiratory Care Inc (P-10629)*

Biotheranostics Inc (HQ).......................................**E...... 877 886-6739**
9640 Towne Centre Dr Ste 200 San Diego (92121) *(P-18540)*

Biotix Inc ....E...... 858 875-5479
6995 Calle De Linea Ste 106 San Diego (92154) *(P-496)*

BIOTIX, INC., San Diego *Also Called: Biotix Inc (P-496)*

Biotone Professional Products, San Diego *Also Called: Natural Thoughts Incorporated (P-4436)*

Biovail Technologies Ltd ....D...... 703 995-2400
1 Enterprise Aliso Viejo (92656) *(P-4075)*

Biovia, San Diego *Also Called: Dassault Systemes Biovia Corp (P-16221)*

BIP Corporation ....F...... 760 591-9822
2951 Norman Strasse Rd San Marcos (92069) *(P-12646)*

Birch Ptrick Convalescent Cntr, Chula Vista *Also Called: Sharp Healthcare (P-18438)*

Birchwood Lighting Inc .... E....... 714 550-7118
   3340 E La Palma Ave Anaheim (92806) *(P-8355)*

Bird, West Hollywood *Also Called: Bird Rides Inc (P-15983)*

Bird B Gone LLC .... D....... 949 472-3122
   1921 E Edinger Ave Santa Ana (92705) *(P-4828)*

Bird Rides Inc .... D....... 866 205-2442
   2501 Colorado Ave Santa Monica (90404) *(P-15982)*

Bird Rides Inc (HQ).. F....... 866 205-2442
   8605 Santa Monica Blvd # 20388 West Hollywood (90069) *(P-15983)*

Birdwell Beach Britches, Irvine *Also Called: Birdwell Enterprises Inc (P-2196)*

Birdwell Enterprises Inc .... E....... 714 557-7040
   8801 Research Dr Irvine (92618) *(P-2196)*

Birmingham Fastener & Sup Inc .... E....... 562 944-9549
   12748 Florence Ave Santa Fe Springs (90670) *(P-5907)*

Birns, Oxnard *Also Called: Birns Oceanographics Inc (P-8356)*

Birns Oceanographics Inc .... F....... 805 487-5393
   1720 Fiske Pl Oxnard (93033) *(P-8356)*

Bis Computer Solutions Inc (PA)...................................... E....... 818 248-4282
   5500 Alta Canyada Rd La Canada Flintridge (91011) *(P-15984)*

Bisco Inc .... C....... 714 693-2901
   5065 E Hunter Ave Anaheim (92807) *(P-12647)*

Bisco Industries Inc (HQ).. D....... 800 323-1232
   5065 E Hunter Ave Anaheim (92807) *(P-12648)*

Biscomerica Corp .... B....... 909 877-5997
   565 West Slover Ave Rialto (92377) *(P-1510)*

Bish Inc .... E....... 619 660-6220
   2820 Via Orange Way Ste G Spring Valley (91978) *(P-9644)*

Bit Medtech LLC .... D....... 858 613-1200
   15870 Bernardo Center Dr San Diego (92127) *(P-19554)*

Bitcentral, Newport Beach *Also Called: Bitcentral Inc (P-12649)*

Bitcentral Inc .... D....... 949 253-9000
   4340 Von Karman Ave # 410 Newport Beach (92660) *(P-12649)*

Bitchin Inc (PA)... E....... 760 224-7447
   6211 Yarrow Dr Ste C Carlsbad (92011) *(P-1858)*

Bitchin Sauce, Carlsbad *Also Called: Bitchin Inc (P-1858)*

Bitchin Sauce LLC .... D....... 737 248-2446
   6211 Yarrow Dr Ste C Carlsbad (92011) *(P-1859)*

Bitchin' Sauce, Carlsbad *Also Called: Bitchin Sauce LLC (P-1859)*

Bitco Cnstr Insur Agcy Inc .... D....... 626 683-5200
   225 S Lake Ave Ste 1050 Pasadena (91101) *(P-14568)*

Bitcoin Ira, Sherman Oaks *Also Called: Alternative Ira Services LLC (P-16774)*

Bitmax .... E....... 323 978-7878
   6600 W Sunset Blvd Los Angeles (90028) *(P-16182)*

Bitmax LLC (PA)... F....... 323 978-7878
   6255 W Sunset Blvd Ste 1515 Los Angeles (90028) *(P-8602)*

Bitscopic Inc .... E....... 650 503-3120
   10866 Wilshire Blvd Ste 400 Los Angeles (90024) *(P-16555)*

Bittree Incorporated .... E....... 818 500-8142
   600 W Elk Ave Glendale (91204) *(P-8499)*

Biu Inc .... D....... 909 556-1311
   9268 1/2 Hall Rd Downey (90241) *(P-16794)*

Bivar, Irvine *Also Called: Bivar Inc (P-9007)*

Bivar Inc .... E....... 949 951-8808
   4 Thomas Irvine (92618) *(P-9007)*

BIW Connector Systems, Irvine *Also Called: ITT Cannon LLC (P-8183)*

Bixolon America Inc .... E....... 858 764-4580
   2575 W 237th St Torrance (90505) *(P-7512)*

BJ's Restaurant & Brewhouse, Huntington Beach *Also Called: BJs Restaurant Operations Co (P-20003)*

Bjarke Ingels Group Nyc LLC .... C....... 347 549-4141
   310 Wilshire Blvd Santa Monica (90401) *(P-19726)*

Bjb Enterprises Inc .... E....... 714 734-8450
   14791 Franklin Ave Tustin (92780) *(P-3929)*

BJs Restaurant Operations Co .... B....... 714 500-2440
   7755 Center Ave Ste 300 Huntington Beach (92647) *(P-20003)*

BJS&t Enterprises Inc .... E....... 619 448-7795
   1702 N Magnolia Ave El Cajon (92020) *(P-6695)*

Bjz LLC .... C....... 760 851-0740
   45150 Club Dr Indian Wells (92210) *(P-18594)*

BK Signs Inc .... F....... 626 334-5600
   1028 W Kirkwall Rd Azusa (91702) *(P-11099)*

Bkf Engineers/Ags .... D....... 949 526-8400
   4675 Macarthur Ct Ste 400 Newport Beach (92660) *(P-19555)*

BKF ENGINEERS/AGS, Newport Beach *Also Called: Bkf Engineers/Ags (P-19555)*

BKM Diablo 227 LLC .... D....... 602 688-6409
   1701 Quail St Ste 100 Newport Beach (92660) *(P-14752)*

BKM Office Environments Inc (PA).................................... F....... 805 339-6388
   816 Via Alondra Camarillo (93012) *(P-13939)*

BKM Total Office of Texas, Santa Fe Springs *Also Called: New Tangram LLC (P-12287)*

Black & Decker, El Toro *Also Called: Black & Decker Corporation (P-7142)*

Black & Decker Corporation .... E....... 949 672-4000
   19701 Da Vinci El Toro (92610) *(P-7142)*

Black Anchor Supply Co LLC .... F....... 661 309-1193
   27636 Avenue Scott Ste A Valencia (91355) *(P-15656)*

Black Box Distribution LLC .... D....... 760 268-1174
   371 2nd St Ste 1 Encinitas (92024) *(P-10978)*

Black Box Inc .... D....... 760 804-3300
   371 2nd St Ste 1 Encinitas (92024) *(P-13098)*

Black Box Network Services, Los Angeles *Also Called: Scottel Voice & Data Inc (P-17073)*

Black Diamond Blade Company (PA).................................. E....... 800 949-9014
   234 E O St Colton (92324) *(P-6926)*

Black Dot Wireless LLC .... D....... 949 502-3800
   23456 Madero Ste 210 Mission Viejo (92691) *(P-11845)*

Black Drop Coffee Inc .... F....... 323 742-5666
   225 W Fairview Ave San Gabriel (91776) *(P-1815)*

Black Gold Pump & Supply Inc .... F....... 323 298-0077
   2459 Lewis Ave Signal Hill (90755) *(P-330)*

Black Jack Farms, Santa Maria *Also Called: Blackjack Frms De La Csta Cntl (P-76)*

Black Knight Infoserv LLC .... C....... 904 854-5100
   2500 Redhill Ave Ste 100 Santa Ana (92705) *(P-16484)*

Black N Gold, Paramount *Also Called: Kum Kang Trading USA Inc (P-4430)*

Black Oxide, Anaheim *Also Called: Black Oxide Industries Inc (P-6591)*

Black Oxide Industries Inc .... E....... 714 870-9610
   1745 N Orangethorpe Park Ste A Anaheim (92801) *(P-6591)*

Black Series Campers, City Of Industry *Also Called: Blackseries Campers Inc (P-9490)*

Blackbaud Internet Solutions, San Diego *Also Called: Kintera Inc (P-16285)*

Blackburn Alton Invstments LLC .... E....... 714 731-2000
   700 E Alton Ave Santa Ana (92705) *(P-3737)*

Blackjack Frms De La Csta Cntl .... C....... 805 347-1333
   2385 A St Santa Maria (93455) *(P-76)*

Blackline, Woodland Hills *Also Called: Blackline Inc (P-16183)*

Blackline Inc (PA).. C....... 818 223-9008
   21300 Victory Blvd Fl 12 Woodland Hills (91367) *(P-16183)*

Blackrock Logistics, Fontana *Also Called: Blackrock Logistics Inc (P-11742)*

Blackrock Logistics Inc .... C....... 909 259-5357
   14601 Slover Ave Fontana (92337) *(P-11742)*

Blackseries Campers Inc .... E....... 833 822-6737
   19501 E Walnut Dr S City Of Industry (91748) *(P-9490)*

Blaga Precision Inc .... E....... 714 891-9509
   11650 Seaboard Cir Stanton (90680) *(P-7784)*

Blair's Metal Polishing, Cerritos *Also Called: Blairs Metal Polsg Pltg Co Inc (P-6592)*

Blairs Metal Polsg Pltg Co Inc .... F....... 562 860-7106
   17760 Crusader Ave Cerritos (90703) *(P-6592)*

Blakely Sokoloff Taylor & Zafman LLP .... C....... 310 207-3800
   12400 Wilshire Blvd Ste 700 Los Angeles (90025) *(P-18829)*

Blanchard Training and Dev Inc (PA)................................. C....... 760 489-5005
   125 State Pl Escondido (92029) *(P-20141)*

Blavity Inc .... C....... 818 669-9162
   600 Wilshire Blvd Ste 1650 Los Angeles (90017) *(P-3431)*

Blazing Industrial Steel Inc .... D....... 951 360-8340
   9040 Jurupa Rd Riverside (92509) *(P-5997)*

Blc Residential Care Inc .... E....... 310 722-7541
   1455 W 112th St Los Angeles (90047) *(P-19029)*

Blc Wc Inc (PA)... C....... 562 926-1452
   13260 Moore St Cerritos (90703) *(P-3738)*

Ble Inc .... E....... 818 504-9577
   11360 Goss St Sun Valley (91352) *(P-278)*

Bleeker Brothers Inc1 .... F....... 310 639-4367
   10868 Drury Ln Lynwood (90262) *(P-6202)*

Blenders Eyewear, San Diego *Also Called: Blenders Eyewear LLC (P-10834)*

Blenders Eyewear LLC .... D....... 858 490-2178
   4683 Cass St San Diego (92109) *(P-10834)*

Mergent email: customerrelations@mergent.com
1016

2024 Southern California
Business Directory and Buyers Guide

(P-0000) Products & Services Section entry number
(PA)=Parent Co (HQ)=Headquarters (DH)=Div Headquarters

Blending Lab Inc .... E....... 323 424-4051
25327 Avenue Stanford Ste 105 Santa Clarita (91355) *(P-1612)*

Blh Construction Company .... C....... 818 905-3837
20750 Ventura Blvd Ste 155 Woodland Hills (91364) *(P-468)*

Blind Squirrel Games Inc .... E....... 714 460-0860
7545 Irvine Center Dr Ste 150 Irvine (92618) *(P-16184)*

Bliss Holdings LLC .... E....... 626 506-8696
745 S Vinewood St Escondido (92029) *(P-8357)*

Blisslights Inc .... E....... 888 868-4603
2625 Temple Heights Dr Ste A Oceanside (92056) *(P-9196)*

Blisterpak, Commerce Also Called: Blisterpak Inc *(P-13530)*

Blisterpak Inc .... E....... 323 728-5555
3020 Supply Ave Commerce (90040) *(P-13530)*

Blitz Rocks Inc .... F....... 310 883-5183
750 B St Ste 3300 San Diego (92101) *(P-16185)*

Blizzard Entertainment Inc (DH) .... D....... 949 955-1380
1 Blizzard Irvine (92618) *(P-16186)*

Blk International LLC (PA) .... E....... 424 282-3443
26565 Agoura Rd Ste 205 Calabasas (91302) *(P-1686)*

Block Tops Inc (PA) .... E....... 714 978-5080
1321 S Sunkist St Anaheim (92806) *(P-2944)*

Blockade Medical, Irvine Also Called: Balt Usa LLC *(P-12475)*

Blois Construction Inc .... C....... 805 485-0011
3201 Sturgis Rd Oxnard (93030) *(P-662)*

Blood Bnk San Brnrdino Rvrside (HQ) .... C....... 909 885-6503
384 W Orange Show Rd San Bernardino (92408) *(P-18747)*

Bloom Designs Corp .... F....... 949 250-4929
3347 Michelson Dr Ste 100 Irvine (92612) *(P-5285)*

Bloomers Metal Stampings Inc .... E....... 661 257-2955
28615 Braxton Ave Valencia (91355) *(P-6500)*

Bloomfield Bakers .... A....... 626 610-2253
10711 Bloomfield St Los Alamitos (90720) *(P-1511)*

Bloomfield Bakers, Los Alamitos Also Called: Bloomfield Bakers *(P-1511)*

Bloomfield Food Inc .... E....... 714 779-7273
4740 E Hunter Ave Anaheim (92807) *(P-1189)*

Bloomios Inc .... E....... 805 222-6330
201 W Montecito St Santa Barbara (93101) *(P-11197)*

Blow Molded Products, Riverside Also Called: Plastic Technologies Inc *(P-5147)*

Blow Molded Products Inc .... E....... 951 360-6055
4720 Felspar St Riverside (92509) *(P-4964)*

Blower-Dempsay Corporation .... E....... 714 547-9266
4044 W Garry Ave Santa Ana (92704) *(P-3083)*

Blower-Dempsay Corporation (PA) .... C....... 714 481-3800
4042 W Garry Ave Santa Ana (92704) *(P-3084)*

Bls Lmsine Svc Los Angeles Inc .... B....... 323 644-7166
2860 Fletcher Dr Los Angeles (90039) *(P-11376)*

BLT, Los Angeles Also Called: BLT & Associates Inc *(P-15657)*

BLT & Associates Inc .... C....... 323 860-4000
6430 W Sunset Blvd Ste 800 Los Angeles (90028) *(P-15657)*

BLT Cmmnctions LLC A Ltd Lblty .... C....... 323 860-4000
6430 W Sunset Blvd Ste 800 Los Angeles (90028) *(P-15590)*

Bltee LLC .... E....... 213 802-1736
7101 Telegraph Rd Montebello (90640) *(P-2231)*

Blu Digital Group Inc (PA) .... C....... 818 527-2763
2233 N Ontario St # 130 Burbank (91504) *(P-15985)*

Blu Heaven, Commerce Also Called: Alliance Apparel Inc *(P-2229)*

Blue and Butter LLC .... F....... 951 763-8808
6828 Ripple Ct Jurupa Valley (91752) *(P-2442)*

Blue Bay Industries, Encino Also Called: Sayari Shahrzad *(P-13110)*

Blue Beacon of Wheeler Ridge, Arvin Also Called: Blue Beacon USA LP *(P-17045)*

Blue Beacon USA LP .... C....... 661 858-2090
5831 Santa Elena Dr Arvin (93203) *(P-17045)*

Blue Chip Stamps Inc .... A....... 626 585-6700
301 E Colorado Blvd Ste 300 Pasadena (91101) *(P-12536)*

Blue Cross, Woodland Hills Also Called: Blue Cross of California *(P-14461)*

Blue Cross Beauty Products Inc .... E....... 818 896-8681
557 Jessie St San Fernando (91340) *(P-4383)*

Blue Cross of California (HQ) .... C....... 805 557-6050
21215 Burbank Blvd Ste 630 Woodland Hills (91367) *(P-14461)*

Blue Desert International Inc .... D....... 951 273-7575
510 N Sheridan St Ste A Corona (92878) *(P-7646)*

Blue Microphone, Westlake Village Also Called: Baltic Ltvian Unvrsal Elec LLC *(P-8398)*

Blue Nalu Inc .... E....... 858 703-8703
6060 Nancy Ridge Dr Ste 100 San Diego (92121) *(P-1800)*

Blue Ocean Marine LLC .... E....... 805 658-2628
2060 Knoll Dr Ste 100 Ventura (93003) *(P-11653)*

Blue Pacific Flavors Inc (PA) .... E....... 626 934-0099
1354 Marion Ct City Of Industry (91745) *(P-1759)*

Blue Ribbon Cont & Display Inc .... E....... 562 944-1217
5450 Dobbs Ave Buena Park (90621) *(P-3085)*

Blue Ribbon Draperies Inc .... E....... 562 425-4637
7341 Adams St Ste A Paramount (90723) *(P-13949)*

Blue Ridge Home Fashions Inc .... E....... 626 960-6069
15761 Tapia St Irwindale (91706) *(P-13080)*

Blue Shield Cal Lf Hlth Insur .... A....... 619 686-4200
2275 Rio Bonito Way Ste 250 San Diego (92108) *(P-14462)*

Blue Shield of California, Long Beach Also Called: California Physicians Service *(P-14463)*

Blue Shield of California, Woodland Hills Also Called: California Physicians Service *(P-14464)*

Blue Sky Elearn LLC .... E....... 877 925-8375
5405 Morehouse Dr Ste 340 San Diego (92121) *(P-20142)*

Blue Sky The Clor Imgntion LLC .... D....... 714 389-7700
410 Exchange Ste 250 Irvine (92602) *(P-12991)*

Blue Sphere Inc .... D....... 714 953-7555
10869 Portal Dr Los Alamitos (90720) *(P-2150)*

Blue Star Steel Inc .... E....... 619 448-5520
12122 Industry Rd Lakeside (92040) *(P-5998)*

Blue-White Industries Ltd (PA) .... D....... 714 893-8529
5300 Business Dr Huntington Beach (92649) *(P-10173)*

Bluebeam Inc (PA) .... C....... 626 788-4100
443 S Raymond Ave Pasadena (91105) *(P-15986)*

Bluebird Office Supplies, Los Angeles Also Called: Image Source Inc *(P-12995)*

Bluecan Company LLC .... E....... 818 450-3290
956 Griswold Ave San Fernando (91340) *(P-1687)*

Bluefield Associates Inc .... E....... 909 476-6027
14900 Hilton Dr Fontana (92336) *(P-4384)*

Bluelab Corporation Usa Inc .... E....... 909 599-1940
437 S Cataract Ave San Dimas (91773) *(P-7383)*

Bluemark Inc .... C....... 323 230-0770
27909 Hancock Pkwy Valencia (91355) *(P-13531)*

Bluenalu, San Diego Also Called: Blue Nalu Inc *(P-1800)*

Blueridge Technology Inc .... E....... 562 762-5914
3375 E Hill St Ste 1 Signal Hill (90755) *(P-10120)*

Bluesky Broadcast, San Diego Also Called: Blue Sky Elearn LLC *(P-20142)*

Bluetriton Brands Inc .... C....... 714 532-6220
619 N Main St Orange (92868) *(P-13355)*

Blufi Lending Corporation C
9909 Mira Mesa Blvd # 160 San Diego (92131) *(P-14303)*

Blufocus, Burbank Also Called: Blu Digital Group Inc *(P-15985)*

Blumenthal Distributing Inc (PA) .... C....... 909 930-2000
1901 S Archibald Ave Ontario (91761) *(P-12278)*

Bluprint Clothing Corp .... D....... 323 780-4347
6013 Randolph St Commerce (90040) *(P-2232)*

Blvd, Los Angeles Also Called: Boulevard Style Inc *(P-2233)*

Blyth/Wndsor Cntry Pk Hlthcare .... D....... 310 385-1090
3232 E Artesia Blvd Long Beach (90805) *(P-18081)*

Blytheco Inc (PA) .... E....... 949 583-9500
530 Technology Dr Ste 100 Irvine (92618) *(P-16556)*

Bm Extrusion Inc .... E....... 951 782-9020
1575 Omaha Ct Riverside (92507) *(P-4965)*

BMC .... E....... 310 321-5555
300 Continental Blvd Ste 570 El Segundo (90245) *(P-16187)*

BMC Group Inc .... D....... 310 321-5555
300 Continental Blvd Ste 570 El Segundo (90245) *(P-18830)*

BMC Industries, Bakersfield Also Called: Bakersfield Machine Co Inc *(P-7773)*

Bmci Inc .... E....... 951 361-8000
1689 S Parco Ave Ontario (91761) *(P-7167)*

Bmi, Temecula Also Called: Bomatic Inc *(P-4967)*

Bmp, Riverside Also Called: Blow Molded Products Inc *(P-4964)*

Bmp, Glendale Also Called: Bunim-Murray Productions *(P-17174)*

Bms Finance Inc .... E....... 619 284-9801
3705 El Cajon Blvd San Diego (92105) *(P-4076)*

Employee Codes: A=Over 500 employees, B=251-500
C=101-250, D=51-100, E=20-50, F=10-19, G=1-9

2024 Southern California
Business Directory and Buyers Guide

© Mergent Inc. 1-800-342-5647

1017

A
L
P
H
A
B
E
T
I
C

Bms Healthcare Inc ....C....... 562 942-7019
8925 Mines Ave Pico Rivera (90660) *(P-18748)*

Bms Investments LLC ....E....... 714 376-2535
12626 Hackberry Ln Moreno Valley (92553) *(P-4077)*

BMW of Palm Springs ....E....... 760 324-7071
3737 E Palm Canyon Dr Palm Springs (92264) *(P-2569)*

BMw Precision Machining Inc ....E....... 760 439-6813
2379 Industry St Oceanside (92054) *(P-7785)*

Bni, Chatsworth *Also Called: Bio-Nutraceuticals Inc (P-4072)*

Bni Enterprises Inc ....A....... 909 305-1818
545 College Commerce Way Upland (91786) *(P-20282)*

Bni Publications Inc ....E....... 760 734-1113
990 Park Center Dr Ste E Vista (92081) *(P-14065)*

Bnk Petroleum (us) Inc ....E....... 805 484-3613
925 Broadbeck Dr Ste 220 Newbury Park (91320) *(P-291)*

Bnl Technologies Inc ....E....... 310 320-7272
22301 S Western Ave Ste 101 Torrance (90501) *(P-7463)*

Bnrg, Irvine *Also Called: Bio-Nutritional RES Group Inc (P-1264)*

Bny Mellon National Assn ....A....... 310 551-7600
10250 Constellation Blvd Ste 2100 Los Angeles (90067) *(P-14160)*

Bny Mellon National Assn ....A....... 877 420-6377
1600 Newport Center Dr Ste 200 Newport Beach (92660) *(P-14180)*

BOa Inc ....E....... 714 256-8960
580 W Lambert Rd Ste L Brea (92821) *(P-2197)*

Boardriders Inc (HQ)...**A....... 714 889-5404**
5600 Argosy Ave Ste 100 Huntington Beach (92649) *(P-2198)*

Boardriders Wholesale LLC ....D....... 949 916-3060
6201 Oak Cyn Ste 100 Irvine (92618) *(P-2307)*

Boardwalk Solutions, Gardena *Also Called: Ocean Direct LLC (P-1810)*

Bob Baker Chrysler-Plymouth, Carlsbad *Also Called: Bob Baker Volkswagen (P-13740)*

Bob Baker Volkswagen ....D....... 760 438-2200
5500 Paseo Del Norte Carlsbad (92008) *(P-13740)*

Bob Hope Health Center, Woodland Hills *Also Called: Motion Picture and TV Fund (P-18347)*

Bob Siemon Designs Inc ....D....... 714 549-0678
3501 W Segerstrom Ave Santa Ana (92704) *(P-11065)*

Bob Stall Chevrolet ....C....... 619 460-1311
7601 Alvarado Rd La Mesa (91942) *(P-13741)*

Bobbi Boss, Cerritos *Also Called: Midway International Inc (P-13548)*

Bobboi Natural Gelato, La Jolla *Also Called: Berenice 2 AM Corp (P-1293)*

Bobit Business Media Inc ....B....... 310 533-2400
3520 Challenger St Torrance (90503) *(P-3346)*

Bobrick Washroom Equipment Inc (HQ)...........................**D....... 818 764-1000**
6901 Tujunga Ave North Hollywood (91605) *(P-2973)*

Bobster Eyewear, San Diego *Also Called: Balboa Manufacturing Co LLC (P-2063)*

Bocchi Laboratories, Santa Clarita *Also Called: Shadow Holdings LLC (P-4454)*

Bocchi Laboratories, Santa Clarita *Also Called: Shadow Holdings LLC (P-4455)*

Body Flex Sports, Walnut *Also Called: Hupa International Inc (P-10999)*

Body Glove, Hollywood *Also Called: Body Glove International LLC (P-2199)*

Body Glove International LLC ....E....... 310 374-3441
6255 W Sunset Blvd Ste 650 Hollywood (90028) *(P-2199)*

Bodycote Thermal Proc Inc ....E....... 714 893-6561
7474 Garden Grove Blvd Westminster (92683) *(P-5826)*

Bodycote Thermal Proc Inc ....D....... 562 946-1717
9921 Romandel Ave Santa Fe Springs (90670) *(P-5827)*

Bodycote Thermal Proc Inc ....E....... 310 604-8000
515 W Apra St Ste A Rancho Dominguez (90220) *(P-5828)*

Bodycote Thermal Proc Inc ....D....... 323 583-1231
3370 Benedict Way Huntington Park (90255) *(P-6593)*

Bodycote Usa Inc ....A....... 323 264-0111
2900 S Sunol Dr Vernon (90058) *(P-5829)*

Bodycote W Cast Anlytcal Svc I ....E....... 562 948-2225
9840 Alburtis Ave Santa Fe Springs (90670) *(P-5830)*

Bodywaves Inc (PA)..**E....... 714 898-9900**
12362 Knott St Garden Grove (92841) *(P-2414)*

Boeing ....E....... 949 623-2222
15320 Barranca Pkwy Irvine (92618) *(P-9511)*

Boeing, El Segundo *Also Called: Boeing Satellite Systems Inc (P-8500)*

Boeing, Long Beach *Also Called: Boeing Company (P-9513)*

Boeing, Carson *Also Called: Boeing Company (P-9514)*

Boeing, Long Beach *Also Called: Boeing Company (P-9515)*

Boeing, San Diego *Also Called: Boeing Company (P-9516)*

Boeing, El Segundo *Also Called: Boeing Satellite Systems Inc (P-9518)*

Boeing, Huntington Beach *Also Called: Boeing Company (P-9892)*

Boeing Coml Satellite Svcs Inc (HQ)................................**F....... 310 335-6682**
900 N Pacific Coast Hwy El Segundo (90245) *(P-9512)*

Boeing Company ....A....... 562 496-1000
4000 N Lakewood Blvd Long Beach (90808) *(P-9513)*

Boeing Company ....C....... 310 522-2809
2220 E Carson St Carson (90810) *(P-9514)*

Boeing Company ....A....... 562 593-5511
4060 N Lakewood Blvd Long Beach (90808) *(P-9515)*

Boeing Company ....A....... 619 545-8382
Bldg-1454 Receiving San Diego (92135) *(P-9516)*

Boeing Company ....B....... 714 896-3311
14441 Astronautics Ln Huntington Beach (92647) *(P-9892)*

Boeing Company, The, El Segundo *Also Called: Boeing Stllite Systems Intl In (P-12903)*

Boeing Encore Interiors LLC ....E....... 949 559-0930
5511 Skylab Rd Huntington Beach (92647) *(P-9645)*

Boeing Intllctual Prprty Lcnsi ....B....... 562 797-2020
14441 Astronautics Ln Huntington Beach (92647) *(P-9517)*

Boeing Satellite Systems Inc (HQ)...................................**E....... 310 791-7450**
900 N Pacific Coast Hwy El Segundo (90245) *(P-8500)*

Boeing Satellite Systems Inc ....A....... 310 568-2735
2300 E Imperial Hwy El Segundo (90245) *(P-9518)*

Boeing Stllite Systems Intl In (HQ)..................................**E....... 310 364-4000**
2260 E Imperial Hwy El Segundo (90245) *(P-12903)*

Boerner Truck Center, Huntington Park *Also Called: Fred M Boerner Motor Co (P-13860)*

Boiling Crab Operations LLC ....B....... 714 636-4885
5811 Mcfadden Ave Huntington Beach (92649) *(P-13985)*

Boiling Crab, The, Huntington Beach *Also Called: Boiling Crab Operations LLC (P-13985)*

Boiling Point Rest S CA Inc ....B....... 626 551-5181
13668 Valley Blvd Unit C2 City Of Industry (91746) *(P-15822)*

Boise Cascade, Riverside *Also Called: Boise Cascade Company (P-13569)*

Boise Cascade Company ....F....... 310 815-2200
3221 Hutchison Ave Los Angeles (90034) *(P-3042)*

Boise Cascade Company ....D....... 951 343-3000
7145 Arlington Ave Riverside (92503) *(P-13569)*

Bojer Inc ....B....... 626 334-1711
177 S Peckham Rd Azusa (91702) *(P-2467)*

Boldyn Networks US Services LL ....B....... 877 999-7070
121 Innovation Dr Ste 200 Irvine (92617) *(P-11872)*

Boldyn Ntwrks US Oprations LLC ....C....... 949 515-1500
121 Innovation Dr Irvine (92617) *(P-11873)*

Bolero Inds Inc A Cal Corp ....E....... 562 693-3000
11850 Burke St Santa Fe Springs (90670) *(P-4966)*

Bolero Plastics, Santa Fe Springs *Also Called: Bolero Inds Inc A Cal Corp (P-4966)*

Bolt Medical Inc ....D....... 949 287-3207
5993 Avenida Encinas Ste 100 Carlsbad (92008) *(P-10460)*

Bolthouse Farms ....A....... 661 366-7205
3200 E Brundage Ln Bakersfield (93304) *(P-7)*

Bolthouse Farms, Bakersfield *Also Called: Wm Bolthouse Farms Inc (P-1381)*

Bomark Inc ....E....... 626 968-1666
601 S 6th Ave La Puente (91746) *(P-4586)*

Bomatic Inc (DH)...**E....... 909 947-3900**
43225 Business Park Dr Temecula (92590) *(P-4967)*

Bomatic Inc ....D....... 909 947-3900
2181 E Francis St Ontario (91761) *(P-4968)*

Bomel Construction Co Inc ....D....... 909 923-3319
939 E Francis St Ontario (91761) *(P-536)*

Bon Appetit, Los Angeles *Also Called: Bon Appetit Management Co (P-20005)*

Bon Appetit Management Co ....C....... 310 440-6209
1200 Getty Center Dr Ste 100 Los Angeles (90049) *(P-20004)*

Bon Appetit Management Co ....C....... 310 440-6052
1200 Getty Center Dr Los Angeles (90049) *(P-20005)*

Bon Appetit Management Co ....C....... 909 607-2788
1050 N Mills Ave Claremont (91711) *(P-20006)*

Bon Appetit Management Co ....C....... 909 748-8970
1259 E Colton Ave Redlands (92374) *(P-20143)*

Bon Suisse Inc ....E....... 714 578-0001
392 W Walnut Ave Fullerton (92832) *(P-20319)*

Bonaventure Brewing Co, Los Angeles *Also Called: Bonaventure Brewing Co Inc (P-13986)*

Bonaventure Brewing Co Inc .... E....... 213 236-0802
404 S Figueroa St Ste 418a Los Angeles (90071) *(P-13986)*

Bonded Carpet, San Diego *Also Called: Bonded Inc (P-15466)*

Bonded Fiberloft Inc .... B....... 323 726-7820
2748 Tanager Ave Commerce (90040) *(P-2013)*

Bonded Inc (PA).. D....... 858 576-8400
7590 Carroll Rd San Diego (92121) *(P-15466)*

Bonded Window Coverings Inc .... E....... 858 576-8400
7831 Ostrow St San Diego (92111) *(P-3001)*

Bonert's Slice of Pie, Santa Ana *Also Called: Bonerts Incorporated (P-1526)*

Bonerts Incorporated .... E....... 714 540-3535
3144 W Adams St Santa Ana (92704) *(P-1526)*

Boneso Brothers Cnstr Inc .... D....... 805 227-4450
2758 Concrete Ct Paso Robles (93446) *(P-745)*

Bonita Golf Club, Bonita *Also Called: Crockett & Coinc (P-17423)*

Bonita Golf Club, Bonita *Also Called: Crockett & Coinc (P-17424)*

Bonne Brdges Mller Okefe Nchol (PA)............................ D....... 213 480-1900
355 S Grand Ave Ste 1750 Los Angeles (90071) *(P-18831)*

Bonterra Psomas, Santa Ana *Also Called: Psomas (P-19749)*

Bony Levy, Los Angeles *Also Called: L & L Diamond Co (P-14077)*

Boochcraft, Chula Vista *Also Called: Boochery Inc (P-1672)*

Boochery Inc .... D....... 619 207-0530
684 Anita St Ste F Chula Vista (91911) *(P-1672)*

Book Binders, Pico Rivera *Also Called: Kater-Crafts Incorporated (P-3847)*

Boom Industrial Inc .... D....... 909 495-3555
2010 Wright Ave La Verne (91750) *(P-7228)*

Boone Printing & Graphics Inc .... D....... 805 683-2349
70 S Kellogg Ave Ste 8 Goleta (93117) *(P-3520)*

Boost Mobile LLC .... A....... 949 451-1563
6316 Irvine Blvd Irvine (92620) *(P-16795)*

Boozak Inc .... E....... 951 245-6045
508 Chaney St Ste A Lake Elsinore (92530) *(P-6203)*

Boral Industries, Oceanside *Also Called: Royal Westlake Roofing LLC (P-1053)*

Borbon Incorporated .... C....... 714 994-0170
2560 W Woodland Dr Anaheim (92801) *(P-843)*

Bordeaux, Vernon *Also Called: Heather By Bordeaux Inc (P-2328)*

Borderview Y M C A, San Diego *Also Called: YMCA of San Diego County (P-19478)*

Borg Produce Sales, Los Angeles *Also Called: Pacific Trellis Fruit LLC (P-13335)*

Borg Produce Sales LLC .... C....... 213 624-2674
1601 E Olympic Blvd Ste 100 Los Angeles (90021) *(P-13313)*

Borges Rock Product, Sun Valley *Also Called: Over & Over Ready Mix Inc (P-5435)*

Borin Manufacturing Inc .... E....... 310 822-1000
5741 Buckingham Pkwy Ste B Culver City (90230) *(P-7270)*

Borrego Cmnty Hlth Foundation .... C....... 951 487-8506
651 N State St Ste 5 San Jacinto (92583) *(P-17602)*

Borrego Cmnty Hlth Foundation .... C....... 760 251-0044
11750 Cholla Dr Ste B Desert Hot Springs (92240) *(P-17603)*

Borrego Cmnty Hlth Foundation .... C....... 760 466-1080
1121 E Washington Ave Escondido (92025) *(P-17604)*

Borrego Cmnty Hlth Foundation (PA)............................ C....... 855 436-1234
587 Palm Canyon Dr Ste 208 Borrego Springs (92004) *(P-17605)*

Borrego Health, San Jacinto *Also Called: Borrego Cmnty Hlth Foundation (P-17602)*

Borrego Medical Center, Borrego Springs *Also Called: Borrego Cmnty Hlth Foundation (P-17605)*

Borrmann Metal Center .... E....... 951 367-1510
12790 Holly St Riverside (92509) *(P-5578)*

Borsos Engineering Inc .... F....... 760 930-0296
5924 Balfour Ct Ste 102 Carlsbad (92008) *(P-7420)*

Boskovich Farms Inc .... C....... 805 987-1443
4224 Pleasant Valley Rd Camarillo (93012) *(P-8)*

Boskovich Farms Inc (PA).. C....... 805 487-2299
711 Diaz Ave Oxnard (93030) *(P-99)*

Boskovich Fresh Cut LLC .... C....... 805 487-2299
711 Diaz Ave Oxnard (93030) *(P-13314)*

Boss, Commerce *Also Called: Norstar Office Products Inc (P-2891)*

Boss Audio Systems, Oxnard *Also Called: Boss International LLC (P-8402)*

Boss International LLC (PA).. E....... 805 988-0192
3451 Lunar Ct Oxnard (93030) *(P-8402)*

Boss Litho Inc .... E....... 626 912-7088
1544 Hauser Blvd Los Angeles (90019) *(P-3521)*

Bostik Inc .... E....... 951 296-6425
27460 Bostik Ct Temecula (92590) *(P-4559)*

Boston Scientific - Valencia, Valencia *Also Called: Boston Scientific Corporation (P-10461)*

Boston Scientific Corporation .... E....... 800 678-2575
25155 Rye Canyon Loop Valencia (91355) *(P-10461)*

Boston Scntfc Nrmdlation Corp (HQ)............................ B....... 661 949-4310
25155 Rye Canyon Loop Valencia (91355) *(P-10639)*

Bostonia Medical Offices, El Cajon *Also Called: Kaiser Foundation Hospitals (P-18310)*

Boswell Properties Inc .... B....... 626 583-3000
101 W Walnut St Pasadena (91103) *(P-96)*

Botanx LLC .... E....... 714 854-1601
3357 E Miraloma Ave Ste 156 Anaheim (92806) *(P-4385)*

Bottaia Wines LP .... E....... 951 252-1799
35601 Rancho California Rd Temecula (92591) *(P-1613)*

Bottle Coatings, Sun Valley *Also Called: Sundial Powder Coatings Inc (P-6741)*

Bottlemate Inc (PA)............................ E....... 323 887-9009
2095 Leo Ave Commerce (90040) *(P-4969)*

Bottling Group LLC .... E....... 951 697-3200
6659 Sycamore Canyon Blvd Riverside (92507) *(P-1688)*

Boudraux Prcsion McHining Corp .... E....... 714 894-4523
11762 Western Ave Ste G Stanton (90680) *(P-7786)*

Boudreau Pipeline Corporation .... B....... 951 493-6780
463 N Smith Ave Corona (92878) *(P-663)*

Boughts Inc .... E....... 619 895-7246
5927 Balfour Ct Carlsbad (92008) *(P-16557)*

BOULDER CREEK POST ACUTE, Poway *Also Called: Pomerado Operations LLC (P-18033)*

Boulevard Automotive Group (PA)............................ D....... 562 492-1000
2850 Cherry Ave Signal Hill (90755) *(P-13742)*

Boulevard Collision Center, Signal Hill *Also Called: Boulevard Automotive Group (P-13742)*

Boulevard Labs Inc .... D....... 323 310-2093
626 Wilshire Blvd Ste 410 Los Angeles (90005) *(P-15987)*

Boulevard Style Inc .... E....... 213 749-1551
1680 E 40th Pl Los Angeles (90011) *(P-2233)*

Bouqs Company .... D....... 888 320-2687
4094 Glencoe Ave Marina Del Rey (90292) *(P-13504)*

Bourns, Riverside *Also Called: Bourns Inc (P-8936)*

Bourns Inc (PA)............................ C....... 951 781-5500
1200 Columbia Ave Riverside (92507) *(P-8936)*

Bowman Pipeline Contractors, Bakersfield *Also Called: Southwest Contractors (P-693)*

Bowman Plating Co Inc .... C....... 310 639-4343
2631 E 126th St Compton (90222) *(P-6594)*

Bowman-Field Inc .... D....... 310 638-8519
2800 Martin Luther King Jr Blvd Lynwood (90262) *(P-6595)*

Boxes R Us Inc .... D....... 626 820-5410
15051 Don Julian Rd City Of Industry (91746) *(P-3086)*

BOY SCOUTS OF AMERICA, Los Angeles *Also Called: Greater Los Angles Area Cncil (P-19449)*

Boy's & Girls Club Bakersfield, Bakersfield *Also Called: Boys Girls Clubs of Kern Cnty (P-19427)*

Boyd and Associates .... D....... 805 988-8298
445 E Esplanade Dr Ste 210 Oxnard (93036) *(P-16625)*

Boyd and Associates (PA)............................ C....... 818 752-1888
2191 E Thompson Blvd Ventura (93001) *(P-16626)*

Boyd Chatsworth Inc .... D....... 818 998-1477
9959 Canoga Ave Chatsworth (91311) *(P-10640)*

Boyd Coddington Wheels, La Habra *Also Called: NRG Motorsports Inc (P-9435)*

Boyd Construction, Yorba Linda *Also Called: Boyd Corporation (P-5999)*

Boyd Corporation (PA)............................ E....... 714 533-2375
5832 Ohio St Yorba Linda (92886) *(P-5999)*

Boyd Dental Corporation .... D....... 909 890-0421
362 E Vanderbilt Way San Bernardino (92408) *(P-17835)*

Boyd Flotation Inc .... E....... 314 997-5222
7551 Cherry Ave Fontana (92336) *(P-13940)*

Boyd Specialties LLC .... D....... 909 219-5120
1016 E Cooley Dr Ste N Colton (92324) *(P-1214)*

Boyd Specialty Sleep, Fontana *Also Called: Boyd Flotation Inc (P-13940)*

Boyle Engineering Corporation .... B....... 949 476-3300
999 W Town And Country Rd Orange (92868) *(P-19556)*

Employee Codes: A=Over 500 employees, B=251-500
C=101-250, D=51-100, E=20-50, F=10-19, G=1-9

2024 Southern California
Business Directory and Buyers Guide

© Mergent Inc. 1-800-342-5647

1019

A
L
P
H
A
B
E
T
I
C

BOYS & GIRLS CLUBS OF HUNTINGT, Fountain Valley *Also Called: Boys Grls Clubs Huntington Vly (P-19430)*

BOYS & GIRLS CLUBS OF SANTA MO, Santa Monica *Also Called: Boys Grls CLB Snta Monica Inc (P-19429)*

Boys & Girls Clubs South Cnty .... D...... 619 424-2266
847 Encina Ave Imperial Beach (91932) *(P-19426)*

Boys Girls Clubs of Kern Cnty .... B...... 661 325-3730
801 Niles St Bakersfield (93305) *(P-19427)*

Boys Grls CLB Brbank Grter E V .... D...... 818 842-9333
300 E Angeleno Ave Burbank (91502) *(P-19428)*

Boys Grls CLB Snta Monica Inc .... D...... 310 361-8500
1220 Lincoln Blvd Santa Monica (90401) *(P-19429)*

Boys Grls Clubs Grdn Grove Inc (PA) .... C...... 714 530-0430
10540 Chapman Ave Garden Grove (92840) *(P-19008)*

Boys Grls Clubs Huntington Vly (PA) .... D...... 714 531-2582
16582 Brookhurst St Fountain Valley (92708) *(P-19430)*

Boys Republic (PA) .... C...... 909 902-6690
1907 Boys Republic Dr Chino Hills (91709) *(P-19241)*

BP Clothing LLC C
3424 Garfield Ave Commerce (90040) *(P-13119)*

Bpi Records, Commerce *Also Called: Bridge Publications Inc (P-3400)*

Bpoms/Hro Inc (HQ) .... D...... 714 974-2670
8175 E Kaiser Blvd # 100 Anaheim (92808) *(P-16188)*

BQE Software Inc .... D...... 310 602-4020
3825 Del Amo Blvd Torrance (90503) *(P-16189)*

BR Building Resources Co .... C...... 626 963-4880
2247 Lindsay Way Glendora (91740) *(P-537)*

Bradco Environmental, Redlands *Also Called: Bradco Industrial Corporation (P-230)*

Bradco Industrial Corporation .... F...... 888 272-3261
1671 Sessums Dr Redlands (92374) *(P-230)*

Bradford Soap Mexico Inc .... B...... 760 768-4539
1778 Zinetta Rd Ste G Calexico (92231) *(P-4334)*

Bradley Court, Chula Vista *Also Called: Healthcare Management Systems Inc (P-17972)*

Bradley Manufacturing Co Inc .... E...... 562 923-5556
9368 Stewart And Gray Rd Downey (90241) *(P-4970)*

Bradley's Plastic Bag Co, Downey *Also Called: Bradley Manufacturing Co Inc (P-4970)*

Bradshaw Home, Rancho Cucamonga *Also Called: Bradshaw International Inc (P-12296)*

Bradshaw International Inc (PA) .... B...... 909 476-3884
9409 Buffalo Ave Rancho Cucamonga (91730) *(P-12296)*

Brady Company/San Diego Inc .... B...... 619 462-2600
8100 Center St La Mesa (91942) *(P-971)*

Brady Socal Incorporated .... D...... 619 462-2600
8100 Center St La Mesa (91942) *(P-972)*

Braemar Country Club, Tarzana *Also Called: Braemar Country Club Inc (P-17476)*

Braemar Country Club Inc .... C...... 323 873-6880
4001 Reseda Blvd Tarzana (91356) *(P-17476)*

Braemar Partnership .... B...... 858 488-1081
3999 Mission Blvd San Diego (92109) *(P-15096)*

Braga Fresh Family Farms Inc .... C...... 760 353-1155
817 W Hackleman Rd El Centro (92243) *(P-77)*

Braga Fresh Imperial, El Centro *Also Called: Braga Fresh Family Farms Inc (P-77)*

Bragel International Inc .... E...... 909 598-8808
3383 Pomona Blvd Pomona (91768) *(P-2394)*

Bragg Crane & Rigging, Long Beach *Also Called: Bragg Investment Company Inc (P-15759)*

Bragg Investment Company Inc .... D...... 805 485-2106
1930 Lockwood St Oxnard (93036) *(P-12235)*

Bragg Investment Company Inc (PA) .... B...... 562 984-2400
6251 N Paramount Blvd Long Beach (90805) *(P-15759)*

Braille Institute, Los Angeles *Also Called: Braille Institute America Inc (P-19030)*

Braille Institute America Inc (PA) .... C...... 323 663-1111
741 N Vermont Ave Los Angeles (90029) *(P-19030)*

Brain Corporation .... C...... 858 689-7600
10182 Telesis Ct Ste 100 San Diego (92121) *(P-15988)*

Brainstorm Corporation .... C...... 888 370-8882
1620 Proforma Ave Ontario (91761) *(P-12400)*

Brainstormproducts LLC .... E...... 760 871-1135
1011 S Andreasen Dr Ste 100 Escondido (92029) *(P-10948)*

Brake Depot Systems Inc .... B...... 714 623-9030
1205 E 1st St Santa Ana (92701) *(P-17029)*

Branan Medical Corporation (PA) .... E...... 949 598-7166
9940 Mesa Rim Rd San Diego (92121) *(P-10462)*

Branch Medical Center, San Diego *Also Called: NAVY UNITED STATES DEPARTMENT (P-17722)*

Brand Therapy LLC .... D...... 415 336-6411
7376 W 88th St Los Angeles (90045) *(P-18674)*

Branded Entrmt Netwrk Inc (PA) .... C...... 310 342-1500
14724 Ventura Blvd Ste 1200 Sherman Oaks (91403) *(P-15654)*

Branded Group Inc .... C...... 323 940-1444
222 S Harbor Blvd Ste 500 Anaheim (92805) *(P-20144)*

Brandes Inv Partners Inc (PA) .... C...... 858 755-0239
11988 El Camino Real Ste 300 San Diego (92131) *(P-14418)*

Brandmd Skin Care, Chatsworth *Also Called: Samuel Raoof (P-4452)*

Brands Republic Inc .... E...... 302 401-1195
10333 Rush St South El Monte (91733) *(P-8230)*

Branlyn Prominence Inc .... C...... 760 843-5655
13334 Amargosa Rd Victorville (92392) *(P-18595)*

Branlyn Prominence Inc (PA) .... D...... 909 476-9030
9213 Archibald Ave Rancho Cucamonga (91730) *(P-18596)*

Brantner and Associates Inc (DH) .... C...... 619 562-7070
1700 Gillespie Way El Cajon (92020) *(P-8961)*

Brass Unique Inc .... E...... 626 444-8977
9948 Hayward Way South El Monte (91733) *(P-6000)*

Brasscraft Corona, Corona *Also Called: Brasscraft Manufacturing Co (P-6788)*

Brasscraft Manufacturing Co .... D...... 951 735-4375
215 N Smith Ave Corona (92878) *(P-6788)*

Brasstech Inc (HQ) .... C...... 949 417-5207
2001 Carnegie Ave Santa Ana (92705) *(P-5963)*

Brasstech Inc .... C...... 714 796-9278
1301 E Wilshire Ave Santa Ana (92705) *(P-5964)*

Brat Inc .... D...... 619 410-3403
913 N Highland Ave Los Angeles (90038) *(P-17274)*

Brault .... C...... 626 447-0296
180 Via Verde Ste 100 San Dimas (91773) *(P-19756)*

Braun Linen Service (PA) .... C...... 909 623-2678
16514 Garfield Ave Paramount (90723) *(P-15449)*

Brava, Pomona *Also Called: Bragel International Inc (P-2394)*

Bravo Highline LLC .... E...... 562 484-5100
3101 Ocean Park Blvd Ste 100 Santa Monica (90405) *(P-10979)*

Bravo Sign & Design Inc .... F...... 714 284-0500
520 S Central Park Ave E Anaheim (92802) *(P-1145)*

Bravo Sports .... E...... 858 408-0083
4370 Jutland Dr San Diego (92117) *(P-10980)*

Bravo Sports (HQ) .... D...... 562 484-5100
12801 Carmenita Rd Santa Fe Springs (90670) *(P-10981)*

Bravo Support, Commerce *Also Called: S Bravo Systems Inc (P-6155)*

Brawley Union High School Dist (PA) .... D...... 760 312-6068
480 N Imperial Ave Brawley (92227) *(P-18964)*

Brax Company Inc .... E...... 760 749-2209
31248 Valley Center Rd Valley Center (92082) *(P-1093)*

Braxton Caribbean Mfg Co Inc .... D...... 714 508-3570
2641 Walnut Ave Tustin (92780) *(P-6501)*

Brazeau Thoroughbred Farms LP .... E...... 951 201-2278
30500 State St Hemet (92543) *(P-6901)*

Brea Canon Oil Co Inc .... F...... 310 326-4002
23903 Normandie Ave Harbor City (90710) *(P-251)*

Bread Bar, El Segundo *Also Called: El Segundo Bread Bar LLC (P-1464)*

Break Media, Beverly Hills *Also Called: Nextpoint Inc (P-11895)*

Breakthru Beverage Cal LLC (HQ) .... B...... 800 331-2829
6550 E Washington Blvd Commerce (90040) *(P-13474)*

Breathe Technologies Inc .... E...... 949 988-7700
15091 Bake Pkwy Irvine (92618) *(P-10641)*

Brecht BMW, Escondido *Also Called: Brecht Enterprises Inc (P-13743)*

Brecht Enterprises Inc .... D...... 760 745-3000
1555 Auto Park Way Escondido (92029) *(P-13743)*

Bree Engineering Corp .... E...... 760 510-4950
135 Vallecitos De Oro Ste G San Marcos (92069) *(P-9008)*

Breeze Air Conditioning LLC .... D...... 760 346-0855
75145 Saint Charles Pl Ste A Palm Desert (92211) *(P-746)*

Breg Inc (HQ) .... C...... 760 599-3000
2382 Faraday Ave Carlsbad (92008) *(P-10463)*

Brehm Communications Inc (PA) .... E...... 858 451-6200
16644 W Bernardo Dr Ste 300 San Diego (92127) *(P-3522)*

Breitburn Energy Holdings LLC .... F...... 213 225-5900
707 Wilshire Blvd Ste 4600 Los Angeles (90017) *(P-292)*

Breitburn Energy Partners LP .... A...... 213 225-5900
707 Wilshire Blvd Ste 4600 Los Angeles (90017) *(P-252)*

Breitburn GP LLC .... E...... 213 225-5900
707 Wilshire Blvd # 4600 Los Angeles (90017) *(P-253)*

Brek Manufacturing Co (HQ) .... D...... 310 329-7638
1513 W 132nd St Gardena (90249) *(P-7787)*

Brek Manufacturing Co .... C...... 310 329-7638
2601 W Ball Rd Ste 105 Anaheim (92804) *(P-7788)*

Bremik International Inc .... D...... 310 715-6622
14403 S Main St Gardena (90248) *(P-3432)*

Bremik Press, Gardena *Also Called: Bremik International Inc (P-3432)*

Brendan Technologies Inc .... E...... 760 929-7500
1947 Camino Vida Roble Ste 215 Carlsbad (92008) *(P-16190)*

Brennan International Trnspt, Long Beach *Also Called: Vanguard Lgistics Svcs USA Inc (P-11814)*

Brenner-Fiedler & Assoc Inc (PA) .... E...... 562 404-2721
4059 Flat Rock Dr Riverside (92505) *(P-10355)*

Brenntag Pacific Inc (DH) .... C...... 562 903-9626
10747 Patterson Pl Santa Fe Springs (90670) *(P-13425)*

Brent-Wood Products Inc .... E...... 800 400-7335
17071 Hercules St Hesperia (92345) *(P-2752)*

Brentwood Appliances Inc .... E...... 323 266-4600
3088 E 46th St Vernon (90058) *(P-8240)*

Brentwood Bmdical RES Inst Inc .... C...... 310 312-1554
11301 Wilshire Blvd Bldg 114 Los Angeles (90073) *(P-19919)*

BRENTWOOD COUNTRY CLUB, Los Angeles *Also Called: Brentwood Country Club Los Angeles (P-17477)*

Brentwood Country Club Los Angeles .... D...... 310 451-8011
590 S Burlingame Ave Los Angeles (90049) *(P-17477)*

Brentwood Home LLC (PA) .... C...... 562 949-3759
701 Burning Tree Rd Ste A Fullerton (92833) *(P-2845)*

Brentwood Originals, Long Beach *Also Called: Brentwood Originals Inc (P-2468)*

Brentwood Originals Inc (PA) .... C...... 310 637-6804
3780 Kilroy Airport Way Ste 540 Long Beach (90806) *(P-2468)*

Brer Affiliates LLC (DH) .... C...... 949 794-7900
18500 Von Karman Ave Ste 400 Irvine (92612) *(P-15008)*

Brethren Hillcrest Homes .... C...... 909 593-4917
2705 Mountain View Dr Ofc La Verne (91750) *(P-19242)*

Bretkeri Corporation .... F...... 858 292-4919
8316 Clairemont Mesa Blvd Ste 105 San Diego (92111) *(P-3739)*

Breville, Torrance *Also Called: Breville Usa Inc (P-8241)*

Breville Usa Inc .... E...... 310 755-3000
19400 S Western Ave Torrance (90501) *(P-8241)*

Brian Guy Electric Ltg Svcs Co, Moorpark *Also Called: Insparation Inc (P-4423)*

Bridge Group Hh Inc .... C...... 858 455-5000
3636 Nobel Dr Ste 450 San Diego (92122) *(P-14925)*

Bridge Home Health LLC .... D...... 858 277-5200
5090 Shoreham Pl Ste 109 San Diego (92122) *(P-18597)*

Bridge Metals, Los Angeles *Also Called: Zia Aamir (P-6095)*

Bridge Publications Inc (PA) .... E...... 323 888-6200
5600 E Olympic Blvd Commerce (90022) *(P-3400)*

Bridgestone Americas .... E...... 909 770-8523
14521 Hawthorne Ave Fontana (92335) *(P-17020)*

Bridgestone Americas Inc .... E...... 858 874-3109
3690 Murphy Canyon Rd San Diego (92123) *(P-4694)*

Bridgestone Hosepower LLC .... E...... 562 699-9500
2865 Pellissier Pl City Of Industry (90601) *(P-12845)*

Bridgestone Living LLC .... D...... 949 487-9500
27101 Puerta Real Ste 450 Mission Viejo (92691) *(P-17893)*

Bridgewave Communications Inc .... E...... 408 567-6900
17034 Camino San Bernardo San Diego (92127) *(P-5732)*

Bridgewest Group, The, San Diego *Also Called: Bridgewest Ventures LLC (P-14976)*

Bridgewest Ventures LLC (PA) .... A...... 858 529-6600
7310 Miramar Rd Ste 500 San Diego (92126) *(P-14976)*

Bridgford Marketing Company (DH) .... D...... 714 526-5533
1308 N Patt St Anaheim (92801) *(P-13291)*

Bridgwter Consulting Group Inc .... D...... 949 535-1755
18881 Von Karman Ave Ste 1450 Irvine (92612) *(P-20145)*

Bridport Erie Aviation Inc .... E...... 714 634-8801
6900 Orangethorpe Ave Buena Park (90620) *(P-17117)*

Bridport-Air Carrier Inc (HQ) .... D...... 253 872-7205
6900 Orangethorpe Ave Ste B Buena Park (90620) *(P-2499)*

Briggs Electric Inc (PA) .... D...... 714 544-2500
14381 Franklin Ave Tustin (92780) *(P-873)*

Briggs Mine The, Trona *Also Called: Dv Natural Resources LLC (P-232)*

Bright Event Rentals LLC (PA) .... C...... 310 202-0011
1640 W 190th St Ste A Torrance (90501) *(P-15772)*

Bright Glow, Covina *Also Called: Bright Glow Candle Company Inc (P-11198)*

Bright Glow Candle Company Inc (PA) .... E...... 909 469-4733
20591 E Via Verde St Covina (91724) *(P-11198)*

Bright Health Physicians (PA) .... C...... 562 947-8478
15725 Whittier Blvd Ste 500 Whittier (90603) *(P-17606)*

Bright Now Dental, Irvine *Also Called: Smile Brands Group Inc (P-20093)*

Brightcloud Inc .... B...... 858 652-4803
4370 La Jolla Village Dr Ste 820 San Diego (92122) *(P-16724)*

Brighton Convalescent Center .... D...... 626 798-9124
1836 N Fair Oaks Ave Pasadena (91103) *(P-18114)*

Brighton Place Spring Valley, Spring Valley *Also Called: B-Spring Valley LLC (P-17885)*

Brightstar Care Lake Forest .... B...... 949 837-7000
26023 Acero Ste 100 Mission Viejo (92691) *(P-18598)*

Brightview Companies LLC .... C...... 714 437-1586
11555 Coley River Cir Fountain Valley (92708) *(P-184)*

Brightview Golf Maint Inc .... D...... 805 968-6400
405 N Glen Annie Rd Santa Barbara (93117) *(P-145)*

Brightview Landscape Dev Inc .... B...... 858 458-9900
8450 Miramar Pl San Diego (92121) *(P-146)*

Brightview Landscape Dev Inc .... C...... 714 546-7975
8 Hughes Ste 125 Irvine (92618) *(P-747)*

Brightview Landscape Svcs Inc .... C...... 858 458-1900
8500 Miramar Pl San Diego (92121) *(P-147)*

Brightview Landscape Svcs Inc .... C...... 619 474-4478
415 W 30th St National City (91950) *(P-148)*

Brightview Landscape Svcs Inc .... C...... 909 946-3196
8726 Calabash Ave Fontana (92335) *(P-149)*

Brightview Landscape Svcs Inc .... C...... 805 642-9300
2064 Eastman Ave Ste 104 Ventura (93003) *(P-150)*

Brightview Landscape Svcs Inc .... C...... 714 546-7843
32202 Paseo Adelanto San Juan Capistrano (92675) *(P-151)*

Brightview Landscape Svcs Inc .... B...... 714 546-7843
1960 S Yale St Santa Ana (92704) *(P-152)*

Brightview Landscape Svcs Inc .... C...... 310 327-8700
17813 S Main St Ste 105 Gardena (90248) *(P-153)*

Brightview Tree Care Svcs Inc .... D...... 951 684-2730
715 W La Cadena Dr Riverside (92501) *(P-154)*

Brightview Tree Company .... D...... 760 955-2560
Apple Valley (92307) *(P-155)*

Brightview Tree Company .... D...... 714 546-7975
3200 W Telegraph Rd Fillmore (93015) *(P-227)*

Brightview Tree Company .... D...... 818 951-5500
9500 Foothill Blvd Sunland (91040) *(P-228)*

Briles Aerospace LLC .... E...... 424 320-3817
1559 W 135th St Gardena (90249) *(P-6433)*

Brill Inc .... C...... 909 825-7343
2111 W Valley Blvd Colton (92324) *(P-1456)*

Brilliant AV, Costa Mesa *Also Called: Walin Group Inc (P-7411)*

Brilliant Solutions, Irvine *Also Called: Meguiars Inc (P-4360)*

Brillstein Entrmt Partners LLC (HQ) .... D...... 310 205-5100
9150 Wilshire Blvd Ste 350 Beverly Hills (90212) *(P-17172)*

Brillstein Grey Entertainment, Beverly Hills *Also Called: Brillstein Entrmt Partners LLC (P-17172)*

Brimad Enterprises Inc .... E...... 951 354-8187
2900 Adams St Ste B16 Riverside (92504) *(P-15585)*

Brimes International, San Diego *Also Called: Cali Resources Inc (P-9012)*

Brinderson LLC (DH) .... C...... 714 466-7100
18841 S Broadwick St Compton (90220) *(P-19557)*

Brink's, Garden Grove *Also Called: Brinks Incorporated (P-16627)*

Brinks Incorporated .... C...... 714 903-9272
7191 Patterson Dr Garden Grove (92841) *(P-16627)*

Brio Water Technology Inc .... E...... 800 781-1680
768 Turnbull Canyon Rd Hacienda Heights (91745) *(P-12761)*

Briotix .... D...... 805 864-2711
515 Marin St Ste 318 Thousand Oaks (91360) *(P-20146)*

A
L
P
H
A
B
E
T
I
C

Brisam Lax (de) LLC ....D....... 310 649-5151
9901 S La Cienega Blvd Los Angeles (90045) *(P-15097)*

Bristol Farms (HQ) ....**D....... 310 233-4700**
915 E 230th St Carson (90745) *(P-1860)*

Bristol Industries LLC ....C....... 714 990-4121
630 E Lambert Rd Brea (92821) *(P-6434)*

Bristol Omega Inc ....E....... 909 794-6862
9441 Opal Ave Ste 2 Mentone (92359) *(P-2945)*

Bristolite, Santa Ana *Also Called: Sundown Liquidating Corp (P-5318)*

Britcan Inc ....E....... 760 722-2300
3809 Ocean Ranch Blvd Ste 110 Oceanside (92056) *(P-2974)*

Brite Plating Co Inc ....E....... 323 263-7593
1313 Mirasol St Los Angeles (90023) *(P-6596)*

Brithinee Electric ....D....... 909 825-7971
620 S Rancho Ave Colton (92324) *(P-12588)*

Brittany House LLC ....C....... 562 421-4717
5401 E Centralia St Long Beach (90808) *(P-19243)*

Brixen & Sons Inc ....E....... 714 566-1444
2100 S Fairview St Santa Ana (92704) *(P-3740)*

Brm Manufacturing, Los Angeles *Also Called: Brush Research Mfg Co Inc (P-11085)*

Broadata Communications Inc ....D....... 310 530-1416
2545 W 237th St Ste K Torrance (90505) *(P-5733)*

Broadband Telecom Inc ....E....... 818 450-5714
515 S Flower St Fl 36 Los Angeles (90071) *(P-20320)*

Broadcast Microwave Svcs LLC (PA)......................**C....... 858 391-3050**
13475 Danielson St Ste 130 Poway (92064) *(P-8501)*

Broadcom Corporation ....D....... 949 926-5000
15101 Alton Pkwy Irvine (92618) *(P-8775)*

Broadcom Corporation ....E....... 714 376-5029
15191 Alton Pkwy Irvine (92618) *(P-8776)*

Broadcom Corporation ....C....... 858 385-8800
16340 W Bernardo Dr Bldg A San Diego (92127) *(P-8777)*

Broadcom Limited Bldg 2, Irvine *Also Called: Broadcom Corporation (P-8776)*

Broadley-James Corporation ....D....... 949 829-5555
19 Thomas Irvine (92618) *(P-10246)*

Broadreach Capitl Partners LLC ....A....... 310 691-5760
6430 W Sunset Blvd Ste 504 Los Angeles (90028) *(P-15022)*

Broadview Networks Inc ....D....... 818 939-0015
7731 Hayvenhurst Ave Van Nuys (91406) *(P-11874)*

Broadway AC Htg & Shtmtl ....E....... 818 781-1477
7855 Burnet Ave Van Nuys (91405) *(P-6204)*

Broadway Auto Parts, Santa Ana *Also Called: United Syatt America Corp (P-13887)*

Broadway Manor Care Center, Glendale *Also Called: Longwood Management Corp (P-18138)*

Broadway Sheet Metal, Van Nuys *Also Called: Broadway AC Htg & Shtmtl (P-6204)*

Broadway Typewriter Co Inc ....D....... 800 998-9199
1055 6th Ave Ste 101 San Diego (92101) *(P-12401)*

Brochure Holders 4u, Santa Ana *Also Called: Clear-Ad Inc (P-4992)*

Broco, Ontario *Also Called: Broco Inc (P-7156)*

Broco Inc ....E....... 909 483-3222
400 S Rockefeller Ave Ontario (91761) *(P-7156)*

Broma Applicators LLC ....E....... 760 351-0101
322 W J St Brawley (92227) *(P-13487)*

Bromack, Los Angeles *Also Called: LA Cabinet & Millwork Inc (P-2959)*

Bromack Company ....E....... 323 227-5000
3005 Humboldt St Los Angeles (90031) *(P-2649)*

Bromic Heating Pty Limited ....D....... 855 552-7432
7595 Irvine Center Dr Ste 100 Irvine (92618) *(P-748)*

Bronze-Way Plating Corporation (PA).....................**E....... 323 266-6933**
3301 E 14th St Los Angeles (90023) *(P-6597)*

Brook & Whittle Limited ....E....... 714 634-3466
1177 N Grove St Anaheim (92806) *(P-3741)*

Brookdale Clairemont, San Diego *Also Called: Emeritus Corporation (P-17932)*

Brookfeld Sthland Holdings LLC ....C....... 714 427-6868
3200 Park Center Dr Ste 1000 Costa Mesa (92626) *(P-422)*

Brookfield Residential, Costa Mesa *Also Called: Brookfeld Sthland Holdings LLC (P-422)*

Brooks Restaurant Group Inc (PA).........................E....... 559 485-8520
220 Five Cities Dr Pismo Beach (93449) *(P-13173)*

Brothers Desserts, Santa Ana *Also Called: Brothers Intl Desserts (P-1295)*

Brothers Intl Desserts (PA) ....**D....... 949 655-0080**
3400 W Segerstrom Ave Santa Ana (92704) *(P-1295)*

Brothers Machine & Tool Inc ....E....... 951 361-9454
11095 Inland Ave Jurupa Valley (91752) *(P-7032)*

Brotherwise Games, Hawthorne *Also Called: Marina Graphic Center Inc (P-3630)*

Brotman Medical Center Inc ....B....... 310 836-7000
3828 Delmas Ter Culver City (90232) *(P-18193)*

Brower Hale, Laguna Hills *Also Called: Valley Insurance Service Inc (P-14639)*

Brown Hnycutt Truss Systems In ....F....... 760 244-8887
16775 Smoke Tree St Hesperia (92345) *(P-2693)*

Brown-Pacific Inc ....E....... 562 921-3471
13639 Bora Dr Santa Fe Springs (90670) *(P-5579)*

Brownco Construction, Anaheim *Also Called: Brownco Construction Co Inc (P-423)*

Brownco Construction Co Inc ....D....... 714 935-9600
1000 E Katella Ave Anaheim (92805) *(P-423)*

Browne Child Development Ctr, Oceanside *Also Called: Marine Corps Community Svcs (P-19216)*

Brownstone Companies Inc ....A....... 310 297-3600
2629 Manhattan Beach Blvd # 100 Redondo Beach (90278) *(P-12650)*

Brownstone Security, Redondo Beach *Also Called: Brownstone Companies Inc (P-12650)*

Browntrout, El Segundo *Also Called: Browntrout Publishers Inc (P-3433)*

Browntrout Publishers Inc (PA).............................**E....... 424 290-6122**
201 Continental Blvd Ste 200 El Segundo (90245) *(P-3433)*

Brownwood Furniture Inc ....C....... 909 945-5613
9805 6th St Ste 104 Rancho Cucamonga (91730) *(P-2769)*

Bruck Lighting Systems, Irvine *Also Called: Ledra Brands Inc (P-12306)*

Brud Inc ....F....... 310 806-2283
837 N Spring St Ste 101 Los Angeles (90012) *(P-3434)*

Bruin Biometrics LLC ....F....... 310 268-9494
10877 Wilshire Blvd Ste 1600 Los Angeles (90024) *(P-10464)*

Bruker Corporation ....F....... 805 388-3326
3601 Calle Tecate Ste C Camarillo (93012) *(P-10247)*

Brunton Enterprises Inc ....C....... 562 945-0013
8815 Sorensen Ave Santa Fe Springs (90670) *(P-6001)*

Brusco Tug & Barge Inc ....C....... 805 986-1600
170 E Port Hueneme Rd Port Hueneme (93041) *(P-11650)*

Brush Research Mfg Co Inc ....C....... 323 261-2193
4642 Floral Dr Los Angeles (90022) *(P-11085)*

Brutoco Engineering, Covina *Also Called: Brutoco Engineering & Construction Inc (P-612)*

Brutoco Engineering & Construction Inc C
1272 Center Court Dr Ste 101 Covina (91724) *(P-612)*

Bryant Elementary School, Garden Grove *Also Called: Garden Grove Unified Schl Dst (P-19211)*

Bryant Fuel Systems LLC ....F....... 661 334-5462
1300 32nd St Bakersfield (93301) *(P-6135)*

Bryant Rubber Corp (PA).....................................**E....... 310 530-2530**
1580 W Carson St Long Beach (90810) *(P-4719)*

Bryant Rubber Corp ....C....... 310 530-2530
1083 W 251st St. Bellflower (90706) *(P-4720)*

Brydenscot Metal Products Inc ....F....... 909 799-0088
1299 Riverview Dr San Bernardino (92408) *(P-6205)*

Bsh Home Appliances Corp (DH)...........................**C....... 949 440-7100**
1901 Main St Ste 600 Irvine (92614) *(P-17069)*

Bsst LLC ....E....... 626 593-4500
5462 Irwindale Ave Ste A Irwindale (91706) *(P-9361)*

Bstz, Los Angeles *Also Called: Blakely Sokoloff Taylor & Zafman LLP (P-18829)*

Bsw Roofing Contractors, Bakersfield *Also Called: Bakersfield Shingles Wholesale Inc (P-12370)*

BT Infonet, El Segundo *Also Called: Infonet Services Corporation (P-11889)*

BTG S CORP (PA)...**D....... 323 582-4444**
2801 E Vernon Ave Vernon (90058) *(P-13532)*

Btg Textiles Inc ....E....... 323 586-9488
710 Union St Montebello (90640) *(P-14109)*

Bti Aerospace & Electronics ....E....... 909 465-1569
13546 Vintage Pl Chino (91710) *(P-7789)*

Btl Machine ....D....... 951 808-9929
1168 Sherborn St Corona (92879) *(P-7790)*

Btrade LLC ....E....... 818 334-4433
701 N Brand Blvd Ste 205 Glendale (91203) *(P-16191)*

BTS Trading Inc ....E....... 213 800-6755
3449 S Main St Los Angeles (90007) *(P-2014)*

Btsi, San Diego *Also Called: Bernardo Technical Services (P-16554)*

Mergent email: customerrelations@mergent.com
1022

2024 Southern California
Business Directory and Buyers Guide

(P-0000) Products & Services Section entry number
(PA)=Parent Co (HQ)=Headquarters (DH)=Div Headquarters

Bu Ru LLC .... F...... 424 316-2878
826 E 3rd St Los Angeles (90013) **(P-14092)**

Bubbles Baking Company .... E...... 818 786-1700
15215 Keswick St Van Nuys (91405) **(P-1457)**

Bubbles Baking Company, Van Nuys *Also Called: Danish Baking Co Inc* **(P-1460)**

Buchanan Street Partners LP .... D...... 949 721-1414
3501 Jamboree Rd Ste 4200 Newport Beach (92660) **(P-14753)**

Buchbinder, Jay Industries, Compton *Also Called: Jbi LLC* **(P-2832)**

Buck Owens Production Co Inc (PA)..................**E...... 661 326-1011**
2800 Buck Owens Blvd Bakersfield (93308) **(P-11920)**

Buddha Teas, Carlsbad *Also Called: Living Wellness Partners LLC* **(P-1936)**

Buddy Bar Casting LLC .... C...... 562 861-9664
10801 Sessler St South Gate (90280) **(P-5783)**

Buddy Group Inc .... D...... 949 468-0042
7 Studebaker Irvine (92618) **(P-15989)**

Budget Enterprises Llc .... E...... 949 697-9544
23042 Mill Creek Dr Laguna Hills (92653) **(P-5311)**

Buds Cotton Inc .... E...... 714 223-7800
1240 N Fee Ana St Anaheim (92807) **(P-4386)**

Buds Ice Cream San Francisco, City Of Industry *Also Called: Berkeley Farms LLC* **(P-1306)**

Buena Ventura Care Center Inc .... D...... 818 247-4476
1505 Colby Dr Glendale (91205) **(P-18115)**

Buena Vista Care Center, Santa Barbara *Also Called: Covenant Care California LLC* **(P-17917)**

Buena Vista Food Products Inc (DH)..................**C...... 626 815-8859**
823 W 8th St Azusa (91702) **(P-13356)**

Buena Vista International Inc .... C...... 818 295-5200
350 S Buena Vista St Burbank (91521) **(P-17173)**

Buena Vista Manor, Duarte *Also Called: Humangood Socal* **(P-19273)**

Buena Vista MGT Svcs LLC .... C...... 619 450-4300
2045 1st Ave San Diego (92101) **(P-18599)**

Buena Vista Television (DH)..............................**C...... 818 560-1878**
500 S Buena Vista St Burbank (91521) **(P-16758)**

Buena Vista TV Advg Sls, Burbank *Also Called: Buena Vista Television* **(P-16758)**

Buff and Shine Mfg Inc .... E...... 310 886-5111
2139 E Del Amo Blvd Rancho Dominguez (90220) **(P-5538)**

Buffalo, Chatsworth *Also Called: Piege Co* **(P-13142)**

Buffalo Market, Los Angeles *Also Called: Buffalo Market Inc* **(P-13174)**

Buffalo Market Inc .... C...... 650 337-0078
1439 N Highland Ave Los Angeles (90028) **(P-13174)**

Buffalo Spot MGT Group LLC .... C...... 949 354-0884
7245 Garden Grove Blvd Ste E Garden Grove (92841) **(P-20007)**

Buffalo Wild Wings, Beverly Hills *Also Called: BW Hotel LLC* **(P-13987)**

Buffini & Company (PA)......................................**C...... 760 827-2100**
6349 Palomar Oaks Ct Carlsbad (92011) **(P-19178)**

Builders Fence Company Inc (PA)......................**E...... 818 768-5500**
8937 San Fernando Rd Sun Valley (91352) **(P-12325)**

Building Elctronic Contrls Inc (PA)...................**E...... 909 305-1600**
2246 Lindsay Way Glendora (91740) **(P-874)**

Building News, Vista *Also Called: Bni Publications Inc* **(P-14065)**

Buk Optics Inc .... E...... 714 384-9620
3600 W Moore Ave Santa Ana (92704) **(P-10309)**

Bumble Bee Foods LLC (HQ)............................**F...... 800 800-8572**
280 10th Ave San Diego (92101) **(P-1792)**

Bumble Bee Foods LLC .... D...... 562 483-7474
13100 Arctic Cir Santa Fe Springs (90670) **(P-1793)**

Bumble Bee Seafoods LP .... C...... 858 715-4000
280 10th Ave San Diego (92101) **(P-1794)**

Bump.me, La Jolla *Also Called: Eventscom Inc* **(P-16242)**

Bunim-Murray Productions .... C...... 818 756-5100
1015 Grandview Ave Glendale (91201) **(P-17174)**

Bunker Corp (PA)...**D...... 949 361-3935**
1131 Via Callejon San Clemente (92673) **(P-9362)**

Bunzl, Anaheim *Also Called: Bunzl Distribution Cal LLC* **(P-13004)**

Bunzl Agrclture Group Chstrfel, Oxnard *Also Called: Cool-Pak LLC* **(P-4995)**

Bunzl Distribution Cal LLC (DH).......................**D...... 714 688-1900**
3310 E Miraloma Ave Anaheim (92806) **(P-13004)**

Burbank Airport Mariott Hotel, Burbank *Also Called: PHF II Burbank LLC* **(P-15303)**

Burbank Dental Laboratory Inc .... C...... 818 841-2256
2101 Floyd St Burbank (91504) **(P-18569)**

Burbank Leader, Glendale *Also Called: California Community News LLC* **(P-3260)**

Burbank Partners LLC .... D...... 818 263-8704
15433 Ventura Blvd Sherman Oaks (91403) **(P-15098)**

Burbank Steel Treating Inc .... E...... 818 842-0975
415 S Varney St Burbank (91502) **(P-5831)**

Burbank Water & Power, Burbank *Also Called: City of Burbank* **(P-12103)**

Burke, Los Angeles *Also Called: Burke Williams & Sorensen LLP* **(P-18832)**

Burke Engineering Co .... D...... 626 579-6763
9700 Factorial Way El Monte (91733) **(P-12737)**

Burke Williams & Sorensen LLP (PA)..................**D...... 213 236-0600**
444 S Flower St Ste 2400 Los Angeles (90071) **(P-18832)**

Burleigh Point LLC .... C...... 949 428-3200
5600 Argosy Ave Ste 100 Huntington Beach (92649) **(P-14754)**

Burleigh Point, Ltd., Huntington Beach *Also Called: Burleigh Point LLC* **(P-14754)**

Burlingame Industries Inc .... C...... 909 355-7000
2352 N Locust Ave Rialto (92377) **(P-5565)**

Burlingame Industries Inc ....* .... C...... 909 887-7038
277 Lytle Creek Rd Lytle Creek (92358) **(P-15440)**

Burlingame Industries Inc (PA).........................**D...... 909 355-7000**
3546 N Riverside Ave Rialto (92377) **(P-15441)**

Burlington Coat Factory, Arcadia *Also Called: Burlington Coat Fctry Whse of* **(P-13921)**

Burlington Coat Fctry Whse of ....* .... C...... 626 447-8784
1201 S Baldwin Ave Arcadia (91007) **(P-13921)**

Burlington Convalescent Hosp (PA)....................**D...... 213 381-5585**
845 S Burlington Ave Los Angeles (90057) **(P-17894)**

Burlington Convalescent Hosp .... C...... 323 295-7737
3737 Don Felipe Dr Los Angeles (90008) **(P-17895)**

Burnett & Son Meat Co Inc .... D...... 626 357-2165
1420 S Myrtle Ave Monrovia (91016) **(P-1190)**

Burnett Fine Foods, Monrovia *Also Called: Burnett & Son Meat Co Inc* **(P-1190)**

Burnham Wgb Insur Solutions, Tustin *Also Called: Wood Gutmann Bogart Insur Brks* **(P-14647)**

Burning Torch Inc .... E...... 323 733-7700
1738 Cordova St Los Angeles (90007) **(P-2308)**

Burns & McDonnell Inc .... D...... 714 256-1595
140 S State College Blvd Ste 100 Brea (92821) **(P-19558)**

Burns and Sons Trucking Inc .... D...... 619 460-5394
9210 Olive Dr Spring Valley (91977) **(P-11445)**

Burns Environmental Svcs Inc .... E...... 800 577-4009
19360 Rinaldi St Ste 381 Northridge (91326) **(P-4345)**

Burrtec, Fontana *Also Called: Burrtec Waste Industries Inc* **(P-12160)**

Burrtec Waste Industries Inc (HQ).....................**C...... 909 429-4200**
9890 Cherry Ave Fontana (92335) **(P-12160)**

Burrtec Waste Industries Inc .... C...... 909 889-1969
5455 Industrial Pkwy San Bernardino (92407) **(P-12161)**

Bursar's Office, Long Beach *Also Called: California State Univ Long Bch* **(P-19759)**

Burton James Inc .... D...... 626 961-7221
428 Turnbull Canyon Rd City Of Industry (91745) **(P-2796)**

Burton Way Hotels LLC .... D...... 310 273-2222
300 S Doheny Dr Los Angeles (90048) **(P-15099)**

Burton Way Htels Ltd A Cal Ltd .... C...... 818 575-3000
2 Dole Dr Westlake Village (91362) **(P-15100)**

Burton-Way House Ltd A CA .... C...... 310 273-2222
300 S Doheny Dr Los Angeles (90048) **(P-15101)**

Bus-Let Inc .... E...... 323 728-6245
2555 Jason Ct Oceanside (92056) **(P-15629)**

Busa Servicing Inc (PA)....................................**C...... 310 203-3400**
787 W 5th St Los Angeles (90071) **(P-14181)**

Bushnell Ribbon Corporation .... E...... 562 948-1410
300 W Brookdale Pl Fullerton (92832) **(P-11053)**

Business Department, Murrieta *Also Called: Southwest Healthcare Sys Aux* **(P-18456)**

Business Information Systems, La Canada Flintridge *Also Called: Bis Computer Solutions Inc* **(P-15984)**

Business Office, Irvine *Also Called: St Joseph Hospital of Orange* **(P-18463)**

Buslink Media, Baldwin Park *Also Called: Global Silicon Electronics Inc* **(P-7470)**

Buster and Punch Inc .... E...... 818 392-3827
10844 Burbank Blvd North Hollywood (91601) **(P-12297)**

Busy Bee LLC .... D...... 951 404-9900
36798 Pictor Ave Murrieta (92563) **(P-15683)**

Busy Bee Tooling, Ontario *Also Called: Phillips Tool & Die Inc* **(P-7087)**

Employee Codes: A=Over 500 employees, B=251-500
C=101-250, D=51-100, E=20-50, F=10-19, G=1-9

2024 Southern California
Business Directory and Buyers Guide

© Mergent Inc. 1-800-342-5647

1023

Butler Inc .... F...... 310 323-3114
2140 S Dupont Dr Anaheim (92806) *(P-6435)*

Butler America Holdings Inc .... B...... 951 563-0020
12625 Frederick St Ste E2 Moreno Valley (92553) *(P-15823)*

Butler America Holdings Inc .... B...... 909 417-3660
8647 Haven Ave Ste 100 Rancho Cucamonga (91730) *(P-15824)*

Butler Home Products LLC .... C...... 909 476-3884
9409 Buffalo Ave Rancho Cucamonga (91730) *(P-11086)*

Butler International Inc (PA)...........................**C...... 805 882-2200**
3820 State St Ste A Santa Barbara (93105) *(P-15825)*

Butler Service Group Inc (HQ).........................**D...... 201 891-5312**
3820 State St Ste A Santa Barbara (93105) *(P-15916)*

Butterfly Imprints LLC .... E...... 657 464-5188
5545 Woodruff Ave # 35 Lakewood (90713) *(P-17857)*

Buy Fresh Produce Inc .... D...... 323 796-0127
6636 E 26th St Commerce (90040) *(P-13315)*

Buyefficient LLC .... C...... 949 382-3129
903 Calle Amanecer Ste 200 San Clemente (92673) *(P-12452)*

Bvi International Inc .... E...... 661 834-1775
4301 Yeager Way Bakersfield (93313) *(P-6755)*

BW Hotel LLC .... A...... 310 275-5200
9500 Wilshire Blvd Beverly Hills (90212) *(P-13987)*

By Referral Only Inc .... D...... 760 707-1300
2035 Corte Del Nogal Ste 200 Carlsbad (92011) *(P-20321)*

By The Blue Sea LLC .... B...... 310 458-0030
1 Pico Blvd Santa Monica (90405) *(P-15102)*

Bycor General Contractors, San Diego *Also Called: Bycor General Contractors Inc (P-538)*

Bycor General Contractors Inc .... D...... 858 587-1901
6490 Marindustry Dr San Diego (92121) *(P-538)*

Byd Motors LLC (HQ).......................................**E...... 213 748-3980**
888 E Walnut St Fl 2 Pasadena (91101) *(P-9363)*

Byer California .... C...... 323 780-7615
1201 Rio Vista Ave Los Angeles (90023) *(P-2064)*

Byrnes & Kiefer Co .... D...... 714 554-4000
501 Airpark Dr Fullerton (92833) *(P-1760)*

Byte, Santa Monica *Also Called: Straight Smile LLC (P-10770)*

Bzya Corporation .... B...... 949 656-3220
100 Spectrum Center Dr Ste 900 Irvine (92618) *(P-15696)*

C & B Delivery Service .... D...... 909 623-4708
1405 E Franklin Ave Pomona (91766) *(P-11566)*

C & C Boats Inc .... F...... 714 969-0900
2124 Main St Ste 145 Huntington Beach (92648) *(P-11654)*

C & C Die Engraving .... E...... 562 944-3399
12510 Mccann Dr Santa Fe Springs (90670) *(P-7791)*

C & D Aerospace, Garden Grove *Also Called: Safran Cabin Inc (P-9785)*

C & D Precision Components Inc .... E...... 626 799-7109
969 S Raymond Ave Pasadena (91105) *(P-7792)*

C & D Wax Inc .... C...... 858 292-5954
9353 Waxie Way San Diego (92123) *(P-14654)*

C & F Foods Inc .... B...... 626 723-1000
12400 Wilshire Blvd Ste 1180 Los Angeles (90025) *(P-1861)*

C & G Mercury Plastics, Sylmar *Also Called: C & G Plastics (P-4971)*

C & G Plastics .... E...... 818 837-3773
12729 Foothill Blvd Sylmar (91342) *(P-4971)*

C & H Machine Inc .... D...... 760 746-6459
943 S Andreasen Dr Escondido (92029) *(P-7708)*

C & H Meat Company, Vernon *Also Called: Eastland Corporation (P-13293)*

C & H Testing Service Inc (PA).........................**E...... 661 589-4030**
6224 Price Way Bakersfield (93308) *(P-331)*

C & J Industries, Santa Fe Springs *Also Called: Custom Steel Fabrication Inc (P-6017)*

C & J Metal Prducts, Paramount *Also Called: Jeffrey Fabrication LLC (P-6256)*

C & J Metal Products Inc .... E...... 562 634-3101
6323 Alondra Blvd Paramount (90723) *(P-6206)*

C & L Graphics Inc .... F...... 818 785-8310
6825 Valjean Ave Van Nuys (91406) *(P-3523)*

C & L Refrigeration Corp .... C...... 800 901-4822
4111 N Palm St Fullerton (92835) *(P-749)*

C & M Manufacturing, Santee *Also Called: C&M Manufacturing Company Inc (P-4829)*

C & M Spring Engrg Co Inc .... F...... 909 597-2030
5244 Las Flores Dr Chino (91710) *(P-6801)*

C & M Wood Industries .... E...... 760 949-3292
17229 Lemon St Ste D Hesperia (92345) *(P-3002)*

C & R Molds Inc .... E...... 805 658-7098
2737 Palma Dr Ventura (93003) *(P-4972)*

C & S Assembly Inc .... E...... 866 779-8939
1150 N Armando St Anaheim (92806) *(P-9009)*

C A A, Los Angeles *Also Called: Creative Artsts Agcy Hldngs LL (P-17314)*

C A Buchen Corp .... E...... 818 767-5408
9231 Glenoaks Blvd Sun Valley (91352) *(P-6002)*

C A Schroeder Inc (PA)....................................**E...... 818 365-9561**
1318 1st St San Fernando (91340) *(P-5552)*

C B Coast Newport Properties .... A...... 949 644-1600
840 Newport Center Dr Ste 100 Newport Beach (92660) *(P-14755)*

C B M, Santa Ana *Also Called: Custom Built Machinery Inc (P-19570)*

C B S, San Marcos *Also Called: Winchster Intrcnnect CM CA Inc (P-5753)*

C B Sheets Inc .... E...... 562 921-1223
13901 Carmenita Rd Santa Fe Springs (90670) *(P-3087)*

C Brewer Company, Ontario *Also Called: Balda C Brewer Inc (P-4954)*

C C Graber Co .... F...... 909 983-1761
315 E 4th St Ontario (91764) *(P-47)*

C C I .... E...... 910 616-7426
22591 Avenida Empresa Rcho Sta Marg (92688) *(P-6756)*

C C I, Orange *Also Called: Coastal Component Inds Inc (P-9020)*

C C I Redlands Inc .... E...... 909 307-6500
721 Nevada St Ste 308 Redlands (92373) *(P-9875)*

C C M P, Anaheim *Also Called: Copper Clad Mltilayer Pdts Inc (P-8666)*

C D C, Costa Mesa *Also Called: Creative Design Consultants (P-16810)*

C D Listening Bar Inc .... A...... 949 225-1170
17822 Gillette Ave Ste A Irvine (92614) *(P-12970)*

C D Lyon Construction Inc (PA).........................**D...... 805 653-0173**
380 W Stanley Ave Ventura (93001) *(P-19559)*

C D R, Oxnard *Also Called: Child Dev Rsrces of Vntura CNT (P-19039)*

C D S, Canyon Country *Also Called: Commercial Display Systems LLC (P-7603)*

C D Video, Santa Ana *Also Called: CD Video Manufacturing Inc (P-9179)*

C Enterprises, San Diego *Also Called: C Enterprises Inc (P-7513)*

C Enterprises Inc .... D...... 760 599-5111
16868 Via Del Campo Ct San Diego (92127) *(P-7513)*

C G Motor Sports Inc .... F...... 909 628-1440
5150 Eucalyptus Ave Ste A Chino (91710) *(P-4973)*

C G Systems Inc .... E...... 714 632-8882
1470 N Hundley St Anaheim (92806) *(P-875)*

C I Container Line, Monterey Park *Also Called: Carmichael International Svc (P-11744)*

C I G A, Glendale *Also Called: Califrnia Insur Guarantee Assn (P-14570)*

C J Foods, Los Angeles *Also Called: CJ America Inc (P-13360)*

C J Instruments Incorporated .... E...... 818 996-4131
Canoga Park (91304) *(P-10356)*

C L A, Van Nuys *Also Called: Clay Lacy Aviation Inc (P-11691)*

C L E, Downey *Also Called: Can Lines Engineering Inc (P-7346)*

C M Automotive Systems Inc (PA).....................**E...... 909 869-7912**
5646 W Mission Blvd Ontario (91762) *(P-7307)*

C M C Steel Fabricators Inc .... F...... 909 899-9993
1455 Auto Center Dr Ste 200 Ontario (91761) *(P-6813)*

C M E Corp .... C...... 714 632-6939
1051 S East St Anaheim (92805) *(P-20322)*

C M G Inc (PA)..**E...... 323 780-8250**
801 S Figueroa St Los Angeles (90017) *(P-2309)*

C M I, Corona *Also Called: Corona Magnetics Inc (P-8939)*

C Magazine, Santa Monica *Also Called: C Publishing LLC (P-3435)*

C N B Real Estate Group, Los Angeles *Also Called: City National Bank (P-14162)*

C N L Hotel Del Partners LP .... D...... 619 522-8299
1500 Orange Ave San Diego (92118) *(P-15103)*

C N P Signs & Graphics, El Cajon *Also Called: California Neon Products (P-11101)*

C P I, Simi Valley *Also Called: Chatsworth Products Inc (P-6858)*

C P S Express .... C...... 951 685-1041
4375 E Lowell St Ste G Ontario (91761) *(P-11446)*

C Preme Limited LLC .... E...... 310 355-0498
1250 E 223rd St Carson (90745) *(P-10982)*

C Publishing LLC .... E...... 310 393-3800
1543 7th St Ste 202 Santa Monica (90401) *(P-3435)*

C R Laurence Co Inc (HQ)................................**B...... 323 588-1281**
2503 E Vernon Ave Vernon (90058) *(P-9364)*

Mergent email: customerrelations@mergent.com
1024

2024 Southern California
Business Directory and Buyers Guide

(P-0000) Products & Services Section entry number
(PA)=Parent Co (HQ)=Headquarters (DH)=Div Headquarters

C R M, Newport Beach *Also Called: Crm Co LLC (P-4749)*

C R T, Santa Fe Springs *Also Called: Crt Color Printing Inc (P-3553)*

C S C, Garden Grove *Also Called: Container Supply Company Incorporated (P-5858)*

C S C, Poway *Also Called: Advanced Machining Tooling Inc (P-7046)*

C S C, Northridge *Also Called: Contemporary Services Corp (P-16633)*

C S I, Santa Fe Springs *Also Called: Csi Electrical Contractors Inc (P-890)*

C S I, Santa Ana *Also Called: Color Science Inc (P-4509)*

C S S, Bakersfield *Also Called: Construction Specialty Svc Inc (P-667)*

C S T, Thousand Oaks *Also Called: Custom Sensors & Tech Inc (P-9026)*

C Squared Social ....D...... 858 386-7400
5963 La Place Ct Ste 105 Carlsbad (92008) *(P-15990)*

C T and F Inc ....D...... 562 927-2339
7228 Scout Ave Bell Gardens (90201) *(P-876)*

C T I, Rancho Cucamonga *Also Called: Collection Technology Inc (P-15610)*

C T L Printing Inds Inc ....E...... 714 635-2980
1741 W Lincoln Ave Ste A Anaheim (92801) *(P-3742)*

C W Cole & Company Inc ....E...... 626 443-2473
2560 Rosemead Blvd South El Monte (91733) *(P-8306)*

C W Driver Incorporated ....C...... 619 696-5100
7588 Metropolitan Dr San Diego (92108) *(P-539)*

C W Hotels Ltd ....C..... 310 395-9700
1740 Ocean Ave Santa Monica (90401) *(P-15104)*

C W S, San Diego *Also Called: Communction Wirg Spcalists Inc (P-883)*

C Wolfe Industries Inc ....E...... 626 443-7185
14420 Marquardt Ave Santa Fe Springs (90670) *(P-6502)*

C-28, Corona *Also Called: Aurelio Felix Barreto III (P-13930)*

C-Cure, Ontario *Also Called: Western States Wholesale Inc (P-5396)*

C-Pak Industries Inc ....E...... 909 880-6017
4925 Hallmark Pkwy San Bernardino (92407) *(P-4974)*

C-Preme, Carson *Also Called: C Preme Limited LLC (P-10982)*

C-Quest Inc ....E...... 323 980-1400
1439 S Herbert Ave Los Angeles (90023) *(P-2234)*

C-Thru Sunrooms, Ontario *Also Called: Stell Industries Inc (P-6391)*

C. W. DRIVER, INCORPORATED, San Diego *Also Called: C W Driver Incorporated (P-539)*

C.A.R ENTERPRISES, INC., Hesperia *Also Called: CAr Enterprises Inc (P-7584)*

C&C Aerol Machining, South Gate *Also Called: Precision Forging Dies Inc (P-7089)*

C&C Jewelry Mfg Inc ....D...... 213 623-6800
323 W 8th St Fl 4 Los Angeles (90014) *(P-12960)*

C&D Aerodesign, San Diego *Also Called: Safran Cabin Inc (P-9791)*

C&D Zodiac Aerospace ....E...... 714 891-0683
7330 Lincoln Way Garden Grove (92841) *(P-9646)*

C&H Hydraulics Inc ....E...... 949 646-6230
1585 Monrovia Ave Newport Beach (92663) *(P-9647)*

C&J Well Services LLC ....A...... 661 589-5220
3752 Allen Rd Bakersfield (93314) *(P-332)*

C&M Manufacturing Inc (PA).................................E...... 619 449-7200
9640b Mission Gorge Rd Ste 165 Santee (92071) *(P-4829)*

C&O Manufacturing Company Inc ....D...... 562 692-7525
9640 Beverly Rd Pico Rivera (90660) *(P-6207)*

C&W Facility Services Inc ....A...... 805 267-7123
3011 Townsgate Rd Ste 410 Westlake Village (91361) *(P-15697)*

C2 Financial Corporation ....C...... 858 220-2112
703 Sunset Ct San Diego (92109) *(P-14419)*

CA Arng 115th Rsg, Los Alamitos *Also Called: Military California Department (P-20296)*

CA Department Development Svc, Cathedral City *Also Called: Califrnia Dept Dvlpmental Svcs (P-18749)*

CA Landscape and Design, Upland *Also Called: California Ldscp & Design Inc (P-186)*

CA Signs, Pacoima *Also Called: California Signs Inc (P-11102)*

CA Station Management Inc ....C...... 909 245-6251
3200 E Guasti Rd Ste 100 Ontario (91761) *(P-664)*

Ca75 Atk, San Diego *Also Called: Northrop Grmman Innvtion Syste (P-10006)*

Caballero & Sons Inc ....E...... 562 368-1644
5753 E Santa Ana Canyon Rd Ste G-380 Anaheim (92807) *(P-14410)*

Cabazon Band Mission Indians ....A...... 760 342-5000
84245 Indio Springs Dr Indio (92203) *(P-15105)*

Cabe Brothers ....D...... 562 595-7411
2895 Long Beach Blvd Long Beach (90806) *(P-13744)*

Cabe Toyota, Long Beach *Also Called: Cabe Brothers (P-13744)*

Cabinets 2000 LLC ....C...... 562 868-0909
11100 Firestone Blvd Norwalk (90650) *(P-2650)*

Cabinets By Prcision Works Inc ....E...... 760 342-1133
81101 Indio Blvd Ste D22 Indio (92201) *(P-2651)*

Cabinets Galore Oc, San Diego *Also Called: Cabinets Glore Orange Cnty Inc (P-2565)*

Cabinets Glore Orange Cnty Inc ....E...... 858 586-0555
9279 Cabot Dr Ste D San Diego (92126) *(P-2565)*

Cabinets R US ....E...... 562 483-6886
1240 N Fee Ana St Anaheim (92807) *(P-2652)*

Cableco ....E...... 562 942-8076
13100 Firestone Blvd Santa Fe Springs (90670) *(P-2130)*

Cableconn, San Diego *Also Called: Cableconn Industries Inc (P-12589)*

Cableconn Industries Inc ....D...... 858 571-7111
7198 Convoy Ct San Diego (92111) *(P-12589)*

Cablesys LLC ....E...... 562 356-3222
2100 E Valencia Dr Ste D Fullerton (92831) *(P-5734)*

Cabo Foods, Laguna Beach *Also Called: Cabo Foods Inc (P-13357)*

Cabo Foods Inc (PA)...E...... 949 463-2373
303 Broadway St Ste 104-105 Laguna Beach (92651) *(P-13357)*

Cabrac Inc ....E...... 818 834-0177
13250 Paxton St Pacoima (91331) *(P-6503)*

Cabrillo Crdolgy Med Group Inc ....D...... 805 983-0922
2241 Wankel Way Ste C Oxnard (93030) *(P-17607)*

Cabrillo Hoist, Fontana *Also Called: Engel Holdings Inc (P-548)*

Cac, Lake Forest *Also Called: Cac Inc (P-9010)*

Cac Inc ....E...... 949 587-3328
20322 Windrow Dr Ste 100 Lake Forest (92630) *(P-9010)*

Cachcach, Santa Ana *Also Called: Funny-Bunny Inc (P-2205)*

Cachet Financial Services ....D...... 626 578-9400
175 S Lake Ave Unit 200 Pasadena (91101) *(P-19757)*

Caci Enterprise Solutions LLC ....B...... 619 881-6000
1455 Frazee Rd Ste 700 San Diego (92108) *(P-16431)*

Cacique, La Puente *Also Called: Cacique Distributors US (P-13251)*

Cacique, La Puente *Also Called: Cacique Foods LLC (P-13252)*

Cacique Distributors US ....C...... 626 961-3399
14923 Proctor Ave La Puente (91746) *(P-13251)*

Cacique Foods LLC ....C...... 626 961-3399
14923 Proctor Ave La Puente (91746) *(P-13252)*

Caco-Pacific Corporation (PA).................................C...... 626 331-3361
813 N Cummings Rd Covina (91724) *(P-7055)*

Cad Works Inc ....E...... 626 336-5491
16366 E Valley Blvd La Puente (91744) *(P-6003)*

Cadence Aerospace, Anaheim *Also Called: Aerospace Parts Holdings Inc (P-9607)*

Cadence Aerospace LLC (HQ).................................C...... 949 877-3630
3150 E Miraloma Ave Anaheim (92806) *(P-9648)*

Cadence Aerospace LLC ....F...... 425 353-0405
3130 E Miraloma Ave Anaheim (92806) *(P-9649)*

Cadence Gourmet LLC (PA)....................................F...... 951 444-9269
155 Klug Cir Corona (92878) *(P-1862)*

Cadence Gourmet Involve Foods, Corona *Also Called: Cadence Gourmet LLC (P-1862)*

Cadillac Motor Div Area ....C...... 805 373-9575
30930 Russell Ranch Rd Westlake Village (91362) *(P-13745)*

Caelus Corporation ....E...... 949 877-7170
20472 Crescent Bay Dr Ste 100 Lake Forest (92630) *(P-20008)*

Caelux Corporation ....E...... 626 502-7033
404 N Halstead St Pasadena (91107) *(P-8778)*

Caer Inc ....E...... 415 879-9864
8070 Melrose Ave Los Angeles (90046) *(P-1320)*

Caes Systems LLC ....C...... 858 560-1301
9404 Chesapeake Dr San Diego (92123) *(P-9961)*

Caesar Hardware Intl Ltd ....E...... 800 306-3829
4985 Hallmark Pkwy San Bernardino (92407) *(P-5908)*

Caesars Entrtnment Oprting Inc ....A...... 760 751-3100
777 Harrahs Rincon Way Valley Center (92082) *(P-17542)*

Cafe 21, San Diego *Also Called: Cafe 21 Gaslamp Inc (P-13988)*

Cafe 21 Gaslamp Inc ....E...... 619 795-0721
2736 Adams Ave San Diego (92116) *(P-13988)*

Cafe Champagne, Temecula *Also Called: Thornton Winery (P-1665)*

Caffe DAmore Inc C
1916 S Tubeway Ave Commerce (90040) *(P-1816)*

A L P H A B E T I C

Cafvina Coffee & Tea, Garden Grove *Also Called: Quoc Viet Foods (P-1972)*

Cageco Inc .... E....... 800 605-4859
16225 Beaver Rd Adelanto (92301) *(P-6902)*

Cahn, Jsph/Miller Kaplan Arase, North Hollywood *Also Called: Miller Kaplan Arase LLP (P-19795)*

Cahuilla Creek Casino, Anza *Also Called: Cahuilla Creek Rest & Casino (P-17543)*

Cahuilla Creek Rest & Casino .... C....... 951 763-1200
52702 Us Highway 371 Anza (92539) *(P-17543)*

Cai, Orange *Also Called: Califrnia Anlytical Instrs Inc (P-10121)*

Cai, Corona *Also Called: Combustion Associates Inc (P-12018)*

Caine & Weiner, Sherman Oaks *Also Called: Caine & Weiner Company Inc (P-15608)*

Caine & Weiner Company Inc (PA)............................. D...... 818 226-6000
5805 Sepulveda Blvd Fl 4 Sherman Oaks (91411) *(P-15608)*

Caitac Garment Processing Inc .... B....... 310 217-9888
14725 S Broadway Gardena (90248) *(P-2087)*

Cal AM Manufacturing Co Inc .... E....... 800 992-0499
1939 Friendship Dr Ste E El Cajon (92020) *(P-11199)*

Cal Coast Acidizing Co .... E....... 805 934-2411
6226 Dominion Rd Santa Maria (93454) *(P-333)*

Cal Coast Acidizing Service, Santa Maria *Also Called: Cal Coast Acidizing Co (P-333)*

Cal Coffee Shop, Lakewood *Also Called: Nationwide Theatres Corp (P-17360)*

Cal Mutual Inc .... D...... 888 700-4650
34077 Temecula Creek Rd Temecula (92592) *(P-14304)*

Cal Pac Sheet Metal, Santa Ana *Also Called: Cal Pac Sheet Metal Inc (P-6208)*

Cal Pac Sheet Metal Inc .... E....... 714 979-2733
2720 S Main St Ste B Santa Ana (92707) *(P-6208)*

Cal Partitions Inc .... E....... 310 539-1911
23814 President Ave Harbor City (90710) *(P-2975)*

Cal Pipe Manufacturing Inc (PA)............................. E....... 562 803-4388
12160 Woodruff Ave Downey (90241) *(P-6840)*

Cal Plate (PA).. D...... 562 403-3000
17110 Jersey Ave Artesia (90701) *(P-7183)*

Cal Simba Inc (PA).. E....... 805 240-1177
1283 Flynn Rd Camarillo (93012) *(P-10915)*

Cal Southern Assn Governments (PA).......................... C....... 213 236-1800
900 Wilshire Blvd Ste 1700 Los Angeles (90017) *(P-20323)*

Cal Southern Braiding Inc .... D...... 562 927-5531
7450 Scout Ave Bell Gardens (90201) *(P-9011)*

Cal Southern Graphics Corp (HQ)............................. D...... 310 559-3600
9655 De Soto Ave Chatsworth (91311) *(P-3524)*

Cal Southern Sound Image Inc (PA)........................... D...... 760 737-3900
2425 Auto Park Way Escondido (92029) *(P-12651)*

Cal Southern United Food .... C....... 714 220-2297
6425 Katella Ave Ste 100 Cypress (90630) *(P-14547)*

Cal State La Univ Aux Svcs Inc .... A....... 323 343-2531
5151 State University Dr Los Angeles (90032) *(P-20009)*

Cal State Site Services .... E....... 800 499-5757
4518 Industrial St Simi Valley (93063) *(P-5611)*

Cal Tape & Label, Anaheim *Also Called: C T L Printing Inds Inc (P-3742)*

Cal Tech Precision Inc .... D...... 714 992-4130
1830 N Lemon St Anaheim (92801) *(P-9650)*

Cal Treehouse Almonds LLC .... C....... 661 725-6334
2115 Road 144 Delano (93215) *(P-100)*

Cal West Designs, Santa Fe Springs *Also Called: K S Designs Inc (P-11128)*

Cal West Enterprises, San Diego *Also Called: Wamc Company Inc (P-14732)*

Cal Western Foreclosure Svcs, El Cajon *Also Called: EC Closing Corp (P-14311)*

Cal-A-Vie, Vista *Also Called: Spa Havens LP (P-17414)*

Cal-Aurum, Huntington Beach *Also Called: Cal-Aurum Industries (P-6598)*

Cal-Aurum Industries .... E....... 714 898-0996
15632 Container Ln Huntington Beach (92649) *(P-6598)*

Cal-AZ Sales & Marketing, Placentia *Also Called: Fruth Custom Plastics Inc (P-5032)*

Cal-Coast Pkg & Crating Inc .... E....... 310 518-7215
2040 E 220th St Carson (90810) *(P-2711)*

Cal-Comp Electronics (usa) Co Ltd .... B....... 858 587-6900
9877 Waples St San Diego (92121) *(P-8171)*

Cal-Comp USA (san Diego) Inc .... C....... 858 587-6900
1940 Camino Vida Roble Carlsbad (92008) *(P-8655)*

Cal-Draulics, Corona *Also Called: Johnson Caldraul Inc (P-9729)*

Cal-India Foods International .... E....... 909 613-1660
13591 Yorba Ave Chino (91710) *(P-4517)*

Cal-June Inc (PA)... E....... 323 877-4164
5238 Vineland Ave North Hollywood (91601) *(P-5909)*

Cal-Med Ambulance, South El Monte *Also Called: California Med Response Inc (P-11377)*

Cal-Mil, Oceanside *Also Called: Cal-Mil Plastic Products Inc (P-4975)*

Cal-Mil Plastic Products Inc (PA)........................... E....... 800 321-9069
4079 Calle Platino Oceanside (92056) *(P-4975)*

Cal-Monarch, Corona *Also Called: California Wire Products Corp (P-6814)*

Cal-Organic Farms, Lamont *Also Called: Grimmway Enterprises Inc (P-13329)*

Cal-Pac Chemical Co Inc .... F....... 323 585-2178
6231 Maywood Ave Huntington Park (90255) *(P-3881)*

Cal-Sign Wholesale Inc .... F....... 209 523-7446
2110 S Anne St Santa Ana (92704) *(P-11100)*

Cal-State Auto Parts Inc (PA)............................... C....... 714 630-5950
1361 N Red Gum St Anaheim (92806) *(P-12236)*

Cal-State Steel Corporation .... C....... 310 632-2772
1397 Lynnmere Dr Thousand Oaks (91360) *(P-1102)*

Cal-Tron Plating Inc .... E....... 562 945-1181
11919 Rivera Rd Santa Fe Springs (90670) *(P-6599)*

Cal-West Nurseries Inc .... C....... 951 270-0667
138 North Dr Norco (92860) *(P-185)*

Cala Action Inc .... E....... 213 272-9759
2440 Troy Ave South El Monte (91733) *(P-2015)*

Calabasas Tms Center .... D...... 805 261-0824
2950 Sycamore Dr Simi Valley (93065) *(P-5580)*

CALABASAS TMS CENTER, Simi Valley *Also Called: Calabasas Tms Center (P-5580)*

CALAMP, Irvine *Also Called: Calamp Corp (P-16192)*

Calamp Corp .... D...... 949 600-5600
1401 N Rice Ave Oxnard (93030) *(P-8502)*

Calamp Corp .... E....... 760 444-0952
2200 Faraday Ave Ste 220 Carlsbad (92008) *(P-8503)*

Calamp Corp (PA).. D...... 949 600-5600
15635 Alton Pkwy Ste 250 Irvine (92618) *(P-16192)*

Calance, Anaheim *Also Called: Partners Information Tech (P-16588)*

Calavo, Santa Paula *Also Called: Calavo Growers Inc (P-1863)*

Calavo Growers Inc (PA)..................................... D...... 805 525-1245
1141 Cummings Rd Ste A Santa Paula (93060) *(P-1863)*

Calbiotech Export Inc .... E....... 619 660-6162
1935 Cordell Ct El Cajon (92020) *(P-10465)*

Caldera Medical Inc .... D...... 818 879-6555
4360 Park Terrace Dr Ste 140 Westlake Village (91361) *(P-10466)*

Calderon Drywall Contrs Inc .... D...... 714 696-2977
1931 E Meats Ave Trlr 127 Orange (92865) *(P-973)*

Caldesso LLC .... D...... 909 888-2882
439 S Stoddard Ave San Bernardino (92401) *(P-14124)*

Caldyn, Chatsworth *Also Called: California Dynamics Corp (P-10357)*

Calenergy LLC .... B....... 402 231-1527
7030 Gentry Rd Calipatria (92233) *(P-877)*

Calex, Northridge *Also Called: Valley Hospital Medical Center Foundation (P-18495)*

Calhot Illinios LLC .... D...... 310 536-9800
5250 W El Segundo Blvd Hawthorne (90250) *(P-15106)*

Cali Chem Inc .... E....... 714 265-3740
14271 Corporate Dr Ste B Garden Grove (92843) *(P-4387)*

Cali Food Company Inc .... E....... 714 821-8630
8258 Saigon Pl Garden Grove (92844) *(P-1321)*

Cali Framing, Chatsworth *Also Called: Cali Framing Supplies LLC (P-17118)*

Cali Framing Supplies LLC .... E....... 818 899-7777
20450 Plummer St Chatsworth (91311) *(P-17118)*

Cali Resources Inc .... E....... 619 661-5741
2310 Michael Faraday Dr San Diego (92154) *(P-9012)*

Cali-Fame Los Angeles Inc .... D...... 310 747-5263
20934 S Santa Fe Ave Carson (90810) *(P-2399)*

Cali-Nat Products Inc .... E....... 626 581-5555
534 S 6th Ave City Of Industry (91746) *(P-1864)*

Caliber Bodyworks Texas Inc .... D...... 714 665-3905
5 Auto Center Dr Tustin (92782) *(P-17009)*

Caliber Collision Centers, Tustin *Also Called: Caliber Bodyworks Texas Inc (P-17009)*

Calibr A Division Scripps RES, La Jolla *Also Called: Scripps Research Institute (P-19944)*

Calibre International LLC (PA)............................... C....... 626 969-4660
6250 N Irwindale Ave Irwindale (91702) *(P-20283)*

Calico, Irvine *Also Called: Calico Building Services Inc (P-15698)*

Mergent email: customerrelations@mergent.com
1026

2024 Southern California
Business Directory and Buyers Guide

(P-0000) Products & Services Section entry number
(PA)=Parent Co (HQ)=Headquarters (DH)=Div Headquarters

Calico Building Services Inc .... C...... 949 380-8707
15550 Rockfield Blvd Ste C Irvine (92618) *(P-15698)*

Calidad Inc .... E...... 909 947-3937
1730 S Balboa Ave Ontario (91761) *(P-5784)*

Calient Technologies, Goleta *Also Called: Calient Technologies Inc (P-8469)*

Calient Technologies Inc (PA) .... E...... 805 695-4800
120 Cremona Dr Ste 160 Goleta (93117) *(P-8469)*

Caliente Farms, Delano *Also Called: M Caratan Disc Inc (P-34)*

California Acti, Irvine *Also Called: Acti Corporation Inc (P-8390)*

California Air Tools Inc .... E...... 619 407-7905
8560 Siempre Viva Rd San Diego (92154) *(P-7143)*

California Amforge, Azusa *Also Called: California Amforge Corporation (P-5581)*

California Amforge Corporation .... C...... 626 334-4931
750 N Vernon Ave Azusa (91702) *(P-5581)*

California Arb, Inc., Lake Forest *Also Called: Arb Inc (P-658)*

California Art Products Co, North Hollywood *Also Called: Capco/Psa (P-4981)*

California Assn Realtors Inc (PA) .... C...... 213 739-8200
525 S Virgil Ave Los Angeles (90020) *(P-19374)*

California Baking Company .... B...... 619 591-8289
681 Anita St Chula Vista (91911) *(P-13358)*

California Bank & Trust .... A...... 801 844-7637
11622 El Camino Real San Diego (92130) *(P-14182)*

California Basic, Santa Fe Springs *Also Called: Mias Fashion Mfg Co Inc (P-13137)*

California Blue Apparel Inc .... E...... 213 745-5400
245 W 28th St Los Angeles (90007) *(P-2278)*

California Box Company Inc .... E...... 562 921-1223
13901 Carmenita Rd Santa Fe Springs (90670) *(P-3088)*

California Box II .... D...... 909 944-9202
8949 Toronto Ave Rancho Cucamonga (91730) *(P-13005)*

California Bread Co., Chula Vista *Also Called: California Baking Company (P-13358)*

California Breakers Inc .... E...... 760 598-1528
2490 Grand Ave Vista (92081) *(P-12590)*

California Broadcast Ctr LLC .... D...... 310 233-2425
3800 Via Oro Ave Long Beach (90810) *(P-11970)*

California Business Bureau Inc (PA) .... C...... 626 303-1515
1711 S Mountain Ave Monrovia (91016) *(P-19758)*

California Cancer Specialists Medical Group Inc .. B...... 626 775-3200
1333 S Mayflower Ave # 200 Monrovia (91016) *(P-19391)*

California Candy, South El Monte *Also Called: California Snack Foods Inc (P-1534)*

California Carbon Company Inc .... E...... 562 436-1962
615 W 17th St Long Beach (90813) *(P-3882)*

California Center Bank, Los Angeles *Also Called: Bbcn Bank (P-14159)*

California Chassis Inc .... C...... 714 666-8511
3356 E La Palma Ave Anaheim (92806) *(P-6209)*

California Childrens Academy .... C...... 323 263-3846
233 N Breed St Los Angeles (90033) *(P-19201)*

California Choice, Orange *Also Called: Choic Admini Insur Servi (P-14576)*

California Churros Corporation .... B...... 909 370-4777
751 Via Lata Colton (92324) *(P-1458)*

California City San Bernardino (PA) .... B...... 909 384-7272
290 N D St San Bernardino (92401) *(P-18833)*

California Classics, Santa Clarita *Also Called: California Millworks Corp (P-2587)*

California Closet Co, Huntington Beach *Also Called: California Closet Company Inc (P-1146)*

California Closet Co, San Diego *Also Called: Dehart Inc (P-1153)*

California Closet Company Inc .... C...... 714 899-4905
5921 Skylab Rd Huntington Beach (92647) *(P-1146)*

California Club .... C...... 213 622-1391
538 S Flower St Los Angeles (90071) *(P-19431)*

California Combining Corp .... E...... 323 589-5727
5607 S Santa Fe Ave Vernon (90058) *(P-2125)*

California Commerce Club Inc .... A...... 323 721-2100
6131 Telegraph Rd Commerce (90040) *(P-15107)*

California Commercial Asp LLC .... F...... 858 513-0611
4211 Ponderosa Ave Ste C San Diego (92123) *(P-5465)*

California Community News LLC .... D...... 818 843-8700
221 N Brand Blvd Fl 2 Glendale (91203) *(P-3260)*

California Community News LLC (DH) .... B...... 626 388-1017
2000 E 8th St Los Angeles (90021) *(P-3261)*

California Composites MGT Inc .... E...... 714 258-0405
1935 E Occidental St Santa Ana (92705) *(P-9651)*

California Control Solutions, Anaheim *Also Called: George T Hall Co Inc (P-12754)*

California Costume Int'l, Los Angeles *Also Called: Califrnia Cstume Cllctions Inc (P-2443)*

California Countertop Inc (PA) .... F...... 619 460-0205
7811 Alvarado Rd La Mesa (91942) *(P-2976)*

California Credit Union (PA) .... C...... 818 291-6700
701 N Brand Blvd Fl 7 Glendale (91203) *(P-14245)*

California Cstm Frt & Flavors, Irwindale *Also Called: Califrnia Cstm Frts Flvors In (P-1761)*

California Dairies Inc .... D...... 562 809-2595
11709 Artesia Blvd Artesia (90701) *(P-1307)*

California Dept Fd Agriculture .... A...... 858 755-1161
2260 Jimmy Durante Blvd Del Mar (92014) *(P-20419)*

California Dept of Pub Hlth .... C...... 714 567-2906
681 S Parker St Ste 200 Orange (92868) *(P-20408)*

California Die Casting Inc .... E...... 909 947-9947
1820 S Grove Ave Ontario (91761) *(P-5772)*

California Digital Inc (PA) .... D...... 310 217-0500
6 Saddleback Rd Rolling Hills (90274) *(P-7514)*

California Dynamics Corp (PA) .... E...... 323 223-3882
20500 Prairie St Chatsworth (91311) *(P-10357)*

California Dynasty, Los Angeles *Also Called: MGT Industries Inc (P-2352)*

California Economizer .... E...... 714 898-9963
5622 Engineer Dr Huntington Beach (92649) *(P-8172)*

California Endowment (PA) .... D...... 213 928-8800
1000 N Alameda St Los Angeles (90012) *(P-19318)*

California Exotic Novlt LLC .... D...... 909 606-1950
1455 E Francis St Ontario (91761) *(P-11200)*

California Fair Plan Assn .... D...... 213 487-0111
725 S Figueroa St Ste 3900 Los Angeles (90017) *(P-14569)*

California Faucets Inc .... E...... 657 400-1639
5231 Argosy Ave Huntington Beach (92649) *(P-5965)*

California Faucets Inc (PA) .... E...... 800 822-8855
5271 Argosy Ave Huntington Beach (92649) *(P-5966)*

California Fine Wire Co (PA) .... E...... 805 489-5144
338 S 4th St Grover Beach (93433) *(P-5735)*

California Flexrake Corp .... E...... 626 443-4026
9620 Gidley St Temple City (91780) *(P-5875)*

California Friends Homes .... B...... 714 530-9100
12151 Dale Ave Stanton (90680) *(P-19244)*

California Garlic Company Inc .... E...... 951 506-8883
7651 Saint Andrews Ave San Diego (92154) *(P-13989)*

California Gasket and Rbr Corp (PA) .... E...... 310 323-4250
533 W Collins Ave Orange (92867) *(P-4758)*

California Gate Entry Systems, Anaheim *Also Called: C G Systems Inc (P-875)*

California Glass & Mirror Div, Santa Ana *Also Called: Twed-Dells Inc (P-5359)*

California Graphics, Chatsworth *Also Called: Cal Southern Graphics Corp (P-3524)*

California Industrial Fabrics .... E...... 619 661-7166
2325 Marconi Ct San Diego (92154) *(P-2046)*

California Institute For, La Jolla *Also Called: California Institute For Biomedical Research (P-19920)*

California Institute For Biomedical Research ..... C...... 858 242-1000
11119 N Torrey Pines Rd La Jolla (92037) *(P-19920)*

California Institute Tech .... A...... 818 354-9154
4800 Oak Grove Dr Pasadena (91109) *(P-19921)*

California Insulated Wire & .... D...... 818 569-4930
3050 N California St Burbank (91504) *(P-5736)*

California Internet LP (PA) .... C...... 805 225-4638
251 Camarillo Ranch Rd Camarillo (93012) *(P-11875)*

California Lab Sciences LLC .... B...... 562 758-6900
10200 Pioneer Blvd Ste 500 Santa Fe Springs (90670) *(P-19960)*

California Ldscp & Design Inc .... C...... 909 949-1601
273 N Benson Ave Upland (91786) *(P-186)*

California Machine Specialties, Chino *Also Called: Young Machine Inc (P-8085)*

California Marine Cleaning Inc (PA) .... C...... 619 231-8788
2049 Main St San Diego (92113) *(P-12162)*

California Marketing, San Diego *Also Called: Mabie Marketing Group Inc (P-16865)*

California Med Response Inc .... D...... 562 968-1818
1557 Santa Anita Ave South El Monte (91733) *(P-11377)*

California Milling Co, Los Angeles *Also Called: Grain Craft Inc (P-1411)*

California Millworks Corp .... E...... 661 294-2345
27772 Avenue Scott Santa Clarita (91355) *(P-2587)*

Employee Codes: A=Over 500 employees, B=251-500
C=101-250, D=51-100, E=20-50, F=10-19, G=1-9

2024 Southern California
Business Directory and Buyers Guide

© Mergent Inc. 1-800-342-5647

1027

ALPHABETIC

California Neon Products .... D...... 619 283-2191
9944 Blossom Valley Rd El Cajon (92021) *(P-11101)*

California Offset Printers Inc (PA) .... D...... **818 291-1100**
5075 Brooks St Montclair (91763) *(P-3525)*

California Pak Intl Inc .... E...... 310 223-2500
17706 S Main St Gardena (90248) *(P-8088)*

California Physicians Service .... D...... 310 744-2668
3840 Kilroy Airport Way Long Beach (90806) *(P-14463)*

California Physicians Service .... C...... 818 598-8000
6300 Canoga Ave Ste A Woodland Hills (91367) *(P-14464)*

California Plasteck, Ontario *Also Called: Paramount Panels Inc (P-5130)*

California Plastics, Riverside *Also Called: Altium Holdings LLC (P-4935)*

California Plastix Inc .... E...... 909 629-8288
1319 E 3rd St Pomona (91766) *(P-3179)*

California Pools, Coachella *Also Called: Teserra (P-1179)*

California Portland Cement, Mojave *Also Called: Calportland Company (P-5364)*

California Poultry, Los Angeles *Also Called: Western Supreme Inc (P-1249)*

California Premium Incentives, Lake Forest *Also Called: Aminco International USA Inc (P-10897)*

California Prtg Solutions Inc .... F...... 909 307-2032
1950 W Park Ave Redlands (92373) *(P-3526)*

California Quality Plas Inc .... E...... 909 930-5667
2104 S Cucamonga Ave Ontario (91761) *(P-4976)*

California Rain, Los Angeles *Also Called: California Rain Company Inc (P-13120)*

California Rain Company Inc .... D...... 213 623-6061
1213 E 14th St Los Angeles (90021) *(P-13120)*

California RE Assn Inc .... D...... 213 739-8200
525 S Virgil Ave Los Angeles (90020) *(P-19375)*

California Real Estate, Los Angeles *Also Called: California RE Assn Inc (P-19375)*

California Redwood Products, Colton *Also Called: Frank Kams & Associates Inc (P-2731)*

California Republic Bank .... B...... 949 270-9700
18400 Von Karman Ave # 630 Irvine (92612) *(P-14183)*

California Resources Corp (PA) .... D...... **888 848-4754**
1 World Trade Ctr Ste 1500 Long Beach (90831) *(P-254)*

California Resources Corp .... E...... 661 395-8000
5000 Stockdale Hwy Bakersfield (93309) *(P-293)*

California Resources Prod Corp (HQ) .... C...... **661 869-8000**
27200 Tourney Rd Ste 200 Santa Clarita (91355) *(P-255)*

California Resources Prod Corp .... E...... 661 869-8000
4900 W Lokern Rd Mc Kittrick (93251) *(P-256)*

California Respiratory Care .... D...... 818 379-9999
16055 Ventura Blvd # 715 Encino (91436) *(P-4598)*

California Ribbon Carbn Co Inc .... D
8420 Quinn St Downey (90241) *(P-11054)*

California Scents LLC .... E
18850 Von Karman Ave Ste 200 Irvine (92612) *(P-4346)*

California Screw Products Corp .... D...... 562 633-6626
14957 Gwenchris Ct Paramount (90723) *(P-5910)*

California Semiconductor Tech .... C...... 310 579-2939
429 Santa Monica Blvd Santa Monica (90401) *(P-19560)*

California Sensor Corporation .... E...... 760 438-0525
2075 Corte Del Nogal Ste P Carlsbad (92011) *(P-10358)*

California Sheet Metal, El Cajon *Also Called: California Shtmtl Works Inc (P-497)*

California Shtmtl Works Inc .... D...... 619 562-7010
1020 N Marshall Ave El Cajon (92020) *(P-497)*

California Signs Inc .... E...... 818 899-1888
10280 Glenoaks Blvd Pacoima (91331) *(P-11102)*

California Silica Products LLC .... D...... 909 947-0028
12808 Rancho Rd Adelanto (92301) *(P-3883)*

California Skateparks .... C...... 909 949-1601
285 N Benson Ave Upland (91786) *(P-156)*

California Snack Foods Inc .... E...... 626 444-4508
2131 Tyler Ave South El Monte (91733) *(P-1534)*

California Specialty Farms, Los Angeles *Also Called: Worldwide Specialties Inc (P-2004)*

California Spirits Company LLC .... E...... 619 677-7066
2946 Norman Strasse Rd San Marcos (92069) *(P-1689)*

California Sportservice Inc .... B...... 619 795-5000
100 Park Blvd San Diego (92101) *(P-17366)*

California State Univ Long Bch .... C...... 562 985-1764
1250 N Bellflower Blvd Bh155 Long Beach (90840) *(P-19759)*

California Steel and Tube .... C...... 626 968-5511
16049 Stephens St City Of Industry (91745) *(P-12537)*

California Steel Inds Inc .... B...... 909 350-6300
1 California Steel Way Fontana (92335) *(P-5582)*

California Steel Inds Inc (HQ) .... B...... **909 350-6300**
14000 San Bernardino Ave Fontana (92335) *(P-5583)*

California Steel Services, San Bernardino *Also Called: California Steel Services Inc (P-12538)*

California Steel Services Inc .... E...... 909 796-2222
1212 S Mountain View Ave San Bernardino (92408) *(P-12538)*

California Strl Concepts Inc .... D...... 661 257-6903
28358 Constellation Rd Ste 660 Valencia (91355) *(P-540)*

California Sulphur Company .... E...... 562 437-0768
2250 E Pacific Coast Hwy Wilmington (90744) *(P-3884)*

California Tool & Die, Azusa *Also Called: Mc William & Son Inc (P-6535)*

California Tool & Engineering, Jurupa Valley *Also Called: Cte California Tl & Engrg Inc (P-7114)*

California Trusframe LLC (HQ) .... D...... **951 350-4880**
23665 Cajalco Rd Perris (92570) *(P-2694)*

California Trusframe LLC .... C...... 951 657-7491
23447 Cajalco Rd Perris (92570) *(P-2695)*

California Truss Company (PA) .... D...... **951 657-7491**
23665 Cajalco Rd Perris (92570) *(P-2696)*

California Waste Services LLC .... C...... 310 538-5998
621 W 152nd St Gardena (90247) *(P-12163)*

California Wire Products Corp .... E...... 951 371-7730
1316 Railroad St Corona (92882) *(P-6814)*

California Woodworking Inc .... E...... 805 982-9090
1726 Ives Ave Oxnard (93033) *(P-2653)*

Californian, The, San Diego *Also Called: North County Times (P-3311)*

Califrnia Anlytical Instrs Inc .... D...... 714 974-5560
1312 W Grove Ave Orange (92865) *(P-10121)*

Califrnia Auto Dalers Exch LLC .... B...... 714 996-2400
1320 N Tustin Ave Anaheim (92807) *(P-12223)*

Califrnia Clnic Plstic Surgery .... C...... 760 346-0611
73180 El Paseo Palm Desert (92260) *(P-16796)*

Califrnia Cstm Frits Flvors In (PA) .... E...... **626 736-4130**
15800 Tapia St Irwindale (91706) *(P-1761)*

Califrnia Cstume Cllctions Inc (PA) .... B...... **323 262-8383**
210 S Anderson St Los Angeles (90033) *(P-2443)*

Califrnia Ctr For Arts Escndid .... C...... 760 839-4138
340 N Escondido Blvd Escondido (92025) *(P-19351)*

Califrnia Dept Dvlpmental Svcs .... B...... 760 770-6248
696 Ramon Cathedral City (92234) *(P-18749)*

Califrnia Dept Dvlpmental Svcs .... A...... 714 957-5151
2501 Harbor Blvd Costa Mesa (92626) *(P-19179)*

Califrnia Dept State Hospitals .... A...... 714 957-5000
2501 Harbor Blvd Costa Mesa (92626) *(P-18506)*

Califrnia Dept State Hospitals .... A...... 909 425-7000
3102 E Highland Ave Patton (92369) *(P-18507)*

Califrnia Dept State Hospitals .... A...... 805 468-2000
10333 El Camino Real Atascadero (93422) *(P-18508)*

Califrnia Dluxe Wndows Inds In (PA) .... E...... **818 349-5566**
20735 Superior St Chatsworth (91311) *(P-2588)*

Califrnia Dsgners Chice Cstm C .... E...... 805 987-5820
547 Constitution Ave Ste F Camarillo (93012) *(P-2654)*

Califrnia Frnsic Med Group Inc .... C...... 805 654-3343
800 S Victoria Ave Ventura (93009) *(P-18750)*

Califrnia Furn Collections Inc .... C...... 619 621-2455
150 Reed Ct Ste A Chula Vista (91911) *(P-2869)*

Califrnia Hosp Med Ctr Fndtion .... A...... 213 742-5867
1401 S Grand Ave Los Angeles (90015) *(P-18194)*

Califrnia Insur Guarantee Assn .... C...... 818 844-4300
330 N Brand Blvd Ste 500 Glendale (91203) *(P-14570)*

Califrnia Nutritional Pdts Inc .... D...... 760 485-3000
64405 Lincoln St Mecca (92254) *(P-1419)*

Califrnia Nwspapers Ltd Partnr (DH) .... B...... **626 962-8811**
605 E Huntington Dr Ste 100 Monrovia (91016) *(P-3262)*

Califrnia Nwspapers Ltd Partnr .... E...... 909 987-6397
3200 E Guasti Rd Ste 100 Ontario (91761) *(P-3263)*

Califrnia Nwspapers Ltd Partnr .... E...... 909 793-3221
19 E Citrus Ave Ste 102 Redlands (92373) *(P-3264)*

Mergent email: customerrelations@mergent.com
1028

2024 Southern California
Business Directory and Buyers Guide

(P-0000) Products & Services Section entry number
(PA)=Parent Co (HQ)=Headquarters (DH)=Div Headquarters

Califrnia Prtland Cem Dispatch, Vernon *Also Called: Calportland Company (P-5467)*

Califrnia Rcrtion Instllations, Corona *Also Called: Playmax Surfacing Inc (P-4784)*

Califrnia Rsrces Elk Hills LLC .... B...... 661 412-0000
27200 Tourney Rd Ste 200 Santa Clarita (91355) *(P-294)*

Califrnia Rsurces Long Bch Inc .... D...... 888 848-4754
27200 Tourney Rd Ste 200 Santa Clarita (91355) *(P-295)*

Califrnia Scnce Ctr Foundation .... B...... 213 744-2545
700 Exposition Park Dr Los Angeles (90037) *(P-19352)*

Califrnia State Univ Chnnel Is .... E...... 805 437-2670
45 Rincon Dr Unit 104a Camarillo (93012) *(P-8089)*

Califrnia Suthland Private SEC .... C...... 714 367-4005
1818 S State College Blvd Anaheim (92806) *(P-16628)*

Califrnia Trade Converters Inc .... E...... 818 899-1455
9816 Variel Ave Chatsworth (91311) *(P-3065)*

Calimesa Operations LLC .... C...... 909 795-2421
13542 2nd St Yucaipa (92399) *(P-17896)*

CALIMESA POST ACUTE, Yucaipa *Also Called: Calimesa Operations LLC (P-17896)*

Calimex Deli .... E...... 323 261-7271
711 1/2 S Kern Ave Los Angeles (90022) *(P-13990)*

Call To Action Partners Llc (PA) .... D...... 310 996-7200
11601 Wilshire Blvd Fl 23 Los Angeles (90025) *(P-15023)*

Call-The-Car .... D...... 855 282-6968
21950 Copley Dr Diamond Bar (91765) *(P-11378)*

Callaway Vineyard & Winery .... D...... 951 676-4001
32720 Rancho California Rd Temecula (92591) *(P-1614)*

Calmat Co .... C...... 661 858-2673
16101 Hwy 156 Maricopa (93252) *(P-399)*

Calmat Co (DH) .... C...... 818 553-8821
500 N Brand Blvd Ste 500 Glendale (91203) *(P-4657)*

Calmet Inc (PA) .... C...... 323 721-8120
7202 Petterson Ln Paramount (90723) *(P-12164)*

Calmex Fireplace Eqp Mfg Inc .... E...... 716 645-2901
13629 Talc St Santa Fe Springs (90670) *(P-5911)*

Calmex Fireplace Equip Mfg, Santa Fe Springs *Also Called: Calmex Fireplace Eqp Mfg Inc (P-5911)*

Calmont Engrg & Elec Corp (PA) .... E...... 714 549-0336
420 E Alton Ave Santa Ana (92707) *(P-5737)*

Calmont Wire & Cable, Santa Ana *Also Called: Calmont Engrg & Elec Corp (P-5737)*

Calnetix Technologies LLC (HQ) .... D...... 562 293-1660
16323 Shoemaker Ave Cerritos (90703) *(P-8136)*

Calnrg Operating LLC (PA) .... E...... 805 477-9805
1536 Eastman Ave Ventura (93003) *(P-257)*

Calpaco Papers Inc (PA) .... C...... 323 767-2800
3155 Universe Dr Jurupa Valley (91752) *(P-3232)*

Calpak Usa Inc .... E...... 310 937-7335
13748 Prairie Ave Hawthorne (90250) *(P-8656)*

Calpi Inc .... E...... 661 589-5648
7141 Downing Ave Bakersfield (93308) *(P-334)*

Calpine Energy Solutions LLC (DH) .... C...... 877 273-6772
401 W A St Ste 500 San Diego (92101) *(P-12102)*

Calpipe Industries LLC .... E...... 562 803-4388
923 Calpipe Rd Santa Paula (93060) *(P-5584)*

Calpipe Security Bollards, Downey *Also Called: Cal Pipe Manufacturing Inc (P-6840)*

Calporta Therapeutics Inc .... E...... 858 750-4700
11099 N Torrey Pines Rd Ste 290 La Jolla (92037) *(P-4078)*

Calportland .... E...... 760 343-3403
2025 E Financial Way Glendora (91741) *(P-5466)*

Calportland Company (DH) .... D...... 626 852-6200
2025 E Financial Way Glendora (91741) *(P-5362)*

Calportland Company .... E...... 760 245-5321
19409 National Trails Hwy Oro Grande (92368) *(P-5363)*

Calportland Company .... C...... 661 824-2401
9350 Oak Creek Rd Mojave (93501) *(P-5364)*

Calportland Company .... F...... 800 272-1891
1862 E 27th St Vernon (90058) *(P-5467)*

Calrad Electronics Inc .... E...... 323 465-2131
819 N Highland Ave Los Angeles (90038) *(P-12652)*

Calsemi, Santa Monica *Also Called: California Semiconductor Tech (P-19560)*

Calstar Systems Group Inc .... E...... 818 922-2000
6345 Balboa Blvd Ste 105 Encino (91316) *(P-9197)*

Calvary Church Santa Ana Inc .... C...... 714 973-4800
1010 N Tustin Ave Santa Ana (92705) *(P-19202)*

Calvillo Construction Corp .... E...... 310 985-3911
1133 Brooks St Ste C Ontario (91762) *(P-424)*

Calwax LLC (DH) .... E...... 626 969-4334
16511 Knott Ave La Mirada (90638) *(P-13426)*

Calwest Galvanizing, Carson *Also Called: Calwest Galvanizing Corp (P-6696)*

Calwest Galvanizing Corp .... E...... 310 549-2200
2226 E Dominguez St Carson (90810) *(P-6696)*

Calwest Mfg and Lsk Suspension, Fontana *Also Called: Lamer Street Kreations Corp (P-19637)*

CAM, Fullerton *Also Called: Consolidated Aerospace Mfg LLC (P-9965)*

Camar Aircraft Parts Co .... E...... 805 389-8944
743 Flynn Rd Camarillo (93012) *(P-9652)*

Camar Aircraft Parts Company, Camarillo *Also Called: Camar Aircraft Parts Co (P-9652)*

Camarillo Family YMCA, Camarillo *Also Called: Channel Islnds Yung MNS Chrstn (P-19438)*

Camarillo Healthcare Center .... D...... 805 482-9805
205 Granada St Camarillo (93010) *(P-20010)*

Cambium Business Group Inc (PA) .... C...... 714 670-1171
6950 Noritsu Ave Buena Park (90620) *(P-12279)*

Cambria Pines Lodge, Cambria *Also Called: Pacific Cambria Inc (P-15284)*

Cambria Winery, Santa Maria *Also Called: Jackson Family Wines (P-1639)*

Cambridge Equities LP .... E...... 858 350-2300
9922 Jefferson Blvd Culver City (90232) *(P-4307)*

Cambridge Sierra Holdings LLC .... B...... 909 370-4411
1350 Reche Canyon Rd Colton (92324) *(P-17897)*

Cambro, Huntington Beach *Also Called: Cambro Manufacturing Company (P-4978)*

Cambro Manufacturing, Huntington Beach *Also Called: Cambro Manufacturing Company (P-4977)*

Cambro Manufacturing Company .... D...... 714 848-1555
5801 Skylab Rd Huntington Beach (92647) *(P-4977)*

Cambro Manufacturing Company (PA) .... B...... 714 848-1555
5801 Skylab Rd Huntington Beach (92647) *(P-4978)*

Cambro Manufacturing Company .... C...... 714 848-1555
7601 Clay Ave Huntington Beach (92648) *(P-4979)*

Cambro Manufacturing Company .... C...... 909 354-8962
21558 Ferrero City Of Industry (91789) *(P-11201)*

Camden Center Inc .... D...... 310 526-3807
10780 Santa Monica Blvd Ste 105 Los Angeles (90025) *(P-18751)*

Camden Development Inc .... E...... 949 427-4674
27261 Las Ramblas Mission Viejo (92691) *(P-14756)*

Camellia Gardens Care Center, Pasadena *Also Called: Highland Hlthcare Cmllia Grdns (P-17974)*

Cameo Technologies Inc .... E...... 949 672-7000
20511 Lake Forest Dr Lake Forest (92630) *(P-7464)*

Camera Ready Cars, Fountain Valley *Also Called: Gaffoglio Fmly Mtlcrafters Inc (P-5340)*

Cameron Health Inc .... D...... 949 940-4000
905 Calle Amanecer # 300 San Clemente (92673) *(P-12479)*

Cameron Intrstate Pipeline LLC .... C...... 619 696-3110
488 8th Ave San Diego (92101) *(P-665)*

Cameron Metal Cutting, Santa Ana *Also Called: Automation West Inc (P-7766)*

Cameron Surface Systems, Bakersfield *Also Called: Cameron West Coast Inc (P-12766)*

Cameron Technologies Us LLC .... E...... 562 222-8440
4040 Capitol Ave Whittier (90601) *(P-10122)*

Cameron Welding, Stanton *Also Called: Cameron Welding Supply (P-17080)*

Cameron Welding Supply (PA) .... E...... 714 530-9353
11061 Dale Ave Stanton (90680) *(P-17080)*

Cameron West Coast Inc ....D
4315 Yeager Way Bakersfield (93313) *(P-12766)*

Cameron's Measurement Systems, Whittier *Also Called: Cameron Technologies Us LLC (P-10122)*

Camfil Farr Inc .... D...... 973 616-7300
3625 Del Amo Blvd Ste 260 Torrance (90503) *(P-7320)*

Camino Neurocare .... E...... 858 455-1115
5955 Pacific Center Blvd San Diego (92121) *(P-10467)*

Camino Real Foods Inc (PA) .... C...... 323 585-6599
2638 E Vernon Ave Vernon (90058) *(P-1865)*

Camino Real Kitchens, Vernon *Also Called: Camino Real Foods Inc (P-1865)*

Camino Ruiz Suite 235, San Diego *Also Called: Operation Samahan Inc (P-17731)*

Camisasca Automotive Mfg Inc (PA) .... E...... 949 452-0195
20352 Hermana Cir Lake Forest (92630) *(P-6504)*

Camisasca Automotive Mfg Inc .... E...... 949 452-0195
20341 Hermana Cir Lake Forest (92630) *(P-6505)*

Employee Codes: A=Over 500 employees, B=251-500
C=101-250, D=51-100, E=20-50, F=10-19, G=1-9

2024 Southern California
Business Directory and Buyers Guide

© Mergent Inc. 1-800-342-5647

1029

Camlever Inc .... F...... 909 629-9669
954 Se End Ave Pomona (91766) *(P-6927)*

Camp Bow Wow, Los Angeles *Also Called: Camp Bow Wow Franchising Inc (P-133)*

Camp Bow Wow Franchising Inc .... C...... 310 571-6500
12401 W Olympic Blvd Los Angeles (90064) *(P-133)*

Camp Pendleton Hospital, Oceanside *Also Called: Marine Corps United States (P-18530)*

Camp Smidgemore Inc (DH) .... E...... 323 634-0333
3641 10th Ave Los Angeles (90018) *(P-2310)*

Campbell Certified Inc .... E...... 760 722-9353
1629 Ord Way Oceanside (92056) *(P-6004)*

Campbell Engineering, Lake Forest *Also Called: Campbell Engineering Inc (P-7109)*

Campbell Engineering Inc .... E...... 949 859-3306
20412 Barents Sea Cir Lake Forest (92630) *(P-7109)*

Campbell Membrane Tech Inc .... E...... 619 938-2481
1168 N Johnson Ave El Cajon (92020) *(P-7384)*

Campbell-Ewald Company .... C...... 310 358-4800
1840 Century Park E Ste 1600 Los Angeles (90067) *(P-15530)*

Campbell-Ewald-West, Los Angeles *Also Called: Campbell-Ewald Company (P-15530)*

Camper Packaging LLC .... F...... 562 239-6167
13208 Arctic Cir Santa Fe Springs (90670) *(P-1265)*

Campo Band Missions Indians .... B...... 619 938-6000
1800 Golden Acorn Way Campo (91906) *(P-17444)*

Campus By The Sea, Avalon *Also Called: Intervrsity Chrstn Fllwshp/Usa (P-15436)*

Campus Images, Anaheim *Also Called: University Frames Inc (P-2765)*

Camston Wrather LLC .... C...... 858 525-9999
2856 Whiptail Loop Carlsbad (92010) *(P-20290)*

Camtech, Irvine *Also Called: Computer Assisted Mfg Tech LLC (P-7806)*

Can Lines Engineering Inc (PA) .... D...... 562 861-2996
9839 Downey Norwalk Rd Downey (90241) *(P-7346)*

Canadas Finest Foods Inc .... D...... 951 296-1040
26090 Ynez Rd Temecula (92591) *(P-1366)*

Canari, San Marcos *Also Called: Leemarc Industries LLC (P-2213)*

Canary Medical USA LLC .... D...... 760 448-5066
2710 Loker Ave W Ste 350 Carlsbad (92010) *(P-10468)*

Candle Crafters, Moorpark *Also Called: Globaluxe Inc (P-11221)*

Candle Lamp Holdings LLC .... B...... 951 682-9600
949 S Coast Dr Ste 650 Costa Mesa (92626) *(P-8244)*

Candy Cane Inn, Anaheim *Also Called: Cinderella Motel (P-15117)*

Canine Caviar Pet Foods Inc .... E...... 714 223-1800
4131 Tigris Way Riverside (92503) *(P-1438)*

Canine Caviar Pet Foods De Inc .... F...... 714 223-1800
4131 Tigris Way Riverside (92503) *(P-1428)*

Cannalogic .... F...... 619 458-0775
5404 Whitsett Ave # 219 Valley Village (91607) *(P-11202)*

Cannasafe, Van Nuys *Also Called: Consumer Safety Analytics LLC (P-19965)*

Cannon Gasket Inc .... E...... 909 355-1547
7784 Edison Ave Fontana (92336) *(P-4721)*

Canoga Perkins Corporation (HQ) .... D...... 818 718-6300
20600 Prairie St Chatsworth (91311) *(P-8603)*

Canon, Ventura *Also Called: Canon Solutions America Inc (P-12383)*

Canon Business Solutions-West Inc .... B...... 310 217-3000
110 W Walnut St Gardena (90248) *(P-12382)*

Canon Medical Systems USA Inc (DH) .... B...... 714 730-5000
2441 Michelle Dr Tustin (92780) *(P-12480)*

Canon Recruiting Group LLC .... B...... 661 252-7400
27651 Lincoln Pl Ste 250 Santa Clarita (91387) *(P-15917)*

Canon Solutions America Inc .... E...... 844 443-4636
6435 Ventura Blvd Ste C007 Ventura (93003) *(P-12383)*

Canon USA Inc .... B...... 949 753-4000
15955 Alton Pkwy Irvine (92618) *(P-12376)*

Canoo Inc (PA) .... E...... 424 271-2144
19951 Mariner Ave Torrance (90503) *(P-9365)*

Canopy Energy, Van Nuys *Also Called: Energy Enterprises USA Inc (P-766)*

Cantare Foods Inc .... E
900 Glenneyre St Laguna Beach (92651) *(P-1866)*

Canteen Vending, Garden Grove *Also Called: Compass Group Usa Inc (P-15777)*

Canteen Vending - San Diego .... A...... 619 527-1900
5515 Market St San Diego (92114) *(P-13265)*

Canterbury Designs Inc .... E...... 323 936-7111
6195 Maywood Ave Huntington Park (90255) *(P-6352)*

Canterbury International, Huntington Park *Also Called: Canterbury Designs Inc (P-6352)*

Canterbury, The, Pls Vrds Pnsl *Also Called: Episcopal Communities & Servic (P-17948)*

Canton Food Co Inc .... C...... 213 688-7707
750 S Alameda St Los Angeles (90021) *(P-13175)*

Canvas Concepts, San Diego *Also Called: Masterpiece Artist Canvas LLC (P-2028)*

Canvas Concepts Inc .... E...... 619 424-3428
649 Anita St Ste A2 Chula Vista (91911) *(P-2500)*

Canvas Specialty Inc .... E
1309 S Eastern Ave Commerce (90040) *(P-2501)*

Canvas Worldwide LLC .... C...... 424 303-4300
12015 Bluff Creek Dr Playa Vista (90094) *(P-15591)*

Canyon Composites Incorporated .... E...... 714 991-8181
1548 N Gemini Pl Anaheim (92801) *(P-9653)*

Canyon Engineering Pdts Inc .... D...... 661 294-0084
28909 Avenue Williams Valencia (91355) *(P-9654)*

Canyon Graphics Inc .... D...... 858 646-0444
3738 Ruffin Rd San Diego (92123) *(P-2589)*

Canyon Plastics LLC .... D...... 800 350-6325
28455 Livingston Ave Valencia (91355) *(P-4980)*

Canyon Ridge Hospital Inc .... B...... 909 590-3700
5353 G St Chino (91710) *(P-18509)*

Canyon Rock & Asphalt, San Diego *Also Called: Superior Ready Mix Concrete LP (P-5512)*

Canyon Steel Fabricators Inc .... E...... 951 683-2352
4280 Patterson Ave Perris (92571) *(P-6005)*

Cap Diagnostics LLC .... C...... 714 966-1221
15545 Sand Canyon Ave Irvine (92618) *(P-18541)*

Cap-Mpt (PA) .... C...... 213 473-8600
333 S Hope St Fl 8 Los Angeles (90071) *(P-14535)*

Cap-Mpt, Los Angeles *Also Called: Coopertive Amrcn Physcians Inc (P-19393)*

Capax Technologies Inc .... E...... 661 257-7666
24842 Avenue Tibbitts Valencia (91355) *(P-8202)*

Capc Adult Services, Whittier *Also Called: Whittier Union High Schl Dist (P-18988)*

Capco/Psa .... F...... 818 762-4276
11125 Vanowen St North Hollywood (91605) *(P-4981)*

Cape Robbin Inc .... E...... 626 810-8080
1943 W Mission Blvd Pomona (91766) *(P-13160)*

Capillary Biomedical Inc .... E...... 949 317-1701
2 Wrigley Ste 101 Irvine (92618) *(P-10248)*

Capistrano Labs Inc .... F...... 949 492-0390
150 Calle Iglesia Ste B San Clemente (92672) *(P-10469)*

Capistrano Volkswagen, San Juan Capistrano *Also Called: Mission Volkswagen Inc (P-13797)*

Capital Brands Distribution L (PA) .... D...... 800 523-5993
10900 Wilshire Blvd Ste 900 Los Angeles (90024) *(P-8231)*

Capital Commercial Property, Culver City *Also Called: Property Management Assoc Inc (P-14852)*

Capital Cooking, Carson *Also Called: Capital Cooking Equipment Inc (P-5978)*

Capital Cooking Equipment Inc .... E...... 562 903-1168
1025 E Bedmar St Carson (90746) *(P-5978)*

Capital Drywall LP .... C...... 909 599-6818
333 S Grand Ave Ste 4070 Los Angeles (90071) *(P-974)*

Capital Engineering, Long Beach *Also Called: Capital Engineering LLC (P-19561)*

Capital Engineering LLC .... D...... 562 612-1302
2830 Temple Ave Long Beach (90806) *(P-19561)*

Capital Group, Irvine *Also Called: American Funds Service Company (P-14433)*

Capital Group Companies Inc (PA) .... A...... 213 486-9200
333 S Hope St Fl 55 Los Angeles (90071) *(P-14420)*

Capital Group, The, Los Angeles *Also Called: Capital Group Companies Inc (P-14420)*

Capital Guardian Trust Company (HQ) .... D...... 213 486-9200
333 S Hope St Fl 52 Los Angeles (90071) *(P-14989)*

Capital Invstmnts Vntures Corp (PA) .... C...... 949 858-0647
30151 Tomas Rcho Sta Marg (92688) *(P-19392)*

Capital Network Funding Svcs, Los Angeles *Also Called: Capnet Financial Services Inc (P-14290)*

Capital Ready Mix Inc .... E...... 818 771-1122
11311 Pendleton St Sun Valley (91352) *(P-5468)*

Capital Research and MGT Co (HQ) .... B...... 213 486-9200
333 S Hope St Fl 55 Los Angeles (90071) *(P-14421)*

Capitalsource Bank .... C...... 714 989-4600
130 S State College Blvd Brea (92821) *(P-14184)*

Capitalsource Inc ....A....... 213 443-7700
633 W 5th St 33rd Fl Los Angeles (90071) *(P-14289)*

Capitol Machine Co, Santa Ana *Also Called: M & W Machine Corporation (P-7911)*

Capitol Records, Los Angeles *Also Called: Medholdings of Newnan LLC (P-16870)*

Capitol Steel Fabricators Inc ....E....... 323 721-5460
3522 Greenwood Ave Commerce (90040) *(P-6006)*

Capitol-Emi Music Inc ....A....... 323 462-6252
1750b Vine St Los Angeles (90028) *(P-8452)*

Caplugs, Rancho Dominguez *Also Called: Caplugs Inc (P-4982)*

Caplugs, Carson *Also Called: Caplugs Inc (P-4983)*

Caplugs Inc ....D....... 310 537-2300
18704 S Ferris Pl Rancho Dominguez (90220) *(P-4982)*

Caplugs Inc ....E....... 310 900-8323
18704 S Ferris Pl Carson (90745) *(P-4983)*

Capna Fabrication ....E....... 888 416-6777
16501 Ventura Blvd Ste 400 Encino (91436) *(P-7193)*

Capna Systems, Encino *Also Called: Capna Fabrication (P-7193)*

Capnet Financial Services Inc (PA) ....D....... 877 980-0558
11901 Santa Monica Blvd Los Angeles (90025) *(P-14290)*

Capo Industries Division, El Cajon *Also Called: Senior Operations LLC (P-8023)*

Capri Tools, Pomona *Also Called: Als Group Inc (P-12786)*

Capricor Therapeutics, San Diego *Also Called: Capricor Therapeutics Inc (P-4079)*

Capricor Therapeutics Inc (PA) ....F....... 310 358-3200
10865 Road To The Cure Ste 150 San Diego (92121) *(P-4079)*

Caps Payroll, Burbank *Also Called: New Talco Enterprises LLC (P-19797)*

CAPSBC, San Bernardino *Also Called: Community Action Prtnr San Brn (P-19322)*

Capsida Biotherapeutics Inc (PA) ....D....... 805 410-2673
3075 Townsgate Rd Westlake Village (91361) *(P-4308)*

Capstone, Van Nuys *Also Called: Capstone Green Energy Corp (P-6878)*

Capstone Fire Management Inc (PA) ....E....... 760 839-2290
2240 Auto Park Way Escondido (92029) *(P-7385)*

Capstone Green Energy Corp (PA) C
16640 Stagg St Van Nuys (91406) *(P-6878)*

Capstone Logistics, Moreno Valley *Also Called: Capstone Logistics LLC (P-11829)*

Capstone Logistics LLC ....C....... 770 414-1929
12661 Aldi Pl Moreno Valley (92555) *(P-11829)*

Capsule Manufacturing Inc ....D....... 949 245-4151
1399 N Miller St Anaheim (92806) *(P-335)*

Capsule Mfg, Anaheim *Also Called: Capsule Manufacturing Inc (P-335)*

Captek Holdings LLC ....F....... 562 921-9511
16218 Arthur St Cerritos (90703) *(P-1266)*

Captek Midco Inc ....D....... 760 734-6800
2710 Progress St Vista (92081) *(P-4080)*

Captek Pharma, La Mirada *Also Called: Captek Softgel Intl Inc (P-4082)*

Captek Softgel Intl Inc (DH) ....B....... 562 921-9511
16218 Arthur St Cerritos (90703) *(P-4081)*

Captek Softgel Intl Inc ....E....... 657 325-0412
14535 Industry Cir La Mirada (90638) *(P-4082)*

Captiva Software Corporation (DH) ....D....... 858 320-1000
10145 Pacific Heights Blvd San Diego (92121) *(P-16432)*

CAr Enterprises Inc ....F....... 760 947-6411
13100 Main St Hesperia (92345) *(P-7584)*

Car Sound Exhaust System Inc ....D....... 949 888-1625
1901 Corporate Centre Dr Oceanside (92056) *(P-3885)*

Car Sound Exhaust System Inc ....C....... 949 858-5900
30142 Avenida De Las Bandera Rcho Sta Marg (92688) *(P-9366)*

Car Sound Exhaust System Inc ....D....... 949 858-5900
23201 Antonio Pkwy Rcho Sta Marg (92688) *(P-9367)*

Car Sound Exhaust System Inc (PA) ....E....... 949 858-5900
1901 Corporate Ctr Oceanside (92056) *(P-9368)*

Car Wash Partners Inc ....C....... 661 377-1020
2619 Mount Vernon Ave Bakersfield (93306) *(P-17046)*

CAR WASH PARTNERS, INC., Bakersfield *Also Called: Car Wash Partners Inc (P-17046)*

Caran Precision Engineering & Manufacturing Corp (PA) .....D....... 714 447-5400
2830 Orbiter St Brea (92821) *(P-6506)*

Carat N Amer Dntsu Ageis Ntwrk ....D....... 310 255-1000
5800 Bristol Pkwy 5th Fl Culver City (90230) *(P-15600)*

Caraustar Industries Inc ....E....... 951 685-5544
4502 E Airport Dr Ontario (91761) *(P-3066)*

Caravan Canopy, Cerritos *Also Called: Caravan Canopy Intl Inc (P-2502)*

Caravan Canopy Intl Inc ....D....... 714 367-3000
17510-17512 Studebaker Rd Cerritos (90703) *(P-2502)*

Caravan Distribution, Los Angeles *Also Called: Reaps Company LLC (P-11274)*

Carberry LLC ....E....... 562 264-5078
3645 Long Beach Blvd Long Beach (90807) *(P-11203)*

Carberry LLC (HQ) ....E....... 800 564-0842
17130 Muskrat Ave Ste B Adelanto (92301) *(P-11204)*

Carbomer Inc ....D....... 858 552-0992
6324 Ferris Sq Ste B San Diego (92121) *(P-3886)*

Carbon 38 Inc ....D....... 888 723-5838
10000 Washington Blvd Ste 100 Culver City (90232) *(P-2311)*

Carbon Activated Corporation (PA) ....E....... 310 885-4555
2250 S Central Ave Compton (90220) *(P-3887)*

Carbon By Design LLC ....D....... 760 643-1300
1491 Poinsettia Ave Ste 136 Vista (92081) *(P-9655)*

Carbon California Company LLC ....E....... 805 933-1901
270 Quail Ct Ste 201 Santa Paula (93060) *(P-258)*

Carbon Health Technologies Inc ....C....... 805 226-4222
500 First St Paso Robles (93446) *(P-17608)*

Carbon Health Technologies Inc ....C....... 714 710-3030
1421 W Macarthur Blvd Ste E Santa Ana (92704) *(P-17609)*

Carbon Health Technologies Inc ....C....... 760 603-3221
6971 El Camino Real Ste 101 Carlsbad (92009) *(P-17850)*

Carbro Company, Lawndale *Also Called: Curry Company LLC (P-7115)*

Cardenas Markets LLC ....B....... 909 923-7426
1621 E Francis St Ontario (91761) *(P-1386)*

Cardiac Noninvasive Laboratory, Los Angeles *Also Called: Cedars-Sinai Medical Center (P-17612)*

Cardiac Unit, Anaheim *Also Called: Anaheim Regional Medical Ctr (P-18180)*

Cardiff Transportation, Palm Desert *Also Called: Gary Cardiff Enterprises Inc (P-11389)*

Cardinal C G, Moreno Valley *Also Called: Cardinal Glass Industries Inc (P-5312)*

Cardinal Glass Industries Inc ....C....... 951 485-9007
24100 Cardinal Ave Moreno Valley (92551) *(P-5312)*

Cardinal Health 414 LLC ....E....... 714 572-9900
640 S Jefferson St Placentia (92870) *(P-4083)*

Cardinal Industrial Finishes (PA) ....D....... 626 444-9274
1329 Potrero Ave Ca South El Monte (91733) *(P-4482)*

Cardinal Paint and Powder Inc ....D....... 626 444-9274
1329 Potrero Ave South El Monte (91733) *(P-4483)*

Cardinal Paint and Powder Inc ....C....... 626 937-6767
15010 Don Julian Rd City Of Industry (91746) *(P-4484)*

Cardinal Point Captains, San Diego *Also Called: Cardinal Point Captains Inc (P-15918)*

Cardinal Point Captains Inc ....D....... 760 438-7361
5005 Texas St Ste 104 San Diego (92108) *(P-15918)*

Cardinal Transportation, Gardena *Also Called: First Student Inc (P-11429)*

Cardionet Inc ....D....... 619 243-7500
750 B St Ste 1400 San Diego (92101) *(P-17610)*

CARDIONET, INC., San Diego *Also Called: Cardionet Inc (P-17610)*

Cardiovascular Systems, Tustin *Also Called: Terumo Americas Holding Inc (P-10295)*

Cardno Eri, Lake Forest *Also Called: Environmental Resolutions Inc (P-20334)*

Cardona Manufacturing Corp ....E....... 818 841-8358
1869 N Victory Pl Burbank (91504) *(P-9656)*

Cardservice International Inc (DH) ....B
5898 Condor Dr # 220 Moorpark (93021) *(P-16797)*

Care 1st Health Plan (PA) ....C....... 323 889-6638
601 Potrero Grande Dr Fl 2 Monterey Park (91755) *(P-14449)*

Care Ambulance, San Diego *Also Called: Care Medical Trnsp Inc (P-11379)*

Care Choice Health Systems Inc ....C....... 760 798-4508
1151 S Santa Fe Ave Vista (92083) *(P-18116)*

Care Choice Home Care, Vista *Also Called: Care Choice Health Systems Inc (P-18116)*

Care Fusion Products, San Diego *Also Called: Becton Dickinson and Company (P-10452)*

Care Medical Trnsp Inc ....C....... 858 653-4520
9770 Candida St San Diego (92126) *(P-11379)*

Care Stffing Professionals Inc ....D....... 909 906-2060
2151 E Convention Center Way Ste 204 Ontario (91764) *(P-15919)*

Care Unlimited Health Svcs Inc ....D....... 626 332-3767
1025 W Arrow Hwy Ste 103 Glendora (91740) *(P-18600)*

Carecredit LLC ....C....... 800 300-3046
555 Anton Blvd Ste 700 Costa Mesa (92626) *(P-16798)*

Career Group Inc (PA) ....A....... 310 277-8188
10100 Santa Monica Blvd Ste 900 Los Angeles (90067) *(P-15826)*

A L P H A B E T I C

Employee Codes: A=Over 500 employees, B=251-500
C=101-250, D=51-100, E=20-50, F=10-19, G=1-9

2024 Southern California
Business Directory and Buyers Guide

© Mergent Inc. 1-800-342-5647

1031

Career Strategies Tmpry Inc .... C....... 714 824-6840
575 Anton Blvd Ste 630 Costa Mesa (92626) *(P-15827)*

Career Strategies Tmpry Inc .... C....... 760 564-5959
78060 Calle Estado La Quinta (92253) *(P-15828)*

Career Strategies Tmpry Inc .... C....... 818 883-0440
21031 Ventura Blvd Ste 1005 Woodland Hills (91364) *(P-15829)*

Career Strategies Tmpry Inc .... C....... 909 230-4504
9267 Haven Ave Ste 225 Rancho Cucamonga (91730) *(P-15830)*

Career Tech Circuit Services, Chatsworth *Also Called: Circuit Services Llc (P-8662)*

Carefree Communities, Newbury Park *Also Called: Carefree Communities Inc (P-14736)*

Carefree Communities Inc .... C....... 805 498-2612
1251 Old Conejo Rd Newbury Park (91320) *(P-14736)*

Carefusion 207 Inc .... B....... 760 778-7200
1100 Bird Center Dr Palm Springs (92262) *(P-10470)*

Carefusion 213 LLC (DH).. **B....... 800 523-0502**
3750 Torrey View Ct San Diego (92130) *(P-10471)*

Carefusion Corporation .... D....... 858 617-4271
10020 Pacific Mesa Blvd Bldg A San Diego (92121) *(P-10472)*

Carefusion Corporation .... D....... 760 778-7200
1100 Bird Center Dr Palm Springs (92262) *(P-10473)*

Carefusion Corporation .... D....... 800 231-2466
22745 Savi Ranch Pkwy Yorba Linda (92887) *(P-10474)*

Carefusion Corporation (HQ).. **B....... 858 617-2000**
3750 Torrey View Ct San Diego (92130) *(P-10795)*

Carefusion Solutions LLC (DH).. **A....... 858 617-2100**
3750 Torrey View Ct San Diego (92130) *(P-10475)*

Careismatic Brands LLC (PA).. C....... 818 671-2100
1119 Colorado Ave Santa Monica (90401) *(P-5272)*

Carelon Bhavioral Hlth Cal Inc .... A....... 800 228-1286
12898 Towne Center Dr Cerritos (90703) *(P-14571)*

Carelon Med Benefits MGT Inc .... A....... 847 310-0366
505 N Brand Blvd Glendale (91203) *(P-14450)*

Caremore AP, Cerritos *Also Called: Caremore Medical Management Company A California Limited Partnership (P-20011)*

Caremore Health Plan (HQ).. C....... 562 622-2950
12900 Park Plaza Dr Ste 150 Cerritos (90703) *(P-14451)*

Caremore Insurance Services, Cerritos *Also Called: Caremore Health Plan (P-14451)*

Caremore Medical Management Company A California Limited Partnership.... 562 741-4300
12900 Park Plaza Dr Ste 150 Cerritos (90703) *(P-20011)*

Cares, San Diego *Also Called: Center For Atism RES Evltion S (P-18675)*

Cargill, Fullerton *Also Called: Cargill Incorporated (P-3994)*

Cargill Incorporated .... D....... 714 449-6708
600 N Gilbert St Fullerton (92833) *(P-3994)*

Cargill Flour Milling Division, San Bernardino *Also Called: Ardent Mills LLC (P-1408)*

Cargill Meat Solutions Corp .... E....... 562 345-5240
13034 Excelsior Dr Norwalk (90650) *(P-1191)*

Cargill Meat Solutions Corp .... D....... 909 476-3120
10602 N Trademark Pkwy Ste 500 Rancho Cucamonga (91730) *(P-1192)*

Cargill Meat Solutions Corp .... C....... 515 735-9800
3501 E Vernon Ave Vernon (90058) *(P-1867)*

Cargo Service Center, Los Angeles *Also Called: Swissport Cargo Services LP (P-11708)*

Cargo Solution Brokerage Inc .... C....... 909 350-1644
14587 Valley Blvd Fontana (92335) *(P-11447)*

Cargo Solution Express Inc (PA).. **C....... 909 350-1644**
14587 Valley Blvd # 89 Fontana (92335) *(P-11473)*

Cargomatic Inc (PA).. **C....... 866 513-2343**
211 E Ocean Blvd Ste 350 Long Beach (90802) *(P-11743)*

Carinet, San Diego *Also Called: Fortitude Technology Inc (P-11877)*

Carl Zeiss Meditec Prod LLC .... D....... 877 644-4657
1040 S Vintage Ave Ste A Ontario (91761) *(P-10310)*

Carl Zeiss Meditec,, Ontario *Also Called: Aaren Scientific Inc (P-10306)*

Carla Senter .... F....... 310 366-7295
515 E Alondra Blvd Gardena (90248) *(P-6210)*

Carley (PA).. **C....... 310 325-8474**
1502 W 228th St Torrance (90501) *(P-5323)*

Carlos Shower Doors Inc .... F....... 661 204-6689
300 Kentucky St Bakersfield (93305) *(P-5335)*

Carlsbad By The Sea, Carlsbad *Also Called: Front Porch Communities & Svcs (P-14710)*

Carlsbad Firefighters Assn .... D....... 760 729-3730
2560 Orion Way Carlsbad (92010) *(P-19527)*

Carlsbad International Export Inc .... E....... 760 438-5323
1954 Kellogg Ave Carlsbad (92008) *(P-12481)*

Carlsbad Manufacturing, Carlsbad *Also Called: Stone Yard Inc (P-2875)*

Carlsbad Medical Supply, Carlsbad *Also Called: Carlsbad International Export Inc (P-12481)*

Carlsbad Premium Outlets, Carlsbad *Also Called: Premium Outlet Partners LP (P-14682)*

Carlsbad Tech, Carlsbad *Also Called: Carlsbad Technology Inc (P-4084)*

Carlsbad Tech, Carlsbad *Also Called: Carlsbad Technology Inc (P-4085)*

Carlsbad Technology Inc .... D....... 760 431-8284
5923 Balfour Ct Carlsbad (92008) *(P-4084)*

Carlsbad Technology Inc (DH).. **E....... 760 431-8284**
5922 Farnsworth Ct Ste 102 Carlsbad (92008) *(P-4085)*

Carlstar Group LLC .... E....... 909 829-1703
10730 Production Ave Fontana (92337) *(P-9369)*

Carlton Forge Works .... B....... 562 633-1131
7743 Adams St Paramount (90723) *(P-6476)*

Carlyle Group Inc (PA).. **D....... 310 550-8656**
9073 Nemo St Ste 100 West Hollywood (90069) *(P-14757)*

Carmax Inc .... C....... 951 387-3887
25560 Madison Ave Murrieta (92562) *(P-13850)*

Carmel Mtn Rhab Healthcare Ctr, San Diego *Also Called: Bernardo Hts Healthcare Inc (P-18113)*

Carmel Partners LLC .... C....... 916 479-5286
530 Wilshire Blvd Ste 203 Santa Monica (90401) *(P-14960)*

Carmi Flavors, Commerce *Also Called: Carmi Flvr & Fragrance Co Inc (P-1762)*

Carmi Flvr & Fragrance Co Inc (PA).. **E....... 323 888-9240**
6030 Scott Way Commerce (90040) *(P-1762)*

Carmichael International Svc (DH).. D....... 213 353-0800
1200 Corporate Center Dr Ste 200 Monterey Park (91754) *(P-11744)*

Carmike Cinemas, Thousand Oaks *Also Called: Carmike Cinemas LLC (P-17288)*

Carmike Cinemas LLC .... D....... 805 494-4702
166 W Hillcrest Dr Thousand Oaks (91360) *(P-17288)*

Carnegie Institution Wash .... D....... 626 577-1122
813 Santa Barbara St Pasadena (91101) *(P-19922)*

Carnegie Mortgage LLC .... B....... 949 379-7000
15480 Laguna Canyon Rd Ste 100 Irvine (92618) *(P-14355)*

Carnevale & Lohr Inc .... E....... 562 927-8311
6521 Clara St Bell Gardens (90201) *(P-5526)*

Carol Anderson Inc (PA).. **E....... 310 638-3333**
18700 S Laurel Park Rd Rancho Dominguez (90220) *(P-2279)*

Carol Anderson By Invitation, Rancho Dominguez *Also Called: Carol Anderson Inc (P-2279)*

Carol Cole Company .... C....... 888 360-9171
1325 Sycamore Ave Ste A Vista (92081) *(P-10476)*

Carol Electric Company Inc .... D....... 562 431-1870
3822 Cerritos Ave Los Alamitos (90720) *(P-878)*

Carol Wior Inc .... E....... 562 927-0052
7533 Garfield Ave Bell (90201) *(P-2312)*

Carolense Entrmt Group LLC .... D....... 405 493-1120
506 S Spring St Los Angeles (90013) *(P-10860)*

Carolina Lquid Chmistries Corp .... E....... 336 722-8910
510 W Central Ave Ste C Brea (92821) *(P-10477)*

Carolyn E Wylie Ctr For Chldre .... D....... 951 683-5193
4164 Brockton Ave Riverside (92501) *(P-19031)*

Carousel Child Care Corp .... C....... 310 216-6641
8333 Airport Blvd Los Angeles (90045) *(P-19203)*

Carpenter Co .... D....... 951 354-7550
7809 Lincoln Ave Riverside (92504) *(P-4877)*

Carpenter E R Co, Riverside *Also Called: Carpenter Co (P-4877)*

Carpenter Group .... E....... 619 233-5625
2380 Main St San Diego (92113) *(P-12846)*

Carpenters Southwest ADM Corp .... C....... 805 688-5581
376 Avenue Of The Flags Buellton (93427) *(P-13991)*

Carr Corporation (PA).. **E....... 310 587-1113**
1547 11th St Santa Monica (90401) *(P-10782)*

Carr Management Inc .... D....... 951 277-4800
22324 Temescal Canyon Rd Corona (92883) *(P-4984)*

Carriage Carpet Mills, Cypress *Also Called: Shaw Industries Group Inc (P-2120)*

Carrier Fire SEC Americas Corp .... C....... 949 737-7800
2955 Red Hill Ave Ste 100 Costa Mesa (92626) *(P-8604)*

Carrington Mortgage Svcs LLC .... C....... 909 226-7963
10370 Commerce Center Dr Ste 140 Rancho Cucamonga (91730) *(P-14373)*

2024 Southern California
Business Directory and Buyers Guide
(P-0000) Products & Services Section entry number
(PA)=Parent Co (HQ)=Headquarters (DH)=Div Headquarters

Carrington Mrtg Holdings LLC .... C..... 888 267-0584
1600 S Douglass Rd Ste 110 Anaheim (92806) *(P-14305)*

Carroll Fulmer Logistics Corp .... B..... 626 435-9940
13773 Algranti Ave Sylmar (91342) *(P-11745)*

Carroll Metal Works Inc .... D..... 619 477-9125
740 W 16th St National City (91950) *(P-6007)*

Carros Americas Inc .... C..... 805 267-7176
2945 Townsgate Rd Ste 200 Westlake Village (91361) *(P-9013)*

Carros Sensors Systems Co LLC (DH) .... C..... 805 968-0782
1461 Lawrence Dr Thousand Oaks (91320) *(P-10359)*

Carson Industries LLC .... A..... 951 788-9720
2434 Rubidoux Blvd Riverside (92509) *(P-4985)*

Carson Kurtzman Consultants (DH) .... C..... 310 823-9000
2335 Alaska Ave El Segundo (90245) *(P-18834)*

Carson Operating Company LLC .... D..... 310 830-9200
2 Civic Plaza Dr Carson (90745) *(P-15108)*

Carson Trailer Inc (PA) .... D..... 310 835-0876
14831 S Maple Ave Gardena (90248) *(P-13905)*

Carson Trailer Sales, Gardena *Also Called: Carson Trailer Inc (P-13905)*

Cartel Electronics LLC .... D..... 714 993-0270
1900 Petra Ln Ste C Placentia (92870) *(P-8657)*

Cartel Industries, Irvine *Also Called: Cartel Industries LLC (P-6211)*

Cartel Industries LLC .... E..... 949 474-3200
17152 Armstrong Ave Irvine (92614) *(P-6211)*

Cartel Marketing Inc .... C..... 818 483-1130
5230 Las Virgenes Rd Ste 250 Calabasas (91302) *(P-14572)*

Carter Aston Inc .... C..... 858 609-2062
9635 Granite Ridge Dr San Diego (92123) *(P-15831)*

Carter Holt Harvey Holdings .... E..... 951 272-8180
1230 Railroad St Corona (92882) *(P-5585)*

Carter Laboratories, Irvine *Also Called: Fluxergy Inc (P-19839)*

Carter Pump & Machine Inc .... F..... 661 393-8620
635 G St Wasco (93280) *(P-7793)*

Carters Metal Fabricators Inc .... E..... 626 815-4225
935 W 5th St Azusa (91702) *(P-2906)*

Carton Design, Pico Rivera *Also Called: CD Container Inc (P-3089)*

Carttronics LLC (HQ) .... E..... 888 696-2278
90 Icon Foothill Ranch (92610) *(P-9198)*

Cartwright Trmt Pest Ctrl Inc .... E..... 619 442-9613
1376 Broadway El Cajon (92021) *(P-15684)*

Caruso MGT Ltd A Cal Ltd Prtnr (PA) .... D..... 323 900-8100
101 The Grove Dr Los Angeles (90036) *(P-14758)*

Carvin Corp .... C..... 858 487-1600
16262 W Bernardo Dr San Diego (92127) *(P-13977)*

Carvin Guitars & Pro Sound, San Diego *Also Called: Carvin Corp (P-13977)*

Cas Medical Systems Inc (HQ) .... E..... 203 488-6056
1 Edwards Way Irvine (92614) *(P-10478)*

Casa Barranca Inc .... E..... 805 640-1255
208 E Ojai Ave Ojai (93023) *(P-1615)*

Casa Clina Hosp Ctrs For Hlthc .... C..... 626 334-8735
910 E Alosta Ave Azusa (91702) *(P-17858)*

Casa Clina Hosp Ctrs For Hlthc (HQ) .... B..... 909 596-7733
255 E Bonita Ave Pomona (91767) *(P-18195)*

Casa Clina Hosp Ctrs For Hlthc .... C..... 760 248-6245
11981 Midway Ave Lucerne Valley (92356) *(P-19032)*

Casa Clina Hosp Ctrs For Hlthc, Pomona *Also Called: Casa Colina Inc (P-19033)*

Casa Colina Inc (PA) .... A..... 909 596-7733
255 E Bonita Ave Pomona (91767) *(P-19033)*

CASA COLINA HOSPITAL AND CENTE, Pomona *Also Called: Casa Clina Hosp Ctrs For Hlthc (P-18195)*

Casa De Hermandad (PA) .... E..... 310 477-8272
1639 11th St Santa Monica (90404) *(P-10983)*

Casa De Las Campanas (PA) .... D..... 858 451-9152
18655 W Bernardo Dr San Diego (92127) *(P-19245)*

Casa De Manana, La Jolla *Also Called: Front Porch Communities & Svcs (P-14709)*

Casa Dorinda, Santa Barbara *Also Called: Montecito Retirement Assn (P-18016)*

Casa Herrera Inc (PA) .... D..... 909 392-3930
2655 Pine St Pomona (91767) *(P-7194)*

CASA PACIFICA, Camarillo *Also Called: Casa Pcfica Ctrs For Chldren F (P-19034)*

Casa Pcfica Ctrs For Chldren F (PA) .... C..... 805 482-3260
1722 S Lewis Rd Camarillo (93012) *(P-19034)*

Casa Raphael, Vista *Also Called: Alpha Project For Homeless (P-19018)*

Casa-Pacifica Inc .... B..... 951 658-3369
2200 W Acacia Ave Ofc Hemet (92545) *(P-19246)*

Casa-Pacifica Inc .... B..... 951 766-5116
2400 W Acacia Ave Hemet (92545) *(P-19247)*

Cascade Pump Company .... D..... 562 946-1414
10107 Norwalk Blvd Santa Fe Springs (90670) *(P-7271)*

Cascade Thermal Solutions LLC (PA) .... E..... 619 562-8852
1890 Cordell Ct Ste 102 El Cajon (92020) *(P-750)*

Casco Mfg, San Fernando *Also Called: C A Schroeder Inc (P-5552)*

Caseworx, Redlands *Also Called: Caseworx Inc (P-2879)*

Caseworx Inc (PA) .... E..... 909 799-8550
1130 Research Dr Redlands (92374) *(P-2879)*

Casey Company (PA) .... C..... 562 436-9685
180 E Ocean Blvd Ste 1010 Long Beach (90802) *(P-13448)*

Cash It Here, Santa Ana *Also Called: Continental Currency Svcs Inc (P-14256)*

Cashcall Inc .... A..... 949 752-4600
1 City Blvd W Ste 102 Orange (92868) *(P-14268)*

Cashmere Agency Inc .... C..... 323 928-5080
5242 W Adams Blvd Los Angeles (90016) *(P-20147)*

Casing Specialties Inc .... E..... 661 399-5522
12454 Snow Rd Bakersfield (93314) *(P-336)*

Cask, San Diego *Also Called: Cask Nx LLC (P-20324)*

Cask Nx LLC .... C..... 858 232-8900
8910 University Center Ln Ste 400 San Diego (92122) *(P-20324)*

Casper Company .... C..... 619 589-6001
3825 Bancroft Dr Spring Valley (91977) *(P-1062)*

Cass, El Cajon *Also Called: Cass Construction Inc (P-666)*

Cass Construction Inc (PA) .... B..... 619 590-0929
1100 Wagner Dr El Cajon (92020) *(P-666)*

Cast & Crew LLC (PA) .... C..... 818 570-6180
2300 W Empire Ave Ste 500 Burbank (91504) *(P-19760)*

Cast and Crew Entrmt Svcs, Burbank *Also Called: Cast & Crew LLC (P-19760)*

Cast Partner Inc .... E..... 323 876-9000
4658 W Washington Blvd Los Angeles (90016) *(P-5808)*

Cast Parts Inc .... C..... 626 937-3444
16800 Chestnut St City Of Industry (91748) *(P-5651)*

Cast Parts Inc (HQ) .... C..... 909 595-2252
4200 Valley Blvd Walnut (91789) *(P-5652)*

Cast-Rite Corporation .... D..... 310 532-2080
515 E Airline Way Gardena (90248) *(P-7056)*

Cast-Rite International Inc (PA) .... D..... 310 532-2080
515 E Airline Way Gardena (90248) *(P-5809)*

Castaic Truck Stop Inc .... E..... 661 295-1374
31611 Castaic Rd Castaic (91384) *(P-4639)*

Castaway Restaurant, The, Burbank *Also Called: Specialty Restaurants Corp (P-14037)*

Caster Civil Inc .... E..... 626 201-1300
1858 Rancho Janet Alpine (91901) *(P-7297)*

Castle & Cooke Investments Inc .... C..... 310 208-3636
1 Dole Dr Westlake Village (91362) *(P-541)*

Castle Importing Inc .... E..... 909 428-9200
14550 Miller Ave Fontana (92336) *(P-13992)*

Castle Industries Inc of California .... E..... 909 390-0899
4056 Easy St El Monte (91731) *(P-6212)*

Castle Metals Aerospace, Paramount *Also Called: Transtar Metals Corp (P-12578)*

Castle Press, Pasadena *Also Called: Grant Dahlstrom Inc (P-3851)*

Caston Inc .... D..... 909 381-1619
354 S Allen St San Bernardino (92408) *(P-975)*

Casualway Home & Garden, Oxnard *Also Called: Casualway Usa LLC (P-2827)*

Casualway Usa LLC .... D..... 805 660-7408
1623 Lola Way Oxnard (93030) *(P-2827)*

Catalent Pharma Solutions Inc .... C..... 858 805-6383
7330 Carroll Rd Ste 200 San Diego (92121) *(P-4086)*

Catalent Pharma Solutions Inc .... E..... 877 587-1835
8926 Ware Ct San Diego (92121) *(P-4087)*

Catalent San Diego Inc .... C..... 858 805-6383
7330 Carroll Rd Ste 200 San Diego (92121) *(P-19961)*

Catalina Canyon Resort, Avalon *Also Called: Pacific Catalina Hotel Inc (P-15285)*

Catalina Carpet Mills Inc (PA) .... E..... 562 926-5811
14418 Best Ave Santa Fe Springs (90670) *(P-2111)*

Employee Codes: A=Over 500 employees, B=251-500
C=101-250, D=51-100, E=20-50, F=10-19, G=1-9

2024 Southern California
Business Directory and Buyers Guide

© Mergent Inc. 1-800-342-5647

1033

ALPHABETIC

Catalina Channel Express Inc (HQ)..................................C...... 310 519-7971
385 E Swinford St San Pedro (90731) *(P-11638)*

Catalina Express Cruises, San Pedro Also Called: Catalina Channel Express Inc *(P-11638)*

Catalina Home, Santa Fe Springs Also Called: Catalina Carpet Mills Inc *(P-2111)*

Catalina Offshore Products Inc...............................D...... 619 297-9797
5202 Lovelock St San Diego (92110) *(P-13277)*

Catalina Pacific Concrete...................................E...... 310 532-4600
19030 Normandie Ave Torrance (90502) *(P-5469)*

Catalina Yachts Inc (PA)..................................**E...... 818 884-7700**
2259 Ward Ave Simi Valley (93065) *(P-9856)*

Catalyst Development Corp.................................E...... 760 228-9653
56925 Yucca Trl Yucca Valley (92284) *(P-16193)*

Catalyst Spech Lngage Pthology, Los Angeles Also Called: Catalyst Speech LLC *(P-20148)*

Catalyst Speech LLC....................................B...... 213 346-9945
205 S Broadway Ste 217 Los Angeles (90012) *(P-20148)*

Catalytic Solutions Inc (HQ)..............................**E...... 805 486-4649**
1700 Fiske Pl Oxnard (93033) *(P-10100)*

Catamaran Resort Hotel, San Diego Also Called: Braemar Partnership *(P-15096)*

Catame Inc (PA)..**F...... 213 749-2610**
1930 Long Beach Ave Los Angeles (90058) *(P-11069)*

Catapult Communications Corp (DH).......................**D...... 818 871-1800**
26601 Agoura Rd Calabasas (91302) *(P-16194)*

Catawba County Schools, Camarillo Also Called: Microsemi Communications Inc *(P-8840)*

Cater Tots Too, Santa Ana Also Called: DAd Investments *(P-13999)*

Catered Fit Corp...C...... 855 400-2348
13631 Saticoy St Van Nuys (91402) *(P-11448)*

Caterpillar Authorized Dealer, Imperial Also Called: Empire Southwest LLC *(P-6932)*

Caterpillar Authorized Dealer, Riverside Also Called: Johnson Machinery Co *(P-12772)*

Caterpillar Authorized Dealer, Bakersfield Also Called: Quinn Company *(P-12777)*

Caterpillar Authorized Dealer, City Of Industry Also Called: Quinn Shepherd Machinery *(P-12778)*

Caterpillar Authorized Dealer, San Diego Also Called: Hawthorne Rent-It Service *(P-15764)*

Cathay Bank (HQ)..C...... 626 279-3698
777 N Broadway Los Angeles (90012) *(P-14185)*

Cathay Capital Trust II..................................D...... 213 625-4700
9650 Flair Dr El Monte (91731) *(P-14186)*

Cathay General Bancorp (PA)............................C...... 213 625-4700
777 N Broadway Los Angeles (90012) *(P-14187)*

Catholic Charities, Ventura Also Called: Catholic Chrties Snta Clara CN *(P-19035)*

Catholic Chrties Snta Clara CN..........................D...... 805 643-4694
303 N Ventura Ave Ste A Ventura (93001) *(P-19035)*

Catholic Education Founda................................D...... 213 637-7475
3424 Wilshire Blvd Ste 24 Los Angeles (90010) *(P-19432)*

Catholic Hlthcare W Sthern Cal (HQ).....................**C...... 562 491-9000**
1050 Linden Ave Long Beach (90813) *(P-18196)*

Catholic Resource Center, West Covina Also Called: Saint Jseph Communications Inc *(P-17216)*

Cathy Ireland Home, Chino Also Called: Omnia Leather Motion Inc *(P-2480)*

Catridge Return Center, Calexico Also Called: 4I Technologies Inc *(P-7181)*

Cats U S A Pest Control, North Hollywood Also Called: Cats USA Inc *(P-15685)*

Cats USA Inc...D...... 818 506-1000
5683 Whitnall Hwy North Hollywood (91601) *(P-15685)*

Cattaneo Bros, San Luis Obispo Also Called: Cattaneo Bros Inc *(P-1215)*

Cattaneo Bros Inc..E...... 805 543-7188
769 Caudill St San Luis Obispo (93401) *(P-1215)*

Causeway Capital MGT LLC...............................C...... 310 231-6100
11111 Santa Monica Blvd Fl 15 Los Angeles (90025) *(P-14961)*

Cavalier Inn Inc...D...... 805 927-4688
9415 Hearst Dr San Simeon (93452) *(P-15109)*

Cavalier Oceanfront Resort, San Simeon Also Called: Cavalier Inn Inc *(P-15109)*

Cavanaugh Machine Works Inc............................E...... 562 437-1126
1540 Santa Fe Ave Long Beach (90813) *(P-7794)*

Cavco Industries Inc.....................................E...... 951 688-5353
7007 Jurupa Ave Riverside (92504) *(P-2734)*

Cavins Oil Well Tools, Signal Hill Also Called: Dawson Enterprises *(P-6956)*

Cavotec Dabico US Inc...................................E...... 714 947-0005
5665 Corporate Ave Cypress (90630) *(P-9657)*

Cavotec Inet, Cypress Also Called: Cavotec US Holdings Inc *(P-6948)*

Cavotec Inet US Inc......................................D...... 714 947-0005
5665 Corporate Ave Cypress (90630) *(P-6928)*

Cavotec US Holdings Inc (HQ)............................F...... 714 545-7900
5665 Corporate Ave Cypress (90630) *(P-6948)*

CAW Cowie Inc (PA)......................................E...... 212 396-9007
7 Ginger Root Ln Rancho Palos Verdes (90275) *(P-16799)*

Caylent Inc..C...... 800 215-9124
4521 Campus Dr Ste 344 Irvine (92612) *(P-16558)*

CB Controls, Jurupa Valley Also Called: Christian Brothers Mechanical Services Inc *(P-752)*

CB Richard Ellis Strgc Prtners...........................D...... 213 683-4200
515 S Flower St Ste 3100 Los Angeles (90071) *(P-14655)*

CB Tang MD Incorporated................................D...... 562 437-0831
1250 Pacific Ave Long Beach (90813) *(P-17611)*

Cbdsd Inc...E...... 760 738-4200
1844 Mission Rd Escondido (92029) *(P-11205)*

Cbec, San Diego Also Called: Clear Blue Energy Corp *(P-8358)*

Cbione, Vista Also Called: California Breakers Inc *(P-12590)*

Cbiz Life Insur Solutions Inc.............................C...... 858 444-3100
13500 Evening Creek Dr N Ste 450 San Diego (92128) *(P-14573)*

Cbj LP..D...... 818 676-1750
11150 Santa Monica Blvd Ste 350 Los Angeles (90025) *(P-3347)*

Cbj LP..E...... 323 549-5225
11150 Santa Monica Blvd Los Angeles (90025) *(P-3348)*

Cbj LP..E...... 949 833-8373
18500 Von Karman Ave Ste 150 Irvine (92612) *(P-3349)*

Cbj LP..E...... 858 277-6359
4909 Murphy Canyon Rd Ste 200 San Diego (92123) *(P-3350)*

Cbol Corporation..C...... 818 704-8200
19850 Plummer St Chatsworth (91311) *(P-12653)*

Cbr Electric Inc...C...... 949 455-0331
22 Rancho Cir Lake Forest (92630) *(P-879)*

Cbre, Newport Beach Also Called: Cbre Globl Value Investors LLC *(P-14761)*

Cbre Inc..C...... 858 546-4600
4301 La Jolla Village Dr # 3000 San Diego (92122) *(P-14759)*

Cbre Globl Value Investors LLC (DH)......................C...... 213 683-4200
601 S Figueroa St Ste 49 Los Angeles (90017) *(P-14760)*

Cbre Globl Value Investors LLC...........................C...... 949 725-8500
3501 Jamboree Rd Ste 100 Newport Beach (92660) *(P-14761)*

CBS, Colton Also Called: Entercom Media Corp *(P-11924)*

CBS, Los Angeles Also Called: Entercom Media Corp *(P-11925)*

CBS, Studio City Also Called: CBS Broadcasting Inc *(P-11940)*

CBS Broadcasting Inc....................................C...... 818 655-8500
4024 Radford Ave Bldg 4 Studio City (91604) *(P-11940)*

CBS Fasteners Inc..E...... 714 779-6368
1345 N Brasher St Anaheim (92807) *(P-6436)*

CBS Network News, Los Angeles Also Called: Merlot Film Productions Inc *(P-17200)*

CBS Studio Center, Studio City Also Called: Radford Studio Center LLC *(P-17326)*

CBS Studios Inc..B...... 661 964-6020
27420 Avenue Scott Ste A Santa Clarita (91355) *(P-11941)*

CBS Studios Inc..C...... 818 655-5160
4024 Radford Ave Studio City (91604) *(P-17175)*

Cbx Software Inc..E...... 858 264-1133
8910 University Center Ln Ste 400 San Diego (92122) *(P-16195)*

CCC Property Holdings LLC...............................C...... 310 609-1957
7223 Alondra Blvd Paramount (90723) *(P-14926)*

Ccd, Anaheim Also Called: Craftsman Cutting Dies Inc *(P-5876)*

Ccd, Los Angeles Also Called: ITI Electro-Optic Corporation *(P-10142)*

Ccf China Operating Corp.................................E...... 818 871-3000
26901 Malibu Hills Rd Calabasas Hills (91301) *(P-13993)*

CCH Incorporated..A...... 310 800-9800
2050 W 190th St Torrance (90504) *(P-16485)*

CCI, Redlands Also Called: C C I Redlands Inc *(P-9875)*

CCI, Vernon Also Called: Cherokee Chemical Co Inc *(P-13430)*

CCI Industries Inc (PA)...................................E...... 714 662-3879
350 Fischer Ave Ste A Costa Mesa (92626) *(P-4986)*

CCL Label Inc...D...... 909 608-2655
576 College Commerce Way Upland (91786) *(P-3743)*

CCL Label (delaware) Inc.................................C...... 909 608-2260
576 College Commerce Way Upland (91786) *(P-3744)*

CCL Tube Inc (HQ).......................................C...... 310 635-4444
2250 E 220th St Carson (90810) *(P-4987)*

CCM Assembly & Mfg Inc (PA)............................E...... 760 560-1310
2275 Michael Faraday Dr Ste 6 San Diego (92154) *(P-9014)*

Mergent email: customerrelations@mergent.com
1034

2024 Southern California
Business Directory and Buyers Guide

(P-0000) Products & Services Section entry number
(PA)=Parent Co (HQ)=Headquarters (DH)=Div Headquarters

CCM Enterprises (PA)....................................D...... 619 562-2605
10848 Wheatlands Ave Santee (92071) *(P-2946)*

Cco Holdings LLC ....C...... 626 500-1214
3106 San Gabriel Blvd Rosemead (91770) *(P-11971)*

Cco Holdings LLC ....C...... 310 589-3008
23841 Malibu Rd Malibu (90265) *(P-11972)*

Cco Holdings LLC ....C...... 562 239-2761
12319 Norwalk Blvd Norwalk (90650) *(P-11973)*

Cco Holdings LLC ....C...... 626 513-0204
1151 N Azusa Ave Azusa (91702) *(P-11974)*

Cco Holdings LLC ....C...... 562 228-1262
2310 N Bellflower Blvd Long Beach (90815) *(P-11975)*

Cco Holdings LLC ....C...... 714 509-5861
2684 N Tustin St Orange (92865) *(P-11976)*

Cco Holdings LLC ....C...... 805 904-1047
1128 W Branch St Arroyo Grande (93420) *(P-11977)*

Cco Holdings LLC ....C...... 805 400-1002
1131 Creston Rd Paso Robles (93446) *(P-11978)*

Cco Holdings LLC ....C...... 805 232-5887
51 W Main St Ste F Ventura (93001) *(P-11979)*

Cco Holdings LLC ....C...... 760 810-4076
21898 Us Highway 18 Apple Valley (92307) *(P-11980)*

Cco Holdings LLC ....C...... 909 742-8273
26827 Baseline St Highland (92346) *(P-11981)*

Ccpu, San Diego *Also Called: Continuous Computing Corp (P-7421)*

Ccsd, San Diego *Also Called: Cal-Comp Electronics (usa) Co Ltd (P-8171)*

Ccts, Santa Ana *Also Called: Satellite Management Co (P-14864)*

CD Container Inc ....D...... 562 948-1910
7343 Paramount Blvd Pico Rivera (90660) *(P-3089)*

CD Digital, Rancho Cucamonga *Also Called: Digital Flex Media Inc (P-8455)*

CD Video Manufacturing Inc ....D...... 714 265-0770
12650 Westminster Ave Santa Ana (92706) *(P-9179)*

Cdc International Inc ....E...... 626 347-7705
1925 E Puente St Covina (91724) *(P-9370)*

Cdcf III PCF Lndmark Scrmnto L ....D...... 310 552-7211
515 S Flower St 44th Fl Los Angeles (90071) *(P-14656)*

CDI, Irvine *Also Called: Concept Development Llc (P-8665)*

CDI, Reseda *Also Called: Child Development Institute (P-19040)*

CDI Torque Products, City Of Industry *Also Called: Consolidated Devices Inc (P-13676)*

CDM Company Inc ....E...... 949 644-2820
12 Corporate Plaza Dr Ste 200 Newport Beach (92660) *(P-11206)*

CDM Constructors Inc ....D...... 909 579-3500
9220 Cleveland Ave Ste 100 Rancho Cucamonga (91730) *(P-19562)*

Cdr Graphics Inc (PA)....................................E...... 310 474-7600
1207 E Washington Blvd Los Angeles (90021) *(P-3527)*

Cds California LLC ....F...... 818 766-5000
3330 Cahuenga Blvd W Ste 200 Los Angeles (90068) *(P-10861)*

CDS Moving Equipment Inc (PA)....................................D...... 310 631-1100
375 W Manville St Rancho Dominguez (90220) *(P-12787)*

Cds Packing Solutions, Rancho Dominguez *Also Called: CDS Moving Equipment Inc (P-12787)*

Cdsnet LLC ....B...... 310 981-9500
6053 W Century Blvd Los Angeles (90045) *(P-20325)*

Cdti, Oxnard *Also Called: Cdti Advanced Materials Inc (P-3888)*

Cdti Advanced Materials Inc (PA)....................................E...... 805 639-9458
1641 Fiske Pl Oxnard (93033) *(P-3888)*

Cdw, Anaheim *Also Called: Consolidated Design West Inc (P-15659)*

CECILLA GONZALEZ DE AL HOYA CA, Los Angeles *Also Called: White Memorial Medical Center (P-18501)*

Ceco, Oxnard *Also Called: Component Equipment Coinc (P-8964)*

Cedar Holdings LLC ....D...... 909 862-0611
7534 Palm Ave Highland (92346) *(P-17898)*

CEDAR HOUSE REHABILITATION CEN, Bloomington *Also Called: Social Science Service Center (P-18536)*

Cedar Mountain Post Acute, Yucaipa *Also Called: Cedar Operations LLC (P-17899)*

Cedar Operations LLC ....C...... 909 790-2273
11970 4th St Yucaipa (92399) *(P-17899)*

Cedarlane Natural Foods Inc (PA)....................................D...... 310 886-7720
717 E Artesia Blvd Ste A Carson (90746) *(P-1868)*

Cedars Surgical Research Ctr, West Hollywood *Also Called: Cedars-Sinai Medical Center (P-18198)*

Cedars-Sinai Home Care, Los Angeles *Also Called: Cedars-Sinai Medical Center (P-18207)*

Cedars-Sinai Medical Center ....B...... 310 423-3849
127 S San Vicente Blvd Rm 3417 Los Angeles (90048) *(P-17612)*

Cedars-Sinai Medical Center ....D...... 310 423-4208
8720 Beverly Blvd Lower Level Ste Ac1010 Los Angeles (90048) *(P-17613)*

Cedars-Sinai Medical Center ....B...... 310 824-3664
8635 W 3rd St Ste 1195 Los Angeles (90048) *(P-18197)*

Cedars-Sinai Medical Center ....B...... 310 855-7701
8700 Beverly Blvd # 4018 West Hollywood (90048) *(P-18198)*

Cedars-Sinai Medical Center ....D...... 310 423-5468
8797 Beverly Blvd Ste 220 West Hollywood (90048) *(P-18199)*

Cedars-Sinai Medical Center ....C...... 310 423-6451
8727 W 3rd St Los Angeles (90048) *(P-18200)*

Cedars-Sinai Medical Center ....C...... 310 423-2587
8730 Alden Dr West 220 Los Angeles (90048) *(P-18201)*

Cedars-Sinai Medical Center ....B...... 310 423-8965
8723 Alden Dr Los Angeles (90048) *(P-18202)*

Cedars-Sinai Medical Center ....C...... 310 423-5841
8700 Beverly Blvd Ste 8211 West Hollywood (90048) *(P-18203)*

Cedars-Sinai Medical Center ....D...... 310 423-5147
8700 Beverly Blvd Ste 2216 West Hollywood (90048) *(P-18204)*

Cedars-Sinai Medical Center ....C...... 310 423-9310
310 N San Vicente Blvd West Hollywood (90048) *(P-18205)*

Cedars-Sinai Medical Center ....C...... 310 967-1884
99 N La Cienega Blvd Ste Mezz Beverly Hills (90211) *(P-18206)*

Cedars-Sinai Medical Center ....B...... 310 423-3277
8635 W 3rd St Ste 1165w Los Angeles (90048) *(P-18207)*

Cedars-Sinai Medical Center ....B...... 310 423-9520
444 S San Vicente Blvd Ste 1001 Los Angeles (90048) *(P-18208)*

Cedars-Sinai Medical Center ....A...... 310 967-1900
4100 W 190th St Torrance (90504) *(P-18209)*

Cedars-Sinai Medical Center ....A...... 310 385-3400
250 N Robertson Blvd # 101 Beverly Hills (90211) *(P-18210)*

Cedars-Sinai Medical Center ....C...... 310 423-8780
8700 Beverly Blvd Ste 1103 West Hollywood (90048) *(P-18211)*

Cedarwood-Young Company (PA)....................................C...... 626 962-4047
14620 Joanbridge St Baldwin Park (91706) *(P-12165)*

Cedarwood-Young Company ....D...... 626 962-4047
14618 Arrow Hwy Baldwin Park (91706) *(P-12952)*

Cee Baileys Aircraft Plastics, Montebello *Also Called: Desser Tire & Rubber Co LLC (P-12906)*

Celebrity Casinos Inc ....B...... 310 631-3838
123 E Artesia Blvd Compton (90220) *(P-15110)*

Celesco Transducer Products ....E...... 818 701-2701
20630 Plummer St Chatsworth (91311) *(P-9015)*

Celesco Transducer Products, Chatsworth *Also Called: Celesco Transducer Products (P-9015)*

Celestial Lighting, Santa Fe Springs *Also Called: Shimada Enterprises Inc (P-8381)*

Celestial-Saturn Parent Inc (PA)....................................C...... 949 214-1000
40 Pacifica Irvine (92618) *(P-16486)*

Celestica Aerospace Tech Corp ....C...... 512 310-7540
895 S Rockefeller Ave Ste 102 Ontario (91761) *(P-8658)*

Celestica LLC ....F...... 760 357-4880
280 Campillo St Ste G Calexico (92231) *(P-8256)*

Celestica-Aerospace, Ontario *Also Called: Celestica Aerospace Tech Corp (P-8658)*

Celex Solutions, Brea *Also Called: Contract Services Group Inc (P-15702)*

Celgene Corporation ....E...... 858 795-4961
10300 Campus Point Dr Ste 100 San Diego (92121) *(P-4088)*

Celgene Signal Research, San Diego *Also Called: Celgene Corporation (P-4088)*

Cell-Crete, Monrovia *Also Called: Cell-Crete Corporation (P-1063)*

Cell-Crete Corporation (PA)....................................D...... 626 357-3500
135 Railroad Ave Monrovia (91016) *(P-1063)*

Cello Jeans, Commerce *Also Called: Hidden Jeans Inc (P-2024)*

Celtic Commercial Finance, Irvine *Also Called: Celtic Leasing Corp (P-15773)*

Celtic Leasing Corp ....D...... 949 263-3880
4 Park Plz Ste 300 Irvine (92614) *(P-15773)*

Cem, Santee *Also Called: Air & Gas Tech Inc (P-9853)*

Cemco LLC (DH)....................................D...... 800 775-2362
13191 Crossroads Pkwy N Ste 325 City Of Industry (91746) *(P-6213)*

Cemco Steel, City Of Industry *Also Called: Cemco LLC (P-6213)*

Employee Codes: A=Over 500 employees, B=251-500
C=101-250, D=51-100, E=20-50, F=10-19, G=1-9

2024 Southern California
Business Directory and Buyers Guide

© Mergent Inc. 1-800-342-5647

1035

Cemcoat Inc .... E....... 323 733-0125
4928 W Jefferson Blvd Los Angeles (90016) *(P-6600)*

Cement Cutting Inc .... D....... 619 296-9592
3610 Hancock St Frnt San Diego (92110) *(P-1064)*

Cemex Cement Inc .... C....... 760 381-7616
25220 Black Mountain Quarry Rd Apple Valley (92307) *(P-5470)*

Cemex Cement Inc .... D....... 626 969-1747
1201 W Gladstone St Azusa (91702) *(P-12349)*

Cemex Cnstr Mtls PCF LLC .... F....... 909 335-3105
8203 Alabama Ave Highland (92346) *(P-5471)*

Cemex Construction Mtls Inc (DH) .... **E....... 909 974-5500**
3990 Concours Ste 200 Ontario (91764) *(P-12350)*

Cemex Materials LLC .... D....... 909 825-1500
1205 S Rancho Ave Colton (92324) *(P-5472)*

Cencal Health, Santa Barbara *Also Called: Santa Brbara San Luis Obspo RG (P-14455)*

Cencora Inc .... C....... 610 727-7000
1368 Metropolitan Dr Orange (92868) *(P-13031)*

Center At Parkwest, The, Reseda *Also Called: Chase Group Llc (P-20149)*

Center Automotive Inc .... D....... 818 907-9995
5201 Van Nuys Blvd Sherman Oaks (91401) *(P-13746)*

Center B M W, Sherman Oaks *Also Called: Center Automotive Inc (P-13746)*

Center For Atism RES Evltion S .... C....... 858 444-8823
8787 Complex Dr Ste 300 San Diego (92123) *(P-18675)*

Center For Discovery, Irvine *Also Called: Discovery Practice MGT Inc (P-18690)*

Center For Dscovery Adoloscent .... D....... 562 425-6404
4136 Ann Arbor Rd Lakewood (90712) *(P-18676)*

CENTER FOR FAMILY SOLUTIONS, El Centro *Also Called: Womanhaven (P-19170)*

Center For Sustainable Energy .... D....... 858 244-1177
3980 Sherman St Ste 170 San Diego (92110) *(P-20326)*

Center Line Performance Wheels, Newport Beach *Also Called: Center Line Wheel Corporation (P-9371)*

Center Line Wheel Corporation .... E....... 562 921-9637
23 Corporate Plaza Dr Ste 150 Newport Beach (92660) *(P-9371)*

Center Thtre Group Los Angeles (PA) .... **C....... 213 972-7344**
601 W Temple St Los Angeles (90012) *(P-17312)*

Centerfield Media, Los Angeles *Also Called: Qology Direct LLC (P-16911)*

Centerline Industrial Inc .... E....... 858 505-0838
2530 Southport Way Ste D National City (91950) *(P-12788)*

Centerline Mortgage Capitl Inc .... B....... 949 221-6685
18300 Von Karman Ave Ste 600 Irvine (92612) *(P-15024)*

Centerline Wood Products .... D....... 760 246-4530
15447 Anacapa Rd Ste 102 Victorville (92392) *(P-12971)*

Centerpoint Mfg Co Inc .... E....... 818 842-2147
2625 N San Fernando Blvd Burbank (91504) *(P-7795)*

Centinela Consulting Group Inc .... F....... 310 674-2115
720 E Florence Ave Inglewood (90301) *(P-5402)*

Centinela Frman Rgonal Med Ctr, Inglewood *Also Called: Cfhs Holdings Inc (P-18212)*

Centinela Frman Rgonal Med Ctr, Marina Del Rey *Also Called: Cfhs Holdings Inc (P-18213)*

Centinela Frman Rgonal Med Ctr, Marina Del Rey *Also Called: Cfhs Holdings Inc (P-18214)*

Centinela Hospital Medical Center, Inglewood *Also Called: Prime Healthcare Centinela LLC (P-18386)*

Centinela Skld Nrng Wlns Cntr, Inglewood *Also Called: West Cntinela Vly Care Ctr Inc (P-18075)*

Centinela Sklled Nrsing Wllnes .... D....... 310 674-3216
950 S Flower St Inglewood (90301) *(P-17900)*

Centon, Aliso Viejo *Also Called: Centon Electronics Inc (P-7465)*

Centon Electronics Inc (PA) .... **D....... 949 855-9111**
27412 Aliso Viejo Pkwy Aliso Viejo (92656) *(P-7465)*

Central Blower Co .... E....... 626 330-3182
3427 Pomona Blvd Pomona (91768) *(P-7321)*

Central California Cnstr Inc .... E....... 661 978-8230
7221 Downing Ave Bakersfield (93308) *(P-337)*

Central California Power .... E....... 661 589-2870
19487 Broken Ct Shafter (93263) *(P-17030)*

Central Cardiology Med Clinic .... C....... 661 395-0000
2901 Sillect Ave Ste 100 Bakersfield (93308) *(P-17614)*

Central Coast Agriculture Inc (PA) .... **E....... 805 694-8594**
8701 Santa Rosa Rd Buellton (93427) *(P-78)*

Central Coast Distributing LLC .... D....... 805 922-2108
815 S Blosser Rd Santa Maria (93458) *(P-13462)*

Central Coast Printing, San Luis Obispo *Also Called: David B Anderson (P-3556)*

Central Coast Seafoods .... C....... 805 462-3474
5495 Traffic Way Atascadero (93422) *(P-13278)*

Central Coast Wine Services, Santa Maria *Also Called: Central Coast Wine Warehouse (P-1616)*

Central Coast Wine Warehouse (PA) .... **F....... 805 928-9210**
2717 Aviation Way Ste 101 Santa Maria (93455) *(P-1616)*

Central Health Plan Cal Inc .... C....... 626 938-7120
1540 Bridgegate Dr Diamond Bar (91765) *(P-18601)*

Central Prcss 4140, Los Angeles *Also Called: US Foods Inc (P-13404)*

Central Purchasing LLC (HQ) .... **B....... 800 444-3353**
26677 Agoura Rd Calabasas (91302) *(P-12847)*

Central Shop, Los Angeles *Also Called: Los Angeles Unified School Dst (P-18990)*

Central States Logistics Inc .... C....... 661 295-7222
28338 Constellation Rd Ste 940 Valencia (91355) *(P-11449)*

Central Tent, Santa Clarita *Also Called: Frametent Inc (P-2504)*

Centre For Neuro Skills (PA) .... **B....... 661 872-3408**
5215 Ashe Rd Bakersfield (93313) *(P-18677)*

Centrescapes Inc .... D....... 909 392-3303
165 Gentry St Pomona (91767) *(P-157)*

Centro De Salud De La Comuni (PA) .... **D....... 619 428-4463**
1601 Precision Park Ln San Diego (92173) *(P-18678)*

Centron Industries Inc .... E....... 310 324-6443
441 W Victoria St Gardena (90248) *(P-8504)*

Centurion Group Inc (PA) .... **C....... 760 471-8536**
365 S Rancho Santa Fe Rd San Marcos (92078) *(P-14374)*

Centurion Group, The, Los Angeles *Also Called: Mulholland SEC & Patrol Inc (P-16659)*

Centurum Information Tech Inc .... E....... 619 224-1100
4250 Pacific Hwy Ste 105 San Diego (92110) *(P-5738)*

Century 21, South Gate *Also Called: Century 21 A Better Svc Rlty (P-14762)*

Century 21, Redlands *Also Called: Lois Lauer Realty (P-14823)*

Century 21 A Better Svc Rlty .... C....... 562 806-1000
5831 Firestone Blvd Ste J South Gate (90280) *(P-14762)*

Century 8, North Hollywood *Also Called: Century Theatres Inc (P-17306)*

Century American Aluminum Inc .... F....... 909 390-2384
1001 S Doubleday Ave Ontario (91761) *(P-5694)*

Century Blinds Inc .... D....... 951 734-3762
300 S Promenade Ave Corona (92879) *(P-3003)*

Century Downtown 10, Ventura *Also Called: Century Theatres Inc (P-17305)*

Century Gaming Management Inc .... A....... 310 330-2800
3883 W Century Blvd Inglewood (90303) *(P-15111)*

Century Hlth Staffing Svcs Inc .... C....... 661 322-0606
1701 Westwind Dr Ste 101 Bakersfield (93301) *(P-15832)*

Century National, Westlake Village *Also Called: Kramer-Wilson Company Inc (P-14511)*

Century Pacific Realty Corp .... C....... 310 729-9922
9401 Wilshire Blvd Ste 1250 Beverly Hills (90212) *(P-14898)*

Century Pallets, Lynwood *Also Called: Roger R Caruso Enterprises Inc (P-2724)*

Century Pk Capitl Partners LLC (PA) .... **C....... 310 867-2210**
2101 Rosecrans Ave Ste 4275 El Segundo (90245) *(P-14977)*

Century Precision Engrg Inc .... E....... 310 538-0015
2141 W 139th St Gardena (90249) *(P-7796)*

Century Snacks LLC .... B....... 323 278-9578
5560 E Slauson Ave Commerce (90040) *(P-13266)*

Century Spring, Commerce *Also Called: Matthew Warren Inc (P-6804)*

Century Theatres Inc .... C....... 714 373-4573
7777 Edinger Ave Ste 170 Huntington Beach (92647) *(P-17289)*

Century Theatres Inc .... B....... 805 641-6555
555 E Main St Ventura (93001) *(P-17305)*

Century Theatres Inc .... B....... 818 508-1943
12827 Victory Blvd North Hollywood (91606) *(P-17306)*

Century Tubes Inc .... E....... 858 586-0550
7910 Dunbrook Rd San Diego (92126) *(P-12539)*

Century West LLC .... D....... 818 432-5800
4245 Lankershim Blvd North Hollywood (91602) *(P-13747)*

Century West Concrete Inc .... B....... 951 712-4065
9782 Indiana Ave Riverside (92503) *(P-1065)*

Century West Plumbing, Westlake Village *Also Called: Sdg Enterprises (P-820)*

Century Wire & Cable Inc .... D....... 800 999-5566
7400 E Slauson Ave Commerce (90040) *(P-5739)*

Century-National Insurance Co (DH) .... **B....... 818 760-0880**
16650 Sherman Way Ste 200 Van Nuys (91406) *(P-14574)*

Cenveo Worldwide Limited .... B...... 626 369-4921
705 Baldwin Park Blvd City Of Industry (91746) *(P-12992)*

Cera Inc .... E...... 626 814-2688
14180 Live Oak Ave Ste I Baldwin Park (91706) *(P-10089)*

Ceradyne Esk LLC .... C...... 714 549-0421
3169 Red Hill Ave M Costa Mesa (92626) *(P-5566)*

Ceramic Decorating Company Inc .... E...... 323 268-5135
4651 Sheila St Commerce (90040) *(P-16800)*

Cerecons, Anaheim *Also Called: Unlimited Innovations Inc (P-16414)*

Ceridian, Fountain Valley *Also Called: Ceridian Tax Service Inc (P-15494)*

Ceridian Tax Service Inc .... B...... 714 963-1311
17390 Brookhurst St Fountain Valley (92708) *(P-15494)*

Cerritos Ctr For Prfrmg Arts, Cerritos *Also Called: City of Cerritos (P-20403)*

Certance LLC (HQ) .... B...... 949 856-7800
141 Innovation Dr Irvine (92617) *(P-7466)*

Certemy Inc .... F...... 866 907-4088
14876 Raymer St Ste 200 Van Nuys (91405) *(P-16196)*

Certified Alloy Products Inc .... C...... 562 595-6621
3245 Cherry Ave Long Beach (90807) *(P-5678)*

Certified Enameling Inc (PA) .... D...... 323 264-4403
3342 Emery St Los Angeles (90023) *(P-6697)*

Certified Frt Logistics Inc (PA) .... C...... 800 592-5906
1344 White Ct Santa Maria (93458) *(P-11474)*

Certified Laboratories LLC .... A...... 818 845-0070
3125 N Damon Way Burbank (91505) *(P-19962)*

Certified Metal Craft Inc .... E...... 619 593-3636
877 Vernon Way El Cajon (92020) *(P-5832)*

Certified Steel Treating Corp .... E...... 323 583-8711
2454 E 58th St Vernon (90058) *(P-6601)*

Certified Thermoplastics Inc .... E...... 661 222-3006
26381 Ferry Ct Santa Clarita (91350) *(P-4988)*

Certified Thermoplastics LLC, Santa Clarita *Also Called: Certified Thermoplastics Inc (P-4988)*

Certified Tire & Svc Ctrs Inc .... E...... 951 656-6466
23920 Alessandro Blvd Ste A Moreno Valley (92553) *(P-13855)*

Certified Wtr Dmage Rstrtion E .... E...... 800 417-1776
5319 University Dr Irvine (92612) *(P-15699)*

Certis USA LLC .... E...... 661 758-8471
720 5th St Wasco (93280) *(P-4547)*

Cesar Chavez Center, San Diego *Also Called: San Diego Cmnty College Dst (P-18983)*

Cetera Financial Group Inc (PA) .... B...... 866 489-3100
655 W Broadway Ste 1680 San Diego (92101) *(P-16801)*

Ceva Logistics LLC .... B...... 310 223-6500
19600 S Western Ave Torrance (90501) *(P-11746)*

Cevians LLC (PA) .... D...... 714 619-5135
3128 Red Hill Ave Costa Mesa (92626) *(P-5313)*

Cexi, Oxnard *Also Called: Cryogenic Experts Inc (P-7231)*

CF&b Manufacturing Inc .... E...... 714 744-8361
1700 Barcelona Cir Placentia (92870) *(P-3180)*

Cfhc, Los Angeles *Also Called: Essential Access Health (P-19325)*

Cfhs Holdings Inc .... A...... 310 673-4660
555 E Hardy St Inglewood (90301) *(P-18212)*

Cfhs Holdings Inc .... A...... 310 823-8911
4650 Lincoln Blvd Marina Del Rey (90292) *(P-18213)*

Cfhs Holdings Inc .... A...... 310 448-7800
4640 Admiralty Way Ste 650 Marina Del Rey (90292) *(P-18214)*

CFI Holdings Corp .... E...... 909 595-2252
4200 Valley Blvd Pomona (91765) *(P-5653)*

Cflute Corp .... C...... 562 404-6221
13220 Molette St Santa Fe Springs (90670) *(P-3090)*

Cforia, Westlake Village *Also Called: Cforia Software LLC (P-16197)*

Cforia Software LLC .... E...... 818 871-9687
4333 Park Terrace Dr Ste 201 Westlake Village (91361) *(P-16197)*

Cfp Chocolate Holdings LLC .... E...... 661 257-3700
1100a John Reed Ct City Of Industry (91745) *(P-1554)*

Cfp Fire Protection Inc .... D...... 949 727-3277
153 Technology Dr Ste 200 Irvine (92618) *(P-751)*

CFS Income Tax, Simi Valley *Also Called: CFS Tax Software Inc (P-16198)*

CFS Tax Software Inc .... F...... 805 522-1157
1445 E Los Angeles Ave Ste 214 Simi Valley (93065) *(P-16198)*

Cfwf Inc .... C...... 310 221-6280
842 Flint Ave Wilmington (90744) *(P-1801)*

Cg Oncology Inc .... E...... 949 409-3700
400 Spectrum Center Dr Ste 2040 Irvine (92618) *(P-4089)*

CGB, Gardena *Also Called: Pulp Studio Incorporated (P-15672)*

Cgm Inc .... E...... 818 609-7088
19611 Ventura Blvd Ste 211 Tarzana (91356) *(P-10917)*

Cgm Findings, Tarzana *Also Called: Cgm Inc (P-10917)*

Cgnfm, Valencia *Also Called: Creatons Grdn Ntral Fd Mkts In (P-3996)*

Cgpc America Corporation .... E...... 951 332-4100
4 Latitude Way Unit 108 Corona (92881) *(P-3930)*

Cgr/Thompson Industries Inc .... E...... 714 678-4200
7155 Fenwick Ln Westminster (92683) *(P-8090)*

CH Laboratories Inc (PA) .... E...... 310 516-8273
1243 W 130th St Gardena (90247) *(P-4090)*

Ch Products, Vista *Also Called: Apem Inc (P-8997)*

Cha Health Systems Inc (PA) .... A...... 213 487-3211
3731 Wilshire Blvd Ste 850 Los Angeles (90010) *(P-17615)*

Cha Hollywood Medical Ctr LP .... A...... 213 413-3000
4636 Fountain Ave Los Angeles (90029) *(P-17901)*

Cha La Mirada LLC .... C...... 714 739-8500
14299 Firestone Blvd La Mirada (90638) *(P-15112)*

Cha Renetative Medicine, Los Angeles *Also Called: Cha Health Systems Inc (P-17615)*

Chaco Flaco Drinks, Jurupa Valley *Also Called: Levecke LLC (P-1644)*

Chad, Anaheim *Also Called: Chad Industries Incorporated (P-8659)*

Chad Industries Incorporated .... E...... 714 938-0080
1565 S Sinclair St Anaheim (92806) *(P-8659)*

Challenge Graphics Inc .... F...... 818 892-0123
7661 Densmore Ave Ste 3 Van Nuys (91406) *(P-3528)*

Challenger Sheet Metal Inc .... D...... 619 596-8040
9353 Abraham Way Ste A Santee (92071) *(P-1038)*

Cham-Cal Engineering Co .... D...... 714 898-9721
12722 Western Ave Garden Grove (92841) *(P-5336)*

Chambers Group Inc (PA) .... D...... 949 261-5414
5 Hutton Centre Dr Ste 750 Santa Ana (92707) *(P-20327)*

Chameleon Beverage Company Inc (PA) .... D...... 323 724-8223
6444 E 26th St Commerce (90040) *(P-1690)*

Champion, La Jolla *Also Called: Champion Home Builders Inc (P-2735)*

Champion Chemical Co, Whittier *Also Called: Champion Chemical Co Cal Inc (P-13427)*

Champion Chemical Co Cal Inc .... E...... 562 945-1456
8319 Greenleaf Ave Whittier (90602) *(P-13427)*

Champion Cooling Systems, Lake Elsinore *Also Called: Champion Motosports Inc (P-13856)*

Champion Home Builders Inc .... D...... 951 256-4617
299 N Smith Ave Corona (92878) *(P-425)*

Champion Home Builders Inc .... D...... 858 456-3507
7825 Fay Ave Ste 200 La Jolla (92037) *(P-2735)*

Champion Investment Corp .... D...... 917 712-7807
12809 Oakfield Way Poway (92064) *(P-15113)*

Champion Mortgage, San Diego *Also Called: Integrity Mortgage Group (P-14329)*

Champion Motosports Inc (PA) .... E...... 951 245-9464
32373 Corydon St Lake Elsinore (92530) *(P-13856)*

Champion-Arrowhead LLC .... E...... 323 221-9137
5147 Alhambra Ave Los Angeles (90032) *(P-5967)*

Championx LLC .... E...... 661 834-0454
6321 District Blvd Bakersfield (93313) *(P-3889)*

Chan Family Partnership LP .... D...... 626 322-7132
801 S Grand Ave Apt 1811 Los Angeles (90017) *(P-20012)*

Chancellor Oil Tools Inc .... E...... 661 324-2213
3521 Gulf St Bakersfield (93308) *(P-6954)*

Chandler Aggregates Inc (PA) .... E...... 951 277-1341
24867 Maitri Rd Corona (92883) *(P-397)*

Chandler Packaging A Transpak Company .... D...... 858 292-5674
7595 Raytheon Rd San Diego (92111) *(P-11819)*

Change Lending LLC .... D...... 949 769-3526
32 Discovery Ste 160 Irvine (92618) *(P-14306)*

Change Lending LLC .... D...... 858 500-3060
6265 Greenwich Dr Ste 215 San Diego (92122) *(P-14356)*

Channel Islands Post Acute, Santa Barbara *Also Called: Powers Park Healthcare Inc (P-18034)*

Channel Islnds Yung MNS Chrstn .... D...... 805 963-8775
301 W Figueroa St Santa Barbara (93101) *(P-19433)*

Channel Islnds Yung MNS Chrstn .... D...... 805 736-3483
201 W College Ave Lompoc (93436) *(P-19434)*

Employee Codes: A=Over 500 employees, B=251-500
C=101-250, D=51-100, E=20-50, F=10-19, G=1-9

2024 Southern California
Business Directory and Buyers Guide

© Mergent Inc. 1-800-342-5647
1037

Channel Islnds Yung MNS Chrstn .... D....... 805 687-7727
36 Hitchcock Way Santa Barbara (93105) *(P-19435)*

Channel Islnds Yung MNS Chrstn .... D....... 805 969-3288
591 Santa Rosa Ln Santa Barbara (93108) *(P-19436)*

Channel Islnds Yung MNS Chrstn .... D....... 805 686-2037
900 N Refugio Rd Santa Ynez (93460) *(P-19437)*

Channel Islnds Yung MNS Chrstn .... D....... 805 484-0423
3111 Village Park Dr Camarillo (93012) *(P-19438)*

Channel Islnds Yung MNS Chrstn .... D....... 805 484-0423
3760 Telegraph Rd Ventura (93003) *(P-19439)*

Channel Technologies Group, Santa Barbara *Also Called: International Tranducer Corp*
(P-10206)

Channel Technologies Group LLC .... A....... 805 967-0171
879 Ward Dr Santa Barbara (93111) *(P-9962)*

Channel Vision Technology, Laguna Hills *Also Called: Djh Enterprises (P-8509)*

Channelwave Software Inc .... D....... 949 448-4500
27081 Aliso Creek Rd Aliso Viejo (92656) *(P-20328)*

Chapala Iron & Manufacturing .... F....... 805 654-9803
1301 Callens Rd Ventura (93003) *(P-5586)*

Chaparral Blend, Paso Robles *Also Called: Halter Winery LLC (P-1635)*

Chaparral Motorsports, San Bernardino *Also Called: Ocelot Engineering Inc (P-13902)*

Chapman Family Health, Orange *Also Called: Chapman Global Medical Ctr Inc (P-18215)*

Chapman Global Medical Ctr Inc .... B....... 714 633-0011
2601 E Chapman Ave Orange (92869) *(P-18215)*

Chapman Golf Development LLC .... D....... 760 564-8723
78505 Avenue 52 La Quinta (92253) *(P-17421)*

Chapmn/Lnard Stdio Eqp Cnada I (PA) .... C....... 323 877-5309
12950 Raymer St North Hollywood (91605) *(P-17245)*

Chapter Seven Lending, Orange *Also Called: Cashcall Inc (P-14268)*

Charades, Walnut *Also Called: Diamond Collection LLC (P-2448)*

Charades LLC (PA) .... C....... 626 435-0077
20579 Valley Blvd Walnut (91789) *(P-2444)*

Charger Investment Partners LP .... D....... 310 372-5525
880 Apollo St Ste 347 El Segundo (90245) *(P-14375)*

Chargie LLC .... E....... 310 621-0024
3947 Landmark St Culver City (90232) *(P-8137)*

Charles & Cynthia Eberly Inc .... D....... 323 937-6468
8383 Wilshire Blvd Ste 906 Beverly Hills (90211) *(P-14705)*

Charles Dunn RE Svcs Inc (PA) .... D....... 213 270-6200
800 W 6th St Ste 600 Los Angeles (90017) *(P-14763)*

Charles Komar & Sons Inc .... B....... 951 934-1377
11850 Riverside Dr Jurupa Valley (91752) *(P-2387)*

Charles Meisner Inc .... E....... 909 946-8216
201 Sierra Pl Ste A Upland (91786) *(P-7057)*

Charles Rver Labs Cell Sltons (HQ) .... D....... 877 310-0717
8500 Balboa Blvd Ste 130 Northridge (91325) *(P-18752)*

Charles Schwab, San Diego *Also Called: Charles Schwab Corporation (P-14376)*

Charles Schwab, Temecula *Also Called: Charles Schwab Corporation (P-14377)*

Charles Schwab, San Diego *Also Called: Charles Schwab Corporation (P-14978)*

Charles Schwab Corporation .... D....... 800 435-4000
7510 Hazard Center Dr Ste 407 San Diego (92108) *(P-14376)*

Charles Schwab Corporation .... C....... 800 435-4000
27580 Ynez Rd Ste A Temecula (92591) *(P-14377)*

Charles Schwab Corporation .... D....... 800 435-4000
10920 Via Frontera Ste 100 San Diego (92127) *(P-14978)*

Charlies Specialties Inc .... C....... 724 346-2350
501 Airpark Dr Fullerton (92833) *(P-1512)*

Charmaine Plastics Inc .... D....... 714 630-8117
2941 E La Jolla St Anaheim (92806) *(P-4989)*

Charman Manufacturing Inc .... F....... 213 489-7000
5681 S Downey Rd Vernon (90058) *(P-5632)*

Charming Trim & Packaging .... A....... 415 302-7021
5889 Rickenbacker Rd Commerce (90040) *(P-13081)*

Chart Sequal Technologies Inc .... D....... 858 202-3100
12230 World Trade Dr Ste 100 San Diego (92128) *(P-10479)*

Charter Bhvral Hlth Sys S C/Ch .... C....... 626 966-1632
1161 E Covina Blvd Covina (91724) *(P-18510)*

Charter Communications, Long Beach *Also Called: Cco Holdings LLC (P-11975)*

Charter Communications, Ventura *Also Called: Cco Holdings LLC (P-11979)*

Charter Hospice Colton LLC .... C....... 909 825-2969
1007 E Cooley Dr Ste 100 Colton (92324) *(P-18082)*

Charter Oak Hospital, Covina *Also Called: Charter Bhvral Hlth Sys S C/Ch (P-18510)*

Chase Group Llc .... B....... 805 522-9155
5270 E Los Angeles Ave Simi Valley (93063) *(P-19890)*

Chase Group Llc .... B....... 818 708-3533
6740 Wilbur Ave Reseda (91335) *(P-20149)*

Chase-Durer Ltd (PA) .... F....... 310 550-7280
8455 Fountain Ave Unit 515 West Hollywood (90069) *(P-10892)*

Chatmeter Inc .... D....... 619 300-1050
225 Broadway Ste 2200 San Diego (92101) *(P-16199)*

CHATSWORTH PARK HEALTH CARE CE, Chatsworth *Also Called: Cpcc Inc (P-18119)*

Chatsworth Products Inc (PA) .... E....... 818 735-6100
4175 Guardian St Simi Valley (93063) *(P-6858)*

Chavers Gasket Corporation .... E....... 949 472-8118
23325 Del Lago Dr Laguna Hills (92653) *(P-4722)*

CHC, Los Angeles *Also Called: Covenant House California (P-19255)*

Che Behavioral Health Services .... C....... 760 300-3664
5838 Edison Pl Ste 100 Carlsbad (92008) *(P-18753)*

CHE Precision Inc .... E....... 805 499-8885
2586 Calcite Cir Newbury Park (91320) *(P-7797)*

Che Snior Psychological Svcs PC .... C....... 888 307-0893
4929 Wilshire Blvd Ste 510 Los Angeles (90010) *(P-17859)*

Check It Out, Los Angeles *Also Called: Nexxen Apparel Inc (P-2355)*

Checkworks Inc .... D....... 626 333-1444
315 Cloverleaf Dr Ste J Baldwin Park (91706) *(P-3835)*

Cheek Machine Corp .... E....... 714 279-9486
1312 S Allec St Anaheim (92805) *(P-7798)*

Cheesecake Factory Bakery Inc .... B....... 818 871-3000
26950 Agoura Rd Calabasas Hills (91301) *(P-13994)*

Cheesecake Factory Inc (PA) .... B....... 818 871-3000
26901 Malibu Hills Rd Calabasas Hills (91301) *(P-13995)*

Cheesecake Factory, The, Calabasas Hills *Also Called: Cheesecake Factory Inc (P-13995)*

Chef Merito LLC (PA) .... E....... 818 787-0100
7915 Sepulveda Blvd Van Nuys (91405) *(P-1869)*

Chef Works Inc (PA) .... C....... 858 643-5600
12325 Kerran St # A Poway (92064) *(P-13099)*

Chefmaster .... E....... 714 554-4000
501 Airpark Dr Fullerton (92833) *(P-1870)*

Chem Arrow Corp .... E....... 626 358-2255
13643 Live Oak Ln Irwindale (91706) *(P-4679)*

Chem-Mark of Orange County, Cerritos *Also Called: Better Beverages Inc (P-1757)*

Chem-Tronics, El Cajon *Also Called: GKN Aerospace Chem-Tronics Inc (P-9570)*

Chemat Technology Inc .... E....... 818 727-9786
9036 Winnetka Ave Northridge (91324) *(P-10090)*

Chemat Vision, Northridge *Also Called: Chemat Technology Inc (P-10090)*

Chembridge Corporation (PA) .... B....... 858 451-7400
11199 Sorrento Valley Rd Ste 206 San Diego (92121) *(P-13428)*

Chemco Products Company, Paramount *Also Called: LMC Enterprises (P-4357)*

Chemdiv Inc .... E....... 858 794-4860
12730 High Bluff Dr San Diego (92130) *(P-4599)*

Chemeor Inc (PA) .... E....... 626 966-3808
727 Arrow Grand Cir Covina (91722) *(P-4372)*

Chemi-Source Inc .... E....... 760 477-8177
2665 Vista Pacific Dr Oceanside (92056) *(P-13032)*

Chemical Diversity Labs, San Diego *Also Called: Chemdiv Inc (P-4599)*

Chemical Methods Assoc LLC (DH) .... E....... 714 898-8781
12700 Knott St Garden Grove (92841) *(P-7647)*

Chemlogics Group LLC .... E....... 805 591-3314
7305 Morro Rd Ste 200 Atascadero (93422) *(P-4518)*

Chemseal, Pacoima *Also Called: Flamemaster Corporation (P-4565)*

Chemsil Silicones Inc .... E....... 818 700-0302
21900 Marilla St Chatsworth (91311) *(P-13429)*

Chemtec Chemical Company, Chatsworth *Also Called: Vijall Inc (P-13443)*

Chemtool Incorporated .... C....... 661 823-7190
1300 Goodrick Dr Tehachapi (93561) *(P-4680)*

Chemtreat Inc .... C....... 804 935-2000
8885 Rehco Rd San Diego (92121) *(P-4600)*

Chemtrol, Santa Barbara *Also Called: Santa Barbara Control Systems (P-10160)*

Chen & Huang Partners LP .... D....... 714 557-8700
1400 S Bristol St Santa Ana (92704) *(P-15114)*

Chen-Tech Industries Inc (DH) .... E....... 949 855-6716
9 Wrigley Irvine (92618) *(P-10480)*

Mergent email: customerrelations@mergent.com
1038

2024 Southern California
Business Directory and Buyers Guide

(P-0000) Products & Services Section entry number
(PA)=Parent Co (HQ)=Headquarters (DH)=Div Headquarters

Chenbro Micom (usa) Inc .... E...... 909 937-0100
  2800 Jurupa St Ontario (91761) *(P-7467)*

Cheque Guard Inc .... D...... 818 563-9335
  512 S Verdugo Dr Burbank (91502) *(P-15991)*

Cherokee Chemical Co Inc (PA).............................. E...... 323 265-1112
  3540 E 26th St Vernon (90058) *(P-13430)*

Cherokee Uniform, Santa Monica *Also Called: Careismatic Brands LLC (P-5272)*

Cherokee Uniforms, Chatsworth *Also Called: Strategic Distribution L P (P-2186)*

Cherry City Electric, City Of Industry *Also Called: Morrow-Meadows Corporation (P-920)*

Chester Paul Company, Anaheim *Also Called: Manitwoc Fdsrvice Cmpanies LLC (P-7618)*

Chestnut Ridge Energy Company C
  18101 Von Karman Ave Ste 920 Irvine (92612) *(P-12017)*

Chevelle Classics Parts & ACC, Seal Beach *Also Called: Original Parts Group Inc (P-13866)*

Chevron, El Segundo *Also Called: Chevron Corporation (P-13890)*

Chevron Corporation .... A...... 310 615-5000
  324 W El Segundo Blvd El Segundo (90245) *(P-13890)*

Chevron Mining Inc .... C...... 760 856-7625
  67750 Bailey Rd Mountain Pass (92366) *(P-240)*

CHG Foundation .... B...... 619 422-0422
  740 Bay Blvd Chula Vista (91910) *(P-19528)*

Chicago Brothers, Vernon *Also Called: Overhill Farms Inc (P-1963)*

Chicago Title, Santa Barbara *Also Called: Chicago Title Insurance Co (P-14538)*

Chicago Title Insurance Co (HQ)............................ C...... 805 565-6900
  4050 Calle Real Santa Barbara (93110) *(P-14538)*

Chick Publications Inc .... E...... 909 987-0771
  8780 Archibald Ave Rancho Cucamonga (91730) *(P-3401)*

Chicken of Sea International, El Segundo *Also Called: Tri-Union Seafoods LLC (P-13288)*

Child & Family Center ....C...... 661 259-9439
  21545 Centre Pointe Pkwy Santa Clarita (91350) *(P-19036)*

Child and Family Guidance Ctr (PA)......................... C...... 818 739-5140
  9650 Zelzah Ave Northridge (91325) *(P-18679)*

Child Care Resource Center Inc ....C...... 661 723-3246
  250 Grand Cypress Ave Ste 601 Palmdale (93551) *(P-19037)*

Child Care Resource Center Inc .... C...... 818 717-1000
  20001 Prairie St Chatsworth (91311) *(P-19038)*

Child Care Resource Center Inc ....C...... 818 837-0097
  454 S Kalisher St San Fernando (91340) *(P-19204)*

Child Dev Rsrces of Vntura CNT (PA)....................... C...... 805 485-7878
  221 Ventura Blvd Oxnard (93036) *(P-19039)*

Child Development Incorporated .... B...... 714 842-4064
  17341 Jacquelyn Ln Huntington Beach (92647) *(P-14764)*

Child Development Incorporated .... B...... 949 854-5060
  5151 Amalfi Dr Irvine (92603) *(P-19205)*

Child Development Institute .... D...... 818 888-4559
  18050 Vanowen St Reseda (91335) *(P-19040)*

Child Guidance Center Inc .... C...... 714 953-4455
  525 Cabrillo Park Dr Ste 300 Santa Ana (92701) *(P-18680)*

Child Help Head Start Center, Beaumont *Also Called: Childhelp Inc (P-19248)*

Child Support Services, Commerce *Also Called: County of Los Angeles (P-19056)*

Childhelp Inc ....C...... 951 845-6737
  14700 Manzanita Rd Beaumont (92223) *(P-19248)*

Childnet, Long Beach *Also Called: Childnet Youth & Fmly Svcs Inc (P-19041)*

Childnet Youth & Fmly Svcs Inc (PA)....................... C...... 562 498-5500
  3545 Long Beach Blvd Ste 200 Long Beach (90807) *(P-19041)*

Children's Hospital, San Diego *Also Called: Rady Childrens Hosp & Hlth Ctr (P-18403)*

CHILDREN'S HOSPITAL, San Diego *Also Called: Rady Chld Hospital-San Diego (P-18404)*

Childrens Associated Med Group, San Diego *Also Called: Childrens Spclsts of San Dego (P-17619)*

Childrens Bureau Southern Cal (PA)........................ C...... 213 342-0100
  1910 Magnolia Ave Los Angeles (90007) *(P-19042)*

Childrens Clnic Srving Chldren .... B...... 562 264-4638
  701 E 28th St Ste 200 Long Beach (90806) *(P-17616)*

Childrens Healthcare Cal .... B...... 714 997-3000
  455 S Main St Orange (92868) *(P-17617)*

Childrens Healthcare Cal (PA)................................ A...... 714 997-3000
  1201 W La Veta Ave Orange (92868) *(P-18523)*

Childrens Hospital Los Angeles .... B...... 323 361-2751
  4661 W Sunset Blvd Los Angeles (90027) *(P-18216)*

Childrens Hospital Los Angeles (PA)........................ A...... 323 660-2450
  4650 W Sunset Blvd Los Angeles (90027) *(P-18524)*

Childrens Hospital Orange Cnty ....B...... 949 365-2416
  455 S Main St Orange (92868) *(P-18217)*

Childrens Hospital Orange Cnty ....C...... 949 387-2586
  980 Roosevelt Irvine (92620) *(P-18213)*

Childrens Hospital Orange Cnty (PA) ....A...... 714 509-8300
  1201 W La Veta Ave Orange (92868) *(P-18219)*

Childrens Hospital Orange Cnty ....B...... 714 638-5990
  10602 Chapman Ave Ste 200 Garden Grove (92840) *(P-18220)*

Childrens Hospital Orange Cnty ....C...... 949 631-2062
  500 Superior Ave Newport Beach (92663) *(P-19206)*

Childrens Inst Los Angeles .... A...... 213 383-2765
  679 S New Hampshire Ave Los Angeles (90005) *(P-19043)*

Childrens Inst Los Angeles (PA).............................. C...... 213 385-5100
  2121 W Temple St Los Angeles (90026) *(P-19923)*

Childrens Institute Inc (PA).................................. C...... 213 385-5100
  2121 W Temple St Los Angeles (90026) *(P-19044)*

Childrens Law Center Cal (PA)................................ D...... 323 980-8700
  101 Centre Plaza Dr Monterey Park (91754) *(P-18835)*

Childrens Oncology Group .... C...... 626 241-1500
  1333 S Mayflower Ave Ste 260 Monrovia (91016) *(P-17618)*

Childrens Spclsts of San Dego (PA).........................B...... 858 576-1700
  3020 Childrens Way San Diego (92123) *(P-17619)*

Chili's, Santa Maria *Also Called: Impo International LLC (P-5276)*

Chilicon Power LLC (PA)...................................... E...... 310 800-1396
  15415 W Sunset Blvd Ste 102 Pacific Palisades (90272) *(P-10189)*

China Airlines Ltd .... C...... 310 484-1818
  5651 W 96th St Los Angeles (90045) *(P-11660)*

China Airlines Ltd .... C...... 310 646-4293
  380 World Way Ste S14 Los Angeles (90045) *(P-11661)*

Chinatown Service Center (PA)............................... D...... 213 808-1701
  767 N Hill St Ste 400 Los Angeles (90012) *(P-19180)*

Chinese Consumer Yellow Pages, Rosemead *Also Called: Chinese Overseas Mktg Svc Corp (P-3436)*

Chinese La Daily News, El Monte *Also Called: LA Web Inc (P-850)*

Chinese Overseas Mktg Svc Corp (PA)......................D...... 626 280-8588
  3940 Rosemead Blvd Rosemead (91770) *(P-3436)*

Chinese-La Daily News, El Monte *Also Called: LAweb Offset Printing Inc (P-3780)*

Chino Medical Group Inc ....D...... 909 591-6446
  5475 Walnut Ave Chino (91710) *(P-17620)*

Chino Valley Medical Center, Chino *Also Called: Veritas Health Services Inc (P-18498)*

Chino Valley YMCA, Chino *Also Called: West End Yung MNS Christn Assn (P-19472)*

Chip-Makers Tooling Supply Inc .... F...... 562 698-5840
  33867 Petunia St Murrieta (92563) *(P-7058)*

Chipton-Ross Inc .... D...... 310 414-7800
  420 Culver Blvd Playa Del Rey (90293) *(P-9519)*

Chiro Inc (PA)... C...... 909 879-1160
  2260 S Vista Ave Bloomington (92316) *(P-12889)*

Chirotech Inc .... C...... 619 528-0040
  9265 Sky Park Ct Ste 200 San Diego (92123) *(P-17854)*

Chirotouch, San Diego *Also Called: Chirotech Inc (P-17854)*

Chivaroli & Assoc Inc .... D...... 208 338-6640
  200 N Westlake Blvd Ste 101 Westlake Village (91362) *(P-14575)*

Chlor Alkali Products & Vinyls, Santa Fe Springs *Also Called: Olin Chlor Alkali Logistics (P-3859)*

Choc, Orange *Also Called: Childrens Hospital Orange Cnty (P-18219)*

Choc Childern's, Garden Grove *Also Called: Childrens Hospital Orange Cnty (P-18220)*

Choc Children's, Orange *Also Called: Childrens Healthcare Cal (P-18523)*

Choc Mission, Orange *Also Called: Childrens Hospital Orange Cnty (P-18217)*

Chocolates A La Carte Inc ....C...... 661 257-3700
  24836 Avenue Rockefeller Valencia (91355) *(P-1535)*

Chocolates and Health, La Verne *Also Called: Vitawest Nutraceuticals Inc (P-1289)*

Choic Admini Insur Servi .... B...... 714 542-4200
  721 S Parker St Ste 200 Orange (92868) *(P-14576)*

Choice Lithographics, Buena Park *Also Called: Cyu Lithographics Inc (P-3554)*

Choicepoint, Irvine *Also Called: Lexisnexis Risk Assets Inc (P-14607)*

Chol Enterprises Inc .... E...... 310 516-1328
  12831 S Figueroa St Los Angeles (90061) *(P-9658)*

Choon Inc (PA).. E...... 213 225-2500
  1443 E 4th St Los Angeles (90033) *(P-2280)*

Choose Manufacturing Co LLC .... E...... 714 327-1698
  24 Passion Flower Irvine (92618) *(P-8660)*

ALPHABETIC

Chop Stop Inc ....D....... 818 369-7350
601 N Glendale Ave Glendale (91206) *(P-13996)*

Choura Events ....D....... 310 320-6200
540 Hawaii Ave Torrance (90503) *(P-15774)*

Choura Venue Services ....D....... 562 426-0555
4101 E Willow St Long Beach (90815) *(P-15500)*

Choura Vnue Svcs At Carson Ctr, Long Beach *Also Called: Choura Venue Services*
(P-15500)

Chownow Inc ....D....... 888 707-2469
12181 Bluff Creek Dr Ste W200 Playa Vista (90094) *(P-16200)*

Chp ....D....... 909 213-3788
11338 Walnut St Redlands (92374) *(P-17275)*

Chris Putrimas ....E....... 877 434-1666
1930 E Carson St Ste 102 Carson (90810) *(P-11207)*

Chrislie Formulations, Azusa *Also Called: Bbeautiful LLC (P-4382)*

Christian Bros Flrg Interiors, Lakeside *Also Called: Christian Bros Flrg Intrors In (P-13950)*

Christian Bros Flrg Intrors In ....D....... 619 443-9500
12086 Woodside Ave Lakeside (92040) *(P-13950)*

Christian Brothers Mechanical Services Inc ....C....... 951 361-2247
11140 Thurston Ln Jurupa Valley (91752) *(P-752)*

Christie Digital Systems Inc (HQ) ....D....... 714 236-8610
10550 Camden Dr Cypress (90630) *(P-10862)*

Christie Medical Holdings Inc ....E....... 714 236-8610
10550 Camden Dr Cypress (90630) *(P-10796)*

Christie Parker & Hale LLP (PA) ....C....... 626 795-9900
655 N Central Ave Ste 2300 Glendale (91203) *(P-18836)*

Christos Engineering Inc ....F....... 562 907-4463
7626 Baldwin Pl Whittier (90602) *(P-7059)*

Chroma Systems Solutions Inc (HQ) ....E....... 949 297-4848
19772 Pauling Foothill Ranch (92610) *(P-10190)*

Chromacode Inc ....E....... 442 244-4369
2330 Faraday Ave Ste 100 Carlsbad (92008) *(P-15992)*

Chromadex, Los Angeles *Also Called: Chromadex Corporation (P-3995)*

Chromadex Corporation (PA) ....E....... 310 388-6706
10900 Wilshire Blvd Ste 600 Los Angeles (90024) *(P-3995)*

Chromal Plating & Grinding, Los Angeles *Also Called: Chromal Plating Company (P-6602)*

Chromal Plating Company ....E....... 323 222-0119
1748 Workman St Los Angeles (90031) *(P-6602)*

Chromalloy Component Svcs Inc ....E....... 858 877-2800
7007 Consolidated Way San Diego (92121) *(P-9564)*

Chromalloy Gas Turbine LLC ....D....... 760 768-3723
1749 Stergios Rd Ste 2 Calexico (92231) *(P-9565)*

Chromalloy San Diego Corp ....C....... 858 877-2800
7007 Consolidated Way San Diego (92121) *(P-17119)*

Chromalloy Southwest, Calexico *Also Called: Chromalloy Gas Turbine LLC (P-9565)*

Chromatic Inc Lithographers ....E....... 818 242-5785
127 Concord St Glendale (91203) *(P-3529)*

Chromavision Medical Systems, San Juan Capistrano *Also Called: Clarient Inc (P-18542)*

Chrome Hearts LLC (PA) ....E....... 323 957-7544
915 N Mansfield Ave Los Angeles (90038) *(P-2426)*

Chrome Nickel Plating, Lynwood *Also Called: Bowman-Field Inc (P-6595)*

Chrome River Technologies Inc ....C....... 888 781-0088
5757 Wilshire Blvd Ste 270 Los Angeles (90036) *(P-16201)*

Chrome Tech Inc ....C....... 714 543-4092
2310 Cape Cod Way Santa Ana (92703) *(P-6603)*

Chromium Dental II LLC ....C....... 949 733-3111
1524 Brookhollow Dr Santa Ana (92705) *(P-17836)*

Chromologic, Monrovia *Also Called: Chromologic LLC (P-10481)*

Chromologic LLC ....E....... 626 381-9974
1225 S Shamrock Ave Monrovia (91016) *(P-10481)*

Chronomite Laboratories Inc ....E....... 310 534-2300
17451 Hurley St City Of Industry (91744) *(P-10101)*

Chua & Sons Co Inc ....E....... 323 588-8044
3300 E 50th St Vernon (90058) *(P-2054)*

Chuaolson Enterprises Inc ....E....... 714 630-4751
1274 N Grove St Anaheim (92806) *(P-12717)*

Chubb, Los Angeles *Also Called: Pacific Indemnity Company (P-14620)*

Chubby Gorilla Inc (PA) ....E....... 844 365-5218
4320 N Harbor Blvd Fullerton (92835) *(P-4990)*

Chugach Government Svcs Inc ....B....... 858 578-0276
9466 Black Mountain Rd Ste 240 San Diego (92126) *(P-20291)*

Church & Dwight Co Inc ....E....... 609 613-1551
17486 Nisqualli Rd Victorville (92395) *(P-4335)*

Church & Larsen Inc ....C....... 626 303-8741
16103 Avenida Padilla Irwindale (91702) *(P-976)*

Churchill Aerospace LLC ....F....... 909 266-3116
5091 G St Chino (91710) *(P-7144)*

Churm Publishing Inc (PA) ....E....... 714 796-7000
1451 Quail St Ste 201 Newport Beach (92660) *(P-3265)*

Chus Packaging Supplies Inc ....E....... 562 944-6411
10011 Santa Fe Springs Rd Santa Fe Springs (90670) *(P-13533)*

Ciao, Camarillo *Also Called: Ciao Wireless Inc (P-9016)*

Ciao Wireless Inc ....D....... 805 389-3224
4000 Via Pescador Camarillo (93012) *(P-9016)*

Ciasons Industrial Inc ....E....... 714 259-0838
1615 Boyd St Santa Ana (92705) *(P-4723)*

Cibaria International Inc ....E....... 951 823-8490
705 Columbia Ave Riverside (92507) *(P-13359)*

Cibus Inc ....C....... 858 450-0008
6455 Nancy Ridge Dr San Diego (92121) *(P-4548)*

Cibus Global Ltd ....C....... 858 450-0008
6455 Nancy Ridge Dr San Diego (92121) *(P-19830)*

Cicoil LLC ....C....... 661 295-1295
24960 Avenue Tibbitts Valencia (91355) *(P-12654)*

Cicon Engineering Inc (PA) ....C....... 818 909-6060
6633 Odessa Ave Van Nuys (91406) *(P-9017)*

Cid Management, Westlake Village *Also Called: Comprhnsive Indus Dsblity MGT (P-18755)*

Cidara, San Diego *Also Called: Cidara Therapeutics Inc (P-4309)*

Cidara Therapeutics Inc (PA) ....D....... 858 752-6170
6310 Nancy Ridge Dr Ste 101 San Diego (92121) *(P-4309)*

Cie Manufacturing LLC ....E....... 877 711-0725
10530 Sessler St South Gate (90280) *(P-9491)*

Cig Financial LLC ....C....... 877 244-4442
6 Executive Cir Ste 100 Irvine (92614) *(P-14269)*

Cigna, Glendale *Also Called: Cigna Behavioral Health of Cal (P-14465)*

Cigna, Glendale *Also Called: Cigna Healthcare Cal Inc (P-14466)*

Cigna Behavioral Health of Cal ....B....... 800 753-0540
450 N Brand Blvd Ste 500 Glendale (91203) *(P-14465)*

Cigna Healthcare Cal Inc (DH) ....B....... 818 500-6262
400 N Brand Blvd Ste 400 Glendale (91203) *(P-14466)*

Cii, Santee *Also Called: Compucraft Industries Inc (P-9663)*

Cilajet LLC ....E....... 310 320-8000
16425 Ishida Ave Gardena (90248) *(P-4347)*

Cim Group LP (PA) ....C....... 323 860-4900
4700 Wilshire Blvd Ste 1 Los Angeles (90010) *(P-15115)*

Cim Services, Compton *Also Called: Circle Industrial Mfg Corp (P-7362)*

Cim/H & H Hotel LP ....B....... 323 856-1200
1755 N Highland Ave Los Angeles (90028) *(P-15116)*

Cimarron Group, The, Los Angeles *Also Called: Cimarron Partner Associates LLC (P-15531)*

Cimarron Partner Associates LLC ....C....... 323 337-0300
6855 Santa Monica Blvd Los Angeles (90038) *(P-15531)*

Cimc Intermodal Equipment, South Gate *Also Called: Cimc Intermodal Equipment LLC*
(P-9492)

Cimc Intermodal Equipment LLC (HQ) ....D....... 562 904-8600
10530 Sessler St South Gate (90280) *(P-9492)*

Cinderella Motel ....D....... 559 432-0118
1747 S Harbor Blvd Anaheim (92802) *(P-15117)*

Cinema Secrets Inc ....D....... 818 846-0579
6639 Odessa Ave Van Nuys (91406) *(P-14125)*

Cinnabar ....C....... 818 842-8190
4571 Electronics Pl Los Angeles (90039) *(P-15658)*

Cintas, Whittier *Also Called: Cintas Corporation No 3 (P-13932)*

Cintas, San Diego *Also Called: Cintas Corporation No 3 (P-13933)*

Cintas, Santa Ana *Also Called: Cintas Sales Corporation (P-15450)*

Cintas Corporation ....D....... 714 646-2550
4320 E Miraloma Ave Anaheim (92807) *(P-13931)*

Cintas Corporation No 3 ....D....... 562 692-8741
2829 Workman Mill Rd Whittier (90601) *(P-13932)*

Cintas Corporation No 3 ....D....... 619 239-1001
675 32nd St San Diego (92102) *(P-13933)*

Cintas Fire, Anaheim *Also Called: Cintas Corporation (P-13931)*

Cintas Sales Corporation .... D....... 714 957-2852
2618 Oak St Santa Ana (92707) *(P-15450)*

Cinton LLC .... E....... 714 961-8808
620 Richfield Rd Placentia (92870) *(P-3168)*

Ciphertex LLC .... F...... 818 773-8989
9301 Jordan Ave Ste 105a Chatsworth (91311) *(P-7515)*

Ciphertex Data Security, Chatsworth Also Called: Ciphertex LLC *(P-7515)*

Circle Industrial Mfg Corp (PA)........................... E..... 310 638-5101
1613 W El Segundo Blvd Compton (90222) *(P-7362)*

Circle W Enterprises Inc .... E..... 661 257-2400
27737 Avenue Hopkins Valencia (91355) *(P-6815)*

Circor Aerospace Inc (DH)................................... C..... 951 270-6200
2301 Wardlow Cir Corona (92878) *(P-6757)*

Circor Instrmentation Tech Inc .... D..... 951 270-6200
2301 Wardlow Cir Corona (92878) *(P-6773)*

CIRCOR INSTRUMENTATION TECHNOLOGIES, INC., Corona Also Called: Circor Instrmentation Tech Inc *(P-6773)*

Circor Naval Solutions LLC (DH)......................... D..... 413 436-7711
656 Marsat Ct Ste A Chula Vista (91911) *(P-7272)*

Circuit Assembly Corp (PA)................................. F..... 949 855-7887
6 Autry St 150 Irvine (92618) *(P-8962)*

Circuit Express Inc .... E..... 805 581-2172
67 W Easy St Ste 129 Simi Valley (93065) *(P-8661)*

Circuit Services Llc .... E..... 818 701-5391
9134 Independence Ave Chatsworth (91311) *(P-8662)*

Circulating Air Inc (PA)....................................... D..... 818 764-0530
7337 Varna Ave North Hollywood (91605) *(P-753)*

Cire Group Inc .... C..... 626 321-8822
3579 E Foothill Blvd # 793 Pasadena (91107) *(P-7516)*

Ciri - Stroup Inc .... C..... 949 488-3104
25135 Park Lantern Dana Point (92629) *(P-15501)*

Cirpa Radiology Management, El Segundo Also Called: Radiology Partners Inc *(P-17747)*

Cirrus Enterprises LLC .... D..... 310 204-6159
18027 Bishop Ave Carson (90746) *(P-13410)*

Cirrus Health II LP .... C..... 949 855-0562
24331 El Toro Rd Ste 150 Laguna Hills (92637) *(P-17621)*

Cirtech Inc .... E..... 714 921-0860
250 E Emerson Ave Orange (92865) *(P-16802)*

Cisco & Brothers Designs, Pasadena Also Called: Cisco Bros Corp *(P-2797)*

Cisco Bros Corp (PA).. C..... 323 778-8612
474 S Arroyo Pkwy Pasadena (91105) *(P-2797)*

Citadel Panda Express Inc .... C..... 626 799-9898
899 El Centro St Ste 201 South Pasadena (91030) *(P-13997)*

Citibank, Long Beach Also Called: Citibank FSB *(P-14161)*

Citibank FSB .... C..... 562 999-3453
1 World Trade Ctr Ste 100 Long Beach (90831) *(P-14161)*

Citifinancial, City Of Industry Also Called: Citifinancial Credit Company *(P-14270)*

Citifinancial Credit Company .... D..... 626 712-8780
2655 Del Vista Dr City Of Industry (91745) *(P-14270)*

Citiguard Inc .... B..... 800 613-5903
22736 Vanowen St Ste 300 West Hills (91307) *(P-16629)*

Citivest Inc .... D..... 949 705-0420
4350 Von Karman Ave Ste 200 Newport Beach (92660) *(P-14765)*

Citizen Watch America, Torrance Also Called: Citizen Watch Company of America Inc *(P-12961)*

Citizen Watch Company of America Inc (HQ)......... C..... 800 321-1023
1000 W 190th St Torrance (90502) *(P-12961)*

Citizens Business Bank (HQ)................................ C..... 909 980-4030
701 N Haven Ave Ste 280 Ontario (91764) *(P-14188)*

Citizens Choice Health Plan, Orange Also Called: Alignment Health Plan *(P-14458)*

Citizens of Humanity LLC (PA)............................ C..... 323 923-1240
5715 Bickett St City Of Huntington Park (90255) *(P-2313)*

Citrix Online Group, Goleta Also Called: Citrix Online LLC *(P-15993)*

Citrix Online LLC .... B..... 805 690-6400
7414 Hollister Ave Goleta (93117) *(P-15993)*

Citrus Ford, Ontario Also Called: Citrus Motors Ontario Inc *(P-13748)*

Citrus Motors Ontario Inc (PA)............................ C..... 909 390-0930
1375 S Woodruff Way Ontario (91761) *(P-13748)*

Citrus North Venture LLC .... D..... 256 428-2000
6591 Collins Dr Ste E11 Moorpark (93021) *(P-15118)*

Citrus Restaurant LLC .... C..... 858 277-8888
8110 Aero Dr San Diego (92123) *(P-13998)*

CITRUS VALLEY HEALTH PARTNERS, INC., Covina Also Called: Citrus Vly Hlth Partners Inc *(P-18754)*

Citrus Vly Hlth Care Partners, Glendora Also Called: Emanate Health *(P-18253)*

Citrus Vly Hlth Partners Inc .... A..... 626 962-4011
1115 S Sunset Ave West Covina (91790) *(P-18221)*

Citrus Vly Hlth Partners Inc .... B..... 626 732-3100
1325 N Grand Ave Ste 300 Covina (91724) *(P-18754)*

Citrusbyte LLC .... E..... 888 969-2983
21550 Oxnard St Ste 300 # 11 Woodland Hills (91367) *(P-15994)*

City Chevrolet of San Diego .... C..... 619 276-6171
2111 Morena Blvd San Diego (92110) *(P-17031)*

City Chevrolet of Volkswagen, San Diego Also Called: City Chevrolet of San Diego *(P-17031)*

City Crane, Bakersfield Also Called: Dunbar Electric Sign Company *(P-11110)*

City Hope National Medical Ctr (HQ).................... A..... 626 256-4673
1500 Duarte Rd Duarte (91010) *(P-18222)*

City National Bank .... C..... 310 888-6500
555 S Flower St 2500 Los Angeles (90071) *(P-14162)*

City National Bank (DH)....................................... B..... 310 888-6000
555 S Flower St Ste 2500 Los Angeles (90071) *(P-14163)*

City National Corporation .... A
555 S Flower St Los Angeles (90071) *(P-14164)*

City National Securities Inc .... C..... 310 888-6393
400 N Roxbury Dr Ste 400 Beverly Hills (90210) *(P-14165)*

City of Anaheim .... D..... 714 254-0125
201 S Anaheim Blvd Anaheim (92805) *(P-12212)*

City of Bakersfield .... C..... 661 852-7300
1001 Truxtun Ave Bakersfield (93301) *(P-19045)*

City of Burbank .... B..... 818 238-3550
164 W Magnolia Blvd Burbank (91502) *(P-12103)*

City of Cerritos .... C..... 562 916-8500
18125 Bloomfield Ave Cerritos (90703) *(P-20403)*

City of Coronado .... C..... 619 522-7380
101 B Ave Coronado (92118) *(P-12104)*

City of Culver City .... D..... 310 253-6525
4343 Duquesne Ave Culver City (90232) *(P-20404)*

City of Delano .... E..... 661 721-3352
1107 Lytle Ave Delano (93215) *(P-7648)*

City of Downey .... C..... 562 861-8211
8435 Firestone Blvd Downey (90241) *(P-17313)*

City of Glendale .... C..... 818 548-3945
633 E Broadway Ste 205 Glendale (91206) *(P-19563)*

City of Hope .... C..... 626 396-2900
209 Fair Oaks Ave South Pasadena (91030) *(P-17622)*

City of Hope .... B..... 213 202-5735
1500 Duarte Rd Duarte (91010) *(P-19319)*

City of Hope (PA)... B..... 626 256-4673
1500 Duarte Rd Duarte (91010) *(P-20013)*

City of Hope Corona, Duarte Also Called: City Hope National Medical Ctr *(P-18222)*

City of Hope Medical Group, South Pasadena Also Called: City of Hope *(P-17622)*

City of Industry, Chino Also Called: Balaji Trading Inc *(P-8468)*

City of Industry Sheet Plant, City Of Industry Also Called: Packaging Corporation America *(P-3123)*

City of Irvine .... C..... 949 724-7600
6427 Oak Cyn Irvine (92618) *(P-20150)*

City of Lancaster .... C..... 661 723-6071
43011 N 10th St W Lancaster (93534) *(P-17447)*

City of Long Beach .... C..... 562 570-4000
2525 Grand Ave Long Beach (90815) *(P-20413)*

City of Los Angeles .... A..... 310 732-3734
425 S Palos Verdes St San Pedro (90731) *(P-20418)*

City of Menifee .... D..... 951 672-6777
29844 Haun Rd Menifee (92586) *(P-20014)*

City of Norco .... D..... 951 270-5617
2870 Clark Ave Norco (92860) *(P-20329)*

City of Oxnard (PA).. C..... 805 385-7803
300 W 3rd St Oxnard (93030) *(P-20151)*

City of Paso Robles .... D..... 805 237-3999
747 Spring St Ste B Paso Robles (93446) *(P-613)*

City of Riverside .... C..... 951 351-6140
5950 Acorn St Riverside (92504) *(P-7649)*

City of San Diego .... C..... 619 527-7482
2781 Caminito Chollas San Diego (92105) *(P-614)*

ALPHABETIC

Employee Codes: A=Over 500 employees, B=251-500
C=101-250, D=51-100, E=20-50, F=10-19, G=1-9

2024 Southern California
Business Directory and Buyers Guide

© Mergent Inc. 1-800-342-5647
1041

City of San Diego .... C....... 619 758-2310
2392 Kincaid Rd San Diego (92101) **(P-10249)**

City of San Diego .... B....... 619 795-5000
100 Park Blvd San Diego (92101) **(P-17367)**

City of Santa Ana .... D....... 714 647-6545
1000 E Santa Ana Blvd Ste 107 Santa Ana (92701) **(P-19181)**

City of Santa Monica .... C....... 310 826-6712
1228 S Bundy Dr Los Angeles (90025) **(P-7650)**

City Orange Police Assn Inc .... C....... 714 457-5340
1107 N Batavia St Orange (92867) **(P-19376)**

CITY RESCUE MISSION, San Diego *Also Called: San Diego Rescue Mission Inc (P-19340)*

City Snta Mnica Wtr Trtmnt Pla, Los Angeles *Also Called: City of Santa Monica (P-7650)*

City Steel Heat Treating, Orange *Also Called: Thermal-Vac Technology Inc (P-5851)*

City Triangles, Los Angeles *Also Called: Jodi Kristopher LLC (P-2283)*

City Wire Cloth, Fontana *Also Called: Daniel Gerard Worldwide Inc (P-12546)*

City-Wide Electronic Systems Inc .... D....... 619 444-0219
440 Highland Ave El Cajon (92020) **(P-880)**

Civco, Rcho Sta Marg *Also Called: Capital Invstmnts Vntures Corp (P-19392)*

CIVIC THEATRE, San Diego *Also Called: San Diego Theatres Inc (P-14683)*

CJ Advisors Inc .... E....... 714 956-3388
6900 8th St Buena Park (90620) **(P-7799)**

CJ America, La Palma *Also Called: CJ Foods Inc (P-1871)*

CJ America Inc (HQ) .... D....... 213 338-2700
300 S Grand Ave Ste 1100 Los Angeles (90071) **(P-13360)**

CJ Berry Well Services MGT LLC .... A....... 661 589-5220
3752 Allen Rd Bakersfield (93314) **(P-338)**

CJ Foods Inc (HQ) .... D....... 714 367-7200
4 Centerpointe Dr Ste 100 La Palma (90623) **(P-1871)**

CJ Foods Mfg Beaumont Corp .... E....... 951 916-9300
415 Nicholas Rd Beaumont (92223) **(P-11208)**

CJ Logistics America LLC .... C....... 909 605-7233
12350 Philadelphia Ave Eastvale (91752) **(P-11450)**

CJ Logistics America LLC .... D....... 909 363-4354
1895 Marigold Ave Redlands (92374) **(P-11475)**

CJ Logistics America LLC .... C....... 540 377-2302
5690 Industrial Pkwy San Bernardino (92407) **(P-11747)**

CJ Precision Industries Inc .... E....... 562 426-3708
2817 Cherry Ave Signal Hill (90755) **(P-7800)**

CJ Wilson BMW Mtcyc Murrieta, Murrieta *Also Called: Wilson Cycles Sports Corp (P-13848)*

CJd Construction Svcs Inc .... E....... 626 335-1116
503 E Route 66 Glendora (91740) **(P-339)**

Cji Process Systems Inc .... D....... 562 777-0614
12000 Clark St Santa Fe Springs (90670) **(P-6136)**

CK Manufacturing & Trading Inc .... E....... 949 529-3400
3 Holland Irvine (92618) **(P-2947)**

CK Technologies Inc (PA) .... E....... 805 987-4801
3629 Vista Mercado Camarillo (93012) **(P-10123)**

Ckd Industries Inc .... F....... 714 871-5600
501 E Jamie Ave La Habra (90631) **(P-6507)**

Ckkm Inc (PA) .... E....... 951 371-8484
265 Radio Rd Corona (92879) **(P-12540)**

Cks Solution Incorporated .... E....... 714 292-6307
556 Vanguard Way Ste C Brea (92821) **(P-9018)**

Ckt, Camarillo *Also Called: CK Technologies Inc (P-10123)*

CL Knox Inc .... D....... 661 837-0477
34933 Imperial Ave Bakersfield (93308) **(P-340)**

CL Solutions LLC .... D....... 714 597-6499
1900 S Susan St Santa Ana (92704) **(P-5314)**

Cla-Val Co, Costa Mesa *Also Called: Griswold Industries (P-5795)*

Clack Corporation .... D....... 562 789-1702
8728 Dice Rd Santa Fe Springs (90670) **(P-4991)**

Claremont Club, The, Claremont *Also Called: Claremont Tennis Club (P-17478)*

Claremont Pl Assisted Living, Claremont *Also Called: Sunrise Senior Living MGT Inc (P-19303)*

Claremont Tennis Club .... C....... 909 625-9515
1777 Monte Vista Ave Claremont (91711) **(P-17478)**

Claremont Toyota, Claremont *Also Called: R&C Motor Corporation (P-17037)*

Clarendon Specialty Fas Inc .... D....... 714 842-2603
2180 Temple Ave Long Beach (90804) **(P-12718)**

Clariant Corporation .... E....... 909 825-1793
926 S 8th St Colton (92324) **(P-3169)**

Clariant Corporation .... F....... 562 322-6647
3355 Olive Ave Signal Hill (90755) **(P-4519)**

Clarient Inc .... C....... 949 445-7300
33171 Paseo Cerveza San Juan Capistrano (92675) **(P-18542)**

Clarient Diagnostic Svcs Inc .... C....... 888 443-3310
31 Columbia Aliso Viejo (92656) **(P-19963)**

Clarion Hotel, Anaheim *Also Called: Comfort California Inc (P-15121)*

Clarios LLC .... E....... 805 522-5555
4100 Guardian St Simi Valley (93063) **(P-2922)**

Clarios LLC .... E....... 760 200-5225
39312 Leopard St Ste A Palm Desert (92211) **(P-2923)**

Clariphy Communications Inc (DH) .... D....... 949 861-3074
15485 Sand Canyon Ave Irvine (92618) **(P-8779)**

Clarity Design Inc .... F....... 858 746-3500
16885 Via Del Campo Ct Ste 200 San Diego (92127) **(P-16433)**

Clark - Pacific Corporation .... E....... 626 962-8755
9367 Holly Rd Adelanto (92301) **(P-5403)**

Clark - Pacific Corporation .... E....... 909 823-1433
4684 Ontario Mills Pkwy Ste 200 Ontario (91764) **(P-5404)**

Clark - Pacific Corporation .... E....... 626 962-8751
131 Los Angeles St Irwindale (91706) **(P-5405)**

Clark Cnstr Group - Cal Inc .... B....... 714 754-0764
18201 Von Karman Ave Ste 800 Irvine (92612) **(P-498)**

Clark Cnstr Group - Cal LP .... B....... 714 429-9779
18201 Von Karman Ave Ste 800 Irvine (92612) **(P-542)**

Clark Steel Fabricators Inc .... E....... 619 390-1502
12610 Vigilante Rd Lakeside (92040) **(P-6353)**

Clarkdietrich Building Systems, Riverside *Also Called: Clarkwestern Dietrich Building (P-6214)*

Clarkwestern Dietrich Building .... E....... 951 360-3500
6510 General Rd Riverside (92509) **(P-6214)**

Clary Corporation .... E....... 626 359-4486
150 E Huntington Dr Monrovia (91016) **(P-9019)**

Classe Party Rentals, Rancho Cucamonga *Also Called: Sunn America Inc (P-15800)*

Classic Bev Southern Cal LLC .... B....... 626 934-3700
120 Puente Ave City Of Industry (91746) **(P-13463)**

Classic Camaro Inc .... C....... 714 847-6887
18460 Gothard St Huntington Beach (92648) **(P-13857)**

Classic Components, Torrance *Also Called: I C Class Components Corp (P-12668)*

Classic Containers Inc .... B....... 909 930-3610
1700 S Hellman Ave Ontario (91761) **(P-4857)**

Classic Cosmetics Inc (PA) .... C....... 818 773-9042
9530 De Soto Ave Chatsworth (91311) **(P-4388)**

Classic Firebird, Huntington Beach *Also Called: Classic Camaro Inc (P-13857)*

Classic Litho & Design Inc .... E....... 310 224-5200
340 Maple Ave Torrance (90503) **(P-3530)**

Classic Party Rentals, Inglewood *Also Called: After-Party2 Inc (P-15769)*

Classic Party Rentals, Inglewood *Also Called: After-Party6 Inc (P-15770)*

Classic Party Rentals, Inglewood *Also Called: Classic Party Rentals Inc (P-15775)*

Classic Party Rentals Inc .... A....... 310 966-4900
901 W Hillcrest Blvd A Inglewood (90301) **(P-15775)**

Classic Slip Covers Inc .... F....... 323 583-0804
4300 District Blvd Vernon (90058) **(P-2469)**

Classic Tents .... E....... 310 328-5060
19119 S Reyes Ave Compton (90221) **(P-7602)**

Classic Tents, Compton *Also Called: Classic Tents (P-7602)*

Classic Tents, Torrance *Also Called: Classic/Prime Inc (P-15776)*

Classic Wire Cut Company Inc .... C....... 661 257-0558
28210 Constellation Rd Valencia (91355) **(P-7801)**

Classic/Prime Inc .... D....... 310 328-5060
540 Hawaii Ave Torrance (90503) **(P-15776)**

Classy, San Diego *Also Called: Classy Inc (P-16202)*

Classy Inc .... C....... 619 961-1892
350 10th Ave Ste 1300 San Diego (92101) **(P-16202)**

Clauss Construction .... D....... 619 390-4940
9911 Maine Ave Lakeside (92040) **(P-1130)**

Clay Corona Company (PA) .... E....... 951 277-2667
22079 Knabe Rd Corona (92883) **(P-543)**

Clay Dunn Enterprises Inc .... C....... 310 549-1698
1606 E Carson St Carson (90745) **(P-754)**

Clay Lacy Aviation Inc (PA).......................................B...... 818 989-2900
7435 Valjean Ave Van Nuys (91406) *(P-11691)*

Claybourne Industries Inc ....E...... 951 675-4508
5055 Western Way Perris (92571) *(P-11209)*

Clayton Industries, City Of Industry Also Called: Clayton Manufacturing Company *(P-7386)*

Clayton Manufacturing Company (PA).....................C...... 626 443-9381
17477 Hurley St City Of Industry (91744) *(P-7386)*

Clayton Manufacturing Inc (HQ).............................D...... 626 443-9381
17477 Hurley St City Of Industry (91744) *(P-7387)*

CLC Work Gear, South Gate Also Called: Custom Leathercraft Mfg LLC *(P-5306)*

Clean Cut Technologies, Anaheim Also Called: Oliver Healthcare Packaging Co *(P-12802)*

Clean Cut Technologies LLC .... D...... 714 864-3500
1145 N Ocean Cir Anaheim (92806) *(P-4878)*

Clean Energy .... A...... 949 437-1000
4675 Macarthur Ct Ste 800 Newport Beach (92660) *(P-12081)*

Clean Wave Management Inc .... E...... 949 370-0740
1291 Puerta Del Sol San Clemente (92673) *(P-7298)*

Cleanroom Film & Bags, Placentia Also Called: CF&b Manufacturing Inc *(P-3180)*

Cleanstreet LLC .... C...... 800 225-7316
1918 W 169th St Gardena (90247) *(P-12208)*

Cleantek Electric Inc .... E...... 424 400-3315
403 W 21st St San Pedro (90731) *(P-881)*

Clear Blue Energy Corp .... D...... 858 451-1549
17150 Via Del Campo Ste 203 San Diego (92127) *(P-8358)*

Clear Channel Entertainment, Beverly Hills Also Called: Live Nation Worldwide Inc *(P-17376)*

Clear Channel Radio Sales, Los Angeles Also Called: Katz Millennium Sls & Mktg Inc *(P-8527)*

Clear Group Inc .... C...... 603 325-5600
408 N Avalon Blvd Los Angeles (90074) *(P-15119)*

Clear Image Printing Inc .... E...... 818 547-4684
12744 San Fernando Rd Sylmar (91342) *(P-3531)*

Clear Sign & Design Inc .... F...... 760 736-8111
170 Navajo St San Marcos (92078) *(P-1147)*

Clear View Sanitarium, Gardena Also Called: Clear View Sanitarium Inc *(P-18117)*

Clear View Sanitarium Inc .... C...... 310 538-2323
15823 S Western Ave Gardena (90247) *(P-18117)*

Clear-Ad Inc .... E...... 866 627-9718
2410 W 3rd St Santa Ana (92703) *(P-4992)*

Clearedge Lending .... D...... 562 708-7706
65 Enterprise Aliso Viejo (92656) *(P-14307)*

Clearlake Capital Group LP (PA).............................B...... 310 400-8800
233 Wilshire Blvd Ste 800 Santa Monica (90401) *(P-14962)*

Clearlake Capital Partners .... A...... 310 400-8800
233 Wilshire Blvd Ste 800 Santa Monica (90401) *(P-16203)*

Clearpath Lending .... C...... 949 502-3577
15635 Alton Pkwy Ste 300 Irvine (92618) *(P-14357)*

Clearpath Lending, Irvine Also Called: Clearpath Lending *(P-14357)*

Clearpathgps, Santa Barbara Also Called: Clearpathgps LLC *(P-8963)*

Clearpathgps LLC .... E...... 805 979-3442
3463 State St # 494 Santa Barbara (93105) *(P-8963)*

Clearpoint Neuro Inc (PA).....................................D...... 949 900-6833
120 S Sierra Ave Ste 100 Solana Beach (92075) *(P-10482)*

Clearview Capital LLC .... A...... 310 806-9555
12100 Wilshire Blvd Ste 800 Los Angeles (90025) *(P-15025)*

Cleatech LLC .... E...... 714 754-6668
2106 N Glassell St Orange (92865) *(P-10091)*

Clegg Industries Inc .... C...... 310 225-3800
19032 S Vermont Ave Gardena (90248) *(P-11103)*

Clegg Promo, Gardena Also Called: Clegg Industries Inc *(P-11103)*

Clemson Distribution Inc (PA)...............................E...... 909 595-2770
20722 Currier Rd City Of Industry (91789) *(P-13253)*

Cleughs Frozen Foods Inc .... E
6571 Altura Blvd Ste 200 Buena Park (90620) *(P-1367)*

Cleveland Tramrail So Calif, Corona Also Called: General Conveyor Inc *(P-17129)*

Clickup, San Diego Also Called: Mango Technologies Inc *(P-16069)*

Cliff View Terrace Inc .... D...... 805 682-7443
623 W Junipero St Santa Barbara (93105) *(P-19249)*

Cliffdale Manufacturing LLC .... C...... 818 341-3344
20409 Prairie St Chatsworth (91311) *(P-9915)*

Cliftonlarsonallen LLP .... D...... 310 273-2501
1925 Century Park E 16th Fl Los Angeles (90067) *(P-19761)*

Clima-Tech Inc .... D...... 909 613-5513
1820 Town And Country Dr Norco (92860) *(P-17062)*

Clinch-On Cornerbead Company, Orange Also Called: Continuous Coating Corp *(P-6608)*

Clinic Inc .... D...... 323 730-1920
3834 S Western Ave Los Angeles (90062) *(P-17623)*

Clinica Sierra Vista .... D...... 661 845-3717
8787 Hall Rd Lamont (93241) *(P-17624)*

Clinica Sierra Vista (PA).......................................D...... 661 635-3050
1430 Truxtun Ave Ste 400 Bakersfield (93301) *(P-17625)*

Clinica Srra Vsta Adult Mntal, Lamont Also Called: Clinica Sierra Vista *(P-17624)*

Clinical Research, Rancho Mirage Also Called: Eisenhower Medical Center *(P-18547)*

Clinical Translational RES Ctr, Los Angeles Also Called: Cedars-Sinai Medical Center *(P-18202)*

Clinicomp International Inc (PA).............................D...... 858 546-8202
9655 Towne Centre Dr San Diego (92121) *(P-16434)*

Clinics On Demand Inc .... D...... 310 709-7355
11000 Wilshire Blvd Los Angeles (90024) *(P-18602)*

Cliniqa, San Marcos Also Called: Cliniqa Corporation *(P-4311)*

Cliniqa Corporation .... D...... 760 744-1900
258 La Moree Rd San Marcos (92078) *(P-4310)*

Cliniqa Corporation (HQ).....................................E...... 760 744-1900
495 Enterprise St San Marcos (92078) *(P-4311)*

Clio Inc .... E...... 562 926-3724
12981 166th St Cerritos (90703) *(P-6802)*

Clipboard Health, Covina Also Called: Twomagnets Inc *(P-15901)*

Clipper Oil Inc .... E...... 619 692-9701
2040 Harbor Island Dr Ste 203 San Diego (92101) *(P-13449)*

Clipper Oil Company, San Diego Also Called: Clipper Oil Inc *(P-13449)*

Clipper Windpower, Carpinteria Also Called: Clipper Windpower PLC *(P-6879)*

Clipper Windpower PLC .... A...... 805 690-3275
6305 Carpinteria Ave Ste 300 Carpinteria (93013) *(P-6879)*

Clique Brands Inc (PA)...E...... 310 623-6916
750 N San Vicente Blvd Ste 800 West Hollywood (90069) *(P-3351)*

Clm Group Inc .... E...... 818 349-2549
20730 Dearborn St Chatsworth (91311) *(P-4389)*

Clockparts, Culver City Also Called: Innovation Specialties *(P-16847)*

Clorox, Redlands Also Called: Clorox Manufacturing Company *(P-4348)*

Clorox Manufacturing Company .... D...... 909 307-2756
2300 W San Bernardino Ave Redlands (92374) *(P-4348)*

Closet Factory Inc (PA)...C...... 310 516-7000
12800 S Bdwy Los Angeles (90061) *(P-1148)*

Closet World Inc .... D...... 626 855-0846
14438 Don Julian Rd City Of Industry (91746) *(P-1008)*

Closet World, The, City Of Industry Also Called: Home Organizers Inc *(P-1015)*

Closets By Design, City Of Industry Also Called: Closets By Design Inc *(P-2948)*

Closets By Design Inc .... E...... 562 699-9945
3860 Capitol Ave City Of Industry (90601) *(P-2948)*

Clothing Illustrated Inc (PA).................................E...... 213 403-9950
836 Traction Ave Los Angeles (90013) *(P-2314)*

Clothng/Pparel/Uniform/ppe Mfg, Vernon Also Called: David Grment Ctng Fsing Svc In *(P-2316)*

Cloud Automation Division, Aliso Viejo Also Called: Quest Software Inc *(P-16363)*

Cloud B Inc .... E...... 310 781-3833
150 W Walnut St Ste 100 Gardena (90248) *(P-10937)*

Cloud Nine Comforts, Los Angeles Also Called: Universal Cushion Company Inc *(P-2489)*

Cloud Sftwr Group Holdings Inc .... F...... 800 424-8749
7414 Hollister Ave Goleta Los Angeles (90074) *(P-16204)*

Cloud9 Esports Inc .... D...... 424 256-8391
2720 Neilson Way Unt 5697 Santa Monica (90405) *(P-20152)*

Cloudbeds, San Diego Also Called: Digital Arbitrage Dist Inc *(P-16225)*

Cloudcover, Irvine Also Called: Cloudcover Iot Inc *(P-16205)*

Cloudcover Iot Inc .... E...... 888 511-2022
14 Goodyear Ste 125b Irvine (92618) *(P-16205)*

Cloudradiant Corp (PA)...C...... 408 256-1527
12 Fuchsia Lake Forest (92630) *(P-13534)*

Cloudstaff LLC .... B...... 888 551-5339
26895 Aliso Creek Rd # B-209 Aliso Viejo (92656) *(P-15502)*

Cloudvirga Inc .... D...... 949 799-2643
5291 California Ave Ste 300 Irvine (92617) *(P-16206)*

Clougherty Packing LLC (DH).................................B...... 323 583-4621
3049 E Vernon Ave Vernon (90058) *(P-1193)*

Employee Codes: A=Over 500 employees, B=251-500
C=101-250, D=51-100, E=20-50, F=10-19, G=1-9

2024 Southern California
Business Directory and Buyers Guide

© Mergent Inc. 1-800-342-5647

1043

ALPHABETIC

Clover Envmtl Solutions LLC .... E...... 760 357-9277
315 Weakley St Bldg 3 Calexico (92231) *(P-10863)*

Clover Envmtl Solutions LLC .... A...... 815 431-8100
9414 Eton Ave Chatsworth (91311) *(P-12848)*

CLP Inc (PA) .... E...... **619 444-3105**
1546 E Main St El Cajon (92021) *(P-17081)*

Cls Landscape Management, Montclair *Also Called: Cls Landscape Management Inc (P-222)*

Cls Landscape Management Inc .... B...... 909 628-3005
4329 State St Ste B Montclair (91763) *(P-222)*

Cls Trnsprttion Los Angles LLC (HQ) .... C...... 310 414-8189
600 S Allied Way El Segundo (90245) *(P-11380)*

Club Car LLC .... E...... 951 735-4675
1203 Hall Ave Riverside (92509) *(P-9932)*

Club Speed LLC (PA) .... E...... **951 817-7073**
300 Spectrum Center Dr Irvine (92618) *(P-16207)*

Clutter Inc (PA) .... C...... **800 805-4023**
3526 Hayden Ave Culver City (90232) *(P-15503)*

Clw Foods LLC .... F...... 323 432-4600
3425 E Vernon Ave Vernon (90058) *(P-1872)*

CM Laundry LLC .... D...... 310 436-6170
14919 S Figueroa St Gardena (90248) *(P-15474)*

CMA Dish Machines, Garden Grove *Also Called: Chemical Methods Assoc LLC (P-7647)*

Cmb Laboratory, Cypress *Also Called: Consolted Med Bo-Analysis Inc (P-18543)*

CMC, Goleta *Also Called: CMC Rescue Inc (P-14126)*

CMC Rebar West .... D...... 714 692-7082
10840 Norwalk Blvd Santa Fe Springs (90670) *(P-499)*

CMC Rebar West .... C...... 858 737-7700
7326 Mission Gorge Rd San Diego (92120) *(P-500)*

CMC Rebar West .... C...... 909 713-1130
5425 Industrial Pkwy San Bernardino (92407) *(P-12541)*

CMC Rescue Inc .... D...... 805 562-9120
6740 Cortona Dr Goleta (93117) *(P-14126)*

CMC Steel California, San Bernardino *Also Called: Tamco (P-5604)*

CMC Steel Us LLC .... E...... 909 646-7827
5425 Industrial Pkwy San Bernardino (92407) *(P-6395)*

Cmf Inc .... D...... 714 637-2409
1317 W Grove Ave Orange (92865) *(P-1039)*

CMH Records Inc .... F...... 323 663-8098
2898 Rowena Ave Ste 201 Los Angeles (90039) *(P-8453)*

CMI, Irvine *Also Called: Cooper Microelectronics Inc (P-8783)*

CMI, San Clemente *Also Called: Composite Manufacturing Inc (P-10484)*

CMI Integrated Tech Inc .... E
11248 Playa Ct Culver City (90230) *(P-8138)*

Cmk Manufacturing LLC .... E
10375 Wilshire Blvd Apt 2h Los Angeles (90024) *(P-2047)*

Cmre Financial Services Inc .... B...... 714 528-3200
3075 E Imperial Hwy Ste 200 Brea (92821) *(P-15609)*

CMS, Simi Valley *Also Called: Computerized Mgt Svcs Inc (P-19762)*

CMS Circuit Solutions Inc .... E...... 951 698-4452
41549 Cherry St Murrieta (92562) *(P-8663)*

CMS Products LLC .... E...... 714 424-5520
29620 Skyline Dr Tehachapi (93561) *(P-7517)*

CN Publishing Group, Irvine *Also Called: Cycle News Inc (P-3268)*

Cnc Machining Inc .... E...... 805 681-8855
510 S Fairview Ave Goleta (93117) *(P-7802)*

Cnet Express .... C...... 949 357-5475
15134 Indiana Ave Apt 38 Paramount (90723) *(P-11451)*

Cni Mfg Inc .... F...... 626 962-6646
15627 Arrow Hwy Irwindale (91706) *(P-7803)*

Cni Thl Propco Fe LLC .... D...... 661 325-9700
5101 California Ave Bakersfield (93309) *(P-15120)*

Cnn, Los Angeles *Also Called: Cnn America Inc (P-11942)*

Cnn America Inc .... C...... 323 993-5000
6430 W Sunset Blvd Ste 300 Los Angeles (90028) *(P-11942)*

Cns Inc .... D...... 661 872-3408
5215 Ashe Rd Bakersfield (93313) *(P-17626)*

CNT Acquisition Corp (DH) .... E...... **949 380-6100**
1 Enterprise Aliso Viejo (92656) *(P-8780)*

Co Ltd, All Nippon Airways, Torrance *Also Called: Nippon Express (P-11788)*

Co-Op Solutions, Rancho Cucamonga *Also Called: CU Cooperative Systems Inc (P-14247)*

Co-Production Intl Inc .... A...... 619 429-4344
8716 Sherwood Ter San Diego (92154) *(P-20153)*

Co-West Commodities, San Bernardino *Also Called: Park West Enterprises Inc (P-1569)*

Coach Usa Inc .... D...... 626 357-7912
5640 Peck Rd Arcadia (91006) *(P-11416)*

Coachella Valley Water Dst, Palm Desert *Also Called: Coachlla Vly Wtr Dst Pub Fclti (P-12116)*

Coachlla Vly Wtr Dst Pub Fclti .... C...... 760 398-2651
75525 Hovley Ln E Palm Desert (92260) *(P-12115)*

Coachlla Vly Wtr Dst Pub Fclti (PA) .... C...... **760 398-2651**
75515 Hovley Ln E Palm Desert (92211) *(P-12116)*

Coachworks Holdings Inc .... F...... 951 684-9585
1863 Service Ct Riverside (92507) *(P-9282)*

Coalition Technologies LLC .... E...... 310 905-8268
445 S Figueroa St Ste 3100 Los Angeles (90071) *(P-15995)*

Coast 2 Coast Cables LLC .... C...... 714 666-1062
3162 E La Palma Ave Ste D Anaheim (92806) *(P-5740)*

Coast Aerospace, Placentia *Also Called: Coast Aerospace Mfg Inc (P-7060)*

Coast Aerospace Mfg Inc .... E...... 714 893-8066
950 Richfield Rd Placentia (92870) *(P-7060)*

Coast Aluminum, Santa Fe Springs *Also Called: Coast Aluminum Inc (P-12542)*

Coast Aluminum Inc (PA) .... C...... **562 946-6061**
10628 Fulton Wells Ave Santa Fe Springs (90670) *(P-12542)*

Coast Citrus Distributors (PA) .... D...... **619 661-7950**
7597 Bristow Ct San Diego (92154) *(P-13316)*

Coast Composites LLC .... E...... 949 455-0665
7 Burroughs Irvine (92618) *(P-7804)*

Coast Composites LLC (PA) .... D...... **949 455-0665**
5 Burroughs Irvine (92618) *(P-9659)*

Coast Custom Cable, Carson *Also Called: Belden Inc (P-5731)*

Coast Flagstone Co .... D...... 310 829-4010
1810 Colorado Ave Santa Monica (90404) *(P-5527)*

Coast Group Financial, San Marcos *Also Called: Centurion Group Inc (P-14374)*

Coast Index 965, Newbury Park *Also Called: Coast Index Co Inc (P-3220)*

Coast Index Co Inc .... D...... 805 499-6844
850 Lawrence Dr Newbury Park (91320) *(P-3220)*

Coast Iron & Steel Co .... E...... 562 946-4421
12300 Lakeland Rd Santa Fe Springs (90670) *(P-1103)*

Coast Label Company, Fountain Valley *Also Called: Moreland Manufacturing Inc (P-3788)*

Coast Magnetics, Los Angeles *Also Called: A M I/Coast Magnetics Inc (P-8932)*

Coast News Inc .... E...... 760 436-9737
531 Encinitas Blvd Ste 204 Encinitas (92024) *(P-3266)*

Coast Packing Company .... D...... 323 277-7700
3275 E Vernon Ave Vernon (90058) *(P-1570)*

Coast Plastics Inc (PA) .... F...... **626 812-9174**
4711 E Guasti Rd Ontario (91761) *(P-13411)*

Coast Plating Inc (PA) .... E...... **323 770-0240**
128 W 154th St Gardena (90248) *(P-6604)*

Coast Produce Company (PA) .... C...... **213 955-4900**
1791 Bay St Los Angeles (90021) *(P-13317)*

Coast Rock Products Inc .... E...... 805 925-2505
1625 E Donovan Rd Santa Maria (93454) *(P-12351)*

Coast Sheet Metal Inc .... C...... 949 645-2224
990 W 17th St Costa Mesa (92627) *(P-6215)*

Coast Sign Display, Anaheim *Also Called: Coast Sign Incorporated (P-11104)*

Coast Sign Incorporated .... C...... 714 520-9144
1500 W Embassy St Anaheim (92802) *(P-11104)*

Coast To Coast Circuits Inc (PA) .... E...... **714 891-9441**
5331 Mcfadden Ave Huntington Beach (92649) *(P-8664)*

Coast To Coast Cmpt Pdts Inc .... D...... 805 244-9500
4277 Valley Fair St Simi Valley (93063) *(P-13970)*

Coast To Coast Met Finshg Corp .... E...... 626 282-2122
401 S Raymond Ave Alhambra (91803) *(P-6605)*

Coast Tropical, San Diego *Also Called: Coast Citrus Distributors (P-13316)*

Coast Wire & Plastic Tech LLC .... A...... 310 639-9473
1048 E Burgrove St Carson (90746) *(P-9199)*

Coast/A C M, Torrance *Also Called: Coast/Dvnced Chip Mgnetics Inc (P-8937)*

Coast/Dvnced Chip Mgnetics Inc .... F...... 310 370-8188
4225 Spencer St Torrance (90503) *(P-8937)*

Coastal Alliance Holdings Inc .... C...... 562 370-1000
1650 Ximeno Ave Ste 120 Long Beach (90804) *(P-14766)*

Mergent email: customerrelations@mergent.com
1044

2024 Southern California
Business Directory and Buyers Guide

(P-0000) Products & Services Section entry number
(PA)=Parent Co (HQ)=Headquarters (DH)=Div Headquarters

Coastal Building Services Inc .... B...... 714 775-2855
1433 W Central Park Ave N Anaheim (92802) *(P-15700)*

Coastal Cmnty Senior Care LLC .... C...... 562 596-4884
5500 E Atherton St Ste 216 Long Beach (90815) *(P-18603)*

Coastal Cnting Indus Scale Inc .... E...... 805 487-0403
270 Quail Ct Ste 100 Santa Paula (93060) *(P-7110)*

Coastal Cocktails Inc (PA).......... **D...... 949 250-8951**
1920 E Deere Ave Ste 100 Santa Ana (92705) *(P-13361)*

Coastal Community Hospital, Santa Ana *Also Called: Health Resources Corp (P-18276)*

Coastal Component Inds Inc .... E...... 714 685-6677
133 E Bristol Ln Orange (92865) *(P-9020)*

Coastal Connections .... E...... 805 644-5051
2085 Sperry Ave Ste B Ventura (93003) *(P-8470)*

Coastal Container Inc .... E...... 562 801-4595
8455 Loch Lomond Dr Pico Rivera (90660) *(P-3091)*

Coastal Doors .... E...... 562 665-5585
21818 S Wilmington Ave Ste 407 Carson (90810) *(P-13570)*

Coastal Enterprises .... E...... 714 771-4969
1925 W Collins Ave Orange (92867) *(P-3931)*

Coastal Enterprises, Fountain Valley *Also Called: Joy Products California Inc (P-11052)*

Coastal Enterprises Company, Orange *Also Called: Coastal Enterprises (P-3931)*

Coastal International, Tustin *Also Called: Coastal Intl Holdings LLC (P-16803)*

Coastal Intl Holdings LLC .... B...... 714 635-1200
2832 Walnut Ave Ste B Tustin (92780) *(P-16803)*

Coastal Pacific Fd Distrs Inc .... D...... 909 947-2066
1520 E Mission Blvd Ste B Ontario (91761) *(P-11567)*

Coastal Pacific Foods, Ontario *Also Called: Coastal Pacific Fd Distrs Inc (P-11567)*

Coastal Rdtion Onclogy Med Gro .... D...... 805 494-4483
1240 S Westlake Blvd Ste 103 Westlake Village (91361) *(P-17627)*

Coastal Tag & Label Inc .... D...... 562 946-4318
13233 Barton Cir Whittier (90605) *(P-3745)*

Coastal The, Sherman Oaks *Also Called: Coastal Tile Inc (P-1004)*

Coastal Tile Inc .... D...... 818 988-6134
13226 Moorpark St Apt 104 Sherman Oaks (91423) *(P-1004)*

Coastal View Halthcare Ctr LLC .... D...... 805 642-4101
4904 Telegraph Rd Ventura (93003) *(P-17902)*

Coastal View Healthcare Center, Ventura *Also Called: Coastal View Halthcare Ctr LLC (P-17902)*

Coastal Wood Products, City Of Industry *Also Called: McConnell Cabinets Inc (P-2667)*

Coasthills Credit Union (PA).......... D...... 805 733-7600
1075 E Betteravia Rd Santa Maria (93454) *(P-14246)*

Coastline Cnstr & Awng Co Inc .... D...... 714 891-9798
5742 Research Dr Huntington Beach (92649) *(P-426)*

Coastline Equipment, Oxnard *Also Called: Bragg Investment Company Inc (P-12235)*

Coastline International .... C...... 888 748-7177
1207 Bangor St San Diego (92106) *(P-10797)*

Coastline Metal Finishing Corp .... D...... 714 895-9099
7061 Patterson Dr Garden Grove (92841) *(P-6606)*

Coastwide Tag & Label Co Inc .... E...... 323 721-1501
7647 Industry Ave Pico Rivera (90660) *(P-3746)*

Coatinc United States Inc .... E...... 619 638-7261
325 W Washington St Ste 2340 San Diego (92103) *(P-4601)*

Coating Specialties Inc .... F...... 310 639-6900
815 E Rosecrans Ave Los Angeles (90059) *(P-9660)*

Coatings Resource, Huntington Beach *Also Called: Laird Coatings Corporation (P-4492)*

Cobe Chemical Co Inc .... D...... 877 691-3590
1016 S Vail Ave Montebello (90640) *(P-4390)*

Cobe Laboratories, Montebello *Also Called: Cobe Chemical Co Inc (P-4390)*

Cobham, San Diego *Also Called: Remec Defense & Space Inc (P-10060)*

Cobrapro, Orange *Also Called: Word & Brown Insurance Administrators Inc (P-14648)*

Coc Inc, Los Angeles *Also Called: Colon Manufacturing Inc (P-2235)*

Coca-Cola, Ontario *Also Called: Coca-Cola Company (P-1691)*

Coca-Cola, Victorville *Also Called: Reyes Coca-Cola Bottling LLC (P-1725)*

Coca-Cola, Ventura *Also Called: Reyes Coca-Cola Bottling LLC (P-1726)*

Coca-Cola, Santa Maria *Also Called: Reyes Coca-Cola Bottling LLC (P-1727)*

Coca-Cola, Santa Maria *Also Called: Reyes Coca-Cola Bottling LLC (P-1728)*

Coca-Cola, El Centro *Also Called: Reyes Coca-Cola Bottling LLC (P-1729)*

Coca-Cola, Rancho Cucamonga *Also Called: Reyes Coca-Cola Bottling LLC (P-1731)*

Coca-Cola, San Diego *Also Called: Reyes Coca-Cola Bottling LLC (P-1732)*

Coca-Cola, Los Angeles *Also Called: Reyes Coca-Cola Bottling LLC (P-1734)*

Coca-Cola, Orange *Also Called: Reyes Coca-Cola Bottling LLC (P-1735)*

Coca-Cola, Irvine *Also Called: Reyes Coca-Cola Bottling LLC (P-1736)*

Coca-Cola, Coachella *Also Called: Reyes Coca-Cola Bottling LLC (P-1737)*

Coca-Cola, Downey *Also Called: Reyes Coca-Cola Bottling LLC (P-1738)*

Coca-Cola, Santa Maria *Also Called: Tognazzini Beverage Service (P-1742)*

Coca-Cola, Sylmar *Also Called: Reyes Coca-Cola Bottling LLC (P-13391)*

Coca-Cola Company .... D...... 909 975-5200
1650 S Vintage Ave Ontario (91761) *(P-1691)*

Cockram Construction Inc .... B...... 818 650-0999
16340 Roscoe Blvd Van Nuys (91406) *(P-20154)*

Cod USA Inc .... E...... 949 381-7367
25954 Commercentre Dr Lake Forest (92630) *(P-2924)*

Coda Automotive Inc .... E...... 949 830-7000
14 Auto Center Dr Irvine (92618) *(P-9372)*

Coda Automotive Inc .... E...... 310 820-3611
12101 W Olympic Blvd Los Angeles (90064) *(P-9373)*

Coda Automotive Inc .... E...... 619 291-2040
1441 Camino Del Rio S San Diego (92108) *(P-9374)*

CODA AUTOMOTIVE INC, Irvine *Also Called: Coda Automotive Inc (P-9372)*

CODA AUTOMOTIVE INC, Los Angeles *Also Called: Coda Automotive Inc (P-9373)*

CODA AUTOMOTIVE INC, San Diego *Also Called: Coda Automotive Inc (P-9374)*

Coda Energy, Glendale *Also Called: Coda Energy Holdings LLC (P-9200)*

Coda Energy Holdings LLC .... F...... 626 775-3900
111 N Artsakh Ave Ste 300 Glendale (91206) *(P-9200)*

Coda Mexico, San Diego *Also Called: Eleanor Rigby Leather Co (P-5308)*

Codan US, Santa Ana *Also Called: Codan US Corporation (P-4993)*

Codan US Corporation .... C...... 714 545-2111
3501 W Sunflower Ave Santa Ana (92704) *(P-4993)*

Codazen, Irvine *Also Called: Codazen Inc (P-15996)*

Codazen Inc .... D...... 949 916-6266
60 Bunsen Irvine (92618) *(P-15996)*

Code Red Fire Inc .... E...... 323 726-0982
544 Montebello Way Montebello (90640) *(P-16725)*

Cody Cylinder Service LLC .... E...... 951 786-3650
1393 Dodson Way Ste A Riverside (92507) *(P-7805)*

Codysales Inc .... F...... 951 786-3650
1393 Dodson Way Ste A Riverside (92507) *(P-7273)*

Cofa Media Group LLC .... D...... 877 293-2007
5650 El Camino Real Ste 100a Carlsbad (92008) *(P-16487)*

Coffee Klatch, Rancho Cucamonga *Also Called: Klatch Coffee Inc (P-14020)*

Coffman Specialties Inc (PA).......... **C...... 858 536-3100**
9685 Via Excelencia Ste 200 San Diego (92126) *(P-1066)*

Cofiroute, Irvine *Also Called: Cofiroute Usa LLC (P-11825)*

Cofiroute Usa LLC .... C...... 949 754-0198
100 Progress Ste 110 Irvine (92618) *(P-11825)*

Cognella Inc .... D...... 858 552-1120
3970 Sorrento Valley Blvd Ste 500 San Diego (92121) *(P-3402)*

Cognizant Trztto Sftwr Group I .... C...... 714 481-0396
3631 S Harbor Blvd Ste 200 Santa Ana (92704) *(P-16435)*

Coherent Aerospace & Def Inc .... D...... 714 247-7100
14192 Chambers Rd Tustin (92780) *(P-10311)*

Coherent Aerospace & Defense Inc (HQ).......... **C...... 951 926-2994**
36570 Briggs Rd Murrieta (92563) *(P-9963)*

Cohu, Poway *Also Called: Cohu Inc (P-10191)*

Cohu Inc (PA).......... **C...... 858 848-8100**
12367 Crosthwaite Cir Poway (92064) *(P-10191)*

Cohu Interface Solutions LLC (HQ).......... **D...... 858 848-8000**
12367 Crosthwaite Cir Poway (92064) *(P-10192)*

Coi Ceramics Inc .... E...... 858 621-5700
7130 Miramar Rd Ste 100b San Diego (92121) *(P-9661)*

Coi Pharmaceuticals Inc .... E...... 858 750-4700
11099 N Torrey Pines Rd Ste 290 La Jolla (92037) *(P-19831)*

Coi Rubber Products Inc .... B...... 626 965-9966
19255 San Jose Ave Unit D-1 City Of Industry (91748) *(P-4759)*

Coic, San Diego *Also Called: Coi Ceramics Inc (P-9661)*

Colbi Technologies Inc .... E...... 714 505-9544
13891 Newport Ave Ste 150 Tustin (92780) *(P-3437)*

Colbrit Manufacturing Co Inc .... E...... 818 709-3608
9666 Owensmouth Ave Ste G Chatsworth (91311) *(P-7061)*

Employee Codes: A=Over 500 employees, B=251-500
C=101-250, D=51-100, E=20-50, F=10-19, G=1-9

2024 Southern California
Business Directory and Buyers Guide

© Mergent Inc. 1-800-342-5647

1045

Cold Steel Inc (PA)..F....... 805 650-8481
  6060 Nicolle St Ventura (93003) *(P-14093)*

Coldwater Care Center LLC ....C..... 818 766-6105
  12750 Riverside Dr North Hollywood (91607) *(P-17903)*

Coldwell Banker, Bakersfield *Also Called: Bakersfield Westwind Corp (P-14748)*

Coldwell Banker, Arcadia *Also Called: Coldwell Banker Residential RE (P-14767)*

Coldwell Banker, Mission Viejo *Also Called: Coldwell Bnkr Rsdntial Rfrral (P-14768)*

Coldwell Banker, Newport Beach *Also Called: Coldwell Bnkr Rsdntial Rfrral (P-14769)*

Coldwell Banker Coastl Aliance, Long Beach *Also Called: Coastal Alliance Holdings Inc (P-14766)*

Coldwell Banker Residential BR, San Diego *Also Called: Dorothy Sarkozy (P-14790)*

Coldwell Banker Residential RE ....C..... 626 445-5500
  15 E Foothill Blvd Arcadia (91006) *(P-14767)*

Coldwell Banker Royal Realty, Chula Vista *Also Called: Palanging International Inc (P-14839)*

Coldwell Bnkr Rsdntial Rfrral (DH).........................B..... 949 367-1800
  27271 Las Ramblas Mission Viejo (92691) *(P-14768)*

Coldwell Bnkr Rsdntial Rfrral ....A..... 949 673-8700
  201 Marine Ave Newport Beach (92662) *(P-14769)*

Coldwell Bnkr Rsdntial Rfrral, Newport Beach *Also Called: C B Coast Newport Properties (P-14755)*

Cole Instrument Corp ....D..... 714 556-3100
  2650 S Croddy Way Santa Ana (92704) *(P-8139)*

Cole Lighting, South El Monte *Also Called: C W Cole & Company Inc (P-8306)*

Cole, Norman Anne, Anaheim *Also Called: House Seven Gables RE Inc (P-14811)*

Colin Cowie Lifestyle, Rancho Palos Verdes *Also Called: CAW Cowie Inc (P-16799)*

Collection Technology Inc ....D..... 800 743-4284
  10801 6th St Ste 200 Rancho Cucamonga (91730) *(P-15610)*

Collective Digital Studio, LLC, Beverly Hills *Also Called: Studio 71 LP (P-15598)*

Collective Management Group, Beverly Hills *Also Called: Collective MGT Group LLC (P-20015)*

Collective MGT Group LLC ....C..... 323 655-8585
  8383 Wilshire Blvd Ste 1050 Beverly Hills (90211) *(P-20015)*

Collectors Universe, Santa Ana *Also Called: Collectors Universe Inc (P-17120)*

Collectors Universe Inc (PA)..................................C..... 949 567-1234
  1610 E Saint Andrew Pl Santa Ana (92705) *(P-17120)*

College Hospital Inc (PA)......................................B..... 562 924-9581
  10802 College Pl Cerritos (90703) *(P-18511)*

COLLEGE HOSPITAL CERRITOS, Costa Mesa *Also Called: College Hospital Costa Mesa Mso Inc (P-18223)*

College Hospital Cerritos, Cerritos *Also Called: College Hospital Inc (P-18511)*

College Hospital Costa Mesa Mso Inc (HQ)..............D..... 949 642-2734
  301 Victoria St Costa Mesa (92627) *(P-18223)*

College Park Realty Inc (PA)..................................D..... 562 594-6753
  10791 Los Alamitos Blvd Los Alamitos (90720) *(P-14770)*

Collicutt Energy Services Inc ....E..... 562 944-4413
  12349 Hawkins St Santa Fe Springs (90670) *(P-5968)*

Collins Aerospace, Chula Vista *Also Called: Goodrich Corporation (P-9705)*

Collins Aerospace, Chula Vista *Also Called: Rohr Inc (P-9779)*

Collins Company, Chino *Also Called: Warren Collins and Assoc Inc (P-721)*

Collins Technologies, Brea *Also Called: Curtiss-Wright Flow Ctrl Corp (P-6761)*

Collinson Law A Prof Corp ....C..... 424 212-7777
  21515 Hawthorne Blvd Ste 800 Torrance (90503) *(P-18837)*

Collwood Ter Stellar Care Inc ....D..... 619 287-2920
  4518 54th St San Diego (92115) *(P-19250)*

Colmol Inc ....E..... 858 693-7575
  8517 Production Ave San Diego (92121) *(P-3747)*

Colon Manufacturing Inc (PA)................................F....... 213 749-6149
  1100 S San Pedro St Ste 0-08 Los Angeles (90015) *(P-2235)*

Colonel Lee's Enterprises, Vernon *Also Called: T & T Foods Inc (P-1333)*

Colonial Care Center, Long Beach *Also Called: Longwood Management Corp (P-18142)*

Colonial Enterprises Inc ....E..... 909 822-8700
  690 Knox St Ste 200 Torrance (90502) *(P-4391)*

Colonial Gardens Nursing Home, Pico Rivera *Also Called: Rivera Sanatarium Inc (P-18039)*

Colonial Home Textiles, Corona *Also Called: Amrapur Overseas Incorporated (P-2137)*

Colonnas Shipyard West LLC ....E..... 757 545-2414
  2890 Faivre St Ste 150 Chula Vista (91911) *(P-9835)*

Colony Dstrssed Cr Spcial Stto, Los Angeles *Also Called: Cdcf III PCF Lndmark Scrmnto L (P-14656)*

Color Inc ....E..... 818 240-1350
  1600 Flower St Glendale (91201) *(P-3532)*

Color Ad Inc ....E..... 310 632-5500
  18601 S Santa Fe Ave Compton (90221) *(P-15532)*

Color Concepts, Canoga Park *Also Called: Rte Enterprises Inc (P-855)*

Color Design Laboratory Inc (PA)...........................D..... 818 341-5100
  21329 Nordhoff St Chatsworth (91311) *(P-19964)*

Color Design Labs, Chatsworth *Also Called: Color Design Laboratory Inc (P-19964)*

Color Laser R&D, Chatsworth *Also Called: Clover Envmtl Solutions LLC (P-12848)*

Color ME Cotton, Los Angeles *Also Called: Jd/Cmc Inc (P-2334)*

Color Science Inc ....E..... 714 434-1033
  1230 E Glenwood Pl Santa Ana (92707) *(P-4509)*

Color Spot Holdings Inc (PA).................................A..... 760 695-1430
  3742 Blue Bird Canyon Rd Vista (92084) *(P-50)*

Color Spot Nurseries, Vista *Also Called: Color Spot Holdings Inc (P-50)*

Color West Inc ....C..... 818 840-8881
  2228 N Hollywood Way Burbank (91505) *(P-3533)*

Color West Printing & Packg, Burbank *Also Called: Color West Inc (P-3533)*

Colorado River Adventures Inc (PA).......................C..... 760 663-3737
  2715 Parker Dam Rd Earp (92242) *(P-15442)*

COLORADO RIVER MEDICAL CENTER, Needles *Also Called: Community Hlthcare Partner Inc (P-17630)*

Colorama Paints, Los Angeles *Also Called: Ennis Traffic Safety Solutions (P-4488)*

Colorama Wholesale Nursery, Azusa *Also Called: Richard Wilson Wellington (P-69)*

Colorcom Inc ....E..... 323 246-4640
  2437 S Eastern Ave Commerce (90040) *(P-3534)*

Coloredge ....C..... 818 842-1121
  3520 W Valhalla Dr Burbank (91505) *(P-16760)*

Colorescience Inc ....C..... 866 426-5673
  2141 Palomar Airport Rd Ste 200 Carlsbad (92011) *(P-13033)*

Colorfast Dye & Print Hse Inc ....E..... 323 581-1656
  5075 Pacific Blvd Vernon (90058) *(P-3535)*

Colorfx Inc ....E..... 818 767-7671
  11050 Randall St Sun Valley (91352) *(P-3536)*

Colorgraphics, Los Angeles *Also Called: Madisn/Grham Clor Graphics Inc (P-3627)*

Colormax Industries Inc (PA).................................E..... 213 748-6600
  1627 Paloma St Los Angeles (90021) *(P-2016)*

Colornet Press, Van Nuys *Also Called: Niknejad Inc (P-3644)*

Colosseum Athletics, Compton *Also Called: Colosseum Athletics Corp (P-13100)*

Colosseum Athletics Corp ....D..... 310 667-8341
  2400 S Wilmington Ave Compton (90220) *(P-13100)*

Colour Concepts Inc C
  1225 Los Angeles St Glendale (91204) *(P-3537)*

Colt Services Inc ....D..... 858 271-9910
  9655 Via Excelencia San Diego (92126) *(P-15467)*

Colton Truck Terminal Garage, Colton *Also Called: Erf Enterprises Inc (P-9325)*

Columbia Aluminum Products LLC ....D..... 323 728-7361
  1150 W Rincon St Corona (92878) *(P-6008)*

Columbia Fabricating Co Inc ....E..... 818 247-4220
  5079 Gloria Ave Encino (91436) *(P-6354)*

Columbia Holding Corp ....B..... 310 327-4107
  14400 S San Pedro St Gardena (90248) *(P-6102)*

Columbia Pictures, Culver City *Also Called: Columbia Pictures Inds Inc (P-17177)*

Columbia Pictures Inds Inc ....D..... 818 655-5820
  4024 Radford Ave Studio City (91604) *(P-17176)*

Columbia Pictures Inds Inc (DH).............................C..... 310 244-4000
  10202 Washington Blvd Culver City (90232) *(P-17177)*

Columbia Products Co, Irvine *Also Called: Columbia Sanitary Products Inc (P-5969)*

Columbia Sanitary Products Inc ....E..... 949 474-0777
  1622 Browning Irvine (92606) *(P-5969)*

Columbia Showcase & Cab Co Inc ....C..... 818 765-9710
  11034 Sherman Way Ste A Sun Valley (91352) *(P-2949)*

Columbia Steel Inc ....D..... 909 874-8840
  2175 N Linden Ave Rialto (92377) *(P-6009)*

Columbia Stone Products ....F..... 760 737-3215
  663 S Rancho Santa Fe Rd San Marcos (92078) *(P-5539)*

Com Dev Usa LLC ....D..... 424 456-8000
  2333 Utah Ave El Segundo (90245) *(P-12904)*

Comac America Corporation ....E..... 760 616-9614
  4350 Von Karman Ave Ste 400 Newport Beach (92660) *(P-9520)*

Comav LLC ....C..... 760 523-5100
  18260 Phantom W Victorville (92394) *(P-11692)*

Mergent email: customerrelations@mergent.com
1046

2024 Southern California
Business Directory and Buyers Guide

(P-0000) Products & Services Section entry number
(PA)=Parent Co (HQ)=Headquarters (DH)=Div Headquarters

Comav LLC (PA)..D...... 760 523-5100
18499 Phantom St Ste 17 Victorville (92394) *(P-12905)*

Comav Aviation, Victorville *Also Called: Comav LLC (P-11692)*

Comav Technical Services LLC ....C....... 760 530-2400
18438 Readiness St Victorville (92394) *(P-11693)*

Combimatrix Corporation (HQ)..............................E....... 949 753-0624
310 Goddard Ste 150 Irvine (92618) *(P-10250)*

Combustion Associates Inc ....E....... 951 272-6999
555 Monica Cir Corona (92878) *(P-12018)*

Comcast, Ontario *Also Called: Comcast Corporation (P-11982)*

Comcast Corporation ....D...... 909 890-0886
1205 S Dupont Ave Ontario (91761) *(P-11982)*

Comco Inc ....E....... 818 333-8500
2151 N Lincoln St Burbank (91504) *(P-7651)*

Come Land Maint Svc Co Inc ....A...... 818 567-2455
1419 N San Fernando Blvd-Ste 250 Burbank (91504) *(P-15701)*

Comedy Club Oxnard LLC ....D...... 805 535-5400
591 Collection Blvd Oxnard (93036) *(P-17479)*

Comet Electric Inc ....C....... 818 340-0965
21625 Prairie St Chatsworth (91311) *(P-882)*

Comet Medical, Ventura *Also Called: Peter Brasseler Holdings LLC (P-12507)*

Comfort California Inc ....C....... 714 750-3131
616 W Convention Way Anaheim (92802) *(P-15121)*

Comfort Industries Inc ....E....... 562 692-8288
301 W Las Tunas Dr San Gabriel (91776) *(P-2048)*

Command Gard Srvces Wsa Srvces, Gardena *Also Called: United Facility Solutions Inc (P-16697)*

Command Guard Services, Torrance *Also Called: Resource Collection Inc (P-15744)*

Command Packaging, Vernon *Also Called: Revoltion Cnsmr Sltions CA LLC (P-13556)*

Commander Packaging West Inc ....E....... 714 921-9350
602 S Rockefeller Ave Ste D Ontario (91761) *(P-3092)*

Commerce, Commerce *Also Called: Alarin Aircraft Hinge Inc (P-5896)*

Commerce Casino, Commerce *Also Called: California Commerce Club Inc (P-15107)*

Commerce On Demand LLC ....D...... 562 360-4819
7121 Telegraph Rd Montebello (90640) *(P-11210)*

Commerce Velocity LLC ....E....... 949 756-8950
1 Technology Dr Ste J725 Irvine (92618) *(P-16208)*

Commercial Crrers Insur Agcy I ....D...... 562 404-4900
4 Centerpointe Dr Ste 300 La Palma (90623) *(P-14577)*

Commercial Cstm Sting Uphl Inc ....D...... 714 850-0520
12601 Western Ave Garden Grove (92841) *(P-3021)*

Commercial Display Systems LLC ....E....... 818 361-8160
17341 Sierra Hwy Canyon Country (91351) *(P-7603)*

Commercial Furniture ....F....... 714 350-7045
1261 N Lakeview Ave Anaheim (92807) *(P-2880)*

Commercial Intr Resources Inc ....D...... 562 926-5885
6077 Rickenbacker Rd Commerce (90040) *(P-2798)*

Commercial Inv MGT Group, Los Angeles *Also Called: Cim Group LP (P-15115)*

Commercial Lbr & Pallet Co Inc (PA).................... C...... 626 968-0631
135 Long Ln City Of Industry (91746) *(P-2715)*

Commercial Metal Forming, Orange *Also Called: Commercial Metal Forming Inc (P-6137)*

Commercial Metal Forming Inc ....E....... 714 532-6321
341 W Collins Ave Orange (92867) *(P-6137)*

Commercial Protective Services, Gardena *Also Called: Construction Protective Services Inc (P-16632)*

Commercial Protective Svcs Inc ....A...... 310 515-5290
17215 Studebaker Rd Ste 205 Cerritos (90703) *(P-16630)*

Commercial RE Exch Inc ....C....... 888 273-0423
5510 Lincoln Blvd Playa Vista (90094) *(P-15997)*

Commercial Shtmtl Works Inc ....E....... 213 748-7321
1800 S San Pedro St Los Angeles (90015) *(P-6010)*

Commercial Truck Eqp Co LLC ....D...... 562 803-4466
12351 Bellflower Blvd Downey (90242) *(P-9317)*

Commercial Truck Equipment Co, Downey *Also Called: Commercial Truck Eqp Co LLC (P-9317)*

Commercial Wood Products Company ....C....... 760 246-4530
10019 Yucca Rd Adelanto (92301) *(P-1009)*

Commodity Resource Envmtl Inc ....E....... 661 824-2416
11847 United St Mojave (93501) *(P-5674)*

Commodity Rsource Enviromental, Mojave *Also Called: Commodity Resource Envmtl Inc (P-5674)*

Commodity Sales Co .... C...... 323 980-5463
517 S Clarence St Los Angeles (90033) *(P-1242)*

Common Collabs LLC (PA).....................................E...... 714 519-3245
1820 E Walnut Ave Fullerton (92831) *(P-1763)*

Common Grounds Holdings LLC ....D...... 760 206-7861
6790 Embarcadero Ln Ste 100 Carlsbad (92011) *(P-14771)*

Commonpath LLC ....F....... 858 922-8116
5963 Olivas Park Dr Ste F Ventura (93003) *(P-5337)*

Commons At Calabasas, The, Los Angeles *Also Called: Caruso MGT Ltd A Cal Ltd Prtnr (P-14758)*

Communction Systms-Wst/Lnkabit, San Diego *Also Called: L3 Technologies Inc (P-8533)*

Communction Wirg Spcalists Inc ....D...... 858 278-4545
8909 Complex Dr Ste F San Diego (92123) *(P-883)*

Communication Tech Svcs LLC ....B....... 508 382-2700
1590 S Milliken Ave Ste H Ontario (91761) *(P-884)*

Communications Supply Corp ....D...... 714 670-7711
6251 Knott Ave Buena Park (90620) *(P-12004)*

Community Action Partnership ....D...... 805 541-4122
3970 Short St San Luis Obispo (93401) *(P-19046)*

Community Action Partnr Kern ....D...... 661 835-5405
315 Stine Rd Bakersfield (93309) *(P-19320)*

Community Action Partnr Kern ....D...... 760 371-1469
814 N Norma St Ridgecrest (93555) *(P-19321)*

Community Action Prtnr Ornge C ....D...... 714 897-6670
11870 Monarch St Garden Grove (92841) *(P-19047)*

Community Action Prtnr Rvrside, Riverside *Also Called: County of Riverside (P-19066)*

Community Action Prtnr San Brn ....D...... 909 723-1500
696 S Tippecanoe Ave San Bernardino (92408) *(P-19322)*

Community Action Prtnr San Lui ....C....... 805 544-2478
705 Grand Ave San Luis Obispo (93401) *(P-18681)*

Community Action Prtnr San Lui ....C....... 805 541-2272
805 Fiero Ln Ste A San Luis Obispo (93401) *(P-19207)*

Community Bank ....B....... 626 577-1700
460 Sierra Madre Villa Ave Pasadena (91107) *(P-14189)*

Community Care Center ....D...... 619 465-0702
8665 La Mesa Blvd La Mesa (91942) *(P-17904)*

Community Care On Palm Rvrside ....D...... 951 686-9001
4768 Palm Ave Riverside (92501) *(P-17905)*

Community Cnvlscent Hosp Mntcl, Montclair *Also Called: US Skillserve Inc (P-18065)*

Community Day School, Beaumont *Also Called: Beaumont Unfied Schl Dst Pub F (P-18963)*

Community Dev Inst Head Start ....B....... 858 668-2985
12988 Bowron Rd Poway (92064) *(P-19208)*

Community Food Connection ....D...... 858 751-4613
14047 Twin Peaks Rd Poway (92064) *(P-19048)*

Community Health Agency, Moreno Valley *Also Called: County of Riverside (P-17637)*

Community Health Agency, Riverside *Also Called: County of Riverside (P-20417)*

COMMUNITY HEALTH CENTER, Bakersfield *Also Called: Omni Family Health (P-17730)*

Community Health Group ....C....... 800 224-7766
2420 Fenton St Ste 100 Chula Vista (91914) *(P-17628)*

Community Health Systems Inc ....C....... 951 571-2300
21801 Alessandro Blvd Moreno Valley (92553) *(P-17629)*

Community Hlth Plan Off MGT Ca, Alhambra *Also Called: County of Los Angeles (P-14467)*

Community Hlthcare Partner Inc ....D...... 760 326-4531
1401 Bailey Ave Needles (92363) *(P-17630)*

Community Hosp San Bernardino (DH).................... B...... 909 887-6333
1805 Medical Center Dr San Bernardino (92411) *(P-18224)*

Community Hospital, Long Beach *Also Called: Community Hospital Long Beach (P-18225)*

Community Hospital Long Beach ....A...... 562 494-0600
1760 Termino Ave Ste 105 Long Beach (90804) *(P-18225)*

Community Interface Services ....D...... 760 729-3866
981 Vale Terrace Dr Vista (92084) *(P-19049)*

Community Media Corporation (PA)..........................E...... 714 220-0292
5119 Ball Rd Cypress (90630) *(P-3267)*

Community Mem Hosp San Bnvntur ....D...... 805 652-5072
147 N Brent St Ventura (93003) *(P-18226)*

Community Memorial Health Sys ....C....... 805 646-1401
1306 Maricopa Hwy Ojai (93023) *(P-18227)*

Community Memorial Health Sys (PA)...................... A...... 805 652-5011
147 N Brent St Ventura (93003) *(P-18228)*

Community Memorial Hospital, Ventura *Also Called: Community Memorial Health Sys (P-18228)*

Employee Codes: A=Over 500 employees, B=251-500
C=101-250, D=51-100, E=20-50, F=10-19, G=1-9

2024 Southern California
Business Directory and Buyers Guide

© Mergent Inc. 1-800-342-5647
1047

ALPHABETIC

Community Partners (PA)....................................C....... 213 346-3200
1000 N Alameda St Ste 240 Los Angeles (90012) *(P-19323)*

Community Patrol Inc ....D....... 657 247-4744
1420 E Edinger Ave Ste 213 Santa Ana (92705) *(P-16631)*

Community Support Options Inc ....C....... 661 758-5331
1401 Poso Dr Wasco (93280) *(P-19050)*

Community Transit Services, El Monte *Also Called: First Student Inc (P-11316)*

Compaction American, Lake Elsinore *Also Called: American Compaction Eqp Inc (P-6925)*

Companion Medical Inc ....D....... 858 522-0252
11011 Via Frontera Ste D San Diego (92127) *(P-10483)*

Compas Health, Templeton *Also Called: Compass Health Inc (P-17906)*

Compass Flooring, Santa Fe Springs *Also Called: Altro Usa Inc (P-11183)*

Compass Group Usa Inc ....C....... 714 899-2520
12640 Knott St Garden Grove (92841) *(P-15777)*

Compass Health Inc ....C....... 805 434-3035
290 Heather Ct Templeton (93465) *(P-17906)*

Compass Health Inc ....C....... 805 543-0210
1425 Woodside Dr San Luis Obispo (93401) *(P-17907)*

Compass Health Inc ....C....... 805 772-7372
1405 Teresa Dr Morro Bay (93442) *(P-17908)*

Compass Health Inc ....C....... 805 489-8137
1212 Farroll Ave Arroyo Grande (93420) *(P-17909)*

Compass Health Inc ....C....... 805 466-9254
10805 El Camino Real Atascadero (93422) *(P-17910)*

Compass Health Inc ....C....... 805 687-6651
3880 Via Lucero Santa Barbara (93110) *(P-17911)*

Compass Health Inc ....C....... 805 474-7260
222 S Elm St Arroyo Grande (93420) *(P-19251)*

Compass Water Solutions Inc (PA).....................E....... 949 222-5777
15542 Mosher Ave Tustin (92780) *(P-7652)*

Compatico Inc ....E....... 616 940-1772
1901 S Archibald Ave Ontario (91761) *(P-2950)*

Competrol A Western Pump Co, San Diego *Also Called: Western Pump Inc (P-17163)*

Compex Legal Services Inc (PA).........................C....... 310 782-1801
325 Maple Ave Torrance (90503) *(P-18838)*

Complete Aquatic Systems, Gardena *Also Called: Wally & Pat Enterprises (P-11305)*

Complete Clothing Company (PA)........................E....... 323 277-1470
4950 E 49th St Vernon (90058) *(P-2281)*

Complete Coach Works ....C....... 800 300-3751
42882 Ivy St Murrieta (92562) *(P-17054)*

Complete Metal Fabrication Inc ....F....... 760 353-0260
596 E Main St El Centro (92243) *(P-6011)*

Complete Truck Body Repair Inc ....E....... 323 445-2675
1217 N Alameda St Compton (90222) *(P-9318)*

Completely Fresh Foods Inc ....C....... 323 722-9136
4401 S Downey Rd Vernon (90058) *(P-13362)*

Compliance Poster, Monrovia *Also Called: Global Compliance Inc (P-3449)*

Complyright Dist Svcs Inc ....E....... 805 981-0992
3451 Jupiter Ct Oxnard (93030) *(P-3830)*

Component Equipment Coinc ....E....... 805 988-8004
3050 Camino Del Sol Oxnard (93030) *(P-8964)*

Componetics Inc ....E....... 805 498-0939
600 Azure Hills Dr Simi Valley (93065) *(P-8938)*

Composite Manufacturing Inc ....E....... 949 361-7580
970 Calle Amanecer Ste D San Clemente (92673) *(P-10484)*

Composite Optics Incorporated ....A....... 937 490-4145
7130 Miramar Rd Ste 100b San Diego (92121) *(P-9916)*

Composites Horizons LLC (DH)...........................C....... 626 331-0861
1629 W Industrial Park St Covina (91722) *(P-3932)*

Composites Horizons LLC ....E....... 626 331-0861
1471 W Industrial Park St Covina (91722) *(P-9662)*

Comprehensive Blood Cancer Ctr, Bakersfield *Also Called: Ravi Patel MD Inc (P-17749)*

Comprehensive Cancer Centers Inc ....C....... 323 966-3400
8201 Beverly Blvd Los Angeles (90048) *(P-18682)*

Comprehensive Dist Svcs Inc ....C....... 310 523-1546
18726 S Western Ave Ste 300 Gardena (90248) *(P-11830)*

Comprehensive Print Group LLC ....E....... 949 255-4067
675 N Main St Orange (92868) *(P-3538)*

Comprhnsve Crdvsclar Spclsts (PA)...................F....... 626 281-8663
220 S 1st St Ste 101 Alhambra (91801) *(P-4091)*

Comprhnsve Indus Dsblity MGT ....D....... 866 301-6568
2555 Townsgate Rd Ste 125 Westlake Village (91361) *(P-18755)*

Compton Service Center, Compton *Also Called: Southern California Edison Co (P-12070)*

COMPTON TRAINING CENTER, Van Nuys *Also Called: Apprentice Jrnymen Trning Tr F (P-19174)*

Compu Aire Inc ....C....... 562 945-8971
8167 Byron Rd Whittier (90606) *(P-7604)*

Compucase Corporation ....A....... 626 336-6588
16720 Chestnut St Ste C City Of Industry (91748) *(P-7468)*

Compucraft Industries Inc ....E....... 619 448-0787
8787 Olive Ln Santee (92071) *(P-9663)*

Compugroup Medical Inc ....E....... 949 789-0500
25b Technology Dr Ste 200 Irvine (92618) *(P-16209)*

Compulink Business Systems Inc (PA)................C....... 805 446-2050
1100 Business Center Cir Newbury Park (91320) *(P-16210)*

Compulink Healthcare Solutions, Newbury Park *Also Called: Compulink Business Systems Inc (P-16210)*

Compulink Management Ctr Inc (PA)...................C....... 562 988-1688
3443 Long Beach Blvd Long Beach (90807) *(P-15998)*

Compumeric Engineering Inc ....E....... 909 605-7666
1390 S Milliken Ave Ontario (91761) *(P-6216)*

Compushare Inc ....C....... 714 427-1000
3 Hutton Centre Dr Ste 700 Santa Ana (92707) *(P-16488)*

Computational Systems Inc ....D....... 661 832-5306
4301 Resnik Ct Bakersfield (93313) *(P-10124)*

Computed Tool & Engrg Inc ....E....... 714 630-3911
2910 E Ricker Way Anaheim (92806) *(P-7062)*

Computer Assisted Mfg Tech LLC ....E....... 949 263-8911
8710 Research Dr 8750 Irvine (92618) *(P-7806)*

Computer Intgrted McHining Inc ....E....... 619 596-9246
10940 Wheatlands Ave Santee (92071) *(P-7807)*

Computer Metal Products Corp ....D....... 805 520-6966
370 E Easy St Simi Valley (93065) *(P-6217)*

Computer Proc Unlimited Inc ....C....... 858 530-0875
9235 Activity Rd Ste 104 San Diego (92126) *(P-15999)*

Computer Service Company ....E....... 951 738-1444
210 N Delilah St Corona (92879) *(P-8605)*

Computer Tech Resources Inc ....C....... 714 665-6507
16 Technology Dr Ste 202 Irvine (92618) *(P-16436)*

Computer-Nozzles, Irwindale *Also Called: Cni Mfg Inc (P-7803)*

Computerized Mgt Svcs Inc ....D....... 805 522-5940
4100 Guardian St Ste 205 Simi Valley (93063) *(P-19762)*

Computerized Security Systems, Costa Mesa *Also Called: Winfield Locks Inc (P-5954)*

Computershare Inc ....B....... 800 522-6645
2335 Alaska Ave El Segundo (90245) *(P-14434)*

Computerworks Technologies, Burbank *Also Called: Global Service Resources Inc (P-16040)*

Computrition Inc (HQ)...D....... 818 961-3999
8521 Fallbrook Ave Ste 100 Canoga Park (91304) *(P-16000)*

Computrus Inc ....E....... 951 245-9103
250 Klug Cir Corona (92878) *(P-6138)*

Comune, Los Angeles *Also Called: Dhouse Brands Inc // Comune (P-13039)*

Con-Tech Plastics, Brea *Also Called: Ramtec Associates Inc (P-5173)*

Conam Management Corporation (PA)..................C....... 858 614-7200
3990 Ruffin Rd Ste 100 San Diego (92123) *(P-14772)*

Conamco SA De CV ....D....... 760 586-4356
3008 Palm Hill Dr Vista (92084) *(P-10733)*

Conax Usa Inc ....C....... 949 690-4880
31102 Via Cristal San Juan Capistrano (92675) *(P-9664)*

Concept Development Llc ....E....... 949 623-8000
1881 Langley Ave Irvine (92614) *(P-8665)*

Concept Packaging Group, Ontario *Also Called: Southland Container Corp (P-3131)*

Concept Technology Inc ....B....... 949 851-6550
2941 W Macarthur Blvd Ste 136 Santa Ana (92704) *(P-19564)*

Concept Technology Inc (PA)..............................D....... 949 854-7047
895 Dove St 3rd Fl Newport Beach (92660) *(P-19565)*

Concepts & Wood, Huntington Park *Also Called: Plycraft Industries Inc (P-2690)*

Concise Fabricators, San Diego *Also Called: Concise Fabricators Inc (P-6218)*

Concise Fabricators Inc ....E....... 520 746-3226
7550 Panasonic Way San Diego (92154) *(P-6218)*

CONCISYS ....E....... 858 292-5888
5452 Oberlin Dr San Diego (92121) *(P-10193)*

Conco Cement Co, Fontana *Also Called: Gonsalves & Santucci Inc (P-1072)*

Mergent email: customerrelations@mergent.com
1048

2024 Southern California
Business Directory and Buyers Guide

(P-0000) Products & Services Section entry number
(PA)=Parent Co (HQ)=Headquarters (DH)=Div Headquarters

Concord Document Services Inc (PA)................E....... 213 745-3175
1407 W 11th St Los Angeles (90015) *(P-15643)*

Concord Foods Inc (HQ)..................................D...... 909 975-2000
4601 E Guasti Rd Ontario (91761) *(P-13176)*

Concorde Career Colleges Inc ....D...... 818 766-8151
12412 Victory Blvd North Hollywood (91606) *(P-19002)*

Concorse Ht At Los Angles Arpr, Los Angeles *Also Called: Humnit Hotel At Lax LLC*
(P-15189)

Concrete Construction, San Diego *Also Called: Ben F Smith Inc (P-1061)*

Concrete Holding Co Cal Inc ....A...... 818 788-4228
15821 Ventura Blvd Ste 475 Encino (91436) *(P-5473)*

Concrete Mold Corporation ....D...... 310 537-5171
2121 E Del Amo Blvd Compton (90220) *(P-7063)*

Concrete Tie, Compton *Also Called: Concrete Tie Industries Inc (P-12352)*

Concrete Tie Industries Inc (PA)......................D...... 310 628-2328
130 E Oris St Compton (90222) *(P-12352)*

Concrete West Construction Inc ....F...... 949 448-9940
1235 N Tustin Ave Anaheim (92807) *(P-20155)*

Concurrent Holdings LLC ....A...... 310 473-3065
11150 Santa Monica Blvd Ste 825 Los Angeles (90025) *(P-8203)*

Condition Monitoring Services, Nipomo *Also Called: Condition Monitoring Svcs Inc (P-10251)*

Condition Monitoring Svcs Inc ....E...... 888 359-3277
855 San Ysidro Ln Nipomo (93444) *(P-10251)*

Condon-Johnson & Assoc Inc ....D...... 858 530-9165
3434 Grove St Lemon Grove (91945) *(P-469)*

Condor, Baldwin Park *Also Called: Condor Outdoor Products Inc (P-10984)*

Condor Outdoor Products Inc (PA)....................E...... 626 358-3270
5268 Rivergrade Rd Baldwin Park (91706) *(P-10984)*

Condor Pacific Industries Inc (PA)....................E...... 818 889-2150
905 Rancho Conejo Blvd Newbury Park (91320) *(P-9964)*

Condor Productions LLC ....D...... 310 449-3000
245 N Beverly Dr Beverly Hills (90210) *(P-17246)*

Conduit Lngage Specialists Inc ....D...... 859 299-3178
22720 Ventura Blvd Ste 100 Woodland Hills (91364) *(P-15504)*

Conesys Inc ....C...... 310 212-0065
548 Amapola Ave Torrance (90501) *(P-8965)*

Conexant Holdings Inc ....A...... 415 983-2706
4000 Macarthur Blvd Newport Beach (92660) *(P-8781)*

Conexant Systems LLC (HQ)..............................E...... 949 483-4600
1901 Main St Ste 300 Irvine (92614) *(P-8782)*

Conexis Bnfts Admnstrators LP (HQ)................C...... 714 835-5006
721 S Parker St Ste 300 Orange (92868) *(P-14578)*

Confab, Van Nuys *Also Called: Consolidated Fabricators Corp (P-6139)*

Confido LLC ....A...... 310 361-8558
1055 E Colorado Blvd Pasadena (91106) *(P-18604)*

Confie, Huntington Beach *Also Called: Confie Holding II Co (P-14579)*

Confie Holding II Co (PA)..................................C...... 714 252-2500
7711 Center Ave Ste 200 Huntington Beach (92647) *(P-14579)*

Congatec Inc ....E...... 858 457-2600
6262 Ferris Sq San Diego (92121) *(P-7518)*

Conglas, Bakersfield *Also Called: Consolidated Fibrgls Pdts Co (P-5553)*

Conleys Greenhouse Mfg & Sales, Montclair *Also Called: John L Conley Inc (P-6380)*

Connect Computers, Anaheim *Also Called: General Procurement Inc (P-12415)*

Connectec Company Inc (PA)............................D...... 949 252-1077
1701 Reynolds Ave Irvine (92614) *(P-8257)*

Connectpoint Inc ....F...... 805 682-8900
175 Cremona Dr Ste 160 Goleta (93117) *(P-16211)*

Connell Processing Inc ....E...... 818 845-7661
3094 N Avon St Burbank (91504) *(P-6607)*

Connelly Machine Wks ....E...... 714 558-6855
420 N Terminal St Santa Ana (92701) *(P-7808)*

Connexity Inc (DH)...C...... 310 571-1235
2120 Colorado Ave Ste 400 Santa Monica (90404) *(P-11876)*

Conquer Nation Inc ....C...... 310 651-5555
6100 Wilmington Ave Los Angeles (90001) *(P-2445)*

Conquest Industries Inc ....E...... 562 906-1111
12740 Lakeland Rd Santa Fe Springs (90670) *(P-12543)*

Conquistador International LLC ....D...... 424 249-9304
21200 Oxnard St Ste 492 Woodland Hills (91365) *(P-13034)*

Consensus Cloud Solutions Inc (PA)................D...... 323 860-9200
700 S Flower St Fl 15 Los Angeles (90017) *(P-16212)*

Conservation Corps Long Beach ....C...... 562 986-1249
340 Nieto Ave Long Beach (90814) *(P-19182)*

Conservice Mtring Slutions Inc ....F...... 858 356-7534
9950 Scripps Lake Dr Ste 101 San Diego (92131) *(P-16213)*

Considine Cnsdine An Accntncy ....C...... 619 231-1977
8989 Rio San Diego Dr Ste 250 San Diego (92108) *(P-19763)*

Consoldted Fire Protection LLC (HQ)...............A...... 949 727-3277
153 Technology Dr Ste 200 Irvine (92618) *(P-16804)*

Consoldted Med Bo-Analysis Inc (PA)..............D...... 714 657-7369
10700 Walker St Cypress (90630) *(P-18543)*

Consoldted Precision Pdts Corp ....D...... 805 488-6451
705 Industrial Way Port Hueneme (93041) *(P-5785)*

Consoldted Precision Pdts Corp ....C...... 909 595-2252
4200 West Valley Blvd Pomona (91769) *(P-5786)*

Consolidated Aerospace Mfg LLC ....D...... 714 989-2802
630 E Lambert Rd Brea (92821) *(P-5912)*

Consolidated Aerospace Mfg LLC (HQ)............E...... 714 989-2797
1425 S Acacia Ave Fullerton (92831) *(P-9965)*

Consolidated Aircraft Coatings, Riverside *Also Called: Poly-Fiber Inc (P-4497)*

Consolidated Color Corporation ....E...... 562 420-7714
12316 Carson St Hawaiian Gardens (90716) *(P-4485)*

Consolidated Design West, Pomona *Also Called: Western Converting Spc Inc (P-3825)*

Consolidated Design West Inc ....E...... 714 999-1476
1345 S Lewis St Anaheim (92805) *(P 15659)*

Consolidated Devices Inc (HQ).........................E...... 626 965-0668
19220 San Jose Ave City Of Industry (91748) *(P-13676)*

Consolidated Fabricators Corp (PA)..................C...... 800 635-8335
14620 Arminta St Van Nuys (91402) *(P-6139)*

Consolidated Fibrgls Pdts Co 661 323-6026
3801 Standard St Bakersfield (93308) *(P-5553)*

Consolidated Foundries, Pomona *Also Called: CFI Holdings Corp (P-5653)*

Consolidated Foundries Inc ....C...... 323 773-2363
8333 Wilcox Ave Cudahy (90201) *(P-5787)*

Consolidated Graphics Inc ....D...... 323 460-4115
3550 Tyburn St Los Angeles (90065) *(P-3748)*

Consolidated Plastics Corp (PA)........................E...... 909 393-8222
14954 La Palma Dr Chino (91710) *(P-13412)*

Consolidated Svc Distrs Inc ....D...... 908 687-5800
777 S Central Ave Los Angeles (90021) *(P-13267)*

Consolidated Trading Co Amer, Cerritos *Also Called: Ctcoa LLC (P-9668)*

Consteel Industrial, Whittier *Also Called: Consteel Industrial Inc (P-6012)*

Consteel Industrial Inc ....E...... 562 806-4575
15435 Woodcrest Dr Whittier (90604) *(P-6012)*

Constrction Instlltion Mint Gr, Anaheim *Also Called: Kesa Incorporated (P-16744)*

Construction, Gardena *Also Called: Best Contracting Services Inc (P-1037)*

Construction Protective Services Inc (PA).........A...... 800 257-5512
436 W Walnut St Gardena (90248) *(P-16632)*

Construction Specialty Svc Inc ....D...... 661 864-7573
4550 Buck Owens Blvd Bakersfield (93308) *(P-667)*

CONSTRUCTION TESTING & ENGINEERING, INC., Riverside *Also Called: Construction Tstg & Engrg Inc (P-19566)*

Construction Tstg & Engrg Inc ....B...... 951 571-4081
14538 Meridian Pkwy Ste A Riverside (92518) *(P-19566)*

Consumer Resource Network LLC ....B...... 800 291-4794
4420 E Miraloma Ave Ste J Anaheim (92807) *(P-20156)*

Consumer Safety Analytics LLC ....D...... 818 922-2416
7027 Hayvenhurst Ave Van Nuys (91406) *(P-19965)*

Container Options ....F...... 909 478-0045
1493 E San Bernardino Ave San Bernardino (92408) *(P-4994)*

Container Supply Company Incorporated ....C...... 714 892-8321
12571 Western Ave Garden Grove (92841) *(P-5858)*

Contech Engnered Solutions Inc ....A...... 714 281-7883
950 S Coast Dr Ste 145 Costa Mesa (92626) *(P-5633)*

Contemporary Services Corp (PA).....................A...... 818 885-5150
17101 Superior St Northridge (91325) *(P-16633)*

Contemporary Services Corp ....C...... 310 320-8418
369 Van Ness Way Ste 702 Torrance (90501) *(P-16726)*

Contessa Liquidating Co Inc C
222 W 6th St Fl 8 San Pedro (90731) *(P-13243)*

Contessa Premium Foods, Vernon *Also Called: F I O Imports Inc (P-1891)*

Contessa Premium Foods Inc ....C...... 310 832-8000
5980 Alcoa Ave Vernon (90058) *(P-13244)*

Employee Codes: A=Over 500 employees, B=251-500
C=101-250, D=51-100, E=20-50, F=10-19, G=1-9

2024 Southern California
Business Directory and Buyers Guide

© Mergent Inc. 1-800-342-5647

1049

ALPHABETIC

Continental Acrylics, Compton *Also Called: Plaskolite West LLC (P-3963)*

Continental Airlines, Los Angeles *Also Called: United Airlines Inc (P-11672)*

Continental Bdr Specialty Corp (PA).....................C..... **310 324-8227**
407 W Compton Blvd Gardena (90248) *(P-3836)*

Continental Colorcraft, Monterey Park *Also Called: Graphic Color Systems Inc (P-3580)*

Continental Controls Corp ....E..... 858 453-9880
7710 Kenamar Ct San Diego (92121) *(P-10125)*

Continental Currency Svcs Inc (PA).................D..... **714 667-6699**
1108 E 17th St Santa Ana (92701) *(P-14256)*

Continental Data Graphics, Rancho Cucamonga *Also Called: Continental Graphics Corp (P-3539)*

Continental Data Graphics, Long Beach *Also Called: Continental Graphics Corp (P-3542)*

Continental Data Graphics, El Segundo *Also Called: Continental Graphics Corp (P-3543)*

Continental Data Graphics, Long Beach *Also Called: Continental Graphics Corp (P-15660)*

Continental Datalabel Inc ....F..... 909 307-3600
211 Business Center Ct Redlands (92373) *(P-3233)*

Continental Engineering Svcs, San Diego *Also Called: Continental Graphics Corp (P-3540)*

Continental Exch Solutions Inc (HQ) ....D..... **714 522-7044**
6565 Knott Ave Buena Park (90620) *(P-14257)*

Continental Forge Company LLC ....D..... 310 603-1014
412 E El Segundo Blvd Compton (90222) *(P-6477)*

Continental Graphics Corp ....E..... 909 758-9800
9302 Pittsburgh Ave Ste 100 Rancho Cucamonga (91730) *(P-3539)*

Continental Graphics Corp ....E..... 858 552-6520
6910 Carroll Rd San Diego (92121) *(P-3540)*

Continental Graphics Corp ....E..... 714 827-1752
4060 N Lakewood Blvd Bldg 801 Long Beach (90808) *(P-3541)*

Continental Graphics Corp ....E..... 714 503-4200
4000 N Lakewood Blvd Long Beach (90808) *(P-3542)*

Continental Graphics Corp ....E..... 310 662-2307
222 N Pacific Coast Hwy Ste 300 El Segundo (90245) *(P-3543)*

Continental Graphics Corp (HQ).....................C..... **714 503-4200**
4060 N Lakewood Blvd Bldg 801 Long Beach (90808) *(P-15660)*

Continental Heat Treating Inc ....D..... 562 944-8808
10643 Norwalk Blvd Santa Fe Springs (90670) *(P-5833)*

Continental Industries, Anaheim *Also Called: International West Inc (P-6254)*

Continental Litho Inc ....E..... 760 598-0291
1360 Park Center Dr Vista (92081) *(P-3544)*

Continental Machine Tool Co, Santa Ana *Also Called: Supreme Abrasives (P-5544)*

Continental Maritime Inds Inc ....B..... 619 234-8851
1995 Bay Front St San Diego (92113) *(P-9836)*

Continental Marketing, City Of Industry *Also Called: Continental Marketing Svc Inc (P-2492)*

Continental Marketing Svc Inc ....F..... 626 626-8888
15381 Proctor Ave City Of Industry (91745) *(P-2492)*

Continental Vitamin Co Inc ....D..... 323 581-0176
4510 S Boyle Ave Vernon (90058) *(P-4092)*

Continental Data Graphics, Long Beach *Also Called: Continental Graphics Corp (P-3541)*

Continuing Lf Communities LLC (PA)...........D..... **760 704-6400**
1940 Levante St Carlsbad (92009) *(P-15833)*

Continuous Coating Corp (PA)........................D..... **714 637-4642**
500 W Grove Ave Orange (92865) *(P-6608)*

Continuous Computing Corp ....C..... 858 882-8800
10431 Wateridge Cir Ste 110 San Diego (92121) *(P-7421)*

Contixo Inc ....E..... 909 465-5668
13947 Central Ave Chino (91710) *(P-3221)*

Contra Costa Electric Inc ....C..... 661 322-4036
3208 Landco Dr Bakersfield (93308) *(P-885)*

CONTRACT FURNITURE AND ANCILLA, Compton *Also Called: Peter Pepper Products Inc (P-8620)*

Contract Labeling Service Inc ....E..... 909 937-0344
13885 Ramona Ave Chino (91710) *(P-16805)*

Contract Resources, Commerce *Also Called: Commercial Intr Resources Inc (P-2798)*

Contract Services Group Inc ....C..... 714 582-1800
480 Capricorn St Brea (92821) *(P-15702)*

Contractor, Anaheim *Also Called: Sunset Signs and Printing Inc (P-11171)*

Contractor, Inglewood *Also Called: L and W Developers LLC (P-14902)*

Contractors Cargo Company (PA)....................D..... 310 609-1957
7223 Alondra Blvd Paramount (90723) *(P-11476)*

Contractors Cargo Company, Paramount *Also Called: CCC Property Holdings LLC (P-14926)*

Contractors Flrg Svc Cal Inc ....C..... 714 556-6100
300 E Dyer Rd Santa Ana (92707) *(P-12298)*

Contractors Rigging & Erectors, Paramount *Also Called: Contractors Cargo Company (P-11476)*

Contractors Wardrobe, Valencia *Also Called: Contractors Wardrobe Inc (P-2590)*

Contractors Wardrobe Inc (PA)......................C..... **661 257-1177**
26121 Avenue Hall Valencia (91355) *(P-2590)*

Contrctor Cmpliance Monitoring ....E..... 619 472-9065
2343 Donnington Way San Diego (92139) *(P-10102)*

Control Air Conditioning Corporation ....B..... 714 777-8600
5200 E La Palma Ave Anaheim (92807) *(P-755)*

Control Air Enterprises LLC ....B..... 760 744-2727
1390 Armorlite Dr San Marcos (92069) *(P-17063)*

Control Group Media Co LLC ....D..... 858 242-1350
375 Camino De La Reina Ste 400 San Diego (92101) *(P-15533)*

Control Switches Intl Inc ....E..... 562 498-7331
2425 Mira Mar Ave Long Beach (90815) *(P-8173)*

Control Systems Intl Inc ....D..... 949 238-4150
35 Parker Irvine (92618) *(P-6955)*

Controlmyspa, Costa Mesa *Also Called: Balboa Water Group LLC (P-8170)*

Convaid Products LLC ....D..... 310 618-0111
2830 California St Torrance (90503) *(P-12482)*

Convention Center, San Diego *Also Called: San Dego Cnvntion Ctr Corp Inc (P-16921)*

Converse Inc ....D..... 310 451-0314
1437 3rd Street Promenade 39 Santa Monica (90401) *(P-13161)*

Conversion Technology Co Inc (PA)...............E..... **805 378-0033**
5360 N Commerce Ave Moorpark (93021) *(P-11049)*

Conversionpoint Holdings Inc ....D..... 888 706-6764
840 Newport Center Dr Ste 450 Newport Beach (92660) *(P-16214)*

Conveyor Concepts, Los Angeles *Also Called: Machine Building Spc Inc (P-7207)*

Conveyor Service & Electric ....E..... 562 777-1221
9550 Ann St Santa Fe Springs (90670) *(P-6971)*

Cook and Cook Incorporated ....E..... 714 680-6669
1000 E Elm Ave Fullerton (92831) *(P-6140)*

Cook Induction Heating Co Inc ....E..... 323 560-1327
4925 Slauson Ave Maywood (90270) *(P-5834)*

Cook Induction Heating Co., Maywood *Also Called: Cook Induction Heating Co Inc (P-5834)*

Cook King, La Mirada *Also Called: Stainless Stl Fabricators Inc (P-12824)*

Cookie Lovers, Vernon *Also Called: Interntnal Desserts Delicacies (P-1519)*

Cookingcom Inc ....C..... 310 664-1283
1960 E Grand Ave Ste 60 El Segundo (90245) *(P-13958)*

Cooksey Tlen Gage Dffy Woog A (PA)............D..... **714 431-1100**
535 Anton Blvd Fl 10 Costa Mesa (92626) *(P-18839)*

Cool Curtain CCI, Costa Mesa *Also Called: CCI Industries Inc (P-4986)*

Cool Things, Santa Ana *Also Called: Ecoolthing Corp (P-6861)*

Cool-Pak LLC ....D..... 805 981-2434
401 N Rice Ave Oxnard (93030) *(P-4995)*

Coola LLC ....D..... 760 940-2125
6134 Innovation Way Carlsbad (92009) *(P-4392)*

Coola Suncare, Carlsbad *Also Called: Coola LLC (P-4392)*

Coolhaus, Culver City *Also Called: Farchitecture Bb LLC (P-1297)*

Cooljet Systems, Placentia *Also Called: Mkt Innovations (P-7942)*

Coolsys Coml Indus Sltions Inc (DH)..............C..... **714 510-9609**
145 S State College Blvd Ste 200 Brea (92821) *(P-756)*

Cooltec Refrigeration Corp ....E..... 909 865-2229
1250 E Franklin Ave Unit B Pomona (91766) *(P-7605)*

Coolwater Generating Station, Daggett *Also Called: NRG California South LP (P-12030)*

Cooner Sales Company LLC (PA).....................F..... **818 882-8311**
9265 Owensmouth Ave Chatsworth (91311) *(P-12544)*

Cooner Wire Company, Chatsworth *Also Called: Cooner Sales Company LLC (P-12544)*

Coop, Pico Rivera *Also Called: Coop Home Goods LLC (P-2470)*

Coop Home Goods LLC ....E..... 888 316-1886
7860 Paramount Blvd Pico Rivera (90660) *(P-2470)*

Cooper, Wilmington *Also Called: Cooper & Brain Inc (P-259)*

Cooper & Brain Inc ....E..... 310 834-4411
655 E D St Wilmington (90744) *(P-259)*

Cooper Crouse-Hinds LLC ....E..... 951 241-8766
3350 Enterprise Dr Bloomington (92316) *(P-9201)*

Cooper Interconnect, Bloomington *Also Called: Cooper Crouse-Hinds LLC (P-9201)*

Cooper Interconnect Inc (DH)........................F..... 805 484-0543
750 W Ventura Blvd Camarillo (93010) *(P-8966)*

Mergent email: customerrelations@mergent.com
1050

2024 Southern California
Business Directory and Buyers Guide

(P-0000) Products & Services Section entry number
(PA)=Parent Co (HQ)=Headquarters (DH)=Div Headquarters

Cooper Interconnect Inc .... D...... 617 389-7080
13039 Crossroads Pkwy S City Of Industry (91746) *(P-9021)*

Cooper Lighting, Bloomington *Also Called: Cooper Lighting LLC (P-8359)*

Cooper Lighting LLC .... C...... 760 357-4760
285 Rood Rd Ste 101 Calexico (92231) *(P-886)*

Cooper Lighting LLC .... A...... 909 605-6615
3350 Enterprise Dr Bloomington (92316) *(P-8359)*

Cooper Microelectronics Inc .... E...... 949 553-8352
1671 Reynolds Ave Irvine (92614) *(P-8783)*

Coopertive Amrcn Physcians Inc (PA) .... D...... 213 473-8600
333 S Hope St Fl 8 Los Angeles (90071) *(P-19393)*

Coordinated Companies, Wilmington *Also Called: Coordnted Wire Rope Rgging Inc (P-13677)*

Coordnted Wire Rope Rgging Inc (HQ) .... E...... 310 834-8535
1707 E Anaheim St Wilmington (90744) *(P-13677)*

Cop Communications, Montclair *Also Called: California Offset Printers Inc (P-3525)*

Cop Shopper, San Diego *Also Called: Krasnes Inc (P-2431)*

Copan Diagnostics Inc (DH) .... F...... 951 696-6957
26055 Jefferson Ave Murrieta (92562) *(P-13035)*

Coplan & Coplan Inc .... E...... 760 268-0583
2270 Camino Vida Roble Ste H Carlsbad (92011) *(P-7111)*

Copley Family YMCA, San Diego *Also Called: YMCA of San Diego County (P-19481)*

Copley Newspapers, La Jolla *Also Called: The Copley Press Inc (P-16759)*

Copp Industrial Mfg Inc .... E...... 909 593-7448
5510 Brooks St Montclair (91763) *(P-9665)*

Copper Clad Mltilayer Pdts Inc .... E...... 714 237-1388
1150 N Hawk Cir Anaheim (92807) *(P-8666)*

Coppersmith Global Logistics, El Segundo *Also Called: L E Coppersmith Inc (P-11777)*

Copy Solutions Inc .... E...... 323 307-0900
919 S Fremont Ave Ste 398 Alhambra (91803) *(P-3545)*

Cor Medica, Irvine *Also Called: Cor Medica Technology (P-17631)*

Cor Medica Technology (PA) .... E...... 949 353-4554
188 Technology Dr Ste F Irvine (92618) *(P-17631)*

Corbell Products, Bloomington *Also Called: Westco Industries Inc (P-6093)*

Corbell Products Inc (PA) .... F...... 909 574-9139
14650 Hawthorne Ave Fontana (92335) *(P-6013)*

Corbett Vineyards LLC .... E...... 805 782-9463
2195 Corbett Canyon Rd Arroyo Grande (93420) *(P-1617)*

Corbin Foods, Santa Ana *Also Called: Corbin-Hill Inc (P-1459)*

Corbin-Hill Inc .... E...... 714 966-6695
2961 W Macarthur Blvd Ste 117 Santa Ana (92704) *(P-1459)*

Corbis, Los Angeles *Also Called: Corbis Images LLC (P-15476)*

Corbis Images LLC (PA) .... F...... 323 602-5700
6060 Center Dr Ste 1000 Los Angeles (90045) *(P-15476)*

Cordelia Lighting Inc .... C...... 310 886-3490
20101 S Santa Fe Ave Compton (90221) *(P-12591)*

Cordoba Corporation .... D...... 213 895-0224
1401 N Broadway Los Angeles (90012) *(P-16437)*

Cordova Industries, Sylmar *Also Called: International Academy of Fin (P-4523)*

Core, Los Angeles *Also Called: Core Cmnty Orgnzed Rlief Effor (P-19051)*

Core Bts Inc .... C...... 818 766-2400
5250 Lankershim Blvd Ste 620 North Hollywood (91601) *(P-16438)*

Core Cmnty Orgnzed Rlief Effor .... B...... 323 934-4400
910 N Hill St Los Angeles (90012) *(P-19051)*

Core Holdings Inc .... C...... 714 969-2342
17291 Irvine Blvd Ste 404 Tustin (92780) *(P-18605)*

Core Realty Holdings MGT Inc .... D...... 949 863-1031
1600 Dove St Ste 450 Newport Beach (92660) *(P-14773)*

Core Systems, Poway *Also Called: Rugged Systems Inc (P-7448)*

Core-Mark International Inc .... C...... 661 366-2673
200 Coremark Ct Bakersfield (93307) *(P-13363)*

Core-Mark International Inc .... C...... 323 583-6531
2311 E 48th St Vernon (90058) *(P-13364)*

Corecare III .... C...... 714 256-8000
800 Morningside Dr Fullerton (92835) *(P-19252)*

Corelation Inc .... C...... 619 876-5074
2305 Historic Decatur Rd Ste 300 San Diego (92106) *(P-16001)*

Corelis Inc .... E...... 562 926-6727
13100 Alondra Blvd Ste 102 Cerritos (90703) *(P-9022)*

Corelogic Credco, Irvine *Also Called: Corelogic Credco LLC (P-15621)*

Corelogic Credco LLC .... B...... 619 938-7028
9645 Granite Ridge Dr Ste 300 San Diego (92123) *(P-15620)*

Corelogic Credco LLC (DH) .... C...... 800 255-0792
40 Pacifica Ste 900 Irvine (92618) *(P-15621)*

Corelogic Dorado, Irvine *Also Called: Dorado Network Systems Corp (P-16228)*

Corenco, Vernon *Also Called: Baker Commodities Inc (P-1566)*

Coresite LLC .... B...... 213 327-1231
624 S Grand Ave Ste 1800 Los Angeles (90023) *(P-15013)*

Coreslab Structures La Inc .... C...... 951 943-9119
150 W Placentia Ave Perris (92571) *(P-5406)*

Corkys Pest Control Inc .... D...... 760 432-8801
909 Rancheros Dr San Marcos (92069) *(P-15686)*

Corn Maiden Foods Inc .... D...... 310 784-0400
24201 Frampton Ave Harbor City (90710) *(P-1322)*

Cornerstone, Valencia *Also Called: Cornerstone Display Group Inc (P-11105)*

Cornerstone, Santa Monica *Also Called: Cornerstone Ondemand Inc (P-16215)*

Cornerstone Apparel Inc .... E...... 949 498-2664
101 W Avenida Vista Hermosa San Clemente (92672) *(P-2138)*

Cornerstone Concrete Inc .... D...... 951 279-2221
255 Benjamin Dr Corona (92879) *(P-1067)*

Cornerstone Display Group Inc .... E...... 661 705-1700
28340 Avenue Crocker Valencia (91355) *(P-11105)*

Cornerstone Ondemand Inc (HQ) .... B...... 310 752-0200
1601 Cloverfield Blvd Ste 620s Santa Monica (90404) *(P-16215)*

Cornerstone Protective Svcs .... C...... 888 848-4791
400 Continental Blvd 6056 El Segundo (90245) *(P-16634)*

Cornerstore Apparel, San Clemente *Also Called: Cornerstone Apparel Inc (P-2138)*

Corningware Corelle & More, Riverside *Also Called: Snapware Corporation (P-5208)*

Cornucopia Tool & Plastics Inc .... E...... 805 238-7660
448 Sherwood Rd Paso Robles (93446) *(P-4996)*

Coromega Company Inc (PA) .... E...... 760 599-6088
2525 Commerce Way Vista (92081) *(P-13726)*

Coron-Rnge Fods Intrmdate Hldn, Fullerton *Also Called: Vanlaw Food Products Inc (P-1365)*

Corona - Cllege Hts Ornge Lmon .... B...... 951 359-6451
8000 Lincoln Ave Riverside (92504) *(P-101)*

Corona Clipper Inc .... D...... 951 737-6515
22440 Temescal Canyon Rd Ste 102 Corona (92883) *(P-12719)*

Corona Magnetics Inc .... C...... 951 735-7558
201 Corporate Terrace St Corona (92879) *(P-8939)*

Corona Millworks Company (PA) .... D...... 909 606-3288
5572 Edison Ave Chino (91710) *(P-2655)*

Corona Regional Med Ctr Hosp, Corona *Also Called: Uhs-Corona Inc (P-18482)*

Corona Regional Med Ctr LLC .... C...... 951 737-4343
800 S Main St Corona (92882) *(P-17632)*

Corona Rgnal Med Ctr Rhbltion, Corona *Also Called: Uhs-Corona Inc (P-18727)*

Corona Tools, Corona *Also Called: Corona Clipper Inc (P-12719)*

Coronado Brewing Company Inc (PA) .... E...... 619 437-4452
170 Orange Ave Coronado (92118) *(P-14047)*

Coronado Hospital, Coronado *Also Called: Sharp Coronado Hospital & Healthcare Center (P-18437)*

Coronado Manufacturing LLC .... E...... 818 768-5010
8991 Glenoaks Blvd Sun Valley (91352) *(P-9666)*

Coronado Stone Products, Rialto *Also Called: Creative Stone Mfg Inc (P-5407)*

Coronet Concrete Products Inc (PA) .... E...... 760 398-2441
83801 Avenue 45 Indio (92201) *(P-5474)*

Coronet Lighting, Beverly Hills *Also Called: Dasol Inc (P-8245)*

Corovan Corporation (PA) .... C...... 858 762-8100
12302 Kerran St Poway (92064) *(P-11516)*

Corovan Moving & Storage Co (HQ) .... D...... 858 748-1100
12302 Kerran St Poway (92064) *(P-11517)*

Corp., R.g Barry, Fontana *Also Called: DSV Solutions LLC (P-11755)*

Corpinfo Services, Santa Monica *Also Called: K-Micro Inc (P-12423)*

Corporate Alnce Strategies Inc .... C...... 877 777-7487
3410 La Sierra Ave Ste F244 Riverside (92503) *(P-16727)*

Corporate Graphics & Printing .... F...... 805 529-5333
335 Science Dr Moorpark (93021) *(P-3546)*

Corporate Graphics Intl Inc .... D...... 323 826-3440
4909 Alcoa Ave Vernon (90058) *(P-3547)*

Corporate Graphics West, Vernon *Also Called: Corporate Graphics Intl Inc (P-3547)*

Corporate Impressions La Inc .... E...... 818 761-9295
10742 Burbank Blvd North Hollywood (91601) *(P-3749)*

Corporate Real Estate Advisors, San Diego *Also Called: Cushman & Wakefield Cal Inc (P-14779)*

ALPHABETIC

Corporate Visions Inc .... C....... 760 458-0914
2705 Avenida De Anita Apt 29 Carlsbad (92010) *(P-20157)*

Corptax LLC .... C....... 818 316-2400
21550 Oxnard St Ste 700 Woodland Hills (91367) *(P-16002)*

Corridor Capital LLC (PA) .... C....... 310 442-7000
12400 Wilshire Blvd Ste 645 Los Angeles (90025) *(P-15026)*

Corrpro Companies Inc .... E....... 562 944-1636
10260 Matern Pl Santa Fe Springs (90670) *(P-5668)*

Corru Kraft Buena Pk Div 5058, Buena Park *Also Called: Orora Packaging Solutions*
(P-13012)

Corru-Kraft IV .... F....... 714 773-0124
1911 E Rosslynn Ave Fullerton (92831) *(P-3093)*

Corrugados De Baja California .... A....... 619 662-8672
2475 Paseo De Las A San Diego (92154) *(P-3094)*

Corsair Elec Connectors Inc .... C....... 949 833-0273
17100 Murphy Ave Irvine (92614) *(P-8967)*

Cortez Pallets Service Inc (PA) .... F....... 626 961-9891
14739 Proctor Ave La Puente (91746) *(P-2716)*

Cortica Healthcare Inc .... B....... 858 304-6440
7090 Miratech Dr San Diego (92121) *(P-18756)*

Cortima Co .... F....... 760 347-5535
83778 Avenue 45 Indio (92201) *(P-5528)*

Cosasco Inc .... D....... 562 949-0123
11841 Smith Ave Santa Fe Springs (90670) *(P-10126)*

Cosco Home & Office Products, Ontario *Also Called: Dorel Juvenile Group Inc (P-5016)*

Cosmedx Science Inc .... E....... 951 371-0509
3550 Vine St Ste 210 Riverside (92507) *(P-4093)*

Cosmetic Enterprises Ltd .... F....... 818 896-5355
12848 Pierce St Pacoima (91331) *(P-4393)*

Cosmetic Group Usa Inc .... C....... 818 767-2889
12708 Branford St Pacoima (91331) *(P-4394)*

Cosmetic Laboratories America, Chatsworth *Also Called: Cosmetic Laboratories of America LLC (P-14127)*

Cosmetic Laboratories of America LLC .... B....... 818 717-6140
20245 Sunburst St Chatsworth (91311) *(P-14127)*

Cosmetic Laboratories-America, Chatsworth *Also Called: Kdc/One Chatsworth Inc (P-4428)*

Cosmetic Technologies LLC .... D....... 805 376-9960
2585 Azurite Cir Newbury Park (91320) *(P-4395)*

Cosmetix West (PA) .... E....... 310 726-3080
2305 Utah Ave El Segundo (90245) *(P-14128)*

Cosmic Plastics Inc (PA) .... E....... 661 257-3274
28410 Industry Dr Valencia (91355) *(P-3933)*

Cosmo, Montclair *Also Called: Cosmo Products LLC (P-8232)*

Cosmo Fiber Corporation (PA) .... F....... 626 256-6098
1802 Santo Domingo Ave Duarte (91010) *(P-3750)*

Cosmo International Corp .... D....... 310 271-1100
9200 W Sunset Blvd Ste 401 West Hollywood (90069) *(P-4396)*

Cosmo International Fragrances, West Hollywood *Also Called: Cosmo International Corp (P-4396)*

Cosmo Products LLC .... F....... 626 416-5411
5431 Brooks St Montclair (91763) *(P-8232)*

Cosmo Textiles Inc .... D....... 562 220-1177
13984 Orange Ave Paramount (90723) *(P-2081)*

Cosmodyne LLC .... E....... 562 795-5990
3010 Old Ranch Pkwy Ste 300 Seal Beach (90740) *(P-7229)*

Cosmos Food Co Inc .... E....... 323 221-9142
16015 Phoenix Dr City Of Industry (91745) *(P-1873)*

Cosmotronic, Ontario *Also Called: Tc Cosmotronic Inc (P-8736)*

Cosrich Group Inc .... E....... 818 686-2500
12243 Branford St Sun Valley (91352) *(P-4397)*

Costa Mesa Country Club, Costa Mesa *Also Called: Mesa Verde Partners (P-17438)*

Costco, Montebello *Also Called: Costco Wholesale Corporation (P-13689)*

Costco Auto Program, San Diego *Also Called: Affinity Auto Programs Inc (P-16769)*

Costco Optical Location 908, National City *Also Called: Costco Wholesale Corporation*
(P-10835)

Costco Wholesale Corporation .... C....... 619 336-3412
1001 W 19th St National City (91950) *(P-10835)*

Costco Wholesale Corporation .... A....... 951 361-3606
11600 Riverside Dr Ste A Jurupa Valley (91752) *(P-11568)*

Costco Wholesale Corporation .... C....... 323 890-1904
1345 N Montebello Blvd Montebello (90640) *(P-13689)*

Cosway Company Inc (PA) .... E....... 310 900-4100
20633 S Fordyce Ave Carson (90810) *(P-4398)*

Cots Journal Magazine, San Clemente *Also Called: R T C Group (P-3384)*

Cott Technologies Inc .... F....... 626 961-3399
14923 Proctor Ave La Puente (91746) *(P-6841)*

Cottage Childrens Medical Ctr, Santa Barbara *Also Called: Santa Brbara Cttage Hosp Fndti*
(P-18422)

Cottage Health .... D....... 805 688-6432
2050 Viborg Rd Solvang (93463) *(P-18229)*

Cottage Health System, Santa Barbara *Also Called: Goleta Valley Cottage Hosp Aux*
(P-18270)

Cotterman Company, Bakersfield *Also Called: Material Control Inc (P-6869)*

Cotton Generation Inc .... F....... 323 581-8555
6051 Maywood Ave Huntington Park (90255) *(P-2406)*

Cotton Links LLC .... E....... 714 444-4700
1360 Ritchey St Santa Ana (92705) *(P-2156)*

Cottrell Paul Enterprises LLC (PA) .... C....... 661 212-2357
16654 Soledad Canyon Rd Ste 233 Santa Clarita (91387) *(P-16635)*

Cougar Biotechnology Inc .... D....... 310 943-8040
10990 Wilshire Blvd Ste 1200 Los Angeles (90024) *(P-4094)*

Council On Aging - Sthern Cal .... D....... 714 479-0107
2 Executive Cir Ste 175 Irvine (92614) *(P-19052)*

Counseling and Research Assoc Inc .... C....... 310 715-2020
108 W Victoria St Gardena (90248) *(P-19253)*

Count Machinery Co, Escondido *Also Called: Count Numbering Machine Inc (P-7184)*

Count Numbering Machine Inc .... E....... 760 739-9357
2128 Auto Park Way Escondido (92029) *(P-7184)*

Country Archer Jerky, San Bernardino *Also Called: S&E Gourmet Cuts Inc (P-13274)*

Country Club Fashions Inc .... E....... 323 965-2707
6083 W Pico Blvd Los Angeles (90035) *(P-13912)*

Country Floral Supply Inc (PA) .... D....... 805 520-8026
3802 Weatherly Cir Westlake Village (91361) *(P-13505)*

Country Furnishings, Westlake Village *Also Called: Country Floral Supply Inc (P-13505)*

Country Hills Health Care Inc .... C....... 619 441-8745
1580 Broadway El Cajon (92021) *(P-17912)*

Country Hills Post Acute, El Cajon *Also Called: Country Hills Health Care Inc (P-17912)*

Country House .... F....... 714 505-8988
2852 Walnut Ave Ste C1 Tustin (92780) *(P-1536)*

Country Suites By Carlson, San Diego *Also Called: Libor Management LLC (P-15227)*

Country Villa E Convalescent, Los Angeles *Also Called: Country Villa Service Corp (P-20020)*

Country Villa Health Services, Anaheim *Also Called: Country Villa Service Corp (P-20021)*

COUNTRY VILLA NURSING & REHABI, Los Angeles *Also Called: Country Villa Nursing Ctr Inc (P-17913)*

Country Villa Nursing Ctr Inc .... C....... 213 484-9730
340 S Alvarado St Los Angeles (90057) *(P-17913)*

Country Villa Service Corp .... C....... 760 340-0053
39950 Vista Del Sol Rancho Mirage (92270) *(P-16806)*

Country Villa Service Corp .... C....... 818 246-5516
1208 S Central Ave Glendale (91204) *(P-17914)*

Country Villa Service Corp .... C....... 310 537-2500
3611 E Imperial Hwy Lynwood (90262) *(P-17915)*

Country Villa Service Corp .... C....... 626 445-2421
400 W Huntington Dr Arcadia (91007) *(P-17916)*

Country Villa Service Corp .... C....... 626 285-2165
112 E Broadway San Gabriel (91776) *(P-18118)*

Country Villa Service Corp .... C....... 562 598-2477
3000 N Gate Rd Seal Beach (90740) *(P-19053)*

Country Villa Service Corp .... C....... 323 734-9122
3233 W Pico Blvd Los Angeles (90019) *(P-20016)*

Country Villa Service Corp .... C....... 323 666-1544
3002 Rowena Ave Los Angeles (90039) *(P-20017)*

Country Villa Service Corp .... C....... 562 597-8817
1730 Grand Ave Long Beach (90804) *(P-20018)*

Country Villa Service Corp .... C....... 626 358-4547
615 W Duarte Rd Monrovia (91016) *(P-20019)*

Country Villa Service Corp .... C....... 323 734-1101
2415 S Western Ave Los Angeles (90018) *(P-20020)*

Country Villa Service Corp (PA) .... D....... 310 574-3733
2400 E Katella Ave Ste 800 Anaheim (92806) *(P-20021)*

COUNTRY VILLA WESTWOOD NURSING, Los Angeles *Also Called: Westwood Healthcare Center LP (P-18077)*

Mergent email: customerrelations@mergent.com
1052

2024 Southern California
Business Directory and Buyers Guide

(P-0000) Products & Services Section entry number
(PA)=Parent Co (HQ)=Headquarters (DH)=Div Headquarters

Country Vlla Mar Vsta Nrsing C, Los Angeles *Also Called: Rrt Enterprises LP (P-18045)*

Country Vlla Rncho Mrage Hlthc .... C....... 760 340-0053
39950 Vista Del Sol Rancho Mirage (92270) *(P-19054)*

Countrywide, Thousand Oaks *Also Called: Countrywide Home Loans Inc (P-14308)*

Countrywide, Glendale *Also Called: Countrywide Home Loans Inc (P-14309)*

Countrywide Home Loans Inc (HQ) .... A
225 W Hillcrest Dr Thousand Oaks (91360) *(P-14308)*

Countrywide Home Loans Inc .... A....... 818 550-8700
801 N Brand Blvd Ste 750 Glendale (91203) *(P-14309)*

County Clothing Company, Irvine *Also Called: Snowmass Apparel Inc (P-13150)*

County Ford North Inc (PA) .... C....... **760 945-9900**
450 W Vista Way Vista (92083) *(P-13749)*

County General Hospital, San Luis Obispo *Also Called: County of San Luis Obispo (P-18235)*

County of Kern .... A....... 661 326-2054
1700 Mount Vernon Ave Bakersfield (93306) *(P-18230)*

County of Kern .... C....... 661 336-6871
1600 E Belle Ter Ste 5 Bakersfield (93307) *(P-20416)*

County of Los Angeles .... E....... 626 968-3312
14959 Proctor Ave La Puente (91746) *(P-6929)*

County of Los Angeles .... E....... 310 456-8014
3637 Winter Canyon Rd Malibu (90265) *(P-6930)*

County of Los Angeles .... C....... 562 945-2581
9402 Greenleaf Ave Whittier (90605) *(P-11420)*

County of Los Angeles .... D....... 626 458-1707
1537 Alcazar St Los Angeles (90033) *(P-11569)*

County of Los Angeles .... D....... 213 367-3176
6801 E 2nd St Long Beach (90803) *(P-12117)*

County of Los Angeles .... B....... 626 458-4000
900 S Fremont Ave Alhambra (91803) *(P-12118)*

County of Los Angeles .... D....... 626 299-5300
1000 S Fremont Ave Unit 4 Alhambra (91803) *(P-14467)*

County of Los Angeles .... C....... 213 922-6210
1 Gateway Plz Los Angeles (90012) *(P-15661)*

County of Los Angeles .... A....... 562 940-4324
1100 N Eastern Ave Los Angeles (90063) *(P-16003)*

County of Los Angeles .... C....... 213 974-0515
320 W Temple St Fl 9 Los Angeles (90012) *(P-16525)*

County of Los Angeles .... D....... 323 267-2771
1100 N Eastern Ave Los Angeles (90063) *(P-16807)*

County of Los Angeles .... C....... 909 231-0549
1875 Fairplex Dr Pomona (91768) *(P-17422)*

County of Los Angeles .... A....... 323 226-7131
1900 Zonal Ave Los Angeles (90033) *(P-17633)*

County of Los Angeles .... D....... 213 744-3919
2829 S Grand Ave Los Angeles (90007) *(P-17634)*

County of Los Angeles .... C....... 310 222-2401
1000 W Carson St 8th Fl Palos Verdes Peninsu (90274) *(P-18231)*

County of Los Angeles .... B....... 310 668-4545
12025 Wilmington Ave Los Angeles (90059) *(P-18232)*

County of Los Angeles .... C....... 323 226-6021
1100 N Mission Rd Rm 236 Los Angeles (90033) *(P-18233)*

County of Los Angeles .... C....... 213 473-6100
450 Bauchet St Los Angeles (90012) *(P-18234)*

County of Los Angeles .... C....... 323 226-3468
1240 N Mission Rd Los Angeles (90033) *(P-18525)*

County of Los Angeles .... D....... 661 223-8700
38200 Lake Hughes Rd Castaic (91384) *(P-18526)*

County of Los Angeles .... C....... 661 223-8700
30500 Arrastre Canyon Rd Acton (93510) *(P-18527)*

County of Los Angeles .... A....... 562 401-7088
7601 Imperial Hwy Downey (90242) *(P-18683)*

County of Los Angeles .... B....... 323 897-6187
5850 S Main St Los Angeles (90003) *(P-18684)*

County of Los Angeles .... C....... 213 974-3512
210 W Temple St Fl 18 Los Angeles (90012) *(P-18840)*

County of Los Angeles .... D....... 661 940-4181
5300 W Avenue I Lancaster (93536) *(P-19055)*

County of Los Angeles .... B....... 323 889-3405
5770 S Eastern Ave 4th Fl Commerce (90040) *(P-19056)*

County of Los Angeles .... D....... 562 497-3500
4060 Watson Plaza Dr Lakewood (90712) *(P-19057)*

County of Los Angeles .... D....... 213 974-9331
320 W Temple St Ste 1101 Los Angeles (90012) *(P-19058)*

County of Los Angeles .... D....... 562 908-3119
8240 Broadway Ave Whittier (90606) *(P-19059)*

County of Los Angeles .... D....... 323 226-8511
1601 Eastlake Ave Los Angeles (90033) *(P-19060)*

County of Los Angeles .... D....... 562 940-6856
7285 Quill Dr Downey (90242) *(P-19061)*

County of Los Angeles .... D....... 818 374-2000
14414 Delano St Van Nuys (91401) *(P-19062)*

County of Los Angeles .... C....... 323 780-2185
4849 Civic Center Way Los Angeles (90022) *(P-19063)*

County of Los Angeles .... D....... 213 351-7257
501 Shatto Pl Ste 301 Los Angeles (90020) *(P-19064)*

County of Los Angeles .... C....... 323 226-8611
1605 Eastlake Ave Los Angeles (90033) *(P-19254)*

County of Los Angeles .... C....... 213 240-8412
313 N Figueroa St 9th Fl Los Angeles (90012) *(P-19394)*

County of Los Angeles .... C....... 661 723-6088
44933 Fern Ave Lancaster (93534) *(P-19567)*

County of Los Angeles .... A....... 323 267-2136
1100 N Eastern Ave Los Angeles (90063) *(P-19764)*

County of Los Angeles .... C....... 323 267-6167
1800 Paseo Rancho Castilla Los Angeles (90032) *(P-19966)*

County of Los Angeles .... C....... 562 940-2907
9150 Imperial Hwy Downey (90242) *(P-20022)*

County of Los Angeles .... D....... 661 974-7700
42011 4th St W Ste 3530 Lancaster (93534) *(P-20412)*

County of Los Angeles .... C....... 213 738-4601
510 S Vermont Ave Fl 1 Los Angeles (90020) *(P-20414)*

County of Orange .... C....... 949 252-5006
3160 Airway Ave Costa Mesa (92626) *(P-11694)*

County of Orange .... D....... 714 647-1552
1631 E Wilshire Ave Santa Ana (92705) *(P-15760)*

County of Orange .... D....... 714 896-7188
8141 13th St Westminster (92683) *(P-19065)*

County of Orange .... E....... 714 567-7444
1300 S Grand Ave Ste B Santa Ana (92705) *(P-20409)*

County of Riverside .... D....... 951 955-4800
3450 14th St Riverside (92501) *(P-427)*

County of Riverside .... D....... 951 955-0840
5256 Mission Blvd Riverside (92509) *(P-17635)*

County of Riverside .... A....... 951 486-4000
26520 Cactus Ave Moreno Valley (92555) *(P-17636)*

County of Riverside .... B....... 951 486-4000
26520 Cactus Ave Moreno Valley (92555) *(P-17637)*

County of Riverside .... C....... 951 955-6000
4075 Main St Riverside (92501) *(P-18841)*

County of Riverside .... D....... 951 955-4900
2038 Iowa Ave Ste 102 Riverside (92507) *(P-19066)*

County of Riverside .... C....... 951 683-7691
4500 Glenwood Dr Ste A Riverside (92501) *(P-19440)*

County of Riverside .... C....... 951 358-5000
4065 County Circle Dr Riverside (92503) *(P-20417)*

County of San Diego .... C....... 858 694-2960
5510 Overland Ave Ste 410 San Diego (92123) *(P-16808)*

County of San Diego .... C....... 619 692-8200
3853 Rosecrans St San Diego (92110) *(P-18512)*

County of San Diego .... C....... 619 531-4040
330 W Broadway Ste 1020 San Diego (92101) *(P-18842)*

County of San Diego .... A....... 619 515-8202
330 W Broadway Ste 1100 San Diego (92101) *(P-19067)*

County of San Diego .... D....... 858 505-6100
5560 Overland Ave Ste 410 San Diego (92123) *(P-20410)*

County of San Luis Obispo .... C....... 805 781-4753
2180 Johnson Ave San Luis Obispo (93401) *(P-18235)*

County of Ventura .... C....... 805 654-2561
800 S Victoria Ave Ventura (93009) *(P-19068)*

County of Ventura .... D....... 805 654-3152
800 S Victoria Ave Ste 1540 Ventura (93009) *(P-19765)*

County of Ventura .... D....... 805 652-6100
3291 Loma Vista Rd Ventura (93003) *(P-20405)*

ALPHABETIC

Employee Codes: A=Over 500 employees, B=251-500
C=101-250, D=51-100, E=20-50, F=10-19, G=1-9

2024 Southern California
Business Directory and Buyers Guide

© Mergent Inc. 1-800-342-5647

1053

County Ventura Human Resources, Ventura *Also Called: County of Ventura (P-19068)*

Countywide Mech Systems LLC ....C...... 619 449-9900
1400 N Johnson Ave Ste 114 El Cajon (92020) *(P-757)*

Courtesy Chevrolet Center ....D...... 619 297-4321
750 Camino Del Rio N San Diego (92108) *(P-13750)*

Courtney Inc (PA)...**D...... 949 222-2050**
16781 Millikan Ave Irvine (92606) *(P-1149)*

Courtside Cellars LLC ....F...... 805 467-2882
2425 Mission St San Miguel (93451) *(P-1618)*

Courtside Cellars LLC (PA)..**E...... 805 782-0500**
4910 Edna Rd San Luis Obispo (93401) *(P-1619)*

Courtyard By Marriott, Baldwin Park *Also Called: Baldwin Hospitality LLC (P-15085)*

Courtyard By Marriott, Sherman Oaks *Also Called: Burbank Partners LLC (P-15098)*

Courtyard By Mrrott Los Angles, Monrovia *Also Called: Sage Hospitality Resources LLC (P-15338)*

Courtyard Marriott Mission Vly, San Diego *Also Called: Mbp Land LLC (P-15245)*

Courtyard Oxnard ....D...... 805 988-3600
600 E Esplanade Dr Oxnard (93036) *(P-15122)*

Courtyard San Dego Mssion Vlly, San Diego *Also Called: Mhf Mv Operating VI LLC (P-15250)*

Cousins Foods LLC ....E...... 818 767-3842
2021 1st St San Fernando (91340) *(P-13695)*

Couts Heating & Cooling Inc ....C...... 951 278-5560
1693 Rimpau Ave Corona (92881) *(P-758)*

Covance Antibody Services, San Diego *Also Called: Biolegend Cns Inc (P-19827)*

Covanta Long Bch Rnwble Enrgy ....C...... 562 436-0636
118 Pier S Ave Long Beach (90802) *(P-12166)*

Covario Inc ....D...... 858 397-1500
9255 Towne Centre Dr Ste 600 San Diego (92121) *(P-20158)*

Covenant Care California LLC ....D...... 805 964-4871
160 S Patterson Ave Santa Barbara (93111) *(P-17917)*

Covenant Care La Jolla LLC ....C...... 858 453-5810
2552 Torrey Pines Rd Ste 1 La Jolla (92037) *(P-17918)*

Covenant Care LLC (PA)..**B...... 949 349-1200**
120 Vantis Dr Ste 200 Aliso Viejo (92656) *(P-17919)*

Covenant House California ....C...... 323 461-3131
1325 N Western Ave Los Angeles (90027) *(P-19255)*

Covenant Living At Mt Miguel, Spring Valley *Also Called: Covenant Living West (P-19257)*

Covenant Living At Samarkand, Santa Barbara *Also Called: Covenant Living West (P-19256)*

Covenant Living West ....D...... 805 687-0701
2550 Treasure Dr Santa Barbara (93105) *(P-19256)*

Covenant Living West ....D...... 619 931-1114
325 Kempton St Spring Valley (91977) *(P-19257)*

COVENANT RETIREMENT COMMUNITIES, Santa Barbara *Also Called: Covenant Rtirement Communities (P-17920)*

Covenant Rtirement Communities ....D...... 805 687-0701
2550 Treasure Dr Santa Barbara (93105) *(P-17920)*

Covenant Transport, Pomona *Also Called: Covenant Transport Inc (P-11477)*

Covenant Transport Inc ....A...... 909 469-0130
1300 E Franklin Ave Pomona (91766) *(P-11477)*

Coventry Court Health Center ....C...... 714 636-2800
2040 S Euclid St Anaheim (92802) *(P-17921)*

Coverance Insur Solutions Inc ....C...... 310 856-9925
1343 6th St Manhattan Beach (90266) *(P-14580)*

Coveris, Ontario *Also Called: Transcontinental US LLC (P-3195)*

Coverking, Anaheim *Also Called: Shrin LLC (P-12261)*

Covid Clinic Inc ....B...... 877 219-8378
16541 Gothard St Huntington Beach (92647) *(P-17638)*

Covidien, Costa Mesa *Also Called: Newport Medical Instrs Inc (P-10577)*

Covidien Holding Inc ....C...... 760 603-5020
2101 Faraday Ave Carlsbad (92008) *(P-10485)*

Covidien Holding Inc ....C...... 619 690-8500
2475 Paseo De Las Americas Ste A San Diego (92154) *(P-10486)*

Covidien Kenmex, San Diego *Also Called: Covidien Holding Inc (P-10486)*

Covidien LP ....C...... 949 837-3700
9775 Toledo Way Irvine (92618) *(P-10487)*

Covina Rehabilitation Center ....C...... 626 967-3874
261 W Badillo St Covina (91723) *(P-17922)*

Covina Service Center, San Dimas *Also Called: Southern California Edison Co (P-12059)*

Covington & Burling LLP ....C...... 424 332-4800
1999 Avenue Of The Stars Ste 3500 Los Angeles (90067) *(P-18843)*

Coway Usa Inc ....E...... 213 486-1600
4221 Wilshire Blvd Ste 210 Los Angeles (90010) *(P-14129)*

Cowboy Direct Response ....E...... 714 824-3780
130 E Alton Ave Santa Ana (92707) *(P-11106)*

Cowelco ....E...... 562 432-5766
1634 W 14th St Long Beach (90813) *(P-6219)*

Cowelco Steel Contractors, Long Beach *Also Called: Cowelco (P-6219)*

Cox Castle & Nicholson LLP (PA).....................................**C...... 310 284-2200**
2029 Century Park E Ste 2100 Los Angeles (90002) *(P-18844)*

Cox Castle, Los Angeles *Also Called: Cox Castle & Nicholson LLP (P-18844)*

Cox Communications Cal LLC ....B...... 619 262-1122
5159 Federal Blvd San Diego (92105) *(P-11983)*

Cox Enterprises LLC ....D...... 858 822-8587
325 W 3rd Ave Ste 101 Escondido (92025) *(P-18606)*

Cox Petroleum Transport, Cudahy *Also Called: HF Cox Inc (P-11460)*

Coy Industries Inc ....D...... 310 603-2970
2970 E Maria St E Rncho Dmngz (90221) *(P-6220)*

Coyle Reproductions Inc (PA)..**C...... 866 269-5373**
2850 Orbiter St Brea (92821) *(P-3548)*

Coyne Companies LLC ....F...... 760 353-1016
2351 S 4th St El Centro (92243) *(P-3438)*

Cozza Inc ....F...... 619 749-5663
9941 Prospect Ave Santee (92071) *(P-7809)*

Cozzia USA LLC (HQ)...**F...... 626 667-2272**
861 S Oak Park Rd Covina (91724) *(P-9202)*

CP Auto Products Inc ....E...... 323 266-3850
3901 Medford St Los Angeles (90063) *(P-6609)*

CP Document Technologies LLC ....E...... 310 575-6640
11835 W Olympic Blvd Ste 145 Los Angeles (90064) *(P-15644)*

CP Kelco, San Diego *Also Called: CP Kelco US Inc (P-412)*

CP Kelco US Inc ....E:..... 619 595-5000
2025 Harbor Dr San Diego (92113) *(P-412)*

CP Kelco US Inc ....E...... 619 652-5326
2031 E Belt St San Diego (92113) *(P-4602)*

CP Manufacturing, San Diego *Also Called: CP Manufacturing Inc (P-7230)*

CP Manufacturing Inc (HQ)..**C...... 619 477-3175**
6795 Calle De Linea San Diego (92154) *(P-7230)*

Cp-Carrillo Inc (DH)..**C...... 949 567-9000**
1902 Mcgaw Ave Irvine (92614) *(P-7699)*

Cp-Carrillo Inc ....E...... 949 567-9000
17401 Armstrong Ave Irvine (92614) *(P-7700)*

Cpaperless LLC ....D...... 949 510-3365
605 1/2 Orchid Ave Corona Del Mar (92625) *(P-8454)*

CPC Fabrication Inc ....E...... 714 549-2426
2904 Oak St Santa Ana (92707) *(P-6221)*

CPC Services Inc ....E...... 626 852-6200
2025 E Financial Way Ste 200 Glendora (91741) *(P-5475)*

Cpcc Inc ....D...... 818 882-3200
10610 Owensmouth Ave Chatsworth (91311) *(P-18119)*

Cpd Industries ....E...... 909 465-5596
4665 State St Montclair (91763) *(P-4997)*

Cpe Hr Inc ....D...... 310 270-9800
9000 W Sunset Blvd Ste 900 West Hollywood (90069) *(P-20159)*

Cph Monarch Hotel LLC ....A...... 949 234-3200
1 Monarch Beach Resort Dana Point (92629) *(P-15123)*

CPI Malibu Division ....D...... 805 383-1829
3623 Old Conejo Rd Ste 205 Newbury Park (91320) *(P-8505)*

CPI Satcom & Antenna Tech Inc ....C...... 310 539-6704
3111 Fujita St Torrance (90505) *(P-8506)*

Cpl Holdings LLC ....C...... 310 348-6800
12181 Bluff Creek Dr Ste 250 Playa Vista (90094) *(P-13685)*

Cpp - Pomona, Pomona *Also Called: Consoldted Precision Pdts Corp (P-5786)*

Cpp Cudahy, Cudahy *Also Called: Consolidated Foundries Inc (P-5787)*

Cpp-Azusa, Azusa *Also Called: Magparts (P-5797)*

Cpp-City of Industry, City Of Industry *Also Called: Cast Parts Inc (P-5651)*

Cpp-Pomona, Walnut *Also Called: Cast Parts Inc (P-5652)*

Cpp-Port Hueneme, Port Hueneme *Also Called: Pac Foundries Inc (P-5806)*

Cpp/Belwin Inc ....B...... 818 891-5999
16320 Roscoe Blvd Ste 100 Van Nuys (91406) *(P-3403)*

Cppg Inc ....F...... 714 572-3662
3905 E Miraloma Ave Anaheim (92806) *(P-16809)*

Mergent email: customerrelations@mergent.com
1054

2024 Southern California
Business Directory and Buyers Guide

(P-0000) Products & Services Section entry number
(PA)=Parent Co (HQ)=Headquarters (DH)=Div Headquarters

CPS Security, Cerritos *Also Called: Commercial Protective Svcs Inc (P-16630)*

Cpu Medical Management Systems, San Diego *Also Called: Computer Proc Unlimited Inc (P-15999)*

Cputer Inc .... D...... 844 394-1538
2110 Artesia Blvd Redondo Beach (90278) *(P-16559)*

Cq Press Fairfax Co, Thousand Oaks *Also Called: Sage Publications Inc (P-3414)*

Cr & A Custom, Los Angeles *Also Called: CR & A Custom Apparel Inc (P-3751)*

CR & A Custom Apparel Inc .... E...... 213 749-4440
312 W Pico Blvd Los Angeles (90015) *(P-3751)*

Cr Print, Westlake Village *Also Called: Earth Print Inc (P-3567)*

Craft, San Diego *Also Called: Elco Rfrgn Solutions LLC (P-7609)*

Craft Labor & Support Svcs LLC .... C...... 619 336-9977
1545 Tidelands Ave Ste C National City (91950) *(P-9837)*

Craftech, Anaheim *Also Called: Sp Craftech I LLC (P-5212)*

Craftech Metal Forming Inc .... E...... 951 940-6444
24100 Water Ave Ste B Perris (92570) *(P-6014)*

Craftsman Cutting Dies Inc (PA) .... E...... 714 776-8995
2273 E Via Burton Anaheim (92806) *(P-5876)*

Craftsman Lath and Plaster Inc .... B...... 951 685-9922
8325 63rd St Riverside (92509) *(P-1010)*

Craftsman Unity LLC .... C...... 714 776-8995
2273 E Via Burton Anaheim (92806) *(P-5877)*

Craftsmen Construction, San Diego *Also Called: Hayes Company Inc (P-15543)*

Crafttech, Anaheim *Also Called: Charmaine Plastics Inc (P-4989)*

Craftwood Industries Inc .... E...... 616 796-1209
222 Shelbourne Irvine (92620) *(P-2907)*

Crafty Apes LLC (PA) .... A...... 310 837-3900
127 Lomita St El Segundo (90245) *(P-17178)*

Craig Kackert Design Tech, Simi Valley *Also Called: Jaxx Manufacturing Inc (P-9070)*

Craig Manufacturing Company (PA) .... D...... 323 726-7355
8129 Slauson Ave Montebello (90640) *(P-9375)*

Craig Tools Inc .... E...... 310 322-0614
142 Lomita St El Segundo (90245) *(P-7112)*

Crane Aerospace Inc .... D...... 818 526-2600
3000 Winona Ave Burbank (91504) *(P-9667)*

Crane Co .... C...... 562 426-2531
3201 Walnut Ave Long Beach (90755) *(P-6774)*

CRANE CO., Long Beach *Also Called: Crane Co (P-6774)*

Craneveyor Corp (PA) .... D...... 626 442-1524
1524 Potrero Ave El Monte (91733) *(P-6980)*

Craneworks Southwest Inc .... F...... 760 735-9793
1312 E Barham Dr San Marcos (92078) *(P-6987)*

Crate Modular Inc .... D...... 310 405-0829
3025 E Dominguez St Carson (90810) *(P-6375)*

Cratex, Encinitas *Also Called: Cratex Manufacturing Co Inc (P-5540)*

Cratex Manufacturing Co Inc .... D...... 760 942-2877
328 Encinitas Blvd Ste 200 Encinitas (92024) *(P-5540)*

Crave Foods, Los Angeles *Also Called: Crave Foods Inc (P-1874)*

Crave Foods Inc .... E...... 562 900-7272
2043 Imperial St Los Angeles (90021) *(P-1874)*

Crawford Associates .... E...... 760 922-6804
2635 E Chanslor Way Blythe (92225) *(P-1068)*

Crazy Industries .... E...... 619 270-9090
8675 Avenida Costa Norte San Diego (92154) *(P-10985)*

CRC, Long Beach *Also Called: California Resources Corp (P-254)*

CRC Health Corporate .... A...... 714 542-3581
2101 E 1st St Santa Ana (92705) *(P-18685)*

CRC Health Group Inc .... C...... 951 784-8010
1021 W La Cadena Dr Riverside (92501) *(P-18686)*

CRC Services LLC .... F...... 888 848-4754
27200 Tourney Rd Ste 200 Santa Clarita (91355) *(P-296)*

Crd Mfg Inc .... E...... 714 871-3300
615 Fee Ana St Placentia (92870) *(P-5913)*

Creation Tech Calexico Inc (HQ) .... E
1778 Zinetta Rd Ste F Calexico (92231) *(P-8667)*

Creative Accents .... E...... 760 373-1222
6294 Curtis Pl California City (93505) *(P-2112)*

Creative Age Publications Inc .... E...... 818 782-7328
15975 High Knoll Rd Encino (91436) *(P-3352)*

Creative Artsts Agcy Hldngs LL (PA) .... A...... 424 288-2000
2000 Avenue Of The Stars Ste 100 Los Angeles (90067) *(P-17314)*

Creative Automation, Sun Valley *Also Called: Jack J Engel Manufacturing Inc (P-9220)*

Creative Baby Inc .... E...... 626 330-2289
2222 Lee Ave South El Monte (91733) *(P-12936)*

Creative Channel Services LLC, Los Angeles *Also Called: Rocky Point Investments LLC (P-20232)*

Creative Costuming & Designs, Huntington Beach *Also Called: Creative Costuming Designs Inc (P-2017)*

Creative Costuming Designs Inc .... E...... 714 895-0982
15402 Electronic Ln Huntington Beach (92649) *(P-2017)*

Creative Design Consultants (PA) .... D...... 714 641-4868
2915 Red Hill Ave Ste G201 Costa Mesa (92626) *(P-16810)*

Creative Design Industries .... C...... 619 710-2525
2587 Otay Center Dr San Diego (92154) *(P-2157)*

Creative Fire Kiln and Kit LLC .... E...... 818 486-3899
13612 Van Nuys Blvd Pacoima (91331) *(P-1875)*

Creative Foods LLC .... E...... 858 748-0070
12622 Poway Rd # A Poway (92064) *(P-1876)*

Creative Graphic Services, Santa Clarita *Also Called: Living Way Industries Inc (P-3625)*

Creative Impressions Inc .... F...... 714 521-4441
7697 9th St Buena Park (90621) *(P-4808)*

Creative Inflatables, South El Monte *Also Called: Promotonal Design Concepts Inc (P-4786)*

Creative Machine Technology, Corona *Also Called: Cremach Tech Inc (P-7006)*

Creative Machine Technology, Corona *Also Called: Cremach Tech Inc (P-7007)*

Creative Maintenance Systems .... D...... 949 852-2871
1340 Reynolds Ave Ste 111 Irvine (92614) *(P-15703)*

Creative Outdoor Advertising, Riverside *Also Called: Brimad Enterprises Inc (P-15585)*

Creative Outdoor Distrs USA, Lake Forest *Also Called: Cod USA Inc (P-2924)*

Creative Park Productions LLC .... C...... 818 622-3702
100 Universal City Plz Universal City (91608) *(P-17179)*

Creative Pathways Inc .... E...... 310 530-1965
20815 Higgins Ct Torrance (90501) *(P-7157)*

Creative Press, Anaheim *Also Called: Creative Press LLC (P-3549)*

Creative Press LLC (PA) .... E...... 714 774-5060
1350 S Caldwell Cir Anaheim (92805) *(P-3549)*

Creative Press LLC .... E...... 714 774-5060
1600 E Ball Rd Anaheim (92805) *(P-3550)*

Creative Solutions Svcs LLC .... C...... 646 495-1558
1745 N Vista St Los Angeles (90046) *(P-15834)*

Creative Stone Mfg Inc (PA) .... C...... 909 357-8295
201 S Cactus Ave Rialto (92376) *(P-5407)*

Creative Teaching Press Inc (PA) .... D...... 714 799-2100
6262 Katella Ave Cypress (90630) *(P-3404)*

Creatons Grdn Ntral Fd Mkts In .... E...... 661 877-4280
24849 Anza Dr Valencia (91355) *(P-3996)*

Credibility Corp .... A...... 310 456-8271
22761 Pacific Coast Hwy Malibu (90265) *(P-16811)*

Credit Card Services Inc (PA) .... D...... 213 365-1122
21281 S Western Ave Torrance (90501) *(P-16812)*

Cremach Tech Inc .... D...... 951 735-3194
400 E Parkridge Ave Corona (92879) *(P-7006)*

Cremach Tech Inc (PA) .... D...... 951 735-3194
369 Meyer Cir Corona (92879) *(P-7007)*

Crenshaw Chrstn Ctr Ch Los Ang (PA) .... B...... 323 758-3777
7901 S Vermont Ave Los Angeles (90044) *(P-19499)*

Crenshaw Die and Mfg Corp .... D...... 949 475-5505
7432 Prince Dr Huntington Beach (92647) *(P-7064)*

Crenshaw Manufacturing Inc .... E...... 949 475-5505
7432 Prince Dr Huntington Beach (92647) *(P-5914)*

Crenshaw Nursing, Los Angeles *Also Called: Longwood Management Corp (P-18001)*

Crescent Inc .... E...... 714 992-6030
670 S Jefferson St Placentia (92870) *(P-3551)*

Crescent Healthcare Inc (DH) .... C...... 714 520-6300
11980 Telegraph Rd Ste 100 Santa Fe Springs (90670) *(P-18607)*

Crescenta-Canada YMCA (PA) .... C...... 818 790-0123
1930 Foothill Blvd La Canada (91011) *(P-19441)*

Crescenta-Canada YMCA .... C...... 818 352-3255
6840 Foothill Blvd Tujunga (91042) *(P-19442)*

Crescentone Inc (HQ) .... C...... 310 563-7000
200 Continental Blvd Fl 3 El Segundo (90245) *(P-16004)*

Cresco Manufacturing Inc .... E...... 714 525-2326
1614 N Orangethorpe Way Anaheim (92801) *(P-7810)*

ALPHABETIC

Crescomfg.com, Anaheim *Also Called: Cresco Manufacturing Inc (P-7810)*

Crest Beverage LLC ....B...... 858 452-2300
1348 47th St San Diego (92102) *(P-13464)*

Crest Beverage Company Inc ....C...... 858 452-2300
3840 Via De La Valle Ste 300 Del Mar (92014) *(P-13465)*

Crest Chevrolet, San Bernardino *Also Called: Harbill Inc (P-13777)*

Crest Coating Inc ....D...... 714 635-7090
1361 S Allec St Anaheim (92805) *(P-6698)*

Crest R E O & Relocation, La Crescenta *Also Called: EAM Enterprises Inc (P-14791)*

Crest Steel, Riverside *Also Called: Crest Steel Corporation (P-12545)*

Crest Steel Corporation ....D...... 951 727-2600
6580 General Rd Riverside (92509) *(P-12545)*

Crestec Los Angeles, Long Beach *Also Called: Crestec Usa Inc (P-3552)*

Crestec Usa Inc ....E...... 310 327-9000
2410 Mira Mar Ave Long Beach (90815) *(P-3552)*

Crestline Hotels & Resorts Inc (HQ)..........................C...... 213 629-1200
120 S Los Angeles St 11 Los Angeles (90012) *(P-15124)*

Crestmont Capital LLC ....C...... 949 537-3882
1422 Edinger Ave Ste 210 Tustin (92780) *(P-15027)*

Creston Village, Paso Robles *Also Called: Emeritus Corporation (P-14707)*

Crestone LLC ....E...... 323 588-8857
2511 S Alameda St Vernon (90058) *(P-2236)*

Crestview Landscape Inc ....D...... 818 962-7771
13915 Saticoy St Panorama City (91402) *(P-158)*

Crestwood Behavioral Hlth Inc ....D...... 661 363-8127
6700 Eucalyptus Dr Ste A Bakersfield (93306) *(P-18120)*

Crestwood Behavioral Hlth Inc ....C...... 619 481-6790
5550 University Ave Ste A San Diego (92105) *(P-18121)*

Crestwood Behavioral Hlth Inc ....C...... 760 451-4165
624 E Elder St Fallbrook (92028) *(P-18122)*

Crestwood Behavioral Hlth Inc ....D...... 805 308-8720
303 S C St Lompoc (93436) *(P-19258)*

Creu LLC ....E...... 909 483-4888
12750 Baltic Ct Rancho Cucamonga (91739) *(P-4998)*

Crevier Classics LLC ....B...... 714 835-3171
1500 Auto Mall Dr Santa Ana (92705) *(P-13751)*

Crew Builders Inc ....C...... 619 587-2033
8130 Commercial St La Mesa (91942) *(P-544)*

Crew Knitwear LLC ....D...... 323 526-3888
2155 E 7th St Ste 125 Los Angeles (90023) *(P-2065)*

Crew Knitwear LLC (PA) ....D...... 323 526-3888
660 S Myers St Los Angeles (90023) *(P-2315)*

Crexi, Playa Vista *Also Called: Commercial RE Exch Inc (P-15997)*

Crh Management, Newport Beach *Also Called: Core Realty Holdings MGT Inc (P-14773)*

Cri 2000 LP (PA)..E...... 619 542-1975
2245 San Diego Ave Ste 125 San Diego (92110) *(P-2753)*

Cri Sub 1 (DH)...E...... 310 537-1657
1715 S Anderson Ave Compton (90220) *(P-2881)*

Crimson Resource Management, Bakersfield *Also Called: Delta Trading LP (P-4658)*

CRINETICS, San Diego *Also Called: Crinetics Pharmaceuticals Inc (P-4095)*

Crinetics Pharmaceuticals Inc (PA)...........................D...... 858 450-6464
10222 Barnes Canyon Rd Ste 200 San Diego (92121) *(P-4095)*

Crislu Corp ....E...... 310 322-3444
20916 Higgins Ct Torrance (90501) *(P-10900)*

Crissair Inc ....C...... 661 367-3300
28909 Avenue Williams Valencia (91355) *(P-7711)*

Cristal Materials Inc ....E...... 323 855-1688
6825 Mckinley Ave Los Angeles (90001) *(P-2846)*

Cristek, Anaheim *Also Called: Cristek Interconnects LLC (P-8968)*

Cristek Interconnects LLC (DH)..................................C...... 714 696-5200
5395 E Hunter Ave Anaheim (92807) *(P-8968)*

Critchfeld Mech Inc Sthern Cal ....D...... 949 390-2900
15391 Springdale St Huntington Beach (92649) *(P-759)*

Criterion Machine Works ....E
765 W 16th St Costa Mesa (92627) *(P-7113)*

Criticalpoint Capital LLC ....D...... 909 987-9533
9433 Hyssop Dr Rancho Cucamonga (91730) *(P-3985)*

CRITTENTON SERVICES FOR CHILDR, Fullerton *Also Called: Florence Crttnton Svcs Ornge C (P-19263)*

Crl, Vernon *Also Called: C R Laurence Co Inc (P-9364)*

Crm Co LLC (PA)..F...... 949 263-9100
1301 Dove St Ste 940 Newport Beach (92660) *(P-4749)*

Crmls LLC ....C...... 909 859-2040
15325 Fairfield Ranch Rd Ste 200 Chino Hills (91709) *(P-14657)*

Crockett & Coinc (PA)...................................E...... 619 267-6410
5120 Robinwood Rd Ste A22 Bonita (91902) *(P-17423)*

Crockett & Coinc ....D...... 619 267-1103
5540 Sweetwater Rd Bonita (91902) *(P-17424)*

Crockett Graphics Inc (PA)...........................D...... 805 987-8577
980 Avenida Acaso Camarillo (93012) *(P-3095)*

Crosby Fruit Products, Fontana *Also Called: Refresco Beverages US Inc (P-1343)*

Crosno Construction Inc ....E...... 805 343-7437
819 Sheridan Rd Arroyo Grande (93420) *(P-6015)*

Crossfield Products Corp (PA)......................E...... 310 886-9100
3000 E Harcourt St Compton (90221) *(P-3934)*

Crossing Guard Company ....A...... 310 202-8284
10440 Pioneer Blvd Ste 5 Santa Fe Springs (90670) *(P-16636)*

Crossport Mocean ....F...... 949 646-1701
1611 Babcock St Newport Beach (92663) *(P-2151)*

Crossrads Adult Day Hlth Care, Rancho Cucamonga *Also Called: Horrigan Enterprises Inc (P-19091)*

Crossrads Chrstn Schols Corona ....C...... 951 278-3199
2380 Fullerton Ave Corona (92881) *(P-19009)*

Crossroads Software Inc ....F...... 714 990-6433
210 W Birch St Ste 207 Brea (92821) *(P-16216)*

Crosstown Elec & Data Inc ....D...... 626 813-6693
5454 Diaz St Baldwin Park (91706) *(P-887)*

Crothall Services Group ....A...... 714 562-9275
14710 Northam St La Mirada (90638) *(P-17121)*

Crowdstrike Inc ....C...... 888 512-8906
400 Continental Blvd Ste 275 El Segundo (90245) *(P-16560)*

Crowdstrike Inc ....C...... 888 512-8906
15440 Laguna Canyon Rd Ste 250 Irvine (92618) *(P-16561)*

Crowdstrike Inc ....C...... 888 512-8906
15441 Laguna Canyon Rd, Ste 260 Irvine (92618) *(P-16562)*

Crowell & Moring LLP ....C...... 949 263-8400
3 Park Plz Ste 2000 Irvine (92614) *(P-18845)*

Crowell & Moring LLP ....C...... 213 622-4750
515 S Flower St Ste 4000 Los Angeles (90071) *(P-18846)*

Crower Cams, San Diego *Also Called: Crower Engrg & Sls Co Inc (P-9376)*

Crower Engrg & Sls Co Inc ....D...... 619 661-6477
6180 Business Center Ct San Diego (92154) *(P-9376)*

Crowley Marine Services Inc ....B...... 310 732-6500
86 Berth 300 S Harbor Blvd San Pedro (90731) *(P-11748)*

Crown Bolt, Aliso Viejo *Also Called: Hd Supply Distribution Services LLC (P-12724)*

Crown Building Maintenance Co ....B...... 714 434-9494
14201 Franklin Ave Tustin (92780) *(P-15704)*

Crown Building Maintenance Co ....B...... 858 560-5785
5482 Complex St Ste 108 San Diego (92123) *(P-15705)*

Crown Carton Company Inc ....E...... 323 582-3053
1820 E 48th Pl Vernon (90058) *(P-3096)*

Crown Circuits Inc ....E...... 949 922-0144
6070 Avenida Encinas Carlsbad (92011) *(P-8668)*

Crown Citrus Company Inc ....E...... 760 344-1930
551 W Main St Brawley (92227) *(P-1368)*

Crown Discount Tools, Sylmar *Also Called: TMW Corporation (P-9817)*

Crown Energy Services Inc ....A...... 213 765-7800
2601 S Figueroa St Bldg 1 Los Angeles (90007) *(P-15706)*

Crown Equipment Corporation ....E...... 909 923-8357
4250 Greystone Dr Ontario (91761) *(P-6988)*

Crown Equipment Corporation ....E...... 626 968-0556
1300 Palomares St La Verne (91750) *(P-6989)*

Crown Equipment Corporation ....D...... 310 952-6600
4061 Via Oro Ave Long Beach (90810) *(P-6990)*

Crown Fence Co ....D...... 562 864-5177
12070 Telegraph Rd Ste 340 Santa Fe Springs (90670) *(P-1150)*

Crown Golf Properties LP ....C...... 714 730-1611
12442 Tustin Ranch Rd Tustin (92782) *(P-20160)*

Crown Lift Trucks, Ontario *Also Called: Crown Equipment Corporation (P-6988)*

Crown Lift Trucks, La Verne *Also Called: Crown Equipment Corporation (P-6989)*

Crown Lift Trucks, Long Beach *Also Called: Crown Equipment Corporation (P-6990)*

Mergent email: customerrelations@mergent.com
1056

2024 Southern California
Business Directory and Buyers Guide

(P-0000) Products & Services Section entry number
(PA)=Parent Co (HQ)=Headquarters (DH)=Div Headquarters

Crown Paper Converting, Ontario *Also Called: Crown Paper Converting Inc (P-3043)*

Crown Paper Converting Inc .... E...... 909 923-5226
   1380 S Bon View Ave Ontario (91761) *(P-3043)*

Crown Pavers Inc .... E...... 323 636-3365
   2434 W Valley Blvd Ste C Alhambra (91803) *(P-6931)*

CROWN PAVERS INC, Alhambra *Also Called: Crown Pavers Inc (P-6931)*

Crown Plaza La Harbor Hotel, San Pedro *Also Called: Spf Capital Real Estate LLC (P-15367)*

Crown Plaza Los Angeles, Los Angeles *Also Called: Ihg Management (maryland) LLC (P-15203)*

Crown Poly Inc .... C...... 323 585-5522
   5700 Bickett St Huntington Park (90255) *(P-3181)*

Crown Printers, San Bernardino *Also Called: Shorett Printing Inc (P-3811)*

Crown Products Inc .... E...... 760 471-1188
   177 Newport Dr Ste A San Marcos (92069) *(P-6222)*

Crown Steel, San Marcos *Also Called: Crown Products Inc (P-6222)*

Crown Technical Systems (PA)................................**C......** **951 332-4170**
   13470 Philadelphia Ave Fontana (92337) *(P-8118)*

Crown Vly Precision Machining, Irwindale *Also Called: Sinecera Inc (P-16930)*

Crownair Aviation, San Diego *Also Called: Air 88 Inc (P-11685)*

Crowne Cold Storage LLC .... E...... 661 725-6458
   786 Road 188 Delano (93215) *(P-20161)*

Crowne Plaza Ventura Beach, Ventura *Also Called: Ventura Hsptality Partners LLC (P-15404)*

Crowne Plz Los Angeles Hbr Ht, Long Beach *Also Called: Nhca Inc (P-15261)*

Crowntonka California Inc .... E...... 909 230-6720
   6514 E 26th St Commerce (90040) *(P-7606)*

CRST Expedited Inc .... C...... 909 563-5606
   9032 Merrill Ave Chino (91708) *(P-11478)*

CRST Expedited Inc .... B...... 909 563-5606
   1219 E Elm St Ontario (91761) *(P-11479)*

Crt Color Printing Inc .... F...... 562 906-1517
   13201 Barton Cir Santa Fe Springs (90670) *(P-3553)*

Crucial Power Products .... F...... 323 721-5017
   14000 S Broadway Los Angeles (90061) *(P-9023)*

Crumbl Cookies .... D...... 949 519-0791
   23702 El Toro Rd Ste B Lake Forest (92630) *(P-1513)*

Crunchyroll LLC (DH)..**D......** **972 355-7300**
   10202 Washington Blvd Culver City (90232) *(P-17180)*

Crush Master Grinding Corp .... E...... 909 595-2249
   755 Penarth Ave Walnut (91789) *(P-7811)*

Cruz Modular Inc (PA)..**D......** **714 283-2890**
   249 W Baywood Ave Ste B Orange (92865) *(P-11518)*

Crydom Inc (DH)..**D......** **619 210-1590**
   2320 Paseo De Las Americas Ste 201 San Diego (92154) *(P-8174)*

Cryogenic Experts, Oxnard *Also Called: Acme Cryogenics Inc (P-7219)*

Cryogenic Experts Inc .... E...... 805 981-4500
   531 Sandy Cir Oxnard (93036) *(P-7231)*

Cryogenic Industries, Murrieta *Also Called: Hexco International (P-7240)*

Cryogenic Industries Inc .... C...... 951 677-2060
   25720 Jefferson Ave Murrieta (92562) *(P-8233)*

Cryomax USA Inc (HQ)...**F......** **626 330-3388**
   127 N California Ave Ste B City Of Industry (91744) *(P-11570)*

Cryostar USA, Whittier *Also Called: Messer LLC (P-3869)*

Cryostar USA LLC .... D...... 562 903-1290
   13117 Meyer Rd Whittier (90605) *(P-7274)*

Cryoworks Inc .... D...... 951 360-0920
   3309 Grapevine St Jurupa Valley (91752) *(P-6842)*

Cryst Mark Inc A Swan Techno C .... E...... 818 240-7520
   613 Justin Ave Glendale (91201) *(P-7232)*

Crystal, Riverside *Also Called: Crystal PCF Win & Door Sys LLC (P-12326)*

Crystal Art Gallery, Vernon *Also Called: Rggd Inc (P-12983)*

Crystal Casino & Hotel, Compton *Also Called: Celebrity Casinos Inc (P-15110)*

Crystal Cathedral Ministries (PA).............................**C......** **714 622-2900**
   12901 Lewis St Garden Grove (92840) *(P-19500)*

Crystal Engineering Corp .... E...... 805 595-5477
   708 Fiero Ln Ste 9 San Luis Obispo (93401) *(P-10127)*

Crystal Geyser Water Company .... D...... 661 323-6296
   1233 E California Ave Bakersfield (93307) *(P-1692)*

Crystal Geyser Water Company .... E...... 661 321-0896
   2351 E Brundage Ln Ste A Bakersfield (93307) *(P-1693)*

Crystal Mark, Glendale *Also Called: Cryst Mark Inc A Swan Techno C (P-7232)*

Crystal Organic Farms LLC .... A...... 661 845-5200
   10000 Stockdale Hwy Ste 200 Bakersfield (93311) *(P-79)*

Crystal PCF Win & Door Sys LLC .... E...... 951 779-9300
   1850 Atlanta Ave Riverside (92507) *(P-12326)*

Crystal Stairs Inc (PA)...**B......** **323 299-8998**
   5110 W Goldleaf Cir Ste 150 Los Angeles (90056) *(P-19069)*

Crystal Tip, Irvine *Also Called: Westside Resources Inc (P-10778)*

Cs Electronics, Irvine *Also Called: Cs Systems Inc (P-7519)*

Cs Systems Inc .... E...... 949 475-9100
   16781 Noyes Ave Irvine (92606) *(P-7519)*

CSCU, Santa Maria *Also Called: Coasthills Credit Union (P-14246)*

Cshg Holdings, Temecula *Also Called: Hines Growers Inc (P-56)*

Csi, Santa Clarita *Also Called: Custom Suppression Inc (P-8940)*

Csi Electrical Contractors Inc .... B...... 661 723-0869
   41769 11th St W Ste B Palmdale (93551) *(P-888)*

Csi Electrical Contractors Inc .... B...... 760 227-0577
   310 Via Vera Cruz Ste 106 San Marcos (92078) *(P-889)*

Csi Electrical Contractors Inc (HQ)..........................**C......** **562 946-0700**
   10623 Fulton Wells Ave Santa Fe Springs (90670) *(P-890)*

Csi Technologies Inc .... F...... 760 682-2222
   2540 Fortune Way Vista (92081) *(P-8926)*

Csi Vegas, Santa Clarita *Also Called: CBS Studios Inc (P-11941)*

CSM Metal Fabricating & Engrg, Los Angeles *Also Called: Commercial Shtmtl Works Inc (P-6010)*

Csr Technology Inc .... E...... 619 823-7919
   815 Alamo Ln Escondido (92025) *(P-9024)*

CTA Fixtures Inc .... D...... 909 390-6744
   5721 Santa Ana St Ste B Ontario (91761) *(P-2977)*

CTA Manufacturing Inc .... E...... 951 280-2400
   1160 California Ave Corona (92881) *(P-2493)*

Ctac Research 60901, Irwindale *Also Called: Southern California Edison Co (P-12062)*

Ctbla Inc .... D...... 323 276-1933
   1740 Albion St Los Angeles (90031) *(P-9319)*

Ctc Global, Irvine *Also Called: Ctc Global Corporation (P-8258)*

Ctc Global Corporation (PA).....................................**C......** **949 428-8500**
   2026 Mcgaw Ave Irvine (92614) *(P-8258)*

Ctc Group Inc (DH)...**C......** **310 540-0500**
   21333 Hawthorne Blvd Torrance (90503) *(P-15125)*

Ctcoa LLC .... E...... 562 407-5375
   16818 Marquardt Ave Cerritos (90703) *(P-9668)*

Ctd Machines Inc .... F...... 213 689-4455
   7355 E Slauson Ave Commerce (90040) *(P-7008)*

Cte California TI & Engrg Inc .... E
   7801 Bolero Dr Jurupa Valley (92509) *(P-7114)*

Ctek Inc .... E...... 310 241-2973
   2425 Golden Hill Rd Ste 106 Paso Robles (93446) *(P-12005)*

Ctf, Perris *Also Called: California Trusframe LLC (P-2694)*

Ctg, Santa Barbara *Also Called: Channel Technologies Group LLC (P-9962)*

CTI Foods Azusa LLC .... C...... 626 633-1609
   1120 W Foothill Blvd Azusa (91702) *(P-1216)*

Ctour Holiday LLC .... B...... 323 261-8811
   222 E Huntington Dr Ste 105 Monrovia (91016) *(P-17544)*

CTS Cement Manufacturing Co, Los Angeles *Also Called: CTS Cement Manufacturing Corp (P-4560)*

CTS Cement Manufacturing Corp .... E...... 310 472-4004
   2077 Linda Flora Dr Los Angeles (90077) *(P-4560)*

CTS Cement Manufacturing Corp (PA).......................**E......** **714 379-8260**
   12442 Knott St Garden Grove (92841) *(P-5365)*

Ctsh LLC .... D...... 949 916-6705
   640 N Tustin Ave Ste 201 Santa Ana (92705) *(P-18608)*

CU Cooperative Systems Inc (PA)............................**B......** **909 948-2500**
   9692 Haven Ave Rancho Cucamonga (91730) *(P-14247)*

CU Direct Corporation (PA).....................................**C......** **833 908-0121**
   2855 E Guasti Rd Ste 500 Ontario (91761) *(P-16005)*

Cubework, City Of Industry *Also Called: Cubeworkcom Inc (P-14774)*

Cubeworkcom Inc .... C...... 909 991-6669
   900 Turnbull Canyon Rd City Of Industry (91745) *(P-14774)*

Cubic, San Diego *Also Called: Cubic Corporation (P-9966)*

Cubic, San Diego *Also Called: Cubic Trnsp Systems Inc (P-16006)*

Cubic Corporation (HQ)...**A......** **858 277-6780**
   9233 Balboa Ave San Diego (92123) *(P-9966)*

A L P H A B E T I C

Employee Codes: A=Over 500 employees, B=251-500
C=101-250, D=51-100, E=20-50, F=10-19, G=1-9

2024 Southern California
Business Directory and Buyers Guide

© Mergent Inc. 1-800-342-5647
1057

Cubic Corporation .... A...... 858 277-6780
  9233 Balboa Ave San Diego (92123) *(P-16439)*

Cubic Defense Applications Inc (DH)............................ **A...... 858 776-5664**
  9233 Balboa Ave San Diego (92123) *(P-9203)*

Cubic Defense Applications Inc .... C...... 858 505-2870
  9233 Balboa Ave San Diego (92123) *(P-9204)*

Cubic Defense Systems, San Diego *Also Called: Cubic Corporation (P-16439)*

Cubic Ground Training, San Diego *Also Called: Cubic Defense Applications Inc (P-9203)*

Cubic Secure Communications I .... B...... 858 505-2000
  9233 Balboa Ave San Diego (92123) *(P-11846)*

Cubic Trnsp Systems Inc (DH)..................................... A...... 858 268-3100
  9233 Balboa Ave San Diego (92123) *(P-16006)*

Cucamonga Valley Water Dst .... D...... 909 987-2591
  10440 Ashford St Rancho Cucamonga (91730) *(P-12119)*

Cudahy Medical Offices, Cudahy *Also Called: Kaiser Foundation Hospitals (P-18297)*

Cudc, Ontario *Also Called: CU Direct Corporation (P-16005)*

Cue Health, San Diego *Also Called: Cue Health Inc (P-10252)*

Cue Health Inc .... A...... 858 412-8151
  4980 Carroll Canyon Rd Ste 110 San Diego (92121) *(P-10252)*

Culinary Brands Inc (PA)... **E...... 626 289-3000**
  3280 E 44th St Vernon (90058) *(P-1387)*

Culinary Hispanic Foods Inc .... A...... 619 955-6101
  805 Bow St Chula Vista (91914) *(P-13365)*

Culinary International LLC (PA)................................... C...... 626 289-3000
  3280 E 44th St Vernon (90058) *(P-1877)*

Culinary Specialties, San Marcos *Also Called: Culinary Specialties Inc (P-1878)*

Culinary Specialties Inc .... D...... 760 744-8220
  1231 Linda Vista Dr San Marcos (92078) *(P-1878)*

Culture AMP Inc (HQ).. **F...... 415 326-8453**
  16501 Ventura Blvd Ste 400 Encino (91436) *(P-16217)*

Culver Personnel Agencies Inc .... C...... 888 600-5733
  445 Marine View Ave Ste 101 Del Mar (92014) *(P-15835)*

Culver Personnel Services, Del Mar *Also Called: Culver Personnel Agencies Inc (P-15835)*

Culver West Health Center LLC .... D...... 310 390-9506
  4035 Grand View Blvd Los Angeles (90066) *(P-17923)*

Cummings Resources LLC .... E...... 951 248-1130
  1495 Columbia Ave Riverside (92507) *(P-11107)*

Cummings Resources LLC .... E...... 951 248-1130
  330 W Citrus St Colton (92324) *(P-11108)*

Cummings Transportation, Shafter *Also Called: Cummings Vacuum Service Inc (P-341)*

Cummings Vacuum Service Inc .... D...... 661 746-1786
  19605 Broken Ct Shafter (93263) *(P-341)*

Cummins, Irvine *Also Called: Cummins Pacific LLC (P-6892)*

Cummins Aerospace, Anaheim *Also Called: Cummins Aerospace LLC (P-9967)*

Cummins Aerospace LLC (PA)..................................... **E...... 714 879-2800**
  2320 E Orangethorpe Ave Anaheim (92806) *(P-9967)*

Cummins Pacific LLC (HQ)... **D...... 949 253-6000**
  1939 Deere Ave Irvine (92606) *(P-6892)*

Cunico Corporation .... E...... 562 733-4600
  1910 W 16th St Long Beach (90813) *(P-6843)*

Curated Image, The, Anaheim *Also Called: Haddads Fine Arts Inc (P-4589)*

Curation Foods Inc (HQ)... **D...... 800 454-1355**
  2811 Airpark Dr Santa Maria (93455) *(P-1879)*

Curative Inc .... A...... 650 713-8928
  605 E Huntington Dr Monrovia (91016) *(P-20023)*

Curative-Korva LLC .... D...... 424 645-7575
  605 E Huntington Dr Monrovia (91016) *(P-18544)*

Curemetrix Inc .... E...... 858 333-5830
  402 W Broadway Ste 400 San Diego (92101) *(P-16218)*

Curiosity Ink Media LLC .... C...... 561 287-5776
  478 Ellis St Pasadena (91105) *(P-12849)*

Curlin Medical Inc (HQ).. **E...... 714 897-9301**
  15662 Commerce Ln Huntington Beach (92649) *(P-7275)*

Curology Inc .... B...... 617 959-2480
  5717 Pacific Center Blvd Ste 200 San Diego (92121) *(P-17639)*

CURRAN ENGINEERING COMPANY I .... E...... 800 643-6353
  28727 Industry Dr Valencia (91355) *(P-6355)*

Current Renewables Engrg Inc .... F...... 951 405-1733
  1760 Chicago Ave Ste J13 Riverside (92507) *(P-19568)*

Currie Enterprises .... D...... 714 528-6957
  382 N Smith Ave Corona (92878) *(P-9377)*

Curry Company LLC .... E...... 310 643-8400
  15724 Condon Ave Lawndale (90260) *(P-7115)*

Curtco Robb Media LLC (PA)..................................... **E...... 310 589-7700**
  29160 Heathercliff Rd Ste 200 Malibu (90265) *(P-3353)*

Curtin Maritime Corp .... B...... 562 983-7257
  725 Pier T Ave Long Beach (90802) *(P-707)*

Curtis Winery, Los Olivos *Also Called: Firestone Vineyard LP (P-1628)*

Curtiss-Wrght Cntrls Elctrnic (DH).............................. **C...... 661 702-1494**
  28965 Avenue Penn Santa Clarita (91355) *(P-8175)*

Curtiss-Wrght Cntrls Elctrnic .... C...... 661 257-4430
  28965 Avenue Penn Santa Clarita (91355) *(P-19569)*

Curtiss-Wrght Cntrls Elctrnic, Santa Clarita *Also Called: Curtiss-Wrght Cntrls Elctrnic (P-8175)*

Curtiss-Wrght Cntrls Intgrted .... D...... 714 982-1860
  210 Ranger Ave Brea (92821) *(P-10642)*

Curtiss-Wrght Nclear Div Enrte, Brea *Also Called: Curtiss-Wright Flow Ctrl Corp (P-6762)*

Curtiss-Wright Controls Inc .... E...... 818 503-0998
  6940 Farmdale Ave North Hollywood (91605) *(P-9669)*

Curtiss-Wright Corporation .... D...... 661 257-4430
  28965 Avenue Penn Santa Clarita (91355) *(P-6758)*

Curtiss-Wright Corporation .... D...... 619 482-3405
  1675 Brandywine Ave Ste F Chula Vista (91911) *(P-6759)*

Curtiss-Wright Corporation .... E...... 619 656-4740
  1675 Brandywine Ave Ste E Chula Vista (91911) *(P-17122)*

Curtiss-Wright Flow Control .... C...... 626 851-3100
  28965 Avenue Penn Valencia (91355) *(P-6760)*

Curtiss-Wright Flow Ctrl Corp .... E...... 949 271-7500
  2950 E Birch St Brea (92821) *(P-6761)*

Curtiss-Wright Flow Ctrl Corp .... D...... 714 528-2301
  260 Ranger Ave Brea (92821) *(P-6762)*

Curtiss-Wright Flow Ctrl Corp (DH)............................. **D...... 714 528-1365**
  2950 E Birch St Brea (92821) *(P-6789)*

Curtiss-Wright Surfc Tech LLC .... F...... 714 546-4160
  2151 S Hathaway St Santa Ana (92705) *(P-5835)*

Curvature LLC (DH).. **B...... 800 230-6638**
  7418 Hollister Ave Ste 110 Santa Barbara (93117) *(P-12402)*

Cusa Properties Inc .... E...... 562 432-7300
  4643 Hackett Ave Lakewood (90713) *(P-1802)*

Cushman & Wakefield, Ontario *Also Called: Cushman & Wakefield Cal Inc (P-14782)*

Cushman & Wakefield Cal Inc .... B...... 310 556-1805
  10250 Constellation Blvd Ste 2200 Los Angeles (90067) *(P-14775)*

Cushman & Wakefield Cal Inc .... B...... 562 276-1400
  3760 Kilroy Airport Way Long Beach (90806) *(P-14776)*

Cushman & Wakefield Cal Inc .... B...... 714 591-0451
  7281 Garden Grove Blvd Ste G Garden Grove (92841) *(P-14777)*

Cushman & Wakefield Cal Inc .... A...... 949 474-4004
  18111 Von Karman Ave Ste 1000 Irvine (92612) *(P-14778)*

Cushman & Wakefield Cal Inc .... A...... 858 452-6500
  12830 El Camino Real Ste 100 San Diego (92130) *(P-14779)*

Cushman & Wakefield Cal Inc .... B...... 805 418-5811
  3011 Townsgate Rd Westlake Village (91361) *(P-14780)*

Cushman & Wakefield Cal Inc .... B...... 805 322-7244
  770 Paseo Camarillo 315 Camarillo (93010) *(P-14781)*

Cushman & Wakefield Cal Inc .... B...... 909 483-0077
  3800 Concours Ste 300 Ontario (91764) *(P-14782)*

Cushman & Wakefield Cal Inc .... B...... 909 980-3781
  901 Via Piemonte Ste 200 Ontario (91764) *(P-14783)*

Cushman & Wakefield California, Garden Grove *Also Called: Cushman & Wakefield Cal Inc (P-14777)*

Cushman Realty Corporation .... C...... 213 627-4700
  601 S Figueroa St Ste 4700 Los Angeles (90017) *(P-14784)*

Cushman Winery Corporation .... E...... 805 688-9339
  6905 Foxen Canyon Rd Los Olivos (93441) *(P-13475)*

Custom Autosound Mfg Inc .... F...... 714 535-1091
  1030 Williamson Ave Fullerton (92833) *(P-8403)*

Custom Aviation Supply, Chatsworth *Also Called: Custom Control Sensors LLC (P-8119)*

Custom Blow Molding, Escondido *Also Called: Tri-Pack Enterprises Inc (P-3160)*

Custom Brands Group .... E...... 213 749-6333
  9255 Customhouse Plz Ste A San Diego (92154) *(P-3004)*

Custom Building Products, Huntington Beach *Also Called: Custom Building Products LLC (P-4561)*

Mergent email: customerrelations@mergent.com
1058

2024 Southern California
Business Directory and Buyers Guide

(P-0000) Products & Services Section entry number
(PA)=Parent Co (HQ)=Headquarters (DH)=Div Headquarters

Custom Building Products LLC (DH)..D...... 800 272-8786
7711 Center Ave Ste 500 Huntington Beach (92647) *(P-4561)*

Custom Building Products LLC..C...... 323 582-0846
6511 Salt Lake Ave Bell (90201) *(P-4562)*

Custom Building Products LLC..D...... 661 393-0422
1900 Norris Rd Bakersfield (93308) *(P-12850)*

Custom Built Machinery Inc..E...... 714 424-9250
2614 S Hickory St Santa Ana (92707) *(P-19570)*

Custom Characters Inc...F...... 818 507-5940
621 Thompson Ave Glendale (91201) *(P-2446)*

Custom Chemical Formulators, Santa Fe Springs *Also Called: Morgan Gallacher Inc*
(P-4361)

Custom Control Sensors Inc..E...... 818 341-4610
21111 Plummer St Chatsworth (91311) *(P-8176)*

Custom Control Sensors LLC (PA)..C...... 818 341-4610
21111 Plummer St Chatsworth (91311) *(P-8119)*

Custom Displays Inc..E...... 323 770-8074
411 W 157th St Gardena (90248) *(P-2951)*

Custom Engineering Plastics, San Diego *Also Called: Custom Engineering Plastics LP*
(P-4999)

Custom Engineering Plastics LP...F...... 858 452-0961
8558 Miramar Pl San Diego (92121) *(P-4999)*

Custom Fibreglass Mfg Co...C...... 562 432-5454
1711 Harbor Ave Long Beach (90813) *(P-9923)*

Custom Flavors, San Clemente *Also Called: Custom Ingredients Inc (P-1764)*

Custom Foods, Santa Fe Springs *Also Called: J & J Processing Inc (P-1777)*

Custom Hardtops, Long Beach *Also Called: Custom Fibreglass Mfg Co (P-9923)*

Custom Hotel, Los Angeles *Also Called: Playa Proper Jv LLC (P-15306)*

Custom Hotel LLC..B...... 310 645-0400
8639 Lincoln Blvd Los Angeles (90045) *(P-15126)*

Custom Industries Inc..E...... 714 779-9101
1371 N Miller St Anaheim (92806) *(P-5338)*

Custom Ingredients Inc (PA)...E...... 949 276-7995
160 Calle Iglesia San Clemente (92672) *(P-1764)*

Custom Iron Corporation...E...... 949 939-4379
26895 Aliso Creek Rd Ste B787 Aliso Viejo (92656) *(P-6016)*

Custom Iron Design..E...... 805 581-3763
270 E Easy St Ste 1 Simi Valley (93065) *(P-6859)*

Custom Laminators Inc...E...... 714 778-0895
1350 S Claudina St Anaheim (92805) *(P-4832)*

Custom Lawn Services, Canoga Park *Also Called: American Landscape MGT Inc (P-140)*

Custom Leathercraft Mfg LLC (DH)..E...... 323 752-2221
10240 Alameda St South Gate (90280) *(P-5306)*

Custom Logos Inc...E...... 858 277-1886
7889 Clairemont Mesa Blvd San Diego (92111) *(P-2088)*

Custom Magnetics Cal Inc...E...... 909 620-3877
15142 Vista Del Rio Ave Chino (91710) *(P-8091)*

Custom Metal Fabricators, Orange *Also Called: Cmf Inc (P-1039)*

Custom Metal Finishing Inc..E...... 310 532-5075
17804 S Western Ave Gardena (90248) *(P-7233)*

Custom Molded Devices, Simi Valley *Also Called: Poly-Tainer Inc (P-4864)*

Custom Packaging Design, Montclair *Also Called: Cpd Industries (P-4997)*

Custom Pipe & Fabrication Inc (HQ)...D...... 800 553-3058
10560 Fern Ave Stanton (90680) *(P-6844)*

Custom Printing, Oxnard *Also Called: Pine Grove Industries Inc (P-3658)*

Custom Quilting Inc..E...... 714 731-7271
2832 Walnut Ave Ste D Tustin (92780) *(P-2471)*

Custom Sensors & Tech Inc...A...... 805 716-0322
2475 Paseo De Las Americas San Diego (92154) *(P-9025)*

Custom Sensors & Tech Inc (HQ)...A...... 805 716-0322
1461 Lawrence Dr Thousand Oaks (91320) *(P-9026)*

Custom Steel Fabrication Inc...F...... 562 907-2777
11966 Rivera Rd Santa Fe Springs (90670) *(P-6017)*

Custom Suppression Inc...F...... 818 718-1040
26470 Ruether Ave Ste 106 Santa Clarita (91350) *(P-8940)*

Custom Truck One Source LP..E...... 316 627-2608
4500 State Rd Bakersfield (93308) *(P-9320)*

Custom Vinyls, Fontana *Also Called: Patrick Industries Inc (P-12360)*

Custom Win & Door Design Inc..E...... 760 439-6213
3242 Production Ave Oceanside (92058) *(P-2591)*

Customer Loan Depot, Foothill Ranch *Also Called: Loandepotcom LLC (P-14339)*

Customfab Inc..C...... 714 891-9119
7345 Orangewood Ave Garden Grove (92841) *(P-5256)*

Customzed Svcs Admnstrtors Inc..C...... 858 810-2004
9797 Aero Dr Ste 300 San Diego (92123) *(P-14581)*

Cut N Clean Greens, Oxnard *Also Called: San Miguel Produce Inc (P-11)*

Cutting Edge Creative LLC..D...... 562 907-7007
9944 Flower St Bellflower (90706) *(P-2978)*

Cutting Edge Supply, Colton *Also Called: Black Diamond Blade Company (P-6926)*

Cv Sciences Inc (PA)..E...... 866 290-2157
9530 Padgett St Ste 107 San Diego (92126) *(P-4096)*

Cvb Financial Corp (PA)...C...... 909 980-4030
701 N Haven Ave Ste 350 Ontario (91764) *(P-14190)*

Cvc Specialties, Vernon *Also Called: Continental Vitamin Co Inc (P-4092)*

Cvc Technologies Inc..E...... 909 355-0311
10861 Business Dr Fontana (92337) *(P-7347)*

Cvr Nitrogen LP (HQ)...E...... 310 571-9800
10877 Wilshire Blvd Fl 10 Los Angeles (90024) *(P-4538)*

Cw Industries...E...... 562 432-5421
1735 Santa Fe Ave Long Beach (90813) *(P-6018)*

Cw Industries Inc (PA)...E...... 562 432-5421
1735 Santa Fe Ave Long Beach (90813) *(P-17082)*

Cw Network LLC (HQ)..C...... 818 977-2500
3300 W Olive Ave Fl 3 Burbank (91505) *(P-11943)*

Cwdre, Irvine *Also Called: Certified Wtr Dmage Rstrtion E (P-15699)*

Cwi Steel Technologies Corporation..E...... 949 476-7600
2415 Campus Dr Ste 100 Irvine (92612) *(P-5661)*

Cwp, Adelanto *Also Called: Commercial Wood Products Company (P-1009)*

Cwp Cabinets Inc...C...... 760 246-4530
15447 Anacapa Rd Ste 102 Victorville (92392) *(P-1011)*

Cwtv, Burbank *Also Called: Cw Network LLC (P-11943)*

Cyber Medical Imaging Inc... 888 937-9729
11300 W Olympic Blvd Ste 710 Los Angeles (90064) *(P-10734)*

Cyber-Pro Systems Inc...C...... 562 256-3800
2121 S Towne Centre Pl Ste 200 Anaheim (92806) *(P-16489)*

Cybercoders Inc...C...... 949 885-5151
6591 Irvine Center Dr Ste 200 Irvine (92618) *(P-15836)*

Cybercopy Inc (PA)..F...... 310 736-1001
2766 S La Cienega Blvd Los Angeles (90034) *(P-15645)*

Cyberdefender Corporation..F...... 323 449-0774
617 W 7th St Fl 10 Los Angeles (90017) *(P-16007)*

Cybernet Manufacturing Inc...A...... 949 600-8000
5 Holland Ste 201 Irvine (92618) *(P-7422)*

Cyberpolicy Inc..C...... 877 626-9991
19584 Pine Valley Ave Porter Ranch (91326) *(P-14582)*

Cyberscientific, Irvine *Also Called: Cybercoders Inc (P-15836)*

Cybertouch, Newbury Park *Also Called: Transparent Devices Inc (P-7574)*

Cycle News Inc (PA)...E...... 949 863-7082
17771 Mitchell N Irvine (92614) *(P-3268)*

Cydea Inc...E...... 800 710-9939
8510 Miralani Dr San Diego (92126) *(P-1620)*

Cydwoq Inc..E...... 818 848-8307
2102 Kenmere Ave Burbank (91504) *(P-5260)*

Cygnet Stampng & Fabrictng Inc (PA)...E...... 818 240-7574
613 Justin Ave Glendale (91201) *(P-6508)*

Cylinder Division, Corona *Also Called: Parker-Hannifin Corporation (P-7713)*

Cymbiotika LLC (PA)..E...... 770 910-4945
5825 Oberlin Dr Ste 5 San Diego (92121) *(P-4097)*

Cymbiotika LLC..D...... 949 652-8177
8885 Rehco Rd San Diego (92121) *(P-4098)*

Cymer LLC (HQ)...A...... 858 385-7300
17075 Thornmint Ct San Diego (92127) *(P-9205)*

Cynergy Prof Systems LLC...E...... 800 776-7978
23187 La Cadena Dr Ste 102 Laguna Hills (92653) *(P-12655)*

Cypress Creek Holdings LLC..D...... 310 581-6299
3250 Ocean Park Blvd Ste 355 Santa Monica (90405) *(P-12019)*

Cys Knship Sneca Tstin Wrprund, Santa Ana *Also Called: Seneca Family of Agencies*
(P-14630)

Cytec, Anaheim *Also Called: Cytec Engineered Materials Inc (P-3935)*

Cytec Engineered Materials Inc..E...... 714 632-8444
1191 N Hawk Cir Anaheim (92807) *(P-3935)*

Employee Codes: A=Over 500 employees, B=251-500
C=101-250, D=51-100, E=20-50, F=10-19, G=1-9

2024 Southern California
Business Directory and Buyers Guide

© Mergent Inc. 1-800-342-5647

1059

ALPHABETIC

Cytec Engineered Materials Inc .... C....... 714 630-9400
645 N Cypress St Orange (92867) *(P-4603)*

Cytec Engineered Materials Inc .... C....... 714 632-1174
1440 N Kraemer Blvd Anaheim (92806) *(P-5788)*

Cytec Solvay Group 714 630-9400
1440 N Kraemer Blvd Anaheim (92806) *(P-3890)*

Cytori Therapeutics Inc .... E....... 858 458-0900
5764 Pacific Center Blvd Ste 110 San Diego (92121) *(P-10488)*

Cyu Lithographics Inc .... E....... 888 878-9898
6951 Oran Cir Buena Park (90621) *(P-3554)*

Czinger Vehicles, Torrance *Also Called: Czv Inc (P-9283)*

Czv Inc .... D....... 424 603-1450
19601 Hamilton Ave Torrance (90502) *(P-9283)*

D - Link, Irvine *Also Called: D-Link Systems Incorporated (P-12403)*

D & D Cremations Service, Vernon *Also Called: D & D Services Inc (P-1567)*

D & D Gear Incorporated .... C....... 714 692-6570
4890 E La Palma Ave Anaheim (92807) *(P-9670)*

D & D Saw Works Inc C
1445 Engineer St Ste 110 Vista (92081) *(P-12851)*

D & D Services Inc .... E....... 323 261-4176
4105 Bandini Blvd Vernon (90058) *(P-1567)*

D & D Tool & Supply, Vista *Also Called: D & D Saw Works Inc (P-12851)*

D & J Printing Inc .... D....... 661 265-1995
600 W Technology Dr Palmdale (93551) *(P-3555)*

D & K Engineering (PA) .... D....... 858 451-8999
16990 Goldentop Rd San Diego (92127) *(P-10174)*

D & M Steel Inc .... E....... 818 896-2070
13020 Pierce St Pacoima (91331) *(P-6019)*

D A C, Carpinteria *Also Called: Dac International Inc (P-7009)*

D A V Industries .... D....... 619 337-9244
1049 Elkelton Blvd Spring Valley (91977) *(P-19443)*

D and J Marketing Inc .... E....... 310 538-1583
580 W 184th St Gardena (90248) *(P-2528)*

D B Specialty Farms, Santa Maria *Also Called: Darensberries LLC (P-13)*

D C Shower Doors Inc .... C....... 661 257-1177
26121 Avenue Hall Valencia (91355) *(P-11480)*

D D N, Chatsworth *Also Called: Datadirect Networks Inc (P-16009)*

D D Wire Co Inc (PA) .... E....... 626 442-0459
4335 Temple City Blvd Temple City (91780) *(P-6020)*

D E I, Chino Hills *Also Called: Dynamic Enterprises Inc (P-7822)*

D E X, Camarillo *Also Called: Data Exchange Corporation (P-12405)*

D F Stauffer Biscuit Co Inc .... E....... 714 546-6855
4041 W Garry Ave Santa Ana (92704) *(P-1514)*

D G A, Los Angeles *Also Called: Directors Guild America Inc (P-17248)*

D G X, E Rncho Dmngz *Also Called: Dependable Global Express Inc (P-11751)*

D I F Group Inc .... E....... 323 231-8800
1942 E 46th St Vernon (90058) *(P-20024)*

D J American Supply Inc .... C....... 323 582-2650
6122 S Eastern Ave Commerce (90040) *(P-12972)*

D K Environmental, Vernon *Also Called: Demenno/Kerdoon Holdings (P-4682)*

D Longo Inc .... B....... 626 580-6000
3534 Peck Rd El Monte (91731) *(P-13752)*

D Mills Grnding Machining Inc .... C....... 951 697-6847
1738 N Neville St Orange (92865) *(P-7812)*

D R I, Irvine *Also Called: Dri Commercial Corporation (P-1041)*

D S T Macdonald, Valencia *Also Called: Whi Solutions Inc (P-12451)*

D V S Mdia Srvces/Intelestream, Burbank *Also Called: Dvs Media Services (P-15647)*

D W Mack Co Inc .... E....... 626 969-1817
900 W 8th St Azusa (91702) *(P-4724)*

D X Communications Inc .... E....... 323 256-3000
8160 Van Nuys Blvd Panorama City (91402) *(P-8507)*

D-Link Systems Incorporated .... C....... 714 885-6000
14420 Myford Rd Ste 100 Irvine (92606) *(P-12403)*

D-Mac Inc .... E....... 714 808-3918
1105 E Discovery Ln Anaheim (92801) *(P-2736)*

D-Tech Optoelectronics Inc .... E....... 626 956-1100
18062 Rowland St City Of Industry (91748) *(P-8606)*

D.F. Industries, Chino *Also Called: Dick Farrell Industries Inc (P-7363)*

D'Andrea Graphics, Cypress *Also Called: DAndrea Graphic Corportion (P-15662)*

D'Veal Family and Youth Svcs, Pasadena *Also Called: DVeal Corporation (P-19324)*

D&A Endeavors Inc .... D....... 310 390-7540
8484 Wilshire Blvd Ste 605 Beverly Hills (90211) *(P-1151)*

D&D Wholesale Distributors LLC .... D....... 626 333-2111
777 Baldwin Park Blvd City Of Industry (91746) *(P-13318)*

D&E Propogators, Encinitas *Also Called: Dramm and Echter Inc (P-52)*

D3 Equipment, El Cajon *Also Called: Denardi Machinery Inc (P-12767)*

D3 Go, Encino *Also Called: D3publisher of America Inc (P-16219)*

D3publisher of America Inc .... D....... 310 268-0820
15910 Ventura Blvd Ste 800 Encino (91436) *(P-16219)*

Da Vinci Schools Fund .... C....... 310 725-5800
201 N Douglas St El Segundo (90245) *(P-16813)*

Dab Inc .... D....... 562 623-4773
13415 Marquardt Ave Santa Fe Springs (90670) *(P-8291)*

Dac Heating and AC .... F....... 661 441-2787
190 Sierra Ct Ste B3 Palmdale (93550) *(P-760)*

Dac Heating and Air, Palmdale *Also Called: Dac Heating and AC (P-760)*

Dac International Inc .... E....... 805 684-8307
6390 Rose Ln Carpinteria (93013) *(P-7009)*

Dacenso Inc .... E....... 888 513-9367
2030 Main St Ste 1300 Irvine (92614) *(P-16220)*

Dacha Enterprises Inc (HQ) .... E....... 951 273-7777
13948 Mountain Ave Chino (91710) *(P-5000)*

Dacha Enterprises Inc .... D....... 951 273-7777
1915 Elise Cir Corona (92879) *(P-5001)*

Dacor (DH) .... D....... 626 799-1000
14425 Clark Ave City Of Industry (91745) *(P-13959)*

DAd Investments .... E....... 714 751-8500
2929 Halladay St Santa Ana (92705) *(P-1880)*

DAd Investments .... E....... 714 751-8500
2929 Halladay St Santa Ana (92705) *(P-13999)*

Dae Shin Usa Inc .... D....... 714 578-8900
610 N Gilbert St Fullerton (92833) *(P-2036)*

Daicel America Holdings Inc .... B....... 480 798-6737
21515 Hawthorne Blvd Ste 600 Torrance (90503) *(P-20025)*

Daico Industries Inc .... D....... 310 507-3242
1070 E 233rd St Carson (90745) *(P-9027)*

Daikin Comfort Tech Mfg LP .... B....... 760 955-7770
15024 Anacapa Rd Victorville (92392) *(P-7607)*

Dailey & Associates .... D....... 323 490-3847
8687 Melrose Ave Ste G300 West Hollywood (90069) *(P-15534)*

Daily Breeze .... E....... 310 540-5622
5215 Torrance Blvd Torrance (90503) *(P-3269)*

Daily Breeze, Torrance *Also Called: Medianews Group Inc (P-3305)*

Daily Journal Corporation (PA) .... D....... 213 229-5300
915 E 1st St Los Angeles (90012) *(P-3270)*

Daily News, Monrovia *Also Called: Medianews Group Inc (P-3304)*

Daily Nexus .... D....... 805 893-4006
Santa Barbara (93107) *(P-3271)*

Daily Transcript, Laguna Niguel *Also Called: San Diego Daily Transcript (P-3061)*

Dailymedia Inc (PA) .... F....... 541 821-5207
8 E Figueroa St Ste 220 Santa Barbara (93101) *(P-3272)*

Dairy Farmers America Inc .... D....... 805 653-0042
4375 N Ventura Ave Ventura (93001) *(P-1308)*

Daisy Publishing Company Inc .... D....... 661 295-1910
25233 Anza Dr Santa Clarita (91355) *(P-3354)*

Dako North America Inc .... B....... 805 566-6655
6392 Via Real Carpinteria (93013) *(P-13036)*

Dalton Trucking Inc (PA) .... C....... 909 823-0663
13560 Whittram Ave Fontana (92335) *(P-11571)*

Damac, Costa Mesa *Also Called: Bdfco Inc (P-8601)*

Damar Plastics Inc .... E....... 619 283-2300
1035 Pioneer Way Ste 160 El Cajon (92020) *(P-5002)*

Dameron Alloy Foundries (PA) .... D....... 310 631-5165
6330 Gateway Dr Ste B Cypress (90630) *(P-5662)*

Damo Clothing Company, Los Angeles *Also Called: Damo Textile Inc (P-13121)*

Damo Textile Inc .... E....... 213 741-1323
12121 Wilshire Blvd Ste 1120 Los Angeles (90025) *(P-13121)*

Dan Gurneys All Amercn Racers, Santa Ana *Also Called: All American Racers Inc (P-9871)*

Dan-Loc Bolt & Gasket, Carson *Also Called: Dan-Loc Group LLC (P-4725)*

Dan-Loc Group LLC .... D...... 310 538-2822
20444 Tillman Ave Carson (90746) *(P-4725)*

Dana Creath Designs Ltd .... E..... 714 662-0111
3030 Kilson Dr Santa Ana (92707) *(P-8360)*

Dana Innovations (PA) .... C...... 949 492-7777
991 Calle Amanecer San Clemente (92673) *(P-8404)*

Danchuk Manufacturing Inc .... D...... 714 540-4363
3211 Halladay St Santa Ana (92705) *(P-9378)*

Danco, Ontario *Also Called: Danco Anodizing Inc (P-6611)*

Danco Anodizing Inc (PA) ....E..... 626 445-3303
44 La Porte St Arcadia (91006) *(P-6610)*

Danco Anodizing Inc .... C...... 909 923-0562
1750 E Monticello Ct Ontario (91761) *(P-6611)*

Danco Metal Surfacing, Arcadia *Also Called: Danco Anodizing Inc (P-6610)*

Danco Valve Company .... E...... 562 925-2588
15230 Lakewood Blvd Bellflower (90706) *(P-6763)*

DAndrea Graphic Corportion .... D...... 310 642-0260
6100 Gateway Dr Cypress (90630) *(P-15662)*

Dandy Don's Gourmet Ice Cream, San Fernando *Also Called: Don Whittemore Corp (P-14003)*

Dane Elec Corp USA (HQ) ....E..... 949 450-2900
17520 Von Karman Ave Irvine (92614) *(P-12404)*

Daniel Gerard Worldwide Inc .... D...... 951 361-1111
13055 Jurupa Ave Fontana (92337) *(P-12546)*

Daniels Inc (PA) .... E...... 801 621-3355
74745 Leslie Ave Palm Desert (92260) *(P-3439)*

Danish Baking Co Inc .... D...... 818 786-1700
15215 Keswick St Van Nuys (91405) *(P-1460)*

Danish Care Center, Atascadero *Also Called: Compass Health Inc (P-17910)*

Danmer Custom Shutters, Van Nuys *Also Called: Danmer Inc (P-2592)*

Danmer Inc .... C...... 516 670-5125
8000 Woodley Ave Van Nuys (91406) *(P-2592)*

Danne Montague-King Co (PA) ....F...... 562 944-0230
10420 Pioneer Blvd Santa Fe Springs (90670) *(P-13037)*

Danny Letner Inc .... C...... 714 633-0030
1490 N Glassell St Orange (92867) *(P-1040)*

Danny Ryan Precision Contg Inc .... D...... 949 642-6664
16782 Millikan Ave Irvine (92606) *(P-1131)*

Danone Us LLC .... E...... 949 474-9670
3500 Barranca Pkwy Ste 240 Irvine (92606) *(P-1296)*

Danrich Welding Co Inc .... E...... 562 634-4811
155 N Eucla Ave San Dimas (91773) *(P-6223)*

Dansereau Health Products .... E...... 951 549-1400
1581 Commerce St Corona (92878) *(P-10735)*

Danville Materials LLC .... E...... 714 399-0334
4020 E Leaverton Ct Anaheim (92807) *(P-10736)*

Danza Del Sol Winery Inc .... E...... 951 302-6363
39050 De Portola Rd Temecula (92592) *(P-1621)*

Daou Family Estates LLC .... D...... 805 226-5460
2777 Hidden Mountain Rd Paso Robles (93446) *(P-1622)*

Dar-Ken Inc .... E...... 760 246-4010
10515 Rancho Rd Adelanto (92301) *(P-4726)*

Darensberries LLC .... C...... 805 937-8000
714 S Blosser Rd Santa Maria (93458) *(P-13)*

Darling Ingredients Inc .... E...... 323 583-6311
2626 E 25th St Los Angeles (90058) *(P-1568)*

Darmark Corporation .... D...... 858 679-3970
13225 Gregg St Poway (92064) *(P-7813)*

Darnell-Rose Inc .... E...... 626 912-1688
1205 Via Roma Colton (92324) *(P-5915)*

DART, Ridgecrest *Also Called: Desert Area Resources Training (P-14060)*

Dart Aerospace, Vista *Also Called: Apical Industries Inc (P-12902)*

Dart Container Corp California (PA) .... B...... 951 735-8115
150 S Maple Center Corona (92880) *(P-4879)*

Dart Entities, Commerce *Also Called: Dart International A Corp (P-11572)*

Dart International A Corp (HQ) .... C...... 323 264-8746
1430 S Eastman Ave Commerce (90023) *(P-11572)*

Dart Warehouse Corporation (HQ) .... B...... 323 264-1011
1430 S Eastman Ave Commerce (90023) *(P-11573)*

Dasco Engineering Corp .... C...... 310 326-2277
24747 Crenshaw Blvd Torrance (90505) *(P-9671)*

Dash Radio, Los Angeles *Also Called: Dash Radio Inc (P-11921)*

Dash Radio Inc .... D...... 310 456-9993
6230 Wilshire Blvd # 118 Los Angeles (90048) *(P-11921)*

Dasol Inc .... C...... 310 327-6700
9004 Meredith Pl Beverly Hills (90210) *(P-8245)*

Dassault Systemes Biovia Corp (DH) ....E..... 858 799-5000
5005 Wateridge Vista Dr San Diego (92121) *(P-16221)*

Data Aire Inc (HQ) .... D...... 800 347-2473
230 W Blueridge Ave Orange (92865) *(P-7608)*

Data Circle Inc .... E...... 949 260-6569
3333 Michelson Dr Ste 735 Irvine (92612) *(P-8784)*

Data Council LLC .... D...... 904 512-3200
15310 Barranca Pkwy Ste 100 Irvine (92618) *(P-16814)*

Data Device Corporation .... E...... 858 503-3300
13000 Gregg St Ste C Poway (92064) *(P-8785)*

Data Display Products, El Segundo *Also Called: Display Products Inc (P-8787)*

Data Exchange, Camarillo *Also Called: Dex Corporation (P-19572)*

Data Exchange Corporation (PA) .... B...... 805 388-1711
3600 Via Pescador Camarillo (93012) *(P-12405)*

Data Lights Rigging LLC .... F...... 818 786-0536
7508 Tyrone Ave Van Nuys (91405) *(P-8120)*

Data Processing Design Inc .... E...... 714 695-1000
1409 Glenneyre St Ste B Laguna Beach (92651) *(P-16008)*

Data Solder Inc .... F...... 714 429-9866
2915 Kilson Dr Santa Ana (92707) *(P-8259)*

Data Trace Info Svcs LLC (HQ) .... D...... 714 250-6700
4 First American Way Santa Ana (92707) *(P-20394)*

Databyte, City Of Industry *Also Called: Databyte Technology Inc (P-12628)*

Databyte Technology Inc (PA) ....E..... 626 305-0500
2300 Peck Rd City Of Industry (90601) *(P-12628)*

Datadirect Networks Inc (PA) .... C...... 818 700-7600
9351 Deering Ave Chatsworth (91311) *(P-16009)*

Datadivider, Carlsbad *Also Called: Exois Inc (P-16567)*

Datallegro Inc .... D...... 949 680-3000
85 Enterprise Ste 200 Aliso Viejo (92656) *(P-12406)*

Datametrics Corporation .... E...... 805 577-9710
25 E Easy St Simi Valley (93065) *(P-7520)*

Datatrace Title .... D...... 800 221-2056
200 Commerce Irvine (92602) *(P-20330)*

Datatronic Distribution Inc ....F
28151 Us Highway 74 Romoland (92585) *(P-8092)*

Datatronics, Menifee *Also Called: Datatronics Romoland Inc (P-8093)*

Datatronics Romoland Inc .... D...... 951 928-7700
28151 Us Highway 74 Menifee (92585) *(P-8093)*

Dauntless Industries Inc .... E...... 626 966-4494
806 N Grand Ave Covina (91724) *(P-7065)*

Dauntless Molds, Covina *Also Called: Dauntless Industries Inc (P-7065)*

Davalan Fresh, Los Angeles *Also Called: Davalan Sales Inc (P-13319)*

Davalan Sales Inc .... C...... 213 623-2500
1601 E Olympic Blvd Ste 325 Los Angeles (90021) *(P-13319)*

Dave Inc (PA) ....C...... 844 857-3283
1265 S Cochran Ave Los Angeles (90019) *(P-16222)*

Dave Whipple Sheet Metal Inc .... E...... 619 562-6962
1077 N Cuyamaca St El Cajon (92020) *(P-6224)*

Dave Williams Plbg & Elec Inc .... C...... 760 296-1397
75140 Saint Charles Pl Ste C Palm Desert (92211) *(P-761)*

Dave's Baking Goods, Santa Monica *Also Called: Bake R Us Inc (P-1451)*

David & Goliath LLC .... C...... 310 445-5200
909 N Pacific Coast Hwy Ste 700 El Segundo (90245) *(P-15535)*

David A Campbell Corporation .... C...... 951 785-4444
3060 Adams St Riverside (92504) *(P-13753)*

David and Margaret Home Inc .... C...... 909 596-5921
1350 3rd St La Verne (91750) *(P-19259)*

David B Anderson .... E...... 805 489-0661
174 Suburban Rd Ste 100 San Luis Obispo (93401) *(P-3556)*

David Engineering & Manufacturing Inc .... C...... 951 735-5200
1230 Quarry St Corona (92879) *(P-7066)*

David Engineering & Mfg, Corona *Also Called: David Engineering & Mfg Inc (P-6509)*

David Engineering & Mfg Inc .... E...... 951 735-5200
1230 Quarry St Corona (92879) *(P-6509)*

Employee Codes: A=Over 500 employees, B=251-500
C=101-250, D=51-100, E=20-50, F=10-19, G=1-9

2024 Southern California
Business Directory and Buyers Guide

© Mergent Inc. 1-800-342-5647

1061

David Grment Ctng Fsing Svc In .... E...... 323 216-1574
5008 S Boyle Ave Vernon (90058) *(P-2316)*

David H Fell & Co Inc (PA) .... **E...... 323 722-9992**
6009 Bandini Blvd Los Angeles (90040) *(P-5679)*

David Haid .... E...... 323 752-8096
8619 Crocker St Los Angeles (90003) *(P-3022)*

David Kopf Instruments .... E...... 818 352-3274
7324 Elmo St Tujunga (91042) *(P-10489)*

David L Manwarren Corp .... E...... 909 989-5883
9146 9th St Rancho Cucamonga (91730) *(P-545)*

David Margaret Youth Fmly Svcs, La Verne *Also Called: David and Margaret Home Inc*
(P-19259)

David Shield Security Inc .... D...... 310 849-4950
23945 Calabasas Rd Ste 102 Calabasas (91302) *(P-16637)*

David Wilson's Villa Ford, Orange *Also Called: Villa Ford Inc (P-13843)*

David-Kleis II LLC .... D...... 951 845-3125
1665 E Eighth St Beaumont (92223) *(P-18757)*

Davids Natural Toothpaste Inc .... E...... 949 933-1185
33360 Zeiders Rd Ste 106 Menifee (92584) *(P-4399)*

Davidson Enterprises Inc .... E...... 661 325-2145
3223 Brittan St Bakersfield (93308) *(P-1152)*

Davidson Hotel Partners Lp .... A...... 818 707-1220
30100 Agoura Rd Agoura Hills (91301) *(P-15127)*

Davidson Optronics Inc .... E...... 626 962-5181
9087 Arrow Rte Ste 180 Rancho Cucamonga (91730) *(P-10360)*

Davidsons AC & Htg Inc .... E...... 909 885-2703
495 S Sierra Way San Bernardino (92408) *(P-762)*

Davidsons AC Htg & Sh, San Bernardino *Also Called: Davidsons AC & Htg Inc (P-762)*

Davis California Industries, North Hollywood *Also Called: Davis California Industries Ltd*
(P-6225)

Davis California Industries Ltd .... E...... 818 980-6178
11323 Hartland St North Hollywood (91605) *(P-6225)*

Davis Gregg Enterprises Inc .... F...... 619 449-4250
8525 Roland Acres Dr Santee (92071) *(P-6141)*

Davis Research LLC .... C...... 818 591-2408
26610 Agoura Rd Ste 240 Calabasas (91302) *(P-19891)*

Davis Wire Corporation (HQ) .... C...... 626 969-7651
5555 Irwindale Ave Irwindale (91706) *(P-5612)*

Davis Wright Tremaine LLP .... C...... 213 633-6800
865 S Figueroa St Ste 2400 Los Angeles (90017) *(P-18847)*

Daviselen Advertising (PA) .... **C...... 213 688-7000**
865 S Figueroa St Ste 1200 Los Angeles (90017) *(P-15536)*

Davita Hesperia Dialysis Ctr, Hesperia *Also Called: Davita Inc (P-18657)*

Davita Inc .... C...... 310 536-2406
14135 Main St Ste 501 Hesperia (92345) *(P-18657)*

Davita Inc .... B...... 949 930-4400
15271 Laguna Canyon Rd Irvine (92618) *(P-18658)*

Davita Magan Management Inc (DH) .... **C...... 626 331-6411**
420 W Rowland St Covina (91723) *(P-17640)*

Dawn Food Products Inc .... C...... 714 258-1223
15601 Mosher Ave Ste 230 Tustin (92780) *(P-1461)*

Dawn Sign Press Inc .... E...... 858 625-0600
6130 Nancy Ridge Dr San Diego (92121) *(P-3405)*

Dawson Enterprises (PA) .... **E...... 562 424-8564**
2853 Cherry Ave Signal Hill (90755) *(P-6956)*

Day Care Center, San Luis Obispo *Also Called: Community Action Prtnr San Lui (P-19207)*

Day Designer, Irvine *Also Called: Blue Sky The Clor Imgntion LLC (P-12991)*

Day Star Industries .... F...... 562 926-8800
13727 Excelsior Dr Santa Fe Springs (90670) *(P-2593)*

Day-Glo, Cudahy *Also Called: Day-Glo Color Corp (P-3874)*

Day-Glo Color Corp .... F...... 323 560-2000
4615 Ardine St Cudahy (90201) *(P-3874)*

Daybreak, San Diego *Also Called: Daybreak Game Company LLC (P-16010)*

Daybreak Game Company LLC .... B...... 858 239-0500
13500 Evening Creek Dr N Ste 300 San Diego (92128) *(P-16010)*

Daylight Defense LLC .... E...... 858 432-7500
16465 Via Esprillo Ste 100 San Diego (92127) *(P-10798)*

Daylight Solutions Inc (DH) .... **C...... 858 432-7500**
16465 Via Esprillo Ste 100 San Diego (92127) *(P-8786)*

Daymark Properties Realty, San Diego *Also Called: Daymark Realty Advisors Inc (P-14785)*

Daymark Realty Advisors Inc .... B...... 714 975-2999
750 B St Ste 2620 San Diego (92101) *(P-14785)*

Dayton Dmh Inc .... C...... 858 350-4400
121 Spinnaker Ct Del Mar (92014) *(P-14735)*

Dayton Rogers of California Inc .... C...... 763 784-7714
13630 Saticoy St Van Nuys Van Nuys (91402) *(P-6510)*

Dayton Superior Corporation .... E...... 951 782-9517
6001 20th St Riverside (92509) *(P-5613)*

Daz, Los Angeles *Also Called: Daz Systems LLC (P-16011)*

Daz Systems LLC .... B...... 310 640-1300
1003 E 4th Pl Ste 800 Los Angeles (90013) *(P-16011)*

Dazpak Flexible Packaging, City Of Industry *Also Called: Signature Flexible Packg LLC*
(P-4581)

Db Building Fasteners, Ontario *Also Called: DB Building Fasteners Inc (P-6396)*

DB Building Fasteners Inc (PA) .... **F...... 909 581-6740**
5555 E Gibralter Ontario (91764) *(P-6396)*

Dbi, Cypress *Also Called: Hilti US Manufacturing Inc (P-5892)*

DC, Huntington Beach *Also Called: DC Shoes Inc (P-2200)*

DC Partners Inc (PA) .... **E...... 714 558-9444**
19329 Bryant St Northridge (91324) *(P-5789)*

DC Shoes Inc (DH) .... **E...... 714 889-4206**
5600 Argosy Ave Ste 100 Huntington Beach (92649) *(P-2200)*

DC Shoes Inc .... E...... 951 361-7712
11310 Cantu Galleano Ranch Rd Mira Loma (91752) *(P-13122)*

Dcatalog Inc .... E...... 408 824-5648
6250 Sagebrush Bend Way San Diego (92130) *(P-16223)*

Dcc General Engrg Contrs Inc .... D...... 760 480-7400
2180 Meyers Ave Escondido (92029) *(P-5408)*

DCH Acura of Temecula .... D...... 877 847-9532
26705 Ynez Rd Temecula (92591) *(P-13754)*

DCH California Motors Inc .... D...... 805 988-7900
1631 Auto Center Dr Oxnard (93036) *(P-13755)*

DCH Gardena Honda .... C...... 310 515-5700
15541 S Western Ave Gardena (90249) *(P-13756)*

DCI Hollow Metal On Demand, Fontana *Also Called: Door Components Inc (P-6103)*

Dcii North America LLC (HQ) .... **E...... 714 817-7000**
200 S Kraemer Blvd Bldg E Brea (92821) *(P-10737)*

Dcl, Ontario *Also Called: Discopylabs (P-8456)*

Dcl Maritime LLC .... C...... 818 560-1000
500 S Buena Vista St Burbank (91521) *(P-20026)*

Dcli, Huntington Beach *Also Called: Direct Chassislink Inc (P-15779)*

Dcor, Oxnard *Also Called: Dcor LLC (P-297)*

Dcor LLC (PA) .... **C...... 805 535-2000**
1000 Town Center Dr Fl 6 Oxnard (93036) *(P-297)*

Dcpi, Glendale *Also Called: Disney Cnsmr Pdts Intrctive MD (P-16014)*

Dcw Dcw Inc .... D...... 310 324-3147
20500 Denker Ave Torrance (90501) *(P-11749)*

Dcx-Chol Enterprises Inc (PA) .... **D...... 310 516-1692**
12821 S Figueroa St Los Angeles (90061) *(P-9028)*

Dda Holdings Inc .... E...... 213 624-5200
834 S Broadway Ste 600 Los Angeles (90014) *(P-2317)*

Ddh Enterprise Inc (PA) .... **D...... 760 599-0171**
2220 Oak Ridge Way Vista (92081) *(P-8260)*

De Berns Company, Long Beach *Also Called: Berns Bros Inc (P-7783)*

De La Mare Engineering Inc .... E...... 818 365-9208
1908 1st St San Fernando (91340) *(P-17247)*

De Leon Enterprises, Sun Valley *Also Called: De Leon Entps Elec Spclist Inc (P-8669)*

De Leon Entps Elec Spclist Inc .... E...... 818 252-6690
11934 Allegheny St Sun Valley (91352) *(P-8669)*

De Menno-Kerdoon Trading Co (HQ) .... **C...... 310 537-7100**
2000 N Alameda St Compton (90222) *(P-4640)*

De Nora Water Technologies LLC .... F...... 310 618-9700
1230 Rosecrans Ave Ste 300 Manhattan Beach (90266) *(P-7653)*

De Vries International Inc (PA) .... **E...... 949 252-1212**
17671 Armstrong Ave Irvine (92614) *(P-342)*

De Well Container Shipping Inc .... D...... 310 735-8600
5553 Bandini Blvd Unit A Bell (90201) *(P-11750)*

Dealership Auto Dtail Rstrtons, Monrovia *Also Called: Executive Auto Reconditioning*
(P-17048)

Deamco Corporation .... E...... 323 890-1190
6520 E Washington Blvd Commerce (90040) *(P-6972)*

Dean Distributors Inc .... E...... 323 587-8147
5015 Hallmark Pkwy San Bernardino (92407) *(P-1881)*

Mergent email: customerrelations@mergent.com
1062

2024 Southern California
Business Directory and Buyers Guide

(P-0000) Products & Services Section entry number
(PA)=Parent Co (HQ)=Headquarters (DH)=Div Headquarters

Dean Hesketh Company Inc .... E 714 236-2138
2551 W La Palma Ave Anaheim (92801) *(P-3752)*

Dean L Davis MD .... E 661 632-5000
2215 Truxtun Ave Bakersfield (93301) *(P-19070)*

Dean Socal LLC .... C 951 734-3950
17637 E Valley Blvd City Of Industry (91744) *(P-1309)*

Deanco Healthcare LLC .... A 818 787-2222
14850 Roscoe Blvd Panorama City (91402) *(P-18236)*

Dear John American Classic, Arcadia *Also Called: Dear John Denim Inc (P-2018)*

Dear John Denim Inc .... F 626 350-5100
12318 Lower Azusa Rd Arcadia (91006) *(P-2018)*

Deasy Penner Podley .... C 626 408-1280
30 N Baldwin Ave Sierra Madre (91024) *(P-14786)*

Debisys Inc (PA) .... D 949 699-1401
27442 Portola Pkwy Ste 150 Foothill Ranch (92610) *(P-14258)*

Dec, Santa Ana *Also Called: Dynasty Electronic Company LLC (P-8670)*

Deca International Corp .... E 714 367-5900
10700 Norwalk Blvd Santa Fe Springs (90670) *(P-9968)*

Decatur Electronics, San Diego *Also Called: D & K Engineering (P-10174)*

Decatur Electronics Inc (HQ) .... D 888 428-4315
15890 Bernardo Center Dr San Diego (92127) *(P-9969)*

Decco Castings Inc .... E 619 444-9437
1596 Pioneer Way El Cajon (92020) *(P-5810)*

Decco Graphics Inc .... F 310 534-2861
24411 Frampton Ave Harbor City (90710) *(P-6511)*

Decco US Post-Harvest Inc (HQ) .... F 800 221-0925
1713 S California Ave Monrovia (91016) *(P-4549)*

Deccofelt Corporation .... E 626 963-8511
555 S Vermont Ave Glendora (91741) *(P-2139)*

Decipher Corp .... D 888 975-4540
6925 Lusk Blvd Ste 200 San Diego (92121) *(P-18545)*

Decision Medical, Poway *Also Called: Decision Sciences Med Co LLC (P-10799)*

Decision Ready, Irvine *Also Called: Decision Ready Solutions Inc (P-14310)*

Decision Ready Solutions Inc .... E 949 400-1126
400 Spectrum Center Dr Ste 2050 Irvine (92618) *(P-14310)*

Decision Sciences Med Co LLC .... E 858 602-1600
12345 First American Way Ste 100 Poway (92064) *(P-10799)*

Decisionlogic LLC .... E 858 586-0202
13500 Evening Creek Dr N Ste 600 San Diego (92128) *(P-16224)*

DECKERS BRANDS, Goleta *Also Called: Deckers Outdoor Corporation (P-2447)*

Deckers Outdoor Corporation (PA) .... A 805 967-7611
250 Coromar Dr Goleta (93117) *(P-2447)*

Deco Enterprises Inc .... D 323 726-2575
2917 Vail Ave Commerce (90040) *(P-8307)*

Deco Lighting, Commerce *Also Called: Deco Enterprises Inc (P-8307)*

Decor Interior Design Inc .... E 818 962-4800
21530 Sherman Way Canoga Park (91303) *(P-16815)*

Decorative Woods Lbr & Molding, Irvine *Also Called: Decwood Inc (P-12327)*

Decore-Ative Spc NC LLC (PA) .... A 626 254-9191
2772 Peck Rd Monrovia (91016) *(P-2594)*

Decore-Ative Spc NC LLC .... C 626 960-7731
4414 Azusa Canyon Rd Irwindale (91706) *(P-2595)*

Decra, Corona *Also Called: Decra Roofing Systems Inc (P-6226)*

Decra Roofing Systems Inc (DH) .... D 951 272-8180
1230 Railroad St Corona (92882) *(P-6226)*

Decurion Corporation (PA) .... D 310 659-9432
120 N Robertson Blvd Fl 3 Los Angeles (90048) *(P-17290)*

Decwood Inc .... F 949 588-9663
3 Oldfield Irvine (92618) *(P-12327)*

Dedicted Dfned Beneft Svcs LLC .... C 415 931-1990
550 N Brand Blvd Ste 1610 Glendale (91203) *(P-14583)*

Dedon Inc .... E 310 388-4721
8687 Melrose Ave Ste B188 West Hollywood (90069) *(P-2770)*

Dee Engineering Inc .... E 909 947-5616
6918 Ed Perkic St Riverside (92504) *(P-9379)*

Deepsea Power & Light Inc .... E 858 576-1261
4033 Ruffin Rd San Diego (92123) *(P-8361)*

Deering Banjo Company Inc .... E 619 464-8252
3733 Kenora Dr Spring Valley (91977) *(P-13978)*

Defender SD Manufacturing LLC .... E 314 697-1330
3443 Tripp Ct San Diego (92121) *(P-4099)*

Defense Solutions, Santa Clarita *Also Called: Curtiss-Wright Corporation (P-6758)*

Defenseweb Technologies Inc .... D 858 272-8505
10188 Telesis Ct Ste 300 San Diego (92121) *(P-16563)*

Dehart Inc .... E 858 695-0882
7550 Miramar Rd Ste 300 San Diego (92126) *(P-1153)*

Dei Headquarters Inc .... B 760 598-6200
3002 Wintergreen Dr Carlsbad (92008) *(P-8607)*

Dei Holdings Inc (HQ) .... E 760 598-6200
5541 Fermi Ct Carlsbad (92008) *(P-8608)*

Dekra Insight, Oxnard *Also Called: Behavioral Science Technology Inc (P-20317)*

Dekra-Lite Industries Inc .... D 714 436-0705
3102 W Alton Ave Santa Ana (92704) *(P-16816)*

Del AMO Hospital, Torrance *Also Called: Del AMO Hospital Inc (P-18687)*

Del AMO Hospital Inc .... B 310 530-1151
23700 Camino Del Sol Torrance (90505) *(P-18687)*

Del Mar Blue Print Co Inc .... E 858 755-5134
2201 San Dieguito Dr Ste E Del Mar (92014) *(P-15646)*

Del Mar Country Club Inc .... D 858 759-5500
6001 Clubhouse Dr Rancho Santa Fe (92067) *(P-17480)*

Del Mar Die Casting Co, Gardena *Also Called: Del Mar Industries (P-5773)*

Del Mar Fair Grounds, Del Mar *Also Called: California Dept Fd Agriculture (P-20419)*

Del Mar Fairgrounds .... D 858 792-4288
2260 Jimmy Durante Blvd Del Mar (92014) *(P-15505)*

Del Mar Holding LLC .... A 313 659-7300
1022 Bay Marina Dr 10 National City (91950) *(P-13292)*

Del Mar Industries (PA) .... D 323 321-0600
12901 S Western Ave Gardena (90249) *(P-5773)*

Del Mar Seafoods Inc .... C 805 850-0421
1449 Spinnaker Dr Ventura (93001) *(P-13279)*

Del Mar Thoroughbred Club .... B 858 755-1141
2260 Jimmy Durante Blvd Del Mar (92014) *(P-17385)*

Del Real LLC (PA) .... D 951 681-0395
11041 Inland Ave Jurupa Valley (91752) *(P-1388)*

Del Real Foods, Jurupa Valley *Also Called: Del Real LLC (P-1388)*

Del Rio Convalescent, Bell Gardens *Also Called: Del Rio Sanitarium Inc (P-17924)*

Del Rio Sanitarium Inc .... C 562 927-6586
7002 Gage Ave Bell Gardens (90201) *(P-17924)*

Del Rosa Villa, San Bernardino *Also Called: Del Rosa Villaidence Opco LLC (P-18083)*

Del Rosa Villa Inc .... D 909 885-3261
2018 Del Rosa Ave San Bernardino (92404) *(P-17925)*

Del Rosa Villaidence Opco LLC .... B 909 885-3261
2018 Del Rosa Ave San Bernardino (92404) *(P-18083)*

Del Taco, Lake Forest *Also Called: Del Taco Restaurants Inc (P-14000)*

Del Taco Restaurants Inc (PA) .... C 949 462-9300
25521 Commercentre Dr Ste 200 Lake Forest (92630) *(P-14000)*

Del West Engineering Inc (PA) .... C 661 295-5700
28128 Livingston Ave Valencia (91355) *(P-9380)*

Del West USA, Valencia *Also Called: Del West Engineering Inc (P-9380)*

Delafield Corporation (PA) .... C 626 303-0740
1520 Flower Ave Duarte (91010) *(P-7814)*

Delafield Fluid Technology, Duarte *Also Called: Delafield Corporation (P-7814)*

Delamo Manufacturing Inc .... D 323 936-3566
7171 Telegraph Rd Montebello (90640) *(P-5003)*

Delano Dst Sklled Nrsng Fclty .... C 661 720-2100
1509 Tokay St Delano (93215) *(P-17926)*

Delano Dst Sklled Nrsing Fclty, Delano *Also Called: North Kern S Tulare Hosp Dst (P-18352)*

Delano Growers Grape Products .... D 661 725-3255
32351 Bassett Ave Delano (93215) *(P-1765)*

Delano Regional Medical Center, Delano *Also Called: Adventist Health Delano (P-18161)*

Delano Regional Medical Center, Delano *Also Called: Adventist Health Delano (P-18162)*

Delano Waste Water Treatment, Delano *Also Called: City of Delano (P-7648)*

Delaware Systems Technology, San Bernardino *Also Called: Systems Technology Inc (P-7354)*

Delfin Design & Mfg Inc .... E 949 888-4644
15672 Producer Ln Huntington Beach (92649) *(P-5004)*

Deliver-It, Anaheim *Also Called: Di Overnite LLC (P-11528)*

Deliverr Inc .... B 213 534-8686
307 S Wilson Ave Apt 6 Pasadena (91106) *(P-13177)*

Delkin Devices, Poway *Also Called: Delkin Devices Inc (P-7521)*

Employee Codes: A=Over 500 employees, B=251-500
C=101-250, D=51-100, E=20-50, F=10-19, G=1-9

2024 Southern California
Business Directory and Buyers Guide

© Mergent Inc. 1-800-342-5647

1063

Delkin Devices Inc (PA) .... D...... 858 391-1234
13350 Kirkham Way Poway (92064) *(P-7521)*

Della Robbia Inc .... E...... 951 372-9199
796 E Harrison St Corona (92879) *(P-2847)*

Dellarise, Pasadena *Also Called: Pak Group LLC (P-1522)*

Dellarobbia Inc (PA) .... E...... 949 251-9532
119 Waterworks Way Irvine (92618) *(P-2799)*

Deloitte & Touche LLP .... A...... 619 232-6500
12830 El Camino Real Ste 600 San Diego (92130) *(P-19766)*

Deloitte & Touche LLP .... A...... 213 688-0800
555 W 5th St Ste 2700 Los Angeles (90013) *(P-19767)*

Deloitte & Touche LLP .... C...... 714 436-7419
695 Town Center Dr Ste 1200 Costa Mesa (92626) *(P-19768)*

Deloitte Consulting LLP .... B...... 212 489-1600
350 S Grand Ave Ste 200 Los Angeles (90071) *(P-20331)*

Deloitte Tax LLP .... C...... 404 885-6754
555 W 5th St Ste 2700 Los Angeles (90013) *(P-19769)*

Delori Foods, City Of Industry *Also Called: Delori-Nutifood Products Inc (P-1882)*

Delori-Nutifood Products Inc .... E...... 626 965-3006
17043 Green Dr City Of Industry (91745) *(P-1882)*

Delphi Display Systems Inc .... D...... 714 825-3400
3550 Hyland Ave Costa Mesa (92626) *(P-7522)*

Delstar Holding Corp .... E...... 619 258-1503
9225 Isaac St Santee (92071) *(P-4809)*

Delstar Technologies Inc .... E...... 619 258-1503
1306 Fayette St El Cajon (92020) *(P-4810)*

Delt Industries Inc .... F...... 805 579-0213
90 W Easy St Ste 2 Simi Valley (93065) *(P-5811)*

Delta Airlines, San Diego *Also Called: Delta Airlines Inc (P-9672)*

Delta Airlines Inc .... E...... 619 491-2886
2357 Airlane Rd San Diego (92101) *(P-9672)*

Delta Computer Consulting .... C...... 310 541-9440
25550 Hawthorne Blvd Ste 106 Torrance (90505) *(P-16564)*

Delta Creative Inc .... C...... 800 423-4135
2690 Pellissier Pl City Of Industry (90601) *(P-12937)*

Delta Design Inc (HQ) .... B...... 858 848-8000
12367 Crosthwaite Cir Poway (92064) *(P-7388)*

Delta Design (littleton) Inc .... A...... 858 848-8100
12367 Crosthwaite Cir Poway (92064) *(P-10194)*

Delta Dvh Circuits, Van Nuys *Also Called: Ambay Circuits Inc (P-8645)*

Delta Fabrication Inc .... D...... 818 407-4000
9600 De Soto Ave Chatsworth (91311) *(P-7815)*

Delta Floral Distributors Inc .... C...... 323 751-8116
6810 West Blvd Los Angeles (90043) *(P-13506)*

Delta Galil USA Inc .... B...... 213 488-4859
777 S Alameda St Fl 3 Los Angeles (90021) *(P-2388)*

Delta Galil USA Inc .... C...... 949 296-0380
16912 Von Karman Ave Irvine (92606) *(P-13123)*

Delta Group Electronics, San Diego *Also Called: Delta Group Electronics Inc (P-9029)*

Delta Group Electronics Inc .... D...... 858 569-1681
10180 Scripps Ranch Blvd San Diego (92131) *(P-9029)*

Delta Hi-Tech .... C...... 818 407-4000
9600 De Soto Ave Chatsworth (91311) *(P-7816)*

Delta Microwave LLC .... D...... 805 751-1100
300 Del Norte Blvd Oxnard (93030) *(P-9030)*

Delta Pacific Activewear Inc .... D...... 714 871-9281
331 S Hale Ave Fullerton (92831) *(P-2066)*

Delta Packaging Products, Los Angeles *Also Called: E & S Paper Co (P-13006)*

Delta Printing Solutions Inc .... C...... 661 257-0584
28210 Avenue Stanford Valencia (91355) *(P-3557)*

Delta Scientific Corporation (PA) .... C...... 661 575-1100
40355 Delta Ln Palmdale (93551) *(P-16728)*

Delta Stag Company, Fullerton *Also Called: Trade Leasing Inc (P-9336)*

Delta Stag Manufacturing .... E...... 562 904-6444
1818 E Rosslynn Ave Fullerton (92831) *(P-9321)*

Delta Tau Data Systems Inc Cal (HQ) .... C...... 818 998-2095
21314 Lassen St Chatsworth (91311) *(P-7389)*

Delta Tech Industries LLC .... E...... 909 673-1900
13860 Benson Ave Chino (91710) *(P-8345)*

Delta Trading LP .... E...... 661 834-5560
17731 Millux Rd Bakersfield (93311) *(P-4658)*

Delta-Stag Truck Body, Fullerton *Also Called: Delta Stag Manufacturing (P-9321)*

Deltronic Corporation .... D...... 714 545-5800
3900 W Segerstrom Ave Santa Ana (92704) *(P-10312)*

Deluxe Building Products, Pomona *Also Called: Wcs Equipment Holdings LLC (P-5665)*

Deluxe Encore Inc .... C...... 323 466-7663
2400 W Empire Ave Ste 400 Burbank (91504) *(P-11916)*

Deluxe Nms Inc .... C...... 310 760-8500
4499 Glencoe Ave Marina Del Rey (90292) *(P-17276)*

Dematic Corp .... E...... 714 388-8803
333 City Blvd W Ste 1820 Orange (92868) *(P-6973)*

Demenno Kerdoon .... E...... 310 537-7100
2000 N Alameda St Compton (90222) *(P-298)*

Demenno-Kerdoon, South Gate *Also Called: Demenno/Kerdoon Holdings (P-4681)*

Demenno/Kerdoon Holdings (DH) .... D...... 562 231-1550
9302 Garfield Ave South Gate (90280) *(P-4681)*

Demenno/Kerdoon Holdings .... E...... 323 268-3387
3650 E 26th St Vernon (90058) *(P-4682)*

Demler Brothers LLC .... D...... 760 789-2457
25818 Highway 78 Ramona (92065) *(P-91)*

Demoldco Plastics Inc .... E...... 714 577-9391
3931 E Miraloma Ave Anaheim (92806) *(P-5005)*

Demor Enterprises Inc .... E...... 858 625-0003
4174 Sorrento Valley Blvd Ste H San Diego (92121) *(P-1154)*

Den Editorial LLC .... E...... 949 292-6475
2332 S Centinela Ave Los Angeles (90064) *(P-3440)*

Den-Mat Corporation (DH) .... B...... 805 922-8491
236 S Bdwy Orcutt (93455) *(P-4400)*

Den-Mat Corporation .... C...... 800 445-0345
21515 Vanowen St Ste 200 Canoga Park (91303) *(P-4401)*

Denardi Machinery Inc .... C...... 619 749-0039
1475 Pioneer Way El Cajon (92020) *(P-12767)*

Dendreon Pharmaceuticals LLC (HQ) .... E...... 562 252-7500
1700 Saturn Way Seal Beach (90740) *(P-4100)*

Denim-Tech LLC .... D...... 323 277-8998
375 E 2nd St Apt 604 Los Angeles (90012) *(P-7592)*

Denken Solutions Inc .... C...... 949 630-5263
9170 Irvine Center Dr Ste 200 Irvine (92618) *(P-20162)*

Denmac Industries Inc .... E...... 562 634-2714
7616 Rosecrans Ave Paramount (90723) *(P-6699)*

Dennis & Leen, Los Angeles *Also Called: EC Group Inc (P-12280)*

Dennis Allen Associates (PA) .... D...... 805 884-8777
201 N Milpas St Santa Barbara (93103) *(P-428)*

Dennis Bolton Enterprises Inc .... F...... 818 982-1800
7285 Coldwater Canyon Ave North Hollywood (91605) *(P-3558)*

Dennis DiGiorgio .... E...... 714 408-7527
333 City Blvd W Ste 1700 Orange (92868) *(P-5339)*

Dennis Foland Inc (PA) .... E...... 909 930-9900
1500 S Hellman Ave Ontario (91761) *(P-12973)*

Dennison Division, Brea *Also Called: Avery Dennison Office Products Co Inc (P-3216)*

Dennison Inc .... E...... 626 965-8917
17901 Railroad St City Of Industry (91748) *(P-6356)*

Denovo, Baldwin Park *Also Called: Denovo Dental Inc (P-10738)*

Denovo Dental Inc .... E...... 626 480-0182
5130 Commerce Dr Baldwin Park (91706) *(P-10738)*

Denso Pdts & Svcs Americas Inc .... C...... 951 698-3379
41673 Corning Pl Murrieta (92562) *(P-9381)*

Denso Pdts & Svcs Americas Inc (DH) .... B...... 310 834-6352
3900 Via Oro Ave Long Beach (90810) *(P-12237)*

Denso Wireless Systems America Inc .... C...... 760 734-4600
2251 Rutherford Rd # 100 Carlsbad (92008) *(P-8508)*

Dentalville, Bell *Also Called: Leonid M Glsman DDS A Dntl Cor (P-17839)*

Dentis USA Corporation .... F...... 323 677-4363
11095 Knott Ave Ste B Cypress (90630) *(P-10739)*

Dentons US LLP .... E...... 213 623-9300
601 S Figueroa St Ste 2500 Los Angeles (90017) *(P-18848)*

Department Children Fmly Svcs, Los Angeles *Also Called: County of Los Angeles (P-19064)*

Department of Arprts of The Cy .... A...... 855 463-5252
1 World Way Los Angeles (90045) *(P-11695)*

Department of Health Services, Los Angeles *Also Called: County of Los Angeles (P-18525)*

Department of Mental Health, Los Angeles *Also Called: County of Los Angeles (P-16525)*

Department of Mental Health, Los Angeles Also Called: County of Los Angeles (P-20414)

Department of Public Health ....C...... 619 338-2493
1500 Capitol Ave 5 Fl Ms 7610 San Diego (92101) **(P-17641)**

Department of Public Works, Alhambra Also Called: County of Los Angeles (P-12118)

Dependable Companies ....C...... 800 548-8608
2555 E Olympic Blvd Los Angeles (90023) **(P-11481)**

Dependable Disposal and Recycl, Spring Valley Also Called: Burns and Sons Trucking Inc **(P-11445)**

Dependable Global Express Inc (PA) ....C...... 310 537-2000
19201 S Susana Rd E Rncho Dmngz (90221) **(P-11751)**

Dependable Highway Express Inc (PA) ....B...... 323 526-2200
2555 E Olympic Blvd Los Angeles (90023) **(P-11482)**

Dependable Logistics Services, Los Angeles Also Called: Dependable Highway Express Inc **(P-11482)**

Dependble Break Rm Sltions Inc ....D...... 909 982-5933
1431 W 9th St Ste B Upland (91786) **(P-12453)**

Depo Auto Parts, Fontana Also Called: Maxzone Vehicle Lighting Corp (P-12246)

Dept Children and Family Svcs, Lakewood Also Called: County of Los Angeles (P-19057)

Dept of Cardiologist, Los Angeles Also Called: Kaiser Fndtion Hosp Gift Shppe (P-14473)

Dept of Public Works, Irvine Also Called: City of Irvine (P-20150)

Derek and Constance Lee Corp (PA) ....D...... 909 595-8831
19355 San Jose Ave City Of Industry (91748) **(P-1217)**

Derm Cosmetic Labs, Buena Park Also Called: Derm Cosmetic Labs Inc (P-13038)

Derm Cosmetic Labs Inc (PA) ....E...... 714 562-8873
6370 Altura Blvd Buena Park (90620) **(P-13038)**

Derma E, Simi Valley Also Called: Stearns Corporation (P-4458)

Dermal Group, The, Carson Also Called: Dermalogica LLC (P-4402)

Dermalogica LLC (HQ) ....C...... 310 900-4000
1535 Beachey Pl Carson (90746) **(P-4402)**

Dermtech Inc (PA) ....E...... 866 450-4223
12340 El Camino Real San Diego (92130) **(P-4271)**

Dermtech Operations Inc ....B...... 866 450-4223
12340 El Camino Real Ste 200 San Diego (92130) **(P-19832)**

DES PERES HOSPITAL, INC., Indio Also Called: John F Kennedy Mem Hosp Aux (P-18292)

Deschner Corporation ....E...... 714 557-1261
3211 W Harvard St Santa Ana (92704) **(P-7390)**

Desco, Chino Also Called: Desco Industries Inc (P-8204)

Desco Industries Inc (PA) ....D...... 909 627-8178
3651 Walnut Ave Chino (91710) **(P-8204)**

Desert ARC ....B...... 760 346-1611
73255 Country Club Dr Palm Desert (92260) **(P-19071)**

Desert Area Resources Training (PA) ....B...... 760 375-9787
201 E Ridgecrest Blvd Ridgecrest (93555) **(P-14060)**

Desert Block Co Inc ....E...... 661 824-2624
11374 Tuxford St Sun Valley (91352) **(P-4659)**

Desert Brand, City Of Industry Also Called: Hill Brothers Chemical Company (P-3857)

Desert Cardiology Cons Med G, Rancho Mirage Also Called: Desert Crdlgy Cons Med Group I **(P-17642)**

Desert Crdlgy Cons Med Group I ....C...... 760 346-0642
39000 Bob Hope Dr Rancho Mirage (92270) **(P-17642)**

Desert Grafics, Palm Springs Also Called: Desert Publications Inc (P-3355)

Desert Haven Enterprises ....A...... 661 948-8402
43437 Copeland Cir Lancaster (93535) **(P-187)**

DESERT HORIZONS COUNTRY CLUB, Indian Wells Also Called: Dhccnp (P-17481)

Desert Hot Springs Spa Hotel, Desert Hot Springs Also Called: Desert Hot Sprng Real Prpts In **(P-14658)**

Desert Hot Sprng Real Prpts In ....D...... 760 329-6000
10805 Palm Dr Desert Hot Springs (92240) **(P-14658)**

Desert Inn & Suites, Anaheim Also Called: SAI Management Co Inc (P-15339)

Desert Knlls Convalescent Hosp, Victorville Also Called: Knolls Convalescent Hosp Inc **(P-17982)**

Desert Mechanical Inc ....A...... 702 873-7333
15870 Olden St Rancho Cascades (91342) **(P-763)**

Desert Medical Group Inc (PA) ....C...... 760 320-8814
275 N El Cielo Rd Ste D-402 Palm Springs (92262) **(P-17643)**

Desert Mountain Fics, Victorville Also Called: Victor Cmnty Support Svcs Inc (P-18732)

Desert Oasis Healthcare, Palm Springs Also Called: Desert Medical Group Inc (P-17643)

Desert Publications Inc (PA) ....E...... 760 325-2333
303 N Indian Canyon Dr Palm Springs (92262) **(P-3355)**

Desert Redi Mix, Indio Also Called: Coronet Concrete Products Inc (P-5474)

Desert Regional Med Ctr Inc (HQ) ....A...... 760 323-6511
1150 N Indian Canyon Dr Palm Springs (92262) **(P-18237)**

Desert Sun Publishing Co (DH) ....C...... 760 322-8889
750 N Gene Autry Trl Palm Springs (92262) **(P-3273)**

Desert Sun The, Palm Springs Also Called: Desert Sun Publishing Co (P-3273)

Desert Trils Prpratory Academy, Adelanto Also Called: Adelanto Elementary School Dst **(P-1846)**

Desert Valley Date LLC ....D...... 760 398-0999
86740 Industrial Way Coachella (92236) **(P-13366)**

Desert Valley Hospital (DH) ....C...... 760 241-8000
16850 Bear Valley Rd Victorville (92395) **(P-18238)**

DESERT VALLEY INDUSTRIES, Palm Desert Also Called: Desert ARC (P-19071)

Desert Valley Med Group Inc (PA) ....B...... 760 241-8000
16850 Bear Valley Rd Victorville (92395) **(P-17644)**

Desert Valley Medical Group, Victorville Also Called: Desert Valley Med Group Inc (P-17644)

Desert Water Agency Fing Corp ....D...... 760 323-4971
1200 S Gene Autry Trl Palm Springs (92264) **(P-12120)**

Desert Willow Golf Course, Palm Desert Also Called: Desert Willow Golf Resort Inc (P-17425)

Desert Willow Golf Resort Inc ....C...... 760 346-0015
38995 Desert Willow Dr Palm Desert (92260) **(P-17425)**

Desiccare Inc ....E...... 909 444-8272
3406 Pomona Blvd Pomona (91768) **(P-5549)**

Design Form Inc ....E...... 714 952-3700
8250 Electric Ave Stanton (90680) **(P-6142)**

Design International Group Inc ....E...... 626 369-2289
755 Epperson Dr City Of Industry (91748) **(P-12938)**

Design Knit Inc ....E...... 213 742-1234
1636 Staunton Ave Los Angeles (90021) **(P-2067)**

Design Made Easy, Los Angeles Also Called: Emser Tile LLC (P-12354)

Design People Inc ....C...... 800 969-5799
1700 E Walnut Ave Ste 400 El Segundo (90245) **(P-16490)**

Design Printing, Los Angeles Also Called: Red Brick Corporation (P-3678)

Design Science Inc ....E...... 562 442-4779
444 W Ocean Blvd Ste 800 Long Beach (90802) **(P-16012)**

Design Shapes In Steel Inc ....E...... 626 579-2032
10315 Rush St South El Monte (91733) **(P-5587)**

Design Synthesis Inc ....E...... 858 271-8480
9855 Black Mountain Rd San Diego (92126) **(P-2596)**

DESIGN THERAPEUTICS, Carlsbad Also Called: Design Therapeutics Inc (P-4101)

Design Therapeutics Inc ....E...... 858 293-4900
6005 Hidden Valley Rd Ste 110 Carlsbad (92011) **(P-4101)**

Design Todays Inc (PA) ....E...... 213 745-3091
11707 Cetona Way Porter Ranch (91326) **(P-2318)**

Design West Technologies Inc ....D...... 714 731-0201
2701 Dow Ave Tustin (92780) **(P-5006)**

Designed Metal Connections Inc (DH) ....B...... 310 323-6200
14800 S Figueroa St Gardena (90248) **(P-9673)**

Designer Fashion Door, Temecula Also Called: Designer Sash and Door Sys Inc (P-5007)

Designer Sash and Door Sys Inc ....E...... 951 657-4179
45899 Via Tornado Temecula (92590) **(P-5007)**

Designory, Long Beach Also Called: Designory Inc (P-15663)

Designory Inc (HQ) ....C...... 562 624-0200
211 E Ocean Blvd Ste 100 Long Beach (90802) **(P-15663)**

Deskmakers Inc ....E...... 323 264-2260
6525 Flotilla St Commerce (90040) **(P-2882)**

Desksite, Irvine Also Called: Qdos Inc (P-16359)

Desmond Ventures Inc ....C...... 949 474-0400
17451 Von Karman Ave Irvine (92614) **(P-4563)**

Desser Holding Company LLC (HQ) ....E...... 323 721-4900
6900 W Acco St Montebello (90640) **(P-14927)**

Desser Tire & Rubber Co, Montebello Also Called: Desser Tire & Rubber Co LLC (P-4695)

Desser Tire & Rubber Co LLC ....E...... 323 837-1497
6900 W Acco St Montebello (90640) **(P-12906)**

Desser Tire & Rubber Co LLC (DH) ....E...... 323 721-4900
6900 W Acco St Montebello (90640) **(P-4695)**

Desser Tire & Rubber Co., Montebello Also Called: Desser Holding Company LLC (P-14927)

Dessert Cancer Care, Yucca Valley Also Called: Eisenhower Medical Center (P-17646)

Destination Residences LLC ....B...... 760 346-4647
45750 San Luis Rey Ave Palm Desert (92260) **(P-15128)**

A
L
P
H
A
B
E
T
I
C

Destination Residences LLC ....B...... 858 550-1000
9700 N Torrey Pines Rd La Jolla (92037) *(P-15506)*

Destinations For Teens ....D...... 818 737-2221
20951 Burbank Blvd Ste D Woodland Hills (91367) *(P-18688)*

Detoronics Corp ....E...... 626 579-7130
13071 Rosecrans Ave Santa Fe Springs (90670) *(P-8969)*

Detroit Diesel Corporation ....D...... 562 929-7016
10645 Studebaker Rd 2nd Fl Downey (90241) *(P-6893)*

Deutsch La Inc ....D...... 310 862-3000
12901 W Jefferson Blvd Los Angeles (90066) *(P-15537)*

Deutsche Bank National Tr Co ....D...... 310 788-6200
1999 Avenue Of The Stars Ste 3750 Los Angeles (90067) *(P-14265)*

Deva, Tustin *Also Called: Distribution Electrnics Vlued (P-9206)*

Devax Inc ....E...... 949 461-0450
13900 Alton Pkwy Ste 125 Irvine (92618) *(P-10490)*

Developlus Inc ....C...... 951 738-8595
1575 Magnolia Ave Corona (92879) *(P-11211)*

DEVELOPMENT DISABILITIES CENTE, Santa Ana *Also Called: Regional Ctr Orange Cnty Inc (P-20415)*

Development Resource Cons Inc (PA) ....D...... 714 685-6860
160 S Old Springs Rd Ste 210 Anaheim (92808) *(P-19571)*

Development Services, Lancaster *Also Called: Lancaster Cmnty Svcs Fndtion I (P-17033)*

Devereux California Center, Goleta *Also Called: Devereux Foundation (P-18689)*

Devereux Foundation ....B...... 805 968-2525
7055 Seaway Dr Goleta (93117) *(P-18689)*

Deviation Games LLC ....D...... 310 873-5225
12100 Wilshire Blvd Ste 1150 Los Angeles (90025) *(P-16013)*

Devil Mountain Whl Nurs LLC ....D...... 949 496-9356
29001 Ortega Hwy San Juan Capistrano (92675) *(P-51)*

Devil Mountain Wholesale Nursery, LLC, San Juan Capistrano *Also Called: Devil Mountain Whl Nurs LLC (P-51)*

Dewitt Stern Group Inc ....C...... 818 933-2700
5990 Sepulveda Blvd Ste 550 Van Nuys (91411) *(P-14584)*

Dex Corporation ....C...... 805 388-1711
3600 Via Pescador Camarillo (93012) *(P-19572)*

Dex-O-Tex Division, Compton *Also Called: Crossfield Products Corp (P-3934)*

DEXCOM, San Diego *Also Called: Dexcom Inc (P-10491)*

Dexcom Inc (PA) ....A...... 858 200-0200
6340 Sequence Dr San Diego (92121) *(P-10491)*

Dext Company, Santa Monica *Also Called: Reconserve Inc (P-1448)*

Dext Company of Maryland (DH) ....E...... 310 458-1574
2811 Wilshire Blvd Ste 410 Santa Monica (90403) *(P-1439)*

Dexter Axle Company ....D...... 760 744-1610
135 Sunshine Ln San Marcos (92069) *(P-9493)*

Dexyp, Glendale *Also Called: Yellowpagescom LLC (P-16968)*

Dezario Shoe Company, North Hollywood *Also Called: Meco-Nag Corporation (P-5277)*

Df One Operator LLC ....D...... 310 961-9739
11 Via Santanella Rancho Mirage (92270) *(P-16817)*

Dfa Dairy Brands Fluid LLC ....B...... 800 395-7004
17851 Railroad St City Of Industry (91748) *(P-13254)*

Dfds International Corporation ....D...... 310 414-1516
898 Sepulveda Blvd, 6th Floor El Segundo (90245) *(P-11752)*

Dfds Transport US, El Segundo *Also Called: Dfds International Corporation (P-11752)*

Dfm Dietary Food Management, Canoga Park *Also Called: Computrition Inc (P-16000)*

Dfndr Armor, Camarillo *Also Called: Engense Inc (P-5589)*

Dg Engineering Corp (PA) ....E...... 818 364-9024
13326 Ralston Ave Sylmar (91342) *(P-9970)*

DG Performance Spc Inc ....D...... 714 961-8850
4100 E La Palma Ave Anaheim (92807) *(P-9933)*

Dg Real Estate Inc ....D...... 818 591-8800
4766 Park Granada Ste 214 Calabasas (91302) *(P-14787)*

Dg-Displays LLC ....E...... 877 358-5976
355 Parkside Dr San Fernando (91340) *(P-11109)*

Dg2, Los Angeles *Also Called: Dg2 Worldwide Group LLC (P-15538)*

Dg2 Worldwide Group LLC ....E...... 310 809-0899
12655 W Jefferson Blvd 4th Fl Los Angeles (90066) *(P-15538)*

Dgl Holdings Inc ....E...... 714 630-7840
3850 E Miraloma Ave Anaheim (92806) *(P-6437)*

DH Caster International Inc ....F...... 909 930-6400
2260 S Haven Ave Ste C Ontario (91761) *(P-12720)*

DH Dental Business Svcs LLC (HQ) ....C...... 714 817-7000
200 S Kraemer Blvd Bldg E Brea (92821) *(P-10740)*

Dha America Inc ....D...... 858 925-3246
5403 Harvest Run Dr San Diego (92130) *(P-6816)*

Dharma Ventures Group Inc (PA) ....B...... 661 294-4200
24700 Avenue Rockefeller Valencia (91355) *(P-14130)*

Dhb Delivery LLC ....D...... 626 588-7562
1134 N Chestnut Ln Azusa (91702) *(P-11527)*

Dhccnp ....D...... 760 340-4646
44900 Desert Horizons Dr Indian Wells (92210) *(P-17481)*

Dhl Global Forwarding, Torrance *Also Called: Air Express Intl USA Inc (P-11737)*

DHm International Corp ....F...... 323 263-3888
901 Monterey Pass Rd Monterey Park (91754) *(P-2319)*

Dhouse Brands Inc // Comune ....E...... 213 291-7576
2301 E 7th St Ste F103 Los Angeles (90023) *(P-13039)*

Dhs Consulting LLC ....C...... 714 276-1135
1820 E 1st St Ste 410 Santa Ana (92705) *(P-20027)*

Dhv Industries Inc ....D...... 661 392-8948
3451 Pegasus Dr Bakersfield (93308) *(P-12852)*

Dhx-Dependable Hawaiian Ex Inc (PA) ....C...... 310 537-2000
19201 S Susana Rd Compton (90221) *(P-11753)*

Di Overnite LLC ....D...... 877 997-7447
1900 S State College Blvd Ste 450 Anaheim (92806) *(P-11528)*

Diack 1 Inc ....E...... 626 961-2491
19437 Windrose Dr Rowland Heights (91748) *(P-5718)*

Diagnostic Health Corporation ....C...... 310 665-7180
6801 Park Ter Los Angeles (90045) *(P-20163)*

Diagnostic Health Los Angeles, Los Angeles *Also Called: Diagnostic Health Corporation (P-20163)*

Diagnostic Labs & Rdlgy, Burbank *Also Called: Kan-Di-Ki LLC (P-18554)*

Diagnostixx of California Corp ....E...... 909 482-0840
829 Towne Center Dr Pomona (91767) *(P-10492)*

Diagnstic Intrvntnal Srgcal CT ....D...... 310 574-0400
13160 Mindanao Way Ste 150 Marina Del Rey (90292) *(P-17645)*

Diakont, Carlsbad *Also Called: Diakont Advanced Tech Inc (P-12377)*

Diakont Advanced Tech Inc 858 551-5551
3193 Lionshead Ave Carlsbad (92010) *(P-12377)*

Dial Communications, Camarillo *Also Called: Dial Security Inc (P-16729)*

Dial Industries Inc ....D...... 323 263-6878
3616 Noakes St Los Angeles (90023) *(P-5008)*

Dial Industries Inc (PA) ....D...... 323 263-6878
3628 Noakes St Los Angeles (90023) *(P-5009)*

Dial Precision Inc ....D...... 760 947-3557
17235 Darwin Ave Hesperia (92345) *(P-7817)*

Dial Security Inc (PA) ....C...... 805 389-6700
760 W Ventura Blvd Camarillo (93010) *(P-16729)*

Diality Inc ....D...... 949 916-5851
181 Technology Dr Ste 150 Irvine (92618) *(P-10493)*

Diamodent Inc ....E...... 888 281-8850
1580 N Harmony Cir Anaheim (92807) *(P-10741)*

Diamond Baseball Company Inc ....E...... 800 366-2999
1880 E Saint Andrew Pl Santa Ana (92705) *(P-10986)*

Diamond Collection LLC ....E...... 626 435-0077
20579 Valley Blvd Walnut (91789) *(P-2448)*

Diamond Contract Services Inc ....E...... 818 565-3554
11432 Vanowen St North Hollywood (91605) *(P-15707)*

Diamond Environmental Services, San Marcos *Also Called: Diamond Environmental Svcs LP (P-15778)*

Diamond Environmental Svcs LP ....D...... 760 744-7191
807 E Mission Rd San Marcos (92069) *(P-15778)*

Diamond Gloves ....E...... 714 667-0506
1100 S Linwood Ave Ste A Santa Ana (92705) *(P-10643)*

Diamond Goldenwest Corporation (PA) ....C...... 714 542-9000
15732 Tustin Village Way Tustin (92780) *(P-14074)*

Diamond Ground Products Inc ....E...... 805 498-3837
2651 Lavery Ct Newbury Park (91320) *(P-7158)*

Diamond K2 ....E...... 310 539-6116
23911 Garnier St Ste C Torrance (90505) *(P-5891)*

Diamond Mattress Company Inc (PA) ....E...... 310 638-0363
3112 E Las Hermanas St Compton (90221) *(P-13941)*

Diamond Mattress Nf, Compton *Also Called: Diamond Mattress Company Inc (P-13941)*

Diamond Multimedia, Chatsworth *Also Called: Best Data Products Inc (P-7511)*

Diamond Peo LLC .... C 714 728-5186
27442 Calle Arroyo Ste A San Juan Capistrano (92675) *(P-15837)*

Diamond Resorts LLC .... D 760 866-1800
2800 S Palm Canyon Dr Palm Springs (92264) *(P-15129)*

Diamond Ridge Corporation .... C 909 949-0605
121 S Mountain Ave Upland (91786) *(P-14788)*

Diamond Sports, Santa Ana *Also Called: Diamond Baseball Company Inc (P-10986)*

Diamond Wipes, Chino *Also Called: Diamond Wipes Intl Inc (P-4406)*

Diamond Wipes Intl Inc .... D 626 309-0033
320 Clary Ave San Gabriel (91776) *(P-4403)*

Diamond Wipes Intl Inc .... D 909 230-9888
4200 E Mission Blvd Ontario (91761) *(P-4404)*

Diamond Wipes Intl Inc .... E 909 230-9888
13775 Ramona Ave Chino (91710) *(P-4405)*

Diamond Wipes Intl Inc (PA) .... **D 909 230-9888**
4651 Schaefer Ave Chino (91710) *(P-4406)*

Diamondcore Tools, El Cajon *Also Called: Lexar Incorporated (P-2575)*

Diamondrock San Dego Tnant LLC .... B 619 239-4500
400 W Broadway San Diego (92101) *(P-15130)*

Diamonds By Design, Los Angeles *Also Called: Stardust Diamond Corp (P-10920)*

Diana Did-It Designs Inc .... E 970 226-5062
20579 Valley Blvd Walnut (91789) *(P-2449)*

Dianas Mexican Food Pdts Inc .... D 626 444-0555
2905 Durfee Ave El Monte (91732) *(P-1883)*

Dianas Mexican Food Pdts Inc (PA) .... **E 562 926-5802**
16330 Pioneer Blvd Norwalk (90650) *(P-1884)*

Dianas Mexican Food Pdts Inc .... E 310 834-4886
300 E Sepulveda Blvd Carson (90745) *(P-13696)*

Diasorin Molecular LLC .... C 562 240-6500
11331 Valley View St Cypress (90630) *(P-4272)*

Diatomaceous Earth.com, Santa Barbara *Also Called: Esperer Webstores LLC (P-1268)*

Diba Fashions Inc .... D 323 232-3775
472 N Bowling Green Way Los Angeles (90049) *(P-16818)*

Dibella, Oceanside *Also Called: Dibella Baking Company Inc (P-1515)*

Dibella Baking Company Inc .... D 951 797-4144
3524 Seagate Way Ste 110 Oceanside (92056) *(P-1515)*

Dicaperl Corporation (DH) .... **D 610 667-6640**
23705 Crenshaw Blvd # 10 Torrance (90505) *(P-416)*

Dick Dewese Chevrolet Inc .... C 909 793-2681
800 Alabama St Redlands (92374) *(P-13757)*

Dick Farrell Industries Inc .... F 909 613-9424
5071 Lindsay Ct Chino (91710) *(P-7363)*

Dick Howells Hole Drlg Svc Inc .... F 562 633-9898
2579 E 67th St Long Beach (90805) *(P-279)*

Dicken Enterprises Inc .... E 760 246-7333
22060 Bear Valley Rd Apple Valley (92308) *(P-7364)*

Dickeys Barbecue Pit, Tustin *Also Called: Dickeys Barbecue Rest Inc (P-14001)*

Dickeys Barbecue Rest Inc .... E 714 602-3874
17245 17th St Tustin (92780) *(P-14001)*

Dickson Testing Co Inc (DH) .... **D 562 862-8378**
11126 Palmer Ave South Gate (90280) *(P-19967)*

Didi Hirsch Psychiatric Svc (PA) .... **C 310 390-6612**
4760 Sepulveda Blvd Culver City (90230) *(P-19072)*

Didi Hrsch Cmnty Mntal Hlth Ct, Culver City *Also Called: Didi Hirsch Psychiatric Svc (P-19072)*

Diego & Son Printing Inc .... E 619 233-5373
2277 National Ave San Diego (92113) *(P-3559)*

Dierberg Starlane Vineyard .... F 805 736-0757
1280 Drum Canyon Rd Lompoc (93436) *(P-1623)*

Dietzgen Corporation .... E 951 278-3259
1522 E Bentley Dr Corona (92879) *(P-3234)*

Dig Corporation .... E 760 727-0914
1210 Activity Dr Vista (92081) *(P-6903)*

Digirad Imaging Solutions Inc .... C 800 947-6134
13100 Gregg St Ste A Poway (92064) *(P-15757)*

Digital Arbitrage Dist Inc (PA) .... **E 888 392-9478**
3033 5th Ave Ste 100 San Diego (92103) *(P-16225)*

Digital Domain, Venice *Also Called: Power Studios Inc (P-17211)*

Digital Domain 30 Inc (PA) .... **B 213 797-3100**
12641 Beatrice St Los Angeles (90066) *(P-17181)*

Digital Domain Media Group Inc .... A
12641 Beatrice St Los Angeles (90066) *(P-15664)*

Digital Film Labs, Los Angeles *Also Called: Point360 (P-17261)*

Digital Flex Media Inc .... D 909 484-8440
11150 White Birch Dr Rancho Cucamonga (91730) *(P-8455)*

Digital Force Technologies, San Diego *Also Called: Raytheon Dgital Force Tech LLC (P-10059)*

Digital Label Solutions LLC .... E 714 982-5000
1177 N Grove St Anaheim (92806) *(P-3235)*

Digital Marketing, San Diego *Also Called: Stn Digital LLC (P-15575)*

Digital One Color .... F 858 576-3600
13367 Kirkham Way Ste 110 Poway (92064) *(P-3560)*

Digital Periph Solutions Inc .... E 714 998-3440
160 S Old Springs Rd Ste 220 Anaheim (92808) *(P-8405)*

Digital Printing Systems Inc (PA) .... **D 626 815-1888**
2350 Panorama Ter Los Angeles (90039) *(P-3561)*

Digital Room Holdings Inc (HQ) .... **D 310 575-4440**
8000 Haskell Ave Van Nuys (91406) *(P-3753)*

Digital Signal Power Mfg, San Bernardino *Also Called: DSPM Inc (P-8941)*

Digital Supercolor Inc .... D 949 622-0010
Irvine (92606) *(P-3562)*

Digital Surgery Systems Inc .... E 805 978-5400
125 Cremona Dr Pmb 110 Goleta (93117) *(P-10494)*

Digitalpro Inc .... D 858 874-7750
13257 Kirkham Way Poway (92064) *(P-3563)*

Digitaria, San Diego *Also Called: Mirum Inc (P-15668)*

Digitas Inc .... C 617 867-1000
13031 W Jefferson Blvd Ste 800 Los Angeles (90094) *(P-15539)*

Digitaslbi, Los Angeles *Also Called: Digitas Inc (P-15539)*

Digitran, Rancho Cucamonga *Also Called: Electro Switch Corp (P-8121)*

Digivision Inc .... E 858 530-0100
9830 Summers Ridge Rd San Diego (92121) *(P-10128)*

Dignified Home Loans LLC .... D 818 421-7753
1 Baxter Way Ste 120 Westlake Village (91362) *(P-14358)*

Dignity Health .... C 805 389-5800
2309 Antonio Ave Camarillo (93010) *(P-18239)*

Dignity Health .... A 805 988-2500
1600 N Rose Ave Oxnard (93030) *(P-18240)*

Dignity Health .... B 805 739-3000
1400 E Church St Santa Maria (93454) *(P-18241)*

Dignity Health .... B 661 663-6000
400 Old River Rd Bakersfield (93311) *(P-18242)*

Dignity Health .... B 805 988-2868
200 Oceangate Long Beach (90802) *(P-18243)*

Dignity Health .... A 818 885-8500
18300 Roscoe Blvd Northridge (91325) *(P-18244)*

Dignity Health .... C 562 491-9000
1050 Linden Ave Long Beach (90813) *(P-18245)*

Diligent Delivery Systems, Valencia *Also Called: Central States Logistics Inc (P-11449)*

Diligent Solutions Inc .... E 760 814-8960
3240 Grey Hawk Ct Carlsbad (92010) *(P-7818)*

Dimar Enterprises Inc .... C 949 492-1100
26021 Pala Ste 150 Mission Viejo (92691) *(P-15708)*

Dimensions In Screen Printing, Irvine *Also Called: Tomorrows Look Inc (P-2093)*

Dimic Steel Tech Inc .... E 909 946-6767
145 N 8th Ave Upland (91786) *(P-6227)*

Dincloud Inc .... D 310 929-1101
27520 Hawthorne Blvd Ste 185 Rlng Hls Est (90274) *(P-16226)*

Dine Brands Global, Pasadena *Also Called: Dine Brands Global Inc (P-14002)*

Dine Brands Global Inc (PA) .... **B 818 240-6055**
10 W Walnut St Fl 5 Pasadena (91103) *(P-14002)*

Dioz Group, The, Beverly Hills *Also Called: Alanic International Corp (P-2133)*

Dip Braze Inc .... E 818 768-1555
9131 De Garmo Ave Sun Valley (91352) *(P-17083)*

Diplomatic Security Services, Rancho Cucamonga *Also Called: Harrison Iyke (P-16740)*

Diplomatic Security Svcs LLC .... D 909 463-8409
7581 Etiwanda Ave Rancho Cucamonga (91739) *(P-16638)*

Direct Chassislink Inc .... A 657 216-5846
7777 Center Ave Ste 325 Huntington Beach (92647) *(P-15779)*

Direct Chemicals, Huntington Beach *Also Called: Home & Body Company (P-4609)*

Employee Codes: A=Over 500 employees, B=251-500
C=101-250, D=51-100, E=20-50, F=10-19, G=1-9

2024 Southern California
Business Directory and Buyers Guide

© Mergent Inc. 1-800-342-5647

1067

Direct Drive Systems Inc ....D....... 714 872-5500
  621 Burning Tree Rd Fullerton (92833) *(P-8140)*

Directed LLC ....C....... 800 876-0800
  1 Viper Way Ste 1 Vista (92081) *(P-11754)*

Directors Guild America Inc (PA)..............................**C....... 310 289-2000**
  7920 W Sunset Blvd Los Angeles (90046) *(P-17248)*

Directv ....D....... 323 810-2032
  1655 W 110th Pl Los Angeles (90047) *(P-11984)*

Directv, El Segundo *Also Called: Directv Group Holdings LLC (P-11847)*

Directv, El Segundo *Also Called: Directv Group Inc (P-11990)*

Directv Inc ....B....... 888 388-4249
  2260 E Imperial Hwy El Segundo (90245) *(P-11985)*

Directv Enterprises LLC ....A....... 310 535-5000
  2230 E Imperial Hwy El Segundo (90245) *(P-11986)*

Directv Group Holdings LLC (HQ)............................**C....... 310 964-5000**
  2260 E Imperial Hwy El Segundo (90245) *(P-11847)*

Directv Group Holdings LLC ....C....... 661 632-6562
  715 E Avenue L8 Ste 101 Lancaster (93535) *(P-11987)*

Directv Group Holdings LLC ....C....... 760 375-8300
  140 Station Ave Ridgecrest (93555) *(P-11988)*

Directv Group Holdings LLC ....C....... 805 207-6675
  360 Cortez Cir Camarillo (93012) *(P-11989)*

Directv Group Inc (DH)...**C....... 310 964-5000**
  2260 E Imperial Hwy El Segundo (90245) *(P-11990)*

Directv International Inc (DH)..................................**C....... 310 964-6460**
  2230 E Imperial Hwy Fl 10 El Segundo (90245) *(P-11991)*

Disaster Rstrtion Prfssnals In ....D....... 310 301-8030
  1517 W 130th St Gardena (90249) *(P-429)*

Disco Print Whl 46 A Ltd Lblty ....E....... 949 261-8457
  1891 Alton Pkwy Ste A Irvine (92606) *(P-16440)*

Discopylabs ....E....... 909 390-3800
  4455 E Philadelphia St Ontario (91761) *(P-8456)*

Discount Tire, Ventura *Also Called: Southern Cal Disc Tire Co Inc (P-13871)*

Discount Tire, Escondido *Also Called: Southern Cal Disc Tire Co Inc (P-13872)*

Discount Tire, San Marcos *Also Called: Southern Cal Disc Tire Co Inc (P-13873)*

Discount Tire, Escondido *Also Called: Southern Cal Disc Tire Co Inc (P-13874)*

Discount Tire, Solana Beach *Also Called: Southern Cal Disc Tire Co Inc (P-13875)*

Discount Tire, Poway *Also Called: Southern Cal Disc Tire Co Inc (P-13876)*

Discount Tire, Oceanside *Also Called: Southern Cal Disc Tire Co Inc (P-13877)*

Discount Tire, Encinitas *Also Called: Southern Cal Disc Tire Co Inc (P-13878)*

Discount Tire, San Diego *Also Called: Southern Cal Disc Tire Co Inc (P-13879)*

Discount Tire, Carson *Also Called: Southern Cal Disc Tire Co Inc (P-13880)*

Discount Tire, Glendora *Also Called: Southern Cal Disc Tire Co Inc (P-13881)*

Discount Tire, Hemet *Also Called: Southern Cal Disc Tire Co Inc (P-13882)*

Discount Tire, Huntington Beach *Also Called: Southern Cal Disc Tire Co Inc (P-13883)*

Discount Tire Center 038, Redlands *Also Called: Akh Company Inc (P-13852)*

Discount Tire Center 077, Moreno Valley *Also Called: Akh Company Inc (P-13853)*

Discounted Wheel Warehouse, Fullerton *Also Called: Wheel and Tire Club Inc (P-5608)*

Discovery Communications Inc (PA).........................B....... 310 975-5906
  10100 Santa Monica Blvd Ste 1500 Los Angeles (90067) *(P-12006)*

Discovery Health Services ....B....... 858 459-0785
  5726 La Jolla Blvd Ste 104 La Jolla (92037) *(P-18758)*

Discovery Medical Staffing, La Jolla *Also Called: Discovery Health Services (P-18758)*

Discovery Practice MGT Inc ....B....... 714 828-1800
  18401 Von Karman Ave Ste 500 Irvine (92612) *(P-18690)*

Discovery Scnce Ctr Ornge Cnty ....C....... 866 552-2823
  2500 N Main St Santa Ana (92705) *(P-19353)*

Discus Dental LLC (PA)..**C....... 310 845-8600**
  1700 S Baker Ave Ontario (91761) *(P-12483)*

Disguise Inc (HQ)..E....... 858 391-3600
  12120 Kear Pl Poway (92064) *(P-2450)*

Dish For All Inc ....E....... 760 690-3869
  148 S Escondido Blvd Escondido (92025) *(P-17060)*

Disney, Anaheim *Also Called: Walt Dsney Imgnring RES Dev In (P-2461)*

Disney, Burbank *Also Called: Disney Enterprises Inc (P-11922)*

Disney, Anaheim *Also Called: Disney Enterprises Inc (P-15131)*

Disney, Anaheim *Also Called: Disney Enterprises Inc (P-17182)*

Disney, Anaheim *Also Called: Disney Enterprises Inc (P-17183)*

Disney, Glendale *Also Called: Disney Enterprises Inc (P-17184)*

Disney, Burbank *Also Called: Disney Incorporated (P-17185)*

Disney, Burbank *Also Called: Walt Disney Music Company (P-17232)*

Disney, Glendale *Also Called: Walt Disney Pictures (P-17233)*

Disney, Burbank *Also Called: Walt Disney Records Direct (P-17234)*

Disney, Glendale *Also Called: Walt Dsney Imgnring RES Dev In (P-17273)*

Disney, Burbank *Also Called: Walt Disney Company (P-17456)*

Disney, Burbank *Also Called: Disney Regional Entrmt Inc (P-17545)*

Disney Book Group LLC (DH)....................................E....... 818 560-1000
  500 S Buena Vista St Burbank (91521) *(P-3406)*

Disney Cnsmr Pdts Intrctive MD ....D....... 818 263-1374
  1201 Flower St Glendale (91201) *(P-16014)*

Disney Cruise Line, Burbank *Also Called: Dcl Maritime LLC (P-20026)*

Disney Editions, Burbank *Also Called: Disney Publishing Worldwide (P-3356)*

Disney Enterprises Inc (DH).....................................**A....... 818 560-1000**
  500 S Buena Vista St Burbank (91521) *(P-11922)*

Disney Enterprises Inc ....A....... 714 778-6600
  1150 W Magic Way Anaheim (92802) *(P-15131)*

Disney Enterprises Inc ....D....... 407 397-6000
  1313 S Harbor Blvd Anaheim (92802) *(P-17182)*

Disney Enterprises Inc ....C....... 714 781-1651
  700 W Ball Rd Anaheim (92802) *(P-17183)*

Disney Enterprises Inc ....D....... 818 553-4103
  1101 Flower St Glendale (91201) *(P-17184)*

Disney Financial Services, Burbank *Also Called: Twdc Enterprises 18 Corp (P-11966)*

Disney Incorporated (DH)..**C....... 818 560-1000**
  500 S Buena Vista St Burbank (91521) *(P-17185)*

Disney Interactive Studios, Burbank *Also Called: Disney Interactive Studios Inc (P-16015)*

Disney Interactive Studios Inc ....B....... 818 553-5000
  681 W Buena Vista St Burbank (91521) *(P-16015)*

Disney Interactive Studios Inc ....B....... 818 560-1000
  601 Circle Seven Dr Glendale (91201) *(P-16016)*

Disney Networks Group LLC (DH).............................D....... 310 369-1000
  10201 W Pico Blvd Bldg 101 Los Angeles (90064) *(P-11944)*

Disney Publishing Worldwide (DH)...........................D....... 212 633-4400
  500 S Buena Vista St Burbank (91521) *(P-3356)*

Disney Regional Entrmt Inc (DH)..............................**C....... 818 560-1000**
  500 S Buena Vista St Burbank (91521) *(P-17545)*

Disney Research Pittsburgh ....C....... 412 623-1800
  532 Paula Ave Glendale (91201) *(P-19833)*

Disneyland, Anaheim *Also Called: Disneyland International (P-15132)*

Disneyland, Anaheim *Also Called: Disneyland International (P-17448)*

Disneyland International ....A....... 714 956-6746
  1580 S Disneyland Dr Anaheim (92802) *(P-15132)*

Disneyland International (DH)....................................**C....... 714 781-4565**
  1313 S Harbor Blvd Anaheim (92802) *(P-17448)*

Disneys Grnd Clifornian Ht Spa, Anaheim *Also Called: Wco Hotels Inc (P-15411)*

Disorderly Kids, Los Angeles *Also Called: Avalon Apparel LLC (P-2276)*

Dispensing Dynamics Intl Inc (PA)............................**D....... 626 961-3691**
  1940 Diamond St San Marcos (92078) *(P-5010)*

Display Fabrication Group Inc ....E....... 714 373-2100
  1231 N Miller St Ste 100 Anaheim (92806) *(P-2548)*

Display Products Inc ....E....... 310 640-0442
  445 S Douglas St El Segundo (90245) *(P-8787)*

Displays & Holders, Anaheim *Also Called: Hippo Corporation (P-13541)*

Disposable Waste System, Santa Ana *Also Called: Jwc Environmental Inc (P-7666)*

Distillery, Manhattan Beach *Also Called: Distillery Tech Inc (P-16017)*

Distillery Tech Inc ....C....... 310 776-6234
  1500 Rosecrans Ave Ste 500 Manhattan Beach (90266) *(P-16017)*

Distinct Indulgence ....E....... 818 546-1700
  5018 Lante St Baldwin Park (91706) *(P-1462)*

Distinctive Inds Texas Inc ....E....... 323 889-5766
  9419 Ann St Santa Fe Springs (90670) *(P-2427)*

Distinctive Inds Texas Inc ....E....... 512 491-3500
  10618 Shoemaker Ave Santa Fe Springs (90670) *(P-2428)*

Distinctive Industries ....B....... 800 421-9777
  10618 Shoemaker Ave Santa Fe Springs (90670) *(P-2529)*

Distinctive Plastics Inc ....D....... 760 599-9100
  1385 Decision St Vista (92081) *(P-5011)*

Distribution, Ontario *Also Called: Index Fasteners Inc (P-12859)*

Distribution Alternatives Inc .... D...... 909 746-5600
10621 6th St Rancho Cucamonga (91730) *(P-11574)*

Distribution Alternatives Inc .... D...... 909 770-8900
1979 Renaissance Pkwy Rialto (92376) *(P-13040)*

Distribution Cente, Calexico *Also Called: Clover Envmtl Solutions LLC (P-10863)*

Distribution Electrnics Vlued .... E...... 714 368-1717
2651 Dow Ave Tustin (92780) *(P-9206)*

District Attorney, Los Angeles *Also Called: County of Los Angeles (P-18840)*

District Attorney, Westminster *Also Called: County of Orange (P-19065)*

District Attorney, Lancaster *Also Called: County of Los Angeles (P-20412)*

Divergent 3d, Torrance *Also Called: Divergent Technologies Inc (P-19573)*

Divergent Technologies Inc .... C...... 424 542-2158
19601 Hamilton Ave Torrance (90502) *(P-19573)*

Diverscape Inc .... D...... 951 245-1686
21730 Bundy Canyon Rd Wildomar (92595) *(P-188)*

Diverse Optics Inc .... E...... 909 593-9330
10339 Dorset St Rancho Cucamonga (91730) *(P-5012)*

Diversfied Mtllrgical Svcs Inc .... E...... 714 895-7777
12101 Industry St Garden Grove (92841) *(P-5836)*

Diversfied Nano Solutions Corp .... E...... 858 924-1013
12140 Community Rd Poway (92064) *(P-4587)*

Diversified Tchncal Systems Inc (HQ)................................**E...... 562 493-0158**
1720 Apollo Ct Seal Beach (90740) *(P-10195)*

Diversified Coatings Linings .... E...... 909 591-6366
4810 Cheyenne Way Chino (91710) *(P-1069)*

Diversified Direct, La Mirada *Also Called: Diversified Mailing Incorporated (P-15630)*

Diversified Images Inc .... F...... 661 702-0003
1230 N Jefferson St Ste J Anaheim (92807) *(P-3754)*

Diversified Landscape Co, Wildomar *Also Called: Diverscape Inc (P-188)*

Diversified Logistic Svcs Inc .... E...... 562 941-3600
13033 Telegraph Rd Santa Fe Springs (90670) *(P-11820)*

Diversified Mailing Incorporated .... C...... 714 994-6245
14407 Alondra Blvd La Mirada (90638) *(P-15630)*

Diversified Metal Works, Orange *Also Called: Rika Corporation (P-1115)*

Diversified Minerals Inc .... E...... 805 247-1069
1100 Mountain View Ave Ste F Oxnard (93030) *(P-5476)*

Diversified Plastics Inc .... E...... 760 598-5333
1333 Keystone Way Vista (92081) *(P-5013)*

Diversified Printers Inc .... D...... 714 994-3400
12834 Maxwell Dr Tustin (92782) *(P-3441)*

Diversified Prj Svcs Intl Inc (PA)...................................**D...... 661 371-2800**
5351 Olive Dr Ste 100 Bakersfield (93308) *(P-19574)*

Diversified Silicone, Santa Fe Springs *Also Called: Rogers Corporation (P-4791)*

Diversified Tool & Die .... E...... 760 598-9100
2585 Birch St Vista (92081) *(P-6512)*

Diversified Utility Svcs Inc .... B...... 661 325-3212
3105 Unicorn Rd Bakersfield (93308) *(P-668)*

Diversity Bus Solutions Inc .... C...... 909 395-0243
3532 Old Archibald Ranch Rd Ontario (91761) *(P-15838)*

Divine Pasta Company .... E...... 818 559-7440
140 W Providencia Ave Burbank (91502) *(P-1885)*

Divine Pasta Company, Burbank *Also Called: Palermo Family LP (P-1966)*

Diving Unlimited Int., San Diego *Also Called: Diving Unlimited Intl Inc (P-10987)*

Diving Unlimited Intl Inc .... D...... 619 236-1203
1148 Delevan Dr San Diego (92102) *(P-10987)*

Division 1, Los Angeles *Also Called: Los Angles Cnty Mtro Trnsp Aut (P-11329)*

Division 7, Venice *Also Called: Los Angles Cnty Mtro Trnsp Aut (P-11337)*

Dixieline Lumber Company LLC .... A...... 951 224-8491
2625 Durahart St Riverside (92507) *(P-13571)*

Dixieline Lumber Company LLC (DH)................................**D...... 619 224-4120**
3250 Sports Arena Blvd San Diego (92110) *(P-13572)*

Dixieline Probuild, San Diego *Also Called: Dixieline Lumber Company LLC (P-13572)*

Djh Enterprises .... E...... 714 424-6500
23011 Moulton Pkwy Ste B6 Laguna Hills (92653) *(P-8509)*

Dji Technology Inc .... D...... 818 235-0789
17301 Edwards Rd Cerritos (90703) *(P-10864)*

DJM Suspension, Gardena *Also Called: D and J Marketing Inc (P-2528)*

Djo LLC .... D...... 760 727-1280
3151 Scott St Vista (92081) *(P-10644)*

Djo LLC .... E...... 800 321-9549
1430 Decision St Vista (92081) *(P-10645)*

Djo LLC .... E...... 800 321-9549
5919 Sea Otter Pl Ste 200 Carlsbad (92010) *(P-10646)*

Djo Consumer LLC .... F...... 760 727-1280
1430 Decision St Vista (92081) *(P-10647)*

Djo Holdings LLC (DH)..**E...... 760 727-1280**
1430 Decision St Vista (92081) *(P-10648)*

Djont Operations LLC .... C...... 310 640-3600
1440 E Imperial Ave El Segundo (90245) *(P-15133)*

Djont/Jpm Hsptlity Lsg Spe LLC .... C...... 805 984-2500
2101 Mandalay Beach Rd Oxnard (93035) *(P-15134)*

DK, Los Angeles *Also Called: Design Knit Inc (P-2067)*

DK Amans Valve & Supply, Long Beach *Also Called: DK Valve & Supply Inc (P-17123)*

DK Valve & Supply Inc .... E...... 562 529-8400
2385 E Artesia Blvd Long Beach (90805) *(P-17123)*

Dkn Hotel LLC (PA)..**B...... 714 427-4320**
42 Corporate Park Ste 200 Irvine (92606) *(P-15135)*

DL Horton Enterprises Inc ....D...... 323 777-1700
12705 Daphne Ave Hawthorne (90250) *(P-7819)*

Dl Imaging, Santa Ana *Also Called: Dekra-Lite Industries Inc (P-16816)*

DL Long Landscaping Inc .... D...... 909 628-5531
5475 G St Chino (91710) *(P-159)*

Dla Piper LLP (us) .... C...... 310 595-3000
2000 Avenue Of The Stars Ste 400n Los Angeles (90067) *(P-18849)*

Dlf Logistics, Los Angeles *Also Called: Dlf Logistics LLC (P-11452)*

Dlf Logistics LLC .... D...... 626 387-3797
1019 S Rimpau Blvd Los Angeles (90019) *(P-11452)*

Dlr Group Inc (HQ)..**C...... 213 800-9400**
700 S Flower St Ste 2200 Los Angeles (90017) *(P-19727)*

Dm Luxury LLC .... C...... 858 366-9721
875 Prospect St Ste 300 La Jolla (92037) *(P-3755)*

Dm Software Inc .... E...... 714 953-2653
1842 Park Skyline Rd Santa Ana (92705) *(P-16227)*

DM SOFTWARE INC, Santa Ana *Also Called: Dm Software Inc (P-16227)*

Dm Technology & Energy Inc .... F...... 909 627-1600
4615 State St Montclair (91763) *(P-8308)*

DMA Enterprises Inc (PA)..**F...... 805 520-2468**
2255 Union Pl Simi Valley (93065) *(P-11212)*

Dmbm LLC .... E...... 714 321-6032
2445 E 12th St Ste C Los Angeles (90021) *(P-2320)*

DMC, Simi Valley *Also Called: Datametrics Corporation (P-7520)*

DMC Power Inc (PA)...**E...... 310 323-1616**
623 E Artesia Blvd Carson (90746) *(P-8261)*

Dmf Inc .... D...... 323 934-7779
1118 E 223rd St Unit 1 Carson (90745) *(P-8292)*

Dmf Lighting, Carson *Also Called: Dmf Inc (P-8292)*

Dmi, Rancho Cascades *Also Called: Desert Mechanical Inc (P-763)*

Dmi Ready Mix, Oxnard *Also Called: Diversified Minerals Inc (P-5476)*

Dmk, Santa Fe Springs *Also Called: Danne Montague-King Co (P-13037)*

DMS, Anaheim *Also Called: DMS Facility Services Inc (P-15709)*

DMS Facility Services Inc ....A...... 949 975-1366
2861 E Coronado St Anaheim (92806) *(P-15709)*

DMS Facility Services LLC ....A...... 949 975-1366
2861 E Coronado St Anaheim (92806) *(P-19575)*

DMS Facility Services LLC ....A...... 858 560-4191
5735 Kearny Villa Rd Ste 108 San Diego (92123) *(P-19576)*

DMS Insurance, San Diego *Also Called: Ue Authority Co (P-15578)*

DMS Ue Acqisition Holdings Inc ....D...... 800 466-4178
225 Broadway Ste 2200 San Diego (92101) *(P-14928)*

Dn Tanks Inc .... C...... 619 440-8181
351 Cypress Ln El Cajon (92020) *(P-9929)*

Dna Motor Inc .... E...... 626 965-8898
801 Sentous Ave City Of Industry (91744) *(P-13858)*

Dna Motoring, City Of Industry *Also Called: Dna Motor Inc (P-13858)*

Dna Specialty Inc .... D...... 310 767-4070
200 W Artesia Blvd Compton (90220) *(P-12238)*

DNam Apparel Industries LLC .... E...... 323 859-0114
4938 Triggs St Commerce (90022) *(P-2321)*

Dnatrix Inc .... E...... 832 930-2401
2659 State St # 100 Carlsbad (92008) *(P-4312)*

ALPHABETIC

Employee Codes: A=Over 500 employees, B=251-500
C=101-250, D=51-100, E=20-50, F=10-19, G=1-9

2024 Southern California
Business Directory and Buyers Guide

© Mergent Inc. 1-800-342-5647
1069

Dneg North America Inc (PA)................D......323 461-7887
5750 Hannum Ave Ste 100 Culver City (90230) *(P-17249)*

Dnib Unwind Inc................................C......213 617-2717
333 S Grand Ave Ste 4070 Los Angeles (90071) *(P-4102)*

Do It Best, Pasadena *Also Called: George L Throop Co (P-13577)*

Do It Right Products LLC..........................E......714 998-8152
1838 N Case St Orange (92865) *(P-11213)*

DO IT RIGHT PRODUCTS LLC, Orange *Also Called: Do It Right Products LLC (P-11213)*

Doctors Hospital W Covina Inc.....................C......626 338-8481
725 S Orange Ave West Covina (91790) *(P-18246)*

Doctors Signature Sales (PA)......................E......800 531-4877
495 Raleigh Ave El Cajon (92020) *(P-3997)*

Documotion Research Inc..........................F......714 662-3800
2020 S Eastwood Ave Santa Ana (92705) *(P-3564)*

Docupace Technologies LLC (PA)....................C......310 445-7722
400 Corporate Pointe Ste 300 Culver City (90230) *(P-16018)*

Docupak Inc.......................................F......714 670-7944
1702 Edinger Ave Tustin (92780) *(P-3837)*

Docusource Inc...................................D......562 447-2600
13100 Alondra Blvd Ste 108 Cerritos (90703) *(P-14131)*

Dodger Stadium, Los Angeles *Also Called: Fox BSB Holdco Inc (P-17370)*

DOE & Ingalls Cal Oper LLC........................E......951 801-7175
1060 Citrus St Riverside (92507) *(P-10253)*

Dogswell, Los Angeles *Also Called: Arthur Dogswell LLC (P-1427)*

Doh Quest LLC....................................E......213 651-3441
8939 S Sepulveda Blvd Los Angeles (90045) *(P-2201)*

Doheny Eye Institute (PA).........................D......323 342-7120
150 N Orange Grove Blvd Pasadena (91103) *(P-19924)*

Doi Venture, Rancho Cucamonga *Also Called: Davidson Optronics Inc (P-10360)*

Dolby Laboratories Inc............................E......818 562-1101
1020 Chestnut St Burbank (91506) *(P-8406)*

Dole Holding Company LLC..........................A......818 879-6600
1 Dole Dr Westlake Village (91362) *(P-48)*

Dole Packaged Foods LLC (HQ)......................A......805 601-5500
3059 Townsgate Rd Ste 400 Westlake Village (91361) *(P-1369)*

Dollar Shave Club Inc (HQ)........................C......310 975-8528
13335 Maxella Ave Marina Del Rey (90292) *(P-7010)*

Dolores Canning Co Inc............................E......323 263-9155
1020 N Eastern Ave Los Angeles (90063) *(P-1323)*

Dolphin Bay Hotel & Residences, Shell Beach *Also Called: Dolphin Bay Ht & Residence Inc (P-15136)*

Dolphin Bay Ht & Residence Inc....................D......805 773-4300
2727 Shell Beach Rd Shell Beach (93449) *(P-15136)*

Dolphin Medical Inc (HQ)..........................D......800 448-6506
12525 Chadron Ave Hawthorne (90250) *(P-10800)*

Dominator Radiology Systems, San Diego *Also Called: DR Systems Inc (P-18546)*

Dominguez Law Group PC............................D......213 388-7788
3250 Wilshire Blvd Ste 1750 Los Angeles (90010) *(P-18850)*

Domino Plastics Mfg Inc...........................E......661 396-3744
601 Gateway Ct Bakersfield (93307) *(P-5014)*

Don Alderson Associates Inc.......................E......310 837-5141
3327 La Cienega Pl Los Angeles (90016) *(P-2870)*

Don Lee Farms, Inglewood *Also Called: Goodman Food Products Inc (P-1907)*

Don Miguel Foods, Orange *Also Called: Don Miguel Mexican Foods Inc (P-1389)*

Don Miguel Mexican Foods Inc (HQ).................E......714 385-4500
333 S Anita Dr Ste 1000 Orange (92868) *(P-1389)*

Don Whittemore Corp...............................E......818 994-0111
501 Library St San Fernando (91340) *(P-14003)*

Donahue Schrber Rlty Group Inc (PA)...............D......714 545-1400
200 Baker St Ste 100 Costa Mesa (92626) *(P-14789)*

Donahue Schriber Rlty Group LP (PA)...............D......714 545-1400
200 Baker St Ste 100 Costa Mesa (92626) *(P-14659)*

Donald T Sterling Corporation.....................D......310 275-5575
10300 Wilshire Blvd Los Angeles (90024) *(P-15137)*

Donaldson Company Inc.............................E......661 295-0800
26235 Technology Dr Valencia (91355) *(P-9382)*

Doncasters Gce Integrated, Chula Vista *Also Called: Integrated Energy Technologies Inc (P-7300)*

Donco & Sons Inc.................................E......714 779-0099
2871 E Blue Star St Anaheim (92806) *(P-891)*

Donco Associates & Sons, Anaheim *Also Called: Donco & Sons Inc (P-891)*

Donoco Industries Inc.............................E......714 893-7889
5642 Research Dr Ste B Huntington Beach (92649) *(P-5324)*

Dool Fna Inc.....................................C......562 483-4100
16624 Edwards Rd Cerritos (90703) *(P-2037)*

Door Components Inc...............................C......909 770-5700
7980 Redwood Ave Fontana (92336) *(P-6103)*

Door Doctor, Anaheim *Also Called: R & S Ovrhd Doors So-Cal Inc (P-6119)*

Doorking, Inglewood *Also Called: Doorking Inc (P-9207)*

Doorking Inc (PA)................................C......310 645-0023
120 S Glasgow Ave Inglewood (90301) *(P-9207)*

Doose Landscape Incorporated......................D......760 591-4500
785 E Mission Rd San Marcos (92069) *(P-189)*

Dorado Network Systems Corp.......................C......650 227-7300
40 Pacifica Irvine (92618) *(P-16228)*

Dorado Pkg, North Hollywood *Also Called: Corporate Impressions La Inc (P-3749)*

Dorel Home Furnishings Inc........................D......909 390-5705
5400 Shea Center Dr Ontario (91761) *(P-2771)*

Dorel Juvenile Group Inc..........................C......909 428-0295
9950 Calabash Ave Fontana (92335) *(P-5015)*

Dorel Juvenile Group Inc..........................C......909 390-5705
5400 Shea Center Dr Ontario (91761) *(P-5016)*

Doremi, Burbank *Also Called: Doremi Labs Inc (P-8407)*

Doremi Labs, Burbank *Also Called: Dolby Laboratories Inc (P-8406)*

Doremi Labs Inc...................................E......818 562-1101
1020 Chestnut St Burbank (91506) *(P-8407)*

Dorothy Sarkozy...................................D......858 259-0555
3810 Valley Centre Dr Ste 906 San Diego (92130) *(P-14790)*

Dos Gringos, Vista *Also Called: Gringo Ventures LLC (P-13508)*

DOT Blue Safes Corporation........................E......909 445-8888
2707 N Garey Ave Pomona (91767) *(P-6860)*

DOT Corp...E......714 708-5960
1801 S Standard Ave Santa Ana (92707) *(P-3565)*

DOT Printer Inc (PA)..............................D......949 474-1100
2424 Mcgaw Ave Irvine (92614) *(P-3566)*

Doty Bros Equipment Co (HQ).......................D......562 864-6566
11232 Firestone Blvd Norwalk (90650) *(P-669)*

Double Eagle Trnsp Corp...........................E......760 956-3770
12135 Scarbrough Ct Oak Hills (92344) *(P-11483)*

Double K Industries, Chatsworth *Also Called: Invelop Inc (P-6906)*

Double K Industries Inc...........................F......818 772-2887
9711 Mason Ave Chatsworth (91311) *(P-6904)*

Doubleco Incorporated.............................D......909 481-0799
9444 9th St Rancho Cucamonga (91730) *(P-6438)*

Doubletree By Hilton, Monrovia *Also Called: Doubltree By Hlton Ht Monrovia (P-15138)*

Doubletree By Hilton, San Diego *Also Called: Gringteam Inc (P-15163)*

Doubletree By Hilton, San Diego *Also Called: San Diego Lessee LLC (P-15343)*

Doubletree By Hilton Carson, Carson *Also Called: Carson Operating Company LLC (P-15108)*

Doubletree Golf Resort, San Diego *Also Called: Gringteam Inc (P-15164)*

Doubletree Hotel, Torrance *Also Called: Ctc Group Inc (P-15125)*

Doubletree Hotel, Santa Barbara *Also Called: Fess Prker-Red Lion Gen Partnr (P-15152)*

Doubletree Hotel, Irvine *Also Called: Spectrum Hotel Group LLC (P-15366)*

Doubletree Hotel Boston, Los Angeles *Also Called: L-O Bedford Operating LLC (P-15216)*

Doubletree Ht San Diego Dwntwn, San Diego *Also Called: Harbor View Hotel Ventures LLC (P-15170)*

Doubletree San Diego Del Mar, San Diego *Also Called: Swvp Del Mar Hotel LLC (P-15383)*

Doubltree By Hlton Ht Monrovia....................C......626 357-1900
924 W Huntington Dr Monrovia (91016) *(P-15138)*

Doubltree Palm Sprng Golf Rsor, Cathedral City *Also Called: T Allance One - Palm Sprng LLC (P-17568)*

Doubltree Stes By Hlton Anheim, Anaheim *Also Called: Orangewood LLC (P-15278)*

Doubltree Stes By Hlton Snta M, Santa Monica *Also Called: Santa Monica Hotel Owner LLC (P-15350)*

Doug Mockett & Company Inc........................D......310 318-2491
1915 Abalone Ave Torrance (90501) *(P-2772)*

Doughpro, Perris *Also Called: Steams Product Dev Corp (P-7410)*

Douglas Fir Holdings LLC..........................C......714 842-5551
8382 Newman Ave Huntington Beach (92647) *(P-17927)*

Douglas Furniture of California LLC................A......310 749-0003
809 Tyburn Rd Palos Verdes Estates (90274) *(P-2828)*

Mergent email: customerrelations@mergent.com
1070

2024 Southern California
Business Directory and Buyers Guide

(P-0000) Products & Services Section entry number
(PA)=Parent Co (HQ)=Headquarters (DH)=Div Headquarters

Douglas Steel Supply Inc (PA)..................................D...... 323 587-7676
4804 Laurel Canyon Blvd Valley Village (91607) *(P-12547)*

DOUGLAS STEEL SUPPLY CO., Valley Village Also Called: Douglas Steel Supply Inc
(P-12547)

Douglas Technologies Group Inc (PA)...................E...... 760 758-5560
42092 Winchester Rd Ste B Temecula (92590) *(P-9383)*

Douglas Wheel, Temecula Also Called: Douglas Technologies Group Inc *(P-9383)*

Douglass Truck Bodies Inc ....E...... 661 327-0258
231 21st St Bakersfield (93301) *(P-9322)*

Doval Industries Inc ....D...... 323 226-0335
3961 N Mission Rd Los Angeles (90031) *(P-5916)*

Doval Industries Co, Los Angeles Also Called: Doval Industries Inc *(P-5916)*

Dow Company Foundation ....C...... 909 476-4127
11266 Jersey Blvd Rancho Cucamonga (91730) *(P-3936)*

Dow Hydraulic Systems Inc ....D...... 909 596-6602
2895 Metropolitan Pl Pomona (91767) *(P-7820)*

Dow-Elco Inc ....E...... 323 723-1288
1313 W Olympic Blvd Montebello (90640) *(P-8094)*

Dow-Key Microwave, Ventura Also Called: Dow-Key Microwave Corporation *(P-8177)*

Dow-Key Microwave Corporation ....C...... 805 650-0260
4822 Mcgrath St Ventura (93003) *(P-8177)*

Dowell Aluminum Foundry Inc ....E...... 323 877-9645
11342 Hartland St North Hollywood (91605) *(P-5790)*

Dowell Schlumberger, Bakersfield Also Called: Schlumberger Technology Corp *(P-384)*

Dowling Advisory Group ....D...... 626 319-1369
3579 E Foothill Blvd Ste 651 Pasadena (91107) *(P-20164)*

Downey Care Center, Downey Also Called: Ensign Group Inc *(P-17942)*

Downey Civic Theatre, Downey Also Called: City of Downey *(P-17313)*

Downey Community Health Center ....C...... 562 862-6506
8425 Iowa St Downey (90241) *(P-17928)*

Downey Grinding Co ....E...... 562 803-5556
12323 Bellflower Blvd Downey (90242) *(P-7011)*

Downey Regional Medical Center, Downey Also Called: Pih Health Hospital - Whitti *(P-18379)*

Downhole Stabilization Inc ....E...... 661 631-1044
3515 Thomas Way Bakersfield (93308) *(P-6957)*

Dozuki ....D...... 805 464-0573
1105 Higuera St Ste 100 San Luis Obispo (93401) *(P-16229)*

Dpa Components International, Simi Valley Also Called: Dpa Labs Inc *(P-8788)*

Dpa Labs Inc ....E...... 805 581-9200
2251 Ward Ave Simi Valley (93065) *(P-8788)*

Dpi Direct, Poway Also Called: Digitalpro Inc *(P-3563)*

DPI Labs Inc ....E...... 909 392-5777
1350 Arrow Hwy La Verne (91750) *(P-9674)*

Dpi Specialty Foods, Ontario Also Called: Dpi Specialty Foods West Inc *(P-13178)*

Dpi Specialty Foods West Inc (DH).......................C...... 909 975-1019
601 S Rockefeller Ave Ontario (91761) *(P-13178)*

Dpi Specialty Foods West Inc ....C...... 909 975-1019
930 S Rockefeller Ave Ontario (91761) *(P-13179)*

Dpi West, Ontario Also Called: Dpi Specialty Foods West Inc *(P-13179)*

Dpp 2020 Inc (DH)...E...... 951 845-3161
533 E Third St Beaumont (92223) *(P-5017)*

Dpp Real Estate, Sierra Madre Also Called: Deasy Penner Podley *(P-14786)*

Dpr Construction A Gen Partnr ....C...... 858 646-0757
5010 Shoreham Pl Ste 100 San Diego (92122) *(P-546)*

Dpr Construction A Gen Partnr ....D...... 626 463-1265
88 W Colorado Blvd Ste 301 Pasadena (91105) *(P-547)*

Dr Pepper Snapple Group, Riverside Also Called: American Bottling Company *(P-1678)*

Dr Smoothie Brands Inc ....E...... 714 449-9787
1730 Raymer Ave Fullerton (92833) *(P-1766)*

Dr Smoothie Enterprises ....E...... 714 449-9787
1730 Raymer Ave Fullerton (92833) *(P-1767)*

Dr Squatch LLC ....C...... 631 229-7068
4065 Glencoe Ave Apt 300b Marina Del Rey (90292) *(P-4407)*

DR Systems Inc ....C...... 858 625-3344
10140 Mesa Rim Rd San Diego (92121) *(P-18546)*

Dr. Bronners Magic Soaps, Vista Also Called: All One God Faith Inc *(P-4332)*

Dr. Bronners Magic Soaps, Vista Also Called: All One God Faith Inc *(P-4333)*

Dr. Fresh, La Palma Also Called: Ranir LLC *(P-10764)*

Draco Broadcast Inc ....E...... 818 736-5788
2000 N Lincoln St Burbank (91504) *(P-8510)*

Dragados Usa Inc ....D...... 657 229-7800
3200 Park Center Dr Ste 600 Costa Mesa (92626) *(P-615)*

Dragon Alliance, San Clemente Also Called: Dragon Alliance Inc *(P-10836)*

Dragon Alliance Inc ....D...... 760 931-4900
971 Calle Amanecer San Clemente (92673) *(P-10836)*

Dragon Herbs, Los Angeles Also Called: Ron Teeguarden Enterprises Inc *(P-4014)*

Dragon Trade Intl Corp ....C...... 619 816-6062
1205 Highland Ave National City (91950) *(P-12629)*

Dramm and Echter Inc ....D...... 760 436-0188
1150 Quail Gardens Dr Encinitas (92024) *(P-52)*

Drapery Affair, Paramount Also Called: Blue Ribbon Draperies Inc *(P-13949)*

Dream Hollywood, Los Angeles Also Called: 6417 Selma Hotel LLC *(P-15066)*

Dream Mortgage Group, Brea Also Called: Emet Lending Group Inc *(P-14312)*

Dreamgear LLC ....E...... 310 222-5522
20001 S Western Ave Torrance (90501) *(P-10949)*

Dreamgirl International, Bell Also Called: Lovin Enterprises Inc *(P-13132)*

Dreamstart Labs Inc ....E...... 408 914-1234
2907 Shelter Island Dr Ste 105 San Diego (92106) *(P-16230)*

Dreamworks Animation Pubg LLC ....A...... 818 695-5000
1000 Flower St Glendale (91201) *(P-17186)*

Drees Wood Products Inc ....E...... 562 633-7337
14020 Orange Ave Paramount (90723) *(P-2597)*

Drees Wood Products Inc (PA)...............................E...... 562 633-7337
14003 Orange Ave Paramount (90723) *(P-2656)*

Dresser-Rand Company ....E...... 310 223-0600
18502 Dominguez Hill Dr Rancho Dominguez (90220) *(P-7308)*

Drew Ford ....C...... 619 464-7777
8970 La Mesa Blvd La Mesa (91942) *(P-13758)*

Drew Hyundai, La Mesa Also Called: Drew Ford *(P-13758)*

Dri Commercial Corporation ....C...... 949 266-1900
2081 Business Center Dr Ste 195 Irvine (92612) *(P-1041)*

Dri Companies ....B...... 949 266-1900
2081 Business Center Dr Ste 195 Irvine (92612) *(P-1042)*

Driftwood Health Care Ctr, Torrance Also Called: Mariner Health Care Inc *(P-18007)*

Drillmec Inc ....D...... 281 885-0777
8140 Rosecrans Ave Paramount (90723) *(P-299)*

Drip Hydration ....D...... 323 333-9634
11948 Gorham Ave Apt 3 Los Angeles (90049) *(P-18759)*

Drip Research Technology Svcs, San Diego Also Called: DRTS Enterprises Ltd *(P-6905)*

Driscoll Inc ....E...... 619 226-2500
2500 Shelter Island Dr San Diego (92106) *(P-9857)*

Driscoll Boat Works, San Diego Also Called: Driscoll Inc *(P-9857)*

Drive Devilbiss Healthcare, Rialto Also Called: Medical Depot Inc *(P-10554)*

Driven Technologies, Santa Ana Also Called: Aerospace Driven Tech Inc *(P-9601)*

Driveshaftpro ....E...... 714 893-4585
7532 Anthony Ave Garden Grove (92841) *(P-9384)*

Dropzone Waterpark ....C...... 951 210-1600
2165 Trumble Rd Perris (92571) *(P-17546)*

Drs Daylight Defense, San Diego Also Called: Daylight Defense LLC *(P-10798)*

Drs Daylight Solutions, San Diego Also Called: Daylight Solutions Inc *(P-8786)*

Drs Network & Imaging Systems, Cypress Also Called: Drs Ntwork Imaging Systems LLC *(P-8789)*

Drs Ntwork Imaging Systems LLC ....D...... 714 220-3800
10600 Valley View St Cypress (90630) *(P-8789)*

Drs Own Inc (PA)...E...... 760 804-0751
5923 Farnsworth Ct Carlsbad (92008) *(P-10649)*

DRTS Enterprises Ltd ....E...... 858 270-7244
7979 Stromesa Ct Ste A San Diego (92126) *(P-6905)*

Drymaster, Mission Viejo Also Called: Dimar Enterprises Inc *(P-15708)*

Ds Fibertech Corp ....E...... 619 562-7001
11015 Mission Park Ct Santee (92071) *(P-7365)*

Ds Lakeshore, Costa Mesa Also Called: Donahue Schriber Rlty Group LP *(P-14659)*

Ds Lakeshore LP ....D...... 916 286-5231
200 Baker St Ste 100 Costa Mesa (92626) *(P-19444)*

DSA Phototech LLC ....E...... 866 868-1602
2321 E Gladwick St Rancho Dominguez (90220) *(P-8309)*

DSA Signage, Rancho Dominguez Also Called: DSA Phototech LLC *(P-8309)*

Dsca, Long Beach Also Called: Denso Pdts & Svcs Americas Inc *(P-12237)*

Dsd Trucking Inc ....D...... 310 338-3395
2411 Santa Fe Ave Redondo Beach (90278) *(P-11696)*

Employee Codes: A=Over 500 employees, B=251-500
C=101-250, D=51-100, E=20-50, F=10-19, G=1-9

2024 Southern California
Business Directory and Buyers Guide

© Mergent Inc. 1-800-342-5647

1071

A
L
P
H
A
B
E
T
I
C

DSI Process Systems LLC .... C....... 314 382-1525
7595 Reynolds Cir Huntington Beach (92647) *(P-12789)*

DSM&t Co Inc .... C...... 909 357-7960
10609 Business Dr Fontana (92337) *(P-9165)*

DSPM Inc .... E...... 714 970-2304
439 S Stoddard Ave San Bernardino (92401) *(P-8941)*

Dss, Calabasas *Also Called: David Shield Security Inc (P-16637)*

DSV, Fontana *Also Called: DSV Solutions LLC (P-11632)*

DSV Solutions LLC .... C...... 909 829-5804
13032 Slover Ave Ste 200 Fontana (92337) *(P-11632)*

DSV Solutions LLC .... C...... 909 349-6100
13230 San Bernardino Ave Fontana (92335) *(P-11755)*

DSV Solutions LLC .... C...... 909 390-4563
1670 Etiwanda Ave Ste A Ontario (91761) *(P-11756)*

DSV Solutions LLC .... D...... 714 630-0110
3454 E Miraloma Ave Anaheim (92806) *(P-11757)*

Dsy Educational Corporation .... E...... 805 684-8111
525 Maple St Carpinteria (93013) *(P-2549)*

DT Mattson Enterprises Inc .... E...... 951 849-9781
201 W Lincoln St Banning (92220) *(P-10950)*

Dtiq Holdings Inc .... C...... 323 576-1400
1755 N Main St Los Angeles (90031) *(P-16730)*

Dtrs Santa Monica LLC .... B...... 310 458-6700
1700 Ocean Ave Santa Monica (90401) *(P-15139)*

Dts Inc (DH) .... C...... 818 436-1000
5220 Las Virgenes Rd Calabasas (91302) *(P-17250)*

Dtt, Los Angeles *Also Called: Dtiq Holdings Inc (P-16730)*

Dtwusa, Hacienda Heights *Also Called: Brio Water Technology Inc (P-12761)*

Dtx, Corona *Also Called: Dart Container Corp California (P-4879)*

Dtz, Westlake Village *Also Called: C&W Facility Services Inc (P-15697)*

Dual Diagnosis Trtmnt Ctr Inc (PA) .... C...... 949 276-5553
1211 Puerta Del Sol # 200 San Clemente (92673) *(P-18691)*

Dual Diagnosis Trtmnt Ctr Inc .... C...... 949 324-4531
69640 Highway 111 Rancho Mirage (92270) *(P-18760)*

Duarte Manor, Los Angeles *Also Called: Emp III Inc (P-15028)*

Dubnoff Ctr For Child Dev Edct (PA) .... D...... 818 755-4950
10526 Dubnoff Way North Hollywood (91606) *(P-18965)*

Duclos Lenses, Chatsworth *Also Called: Duclos Lenses Inc (P-17124)*

Duclos Lenses Inc .... F...... 818 773-0600
20222 Bahama St Chatsworth (91311) *(P-17124)*

Ducommun, Santa Ana *Also Called: Ducommun Incorporated (P-9679)*

Ducommun Aerostructures Inc (HQ) .... B...... 310 380-5390
268 E Gardena Blvd Gardena (90248) *(P-9566)*

Ducommun Aerostructures Inc .... C...... 714 637-4401
1885 N Batavia St Orange (92865) *(P-9567)*

Ducommun Aerostructures Inc .... C...... 310 513-7200
23301 Wilmington Ave Carson (90745) *(P-9675)*

Ducommun Aerostructures Inc .... D...... 760 246-4191
4001 El Mirage Rd Adelanto (92301) *(P-9676)*

Ducommun Aerostructures Inc .... E...... 626 358-3211
801 Royal Oaks Dr Monrovia (91016) *(P-9677)*

Ducommun Arostructures-Gardena, Gardena *Also Called: Ahf-Ducommun Incorporated (P-9608)*

Ducommun Incorporated .... F...... 626 358-3211
801 Royal Oaks Dr Monrovia (91016) *(P-9678)*

Ducommun Incorporated (PA) .... C...... 657 335-3665
200 Sandpointe Ave Ste 700 Santa Ana (92707) *(P-9679)*

Ducommun Labarge Tech Inc (HQ) .... C...... 310 513-7200
23301 Wilmington Ave Carson (90745) *(P-9680)*

Dudek Inc (PA) .... D...... 760 942-5147
605 3rd St Encinitas (92024) *(P-19577)*

Dudes Brewing Company .... E...... 424 271-2915
1840 W 208th St Somis (93066) *(P-1586)*

Dudleys Bakery Inc .... E...... 760 765-0488
30218 Hwy 78 Santa Ysabel (92070) *(P-13715)*

Duhig and Co Inc .... E
5071 Telegraph Rd Los Angeles (90022) *(P-12853)*

Duhig Stainless, Los Angeles *Also Called: Duhig and Co Inc (P-12853)*

Duke Pacific Inc .... D...... 909 591-0191
13950 Monte Vista Ave Chino (91710) *(P-1043)*

Dunbar Electric Sign Company .... E...... 661 323-2600
4020 Rosedale Hwy Bakersfield (93308) *(P-11110)*

Duncan Bolt Co .... F...... 909 581-6740
5555 E Gibralter Ontario (91764) *(P-6439)*

Duncan Bros Inc .... E...... 909 877-1904
21516 Main St Grand Terrace (92313) *(P-6021)*

Duncan Carter Corporation (PA) .... D...... 805 964-9749
5427 Hollister Ave Santa Barbara (93111) *(P-10922)*

Duncan McIntosh Company Inc (PA) .... E...... 949 660-6150
18475 Bandilier Cir Fountain Valley (92708) *(P-3357)*

Dunham Metal Processing Inc .... E...... 714 532-5551
936 N Parker St Orange (92867) *(P-6612)*

Dunkel Bros. Machinery Moving, La Mirada *Also Called: MEI Rigging & Crating LLC (P-7248)*

Dunn & Berger Inc .... B...... 818 986-1234
5955 De Soto Ave Ste 160 Woodland Hills (91367) *(P-18609)*

Dunn-Dwrds Pints Wallcoverings, Commerce *Also Called: Dunn-Edwards Corporation (P-13673)*

Dunn-Edwards Corporation (DH) .... C...... 888 337-2468
6119 E Washington Blvd Commerce (90040) *(P-13673)*

Dupaco Inc .... E...... 760 758-4550
4144 Avenida De La Plata Ste B Oceanside (92056) *(P-10495)*

Duplan Industries .... E...... 760 744-4047
1265 Stone Dr San Marcos (92078) *(P-7821)*

Dupont Displays Inc .... C...... 805 562-5400
600 Ward Dr Ste C Santa Barbara (93111) *(P-19834)*

Dupree Inc .... E...... 909 597-4889
14395 Ramona Ave Chino (91710) *(P-6440)*

Dur-Red Products .... E...... 323 771-9000
5634 Costa Dr Chino Hills (91709) *(P-6228)*

Dura Coat Products Inc (PA) .... D...... 951 341-6500
5361 Via Ricardo Riverside (92509) *(P-6700)*

Dura Technologies Inc .... C...... 909 877-8477
2720 S Willow Ave Ste A Bloomington (92316) *(P-4486)*

Durabag Company Inc .... D...... 714 259-8811
1432 Santa Fe Dr Tustin (92780) *(P-3182)*

Duraco Express, Walnut *Also Called: Essentra International LLC (P-4564)*

Duracold Refrigeration Mfg LLC .... E...... 626 358-1710
1551 S Primrose Ave Monrovia (91016) *(P-6376)*

Duramax Building Products, Montebello *Also Called: US Polymers Inc (P-5240)*

Durasafe Inc .... F...... 626 965-1588
18999 Railroad St City Of Industry (91748) *(P-12484)*

Duray, Vernon *Also Called: J F Duncan Industries Inc (P-7663)*

Durham School Services L P .... C...... 310 767-5820
723 S Alameda St Compton (90220) *(P-11421)*

Durham School Services L P .... C...... 562 408-1206
8555 Flower Ave Paramount (90723) *(P-11422)*

Durham School Services L P .... C...... 818 880-4257
4029 Las Virgenes Rd Calabasas (91302) *(P-11423)*

Durham School Services L P .... A...... 626 573-3769
2713 River Ave Rosemead (91770) *(P-11424)*

Durham School Services L P .... C...... 909 899-1809
12999 Victoria St Rancho Cucamonga (91739) *(P-11425)*

Durham School Services L P .... C...... 805 483-6076
3151 W 5th St Ste A Oxnard (93030) *(P-11426)*

Durham School Services L P .... C...... 949 376-0376
2003 Laguna Canyon Rd Laguna Beach (92651) *(P-11427)*

Durham School Services L P .... B...... 714 542-8989
2818 W 5th St Santa Ana (92703) *(P-11434)*

Durkan Patterned Carpets Inc .... C...... 310 838-2898
3633 Lenawee Ave # 120 Los Angeles (90016) *(P-2113)*

Duro-Flex Rubber Products Inc .... E...... 562 946-5533
13215 Lakeland Rd Santa Fe Springs (90670) *(P-4760)*

Durston Manufacturing Company .... F...... 909 593-1506
1395 Palomares St La Verne (91750) *(P-5878)*

Dust Collector Services Inc .... E...... 714 237-1690
1280 N Sunshine Way Anaheim (92806) *(P-12751)*

Dutek Incorporated .... E...... 760 566-8888
2228 Oak Ridge Way Vista (92081) *(P-9208)*

Dux Dental Products, Orange *Also Called: Dux Industries Inc (P-10742)*

Dux Industries Inc .... D...... 805 488-1122
1717 W Collins Ave Orange (92867) *(P-10742)*

Dv Custom Farming LLC ....D...... 661 858-2888
2101 Mettler Frontage Rd E Bakersfield (93307) *(P-80)*

Dv Natural Resources LLC ....F
8 Miles S Ballarat Wingate Rd Trona (93562) *(P-232)*

DVeal Corporation ....C...... 626 296-8900
2750 E Washington Blvd Ste 230 Pasadena (91107) *(P-19324)*

Dvele Inc ....E...... 909 796-2561
25525 Redlands Blvd Loma Linda (92354) *(P-2737)*

Dvele Omega Corporation ....D...... 909 796-2561
25525 Redlands Blvd Loma Linda (92354) *(P-2738)*

Dvm Insurance Agency, Brea Also Called: Veterinary Pet Insurance Services Inc *(P-14640)*

Dvs Media Services (PA) ....**E...... 818 841-6750**
2625 W Olive Ave Burbank (91505) *(P-15647)*

Dw and Bb Consulting Inc ....D...... 818 896-9899
11381 Bradley Ave Pacoima (91331) *(P-9917)*

DWA, Palm Springs Also Called: Desert Water Agency Fing Corp *(P-12120)*

Dwa Alminum Composites USA Inc ....E...... 818 998-1504
21100 Superior St Chatsworth (91311) *(P-5791)*

Dwa Aluminum Composites, Chatsworth Also Called: Dwa Composite Specialties Inc
(P-5695)

Dwa Composite Specialties Inc ....F...... 818 885-8654
21100 Superior St Chatsworth (91311) *(P-5695)*

Dwa Holdings LLC (DH) ....**D...... 818 695-5000**
1000 Flower St Glendale (91201) *(P-17187)*

Dwaynes Engineering & Cnstr ....E...... 661 762-7261
3559 Addie Ave Fellows (93224) *(P-343)*

Dwell Records, Los Angeles Also Called: CMH Records Inc *(P-8453)*

Dwi Enterprises ....E...... 714 842-2236
11081 Winners Cir Ste 100 Los Alamitos (90720) *(P-8408)*

Dxray Inc ....C...... 818 280-0177
19355 Business Center Dr Northridge (91324) *(P-9031)*

Dxterity Diagnostics Inc (PA) ....E...... 310 537-7857
19500 S Rancho Way Ste 116 Compton (90220) *(P-19925)*

Dyk, El Cajon Also Called: Dn Tanks Inc *(P-9929)*

Dyk Incorporated (HQ) ....**E...... 619 440-8181**
351 Cypress Ln El Cajon (92020) *(P-9930)*

Dyk Prestressed Tanks, El Cajon Also Called: Dyk Incorporated *(P-9930)*

Dynabook Americas Inc (HQ) ....**B...... 949 583-3000**
5241 California Ave Ste 100 Irvine (92617) *(P-7423)*

Dynacast LLC ....C...... 949 707-1211
25952 Commercentre Dr Lake Forest (92630) *(P-5774)*

Dynacast, LLC, Lake Forest Also Called: Dynacast LLC *(P-5774)*

Dynaco Equipment Co, Pismo Beach Also Called: Brooks Restaurant Group Inc *(P-13173)*

Dynaflex Products (PA) ....**D...... 323 724-1555**
6466 Gayhart St Commerce (90040) *(P-9323)*

Dynalectric Company ....B...... 619 328-4007
1111 Pioneer Way El Cajon (92020) *(P-892)*

Dynalloy Inc ....E...... 714 436-1206
2801 Mcgaw Ave Irvine (92614) *(P-9032)*

Dynamation Research, Los Angeles Also Called: Gali Corporation *(P-9696)*

Dynamet Incorporated ....E...... 714 375-3150
16052 Beach Blvd Ste 221 Huntington Beach (92647) *(P-5723)*

Dynamex Corporation ....D...... 310 329-0399
155 E Albertoni St Carson (90746) *(P-2131)*

Dynamic Auto Images Inc ....B...... 714 771-3400
2860 Michelle Ste 140 Irvine (92606) *(P-17047)*

Dynamic Chiropractic, Huntington Beach Also Called: Maxwell Petersen Associates *(P-3369)*

Dynamic Cooking Systems Inc ....A...... 714 372-7000
695 Town Center Dr Ste 180 Costa Mesa (92626) *(P-7654)*

Dynamic Detail, Irvine Also Called: Dynamic Auto Images Inc *(P-17047)*

Dynamic Enterprises Inc ....E...... 562 944-0271
2081 Rancho Hills Dr Chino Hills (91709) *(P-7822)*

Dynamic Fabrication Inc ....E...... 714 662-2440
890 Mariner St Brea (92821) *(P-9681)*

Dynamic Home Care, Sherman Oaks Also Called: Dynamic Home Care Service Inc *(P-18610)*

Dynamic Home Care Service Inc (PA) ....D...... 818 981-4446
14260 Ventura Blvd Ste 301 Sherman Oaks (91423) *(P-18610)*

Dynamic Plumbing Systems Inc ....B...... 951 343-1200
5920 Winterhaven Ave Riverside (92504) *(P-764)*

Dynamic Resources Inc ....D...... 619 268-3070
7894 Dagget St Ste 202e San Diego (92111) *(P-3044)*

Dynamic Sciences Intl Inc ....E...... 818 226-6262
9400 Lurline Ave Unit B Chatsworth (91311) *(P-8511)*

Dynamics O&P, Los Angeles Also Called: Dynamics Orthtics Prsthtics In *(P-10650)*

Dynamics Orthtics Prsthtics In ....E...... 213 383-9212
1830 W Olympic Blvd Ste 123 Los Angeles (90006) *(P-10650)*

Dynamo Aviation Inc ....D...... 818 785-9561
9601 Mason Ave # A Chatsworth (91311) *(P-6229)*

Dynaroll, Sylmar Also Called: Providien Machining & Metals Corporation *(P-10592)*

Dynasty Electronic Company LLC ....D...... 714 550-1197
1790 E Mcfadden Ave Ste 105 Santa Ana (92705) *(P-8670)*

Dynasty Marketplace Inc ....B...... 804 837-0119
716 Hampton Dr Venice (90291) *(P-16019)*

Dynatrac Products LLC ....E...... 714 596-4461
7392 Count Cir Huntington Beach (92647) *(P-9385)*

Dynovas, Poway Also Called: Dynovas Inc *(P-16819)*

Dynovas Inc ....F...... 508 717-7494
12250 Iavelli Way Poway (92064) *(P-16819)*

Dyntek Inc (PA) ....**C...... 949 271-6700**
5241 California Ave Ste 150 Irvine (92617) *(P-16565)*

Dytran Instruments Inc ....C...... 818 700-7818
21592 Marilla St Chatsworth (91311) *(P-9033)*

E & B Ntral Resources Mgt Corp (PA) ....**D...... 661 679-1714**
1608 Norris Rd Bakersfield (93308) *(P-300)*

E & B Ntral Resources MGT Corp ....E...... 661 766-2501
1848 Perkins Rd New Cuyama (93254) *(P-301)*

E & C Fashion Inc ....B...... 323 262-0099
1420 Esperanza St Los Angeles (90023) *(P-16820)*

E & L Electric ....F...... 562 903-9272
12322 Los Nietos Rd Santa Fe Springs (90670) *(P-17103)*

E & S International Entps Inc (PA) ....**C...... 818 887-0700**
7801 Hayvenhurst Ave Van Nuys (91406) *(P-12630)*

E & S Paper Co ....D...... 310 538-8700
14110 S Broadway Los Angeles (90061) *(P-13006)*

E Alko Inc ....E...... 818 587-9700
8201 Woodley Ave Van Nuys (91406) *(P-11055)*

E B Bradley Co (PA) ....**E...... 323 585-9917**
5602 Bickett St Vernon (90058) *(P-12721)*

E B Bradley Co ....F...... 800 533-3030
10903 Vanowen St North Hollywood (91605) *(P-12722)*

E C R M C, El Centro Also Called: El Centro Rgnal Med Ctr Fndtio *(P-18252)*

E D Q Inc ....E...... 714 546-6010
2920 Halladay St Santa Ana (92705) *(P-10129)*

E Entertainment Television Inc ....A...... 323 954-2400
5750 Wilshire Blvd # 500 Los Angeles (90036) *(P-11992)*

E Film Digital Labratories, Los Angeles Also Called: Efilm LLC *(P-17188)*

E J Harrison & Sons Inc ....C...... 805 647-1414
1589 Lirio Ave Ventura (93004) *(P-12167)*

E J Lauren LLC ....E...... 562 803-1113
2690 Pellissier Pl City Of Industry (90601) *(P-2800)*

E L I, San Diego Also Called: Energy Labs Inc *(P-7610)*

E L S, Los Angeles Also Called: J C Entertainment Ltg Svcs Inc *(P-17316)*

E M D, Los Angeles Also Called: Capitol-Emi Music Inc *(P-8452)*

E M E Inc ....C...... 310 639-1621
500 E Pine St Compton (90222) *(P-6613)*

E M S, Santa Ana Also Called: Sandberg Industries Inc *(P-9113)*

E O C, Compton Also Called: Cri Sub 1 *(P-2881)*

E O C Health Services, San Luis Obispo Also Called: Community Action Prtnr San Lui
(P-18681)

E O I, Walnut Also Called: Excellence Opto Inc *(P-8346)*

E O S International, Carlsbad Also Called: Electronic Online Systems International *(P-16441)*

E P I, Irvine Also Called: Asian European Products Inc *(P-12232)*

E P I, San Diego Also Called: Engineering Partners Inc *(P-19583)*

E R C Company, E Rncho Dmngz Also Called: Coy Industries Inc *(P-6220)*

E R G International, Oxnard Also Called: Ergonom Corporation *(P-3024)*

E R I T Inc (PA) ....**D...... 760 433-6024**
251 Airport Rd Oceanside (92058) *(P-19260)*

E S 3, San Diego Also Called: Enginring Sftwr Sys Sltons Inc *(P-19584)*

E S T, Carlsbad Also Called: Electro Surface Tech Inc *(P-8671)*

E Sales, Garden Grove Also Called: Elasco Inc *(P-3938)*

Employee Codes: A=Over 500 employees, B=251-500
C=101-250, D=51-100, E=20-50, F=10-19, G=1-9

2024 Southern California
Business Directory and Buyers Guide

© Mergent Inc. 1-800-342-5647
1073

ALPHABETIC

E V G, Anaheim *Also Called: Emergency Vehicle Group Inc (P-13762)*

E Vasquez Distributors Inc .... E....... 805 487-8458
4524 E Pleasant Valley Rd Oxnard (93033) *(P-2717)*

E Z Buy & E Z Sell Recycl Corp (DH)........................... C....... 310 886-7808
4954 Van Nuys Blvd Ste 201 Sherman Oaks (91403) *(P-3274)*

E Z Services .... D....... 714 635-7599
1101 W Lincoln Ave Ste 145 Anaheim (92805) *(P-14259)*

E Z Staffing Inc (PA)... B....... 818 845-2500
200 N Maryland Ave Ste 303 Glendale (91206) *(P-15839)*

E-Band Communications LLC .... E....... 858 408-0660
17034 Camino San Bernardo San Diego (92127) *(P-8512)*

E-Scepter, City Of Industry *Also Called: Sceptre Inc (P-9115)*

E-Times Corporation (PA)... B....... 213 452-6720
601 S Figueroa St Ste 5000 Los Angeles (90017) *(P-16526)*

E-Z Lok Division, Gardena *Also Called: Tool Components Inc (P-12576)*

E-Z Mix Inc (PA).. E....... 818 768-0568
11450 Tuxford St Sun Valley (91352) *(P-3198)*

E-Z-Hook Test Products Div, Baldwin Park *Also Called: Tektest Inc (P-8984)*

E.V. Roberts, Carson *Also Called: Cirrus Enterprises LLC (P-13410)*

E/G Electro-Graph, Vista *Also Called: Plansee USA LLC (P-8865)*

Ea Mobile Inc .... D....... 310 754-7125
5510 Lincoln Blvd Los Angeles (90094) *(P-11848)*

Eagle Access Ctrl Systems Inc .... E....... 818 837-7900
12953 Foothill Blvd Sylmar (91342) *(P-8178)*

Eagle Dominion Energy Corp .... E....... 805 272-9557
200 N Hayes Ave Oxnard (93030) *(P-302)*

Eagle Dominion Trust, Oxnard *Also Called: Eagle Dominion Energy Corp (P-302)*

Eagle Labs, Rancho Cucamonga *Also Called: Eagle Labs LLC (P-10496)*

Eagle Labs LLC .... D....... 909 481-0011
10201a Trademark St Ste A Rancho Cucamonga (91730) *(P-10496)*

Eagle Med Packg Sterilization, Paso Robles *Also Called: Eagle Med Pckg Strlization Inc (P-16821)*

Eagle Med Pckg Strlization Inc .... E....... 805 238-7401
2921 Union Rd Ste A Paso Robles (93446) *(P-16821)*

Eagle Mold Technologies Inc .... E....... 858 530-0888
12330 Crosthwaite Cir Poway (92064) *(P-5018)*

Eagle One Golf Products, Anaheim *Also Called: Golf Supply House Usa Inc (P-10995)*

Eagle Roofing Products, Rialto *Also Called: Burlingame Industries Inc (P-15441)*

Eagle Roofing Products Co, Rialto *Also Called: Burlingame Industries Inc (P-5565)*

Eagle Roofing Products Fla LLC .... E....... 909 822-6000
3546 N Riverside Ave Rialto (92377) *(P-5374)*

Eagle Security Services Inc .... C....... 310 642-0656
12903 S Normandie Ave Gardena (90249) *(P-16639)*

Eagle Topco LP .... A....... 949 585-4329
18200 Von Karman Ave Irvine (92612) *(P-16231)*

Eaglerise E&E Inc .... E....... 215 675-5953
13405 Benson Ave Chino (91710) *(P-9034)*

Eagleware Manufacturing Co Inc .... E....... 562 320-3100
12683 Corral Pl Santa Fe Springs (90670) *(P-6513)*

EAM Enterprises Inc (PA).. D....... 818 248-9100
4005 Foothill Blvd La Crescenta (91214) *(P-14791)*

Earle M Jorgensen Company .... D....... 323 567-1122
350 S Grand Ave Ste 5100 Los Angeles (90071) *(P-12548)*

Earle M Jorgensen Company (HQ)................................. C....... 323 567-1122
10650 Alameda St Lynwood (90262) *(P-12549)*

Early Childhood Resources, San Diego *Also Called: Ecr4kids LP (P-2925)*

Early Learning Center, Los Angeles *Also Called: California Childrens Academy (P-19201)*

Earth Print Inc .... F....... 818 879-6050
31115 Via Colinas Ste 301 Westlake Village (91362) *(P-3567)*

Earthlite, Vista *Also Called: Earthlite LLC (P-2829)*

Earthlite LLC (DH)... D....... 760 599-1112
990 Joshua Way Vista (92081) *(P-2829)*

Earthrise Nutritionals LLC (HQ)..................................... E....... 949 623-0980
2151 Michelson Dr Ste 262 Irvine (92612) *(P-81)*

Earthrise Nutritionals LLC .... E....... 760 348-5027
113 E Hoober Rd Calipatria (92233) *(P-1886)*

East Cast Repr Fabrication LLC .... E....... 619 591-9577
280 Trousdale Dr Ste E Chula Vista (91910) *(P-6022)*

East Los Angles Dctors Hosp In .... B
4060 Whittier Blvd Los Angeles (90023) *(P-18247)*

East Los Angles Rmrkble Ctzens .... D....... 323 223-3079
3839 Selig Pl Los Angeles (90031) *(P-19073)*

East Penn Manufacturing .... E....... 619 660-0016
2709 Via Orange Way Ste B Spring Valley (91978) *(P-9144)*

East Shore Garment Company LLC .... E....... 323 923-4454
3250 E Olympic Blvd Los Angeles (90023) *(P-2019)*

East Valley Glendora Hosp LLC .... B....... 626 852-5000
150 W Route 66 Glendora (91740) *(P-18248)*

East Valley Tourist Dev Auth .... A....... 760 342-5000
84245 Indio Springs Dr Indio (92203) *(P-17547)*

East West, Pasadena *Also Called: East West Bancorp Inc (P-14191)*

EAST WEST, Pasadena *Also Called: East West Bank (P-14192)*

East West Bancorp Inc (PA).. B....... 626 768-6000
135 N Los Robles Ave Fl 7 Pasadena (91101) *(P-14191)*

East West Bank (HQ)... B....... 626 768-6000
135 N Los Robles Ave Ste 100 Pasadena (91101) *(P-14192)*

East West Enterprises .... E....... 310 632-9933
20545 Belshaw Ave Carson (90746) *(P-5614)*

East West Tea Company LLC .... C....... 310 275-9891
1616 Preuss Rd Los Angeles (90035) *(P-1420)*

Eastbiz Corporation .... C....... 310 212-7134
3501 Jack Northrop Ave Hawthorne (90250) *(P-17548)*

Eastern District Office, El Cajon *Also Called: San Diego Gas & Electric Co (P-12042)*

Eastern Goldfields Inc .... C....... 619 497-2555
1660 Hotel Cir N Ste 207 San Diego (92108) *(P-20165)*

Eastern Los Angles Rgnal Ctr F (PA)............................. C....... 626 299-4700
1000 S Fremont Ave Unit 23 Alhambra (91803) *(P-19074)*

Eastern Municipal Water Dst .... C....... 951 657-7469
19750 Evans Rd Perris (92571) *(P-12121)*

Eastern Municipal Water Dst (PA).................................. B....... 951 928-3777
2270 Trumble Rd Perris (92572) *(P-12122)*

Eastern Sports, Thousand Oaks *Also Called: Easton Hockey Inc (P-10988)*

Eastern Staffing LLC .... A....... 805 882-2200
301 Mentor Dr # 210 Santa Barbara (93111) *(P-15840)*

Easterncctv (usa) LLC .... C....... 626 961-8999
525 Parriott Pl W City Of Industry (91745) *(P-16731)*

Eastland Corporation .... E....... 323 261-5388
3017 Bandini Blvd Vernon (90058) *(P-13293)*

Easton Baseball / Softball Inc .... E....... 800 632-7866
3500 Willow Ln Thousand Oaks (91361) *(P-12927)*

Easton Diamond Sports LLC .... D....... 800 632-7866
3500 Willow Ln Thousand Oaks (91361) *(P-12928)*

Easton Hockey Inc .... A....... 818 782-6445
3500 Willow Ln Thousand Oaks (91361) *(P-10988)*

Eastridge Workforce Solutions, San Diego *Also Called: Eplica Corporate Services Inc (P-15843)*

Eastridge Workforce Solutions, San Diego *Also Called: Teg Staffing Inc (P-15898)*

Eastridge Workforce Solutions, San Diego *Also Called: Eplica Inc (P-15921)*

Eastwest Clothing Inc (PA)... F....... 323 980-1177
40 E Verdugo Ave Burbank (91502) *(P-2237)*

Eastwest Container Group Inc .... E....... 626 523-1523
5521 Schaefer Ave Chino (91710) *(P-3067)*

Eastwestproto Inc .... B....... 888 535-5728
6605 E Washington Blvd Commerce (90040) *(P-11381)*

Easy Care Mso LLC .... C....... 562 676-9600
3780 Kilroy Airport Way Ste 530 Long Beach (90806) *(P-18761)*

Easy Flex, Santa Ana *Also Called: Easyflex Inc (P-5588)*

Easy Fuel, Aliso Viejo *Also Called: Efuel LLC (P-13450)*

Easy Reach Supply LLC .... E....... 601 582-7866
3737 Capitol Ave City Of Industry (90601) *(P-11087)*

Easy Reader Inc .... E....... 310 372-4611
832 Hermosa Ave Hermosa Beach (90254) *(P-3275)*

Easydial Inc .... E....... 949 916-5851
181 Technology Dr Ste 150 Irvine (92618) *(P-10497)*

Easyflex Inc .... E....... 888 577-8999
2700 N Main St Ste 800 Santa Ana (92705) *(P-5588)*

Eat Like A Woman, Burbank *Also Called: Staness Jonekos Entps Inc (P-1991)*

Eaton, Irvine *Also Called: Eaton Aerospace LLC (P-9971)*

Eaton Aerospace LLC .... E....... 949 452-9500
9650 Jeronimo Rd Irvine (92618) *(P-9971)*

Eaton Aerospace LLC .... B...... 818 409-0200
4690 Colorado Blvd Los Angeles (90039) *(P-12592)*

Eaton Corporation .... F...... 714 272-4700
9650 Jeronimo Rd Irvine (92618) *(P-9682)*

Eaton Electrical Inc .... C...... 951 685-5788
13201 Dahlia St Fontana (92337) *(P-8179)*

Ebatts.com, Camarillo *Also Called: Battery-Biz Inc (P-9164)*

Ebc Inc (PA)... **D...... 310 753-6407**
219 Manhattan Beach Blvd Ste 3 Manhattan Beach (90266) *(P-430)*

EBEN-EZER CHILDREN'S DAY CARE CENTER, Baldwin Park *Also Called: Eben-Ezer Chld Day Care Ctr (P-19209)*

Eben-Ezer Chld Day Care Ctr .... D...... 626 960-7100
3970 Maine Ave Bldg B Baldwin Park (91706) *(P-19209)*

Eberhard .... C...... 818 782-4604
15220 Raymer St Van Nuys (91405) *(P-1044)*

Eberine Enterprises Inc .... E...... 323 587-1111
3360 Fruitland Ave Vernon (90058) *(P-1817)*

Ebioscience Inc .... C...... 858 642-2058
10255 Science Center Dr San Diego (92121) *(P-19835)*

Ebs General Engineering Inc .... D...... 951 279-6869
1345 Quarry St Ste 101 Corona (92879) *(P-616)*

Ebus Inc .... E...... 562 904-3474
9250 Washburn Rd Downey (90242) *(P-9324)*

EC Closing Corp .... D...... 800 546-1531
525 E Main St El Cajon (92020) *(P-14311)*

EC Design LLC .... E...... 310 220-2362
4860 W 147th St Hawthorne (90250) *(P-14070)*

EC Group Inc (PA).. **D...... 310 815-2700**
5960 Bowcroft St Los Angeles (90016) *(P-12280)*

Eca, Brea *Also Called: Energy Cnvrsion Applctions Inc (P-8095)*

Eca Medical Instruments (DH)...................................... **E...... 805 376-2509**
1107 Tourmaline Dr Newbury Park (91320) *(P-10498)*

ECB Corp (PA)... **D...... 714 385-8900**
6400 Artesia Blvd Buena Park (90620) *(P-765)*

ECCU, Brea *Also Called: Adelfi Credit Union (P-14244)*

Ecg Management Consultant .... C...... 206 689-2200
11512 El Camino Real Ste 200 San Diego (92130) *(P-20166)*

Echelon Fine Printing, Vernon *Also Called: The Ligature Inc (P-3697)*

Echo Bridge Home Entertainment, Los Angeles *Also Called: Platinum Disc LLC (P-12982)*

Eci Water Ski Products Inc .... E...... 951 940-9999
224 Malbert St Perris (92570) *(P-14063)*

Eckert Zegler Isotope Pdts Inc (HQ)............................. **E...... 661 309-1010**
24937 Avenue Tibbitts Valencia (91355) *(P-10361)*

Eckert Zegler Isotope Pdts Inc .... E...... 661 309-1010
1800 N Keystone St Burbank (91504) *(P-10362)*

Ecko Print & Packaging, Ontario *Also Called: Ecko Products Group LLC (P-3097)*

Ecko Products Group LLC .... E...... 909 628-5678
740 S Milliken Ave Ste C Ontario (91761) *(P-3097)*

Eclectic Printing & Design LLC .... F...... 714 528-8040
1030 Ortega Way Ste A Placentia (92870) *(P-3756)*

Eclipse Berry Farms LLC .... D...... 310 207-7879
11812 San Vicente Blvd Ste 250 Los Angeles (90049) *(P-14)*

Eclipse Prtg & Graphics LLC .... E...... 909 390-2452
4462 E Airport Dr Ontario (91761) *(P-3568)*

Ecliptek Inc .... E...... 714 433-1200
24422 Avenida De La Carlota Ste 290 Laguna Hills (92653) *(P-9035)*

Ecmd Inc .... D...... 909 980-1775
10863 Jersey Blvd 100 Rancho Cucamonga (91730) *(P-2598)*

Ecmm Services Inc .... C...... 714 988-9388
1320 Valley Vista Dr # 204 Diamond Bar (91765) *(P-11056)*

Eco Services Operations Corp .... D...... 310 885-6719
20720 S Wilmington Ave Long Beach (90810) *(P-3891)*

Ecoatm LLC (DH)... **C...... 858 999-3200**
10121 Barnes Canyon Rd San Diego (92121) *(P-8634)*

Ecoflow Technology Inc .... E...... 407 247-6023
245 E Main St Ste 107 Alhambra (91801) *(P-12020)*

Ecolab .... D...... 323 292-7752
5640 S Fairfax Ave Los Angeles (90056) *(P-4336)*

Ecolink Intelligent Tech Inc .... F...... 855 432-6546
2055 Corte Del Nogal Carlsbad (92011) *(P-8409)*

Ecology Recycling Services LLC .... C...... 909 370-1318
785 E M St Colton (92324) *(P-12168)*

Econo Air, Placentia *Also Called: Mddr Inc (P-792)*

Econocold Refrigerators, Cerritos *Also Called: Refrigerator Manufacters Inc (P-8228)*

Econolite Control Products Inc (PA).............................. **C...... 714 630-3700**
1250 N Tustin Ave Anaheim (92807) *(P-8609)*

Ecoolthing Corp .... E...... 714 368-4791
1321 E Saint Gertrude Pl Ste A Santa Ana (92705) *(P-6861)*

Ecosense Lighting Inc (PA).. **D...... 855 632-6736**
837 N Spring St Ste 103 Los Angeles (90012) *(P-12593)*

Ecosense Lighting Inc .... C...... 714 823-1014
14811 Myford Rd Tustin (92780) *(P-12594)*

Ecosmart Technologies Inc .... E...... 770 667-0006
1585 W Mission Blvd Pomona (91766) *(P-4550)*

Ecowater Systems, Vista *Also Called: Yanchewski & Wardell Entps Inc (P-7694)*

Ecowise Inc .... E...... 626 759-3997
13538 Excelsior Dr Unit B Santa Fe Springs (90670) *(P-3937)*

Ecr4kids LP .... E...... 619 323-2005
5630 Kearny Mesa Rd Ste B San Diego (92111) *(P-2925)*

Ecs-National City Head Start, National City *Also Called: Episcopal Community Services (P-19077)*

Ect News Network Inc .... E...... 818 461-9700
16133 Ventura Blvd Ste 700 Encino (91436) *(P-3442)*

Ectron Corporation .... E...... 858 278-0600
9340 Hazard Way Ste B2 San Diego (92123) *(P-8513)*

Ed Hardy, Commerce *Also Called: DNam Apparel Industries LLC (P-2321)*

Ed Stiglic .... F...... 760 744-7239
1125 Linda Vista Dr Ste 110 San Marcos (92078) *(P-7823)*

Edco Disposal Corporation (PA).................................... **C...... 619 287-7555**
2755 California Ave Signal Hill (90755) *(P-12169)*

Edco Plastics Inc .... E...... 714 772-1986
2110 E Winston Rd Anaheim (92806) *(P-5019)*

Edelbrock LLC .... E...... 310 781-2290
501 Amapola Ave Torrance (90501) *(P-9386)*

Edelbrock Foundry Corp .... E...... 951 654-6677
1320 S Buena Vista St San Jacinto (92583) *(P-5758)*

Edelmann Usa Inc (DH).. **F...... 323 669-5700**
2150 S Parco Ave Ontario (91761) *(P-11111)*

Eden Beauty Concepts Inc .... E...... 760 330-9941
5876 Owens Ave Ste 200 Carlsbad (92008) *(P-4408)*

Edf Renewables Inc (PA)... **C...... 858 521-3300**
15445 Innovation Dr San Diego (92128) *(P-12021)*

Edgate Holdings Inc .... E...... 858 712-9341
4655 Cass St San Diego (92109) *(P-16232)*

Edge Autonomy Slo LLC .... E...... 805 544-0932
831 Buckley Rd San Luis Obispo (93401) *(P-9972)*

Edge Mortgage Advisory Co LLC .... D...... 714 564-5800
2125 E Katella Ave Ste 350 Anaheim (92806) *(P-20332)*

Edge Plastics Inc (PA).. **E...... 951 786-4750**
3016 Kansas Ave Bldg 3 Riverside (92507) *(P-5020)*

Edge Solutions Consulting Inc (PA).............................. **E...... 818 591-3500**
5126 Clareton Dr Ste 160 Agoura Hills (91301) *(P-7424)*

Edgemine Inc .... C...... 323 267-8222
1801 E 50th St Los Angeles (90058) *(P-13124)*

Edgewave Inc .... D...... 800 782-3762
4225 Executive Sq Ste 1600 La Jolla (92037) *(P-16233)*

Edgewood Partners Insur Ctr .... E...... 949 263-0606
4675 Macarthur Ct Newport Beach (92660) *(P-14585)*

Edgeworth Integration LLC .... D...... 805 915-0211
2360 Shasta Way Ste F Simi Valley (93065) *(P-16732)*

Edi Ideas, Fountain Valley *Also Called: Freightgate Inc (P-16252)*

Edie Lee, Commerce *Also Called: J Michelle of California (P-2102)*

Edison Capital .... C...... 909 594-3789
18101 Von Karman Ave Ste 1700 Irvine (92612) *(P-12022)*

Edison Energy LLC .... C...... 949 491-1633
2 Park Plz Ste 200 Irvine (92614) *(P-16822)*

Edison International (PA).. **A...... 626 302-2222**
2244 Walnut Grove Ave Rosemead (91770) *(P-12023)*

Edison Mission, Rosemead *Also Called: Edison Mission Energy (P-12024)*

Edison Mission Energy (PA)... **C...... 626 302-5778**
2244 Walnut Grove Ave Rosemead (91770) *(P-12024)*

Edison Mssion Midwest Holdings .... A...... 626 302-2222
2244 Walnut Grove Ave Rosemead (91770) *(P-12025)*

Employee Codes: A=Over 500 employees, B=251-500
C=101-250, D=51-100, E=20-50, F=10-19, G=1-9

2024 Southern California
Business Directory and Buyers Guide

© Mergent Inc. 1-800-342-5647

1075

Edison Price Lighting Inc (PA)..C...... 718 685-0700
5424 E Slauson Ave Commerce (90040) *(P-8310)*

Edje-Enterprises..D...... 951 245-7070
18500 Pasadena St Ste B Lake Elsinore (92530) *(P-1045)*

Edmund A Gray Co (PA)..D...... 213 625-0376
2277 E 15th St Los Angeles (90021) *(P-6845)*

Edmund A Gray Co..E...... 213 625-2725
1901 Imperial St Los Angeles (90021) *(P-11575)*

Edmund Kim International Inc (PA)..E...... 310 604-1100
2880 E Ana St Compton (90221) *(P-2202)*

Edmunds Holding Company (PA)..A...... 310 309-6300
2401 Colorado Ave Santa Monica (90404) *(P-16527)*

Edmunds.com, Santa Monica *Also Called: Edmunds Holding Company (P-16527)*

Edmundscom Inc (HQ)..A...... 310 309-6300
2401 Colorado Ave Ste P1 Santa Monica (90404) *(P-15592)*

EDN Aviation Inc..E...... 818 988-8826
6720 Valjean Ave Van Nuys (91406) *(P-17125)*

Edna H Pagel Inc..D...... 323 234-2200
2050 E 38th St Vernon (90058) *(P-501)*

Edo Communications and Countermeasures Systems Inc..D...... 818 464-2475
7821 Orion Ave Van Nuys (91406) *(P-9973)*

Edris Plastics Mfg Inc..E...... 323 581-7000
4560 Pacific Blvd Vernon (90058) *(P-5021)*

Edro Engineering LLC (DH)..E...... 909 594-5751
20500 Carrey Rd Walnut (91789) *(P-7067)*

Edsi..D...... 760 731-3501
700 Ammunition Rd Bldg 103 Fallbrook (92028) *(P-19578)*

Education Systems Inc..E...... 858 454-9765
1111 Torrey Pines Rd La Jolla (92037) *(P-16020)*

Educational Ideas Incorporated..E...... 714 990-4332
471 Atlas St Brea (92821) *(P-3443)*

Educational Insights, Torrance *Also Called: Learning Resources Inc (P-11242)*

Edward Thomas Companies..C...... 714 782-7500
640 W Katella Ave Anaheim (92802) *(P-15140)*

Edward Thomas Hospitality Corp..B...... 310 458-0030
1 Pico Blvd Santa Monica (90405) *(P-15141)*

EDWARDS, Irvine *Also Called: Edwards Lifesciences Corp (P-10653)*

Edwards, Irvine *Also Called: Edwards Lifesciences US Inc (P-10801)*

Edwards Assoc Cmmnications Inc (PA)..C...... 805 658-2626
2277 Knoll Dr Ste A Ventura (93003) *(P-3170)*

Edwards Cinemas University, Irvine *Also Called: Edwards Theatres Circuit Inc (P-17297)*

Edwards Label, Ventura *Also Called: Edwards Assoc Cmmnications Inc (P-3170)*

Edwards Lfsciences Cardiaq LLC..D...... 949 387-2615
1 Edwards Way Irvine (92614) *(P-10499)*

Edwards Life Sciences Cardio V, Irvine *Also Called: Edwards Lifesciences Corp (P-10654)*

Edwards Lifesciences..E...... 951 749-3316
11811 Landon Dr Eastvale (91752) *(P-10651)*

Edwards Lifesciences Corp..F...... 949 250-3522
1402 Alton Pkwy Irvine (92606) *(P-10652)*

Edwards Lifesciences Corp (PA)..A...... 949 250-2500
1 Edwards Way Irvine (92614) *(P-10653)*

Edwards Lifesciences Corp..C...... 949 250-2500
17221 Red Hill Ave Irvine (92614) *(P-10654)*

Edwards Lifesciences Corp PR..E...... 949 250-2500
1 Edwards Way Irvine (92614) *(P-10655)*

Edwards Lifesciences Fing LLC..E...... 949 250-3480
1 Edwards Way Irvine (92614) *(P-11214)*

Edwards Lifesciences LLC (HQ)..A...... 949 250-2500
1 Edwards Way Irvine (92614) *(P-4103)*

Edwards Lifesciences US Inc (HQ)..D...... 949 250-2500
1 Edwards Way Irvine (92614) *(P-10801)*

Edwards Sheet Metal Supply Inc..E...... 818 785-8600
7810 Burnet Ave Van Nuys (91405) *(P-6230)*

Edwards Theatres Inc..C...... 949 582-4078
27741 Crown Valley Pkwy Ste 301 Mission Viejo (92691) *(P-17291)*

Edwards Theatres Inc (DH)..C...... 949 640-4600
300 Newport Center Dr Newport Beach (92660) *(P-17292)*

Edwards Theatres Inc..C...... 844 462-7342
1950 Foothill Blvd La Verne (91750) *(P-17293)*

Edwards Theatres Circuit Inc..C...... 619 660-3460
2951 Jamacha Rd El Cajon (92019) *(P-17294)*

Edwards Theatres Circuit Inc..C...... 858 635-7716
10733 Westview Pkwy San Diego (92126) *(P-17295)*

Edwards Theatres Circuit Inc..C...... 714 428-0962
901 S Coast Dr Costa Mesa (92626) *(P-17296)*

Edwards Theatres Circuit Inc..C...... 949 854-8811
4245 Campus Dr Irvine (92612) *(P-17297)*

Edwards Theatres Circuit Inc..C...... 951 296-0144
40750 Winchester Rd Temecula (92591) *(P-17298)*

Edwards Theatres Circuit, Inc., Newport Beach *Also Called: Edwards Theatres , Inc (P-17292)*

Eeco Switch, Brea *Also Called: Transico Inc (P-9131)*

Eema Industries Inc..E...... 323 904-0200
5461 W Jefferson Blvd Los Angeles (90016) *(P-8362)*

Eevelle LLC..E...... 760 434-2231
5928 Balfour Ct Carlsbad (92008) *(P-2550)*

Efax Corporate, Los Angeles *Also Called: J2 Cloud Services LLC (P-11917)*

Efaxcom (DH)..D...... 323 817-3207
6720 Hollywood Blvd Fl 5 Los Angeles (90028) *(P-7523)*

Efaxcom..E...... 805 692-0064
5385 Hollister Ave Ste 208 Santa Barbara (93111) *(P-7524)*

Effective Graphics NC Inc..E...... 310 323-2223
40 E Verdugo Ave Burbank (91502) *(P-3852)*

Efficient Pwr Conversion Corp (PA)..D...... 310 615-0279
909 N Pacific Coast Hwy El Segundo (90245) *(P-8790)*

Efilm LLC..C...... 323 463-7041
1144 N Las Palmas Ave Los Angeles (90038) *(P-17188)*

Efuel LLC..D...... 949 330-7145
65 Enterprise 3rd Fl Aliso Viejo (92656) *(P-13450)*

Egge Machine Company Inc (PA)..E...... 562 945-3419
8403 Allport Ave Santa Fe Springs (90670) *(P-12239)*

Eggleston Youth Centers Inc (PA)..D...... 626 480-8107
256 W Badillo St Covina (91723) *(P-19075)*

Eggs West..F...... 909 947-6207
13610 S Archibald Ave Ontario (91761) *(P-13690)*

Egl Holdco Inc..A...... 800 678-7423
18200 Von Karman Ave # 1000 Irvine (92612) *(P-16234)*

Ego Inc..C...... 626 447-0296
180 Via Verde Ste 100 San Dimas (91773) *(P-19770)*

Egon Zehnder International..B...... 213 337-1500
350 S Grand Ave Ste 3580 Los Angeles (90071) *(P-20167)*

Egr Incorporated (DH)..E...... 909 923-7075
4000 Greystone Dr Ontario (91761) *(P-9387)*

Egs Financial Care Inc (DH)..B...... 877 217-4423
5 Park Plz Ste 1100 Irvine (92614) *(P-15611)*

Eharmony Inc (HQ)..C...... 424 258-1199
10900 Wilshire Blvd Fl 17 Los Angeles (90024) *(P-15507)*

Eharmony.com, Los Angeles *Also Called: Eharmony Inc (P-15507)*

Ehmcke Sheet Metal Corp..D...... 619 477-6484
840 W 19th St National City (91950) *(P-1046)*

Eibach Inc..D...... 951 256-8300
264 Mariah Cir Corona (92879) *(P-6781)*

Eibach Springs, Inc., Corona *Also Called: Eibach Inc (P-6781)*

Eichleay Inc..C...... 562 256-8600
500 N State College Blvd Orange (92868) *(P-19579)*

Eide Bailly LLP..B...... 909 466-4410
10681 Foothill Blvd Ste 300 Rancho Cucamonga (91730) *(P-19771)*

Eide Industries Inc..D...... 562 402-8335
16215 Piuma Ave Cerritos (90703) *(P-2503)*

Eight Point Trailer Corp..F...... 909 357-9227
14770 Slover Ave Fontana (92337) *(P-17042)*

Eight Star Equipment, El Centro *Also Called: Noblesse Oblige Inc (P-97)*

Eighteenth Meridian Inc..B...... 714 706-3643
200 Spectrum Center Dr Ste 300 Irvine (92618) *(P-16021)*

Einfochips Inc..D...... 949 527-6459
2361 Campus Dr Ste 105 Irvine (92612) *(P-16022)*

Einstein Dental, San Diego *Also Called: Einstein Industries Inc (P-16023)*

Einstein Industries Inc..C...... 858 459-1182
6825 Flanders Dr San Diego (92121) *(P-16023)*

Einstein Noah Rest Group Inc..C...... 714 847-4609
16304 Beach Blvd Westminster (92683) *(P-1253)*

Eisel Enterprises Inc..E...... 714 993-1706
714 Fee Ana St Placentia (92870) *(P-5409)*

Mergent email: customerrelations@mergent.com
1076

2024 Southern California
Business Directory and Buyers Guide

(P-0000) Products & Services Section entry number
(PA)=Parent Co (HQ)=Headquarters (DH)=Div Headquarters

Eisenberg Village, Reseda Also Called: Los Angles Jewish HM For Aging *(P-18002)*

Eisenberg Vlg of The Los Angle .... D...... 818 774-3372
18855 Victory Blvd Reseda (91335) *(P-17929)*

Eisenhower Health, Rancho Mirage Also Called: Eisenhower Medical Center *(P-18251)*

Eisenhower Health Services, Rancho Mirage Also Called: Eisenhower Medical Center *(P-18611)*

Eisenhower Medical Center .... D...... 760 228-9900
57475 29 Palms Hwy Ste 104 Yucca Valley (92284) *(P-17646)*

Eisenhower Medical Center .... C...... 760 836-0232
34450 Gateway Dr Palm Desert (92211) *(P-17647)*

Eisenhower Medical Center .... C...... 760 610-7200
45280 Seeley Dr La Quinta (92253) *(P-18249)*

Eisenhower Medical Center .... C...... 760 325-6621
555 E Tachevah Dr Palm Springs (92262) *(P-18250)*

Eisenhower Medical Center (PA) .... **A**...... **760 340-3911**
39000 Bob Hope Dr Rancho Mirage (92270) *(P-18251)*

Eisenhower Medical Center .... C...... 760 773-1364
39000 Bob Hope Dr Frnt Rancho Mirage (92270) *(P-18547)*

Eisenhower Medical Center .... C...... 760 773-1888
39000 Bob Hope Dr Ste 102 Rancho Mirage (92270) *(P-18611)*

Eisenhower-Memory-Care-center, Palm Desert Also Called: Eisenhower Medical Center *(P-17647)*

EISNER PEDIATRIC & FAMILY MEDI, Los Angeles Also Called: Pediatric & Family Medical Ctr *(P-17735)*

Eiu of California, Bakersfield Also Called: Electrical & Instrumentation Unlimited of California Inc *(P-893)*

Ejay Filtration Inc .... E...... 951 683-0805
3036 Durahart St Riverside (92507) *(P-6817)*

Ejays Machine Co Inc .... E...... 714 879-0558
1108 E Valencia Dr Fullerton (92831) *(P-7824)*

Ejl, City Of Industry Also Called: E J Lauren LLC *(P-2800)*

Ekedal Concrete Inc .... D...... 949 729-8082
19600 Fairchild Ste 123 Irvine (92612) *(P-1070)*

Eklin Medical Systems Inc .... E...... 760 918-9626
6359 Paseo Del Lago Carlsbad (92011) *(P-10500)*

Eknowledge Group Inc .... E...... 951 256-4076
160 W Fthill Pkwy Ste 105 Corona (92882) *(P-16235)*

El & El Wood Products Corp (DH) .... **D**...... **909 591-0339**
6011 Schaefer Ave Chino (91710) *(P-2599)*

EL ARCA, Los Angeles Also Called: East Los Angles Rmrkble Ctzens *(P-19073)*

El Aviso Magazine .... D...... 323 586-9199
4850 Gage Ave Bell (90201) *(P-13494)*

El Caballero Country Club .... C...... 818 654-3000
18300 Tarzana Dr Tarzana (91356) *(P-17482)*

El Cajon Ford, El Cajon Also Called: El Cajon Motors *(P-16984)*

El Cajon Medical Offices, El Cajon Also Called: Kaiser Foundation Hospitals *(P-17678)*

El Cajon Motors (PA) .... **D**...... **619 579-8888**
1595 E Main St El Cajon (92021) *(P-16984)*

El Camino Rental .... E...... 760 438-7368
5701 El Camino Real Carlsbad (92008) *(P-16969)*

El Centro Hospitality LLC .... C...... 760 353-2600
503 E Danenberg Dr El Centro (92243) *(P-15142)*

El Centro Hospitality 2 LLC .... C...... 760 370-3800
3003 S Dogwood Rd El Centro (92243) *(P-15143)*

El Centro Motors .... D...... 760 336-2100
1520 Ford Dr El Centro (92243) *(P-13759)*

El Centro Rgnal Med Ctr Fndtio (PA) .... A...... 760 339-7100
1415 Ross Ave El Centro (92243) *(P-18252)*

El Clasificado (PA) .... E...... 323 837-4095
11205 Imperial Hwy Norwalk (90650) *(P-3276)*

El Dorado Broadcasters LLC .... D...... 760 241-1313
11920 Hesperia Rd Hesperia (92345) *(P-11923)*

El Dorado Enterprises Inc .... E...... 310 719-9800
1000 W Redondo Beach Blvd Gardena (90247) *(P-15144)*

El Gallito Market Inc .... E...... 626 442-1190
12242 Valley Blvd El Monte (91732) *(P-1887)*

El Guapo Spices Inc (PA) .... **D**...... **213 312-1300**
6200 E Slauson Ave Commerce (90040) *(P-13367)*

El Guapo Spices and Herbs Pkg, Commerce Also Called: El Guapo Spices Inc *(P-13367)*

El Indio Mexican Restaurant, San Diego Also Called: El Indio Shops Incorporated *(P-1267)*

El Indio Shops Incorporated .... D...... 619 299-0333
3695 India St San Diego (92103) *(P-1267)*

El Jinete Leather & Western .... F...... 951 264-8396
2001 S Garey Ave Pomona (91766) *(P-5307)*

El Latino Newspaper, Chula Vista Also Called: Latina & Associates Inc *(P-3296)*

El Metate Inc .... C...... 949 646-9362
817 W 19th St Costa Mesa (92627) *(P-1463)*

El Metate Market, Costa Mesa Also Called: El Metate Inc *(P-1463)*

El Monte Automotive Group Inc .... C...... 626 580-6200
3530 Peck Rd El Monte (91731) *(P-13760)*

El Monte Automotive Group LLC .... D...... 626 444-0321
3464 Peck Rd El Monte (91731) *(P-13761)*

El Monte Rents Inc (HQ) .... **C**...... **562 404-9300**
12818 Firestone Blvd Santa Fe Springs (90670) *(P-16986)*

El Monte Rv, Santa Fe Springs Also Called: El Monte Rents Inc *(P-16986)*

El Nido Family Centers (PA) .... **C**...... **818 830-3646**
10200 Sepulveda Blvd Ste 350 Mission Hills (91345) *(P-19076)*

El Nopalito Inc (PA) .... **E**...... **760 436-5775**
560 Santa Fe Dr Encinitas (92024) *(P-13697)*

El Nopalito Mexican Food, Encinitas Also Called: El Nopalito Inc *(P-13697)*

El Pollo Loco, Cypress Also Called: WKS Restaurant Corporation *(P-14045)*

El Pollo Loco Holdings Inc (PA) .... **C**...... **714 599-5000**
3535 Harbor Blvd Ste 100 Costa Mesa (92626) *(P-14004)*

El Prado Golf Course LP .... D...... 909 597-1751
6555 Pine Ave Chino (91708) *(P-17426)*

El Primo Foods Inc .... C...... 626 289-5054
608 Monterey Pass Rd Monterey Park (91754) *(P-13245)*

El Rancho Vista Hlth Care Ctr, Pico Rivera Also Called: Mariner Health Care Inc *(P-18005)*

El Segundo Bread Bar LLC .... E...... 310 615-9898
701 E El Segundo Blvd El Segundo (90245) *(P-1464)*

El Super Leon Pnchin Sncks Inc .... E...... 619 426-2968
2545 Britannia Blvd Ste A San Diego (92154) *(P-1537)*

El Tigre Inc .... E...... 619 429-8212
2909 Coronado Ave San Diego (92154) *(P-13698)*

El Tigre Warehouse 2, San Diego Also Called: El Tigre Inc *(P-13698)*

El Torito Franchising Company, Cypress Also Called: Real Mex Foods Inc *(P-13193)*

Elasco Inc .... D...... 714 373-4767
11377 Markon Dr Garden Grove (92841) *(P-3938)*

Elasco Urethane Inc .... E...... 714 895-7031
11377 Markon Dr Garden Grove (92841) *(P-3939)*

Elastpro Silicone Sheeting LLC .... F...... 562 348-2348
13937 Rosecrans Ave Santa Fe Springs (90670) *(P-5022)*

Elation Lighting Inc .... D...... 323 582-3322
6122 S Eastern Ave Commerce (90040) *(P-8363)*

Elation Professional, Commerce Also Called: Elation Lighting Inc *(P-8363)*

Elavon Inc .... B...... 865 403-7000
700 S Western Ave Los Angeles (90005) *(P-16528)*

Elba Company, San Dimas Also Called: Elba Jewelry Inc *(P-10901)*

Elba Jewelry Inc .... F...... 909 394-5803
910 N Amelia Ave San Dimas (91773) *(P-10901)*

Elco Lighting, Vernon Also Called: AMP Plus Inc *(P-8344)*

Elco Rfrgn Solutions LLC .... A...... 858 888-9447
2554 Commercial St San Diego (92113) *(P-7609)*

Eldorado Care Center LP .... B...... 619 440-1211
510 E Washington Ave El Cajon (92020) *(P-17930)*

Eldorado Country Club .... C...... 760 346-8081
46000 E Eldorado Dr Indian Wells (92210) *(P-17483)*

Eldorado National Cal Inc (HQ) .... **B**...... **951 727-9300**
9670 Galena St Riverside (92509) *(P-9284)*

Eldorado Stone LLC (DH) .... **E**...... **800 925-1491**
3817 Ocean Ranch Blvd Oceanside (92056) *(P-5410)*

Eldorado Stone LLC .... A...... 951 601-3838
24100 Orange Ave Perris (92570) *(P-12353)*

Eleanor Rigby Leather Co .... D...... 619 356-5590
4660 La Jolla Village Dr Ste 500 Pmb 50054 San Diego (92122) *(P-5308)*

Electra Craft, Westlake Village Also Called: Toller Enterprises Inc *(P-13894)*

Electra Owners Assoc .... C...... 619 236-3310
700 W E St San Diego (92101) *(P-19377)*

Electrasem Corp .... C...... 951 371-6140
372 Elizabeth Ln Corona (92878) *(P-10103)*

Electrcal Instrmnttion Cntrls, Bakersfield Also Called: Measurment Instrmnttion Cntrls *(P-12799)*

ALPHABETIC

Employee Codes: A=Over 500 employees, B=251-500
C=101-250, D=51-100, E=20-50, F=10-19, G=1-9

2024 Southern California
Business Directory and Buyers Guide

© Mergent Inc. 1-800-342-5647

1077

Electric, San Clemente *Also Called: Electric Visual Evolution LLC (P-10837)*

Electric Designs, Gardena *Also Called: Gloria Lance Inc (P-2241)*

Electric Gate Store Inc ....C...... 818 361-6872
   15342 Chatsworth St Mission Hills (91345) *(P-9209)*

Electric Motor Works Inc ....E...... 661 327-4271
   803 Inyo Street At 21st St Bakersfield (93305) *(P-17104)*

Electric Motors, Santa Ana *Also Called: Advantage Manufacturing Inc (P-12583)*

Electric Solidus LLC ....E...... 917 692-7764
   26565 Agoura Rd Ste 200 Calabasas (91302) *(P-3444)*

Electric Visual Evolution LLC (PA) ....**E...... 949 940-9125**
   950 Calle Amanecer Ste 101 San Clemente (92673) *(P-10837)*

Electrical & Instrumentation Unlimited of California Inc C
   6950 District Blvd Bakersfield (93313) *(P-893)*

Electrical Products Rep, Irvine *Also Called: Agents West Inc (P-9192)*

Electrical Rebuilders Sls Inc (PA) ....**D...... 323 249-7545**
   7603 Willow Glen Rd Los Angeles (90046) *(P-9166)*

Electrical Systems, Corona *Also Called: Panel Shop Inc (P-8127)*

Electro Adapter Inc ....D...... 818 998-1198
   20640 Nordhoff St Chatsworth (91311) *(P-8262)*

Electro Kinetics Division, Simi Valley *Also Called: Pacific Scientific Company (P-10049)*

Electro Machine & Engrg Co, Compton *Also Called: E M E Inc (P-6613)*

Electro Surface Tech Inc ....E...... 760 431-8306
   2281 Las Palmas Dr # 101 Carlsbad (92011) *(P-8671)*

Electro Switch Corp ....D...... 909 581-0855
   10410 Trademark St Rancho Cucamonga (91730) *(P-8121)*

Electro Switch Corp ....E...... 909 581-0855
   10410 Trademark St Rancho Cucamonga (91730) *(P-9036)*

Electro Tech Coatings Inc ....E...... 760 746-0292
   836 Rancheros Dr Ste A San Marcos (92069) *(P-6701)*

Electro Tech Powder Coating, San Marcos *Also Called: Electro Tech Coatings Inc (P-6701)*

Electro-Optical Industries LLC ....E...... 805 964-6701
   859 Ward Dr Santa Barbara (93111) *(P-10313)*

Electro-Support Systems Corp ....E...... 951 676-2751
   27449 Colt Ct Temecula (92590) *(P-9037)*

Electro-Tech Machining Div, Long Beach *Also Called: Kbr Inc (P-8164)*

Electro-Tech Products, Glendora *Also Called: Electro-Tech Products Inc (P-9038)*

Electro-Tech Products Inc ....E...... 909 592-1434
   2001 E Gladstone St Ste A Glendora (91740) *(P-9038)*

Electro-Tech's, Corona *Also Called: R&M Deese Inc (P-11148)*

Electrocube Inc (PA) ....**E...... 909 595-1821**
   3366 Pomona Blvd Pomona (91768) *(P-9039)*

Electrode Technologies Inc ....E...... 714 549-3771
   3110 W Harvard St Ste 14 Santa Ana (92704) *(P-6614)*

Electrofilm Mfg Co LLC ....D...... 661 257-2242
   28150 Industry Dr Valencia (91355) *(P-6775)*

Electrolizing Inc ....E...... 213 749-7876
   1947 Hooper Ave Los Angeles (90011) *(P-6615)*

Electrolurgy Inc ....D...... 949 250-4494
   1121 Duryea Ave Irvine (92614) *(P-6616)*

Electromed Inc ....D...... 805 523-7500
   4590 Ish Dr Simi Valley (93063) *(P-12485)*

Electron Devices, Torrance *Also Called: Stellant Systems Inc (P-10073)*

Electron Plating, Garden Grove *Also Called: Electron Plating III Inc (P-6617)*

Electron Plating III Inc ....E...... 714 554-2210
   13932 Enterprise Dr Garden Grove (92843) *(P-6617)*

Electronic Chrome Grinding Inc ....E...... 562 946-6671
   9128 Dice Rd Santa Fe Springs (90670) *(P-6618)*

Electronic Clearing House Inc (HQ) ....D...... 805 419-8700
   730 Paseo Camarillo Camarillo (93010) *(P-16236)*

Electronic Commerce, Newport Beach *Also Called: Electronic Commerce LLC (P-14291)*

Electronic Commerce LLC ....D...... 800 770-5520
   4100 Newport Place Dr Ste 500 Newport Beach (92660) *(P-14291)*

Electronic Control Systems LLC ....C...... 858 513-1911
   12575 Kirkham Ct Ste 1 Poway (92064) *(P-894)*

Electronic Hardware Limited (PA) ....**E...... 818 982-6100**
   13257 Saticoy St North Hollywood (91605) *(P-12656)*

Electronic Online Systems International ....D...... 760 431-8400
   2292 Faraday Ave Frnt Carlsbad (92008) *(P-16441)*

Electronic Precision Spc Inc ....E...... 714 256-8950
   545 Mercury Ln Brea (92821) *(P-6619)*

Electronic Prtg Solutions LLC ....E...... 858 576-3000
   4879 Ronson Ct Ste C San Diego (92111) *(P-3757)*

Electronic Services, Los Angeles *Also Called: Esi Inc (P-8794)*

Electronic Source Company, Van Nuys *Also Called: Alyn Industries Inc (P-8994)*

Electronic Surfc Mounted Inds ....E...... 858 455-1710
   6731 Cobra Way San Diego (92121) *(P-8672)*

Electronic Waveform Lab Inc ....E...... 714 843-0463
   5702 Bolsa Ave Huntington Beach (92649) *(P-10501)*

Electrorack, Anaheim *Also Called: Ortronics Inc (P-6279)*

Element Anheim Rsort Cnvntion, Anaheim *Also Called: Singod Investors Vi LLC (P-3909)*

Element Materials (DH) ....**D...... 714 892-1961**
   15062 Bolsa Chica St Huntington Beach (92649) *(P-19968)*

Element Mtrls Tech HB Inc ....D...... 310 632-8500
   18100 S Wilmington Ave Compton (90220) *(P-19969)*

Element Rancho Dominguez, Compton *Also Called: Element Mtrls Tech HB Inc (P-19969)*

Elementis Specialties Inc ....D...... 760 257-9112
   31763 Mountain View Rd Newberry Springs (92365) *(P-3892)*

Elements Food Group Inc ....D...... 909 983-2011
   5560 Brooks St Montclair (91763) *(P-1516)*

Elers Medical Usa Inc ....E...... 858 336-4900
   21707 Hawthorne Blvd Ste 206 Torrance (90503) *(P-12486)*

Elevate Dynamics, Carlsbad *Also Called: Thorwear Inc (P-12519)*

Elevated Resources Inc (PA) ....**C...... 949 419-6632**
   3990 Westerly Pl Ste 270 Newport Beach (92660) *(P-16491)*

Elevator Research & Mfg Co ....E...... 213 746-1914
   1417 Elwood St Los Angeles (90021) *(P-6965)*

Eleven Western Builders Inc (PA) ....**D...... 760 796-6346**
   2862 Executive Pl Escondido (92029) *(P-431)*

Eliel & Co ....E...... 760 877-8469
   2215 La Mirada Dr Vista (92081) *(P-13101)*

Eliel Cycling, Vista *Also Called: Eliel & Co (P-13101)*

Elijah Textiles Inc ....D...... 310 666-3443
   1251 E Olympic Blvd Ste 108 Los Angeles (90021) *(P-12299)*

Elite, Culver City *Also Called: West Publishing Corporation (P-16478)*

Elite 4 Print Inc ....E...... 310 366-1344
   851 E Walnut St Carson (90746) *(P-3569)*

Elite Craftsman (PA) ....**C...... 562 989-3511**
   2763 Saint Louis Ave Long Beach (90755) *(P-15710)*

Elite Electric ....D...... 951 681-5811
   9415 Bellegrave Ave Riverside (92509) *(P-895)*

Elite Enfrcment SEC Sltons Inc ....C...... 866 354-8308
   29970 Technology Dr Ste 117d Murrieta (92563) *(P-16640)*

Elite Engineering Contrs Inc ....E...... 310 465-8333
   16619 S Broadway Gardena (90248) *(P-19580)*

Elite Gates, Los Angeles *Also Called: United Marketing Group Inc (P-1026)*

Elite Intractive Solutions Inc ....E...... 310 740-5426
   1200 W 7th St Ste L1-180 Los Angeles (90017) *(P-16733)*

Elite Leather LLC ....D...... 909 548-8600
   1620 5th Ave Ste 400 San Diego (92101) *(P-2801)*

Elite Lighting ....C...... 323 888-1973
   5424 E Slauson Ave Commerce (90040) *(P-8364)*

Elite Lighting, Commerce *Also Called: Elite Lighting (P-8364)*

Elite Metal Finishing, Oceanside *Also Called: Rose Manufacturing Group Inc (P-6657)*

Elite Metal Finishing LLC (PA) ....**C...... 805 983-4320**
   540 Spectrum Cir Oxnard (93030) *(P-6620)*

Elite Mfg Corp ....C...... 888 354-8356
   12143 Altamar Pl Santa Fe Springs (90670) *(P-2908)*

Elite Modern, Santa Fe Springs *Also Called: Elite Mfg Corp (P-2908)*

Elite Optical, Compton *Also Called: Essilor Laboratories Amer Inc (P-10839)*

Elite Screens Inc ....E...... 877 511-1211
   12282 Knott St Garden Grove (92841) *(P-10865)*

Elite Show Services Inc ....A...... 619 574-1589
   2878 Camino Del Rio S Ste 260 San Diego (92108) *(P-16641)*

Elite Stone & Cabinet Inc ....E...... 909 629-6988
   1655 E Mission Blvd Pomona (91766) *(P-2657)*

Elitra Pharmaceuticals ....D...... 858 410-3030
   3510 Dunhill St Ste A San Diego (92121) *(P-4104)*

Elixir Industries ....D...... 949 860-5000
   24800 Chrisanta Dr Ste 210 Mission Viejo (92691) *(P-6514)*

Elizabeth Glaser Pedia ....B...... 310 231-0400
   16130 Ventura Blvd Ste 250 Encino (91436) *(P-18762)*

Elizabeth Glser Pdtric Aids FN .... B...... 310 593-0047
2950 31st St Ste 125 Santa Monica (90405) *(P-19445)*

Elizabeth Hospice Inc (PA)... C...... 760 737-2050
800 W Valley Pkwy Escondido (92025) *(P-18612)*

Elizabeth Shutters, Colton *Also Called: Elizabeth Shutters Inc (P-6104)*

Elizabeth Shutters Inc .... E...... 909 825-1531
525 S Rancho Ave Colton (92324) *(P-6104)*

Elk, Shafter *Also Called: Elk Corporation of Texas (P-5411)*

Elk Corporation of Texas .... C...... 661 391-3900
6200 Zerker Rd Shafter (93263) *(P-5411)*

Elk Hills Power LLC .... E...... 661 763-2730
101 Ash St San Diego (92101) *(P-303)*

Elkay Plastics Co Inc (PA)... D...... 323 722-7073
6000 Sheila St Commerce (90040) *(P-13413)*

Elkins Kalt Wntraub Rben Grtsi .... D...... 310 746-4431
10345 W Olympic Blvd Los Angeles (90064) *(P-18851)*

Ellens Silk Screening Inc .... E...... 626 441-4415
1500 Mission St South Pasadena (91030) *(P-15665)*

Ellie Mae Inc .... B...... 818 223-2000
24025 Park Sorrento Ste 210 Calabasas (91302) *(P-16024)*

ELLIE MAE, INC., Calabasas *Also Called: Ellie Mae Inc (P-16024)*

Ellingson Inc .... E...... 714 773-1923
119 W Santa Fe Ave Fullerton (92832) *(P-7825)*

Elliotts Designs Inc .... E...... 310 631-4931
2473 E Rancho Del Amo Pl Compton (90220) *(P-2830)*

Ellis Building Contractors, Manhattan Beach *Also Called: Ebc Inc (P-430)*

Ellis Grge Cpllone Obrien Anng .... D...... 310 274-7100
2121 Avenue Of The Stars Fl 30 Los Angeles (90067) *(P-18852)*

Ellison Educational Eqp Inc (PA)................................... E...... 949 598-8822
25862 Commercentre Dr Lake Forest (92630) *(P-7180)*

Ellison Institute LLC (PA)... C...... 310 228-6400
12414 Exposition Blvd Los Angeles (90064) *(P-19970)*

Ellisson Institute Technology, Los Angeles *Also Called: Ellison Institute LLC (P-19970)*

Elm System Inc .... F...... 408 694-2750
11622 El Camino Real Ste 100 San Diego (92130) *(P-9180)*

Elmco Sales Inc (PA)... D...... 626 855-4831
15070 Proctor Ave City Of Industry (91746) *(P-12738)*

Elotek Systems Inc (PA)... E...... 949 366-4404
216 Avenida Fabricante Ste 112 San Clemente (92672) *(P-12407)*

Elro Manufacturing Company (PA)................................. E...... 310 380-7444
400 W Walnut St Gardena (90248) *(P-11112)*

Elro Sign Company, Gardena *Also Called: Elro Manufacturing Company (P-11112)*

Elrob LLC, Garden Grove *Also Called: Winchester Interconnect EC LLC (P-12711)*

Elsevier, San Diego *Also Called: Elsevier Inc (P-3445)*

Elsevier Academic Press, San Diego *Also Called: Elsevier Inc (P-3446)*

Elsevier Inc .... D...... 619 231-6616
10620 Treena St San Diego (92131) *(P-3445)*

Elsevier Inc .... E...... 619 231-6616
525 B St San Diego (92101) *(P-3446)*

Eltron International, Agoura Hills *Also Called: Zebra Technologies Corporation (P-7582)*

Elum, San Diego *Also Called: Elum Designs Inc (P-3570)*

Elum Designs Inc .... E...... 858 650-3586
8969 Kenamar Dr Ste 113 San Diego (92121) *(P-3570)*

Elwin Inc .... E...... 714 752-6962
6910 8th St Buena Park (90620) *(P-3005)*

Ely Co Inc .... E...... 310 539-5831
3046 Kashiwa St Torrance (90505) *(P-7826)*

Elysium Ceramics, Anaheim *Also Called: Elysium Tiles Inc (P-5372)*

Elysium Jennings LLC .... C...... 661 679-1700
1600 Norris Rd Bakersfield (93308) *(P-280)*

Elysium Tiles Inc .... F...... 714 991-7885
1160 N Anaheim Blvd Anaheim (92801) *(P-5372)*

Elyte Inc .... F...... 661 832-1000
4516 District Blvd Bakersfield (93313) *(P-6702)*

Ema, City Of Industry *Also Called: Engineering Model Assoc Inc (P-5024)*

Emanate Health .... C...... 626 912-5282
1722 Desire Ave Ste 206 Rowland Heights (91748) *(P-17648)*

Emanate Health .... B...... 626 857-3477
427 W Carroll Ave Glendora (91741) *(P-18253)*

Emanate Health, Rowland Heights *Also Called: Emanate Health (P-17648)*

Emanate Health, West Covina *Also Called: Emanate Health Medical Center (P-18257)*

Emanate Health Medical Center ....B...... 626 858-8515
140 W College St Covina (91723) *(P-18254)*

Emanate Health Medical Center .... B...... 626 963-8411
1115 S Sunset Ave West Covina (91790) *(P-18255)*

Emanate Health Medical Center .... A...... 626 331-7331
210 W San Bernardino Rd Covina (91723) *(P-18256)*

Emanate Health Medical Center (PA)............................. A...... 626 962-4011
1115 S Sunset Ave West Covina (91790) *(P-18257)*

Emanate Health Medical Group (PA)............................... A...... 626 331-7331
210 W San Bernardino Rd Covina (91723) *(P-18258)*

Emanate Hlth Fthill Prsbt Hosp (PA)............................. D...... 626 857-3145
250 S Grand Ave Glendora (91741) *(P-18259)*

Emanate Hlth Intr-Cmmnity Hosp, Covina *Also Called: Emanate Health Medical Group (P-18258)*

Emazing Lights LLC ....E...... 626 628-6482
240 S Loara St Anaheim (92802) *(P-8365)*

Embassy Stes - Mndlay Bch Rsor, Oxnard *Also Called: Djont/Jpm Hsptlity Lsg Spe LLC (P-15134)*

Embassy Suites, Garden Grove *Also Called: Embassy Suites & Hotel (P-15145)*

Embassy Suites, San Diego *Also Called: Sunstone Top Gun Lessee Inc (P-15382)*

Embassy Suites, Lompoc *Also Called: Windsor Capital Group Inc (P-15420)*

Embassy Suites, Temecula *Also Called: Windsor Capital Group Inc (P-15421)*

Embassy Suites, Brea *Also Called: Windsor Capital Group Inc (P-15422)*

Embassy Suites, Santa Ana *Also Called: Windsor Capital Group Inc (P-15423)*

Embassy Suites - Lax Airport S, El Segundo *Also Called: Djont Operations LLC (P-15133)*

Embassy Suites & Hotel .... C...... 714 539-3300
11767 Harbor Blvd Garden Grove (92840) *(P-15145)*

Embedded Designs Inc ....E...... 858 673-6050
16120 W Bernardo Dr Ste A San Diego (92127) *(P-10130)*

Embedded Systems Inc .... E...... 805 624-6030
2250a Union Pl Simi Valley (93065) *(P-8180)*

Embee Performance LLC .... E...... 714 540-1354
2100 Ritchey St Santa Ana (92705) *(P-13431)*

Embee Plating, Santa Ana *Also Called: Embee Processing LLC (P-19581)*

Embee Powder Coating, Santa Ana *Also Called: Embee Performance LLC (P-13431)*

Embee Processing LLC .... B...... 714 546-9842
2158 S Hathaway St Santa Ana (92705) *(P-19581)*

Ember Technologies Inc .... E...... 520 400-9337
880 Hampshire Rd Westlake Village (91361) *(P-5023)*

Emcor Facilities Services Inc ....C...... 949 475-6020
2 Cromwell Irvine (92618) *(P-10175)*

Emcor Services Mesa Energy, Irvine *Also Called: Mesa Energy Systems Inc (P-794)*

Emcore, Alhambra *Also Called: Emcore Corporation (P-8792)*

Emcore Corporation .... C...... 626 293-3400
2015 Chestnut St Alhambra (91803) *(P-8791)*

Emcore Corporation (PA)... C...... 626 293-3400
2015 Chestnut St Alhambra (91803) *(P-8792)*

EMD Millipore Corporation .... D...... 951 676-8080
28820 Single Oak Dr Temecula (92590) *(P-4313)*

EMD Millipore Corporation .... D...... 951 676-8080
28835 Single Oak Dr Temecula (92590) *(P-10254)*

EMD Millipore Corporation .... E...... 760 788-9692
26578 Old Julian Hwy Ramona (92065) *(P-10255)*

Eme Fan & Motor, Brea *Also Called: Sunon Inc (P-7333)*

Emerald Acquisition LLC .... C...... 714 891-8752
6381 Industry Way Westminster (92683) *(P-617)*

Emerald Connect LLC (HQ).. D...... 800 233-2834
15050 Avenue Of Science Ste 200 San Diego (92128) *(P-16492)*

Emerald Paving Company, Westminster *Also Called: Emerald Acquisition LLC (P-617)*

Emergency Ambulance Svc Inc .... D...... 714 990-1331
3200 E Birch St Ste A Brea (92821) *(P-11382)*

Emergency Dept Dignity Hlth, Arroyo Grande *Also Called: Arroyo Grande Community Hospital (P-18187)*

Emergency Groups Office, San Dimas *Also Called: Ego Inc (P-19770)*

Emergency Groups' Office, San Dimas *Also Called: Brault (P-19756)*

Emergency Vehicle Group Inc .... E...... 714 238-0110
2883 E Coronado St Ste A Anaheim (92806) *(P-13762)*

Emergent Group Inc (DH)... D...... 818 394-2800
10939 Pendleton St Sun Valley (91352) *(P-10656)*

Employee Codes: A=Over 500 employees, B=251-500
C=101-250, D=51-100, E=20-50, F=10-19, G=1-9

2024 Southern California
Business Directory and Buyers Guide

© Mergent Inc. 1-800-342-5647
1079

Emergent Medical Associates .... D 818 995-5350
16237 Ventura Blvd Encino (91436) *(P-17649)*

Emergncy Mdcine Spclist Ornge 714 543-8911
1310 W Stewart Dr Ste 212 Orange (92868) *(P-15920)*

Emerik Hotel Corp .... D 213 748-1291
1020 S Figueroa St Los Angeles (90015) *(P-15146)*

Emeritus At Casa Glendale, Glendale *Also Called: Emeritus Corporation (P-17937)*

Emeritus At San Dimas, San Dimas *Also Called: Emeritus Corporation (P-17936)*

Emeritus At Villa Colima, Walnut *Also Called: Emeritus Corporation (P-17938)*

Emeritus Corporation .... C 760 741-3055
1351 E Washington Ave Escondido (92027) *(P-14706)*

Emeritus Corporation .... C 805 239-1313
1919 Creston Rd Ofc Paso Robles (93446) *(P-14707)*

Emeritus Corporation .... C 909 420-0153
22325 Barton Rd Grand Terrace (92313) *(P-17931)*

Emeritus Corporation .... C 858 292-8044
5219 Clairemont Mesa Blvd San Diego (92117) *(P-17932)*

Emeritus Corporation .... C 714 639-3590
142 S Prospect St Orange (92869) *(P-17933)*

Emeritus Corporation .... C 714 441-0644
411 E Commonwealth Ave Fullerton (92832) *(P-17934)*

Emeritus Corporation .... C 951 744-9861
1001 N Lyon Ave Hemet (92545) *(P-17935)*

Emeritus Corporation .... C 909 394-0304
1740 S San Dimas Ave San Dimas (91773) *(P-17936)*

Emeritus Corporation .... C 818 246-7457
426 Piedmont Ave Glendale (91206) *(P-17937)*

Emeritus Corporation .... C 909 595-5030
19850 Colima Rd Walnut (91789) *(P-17938)*

Emet Lending Group Inc .... D 714 933-9800
2601 Saturn St Ste 200 Brea (92821) *(P-14312)*

EMI Solutions Inc .... F 949 206-9960
13805 Alton Pkwy Ste B Irvine (92618) *(P-9040)*

Emida Technologies, Foothill Ranch *Also Called: Debisys Inc (P-14258)*

Emids Tech Private Ltd Corp .... A 805 304-5986
6320 Canoga Ave Woodland Hills (91367) *(P-16025)*

EMJ Corporate, Lynwood *Also Called: Earle M Jorgensen Company (P-12549)*

Emp Connectors Inc .... E 310 533-6799
2280 W 208th St Torrance (90501) *(P-8263)*

Emp III Inc .... D 323 231-4174
1755 Mrtn Lthr Kng Jr Blv Los Angeles (90058) *(P-15028)*

Empcc Inc .... B 888 278-8200
1682 Langley Ave Fl 2 Irvine (92614) *(P-844)*

Empi Inc .... D 714 446-9606
301 E Orangethorpe Ave Anaheim (92801) *(P-12240)*

Empire Cls Wrldwide Chffred Sv, El Segundo *Also Called: Cls Trnsprttion Los Angles LLC (P-11380)*

Empire Community Painting, Irvine *Also Called: Empcc Inc (P-844)*

Empire Container Corporation .... D 310 537-8190
1161 E Walnut St Carson (90746) *(P-3098)*

Empire Demolition Inc .... D 909 393-8300
137 N Joy St Corona (92879) *(P-1132)*

Empire Med Transportations LLC .... D 877 473-6029
1433 W Linden St Ste M Riverside (92507) *(P-11758)*

Empire Oil Co .... C 909 877-0226
2756 S Riverside Ave Bloomington (92316) *(P-13451)*

Empire Products Inc .... D 909 399-3355
5061 Brooks St Montclair (91763) *(P-5979)*

Empire Sheet Metal Inc .... E 909 923-2927
1215 S Bon View Ave Ontario (91761) *(P-6231)*

Empire Southwest LLC .... E 760 545-6200
3393 Us Highway 86 Imperial (92251) *(P-6932)*

Empire Transportation Inc .... B 562 529-2676
8800 Park St Bellflower (90706) *(P-11415)*

Empirical Systems Arospc Inc (PA) .... C 805 474-5900
3580 Sueldo St San Luis Obispo (93401) *(P-9521)*

Employee Owned PCF Cast Pdts I .... E 562 633-6673
520 S Palmetto Ave Ontario (91762) *(P-5792)*

Employer Defense Group .... F 949 200-0137
2390 E Orangewood Ave Ste 520 Anaheim (92806) *(P-9974)*

Employers Training Resource, Bakersfield *Also Called: County of Kern (P-20416)*

Employnet Inc .... A 909 458-0961
123 E 9th St Ste 103 Upland (91786) *(P-15841)*

Empower Our Youth .... D 323 203-5436
6767 W Sunset Blvd 8-188 Los Angeles (90028) *(P-14983)*

Empower Rf, Inglewood *Also Called: Empower Rf Systems Inc (P-8514)*

Empower Rf Systems Inc (PA) .... D 310 412-8100
316 W Florence Ave Inglewood (90301) *(P-8514)*

Emser Tile LLC .... E 951 296-3671
42092 Winchester Rd Temecula (92590) *(P-13573)*

Emser Tile LLC .... E 661 837-4400
4546 Stine Rd Bakersfield (93313) *(P-13574)*

Emser Tile LLC (PA) .... B 323 650-2000
8431 Santa Monica Blvd Los Angeles (90069) *(P-12354)*

Emsoc, Orange *Also Called: Emergncy Mdcine Spclist Ornge (P-15920)*

Emtek Products, Irwindale *Also Called: Assa Abloy Rsdential Group Inc (P-12715)*

Emulex Corporation (DH) C
5300 California Ave Irvine (92617) *(P-7525)*

En Pointe Technologies Sls LLC .... C 310 337-6151
200 N Pacific Coast Hwy Ste 1050 El Segundo (90245) *(P-12408)*

Enagic Usa Inc (PA) .... D 310 542-7700
4115 Spencer St Torrance (90503) *(P-14110)*

Enaqua .... E 760 599-2644
1350 Specialty Dr Ste D Vista (92081) *(P-7655)*

Enas Media Inc .... F 626 962-1115
1316 Michillinda Ave Arcadia (91006) *(P-8457)*

Enbio Corp .... C 818 953-9976
150 E Olive Ave Ste 114 Burbank (91502) *(P-20168)*

Enbiz International, Lake Forest *Also Called: Cloudradiant Corp (P-13534)*

Enchannel Medical Ltd .... E 949 694-6802
555 Corporate Dr Ste 165 Ladera Ranch (92694) *(P-10502)*

Encina Pepper Tree Joint Ventr .... D 805 682-7277
2220 Bath St Santa Barbara (93105) *(P-15147)*

Encinitas Ford, Encinitas *Also Called: Wayne Gossett Ford Inc (P-13847)*

Encinitas Ranch Golf Course, San Diego *Also Called: JC Resorts LLC (P-20043)*

Encino Financial Center, Encino *Also Called: Lowe Enterprises Rlty Svcs Inc (P-14824)*

Encino Living LLC .... C 818 907-1343
16710 Magnolia Blvd Encino (91436) *(P-17396)*

Enclarity Inc .... B 949 797-7160
16815 Von Karman Ave Ste 125 Irvine (92606) *(P-16493)*

Encore, San Diego *Also Called: Encore Capital Group Inc (P-14281)*

Encore Capital Group Inc (PA) .... A 877 445-4581
350 Camino De La Reina Ste 100 San Diego (92108) *(P-14281)*

Encore Cases Inc .... E 818 768-8803
5260 Vineland Ave North Hollywood (91601) *(P-5286)*

Encore Image, Torrance *Also Called: Encore Image Group Inc (P-11114)*

Encore Image Inc .... E 909 986-4632
303 W Main St Ontario (91762) *(P-11113)*

Encore Image Group Inc (PA) .... D 310 534-7500
1445 Sepulveda Blvd Torrance (90501) *(P-11114)*

Encore Plastics, Huntington Beach *Also Called: Donoco Industries Inc (P-5324)*

Encore Seats Inc .... E 949 559-0930
5511 Skylab Rd Huntington Beach (92647) *(P-9683)*

Encore Semi Inc .... D 858 225-4993
7310 Miramar Rd Ste 410 San Diego (92126) *(P-19582)*

Encore Tex Inc, Huntington Park *Also Called: Kuk Rim USA Inc (P-2122)*

Encorr Sheets LLC .... E 626 523-4661
5171 E Francis St Ontario (91761) *(P-3236)*

Encrypted Access Corporation .... C 714 371-4125
1730 Redhill Ave Irvine (92697) *(P-7526)*

Endeavor Group Holdings Inc (PA) .... D 310 285-9000
9601 Wilshire Blvd Fl 3 Beverly Hills (90210) *(P-17368)*

Endemol Shine North America .... D 747 529-8000
5161 Lankershim Blvd Ste 400 North Hollywood (91601) *(P-17189)*

Enderle Fuel Injection .... E 805 526-3838
1830 Voyager Ave Simi Valley (93063) *(P-9388)*

Enderle Vault Co, Inglewood *Also Called: Centinela Consulting Group Inc (P-5402)*

Endo Pharmaceuticals Inc .... E 949 767-9420
9601 Jeronimo Rd Irvine (92618) *(P-4105)*

Endologix, Irvine *Also Called: Endologix Inc (P-10503)*

Endologix Inc (PA) .... D 949 595-7200
2 Musick Irvine (92618) *(P-10503)*

2024 Southern California
Business Directory and Buyers Guide

(P-0000) Products & Services Section entry number
(PA)=Parent Co (HQ)=Headquarters (DH)=Div Headquarters

Endologix Canada LLC .... D....... 949 595-7200
2 Musick Irvine (92618) *(P-10504)*

Endotec Inc .... E....... 714 681-6306
14525 Valley View Ave Ste H Santa Fe Springs (90670) *(P-10657)*

Endpak Packaging Inc .... D....... 562 801-0281
9101 Perkins St Pico Rivera (90660) *(P-3199)*

Endress & Hauser Conducta Inc .... E....... 800 835-5474
4123 E La Palma Ave St200 Anaheim (92807) *(P-10256)*

Endress+hser Optcal Analis Inc .... E....... 909 477-2329
11027 Arrow Rte Rancho Cucamonga (91730) *(P-10257)*

Endresshauser Conducta, Anaheim *Also Called: Endress & Hauser Conducta Inc (P-10256)*

Endura Healthcare Inc .... C....... 949 487-9500
29222 Rancho Viejo Rd Ste 127 San Juan Capistrano (92675) *(P-17939)*

Endura Steel Inc (HQ) .... F....... 760 244-9325
17671 Bear Valley Rd Hesperia (92345) *(P-12550)*

Enduratex, Corona *Also Called: Cgpc America Corporation (P-3930)*

Ener-Tech Metals Inc .... D....... 562 529-5034
7815 Somerset Blvd Paramount (90723) *(P-5663)*

Energetic Lighting, Chino *Also Called: Yankon Industries Inc (P-8343)*

Energy Club, Pacoima *Also Called: Energy Club Inc (P-13268)*

Energy Club Inc .... D
12950 Pierce St Pacoima (91331) *(P-13268)*

Energy Cnvrsion Applctions Inc .... F....... 714 256-2166
582 Explorer St Brea (92821) *(P-8095)*

Energy Enterprises USA Inc (PA) .... D....... 424 339-0005
6842 Van Nuys Blvd Ste 800 Van Nuys (91405) *(P-766)*

Energy Labs Inc (DH) .... B....... 619 671-0100
1695 Cactus Rd San Diego (92154) *(P-7610)*

Energy Link Indus Svcs Inc .... E....... 661 765-4444
11439 S Enos Ln Bakersfield (93311) *(P-7827)*

Energy Suspension, San Clemente *Also Called: Bunker Corp (P-9362)*

Energy Watch .... D....... 661 324-0930
3555 Landco Dr Bakersfield (93308) *(P-896)*

Enerpath Services Inc .... D....... 909 335-1699
1758 Orange Tree Ln Redlands (92374) *(P-897)*

Enerpro Inc .... E....... 805 683-2114
99 Aero Camino Goleta (93117) *(P-12657)*

Enersponse Inc .... E....... 949 829-3901
1148 Manhattan Ave Manhattan Beach (90266) *(P-10196)*

Enersys .... E....... 909 464-8251
5580 Edison Ave Chino (91710) *(P-9145)*

Enertron Technologies Inc .... E....... 800 537-7649
3525 Del Mar Heights Rd San Diego (92130) *(P-8311)*

Enervee Corporation .... C....... 844 363-7833
11845 W Olympic Blvd Ste 1100w Los Angeles (90064) *(P-16494)*

Enevate, Irvine *Also Called: Enevate Corporation (P-9146)*

Enevate Corporation .... D....... 949 243-0399
101 Theory Ste 200 Irvine (92617) *(P-9146)*

Enfora Inc .... E....... 972 234-1689
9645 Scranton Rd Ste 205 San Diego (92121) *(P-9041)*

Engel & Gray Inc .... E....... 805 925-2771
745 W Betteravia Rd Ste A Santa Maria (93455) *(P-344)*

Engel Holdings Inc .... C....... 866 950-9862
14754 Ceres Ave Fontana (92335) *(P-548)*

Engense Inc .... F....... 805 484-8317
2255 Pleasant Valley Rd Ste G Camarillo (93012) *(P-5589)*

Engersall, Riverside *Also Called: Club Car LLC (P-9932)*

Engineered Coating Tech Inc .... E....... 323 588-0260
2838 E 54th St Vernon (90058) *(P-4487)*

Engineered Food Systems .... E....... 714 921-9913
2490 Anselmo Dr Corona (92879) *(P-7656)*

Engineered Lighting Products, El Monte *Also Called: R W Swarens Associates Inc (P-8329)*

Engineered Machinery Group Inc .... F....... 909 579-0088
1042 N Mountain Ave Ste B561 Upland (91786) *(P-7150)*

Engineered Magnetics Inc .... E....... 310 649-9000
10524 S La Cienega Blvd Inglewood (90304) *(P-8205)*

Engineered Well Svc Intl Inc .... F....... 866 913-6283
3120 Standard St Bakersfield (93308) *(P-345)*

Engineering Division, Lancaster *Also Called: County of Los Angeles (P-19567)*

Engineering Jk Aerospace & Def .... E....... 714 499-9092
23231 La Palma Ave Yorba Linda (92887) *(P-9684)*

Engineering Model Assoc Inc (PA) .... E....... 626 912-7011
1020 Wallace Way City Of Industry (91748) *(P-5024)*

Engineering Partners Inc .... D....... 858 824-1761
10150 Meanley Dr Ste 200 San Diego (92131) *(P-19583)*

Engineering Public Works, Glendale *Also Called: City of Glendale (P-19563)*

Enginring Sftwr Sys Sltons Inc (PA) .... D....... 619 338-0380
600 B St San Diego (92101) *(P-19584)*

Enhance America Inc .... E....... 951 361-3000
3463 Grapevine St Jurupa Valley (91752) *(P-11115)*

Enhanced Vision Systems Inc (HQ) .... D....... 800 440-9476
15301 Springdale St Huntington Beach (92649) *(P-10314)*

Enjoy Food, Colton *Also Called: Saab Enterprises Inc (P-1234)*

Enjoy Haircare, Oceanside *Also Called: USP Inc (P-4465)*

Enkeboll Design, Carson *Also Called: The Enkeboll Co (P-2637)*

Enki Health and RES Systems .... D....... 626 961-8971
160 S 7th Ave La Puente (91746) *(P-17650)*

Enki Health Care, La Puente *Also Called: Enki Health and RES Systems (P-17650)*

Enlink Geoenergy Services Inc .... E....... 424 242-1200
2630 Homestead Pl Rancho Dominguez (90220) *(P-7611)*

Enlyte, San Diego *Also Called: Mitchell International Inc (P-16076)*

Ennis Traffic Safety Solutions .... E....... 323 758-1147
6624 Stanford Ave Los Angeles (90001) *(P-4488)*

Enniss Inc .... E....... 619 561-1101
12535 Vigilante Rd Lakeside (92040) *(P-405)*

Eno Brands Inc .... E....... 714 220-1318
6481 Global Dr Cypress (90630) *(P-14075)*

Enovis Consumer, Vista *Also Called: Djo Consumer LLC (P-10647)*

Ens Security, City Of Industry *Also Called: Easterncctv (usa) LLC (P-16731)*

Ensemble Communications Inc .... C....... 858 458-1400
2223 Avenida De La Playa La Jolla (92037) *(P-8515)*

ENSIGN, Palm Springs *Also Called: Ensign Palm I LLC (P-17944)*

ENSIGN, Whittier *Also Called: Ensign Whittier East LLC (P-17947)*

ENSIGN, San Diego *Also Called: La Jolla Skilled Inc (P-17984)*

ENSIGN, Upland *Also Called: Upland Community Care Inc (P-18064)*

Ensign Group Inc .... C....... 818 893-6385
9541 Van Nuys Blvd Panorama City (91402) *(P-17940)*

Ensign Group Inc .... C....... 562 947-7817
10426 Bogardus Ave Whittier (90603) *(P-17941)*

Ensign Group Inc .... C....... 562 923-9301
13007 Paramount Blvd Downey (90242) *(P-17942)*

Ensign Group Inc .... C....... 626 607-2400
4800 Delta Ave Rosemead (91770) *(P-17943)*

Ensign Group Inc .... C....... 805 925-8713
1405 E Main St Santa Maria (93454) *(P-19261)*

Ensign Palm I LLC .... C....... 760 323-2638
2990 E Ramon Rd Palm Springs (92264) *(P-17944)*

Ensign San Dimas LLC .... C....... 626 963-7531
1033 E Arrow Hwy Glendora (91740) *(P-18123)*

Ensign Services Inc .... C....... 949 487-9500
29222 Rancho Viejo Rd Ste 127 San Juan Capistrano (92675) *(P-17945)*

Ensign Southland LLC .... C....... 949 487-9500
29222 Rancho Viejo Rd Ste 127 San Juan Capistrano (92675) *(P-17946)*

Ensign US Drlg Cal Inc .... C....... 661 387-8400
3701 Fruitvale Ave Bakersfield (93308) *(P-898)*

Ensign US Drlg Cal Inc (HQ) .... E....... 661 589-0111
7001 Charity Ave Bakersfield (93308) *(P-7012)*

Ensign Whittier East LLC .... C....... 562 947-7817
10426 Bogardus Ave Whittier (90603) *(P-17947)*

Ensign-Bickford Arospc Def Co .... C....... 805 292-4000
14370 White Sage Rd Moorpark (93021) *(P-9975)*

Enstrom Mold & Engineering Inc .... F....... 760 744-1880
235 Trade St San Marcos (92078) *(P-7068)*

Entech Instruments Inc .... D....... 805 527-5939
2207 Agate Ct Simi Valley (93065) *(P-10258)*

Entegris Inc .... D....... 805 541-9299
4175 Santa Fe Rd San Luis Obispo (93401) *(P-20028)*

Entegris Gp Inc .... C....... 805 541-9299
4175 Santa Fe Rd San Luis Obispo (93401) *(P-7391)*

Entercom Media Corp .... D....... 909 825-9525
900 E Washington St Ste 315 Colton (92324) *(P-11924)*

Employee Codes: A=Over 500 employees, B=251-500
C=101-250, D=51-100, E=20-50, F=10-19, G=1-9

2024 Southern California
Business Directory and Buyers Guide

© Mergent Inc. 1-800-342-5647
1081

A
L
P
H
A
B
E
T
I
C

Entercom Media Corp .... C 323 930-7317
  5670 Wilshire Blvd Ste 200 Los Angeles (90036) *(P-11925)*

Enterprise Bank & Trust .... C 858 432-7000
  11939 Rancho Bernardo Rd Ste 200 San Diego (92128) *(P-14193)*

Enterprise Bank & Trust .... C 562 345-9092
  17785 Center Court Dr N # 750 Cerritos (90703) *(P-14194)*

Enterprise Rent-A-Car, Orange *Also Called: Enterprise Rnt--car Los Angles (P-16981)*

Enterprise Rnt--car Los Angles (DH) .... D 657 221-4400
  333 City Blvd W Ste 1000 Orange (92868) *(P-16981)*

Enterprise Security Inc (PA) .... D 714 630-9100
  22860 Savi Ranch Pkwy Yorba Linda (92887) *(P-16734)*

Enterprise Security Solutions, Yorba Linda *Also Called: Enterprise Security Inc (P-16734)*

Enterprises Industries Inc .... C 818 989-6103
  7500 Tyrone Ave Van Nuys (91405) *(P-6515)*

Entertainment Partners Inc (PA) .... B 818 955-6000
  2950 N Hollywood Way Burbank (91505) *(P-19772)*

Entos Pharmaceuticals Inc .... F 800 727-0884
  3040 Science Park Rd San Diego (92121) *(P-4106)*

Entrance Tech, El Monte *Also Called: Santoshi Corporation (P-6660)*

Entravsion Communications Corp (PA) .... C 310 447-3870
  2425 Olympic Blvd Ste 6000w Santa Monica (90404) *(P-11945)*

Entravsion Communications Corp .... D 323 900-6100
  5700 Wilshire Blvd Ste 250 Los Angeles (90036) *(P-11946)*

Entrepeneur Magazine, Irvine *Also Called: Entrepreneur Media Inc (P-3358)*

Entrepreneur Media Inc (PA) .... D 949 261-2325
  18061 Fitch Irvine (92614) *(P-3358)*

Entrepreneurial Capital Corp .... C 949 809-3900
  4100 Newport Place Dr Ste 400 Newport Beach (92660) *(P-14660)*

Envelopments Inc .... E 714 569-3300
  13091 Sandhurst Pl Santa Ana (92705) *(P-3045)*

Envent Corporation (PA) .... D 562 997-9465
  3220 E 29th St Long Beach (90806) *(P-20333)*

Envion LLC .... D 818 217-2500
  14724 Ventura Blvd Fl 200 Sherman Oaks (91403) *(P-7322)*

Envirnmental Catalyst Tech LLC .... E 949 459-3870
  3937 Ocean Ranch Blvd Oceanside (92056) *(P-3893)*

Envirnmntal Systems RES Inst I .... E 909 793-2853
  1411 W State St Redlands (92373) *(P-16237)*

Enviro-Intercept Inc .... E 818 982-6063
  7327 Varna Ave Unit 5 North Hollywood (91605) *(P-7612)*

Envirochem Technologies, Atascadero *Also Called: Chemlogics Group LLC (P-4518)*

Envirofabrics, Los Angeles *Also Called: Roshan Trading Inc (P-2051)*

Envirogenics Systems Company .... D 818 573-9220
  9255 Telstar Ave El Monte (91731) *(P-708)*

Enviroguard, Montclair *Also Called: Expo Power Systems Inc (P-12595)*

Environmental Catalyst Tech .... E 949 888-1625
  22961 Arroyo Vis Rcho Sta Marg (92688) *(P-3894)*

Environmental Construction Inc .... D 818 449-8920
  21550 Oxnard St Ste 1060 Woodland Hills (91367) *(P-549)*

Environmental Industries, Fillmore *Also Called: Brightview Tree Company (P-227)*

Environmental Resolutions Inc .... B 949 457-8950
  25371 Commercentre Dr Ste 250 Lake Forest (92630) *(P-20334)*

Environmental Science Assoc .... C 213 599-4300
  626 Wilshire Blvd Ste 1100 Los Angeles (90017) *(P-19836)*

Environmental Science Assoc .... C 858 638-0900
  9191 Towne Centre Dr Ste 340 San Diego (92122) *(P-20335)*

Environmental Systems Research Institute Inc (PA) .... A 909 793-2853
  380 New York St Redlands (92373) *(P-12409)*

Envise (HQ) .... C 800 613-6240
  12131 Western Ave Garden Grove (92841) *(P-767)*

Envise, Garden Grove *Also Called: Envise (P-767)*

Envision Plastics, Chino *Also Called: Envision Plastics Industries LLC (P-5025)*

Envision Plastics Industries LLC .... E 909 590-7334
  14312 Central Ave Chino (91710) *(P-5025)*

Envista, Brea *Also Called: Envista Holdings Corporation (P-10743)*

Envista Holdings Corporation (PA) .... D 714 817-7000
  200 S Kraemer Blvd Bldg E Brea (92821) *(P-10743)*

Envveno Medical Corporation .... F 949 261-2900
  70 Doppler Irvine (92618) *(P-10505)*

Eos, Paso Robles *Also Called: Eos Estate Winery (P-1624)*

Eos Estate Winery .... E 805 239-2562
  2300 Airport Rd Paso Robles (93446) *(P-1624)*

Eoy, Los Angeles *Also Called: Empower Our Youth (P-14983)*

Ep Holdings Inc .... E 949 713-4600
  30442 Esperanza Rcho Sta Marg (92688) *(P-7469)*

Ep Memory, Rcho Sta Marg *Also Called: Ep Holdings Inc (P-7469)*

EPC Power Corp (PA) .... C 858 748-5590
  13250 Gregg St Ste A2 Poway (92064) *(P-8206)*

Epe Industries Usa Inc (HQ) .... F 800 315-0336
  17835 Newhope St Ste G Fountain Valley (92708) *(P-4880)*

Epe USA, Fountain Valley *Also Called: Epe Industries Usa Inc (P-4880)*

Epic Management LP (PA) .... D 909 799-1818
  1615 Orange Tree Ln Redlands (92374) *(P-20029)*

Epic Sciences Inc .... D 858 356-6610
  9381 Judicial Dr Ste 200 San Diego (92121) *(P-18548)*

Epic Technologies LLC .... A 908 707-4085
  9340 Owensmouth Ave Chatsworth (91311) *(P-8471)*

Epica Medical Innovations LLC .... E 949 238-6323
  901 Calle Amanecer Ste 150 San Clemente (92673) *(P-10506)*

EPICENTRE, San Diego *Also Called: Harmonium Inc (P-19212)*

Epicuren Discovery .... D 949 588-5807
  31 Journey Ste 100 Aliso Viejo (92656) *(P-4273)*

Epidaurus .... B 213 743-9075
  3745 S Grand Ave Los Angeles (90007) *(P-14990)*

Epilogue and Arrested, Los Angeles *Also Called: Rhapsody Clothing Inc (P-2366)*

Epirus Inc .... E 310 620-8678
  19145 Gramercy Pl Torrance (90501) *(P-16238)*

Episcopal Communities & Servic .... D 310 544-2204
  5801 Crestridge Rd Pls Vrds Pnsl (90275) *(P-17948)*

Episcopal Community Services .... D 619 470-0720
  2432 E 18th St National City (91950) *(P-19077)*

Episource LLC .... A 714 452-1961
  500 W 190th St Ste 400 Gardena (90248) *(P-14586)*

Epitec Inc .... A 760 650-2515
  515 Olive Ave Vista (92083) *(P-16026)*

Epl, Commerce *Also Called: Edison Price Lighting Inc (P-8310)*

Eplastics, San Diego *Also Called: Laird Plastics Inc (P-4813)*

Eplastics, San Diego *Also Called: Ridout Plastics Company (P-4819)*

Eplica Inc .... C 562 977-4300
  17785 Center Court Dr N Cerritos (90703) *(P-15842)*

Eplica Inc (PA) .... C 619 260-2000
  2385 Northside Dr Ste 250 San Diego (92108) *(P-15921)*

Eplica Corporate Services Inc .... A 619 282-1400
  2385 Northside Dr Ste 250 San Diego (92108) *(P-15843)*

Epmar Corporation .... E 562 946-8781
  9930 Painter Ave Whittier (90605) *(P-4489)*

Epoca Yocool, South Gate *Also Called: Win Soon Inc (P-1317)*

Epoch.com, Santa Monica *Also Called: Epochcom LLC (P-16495)*

Epochcom LLC .... C 310 664-5700
  3110 Main St Ste 220 Santa Monica (90405) *(P-16495)*

Eppig Brewing, Vista *Also Called: J&L Eppig Brewing LLC (P-1592)*

Eps Corporate Holdings Inc .... F 562 698-7774
  12468 Lambert Rd Whittier (90606) *(P-12739)*

Epsilon Systems Sltons Mssion .... D 619 702-1700
  9242 Lightwave Ave Ste 100 San Diego (92123) *(P-19585)*

Epsilon Systems Solutions Inc .... C 619 474-3252
  2101 Haffley Ave # A National City (91950) *(P-19378)*

Epsilon Systems Solutions Inc (PA) .... D 619 702-1700
  9444 Balboa Ave Ste 100 San Diego (92123) *(P-19586)*

Epson America Inc (DH) .... A 800 463-7766
  3131 Katella Ave Los Alamitos (90720) *(P-7527)*

Epson Electronics America Inc (DH) .... E 408 922-0200
  3131 Katella Ave Los Alamitos (90720) *(P-8793)*

Epstein Becker & Green PC .... C 310 556-8861
  1875 Century Park E Ste 500 Los Angeles (90067) *(P-18853)*

Epworth Morehouse Cowles, Chino *Also Called: Morehouse-Cowles LLC (P-7250)*

Equal Exchange Inc .... D 619 335-6259
  2920 Norman Strasse Rd San Marcos (92069) *(P-1818)*

Equator LLC (HQ) .... C 310 469-9500
  6060 Center Dr Ste 500 Los Angeles (90045) *(P-16027)*

Mergent email: customerrelations@mergent.com
1082

2024 Southern California
Business Directory and Buyers Guide

(P-0000) Products & Services Section entry number
(PA)=Parent Co (HQ)=Headquarters (DH)=Div Headquarters

Equator Business Solutions, Los Angeles *Also Called: Equator LLC (P-16027)*

Equillium Inc (PA).. F...... **858 412-5302**
2223 Avenida De La Playa Ste 105 La Jolla (92037) *(P-4107)*

Equimine .... E...... 877 204-9040
26457 Rancho Pkwy S Lake Forest (92630) *(P-16239)*

Equine Comfort Products, Simi Valley *Also Called: Eurow and OReilly Corp (P-13536)*

Equinox Fitness Club, Los Angeles *Also Called: Equinox-76th Street Inc (P-17398)*

Equinox Fitness Club, Irvine *Also Called: Equinox-76th Street Inc (P-17399)*

Equinox-76th Street Inc .... D...... 310 479-5200
1835 S Sepulveda Blvd Los Angeles (90025) *(P-17397)*

Equinox-76th Street Inc .... D...... 310 552-0420
10250 Santa Monica Blvd Los Angeles (90067) *(P-17398)*

Equinox-76th Street Inc .... D...... 949 296-1700
19540 Jamboree Rd Irvine (92612) *(P-17399)*

Equipment & Tool Institute, Irvine *Also Called: Innova Electronics Corporation (P-9406)*

Equipment Brokers Unlimited, Cerritos *Also Called: Docusource Inc (P-14131)*

Equipment Depot Inc .... C...... 562 949-1000
12393 Slauson Ave Whittier (90606) *(P-12790)*

Equipment Design & Mfg Inc .... D...... 909 594-2229
119 Explorer St Pomona (91768) *(P-6232)*

Equity Ford Research .... E...... 858 755-1327
11722 Sorrento Valley Rd Ste I San Diego (92121) *(P-3447)*

Equity International Inc .... A...... 978 664-2712
5541 Fermi Ct Carlsbad (92008) *(P-12658)*

Equity Smart Home Loans Inc .... D...... 626 864-8774
1499 Huntington Dr Ste 500 South Pasadena (91030) *(P-14313)*

Equity Title Company (DH)..................................... D...... **818 291-4400**
801 N Brand Blvd Ste 400 Glendale (91203) *(P-14888)*

Equus Products Inc .... E...... 714 424-6779
17352 Von Karman Ave Irvine (92614) *(P-10197)*

Erasca Inc .... C...... 858 465-6511
10835 Road To The Cure Ste 140 San Diego (92121) *(P-4108)*

Erba Organics, Chatsworth *Also Called: Erbaviva Inc (P-3998)*

Erbaviva Inc .... E...... 818 998-7112
19831 Nordhoff Pl Ste 116 Chatsworth (91311) *(P-3998)*

Ereplacements LLC .... E...... 714 361-2652
16885 W Bernardo Dr Ste 370 San Diego (92127) *(P-9147)*

Erf Enterprises Inc .... F...... 909 825-4080
863 E Valley Blvd Colton (92324) *(P-9325)*

Erg International, Oxnard *Also Called: Ergonom Corporation (P-3023)*

Ergo Baby Carrier Inc (HQ)................................... E...... **213 283-2090**
680 Knox St Ste 125 Torrance (90502) *(P-10951)*

Ergocraft Contract Solutions ....E
6055 E Washington Blvd Ste 500 Commerce (90040) *(P-2909)*

Ergocraft Office Furniture, Commerce *Also Called: Ergocraft Contract Solutions (P-2909)*

Ergonom Corporation .... D...... 805 981-9978
390 Lombard St Oxnard (93030) *(P-3023)*

Ergonom Corporation (PA)..................................... D...... **805 981-9978**
361 Bernoulli Cir Oxnard (93030) *(P-3024)*

Ergononmic Comfort Design Inc .... F...... 951 277-1558
9140 Stellar Ct Ste B Corona (92883) *(P-2910)*

Erickson-Hall Construction Co (PA)....................... D...... **760 796-7700**
500 Corporate Dr Escondido (92029) *(P-550)*

Erika Records Inc .... E...... 714 228-5420
6300 Caballero Blvd Buena Park (90620) *(P-8458)*

Eriks North America Inc .... D...... 562 802-7782
15500 Blackburn Ave Norwalk (90650) *(P-4727)*

Erin Condren, Hawthorne *Also Called: EC Design LLC (P-14070)*

Ernest Packaging Inc .... C...... **800 233-7788**
5777 Smithway St Commerce (90040) *(P-13535)*

Ernest Paper, Commerce *Also Called: Ernest Packaging (P-13535)*

Ernie Ball, San Luis Obispo *Also Called: Ernie Ball Inc (P-10923)*

Ernie Ball Inc (PA).. E...... **805 544-7726**
4117 Earthwood Ln San Luis Obispo (93401) *(P-10923)*

Ernst & Young LLP .... B...... 949 794-2300
18101 Von Karman Ave Ste 1700 Irvine (92612) *(P-19773)*

Ernst & Young LLP .... A...... 213 977-3200
725 S Figueroa St Ste 200 Los Angeles (90017) *(P-19774)*

Ernst & Young LLP .... C...... 858 535-7200
4365 Executive Dr Ste 1600 San Diego (92121) *(P-19775)*

Eros Stx Global Corporation ....A...... 818 524-7000
3900 W Alameda Ave Fl 32 Burbank (91505) *(P-17307)*

Erp, Rancho Dominguez *Also Called: Expanded Rubber & Plastics Corp (P-5026)*

Erp Integrated Solutions LLC .... D...... 562 425-7800
5000 Airport Plaza Dr Ste 230 Long Beach (90815) *(P-16028)*

Erp Power LLC (PA) .... F...... **805 517-1300**
2625 Townsgate Rd Westlake Village (91361) *(P-10198)*

Es Engineering Services LLC .... D...... 949 988-3500
4 Park Plz Ste 790 Irvine (92614) *(P-19587)*

ES Kluft & Company Inc (DH)................................ C...... **909 373-4211**
11096 Jersey Blvd Ste 101 Rancho Cucamonga (91730) *(P-2848)*

ESA, Los Angeles *Also Called: Environmental Science Assoc (P-19836)*

Esaero, San Luis Obispo *Also Called: Empirical Systems Arospc Inc (P-9521)*

Esaloncom LLC .... D...... 866 550-2424
1910 E Maple Ave El Segundo (90245) *(P-15480)*

Escape Communications Inc .... F...... 310 997-1300
2790 Skypark Dr Ste 203 Torrance (90505) *(P-8516)*

Eschat .... D...... 805 541-5044
3450 Broad St Ste 106 San Luis Obispo (93401) *(P-11849)*

Esco Technologies Inc .... E...... 805 604-3875
501 Del Norte Blvd Oxnard (93030) *(P-8610)*

Escondido Medical Offices, Escondido *Also Called: Kaiser Foundation Hospitals (P-17679)*

Escondido Motors LLC .... D...... 760 745-5000
1101 W 9th Ave Escondido (92025) *(P-13763)*

Escondido Post Acute Rehab, Escondido *Also Called: Mek Escondido LLC (P-18012)*

Escondido Roof Truss Co Inc .... F...... 760 744-4040
430 Via Vera Cruz San Marcos (92078) *(P-2697)*

Ese, El Segundo *Also Called: Mod-Electronics Inc (P-10893)*

Ese, Los Angeles *Also Called: ESE INC (P-13432)*

ESE INC .... E...... 213 614-0102
1111 S Central Ave Los Angeles (90021) *(P-13432)*

Eset LLC (HQ)... C...... **619 876-5400**
610 W Ash St Ste 1700 San Diego (92101) *(P-12410)*

Eset North America, San Diego *Also Called: Eset LLC (P-12410)*

Esi Inc .... D...... 310 670-4974
5710 W Manchester Ave Ste 109 Los Angeles (90045) *(P-8794)*

Esi Motion, Simi Valley *Also Called: Embedded Systems Inc (P-8180)*

Esign Emcee, Moorpark *Also Called: Topaz Systems Inc (P-7572)*

Esl, Burbank *Also Called: Esl Gaming America Inc (P-17336)*

Esl Gaming America Inc .... D...... 818 861-7315
1212 Chestnut St Burbank (91506) *(P-17336)*

Esl Power Systems Inc .... D...... 800 922-4188
2800 Palisades Dr Corona (92878) *(P-8264)*

ESM Aerospace Inc .... E...... 818 841-3653
1203 W Isabel St Burbank (91506) *(P-6233)*

Esmi, San Diego *Also Called: Electronic Surfc Mounted Inds (P-8672)*

Esmond Natural Inc .... E...... 626 337-1588
5316 Irwindale Ave Ste B Irwindale (91706) *(P-3999)*

ESP Corp .... E...... 310 639-2535
1175 W Victoria St Compton (90220) *(P-9042)*

Esparza Enterprises Inc .... A...... 760 344-2031
251 W Main St Ste G&F Brawley (92227) *(P-135)*

Esparza Enterprises Inc .... A...... 661 631-0347
500 Workman St Bakersfield (93307) *(P-11484)*

Esparza Enterprises Inc .... A...... 760 398-0349
51335 Cesar Chavez St Ste 112 Coachella (92236) *(P-15844)*

Esparza Enterprises Inc .... A...... 661 631-0347
222 S Union Ave Bakersfield (93307) *(P-15845)*

Especial T Hvac Shtmtl Fttngs .... E...... 909 869-9150
1239 E Franklin Ave Pomona (91766) *(P-12752)*

Especializados Del Aire, San Diego *Also Called: Alliance Air Products Llc (P-7596)*

Esperanzas Tortilleria .... E...... 760 743-5908
750 Rock Springs Rd Escondido (92025) *(P-1888)*

Esperer Webstores LLC .... F...... 805 880-1900
3820 State St Ste B Santa Barbara (93105) *(P-1268)*

Esri, Redlands *Also Called: Environmental Systems Research Institute Inc (P-12409)*

Esri, Redlands *Also Called: Envirmnntal Systems RES Inst I (P-16237)*

Esri International LLC .... E...... 909 793-2853
380 New York St Redlands (92373) *(P-12411)*

Ess LLC .... D...... 888 303-6424
5227 Dantes View Dr Agoura Hills (91301) *(P-768)*

Employee Codes: A=Over 500 employees, B=251-500
C=101-250, D=51-100, E=20-50, F=10-19, G=1-9

2024 Southern California
Business Directory and Buyers Guide

© Mergent Inc. 1-800-342-5647
1083

ALPHABETIC

Essence of America .... E...... 312 805-9365
1855 1st Ave Ste 103 San Diego (92101) *(P-19078)*

Essendant Co .... C...... 626 961-0011
918 S Stimson Ave City Of Industry (91745) *(P-12993)*

Essense .... A...... 323 202-4650
6300 Wilshire Blvd Ste 720 Los Angeles (90048) *(P-20395)*

Essential Access Health (PA) .... **D...... 213 386-5614**
3600 Wilshire Blvd Ste 600 Los Angeles (90010) *(P-19325)*

Essential Pharmaceutical Corp .... E...... 909 623-4565
1906 W Holt Ave Pomona (91768) *(P-4109)*

Essentra International LLC .... A...... 708 315-7498
21303 Ferrero Walnut (91789) *(P-4564)*

Essex Electronics Inc .... E...... 805 684-7601
1130 Mark Ave Carpinteria (93013) *(P-8795)*

Essex Industries, Huntington Beach *Also Called: Momeni Engineering LLC (P-7945)*

Essilor Laboratories Amer Inc .... E...... 858 565-0751
9560 Ridgehaven Ct Ste B San Diego (92123) *(P-10838)*

Essilor Laboratories Amer Inc .... E...... 310 604-8668
1450 W Walnut St Compton (90220) *(P-10839)*

Essilor Laboratories Amer Inc .... E...... 626 969-6181
1300 W Optical Dr Irwindale (91702) *(P-12524)*

Esslinger Engineering Inc .... E...... 909 539-0544
5946 Freedom Dr Chino (91710) *(P-9389)*

Estancia Hotel LLC .... C...... 949 474-7368
9700 N Torrey Pines Rd La Jolla (92037) *(P-15148)*

Estancia La Jolla Hotel & Spa, La Jolla *Also Called: Estancia Hotel LLC (P-15148)*

Estates At Trump Nat Golf CLB .... C...... 310 265-5000
1 Trump National Dr Rancho Palos Verdes (90275) *(P-17427)*

Esterline Mason, Rancho Cascades *Also Called: Janco Corporation (P-9068)*

Esterline Technologies Corp .... E...... 805 238-2840
1740 Commerce Way Paso Robles (93446) *(P-9685)*

Estes, City Of Industry *Also Called: Estes Express Lines (P-11486)*

Estes Express Lines .... C...... 714 994-3770
14727 Alondra Blvd La Mirada (90638) *(P-11485)*

Estes Express Lines .... D...... 626 333-9090
13327 Temple Ave City Of Industry (91746) *(P-11486)*

Estes Express Lines .... C...... 909 427-9850
10736 Cherry Ave Fontana (92337) *(P-11487)*

Estes Express Lines .... D...... 619 425-4040
120 Press Ln Chula Vista (91910) *(P-11488)*

Estify Inc .... E...... 801 341-1911
5023 Parkway Calabasas Calabasas (91302) *(P-16240)*

Estrella Inc .... C...... 562 925-6418
1340 Highland Ave # 12 Duarte (91010) *(P-17949)*

Estudysite .... C...... 619 955-5246
752 Medical Center Ct Ste 304 Chula Vista (91911) *(P-19837)*

Et Whitehall Seascape LLC .... C...... 310 581-5533
1910 Ocean Way Santa Monica (90405) *(P-15149)*

Etap, Irvine *Also Called: Operation Technology Inc (P-16090)*

Etchandy Farms LLC .... D...... 805 983-4700
4324 E Vineyard Ave Oxnard (93036) *(P-15)*

Etekcity, Anaheim *Also Called: Etekcity Corporation (P-12631)*

Etekcity Corporation .... C...... 855 686-3835
1202 N Miller St Unit A Anaheim (92806) *(P-12631)*

Eternity Floors, Pacoima *Also Called: LA Hardwood Flooring Inc (P-2574)*

Etherwan Systems Inc .... D...... 714 779-3800
2301 E Winston Rd Anaheim (92806) *(P-16566)*

Ethicon Inc .... B...... 949 581-5799
33 Technology Dr Irvine (92618) *(P-10658)*

Ethos Seafood Group LLC .... D...... 312 858-3474
18531 S Broadwick St Rancho Dominguez (90220) *(P-1803)*

Ethosenergy Field Services LLC (DH) .... E...... 310 639-3523
10455 Slusher Dr # 12 Santa Fe Springs (90670) *(P-346)*

Eti B Si Professional, Commerce *Also Called: Eti Sound Systems Inc (P-8410)*

Eti Partners IV LLC .... E...... 949 273-4990
901 Wshngton Blvd Ste 208 Marina Del Rey (90292) *(P-8673)*

Eti Sound Systems Inc .... E...... 323 835-6660
5300 Harbor St Commerce (90040) *(P-8410)*

Eti Systems .... D...... 310 684-3664
1800 Century Park E Ste 600 Los Angeles (90067) *(P-10131)*

Etiwanda Power Plant, Rancho Cucamonga *Also Called: NRG California South LP (P-12029)*

Etnies, Lake Forest *Also Called: Sole Technology Inc (P-5282)*

Etrade 24 Inc .... E...... 818 712-0574
16600 Calneva Dr Encino (91436) *(P-2140)*

Etro USA Incorporated .... F...... 310 248-2855
9501 Wilshire Blvd Beverly Hills (90212) *(P-2238)*

Ets Express, Oxnard *Also Called: Ets Express LLC (P-6703)*

Ets Express LLC (DH) .... **E...... 805 278-7771**
420 Lombard St Oxnard (93030) *(P-6703)*

Eturns Inc .... E...... 949 265-2626
19700 Fairchild Ste 290 Irvine (92612) *(P-16241)*

Eubanks Engineering Co (PA) .... **E...... 909 483-2456**
1921 S Quaker Ridge Pl Ontario (91761) *(P-7168)*

Eufora, Carlsbad *Also Called: Eden Beauty Concepts Inc (P-4408)*

Eugenios Sheet Metal Inc .... E...... 909 923-2002
2151 Maple Privado Ontario (91761) *(P-6234)*

Euhomy LLC .... E...... 213 265-5081
1230 Santa Anita Ave South El Monte (91733) *(P-4696)*

Euro Bello USA .... E...... 213 446-2818
10660 Wilshire Blvd Apt 601 Los Angeles (90024) *(P-2429)*

Euro Coffee, Vernon *Also Called: Eberine Enterprises Inc (P-1817)*

Euroamerican Propagators LLC .... B...... 760 731-6029
32149 Aquaduct Rd Bonsall (92003) *(P-53)*

Eurobizusa Inc .... F...... 626 793-0032
572 E Green St Ste 301 Pasadena (91101) *(P-1625)*

Eurocraft Archtectural Met Inc .... E...... 323 771-1323
5619 Watcher St Bell Gardens (90201) *(P-6357)*

Eurodrip USA Inc .... D...... 559 674-2670
7545 Carroll Rd San Diego (92121) *(P-12780)*

Eurofins Eaton Analytical LLC (DH) .... **D...... 626 386-1100**
750 Royal Oaks Dr Ste 100 Monrovia (91016) *(P-19971)*

Euroline Steel Windows .... E...... 877 590-2741
22600 Savi Ranch Pkwy Ste E Yorba Linda (92887) *(P-6105)*

Euroline Steel Windows & Doors, Yorba Linda *Also Called: Euroline Steel Windows (P-6105)*

Europa Auto Imports Inc .... C...... 858 569-6900
4750 Kearny Mesa Rd San Diego (92111) *(P-13764)*

Europcar, Los Angeles *Also Called: Fox Rent A Car Inc (P-16982)*

European Ht Invstors I I A Cal .... D...... 949 474-7368
2532 Dupont Dr Irvine (92612) *(P-15150)*

European Wholesale Counter .... C...... 619 562-0565
10051 Prospect Ave Santee (92071) *(P-2952)*

Eurotec Seating, La Habra *Also Called: Orbo Corporation (P-2934)*

Eurotec Seating Incorporated .... E...... 562 806-6171
1000 S Euclid St La Habra (90631) *(P-2926)*

Eurotech Luxury Shower Doors, Laguna Hills *Also Called: Eurotech Showers Inc (P-4914)*

Eurotech Showers Inc .... E...... 949 716-4099
23552 Commerce Center Dr Ste B Laguna Hills (92653) *(P-4914)*

Eurow and OReilly Corp .... E...... 800 747-7452
51 Moreland Rd Simi Valley (93065) *(P-13536)*

Eurton Electric Company Inc .... E...... 562 946-4477
9920 Painter Ave Whittier (90605) *(P-17105)*

Ev R Inc .... E...... 323 312-5400
3400 Slauson Ave Maywood (90270) *(P-2322)*

Ev Ray Inc .... E...... 818 346-5381
6400 Variel Ave Woodland Hills (91367) *(P-12300)*

Ev3 Neurovascular, Irvine *Also Called: Micro Therapeutics Inc (P-10566)*

Evans Alloys .... E...... 714 373-2515
15701 Graham St Huntington Beach (92649) *(P-6235)*

Evans Hydro, Compton *Also Called: Evans Hydro Inc (P-17126)*

Evans Hydro Inc .... E...... 310 608-5801
18128 S Santa Fe Ave Compton (90221) *(P-17126)*

Evans Industries Inc .... D...... 626 912-1688
17915 Railroad St City Of Industry (91748) *(P-6862)*

Evans Manufacturing, Garden Grove *Also Called: Evans Manufacturing Inc (P-11116)*

Evans Manufacturing Inc (HQ) .... **C...... 714 379-6100**
7422 Chapman Ave Garden Grove (92841) *(P-11116)*

Evans Walker Enterprises .... E...... 951 784-7223
2304 Fleetwood Dr Riverside (92509) *(P-9390)*

Evans, Walker Racing, Riverside *Also Called: Evans Walker Enterprises (P-9390)*

Eve, Lakewood *Also Called: Eve Hair Inc (P-13537)*

Eve Hair Inc (PA) .... **E...... 562 377-1020**
3935 Paramount Blvd Lakewood (90712) *(P-13537)*

Mergent email: customerrelations@mergent.com
1084

2024 Southern California
Business Directory and Buyers Guide

(P-0000) Products & Services Section entry number
(PA)=Parent Co (HQ)=Headquarters (DH)=Div Headquarters

Event Intelligence Group .... D....... 310 237-5375
   4140 Jackson Ave Culver City (90232) *(P-16735)*

Eventscom Inc .... E...... 858 257-2300
   811 Prospect St La Jolla (92037) *(P-16242)*

Ever Blue, Los Angeles *Also Called: California Blue Apparel Inc (P-2278)*

Ever Increasing Faith Ministry, Los Angeles *Also Called: Crenshaw Chrstn Ctr Ch Los Ang (P-19499)*

Everbrands Inc .... E...... 855 595-2999
   401 N Oak St Inglewood (90302) *(P-4409)*

Everbridge Inc (PA) .... **C....... 818 230-9700**
   155 N Lake Ave Ste 900 Pasadena (91101) *(P-16243)*

Everde Growers, Fallbrook *Also Called: Treesap Farms LLC (P-88)*

Everest Group USA Inc .... E...... 909 923-1818
   2030 S Carlos Ave Ontario (91761) *(P-5879)*

Everfilt, Jurupa Valley *Also Called: Puri Tech Inc (P-7681)*

Everfocus Electronics Corp (HQ) .... **E...... 626 844-8888**
   324 W Blueridge Ave Orange (92865) *(P-12659)*

Evergreen At Lakeport LLC .... D...... 661 871-3133
   6212 Tudor Way Bakersfield (93306) *(P-17950)*

Evergreen Environmental Svcs, Gardena *Also Called: Evergreen Oil Inc (P-4684)*

Evergreen Fullerton Healthcare, Fullerton *Also Called: Fullerton Hlthcare Wllness CNT (P-17956)*

Evergreen Health Care LLC .... A...... 661 854-4475
   323 Campus Dr Arvin (93203) *(P-17951)*

Evergreen Healthcare Center, Bakersfield *Also Called: Evergreen At Lakeport LLC (P-17950)*

Evergreen Holdings Inc (PA) .... **E... 949 757-7770**
   18952 Macarthur Blvd Ste 410 Irvine (92612) *(P-4683)*

Evergreen Industries Inc (DH) .... D..... 323 583-1331
   2254 E 49th St Vernon (90058) *(P-10092)*

Evergreen Lighting, Pomona *Also Called: Yawitz Inc (P-8301)*

Evergreen Oil Inc (HQ) .... **E... 949 757-7770**
   18025 S Broadway Gardena (90248) *(P-4684)*

Evergreen Scientific, Vernon *Also Called: Evergreen Industries Inc (P-10092)*

Evergreen Solar Services, Agoura Hills *Also Called: Ess LLC (P-768)*

Everidge Inc .... E...... 909 605-6419
   8886 White Oak Ave Rancho Cucamonga (91730) *(P-7613)*

Everleigh, Los Angeles *Also Called: J Heyri Inc (P-2245)*

Evernote Corporation (PA) .... **B..... 650 216-7700**
   12671 High Bluff Dr San Diego (92130) *(P-16029)*

Everpark Inc .... C...... 310 987-6922
   3470 Wilshire Blvd Ste 940 Los Angeles (90010) *(P-16990)*

Everson Spice Company Inc .... E...... 562 595-4785
   2667 Gundry Ave Long Beach (90755) *(P-1889)*

Everspring, Los Angeles *Also Called: Everspring Chemical Inc (P-4604)*

Everspring Chemical Inc .... E...... 310 707-1600
   11577 W Olympic Blvd Los Angeles (90064) *(P-4604)*

Everytable, Los Angeles *Also Called: Everytable Pbc (P-1890)*

Everytable Pbc .... E...... 323 296-0311
   3650 W Martin Luther King Jr Blvd Los Angeles (90008) *(P-1890)*

Evgo Montgomery Co, Los Angeles *Also Called: Evgo Services LLC (P-13891)*

Evgo Services LLC .... B..... 310 954-2900
   11835 W Olympic Blvd Ste 900e Los Angeles (90064) *(P-13891)*

Evocative Inc .... D...... 888 365-2656
   600 W 7th St Ste 510 Los Angeles (90017) *(P-16244)*

Evofem, San Diego *Also Called: Evofem Biosciences Inc (P-4110)*

Evofem Biosciences Inc (PA) .... **E...... 858 550-1900**
   12400 High Bluff Dr Ste 600 San Diego (92130) *(P-4110)*

Evolife Scientific Llc .... E...... 888 750-0310
   3150 Long Beach Blvd Long Beach (90807) *(P-4000)*

EVOLUS, Newport Beach *Also Called: Evolus Inc (P-4111)*

Evolus Inc (PA) .... **D... 949 284-4555**
   520 Newport Center Dr Ste 1200 Newport Beach (92660) *(P-4111)*

Evolution Design Lab Inc .... E...... 626 960-8388
   144 W Colorado Blvd Pasadena (91105) *(P-5275)*

Evolution Fresh Inc .... C...... 800 794-9986
   11655 Jersey Blvd Ste A Rancho Cucamonga (91730) *(P-13320)*

Evolution Juice, Rancho Cucamonga *Also Called: Evolution Fresh Inc (P-13320)*

Evolution Robotics Inc .... C...... 626 993-3300
   1055 E Colorado Blvd Ste 320 Pasadena (91106) *(P-16245)*

Evolve Dental Technologies Inc .... E...... 949 713-0909
   5 Vanderbilt Irvine (92618) *(P-10744)*

Evolve Treatment Centers .... D....... 310 622-1420
   600 N Sepulveda Blvd Los Angeles (90049) *(P-18692)*

Evonik Corporation .... C...... 323 264-0311
   3305 E 26th St Vernon (90058) *(P-4605)*

Evoq Properties Inc .... D...... 213 988-8890
   1318 E 7th St Ste 200 Los Angeles (90021) *(P-14792)*

Evoqua Water Technologies LLC .... E...... 213 748-8511
   1441 E Washington Blvd Los Angeles (90021) *(P-14132)*

Evoralight, Costa Mesa *Also Called: Flexfire Leds Inc (P-8312)*

Evy of California Inc .... C...... 213 746-4647
   2042 Garfield Ave Commerce (90040) *(P-2407)*

Ew Corprtion Indus Fabricators (PA) .... **D....... 760 337-0020**
   1002 E Main St El Centro (92243) *(P-6023)*

EW Scripps Company .... C...... 619 237-1010
   4600 Air Way San Diego (92102) *(P-11947)*

Eworkplace Manufacturing Inc .... C...... 949 583-1646
   9861 Irvine Center Dr Irvine (92618) *(P-12412)*

Exagen Inc .... C...... 505 272-7966
   1261 Liberty Way Ste C Vista (92081) *(P-18549)*

Examone, San Diego *Also Called: Examone World Wide Inc (P-18763)*

Examone World Wide Inc .... D...... 619 299-3926
   7480 Mission Valley Rd Ste 101 San Diego (92108) *(P-18763)*

Excalibur Extrusion Inc .... E...... 714 528-8834
   110 E Crowther Ave Placentia (92870) *(P-4847)*

Excalibur International, Long Beach *Also Called: A W Chang Corporation (P-13078)*

Excalibur Well Services Corp .... C...... 661 589-5338
   22034 Rosedale Hwy Bakersfield (93314) *(P-281)*

Excel Bridge Manufacturing Co., Santa Fe Springs *Also Called: Excel Sheet Metal Inc (P-6236)*

Excel Cabinets Inc .... E...... 951 279-4545
   225 Jason Ct Corona (92879) *(P-2658)*

Excel Contractors Inc .... D...... 661 942-6944
   348 E Avenue K8 Ste B Lancaster (93535) *(P-432)*

Excel Landscape Inc .... C...... 951 735-9650
   710 Rimpau Ave Ste 108 Corona (92879) *(P-190)*

Excel Mdular Scaffold Lsg Corp .... A...... 760 598-0050
   2555 Birch St Vista (92081) *(P-1155)*

Excel Paving Co, Long Beach *Also Called: Palp Inc (P-638)*

Excel Picture Frames Inc .... E...... 323 231-0244
   647 E 59th St Los Angeles (90001) *(P-17127)*

Excel Scientific LLC .... E...... 760 246-4545
   18350 George Blvd Victorville (92394) *(P-12526)*

Excel Sheet Metal Inc (PA) .... **D...... 562 944-0701**
   12001 Shoemaker Ave Santa Fe Springs (90670) *(P-6236)*

Excelity .... D...... 818 767-1000
   11127 Dora St Sun Valley (91352) *(P-5812)*

Excell Staffing & SEC Svcs, El Cajon *Also Called: Xl Staffing Inc (P-15908)*

Excellence Opto Inc (PA) .... **E...... 909 468-0550**
   21858 Garcia Ln Walnut (91789) *(P-8346)*

Excelline Food Products LLC .... E...... 818 701-7710
   833 N Hollywood Way Burbank (91505) *(P-1390)*

Excello Circuits Inc .... D...... 714 993-0560
   5330 E Hunter Ave Anaheim (92807) *(P-8674)*

Excellon Acquisition LLC (HQ) .... **E...... 310 668-7700**
   16130 Gundry Ave Paramount (90723) *(P-7234)*

Excellon Automation Co, Paramount *Also Called: Excellon Acquisition LLC (P-7234)*

Excellos Incorporated .... E...... 619 400-8235
   1155 Island Ave San Diego (92101) *(P-4314)*

Excelpro Inc (PA) .... **F....... 323 415-8544**
   1630 Amapola Ave Torrance (90501) *(P-1254)*

Excelsior Nutrition Inc .... D....... 657 999-5188
   1206 N Miller St Unit D Anaheim (92806) *(P-4001)*

Exclsus A Division of Pulse .... E...... 760 476-1511
   2875 Loker Ave E Carlsbad (92010) *(P-8472)*

Exceptional Chld Foundation .... C...... 213 748-3556
   1430 Venice Blvd Los Angeles (90006) *(P-19183)*

Exceptional Chld Foundation (PA) .... **C...... 310 204-3300**
   5350 Machado Ln Culver City (90230) *(P-19184)*

Exceptional Chld Foundation .... C...... 310 915-6606
   11124 Fairbanks Way Culver City (90230) *(P-19446)*

Execuprint Inc .... F...... 818 993-8184
   24963 Avenue Tibbitts Santa Clarita (91355) *(P-16496)*

Employee Codes: A=Over 500 employees, B=251-500
C=101-250, D=51-100, E=20-49, F=10-19, G=1-9

2024 Southern California
Business Directory and Buyers Guide

© Mergent Inc. 1-800-342-5647
1085

A
L
P
H
A
B
E
T
I
C

Executive Auto Reconditioning .... E...... 626 416-3322
522 E Duarte Rd Monrovia (91016) *(P-17048)*

Executive Car Leasing Company (PA).............. D...... 800 800-3932
7807 Santa Monica Blvd West Hollywood (90046) *(P-16985)*

Executive Committee, The, San Diego *Also Called: Vistage International Inc (P-20268)*

Executive Landscape Inc .... C...... 760 731-9036
2131 Huffstatler St Fallbrook (92028) *(P-160)*

Executive Network Entps Inc (PA).............. D...... 310 447-2759
13440 Beach Ave Marina Del Rey (90292) *(P-11383)*

Executive Network Entps Inc .... A...... 310 457-8822
1224 21st St Apt E Santa Monica (90404) *(P-11384)*

Executive Personnel Services .... B...... 714 310-9506
1526 Brookhollow Dr Ste 83 Santa Ana (92705) *(P-15846)*

Executive Safe and SEC Corp .... E...... 909 947-7020
10722 Edison Ct Rancho Cucamonga (91730) *(P-6863)*

Exemplis LLC .... E...... 714 995-4800
6280 Artesia Blvd Buena Park (90620) *(P-2911)*

Exemplis LLC (PA).............. E...... 714 995-4800
6415 Katella Ave Cypress (90630) *(P-2912)*

Exemptax, Irvine *Also Called: Dacenso Inc (P-16220)*

Exer, Simi Valley *Also Called: Providnce Facey Med Foundation (P-17851)*

Exer Holding Company LLC .... C...... 818 287-0894
15503 Ventura Blvd Encino (91436) *(P-17651)*

Exeter Packers Inc .... C...... 626 993-6245
1095 E Green St Pasadena (91106) *(P-42)*

Exeter Packers Inc .... C...... 661 399-0416
33374 Lerdo Hwy Bakersfield (93308) *(P-11551)*

Exhaust Tech, Commerce *Also Called: Dynaflex Products (P-9323)*

Exigent Sensors LLC .... E...... 949 439-1321
11441 Markon Dr Garden Grove (92841) *(P-8611)*

Exois Inc .... C...... 408 777-6630
2567 Ingleton Ave Carlsbad (92009) *(P-16567)*

Expak Logistics, Los Angeles *Also Called: Kxp Carrier Services LLC (P-11532)*

Expand Machinery LLC .... F...... 818 349-9166
20869 Plummer St Chatsworth (91311) *(P-7828)*

Expanded Rubber & Plastics Corp .... E...... 310 324-6692
19200 S Laurel Park Rd Rancho Dominguez (90220) *(P-5026)*

Expeditors International, Hawthorne *Also Called: Expeditors Intl Wash Inc (P-11760)*

Expeditors Intl Wash Inc .... B...... 310 343-6200
19701 Hamilton Ave Torrance (90502) *(P-11759)*

Expeditors Intl Wash Inc .... D...... 310 343-6200
12200 Wilkie Ave # 100 Hawthorne (90250) *(P-11760)*

Experian, Costa Mesa *Also Called: Experian Info Solutions Inc (P-15622)*

Experian Info Solutions Inc (DH).............. A...... 714 830-7000
475 Anton Blvd Costa Mesa (92626) *(P-15622)*

Experian Marketing, Costa Mesa *Also Called: Experian Mktg Solutions LLC (P-15623)*

Experian Mktg Solutions LLC .... A...... 714 830-7000
475 Anton Blvd Costa Mesa (92626) *(P-15623)*

Experian Qas, Costa Mesa *Also Called: Marigold Usa Inc (P-16070)*

Expert Assembly Services Inc .... E...... 714 258-8880
14312 Chambers Rd Ste B Tustin (92780) *(P-8675)*

Expert Ems, Tustin *Also Called: Expert Assembly Services Inc (P-8675)*

Exploding Kittens LLC .... E...... 310 788-8699
101 S La Brea Ave S A Los Angeles (90036) *(P-10952)*

Expo Builders Supply, San Diego *Also Called: Expo Industries Inc (P-12328)*

Expo Dyeing & Finishing Inc .... C...... 714 220-9583
1365 N Knollwood Cir Anaheim (92801) *(P-2100)*

Expo Industries Inc .... D...... 858 566-3110
7455 Carroll Rd San Diego (92121) *(P-12328)*

Expo Power Systems Inc .... E...... 800 506-9884
5534 Olive St Montclair (91763) *(P-12595)*

Expo-3 International Inc .... E...... 714 379-8383
12350 Edison Way 60 Garden Grove (92841) *(P-11117)*

Express, San Diego *Also Called: Express Business Systems Inc (P-3758)*

Express Business Systems Inc .... E...... 858 549-9828
9155 Trade Pl San Diego (92126) *(P-3758)*

Express Container Inc .... E...... 909 798-3857
5450 Dodds Ave Buena Park (90621) *(P-3099)*

Express Contractors Inc .... D...... 951 360-6500
3810 Wacker Dr Jurupa Valley (91752) *(P-15468)*

Express Die Supply Inc .... E...... 562 903-1700
10020 Freeman Ave Santa Fe Springs (90670) *(P-7069)*

Express Imaging Services Inc .... D...... 888 846-8804
1805 W 208th St Ste 202 Torrance (90501) *(P-11633)*

Express Manufacturing Inc (PA).............. B...... 714 979-2228
3519 W Warner Ave Santa Ana (92704) *(P-9043)*

Expro Manufacturing Corporation .... E...... 323 415-8544
2800 Ayers Ave Vernon (90058) *(P-1324)*

Exrox Inc .... E...... 213 536-5290
535 Ceres Ave Los Angeles (90013) *(P-4761)*

Extensions Plus, Tarzana *Also Called: Extensions Plus Inc (P-12890)*

Extensions Plus Inc .... E...... 818 881-5611
5428 Reseda Blvd Tarzana (91356) *(P-12890)*

Extreme Group Holdings LLC .... E...... 310 899-3200
1531 14th St Santa Monica (90404) *(P-8459)*

Extreme Production Music, Santa Monica *Also Called: Extreme Group Holdings LLC (P-8459)*

Extron Electronics, Anaheim *Also Called: Rgb Systems Inc (P-7567)*

Extrude Hone Abrsive Flow McHn, Paramount *Also Called: Extrude Hone Deburring Svc Inc (P-7829)*

Extrude Hone Deburring Svc Inc .... E...... 562 531-2976
8800 Somerset Blvd Paramount (90723) *(P-7829)*

Extrumed Inc (DH).............. E...... 951 547-7400
547 Trm Cir Corona (92879) *(P-5027)*

Exult Inc .... A...... 949 856-8800
121 Innovation Dr Ste 200 Irvine (92617) *(P-20169)*

Exxel Outdoors Inc .... C...... 626 369-7278
343 Baldwin Park Blvd City Of Industry (91746) *(P-2551)*

Exxon, Goleta *Also Called: Exxon Mobil Corporation (P-13892)*

Exxon Mobil Corporation .... E...... 805 961-4093
12000 Calle Real Goleta (93117) *(P-13892)*

Ey, Irvine *Also Called: Ernst & Young LLP (P-19773)*

Ey, Los Angeles *Also Called: Ernst & Young LLP (P-19774)*

Ey, San Diego *Also Called: Ernst & Young LLP (P-19775)*

Eye Exam of California, San Diego *Also Called: James G Meyers & Associates (P-17855)*

Eyeline Studios, Los Angeles *Also Called: Scanlinevfx La LLC (P-17218)*

Eyeonics Inc .... E...... 949 788-6000
15273 Alton Pkwy Ste 100 Irvine (92618) *(P-10840)*

Eyeshadow, Los Angeles *Also Called: Stony Apparel Corp (P-2264)*

EZ Lube LLC .... D...... 951 766-1996
532 W Florida Ave Hemet (92543) *(P-4685)*

EZ Lube LLC .... C...... 714 966-1647
3599 Harbor Blvd Costa Mesa (92626) *(P-17055)*

EZ Lube LLC .... C...... 310 821-2517
13421 Washington Blvd Marina Del Rey (90292) *(P-17056)*

EZ Lube- Costco, Marina Del Rey *Also Called: EZ Lube LLC (P-17056)*

Ezaki Glico, Irvine *Also Called: Ezaki Glico USA Corporation (P-1538)*

Ezaki Glico USA Corporation .... F...... 949 251-0144
18022 Cowan Ste 110 Irvine (92614) *(P-1538)*

Ezcaretech Usa Inc .... B...... 424 558-3191
21081 S Western Ave Ste 130 Torrance (90501) *(P-13538)*

Ezekiel, Costa Mesa *Also Called: 3 Point Distribution LLC (P-2188)*

Ezviz Inc .... C...... 855 693-9849
18639 Railroad St City Of Industry (91748) *(P-16736)*

F & D Flores Enterprises Inc .... E...... 909 975-4853
761 E Francis St Ontario (91761) *(P-10363)*

F & E Arcft Mint Los Angles LL .... B...... 310 338-0063
531 Main St Ste 672 El Segundo (90245) *(P-11697)*

F & L Industrial Solutions, Poway *Also Called: Motion Industries Inc (P-12866)*

F & L Tls Precision Machining, Corona *Also Called: F & L Tools Corporation (P-7830)*

F & L Tools Corporation .... F...... 951 279-1555
245 Jason Ct Corona (92879) *(P-7830)*

F C I, San Marcos *Also Called: Fluid Components Intl LLC (P-10132)*

F C I, Anaheim *Also Called: Fci Lender Services Inc (P-15612)*

F Gavina & Sons Inc .... B...... 323 582-0671
2700 Fruitland Ave Vernon (90058) *(P-1819)*

F I N, Granada Hills *Also Called: Financial Info Netwrk Inc (P-16033)*

F I O Imports Inc .... C...... 323 263-5100
5980 Alcoa Ave Vernon (90058) *(P-1891)*

F I T, Compton *Also Called: Fastener Innovation Tech Inc (P-6414)*

F J & J Corporation ....F...... 505 452-1700
6938 Shadygrove St Tujunga (91042) *(P-17251)*

F M H, Irvine *Also Called: Fmh Aerospace Corp (P-9692)*

F M I, Santa Ana *Also Called: Flexible Manufacturing LLC (P-8970)*

F M P, Downey *Also Called: Florence Meat Packing Co Inc (P-14009)*

F M Tarbell Co (HQ) ....C...... 714 972-0988
1403 N Tustin Ave Ste 380 Santa Ana (92705) *(P-14793)*

F O X, Los Angeles *Also Called: Fox Sports Inc (P-11950)*

F R T International Inc (PA) ....D...... 310 604-8208
1700 N Alameda St Compton (90222) *(P-11576)*

F T B & Son Inc ....E...... 714 891-8003
11551 Markon Dr Garden Grove (92841) *(P-6237)*

F T I, Long Beach *Also Called: Fundamental Tech Intl Inc (P-10133)*

F-J-E Inc ....E...... 562 437-7466
546 W Esther St Long Beach (90813) *(P-2953)*

F&M Bank, Long Beach *Also Called: Farmers Merchants Bnk Long Bch (P-14195)*

F6s Network Limited ....D...... 619 818-4363
16935 Encino Hills Dr Encino (91436) *(P-19838)*

FAA Beverly Hills Inc ....D...... 323 801-1430
5070 Wilshire Blvd Los Angeles (90036) *(P-13765)*

Fab Services West Inc ....D...... 909 350-7500
10007 Elm Ave Fontana (92335) *(P-6397)*

Fabco Steel Fabrication Inc ....E...... 909 350-1535
14688 San Bernardino Ave Fontana (92335) *(P-6024)*

Fabcon, Santa Ana *Also Called: Fabrication Concepts Corporation (P-6238)*

Fabcon, Valencia *Also Called: Bayless Manufacturing LLC (P-7777)*

Faber Enterprises Inc ....C...... 310 323-6200
14800 S Figueroa St Gardena (90248) *(P-6776)*

Fabfad LLC ....F...... 213 488-0456
1901 E 7th Pl Los Angeles (90021) *(P-3759)*

Fabri Cote, Los Angeles *Also Called: Rdmm Legacy Inc (P-13091)*

Fabric8labs Inc ....D...... 858 215-1142
10788 Roselle St Ste 101 San Diego (92121) *(P-7185)*

Fabrica Fine Carpet, Santa Ana *Also Called: Fabrica International Inc (P-2114)*

Fabrica International Inc ....C...... 949 261-7181
3201 S Susan St Santa Ana (92704) *(P-2114)*

Fabricast Inc (PA) ....E...... 626 443-3247
2517 Seaman Ave South El Monte (91733) *(P-9044)*

Fabricated Components Corp ....C...... 714 974-8590
130 W Bristol Ln Orange (92865) *(P-8676)*

Fabrication Concepts Corporation ....C...... 714 881-2000
1800 E Saint Andrew Pl Santa Ana (92705) *(P-6238)*

Fabrication Tech Inds Inc ....D...... 619 477-4141
2200 Haffley Ave National City (91950) *(P-6025)*

Fabricmate, Ventura *Also Called: Fabricmate Systems Inc (P-2038)*

Fabricmate Systems Inc ....E...... 805 642-7470
2781 Golf Course Dr Unit A Ventura (93003) *(P-2038)*

Fabritec Structures, Tustin *Also Called: Shade Structures Inc (P-6312)*

Fabtex Inc ....C...... 714 538-0877
615 S State College Blvd Fullerton (92831) *(P-2039)*

Fabtronics Inc ....E...... 626 962-3293
5026 Calmview Ave Baldwin Park (91706) *(P-6239)*

Facefirst LLC ....E...... 805 482-8428
31416 Agoura Rd Ste 250 Westlake Village (91361) *(P-16246)*

Facey Medical Group, Santa Clarita *Also Called: Providnce Facey Med Foundation (P-18791)*

Facilitec West, Covina *Also Called: Stavros Enterprises Inc (P-17154)*

Facilities MGT & Coml RPS Svcs, Anaheim *Also Called: Branded Group Inc (P-20144)*

Facility Makers Inc ....E...... 714 544-1702
345 W Freedom Ave Orange (92865) *(P-6240)*

Facter Direct Ltd ....B...... 323 634-1999
4751 Wilshire Blvd Ste 140 Los Angeles (90010) *(P-16823)*

Factory One Studio Inc ....D...... 323 752-1670
6700 Avalon Blvd Ste 101 Los Angeles (90003) *(P-2020)*

Factory Showroom Exchange, Los Angeles *Also Called: Sofa U Love LLC (P-2818)*

Factron Test Fixtures, Poway *Also Called: Cohu Interface Solutions LLC (P-10192)*

Fahetas LLC (PA) ....D...... 949 280-1983
1419 N Tustin St Ste A Orange (92867) *(P-14005)*

Fair Financial Corp (PA) ....B...... 800 584-5000
1540 2nd St Ste 200 Santa Monica (90401) *(P-16030)*

Fair Price Carpets, Riverside *Also Called: Fairprice Enterprises Inc (P-13951)*

Fairbanks Ranch Cntry CLB Inc ....C...... 858 259-8811
15150 San Dieguito Rd Rancho Santa Fe (92067) *(P-17484)*

Fairfeld Inn By Mrrott Ltd Prt ....C...... 714 772-6777
1460 S Harbor Blvd Anaheim (92802) *(P-15151)*

Fairfield Development Inc (PA) ....C...... 858 457-2123
5355 Mira Sorrento Pl Ste 100 San Diego (92121) *(P-470)*

Fairfield Inn, El Centro *Also Called: El Centro Hospitality LLC (P-15142)*

Fairfield Properties, San Diego *Also Called: Ffrt Residential LLC (P-14708)*

Fairmont Designs, Buena Park *Also Called: Cambium Business Group Inc (P-12279)*

Fairmont Miramar Hotel, Santa Monica *Also Called: Ocean Avenue LLC (P-15268)*

Fairplex Enterprises Inc ....C...... 909 623-3111
1101 W Mckinley Ave Pomona (91768) *(P-17549)*

Fairplex Rv Park, Pomona *Also Called: Los Angeles County Fair Assn (P-17556)*

Fairprice Enterprises Inc ....D...... 951 684-8578
1070 Center St Riverside (92507) *(P-13951)*

Fairview Developmental Center, Costa Mesa *Also Called: Califrnia Dept State Hospitals (P-18506)*

Fairview Developmental Center, Costa Mesa *Also Called: Califrnia Dept Dvlpmental Svcs (P-19179)*

Fairway Import-Export Inc ....E...... 262 788-7313
2130 E Gladwick St Rancho Dominguez (90220) *(P-10989)*

Fairway Injection Molds Inc ....D...... 909 595-2201
20109 Paseo Del Prado Walnut (91789) *(P-7070)*

Fairway Technologies LLC (PA) ....D...... 858 454-4471
4370 La Jolla Village Dr Ste 500 San Diego (92122) *(P-20170)*

Fairwinds-West Hills, West Hills *Also Called: Leisure Care LLC (P-18089)*

Faith Electric LLC ....C...... 909 767-2682
1980 Orange Tree Ln Ste 106 Redlands (92374) *(P-899)*

Faith Jones & Associates Inc (PA) ....D...... 619 297-9601
7801 Mission Center Ct Ste 106 San Diego (92108) *(P-18613)*

Falck Mobile Health Corp ....B...... 323 720-1578
212 S Atlantic Blvd Ste 102 Los Angeles (90022) *(P-11385)*

Falck Mobile Health Corp ....B...... 714 828-7750
8932 Katella Ave Ste 201 Anaheim (92804) *(P-11386)*

Falcon Abrasive Mfg Inc ....F...... 909 598-3078
5490 Brooks St Montclair (91763) *(P-5541)*

Falcon Aerospace Holdings LLC ....A...... 661 775-7200
27727 Avenue Scott Valencia (91355) *(P-12907)*

Falcon Waterfree Tech LLC (HQ) ....E...... 310 209-7250
2255 Barry Ave Los Angeles (90064) *(P-4762)*

Falken Tire, Rancho Cucamonga *Also Called: Sumitomo Rubber North Amer Inc (P-12273)*

Falken Tire Holdings Inc ....D...... 800 723-2553
8656 Haven Ave Rancho Cucamonga (91730) *(P-12268)*

Falken Tires, Rancho Cucamonga *Also Called: Falken Tire Holdings Inc (P-12268)*

Falkner Winery Inc ....D...... 951 676-6741
40620 Calle Contento Temecula (92591) *(P-1626)*

Falkor Partners LLC ....E...... 714 721-8772
333 Mccormick Ave Costa Mesa (92626) *(P-8796)*

Fallas Discount Stores, Gardena *Also Called: J & M Sales Inc (P-13922)*

Fallbrook Bonsall Village News, Temecula *Also Called: Village News Inc (P-3334)*

Fallbrook Industries Inc ....E...... 760 728-7229
323 Industrial Way Ste 1 Fallbrook (92028) *(P-6516)*

Falltech, Compton *Also Called: Andrew Alexander Inc (P-5254)*

Fam LLC (PA) ....D...... 323 888-7755
5553 Bandini Blvd B Bell (90201) *(P-2049)*

Fam Brands, Bell *Also Called: Fam LLC (P-2049)*

Fam Ppe LLC ....C...... 323 888-7755
5553-B Bandini Blvd B Bell (90201) *(P-12974)*

Family Assistance Program ....D...... 760 843-0701
15075 Seventh St Victorville (92395) *(P-19079)*

Family Care Center, Ventura *Also Called: County of Ventura (P-20405)*

Family Health Center San Diego, Spring Valley *Also Called: Family Hlth Ctrs San Diego Inc (P-17655)*

Family Hlth Ctrs San Diego Inc ....B...... 619 515-2526
1845 Logan Ave San Diego (92113) *(P-17652)*

Family Hlth Ctrs San Diego Inc ....B...... 619 515-2435
2391 Island Ave San Diego (92102) *(P-17653)*

Family Hlth Ctrs San Diego Inc ....B...... 619 515-2400
5379 El Cajon Blvd San Diego (92115) *(P-17654)*

Employee Codes: A=Over 500 employees, B=251-500
C=101-250, D=51-100, E=20-50, F=10-19, G=1-9

2024 Southern California
Business Directory and Buyers Guide

© Mergent Inc. 1-800-342-5647
1087

Family Hlth Ctrs San Diego Inc .... B...... 619 515-2555
8788 Jamacha Rd Spring Valley (91977) *(P-17655)*

Family Hlth Ctrs San Diego Inc .... B...... 619 515-2444
3705 Mission Blvd San Diego (92109) *(P-17656)*

Family Hlth Ctrs San Diego Inc .... B...... 619 515-2300
1809 National Ave San Diego (92113) *(P-17837)*

Family Hlth Ctrs San Diego Inc .... B...... 619 515-2550
7592 Broadway Lemon Grove (91945) *(P-18764)*

Family Loompya Corporation .... E...... 619 477-2125
2626 Southport Way Ste F National City (91950) *(P-1892)*

Family Svc Agcy Snta Brbara CN .... D....... 805 965-1001
123 W Gutierrez St Santa Barbara (93101) *(P-19080)*

Family Tree Produce Inc .... C...... 714 693-5688
5510 E La Palma Ave Anaheim (92807) *(P-13321)*

Famoso Nut, Mc Farland *Also Called: Amaretto Orchards LLC (P-11188)*

Fan Fave Inc .... E...... 909 975-4999
10329 Dorset St Rancho Cucamonga (91730) *(P-11118)*

Fanboys Window Factory Inc (PA) .... E...... 626 280-8787
10750 Saint Louis Dr El Monte (91731) *(P-6106)*

Fancy Life Enterprises LLC (PA) .... C...... 619 560-9890
8030 La Mesa Blvd Pmb 3039 La Mesa (91942) *(P-17190)*

Fancy Life Studios, La Mesa *Also Called: Fancy Life Enterprises LLC (P-17190)*

Fanfave, Rancho Cucamonga *Also Called: Fan Fave Inc (P-11118)*

Fantasia Distribution Inc .... F...... 714 817-8300
1566 W Embassy St Anaheim (92802) *(P-2008)*

Fantasia Hookah Tobacco, Anaheim *Also Called: Fantasia Distribution Inc (P-2008)*

Fantasy Activewear Inc (PA) .... E...... 213 705-4111
5383 Alcoa Ave Vernon (90058) *(P-2068)*

Fantasy Cookie Company, Sylmar *Also Called: Fantasy Cookie Corporation (P-1517)*

Fantasy Cookie Corporation (PA) .... E...... 818 361-6901
12322 Gladstone Ave Sylmar (91342) *(P-1517)*

Fantasy Dyeing & Finishing Inc .... E...... 323 983-9988
5383 Alcoa Ave Vernon (90058) *(P-2069)*

Fantasy Manufacturing, Vernon *Also Called: Fantasy Activewear Inc (P-2068)*

Fantasy Springs Resort Casino, Indio *Also Called: East Valley Tourist Dev Auth (P-17547)*

Fantom Drives, Torrance *Also Called: Bnl Technologies Inc (P-7463)*

Far East National Bank .... B...... 213 687-1300
977 N Broadway Ste 306 Los Angeles (90012) *(P-20030)*

Far Out Toys Inc .... E...... 310 480-7554
300 N Pacific Coast Hwy Ste 1050 El Segundo (90245) *(P-10938)*

Far West Bond Services Cal Inc (PA) .... B...... 818 704-1111
5230 Las Virgenes Rd Calabasas (91302) *(P-14536)*

Far West Meats, Highland *Also Called: Raemica Inc (P-1232)*

Far West Technology Inc .... F...... 805 964-3615
330 S Kellogg Ave Ste B Goleta (93117) *(P-10364)*

Farchitecture Bb LLC .... E...... 917 701-2777
8588 Washington Blvd Culver City (90232) *(P-1297)*

Farley Interlocking Pav Stones, Palm Desert *Also Called: Farley Paving Stone Co Inc (P-5412)*

Farley Paving Stone Co Inc .... D...... 760 773-3960
39301 Badger St Palm Desert (92211) *(P-5412)*

Farm Street Designs Inc .... E...... 562 985-0026
2520 Mira Mar Ave Long Beach (90815) *(P-13476)*

Farmdale, San Bernardino *Also Called: Farmdale Creamery Inc (P-1310)*

Farmdale Creamery Inc .... D...... 909 888-4938
1049 W Base Line St San Bernardino (92411) *(P-1310)*

Farmers Group Inc (HQ) .... A...... 323 932-3200
6301 Owensmouth Ave Woodland Hills (91367) *(P-14587)*

Farmers Insurance .... C...... 951 681-1068
3600 Lime St Ste 122 Riverside (92501) *(P-14588)*

Farmers Insurance .... C...... 626 288-0870
113 Avondale Ave Monterey Park (91754) *(P-14589)*

Farmers Insurance .... B...... 818 876-3400
6303 Owensmouth Ave Fl 1 Woodland Hills (91367) *(P-14590)*

Farmers Insurance .... C...... 661 257-0844
27433 Tourney Rd Ste 170 Valencia (91355) *(P-14591)*

Farmers Insurance, Woodland Hills *Also Called: Farmers Group Inc (P-14587)*

Farmers Insurance, Woodland Hills *Also Called: Farmers Insurance (P-14590)*

Farmers Insurance, Woodland Hills *Also Called: Farmers Insurance Exchange (P-14592)*

Farmers Insurance Exchange (DH) .... A...... 888 327-6335
6301 Owensmouth Ave Woodland Hills (91367) *(P-14592)*

Farmers Link Inc .... D...... 213 623-5242
2858 E 26th St Vernon (90058) *(P-13322)*

Farmers Merchants Bnk Long Bch (HQ) .... C...... 562 437-0011
302 Pine Ave Long Beach (90802) *(P-14195)*

Farrar Grinding Company .... E...... 323 678-4879
347 E Beach Ave Inglewood (90302) *(P-9686)*

Farstone Technology Inc .... C...... 949 336-4321
184 Technology Dr Ste 205 Irvine (92618) *(P-9181)*

Farwest Insulation Contracting .... D...... 310 634-2800
2741 Yates Ave Commerce (90040) *(P-977)*

Fashion Logistics Inc .... C...... 424 201-4100
20550 Denker Ave Torrance (90501) *(P-11577)*

Fashion Resources, Vernon *Also Called: Tarrant Apparel Group (P-13153)*

Fashion World Incorporated .... C...... 310 273-6544
420 N Rodeo Dr Beverly Hills (90210) *(P-13102)*

Fashiongo .... F...... 213 745-2667
2250 Maple Ave Los Angeles (90011) *(P-2166)*

Fashiongo.com, Los Angeles *Also Called: Nhn Global Inc (P-13139)*

Fast Undercar, Ventura *Also Called: Parts Authority LLC (P-12251)*

Fastclick Inc .... A...... 805 689-9839
530 E Montecito St Santa Barbara (93103) *(P-15601)*

Fastclick.com, Santa Barbara *Also Called: Fastclick Inc (P-15601)*

Fastcor, Anaheim *Also Called: Bisco Industries Inc (P-12648)*

Fastec Imaging Corporation .... E...... 858 592-2342
17150 Via Del Campo Ste 301 San Diego (92127) *(P-10866)*

Fastener Dist Holdings LLC .... E...... 213 620-9950
5200 Sheila St Commerce (90040) *(P-9522)*

Fastener Dist Holdings LLC (HQ) .... E...... 213 620-9950
5200 Sheila St Commerce (90040) *(P-12854)*

Fastener Innovation Tech Inc .... D...... 310 538-1111
19300 S Susana Rd Compton (90221) *(P-6414)*

Fastener Technology Corp .... C...... 818 764-6467
7415 Fulton Ave North Hollywood (91605) *(P-12855)*

Fasthouse Inc .... E...... 661 775-5963
28757 Industry Dr Valencia (91355) *(P-10990)*

Fat Brands Inc (PA) .... B...... 310 319-1850
9720 Wilshire Blvd Ste 500 Beverly Hills (90212) *(P-14006)*

Fattail Inc (PA) .... E...... 818 615-0380
23586 Calabasas Rd Ste 102 Calabasas (91302) *(P-16031)*

Fax Star, Costa Mesa *Also Called: Sepe Inc (P-7449)*

Faze Clan Inc .... B...... 818 688-6373
720 N Cahuenga Blvd Los Angeles (90038) *(P-17550)*

Faze Holdings Inc (PA) .... C...... 818 688-6373
720 N Cahuenga Blvd Los Angeles (90038) *(P-17551)*

FB Corporation .... B...... 626 300-0880
1211 E Valley Blvd Alhambra (91801) *(P-14196)*

FB Productions Inc .... E...... 818 773-9337
12722 Riverside Dr Ste 204 Valley Village (91607) *(P-3571)*

Fc Management Services .... E...... 805 499-0050
2001 Anchor Ct Ste B Newbury Park (91320) *(P-7235)*

Fci Lender Services Inc .... C...... 800 931-2424
8180 E Kaiser Blvd Anaheim (92808) *(P-15612)*

FCKingston Co .... E...... 310 326-8287
23201 Normandie Ave Torrance (90501) *(P-6764)*

Fcp Inc (PA) .... D...... 951 678-4571
23100 Wildomar Trl Wildomar (92595) *(P-6377)*

Fcti Inc (PA) .... D...... 310 405-0022
11766 Wilshire Blvd Ste 300 Los Angeles (90025) *(P-14260)*

Fdh Aero, Commerce *Also Called: Fastener Dist Holdings LLC (P-9522)*

FDS Manufacturing Company (PA) .... D...... 909 591-1733
2200 S Reservoir St Pomona (91766) *(P-3237)*

FDS Manufacturing Company Svcs, Pomona *Also Called: Federated Diversified Sls Inc (P-3151)*

Fear of God LLC .... E...... 310 466-9751
558 S Alameda St Los Angeles (90013) *(P-2203)*

Federal Express Corporation .... D...... 800 463-3339
3333 S Grand Ave Los Angeles (90007) *(P-11676)*

Federal Heath Sign Company LLC .... C...... 760 941-0715
3609 Ocean Ranch Blvd Ste 204 Oceanside (92056) *(P-11119)*

Federal Home Loan Mrtg Corp .... A...... 213 337-4200
444 S Flower St Fl 44 Los Angeles (90071) *(P-14314)*

Federal Manufacturing Corp .... E....... 818 341-9825
9825 De Soto Ave Chatsworth (91311) *(P-6441)*

Federal Prison Industries .... F....... 805 735-2771
3901 Klein Blvd Lompoc (93436) *(P-11120)*

Federal Rsrve Bnk San Frncisco .... A....... 213 683-2300
950 S Grand Ave Fl 1 Los Angeles (90015) *(P-14154)*

Federated Diversified Sls Inc .... D....... 909 591-1733
2200 S Reservoir St Pomona (91766) *(P-3151)*

Fedex, Los Angeles *Also Called: Federal Express Corporation (P-11676)*

Fedex Services .... D....... 323 881-3400
5391 Rickenbacker Rd Bell (90201) *(P-16824)*

Feemster Co Inc .... F....... 909 621-9772
119 Yale Ave Claremont (91711) *(P-1465)*

Fei-Zyfer Inc (HQ) .... E....... 714 933-4000
7321 Lincoln Way Garden Grove (92841) *(P-8517)*

Feihe International Inc (PA) .... A....... 626 757-8885
2275 Huntington Dr Ste 278 San Marino (91108) *(P-1269)*

Feit Electric, Pico Rivera *Also Called: Feit Electric Company Inc (P-8293)*

Feit Electric Company Inc (PA) .... C....... 562 463-2852
4901 Gregg Rd Pico Rivera (90660) *(P-8293)*

Felbro, Los Angeles *Also Called: Felbro Food Products Inc (P-1768)*

Felbro Inc .... C....... 323 263-8686
3666 E Olympic Blvd Los Angeles (90023) *(P-2979)*

Felbro Food Products Inc .... E....... 323 936-5266
5700 W Adams Blvd Los Angeles (90016) *(P-1768)*

Felix Chevrolet, Los Angeles *Also Called: Felix Chevrolet LP (P-13766)*

Felix Chevrolet LP (PA) .... C....... 213 748-6141
714 W Olympic Blvd Ste 1124 Los Angeles (90015) *(P-13766)*

Felix Schoeller North Amer Inc .... E....... 315 298-8425
1260 N Lakeview Ave Anaheim (92807) *(P-3171)*

Fellow, Venice *Also Called: Fellow Industries Inc (P-8234)*

Fellow Industries Inc .... E....... 415 649-0361
1342 1/2 Abbot Kinney Blvd Venice (90291) *(P-8234)*

Fema Electronics Corporation .... E....... 714 825-0140
22 Corporate Park Irvine (92606) *(P-9045)*

Femto Blanc Inc .... D....... 408 409-2900
9267 Research Dr Irvine (92618) *(P-9210)*

Fencecorp Inc .... D....... 760 721-2101
3045 Industry St Oceanside (92054) *(P-1156)*

Fencecorp Inc (HQ) .... C....... 951 686-3170
18440 Van Buren Blvd Riverside (92508) *(P-1157)*

Fenceworks Inc (PA) .... C....... 951 788-5620
870 Main St Riverside (92501) *(P-1158)*

Fenchem, Chino *Also Called: Fenchem Inc (P-1270)*

Fenchem Inc (HQ) .... E....... 909 597-8880
15308 El Prado Rd Bldg 8 Chino (91710) *(P-1270)*

Fender Musical Instrs Corp .... A....... 480 596-9690
311 Cessna Cir Corona (92878) *(P-10924)*

Fenderscape Incorporated .... C....... 562 988-2228
1446 E Hill St Signal Hill (90755) *(P-191)*

Fenico Precision Castings Inc .... D....... 562 634-5000
7805 Madison St Paramount (90723) *(P-5813)*

Ferco Color Inc (PA) .... E....... 909 930-0773
5498 Vine St Chino (91710) *(P-3940)*

Ferco Plastic Products, Chino *Also Called: Ferco Color Inc (P-3940)*

Fergadis Enterprises, Bell *Also Called: Perrin Bernard Supowitz LLC (P-13022)*

Ferguson Co .... F....... 562 428-3300
6226 Cherry Ave Long Beach (90805) *(P-7614)*

Ferguson Fire Fabrication Inc (DH) .... D....... 909 517-3085
2750 S Towne Ave Pomona (91766) *(P-12740)*

Fermented Sciences Inc .... E....... 818 427-8442
3200 Golf Course Dr Ventura (93003) *(P-1587)*

Ferra Aerospace Inc .... E....... 918 787-2220
940 E Orangethorpe Ave Ste A Anaheim (92801) *(P-9687)*

Ferraco Inc (HQ) .... E....... 562 988-2414
2933 Long Beach Blvd Long Beach (90806) *(P-10659)*

Ferrante Paul Cstm Lmps & Shds, West Hollywood *Also Called: Paul Ferrante Inc (P-11262)*

Fertile Soil LLC .... F....... 949 981-9026
79 Dunmore Irvine (92620) *(P-1627)*

Fess Prker-Red Lion Gen Partnr .... C....... 805 564-4333
633 E Cabrillo Blvd Santa Barbara (93103) *(P-15152)*

Fetish Group Inc (PA) .... E....... 323 587-7873
1013 S Los Angeles St Ste 700 Los Angeles (90015) *(P-2204)*

Ffd II, San Diego *Also Called: Fairfield Development Inc (P-470)*

FFF Enterprises Inc (PA) .... B....... 951 296-2500
44000 Winchester Rd Temecula (92590) *(P-13041)*

FFI, Irvine *Also Called: First Foundation Inc (P-14197)*

Ffna, Irvine *Also Called: Frontech N Fujitsu Amer Inc (P-16035)*

Ffrt Residential LLC .... C....... 858 457-2123
5510 Morehouse Dr Ste 200 San Diego (92121) *(P-14708)*

Fgr 1 LLC .... E....... 800 653-3517
3191 Red Hill Ave Ste 100 Costa Mesa (92626) *(P-14007)*

Fgs-Wi LLC .... E....... 909 467-8300
5401 Jurupa St Ontario (91761) *(P-3572)*

Fhi Brands, Norwalk *Also Called: AG Global Products LLC (P-8229)*

Fht Printing, Fullerton *Also Called: Advanced Image Direct LLC (P-15626)*

Fiber Care Baths Inc .... B....... 760 246-0019
9832 Yucca Rd Ste A Adelanto (92301) *(P-4915)*

Fiber Optic Technologies, Torrance *Also Called: ACS Communications Inc (P-861)*

Fiberoptic Systems Inc .... E....... 805 579-6600
60 Moreland Rd Ste A Simi Valley (93065) *(P-5741)*

Fibreform Electronics Inc .... E....... 714 898-9641
5341 Argosy Ave Huntington Beach (92649) *(P-7831)*

Fibreform Precision Machining, Huntington Beach *Also Called: Fibreform Electronics Inc (P-7831)*

Ficto, West Hollywood *Also Called: Ficto Holdings LLC (P-16032)*

Ficto Holdings LLC .... F....... 424 250-2400
1049 Havenhurst Dr Ste 236 West Hollywood (90046) *(P-16032)*

Fidelity Nat Title Insur Co NY .... A....... 805 370-1400
950 Hampshire Rd Westlake Village (91361) *(P-14889)*

Fidelity National, Westlake Village *Also Called: Fidelity Nat Title Insur Co NY (P-14889)*

Field Fresh Foods Incorporated .... A....... 310 719-8422
14805 S San Pedro St Gardena (90248) *(P-13323)*

Field Manufacturing Corp (PA) .... E....... 310 781-9292
1751 Torrance Blvd Ste N Torrance (90501) *(P-2980)*

Field Time Target Training LLC .... E....... 714 677-2841
8230 Electric Ave Stanton (90680) *(P-6747)*

Fieldpiece, Orange *Also Called: Fieldpiece Instruments Inc (P-10199)*

Fieldpiece Instruments Inc (PA) .... D....... 714 634-1844
1636 W Collins Ave Orange (92867) *(P-10199)*

Fieldstone Communities Inc (PA) .... C....... 949 790-5400
16 Technology Dr Ste 125 Irvine (92618) *(P-483)*

Fiesta Concession, Vernon *Also Called: Mahar Manufacturing Corp (P-10939)*

Fiesta De Reyes, San Diego *Also Called: Old Town Fmly Hospitality Corp (P-15273)*

Fiesta Fashion Co Inc (PA) .... E....... 213 748-5775
1100 Wall St Ste 106 Los Angeles (90015) *(P-13125)*

Fiesta Ford Inc .... C....... 760 775-7777
79015 Avenue 40 Indio (92203) *(P-13767)*

Fiesta Ford Lincoln-Mercury, Indio *Also Called: Fiesta Ford Inc (P-13767)*

Fiesta Mexican Foods Inc .... E....... 760 344-3580
979 G St Brawley (92227) *(P-1466)*

Fig313 Inc .... E....... 949 218-4406
313 N El Camino Real San Clemente (92672) *(P-1804)*

Figs Inc .... B....... 424 300-8330
2834 Colorado Ave Ste 100 Santa Monica (90404) *(P-2173)*

Figure 8, Torrance *Also Called: Nothing To Wear Inc (P-2261)*

Filenet Corporation .... A....... 800 345-3638
3565 Harbor Blvd Costa Mesa (92626) *(P-16442)*

Film Payroll Services Inc (PA) .... D....... 310 440-9600
500 S Sepulveda Blvd Fl 4 Los Angeles (90049) *(P-19776)*

Film Roman Llc .... C....... 818 748-4000
6320 Canoga Ave Ste 450 Woodland Hills (91367) *(P-17191)*

Filmetrics Inc (HQ) .... E....... 858 573-9300
10655 Roselle St Ste 200 San Diego (92121) *(P-10259)*

Filml.a, Los Angeles *Also Called: A Filml Inc (P-17242)*

Filmtools Inc (PA) .... E....... 323 467-1116
1015 N Hollywood Way Burbank (91505) *(P-14082)*

Filtec, Torrance *Also Called: Industrial Dynamics Co Ltd (P-7241)*

Filter Concepts Incorporated .... E....... 714 545-7003
22895 Eastpark Dr Yorba Linda (92887) *(P-8942)*

Filter Pump Industries, Sun Valley *Also Called: Penguin Pumps Incorporated (P-7285)*

Employee Codes: A=Over 500 employees, B=251-500
C=101-250, D=51-100, E=20-50, F=10-19, G=1-9

2024 Southern California
Business Directory and Buyers Guide

© Mergent Inc. 1-800-342-5647

1089

A
L
P
H
A
B
E
T
I
C

Filtronics Inc .... F...... 714 630-5040
16872 Hale Ave Ste B Irvine (92606) *(P-7657)*

Filyn Corporation .... C...... 714 632-0225
2950 E La Jolla St Anaheim (92806) *(P-11387)*

Fin-West Group .... B...... 805 658-7435
5740 Ralston St Ste 130 Ventura (93003) *(P-14315)*

Final Finish Inc .... F...... 562 777-7774
10910 Norwalk Blvd Santa Fe Springs (90670) *(P-2095)*

Final Touch Apparel, Vernon *Also Called: Final Touch Apparel Inc (P-2239)*

Final Touch Apparel Inc .... F...... 323 484-9621
4801 Pacific Blvd Vernon (90058) *(P-2239)*

Finan Group, North Hollywood *Also Called: Financial Group Inc (P-14593)*

Financial Fitness Group, San Diego *Also Called: Precision Information LLC (P-16352)*

Financial Group Inc .... C...... 818 308-8527
12432 Oxnard St North Hollywood (91606) *(P-14593)*

Financial Group Inc .... C...... 805 646-7974
1991 Country Pl Ojai (93023) *(P-20031)*

Financial Info Netwrk Inc .... B...... 818 782-0331
11164 Bertrand Ave Granada Hills (91344) *(P-16033)*

Financial Statement Svcs Inc (PA) .... C...... 714 436-3326
3300 S Fairview St Santa Ana (92704) *(P-15631)*

Financial Svc Ctrs Coop Inc .... C...... 909 753-1213
924 Overland Ct San Dimas (91773) *(P-16825)*

Financial Tech Sltons Intl Inc .... B...... 818 241-9571
406 E Huntington Dr Ste 100 Monrovia (91016) *(P-20171)*

Fine Line Circuits & Tech Inc .... E...... 714 529-2942
594 Apollo St Ste A Brea (92821) *(P-8677)*

Fine Pitch, Irwindale *Also Called: Fine Ptch Elctrnic Assmbly LLC (P-8678)*

Fine Ptch Elctrnic Assmbly LLC .... E...... 626 337-2800
5106 Azusa Canyon Rd Irwindale (91706) *(P-8678)*

Fineline Architectural Mllwk, Costa Mesa *Also Called: Fineline Woodworking Inc (P-2600)*

Fineline Settings LLC .... E...... 845 369-6100
2041 S Turner Ave Unit 30 Ontario (91761) *(P-3142)*

Fineline Woodworking Inc .... D...... 714 540-5468
1139 Baker St Costa Mesa (92626) *(P-2600)*

Finesse, South Pasadena *Also Called: Finesse Apparel Inc (P-2323)*

Finesse Apparel Inc .... E...... 213 747-7077
815 Fairview Ave Unit 101 South Pasadena (91030) *(P-2323)*

Finest Hour Holdings Inc .... E...... 310 533-9966
3203 Kashiwa St Torrance (90505) *(P-10660)*

Finis LLC .... D...... 949 250-4929
3347 Michelson Dr Ste 100 Irvine (92612) *(P-7528)*

Finishing Touch Moulding Inc .... D...... 760 444-1019
6190 Corte Del Cedro Carlsbad (92011) *(P-2659)*

Finleys Tree & Landcare Inc .... C...... 310 326-9818
1209 W 228th St Torrance (90502) *(P-161)*

Fiore Stone Inc .... E...... 909 424-0221
1814 Commercenter W Ste E San Bernardino (92408) *(P-5413)*

Firan Tech Group USA Corp (HQ) .... D...... 818 407-4024
20750 Marilla St Chatsworth (91311) *(P-9976)*

Fire Insurance Exchange (PA) .... A...... 323 932-3200
6301 Owensmouth Ave Woodland Hills (91367) *(P-14594)*

Fire Protection Group Amer Inc .... E...... 323 732-4200
3712 W Jefferson Blvd Los Angeles (90016) *(P-19588)*

Fire Sprnklr Fire Alarm Dsign, San Diego *Also Called: Symons Fire Protection Inc (P-16756)*

Fire Systems, Los Angeles *Also Called: First Fire Systems Inc (P-900)*

Fireblast, Murrieta *Also Called: Fireblast Global Inc (P-7392)*

Fireblast Global Inc .... E...... 951 277-8319
41633 Eastman Dr Murrieta (92562) *(P-7392)*

Firebrand Media LLC .... F...... 949 715-4100
900 Glenneyre St Laguna Beach (92651) *(P-3573)*

Firefighters First Credit Un (PA) .... C...... 323 254-1700
1520 W Colorado Blvd Pasadena (91105) *(P-14224)*

Firestone Cmplete Auto Care 79, San Diego *Also Called: Bridgestone Americas Inc (P-4694)*

Firestone Vineyard LP .... D...... 805 688-3940
5000 Zaca Station Rd Los Olivos (93441) *(P-1628)*

Firestone Walker Inc .... D...... 805 226-8514
1332 Vendels Cir Paso Robles (93446) *(P-1588)*

Firestone Walker Inc (PA) .... C...... 805 225-5911
1400 Ramada Dr Paso Robles (93446) *(P-1589)*

Firestone Walker Inc .... D...... 805 254-4205
620 Mcmurray Rd Buellton (93427) *(P-1590)*

Firestone Walker Brewing Co, Paso Robles *Also Called: Firestone Walker Inc (P-1589)*

Firestone Walker Brewing Co, Buellton *Also Called: Firestone Walker Inc (P-1590)*

Firma Plastic Co Inc .... C...... 323 567-7767
9309 Rayo Ave South Gate (90280) *(P-12953)*

Firmenich .... D...... 714 535-2871
424 S Atchison St Anaheim (92805) *(P-4520)*

Firmenich Inc, Anaheim *Also Called: Firmenich Incorporated (P-4521)*

Firmenich Incorporated .... D...... 714 535-2871
424 S Atchison St Anaheim (92805) *(P-4521)*

Firmenich Incorporated .... E...... 858 646-8323
10636 Scripps Summit Ct San Diego (92131) *(P-4606)*

First 5 La .... C...... 213 482-5920
750 N Alameda St Ste 300 Los Angeles (90012) *(P-19081)*

First Amercn HM Warranty Corp .... B...... 818 781-5050
8511 Fallbrook Ave West Hills (91304) *(P-14890)*

First Amercn Prof RE Svcs Inc (HQ) .... C...... 714 250-1400
200 Commerce Irvine (92602) *(P-14794)*

First American Financial Corp (PA) .... A...... 714 250-3000
1 First American Way Santa Ana (92707) *(P-14539)*

First American Mortgage Svcs .... B...... 714 250-4210
3 First American Way Santa Ana (92707) *(P-14540)*

First American Mortgage Svcs, Santa Ana *Also Called: First American Title Insur Co (P-14541)*

First American Team Realty Inc (PA) .... C...... 562 427-7765
2501 Cherry Ave Ste 100 Signal Hill (90755) *(P-14795)*

First American Title Company .... A...... 714 250-3109
1 First American Way Santa Ana (92707) *(P-14891)*

First American Title Insur Co (HQ) .... B...... 800 854-3643
1 First American Way Santa Ana (92707) *(P-14541)*

First Amrcn Prprty Insur Cslty .... C...... 949 474-7500
114 E 5th St Santa Ana (92701) *(P-14595)*

First Assmbly of God Bkrsfield .... D...... 661 327-2227
4901 California Ave Bakersfield (93309) *(P-18966)*

First Class Foods, Hawthorne *Also Called: Firstclass Foods - Trojan Inc (P-1194)*

First Class Packaging Inc .... E...... 619 579-7166
280 Cypress Ln Ste D El Cajon (92020) *(P-3068)*

First Community Bancorp .... D...... 858 756-3023
5900 La Place Ct Ste 200 Carlsbad (92008) *(P-14166)*

First Energy Services Inc .... E...... 661 387-1972
1031 Carrier Parkway Ave Bakersfield (93308) *(P-347)*

First Entertainment Credit Un (PA) .... D...... 323 851-3673
6735 Forest Lawn Dr Ste 100 Los Angeles (90068) *(P-14225)*

First Financial Federal Cr Un .... C...... 800 537-8491
650 Sierra Madre Villa Ave Ste 300 Pasadena (91107) *(P-14226)*

First Finish Inc .... E...... 310 631-6717
11126 Wright Rd Lynwood (90262) *(P-2021)*

First Fire Systems Inc (PA) .... D...... 310 559-0900
5947 Burchard Ave Los Angeles (90034) *(P-900)*

First Foundation Inc (PA) .... C...... 949 202-4160
18101 Von Karman Ave Ste 700 Irvine (92612) *(P-14197)*

First Foundation Inc .... C...... 626 993-1300
301 N Lake Ave Ste 100 Pasadena (91101) *(P-14212)*

First Group, Inglewood *Also Called: First Transit Inc (P-11318)*

First Legal Network .... E...... 213 250-1111
1517 Beverly Blvd Los Angeles (90026) *(P-10200)*

First Mortgage Corporation .... B...... 909 595-1996
1131 W 6th St Ste 300 Ontario (91762) *(P-14316)*

First National Bank .... B...... 858 756-3023
6110 El Tordo Rancho Santa Fe (92067) *(P-14167)*

First National Bank, Rancho Santa Fe *Also Called: First National Bank (P-14167)*

First Reprographic, Los Angeles *Also Called: Lasr Inc (P-15649)*

First Student Inc .... C...... 626 448-9446
4337 Rowland Ave El Monte (91731) *(P-11316)*

First Student Inc .... B...... 760 320-4659
5006 E Calle San Raphael Palm Springs (92264) *(P-11428)*

First Student Inc .... A...... 310 769-2400
14800 S Avalon Blvd Gardena (90248) *(P-11429)*

First Team RE - Orange Cnty .... B...... 949 240-7979
32451 Golden Lantern Ste 210 Laguna Niguel (92677) *(P-14796)*

Mergent email: customerrelations@mergent.com
1090

2024 Southern California
Business Directory and Buyers Guide

(P-0000) Products & Services Section entry number
(PA)=Parent Co (HQ)=Headquarters (DH)=Div Headquarters

First Team RE - Orange Cnty .... B...... 714 544-5456
17240 17th St Tustin (92780) *(P-14797)*

First Team RE - Orange Cnty .... C...... 714 974-9191
8028 E Santa Ana Canyon Rd Anaheim (92808) *(P-14798)*

First Team RE - Orange Cnty .... C...... 949 389-0004
26711 Aliso Creek Rd Ste 200a Aliso Viejo (92656) *(P-14799)*

First Team RE - Orange Cnty (PA) .... **C...... 949 988-3000**
108 Pacifica Ste 300 Irvine (92618) *(P-14800)*

First Team RE - Orange Cnty .... C...... 562 596-9911
12501 Seal Beach Blvd Ste 100 Seal Beach (90740) *(P-14801)*

First Team Real Estate, Anaheim *Also Called: First Team RE - Orange Cnty (P-14798)*

First Team Real Estate, Aliso Viejo *Also Called: First Team RE - Orange Cnty (P-14799)*

First Team Walk-In Realty, Irvine *Also Called: First Team RE - Orange Cnty (P-14800)*

First Transit Inc .... D...... 323 222-0010
15730 S Figueroa St Gardena (90248) *(P-11317)*

First Transit Inc .... D...... 310 216-9584
1213 W Arbor Vitae St Inglewood (90301) *(P-11318)*

First Transit Inc .... C...... 805 544-2730
29 Prado Rd San Luis Obispo (93401) *(P-11319)*

Firstat Nursing Services Inc .... C...... 619 220-7600
411 Camino Del Rio S Ste 100 San Diego (92108) *(P-18614)*

Firstclass Foods - Trojan Inc .... C...... 310 676-2500
12500 Inglewood Ave Hawthorne (90250) *(P-1194)*

Firstsrvice Rsidential Cal LLC (HQ) .... **C...... 949 448-6000**
15241 Laguna Canyon Rd Irvine (92618) *(P-14802)*

Firstsrvice Rsidential Cal LLC .... C...... 213 213-0886
3415 S Sepulveda Blvd Ste 720 Los Angeles (90034) *(P-20032)*

Fisa, Laguna Beach *Also Called: Flavor Infusion LLC (P-1770)*

Fischer Cstm Cmmunications Inc (PA) .... E...... 310 303-3300
19220 Normandie Ave Unit B Torrance (90502) *(P-10201)*

Fischer Mold Incorporated .... D...... 951 279-1140
393 Meyer Cir Corona (92879) *(P-5028)*

Fish & Richardson PC .... C...... 858 678-5070
12390 El Camino Real San Diego (92130) *(P-18854)*

Fish Bowl, Woodland Hills *Also Called: Second Generation Inc (P-2369)*

Fish House Foods Inc .... B...... 760 597-1270
1263 Linda Vista Dr San Marcos (92078) *(P-1805)*

Fish House Partners One LLC .... D...... 323 460-4170
5955 Melrose Ave Los Angeles (90038) *(P-14008)*

Fishel Company .... C...... 858 658-0830
5878 Autoport Mall San Diego (92121) *(P-901)*

Fisher & Paykel, Costa Mesa *Also Called: Dynamic Cooking Systems Inc (P-7654)*

Fisher & Paykel Appliances Inc (DH) .... **E...... 949 790-8900**
695 Town Center Dr Ste 180 Costa Mesa (92626) *(P-8242)*

Fisher & Paykel Healthcare Inc .... C...... 949 453-4000
17400 Laguna Canyon Rd Ste 300 Irvine (92618) *(P-12487)*

Fisher & Phillips LLP .... C...... 949 851-2424
2050 Main St Ste 1000 Irvine (92614) *(P-18855)*

Fisher Printing Inc (PA) .... **C...... 714 998-9200**
2257 N Pacific St Orange (92865) *(P-3574)*

Fisher Ranch LLC .... D...... 760 922-4151
10610 Ice Plant Rd Blythe (92225) *(P-102)*

Fisheries Resource VIntr Corps .... C...... 562 596-9261
109 Stanford Ln Seal Beach (90740) *(P-20172)*

Fishermans Pride Prcessors Inc .... B...... 323 232-1980
4510 S Alameda St Vernon (90058) *(P-1806)*

Fisk Electric Company .... C...... 818 884-1166
15870 Olden St Rancho Cascades (91342) *(P-902)*

Fisker, Manhattan Beach *Also Called: Fisker Inc (P-9287)*

Fisker Automotive Inc .... D
3080 Airway Ave Costa Mesa (92626) *(P-9285)*

Fisker Group Inc (HQ) .... **E...... 833 434-7537**
1888 Rosecrans Ave Manhattan Beach (90266) *(P-9286)*

Fisker Inc (PA) .... **E...... 833 434-7537**
1888 Rosecrans Ave Manhattan Beach (90266) *(P-9287)*

Fit Athletic Club .... D...... 858 592-2440
12171 World Trade Dr San Diego (92128) *(P-17552)*

Fit-Line Inc .... E...... 714 549-9091
2901 S Tech Center Dr Santa Ana (92705) *(P-5029)*

Fit-Line Global, Santa Ana *Also Called: Fit-Line Inc (P-5029)*

Fitbit Inc .... D...... 415 513-1000
15255 Innovation Dr Ste 200 San Diego (92128) *(P-10365)*

Fitbit, Inc., San Diego *Also Called: Fitbit Inc (P-10365)*

Fitness Warehouse LLC (PA) .... **E...... 858 578-7676**
9990 Alesmith Ct Ste 130 San Diego (92126) *(P-10991)*

Fitzgerald Formliners, Santa Ana *Also Called: Prime Forming & Cnstr Sups Inc (P-5440)*

FIVE ACRES, Altadena *Also Called: Five Acres - The Bys Grls Aid (P-19262)*

Five Acres - The Bys Grls Aid .... B...... 626 798-6793
760 Mountain View St Altadena (9100 i) *(P-19262)*

Five Star Food Containers Inc .... D...... 626 437-6219
250 Eastgate Rd Barstow (92311) *(P-4881)*

Five Star Gourmet Foods Inc (PA) .... **C...... 909 390-0032**
3880 Ebony St Ontario (91761) *(P-1893)*

Five Star Plastering Inc .... D...... 949 683-5091
23022 La Cadena Dr Ste 200 Laguna Hills (92653) *(P-978)*

Five Star Senior Living Inc .... C...... 858 673-6300
16925 Hierba Dr San Diego (92128) *(P-17952)*

Fivesixtwo Inc, Long Beach *Also Called: Traffic Management Pdts Inc (P-16410)*

Fixd Construction Co., Ontario *Also Called: Nhs Western Division Inc (P-448)*

FJ Willert Contracting Co .... C...... 619 421-1980
1869 Nirvana Ave Chula Vista (91911) *(P-551)*

Fjs Inc .... C...... 714 905-1050
888 S Disneyland Dr Ste 400 Anaheim (92802) *(P-15153)*

Flagship Credit Acceptance LLC .... C...... 949 748-7172
7525 Irvine Center Dr Irvine (92618) *(P-16826)*

Flame and Wax Inc .... C...... 949 752-4000
2900 Mccabe Way Irvine (92614) *(P-11215)*

Flame-Spray Inc .... E...... 619 283-2007
4674 Alvarado Canyon Rd San Diego (92120) *(P-6704)*

Flamemaster Corporation .... E...... 818 890-1401
13576 Desmond St Pacoima (91331) *(P-4565)*

Flare Group .... E...... 714 549-0202
1571 Macarthur Blvd Costa Mesa (92626) *(P-6621)*

Flare Group .... E...... 714 850-2080
1571 Macarthur Blvd Costa Mesa (92626) *(P-9688)*

Flash Code Solutions LLC .... F...... 800 633-7467
4727 Wilshire Blvd Ste 302 Los Angeles (90010) *(P-16247)*

Flat Planet Inc .... E...... 888 656-6872
618 Hampton Dr Venice (90291) *(P-7236)*

Flat White Economy Inv USA LLC .... E...... 949 344-5013
5151 California Ave Ste 100 Costa Mesa (92626) *(P-12170)*

Flatiron West Inc .... C...... 909 597-8413
16341 Chino Corona Rd Chino (91708) *(P-652)*

Flaunt Magazine .... F...... 323 836-1044
1418 N Highland Ave Los Angeles (90028) *(P-3359)*

Flavor House Inc .... E...... 760 246-9131
16378 Koala Rd Adelanto (92301) *(P-1769)*

Flavor Infusion LLC .... E...... 949 715-4369
332 Forest Ave Ste 19 Laguna Beach (92651) *(P-1770)*

Flavor Producers, West Hills *Also Called: Flavor Producers LLC (P-1771)*

Flavor Producers LLC (PA) .... **E...... 661 257-3400**
8521 Fallbrook Ave Ste 380 West Hills (91304) *(P-1771)*

Fleet Management Solutions Inc .... E...... 800 500-6009
310 Commerce Ste 100 Irvine (92602) *(P-8518)*

Fleet Mangement Solutions, Irvine *Also Called: Teletrac Inc (P-12013)*

Fleetwood Aluminum Products Inc .... C...... 800 736-7363
1 Fleetwood Way Corona (92879) *(P-12329)*

Fleetwood Continental Inc .... D...... 310 609-1477
19451 S Susana Rd Compton (90221) *(P-5802)*

Fleetwood Fibre LLC .... C...... 626 968-8503
15250 Don Julian Rd City Of Industry (91745) *(P-3100)*

Fleetwood Fibre Pkg & Graphics, City Of Industry *Also Called: Fleetwood Fibre LLC (P-3100)*

Fleetwood Homes, Riverside *Also Called: Cavco Industries Inc (P-2734)*

Fleetwood Homes, Riverside *Also Called: Fleetwood Homes California Inc (P-2739)*

Fleetwood Homes, Riverside *Also Called: Fleetwood Homes of Florida (P-2740)*

Fleetwood Homes, Corona *Also Called: Fleetwood Homes of Kentucky (P-2741)*

Fleetwood Homes, Riverside *Also Called: Fleetwood Motor Homes-Califinc (P-9501)*

Fleetwood Homes, Riverside *Also Called: Fleetwood Motor Homes-Califinc (P-17128)*

Fleetwood Homes California Inc (DH) .... **C...... 951 351-2494**
7007 Jurupa Ave Riverside (92504) *(P-2739)*

Fleetwood Homes of Florida (DH) .... **C...... 909 261-4274**
3125 Myers St Riverside (92503) *(P-2740)*

A L P H A B E T I C

Fleetwood Homes of Kentucky (DH)..............................E...... 800 688-1745
1351 Pomona Rd Ste 230 Corona (92882) *(P-2741)*

Fleetwood Motor Homes-Califinc (DH)...........................C...... 951 354-3000
3125 Myers St Riverside (92503) *(P-9501)*

Fleetwood Motor Homes-Califinc ....C...... 951 274-2000
2350 Fleetwood Dr Riverside (92509) *(P-17128)*

Fleetwood Travel Trlrs Ind Inc (DH)............................C...... 951 354-3000
3125 Myers St Riverside (92503) *(P-9924)*

Fleetwood Travel Trlrs of MD (DH)..............................E...... 951 351-3500
3125 Myers St Riverside (92503) *(P-9925)*

Fleetwood Windows and Doors, Corona *Also Called: Fleetwood Aluminum Products Inc*
(P-12329)

Fleis Chmanns Vinegar, Cerritos *Also Called: AB Mauri Food Inc (P-1845)*

Fleischmanns Vinegar Company Inc (DH) ....E...... 562 483-4619
12604 Hiddencreek Way Ste A Cerritos (90703) *(P-1894)*

Fleming Metal Fabricators ....E...... 323 723-8203
874 Camino De Los Mares San Clemente (92673) *(P-9326)*

Fletcher Bldg Holdings USA Inc (DH)............................D...... 951 272-8180
1230 Railroad St Corona (92882) *(P-6241)*

Fletcher Coating, Orange *Also Called: Fletcher Coating Co (P-6705)*

Fletcher Coating Co ....E...... 714 637-4763
426 W Fletcher Ave Orange (92865) *(P-6705)*

Flex Company (PA)..E...... 424 209-2711
318 Lincoln Blvd Ste 204 Venice (90291) *(P-4763)*

Flexco Inc ....E...... 562 927-2525
6855 Suva St Bell Gardens (90201) *(P-9689)*

Flexcon Company Inc ....C...... 909 465-0408
12840 Reservoir St Chino (91710) *(P-4811)*

Flexfire Leds Inc ....E...... 925 273-9080
3554 Business Park Dr Ste F Costa Mesa (92626) *(P-8312)*

Flexi-Liner, Chino *Also Called: Liner Technologies Inc (P-5085)*

Flexible Manufacturing LLC ....D...... 714 259-7996
1719 S Grand Ave Santa Ana (92705) *(P-8970)*

Flexible Metal Inc ....C...... 734 516-3017
1685 Brandywine Ave Chula Vista (91911) *(P-6846)*

Flexible Video Systems, Marina Del Rey *Also Called: Sewer Rodding Equipment Co (P-7684)*

Flexicare Incorporated ....E...... 949 450-9999
15281 Barranca Pkwy Ste D Irvine (92618) *(P-10802)*

Flexline Incorporated ....E...... 562 921-4141
3727 S Meyler St San Pedro (90731) *(P-3853)*

Flexrake, Temple City *Also Called: California Flexrake Corp (P-5875)*

Flexsystems Usa Inc ....F...... 619 401-1858
1308 N Magnolia Ave Ste J El Cajon (92020) *(P-2552)*

Flexy Foam, Chino *Also Called: Inter-Packing Inc (P-4891)*

Flight Environments Inc ....E
570 Linne Rd Ste 100 Paso Robles (93446) *(P-9690)*

Flight Line Products Inc ....E...... 661 775-8366
28732 Witherspoon Pkwy Valencia (91355) *(P-9691)*

Flight Microwave Corporation ....E...... 310 607-9819
410 S Douglas St El Segundo (90245) *(P-7237)*

Flight Suits ....D...... 619 440-2700
1900 Weld Blvd Ste 140 El Cajon (92020) *(P-2430)*

Flightways Manufacturing, Valencia *Also Called: Flight Line Products Inc (P-9691)*

Flint Energy Services Inc ....C...... 213 593-8000
1999 Avenue Of The Stars Ste 2600 Los Angeles (90067) *(P-19589)*

Flir Motion Ctrl Systems Inc ....E...... 650 692-3900
6769 Hollister Ave Goleta (93117) *(P-7238)*

Flirt Inc ....E...... 213 748-4442
141 E Jefferson Blvd Los Angeles (90011) *(P-13126)*

Flixbus Inc ....C...... 925 577-4164
12575 Beatrice St Los Angeles (90066) *(P-11388)*

Flo Dynamics, Compton *Also Called: Norco Industries Inc (P-7402)*

Flo TV Incorporated ....E...... 858 651-1645
5775 Morehouse Dr San Diego (92121) *(P-8519)*

Flo-CHI, Los Angeles *Also Called: Lindsey & Sons (P-16862)*

Flo-Kem, Compton *Also Called: LMC Enterprises (P-4358)*

Flo-Kem Inc ....E...... 310 632-7124
19402 S Susana Rd Compton (90221) *(P-4349)*

Flock Freight Inc ....C...... 855 744-7585
701 S Coast Highway 101 Encinitas (92024) *(P-11761)*

Flood Ranch Company ....E...... 805 937-3616
6600 Foxen Canyon Rd Santa Maria (93454) *(P-1629)*

Floor Covering Soft ....E...... 626 683-9188
221 E Walnut St Ste 110 Pasadena (91101) *(P-16248)*

Floral Gift HM Decor Intl Inc ....E...... 818 849-8832
3200 Golf Course Dr Ste B Ventura (93003) *(P-54)*

Florence Crttnton Svcs Ornge C ....B...... 714 680-9000
801 E Chapman Ave Ste 203 Fullerton (92831) *(P-19263)*

Florence Filter Corporation ....D...... 310 637-1137
530 W Manville St Compton (90220) *(P-12753)*

Florence Meat Packing Co Inc ....E...... 562 401-0760
9840 Everest St Downey (90242) *(P-14009)*

Florence Wstn Med Clinic Inc ....C...... 818 896-2999
13500 Van Nuys Blvd Pacoima (91331) *(P-17657)*

Flotron ....E...... 760 727-2700
2630 Progress St Vista (92081) *(P-7071)*

Flowers Bkg Co Henderson LLC ....D...... 818 884-8970
21540 Blythe St Canoga Park (91304) *(P-1467)*

Flowers Bkg Co Henderson LLC ....D...... 310 695-9846
3800 W Century Blvd Inglewood (90303) *(P-1468)*

Flowline Inc ....E...... 562 598-3015
10500 Humbolt St Los Alamitos (90720) *(P-10366)*

Flowline Liquid Intelligence, Los Alamitos *Also Called: Flowline Inc (P-10366)*

Flowserve Corporation ....D...... 951 296-2464
27455 Tierra Alta Way Ste C Temecula (92590) *(P-7276)*

Flowserve Corporation ....B...... 323 584-1890
2300 E Vernon Ave Stop 76 Vernon (90058) *(P-7277)*

Flowserve Corporation ....D...... 310 667-4220
1909 E Cashdan St Compton (90220) *(P-7278)*

Flowspace Inc ....D...... 323 741-1325
660 Baker St Ste B201 Costa Mesa (92626) *(P-11578)*

Fluid Components Intl LLC (PA)..................................C...... 760 744-6950
1755 La Costa Meadows Dr San Marcos (92078) *(P-10132)*

Fluid Line Technology Corp ....E...... 818 998-8848
4590 Ish Dr Simi Valley (93063) *(P-10507)*

Fluidmaster Inc (PA)..C...... 949 728-2000
30800 Rancho Viejo Rd San Juan Capistrano (92675) *(P-5030)*

Fluidra Usa LLC (PA)..E...... 904 378-0999
2882 Whiptail Loop Ste 100 Carlsbad (92010) *(P-7658)*

Fluids Manufacturing Inc ....C...... 818 264-4657
11941 Vose St North Hollywood (91605) *(P-13407)*

Fluor Corporation ....D...... 949 349-2000
3 Polaris Way Aliso Viejo (92656) *(P-19590)*

Fluor Daniel, Aliso Viejo *Also Called: Fluor Plant Services Intl Inc (P-19592)*

Fluor Daniel Construction, Aliso Viejo *Also Called: Fluor Daniel Construction Co (P-653)*

Fluor Daniel Construction Co (DH)..............................B...... 949 349-2000
3 Polaris Way Aliso Viejo (92656) *(P-653)*

Fluor Daniel Eurasia Inc (DH)....................................E...... 949 349-2000
1 Fluor Daniel Dr Aliso Viejo (92698) *(P-19591)*

Fluor Fltron Blfour Btty Drgdo ....D...... 949 420-5000
5901 W Century Blvd Los Angeles (90045) *(P-11831)*

Fluor Plant Services Intl Inc ....D...... 949 349-2000
1 Enterprise Aliso Viejo (92656) *(P-19592)*

Fluorescent Supply Co Inc ....E...... 909 948-8878
9120 Center Ave Rancho Cucamonga (91730) *(P-8313)*

Flux Power Holdings Inc (PA).....................................C...... 877 505-3589
2685 S Melrose Dr Vista (92081) *(P-9148)*

Fluxergy Inc ....F...... 949 305-4201
15 Musick Irvine (92618) *(P-10508)*

Fluxergy Inc ....F...... 949 305-4201
13766 Alton Pkwy Irvine (92618) *(P-10509)*

Fluxergy Inc (PA)..E...... 949 305-4201
30 Fairbanks Irvine (92618) *(P-19839)*

Flyer Defense LLC ....D...... 310 324-5650
151 W 135th St Los Angeles (90061) *(P-9288)*

Flying Colors, Walnut *Also Called: Jakks Pacific Inc (P-10958)*

Flying Machine Factory, Compton *Also Called: Fmf Racing (P-9876)*

Flynt, Larry Publishing, Beverly Hills *Also Called: L F P Inc (P-3364)*

FMC Metals, Los Angeles *Also Called: 75s Corp (P-12949)*

Fmf Racing ....C...... 310 631-4363
18033 S Santa Fe Ave Compton (90221) *(P-9876)*

Mergent email: customerrelations@mergent.com
1092

2024 Southern California
Business Directory and Buyers Guide

(P-0000) Products & Services Section entry number
(PA)=Parent Co (HQ)=Headquarters (DH)=Div Headquarters

Fmh Aerospace Corp ....D...... 714 751-1000
17072 Daimler St Irvine (92614) *(P-9692)*

FMI, Chula Vista Also Called: Flexible Metal Inc *(P-6846)*

FMI International West 2, San Pedro Also Called: Toll Global Fwdg Scs USA Inc *(P-11809)*

Fmsinfoserv, Los Angeles Also Called: Cdsnet LLC *(P-20325)*

FN Logistics Llc ....A...... 213 625-5900
12588 Florence Ave Santa Fe Springs (90670) *(P-11519)*

Fnc Medical Corporation ....E...... 805 644-7576
6000 Leland St Ventura (93003) *(P-4410)*

FNS, Torrance Also Called: Fns Inc *(P-11762)*

Fns Inc (PA) ....D...... 661 615-2300
1545 Francisco St Torrance (90501) *(P-11762)*

Fntech ....D...... 714 429-7833
3000 W Segerstrom Ave Santa Ana (92704) *(P-16827)*

Foam Concepts Inc ....E...... 714 693-1037
4729 E Wesley Dr Anaheim (92807) *(P-4882)*

Foam Depot, City Of Industry Also Called: American Foam Fiber & Sups Inc *(P-2135)*

Foam Factory Inc ....E...... 310 603-9808
17515 S Santa Fe Ave Compton (90221) *(P-4883)*

Foam Molders and Specialties ....E...... 562 924-7757
20004 State Rd Cerritos (90703) *(P-4884)*

Foam Molders and Specialties (PA) ....E... 562 924-7757
11110 Business Cir Cerritos (90703) *(P-4885)*

Foam Specialties, Cerritos Also Called: Foam Molders and Specialties *(P-4885)*

Foam-Craft Inc ....C...... 714 459-9971
2441 Cypress Way Fullerton (92831) *(P-4886)*

Foamex, San Bernardino Also Called: Foamex LP *(P-4887)*

Foamex LP ....E...... 909 824-8981
1400 E Victoria Ave San Bernardino (92408) *(P-4887)*

Foamex LP ....C...... 323 774-5600
19201 S Reyes Ave Compton (90221) *(P-11579)*

Foampro Manufacturing, Irvine Also Called: Foampro Mfg Inc *(P-11088)*

Foampro Mfg Inc ....D...... 949 252-0112
1781 Langley Ave Irvine (92614) *(P-11088)*

Focus Diagnostics, Cypress Also Called: Focus Diagnostics Inc *(P-18550)*

Focus Diagnostics Inc ....B...... 714 220-1900
11331 Valley View St Ste 150 Cypress (90630) *(P-18550)*

Focus Features LLC (DH) ....D
1540 2nd St Ste 200 Santa Monica (90401) *(P-17192)*

Focus Industries Inc ....D...... 949 830-1350
25301 Commercentre Dr Lake Forest (92630) *(P-8314)*

Focus Landscape, Lake Forest Also Called: Focus Industries Inc *(P-8314)*

Focus One Home, Corona Also Called: Della Robbia Inc *(P-2847)*

Focus Technologies Holding Co ....E...... 800 838-4548
10703 Progress Way Cypress (90630) *(P-10260)*

Foh Group Inc (PA) ....E
6255 W Sunset Blvd Ste 2212 Los Angeles (90028) *(P-2395)*

Foldimate Inc ....E...... 805 876-4418
879 White Pine Ct Oak Park (91377) *(P-8235)*

Folding Cartons, Camarillo Also Called: Crockett Graphics Inc *(P-3095)*

Foley Fmly Wines Holdings Inc ....D...... 805 450-7225
90 Easy St Buellton (93427) *(P-1630)*

Fonco Creative Services ....F...... 415 254-5460
1310 N San Fernando Rd Los Angeles (90065) *(P-17193)*

Fonco Studios, Los Angeles Also Called: Fonco Creative Services *(P-17193)*

Fontana Foundry Corporation ....F...... 909 822-6128
8306 Cherry Ave Fontana (92335) *(P-5793)*

Fontana Paper Mills Inc ....D...... 909 823-4100
13733 Valley Blvd Fontana (92335) *(P-4668)*

Fontana Resources At Work ....E...... 909 428-3833
9460 Sierra Ave Fontana (92335) *(P-19185)*

Fontana Steel, Ontario Also Called: C M C Steel Fabricators Inc *(P-6813)*

Fontana Water Company, El Monte Also Called: San Gabriel Valley Water Co *(P-12144)*

Food 4 Less, Paso Robles Also Called: Paq Inc *(P-13893)*

Food For Life Baking Co Inc (PA) ....D...... 951 273-3031
2991 Doherty St Corona (92879) *(P-1469)*

Food Pharma, Santa Fe Springs Also Called: Food Technology and Design LLC *(P-1539)*

Food Processing Equipment Co, Santa Fe Springs Also Called: FPec Corporation A Cal Corp *(P-7197)*

Food Sales West Inc ....D...... 714 966-2900
235 Baker St Costa Mesa (92626) *(P-13180)*

Food Technology and Design LLC (PA) ....E...... 562 944-7821
10012 Painter Ave Santa Fe Springs (90670) *(P-1539)*

Foodology LLC ....D...... 818 252-1888
8920 Norris Ave Sun Valley (91352) *(P-1895)*

Foods On Fly LLC ....E...... 858 404-0642
7004 Carroll Rd San Diego (92121) *(P-1896)*

Foodtools Consolidated Inc (PA) ....E...... 805 962-8383
315 Laguna St Santa Barbara (93101) *(P-7195)*

Fooma America Inc ....E...... 310 921-0717
12735 Stanhill Dr La Mirada (90638) *(P-7169)*

Foote Axle & Forge LLC ....E...... 323 268-4151
250 W Duarte Rd Ste A Monrovia (91016) *(P-9391)*

Foothill Electric Motors, Santa Clarita Also Called: Wrights Supply Inc *(P-17110)*

Foothill Family Service ....C...... 626 246-1240
3629 Santa Anita Ave Ste 201 El Monte (91731) *(P-19082)*

Foothill Family Service ....C...... 626 795-6907
2500 E Foothill Blvd Ste 300 Pasadena (91107) *(P-19083)*

Foothill Packing Inc ....B...... 805 925-7900
2255 S Broadway Santa Maria (93454) *(P-13181)*

Foothill Presbyterian Hospital, Glendora Also Called: Emanate Hlth Fthill Prsbt Hosp *(P-18259)*

Foothill Regional Medical Ctr ....C...... 310 943-4500
14662 Newport Ave Tustin (92780) *(P-18260)*

Foothill Regional Medical Ctr, Tustin Also Called: Alta Hospitals System LLC *(P-18174)*

Foothill Transit West Covina, Arcadia Also Called: Coach Usa Inc *(P-11416)*

Foothill Vctonal Opportunities, Pasadena Also Called: Fvo Solutions Inc *(P-6706)*

For Cali Productions LLC ....B...... 323 956-9500
5555 Melrose Ave Bldg 213 Los Angeles (90038) *(P-17252)*

Forbes Industries Div ....C...... 909 923-4559
1933 E Locust St Ontario (91761) *(P-3025)*

Force Protection Systems, Van Nuys Also Called: Edo Communications and Countermeasures Systems Inc *(P-9973)*

Ford, Santa Monica Also Called: Ford of Santa Monica Inc *(P-13768)*

Ford, Upland Also Called: Park Place Ford LLC *(P-13811)*

Ford, Irvine Also Called: Ford Motor Land Dev Corp *(P-14661)*

Ford Lincoln Mercury, El Centro Also Called: El Centro Motors *(P-13759)*

Ford Motor Land Dev Corp ....C...... 949 242-6606
3 Glen Bell Way Ste 100 Irvine (92618) *(P-14661)*

Ford of Santa Monica Inc ....D...... 310 451-1588
1402 Santa Monica Blvd Santa Monica (90404) *(P-13768)*

Fordon Grind Industries, Torrance Also Called: Aeroliant Manufacturing Inc *(P-7746)*

Forecast 3d, Carlsbad Also Called: Product Slingshot Inc *(P-7091)*

Foreign Trade Corporation ....C...... 805 823-8400
685 Cochran St Ste 200 Simi Valley (93065) *(P-12660)*

Foremay Inc (PA) ....E...... 408 228-3468
225 S Lake Ave Ste 300 Pasadena (91101) *(P-16034)*

Forensic Analytical, Carson Also Called: Forensic Analytical Spc Inc *(P-19972)*

Forensic Analytical Spc Inc ....D...... 310 763-2374
20535 Belshaw Ave Carson (90746) *(P-19972)*

Foreseeson Custom Displays Inc (PA) ....E...... 714 300-0540
2210 E Winston Rd Anaheim (92806) *(P-7529)*

Forespar, Rcho Sta Marg Also Called: Light Composite Corporation *(P-5927)*

Forespar Products Corp (PA) ....E...... 949 858-8820
22322 Gilberto Rcho Sta Marg (92688) *(P-5917)*

Forest Home Inc ....C...... 909 389-2300
40000 Valley Of The Falls Dr Forest Falls (92339) *(P-15435)*

Forest Home Ministries, Forest Falls Also Called: Forest Home Inc *(P-15435)*

Forest Lawn Co ....C...... 818 241-4151
1712 S Glendale Ave Glendale (91205) *(P-14915)*

Forest Lawn Mem Parks Mortuary, Glendale Also Called: Forest Lawn Memorial-Park Assn *(P-14113)*

Forest Lawn Memorial-Park Assn (PA) ....B...... 323 254-3131
1712 S Glendale Ave Glendale (91205) *(P-14113)*

Forest Lawn Mortuary ....B...... 760 329-8737
66272 Pierson Blvd Desert Hot Springs (92240) *(P-15487)*

Forever 21 Logistics LLC ....B...... 888 494-3837
110 E 9th St Ste C910 Los Angeles (90079) *(P-16828)*

Forever Rich International LLC ....E...... 310 867-4723
14622 Ventura Blvd Sherman Oaks (91403) *(P-1271)*

A L P H A B E T I C

Employee Codes: A=Over 500 employees, B=251-500
C=101-250, D=51-100, E=20-50, F=10-19, G=1-9
2024 Southern California
Business Directory and Buyers Guide
© Mergent Inc. 1-800-342-5647
1093

Forged Metals Inc ....C...... 909 350-9260
10685 Beech Ave Fontana (92337) *(P-6459)*

Forgiato, Sun Valley *Also Called: Forgiato Inc* *(P-9392)*

Forgiato Inc ....D...... 818 771-9779
11915 Wicks St Sun Valley (91352) *(P-9392)*

Foria International Inc ....C...... 626 912-8836
18689 Arenth Ave City Of Industry (91748) *(P-13103)*

Form Grind Corporation ....E...... 949 858-7000
30062 Aventura Rcho Sta Marg (92688) *(P-7832)*

Form Products, Rcho Sta Marg *Also Called: Form Grind Corporation (P-7832)*

Former Luna Subsidiary Inc (HQ)...............................D
Camarillo (93012) *(P-8797)*

Formex LLC ....E...... 858 529-6600
9601 Jeronimo Rd Irvine (92618) *(P-4112)*

Forming Specialties Inc ....E...... 310 639-1122
3262 Falkland Cir Huntington Beach (92649) *(P-9693)*

Formology Lab Inc ....E...... 424 452-0377
9174 Deering Ave Chatsworth (91311) *(P-4411)*

Formosa Meat Company Inc ....E...... 909 987-0470
10646 Fulton Ct Rancho Cucamonga (91730) *(P-1218)*

Forms and Surfaces Inc ....D...... 805 684-8626
6395 Cindy Ln Carpinteria (93013) *(P-6358)*

Forms and Surfaces Company LLC ....E...... 805 684-8626
6395 Cindy Ln Carpinteria (93013) *(P-5414)*

Formula Plastics Inc ....B...... 866 307-1362
451 Tecate Rd Ste 2b Tecate (91980) *(P-5031)*

Fornaca Inc (PA)...**C...... 866 308-9461**
2400 National City Blvd National City (91950) *(P-13859)*

Forrest Group LLC (PA)...**D...... 619 808-9798**
1422 N Curson Ave Apt 9 Los Angeles (90046) *(P-11320)*

Forrest Machining LLC ....C...... 661 257-0231
27756 Avenue Mentry Valencia (91355) *(P-9694)*

Forrester Eastland Corporation ....E...... 310 784-2464
1320 Storm Pkwy Torrance (90501) *(P-11216)*

Forrestmachining.com, Valencia *Also Called: Forrest Machining LLC (P-9694)*

Fortanasce & Associates, Murrieta *Also Called: Michael G Frtnsce Physcl Thrap (P-17869)*

Fortel Traffic Inc ....F...... 714 701-9800
5310 E Hunter Ave Anaheim (92807) *(P-19593)*

Forterra Pipe & Precast LLC ....E...... 858 715-5600
9229 Harris Plant Rd San Diego (92145) *(P-5415)*

Forterra Pipe & Precast LLC ....E...... 951 523-7039
26380 Palomar Rd Sun City (92585) *(P-5416)*

Fortiss LLC ....D...... 323 415-4900
1100 S Flower St Ste 3100 Los Angeles (90015) *(P-17553)*

Fortitude Technology Inc ....D...... 858 974-5080
8929 Complex Dr Ste A San Diego (92123) *(P-11877)*

Fortner Eng & Mfg Inc ....E...... 818 240-7740
2927 N Ontario St Burbank (91504) *(P-7833)*

Fortress Inc ....E...... 909 593-8600
1721 Wright Ave La Verne (91750) *(P-2883)*

Fortress Holding Group LLC ....D...... 714 202-8710
5500 E Santa Ana Canyon Rd Ste 220 Anaheim (92807) *(P-14929)*

Fortuna Enterprises LP ....B...... 310 410-4000
5711 W Century Blvd Los Angeles (90045) *(P-15154)*

Fortune Casuals LLC (PA)..**D...... 310 733-2100**
10119 Jefferson Blvd Culver City (90232) *(P-2240)*

Fortune Dynamic Inc ....D...... 909 979-8318
21923 Ferrero City Of Industry (91789) *(P-13162)*

Fortune Energy USA, Simi Valley *Also Called: Williams East Heating A & Plbg (P-837)*

Fortune Manufacturing Inc ....E...... 909 591-1547
13849 Magnolia Ave Chino (91710) *(P-7834)*

Fortune Swimwear LLC (HQ)......................................**E...... 310 733-2130**
2340 E Olympic Blvd Ste A Los Angeles (90021) *(P-2070)*

Forty-Niner Shops Inc ....A...... 562 985-5093
6049 E 7th St Long Beach (90840) *(P-14066)*

Forward Slope Incorporated (PA)..............................**C...... 619 299-4400**
2020 Camino Del Rio N Ste 400 San Diego (92108) *(P-19594)*

Forward Slope., San Diego *Also Called: Forward Slope Incorporated (P-19594)*

Foshay Electric Co Inc ....D...... 858 277-7676
950 Industrial Blvd Chula Vista (91911) *(P-903)*

Foss Maritime Company ....F...... 562 437-6098
49 W Pier D St Long Beach (90802) *(P-6026)*

FOSS MARITIME COMPANY, Long Beach *Also Called: Foss Maritime Company (P-6026)*

Foster Poultry Farms ....A...... 310 223-1499
1805 N Santa Fe Ave Compton (90221) *(P-1243)*

FOSTER POULTRY FARMS, Compton *Also Called: Foster Poultry Farms (P-1243)*

Foster Print, Santa Ana *Also Called: Blackburn Alton Invstments LLC (P-3737)*

Foster Printing Company Inc ....E...... 714 731-2000
700 E Alton Ave Santa Ana (92705) *(P-3575)*

Foster Sand & Gravel, Corona *Also Called: Werner Corporation (P-5518)*

Fotis and Son Imports Inc (PA)..................................**E...... 714 894-9022**
15451 Electronic Ln Huntington Beach (92649) *(P-7196)*

Foto Kem Film & Video, Burbank *Also Called: Foto-Kem Industries Inc (P-17253)*

Foto-Kem Industries Inc (PA).....................................**C...... 818 846-3102**
2801 W Alameda Ave Burbank (91505) *(P-17253)*

Foundation 9 Entertainment Inc (PA)..........................**C...... 949 698-1500**
30211 Avenida De Las Bandera Ste 200 Rancho Santa Margari (92688) *(P-16249)*

Foundation Ai, Irvine *Also Called: Foundation Inc (P-16250)*

Foundation Building Materials, Santa Ana *Also Called: Foundation Building Mtls Inc (P-12330)*

Foundation Building Mtls Inc (HQ).............................**C...... 714 380-3127**
2520 Redhill Ave Santa Ana (92705) *(P-12330)*

Foundation Inc ....E...... 310 294-8955
19800 Macarthur Blvd Ste 300 Irvine (92612) *(P-16250)*

Foundation Laboratory, Pomona *Also Called: Latara Enterprise Inc (P-18555)*

Foundation Pile Inc ....D...... 909 350-1584
8375 Almeria Ave Fontana (92335) *(P-709)*

Foundry Med Innovations Inc ....F...... 888 445-2333
1965 Kellogg Ave Carlsbad (92008) *(P-10510)*

Foundry Service & Supplies Inc ....E...... 909 284-5000
2029 S Parco Ave Ontario (91761) *(P-5567)*

Foundstone Inc ....E...... 949 297-5600
27201 Puerta Real Ste 400 Mission Viejo (92691) *(P-16251)*

Fountain View Cnvalescent Hosp, Los Angeles *Also Called: Genesis Healthcare LLC (P-18126)*

Fountain Vly Rgnal Hosp Med CT ....A...... 714 966-7200
17100 Euclid St Fountain Valley (92708) *(P-18261)*

Fountainhead Industries ....E...... 310 248-2444
700 N San Vicente Blvd Ste G410 West Hollywood (90069) *(P-11217)*

Fountains At The Carlotta, The, Palm Desert *Also Called: Watermark Rtrment Cmmnties Inc (P-18074)*

Four Pnts By Shrton La Intl Ar, Los Angeles *Also Called: Irp Lax Hotel LLC (P-15205)*

Four Points Bakersfield, Bakersfield *Also Called: Cni Thl Propco Fe LLC (P-15120)*

Four Seasons Design Inc (PA).....................................**E...... 619 761-5151**
2451 Britannia Blvd San Diego (92154) *(P-2530)*

Four Seasons General Mdse, Vernon *Also Called: BTG S CORP (P-13532)*

Four Seasons Hotel, Los Angeles *Also Called: Burton-Way House Ltd A CA (P-15101)*

Four Seasons Hotels Limited, Los Angeles *Also Called: Burton Way Hotels LLC (P-15099)*

Four Seasons Ht Westlake Vlg, Westlake Village *Also Called: Burton Way Htels Ltd A Cal Ltd (P-15100)*

Four Seasons Hummus Inc ....F...... 305 409-0449
11030 Randall St Sun Valley (91352) *(P-1897)*

Four Seasons Rest Eqp Inc ....E...... 951 278-9100
412 Jenks Cir Corona (92878) *(P-6242)*

Four Ssons Rsort Santa Barbara, Santa Barbara *Also Called: 1260 Bb Property LLC (P-15062)*

Four Star Chemical, Vernon *Also Called: Starco Enterprises Inc (P-7259)*

Four Star Distribution ....E...... 949 369-4420
206 Calle Conchita San Clemente (92672) *(P-4702)*

Four Wheel Parts Wholesalers, Compton *Also Called: Transamerican Dissolution LLC (P-13886)*

Foursquare International, Los Angeles *Also Called: Interntnal Ch of Frsqare Gospl (P-19502)*

Fourthfloor Fashion Talent, Los Angeles *Also Called: Career Group Inc (P-15826)*

Foutains Executive Course, Escondido *Also Called: Welk Group Inc (P-17443)*

Fovell Enterprises Inc ....E...... 951 734-6275
1852 Pomona Rd Corona (92878) *(P-11121)*

Fox, Los Angeles *Also Called: Twentieth Cntury Fox Intl Corp (P-17280)*

Fox Inc (DH)...**A...... 310 369-1000**
10201 W Pico Blvd Los Angeles (90064) *(P-11948)*

Fox Baseball Holdings Inc ....C...... 323 224-1500
1000 Vin Scully Ave Los Angeles (90012) *(P-17369)*

Fox Broadcasting Company LLC (HQ)....................................C...... 310 369-1000
  10201 W Pico Blvd Bldg 1003220 Los Angeles (90064) *(P-11949)*

Fox BSB Holdco Inc (HQ)...B...... 323 224-1500
  1000 Vin Scully Ave Los Angeles (90012) *(P-17370)*

Fox Electronics, Laguna Hills *Also Called: Fox Enterprises LLC (P-9046)*

Fox Enterprises LLC (HQ)..E...... 239 693-0099
  24422 Avenida De La Carlota Ste 290 Laguna Hills (92653) *(P-9046)*

Fox Family Channel, Burbank *Also Called: International Fmly Entrmt Inc (P-11996)*

Fox Head Inc (HQ)...B...... 949 757-9500
  16752 Armstrong Ave Irvine (92606) *(P-13127)*

Fox Hills Auto Inc (PA)...C...... 310 649-3673
  5880 W Centinela Ave Los Angeles (90045) *(P-13769)*

Fox Hills Industries...E...... 714 893-1940
  5831 Research Dr Huntington Beach (92649) *(P-5644)*

Fox Interactive Media Inc...C...... 310 969-7000
  6100 Center Dr Ste 800 Los Angeles (90045) *(P-11878)*

Fox Net Inc..A...... 310 369-1000
  10201 W Pico Blvd Los Angeles (90064) *(P-17194)*

Fox Network Center, Los Angeles *Also Called: Disney Networks Group LLC (P-11944)*

Fox Racing, Irvine *Also Called: Fox Head Inc (P-13127)*

Fox Rent A Car Inc..C...... 310 342-5155
  5500 W Century Blvd Los Angeles (90045) *(P-16982)*

Fox Rent A Car Inc..D...... 909 635-6390
  1776 E Holt Blvd Ontario (91761) *(P-16983)*

Fox Sports Inc (DH)..C...... 310 369-1000
  10201 W Pico Blvd Los Angeles (90064) *(P-11950)*

Fox Television Center, Los Angeles *Also Called: Fox Television Stations Inc (P-11951)*

Fox Television Stations Inc (HQ)...B...... 310 584-2000
  1999 S Bundy Dr Los Angeles (90025) *(P-11951)*

Fox Transportation Inc...C...... 310 971-0867
  18408 S Laurel Park Rd Compton (90220) *(P-11520)*

Fox US Productions 27 Inc...C...... 310 727-2550
  1600 Rosecrans Ave Bldg 5a Manhattan Beach (90266) *(P-11952)*

Foxen Canyon Winery & Vineyard, Santa Maria *Also Called: Foxen Vineyard Inc (P-1631)*

Foxen Vineyard Inc...E...... 805 937-4251
  7600 Foxen Canyon Rd Santa Maria (93454) *(P-1631)*

Foxfury Lighting Solution, Oceanside *Also Called: Foxfury LLC (P-8366)*

Foxfury LLC...E...... 760 945-4231
  3544 Seagate Way Oceanside (92056) *(P-8366)*

Foxlink International Inc (HQ)..E...... 714 256-1777
  3010 Saturn St Ste 200 Brea (92821) *(P-8265)*

FP Nutraceuticals LLC...D...... 562 944-7821
  3851 Schaufele Ave Long Beach (90808) *(P-4113)*

Fpc Inc...E...... 323 468-5778
  1017 N Las Palmas Ave Los Angeles (90038) *(P-10867)*

FPec Corporation A Cal Corp (PA)...F...... 562 802-3727
  13623 Pumice St Santa Fe Springs (90670) *(P-7197)*

Fpg Oc Inc..E...... 714 692-2950
  24855 Corbit Pl Ste B Yorba Linda (92887) *(P-1772)*

Fpg Services LLC..C...... 818 858-1080
  15821 Ventura Blvd Ste 625 Encino (91436) *(P-20173)*

Fpk Investigaions, Valencia *Also Called: Fpk Security Inc (P-16642)*

Fpk Security Inc..B...... 661 702-9091
  28348 Constellation Rd Ste 880 Valencia (91355) *(P-16642)*

Fragile Handle With Care, San Diego *Also Called: Chandler Packaging A Transpak Company (P-11819)*

Fralock, Valencia *Also Called: Lockwood Industries LLC (P-8829)*

Frameless Hardware Company LLC...E...... 888 295-4531
  4361 Firestone Blvd South Gate (90280) *(P-5918)*

Frametent Inc...E...... 661 290-3375
  26480 Summit Cir Santa Clarita (91350) *(P-2504)*

Franchise Services Inc (PA)...E...... 949 348-5400
  26722 Plaza Mission Viejo (92691) *(P-3576)*

FRANK D LANTERMAN REGIONAL CEN, Los Angeles *Also Called: Los Angles Cnty Dvlpmntal Svcs (P-18778)*

Frank Kams & Associates Inc...E...... 909 382-0047
  242 W Hanna St Colton (92324) *(P-2731)*

Frank Russell Inc..F...... 661 324-5575
  341 Pacific Ave Shafter (93263) *(P-7835)*

Frank S Smith Masonry Inc...D...... 909 468-0525
  2830 Pomona Blvd Pomona (91768) *(P-956)*

Frank Stubbs Co Inc...E...... 805 278-4300
  1830 Eastman Ave Oxnard (93030) *(P-10661)*

Frank Toyota & Scion, National City *Also Called: Fornaca Inc (P-13859)*

Frankies Bikinis, Venice *Also Called: Frankies Bikinis LLC (P-2415)*

Frankies Bikinis LLC...E...... 323 354-4133
  4030 Del Rey Ave Venice (90292) *(P-2415)*

Franklin Wireless, San Diego *Also Called: Franklin Wireless Corp (P-8473)*

Franklin Wireless Corp...D...... 858 623-0000
  9707 Waples St Ste 150 San Diego (92121) *(P-8473)*

Franklins Inds San Diego Inc..E...... 858 486-9399
  12135 Dearborn Pl Poway (92064) *(P-7836)*

Frans Manufacturing Inc...E...... 760 741-9135
  126 N Vinewood St Escondido (92029) *(P-7837)*

Franz Family Bakeries, Los Angeles *Also Called: United States Bakery (P-1496)*

Frazee Industries Inc..A...... 858 626-3600
  6625 Miramar Rd San Diego (92121) *(P-4490)*

Frazee Paint & Wallcovering, San Diego *Also Called: Frazee Industries Inc (P-4490)*

Frazier Aviation Inc..E...... 818 898-1998
  445 N Fox St San Fernando (91340) *(P-9695)*

Fred M Boerner Motor Co (PA)..D...... 323 560-3882
  3620 E Florence Ave Huntington Park (90255) *(P-13860)*

Fred R Rippy Inc...E...... 562 698-9801
  12450 Whittier Blvd Whittier (90602) *(P-6517)*

Freddie Mac, Los Angeles *Also Called: Federal Home Loan Mrtg Corp (P-14314)*

Fredericka Manor Care Center, Chula Vista *Also Called: Front Porch Communities & Svcs (P-17955)*

FREDERICKA MANOR CARE CENTER, Glendale *Also Called: Front Prch Cmmnties Oprting Gr (P-18125)*

Fredericks.com, Los Angeles *Also Called: Foh Group Inc (P-2395)*

Free Conferencing Corporation..C...... 562 437-1411
  4300 E Pacific Coast Hwy Long Beach (90804) *(P-11879)*

Free Motion Wakeboards, Carlsbad *Also Called: Liquid Force Wakeboards (P-11009)*

Freeberg Indus Fbrication Corp..D...... 760 737-7614
  2874 Progress Pl Escondido (92029) *(P-6027)*

Freeberg Industrial, Escondido *Also Called: Freeberg Indus Fbrication Corp (P-6027)*

Freeconferencecall.com, Long Beach *Also Called: Free Conferencing Corporation (P-11879)*

Freedom Communications Inc..A...... 714 796-7000
  625 N Grand Ave Santa Ana (92701) *(P-3277)*

Freedom Designs Inc..C...... 805 582-0077
  2241 N Madera Rd Simi Valley (93065) *(P-10662)*

Freedom Forever, Temecula *Also Called: Freedom Solar Services (P-771)*

Freedom Forever LLC..A...... 714 955-8735
  3322 Garfield Ave Commerce (90040) *(P-769)*

Freedom Forever LLC (PA)..D...... 888 557-6431
  43445 Business Park Dr Ste 104 Temecula (92590) *(P-770)*

Freedom Newspapers, Santa Ana *Also Called: Freedom Communications Inc (P-3277)*

Freedom Photonics LLC..E...... 805 967-4900
  41 Aero Camino Santa Barbara (93117) *(P-9211)*

Freedom Prfmce Exhaust Inc..E...... 951 898-4733
  1255 Railroad St Corona (92882) *(P-13861)*

Freedom Properties, Hemet *Also Called: Casa-Pacifica Inc (P-19246)*

Freedom Properties Village, Hemet *Also Called: Casa-Pacifica Inc (P-19247)*

Freedom Properties-Hemet LLC..C...... 949 489-0430
  27122b Paseo Espada Ste 1024 San Juan Capistrano (92675) *(P-14662)*

Freedom Solar Services..C...... 888 557-6431
  43445 Business Park Dr Ste 110 Temecula (92590) *(P-771)*

Freedom Village Healthcare Ctr...C...... 949 472-4733
  23442 El Toro Rd Bldg 2 Lake Forest (92630) *(P-17953)*

Freeman, Anaheim *Also Called: Freeman Expositions LLC (P-16829)*

Freeman Expositions LLC...C...... 714 254-3400
  2170 S Towne Centre Pl Ste 100 Anaheim (92806) *(P-16829)*

Freeport-Mcmoran Oil & Gas LLC..F...... 805 567-1601
  760 W Hueneme Rd Oxnard (93033) *(P-304)*

Freeport-Mcmoran Oil & Gas LLC..E...... 323 298-2200
  5640 S Fairfax Ave Los Angeles (90056) *(P-305)*

Freeport-Mcmoran Oil & Gas LLC..E...... 661 322-7600
  1200 Discovery Dr Ste 500 Bakersfield (93309) *(P-306)*

Freestyle, Santa Fe Springs *Also Called: Freestyle Sales Co Ltd Partnr (P-14083)*

Freestyle Sales Co Ltd Partnr...D...... 323 660-3460
  12231 Florence Ave Santa Fe Springs (90670) *(P-14083)*

A L P H A B E T I C

Employee Codes: A=Over 500 employees, B=251-500
C=101-250, D=51-100, E=20-50, F=10-19, G=1-9

2024 Southern California
Business Directory and Buyers Guide

© Mergent Inc. 1-800-342-5647

1095

Freeway Insurance (PA)..C...... 714 252-2500
7711 Center Ave Ste 200 Huntington Beach (92647) *(P-14596)*

Freightgate Inc ....E....... 714 799-2833
10055 Slater Ave Ste 231 Fountain Valley (92708) *(P-16252)*

Fremantle Media, Burbank *Also Called: Prdctions N Fremantle Amer Inc (P-17324)*

Fremarc Designs, City Of Industry *Also Called: Fremarc Industries Inc (P-2773)*

Fremarc Industries Inc (PA)..D...... 626 965-0802
18810 San Jose Ave City Of Industry (91748) *(P-2773)*

Fremont, Pasadena *Also Called: Fremont & Purdon Inc (P-17021)*

Fremont & Purdon Inc ....E....... 626 795-6282
836 E Orange Grove Blvd Pasadena (91104) *(P-17021)*

Fremont Office, Irvine *Also Called: Western Digital Corporation (P-7493)*

French Hospital Medical Center (DH)..............................B....... 805 543-5353
1911 Johnson Ave San Luis Obispo (93401) *(P-18262)*

Fresenius Kidney Care Lynwood, Downey *Also Called: Rai Care Centers Lynwood LLC (P-18661)*

Fresh & Ready, San Fernando *Also Called: Lehman Foods Inc (P-1933)*

Fresh & Ready Foods LLC (PA)...D...... 818 837-7600
1145 Arroyo St Ste B San Fernando (91340) *(P-1898)*

Fresh Creative Foods, Vista *Also Called: Rmjv LP (P-7214)*

Fresh Grill LLC ....C...... 714 444-2126
111 E Garry Ave Santa Ana (92707) *(P-16830)*

Fresh Griller, Costa Mesa *Also Called: Fgr 1 LLC (P-14007)*

Fresh Innovations LLC ....E....... 805 483-2265
908 E 3rd St Oxnard (93030) *(P-1836)*

Fresh Origins, San Marcos *Also Called: San Diego Farms LLC (P-86)*

Fresh Packing Corporation ....E....... 213 612-0136
4333 S Maywood Ave Vernon (90058) *(P-1325)*

Fresh Start Bakeries, Ontario *Also Called: Aspire Bakeries LLC (P-13351)*

Fresh Start Bakeries Inc ....A....... 714 256-8900
145 S State College Blvd Ste 200 Brea (92821) *(P-1470)*

Fresh Start Bakeries N Amer, Brea *Also Called: Fresh Start Bakeries Inc (P-1470)*

Fresh Venture Farms LLC ....D...... 805 754-4449
1181 S Wolff Rd Oxnard (93033) *(P-9)*

Fresh Venture Foods LLC ....C...... 805 928-3374
1205 Craig Dr Santa Maria (93458) *(P-7198)*

Freshpoint Inc ....C...... 626 855-1400
155 N Orange Ave City Of Industry (91744) *(P-13324)*

Freshpoint Las Vegas, City Of Industry *Also Called: Freshpoint Inc (P-13324)*

Freshpoint Southern Cal Inc ....C...... 626 855-1400
155 N Orange Ave City Of Industry (91744) *(P-13325)*

Freshpoint Southern California, City Of Industry *Also Called: Freshpoint Southern Cal Inc (P-13325)*

Freshrealm Inc (PA)..C...... 800 264-1297
1330 Calle Avanzado San Clemente (92673) *(P-1899)*

Freshway Farms LLC ....C...... 805 349-7170
2165 W Main St Santa Maria (93458) *(P-16)*

Freudenberg Medical LLC ....C...... 626 814-9684
5050 Rivergrade Rd Baldwin Park (91706) *(P-10511)*

Freudenberg Medical LLC (DH)..C...... 805 684-3304
1110 Mark Ave Carpinteria (93013) *(P-10663)*

Freudenberg Medical LLC ....D...... 805 576-5308
6385 Rose Ln Ste A Carpinteria (93013) *(P-10664)*

Freudenberg Medical LLC ....E....... 805 684-3304
1009 Cindy Ln Carpinteria (93013) *(P-10665)*

Freudenberg-Nok General Partnr ....C...... 714 834-0602
2041 E Wilshire Ave Santa Ana (92705) *(P-4728)*

Freund Baking, Commerce *Also Called: Oakhurst Industries Inc (P-1487)*

Frick Paper Company LLC ....C...... 714 787-4900
2164 N Batavia St Orange (92865) *(P-13007)*

Friction Materials LLC ....C...... 248 362-3600
2525 W 190th St Torrance (90504) *(P-19595)*

Friendly Hlls Cntry CLB Fndtio ....C...... 562 698-0331
8500 Villaverde Dr Whittier (90605) *(P-17485)*

Friends of Cultural Center Inc ....D...... 760 346-6505
73000 Fred Waring Dr Palm Desert (92260) *(P-17315)*

Fringe Studio LLC ....E....... 310 390-9900
17909 Fitch Irvine (92614) *(P-11218)*

Frisco Baking Company, Los Angeles *Also Called: Frisco Baking Company Inc (P-1471)*

Frisco Baking Company Inc ....C...... 323 225-6111
621 W Avenue 26 Los Angeles (90065) *(P-1471)*

Frito-Lay, Bloomington *Also Called: Frito-Lay North America Inc (P-1825)*

Frito-Lay, Bakersfield *Also Called: Frito-Lay North America Inc (P-13269)*

Frito-Lay, Torrance *Also Called: Frito-Lay North America Inc (P-13270)*

Frito-Lay, Rancho Cucamonga *Also Called: Frito-Lay North America Inc (P-13271)*

Frito-Lay, Rancho Cucamonga *Also Called: Frito-Lay North America Inc (P-13272)*

Frito-Lay North America Inc ....E....... 909 877-0902
635 W Valley Blvd Bloomington (92316) *(P-1825)*

Frito-Lay North America Inc ....C...... 661 328-6034
28801 Highway 58 Bakersfield (93314) *(P-13269)*

Frito-Lay North America Inc ....E....... 310 224-5600
1500 Francisco St Torrance (90501) *(P-13270)*

Frito-Lay North America Inc ....E....... 909 941-6214
9535 Archibald Ave Rancho Cucamonga (91730) *(P-13271)*

Frito-Lay North America Inc ....E....... 909 941-6218
9846 4th St Rancho Cucamonga (91730) *(P-13272)*

Frize Corporation ....D...... 800 834-2127
16605 Gale Ave City Of Industry (91745) *(P-502)*

Front Edge Technology Inc ....E....... 626 856-8979
13455 Brooks Dr Ste A Baldwin Park (91706) *(P-9149)*

Front Porch Communities & Svcs 858 454-2151
849 Coast Blvd La Jolla (92037) *(P-14709)*

Front Porch Communities & Svcs ....C...... 760 729-4983
2855 Carlsbad Blvd Carlsbad (92008) *(P-14710)*

Front Porch Communities & Svcs ....C...... 323 661-1128
1055 N Kingsley Dr Los Angeles (90029) *(P-17954)*

Front Porch Communities & Svcs 619 427-2777
111 Third Ave Chula Vista (91910) *(P-17955)*

Front Porch Communities & Svcs ....D...... 805 687-0793
3775 Modoc Rd Santa Barbara (93105) *(P-18124)*

Front Prch Cmmnties Oprting Gr ....C...... 800 233-3709
800 N Brand Blvd Fl 19 Glendale (91203) *(P-18125)*

Frontech N Fujitsu Amer Inc (DH)......................................C...... 877 766-7545
36 Technology Dr Ste 150 Irvine (92618) *(P-16035)*

Frontera Solutions Inc ....E....... 714 368-1631
1913 E 17th St Ste 210 Santa Ana (92705) *(P-8163)*

Frontier California Inc ....B....... 818 365-0542
510 Park Ave San Fernando (91340) *(P-11880)*

Frontier California Inc ....B....... 805 372-6000
1 Wellpoint Way Westlake Village (91362) *(P-11881)*

Frontier California Inc ....B....... 805 925-0000
200 W Church St Santa Maria (93458) *(P-11882)*

Frontier California Inc ....B....... 714 375-6713
7352 Slater Ave Huntington Beach (92647) *(P-11883)*

Frontier California Inc ....B....... 760 342-0500
83793 Doctor Carreon Blvd Indio (92201) *(P-11884)*

Frontier Electronics Corp ....F....... 805 522-9998
667 Cochran St Simi Valley (93065) *(P-8943)*

Frontier Engrg & Mfg Tech Inc ....E....... 562 606-2655
800 W 16th St Long Beach (90813) *(P-7838)*

Frontier Logistics Services, Compton *Also Called: F R T International Inc (P-11576)*

Frontier Mechanical Inc ....D...... 661 589-6203
6309 Seven Seas Ave Bakersfield (93308) *(P-772)*

Frontier Plumbing, Bakersfield *Also Called: Frontier Mechanical Inc (P-772)*

Frontier Technologies, Long Beach *Also Called: Frontier Engrg & Mfg Tech Inc (P-7838)*

Frontwave Credit Union (PA)..C...... 760 430-7511
1278 Rocky Point Dr Oceanside (92056) *(P-14227)*

Frozen Bean Inc ....E....... 855 837-6936
9238 Bally Ct Rancho Cucamonga (91730) *(P-1773)*

Fruit Growers Supply Company (PA)..................................E....... 888 997-4855
27770 Entertainment Dr Ste 120 Valencia (91355) *(P-3101)*

Frutarom ....E....... 951 734-6620
790 E Harrison St Corona (92879) *(P-1774)*

Fruth Custom Plastics Inc ....D...... 714 993-9955
701 Richfield Rd Placentia (92870) *(P-5032)*

Fry Reglet Corporation (PA)..D...... 800 237-9773
14013 Marquardt Ave Santa Fe Springs (90670) *(P-5696)*

Fry Steel Company ....C...... 562 802-2721
13325 Molette St Santa Fe Springs (90670) *(P-12551)*

Fryman Management Inc ....D...... 949 481-5211
18 Goodyear Ste 105 Irvine (92618) *(P-20336)*

Fs - Precision Tech Co LLC ....D...... 310 638-0595
3025 E Victoria St Compton (90221) *(P-5814)*

Mergent email: customerrelations@mergent.com
1096

2024 Southern California
Business Directory and Buyers Guide

(P-0000) Products & Services Section entry number
(PA)=Parent Co (HQ)=Headquarters (DH)=Div Headquarters

FSA Arlanza Child Dev Ctr .... D...... 951 353-0129
8172 Magnolia Ave Riverside (92504) *(P-19210)*

Fsc, Rancho Cucamonga *Also Called: Fluorescent Supply Co Inc (P-8313)*

FSI Coating Technologies Inc .... E...... 949 540-1140
45 Parker Ste 100 Irvine (92618) *(P-4491)*

Fssi, Santa Ana *Also Called: Financial Statement Svcs Inc (P-15631)*

Ft 2 Inc .... C...... 714 765-5555
1211 N Miller St Anaheim (92806) *(P-12975)*

Ft Textiles, Fullerton *Also Called: Fabtex Inc (P-2039)*

Ft3 Tactical, Stanton *Also Called: Field Time Target Training LLC (P-6747)*

Ftdi West Inc .... D...... 909 473-1111
3375 Enterprise Dr Bloomington (92316) *(P-11580)*

Ftg Aerospace Inc (DH) .... **E**...... **818 407-4024**
20740 Marilla St Chatsworth (91311) *(P-5775)*

Ftg Circuits Inc (DH) .... **E**...... **818 407-4024**
20750 Marilla St Chatsworth (91311) *(P-8679)*

Fti Consulting Inc .... D...... 213 689-1200
350 S Grand Ave Ste 3000 Los Angeles (90071) *(P-19596)*

Ftr Associates Inc .... E...... 562 945-7504
11862 Burke St Santa Fe Springs (90670) *(P-6518)*

Ftsi, Monrovia *Also Called: Financial Tech Sltons Intl Inc (P-20171)*

Fuego Living LLC .... E...... 415 558-7151
1714 Alta Mura Rd Pacific Palisades (90272) *(P-8217)*

Fuji Food Products Inc (PA) .... **D**...... **562 404-2590**
14420 Bloomfield Ave Santa Fe Springs (90670) *(P-1900)*

Fuji Food Products Inc .... C...... 619 268-3118
8660 Miramar Rd Ste N San Diego (92126) *(P-1901)*

Fuji Natural Foods Inc (HQ) .... **D**...... **909 947-1008**
13500 S Hamner Ave Ontario (91761) *(P-1902)*

Fujifilm Dsynth Btchnlgies Cal .... E...... 914 789-8100
2430 Conejo Spectrum St Thousand Oaks (91320) *(P-4315)*

Fujifilm Dsynth Btchnlgies USA .... E...... 805 699-5579
2430 Conejo Spectrum St Thousand Oaks (91320) *(P-4316)*

Fujifilm Irvine Scientific Inc (DH) .... **E**...... **949 261-7800**
1830 E Warner Ave Santa Ana (92705) *(P-4317)*

Fujikura Composite America Inc .... E...... 760 598-6060
1819 Aston Ave Ste 101 Carlsbad (92008) *(P-10992)*

Fujikuria Composits, Carlsbad *Also Called: Fujikura Composite America Inc (P-10992)*

Fujitec America Inc .... C...... 310 464-8270
12170 Mora Dr Ste 1 Santa Fe Springs (90670) *(P-20033)*

Fujitsu Glovia, Inc., El Segundo *Also Called: Crescentone Inc (P-16004)*

Fulcrum Microsystems Inc .... D...... 818 871-8100
26630 Agoura Rd Calabasas (91302) *(P-8798)*

Fulgent Genetics Inc (PA) .... **A**...... **626 350-0537**
4399 Santa Anita Ave El Monte (91731) *(P-18551)*

Fulham Co Inc .... E...... 323 779-2980
12705 S Van Ness Ave Hawthorne (90250) *(P-8096)*

Full Scale Logistics LLC .... D...... 805 279-6799
2722 Rocky Point Ct Thousand Oaks (91362) *(P-11832)*

Full-Swing Golf Inc .... E...... 858 675-1100
1905 Aston Ave Ste 100 Carlsbad (92008) *(P-12929)*

Full/Tech Systems Inc .... E...... 619 297-0454
5525 Market St San Diego (92114) *(P-15632)*

Fullerton College Bookstore, Fullerton *Also Called: North Ornge Cnty Cmnty Cllege (P-14068)*

Fullerton Hlthcare Wllness CNT .... C...... 714 992-5701
2222 N Harbor Blvd Fullerton (92835) *(P-17956)*

Fullmer Construction .... C...... 909 947-9467
1725 S Grove Ave Ontario (91761) *(P-503)*

Fulwider and Patton LLP .... D...... 310 824-5555
111 W Ocean Blvd Ste 1510 Long Beach (90802) *(P-18856)*

Fun Flex, Big Bear Lake *Also Called: Big Bear Bowling Barn Inc (P-1144)*

Fun Furnishings, La Verne *Also Called: G & M Mattress and Foam Corporation (P-2849)*

Fun Properties Inc (PA) .... **D**...... **310 787-4500**
2645 Maricopa St Torrance (90503) *(P-5880)*

Funai Corporation Inc (HQ) .... **E**...... **310 787-3000**
12489 Lakeland Rd Santa Fe Springs (90670) *(P-8411)*

Funai Corporation Inc .... D...... 201 727-4560
19900 Van Ness Ave Torrance (90501) *(P-8412)*

Funai Electric Co., Torrance *Also Called: Funai Corporation Inc (P-8412)*

Fundamental Tech Intl Inc .... E...... 562 595-0661
2900 E 29th St Long Beach (90806) *(P-10133)*

Fungs Village Inc .... E...... 323 881-1600
5339 E Washington Blvd Commerce (90040) *(P-1839)*

Funimation Entertainment, Culver City *Also Called: Crunchyroll LLC (P-17180)*

Funnelcloudsales .... D...... 661 284-6032
21758 Placeritos Blvd Santa Clarita (91321) *(P-11529)*

Funny-Bunny Inc (PA) .... **D**...... **714 957-1114**
1513b E Saint Gertrude Pl Santa Ana (92705) *(P-2205)*

Furniture America Cal Inc (PA) .... **E**...... **866 923-8500**
20300 Business Pkwy City Of Industry (91789) *(P-12281)*

Furniture America Cal Inc .... E...... 909 718-7276
19635 E Walnut Dr N City Of Industry (91789) *(P-12282)*

Furniture Solutions Inc .... E...... 714 666-0424
1347 N Blue Gum St Anaheim (92806) *(P-2884)*

Furniture Technics Inc .... E...... 562 802-0261
2900 Supply Ave Commerce (90040) *(P-2774)*

Furniture Techniques, Commerce *Also Called: Furniture Technics Inc (P-2774)*

Furniture Technologies Inc .... E...... 760 246-9180
17227 Columbus St Adelanto (92301) *(P-2570)*

Furst, Marina Del Rey *Also Called: Lf Sportswear Inc (P-2253)*

Fuscoe Engineering Inc (PA) .... **D**...... **949 474-1960**
15535 Sand Canyon Ave Irvine (92618) *(P-19597)*

Fusefx, Van Nuys *Also Called: Fusefx LLC (P-17254)*

Fusefx LLC .... B...... 818 237-5052
14823 Califa St Van Nuys (91411) *(P-17254)*

Fusion Biotec Inc .... E...... 949 264-3437
160 S Cypress St Ste 400 Orange (92866) *(P-10512)*

Fusion Food Factory .... F...... 858 578-8001
8980 Crestmar Pt San Diego (92121) *(P-1472)*

Fusion Product Mfg Inc .... D...... 619 819-5521
24024 Humphries Rd Bldg 1 Tecate (91980) *(P-7072)*

Fusion Sign & Design Inc (PA) .... **F**...... **877 477-8777**
680 Columbia Ave Riverside (92507) *(P-11122)*

Futek Advanced Sensor Tech, Irvine *Also Called: Futek Advanced Sensor Tech Inc (P-10134)*

Futek Advanced Sensor Tech Inc .... C...... 949 465-0900
10 Thomas Irvine (92618) *(P-10134)*

Future Commodities Intl Inc .... E...... 888 588-2378
1425 S Campus Ave Ontario (91761) *(P-7348)*

Future Foam, Fullerton *Also Called: Future Foam Inc (P-4888)*

Future Foam Inc .... C...... 714 459-9971
2441 Cypress Way Fullerton (92831) *(P-4888)*

Future Foam Inc .... E...... 714 871-2344
2451 Cypress Way Fullerton (92831) *(P-4889)*

Future Tech Metals Inc .... E...... 951 781-4801
719 Palmyrita Ave Riverside (92507) *(P-7839)*

Futuristics Machine Inc .... E...... 858 450-0644
7014 Carroll Rd San Diego (92121) *(P-7840)*

Fvo Solutions Inc .... D...... 626 449-0218
789 N Fair Oaks Ave Pasadena (91103) *(P-6706)*

Fw, Paramount *Also Called: Carlton Forge Works (P-6476)*

Fx Networks LLC .... C...... 310 369-1000
10201 W Pico Blvd Bldg 103 Los Angeles (90064) *(P-11993)*

Fxc Corporation .... D...... 714 557-8032
3050 Red Hill Ave Costa Mesa (92626) *(P-2553)*

Fxc Corporation (PA) .... **E**...... **714 556-7400**
3050 Red Hill Ave Costa Mesa (92626) *(P-5919)*

Fxp Technologies, Brea *Also Called: S&B Industry Inc (P-5194)*

Fziomed Inc (PA) .... **E**...... **805 546-0610**
231 Bonetti Dr San Luis Obispo (93401) *(P-10513)*

G - L Veneer Co Inc (PA) .... **D**...... **323 582-5203**
2224 E Slauson Ave Huntington Park (90255) *(P-2687)*

G & G Door Products Inc .... E...... 714 228-2008
7600 Stage Rd Buena Park (90621) *(P-13575)*

G & G Quality Case Co Inc .... D...... 323 233-2482
2025 E 25th St Vernon (90058) *(P-5287)*

G & I Industries, Baldwin Park *Also Called: G & I Islas Industries Inc (P-7199)*

G & I Islas Industries Inc (PA) .... **E**...... **626 960-5020**
12860 Schabarum Ave Baldwin Park (91706) *(P-7199)*

G & L Musical Instruments, Fullerton *Also Called: Bbe Sound Inc (P-10921)*

Employee Codes: A=Over 500 employees, B=251-500
C=101-250, D=51-100, E=20-50, F=10-19, G=1-9

2024 Southern California
Business Directory and Buyers Guide

© Mergent Inc. 1-800-342-5647

1097

G & M Mattress and Foam Corporation .... D....... 909 593-1000
 1943 N White Ave La Verne (91750) *(P-2849)*

G A Systems, Orange *Also Called: SA Serving Lines Inc (P-6309)*

G A Systems Inc .... F....... 714 848-7529
 226 W Carleton Ave Orange (92867) *(P-7659)*

G B Remanufacturing Inc .... D....... 562 272-7333
 2040 E Cherry Industrial Cir Long Beach (90805) *(P-5033)*

G C Pallets Inc .... E....... 909 357-8515
 5490 26th St Riverside (92509) *(P-2718)*

G C S, Torrance *Also Called: Global Comm Semiconductors LLC (P-8799)*

G F Cole Corporation (PA) .... F....... 310 320-0601
 21735 S Western Ave Torrance (90501) *(P-4729)*

G F I, Vernon *Also Called: Good Fellas Industries Inc (P-13960)*

G Girl Clothing, Vernon *Also Called: LAT LLC (P-2346)*

G Kagan and Sons Inc (PA) .... E....... 323 583-1400
 3957 S Hill St Los Angeles (90037) *(P-2022)*

G M I, Anaheim *Also Called: Gear Manufacturing Inc (P-9698)*

G M I, San Diego *Also Called: Guard Management Inc (P-16646)*

G M S, Carlsbad *Also Called: Global Microwave Systems Inc (P-8520)*

G P H Medical Services, Beverly Hills *Also Called: GPh Medical & Legal Services (P-17966)*

G P Resources, Compton *Also Called: General Petroleum LLC (P-13452)*

G P S, Taft *Also Called: General Production Svc Cal Inc (P-670)*

G Printing Inc .... F....... 818 246-1156
 1815 Ayers Way Burbank (91501) *(P-3577)*

G R C, Chatsworth *Also Called: General Ribbon Corp (P-11057)*

G R Leonard & Co Inc .... E....... 847 797-8101
 181 N Vermont Ave Glendora (91741) *(P-3448)*

G S N, Santa Monica *Also Called: Game Show Network Music LLC (P-11994)*

G T C, Whittier *Also Called: General Transistor Corporation (P-12661)*

G T Water Products Inc .... F....... 805 529-2900
 5239 N Commerce Ave Moorpark (93021) *(P-5970)*

G V Industries Inc .... E....... 619 474-3013
 1346 Cleveland Ave National City (91950) *(P-7841)*

G W Surfaces (PA) .... D....... 805 642-5004
 2432 Palma Dr Ventura (93003) *(P-1159)*

G-2 Graphic Service Inc .... D....... 818 623-3100
 5510 Cleon Ave North Hollywood (91601) *(P-3760)*

G-G Distribution & Dev Co Inc .... C....... 661 257-5700
 28545 Livingston Ave Valencia (91355) *(P-6790)*

G/G Industries, Valencia *Also Called: G-G Distribution & Dev Co Inc (P-6790)*

G/M Business Interiors, San Diego *Also Called: Goforth & Marti (P-12283)*

G&L Penasquitos Inc .... A....... 858 538-0802
 10584 Rancho Carmel Dr San Diego (92128) *(P-19084)*

G2 Software Systems Inc .... C....... 619 222-8025
 4025 Hancock St Ste 105 San Diego (92110) *(P-16036)*

G4s Government Services, Anaheim *Also Called: G4s Justice Services LLC (P-16737)*

G4s Justice Services LLC .... D....... 800 589-6003
 1290 N Hancock St Ste 103 Anaheim (92807) *(P-16737)*

GA Gertmenian and Sons LLC (PA) .... C....... 213 250-7777
 300 W Avenue 33 Los Angeles (90031) *(P-12301)*

Ga-Asi, Poway *Also Called: General Atmics Arntcal Systems (P-9523)*

Gable House Inc .... D....... 310 378-2265
 1611 S Pacific Coast Hwy Redondo Beach (90277) *(P-17356)*

Gable House Bowl, Redondo Beach *Also Called: Gable House Inc (P-17356)*

Gabriel Container (PA) .... C....... 562 699-1051
 8844 Millergrove Dr Santa Fe Springs (90670) *(P-3102)*

Gachupin Enterprises LLC .... F....... 714 375-4111
 5671 Engineer Dr Huntington Beach (92649) *(P-3761)*

GAF Materials, Shafter *Also Called: Standard Industries Inc (P-12369)*

Gaffoglio Fmly Mtlcrafters Inc (PA) .... C....... 714 444-2000
 11161 Slater Ave Fountain Valley (92708) *(P-5340)*

Gaikai Inc .... D
 65 Enterprise Aliso Viejo (92656) *(P-16253)*

Gail Materials Inc .... E....... 951 667-6106
 10060 Dawson Canyon Rd Corona (92883) *(P-406)*

Gaines Manufacturing Inc .... E....... 858 486-7100
 12200 Kirkham Rd Poway (92064) *(P-6243)*

Gainey Ceramics Inc .... E....... 909 596-4464
 1200 Arrow Hwy La Verne (91750) *(P-5384)*

Gainey Vineyard .... E....... 805 688-0558
 3950 E Highway 246 Santa Ynez (93460) *(P-1632)*

Gaju Market Corporation .... C....... 213 382-9444
 450 S Western Ave Los Angeles (90020) *(P-13539)*

Galactic Co LLC (DH) .... F....... 661 824-6600
 16555 Spaceship Landing Way Mojave (93501) *(P-9893)*

Galasso's Bakery, Jurupa Valley *Also Called: Galassos Bakery (P-13368)*

Galassos Bakery (PA) .... C....... 951 360-1211
 10820 San Sevaine Way Jurupa Valley (91752) *(P-13368)*

Galaxy Bearing Company, Valencia *Also Called: Galaxy Die and Engineering Inc (P-5803)*

Galaxy Die and Engineering Inc .... E....... 661 775-9301
 24910 Avenue Tibbitts Valencia (91355) *(P-5803)*

Gale Banks Engineering .... C....... 626 969-9600
 546 S Duggan Ave Azusa (91702) *(P-6894)*

Gale/Triangle Inc (PA) .... D....... 562 741-1300
 12816 Shoemaker Ave Santa Fe Springs (90670) *(P-11453)*

Gali Corporation .... E....... 310 477-1224
 2301 Pontius Ave Los Angeles (90064) *(P-9696)*

Galkos Construction Inc .... D....... 714 373-8545
 15262 Pipeline Ln Huntington Beach (92649) *(P-552)*

Gallagher Rental Inc .... E....... 714 690-1559
 15701 Heron Ave La Mirada (90638) *(P-8367)*

Gallegos United, Huntington Beach *Also Called: Grupo Gallegos (P-15541)*

Galleher, Santa Fe Springs *Also Called: Galleher LLC (P-12302)*

Galleher Acquisition Corp .... E....... 909 623-5888
 1384 S Signal Dr Pomona (91766) *(P-6442)*

Galleher Industries, Pomona *Also Called: Galleher Acquisition Corp (P-6442)*

Galleher LLC (PA) .... C....... 562 944-8885
 9303 Greenleaf Ave Santa Fe Springs (90670) *(P-12302)*

Galley Solutions Inc .... F....... 818 636-1538
 712 Archer St San Diego (92109) *(P-16254)*

Galpin Ford, North Hills *Also Called: Galpin Motors Inc (P-13770)*

Galpin Motors Inc (PA) .... B....... 818 787-3800
 15505 Roscoe Blvd North Hills (91343) *(P-13770)*

Galt, San Diego *Also Called: Global A Lgistics Training Inc (P-9979)*

Galtech Computer Corporation .... E....... 805 376-1060
 501 Flynn Rd Camarillo (93012) *(P-2885)*

Galtech International, Camarillo *Also Called: Galtech Computer Corporation (P-2885)*

Gama Contracting Services Inc .... C....... 626 442-7200
 1835 Floradale Ave South El Monte (91733) *(P-12768)*

Gambol Industries Inc .... E....... 562 901-2470
 1880 Century Park E Ste 950 Los Angeles (90067) *(P-9858)*

Gamco, North Hollywood *Also Called: Bobrick Washroom Equipment Inc (P-2973)*

Game Show Network Music LLC (DH) .... C....... 310 255-6800
 2150 Colorado Ave Ste 100 Santa Monica (90404) *(P-11994)*

Gamebreaker Inc (PA) .... E....... 818 224-7424
 31324 Via Colinas Ste 102 Westlake Village (91362) *(P-10993)*

Gamemine LLC .... E....... 310 310-3105
 439 Carroll Canal Venice (90291) *(P-16255)*

Gameworks Entertainment LLC (PA) .... A....... 206 521-0952
 9737 Lurline Ave Chatsworth (91311) *(P-14010)*

Gamma, Vernon *Also Called: Rotax Incorporated (P-2367)*

Gamma Aerospace LLC .... E....... 310 532-4480
 1461 S Balboa Ave Ontario (91761) *(P-7842)*

Gamma Scientific Inc .... E....... 858 635-9008
 9925 Carroll Canyon Rd San Diego (92131) *(P-10367)*

Gan Limited .... B....... 702 964-5777
 400 Spectrum Center Dr Ste 1900 Irvine (92618) *(P-16037)*

Ganahl Lumber Company .... D....... 951 278-4000
 150 W Blaine St Corona (92878) *(P-13576)*

Gans Ink and Supply Co Inc (PA) .... E....... 323 264-2200
 1441 Boyd St Los Angeles (90033) *(P-4588)*

Gantner Instruments Inc .... E....... 888 512-5788
 402 W Broadway Ste 400 San Diego (92101) *(P-10368)*

Ganz USA LLC .... C....... 818 901-0077
 16525 Sherman Way Ste C5 Van Nuys (91406) *(P-20174)*

Gar Enterprises .... E....... 909 985-4575
 1396 W 9th St Upland (91786) *(P-9047)*

Gar Enterprises (PA) .... D....... 626 574-1175
 418 E Live Oak Ave Arcadia (91006) *(P-12413)*

Gar Laboratories Inc .... C....... 951 788-0700
1844 Massachusetts Ave Riverside (92507) *(P-4412)*

Gard Inc .... E....... 714 738-5891
524 E Walnut Ave Fullerton (92832) *(P-6244)*

Garda CL West Inc (HQ).. B....... 213 383-3611
1612 W Pico Blvd Los Angeles (90015) *(P-16643)*

Garden Crest Cnvlscent Hosp In .... D....... 323 663-8281
909 Lucile Ave Los Angeles (90026) *(P-17957)*

GARDEN CREST RETIREMENT RESIDE, Los Angeles *Also Called: Garden Crest Cnvlscent Hosp In (P-17957)*

Garden Grove Advanced Imaging .... C....... 310 445-2800
1510 Cotner Ave Los Angeles (90025) *(P-17658)*

Garden Grove Hospital, Garden Grove *Also Called: Kenneth Corp (P-18314)*

Garden Grove Medical Investors (HQ)..................... D....... 714 534-1041
12332 Garden Grove Blvd Garden Grove (92843) *(P-17958)*

Garden Grove Rehabilitation, Garden Grove *Also Called: Garden Grove Medical Investors (P-17958)*

Garden Grove Unified Schl Dst .... E....... 714 663-6101
12381 Dale St Garden Grove (92841) *(P-18967)*

Garden Grove Unified Schl Dst .... D....... 714 663-6437
8371 Orangewood Ave Garden Grove (92841) *(P-19211)*

Garden Pals Inc .... E....... 909 605-0200
3632 E Moonlight St Unit 91 Ontario (91761) *(P-5881)*

Gardena Honda, Gardena *Also Called: DCH Gardena Honda (P-13756)*

Gardena Hospital LP .... A....... 310 532-4200
1145 W Redondo Beach Blvd Gardena (90247) *(P-18263)*

Gardena Medical Offices, Gardena *Also Called: Kaiser Foundation Hospitals (P-18298)*

Gardena Retirement Center Inc .... C....... 310 327-4091
14741 S Vermont Ave Gardena (90247) *(P-17959)*

Gardena Valley News Inc .... E....... 310 329-6351
15005 S Vermont Ave Gardena (90247) *(P-3278)*

Gardens Regional Hosp Med Ctr, Hawaiian Gardens *Also Called: Gardens Regional Hospital and Medical Center Incorporated (P-18264)*

Gardens Regional Hospital and Medical Center Incorporated .... B....... 877 877-1104
21530 Pioneer Blvd Hawaiian Gardens (90716) *(P-18264)*

Gardner Logistics, Chino *Also Called: CRST Expedited Inc (P-11478)*

Garfield Imaging Center Inc .... C....... 626 572-0912
555 N Garfield Ave Monterey Park (91754) *(P-17659)*

Garfield Medical Center, Monterey Park *Also Called: Ahmc Garfield Medical Ctr LP (P-17876)*

Garich Inc (PA).. B....... 858 453-1331
6050 Santo Rd Ste 200 San Diego (92124) *(P-15847)*

Garich Inc .... B....... 951 302-4750
504 E Alvarado St Ste 201 Fallbrook (92028) *(P-15848)*

Garlic Company .... C....... 661 393-4212
18602 Zerker Rd Shafter (93263) *(P-4)*

Garlic King, San Diego *Also Called: California Garlic Company Inc (P-13989)*

Garmin International Inc .... B....... 909 444-5000
135 S State College Blvd Ste 110 Brea (92821) *(P-9977)*

Garmon Corporation (PA).......................................D....... 888 628-8783
27461 Via Industria Temecula (92590) *(P-1440)*

Garner Holt Productions, Redlands *Also Called: Garner Holt Productions Inc (P-7425)*

Garner Holt Productions Inc .... E....... 909 799-3030
1255 Research Dr Redlands (92374) *(P-7425)*

Garrett J Gentry Gen Engrg Inc .... D....... 909 693-3391
1297 W 9th St Upland (91786) *(P-19598)*

Garrett Motion Inc .... C....... 973 867-7016
290 E Cole Blvd Calexico (92231) *(P-9393)*

Garrett Motion Inc .... D....... 760 357-3297
1778 Zinetta Rd Ste A Calexico (92231) *(P-9568)*

Garrett Motion Inc .... C....... 310 512-5424
2525 W 190th St Torrance (90504) *(P-19840)*

Garrett Precision Inc .... F....... 949 855-9710
25082 La Suen Rd Laguna Hills (92653) *(P-7843)*

Garrett Transportation I Inc (HQ)............................D....... 973 455-2000
2525 W 190th St Torrance (90504) *(P-9569)*

Garris Plastering, Orange *Also Called: Padilla Construction Company (P-990)*

Garrison Manufacturing Inc .... E....... 714 549-4880
3320 S Yale St Santa Ana (92704) *(P-9394)*

Garvey Nut & Candy, Pico Rivera *Also Called: Genesis Foods Corporation (P-1540)*

Gary Bale Redi-Mix Con Inc .... D....... 949 786-9441
16131 Construction Cir W Irvine (92606) *(P-5477)*

Gary Cardiff Enterprises Inc .... D....... 760 568-1403
75255 Sheryl Ave Palm Desert (92211) *(P-11389)*

Gary Manufacturing, National City *Also Called: Gmi Inc (P-2494)*

Gary Manufacturing Inc .... E....... 619 429-4479
2626 Southport Way Ste E National City (91950) *(P-5034)*

Gas Company, The, Los Angeles *Also Called: Southern California Gas Co (P-12084)*

Gas Company, The, Downey *Also Called: Southern California Gas Co (P-12095)*

Gasket Associates LP (PA)...................................... F....... 310 217-5630
10816 Kurt St Sylmar (91342) *(P-4730)*

Gasket Manufacturing Co .... E....... 310 217-5600
8427 Secura Way Santa Fe Springs (90670) *(P-4731)*

Gasketfab Division, Torrance *Also Called: Industrial Gasket and Sup Co (P-4734)*

Gat - Arln Ground Support Inc .... C....... 818 847-9127
2627 N Hollywood Way Burbank (91505) *(P-11698)*

Gatc Ghq, Rancho Dominguez *Also Called: Global Agri-Trade (P-1564)*

Gate City Beverage Distrs (PA)................................ B....... 909 799-0281
2505 Steele Rd San Bernardino (92408) *(P-13466)*

Gate Three Healthcare LLC .... C....... 949 587-9000
24962 Calle Aragon Laguna Hills (92637) *(P-17960)*

Gateb Consulting Inc .... C....... 310 526-8323
815 Hampton Dr Unit 1b Venice (90291) *(P-20337)*

Gatekeeper Systems Inc (PA)..................................D....... 888 808-9433
90 Icon Foothill Ranch (92610) *(P-9212)*

Gateway, Poway *Also Called: Gateway Inc (P-7426)*

Gateway, Irvine *Also Called: Gateway Inc (P-7427)*

Gateway, Los Angeles *Also Called: County of Los Angeles (P-15661)*

Gateway Inc .... E....... 858 451-9933
12750 Gateway Park Rd # 124 Poway (92064) *(P-7426)*

Gateway Inc (DH)... C....... 949 471-7000
7565 Irvine Center Dr Ste 150 Irvine (92618) *(P-7427)*

Gateway Fresh LLC .... C....... 951 378-5439
3660 Grand Ave Ste A Chino Hills (91709) *(P-14930)*

Gateway Genomics LLC ....D....... 858 886-7250
11436 Sorrento Valley Rd San Diego (92121) *(P-4274)*

Gateway Hardware, Inyokern *Also Called: Herbert Rizzardini (P-13678)*

Gateway Home Realty, Brea *Also Called: American Financial Network Inc (P-14294)*

Gateway Logistics Tech LLC .... C....... 732 750-9000
11400 W Olympic Blvd Los Angeles (90064) *(P-11454)*

Gateway Manufacturing LLC ....D....... 949 471-7000
7565 Irvine Center Dr Irvine (92618) *(P-7495)*

Gateway Mattress Co Inc .... C....... 323 725-1923
624 S Vail Ave Montebello (90640) *(P-2850)*

Gateway US Retail Inc .... C....... 949 471-7000
7565 Irvine Center Dr Irvine (92618) *(P-7428)*

Gateways Hosp Mental Hlth Ctr (PA)...................... C....... 323 644-2000
1891 Effie St Los Angeles (90026) *(P-18513)*

Gavia, Vernon *Also Called: F Gavina & Sons Inc (P-1819)*

Gavial Engineering & Mfg Inc .... E....... 805 614-0060
1435 W Mccoy Ln Santa Maria (93455) *(P-8680)*

Gavin De Becker & Assoc GP LLC .... C....... 818 505-0177
350 N Glendale Ave Ste 517 Glendale (91206) *(P-20175)*

Gavin De Becker & Associates, Glendale *Also Called: Gavin De Becker & Assoc GP LLC (P-20175)*

Gaylord's Meat Co, Fullerton *Also Called: Gaylords HRI Meats (P-1195)*

Gaylords HRI Meats .... F....... 714 526-2278
1100 E Ash Ave Ste C Fullerton (92831) *(P-1195)*

Gaytan Foods LLC ....D....... 626 330-4553
15430 Proctor Ave City Of Industry (91745) *(P-1219)*

Gaze USA Inc .... E....... 213 622-0022
2011 E 25th St Vernon (90058) *(P-2324)*

Gazelle Transportation LLC .... C....... 661 322-8868
34915 Gazelle Ct Bakersfield (93308) *(P-11455)*

Gb007 Inc .... E....... 858 684-1300
3013 Science Park Rd San Diego (92121) *(P-4318)*

Gbc Concrete Masnry Cnstr Inc .... C....... 951 245-2355
561 Birch St Lake Elsinore (92530) *(P-957)*

GBF Enterprises Inc .... E....... 714 979-7131
2709 Halladay St Santa Ana (92705) *(P-7844)*

Gbl Systems Corporation .... E....... 805 987-4345
760 Paseo Camarillo Ste 401 Camarillo (93010) *(P-16443)*

Employee Codes: A=Over 500 employees, B=251-500
C=101-250, D=51-100, E=20-50, F=10-19, G=1-9

2024 Southern California
Business Directory and Buyers Guide

© Mergent Inc. 1-800-342-5647

1099

A L P H A B E T I C

Gbm, Alhambra *Also Called: Gracing Brand Management Inc (P-2416)*

GBS Linens Inc (PA)..D....... 714 778-6448
305 N Muller St Anaheim (92801) *(P-15451)*

GBS Party Linens, Anaheim *Also Called: GBS Linens Inc (P-15451)*

GBT Inc ....C....... 626 854-9338
17358 Railroad St City Of Industry (91748) *(P-12414)*

Gc International Inc (PA).....................................E....... 805 389-4631
4671 Calle Carga Camarillo (93012) *(P-5794)*

Gc International Inc ....E....... 805 389-4631
4671 Calle Carga Camarillo (93012) *(P-8460)*

Gciu Employer Retirement Fund, City Of Industry *Also Called: Benefits Prgram Adminsitration (P-14988)*

Gcl W, Los Angeles *Also Called: Garda CL West Inc (P-16643)*

Gcn Supply LLC ....E....... 909 643-4603
9070 Bridgeport Pl Rancho Cucamonga (91730) *(P-6378)*

Gcorp Consulting ....C....... 619 587-3160
2831 Camino Del Rio S Ste 311 San Diego (92108) *(P-20176)*

GCR Tires & Service 185, Fontana *Also Called: Bridgestone Americas (P-17020)*

GD Heil Inc ....C....... 714 687-9100
1031 Segovia Cir Placentia (92870) *(P-1133)*

Gda Inc ....F....... 702 260-1949
13563 Alondra Blvd Santa Fe Springs (90670) *(P-2023)*

GE, Victorville *Also Called: General Electric Company (P-9535)*

GE, Walnut *Also Called: General Electric Company (P-11581)*

GE, Chino *Also Called: General Electric Company (P-13433)*

GE Aviation Systems LLC ....E....... 714 692-0200
23695 Via Del Rio Yorba Linda (92887) *(P-9697)*

GE Energy, Diamond Bar *Also Called: Motech Americas LLC (P-19861)*

GE Water & Process Tech, Avila Beach *Also Called: Veolia Wts Usa Inc (P-4637)*

GE Wind Energy LLC ....C....... 661 823-6423
13681 Chantico Rd Tehachapi (93561) *(P-6880)*

GE Wind Energy LLC (HQ)..................................B....... 661 822-6835
13000 Jameson Rd Tehachapi (93561) *(P-6881)*

Gear Manufacturing Inc ....E....... 714 792-2895
3701 E Miraloma Ave Anaheim (92806) *(P-9698)*

Gear Technology, Rancho Cucamonga *Also Called: Marino Enterprises Inc (P-9742)*

Gear Vendors, El Cajon *Also Called: Gear Vendors Inc (P-9395)*

Gear Vendors Inc ....E....... 619 562-0060
1717 N Magnolia Ave El Cajon (92020) *(P-9395)*

GEARMENT, Huntington Beach *Also Called: Gearment Inc (P-2101)*

Gearment Inc (PA)...C....... 866 236-5476
14801 Able Ln Ste 102 Huntington Beach (92647) *(P-2101)*

Gedney Foods Company ....C....... 952 448-2612
12243 Branford St Sun Valley (91352) *(P-1359)*

Geek Squad, Cerritos *Also Called: Geek Squad Inc (P-16568)*

Geek Squad Inc ....D....... 562 402-1555
12989 Park Plaza Dr Cerritos (90703) *(P-16568)*

Geeriraj Inc ....E....... 760 244-6149
7042 Santa Fe Ave E Ste A1 Hesperia (92345) *(P-8681)*

Gehr Group, Commerce *Also Called: Gehr Industries Inc (P-5742)*

Gehr Industries Inc (HQ)....................................C....... 323 728-5558
7400 E Slauson Ave Commerce (90040) *(P-5742)*

Gehry Partners LLP ....C....... 310 482-3000
12541 Beatrice St Los Angeles (90066) *(P-19728)*

Gehry Technologies Inc ....D....... 310 862-1200
12181 Bluff Creek Dr Los Angeles (90094) *(P-16038)*

Geico, Poway *Also Called: Geico General Insurance Co (P-14597)*

Geico General Insurance Co ....A....... 858 848-8200
14111 Danielson St Poway (92064) *(P-14597)*

Geiger Plastics Inc ....E....... 310 327-9926
16150 S Maple Ave # A Gardena (90248) *(P-5035)*

Gel Industries Inc ....C....... 714 639-8191
810 N Lemon St Orange (92867) *(P-6478)*

Gelato Love, Carlsbad *Also Called: Skylar Creations Inc (P-14036)*

Gelfand Rennert & Feldman LLP (PA)...................C....... 310 553-1707
1880 Century Park E Ste 1600 Los Angeles (90067) *(P-16831)*

Gelsons Markets ....D....... 310 306-3192
13455 Maxella Ave Marina Del Rey (90292) *(P-13699)*

Geltman Industries, Vernon *Also Called: Rezex Corporation (P-2106)*

Gem, Palmdale *Also Called: Golden Empire Mortgage Inc (P-14319)*

Gem Mortgage, Bakersfield *Also Called: Golden Empire Mortgage Inc (P-14321)*

Gemalto Cogent Inc (HQ)...................................D....... 626 325-9600
2964 Bradley St Pasadena (91107) *(P-16444)*

Gemco Display and Str Fixs LLC (PA)....................E....... 800 262-1126
2640 E Del Amo Blvd Compton (90221) *(P-12454)*

Gemini Aluminum, Pomona *Also Called: Gemini Aluminum Corporation (P-5697)*

Gemini Aluminum Corporation ....E....... 909 595-7403
3255 Pomona Blvd Pomona (91768) *(P-5697)*

Gemini Basketball LLC ....D....... 213 929-1300
9100 Wilshire Blvd Ste 700e Beverly Hills (90212) *(P-17371)*

Gemini Film & Bag Inc (PA)................................E....... 323 582-0901
3574 Fruitland Ave Maywood (90270) *(P-5036)*

Gemini GEL Llc ....E....... 323 651-0513
8365 Melrose Ave Los Angeles (90069) *(P-3854)*

Gemini Industries Inc ....D....... 949 250-4011
2311 Pullman St Santa Ana (92705) *(P-5680)*

Gemini Mfg & Engrg Inc ....E....... 714 999-0010
1020 E Vermont Ave Anaheim (92805) *(P-7073)*

Gemini Plastics, Maywood *Also Called: Gemini Film & Bag Inc (P-5036)*

Gemini Superfoods, Beverly Hills *Also Called: Organic Gemini LLC (P-1414)*

Gemmm Corporation (PA)...................................D....... 805 496-0555
2860 E Thousand Oaks Blvd Thousand Oaks (91362) *(P-14803)*

Gemological Institute Amer Inc (PA).....................A....... 760 603-4000
5345 Armada Dr Carlsbad (92008) *(P-19003)*

Gemological Institute America, Carlsbad *Also Called: Gemological Institute Amer Inc (P-19003)*

Gemsa Enterprises LLC ....E....... 714 521-1736
14370 Gannet St La Mirada (90638) *(P-1571)*

Gemsa Oils, La Mirada *Also Called: Gemsa Enterprises LLC (P-1571)*

Gemtech Inds Good Earth Mfg ....E....... 714 848-2517
2737 S Garnsey St Santa Ana (92707) *(P-6707)*

Gemtech International, Santa Ana *Also Called: Gemtech Inds Good Earth Mfg (P-6707)*

Gen-Probe Incorporated ....D....... 858 410-8000
10210 Genetic Center Dr San Diego (92121) *(P-4275)*

Gen-Probe Sales & Service Inc ....E....... 858 410-8000
10210 Genetic Center Dr San Diego (92121) *(P-10803)*

Genalyte Inc (PA)..F....... 858 956-1200
6620 Mesa Ridge Rd San Diego (92121) *(P-10514)*

Genasys, San Diego *Also Called: Genasys Inc (P-8413)*

Genasys Inc (PA)...D....... 858 676-1112
16262 W Bernardo Dr San Diego (92127) *(P-8413)*

Genbody America LLC ....E....... 949 561-0664
3420 De Forest Cir Jurupa Valley (91752) *(P-10515)*

Genea Energy Partners Inc ....C....... 714 694-0536
19100 Von Karman Ave Ste 550 Irvine (92612) *(P-16445)*

Genentech Inc ....A....... 760 231-2440
1 Antibody Way Oceanside (92056) *(P-4114)*

General Acute Care Hospital, Downey *Also Called: Pih Health Downey Hospital (P-18377)*

General Acute Care Hospital, Whittier *Also Called: Pih Health Whittier Hospital (P-18380)*

General Atmics Arntcal Systems (DH)....................B....... 858 312-2810
14200 Kirkham Way Poway (92064) *(P-9523)*

General Atmics Arntcal Systems ....C....... 858 455-3358
11906 Tech Center Ct Poway (92064) *(P-9524)*

General Atmics Arntcal Systems ....B....... 858 964-6700
13330 Evening Creek Dr N San Diego (92128) *(P-9525)*

General Atmics Arntcal Systems ....B....... 858 312-4247
13550 Stowe Dr Poway (92064) *(P-9526)*

General Atmics Arntcal Systems ....C....... 858 455-3000
12220 Parkway Centre Dr Poway (92064) *(P-9527)*

General Atmics Arntcal Systems ....A....... 858 762-6700
16761 Via Del Campo Ct San Diego (92127) *(P-9528)*

General Atmics Arntcal Systems ....B....... 858 455-2810
3550 General Atomics Ct San Diego (92121) *(P-9529)*

General Atmics Arntcal Systems ....B....... 858 762-6700
12365 Crosthwaite Cir Poway (92064) *(P-9530)*

General Atomic Aeron ....C....... 858 455-4560
14040 Danielson St Poway (92064) *(P-9531)*

General Atomic Aeron ....C....... 858 312-3428
13950 Stowe Dr Poway (92064) *(P-9532)*

Mergent email: customerrelations@mergent.com
1100

2024 Southern California
Business Directory and Buyers Guide

(P-0000) Products & Services Section entry number
(PA)=Parent Co (HQ)=Headquarters (DH)=Div Headquarters

General Atomic Aeron .... B...... 858 312-2543
14115 Stowe Dr Poway (92064) *(P-9533)*

General Atomic Aeron .... C...... 760 388-8208
73 El Mirage Airport Rd Ste B Adelanto (92301) *(P-9534)*

General Atomics .... D...... 858 455-4141
3483 Dunhill St San Diego (92121) *(P-19841)*

General Atomics .... D...... 858 676-7100
16969 Mesamint St San Diego (92127) *(P-19842)*

General Atomics .... C...... 858 455-4000
4949 Greencraig Ln San Diego (92123) *(P-19843)*

General Atomics (HQ) .... A...... 858 455-2810
3550 General Atomics Ct San Diego (92121) *(P-19892)*

General Atomics, San Diego *Also Called: General Atmics Arntcal Systems (P-9529)*

General Atomics, Adelanto *Also Called: General Atomic Aeron (P-9534)*

General Atomics Electronic Systems Inc .... B...... 858 522-8495
4949 Greencraig Ln San Diego (92123) *(P-8927)*

General Atomics Energy Pdts, San Diego *Also Called: General Atomics (P-19843)*

General Coatings Corporation .... D...... 858 587-1277
600 W Freedom Ave Orange (92865) *(P-845)*

General Coatings Corporation (PA) .... C...... 858 587-1277
6711 Nancy Ridge Dr San Diego (92121) *(P-846)*

General Coatings Corporation .... D...... 909 204-4150
9349 Feron Blvd Rancho Cucamonga (91730) *(P-847)*

General Cold Stg 4145, Bell Gardens *Also Called: US Foods Inc (P-13403)*

General Container .... D...... 714 562-8700
235 Radio Rd Corona (92879) *(P-3103)*

General Conveyor Inc .... E...... 951 734-3460
13385 Estelle St Corona (92879) *(P-17129)*

General Dynamics Mission .... D...... 619 671-5400
7603 Saint Andrews Ave Ste H San Diego (92154) *(P-8181)*

GENERAL DYNAMICS OTS (CALIFORNIA), INC., San Diego *Also Called: General Dynamics Ots Cal Inc (P-9699)*

General Dynamics Ots Cal Inc .... C...... 619 671-5411
7603 Saint Andrews Ave Ste H San Diego (92154) *(P-9699)*

General Electric Company .... E...... 760 530-5200
18000 Phantom St Victorville (92394) *(P-9535)*

General Electric Company .... D...... 909 869-7404
20005 Business Pkwy Walnut (91789) *(P-11581)*

General Electric Company .... F...... 909 517-2560
4045 Cheyenne Ct Chino (91710) *(P-13433)*

General Forming Corporation .... E...... 310 326-0624
640 Alaska Ave Torrance (90503) *(P-9978)*

General Industrial Repair .... E...... 323 278-0873
6865 Washington Blvd Montebello (90640) *(P-7845)*

General Lgstics Systems US Inc .... C...... 562 577-6037
12300 Bell Ranch Dr Santa Fe Springs (90670) *(P-11456)*

General Lgstics Systems US Inc .... C...... 951 677-3972
24305 Prielipp Rd Wildomar (92595) *(P-11457)*

General Linear Systems Inc .... F...... 714 994-4822
4332 Artesia Ave Fullerton (92833) *(P-8944)*

General Mills, Carson *Also Called: General Mills Inc (P-1311)*

General Mills, Vernon *Also Called: General Mills Inc (P-1409)*

General Mills Inc .... D...... 310 605-6108
1055 Sandhill Ave Carson (90746) *(P-1311)*

General Mills Inc .... E...... 323 584-3433
4309 Fruitland Ave Vernon (90058) *(P-1409)*

General Monitors Inc (DH) .... C...... 949 581-4464
16782 Von Karman Ave Ste 14 Irvine (92606) *(P-8612)*

General Motors, Torrance *Also Called: General Motors LLC (P-13771)*

General Motors LLC .... E...... 313 556-5000
3050 Lomita Blvd Ste 237 Torrance (90505) *(P-13771)*

General Networks Corporation .... D...... 818 249-1962
3524 Ocean View Blvd Glendale (91208) *(P-16569)*

General Newsprint, Placentia *Also Called: General Rewinding Inc (P-3845)*

General Pavement Management Inc .... D...... 805 933-0909
850 Lawrence Dr Ste 100 Thousand Oaks (91320) *(P-1071)*

General Petroleum LLC (HQ) .... C...... 562 983-7300
19501 S Santa Fe Ave Compton (90221) *(P-13452)*

General Photonics, Chino *Also Called: General Photonics Corp (P-8474)*

General Photonics Corp .... D...... 909 590-5473
14351 Pipeline Ave Chino (91710) *(P-8474)*

General Plastics, Sun Valley *Also Called: Plastic Services and Products (P-4896)*

General Plating, Los Angeles *Also Called: Alpha Polishing Corporation (P-6581)*

General Power Systems, Anaheim *Also Called: General Power Systems Inc (P-9048)*

General Power Systems Inc .... E...... 714 956-9321
955 E Ball Rd Anaheim (92805) *(P-9048)*

General Procurement Inc (PA) .... D...... 949 679-7960
1964 W Corporate Way Anaheim (92801) *(P-12415)*

General Produce, Vernon *Also Called: V & L Produce Inc (P-13344)*

General Production Services .... E...... 818 365-4211
670 Arroyo St San Fernando (91340) *(P-7846)*

General Production Svc Cal Inc .... C...... 661 765-5330
1333 Kern St Taft (93268) *(P-670)*

General Restaurant Equipment, Los Angeles *Also Called: South China Sheet Metal Inc (P-828)*

General Rewinding Inc .... E...... 714 776-5561
888 W Crowther Ave Placentia (92870) *(P-3845)*

General Ribbon Corp .... B...... 818 709-1234
5775 E Los Angeles Ave Ste 230 Chatsworth (91311) *(P-11057)*

General Sealants .... C...... 626 961-0211
300 Turnbull Canyon Rd City Of Industry (91745) *(P-4566)*

General Switchgear Inc .... E
14729 Spring Ave Santa Fe Springs (90670) *(P-8122)*

General Tool Inc .... D...... 949 261-2322
2025 Alton Pkwy Irvine (92606) *(P-12356)*

General Transistor Corporation (PA) .... E...... 310 578-7344
12449 Putnam St Whittier (90602) *(P-12661)*

General Underground .... C...... 714 632-8646
701 W Grove Ave Orange (92865) *(P-773)*

General Veneer Mfg Co .... E...... 323 564-2661
8652 Otis St South Gate (90280) *(P-2688)*

General Water Systems .... F...... 951 278-8992
1525 E 6th St Corona (92879) *(P-16832)*

General Wax & Candle Co, North Hollywood *Also Called: General Wax Co Inc (P-11219)*

General Wax Co Inc (PA) .... D...... 818 765-5800
6863 Beck Ave North Hollywood (91605) *(P-11219)*

Generation Construction Inc .... C...... 909 923-2077
15650 El Prado Rd Chino (91710) *(P-433)*

Generational Properties Inc .... B...... 323 583-3163
3141 E 44th St Vernon (90058) *(P-11582)*

Generis Holdings LP (PA) .... C...... 661 366-7209
7200 E Brundage Ln Bakersfield (93307) *(P-10)*

Genes Plating Works Inc (PA) .... E...... 323 269-8748
3498 E 14th St Los Angeles (90023) *(P-6622)*

Genesis 2000, La Puente *Also Called: Genesis Tc Inc (P-2802)*

Genesis Computer Systems Inc .... E...... 714 632-3648
4055 E La Palma Ave Ste C Anaheim (92807) *(P-12416)*

Genesis Foods Corporation .... D...... 323 890-5890
8825 Mercury Ln Pico Rivera (90660) *(P-1540)*

Genesis Health Care, Orange *Also Called: Prospect Medical Systems Inc (P-20085)*

GENESIS HEALTHCARE CORPORATION, Los Angeles *Also Called: Sharon Care Center LLC (P-18052)*

Genesis Healthcare LLC .... A...... 805 922-3558
425 Barcellus Ave Santa Maria (93454) *(P-17961)*

Genesis Healthcare LLC .... C...... 310 370-3594
20900 Earl St Ste 100 Torrance (90503) *(P-17962)*

Genesis Healthcare LLC .... A...... 323 461-9961
5310 Fountain Ave Los Angeles (90029) *(P-18126)*

Genesis Tc Inc .... E...... 626 968-4455
524 Hofgaarden St La Puente (91744) *(P-2802)*

Genesis Tech Partners LLC .... C...... 800 950-2647
21540 Plummer St Ste A Chatsworth (91311) *(P-17130)*

Genetronics Inc .... E...... 858 597-6006
11494 Sorrento Valley Rd Ste A San Diego (92121) *(P-10093)*

Genetronics Inc .... C...... 858 410-3112
10480 Wateridge Cir San Diego (92121) *(P-4115)*

Genex (DH) .... C...... 424 672-9500
800 Corporate Pointe Ste 100 Culver City (90230) *(P-16039)*

Genica Corporation .... B...... 855 433-5747
43195 Business Park Dr Temecula (92590) *(P-12417)*

Genius Products Inc .... C...... 310 453-1222
3301 Exposition Blvd Ste 100 Santa Monica (90404) *(P-12976)*

ALPHABETIC

Employee Codes: A=Over 500 employees, B=251-500
C=101-250, D=51-100, E=20-50, F=10-19, G=1-9

2024 Southern California
Business Directory and Buyers Guide

© Mergent Inc. 1-800-342-5647

1101

Genius Products Nt Inc .... C 510 671-0219
556 N Diamond Bar Blvd Ste 101 Diamond Bar (91765) *(P-1694)*

Genlabs (PA) .... **C 909 591-8451**
5568 Schaefer Ave Chino (91710) *(P-4350)*

Genmark, Carlsbad *Also Called: Genmark Diagnostics Inc (P-10516)*

Genmark Diagnostics Inc (DH) .... **B 760 448-4300**
5964 La Place Ct Ste 100 Carlsbad (92008) *(P-10516)*

Gensler, Newport Beach *Also Called: M Arthur Gensler Jr Assoc Inc (P-19736)*

Gensler and Associates, Los Angeles *Also Called: M Arthur Gensler Jr Assoc Inc (P-19737)*

Gentex Corporation .... D 909 481-7667
9859 7th St Rancho Cucamonga (91730) *(P-19844)*

Genuine Parts Distributors, Ontario *Also Called: Tracy Industries Inc (P-6896)*

Genvivo Incorporated .... D 626 441-6695
1981 E Locust St Ontario (91761) *(P-4116)*

Genvivo Incorporated, Ontario *Also Called: Genvivo Incorporated (P-4116)*

Genzyme Corporation .... D 626 471-9922
655 E Huntington Dr Monrovia (91016) *(P-4117)*

Genzyme Genetics, Monrovia *Also Called: Genzyme Corporation (P-4117)*

Geo Drilling Fluids Inc (PA) .... **E 661 325-5919**
1431 Union Ave Bakersfield (93305) *(P-13434)*

Geo Guidance Drilling Svcs Inc (PA) .... **E 661 833-9999**
200 Old Yard Dr Bakersfield (93307) *(P-282)*

Geo Plastics .... E 323 277-8106
2200 E 52nd St Vernon (90058) *(P-5037)*

Geo Sales-Courtesy Chevrolet, San Diego *Also Called: Courtesy Chevrolet Center (P-13750)*

Geocon, San Diego *Also Called: Geocon Consultants Inc (P-20338)*

Geocon Consultants Inc (PA) .... **D 858 558-6900**
6960 Flanders Dr San Diego (92121) *(P-20338)*

Geocon Incorporated .... D 858 558-6900
6960 Flanders Dr San Diego (92121) *(P-19599)*

Geolabs Westlake Village, Newbury Park *Also Called: R & R Services Corporation (P-4789)*

Geolinks, Camarillo *Also Called: California Internet LP (P-11875)*

Geologics Corporation .... B 661 259-5767
25375 Orchard Village Rd Ste 102 Valencia (91355) *(P-20339)*

Georg Fischer Harvel LLC .... E 661 396-0653
7001 Schirra Ct Bakersfield (93313) *(P-4848)*

Georg Fischer Signet LLC .... D 626 571-2770
5462 Irwindale Ave Ste A Baldwin Park (91706) *(P-10135)*

George Brazil Plbg Htg & AC, Santa Ana *Also Called: Orange County Services Inc (P-803)*

George Chevrolet .... D 562 925-2500
17000 Lakewood Blvd Bellflower (90706) *(P-13772)*

George Chevrolet, Bellflower *Also Called: George Chevrolet (P-13772)*

George Coriaty .... E 562 698-7513
7240 Greenleaf Ave Whittier (90602) *(P-3578)*

George Fischer Inc (HQ) .... **C 626 571-2770**
5462 Irwindale Ave Ste A Baldwin Park (91706) *(P-7847)*

George Jue Mfg Co Inc .... D 562 634-8181
8140 Rosecrans Ave Paramount (90723) *(P-7145)*

George L Throop Co .... E 626 796-0285
444 N Fair Oaks Ave Pasadena (91103) *(P-13577)*

George P Johnson Company .... E 310 965-4300
18500 Crenshaw Blvd Torrance (90504) *(P-11123)*

George T Hall Co Inc (PA) .... **E 909 825-9751**
1605 E Gene Autry Way Anaheim (92805) *(P-12754)*

Georgetown Mortgage, Rancho Cucamonga *Also Called: Thrive Mortgage LLC (P-14352)*

Georgia Atkison Snf LLC .... D 626 444-2535
3825 Durfee Ave El Monte (91732) *(P-17963)*

Georgia Pacific Holdings Inc .... A 626 926-1474
13208 Hadley St Apt 1 Whittier (90601) *(P-3205)*

Georgia-Pacific, Santa Fe Springs *Also Called: Georgia-Pacific LLC (P-13008)*

Georgia-Pacific, La Mirada *Also Called: Georgia-Pacific LLC (P-14133)*

Georgia-Pacific LLC .... B 562 861-6226
9206 Santa Fe Springs Rd Santa Fe Springs (90670) *(P-13008)*

Georgia-Pacific LLC .... E 562 926-8888
15500 Valley View Ave La Mirada (90638) *(P-14133)*

Gerard Roof Products LLC (DH) .... **E 714 529-0407**
721 Monroe Way Placentia (92870) *(P-6245)*

Gerard Roofing Technologies, Placentia *Also Called: Gerard Roof Products LLC (P-6245)*

Gerdau Ameristeel, San Bernardino *Also Called: CMC Steel Us LLC (P-6395)*

Gerdau Rancho Cucamonga, Newport Beach *Also Called: Tamco (P-6406)*

Gerhardt Gear Co Inc .... E 818 842-6700
133 E Santa Anita Ave Burbank (91502) *(P-9396)*

Geri-Care Inc .... D 310 320-0961
21521 S Vermont Ave Torrance (90502) *(P-17964)*

Geri-Care II Inc .... C 310 328-0812
22035 S Vermont Ave Torrance (90502) *(P-18127)*

Gerlait Group Inc .... E 858 587-0400
9255 Towne Centre Dr San Diego (92121) *(P-1272)*

German Machine Products, Gardena *Also Called: German Machined Products Inc (P-7848)*

German Machined Products Inc .... E 310 532-4480
1415 W 178th St Gardena (90248) *(P-7848)*

Ges, Huntington Beach *Also Called: Global Exprnce Specialists Inc (P-16834)*

Ges US (new England) Inc .... C 978 459-4434
1051 S East St Anaheim (92805) *(P-9049)*

Get Engineering, El Cajon *Also Called: Get Engineering Corp (P-10136)*

Get Engineering Corp .... F 619 443-8295
9350 Bond Ave El Cajon (92021) *(P-10136)*

Get-A-Lift Handicap Bus Trnsp, Bakersfield *Also Called: Golden Empire Transit District (P-11321)*

Getac Inc .... D 949 681-2900
15495 Sand Canyon Ave Ste 350 Irvine (92618) *(P-12418)*

Getac North America, Irvine *Also Called: Getac Inc (P-12418)*

Getmedlegal, San Dimas *Also Called: Legal Solutions Holdings Inc (P-18894)*

Getpart La Inc .... E 424 331-9599
13705 Cimarron Ave Gardena (90249) *(P-5038)*

Getty Center, Los Angeles *Also Called: Bon Appetit Management Co (P-20004)*

Getty Publications, Los Angeles *Also Called: The J Paul Getty Trust (P-19365)*

Gff Inc .... D 323 232-6255
145 Willow Ave City Of Industry (91746) *(P-1360)*

Gfk Etilize Inc .... D 888 608-1212
34145 Pacific Coast Hwy 636 Dana Point (92629) *(P-19893)*

GFS Capital Holdings .... B 714 720-3918
6499 Havenwood Cir Ste 720 Huntington Beach (92648) *(P-14317)*

Ggg Demolition Inc (PA) .... **D 714 699-9350**
1130 W Trenton Ave Orange (92867) *(P-553)*

Ggtw LLC .... E 619 423-3388
1470 Bay Blvd Chula Vista (91911) *(P-4607)*

Gh Group Inc .... C 562 264-5078
3645 Long Beach Blvd Long Beach (90807) *(P-14931)*

Ghost Management Group LLC .... C 949 870-1400
41 Discovery Irvine (92618) *(P-15593)*

Ghp Management Corporation .... C 310 432-1441
270 N Canon Dr Beverly Hills (90210) *(P-20034)*

Giant Inland Empire Rv Ctr Inc (PA) .... **C 909 981-0444**
9150 Benson Ave Montclair (91763) *(P-13895)*

Giant Mgllan Tlscope Orgnztion, Pasadena *Also Called: Gmto Corporation (P-10315)*

Giant Rv, Montclair *Also Called: Giant Inland Empire Rv Ctr Inc (P-13895)*

Giant Sportz Paintball Park, Bellflower *Also Called: Hollywood Sports Park LLC (P-16841)*

Gibbel Bros Inc .... F 323 875-1367
11145 Tuxford St Sun Valley (91352) *(P-5478)*

Gibo/Kodama Chairs, Garden Grove *Also Called: Intra Storage Systems Inc (P-6865)*

Gibraltar, Jurupa Valley *Also Called: Pacific Award Metals Inc (P-12368)*

Gibraltar Cnvalescent Hosp Inc .... D 626 443-9425
2720 Nevada Ave El Monte (91733) *(P-18128)*

Gibraltar Plastic Pdts Corp .... E 818 365-9318
12885 Foothill Blvd Sylmar (91342) *(P-5039)*

Gibson Dunn & Crutcher Inc .... C 213 229-7000
333 S Grand Ave Los Angeles (90071) *(P-18857)*

Gibson Dunn & Crutcher LLP (PA) .... **B 213 229-7000**
333 S Grand Ave Ste 4600 Los Angeles (90071) *(P-18858)*

Gibson Dunn & Crutcher LLP .... D 310 552-8500
2029 Century Park E Ste 4000 Los Angeles (90002) *(P-18859)*

Gibson Dunn & Crutcher LLP .... D 949 451-3800
3161 Michelson Dr Ste 1200 Irvine (92612) *(P-18860)*

Gibson & Barnes, El Cajon *Also Called: Flight Suits (P-2430)*

Gibson & Schaefer Inc (PA) .... **E 619 352-3535**
1126 Rock Wood Rd Heber (92249) *(P-5479)*

Gibson Exhaust Systems, Corona *Also Called: Gibson Performance Corporation (P-9397)*

Gibson Homeware, Commerce *Also Called: Gibson Overseas Inc (P-12303)*

Gibson Overseas Inc (PA).................................B...... 323 832-8900
2410 Yates Ave Commerce (90040) *(P-12303)*

Gibson Overseas Inc ....C...... 323 832-8900
7776 Tippecanoe Ave San Bernardino (92410) *(P-20340)*

Gibson Performance Corporation ....D...... 951 372-1220
1270 Webb Cir Corona (92879) *(P-9397)*

Giddens Industries Inc (DH).............................C...... 425 353-0405
3130 E Miraloma Ave Anaheim (92806) *(P-9700)*

Gigabyte Technology, City Of Industry *Also Called: GBT Inc (P-12414)*

Gigastone America, Irvine *Also Called: Dane Elec Corp USA (P-12404)*

Gigatera Communications ....D...... 714 515-1100
1818 E Orangethorpe Ave Fullerton (92831) *(P-9050)*

Gilbert Machine & Mfg, San Marcos *Also Called: Duplan Industries (P-7821)*

Gilbert Martin Wdwkg Co Inc (PA).....................E...... 800 268-5669
2345 Britannia Blvd San Diego (92154) *(P-2866)*

Gildan USA Inc ....F...... 909 485-1475
28200 Highway 189 Lake Arrowhead (92352) *(P-2058)*

GILDAN USA INC., Lake Arrowhead *Also Called: Gildan USA Inc (P-2058)*

Gilead Palo Alto Inc ....C...... 909 394-4000
550 Cliffside Dr San Dimas (91773) *(P-4118)*

Gilead Palo Alto Inc ....C...... 760 945-7701
4049 Avenida De La Plata Oceanside (92056) *(P-4119)*

Gilead Sciences Inc ....E...... 909 394-4000
650 Cliffside Dr San Dimas (91773) *(P-4120)*

Gilead Sciences Inc ....D...... 650 522-2771
1800 Wheeler St La Verne (91750) *(P-4121)*

Gilead Scientist, San Dimas *Also Called: Gilead Palo Alto Inc (P-4118)*

Gill Corporation (PA)...C...... 626 443-6094
4056 Easy St El Monte (91731) *(P-5040)*

Gilli Inc ....F...... 213 744-9808
1100 S San Pedro St Ste C07 Los Angeles (90015) *(P-2451)*

Gils Distributing Service ....C...... 213 627-0539
718 E 8th St Los Angeles (90021) *(P-15602)*

Gin'l Fabrics, Los Angeles *Also Called: Ax II Inc (P-2053)*

Gingi Pak, Camarillo *Also Called: Belport Company Inc (P-10730)*

Gino Corporation ....E...... 323 234-7979
555 E Jefferson Blvd Los Angeles (90011) *(P-2158)*

Giovanni Cosmetics Inc ....D...... 310 952-9960
2064 E University Dr Rancho Dominguez (90220) *(P-4413)*

Giovanni Hair Care & Cosmetics, Rancho Dominguez *Also Called: Giovanni Cosmetics Inc (P-4413)*

Girard Food Service, City Of Industry *Also Called: Gff Inc (P-1360)*

Girardi Keese (PA)..D...... 213 977-0211
1126 Wilshire Blvd Los Angeles (90017) *(P-18861)*

GIRL SCOUTS SAN DIEGO, San Diego *Also Called: Girl Scuts San Dg-Mprial Cncil (P-19448)*

Girl Scuts Greater Los Angeles (PA)..................C...... 626 677-2265
423 N La Brea Ave Inglewood (90302) *(P-19447)*

Girl Scuts San Dg-Mprial Cncil (PA)...................D...... 619 610-0751
1231 Upas St San Diego (92103) *(P-19448)*

GIRLS REPUBLIC, Chino Hills *Also Called: Boys Republic (P-19241)*

Giroux, Los Angeles *Also Called: Giroux Glass Inc (P-1118)*

Giroux Glass Inc (PA)...C...... 213 747-7406
850 W Washington Blvd Ste 200 Los Angeles (90015) *(P-1118)*

Giuliano-Pagano Corporation ....D...... 310 537-7700
1264 E Walnut St Carson (90746) *(P-1473)*

Giuliano's Bakery, Carson *Also Called: Giuliano-Pagano Corporation (P-1473)*

Giumarra Agricom Intl LLC ....A...... 760 480-8502
15651 Old Milky Way Escondido (92027) *(P-13326)*

Giumarra Vineyards Corporation ....C...... 661 395-7071
11220 Edison Hwy Bakersfield (93307) *(P-30)*

Giumarra Vineyards Corporation (PA)..................B...... 661 395-7000
11220 Edison Hwy Edison (93220) *(P-31)*

Giumarra Vineyards Corporation ....D...... 661 395-7000
11220 Edison Hwy Bakersfield (93307) *(P-1633)*

Given Imaging Los Angeles LLC ....C...... 310 641-8492
5860 Uplander Way Culver City (90230) *(P-10804)*

Giving Keys Inc ....E...... 213 935-8791
836 Traction Ave Los Angeles (90013) *(P-10902)*

GK Foods Inc ....E...... 760 752-5230
133 Mata Way Ste 101 San Marcos (92069) *(P-1410)*

GK Management Co Inc (PA)..............................C...... 310 204-2050
5150 Overland Ave Culver City (90230) *(P-14804)*

Gkk Corporation (PA)...D...... 949 250-1500
2355 Main St Ste 220 Irvine (92614) *(P-19729)*

Gkkworks, Irvine *Also Called: Gkk Corporation (P-19729)*

GKN Aerospace ....E...... 714 653-7531
12242 Western Ave Garden Grove (92841) *(P-9536)*

GKN Aerospace Camarillo Inc ....F...... 805 383-6684
3030 Redhll Ave Santa Ana (92705) *(P-6246)*

GKN Aerospace Chem-Tronics Inc (DH)..............A...... 619 258-5000
1150 W Bradley Ave El Cajon (92020) *(P-9570)*

GKN Arspace Trnsprncy Systems ....B...... 714 893-7531
12122 Western Ave Garden Grove (92841) *(P-5041)*

GL Nemirow Inc ....D...... 818 562-9433
2550 N Hollywood Way Ste 502 Burbank (91505) *(P-15540)*

GL Woodworking Inc ....D...... 949 515-2192
14341 Franklin Ave Tustin (92780) *(P-2601)*

Glacier Foods Division, Westlake Village *Also Called: Dole Packaged Foods LLC (P-1369)*

Glad-A-Way Gardens Inc ....C...... 805 938-0569
2669 E Clark Ave Santa Maria (93455) *(P-55)*

Glam and Glits Nail Design Inc ....D...... 661 393-4800
8700 Swigert Ct Unit 209 Bakersfield (93311) *(P-4414)*

Glamour Industries Co ....D...... 213 687-8600
100 Wilshire Blvd Ste 700 Santa Monica (90401) *(P-12891)*

Glamour Industries Co (PA)................................B...... 323 728-2999
2220 Gaspar Ave Commerce (90040) *(P-13042)*

Glare Technology Usa Inc ....C...... 909 437-6999
30898 Wealth St Murrieta (92563) *(P-16738)*

Glas Werk Inc ....E...... 949 766-1296
29710 Avenida De Las Bandera Rancho Santa Margari (92688) *(P-5325)*

Glaser Weil Fink Jacobs (PA)...............................C...... 310 553-3000
10250 Constellation Blvd Fl 19 Los Angeles (90067) *(P-18862)*

Glaspro, Santa Fe Springs *Also Called: GP Merger Sub Inc (P-5342)*

Glass Fabrication and Dist, Stanton *Also Called: Newport Industrial Glass Inc (P-5350)*

Glass House Group, Long Beach *Also Called: Gh Group Inc (P-14931)*

Glasswerks Group, South Gate *Also Called: Glasswerks La Inc (P-5341)*

Glasswerks La Inc (HQ).......................................B...... 888 789-7810
8600 Rheem Ave South Gate (90280) *(P-5341)*

Glastar, Canoga Park *Also Called: Glastar Corporation (P-7239)*

Glastar Corporation ....E...... 818 341-0301
8425 Canoga Ave Canoga Park (91304) *(P-7239)*

Glaukos Corporation (PA).....................................C...... 949 367-9600
1 Glaukos Way Aliso Viejo (92656) *(P-10517)*

GLAZA, Los Angeles *Also Called: Greater Los Angeles Zoo Assn (P-19326)*

Gleason Industrial Pdts Inc ....C...... 574 533-1141
10474 Santa Monica Blvd Ste 400 Los Angeles (90025) *(P-6991)*

Gledhill/Lyons Inc ....E...... 714 502-0274
1521 N Placentia Ave Anaheim (92806) *(P-9701)*

Glen - Mac Swiss Co ....E...... 310 978-4555
12848 Weber Way Hawthorne (90250) *(P-8971)*

Glen Annie Golf Club ....D...... 805 968-6400
405 Glen Annie Rd Goleta (93117) *(P-17428)*

Glen Ivy Hot Springs ....C...... 714 990-2090
1001 Brea Mall Brea (92821) *(P-15508)*

Glenair Inc (PA)...A...... 818 247-6000
1211 Air Way Glendale (91201) *(P-8266)*

Glendale Adventist Medical Ctr (HQ)....................A...... 818 409-8000
1509 Wilson Ter Glendale (91206) *(P-18265)*

Glendale Associates Ltd ....D...... 818 246-6737
100 W Broadway Ste 100 Glendale (91210) *(P-14663)*

Glendale Medical Offices, Glendale *Also Called: Kaiser Foundation Hospitals (P-17693)*

Glendale Mem Hlth Foundation ....C...... 818 502-2375
1420 S Central Ave Glendale (91204) *(P-18266)*

Glendale Memorial Breast Ctr, Glendale *Also Called: Glendale Memorial Health Corp (P-18267)*

Glendale Memorial Center, Glendale *Also Called: Glendale Memorial Health Corporation (P-18268)*

Glendale Memorial Health Corp ....A...... 818 502-2323
222 W Eulalia St Glendale (91204) *(P-18267)*

Glendale Memorial Health Corporation ....A...... 818 502-1900
1420 S Central Ave Glendale (91204) *(P-18268)*

Employee Codes: A=Over 500 employees, B=251-500
C=101-250, D=51-100, E=20-50, F=10-19, G=1-9

2024 Southern California
Business Directory and Buyers Guide

© Mergent Inc. 1-800-342-5647
1103

GLENDALE YMCA SWIM SCHOOL, Glendale *Also Called: Young MNS Chrstn Assn Glndale* *(P-19493)*

Glendee Corp ....E....... 805 523-2422
5151 N Commerce Ave Moorpark (93021) *(P-7849)*

Glendee Corp (PA) ....**E....... 805 523-2422**
5390 Gabbert Rd Moorpark (93021) *(P-7850)*

Glendora Country Club ....D....... 626 335-4051
2400 Country Club Drive Glendora (91741) *(P-17486)*

Glendora Oaks Bhvral Hlth Hosp, Glendora *Also Called: East Valley Glendora Hosp LLC* *(P-18248)*

Glenn A Rick Engrg & Dev Co (PA) ....**C....... 619 291-0708**
5620 Friars Rd San Diego (92110) *(P-19600)*

Glenoaks Convalescent Hospital ....D....... 818 240-4300
409 W Glenoaks Blvd Glendale (91202) *(P-18269)*

Glenoaks Food Inc ....E....... 818 768-9091
11030 Randall St Sun Valley (91352) *(P-1244)*

Glentek Inc ....D....... 310 322-3026
208 Standard St El Segundo (90245) *(P-8141)*

Glidewell Laboratories, Newport Beach *Also Called: James R Gldwell Dntl Crmics In* *(P-18570)*

Global A Lgistics Training Inc ....E....... 760 688-0365
3860 Calle Fortunada Ste 100 San Diego (92123) *(P-9979)*

Global Aerospace Tech Corp ....E....... 818 407-5600
29077 Avenue Penn Valencia (91355) *(P-9702)*

Global Agri-Trade (PA) ....**E....... 562 320-8550**
15500 S Avalon Blvd Rancho Dominguez (90220) *(P-1564)*

Global Bakeries, Pacoima *Also Called: Surge Globl Bkries Hldings LLC (P-13397)*

Global Care Travel, San Diego *Also Called: Customzed Svcs Admnstrtors Inc (P-14581)*

Global Cash Card Inc ....C....... 949 751-0360
3972 Barranca Pkwy Ste J610 Irvine (92606) *(P-16256)*

Global Casuals Inc ....D....... 310 817-2828
18505 S Broadway Gardena (90248) *(P-2206)*

Global Comm Semiconductors LLC ....E....... 310 530-7274
23155 Kashiwa Ct Torrance (90505) *(P-8799)*

Global Compliance Inc ....E....... 626 303-6855
438 W Chestnut Ave Ste A Monrovia (91016) *(P-3449)*

Global Customer Services Inc ....D....... 760 995-7949
17373 Lilac St Hesperia (92345) *(P-16833)*

Global Elastomeric Pdts Inc ....D....... 661 831-5380
5551 District Blvd Bakersfield (93313) *(P-6958)*

Global Environmental Pdts Inc ....D....... 909 713-1600
5405 Industrial Pkwy San Bernardino (92407) *(P-9289)*

Global Exprnce Specialists Inc ....C....... 619 498-6300
18504 Beach Blvd Unit 511 Huntington Beach (92648) *(P-16834)*

Global Fabricators, Shafter *Also Called: McM Fabricators Inc (P-6047)*

Global Impact Inv Partners LLC ....E....... 310 592-2000
1410 Westwood Blvd Apt 260 Los Angeles (90024) *(P-1474)*

Global Innovation Partner, Los Angeles *Also Called: Cbre Globl Value Investors LLC* *(P-14760)*

Global Integrated Logistics, Irvine *Also Called: Agility Logistics Corp (P-11736)*

Global Lab Supply, Orange *Also Called: Cleatech LLC (P-10091)*

Global Language Solutions LLC ....D....... 949 798-1400
19800 Macarthur Blvd Irvine (92612) *(P-16835)*

Global Link Sourcing Inc ....D....... 951 698-1977
41690 Corporate Center Ct Murrieta (92562) *(P-3152)*

Global Locate Inc ....E....... 949 926-5000
5300 California Ave Irvine (92617) *(P-8800)*

Global Mail Inc ....C....... 310 735-0800
921 W Artesia Blvd Compton (90220) *(P-11763)*

Global Metal Solutions Inc ....E....... 949 872-2995
2150 Mcgaw Ave Irvine (92614) *(P-6623)*

Global Microwave Systems Inc ....E....... 760 496-0046
1916 Palomar Oaks Way Ste 100 Carlsbad (92008) *(P-8520)*

Global Packaging Solutions Inc ....B....... 619 710-2661
6259 Progressive Dr Ste 200 San Diego (92154) *(P-3104)*

Global Paper Solutions Inc ....E....... 714 687-6102
100 S Anaheim Blvd Ste 250 Anaheim (92805) *(P-3046)*

Global Paratransit Inc ....B....... 310 715-7550
400 W Compton Blvd Gardena (90248) *(P-11390)*

Global Pcci (gpc) (PA) ....**C....... 757 637-9000**
2465 Campus Dr Ste 100 Irvine (92612) *(P-6519)*

Global Plastics Inc ....C....... 951 657-5466
145 Malbert St Perris (92570) *(P-12954)*

Global Plumbing & Fire Supply ....C....... 818 550-8444
723 Sonora Ave Glendale (91201) *(P-12741)*

Global Rental Co Inc ....C....... 909 469-5160
1253 Price Ave Pomona (91767) *(P-15761)*

Global Sales Inc ....E....... 310 474-7700
1732 Westwood Blvd Los Angeles (90024) *(P-4415)*

Global Service Resources Inc ....D....... 800 679-7658
711 S Victory Blvd Burbank (91502) *(P-16040)*

Global Silicon Electronics Inc ....E....... 626 336-1888
440 Cloverleaf Dr Baldwin Park (91706) *(P-7470)*

Global Sweeping Solutions, San Bernardino *Also Called: Global Environmental Pdts Inc* *(P-9289)*

Global Trade Alliance Inc ....C....... 562 944-6422
13642 Orden Dr Santa Fe Springs (90670) *(P-13862)*

Global Truss, Vernon *Also Called: Global Truss America LLC (P-5698)*

Global Truss America LLC ....D....... 323 415-6225
4295 Charter St Vernon (90058) *(P-5698)*

Global Uxe Inc ....E....... 805 583-4600
405 Science Dr Moorpark (93021) *(P-11220)*

Global Wave Group ....E....... 949 916-9800
26970 Aliso Viejo Pkwy Ste 250 Aliso Viejo (92656) *(P-16257)*

Global-Dining Inc California ....D....... 310 576-9922
1212 3rd Street Promenade Santa Monica (90401) *(P-20035)*

Globaluxe Inc ....E....... 805 583-4600
405 Science Dr Moorpark (93021) *(P-11221)*

Globalvision Systems Inc ....E....... 888 227-7967
9401 Oakdale Ave Ste 100 Chatsworth (91311) *(P-7471)*

Globe Iron Foundry Inc ....D....... 323 723-8983
5649 Randolph St Commerce (90040) *(P-5645)*

Globe Plastics, Chino *Also Called: PRC Composites LLC (P-5156)*

Globe Shoes, Carson *Also Called: Osata Enterprises Inc (P-13163)*

Globecast America Incorporated ....C....... 310 845-3900
10525 Washington Blvd Culver City (90232) *(P-11995)*

Gloria Lance Inc (PA) ....**D....... 310 767-4400**
15616 S Broadway Gardena (90248) *(P-2241)*

Gloves In A Bottle Inc ....E....... 818 248-9980
3720 Park Pl Montrose (91020) *(P-13043)*

Glovis America Inc (HQ) ....**C....... 714 427-0944**
17305 Von Karman Ave Ste 200 Irvine (92614) *(P-11764)*

GLS US Freight Inc ....E....... 909 627-2538
3561 Philadelphia St Chino (91710) *(P-3450)*

Gluten Free Foods Mfg LLC (PA) ....**E....... 909 823-8230**
5010 Eucalyptus Ave Chino (91710) *(P-1903)*

Glysens Incorporated ....E....... 858 638-7708
3931 Sorrento Valley Blvd Ste 110 San Diego (92121) *(P-10518)*

Gma Cover Corp C
1170 Somera Rd Los Angeles (90077) *(P-2505)*

Gmi Inc ....E....... 619 429-4479
2626 Southport Way Ste E National City (91950) *(P-2494)*

GMI Building Services Inc ....C....... 858 279-6262
8001 Vickers St San Diego (92111) *(P-15711)*

Gmp Laboratories America Inc (PA) ....**D....... 714 630-2467**
2931 E La Jolla St Anaheim (92806) *(P-4122)*

Gmp Labratories of America, Anaheim *Also Called: Gmp Laboratories America Inc (P-4122)*

Gms Elevator Services, San Dimas *Also Called: Gms Elevator Services Inc (P-6966)*

Gms Elevator Services Inc ....E....... 909 599-3904
401 Borrego Ct San Dimas (91773) *(P-6966)*

Gms Landscapes Inc ....D....... 805 402-3925
207 Camino Leon Camarillo (93012) *(P-5971)*

Gms Molds ....E....... 310 403-9870
732 Avenue C Redondo Beach (90277) *(P-2602)*

Gmto Corporation ....D....... 626 204-0500
300 N Lake Ave Fl 14 Pasadena (91101) *(P-10315)*

Gnet Agency ....D....... 323 951-9399
5455 Wilshire Blvd Ste 2200 Los Angeles (90036) *(P-14598)*

Go Sales.us, West Covina *Also Called: Ola Nation LLC (P-2286)*

Go-Staff Inc ....A....... 760 730-8520
9878 Complex Dr Oceanside (92054) *(P-15849)*

Go-Staff Inc ....A....... 657 242-9350
240 W Lincoln Ave Anaheim (92805) *(P-15850)*

Mergent email: customerrelations@mergent.com
1104
2024 Southern California
Business Directory and Buyers Guide
(P-0000) Products & Services Section entry number
(PA)=Parent Co (HQ)=Headquarters (DH)=Div Headquarters

Goal Financial LLC .... C...... 619 684-7600
401 W A St Ste 1300 San Diego (92101) *(P-14318)*

Gobbler, Los Angeles *Also Called: Media Gobbler Inc (P-16303)*

Goeppner Industries Inc .... E...... 310 784-2800
22924 Lockness Ave Torrance (90501) *(P-7851)*

Goetzman Group Inc .... D...... 818 595-1112
21333 Oxnard St Ste 200 Woodland Hills (91367) *(P-20177)*

Goforth & Marti (PA) .... D...... **800 686-6583**
110 W A St Ste 140 San Diego (92101) *(P-12283)*

Goglanian, Santa Ana *Also Called: Goglanian Bakeries Inc (P-13369)*

Goglanian Bakeries Inc (HQ) .... B...... **714 338-1145**
3401 W Segerstrom Ave Santa Ana (92704) *(P-13369)*

Goguardian, El Segundo *Also Called: Liminex Inc (P-16065)*

Gohz Inc .... E...... 800 603-1219
23555 Golden Springs Dr Ste K1 Diamond Bar (91765) *(P-8142)*

Gold Coast Baking Company LLC (PA) .... D...... **818 575-7280**
21250 Califa St Ste 104 Woodland Hills (91367) *(P-1475)*

Gold Coast Baking Company Inc .... E...... 714 545-2253
1590 E Saint Gertrude Pl Santa Ana (92705) *(P-1476)*

Gold Coast Baking Company, Inc., Santa Ana *Also Called: Gold Coast Baking Company Inc (P-1476)*

Gold Coast Health Plan, Camarillo *Also Called: Ventura Cnty Md-Cal Mnged Care (P-18815)*

Gold Coast Ingredients Inc .... D...... 323 724-8935
2429 Yates Ave Commerce (90040) *(P-1904)*

Gold Coast Sunwear, San Marcos *Also Called: Peter Grimm Ltd (P-2403)*

Gold Coast Tours, Brea *Also Called: Hot Dogger Tours Inc (P-11417)*

Gold Crest Industries Inc .... E...... 909 930-9069
1018 E Acacia St Ontario (91761) *(P-2495)*

Gold Cross Ambulance, Los Angeles *Also Called: Schaefer Ambulance Service Inc (P-11404)*

Gold Parent LP .... A...... 310 954-0444
11111 Santa Monica Blvd Los Angeles (90025) *(P-14378)*

Gold Peak Industries (north America) Inc .... E...... 858 674-6099
11245 W Bernardo Ct Ste 104 San Diego (92127) *(P-9150)*

Gold Prospectors Assn Amer, Murrieta *Also Called: Gold Prospectors Assn Amer LLC (P-3360)*

Gold Prospectors Assn Amer LLC .... E...... 951 699-4749
25819 Jefferson Ave Ste 110 Murrieta (92562) *(P-3360)*

Gold Star Foods Inc (HQ) .... D...... **909 843-9600**
3781 E Airport Dr Ontario (91761) *(P-1905)*

Gold's Gym, West Hollywood *Also Called: Rsg Group USA Inc (P-14943)*

Goldak Inc .... E...... 818 240-2666
15835 Monte St Ste 104 Sylmar (91342) *(P-9980)*

Goldberg and Solovy Foods Inc, Vernon *Also Called: Palisades Ranch Inc (P-13190)*

Goldco, Calabasas *Also Called: Goldco Direct LLC (P-12962)*

Goldco Direct LLC .... D...... 818 343-0186
24025 Park Sorrento Ste 210 Calabasas (91302) *(P-12962)*

Golden Acorn Casino & Trvl Ctr, Campo *Also Called: Campo Band Missions Indians (P-17444)*

Golden Applexx Co Inc .... E...... 909 594-9788
19805 Harrison Ave Walnut (91789) *(P-3762)*

Golden Bolt LLC .... D...... 818 626-8261
9361 Canoga Ave Chatsworth (91311) *(P-6443)*

Golden Brands, Huntington Beach *Also Called: Harbor Distributing LLc (P-13468)*

Golden Care Inc .... D...... 818 763-6275
6120 Vineland Ave North Hollywood (91606) *(P-18129)*

Golden Color Printing Inc .... F...... 626 455-0850
9353 Rush St South El Monte (91733) *(P-3579)*

Golden Door, San Marcos *Also Called: Golden Door Properties LLC (P-15155)*

Golden Door Properties LLC .... C...... 760 744-5777
777 Deer Springs Rd San Marcos (92069) *(P-15155)*

Golden Eagle, San Diego *Also Called: Golden Eagle Insurance Corp (P-14508)*

Golden Eagle Insurance Corp (DH) .... C...... **619 744-6000**
525 B St Ste 1300 San Diego (92101) *(P-14508)*

Golden Empire Con Pdts Inc .... D...... 661 833-4490
8261 Mccutchen Rd Bakersfield (93311) *(P-5417)*

Golden Empire Mortgage Inc .... B...... 661 949-3388
41331 12th St W Ste 102 Palmdale (93551) *(P-14319)*

Golden Empire Mortgage Inc (PA) .... D...... **661 328-1600**
2130 Chester Ave Bakersfield (93301) *(P-14320)*

Golden Empire Mortgage Inc (PA) .... D...... **661 328-1600**
1200 Discovery Dr Ste 300 Bakersfield (93309) *(P-14321)*

Golden Empire Transit District (PA) .... C...... **661 869-2438**
1830 Golden State Ave Bakersfield (93301) *(P-11321)*

Golden Eye Media Usa Inc .... F...... 760 688-9962
1000 Camino De Las Ondas Carlsbad (92011) *(P-13009)*

Golden Hotels Ltd Partnership .... C...... 949 833-2770
18700 Macarthur Blvd Irvine (92612) *(P-15156)*

Golden Hour Data Systems Inc .... C...... 858 768-2500
10052 Mesa Ridge Ct Ste 200 San Diego (92121) *(P-11765)*

Golden International .... A...... 213 628-1388
424 S Los Angeles St Ste 2 Los Angeles (90013) *(P-15029)*

Golden Island Jerky Co Inc, Rancho Cucamonga *Also Called: Tfi of California Inc (P-1240)*

Golden Kraft Inc .... B...... 562 926-8888
15500 Valley View Ave La Mirada (90638) *(P-3238)*

Golden Mattress Co Inc .... D...... 323 887-1888
11680 Wright Rd Lynwood (90262) *(P-2851)*

Golden Pacific, Pomona *Also Called: Travelers Choice Travelware (P-5297)*

Golden Pacific Seafoods Inc .... E...... 714 589-8888
700 S Raymond Ave Fullerton (92831) *(P-7200)*

Golden Queen Mining Co LLC .... C...... 661 824-4300
2818 Silver Queen Rd Mojave (93501) *(P-233)*

Golden Rule Bindery Inc .... E...... 760 471-2013
1315 Hot Springs Way Ste 102 Vista (92081) *(P-3846)*

Golden Rule Packaging, Vista *Also Called: Golden Rule Bindery Inc (P-3846)*

Golden Specialty Foods LLC .... E...... 562 802-2537
14605 Best Ave Norwalk (90650) *(P-1906)*

Golden State Care Center, Baldwin Park *Also Called: Golden State Habilitation Conv (P-17965)*

Golden State Company LLC .... E...... 310 376-7800
200 N Pacific Coast Hwy Ste 110 El Segundo (90245) *(P-3451)*

Golden State Drilling Inc .... D...... 661 589-0730
3500 Fruitvale Ave Bakersfield (93308) *(P-283)*

Golden State Engineering Inc .... C...... 562 634-3125
15338 Garfield Ave Paramount (90723) *(P-7170)*

Golden State Fence Co., Riverside *Also Called: Fenceworks Inc (P-1158)*

Golden State Foods, Irvine *Also Called: Golden State Foods Corp (P-1775)*

Golden State Foods Corp .... B...... 626 465-7500
640 S 6th Ave City Of Industry (91746) *(P-1391)*

Golden State Foods Corp (PA) .... E...... **949 247-8000**
18301 Von Karman Ave Ste 1100 Irvine (92612) *(P-1775)*

Golden State Graphics, Carlsbad *Also Called: Gsg Printing Inc (P-3582)*

Golden State Habilitation Conv (PA) .... C...... **626 962-3274**
1758 Big Dalton Ave Baldwin Park (91706) *(P-17965)*

Golden State Health Ctrs Inc .... C...... 310 451-9706
1340 15th St Santa Monica (90404) *(P-18130)*

Golden State Medical Sup Inc .... C...... 805 477-9866
5187 Camino Ruiz Camarillo (93012) *(P-12488)*

Golden State Medical Supply .... D...... 805 477-8966
5247 Camino Ruiz Camarillo (93012) *(P-12977)*

Golden State Mutl Lf Insur Co (PA) .... D...... **713 526-4361**
1999 W Adams Blvd Los Angeles (90018) *(P-14435)*

Golden Supreme Inc .... E...... 562 903-1063
12304 Mccann Dr Santa Fe Springs (90670) *(P-11222)*

Golden Temple, Los Angeles *Also Called: East West Tea Company LLC (P-1420)*

Golden West Casino, Bakersfield *Also Called: Golden West Partners Inc (P-15157)*

Golden West Food Group Inc (PA) .... E...... **888 807-3663**
4401 S Downey Rd Vernon (90058) *(P-1196)*

Golden West K-9, Pacoima *Also Called: Golden West Security (P-16644)*

Golden West Machine Inc .... E...... 562 903-1111
9930 Jordan Cir Santa Fe Springs (90670) *(P-7852)*

Golden West Packg Group LLC (PA) .... B...... **888 501-5893**
15400 Don Julian Rd City Of Industry (91745) *(P-3105)*

Golden West Partners Inc .... C...... 661 324-6936
1001 S Union Ave Bakersfield (93307) *(P-15157)*

Golden West Refining Company .... E...... 562 921-3581
13116 Imperial Hwy Santa Fe Springs (90670) *(P-4641)*

Golden West Security .... C...... 818 897-5965
12502 Van Nuys Blvd Ste 215 Pacoima (91331) *(P-16644)*

Golden West Shutters, Lake Forest *Also Called: ABC Custom Wood Shutters Inc (P-2581)*

Golden West Technology .... D...... 714 738-3775
1180 E Valencia Dr Fullerton (92831) *(P-8682)*

ALPHABETIC

Employee Codes: A=Over 500 employees, B=251-500
C=101-250, D=51-100, E=20-50, F=10-19, G=1-9

2024 Southern California
Business Directory and Buyers Guide

© Mergent Inc. 1-800-342-5647

1105

Golden West Trading Inc .... C...... 323 581-3663
4401 S Downey Rd Vernon (90058) *(P-13246)*

Goldencorr Sheets LLC .... C...... 626 369-6446
13890 Nelson Ave City Of Industry (91746) *(P-3106)*

Goldenwood Truss Corporation .... D...... 805 659-2520
11032 Nardo St Ventura (93004) *(P-2698)*

Goldfax, Laguna Beach *Also Called: Data Processing Design Inc (P-16008)*

Goldman Data LLC .... D...... 714 283-5889
2156 N Shaffer St Orange (92865) *(P-20341)*

Goldman Sachs, Los Angeles *Also Called: Goldman Sachs & Co LLC (P-14379)*

Goldman Sachs & Co LLC .... C...... 310 407-5700
2121 Avenue Of The Stars Ste 2600 Los Angeles (90067) *(P-14379)*

Goldrich & Kest Industries LLC (PA) .... A...... 310 204-2050
5150 Overland Ave Culver City (90230) *(P-14899)*

Goldrich Kest Hirsch Stern LLC (PA) .... C...... 310 204-2050
5150 Overland Ave Culver City (90230) *(P-14900)*

Golds Gym, Northridge *Also Called: Musclebound Inc (P-17408)*

Goldsign, Huntington Park *Also Called: Citizens of Humanity LLC (P-2313)*

Goldstar, Irvine *Also Called: Spireon Inc (P-16121)*

Goldstar Asphalt Products, Perris *Also Called: Npg Inc (P-4662)*

Goldstar Asphalt Products Inc .... E...... 951 940-1610
1354 Jet Way Perris (92571) *(P-4660)*

Goleta Valley Cottage Hosp Aux .... B...... 805 681-6468
351 S Patterson Ave Santa Barbara (93111) *(P-18270)*

Golf Buddy, Santa Fe Springs *Also Called: Deca International Corp (P-9968)*

Golf Management Operating LLC .... A...... 760 777-4839
50200 Avnida Vista Bonita La Quinta (92253) *(P-17429)*

Golf Sales West, Oxnard *Also Called: Golf Sales West Inc (P-10994)*

Golf Sales West Inc .... E...... 805 988-3363
1901 Eastman Ave Oxnard (93030) *(P-10994)*

Golf Supply House Usa Inc .... D...... 714 983-0050
1340 N Jefferson St Anaheim (92807) *(P-10995)*

Gomen Furniture Mfg Inc .... E...... 310 635-4894
11612 Wright Rd Lynwood (90262) *(P-2803)*

Gonsalves & Santucci Inc .... B...... 909 350-0474
13052 Dahlia St Fontana (92337) *(P-1072)*

Gooch and Housego Cal LLC .... D...... 805 529-3324
5390 Kazuko Ct Moorpark (93021) *(P-10316)*

Good American LLC (PA) .... E...... 213 357-5100
3125 S La Cienega Blvd Los Angeles (90016) *(P-2325)*

Good Culture LLC .... E...... 949 545-9945
22 Corporate Park Irvine (92606) *(P-1312)*

Good Feet, Carlsbad *Also Called: Drs Own Inc (P-10649)*

Good Fellas Industries Inc .... D...... 323 924-9495
4400 Bandini Blvd Vernon (90058) *(P-13960)*

Good Health Inc .... C...... 714 961-7930
410 Cloverleaf Dr Baldwin Park (91706) *(P-18765)*

Good Samaritan Hospital Aux .... B...... 213 977-2121
1225 Wilshire Blvd Los Angeles (90017) *(P-17660)*

Good Shepherd Lutheran HM of W .... C...... 805 526-2482
2949 Alamo St Simi Valley (93063) *(P-19264)*

Good Smrtan Hosp A Cal Ltd Prt .... B...... 661 903-9555
901 Olive Dr Bakersfield (93308) *(P-18271)*

Good Sports Plus Ltd .... B...... 310 671-4400
370 Amapola Ave Ste 208 Torrance (90501) *(P-16041)*

Good Tree, Montebello *Also Called: Commerce On Demand LLC (P-11210)*

Good Worldwide LLC .... E...... 323 206-6495
6380 Wilshire Blvd # 15 Los Angeles (90048) *(P-3452)*

Good-West Rubber Corp (PA) .... C...... 909 987-1774
9615 Feron Blvd Rancho Cucamonga (91730) *(P-4764)*

Gooden Center .... D...... 626 356-0078
191 N El Molino Ave Pasadena (91101) *(P-18528)*

Goodix Technology Inc .... E...... 858 554-0352
133 Technology Dr Ste 200 Irvine (92618) *(P-7530)*

Goodleap, Irvine *Also Called: Goodleap LLC (P-14322)*

Goodleap LLC .... D...... 916 290-9999
22 Executive Park Ste 100 Irvine (92614) *(P-14322)*

Goodman Food Products Inc (PA) .... C...... 310 674-3180
200 E Beach Ave Fl 1 Inglewood (90302) *(P-1907)*

Goodrich Corporation .... D...... 562 944-4441
9920 Freeman Ave Santa Fe Springs (90670) *(P-9703)*

Goodrich Corporation .... C...... 714 984-1461
3355 E La Palma Ave Anaheim (92806) *(P-9704)*

Goodrich Corporation .... C...... 619 691-4111
850 Lagoon Dr Chula Vista (91910) *(P-9705)*

Goodrx, Santa Monica *Also Called: Goodrx Holdings Inc (P-16497)*

Goodrx Holdings Inc (PA) .... B...... 855 268-2822
2701 Olympic Blvd Santa Monica (90404) *(P-16497)*

Goodwest Linings & Coatings, Rancho Cucamonga *Also Called: Goodwest Rubber Linings Inc (P-4765)*

Goodwest Rubber Linings Inc .... E...... 888 499-0085
8814 Industrial Ln Rancho Cucamonga (91730) *(P-4765)*

Goodwill Central Coast .... C...... 805 544-0542
880 Industrial Way San Luis Obispo (93401) *(P-14061)*

Goodwill Inds Orange Cnty Cal .... C...... 714 881-3986
5880 Edinger Ave Huntington Beach (92649) *(P-19186)*

Goodwill Inds San Diego Cnty .... D...... 760 806-7670
3841 Plaza Dr Ste 902 Oceanside (92056) *(P-19529)*

Goodwill Inds San Luis Obispo, San Luis Obispo *Also Called: Goodwill Central Coast (P-14061)*

Goodwill Inds Southern Cal (PA) .... A...... 323 223-1211
342 N San Fernando Rd Los Angeles (90031) *(P-13686)*

Goodwill Industries, Huntington Beach *Also Called: Goodwill Inds Orange Cnty Cal (P-19186)*

Goodwill Industries, Oceanside *Also Called: Goodwill Inds San Diego Cnty (P-19529)*

Goodwill Srving The Pple Sther (PA) .... D...... 562 435-3411
800 W Pacific Coast Hwy Long Beach (90806) *(P-16836)*

Goodwin Ammonia Company LLC .... D...... 714 894-0531
12361 Monarch St Garden Grove (92841) *(P-4337)*

Goodyear, Moreno Valley *Also Called: Certified Tire & Svc Ctrs Inc (P-13855)*

Goodyear Rbr Co Southern Cal, Rancho Cucamonga *Also Called: Good-West Rubber Corp (P-4764)*

Google International LLC (DH) .... D...... 650 253-0000
35018 Avenue D Yucaipa (92399) *(P-11885)*

Goproto, San Diego *Also Called: Higgs Fletcher & Mack Llp (P-18868)*

Gordian Medical Inc .... B...... 714 556-0200
17595 Cartwright Rd Irvine (92614) *(P-12489)*

Gordon Brush Mfg Co Inc (PA) .... E...... 323 724-7777
3737 Capitol Ave City Of Industry (90601) *(P-11089)*

Gordon Rees Scully Mansukhani .... C...... 213 576-5000
633 W 5th St 52nd Fl Los Angeles (90071) *(P-18863)*

Gordon Rees Scully Mansukhani .... C...... 619 696-6700
101 W Broadway Ste 1600 San Diego (92101) *(P-18864)*

Gores Group LLC (PA) .... D...... 310 209-3010
9800 Wilshire Blvd Beverly Hills (90212) *(P-14380)*

Gores Radio Holdings LLC .... D...... 310 209-3010
10877 Wilshire Blvd Ste 1805 Los Angeles (90024) *(P-9213)*

Gorilla Automotive Products, Buena Park *Also Called: Amcor Industries Inc (P-9350)*

Gorlitz Sewer & Drain Inc .... E...... 562 944-3060
10132 Norwalk Blvd Santa Fe Springs (90670) *(P-7660)*

Gosch Ford Lincoln Mercury, Hemet *Also Called: Jack Gosch Ford Inc (P-13782)*

Gosecure Inc (PA) .... C...... 301 442-3432
13220 Evening Creek Dr S Ste 107 San Diego (92128) *(P-13971)*

Gossamer Bio Inc (PA) .... E...... 858 684-1300
3013 Science Park Rd Ste 200 San Diego (92121) *(P-4123)*

Gothic Ground Management, Santa Clarita *Also Called: Gothic Landscaping Inc (P-192)*

Gothic Grounds Mgmt, Valencia *Also Called: Gothic Landscaping Inc (P-162)*

Gothic Landscaping Inc .... C...... 661 257-5085
27413 Tourney Rd Ste 200 Valencia (91355) *(P-162)*

Gothic Landscaping Inc (PA) .... C...... 661 678-1400
27413 Tourney Rd Santa Clarita (91355) *(P-192)*

Gottstein Corporation .... E...... 661 322-8934
3500 Chester Ave Bakersfield (93301) *(P-12769)*

Goudy Honda, Alhambra *Also Called: Alhambra Motors Inc (P-13737)*

Gould & Bass Company Inc .... E...... 909 623-6793
1431 W 2nd St Pomona (91766) *(P-10202)*

Gould Electric Inc .... C...... 858 486-1727
12975 Brookprinter Pl Ste 280 Poway (92064) *(P-904)*

Gourmet Coffee Warehouse Inc (PA) .... E...... 323 871-8930
920 N Formosa Ave Los Angeles (90046) *(P-1820)*

Gourmet Foods Inc (PA) .... D...... 310 632-3300
2910 E Harcourt St Compton (90221) *(P-13182)*

Mergent email: customerrelations@mergent.com
1106

2024 Southern California
Business Directory and Buyers Guide

(P-0000) Products & Services Section entry number
(PA)=Parent Co (HQ)=Headquarters (DH)=Div Headquarters

Governmentjobscom Inc .... C...... 310 426-6304
2120 Park Pl Ste 100 El Segundo (90245) *(P-16258)*

GP Batteries, San Diego *Also Called: Gold Peak Industries (north America) Inc (P-9150)*

GP Color Imaging Group, North Hollywood *Also Called: Wes Go Inc (P-3824)*

GP Merger Sub Inc .... D...... 562 946-7722
9401 Ann St Santa Fe Springs (90670) *(P-5342)*

Gpc, Irvine *Also Called: Global Pcci (gpc) (P-6519)*

GPde Slva Spces Incrporation (PA)................................**D...... 562 407-2643**
8531 Loch Lomond Dr Pico Rivera (90660) *(P-1908)*

GPh Medical & Legal Services (PA)..................................**C...... 213 207-2700**
468 N Camden Dr Beverly Hills (90210) *(P-17966)*

Gpi Ca-Niii Inc .... D...... 626 305-3000
1434 Buena Vista St Duarte (91010) *(P-13773)*

GPM, Thousand Oaks *Also Called: General Pavement Management Inc (P-1071)*

Gps Associates Inc .... E....... 949 408-3162
1803 Carnegie Ave Santa Ana (92705) *(P-4351)*

Gps Painting Wallcovering Inc ....C...... 714 730-8904
1307 E Saint Gertrude Pl Ste C Santa Ana (92705) *(P-848)*

Graber Olive House, Ontario *Also Called: C C Graber Co (P-47)*

Grabit Interactive Inc .... E....... 844 472-2488
14724 Ventura Blvd Sherman Oaks (91403) *(P-15594)*

Grace Communications Inc (PA).................................**E... 213 628-4384**
210 S Spring St Los Angeles (90012) *(P-3279)*

Grace Dvson Discovery Sciences, Hesperia *Also Called: W R Grace & Co-Conn (P-10304)*

Gracek Jewelry, Newport Coast *Also Called: Krystal Ventures LLC (P-10904)*

Gracing Brand Management Inc ....B...... 626 297-2472
1108 W Valley Blvb Ste 660 Alhambra (91803) *(P-2416)*

Graco Childrens Products Inc ....B...... 770 418-7200
17182 Nevada St Victorville (92394) *(P-2831)*

Gradient Engineers Inc .... C...... 949 477-0555
17781 Cowan Ste 140 Irvine (92614) *(P-19601)*

Graffiti Shield Inc .... E....... 714 575-1100
2940 E La Palma Ave Ste D Anaheim (92806) *(P-4812)*

Graham Webb International Inc (HQ)..............................D...... 760 918-3600
6109 De Soto Ave Woodland Hills (91367) *(P-4416)*

Grain Craft Inc .... D...... 323 585-0131
1861 E 55th St Los Angeles (90058) *(P-1411)*

Grain To Green Inc .... C...... 760 845-6107
301 N El Camino Real San Clemente (92672) *(P-13406)*

Gramercy Productions LLC .... D...... 818 777-1677
100 Universal City Plz Bldg 2150 Universal City (91608) *(P-17277)*

Granatelli Motor Sports Inc .... E....... 805 486-6644
1000 Yarnell Pl Oxnard (93033) *(P-9398)*

Granath & Granath Inc ....F....... 310 327-5740
1930 W Rosecrans Ave Gardena (90249) *(P-6624)*

Grancell Village, Reseda *Also Called: Los Angles Jewish HM For Aging (P-18003)*

Grand Avenue Hlth Holdings LLC ....D...... 949 487-9500
29222 Rancho Viejo Rd Ste 127 San Juan Capistrano (92675) *(P-17967)*

Grand Del Mar, San Diego *Also Called: Grand Del Mar Resort LP (P-15158)*

Grand Del Mar Resort LP ....A...... 858 314-2000
5300 Grand Del Mar Ct San Diego (92130) *(P-15158)*

Grand Fusion Housewares Inc ....E....... 909 292-5776
9375 Customhouse Plz San Diego (92154) *(P-5042)*

GRAND FUSION HOUSEWARES, INC, San Diego *Also Called: Grand Fusion Housewares Inc (P-5042)*

Grand General, Rancho Dominguez *Also Called: Grand General Accessories LLC (P-8097)*

Grand General Accessories LLC ....E....... 310 631-2589
1965 E Vista Bella Way Rancho Dominguez (90220) *(P-8097)*

Grand Pacific Carlsbad Ht LP ....B...... 760 827-2400
5480 Grand Pacific Dr Carlsbad (92008) *(P-15159)*

Grand Pacific Resorts Inc (PA)....................................**C...... 760 431-8500**
5900 Pasteur Ct Ste 200 Carlsbad (92008) *(P-14805)*

Grand Pacific Resorts Inc ....A...... 760 431-8500
5900 Pasteur Ct Ste 200 Carlsbad (92008) *(P-15160)*

Grand Pacific Resorts Svcs LP ....C...... 760 431-8500
5900 Pasteur Ct Ste 200 Carlsbad (92008) *(P-15161)*

Grand Prix Performance, Costa Mesa *Also Called: Grand Prix Road Trends Inc (P-13863)*

Grand Prix Road Trends Inc (PA)..................................**F...... 323 962-8600**
1718 Newport Blvd Costa Mesa (92627) *(P-13863)*

Grand Slam Tennis Program, Pacific Palisades *Also Called: Riviera Country Club Inc (P-17562)*

Grand Supercenter Inc .... D...... 562 318-3451
8550 Chetle Ave Ste B Whittier (90606) *(P-13183)*

Grand Textile, Cerritos *Also Called: Dool Fna Inc (P-2037)*

Grand Vista Hotel, Simi Valley *Also Called: Simi West Inc (P-15357)*

Grandall Distributing Co Inc .... E....... 818 242-6640
321 El Bonito Ave Glendale (91204) *(P-16837)*

Grandcare Health Services LLC (PA)............................**C...... 866 554-2447**
3452 E Foothill Blvd Ste 700 Pasadena (91107) *(P-18615)*

Grandma Lucys LLC ....F...... 949 206-8547
30432 Esperanza Rcho Sta Marg (92688) *(P-14134)*

Grandville Llc .... E....... 213 382-3878
1670 Cordova St Los Angeles (90007) *(P-1518)*

Grani Installation Inc (PA)...**D...... 714 898-0441**
5411 Commercial Dr Huntington Beach (92649) *(P-554)*

Granite Construction Company ....B...... 760 775-7500
38000 Monroe St Indio (92203) *(P-618)*

Granite Construction Company ....C...... 805 964-9951
5335 Debbie Rd Santa Barbara (93111) *(P-619)*

Granite Construction Inc .... D...... 805 667-8210
213 Columbia Way Lancaster (93535) *(P-620)*

Granite Gold Inc .... D...... 858 499-8933
12780 Danielson Ct Ste A Poway (92064) *(P-4352)*

Granitize Products Inc .... D...... 562 923-5438
11022 Vulcan St South Gate (90280) *(P-4353)*

Granlund Candies, Yucaipa *Also Called: B B G Management Group (P-13263)*

Grant & Weber (PA)...**D...... 818 878-7700**
26610 Agoura Rd Ste 209 Calabasas (91302) *(P-15613)*

Grant & Weber Travel, Calabasas *Also Called: Grant & Weber (P-15613)*

Grant Construction Inc .... D...... 661 588-4586
7702 Meany Ave Ste 103 Bakersfield (93308) *(P-1012)*

Grant Dahlstrom Inc ....F...... 626 798-0858
1222 N Fair Oaks Ave Pasadena (91103) *(P-3851)*

Grant Piston Rings, Anaheim *Also Called: Rtr Industries LLC (P-7705)*

Grapheex, Agoura Hills *Also Called: Pars Publishing Corp (P-3653)*

Graphic Business Solutions Inc ....E....... 619 258-4081
1912 John Towers Ave El Cajon (92020) *(P-12994)*

Graphic Color Systems Inc .... D...... 323 283-3000
1166 W Garvey Ave Monterey Park (91754) *(P-3580)*

Graphic Ink Corp .... E....... 714 901-2805
5382 Industrial Dr Huntington Beach (92649) *(P-15666)*

Graphic Ink and Graphic Ink, Huntington Beach *Also Called: Graphic Ink Corp (P-15666)*

Graphic Packaging Intl LLC ....D...... 949 250-0900
1600 Barranca Pkwy Irvine (92606) *(P-13540)*

Graphic Prints Inc .... E....... 310 870-1239
904 Silver Spur Rd Ste 415 Rllng Hls Est (90274) *(P-2531)*

Graphic Research Inc .... E....... 818 886-7340
3339 Durham Ct Burbank (91504) *(P-8683)*

Graphic Trends Incorporated ....E....... 562 531-2339
7301 Adams St Paramount (90723) *(P-3763)*

Graphic Visions Inc .... E....... 818 845-8393
7119 Fair Ave North Hollywood (91605) *(P-3581)*

Graphics 2000 LLC .... D...... 714 879-1188
1600 E Valencia Dr Fullerton (92831) *(P-3764)*

Graphics Department, La Jolla *Also Called: University Cal San Diego (P-15678)*

Graphiq LLC .... C...... 805 335-2433
101a Innovation Pl Santa Barbara (93108) *(P-3453)*

Graphtec, Irvine *Also Called: Graphtec America Inc (P-10137)*

Graphtec America Inc (DH)...**E....... 949 770-6010**
17462 Armstrong Ave Irvine (92614) *(P-10137)*

Grasshopper House Partners LLC ....C...... 310 589-2880
6428 Meadows Ct Malibu (90265) *(P-19085)*

Grating Pacific Inc (PA)..**E....... 562 598-4314**
3651 Sausalito St Los Alamitos (90720) *(P-6028)*

Gray Construction Inc .... C...... 714 491-1315
421 E Cerritos Ave Anaheim (92805) *(P-434)*

Gray Wc, Anaheim *Also Called: Gray West Construction Inc (P-504)*

Gray West Construction Inc ....C...... 714 491-1317
421 E Cerritos Ave Anaheim (92805) *(P-504)*

Graybar, Diamond Bar *Also Called: Graybar Electric Company Inc (P-12596)*

Graybar Electric Company Inc ....C...... 909 451-4300
1370 Valley Vista Dr Ste 100 Diamond Bar (91765) *(P-12596)*

Employee Codes: A=Over 500 employees, B=251-500
C=101-250, D=51-100, E=20-50, F=10-19, G=1-9

2024 Southern California
Business Directory and Buyers Guide

© Mergent Inc. 1-800-342-5647
1107

Graybar Electric Company Inc ....D...... 858 578-8606
8606 Miralani Dr San Diego (92126) *(P-12597)*

Graybill Medical Group Inc (PA) ....C...... 866 228-2236
225 E 2nd Ave Escondido (92025) *(P-17661)*

Grayd-A Prcsion Met Fbricators ....E...... 562 944-8951
13233 Florence Ave Santa Fe Springs (90670) *(P-6247)*

Grayson Service Inc ....F...... 661 589-5444
1845 Greeley Rd Bakersfield (93314) *(P-348)*

Great Amercn Seafood Import Co, Carson *Also Called: Southwind Foods LLC (P-1796)*

Great American Packaging ....E...... 323 582-2247
4361 S Soto St Vernon (90058) *(P-3183)*

Great Amrcn Logistics Dist Inc ....D...... 562 229-3601
13565 Larwin Cir Santa Fe Springs (90670) *(P-11521)*

Great Atlantic News LLC ....C...... 770 863-9000
1575 N Main St Orange (92867) *(P-13495)*

Great Eastern Entertainment Co (PA) ....E...... 310 638-5058
610 W Carob St Compton (90220) *(P-3454)*

Great Pacific Elbow LLC ....E...... 909 606-5551
13900 Sycamore Way Chino (91710) *(P-6248)*

Great Pacific Elbow Company, Chino *Also Called: Great Pacific Elbow LLC (P-6248)*

Great Pacific Patagonia, Ventura *Also Called: Patagonia Inc (P-2217)*

Great River Food, City Of Industry *Also Called: Derek and Constance Lee Corp (P-1217)*

Great Western Distributing Svc, Los Angeles *Also Called: Gils Distributing Service (P-15602)*

Great Western Malting Co ....D...... 360 991-0888
995 Joshua Way Ste B Vista (92081) *(P-1609)*

Great Western Packaging LLC ....D...... 818 464-3800
8230 Haskell Ave 8240 Van Nuys (91406) *(P-3765)*

Greatbatch Medical, San Diego *Also Called: Integer Holdings Corporation (P-10533)*

Greatcall Inc ....A...... 800 733-6632
10945 Vista Sorrento Pkwy Ste 120 San Diego (92130) *(P-14135)*

Greater El Monte Cmnty Hosp, El Monte *Also Called: Ahm Gemch Inc (P-18165)*

Greater Los Angeles Zoo Assn ....D...... 323 644-4200
5333 Zoo Dr Los Angeles (90027) *(P-19326)*

Greater Los Angles Area Cncil (PA) ....D...... 213 413-4400
2333 Scout Way Los Angeles (90026) *(P-19449)*

Greater Los Angles Cnty Vctor ....C...... 562 944-7976
12545 Florence Ave Santa Fe Springs (90670) *(P-20342)*

Greater Los Angles Vtrans RES ....D...... 310 312-1554
11301 Wilshire Blvd Bldg 114 Los Angeles (90073) *(P-14984)*

Greater San Diego AC Co Inc ....C...... 619 469-7818
3883 Ruffin Rd Ste C San Diego (92123) *(P-774)*

Greater Valley Medical Group ....C...... 818 781-7097
14600 Sherman Way Ste 300 Van Nuys (91405) *(P-18693)*

Grech Motors LLC (PA) ....E...... 951 688-8347
6915 Arlington Ave Riverside (92504) *(P-17106)*

Green Acres Lodge, Rosemead *Also Called: Longwood Management Corp (P-17999)*

Green Convergence (PA) ....D...... 661 294-9495
28476 Westinghouse Pl Valencia (91355) *(P-12742)*

Green Dragon, Los Angeles *Also Called: Cmk Manufacturing LLC (P-2047)*

Green Energy Innovations, Buena Park *Also Called: Sfadia Inc (P-934)*

Green Farms Inc ....D...... 858 831-7701
2652 Long Beach Ave Los Angeles (90058) *(P-13327)*

Green Hasson & Janks LLP ....C...... 310 873-1600
700 S Flower St Ste 3300 Los Angeles (90017) *(P-19777)*

Green Hills Software, Santa Barbara *Also Called: Green Hills Software LLC (P-16259)*

Green Hills Software LLC (HQ) ....C...... 805 965-6044
30 W Sola St Santa Barbara (93101) *(P-16259)*

Green Line Rail Eqp Maint, Lawndale *Also Called: Los Angles Cnty Mtro Trnsp Aut (P-11335)*

Green River Golf Corporation ....D...... 714 970-8411
5215 Green River Rd Corona (92878) *(P-17430)*

Green River Golf Course, Corona *Also Called: Green River Golf Corporation (P-17430)*

Green Spot Packaging Inc ....E...... 909 625-8771
100 S Cambridge Ave Claremont (91711) *(P-1695)*

Green Spot USA, Claremont *Also Called: Green Spot Packaging Inc (P-1695)*

Green Thumb International Inc ....D...... 818 340-6400
21812 Sherman Way Canoga Park (91303) *(P-13507)*

Green Thumb International Inc ....D...... 661 259-1071
23734 Newhall Ave Newhall (91321) *(P-13679)*

Green Thumb Nurseries, Newhall *Also Called: Green Thumb International Inc (P-13679)*

Green Thumb Produce Inc ....C...... 951 849-4711
2648 W Ramsey St Banning (92220) *(P-13328)*

Green Tomato Grill, Orange *Also Called: Fahetas LLC (P-14005)*

Greenball Corp (PA) ....E...... 714 782-3060
222 S Harbor Blvd Ste 700 Anaheim (92805) *(P-12269)*

Greenberg Glsker Flds Clman Mc ....C...... 310 553-3610
2049 Century Park E Ste 2600 Los Angeles (90067) *(P-18865)*

Greenberg Traurig, Irvine *Also Called: Greenberg Traurig LLP (P-18866)*

Greenberg Traurig LLP ....D...... 949 732-6500
18565 Jamboree Rd Ste 500 Irvine (92612) *(P-18866)*

Greenbox, Los Angeles *Also Called: Greenbox Loans Inc (P-14215)*

Greenbox Art and Culture, San Diego *Also Called: No Boundaries Inc (P-3645)*

Greenbox Loans Inc ....D...... 800 919-1086
3250 Wilshire Blvd 1900 Los Angeles (90010) *(P-14215)*

Greenbridge Technology Inc ....E...... 714 991-0200
1335 S Acacia Ave Fullerton (92831) *(P-7366)*

Greenbrier Rail, San Bernardino *Also Called: Meridian Rail Acquisition (P-11836)*

Greenbrier Rail Services, San Bernardino *Also Called: Gunderson Rail Services LLC (P-11833)*

Greene Group Industries, Oceanside *Also Called: Southwest Greene Intl Inc (P-6556)*

Greenheart, Arroyo Grande *Also Called: Greenheart Farms Inc (P-82)*

Greenheart Farms Inc ....B...... 805 481-2234
902 Zenon Way Arroyo Grande (93420) *(P-82)*

Greenhedge Escrow ....C...... 310 640-3040
2015 Manhattan Beach Blvd Redondo Beach (90278) *(P-14892)*

Greenhouse Agency Inc ....C...... 949 752-7542
4100 Birch St Ste 500 Newport Beach (92660) *(P-20178)*

Greenkraft Inc ....F...... 714 545-7777
2530 S Birch St Santa Ana (92707) *(P-9290)*

Greenlots, Los Angeles *Also Called: Zeco Systems Inc (P-13446)*

Greenpath Recovery Recycl Svcs, Colton *Also Called: Greenpath Recovery West Inc (P-12955)*

Greenpath Recovery West Inc ....D...... 909 954-0686
330 W Citrus St Ste 250 Colton (92324) *(P-12955)*

Greenpower Motor Company Inc ....D...... 909 308-0960
8885 Haven Ave Rancho Cucamonga (91730) *(P-9291)*

Greens Group Inc ....C...... 949 829-4902
16530 Bake Pkwy Ste 200 Irvine (92618) *(P-15162)*

Greenscreen ....E...... 310 837-0526
725 S Figueroa St Ste 1825 Los Angeles (90017) *(P-163)*

Greenshine New Energy LLC ....D...... 949 609-9636
23661 Birtcher Dr Lake Forest (92630) *(P-8368)*

Greensoft Technology Inc ....C...... 323 254-5961
155 S El Molino Ave Ste 100 Pasadena (91101) *(P-16498)*

Greenwave Reality Inc ....E...... 714 805-9283
15420 Laguna Canyon Rd Ste 150 Irvine (92618) *(P-16446)*

Greenwave Systems, Irvine *Also Called: Greenwave Reality Inc (P-16446)*

Greenwich Biosciences LLC (DH) ....E...... 760 795-2200
5750 Fleet St Ste 200 Carlsbad (92008) *(P-4124)*

Greenwich Biosciences, Inc., Carlsbad *Also Called: Greenwich Biosciences LLC (P-4124)*

Greenwood & Hall, Los Angeles *Also Called: Pcs Link Inc (P-20371)*

Greenwood Hall Inc ....C...... 310 905-8300
6230 Wilshire Blvd Ste 136 Los Angeles (90048) *(P-19010)*

Grefco Dicaperl, Torrance *Also Called: Dicaperl Corporation (P-416)*

Gregg Drilling LLC ....C...... 562 427-6899
2726 Walnut Ave Signal Hill (90755) *(P-1094)*

Gregg Electric Inc ....C...... 909 983-1794
608 W Emporia St Ontario (91762) *(P-905)*

Gregg Hammork Enterprises Inc ....E...... 949 586-7902
23002 Alicia Pkwy Mission Viejo (92692) *(P-260)*

Gregg's Mission Viejo Mobile, Mission Viejo *Also Called: Gregg Hammork Enterprises Inc (P-260)*

Gregory Consulting Inc (PA) ....C...... 805 642-0111
6350 Leland St Ventura (93003) *(P-13774)*

Greif Inc ....E...... 323 724-7500
6001 S Eastern Ave Commerce (90040) *(P-2732)*

Greif Inc ....D...... 909 350-2112
8250 Almeria Ave Fontana (92335) *(P-5867)*

Greif Bros Corp ....E...... 909 941-4570
3042 Inland Empire Blvd Ontario (91764) *(P-3136)*

Greka, Santa Maria *Also Called: Greka Integrated Inc (P-307)*

Greka Integrated Inc (PA) ....C...... 805 347-8700
1700 Sinton Rd Santa Maria (93458) *(P-307)*

Gremlin Inc .... D...... 408 214-9885
440 N Barranca Ave Ste 3101 Walnut (91789) *(P-16260)*

Greneker Solutions, Los Angeles *Also Called: Pacific Manufacturing MGT Inc (P-2985)*

Gresean Industries Inc .... E
6320 Caballero Blvd Buena Park (90620) *(P-1013)*

Greyhound Lines Inc .... D...... 213 629-8400
1716 E 7th St Los Angeles (90021) *(P-11435)*

Greystar, Newport Beach *Also Called: Greystar Management Svcs LP (P-14806)*

Greystar Management Svcs LP .... A...... 949 705-0010
620 Newport Center Dr 15th Fl Newport Beach (92660) *(P-14806)*

Greystar Management Svcs LP .... C...... 818 596-2180
6320 Canoga Ave Ste 1512 Woodland Hills (91367) *(P-14807)*

Griff Industries Inc .... F...... 661 728-0111
4515 Runway Dr Lancaster (93536) *(P-5043)*

Griffith Company .... B...... 661 392-6640
1128 Carrier Parkway Ave Bakersfield (93308) *(P-621)*

Griffith Company (PA)......................................**C.... 714 984-5500**
3050 E Birch St Brea (92821) *(P-622)*

Grifols Bio Supplies Inc .... C...... 760 651-4042
980 Park Center Dr Ste F Vista (92081) *(P-18766)*

Grifols Biologicals LLC (DH)...........................**D.... 323 225-2221**
5555 Valley Blvd Los Angeles (90032) *(P-4319)*

Grifols Usa LLC .... D...... 760 931-8444
995 Park Center Dr Vista (92081) *(P-4320)*

Grifols Usa LLC .... A...... 626 435-2600
13111 Temple Ave City Of Industry (91746) *(P-12490)*

Griley Air Freight, Los Angeles *Also Called: Southern Counties Terminals (P-11465)*

Grimmway Enterprises Inc .... B...... 661 393-3320
6101 Zerker Rd Shafter (93263) *(P-103)*

Grimmway Enterprises Inc .... B...... 661 854-6250
830 Sycamore Rd Arvin (93203) *(P-104)*

Grimmway Enterprises Inc .... A...... 661 854-6200
11412 Malaga Rd Arvin (93203) *(P-105)*

Grimmway Enterprises Inc .... C...... 661 845-5200
6900 Mountain View Rd Bakersfield (93307) *(P-106)*

Grimmway Enterprises Inc .... C...... 661 854-6240
12020 Malaga Rd Arvin (93203) *(P-505)*

Grimmway Enterprises Inc .... D...... 307 302-0090
11646 Malaga Rd Arvin (93203) *(P-11458)*

Grimmway Enterprises Inc .... B...... 661 845-3758
12000 Main St Lamont (93241) *(P-13329)*

Grimmway Enterprises Inc .... D...... 661 854-6200
14141 Di Giorgio Rd Arvin (93203) *(P-20036)*

Grimmway Farms, Arvin *Also Called: Grimmway Enterprises Inc (P-105)*

Grimmway Farms, Bakersfield *Also Called: Grimmway Enterprises Inc (P-106)*

Grimmway Frozen Foods, Arvin *Also Called: Grimmway Enterprises Inc (P-104)*

Grindr LLC .... C...... 310 776-6680
750 N San Vicente Blvd West Hollywood (90069) *(P-16042)*

Gringo Ventures LLC .... B...... 760 477-7999
3260 Corporate Vw Vista (92081) *(P-13508)*

Gringteam Inc .... B...... 619 297-5466
7450 Hazard Center Dr San Diego (92108) *(P-15163)*

Gringteam Inc .... D...... 858 485-4145
800 W Ivy St Ste D San Diego (92101) *(P-15164)*

Griswald Industries, Perris *Also Called: Griswold Industries (P-12857)*

Griswold Controls, Irvine *Also Called: Griswold Controls LLC (P-6791)*

Griswold Controls LLC (PA)............................ D...... 949 559-6000
1700 Barranca Pkwy Irvine (92606) *(P-6791)*

Griswold Industries (PA)................................ B...... 949 722-4800
1701 Placentia Ave Costa Mesa (92627) *(P-5795)*

Griswold Industries .... F...... 949 722-4831
1731 Placentia Ave Costa Mesa (92627) *(P-6777)*

Griswold Industries .... F...... 951 657-1718
24100 Water Ave Perris (92570) *(P-12857)*

Griswold Pump Company .... E...... 909 422-1700
22069 Van Buren St Grand Terrace (92313) *(P-7279)*

Gro-Power Inc .... E...... 909 393-3744
15065 Telephone Ave Chino (91710) *(P-4539)*

Grolink, Oxnard *Also Called: Grolink Plant Company Inc (P-13509)*

Grolink Plant Company Inc (PA)......................:..**C.... 805 984-7958**
4107 W Gonzales Rd Oxnard (93036) *(P-13509)*

Grossmont Home Hlth & Hospice, La Mesa *Also Called: Grossmont Hospital Corporation (P-18273)*

Grossmont Hospital Corporation (HQ)................**A...... 619 740-6000**
5555 Grossmont Center Dr La Mesa (91942) *(P-18272)*

Grossmont Hospital Corporation .... B...... 619 667-1900
8881 Fletcher Pkwy Ste 105 La Mesa (91942) *(P-18273)*

Grosvenor Inv MGT US Inc ....D...... 310 265-0297
2308 Chelsea Rd Palos Verdes Estates (90274) *(P-14599)*

Ground Control Business MGT (DH)....................**F.... 310 315-6200**
2049 Century Park E Ste 1400 Los Angeles (90067) *(P-2040)*

Ground Force One, Redondo Beach *Also Called: Cputer Inc (P-16559)*

Ground Fueling, Irvine *Also Called: Eaton Corporation (P-9682)*

Ground Hog Inc .... E...... 909 478-5700
1470 Victoria Ct San Bernardino (92408) *(P-6933)*

Groundwork Coffee, North Hollywood *Also Called: Groundwork Coffee Roasters LLC (P-1821)*

Groundwork Coffee Company, Los Angeles *Also Called: Gourmet Coffee Warehouse Inc (P-1820)*

Groundwork Coffee Roasters LLC .... C...... 818 506-6020
5457 Cleon Ave North Hollywood (91601) *(P-1821)*

Groundwork Open Source Inc .... D...... 415 992-4500
23332 Mill Creek Dr Ste 155 Laguna Hills (92653) *(P-16529)*

Group Five, Whittier *Also Called: Russ Bassett Corp (P-2787)*

Group H Engineering .... E...... 818 999-0999
2030 Vista Ave Sierra Madre (91024) *(P-349)*

Grove Diagnstc Imaging Ctr Inc .... B...... 909 982-8638
8805 Haven Ave Ste 120 Rancho Cucamonga (91730) *(P-17662)*

Grove Lumber & Bldg Sups Inc (PA)...................**C.... 909 947-0277**
27126 Watson Rd Menifee (92585) *(P-12331)*

Grover Manufacturing, South El Monte *Also Called: Grover Smith Mfg Corp (P-7280)*

Grover Products Co .... D...... 323 263-9981
3424 E Olympic Blvd Los Angeles (90023) *(P-9399)*

Grover Smith Mfg Corp .... E...... 323 724-3444
9717 Factorial Way South El Monte (91733) *(P-7280)*

Groves Capital Inc ....C...... 619 519-4453
4025 Stonebridge Ln Rancho Santa Fe (92091) *(P-15030)*

Grow More Inc .... D...... 310 515-1700
15600 New Century Dr Gardena (90248) *(P-4551)*

Grubb & Ellis Company .... A...... 714 667-8252
1551 N Tustin Ave Ste 300 Santa Ana (92705) *(P-14808)*

Grubb & Ellis Management Services Inc .... A...... 412 201-8200
1551 N Tustin Ave Ste 300 Santa Ana (92705) *(P-14809)*

Gruber Systems Inc .... E...... 661 257-0464
29071 The Old Rd Valencia (91355) *(P-7074)*

Gruma Corporation .... C...... 909 980-3566
11559 Jersey Blvd Ste A Rancho Cucamonga (91730) *(P-1826)*

Gruma Corporation .... B...... 323 803-1400
5505 E Olympic Blvd Commerce (90022) *(P-1827)*

Grupo Gallegos .... D...... 562 256-3600
300 Pacific Coast Hwy Ste 200 Huntington Beach (92648) *(P-15541)*

Grupoex, La Mirada *Also Called: Mejico Express Inc (P-11677)*

Gryphon, Chula Vista *Also Called: Gryphon Marine LLC (P-19602)*

Gryphon Marine LLC ....D...... 619 407-4010
694 Moss St Chula Vista (91911) *(P-19602)*

Gs Brothers Inc (PA)......................................**C.... 310 833-1369**
20331 Main St Carson (90745) *(P-193)*

Gscm Ventures Inc .... E...... 818 303-2600
12924 Pierce St Pacoima (91331) *(P-4417)*

Gsg Printing Inc (PA)......................................**E.... 760 752-9500**
2304 Faraday Ave Carlsbad (92008) *(P-3582)*

Gsg Protective Services CA Inc ....C...... 310 371-5300
15901 Hawthorne Blvd Ste 324 Redondo Beach (90278) *(P-16645)*

Gsms Inc (PA)..**E...... 805 477-9866**
5187 Camino Ruiz Camarillo (93012) *(P-4125)*

Gsp Metal Finishing Inc .... E...... 818 744-1328
16520 S Figueroa St Gardena (90248) *(P-6625)*

GSP Precision Inc .... E...... 818 845-2212
650 Town Center Dr Ste 950 Costa Mesa (92626) *(P-7853)*

Gst Inc .... E...... 949 510-1142
3419 Via Lido Ste 164 Newport Beach (92663) *(P-7472)*

Gt Diamond, Irvine *Also Called: General Tool Inc (P-12856)*

Employee Codes: A=Over 500 employees, B=251-500
C=101-250, D=51-100, E=20-50, F=10-19, G=1-9

2024 Southern California
Business Directory and Buyers Guide

© Mergent Inc. 1-800-342-5647

1109

ALPHABETIC

GT Precision Inc ....C...... 310 323-4374
1629 W 132nd St Gardena (90249) *(P-6415)*

GT Styling Corp ....E...... 714 644-9214
2830 E Via Martens Anaheim (92806) *(P-5044)*

Gtr, Carlsbad *Also Called: Gtr Enterprises Incorporated (P-7854)*

Gtr Enterprises Incorporated ....E...... 760 931-1192
6352 Corte Del Abeto Ste E Carlsbad (92011) *(P-7854)*

Gtran Inc (PA)...**E...... 805 445-4500**
829 Flynn Rd Camarillo (93012) *(P-9051)*

Gts Living Foods LLC ....E...... 323 581-7787
4646 Hampton St Vernon (90058) *(P-1696)*

Gts Living Foods LLC (PA).....................................**A...... 323 581-7787**
4415 Bandini Blvd Vernon (90058) *(P-1697)*

Gtt International Inc ....E...... 951 788-8729
1615 Eastridge Ave Riverside (92507) *(P-12304)*

Guadalupe Union School Dst (PA).........................**C...... 805 343-2114**
4465 9th St Guadalupe (93434) *(P-18968)*

Guarachi Wine Partners Inc ....D...... 818 225-5100
27001 Agoura Rd Ste 285 Calabasas (91301) *(P-13477)*

Guaranteed Rate Inc ....C...... 424 354-5344
230 Commerce Irvine (92602) *(P-14323)*

Guaranteed Rate Inc ....C...... 760 310-6008
1455 Frazee Rd Ste 500 San Diego (92108) *(P-14324)*

Guaranteed Rate Inc ....C...... 805 550-6933
1065 Higuera St Ste 100 San Luis Obispo (93401) *(P-14325)*

Guard Management Inc ....C...... 858 279-8282
8001 Vickers St San Diego (92111) *(P-16646)*

Guard Systems District 1, Monterey Park *Also Called: Guard-Systems Inc (P-16648)*

Guard-Systems Inc ....A...... 909 947-5400
1910 S Archibald Ave Ste M2 Ontario (91761) *(P-16647)*

Guard-Systems Inc ....A...... 323 881-6715
1190 Monterey Pass Rd Monterey Park (91754) *(P-16648)*

Guardian Integrated SEC Inc (PA).........................**C...... 800 400-3167**
21828 Lassen St Ste A Chatsworth (91311) *(P-16739)*

Guardian Intl Solutions ....D...... 323 528-6555
3415 S Sepulveda Blvd Ste 1100 Los Angeles (90034) *(P-16649)*

Guardian Solutions, Orange *Also Called: Lres Corporation (P-14825)*

Guardian Title Company ....D...... 949 495-9306
300 Commerce Irvine (92602) *(P-14893)*

Guardsmark LLC (DH)...**C...... 714 619-9700**
1551 N Tustin Ave Ste 650 Santa Ana (92705) *(P-16650)*

Guckenheimer Enterprises Inc ....D...... 760 414-3659
4010 Ocean Ranch Blvd Oceanside (92056) *(P-4126)*

Guelaguetza, Los Angeles *Also Called: Pbf & E LLC (P-14030)*

Guess, Los Angeles *Also Called: Baby Guess Inc (P-2413)*

Guess Inc (PA)..**A...... 213 765-3100**
1444 S Alameda St Los Angeles (90021) *(P-2389)*

GUESS?, Los Angeles *Also Called: Guess Inc (P-2389)*

Guggenheim Prtners Inv MGT LLC ....C...... 310 576-1270
100 Wilshire Blvd 5th Fl Santa Monica (90401) *(P-14963)*

Guhring Inc ....E...... 714 841-3582
15581 Computer Ln Huntington Beach (92649) *(P-7116)*

Guidance Software Inc (HQ)....................................C...... 626 229-9191
1055 E Colorado Blvd Ste 400 Pasadena (91106) *(P-16261)*

Guided Wave Inc ....E...... 919 264-9651
2121 Aviation Dr Upland (91786) *(P-10138)*

Guild Holdings Company (PA)..................................**B...... 858 560-6330**
5887 Copley Dr San Diego (92111) *(P-14326)*

Guild Mortgage, San Diego *Also Called: Guild Holdings Company (P-14326)*

Guild Mortgage, San Diego *Also Called: Guild Mortgage Company LLC (P-14991)*

Guild Mortgage Company LLC (HQ).........................**C...... 800 365-4441**
5887 Copley Dr San Diego (92111) *(P-14991)*

Gulf Development, Torrance *Also Called: Signtronix Inc (P-11166)*

Gulf Enterprises, Chatsworth *Also Called: Mercury Magnetics Inc (P-8947)*

Gulf Streams ....E...... 562 420-1818
4150 E Donald Douglas Dr Long Beach (90808) *(P-9537)*

Gulfstream, Van Nuys *Also Called: Gulfstream Aerospace Corp GA (P-9540)*

Gulfstream Aerospace Corp GA ....A...... 562 420-1818
4150 E Donald Douglas Dr Long Beach (90808) *(P-9538)*

Gulfstream Aerospace Corp GA ....B...... 562 907-9300
9818 Mina Ave Whittier (90605) *(P-9539)*

Gulfstream Aerospace Corp GA ....B...... 805 236-5755
16644 Roscoe Blvd Van Nuys (91406) *(P-9540)*

Gumbiner Savett Inc ....D...... 310 828-9798
1723 Cloverfield Blvd Santa Monica (90404) *(P-14664)*

Gumbiner Svett Fnkel Fnglson R, Santa Monica *Also Called: Gumbiner Savett Inc (P-14664)*

Gumgum Inc (PA)..**E...... 310 260-9666**
1314 7th St Fl 5 Santa Monica (90401) *(P-16262)*

Gunderson Rail Services LLC ....C...... 909 478-0541
1475 Cooley Ct San Bernardino (92408) *(P-11833)*

Gunjoy Inc ....E...... 714 289-0055
22895 Eastpark Dr Yorba Linda (92887) *(P-9052)*

Gunnar Optiks LLC ....E...... 858 769-2500
2236 Rutherford Rd Ste 123 Carlsbad (92008) *(P-14118)*

Gursey Schneider & Co LLC (PA)............................**C...... 310 552-0960**
1888 Century Park E Ste 900 Los Angeles (90067) *(P-19778)*

Guru Denim LLC (DH)...**C...... 323 266-3072**
500 W 190th St Ste 300 Gardena (90248) *(P-13908)*

Guru Knits Inc ....D...... 323 235-9424
225 W 38th St Los Angeles (90037) *(P-2242)*

Gurucul Solutions LLC ....E...... 213 291-6888
222 N Pacific Coast Hwy Ste 1322 El Segundo (90245) *(P-13972)*

Guthy-Renker Direct, Santa Monica *Also Called: Guthy-Renker LLC (P-12978)*

Guthy-Renker LLC ....D...... 310 581-6250
3340 Ocean Park Blvd Fl 2 Santa Monica (90405) *(P-12978)*

Guy Yocom Construction Inc (PA)............................**C...... 951 284-3456**
3299 Horseless Carriage Rd Ste H Norco (92860) *(P-1073)*

Guys Patio Inc ....E...... 844 968-7485
2907 Oak St Santa Ana (92707) *(P-17077)*

Guzman Grading and Paving Corp ....D...... 909 428-5960
14030 Rose Ave Fontana (92337) *(P-15780)*

Guzzler Manufacturing Inc ....E...... 562 436-0250
1510 Hayes Ave Long Beach (90813) *(P-11223)*

Gvs Italy ....D...... 424 382-4343
8616 La Tijera Blvd Los Angeles (90045) *(P-12552)*

GW Reed Printing Inc ....E...... 909 947-0599
4071 Greystone Dr Ontario (91761) *(P-3583)*

Gwla Acquisition Corp (PA)......................................**F...... 323 789-7800**
8600 Rheem Ave South Gate (90280) *(P-5315)*

Gxo Logistics Supply Chain Inc ....A...... 336 309-6201
3520 S Cactus Ave Bloomington (92316) *(P-11583)*

Gxo Logistics Supply Chain Inc ....D...... 951 512-1201
2163 S Riverside Ave Colton (92324) *(P-11584)*

Gxo Logistics Supply Chain Inc ....D...... 909 838-5631
7140 Cajon Blvd San Bernardino (92407) *(P-11766)*

Gynecologic Oncology Assoc, Newport Beach *Also Called: Micha-Rettenmaier Partnership (P-17712)*

Gypsy 05 Inc ....E...... 323 265-2700
3200 Union Pacific Ave Los Angeles (90023) *(P-2326)*

Gyre Therapeutics Inc (PA)......................................**D...... 650 266-8674**
12730 High Bluff Dr Ste 250 San Diego (92130) *(P-4127)*

H & A Transmissions Inc ....E...... 909 941-9020
8727 Rochester Ave Rancho Cucamonga (91730) *(P-17025)*

H & H LLC (PA)...**D...... 805 925-2036**
1131 S Russell Ave Santa Maria (93458) *(P-15165)*

H & H Agency Inc (PA)...**D...... 949 260-8840**
1403 N Tustin Ave Ste 280 Santa Ana (92705) *(P-14600)*

H & H Manufacturing, Pomona *Also Called: Holland & Herring Mfg Inc (P-7866)*

H & H Specialties Inc ....E...... 626 575-0776
14850 Don Julian Rd Ste B City Of Industry (91746) *(P-11224)*

H & L Forge Company, Montebello *Also Called: H & L Tooth Company (P-6934)*

H & L Tooth Company (PA)..D...... 323 721-5146
1540 S Greenwood Ave Montebello (90640) *(P-6934)*

H & M Four-Slide Inc ....E...... 951 461-8244
498 Melbourne Gln Escondido (92026) *(P-7855)*

H & N Fish Co., Vernon *Also Called: H & N Foods International Inc (P-13280)*

H & N Foods International Inc (HQ)...........................**C...... 323 586-9300**
5580 S Alameda St Vernon (90058) *(P-13280)*

H & R Accounts Inc ....C...... 619 819-8844
3131 Camino Del Rio N Ste 1500 San Diego (92108) *(P-16043)*

H & T Seafood Inc ....E...... 323 526-0888
5598 Lindbergh Ln Bell (90201) *(P-13281)*

H and H Drug Stores Inc .... D...... 909 890-9700
114 E Airport Dr San Bernardino (92408) *(P-12491)*

H C I, Riverside *Also Called: Hci LLC (P-671)*

H C V T, Los Angeles *Also Called: Holthouse Carlin Van Trigt LLP (P-19780)*

H Co Computer Products (PA)................................... E...... **949 833-3222**
16812 Hale Ave Irvine (92606) *(P-7473)*

H D G Associates .... C...... 805 963-0744
1111 E Cabrillo Blvd Santa Barbara (93103) *(P-15166)*

H D Smith LLC .... D...... 310 641-1885
1370 E Victoria St Carson (90746) *(P-13044)*

H G Group Inc .... B...... 805 486-6463
4225 Saviers Rd Oxnard (93033) *(P-15495)*

H J Harkins Company Inc .... E...... 805 929-1333
1400 W Grand Ave Ste F Grover Beach (93433) *(P-4128)*

H K Prcision Turning Machining, Oceanside *Also Called: Balda HK Plastics Inc (P-6412)*

H L Moe Co Inc (PA).. C...... **818 572-2100**
526 Commercial St Glendale (91203) *(P-775)*

H M C, Chula Vista *Also Called: Heartland Meat Company Inc (P-13296)*

H M E, Carlsbad *Also Called: HM Electronics Inc (P-12666)*

H M Electronics Inc .... E...... 858 535-6139
2848 Whiptail Loop Carlsbad (92010) *(P-8613)*

H M F, Anaheim *Also Called: Hitech Metal Fabrication Corp (P-6029)*

H Rauvel Inc .... C...... 562 989-3333
501 W Walnut St Compton (90220) *(P-11489)*

H Roberts Construction .... D...... 562 590-4825
2165 W Gaylord St Long Beach (90813) *(P-6379)*

H W Hunter Inc (PA) .... D...... **661 948-8411**
1130 Auto Mall Dr Lancaster (93534) *(P-13775)*

H Wayne Lewis Inc .... E...... 909 874-2213
312 S Willow Ave Rialto (92376) *(P-6398)*

H. M. ELECTRONICS, INC., Carlsbad *Also Called: H M Electronics Inc (P-8613)*

H2o Innovation Operation Maint, Valencia *Also Called: H2o Innovation USA Holding Inc (P-12743)*

H2o Innovation USA Holding Inc .... D...... 418 688-0170
1048 La Mirada Ct Valencia (91355) *(P-12743)*

H2scan Corporation (PA).. E...... **661 775-9575**
27215 Turnberry Ln Unit A Valencia (91355) *(P-10369)*

H2u Technologies Inc .... E...... 626 344-0505
20360 Plummer St Chatsworth (91311) *(P-3866)*

H2w .... E...... 800 578-3088
7660 Alabama Ave Canoga Park (91304) *(P-12979)*

Haas Automation Inc (PA).. A...... **805 278-1800**
2800 Sturgis Rd Oxnard (93030) *(P-7013)*

Haberfelde Ford (PA).. C...... **661 328-3600**
2001 Oak St Bakersfield (93301) *(P-13776)*

Hacienda Golf Club .... D...... 562 694-1081
718 East Rd La Habra Heights (90631) *(P-17487)*

Haddads Fine Arts Inc .... E...... 714 996-2100
3855 E Miraloma Ave Anaheim (92806) *(P-4589)*

Hadley Fruit Orchards Inc (PA).................................. E...... **951 849-5255**
48980 Seminole Dr Cabazon (92230) *(P-14094)*

Hadrian, Torrance *Also Called: Hadrian Automation Inc (P-8521)*

Hadrian Automation Inc .... D...... 503 807-4490
19501 S Western Ave Torrance (90501) *(P-8521)*

Hadronex Inc .... E...... 760 291-1980
2110 Enterprise St Escondido (92029) *(P-12152)*

Haea, Fountain Valley *Also Called: Hyundai Autoever America LLC (P-16542)*

Haemonetics Manufacturing Inc (HQ)....................... E...... **626 339-7388**
1630 W Industrial Park St Covina (91722) *(P-10519)*

Hagen Streiff Newton & Oshiro Accountants PC .... D...... 949 390-7647
4667 Macarthur Blvd Ste 400 Newport Beach (92660) *(P-19779)*

Hagen-Renaker Inc (PA)... D...... **909 599-2341**
914 W Cienega Ave San Dimas (91773) *(P-5385)*

HAID, DAVID, Los Angeles *Also Called: David Haid (P-3022)*

Haight, Los Angeles *Also Called: Haight Brown & Bonesteel LLP (P-18867)*

Haight Brown & Bonesteel LLP (PA)......................... D...... **213 542-8000**
555 S Flower St Ste 4500 Los Angeles (90071) *(P-18867)*

Haimetal Duct Inc .... E...... 818 768-2315
625 Arroyo St San Fernando (91340) *(P-6249)*

Hain Celestial Group Inc .... C...... 323 859-0553
5630 Rickenbacker Rd Bell (90201) *(P-4418)*

Hakes Sash & Door Inc .... C...... 951 674-2414
31945 Corydon St Lake Elsinore (92530) *(P-1014)*

Hal Hays Construction Inc (PA).................................. C...... **951 788-0703**
4181 Latham St Riverside (92501) *(P-506)*

Halcore Group Inc .... E...... 626 575-0880
10941 Weaver Ave South El Monte (91733) *(P-9292)*

Halcyon Microelectronics Inc .... F...... 626 814-4688
5467 2nd St Irwindale (91706) *(P-8801)*

Hales Engineering Coinc .... E
18 Wood Rd Camarillo (93010) *(P-7856)*

Halex Corporation (DH).. E...... **909 629-6219**
4200 Santa Ana St Ste A Ontario (91761) *(P-5882)*

Haley Bros, Riverside *Also Called: T M Cobb Company (P-2634)*

Haley Bros Inc .... C...... 800 854-5951
1575 Riverview Dr San Bernardino (92408) *(P-2603)*

Haley Bros Inc (HQ).. D...... **714 670-2112**
6291 Orangethorpe Ave Buena Park (90620) *(P-2604)*

Haley Indus Ctings Linings Inc .... E...... 323 588-8086
2919 Tanager Ave Commerce (90040) *(P-6708)*

Haliburton International Foods Inc .... B...... 909 428-8520
3855 Jurupa St Ontario (91761) *(P-1909)*

Hall Associates Racg Pdts Inc .... F...... 310 326-4111
2711 Plaza Del Amo Ste 503 Torrance (90503) *(P-9934)*

Halliburton Company .... D...... 661 393-8111
34722 7th Standard Rd Bakersfield (93314) *(P-350)*

Hallmark Channel, Studio City *Also Called: Hallmark Media US LLC (P-11953)*

Hallmark Floors, Ontario *Also Called: Hallmark Home Interiors Inc (P-2571)*

Hallmark Home Interiors Inc (PA)............................. F...... **909 947-7736**
2360 S Archibald Ave Ontario (91761) *(P-2571)*

Hallmark Labs LLC .... C...... 424 210-3600
3130 Wilshire Blvd Ste 400 Santa Monica (90403) *(P-14086)*

Hallmark Lighting, Commerce *Also Called: Hallmark Lighting LLC (P-8315)*

Hallmark Lighting LLC .... D...... 818 885-5010
1945 S Tubeway Ave Commerce (90040) *(P-8315)*

Hallmark Media US LLC (DH)................................... D...... **818 755-2400**
12700 Ventura Blvd Ste 100 Studio City (91604) *(P-11953)*

Hallmark Metals Inc .... E...... 626 335-1263
600 W Foothill Blvd Glendora (91741) *(P-6250)*

Hallmark Southwest, Loma Linda *Also Called: Dvele Omega Corporation (P-2738)*

Halonus Inc .... B...... 714 345-0822
6855 E Swarthmore Dr Anaheim (92807) *(P-11225)*

Halozyme, San Diego *Also Called: Halozyme Therapeutics Inc (P-4321)*

Halozyme Inc .... C...... 858 794-8889
12390 El Camino Real San Diego (92130) *(P-19845)*

Halozyme Therapeutics, San Diego *Also Called: Halozyme Inc (P-19845)*

Halozyme Therapeutics Inc (PA)................................ D...... **858 794-8889**
12390 El Camino Real San Diego (92130) *(P-4321)*

Halsteel Inc (DH).. E...... **909 937-1001**
4190 Santa Ana St Ste A Ontario (91761) *(P-5615)*

Halter Properties LLC .... E...... 805 226-9455
8910 Adelaida Rd Paso Robles (93446) *(P-1634)*

Halter Ranch Vineyard, Paso Robles *Also Called: Halter Properties LLC (P-1634)*

Halter Winery LLC (PA)... E...... **805 226-9455**
8910 Adelaida Rd Paso Robles (93446) *(P-1635)*

Hamburger Home (PA)... D...... **323 876-0550**
7120 Franklin Ave Los Angeles (90046) *(P-19265)*

Hamby Corporation .... E...... 661 257-1924
27704 Avenue Scott Valencia (91355) *(P-8684)*

Hamilton Metalcraft Inc .... E...... 626 795-4811
848 N Fair Oaks Ave Pasadena (91103) *(P-6251)*

Hamilton Sundstrand Corp .... C...... 909 593-5300
960 Overland Ct San Dimas (91773) *(P-10261)*

Hamilton Sundstrand Spc Systms .... D...... 909 288-5300
960 Overland Ct San Dimas (91773) *(P-10370)*

Hammer Collection Inc .... F...... 310 515-0276
14427 S Main St Gardena (90248) *(P-2804)*

HAMMER MUSEUM, Los Angeles *Also Called: Armand Hmmer Mseum of Art Cltr (P-19349)*

Hammitt Inc .... D...... 310 292-5200
2101 Pacific Coast Hwy Hermosa Beach (90254) *(P-5288)*

Hammond Inc Which Will Do Bus .... E...... 925 381-5392
404 S Coast Hwy Oceanside (92054) *(P-1673)*

Employee Codes: A=Over 500 employees, B=251-500
C=101-250, D=51-100, E=20-50, F=10-19, G=1-9

2024 Southern California
Business Directory and Buyers Guide

© Mergent Inc. 1-800-342-5647

1111

A
L
P
H
A
B
E
T
I
C

Hamo Constraction .... E...... 818 415-3334
3650 Altura Ave La Crescenta (91214) *(P-351)*

Hampstead Lafayette Hotel LLC .... C...... 619 296-2101
2223 El Cajon Blvd San Diego (92104) *(P-15167)*

Hampton Inn, Foothill Ranch *Also Called: Stonebridge Rlty Advisors Inc (P-15375)*

Hampton Products Intl Corp (PA).......................... D...... **949 472-4256**
50 Icon Foothill Ranch (92610) *(P-12723)*

Hampton Tdder Tchncal Svcs Inc .... F...... 909 628-1256
4571 State St Montclair (91763) *(P-19973)*

Hamrock Inc .... C...... 562 944-0255
3019 Wilshire Blvd Santa Monica (90403) *(P-5616)*

Hana Commercial Finance LLC .... D...... 213 240-1234
1000 Wilshire Blvd Ste 570 Los Angeles (90017) *(P-14282)*

Hana Financial Inc (PA)...................................... D...... **213 240-1234**
1000 Wilshire Blvd Ste 2000 Los Angeles (90017) *(P-15781)*

Hancor Inc .... E...... 661 366-1520
140 Vineland Rd Bakersfield (93307) *(P-4849)*

Handbill Printers, Corona *Also Called: Handbill Printers LP (P-3584)*

Handbill Printers LP .... E...... 951 547-5910
820 E Parkridge Ave Corona (92879) *(P-3584)*

Handel's Ice Cream, Rancho Cucamonga *Also Called: Handels Homemade Ice Cream (P-14011)*

Handels Homemade Ice Cream .... E...... 909 989-7065
6403 Haven Ave Rancho Cucamonga (91737) *(P-14011)*

Handlery Hotels, San Diego *Also Called: Handlery Hotels Inc (P-15168)*

Handlery Hotels Inc .... C...... 415 781-4550
950 Hotel Cir N San Diego (92108) *(P-15168)*

Handpiece Parts & Products Inc .... E...... 714 997-4331
707 W Angus Ave Orange (92868) *(P-10745)*

Hanford Hotels Inc .... C...... 714 557-3000
3131 Bristol St Costa Mesa (92626) *(P-15169)*

Hangar 1, Fullerton *Also Called: Common Collabs LLC (P-1763)*

Hanger Prsthtics Orthtics W In .... D...... 213 250-7850
1127 Wilshire Blvd Ste 310 Los Angeles (90017) *(P-10666)*

Hanger Prsthtics Orthtics W In (HQ)..................... E...... **714 961-2112**
4155 E La Palma Ave Ste 400 Anaheim (92807) *(P-10667)*

Hanjin Global Logistics, Gardena *Also Called: Hanjin Transportation Co Ltd (P-11767)*

Hanjin Shipping Co Ltd .... A...... 201 291-4600
301 Hanjin Rd Long Beach (90802) *(P-11655)*

Hanjin Transportation Co Ltd .... D...... 310 522-5030
15913 S Main St Gardena (90248) *(P-11767)*

Hanken Cono Assad & Co Inc .... C...... 619 575-3100
1504 Oro Vista Rd Apt 145 San Diego (92154) *(P-14810)*

Hankey Group, Los Angeles *Also Called: Nowcom LLC (P-16582)*

Hanley Wood Media Inc (HQ).............................. F...... **202 736-3300**
4000 Macarthur Blvd Ste 400 Newport Beach (92660) *(P-3455)*

Hanmar LLC (PA)... D...... **818 890-2802**
11441 Bradley Ave Pacoima (91331) *(P-6520)*

Hanna Fuji Sushi, Santa Fe Springs *Also Called: Nikko Enterprise Corporation (P-1809)*

Hannahmax Baking Inc .... C...... 310 380-6778
14601 S Main St Gardena (90248) *(P-1477)*

Hannam Chain Super 1 Market, Los Angeles *Also Called: Hannam Chain USA Inc (P-12455)*

Hannam Chain USA Inc (PA)............................... C...... **213 382-2922**
2740 W Olympic Blvd Los Angeles (90006) *(P-12455)*

Hannspree North America Inc .... D...... 909 992-5025
13223 Black Mountain Rd San Diego (92129) *(P-9053)*

Hanover Accessories Corp C
6049 E Slauson Ave Commerce (90040) *(P-3838)*

Hansen Engineering Co .... D...... 310 534-3870
24020 Frampton Ave Harbor City (90710) *(P-7857)*

Hansens Welding Inc .... E...... 310 329-6888
358 W 168th St Gardena (90248) *(P-17084)*

Hanson Aggrgtes Md-Pacific Inc .... F...... 805 967-2371
50 S Kellogg Ave Goleta (93117) *(P-11459)*

Hanson Distributing Company (PA)........................ C...... **626 224-9800**
975 W 8th St Azusa (91702) *(P-12241)*

Hanson Lab Solutions Inc .... E...... 805 498-3121
747 Calle Plano Camarillo (93012) *(P-10094)*

Hanson Roof Tile Inc .... B...... 888 509-4787
10651 Elm Ave Fontana (92337) *(P-5418)*

Hanson Tank, Los Angeles *Also Called: Roy E Hanson Jr Mfg (P-6154)*

Hanson Truss Inc .... B...... 909 591-9256
13950 Yorba Ave Chino (91710) *(P-2699)*

Hanwha Q Cells America Inc (DH)......................... F...... **949 748-5996**
400 Spectrum Center Dr Ste 1400 Irvine (92618) *(P-8802)*

Hanwha Q Cells USA Corp .... D...... 949 748-5996
300 Spectrum Center Dr Ste 1250 Irvine (92618) *(P-12026)*

Hapag-Lloyd (america) LLC .... C...... 562 435-0771
555 E Ocean Blvd Ste 300 Long Beach (90802) *(P-11768)*

Happy Money, Costa Mesa *Also Called: Payoff Inc (P-14277)*

Happy Money Inc .... B...... 949 430-0630
21515 Hawthorne Blvd Ste 200 Torrance (90503) *(P-14261)*

Happy Planner, The, Cypress *Also Called: ME & My Big Ideas LLC (P-12939)*

Happyco Inc (PA)... C...... **415 230-9832**
5857 Owens Ave Ste 300 Carlsbad (92008) *(P-16044)*

Har-Bro LLC (HQ)... D...... **562 528-8000**
2750 Signal Pkwy Signal Hill (90755) *(P-555)*

Haralambos Beverage Co .... B...... 562 347-4300
26717 Palmetto Ave Redlands (92374) *(P-13467)*

Harari Inc (PA).. E...... **323 734-5302**
9646 Brighton Way Los Angeles (90016) *(P-2243)*

Harbill Inc .... D...... 909 883-8833
909 W 21st St San Bernardino (92405) *(P-13777)*

Harbinger Motors Inc .... E...... 914 299-3998
15700 S Figueroa St Gardena (90248) *(P-9293)*

Harbor Distributing LLc (HQ)............................... C...... **714 933-2400**
5901 Bolsa Ave Huntington Beach (92647) *(P-13468)*

Harbor Distributing LLC .... D...... 310 538-5483
16407 S Main St Gardena (90248) *(P-13469)*

Harbor Distributing Co, Gardena *Also Called: Harbor Distributing LLC (P-13469)*

Harbor Dvlpmntal Dsblties Fndt .... C...... 310 540-1711
21231 Hawthorne Blvd Torrance (90503) *(P-19327)*

Harbor Freight Tools, Calabasas *Also Called: Central Purchasing LLC (P-12847)*

Harbor Furniture Mfg Inc (PA)............................. E...... **323 636-1201**
15817 Whitepost Ln La Mirada (90638) *(P-2805)*

Harbor Glen Care Center .... C...... 626 963-7531
1033 E Arrow Hwy Glendora (91740) *(P-17968)*

Harbor Green Grain LP .... E...... 310 991-8089
13181 Crossroads Pkwy N Ste 200 City Of Industry (91746) *(P-1441)*

Harbor Health Care Inc .... C...... 562 866-7054
9461 Flower St Bellflower (90706) *(P-19266)*

Harbor Health Systems LLC .... C...... 949 273-7020
3501 Jamboree Rd Ste 540 Newport Beach (92660) *(P-18767)*

Harbor House, La Mirada *Also Called: Harbor Furniture Mfg Inc (P-2805)*

Harbor Industrial, Wilmington *Also Called: Harbor Industrial Svcs Corp (P-15762)*

Harbor Industrial Svcs Corp .... D...... 310 522-1193
211 N Marine Ave Wilmington (90744) *(P-15762)*

Harbor Packaging, Poway *Also Called: Liberty Diversified Intl Inc (P-3115)*

Harbor Pipe and Steel Inc .... C...... 951 369-3990
1495 Columbia Ave Bldg 10 Riverside (92507) *(P-12553)*

Harbor Post Accute Care Center, Torrance *Also Called: Geri-Care Inc (P-17964)*

HARBOR REGIONAL CENTER, Torrance *Also Called: Harbor Dvlpmntal Dsblties Fndt (P-19327)*

Harbor Truck Bodies Inc .... D...... 714 996-0411
255 Voyager Ave Brea (92821) *(P-9327)*

Harbor Truck Body, Brea *Also Called: Harbor Truck Bodies Inc (P-9327)*

Harbor Ucla Med Foundation, Torrance *Also Called: Harbor-Ucla Med Foundation Inc (P-20037)*

Harbor View Hotel Ventures LLC .... D...... 619 239-6800
1646 Front St San Diego (92101) *(P-15170)*

Harbor View House, San Pedro *Also Called: Healthview Inc (P-19269)*

Harbor-Ucla Med Foundation Inc .... B...... 310 533-0413
21602 S Vermont Ave Torrance (90502) *(P-18659)*

Harbor-Ucla Med Foundation Inc (PA)................... D...... **310 222-5015**
21840 Normandie Ave Ste 100 Torrance (90502) *(P-20037)*

Harcon Precision Metals Inc .... E...... 619 423-5544
1790 Dornoch Ct Chula Vista (91910) *(P-6935)*

Harcourt Trade Publishers, San Diego *Also Called: Houghton Mifflin Harcourt Pubg (P-3407)*

Hard Candy LLC .... E...... 949 515-3923
833 W 16th St Newport Beach (92663) *(P-13045)*

Hard Rock Hotel, San Diego *Also Called: T-12 Three LLC (P-15387)*

Mergent email: customerrelations@mergent.com
1112

2024 Southern California
Business Directory and Buyers Guide

(P-0000) Products & Services Section entry number
(PA)=Parent Co (HQ)=Headquarters (DH)=Div Headquarters

Harding Containers Intl Inc .... E 310 549-7272
4000 Santa Fe Ave Long Beach (90810) *(P-2719)*

Hardware Imports Inc .... E 909 595-6201
161 Commerce Way Walnut (91789) *(P-9328)*

Hardware Specialties, Ontario *Also Called: F & D Flores Enterprises Inc (P-10363)*

Hardwood Flrg Liquidators Inc (PA) .... D 323 201-4200
7227 Telegraph Rd Montebello (90640) *(P-2572)*

Hardy & Harper Inc .... E 714 444-1851
32 Rancho Cir Lake Forest (92630) *(P-623)*

Hardy Diagnostics Inc (PA) .... B 805 346-2766
1430 W Mccoy Ln Santa Maria (93455) *(P-12492)*

Hardy Frames Inc .... D 951 245-9525
250 Klug Cir Corona (92878) *(P-5590)*

Hardy Process Solutions .... E 858 278-2900
10075 Mesa Rim Rd San Diego (92121) *(P-10139)*

Hardy Process Solutions, San Diego *Also Called: Hardy Process Solutions (P-10139)*

Hardy Window Company (PA) .... C 714 996-1807
1639 E Miraloma Ave Placentia (92870) *(P-12332)*

Harkham Industries Inc (PA) .... E 323 586-4600
857 S San Pedro St Ste 300 Los Angeles (90014) *(P-2244)*

Harkins Theatres Inc .... D 909 627-8010
3100 Chino Ave Chino Hills (91709) *(P-17299)*

Harkins Theatres Inc .... D 909 793-7993
27481 San Bernardino Ave Redlands (92374) *(P-17300)*

Harland Brewing Co LLC .... E 858 800-4566
10115 Carroll Canyon Rd San Diego (92131) *(P-14048)*

Harman Envelopes, North Hollywood *Also Called: Harman Press Inc (P-3585)*

Harman International Inds Inc .... A 818 893-8411
8500 Balboa Blvd Northridge (91325) *(P-12662)*

Harman Press Inc .... E 818 432-0570
6840 Vineland Ave North Hollywood (91605) *(P-3585)*

Harman Professional, Northridge *Also Called: Harman Professional Inc (P-8416)*

Harman Professional Inc .... C 844 776-4899
14780 Bar Harbor Rd Fontana (92336) *(P-8414)*

Harman Professional Inc .... C 951 242-2927
24950 Grove View Rd Moreno Valley (92551) *(P-8415)*

Harman Professional Inc (DH) .... B 818 893-8411
8500 Balboa Blvd Northridge (91325) *(P-8416)*

Harman-Kardon, Northridge *Also Called: Harman-Kardon Incorporated (P-12632)*

Harman-Kardon Incorporated .... B 818 841-4600
8500 Balboa Blvd Northridge (91329) *(P-12632)*

Harmonium Inc (PA) .... C 858 684-3080
5440 Morehouse Dr Ste 1000 San Diego (92121) *(P-19212)*

Harmony Kids, San Fernando *Also Called: Newco International Inc (P-2783)*

Harper & Two Inc (PA) .... F 562 424-3030
2937 Cherry Ave Signal Hill (90755) *(P-9054)*

Harper Federal Cnstr LLC .... D 619 543-1296
14130 Biscayne Pl Poway (92064) *(P-624)*

Harper Wilde Inc .... E 213 510-1608
10866 Wilshire Blvd Ste 1650 Los Angeles (90024) *(P-2390)*

Harpers Pharmacy Inc .... C 877 778-3773
132 S Anita Dr Ste 210 Orange (92868) *(P-4129)*

Harpo Entertainment Group, Van Nuys *Also Called: Harpo Productions Inc (P-17195)*

Harpo Productions Inc .... C 312 633-1000
7619 N Patriot Way Van Nuys (91405) *(P-17195)*

Harrah's, Valley Center *Also Called: Caesars Entrtnment Oprtng Inc (P-17542)*

Harrahs Resort Southern Cal, Valley Center *Also Called: Hcal LLC (P-15174)*

Harrell Holdings (PA) .... C 661 322-5627
1707 Eye St Ste 102 Bakersfield (93301) *(P-3280)*

Harrington & Sons Inc .... E 951 674-0998
590 Crane St Lake Elsinore (92530) *(P-5568)*

Harrington Industrial Plas LLC (PA) .... D 909 597-8641
14480 Yorba Ave Chino (91710) *(P-12744)*

Harris, Van Nuys *Also Called: L3harris Technologies Inc (P-9989)*

Harris, Los Angeles *Also Called: L3harris Technologies Inc (P-9990)*

Harris Freeman & Co Inc (PA) .... B 714 765-7525
3110 E Miraloma Ave Anaheim (92806) *(P-13370)*

Harris Industries Inc (PA) .... E 714 898-8048
5181 Argosy Ave Huntington Beach (92649) *(P-3172)*

Harris Organs Inc .... E 562 693-3442
7047 Comstock Ave Whittier (90602) *(P-10925)*

Harris Spice Company Inc (HQ) .... E 714 507-1919
3110 E Miraloma Ave Anaheim (92806) *(P-13727)*

Harris Tea Company, Anaheim *Also Called: Harris Freeman & Co Inc (P-13370)*

Harris' Precision Products, Whittier *Also Called: Harris Organs Inc (P-10925)*

Harrison Iyke .... D 909 463-8409
7611 Etiwanda Ave Rancho Cucamonga (91739) *(P-16740)*

Harrison, E J & Sons Recycling, Ventura *Also Called: E J Harrison & Sons Inc (P-12167)*

Harry's Dye & Wash, Anaheim *Also Called: Harrys Dye and Wash Inc (P-2089)*

Harrys Dye and Wash Inc .... E 714 446-0300
1015 E Orangethorpe Ave Anaheim (92801) *(P-2089)*

Hartley Company .... E 949 646-9643
1987 Placentia Ave Costa Mesa (92627) *(P-11046)*

Hartley-Racon, Costa Mesa *Also Called: Hartley Company (P-11046)*

Hartman Slicer Div, Santa Fe Springs *Also Called: United Bakery Equipment Co Inc (P-7355)*

Hartmark Cab Design & Mfg Inc .... E 909 591-9153
3575 Grapevine St Jurupa Valley (91752) *(P-1160)*

Hartmark Cabinet Design, Jurupa Valley *Also Called: Hartmark Cab Design & Mfg Inc (P-1160)*

Hartwell Corporation (DH) .... C 714 993-4200
900 Richfield Rd Placentia (92870) *(P-5920)*

Hartzell Aerospace, Valencia *Also Called: Electrofilm Mfg Co LLC (P-6775)*

Harvard Card Systems, City Of Industry *Also Called: Harvard Label LLC (P-3047)*

Harvard Label LLC .... C 626 333-8881
111 Baldwin Park Blvd City Of Industry (91746) *(P-3047)*

Harvest Farms Inc .... D 661 945-3636
45000 Yucca Ave Lancaster (93534) *(P-1392)*

Harvest Food Distributors, National City *Also Called: Harvest Meat Company Inc (P-13295)*

Harvest Landscape Entps Inc (PA) .... C 714 693-8100
8030 E Crystal Dr Anaheim (92807) *(P-164)*

Harvest Landscape Maintenance, Anaheim *Also Called: Harvest Landscape Entps Inc (P-164)*

Harvest Management Sub LLC .... A 805 543-0187
1299 Briarwood Dr San Luis Obispo (93401) *(P-14711)*

Harvest Meat Company Inc .... D 619 477-0185
1022 Bay Marina Dr Ste 106 National City (91950) *(P-13294)*

Harvest Meat Company Inc (HQ) .... D 619 477-0185
1000 Bay Marina Dr National City (91950) *(P-13295)*

HARVEST MEAT COMPANY, INC., National City *Also Called: Harvest Meat Company Inc (P-13294)*

Harvest Pack Inc .... F 888 727-7225
12336 Lower Azusa Rd Arcadia (91006) *(P-3143)*

Harvey Inc .... C 858 769-4000
9455 Ridgehaven Ct Ste 200 San Diego (92123) *(P-556)*

Harvey General Contracting, San Diego *Also Called: Harvey Inc (P-556)*

Harwil, Oxnard *Also Called: Harwil Precision Products (P-9055)*

Harwil Precision Products .... E 805 988-6800
541 Kinetic Dr Oxnard (93030) *(P-9055)*

Hasa Inc (PA) .... D 661 259-5848
23119 Drayton St Saugus (91350) *(P-3856)*

Hasco, Placentia *Also Called: Hartwell Corporation (P-5920)*

Haskel International LLC (HQ) .... C 818 843-4000
100 E Graham Pl Burbank (91502) *(P-7281)*

Haskon, Div of, Brea *Also Called: Kirkhill Inc (P-4737)*

Hatchbeauty, Los Angeles *Also Called: Hatchbeauty Products LLC (P-13046)*

Hatchbeauty Agency LLC (PA) .... E 310 396-7070
355 S Grand Ave Los Angeles (90071) *(P-20179)*

Hatchbeauty Products LLC (PA) .... D 310 396-7070
355 S Grand Ave Los Angeles (90071) *(P-13046)*

Hathaway Children and Family, Pacoima *Also Called: Hathaway-Sycmres Child Fmly Svc (P-19086)*

Hathaway LLC .... E 661 393-2004
4205 Atlas Ct Bakersfield (93308) *(P-261)*

Hathawy-Sycmres Child Fmly Svc .... C 626 395-7100
12502 Van Nuys Blvd Ste 120 Pacoima (91331) *(P-19086)*

Hathawy-Sycmres Child Fmly Svc .... C 323 733-0322
3741 Stocker St Ste 101 View Park (90008) *(P-19087)*

Hathawy-Sycmres Child Fmly Svc .... D 323 257-9600
840 N Avenue 66 Los Angeles (90042) *(P-19267)*

Haulaway Storage Cntrs Inc .... B 800 826-9040
11292 Western Ave Stanton (90680) *(P-11585)*

Hav Holdings & Subsidiaries, Sun Valley *Also Called: Hollywood Film Company (P-10869)*

Employee Codes: A=Over 500 employees, B=251-500
C=101-250, D=51-100, E=20-50, F=10-19, G=1-9

2024 Southern California
Business Directory and Buyers Guide

© Mergent Inc. 1-800-342-5647

1113

Havaianas, Venice *Also Called: Alpargatas Usa Inc (P-5274)*

Havas Edge LLC (DH) .... D....... 760 929-0041
1525 Faraday Ave Ste 250 Carlsbad (92008) *(P-15542)*

Havas Formula LLC .... D....... 619 234-0345
1215 Cushman Ave San Diego (92110) *(P-20284)*

Havuni LLC .... E....... 917 428-1183
11321 Iowa Ave Los Angeles (90025) *(P-2452)*

Hawa Corporation (PA) .... F....... 909 825-8882
125 E Laurel St Colton (92324) *(P-1220)*

Hawaiian Gardens Casino .... A....... 562 860-5887
11871 Carson St Hawaiian Gardens (90716) *(P-15171)*

Hawaiian Gardens Casino .... A....... 562 860-5887
11871 Carson St Hawaiian Gardens (90716) *(P-17554)*

Hawaiian Hotels & Resorts Inc .... C....... 805 480-0052
2830 Borchard Rd Newbury Park (91320) *(P-15172)*

Hawker Pacific Aerospace .... B....... 818 765-6201
11240 Sherman Way Sun Valley (91352) *(P-17131)*

Hawkins Brown USA Inc .... B....... 310 600-2695
8500 Steller Dr Ste 1 Culver City (90232) *(P-19730)*

Hawthorne Cat, San Diego *Also Called: Hawthorne Machinery Co (P-15763)*

Hawthorne Lift Systems, Coachella *Also Called: Naumann/Hobbs Mtl Hdlg Corp II (P-12775)*

Hawthorne Lowe's, Hawthorne *Also Called: Lowes Home Centers LLC (P-13630)*

Hawthorne Machinery Co (PA) .... C....... 858 674-7000
16945 Camino San Bernardo San Diego (92127) *(P-15763)*

Hawthorne Rent-It Service (HQ) .... D....... 858 674-7000
16945 Camino San Bernardo San Diego (92127) *(P-15764)*

Hay Group, Los Angeles *Also Called: Korn Ferry (us) (P-20188)*

Hayden Industrial Products, San Bernardino *Also Called: Hayden Products LLC (P-6143)*

Hayden Products LLC .... D....... 951 736-2600
5199 N Mingo Rd San Bernardino (92408) *(P-6143)*

Hayes Company Inc .... E....... 949 375-3113
5663 Balboa Ave San Diego (92111) *(P-15543)*

Hayes Protective Services Inc .... C....... 323 755-2282
2930 W Imperial Hwy 200b Inglewood (90303) *(P-16651)*

Hayes Welding Inc (PA) .... D....... 760 246-4878
12522 Violet Rd Adelanto (92301) *(P-17085)*

Haymarket Worldwide Inc .... E....... 949 417-6700
17030 Red Hill Ave Irvine (92614) *(P-3361)*

Haynes Building Service LLC .... C....... 626 359-6100
16027 Arrow Hwy Ste I Baldwin Park (91706) *(P-15712)*

Haynes Family Programs Inc .... C....... 909 593-2581
233 Baseline Rd La Verne (91750) *(P-19268)*

Haynes Publications, Westlake Village *Also Called: Odcombe Press (nashville) (P-3647)*

Hayward Gordon Us Inc .... B....... 760 246-3430
9351 Industrial Way Adelanto (92301) *(P-7201)*

Hazard Construction, Lakeside *Also Called: Hazard Construction Company (P-654)*

Hazard Construction Company .... D....... 858 587-3600
10529 Vine St Ste 1 Lakeside (92040) *(P-654)*

Hazel Clothes, Vernon *Also Called: Crestone LLC (P-2236)*

Hazens Investment LLC .... B....... 310 642-1111
6101 W Century Blvd Los Angeles (90045) *(P-15173)*

HB Parkco Construction Inc (PA) .... B....... 714 567-4752
24795 State Highway 74 Perris (92570) *(P-1074)*

HB Products LLC .... D....... 714 799-6967
5671 Engineer Dr Huntington Beach (92649) *(P-3766)*

Hba Incorporated .... D....... 714 635-8602
512 E Vermont Ave Anaheim (92805) *(P-958)*

Hbc Solutions Holdings LLC .... E....... 321 727-9100
10877 Wilshire Blvd Fl 18 Los Angeles (90024) *(P-8522)*

Hc West LLC .... B....... 858 277-3473
7130 Convoy Ct San Diego (92111) *(P-9214)*

Hcal LLC .... B....... 760 751-3100
777 S Resort Dr Valley Center (92082) *(P-15174)*

HCC Surety Group, Los Angeles *Also Called: American Contrs Indemnity Co (P-14534)*

Hci, San Marcos *Also Called: Hughes Circuits Inc (P-8687)*

Hci LLC (HQ) .... B....... 951 520-4200
6830 Airport Dr Riverside (92504) *(P-671)*

Hco Holding I Corporation (HQ) .... D....... 323 583-5000
999 N Pacific Coast Hwy Ste 800 El Segundo (90245) *(P-14932)*

Hco Holding II Corporation .... A....... 310 955-9200
999 N Pacific Coast Hwy Ste 800 El Segundo (90245) *(P-4669)*

Hcr Manorcare Med Svcs Fla LLC .... C....... 949 587-9000
24962 Calle Aragon Aliso Viejo (92653) *(P-17969)*

Hct Group, Santa Monica *Also Called: Hct Packaging Inc (P-16838)*

Hct Packaging Inc (PA) .... C....... 310 260-7680
2800 28th St Ste 240 Santa Monica (90405) *(P-16838)*

Hd Supply Distribution Services LLC .... A....... 949 643-4700
26940 Aliso Viejo Pkwy Aliso Viejo (92656) *(P-12724)*

Hd Window Fashions Inc (DH) .... B....... 213 749-6333
1818 Oak St Los Angeles (90015) *(P-3006)*

Hdmc Holdings LLC .... C....... 760 366-3711
6601 White Feather Rd Joshua Tree (92252) *(P-18274)*

Hdp Holdings, San Diego *Also Called: Wd-40 Company (P-4656)*

Hdz Brothers Inc .... E....... 714 953-4010
1924 E Mcfadden Ave Santa Ana (92705) *(P-4732)*

Headwaters Construction Inc .... E....... 714 523-1530
16005 Phoebe Ave La Mirada (90638) *(P-5366)*

Headwaters Incorporated .... E....... 909 627-9066
1345 Philadelphia St Pomona (91766) *(P-5419)*

Health & Human Services, San Diego *Also Called: County of San Diego (P-18512)*

Health Advocates, Chatsworth *Also Called: Health Advocates LLC (P-19328)*

Health Advocates LLC .... B....... 818 995-9500
21540 Plummer St Ste B Chatsworth (91311) *(P-19328)*

Health Dept, Los Angeles *Also Called: County of Los Angeles (P-18684)*

Health Investment Corporation .... A....... 714 669-2085
14642 Newport Ave Ste 388 Tustin (92780) *(P-18275)*

Health Mate, Los Alamitos *Also Called: Samick Music Corp (P-12986)*

Health Net LLC .... C....... 661 321-3904
6013 Niles St Bakersfield (93306) *(P-14468)*

Health Net LLC (HQ) .... C....... 818 676-6000
21650 Oxnard St Woodland Hills (91367) *(P-14469)*

Health Net Inc .... A....... 818 676-6000
21650 Oxnard St Fl 25 Woodland Hills (91367) *(P-14470)*

Health Resources Corp .... B....... 714 754-5454
2701 S Bristol St Santa Ana (92704) *(P-18276)*

Health Services Advisory Group .... C....... 818 409-9220
700 N Brand Blvd Fl 1 Glendale (91203) *(P-18768)*

Health Services Dept, Palos Verdes Peninsu *Also Called: County of Los Angeles (P-18231)*

Health Services Dept, Los Angeles *Also Called: County of Los Angeles (P-18233)*

Health Services, Dept of, Los Angeles *Also Called: County of Los Angeles (P-17633)*

Health Services, Dept of, Los Angeles *Also Called: County of Los Angeles (P-18232)*

Health Services, Dept of, Castaic *Also Called: County of Los Angeles (P-18526)*

Health Services, Dept of, Acton *Also Called: County of Los Angeles (P-18527)*

Health Services, Dept of, Downey *Also Called: County of Los Angeles (P-18683)*

Health Smart Clinic, Long Beach *Also Called: Healthsmart Pacific Inc (P-17663)*

Health System Medical Network, Beverly Hills *Also Called: Cedars-Sinai Medical Center (P-18210)*

Healthcare, Oxnard *Also Called: Amigo Baby Inc (P-19023)*

Healthcare Ctr of Downey LLC .... C....... 562 869-0978
12023 Lakewood Blvd Downey (90242) *(P-17970)*

Healthcare Finance Direct LLC .... D....... 661 616-4400
1707 Eye St Ste 300 Bakersfield (93301) *(P-20180)*

Healthcare Investments Inc (PA) .... D....... 310 323-3194
1140 W Rosecrans Ave Gardena (90247) *(P-17971)*

Healthcare Management Systems Inc .... C....... 619 521-9641
900 Lane Ave Ste 190 Chula Vista (91914) *(P-17972)*

Healthcare Partners, Van Nuys *Also Called: Greater Valley Medical Group (P-18693)*

Healthcare Partners Med Group, El Segundo *Also Called: Optumcare Management LLC (P-17732)*

Healthcare Resource Group .... C....... 562 945-7224
6571 Altura Blvd Ste 200 Buena Park (90620) *(P-15922)*

Healthcare Services Group Inc .... A....... 562 494-7939
5199 E Pacific Coast Hwy Ste 402 Long Beach (90804) *(P-20396)*

Healthcare Talent .... D....... 714 341-1197
26090 Towne Centre Dr Foothill Ranch (92610) *(P-18769)*

Healthpoint Capital LLC (PA) .... C....... 212 935-7780
9920 Pacific Heights Blvd Ste 150 San Diego (92121) *(P-19926)*

Healthquest Clinical Lab Inc .... D....... 909 445-9727
9805 Research Dr Irvine (92618) *(P-18552)*

Healthsmart Management Service .... D....... 714 947-8600
10855 Business Center Dr Ste C Cypress (90630) *(P-14601)*

Mergent email: customerrelations@mergent.com
1114

2024 Southern California
Business Directory and Buyers Guide

(P-0000) Products & Services Section entry number
(PA)=Parent Co (HQ)=Headquarters (DH)=Div Headquarters

Healthsmart Pacific Inc .... B...... 562 595-1911
2683 Pacific Ave Long Beach (90806) *(P-17663)*

Healthsmart Pacific Inc (PA) .... A...... 562 595-1911
5150 E Pacific Coast Hwy Ste 200 Long Beach (90804) *(P-18277)*

HealthSouth, Oxnard *Also Called: N S C Channel Islands Inc (P-17721)*

Healthview Inc (PA) .... C...... 310 638-4113
921 S Beacon St San Pedro (90731) *(P-19269)*

Healtth Sanitation Services, Santa Maria *Also Called: Valley Garbage Rubbish Co Inc (P-12191)*

Hearst Ranch Winery .... F...... 805 467-2241
7300 N River Rd Paso Robles (93446) *(P-1636)*

Heart N Soul, La Puente *Also Called: Living Doll LLC (P-13913)*

Heart Rate Inc .... E...... 714 850-9716
1411 E Wilshire Ave Santa Ana (92705) *(P-10996)*

Heartland Express, Fontana *Also Called: Heartland Express Inc Iowa (P-11490)*

Heartland Express Inc Iowa .... A...... 319 626-3600
10131 Redwood Ave Fontana (92335) *(P-11490)*

Heartland Farms, City Of Industry *Also Called: Sbm Dairies Inc (P-1739)*

Heartland Label Printers LLC .... A...... 909 243-7151
9817 7th St Ste 703 Rancho Cucamonga (91730) *(P-3767)*

Heartland Meat Company Inc .... D...... 619 407-3668
3461 Main St Chula Vista (91911) *(P-13296)*

Hearts Delight .... E...... 805 648-7123
4035 N Ventura Ave Ventura (93001) *(P-2327)*

Heat Software, Newport Beach *Also Called: Heat Waves LLC (P-16045)*

Heat Transfer Pdts Group LLC .... C...... 909 786-3669
1933 S Vineyard Ave Ontario (91761) *(P-12755)*

Heat Waves LLC .... C...... 719 651-4942
4201 Jamboree Rd Unit 518 Newport Beach (92660) *(P-16045)*

Heater Designs Inc .... E...... 909 421-0971
2211 S Vista Ave Bloomington (92316) *(P-7367)*

Heather By Bordeaux Inc .... E...... 213 622-0555
5983 Malburg Way Vernon (90058) *(P-2328)*

Heatherfield Foods Inc .... E...... 877 460-3060
1150 Brooks St Ontario (91762) *(P-1197)*

Heatshield Products Inc .... E...... 760 751-0441
1040 S Andreasen Dr Ste 110 Escondido (92029) *(P-9400)*

Heatwave LLC .... D...... 949 717-7588
1308 Bison Ave Newport Beach (92660) *(P-17400)*

Heaviland Enterprises Inc .... C...... 858 412-1576
8710 Miramar Pl San Diego (92121) *(P-194)*

Heavy Civil - Gen Engrg Cnstr, Chatsworth *Also Called: Maloof Naman Builders (P-12774)*

Heavy Equipment Rentals, Corona *Also Called: Porter Hire Ltd (P-15793)*

Heavy Metal Steel Company Inc .... E...... 858 433-4800
12130 Lomica Dr San Diego (92128) *(P-1104)*

Hec Asset Management Inc .... D...... 661 587-2250
29341 Kimberlina Rd Wasco (93280) *(P-12456)*

Hec Inc .... B...... 818 879-7414
30961 Agoura Rd Ste 311 Westlake Village (91361) *(P-12663)*

Hedman Hedders, Whittier *Also Called: Hedman Manufacturing (P-9401)*

Hedman Manufacturing (PA) .... E...... 562 204-1031
12438 Putnam St Whittier (90602) *(P-9401)*

Hee Environmental Engineering LLC ...... E...... 760 530-1409
16605 Koala Rd Adelanto (92301) *(P-5045)*

Hehr International Inc .... C...... 323 663-1261
Los Angeles (90039) *(P-6107)*

Hehr International Polymers, Los Angeles *Also Called: Hehr International Inc (P-6107)*

HEI Hospitality LLC .... C...... 818 887-4800
21850 Oxnard St Woodland Hills (91367) *(P-15175)*

HEI Long Beach LLC .... C...... 562 983-3400
701 W Ocean Blvd Long Beach (90831) *(P-15176)*

Heidelberg Investment Group In .... C...... 213 884-7747
4957 Onaknoll Ave Los Angeles (90043) *(P-20181)*

HEIDELBERG MATERIALS SOUTHWEST AGG LLC, Inglewood *Also Called: Heidelberg Mtls Sthwest Agg LL (P-5480)*

Heidelberg Mtls Sthwest Agg LL .... E...... 310 419-1520
1050 S Prairie Ave Inglewood (90301) *(P-5480)*

Heimark Distributing, Santa Fe Springs *Also Called: Triangle Distributing Co (P-13473)*

Helendale Lckheed Plant Prtcti, Helendale *Also Called: Lockheed Martin Corporation (P-9993)*

Helfer Enterprises .... E...... 714 557-2733
3030 Oak St Santa Ana (92707) *(P-7858)*

Helfer Tool Co, Santa Ana *Also Called: Helfer Enterprises (P-7858)*

Helica Biosystems Inc .... F...... 714 578-7830
3310 W Macarthur Blvd Santa Ana (92704) *(P-4276)*

Helical Products, Santa Maria *Also Called: Matthew Warren Inc (P-6783)*

Helical Products Company Inc .... C...... 805 928-3851
901 W Mccoy Ln Santa Maria (93455) *(P-7377)*

Helicopter Tech Co Ltd Partnr .... E...... 310 523-2750
12902 S Broadway Los Angeles (90061) *(P-9706)*

Helicopter Technology Company, Los Angeles *Also Called: Helicopter Tech Co Ltd Partnr (P-9706)*

Helistrand Inc .... E...... 805 963-4518
707 E Yanonali St Santa Barbara (93103) *(P-5743)*

Helium 10, Irvine *Also Called: Pixel Labs LLC (P-19981)*

Helix Electric Inc .... A...... 562 941-7200
13100 Alondra Blvd Ste 108 Cerritos (90703) *(P-906)*

Helix Electric Inc (PA) .... C...... 858 535-0505
6795 Flanders Dr San Diego (92121) *(P-907)*

Helix Healthcare Inc .... B...... 619 465-4411
7050 Parkway Dr La Mesa (91942) *(P-18694)*

Helix Mechanical Inc .... C...... 619 440-1518
1100 N Magnolia Ave Ste L El Cajon (92020) *(P-776)*

Helix Medical, Carpinteria *Also Called: Freudenberg Medical LLC (P-10663)*

Helix Renewables, San Diego *Also Called: Helix Electric Inc (P-907)*

Hellas Construction Inc .... B...... 760 891-8090
5135 Avenida Encinas Ste A Carlsbad (92008) *(P-710)*

Hellman Properties LLC .... E...... 562 431-6022
711 First St Seal Beach (90740) *(P-262)*

Hellmuth Obata & Kassabaum Inc .... D...... 310 838-9555
757 S Alameda St Los Angeles (90021) *(P-19731)*

Helloworld Travel Svcs USA Inc .... D...... 310 535-1005
6171 W Century Blvd Ste 160 Los Angeles (90045) *(P-11715)*

Helmet House LLC (PA) .... D...... 800 421-7247
26855 Malibu Hills Rd Calabasas Hills (91301) *(P-13104)*

Help Children World Foundation .... B...... 818 706-9848
26500 Agoura Rd Ste 657 Calabasas (91302) *(P-19088)*

Help Group West (PA) .... C...... 818 781-0360
13130 Burbank Blvd Sherman Oaks (91401) *(P-18695)*

Help Unlimited, Ojai *Also Called: Help Unlmted Personnel Svc Inc (P-18616)*

Help Unlmted Personnel Svc Inc .... A...... 805 962-4646
3202 E Ojai Ave Ojai (93023) *(P-18616)*

Heluna Health, City Of Industry *Also Called: Public Hlth Fndation Entps Inc (P-19458)*

Hely & Weber Orthopedic, Santa Paula *Also Called: Weber Orthopedic LP (P-10722)*

Hemacare Corporation, Northridge *Also Called: Charles Rver Labs Cell Sltons (P-18752)*

Hemet Ready Mix, Hemet *Also Called: Superior Ready Mix Concrete LP (P-5508)*

Hemet Unified School District .... D...... 951 765-5100
2075 W Acacia Ave Hemet (92545) *(P-18969)*

Hemet Unified School District .... D...... 951 765-6287
985 N Cawston Ave Hemet (92545) *(P-18970)*

Hemet Valley Medical Center, Hemet *Also Called: Hemet Valley Medical Center-Education (P-18278)*

Hemet Valley Medical Center-Education ... A...... 951 652-2811
1117 E Devonshire Ave Hemet (92543) *(P-18278)*

Hemodialysis Inc .... D...... 626 792-0548
806 S Fair Oaks Ave Pasadena (91105) *(P-10520)*

Hemosure Inc .... E...... 888 436-6787
5358 Irwindale Ave Baldwin Park (91706) *(P-4608)*

Henkel Chemical Management LLC .... C...... 888 943-6535
14000 Jamboree Rd Irvine (92606) *(P-4567)*

Henkel Corporation .... C...... 714 368-8000
14000 Jamboree Rd Irvine (92606) *(P-4568)*

Henkel Electronic Mtls LLC, Irvine *Also Called: Henkel Chemical Management LLC (P-4567)*

Henkel US Operations Corp .... E...... 818 435-0889
21551 Prairie St Chatsworth (91311) *(P-4373)*

Henkel US Operations Corp .... C...... 562 297-6840
20021 S Susana Rd Compton (90221) *(P-4374)*

Henkel US Operations Corp .... E...... 626 321-4100
5800 Bristol Pkwy Culver City (90230) *(P-4419)*

Henkel US Operations Corp .... E...... 203 655-8911
12155 Paine Pl Poway (92064) *(P-4420)*

Henkel US Operations Corp .... D...... 626 968-6511
15051 Don Julian Rd City Of Industry (91746) *(P-4569)*

Employee Codes: A=Over 500 employees, B=251-500
C=101-250, D=51-100, E=20-50, F=10-19, G=1-9

2024 Southern California
Business Directory and Buyers Guide

© Mergent Inc. 1-800-342-5647
1115

Henkel US Operations Corp .... C....... 714 368-8000
14000 Jamboree Rd Irvine (92606) *(P-19894)*

Henkels & McCoy Inc .... B....... 909 517-3011
2840 Ficus St Pomona (91766) *(P-672)*

Hennis Enterprises Inc .... E....... 805 477-0257
2646 Palma Dr Ste 430 Ventura (93003) *(P-3941)*

Henry Building Products, El Segundo *Also Called: Henry Company LLC (P-4670)*

Henry Call Inc .... C....... 805 734-2762
Bldg 861 Clark And Arguello Vandenberg Afb (93437) *(P-20292)*

Henry Company LLC (HQ) .... D....... 310 955-9200
999 N Pacific Coast Hwy Ste 800 El Segundo (90245) *(P-4670)*

Henry Mayo Newhall Mem Hosp (PA) .... A....... 661 253-8000
23845 Mcbean Pkwy Valencia (91355) *(P-18279)*

Henry Mayo Nwhall Mem Hlth Fnd .... A....... 661 253-8000
23845 Mcbean Pkwy Valencia (91355) *(P-18280)*

Henry Samueli School Engrg, Irvine *Also Called: University California Irvine (P-19887)*

Henrymayo Newhall Mem Hosp, Valencia *Also Called: Henry Mayo Nwhall Mem Hlth Fnd (P-18280)*

Henrys Adio Vsual Slutions Inc .... E....... 714 258-7238
18002 Cowan Irvine (92614) *(P-8417)*

Henway Inc .... F....... 661 822-6873
1314 Goodrick Dr Tehachapi (93561) *(P-11070)*

Hepa Corporation .... D....... 714 630-5700
3071 E Coronado St Anaheim (92806) *(P-7323)*

Hera Technologies LLC .... E....... 951 751-6191
1055 E Francis St Ontario (91761) *(P-7859)*

Heraeus Prcous Mtls N Amer LLC (DH) .... C....... 562 921-7464
15524 Carmenita Rd Santa Fe Springs (90670) *(P-5681)*

Herald Christian Health Center (PA) .... D....... 626 286-8700
3401 Aero Jet Ave El Monte (91731) *(P-17664)*

Herbalife Manufacturing LLC (DH) .... E....... 866 866-4744
800 W Olympic Blvd Ste 406 Los Angeles (90015) *(P-1776)*

Herbert Rizzardini .... F....... 760 377-4571
6259 Highway 178 Inyokern (93527) *(P-13678)*

Herca Construction Services, Perris *Also Called: Herca Telecomm Services Inc (P-12770)*

Herca Telecomm Services Inc .... D....... 951 940-5941
18610 Beck St Perris (92570) *(P-12770)*

Heritage Auctions Inc .... D....... 310 300-8390
9478 W Olympic Blvd Beverly Hills (90212) *(P-16839)*

Heritage Cabinet Co Inc .... F....... 818 786-4900
21740 Marilla St Chatsworth (91311) *(P-2954)*

Heritage California Aco, Northridge *Also Called: Regal Medical Group Inc (P-19402)*

Heritage Container Inc .... D....... 951 360-1900
4777 Felspar St Riverside (92509) *(P-3107)*

Heritage Distributing Company .... E....... 626 333-9526
425 S 9th Ave City Of Industry (91746) *(P-1273)*

Heritage Distributing Company (PA) .... E....... 323 838-1225
5743 Smithway St Ste 105 Commerce (90040) *(P-1313)*

Heritage Foods, Santa Ana *Also Called: Stremicks Heritage Foods LLC (P-1316)*

Heritage Gardens Hlth Care Ctr, Loma Linda *Also Called: Heritage Health Care Inc (P-17973)*

Heritage Golf Group LLC .... D....... 949 369-6226
990 Avenida Talega San Clemente (92673) *(P-17431)*

Heritage Golf Group LLC .... C....... 661 254-4401
27330 Tourney Rd Valencia (91355) *(P-17432)*

Heritage Health Care, Lancaster *Also Called: High Dsert Med Corp A Med Grou (P-17665)*

Heritage Health Care Inc .... C....... 909 796-0216
25271 Barton Rd Loma Linda (92354) *(P-17973)*

Heritage Leather Company Inc .... E....... 323 983-0420
4011 E 52nd St Maywood (90270) *(P-5257)*

Heritage Medical Group .... B....... 760 956-1286
12370 Hesperia Rd Ste 6 Victorville (92395) *(P-18770)*

HERITAGE MEDICAL GROUP, Victorville *Also Called: Heritage Medical Group (P-18770)*

Heritage Oak Prvate Elmntary S, Yorba Linda *Also Called: Rgbx Inc (P-19227)*

Heritage Oaks Bancorp .... B....... 805 369-5200
1222 Vine St Paso Robles (93446) *(P-14198)*

Heritage Oaks Bank .... C....... 805 239-5200
1222 Vine St Paso Robles (93446) *(P-14199)*

Heritage Paper Co (HQ) .... D....... 714 540-9737
2400 S Grand Ave Santa Ana (92705) *(P-3108)*

Heritage Pointe, Rancho Cucamonga *Also Called: National Community Renaissance (P-14728)*

HERITAGE POINTE, Mission Viejo *Also Called: Jewish HM For The Aging Ornge (P-17980)*

Heritage Security Services, Temecula *Also Called: Richman Management Corporation (P-16675)*

Herman Weissker Inc (HQ) .... C....... 951 826-8800
1645 Brown Ave Riverside (92509) *(P-673)*

Hermes-Microvision Inc .... E....... 858 385-6500
17075 Thornmint Ct San Diego (92127) *(P-8803)*

Hermetic Seal Corporation (DH) .... C....... 626 443-8931
4232 Temple City Blvd Rosemead (91770) *(P-9056)*

Heron Therapeutics Inc (PA) .... C....... 858 251-4400
4242 Campus Point Ct Ste 200 San Diego (92121) *(P-4130)*

Herring Networks Inc .... C....... 858 270-6900
4757 Morena Blvd San Diego (92117) *(P-11954)*

Hertz Entertainment Services, Burbank *Also Called: 24/7 Studio Equipment Inc (P-8487)*

Hertzbrg-Dvis Frnsic Scnce Ctr, Los Angeles *Also Called: County of Los Angeles (P-19966)*

Herzog Contracting Corp .... D....... 562 595-7414
3760 Kilroy Airport Way Ste 120 Long Beach (90806) *(P-711)*

Herzog Contracting Corp .... D....... 619 849-6990
2155 Hancock St San Diego (92110) *(P-1161)*

Herzog Wine Cellars, Oxnard *Also Called: Royal Wine Corporation (P-1658)*

Hesperia Holding Inc .... D....... 760 244-8787
9780 E Ave Hesperia (92345) *(P-2700)*

Hesperia Unified School Dst .... D....... 760 948-1051
11176 G Ave Hesperia (92345) *(P-1910)*

Hesperia Usd Food Service, Hesperia *Also Called: Hesperia Unified School Dst (P-1910)*

Hess Contracting Inc .... E....... 619 442-6333
1024 Pine Dr El Cajon (92020) *(P-308)*

Hestan Commercial Corporation .... C....... 714 869-2380
3375 E La Palma Ave Anaheim (92806) *(P-8243)*

Hetherington Engineering (PA) .... C....... 760 931-1917
4333 Apache St Oceanside (92056) *(P-19603)*

Hexagon Agility Inc .... D....... 949 236-5520
3335 Susan St Ste 100 Costa Mesa (92626) *(P-274)*

Hexagon Mfg Intelligence Inc .... D....... 760 994-1401
3536 Seagate Way Ste 100 Oceanside (92056) *(P-10203)*

Hexco International .... C....... 951 677-2081
25720 Jefferson Ave Murrieta (92562) *(P-7240)*

Hexoden Holdings Inc (PA) .... D....... 858 201-3412
1219 Linda Vista Dr San Marcos (92078) *(P-11226)*

HF Cox Inc .... B....... 323 587-2359
8330 Atlantic Ave Cudahy (90201) *(P-11460)*

Hf Group Inc (PA) .... E....... 310 605-0755
203 W Artesia Blvd Compton (90220) *(P-10868)*

HG Fenton Company .... C....... 619 400-0120
7577 Mission Valley Rd Ste 200 San Diego (92108) *(P-14712)*

HG Fenton Property Company (PA) .... C....... 619 400-0120
7577 Mission Valley Rd Ste 200 San Diego (92108) *(P-14737)*

Hgc Holdings Inc .... E....... 323 567-2226
3303 Martin Luther King Jr Blvd Lynwood (90262) *(P-1541)*

HI LLC (PA) .... D....... 757 655-4113
10361 Jefferson Blvd Culver City (90232) *(P-19895)*

HI Perfrmnce Elc Vhcl Systems .... E....... 909 923-1973
620 S Magnolia Ave Ste B Ontario (91762) *(P-8143)*

HI Pro Inc .... C....... 760 367-7734
4584 Adobe Rd Twentynine Palms (92277) *(P-11491)*

HI Rel Connectors Inc .... B....... 909 626-1820
760 Wharton Dr Claremont (91711) *(P-8267)*

HI Tech Electronic Mfg Corp .... D....... 858 657-0908
1938 Avenida Del Oro Oceanside (92056) *(P-8685)*

HI Tech Honeycomb Inc .... C....... 858 974-1600
9355 Ruffin Ct San Diego (92123) *(P-6521)*

HI Temp Forming Co .... E....... 714 529-6556
315 Arden Ave Ste 28 Glendale (91203) *(P-7860)*

HI Torque Publicatio .... E....... 661 367-2134
25233 Anza Dr Valencia (91355) *(P-3456)*

Hi-Craft Metal Products .... E....... 310 323-6949
606 W 184th St Gardena (90248) *(P-6252)*

Hi-Desert Medical Center, Joshua Tree *Also Called: Hdmc Holdings LLC (P-18274)*

Hi-Desert Publishing Company .... E....... 909 795-8145
35154 Yucaipa Blvd Yucaipa (92399) *(P-3281)*

Hi-Desert Publishing Company .... E....... 909 336-3555
28200 Highway 189 Bldg O-1 Lake Arrowhead (92352) *(P-3282)*

Mergent email: customerrelations@mergent.com
1116

2024 Southern California
Business Directory and Buyers Guide

(P-0000) Products & Services Section entry number
(PA)=Parent Co (HQ)=Headquarters (DH)=Div Headquarters

Hi-Desert Publishing Company (HQ) ....D...... 760 365-3315
56445 29 Palms Hwy Yucca Valley (92284) *(P-3283)*

Hi-Desert Publishing Company ....E...... 909 866-3456
42007 Fox Farm Rd Ste 3b Big Bear Lake (92315) *(P-14117)*

Hi-Grade Materials Co ....D...... 661 533-3100
6500 E Avenue T Littlerock (93543) *(P-5481)*

Hi-Lite Manufacturing Co Inc ....D...... 909 465-1999
13450 Monte Vista Ave Chino (91710) *(P-8316)*

Hi-Plas, Jurupa Valley *Also Called: Highland Plastics Inc (P-5048)*

Hi-Precision Grinding, Santa Ana *Also Called: Deltronic Corporation (P-10312)*

Hi-Rel Plastics & Molding Corp ....E...... 951 354-0258
7575 Jurupa Ave Riverside (92504) *(P-5046)*

Hi-Shear Corporation (DH) ....A...... 310 326-8110
2600 Skypark Dr Torrance (90505) *(P-6444)*

Hi-Tech Engineering, Camarillo *Also Called: Hte Acquisition LLC (P-7868)*

Hi-Tech Iron Works, Commerce *Also Called: Architectural Enterprises Inc (P-6351)*

Hi-Tech Labels Incorporated ....E...... 714 670-2150
8530 Roland St Buena Park (90621) *(P-7861)*

Hi-Tech Products, Buena Park *Also Called: Hi-Tech Labels Incorporated (P-7861)*

Hi-Tech Welding & Forming Inc ....E...... 619 562-5929
1327 Fayette St El Cajon (92020) *(P-7862)*

Hi-Temp Insulation Inc ....B...... 805 484-2774
4700 Calle Alto Camarillo (93012) *(P-979)*

Hi-Torque Publications, Santa Clarita *Also Called: Daisy Publishing Company Inc (P-3354)*

Hi-Way Safety, Chino *Also Called: Myers & Sons Hi-Way Safety Inc (P-11139)*

Hiatus, Los Angeles *Also Called: Crew Knitwear LLC (P-2315)*

Hibernia Woolen Mills, Manhattan Beach *Also Called: Stanton Carpet Corp (P-2121)*

Hid Global Corporation ....E...... 949 732-2000
15370 Barranca Pkwy Irvine (92618) *(P-10204)*

Hidden Jeans Inc ....E...... 213 746-4223
7210 Dominion Cir Commerce (90040) *(P-2024)*

Hidden Villa Ranch, Fullerton *Also Called: Hidden Villa Ranch Produce Inc (P-13258)*

Hidden Villa Ranch Produce Inc (HQ) ....B...... 714 680-3447
310 N Harbor Blvd Ste 205 Fullerton (92832) *(P-13258)*

Hideaway ....C...... 760 777-7400
80440 Hideaway Club Ct La Quinta (92253) *(P-14012)*

Hideaway, La Quinta *Also Called: Hideaway Club (P-17488)*

Hideaway Club ....B...... 760 777-7400
80440 Hideaway Club Ct La Quinta (92253) *(P-17488)*

Higgins Hardwood Inc ....F...... 775 856-1653
450 B St Ste 1900 San Diego (92101) *(P-5047)*

Higgs Fletcher & Mack Llp ....C...... 619 236-1551
401 W A St Ste 2600 San Diego (92101) *(P-18868)*

High Caliber Line, Irwindale *Also Called: Calibre International LLC (P-20283)*

High Dsert Med Corp A Med Grou (PA) ....C...... 661 945-5984
43839 15th St W Lancaster (93534) *(P-17665)*

High Dsert Prtnr In Acdmic Exc ....B...... 760 946-5414
17500 Mana Rd Apple Valley (92307) *(P-19896)*

High Five Inc ....E...... 714 847-2200
625 Fee Ana St Placentia (92870) *(P-3586)*

High Moon Studios LLC ....C...... 760 448-3000
2051 Palomar Airport Rd Ste 250 Carlsbad (92011) *(P-15509)*

High Performance Seals, Garden Grove *Also Called: Saint-Gobain Prfmce Plas Corp (P-3969)*

High Prcsion Grnding McHning I ....E...... 619 440-0303
1130 Pioneer Way El Cajon (92020) *(P-7863)*

High Road Craft Ice Cream Inc (PA) ....E...... 678 701-7623
12243 Branford St Sun Valley (91352) *(P-1298)*

High Tech Pet Products ....D...... 805 644-1797
2111 Portola Rd # A Ventura (93003) *(P-12664)*

High Times Productions Inc ....C...... 844 933-3287
10990 Wilshire Blvd Los Angeles (90024) *(P-16840)*

Higher Ground Education Inc (PA) ....B...... 949 836-9401
10 Orchard Ste 200 Lake Forest (92630) *(P-20343)*

Higher Talent, Los Angeles *Also Called: Creative Solutions Svcs LLC (P-15834)*

Highland Hlthcare Cmllia Grdns ....C...... 626 798-6777
1920 N Fair Oaks Ave Pasadena (91103) *(P-17974)*

Highland Lumber Sales Inc ....E...... 714 778-2293
300 E Santa Ana St Anaheim (92805) *(P-2605)*

Highland Palms Healthcare Ctr, Highland *Also Called: Cedar Holdings LLC (P-17898)*

Highland Plastics Inc ....C...... 951 360-9587
3650 Dulles Dr Jurupa Valley (91752) *(P-5048)*

Highlander Home Inc ....E...... 858 261-4068
6679 Tierra Vista Ct San Diego (92130) *(P-13578)*

Highlander Newspaper 951 827-3457
4158 Chestnut St Riverside (92501) *(P-3284)*

Highline Aftermarket LLC ....D...... 951 361-0331
10385 San Sevaine Way Ste B Jurupa Valley (91752) *(P-12242)*

Highmark, Huntington Beach *Also Called: Highmark Smart Reliable Seating Inc (P-2913)*

Highmark Smart Reliable Seating Inc ....C...... 714 903-2257
5559 Mcfadden Ave Huntington Beach (92649) *(P-2913)*

Hightower Metal Products ....D...... 714 637-7000
2090 N Glassell St Orange (92865) *(P-7075)*

Hightower Plating & Mfg Co ....E...... 714 637-9110
2090 N Glassell St Orange (92865) *(P-6626)*

Highways Magazine, Oxnard *Also Called: TI Enterprises LLC (P-3391)*

Hii Fleet Support Group LLC ....C...... 619 474-8820
131 W 33rd St Ste 100a National City (91950) *(P-19604)*

Hii Fleet Support Group LLC ....B...... 858 522-6319
9444 Balboa Ave Ste 400 San Diego (92123) *(P-19846)*

Hii San Diego Shipyard Inc ....B...... 619 234-8851
1995 Bay Front St San Diego (92101) *(P-9838)*

Hikma Pharmaceuticals USA Inc ....E...... 760 683-0901
2325 Camino Vida Roble Ste B Carlsbad (92011) *(P-4131)*

Hikvision USA Inc (HQ) ....C...... 909 895-0400
18639 Railroad St City Of Industry (91748) *(P-16741)*

Hill Brothers Chemical, Brea *Also Called: Hill Brothers Chemical Company (P-13435)*

Hill Brothers Chemical Company ....F...... 626 333-2251
15017 Clark Ave City Of Industry (91745) *(P-3857)*

Hill Brothers Chemical Company (PA) ....C...... 714 998-8800
3000 E Birch St Ste 108 Brea (92821) *(P-13435)*

Hill Farrer & Burrill ....D...... 213 620-0460
300 S Grand Ave Fl 37 Los Angeles (90071) *(P-18869)*

Hill Phoenix Inc ....D...... 909 592-8830
14680 Monte Vista Ave Chino (91710) *(P-12762)*

Hillcor Distribution Inc ....F...... 626 960-8789
5100 Commerce Dr Baldwin Park (91706) *(P-5049)*

HILLCREST, La Verne *Also Called: Brethren Hillcrest Homes (P-19242)*

Hillcrest Country Club ....C...... 310 553-8911
10000 W Pico Blvd Los Angeles (90064) *(P-17489)*

Hillcrest Manor Sanitarium, National City *Also Called: Imaginative Horizons Inc (P-17976)*

Hilliard Bruce Vineyards LLC (PA) ....F...... 805 736-5366
2097 Vineyard View Ln Lompoc (93436) *(P-1637)*

Hills Wldg & Engrg Contr Inc ....D...... 661 746-5400
22038 Stockdale Hwy Bakersfield (93314) *(P-352)*

Hillsdale Group LP ....C...... 818 623-2170
12750 Riverside Dr North Hollywood (91607) *(P-18131)*

Hillside Capital Inc ....C...... 650 367-2011
6222 Fallbrook Ave Woodland Hills (91367) *(P-8523)*

HILLSIDE ENTERPRISES - AR & C, Long Beach *Also Called: Advocacy For Rspect Chice - Lo (P-19173)*

Hillside House ....D...... 805 687-0788
1235 Veronica Springs Rd Santa Barbara (93105) *(P-18084)*

Hillsides ....B...... 323 254-2274
940 Avenue 64 Pasadena (91105) *(P-19089)*

Hillview Mental Health Ctr Inc ....D...... 818 896-1161
12450 Van Nuys Blvd Ste 200 Pacoima (91331) *(P-18696)*

Hilti US Manufacturing Inc ....E...... 714 230-7410
6601 Darin Way Cypress (90630) *(P-5892)*

Hilton, Los Angeles *Also Called: Fortuna Enterprises LP (P-15154)*

Hilton, Carlsbad *Also Called: Hilton Garden Inns MGT LLC (P-15177)*

Hilton, San Diego *Also Called: Lho Mssion Bay Rsie Lessee Inc (P-15225)*

Hilton, Anaheim *Also Called: Makar Anaheim LLC (P-15237)*

Hilton, Long Beach *Also Called: Merritt Hospitality LLC (P-15247)*

Hilton, Beverly Hills *Also Called: Park Hotels & Resorts Inc (P-15297)*

Hilton, San Bernardino *Also Called: San Bernardino Hilton (P-15341)*

Hilton, Huntington Beach *Also Called: Waterfront Hotel LLC (P-15410)*

Hilton, San Diego *Also Called: Ww San Diego Harbor Island LLC (P-15428)*

Hilton Garden Inns MGT LLC ....A...... 760 476-0800
6450 Carlsbad Blvd Carlsbad (92011) *(P-15177)*

Hilton Grdn Inn San Dego Dwntw, San Diego *Also Called: M4dev LLC (P-15235)*

Hilton Hotels, Long Beach *Also Called: HEI Long Beach LLC (P-15176)*

A L P H A B E T I C

Hilton Los Angles Universal Cy ....C...... 818 506-2500
555 Universal Hollywood Dr Universal City (91608) *(P-15178)*

Hilton Los Angls/Nversal Cy Ht, Universal City *Also Called: Sun Hill Properties Inc (P-15377)*

Hilton Port Los Angls-San Pdro, San Pedro *Also Called: Meristar San Pedro Hilton LLC (P-15246)*

Hilton Resort In Palm Spring, Palm Springs *Also Called: Walters Family Partnership (P-15409)*

Hilton San Diego Airport/Hrbr, San Diego *Also Called: Bartell Hotels (P-15087)*

Hilton San Diego/Del Mar, Del Mar *Also Called: Sunstone Durante LLC (P-15378)*

Hilton Woodland Hills & Towers ....D...... 818 595-1000
6360 Canoga Ave Woodland Hills (91367) *(P-15179)*

Hines Growers Inc ....A...... 800 554-4065
27368 Via Industria Ste 201 Temecula (92590) *(P-56)*

Hines Horticulture Inc (PA) ....B...... 949 559-4444
12621 Jeffery Rd Irvine (92620) *(P-57)*

Hines Nurseries, Irvine *Also Called: Hines Horticulture Inc (P-57)*

Hino Motors Mfg USA Inc ....D...... 951 727-0286
4550 Wineville Ave Jurupa Valley (91752) *(P-12243)*

Hinoichi Tofu, Garden Grove *Also Called: House Foods America Corp (P-1913)*

Hintex ....F...... 320 400-0009
1230 S Glendale Ave Glendale (91205) *(P-5420)*

Hippo Corporation ....F...... 714 229-9152
2535 W Via Palma Anaheim (92801) *(P-13541)*

Hira Paris Inc ....C...... 909 634-3900
3811 Schaefer Ave Ste B Chino (91710) *(P-1542)*

Hire Elegance ....F...... 858 740-7862
8333 Arjons Dr Ste E San Diego (92126) *(P-3026)*

Hirel Connectors, Claremont *Also Called: HI Rel Connectors Inc (P-8267)*

Hirok Inc ....E...... 619 713-5066
5644 Kearny Mesa Rd Ste H San Diego (92111) *(P-6936)*

Hirsch Electronics LLC ....D...... 949 250-8888
1900 Carnegie Ave Ste B Santa Ana (92705) *(P-12665)*

Hirsch3667 Corp ....C...... 310 641-6690
5700 Hannum Ave Ste 250 Culver City (90230) *(P-14933)*

Hirsh Inc ....E...... 213 622-9441
860 S Los Angeles St # 900 Los Angeles (90014) *(P-353)*

His Company Inc ....F...... 858 513-7748
2215 Paseo De Las Americas Ste 29 San Diego (92154) *(P-8098)*

His Industries Inc ....E...... 949 383-4308
1202 W Shelley Ct Orange (92868) *(P-7349)*

His Life Woodworks ....E...... 310 756-0170
22651 Gaycrest Ave Torrance (90505) *(P-2606)*

Hisamitsu Pharmaceutical Co Inc ....A...... 760 931-1756
2730 Loker Ave W Carlsbad (92010) *(P-19927)*

Hisco, San Diego *Also Called: His Company Inc (P-8098)*

Historic Mission Inn Corp ....B...... 951 784-0300
3649 Mission Inn Ave Riverside (92501) *(P-15180)*

Historical Properties Inc (PA) ....D...... 619 230-8417
311 Island Ave San Diego (92101) *(P-15181)*

Hitachi Automotive Systems ....D...... 310 212-0200
6200 Gateway Dr Cypress (90630) *(P-8144)*

Hitachi Solutions America Ltd (DH) ....E...... 949 242-1300
100 Spectrum Center Dr Ste 350 Irvine (92618) *(P-12419)*

Hitachi Transport System (america) Ltd ....B...... 310 787-3420
21061 S Wstn Ave Ste 300 Torrance (90501) *(P-11769)*

Hitech Metal Fabrication Corp ....D...... 714 635-3505
1705 S Claudina Way Anaheim (92805) *(P-6029)*

Hitem, Oceanside *Also Called: HI Tech Electronic Mfg Corp (P-8685)*

Hitex Dyeing & Finishing Inc ....E...... 626 363-0160
355 Vineland Ave City Of Industry (91746) *(P-2554)*

Hitt Companies ....E...... 714 979-1405
3231 W Macarthur Blvd Santa Ana (92704) *(P-4766)*

Hitt Contracting Inc ....B...... 424 326-1042
3733 Motor Ave Ste 200 Los Angeles (90034) *(P-557)*

Hitt Marking Devices I D Tech, Santa Ana *Also Called: Hitt Companies (P-4766)*

Hixson Metal Finishing ....C...... 800 900-9798
829 Production Pl Newport Beach (92663) *(P-6627)*

Hizco Truck Body, Los Angeles *Also Called: A A Cater Truck Mfg Co Inc (P-2824)*

HK Precision Turning Machining, Oceanside *Also Called: Balda Precision Inc (P-6413)*

Hkf Inc (PA) ....D...... 323 225-1318
5983 Smithway St Commerce (90040) *(P-12756)*

HI Welding Inc ....E...... 619 336-9231
2434 Southport Way Ste L National City (91950) *(P-17086)*

HM Electronics Inc (PA) ....B...... 858 535-6000
2848 Whiptail Loop Carlsbad (92010) *(P-12666)*

HMC Architects, Ontario *Also Called: HMC Group (P-19732)*

HMC Assets LLC ....D...... 310 535-9293
2015 Manhattan Beach Blvd Ste 200 Redondo Beach (90278) *(P-14509)*

HMC Group (HQ) ....C...... 909 989-9979
3546 Concours Ontario (91764) *(P-19732)*

HMcompany ....F...... 805 650-2651
4464 Mcgrath St Ste 111 Ventura (93003) *(P-7864)*

Hmr Building Systems LLC ....D...... 951 749-4700
620 Newport Center Dr Fl 12 Newport Beach (92660) *(P-2566)*

Hmt Electric Inc ....D...... 858 458-9771
2340 Meyers Ave Escondido (92029) *(P-908)*

Hnc Parent Inc (PA) ....D...... 310 955-9200
999 N Pacific Coast Hwy Ste 800 El Segundo (90245) *(P-4671)*

Hntb Corporation ....C...... 619 684-6586
401 B St Ste 510 San Diego (92101) *(P-19605)*

Hntb Corporation ....D...... 909 727-5600
3633 Inland Empire Blvd Ontario (91764) *(P-19606)*

Hntb Corporation ....C...... 714 460-1600
6 Hutton Centre Dr Ste 500 Santa Ana (92707) *(P-19607)*

Hntb Gerwick Water Solutions ....C...... 714 460-1600
200 Sandpointe Ave Santa Ana (92707) *(P-19608)*

Hoag Clinic ....B...... 949 764-1888
1 Hoag Dr Newport Beach (92663) *(P-18281)*

HOAG CORPORATE HEALTH, Newport Beach *Also Called: Hoag Clinic (P-18281)*

Hoag Family Cancer Institute ....C...... 949 764-7777
1190 Baker St Costa Mesa (92626) *(P-18282)*

Hoag Hospital Irvine ....D...... 949 764-4624
16200 Sand Canyon Ave Irvine (92618) *(P-18283)*

Hoag Memorial Hospital Presbt (PA) ....A...... 949 764-4624
1 Hoag Dr Newport Beach (92663) *(P-18284)*

Hoag Orthopedic Institute LLC ....B...... 949 515-0708
22 Corporate Plaza Dr Ste 150 Newport Beach (92660) *(P-18285)*

Hoag Orthpd Inst Srgery Ctr -, Newport Beach *Also Called: Hoag Orthopedic Institute LLC (P-18285)*

Hob Entertainment LLC ....C...... 714 520-2310
400 W Disney Way Ste 337 Anaheim (92802) *(P-17337)*

Hob Entertainment LLC (DH) ....C...... 323 769-4600
7060 Hollywood Blvd Los Angeles (90028) *(P-17338)*

Hobie Cat Company (PA) ....C...... 760 758-9100
4925 Oceanside Blvd Oceanside (92056) *(P-9859)*

Hobie Cat Company II LLC ....C...... 760 758-9100
4925 Oceanside Blvd Oceanside (92056) *(P-10997)*

Hochiki, Buena Park *Also Called: Hochiki America Corporation (P-12598)*

Hochiki America Corporation (HQ) ....D...... 714 522-2246
7051 Village Dr Ste 100 Buena Park (90621) *(P-12598)*

Hodge Products Inc ....E...... 800 778-2217
7365 Mission Gorge Rd Ste F San Diego (92120) *(P-5921)*

Hoefner Corporation ....E...... 626 443-3258
9722 Rush St South El Monte (91733) *(P-7865)*

Hoehn Company Inc ....D...... 760 438-1818
5454 Paseo Del Norte Carlsbad (92008) *(P-13778)*

Hoehn Honda, Carlsbad *Also Called: Hoehn Company Inc (P-13778)*

Hoffman Medical Research Ctr, Los Angeles *Also Called: Keck School (P-18313)*

Hoffman Plastic Compounds Inc ....E...... 323 636-3346
16616 Garfield Ave Paramount (90723) *(P-3942)*

Hogan Co Inc ....E...... 909 421-0245
2741 S Lilac Ave Bloomington (92316) *(P-5617)*

Hogue Bros Inc ....E...... 805 239-1440
550 Linne Rd Paso Robles (93446) *(P-2573)*

Hogue Grips, Paso Robles *Also Called: Hogue Bros Inc (P-2573)*

Hoist Fitness, Poway *Also Called: Hoist Fitness Systems Inc (P-10998)*

Hoist Fitness Systems, San Diego *Also Called: Fitness Warehouse LLC (P-10991)*

Hoist Fitness Systems Inc ....D...... 858 578-7676
11900 Community Rd Poway (92064) *(P-10998)*

Hokto Kinoko Company ....D...... 323 526-1155
130 S Myers St Los Angeles (90033) *(P-74)*

Holdrite, Poway *Also Called: Securus Inc (P-6369)*

Mergent email: customerrelations@mergent.com
1118

2024 Southern California
Business Directory and Buyers Guide

(P-0000) Products & Services Section entry number
(PA)=Parent Co (HQ)=Headquarters (DH)=Div Headquarters

Holguin & Holguin Inc .... E...... 626 815-0168
968 W Foothill Blvd Azusa (91702) *(P-2927)*

Holiday Foliage, San Diego *Also Called: Holiday Foliage Inc (P-11227)*

Holiday Foliage Inc .... E...... 619 661-9094
2592 Otay Center Dr San Diego (92154) *(P-11227)*

Holiday Inn, Los Angeles *Also Called: Brisam Lax (de) LLC (P-15097)*

Holiday Inn, Simi Valley *Also Called: Holiday Inn Express (P-15182)*

Holiday Inn, North Hollywood *Also Called: Marcus Hotels Inc (P-15239)*

Holiday Inn, Bakersfield *Also Called: Newport Hospitality Group Inc (P-15260)*

Holiday Inn, Chula Vista *Also Called: Otay Hospitality Inc (P-15280)*

Holiday Inn, North Hollywood *Also Called: Rio Vista Development Co Inc (P-15326)*

Holiday Inn, Santa Ana *Also Called: S W K Properties LLC (P-15337)*

Holiday Inn, Los Angeles *Also Called: Seattle Arprt Hospitality LLC (P-15352)*

Holiday Inn, Lebec *Also Called: Six Continents Hotels Inc (P-15358)*

Holiday Inn, Buena Park *Also Called: Uniwell Corporation (P-15397)*

Holiday Inn, Torrance *Also Called: V Todays Inc (P-15401)*

Holiday Inn, Los Angeles *Also Called: W&J Business Ventures LLC (P-15408)*

Holiday Inn, Long Beach *Also Called: Yhb Long Beach LLC (P-15429)*

Holiday Inn Express .... C...... 805 584-6006
2550 Erringer Rd Simi Valley (93065) *(P-15182)*

Holiday Inn Express, San Diego *Also Called: Win Time Ltd (P-15419)*

Holiday Inn La Mirada, La Mirada *Also Called: Cha La Mirada LLC (P-15112)*

Holiday Manor Care Center, Canoga Park *Also Called: Sela Healthcare Inc (P-18050)*

Holiday Manor Care Center, Upland *Also Called: Sela Healthcare Inc (P-18051)*

Holiday Transportation, Van Nuys *Also Called: Rwh Inc (P-5501)*

Holiday Tree Farms Inc .... C...... 323 276-1900
329 Van Norman Rd Montebello (90640) *(P-229)*

Holland & Herring Mfg Inc .... E...... 909 469-4700
661 E Monterey Ave Pomona (91767) *(P-7866)*

Holland & Knight LLP .... D...... 213 896-2400
400 S Hope St Ste 800 Los Angeles (90071) *(P-18870)*

Holland Electronics, Ventura *Also Called: Holland Electronics LLC (P-8972)*

Holland Electronics LLC .... E...... 805 339-9060
2935 Golf Course Dr Ventura (93003) *(P-8972)*

Hollandia Dairy Inc (PA) .... C...... 760 744-3222
622 E Mission Rd San Marcos (92069) *(P-90)*

Hollands Custom Cabinets Inc .... E...... 619 443-6081
14511 Olde Highway 80 El Cajon (92021) *(P-2660)*

HOLLENBECK HOME FOR THE AGED, Newhall *Also Called: Hollenbeck Palms (P-19270)*

Hollenbeck Palms .... C...... 323 263-6195
24431 Lyons Ave Apt 336 Newhall (91321) *(P-19270)*

Holliday Rock Trucking Inc .... D...... 888 273-2200
2300 W Base Line St San Bernardino (92410) *(P-5482)*

HOLLIDAY ROCK TRUCKING INC, San Bernardino *Also Called: Holliday Rock Trucking Inc (P-5482)*

Holliday Trucking Inc (PA) .... D...... 909 982-1553
1401 N Benson Ave Upland (91786) *(P-5483)*

Hollingshead Management, Los Angeles *Also Called: Proland Property Managment LLC (P-14851)*

Hollywood Bed & Spring Mfg, Commerce *Also Called: Hollywood Bed Spring Mfg Inc (P-5922)*

Hollywood Bed Spring Mfg Inc (PA) .... D...... 323 887-9500
5959 Corvette St Commerce (90040) *(P-5922)*

Hollywood Bowl, Los Angeles *Also Called: Los Angeles Philharmonic Assn (P-17345)*

Hollywood Chairs .... E...... 760 471-6600
1880 Diamond St San Marcos (92078) *(P-2775)*

Hollywood Cmnty Hosp Hollywood, Los Angeles *Also Called: Hollywood Cmnty Hosp Med Ctr I (P-18286)*

Hollywood Cmnty Hosp Med Ctr I .... C...... 323 462-2271
6245 De Longpre Ave Los Angeles (90028) *(P-18286)*

Hollywood Film Company .... E...... 818 683-1130
9265 Borden Ave Sun Valley (91352) *(P-10869)*

Hollywood Lamp & Shade Co .... E...... 323 585-3999
2838 E 54th St Vernon (90058) *(P-8246)*

Hollywood Medical Center LP .... A...... 213 413-3000
1300 N Vermont Ave Los Angeles (90027) *(P-18287)*

Hollywood Park Casino, Inglewood *Also Called: Century Gaming Management Inc (P-15111)*

Hollywood Park Casino Co Inc .... C...... 310 330-2800
3883 W Century Blvd Inglewood (90303) *(P-15183)*

Hollywood Presbyterian Med Ctr, Los Angeles *Also Called: Hollywood Medical Center LP (P-18287)*

Hollywood Records Inc .... E...... 818 560-5670
500 S Buena Vista St Burbank (91521) *(P-8461)*

Hollywood Reporter .... C...... 323 525-2000
6715 W Sunset Blvd Los Angeles (90028) *(P-3285)*

Hollywood Reporter .... E...... 323 525-2150
100 N Crescent Dr Ste Gl-1 Beverly Hills (90210) *(P-3286)*

Hollywood Reporter LLC .... E...... 323 525-2000
100 N Crescent Dr Ste Gl-1 Beverly Hills (90210) *(P-3287)*

Hollywood Ribbon Industries Inc .... B...... 323 266-0670
9000 Rochester Ave Rancho Cucamonga (91730) *(P-2055)*

Hollywood Rntals Prod Svcs LLC (PA) .... D...... 818 407-7800
5300 Melrose Ave Los Angeles (90038) *(P-17255)*

Hollywood Roosevelt Hotel, Los Angeles *Also Called: Roosevelt Hotel LLC (P-15332)*

Hollywood Software Inc .... E...... 818 205-2121
5000 Van Nuys Blvd Ste 300 Van Nuys (91403) *(P-16263)*

Hollywood Sports Park LLC .... D...... 562 867-9600
9030 Somerset Blvd Bellflower (90706) *(P-16841)*

Holmes & Narver Inc (HQ) .... C...... 714 567-2400
999 W Town And Country Rd Orange (92868) *(P-19609)*

Holmes Body Shop-Alhambra .... E...... 626 282-6173
1130 E Main St Alhambra (91801) *(P-17010)*

Hologic Inc .... E...... 858 410-8792
9393 Waples St San Diego (92121) *(P-10805)*

Hologic Inc .... C...... 858 410-8000
10210 Genetic Center Dr San Diego (92121) *(P-10806)*

Holt Integrated Circuits, Aliso Viejo *Also Called: W G Holt Inc (P-8921)*

Holthouse Carlin Van Trigt LLP (PA) .... C...... 310 566-1900
11444 W Olympic Blvd Fl 11 Los Angeles (90064) *(P-19780)*

Holy Cross Cemetary, San Diego *Also Called: Roman Cthlic Bshp of San Diego (P-14862)*

Holy Sepulcher Cemetery, Orange *Also Called: Roman Cthlic Diocese of Orange (P-14917)*

Holzheus El Rancho Market Inc .... D...... 805 688-4300
2886 Mission Dr Solvang (93463) *(P-13700)*

Home & Body Company (PA) .... B...... 714 842-8000
5800 Skylab Rd Huntington Beach (92647) *(P-4609)*

Home Brew Mart Inc .... B...... 858 790-6900
9045 Carroll Way San Diego (92121) *(P-1591)*

Home Carpet Investment Inc (PA) .... D...... 619 262-8040
730 Design Ct Ste 401 Chula Vista (91911) *(P-1030)*

Home Comfort USA, Anaheim *Also Called: Ken Starr Inc (P-783)*

Home Concepts Products Inc .... E...... 866 981-0500
4199 Bandini Blvd Vernon (90058) *(P-5050)*

Home Decor Wholesaler, City Of Industry *Also Called: Pacific Heritg HM Fashion Inc (P-12313)*

Home Depot USA Inc .... C...... 951 361-1235
11650 Venture Dr Jurupa Valley (91752) *(P-11586)*

Home Depot USA Inc .... C...... 909 483-8115
8535 Oakwood Pl Ste B Rancho Cucamonga (91730) *(P-11587)*

Home Depot USA Inc .... C...... 858 859-4143
13250 Gregg St Ste A2 Poway (92064) *(P-11588)*

Home Depot USA Inc .... D...... 714 522-8651
14659 Alondra Blvd Ste B La Mirada (90638) *(P-11589)*

Home Depot USA Inc .... C...... 951 358-1370
3323 Madison St Riverside (92504) *(P-13579)*

Home Depot USA Inc .... C...... 951 727-0324
6140 Hamner Ave Eastvale (91752) *(P-13580)*

Home Depot USA Inc .... D...... 951 485-5400
15975 Perris Blvd Moreno Valley (92551) *(P-13581)*

Home Depot USA Inc .... C...... 951 698-1555
25100 Madison Ave Murrieta (92562) *(P-13582)*

Home Depot USA Inc .... C...... 951 808-0327
1355 E Ontario Ave Corona (92881) *(P-13583)*

Home Depot USA Inc .... C...... 949 831-3698
27401 La Paz Rd Laguna Niguel (92677) *(P-13584)*

Home Depot USA Inc .... C...... 714 459-4909
625 S Placentia Ave Fullerton (92831) *(P-13585)*

Home Depot USA Inc .... D...... 714 921-1215
1095 N Pullman St Anaheim (92807) *(P-13586)*

Home Depot USA Inc .... D...... 562 690-6006
600 S Harbor Blvd La Habra (90631) *(P-13587)*

Employee Codes: A=Over 500 employees, B=251-500
C=101-250, D=51-100, E=20-50, F=10-19, G=1-9

2024 Southern California
Business Directory and Buyers Guide

© Mergent Inc. 1-800-342-5647

1119

A
L
P
H
A
B
E
T
I
C

Home Depot USA Inc .... C...... 714 966-8551
3500 W Macarthur Blvd Santa Ana (92704) *(P-13588)*

Home Depot USA Inc .... C...... 714 538-9600
435 W Katella Ave Orange (92867) *(P-13589)*

Home Depot USA Inc .... C...... 949 646-4220
2300 Harbor Blvd Ste F Costa Mesa (92626) *(P-13590)*

Home Depot USA Inc .... C...... 949 609-0221
20021 Lake Forest Dr Lake Forest (92630) *(P-13591)*

Home Depot USA Inc .... D...... 949 364-1900
27952 Hillcrest Mission Viejo (92692) *(P-13592)*

Home Depot USA Inc .... C...... 714 539-0319
10801 Garden Grove Blvd Garden Grove (92843) *(P-13593)*

Home Depot USA Inc .... D...... 714 259-1030
1750 E Edinger Ave Santa Ana (92705) *(P-13594)*

Home Depot USA Inc .... D...... 619 263-1533
355 Marketplace Ave San Diego (92113) *(P-13595)*

Home Depot USA Inc .... C...... 760 233-1285
1475 E Valley Pkwy Escondido (92027) *(P-13596)*

Home Depot USA Inc .... C...... 619 421-0639
1320 Eastlake Pkwy Chula Vista (91915) *(P-13597)*

Home Depot USA Inc .... D...... 619 401-6610
298 Fletcher Pkwy El Cajon (92020) *(P-13598)*

Home Depot USA Inc .... C...... 619 589-2999
7530 Broadway Lemon Grove (91945) *(P-13599)*

Home Depot USA Inc .... B...... 805 389-9918
401 W Ventura Blvd Camarillo (93010) *(P-13600)*

Home Depot USA Inc .... C...... 805 983-0653
401 W Esplanade Dr Oxnard (93036) *(P-13601)*

Home Depot USA Inc .... C...... 909 748-0505
1151 W Lugonia Ave Redlands (92374) *(P-13602)*

Home Depot USA Inc .... C...... 760 955-2999
15150 Bear Valley Rd Victorville (92395) *(P-13603)*

Home Depot USA Inc .... C...... 909 393-5205
14549 Ramona Ave Chino (91710) *(P-13604)*

Home Depot USA Inc .... C...... 909 948-9200
11884 Foothill Blvd Rancho Cucamonga (91730) *(P-13605)*

Home Depot USA Inc .... C...... 323 292-1397
1830 W Slauson Ave Los Angeles (90047) *(P-13606)*

Home Depot USA Inc .... C...... 323 342-9495
2055 N Figueroa St Los Angeles (90065) *(P-13607)*

Home Depot USA Inc .... C...... 562 272-8055
6400 Alondra Blvd Paramount (90723) *(P-13608)*

Home Depot USA Inc .... C...... 626 813-7131
3200 Puente Ave Baldwin Park (91706) *(P-13609)*

Home Depot USA Inc .... C...... 310 835-7547
110 E Sepulveda Blvd Carson (90745) *(P-13610)*

Home Depot USA Inc .... C...... 562 789-4121
12322 Washington Blvd Whittier (90606) *(P-13611)*

Home Depot USA Inc .... C...... 310 644-9600
14603 Ocean Gate Ave Hawthorne (90250) *(P-13612)*

Home Depot USA Inc .... C...... 323 727-9600
7015 Telegraph Rd Commerce (90040) *(P-13613)*

Home Depot USA Inc .... C...... 310 822-3330
12975 W Jefferson Blvd Los Angeles (90066) *(P-13614)*

Home Depot USA Inc .... C...... 818 365-7662
12960 Foothill Blvd Sylmar (91342) *(P-13615)*

Home Depot USA Inc .... C...... 661 252-7800
20642 Golden Triangle Rd Santa Clarita (91351) *(P-13616)*

Home Depot USA Inc .... D...... 562 595-9200
2450 Cherry Ave Long Beach (90755) *(P-13617)*

Home Depot USA Inc .... C...... 760 375-4614
575 N China Lake Blvd Ridgecrest (93555) *(P-13618)*

Home Depot USA Inc .... C...... 562 776-2200
7121 Firestone Blvd Downey (90241) *(P-13619)*

Home Depot USA Inc .... C...... 818 780-5448
16800 Roscoe Blvd Van Nuys (91406) *(P-13620)*

Home Depot USA Inc .... C...... 323 587-5520
3040 E Slauson Ave Huntington Park (90255) *(P-13621)*

Home Depot USA Inc .... C...... 310 677-1944
3363 W Century Blvd Inglewood (90303) *(P-13622)*

Home Depot USA Inc .... C...... 626 256-0580
1625 S Mountain Ave Monrovia (91016) *(P-13623)*

Home Depot, The, Jurupa Valley *Also Called: Home Depot USA Inc (P-11586)*

Home Depot, The, Rancho Cucamonga *Also Called: Home Depot USA Inc (P-11587)*

Home Depot, The, Poway *Also Called: Home Depot USA Inc (P-11588)*

Home Depot, The, La Mirada *Also Called: Home Depot USA Inc (P-11589)*

Home Depot, The, Riverside *Also Called: Home Depot USA Inc (P-13579)*

Home Depot, The, Eastvale *Also Called: Home Depot USA Inc (P-13580)*

Home Depot, The, Moreno Valley *Also Called: Home Depot USA Inc (P-13581)*

Home Depot, The, Murrieta *Also Called: Home Depot USA Inc (P-13582)*

Home Depot, The, Corona *Also Called: Home Depot USA Inc (P-13583)*

Home Depot, The, Laguna Niguel *Also Called: Home Depot USA Inc (P-13584)*

Home Depot, The, Fullerton *Also Called: Home Depot USA Inc (P-13585)*

Home Depot, The, Anaheim *Also Called: Home Depot USA Inc (P-13586)*

Home Depot, The, La Habra *Also Called: Home Depot USA Inc (P-13587)*

Home Depot, The, Santa Ana *Also Called: Home Depot USA Inc (P-13588)*

Home Depot, The, Orange *Also Called: Home Depot USA Inc (P-13589)*

Home Depot, The, Costa Mesa *Also Called: Home Depot USA Inc (P-13590)*

Home Depot, The, Lake Forest *Also Called: Home Depot USA Inc (P-13591)*

Home Depot, The, Mission Viejo *Also Called: Home Depot USA Inc (P-13592)*

Home Depot, The, Garden Grove *Also Called: Home Depot USA Inc (P-13593)*

Home Depot, The, Santa Ana *Also Called: Home Depot USA Inc (P-13594)*

Home Depot, The, San Diego *Also Called: Home Depot USA Inc (P-13595)*

Home Depot, The, Escondido *Also Called: Home Depot USA Inc (P-13596)*

Home Depot, The, Chula Vista *Also Called: Home Depot USA Inc (P-13597)*

Home Depot, The, El Cajon *Also Called: Home Depot USA Inc (P-13598)*

Home Depot, The, Lemon Grove *Also Called: Home Depot USA Inc (P-13599)*

Home Depot, The, Camarillo *Also Called: Home Depot USA Inc (P-13600)*

Home Depot, The, Oxnard *Also Called: Home Depot USA Inc (P-13601)*

Home Depot, The, Redlands *Also Called: Home Depot USA Inc (P-13602)*

Home Depot, The, Victorville *Also Called: Home Depot USA Inc (P-13603)*

Home Depot, The, Chino *Also Called: Home Depot USA Inc (P-13604)*

Home Depot, The, Rancho Cucamonga *Also Called: Home Depot USA Inc (P-13605)*

Home Depot, The, Los Angeles *Also Called: Home Depot USA Inc (P-13606)*

Home Depot, The, Los Angeles *Also Called: Home Depot USA Inc (P-13607)*

Home Depot, The, Paramount *Also Called: Home Depot USA Inc (P-13608)*

Home Depot, The, Baldwin Park *Also Called: Home Depot USA Inc (P-13609)*

Home Depot, The, Carson *Also Called: Home Depot USA Inc (P-13610)*

Home Depot, The, Whittier *Also Called: Home Depot USA Inc (P-13611)*

Home Depot, The, Hawthorne *Also Called: Home Depot USA Inc (P-13612)*

Home Depot, The, Commerce *Also Called: Home Depot USA Inc (P-13613)*

Home Depot, The, Los Angeles *Also Called: Home Depot USA Inc (P-13614)*

Home Depot, The, Sylmar *Also Called: Home Depot USA Inc (P-13615)*

Home Depot, The, Santa Clarita *Also Called: Home Depot USA Inc (P-13616)*

Home Depot, The, Long Beach *Also Called: Home Depot USA Inc (P-13617)*

Home Depot, The, Ridgecrest *Also Called: Home Depot USA Inc (P-13618)*

Home Depot, The, Downey *Also Called: Home Depot USA Inc (P-13619)*

Home Depot, The, Van Nuys *Also Called: Home Depot USA Inc (P-13620)*

Home Depot, The, Huntington Park *Also Called: Home Depot USA Inc (P-13621)*

Home Depot, The, Inglewood *Also Called: Home Depot USA Inc (P-13622)*

Home Depot, The, Monrovia *Also Called: Home Depot USA Inc (P-13623)*

Home Entertainment Div, Los Angeles *Also Called: Fox Inc (P-11948)*

Home Express Delivery Svc LLC .... A...... 949 715-9844
25361 Commercentre Dr Ste 250 Lake Forest (92630) *(P-11770)*

Home Guiding Hands Corporation (PA) .... B...... 619 938-2850
1908 Friendship Dr El Cajon (92020) *(P-19271)*

Home Helpers of North County, Escondido *Also Called: Cox Enterprises LLC (P-18606)*

Home Instead Senior Care, Victorville *Also Called: Branlyn Prominence Inc (P-18595)*

Home Instead Senior Care, Rancho Cucamonga *Also Called: Branlyn Prominence Inc (P-18596)*

Home Instead Senior Care, Long Beach *Also Called: Coastal Cmnty Senior Care LLC (P-18603)*

Home Junction Inc .... D...... 858 777-9533
1 Venture Ste 300 Irvine (92618) *(P-16046)*

Home Mrtg Aliance Corp Hmac (PA) .... B...... 800 900-7040
4 Hutton Centre Dr Ste 500 Santa Ana (92707) *(P-14327)*

Home Organizers Inc .... A...... 562 699-9945
3860 Capitol Ave City Of Industry (90601) *(P-1015)*

Home Security and HM Ctrl Svcs, Anaheim *Also Called: ADT LLC (P-16717)*

Home Security Stores Inc ....E..... 951 782-8494
12660 Magnolia Ave Riverside (92503) *(P-12667)*

Home Street Operations LLC ....D..... 949 449-2500
114 Pacifica Ste 230 Irvine (92618) *(P-18085)*

Home-Flex, Valencia *Also Called: Valencia Pipe Company (P-4855)*

Home2 Sites By Hilton Temecula, Temecula *Also Called: Temecula Hhg Hotel Dev LP (P-15388)*

Homeboy Bakery, Los Angeles *Also Called: Homeboy Industries (P-19090)*

Homeboy Industries (PA) ....**B.....** **323 526-1254**
130 Bruno St Los Angeles (90012) *(P-19090)*

Homebridge Financial Svcs Inc ....A..... 818 981-0606
15301 Ventura Blvd Ste D300 Sherman Oaks (91403) *(P-14359)*

Homeland Housewares LLC ....D..... 310 996-7200
10900 Wilshire Blvd Ste 900 Los Angeles (90024) *(P-12633)*

Homeowners Association, Helendale *Also Called: Silver Lakes Association (P-19464)*

Homes Media Solutions LLC ....D..... 888 510-8795
5510 Morehouse Dr Ste 100 San Diego (92121) *(P-15544)*

Homestead Sheet Metal ....E..... 619 469-4373
9031 Memory Ln Spring Valley (91977) *(P-6030)*

Homewatch Caregivers, Carlsbad *Also Called: North Coast Home Care Inc (P-18631)*

Homewood Suites, Palm Desert *Also Called: Palm Desert Hospitality LLC (P-15294)*

Honav Usa Inc ....F..... 858 634-0617
3030 W Warner Ave Santa Ana (92704) *(P-8418)*

Honda, Torrance *Also Called: Honda R&D Americas LLC (P-19897)*

Honda R&D Americas LLC ....A..... 310 781-5500
1900 Harpers Way Torrance (90501) *(P-19897)*

Honda World Westminster ....C..... 714 890-8900
13600 Beach Blvd Westminster (92683) *(P-13779)*

Honest, Los Angeles *Also Called: Honest Company Inc (P-2391)*

Honest Company Inc (PA) ....**C.....** **310 917-9199**
12130 Millennium Ste 500 Los Angeles (90094) *(P-2391)*

Honest Kitchen Inc ....D..... 619 544-0018
350 Camino De La Reina Ste 140 San Diego (92108) *(P-1429)*

Honey ....F..... 805 963-8300
333 E Haley St Santa Barbara (93101) *(P-1911)*

Honey, Los Angeles *Also Called: Honey Science LLC (P-16047)*

Honey Bennetts Farm ....E..... 805 521-1375
3176 Honey Ln Fillmore (93015) *(P-1912)*

Honey Isabells Inc ....E..... 800 708-8485
539 N Glenoaks Blvd Ste 207b Burbank (91502) *(P-92)*

Honey Punch, Los Angeles *Also Called: Klk Forte Industry Inc (P-2342)*

Honey Science LLC ....C..... 949 795-1695
963 E 4th St Ste 100 Los Angeles (90013) *(P-16047)*

Honeybee Robotics LLC ....E..... 303 774-7613
2408 Lincoln Ave Altadena (91001) *(P-7393)*

Honeybee Robotics LLC ....E..... 510 207-4555
398 W Washington Blvd Ste 200 Pasadena (91103) *(P-7394)*

Honeymoon Real Estate LP ....D..... 310 277-5221
9400 W Olympic Blvd Beverly Hills (90212) *(P-15184)*

Honeyville Inc ....D..... 909 980-9500
11600 Dayton Dr Rancho Cucamonga (91730) *(P-11548)*

Honeyville Grain Inc ....E..... 909 243-1050
9175 Milliken Ave Rancho Cucamonga (91730) *(P-1412)*

Honeywell, Calexico *Also Called: Honeywell International Inc (P-9571)*

Honeywell, Torrance *Also Called: Honeywell International Inc (P-9572)*

Honeywell, San Diego *Also Called: Honeywell International Inc (P-10104)*

Honeywell Authorized Dealer, Riverside *Also Called: 20/20 Plumbing & Heating Inc (P-722)*

Honeywell Authorized Dealer, San Diego *Also Called: Atlas Mechanical Inc (P-738)*

HONEYWELL AUTHORIZED DEALER, Fullerton *Also Called: C & L Refrigeration Corp (P-749)*

Honeywell Authorized Dealer, North Hollywood *Also Called: Circulating Air Inc (P-753)*

Honeywell Authorized Dealer, Anaheim *Also Called: Control Air Conditioning Corporation (P-755)*

Honeywell Authorized Dealer, San Diego *Also Called: Greater San Diego AC Co Inc (P-774)*

Honeywell Authorized Dealer, Corona *Also Called: LDI Mechanical Inc (P-785)*

Honeywell Authorized Dealer, San Diego *Also Called: Pacific Rim Mech Contrs Inc (P-805)*

Honeywell Authorized Dealer, Paramount *Also Called: Reliable Energy Management Inc (P-817)*

Honeywell Authorized Dealer, Santa Fe Springs *Also Called: Western Allied Corporation (P-835)*

Honeywell Authorized Dealer, Santa Clarita *Also Called: Tri-Signal Integration Inc (P-947)*

Honeywell International Inc ....F..... 760 312-5300
233 Paulin Ave Box 8500 Calexico (92231) *(P-9571)*

Honeywell International Inc ....A..... 310 323-9500
2525 W 190th St Torrance (90504) *(P-9572)*

Honeywell International Inc ....C..... 619 671-5612
2055 Dublin Dr San Diego (92154) *(P-10104)*

Honeywell Safety Pdts USA Inc ....C..... 619 661-8383
7828 Waterville Rd San Diego (92154) *(P-10668)*

Hongfa America Inc ....E..... 714 669-2888
20381 Hermana Cir Lake Forest (92630) *(P-8182)*

Honk Technologies Inc ....C..... 800 979-3162
2251 Barry Ave Los Angeles (90064) *(P-16499)*

Honor Life, Vista *Also Called: Rayzist Photomask Inc (P-11061)*

Honor Plastics, Pomona *Also Called: Performnce Engineered Pdts Inc (P-5134)*

Honor Rancho Station, Valencia *Also Called: Southern California Gas Co (P-12087)*

Honulua Surf Co, Irvine *Also Called: Veezee Inc (P-2269)*

Hood Manufacturing Inc ....D..... 714 979-7681
2621 S Birch St Santa Ana (92707) *(P-5051)*

Hook It Up ....E..... 714 600-0100
1513 S Grand Ave Santa Ana (92705) *(P-2005)*

Hooked ....E..... 805 551-4981
1524 11th St Unit C Santa Monica (90401) *(P-16264)*

Hoosier Inc ....D..... 951 272-3070
1152 California Ave Corona (92881) *(P-5052)*

Hoover Containers Inc ....E..... 909 444-9454
19570 San Jose Ave City Of Industry (91748) *(P-3109)*

Hoover Treated Wood Pdts Inc ....E..... 661 833-0429
5601 District Blvd Bakersfield (93313) *(P-2746)*

Hoover Treated Wood Pdts Plant, Bakersfield *Also Called: Hoover Treated Wood Pdts Inc (P-2746)*

Hope Bancorp Inc (PA) ....**D.....** **213 639-1700**
3200 Wilshire Blvd Ste 1400 Los Angeles (90010) *(P-14168)*

Hope Hse For Mltple Hndcpped I (PA) ....**D.....** **626 443-1313**
4215 Peck Rd El Monte (91732) *(P-19272)*

Hope Plastics Co Inc ....E..... 818 769-5560
5353 Strohm Ave North Hollywood (91601) *(P-5053)*

Hopkins Labratory Co, Irwindale *Also Called: Esmond Natural Inc (P-3999)*

Horiba Americas Holding Inc (HQ) ....**A.....** **949 250-4811**
9755 Research Dr Irvine (92618) *(P-10262)*

Horiba Automotive Test Systems, Irvine *Also Called: Horiba Instruments Inc (P-10263)*

Horiba Instruments Inc (DH) ....**C.....** **949 250-4811**
9755 Research Dr Irvine (92618) *(P-10263)*

Horiba International Corp ....A..... 949 250-4811
9755 Research Dr Irvine (92618) *(P-10371)*

Horiba Medical, Irvine *Also Called: Horibaabx Inc (P-12493)*

Horibaabx Inc ....C..... 949 453-0500
34 Bunsen Irvine (92618) *(P-12493)*

Horizon Communication, Irvine *Also Called: Horizon Communication Tech Inc (P-12007)*

Horizon Communication Tech Inc ....D..... 714 982-3900
13700 Alton Pkwy Ste 154-278 Irvine (92618) *(P-12007)*

Horizon Hobby LLC ....D..... 909 390-9595
4710 E Guasti Rd Ste A Ontario (91761) *(P-10953)*

Horizon Media Inc ....B..... 310 282-0909
1888 Century Park E Ste 700 Los Angeles (90067) *(P-15545)*

HORIZON MEDIA, INC., Los Angeles *Also Called: Horizon Media Inc (P-15545)*

Horizon Solar Power, Hemet *Also Called: Lpsh Holdings Inc (P-788)*

Horizon Solar Power, Hemet *Also Called: Lpsh Holdings Inc (P-789)*

Horizon Well Logging Inc ....E..... 805 733-0972
711 Saint Andrews Way Lompoc (93436) *(P-354)*

Hormel, Irvine *Also Called: Hormel Foods Corp Svcs LLC (P-1221)*

Hormel Foods Corp Svcs LLC ....E..... 949 753-5350
2 Venture Ste 250 Irvine (92618) *(P-1221)*

Hornblower Cruisers and Events, Newport Beach *Also Called: Hornblower Yachts LLC (P-11716)*

Hornblower Cruises & Events, San Diego *Also Called: Hornblower Yachts LLC (P-11639)*

Hornblower Yachts LLC ....D..... 619 686-8700
2825 5th Ave San Diego (92103) *(P-11639)*

Hornblower Yachts LLC ....A..... 949 650-2412
2527 W Coast Hwy Newport Beach (92663) *(P-11716)*

ALPHABETIC

Employee Codes: A=Over 500 employees, B=251-500
C=101-250, D=51-100, E=20-50, F=10-19, G=1-9

2024 Southern California
Business Directory and Buyers Guide

© Mergent Inc. 1-800-342-5647
1121

Horrigan Cole Enterprises, Murrieta *Also Called: National Mentor Holdings Inc* *(P-19289)*

Horrigan Enterprises Inc .... C...... 909 481-9663
7945 Cartilla Ave Rancho Cucamonga (91730) *(P-19091)*

Horsemen Inc .... D...... 714 847-4243
16911 Algonquin St Huntington Beach (92649) *(P-16652)*

Horstman Manufacturing Co Inc .... F...... 760 598-2100
1970 Peacock Blvd Oceanside (92056) *(P-9402)*

Horton Grand Hotel, San Diego *Also Called: Historical Properties Inc* *(P-15181)*

Hose Power USA, City Of Industry *Also Called: Bridgestone Hosepower LLC* *(P-12845)*

Hospital of Barstow Inc (DH) .... D...... 760 256-1761
820 E Mountain View St Barstow (92311) *(P-18288)*

Hospitality Wood Products Inc .... F...... 562 806-5564
7206 E Gage Ave Commerce (90040) *(P-2607)*

Hospitler Order of St John Go .... B...... 323 731-0641
2468 S St Andrews Pl Los Angeles (90018) *(P-19501)*

Host Healthcare Inc ....A...... 858 999-3579
4225 Executive Sq Ste 1500 La Jolla (92037) *(P-15923)*

Hot Dogger Tours Inc .... C...... 714 988-4088
105 Gemini Ave Brea (92821) *(P-11417)*

Hot Topic Inc (DH) .... A...... 626 839-4681
18305 San Jose Ave City Of Industry (91748) *(P-13934)*

Hotchkis Wiley Capitl MGT LLC (PA) .... C...... 213 430-1000
725 S Figueroa St Ste 3900 Los Angeles (90017) *(P-20038)*

Hotel Angeleno, Los Angeles *Also Called: Ascot Hotel LP* *(P-15078)*

Hotel Associates Palm Springs, La Quinta *Also Called: Msr Desert Resort LP* *(P-14027)*

Hotel Bel-Air .... B...... 310 472-1211
701 Stone Canyon Rd Los Angeles (90077) *(P-15185)*

Hotel Bel-Air, Los Angeles *Also Called: Kava Holdings Inc* *(P-15207)*

Hotel Casa Del Mar, Santa Monica *Also Called: Et Whitehall Seascape LLC* *(P-15149)*

Hotel Circle Property LLC .... B...... 619 291-7131
500 Hotel Cir N San Diego (92108) *(P-15186)*

Hotel Company, El Segundo *Also Called: Uhg Lax Prop Llc* *(P-15395)*

Hotel Del Coronado, Coronado *Also Called: Ksl Resorts Hotel Del Coronado* *(P-15213)*

Hotel Fullerton Anaheim, The, Fullerton *Also Called: Huoyen International Inc* *(P-15191)*

Hotel Hanford, The, Costa Mesa *Also Called: Hanford Hotels Inc* *(P-15169)*

Hotel Indigo Del Mar, Del Mar *Also Called: Pacifica Hosts Inc* *(P-15290)*

Hotel Indigo Los Angles Dwntwn, Los Angeles *Also Called: Metropolis Hotel MGT LLC* *(P-15249)*

Hotel June, The, Los Angeles *Also Called: Custom Hotel LLC* *(P-15126)*

Hotel Managers Group, San Diego *Also Called: Hotel Managers Group Llc* *(P-20039)*

Hotel Managers Group Llc .... B...... 858 673-1534
11590 W Bernardo Ct Ste 211 San Diego (92127) *(P-20039)*

Hotel Marmonte, Santa Barbara *Also Called: H D G Associates* *(P-15166)*

Hotel Maya, Long Beach *Also Called: Queensbay Hotel LLC* *(P-15313)*

Hotel Palomar, Los Angeles *Also Called: Behringer Harvard Wilshire Blv* *(P-15089)*

Hotel Portofino, Redondo Beach *Also Called: Portofino Hotel Partners LP* *(P-15307)*

Hotel Solamar, San Diego *Also Called: Souldriver Lessee Inc* *(P-15363)*

Hotlix (PA) .... E...... 805 473-0596
966 Griffin St Grover Beach (93433) *(P-1543)*

Hotlix Candy, Grover Beach *Also Called: Hotlix* *(P-1543)*

Houalla Enterprises Ltd .... D...... 949 515-4350
2610 Avon St Newport Beach (92663) *(P-558)*

Houghton Mifflin Harcourt Pubg .... E...... 617 351-5000
525 B St Ste 1900 San Diego (92101) *(P-3407)*

Houlihan Lokey Inc (PA) .... B...... 310 788-5200
10250 Constellation Blvd Fl 5 Los Angeles (90067) *(P-14422)*

House Ear, Los Angeles *Also Called: House Ear Clinic Inc* *(P-17666)*

House Ear Clinic Inc (PA) .... D...... 213 483-9930
1245 Wilshire Blvd Ste 812 Los Angeles (90017) *(P-17666)*

House Foods America Corp (HQ) .... E...... 714 901-4350
7351 Orangewood Ave Garden Grove (92841) *(P-1913)*

House of Blues, Los Angeles *Also Called: Hob Entertainment LLC* *(P-17338)*

House of Blues Anaheim, Anaheim *Also Called: Hob Entertainment LLC* *(P-17337)*

House of Blues Concerts Inc (DH) .... C...... 323 769-4977
6255 W Sunset Blvd Fl 16 Los Angeles (90028) *(P-17339)*

House of Magnets, El Cajon *Also Called: Graphic Business Solutions Inc* *(P-12994)*

House of Printing Inc .... E...... 626 793-7034
3336 E Colorado Blvd Pasadena (91107) *(P-3587)*

House Research Institute .... C...... 213 353-7012
2100 W 3rd St Ste 500 Los Angeles (90057) *(P-19928)*

House Seven Gables RE Inc .... D...... 714 282-0306
5753 E Santa Ana Canyon Rd Ste P Anaheim (92807) *(P-14811)*

Housewares International Inc .... E...... 323 581-3000
1933 S Broadway Ste 867 Los Angeles (90007) *(P-5054)*

Houston Bazz Co .... D...... 714 898-2666
12700 Western Ave Garden Grove (92841) *(P-6522)*

Houston Cheesecake Fctry Corp .... D...... 818 871-3000
26901 Malibu Hills Rd Calabasas Hills (91301) *(P-14013)*

Houston Fearless 76, Compton *Also Called: Hf Group Inc* *(P-10868)*

Houston Ontic Inc .... F...... 818 678-6555
20400 Plummer St Chatsworth (91311) *(P-7867)*

Houwelings Camarillo Inc .... B...... 805 250-1600
645 Laguna Rd Camarillo (93012) *(P-75)*

Howard Johnson, Anaheim *Also Called: Northwest Hotel Corporation* *(P-15264)*

Howell Drilling, Long Beach *Also Called: Dick Howells Hole Drlg Svc Inc* *(P-279)*

Howmedica Osteonics Corp .... D...... 800 621-6104
6885 Flanders Dr Ste G San Diego (92121) *(P-10669)*

Howmet Aerospace Inc .... B...... 212 836-2674
3016 Lomita Blvd Torrance (90505) *(P-5670)*

Howmet Aerospace Inc .... C...... 323 728-3901
1550 Gage Rd Montebello (90640) *(P-5687)*

Howmet Aerospace Inc, Montebello *Also Called: Howmet Aerospace Inc* *(P-5687)*

Howmet Corporation ....A...... 310 847-8152
900 E Watson Center Rd Carson (90745) *(P-5654)*

Howmet Fastening Systems, Simi Valley *Also Called: Howmet Globl Fstning Systems I* *(P-12858)*

Howmet Globl Fstning Systems I .... D...... 714 871-1550
800 S State College Blvd Fullerton (92831) *(P-5655)*

Howmet Globl Fstning Systems I (HQ) .... C...... 805 426-2270
3990a Heritage Oak Ct Simi Valley (93063) *(P-12858)*

Hoya Corporation .... E...... 858 309-6050
4255 Ruffin Rd San Diego (92123) *(P-10841)*

Hoya Holdings Inc .... D...... 626 739-5200
425 E Huntington Dr Monrovia (91016) *(P-10317)*

Hoya San Diego, San Diego *Also Called: Hoya Corporation* *(P-10841)*

Hoya Surgical Optics Inc .... E...... 909 680-3900
110 Progress Irvine (92618) *(P-10521)*

Hoylu Inc .... F...... 213 440-2499
6121 W Sunset Blvd Los Angeles (90028) *(P-16265)*

Hoylu La, Los Angeles *Also Called: Hoylu Inc* *(P-16265)*

HP, San Diego *Also Called: HP Inc* *(P-7429)*

HP Communications Inc (PA) .... D...... 951 572-1200
13341 Temescal Canyon Rd Corona (92883) *(P-674)*

HP Core Co Inc .... F...... 323 582-1688
1264 Indian Springs Dr Glendora (91741) *(P-7043)*

HP Inc .... B...... 858 924-5117
16399 W Bernardo Dr Bldg 61 San Diego (92127) *(P-7429)*

HP It Services Incorporated .... E...... 714 844-7737
1506 W Flower Ave Fullerton (92833) *(P-7531)*

HP Lq Investment LP .... C...... 760 564-4111
49499 Eisenhower Dr La Quinta (92253) *(P-15187)*

Hpa-USA, Compton *Also Called: Hydroprocessing Associates LLC* *(P-16842)*

Hpcwire, San Diego *Also Called: Tabor Communications Inc* *(P-3490)*

Hpi Liquidations Inc .... C...... 858 391-7302
13100 Danielson St Poway (92064) *(P-3110)*

Hpi Racing, Lake Forest *Also Called: SMC Products Inc* *(P-12945)*

Hpp Food Services, Wilmington *Also Called: Icpk Corporation* *(P-13184)*

Hps Mechanical Inc (PA) .... C...... 661 397-2121
3100 E Belle Ter Bakersfield (93307) *(P-777)*

Hqe Systems Inc .... D...... 800 967-3036
27419 Via Industria Temecula (92590) *(P-20344)*

Hr Cloud Inc .... E...... 510 909-1993
222 N Pacific Coast Hwy Ste 2000 El Segundo (90245) *(P-16266)*

Hrc Consultants, Carlsbad *Also Called: Human Resource Capitl Cons Inc* *(P-20182)*

Hrd Aero Systems Inc (PA) .... C...... 661 295-0670
25555 Avenue Stanford Valencia (91355) *(P-17132)*

Hre Performance Wheels, Vista *Also Called: Phoenix Wheel Company Inc* *(P-12252)*

Hrk Pet Food Products Inc .... F...... 818 897-2521
12924 Pierce St Pacoima (91331) *(P-1442)*

Hrl Laboratories LLC .... A 310 317-5000
3011 Malibu Canyon Rd Malibu (90265) *(P-19898)*

Hrn Services Inc .... D 323 951-1450
520 N Brand Blvd Ste 200 Glendale (91203) *(P-15851)*

Hronis Inc A California Corp (PA) .... C 661 725-2503
10443 Hronis Rd Delano (93215) *(P-43)*

Hsb Holdings Inc .... E 951 214-6590
14050 Day St Moreno Valley (92553) *(P-4697)*

Hsf Affiliates LLC (PA) .... D 949 794-7900
18500 Von Karman Ave Ste 400 Irvine (92612) *(P-14812)*

Hsiao & Montano Inc .... E 626 588-2528
809 W Santa Anita Ave San Gabriel (91776) *(P-5289)*

Hsssi, San Dimas Also Called: Hamilton Sundstrand Spc Systms *(P-10370)*

Hst Lessee Mission Hills LP .... D 760 328-5955
71333 Dinah Shore Dr Rancho Mirage (92270) *(P-15188)*

Ht Multinational Inc .... E 909 325-8582
15780 El Prado Rd Chino (91708) *(P-9403)*

Hte Acquisition LLC .... E 805 987-5449
4610 Calle Quetzal Camarillo (93012) *(P-7868)*

Htl Manufacturing Div, Simi Valley Also Called: Meggitt Safety Systems Inc *(P-9750)*

Htpghnl, Ontario Also Called: Heat Transfer Pdts Group LLC *(P-12755)*

Hub City, Fullerton Also Called: Hub Group Los Angeles LLC *(P-11771)*

Hub Distributing Inc (HQ) .... B **951 340-3149**
1260 Corona Pointe Ct Corona (92879) *(P-13909)*

Hub Group Los Angeles LLC .... D 714 449-6300
1400 N Harbor Blvd # 300 Fullerton (92835) *(P-11771)*

Hub Group Trucking Inc .... B 909 770-8950
13867 Valley Blvd Fontana (92335) *(P-11461)*

Huck International Inc .... C 310 830-8200
900 E Watson Center Rd Carson (90745) *(P-6445)*

Hudson H Clude Cmplete Hlth Ct, Los Angeles Also Called: County of Los Angeles *(P-17634)*

Hudson Printing, Carlsbad Also Called: Hudson Printing Inc *(P-3768)*

Hudson Printing Inc .... E 760 602-1260
2780 Loker Ave W Carlsbad (92010) *(P-3768)*

Hueston Hennigan LLP .... D 213 788-4340
523 W 6th St Ste 400 Los Angeles (90014) *(P-18871)*

Hughes Bros Aircrafters Inc .... E 323 773-4541
11010 Garfield Pl South Gate (90280) *(P-7076)*

Hughes Circuits Inc .... C 760 744-0300
540 S Pacific St San Marcos (92078) *(P-8686)*

Hughes Circuits Inc (PA) .... D **760 744-0300**
546 S Pacific St San Marcos (92078) *(P-8687)*

Hughes Research Laboratories, Malibu Also Called: Hrl Laboratories LLC *(P-19898)*

Huhtamaki Inc .... C 323 269-0151
4209 Noakes St Commerce (90023) *(P-4890)*

Hulsey Contracting Inc .... E 951 549-3665
1740 Howard Pl Redlands (92373) *(P-12771)*

Hulu LLC .... A 888 631-4858
12312 W Olympic Blvd Los Angeles (90064) *(P-11886)*

Hulu LLC (HQ) .... B **310 571-4700**
2500 Broadway Ste 200 Santa Monica (90404) *(P-11887)*

Human Capital Select, LLC, San Diego Also Called: Lotus Workforce LLC *(P-20191)*

Human Dsgns Prsthtic Orthtic L, Long Beach Also Called: Ferraco Inc *(P-10659)*

Human Resource Capitl Cons Inc .... C 760 518-8816
6236 Paseo Colina Carlsbad (92009) *(P-20182)*

Human Resources, Anaheim Also Called: L3harris Interstate Elec Corp *(P-10210)*

Human Resources Department, Covina Also Called: Emanate Health Medical Center *(P-18254)*

Human Resources Services, Los Angeles Also Called: Los Angeles World Airports *(P-11700)*

Humangood (PA) .... C **602 906-4024**
1900 Huntington Dr Duarte (91010) *(P-18132)*

HUMANGOOD, Duarte Also Called: Bay Vista Senior Housing *(P-14704)*

Humangood Norcal .... C 661 834-0620
1401 New Stine Rd Bakersfield (93309) *(P-18133)*

Humangood Norcal .... C 909 793-1233
900 Salem Dr Redlands (92373) *(P-18134)*

Humangood Socal .... C 818 244-7219
1230 E Windsor Rd Ofc Glendale (91205) *(P-14713)*

Humangood Socal .... D 626 357-1632
1763 Royal Oaks Dr Ofc Duarte (91010) *(P-14714)*

Humangood Socal .... C 949 854-9500
19191 Harvard Ave Ofc Irvine (92612) *(P-14715)*

Humangood Socal .... C 626 359-8141
802 Buena Vista St Duarte (91010) *(P-19273)*

Humangood Socal .... C 858 454-4201
7450 Olivetas Ave Ofc La Jolla (92037) *(P-19274)*

Humangood Socal .... C 760 747-4306
710 W 13th Ave Escondido (92025) *(P-19275)*

Humano LLC .... D 844 448-6266
4231 Balboa Ave San Diego (92117) *(P-20345)*

Humetrix Holdings Inc .... E 858 259-8987
1155 Camino Del Mar Ste 5 Del Mar (92014) *(P-20183)*

Hummus Guy, The, Torrance Also Called: Thg Brands Inc *(P-1998)*

Humnit Hotel At Lax LLC .... D 424 702-1234
6225 W Century Blvd Los Angeles (90045) *(P-15189)*

Hungry Heart Media Inc .... C 323 951-0010
5450 W Washington Blvd Los Angeles (90016) *(P-17196)*

Hunnington Dialysis Center, Pasadena Also Called: Hemodialysis Inc *(P-10520)*

Hunsaker & Assoc Irvine Inc .... B 951 352-7200
2900 Adams St Ste A15 Riverside (92504) *(P-19610)*

Hunsaker & Assoc Irvine Inc (PA) .... D **949 583-1010**
3 Hughes Irvine (92618) *(P-19611)*

Hunsaker & Associates, Irvine Also Called: Hunsaker & Assoc Irvine Inc *(P-19611)*

Hunt Electronic, Rancho Cucamonga Also Called: Hunt Electronic Usa Inc *(P-9215)*

Hunt Electronic Usa Inc .... F 909 987-6999
11790 Jersey Blvd Rancho Cucamonga (91730) *(P-9215)*

Hunter, San Marcos Also Called: Hunter Industries Incorporated *(P-12213)*

Hunter Dodge Chrysler Jeep Ram, Lancaster Also Called: H W Hunter Inc *(P-13775)*

Hunter Douglas Inc .... B 858 679-7500
9900 Gidley St El Monte (91731) *(P-3007)*

Hunter Easterday Corporation .... C 714 238-3400
1475 N Hundley St Anaheim (92806) *(P-15713)*

Hunter Industries Incorporated (PA) .... C **760 744-5240**
1940 Diamond St San Marcos (92078) *(P-12213)*

Huntington Bch Senior Hsing LP .... C 714 842-4006
18765 Florida St Huntington Beach (92648) *(P-14716)*

Huntington Beach Ford, Huntington Beach Also Called: York Enterprises South Inc *(P-13849)*

Huntington Beach Hospital, Huntington Beach Also Called: Prime Hlthcare Hntngtn Bch LL *(P-18388)*

Huntington Beach Union High .... C 714 478-7684
7180 Yorktown Ave Huntington Beach (92648) *(P-15852)*

Huntington Care LLC .... C 877 405-6990
3452 E Foothill Blvd Ste 760 Pasadena (91107) *(P-18617)*

Huntington Extended Care Ctr, Pasadena Also Called: Pasadena Hospital Assn Ltd *(P-18028)*

Huntington Gardens, Huntington Beach Also Called: Huntington Bch Senior Hsing LP *(P-14716)*

Huntington Home Care, Pasadena Also Called: Huntington Care LLC *(P-18617)*

Huntington Hotel Company .... D 858 756-1131
5951 Linea Del Cielo Rancho Santa Fe (92067) *(P-15190)*

Huntington Industries Inc .... C 323 772-5575
12520 Chadron Ave Hawthorne (90250) *(P-2806)*

Huntington Ingalls Industries .... E 858 522-6000
9444 Balboa Ave Ste 400 San Diego (92123) *(P-11228)*

Huntington Lib Art Clictons BT .... B 626 405-2100
1151 Oxford Rd San Marino (91108) *(P-18999)*

Huntington Medical Foundation .... D 626 795-4210
10 Congress St Ste 208 Pasadena (91105) *(P-17667)*

Huntington Medical Foundation .... C 626 792-3141
65 N Madison Ave Ste 800 Pasadena (91101) *(P-18289)*

Huntington Memorial Hospital, Pasadena Also Called: Pasadena Hospital Assn Ltd *(P-18374)*

Huntington Memory Care Cmnty, Alhambra Also Called: Silverado Senior Living Inc *(P-18053)*

Huntington Vly Healthcare Ctr, Huntington Beach Also Called: Douglas Fir Holdings LLC *(P-17927)*

Huntley Hotel Santa Monica Bch, Santa Monica Also Called: Second Street Corporation *(P-15353)*

Huntsman, Los Angeles Also Called: Huntsman Advanced Materials AM *(P-3943)*

Huntsman Advanced Materials AM .... C 818 265-7221
5121 W San Fernando Rd Los Angeles (90039) *(P-3943)*

Employee Codes: A=Over 500 employees, B=251-500
C=101-250, D=51-100, E=20-50, F=10-19, G=1-9

2024 Southern California
Business Directory and Buyers Guide

© Mergent Inc. 1-800-342-5647
1123

Huoyen International Inc .... D...... 714 635-9000
1500 S Raymond Ave Fullerton (92831) *(P-15191)*

Hupa International Inc .... E...... 909 598-9876
21717 Ferrero Walnut (91789) *(P-10999)*

Hurley, Costa Mesa *Also Called: Hurley International LLC (P-2207)*

Hurley International LLC (PA)................................. C...... **949 548-9375**
3080 Bristol St Costa Mesa (92626) *(P-2207)*

Hurst International, Chatsworth *Also Called: Labeling Hurst Systems LLC (P-3778)*

Husks Unlimited (PA)... E...... **619 476-8301**
9925 Airway Rd # C San Diego (92154) *(P-1370)*

Husky Injction Mlding Systems .... D...... 805 523-9593
5245 Maureen Ln Moorpark (93021) *(P-5055)*

Husky Injction Mlding Systems .... D...... 714 545-8200
3505 Cadillac Ave Ste N4 Costa Mesa (92626) *(P-5056)*

Hussmann Corporation .... B...... 909 590-4910
13770 Ramona Ave Chino (91710) *(P-7615)*

Hussmann Tech Corp Amer .... D...... 619 661-1134
2001 Sanyo Ave San Diego (92154) *(P-7616)*

Hustler Casino, Gardena *Also Called: El Dorado Enterprises Inc (P-15144)*

Hutchins Healthcare Inc .... D...... 949 487-9500
27101 Puerta Real Ste 450 Mission Viejo (92691) *(P-17668)*

Hutchinson Arospc & Indust Inc .... C...... 818 843-1000
4510 W Vanowen St Burbank (91505) *(P-4767)*

Hutchinson Arospc & Indust Inc .... C...... 818 843-1000
4510 W Vanowen St Burbank (91505) *(P-9707)*

Hutchinson Seal Corporation (DH)........................ C...... **248 375-4190**
11634 Patton Rd Downey (90241) *(P-4733)*

Huxtable's, Vernon *Also Called: Huxtables Kitchen Inc (P-14014)*

Huxtables Kitchen Inc .... D...... 323 923-2900
2100 E 49th St Vernon (90058) *(P-14014)*

Huy Fong Foods Inc .... E...... 626 286-8328
4800 Azusa Canyon Rd Irwindale (91706) *(P-1337)*

HV Randall Foods LLC .... C...... 323 261-6565
2900 Ayers Ave Vernon (90058) *(P-13297)*

Hvac Installation and Repair, Los Angeles *Also Called: Precise Air Systems Inc (P-810)*

Hvantage Technologies Inc (PA)........................... D...... **818 661-6301**
22048 Sherman Way Ste 306 Canoga Park (91303) *(P-16048)*

Hwe Mechanical, Bakersfield *Also Called: Hills Wldg & Engrg Contr Inc (P-352)*

Hwood Group .... D...... 310 859-1011
9229 W Sunset Blvd Ste 305 West Hollywood (90069) *(P-12284)*

Hy-Tech Tile Inc .... C...... 951 788-0550
1130 Palmyrita Ave Ste 350 Riverside (92507) *(P-1031)*

Hyatt Corp As Agt Brcp Hef Ht .... D...... 760 603-6851
7100 Aviara Resort Dr Carlsbad (92011) *(P-15192)*

Hyatt Corporation .... C...... 858 453-0018
3777 La Jolla Village Dr San Diego (92122) *(P-15193)*

Hyatt Corporation .... C...... 619 232-1234
1 Market Pl San Diego (92101) *(P-15194)*

Hyatt Corporation .... C...... 619 849-1234
600 F St San Diego (92101) *(P-15195)*

Hyatt Corporation .... B...... 312 750-1234
6225 W Century Blvd Los Angeles (90045) *(P-15196)*

Hyatt Corporation .... C...... 323 656-1234
8401 W Sunset Blvd Los Angeles (90069) *(P-15197)*

Hyatt Corporation .... B...... 562 432-0161
200 S Pine Ave Long Beach (90802) *(P-15198)*

Hyatt Corporation .... D...... 949 975-1234
17900 Jamboree Rd Irvine (92614) *(P-15199)*

Hyatt Corporation .... B...... 949 729-1234
1107 Jamboree Rd Newport Beach (92660) *(P-15200)*

Hyatt Corporation .... A...... 760 341-1000
44600 Indian Wells Ln Indian Wells (92210) *(P-15201)*

Hyatt Die Cast and Engineering Corporation - South (PA)...D...... **714 826-7550**
4656 Lincoln Ave Cypress (90630) *(P-5759)*

Hyatt Die Cast Engrg Corp - S .... E...... 714 622-2131
12250 Industry St Garden Grove (92841) *(P-5760)*

Hyatt Grand Champion Resort, Indian Wells *Also Called: Hyatt Corporation (P-15201)*

Hyatt Hotel, Carlsbad *Also Called: Hyatt Corp As Agt Brcp Hef Ht (P-15192)*

Hyatt Hotel, Los Angeles *Also Called: Hyatt Corporation (P-15197)*

Hyatt Hotel, Long Beach *Also Called: Hyatt Corporation (P-15198)*

Hyatt Hotel, Irvine *Also Called: Hyatt Corporation (P-15199)*

Hyatt Hotel, Newport Beach *Also Called: Hyatt Corporation (P-15200)*

Hyatt Hotel, Westlake Village *Also Called: Sky Court USA Inc (P-15359)*

Hyatt Los Angeles Airport, Los Angeles *Also Called: Hyatt Corporation (P-15196)*

Hyatt Regency Century Plaza .... A...... 310 228-1234
2025 Avenue Of The Stars Los Angeles (90067) *(P-15202)*

Hyatt Regency Lajolla, San Diego *Also Called: Hyatt Corporation (P-15193)*

Hyatt Westlake, Westlake Village *Also Called: Swvp Westlake LLC (P-15384)*

Hybrid Promotions, Cypress *Also Called: Hybrid Promotions LLC (P-13105)*

Hybrid Promotions LLC (PA)................................ C...... **714 952-3866**
10700 Valley View St Cypress (90630) *(P-13105)*

Hycor, Garden Grove *Also Called: Hycor Biomedical LLC (P-10522)*

Hycor Biomedical LLC .... C...... 714 933-3000
7272 Chapman Ave Ste A Garden Grove (92841) *(P-10522)*

Hyde, Vernon *Also Called: Streets Ahead Inc (P-2435)*

Hyde Pk Rehabilitation Ctr LLC .... D...... 323 753-1354
6520 West Blvd Los Angeles (90043) *(P-17975)*

Hydra-Electric Company (PA)............................... C...... **818 843-6211**
3151 N Kenwood St Burbank (91505) *(P-8123)*

Hydrafacial Company, The, Long Beach *Also Called: Hydrafacial LLC (P-10523)*

Hydrafacial Company, The, Long Beach *Also Called: Hydrafacial LLC (P-11590)*

Hydrafacial LLC (HQ)... D...... **800 603-4996**
2165 E Spring St Long Beach (90806) *(P-10523)*

Hydrafacial LLC .... E...... 562 391-2052
3600 E Burnett St Long Beach (90815) *(P-11590)*

Hydraflow .... B...... 714 773-2600
1881 W Malvern Ave Fullerton (92833) *(P-9708)*

Hydraflow, Fullerton *Also Called: Hydraflow (P-9708)*

Hydralic Systems Cmponents Inc .... E...... 760 744-9350
725 N Twin Oaks Valley Rd San Marcos (92069) *(P-17133)*

Hydranautics (DH).. B...... **760 901-2500**
401 Jones Rd Oceanside (92058) *(P-4610)*

Hydraulic Shop Inc .... E...... 909 875-9336
2753 S Vista Ave Bloomington (92316) *(P-6992)*

Hydraulics International Inc (PA).......................... B...... **818 998-1231**
20961 Knapp St Chatsworth (91311) *(P-9709)*

Hydraulics International Inc .... E...... 818 998-1236
9000 Mason Ave Chatsworth (91311) *(P-9710)*

Hydraulics International Inc .... E...... 818 998-1231
9261 Independence Ave Chatsworth (91311) *(P-9711)*

Hydril Company .... D...... 661 588-9332
3237 Patton Way Bakersfield (93308) *(P-6959)*

Hydro Extrusion Usa LLC .... B...... 626 964-3411
18111 Railroad St City Of Industry (91748) *(P-5699)*

Hydro Quip, Corona *Also Called: Blue Desert International Inc (P-7646)*

Hydro Systems Inc (PA).. D...... **661 775-0686**
29132 Avenue Paine Valencia (91355) *(P-5958)*

Hydro Tek, Redlands *Also Called: Hydro Tek Systems Inc (P-12892)*

Hydro Tek Systems Inc .... D...... 909 799-9222
2353 Almond Ave Redlands (92374) *(P-12892)*

Hydro-Aire Inc (HQ)... B...... **818 526-2600**
3000 Winona Ave Burbank (91504) *(P-9712)*

Hydro-Aire Aerospace Corp .... C...... 818 526-2600
3000 Winona Ave Burbank (91504) *(P-9713)*

Hydro-Pressure Systems, North Hollywood *Also Called: Woods Maintenance Services Inc (P-1186)*

Hydrochempsc, Bakersfield *Also Called: PSC Industrial Outsourcing LP (P-381)*

Hydrodex LLC .... E...... 800 218-8813
31225 La Baya Dr Westlake Village (91362) *(P-7661)*

Hydroform USA Incorporated .... C...... 310 632-6353
2848 E 208th St Carson (90810) *(P-9714)*

Hydromach Inc .... E...... 818 341-0915
20400 Prairie St Chatsworth (91311) *(P-9918)*

Hydroprocessing Associates LLC .... D...... 310 667-6456
19122 S Santa Fe Ave Compton (90221) *(P-16842)*

Hydrotech Construction Group, Newport Beach *Also Called: Citivest Inc (P-14765)*

Hygeia II Medical Group Inc .... E...... 714 515-7571
6241 Yarrow Dr Ste A Carlsbad (92011) *(P-10807)*

Hygenia, Camarillo *Also Called: Medical Packaging Corporation (P-10680)*

Hyland's Homeopathic, Los Angeles *Also Called: Hylands Consumer Health Inc (P-4132)*

Hylands Consumer Health Inc (PA)........................B....... 310 768-0700
  13301 S Main St Los Angeles (90061) *(P-4132)*

Hylete, San Diego *Also Called: Hylete Inc (P-2329)*

Hylete Inc ....E....... 858 225-8998
  11622 El Camino Real Ste 100 San Diego (92130) *(P-2329)*

Hyper Ice Inc (PA)..E....... 949 565-4994
  525 Technology Dr Ste 100 Irvine (92618) *(P-11000)*

Hyper-Tech LLC ....F....... 805 988-2000
  2993 Yucca Dr Santa Rosa Valley (93012) *(P-16843)*

Hyperbaric Technologies Inc ....D....... 619 336-2022
  3224 Hoover Ave National City (91950) *(P-10808)*

Hyperfly Inc ....E....... 760 300-0909
  2251 Las Palmas Dr Carlsbad (92011) *(P-11001)*

Hyperice, Irvine *Also Called: Hyper Ice Inc (P-11000)*

Hyperion Books For Children, Burbank *Also Called: Disney Book Group LLC (P-3406)*

Hyperion Motors LLC ....E....... 714 363-5858
  1032 W Taft Ave Orange (92865) *(P-7712)*

Hyperloop One, Los Angeles *Also Called: Hyperloop Technologies Inc (P-11834)*

Hyperloop Technologies Inc ....C....... 213 800-3270
  777 S Alameda St Ste 400 Los Angeles (90021) *(P-11834)*

Hyponex Corporation ....B....... 909 597-2811
  12273 Brown Ave Jurupa Valley (92509) *(P-4540)*

Hyspan, Chula Vista *Also Called: Hyspan Precision Products Inc (P-7378)*

Hyspan Precision Products Inc (PA)......................D....... 619 421-1355
  1685 Brandywine Ave Chula Vista (91911) *(P-7378)*

Hytron Mfg Co Inc ....E....... 714 903-6701
  15582 Chemical Ln Huntington Beach (92649) *(P-7869)*

Hyundai ABS Funding LLC ....C....... 949 732-2697
  3161 Michelson Dr Irvine (92612) *(P-14381)*

Hyundai Amer Technical Ctr Inc ....C....... 734 337-2500
  101 Peters Canyon Rd Irvine (92606) *(P-19612)*

Hyundai Amer Technical Ctr Inc ....C....... 909 627-3525
  12610 Eastend Ave Chino (91710) *(P-19974)*

Hyundai America/Tech Center, Chino *Also Called: Hyundai Amer Technical Ctr Inc (P-19974)*

Hyundai Autoever America LLC ....B....... 714 965-3000
  10550 Talbert Ave 3rd Fl Fountain Valley (92708) *(P-16542)*

Hyundai Motor America (HQ)....................................B....... 714 965-3000
  10550 Talbert Ave Fountain Valley (92708) *(P-12224)*

Hyundai Protection Plan Inc ....B....... 949 468-4000
  3161 Michelson Dr Ste 1900 Irvine (92612) *(P-14271)*

Hyundai Translead (HQ)...D....... 619 574-1500
  8880 Rio San Diego Dr Ste 600 San Diego (92108) *(P-6144)*

I & I Sports Supply Company (PA)...........................E....... 310 715-6800
  435 W Alondra Blvd Gardena (90248) *(P-11002)*

I A C, Irvine *Also Called: Irvine APT Communities LP (P-14722)*

I A D S, Palmdale *Also Called: Teletronics Technology Corp (P-10081)*

I and E Cabinets Inc ....E....... 818 933-6480
  14660 Raymer St Van Nuys (91405) *(P-2661)*

I B E, Sun Valley *Also Called: Industrial Battery Engrg Inc (P-9151)*

I Brands LLC ....C....... 424 336-5216
  2617 N Sepulveda Blvd Manhattan Beach (90266) *(P-12781)*

I C C, Fullerton *Also Called: Interntnal Cnnctors Cable Corp (P-8475)*

I C Class Components Corp (PA)............................D....... 310 539-5500
  23605 Telo Ave Torrance (90505) *(P-12668)*

I C S, Ventura *Also Called: Instrument Control Services (P-355)*

I C W, San Diego *Also Called: Insurance Company of West (P-14602)*

I Copy Inc ....E....... 562 921-0202
  11266 Monarch St Ste B Garden Grove (92841) *(P-7870)*

I D Brand LLC ....E....... 949 422-7057
  3185 Airway Ave Ste A Costa Mesa (92626) *(P-2532)*

I D C, Bakersfield *Also Called: Industrial Data Communications (P-12791)*

I D Property Corporation ....C....... 213 625-0100
  1001 Wilshire Blvd Ste 100 Los Angeles (90017) *(P-14813)*

I D W, Rancho Cucamonga *Also Called: Innovative Displayworks Inc (P-12457)*

I I D, Imperial *Also Called: Imperial Irrigation District (P-12027)*

I J S, San Dimas *Also Called: Industrial Janitor Service (P-15714)*

I M S Electonics Recycling, Poway *Also Called: IMS Electronics Recycling Inc (P-12171)*

I M T, Burbank *Also Called: Integrated Media Tech Inc (P-16571)*

I N C Builders Inc ....B....... 760 352-4200
  1560 Ocotillo Dr Ste L El Centro (92243) *(P-15924)*

I O Interconnect Ltd (PA)..E....... 714 564-1111
  1041 W 18th St Ste A101 Costa Mesa (92627) *(P-8973)*

I P, Chatsworth *Also Called: International Precision Inc (P-7874)*

I P S, Mentone *Also Called: International Paving Svcs Inc (P-626)*

I Pwlc Inc ....D....... 760 630-0231
  408 Olive Ave Vista (92083) *(P-165)*

I S E, Hawthorne *Also Called: Interntonal Strl Engineers Inc (P-19616)*

I S E, Poway *Also Called: ISE Corporation (P-19849)*

I T C, Buellton *Also Called: Infraredvision Technology Corp (P-8810)*

I-Coat Company LLC ....E....... 562 941-9989
  12020 Mora Dr Ste 2 Santa Fe Springs (90670) *(P-10318)*

I-Flow LLC ....A....... 800 448-3569
  43 Discovery Ste 100 Irvine (92618) *(P-10524)*

I.C.O.N. Salon, Woodland Hills *Also Called: ICON Line Inc (P-11229)*

I.V. League Medical, Camarillo *Also Called: Western Mfg & Distrg LLC (P-9889)*

I/O Interconnect, Costa Mesa *Also Called: I O Interconnect Ltd (P-8973)*

I/O Magic Corporation ....E....... 949 707-4800
  4 Marconi Irvine (92618) *(P-7430)*

I/Omagic Corporation (PA).......................................E....... 949 707-4800
  20512 Crescent Bay Dr Lake Forest (92630) *(P-7474)*

I2k LLC ....E....... 626 969-7780
  748 N Mckeever Ave Azusa (91702) *(P-17308)*

I3dnet LLC ....A....... 800 482-6910
  7 N Fair Oaks Ave Pasadena (91103) *(P-16447)*

Iaba, Culver City *Also Called: Institute For Applied Bhvior A (P-17862)*

Iaba, Camarillo *Also Called: Institute For Applied Bhvior A (P-17864)*

Iaccess Technologies Inc (PA)...............................E....... 714 922-9158
  1251 E Dyer Rd Ste 160 Santa Ana (92705) *(P-20346)*

Iamplus LLC ....D....... 323 210-3852
  809 N Cahuenga Blvd Los Angeles (90038) *(P-8207)*

IaMplus Electronics Inc (PA)..................................323 210-3852
  809 N Cahuenga Blvd Los Angeles (90038) *(P-16267)*

Iatse Affl Prprty Crftsprson L 818 769-2500
  12021 Riverside Dr North Hollywood (91607) *(P-19409)*

Ibaset Inc (PA)..E....... 949 598-5200
  26812 Vista Ter Lake Forest (92630) *(P-20347)*

Ibe Digital, Garden Grove *Also Called: I Copy Inc (P-7870)*

Ibftech Inc ....D....... 424 217-8010
  343 Main St El Segundo (90245) *(P-15853)*

Ibg Holdings Inc ....E....... 661 702-8680
  24841 Avenue Tibbitts Valencia (91355) *(P-4421)*

IBM, Glendale *Also Called: International Bus Mchs Corp (P-7433)*

IBM, Irvine *Also Called: Neudesic LLC (P-16081)*

Ibuypower, City Of Industry *Also Called: American Future Tech Corp (P-12395)*

Icann, Los Angeles *Also Called: Internet Corp For Assgned Nmes (P-16450)*

Icarcover Inc ....E....... 714 469-7759
  15529 Blackburn Ave Norwalk (90650) *(P-9404)*

ICC, Riverside *Also Called: Inland Cc Inc (P-1075)*

ICC Networking, Riverside *Also Called: Interntnal Communications Corp (P-16451)*

Ice Management Systems Inc ....E....... 951 676-2751
  27449 Colt Ct Temecula (92590) *(P-9715)*

Iced Out Gear, Canoga Park *Also Called: H2w (P-12979)*

Icf Jones & Stokes Inc 858 578-8964
  525 B St Ste 1700 San Diego (92101) *(P-20348)*

Ichia USA Inc ....D....... 619 482-2222
  509 Telegraph Canyon Rd Chula Vista (91910) *(P-8804)*

Icl Systems Inc 877 425-8725
  19782 Macarthur Blvd Ste 260 Irvine (92612) *(P-16448)*

ICON Line Inc ....F....... 818 709-4266
  20600 Ventura Blvd Ste C Woodland Hills (91364) *(P-11229)*

Icon Media Direct Inc (PA).......................................D....... 818 995-6400
  5910 Lemona Ave Van Nuys (91411) *(P-15546)*

Iconn Inc ....D....... 800 286-6742
  8909 Irvine Center Dr Irvine (92618) *(P-8124)*

Iconn Engineering LLC ....E....... 714 696-8826
  6882 Preakness Dr Huntington Beach (92648) *(P-6803)*

Iconn Technologies, Irvine *Also Called: Iconn Inc (P-8124)*

Employee Codes: A=Over 500 employees, B=251-500
C=101-250, D=51-100, E=20-50, F=10-19, G=1-9

2024 Southern California
Business Directory and Buyers Guide

© Mergent Inc. 1-800-342-5647

1125

A
L
P
H
A
B
E
T
I
C

ICP West, Buena Park *Also Called: Interntional Color Posters Inc (P-3771)*

Icpk Corporation ....D....... 310 830-8020
1130 W C St Wilmington (90744) *(P-13184)*

ICU MEDICAL, San Clemente *Also Called: Icu Medical Inc (P-10525)*

Icu Medical Inc (PA) ....B....... 949 366-2183
951 Calle Amanecer San Clemente (92673) *(P-10525)*

Icu Medical Sales Inc (HQ) ....D....... 949 366-2183
951 Calle Amanecer San Clemente (92673) *(P-10526)*

Icw Group Holdings Inc (PA) ....C....... 858 350-2400
15025 Innovation Dr San Diego (92128) *(P-14510)*

Icw Valencia LLC ....C....... 858 350-2600
11455 El Camino Real Ste 200 San Diego (92130) *(P-14665)*

ID Analytics LLC ....C....... 858 312-6200
10089 Willow Creek Rd Ste 120 San Diego (92131) *(P-16049)*

ID Supply ....E....... 714 728-6478
3183 Red Hill Ave Costa Mesa (92626) *(P-3769)*

ID&c, Brea *Also Called: Avery Products Corporation (P-3218)*

Idea, Brea *Also Called: Instrment Dsign Engrg Assoc In (P-9060)*

Idea Tooling and Engrg Inc ....D....... 310 608-7488
13915 S Main St Los Angeles (90061) *(P-7077)*

Ideal Mattress Company Inc ....E....... 619 595-0003
1901 Main St San Diego (92113) *(P-2852)*

Ideal Printing Company ....E....... 626 964-2019
17855 Maclaren St City Of Industry (91744) *(P-3588)*

Ideal Products Inc ....E....... 951 727-8600
4025 Garner Rd Riverside (92501) *(P-2955)*

Idealab (HQ) ....D....... 626 356-3654
130 W Union St Pasadena (91103) *(P-13780)*

Idealab Holdings LLC (PA) ....A....... 626 585-6900
130 W Union St Pasadena (91103) *(P-15031)*

Idemia America Corp ....C....... 310 884-7900
3150 E Ana St Compton (90221) *(P-5057)*

Identigraphix Inc ....E....... 909 468-4741
19866 Quiroz Ct Walnut (91789) *(P-15667)*

Identity Intlligence Group LLC ....C....... 626 522-7993
43454 Business Park Dr Temecula (92590) *(P-16742)*

Idex Health & Science LLC ....C....... 760 438-2131
2051 Palomar Airport Rd Ste 200 Carlsbad (92011) *(P-10319)*

Idiq, Temecula *Also Called: Identity Intlligence Group LLC (P-16742)*

Idirect Home Loans, San Diego *Also Called: Iserve Residential Lending LLC (P-14330)*

IDS Inc ....D....... 866 297-5757
20300 Ventura Blvd Ste 200 Woodland Hills (91364) *(P-11717)*

IDS Technology, Woodland Hills *Also Called: IDS Inc (P-11717)*

Idx Los Angeles LLC ....C....... 909 212-8333
5005 E Philadelphia St Ontario (91761) *(P-2981)*

IEC, Commerce *Also Called: Interstate Electric Co Inc (P-12458)*

Iecp, Oxnard *Also Called: Inclusive Edcatn Cmnty Prtnr I (P-18971)*

Iee, Van Nuys *Also Called: Industrial Elctrnic Engners In (P-7533)*

Ieee Computer Society, Los Alamitos *Also Called: Institute of Elec Elec Engners (P-19379)*

Iehp, Rancho Cucamonga *Also Called: Inland Empire Health Plan (P-14452)*

Ies, San Diego *Also Called: Ies Commercial Inc (P-625)*

Ies, Irvine *Also Called: Ies Commercial Inc (P-20349)*

Ies Commercial Inc ....C....... 858 210-4900
6885 Flanders Dr Ste A San Diego (92121) *(P-625)*

Ies Commercial Inc ....D....... 949 222-0320
9211 Irvine Blvd Irvine (92618) *(P-20349)*

Ies Engineering, Bakersfield *Also Called: Innovative Engrg Systems Inc (P-19614)*

Ifco Systems Us LLC ....D....... 909 484-4332
8950 Rochester Ave Ste 150 Rancho Cucamonga (91730) *(P-2720)*

Ifiber Optix Inc ....E....... 714 665-9796
14450 Chambers Rd Tustin (92780) *(P-5326)*

Ifit Inc ....A....... 909 335-2888
2220 Almond Ave Redlands (92374) *(P-11003)*

Igenomix Usa LLC ....E....... 818 919-1657
383 Van Ness Ave Ste 1605 Torrance (90501) *(P-10527)*

Ignite Health LLC (PA) ....D....... 949 861-3200
7535 Irvine Center Dr Ste 200 Irvine (92618) *(P-15547)*

Ignited LLC (PA) ....C....... 310 773-3100
111 Penn St El Segundo (90245) *(P-15548)*

Ignitenet, Irvine *Also Called: SMC Networks Inc (P-12438)*

Ignition Creative LLC ....D....... 310 315-6300
1201 W 5th St Ste T1100 Los Angeles (90017) *(P-17197)*

Igrad Inc ....E....... 858 705-2917
2163 Newcastle Ave Ste 100 Cardiff By The Sea (92007) *(P-16268)*

Ihealth Manufacturing Inc ....D....... 216 785-0107
15715 Arrow Hwy Irwindale (91706) *(P-12494)*

Iheartraves LLC ....F....... 626 628-6482
250 S Glendora Ave West Covina (91790) *(P-13919)*

Iherb LLC (PA) ....A....... 951 616-3600
22780 Harley Knox Blvd Unit 101 Perris (92570) *(P-13728)*

Iherb House Brands, Perris *Also Called: Iherb LLC (P-13728)*

Ihg Management (maryland) LLC ....D....... 310 642-7500
5985 W Century Blvd Los Angeles (90045) *(P-15203)*

Ihg Management (maryland) LLC ....D....... 213 688-7777
900 Wilshire Blvd Los Angeles (90017) *(P-15204)*

Ii-VI Aerospace & Defense Inc, Murrieta *Also Called: Coherent Aerospace & Defense Inc (P-9963)*

IJ Research Inc ....E....... 714 546-8522
2919 S Tech Center Dr Santa Ana (92705) *(P-9057)*

Ikano Communications Inc (PA) ....D....... 801 924-0900
9221 Corbin Ave Ste 260 Northridge (91324) *(P-16500)*

Ikanos Communications Inc (DH) ....F....... 858 587-1121
5775 Morehouse Dr San Diego (92121) *(P-8805)*

IKEA Purchasing Svcs US Inc ....C....... 818 841-3500
600 N San Fernando Blvd Burbank (91502) *(P-20040)*

Ikegami Mold Corp America ....F....... 619 858-6855
4025 Camino Del Rio S # 301 San Diego (92108) *(P-5058)*

Ikhana Aircraft Services, Murrieta *Also Called: Ikhana Group LLC (P-9716)*

Ikhana Group LLC ....C....... 951 600-0009
37260 Sky Canyon Dr Hngr 20 Murrieta (92563) *(P-9716)*

Ikonick LLC ....E....... 516 680-7765
705 W 9th St Apt 1404 Los Angeles (90015) *(P-3589)*

Ikrusher Inc ....D....... 626 256-3449
11818 Clark St Arcadia (91006) *(P-14115)*

IL Fornaio (america) LLC ....C....... 714 752-7052
16932 Valley View Ave Ste A La Mirada (90638) *(P-14015)*

Ilco Industries, Compton *Also Called: Ilco Industries Inc (P-6847)*

Ilco Industries Inc ....E....... 310 631-8655
1308 W Mahalo Pl Compton (90220) *(P-6847)*

Illah Sports Inc ....E....... 805 240-7790
1610 Fiske Pl Oxnard (93033) *(P-11004)*

Illume Agriculture LLC ....C....... 661 587-5198
9100 Ming Ave Ste 200 Bakersfield (93311) *(P-136)*

Illumina, San Diego *Also Called: Illumina Inc (P-10265)*

Illumina Inc ....E....... 800 809-4566
9885 Towne Centre Dr San Diego (92121) *(P-10264)*

Illumina Inc (PA) ....A....... 858 202-4500
5200 Illumina Way San Diego (92122) *(P-10265)*

Illumination Entertainment ....C....... 626 298-1879
2043 Colorado Ave Santa Monica (90404) *(P-17340)*

Illumnate Educatn Holdings Inc (PA) ....E....... 949 656-3133
6531 Irvine Center Dr Ste 100 Irvine (92618) *(P-16269)*

Ilts California, Vista *Also Called: International Lottery & Totalizator Systems Inc (P-16056)*

Ilts Delaware, Vista *Also Called: Interntnal Lttery Ttlztor Syst (P-16057)*

Im-Logstics An Ingram McRo Div, Irvine *Also Called: Ingram Micro Inc (P-12420)*

Image Apparel For Business Inc ....E....... 714 541-5247
1618 E Edinger Ave Santa Ana (92705) *(P-2174)*

Image Business Forms, El Segundo *Also Called: Ibftech Inc (P-15853)*

Image Micro Spare Parts Inc ....F....... 562 776-9808
7225 Oxford Way Commerce (90040) *(P-8145)*

Image Options (PA) ....D....... 949 586-7665
80 Icon Foothill Ranch (92610) *(P-15603)*

Image Options Painting & Dctg, Foothill Ranch *Also Called: Image Options (P-15603)*

Image Solutions, Torrance *Also Called: Image Solutions Apparel Inc (P-2175)*

Image Solutions Apparel Inc ....C....... 310 464-8991
19571 Magellan Dr Torrance (90502) *(P-2175)*

Image Source Inc (PA) ....C....... 310 477-0700
2110 Pontius Ave Los Angeles (90025) *(P-12995)*

Image Transfer, Valencia *Also Called: D C Shower Doors Inc (P-11480)*

Image X, Goleta *Also Called: Image-X Enterprises Inc (P-16050)*

Mergent email: customerrelations@mergent.com
1126

2024 Southern California
Business Directory and Buyers Guide

(P-0000) Products & Services Section entry number
(PA)=Parent Co (HQ)=Headquarters (DH)=Div Headquarters

Image-X Enterprises Inc ....F...... 805 964-3535
  6464 Hollister Ave Ste 7g Goleta (93117) *(P-16050)*

Imagegrid Inc ....E...... 949 852-1000
  5010 Campus Dr Newport Beach (92660) *(P-10372)*

Imagemover Inc ....F...... 818 485-8840
  13031 Bradley Ave Sylmar (91342) *(P-3590)*

Imagic ....D...... 818 333-1670
  2810 N Lima St Burbank (91504) *(P-3591)*

Imaginative Horizons Inc ....D...... 619 477-1176
  1889 National City Blvd National City (91950) *(P-17976)*

Imagine This, Irvine Also Called: Shye West Inc *(P-11157)*

Imaging Hlthcare Spcalists LLC ....C...... 619 229-2299
  6386 Alvarado Ct San Diego (92120) *(P-17669)*

IMC, Canoga Park Also Called: Azimc Investments Inc *(P-12233)*

IMC, Los Angeles Also Called: International Medical Corps *(P-19098)*

IMC Networks Corp (PA) ....E...... 949 465-3000
  25531 Commercentre Dr Ste 200 Lake Forest (92630) *(P-7496)*

Imcd Us LLC ....D...... 714 562-7660
  16050 Canary Ave La Mirada (90638) *(P-4133)*

Imcsd, San Diego Also Called: Integrated Microwave Corp *(P-9061)*

Imdex Technology Usa LLC ....E...... 805 540-2017
  179 Cross St San Luis Obispo (93401) *(P-10373)*

Imerys Minerals California Inc (HQ) ....D...... 805 736-1221
  2500 San Miguelito Rd Lompoc (93436) *(P-417)*

Imhoff & Associates PC ....D...... 310 691-2200
  12424 Wilshire Blvd Ste 770 Los Angeles (90025) *(P-18872)*

IMI CCI, Rcho Sta Marg Also Called: IMI Critical Engineering LLC *(P-6765)*

IMI Critical Engineering LLC (DH) ....B...... 949 858-1877
  22591 Avenida Empresa Rcho Sta Marg (92688) *(P-6765)*

Immco, El Monte Also Called: Industrial Machine & Mfg Co *(P-6032)*

IMMDEF, Los Angeles Also Called: Immigrant Defenders Law Center *(P-18873)*

Immigrant Defenders Law Center ....D...... 213 634-0999
  634 S Spring St Fl 10 Los Angeles (90014) *(P-18873)*

Immortals LLC ....D...... 310 554-8267
  11460 W Washington Blvd Los Angeles (90066) *(P-17372)*

Immport Therapeutics Inc ....F...... 949 679-4068
  1 Technology Dr Ste E309 Irvine (92618) *(P-10783)*

Immunalysis, Pomona Also Called: Alere San Diego Inc *(P-4265)*

Immunalysis, Pomona Also Called: Diagnostixx of California Corp *(P-10492)*

Immunalysis Corporation ....D...... 909 482-0840
  829 Towne Center Dr Pomona (91767) *(P-18553)*

Immunitybio Inc (PA) ....D...... 844 696-5235
  3530 John Hopkins Ct San Diego (92121) *(P-4322)*

Impac International, Ontario Also Called: LLC Walker West *(P-2984)*

Impac Mortgage, Irvine Also Called: Impac Mortgage Corp *(P-14328)*

Impac Mortgage Corp ....B...... 949 475-3600
  19500 Jamboree Rd Ste 100 Irvine (92612) *(P-14328)*

Impac Secured Assets Corp ....D...... 949 475-3600
  19500 Jamboree Rd Irvine (92612) *(P-14992)*

Impac Technologies, Costa Mesa Also Called: Impac Technologies Inc *(P-8524)*

Impac Technologies Inc ....E...... 714 427-2000
  3050 Red Hill Ave Costa Mesa (92626) *(P-8524)*

Impact Bearing, San Clemente Also Called: Clean Wave Management Inc *(P-7298)*

Impact Components A California Limited Partnership ....E...... 858 634-4800
  6010 Cornerstone Ct W Ste 200 San Diego (92121) *(P-12669)*

Impact LLC ....E...... 714 546-6000
  22521 Avenida Empresa Ste 107 Rcho Sta Marg (92688) *(P-9058)*

Impact Printing & Graphics ....E...... 909 614-1678
  15150 Sierra Bonita Ln Chino (91710) *(P-3592)*

Impact Project Management Inc ....E...... 760 747-6616
  2872 S Santa Fe Ave San Marcos (92069) *(P-8688)*

Impco, Santa Ana Also Called: Impco Technologies Inc *(P-9405)*

Impco Technologies Inc (HQ) ....C...... 714 656-1200
  3030 S Susan St Santa Ana (92704) *(P-9405)*

Impedimed Inc (HQ) ....E...... 760 585-2100
  5900 Pasteur Ct Ste 125 Carlsbad (92008) *(P-10528)*

Imperfect Foods Inc (HQ) ....D...... 510 595-6683
  351 Cheryl Ln Walnut (91789) *(P-1914)*

Imperfect Produce, Walnut Also Called: Imperfect Foods Inc *(P-1914)*

Imperial Bag & Paper Co LLC ....D...... 800 834-6248
  2825 Warner Ave Irvine (92606) *(P-13010)*

Imperial Cal Products Inc ....E...... 714 990-9100
  425 Apollo St Brea (92821) *(P-6523)*

Imperial Capital LLC (PA) ....D...... 310 246-3700
  10100 Santa Monica Blvd Ste 2400 Los Angeles (90067) *(P-14382)*

Imperial Care Center, Studio City Also Called: Longwood Management Corp *(P-18140)*

Imperial Coml Cooking Eqp, Corona Also Called: Spenuzza Inc *(P-7688)*

Imperial Convalescent, La Mirada Also Called: Life Care Centers America Inc *(P-17990)*

Imperial Crest Healthcare Ctr, Hawthorne Also Called: Longwood Management Corp *(P-17997)*

Imperial Irrigation District (PA) ....A...... 800 303-7756
  333 E Barioni Blvd Imperial (92251) *(P-12027)*

Imperial Irrigation District ....C...... 760 398-5811
  81600 58th Ave La Quinta (92253) *(P-12110)*

Imperial Marking Systems, Cerritos Also Called: Blc Wc Inc *(P-3738)*

Imperial Mfg Co, Duarte Also Called: Spenuzza Inc *(P-7687)*

Imperial Pipe Services LLC ....E...... 951 682-3307
  12375 Brown Ave Riverside (92509) *(P-5634)*

Imperial Printers (PA) ....F...... 760 352-4374
  430 W Main St El Centro (92243) *(P-3593)*

Imperial Printers Rocket Copy, El Centro Also Called: Imperial Printers *(P-3593)*

Imperial Rfrgn & Ice Mchs, Huntington Beach Also Called: Aire-Rite AC & Rfrgn LLC *(P-728)*

Imperial Rubber Products Inc ....E...... 909 393-0528
  5691 Gates St Chino (91710) *(P-7186)*

Imperial Toy LLC (PA) ....C...... 818 536-6500
  16641 Roscoe Pl North Hills (91343) *(P-10954)*

Imperial Valley Foods Inc ....B...... 760 203-1896
  1961 Buchanan Ave Calexico (92231) *(P-1371)*

Imperial Valley Press, El Centro Also Called: Associated Desert Newspaper *(P-3258)*

Imperial Valley Steel Company ....E...... 858 900-2011
  8516 La Jolla Shores Dr La Jolla (92037) *(P-6031)*

Imperial Western Products Inc A California Corporation (HQ) ....E...... 760 398-0815
  86600 Avenue 54 Coachella (92236) *(P-13408)*

Imperials Sand Dunes, Brea Also Called: Worldwide Envmtl Pdts Inc *(P-10170)*

Implant Direct, Westlake Village Also Called: Implant Direct Sybron Mfg LLC *(P-10747)*

Implant Direct Sybron Intl LLC (HQ) ....E...... 818 444-3000
  3050 E Hillcrest Dr Ste 100 Westlake Village (91362) *(P-10746)*

Implant Direct Sybron Mfg LLC ....C...... 818 444-3300
  3050 E Hillcrest Dr Westlake Village (91362) *(P-10747)*

Implantech Associates Inc ....E...... 805 289-1665
  6025 Nicolle St Ste B Ventura (93003) *(P-10670)*

Impo International LLC ....E...... 805 922-7753
  3510 Black Rd Santa Maria (93455) *(P-5276)*

Import, Vernon Also Called: Brentwood Appliances Inc *(P-8240)*

Import Direct, City Of Industry Also Called: Furniture America Cal Inc *(P-12281)*

Import Direct, Van Nuys Also Called: E & S International Entps Inc *(P-12630)*

Impresa Aerospace LLC ....C...... 310 354-1200
  344 W 157th St Gardena (90248) *(P-9717)*

Impress Communications Inc ....D...... 818 701-8800
  9320 Lurline Ave Chatsworth (91311) *(P-3594)*

Impressions Vanity Company (PA) ....E...... 844 881-0790
  17353 Derian Ave Irvine (92614) *(P-13961)*

Imprimisrx LLC ....D...... 844 446-6979
  1000 Aviara Dr Ste 220 Carlsbad (92011) *(P-4134)*

Impulse Amusement, Sun Valley Also Called: Impulse Industries Inc *(P-7591)*

Impulse Industries Inc ....E...... 818 767-4258
  9281 Borden Ave Sun Valley (91352) *(P-7591)*

Impulse Space Inc ....E...... 949 315-5540
  2651 Manhattan Beach Blvd Redondo Beach (90278) *(P-9894)*

Imri, Aliso Viejo Also Called: Information MGT Resources Inc *(P-16449)*

IMS, South El Monte Also Called: Interntnal Mdction Systems Ltd *(P-4138)*

IMS, Chula Vista Also Called: Integrated Marine Services Inc *(P-9839)*

IMS Electronics Recycling Inc ....C...... 858 679-1555
  12455 Kerran St Ste 300 Poway (92064) *(P-12171)*

IMS-Ess, Temecula Also Called: Electro-Support Systems Corp *(P-9037)*

IMS-Ess, Temecula Also Called: Ice Management Systems Inc *(P-9715)*

IMT Analytical, Goleta Also Called: Atomica Corp *(P-8771)*

In Montrose Wtr Sstnblity Svcs ....D...... 949 988-3500
  4 Park Plz Ste 790 Irvine (92614) *(P-20350)*

In Stepps Inc ....D...... 949 474-1493
  10 Skypark Circle, Suite 110 Irvine (92614) *(P-17860)*

A L P H A B E T I C

Employee Codes: A=Over 500 employees, B=251-500
C=101-250, D=51-100, E=20-50, F=10-19, G=1-9

2024 Southern California
Business Directory and Buyers Guide

© Mergent Inc. 1-800-342-5647

1127

In Win Development USA Inc .... E...... 909 348-0588
188 Brea Canyon Rd Walnut (91789) *(P-7475)*

In-Line Construction, Ramona *Also Called: In-Line Fence & Railing Co Inc (P-1162)*

In-Line Fence & Railing Co Inc ....E...... 760 789-0282
1307 Walnut St Ramona (92065) *(P-1162)*

In-Roads Creative Programs ....B...... 909 989-9944
9057 Arrow Rte Ste 120 Rancho Cucamonga (91730) *(P-19092)*

In-Roads Creative Programs ....B...... 909 947-9142
1951 E Saint Andrews Dr Ontario (91761) *(P-19093)*

Inari, Irvine *Also Called: Inari Medical Inc (P-10529)*

Inari Medical Inc (PA)..D...... **877 927-4747**
6001 Oak Cyn Ste 100 Irvine (92618) *(P-10529)*

Inbody, Cerritos *Also Called: Biospace Inc (P-19829)*

Inc Polycarbon, Valencia *Also Called: Sgl Technic LLC (P-5551)*

Inca One Corporation .... E...... 310 808-0001
1632 1/2 W 134th St Gardena (90249) *(P-8928)*

Inca Plastics Molding Co Inc .... F...... 760 246-8087
17129 Koala Rd Adelanto (92301) *(P-5059)*

Inca Plastics Molding Co Inc .... F...... 909 923-3235
948 E Belmont St Ontario (91761) *(P-5060)*

Incipio Group, Irvine *Also Called: Incipio Technologies Inc (P-7532)*

Incipio Technologies Inc (PA)...........................E...... **888 893-1638**
3347 Michelson Dr Ste 100 Irvine (92612) *(P-7532)*

Incircle LLC ....A...... 800 843-7477
44000 Winchester Rd Temecula (92590) *(P-16844)*

Inclinator of California, San Fernando *Also Called: TL Shield & Associates Inc (P-6967)*

Inclusion Services, Whittier *Also Called: Inclusion Services LLC (P-19094)*

Inclusion Services LLC ....C...... 562 945-2000
7255 Greenleaf Ave Ste 20 Whittier (90602) *(P-19094)*

Inclusive Edcatn Cmnty Prtnr I ....B...... 805 985-4808
2323 Roosevelt Blvd Apt 3 Oxnard (93035) *(P-18971)*

Incomnet Communications Corp ....D...... 949 251-8000
2801 Main St Irvine (92614) *(P-11888)*

Incotec, Mojave *Also Called: Innovative Coatings Technology Corporation (P-6711)*

Indel Engineering Inc .... E...... 562 594-0995
6400 E Marina Dr Long Beach (90803) *(P-9860)*

Independent, Santa Barbara *Also Called: Santa Barbara Independent Inc (P-3322)*

Independent Energy Solutions Inc .... E...... 760 752-9706
663 S Rancho Santa Fe Rd Ste 682 San Marcos (92078) *(P-5980)*

Independent Fincl Group LLC ....C...... 858 436-3180
12671 High Bluff Dr Ste 200 San Diego (92130) *(P-20184)*

Independent Forge Company .... E...... 714 997-7337
692 N Batavia St Orange (92868) *(P-6460)*

Independent Options Inc ....D...... 858 598-5260
5095 Murphy Canyon Rd San Diego (92123) *(P-19276)*

Independent Options Inc ....D...... 714 738-4991
2625 Sherwood Ave Fullerton (92831) *(P-19277)*

Indepndnt Asstd Lvng & Memory, Arcadia *Also Called: Arcadia Gardens MGT Corp (P-18080)*

Index Fasteners Inc (PA).....................................F...... **909 923-5002**
945 E Grevillea Ct Ontario (91761) *(P-12859)*

Index Fresh Inc (PA)...D...... **909 877-0999**
1250 Corona Pointe Ct Ste 401 Corona (92879) *(P-13330)*

India Tea Importers, Commerce *Also Called: Interntional Tea Importers Inc (P-1916)*

Indian Health Council Inc (PA)............................D...... **760 749-1410**
50100 Golsh Rd Valley Center (92082) *(P-17670)*

Indian Summer, Rancho Cucamonga *Also Called: Mizkan America Inc (P-1947)*

Indian Wells Golf Resort, Indian Wells *Also Called: Troon Golf LLC (P-20110)*

Indie, Aliso Viejo *Also Called: Indie Semiconductor Inc (P-8806)*

Indie LLC ....C...... 949 608-0854
32 Journey Ste 100 Aliso Viejo (92656) *(P-20351)*

Indie Semiconductor Inc (PA).............................E...... **949 608-0854**
32 Journey Ste 100 Aliso Viejo (92656) *(P-8806)*

Indie Source .... E...... 424 200-2027
940 Venice Blvd Venice (90291) *(P-2176)*

Indio Products Inc .... E...... 323 720-9117
5331 E Slauson Ave Commerce (90040) *(P-4611)*

Indio Products Inc (PA).......................................C...... **323 720-1188**
12910 Mulberry Dr Unit A Whittier (90602) *(P-12527)*

Indizen Optical Tech Amer LLC ....F...... 310 783-1533
2925 California St Ste 201 Torrance (90503) *(P-16051)*

Indorama Vntres Sstnble Sltion ....D...... 951 727-8318
11591 Etiwanda Ave Fontana (92337) *(P-3944)*

Indu-Electric North Amer Inc (PA)......................E...... **310 578-2144**
27756 Avenue Hopkins Valencia (91355) *(P-7379)*

Indus Technology Inc ....C...... 619 299-2555
2243 San Diego Ave Ste 200 San Diego (92110) *(P-19613)*

Induspac California Inc .... E...... 909 390-4422
1550 Champagne Ave Ontario (91761) *(P-3945)*

Industrial Battery Engrg Inc .... E...... 818 767-7067
9121 De Garmo Ave Sun Valley (91352) *(P-9151)*

Industrial Coatings Division, Huntington Beach *Also Called: PPG Industries Inc (P-4498)*

Industrial Coml Systems Inc ....C...... 760 300-4094
1165 Joshua Way Vista (92081) *(P-778)*

Industrial Components Div, Simi Valley *Also Called: Rexnord Industries LLC (P-7213)*

Industrial Data Communications .... E...... 661 589-4477
4000 Fruitvale Ave Ste 16 Bakersfield (93308) *(P-12791)*

Industrial Design Products Inc .... E...... 909 468-0693
2700 Pomona Blvd Pomona (91768) *(P-6993)*

Industrial Dynamics Co Ltd (PA).........................C...... **310 325-5633**
3100 Fujita St Torrance (90505) *(P-7241)*

Industrial Elctrnic Engners In ....D...... 818 787-0311
7723 Kester Ave Van Nuys (91405) *(P-7533)*

Industrial Fire Sprnklr Co Inc .... E...... 619 266-6030
3845 Imperial Ave San Diego (92113) *(P-7395)*

Industrial Gasket and Sup Co .... E...... 310 530-1771
23018 Normandie Ave Torrance (90502) *(P-4734)*

Industrial Janitor Service ....D...... 818 782-5658
221 N San Dimas Ave Ste 217 San Dimas (91773) *(P-15714)*

Industrial Machine & Mfg Co .... E...... 626 444-0181
2626 Seaman Ave El Monte (91733) *(P-6032)*

Industrial Medical Support Inc ....A...... 877 878-9185
3320 E Airport Way Long Beach (90806) *(P-18771)*

Industrial Metal Cleaning Co ....F...... 314 621-4209
339 Palm Ave Coronado (92118) *(P-5837)*

Industrial Metal Finishing Inc ....F...... 714 628-8808
1941 Petra Ln Placentia (92870) *(P-6628)*

Industrial Metal Supply Co, Irvine *Also Called: Norman Industrial Mtls Inc (P-12562)*

Industrial Metal Supply Co, Sun Valley *Also Called: Norman Industrial Mtls Inc (P-12563)*

Industrial Minerals Company, Bakersfield *Also Called: Geo Drilling Fluids Inc (P-13434)*

Industrial Parts Depot LLC (HQ)........................D...... **310 530-1900**
1550 Charles Willard St Carson (90746) *(P-12792)*

Industrial Sprockets Gears Inc .... E...... 323 233-7221
13650 Rosecrans Ave Santa Fe Springs (90670) *(P-7380)*

Industrial Stitchtech Inc ....C...... 818 361-6319
520 Library St San Fernando (91340) *(P-16845)*

Industrial Strength Corp ....F...... 760 795-1068
6115 Corte Del Cedro Carlsbad (92011) *(P-12963)*

Industrial Tctnics Brings Corp (DH).....................C...... **310 537-3750**
18301 S Santa Fe Ave E Rncho Dmngz (90221) *(P-7299)*

Industrial Tools Inc .... E...... 805 483-1111
1800 Avenue Of The Stars Los Angeles (90067) *(P-7242)*

Industrial Tube Company, Valencia *Also Called: Industrial Tube Company LLC (P-6778)*

Industrial Tube Company LLC ....D...... 661 295-4000
28150 Industry Dr Valencia (91355) *(P-6778)*

Industrial Valco, Compton *Also Called: Industrial Valco Inc (P-12860)*

Industrial Valco Inc (PA).....................................E...... **310 635-0711**
3135 E Ana St Compton (90221) *(P-12860)*

Industrial Wood Products Inc ....F...... 909 625-1247
5123 Brooks St Montclair (91763) *(P-13624)*

Industry Station, City Of Industry *Also Called: Southern California Gas Co (P-12097)*

Indyme Solutions LLC .... E...... 858 268-0717
8295 Aero Pl Ste 260 San Diego (92123) *(P-8614)*

Indyme Solutions LLC ....D...... 858 268-0717
8295 Aero Pl Ste 260 San Diego (92123) *(P-8615)*

Indyne Inc ....B...... 805 606-7225
1036 California Blvd Bldg 11013 Vandenberg Afb (93437) *(P-20293)*

Ineos, Carson *Also Called: Ineos Polypropylene LLC (P-3947)*

Ineos Composites Us LLC ....D...... 323 767-1300
6608 E 26th St Commerce (90040) *(P-3946)*

Ineos Polypropylene LLC .... E...... 310 847-8523
2384 E 223rd St Carson (90810) *(P-3947)*

Inertech, Monterey Park *Also Called: Inertech Supply Inc (P-4735)*

Inertech Supply Inc ....D..... 626 282-2000
641 Monterey Pass Rd Monterey Park (91754) *(P-4735)*

Inet, Cypress *Also Called: Inet Airport Systems Inc (P-9718)*

Inet Airport Systems Inc ....E..... 714 888-2700
5665 Corporate Ave Cypress (90630) *(P-9718)*

Infab LLC ....D..... 805 987-5255
1040 Avenida Acaso Camarillo (93012) *(P-10671)*

Infineon Tech Americas Corp ....A..... 951 375-6008
41915 Business Park Dr Temecula (92590) *(P-7534)*

Infineon Tech Americas Corp (HQ)...............................A..... 310 726-8200
101 N Pacific Coast Hwy El Segundo (90245) *(P-8807)*

Infineon Tech Americas Corp ....C..... 310 252-7116
1521 E Grand Ave El Segundo (90245) *(P-8808)*

Infineon Tech Americas Corp ....E..... 310 726-8000
233 Kansas St El Segundo (90245) *(P-8809)*

Infineon Tech Americas Corp ....A..... 310 726-8000
222 Kansas St El Segundo (90245) *(P-19781)*

Infinite Electronics Inc (HQ)..E..... **949 261-1920**
17792 Fitch Irvine (92614) *(P-9059)*

Infinite Electronics Intl Inc (DH).................................D..... **949 261-1920**
17792 Fitch Irvine (92614) *(P-8974)*

Infinite Engineering Inc ....F..... 714 534-4688
13682 Newhope St Garden Grove (92843) *(P-7871)*

Infinite Optics Inc ....E..... 714 557-2299
1712 Newport Cir Ste F Santa Ana (92705) *(P-10320)*

Infinite Technologies LLC ....C..... 786 408-7995
1667 N Batavia St Orange (92867) *(P-16052)*

Infinity Aerospace Inc (PA)..E..... **818 998-9811**
9060 Winnetka Ave Northridge (91324) *(P-9719)*

Infinity Plumbing Designs Inc ....B..... 951 737-4436
9182 Stellar Ct Corona (92883) *(P-779)*

Infinity Watch Corporation ....E..... 626 289-9878
21078 Commerce Point Dr Walnut (91789) *(P-11124)*

Inflight Entrmt & Connectivity, Irvine *Also Called: Thales Avionics Inc (P-9813)*

Inflight Warning Systems Inc ....F..... 714 993-9394
3940 Prospect Ave Ste P Yorba Linda (92886) *(P-9720)*

Infocast, Woodland Hills *Also Called: Information Forecast Inc (P-20185)*

Infocus Cnc Machining Inc ....E..... 714 979-1253
11245 Young River Ave Fountain Valley (92708) *(P-7872)*

Infomagnus LLC ....D..... 714 810-3430
5882 Bolsa Ave Ste 210 Huntington Beach (92649) *(P-16053)*

Infonet Services Corporation (DH)...............................A..... **310 335-2600**
2160 E Grand Ave El Segundo (90245) *(P-11889)*

Inform Solution Incorporated ....E..... 805 879-6000
201 Mentor Dr Santa Barbara (93111) *(P-16270)*

Informa Business Media Inc ....E..... 949 252-1146
16815 Von Karman Ave # 150 Irvine (92606) *(P-3457)*

Informa Research Services Inc (HQ)............................C..... **818 880-8877**
26565 Agoura Rd Ste 300 Calabasas (91302) *(P-19899)*

Information Forecast Inc ....E..... 818 888-4445
22144 Clarendon St Ste 280 Woodland Hills (91367) *(P-20185)*

Information MGT Resources Inc (PA)............................C..... **949 215-8889**
85 Argonaut Ste 215 Aliso Viejo (92656) *(P-16449)*

Information Systems, Orange *Also Called: St Joseph Hospital of Orange (P-18462)*

Informs, Anaheim *Also Called: Rush Business Forms Inc (P-14071)*

Informtion Intgrtion Group Inc ....E..... 818 956-3744
457 Palm Dr Ste 200 Glendale (91202) *(P-16271)*

Informtion Rfrral Fdrtion of L ....D..... 626 350-1841
526 W Las Tunas Dr San Gabriel (91776) *(P-15510)*

Infosend Inc (PA)...E..... **714 993-2690**
4240 E La Palma Ave Anaheim (92807) *(P-15680)*

Infospan ....A..... 949 260-9990
31878 Del Obispo St Ste 118 San Juan Capistrano (92675) *(P-20186)*

Infrared Dynamics Inc ....E..... 714 572-4050
3830 Prospect Ave Yorba Linda (92886) *(P-5981)*

Infraredvision Technology Corp ....D..... 805 686-8848
140 Industrial Way Buellton (93427) *(P-8810)*

Infusion Care, Long Beach *Also Called: Long Beach Medical Center (P-18334)*

Ingalls Conveyors Inc ....E..... 323 837-9900
1005 W Olympic Blvd Montebello (90640) *(P-6974)*

Ingardia Bros Produce Inc ....C..... 949 645-1365
700 S Hathaway St Santa Ana (92705) *(P-13331)*

Ingenu, San Diego *Also Called: Ingenu Inc (P-8525)*

Ingenu Inc (PA)..E
10301 Meanley Dr San Diego (92131) *(P-8525)*

Ingenue Inc ....D..... 323 726-8084
1111 W Olympic Blvd Montebello (90640) *(P-1245)*

Ingenuity Studios Intl Inc ....C..... 323 460-6096
941 N Highland Ave 2nd Fl Los Angeles (90038) *(P-16846)*

Ingersoll-Rand, City Of Industry *Also Called: Trane Technologies Company LLC (P-7293)*

Ingla Rubber Products, Bellflower *Also Called: Bryant Rubber Corp (P-4720)*

Inglewood Park Cemetery (PA)......................................C..... **310 412-6500**
720 E Florence Ave Inglewood (90301) *(P-14916)*

Ingram Micro Inc (HQ)...A..... **714 566-1000**
3351 Michelson Dr Ste 100 Irvine (92612) *(P-12420)*

Ingram Micro Services LLC ....D..... 714 566-1000
3351 Michelson Dr Ste 100 Irvine (92612) *(P-12421)*

Ingredients By Nature LLC ....E..... 909 230-6200
5555 Brooks St Montclair (91763) *(P-1915)*

Inhealth Technologies ....E..... 800 477-5969
1110 Mark Ave Carpinteria (93013) *(P-10672)*

Inhibrx, La Jolla *Also Called: Inhibrx Inc (P-4323)*

Inhibrx Inc (PA)...E..... **858 795-4220**
11025 N Torrey Pines Rd Ste 200 La Jolla (92037) *(P-4323)*

Initiative Media North America, Los Angeles *Also Called: Mediabrands Worldwide Inc (P-15557)*

Initium Aerospace LLC ....F..... 818 324-3684
4255 Ruffin Rd Ste 100 San Diego (92123) *(P-5656)*

Injen Technology Company Ltd ....E..... 909 839-0706
244 Pioneer Pl Pomona (91768) *(P-12757)*

Ink & Color Inc ....E..... 310 280-6060
5920 Bowcroft St Los Angeles (90016) *(P-3595)*

Ink Fx Corporation ....E..... 909 673-1950
513 S La Serena Dr Covina (91723) *(P-3770)*

Ink Spot Inc ....E..... 626 338-4500
9737 Bell Ranch Dr Santa Fe Springs (90670) *(P-3596)*

Ink Systems Inc (PA)...D..... **323 720-4000**
2311 S Eastern Ave Commerce (90040) *(P-4590)*

Inkovation Inc ....F..... 800 465-4174
13659 Excelsior Dr Santa Fe Springs (90670) *(P-3597)*

Inkwright LLC ....E..... 714 892-3300
5882 Research Dr Huntington Beach (92649) *(P-3598)*

Inland Cc Inc ....C..... 909 355-1318
7010 Wyndham Hill Dr Riverside (92506) *(P-1075)*

Inland Chrstn HM Fundation Inc ....C..... 909 395-9322
1950 S Mountain Ave Ofc Ontario (91762) *(P-17977)*

Inland Cnties Regional Ctr Inc (PA)...............................C..... **909 890-3000**
1365 S Waterman Ave San Bernardino (92408) *(P-19095)*

Inland Cnties Regional Ctr Inc ....E..... 951 826-2600
1500 Iowa Ave Ste 100 Riverside (92507) *(P-20041)*

Inland Cold Storage ....E..... 951 369-0230
2356 Fleetwood Dr Riverside (92509) *(P-1807)*

Inland Empire 66ers Bsbal CLB ....C..... 909 888-9922
280 Se St San Bernardino (92401) *(P-17373)*

Inland Empire Chptr-Ssction Cr ....D..... 512 478-9000
2210 E Route 66 Glendora (91740) *(P-19530)*

Inland Empire Foods Inc (PA)..E..... **951 682-8222**
5425 Wilson St Riverside (92509) *(P-1355)*

Inland Empire Health Plan (PA)......................................A..... **909 890-2000**
10801 6th St Ste 120 Rancho Cucamonga (91730) *(P-14452)*

Inland Empire Health Plan ....A..... 866 228-4347
805 W 2nd St Ste C San Bernardino (92410) *(P-14471)*

Inland Empire Heart Institute, San Bernardino *Also Called: St Bernardine Med Ctr Aux Inc (P-18458)*

Inland Empire Magazine, Temecula *Also Called: Inland Empire Media Group Inc (P-3362)*

Inland Empire Media Group Inc ....E..... 951 682-3026
36095 Monte De Oro Rd Temecula (92592) *(P-3362)*

Inland Empire Utlties Agcy A M (PA)..............................D..... **909 993-1600**
6075 Kimball Ave Chino (91708) *(P-12123)*

Inland Envelope Company ....D..... 909 622-2016
150 N Park Ave Pomona (91768) *(P-3211)*

Employee Codes: A=Over 500 employees, B=251-500
C=101-250, D=51-100, E=20-50, F=10-19, G=1-9

2024 Southern California
Business Directory and Buyers Guide

© Mergent Inc. 1-800-342-5647
1129

Inland Group, Anaheim *Also Called: Inland Litho LLC (P-3599)*

Inland Kenworth Inc (HQ) .... C....... 909 823-9955
9730 Cherry Ave Fontana (92335) *(P-12225)*

Inland Litho LLC .... D....... 714 993-6000
4305 E La Palma Ave Anaheim (92807) *(P-3599)*

Inland Metal Trading Inc .... F....... 833 396-0740
41187 Sandalwood Cir Murrieta (92562) *(P-6253)*

Inland Pacific Coatings Inc .... E....... 909 822-0594
3556 Lytle Creek Rd Lytle Creek (92358) *(P-6709)*

Inland Powder Coating Corp .... C....... 909 947-1122
1656 S Bon View Ave Ste F Ontario (91761) *(P-6710)*

Inland Regional Center, San Bernardino *Also Called: Inland Cnties Regional Ctr Inc (P-19095)*

Inland Regional Center, Riverside *Also Called: Inland Cnties Regional Ctr Inc (P-20041)*

Inland Sports Group, Menifee *Also Called: Tea Financial Services (P-12932)*

Inland Truss Inc (PA) .... D....... 951 300-1758
275 W Rider St Perris (92571) *(P-2701)*

Inland Valley Care & Rehab Ctr, Pomona *Also Called: Inland Valley Partners LLC (P-17861)*

Inland Valley Daily Bulletin, Monrovia *Also Called: Califrnia Nwspapers Ltd Partnr (P-3262)*

Inland Valley Daily Bulletin, Ontario *Also Called: Califrnia Nwspapers Ltd Partnr (P-3263)*

Inland Valley Hospice Co .... D....... 760 243-2501
19167 Us Highway 18 Ste 6 Apple Valley (92307) *(P-18086)*

Inland Valley Partners LLC .... C....... 909 623-7100
250 W Artesia St Pomona (91768) *(P-17861)*

Inland Vly Rgional Med Ctr Inc .... B....... 951 677-1111
36485 Inland Valley Dr Wildomar (92595) *(P-18290)*

Inline Plastics Inc .... E....... 909 923-1033
1950 S Baker Ave Ontario (91761) *(P-5061)*

Inlog Inc .... D....... 949 212-3867
6765 Westminster Blvd Ste 424 Westminster (92683) *(P-11772)*

Inmode Aesthetic Solutions, Irvine *Also Called: Invasix Inc (P-19848)*

Inmotion Entrmt Group LLC .... C....... 904 332-0459
3225 N Harbor Dr San Diego (92101) *(P-17341)*

Inn At Mssion San Juan Cpstran, San Juan Capistrano *Also Called: Marriott International Inc (P-15241)*

Innercool Therapies, San Diego *Also Called: Philips North America LLC (P-12635)*

Inners Tasks LLC .... E....... 951 225-9696
27708 Jefferson Ave Ste 201 Temecula (92590) *(P-7431)*

Innerspace Cases, North Hollywood *Also Called: Armored Group Inc (P-2708)*

Inno Tech Manufacturing Inc .... F....... 858 565-4556
10109 Carroll Canyon Rd San Diego (92131) *(P-7873)*

Innocean USA, Huntington Beach *Also Called: Innocean Wrldwide Americas LLC (P-15549)*

Innocean Wrldwide Americas LLC (HQ) .... C....... 714 861-5200
180 5th St Ste 200 Huntington Beach (92648) *(P-15549)*

Innocor West LLC .... B....... 909 307-3737
300 S Tippecanoe Ave 310 San Bernardino (92408) *(P-4768)*

Innophase, San Diego *Also Called: Innophase Inc (P-8811)*

Innophase Inc .... D....... 619 541-8280
5880 Oberlin Dr San Diego (92121) *(P-8811)*

Innov8v, Irvine *Also Called: Innovative Tech & Engrg Inc (P-7535)*

Innova Design Inc .... F....... 858 535-9389
13230 Evening Creek Dr S Ste 216 San Diego (92128) *(P-7176)*

Innova Electronics Corporation .... E....... 714 241-6800
17352 Von Karman Ave Irvine (92614) *(P-9406)*

Innovacon Inc .... D....... 858 805-8900
9975 Summers Ridge Rd San Diego (92121) *(P-4277)*

Innovasystems Intl LLC .... C....... 619 955-5890
850 Beech St Unit 1006 San Diego (92101) *(P-16054)*

Innovation Specialties .... C....... 888 827-2387
11869 Teale St Ste 302 Culver City (90230) *(P-16847)*

Innovations Building Svcs LLC .... D....... 323 787-6068
402 S Orange Ave Apt D Monterey Park (91755) *(P-15715)*

Innovative Biosciences Corp .... E....... 760 603-0772
1849 Diamond St San Marcos (92078) *(P-4422)*

Innovative Body Science, San Marcos *Also Called: Innovative Biosciences Corp (P-4422)*

Innovative Casework Mfg Inc .... E....... 714 890-9100
12261 Industry St Garden Grove (92841) *(P-11230)*

Innovative Cleaning Svcs LLC .... B....... 949 251-9188
44 Waterworks Way Irvine (92618) *(P-15716)*

Innovative Cnstr Solutions .... C....... 714 893-6366
575 Anton Blvd Ste 850 Costa Mesa (92626) *(P-20294)*

Innovative Coatings Technology Corporation .... C....... 661 824-8101
1347 Poole St 106 Mojave (93501) *(P-6711)*

Innovative Communities Inc (PA) .... D....... 760 690-5225
1282 Pacific Oaks Pl Escondido (92029) *(P-435)*

Innovative Control Systems Inc .... E....... 800 246-3469
20992 Bake Pkwy Ste 106 Lake Forest (92630) *(P-7662)*

Innovative Dialysis Partners Inc .... B....... 562 495-8075
1 World Trade Ctr Ste 2500 Long Beach (90831) *(P-14136)*

Innovative Displayworks Inc .... E....... 909 447-8254
8825 Boston Pl Rancho Cucamonga (91730) *(P-12457)*

Innovative Emergency Equipment .... E....... 951 222-2270
1616 Marlborough Ave Riverside (92507) *(P-17134)*

Innovative Engrg Systems Inc (PA) .... D....... 661 381-7800
8800 Crippen St Bakersfield (93311) *(P-19614)*

Innovative Integration Inc .... E....... 805 520-3300
741 Flynn Rd Camarillo (93012) *(P-10140)*

Innovative Metal Designs Inc .... E....... 714 799-6700
12691 Monarch St Garden Grove (92841) *(P-12244)*

Innovative Metal Inds Inc .... D....... 909 796-6200
1330 Riverview Dr San Bernardino (92408) *(P-6399)*

Innovative Organics Inc .... F....... 714 701-3900
4905 E Hunter Ave Anaheim (92807) *(P-4522)*

Innovative Placements Inc .... C....... 800 322-9796
12400 High Bluff Dr Ste 100 San Diego (92130) *(P-15854)*

Innovative Plastics Inc .... E....... 714 891-8800
5502 Buckingham Dr Huntington Beach (92649) *(P-4833)*

Innovative Product Brands Inc .... E....... 909 864-7477
7045 Palm Ave Highland (92346) *(P-10530)*

Innovative Skin Care, Burbank *Also Called: Science of Skincare LLC (P-13067)*

Innovative Stamping Inc .... E....... 310 537-6996
2068 E Gladwick St Compton (90220) *(P-6524)*

Innovative Systems, Compton *Also Called: Innovative Stamping Inc (P-6524)*

Innovative Tech & Engrg Inc .... E....... 949 955-2501
2691 Richter Ave Ste 124 Irvine (92606) *(P-7535)*

Innovative Vhcl Solutions LLC .... C....... 714 896-8267
5831 Research Dr Huntington Beach (92649) *(P-20352)*

Innovel Solutions Inc .... A....... 909 605-1446
5691 E Philadelphia St Ste 200 Ontario (91761) *(P-11773)*

Innovel Solutions Inc .... A....... 619 497-1123
960 Sherman St San Diego (92110) *(P-11774)*

Innovista Sensors, Westlake Village *Also Called: Carros Americas Inc (P-9013)*

Innovive LLC (PA) .... E....... 858 309-6620
10019 Waples Ct San Diego (92121) *(P-6818)*

Innsuites Hotels, San Diego *Also Called: Hampstead Lafayette Hotel LLC (P-15167)*

Inogen Inc (PA) .... C....... 805 562-0500
301 Coromar Dr Goleta (93117) *(P-10531)*

Inova Diagnostics Inc .... C....... 858 586-9900
9889 Willow Creek Rd San Diego (92131) *(P-4135)*

Inova Diagnostics Inc .... C....... 858 586-9900
9675 Businesspark Ave San Diego (92131) *(P-4278)*

Inova Diagnostics Inc (HQ) .... B....... 858 586-9900
9900 Old Grove Rd San Diego (92131) *(P-19847)*

Inova Labs Inc .... D....... 866 647-0691
9001 Spectrum Center Blvd Ste 200 San Diego (92123) *(P-10532)*

Inovativ Inc .... E....... 626 969-5300
1500 W Mckinley St Azusa (91702) *(P-5671)*

Inphi International Pte Ltd .... E....... 805 719-2300
112 S Lakeview Canyon Rd Westlake Village (91362) *(P-8812)*

Input 1 LLC .... C....... 818 340-0033
6200 Canoga Ave Ste 400 Woodland Hills (91367) *(P-14283)*

Input/Output Technology Inc .... E....... 661 257-1000
28415 Industry Dr Ste 520 Valencia (91355) *(P-7536)*

Inseat Solutions LLC .... E....... 562 447-1780
1871 Wright Ave La Verne (91750) *(P-8236)*

Insignia/Esg Ht Partners Inc (DH) .... B....... 310 765-2600
11150 Santa Monica Blvd Ste 220 Los Angeles (90025) *(P-14666)*

Insite Digestive Health Care .... E....... 626 817-2900
225 W Broadway Ste 350 Glendale (91204) *(P-17671)*

Insomniac, Calabasas *Also Called: Insomniac Inc (P-17342)*

Insomniac Inc .... C....... 323 874-7020
5023 Parkway Calabasas Calabasas (91302) *(P-17342)*

Mergent email: customerrelations@mergent.com
1130

2024 Southern California
Business Directory and Buyers Guide

(P-0000) Products & Services Section entry number
(PA)=Parent Co (HQ)=Headquarters (DH)=Div Headquarters

Insomniac Games Inc (PA) .... D 818 729-2400
2255 N Ontario St Ste 550 Burbank (91504) *(P-10955)*

Insparation Inc .... E 805 553-0820
11950 Hertz Ave Moorpark (93021) *(P-4423)*

Inspectorate America Corp .... C 800 424-0099
3401 Jack Northrop Ave Hawthorne (90250) *(P-16848)*

INSPECTORATE AMERICA CORPORATION, Hawthorne *Also Called: Inspectorate America Corp (P-16848)*

Inspire Energy, Santa Monica *Also Called: Inspire Energy Holdings LLC (P-12028)*

Inspire Energy Holdings LLC .... C 866 403-2620
3402 Pico Blvd Ste 300 Santa Monica (90405) *(P-12028)*

Inspired Flight, San Luis Obispo *Also Called: Inspired Flight Tech Inc (P-5923)*

Inspired Flight Tech Inc .... E 805 776-3640
225 Suburban Rd Ste A San Luis Obispo (93401) *(P-5923)*

Insta Graphic Systems, Cerritos *Also Called: Insta-Lettering Machine Co (P-2071)*

Insta-Lettering Machine Co (PA) .... D 562 404-3000
13925 166th St Cerritos (90703) *(P-2071)*

Instacure Healing Products .... E 818 222-9600
235 N Moorpark Rd Unit 2022 Thousand Oaks (91358) *(P-4136)*

Instant Checkmate, San Diego *Also Called: Instant Checkmate LLC (P-15511)*

Instant Checkmate LLC .... C 800 222-8985
375 Camino De La Reina Ste 400 San Diego (92108) *(P-15511)*

Instant Imprints Franchising .... F 858 642-4848
7310 Miramar Rd San Diego (92126) *(P-3600)*

Instant Tuck Inc .... E 310 955-8824
9663 Santa Monica Blvd Beverly Hills (90210) *(P-2472)*

Instant Web LLC .... C 562 658-2020
7300 Flores St Downey (90242) *(P-3601)*

Instantly Inc .... C 866 872-4006
16501 Ventura Blvd # 300 Encino (91436) *(P-19900)*

Institute For Applied Bhvior A (PA) .... C 310 649-0499
5601 W Slauson Ave Culver City (90230) *(P-17862)*

Institute For Applied Bhvior A .... D 818 341-1933
9221 Corbin Ave Northridge (91324) *(P-17863)*

Institute For Applied Bhvior A .... D 805 987-5886
2310 E Ponderosa Dr Ste 1 Camarillo (93010) *(P-17864)*

Institute For Bhvoral Hlth Inc .... B 909 289-1041
1905 Business Center Dr Ste 100 San Bernardino (92408) *(P-18697)*

Institute For Defense Analyses .... C 858 622-5439
4320 Westerra Ct San Diego (92121) *(P-19929)*

Institute of Elec Elec Engners .... D 714 821-8380
10662 Los Vaqueros Cir Los Alamitos (90720) *(P-19379)*

Instride, Los Angeles *Also Called: Attainment Holdco LLC (P-19390)*

Instrment Dsign Engrg Assoc In .... E 714 525-3302
2923 Saturn St Ste F Brea (92821) *(P-9060)*

Instrument Bearing Factory USA .... E 818 989-5052
19360 Rinaldi St Northridge (91326) *(P-6446)*

Instrument Control Services .... E 805 642-1999
6085 King Dr Unit 100 Ventura (93003) *(P-355)*

Instrumentation Tech Systems .... F 818 886-2034
11949 Wood Ranch Rd Granada Hills (91344) *(P-7537)*

Instruments Incorporated .... E 858 571-1111
7263 Engineer Rd Ste G San Diego (92111) *(P-9216)*

Instyler, Torrance *Also Called: Tre Milano LLC (P-11299)*

Insua Graphics Incorporated .... E 818 767-7007
9121 Glenoaks Blvd Sun Valley (91352) *(P-3602)*

Insul-Therm, Commerce *Also Called: Insul-Therm International Inc (P-12367)*

Insul-Therm International Inc (PA) .... E 323 728-0558
6651 E 26th St Commerce (90040) *(P-12367)*

Insultech, Santa Ana *Also Called: Insultech LLC (P-4612)*

Insultech LLC (PA) .... E 714 384-0506
3530 W Garry Ave Santa Ana (92704) *(P-4612)*

Insurance Company of West (HQ) .... D 858 350-2400
15025 Innovation Dr San Diego (92128) *(P-14602)*

Insurance Inc Southern Cal .... E 951 300-9333
3400 Central Ave Ste 220 Riverside (92506) *(P-14603)*

Insurance Journal, San Diego *Also Called: Wells Media Group Inc (P-18955)*

Insure Express Insurance Svc, Calabasas *Also Called: Cartel Marketing Inc (P-14572)*

Integer Holdings Corporation .... D 619 498-9448
8830 Siempre Viva Rd Ste 100 San Diego (92154) *(P-10533)*

Integra Lfscnces Holdings Corp .... E 609 529-9748
5955 Pacific Center Blvd San Diego (92121) *(P-10534)*

Integra Lifesciences, Carlsbad *Also Called: Seaspine Inc (P-10700)*

Integra Technologies Inc .... E 310 606-0855
321 Coral Cir El Segundo (90245) *(P-8813)*

Integral Aerospace LLC .... C 949 250-3123
2040 E Dyer Rd Santa Ana (92705) *(P-9721)*

Integral Engrg Fabrication Inc .... E 626 369-0958
520 Hofgaarden St City Of Industry (91744) *(P-6033)*

Integral Senior Living (PA) .... E 760 547-2863
2333 State St Ste 300 Carlsbad (92008) *(P-14717)*

Integrated Associates Inc .... C 858 412-6189
4010 Morena Blvd Ste 222 San Diego (92117) *(P-15855)*

Integrated Communications Inc .... E 310 851-8066
208 N Broadway Santa Ana (92701) *(P-3603)*

Integrated Energy Group LLC .... C 605 381-7859
3929 E Guasti Rd Ste F Ontario (91761) *(P-780)*

Integrated Energy Technologies Inc .... C 619 421-1151
1478 Santa Sierra Dr Chula Vista (91913) *(P-7300)*

Integrated Food Service, Gardena *Also Called: Lets Do Lunch (P-1934)*

INTEGRATED HEALTHCARE DELIVERY, Los Angeles *Also Called: Pih Health Good Samaritan Hosp (P-18378)*

Integrated Intermodal Svcs Inc .... D 909 355-4100
8600 Banana Ave Fontana (92335) *(P-16570)*

Integrated Magnetics, Culver City *Also Called: Magnet Sales & Mfg Co Inc (P-5381)*

Integrated Magnetics Inc .... E 310 391-7213
11250 Playa Ct Culver City (90230) *(P-8146)*

Integrated Marine Services Inc .... D 619 429-0300
2320 Main St Chula Vista (91911) *(P-9839)*

Integrated Media Tech Inc (PA) .... D 818 761-9770
832 N Victory Blvd Burbank (91502) *(P-16571)*

Integrated Mfg Solutions LLC .... E 760 599-4300
2590 Pioneer Ave Ste C Vista (92081) *(P-11231)*

Integrated Microwave Corp .... D 858 259-2600
11353 Sorrento Valley Rd San Diego (92121) *(P-9061)*

Integrated Parcel Network .... B 714 278-6100
11135 Rush St Ste A South El Monte (91733) *(P-11530)*

Integrated Procurement Tech (PA) .... D 805 682-0842
7230 Hollister Ave Goleta (93117) *(P-12908)*

Integrated Sign Associates .... E 619 579-2229
1160 Pioneer Way Ste M El Cajon (92020) *(P-11125)*

Integrated Tech Group Inc (PA) .... E 310 391-7213
11250 Playa Ct Culver City (90230) *(P-6864)*

Integrated Technical Services, Anaheim *Also Called: L3harris Interstate Elec Corp (P-10211)*

Integrity Mortgage Group .... D 858 225-5000
9747 Businesspark Ave San Diego (92131) *(P-14329)*

Integrity Rebar Placers .... C 951 696-6843
1345 Nandina Ave Perris (92571) *(P-1105)*

Integrted Crygnic Slutions LLC .... E 951 234-0899
2835 Progress Pl Escondido (92029) *(P-7243)*

Integrted Healthcare Dlvry Sys, Whittier *Also Called: Pih Health Inc (P-18376)*

Integrus LLC .... D 949 538-9211
14370 Myford Rd Ste 100 Irvine (92606) *(P-12384)*

Intelex Systems Inc .... D 818 992-2969
21900 Burbank Blvd Ste 3087 Woodland Hills (91367) *(P-16055)*

Intelicare Direct Llc .... D 858 299-3636
8885 Rio San Diego Dr San Diego (92108) *(P-15512)*

Intelius, San Diego *Also Called: Intelius LLC (P-15513)*

Intelius LLC .... C 888 245-1655
375 Camino De La Reina San Diego (92108) *(P-15513)*

Intell Set, Long Beach *Also Called: Intelsat US LLC (P-12008)*

Intellgard Inventory Solutions, San Diego *Also Called: Meps Real-Time Inc (P-10383)*

Intelligent Beauty LLC .... A 310 683-0940
2301 Rosecrans Ave Ste 5000 El Segundo (90245) *(P-14137)*

Intelligent Blends LP .... E 858 888-7937
5330 Eastgate Mall San Diego (92121) *(P-1421)*

Intelligent Cmpt Solutions Inc (PA) .... E 818 998-5805
8968 Fullbright Ave Chatsworth (91311) *(P-10205)*

Intelligent Technologies LLC .... C 858 458-1500
9454 Waples St San Diego (92121) *(P-8208)*

Intelliloan, Costa Mesa *Also Called: Metropolitan Home Mortgage Inc (P-14340)*

Employee Codes: A=Over 500 employees, B=251-500
C=101-250, D=51-100, E=20-50, F=10-19, G=1-9

2024 Southern California
Business Directory and Buyers Guide

© Mergent Inc. 1-800-342-5647

1131

A
L
P
H
A
B
E
T
I
C

Intellipower Inc .... D....... 714 921-1580
1746 N Saint Thomas Cir Orange (92865) *(P-12670)*

Intellisense Systems Inc .... C....... 310 320-1827
21041 S Western Ave Torrance (90501) *(P-9981)*

Intelsat US LLC .... C....... 310 525-5500
1600 Forbes Way Long Beach (90810) *(P-12008)*

Intense Lighting LLC .... D....... 714 630-9877
3340 E La Palma Ave Anaheim (92806) *(P-8317)*

Intention Financial Group, Irvine *Also Called: Mission Loans LLC (P-14342)*

Inter Community Hospital, Covina *Also Called: Emanate Health Medical Center (P-18256)*

Inter-Con Security Systems Inc (PA)........................ A....... 626 535-2200
210 S De Lacey Ave Pasadena (91105) *(P-16653)*

Inter-Packing Inc .... F....... 909 465-5555
12315 Colony Ave Chino (91710) *(P-4891)*

Interactive Display Solutions, Irvine *Also Called: Interctive Dsplay Slutions Inc (P-9063)*

Interactive Media Holdings Inc .... C....... 949 861-8888
2722 Michelson Dr Ste 100 Irvine (92612) *(P-15550)*

Intercare Therapy Inc .... C....... 323 866-1880
4221 Wilshire Blvd Ste 300a Los Angeles (90010) *(P-17865)*

Intercntnntal Los Angles Dwntw, Los Angeles *Also Called: Ihg Management (maryland) LLC (P-15204)*

Intercommunity Care Center, Long Beach *Also Called: Intercommunity Care Ctrs Inc (P-17978)*

Intercommunity Care Ctrs Inc .... C....... 562 427-8915
2626 Grand Ave Long Beach (90815) *(P-17978)*

Interconnect Solutions Co LLC (PA).......................... D....... 909 545-6140
17595 Mount Herrmann St Fountain Valley (92708) *(P-8209)*

Interconnect Solutions Co LLC .... D....... 661 295-0020
25358 Avenue Stanford Valencia (91355) *(P-9062)*

Interconnect Systems Intl LLC (DH).......................... D....... 805 482-2870
741 Flynn Rd Camarillo (93012) *(P-8814)*

Interconnect Systems, Inc., Camarillo *Also Called: Interconnect Systems Intl LLC (P-8814)*

Intercontinental Art, Compton *Also Called: Artboxx Framing Inc (P-11191)*

Intercontinental San Diego, San Diego *Also Called: Lfs Development LLC (P-15222)*

Interctive Dsplay Slutions Inc .... E....... 949 727-1959
490 Wald Irvine (92618) *(P-9063)*

Interdigital Inc .... E....... 858 210-4800
9276 Scranton Rd Ste 300 San Diego (92121) *(P-8526)*

INTERDIGITAL, INC., San Diego *Also Called: Interdigital Inc (P-8526)*

Interface Associates Inc .... C....... 949 448-7056
27721 La Paz Rd Laguna Niguel (92677) *(P-10535)*

Interface Catheter Solutions, Laguna Niguel *Also Called: Interface Associates Inc (P-10535)*

INTERFACE CHILDREN FAMILY SERV, Camarillo *Also Called: Interface Community (P-19096)*

Interface Community (PA)... D....... 805 485-6114
4001 Mission Oaks Blvd Ste I Camarillo (93012) *(P-19096)*

Interface Rehab Inc .... A....... 714 646-8300
774 S Placentia Ave Ste 200 Placentia (92870) *(P-17866)*

Interface Welding .... E....... 310 323-4944
20722 Belshaw Ave Carson (90746) *(P-17135)*

Interfaceflor LLC .... D....... 213 741-2139
1111 S Grand Ave Ste 103 Los Angeles (90015) *(P-2115)*

Interfaith Community Services, Escondido *Also Called: Interfaith Community Svcs Inc (P-19097)*

Interfaith Community Svcs Inc .... D....... 760 489-6380
250 N Ash St Escondido (92027) *(P-19097)*

Interglobal Waste MGT Inc .... D....... 805 388-1588
820 Calle Plano Camarillo (93012) *(P-10266)*

Intergro Rehab Service .... D....... 714 901-4200
13211 Foothill Blvd Santa Ana (92705) *(P-17867)*

Interhealth Services Inc (HQ)................................... C....... 562 698-0811
12401 Washington Blvd Whittier (90602) *(P-18618)*

Interim Healthcare Inc .... C....... 951 684-6111
7000 Indiana Ave Ste 107 Riverside (92506) *(P-18619)*

Interim Hlthcare San Diego LLC .... B....... 858 576-9501
5625 Ruffin Rd Ste 225 San Diego (92123) *(P-18620)*

Interim Services, Riverside *Also Called: Interim Healthcare Inc (P-18619)*

Interior Experts Gen Bldrs Inc .... D....... 909 203-4922
4534 Carter Ct Chino (91710) *(P-980)*

Interior Lgic Group Hldngs IV (PA)........................... D....... 800 959-8333
10 Bunsen Irvine (92618) *(P-559)*

Interior Logic Group HM Rmdlg, Irvine *Also Called: Interior Specialists Inc (P-1032)*

Interior Rmoval Specialist Inc .... C....... 323 357-6900
8990 Atlantic Ave South Gate (90280) *(P-1134)*

Interior Specialists Inc .... B....... 800 959-8333
18565 Jamboree Rd Ste 125 Irvine (92612) *(P-1032)*

Interior Specialists Inc .... B....... 909 983-5386
15822 Bernardo Center Dr Ste 1 San Diego (92127) *(P-16849)*

Interior Wood of San Diego .... F....... 619 295-6469
1215 W Nutmeg St San Diego (92101) *(P-2886)*

Interlink Inc .... D....... 714 905-7700
3845 E Coronado St Anaheim (92807) *(P-3604)*

Interlink Electronics Inc (PA)................................... E....... 805 484-8855
1 Jenner Ste 200 Irvine (92618) *(P-9064)*

Interlink Securities Corp .... D....... 818 992-6700
20750 Ventura Blvd Ste 300 Woodland Hills (91364) *(P-14383)*

Interlog Construction, Anaheim *Also Called: Interlog Corporation (P-9065)*

Interlog Corporation .... E....... 714 529-7808
1295 N Knollwood Cir Anaheim (92801) *(P-9065)*

Intermountain Specialty Eqp, La Palma *Also Called: Isec Incorporated (P-1016)*

Internal Services, Los Angeles *Also Called: County of Los Angeles (P-16003)*

Internal Services Department, Los Angeles *Also Called: County of Los Angeles (P-19764)*

Internal Services Department, Downey *Also Called: County of Los Angeles (P-20022)*

Internal Services Dept, Los Angeles *Also Called: County of Los Angeles (P-16807)*

International Academy of Fin (PA)............................. E....... 818 361-7724
13177 Foothill Blvd Sylmar (91342) *(P-4523)*

International Bay Clubs LLC (PA).............................. C....... 949 645-5000
1221 W Coast Hwy Ste 145 Newport Beach (92663) *(P-17490)*

International Bus Mchs Corp .... E....... 714 472-2237
600 Anton Blvd Ste 400 Costa Mesa (92626) *(P-7432)*

International Bus Mchs Corp .... A....... 818 553-8100
400 N Brand Blvd Fl 7 Glendale (91203) *(P-7433)*

INTERNATIONAL CHILDREN'S CHARI, Calabasas *Also Called: Help Children World Foundation (P-19088)*

International Coatings, Cerritos *Also Called: International Coatings Co Inc (P-4570)*

International Coatings Co Inc (PA)............................ E....... 562 926-1010
13929 166th St Cerritos (90703) *(P-4570)*

International Component Tech, Santa Ana *Also Called: Nivek Industries Inc (P-8272)*

International Consulting Unltd .... C....... 657 256-1761
10542 Calle Lee Los Alamitos (90720) *(P-5635)*

International Daily News Inc (PA).............................. E....... 323 265-1317
870 Monterey Pass Rd Monterey Park (91754) *(P-3288)*

International Die Casting Inc .... E....... 310 324-2278
515 E Airline Way Gardena (90248) *(P-5815)*

International E-Z Up Inc (PA).................................... D....... 800 457-4233
1900 2nd St Norco (92860) *(P-2506)*

International Energy Services USA Inc .... C....... 310 257-8222
3445 Kashiwa St Torrance (90505) *(P-19615)*

International Energy Svcs Co, Torrance *Also Called: International Energy Services USA Inc (P-19615)*

International Fmly Entrmt Inc (DH)............................ C....... 818 560-1000
3800 W Alameda Ave Burbank (91505) *(P-11996)*

International Iron Products, San Diego *Also Called: Price Industries Inc (P-5597)*

International Lottery & Totalizator Systems Inc ...... E....... 760 598-1655
2310 Cousteau Ct Vista (92081) *(P-16056)*

International Medical Corps (PA).............................. A....... 310 826-7800
12400 Wilshire Blvd Ste 1500 Los Angeles (90025) *(P-19098)*

International Merchandising, Beverly Hills *Also Called: Wme Img LLC (P-17384)*

International Mfg Tech Inc (DH)................................ D....... 619 544-7741
2798 Harbor Dr San Diego (92113) *(P-5591)*

International Paper, Santa Fe Springs *Also Called: International Paper Company (P-3049)*

International Paper, Carson *Also Called: International Paper Company (P-3050)*

International Paper, Compton *Also Called: International Paper Company (P-3051)*

International Paper, Ontario *Also Called: New-Indy Containerboard LLC (P-3055)*

International Paper, Santa Fe Springs *Also Called: International Paper Company (P-3111)*

International Paper Company .... D....... 714 776-6060
601 E Ball Rd Anaheim (92805) *(P-3048)*

International Paper Company .... E....... 562 692-9465
9211 Norwalk Blvd Santa Fe Springs (90670) *(P-3049)*

International Paper Company .... E....... 310 549-5525
1350 E 223rd St Carson (90745) *(P-3050)*

Mergent email: customerrelations@mergent.com
1132
2024 Southern California
Business Directory and Buyers Guide
(P-0000) Products & Services Section entry number
(PA)=Parent Co (HQ)=Headquarters (DH)=Div Headquarters

International Paper Company .... E...... 310 639-2310
19615 S Susana Rd Compton (90221) *(P-3051)*

International Paper Company .... E...... 323 946-6100
11211 Greenstone Ave Santa Fe Springs (90670) *(P-3111)*

International Paving Svcs Inc .... D...... 909 794-2101
1199 Opal Ave Mentone (92359) *(P-626)*

International Plating Svc LLC (PA).......................... E...... 619 454-2135
4045 Bonita Rd Ste 309 Bonita (91902) *(P-6629)*

International Precision Inc .... F...... 818 882-3933
9526 Vassar Ave Chatsworth (91311) *(P-7874)*

International Processing Corp (DH) .... E...... 310 458-1574
233 Wilshire Blvd Ste 310 Santa Monica (90401) *(P-1443)*

International Research Labs, Moorpark *Also Called: Lifetech Resources LLC (P-13051)*

International Rite-Way Pdts, Ontario *Also Called: AMD International Tech LLC (P-6185)*

International Rubber Pdts Inc (HQ).......................... D...... 909 947-1244
1035 Calle Amanecer San Clemente (92673) *(P-4769)*

International Seal Company, Santa Ana *Also Called: Freudenberg-Nok General Partnr (P-4728)*

International Sensor Tech .... E...... 949 452-9000
3 Whatney Ste 100 Irvine (92618) *(P-10374)*

International Skylights .... C...... 800 325-4355
1831 Ritchey St Santa Ana (92705) *(P-5316)*

International Technidyne Corp (DH) .... C...... 858 263-2300
6260 Sequence Dr San Diego (92121) *(P-10536)*

International Tranducer Corp .... C...... 805 683-2575
869 Ward Dr Santa Barbara (93111) *(P-10206)*

International Trnsp Svc LLC (PA)............................ C...... 562 435-7781
1281 Pier G Way Long Beach (90802) *(P-11641)*

International Vitamin Corp .... C...... 951 361-1120
1 Park Plz Ste 800 Irvine (92614) *(P-4137)*

International West Inc .... E...... 714 632-9190
1025 N Armando St Anaheim (92806) *(P-6254)*

International Wind Inc (PA)...................................... E...... 562 240-3963
137 N Joy St Corona (92879) *(P-9573)*

International Wood Products, San Diego *Also Called: Jeld-Wen Inc (P-2608)*

Internet Brands, El Segundo *Also Called: Mh Sub I LLC (P-15558)*

Internet Corp For Assgned Nmes (PA)..................C...... 310 823-9358
12025 Waterfront Dr Ste 300 Los Angeles (90094) *(P-16450)*

Internet Machines Corporation (PA)........................ D...... 818 575-2100
30501 Agoura Rd Ste 203 Agoura Hills (91301) *(P-7538)*

Interntional Color Posters Inc .... E...... 949 768-1005
8081 Orangethorpe Ave Buena Park (90621) *(P-3771)*

Interntional Photo Plates Corp .... E...... 805 496-5031
2641 Townsgate Rd Ste 100 Westlake Village (91361) *(P-6630)*

Interntional Tea Importers Inc (PA)........................ E...... 562 801-9600
2140 Davie Ave Commerce (90040) *(P-1916)*

Interntional Tech Systems Corp .... E...... 714 761-8886
10721 Walker St Cypress (90630) *(P-12671)*

Interntional Un Oper Engineers .... A...... 909 307-8700
1647 W Lugonia Ave Redlands (92374) *(P-19410)*

Interntional Un Oper Engineers .... A...... 619 295-3186
3935 Normal St San Diego (92103) *(P-19411)*

Interntnal Ch of Frsqare Gospl (PA)...................... D...... 714 701-1818
1910 W Sunset Blvd Los Angeles (90026) *(P-19502)*

Interntnal Cnnctors Cable Corp .... C...... 888 275-4422
2100 E Valencia Dr Ste D Fullerton (92831) *(P-8475)*

Interntnal Communications Corp .... E...... 951 934-0531
11801 Pierce St Fl 2 Riverside (92505) *(P-16451)*

Interntnal Desserts Delicacies (PA)...................... F...... 818 549-0056
4700 District Blvd Vernon (90058) *(P-1519)*

Interntnal Fndtion For Krea Un .... B...... 213 550-2182
3435 Wilshire Blvd Ste 480 Los Angeles (90010) *(P-19329)*

Interntnal Lttery Ttlztor Syst .... E...... 760 598-1655
2310 Cousteau Ct Vista (92081) *(P-16057)*

Interntnal Mdction Systems Ltd ....A...... 626 442-6757
1886 Santa Anita Ave South El Monte (91733) *(P-4138)*

Interntnal Plymr Solutions Inc .... E...... 949 458-3731
5 Studebaker Irvine (92618) *(P-6766)*

Interntnal Metallurgical Svcs .... F...... 310 645-7300
6371 Arizona Cir Los Angeles (90045) *(P-5838)*

Interntnal Strl Engineers Inc .... E...... 310 643-7310
11926 S La Cienega Blvd Hawthorne (90250) *(P-19616)*

Interntonal Thermoproducts Div, Santee *Also Called: Ds Fibertech Corp (P-7365)*

Interocean Industries Inc .... E...... 858 292-0808
9201 Isaac St Ste C Santee (92071) *(P-9982)*

Interocean Systems, Santee *Also Called: Interocean Industries Inc (P-9982)*

Interocean Systems LLC .... E...... 858 565-8400
9201 Isaac St Ste C Santee (92071) *(P-9983)*

Interplastic, Ontario *Also Called: North American Composites Co (P-3959)*

Interpore Cross Intl Inc (DH) .... D...... 949 453-3200
181 Technology Dr Irvine (92618) *(P-10673)*

Interscan Corporation .... E...... 805 823-8301
4590 Ish Dr Ste 110 Simi Valley (93063) *(P-10176)*

Interspace Battery Inc (PA).................................... E...... 626 813-1234
2009 W San Bernardino Rd West Covina (91790) *(P-5724)*

Interstate Cabinet Inc .... E...... 951 736-0777
1631 Pomona Rd Ste B Corona (92878) *(P-11232)*

Interstate Design Industry, Corona *Also Called: Interstate Cabinet Inc (P-11232)*

Interstate Electric Co Inc .... D...... 800 225-5432
2240 Yates Ave Commerce (90040) *(P-12458)*

Interstate Foods Inc .... E...... 310 635-2442
310 S Long Beach Blvd Compton (90221) *(P-13259)*

Interstate Meat Co Inc .... D...... 323 838-9400
6114 Scott Way Commerce (90040) *(P-7202)*

Interstate Mnroe McHy Sups Div, Huntington Beach *Also Called: Statco Engrg & Fabricators LLC (P-12825)*

Interstate Rhbltation Svcs LLC .... C...... 818 244-5656
333 E Glenoaks Blvd Ste 204 Glendale (91207) *(P-18698)*

Interstate Steel Center Co Inc .... E...... 323 583-0855
7001 S Alameda St Los Angeles (90001) *(P-5719)*

Intertek Pharmaceutical Svcs, San Diego *Also Called: Intertek USA Inc (P-19975)*

Intertek USA Inc .... D...... 858 558-2599
10420 Wateridge Cir San Diego (92121) *(P-19975)*

Intertrade Industries Ltd .... D...... 714 894-5566
14600 Hoover St Westminster (92683) *(P-5062)*

Interval House .... D...... 562 594-4555
6615 E Pacific Coast Hwy Ste 170 Long Beach (90803) *(P-19099)*

Interviewing Service Amer LLC (PA)...................... C...... 818 989-1044
15400 Sherman Way Ste 400 Van Nuys (91406) *(P-19901)*

Intervrsity Chrstn Fllwshp/Usa ....A...... 310 510-0015
Gallager&Apos;S Cove Avalon (90704) *(P-15436)*

Intevac Photonics Inc .... E...... 760 476-0339
5909 Sea Lion Pl Ste A Carlsbad (92010) *(P-10321)*

Intevac Vision Systems, Carlsbad *Also Called: Intevac Photonics Inc (P-10321)*

Intex Properties S Bay Corp (PA) .... D...... 310 549-5400
4001 Via Oro Ave Ste 210 Long Beach (90810) *(P-12930)*

Intex Recreation Corp .... D...... 310 549-5400
4001 Via Oro Ave Long Beach (90810) *(P-12285)*

Intex Recreation Corp .... C...... 310 549-5400
1665 Hughes Way Long Beach (90810) *(P-14667)*

INTEX RECREATION CORP, Long Beach *Also Called: Intex Recreation Corp (P-14667)*

Intimo Industry, Vernon *Also Called: Pjy LLC (P-2030)*

Intouch Health, Goleta *Also Called: Intouch Technologies Inc (P-19330)*

Intouch Technologies Inc (HQ)................................ C...... 805 562-8686
7402 Hollister Ave Goleta (93117) *(P-19330)*

Intra Aerospace LLC .... E...... 909 476-0343
10671 Civic Center Dr Rancho Cucamonga (91730) *(P-7875)*

Intra Storage Systems Inc .... E...... 714 373-2346
7100 Honold Cir Garden Grove (92841) *(P-6865)*

Intrepid Inv Bankers LLC ....A...... 310 478-9000
11755 Wilshire Blvd Ste 2200 Los Angeles (90025) *(P-15032)*

Intri-Plex Technologies Inc (HQ)............................ C...... 805 683-3414
751 S Kellogg Ave Goleta (93117) *(P-7876)*

Intuit Inc .... C...... 858 780-2846
7535 Torrey Santa Fe Rd San Diego (92129) *(P-16272)*

Intuit Inc .... B...... 858 215-8000
7545 Torrey Santa Fe Rd San Diego (92129) *(P-16273)*

Intuit Inc .... C...... 818 436-7800
21650 Oxnard St Ste 2200 Woodland Hills (91367) *(P-16274)*

Invapharm Inc .... E...... 909 757-1818
1320 W Mission Blvd Ontario (91762) *(P-14411)*

Invasix Inc .... D...... 855 418-5306
17 Hughes Irvine (92618) *(P-19848)*

A
L
P
H
A
B
E
T
I
C

Employee Codes: A=Over 500 employees, B=251-500
C=101-250, D=51-100, E=20-50, F=10-19, G=1-9

2024 Southern California
Business Directory and Buyers Guide

© Mergent Inc. 1-800-342-5647

1133

Inveco Inc .... E...... 949 378-3850
440 Fair Dr Ste 200 Costa Mesa (92626) *(P-6631)*

Invelop Inc .... E...... 818 772-2887
9711 Mason Ave Chatsworth (91311) *(P-6906)*

Invenios, Santa Barbara *Also Called: Picosys Incorporated (P-7124)*

Invenios LLC .... D...... 805 962-3333
320 N Nopal St Santa Barbara (93103) *(P-5343)*

Invenlux Corporation .... E...... 626 277-4163
168 Mason Way Ste B5 City Of Industry (91746) *(P-8815)*

Invensys Climate Controls, Long Beach *Also Called: Schneider Elc Buildings LLC (P-9252)*

Inventure Capital Corporation (PA) .... A...... 213 262-6903
429 Santa Monica Blvd Ste 450 Santa Monica (90401) *(P-15033)*

Inveserve Corporation .... D...... 626 458-3435
812 W Las Tunas Dr San Gabriel (91776) *(P-14814)*

Investment Enterprises Inc (PA) .... E...... 818 464-3800
8230 Haskell Ave Ste 8240 Van Nuys (91406) *(P-3772)*

Investors Business Daily Inc (HQ) .... C...... 800 831-2525
5900 Wilshire Blvd Ste 2950 Los Angeles (90036) *(P-3289)*

Invisble Prtection Systems Inc .... E...... 213 254-0463
8847 S Halldale Ave Los Angeles (90047) *(P-16275)*

Invision Networking LLC .... C...... 949 309-3441
333 City Blvd W Ste 1700 Orange (92868) *(P-16572)*

Invitation Homes Inc .... D...... 805 372-2900
680 E Colorado Blvd Pasadena (91101) *(P-14815)*

Invitrogen Ip Holdings Inc (DH) .... D...... 760 603-7200
5791 Van Allen Way Carlsbad (92008) *(P-10267)*

Inwesco Incorporated (PA) .... D...... 626 334-7115
746 N Coney Ave Azusa (91702) *(P-5618)*

INX Prints Inc .... D...... 949 660-9190
1802 Kettering Irvine (92614) *(P-2096)*

Io Semiconductor Incorporated .... E...... 858 362-4074
4795 Eastgate Mall San Diego (92121) *(P-8816)*

Iog Products LLC .... E...... 818 350-5077
9735 Lurline Ave Chatsworth (91311) *(P-8817)*

Iogear, Irvine *Also Called: Aten Technology Inc (P-12397)*

Ionis, Carlsbad *Also Called: Ionis Pharmaceuticals Inc (P-4141)*

Ionis Pharmaceuticals Inc .... E...... 760 603-3567
2282 Faraday Ave Carlsbad (92008) *(P-4139)*

Ionis Pharmaceuticals Inc .... D...... 760 931-9200
1896 Rutherford Rd Carlsbad (92008) *(P-4140)*

Ionis Pharmaceuticals Inc (PA) .... B...... 760 931-9200
2855 Gazelle Ct Carlsbad (92010) *(P-4141)*

Iosemi, San Diego *Also Called: Io Semiconductor Incorporated (P-8816)*

Iot Photochromics, Torrance *Also Called: Indizen Optical Tech Amer LLC (P-16051)*

Ip Corporation .... E...... 323 757-1801
12335 S Van Ness Ave Hawthorne (90250) *(P-3948)*

Ipayment Inc .... B...... 213 387-1353
3325 Wilshire Blvd Ste 535 Los Angeles (90010) *(P-16850)*

Ipb, Highland *Also Called: Innovative Product Brands Inc (P-10530)*

IPC Cal Flex Inc .... E...... 714 952-0373
13337 South St 307 Cerritos (90703) *(P-8689)*

IPC Healthcare Inc (DH) .... C...... 888 447-2362
4605 Lankershim Blvd Ste 617 North Hollywood (91602) *(P-17672)*

Ipd, Carson *Also Called: Industrial Parts Depot LLC (P-12792)*

Ipi Travel, San Diego *Also Called: Innovative Placements Inc (P-15854)*

Ipitek, Carlsbad *Also Called: Ipitek Inc (P-909)*

Ipitek Inc .... C...... 760 438-1010
2461 Impala Dr Carlsbad (92010) *(P-909)*

Ipolymer, Irvine *Also Called: Interntnal Plymr Solutions Inc (P-6766)*

Ipr Software, Encino *Also Called: Ipr Software Inc (P-16276)*

Ipr Software Inc .... E...... 310 499-0544
16501 Ventura Blvd Ste 424 Encino (91436) *(P-16276)*

Ips Corporation (HQ) .... C...... 310 898-3300
455 W Victoria St Compton (90220) *(P-4571)*

Ips Group Inc (PA) .... E...... 858 404-0607
7737 Kenamar Ct San Diego (92121) *(P-12009)*

Ips Industries Inc .... D...... 562 623-2555
12641 166th St Cerritos (90703) *(P-5063)*

Ipsos Otx Corporation (HQ) .... C...... 310 736-3400
300 Corporate Pointe Ste 500 Culver City (90230) *(P-19902)*

Ipt, Goleta *Also Called: Integrated Procurement Tech (P-12908)*

Ipt Holding Inc (PA) .... F...... 805 683-3414
751 S Kellogg Ave Goleta (93117) *(P-6525)*

Iq Cosmetics, El Segundo *Also Called: Intelligent Beauty LLC (P-14137)*

Iq Power Tools, Perris *Also Called: Jpl Global LLC (P-12773)*

Iq-Analog Corporation .... E...... 858 200-0388
12348 High Bluff Dr Ste 110 San Diego (92130) *(P-8818)*

Iqair North America Inc .... E...... 877 715-4247
14351 Firestone Blvd La Mirada (90638) *(P-7324)*

Iqd Frequency Products Inc .... E...... 408 250-1435
592 N Tercero Cir Palm Springs (92262) *(P-9066)*

Iqms LLC (DH) .... C...... 805 227-1122
2231 Wisteria Ln Paso Robles (93446) *(P-16277)*

Iqvia Inc (DH) .... D...... 866 267-4479
2601 Main St Ste 650 Irvine (92614) *(P-19903)*

Ircamera LLC .... E...... 805 965-9650
30 S Calle Cesar Chavez Santa Barbara (93103) *(P-10322)*

Irell & Manella LLP .... E...... 949 760-0991
840 Newport Center Dr Ste 400 Newport Beach (92660) *(P-18874)*

Irell & Manella LLP (PA) .... C...... 310 277-1010
1800 Avenue Of The Stars Ste 900 Los Angeles (90067) *(P-18875)*

Iris Group Inc .... C...... 760 431-1103
1675 Faraday Ave Carlsbad (92008) *(P-3773)*

Irise (PA) .... D...... 800 556-0399
2381 Rosecrans Ave Ste 100 El Segundo (90245) *(P-16058)*

Irish Communication Company (DH) .... D...... 626 288-6170
2649 Stingle Ave Rosemead (91770) *(P-675)*

Irish Construction (HQ) .... C...... 626 288-8530
2641 River Ave Rosemead (91770) *(P-676)*

Irish Interiors Inc .... C...... 562 344-1700
5511 Skylab Rd Ste 101 Huntington Beach (92647) *(P-9722)*

Irish Interiors Inc (HQ) .... C...... 949 559-0930
5511 Skylab Rd Ste 101 Huntington Beach (92647) *(P-9723)*

Irish Interiors Holdings Inc .... E...... 949 559-0930
1729 Apollo Ct Seal Beach (90740) *(P-9724)*

IRISH INTERIORS HOLDINGS, INC., Seal Beach *Also Called: Irish Interiors Holdings Inc (P-9724)*

Irish International .... C...... 949 559-0930
5511 Skylab Rd Huntington Beach (92647) *(P-9574)*

Irisys Inc .... D...... 858 623-1520
6828 Nancy Ridge Dr Ste 100 San Diego (92121) *(P-13047)*

Iron Beds of America, Los Angeles *Also Called: Wesley Allen Inc (P-2840)*

Iron Grip Barbell Company Inc .... D...... 714 850-6900
11377 Markon Dr Garden Grove (92841) *(P-11005)*

Iron Mountain Info MGT LLC .... D...... 818 848-9766
441 N Oak St Inglewood (90302) *(P-11775)*

Ironman Inc .... E...... 818 341-0980
20555 Superior St Chatsworth (91311) *(P-17087)*

Ironman Renewal LLC .... D...... 951 735-3710
2535 Anselmo Dr Corona (92879) *(P-17032)*

Ironwood Electric Inc .... E...... 714 630-2350
13 Ashton Mission Viejo (92692) *(P-9217)*

Ironwood Fabrication Inc .... F...... 714 576-7320
761 Monroe Way Placentia (92870) *(P-6461)*

Ironwood Packaging LLC .... E...... 909 581-0077
8975 Cottage Ave Rancho Cucamonga (91730) *(P-3153)*

Irp, San Clemente *Also Called: International Rubber Pdts Inc (P-4769)*

Irp Lax Hotel LLC .... C...... 310 645-4600
9750 Airport Blvd Los Angeles (90045) *(P-15205)*

Irriscape Construction Inc .... D...... 951 694-6936
20182 Carancho Rd Temecula (92590) *(P-195)*

Irrometer Company Inc .... F...... 951 682-9505
1425 Palmyrita Ave Riverside (92507) *(P-10375)*

Irvine APT Communities LP .... C...... 714 537-8500
13212 Magnolia St Ofc Garden Grove (92844) *(P-14718)*

Irvine APT Communities LP .... B...... 714 505-7181
100 Robinson Dr Tustin (92782) *(P-14719)*

Irvine APT Communities LP .... C...... 714 937-8900
299 N State College Blvd Orange (92868) *(P-14720)*

Irvine APT Communities LP .... C...... 949 854-4942
146 Berkeley Irvine (92612) *(P-14721)*

Irvine APT Communities LP (HQ).................................C....... 949 720-5600
110 Innovation Dr Irvine (92617) *(P-14722)*

Irvine APT Communities LP ....C....... 310 255-1221
1221 Ocean Ave Santa Monica (90401) *(P-14723)*

Irvine Biomedical Inc ....C....... 949 851-3053
2375 Morse Ave Irvine (92614) *(P-10537)*

Irvine Company Office Property, Newport Beach *Also Called: Irvine Eastgate Office II LLC (P-15014)*

Irvine Eastgate Office II LLC ....A....... 949 720-2000
550 Newport Center Dr Newport Beach (92660) *(P-15014)*

Irvine Electronics LLC ....D....... 949 250-0315
1601 Alton Pkwy Ste A Irvine (92606) *(P-8690)*

Irvine Electronics Inc, Irvine *Also Called: Irvine Electronics LLC (P-8690)*

Irvine Medical Center, Orange *Also Called: University California Irvine (P-18489)*

Irvine Ranch Water District ....C....... 949 453-5300
3512 Michelson Dr Irvine (92612) *(P-12124)*

Irvine Ranch Water District (PA).................................C....... 949 453-5300
15600 Sand Canyon Ave Irvine (92618) *(P-12125)*

Irvine Regional Hospital, Anaheim *Also Called: Tenet Healthsystem Medical Inc (P-18473)*

Irvine Scientific, Santa Ana *Also Called: Fujifilm Irvine Scientific Inc (P-4317)*

Irvine Sensors, Costa Mesa *Also Called: Isc8 Inc (P-9218)*

Irvine Sensors Corporation ....E....... 714 444-8700
3000 Airway Ave Ste A1 Costa Mesa (92626) *(P-8819)*

Irvine Technology Corporation ....C....... 714 445-2624
2850 Redhill Ave Ste 230 Santa Ana (92705) *(P-20353)*

Irwin Aviation Inc ....E....... 951 372-9555
225 Airport Cir Corona (92878) *(P-9725)*

Irwin Industries Inc ....A....... 704 457-5117
2301 Rosecrans Ave Ste 3185 El Segundo (90245) *(P-712)*

Irwin International Inc (PA).................................D....... 951 372-9555
225 Airport Cir Corona (92878) *(P-13906)*

Irwindale 6000, Irwindale *Also Called: Southern California Edison Co (P-12068)*

ISA, Van Nuys *Also Called: Interviewing Service Amer LLC (P-19901)*

Isaac Fair Corporation ....D....... 858 369-8000
3661 Valley Centre Dr San Diego (92130) *(P-16059)*

Isabell's Honey Farm, Burbank *Also Called: Honey Isabells Inc (P-92)*

Isabelle Handbag Inc ....E....... 323 277-9888
3155 Bandini Blvd Unit A Vernon (90058) *(P-5298)*

Isc8 Inc ....E....... 714 549-8211
151 Kalmus Dr Ste A203 Costa Mesa (92626) *(P-9218)*

ISE Corporation ....C....... 858 413-1720
12302 Kerran St Poway (92064) *(P-19849)*

Isec Incorporated ....C....... 858 279-9085
10105 Carroll Canyon Rd San Diego (92131) *(P-507)*

Isec Incorporated ....D....... 858 279-9085
5735 Kearny Villa Rd Ste 105 San Diego (92123) *(P-10095)*

Isec Incorporated ....C....... 714 761-5151
20 Centerpointe Dr Ste 140 La Palma (90623) *(P-1016)*

Iserve Residential Lending LLC ....D....... 858 486-4169
10920 Via Frontera Ste 520 San Diego (92127) *(P-14330)*

ISI Detention Contg Group Inc ....D....... 714 288-1770
577 N Batavia St Orange (92868) *(P-7877)*

Isiqalo LLC ....B....... 714 683-2820
5610 Daniels St Chino (91710) *(P-2072)*

Island Powder Coating ....E....... 626 279-2460
1830 Tyler Ave South El Monte (91733) *(P-6712)*

Island Products, Buena Park *Also Called: Island Snacks Inc (P-1544)*

Island Snacks Inc ....E....... 714 994-1228
7650 Stage Rd Buena Park (90621) *(P-1544)*

Isolatek International, San Bernardino *Also Called: United States Mineral Pdts Co (P-5559)*

Isolutecom Inc (PA).................................E....... 805 498-6259
9 Northam Ave Newbury Park (91320) *(P-16278)*

Isomedix Operations Inc ....D....... 951 694-9340
43425 Business Park Dr Temecula (92590) *(P-10674)*

Isomedix Operations Inc ....E....... 909 390-9942
1000 Sarah Pl Ontario (91761) *(P-10675)*

Isotis Orthobiologics Inc ....C....... 949 595-8710
2 Goodyear Ste A Irvine (92618) *(P-19850)*

Isotope Products Lab, Valencia *Also Called: Eckert Zegler Isotope Pdts Inc (P-10361)*

Isound, Torrance *Also Called: Dreamgear LLC (P-10949)*

Isovac Engineering Inc ....E....... 818 552-6200
614 Justin Ave Glendale (91201) *(P-16851)*

Ispace Inc ....C....... 310 563-3800
840 Apollo St Ste 100 El Segundo (90245) *(P-16573)*

Issac, Tustin *Also Called: Trellborg Sling Sltions US Inc (P-10619)*

Issac Medical Inc ....B....... 805 239-4284
2761 Walnut Ave Tustin (92780) *(P-10538)*

Ista Pharmaceuticals Inc ....B....... 949 788-6000
50 Technology Dr Irvine (92618) *(P-4142)*

ISU Petasys Corp ....B....... 818 833-5800
12930 Bradley Ave Sylmar (91342) *(P-8691)*

Isuzu North America Corp (HQ).................................C....... 714 935-9300
1400 S Douglass Rd Ste 100 Anaheim (92806) *(P-13781)*

Isuzu Truck Services, Santa Ana *Also Called: Toms Truck Center Inc (P-13837)*

It Campus, Vernon *Also Called: It Jeans Inc (P-2330)*

It Division Inc ....C....... 678 648-2709
9170 Irvine Center Dr Ste 200 Irvine (92618) *(P-19000)*

It Is Written, Riverside *Also Called: Adventist Media Center Inc (P-17309)*

It Jeans Inc ....E....... 323 588-2156
2425 E 38th St Vernon (90058) *(P-2330)*

It's Delish, North Hollywood *Also Called: Mave Enterprises Inc (P-1545)*

Itc, San Diego *Also Called: International Technidyne Corp (P-10536)*

Itc Nexus Holding Company, San Diego *Also Called: Accriva Dgnostics Holdings Inc (P-10414)*

Itc Sftware Slutions Group LLC (PA).................................E....... 877 248-2774
201 Sandpointe Ave Ste 305 Santa Ana (92707) *(P-16279)*

Itc Solutions & Services Group, Santa Ana *Also Called: Itc Sftware Slutions Group LLC (P-16279)*

ITD Arizona Inc ....D....... 323 722-8542
6737 E Washington Blvd Commerce (90040) *(P-12270)*

Itech, San Diego *Also Called: Intelligent Technologies LLC (P-8208)*

Itek Services Inc ....D....... 949 770-4835
25501 Arctic Ocean Dr Lake Forest (92630) *(P-16574)*

ITI Electro-Optic Corporation ....E....... 310 312-4526
1500 Olympia Blvd Ste 400 Los Angeles (90021) *(P-10141)*

ITI Electro-Optic Corporation (PA).................................E....... 310 445-8900
11500 W Olympic Blvd Ste 400 Los Angeles (90064) *(P-10142)*

Itochu Aviation Inc (DH).................................E....... 310 640-2770
222 N Pacific Coast Hwy Ste 2200 El Segundo (90245) *(P-12909)*

Itrex Group USA Corporation ....B....... 213 436-7785
120 Vantis Dr Ste 545 Aliso Viejo (92656) *(P-16060)*

Its, Granada Hills *Also Called: Instrumentation Tech Systems (P-7537)*

Itsco, Cypress *Also Called: Interntional Tech Systems Corp (P-12671)*

ITT Aerospace Controls LLC (HQ).................................D....... 315 568-7258
28150 Industry Dr Valencia (91355) *(P-9726)*

ITT Aerospace Controls LLC ....B....... 661 295-4000
28150 Industry Dr Valencia (91355) *(P-9727)*

ITT Cannon LLC ....C....... 714 557-4700
56 Technology Dr Irvine (92618) *(P-8183)*

ITT LLC ....D....... 562 908-4144
3951 Capitol Ave City Of Industry (90601) *(P-8184)*

ITW Global Tire Repair Inc ....D....... 805 489-0490
125 Venture Dr Ste 210 San Luis Obispo (93401) *(P-4698)*

ITW Space Bag, San Diego *Also Called: New West Products Inc (P-5113)*

Ivar's Displays, Ontario *Also Called: Ivars Display (P-2956)*

Ivars Display (PA).................................D....... 909 923-2761
2314 E Locust Ct Ontario (91761) *(P-2956)*

Ivera Medical LLC ....E....... 888 861-8228
10805 Rancho Bernardo Rd Ste 100 San Diego (92127) *(P-10539)*

Ivigen, Torrance *Also Called: Igenomix Usa LLC (P-10527)*

Ivy Enterprises Inc ....B....... 323 887-8661
5564 E 61st St Commerce (90040) *(P-20354)*

Iwco Direct - Downey, Downey *Also Called: Instant Web LLC (P-3601)*

Iwcus, Walnut *Also Called: Infinity Watch Corporation (P-11124)*

Iwerks Entertainment Inc ....D....... 661 678-1800
25040 Avenue Tibbitts Ste F Valencia (91355) *(P-9219)*

Iworks, Commerce *Also Called: Iworks Us Inc (P-8247)*

Iworks Us Inc ....D....... 323 278-8363
2501 S Malt Ave Commerce (90040) *(P-8247)*

Iws Predictive Technologies, Yorba Linda *Also Called: Inflight Warning Systems Inc (P-9720)*

Employee Codes: A=Over 500 employees, B=251-500
C=101-250, D=51-100, E=20-50, F=10-19, G=1-9

2024 Southern California
Business Directory and Buyers Guide

© Mergent Inc. 1-800-342-5647
1135

Ixi Technology, Yorba Linda *Also Called: Ixi Technology Inc* **(P-7434)**

Ixi Technology Inc .... E...... 714 221-5000
22705 Savi Ranch Pkwy Ste 200 Yorba Linda (92887) **(P-7434)**

Ixia .... E...... 818 871-1800
26701 Agoura Rd Calabasas (91302) **(P-10207)**

Ixia (HQ) .... B...... **818 871-1800**
26601 Agoura Rd Calabasas (91302) **(P-10208)**

Ixia Communications, Calabasas *Also Called: Ixia* **(P-10207)**

Ixys Intgrted Crcits Div AV In .... A...... 949 831-4622
145 Columbia Aliso Viejo (92656) **(P-8820)**

Ixys Long Beach Inc (DH) .... E...... **562 296-6584**
2500 Mira Mar Ave Long Beach (90815) **(P-8821)**

Iyuno-Sdi Group, Los Angeles *Also Called: SDI Media USA Inc* **(P-17219)**

Izola, San Diego *Also Called: Tallgrass Pictures LLC* **(P-1495)**

J-TECH .... C...... 310 533-6700
548 Amapola Ave Torrance (90501) **(P-8975)**

J & B Manufacturing Corp .... E...... 760 846-6316
2780 La Mirada Dr Ste C Vista (92081) **(P-5344)**

J & D Laboratories Inc .... B...... 760 734-6800
2710 Progress St Vista (92081) **(P-4002)**

J & F Design Inc .... D...... 323 526-4444
2042 Garfield Ave Commerce (90040) **(P-2331)**

J & F Machine Inc .... E...... 714 527-3499
6401 Global Dr Cypress (90630) **(P-7878)**

J & H Production .... E...... 323 261-6600
4481 S Santa Fe Ave Vernon (90058) **(P-2533)**

J & J Processing Inc .... E...... 562 926-2333
14715 Anson Ave Santa Fe Springs (90670) **(P-1777)**

J & J Snack Foods Corp Cal (HQ) .... C...... **323 581-0171**
5353 S Downey Rd Vernon (90058) **(P-1520)**

J & L Cstm Plstic Extrsons Inc .... E...... 626 442-0711
850 Lawson St City Of Industry (91748) **(P-5064)**

J & L Vineyards .... D...... 559 268-1627
1850 Ramada Dr Ste 3 Paso Robles (93446) **(P-32)**

J & M Products Inc .... D...... 818 837-0205
1647 Truman St San Fernando (91340) **(P-5924)**

J & M Realty Company (PA) .... C...... **949 261-2727**
41 Corporate Park Ste 240 Irvine (92606) **(P-14816)**

J & M Richman Corporation .... E...... 800 422-9646
1501 Beach St Montebello (90640) **(P-2515)**

J & M Sales Inc .... A...... 310 324-9962
15001 S Figueroa St Gardena (90248) **(P-13922)**

J & R Bottling and Distributing Inc .... E...... 323 724-4076
1130 S Vail Ave Montebello (90640) **(P-1698)**

J & R Concrete Products Inc .... E...... 951 943-5855
440 W Markham St Perris (92571) **(P-5421)**

J & R Machine Works .... E...... 661 945-8826
45420 60th St W Lancaster (93536) **(P-7879)**

J & S Inc .... E...... 310 719-7144
229 E Gardena Blvd Gardena (90248) **(P-7880)**

J A English II Inc .... E...... 760 598-5333
1333 Keystone Way Vista (92081) **(P-5065)**

J and D Stl Fbrication Repr LP .... F...... 805 928-9674
2360 Westgate Rd Santa Maria (93455) **(P-17088)**

J and K Manufacturing Inc .... E...... 562 630-8417
14701 Garfield Ave Paramount (90723) **(P-7881)**

J and L Industries, El Segundo *Also Called: Aerospace Engrg Support Corp* **(P-9606)**

J B Tool Inc .... F...... 714 993-7173
350 E Orangethorpe Ave Ste 6 Placentia (92870) **(P-7882)**

J B3d, Orange *Also Called: John Bishop Design Inc* **(P-11126)**

J C Entertainment Ltg Svcs Inc .... C...... 818 252-7481
5435 W San Fernando Rd Los Angeles (90039) **(P-17316)**

J C Ford Company (HQ) .... D...... 714 871-7361
901 S Leslie St La Habra (90631) **(P-7203)**

J C Precision, Rancho Cucamonga *Also Called: JCPM Inc* **(P-7886)**

J C Sales, Vernon *Also Called: Shims Bargain Inc* **(P-13561)**

J C Trimming Company Inc .... D...... 323 235-4458
3800 S Hill St Los Angeles (90037) **(P-2282)**

J Cloud Incorporated .... E...... 619 593-9020
2094 Willow Glen Dr El Cajon (92019) **(P-713)**

J Craig Venter Institute Inc (PA) .... B...... **301 795-7000**
4120 Capricorn Ln La Jolla (92037) **(P-19930)**

J Deluca Fish Company Inc .... E...... 310 221-6500
505 E Harry Bridges Blvd Wilmington (90744) **(P-1808)**

J F Duncan Industries Inc (PA) .... D...... **562 862-4269**
4380 Ayers Ave Vernon (90058) **(P-7663)**

J F I, Los Angeles *Also Called: Jet Fleet International Corp* **(P-15515)**

J Flying Machine Inc .... F...... 760 504-0323
701 S Andreasen Dr Ste C Escondido (92029) **(P-7883)**

J G Boswell Company .... B...... 661 327-7721
21101 Bear Mountain Blvd Bakersfield (93311) **(P-1)**

J G Boswell Company .... B...... 661 764-9000
36889 Hwy 58 Buttonwillow (93206) **(P-37)**

J Ginger Masonry LP (PA) .... B...... **951 688-5050**
8188 Lincoln Ave Ste 100 Riverside (92504) **(P-959)**

J H Textiles Inc .... E...... 323 585-4124
2301 E 55th St Vernon (90058) **(P-2141)**

J Hellman Frozen Foods Inc (PA) .... E...... **213 243-9105**
1601 E Olympic Blvd Ste 200 Los Angeles (90021) **(P-1372)**

J Heyri Inc .... E...... 323 588-1234
219 E 32nd St Los Angeles (90011) **(P-2245)**

J I Machine Company Inc .... E...... 858 695-1787
9720 Distribution Ave San Diego (92121) **(P-7884)**

J J Foil Company Inc .... E...... 714 998-9920
1734 W Sequoia Ave Orange (92868) **(P-3202)**

J L Cooper Electronics Inc .... E...... 310 322-9990
142 Arena St El Segundo (90245) **(P-9067)**

J L F/Lone Meadow, San Diego *Also Called: J L Furnishings LLC* **(P-2928)**

J L Fisher Inc .... D...... 818 846-8366
1000 W Isabel St Burbank (91506) **(P-15782)**

J L Furnishings LLC .... B...... 310 605-6600
1620 5th Ave Ste 400 San Diego (92101) **(P-2928)**

J L Industries, Commerce *Also Called: Samson Products Inc* **(P-2992)**

J L M C Inc .... E...... 909 947-2980
1944 S Bon View Ave Ontario (91761) **(P-6034)**

J L Shepherd and Assoc Inc .... E...... 818 898-2361
1010 Arroyo St San Fernando (91340) **(P-10376)**

J L Wingert Company .... D...... 714 379-5519
1298 N Blue Gum St Anaheim (92806) **(P-7664)**

J Lohr Winery Corporation .... E...... 805 239-8900
6169 Airport Rd Paso Robles (93446) **(P-1638)**

J M Smucker Company .... D...... 805 487-5483
800 Commercial Ave Oxnard (93030) **(P-1338)**

J M V B Inc .... D...... 714 288-9797
12118 Severn Way Riverside (92503) **(P-849)**

J Michelle of California .... F...... 323 585-8500
6409 Gayhart St Commerce (90040) **(P-2102)**

J Miller Canvas LLC .... E...... 714 641-0052
2429 S Birch St Santa Ana (92707) **(P-2126)**

J Miller Co Inc .... E...... 818 837-0181
11537 Bradley Ave San Fernando (91340) **(P-4736)**

J P H Consulting Inc .... C...... 323 934-5660
4515 Huntington Dr S Los Angeles (90032) **(P-17979)**

J P Sportswear, Lynwood *Also Called: Aaron Corporation* **(P-2297)**

J R C Industries Inc .... E...... 562 698-0171
11804 Wakeman St Santa Fe Springs (90670) **(P-3052)**

J R Industries, Westlake Village *Also Called: Jri Inc* **(P-12673)**

J Robert Scott Inc (PA) C
722 N La Cienega Blvd West Hollywood (90069) **(P-13082)**

J Spices, City Of Industry *Also Called: Cali-Nat Products Inc* **(P-1864)**

J T Walker Industries Inc .... A...... 909 481-1909
9322 Hyssop Dr Rancho Cucamonga (91730) **(P-6108)**

J Talley Corporation (PA) .... D...... **951 654-2123**
989 W 7th St San Jacinto (92582) **(P-6359)**

J W Floor Covering Inc (PA) .... C...... **858 536-8565**
9881 Carroll Centre Rd San Diego (92126) **(P-1033)**

J-M Manufacturing Company Inc .... D...... 909 822-3009
10990 Hemlock Ave Fontana (92337) **(P-3949)**

J-M Manufacturing Company Inc .... E...... 951 657-7400
23711 Rider St Perris (92570) **(P-3950)**

J-M Manufacturing Company Inc (PA) .... C...... **310 693-8200**
5200 W Century Blvd Los Angeles (90045) **(P-4850)**

J-Mark Company, Vista *Also Called: J-Mark Manufacturing Inc* **(P-6526)**

J-Mark Manufacturing Inc ....E....... 760 727-6956
2480 Coral St Vista (92081) *(P-6526)*

J. W. Floor Covering, San Diego *Also Called: J W Floor Covering Inc (P-1033)*

J&C Apparel ....E....... 323 490-8260
757 Towne Ave Unit B Los Angeles (90021) *(P-2168)*

J&E Conveyor Services, Eastvale *Also Called: Jose Perez (P-6975)*

J&G Berry Farms LLC ....C...... 831 750-9408
720 Rosemary Rd Santa Maria (93454) *(P-17)*

J&K Welding, Rancho Cucamonga *Also Called: Kathleen Brugger (P-17092)*

J&L Eppig Brewing LLC ....F....... 760 295-2009
1347 Keystone Way Ste C Vista (92081) *(P-1592)*

J&M Keystone Inc ....C...... 619 466-9876
2709 Via Orange Way Ste A Spring Valley (91978) *(P-1163)*

J&R Taylor Brothers Assoc Inc ....D....... 626 334-9301
16321 Arrow Hwy Irwindale (91706) *(P-1430)*

J&S Goodwin Inc (HQ)...D....... 714 956-4040
5753 E Santa Ana Canyon Rd Ste G-355 Anaheim (92807) *(P-6994)*

J&S Machine Works, Sylmar *Also Called: Kay & James Inc (P-7895)*

J2 Cloud Services LLC (HQ)...D....... 323 860-9200
700 S Flower St Fl 15 Los Angeles (90017) *(P-11917)*

J2 Global Communications, Santa Barbara *Also Called: Efaxcom (P-7524)*

JA Ferrari Print Imaging LLC ....F....... 619 295-8307
7515 Metropolitan Dr Ste 405 San Diego (92108) *(P-3605)*

Jabil Chad Automation, Anaheim *Also Called: Jabil Inc (P-8692)*

Jabil Inc ....E....... 714 938-0080
1565 S Sinclair St Anaheim (92806) *(P-8692)*

Jack Gosch Ford Inc ....D....... 951 658-3181
150 Carriage Cir Hemet (92545) *(P-13782)*

Jack In Box Inc (PA)..A....... 858 571-2121
9357 Spectrum Center Blvd San Diego (92123) *(P-14016)*

Jack In The Box, San Diego *Also Called: Jack In Box Inc (P-14016)*

Jack J Engel Manufacturing Inc ....E....... 818 767-6220
11641 Pendleton St Sun Valley (91352) *(P-9220)*

Jack Jones Trucking Inc ....D....... 909 456-2500
1090 E Belmont St Ontario (91761) *(P-11492)*

Jack Pwell Chrysler - Ddge Inc ....D....... 760 745-2880
1625 Auto Park Way Escondido (92029) *(P-13783)*

Jack Pwell Chrysler Ddge Jeep, Escondido *Also Called: Jack Pwell Chrysler - Ddge Inc (P-13783)*

Jack Rubin & Sons Inc (PA).......................................E....... 310 635-5407
13103 S Alameda St Compton (90222) *(P-12554)*

Jack's Disposal Inc, San Bernardino *Also Called: Burrtec Waste Industries Inc (P-12161)*

Jackie Robinson Family YMCA, San Diego *Also Called: YMCA of San Diego County (P-19485)*

Jackoway Tyrman Wrthmer Asten ....D....... 310 553-0305
1925 Century Park E 2nd Fl Los Angeles (90067) *(P-18876)*

Jacks Candy, Los Angeles *Also Called: Consolidated Svc Distrs Inc (P-13267)*

Jacksam Corp Blackout, Newport Beach *Also Called: Jacksam Corporation (P-7350)*

Jacksam Corporation ....E....... 800 605-3580
4440 Von Karman Ave Ste 220 Newport Beach (92660) *(P-7350)*

Jackson & Blanc ....C...... 858 831-7900
7929 Arjons Dr San Diego (92126) *(P-781)*

Jackson Engineering Co Inc ....E....... 818 886-9567
9411 Winnetka Ave # A Chatsworth (91311) *(P-8099)*

Jackson Family Wines Inc ....E....... 805 938-7300
5475 Chardonnay Ln Santa Maria (93454) *(P-1639)*

Jackson Manufacturing LLC ....F....... 213 399-9300
3515 W Washington Blvd Los Angeles (90018) *(P-1339)*

Jacmar Companies, The, Alhambra *Also Called: Pacific Ventures Ltd (P-20076)*

Jaco Engineering ....E....... 714 991-1680
879 S East St Anaheim (92805) *(P-7885)*

Jacobellis, Burbank *Also Called: V J Provision Inc (P-1206)*

Jacobs Atcs Fema A Joint Ventr ....D....... 571 218-1115
155 N Lake Ave Fl 5 Pasadena (91101) *(P-19617)*

Jacobs Civil Inc ....C...... 310 847-2500
1500 Hughes Way Ste B400 Long Beach (90810) *(P-19618)*

Jacobs Engineering Company ....A....... 626 449-2171
1111 S Arroyo Pkwy Pasadena (91105) *(P-19619)*

Jacobs Engineering Group Inc ....D....... 949 224-7500
2600 Michelson Dr Ste 500 Irvine (92612) *(P-19620)*

Jacobs Engineering Group Inc ....D....... 626 578-3500
1111 S Arroyo Pkwy Pasadena (91105) *(P-19621)*

Jacobs Engineering Inc (DH).....................................C...... 626 578-3500
155 N Lake Ave Pasadena (91101) *(P-19622)*

Jacobs Government Services Co ....C...... 949 224-7500
2600 Michelson Dr Ste 500 Irvine (92612) *(P-19623)*

Jacobs International Ltd Inc ....B...... 626 578-3500
155 N Lake Ave Ste 800 Pasadena (91101) *(P-19624)*

Jacobs Project Management Co ....D....... 949 224-7695
2600 Michelson Dr Ste 500 Irvine (92612) *(P-19625)*

Jacobson Plastics Inc ....D....... 562 433-4911
1401 Freeman Ave Long Beach (90804) *(P-5066)*

Jacoby & Meyers Attys LLP ....D....... 310 312-3300
10900 Wilshire Blvd Ste 930 Los Angeles (90024) *(P-18877)*

Jacuzzi Brands LLC ....E....... 909 606-1416
14525 Monte Vista Ave Chino (91710) *(P-11233)*

Jacuzzi Inc (DH)..C...... 909 606-7733
17872 Gillette Ave Ste 300 Irvine (92614) *(P-7665)*

Jacuzzi Outdoor Products, Irvine *Also Called: Jacuzzi Inc (P-7665)*

Jacuzzi Products Co (DH)..C...... 909 606-1416
13925 City Center Dr Ste 200 Chino Hills (91709) *(P-4916)*

Jacuzzi Products Co ....B...... 909 548-7732
14525 Monte Vista Ave Chino (91710) *(P-4917)*

Jada Group Inc (DH)..E....... 626 810-8382
18521 Railroad St City Of Industry (91748) *(P-10956)*

Jada Toys, City Of Industry *Also Called: Jada Group Inc (P-10956)*

Jade Products, Brea *Also Called: Jade Range LLC (P-8218)*

Jade Range LLC ....C...... 714 961-2400
2650 Orbiter St Brea (92821) *(P-8218)*

Jae Electronics Inc (HQ)..E....... 949 753-2600
142 Technology Dr Ste 100 Irvine (92618) *(P-12672)*

Jafra Cosmetics, Westlake Village *Also Called: Jafra Cosmetics Intl Inc (P-14138)*

Jafra Cosmetics Intl Inc (DH)....................................D....... 805 449-3000
1 Baxter Way Ste 150 Westlake Village (91362) *(P-14138)*

Jag Professional Services Inc ....C...... 310 945-5648
2008 Walnut Ave Manhattan Beach (90266) *(P-20355)*

Jake Hey Incorporated ....C...... 323 856-5280
257 S Lake St Burbank (91502) *(P-16761)*

Jakks, Santa Monica *Also Called: Jakks Pacific Inc (P-10957)*

Jakks Pacific Inc (PA)...D....... 424 268-9444
2951 28th St Santa Monica (90405) *(P-10957)*

Jakks Pacific Inc ....E....... 909 594-7771
21749 Baker Pkwy Walnut (91789) *(P-10958)*

Jakov Dulcich and Sons LLC ....C...... 661 792-6360
31956 Peterson Rd Mc Farland (93250) *(P-33)*

Jal Avionet USA (HQ)...E....... 310 606-1000
300 Continental Blvd # 190 El Segundo (90245) *(P-12422)*

Jam City Inc (PA)...E....... 310 205-4800
3562 Eastham Dr Culver City (90232) *(P-13973)*

Jam City Inc ....D....... 804 920-8760
2255 N Ontario St Burbank (91504) *(P-16280)*

Jamboree Management, Laguna Hills *Also Called: Jamboree Realty Corp (P-14817)*

Jamboree Realty Corp (PA)..C...... 949 380-0300
22982 Mill Creek Dr Laguna Hills (92653) *(P-14817)*

James Allison Estates & Homes ....C...... 866 463-5780
1902 Wright Pl Carlsbad (92008) *(P-436)*

James G Meyers & Associates ....E....... 858 622-2165
4353 La Jolla Village Dr Ste 180 San Diego (92122) *(P-17855)*

James H Cowan & Associates Inc ....D....... 310 457-2574
5126 Clareton Dr Ste 200 Agoura Hills (91301) *(P-196)*

James Hardie Building Pdts Inc ....C...... 909 355-6500
10901 Elm Ave Fontana (92337) *(P-12333)*

James Hardie Trading Co Inc ....C...... 949 582-2378
26300 La Alameda Ste 400 Mission Viejo (92691) *(P-4672)*

James Jones Company ....A....... 909 418-2558
1470 S Vintage Ave Ontario (91761) *(P-6767)*

James Litho, Ontario *Also Called: Eclipse Prtg & Graphics LLC (P-3568)*

James M Lally Do ....D....... 909 464-8600
5451 Walnut Ave Chino (91710) *(P-17673)*

James Magna Ltd ....F....... 909 391-2025
8782 Lanyard Ct Rancho Cucamonga (91730) *(P-17043)*

Employee Codes: A=Over 500 employees, B=251-500
C=101-250, D=51-100, E=20-50, F=10-19, G=1-9

2024 Southern California
Business Directory and Buyers Guide

© Mergent Inc. 1-800-342-5647
1137

James Metals, Riverside *Also Called: Harbor Pipe and Steel Inc (P-12553)*

James R Gldwell Dntl Crmics In (PA)..................................A...... **949 440-2600**
    4141 Macarthur Blvd Newport Beach (92660) *(P-18570)*

James Rebecca Prouty Entps Inc............................D...... 951 292-9777
    43980 Margarita Rd Ste 102 Temecula (92592) *(P-18621)*

James Tobin Cellars Inc............................E...... 805 239-2204
    8950 Union Rd Paso Robles (93446) *(P-1640)*

Jameson Inn, North Hollywood *Also Called: Park Management Group LLC (P-15298)*

Jan-Al Cases, Los Angeles *Also Called: Jan-Al Innerprizes Inc (P-5290)*

Jan-Al Innerprizes Inc............................E...... 323 260-7212
    3339 Union Pacific Ave Los Angeles (90023) *(P-5290)*

Jan-Kens Enameling Company Inc............................E...... 626 358-1849
    715 E Cypress Ave Monrovia (91016) *(P-6713)*

Janco Corporation............................C...... 818 361-3366
    13955 Balboa Blvd Rancho Cascades (91342) *(P-9068)*

Jandy Pool Products, Carlsbad *Also Called: Zodiac Pool Systems LLC (P-7698)*

Janin............................C...... 323 564-0995
    10031 Hunt Ave South Gate (90280) *(P-2332)*

Jano Graphics, Oxnard *Also Called: National Graphics LLC (P-3642)*

Jans Enterprises Corporation............................E...... 626 575-2000
    4181 Temple City Blvd Ste A El Monte (91731) *(P-13371)*

Jans Towing Inc............................C...... 909 596-9060
    134 N Valencia Ave Glendora (91741) *(P-17057)*

Jansen Ornamental Supply Co............................E...... 626 442-0271
    10926 Schmidt Rd El Monte (91733) *(P-6360)*

Janssen Research & Dev LLC............................C...... 858 450-2000
    3210 Merryfield Row San Diego (92121) *(P-4143)*

Janus Et Cie (PA)............................C...... **310 601-2958**
    12310 Greenstone Ave Santa Fe Springs (90670) *(P-12286)*

Janux Therapeutics Inc............................E...... 858 751-4493
    10955 Vista Sorrento Pkwy Ste 300 San Diego (92130) *(P-4144)*

Jariet Technologies Inc............................E...... 310 698-1001
    103 W Torrance Blvd Redondo Beach (90277) *(P-9984)*

Jarrow Formulas Inc (PA)............................D...... **310 204-6936**
    15233 Ventura Blvd Fl 900 Sherman Oaks (91403) *(P-13048)*

Jarrow Industries LLC (PA)............................D...... **562 906-1919**
    12246 Hawkins St Santa Fe Springs (90670) *(P-4145)*

Jarrow Industries LLC............................E...... 562 631-9330
    12342 Hawkins St Santa Fe Springs (90670) *(P-4146)*

Jarrow Industries LLC............................E...... 562 631-9330
    10226 Palm Dr Santa Fe Springs (90670) *(P-4147)*

Jarrow Industries LLC............................E...... 562 631-9330
    12328 Hawkins St Santa Fe Springs (90670) *(P-4148)*

Jason Incorporated............................E...... 562 921-9821
    13006 Philadelphia St Ste 305 Whittier (90601) *(P-5542)*

Jason Markk Inc (PA)............................E...... **213 687-7060**
    15325 Blackburn Ave Norwalk (90650) *(P-4354)*

Jason Tool and Engineering Inc............................E...... 714 895-5067
    7101 Honold Cir Garden Grove (92841) *(P-5067)*

Jason's Natural, Bell *Also Called: Hain Celestial Group Inc (P-4418)*

Jasper Electronics............................E...... 714 917-0749
    1580 N Kellogg Dr Anaheim (92807) *(P-9069)*

Javanan Inc............................E...... 310 741-0011
    24629 Calvert St Woodland Hills (91367) *(P-16061)*

Javanan Magazine, Woodland Hills *Also Called: Javanan Inc (P-16061)*

Javo Beverage Company Inc............................D...... 760 560-5286
    1311 Specialty Dr Vista (92081) *(P-1778)*

Jaxx Manufacturing Inc............................E...... 805 526-4979
    1912 Angus Ave Simi Valley (93063) *(P-9070)*

Jay's Catering, Garden Grove *Also Called: Mastroianni Family Entps Ltd (P-15517)*

Jaya Apparel Group LLC (PA)............................D...... **323 584-3500**
    5175 S Soto St Vernon (90058) *(P-2333)*

Jayco Interface Technology Inc............................E...... 951 738-2000
    1351 Pico St Corona (92881) *(P-9071)*

Jayco/Mmi Inc............................E...... 951 738-2000
    1351 Pico St Corona (92881) *(P-9072)*

Jayone Foods Inc............................E...... 562 633-7400
    7212 Alondra Blvd Paramount (90723) *(P-1917)*

Jaz Distribution Inc............................F...... 714 521-3888
    8485 Artesia Blvd Ste B Buena Park (90621) *(P-6462)*

Jazz Semiconductor, Newport Beach *Also Called: Newport Fab LLC (P-8851)*

Jazzercise, Carlsbad *Also Called: Jazzercise Inc (P-17401)*

Jazzercise Inc (PA)............................D...... **760 476-1750**
    2460 Impala Dr Carlsbad (92010) *(P-17401)*

JB Brananne Inc............................E...... 949 215-7704
    6 Orchard Lake Forest (92630) *(P-5068)*

JB Dental Supply Co Inc (PA)............................C...... **310 202-8855**
    17000 Kingsview Ave Carson (90746) *(P-12495)*

JB Plastics Inc............................E...... 714 541-8500
    1921 E Edinger Ave Santa Ana (92705) *(P-5069)*

JB Rogers Consulting Inc............................F...... 661 397-4987
    7800 Davin Park Dr Bakersfield (93308) *(P-6960)*

JBA Brands, Garden Grove *Also Called: Advanced Phrm Svcs Inc (P-13027)*

Jbb Inc............................E...... 888 538-9287
    4900 E Hunter Ave Anaheim (92807) *(P-9221)*

Jbi LLC............................E...... 310 537-2910
    18521 S Santa Fe Ave Compton (90221) *(P-2832)*

Jbi LLC (PA)............................C...... **310 886-8034**
    2650 E El Presidio St Long Beach (90810) *(P-3027)*

Jbi Interiors, Long Beach *Also Called: Jbi LLC (P-3027)*

JBL Enterprises Inc............................E...... 760 754-2727
    3219 Roymar Rd Oceanside (92058) *(P-11006)*

Jbs Case Ready, Riverside *Also Called: Swift Beef Company (P-1237)*

JBW Precision Inc............................E...... 805 499-1973
    2650 Lavery Ct Newbury Park (91320) *(P-6255)*

JC Ford, La Habra *Also Called: J C Ford Company (P-7203)*

JC Hanscom Inc............................F...... 562 789-9955
    10472 Caribou Way Tustin (92782) *(P-2689)*

JC Industries, Los Angeles *Also Called: J C Trimming Company Inc (P-2282)*

JC Penney, Arcadia *Also Called: Penney Opco LLC (P-13681)*

JC Penney, Thousand Oaks *Also Called: Penney Opco LLC (P-13683)*

JC Penney 1505, West Covina *Also Called: Penney Opco LLC (P-13682)*

JC Resorts LLC............................A...... 949 376-2779
    1555 S Coast Hwy Laguna Beach (92651) *(P-20042)*

JC Resorts LLC............................B...... 760 944-1936
    4154 Maryland St San Diego (92103) *(P-20043)*

JC Resorts LLC............................C...... 858 675-8500
    17550 Bernardo Oaks Dr San Diego (92128) *(P-20044)*

JC Sales, Commerce *Also Called: Shims Bargain Inc (P-516)*

JC Supply & Manufacturing, Ontario *Also Called: Lightcap Industries Inc (P-6040)*

JC Weight Loss Centres Inc (PA)............................C...... **760 696-4000**
    5770 Fleet St Carlsbad (92008) *(P-15514)*

JC Window Fashions, Whittier *Also Called: JC Window Fashions Inc (P-3008)*

JC Window Fashions Inc............................E...... 909 364-8888
    2438 Peck Rd Whittier (90601) *(P-3008)*

Jc's Pie Pops, Chatsworth *Also Called: We The Pie People LLC (P-1302)*

Jci Jones Chemicals Inc............................F...... 310 523-1629
    1401 Del Amo Blvd Torrance (90501) *(P-3858)*

Jci Metal Products (PA)............................D...... **619 229-8206**
    6540 Federal Blvd Lemon Grove (91945) *(P-6035)*

Jcm Engineering Corp............................D...... 909 923-3730
    2690 E Cedar St Ontario (91761) *(P-12910)*

JCM Industries Inc (PA)............................E...... **714 902-9000**
    15302 Pipeline Ln Huntington Beach (92649) *(P-2982)*

JCPM Inc............................E...... 909 484-9040
    8576 Red Oak St Rancho Cucamonga (91730) *(P-7886)*

Jcr Aircraft Deburring LLC............................D...... 714 870-4427
    221 Foundation Ave La Habra (90631) *(P-6632)*

Jcr Deburring, La Habra *Also Called: Jcr Aircraft Deburring LLC (P-6632)*

JD Business Solutions Inc............................E...... 805 962-8193
    1351 Holiday Hill Rd Goleta (93117) *(P-3606)*

JD Power and Associates Inc............................C...... 805 418-8000
    2625 Townsgate Rd Ste 100 Westlake Village (91361) *(P-19904)*

JD Processing Inc............................E...... 714 972-8161
    2220 Cape Cod Way Santa Ana (92703) *(P-6633)*

Jd/Cmc Inc............................E...... 818 767-2260
    2834 E 11th St Los Angeles (90023) *(P-2334)*

Jdh Pacific Inc (PA)............................E...... **818 269-6274**
    14821 Artesia Blvd La Mirada (90638) *(P-5646)*

Jdi Distribution, Loma Linda *Also Called: Bakell LLC (P-494)*

Jdr Engineering Cons Inc (PA)............................D...... **714 751-7084**
    3122 Maple St Santa Ana (92707) *(P-5070)*

Jdz Inc .... D....... 858 549-9888
9990 Alesmith Ct San Diego (92126) *(P-1593)*

JE Rich Company ....E....... 909 464-1872
7225 Edison Ave Ontario (91762) *(P-1431)*

Jeanne Jugan, A Residence, San Pedro *Also Called: Little Ssters of The Poor Los (P-17995)*

Jeannine's Bakery, Santa Barbara *Also Called: Jeannines Bkg Co Santa Barbara (P-1478)*

Jeannines Bkg Co Santa Barbara (PA)......................F....... 805 687-8701
3607 State St Santa Barbara (93105) *(P-1478)*

Jeb Holdings Corp .... E....... 951 296-9900
42033 Rio Nedo Temecula (92590) *(P-5744)*

Jeep Chrysler Ddge Ram Ontario, Ontario *Also Called: Jeep Chrysler of Ontario (P-13784)*

Jeep Chrysler of Ontario .... D....... 909 390-9898
1202 Auto Center Dr Ontario (91761) *(P-13784)*

Jeep Gear, Irvine *Also Called: Alcone Marketing Group Inc (P-15529)*

Jeff Lane ....E....... 714 779-8484
1530 Lakeview Loop Anaheim (92807) *(P-3607)*

Jeffer Mngels Btlr Mtchell LLP (PA)......................C....... 310 203-8080
1900 Avenue Of The Stars Fl 7 Los Angeles (90067) *(P-18878)*

Jeffrey Fabrication LLC ....E....... 562 634-3101
6323 Alondra Blvd Paramount (90723) *(P-6256)*

Jeffries Global Inc ....D....... 888 255-3488
8484 Wilshire Blvd Ste 605 Beverly Hills (90211) *(P-1164)*

Jeld-Wen Inc ....C....... 800 468-3667
3760 Convoy St Ste 111 San Diego (92111) *(P-2608)*

Jeld-Wen Inc ....C....... 909 879-8700
120 S Cedar Ave Rialto (92376) *(P-12334)*

Jeld-Wen Inc ....B....... 760 597-4201
2760 Progress St Ste B Vista (92081) *(P-12335)*

Jeld-Wen Windows, Vista *Also Called: Jeld-Wen Inc (P-12335)*

Jelenko, San Diego *Also Called: Argen Corporation (P-5673)*

Jellco Container Inc ....D....... 714 666-2728
1151 N Tustin Ave Anaheim (92807) *(P-3112)*

Jellypop, Pasadena *Also Called: Evolution Design Lab Inc (P-5275)*

JEM SPORTSWEAR, Cypress *Also Called: Awake Inc (P-2277)*

Jem Unlimited Iron, Anaheim *Also Called: Jorge Ulloa (P-11235)*

Jem-Hd Co Inc ....E....... 619 710-1443
10030 Via De La Amistad Ste F San Diego (92154) *(P-5071)*

Jenco Productions Inc (PA)......................C....... 909 381-9453
401 S J St San Bernardino (92410) *(P-16852)*

Jeneric/Pentron Incorporated (HQ)......................C....... 203 265-7397
1717 W Collins Ave Orange (92867) *(P-10748)*

Jenny Craig, Carlsbad *Also Called: JC Weight Loss Centres Inc (P-15514)*

Jenny Silks, Santa Ana *Also Called: Jenny Silks Inc (P-13510)*

Jenny Silks Inc ....F....... 714 597-7272
2101 S Grand Ave Santa Ana (92705) *(P-13510)*

Jensen Enterprises Inc ....B....... 909 357-7264
14221 San Bernardino Ave Fontana (92335) *(P-5422)*

Jensen Meat Company Inc ....D....... 619 754-6400
2550 Britannia Blvd Ste 101 San Diego (92154) *(P-13298)*

Jensen Precast, Fontana *Also Called: Jensen Enterprises Inc (P-5422)*

Jeremywell International Inc ....F....... 949 588-6888
14 Vanderbilt Irvine (92618) *(P-7396)*

Jericho Foods, San Fernando *Also Called: Cousins Foods LLC (P-13695)*

Jerry Leigh Entertainment AP, Van Nuys *Also Called: Leigh Jerry California Inc (P-2410)*

Jerry Melton & Sons Cnstr, Taft *Also Called: Jerry Melton & Sons Cnstr Inc (P-356)*

Jerry Melton & Sons Cnstr Inc ....D....... 661 765-5546
100 Jamison Ln Taft (93268) *(P-356)*

Jessie & Jenna, Gardena *Also Called: Lily Bleu Inc (P-13131)*

Jessie Lord, Torrance *Also Called: Jessie Lord Bakery LLC (P-13716)*

Jessie Lord Bakery LLC ....E....... 310 533-6010
21100 S Western Ave Torrance (90501) *(P-13716)*

Jet Air Fbo LLC ....E....... 619 448-5991
681 Kenney St El Cajon (92020) *(P-9728)*

Jet Blue, Long Beach *Also Called: Jetblue Airways Inc (P-11662)*

Jet Cutting Solutions Inc ....E....... 909 948-2424
10853 Bell Ct Rancho Cucamonga (91730) *(P-7887)*

Jet Delivery Inc (PA)......................D....... 800 716-7177
2169 Wright Ave La Verne (91750) *(P-11531)*

Jet Fleet International Corp ....E....... 310 440-3820
2370 Westwood Blvd Ste K Los Angeles (90064) *(P-15515)*

Jet I, Fontana *Also Called: Jeti Inc (P-17089)*

Jet Manufacturing Inc ....E....... 951 736-9316
13445 Estelle St Corona (92879) *(P-6257)*

Jet Plastics (PA)......................E....... 323 268-6706
941 N Eastern Ave Los Angeles (90063) *(P-5072)*

Jet Products, San Diego *Also Called: Senior Operations LLC (P-8024)*

Jet Propulsion Laboratory, Pasadena *Also Called: California Institute Tech (P-19921)*

Jet Sets, North Hollywood *Also Called: M Gaw Inc (P-1168)*

Jetblue Airways Inc ....D....... 562 394-4397
4100 E Donald Douglas Dr Long Beach (90808) *(P-11662)*

Jetfax, Los Angeles *Also Called: Efaxcom (P-7523)*

Jeti Inc ....F....... 909 357-2966
14578 Hawthorne Ave Fontana (92335) *(P-17089)*

Jetro Cash and Carry Entps LLC ....D....... 619 233-0200
1709 Main St San Diego (92113) *(P-13299)*

Jetro Holdings LLC ....B....... 213 516-0301
1611 E Washington Blvd Los Angeles (90021) *(P-12459)*

Jetro Holdings LLC ....B....... 858 564-0466
7466 Carroll Rd Ste 100 San Diego (92121) *(P-12460)*

Jetzero Inc ....E....... 949 474-8222
4301 E Donald Douglas Dr Long Beach (90808) *(P-9541)*

Jewelers Touch ....E....... 714 579-1616
2535 E Imperial Hwy Brea (92821) *(P-14076)*

Jewelry Exchange, The, Tustin *Also Called: Diamond Goldenwest Corporation (P-14074)*

Jewelscent Inc ....D....... 800 550-1762
955 W Imperial Hwy Ste 120 Brea (92821) *(P-13542)*

Jewish Cmnty Fndtion Los Angle (PA)......................C....... 323 761-8700
6505 Wilshire Blvd Ste 1150 Los Angeles (90048) *(P-19450)*

Jewish Community Ctr Long Bch ....C....... 562 426-7601
3801 E Willow St Long Beach (90815) *(P-19100)*

Jewish Family Service, San Diego *Also Called: Jewish Family Svc San Diego (P-19102)*

Jewish Family Svc Los Angeles ....C....... 323 937-5900
330 N Fairfax Ave Los Angeles (90036) *(P-19101)*

Jewish Family Svc San Diego (PA)......................C....... 858 637-3000
8804 Balboa Ave San Diego (92123) *(P-19102)*

Jewish HM For The Aging Ornge ....C....... 949 364-9685
27356 Bellogente Mission Viejo (92691) *(P-17980)*

Jewish Journal, The, Los Angeles *Also Called: Tribe Mdia Corp A Cal Nnprfit (P-3332)*

Jewish Synagogue, Los Angeles *Also Called: Temple Israel of Hollywood (P-15491)*

Jezowski & Markel Contrs Inc ....E....... 714 978-2222
749 N Poplar St Orange (92868) *(P-1076)*

Jf Fixtures & Design, Long Beach *Also Called: F-J-E Inc (P-2953)*

JF Shea Construction Inc (HQ)......................C....... 909 594-9500
655 Brea Canyon Rd Walnut (91789) *(P-437)*

Jfc International Inc (HQ)......................C....... 323 721-6100
7101 E Slauson Ave Commerce (90040) *(P-13372)*

Jfc International Inc ....C....... 323 721-6900
7140 Bandini Blvd Commerce (90040) *(P-13373)*

Jfe Shoji America Holdings Inc (DH)......................D....... 562 637-3500
301 E Ocean Blvd Ste 1750 Long Beach (90802) *(P-12555)*

Jff Uniforms, Torrance *Also Called: Just For Fun Inc (P-2160)*

JFK Memorial Hospital Inc ....C....... 760 347-6191
47111 Monroe St Indio (92201) *(P-18291)*

JG Plastics Group LLC ....E....... 714 751-4266
335 Fischer Ave Costa Mesa (92626) *(P-5073)*

JGM Automotive Tooling Inc ....F....... 714 895-7001
5355 Industrial Dr Huntington Beach (92649) *(P-7244)*

Jh Biotech, Ventura *Also Called: Jh Biotech Inc (P-4544)*

Jh Biotech Inc (PA)......................E....... 805 650-8933
4951 Olivas Park Dr Ventura (93003) *(P-4544)*

Jh Design Group ....D....... 213 747-5700
940 W Washington Blvd Los Angeles (90015) *(P-2208)*

Jhawar Industries LLC ....E....... 951 340-4646
525 Klug Cir Corona (92878) *(P-7368)*

Jif-Pak Manufacturing Inc (PA)......................D....... 760 597-2665
1451 Engineer St Ste A Vista (92081) *(P-2082)*

Jiffy Lube, Moreno Valley *Also Called: Bms Investments LLC (P-4077)*

Jiffy Lube, Tustin *Also Called: Allied Lube Inc (P-17027)*

Jihwaja Rice Bakery, Los Angeles *Also Called: Grandville Llc (P-1518)*

Jim Burke Ford, Bakersfield *Also Called: Haberfelde Ford (P-13776)*

ALPHABETIC

Employee Codes: A=Over 500 employees, B=251-500
C=101-250, D=51-100, E=20-50, F=10-19, G=1-9

2024 Southern California
Business Directory and Buyers Guide

© Mergent Inc. 1-800-342-5647
1139

Jim ONeal Distributing Inc .... E....... 805 426-3300
799 Camarillo Springs Rd Camarillo (93012) *(P-13900)*

Jim-Buoy, North Hollywood *Also Called: Cal-June Inc (P-5909)*

Jim's Machining, Camarillo *Also Called: Thiessen Products Inc (P-8046)*

Jim's Tire Center Simi Valley, Simi Valley *Also Called: Jims Tire Center Simi Vly Inc (P-17022)*

Jimenes Food Inc .... E....... 562 602-2505
7046 Jackson St Paramount (90723) *(P-1918)*

Jimenez Mexican Foods Inc .... E....... 951 351-0102
20343 Harvill Ave Perris (92570) *(P-1326)*

Jimenez Nursery Inc .... D....... 805 684-7955
3800 Via Real Carpinteria (93013) *(P-58)*

Jimenez Nursery and Landscapes, Carpinteria *Also Called: Jimenez Nursery Inc (P-58)*

Jims Supply Co Inc (PA) ....**D....... 661 616-6977**
3500 Buck Owens Blvd Bakersfield (93308) *(P-12556)*

Jims Tire Center Simi Vly Inc .... F....... 805 581-1104
1525 E Los Angeles Ave Simi Valley (93065) *(P-17022)*

Jimway Inc .... D....... 310 886-3718
20101 S Santa Fe Ave Compton (90221) *(P-8369)*

Jipc Management Inc .... A....... 949 916-2000
22342 Avenida Empresa Ste 220 Rancho Santa Margari (92688) *(P-20045)*

JIT Manufacturing Inc .... E....... 805 238-5000
1610 Commerce Way Paso Robles (93446) *(P-10540)*

Jitterbug, San Diego *Also Called: Greatcall Inc (P-14135)*

Jj Acquisitions LLC .... E....... 818 772-0100
8501 Fllbrook Ave Ste 370 West Hills (91304) *(P-4770)*

JJ Mac Intyre Co Inc (PA) ....**C....... 951 898-4300**
4160 Temescal Canyon Rd Ste 601 Corona (92883) *(P-15614)*

Jk Imaging Ltd .... D....... 310 755-6848
17239 S Main St Gardena (90248) *(P-12378)*

JKL Components Corporation .... E....... 818 896-0019
13343 Paxton St Pacoima (91331) *(P-8347)*

Jkv Inc .... E....... 562 948-3000
8343 Loch Lomond Dr Pico Rivera (90660) *(P-3113)*

Jl Design Enterprises Inc .... D....... 714 479-0240
1451 Edinger Ave Ste C Tustin (92780) *(P-2159)*

Jl Racing.com, Tustin *Also Called: Jl Design Enterprises Inc (P-2159)*

Jlabs, San Diego *Also Called: Johnson Johnson Innovation LLC (P-20356)*

Jlcooper, El Segundo *Also Called: J L Cooper Electronics Inc (P-9067)*

Jlg Industries Inc .... D....... 951 358-1915
7820 Lincoln Ave Riverside (92504) *(P-6937)*

Jlg Serviceplus, Riverside *Also Called: Jlg Industries Inc (P-6937)*

Jlo Beauty & Lifestyle LLC .... E....... 888 853-3169
100 N Pacific Coast Hwy Ste 1900 El Segundo (90245) *(P-13049)*

JM Eagle, Perris *Also Called: J-M Manufacturing Company Inc (P-3950)*

JM Eagle, Los Angeles *Also Called: J-M Manufacturing Company Inc (P-4850)*

JM Eagle, Los Angeles *Also Called: Pw Eagle Inc (P-4853)*

JM Huber Micropowders Inc .... E....... 714 994-7855
16024 Phoebe Ave La Mirada (90638) *(P-3895)*

Jmbm, Los Angeles *Also Called: Jeffer Mngels Btlr Mtchell LLP (P-18878)*

Jme Inc (PA) ....**D....... 201 896-8600**
527 Park Ave San Fernando (91340) *(P-12599)*

Jmg Machine Inc .... E....... 714 522-6221
17037 Industry Pl La Mirada (90638) *(P-7888)*

Jmh Engineering and Cnstr .... D....... 562 317-1700
2457 Brayton Ave Signal Hill (90755) *(P-438)*

JMI Steel Inc .... E....... 818 768-3955
8983 San Fernando Rd Sun Valley (91352) *(P-6361)*

JMJ Enterprises Inc .... C....... 818 343-5151
5973 Reseda Blvd Tarzana (91356) *(P-14017)*

Jml Textile Inc .... F....... 323 584-2323
5801 S 2nd St Vernon (90058) *(P-2025)*

Jmmca Inc (PA) ....**D....... 619 448-2711**
850 W Bradley Ave El Cajon (92020) *(P-6463)*

Jmp Electronics Inc .... E....... 714 730-2086
2685 Dow Ave Ste A1 Tustin (92780) *(P-8693)*

Jmw Truss and Components, San Diego *Also Called: Trademark Construction Co Inc (P-9175)*

JNJ Apparel Inc .... E....... 323 584-9700
18788 Fairfield Rd Porter Ranch (91326) *(P-2335)*

Joanka Inc .... F....... 310 326-8940
25510 Frampton Ave Harbor City (90710) *(P-6109)*

Job Options Incorporated .... A....... 909 890-4612
1110 S Washington Ave San Bernardino (92408) *(P-15475)*

Jobbers Meat Packing Co LLC .... C....... 323 585-6328
3336 Fruitland Ave Vernon (90058) *(P-1198)*

Jobsite Stud Welding .... E....... 855 885-7883
9445 Washburn Rd Downey (90242) *(P-17090)*

Jodi Kristopher LLC (PA) ....**D....... 323 890-8000**
1950 Naomi Ave Los Angeles (90011) *(P-2283)*

Jody of California, Los Angeles *Also Called: Private Brand Mdsg Corp (P-2287)*

Joe & Mary Mottino YMCA, Encinitas *Also Called: YMCA of San Diego County (P-19489)*

Joe Blasco Cosmetics, Palm Springs *Also Called: Joe Blasco Enterprises Inc (P-11234)*

Joe Blasco Enterprises Inc .... E....... 323 467-4949
1285 N Valdivia Way # A Palm Springs (92262) *(P-11234)*

Joe Heger Farms LLC .... C....... 760 353-5111
1625 Drew Rd El Centro (92243) *(P-83)*

Joe Wells Enterprises Inc .... E
1500 S Sunkist St Ste D Anaheim (92806) *(P-2209)*

Joe's Auto Parks, Los Angeles *Also Called: L and R Auto Parks Inc (P-16991)*

Joes Plastics, Vernon *Also Called: Joes Plastics Inc (P-3951)*

Joes Plastics Inc .... E....... 323 771-8433
5725 District Blvd Vernon (90058) *(P-3951)*

Johanson Technology Inc .... C....... 805 575-0124
4001 Calle Tecate Camarillo (93012) *(P-8929)*

Johasee Rebar, Corona *Also Called: Johasee Rebar Inc (P-6036)*

Johasee Rebar Inc .... E....... 661 589-0972
26365 Earthmover Cir Corona (92883) *(P-6036)*

John Alden Life Insurance Co .... C....... 818 595-7600
20950 Warner Center Ln Ste A Woodland Hills (91367) *(P-14436)*

John Bean Technologies Corp .... D....... 951 222-2300
1660 Iowa Ave Ste 100 Riverside (92507) *(P-7204)*

John Bishop Design Inc .... E....... 714 744-2300
731 N Main St Orange (92868) *(P-11126)*

John Collins Co Inc .... D....... 818 227-2190
5155 Cedarwood Rd Bonita (91902) *(P-14724)*

John Currie Performance Group .... E....... 714 367-1580
1592 Jenks Dr Corona (92878) *(P-7245)*

John Deere Authorized Dealer, Colton *Also Called: A-Z Bus Sales Inc (P-12217)*

John Deere Authorized Dealer, Poway *Also Called: Bay City Equipment Inds Inc (P-12587)*

John Deere Authorized Dealer, City Of Industry *Also Called: Valley Power Systems Inc (P-12832)*

John Deere Water, San Diego *Also Called: Rivulis Irrigation Inc (P-6912)*

John F Kennedy Mem Hosp Aux .... A....... 760 347-6191
47111 Monroe St Indio (92201) *(P-18292)*

John Hancock, Los Angeles *Also Called: John Hancock Life Insur Co USA (P-14604)*

John Hancock, San Diego *Also Called: John Hancock Life Insur Co USA (P-14605)*

John Hancock Life Insur Co USA .... D....... 949 254-1440
5000 Birch St Ste 120 Newport Beach (92660) *(P-14437)*

John Hancock Life Insur Co USA (DH) ....**A....... 213 689-0813**
865 S Figueroa St Ste 3320 Los Angeles (90017) *(P-14604)*

John Hancock Life Insur Co USA .... C....... 858 292-1667
10180 Telesis Ct San Diego (92121) *(P-14605)*

John Jory Corporation (PA) ....**B....... 714 279-7901**
2180 N Glassell St Orange (92865) *(P-981)*

John L Conley Inc .... D....... 909 627-0981
4344 Mission Blvd Montclair (91763) *(P-6380)*

John List Corporation .... E....... 818 882-7848
9732 Cozycroft Ave Chatsworth (91311) *(P-7151)*

John M Frank Construction Inc .... D....... 714 210-3600
913 E 4th St Santa Ana (92701) *(P-560)*

John M Frank Service Group, Santa Ana *Also Called: John M Frank Construction Inc (P-560)*

John M Phillips LLC .... E....... 661 327-3118
2800 Gibson St Bakersfield (93308) *(P-357)*

John M Phillips Oil Field Eqp, Bakersfield *Also Called: John M Phillips LLC (P-357)*

JOHN TILLMAN COMPANY (DH) ....**D....... 310 764-0110**
1300 W Artesia Blvd Compton (90220) *(P-12793)*

John Wayne Airport, Costa Mesa *Also Called: County of Orange (P-11694)*

John's Incredible Pizza Co, Rancho Santa Margari *Also Called: Jipc Management Inc (P-20045)*

Johnny Was LLC .... D....... 310 656-0600
395 Santa Monica Pl Ste 124 Santa Monica (90401) *(P-13128)*

Mergent email: customerrelations@mergent.com
1140

2024 Southern California
Business Directory and Buyers Guide

(P-0000) Products & Services Section entry number
(PA)=Parent Co (HQ)=Headquarters (DH)=Div Headquarters

Johnny Was Showroom, Los Angeles *Also Called: Jwc Studio Inc (P-2284)*

Johns Manville Corporation ....D...... 323 568-2220
4301 Firestone Blvd South Gate (90280) *(P-5554)*

Johnson & Johnson ....B...... 909 839-8650
15715 Arrow Hwy Irwindale (91706) *(P-10676)*

Johnson & Johnson, Irwindale *Also Called: Johnson & Johnson (P-10676)*

Johnson & Johnson Consumer Inc ....D...... 310 642-1150
5760 W 96th St Los Angeles (90045) *(P-4424)*

Johnson & Johnson Vision, Irvine *Also Called: Johnson Jhnson Srgcal Vsion In (P-10809)*

Johnson Caldraul Inc ....E...... 951 340-1067
220 N Delilah St Ste 101 Corona (92879) *(P-9729)*

Johnson Cntrls Fire Prtction L ....C...... 858 633-9100
3568 Ruffin Rd San Diego (92123) *(P-8616)*

Johnson Contrls Authorized Dlr, Montebello *Also Called: Johnstone Supply Inc (P-13968)*

Johnson Controls ....C...... 562 405-3817
12728 Shoemaker Ave Santa Fe Springs (90670) *(P-16743)*

Johnson Controls, Simi Valley *Also Called: Clarios LLC (P-2922)*

Johnson Controls, Palm Desert *Also Called: Clarios LLC (P-2923)*

Johnson Controls, Whittier *Also Called: Johnson Controls Inc (P-2929)*

Johnson Controls, Cypress *Also Called: Johnson Controls Inc (P-2930)*

Johnson Controls Inc ....E...... 562 698-8301
12393 Slauson Ave Whittier (90606) *(P-2929)*

Johnson Controls Inc ....C...... 562 594-3200
5770 Warland Dr Ste A Cypress (90630) *(P-2930)*

Johnson Fain Inc ....D...... 323 224-6000
1201 N Broadway Los Angeles (90012) *(P-19733)*

Johnson Ford (PA)...C...... 888 483-0454
1155 Auto Mall Dr Lancaster (93534) *(P-13785)*

Johnson Jhnson Srgcal Vsion In (HQ)..........................B...... 949 581-5799
31 Technology Dr Bldg 29a Irvine (92618) *(P-10809)*

Johnson Johnson Innovation LLC ....A...... 858 242-1504
3210 Merryfield Row San Diego (92121) *(P-20356)*

Johnson Laminating Coating Inc ....D...... 310 635-4929
20631 Annalee Ave Carson (90746) *(P-4834)*

Johnson Machinery Co (PA)..C...... 951 686-4560
800 E La Cadena Dr Riverside (92507) *(P-12772)*

Johnson Manufacturing Inc ....E...... 714 903-0393
15201 Connector Ln Huntington Beach (92649) *(P-7889)*

Johnson Matthey Inc ....C...... 858 716-2400
12205 World Trade Dr San Diego (92128) *(P-5682)*

Johnson Outdoors Inc ....C...... 619 402-1023
1166 Fesler St Ste A El Cajon (92020) *(P-11007)*

Johnson Precision Products Inc ....F...... 714 824-6971
1308 E Wakeham Ave Santa Ana (92705) *(P-7890)*

Johnson Racing, Santa Maria *Also Called: Alan Johnson Prfmce Engrg Inc (P-9274)*

Johnson Wilshire Inc ....E...... 562 777-0088
17343 Freedom Way City Of Industry (91748) *(P-10677)*

Johnston International Corporation ....E...... 714 542-4487
14272 Chambers Rd Tustin (92780) *(P-7397)*

Johnstone Supply Inc ....D...... 323 722-2859
8040 Slauson Ave Montebello (90640) *(P-13968)*

Joico Laboratories Inc ....C...... 626 321-4100
5800 Bristol Pkwy Culver City (90230) *(P-4425)*

Jolly Roger Games, Commerce *Also Called: Ultra Pro International LLC (P-12946)*

Jolly Roger Inn, Anaheim *Also Called: Edward Thomas Companies (P-15140)*

Jolo Industries Inc ....F...... 714 554-6840
10432 Brightwood Dr Santa Ana (92705) *(P-9073)*

Jolyn Clothing Company LLC ....E...... 714 794-2149
16390 Pacific Coast Hwy Ste 201 Huntington Beach (92649) *(P-2336)*

Jomar Table Linens Inc ....D...... 909 390-1444
4000 E Airport Dr Ste A Ontario (91761) *(P-2473)*

Jon Brooks Inc (PA)...D...... 626 330-0631
14400 Lomitas Ave City Of Industry (91746) *(P-5550)*

Jon Davler Inc ....E...... 626 941-6558
9440 Gidley St Temple City (91780) *(P-14139)*

Jon Renau Collection Inc ....D...... 760 598-0067
2842 Whiptail Loop Carlsbad (92010) *(P-15516)*

Jon Steel Erectors Inc ....E...... 909 799-0005
1431 S Gage St San Bernardino (92408) *(P-17091)*

Jon-Lin Foods, Colton *Also Called: Jon-Lin Frozen Foods (P-13247)*

Jon-Lin Frozen Foods (PA)..D...... 909 825-8542
1620 N 8th St Colton (92324) *(P-13247)*

Jonathan Beach Club, Santa Monica *Also Called: Jonathan Club (P-17491)*

Jonathan Club ....D...... 310 393-9245
850 Palisades Beach Rd Santa Monica (90403) *(P-17491)*

Jonathan Club (PA)..C...... 213 624-0881
545 S Figueroa St Los Angeles (90071) *(P-19451)*

Jonathan Engnred Slutions Corp (HQ)..........................E...... 714 665-4400
250 Commerce Ste 100 Irvine (92602) *(P-5925)*

Jonathan Martin, Los Angeles *Also Called: Harkham Industries Inc (P-2244)*

Jondo Ltd (HQ)..D...... 714 279-2300
22700 Savi Ranch Pkwy Yorba Linda (92887) *(P-10870)*

Jonel Engineering ....E...... 714 879-2360
500 E Walnut Ave Fullerton (92832) *(P-7716)*

Jones Brothers Cnstr Corp (PA).....................................D...... 310 470-1885
1601 Cloverfield Blvd Santa Monica (90404) *(P-561)*

Jones Chemicals, Torrance *Also Called: Jci Jones Chemicals Inc (P-3858)*

Jones Day, Los Angeles *Also Called: Jones Day Limited Partnership (P-18879)*

Jones Day Limited Partnership ....C...... 213 489-3939
555 S Flower St Fl 50 Los Angeles (90071) *(P-18879)*

Jones Sign Co Inc ....C...... 858 569-1400
9474 Chesapeake Dr Ste 902 San Diego (92123) *(P-11127)*

Jones Signs Co Inc ....C...... 858 569-1400
9025 Balboa Ave Ste 150 San Diego (92123) *(P-12461)*

Joni and Friends Foundation (PA)..................................D...... 818 707-5664
30009 Ladyface Ct Agoura (91301) *(P-19103)*

Jonset LLC ....D...... 949 551-5151
16251 Construction Cir W Irvine (92606) *(P-12209)*

Joong-Ang Daily News Cal Inc ....D...... 858 573-1111
7750 Dagget St Ste 208 San Diego (92111) *(P-3290)*

Joong-Ang Daily News Cal Inc, Los Angeles *Also Called: Joongangilbo Usa Inc (P-3291)*

Joong-Ang Daily News California, Inc., San Diego *Also Called: Joong-Ang Daily News Cal Inc (P-3290)*

Joongangilbo Usa Inc (DH)...C...... 213 368-2512
690 Wilshire Pl Los Angeles (90005) *(P-3291)*

Joor Bros Metal Supply, Corona *Also Called: Joor Bros Welding Inc (P-12557)*

Joor Bros Welding Inc ....E...... 951 737-3950
2818 Garretson Ave Corona (92881) *(P-12557)*

Jordahl USA Inc ....C...... 866 332-6687
34420 Gateway Dr Palm Desert (92211) *(P-6258)*

Jordano's Food Service, Santa Barbara *Also Called: Jordanos Inc (P-13470)*

Jordanos Inc (PA)..C...... 805 964-0611
550 S Patterson Ave Santa Barbara (93111) *(P-13470)*

Jorge Ulloa ....F...... 714 630-0499
3162 E La Palma Ave Ste F Anaheim (92806) *(P-11235)*

Jose Perez ....E...... 920 318-6527
5869 Silveira St Eastvale (92880) *(P-6975)*

Joseph Company Intl Inc ....E...... 949 474-2200
1711 Langley Ave Irvine (92614) *(P-5859)*

Joslyn Sunbank Company LLC ....B...... 805 238-2840
1740 Commerce Way Paso Robles (93446) *(P-8976)*

Jowett Garments Factory Inc ....E...... 626 350-0515
10359 Rush St South El Monte (91733) *(P-2337)*

Jowett Group, South El Monte *Also Called: Jowett Garments Factory Inc (P-2337)*

Joy Products California Inc ....E...... 714 437-7250
17281 Mount Wynne Cir Fountain Valley (92708) *(P-11052)*

Joybird, Los Angeles *Also Called: Stitch Industries Inc (P-2820)*

JP Gunite Inc ....E...... 619 938-0228
9458 New Colt Ct El Cajon (92021) *(P-5484)*

JP Products LLC ....E...... 310 237-6237
2054 Davie Ave Commerce (90040) *(P-2776)*

JP Weaver & Company ....E...... 818 500-1740
941 Air Way Glendale (91201) *(P-5569)*

Jpl Global LLC ....E...... 888 274-7744
4635 Wade Ave Perris (92571) *(P-12773)*

JR Filanc Cnstr Co Inc (PA)...D...... 760 941-7130
740 N Andreasen Dr Escondido (92029) *(P-677)*

JR Machine Company Inc ....E...... 562 903-9477
13245 Florence Ave Santa Fe Springs (90670) *(P-7891)*

Jri Inc ....E...... 818 706-2424
31280 La Baya Dr Westlake Village (91362) *(P-12673)*

Employee Codes: A=Over 500 employees, B=251-500
C=101-250, D=51-100, E=20-50, F=10-19, G=1-9

2024 Southern California
Business Directory and Buyers Guide

© Mergent Inc. 1-800-342-5647

1141

A
L
P
H
A
B
E
T
I
C

Js Apparel Inc ....D...... 310 631-6333
1751 E Del Amo Blvd Carson (90746) *(P-2210)*

JS Held LLC ....D...... 949 390-7647
4667 Macarthur Blvd Ste 400 Newport Beach (92660) *(P-19782)*

Jsl Foods Inc (PA) ....**D...... 323 223-2484**
3550 Pasadena Ave Los Angeles (90031) *(P-1919)*

Jsl Technologies Inc ....B...... 805 985-7700
1451 N Rice Ave Ste A Oxnard (93030) *(P-19626)*

Jsn Industries Inc ....D...... 949 458-0050
9700 Jeronimo Rd Irvine (92618) *(P-5074)*

Jsn Packaging Products Inc ....D...... 949 458-0050
9700 Jeronimo Rd Irvine (92618) *(P-4830)*

JT Design Studio Inc (PA) ....**E...... 213 891-1500**
860 S Los Angeles St Ste 912 Los Angeles (90014) *(P-2338)*

Jt Resources Inc ....C...... 661 367-6827
26372 Ruether Ave Santa Clarita (91350) *(P-15856)*

JT Wimsatt Contg Co Inc (PA) ....**B...... 661 775-8090**
28064 Avenue Stanford Unit B Valencia (91355) *(P-1077)*

Jt Windows Inc ....E...... 818 709-7950
9261 Independence Ave Chatsworth (91311) *(P-1017)*

Jt3 LLC ....A...... 661 277-4900
190 S Wolfe Ave Bldg 1260 Edwards (93524) *(P-19627)*

Jtb Americas Ltd (HQ) ....**D...... 310 406-3121**
3625 Del Amo Blvd Ste 260 Torrance (90503) *(P-11718)*

Jtb Supply Company Inc ....F...... 714 639-9558
1030 N Batavia St Ste A Orange (92867) *(P-8617)*

Jts Modular Inc ....E...... 661 835-9270
7001 Mcdivitt Dr Ste B Bakersfield (93313) *(P-6381)*

Juanitas Foods ....C...... 310 834-5339
645 N. Eubank Ave Wilmington (90744) *(P-1327)*

Judco Manufacturing Inc (PA) ....**C...... 310 534-0959**
1429 240th St Harbor City (90710) *(P-8268)*

Judith Von Hopf Inc ....E...... 909 481-1884
1525 W 13th St Ste H Upland (91786) *(P-2957)*

Judson Studios Inc ....E...... 323 255-0131
200 S Avenue 66 Los Angeles (90042) *(P-5345)*

Judy Ann, Culver City *Also Called: Fortune Casuals LLC (P-2240)*

Judy Ann of California Inc ....C...... 213 623-9233
1936 Mateo St Los Angeles (90021) *(P-2246)*

Judy O Productions Inc ....E...... 323 938-8513
4858 W Pico Blvd Ste 331 Los Angeles (90019) *(P-3408)*

Juengermann Inc ....E...... 805 644-7165
1899 Palma Dr Ste A Ventura (93003) *(P-6782)*

Juice Division, Pacoima *Also Called: American Fruits & Flavors LLC (P-1754)*

Juicy Couture Inc ....C...... 888 824-8826
1580 Jesse St Los Angeles (90021) *(P-2041)*

Juicy Whip Inc ....E...... 909 392-7500
1668 Curtiss Ct La Verne (91750) *(P-7205)*

Julian Bakery Inc ....E...... 760 721-5200
624 Garrison St Ste1-2 Oceanside (92054) *(P-13717)*

Julians Foods LLC ....E...... 760 583-9358
3021 Industry St Oceanside (92054) *(P-1422)*

Jumper Media, La Jolla *Also Called: Jumper Media LLC (P-3458)*

Jumper Media LLC ....D...... 831 333-6202
1719 Alta La Jolla Dr La Jolla (92037) *(P-3458)*

June Group LLC ....D...... 858 450-4290
9909 Mira Mesa Blvd Ste 240 San Diego (92131) *(P-15925)*

Juneshine Inc ....C...... 619 501-8311
10051 Old Grove Rd Ste A San Diego (92131) *(P-1920)*

Jungle Jumps, Pacoima *Also Called: Twin Peak Industries Inc (P-11037)*

Jungotv LLC ....D...... 650 207-6227
4605 Lankershim Blvd Ste 180 North Hollywood (91602) *(P-3459)*

Juniper Publishers ....E...... 909 563-8215
1890 W Hillcrest Dr Newbury Park (91320) *(P-3460)*

Juniper Rock Corporation ....F...... 949 500-1797
26000 Commercentre Dr Lake Forest (92630) *(P-400)*

Juntee of California Inc ....E...... 213 742-0246
1031 S Broadway Rm 327 Los Angeles (90015) *(P-2247)*

Jupiter Bellflower Doctors Hospital ....B
3699 Wilshire Blvd Ste 540 Los Angeles (90010) *(P-18293)*

Jurny Inc ....E...... 888 875-8769
6600 W Sunset Blvd Los Angeles (90028) *(P-16281)*

Jurupa Community Services Dst ....D...... 951 685-7073
11201 Harrel St Riverside (92509) *(P-12126)*

Jurupa Hills Post Acute, Riverside *Also Called: Mt Rubidouxidence Opco LLC (P-18018)*

Just For Fun Inc ....E...... 310 320-1327
557 Van Ness Ave Torrance (90501) *(P-2160)*

Just For Wraps Inc (PA) ....**C...... 213 239-0503**
4871 S Santa Fe Ave Vernon (90058) *(P-2339)*

Justenough Software Corp Inc (HQ) ....**E...... 949 706-5400**
15440 Laguna Canyon Rd Ste 100 Irvine (92618) *(P-16282)*

Justfoodfordogs LLC (PA) ....**F...... 866 726-9509**
17851 Sky Park Cir Ste A Irvine (92614) *(P-1432)*

Justice Bros Dist Co Inc ....E...... 626 359-9174
2734 Huntington Dr Duarte (91010) *(P-4375)*

Justice Bros-J B Car Care Pdts, Duarte *Also Called: Justice Bros Dist Co Inc (P-4375)*

Justin, El Monte *Also Called: Justin Inc (P-8100)*

Justin Inc ....E...... 626 444-4516
2663 Lee Ave El Monte (91733) *(P-8100)*

Justman Packaging & Display (PA) ....**D...... 323 728-8888**
5819 Telegraph Rd Commerce (90040) *(P-12462)*

Juvenile Justice Division Cal ....A...... 805 485-7951
3100 Wright Rd Camarillo (93010) *(P-20046)*

Jvckenwood USA Corporation (HQ) ....**C...... 310 639-9000**
4001 Worsham Ave Long Beach (90808) *(P-12674)*

Jvr Sheetmetal Fabrication Inc ....E...... 714 841-2464
7101 Patterson Dr Garden Grove (92841) *(P-9542)*

Jvs Socal ....B...... 323 761-8879
6505 Wilshire Blvd Los Angeles (90048) *(P-19104)*

JW Manufacturing Inc ....E...... 805 498-4594
12989 Bradley Ave Sylmar (91342) *(P-6447)*

JW Marriott Le Merigot, Santa Monica *Also Called: C W Hotels Ltd (P-15104)*

Jwc Environmental Inc ....D...... 714 662-5829
2600 S Garnsey St Santa Ana (92707) *(P-7666)*

Jwc Environmental Inc (DH) ....**E...... 949 833-3888**
2850 Redhill Ave Ste 125 Santa Ana (92705) *(P-12794)*

Jwc Studio Inc (PA) ....**E...... 323 231-8222**
2423 E 23rd St Los Angeles (90058) *(P-2284)*

Jwch Institute Inc ....C...... 562 867-7999
14371 Clark Ave Bellflower (90706) *(P-18772)*

Jwch Institute Inc ....C...... 562 862-1000
8530 Firestone Blvd Downey (90241) *(P-18773)*

Jwch Institute Inc ....C...... 310 223-1035
3591 E Imperial Hwy Lynwood (90262) *(P-19105)*

Jwch Institute Inc ....C...... 323 562-5813
6912 Ajax Ave Bell (90201) *(P-19931)*

Jwch Institute Inc ....C...... 562 281-0306
12360 Firestone Blvd Norwalk (90650) *(P-19932)*

Jwch Medical Center, Lynwood *Also Called: Jwch Institute Inc (P-19105)*

Jwilliams Staffing Inc ....C...... 949 250-1923
18022 Cowan Ste 105 Irvine (92614) *(P-15857)*

Jynormus LLC ....F...... 949 436-2112
19800 Macarthur Blvd 3rd Fl Irvine (92612) *(P-11890)*

K & D Graphics ....E...... 714 639-8900
1432 N Main St Ste C Orange (92867) *(P-3203)*

K & D Graphics Prtg & Packg, Orange *Also Called: K & D Graphics (P-3203)*

K & G Latirovian Inc ....D...... 818 319-2862
11182 Penrose St Sun Valley (91352) *(P-9407)*

K & J Wire Products Corp ....E...... 714 816-0360
1220 N Lance Ln Anaheim (92806) *(P-6362)*

K & L Shutters, Bellflower *Also Called: Kl Decorator Sales (P-2610)*

K & M Meat Co, Vernon *Also Called: K & M Packing Co Inc (P-1199)*

K & M Packing Co Inc ....E...... 323 585-5318
2443 E 27th St Vernon (90058) *(P-1199)*

K & N Engineering Inc (PA) ....**A...... 951 826-4000**
1455 Citrus St Riverside (92507) *(P-9877)*

K & P Janitorial Services ....D...... 310 540-8878
412 S Pacific Coast Hwy Ste 200 Redondo Beach (90277) *(P-15717)*

K & S Air Conditioning Inc ....C...... 714 685-0077
143 E Meats Ave Orange (92865) *(P-782)*

K & S Enterprises, Adelanto *Also Called: Dar-Ken Inc (P-4726)*

K & Z Cabinet Co Inc ....D...... 909 947-3567
1450 S Grove Ave Ontario (91761) *(P-2662)*

Mergent email: customerrelations@mergent.com
1142

2024 Southern California
Business Directory and Buyers Guide

(P-0000) Products & Services Section entry number
(PA)=Parent Co (HQ)=Headquarters (DH)=Div Headquarters

K A McNair Brewing Co LLC .... E...... 858 254-3238
3038 University Ave San Diego (92104) *(P-1594)*

K B Socks Inc (DH) ....D...... 310 670-3235
550 N Oak St Inglewood (90302) *(P-2059)*

K Bell, Inglewood Also Called: *K B Socks Inc (P-2059)*

K C C, El Segundo Also Called: *Carson Kurtzman Consultants (P-18834)*

K C Restoration Co Inc .... E...... 310 280-0597
1514 W 130th St Gardena (90249) *(P-358)*

K E, Irvine Also Called: *Kite Electric Incorporated (P-911)*

K E S, San Diego Also Called: *Koam Engineering Systems Inc (P-16452)*

K I C, San Diego Also Called: *Embedded Designs Inc (P-10130)*

K L Electronic Inc .... E...... 714 751-5611
3083 S Harbor Blvd Santa Ana (92704) *(P-8694)*

K M I, Dana Point Also Called: *Kanstul Musical Instrs Inc (P-10926)*

K Mars, Van Nuys Also Called: *Kazak-Mars Inc (P-10842)*

K Motors Inc .... C...... 619 270-3000
965 Arnele Ave El Cajon (92020) *(P-13851)*

K P B S, San Diego Also Called: *San Diego State University (P-18992)*

K S Designs Inc .... E...... 562 929-3973
9515 Sorensen Ave Santa Fe Springs (90670) *(P-11128)*

K S Fabrication & Machine Inc .... C...... 661 617-1700
6205 District Blvd Bakersfield (93313) *(P-678)*

K S I, Bakersfield Also Called: *KS Industries LP (P-680)*

K S S C - F M, Los Angeles Also Called: *Entravsion Communications Corp (P-11946)*

K Squared Metals, Lake Elsinore Also Called: *Boozak Inc (P-6203)*

K Too .... E...... 213 747-7766
800 E 12th St Ste 117 Los Angeles (90021) *(P-2248)*

K Tube Technologies, Poway Also Called: *K-Tube Corporation (P-5636)*

K-1 Packaging Group .... C...... 626 964-9384
2001 W Mission Blvd Pomona (91766) *(P-3608)*

K-1 Packaging Group, Pomona Also Called: *K-1 Packaging Group (P-3608)*

K-1 Packaging Group LLC (PA) ....D...... 626 964-9384
17989 Arenth Ave City Of Industry (91748) *(P-3609)*

K-Jack Engineering Co Inc ....D...... 310 327-8389
5672 Buckingham Dr Huntington Beach (92649) *(P-2983)*

K-Max Health Products Corp .... F...... 909 455-0158
1468 E Mission Blvd Pomona (91766) *(P-4149)*

K-Micro Inc ....D...... 310 442-3200
1618 Stanford St Santa Monica (90404) *(P-12423)*

K-P Engineering Corp .... E...... 714 545-7045
2126 S Lyon St Ste A Santa Ana (92705) *(P-7892)*

K-Swiss, Los Angeles Also Called: *K-Swiss Inc (P-4703)*

K-Swiss Inc (DH) ....E...... 323 675-2700
523 W 6th St Ste 534 Los Angeles (90014) *(P-4703)*

K-Swiss Sales Corp .... C...... 323 675-2700
523 W 6th St Ste 534 Los Angeles (90014) *(P-4704)*

K-Tech Machine Inc .... C...... 800 274-9424
1377 Armorlite Dr San Marcos (92069) *(P-7893)*

K-Tek, Vista Also Called: *M Klemme Technology Corp (P-8420)*

K-Too, Los Angeles Also Called: *K Too (P-2248)*

K-Tube Corporation ....D...... 858 513-9229
13400 Kirkham Way Frnt Poway (92064) *(P-5636)*

K-V Engineering Inc ....D...... 714 229-9977
2411 W 1st St Santa Ana (92703) *(P-7014)*

K.G.S.electronics, Upland Also Called: *Gar Enterprises (P-9047)*

K&B Electric LLC .... C...... 951 808-9501
290 Corporate Terrace Cir Ste 200 Corona (92879) *(P-19628)*

K&B Engineering .... C...... 951 808-9501
290 Corporate Terrace Cir Ste 200 Corona (92879) *(P-19629)*

K&B Engineering, Corona Also Called: *K&B Electric LLC (P-19628)*

K&L Gates LLP ....D...... 310 552-5000
10100 Santa Monica Blvd Ste 700 Los Angeles (90067) *(P-18880)*

K&N, Riverside Also Called: *K & N Engineering Inc (P-9877)*

K&S, Orange Also Called: *K & S Air Conditioning Inc (P-782)*

K2 Label & Printing Inc .... E...... 626 922-8108
633 Great Bend Dr Diamond Bar (91765) *(P-3610)*

K31, Laguna Beach Also Called: *K31 Road Engineering LLC (P-11236)*

K31 Road Engineering LLC .... E...... 305 928-1968
1968 S Coast Hwy Pmb 593 Laguna Beach (92651) *(P-11236)*

Ka Management II Inc ....D...... 858 404-6080
5820 Oberlin Dr Ste 201 San Diego (92121) *(P-20047)*

Kaar Drect Mail Flfillment LLC .... E...... 619 382-3670
1225 Exposition Way Ste 160 San Diego (92154) *(P-3292)*

Kafco Sales Company ....E...... 323 588-7141
2300 E 37th St Vernon (90058) *(P-12795)*

Kafp, Foothill Ranch Also Called: *Kaiser Aluminum Fab Pdts LLC (P-5688)*

Kaga (usa) Inc ....E...... 714 540-2697
2620 S Susan St Santa Ana (92704) *(P-6527)*

Kagan Trim Center, Los Angeles Also Called: *G Kagan and Sons Inc (P-2022)*

Kahgo Truck Parts, Sun Valley Also Called: *K & G Latirovian Inc (P-9407)*

Kai USA Ltd ....E...... 323 589-2600
6031 Malburg Way Vernon (90058) *(F-5868)*

Kainalu Blue Inc ....E...... 760 806-6400
4675 North Ave Oceanside (92056) *(F-5555)*

Kair Harbor Express LLC (PA) ....D...... 562 432-6800
1129 Canal Ave Long Beach (90813) *(P-11591)*

Kairos Manufacturing Inc ....F...... 805 544-2216
201 Bridge St San Luis Obispo (93401) *(P-11237)*

Kaiser Air Conditioning, Oxnard Also Called: *Kaiser Air Conditioning and Sheet Metal Inc (P-1047)*

Kaiser Air Conditioning and Sheet Metal Inc .....E...... 805 988-1800
600 Pacific Ave Oxnard (93030) *(P-1047)*

Kaiser Aluminum Corporation .... B...... 323 726-8011
6250 Bandini Blvd Commerce (90040) *(P-5700)*

Kaiser Aluminum Fab Pdts LLC (HQ) ....A...... 949 614-1740
27422 Portola Pkwy Ste 200 Foothill Ranch (92610) *(P-5688)*

Kaiser Aluminum Fab Pdts LLC ....F...... 323 722-7151
6250 E Bandini Blvd Commerce (90040) *(P-5701)*

Kaiser Fndtion Hlth Plan GA In .... B...... 951 270-1200
1850 California Ave Corona (92881) *(P-14472)*

Kaiser Fndtion Hosp Gift Shppe .... C...... 323 857-3290
6041 Cadillac Ave Los Angeles (90034) *(P-14473)*

Kaiser Foundation Health Plan, West Covina Also Called: *Kaiser Foundation Hospitals (P-14477)*

Kaiser Foundation Health Plan, Downey Also Called: *Kaiser Foundation Hospitals (P-14478)*

Kaiser Foundation Health Plan, North Hollywood Also Called: *Kaiser Foundation Hospitals (P-14479)*

Kaiser Foundation Health Plan, Fontana Also Called: *Kaiser Foundation Hospitals (P-14481)*

Kaiser Foundation Health Plan, San Diego Also Called: *Southern Cal Prmnnte Med Group (P-14497)*

Kaiser Foundation Hospitals .... C...... 323 264-4310
3355 E 26th St Vernon (90058) *(P-13942)*

Kaiser Foundation Hospitals .... A...... 626 851-1011
1011 Baldwin Park Blvd Baldwin Park (91706) *(P-14474)*

Kaiser Foundation Hospitals .... B...... 562 657-9000
9333 Imperial Hwy Downey (90242) *(P-14475)*

Kaiser Foundation Hospitals .... C...... 866 340-5974
12470 Whittier Blvd Whittier (90602) *(P-14476)*

Kaiser Foundation Hospitals ....D...... 626 856-3045
1539 W Garvey Ave N West Covina (91790) *(P-14477)*

Kaiser Foundation Hospitals .... C...... 562 622-4190
12200 Bellflower Blvd Downey (90242) *(P-14478)*

Kaiser Foundation Hospitals .... C...... 818 503-7082
11666 Sherman Way North Hollywood (91605) *(P-14479)*

Kaiser Foundation Hospitals .... C...... 888 750-0036
3750 Grand Ave Chino (91710) *(P-14480)*

Kaiser Foundation Hospitals .... B...... 909 427-3910
9961 Sierra Ave Fontana (92335) *(P-14481)*

Kaiser Foundation Hospitals .... C...... 619 528-5000
8080 Parkway Dr La Mesa (91942) *(P-14482)*

Kaiser Foundation Hospitals .... B...... 949 932-5000
6640 Alton Pkwy Irvine (92618) *(P-14993)*

Kaiser Foundation Hospitals ....D...... 951 601-6174
12815 Heacock St Moreno Valley (92553) *(P-14994)*

Kaiser Foundation Hospitals .... A...... 619 528-5888
4647 Zion Ave San Diego (92120) *(P-14995)*

Kaiser Foundation Hospitals ....D...... 323 881-5516
5119 Pomona Blvd Los Angeles (90022) *(P-14996)*

Kaiser Foundation Hospitals .... C...... 888 750-0036
1301 California St Redlands (92374) *(P-17674)*

ALPHABETIC

Employee Codes: A=Over 500 employees, B=251-500
C=101-250, D=51-100, E=20-50, F=10-19, G=1-9

2024 Southern California
Business Directory and Buyers Guide

© Mergent Inc. 1-800-342-5647

1143

Kaiser Foundation Hospitals .... C...... 909 724-5000
2295 S Vineyard Ave Ontario (91761) *(P-17675)*

Kaiser Foundation Hospitals .... A...... 909 427-5000
9961 Sierra Ave Fontana (92335) *(P-17676)*

Kaiser Foundation Hospitals .... D...... 619 528-5000
780 Shadowridge Dr Vista (92083) *(P-17677)*

Kaiser Foundation Hospitals .... D...... 619 528-5000
250 Travelodge Dr El Cajon (92020) *(P-17678)*

Kaiser Foundation Hospitals .... C...... 619 528-5000
732 N Broadway Escondido (92025) *(P-17679)*

Kaiser Foundation Hospitals .... D...... 951 353-3790
10800 Magnolia Ave Riverside (92505) *(P-17680)*

Kaiser Foundation Hospitals .... A...... 951 353-2000
10800 Magnolia Ave Riverside (92505) *(P-17681)*

Kaiser Foundation Hospitals .... A...... 951 243-0811
27300 Iris Ave Moreno Valley (92555) *(P-17682)*

Kaiser Foundation Hospitals .... C...... 714 279-4675
411 N Lakeview Ave Anaheim (92807) *(P-17683)*

Kaiser Foundation Hospitals .... C...... 714 741-3448
12100 Euclid St Garden Grove (92840) *(P-17684)*

Kaiser Foundation Hospitals .... C...... 714 562-3420
5 Centerpointe Dr La Palma (90623) *(P-17685)*

Kaiser Foundation Hospitals .... C...... 714 967-4700
1900 E 4th St Santa Ana (92705) *(P-17686)*

Kaiser Foundation Hospitals .... C...... 818 375-4023
13652 Cantara St Panorama City (91402) *(P-17687)*

Kaiser Foundation Hospitals .... C...... 323 857-2000
6041 Cadillac Ave Los Angeles (90034) *(P-17688)*

Kaiser Foundation Hospitals .... A...... 323 857-2000
6041 Cadillac Ave Los Angeles (90034) *(P-17689)*

Kaiser Foundation Hospitals .... A...... 818 375-2000
13651 Willard St Panorama City (91402) *(P-17690)*

Kaiser Foundation Hospitals .... A...... 310 325-5111
25825 Vermont Ave Harbor City (90710) *(P-17691)*

Kaiser Foundation Hospitals .... D...... 323 783-7955
1550 N Edgemont St Los Angeles (90027) *(P-17692)*

Kaiser Foundation Hospitals .... C...... 818 552-3000
444 W Glenoaks Blvd Glendale (91202) *(P-17693)*

Kaiser Foundation Hospitals .... C...... 626 440-5639
3280 E Foothill Blvd Pasadena (91107) *(P-17694)*

Kaiser Foundation Hospitals .... C...... 323 783-8306
1515 N Vermont Ave Fl 3 Los Angeles (90027) *(P-17695)*

Kaiser Foundation Hospitals .... D...... 310 419-3303
110 N La Brea Ave Inglewood (90301) *(P-17696)*

Kaiser Foundation Hospitals .... C...... 661 398-5011
3501 Stockdale Hwy Bakersfield (93309) *(P-17697)*

Kaiser Foundation Hospitals .... D...... 661 334-2020
5055 California Ave Ste 110 Bakersfield (93309) *(P-17698)*

Kaiser Foundation Hospitals .... C...... 310 937-4311
400 S Sepulveda Blvd Manhattan Beach (90266) *(P-18294)*

Kaiser Foundation Hospitals .... C...... 323 783-4011
4733 W Sunset Blvd Fl 2 Los Angeles (90027) *(P-18295)*

Kaiser Foundation Hospitals .... C...... 909 394-2530
1255 W Arrow Hwy San Dimas (91773) *(P-18296)*

Kaiser Foundation Hospitals .... C...... 323 562-6400
7825 Atlantic Ave Cudahy (90201) *(P-18297)*

Kaiser Foundation Hospitals .... C...... 310 517-2956
15446 S Western Ave Gardena (90249) *(P-18298)*

Kaiser Foundation Hospitals .... D...... 833 574-2273
20000 Rinaldi St Porter Ranch (91326) *(P-18299)*

Kaiser Foundation Hospitals .... B...... 626 440-5659
1055 E Colorado Blvd Ste 100 Pasadena (91106) *(P-18300)*

Kaiser Foundation Hospitals .... C...... 661 412-6777
8800 Ming Ave Bakersfield (93311) *(P-18301)*

Kaiser Foundation Hospitals .... A...... 818 719-2000
5601 De Soto Ave Woodland Hills (91367) *(P-18302)*

Kaiser Foundation Hospitals .... A...... 661 726-2500
43112 15th St W Lancaster (93534) *(P-18303)*

Kaiser Foundation Hospitals .... C...... 951 353-2000
36450 Inland Valley Dr Ste 204 Wildomar (92595) *(P-18304)*

Kaiser Foundation Hospitals .... C...... 949 262-5780
6 Willard Irvine (92604) *(P-18305)*

Kaiser Foundation Hospitals .... C...... 951 353-4000
12620 Prescott Ave Tustin (92782) *(P-18306)*

Kaiser Foundation Hospitals .... A...... 714 644-2000
3440 E La Palma Ave Anaheim (92806) *(P-18307)*

Kaiser Foundation Hospitals .... C...... 619 528-2583
4405 Vandever Ave Fl 5 San Diego (92120) *(P-18308)*

Kaiser Foundation Hospitals .... C...... 858 573-1504
9455 Clairemont Mesa Blvd San Diego (92123) *(P-18309)*

Kaiser Foundation Hospitals .... C...... 619 528-5000
1630 E Main St El Cajon (92021) *(P-18310)*

Kaiser Foundation Hospitals .... C...... 213 580-7200
765 W College St Los Angeles (90012) *(P-18514)*

Kaiser Foundation Hospitals .... C...... 310 513-6707
23621 Main St Carson (90745) *(P-18699)*

Kaiser Mental Health Center, Los Angeles *Also Called: Kaiser Foundation Hospitals* *(P-18514)*

Kaiser Permanente .... C...... 909 427-3910
9985 Sierra Ave Fontana (92335) *(P-14483)*

Kaiser Permanente, Baldwin Park *Also Called: Kaiser Foundation Hospitals (P-14474)*

Kaiser Permanente, Whittier *Also Called: Kaiser Foundation Hospitals (P-14476)*

Kaiser Permanente, Chino *Also Called: Kaiser Foundation Hospitals (P-14480)*

Kaiser Permanente, San Diego *Also Called: Kaiser Foundation Hospitals (P-14995)*

Kaiser Permanente, Los Angeles *Also Called: Kaiser Foundation Hospitals (P-14996)*

Kaiser Permanente, Redlands *Also Called: Kaiser Foundation Hospitals (P-17674)*

Kaiser Permanente, Fontana *Also Called: Kaiser Foundation Hospitals (P-17676)*

Kaiser Permanente, Vista *Also Called: Kaiser Foundation Hospitals (P-17677)*

Kaiser Permanente, Garden Grove *Also Called: Kaiser Foundation Hospitals (P-17684)*

Kaiser Permanente, Santa Ana *Also Called: Kaiser Foundation Hospitals (P-17686)*

Kaiser Permanente, Panorama City *Also Called: Kaiser Foundation Hospitals (P-17690)*

Kaiser Permanente, Harbor City *Also Called: Kaiser Foundation Hospitals (P-17691)*

Kaiser Permanente, Los Angeles *Also Called: Kaiser Foundation Hospitals (P-17695)*

Kaiser Permanente, Inglewood *Also Called: Kaiser Foundation Hospitals (P-17696)*

Kaiser Permanente, Bakersfield *Also Called: Kaiser Foundation Hospitals (P-17698)*

Kaiser Permanente, San Diego *Also Called: Southern Cal Prmnnte Med Group (P-17785)*

Kaiser Permanente, San Dimas *Also Called: Kaiser Foundation Hospitals (P-18296)*

Kaiser Permanente, Pasadena *Also Called: Kaiser Foundation Hospitals (P-18300)*

Kaiser Permanente, Bakersfield *Also Called: Kaiser Foundation Hospitals (P-18301)*

Kaiser Permanente, Woodland Hills *Also Called: Kaiser Foundation Hospitals (P-18302)*

Kaiser Permanente, Lancaster *Also Called: Kaiser Foundation Hospitals (P-18303)*

Kaiser Permanente, Tustin *Also Called: Kaiser Foundation Hospitals (P-18306)*

Kaiser Permanente, San Diego *Also Called: Kaiser Foundation Hospitals (P-18308)*

Kaiser Permanente, San Diego *Also Called: Kaiser Foundation Hospitals (P-18309)*

Kaiser Permanente, Downey *Also Called: Southern Cal Prmnnte Med Group (P-18451)*

Kaiser Permanente, Carson *Also Called: Kaiser Foundation Hospitals (P-18699)*

Kaiser Permanente Watts C .... D...... 323 564-7911
1465 E 103rd St Los Angeles (90002) *(P-18311)*

Kaiser Prmnente Downey Med Ctr, Downey *Also Called: Kaiser Foundation Hospitals* *(P-14475)*

Kaiser Prmnnte Mreno Vly Med C, Moreno Valley *Also Called: Kaiser Foundation Hospitals* *(P-17682)*

Kaiser Prmnnte Nat Fclties Svc, Vernon *Also Called: Kaiser Foundation Hospitals (P-13942)*

Kaiser Prmnnte Ornge Cnty-Nhei, Anaheim *Also Called: Kaiser Foundation Hospitals* *(P-18307)*

Kaiser Prmnnte Psadena Med Off, Pasadena *Also Called: Kaiser Foundation Hospitals* *(P-17694)*

Kaiser Prmnnte Schl Anesthesia .... C...... 626 564-3016
100 S Los Robles Ste 501 Pasadena (91101) *(P-17699)*

Kaiser Prmnnte W Los Angles Me, Los Angeles *Also Called: Kaiser Foundation Hospitals* *(P-17689)*

Kaizen Syndicate LLC .... C...... 858 309-2028
10413 Magical Waters Ct Spring Valley (91978) *(P-16575)*

Kakuichi America Inc .... D...... 310 539-1590
23540 Telo Ave Torrance (90505) *(P-4851)*

Kal Plastics, Vernon *Also Called: Tom York Enterprises Inc (P-5229)*

Kal-Cameron Manufacturing Corp (HQ) .... D...... **626 338-7308**
4265 Puente Ave Baldwin Park (91706) *(P-5883)*

Kalap Inc .... F...... 818 332-6916
401 N Brand Blvd Ste 814 Glendale (91203) *(P-10871)*

Kalaydjian Shahe Inc .... F...... 818 988-3700
7032 Valjean Ave Van Nuys (91406) *(P-9408)*

Kaleidioscope Stadium Cinema, Mission Viejo *Also Called: Edwards Theatres Inc (P-17291)*

Kama Sutra, Moorpark *Also Called: Kamsut Incorporated (P-4426)*

Kamm Industries Inc ....E...... 800 317-6253
43352 Business Park Dr Temecula (92590) *(P-2534)*

Kammerer Enterprises Inc ....D...... 760 560-0550
1280 N Melrose Dr Vista (92083) *(P-5529)*

Kamsut Incorporated ....E...... 805 495-7479
5260 Kazuko Ct Moorpark (93021) *(P-4426)*

Kan-Di-Ki LLC (HQ)...D...... 818 549-1880
2820 N Ontario St Burbank (91504) *(P-18554)*

Kana Pipeline Inc ....D...... 714 986-1400
12620 Magnolia Ave Riverside (92503) *(P-679)*

Kanan Baking Company, Woodland Hills *Also Called: Gold Coast Baking Company LLC (P-1475)*

Kandy Kiss of California Inc ....D
14761 Califa St Van Nuys (91411) *(P-2249)*

Kanex ....E...... 714 332-1681
4295 Jurupa St Ste 111 Ontario (91761) *(P-9222)*

Kaney Foods, San Luis Obispo *Also Called: Amk Foodservices Inc (P-13171)*

Kang Family Partners LLC ....C...... 805 688-1000
555 Mcmurray Rd Buellton (93427) *(P-15206)*

Kanstul Musical Instrs Inc ....E...... 714 563-1000
23772 Perth Bay Dana Point (92629) *(P-10926)*

Kap Manufacturing Inc ....E...... 909 599-2525
327 W Allen Ave San Dimas (91773) *(P-7894)*

Kap Medical ....E...... 951 340-4360
1395 Pico St Corona (92881) *(P-10377)*

Kapan - Kent Company Inc ....E...... 760 631-1716
3540 Seagate Way Ste 100 Oceanside (92056) *(P-2535)*

Kar Ice Service Inc (PA)...F...... 760 256-2648
2521 Solar Way Barstow (92311) *(P-1837)*

Karat, Chino *Also Called: Karat Packaging Inc (P-5075)*

Karat Packaging Inc (PA)..E...... 626 965-8882
6185 Kimball Ave Chino (91708) *(P-5075)*

Karbide Inc ....E...... 951 354-0900
12650 Magnolia Ave Ste B Riverside (92503) *(P-7117)*

Kare Klub ....D...... 858 538-5437
9995 Carmel Mountain Rd Ste B8 San Diego (92129) *(P-19213)*

Karel Manufacturing, Calexico *Also Called: Lorenz Inc (P-9227)*

Karem Aircraft Inc ....E...... 949 859-4444
1 Capital Dr Lake Forest (92630) *(P-9730)*

Karen Kane Inc (PA)..C...... 323 588-0000
2275 E 37th St Vernon (90058) *(P-13129)*

Kareo PM, Corona Del Mar *Also Called: Tebra Technologies Inc (P-16133)*

Kargo Global Inc ....C...... 212 979-9000
1437 4th St Ste 200 Santa Monica (90401) *(P-15595)*

Karl Storz Endscpy-America Inc ....D...... 800 964-5563
1 N Los Carneros Dr Goleta (93117) *(P-10541)*

Karl Storz Endscpy-America Inc (HQ).....................B...... 424 218-8100
2151 E Grand Ave El Segundo (90245) *(P-10542)*

Karl Storz Imaging Inc (HQ).....................................B...... 805 968-5563
1 S Los Carneros Rd Goleta (93117) *(P-10378)*

Karl Storz Imaging Inc ....E...... 805 968-5563
32 Aero Camino Goleta (93117) *(P-10543)*

Karl Strauss Brewery & Rest, San Diego *Also Called: Associated Microbreweries Inc (P-1582)*

Karl Strauss Brewery Garden, San Diego *Also Called: Associated Microbreweries Inc (P-1583)*

Karl Strauss Brewing Company (PA) ....E...... 858 273-2739
5985 Santa Fe St San Diego (92109) *(P-1595)*

Karl Strauss Brewing Company, San Diego *Also Called: Assocted McRbrwries Ltd A Cal (P-1585)*

Karma Automotive LLC ....A...... 855 565-2762
9950 Jeronimo Rd Irvine (92618) *(P-9294)*

Karoun Cheese, San Fernando *Also Called: Karoun Dairies Inc (P-1255)*

Karoun Dairies Inc (PA)...E...... 818 767-7000
13023 Arroyo St San Fernando (91340) *(P-1255)*

Kas Engineering Inc (PA)...E...... 310 450-8925
1714 14th St Santa Monica (90404) *(P-5076)*

Kastle Stair Inc (PA)...E...... 714 596-2600
7422 Mountjoy Dr Huntington Beach (92648) *(P-2609)*

Kate Farms Inc ....C...... 805 845-2446
101 Innovation Pl Santa Barbara (93108) *(P-1921)*

Kate Smrvlle Skin Hlth Experts, Beverly Hills *Also Called: Kate Somerville Skincare LLC (P-4150)*

Kate Somerville Skincare LLC (HQ).........................D...... 323 655-7546
144 S Beverly Dr Ste 500 Beverly Hills (90212) *(P-4150)*

Katella Properties ....D...... 562 704-8695
10140 Grayling Ave Whittier (90603) *(P-14668)*

Katella Properties ....D...... 562 596-5561
3902 Katella Ave Los Alamitos (90720) *(P-17981)*

Kater-Crafts Incorporated ....E...... 562 692-0665
4860 Gregg Rd Pico Rivera (90660) *(P-3847)*

Katerra ....D...... 720 449-3909
1950 W Corporate Way Anaheim (92801) *(P-439)*

Katerra Construction LLC ....A...... 720 449-3909
1950 W Corporate Way Anaheim (92801) *(P-440)*

Kathleen Brugger ....E...... 909 226-1372
6815 Foxtail Ct Rancho Cucamonga (91739) *(P-17092)*

Katolec Development Inc ....E...... 619 710-0075
6120 Business Center Ct San Diego (92154) *(P-9074)*

Katz Millennium Sls & Mktg Inc ....C...... 323 966-5066
5700 Wilshire Blvd Ste 100 Los Angeles (90036) *(P-8527)*

Katzirs Floor & HM Design Inc (PA).........................E...... 818 988-9663
14959 Delano St Van Nuys (91411) *(P-12305)*

Katzkin Leather Inc (PA)...C...... 323 725-1243
6868 W Acco St Montebello (90640) *(P-13543)*

Kava Holdings Inc (DH)...C...... 310 472-1211
701 Stone Canyon Rd Los Angeles (90077) *(P-15207)*

Kavlico Corporation (DH)..A...... 805 523-2000
1461 Lawrence Dr Thousand Oaks (91320) *(P-9075)*

Kawasaki Motors Corp USA (HQ).............................B...... 949 837-4683
26972 Burbank Foothill Ranch (92610) *(P-13901)*

Kawneer Company Inc ....D...... 951 410-4779
925 Marlborough Ave Riverside (92507) *(P-6110)*

Kay & James Inc ....D...... 818 998-0357
14062 Balboa Blvd Sylmar (91342) *(P-7895)*

Kaydan Logistics LLC ....D...... 951 961-9000
45562 Ponderosa Ct Temecula (92592) *(P-11835)*

Kaylas Cake Corporation ....E...... 714 869-1522
1311 S Gilbert St Fullerton (92833) *(P-13718)*

Kayo Clothing Company, Lynwood *Also Called: Kayo of California (P-2340)*

Kayo of California (PA)..E...... 323 233-6107
11854 Alameda St Lynwood (90262) *(P-2340)*

Kazak-Mars Inc ....E...... 818 375-1033
16430 Vanowen St Van Nuys (91406) *(P-10842)*

Kazuhm Inc ....E...... 858 771-3861
6450 Lusk Blvd Ste E208 San Diego (92121) *(P-16283)*

KB Delta Inc ....E...... 310 530-1539
3340 Fujita St Torrance (90505) *(P-6528)*

KB Delta Comprsr Valve Parts, Torrance *Also Called: KB Delta Inc (P-6528)*

KB Foam Inc ....F...... 619 661-1870
2525 Camino Del Rio S Ste 145 San Diego (92108) *(P-4892)*

KB Home (PA)...D...... 310 231-4000
10990 Wilshire Blvd Fl 7 Los Angeles (90024) *(P-484)*

KB Home Grater Los Angeles Inc (HQ).....................D...... 310 231-4000
10990 Wilshire Blvd Ste 700 Los Angeles (90024) *(P-441)*

KB Home Grater Los Angeles Inc ....C...... 951 691-5300
36310 Inland Valley Dr Wildomar (92595) *(P-442)*

KB Sheetmetal Fabrication Inc ....E...... 714 979-1780
17371 Mount Wynne Cir # B Fountain Valley (92708) *(P-6259)*

Kba Engineering LLC ....D...... 661 323-0487
2157 Mohawk St Bakersfield (93308) *(P-6961)*

Kbkg Inc ....C...... 626 449-4225
225 S Lake Ave Ste 400 Pasadena (91101) *(P-19783)*

Kbm Building Services, San Diego *Also Called: Kbm Fclity Sltons Holdings LLC (P-15718)*

Kbm Fclity Sltons Holdings LLC ....B...... 858 467-0202
7976 Engineer Rd Ste 200 San Diego (92111) *(P-15718)*

Kbr Inc ....E...... 562 436-9281
2000 W Gaylord St Long Beach (90813) *(P-8164)*

Kc Hilites Inc ....E...... 928 635-2607
13637 Cimarron Ave Gardena (90249) *(P-8348)*

Kc Pharmaceuticals Inc (PA)....................................D...... 909 598-9499
3201 Producer Way Pomona (91768) *(P-4151)*

Employee Codes: A=Over 500 employees, B=251-500
C=101-250, D=51-100, E=20-50, F=10-19, G=1-9

2024 Southern California
Business Directory and Buyers Guide

© Mergent Inc. 1-800-342-5647

1145

Kc Services, Anaheim *Also Called: Korean Community Services Inc (P-18529)*

Kca Electronics Inc ....C....... 714 239-2433
223 N Crescent Way Anaheim (92801) *(P-8695)*

Kcb Towers Inc ....D...... 909 862-0322
27260 Meines St Highland (92346) *(P-1106)*

Kdc Inc (HQ)..**C....... 714 828-7000**
4462 Corporate Center Dr Los Alamitos (90720) *(P-910)*

Kdc Systems, Los Alamitos *Also Called: Kdc Inc (P-910)*

Kdc/One Chatsworth Inc (DH)...........................**C....... 818 709-1345**
20245 Sunburst St Chatsworth (91311) *(P-4427)*

Kdc/One Chatsworth Inc ....C....... 818 709-1345
20320 Prairie St Chatsworth (91311) *(P-4428)*

Kdg Construction Consulting, Glendale *Also Called: Kennard Development Group (P-471)*

Keating Dental Arts Inc ....C....... 949 955-2100
16881 Hale Ave Ste A Irvine (92606) *(P-18571)*

Keating Dental Lab, Irvine *Also Called: Keating Dental Arts Inc (P-18571)*

Kec Engineering ....C....... 951 734-3010
26320 Lester Cir Corona (92883) *(P-627)*

Kechika, Rcho Sta Marg *Also Called: Point Conception Inc (P-2360)*

Keck Hospital of Usc ....A....... 800 872-2273
1500 San Pablo St Los Angeles (90033) *(P-18312)*

Keck Medical Center of Usc ....D...... 323 371-9535
1520 San Pablo St Los Angeles (90033) *(P-17700)*

Keck School ....D...... 323 442-1179
2011 Zonal Ave Los Angeles (90089) *(P-18313)*

Keco Inc ....E....... 619 298-3800
3475 Kurtz St San Diego (92110) *(P-12796)*

Kedren Acute Psychtric Hosp Cm, Los Angeles *Also Called: Kedren Community Hlth Ctr Inc (P-18515)*

Kedren Community Hlth Ctr Inc (PA)....................**B....... 323 233-0425**
4211 Avalon Blvd Los Angeles (90011) *(P-18515)*

Kedren Community Hlth Ctr Inc ....C....... 323 524-0634
3800 S Figueroa St Los Angeles (90037) *(P-19106)*

Keefe Plumbing Services, Glendale *Also Called: H L Moe Co Inc (P-775)*

Keenan & Associates (HQ)...................................**B....... 310 212-3344**
2355 Crenshaw Blvd Ste 200 Torrance (90501) *(P-14606)*

Keesal Young Logan A Prof Corp (PA)...................**D...... 562 436-2000**
400 Oceangate Long Beach (90802) *(P-18881)*

KEIRO SENIOR HEALTH CARE, Los Angeles *Also Called: Keiro Services (P-20048)*

Keiro Services ....B....... 213 873-5700
420 E 3rd St Ste 1000 Los Angeles (90013) *(P-20048)*

Keith Co, Pico Rivera *Also Called: W P Keith Co Inc (P-7374)*

Keith E Archambeau Sr Inc ....E....... 818 718-6110
20615 Plummer St Chatsworth (91311) *(P-6260)*

Kelco, Oxnard *Also Called: Kim Laube & Company Inc (P-4429)*

Kelcourt Plastics Inc (DH)...................................**D...... 949 361-0774**
1000 Calle Recodo San Clemente (92673) *(P-5077)*

Keller Classics Inc (PA).......................................**E....... 805 524-1322**
102 S Robinson St Tehachapi (93561) *(P-2293)*

Keller North America Inc ....D...... 805 933-1331
1780 E Lemonwood Dr Santa Paula (93060) *(P-1165)*

Keller Williams ....D...... 323 300-1700
2150 Hillhurst Ave Los Angeles (90027) *(P-14818)*

Keller Williams Realtors, Los Angeles *Also Called: Keller Williams (P-14818)*

Keller Williams Realtors, Beverly Hills *Also Called: Keller Wllams Rlty Bvrly Hills (P-14819)*

Keller Williams Realtors, Corona *Also Called: Pro Group Inc (P-14845)*

Keller Wllams Rlty Bvrly Hills ....D...... 310 432-6400
439 N Canon Dr Ste 300 Beverly Hills (90210) *(P-14819)*

Kellermyer Bergensons Svcs LLC (PA)...................**E....... 760 631-5111**
3605 Ocean Ranch Blvd Ste 200 Oceanside (92056) *(P-7667)*

Kelley Blue Book Co Inc (DH)...............................**D...... 949 770-7704**
195 Technology Dr Irvine (92618) *(P-3363)*

Kelly Pneumatics Inc ....E....... 800 704-7552
1611 Babcock St Newport Beach (92663) *(P-9223)*

Kelly Services, Costa Mesa *Also Called: Southern Home Care Svcs Inc (P-15943)*

Kelly Spicers Inc (HQ)...**C....... 562 698-1199**
12310 Slauson Ave Santa Fe Springs (90670) *(P-12990)*

Kelly Spicers Packaging North, Santa Fe Springs *Also Called: Kelly Spicers Inc (P-12990)*

Kelly Thomas MD Ucsd Hlth Care ....C....... 619 543-2885
200 W Arbor Dr San Diego (92103) *(P-18774)*

Kelly Toys, Vernon *Also Called: Kelly Toys Holdings LLC (P-14934)*

Kelly Toys Holdings LLC ....D...... 323 923-1300
4811 S Alameda St Vernon (90058) *(P-14934)*

Kelly-Wright Hardwoods Inc ....F....... 714 632-9930
450 Delta Ave Brea (92821) *(P-12336)*

Kelmscott Communications LLC ....B....... 949 475-1900
2485 Da Vinci Irvine (92614) *(P-3611)*

Kelpac Medical, San Clemente *Also Called: Kelcourt Plastics Inc (P-5077)*

Kemac Technology Inc ....E....... 626 334-1519
503 S Vincent Ave Azusa (91702) *(P-7896)*

Kemco, Ontario *Also Called: Kitchen Equipment Mfg Co Inc (P-6529)*

Kemira Water Solutions Inc ....E....... 909 350-5678
14000 San Bernardino Ave Fontana (92335) *(P-3896)*

Kemira Water Solutions Inc ....E....... 909 350-5678
14000 San Bernardino Ave Fontana (92335) *(P-4613)*

Kemiron Pacific, Fontana *Also Called: Kemira Water Solutions Inc (P-4613)*

Kemper Enterprises Inc ....E....... 909 627-6191
13595 12th St Chino (91710) *(P-5884)*

Kempton Machine Works Inc ....E....... 714 990-0596
4070 E Leaverton Ct Anaheim (92807) *(P-7118)*

Ken Blanchard Companies, The, Escondido *Also Called: Blanchard Training and Dev Inc (P-20141)*

Ken Grody Ford, Carlsbad *Also Called: Ted Ford Jones Inc (P-13835)*

Ken Grody Ford, Buena Park *Also Called: Ted Ford Jones Inc (P-17039)*

Ken Grody Ford - Redlands, Redlands *Also Called: Ken Grody Redlands LLC (P-13786)*

Ken Grody Redlands LLC ....D...... 909 793-3211
1121 W Colton Ave Redlands (92374) *(P-13786)*

Ken Real Estate Lease Ltd ....D...... 714 778-1700
900 S Disneyland Dr Anaheim (92802) *(P-15208)*

Ken Starr Inc ....D...... 714 632-8789
1120 N Tustin Ave Anaheim (92807) *(P-783)*

Kenai Drilling Limited ....C....... 661 587-0117
2651 Patton Way Bakersfield (93308) *(P-1095)*

Kendal Floral Supply LLC (PA).............................**D...... 888 828-9875**
1960 Kellogg Ave Carlsbad (92008) *(P-13511)*

Kendal North Bouquet Co, Carlsbad *Also Called: Kendal Floral Supply LLC (P-13511)*

Kendon Industries LLC ....F....... 714 630-7144
2990 E Miraloma Ave Anaheim (92806) *(P-13896)*

Kennard Development Group ....D...... 818 241-0800
1025 N Brand Blvd Ste 300 Glendale (91202) *(P-471)*

Kennedy Athletics, Carson *Also Called: Cali-Fame Los Angeles Inc (P-2399)*

Kennedy Engineered Pdts Inc ....F....... 661 272-1147
38830 17th St E Palmdale (93550) *(P-9409)*

Kennedy Name Plate Co ....E....... 323 585-0121
4501 Pacific Blvd Vernon (90058) *(P-6714)*

Kennedy-Wilson Inc (PA)......................................**C....... 310 887-6400**
151 El Camino Dr Beverly Hills (90212) *(P-14820)*

Kenneth Corp ....A....... 714 537-5160
12601 Garden Grove Blvd Garden Grove (92843) *(P-18314)*

KENNETH NORRIS CANCER HOSPITAL, Los Angeles *Also Called: Tenet Health Systems Norris (P-18472)*

Kenny The Printer, Orange *Also Called: American PCF Prtrs College Inc (P-3509)*

Kens Spray Equipment Inc ....C....... 310 635-9995
1900 W Walnut St Compton (90220) *(P-6715)*

Kenwait Die Casting Company, Sun Valley *Also Called: Kenwalt Die Casting Corp (P-5761)*

Kenwalt Die Casting Corp ....E....... 818 768-5800
8719 Bradley Ave Sun Valley (91352) *(P-5761)*

Keolis Transit America Inc ....C....... 818 616-5254
14663 Keswick St Van Nuys (91405) *(P-11322)*

Keolis Transit America Inc ....D...... 661 341-3910
660 W Avenue L Lancaster (93534) *(P-11323)*

Kepner Plas Fabricators Inc ....E....... 310 325-3162
3131 Lomita Blvd Torrance (90505) *(P-5078)*

Kerleylegacy63 Inc ....D...... 714 630-7286
3000-3010 La Jolla St Anaheim (92806) *(P-7897)*

Kern County Hospital Authority (PA)......................**B....... 661 326-2102**
1700 Mount Vernon Ave Bakersfield (93306) *(P-18315)*

Kern County Hospital Authority ....A....... 661 843-7980
1902 B St Bakersfield (93301) *(P-18700)*

Kern Direct Marketing, Woodland Hills *Also Called: Kern Organization Inc (P-15551)*

Mergent email: customerrelations@mergent.com
1146

2024 Southern California
Business Directory and Buyers Guide

(P-0000) Products & Services Section entry number
(PA)=Parent Co (HQ)=Headquarters (DH)=Div Headquarters

Kern Energy, Bakersfield *Also Called: Kern Oil & Refining Co (P-4642)*

Kern Engineering, Chino *Also Called: R Kern Engineering & Mfg Corp (P-8980)*

Kern Family Helathcare, Bakersfield *Also Called: Kern Health Systems Inc (P-17701)*

Kern Federal Credit Union ....D...... 661 327-9461
1717 Truxtun Ave Bakersfield (93301) *(P-14228)*

Kern Health Systems Inc ....D...... 661 664-5000
2900 Buck Owens Blvd Bakersfield (93308) *(P-17701)*

Kern Oil & Refining Co (HQ)...C...... 661 845-0761
7724 E Panama Ln Bakersfield (93307) *(P-4642)*

Kern Organization Inc ....D...... 818 703-8775
20955 Warner Center Ln Woodland Hills (91367) *(P-15551)*

Kern Regional Center (PA)..C...... 661 327-8531
3200 N Sillect Ave Bakersfield (93308) *(P-19331)*

Kern Ridge Growers LLC ....B...... 661 854-3141
25429 Barbara St Arvin (93203) *(P-107)*

KERN RIVER HEALTH CENTER, Bakersfield *Also Called: Clinica Sierra Vista (P-17625)*

Kern River Transitional Care, Bakersfield *Also Called: Bakersfieldidence Opco LLC (P-17887)*

Kern Steel Fabrication Inc (PA)......................................D...... 661 327-9588
627 Williams St Bakersfield (93305) *(P-6037)*

Kern Valley Hosp Foundation (PA)...............................B...... 760 379-2681
6412 Laurel Ave Lake Isabella (93240) *(P-14055)*

KERN VALLEY HOSPITAL, Lake Isabella *Also Called: Kern Valley Hosp Foundation (P-14055)*

Kern Valley Sun, Lake Isabella *Also Called: Wick Communications Co (P-3338)*

Kern Valleyidence Opco LLC ....C...... 661 323-2894
3601 San Dimas St Bakersfield (93301) *(P-18087)*

Kernel, Culver City *Also Called: HI LLC (P-19895)*

Kernridge Division, Mc Kittrick *Also Called: Aera Energy LLC (P-244)*

Kerns Beverages LLC (DH) ....E...... 888 655-3767
4002 Westminster Ave Santa Ana (92703) *(P-1699)*

Kerr Corporation (HQ)...C...... 714 516-7400
1717 W Collins Ave Orange (92867) *(P-10749)*

Kerry Inc ....D...... 760 396-2116
64405 Lincoln St Mecca (92254) *(P-1274)*

Kerv Interactive, Sherman Oaks *Also Called: Grabit Interactive Inc (P-15594)*

Kesa Incorporated ....E...... 714 956-2827
960 E Discovery Ln Anaheim (92801) *(P-16744)*

Kesmor Associates ....E...... 213 629-2300
610 S Broadway Ste 717 Los Angeles (90014) *(P-10903)*

Ketab Corporation ....E...... 310 477-7477
12701 Van Nuys Blvd Ste H Pacoima (91331) *(P-14067)*

Kettenbach LP ....E...... 877 532-2123
16052 Beach Blvd Ste 221 Huntington Beach (92647) *(P-10750)*

Kettenburg Marine Corporation ....C...... 619 224-8211
2810 Carleton St San Diego (92106) *(P-12911)*

Keurig Green Mountain Inc ....E...... 909 557-6513
26875 Pioneer Ave Redlands (92374) *(P-1700)*

Kev-Ton Inc ....E...... 619 482-2600
925 Hale Pl Ste A10 Chula Vista (91914) *(P-9076)*

Kevcon Inc ....D...... 760 432-0307
10679 Westview Pkwy San Diego (92126) *(P-508)*

Kevin Whaley ....E...... 619 596-4000
9565 Pathway St Santee (92071) *(P-6819)*

Kevita, Oxnard *Also Called: Kevita Inc (P-1701)*

Kevita Inc (HQ)...D...... 805 200-2250
2220 Celsius Ave Ste A Oxnard (93030) *(P-1701)*

Key Code Media Inc (PA)...E...... 818 303-3900
270 S Flower St Burbank (91502) *(P-7435)*

Key Container, South Gate *Also Called: Liberty Container Company (P-3114)*

Key Essentials Inc ....D
1916 S Tubeway Ave Commerce (90040) *(P-1779)*

Key-Bak, Ontario *Also Called: West Coast Chain Mfg Co (P-9270)*

Keyes Lexus, Van Nuys *Also Called: Keylex Inc (P-13788)*

Keyes Motors Inc (PA)...D...... 818 782-0122
5855 Van Nuys Blvd Van Nuys (91401) *(P-13787)*

Keyes Toyota, Van Nuys *Also Called: Keyes Motors Inc (P-13787)*

Keylex Inc (PA)...D...... 818 379-4000
5905 Van Nuys Blvd Van Nuys (91401) *(P-13788)*

Keyline Sales Inc ....E...... 562 904-3910
9768 Firestone Blvd Downey (90241) *(P-12745)*

Keystone Automotive Warehouse ....D...... 951 277-5237
15640 Cantu Galleano Ranch Rd Eastvale (91752) *(P-12245)*

KEYSTONE AUTOMOTIVE WAREHOUSE, Eastvale *Also Called: Keystone Automotive Warehouse (P-12245)*

Keystone Dental Inc ....E...... 781 328-3324
5 Holland Ste 209 Irvine (92618) *(P-10751)*

Keystone Dental Inc ....E...... 781 328-3382
13645 Alton Pkwy Ste A Irvine (92618) *(P-10752)*

Keystone Educatn & Youth Svcs, Riverside *Also Called: Keystone NPS LLC (P-19332)*

Keystone Ford Inc (PA)...C...... 562 868-0825
12000 Firestone Blvd Norwalk (90650) *(P-13789)*

Keystone NPS LLC ....C...... 951 785-0504
9994 County Farm Rd Riverside (92503) *(P-19332)*

Keystone NPS LLC (DH)..D...... 909 633-6354
11980 Mount Vernon Ave Grand Terrace (92313) *(P-19333)*

Keystone Schools-Ramona, Grand Terrace *Also Called: Keystone NPS LLC (P-19333)*

Keyt Television, Santa Barbara *Also Called: Smith Broadcasting Group Inc (P-11964)*

Keytonex Inc ....E...... 310 828-2207
5957 Pat Ave Woodland Hills (91367) *(P-11058)*

Kgs Electronics, Arcadia *Also Called: Gar Enterprises (P-12413)*

Kgtv, San Diego *Also Called: EW Scripps Company (P-11947)*

Khyber Foods Incorporated ....F...... 714 879-0900
500 S Acacia Ave Fullerton (92831) *(P-1922)*

Ki-P C USA Jeans Inc ....D...... 310 234-8185
6738 Los Verdes Dr Apt 2 Rancho Palos Verdes (90275) *(P-2169)*

Kia Design Center America, Irvine *Also Called: Hyundai Amer Technical Ctr Inc (P-19612)*

Kiara Sky Professional Nails, Bakersfield *Also Called: Glam and Glits Nail Design Inc (P-4414)*

Kids Empire, West Hollywood *Also Called: Kids Empire USA LLC (P-17555)*

Kids Empire USA LLC ....D...... 424 527-1039
8605 Santa Monica Blvd West Hollywood (90069) *(P-17555)*

Kids Healthy Foods LLC ....E...... 949 260-4950
2030 Main St Ste 1300 Irvine (92614) *(P-13374)*

Kids Line LLC ....C...... 310 660-0110
10541 Humbolt St Los Alamitos (90720) *(P-2474)*

KIDSPACE, Pasadena *Also Called: Kidspce A Prticipatory Museum (P-19354)*

Kidspce A Prticipatory Museum ....D...... 626 449-9144
480 N Arroyo Blvd Pasadena (91103) *(P-19354)*

Kieran Label Corp ....E...... 619 449-4457
2321 Siempre Viva Ct Ste 101 San Diego (92154) *(P-3774)*

Kiewit Corporation ....D...... 858 208-4285
12700 Stowe Dr Ste 180 Poway (92064) *(P-562)*

Kiewit Infrastructure West Co ....C...... 562 946-1816
10704 Shoemaker Ave Santa Fe Springs (90670) *(P-628)*

Kifm Smooth Jazz 981 Inc ....C...... 619 297-3698
1615 Murray Canyon Rd San Diego (92108) *(P-11926)*

Kifuki USA Co Inc (HQ)...D...... 626 334-8090
15547 1st St Irwindale (91706) *(P-1246)*

Kik, Santa Fe Springs *Also Called: Kik-Socal Inc (P-4355)*

Kik Custom Products, Torrance *Also Called: Prestone Products Corporation (P-4627)*

Kik Pool Additives Inc ....C...... 909 390-9912
5160 E Airport Dr Ontario (91761) *(P-4614)*

Kik-Socal Inc ....A...... 562 946-6427
9028 Dice Rd Santa Fe Springs (90670) *(P-4355)*

Kilgore Machine Company Inc ....E...... 714 540-3659
2312 S Susan St Santa Ana (92704) *(P-7898)*

Killion Industries Inc (PA)...D...... 760 727-5102
1380 Poinsettia Ave Vista (92081) *(P-2958)*

Kilovac, Carpinteria *Also Called: Te Connectivity Corporation (P-8194)*

Kim & Cami Productions Inc ....E...... 323 584-1300
2950 Leonis Blvd Vernon (90058) *(P-2341)*

Kim Chong ....E...... 323 581-4700
2105 E 25th St Los Angeles (90058) *(P-16853)*

Kim Laube & Company Inc ....E...... 805 240-1300
2221 Statham Blvd Oxnard (93033) *(P-4429)*

Kim Lighting & Mfg, City Of Industry *Also Called: Kim Lighting Inc (P-8370)*

Kim Lighting Inc ....A...... 626 968-5666
16555 Gale Ave City Of Industry (91745) *(P-8370)*

Kim's Fence, Fullerton *Also Called: Kims Welding and Iron Works (P-6464)*

Kimberly Lighting, Vernon *Also Called: Hollywood Lamp & Shade Co (P-8246)*

Employee Codes: A=Over 500 employees, B=251-500
C=101-250, D=51-100, E=20-50, F=10-19, G=1-9

2024 Southern California
Business Directory and Buyers Guide

© Mergent Inc. 1-800-342-5647

1147

ALPHABETIC

Kimberly Machine Inc .... E....... 714 539-0151
12822 Joy St Garden Grove (92840) *(P-7899)*

Kimco Services, Ontario *Also Called: Kimco Staffing Services Inc (P-15859)*

Kimco Staffing Services Inc .... A....... 951 686-3800
1770 Iowa Ave Ste 160 Riverside (92507) *(P-15858)*

Kimco Staffing Services Inc .... A....... 909 390-9881
4295 Jurupa St Ste 107 Ontario (91761) *(P-15859)*

Kimco Staffing Services Inc .... A....... 310 622-1616
3415 S Sepulveda Blvd Ste 1100 Los Angeles (90034) *(P-15860)*

Kimco Staffing Solutions, Riverside *Also Called: Kimco Staffing Services Inc (P-15858)*

Kimpton Hotel & Rest Group LLC .... C....... 323 852-6000
6317 Wilshire Blvd Los Angeles (90048) *(P-15209)*

Kims Welding and Iron Works .... F....... 714 680-7700
2331 E Orangethorpe Ave Fullerton (92831) *(P-6464)*

Kinamed Inc .... E....... 805 384-2748
820 Flynn Rd Camarillo (93012) *(P-10678)*

Kindeva Drug Delivery LP .... B....... 818 341-1300
19901 Nordhoff St Northridge (91324) *(P-4152)*

Kindred Hospital - Rancho, Rancho Cucamonga *Also Called: Knd Development 55 LLC (P-18316)*

Kindred Hospital La Mirata, West Covina *Also Called: Southern Cal Spcialty Care Inc (P-18453)*

Kindred Hospital Santa Ana, Santa Ana *Also Called: Southern Cal Spcialty Care Inc (P-18454)*

Kindred Litho Incorporated .... E....... 909 944-4015
10833 Bell Ct Rancho Cucamonga (91730) *(P-3612)*

KINECTA, Manhattan Beach *Also Called: Kinecta Federal Credit Union (P-14229)*

Kinecta Federal Credit Union (PA) .... C....... 310 643-5400
1440 Rosecrans Ave Manhattan Beach (90266) *(P-14229)*

Kinemetrics Inc (DH) .... D....... 626 795-2220
222 Vista Ave Pasadena (91107) *(P-19630)*

Kineticom Inc (PA) .... D....... 619 330-3100
333 H St Chula Vista (91910) *(P-15861)*

King Bros Enterprises LLC .... C....... 661 257-3262
29101 The Old Rd Valencia (91355) *(P-4918)*

King Bros Industries C
29101 The Old Rd Valencia (91355) *(P-5079)*

King Ex Chinese Fd & Donut, North Hollywood *Also Called: King Express Inc (P-14018)*

King Express Inc .... F....... 818 503-2772
12053 Vanowen St North Hollywood (91605) *(P-14018)*

King Graphics, San Diego *Also Called: Colmol Inc (P-3747)*

King Henrys Inc .... E....... 818 536-3692
29124 Hancock Pkwy 1 Valencia (91355) *(P-1828)*

King Holding Corporation .... A....... 586 254-3900
360 N Crescent Dr Beverly Hills (90210) *(P-6448)*

King Instrument Company Inc .... E....... 714 891-0008
12700 Pala Dr Garden Grove (92841) *(P-10143)*

King Nutronics LLC .... E....... 818 887-5460
6421 Independence Ave Woodland Hills (91367) *(P-10144)*

King Nutronics Corporation, Woodland Hills *Also Called: King Nutronics LLC (P-10144)*

King Plastics Inc .... D....... 714 997-7540
840 N Elm St Orange (92867) *(P-5080)*

King Shock Technology Inc .... D....... 719 394-3754
12472 Edison Way Garden Grove (92841) *(P-9410)*

King Ventures .... C....... 805 544-4444
285 Bridge St San Luis Obispo (93401) *(P-14901)*

King Wire Partitions Inc .... E....... 323 256-4848
6044 N Figueroa St Los Angeles (90042) *(P-6400)*

King World, Los Angeles *Also Called: King World Productions Inc (P-11955)*

King World Productions Inc .... C....... 310 264-3549
1575 N Gower St Ste 100 Los Angeles (90028) *(P-11955)*

Kingcom(us) LLC (DH) .... E....... 424 744-5697
3100 Ocean Park Blvd Santa Monica (90405) *(P-16284)*

Kingdom Matress Company, Commerce *Also Called: Kingdom Mattress Co Inc (P-2853)*

Kingdom Mattress Co Inc .... E....... 562 630-5531
2425 S Malt Ave Commerce (90040) *(P-2853)*

Kingman Industries, Tustin *Also Called: Johnston International Corporation (P-7397)*

Kingman Industries .... E....... 951 698-1812
26370 Beckman Ct Ste A Murrieta (92562) *(P-4338)*

Kings & Convicts Bp LLC .... C....... 619 255-7213
2215 India St San Diego (92101) *(P-1596)*

Kings & Convicts Bp LLC .... E....... 619 295-2337
5401 Linda Vista Rd Ste 406 San Diego (92110) *(P-1597)*

Kings Garden LLC .... C....... 760 275-4969
3540 N Anza Rd Palm Springs (92262) *(P-20187)*

Kings Garden Royal Deliveries, Palm Springs *Also Called: Kings Garden LLC (P-20187)*

Kings Hawaiian Bakery, Gardena *Also Called: Kings Hawaiian Bakery W Inc (P-14019)*

Kings Hawaiian Bakery W Inc (HQ) .... E....... 310 533-3250
1411 W 190th St Gardena (90248) *(P-14019)*

Kings Oil Tools Inc (PA) .... E....... 805 238-9311
2235 Spring St Paso Robles (93446) *(P-15765)*

Kings Seafood Company LLC .... A....... 714 793-1177
7691 Edinger Ave Huntington Beach (92647) *(P-13282)*

Kingsley Manor, Los Angeles *Also Called: Front Porch Communities & Svcs (P-17954)*

Kingsolver Inc .... F....... 562 945-7590
8417 Secura Way Santa Fe Springs (90670) *(P-11090)*

Kingson Mold & Machine Inc .... E....... 714 871-0221
1350 Titan Way Brea (92821) *(P-7078)*

Kingston Digital Inc (HQ) .... E....... 714 435-2600
17600 Newhope St Fountain Valley (92708) *(P-7539)*

Kingston Technology Company Inc (PA) .... A....... 714 435-2600
17600 Newhope St Fountain Valley (92708) *(P-12424)*

Kingston Technology Corp (PA) .... B....... 714 435-2600
17600 Newhope St Fountain Valley (92708) *(P-7540)*

Kingswood Capital MGT LP .... C....... 424 744-8238
11111 Santa Monica Blvd Ste 1700 Los Angeles (90025) *(P-14979)*

Kinkisharyo (usa) Inc .... C....... 424 276-1803
300 Continental Blvd Ste 300 El Segundo (90245) *(P-9869)*

Kinkisharyo Int LLC (HQ) .... F....... 424 276-1803
1960 E Grand Ave Ste 1210 El Segundo (90245) *(P-9870)*

Kinkisharyo International .... C....... 661 265-1647
2825 E Avenue P Palmdale (93550) *(P-20357)*

Kino Flo Lighting Systems, Burbank *Also Called: Nomoflo Enterprises Inc (P-8323)*

Kintera Inc (HQ) .... D....... 858 795-3000
9605 Scranton Rd Ste 200 San Diego (92121) *(P-16285)*

Kintetsu Enterprises Co Amer (HQ) .... C....... 310 782-9300
21241 S Western Ave Ste 100 Torrance (90501) *(P-15210)*

Kintetsu Enterprises Co Amer, Torrance *Also Called: Kintetsu Enterprises Co Amer (P-15210)*

Kip Steel Inc .... E....... 714 461-1051
1650 Valley Ln Fullerton (92833) *(P-5629)*

Kirby Industries Inc .... F....... 714 437-0789
2109 S Lyon St Santa Ana (92705) *(P-1005)*

Kirk Containers, Commerce *Also Called: Arthurmade Plastics Inc (P-4949)*

Kirkhill Inc .... A....... 714 529-4901
300 E Cypress St Brea (92821) *(P-4737)*

Kirkhill Inc .... D....... 562 803-1117
1451 S Carlos Ave Ontario (91761) *(P-4771)*

Kirkhill Inc (HQ) .... C....... 714 529-4901
300 E Cypress St Brea (92821) *(P-9731)*

Kirkhill Manufacturing Company, Ontario *Also Called: KMC Acquisition LLC (P-4773)*

Kirkhill Rubber Company .... D....... 562 803-1117
2500 E Thompson St Long Beach (90805) *(P-4772)*

Kirkland & Ellis LLP .... D....... 310 552-4200
2049 Century Park E Ste 3700 Los Angeles (90067) *(P-18882)*

Kirkland & Ellis LLP .... C....... 213 680-8400
555 S Flower St Ste 3700 Los Angeles (90071) *(P-18883)*

Kirkland & Ellis LLP .... B....... 213 680-8400
333 S Hope St Ste 3000 Los Angeles (90071) *(P-18884)*

Kirschenman Enterprises Sls LP .... C....... 661 366-5736
12826 Edison Hwy Edison (93220) *(P-16854)*

Kisca, Los Angeles *Also Called: Komarov Enterprises Inc (P-2294)*

Kisco Senior Living LLC .... C....... 714 997-5355
620 S Glassell St Orange (92866) *(P-14725)*

Kiss Packaging Systems, Vista *Also Called: Accutek Packaging Equipment Co (P-7343)*

Kitch Engineering Inc .... E....... 818 897-7133
12320 Montague St Pacoima (91331) *(P-7900)*

Kitchen and Rail, Arroyo Grande *Also Called: Corbett Vineyards LLC (P-1617)*

Kitchen Cuts LLC .... D....... 323 560-7415
6045 District Blvd Maywood (90270) *(P-1222)*

Kitchen Equipment Mfg Co Inc .... E....... 909 923-3153
2102 Maple Privado Ontario (91761) *(P-6529)*

Mergent email: customerrelations@mergent.com
1148

2024 Southern California
Business Directory and Buyers Guide

(P-0000) Products & Services Section entry number
(PA)=Parent Co (HQ)=Headquarters (DH)=Div Headquarters

Kitchen Expo ....F
7458 La Jolla Blvd La Jolla (92037) *(P-1166)*

Kitchen Pro Cabinetry Inc ....E...... 877 210-6361
8910 Quartz Ave Northridge (91324) *(P-2663)*

Kitcor Corporation ....E...... 323 875-2820
9959 Glenoaks Blvd Sun Valley (91352) *(P-6530)*

Kite Electric Incorporated ....C...... 949 380-7471
2 Thomas Irvine (92618) *(P-911)*

Kite Pharma (HQ).................................D....... 310 824-9999
2400 Broadway Ste 100 Santa Monica (90404) *(P-19851)*

Kite, A Gilead Company, Santa Monica *Also Called: Kite Pharma Inc (P-19851)*

Kitson Landscape MGT Inc ....D...... 805 681-9460
5787 Thornwood Dr Goleta (93117) *(P-197)*

Kittrich Corporation (PA).......................C...... 714 736-1000
1585 W Mission Blvd Pomona (91766) *(P-3009)*

Kittyhawk Products, Garden Grove *Also Called: Kpi Services Inc (P-5840)*

Kittyhawk Products CA LLC ....E...... 714 895-5024
11651 Monarch St Garden Grove (92841) *(P-5839)*

Kjos Music, San Diego *Also Called: Neil A Kjos Music Company (P-3468)*

Kkw Trucking Inc (PA)...........................A...... 909 869-1200
3100 Pomona Blvd Pomona (91768) *(P-11592)*

Kl Decorator Sales ....E...... 562 920-0268
10120 Artesia Pl Bellflower (90706) *(P-2610)*

Klatch Coffee Inc (PA)...........................E...... 909 981-4031
8767 Onyx Ave Rancho Cucamonga (91730) *(P-14020)*

Klein Electronics, Escondido *Also Called: Klein Electronics Inc (P-12675)*

Klein Electronics Inc ....E...... 760 781-3220
349 N Vinewood St Escondido (92029) *(P-12675)*

Kleinfelder, San Diego *Also Called: Kleinfelder Inc (P-19631)*

Kleinfelder Inc (HQ)..............................C...... 619 831-4600
770 1st Ave Ste 400 San Diego (92101) *(P-19631)*

Kleinfelder Associates ....C...... 619 831-4600
550 W C St Ste 1200 San Diego (92101) *(P-19632)*

Kleinfelder Group Inc (PA)....................C...... 619 831-4600
770 1st Ave Ste 400 San Diego (92101) *(P-19633)*

Klientboost LLC ....C...... 657 203-7866
2787 Bristol St Ste 100 Costa Mesa (92626) *(P-15552)*

Klk Forte Industry Inc (PA)...................E...... 323 415-9181
1535 Rio Vista Ave Los Angeles (90023) *(P-2342)*

Klm Laboratories Inc ....D...... 661 295-2600
28280 Alta Vista Ave Valencia (91355) *(P-12496)*

Klm Orthotic, Valencia *Also Called: Klm Laboratories Inc (P-12496)*

Klooma Holdings Inc ....E...... 305 747-3315
113 N San Vicente Blvd Beverly Hills (90211) *(P-16286)*

Kls Doors LLC ....D...... 909 605-6468
501 Kettering Dr Ontario (91761) *(P-2611)*

Klune Industries Inc (DH)......................B...... 818 503-8100
7323 Coldwater Canyon Ave North Hollywood (91605) *(P-9732)*

Km Printing Production Inc ....F...... 626 821-0008
218 Longden Ave Irwindale (91706) *(P-3613)*

Kmb Foods Inc (PA)...............................E...... 626 447-0545
1010 S Sierra Way San Bernardino (92408) *(P-1223)*

KMC Acquisition LLC (PA).....................D...... 562 396-0121
1451 S Carlos Ave Ontario (91761) *(P-4773)*

Kme Fire, Fontana *Also Called: Kovatch Mobile Equipment Corp (P-9295)*

Kmp Numatech Pacific, Pomona *Also Called: Numatech West (kmp) LLC (P-3119)*

Kmr Label LLC ....E...... 310 603-8910
1360 W Walnut Pkwy Compton (90220) *(P-3719)*

KMW Communications, Fullerton *Also Called: Gigatera Communications (P-9050)*

Knd Development 55 LLC ....C...... 909 581-6400
10841 White Oak Ave Rancho Cucamonga (91730) *(P-18316)*

Knight Law Group LLP ....D...... 424 355-1155
10250 Constellation Blvd Ste 2500 Los Angeles (90067) *(P-18885)*

Knight LLC (HQ).....................................D...... 949 595-4800
15340 Barranca Pkwy Irvine (92618) *(P-7398)*

Knit Generation Group Inc ....E...... 213 221-5081
3818 S Broadway Los Angeles (90037) *(P-2026)*

Knk Apparel Inc ....F...... 310 768-3333
223 W Rosecrans Ave Gardena (90248) *(P-2177)*

Knobbe Martens Olson Bear LLP (PA)......B...... 949 760-0404
2040 Main St Fl 14 Irvine (92614) *(P-18886)*

Knolls Convalescent Hosp Inc (PA)........C...... 760 245-5361
16890 Green Tree Blvd Victorville (92395) *(P-17982)*

Knolls West Enterprise ....C...... 760 245-0107
16890 Green Tree Blvd Victorville (92395) *(P-17983)*

Knolls West Residential Care, Victorville *Also Called: Knolls West Enterprise (P-17983)*

Knott's Berry Farm, Buena Park *Also Called: Knotts Berry Farm LLC (P-17449)*

Knott's Berry Farm Hotel, Buena Park *Also Called: Knotts Berry Farm LLC (P-15211)*

Knotts Berry Farm LLC ....D...... 714 995-1111
7675 Crescent Ave Buena Park (90620) *(P-15211)*

Knotts Berry Farm LLC (HQ)...................B...... 714 827-1776
8039 Beach Blvd Buena Park (90620) *(P-17449)*

Knox Attorney Service Inc (PA)..............C...... 619 233-9700
1550 Hotel Cir N Ste 440 San Diego (92108) *(P-15648)*

Knox Services, San Diego *Also Called: Knox Attorney Service Inc (P-15648)*

Kns Industrial Supply, Los Alamitos *Also Called: International Consulting Unltd (P-5635)*

Koam Engineering Systems Inc ....C...... 858 292-0922
7807 Convoy Ct Ste 200 San Diego (92111) *(P-16452)*

Kobelco Compressors Amer Inc ....D...... 951 739-3030
301 N Smith Ave Corona (92878) *(P-7309)*

Kobelco Compressors Amer Inc (DH).......B...... 951 739-3030
1450 W Rincon St Corona (92878) *(P-7310)*

Kobert & Company Inc ....D...... 323 725-1000
6131 Garfield Ave Commerce (90040) *(P-12600)*

Kobis Windows & Doors Mfg Inc ....E...... 818 764-6400
7326 Laurel Canyon Blvd North Hollywood (91605) *(P-2664)*

Kodella LLC ....C...... 844 563-3552
17922 Fitch Ste 200 Irvine (92614) *(P-16576)*

Kofax Inc (PA)...B...... 949 783-1000
15211 Laguna Canyon Rd Irvine (92618) *(P-16062)*

Kofax Limited (PA)..................................E...... 949 783-1000
15211 Laguna Canyon Rd Irvine (92618) *(P-16287)*

Koll Construction LP ....D...... 949 833-3030
4343 Von Karman Ave Ste 150 Newport Beach (92660) *(P-563)*

Kollmorgen Corporation ....D...... 805 696-1236
33 S La Patera Ln Santa Barbara (93117) *(P-8147)*

Koltov Inc (PA).......................................E...... 805 764-0280
300 S Lewis Rd Ste A Camarillo (93012) *(P-5301)*

Komar Apparel Supply, Los Angeles *Also Called: Mdc Interior Solutions LLC (P-2455)*

Komar Distribution Services, Jurupa Valley *Also Called: Charles Komar & Sons Inc (P-2387)*

Komarov Enterprises Inc ....D...... 213 244-7000
10939 Venice Blvd Los Angeles (90034) *(P-2294)*

Kona Bay Hotel, Manhattan Beach *Also Called: Oka & Oka Hawaii LLC (P-15272)*

Kona Kai Resort Hotel, San Diego *Also Called: Westgroup Kona Kai LLC (P-17536)*

Kone Inc ....E...... 714 890-7080
1540 Scenic Ave # 100 Costa Mesa (92626) *(P-17136)*

Konecranes Inc ....E...... 562 903-1371
10310 Pioneer Blvd Ste 2 Santa Fe Springs (90670) *(P-6981)*

Konecranes Inc ....E...... 909 930-0108
1620 S Carlos Ave Ontario (91761) *(P-6982)*

Konigsberg Instruments Inc ....E...... 626 775-6500
1017 S Mountain Ave Monrovia (91016) *(P-10544)*

Kontron America Incorporated ....D...... 800 822-7522
9477 Waples St Ste 150 San Diego (92121) *(P-7436)*

Kool Star, Long Beach *Also Called: Three Star Rfrgn Engrg Inc (P-7626)*

Koos Manufacturing Inc ....A:..... 323 249-1000
2741 Seminole Ave South Gate (90280) *(P-16855)*

Kopykake Enterprises Inc (PA)...............F...... 310 373-8906
3699 W 240th St Torrance (90505) *(P-6531)*

Kor Realty Group LLC (PA).....................D...... 323 930-3700
1212 S Flower St Fl 5 Los Angeles (90015) *(P-14821)*

Kor Shots Inc ....E...... 805 351-0700
29160 Heathercliff Rd Unit 4273 Malibu (90264) *(P-1373)*

Koral Activewear, Santa Monica *Also Called: Koral LLC (P-2211)*

Koral Industries LLC (PA).......................E...... 323 585-5343
1334 3rd Street Promenade Ste 200 Santa Monica (90401) *(P-2343)*

Koral LLC ....E...... 323 391-1060
1334 3rd Street Promenade Ste 200 Santa Monica (90401) *(P-2211)*

Koral Los Angeles, Santa Monica *Also Called: Koral Industries LLC (P-2343)*

Korden Inc ....E...... 909 988-8979
601 S Milliken Ave Ontario (91761) *(P-2914)*

Employee Codes: A=Over 500 employees, B=251-500
C=101-250, D=51-100, E=20-50, F=10-19, G=1-9

2024 Southern California
Business Directory and Buyers Guide

© Mergent Inc. 1-800-342-5647
1149

Kore1 Inc .... D...... 949 706-6990
530 Technology Dr Ste 150 Irvine (92618) *(P-16577)*

Kore1 LLC .... C...... 949 706-6990
530 Technology Dr Ste 150 Irvine (92618) *(P-15862)*

Korea Times, Los Angeles *Also Called: The Korea Times Los Angeles Inc (P-3329)*

Korean Air, Los Angeles *Also Called: Korean Air Lines Co Ltd (P-11663)*

Korean Air, Los Angeles *Also Called: Korean Airlines Co Ltd (P-11665)*

Korean Air, Los Angeles *Also Called: Korean Airlines Co Ltd (P-11732)*

Korean Air Lines Co Ltd .... C...... 310 646-4866
380 World Way Ste S4 Los Angeles (90045) *(P-11663)*

Korean Airlines Co Ltd .... C...... 310 410-2000
6101 W Imperial Hwy Los Angeles (90045) *(P-11664)*

Korean Airlines Co Ltd .... B...... 213 484-5700
900 Wilshire Blvd Ste 1100 Los Angeles (90017) *(P-11732)*

Korean Airlines Co Ltd .... D...... 213 484-1900
1813 Wilshire Blvd Ste 400 Los Angeles (90057) *(P-11665)*

Korean Arln Crgo Reservations, Los Angeles *Also Called: Korean Airlines Co Ltd (P-11664)*

Korean Community Services Inc .... C...... 714 527-6561
451 W Lincoln Ave Ste 100 Anaheim (92805) *(P-18529)*

Korn Ferry (PA)... **C...... 310 552-1834**
1900 Avenue Of The Stars Ste 1500 Los Angeles (90067) *(P-15863)*

Korn Ferry, Los Angeles *Also Called: Korn Ferry (P-15863)*

Korn Ferry (us) (HQ) .... C...... 310 552-1834
1900 Avenue Of The Stars Ste 2600 Los Angeles (90067) *(P-20188)*

Koros USA Inc .... E...... 805 529-0825
610 Flinn Ave Moorpark (93021) *(P-10545)*

Kosakura Associates, Irvine *Also Called: CK Manufacturing & Trading Inc (P-2947)*

Kota Construction LLC .... D...... 855 800-5682
1200 Lawrence Dr Ste 180 Newbury Park (91320) *(P-443)*

Kovatch Mobile Equipment Corp .... E...... 951 685-1224
14562 Manzanita Dr Fontana (92335) *(P-9295)*

Kovin Corporation Inc .... E...... 858 558-0100
9240 Mira Este Ct San Diego (92126) *(P-3614)*

Kpc Global Medical Centers Inc (DH)........... **C...... 714 953-3500**
1117 E Devonshire Ave Hemet (92543) *(P-18317)*

Kpc Group Inc (PA)...................................... **C...... 951 782-8812**
9 Kpc Pkwy # 301 Corona (92879) *(P-20189)*

Kpff Inc .... D...... 949 252-1022
18500 Von Karman Ave Ste 1000 Irvine (92612) *(P-19634)*

Kpi Services Inc .... E...... 714 895-5024
11651 Monarch St Garden Grove (92841) *(P-5840)*

Kpmg LLP .... D...... 703 286-8175
4464 Jasmine Ave Culver City (90232) *(P-19784)*

Kpmg LLP .... C...... 949 885-5400
20 Pacifica Ste 700 Irvine (92618) *(P-19785)*

Kprs, Brea *Also Called: Kprs Construction Services Inc (P-564)*

Kprs Construction Services Inc (PA)............. **D...... 714 672-0800**
2850 Saturn St Ste 110 Brea (92821) *(P-564)*

Kpwr Radio LLC .... C...... 562 745-2300
9550 Firestone Blvd Ste 105 Downey (90241) *(P-16856)*

Kraco Enterprises LLC .... C...... 310 639-0666
505 E Euclid Ave Compton (90222) *(P-13864)*

Kraft Foods, Buena Park *Also Called: Mondelez Global LLC (P-1226)*

Kraft Foods, Fullerton *Also Called: Kraft Heinz Foods Company (P-1340)*

Kraft Heinz Foods Company .... E...... 949 250-4080
2450 White Rd Irvine (92614) *(P-1328)*

Kraft Heinz Foods Company .... D...... 714 870-8235
1500 E Walnut Ave Fullerton (92831) *(P-1340)*

Kramer-Wilson Company Inc (PA)................ **C...... 818 760-0880**
340 N Westlake Blvd Ste 210 Westlake Village (91362) *(P-14511)*

Krasnes Inc .... D...... 619 232-2066
2222 Commercial St San Diego (92113) *(P-2431)*

Kratos, San Diego *Also Called: Kratos Def & SEC Solutions Inc (P-9895)*

Kratos Def & SEC Solutions Inc (PA)............ **C...... 858 812-7300**
10680 Treena St Ste 600 San Diego (92131) *(P-9895)*

Kratos Public Safety & Security Solutions Inc ... D...... 858 812-7300
4820 Eastgate Mall Ste 200 San Diego (92121) *(P-16745)*

Kratos Tech Trning Sltions Inc (HQ)............. **D...... 858 812-7300**
10680 Treena St Ste 600 San Diego (92131) *(P-19635)*

KRC Orange, Orange *Also Called: Kisco Senior Living LLC (P-14725)*

Krca License LLC .... C...... 818 840-1400
1845 W Empire Ave Burbank (91504) *(P-11927)*

Kretek International Inc (DH)...................... **D...... 805 531-8888**
5449 Endeavour Ct Moorpark (93021) *(P-13522)*

Kretus Group Inc (PA)................................ **E...... 714 738-6640**
1129 N Patt St Anaheim (92801) *(P-12355)*

Krg Technologies Inc (PA)........................... **B...... 661 257-9967**
25000 Avenue Stanford Ste 243 Valencia (91355) *(P-16063)*

Krieger Speciality Products, Pico Rivera *Also Called: Metal Tite Products (P-6112)*

Krikorian Premiere Theatre LLC .... D...... 760 945-7469
25 Main St Vista (92083) *(P-17301)*

Krikorian Premiere Theatre LLC .... D...... 562 205-3456
8540 Whittier Blvd Pico Rivera (90660) *(P-17302)*

Krikorian Premiere Theatre LLC .... D...... 714 826-7469
8290 La Palma Ave Buena Park (90620) *(P-17303)*

Kroger Co .... B...... 859 630-6959
2201 S Wilmington Ave Compton (90220) *(P-11593)*

Kros-Wise .... C...... 619 607-2899
435 E Carmel St San Marcos (92078) *(P-20358)*

Krost (PA)... **C...... 626 449-4225**
225 S Lake Ave Ste 400 Pasadena (91101) *(P-19786)*

Krost Bumgarten Kniss Guerrero, Pasadena *Also Called: Krost (P-19786)*

Krueger International Inc .... E...... 949 748-7000
16510 Bake Pkwy Ste 100 Irvine (92618) *(P-2931)*

Kruse and Son Inc .... E...... 626 358-4536
235 Kruse Ave Monrovia (91016) *(P-1224)*

Kryler Corp .... E...... 714 871-9611
1217 E Ash Ave Fullerton (92831) *(P-6634)*

Krystal Enterprises, Riverside *Also Called: Krystal Infinity LLC (P-9329)*

Krystal Infinity LLC .... B
6915 Arlington Ave Riverside (92504) *(P-9329)*

Krystal Ventures LLC .... E...... 213 507-2215
17 Shell Bch Newport Coast (92657) *(P-10904)*

KS Fabrication & Machine, Bakersfield *Also Called: K S Fabrication & Machine Inc (P-678)*

KS Industries LP (PA)................................. **A...... 661 617-1700**
6205 District Blvd Bakersfield (93313) *(P-680)*

Ksby Communications LLC .... C...... 805 541-6666
1772 Calle Joaquin San Luis Obispo (93405) *(P-11956)*

Ksc Industries Inc .... E...... 619 671-0110
9771 Clairemont Mesa Blvd Ste E San Diego (92124) *(P-8419)*

Ksl Rancho Mirage Operating Co Inc .... B...... 760 568-2727
41000 Bob Hope Dr Rancho Mirage (92270) *(P-15212)*

Ksl Recreation Management Operations LLC ... A...... 760 564-8000
50905 Avenida Bermudas La Quinta (92253) *(P-17433)*

Ksl Resorts Hotel Del Coronado .... C...... 619 435-6611
1500 Orange Ave Coronado (92118) *(P-15213)*

KSM Garment Inc .... E...... 323 585-8811
5613 Maywood Ave Maywood (90270) *(P-2250)*

Kt Hotels LLC .... C...... 949 715-5000
3 Ada Ste 100 Irvine (92618) *(P-15214)*

Ktb Software LLC .... D...... 213 935-0902
11101 W Olympic Blvd Los Angeles (90064) *(P-16064)*

Ktc-Tu Corporation .... E...... 714 435-2600
17600 Newhope St Fountain Valley (92708) *(P-8822)*

Kti Incorporated .... D...... 909 434-1888
3011 N Laurel Ave Rialto (92377) *(P-5423)*

Kts Kitchens Inc .... C...... 310 764-0850
1065 E Walnut St Ste C Carson (90746) *(P-1923)*

Kuehne + Nagel Inc .... C...... 310 641-5500
20000 S Western Ave Torrance (90501) *(P-11776)*

Kugler Wines LLC .... E...... 630 306-4634
300 N 12th St Ste 4b Lompoc (93436) *(P-1641)*

Kui Co Inc .... E...... 949 369-7949
266 Calle Pintoresco San Clemente (92672) *(P-3053)*

Kuk Rim USA Inc .... C...... 323 277-9256
7507 Roseberry Ave Huntington Park (90255) *(P-2122)*

Kukdong Apparel America Inc .... E...... 562 403-0044
17100 Pioneer Blvd Ste 230 Artesia (90701) *(P-16857)*

Kulicke & Soffa Industries, Santa Ana *Also Called: Kulicke Sffa Wedge Bonding Inc (P-9224)*

Kulicke Sffa Wedge Bonding Inc .... C...... 949 660-0440
1821 E Dyer Rd Ste 200 Santa Ana (92705) *(P-9224)*

Kulr Technology Corporation ....E...... 408 675-7002
4863 Shawline St Ste B San Diego (92111) *(P-8823)*

Kum Kang Trading USA Inc ....E...... 562 531-6111
6433 Alondra Blvd Paramount (90723) *(P-4430)*

Kumar Industries ....E...... 909 591-0722
4775 Chino Ave Chino (91710) *(P-6038)*

Kura Oncology Inc (PA) ....**E...... 858 500-8800**
12730 High Bluff Dr Ste 400 San Diego (92130) *(P-4153)*

Kurz Transfer Products LP ....D...... 951 738-9521
415 N Smith Ave Corona (92878) *(P-11238)*

Kush Supply Co LLC ....D...... 714 243-4023
7375 Chapman Ave Garden Grove (92841) *(P-13050)*

Kushwood Chair Inc ....E...... 909 930-2100
1290 E Elm St Ontario (91761) *(P-2887)*

Kuster Co Oil Well Services ....E...... 562 595-0661
2900 E 29th St Long Beach (90806) *(P-284)*

Kuster Company, Long Beach *Also Called: Kuster Co Oil Well Services (P-284)*

Kustom Kanopies Inc ....E...... 801 399-3400
210 Senior Cir Lompoc (93436) *(P-509)*

Kut From The Kloth, City Of Industry *Also Called: Swatfame Inc (P-13152)*

Kuzz FM, Bakersfield *Also Called: Buck Owens Production Co Inc (P-11920)*

Kvcr, TV & FM, San Bernardino *Also Called: San Brnrdino Cmnty College Dst (P-11935)*

Kvr Investment Group Inc ....D...... 818 896-1102
12113 Branford St Sun Valley (91352) *(P-7246)*

Kwdz Manufacturing LLC (PA) ....**D...... 323 526-3526**
337 S Anderson St Los Angeles (90033) *(P-2408)*

Kwikparts.com, Torrance *Also Called: Probe Racing Components Inc (P-7703)*

Kwikset Corporation ....A...... 949 672-4000
19701 Da Vinci Foothill Ranch (92610) *(P-5926)*

KWJ ENGINEERING, Irvine *Also Called: Interlink Electronics Inc (P-9064)*

Kworld (usa) Computer Inc ....E...... 626 581-0867
499 Nibus Ste D Brea (92821) *(P-8528)*

Kxp Carrier Services LLC ....C...... 424 320-5300
11777 San Vicente Blvd Los Angeles (90049) *(P-11532)*

Kyoceara, Costa Mesa *Also Called: Kyocera Tycom Corporation (P-7015)*

Kyocera America Inc ....E...... 858 576-2600
8611 Balboa Ave San Diego (92123) *(P-8824)*

Kyocera AVX Cmpnnts San Dego I (DH) ....**E...... 858 550-3820**
5501 Oberlin Dr Ste 100 San Diego (92121) *(P-8529)*

Kyocera Dcment Solutions W LLC ....C...... 800 996-9591
14101 Alton Pkwy Irvine (92618) *(P-12385)*

Kyocera International Inc (HQ) ....**D...... 858 492-1456**
8611 Balboa Ave San Diego (92123) *(P-8825)*

Kyocera Medical Tech Inc ....E...... 909 557-2360
1200 California St Ste 210 Redlands (92374) *(P-10679)*

Kyocera Sld Laser Inc (HQ) ....**E...... 805 696-6999**
485 Pine Ave Goleta (93117) *(P-9225)*

Kyocera Tycom Corporation ....B...... 714 428-3600
3565 Cadillac Ave Costa Mesa (92626) *(P-7015)*

Kyolic, Mission Viejo *Also Called: Wakunaga of America Co Ltd (P-4255)*

Kyoto Grand Hotel and Gardens, Los Angeles *Also Called: Crestline Hotels & Resorts Inc (P-15124)*

Kyowa Kirin Phrm RES Inc (DH) ....**E...... 858 952-7000**
9420 Athena Cir La Jolla (92037) *(P-4154)*

Kyriba Corp (PA) ....**E...... 858 210-3560**
4435 Eastgate Mall Ste 200 San Diego (92121) *(P-16288)*

Kythera Biopharmaceuticals Inc ....C...... 818 587-4500
30930 Russell Ranch Rd Fl 3 Westlake Village (91362) *(P-4155)*

L & A Care Corporation ....C...... 310 202-7693
5000 Overland Ave Ste 101 Culver City (90230) *(P-18088)*

L & A Plastics, Yorba Linda *Also Called: Loritz & Associates Inc (P-5087)*

L & H Mold & Engineering Inc (PA) ....**E...... 909 930-1547**
140 Atlantic St Pomona (91768) *(P-5081)*

L & H Molds, Pomona *Also Called: L & H Mold & Engineering Inc (P-5081)*

L & L Custom Shutters Inc ....F...... 714 996-9539
3133 Yukon Ave Costa Mesa (92626) *(P-2612)*

L & L Diamond Co ....E...... 213 622-5752
1801 Beverly Blvd Los Angeles (90057) *(P-14077)*

L & L Distributors, Los Angeles *Also Called: L&L Manufacturing Co Inc (P-2345)*

L & L Nursery Supply Inc (HQ) ....**C...... 909 591-0461**
2552 Shenandoah Way San Bernardino (92407) *(P-13488)*

L & L Printers Carlsbad LLC ....E...... 760 477-0321
6200 Yarrow Dr Carlsbad (92011) *(P-3615)*

L & M Machining Corporation ....D...... 714 414-0923
550 S Melrose St Placentia (92870) *(P-8977)*

L & O Aliso Viejo LLC ....D...... 949 643-6700
50 Enterprise Aliso Viejo (92656) *(P-15215)*

L & R Distributors Inc ....B...... 909 980-3807
9292 9th St Rancho Cucamonga (91730) *(P-13083)*

L & S Stone and Fireplace Shop, San Marcos *Also Called: L&S Stone LLC (P-5530)*

L & T Meat Co ....D...... 323 262-2815
3050 E 11th St Los Angeles (90023) *(P-13300)*

L & T Precision LLC ....C...... 858 513-7874
12105 Kirkham Rd Poway (92064) *(P-6261)*

L A Air Inc ....C...... 310 215-8245
5933 W Century Blvd 500 Los Angeles (90045) *(P-11666)*

L A Cstm AP & Promotions Inc (PA) ....**E...... 562 595-1770**
2680 Temple Ave Long Beach (90806) *(P-2212)*

L A Gauge Company Inc ....D...... 818 767-7193
7440 San Fernando Rd Sun Valley (91352) *(P-7901)*

L A Girl, Ontario *Also Called: Beauty 21 Cosmetics Inc (P-13030)*

L A H S A, Los Angeles *Also Called: Los Angeles Homeless Svcs Auth (P-19110)*

L A Hq Inc ....E...... 310 880-7433
5363 Wilshire Blvd Los Angeles (90036) *(P-11239)*

L A Japanese Daily News, Los Angeles *Also Called: Rafu Shimpo (P-3317)*

L A Lighting, El Monte *Also Called: Los Angeles Ltg Mfg Co Inc (P-12602)*

L A P F C U, Van Nuys *Also Called: Los Angeles Police Credit Un (P-14249)*

L A Party Rents Inc ....D...... 818 989-4300
13520 Saticoy St Van Nuys (91402) *(P-15783)*

L A PHILHARMONIC, Los Angeles *Also Called: Los Angeles Philharmonic Assn (P-17344)*

L A Press, Los Angeles *Also Called: LA Printing & Graphics Inc (P-3617)*

L A Propoint Inc ....E...... 818 767-6800
10870 La Tuna Canyon Rd Sun Valley (91352) *(P-6866)*

L A S A M Inc ....F...... 323 586-8717
3844 S Santa Fe Ave Vernon (90058) *(P-2409)*

L A Steel Craft Products (PA) ....**E...... 626 798-7401**
1975 Lincoln Ave Pasadena (91103) *(P-11008)*

L A Supply Co ....E...... 949 470-9900
4241 E Brickell St Ontario (91761) *(P-3775)*

L A U S D, Pico Rivera *Also Called: Los Angeles Unified School Dst (P-16864)*

L and R Auto Parks Inc ....C...... 213 784-3018
707 Wilshire Blvd Ste 4300 Los Angeles (90017) *(P-16991)*

L and W Developers LLC ....E...... 310 654-8428
1635 Centinela Ave Inglewood (90302) *(P-14902)*

L C Miller Company ....E...... 323 268-3611
717 Monterey Pass Rd Monterey Park (91754) *(P-7369)*

L C Pringle Sales Inc (PA) ....**E...... 714 892-1524**
12020 Western Ave Garden Grove (92841) *(P-3010)*

L E Coppersmith Inc (PA) ....**D...... 310 607-8000**
525 S Douglas St Ste 100 El Segundo (90245) *(P-11777)*

L F P Inc (PA) ....**D...... 323 651-3525**
8484 Wilshire Blvd Ste 900 Beverly Hills (90211) *(P-3364)*

L J B, San Diego *Also Called: Tanvex Biopharma Usa Inc (P-19879)*

L M I, Ontario *Also Called: Larry Mthvin Installations Inc (P-5346)*

L M S, Irvine *Also Called: Ovation Tech Inc (P-16587)*

L M Scofield Company (DH) ....**E...... 323 720-3000**
12767 Imperial Hwy Santa Fe Springs (90670) *(P-4615)*

L S A, Irvine *Also Called: Lsa Associates Inc (P-20360)*

L Space, Irvine *Also Called: Lspace America LLC (P-2255)*

L Spark ....E...... 805 626-0511
1140 Kendall Rd Ste A San Luis Obispo (93401) *(P-10905)*

L T Litho & Printing Co ....E...... 949 466-8584
16811 Noyes Ave Irvine (92606) *(P-3616)*

L W Lefort, Placentia *Also Called: Richfield Engineering Inc (P-6152)*

L Y A Group Inc ....E...... 213 683-1123
1317 S Grand Ave Los Angeles (90015) *(P-2344)*

L-3 Interstate Electronics, Anaheim *Also Called: L3harris Interstate Elec Corp (P-10212)*

L-3 Telemetry & Rf Products, San Diego *Also Called: L3 Technologies Inc (P-8531)*

L-Com, Irvine *Also Called: Infinite Electronics Inc (P-9059)*

L-O Bedford Operating LLC ....C...... 781 275-5500
11755 Wilshire Blvd Ste 1350 Los Angeles (90025) *(P-15216)*

Employee Codes: A=Over 500 employees, B=251-500
C=101-250, D=51-100, E=20-50, F=10-19, G=1-9

2024 Southern California
Business Directory and Buyers Guide

© Mergent Inc. 1-800-342-5647
1151

ALPHABETIC

L.A. Care Health Plan, Los Angeles *Also Called: Local Inttive Hlth Auth For Lo (P-14486)*

L.A. Cold Storage, Los Angeles *Also Called: Standard-Southern Corporation (P-11558)*

L.A. GAY & LESBIAN CENTER, Los Angeles *Also Called: Los Angeles Lgbt Center (P-19335)*

L.a. Gem And Jewelry Design, Inc., Vernon *Also Called: LA Gem and Jwly Design Inc (P-10907)*

L.A. Inflight Service Company, Gardena *Also Called: World Svc Wst/La Inflght Svc L (P-11709)*

L.A. Sleeve, Santa Fe Springs *Also Called: Los Angeles Sleeve Co Inc (P-9415)*

L.A.cO., Whittier *Also Called: Los Angles Cnty Snttion Dstrct (P-12210)*

L.H. Dottie Co, Commerce *Also Called: Kobert & Company Inc (P-12600)*

L'Auberge Del Mar, Del Mar *Also Called: Lhoberge Lessee Inc (P-15226)*

L'Ermitage Hotel, Beverly Hills *Also Called: Raffles Lrmitage Beverly Hills (P-15316)*

L&L Foods Holdings LLC ....C....... 714 254-1430
333 N Euclid Way Anaheim (92801) *(P-11821)*

L&L Manufacturing Co Inc ....B
12400 Wilshire Blvd Ste 360 Los Angeles (90025) *(P-2345)*

L&S Stone LLC (DH) ....**E....... 760 736-3232**
1370 Grand Ave Ste B San Marcos (92078) *(P-5530)*

L&T Staffing Inc ....B....... 323 727-9056
2122 W Whittier Blvd Montebello (90640) *(P-15864)*

L3 Applied Technologies Inc (DH) ....**E....... 858 404-7824**
10180 Barnes Canyon Rd Ste 100 San Diego (92121) *(P-8530)*

L3 Maripro Inc ....D....... 805 683-3881
1522 Cook Pl Goleta (93117) *(P-19636)*

L3 Technologies Inc ....B....... 858 279-0411
9020 Balboa Ave San Diego (92123) *(P-8531)*

L3 Technologies Inc ....D....... 858 552-9716
10180 Barnes Canyon Rd San Diego (92121) *(P-8532)*

L3 Technologies Inc ....B....... 858 552-9500
9020 Balboa Ave San Diego (92123) *(P-8533)*

L3 Technologies Inc ....D....... 805 683-3881
7414 Hollister Ave Goleta (93117) *(P-8534)*

L3 Technologies Inc ....C....... 818 367-0111
15825 Roxford St Sylmar (91342) *(P-8535)*

L3 Technologies Inc ....C....... 714 758-4222
602 E Vermont Ave Anaheim (92805) *(P-8536)*

L3 Technologies Inc ....C....... 760 431-6800
5957 Landau Ct Carlsbad (92008) *(P-9985)*

L3 Technologies Inc ....D....... 805 584-1717
200 W Los Angeles Ave Simi Valley (93065) *(P-9986)*

L3 Technologies Inc ....E....... 714 956-9200
901 E Ball Rd Anaheim (92805) *(P-9987)*

L3 Technologies Inc ....C....... 818 367-0111
28022 Industry Dr Valencia (91355) *(P-9988)*

L3harris Interstate Elec Corp ....E....... 714 758-3395
604 E Vermont Ave Anaheim (92805) *(P-8537)*

L3harris Interstate Elec Corp ....D....... 858 552-9500
3033 Science Park Rd San Diego (92121) *(P-10209)*

L3harris Interstate Elec Corp ....E....... 714 758-0500
708 E Vermont Ave Anaheim (92805) *(P-10210)*

L3harris Interstate Elec Corp ....E....... 714 758-0500
600 E Vermont Ave Anaheim (92805) *(P-10211)*

L3harris Interstate Elec Corp (DH) ....**B....... 714 758-0500**
602 E Vermont Ave Anaheim (92805) *(P-10212)*

L3harris Interstate Elec Corp ....C....... 714 758-0500
707 E Vermont Ave A Anaheim (92805) *(P-12676)*

L3harris Technologies Inc ....B....... 818 901-2523
7821 Orion Ave Van Nuys (91406) *(P-9989)*

L3harris Technologies Inc ....E....... 310 481-6000
12121 Wilshire Blvd Ste 910 Los Angeles (90025) *(P-9990)*

L3harris Technologies Inc ....D....... 626 305-6230
1400 S Shamrock Ave Monrovia (91016) *(P-9991)*

La 1000 Santa Fe LLC ....C....... 213 205-1000
1000 S Santa Fe Ave Los Angeles (90021) *(P-20049)*

La Aloe LLC ....E....... 888 968-2563
2301 E 7th St Ste A152 Los Angeles (90023) *(P-1374)*

La Apparel, Los Angeles *Also Called: Los Angeles Apparel Inc (P-2454)*

La Asccion Ncnal Pro Prsnas My ....A....... 213 202-5900
1452 W Temple St Ste 100 Los Angeles (90026) *(P-19107)*

La Barca Tortilleria Inc ....E....... 323 268-1744
3047 Whittier Blvd Los Angeles (90023) *(P-1924)*

La Bath Vanity Inc (PA) ....**F....... 909 303-3323**
1071 W 9th St Upland (91786) *(P-2665)*

LA BIOMED, Torrance *Also Called: Lundquist Institute For Biomedical Innovation At Harbor-Ucla Medical Center (P-19934)*

La Bonita, Norwalk *Also Called: Dianas Mexican Food Pdts Inc (P-1884)*

La Bonne Vie Inc ....D....... 805 773-5003
2723 Shell Beach Rd Shell Beach (93449) *(P-17402)*

La Bottleworks Inc ....E....... 323 724-4076
1605 Beach St Montebello (90640) *(P-1702)*

La Boxing Franchise Corp ....B....... 714 668-0911
1241 E Dyer Rd Ste 100 Santa Ana (92705) *(P-17403)*

LA Cabinet & Millwork Inc ....E....... 323 227-5000
3005 Humboldt St Los Angeles (90031) *(P-2959)*

La Canada Flintridge Cntry CLB ....D....... 818 790-0611
5500 Godbey Dr La Canada (91011) *(P-17492)*

La Capital, Los Angeles *Also Called: Los Angeles Capital MGT LLC (P-14964)*

La Casa Mhrc, Long Beach *Also Called: Telecare Corporation (P-18725)*

La Chapalita Inc (PA) ....**E....... 626 443-8556**
1724 Chico Ave El Monte (91733) *(P-1925)*

La Clippers LLC ....C....... 213 742-7500
1212 S Flower St Fl 5 Los Angeles (90015) *(P-17374)*

La Colonial Mexican Foods, Monterey Park *Also Called: La Colonial Tortilla Pdts Inc (P-1926)*

La Colonial Tortilla Pdts Inc ....C....... 626 289-3647
543 Monterey Pass Rd Monterey Park (91754) *(P-1926)*

La Copa De Oro ....E....... 714 554-9925
3321 W 1st St Santa Ana (92703) *(P-1927)*

La Costa Coffee Roasting Co (PA) ....**E....... 760 438-8160**
6965 El Camino Real Ste 208 Carlsbad (92009) *(P-13729)*

La Costa Glen, Carlsbad *Also Called: Continuing Lf Communities LLC (P-15833)*

La Costa Resort & Spa, Carlsbad *Also Called: Lc Trs Inc (P-15221)*

La Costa Urgent Care, Carlsbad *Also Called: Carbon Health Technologies Inc (P-17850)*

La County ....D....... 310 417-5184
5530 W 83rd St Los Angeles (90045) *(P-14669)*

La County Museum of Art, Los Angeles *Also Called: Museum Associates (P-19356)*

La County Probation, Whittier *Also Called: County of Los Angeles (P-19059)*

La County Sheriff PDC No ....C....... 661 294-6312
211 W Temple St Los Angeles (90012) *(P-19452)*

La Cumbre Country Club ....D....... 805 687-2421
4015 Via Laguna Santa Barbara (93110) *(P-17493)*

La Dye & Print Inc ....E....... 310 327-3200
13416 Estrella Ave Gardena (90248) *(P-13130)*

LA Envelope Incorporated ....E....... 323 838-9300
1053 S Vail Ave Montebello (90640) *(P-3212)*

La Espanola Meats Inc ....E....... 310 539-0455
25020 Doble Ave Harbor City (90710) *(P-1225)*

La Fe Tortilla Factory Inc (PA) ....**E....... 760 752-8350**
1512 Linda Vista Dr San Marcos (92078) *(P-13719)*

La Fe Tortilleria Factory, San Marcos *Also Called: La Fe Tortilla Factory Inc (P-13719)*

La Flora Del Sur, Los Angeles *Also Called: Walker Foods Inc (P-1352)*

La Folette Johnson Dehass Sesl ....D....... 213 426-3600
865 S Figueroa St # 3200 Los Angeles (90017) *(P-18887)*

La Folltte Jhnson De Haas Fsle (PA) ....**C....... 213 426-3600**
701 N Brand Blvd Ste 600 Glendale (91203) *(P-18888)*

La Fortaleza Inc ....D....... 323 261-1211
525 N Ford Blvd Los Angeles (90022) *(P-1928)*

LA Gem and Jewelry Design (PA) ....**E....... 213 488-1290**
659 S Broadway Fl 7 Los Angeles (90014) *(P-10906)*

LA Gem and Jwly Design Inc ....D....... 213 488-1290
3232 E Washington Blvd Vernon (90058) *(P-10907)*

La Gloria Flour Tortillas, Los Angeles *Also Called: La Gloria Foods Corp (P-1929)*

La Gloria Foods Corp ....E....... 323 263-6755
3285 E Cesar E Chavez Ave Los Angeles (90063) *(P-1929)*

La Gloria Foods Corp (PA) ....D....... 323 262-0410
3455 E 1st St Los Angeles (90063) *(P-1930)*

La Gloria Tortilleria, Los Angeles *Also Called: La Gloria Foods Corp (P-1930)*

La Habra Stucco, Riverside *Also Called: Parex Usa Inc (P-13669)*

LA Hardwood Flooring Inc (PA) ....**F....... 818 361-0099**
9880 San Fernando Rd Pacoima (91331) *(P-2574)*

La Jolla Baking Co, San Diego *Also Called: Fusion Food Factory (P-1472)*

La Jolla Bch & Tennis CLB Inc ....B....... 858 459-8271
8110 Camino Del Oro La Jolla (92037) *(P-15217)*

Mergent email: customerrelations@mergent.com
1152

2024 Southern California
Business Directory and Buyers Guide

(P-0000) Products & Services Section entry number
(PA)=Parent Co (HQ)=Headquarters (DH)=Div Headquarters

La Jolla Bch & Tennis CLB Inc (PA).................................C....... 858 454-7126
  2000 Spindrift Dr La Jolla (92037) *(P-17494)*

La Jolla Country Club Inc ....D....... 858 454-9601
  7301 High Ave La Jolla (92037) *(P-17495)*

La Jolla Group Inc (PA)..B....... 949 428-2800
  14350 Myford Rd Irvine (92606) *(P-16858)*

La Jolla Inst For Allrgy Immnl, La Jolla *Also Called: La Jolla Inst For Immunology (P-19933)*

La Jolla Inst For Immunology ....B....... 858 752-6500
  9420 Athena Cir La Jolla (92037) *(P-19933)*

La Jolla Nrsing Rhbltation Ctr, La Jolla *Also Called: Covenant Care La Jolla LLC (P-17918)*

La Jolla Orthpdic Srgery Ctr L ....D....... 858 657-0055
  4120 La Jolla Village Dr La Jolla (92037) *(P-17702)*

LA JOLLA PLAYHOUSE, La Jolla *Also Called: Theater Arts Fndtion San Dego (P-19466)*

La Jolla Skilled Inc ....C....... 858 625-8700
  3884 Nobel Dr San Diego (92122) *(P-17984)*

La Jolla Station, Anaheim *Also Called: Southern California Gas Co (P-12086)*

La Jolla YMCA, La Jolla *Also Called: YMCA of San Diego County (P-19477)*

La La Land Production & Design ....E....... 323 406-9223
  1701 S Santa Fe Ave Los Angeles (90021) *(P-5258)*

La Linen Inc ....E....... 213 745-4004
  1760 E 15th St Los Angeles (90021) *(P-13962)*

LA MAESTRA COMMUNITY HEALTH CE, San Diego *Also Called: La Maestra Family Clinic Inc (P-17703)*

La Maestra Family Clinic Inc (PA)...............................C....... 619 584-1612
  4060 Fairmount Ave San Diego (92105) *(P-17703)*

La Mamba LLC ....E....... 323 526-3526
  150 N Myers St Los Angeles (90033) *(P-2251)*

La Mesa Disposal, Signal Hill *Also Called: Edco Disposal Corporation (P-12169)*

La Mesa Medical Offices, La Mesa *Also Called: Kaiser Foundation Hospitals (P-14482)*

La Mesa R V Center Inc (PA)......................................C....... 858 874-8000
  7430 Copley Park Pl San Diego (92111) *(P-13897)*

LA Metropolitan Medical Center ....A....... 323 730-7300
  2231 Southwest Dr Los Angeles (90043) *(P-18318)*

La Mexicana LLC ....E....... 323 277-3660
  6535 Caballero Blvd A Buena Park (90620) *(P-1393)*

La Mousse, Gardena *Also Called: La Mousse Desserts Inc (P-1394)*

La Mousse Desserts Inc ....E....... 310 478-6051
  18211 S Broadway Gardena (90248) *(P-1394)*

La Opinion LP ....B....... 213 896-2222
  210 E Washington Blvd Los Angeles (90015) *(P-3293)*

La Opinion LP (HQ)...D....... 213 891-9191
  915 Wilshire Blvd Ste 915 Los Angeles (90017) *(P-3294)*

La Palm Furnitures & ACC Inc (PA)..............................E....... 310 217-2700
  1650 W Artesia Blvd Gardena (90248) *(P-2516)*

La Palma Hospital Medical Center ....B....... 714 670-7400
  7901 Walker St La Palma (90623) *(P-18319)*

La Palma Intercommunity Hosp, La Palma *Also Called: La Palma Hospital Medical Center (P-18319)*

La Palma Medical Offices, La Palma *Also Called: Kaiser Foundation Hospitals (P-17685)*

La Paz Products Inc ....F....... 714 990-0982
  345 Oak Pl Brea (92821) *(P-1780)*

La Princesita Tortilleria Inc (PA)..................................F....... 323 267-0673
  3432 E Cesar E Chavez Ave Los Angeles (90063) *(P-1931)*

LA Printing & Graphics Inc ....E....... 310 527-4526
  13951 S Main St Los Angeles (90061) *(P-3617)*

La Provence Inc ....D....... 760 736-3299
  1370 W San Marcos Blvd Ste 130 San Marcos (92078) *(P-13375)*

La Provence Bakery, San Marcos *Also Called: La Provence Inc (P-13375)*

La Quinta Brewing Company LLC ....D....... 760 200-2597
  74714 Technology Dr Palm Desert (92211) *(P-1598)*

La Quinta Cliff House, La Quinta *Also Called: TS Enterprises Inc (P-14040)*

La Quinta Resort & Club, La Quinta *Also Called: HP Lq Investment LP (P-15187)*

La Quinta Resort & Club, La Quinta *Also Called: Lqr Property LLC (P-15233)*

La Rams Football Club, Los Angeles *Also Called: Los Angeles Rams LLC (P-20057)*

La Rancherita Tortilleria Deli, Santa Ana *Also Called: MRS Foods Incorporated (P-1952)*

La Rocks, Los Angeles *Also Called: LA Gem and Jewelry Design (P-10906)*

La Sentinel Newspaper, Los Angeles *Also Called: Los Angeles Sentinel Inc (P-3298)*

LA SOLAR GROUP, San Fernando *Also Called: La Solar Group Inc (P-784)*

La Solar Group Inc ....D....... 818 373-0077
  560 Library St San Fernando (91340) *(P-784)*

LA Spas Inc ....C....... 714 630-1150
  1325 N Blue Gum St Anaheim (92806) *(P-11240)*

LA Specialty Produce Co (PA)....................................B....... 562 741-2200
  13527 Orden Dr Santa Fe Springs (90670) *(P-13332)*

La Sports Arena, Los Angeles *Also Called: Los Angeles Mem Coliseum Comm (P-19531)*

LA Sports Properties Inc ....C....... 213 742-7500
  1212 S Flower St Fl 5 Los Angeles (90015) *(P-17375)*

La Times ....E....... 213 237-2279
  202 W 1st St Ste 500 Los Angeles (90012) *(P-3295)*

La Tolteca Mexican Foods, Azusa *Also Called: Arrietta Incorporated (P-13694)*

LA Triumph Inc ....E....... 562 404-7657
  13336 Alondra Blvd Cerritos (90703) *(P-2178)*

LA Turbine (HQ)...D....... 661 294-8290
  28557 Industry Dr Valencia (91355) *(P-6882)*

La Ventana Treatment Programs ....D....... 805 644-5745
  1408 E Thousand Oaks Blvd Thousand Oaks (91362) *(P-18701)*

La Verne Cinema 12, La Verne *Also Called: Edwards Theatres Inc (P-17293)*

La Verne Nursery Inc ....D....... 805 521-0111
  3653 Center St Piru (93040) *(P-13512)*

La Vida Del Mar Associates, Solana Beach *Also Called: Senior Resource Group LLC (P-14730)*

LA Web Inc ....F....... 626 453-8800
  9645 Telstar Ave El Monte (91731) *(P-850)*

La Workout Inc ....C....... 805 482-8884
  500 Paseo Camarillo Camarillo (93010) *(P-17404)*

La Workout Camarillo West, Camarillo *Also Called: La Workout Inc (P-17404)*

La Xpress Air & Heating Svcs ....D....... 310 856-9678
  6400 E Washington Blvd Ste 121 Commerce (90040) *(P-3461)*

La's Totally Awesome, Buena Park *Also Called: Awesome Products Inc (P-4343)*

La6721 LLC ....F....... 323 484-4070
  1275 E 6th St Los Angeles (90021) *(F-11129)*

Laaco Ltd (HQ)..C....... 213 622-1254
  4469 Admiralty Way Marina Del Rey (30292) *(P-14738)*

Lab Clean Inc ....E....... 714 689-0063
  3627 Briggeman Dr Los Alamitos (90720) *(P-4356)*

Labarge/Stc Inc ....B....... 281 207-1400
  200 Sandpointe Ave Ste 700 Santa Ana (92707) *(P-8826)*

Label House, Ontario *Also Called: L A Supply Co (P-3775)*

Label Impressions, Anaheim *Also Called: Brook & Whittle Limited (P-3741)*

Label Impressions Inc ....E....... 714 634-3466
  1831 W Sequoia Ave Orange (92868) *(P-3776)*

Label Shoppe, The, City Of Industry *Also Called: Labels-R-Us Inc (P-14062)*

Label Specialties Inc ....E....... 714 961-8074
  704 Dunn Way Placentia (92870) *(P-3777)*

Label-Aire, Fullerton *Also Called: Label-Aire Inc (P-7351)*

Label-Aire Inc (PA)..D....... 714 449-5155
  550 Burning Tree Rd Fullerton (92833) *(P-7351)*

Labeling Hurst Systems LLC ....F....... 818 701-0710
  20747 Dearborn St Chatsworth (91311) *(P-3778)*

Labels-R-Us Inc ....E....... 626 333-4001
  1121 Fullerton Rd City Of Industry (91748) *(P-14062)*

Labeltex Mills Inc (PA)..C....... 323 582-0228
  5301 S Santa Fe Ave Vernon (90058) *(P-11071)*

Labeltronix LLC (HQ)...D....... 800 429-4321
  2419 E Winston Rd Anaheim (92806) *(P-3779)*

Labonita Diana's Mexican Food, Carson *Also Called: Dianas Mexican Food Pdts Inc (P-13696)*

Laborlawcenter LLC ....E....... 800 745-9970
  1651 E Saint Andrew Pl Santa Ana (92705) *(P-3618)*

Laborlawcenter.com, Santa Ana *Also Called: Laborlawcenter LLC (P-3618)*

Labrucherie Produce LLC ....E....... 760 352-2170
  1407 S La Brucherie Rd El Centro (92243) *(P-1932)*

Labs.dental, Santa Ana *Also Called: Chromium Dental II LLC (P-17836)*

Lac & Usc Medical Center ....D....... 323 409-2345
  2051 Marengo St Los Angeles (90033) *(P-17704)*

Lac Usc County Hospital ....D....... 323 226-2622
  2051 Marengo St Los Angeles (90033) *(P-18320)*

Lac Usc Medical Center C
  1200 N State St Rm 5250 Los Angeles (90089) *(P-18321)*

Lacera, Pasadena *Also Called: Los Angles Cnty Employees Rtrme (P-14548)*

**A
L
P
H
A
B
E
T
I
C**

Employee Codes: A=Over 500 employees, B=251-500
C=101-250, D=51-100, E=20-50, F=10-19, G=1-9

2024 Southern California
Business Directory and Buyers Guide

© Mergent Inc. 1-800-342-5647

1153

Laclede Inc ....E....... 310 605-4280
2103 E University Dr Rancho Dominguez (90220) *(P-10753)*

Laclede Research Center, Rancho Dominguez *Also Called: Laclede Inc (P-10753)*

Lacma, Los Angeles *Also Called: Los Angeles Cnty Mseum of Art (P-19355)*

Lacmta, Los Angeles *Also Called: Los Angles Cnty Mtro Trnsp Aut (P-11336)*

Ladwp, Los Angeles *Also Called: Los Angeles Dept Wtr & Pwr (P-12128)*

Laetitia Vineyard & Winery Inc ....D....... 805 481-1772
453 Laetitia Vineyard Dr Arroyo Grande (93420) *(P-1642)*

Laetitia Winery, Arroyo Grande *Also Called: Laetitia Vineyard & Winery Inc (P-1642)*

Lafc Partners Lllp ....B....... 213 334-4239
818 W 7th St Ste 1200 Los Angeles (90017) *(P-17496)*

Lagun Engineering Solutions, Harbor City *Also Called: Republic Machinery Co Inc (P-7020)*

Laguna Beach Magazine, Laguna Beach *Also Called: Firebrand Media LLC (P-3573)*

Laguna Blanca School (PA) ....D....... 805 687-2461
4125 Paloma Dr Santa Barbara (93110) *(P-18972)*

Laguna Clay Company, City Of Industry *Also Called: Jon Brooks Inc (P-5550)*

Laguna Cookie Company Inc ....D....... 714 546-6855
4041 W Garry Ave Santa Ana (92704) *(P-1521)*

Laguna Hills Surgery Center, Laguna Hills *Also Called: Cirrus Health II LP (P-17621)*

Laguna Home Health Svcs LLC ....C....... 949 707-5023
25411 Cabot Rd Ste 205 Laguna Hills (92653) *(P-18622)*

Laguna Playhouse Inc ....C....... 949 497-2787
606 Laguna Canyon Rd Laguna Beach (92651) *(P-17317)*

Laguna Woods Village ....A....... 949 597-4267
24351 El Toro Rd Laguna Woods (92637) *(P-14822)*

Laidlaw Educational Services, Palm Springs *Also Called: First Student Inc (P-11428)*

Laird Coatings Corporation ....D....... 714 894-5252
15541 Commerce Ln Huntington Beach (92649) *(P-4492)*

Laird Plastics Inc ....D....... 858 560-1551
5535 Ruffin Rd San Diego (92123) *(P-4813)*

Laird Plastics Inc ....E....... 562 464-9929
12991 Marquardt Ave Santa Fe Springs (90670) *(P-13414)*

Laird R & F Products Inc (DH) ....E....... 760 916-9410
2091 Rutherford Rd Carlsbad (92008) *(P-9992)*

Lake Arrwhead Rsort Oprtor Inc (HQ) ....C....... 909 336-1511
27984 Hwy 189 Lake Arrowhead (92352) *(P-15218)*

Lake Chevrolet ....C....... 951 674-3116
31201 Auto Center Dr Lake Elsinore (92530) *(P-13790)*

Lake Frest No II Mstr Hmwners ....D....... 949 586-0860
24752 Toledo Ln Lake Forest (92630) *(P-19453)*

Lake Mission Viejo Association ....D....... 949 770-1313
22555 Olympiad Rd Mission Viejo (92692) *(P-19454)*

Lakes Country Club Assn Inc (PA) ....C....... 760 568-4321
161 Old Ranch Rd Palm Desert (92211) *(P-17497)*

Lakes Country Club, The, Palm Desert *Also Called: Lakes Country Club Assn Inc (P-17497)*

Lakeshirts LLC ....E....... 805 239-1290
1400 Railroad St Ste 104 Paso Robles (93446) *(P-2517)*

Lakeside Golf Club ....D....... 818 984-0601
4500 W Lakeside Dr Burbank (91505) *(P-17434)*

Lakeside Medical Systems, Northridge *Also Called: Lakeside Systems Inc (P-20050)*

Lakeside Systems Inc ....A....... 866 654-3471
8510 Balboa Blvd Ste 150 Northridge (91325) *(P-20050)*

Lakeview Medical Offices, Anaheim *Also Called: Kaiser Foundation Hospitals (P-17683)*

Lakewood Healthcare Center, Downey *Also Called: Healthcare Ctr of Downey LLC (P-17970)*

Lakewood Park Health Ctr Inc (PA) ....B....... 562 869-0978
12023 Lakewood Blvd Downey (90242) *(P-16859)*

Lakewood Regional Med Ctr Inc ....A....... 562 531-2550
3700 South St Lakewood (90712) *(P-18322)*

Lakewood Regional Medical Ctr, Lakewood *Also Called: Tenet Healthsystem Medical Inc (P-17801)*

Lakewood Regional Medical Ctr, Lakewood *Also Called: Lakewood Regional Med Ctr Inc (P-18322)*

Lakim Industries Incorporated (PA) ....E....... 310 637-8900
389 Rood Rd Calexico (92231) *(P-11091)*

Lakin Tire of Calif, Santa Fe Springs *Also Called: Lakin Tire West Incorporated (P-12271)*

Lakin Tire West Incorporated (PA) ....C....... 562 802-2752
15305 Spring Ave Santa Fe Springs (90670) *(P-12271)*

Lamar Jhnson Collaborative Inc ....C....... 424 361-3960
8590 National Blvd Culver City (90232) *(P-19734)*

Lamart California Inc ....E....... 973 772-6262
7560 Bristow Ct Ste C San Diego (92154) *(P-5556)*

Lamb Fuels Inc ....E....... 619 777-9135
725 Main St Ste B Chula Vista (91911) *(P-4524)*

Lambda Research Optics Inc ....D....... 714 327-0600
1695 Macarthur Blvd Costa Mesa (92626) *(P-10268)*

Lambs & Ivy Inc ....E....... 310 322-3800
2042 E Maple Ave El Segundo (90245) *(P-2475)*

Lamer Street Kreations Corp ....E....... 909 305-4824
13815 Arrow Blvd Fontana (92335) *(P-19637)*

Laminated Shim Company Inc ....E....... 951 273-3900
1691 California Ave Corona (92881) *(P-6867)*

Laminating Company of America ....E....... 949 587-3300
20322 Windrow Dr Ste 100 Lake Forest (92630) *(P-8696)*

Laminating Company of America, Lake Forest *Also Called: Tri-Star Laminates Inc (P-8741)*

Lamkin Corporation (PA) ....E....... 619 661-7090
6530 Gateway Park Dr San Diego (92154) *(P-3952)*

Lamp Inc ....C....... 213 488-9559
2116 Arlington Ave Lbby Los Angeles (90018) *(P-19278)*

Lamp Community, Los Angeles *Also Called: Lamp Inc (P-19278)*

Lamps Plus Inc ....E....... 805 642-9007
4723 Telephone Rd Ventura (93003) *(P-8318)*

Lamsco West Inc ....D....... 661 295-8620
29101 The Old Rd Santa Clarita (91355) *(P-5082)*

Lancaster Cmnty Svcs Fndtion I ....C....... 661 723-6230
46008 7th St W Lancaster (93534) *(P-17033)*

Lancaster Crdlgy Med Group Inc (PA) ....D....... 661 726-3058
43847 Heaton Ave Ste B Lancaster (93534) *(P-17705)*

Lance Soll & Lunghard LLP ....D....... 714 672-0022
203 N Brea Blvd Ste 203 Brea (92821) *(P-19787)*

Lance Rygg Dental Corp ....C....... 858 492-9300
10405 Tierrasanta Blvd San Diego (92124) *(P-17838)*

Lancer Orthodontics Inc (PA) ....E....... 760 744-5585
2726 Loker Ave W Carlsbad (92010) *(P-10754)*

Land Disposition Company, Irvine *Also Called: NRLL LLC (P-15044)*

Landcare USA LLC ....C....... 858 453-1755
5248 Governor Dr San Diego (92122) *(P-198)*

Landcare USA LLC ....C....... 949 559-7771
216 N Clara St Santa Ana (92703) *(P-199)*

Landforce Corporation ....C....... 760 843-7839
17201 N D St Victorville (92394) *(P-11493)*

Landing Gear, Los Angeles *Also Called: Judy Ann of California Inc (P-2246)*

Landjet (PA) ....C....... 909 873-4636
1090 Hall Ave Jurupa Valley (92509) *(P-11391)*

Landmark Electronics Inc ....E....... 626 967-2857
990 N Amelia Ave San Dimas (91773) *(P-9077)*

Landmark Event Staffing ....A....... 714 293-4248
4790 Irvine Blvd Ste 105 Irvine (92620) *(P-16654)*

Landmark Health LLC ....B....... 657 237-2450
7755 Center Ave Ste 630 Huntington Beach (92647) *(P-18623)*

Landmark Medical Center, Pomona *Also Called: Landmark Medical Services Inc (P-18516)*

Landmark Medical Services Inc ....D....... 909 593-2585
2030 N Garey Ave Pomona (91767) *(P-18516)*

Landmark Mfg Inc ....E....... 760 941-6626
4112 Avenida De La Plata Oceanside (92056) *(P-7902)*

Landmark Motor Cycle ACC, Oceanside *Also Called: Landmark Mfg Inc (P-7902)*

Landor Associates, Irvine *Also Called: Young & Rubicam LLC (P-15583)*

Landsberg Flfilment Sltons Div, Fontana *Also Called: Orora Packaging Solutions (P-13014)*

Landsberg Los Angeles Div 1001, Montebello *Also Called: Orora Packaging Solutions (P-13017)*

Landsberg Orange Cnty Div 1025, Buena Park *Also Called: Orora Packaging Solutions (P-13019)*

Landsberg Snta Brbara Div 1046, Oxnard *Also Called: Orora Packaging Solutions (P-13016)*

Landscape Center, Riverside *Also Called: B & B Nurseries Inc (P-13501)*

Landscape Communications Inc ....E....... 714 979-5276
14771 Plaza Dr Ste A Tustin (92780) *(P-3365)*

Landscape Contract National, Tustin *Also Called: Landscape Communications Inc (P-3365)*

Landscape Development Inc (PA) ....B....... 661 295-1970
28447 Witherspoon Pkwy Valencia (91355) *(P-200)*

Landscape Development Inc ....C....... 951 371-9370
1290 Carbide Dr Corona (92881) *(P-201)*

Landtec North America Inc ....E....... 909 783-3636
850 Via Lata Ste 112 Colton (92324) *(P-20359)*

Mergent email: customerrelations@mergent.com
1154

2024 Southern California
Business Directory and Buyers Guide

(P-0000) Products & Services Section entry number
(PA)=Parent Co (HQ)=Headquarters (DH)=Div Headquarters

Lange Precision Inc .... F....... 714 870-5420
  1106 E Elm Ave Fullerton (92831) *(P-7903)*

Langer Juice Company Inc .... B....... 626 336-3100
  16195 Stephens St City Of Industry (91745) *(P-13730)*

Langers Juice, City Of Industry *Also Called: Langer Juice Company Inc (P-13730)*

Langers Juice Company Inc .... B....... 626 336-3100
  129 Stephen St City Of Industry (91744) *(P-1375)*

Langham Hotels International, Pasadena *Also Called: Langham Hotels Pacific Corp (P-15219)*

Langham Hotels Pacific Corp .... C....... 617 451-1900
  1401 S Oak Knoll Ave Pasadena (91106) *(P-15219)*

Langham Huntington Hotel & Spa, Pasadena *Also Called: Pacific Huntington Hotel Corp (P-15288)*

Langlois Company .... E....... 951 360-3900
  10810 San Sevaine Way Jurupa Valley (91752) *(P-1424)*

Langlois Fancy Frozen Foods Inc .... E....... 949 497-1741
  2975 Laguna Canyon Rd Laguna Beach (92651) *(P-1395)*

Langlois Flour Company, Jurupa Valley *Also Called: Langlois Company (P-1424)*

Language Los Angeles, Burbank *Also Called: Eastwest Clothing Inc (P-2237)*

Lani, Irvine *Also Called: Loan Administration Netwrk Inc (P-15865)*

Lanic Aerospace, Rancho Cucamonga *Also Called: Lanic Engineering Inc (P-9733)*

Lanic Engineering Inc (PA).. E....... 877 763-0411
  12144 6th St Rancho Cucamonga (91730) *(P-9733)*

Lanpar Inc .... E....... 541 484-1962
  1333 S Bon View Ave Ontario (91761) *(P-2777)*

Lansair Corporation .... E....... 661 294-9503
  25228 Anza Dr Santa Clarita (91355) *(P-7904)*

Lantz Security Systems Inc .... C....... 805 496-5775
  101 N Westlake Blvd Ste 200 Westlake Village (91362) *(P-16655)*

Lanza Research International .... E....... 310 393-5227
  429 Santa Monica Blvd Ste 510 Santa Monica (90401) *(P-4431)*

Lao-Hmong Security Agency Inc .... D....... 714 533-6776
  10682 Trask Ave Garden Grove (92843) *(P-16656)*

Lapco West, Cerritos *Also Called: Lapco West LLC (P-9411)*

Lapco West LLC .... E....... 562 348-4850
  13140 Midway Pl Cerritos (90703) *(P-9411)*

Largo Concrete Inc .... C....... 619 356-2142
  591 Camino De La Reina Ste 620 San Diego (92108) *(P-444)*

Largo Concrete Inc .... C....... 909 981-7844
  1690 W Foothill Blvd Ste B Upland (91786) *(P-1078)*

Larin Corp .... E....... 909 464-0605
  5651 Schaefer Ave Chino (91710) *(P-5885)*

Laritech Inc .... C....... 805 529-5000
  5898 Condor Dr Moorpark (93021) *(P-8697)*

Lark Engineering, Anaheim *Also Called: Secure Technology Company (P-8729)*

LARK Industries Inc (DH).. D....... 714 701-4200
  18565 Jamboree Rd Ste 125 Irvine (92612) *(P-16860)*

Larry Jacinto Construction Inc .... D....... 909 794-2151
  9555 N Wabash Ave Redlands (92374) *(P-629)*

Larry Jacinto Farming Inc .... D....... 909 794-2276
  9555 N Wabash Ave Redlands (92374) *(P-137)*

Larry Mthvin Installations Inc (HQ)............................... C....... 909 563-1700
  501 Kettering Dr Ontario (91761) *(P-5346)*

Larry Spun Products Inc .... E....... 323 881-6300
  1533 S Downey Rd Los Angeles (90023) *(P-6532)*

Larsen Supply Co (PA).. D....... 562 698-0731
  12055 Slauson Ave Santa Fe Springs (90670) *(P-12746)*

Larson Al Boat Shop .... D....... 310 514-4100
  1046 S Seaside Ave San Pedro (90731) *(P-9840)*

Larson Picture Frames, Santa Fe Springs *Also Called: Larson-Juhl US LLC (P-2754)*

Larson-Juhl US LLC .... E....... 562 946-6873
  12206 Bell Ranch Dr Santa Fe Springs (90670) *(P-2754)*

Las Brisas, San Luis Obispo *Also Called: Harvest Management Sub LLC (P-14711)*

Las Colinas Post Acute, Ontario *Also Called: Ontarioidence Opco LLC (P-18093)*

Las Glondrinas Mexican Fd Pdts (PA)........................... F....... 949 240-3440
  27124 Paseo Espada Ste 803 San Juan Capistrano (92675) *(P-14021)*

Las Posas Berry Farms LLC .... D....... 805 483-1000
  730 S A St Oxnard (93030) *(P-18)*

Las Posas Country Club .... C....... 805 482-4518
  955 Fairway Dr Camarillo (93010) *(P-17498)*

Las Vegas / LA Express Inc (PA)................................. C....... 909 972-3100
  1000 S Cucamonga Ave Ontario (91761) *(P-11494)*

Las Villas De Carlsbad, Oceanside *Also Called: Villas De Crlsbad Ltd A Cal Lt (P-19308)*

Las Villas Del Norte .... C....... 760 741-1047
  1325 Las Villas Way Escondido (92026) *(P-19279)*

Las Virgenes Municipal Wtr Dst .... C....... 818 251-2100
  4232 Las Virgenes Rd Lbby Calabasas (91302) *(P-12127)*

Lasco, Santa Fe Springs *Also Called: Larsen Supply Co (P-12746)*

Laser Electric Inc .... C....... 760 658-6626
  650 Opper St Escondido (92029) *(P-912)*

Laser Image Plus, Tustin *Also Called: Robert Pool (P-16594)*

Laser Imaging International, Van Nuys *Also Called: E Alko Inc (P-11055)*

Laser Industries Inc .... D....... 714 532-3271
  1351 Manhattan Ave Fullerton (92831) *(P-7905)*

Laser Operations LLC .... E....... 818 986-0000
  15632 Roxford St Rancho Cascades (91342) *(P-8827)*

Laser Spectrum Inc .... E....... 949 726-2978
  15 Mira Mesa Rcho Sta Marg (92688) *(P-9226)*

Laser Technologies, San Fernando *Also Called: Laser Technologies & Services LLC (P-10872)*

Laser Technologies & Services LLC ....D
  1175 Aviation Pl San Fernando (91340) *(P-10872)*

Lasercare, Irvine *Also Called: Lasercare Technologies Inc (P-11059)*

Lasercare Technologies Inc (PA).................................. E....... 310 202-4200
  14370 Myford Rd Ste 100 Irvine (92606) *(P-11059)*

Laserfiche Document Imaging, Long Beach *Also Called: Compulink Management Ctr Inc (P-15998)*

Lasergraphics Inc .... E....... 949 753-8282
  20 Ada Irvine (92618) *(P-7541)*

Lasergraphics General Business, Irvine *Also Called: Lasergraphics Inc (P-7541)*

Laserod Technologies LLC .... E....... 310 328-5869
  20312 Gramercy Pl Torrance (90501) *(P-7906)*

Lash Construction Inc .... D....... 805 963-3553
  721 Carpinteria St Santa Barbara (93103) *(P-19638)*

Lasr Inc .... C....... 877 591-9979
  1517 Beverly Blvd Los Angeles (90026) *(P-15649)*

LAT LLC .... E....... 323 233-3017
  2618 Fruitland Ave Vernon (90058) *(P-2346)*

Latara Enterprise Inc (PA)... C....... 909 623-9301
  1716 W Holt Ave Pomona (91768) *(P-18555)*

Latexco West, Santa Fe Springs *Also Called: Sleepcomp West LLC (P-4905)*

Latham & Watkins LLP .... B....... 213 891-7108
  555 W 5th St Ste 300 Los Angeles (90013) *(P-18889)*

Latham & Watkins LLP .... B....... 714 540-1235
  650 Town Center Dr Ste 2000 Costa Mesa (92626) *(P-18890)*

Latham & Watkins LLP (PA).. A....... 213 485-1234
  555 W 5th St Ste 300 Los Angeles (90013) *(P-18891)*

Latham & Watkins LLP .... B....... 858 523-5400
  12670 High Bluff Dr Ste 100 San Diego (92130) *(P-18892)*

Latigo Inc .... E....... 323 583-8000
  4371 E 49th St Vernon (90058) *(P-2073)*

Latina & Associates Inc (PA).. E....... 619 426-1491
  1105 Broadway Chula Vista (91911) *(P-3296)*

Laumiere Gourmet Fruits Co LLC .... F....... 661 218-9768
  3331 Pegasus Dr Ste 101 Bakersfield (93308) *(P-1356)*

Launchpad Communications, Anaheim *Also Called: Consumer Resource Network LLC (P-20156)*

Launchpint Elc Prplsion Sltons .... E....... 805 683-9659
  320 Storke Rd Goleta (93117) *(P-9734)*

Launchpoint Eps, Goleta *Also Called: Launchpint Elc Prplsion Sltons (P-9734)*

Laundry Design LLC .... C....... 323 933-2800
  4079 Redwood Ave Ste A Los Angeles (90066) *(P-16861)*

Lauras House .... D....... 949 361-3775
  33 Journey Ste 150 Aliso Viejo (92656) *(P-19108)*

Lauras Orgnal Bston Brwnies In .... F....... 619 855-3258
  2735 Cactus Rd Ste 101 San Diego (92154) *(P-1479)*

Laurelwood Industries Inc .... F....... 760 705-1649
  1939 Palomar Oaks Way Ste B Carlsbad (92011) *(P-7907)*

Lauren Anthony & Co Inc .... E....... 619 590-1141
  11425 Woodside Ave Ste B Santee (92071) *(P-2778)*

Laurence-Hovenier Inc .... C....... 951 736-2990
  179 N Maple St Corona (92878) *(P-1018)*

Lav Hotel Corp .... C....... 858 454-0771
  1132 Prospect St La Jolla (92037) *(P-15220)*

Employee Codes: A=Over 500 employees, B=251-500
C=101-250, D=51-100, E=20-50, F=10-19, G=1-9

2024 Southern California
Business Directory and Buyers Guide

© Mergent Inc. 1-800-342-5647
1155

ALPHABETIC

Lava Products, Fullerton *Also Called: Lava Products Inc (P-3619)*

Lava Products Inc .... E..... 949 951-7191
2358 E Walnut Ave Fullerton (92831) *(P-3619)*

Lavash Corporation of America .... E..... 323 663-5249
2835 Newell St Los Angeles (90039) *(P-1480)*

Lavi Industries (PA) .... D..... 877 275-5284
27810 Avenue Hopkins Valencia (91355) *(P-6363)*

Law Offces Les Zeve A Prof Cor .... C..... 714 848-7920
30 Corporate Park Ste 450 Irvine (92606) *(P-18893)*

Law Offices Juan J. Dominguez, Los Angeles *Also Called: Dominguez Law Group PC (P-18850)*

Law School Financial Inc .... C..... 626 243-1800
175 S Lake Ave Unit 200 Pasadena (91101) *(P-14266)*

Law School Loans, Pasadena *Also Called: Law School Financial Inc (P-14266)*

LAweb Offset Printing Inc .... F..... 626 454-2469
9645 Telstar Ave El Monte (91731) *(P-3780)*

Lawinfocom Inc .... E..... 800 397-3743
5901 Priestly Dr Ste 200 Carlsbad (92008) *(P-16289)*

Lawrence Berkeley National Lab, Brea *Also Called: United Sttes Dept Enrgy Brkley (P-19950)*

Lawrence Equipment, El Monte *Also Called: Lawrence Equipment Leasing Inc (P-7206)*

Lawrence Equipment Leasing Inc (PA) .... C..... 626 442-2894
2034 Peck Rd El Monte (91733) *(P-7206)*

Lawrence Fmly Jwish Cmnty Ctrs (PA) .... C..... 858 362-1144
4126 Executive Dr La Jolla (92037) *(P-19334)*

Lawrence Roll Up Doors Inc (PA) .... E..... 626 962-4163
4525 Littlejohn St Baldwin Park (91706) *(P-6111)*

Lawrence Welk Desert Oasis, Cathedral City *Also Called: Whv Resort Group Inc (P-15418)*

Lawrys Restaurants II Inc .... C..... 323 664-0228
2980 Los Feliz Blvd Los Angeles (90039) *(P-14022)*

Lawyers Title Escrow, Newport Beach *Also Called: Lawyers Title Insurance Corp (P-14542)*

Lawyers Title Insurance Corp .... C..... 949 223-5575
5000 Birch St Newport Beach (92660) *(P-14542)*

Lawyers Title Insurance Corp .... C..... 949 223-5575
18551 Von Karman Ave Ste 100 Irvine (92612) *(P-14543)*

Lawyers Title Insurance Corp .... A..... 805 484-2701
2751 Park View Ct Oxnard (93036) *(P-14544)*

Layfield USA Corporation (DH) .... D..... 619 562-1200
10038 Marathon Pkwy Lakeside (92040) *(P-1167)*

Laymon Candy Co Inc .... E..... 909 825-4408
276 Commercial Rd San Bernardino (92408) *(P-13273)*

Layton Printing, La Verne *Also Called: Layton Printing & Mailing (P-3620)*

Layton Printing & Mailing .... F..... 909 592-4419
1538 Arrow Hwy La Verne (91750) *(P-3620)*

Laz Karp Associates LLC .... C..... 323 464-4190
1400 Ivar Ave Los Angeles (90028) *(P-16992)*

Lb3 Enterprises Inc .... D..... 619 579-6161
12485 Highway 67 # 3 Lakeside (92040) *(P-630)*

Lbct LLC .... D..... 562 951-6000
1171 Pier F Ave Long Beach (90802) *(P-11642)*

Lbf Travel Inc .... B..... 858 429-7599
4545 Murphy Canyon Rd Ste 210 San Diego (92123) *(P-11719)*

Lbi - USA, Chatsworth *Also Called: Lehrer Brllnprfktion Werks Inc (P-5084)*

Lbi Media Holdings Inc .... B..... 714 554-5000
3101 W 5th St Santa Ana (92703) *(P-11928)*

Lbs Financial Credit Union (PA) .... C..... 562 598-9007
5505 Garden Grove Blvd Ste 500 Westminster (92683) *(P-14248)*

Lc Trs Inc .... A..... 760 438-9111
2100 Costa Del Mar Rd Carlsbad (92009) *(P-15221)*

Lca Promotions Inc .... E..... 818 773-9170
3073 Cicero Ct Simi Valley (93063) *(P-3781)*

LCD&d, Chatsworth *Also Called: Lighting Control & Design Inc (P-8373)*

Lcoa, Lake Forest *Also Called: Laminating Company of America (P-8696)*

Lcptracker Inc .... E..... 714 669-0052
117 E Chapman Ave Orange (92866) *(P-16290)*

Ld Acquisition Company 16 LLC .... D..... 310 294-8160
400 Continental Blvd Ste 500 El Segundo (90245) *(P-15034)*

Ld Products Inc .... C..... 888 321-2552
3700 Cover St Long Beach (90808) *(P-3054)*

LDI Mechanical Inc (PA) .... C..... 951 340-9685
1587 E Bentley Dr Corona (92879) *(P-785)*

LDI Operations LLC .... C..... 818 240-7500
450 N Brand Blvd Ste 900 Glendale (91203) *(P-11241)*

Le Elegant Bath Inc .... C..... 951 734-0238
13405 Estelle St Corona (92879) *(P-4919)*

Le Parc Suite Hotel, West Hollywood *Also Called: Ols Hotels & Resorts LLC (P-15275)*

Leach Grain & Milling Co Inc .... E..... 562 869-4451
8131 Pivot St Downey (90241) *(P-13489)*

Leach International Corp (DH) .... B..... 714 736-7537
6900 Orangethorpe Ave Buena Park (90620) *(P-9735)*

Leadcrunch, San Diego *Also Called: Leadcrunch Inc (P-16291)*

Leadcrunch Inc (PA) .... E..... 888 708-6649
750 B St Ste 1630 San Diego (92101) *(P-16291)*

Leader Drug Store, Torrance *Also Called: Little Company Mary Hospital (P-18324)*

Leader Electronics (na) Inc .... F..... 714 435-0505
2901 S Harbor Blvd Santa Ana (92704) *(P-8476)*

Leader Emergency Vehicles, South El Monte *Also Called: Leader Industries Inc (P-11392)*

Leader Industries Inc .... C..... 626 575-0880
10941 Weaver Ave South El Monte (91733) *(P-11392)*

Leading Edge Aviation Svcs Inc .... A..... 714 556-0576
5251 California Ave # 170 Irvine (92617) *(P-851)*

Leading Industry Inc .... D..... 805 385-4100
1151 Pacific Ave Oxnard (93033) *(P-5083)*

Leadingway Corporation (PA) .... F..... 949 509-6589
4199 Campus Dr Ste 550 Irvine (92612) *(P-16453)*

Leadingway Knowledge Systems, Irvine *Also Called: Leadingway Corporation (P-16453)*

Leadmmatic LLC .... E..... 310 857-4511
5154 Don Pio Dr Woodland Hills (91364) *(P-3462)*

Leads360 LLC .... E..... 888 843-1777
207 Hindry Ave Inglewood (90301) *(P-16292)*

Leaf Group, Santa Monica *Also Called: Leaf Group Ltd (P-16501)*

Leaf Group Ltd (HQ) .... C..... 310 394-6400
1655 26th St Santa Monica (90404) *(P-16501)*

Lean Merch, Huntington Beach *Also Called: HB Products LLC (P-3766)*

Learjet Inc .... E..... 818 894-8241
16750 Schoenborn St North Hills (91343) *(P-9543)*

Learning Explorer Inc .... F..... 888 909-9035
924 Anacapa St Ste 4i Santa Barbara (93101) *(P-16293)*

Learning Ovations Inc .... E..... 734 904-1459
16 Coltrane Ct Irvine (92617) *(P-19011)*

Learning Resources Inc .... E..... 800 995-4436
19700 S Vermont Ave Torrance (90502) *(P-11242)*

Learning Tree Pre-School, Tujunga *Also Called: Crescenta-Canada YMCA (P-19442)*

Leather Pro Inc .... E..... 818 833-8822
12900 Bradley Ave Sylmar (91342) *(P-5302)*

Leather.com, National City *Also Called: San Diego Leather Inc (P-13936)*

Lebata Inc .... E..... 949 253-2800
4621 Teller Ave Ste 130 Newport Beach (92660) *(P-5485)*

Leda Corporation .... E..... 714 841-7821
7080 Kearny Dr Huntington Beach (92648) *(P-9919)*

Leda Multimedia, Chino *Also Called: Shop4techcom (P-7485)*

Ledconn, Brea *Also Called: Ledconn Corp (P-8371)*

Ledconn Corp .... E..... 714 256-2111
301 Thor Pl Brea (92821) *(P-8371)*

Ledcor CMI Inc .... D..... 602 595-3017
6405 Mira Mesa Blvd Ste 100 San Diego (92121) *(P-510)*

Ledra Brands Inc .... C..... 714 259-9959
88 Maxwell Irvine (92618) *(P-12306)*

Ledtronics Inc (PA) .... E..... 310 534-1505
23105 Kashiwa Ct Torrance (90505) *(P-8828)*

Ledvance LLC .... E..... 909 923-3003
1651 S Archibald Ave Ontario (91761) *(P-8248)*

Lee .... E..... 213 200-1000
111 Pacifica Ste 310 Irvine (92618) *(P-2170)*

Lee Kum Kee (usa) Foods Inc (PA) .... D..... 626 709-1888
14455 Don Julian Rd City Of Industry (91746) *(P-1361)*

Lee Kum Kee (usa) Inc (DH) .... E..... 626 709-1888
14841 Don Julian Rd City Of Industry (91746) *(P-13376)*

Lee Mar Aquarium & Pet Sups, Vista *Also Called: Lee-Mar Aquarium & Pet Sups (P-13544)*

Lee Pharmaceuticals .... D..... 626 442-3141
1434 Santa Anita Ave South El Monte (91733) *(P-4432)*

Mergent email: customerrelations@mergent.com
1156

2024 Southern California
Business Directory and Buyers Guide

(P-0000) Products & Services Section entry number
(PA)=Parent Co (HQ)=Headquarters (DH)=Div Headquarters

Lee Ray Sandblasting, Santa Fe Springs *Also Called: Cji Process Systems Inc (P-6136)*

Lee Thomas Inc (PA)...E....... 310 532-7560
13800 S Figueroa St Los Angeles (90061) *(P-2347)*

Lee-Mar Aquarium & Pet Sups ....D....... 760 727-1300
2459 Dogwood Way Vista (92081) *(P-13544)*

Lee's Enterprise, Chatsworth *Also Called: Molnar Engineering Inc (P-7944)*

Lee's Kitchen, City Of Industry *Also Called: Lee Kum Kee (usa) Inc (P-13376)*

Leebe, Los Angeles *Also Called: Leebe Apparel Inc (P-2252)*

Leebe Apparel Inc ....E....... 323 897-5585
3499 S Main St Los Angeles (90007) *(P-2252)*

Leed Electric Inc ....C....... 562 270-9500
13138 Arctic Cir Santa Fe Springs (90670) *(P-913)*

Leemarc Industries LLC ....D....... 760 598-0505
340 Rancheros Dr Ste 172 San Marcos (92069) *(P-2213)*

Leeper's Stair Products, Corona *Also Called: Leepers Wood Turning Co Inc (P-2613)*

Leepers Wood Turning Co Inc (PA)....................E....... 562 422-6525
341 Bonnie Cir Ste 104 Corona (92878) *(P-2613)*

Lees Maintenance Service Inc ....B....... 818 988-6644
14740 Keswick St Van Nuys (91405) *(P-15719)*

Leet Technology Inc ....F....... 877 238-4492
1427 S Robertson Blvd Los Angeles (90035) *(P-9412)*

Lefiell, Santa Fe Springs *Also Called: Lefiell Manufacturing Company (P-9736)*

Lefiell Manufacturing Company ....C....... 562 921-3411
13700 Firestone Blvd Santa Fe Springs (90670) *(P-9736)*

Leftbank Art, La Mirada *Also Called: Outlook Resources Inc (P-2523)*

Lefty Production Co LLC ....E....... 323 515-9266
318 W 9th St Ste 1010 Los Angeles (90015) *(P-2348)*

Legacy Commercial Holdings Inc ....E....... 818 767-6626
28939 Avenue Williams Valencia (91355) *(P-2779)*

Legacy Epoch LLC ....D....... 844 673-7305
21011 Warner Center Ln Ste A Woodland Hills (91367) *(P-1444)*

Legacy Farms LLC ....D....... 714 736-1800
1765 W Penhall Way Anaheim (92801) *(P-13333)*

Legacy Healthcare Center LLC ....D....... 626 798-0558
1570 N Fair Oaks Ave Pasadena (91103) *(P-18775)*

Legacy Prtners Residential Inc ....C....... 949 930-6600
5141 California Ave Ste 100 Irvine (92617) *(P-20051)*

Legacy Reinforcing Steel LLC ....C....... 619 646-0205
1057 Tierra Del Rey Ste F Chula Vista (91910) *(P-1107)*

Legal Solutions Holdings Inc ....C....... 800 244-3495
955 Overland Ct Ste 200 San Dimas (91773) *(P-18894)*

Legal Vision Group LLC ....E....... 310 945-5550
2030 Paddock Ln Norco (92860) *(P-3621)*

LEGALZOOM, Glendale *Also Called: Legalzoomcom Inc (P-16502)*

Legalzoomcom Inc (PA).................................B....... 323 962-8600
101 N Brand Blvd Fl 11 Glendale (91203) *(P-16502)*

Legend Films ....B....... 858 793-4420
2200 Faraday Ave Ste 100 Carlsbad (92008) *(P-17256)*

Legend Pump & Well Service Inc ....E....... 909 384-1000
1324 W Rialto Ave San Bernardino (92410) *(P-285)*

Legendary Headwear, San Diego *Also Called: Legendary Holdings Inc (P-2400)*

Legendary Holdings Inc ....E....... 619 872-6100
2295 Paseo De Las Americas Ste 19 San Diego (92154) *(P-2400)*

Legendary Pictures Films LLC ....C....... 818 688-7003
2900 W Alameda Ave Burbank (91505) *(P-15553)*

Leggett & Platt Incorporated ....D....... 909 937-1010
1050 S Dupont Ave Ontario (91761) *(P-2854)*

Leggett & Platt 0768, Poway *Also Called: Valley Metals LLC (P-5642)*

Legion Creative Group ....E....... 323 498-1100
500 N Brand Blvd Ste 1800 Glendale (91203) *(P-3782)*

Legoland California LLC ....B....... 760 450-3661
1 Legoland Dr Carlsbad (92008) *(P-17450)*

Legoland California Resort, Carlsbad *Also Called: Legoland California LLC (P-17450)*

Leham Millet West, Santa Ana *Also Called: Lehman Millet Incorporated (P-4279)*

Lehman Foods Inc ....E....... 818 837-7600
1145 Arroyo St Ste B San Fernando (91340) *(P-1933)*

Lehman Millet Incorporated ....E....... 714 850-7900
3 Macarthur Pl Ste 700 Santa Ana (92707) *(P-4279)*

Lehrer Brllnprfktion Werks Inc ....D....... 818 407-1890
20801 Nordhoff St Chatsworth (91311) *(P-5084)*

Lei AG Seattle, Los Angeles *Also Called: Lowe Enterprises Inc (P-15232)*

Leica Biosystems Imaging Inc (HQ)..................C....... 760 539-1100
1360 Park Center Dr Vista (92081) *(P-10269)*

LEICHTAG ASSISTED LIVING, Encinitas *Also Called: San Diego Hebrew Homes (P-18046)*

Leidos Inc ....D....... 858 826-6000
Naval Air Station San Diego (92135) *(P-19852)*

Leidos Inc ....C....... 858 826-9416
4161 Campus Point Ct Stop Em3 San Diego (92121) *(P-19853)*

Leidos Inc ....C....... 858 826-9090
2985 Scott St Vista (92081) *(P-19854)*

Leidos Inc ....C....... 703 676-4300
10260 Campus Point Dr Bldg C San Diego (92121) *(P-19855)*

Leidos Engrg & Sciences LLC ....C....... 619 542-3130
1330 30th St Ste A San Diego (92154) *(P-19856)*

Leidos Government Services Inc ....C....... 323 721-6979
500 N Via Val Verde Montebello (90640) *(P-16578)*

Leigh Jerry California Inc (PA).........................B....... 818 909-6200
7860 Nelson Rd Van Nuys (91402) *(P-2410)*

Leighton & Associates, Irvine *Also Called: Gradient Engineers Inc (P-19601)*

Leighton Group Inc ....C....... 760 776-4192
75450 Gerald Ford Dr Ste 301 Palm Desert (92211) *(P-19395)*

Leiner Health Products, Carson *Also Called: Leiner Health Products Inc (P-4156)*

Leiner Health Products, Garden Grove *Also Called: Leiner Health Products Inc (P-4157)*

Leiner Health Products Inc (DH)......................C....... 631 200-2000
901 E 233rd St Carson (90745) *(P-4156)*

Leiner Health Products Inc ....E....... 714 898-9936
7366 Orangewood Ave Garden Grove (92841) *(P-4157)*

Leisure Care LLC ....C....... 818 713-0900
8138 Woodlake Ave West Hills (91304) *(P-18089)*

Leisure Care LLC ....C....... 626 447-0106
601 Sunset Blvd Arcadia (91007) *(P-19280)*

Leisure Care LLC ....C....... 714 974-1616
380 S Anaheim Hills Rd Ofc Anaheim (92807) *(P-19281)*

Leisure Components, Cerritos *Also Called: Sedenquist-Fraser Entps Inc (P-9458)*

Leisure Glen Convalescent Ctr, Glendale *Also Called: Buena Ventura Care Center Inc (P-18115)*

Leisure World Pharmacy, Seal Beach *Also Called: Tenet Healthsystem Medical Inc (P-17803)*

Leisure World Resales, Laguna Hills *Also Called: Professional Cmnty MGT Cal Inc (P-14849)*

Lejon of California Inc ....E....... 951 736-1229
1229 Railroad St Corona (92882) *(P-2434)*

Lejon Tulliani, Corona *Also Called: Lejon of California Inc (P-2434)*

Lekos Dye & Finishing Inc (PA).......................D....... 310 763-0900
3131 E Harcourt St Compton (90221) *(P-2050)*

Lemon Grove Care Rhbltttion Ctr, Lemon Grove *Also Called: Lemon Grove Health Assoc LLC (P-17985)*

Lemon Grove Health Assoc LLC ....B....... 619 463-0294
8351 Broadway Lemon Grove (91945) *(P-17985)*

Lenco Racing Transmissions Inc ....F....... 909 673-9080
1326 E Francis St Ontario (91761) *(P-9413)*

Lenders Investment Corp ....D....... 714 540-4747
18101 Von Karman Ave Ste 400 Irvine (92612) *(P-14331)*

Lendsure Mortgage Corp ....C....... 888 707-7811
12230 World Trade Dr San Diego (92128) *(P-14332)*

Lennar Corporation ....D....... 949 349-8000
15131 Alton Pkwy Ste 190 Irvine (92618) *(P-485)*

Lennar Multi Family Community, Aliso Viejo *Also Called: LMC Hollywood Highland (P-565)*

Lenntek Corporation ....E....... 310 534-2738
1610 Lockness Pl Torrance (90501) *(P-8538)*

Lenore John & Co (PA)...................................C....... 619 232-6136
1250 Delevan Dr San Diego (92102) *(P-13377)*

Lenox Financial Mortgage Corp ....B....... 949 428-5100
200 Sandpointe Ave Ste 800 Santa Ana (92707) *(P-14333)*

Leoben Company ....E....... 951 284-9653
16692 Burke Ln Huntington Beach (92647) *(P-11243)*

Leoch Battery Corporation (DH)......................D....... 949 588-5853
20322 Valencia Cir Lake Forest (92630) *(P-8148)*

Leon Krous Drilling Inc ....E....... 818 833-4654
9300 Borden Ave Sun Valley (91352) *(P-286)*

Leonard Craft Co LLC ....D....... 714 549-0678
1815 Ritchey St Ste B Santa Ana (92705) *(P-10908)*

Employee Codes: A=Over 500 employees, B=251-500
C=101-250, D=51-100, E=20-50, F=10-19, G=1-9

2024 Southern California
Business Directory and Buyers Guide

© Mergent Inc. 1-800-342-5647

1157

A
L
P
H
A
B
E
T
I
C

Leonard Green & Partners LP (PA)......................................D...... 310 954-0444
  11111 Santa Monica Blvd Ste 2000 Los Angeles (90025) *(P-14384)*

Leonard Roofing Inc ....D...... 951 506-3811
  43280 Business Park Dr Ste 107 Temecula (92590) *(P-1048)*

Leonard's Guide, Glendora *Also Called: G R Leonard & Co Inc (P-3448)*

Leonards Carpet Service Inc (PA)...............................D...... 714 630-1930
  1121 N Red Gum St Anaheim (92806) *(P-2960)*

Leonards Molded Products Inc ....E...... 661 253-2227
  25031 Anza Dr Valencia (91355) *(P-4774)*

Leonesse Cellars, Temecula *Also Called: Temecula Valley Winery MGT LLC (P-1662)*

Leonesse Cellars LLC ....E...... 951 302-7601
  38311 De Portola Rd Temecula (92592) *(P-1643)*

Leonetti Company, Tujunga *Also Called: F J & J Corporation (P-17251)*

Leonid M Glsman DDS A Dntl Cor ....C...... 323 560-4514
  5021 Florence Ave Bell (90201) *(P-17839)*

Leport Educational Inst Inc ....B...... 914 374-8860
  1 Technology Dr Bldg A Irvine (92618) *(P-19214)*

Leport Schools ....D...... 714 377-6035
  1 Technology Dr Ste H100 Irvine (92618) *(P-19215)*

Leport Schools, Irvine *Also Called: Leport Educational Inst Inc (P-19214)*

Lereta LLC (PA)...B...... 626 543-1765
  901 Corporate Center Dr Pomona (91768) *(P-14385)*

Lereta LLC ....C...... 626 332-1942
  10760 4th St Rancho Cucamonga (91730) *(P-14670)*

LEROY HAYNES CENTER, La Verne *Also Called: Haynes Family Programs Inc (P-19268)*

Lesco, Torrance *Also Called: American Ultraviolet West Inc (P-6969)*

Lester Lithograph Inc ....E...... 714 491-3981
  1128 N Gilbert St Anaheim (92801) *(P-3622)*

Lestonnac Preschool, Tustin *Also Called: Tustin Unified School District (P-18985)*

Letner Roofing Company, Orange *Also Called: Danny Letner Inc (P-1040)*

Lets Do Lunch ....B...... 310 523-3664
  310 W Alondra Blvd Gardena (90248) *(P-1934)*

Lets Go Apparel Inc (PA)..E...... 213 863-1767
  1729 E Washington Blvd Los Angeles (90021) *(P-2453)*

Levecke LLC ....E...... 951 681-8600
  10810 Inland Ave Jurupa Valley (91752) *(P-1644)*

Level 99, Gardena *Also Called: Phoenix Textile Inc (P-13088)*

Level Furnished Living, Los Angeles *Also Called: Onni Properties LLC (P-20071)*

Levena Biopharma Us Inc ....E...... 858 720-1439
  11760 Sorrento Valley Rd Ste N San Diego (92121) *(P-4158)*

Levity Live, Oxnard *Also Called: Comedy Club Oxnard LLC (P-17479)*

Levity of Brea LLC ....D...... 714 482-0700
  180 S Brea Blvd Brea (92821) *(P-14049)*

Levlad LLC ....C...... 818 882-2951
  9200 Mason Ave Chatsworth (91311) *(P-12497)*

Lewis Barricade Inc ....E...... 661 363-0912
  4000 Westerly Pl Ste 100 Newport Beach (92660) *(P-4661)*

Lewis Brsbois Bsgard Smith LLP ....C...... 714 545-9200
  650 Town Center Dr Ste 1400 Costa Mesa (92626) *(P-18895)*

Lewis Brsbois Bsgard Smith LLP (PA)..........................A...... 213 250-1800
  633 W 5th St Ste 4000 Los Angeles (90071) *(P-18896)*

Lewis Brsbois Bsgard Smith LLP ....C...... 619 233-1006
  701 B St Ste 1900 San Diego (92101) *(P-18897)*

Lewis Center For Eductl RES, Apple Valley *Also Called: High Dsert Prtnr In Acdmic Exc (P-19896)*

Lewis Companies (PA)...C...... 909 985-0971
  1156 N Mountain Ave Upland (91786) *(P-486)*

Lewis Lifetime Tools, Poway *Also Called: Richmond Engineering Co Inc (P-215)*

Lewis Management Corp ....C...... 909 985-0971
  1154 N Mountain Ave Upland (91786) *(P-20052)*

Lexani, Corona *Also Called: Lexani Wheel Corporation (P-5592)*

Lexani Wheel Corporation ....E...... 951 808-4220
  1121 Olympic Dr Corona (92881) *(P-5592)*

Lexar Incorporated ....F...... 619 252-8265
  380 Vernon Way Ste J El Cajon (92020) *(P-2575)*

Lexco Imports Inc ....E...... 800 883-1454
  1455 S Campus Ave Ontario (91761) *(P-6820)*

Lexicon Marketing, Los Angeles *Also Called: Lexicon Marketing (usa) Inc (P-12528)*

Lexicon Marketing (usa) Inc (PA)................................D...... 323 782-8282
  640 S San Vicente Blvd Los Angeles (90048) *(P-12528)*

Lexington, North Hollywood *Also Called: Lexington Acquisition Inc (P-6039)*

Lexington Acquisition Inc ....C...... 818 768-5768
  11125 Vanowen St North Hollywood (91605) *(P-6039)*

Lexington Group International ....C...... 562 428-4681
  260 E Market St Long Beach (90805) *(P-18135)*

Lexisnexis Risk Assets Inc ....C...... 949 222-0028
  2112 Business Center Dr Ste 150 Irvine (92614) *(P-14607)*

Lexor Inc ....D...... 714 444-4144
  7400 Hazard Ave Westminster (92683) *(P-11244)*

Lexus of Cerritos, Cerritos *Also Called: Bargain Rent-A-Car (P-13739)*

Lexus Santa Monica, Santa Monica *Also Called: Volkswagen Santa Monica Inc (P-13845)*

Lexxiom Inc ....B...... 909 581-7313
  99 N San Antonio Ave Ste 330 Upland (91786) *(P-20053)*

Ley Grand Foods Corporation ....E...... 626 336-2244
  287 S 6th Ave La Puente (91746) *(P-1935)*

Lf Illumination LLC ....D...... 818 885-1335
  9200 Deering Ave Chatsworth (91311) *(P-8319)*

Lf Sportswear Inc (PA)..E...... 310 437-4100
  13336 Beach Ave Marina Del Rey (90292) *(P-2253)*

LFC Corporate Services Inc ....D...... 949 640-4950
  17 Corporate Plaza Dr Ste 200 Newport Beach (92660) *(P-20054)*

Lfs Development LLC ....C...... 619 501-5400
  901 Bayfront Ct Ste 1 San Diego (92101) *(P-15222)*

Lg Nanoh2o LLC ....E...... 424 218-4000
  21250 Hawthorne Blvd Ste 330 Torrance (90503) *(P-4616)*

Lg Nanoh2o, Inc., Torrance *Also Called: Lg Nanoh2o LLC (P-4616)*

Lg-Ericsson USA Inc ....E...... 877 828-2673
  20 Mason Irvine (92618) *(P-8477)*

Lg-Led Solutions Limited ....E...... 626 587-8506
  15902 Halliburton Rd Ste A Hacienda Heights (91745) *(P-8372)*

LGarde Inc ....E...... 714 259-0771
  15181 Woodlawn Ave Tustin (92780) *(P-7476)*

Lh Indian Wells Operating LLC ....C...... 760 341-2200
  4500 Indian Wells Ln Indian Wells (92210) *(P-15223)*

Lh Universal Operating LLC ....B...... 818 980-1212
  333 Universal Hollywood Dr Universal City (91608) *(P-15224)*

Lho Mssion Bay Rsie Lessee Inc ....B...... 619 276-4010
  1775 E Mission Bay Dr San Diego (92109) *(P-15225)*

Lhoberge Lessee Inc ....C...... 858 259-1515
  1540 Camino Del Mar Del Mar (92014) *(P-15226)*

Lhv Power Corporation (PA)..E...... 619 258-7700
  10221 Buena Vista Ave Ste A Santee (92071) *(P-9078)*

Liberman Broadcasting Inc ....D...... 818 729-5300
  1845 W Empire Ave Burbank (91504) *(P-11929)*

Liberty Ambulance LLC ....C...... 562 741-6230
  9441 Washburn Rd Downey (90242) *(P-11393)*

Liberty Container Company ....C...... 323 564-4211
  4224 Santa Ana St South Gate (90280) *(P-3114)*

Liberty Dental Plan Cal Inc ....B...... 949 223-0007
  340 Commerce Ste 100 Irvine (92602) *(P-14484)*

Liberty Dental Plan Corp (PA).......................................D...... 888 703-6999
  340 Commerce Ste 100 Irvine (92602) *(P-14485)*

Liberty Diversified Intl Inc ....C...... 858 391-7302
  13100 Danielson St Poway (92064) *(P-3115)*

Liberty Film, Commerce *Also Called: Liberty Packg & Extruding Inc (P-3184)*

Liberty Landscaping Inc (PA).......................................C...... 951 683-2999
  5212 El Rivino Rd Riverside (92509) *(P-202)*

Liberty Packg & Extruding Inc ....E...... 323 722-5124
  3015 Supply Ave Commerce (90040) *(P-3184)*

Liberty Photo Products, San Clemente *Also Called: Liberty Synergistics Inc (P-12861)*

Liberty Residential Svcs Inc ....D...... 858 500-0852
  12700 Stowe Dr Ste 110 Poway (92064) *(P-18624)*

Liberty School, Paso Robles *Also Called: Treana Winery LLC (P-1666)*

Liberty Synergistics Inc ....D...... 949 361-1100
  1041 Calle Trepadora San Clemente (92673) *(P-12861)*

Liberty Vegetable Oil Company ....E...... 562 921-3567
  15306 Carmenita Rd Santa Fe Springs (90670) *(P-1572)*

Libor Management LLC ....C...... 858 450-7175
  5975 Lusk Blvd San Diego (92121) *(P-15227)*

Library Reproduction Service, Los Angeles *Also Called: Microfilm Company of Cal Inc (P-3410)*

Mergent email: customerrelations@mergent.com
1158

2024 Southern California
Business Directory and Buyers Guide

(P-0000) Products & Services Section entry number
(PA)=Parent Co (HQ)=Headquarters (DH)=Div Headquarters

Licher Direct Mail Inc .... E....... 626 795-3333
980 Seco St Pasadena (91103) *(P-3623)*

Lidlaw Educational Services, Rancho Cucamonga Also Called: Durham School Services L P *(P-11425)*

Lief Labs, Valencia Also Called: Lief Organics LLC *(P-1275)*

Lief Organics LLC (PA)................................. E....... 661 775-2500
28903 Avenue Paine Valencia (91355) *(P-1275)*

Life Alert, Encino Also Called: Life Alert Emrgncy Rsponse Inc *(P-16746)*

Life Alert Emrgncy Rsponse Inc (PA).............C....... 800 247-0000
16027 Ventura Blvd Ste 400 Encino (91436) *(P-16746)*

Life Care Center of La Habra, La Habra Also Called: Life Care Centers America Inc *(P-17992)*

Life Care Center of Norwalk, Norwalk Also Called: Life Care Centers America Inc *(P-17989)*

Life Care Centers America Inc ....C....... 760 252-2515
27555 Rimrock Rd Barstow (92311) *(P-17986)*

Life Care Centers America Inc ....C....... 760 741-6109
1980 Felicita Rd Escondido (92025) *(P-17987)*

Life Care Centers America Inc ....C....... 562 947-8691
12200 La Mirada Blvd La Mirada (90638) *(P-17988)*

Life Care Centers America Inc ....D....... 562 921-6624
12350 Rosecrans Ave Norwalk (90650) *(P-17989)*

Life Care Centers America Inc ....C....... 562 943-7156
11926 La Mirada Blvd La Mirada (90638) *(P-17990)*

Life Care Centers America Inc ....C....... 562 867-1761
16910 Woodruff Ave Bellflower (90706) *(P-17991)*

Life Care Centers America Inc ....C....... 562 690-0852
1233 W La Habra Blvd La Habra (90631) *(P-17992)*

Life Care Centers America Inc ....C....... 760 724-8222
304 N Melrose Dr Vista (92083) *(P-18136)*

Life Care Centers of Escondido, Escondido Also Called: Life Care Centers America Inc *(P-17987)*

Life Care Residences Inc ....E....... 760 743-8843
612 Tranquility Gln Escondido (92027) *(P-17993)*

Life Cycle Engineering Inc ....C....... 619 785-5990
7510 Airway Rd Ste 2 San Diego (92154) *(P-15720)*

Life Force International, El Cajon Also Called: Doctors Signature Sales *(P-3997)*

Life Guard Gloves, City Of Industry Also Called: Durasafe Inc *(P-12484)*

Life Is Life LLC ....E....... 310 584-7541
2611 Cottonwood Ave Moreno Valley (92553) *(P-1256)*

Life Science Outsourcing Inc ....D....... 714 672-1090
830 Challenger St Brea (92821) *(P-10546)*

Life Steps Foundation Inc ....D....... 562 436-0751
500 E 4th St Long Beach (90802) *(P-19109)*

Life Technologies, Carlsbad Also Called: Life Technologies Corporation *(P-10270)*

Life Technologies Corporation (HQ)...............C....... 760 603-7200
5781 Van Allen Way Carlsbad (92008) *(P-4280)*

Life Technologies Corporation ....C....... 760 918-0135
5791 Van Allen Way Carlsbad (92008) *(P-10270)*

Life Technologies Corporation ....E....... 760 918-4259
5791 Van Allen Way Carlsbad (92008) *(P-10271)*

Life Time Inc ....D....... 858 459-0281
1055 Wall St La Jolla (92037) *(P-17405)*

Life Time Inc ....D....... 949 492-1515
111 Avenida Vista Montana San Clemente (92672) *(P-17406)*

Life Time Fitness, San Clemente Also Called: Life Time Inc *(P-17406)*

Life Time Fitness Inc ....C....... 949 238-2700
28221 Crown Valley Pkwy Laguna Niguel (92677) *(P-18776)*

LIFE TIME FITNESS, INC., Laguna Niguel Also Called: Life Time Fitness Inc *(P-18776)*

Lifebloom Corporation ....E....... 562 944-6800
970 Challenger St Brea (92821) *(P-4159)*

Lifecare Assurance Company ....C....... 818 887-4436
21600 Oxnard St Fl 16 Woodland Hills (91367) *(P-14453)*

Lifecare Assurance Company, Woodland Hills Also Called: 21st Century Lf & Hlth Co Inc *(P-14445)*

Lifeline Ambulance, Commerce Also Called: Eastwestproto Inc *(P-11381)*

Lifeome Biolabs Inc ....E....... 619 302-0129
10054 Mesa Ridge Ct San Diego (92121) *(P-4281)*

Liferay, Diamond Bar Also Called: Liferay Inc *(P-16454)*

Liferay Inc (PA)..A....... 877 543-3729
1400 Montefino Ave Ste 100 Diamond Bar (91765) *(P-16454)*

Lifescript, Newport Beach Also Called: Lifescript Inc *(P-16530)*

Lifescript Inc ....C....... 949 454-0422
4000 Macarthur Blvd Ste 800 Newport Beach (92660) *(P-16530)*

Lifesinnovations Inc ....E....... 866 603-8456
6312 W 77th St Los Angeles (90045) *(P-8539)*

Lifesource Water Systems Inc (PA)...............E....... 626 792-9996
523 S Fair Oaks Ave Pasadena (91105) *(P-7668)*

Lifestream, San Bernardino Also Called: Blood Bnk San Brnrdino Rvrside *(P-18747)*

Lifetech Resources LLC ....D....... 805 944-1199
700 Science Dr Moorpark (93021) *(P-13051)*

Lifetime Entrmt Svcs LLC ....B....... 310 556-7500
2049 Century Park E Ste 840 Los Angeles (90067) *(P-11957)*

Lifetime Memory Products Inc ....E....... 949 794-9000
2505 Da Vinci Ste A Irvine (92614) *(P-8698)*

Lifetime TV Network, Los Angeles Also Called: Lifetime Entrmt Svcs LLC *(P-11957)*

Lifoam Industries LLC ....E....... 714 891-5035
15671 Industry Ln Huntington Beach (92649) *(P-3116)*

Lift Aviation, Rancho Dominguez Also Called: Fairway Import-Export Inc *(P-10989)*

Lift By Encore, Huntington Beach Also Called: Encore Seats Inc *(P-9683)*

Lift By Encore, Huntington Beach Also Called: Irish Interiors Inc *(P-9723)*

Lift It, Pomona Also Called: Lift-It Manufacturing Co Inc *(P-2132)*

Lift-It Manufacturing Co Inc ....E....... 909 469-2251
1603 W 2nd St Pomona (91766) *(P-2132)*

Light Composite Corporation ....E....... 949 858-8820
22322 Gilberto Rcho Sta Marg (92688) *(P-5927)*

Light Helmets, Carlsbad Also Called: Safer Sports Inc *(P-11022)*

Lightcap Industries Inc ....E....... 909 930-3772
1612 S Cucamonga Ave Ontario (91761) *(P-6040)*

Lightform, Carpinteria Also Called: Forms and Surfaces Company LLC *(P-5414)*

Lighthouse Healthcare Ctr LLC ....D....... 323 564-4461
2222 Santa Ana S Los Angeles (90059) *(P-17994)*

Lighthouse Trucking, Montebello Also Called: Beacon Concrete Inc *(P-5463)*

Lighting Control & Design Inc ....E....... 323 226-0000
9144 Deering Ave Chatsworth (91311) *(P-8373)*

Lighting Technologies Intl LLC ....C....... 626 480-0755
13700 Live Oak Ave Baldwin Park (91706) *(P-12601)*

Lightpointe Communications Inc ....E....... 858 834-4083
8515 Arjons Dr Ste G San Diego (92126) *(P-12677)*

Lightpointe Wireless, San Diego Also Called: Lightpointe Communications Inc *(P-12677)*

Lights of America Inc (PA)............................B....... 909 594-7883
13602 12th St Ste B Chino (91710) *(P-8294)*

Lightspeed Software Inc ....E....... 661 716-7600
1800 19th St Bakersfield (93301) *(P-16294)*

Lightstone Dt La LLC ....B....... 310 669-9252
1260 S Figueron St Los Angeles (90015) *(P-15228)*

Lightthipe Substation, Long Beach Also Called: Southern California Edison Co *(P-12057)*

Lightway Industries ....E....... 661 257-0286
28435 Industry Dr Valencia (91355) *(P-8320)*

Lightworks Optics Inc ....D....... 714 247-7100
14192 Chambers Rd Tustin (92780) *(P-10323)*

Lily Bleu Inc ....E....... 310 225-2522
1406 W 178th St Gardena (90248) *(P-13131)*

Liminex Inc (PA)..C....... 888 310-0410
2030 E Maple Ave Ste 100 El Segundo (90245) *(P-16065)*

Limos By Tiffany Inc ....E....... 951 657-2680
23129 Cajalco Rd Perris (92570) *(P-9330)*

Lincoln Prprty No 2087 Ltd Prt ....C....... 214 740-3300
7777 Center Ave Ste 150 Huntington Beach (92647) *(P-14903)*

LINCOLN TRAINING CENTER, South El Monte Also Called: Lincoln Trning Ctr Rhbltion W *(P-19187)*

Lincoln Trning Ctr Rhbltion W ....D....... 626 442-0621
2643 Loma Ave South El Monte (91733) *(P-19187)*

Linda Loma Univ Hlth Care (PA)....................A....... 909 558-4729
11175 Campus St A-1108 Loma Linda (92350) *(P-17706)*

Linda Loma Univ Hlth Care (HQ)....................C....... 909 558-2806
11370 Anderson St Ste 3900 Loma Linda (92354) *(P-18323)*

LINDA VISTA HEALTH CARE CENTER, San Diego Also Called: San Diego Family Care *(P-17757)*

Lindamar Industries Inc ....D....... 805 237-1910
1603 Commerce Way Paso Robles (93446) *(P-3185)*

Lindbergh Child Care Center, Lynwood Also Called: Lynwood Unified School Dst *(P-18975)*

Employee Codes: A=Over 500 employees, B=251-500
C=101-250, D=51-100, E=20-50, F=10-19, G=1-9

2024 Southern California
Business Directory and Buyers Guide

© Mergent Inc. 1-800-342-5647

1159

A
L
P
H
A
B
E
T
I
C

Lindblade Metal Works, La Mirada *Also Called: Lindblade Metalworks Inc (P-6041)*

Lindblade Metalworks Inc ....E...... 714 670-7172
14355 Macaw St La Mirada (90638) *(P-6041)*

Linde Inc ....E...... 909 390-0283
5705 E Airport Dr Ontario (91761) *(P-3867)*

Lindsey & Sons ....D...... 657 306-5369
1226 E 76th St Los Angeles (90001) *(P-16862)*

Lindsey Doors Inc ....E...... 760 775-1959
81101 Indio Blvd Ste D16 Indio (92201) *(P-4835)*

Lindsey Manufacturing Co ....C...... 626 969-3471
760 N Georgia Ave Azusa (91702) *(P-6479)*

Lindsey Mfg, Indio *Also Called: Lindsey Doors Inc (P-4835)*

Lindsey Systems, Azusa *Also Called: Lindsey Manufacturing Co (P-6479)*

Line Hotel, The, Los Angeles *Also Called: Sydell Hotels LLC (P-15386)*

Line One Laboratories, Chatsworth *Also Called: Line One Laboratories Inc USA (P-4775)*

Line One Laboratories Inc USA ....F...... 818 886-2288
9600 Lurline Ave Chatsworth (91311) *(P-4775)*

Linea Pelle, Van Nuys *Also Called: Linea Pelle Inc (P-5259)*

Linea Pelle Inc (PA) ....**F...... 310 231-9950**
7107 Valjean Ave Van Nuys (91406) *(P-5259)*

Lineage, Vernon *Also Called: American Fruits & Flavors LLC (P-1752)*

LINEAGE, Carlsbad *Also Called: Lineage Cell Therapeutics Inc (P-4324)*

Lineage Cell Therapeutics Inc (PA) ....**E...... 510 521-3390**
2173 Salk Ave Ste 200 Carlsbad (92008) *(P-4324)*

Linen Lovers, Ontario *Also Called: Jomar Table Linens Inc (P-2473)*

Linen Salvage Et Cie LLC ....E...... 323 904-3100
1073 Stearns Dr Los Angeles (90035) *(P-13963)*

Liner Law, Los Angeles *Also Called: Liner LLP (P-18898)*

Liner LLP ....C...... 310 500-3500
1100 Glendon Ave 14th Los Angeles (90024) *(P-18898)*

Liner Technologies Inc ....E...... 909 594-6610
4821 Chino Ave Chino (91710) *(P-5085)*

Linfinity Microelectronics, Garden Grove *Also Called: Microsemi Corp - Anlog Mxed Sg (P-8841)*

Ling's, South El Monte *Also Called: Out of Shell LLC (P-1962)*

Links Medical Products Inc (PA) ....**E...... 949 753-0001**
9249 Research Dr Irvine (92618) *(P-10547)*

Links Sign Lngage Intrprting S, Long Beach *Also Called: Goodwill Srving The Pple Sther (P-16836)*

Linksoul LLC ....E...... 760 231-7069
530 S Coast Hwy Oceanside (92054) *(P-2027)*

Linksys LLC ....C...... 408 526-4000
120 Theory Irvine (92617) *(P-12678)*

Linksys LLC ....C...... 310 751-5100
121 Theory Ste 150 Irvine (92617) *(P-12679)*

Linksys Usa Inc ....D...... 949 270-8500
121 Theory Irvine (92617) *(P-12680)*

Linn Energy LLC ....E...... 714 257-1600
2000 Tonner Canyon Rd Brea (92821) *(P-309)*

Linn Western Operating, Brea *Also Called: Linn Energy LLC (P-309)*

Linn's Main Bin, Cambria *Also Called: Linns Fruit Bin Inc (P-13714)*

Linnco LLC ....A...... 661 616-3900
5201 Truxtun Ave Bakersfield (93309) *(P-310)*

Linns Fruit Bin Inc (PA) ....**E...... 805 927-1499**
2535 Village Ln Ste A Cambria (93428) *(P-13714)*

Linquest Corporation (PA) ....**C...... 323 924-1600**
5140 W Goldleaf Cir Ste 400 Los Angeles (90056) *(P-19639)*

Linzer Products, San Fernando *Also Called: Ahi Investment Inc (P-13525)*

Lion Tank Line Inc ....F...... 323 726-1966
5801 Randolph St Commerce (90040) *(P-4643)*

Lion-Vallen Ltd Partnership ....D...... 760 385-4885
22 Area Aven A Bldg #2234 Camp Pendleton (92055) *(P-20055)*

Lions Gate Films Inc ....C...... 310 449-9200
2700 Colorado Ave Santa Monica (90404) *(P-17198)*

Lionsgate Productions Inc ....B...... 310 255-3937
2700 Colorado Ave Ste 200 Santa Monica (90404) *(P-17278)*

Lip Service, Burbank *Also Called: The Original Cult Inc (P-2378)*

Lippert Components Inc ....E...... 909 873-0061
168 S Spruce Ave Rialto (92376) *(P-9296)*

Lippert Components Mfg Inc ....E...... 909 628-5557
1021 Walnut Ave Pomona (91766) *(P-5347)*

Liqui-Box Corporation ....E...... 909 390-4646
5772 Jurupa St Ste C Ontario (91761) *(P-4858)*

Liquid Advertising Inc ....D...... 310 450-2653
138 Eucalyptus Dr El Segundo (90245) *(P-15554)*

Liquid Death Mountain Water ....E...... 818 521-5500
1447 2nd St Ste 200 Santa Monica (90401) *(P-1703)*

Liquid Force Wakeboards ....E...... 760 943-8364
1815 Aston Ave Ste 105 Carlsbad (92008) *(P-11009)*

Liquid Graphics Inc ....C...... 949 486-3588
2701 S Harbor Blvd Unit A Santa Ana (92704) *(P-2214)*

Liquid Investments Inc (PA) ....**C...... 858 509-8510**
3840 Via De La Valle Ste 300 Del Mar (92014) *(P-13471)*

Lisa Factory Inc ....D...... 213 536-5326
144 N Swall Dr Beverly Hills (90211) *(P-2161)*

Lisi Aerospace ....E...... 310 326-8110
2600 Skypark Dr Torrance (90505) *(P-10548)*

Lisi Aerospace, City Of Industry *Also Called: Monadnock Company (P-5934)*

Lisi Aerospace North Amer Inc ....A...... 310 326-8110
2600 Skypark Dr Torrance (90505) *(P-5657)*

Lite Extrusions, Gardena *Also Called: Lite Extrusions Mfg Inc (P-4836)*

Lite Extrusions Mfg Inc ....E...... 323 770-4298
15025 S Main St Gardena (90248) *(P-4836)*

Lite Solar, Long Beach *Also Called: Lite Solar Corp (P-786)*

Lite Solar Corp ....C...... 562 256-1249
3553 Atlantic Ave Long Beach (90807) *(P-786)*

Litegear Inc ....E...... 818 358-8542
4406 W Vanowen St Burbank (91505) *(P-8249)*

Litel Instruments Inc ....E...... 858 546-3788
10650 Scripps Ranch Blvd Ste 105 San Diego (92131) *(P-10213)*

Litepanels Inc ....E...... 818 752-7009
20600 Plummer St Chatsworth (91311) *(P-8250)*

Lith-O-Roll Corporation ....E...... 626 579-0340
9521 Telstar Ave El Monte (91731) *(P-7187)*

Lithia, Temecula *Also Called: DCH Acura of Temecula (P-13754)*

Lithocraft Co, Anaheim *Also Called: Man-Grove Industries Inc (P-3629)*

Lithographix Inc (PA) ....**B...... 323 770-1000**
12250 Crenshaw Blvd Hawthorne (90250) *(P-3624)*

Liton Lighting, Los Angeles *Also Called: Eema Industries Inc (P-8362)*

Little Brothers Bakery, Gardena *Also Called: Little Brothers Bakery LLC (P-1481)*

Little Brothers Bakery LLC ....D...... 310 225-3790
320 W Alondra Blvd Gardena (90248) *(P-1481)*

Little Co Mary- San Pedro Hosp, San Pedro *Also Called: San Pedro Peninsula Hospital (P-18418)*

Little Company Mary Hospital ....A...... 310 540-7676
4101 Torrance Blvd Torrance (90503) *(P-18324)*

Little Company Mary Svc Area, Torrance *Also Called: Little Company of Mary Health Services (P-18325)*

Little Company of Mary Health Services ....A...... 310 540-7676
4101 Torrance Blvd Torrance (90503) *(P-18325)*

Little Ssters of The Poor Los ....D...... 310 548-0625
2100 S Western Ave San Pedro (90732) *(P-17995)*

Littlefeet Inc ....E...... 858 375-6400
13000 Gregg St Poway (92064) *(P-8478)*

Littlejohn-Reuland Corporation ....E...... 323 587-5255
4575 Pacific Blvd Vernon (90058) *(P-914)*

Live Fresh Corporation ....C...... 909 478-0895
1055 E Cooley Ave San Bernardino (92408) *(P-1376)*

Live Nation, Beverly Hills *Also Called: Live Nation Entertainment Inc (P-16863)*

Live Nation Entertainment Inc (PA) ....**C...... 310 867-7000**
9348 Civic Center Dr Lbby Beverly Hills (90210) *(P-16863)*

Live Nation Worldwide Inc (HQ) ....**A...... 310 867-7000**
9348 Civic Center Dr Lbby Beverly Hills (90210) *(P-17343)*

Live Nation Worldwide Inc ....B...... 310 867-7000
325 N Maple Dr Beverly Hills (90210) *(P-17376)*

Live Oak Rehab, San Gabriel *Also Called: Longwood Management Corp (P-18141)*

Liveoffice LLC ....D...... 877 253-2793
900 Corporate Pointe Culver City (90230) *(P-16295)*

Livescribe Inc ....E
930 Roosevelt Irvine (92620) *(P-7542)*

Livhome Inc (PA) ....**A...... 800 807-5854**
5670 Wilshire Blvd Ste 500 Los Angeles (90036) *(P-18625)*

Living Desert .... C...... 760 346-5694
47900 Portola Ave Palm Desert (92260) *(P-19367)*

Living Doll LLC .... F...... 213 222-1010
13071 Temple Ave La Puente (91746) *(P-13913)*

Living Spaces Furniture LLC .... C...... 760 945-6805
1900 University Dr Vista (92083) *(P-13943)*

Living Spaces Furniture LLC (PA) .... C...... 877 266-7300
14501 Artesia Blvd La Mirada (90638) *(P-13944)*

Living Way Industries Inc .... F...... 661 298-3200
20734 Centre Pointe Pkwy Santa Clarita (91350) *(P-3625)*

Living Wellness Partners LLC .... E...... 800 642-3754
3305 Tyler St Carlsbad (92008) *(P-1936)*

Livingston Mem Vna Hlth Corp .... B...... 805 642-0239
1996 Eastman Ave Ste 101 Ventura (93003) *(P-20056)*

Livingston Mem Vsting Nrse Ass, Ventura *Also Called: Livingston Mem Vna Hlth Corp*
(P-20056)

Ljg, Irvine *Also Called: La Jolla Group Inc (P-16858)*

Llamas Plastics Inc .... C...... 818 362-0371
12970 Bradley Ave Sylmar (91342) *(P-9737)*

LLC Bates White .... C...... 858 523-2150
322 8th St Del Mar (92014) *(P-18899)*

LLC Walker West .... D...... 800 767-9378
5500 Jurupa St Ontario (91761) *(P-2984)*

LLC Walker West .... C...... 909 390-4300
1555 S Vintage Ave Ontario (91761) *(P-5086)*

LLC Walker West .... D...... 951 685-9660
11445 Pacific Ave Fontana (92337) *(P-6262)*

LLC Woodward West .... C...... 661 822-7900
28400 Stallion Springs Dr Tehachapi (93561) *(P-15437)*

Lloyd Design Corporation .... D...... 818 768-6001
19731 Nordhoff St Northridge (91324) *(P-9414)*

Lloyd Mats, Northridge *Also Called: Lloyd Design Corporation (P-9414)*

Lloyd Staffing Inc .... A...... 631 777-7600
18000 Studebaker Rd Ste 700 Cerritos (90703) *(P-15926)*

LLP Mayer Brown .... B...... 213 229-9500
350 S Grand Ave Ste 2500 Los Angeles (90071) *(P-18900)*

LLP Moss Adams .... C...... 949 221-4000
2040 Main St Ste 900 Irvine (92614) *(P-19788)*

LLP Moss Adams .... C...... 310 477-0450
21700 Oxnard St Ste 300 Woodland Hills (91367) *(P-19789)*

LLP Moss Adams .... D...... 858 627-1400
4747 Executive Dr Ste 1300 San Diego (92121) *(P-19790)*

LLUCH, Loma Linda *Also Called: Loma Linda Univ Chld Hosp (P-14997)*

LLUMC, Loma Linda *Also Called: Loma Linda University Med Ctr (P-18326)*

Lmb Opco LLC .... B...... 310 348-6800
12181 Bluff Creek Dr Ste 250 Playa Vista (90094) *(P-14360)*

LMC Enterprises (PA) .... D...... 562 602-2116
6401 Alondra Blvd Paramount (90723) *(P-4357)*

LMC Enterprises .... E...... 310 632-7124
19402 S Susana Rd Compton (90221) *(P-4358)*

LMC Hollywood Highland .... B...... 949 448-1600
95 Enterprise Ste 200 Aliso Viejo (92656) *(P-565)*

LMS Reinforcing Steel Group, Corona *Also Called: LMS Reinforcing Steel Usa LP (P-6401)*

LMS Reinforcing Steel Usa LP (HQ) .... E...... 604 598-9930
26365 Earthmover Cir Corona (92883) *(P-6401)*

Lmw Enterprises LLC .... E...... 562 944-1969
10558 Norwalk Blvd Santa Fe Springs (90670) *(P-7617)*

Lni Custom Manufacturing Inc .... E...... 310 978-2000
15542 Broadway Center St Gardena (90248) *(P-6364)*

Load Delivered Logistics LLC .... C...... 310 822-0215
214 Main St Venice (90291) *(P-11495)*

Loaded Boards Inc .... F...... 310 839-1800
10575 Virginia Ave Culver City (90232) *(P-9878)*

Loan Administration Netwrk Inc 949 752-5246
2082 Business Center Dr Ste 250 Irvine (92612) *(P-15865)*

Loandepot, Irvine *Also Called: Loandepot Inc (P-14334)*

Loandepot Inc (PA) .... B...... 888 337-6888
6561 Irvine Center Dr Irvine (92618) *(P-14334)*

Loandepot Inc .... B...... 949 470-6263
25500 Commercentre Dr Lake Forest (92630) *(P-14335)*

Loandepot Inc 619 245-0115
2080 Otay Lakes Rd # 101 Chula Vista (91913) *(P-14336)*

Loandepotcom LLC .... A...... 661 202-1700
42455 10th St W Ste 109 Lancaster (93534) *(P-14337)*

Loandepotcom LLC .... A...... 760 797-6000
901 N Palm Canyon Dr Ste 107 Palm Springs (92262) *(P-14338)*

Loandepotcom LLC (DH) .... A...... 888 337-6888
26642 Towne Centre Dr Foothill Ranch (92610) *(P-14339)*

Lobue Laser & Eye Medical Ctrs .... E...... 951 696-1135
40740 California Oaks Rd Murrieta (92562) *(P-10810)*

Local 12, Redlands *Also Called: Interntional Un Oper Engineers (P-19410)*

Local 12, San Diego *Also Called: Interntional Un Oper Engineers (P-19411)*

Local Corporation (PA) .... D...... 949 784-0800
7555 Irvine Center Dr Irvine (92618) *(P-15555)*

Local Inttive Hlth Auth For Lo (PA) .... A...... 213 694-1250
1055 W 7th St Fl 10 Los Angeles (90017) *(P-14486)*

Local Media San Diego LLC .... D...... 858 888-7000
6160 Cornerstone Ct E Ste 150 San Diego (92121) *(P-11930)*

Local Neon Company Inc .... E...... 310 978-2000
12536 Chadron Ave Hawthorne (90250) *(P-11130)*

Local.com, Irvine *Also Called: Local Corporation (P-15555)*

Locale Lifestyle Magazine LLC .... E...... 949 436-8910
2755 Bristol St Ste 295 Costa Mesa (92626) *(P-3366)*

Locale Magazine, Costa Mesa *Also Called: Locale Lifestyle Magazine LLC (P-3366)*

Locator Services Inc .... C...... 619 229-6100
4616 Mission Gorge Pl San Diego (92120) *(P-16657)*

Lock America Inc .... F...... 951 277-5180
9168 Stellar Ct Corona (92883) *(P-5928)*

Lock People, The, San Diego *Also Called: Hodge Products Inc (P-5921)*

Lock-Ridge Tool Company Inc .... D...... 909 865-8309
145 N 8th Ave Upland (91786) *(P-6533)*

Lockheed Martin, Coronado *Also Called: Lockheed Martin Corporation (P-9994)*

Lockheed Martin, Chula Vista *Also Called: Lockheed Martin Services LLC (P-19640)*

Lockheed Martin Aeronautics Co, Palmdale *Also Called: Lockheed Martin Corporation*
(P-9996)

Lockheed Martin Corporation .... D...... 760 952-4200
17452 Wheeler Rd Helendale (92342) *(P-9993)*

Lockheed Martin Corporation .... C...... 619 437-7230
Nas North Island Coronado (92118) *(P-9994)*

Lockheed Martin Corporation .... E...... 805 571-2346
346 Bollay Dr Goleta (93117) *(P-9995)*

Lockheed Martin Corporation .... A...... 661 572-7428
1011 Lockheed Way Palmdale (93599) *(P-9996)*

Lockheed Martin Corporation .... C...... 760 386-2572
Bldg 821 South Loop Fort Irwin (92310) *(P-11594)*

Lockheed Martin Orincon Corp (HQ) .... C...... 858 455-5530
10325 Meanley Dr San Diego (92131) *(P-9997)*

Lockheed Martin Services LLC .... E...... 619 271-9831
645 Marsat Ct Ste D Chula Vista (91911) *(P-19640)*

Lockheed Martin Unmanned .... D...... 805 503-4340
125 Venture Dr Ste 110 San Luis Obispo (93401) *(P-16455)*

Lockheed Martin Unmndd, San Luis Obispo *Also Called: AME Unmanned Air Systems Inc*
(P-19545)

Lockton Cmpnies LLC - PCF Srie (HQ) .... B...... 213 689-0500
777 S Figueroa St Ste 5200 Los Angeles (90017) *(P-14608)*

Lockton Insurance Brokers, Los Angeles *Also Called: Lockton Cmpnies LLC - PCF Srie*
(P-14608)

Lockwood Industries LLC (HQ) .... D...... 661 702-6999
28525 Industry Dr Valencia (91355) *(P-8829)*

Locums Unlimited LLC .... A...... 619 550-3763
4141 Jutland Dr Ste 305 San Diego (92117) *(P-17868)*

Loeb & Loeb, Los Angeles *Also Called: Loeb & Loeb LLP (P-18901)*

Loeb & Loeb LLP (PA) .... C...... 310 282-2000
10100 Santa Monica Blvd Ste 2200 Los Angeles (90067) *(P-18901)*

Loews Coronado Bay Resort, Coronado *Also Called: 51st St & 8th Ave Corp (P-15065)*

Loews Hollywood Hotel LLC .... B...... 323 450-2235
1755 N Highland Ave Hollywood (90028) *(P-15229)*

Loews Santa Monica Beach Hotel, Santa Monica *Also Called: Dtrs Santa Monica LLC*
(P-15139)

Lofta .... E...... 858 299-8000
9225 Brown Deer Rd San Diego (92121) *(P-2476)*

Lofty Coffee Inc .... D...... 760 230-6747
97 N Coast Highway 101 Ste 101 Encinitas (92024) *(P-14023)*

ALPHABETIC

Employee Codes: A=Over 500 employees, B=251-500
C=101-250, D=51-100, E=20-50, F=10-19, G=1-9

2024 Southern California
Business Directory and Buyers Guide

© Mergent Inc. 1-800-342-5647

1161

Logicmonitor Inc (PA) .... C....... 805 394-8632
820 State St Fl 5 Santa Barbara (93101) *(P-16531)*

Logicube, Chatsworth Also Called: Logicube Inc *(P-7543)*

Logicube Inc (PA) .... E....... 888 494-8832
19755 Nordhoff Pl Chatsworth (91311) *(P-7543)*

Logility Inc .... D....... 858 565-4238
4885 Greencraig Ln 200 San Diego (92123) *(P-16066)*

Logisteed America Inc .... D....... 323 263-8100
1000 Corporate Center Dr Ste 400 Monterey Park (91754) *(P-11778)*

Logisteed Monterey Park, Monterey Park Also Called: Logisteed America Inc *(P-11778)*

Logistical Support LLC .... C....... 818 341-3344
20409 Prairie St Chatsworth (91311) *(P-9575)*

Logistical Support LLC .... C....... 818 341-3344
20409 Prairie St Chatsworth (91311) *(P-12912)*

Logistics, Bell Also Called: De Well Container Shipping Inc *(P-11750)*

Logitech Inc .... A....... 510 795-8500
3 Jenner Ste 180 Irvine (92618) *(P-7544)*

Logix Federal Credit Union (PA) .... C....... 888 718-5328
2340 N Hollywood Way Burbank (91505) *(P-14230)*

Logix3, Irvine Also Called: Data Council LLC *(P-16814)*

Logo Expressions, Ontario Also Called: Dennis Foland Inc *(P-12973)*

Logomark Inc .... C....... 714 675-6100
1201 Bell Ave Tustin (92780) *(P-13545)*

Lois Lauer Realty (PA) .... C....... 909 748-7000
1998 Orange Tree Ln Redlands (92374) *(P-14823)*

Lola Belle Brands LLC .... F....... 855 226-3526
631 S Palm Ave Alhambra (91803) *(P-13914)*

Lollicup Franchising LLC .... C....... 626 965-8882
6185 Kimball Ave Chino (91708) *(P-20190)*

Loma Linda Healthcare Sys 605, Loma Linda Also Called: Veterans Health Administration *(P-17829)*

Loma Linda Univ Chld Hosp .... C....... 909 558-8000
11234 Anderson St Loma Linda (92354) *(P-14997)*

Loma Linda University Med Ctr (DH) .... A....... 909 558-4000
11234 Anderson St Loma Linda (92354) *(P-18326)*

Loma Linda University Med Ctr .... D....... 909 558-4000
26780 Barton Rd Redlands (92373) *(P-18327)*

Loma Linda University Med Ctr .... D....... 909 558-9275
1710 Barton Rd Redlands (92373) *(P-18328)*

Loma Linda University Med Ctr .... C....... 909 558-4385
11370 Anderson St Loma Linda (92354) *(P-18329)*

Loma Linda University Med Ctr, Loma Linda Also Called: Loma Lnda - Inland Empire Cnsr *(P-18330)*

Loma Lnda - Inland Empire Cnsr .... C....... 909 558-4000
11234 Anderson St Loma Linda (92354) *(P-18330)*

Loma Lnda Univ Fmly Med Group .... D....... 909 558-6600
25455 Barton Rd Ste 204b Loma Linda (92354) *(P-17707)*

Lombard Enterprises Inc .... E....... 562 692-7070
3619 San Gabriel River Pkwy Pico Rivera (90660) *(P-3626)*

Lombard Graphics, Pico Rivera Also Called: Lombard Enterprises Inc *(P-3626)*

Lombardy Holdings Inc (PA) .... C....... 951 808-4550
151 Kalmus Dr Ste F6 Costa Mesa (92626) *(P-681)*

Lomita Logistics LLC .... D....... 310 784-8485
3541 Lomita Blvd Torrance (90505) *(P-15633)*

Lompoc Family YMCA, Lompoc Also Called: Channel Islnds Yung MNS Chrstn *(P-19434)*

Lompoc Skilled Care Center, Lompoc Also Called: Lompoc Valley Medical Center *(P-18332)*

Lompoc Valley Medical Center .... C....... 805 735-9229
1111 E Ocean Ave Ste 2 Lompoc (93436) *(P-18331)*

Lompoc Valley Medical Center (PA) .... B....... 805 737-3300
1515 E Ocean Ave Lompoc (93436) *(P-18332)*

London Spitfire, Santa Monica Also Called: Cloud9 Esports Inc *(P-20152)*

Lonestar Sierra LLC .... C....... 866 575-5680
1820 W Orangewood Ave Orange (92868) *(P-12862)*

Long Bch Dept Hlth & Humn Svcs, Long Beach Also Called: City of Long Beach *(P-20413)*

Long Beach Care Center Inc .... C....... 562 426-6141
2615 Grand Ave Long Beach (90815) *(P-17996)*

Long Beach Golden Sails Inc .... D....... 562 596-1631
23545 Crenshaw Blvd Ste 100 Torrance (90505) *(P-15230)*

Long Beach Hilton, The, Long Beach Also Called: World Trade Ctr Ht Assoc Ltd *(P-15426)*

Long Beach Marriott, Long Beach Also Called: Ruffin Hotel Corp of Cal *(P-15335)*

Long Beach Medical Center .... C....... 562 933-0085
1720 Termino Ave Long Beach (90804) *(P-18333)*

Long Beach Medical Center .... C....... 562 933-7701
450 E Spring St Ste 11 Long Beach (90806) *(P-18334)*

Long Beach Medical Center (HQ) .... A....... 562 933-2000
2801 Atlantic Ave Fl 2 Long Beach (90806) *(P-18335)*

Long Beach Medical Clinic, Long Beach Also Called: CB Tang MD Incorporated *(P-17611)*

Long Beach Memorial Med Ctr .... C....... 562 933-0432
1057 Pine Ave Long Beach (90813) *(P-18336)*

LONG BEACH MEMORIAL MEDICAL CENTER, Long Beach Also Called: Long Beach Memorial Med Ctr *(P-18336)*

Long Beach Pain Center, Long Beach Also Called: Healthsmart Pacific Inc *(P-18277)*

Long Beach Public Trnsp Co .... D....... 562 591-2301
1300 Gardenia Ave Long Beach (90804) *(P-11324)*

Long Beach Public Trnsp Co (PA) .... A....... 562 599-8571
1963 E Anaheim St Long Beach (90813) *(P-11325)*

Long Beach Transit, Long Beach Also Called: Long Beach Public Trnsp Co *(P-11325)*

Long Beach Unified School Dst .... C....... 562 426-6176
2700 Pine Ave Long Beach (90806) *(P-11430)*

Long Beach Unified School Dst .... D....... 562 426-5571
3038 Delta Ave Long Beach (90810) *(P-18973)*

Long Machine Inc .... E....... 951 296-0194
27450 Colt Ct Temecula (92590) *(P-7908)*

Long Point Development LLC .... A....... 310 265-2800
100 Terranea Way Rancho Palos Verdes (90275) *(P-15231)*

Long-Lok LLC .... E....... 424 209-8726
20531 Belshaw Ave Carson (90746) *(P-9738)*

Long-Lok Fasteners Corporation .... F....... 424 213-4570
20531 Belshaw Ave Carson (90746) *(P-12725)*

Longboard Pharmaceuticals Inc .... E....... 619 592-9775
4275 Executive Sq Ste 950 La Jolla (92037) *(P-4160)*

Longo Lexus, El Monte Also Called: El Monte Automotive Group Inc *(P-13760)*

Longo Scion, El Monte Also Called: D Longo Inc *(P-13752)*

Longwood Management Corp .... C....... 310 679-1461
11834 Inglewood Ave Hawthorne (90250) *(P-17997)*

Longwood Management Corp .... D....... 818 360-1864
17922 San Fernando Mission Blvd Granada Hills (91344) *(P-17998)*

Longwood Management Corp .... C....... 626 280-2293
8101 Hill Dr Rosemead (91770) *(P-17999)*

Longwood Management Corp .... C....... 626 280-4820
8035 Hill Dr Rosemead (91770) *(P-18000)*

Longwood Management Corp .... C....... 323 933-1560
1900 S Longwood Ave Los Angeles (90016) *(P-18001)*

Longwood Management Corp .... D....... 323 735-5146
2000 W Washington Blvd Los Angeles (90018) *(P-18137)*

Longwood Management Corp .... D....... 818 246-7174
605 W Broadway Glendale (91204) *(P-18138)*

Longwood Management Corp .... C....... 213 382-8461
1240 S Hoover St Los Angeles (90006) *(P-18139)*

Longwood Management Corp .... D....... 818 980-8200
11429 Ventura Blvd Studio City (91604) *(P-18140)*

Longwood Management Corp .... C....... 626 289-3763
537 W Live Oak St San Gabriel (91776) *(P-18141)*

Longwood Management Corp .... C....... 562 432-5751
1913 E 5th St Long Beach (90802) *(P-18142)*

Longwood Management Corp .... D....... 562 693-5240
7716 Pickering Ave Whittier (90602) *(P-18337)*

Longwood Management Corp .... D....... 310 675-9163
14110 Cordary Ave Hawthorne (90250) *(P-19282)*

Lonix Pharmaceutical Inc .... F....... 626 287-4700
5001 Earle Ave Rosemead (91770) *(P-1276)*

Loomworks Apparel, Irvine Also Called: Delta Galil USA Inc *(P-13123)*

Loop Inc .... E....... 888 385-6674
115 Eucalyptus Dr El Segundo (90245) *(P-9167)*

Lopez & Associates Engineers, El Monte Also Called: R and L Lopez Associates Inc *(P-19676)*

Lorber Industries California .... F....... 310 275-1568
823 N Roxbury Dr Beverly Hills (90210) *(P-2090)*

Lorber Industries of Claif, Beverly Hills Also Called: Lorber Industries California *(P-2090)*

Lord & Sons Inc .... D....... 562 529-2500
10504 Pioneer Blvd Santa Fe Springs (90670) *(P-12863)*

Mergent email: customerrelations@mergent.com
1162

2024 Southern California
Business Directory and Buyers Guide

(P-0000) Products & Services Section entry number
(PA)=Parent Co (HQ)=Headquarters (DH)=Div Headquarters

Lorem Cytori Usa Inc .... E...... 858 746-8696
8659 Production Ave San Diego (92121) *(P-4161)*

Loren Electric Sign & Lighting, Whittier Also Called: Loren Industries *(P-11131)*

Loren Industries .... E...... 562 699-1122
12226 Coast Dr Whittier (90601) *(P-11131)*

Lorenz Inc .... E...... 760 427-1815
1749 Stergios Rd Calexico (92231) *(P-9227)*

Lorenzo USA, Solana Beach Also Called: Simon Golub & Sons Inc *(P-12968)*

Lorimar Winery .... E...... 951 240-5177
42031 Main St Ste C Temecula (92590) *(P-1645)*

Loritz & Associates Inc .... E...... 714 694-0200
24895 La Palma Ave Yorba Linda (92887) *(P-5087)*

Lorser Industries Inc .... E...... 619 917-4298
9636 Arby Dr Beverly Hills (90210) *(P-8699)*

Los Alamitos Medical Ctr Inc (HQ) .... A...... 714 826-6400
3751 Katella Ave Los Alamitos (90720) *(P-18338)*

Los Alamitos Race Course .... C...... 714 820-2800
4961 Katella Ave Cypress (90720) *(P-14024)*

Los Altos, City Of Industry Also Called: Los Altos Food Products LLC *(P-13255)*

Los Altos Food Products LLC .... C...... 626 330-6555
450 Baldwin Park Blvd City Of Industry (91746) *(P-13255)*

Los Angeles Angels of Anaheim, Anaheim Also Called: Angels Baseball LP *(P-17363)*

Los Angeles Apparel Inc (PA) .... B...... 213 275-3120
1020 E 59th St Los Angeles (90001) *(P-2454)*

Los Angeles Athletic Club Inc .... C...... 213 625-2211
431 W 7th St Los Angeles (90014) *(P-17407)*

Los Angeles Branch, Commerce Also Called: Jfc International Inc *(P-13373)*

Los Angeles Branch, Los Angeles Also Called: Federal Rsrve Bnk San Frncisco *(P-14154)*

Los Angeles Brass Products, Huntington Park Also Called: Los Angles Pump Valve Pdts Inc *(P-7282)*

Los Angeles Bus Jurnl Assoc .... E...... 323 549-5225
11150 Santa Monica Blvd Ste 350 Los Angeles (90025) *(P-3367)*

Los Angeles Business Journal, Los Angeles Also Called: Cbj LP *(P-3348)*

Los Angeles Capital MGT LLC (PA) .... D...... 310 479-9998
11150 Santa Monica Blvd Ste 200 Los Angeles (90025) *(P-14964)*

Los Angeles Church of Christ, Santa Monica Also Called: Los Angeles Intl Ch Chrst *(P-19503)*

Los Angeles City Hauling, Sun Valley Also Called: USA Waste of California Inc *(P-12190)*

Los Angeles Clippers, Los Angeles Also Called: LA Sports Properties Inc *(P-17375)*

Los Angeles Cnty Mseum of Art .... B...... 323 857-6000
5905 Wilshire Blvd Los Angeles (90036) *(P-19355)*

Los Angeles Cold Storage, Los Angeles Also Called: Standard-Southern Corporation *(P-11559)*

Los Angeles Cold Storage Co, Los Angeles Also Called: Standard-Southern Corporation *(P-11557)*

LOS ANGELES COMMUNITY HOSPITAL, Los Angeles Also Called: Paraclsus Los Angles Cmnty Hos *(P-18370)*

Los Angeles Conven and Exh .... B...... 213 741-1151
1201 S Figueroa St Los Angeles (90015) *(P-14671)*

Los Angeles Convention Center, Los Angeles Also Called: AEG Management Lacc LLC *(P-19989)*

Los Angeles Country Club .... C...... 310 276-6104
10101 Wilshire Blvd Los Angeles (90024) *(P-17499)*

Los Angeles County Bar Assn (PA) .... D...... 213 627-2727
444 S Flower St Los Angeles (90071) *(P-19396)*

Los Angeles County Fair Assn (PA) .... D...... 909 623-3111
1101 W Mckinley Ave Pomona (91768) *(P-17556)*

Los Angeles County Hospital, Los Angeles Also Called: Lac Usc Medical Center *(P-18321)*

Los Angeles Daily News Pubg Co .... E...... 818 713-3883
21860 Burbank Blvd Ste 200 Woodland Hills (91367) *(P-3297)*

Los Angeles Dept Convetion Tou, Los Angeles Also Called: Los Angeles Conven and Exh *(P-14671)*

Los Angeles Dept Wtr & Pwr .... A...... 310 524-8500
12700 Vista Del Mar Playa Del Rey (90293) *(P-12111)*

Los Angeles Dept Wtr & Pwr (HQ) .... A...... 213 367-1320
111 N Hope St Los Angeles (90012) *(P-12128)*

Los Angeles Dept Wtr & Pwr .... A...... 213 367-5706
1141 W 2nd St Bldg D Los Angeles (90012) *(P-12129)*

Los Angeles Dept Wtr & Pwr .... A...... 323 256-8079
4030 Crenshaw Blvd Los Angeles (90008) *(P-12130)*

Los Angeles Dept Wtr & Pwr .... A...... 213 367-1342
11801 Sheldon St Sun Valley (91352) *(P-12131)*

Los Angeles Dept Wtr & Pwr .... A...... 213 367-4211
1630 N Main St Los Angeles (90012) *(P-12132)*

Los Angeles Engineering Inc .... C...... 626 869-1400
633 N Barranca Ave Covina (91723) *(P-19641)*

Los Angeles Federal Credit Un (PA) .... D...... 818 242-8640
300 S Glendale Ave Ste 100 Glendale (91205) *(P-14231)*

Los Angeles Federal Credit Un, Glendale Also Called: Los Angeles Federal Credit Un *(P-14231)*

Los Angeles Fiber Co, Vernon Also Called: Marspring Corporation *(P-2855)*

Los Angeles Free Clinic .... C...... 323 653-1990
5205 Melrose Ave Los Angeles (90038) *(P-17708)*

Los Angeles Freightliner, Fontana Also Called: Los Angeles Truck Centers LLC *(P-12226)*

Los Angeles Galvanizing Co .... D...... 323 583-2263
2518 E 53rd St Huntington Park (90255) *(P-6716)*

Los Angeles Homeless Svcs Auth .... A...... 213 683-3333
707 Wilshire Blvd Ste 1000 Los Angeles (90017) *(P-19110)*

Los Angeles Intl Ch Chrst .... C...... 213 351-2300
2716 Ocean Park Blvd Ste 2006 Santa Monica (90405) *(P-19503)*

Los Angeles Junction Rlwy Co .... C...... 323 277-2004
4433 Exchange Ave Vernon (90058) *(P-11311)*

LOS ANGELES LAWYER MAGAZINE, Los Angeles Also Called: Los Angeles County Bar Assn *(P-19396)*

Los Angeles Lgbt Center (PA) .... C...... 323 993-7618
1625 Schrader Blvd Los Angeles (90028) *(P-19335)*

Los Angeles Ltg Mfg Co Inc .... D...... 626 454-8300
10141 Olney St El Monte (91731) *(P-12602)*

Los Angeles Mem Coliseum Comm .... B...... 213 747-7111
3911 S Figueroa St Los Angeles (90037) *(P-19531)*

Los Angeles Opera Company .... B...... 213 972-7219
135 N Grand Ave Ste 327 Los Angeles (90012) *(P-17318)*

Los Angeles Philharmonic Assn (PA) .... C...... 213 972-7300
151 S Grand Ave Los Angeles (90012) *(P-17344)*

Los Angeles Philharmonic Assn .... A...... 323 850-2060
2301 N Highland Ave Los Angeles (90068) *(P-17345)*

Los Angeles Plant, Cypress Also Called: Hitachi Automotive Systems *(P-8144)*

Los Angeles Police Credit Un (PA) .... D...... 818 787-6520
16150 Sherman Way Van Nuys (91406) *(P-14249)*

Los Angeles Poultry Co Inc .... D...... 323 232-1619
4816 Long Beach Ave Los Angeles (90058) *(P-1247)*

Los Angeles Rams LLC (PA) .... D...... 314 982-7267
29899 Agoura Rd Agoura Hills (91301) *(P-17377)*

Los Angeles Rams LLC .... D...... 310 277-4700
10271 W Pico Blvd Los Angeles (90064) *(P-20057)*

Los Angeles Regional Food Bank .... C...... 323 234-3030
1734 E 41st St Vernon (90058) *(P-19111)*

Los Angeles Residential Comm F .... D...... 661 296-8636
29890 Bouquet Canyon Rd Santa Clarita (91390) *(P-19283)*

Los Angeles Sales Office, Northridge Also Called: Harman International Inds Inc *(P-12662)*

Los Angeles Sentinel Inc .... D...... 323 299-3800
3800 Crenshaw Blvd Los Angeles (90008) *(P-3298)*

Los Angeles Sleeve Co Inc .... E...... 562 945-7578
12051 Rivera Rd Santa Fe Springs (90670) *(P-9415)*

Los Angeles Sparks, Beverly Hills Also Called: Gemini Basketball LLC *(P-17371)*

Los Angeles Times, El Segundo Also Called: Los Angles Tmes Cmmnctions LLC *(P-3299)*

Los Angeles Truck Centers LLC .... C...... 909 510-4000
13800 Valley Blvd Fontana (92335) *(P-12226)*

Los Angeles Truck Centers LLC (PA) .... D...... 562 447-1200
2429 Peck Rd Whittier (90601) *(P-17034)*

Los Angeles Turf Club Inc (DH) .... C...... 626 574-6330
285 W Huntington Dr Arcadia (91007) *(P-17386)*

Los Angeles Unified School Dst .... D...... 310 808-1500
17729 S Figueroa St Gardena (90248) *(P-15721)*

Los Angeles Unified School Dst .... C...... 562 654-9007
8525 Rex Rd Pico Rivera (90660) *(P-16864)*

Los Angeles Unified School Dst .... C...... 818 346-3540
6200 Winnetka Ave Woodland Hills (91367) *(P-18974)*

Los Angeles Unified School Dst .... D...... 213 763-2900
1240 Naomi Ave Los Angeles (90021) *(P-18990)*

Los Angeles World Airports .... C...... 424 646-9118
5312 W 99th Pl Los Angeles (90045) *(P-11699)*

ALPHABETIC

Los Angeles World Airports ....B...... 424 646-5900
7301 World Way W Fl 5 Los Angeles (90045) *(P-11700)*

Los Angeles World Airports (PA) ....**C......** **855 463-5252**
1 World Way Los Angeles (90045) *(P-11701)*

Los Angles Area Chmber Cmmerce ....D...... 213 580-7500
350 S Bixel St Los Angeles (90017) *(P-19380)*

Los Angles Cnty Cntl Jail Hosp, Los Angeles *Also Called: County of Los Angeles (P-18234)*

Los Angles Cnty Dept Mntal HLT ....D...... 213 738-4431
3205 N Lakewood Blvd Long Beach (90808) *(P-18777)*

Los Angles Cnty Dvlpmntal Svcs ....C...... 213 383-1300
3303 Wilshire Blvd Ste 700 Los Angeles (90010) *(P-18778)*

Los Angles Cnty Emplyees Rtrme (PA) ....**C......** **626 564-6000**
300 N Lake Ave Ste 720 Pasadena (91101) *(P-14548)*

Los Angles Cnty Mseum Ntral Hs (PA) ....**C......** **213 763-3466**
900 Exposition Blvd Los Angeles (90007) *(P-20406)*

Los Angles Cnty Mtro Trnsp Aut (PA) ....**A......** **323 466-3876**
1 Gateway Plz Fl 25 Los Angeles (90012) *(P-11326)*

Los Angles Cnty Mtro Trnsp Aut ....A...... 213 922-6308
9201 Canoga Ave Chatsworth (91311) *(P-11327)*

Los Angles Cnty Mtro Trnsp Aut ....A...... 213 922-5887
900 Lyon St Los Angeles (90012) *(P-11328)*

Los Angles Cnty Mtro Trnsp Aut ....B...... 213 922-6301
1130 E 6th St Los Angeles (90021) *(P-11329)*

Los Angles Cnty Mtro Trnsp Aut ....B...... 213 922-6203
630 W Avenue 28 Los Angeles (90065) *(P-11330)*

Los Angles Cnty Mtro Trnsp Aut ....A...... 213 922-6202
1 Gateway Plaza Dr Los Angeles (90012) *(P-11331)*

Los Angles Cnty Mtro Trnsp Aut ....A...... 213 922-6207
8800 Santa Monica Blvd Los Angeles (90069) *(P-11332)*

Los Angles Cnty Mtro Trnsp Aut ....A...... 213 922-6215
11900 Branford St Sun Valley (91352) *(P-11333)*

Los Angles Cnty Mtro Trnsp Aut ....B...... 213 533-1506
720 E 15th St Los Angeles (90021) *(P-11334)*

Los Angles Cnty Mtro Trnsp Aut ....B...... 310 643-3804
14724 Aviation Blvd Lawndale (90260) *(P-11335)*

Los Angles Cnty Mtro Trnsp Aut ....A...... 213 922-5012
470 Bauchet St Los Angeles (90012) *(P-11336)*

Los Angles Cnty Mtro Trnsp Aut ....A...... 310 392-8636
100 Sunset Ave Venice (90291) *(P-11337)*

Los Angles Cnty Mtro Trnsp Aut ....A...... 213 244-6783
818 W 7th St Ste 500 Los Angeles (90017) *(P-11338)*

Los Angles Cnty Mtro Trnsp Aut ....A...... 213 626-4455
320 S Santa Fe Ave Los Angeles (90013) *(P-11339)*

Los Angles Cnty Rncho Los Amgo ....A...... 562 385-7111
7601 Imperial Hwy Downey (90242) *(P-18090)*

Los Angles Cnty Snttion Dstrct (PA) ....**A......** **562 699-7411**
1955 Workman Mill Rd Whittier (90601) *(P-12210)*

Los Angles Dst Off Policy Svcs, Monterey Park *Also Called: State Compensation Insur Fund (P-14527)*

Los Angles Jewish HM For Aging ....B...... 818 774-3000
18855 Victory Blvd Reseda (91335) *(P-18002)*

Los Angles Jewish HM For Aging (PA) ....B...... 818 774-3000
7150 Tampa Ave Reseda (91335) *(P-18003)*

Los Angles Pump Valve Pdts Inc ....E...... 323 277-7788
2528 E 57th St Huntington Park (90255) *(P-7282)*

Los Angles Tmes Cmmnctions LLC (PA) ....**A......** **213 237-5000**
2300 E Imperial Hwy El Segundo (90245) *(P-3299)*

Los Cabos Mexican Foods, Santa Fe Springs *Also Called: MCI Foods Inc (P-1943)*

Los Feliz Ford Inc (PA) ....**D......** **818 502-1901**
1101 S Brand Blvd Glendale (91204) *(P-13791)*

Los Palos Convalescent Hosp, San Pedro *Also Called: San Pedro Convalescent HM Inc (P-18047)*

Los Pericos Food Products LLC ....E...... 909 623-5625
2301 Valley Blvd Pomona (91768) *(P-1937)*

Los Robles Hospital & Med Ctr, Thousand Oaks *Also Called: Los Robles Regional Med Ctr (P-18339)*

Los Robles Regional Med Ctr ....B...... 805 370-4531
150 Via Merida Westlake Village (91362) *(P-17709)*

Los Robles Regional Med Ctr ....B...... 805 494-0880
2200 Lynn Rd Thousand Oaks (91360) *(P-17710)*

Los Robles Regional Med Ctr (DH) ....**A......** **805 497-2727**
215 W Janss Rd Thousand Oaks (91360) *(P-18339)*

Los Serranos Golf & Cntry CLB, Chino Hills *Also Called: Los Serranos Golf Club (P-17435)*

Los Serranos Golf Club ....C...... 909 597-1769
15656 Yorba Ave Chino Hills (91709) *(P-17435)*

Loss and Risk Advisors, San Diego *Also Called: Barney & Barney Inc (P-14567)*

Lost & Wander, Vernon *Also Called: Vxb & Orfwid Inc (P-2382)*

Lost Dutchmans Minings Assn (DH) ....**E......** **951 699-4749**
43445 Bus Pk Dr Ste 113 Temecula (92590) *(P-234)*

Lost International LLC ....D...... 949 600-6950
170 Technology Dr Irvine (92618) *(P-2215)*

Lotus and Luna ....E...... 805 216-4451
5780 Chesapeake Ct Ste 5 San Diego (92123) *(P-11245)*

Lotus Clinical Research LLC ....D...... 626 381-9830
100 W California Blvd Pasadena (91105) *(P-18556)*

Lotus Hygiene Systems Inc ....E...... 714 259-8805
1621 E Saint Andrew Pl Santa Ana (92705) *(P-5377)*

Lotus Labels, Brea *Also Called: President Enterprise LLC (P-3797)*

Lotus Orient Corp (PA) ....**F......** **626 285-5796**
411 S California St San Gabriel (91776) *(P-2285)*

Lotus Trolley Bags, Carlsbad *Also Called: Golden Eye Media Usa Inc (P-13009)*

Lotus Workforce LLC ....A...... 480 264-0773
5930 Cornerstone Ct W Ste 300 San Diego (92121) *(P-20191)*

Lou Ana Foods, Brea *Also Called: Ventura Foods LLC (P-1574)*

Louden Madelon, Vernon *Also Called: National Corset Supply House (P-2392)*

Loudlabs News LLC ....F...... 310 877-8374
11932 Heritage Cir Downey (90241) *(P-3300)*

Louidar LLC ....E...... 951 676-5047
33820 Rancho California Rd Temecula (92591) *(P-1646)*

Louis F Mascola DDS ....C...... 310 986-2930
3660 Lomita Blvd Torrance (90505) *(P-17840)*

Louis Sardo Upholstery Inc (PA) ....**D......** **310 327-0532**
512 W Rosecrans Ave Gardena (90248) *(P-2932)*

Louis W Osborn Co., La Mirada *Also Called: Headwaters Construction Inc (P-5366)*

Lounge Fly, Walnut *Also Called: Loungefly LLC (P-11066)*

Loungefly LLC ....E...... 818 718-5600
108 S Mayo Ave Walnut (91789) *(P-11066)*

Louroe Electronics Inc ....E...... 818 994-6498
6955 Valjean Ave Van Nuys (91406) *(P-16747)*

Lovco Construction, Signal Hill *Also Called: Lovco Construction Inc (P-1123)*

Lovco Construction Inc ....C...... 562 595-1601
1300 E Burnett St Signal Hill (90755) *(P-1123)*

Love Stitch, Los Angeles *Also Called: Clothing Illustrated Inc (P-2314)*

Lovemarks Inc ....D...... 213 514-5888
2050 E 51st St Vernon (90058) *(P-2254)*

Lovin Enterprises Inc ....D...... 323 268-0220
5548 Lindbergh Ln Bell (90201) *(P-13132)*

Low Cost Interlock Inc ....E...... 844 387-0326
2038 W Park Ave Redlands (92373) *(P-9168)*

Lowe Enterprises, Los Angeles *Also Called: Lowe Enterprises RE Group (P-14904)*

Lowe Enterprises Inc (PA) ....C...... 310 820-6661
11777 San Vicente Blvd Ste 900 Los Angeles (90049) *(P-15232)*

Lowe Enterprises RE Group ....C...... 310 820-6661
11777 San Vicente Blvd Ste 900 Los Angeles (90049) *(P-14904)*

Lowe Enterprises Rlty Svcs Inc ....A...... 818 990-9555
16133 Ventura Blvd Ste 535 Encino (91436) *(P-14824)*

Lowe's, Perris *Also Called: Lowes Home Centers LLC (P-11595)*

Lowe's, El Centro *Also Called: Lowes Home Centers LLC (P-13625)*

Lowe's, Bakersfield *Also Called: Lowes Home Centers LLC (P-13626)*

Lowe's, Pacoima *Also Called: Lowes Home Centers LLC (P-13627)*

Lowe's, West Hills *Also Called: Lowes Home Centers LLC (P-13628)*

Lowe's, Burbank *Also Called: Lowes Home Centers LLC (P-13629)*

Lowe's, Pico Rivera *Also Called: Lowes Home Centers LLC (P-13631)*

Lowe's, Palmdale *Also Called: Lowes Home Centers LLC (P-13632)*

Lowe's, Torrance *Also Called: Lowes Home Centers LLC (P-13633)*

Lowe's, Northridge *Also Called: Lowes Home Centers LLC (P-13634)*

Lowe's, Norwalk *Also Called: Lowes Home Centers LLC (P-13635)*

Lowe's, Santa Clarita *Also Called: Lowes Home Centers LLC (P-13636)*

Lowe's, Rancho Cucamonga *Also Called: Lowes Home Centers LLC (P-13637)*

Lowe's, Victorville *Also Called: Lowes Home Centers LLC (P-13638)*

Mergent email: customerrelations@mergent.com
1164

2024 Southern California
Business Directory and Buyers Guide

(P-0000) Products & Services Section entry number
(PA)=Parent Co (HQ)=Headquarters (DH)=Div Headquarters

Lowe's, Upland *Also Called: Lowes Home Centers LLC (P-13639)*

Lowe's, Fontana *Also Called: Lowes Home Centers LLC (P-13640)*

Lowe's, Redlands *Also Called: Lowes Home Centers LLC (P-13641)*

Lowe's, Apple Valley *Also Called: Lowes Home Centers LLC (P-13642)*

Lowe's, Ontario *Also Called: Lowes Home Centers LLC (P-13643)*

Lowe's, Chino Hills *Also Called: Lowes Home Centers LLC (P-13644)*

Lowe's, Highland *Also Called: Lowes Home Centers LLC (P-13645)*

Lowe's, Oceanside *Also Called: Lowes Home Centers LLC (P-13646)*

Lowe's, Vista *Also Called: Lowes Home Centers LLC (P-13647)*

Lowe's, Chula Vista *Also Called: Lowes Home Centers LLC (P-13648)*

Lowe's, Santee *Also Called: Lowes Home Centers LLC (P-13649)*

Lowe's, Escondido *Also Called: Lowes Home Centers LLC (P-13650)*

Lowe's, Ventura *Also Called: Lowes Home Centers LLC (P-13651)*

Lowe's, Simi Valley *Also Called: Lowes Home Centers LLC (P-13652)*

Lowe's, Paso Robles *Also Called: Lowes Home Centers LLC (P-13653)*

Lowe's, San Diego *Also Called: Lowes Home Centers LLC (P-13654)*

Lowe's, San Clemente *Also Called: Lowes Home Centers LLC (P-13655)*

Lowe's, Anaheim *Also Called: Lowes Home Centers LLC (P-13656)*

Lowe's, La Habra *Also Called: Lowes Home Centers LLC (P-13657)*

Lowe's, Tustin *Also Called: Lowes Home Centers LLC (P-13658)*

Lowe's, Menifee *Also Called: Lowes Home Centers LLC (P-13659)*

Lowe's, Riverside *Also Called: Lowes Home Centers LLC (P-13660)*

Lowe's, La Quinta *Also Called: Lowes Home Centers LLC (P-13661)*

Lowe's, Palm Springs *Also Called: Lowes Home Centers LLC (P-13662)*

Lowe's, Murrieta *Also Called: Lowes Home Centers LLC (P-13663)*

Lowe's, Moreno Valley *Also Called: Lowes Home Centers LLC (P-13664)*

Lowe's, Temecula *Also Called: Lowes Home Centers LLC (P-13665)*

Lowe's, Corona *Also Called: Lowes Home Centers LLC (P-13666)*

Lowe's, Lake Elsinore *Also Called: Lowes Home Centers LLC (P-13667)*

Lowermybills Inc .... C....... 310 348-6800
12181 Bluff Creek Dr Ste 250 Playa Vista (90094) *(P-16532)*

Lowermybills.com, Playa Vista *Also Called: Lmb Opco LLC (P-14360)*

Lowermybills.com, Playa Vista *Also Called: Lowermybills Inc (P-16532)*

Lowes Home Centers LLC .... B....... 951 443-2500
3984 Indian Ave Perris (92571) *(P-11595)*

Lowes Home Centers LLC .... D....... 760 337-6700
2053 N Imperial Ave El Centro (92243) *(P-13625)*

Lowes Home Centers LLC .... C....... 661 889-9000
1601 Columbus St Bakersfield (93305) *(P-13626)*

Lowes Home Centers LLC .... C....... 818 686-4300
13500 Paxton St Pacoima (91331) *(P-13627)*

Lowes Home Centers LLC .... D....... 818 610-1960
8383 Topanga Canyon Blvd West Hills (91304) *(P-13628)*

Lowes Home Centers LLC .... C....... 818 557-2300
2000 W Empire Ave Burbank (91504) *(P-13629)*

Lowes Home Centers LLC .... C....... 323 327-4000
2800 W 120th St Hawthorne (90250) *(P-13630)*

Lowes Home Centers LLC .... C....... 562 942-9909
8600 Washington Blvd Pico Rivera (90660) *(P-13631)*

Lowes Home Centers LLC .... D....... 661 267-9888
39500 Lowes Dr Palmdale (93551) *(P-13632)*

Lowes Home Centers LLC .... C....... 310 787-1469
22255 S Western Ave Torrance (90501) *(P-13633)*

Lowes Home Centers LLC .... C....... 818 477-9022
19601 Nordhoff St Northridge (91324) *(P-13634)*

Lowes Home Centers LLC .... D....... 562 926-0826
14873 Carmenita Rd Norwalk (90650) *(P-13635)*

Lowes Home Centers LLC .... C....... 661 678-4430
19001 Golden Valley Rd Santa Clarita (91387) *(P-13636)*

Lowes Home Centers LLC .... C....... 909 476-9697
11399 Foothill Blvd Rancho Cucamonga (91730) *(P-13637)*

Lowes Home Centers LLC .... D....... 760 949-9565
14333 Bear Valley Rd Victorville (92392) *(P-13638)*

Lowes Home Centers LLC .... C....... 909 982-4795
1659 W Foothill Blvd Upland (91786) *(P-13639)*

Lowes Home Centers LLC .... C....... 909 350-7900
16851 Sierra Lakes Pkwy Fontana (92336) *(P-13640)*

Lowes Home Centers LLC .... D....... 909 307-8883
1725 W Redlands Blvd Redlands (92373) *(P-13641)*

Lowes Home Centers LLC .... C....... 760 961-3000
12189 Apple Valley Rd Apple Valley (92308) *(P-13642)*

Lowes Home Centers LLC .... C....... 909 969-9053
2390 S Grove Ave Ontario (91761) *(P-13643)*

Lowes Home Centers LLC .... C....... 909 438-9000
4777 Chino Hills Pkwy Chino Hills (91709) *(P-13644)*

Lowes Home Centers LLC .... D....... 909 557-9010
27847 Greenspot Rd Highland (92346) *(P-13645)*

Lowes Home Centers LLC .... C....... 760 966-7140
155 Old Grove Rd Oceanside (92057) *(P-13646)*

Lowes Home Centers LLC .... D....... 760 631-6255
151 Vista Village Dr Vista (92083) *(P-13647)*

Lowes Home Centers LLC .... C....... 619 739-9060
2225 Otay Lakes Rd Chula Vista (91915) *(P-13648)*

Lowes Home Centers LLC .... C....... 619 212-4100
9416 Mission Gorge Rd Santee (92071) *(P-13649)*

Lowes Home Centers LLC .... D....... 760 484-5113
620 W Mission Ave Escondido (92025) *(P-13650)*

Lowes Home Centers LLC .... C....... 805 675-8800
500 S Mills Rd Ventura (93003) *(P-13651)*

Lowes Home Centers LLC .... C....... 805 426-2780
1275 Simi Town Center Way Simi Valley (93065) *(P-13652)*

Lowes Home Centers LLC .... C....... 805 602-9051
2445 Golden Hill Rd Paso Robles (93446) *(P-13653)*

Lowes Home Centers LLC .... C....... 619 584-5500
2318 Northside Dr San Diego (92108) *(P-13654)*

Lowes Home Centers LLC .... D....... 949 369-4644
907 Avenida Pico San Clemente (92673) *(P-13655)*

Lowes Home Centers LLC .... C....... 714 447-6140
1500 N Lemon St Anaheim (92801) *(P-13656)*

Lowes Home Centers LLC .... C....... 562 690-5122
1380 S Beach Blvd La Habra (90631) *(P-13657)*

Lowes Home Centers LLC .... C....... 714 913-2663
2500 Park Ave Tustin (92782) *(P-13658)*

Lowes Home Centers LLC .... C....... 951 723-1930
30472 Haun Rd Menifee (92584) *(P-13659)*

Lowes Home Centers LLC .... C....... 951 509-5500
9851 Magnolia Ave Riverside (92503) *(P-13660)*

Lowes Home Centers LLC .... C....... 760 771-5566
78865 Highway 111 La Quinta (92253) *(P-13661)*

Lowes Home Centers LLC .... C....... 760 866-1901
5201 E Ramon Rd Palm Springs (92264) *(P-13662)*

Lowes Home Centers LLC .... C....... 951 461-8916
24701 Madison Ave Murrieta (92562) *(P-13663)*

Lowes Home Centers LLC .... D....... 951 656-1859
12400 Day St Moreno Valley (92553) *(P-13664)*

Lowes Home Centers LLC .... C....... 951 296-1618
40390 Winchester Rd Temecula (92591) *(P-13665)*

Lowes Home Centers LLC .... C....... 951 256-9004
1285 Magnolia Ave Corona (92879) *(P-13666)*

Lowes Home Centers LLC .... C....... 951 253-6000
29335 Central Ave Lake Elsinore (92532) *(P-13667)*

Lowratscom 1st Lbrty Cal State, Cerritos *Also Called: Sun West Mortgage Company Inc (P-14350)*

Lozano Caseworks Inc .... D....... 909 783-7530
242 W Hanna St Colton (92324) *(P-1019)*

Lozano Enterprises, Los Angeles *Also Called: La Opinion LP (P-3294)*

Lozano Plumbing Services Inc .... C....... 951 683-4840
3615 Presley Ave Riverside (92507) *(P-787)*

LPA Inc (PA) .... C....... 949 261-1001
5301 California Ave Ste 100 Irvine (92617) *(P-19735)*

LPC Commercial Services Inc .... C....... 213 362-9080
915 Wilshire Blvd Ste 250 Los Angeles (90017) *(P-14905)*

LPC COMMERCIAL SERVICES, INC., Los Angeles *Also Called: LPC Commercial Services Inc (P-14905)*

Lpcc, Camarillo *Also Called: Las Posas Country Club (P-17498)*

Lpcc 6008, Ontario *Also Called: Leggett & Platt Incorporated (P-2854)*

Lpl Financial Holdings Inc (PA) .... B....... 800 877-7210
4707 Executive Dr San Diego (92121) *(P-14386)*

Lpl Holdings, San Diego *Also Called: Lpl Holdings Inc (P-20192)*

Lpl Holdings Inc (HQ) .... D....... 858 450-9606
4707 Executive Dr San Diego (92121) *(P-20192)*

Employee Codes: A=Over 500 employees, B=251-500
C=101-250, D=51-100, E=20-50, F=10-19, G=1-9

2024 Southern California
Business Directory and Buyers Guide

© Mergent Inc. 1-800-342-5647
1165

ALPHABETIC

Lplfh, San Diego *Also Called: Lpl Financial Holdings Inc (P-14386)*

Lps Agency Sales & Posting Inc .... D...... 714 247-7500
3210 El Camino Real Ste 200 Irvine (92602) *(P-3783)*

Lpsh Holdings Inc .... B...... 951 926-1176
3570 W Florida Ave Ste 168 Hemet (92545) *(P-788)*

Lpsh Holdings Inc (PA)... D...... 855 647-5061
7100 W Florida Ave Hemet (92545) *(P-789)*

Lqr Property LLC .... C...... 760 564-4111
49499 Eisenhower Dr La Quinta (92253) *(P-15233)*

LR Baggs Corporation .... E...... 805 929-3545
483 N Frontage Rd Nipomo (93444) *(P-10927)*

Lrc Coil Company, Santa Fe Springs *Also Called: Lmw Enterprises LLC (P-7617)*

Lres Corporation (PA).. D...... 714 520-5737
765 The City Dr S Orange (92868) *(P-14825)*

Lrw Group, Los Angeles *Also Called: Material Holdings LLC (P-19906)*

Lsa Associates Inc (PA)... C...... 949 553-0666
3210 El Camino Real Ste 100 Irvine (92602) *(P-20360)*

Lsf9 Cypress LP (PA)... C...... 714 380-3127
2741 Walnut Ave Ste 200 Tustin (92780) *(P-12371)*

Lsf9 Cypress Parent 2 LLC .... A...... 714 380-3127
2741 Walnut Ave Ste 200 Tustin (92780) *(P-12372)*

LSI Products Inc .... F...... 951 343-9270
12885 Wildflower Ln Riverside (92503) *(P-9416)*

Lso, San Diego *Also Called: Cri 2000 LP (P-2753)*

Lspace America LLC .... D...... 949 750-2292
14420 Myford Rd Irvine (92606) *(P-2255)*

Lt Foods Americas Inc (HQ).. F...... 562 340-4040
11130 Warland Dr Cypress (90630) *(P-1413)*

Ltl Pros Inc .... D...... 909 350-1600
13610 S Archibald Ave Ontario (91761) *(P-11496)*

Ltr, South Gate *Also Called: Lunday-Thagard Company (P-4690)*

Lubeco Inc .... E...... 562 602-1791
6859 Downey Ave Long Beach (90805) *(P-4686)*

Lubricating Specialties Company .... C...... 562 776-4000
8015 Paramount Blvd Pico Rivera (90660) *(P-4687)*

Lubrication Scientifics LLC .... E...... 714 557-0664
17651 Armstrong Ave Irvine (92614) *(P-7399)*

Lubrizol Global Management Inc .... E...... 805 239-1550
3115 Propeller Dr Paso Robles (93446) *(P-4617)*

Lucas & Lewellen Vineyards Inc (PA).. E...... 805 686-9336
1645 Copenhagen Dr Solvang (93463) *(P-13478)*

Lucas Lwllen Vnyrds Tasting Rm, Solvang *Also Called: Lucas & Lewellen Vineyards Inc (P-13478)*

Lucent Diamonds Inc .... E...... 424 781-7127
6303 Owensmouth Ave Fl 10 Woodland Hills (91367) *(P-10918)*

Lucite Intl Prtnr Holdings Inc .... D...... 760 929-0001
5441 Avenida Encinas Ste B Carlsbad (92008) *(P-11010)*

Lucix, Camarillo *Also Called: Lucix Corporation (P-9079)*

Lucix Corporation (HQ)... D...... 805 987-6645
800 Avenida Acaso Ste E Camarillo (93012) *(P-9079)*

Lucky Line Products Inc .... E...... 858 549-6699
7890 Dunbrook Rd San Diego (92126) *(P-5929)*

Lucky Strike, Sherman Oaks *Also Called: Lucky Strike Entertainment Inc (P-11011)*

Lucky Strike Entertainment Inc (PA).. E...... 818 933-3752
15260 Ventura Blvd Ste 1110 Sherman Oaks (91403) *(P-11011)*

Lucky Strike Entertainment Inc .... B...... 213 542-4880
800 W Olympic Blvd Ste 250 Los Angeles (90015) *(P-17357)*

Lucky Strike Entertainment Inc .... D...... 248 374-3420
15260 Ventura Blvd Ste 1110 Sherman Oaks (91403) *(P-17358)*

Lucky Strike Entertainment LLC .... D...... 248 374-3420
20 City Blvd W Ste G2 Orange (92868) *(P-17359)*

Lucky Strike Novi, Sherman Oaks *Also Called: Lucky Strike Entertainment LLC (P-17358)*

Lucky-13 Apparel, Los Alamitos *Also Called: Blue Sphere Inc (P-2150)*

Ludfords Inc .... E...... 909 948-0797
3038 Pleasant St Riverside (92507) *(P-1341)*

Luma Comfort, Cypress *Also Called: Luma Comfort LLC (P-8237)*

Luma Comfort LLC .... E...... 855 963-9247
6600 Katella Ave Cypress (90630) *(P-8237)*

Luma Pictures Inc .... C...... 310 888-8738
1453 3rd Street Promenade Ste 400 Santa Monica (90401) *(P-17199)*

Lumificient Corporation .... E...... 763 424-3702
2280 Ward Ave Simi Valley (93065) *(P-8321)*

Luminance, Rancho Cucamonga *Also Called: American De Rosa Lamparts LLC (P-493)*

Luminit LLC (PA) .... E...... 310 320-1066
1850 W 205th St Torrance (90501) *(P-10324)*

Lumio Inc .... E...... 586 861-2408
6355 Topanga Canyon Blvd Ste 335 Woodland Hills (91367) *(P-8830)*

Lumiradx Inc .... C...... 951 201-9384
444 S Cedros Ave Ste 101 Solana Beach (92075) *(P-16067)*

Luna Imaging Inc .... E...... 323 908-1400
2702 Media Center Dr Los Angeles (90065) *(P-16296)*

Lund Motion Products Inc .... E...... 888 983-2204
3172 Nasa St Brea (92821) *(P-9417)*

Lunday-Thagard Company .... B...... 562 928-6990
9301 Garfield Ave South Gate (90280) *(P-4673)*

Lunday-Thagard Company (HQ).. C...... 562 928-7000
9302 Garfield Ave South Gate (90280) *(P-4690)*

Lundberg Survey Incorporated .... E...... 805 383-2400
911 Via Alondra Camarillo (93012) *(P-3368)*

Lundquist Institute For Biomedical Innovation At Harbor-Ucla Medical Center 877 452-2674
1124 W Carson St Torrance (90502) *(P-19934)*

Lupitas Bakery Inc (PA).. F...... 323 752-2391
1848 W Florence Ave Los Angeles (90047) *(P-1482)*

Luppen Holdings Inc (PA)... E...... 323 581-8121
3050 Leonis Blvd Vernon (90058) *(P-6534)*

Luran Inc .... F...... 661 257-6303
24927 Avenue Tibbitts Ste K Valencia (91355) *(P-7909)*

Lusive Decor .... E...... 323 227-9207
3400 Medford St Los Angeles (90063) *(P-20361)*

Lusk Quality Machine Products .... E...... 661 272-0630
39457 15th St E Palmdale (93550) *(P-7910)*

Lustros Inc .... E...... 619 449-4800
9025 Carlton Hills Blvd Ste A Santee (92071) *(P-231)*

Lutema, San Diego *Also Called: MI Technologies Inc (P-5098)*

Luth Research Inc (PA)... B...... 619 234-5884
404 Camino Del Rio S Ste 505 San Diego (92108) *(P-19905)*

Lux LLC .... E...... 661 479-2926
5206 Phisto Pl Bakersfield (93313) *(P-5531)*

Luxe City Center, Los Angeles *Also Called: Emerik Hotel Corp (P-15146)*

Luxe Light and Home, Los Angeles *Also Called: Lusive Decor (P-20361)*

Luxfer Gas Cylinder, Riverside *Also Called: Luxfer Inc (P-9739)*

Luxfer Inc .... E...... 951 684-5110
1995 3rd St Riverside (92507) *(P-5702)*

Luxfer Inc .... E...... 951 351-4100
6825 Jurupa Ave Riverside (92504) *(P-6480)*

Luxfer Inc (DH).. D...... 951 684-5110
3016 Kansas Ave Bldg 1 Riverside (92507) *(P-9739)*

Luxtera LLC .... C...... 760 448-3520
2320 Camino Vida Roble Ste 100 Carlsbad (92011) *(P-8831)*

Luxury Presence Inc .... C...... 310 955-1077
2805 W 233rd St Torrance (90505) *(P-16456)*

Luxury Signs Inc .... E...... 951 446-9303
7525 Jurupa Ave Ste E Riverside (92504) *(P-11132)*

Lymi Inc (PA).. D...... 855 756-0560
2744 E 11th St Los Angeles (90023) *(P-13133)*

Lynam Industries Inc (PA).. D...... 951 360-1919
11027 Jasmine St Fontana (92337) *(P-6263)*

Lynch Ambulance Service, Anaheim *Also Called: Filyn Corporation (P-11387)*

Lyncole Grunding Solutions LLC .... E...... 310 214-4000
3547 Voyager St Ste 204 Torrance (90503) *(P-8269)*

Lyncole Xit Grounding, Torrance *Also Called: Lyncole Grunding Solutions LLC (P-8269)*

Lynde-Ordway Company Inc .... F...... 714 957-1311
5402 Commercial Dr Huntington Beach (92649) *(P-7586)*

Lynn Products Inc .... A...... 310 530-5966
2645 W 237th St Torrance (90505) *(P-7545)*

Lynwood Pattern Service Inc .... E...... 310 631-2225
603 S Hope Ave Ontario (91761) *(P-5796)*

Lynwood Unified School Dst .... D...... 310 631-7308
12120 Lindbergh Ave Lynwood (90262) *(P-18975)*

Lynx Phtnic Ntworks A Del Corp .... F...... 818 802-0244
6303 Owensmouth Ave Fl 10 Woodland Hills (91367) *(P-8479)*

Lyon Stahl Investment RE Inc .... D 310 425-9838
239 Oregon St El Segundo (90245) *(P-14826)*

Lyon Technologies Inc .... E
1690 Brandywine Ave Ste A Chula Vista (91911) *(P-6907)*

Lytle Screen Printing Inc .... F 714 969-2424
21572 Surveyor Cir Huntington Beach (92646) *(P-7177)*

Lytx Inc (PA) .... B 858 430-4000
9785 Towne Centre Dr San Diego (92121) *(P-9998)*

M & A Custom Doors, Harbor City Also Called: Joanka Inc *(P-6109)*

M & A Plastics Inc .... F 818 768-0479
11735 Sheldon St Sun Valley (91352) *(P-5088)*

M & B Window Fashions, Los Angeles Also Called: Hd Window Fashions Inc *(P-3006)*

M & C, Los Angeles Also Called: Murchison & Cumming LLP *(P-18915)*

M & E Technical Services L L C .... D 256 964-6486
3601 Bayview Dr Manhattan Beach (90266) *(P-20295)*

M & G Jewelers Inc .... D 909 989-2929
10823 Edison Ct Rancho Cucamonga (91730) *(P-14078)*

M & H Electric Fabricators Inc .... E 562 926-9552
13537 Alondra Blvd Santa Fe Springs (90670) *(P-9169)*

M & M Plumbing Inc .... D 951 354-5388
6782 Columbus St Riverside (92504) *(P-790)*

M & O Perry Industries Inc .... E 951 734-9838
412 N Smith Ave Corona (92878) *(P-7352)*

M & R Plating Corporation .... F 818 896-2700
12375 Montague St Pacoima (91331) *(P-6635)*

M & S Acquisition Corporation (PA) .... C 213 385-1515
707 Wilshire Blvd Ste 5200 Los Angeles (90017) *(P-14827)*

M & S Security Services Inc .... D 661 397-9616
2900 L St Bakersfield (93301) *(P-16658)*

M & W Machine Corporation .... E 714 541-2652
1642 E Edinger Ave Ste A Santa Ana (92705) *(P-7911)*

M A A C Project, Chula Vista Also Called: Metroplitan Area Advsory Cmmtte *(P-19188)*

M A G, Santa Maria Also Called: Microwave Applications Group *(P-19647)*

M A G Engineering Mfg Co .... E
17305 Demler St Irvine (92614) *(P-5930)*

M Argeso & Co Inc .... E 626 573-3000
2628 River Ave Rosemead (91770) *(P-4644)*

M Arthur Gensler Jr Assoc Inc .... C 949 863-9434
4675 Macarthur Ct Ste 100 Newport Beach (92660) *(P-19736)*

M Arthur Gensler Jr Assoc Inc .... C 213 927-3600
500 S Figueroa St Los Angeles (90071) *(P-19737)*

M Bar C Construction Inc .... D 760 744-4131
1770 La Costa Meadows Dr San Marcos (92078) *(P-1108)*

M C, Los Angeles Also Called: Muir-Chase Plumbing Co Inc *(P-795)*

M C C, Torrance Also Called: Medical Chemical Corporation *(P-4621)*

M C C, Brea Also Called: Mercury Casualty Company *(P-14512)*

M C E, Torrance Also Called: Magnetic Component Engrg LLC *(P-6868)*

M Caratan Disc Inc .... C 661 725-2566
33787 Cecil Ave Delano (93215) *(P-34)*

M D H, Monrovia Also Called: Radcal Corporation *(P-10393)*

M D H Burner & Boiler Co Inc .... F 562 630-2875
12106 Center St South Gate (90280) *(P-7325)*

M D Manufacturing Inc .... F 661 283-7550
34970 Mcmurtrey Ave Bakersfield (93308) *(P-7669)*

M E D Inc .... D 562 921-0464
14001 Marquardt Ave Santa Fe Springs (90670) *(P-9418)*

M E I, Santa Barbara Also Called: Motion Engineering Inc *(P-7553)*

M E T, Murrieta Also Called: Medical Extrusion Tech Inc *(P-5094)*

M F G West, Adelanto Also Called: Molded Fiber GL Companies - W *(P-5105)*

M Gaw Inc .... D 818 503-7997
6910 Farmdale Ave North Hollywood (91605) *(P-1168)*

M I E, Temecula Also Called: Molding Intl & Engrg Inc *(P-5107)*

M I P, Covina Also Called: Moores Ideal Products LLC *(P-10962)*

M I T Inc .... E 714 899-6066
15202 Pipeline Ln Huntington Beach (92649) *(P-7079)*

M K Products Inc .... D 949 798-1234
16882 Armstrong Ave Irvine (92606) *(P-7159)*

M K Smith Chevrolet .... C 909 628-8961
12845 Central Ave Chino (91710) *(P-13792)*

M Klemme Technology Corp .... E 760 727-0593
1384 Poinsettia Ave Ste F Vista (92081) *(P-8420)*

M L Stern & Co LLC (DH) .... C 323 658-4400
8350 Wilshire Blvd Ste 300 Beverly Hills (90211) *(P-14387)*

M M C, Covina Also Called: Davita Magan Management Inc *(P-17640)*

M M Fab Inc .... D 310 763-3800
2300 E Gladwick St Compton (90220) *(P-13084)*

M M S, Claremont Also Called: Micro Matrix Systems *(P-6538)*

M M S Trading Inc .... E 323 587-1082
100 Corporate Pointe Culver City (90230) *(P-13546)*

M Nexon Inc .... E 213 858-5930
222 N Pacific Coast Hwy Ste 300 El Segundo (90245) *(P-16297)*

M P C Industrial Products Inc .... E 949 863-0106
2150 Mcgaw Ave Irvine (92614) *(P-6636)*

M P C Industries, Irvine Also Called: M P C Industrial Products Inc *(P-6636)*

M R I, Chatsworth Also Called: Medical Research Institute *(P-13054)*

M S E, Sylmar Also Called: Matthews Studio Equipment Inc *(P-10873)*

M S International Inc (PA) .... B 714 685-7500
2095 N Batavia St Orange (92865) *(P-12356)*

M T C, City Of Industry Also Called: Micro-Technology Concepts Inc *(P-12427)*

M T D, Santa Barbara Also Called: Santa Barbara Metro Trnst Dst *(P-11364)*

M W Reid Welding Inc .... D 619 401-5880
781 Oconner St El Cajon (92020) *(P-6042)*

M W Sausse & Co Inc (PA) .... D 661 257-3311
28744 Witherspoon Pkwy Valencia (91355) *(P-8185)*

M Z J, Chino Hills Also Called: Victory Intl Group LLC *(P-12947)*

M Z T, Santa Ana Also Called: Macro-Z-Technology Company *(P-631)*

M-5 Steel Mfg Inc (PA) .... E 323 263-9383
11778 San Marino St Ste A Rancho Cucamonga (91730) *(P-6264)*

M-7 Consolidation Inc .... D 310 898-3456
475 W Apra St Compton (90220) *(P-11779)*

M-Aurora Worldwide (us) LP (PA) .... C 800 888-0808
2222 Corinth Ave Los Angeles (90064) *(P-15430)*

M-H Ironworks Inc .... D
1000 S Seaward Ave Ventura (93001) *(P-12558)*

M-I LLC .... E 661 321-5400
4400 Fanucchi Way Shafter (93263) *(P-359)*

M-I Swaco, Shafter Also Called: M-I LLC *(P-359)*

M-Industrial Enterprises LLC .... E 949 413-7513
11 Via Onagro Rcho Sta Marg (92688) *(P-7912)*

M-N-Z Janitorial Services Inc .... C 323 851-4115
2109 W Burbank Blvd Burbank (91506) *(P-15722)*

M.A.g Engineering & Mfg, Irvine Also Called: M A G Engineering Mfg Co *(P-5930)*

M.C. Gill, El Monte Also Called: Castle Industries Inc of California *(P-6212)*

M&B Sciences Inc .... E 858 812-8735
4445 Eastgate Mall San Diego (92121) *(P-19857)*

M&C Hotel Interests Inc .... B 310 399-9344
530 Pico Blvd Santa Monica (90405) *(P-15234)*

M&J Design Inc .... E 714 687-9918
1303 S Claudina St Anaheim (92805) *(P-2807)*

M&J Design Furniture, Anaheim Also Called: M&J Design Inc *(P-2807)*

M2 Automotive .... A 310 399-3887
1100 Colorado Ave 2nd Fl Santa Monica (90401) *(P-17011)*

M2 Marketplace Inc .... E
2555 W 190th St 201 Torrance (90504) *(P-7437)*

M4dev LLC .... D 619 696-6300
2137 Pacific Hwy Ste A San Diego (92101) *(P-15235)*

M724 Inc .... F 951 314-1333
949 N Cataract Ave Ste E San Dimas (91773) *(P-2833)*

Maas-Hansen Steel, Westminster Also Called: Neighborhood Steel LLC *(P-12561)*

Mabel Baas Inc .... E 805 520-8075
3960 Royal Ave Simi Valley (93063) *(P-6717)*

Mabie Marketing Group Inc .... C 858 279-5585
8352 Clairemont Mesa Blvd San Diego (92111) *(P-16865)*

Mac M Mc Cully Corporation .... E 805 529-0661
5316 Kazuko Ct Moorpark (93021) *(P-8149)*

Mac M McCully Co, Moorpark Also Called: Mac M Mc Cully Corporation *(P-8149)*

Mac Performance Exhaust, Temecula Also Called: MAC Products Inc *(P-5593)*

MAC Products Inc .... E 951 296-3077
43214 Black Deer Loop Ste 113 Temecula (92590) *(P-5593)*

Macbee Engineering, Upland Also Called: Engineered Machinery Group Inc *(P-7150)*

ALPHABETIC

Employee Codes: A=Over 500 employees, B=251-500
C=101-250, D=51-100, E=20-50, F=10-19, G=1-9

2024 Southern California
Business Directory and Buyers Guide

© Mergent Inc. 1-800-342-5647

1167

Macdonald Carbide Co .... E....... 626 960-4034
525 S Prospero Dr West Covina (91791) *(P-7080)*

MACERICH, Santa Monica *Also Called: Macerich Company (P-15015)*

Macerich Company (PA) .... D....... 310 394-6000
401 Wilshire Blvd Ste 700 Santa Monica (90401) *(P-15015)*

Macgregor Yacht Corporation .... E....... 310 621-2206
1631 Placentia Ave Costa Mesa (92627) *(P-9861)*

Machine Building Spc Inc .... E....... 323 666-8289
1977 Blake Ave Los Angeles (90039) *(P-7207)*

Machine Craft of San Diego .... F....... 858 642-0509
7204 Babilonia St Carlsbad (92009) *(P-7913)*

Machine Precision Components .... F....... 562 404-0500
14014 Dinard Ave Santa Fe Springs (90670) *(P-7914)*

Machine Vision Products Inc (PA) .... E....... 760 438-1138
3270 Corporate Vw Ste D Vista (92081) *(P-10325)*

Machinetek LLC .... F....... 760 438-6644
1985 Palomar Oaks Way Carlsbad (92011) *(P-9740)*

Macias Gini & OConnell LLP .... C....... 213 408-8700
700 S Flower St Ste 800 Los Angeles (90017) *(P-19791)*

Macias Gini & OConnell LLP .... C....... 323 653-8300
2121 Avenue Of The Stars Ste 2200 Los Angeles (90067) *(P-19792)*

Macias Gini & OConnell LLP .... C....... 916 928-4600
2121 Avenue Of The Stars Ste 2200 Los Angeles (90067) *(P-19793)*

Mack Packaging Inc .... E....... 760 752-3500
1239 Linda Vista Dr San Marcos (92078) *(P-13547)*

Mackenzie Laboratories Inc .... E....... 909 394-9007
1163 Nicole Ct Glendora (91740) *(P-8832)*

Mackie International Inc (PA) .... E....... 951 346-0530
4193 Flat Rock Dr Ste 200 Riverside (92505) *(P-1299)*

Macpherson Oil Company LLC .... E....... 661 556-6096
24118 Round Mountain Rd Bakersfield (93308) *(P-311)*

Macpherson Wstn TI Sup Co LLC .... F....... 714 666-4100
1160 N Tustin Ave Anaheim (92807) *(P-12726)*

Macro Air Technologies, San Bernardino *Also Called: Macroair Technologies Inc (P-7326)*

Macro Industries Inc .... F....... 909 606-2218
14178 Albers Way Chino (91710) *(P-11246)*

Macro-Pro Inc (PA) .... C....... 562 595-0900
2400 Grand Ave Long Beach (90815) *(P-16866)*

Macro-Z-Technology Company (PA) .... D....... 714 564-1130
841 E Washington Ave Santa Ana (92701) *(P-631)*

Macroair Technologies Inc (PA) .... E....... 909 890-2270
794 S Allen St San Bernardino (92408) *(P-7326)*

Macs Lift Gate Inc (PA) .... E....... 562 529-3465
2801 E South St Long Beach (90805) *(P-11247)*

Mactech Magazine, Westlake Village *Also Called: Xplain Corporation (P-3396)*

Mad Catz, San Diego *Also Called: Mad Catz Inc (P-7546)*

Mad Catz Inc .... C....... 858 790-5008
10680 Treena St Ste 500 San Diego (92131) *(P-7546)*

Mad Engine, San Diego *Also Called: Mad Engine Global LLC (P-2074)*

Mad Engine Global LLC (HQ) .... D....... 858 558-5270
6740 Cobra Way Ste 100 San Diego (92121) *(P-2074)*

Mad Engine Global LLC .... B....... 858 558-5270
6740 Cobra Way Ste 100 San Diego (92121) *(P-13134)*

Madden Corporation .... D....... 714 922-1670
2301 E Pacifica Pl Compton (90220) *(P-11533)*

Mader News Inc .... D....... 818 551-5000
508 S Varney St Burbank (91502) *(P-13496)*

Madewell Inc .... E....... 619 491-0549
7007 Friars Rd Ste 820 San Diego (92108) *(P-13923)*

Madisn/Grham Clor Graphics Inc .... B....... 323 261-7171
150 N Myers St Los Angeles (90033) *(P-3627)*

Madison Inc of Oklahoma .... D....... 918 224-6990
18000 Studebaker Rd Cerritos (90703) *(P-6043)*

Madison Club Owners Assn .... C....... 760 777-9320
53035 Meriwether Way La Quinta (92253) *(P-17436)*

Madison Club, The, La Quinta *Also Called: Madison Club Owners Assn (P-17436)*

Madison Industries (HQ) .... E....... 323 583-4061
2961 W Macarthur Blvd Ste 211 Santa Ana (92704) *(P-6382)*

Madn Aircraft Hinge .... E....... 661 257-3430
26911 Ruether Ave Ste Q Santa Clarita (91351) *(P-9544)*

Madonna Inn Inc .... C....... 805 543-3000
100 Madonna Rd San Luis Obispo (93405) *(P-13720)*

Maersk Whsng Dist Svcs USA LLC (HQ) .... C....... 562 345-2200
2240 E Maple Ave El Segundo (90245) *(P-11780)*

Maersk Whsng Dist Svcs USA LLC .... C....... 801 301-1732
1651 California St Ste A Redlands (92374) *(P-11781)*

Mag Aerospace Industries LLC .... B....... 801 400-7944
1500 Glenn Curtiss St Carson (90746) *(P-5959)*

Mag Instrument Inc (PA) .... A....... 909 947-1006
2001 S Hellman Ave Ontario (91761) *(P-8374)*

Magdalena Ecke Family YMCA, Encinitas *Also Called: YMCA of San Diego County (P-19482)*

Magic 92.5, San Diego *Also Called: Local Media San Diego LLC (P-11930)*

Magic Acquisition Corp .... B....... 661 382-4700
23920 Creekside Rd Valencia (91355) *(P-13793)*

Magic Apparel & Magic Headwear, Compton *Also Called: Magic Apparel Group Inc (P-2401)*

Magic Apparel Group Inc .... E....... 310 223-4000
1100 W Walnut St Compton (90220) *(P-2401)*

Magic Bullet, Los Angeles *Also Called: Homeland Housewares LLC (P-12633)*

Magic Castles Inc .... D....... 323 851-3313
7001 Franklin Ave Los Angeles (90028) *(P-14025)*

Magic International, Santa Monica *Also Called: Mens Apparel Guild In Cal Inc (P-19381)*

Magic Jump Inc .... E....... 818 847-1313
9165 Glenoaks Blvd Sun Valley (91352) *(P-15784)*

Magic Mountain LLC .... C....... 661 255-4100
26101 Magic Mountain Pkwy Valencia (91355) *(P-17319)*

Magic Plastics Inc (PA) .... E....... 800 369-0303
25215 Avenue Stanford Santa Clarita (91355) *(P-5089)*

Magic Software Enterprises Inc .... E....... 949 250-1718
530 Technology Dr Ste 100 Irvine (92618) *(P-16298)*

Magic Touch Software Intl .... E....... 800 714-6490
950 Boardwalk Ste 200 San Marcos (92078) *(P-16299)*

Magic Workforce Solutions LLC .... A....... 310 246-6153
9100 Wilshire Blvd Ste 700e Beverly Hills (90212) *(P-20285)*

Magic-Flight General Mfg Inc .... E....... 619 288-4638
3417 Hancock St San Diego (92110) *(P-2755)*

Magicall Inc .... E....... 805 484-4300
4550 Calle Alto Camarillo (93012) *(P-8150)*

Magma, San Diego *Also Called: Mission Technology Group Inc (P-7551)*

Magma, Escondido *Also Called: One Stop Systems Inc (P-7558)*

Magma Inc .... E....... 858 530-2511
9918 Via Pasar San Diego (92126) *(P-7547)*

Magma Products LLC .... D....... 562 627-0500
3940 Pixie Ave Lakewood (90712) *(P-8219)*

Magna Tool Inc .... E....... 714 826-2500
5594 Market Pl Cypress (90630) *(P-7915)*

Magnabiosciences LLC .... E....... 858 481-4400
6325 Lusk Blvd San Diego (92121) *(P-10549)*

Magnaflow Performance, Oceanside *Also Called: Car Sound Exhaust System Inc (P-9368)*

Magnaslow, Rcho Sta Marg *Also Called: Car Sound Exhaust System Inc (P-9366)*

Magnasync-Moviola, Burbank *Also Called: Magnasync/Moviola Corporation (P-8421)*

Magnasync/Moviola Corporation .... E....... 818 845-8066
1400 W Burbank Blvd Burbank (91506) *(P-8421)*

Magnebit Holding Corp .... E....... 858 573-0727
9474 La Cuesta Dr La Mesa (91941) *(P-10214)*

Magnell Associate Inc (DH) .... C....... 800 685-3471
17560 Rowland St City Of Industry (91748) *(P-12425)*

Magnesium Alloy Pdts Co Inc .... E....... 310 605-1440
2420 N Alameda St Compton (90222) *(P-5762)*

Magnesium Alloy Products Co LP .... E....... 323 636-2276
2420 N Alameda St Compton (90222) *(P-5763)*

Magnet Sales & Mfg Co Inc (HQ) .... D....... 310 391-7213
11250 Playa Ct Culver City (90230) *(P-5381)*

Magnetic Component Engrg LLC (PA) .... D....... 310 784-3100
2830 Lomita Blvd Torrance (90505) *(P-6868)*

Magnetic Sensors Corporation .... E....... 714 630-8380
1365 N Mccan St Anaheim (92806) *(P-9080)*

Magnetika Inc (PA) .... D....... 310 527-8100
2041 W 139th St Gardena (90249) *(P-12603)*

Magnetron Power Inventions Inc .... E....... 310 462-6970
2226 W 232nd St Torrance (90501) *(P-312)*

Magnolia Convalescent Hospital, Riverside *Also Called: Magnolia Rhbltion Nursing Ctr (P-18143)*

Mergent email: customerrelations@mergent.com
1168

2024 Southern California
Business Directory and Buyers Guide

(P-0000) Products & Services Section entry number
(PA)=Parent Co (HQ)=Headquarters (DH)=Div Headquarters

Magnolia Grdns Convalescent HM, Granada Hills *Also Called: Longwood Management Corp (P-17998)*

Magnolia Rhbltton Nursing Ctr .... C...... 951 688-4321
8133 Magnolia Ave Riverside (92504) *(P-18143)*

Magnuson Products LLC .... E...... 805 642-8833
1990 Knoll Dr Ste A Ventura (93003) *(P-9419)*

Magnuson Superchargers, Ventura *Also Called: Magnuson Products LLC (P-9419)*

Magor Mold LLC .... D...... 909 592-3663
420 S Lone Hill Ave San Dimas (91773) *(P-7081)*

Magparts (HQ) .... **C...... 626 334-7897**
1545 W Roosevelt St Azusa (91702) *(P-5797)*

Magtech & Power Conversion Inc .... E...... 714 451-0106
1146 E Ash Ave Fullerton (92831) *(P-8945)*

Magtek Inc (PA) .... **C...... 562 546-6400**
1710 Apollo Ct Seal Beach (90740) *(P-7548)*

Mahar Manufacturing Corp (PA) .... **E...... 323 581-9988**
2834 E 46th St Vernon (90058) *(P-10939)*

Mail Boxes Etc, San Diego *Also Called: UPS Store Inc (P-16955)*

Mail Handling Group Inc .... C...... 952 975-5000
2840 Madonna Dr Fullerton (92835) *(P-3628)*

Mail Handling Services, Fullerton *Also Called: Mail Handling Group Inc (P-3628)*

Mailers Software, Rcho Sta Marg *Also Called: Melissa Data Corporation (P-16073)*

Maimone Liquidating Corp (PA) .... D...... 626 286-5691
1390 E Palm St Altadena (91001) *(P-17012)*

Main Electric Supply Co LLC .... E...... 323 753-5131
8146 Byron Rd Whittier (90606) *(P-12604)*

Main Electric Supply Co LLC .... E...... 858 737-7000
4674 Cardin St San Diego (92111) *(P-12605)*

Main Steel LLC .... D...... 951 231-4949
3100 Jefferson St Riverside (92504) *(P-6637)*

Main Street Banner, Carpinteria *Also Called: Dsy Educational Corporation (P-2549)*

Mainfreight Inc (HQ) .... **D...... 310 900-1974**
1400 Glenn Curtiss St Carson (90746) *(P-11782)*

Mainline, Torrance *Also Called: Mainline Equipment Inc (P-8540)*

Mainline Equipment Inc .... D...... 800 444-2288
20917 Higgins Ct Torrance (90501) *(P-8540)*

Mainplace Senior Living, Orange *Also Called: Pennant Group Inc (P-18030)*

MainStay Medical Limited .... D...... 619 261-9144
2159 India St Ste 200 San Diego (92101) *(P-17711)*

Mainstream Energy Corporation .... B...... 805 528-9705
775 Fiero Ln Ste 200 San Luis Obispo (93401) *(P-791)*

Maintech Incorporated .... C...... 714 921-8000
2401 N Glassell St Orange (92865) *(P-16068)*

Maintech Resources Inc .... E...... 562 804-0664
5042 Northwestern Way Westminster (92683) *(P-1137)*

Maintenace Operations Svc Ctr, National City *Also Called: National School District (P-18976)*

Maintenance & Operation Dept, Montebello *Also Called: Montebello Unified School Dst (P-15729)*

Maintenance Dept, Gardena *Also Called: Los Angeles Unified School Dst (P-15721)*

Maintenance Dept, Port Hueneme *Also Called: NAVY UNITED STATES DEPARTMENT (P-17140)*

Maintex Inc (PA) .... **C...... 800 446-1888**
13300 Nelson Ave City Of Industry (91746) *(P-4359)*

Majestic Industry Hills LLC .... A...... 626 810-4455
1 Industry Hills Pkwy City Of Industry (91744) *(P-15236)*

Majestic Management Co., City Of Industry *Also Called: Majestic Realty Co (P-14828)*

Majestic Realty Co (PA) .... **C...... 562 692-9581**
13191 Crossroads Pkwy N Ste 600 City Of Industry (91746) *(P-14828)*

Major Gloves & Safety Inc .... E...... 626 330-8022
250 Turnbull Canyon Rd City Of Industry (91745) *(P-15469)*

Major Market Inc .... C...... 760 723-0857
845 S Main Ave Fallbrook (92028) *(P-13701)*

Major Market-Ftd Florist, Fallbrook *Also Called: Major Market Inc (P-13701)*

Makabi 26 Inc .... F...... 323 588-7666
2850 E 44th St Vernon (90058) *(P-5090)*

Makar Anaheim LLC .... A...... 714 740-4431
777 W Convention Way Anaheim (92802) *(P-15237)*

Maker Studios LLC (DH) .... **C...... 310 606-2182**
3515 Eastham Dr Culver City (90232) *(P-17346)*

Makespace Labs Inc .... C...... 800 920-9440
3526 Hayden Ave Culver City (90232) *(P-11596)*

Makesy, Irvine *Also Called: Wood Candle Wick Tech Inc (P-11309)*

Makita, La Mirada *Also Called: Makita USA Inc (P-12727)*

Makita USA Inc (HQ) .... **C...... 714 522-8088**
14930 Northam St La Mirada (90638) *(P-12727)*

Mako Industries SC Inc .... E...... 714 632-1400
1280 N Red Gum St Anaheim (92806) *(P-10272)*

Malcolm & Cisneros A Law Corp .... C...... 949 252-9400
2112 Business Center Dr Ste 100 Irvine (92612) *(P-18902)*

Malcolm Cisneros, Irvine *Also Called: Malcolm & Cisneros A Law Corp (P-18902)*

Malibu Conference Center Inc .... B...... 818 889-6440
327 Latigo Canyon Rd Malibu (90265) *(P-14672)*

Malibu Leather Inc .... C...... 310 985-0707
510 W 6th St Ste 1002 Los Angeles (90014) *(P-5303)*

Malibu Limousine Service, Marina Del Rey *Also Called: Executive Network Entps Inc (P-11383)*

Malibu Times Inc .... F...... 310 456-5507
3864 Las Flores Canyon Rd Malibu (90265) *(P-3301)*

Malk Partners .... D...... 858 914-1125
7911 Herschel Ave Ste 400 La Jolla (92037) *(P-14965)*

Mallin Casual Furniture, Los Angeles *Also Called: Minson Corporation (P-2811)*

Malmberg Engineering Inc .... E...... 925 606-6500
655 Deep Valley Dr Ste 125 Rlling Hls Est (90274) *(P-7916)*

Maloof Naman Builders .... D...... 818 775-0040
9614 Cozycroft Ave Chatsworth (91311) *(P-12774)*

Malys of California Inc .... B...... 661 295-8317
28145 Harrison Pkwy Valencia (91355) *(P-12893)*

Mama Mellaces Old World Treats, Carlsbad *Also Called: Mfb Liquidation Inc (P-1558)*

Mamco Inc (PA) .... **C...... 951 776-9300**
764 Ramona Expy Ste C Perris (92571) *(P-632)*

Mammography Center, Lompoc *Also Called: Lompoc Valley Medical Center (P-18331)*

Mammoth Media Inc .... D...... 832 315-0833
1447 2nd St Santa Monica (90401) *(P-3302)*

Mammoth Water, Montebello *Also Called: Unix Packaging LLC (P-1743)*

Mamolos Cntntl Bailey Bakeries .... C...... 805 496-0045
2734 Townsgate Rd Westlake Village (91361) *(P-13721)*

Man Theateres, Westlake Village *Also Called: Weststar Cinemas Inc (P-17304)*

Man-Grove Industries Inc .... D...... 714 630-3020
1201 N Miller St Anaheim (92806) *(P-3629)*

Managed Dental Care .... C...... 818 598-6599
6200 Canoga Ave Ste 100 Woodland Hills (91367) *(P-14487)*

Managed Dental Care California, Woodland Hills *Also Called: Managed Dental Care (P-14487)*

Managed Health, Huntington Beach *Also Called: Managed Health Network (P-14488)*

Managed Health Network .... B...... 714 934-5519
7755 Center Ave Ste 700 Huntington Beach (92647) *(P-14488)*

Management 360 .... D...... 310 272-7000
9111 Wilshire Blvd Beverly Hills (90210) *(P-17320)*

Management Applied Prgrm Inc (PA) .... **D...... 562 463-5000**
13191 Crossroads Pkwy N Ste 205 City Of Industry (91746) *(P-16503)*

Management Trust Assn Inc .... C...... 562 926-3372
12607 Hiddencreek Way Ste R Cerritos (90703) *(P-20193)*

Manatt Phelps & Phillips LLP (PA) .... **B...... 310 312-4000**
2049 Century Park E Ste 1700 Los Angeles (90067) *(P-18903)*

Manchester Feeds Inc (PA) .... **F...... 714 637-7062**
1520 E Barham Dr San Marcos (92078) *(P-1445)*

Manchester Feeds San Marcos, San Marcos *Also Called: Manchester Feeds Inc (P-1445)*

Manchester Grand Resorts LP .... C...... 619 232-1234
1 Market Pl Fl 33 San Diego (92101) *(P-15238)*

Manchster Grnd Hyatt San Diego, San Diego *Also Called: Hyatt Corporation (P-15194)*

Manchster Grnd Hyatt San Diego, San Diego *Also Called: Manchester Grand Resorts LP (P-15238)*

Mandala, Carlsbad *Also Called: Oceanside Glasstile Company (P-5373)*

Mandalay Generating Station, Oxnard *Also Called: NRG California South LP (P-12031)*

Maneri Sign Co Inc .... E...... 310 327-6261
1928 W 135th St Gardena (90249) *(P-11133)*

Maney Aircraft, Ontario *Also Called: Maney Aircraft Inc (P-9741)*

Maney Aircraft Inc .... E...... 909 390-2500
1305 S Wanamaker Ave Ontario (91761) *(P-9741)*

Mangan Inc (PA) .... **D...... 310 835-8080**
3901 Via Oro Ave Long Beach (90810) *(P-19642)*

Employee Codes: A=Over 500 employees, B=251-500
C=101-250, D=51-100, E=20-50, F=10-19, G=1-9

2024 Southern California
Business Directory and Buyers Guide

© Mergent Inc. 1-800-342-5647

1169

ALPHABETIC

Mango Technologies Inc (PA).....................................A...... 888 625-4258
350 10th Ave Ste 500 San Diego (92101) *(P-16069)*

Mangomint Inc ....E...... 310 496-8677
10401 Venice Blvd 497 Los Angeles (90034) *(P-16300)*

Manhattan Bancorp ....C...... 310 606-8000
2141 Rosecrans Ave # 1100 El Segundo (90245) *(P-14169)*

Manhattan Beachwear LLC (PA).........................D...... 657 384-2110
10855 Business Center Dr Ste C Cypress (90630) *(P-2417)*

Manhattan Country Club, Manhattan Beach Also Called: 1334 Partners LP *(P-17457)*

Manhattan Stitching Co, Buena Park Also Called: Manhattan Stitching Co Inc *(P-2518)*

Manhattan Stitching Co Inc ....E...... 714 521-9479
8362 Artesia Blvd Ste E Buena Park (90621) *(P-2518)*

Manitwoc Fdsrvice Cmpanies LLC ....B...... 323 245-3761
1210 N Red Gum St Anaheim (92806) *(P-7618)*

Manley Laboratories Inc ....E...... 909 627-4256
13880 Magnolia Ave Chino (91710) *(P-8541)*

Mann+hmmel Wtr Fluid Sltons In (DH)................D..... 805 964-8003
93 S La Patera Ln Goleta (93117) *(P-7670)*

Manna, La Jolla Also Called: Manna Health LLC *(P-4162)*

Manna Health LLC ....E...... 877 576-2662
216 Nautilus St La Jolla (92037) *(P-4162)*

Manning Kass Ellrod Rmrez Trst (PA)..................C...... 213 624-6900
801 S Figueroa St 15th Fl Los Angeles (90017) *(P-18904)*

MANOR AT SANTA TERESITA HOSPIT, Duarte Also Called: Santa Teresita Inc *(P-18423)*

Manorcare Health Services, Aliso Viejo Also Called: Hcr Manorcare Med Svcs Fla LLC *(P-17969)*

Manson Western LLC ....C...... 424 201-8800
625 Alaska Ave Torrance (90503) *(P-3409)*

Manti - Machine Co Inc ....E...... 714 902-1465
11782 Western Ave Ste 15 Stanton (90680) *(P-7917)*

Manufacture, Los Angeles Also Called: BTS Trading Inc *(P-2014)*

Manufacture, Vernon Also Called: D I F Group Inc *(P-20024)*

Manufactured Solutions LLC ....E...... 714 548-6915
9601 Janice Cir Villa Park (92861) *(P-11248)*

Manufacturer, Paramount Also Called: Z-Tronix Inc *(P-9142)*

Manufacturer, Irvine Also Called: Sonnet Technologies Inc *(P-9255)*

Manufacturer, Riverside Also Called: Aleph Group Inc *(P-9275)*

Manufacturer and Distributor, Corona Also Called: Approved Aeronautics LLC *(P-9628)*

Manufacturers Bank, Los Angeles Also Called: Smbc Manubank *(P-14207)*

Manufacturers of Wood Products, Santa Barbara Also Called: Architctral Mllwk Snta Barbara *(P-2584)*

Manufacturing, Anaheim Also Called: Bloomfield Food Inc *(P-1189)*

Manufacturing, Valencia Also Called: King Henrys Inc *(P-1828)*

Manufacturing, Temecula Also Called: Marathon Finishing Systems Inc *(P-6265)*

Manufacturing, Chino Also Called: Manley Laboratories Inc *(P-8541)*

Manufacturing, San Diego Also Called: Continental Controls Corp *(P-10125)*

Maof, Montebello Also Called: Mexican Amrcn Oprtnty Fndation *(P-19112)*

Maof Commerce, Commerce Also Called: Mexican Amrcn Oprtnty Fndation *(P-19113)*

Mapcargo Global Logistics (PA).............................D...... 310 297-8300
2501 Santa Fe Ave Redondo Beach (90278) *(P-11783)*

Mapei Corporation ....E...... 909 475-4100
5415 Industrial Pkwy San Bernardino (92407) *(P-3953)*

Maple Imaging LLC (HQ)...E...... 805 373-4545
1049 Camino Dos Rios Thousand Oaks (91360) *(P-9081)*

Mapp Digital Us LLC ....B...... 619 342-4340
4660 La Jolla Village Dr Ste 100 San Diego (92122) *(P-20194)*

Mar Cor Purification Inc ....E...... 800 633-3080
6351 Orangethorpe Ave Buena Park (90620) *(P-7671)*

Mar Engineering Company ....E...... 818 765-4805
7350 Greenbush Ave North Hollywood (91605) *(P-7918)*

Marathon Finishing Systems Inc ....E...... 310 791-5601
42355 Rio Nedo Temecula (92590) *(P-6265)*

Marathon General Inc ....D...... 760 738-9714
1728 Mission Rd Escondido (92029) *(P-633)*

Marathon Industries Inc ....C...... 661 286-1520
25597 Springbrook Ave Santa Clarita (91350) *(P-12227)*

Marathon Land Inc ....C...... 805 488-3585
2599 E Hueneme Rd Oxnard (93033) *(P-59)*

Marathon Truck Bodies, Santa Clarita Also Called: Marathon Industries Inc *(P-12227)*

Maravai Lf Scnces Holdings LLC (HQ)....................C...... 650 697-3600
10770 Wateridge Cir Ste 100 San Diego (92121) *(P-19858)*

Maravai Lfscences Holdings Inc (PA)......................E...... 858 546-0004
10770 Wateridge Cir Ste 200 San Diego (92121) *(P-4163)*

Maravai Lifesciences, San Diego Also Called: Maravai Lfscences Holdings Inc *(P-4163)*

Maravilla Foundation (PA)......................................C...... 323 721-4162
5729 Union Pacific Ave Commerce (90022) *(P-19455)*

Marbleworks, Huntington Beach Also Called: Tile & Marble Design Co Inc *(P-1007)*

Marborg Industries (PA)...C...... 805 963-1852
728 E Yanonali St Santa Barbara (93103) *(P-12172)*

Marborg Recovery LP ....C...... 805 963-1852
14470 Calle Real Goleta (93117) *(P-12173)*

Marcea Inc ....F...... 213 746-5191
1742 Crenshaw Blvd Torrance (90501) *(P-2349)*

March Products Inc ....D...... 909 622-4800
4645 Troy Ct Jurupa Valley (92509) *(P-11249)*

March Vision Care Inc ....E...... 310 665-0975
6701 Center Dr W Ste 790 Los Angeles (90045) *(P-10843)*

Marchem Solvay Group, Long Beach Also Called: Solvay USA Inc *(P-3914)*

Marchem Technologies LLC ....E...... 310 638-9352
20851 S Santa Fe Ave Carson (90810) *(P-3897)*

Marco Fine Arts Galleries Inc ....E...... 310 615-1818
4860 W 147th St Hawthorne (90250) *(P-3784)*

Marco Products, Los Angeles Also Called: Augerscope Inc *(P-5874)*

Marco's Auto Body, Altadena Also Called: Maimone Liquidating Corp *(P-17012)*

Marcoa Media LLC (PA)..E...... 858 635-9627
9955 Black Mountain Rd San Diego (92126) *(P-3463)*

Marcoa Quality Publishing LLC ....F...... 858 695-9600
9955 Black Mountain Rd San Diego (92126) *(P-3464)*

Marcom Eng'g System, Irvine Also Called: Mgc Systems Corp *(P-19645)*

Marcum LLP ....D...... 949 236-5600
600 Anton Blvd Ste 1600 Costa Mesa (92626) *(P-19794)*

Marcus & Millichap, Calabasas Also Called: Marcus & Millichap Inc *(P-14829)*

Marcus & Millichap Inc (PA)...................................C...... 818 212-2250
23975 Park Sorrento Ste 400 Calabasas (91302) *(P-14829)*

Marcus Hotels Inc ....C...... 818 980-8000
4222 Vineland Ave North Hollywood (91602) *(P-15239)*

Mareblu Naturals, Anaheim Also Called: 180 Snacks Inc *(P-1532)*

Marflex, Vernon Also Called: Marspring Corporation *(P-2116)*

Marfred Industries ....B
12708 Branford St Sun Valley (91353) *(P-3117)*

Margartville Resort Palm Sprng, Palm Springs Also Called: Margartvlle Rsort Orlndo Rsort *(P-15240)*

Margartvlle Rsort Orlndo Rsort ....C...... 760 327-8311
1600 N Indian Canyon Dr Palm Springs (92262) *(P-15240)*

Marge Carson Inc (PA)..D...... 626 571-1111
555 W 5th St Los Angeles (90013) *(P-2808)*

Mariak Industries Inc ....B...... 310 661-4400
879 W 190th St Ste 1050 Gardena (90248) *(P-12307)*

Mariak Window Fashion, Gardena Also Called: Mariak Industries Inc *(P-12307)*

Marian Community Clinic ....D...... 805 739-3867
117 W Bunny Ave Santa Maria (93458) *(P-18340)*

Marian Medical Center ....A...... 805 739-3000
1400 E Church St Santa Maria (93454) *(P-18341)*

Marian Regional Medical Center, Santa Maria Also Called: Dignity Health *(P-18241)*

Marian Regional Medical Center, Santa Maria Also Called: Marian Medical Center *(P-18341)*

Marie Callender's Pie Shops, Rancho Palos Verdes Also Called: Pie Rise Ltd *(P-14031)*

Marie Cllender Wholesalers Inc ....A...... 951 737-6760
170 E Rincon St Corona (92879) *(P-13248)*

Marie Edward Vineyards Inc ....E...... 661 363-5038
6901 E Brundage Ln Bakersfield (93307) *(P-6908)*

Marigold Usa Inc ....C...... 617 385-6786
475 Anton Blvd Costa Mesa (92626) *(P-16070)*

Marika LLC ....D...... 323 888-7755
5553 Bandini Blvd B Bell (90201) *(P-2350)*

Marika Group Inc ....E...... 858 537-5300
8960 Carroll Way San Diego (92121) *(P-13135)*

Marina, Orange Also Called: Marina Landscape Inc *(P-203)*

Marina City Club LP A Cali ....C...... 310 822-0611
4333 Admiralty Way Marina Del Rey (90292) *(P-14726)*

Mergent email: customerrelations@mergent.com
1170

2024 Southern California
Business Directory and Buyers Guide

(P-0000) Products & Services Section entry number
(PA)=Parent Co (HQ)=Headquarters (DH)=Div Headquarters

Marina Graphic Center Inc .... C....... 310 970-1777
12901 Cerise Ave Hawthorne (90250) *(P-3630)*

Marina Landscape Inc .... B....... 714 939-6600
3707 W Garden Grove Blvd Orange (92868) *(P-203)*

Marina Landscape Maint Inc, Anaheim *Also Called: Marina Maintenance Group Inc (P-166)*

Marina Maintenance Group Inc .... B....... 714 939-6600
1900 S Lewis St Anaheim (92805) *(P-166)*

Marina Shipyard, Long Beach *Also Called: Indel Engineering Inc (P-9860)*

Marina Village, San Diego *Also Called: Southern Cal Pipe Trades ADM (P-14865)*

Marine & Rest Fabricators Inc .... E....... 619 232-7267
3768 Dalbergia St San Diego (92113) *(P-6266)*

Marine Aviation Logistics, Oceanside *Also Called: United States Marine Corps (P-12922)*

Marine Corps United States .... A....... 760 725-1304
Camp Pendleton Oceanside (92055) *(P-18530)*

Marine Corps Cmnty Svcs Dept, San Diego *Also Called: Marine Corps Community Svcs (P-17558)*

Marine Corps Community Svcs .... C....... 760 725-6195
Acs Mccs Attn Semper Fi Box 555020 Marine Corp Base Camp Pendleton (92055) *(P-17557)*

Marine Corps Community Svcs .... B....... 858 577-1061
2273 Elrod Ave San Diego (92145) *(P-17558)*

Marine Corps Community Svcs .... C....... 760 725-5187
Camp Pendleton Marine Corps Base Oceanside (92055) *(P-17841)*

Marine Corps Community Svcs .... C....... 760 725-2817
202860 San Jacinto Rd Oceanside (92054) *(P-19216)*

Marine Corps Community Svcs .... C....... 760 725-7311
Basilone Rd Bldg 51080 Camp Pendleton (92055) *(P-19217)*

Marine Group Boat Works, Chula Vista *Also Called: Marine Group Boat Works LLC (P-17137)*

Marine Group Boat Works LLC .... C....... 619 427-6767
997 G St Chula Vista (91910) *(P-17137)*

Marine Interiors, San Diego *Also Called: US Joiner LLC (P-719)*

Marine Outfitters, Carlsbad *Also Called: Matthew Smith Crampton (P-9862)*

Marine Room Restaurant, La Jolla *Also Called: La Jolla Bch & Tennis CLB Inc (P-17494)*

Marine Terminals Corporation .... B....... 310 519-2300
389 Terminal Way San Pedro (90731) *(P-11643)*

Mariner Health Care Inc .... D....... 818 246-5677
430 N Glendale Ave Glendale (91206) *(P-18004)*

Mariner Health Care Inc .... D....... 562 942-7019
8925 Mines Ave Pico Rivera (90660) *(P-18005)*

Mariner Health Care Inc .... D....... 818 957-0850
3050 Montrose Ave La Crescenta (91214) *(P-18006)*

Mariner Health Care Inc .... C....... 310 371-4628
4109 Emerald St Torrance (90503) *(P-18007)*

Mariner Health Care Inc .... C....... 760 776-7700
44610 Monterey Ave Palm Desert (92260) *(P-18008)*

Mariner Health Care Inc .... D....... 760 327-8541
277 S Sunrise Way Palm Springs (92262) *(P-20058)*

Mariner Systems Inc (PA) .... E....... 305 266-7255
114 C Ave Coronado (92118) *(P-16867)*

Marino Enterprises Inc .... E....... 909 476-0343
10671 Civic Center Dr Rancho Cucamonga (91730) *(P-9742)*

Mariposa Horticultural Entps, Irwindale *Also Called: Mariposa Landscapes Inc (P-204)*

Mariposa Landscapes Inc (PA) .... D....... 626 960-0196
6232 Santos Diaz St Irwindale (91702) *(P-204)*

Maripro, Goleta *Also Called: L3 Technologies Inc (P-8534)*

Maritime Telecom Netwrk Inc (DH) C
6080 Center Dr Ste 1200 Los Angeles (90045) *(P-8542)*

Marjan Stone Inc .... E....... 619 825-6000
2758 Via Orange Way Spring Valley (91978) *(P-12357)*

Mark & Fred Enterprises .... C....... 714 821-1993
645 S Beach Blvd Anaheim (92804) *(P-18009)*

Mark Christopher Chevrolet Inc (PA) .... C....... 909 321-5860
2131 E Convention Center Way Ontario (91764) *(P-13794)*

Mark Christopher Hummer, Ontario *Also Called: Mark Christopher Chevrolet Inc (P-13794)*

Mark Clemons .... C....... 760 361-1531
4584 Adobe Rd Twentynine Palms (92277) *(P-11497)*

Mark Company, Orange *Also Called: Santa Ana Creek Development Company (P-1085)*

Mark IV Metal Products Inc .... E....... 310 217-9700
544 W 132nd St Gardena (90248) *(P-6848)*

Mark Land Electric Inc .... C....... 818 883-5110
7876 Deering Ave Canoga Park (91304) *(P-915)*

Mark Optics Inc .... E....... 714 545-6684
1424 E Saint Gertrude Pl Santa Ana (92705) *(P-10326)*

Mark Sheffield Cnstr Inc .... F....... 661 589-8520
9105 Langley Rd Bakersfield (93312) *(P-360)*

Markar & Pemko Products, Ventura *Also Called: Assa Abloy ACC Door Cntrls Gro (P-5898)*

Markel Corp .... B....... 818 595-0600
21600 Oxnard St Ste 900 Woodland Hills (91367) *(P-14609)*

Market Scan, Camarillo *Also Called: Market Scan Info Systems Inc (P-16071)*

Market Scan Info Systems Inc .... D....... 800 658-7226
815 Camarillo Springs Rd Camarillo (93012) *(P-16071)*

Marketing Design Group, San Diego *Also Called: Phase Ten Strategic Corp (P-14843)*

Marketspark, San Diego *Also Called: Marketspark Sub Inc (P-8543)*

Marketspark Sub Inc .... D....... 844 900-0599
750 B St Ste 1630 San Diego (92101) *(P-8543)*

Markland Industries Inc (PA) .... D....... 714 245-2850
1111 E Mcfadden Ave Santa Ana (92705) *(P-9879)*

Marko Foam Products, Huntington Beach *Also Called: Marko Foam Products Inc (P-4893)*

Marko Foam Products Inc (PA) .... E....... 949 417-3307
7441 Vincent Cir Huntington Beach (92648) *(P-4893)*

Markwins Beauty Brands Inc (PA) .... C....... 909 595-8898
22067 Ferrero City Of Industry (91789) *(P-13052)*

Marlee Manufacturing Inc .... E....... 909 390-3222
4711 E Guasti Rd Ontario (91761) *(P-10550)*

Marleon Inc .... F....... 310 679-1242
3202 W Rosecrans Ave Hawthorne (90250) *(P-17093)*

Marlin Designs LLC .... C....... 949 637-7257
13845 Alton Pkwy Ste C Irvine (92618) *(P-2809)*

Marlin Equity Partners LLC (PA) .... D....... 310 364-0100
1301 Manhattan Ave Hermosa Beach (90254) *(P-14423)*

Marlinda Imperial Hospital, Pasadena *Also Called: Two Palms Nursing Center Inc (P-18155)*

Marlinda Management Inc (PA) .... C....... 310 631-6122
3351 E Imperial Hwy Lynwood (90262) *(P-18144)*

Marlora Investments LLC .... D....... 562 494-3311
3801 E Anaheim St Long Beach (90804) *(P-18010)*

Marlora Post Accute Rhbltton, Long Beach *Also Called: Marlora Investments LLC (P-18010)*

Marman Industries Inc .... D....... 909 392-2136
1701 Earhart La Verne (91750) *(P-7082)*

Maroney Company .... F....... 818 882-2722
9016 Winnetka Ave Northridge (91324) *(P-7919)*

Marples Gears Inc .... E....... 626 570-1744
1310 Mountain View Cir Azusa (91702) *(P-7357)*

Marquez & Marquez Food PR, South Gate *Also Called: Marquez Marquez Inc (P-1829)*

Marquez Brothers Entps Inc .... C....... 626 330-3310
15480 Valley Blvd City Of Industry (91746) *(P-13185)*

Marquez Marquez Inc .... E....... 562 408-0960
11821 Industrial Ave South Gate (90280) *(P-1829)*

Marriott, Anaheim *Also Called: Fairfeld Inn By Mrrott Ltd Prt (P-15151)*

Marriott, Woodland Hills *Also Called: HEI Hospitality LLC (P-15175)*

Marriott, Lake Arrowhead *Also Called: Lake Arrwhead Rsort Oprtor Inc (P-15218)*

Marriott, Irvine *Also Called: Marriott International Inc (P-15242)*

Marriott, Los Angeles *Also Called: Marriott International Inc (P-15243)*

Marriott, La Jolla *Also Called: Marriott International Inc (P-15244)*

Marriott, Fullerton *Also Called: Merritt Hospitality LLC (P-15248)*

Marriott, Baldwin Park *Also Called: Ols Hotels & Resorts LLC (P-15274)*

Marriott, Los Angeles *Also Called: Renaissance Hotel Operating Co (P-15321)*

Marriott, Newport Beach *Also Called: Wj Newport LLC (P-15425)*

Marriott International, Coronado *Also Called: Sanci Marriott Hotels (P-15348)*

Marriott International Inc .... D....... 949 503-5700
31692 El Camino Real San Juan Capistrano (92675) *(P-15241)*

Marriott International Inc .... B....... 949 724-3606
18000 Von Karman Ave Irvine (92612) *(P-15242)*

Marriott International Inc .... A....... 310 641-5700
5855 W Century Blvd Los Angeles (90045) *(P-15243)*

Marriott International Inc .... B....... 858 587-1414
4240 La Jolla Village Dr La Jolla (92037) *(P-15244)*

Marriott San Dego Gslamp Qrter, San Diego *Also Called: San Diego Hotel Company LLC (P-15342)*

Marrs Printing Inc .... D....... 909 594-9459
860 Tucker Ln City Of Industry (91789) *(P-3631)*

ALPHABETIC

Employee Codes: A=Over 500 employees, B=251-500
C=101-250, D=51-100, E=20-50, F=10-19, G=1-9

2024 Southern California
Business Directory and Buyers Guide

© Mergent Inc. 1-800-342-5647
1171

Mars Air Curtains, Gardena *Also Called: Mars Air Systems LLC (P-7327)*

Mars Air Systems LLC ....D...... 310 532-1555
14716 S Broadway Gardena (90248) *(P-7327)*

Mars Food North America, Rancho Dominguez *Also Called: Mars Food Us LLC (P-1938)*

Mars Food Us LLC (HQ)..**B...... 310 933-0670**
2001 E Cashdan St Ste 201 Rancho Dominguez (90220) *(P-1938)*

Mars Petcare Us Inc ....E...... 909 887-8131
2765 Lexington Way San Bernardino (92407) *(P-1433)*

Mars Petcare Us Inc ....D...... 760 261-7900
13243 Nutro Way Victorville (92395) *(P-1434)*

Mars Printing and Packaging, City Of Industry *Also Called: Marrs Printing Inc (P-3631)*

Marsh, San Diego *Also Called: Marsh & McLennan Agency LLC (P-14610)*

Marsh & McLennan Agency LLC ....C..... 858 457-3414
9171 Towne Centre Dr Ste 500 San Diego (92122) *(P-14610)*

Marsh Risk & Insurance Svcs ....A..... 213 624-5555
633 W 5th St Ste 1200 Los Angeles (90071) *(P-14611)*

Marsha Vicki Originals Inc ....F..... 714 895-6371
5292 Production Dr Huntington Beach (92649) *(P-2179)*

Marshall Advertising and Design Inc ....E..... 714 545-5757
2729 Bristol St Ste 100 Costa Mesa (92626) *(P-15556)*

Marshall B Ketchum University (PA)............................C..... 714 463-7567
2575 Yorba Linda Blvd Fullerton (92831) *(P-18991)*

Marshall Electronics Inc (PA).....................................D..... 310 333-0606
20608 Madrona Ave Torrance (90503) *(P-8422)*

Marshall Reddick RE Netwrk, Newport Beach *Also Called: Marshall Reddick Realty Inc (P-14830)*

Marshall Reddick Realty Inc ....C..... 949 885-8180
4299 Macarthur Blvd Ste 102 Newport Beach (92660) *(P-14830)*

Marshall S Ezralow & Assoc, Calabasas *Also Called: MSE Enterprises Inc (P-14834)*

Marspring Corporation (PA)...E..... 323 589-5637
4920 S Boyle Ave Vernon (90058) *(P-2116)*

Marspring Corporation ....D..... 310 484-6849
5190 S Santa Fe Ave Vernon (90058) *(P-2855)*

Martek Power, Torrance *Also Called: Sure Power Inc (P-9124)*

Martin AC Partners Inc ....C..... 213 683-1900
444 S Flower St Ste 1200 Los Angeles (90071) *(P-19738)*

Martin Archery, Los Angeles *Also Called: Martin Sports Inc (P-11012)*

Martin Bros/Marcowall Inc (PA)..................................C..... 310 532-5335
17104 S Figueroa St Gardena (90248) *(P-982)*

Martin Brown Construction Inc ....F..... 619 660-0988
10777 Eureka Rd Spring Valley (91978) *(P-445)*

Martin Chancey Corporation ....E..... 510 972-6300
525 Malloy Ct Corona (92878) *(P-5091)*

Martin Chevrolet ....D..... 323 772-6494
23505 Hawthorne Blvd Torrance (90505) *(P-13795)*

Martin E-Z Stick Labels ....E..... 562 906-1577
12921 Sunnyside Pl Santa Fe Springs (90670) *(P-3785)*

Martin Erattrud Co, Gardena *Also Called: Baxstra Inc (P-2568)*

Martin Furniture, San Diego *Also Called: Gilbert Martin Wdwkg Co Inc (P-2866)*

Martin Integrated, Orange *Also Called: Martin Integrated Systems (P-983)*

Martin Integrated Systems ....E..... 714 998-9100
1525 W Orange Grove Ave Ste D Orange (92868) *(P-983)*

Martin Lther King Jr Cmnty Hos, Los Angeles *Also Called: Martin Lther King Jr-Los Angle (P-18779)*

Martin Lther King Jr-Los Angle ....B..... 424 338-8000
1680 E 120th St Los Angeles (90059) *(P-18779)*

Martin Sports Inc (PA)...E..... 509 529-2554
1100 Glendon Ave Ste 920 Los Angeles (90024) *(P-11012)*

Martin Sprocket & Gear Inc ....F..... 323 728-8117
5920 Triangle Dr Commerce (90040) *(P-7358)*

Martin/Brattrud Inc ....D..... 323 770-4171
1231 W 134th St Gardena (90247) *(P-2810)*

Martinez & Turek, Rialto *Also Called: Martinez and Turek Inc (P-7920)*

Martinez and Turek Inc ....C..... 909 820-6800
300 S Cedar Ave Rialto (92376) *(P-7920)*

Martinez Steel Corporation ....C..... 909 946-0686
1500 S Haven Ave Ste 150 Ontario (91761) *(P-1109)*

Martins Quality Truck Body Inc ....F..... 310 632-5978
1831 W El Segundo Blvd Compton (90222) *(P-9297)*

Marton Precision Mfg LLC ....E..... 714 808-6523
1365 S Acacia Ave Fullerton (92831) *(P-9576)*

Maruchan Inc ....C...... 949 789-2300
1902 Deere Ave Irvine (92606) *(P-1840)*

Maruchan Inc (HQ)...**B...... 949 789-2300**
15800 Laguna Canyon Rd Irvine (92618) *(P-1939)*

Maruhachi Ceramics America Inc ....E..... 800 736-6221
1985 Sampson Ave Corona (92879) *(P-5375)*

Maruichi American Corporation ....D..... 562 903-8600
11529 Greenstone Ave Santa Fe Springs (90670) *(P-5637)*

Marukan Vinegar, Paramount *Also Called: Marukan Vinegar U S A Inc (P-1940)*

Marukan Vinegar U S A Inc (HQ).................................**E...... 562 630-6060**
16203 Vermont Ave Paramount (90723) *(P-1940)*

Marukan Vinegar U S A Inc ....E..... 562 630-6060
7755 Monroe St Paramount (90723) *(P-1941)*

Marukome USA Inc ....F..... 949 863-0110
17132 Pullman St Irvine (92614) *(P-1942)*

Marvell Semiconductor Inc ....A..... 949 614-7700
15485 Sand Canyon Ave Irvine (92618) *(P-8833)*

Marvin Engineering Co Inc (PA)..................................**A...... 310 674-5030**
261 W Beach Ave Inglewood (90302) *(P-19643)*

Marvin Group The, Inglewood *Also Called: Marvin Land Systems Inc (P-9298)*

Marvin Group, The, Inglewood *Also Called: Marvin Engineering Co Inc (P-19643)*

Marvin Land Systems Inc ....E..... 310 674-5030
261 W Beach Ave Inglewood (90302) *(P-9298)*

Marvin Test Solutions Inc ....D..... 949 263-2222
1770 Kettering Irvine (92614) *(P-10215)*

Marway Power Solutions, Santa Ana *Also Called: Marway Power Systems Inc (P-7549)*

Marway Power Systems Inc (PA)..................................**E...... 714 917-6200**
1721 S Grand Ave Santa Ana (92705) *(P-7549)*

Marwell Corporation ....F..... 909 794-4192
1094 Wabash Ave Mentone (92359) *(P-8125)*

Mary Hlth of Sick Cnvlscent Nr ....D..... 805 498-3644
2929 Theresa Dr Newbury Park (91320) *(P-18011)*

Marycrest Manor ....D..... 310 838-2778
10664 Saint James Dr Culver City (90230) *(P-18145)*

Maryvale ....C..... 626 280-6510
7600 Graves Ave Rosemead (91770) *(P-19284)*

Maryvale Day Care Center ....C..... 626 357-1514
2502 Huntington Dr Duarte (91010) *(P-19218)*

Maryvale Edcatn Fmly Rsrce Ctr, Duarte *Also Called: Maryvale Day Care Center (P-19218)*

MASADA HOMES, Gardena *Also Called: Counseling and Research Assoc (P-19253)*

MASCOLA, LOUIS F DDS, Torrance *Also Called: Louis F Mascola DDS (P-17840)*

Mascorro Leather Inc ....E..... 323 724-6759
1303 S Gerhart Ave Commerce (90022) *(P-5309)*

Mashburn Trnsp Svcs Inc ....C..... 661 763-5724
1423 Kern St Taft (93268) *(P-11498)*

Mashindustries Inc ....E..... 714 736-9600
7150 Village Dr Buena Park (90621) *(P-3028)*

Masimo, Irvine *Also Called: Masimo Corporation (P-10811)*

Masimo Americas Inc ....D..... 949 297-7000
52 Discovery Irvine (92618) *(P-10551)*

Masimo Consumer, Carlsbad *Also Called: Dei Holdings Inc (P-8608)*

Masimo Corporation (PA)..**B...... 949 297-7000**
52 Discovery Irvine (92618) *(P-10811)*

Masimo Corporation ....E..... 949 297-7000
40 Parker Irvine (92618) *(P-10812)*

Masimo Corporation ....E..... 949 297-7000
9600 Jeronimo Rd Irvine (92618) *(P-10813)*

Masimo Corporation ....F..... 949 297-7000
15776 Laguna Canyon Rd Irvine (92618) *(P-10814)*

Masimo Semiconductor Inc ....E..... 603 595-8900
52 Discovery Irvine (92618) *(P-8834)*

Mask Technology Inc ....F..... 714 557-3383
2601 Oak St Santa Ana (92707) *(P-9082)*

Mask-Off Company Inc ....F..... 626 359-3261
345 W Maple Ave Monrovia (91016) *(P-4572)*

Mason Electric Co ....B..... 818 361-3366
13955 Balboa Blvd Rancho Cascades (91342) *(P-9743)*

Masongate Inc ....E..... 323 415-8544
2800 Ayers Ave Vernon (90058) *(P-1329)*

Masonite Entry Door Corp ....F..... 951 243-2261
25100 Globe St Moreno Valley (92551) *(P-2614)*

Mergent email: customerrelations@mergent.com
1172

2024 Southern California
Business Directory and Buyers Guide

(P-0000) Products & Services Section entry number
(PA)=Parent Co (HQ)=Headquarters (DH)=Div Headquarters

Masonry Concepts Inc .... D....... 562 802-3700
  15408 Cornet St Santa Fe Springs (90670) **(P-960)**

Masonry Group Nevada Inc .... D....... 951 509-5300
  8188 Lincoln Ave Ste 99 Riverside (92504) **(P-961)**

Mass Systems, Baldwin Park *Also Called: Ametek Ameron LLC* **(P-10116)**

Mast Biosurgery, San Diego *Also Called: Mast Biosurgery USA Inc* **(P-10552)**

Mast Biosurgery USA Inc .... E....... 858 550-8050
  6749 Top Gun St Ste 108 San Diego (92121) **(P-10552)**

Mast Technologies Inc .... F....... 858 452-1700
  8380 Camino Santa Fe Ste 200 San Diego (92121) **(P-4493)**

Masten Space, Mojave *Also Called: Masten Space Systems Inc* **(P-9896)**

Masten Space Systems Inc .... E....... 888 488-8455
  1570 Sabovich St 25 Mojave (93501) **(P-9896)**

Master Builders LLC .... A....... 909 987-1758
  9060 Haven Ave Rancho Cucamonga (91730) **(P-4618)**

Master Enterprises Inc .... E....... 626 442-1821
  2025 Lee Ave South El Monte (91733) **(P-6267)**

Master Machine Products, Riverside *Also Called: Metric Machining* **(P-7931)**

Master Powder Coating Inc .... E....... 562 863-4135
  13721 Bora Dr Santa Fe Springs (90670) **(P-4494)**

Master Research & Mfg Inc .... D....... 562 483-8789
  13528 Pumice St Norwalk (90650) **(P-9744)**

Master-Chef's Linen Rental, Los Angeles *Also Called: American Textile Maint Co* **(P-15447)**

Masterbilt Atmtn Solutions Inc .... E....... 858 748-6700
  12568 Kirkham Ct Poway (92064) **(P-7171)**

Masterbrand Cabinets LLC .... E....... 951 682-1535
  3700 S Riverside Ave Colton (92324) **(P-2666)**

Masterpiece Artist Canvas LLC .... E....... 619 710-2500
  1401 Air Wing Rd San Diego (92154) **(P-2028)**

Masters In Metal Inc .... E....... 805 988-1992
  131 Lombard St Oxnard (93030) **(P-5380)**

Mastey De Paris Inc .... E....... 661 257-4814
  24841 Avenue Tibbitts Valencia (91355) **(P-4433)**

Mastroianni Family Entps Ltd .... B....... 310 952-1700
  10581 Garden Grove Blvd Garden Grove (92843) **(P-15517)**

Mat Cactus Mfg Co .... E....... 626 969-0444
  930 W 10th St Azusa (91702) **(P-2117)**

Matches Inc .... B....... 760 899-1919
  1700 E Araby St Ste 64 Palm Springs (92264) **(P-3986)**

Matchmaster Dyg & Finshg Inc (PA) .... C....... 323 232-2061
  3750 S Broadway Los Angeles (90007) **(P-2103)**

Materals MGT At St Mary Med Ct, Apple Valley *Also Called: St Mary Medical Center LLC* **(P-18469)**

Materia Inc (DH) .... C....... 626 584-8400
  60 N San Gabriel Blvd Pasadena (91107) **(P-3898)**

Material Control Inc .... D....... 661 617-6033
  6901 District Blvd Ste A Bakersfield (93313) **(P-6869)**

Material Handling Supply Inc (HQ) .... D....... 562 921-7715
  12900 Firestone Blvd Santa Fe Springs (90670) **(P-12797)**

Material Holdings LLC (PA) .... C....... 310 553-0550
  1900 Avenue Of The Stars Ste 1600 Los Angeles (90067) **(P-19906)**

Material Sciences Corporation .... E....... 562 699-4550
  3730 Capitol Ave City Of Industry (90601) **(P-5689)**

Materion Prcsion Optics Thin F .... D....... 805 688-4949
  153 Industrial Way Buellton (93427) **(P-8835)**

Matesta Corporation .... E....... 949 874-6052
  5620 Knott Ave Buena Park (90621) **(P-13136)**

Math Holdings Inc (PA) .... C....... 909 517-2200
  15820 Euclid Ave Chino (91708) **(P-16868)**

Matheson Tri-Gas Inc .... E....... 626 334-2905
  16125 Ornelas St Irwindale (91706) **(P-3868)**

Mathy Machine Inc .... E....... 619 448-0404
  9315 Wheatlands Rd Santee (92071) **(P-7921)**

Matich Corporation (PA) .... D....... 909 382-7400
  1596 E Harry Shepard Blvd San Bernardino (92408) **(P-634)**

Matri Kart .... E....... 858 609-0933
  448 W Market St San Diego (92101) **(P-7438)**

Matrix, Commerce *Also Called: Matrix International Tex Inc* **(P-13085)**

Matrix, Palmdale *Also Called: Africajun LLC* **(P-17167)**

Matrix Aviation Services Inc .... C....... 310 337-3037
  6171 W Century Blvd Ste 100 Los Angeles (90045) **(P-11733)**

Matrix Direct Insurance Svcs, San Diego *Also Called: AIG Direct Insurance Svcs Inc* **(P-14555)**

Matrix Document Imaging Inc .... F....... 626 966-9959
  527 E Rowland St Ste 214 Covina (91723) **(P-3786)**

Matrix International Tex Inc .... E....... 323 582-9100
  1363 S Bonnie Beach Pl Commerce (90023) **(P-13085)**

Matrix USA Inc .... E....... 714 825-0404
  2730 S Main St Santa Ana (92707) **(P-8700)**

Matrix-Focalspot Inc .... E....... 858 536-5050
  2747 Loker Ave W Carlsbad (92010) **(P-12681)**

Matsuda House Printing Inc .... E....... 310 532-1533
  1825 W 169th St Ste A Gardena (90247) **(P-3632)**

Matsui International Co Inc (HQ) .... C....... 310 767-7812
  1501 W 178th St Gardena (90248) **(P-4619)**

Matsushita International Corp (PA) .... D....... 949 498-1000
  1141 Via Callejon San Clemente (92673) **(P-15035)**

Matt Construction Corporation (PA) .... C....... 562 903-2277
  9814 Norwalk Blvd Ste 100 Santa Fe Springs (90670) **(P-20195)**

Mattco Forge Inc .... E....... 562 634-8635
  7530 Jackson St Paramount (90723) **(P-6465)**

Mattco Forge Inc (HQ) .... F....... 562 634-8635
  16443 Minnesota Ave Paramount (90723) **(P-6466)**

MATTEL, El Segundo *Also Called: Mattel Inc* **(P-10940)**

Mattel, El Segundo *Also Called: Mattel Direct Import Inc* **(P-10959)**

Mattel Inc (PA) .... A....... 310 252-2000
  333 Continental Blvd El Segundo (90245) **(P-10940)**

Mattel Direct Import Inc (HQ) .... E....... 310 252-2000
  333 Continental Blvd El Segundo (90245) **(P-10959)**

Mattel Investment Inc .... E....... 310 252-2000
  333 Continental Blvd El Segundo (90245) **(P-10941)**

Mattel Operations Inc .... E....... 310 252-2000
  333 Continental Blvd El Segundo (90245) **(P-10960)**

Matteo LLC .... E....... 213 617-2813
  1000 E Cesar E Chavez Ave Los Angeles (90033) **(P-2477)**

Matthew Smith Crampton .... E....... 760 840-8404
  300 Carlsbad Village Dr # 10 Carlsbad (92008) **(P-9862)**

Matthew Warren Inc .... E....... 805 928-3851
  901 W Mccoy Ln Santa Maria (93455) **(P-6783)**

Matthew Warren Inc .... D....... 800 237-5225
  5959 Triumph St Commerce (90040) **(P-6804)**

Matthew Warren Inc .... E....... 714 630-7840
  3850 E Miraloma Ave Anaheim (92806) **(P-11072)**

Matthews International Corp .... F....... 951 537-6615
  442 W Esplanade Ave # 105 San Jacinto (92583) **(P-5804)**

Matthews Studio Equipment Inc .... E....... 818 843-6715
  15148 Bledsoe St Sylmar (91342) **(P-10873)**

Matz Rubber Company Inc .... E....... 323 849-5170
  1209 Chestnut St Burbank (91506) **(P-4776)**

Maud Booth Family Center, North Hollywood *Also Called: Volunteers of Amer Los Angeles* **(P-19163)**

Maul Mfg Inc (PA) .... E....... 714 641-0727
  3041 S Shannon St Santa Ana (92704) **(P-7922)**

Maurer Marine Inc .... F....... 949 645-7673
  873 W 17th St Costa Mesa (92627) **(P-9863)**

Maurice & Maurice Engrg Inc .... E....... 760 949-5151
  17579 Mesa St Ste B4 Hesperia (92345) **(P-5672)**

Maurice Carrie Winery .... F....... 951 676-1711
  34225 Rancho California Rd Temecula (92591) **(P-1647)**

Maurice Kraiem & Company .... E....... 213 629-0038
  228 S Beverly Dr Beverly Hills (90212) **(P-12964)**

Maury Microwave Inc (PA) .... C....... 909 987-4715
  2900 Inland Empire Blvd Ontario (91764) **(P-12682)**

Mave Enterprises Inc .... E....... 818 767-4533
  11555 Cantara St Ste B-E North Hollywood (91605) **(P-1545)**

Maverick Abrasives Corporation .... D....... 714 854-9531
  4340 E Miraloma Ave Anaheim (92807) **(P-5543)**

Maverick Aerospace LLC .... D....... 714 578-1700
  3718 Capitol Ave City Of Industry (90601) **(P-9745)**

Maverick Desk, Gardena *Also Called: New Maverick Desk Inc* **(P-2890)**

Max Leon Inc (PA) .... D....... 626 797-6886
  3100 New York Dr Ste 100 Pasadena (91107) **(P-2351)**

A L P H A B E T I C

Employee Codes: A=Over 500 employees, B=251-500
C=101-250, D=51-100, E=20-50, F=10-19, G=1-9

2024 Southern California
Business Directory and Buyers Guide

© Mergent Inc. 1-800-342-5647

1173

Max Muscle, Anaheim *Also Called: Joe Wells Enterprises Inc (P-2209)*

Max Q, Ontario *Also Called: Maximum Quality Metal Pdts Inc (P-6044)*

Max Studio.com, Pasadena *Also Called: Max Leon Inc (P-2351)*

Max Windsor Floors, Rancho Cucamonga *Also Called: Three Wise Men Inc (P-12317)*

Maxair Systems, Irvine *Also Called: Bio-Medical Devices Inc (P-10453)*

Maxim Healthcare Services Inc ....C...... 310 329-9115
1515 W 190th St Gardena (90248) *(P-15927)*

Maxim Healthcare Services Inc ....D...... 661 322-3039
5201 California Ave Ste 200 Bakersfield (93309) *(P-15928)*

Maxim Healthcare Services Inc ....D...... 661 964-6350
28470 Avenue Stanford Ste 250 Valencia (91355) *(P-15929)*

Maxim Healthcare Services Inc ....D...... 626 962-6453
801 Corporate Center Dr Ste 210 Pomona (91768) *(P-15930)*

Maxim Healthcare Services Inc ....D...... 951 684-4148
1845 Business Center Dr Ste 112 San Bernardino (92408) *(P-15931)*

Maxim Healthcare Services Inc ....C...... 951 694-0100
27555 Ynez Rd Temecula (92591) *(P-15932)*

Maxim Healthcare Services Inc ....B...... 866 465-5678
3580 Wilshire Blvd Ste 1000 Los Angeles (90010) *(P-18626)*

Maxim Healthcare Services Inc ....B...... 619 299-9350
3111 Camino Del Rio N Ste 1200 San Diego (92108) *(P-18627)*

Maxim Healthcare Services Inc ....C...... 760 243-3377
560 E Hospitality Ln Ste 400 San Bernardino (92408) *(P-18628)*

Maxim Lighting, City Of Industry *Also Called: Maxim Lighting Intl Inc (P-12606)*

Maxim Lighting Intl Inc ....E...... 626 956-4200
247 Vineland Ave City Of Industry (91746) *(P-8295)*

Maxim Lighting Intl Inc (PA).................................**C...... 626 956-4200**
253 Vineland Ave City Of Industry (91746) *(P-12606)*

Maxima Racing Oils, Santee *Also Called: South West Lubricants Inc (P-4688)*

Maximum Quality Metal Pdts Inc ....E...... 909 902-5018
1017 E Acacia St Ontario (91761) *(P-6044)*

Maxin, Tustin *Also Called: Core Holdings Inc (P-18605)*

Maxlinear Inc (PA).................................**E...... 760 692-0711**
5966 La Place Ct Ste 100 Carlsbad (92008) *(P-8836)*

Maxlinear Technologies LLC (HQ).................................C...... 760 692-0711
5966 La Place Ct Ste 100 Carlsbad (92008) *(P-8837)*

Maxon Industries Inc ....D...... 562 464-0099
11921 Slauson Ave Santa Fe Springs (90670) *(P-9420)*

Maxon Lift Corp (PA).................................**C...... 562 464-0099**
11921 Slauson Ave Santa Fe Springs (90670) *(P-12798)*

Maxtrol Corporation ....E...... 714 245-0506
1701 E Edinger Ave Ste B6 Santa Ana (92705) *(P-8701)*

Maxus USA, Los Angeles *Also Called: Essense (P-20395)*

Maxwell, San Diego *Also Called: Maxwell Technologies Inc (P-9170)*

Maxwell Alarm Screen Mfg Inc ....E...... 818 773-5533
20327 Nordhoff St Chatsworth (91311) *(P-11134)*

Maxwell Petersen Associates ....E...... 714 230-3150
412 Olive Ave Ste 208 Huntington Beach (92648) *(P-3369)*

Maxwell Sign and Decal Div, Chatsworth *Also Called: Maxwell Alarm Screen Mfg Inc (P-11134)*

Maxwell Technologies Inc ....D...... 858 503-3493
3912 Calle Fortunada San Diego (92123) *(P-8210)*

Maxwell Technologies Inc (HQ).................................D...... 858 503-3300
3888 Calle Fortunada San Diego (92123) *(P-9170)*

Maxxess Systems Inc (PA).................................**F...... 714 772-1000**
135 S State College Blvd Ste 200 Brea (92821) *(P-16301)*

Maxxon Company, City Of Industry *Also Called: Dennison Inc (P-6356)*

Maxzone Vehicle Lighting Corp (HQ).................................E...... 909 822-3288
15889 Slover Ave Unit A Fontana (92337) *(P-12246)*

Maya Steel Fabrications Inc ....D...... 310 532-8830
301 E Compton Blvd Gardena (90248) *(P-6045)*

Mayer Baking Co, Torrance *Also Called: Kopykake Enterprises Inc (P-6531)*

Mayer Brown & Platt, Los Angeles *Also Called: LLP Mayer Brown (P-18900)*

Mayoni Enterprises ....D...... 818 896-0026
10320 Glenoaks Blvd Pacoima (91331) *(P-6268)*

MAYWOOD ACRES HEALTHCARE, Oxnard *Also Called: Milwood Healthcare Inc (P-14674)*

Mazda Motor of America Inc (HQ).................................B...... 949 727-1990
200 Spectrum Center Dr Ste 100 Irvine (92618) *(P-9299)*

Mazda North Amercn Operations, Irvine *Also Called: Mazda Motor of America Inc (P-9299)*

Mazzei Injector Company LLC ....E...... 661 363-6500
500 Rooster Dr Bakersfield (93307) *(P-7672)*

MB Coatings Inc ....D...... 714 625-2118
1540 S Lewis St Anaheim (92805) *(P-16869)*

MB Herzog Electric Inc ....C...... 562 531-2002
15709 Illinois Ave Paramount (90723) *(P-916)*

MBC Systems, Santa Ana *Also Called: Medical Network Inc (P-20059)*

Mbe, Pasadena *Also Called: Ttg Engineers (P-19710)*

Mbit Wireless Inc (PA).................................**C...... 949 205-4559**
4340 Von Karman Ave Ste 140 Newport Beach (92660) *(P-11850)*

Mbp Land LLC ....A...... 619 291-5720
595 Hotel Cir S San Diego (92108) *(P-15245)*

Mc Allister Industries Inc (PA).................................**E...... 858 755-0683**
731 S Highway 101 Ste 2 Solana Beach (92075) *(P-3720)*

Mc Cann's Engineering & Mfg Co, La Mirada *Also Called: MEMC Liquidating Corporation (P-7209)*

Mc Products Inc ....E...... 949 888-7100
23331 Antonio Pkwy Rcho Sta Marg (92688) *(P-4620)*

Mc William & Son Inc ....F...... 626 969-1821
421 S Irwindale Ave Azusa (91702) *(P-6535)*

Mc-40 (PA).................................**C...... 323 225-4111**
777 N Georgia Ave Azusa (91702) *(P-15723)*

MC&a Usa LLC ....D...... 504 267-8145
19700 Mariner Ave Torrance (90503) *(P-446)*

McBain Systems A Cal Ltd Prtnr ....E...... 805 581-6800
810 Lawrence Dr Newbury Park (91320) *(P-12529)*

McCain Manufacturing Inc ....D...... 760 295-9290
2633 Progress St Vista (92081) *(P-6046)*

McCallum Theatre, Palm Desert *Also Called: Friends of Cultural Center Inc (P-17315)*

McCarthy Bldg Companies Inc ....B...... 949 851-8383
20401 Sw Birch St Ste 200 Newport Beach (92660) *(P-566)*

McCarthy Bldg Companies Inc ....D...... 949 851-8383
1113 Bush Orange (92868) *(P-567)*

McConnell Cabinets Inc ....A...... 626 937-2200
13110 Louden Ln City Of Industry (91746) *(P-2667)*

McConnells Fine Ice Creams LLC ....E...... 805 963-8813
800 Del Norte Blvd Oxnard (93030) *(P-13256)*

McCoppin Enterprises ....E...... 818 240-4840
6641 San Fernando Rd Glendale (91201) *(P-7923)*

McCrometer Inc (HQ).................................**C...... 951 652-6811**
3255 W Stetson Ave Hemet (92545) *(P-10145)*

McDonald Packaging Inc C
2601 S Garnsey St Santa Ana (92707) *(P-3118)*

McDowell Craig Off Systems Inc ....D...... 562 921-4441
13146 Firestone Blvd Norwalk (90650) *(P-2915)*

McDowell-Craig Office Furn, Norwalk *Also Called: McDowell Craig Off Systems Inc (P-2915)*

McElroy Metal, Adelanto *Also Called: McElroy Metal Mill Inc (P-6383)*

McElroy Metal Mill Inc ....E...... 760 246-5545
17031 Koala Rd Adelanto (92301) *(P-6383)*

McGuff Otsurcing Solutions Inc ....E...... 800 603-4795
2921 W Macarthur Blvd # 1 Santa Ana (92704) *(P-4164)*

MCI Foods Inc ....C...... 562 977-4000
13013 Molette St Santa Fe Springs (90670) *(P-1943)*

McK Enterprises Inc ....D...... 805 483-5292
910 Commercial Ave Oxnard (93030) *(P-1944)*

McKeever Danlee Confectionary ....D...... 626 334-8964
760 N Mckeever Ave Azusa (91702) *(P-1546)*

McKenna Boiler Works Inc ....E...... 323 221-1171
2601 Industry St Oceanside (92054) *(P-17138)*

McKenna Labs Inc (PA).................................**E...... 714 687-6888**
1601 E Orangethorpe Ave Fullerton (92831) *(P-4165)*

McKesson Corporation ....C...... 562 463-2100
9501 Norwalk Blvd Santa Fe Springs (90670) *(P-13053)*

McKesson Drug Company, Santa Fe Springs *Also Called: McKesson Corporation (P-13053)*

McKesson Mdcl-Srgcal Top Hldng ....B...... 800 300-4350
1938 W Malvern Ave Fullerton (92833) *(P-12498)*

McKinley Child Development Ctr ....D...... 562 531-6182
6822 N Paramount Blvd Long Beach (90805) *(P-19219)*

McKinley Childrens Center Inc (PA).................................**C...... 909 599-1227**
180 Via Verde Ste 200 San Dimas (91773) *(P-19285)*

McKinnon Enterprises ....F...... 858 571-1818
4577 Viewridge Ave San Diego (92123) *(P-3370)*

McKinnon Publishing Company ....A...... 858 571-5151
4575 Viewridge Ave San Diego (92123) *(P-11958)*

Mergent email: customerrelations@mergent.com
1174

2024 Southern California
Business Directory and Buyers Guide

(P-0000) Products & Services Section entry number
(PA)=Parent Co (HQ)=Headquarters (DH)=Div Headquarters

McL Fresh, Commerce *Also Called: 4 Earth Farms LLC (P-13311)*

McLane Foodservice Inc .... C....... 951 867-3727
14813 Meridian Pkwy Riverside (92518) *(P-13186)*

McLane Manufacturing Inc ....D..... 562 633-8158
6814 Foster Bridge Blvd Bell Gardens (90201) *(P-6919)*

McLane Riverside, Riverside *Also Called: McLane Foodservice Inc (P-13186)*

McLaren Strategic Solutions ....D..... 310 564-6754
1 Park Plz Ste 600 Irvine (92614) *(P-16579)*

McLeod Racing, Anaheim *Also Called: McLeod Racing LLC (P-9421)*

McLeod Racing LLC .... E....... 714 630-2764
1570 Lakeview Loop Anaheim (92807) *(P-9421)*

McM Fabricators Inc .... C....... 661 589-2774
720 Commerce Way Shafter (93263) *(P-6047)*

MCM Harvesters Inc .... B....... 805 659-6833
1585 Lirio Ave Ventura (93004) *(P-15866)*

McMahon Steel Company Inc .... C....... 619 671-9700
1880 Nirvana Ave Chula Vista (91911) *(P-5931)*

McMaster-Carr Supply Company .... B....... 562 692-5911
9630 Norwalk Blvd Santa Fe Springs (90670) *(P-12864)*

McMillin Communities Inc .... A....... 951 506-3303
41687 Temeku Dr Temecula (92591) *(P-17437)*

McMillin Companies LLC (PA).. **D..... 619 477-4117**
2750 Womble Rd Ste 102 San Diego (92106) *(P-15036)*

McMillin Homes, San Diego *Also Called: McMillin Companies LLC (P-15036)*

McMurtrie & Mcmurtrie Inc .... E....... 626 815-0177
915 W 5th St Azusa (91702) *(P-2576)*

McNeilus Truck and Mfg Inc .... E....... 909 370-2100
401 N Pepper Ave Colton (92324) *(P-9331)*

McNichols, Cerritos *Also Called: McNichols Company (P-12559)*

McNichols Company ....F....... 562 921-3344
14108 Arbor Pl Cerritos (90703) *(P-12559)*

McO Inc .... E....... 909 627-3574
13925 Benson Ave Chino (91710) *(P-9422)*

McQ, Burbank *Also Called: Silver Saddle Ranch & Club Inc (P-14911)*

MCR Printing and Packg Corp .... C....... 619 488-3012
8830 Siempre Viva Rd San Diego (92154) *(P-11597)*

McStarlite, Harbor City *Also Called: Basmat Inc (P-6198)*

McWhirter Steel Inc ....D..... 661 951-8998
42211 7th St E Lancaster (93535) *(P-6048)*

MD Engineering Inc .... E....... 951 736-5390
1550 Consumer Cir Corona (92878) *(P-7924)*

MD Stainless Services .... E....... 562 904-7022
8241 Phlox St Downey (90241) *(P-6849)*

Md-Staff, Temecula *Also Called: Applied Statistics & MGT Inc (P-16174)*

Mdc Interior Solutions LLC .... E....... 800 621-4006
6900 E Washington Blvd Los Angeles (90040) *(P-2455)*

Mddr Inc .... C....... 714 792-1993
1921 Petra Ln Placentia (92870) *(P-792)*

Mdm Solutions LLC .... B....... 800 669-6361
575 Anton Blvd Ste 300 Costa Mesa (92626) *(P-361)*

ME & My Big Ideas LLC .... C....... 240 348-5240
6261 Katella Ave Cypress (90630) *(P-12939)*

Meadow Lake Country Club, Escondido *Also Called: Welk Group Inc (P-17535)*

Meadowbrook Vlg Chrstn Rtrment .... C....... 760 746-2500
100 Holland Gln Escondido (92026) *(P-19286)*

Meadows Mechanical, Gardena *Also Called: Meadows Sheet Metal and AC Inc (P-6269)*

Meadows Sheet Metal and AC Inc .... E....... 310 615-1125
333 Crown Vista Dr Gardena (90248) *(P-6269)*

Means Engineering Inc ....D..... 760 931-9452
5927 Geiger Ct Carlsbad (92008) *(P-10273)*

Mearsk, San Pedro *Also Called: APM Terminals Pacific LLC (P-11741)*

Measure of Excellence Cabinets, Poway *Also Called: Kiewit Corporation (P-562)*

Measure Uas Inc .... E....... 714 916-6166
5862 Bolsa Ave Ste 104 Huntington Beach (92649) *(P-10379)*

Measurement Specialties Inc ....D..... 818 701-2750
9131 Oakdale Ave Ste 170 Chatsworth (91311) *(P-10380)*

Measurment Instrmnttion Cntrls .... E....... 661 401-0070
2960 Pacini St Bakersfield (93314) *(P-12799)*

Meat Packers Butchers Sup Inc ....F....... 323 268-8514
2820 E Washington Blvd Los Angeles (90023) *(P-7208)*

Mec-CCC S All N One .... E....... 909 529-0013
13800 Parkcenter Ln Apt 304 Tustin (92782) *(P-362)*

Mechancal Systm-Rial Refueling, Yorba Linda *Also Called: GE Aviation Systems LLC (P-9697)*

Mechanix Wear, Valencia *Also Called: Mechanix Wear LLC (P-2422)*

Mechanix Wear LLC (PA).. **E....... 800 222-4296**
27335 Tourney Rd Valencia (91355) *(P-2422)*

Mechanized Science Seals Inc .... E....... 714 898-5602
5322 Mcfadden Ave Huntington Beach (92649) *(P-10381)*

Meco-Nag Corporation .... E....... 818 764-2020
7306 Laurel Canyon Blvd North Hollywood (91605) *(P-5277)*

Med Couture Inc ....D..... 214 231-2500
9800 De Soto Ave Chatsworth (91311) *(P-2180)*

Med-Fit Systems Inc ....F....... 760 723-3618
3553 Rosa Way Fallbrook (92028) *(P-11013)*

Med-Legal LLC .... C....... 626 653-5160
955 Overland Ct Ste 200 San Dimas (91773) *(P-18905)*

Med-Pharmex Inc .... C....... 909 593-7875
2727 Thompson Creek Rd Pomona (91767) *(P-4166)*

Med-Safe Systems Inc .... E....... 855 236-2772
10975 Torreyana Rd San Diego (92121) *(P-10553)*

Medasend Biomedical Inc (PA)...................................... **E....... 800 200-3581**
1402 Daisy Ave Long Beach (90813) *(P-18780)*

Medata Inc (PA).. **D..... 714 918-1310**
5 Peters Canyon Rd Ste 250 Irvine (92606) *(P-16302)*

Medegen LLC (DH).. **E....... 909 390-9080**
4501 E Wall St Ontario (91761) *(P-5092)*

Medegen Inc .... C....... 909 390-9080
930 S Wanamaker Ave Ontario (91761) *(P-5093)*

Medennium Inc (PA).. **E....... 949 789-9000**
9 Parker Ste 150 Irvine (92618) *(P-10844)*

Medgear, Cerritos *Also Called: LA Triumph Inc (P-2178)*

Medholdings of Newnan LLC .... A....... 213 462-6252
1750 Vine St Los Angeles (90028) *(P-16870)*

Media Blast & Abrasive Inc ....F....... 714 257-0484
591 Apollo St Brea (92821) *(P-7673)*

Media Gobbler Inc ....F....... 323 203-3222
6427 W Sunset Blvd Los Angeles (90028) *(P-16303)*

Media Nation, Lake Forest *Also Called: Media Nation Enterprises LLC (P-11135)*

Media Nation Enterprises LLC .... E....... 714 371-9494
25361 Commercentre Dr Ste 100 Lake Forest (92630) *(P-11135)*

Media Nation Enterprises LLC (PA)................................ **E....... 888 502-8222**
15271 Barranca Pkwy Irvine (92618) *(P-11136)*

Media Nation USA, Irvine *Also Called: Media Nation Enterprises LLC (P-11136)*

Media Services, Los Angeles *Also Called: Oberman Tivoli & Pickert Inc (P-16464)*

Media Temple Inc .... C....... 877 578-4000
12655 W Jefferson Blvd # 400 Los Angeles (90066) *(P-11891)*

Mediaalpha Inc (PA)... **D..... 213 316-6256**
700 S Flower St Ste 640 Los Angeles (90017) *(P-15596)*

Mediabrands Worldwide Inc .... B....... 323 370-8000
1840 Century Park E Los Angeles (90067) *(P-15557)*

Mediamorph Inc (HQ)... **E....... 212 643-0762**
1841 Centinela Ave Santa Monica (90404) *(P-16304)*

Medianews Group Inc .... E....... 562 435-1161
300 Oceangate Ste 150 Long Beach (90802) *(P-3303)*

Medianews Group Inc .... C....... 818 713-3000
605 E Huntington Dr Ste 100 Monrovia (91016) *(P-3304)*

Medianews Group Inc .... E....... 310 540-5511
5215 Torrance Blvd Torrance (90503) *(P-3305)*

Mediapointe Inc .... E....... 805 480-3700
3952 Camino Ranchero Camarillo (93012) *(P-8423)*

Mediatek USA Inc .... C....... 408 526-1899
1 Ada Ste 200 Irvine (92618) *(P-7439)*

Mediatek USA Inc .... C....... 858 731-9200
10188 Telesis Ct Ste 500 San Diego (92121) *(P-12426)*

Medic-1 Ambulance Service Inc ....D..... 909 592-8840
1305 W Arrow Hwy Ste 206 San Dimas (91773) *(P-11394)*

Medical Billing Services, Monrovia *Also Called: California Business Bureau Inc (P-19758)*

Medical Brkthrugh Mssage Chirs .... E....... 408 677-7702
24971 Avenue Stanford Valencia (91355) *(P-11250)*

Medical Center, San Diego *Also Called: University Cal San Diego (P-18486)*

Employee Codes: A=Over 500 employees, B=251-500
C=101-250, D=51-100, E=20-50, F=10-19, G=1-9

2024 Southern California
Business Directory and Buyers Guide

© Mergent Inc. 1-800-342-5647
1175

Medical Chemical Corporation ....E...... 310 787-6800
19250 Van Ness Ave Torrance (90501) *(P-4621)*

Medical Data Exchange, Anaheim *Also Called: Cyber-Pro Systems Inc (P-16489)*

Medical Depot Inc ....E...... 877 224-0946
548 W Merrill Ave Rialto (92376) *(P-10554)*

Medical Device Manufacturing, Brea *Also Called: Life Science Outsourcing Inc (P-10546)*

Medical Extrusion Tech Inc (PA).................................**E... 951 698-4346**
26608 Pierce Cir Ste A Murrieta (92562) *(P-5094)*

Medical Eye Services Inc ....D...... 714 619-4660
345 Baker St Costa Mesa (92626) *(P-14612)*

Medical Genetics, Los Angeles *Also Called: Cedars-Sinai Medical Center (P-18208)*

Medical Illumination International Inc (PA).........**F... 818 838-3025**
19749 Dearborn St Chatsworth (91311) *(P-8322)*

Medical Management Cons Inc ....A...... 858 587-0609
6046 Cornerstone Ct W San Diego (92121) *(P-20196)*

Medical Network Inc ....D...... 949 863-0022
1809 E Dyer Rd Ste 311 Santa Ana (92705) *(P-20059)*

Medical Packaging Corporation ....D...... 805 388-2383
941 Avenida Acaso Camarillo (93012) *(P-10680)*

Medical Research Institute ....C...... 818 739-6000
21411 Prairie St Chatsworth (91311) *(P-13054)*

Medical Spc Managers Inc ....C...... 714 571-5000
1 City Blvd W Ste 1100 Orange (92868) *(P-20197)*

Medical Specialty Billing, Orange *Also Called: Medical Spc Managers Inc (P-20197)*

Medical Tactile Inc ....E...... 310 641-8228
5500 W Rosecrans Ave Ste A Hawthorne (90250) *(P-10555)*

Medico Professional Linen Svc, Los Angeles *Also Called: American Textile Maint Co (P-15446)*

Medicool Inc ....F...... 310 782-2200
20460 Gramercy Pl Torrance (90501) *(P-10556)*

Medieval Times Entrmt Inc (HQ).................................**A... 714 523-1100**
7662 Beach Blvd Buena Park (90620) *(P-15443)*

Mediland Corporation ....D...... 562 630-9696
15 Longitude Way Corona (92881) *(P-5317)*

Medimizer, San Diego *Also Called: Medimizer Software (P-16072)*

Medimizer Software ....E...... 760 642-2000
9920 Pacific Heights Blvd Ste 150 San Diego (92121) *(P-16072)*

Medimpact Hlthcare Systems Inc (HQ).................**C... 858 566-2727**
10181 Scripps Gateway Ct San Diego (92131) *(P-19397)*

Medimpact Holdings Inc (PA).................................**A... 858 566-2727**
10181 Scripps Gateway Ct San Diego (92131) *(P-15037)*

Medina Construction, Riverside *Also Called: Bens Asphalt & Maint Co Inc (P-611)*

Mediscan Diagnostic Svcs LLC ....D...... 818 758-4224
21050 Califa St Ste 100 Woodland Hills (91367) *(P-15867)*

Mediscan Staffing Services, Woodland Hills *Also Called: Mediscan Diagnostic Svcs LLC (P-15867)*

Medix Ambulance Service Inc (PA).................................**C... 949 470-8915**
26021 Pala Mission Viejo (92691) *(P-11395)*

Medley Communications Inc (PA).................................**C... 951 245-5200**
43015 Black Deer Loop Ste 203 Temecula (92590) *(P-917)*

Medlin & Sons, Whittier *Also Called: Medlin and Son Engrg Svc Inc (P-7925)*

Medlin and Son Engrg Svc Inc ....E...... 562 464-5889
12484 Whittier Blvd Whittier (90602) *(P-7925)*

Medlin Ramps ....E...... 877 463-3546
14903 Marquardt Ave Santa Fe Springs (90670) *(P-7033)*

Medline Industries LP ....E...... 951 296-2600
42500 Winchester Rd Temecula (92590) *(P-10681)*

Medresponse (PA).................................**C... 818 442-9222**
7040 Hayvenhurst Ave Van Nuys (91406) *(P-11396)*

Medsco Fabrication & Dist Inc ....D...... 323 263-0511
938 N Eastern Ave Los Angeles (90063) *(P-6049)*

Medterra Cbd LLC ....D...... 800 971-1288
18500 Von Karman Ave Irvine (92612) *(P-5)*

Medtronic, San Diego *Also Called: Medtronic Inc (P-10557)*

Medtronic, Carlsbad *Also Called: Medtronic Inc (P-10558)*

Medtronic, Irvine *Also Called: Medtronic Inc (P-10559)*

Medtronic, Northridge *Also Called: Medtronic Minimed Inc (P-10562)*

Medtronic, Irvine *Also Called: Medtronic PS Medical Inc (P-10563)*

Medtronic Inc ....E...... 949 798-3934
1659 Gailes Blvd San Diego (92154) *(P-10557)*

Medtronic Inc ....E...... 760 214-3009
2101 Faraday Ave Carlsbad (92008) *(P-10558)*

Medtronic Inc ....C...... 949 837-3700
9775 Toledo Way Irvine (92618) *(P-10559)*

Medtronic Inc ....B...... 949 474-3943
1851 E Deere Ave Santa Ana (92705) *(P-10560)*

Medtronic 3f Therapeutics Inc ....C...... 949 399-1675
1851 E Deere Ave Santa Ana (92705) *(P-10815)*

Medtronic Ats Medical Inc ....C...... 949 380-9333
1851 E Deere Ave Santa Ana (92705) *(P-10561)*

Medtronic Minimed Inc (DH).................................**A... 800 646-4633**
18000 Devonshire St Northridge (91325) *(P-10562)*

Medtronic PS Medical Inc (DH).................................**C... 805 571-3769**
5290 California Ave # 100 Irvine (92617) *(P-10563)*

Medusind Solutions Inc (PA).................................**D... 949 240-8895**
31103 Rancho Viejo Rd Ste 2150 San Juan Capistrano (92675) *(P-16871)*

Medway Plastics Corporation ....C...... 562 630-1175
2250 E Cherry Industrial Cir Long Beach (90805) *(P-5095)*

Meeder Equipment Company ....F...... 909 463-0600
12323 6th St Rancho Cucamonga (91739) *(P-19644)*

Meeting Services Inc ....D...... 858 348-0100
1125 Joshua Way Vista (92081) *(P-15785)*

Mega Appraisers Inc ....A...... 818 246-7370
14724 Ventura Blvd Ste 800 Sherman Oaks (91403) *(P-16872)*

Mega Brands America Inc (DH).................................**D... 949 727-9009**
333 Continental Blvd El Segundo (90245) *(P-10961)*

Mega Machinery Inc ....E...... 951 300-9300
6688 Doolittle Ave Riverside (92503) *(P-7247)*

Mega Toys, Commerce *Also Called: PC Woo Inc (P-12942)*

Meganutra Inc ....E...... 949 331-2503
17332 Irvine Blvd Ste 232 Tustin (92780) *(P-1277)*

Meggitt (orange County) Inc (DH).................................**B... 949 493-8181**
4 Marconi Irvine (92618) *(P-10382)*

Meggitt (san Diego) Inc (HQ).................................**C... 858 824-8976**
6650 Top Gun St San Diego (92121) *(P-9746)*

Meggitt Arcft Braking Systems, Gardena *Also Called: Nasco Aircraft Brake Inc (P-9755)*

Meggitt Control Systems, North Hollywood *Also Called: Meggitt North Hollywood Inc (P-9748)*

Meggitt Ctrl Systms-Vntura Cnt, Simi Valley *Also Called: Meggitt Safety Systems Inc (P-9228)*

Meggitt Defense Systems Inc ....B...... 949 465-7700
9801 Muirlands Blvd Irvine (92618) *(P-9747)*

Meggitt North Hollywood Inc (DH).................................**C... 818 765-8160**
12838 Saticoy St North Hollywood (91605) *(P-9748)*

Meggitt North Hollywood Inc ....E...... 818 691-6258
10092 Foxrun Rd Santa Ana (92705) *(P-9749)*

Meggitt Polymers & Composites, San Diego *Also Called: Meggitt (san Diego) Inc (P-9746)*

Meggitt Polymers & Composites, Simi Valley *Also Called: Meggitt-Usa Inc (P-9752)*

Meggitt Safety Systems Inc (DH).................................**C... 805 584-4100**
1785 Voyager Ave Simi Valley (93063) *(P-9228)*

Meggitt Safety Systems Inc ....D...... 805 584-4100
1785 Voyager Ave Simi Valley (93063) *(P-9750)*

Meggitt Safety Systems Inc ....C...... 805 584-4100
1785 Voyager Ave Simi Valley (93063) *(P-9751)*

Meggitt Sensing Systems, Irvine *Also Called: Meggitt (orange County) Inc (P-10382)*

Meggitt Western Design Inc ....C...... 949 465-7700
9801 Muirlands Blvd Irvine (92618) *(P-10105)*

Meggitt-Usa Inc (DH).................................**B... 805 526-5700**
1955 Surveyor Ave Simi Valley (93063) *(P-9752)*

Megiddo Global LLC ....E...... 844 477-7007
17101 Central Ave Ste 1c Carson (90746) *(P-10682)*

Meguiars Inc (HQ).................................**E... 949 752-8000**
213 Technology Dr Irvine (92618) *(P-4360)*

MEI Pharma, San Diego *Also Called: MEI Pharma Inc (P-4167)*

MEI Pharma Inc ....E...... 858 369-7100
11455 El Camino Real Ste 250 San Diego (92130) *(P-4167)*

MEI Rigging & Crating LLC ....D...... 714 712-5888
14555 Alondra Blvd La Mirada (90638) *(P-7248)*

Meissner Filtration Pdts Inc (PA).................................**E... 805 388-9911**
1001 Flynn Rd Camarillo (93012) *(P-8946)*

Meissner Mfg Co Inc (PA).................................**D... 818 678-0400**
21701 Prairie St Chatsworth (91311) *(P-7674)*

Mergent email: customerrelations@mergent.com
1176

2024 Southern California
Business Directory and Buyers Guide

(P-0000) Products & Services Section entry number
(PA)=Parent Co (HQ)=Headquarters (DH)=Div Headquarters

Mejico Express Inc (PA)..C...... 714 690-8300
  14849 Firestone Blvd Fl 1 La Mirada (90638) *(P-11677)*

Mek Enterprises Inc ....D...... 619 527-0957
  3517 Camino Del Rio S Ste 215 San Diego (92108) *(P-11822)*

Mek Escondido LLC ....C...... 760 747-0430
  421 E Mission Ave Escondido (92025) *(P-18012)*

Mek Industries Inc ....C...... 858 610-9601
  3517 Camino Del Rio S Ste 215 San Diego (92108) *(P-15933)*

Mekong Printing Inc ....E...... 714 558-9595
  2421 W 1st St Santa Ana (92703) *(P-3633)*

Mel Bernie and Company Inc (PA)..........................C...... 818 841-1928
  3000 W Empire Ave Burbank (91504) *(P-12965)*

Melan Inc ....D...... 818 489-1745
  13700 Alton Pkwy Ste 154-2 Irvine (92618) *(P-17139)*

Melano Enterprises, Oceanside *Also Called: Mellano & Co (P-13513)*

Melcast, Cerritos *Also Called: Molino Company (P-3640)*

Melco Steel Inc ....E...... 626 334-7875
  1100 W Foothill Blvd Azusa (91702) *(P-6145)*

Melfred Borzall Inc ....E...... 805 614-4344
  2712 Airpark Dr Santa Maria (93455) *(P-7016)*

Melin LLC ....E...... 323 489-3274
  10 Faraday Irvine (92618) *(P-11014)*

Melissa Data Corporation (PA)..............................D...... 949 858-3000
  22382 Avenida Empresa Rcho Sta Marg (92688) *(P-16073)*

Melissa Trinidad ....E...... 805 536-0954
  3589 Vine St Paso Robles (93446) *(P-4434)*

Melissas World Variety Produce, Vernon *Also Called: World Variety Produce Inc (P-13349)*

Melkes Machine Inc ....E...... 626 448-5062
  9928 Hayward Way South El Monte (91733) *(P-7926)*

Mellace Family Brands Inc ....E...... 760 448-1940
  6195 El Camino Real Carlsbad (92009) *(P-1556)*

Mellace Family Brands Cal Inc ....E...... 760 448-1940
  6195 El Camino Real Carlsbad (92009) *(P-1557)*

Mellano & Co ....C...... 760 433-9550
  734 Wilshire Rd Oceanside (92057) *(P-13513)*

Melles Griot Inc ....E...... 760 438-2131
  2072 Corte Del Nogal Carlsbad (92011) *(P-10327)*

Melles Griot Inc ....D...... 760 438-2254
  2051 Palomar Airport Rd # 200 Carlsbad (92011) *(P-10328)*

Melling Sintered Metals, Gardena *Also Called: Melling Tool Rush Metals LLC (P-5854)*

Melling Tool Rush Metals LLC ....E...... 580 725-3295
  16100 S Figueroa St Gardena (90248) *(P-5854)*

Mellmo Inc ....C...... 858 847-3272
  131 Aberdeen Dr Cardiff By The Sea (92007) *(P-16074)*

Mellon, Los Angeles *Also Called: Bny Mellon National Assn (P-14160)*

Mellon, Newport Beach *Also Called: Bny Mellon National Assn (P-14180)*

Melmarc Products Inc ....C...... 714 549-2170
  752 S Campus Ave Ontario (91761) *(P-2519)*

Melton Intl Tackle Inc ....E...... 714 978-9192
  1375 S State College Blvd Anaheim (92806) *(P-14095)*

MEMC Liquidating Corporation ....D...... 818 637-7200
  4570 Colorado Blvd La Mirada (90638) *(P-7209)*

Memco Holdings Inc ....C...... 310 277-0057
  10390 Santa Monica Blvd # 210 Los Angeles (90025) *(P-14831)*

Memeged Tevuot Shemesh (PA)............................C...... 866 575-1211
  5550 Topanga Canyon Blvd Ste 280 Woodland Hills (91367) *(P-793)*

Memorex Products Inc ....C...... 562 653-2800
  17777 Center Court Dr N Ste 800 Cerritos (90703) *(P-12634)*

Memorial Care Medical Centers, Fountain Valley *Also Called: Memorial Health Services (P-18342)*

Memorial Center, Bakersfield *Also Called: Bakersfield Memorial Hospital (P-18189)*

Memorial Health Services (PA)...............................B...... 714 377-2900
  17360 Brookhurst St Ste 160 Fountain Valley (92708) *(P-18342)*

Memorial Healthtec Labratories ....A...... 714 962-4677
  9920 Talbert Ave Fountain Valley (92708) *(P-19859)*

Memorial Hlth Svcs - Univ Cal (PA).........................A...... 562 933-2000
  2801 Atlantic Ave Long Beach (90806) *(P-18343)*

Memorial Hospital of Gardena ....B...... 323 268-5514
  4060 Woody Blvd Los Angeles (90023) *(P-18344)*

Memorial Hospital of Gardena, Gardena *Also Called: Gardena Hospital LP (P-18263)*

Memorial Medical Center Foundation ....A...... 562 933-2273
  2801 Atlantic Ave Long Beach (90806) *(P-19532)*

Memorlcare Heart Vascular Inst, Laguna Hills *Also Called: Saddleback Memorial Med Ctr (P-18411)*

Memory Experts Intl USA Inc (HQ)..........................E...... **714 258-3000**
  2102 Business Center Dr Irvine (92612) *(P-7477)*

Menke Marketing Devices, Santa Fe Springs *Also Called: Menke Marking Devices Inc (P-12800)*

Menke Marking Devices Inc ....E...... 562 921-1380
  10440 Pioneer Blvd Ste 4 Santa Fe Springs (90670) *(P-12800)*

Mens Apparel Guild In Cal Inc ....D...... 310 857-7500
  2901 28th St Ste 100 Santa Monica (90405) *(P-19381)*

Mentor California, Bakersfield *Also Called: Alliance Childrens Services (P-19236)*

Mentor Mdia USA Sup Chain MGT ....D...... 909 930-0800
  865 S Washington Ave San Bernardino (92408) *(P-20060)*

Mentor Worldwide LLC (DH).................................C...... **800 636-8678**
  31 Technology Dr Ste 200 Irvine (92618) *(P-10683)*

Mentor Worldwide LLC ....B...... 805 681-6000
  5425 Hollister Ave Santa Barbara (93111) *(P-12499)*

Meow Logistics, Walnut *Also Called: Straight Forwarding Inc (P-11806)*

Meps Real-Time Inc ....E...... 760 448-9500
  12220 World Trade Dr Ste 210 San Diego (92128) *(P-10383)*

Mer-Kote Products Inc ....E...... 714 778-2266
  4125 E La Palma Ave Ste 250 Anaheim (92807) *(P-3954)*

Mer-Mar Electronics, Hesperia *Also Called: Geeriraj Inc (P-8681)*

Mercado Latino Inc ....D...... 310 537-1062
  1420 W Walnut St Compton (90220) *(P-11251)*

Mercado Latino Inc (PA).......................................D...... **626 333-6862**
  245 Baldwin Park Blvd City Of Industry (91746) *(P-13187)*

Mercedes Benz of Bakersfield, Bakersfield *Also Called: Sangera Buick Inc (P-17038)*

Mercedes Benz of Escondido, Escondido *Also Called: Escondido Motors LLC (P-13763)*

Mercedes Benz of Riverside, Riverside *Also Called: Walters Auto Sales and Svc Inc (P-13846)*

Mercedes Benz of San Diego, San Diego *Also Called: Europa Auto Imports Inc (P-13764)*

Mercfuel LLC ....F...... 310 827-5778
  2780 Skypark Dr Ste 300 Torrance (90505) *(P-4525)*

Merchant of Tennis Inc ....A...... 909 923-3388
  1625 Proforma Ave Ontario (91761) *(P-16873)*

Merchant Services, Irvine *Also Called: Universal Card Inc (P-16949)*

Merchants Building Maint Co ....A...... 909 622-8260
  1995 W Holt Ave Pomona (91768) *(P-15724)*

Merchants Building Maint Co ....C...... 323 881-8902
  606 Monterey Pass Rd Ste 202 Monterey Park (91754) *(P-15725)*

Merchants Building Maint Co ....B...... 858 455-0163
  9555 Distribution Ave Ste 102 San Diego (92121) *(P-15726)*

Merchants Building Maint Co ....B...... 714 973-9272
  1639 E Edinger Ave Ste C Santa Ana (92705) *(P-15727)*

Merchants Building Maintenance, Pomona *Also Called: Merchants Building Maint Co (P-15724)*

Merchants Building Maintenance, Santa Ana *Also Called: Merchants Building Maint Co (P-15727)*

Merchants Landscape Services ....D...... 909 981-1022
  8748 Industrial Ln # 1 Rancho Cucamonga (91730) *(P-167)*

Merchants Landscape Services ....D...... 619 778-6239
  2865 Main St Ste A Chula Vista (91911) *(P-205)*

Merchants Metals, Riverside *Also Called: Merchants Metals LLC (P-5619)*

Merchants Metals LLC ....D...... 951 686-1888
  6466 Mission Blvd Riverside (92509) *(P-5619)*

Merchsource LLC (DH)...C...... **800 374-2744**
  7755 Irvine Center Dr Irvine (92618) *(P-12940)*

Merco Manufacturing Co, Walnut *Also Called: Aero Pacific Corporation (P-9598)*

Mercotac Inc ....F...... 760 431-7723
  6195 Corte Del Cedro Ste 100 Carlsbad (92011) *(P-8270)*

Mercury Broach Co Inc ....F...... 626 443-5904
  2546 Seaman Ave El Monte (91733) *(P-7119)*

Mercury Casualty Company (HQ).............................A...... 323 937-1060
  555 W Imperial Hwy Brea (92821) *(P-14512)*

Mercury Computer System Inc ....E...... 760 494-9600
  1815 Aston Ave Ste 107 Carlsbad (92008) *(P-7440)*

Mercury Defense Systems Inc ....D...... 714 898-8200
  10855 Business Center Dr Ste A Cypress (90630) *(P-16504)*

Mercury Engineering Corp ....E...... 562 861-7816
  5630 Imperial Hwy South Gate (90280) *(P-7927)*

Employee Codes: A=Over 500 employees, B=251-500
C=101-250, D=51-100, E=20-50, F=10-19, G=1-9

2024 Southern California
Business Directory and Buyers Guide

© Mergent Inc. 1-800-342-5647

1177

A
L
P
H
A
B
E
T
I
C

Mercury General, Los Angeles *Also Called: Mercury General Corporation (P-14513)*

Mercury General Corporation (PA)..........................**A......323 937-1060**
4484 Wilshire Blvd Los Angeles (90010) *(P-14513)*

Mercury Insurance Broker, Santa Monica *Also Called: Mercury Insurance Company (P-14519)*

Mercury Insurance Company (HQ)...........................**C......323 937-1060**
4484 Wilshire Blvd Los Angeles (90010) *(P-14514)*

Mercury Insurance Company ....D......714 671-6700
555 W Imperial Hwy Brea (92821) *(P-14515)*

Mercury Insurance Company ....A......714 255-5000
1700 Greenbriar Ln Brea (92821) *(P-14516)*

Mercury Insurance Company ....A......858 694-4100
9635 Granite Ridge Dr Ste 200 San Diego (92123) *(P-14517)*

Mercury Insurance Company ....A......661 291-6470
27200 Tourney Rd Ste 400 Valencia (91355) *(P-14518)*

Mercury Insurance Company ....B......310 451-4943
1433 Santa Monica Blvd Santa Monica (90404) *(P-14519)*

Mercury Insurance Group, Brea *Also Called: Mercury Insurance Company (P-14515)*

Mercury Insurance Services LLC (PA)......................A......323 937-1060
4484 Wilshire Blvd Los Angeles (90010) *(P-14520)*

Mercury LLC - Rf Integrated Solutions ....C......805 388-1345
1000 Avenida Acaso Camarillo (93012) *(P-9083)*

Mercury Magnetics Inc ....E......818 998-7791
10050 Remmet Ave Chatsworth (91311) *(P-8947)*

Mercury Mission Systems LLC ....E......310 320-3088
20701 Manhattan Pl Torrance (90501) *(P-19860)*

Mercury Plastics Inc (HQ)....................................**B......626 961-0165**
14825 Salt Lake Ave City Of Industry (91746) *(P-3186)*

Mercury Plastics Inc ....D......323 264-2400
2939 E Washington Blvd Los Angeles (90023) *(P-4814)*

Mercury Security Products LLC ....F......562 986-9105
4811 Airport Plaza Dr Ste 300 Long Beach (90815) *(P-9229)*

Mercury Systems, Cypress *Also Called: Mercury Defense Systems Inc (P-16504)*

Mercury Systems Inc ....C......805 388-1345
400 Del Norte Blvd Oxnard (93030) *(P-8702)*

Mercury Systems Inc ....C......805 751-1100
300 Del Norte Blvd Oxnard (93030) *(P-8703)*

Mercury Systems Inc ....D......714 898-8200
10855 Business Center Dr Ste A Cypress (90630) *(P-16505)*

Mercy Air Tri-County LLC ....C......909 829-1051
1670 Miro Way Rialto (92376) *(P-17064)*

Mercy For Animals Inc ....C......347 839-6464
8033 W Sunset Blvd Ste 864 Los Angeles (90046) *(P-123)*

Mercy Hospital, Bakersfield *Also Called: Dean L Davis MD (P-19070)*

Mercy House Living Centers ....C......714 836-7188
807 N Garfield St Santa Ana (92701) *(P-19382)*

Mercy Hse Trnstnal Living Ctrs, Santa Ana *Also Called: Mercy House Living Centers (P-19382)*

Mercy Medical Trnsp Inc ....C......760 739-8026
27350 Valley Center Rd Ste A Valley Center (92082) *(P-11397)*

Meredith Baer & Associates, South Gate *Also Called: Meribear Productions Inc (P-16874)*

Merelex Corporation ....E......310 208-0551
10884 Weyburn Ave Los Angeles (90024) *(P-3899)*

Merex Inc ....E......805 446-2700
1283 Flynn Rd Camarillo (93012) *(P-10216)*

Merger Sub Gotham 2 LLC ....C......714 462-4603
6261 Katella Ave Ste 250 Cypress (90630) *(P-5096)*

Meribear Productions Inc ....D......310 204-5353
4100 Ardmore Ave South Gate (90280) *(P-16874)*

Merical, Anaheim *Also Called: B & C Nutritional Products Inc (P-3991)*

Merical LLC ....C......714 685-0977
447 W Freedom Ave Orange (92865) *(P-16875)*

Merical LLC ....B......714 283-9551
233 E Bristol Ln Orange (92865) *(P-16876)*

Merical LLC ....C......714 238-7225
445 W Freedom Ave Orange (92865) *(P-16877)*

Merical/Vita-Pak, Orange *Also Called: Merical LLC (P-16876)*

Meridian, San Diego *Also Called: Meridian Rack & Pinion Inc (P-12247)*

Meridian Graphics Inc ....D......949 833-3500
2652 Dow Ave Tustin (92780) *(P-3634)*

Meridian Optical, San Diego *Also Called: Essilor Laboratories Amer Inc (P-10838)*

Meridian Rack & Pinion Inc ....C......888 875-0026
9980 Huennekens St Ste 200 San Diego (92121) *(P-12247)*

Meridian Rail Acquisition ....C......909 478-0541
1475 Cooley Ct San Bernardino (92408) *(P-11836)*

Meridian Vineyards, Paso Robles *Also Called: Treasury Wine Estates Americas (P-36)*

Meristar San Pedro Hilton LLC ....D......310 514-3344
2800 Via Cabrillo Marina San Pedro (90731) *(P-15246)*

Merit Aluminum Inc (PA)......................................**C......951 735-1770**
2480 Railroad St Corona (92878) *(P-5703)*

Merit Companies The, Irvine *Also Called: Firstsrvice Rsidential Cal LLC (P-14802)*

Merit Day Food Service, Pico Rivera *Also Called: Three Sons Inc (P-13309)*

Merit Medical Systems Inc ....E......801 208-4793
6 Journey Ste 125 Aliso Viejo (92656) *(P-10564)*

Meritek Electronics Corp (PA).............................**D......626 373-1728**
5160 Rivergrade Rd Baldwin Park (91706) *(P-7249)*

Merito.com, Van Nuys *Also Called: Chef Merito LLC (P-1869)*

Merle Norman Cosmetics, Los Angeles *Also Called: Merle Norman Cosmetics Inc (P-4435)*

Merle Norman Cosmetics Inc (PA)........................**B......310 641-3000**
9130 Bellanca Ave Los Angeles (90045) *(P-4435)*

Merlex Stucco Inc ....E......877 547-8822
2911 N Orange Olive Rd Orange (92865) *(P-5570)*

Merlex Stucco Mfg, Orange *Also Called: Merlex Stucco Inc (P-5570)*

Merlot Film Productions Inc ....D......323 575-2906
7800 Beverly Blvd Los Angeles (90036) *(P-17200)*

Merqbiz LLC ....E......855 637-7249
300 Continental Blvd Ste 640 El Segundo (90245) *(P-14096)*

Merrick Engineering Inc (PA)...............................**C......951 737-6040**
1275 Quarry St Corona (92879) *(P-5097)*

Merrill Lynch, Costa Mesa *Also Called: Merrill Lynch Prce Fnner Smith (P-14388)*

Merrill Lynch, Pasadena *Also Called: Merrill Lynch Prce Fnner Smith (P-14390)*

Merrill Lynch Carlsbad Office, Carlsbad *Also Called: Merrill Lynch Prce Fnner Smith (P-14389)*

Merrill Lynch Prce Fnner Smith ....D......714 429-2800
650 Town Center Dr # 500 Costa Mesa (92626) *(P-14388)*

Merrill Lynch Prce Fnner Smith ....D......760 930-3100
1000 Aviara Dr Ste 200 Carlsbad (92011) *(P-14389)*

Merrill Lynch Prce Fnner Smith ....C......800 637-7455
800 E Colorado Blvd Ste 400 Pasadena (91101) *(P-14390)*

Merrimans Incorporated ....E......909 795-5301
32195 Dunlap Blvd Yucaipa (92399) *(P-6050)*

Merritt Hawkins & Assoc LLC (HQ)......................**C......858 792-0711**
12400 High Bluff Dr Ste 100 San Diego (92130) *(P-15868)*

Merritt Hospitality LLC ....C......562 983-3400
701 W Ocean Blvd Long Beach (90831) *(P-15247)*

Merritt Hospitality LLC ....C......714 738-7800
2701 Nutwood Ave Fullerton (92831) *(P-15248)*

Merry An Cejka ....E......323 560-3949
4601 Cecilia St Cudahy (90201) *(P-7928)*

Meruelo Enterprises Inc (PA)...............................**A......562 745-2300**
9550 Firestone Blvd Ste 105 Downey (90241) *(P-568)*

Mesa Contracting Corporation C
22845 Savi Ranch Pkwy Ste D Yorba Linda (92887) *(P-635)*

Mesa Energy Systems Inc (HQ)............................**C......949 460-0460**
2 Cromwell Irvine (92618) *(P-794)*

Mesa Industries Inc ....E......626 712-1708
1419 Palomares St La Verne (91750) *(P-6938)*

Mesa Insurance Solutions Inc ....C......805 308-6308
50 Castilian Dr Goleta (93117) *(P-14613)*

Mesa Pointe Stadium 12, Costa Mesa *Also Called: Edwards Theatres Circuit Inc (P-17296)*

Mesa Reprographics, San Diego *Also Called: San Diego Printing Group Inc (P-3682)*

Mesa Verde Country Club ....C......714 549-0377
3000 Club House Rd Costa Mesa (92626) *(P-17500)*

Mesa Verde Partners ....C......714 540-7500
1701 Golf Course Dr Costa Mesa (92626) *(P-17438)*

Mesa Verde Prosecute Care, Costa Mesa *Also Called: Mesa Vrde Cnvalescent Hosp Inc (P-18013)*

Mesa Vrde Cnvalescent Hosp Inc ....C......949 548-5584
661 Center St Costa Mesa (92627) *(P-18013)*

Mesfin Enterprises ....B......310 615-0881
222 N Pacific Coast Hwy Ste 1570 El Segundo (90245) *(P-16457)*

Messenger Express (PA)..C....... 213 614-0475
5435 Cahuenga Blvd Ste C North Hollywood (91601) *(P-11534)*

Messer LLC ....D..... 562 903-1290
13117 Meyer Rd Whittier (90605) *(P-3869)*

Messer LLC ....D..... 310 533-8394
2535 Del Amo Blvd Torrance (90503) *(P-3870)*

Mestek Inc ....C..... 310 835-7500
1220 E Watson Center Rd Carson (90745) *(P-7619)*

Mesvision, Costa Mesa *Also Called: Medical Eye Services Inc (P-14612)*

Met News ....E..... 310 346-0033
210 S Spring St Los Angeles (90012) *(P-3306)*

Metabasis Therapeutics Inc ....E..... 858 550-7500
11085 N Torrey Pines Rd Ste 300 La Jolla (92037) *(P-4168)*

Metabolic Response Modifiers, Oceanside *Also Called: Chemi-Source Inc (P-13032)*

Metacrine, San Diego *Also Called: Metacrine Inc (P-4169)*

Metacrine Inc ....E..... 858 369-7800
3985 Sorrento Valley Blvd Ste C San Diego (92121) *(P-4169)*

Metagenics LLC (PA)..C..... 949 366-0818
25 Enterprise Ste 200 Aliso Viejo (92656) *(P-13055)*

Metal Analysis, Santa Fe Springs *Also Called: Bodycote W Cast Anlytcal Svc I (P-5830)*

Metal Art of California Inc (PA)..................................D....... 714 532-7100
640 N Cypress St Orange (92867) *(P-11137)*

Metal Cast Inc ....E..... 714 285-9792
2002 W Chestnut Ave Santa Ana (92703) *(P-5664)*

Metal Chem, Chatsworth *Also Called: Metal Chem Inc (P-6638)*

Metal Chem Inc ....E..... 818 727-9951
21514 Nordhoff St Chatsworth (91311) *(P-6638)*

Metal Coaters, Rancho Cucamonga *Also Called: Nci Group Inc (P-6387)*

Metal Coaters California Inc ....D..... 909 987-4681
9123 Center Ave Rancho Cucamonga (91730) *(P-6718)*

Metal Coaters System, Rancho Cucamonga *Also Called: Metal Coaters California Inc (P-6718)*

Metal Container Corporation ....C..... 951 354-0444
7155 Central Ave Riverside (92504) *(P-5860)*

Metal Container Corporation ....C..... 951 360-4500
10980 Inland Ave Jurupa Valley (91752) *(P-5861)*

Metal Cutting Service ....F..... 626 968-4764
16233 Gale Ave City Of Industry (91745) *(P-7929)*

Metal Engineering Inc ....E..... 626 334-1819
1642 S Sacramento Ave Ontario (91761) *(P-6270)*

Metal Finishing Division, South Gate *Also Called: Anadite Cal Restoration Tr (P-6582)*

Metal Finishing Pntg Lab Tstg, Oxnard *Also Called: Elite Metal Finishing LLC (P-6620)*

Metal Improvement Company LLC ....E..... 949 855-8010
35 Argonaut Ste A1 Laguna Hills (92656) *(P-5841)*

Metal Improvement Company LLC ....E..... 714 546-4160
2151 S Hathaway St Santa Ana (92705) *(P-5842)*

Metal Improvement Company LLC ....D..... 323 585-2168
2588 Industry Way Ste A Lynwood (90262) *(P-5843)*

Metal Improvement Company LLC ....D..... 818 983-1952
6940 Farmdale Ave North Hollywood (91605) *(P-5844)*

Metal Improvement Company LLC ....D..... 818 407-6280
20751 Superior St Chatsworth (91311) *(P-5845)*

Metal Master Inc ....E..... 858 292-8880
4611 Overland Ave San Diego (92123) *(P-6271)*

Metal Products Engineering, Vernon *Also Called: Luppen Holdings Inc (P-6534)*

Metal Supply LLC ....D..... 562 634-9940
11810 Center St South Gate (90280) *(P-6051)*

Metal Surfaces Intl LLC ....C..... 562 927-1331
6060 Shull St Bell Gardens (90201) *(P-6639)*

Metal Tek Company ....E..... 661 832-6011
3801 S H St Bakersfield (93304) *(P-6052)*

Metal Tite Products (PA)...D..... 562 695-0645
4880 Gregg Rd Pico Rivera (90660) *(P-6112)*

Metal-Fab Services Indust Inc ....E..... 714 630-7771
2500 E Miraloma Way Anaheim (92806) *(P-6272)*

Metalagraphics, Moorpark *Also Called: Glendee Corp (P-7849)*

Metalagraphics, Moorpark *Also Called: Glendee Corp (P-7850)*

Metalcast, Santa Ana *Also Called: Metal Cast Inc (P-5664)*

Metalite Manufacturing, Pacoima *Also Called: Hanmar LLC (P-6520)*

Metalite Manufacturing Company ....E..... 818 890-2802
11441 Bradley Ave Pacoima (91331) *(P-6536)*

Metalite Mfg Companys, Pacoima *Also Called: Metalite Manufacturing Company (P-6536)*

Metalore Inc ....E..... 310 643-0360
750 S Douglas St El Segundo (90245) *(P-7930)*

Metals USA, Brea *Also Called: Metals USA Building Pdts LP (P-5720)*

Metals USA Building Pdts LP (DH)..............................A....... 713 946-9000
955 Columbia St Brea (92821) *(P-5720)*

Metals USA Building Pdts LP ....D..... 800 325-1305
1951 S Parco Ave Ste C Ontario (91761) *(P-5721)*

Metals USA Building Pdts LP ....C..... 714 522-7852
6450 Caballero Blvd Ste A Buena Park (90620) *(P-6053)*

Metcal, Cypress *Also Called: OK International Inc (P-7160)*

Metco Fourslide Manufacturing, Gardena *Also Called: Metco Manufacturing Inc (P-6537)*

Metco Manufacturing Inc ....E..... 310 516-6547
17540 S Denver Ave Gardena (90248) *(P-6537)*

Metcoe Skylight Specialites, Gardena *Also Called: Weiss Sheet Metal Company (P-1056)*

Methodist Hospital, Arcadia *Also Called: Usc Arcadia Hospital (P-18492)*

Metra Electronics Corporation ....E..... 562 470-6601
3201 E 59th St Long Beach (90805) *(P-9423)*

Metric Machining (PA)...E..... 909 947-9222
3263 Trade Center Dr Riverside (92507) *(P-7931)*

Metric Precision, Huntington Beach *Also Called: AMG Torrance LLC (P-9623)*

Metric Products Inc (PA)...E..... 310 815-9000
4630 Leahy St Culver City (90232) *(P-2396)*

Metro, Los Angeles *Also Called: Los Angles Cnty Mtro Trnsp Aut (P-11326)*

Metro, Sun Valley *Also Called: Los Angles Cnty Mtro Trnsp Aut (P-11333)*

Metro, Los Angeles *Also Called: Los Angles Cnty Mtro Trnsp Aut (P-11334)*

Metro Bldrs & Engineers Group, Newport Beach *Also Called: Houalla Enterprises Ltd (P-558)*

Metro Digital, Santa Ana *Also Called: Metro Digital Printing Inc (P-3635)*

Metro Digital Printing Inc ....E..... 714 545-8400
3311 W Macarthur Blvd Santa Ana (92704) *(P-3635)*

Metro Ports, Long Beach *Also Called: Suderman Contg Stevedores Inc (P-11648)*

Metro Truck Body Inc ....E..... 310 532-5570
240 Citation Cir Corona (92878) *(P-17013)*

Metro-Goldwyn-Mayer Inc (DH)...................................B....... 310 449-3000
245 N Beverly Dr Beverly Hills (90210) *(P-17201)*

Metrolink, Los Angeles *Also Called: Southern Cal Rgional Rail Auth (P-11368)*

Metrolink Doc, Pomona *Also Called: Southern Cal Rgional Rail Auth (P-11367)*

Metromedia Technologies Inc ....E..... 818 552-6500
311 Parkside Dr San Fernando (91340) *(P-7550)*

Metropltan Area Advsory Cmmtte (PA)........................D....... 619 426-3595
1355 Third Ave Chula Vista (91911) *(P-19188)*

Metropltan Wtr Dst of Sthern C ....B....... 909 593-7474
700 Moreno Ave La Verne (91750) *(P-12133)*

Metropltan Wtr Dst of Sthern C ....D..... 714 577-5031
3972 Valley View Ave Yorba Linda (92886) *(P-12134)*

Metropolis Hotel MGT LLC ....C..... 213 683-4855
899 Francisco St Los Angeles (90017) *(P-15249)*

Metropolitan Automotive Warehouse ....A....... 909 885-2886
535 Tennis Court Ln San Bernardino (92408) *(P-12248)*

Metropolitan Home Mortgage Inc ....D..... 949 428-0161
3090 Bristol St Ste 600 Costa Mesa (92626) *(P-14340)*

Metropolitan Imports LLC ....C..... 646 980-5343
16311 Ventura Blvd Encino (91436) *(P-16878)*

Metropolitan News Company ....E..... 951 369-5890
3540 12th St Riverside (92501) *(P-3307)*

Metropolitan News Company, Los Angeles *Also Called: Grace Communications Inc (P-3279)*

Metropolitan Waste Disposal, Paramount *Also Called: Calmet Inc (P-12164)*

Metropolitan Water Lavern, La Verne *Also Called: Metropltan Wtr Dst of Sthern C (P-12133)*

Metropro Road Services Inc ....D..... 714 556-7600
957 W 17th St Costa Mesa (92627) *(P-17058)*

Metrostudy Inc ....C..... 714 619-7800
4000 Macarthur Blvd Ste 40 Newport Beach (92660) *(P-20198)*

Mets//, Manhattan Beach *Also Called: M & E Technical Services L L C (P-20295)*

Mettler Electronics Corp ....E..... 714 533-2221
1333 S Claudina St Anaheim (92805) *(P-10565)*

Meundies Inc ....B....... 888 552-6775
3650 Holdrege Ave Los Angeles (90016) *(P-13910)*

Meus, Cypress *Also Called: Mitsubishi Electric Us Inc (P-12683)*

Mevsa, Cypress *Also Called: Mitsubshi Elc Vsual Sltons AME (P-9086)*

Employee Codes: A=Over 500 employees, B=251-500
C=101-250, D=51-100, E=20-50, F=10-19, G=1-9

2024 Southern California
Business Directory and Buyers Guide

© Mergent Inc. 1-800-342-5647

1179

ALPHABETIC

Mexapparel Inc (PA) .... E 323 364-8600
2344 E 38th St Vernon (90058) *(P-2181)*

Mexicali Inc .... C 661 327-3861
631 18th St Bakersfield (93301) *(P-14026)*

Mexicali Restaurant, Bakersfield *Also Called: Mexicali Inc (P-14026)*

Mexican Amrcn Oprtnty Fndation (PA) .... D 323 890-9600
401 N Garfield Ave Montebello (90640) *(P-19112)*

Mexican Amrcn Oprtnty Fndation .... D 323 890-1555
5657 E Washington Blvd Commerce (90040) *(P-19113)*

Meyco Machine and Tool Inc .... E 714 435-1546
11579 Martens River Cir Fountain Valley (92708) *(P-7120)*

Meziere Enterprises Inc .... E 800 208-1755
220 S Hale Ave Ste A Escondido (92029) *(P-7932)*

Mf Inc .... C 213 627-2498
2010 E 15th St Los Angeles (90021) *(P-2256)*

Mfb Liquidation Inc .... E 760 448-1940
6195 El Camino Real Carlsbad (92009) *(P-1558)*

Mflex, Irvine *Also Called: Multi-Fineline Electronix Inc (P-8705)*

Mflex Delaware Inc .... A 949 453-6800
101 Academy Ste 250 Irvine (92617) *(P-8704)*

MGA Entertainment Inc .... A 800 222-4685
9220 Winnetka Ave Chatsworth (91311) *(P-12941)*

MGB Construction Inc .... C 951 342-0303
91 Commercial Ave Riverside (92507) *(P-447)*

Mgc Systems Corp .... E 714 442-2064
73 Bunsen Irvine (92618) *(P-19645)*

Mge Underground Inc .... B 805 238-3510
2501 Golden Hill Rd Paso Robles (93446) *(P-1124)*

Mgid Inc .... D 424 322-8059
1149 3rd St Ste 210 Santa Monica (90403) *(P-20199)*

Mgl, Santa Ana *Also Called: Michael Gerald Ltd (P-13106)*

MGM, Beverly Hills *Also Called: Metro-Goldwyn-Mayer Inc (P-17201)*

MGM and Ua Services Company .... A 310 449-3000
245 N Beverly Dr Beverly Hills (90210) *(P-20397)*

MGM Transformer Co .... D 323 726-0888
5701 Smithway St Commerce (90040) *(P-8101)*

Mgo, Los Angeles *Also Called: Macias Gini & OConnell LLP (P-19793)*

Mgp Exhausts Usa Inc .... E 760 445-1235
2225 Meyers Ave Escondido (92029) *(P-9424)*

MGP Exhausts USA, Inc., Escondido *Also Called: Mgp Exhausts Usa Inc (P-9424)*

Mgr Design International Inc .... C 805 981-6400
1950 Williams Dr Oxnard (93036) *(P-11252)*

MGT Industries Inc (PA) .... D 310 516-5900
13889 S Figueroa St Los Angeles (90061) *(P-2352)*

Mh Sub I LLC (PA) .... C 310 280-4000
909 N Pacific Coast Hwy Fl 11 El Segundo (90245) *(P-15558)*

Mhf Mv Operating VI LLC .... D 619 481-5881
595 Hotel Cir S San Diego (92108) *(P-15250)*

Mhh Holdings Inc .... C 949 651-9903
5653 Alton Pkwy Irvine (92618) *(P-13378)*

Mhh Holdings Inc .... C 626 744-9370
415 S Lake Ave Ste 108 Pasadena (91101) *(P-13379)*

Mhk Investment Holdings Inc .... E 562 699-3578
4845 Pioneer Blvd Whittier (90601) *(P-5424)*

Mhm Services Inc .... C 805 904-6678
230 Station Way Arroyo Grande (93420) *(P-18702)*

MHRP Resort Inc .... D 760 249-5808
24510 Highway 2 Wrightwood (92397) *(P-15251)*

MI Technologies Inc .... A 619 710-2637
2215 Paseo De Las Americas Ste 30 San Diego (92154) *(P-5098)*

Mias Fashion Mfg Co Inc .... B 562 906-1060
12623 Cisneros Ln Santa Fe Springs (90670) *(P-13137)*

Micha-Rettenmaier Partnership .... D 714 280-1645
351 Hospital Rd Ste 507 Newport Beach (92663) *(P-17712)*

Michael Baker International Inc (DH) .... B 949 472-3505
5 Hutton Centre Dr Ste 500 Santa Ana (92707) *(P-19646)*

Michael G Frtnsce Physcl Thrap .... C 626 446-7027
24630 Washington Ave Ste 200 Murrieta (92562) *(P-17869)*

Michael Gerald Ltd .... E 562 921-9611
1852 Carnegie Ave Santa Ana (92705) *(P-13106)*

Michael Nicholas Designs Inc .... C 714 562-8101
2330 Raymer Ave Fullerton (92833) *(P-2871)*

Michael Sullivan & Assoc LLP .... C 310 337-4480
2401 E El Segundo Blvd El Segundo (90245) *(P-18906)*

Michaelson Connor & Boul (PA) .... D 714 230-3600
5312 Bolsa Ave Huntington Beach (92649) *(P-20200)*

Micro Analog Inc .... C 909 392-8277
1861 Puddingstone Dr La Verne (91750) *(P-8838)*

Micro Matrix Systems (PA) .... E 909 626-8544
1899 Salem Ct Claremont (91711) *(P-6538)*

Micro Plastics Inc .... F 818 882-0244
20821 Dearborn St Chatsworth (91311) *(P-8271)*

Micro Prcision Calibration Inc .... C 714 901-5659
2165 N Glassell St Orange (92865) *(P-19976)*

Micro Precision, Orange *Also Called: Micro Prcision Calibration Inc (P-19976)*

Micro Steel Inc .... E 818 348-8701
7850 Alabama Ave Canoga Park (91304) *(P-9920)*

Micro Surface Engr Inc (PA) .... E 323 582-7348
1550 E Slauson Ave Los Angeles (90011) *(P-5855)*

Micro Therapeutics Inc (HQ) .... E 949 837-3700
9775 Toledo Way Irvine (92618) *(P-10566)*

Micro Tool & Manufacturing Inc .... E 619 582-2884
6494 Federal Blvd Lemon Grove (91945) *(P-7121)*

Micro-Mode Products Inc .... C 619 449-3844
1870 John Towers Ave El Cajon (92020) *(P-8544)*

Micro-Polish, Anaheim *Also Called: Stainless Micro-Polish Inc (P-6666)*

Micro-Pro Microfilming Svcs, Long Beach *Also Called: Macro-Pro Inc (P-16866)*

Micro-TEC, Chatsworth *Also Called: Wallace E Miller Inc (P-8071)*

Micro-Technology Concepts Inc .... D 626 839-6800
17837 Rowland St City Of Industry (91748) *(P-12427)*

Micro/Sys Inc .... E 818 244-4600
158 W Pomona Ave Monrovia (91016) *(P-7441)*

Microblend Inc .... E 330 998-4602
543 Country Club Dr Simi Valley (93065) *(P-4495)*

Microblend Technologies, Simi Valley *Also Called: Microblend Inc (P-4495)*

Microcosm Inc .... E 310 219-2700
3111 Lomita Blvd Torrance (90505) *(P-9909)*

Microdyne Plastics Inc .... D 909 503-4010
1901 E Cooley Dr Colton (92324) *(P-5099)*

Microfabrica Inc .... E 888 964-2763
7911 Haskell Ave Van Nuys (91406) *(P-9084)*

Microfilm Company of Cal Inc .... F 310 354-2610
14214 S Figueroa St Los Angeles (90061) *(P-3410)*

Microfinancial Incorporated .... C 805 367-8900
2801 Townsgate Rd Westlake Village (91361) *(P-15786)*

Microlease Inc (DH) .... D 866 520-0200
6060 Sepulveda Blvd Van Nuys (91411) *(P-15787)*

Micrometals Inc (PA) .... C 714 970-9400
5615 E La Palma Ave Anaheim (92807) *(P-9085)*

Micron Instruments, Simi Valley *Also Called: Piezo-Metrics Inc (P-8864)*

Micron Machine Company .... E 858 486-5900
3337 Highway 67 Ramona (92065) *(P-7933)*

Micronova Manufacturing Inc .... E 310 784-6990
3431 Lomita Blvd Torrance (90505) *(P-2478)*

Microplate, Inglewood *Also Called: Multichrome Company Inc (P-6641)*

Microplex Inc .... F 714 630-8220
1070 Ortega Way Placentia (92870) *(P-8839)*

Microscale Industries Inc .... F 714 593-1422
18435 Bandilier Cir Fountain Valley (92708) *(P-3636)*

Microsemi, Garden Grove *Also Called: Microsemi Corporation (P-8843)*

Microsemi Communications Inc (DH) .... D 805 388-3700
4721 Calle Carga Camarillo (93012) *(P-8840)*

Microsemi Corp - Anlog Mxed Sg (DH) .... D 714 898-8121
11861 Western Ave Garden Grove (92841) *(P-8841)*

Microsemi Corp - High Prfmce T (DH) .... D 949 380-6100
11861 Western Ave Garden Grove (92841) *(P-8842)*

Microsemi Corp - Santa Ana, Garden Grove *Also Called: Microsemi Corporation (P-8844)*

Microsemi Corp-Power MGT Group .... C 714 994-6500
11861 Western Ave Garden Grove (92841) *(P-8186)*

Microsemi Corporation (HQ) .... E 949 380-6100
11861 Western Ave Garden Grove (92841) *(P-8843)*

Microsemi Corporation .... C 714 898-7112
11861 Western Ave Garden Grove (92841) *(P-8844)*

Micross Holdings Inc ....D..... 215 997-3200
11150 Santa Monica Blvd Los Angeles (90025) *(P-8845)*

Microtek Lab Inc (HQ)..C..... **310 687-5823**
13337 South St Cerritos (90703) *(P-12386)*

Microvention Inc (DH)..C..... **714 258-8000**
35 Enterprise Aliso Viejo (92656) *(P-10567)*

Microvention Inc ....E..... 714 258-8001
1311 Valencia Ave Tustin (92780) *(P-10568)*

Microvention Terumo, Aliso Viejo Also Called: Microvention Inc *(P-10567)*

Microvision Development Inc ....E..... 760 438-7781
1734 Oriole Ct Carlsbad (92011) *(P-16305)*

Microwave Applications Group ....E..... 805 928-5711
3030 Industrial Pkwy Santa Maria (93455) *(P-19647)*

Microwave Dynamics LLC ....F..... 949 679-7788
16541 Scientific Irvine (92618) *(P-8545)*

Mid-Century Insurance Company ....C..... 323 932-7116
6303 Owensmouth Ave Fl 1 Woodland Hills (91367) *(P-14521)*

Mid-State Concrete Pdts Inc ....E..... 805 928-2855
1625 E Donovan Rd Ste C Santa Maria (93454) *(P-5425)*

Mid-West Fabricating Co ....E..... 562 698-9615
8623 Dice Rd Santa Fe Springs (90670) *(P-9425)*

Mid-West Wholesale Hardware Co ....E..... 714 630-4751
1641 S Sunkist St Anaheim (92806) *(P-5932)*

Mida Industries Inc ....C..... 562 616-1020
6101 Obispo Ave Long Beach (90805) *(P-15728)*

Midas Express Los Angeles Inc ....C..... 310 609-0366
11854 Alameda St Lynwood (90262) *(P-11598)*

Midi Association, The, Aliso Viejo Also Called: Midi Manufacturers Assn Inc *(P-19383)*

Midi Manufacturers Assn Inc ....D..... 714 227-0068
85 Matisse Cir Aliso Viejo (92656) *(P-19383)*

Midland Credit Management, San Diego Also Called: Midland Credit Management Inc
(P-14284)

Midland Credit Management Inc ....A..... 877 240-2377
350 Camino De La Reina Ste 100 San Diego (92108) *(P-14284)*

Midland Industries ....D..... 800 821-5725
659 E Ball Rd Anaheim (92805) *(P-12865)*

Midnight Manufacturing LLC ....E..... 714 833-6130
2535 Conejo Spectrum St Bldg 4 Thousand Oaks (91320) *(P-4003)*

Midnight Oil Agency LLC ....B..... 818 295-6100
3800 W Vanowen St Ste 101 Burbank (91505) *(P-3637)*

Midnight Oil Agency, Inc., Burbank Also Called: Midnight Oil Agency LLC *(P-3637)*

Midnight Sun Enterprises Inc ....D..... 310 532-2427
19900 Normandie Ave Torrance (90502) *(P-20362)*

Midstream Energy Partners USA ....E..... 661 765-4087
9224 Tupman Rd Tupman (93276) *(P-241)*

Midthrust, Los Angeles Also Called: Midthrust Imports Inc *(P-2084)*

Midthrust Imports Inc ....E..... 213 749-6651
830 E 14th Pl Los Angeles (90021) *(P-2084)*

Midway International Inc ....D..... 800 826-2383
13131 166th St Cerritos (90703) *(P-13548)*

Mig Management Services LLC ....D..... 949 474-5800
660 Newport Center Dr Ste 1300 Newport Beach (92660) *(P-20061)*

Mighty Green, Costa Mesa Also Called: Inveco Inc *(P-6631)*

Mikada Cabinets, Los Angeles Also Called: Mikada Cabinets LLC *(P-2668)*

Mikada Cabinets LLC ....D..... 713 681-6116
11777 San Vicente Blvd Los Angeles (90049) *(P-2668)*

Mikawaya, Vernon Also Called: Mochi Ice Cream Company LLC *(P-1483)*

Mike Campbell & Associates Ltd ....A..... 626 369-3981
10907 Downey Ave Ste 203 Downey (90241) *(P-11552)*

Mike Campbell Assoc Logictics, Downey Also Called: Mike Campbell & Associates Ltd
(P-11552)

Mike Dyell Machine Shop Inc (PA)...........................F..... **909 350-4101**
160 S Linden Ave Rialto (92376) *(P-7934)*

Mike Kenney Tool Inc ....E..... 714 577-9262
588 Porter Way Placentia (92870) *(P-7935)*

Mike Parker Landscape, Santa Ana Also Called: Mpl Enterprises Inc *(P-206)*

Mike Rovner Construction Inc ....C..... 949 458-1562
22600 Lambert St Lake Forest (92630) *(P-20062)*

Mikelson Machine Shop Inc ....E..... 626 448-3920
2546 Merced Ave South El Monte (91733) *(P-7936)*

Mikes Metal Works Inc ....F..... 619 440-8804
3552 Fowler Canyon Rd Jamul (91935) *(P-6054)*

Mikhail Darafeev Inc (PA)..E..... **909 613-1818**
5075 Edison Ave Chino (91710) *(P-2780)*

Mikkeller Brewing San Diego ....E..... 858 381-3500
9368 Cabot Dr San Diego (92126) *(P-1599)*

Mikron Products Inc ....E..... 909 545-8600
3701 E Conant St Long Beach (90808) *(P-4750)*

Mil-Spec Magnetics Inc ....E..... 909 598-8116
169 Pacific St Pomona (91768) *(P-8948)*

Milani Cosmetics, Culver City Also Called: New Milani Group LLC *(P-13059)*

Milbank Global Securities, Los Angeles Also Called: Milbank Tweed Hdley McCloy LLP
(P-18907)

Milbank Tweed Hdley McCloy LLP ....C..... 424 386-4000
2029 Century Park E Los Angeles (90002) *(P-18907)*

Milco Waterjet, Huntington Beach Also Called: Milco Wire Edm Inc *(P-7937)*

Milco Wire Edm Inc ....F..... 714 373-0098
15221 Connector Ln Huntington Beach (92649) *(P-7937)*

Mile High Valet, Dana Point Also Called: Ciri - Stroup Inc *(P-15501)*

Mile Square Golf Course ....C..... 714 962-5541
10401 Warner Ave Fountain Valley (92708) *(P-17439)*

Milgard Manufacturing LLC ....B..... 480 763-6000
26879 Diaz Rd Temecula (92590) *(P-5100)*

Milgard Manufacturing LLC ....C..... 805 581-6325
355 E Easy St Simi Valley (93065) *(P-5348)*

Milgard Windows, Temecula Also Called: Milgard Manufacturing LLC *(P-5100)*

Milgard-Simi Valley, Simi Valley Also Called: Milgard Manufacturing LLC *(P-5348)*

Military California Department ....B..... 562 795-2065
11300 Lexington Dr Bldg 1000 Los Alamitos (90720) *(P-20296)*

Milken Family Foundation ....C..... 310 570-4800
1250 4th St Fl 1 Santa Monica (90401) *(P-19456)*

Millcraft Inc ....D..... 714 632-9621
2850 E White Star Ave Anaheim (92806) *(P-2615)*

Millennial Brands LLC ....E..... 925 230-0617
126 W 9th St Los Angeles (90015) *(P-5278)*

Millennium Biltmore Hotel, Los Angeles Also Called: Whb Corporation *(P-15417)*

Millennium Health LLC ....B..... 877 451-3534
16981 Via Tazon Ste F San Diego (92127) *(P-19977)*

Millennium Reinforcing Inc ....B..... 949 361-9730
1046 Calle Recodo San Clemente (92673) *(P-1110)*

Millennium Space Systems Inc (HQ)........................E..... **310 683-5840**
2265 E El Segundo Blvd El Segundo (90245) *(P-8546)*

Millenworks ....D..... 714 426-5500
1361 Valencia Ave Tustin (92780) *(P-9300)*

Miller and Associates, Los Angeles Also Called: Imhoff & Associates PC *(P-18872)*

Miller Automotive Group Inc (HQ)............................B..... **818 787-8400**
5425 Van Nuys Blvd Sherman Oaks (91401) *(P-13796)*

Miller Brewing Co ....E..... 626 353-1604
15801 1st St Irwindale (91706) *(P-1600)*

Miller Castings Inc (PA)..B..... **562 695-0461**
2503 Pacific Pk Dr Whittier (90601) *(P-5658)*

Miller Children's Hospital, Long Beach Also Called: Long Beach Medical Center *(P-18335)*

MILLER CHILDREN'S HOSPITAL, Long Beach Also Called: Memorial Medical Center
Foundation *(P-19532)*

Miller Cnc, Chula Vista Also Called: Miller Machine Works LLC *(P-7938)*

Miller Environmental Inc ....C..... 714 385-0099
1130 W Trenton Ave Orange (92867) *(P-1135)*

Miller Gasket Co, San Fernando Also Called: J Miller Co Inc *(P-4736)*

Miller Kaplan Arase LLP (PA)....................................C..... **818 769-2010**
4123 Lankershim Blvd North Hollywood (91602) *(P-19795)*

Miller Machine Works LLC ....F..... 619 501-9866
789 Anita St Chula Vista (91911) *(P-7938)*

Miller Marine ....E..... 619 791-1500
2275 Manya St San Diego (92154) *(P-9841)*

Miller Nissan, Sherman Oaks Also Called: Miller Automotive Group Inc *(P-13796)*

Miller Woodworking Inc ....E..... 310 257-6806
1429 259th St Harbor City (90710) *(P-2616)*

Millers American Honey Inc ....F..... 909 825-1722
1455 Riverview Dr San Bernardino (92408) *(P-1945)*

Millers Fab & Weld Corp ....E..... 951 359-3100
6100 Industrial Ave Riverside (92504) *(P-6055)*

Millers Woodworking, Tustin Also Called: GL Woodworking Inc *(P-2601)*

ALPHABETIC

Million Corporation .... D...... 626 969-1888
1300 W Optical Dr Ste 600 Irwindale (91702) *(P-3787)*

Millipart Inc (PA)...F...... **626 963-4101**
412 W Carter Dr Glendora (91740) *(P-7939)*

Mills Corporation ....D...... 909 484-8300
1 Mills Cir Ste 1 Ontario (91764) *(P-14673)*

Millworks Etc Inc ....E...... 805 499-3400
2230 Statham Blvd Ste 100 Oxnard (93033) *(P-6113)*

Millworks By Design Inc ....E...... 818 597-1326
4525 Runway St Simi Valley (93063) *(P-2617)*

Millworx, Corona Also Called: Millworx Prcsion Machining Inc *(P-7940)*

Millworx Prcsion Machining Inc ....E...... 951 371-2683
506 Malloy Ct Corona (92878) *(P-7940)*

Milodon Incorporated ....E...... 805 577-5950
2250 Agate Ct Simi Valley (93065) *(P-9426)*

Milwaukee Hand Truck, Los Angeles Also Called: Gleason Industrial Pdts Inc *(P-6991)*

Milwood Healthcare Inc ....D...... 626 274-4345
2641 S C St Oxnard (93033) *(P-14674)*

Min-E-Con LLC ....D...... 949 250-0087
17312 Eastman Irvine (92614) *(P-8978)*

Mind Research Institute ....C...... 949 345-8700
5281 California Ave Ste 300 Irvine (92617) *(P-19935)*

Mindbody, San Luis Obispo Also Called: Mindbody Inc *(P-16506)*

Mindbody Inc (PA)...C...... **877 755-4279**
651 Tank Farm Rd San Luis Obispo (93401) *(P-16506)*

Mindgruve Holdings Inc ....C...... 619 757-1325
627 8th Ave Ste 300 San Diego (92101) *(P-15559)*

Mindlance Inc ....A...... 858 433-9298
10679 Westview Pkwy Fl 2 San Diego (92126) *(P-20201)*

MINDLANCE INC., San Diego Also Called: Mindlance Inc *(P-20201)*

Mindrum Precision Inc ....E...... 909 989-1728
10000 4th St Rancho Cucamonga (91730) *(P-10177)*

Mindrum Precision Products, Rancho Cucamonga Also Called: Mindrum Precision Inc *(P-10177)*

Mindshow ....E...... 213 531-0277
811 W 7th St Ste 400 Los Angeles (90017) *(P-16306)*

Mindspeed Technologies LLC (HQ)....................D...... **949 579-3000**
4000 Macarthur Blvd Newport Beach (92660) *(P-8846)*

Mindspeed Technologies, Inc., Newport Beach Also Called: Mindspeed Technologies LLC *(P-8846)*

Mindwave Software, San Diego Also Called: Isaac Fair Corporation *(P-16059)*

Mine, Los Angeles Also Called: Edgemine Inc *(P-13124)*

Miniluxe, Los Angeles Also Called: Miniluxe Inc *(P-15481)*

Miniluxe Inc ....D...... 424 442-1630
11965 San Vicente Blvd Los Angeles (90049) *(P-15481)*

Minorities & Success, Torrance Also Called: Minority Success Pubg Group *(P-3371)*

Minority Success Pubg Group ....E...... 310 736-2462
23505 Crenshaw Blvd Torrance (90505) *(P-3371)*

Minshew Brothers Stl Cnstr Inc C
12578 Vigilante Rd Lakeside (92040) *(P-511)*

Minsley Inc ....E...... 909 458-1100
989 S Monterey Ave Ontario (91761) *(P-1946)*

Minson Corporation ....B...... 323 513-1041
11701 Wilshire Blvd Ste 15a Los Angeles (90025) *(P-2811)*

Mintie Technologies, Azusa Also Called: Mc-40 *(P-15723)*

Mintle Enterprises Inc ....F...... 951 506-4005
41571 Date St Murrieta (92562) *(P-16307)*

Mintz Levin Cohn Ferris GL ....D...... 858 314-1500
3580 Carmel Mountain Rd Ste 300 San Diego (92130) *(P-18908)*

Minus K Technology Inc ....C...... 310 348-9656
460 Hindry Ave Ste C Inglewood (90301) *(P-10384)*

Mir3 Inc ....D...... 858 724-1200
3398 Carmel Mountain Rd # 100 San Diego (92121) *(P-16075)*

Mira Loma Dry Depot, Jurupa Valley Also Called: Costco Wholesale Corporation *(P-11568)*

Mira Mesa Stadium 18, San Diego Also Called: Edwards Theatres Circuit Inc *(P-17295)*

Miracle Bedding Corporation ....E...... 562 908-2370
3700 Capitol Ave City Of Industry (90601) *(P-2856)*

Mirada, Long Beach Also Called: Motion Theory Inc *(P-15669)*

Mirada Hlls Rehb Cnvlscent Hos, La Mirada Also Called: Life Care Centers America Inc *(P-17988)*

Miramar Acquisition Co LLC ....C...... 805 900-8338
1759 S Jameson Ln Santa Barbara (93108) *(P-15038)*

Miramar Hotel, Santa Barbara Also Called: Morgans Hotel Group MGT LLC *(P-15255)*

Miramar Plant 33, San Diego Also Called: Robertsons Ready Mix Ltd *(P-5498)*

Miramar Transportation Inc ....D...... 858 693-0071
9340 Cabot Dr Ste I San Diego (92126) *(P-11784)*

Miramonte Enterprises LLC ....C...... 951 658-9441
275 N San Jacinto St Hemet (92543) *(P-18014)*

Mirati, San Diego Also Called: Mirati Therapeutics Inc *(P-4170)*

Mirati Therapeutics Inc (PA).............................A...... **858 332-3410**
3545 Cray Ct San Diego (92121) *(P-4170)*

Miro Technologies Inc ....C...... 858 677-2100
5643 Copley Dr San Diego (92111) *(P-16458)*

Mirth Corporation ....D...... 714 389-1200
611 Anton Blvd Ste 500 Costa Mesa (92626) *(P-16308)*

Mirum Inc ....C...... 619 237-5552
350 10th Ave Ste 1200 San Diego (92101) *(P-15668)*

Mis Sciences Corp ....C...... 818 847-0213
2550 N Hollywood Way Ste 404 Burbank (91505) *(P-11892)*

Misa Imports Inc ....D...... 562 281-6773
2343 Saybrook Ave Commerce (90040) *(P-13549)*

MISSION, Oxnard Also Called: Mission Produce Inc *(P-108)*

Mission Ambulance Inc ....D...... 951 272-2300
400 Ramona Ave Corona (92879) *(P-11398)*

Mission Bay Aquatic Center, San Diego Also Called: Associted Stdnts San Dego State *(P-19511)*

Mission Brewery Inc ....E...... 619 818-7147
1441 L St San Diego (92101) *(P-14050)*

Mission Care Center, Rosemead Also Called: Ensign Group Inc *(P-17943)*

Mission Cloud Services Inc (PA)........................C...... **855 647-7466**
9350 Wilshire Blvd Ste 203 Beverly Hills (90212) *(P-16580)*

Mission Community Bancorp ....C...... 805 782-5000
3380 S Higuera St San Luis Obispo (93401) *(P-14170)*

MISSION COMMUNITY HOSPITAL, Panorama City Also Called: Deanco Healthcare LLC *(P-18236)*

Mission Crtical Composites LLC ....E...... 714 831-2100
15400 Graham St Ste 102 Huntington Beach (92649) *(P-9753)*

Mission Custom Extrusion Inc ....E...... 909 822-1581
10904 Beech Ave Fontana (92337) *(P-5101)*

Mission Federal Credit Union ....C...... 858 531-5106
4250 Clairemont Mesa Blvd Ste B San Diego (92117) *(P-14232)*

Mission Federal Services LLC (PA).....................C...... **858 524-2850**
10325 Meanley Dr San Diego (92131) *(P-14233)*

Mission Foods, Rancho Cucamonga Also Called: Gruma Corporation *(P-1826)*

Mission Foods, Commerce Also Called: Gruma Corporation *(P-1827)*

Mission Healthcare, San Diego Also Called: Mission HM Hlth San Diego LLC *(P-18629)*

Mission Hills Country Club Inc ....C...... 760 324-9400
34600 Mission Hills Dr Rancho Mirage (92270) *(P-17501)*

Mission Hills Health Care Inc ....D...... 619 297-4086
726 Torrance St San Diego (92103) *(P-18015)*

Mission Hills Healthcare Ctr, San Diego Also Called: Mission Hills Health Care Inc *(P-18015)*

Mission Hills Mortgage Bankers, Irvine Also Called: Mission Hills Mortgage Corp *(P-14341)*

Mission Hills Mortgage Corp (HQ)......................C...... **714 972-3832**
18500 Von Karman Ave Ste 1100 Irvine (92612) *(P-14341)*

Mission HM Hlth San Diego LLC ....D...... 619 757-2700
2365 Northside Dr Ste 200 San Diego (92108) *(P-18629)*

Mission Hockey Company (PA)..........................F...... **949 585-9390**
12 Goodyear Ste 100 Irvine (92618) *(P-11015)*

Mission Hosp Regional Med Ctr (PA)..................A...... **949 364-1400**
27700 Medical Center Rd Mission Viejo (92691) *(P-18345)*

Mission Hospital, Mission Viejo Also Called: Auxilary of Mssion Hosp Mssion *(P-18188)*

Mission Hospital, Mission Viejo Also Called: Mission Hosp Regional Med Ctr *(P-18345)*

Mission Inn Hotel and Spa, The, Riverside Also Called: Historic Mission Inn Corp *(P-15180)*

Mission Internal Med Group Inc ....D...... 949 364-3605
27882 Forbes Rd Ste 110 Laguna Niguel (92677) *(P-17713)*

Mission Internal Med Group Inc ....D...... 949 364-3570
26800 Crown Valley Pkwy Ste 103 Mission Viejo (92691) *(P-17714)*

Mission Kleensweep Prod Inc ....D...... 323 223-1405
13644 Live Oak Ln Baldwin Park (91706) *(P-4339)*

Mission Laboratories, Baldwin Park Also Called: Mission Kleensweep Prod Inc *(P-4339)*

Mergent email: customerrelations@mergent.com
1182

2024 Southern California
Business Directory and Buyers Guide

(P-0000) Products & Services Section entry number
(PA)=Parent Co (HQ)=Headquarters (DH)=Div Headquarters

Mission Ldscp Companies Inc ....C..... 714 545-9962
536 E Dyer Rd Santa Ana (92707) *(P-168)*

Mission Ldscp Companies Inc ....D...... 800 545-9963
16672 Millikan Ave Irvine (92606) *(P-169)*

Mission Linen & Uniform Svc, Lancaster *Also Called: Mission Linen Supply (P-15452)*

Mission Linen & Uniform Svc, Chino *Also Called: Mission Linen Supply (P-15453)*

Mission Linen & Uniform Svc, Oceanside *Also Called: Mission Linen Supply (P-15454)*

Mission Linen & Uniform Svc, Oxnard *Also Called: Mission Linen Supply (P-15455)*

Mission Linen & Uniform Svc, Santa Barbara *Also Called: Mission Linen Supply (P-15456)*

Mission Linen & Uniform Svc, Santa Maria *Also Called: Mission Linen Supply (P-15457)*

Mission Linen Supply ....D...... 661 948-5052
619 W Avenue I Lancaster (93534) *(P-15452)*

Mission Linen Supply ....C...... 909 393-6857
5400 Alton Way Chino (91710) *(P-15453)*

Mission Linen Supply ....C...... 760 757-9099
2727 Industry St Oceanside (92054) *(P-15454)*

Mission Linen Supply ....D...... 805 485-6794
505 Maulhardt Ave Oxnard (93030) *(P-15455)*

Mission Linen Supply ....C...... 805 962-7687
712 E Montecito St Santa Barbara (93103) *(P-15456)*

Mission Linen Supply ....D...... 805 922-3579
602 S Western Ave Santa Maria (93458) *(P-15457)*

Mission Loans LLC ....C...... 855 959-4500
5 Park Plz Ste 900 Irvine (92614) *(P-14342)*

Mission Microwave Tech LLC ....D...... 951 893-4925
6060 Phyllis Dr Cypress (90630) *(P-8547)*

Mission Plastics Inc ....C...... 909 947-7287
1930 S Parco Ave Ontario (91761) *(P-5102)*

Mission Pools of Escondido ....C...... 949 588-0100
22600 Lambert St Ste 1104 Lake Forest (92630) *(P-1169)*

Mission Pools of Lake Forest, Lake Forest *Also Called: Mission Pools of Escondido (P-1169)*

Mission Produce Inc (PA) ....C...... 805 981-3650
2710 Camino Del Sol Oxnard (93030) *(P-108)*

Mission Research Corporation (DH) ....D...... 805 690-2447
6750 Navigator Way Ste 200 Goleta (93117) *(P-9999)*

Mission Rubber Company LLC ....C...... 951 736-1313
1660 Leeson Ln Corona (92879) *(P-6792)*

Mission Service Inc ....A...... 323 266-2593
1800 Avenue Of The Stars Ste 1400 Los Angeles (90067) *(P-17035)*

Mission Technology Group Inc ....E...... 858 530-2511
9918 Via Pasar San Diego (92126) *(P-7551)*

Mission Terrace, Santa Barbara *Also Called: Cliff View Terrace Inc (P-19249)*

Mission Valley YMCA, San Diego *Also Called: YMCA of San Diego County (P-19488)*

Mission Viejo Country Club ....C...... 949 582-1550
26200 Country Club Dr Mission Viejo (92691) *(P-17502)*

Mission View Health Center, San Luis Obispo *Also Called: Compass Health Inc (P-17907)*

Mission Vly Cab / Counter Tech, Poway *Also Called: B Young Enterprises Inc (P-2648)*

Mission Volkswagen Inc ....D...... 949 493-4511
32922 Valle Rd San Juan Capistrano (92675) *(P-13797)*

Misyd Corp (PA) ....D...... 213 742-1800
30 Fremont Pl Los Angeles (90005) *(P-2411)*

Mitchell Fabrication ....E...... 909 590-0393
4564 Mission Blvd Montclair (91763) *(P-6056)*

Mitchell International Inc (PA) ....C...... 858 368-7000
9771 Clairemont Mesa Blvd Ste A San Diego (92124) *(P-16076)*

Mitchell Processing LLC ....E...... 909 519-5759
2778 Pomona Blvd Pomona (91768) *(P-4777)*

Mitchell Repair Info Co LLC (HQ) ....E...... 858 391-5000
16067 Babcock St San Diego (92127) *(P-3465)*

Mitchell Rubber Products LLC (PA) ....C...... 951 681-5655
1880 Iowa Ave Ste 400 Riverside (92507) *(P-4778)*

Mitchell Silberberg Knupp LLP (PA) ....C...... 310 312-2000
2049 Century Park E Fl 18 Los Angeles (90067) *(P-18909)*

Mitchell Slbrberg Knupp Fndtio, Los Angeles *Also Called: Mitchell Silberberg Knupp LLP (P-18909)*

Mitchell1, San Diego *Also Called: Mitchell Repair Info Co LLC (P-3465)*

Mitchellamazing, Montclair *Also Called: Amazing Steel Company (P-5991)*

Mitco Industries Inc (PA) ....E...... 909 877-0800
2235 S Vista Ave Bloomington (92316) *(P-7941)*

Mitek, San Diego *Also Called: Mitek Systems Inc (P-7552)*

Mitek Systems Inc (PA) ....C...... 619 269-6800
600 B St Ste 100 San Diego (92101) *(P-7552)*

Mitratech Holdings Inc ....C...... 323 964-0000
5900 Wilshire Blvd Ste 1500 Los Angeles (90036) *(P-16309)*

Mitre Corporation ....D...... 619 758-7818
2756 Locust St San Diego (92106) *(P-19936)*

Mitsubishi Cement Corporation ....B...... 562 495-0600
1150 Pier F Ave Long Beach (90802) *(P-5367)*

Mitsubishi Cement Corporation ....C...... 760 248-7373
5808 State Highway 18 Lucerne Valley (92356) *(P-5368)*

Mitsubishi Chemical Carbon Fiber and Composites, Inc., Irvine *Also Called: Mitsubishi Chemical Crbn Fbr (P-4573)*

Mitsubishi Chemical Crbn Fbr ....C...... 800 929-5471
1822 Reynolds Ave Irvine (92614) *(P-4573)*

Mitsubishi Electric Us Inc (DH) ....C...... 714 220-2500
5900 Katella Ave Ste A Cypress (90630) *(P-12683)*

Mitsubishi Motors Cr Amer Inc (DH) ....B...... 714 799-4730
6400 Katella Ave Cypress (90630) *(P-14272)*

Mitsubshi Elc Vsual Sltons AME ....C...... 800 553-7278
10833 Valley View St Ste 300 Cypress (90630) *(P-9086)*

Mittal Ram ....D...... 310 769-6669
100 E Hillcrest Blvd Inglewood (90301) *(P-12747)*

Mittera Group Inc ....E...... 562 598-2446
3791 Catalina St Los Alamitos (90720) *(P-3638)*

Mittera-CA, Los Alamitos *Also Called: Mittera Group Inc (P-3638)*

Miva Inc ....C...... 858 490-2570
16870 W Bernardo Dr Ste 100 San Diego (92127) *(P-16459)*

Miva Merchant, San Diego *Also Called: Miva Inc (P-16459)*

Mixed Nuts Inc ....E...... 323 587-6887
7909 Crossway Dr Pico Rivera (90660) *(P-1559)*

Mixmode Inc ....E...... 858 225-2352
111 W Micheltorena St Ste 300-A Santa Barbara (93101) *(P-16310)*

Mixmor Inc ....F...... 323 664-1941
3131 Casitas Ave Los Angeles (90039) *(P-6939)*

Mizari Enterprises Inc (PA) ....E...... 323 549-9400
5455 Wilshire Blvd Ste 1410 Los Angeles (90036) *(P-12980)*

Mizkan America Inc ....C...... 909 484-8743
10037 8th St Rancho Cucamonga (91730) *(P-1947)*

Mizuho Bank Ltd ....C...... 213 243-4500
350 S Grand Ave Ste 1500 Los Angeles (90071) *(P-14220)*

MIZUHO BANK LTD, Los Angeles *Also Called: Mizuho Bank Ltd (P-14220)*

Mj Best Videographer LLC ....C...... 209 208-8432
14005 S Berendo Ave Apt 3 Gardena (90247) *(P-8424)*

Mjc America Ltd (PA) ....E...... 888 876-5387
20035 E Walnut Dr N Walnut (91789) *(P-8238)*

Mjc Engineering and Tech Inc ....F...... 714 890-0618
15401 Assembly Ln Huntington Beach (92649) *(P-7034)*

Mjw Inc ....D...... 323 778-8900
1328 W Slauson Ave Los Angeles (90044) *(P-7283)*

Mk Diamond Products Inc (PA) ....D...... 310 539-5221
1315 Storm Pkwy Torrance (90501) *(P-7146)*

Mk Luxury Group, Beverly Hills *Also Called: Maurice Kraiem & Company (P-12964)*

Mk Magnetics Inc ....D...... 760 246-6373
17030 Muskrat Ave Adelanto (92301) *(P-5620)*

Mk Manufacturing, Irvine *Also Called: M K Products Inc (P-7159)*

Mk Printing, Santa Ana *Also Called: Mekong Printing Inc (P-3633)*

Mkt Innovations ....D...... 714 524-7668
588 Porter Way Placentia (92870) *(P-7942)*

Mkt Innovations, Placentia *Also Called: Mike Kenney Tool Inc (P-7935)*

Mktg Inc ....B...... 310 972-7900
5800 Bristol Pkwy Ste 500 Culver City (90230) *(P-16879)*

MKTG, INC., Culver City *Also Called: Mktg Inc (P-16879)*

ML Kishigo Mfg Co LLC ....D...... 949 852-1963
11250 Slater Ave Fountain Valley (92708) *(P-2456)*

Mlim Holdings LLC ....A...... 619 299-3131
350 Camino De La Reina San Diego (92108) *(P-14935)*

MMC, Los Angeles *Also Called: Marsh Risk & Insurance Svcs (P-14611)*

MMC, San Diego *Also Called: Medical Management Cons Inc (P-20196)*

Mmca, Cypress *Also Called: Mitsubishi Motors Cr Amer Inc (P-14272)*

Mmd Equipment, Simi Valley *Also Called: Rajysan Incorporated (P-12814)*

ALPHABETIC

Employee Codes: A=Over 500 employees, B=251-500
C=101-250, D=51-100, E=20-50, F=10-19, G=1-9

2024 Southern California
Business Directory and Buyers Guide

© Mergent Inc. 1-800-342-5647
1183

Mmi Services Inc .... C...... 661 589-9366
4042 Patton Way Bakersfield (93308) *(P-363)*

Mmp Sheet Metal Inc .... E...... 562 691-1055
501 Commercial Way La Habra (90631) *(P-6273)*

Mmxviii Holdings Inc .... E...... 800 672-3974
20251 Sw Acacia St Ste 120 Newport Beach (92660) *(P-11138)*

Mnm Corporation (PA) .... **E...... 213 627-3737**
110 E 9th St Ste A777 Los Angeles (90079) *(P-3372)*

Mnm Manufacturing Inc .... D...... 310 898-1099
3019 E Harcourt St Compton (90221) *(P-6114)*

MNS Engineers Inc (PA) .... D...... 805 692-6921
201 N Calle Cesar Chavez Ste 300 Santa Barbara (93103) *(P-19648)*

Mob Scene LLC (PA) .... C...... 323 648-7200
8447 Wilshire Blvd Ste 100 Beverly Hills (90211) *(P-15560)*

Mob Scene Creative Productions, Beverly Hills *Also Called: Mob Scene LLC (P-15560)*

Mobile Equipment Appraisers, Bakersfield *Also Called: Mobile Equipment Company (P-6983)*

Mobile Equipment Company .... E...... 661 327-8476
3610 Gilmore Ave Bakersfield (93308) *(P-6983)*

Mobile Mini Inc .... F...... 909 356-1690
42207 3rd St E Lancaster (93535) *(P-6384)*

Mobile Modular Management Corp .... D...... 800 819-1084
11450 Mission Blvd Jurupa Valley (91752) *(P-6385)*

Mobilenet Services Inc (PA) .... **C...... 949 951-4444**
18 Morgan Ste 200 Irvine (92618) *(P-19649)*

Mobilitie Services, LLC, Irvine *Also Called: Boldyn Networks US Services LL (P-11872)*

Mobility Solutions Inc (PA) .... **E...... 858 278-0591**
7895 Convoy Ct Ste 11 San Diego (92111) *(P-12500)*

Mobilityware, Irvine *Also Called: Upstanding LLC (P-16415)*

Mobis, Fountain Valley *Also Called: Mobis Parts America LLC (P-9427)*

Mobis Parts America LLC .... E...... 949 450-0014
10550 Talbert Ave # 4 Fountain Valley (92708) *(P-9427)*

Mobis Parts America LLC (HQ) .... D...... 786 515-1101
10550 Talbert Ave 4th Fl Fountain Valley (92708) *(P-12249)*

Mobis Ventures Sv, Fountain Valley *Also Called: Mobis Parts America LLC (P-12249)*

Mobisystems Inc .... C...... 858 350-0315
4501 Mission Bay Dr Ste 3a San Diego (92109) *(P-16460)*

Mobiz, Redlands *Also Called: Mobiz It Inc (P-918)*

Mobiz It Inc .... D...... 909 453-6700
1175 Idaho St Ste 103 Redlands (92374) *(P-918)*

Moc Products Company Inc (PA) .... D...... 818 794-3500
12306 Montague St Pacoima (91331) *(P-4622)*

Mocean, Newport Beach *Also Called: Crossport Mocean (P-2151)*

Mocean, Los Angeles *Also Called: Mocean LLC (P-16507)*

Mocean LLC .... C...... 310 481-0808
2440 S Sepulveda Blvd Ste 150 Los Angeles (90064) *(P-16507)*

Mochi Ice Cream Company LLC (PA) .... **E...... 323 587-5504**
5563 Alcoa Ave Vernon (90058) *(P-1483)*

Mod 2, Los Angeles *Also Called: Mod2 Inc (P-16311)*

Mod-Electronics Inc .... E...... 310 322-2136
142 Sierra St El Segundo (90245) *(P-10893)*

Mod2 Inc .... F...... 213 747-8424
3317 S Broadway Los Angeles (90007) *(P-16311)*

Model Match Inc .... F...... 949 525-9405
209 Avenida Fabricante Ste 150 San Clemente (92672) *(P-16312)*

Modelo Group Inc .... E...... 562 446-5091
16751 Millikan Ave Irvine (92606) *(P-19650)*

Modern Aire Ventilating, North Hollywood *Also Called: Modern-Aire Ventilating Inc (P-6274)*

Modern Campus USA Inc (PA) .... D...... 805 484-9400
1320 Flynn Rd Ste 100 Camarillo (93012) *(P-16077)*

Modern Candle Co Inc .... E...... 323 441-0104
12884 Bradley Ave Sylmar (91342) *(P-13550)*

Modern Candles, Sylmar *Also Called: Modern Candle Co Inc (P-13550)*

Modern Concepts Inc .... D...... 310 637-0013
3121 E Ana St E Rncho Dmngz (90221) *(P-5103)*

Modern Dev Co A Ltd Partnr .... D...... 949 646-6400
7900 All America City Way Paramount (90723) *(P-16880)*

Modern Embroidery Inc .... E...... 714 436-9960
3701 W Moore Ave Santa Ana (92704) *(P-2520)*

Modern Engine Inc .... E...... 818 409-9494
701 Sonora Ave Glendale (91201) *(P-7943)*

Modern Gourmet Foods, Santa Ana *Also Called: Coastal Cocktails Inc (P-13361)*

Modern Hr Inc .... D...... 877 842-4988
7590 N Glenoaks Blvd Burbank (91504) *(P-20202)*

Modern Parking Inc .... C...... 310 271-1125
415 N Bedford Dr Beverly Hills (90210) *(P-16993)*

Modern Parking Inc .... C...... 310 821-1081
14110 Palawan Way Marina Del Rey (90292) *(P-16994)*

Modern Parking Inc .... C...... 818 783-3143
4955 Van Nuys Blvd Frnt Van Nuys (91403) *(P-16995)*

Modern Parking Inc .... C...... 619 233-0412
1025 W Laurel St Ste 105 San Diego (92101) *(P-16996)*

Modern Plating, Los Angeles *Also Called: Alco Plating Corp (P-6576)*

Modern Postcard, Carlsbad *Also Called: Iris Group Inc (P-3773)*

Modern Printing & Mailing Inc .... E...... 619 222-0535
3535 Enterprise St San Diego (92110) *(P-3639)*

Modern Stairways Inc .... E...... 619 466-1484
3239 Bancroft Dr Spring Valley (91977) *(P-5426)*

Modern Studio Equipment Inc .... F...... 818 764-8574
16200 Stagg St Van Nuys (91406) *(P-10874)*

Modern Woodworks, Canoga Park *Also Called: Modern Woodworks Inc (P-2756)*

Modern Woodworks Inc .... E...... 800 575-3475
7949 Deering Ave Canoga Park (91304) *(P-2756)*

Modern-Aire Ventilating Inc .... E...... 818 765-9870
7319 Lankershim Blvd North Hollywood (91605) *(P-6274)*

Modernica, Vernon *Also Called: Modernica Inc (P-13945)*

Modernica Inc (PA) .... **E...... 323 826-1600**
2901 Saco St Vernon (90058) *(P-13945)*

Modified Plastics Inc (PA) .... **E...... 714 546-4667**
1240 E Glenwood Pl Santa Ana (92707) *(P-5104)*

Modis, Glendale *Also Called: Akkodis Inc (P-15959)*

Modivcare Solutions LLC .... C...... 714 503-6871
7441 Lincoln Way # 225 Garden Grove (92841) *(P-11785)*

Moducom, La Crescenta *Also Called: Modular Communications Systems (P-8548)*

Modular Communications Systems .... E...... 818 764-1333
2629 Foothill Blvd La Crescenta (91214) *(P-8548)*

MODULAR MEDICAL, San Diego *Also Called: Modular Medical Inc (P-10569)*

Modular Medical Inc .... E...... 858 800-3500
10740 Thornmint Rd San Diego (92127) *(P-10569)*

Modular Metal Fabricators Inc .... C...... 951 242-3154
24600 Nandina Ave Moreno Valley (92551) *(P-6275)*

Modular Office Solutions Inc .... E...... 909 476-4200
11701 6th St Rancho Cucamonga (91730) *(P-2916)*

Modular Wind Energy Inc .... D...... 562 304-6782
1709 Apollo Ct Seal Beach (90740) *(P-6883)*

Modus Advanced Inc .... D...... 925 960-8700
2772 Loker Ave W Carlsbad (92010) *(P-4779)*

Moelis & Company LLC .... C...... 310 443-2300
1999 Avenue Of The Stars Ste 1900 Los Angeles (90067) *(P-14998)*

Moeller Mfg & Sup LLC .... E...... 714 999-5551
630 E Lambert Rd Brea (92821) *(P-5933)*

Mogami, Torrance *Also Called: Marshall Electronics Inc (P-8422)*

Mohawk Industries Inc .... E...... 909 357-1064
9687 Transportation Way Fontana (92335) *(P-2118)*

Mohawk Medical Group Inc .... D...... 661 324-4747
9500 Stockdale Hwy Ste 200 Bakersfield (93311) *(P-17715)*

Mohawk Western Plastics Inc .... E...... 909 593-7547
1496 Arrow Hwy La Verne (91750) *(P-3187)*

Mojave Foods Corporation (HQ) .... **C...... 323 890-8900**
6200 E Slauson Ave Commerce (90040) *(P-1948)*

Molded Fiber GL Companies - W .... D...... 760 246-4042
9400 Holly Rd Adelanto (92301) *(P-5105)*

Moldex, Culver City *Also Called: Moldex-Metric Inc (P-10684)*

Moldex-Metric Inc .... B...... 310 837-6500
10111 Jefferson Blvd Culver City (90232) *(P-10684)*

Molding Corporation America .... E...... 818 890-7877
10349 Norris Ave Pacoima (91331) *(P-5106)*

Molding Intl & Engrg Inc .... E...... 951 296-5010
42136 Avenida Alvarado Temecula (92590) *(P-5107)*

Moldings Plus Inc .... E...... 909 947-3310
1856 S Grove Ave Ontario (91761) *(P-2618)*

Mole-Richardson Co Ltd (PA).................D....... 323 851-0111
12154 Montague St Pacoima (91331) *(P-8375)*

Moleaer Inc ....D....... 424 558-3567
3232 W El Segundo Blvd Hawthorne (90250) *(P-7284)*

Molecular Bio Products, San Diego Also Called: Thermo Fisher Scientific Inc *(P-10298)*

Molecular Bioproducts Inc (DH)..............C....... 858 453-7551
9389 Waples St San Diego (92121) *(P-10274)*

Molecular Bioproducts Svc Corp (HQ)........E....... 858 875-7696
10636 Scripps Summit Ct San Diego (92131) *(P-12530)*

Molecular Probes Inc ....D....... 760 603-7200
5781 Van Allen Way Carlsbad (92008) *(P-4282)*

Moleculum ....F....... 714 619-5139
3128 Red Hill Ave Costa Mesa (92626) *(P-4645)*

Molina Healthcare, Long Beach Also Called: Molina Healthcare Inc *(P-17716)*

Molina Healthcare Inc (PA)....................A....... 562 435-3666
200 Oceangate Ste 100 Long Beach (90802) *(P-17716)*

Molina Healthcare Inc ....C....... 562 435-3666
1 Golden Shore Long Beach (90802) *(P-18781)*

Molina Healthcare California ....A....... 800 526-8196
200 Oceangate Ste 100 Long Beach (90802) *(P-17717)*

Molina Hlthcare Cal Prtner Pla ....B....... 562 435-3666
200 Oceangate Ste 100 Long Beach (90802) *(P-14454)*

Molina Pathways LLC ....B....... 562 491-5773
200 Oceangate Ste 100 Long Beach (90802) *(P-17718)*

Molino Company ....D....... 323 726-1000
13712 Alondra Blvd Cerritos (90703) *(P-3640)*

Molnar Engineering Inc ....E....... 818 993-3495
20731 Marilla St Chatsworth (91311) *(P-7944)*

Momco App Inc ....E....... 619 450-6340
5598 Elgin Ave San Diego (92120) *(P-16313)*

Momeni Engineering LLC ....E....... 714 897-9301
5451 Argosy Ave Huntington Beach (92649) *(P-7945)*

Momentum Textiles LLC (PA)....................E....... 949 833-8886
17811 Fitch Irvine (92614) *(P-13086)*

Momentum Textiles Wallcovering, Irvine Also Called: Momentum Textiles LLC *(P-13086)*

Monaco Baking Company, Fullerton Also Called: Phenix Gourmet LLC *(P-1523)*

Monadnock Company ....C....... 626 964-6581
16728 Gale Ave City Of Industry (91745) *(P-5934)*

Monarch Beach Golf Links (HQ).................D....... 949 240-8247
50 Monarch Beach Resort N Dana Point (92629) *(P-17440)*

Monarch Healthcare A Medical ....C....... 949 489-1960
675 Camino De Los Mares Ste 300 San Clemente (92673) *(P-17719)*

Monarch Healthcare A Medical (HQ).............D....... 949 923-3200
11 Technology Dr Irvine (92618) *(P-17720)*

Monarch Hlthcare A Med Group I ....C....... 760 730-9448
2562 State St Carlsbad (92008) *(P-18782)*

Monarch Litho Inc (PA).........................E....... 323 727-0300
1501 Date St Montebello (90640) *(P-3641)*

Monarch Nut Company LLC ....C....... 661 725-6458
786 Road 188 Delano (93215) *(P-109)*

Monark LP ....D....... 310 769-6669
2804 W El Segundo Blvd Gardena (90249) *(P-14727)*

Monco Products Inc ....E....... 714 891-2788
7562 Acacia Ave Garden Grove (92841) *(P-5108)*

Mondelez Global LLC ....F....... 714 690-7428
6201 Knott Ave Buena Park (90620) *(P-1226)*

Mondelez Global LLC ....D....... 909 605-0140
5815 Clark St Ontario (91761) *(P-13380)*

Mondrian Holdings LLC ....B....... 323 848-6004
8440 W Sunset Blvd West Hollywood (90069) *(P-15252)*

Mondrian Hotel, Los Angeles Also Called: Morgans Hotel Group MGT LLC *(P-15256)*

Monex, Newport Beach Also Called: Monex Deposit A Cal Ltd Partnr *(P-14079)*

Monex Deposit A Cal Ltd Partnr ....D....... 800 444-8317
4910 Birch St Newport Beach (92660) *(P-14079)*

Moneyjet, San Diego Also Called: National Funding Inc *(P-14285)*

Monier Lifetile, Rialto Also Called: Royal Westlake Roofing LLC *(P-5447)*

Mono Engineering Corp ....E....... 818 772-4998
20977 Knapp St Chatsworth (91311) *(P-7946)*

Monobind Sales Inc (PA)........................E....... 949 951-2665
100 N Pointe Dr Lake Forest (92630) *(P-10570)*

Monocent, Northridge Also Called: Monocent Inc *(P-4283)*

Monocent Inc ....F....... 424 310-0777
8920 Quartz Ave Northridge (91324) *(P-4283)*

Monogram Aerospace Fas Inc ....C....... 323 722-4760
3423 Garfield Ave Commerce (90040) *(P-5935)*

Monogram Systems, Carson Also Called: Mag Aerospace Industries LLC *(P-5959)*

Monogram Systems, Carson Also Called: Zodiac Wtr Waste Aero Systems *(P-9832)*

Monrovia Growes, Azusa Also Called: Monrovia Nursery Company *(P-60)*

MONROVIA MEMORIAL HOSPITAL, Monrovia Also Called: Alakor Healthcare LLC *(P-18171)*

Monrovia Nursery Company (PA).................A....... 626 334-9321
817 E Monrovia Pl Azusa (91702) *(P-60)*

Monrovia Ranch Market, Victorville Also Called: Baja Fresh Supermarket *(P-93)*

Monrovia Service Center, Monrovia Also Called: Southern California Edison Co *(P-12067)*

Monrow, Los Angeles Also Called: Monrow Inc *(P-2257)*

Monrow Inc ....E....... 213 741-6007
1404 S Main St Ste C Los Angeles (90015) *(P-2257)*

Monsanto, Oxnard Also Called: Monsanto Company *(P-4552)*

Monsanto Company ....E....... 805 827-2341
2700 Camino Del Sol Oxnard (93030) *(P-4552)*

Monsieur Marcel, Los Angeles Also Called: Strouk Group LLC *(P-13307)*

Monster Beverage 1990 Corporation ....A....... 951 739-6200
1 Monster Way Corona (92879) *(P-1704)*

Monster Beverage Company ....E....... 866 322-4466
1990 Pomona Rd Corona (92878) *(P-1705)*

Monster Beverage Corporation (PA).............A....... 951 739-6200
1 Monster Way Corona (92879) *(P-1706)*

Monster Energy, Corona Also Called: Monster Energy Company *(P-13381)*

Monster Energy Company (HQ)..................B....... 866 322-4466
1 Monster Way Corona (92879) *(P-13381)*

Monster Tool LLC ....C....... 760 477-1000
2470 Ash St U 2 Vista (92081) *(P-5886)*

Montage Hotels & Resorts LLC (PA)............A....... 949 715-5002
3 Ada Ste 100 Irvine (92618) *(P-15253)*

Montage Hotels & Resorts LLC ....A....... 949 715-6000
30801 Coast Hwy Laguna Beach (92651) *(P-20063)*

Montage Laguna Beach, Irvine Also Called: Montage Hotels & Resorts LLC *(P-15253)*

Montage Laguna Beach, Laguna Beach Also Called: Montage Hotels & Resorts LLC *(P-20063)*

Montbleau & Associates Inc (PA)................D....... 619 263-5550
555 Raven St San Diego (92102) *(P-2888)*

Montclair Bronze Inc (PA).......................E....... 909 986-2664
2535 E 57th St Huntington Park (90255) *(P-5805)*

Montclair Hospital Medical Center, Montclair Also Called: Prime Hlthcare Srvcs-Mntclair *(P-18389)*

Montclair Wood Corporation ....E....... 909 985-0302
545 N Mountain Ave Ste 104 Upland (91786) *(P-2577)*

Monte Vista Child Care Ctr Inc ....D....... 909 476-6780
7976 Beechwood Dr Rancho Cucamonga (91701) *(P-19220)*

Monte Vista Grove Homes ....D....... 626 796-6135
2889 San Pasqual St Pasadena (91107) *(P-19287)*

Montebello Container, Santa Fe Springs Also Called: Cflute Corp *(P-3090)*

Montebello Plastics LLC ....E....... 323 728-6814
601 W Olympic Blvd Montebello (90640) *(P-4815)*

Montebello Unified School Dst ....D....... 323 887-2140
500 Hendricks St 2nd Fl Montebello (90640) *(P-15729)*

Montebello Unified School Dst ....D....... 323 440-2899
831 Perry Ave Montebello (90640) *(P-16881)*

Montecito Country Club Inc ....D....... 805 969-0800
920 Summit Rd Santa Barbara (93108) *(P-17503)*

Montecito Family YMCA, Santa Barbara Also Called: Channel Islnds Yung MNS Chrstn *(P-19436)*

Montecito Retirement Assn ....B....... 805 969-8011
300 Hot Springs Rd Santa Barbara (93108) *(P-18016)*

Monterey Canyon LLC (PA)......................D....... 213 741-0209
1515 E 15th St Los Angeles (90021) *(P-2353)*

Monterey Collection Services, Oceanside Also Called: Monterey Financial Svcs Inc *(P-14273)*

Monterey Financial Svcs Inc (PA)................C....... 760 639-3500
4095 Avenida De La Plata Oceanside (92056) *(P-14273)*

Monterey Palms Health Care Ctr, Palm Desert Also Called: Mariner Health Care Inc *(P-18008)*

Monterey Park Hospital ....C....... 626 570-9000
900 S Atlantic Blvd Monterey Park (91754) *(P-18346)*

ALPHABETIC

Employee Codes: A=Over 500 employees, B=251-500
C=101-250, D=51-100, E=20-50, F=10-19, G=1-9

2024 Southern California
Business Directory and Buyers Guide

© Mergent Inc. 1-800-342-5647
1185

Monterey Park Hospital, Monterey Park *Also Called: Monterey Park Hospital* **(P-18346)**

Monterrey The Natural Choice, San Diego *Also Called: Mpci Holdings Inc* **(P-13301)**

Montesquieu Corp ....D...... 877 705-5669
888 W E St San Diego (92101) **(P-13479)**

Montesquieu Vins & Domaines, San Diego *Also Called: Montesquieu Corp* **(P-13479)**

Montesquieu Winery, San Diego *Also Called: WG Best Weinkellerei Inc* **(P-1667)**

Monzu Holdings LLC ....D...... 619 255-5032
780 Hollister St San Diego (92154) **(P-1841)**

Moog Aircraft Group, Torrance *Also Called: Moog Inc* **(P-10002)**

Moog Inc .... B...... 310 533-1178
1218 W Jon St Torrance (90502) **(P-8187)**

Moog Inc .... B...... 805 618-3900
7406 Hollister Ave Goleta (93117) **(P-10000)**

Moog Inc .... C...... 818 341-5156
21339 Nordhoff St Chatsworth (91311) **(P-10001)**

Moog Inc .... B...... 310 533-1178
20263 S Western Ave Torrance (90501) **(P-10002)**

Moog Jon Street Warehouse, Torrance *Also Called: Moog Inc* **(P-8187)**

Mooney International, Chino *Also Called: Soaring America Corporation* **(P-9553)**

Moonstone Bch Innvstors A Cal ....C...... 805 927-8661
6700 Moonstone Beach Dr Cambria (93428) **(P-15254)**

Moonstone Hotel Properties, Cambria *Also Called: Moonstone Management Corp* **(P-14832)**

Moonstone Management Corp (PA)..................................C...... **805 927-4200**
2905 Burton Dr Cambria (93428) **(P-14832)**

Moore Business Forms, Temecula *Also Called: R R Donnelley & Sons Company* **(P-12999)**

Moore Farms Inc ....E...... 661 854-5588
916 S Derby St Arvin (93203) **(P-1949)**

Moore Industries, North Hills *Also Called: Moore Industries-International Inc* **(P-10146)**

Moore Industries-International Inc (PA) ....C...... **818 894-7111**
16650 Schoenborn St North Hills (91343) **(P-10146)**

Moores Ideal Products LLC ....E...... 626 339-9007
830 W Golden Grove Way Covina (91722) **(P-10962)**

Moose, El Segundo *Also Called: Moose Toys LLC* **(P-10942)**

Moose Toys LLC ....D...... 310 341-4642
737 Campus Sq W El Segundo (90245) **(P-10942)**

Mophie Inc (DH)..F...... **888 866-7443**
15495 Sand Canyon Ave Ste 400 Irvine (92618) **(P-8549)**

Moral Welfare and Recreation, Camp Pendleton *Also Called: Marine Corps Community Svcs* **(P-17557)**

Moravek, Brea *Also Called: Moravek Biochemicals Inc* **(P-3900)**

Moravek Biochemicals Inc (PA).......................................E...... **714 990-2018**
577 Mercury Ln Brea (92821) **(P-3900)**

Morehouse Foods Inc ....E...... 626 854-1655
760 Epperson Dr City Of Industry (91748) **(P-1362)**

Morehouse-Cowles LLC ....E...... 909 627-7222
13930 Magnolia Ave Chino (91710) **(P-7250)**

Moreland Manufacturing Inc ....E...... 714 426-1411
17406 Mount Cliffwood Cir Fountain Valley (92708) **(P-3788)**

Morelends.com, San Diego *Also Called: Synergy One Lending Inc* **(P-14351)**

MORENO VALLEY FAMILY HEALTH CE, Moreno Valley *Also Called: Community Health Systems Inc* **(P-17629)**

Moreno Valley Heacock Med Offs, Moreno Valley *Also Called: Kaiser Foundation Hospitals* **(P-14994)**

Morettis Design Collection Inc ....E...... 310 638-5555
16926 Keegan Ave Ste C Carson (90746) **(P-2781)**

Morgan Fabrics, Vernon *Also Called: Morgan Fabrics Corporation* **(P-13087)**

Morgan Fabrics Corporation (PA)....................................D...... 323 583-9981
4265 Exchange Ave Vernon (90058) **(P-13087)**

Morgan Gallacher Inc ....E...... 562 695-1232
8707 Millergrove Dr Santa Fe Springs (90670) **(P-4361)**

Morgan Linen Service, Los Angeles *Also Called: Morgan Services Inc* **(P-15458)**

Morgan Marine, Simi Valley *Also Called: Catalina Yachts Inc* **(P-9856)**

Morgan Polymer Seals LLC (PA).....................................B...... 619 498-9221
2475a Paseo De Las Americas Ste 3303 San Diego (92154) **(P-4738)**

Morgan Polymer Seals LLC ....B...... 619 498-9221
3303 2475a Paseo De Las Americas San Diego (92154) **(P-7251)**

Morgan Services Inc ....D...... 213 485-9666
905 Yale St Los Angeles (90012) **(P-15458)**

Morgan Stanley Smith Barney, San Diego *Also Called: Morgan Stnley Smith Barney LLC* **(P-14393)**

Morgan Stnley Smith Barney LLC ....C...... 760 568-3500
74199 El Paseo Ste 201 Palm Desert (92260) **(P-14200)**

Morgan Stnley Smith Barney LLC ....C...... 818 715-1800
21650 Oxnard St Ste 1800 Woodland Hills (91367) **(P-14391)**

Morgan Stnley Smith Barney LLC ....C...... 213 891-3200
444 S Flower St Ste 2700 Los Angeles (90071) **(P-14392)**

Morgan Stnley Smith Barney LLC ....C...... 619 238-1226
101 W Broadway Ste 1800 San Diego (92101) **(P-14393)**

Morgan Stnley Smith Barney LLC ....C...... 805 963-3381
1014 Santa Barbara St Santa Barbara (93101) **(P-14394)**

Morgan Stnley Smith Barney LLC ....C...... 760 438-5100
5796 Armada Dr Ste 200 Carlsbad (92008) **(P-14395)**

Morgan Stnley Smith Barney LLC ....C...... 212 761-4000
1225 Prospect St Ste 202 La Jolla (92037) **(P-14396)**

Morgan Stnley Smith Barney LLC ....C...... 714 674-4100
10 Pointe Dr Ste 400 Brea (92821) **(P-14397)**

Morgan Stnley Smith Barney LLC ....C...... 951 682-1181
3750 University Ave Ste 600 Riverside (92501) **(P-14398)**

Morgans Hotel Group MGT LLC ....C...... 805 969-2203
1555 S Jameson Ln Santa Barbara (93108) **(P-15255)**

Morgans Hotel Group MGT LLC ....C...... 323 650-8999
8440 W Sunset Blvd Los Angeles (90069) **(P-15256)**

Morin Corporation ....E...... 909 428-3747
10707 Commerce Way Fontana (92337) **(P-6386)**

Morin Industrial Technology, Huntington Beach *Also Called: M I T Inc* **(P-7079)**

Morin West, Fontana *Also Called: Morin Corporation* **(P-6386)**

Morinaga Nutritional Foods Inc (HQ)..............................F...... **310 787-0200**
3838 Del Amo Blvd Ste 201 Torrance (90503) **(P-1950)**

Morley Builders Inc (PA)..C...... 310 399-1600
3330 Ocean Park Blvd Santa Monica (90405) **(P-512)**

Morley Construction Company (HQ)..................................D...... 310 399-1600
3330 Ocean Park Blvd Santa Monica (90405) **(P-1079)**

Morningside of Fullerton, Fullerton *Also Called: Corecare I I I* **(P-19252)**

Morningstar of Mission Viejo, Mission Viejo *Also Called: Morningstar Senior MGT LLC* **(P-19288)**

Morningstar Senior MGT LLC ....C...... 949 298-3675
28570 Marguerite Pkwy Mission Viejo (92692) **(P-19288)**

Morongo Band Mission Indians ....C...... 951 849-3080
49500 Seminole Dr Cabazon (92230) **(P-17559)**

Morongo Casino Resort Spa, Cabazon *Also Called: Morongo Band Mission Indians* **(P-17559)**

Morpheus Space Inc (PA)...F...... **562 766-8470**
300 Continental Blvd Ste 350 El Segundo (90245) **(P-9910)**

Morphotrak LLC (DH)...C...... **714 238-2000**
5515 E La Palma Ave Ste 100 Anaheim (92807) **(P-16461)**

Morrell's Metal Finishing, Compton *Also Called: Morrells Electro Plating Inc* **(P-6640)**

Morrells Electro Plating Inc ....E...... 310 639-1024
432 E Euclid Ave Compton (90222) **(P-6640)**

Morris & Willner Partners ....D...... 949 705-0682
2151 Michelson Dr Ste 185 Irvine (92612) **(P-20203)**

Morris Crullo World Evangelism (PA)...............................D...... **858 277-2200**
875 Hotel Cir S # 2 San Diego (92108) **(P-19504)**

Morris Enterprises Inc ....F...... 818 894-9103
16799 Schoenborn St North Hills (91343) **(P-5109)**

Morris Group International, City Of Industry *Also Called: Acorn Engineering Company* **(P-4593)**

Morris Grritano Insur Agcy Inc ....D...... 805 543-6887
1122 Laurel Ln San Luis Obispo (93401) **(P-14614)**

Morris Polich & Purdy LLP (PA)......................................D...... **213 891-9100**
1055 W 7th St Ste 2400 Los Angeles (90017) **(P-18910)**

Morrison & Foerster, Los Angeles *Also Called: Morrison & Foerster LLP* **(P-18911)**

Morrison & Foerster LLP ....C...... 213 892-5200
707 Wilshire Blvd Ste 6000 Los Angeles (90017) **(P-18911)**

Morrison & Foerster LLP ....B...... 858 720-5100
12531 High Bluff Dr Ste 100 San Diego (92130) **(P-18912)**

Morrow-Meadows Corporation ....B...... 858 974-3650
13000 Kirkham Way Ste 101 Poway (92064) **(P-919)**

Morrow-Meadows Corporation (PA).................................A...... **858 974-3650**
231 Benton Ct City Of Industry (91789) **(P-920)**

Morse Micro Inc ....D...... 949 501-7080
40 Waterworks Way Irvine (92618) **(P-8847)**

Mortech Manufacturing ....D...... 626 334-1471
411 N Aerojet Dr Azusa (91702) **(P-2933)**

Mergent email: customerrelations@mergent.com
1186

2024 Southern California
Business Directory and Buyers Guide

(P-0000) Products & Services Section entry number
(PA)=Parent Co (HQ)=Headquarters (DH)=Div Headquarters

Mortex Apparel, Burbank *Also Called: Mortex Corporation (P-2216)*

Mortex Corporation C
40 E Verdugo Ave Burbank (91502) *(P-2216)*

Mortgage Works Financial, Redlands *Also Called: Mountain West Financial Inc (P-14343)*

Morton Grinding Inc ....C...... 661 298-0895
201 E Avenue K15 Lancaster (93535) *(P-11073)*

Morton Manufacturing, Lancaster *Also Called: Morton Grinding Inc (P-11073)*

Morton Salt Inc ....C...... 562 437-0071
1050 Pier F Ave Long Beach (90802) *(P-4623)*

Moseley, Goleta *Also Called: Moseley Associates Inc (P-8550)*

Moseley Associates Inc (HQ) ....D...... 805 968-9621
82 Coromar Dr Goleta (93117) *(P-8550)*

Moseys Production Machinists Inc (PA) .... E...... 714 693-4840
1550 Lakeview Loop Anaheim (92807) *(P-7947)*

Moss Management Services Inc ....C...... 818 990-5999
15300 Ventura Blvd Ste 405 Sherman Oaks (91403) *(P-14833)*

Moss Motors Ltd (PA) ....C...... 805 967-4546
400 Rutherford St Goleta (93117) *(P-13865)*

Mossy Automotive Group Inc (PA) ....D...... 858 581-4000
4555 Mission Bay Dr San Diego (92109) *(P-13798)*

Mossy Ford Inc ....C...... 858 273-7500
4570 Mission Bay Dr San Diego (92109) *(P-13799)*

Mossy Nissan Inc ....D...... 858 565-6608
8118 Clairemont Mesa Blvd San Diego (92111) *(P-13800)*

Mossy Nissan Kearny Mesa, San Diego *Also Called: Mossy Nissan Inc (P-13800)*

Mossy Toyota, San Diego *Also Called: Mossy Automotive Group Inc (P-13798)*

Motec USA, Huntington Beach *Also Called: JGM Automotive Tooling Inc (P-7244)*

Motech Americas LLC ....B...... 302 451-7500
1300 Valley Vista Dr Ste 207 Diamond Bar (91765) *(P-19861)*

Motion Engineering Inc (DH) ....D...... 805 696-1200
33 S La Patera Ln Santa Barbara (93117) *(P-7553)*

Motion Industries Inc ....E...... 858 602-1500
12550 Stowe Dr Poway (92064) *(P-12866)*

Motion Pcture Indust Pnsion HI ....C...... 818 769-0007
11365 Ventura Blvd Ste 300 Studio City (91604) *(P-14549)*

Motion Picture and TV Fund (PA) ....A...... 818 876-1777
23388 Mulholland Dr Ste 200 Woodland Hills (91364) *(P-18347)*

Motion Theory Inc ....C...... 310 396-9433
444 W Ocean Blvd Ste 1400 Long Beach (90802) *(P-15669)*

Motionloft Inc ....E...... 415 580-7671
13681 Newport Ave Ste 8 Tustin (92780) *(P-10275)*

Motivational Systems Inc (PA) ....D...... 619 474-8246
2200 Cleveland Ave National City (91950) *(P-15670)*

Motive Energy Inc (PA) ....D...... 714 888-2525
17260 Newhope St Fountain Valley (92708) *(P-12607)*

Motive Nation, Downey *Also Called: Rockview Dairies Inc (P-13392)*

Motivtnal Flfllment Lgstics Sv, Chino *Also Called: Math Holdings Inc (P-16868)*

Motor City GMC Buick Pontiac, Bakersfield *Also Called: Motor City Sales & Service (P-13801)*

Motor City Sales & Service (PA) ....C...... 661 836-9000
3101 Pacheco Rd Bakersfield (93313) *(P-13801)*

Motor Technology Inc ....D...... 951 270-6200
2301 Wardlow Cir Corona (92878) *(P-8151)*

Motorcar Parts of America Inc (PA) ....A...... 310 212-7910
2929 California St Torrance (90503) *(P-9428)*

Motorola, San Diego *Also Called: Motorola Mobility LLC (P-12684)*

Motorola Mobility LLC ....D...... 858 455-1500
6450 Sequence Dr San Diego (92121) *(P-12684)*

Motorola Sltons Cnnctivity Inc (HQ) ....C...... 951 719-2100
42555 Rio Nedo Temecula (92590) *(P-8480)*

Motors & Controls Whse Inc ....E...... 714 956-0480
1440 N Burton Pl Anaheim (92806) *(P-12685)*

Motorvac Technologies Inc ....E...... 714 558-4822
1431 Village Way Santa Ana (92705) *(P-7948)*

Moulton Logistics Management ....C...... 818 997-1800
7855 Hayvenhurst Ave Van Nuys (91406) *(P-11599)*

Moulton Nguel Wtr Dst Pub Fclt ....D...... 949 831-2500
26161 Gordon Rd Laguna Hills (92653) *(P-12135)*

Moulton Niguel Water District, Laguna Hills *Also Called: Moulton Nguel Wtr Dst Pub Fclt (P-12135)*

Mount Palomar Winery, Temecula *Also Called: Louidar LLC (P-1646)*

Mountain Gear Corporation ....C...... 626 851-2488
4889 4th St Irwindale (91706) *(P-13107)*

Mountain High Ski Resort, Wrightwood *Also Called: MHRP Resort Inc (P-15251)*

Mountain Materials Inc ....E...... 619 445-4150
1117 Tavern Rd Alpine (91901) *(P-5486)*

Mountain News & Shopper, Lake Arrowhead *Also Called: Hi-Desert Publishing Company (P-3282)*

Mountain View Child Care Inc (PA) ....B...... 909 796-6915
1720 Mountain View Ave Loma Linda (92354) *(P-18348)*

Mountain View Child Care Inc ....C...... 818 252-5863
10716 La Tuna Canyon Rd Sun Valley (91352) *(P-19221)*

Mountain View Transportation, Oxnard *Also Called: AG Rx (P-13486)*

Mountain Vista Golf Course At ....D...... 760 200-2200
38180 Del Webb Blvd Palm Desert (92211) *(P-17560)*

Mountain Water Ice Company ....E...... 760 722-7611
2843 Benet Rd Oceanside (92058) *(P-11553)*

Mountain Water Ice Company Inc (PA) ....D...... 310 638-0321
17011 Central Ave Carson (90746) *(P-1838)*

Mountain West Financial Inc (PA) ....B...... 909 793-1500
31 W Stuart Ave Redlands (92374) *(P-14343)*

Mountains Community Hosp Fndtn ....C...... 909 336-3651
29101 Hospital Rd Lake Arrowhead (92352) *(P-18349)*

Mountains Community Hospital, Lake Arrowhead *Also Called: Mountains Community Hosp Fndtn (P-18349)*

Mouse Graphics, Costa Mesa *Also Called: Orange Coast Reprographics Inc (P-3648)*

Mousepad Designs, Cerritos *Also Called: Mpd Holdings Inc (P-7555)*

Movers and Shakers LLC ....D...... 310 893-7051
1217 Wilshire Blvd Santa Monica (90403) *(P-15561)*

Movieclips.com, Los Angeles *Also Called: Zefr Inc (P-19916)*

Moving Image Technologies LLC ....E...... 714 751-7998
17760 Newhope St Ste B Fountain Valley (92708) *(P-10875)*

Moviola Digital, Burbank *Also Called: Filmtools Inc (P-14082)*

Mowery Thomason Inc ....C...... 714 666-1717
1225 N Red Gum St Anaheim (92806) *(P-984)*

Moxa Americas Inc ....E...... 714 528-6777
601 Valencia Ave Ste 100 Brea (92823) *(P-7554)*

Moxy AC Ht Dwntwn Los Angeles, Los Angeles *Also Called: Lightstone Dt La LLC (P-15228)*

Moyes Custom Furniture Inc ....E...... 714 729-0234
1884 Pomona Rd Corona (92878) *(P-17078)*

Mozaik LLC ....E...... 562 207-1900
245 W Carl Karcher Way Anaheim (92801) *(P-3076)*

Mp Aero LLC ....D...... 818 901-9828
7701 Woodley Ave Van Nuys (91406) *(P-1170)*

Mp Biomedicals, Irvine *Also Called: Mp Biomedicals LLC (P-10276)*

Mp Biomedicals LLC (HQ) ....E...... 949 833-2500
9 Goddard Irvine (92618) *(P-10276)*

MP Environmental Svcs Inc (PA) ....C...... 800 458-3036
3400 Manor St Bakersfield (93308) *(P-12174)*

Mp Materials Corp ....E...... 702 844-6111
67750 Bailey Rd Mountain Pass (92366) *(P-239)*

Mp Mine Operations LLC ....C...... 702 277-0848
67750 Bailey Rd Mountain Pass (92366) *(P-414)*

Mp Solutions Inc ....E
21818 S Wilmington Ave Ste 411 Carson (90810) *(P-10003)*

Mp3com Inc ....D...... 858 623-7000
4790 Eastgate Mall San Diego (92121) *(P-11893)*

MPA, Torrance *Also Called: Motorcar Parts of America Inc (P-9428)*

Mpb Furniture Corporation ....E...... 760 375-4800
414 W Ridgecrest Blvd Ridgecrest (93555) *(P-2812)*

Mpbs Industries, Los Angeles *Also Called: Meat Packers Butchers Sup Inc (P-7208)*

Mpci Holdings Inc ....C...... 619 294-2222
7850 Waterville Rd San Diego (92154) *(P-13301)*

Mpd Holdings Inc ....E...... 213 210-2591
16200 Commerce Way Cerritos (90703) *(P-7555)*

Mpi, Camarillo *Also Called: Multilayer Prototypes Inc (P-8706)*

Mpl Enterprises Inc ....D...... 714 545-1717
2302 S Susan St Santa Ana (92704) *(P-206)*

Mpm & Associates, Van Nuys *Also Called: Mpm Building Services Inc (P-4362)*

Mpm Building Services Inc ....E...... 818 708-9676
7011 Hayvenhurst Ave Ste F Van Nuys (91406) *(P-4362)*

Employee Codes: A=Over 500 employees, B=251-500
C=101-250, D=51-100, E=20-50, F=10-19, G=1-9

2024 Southern California
Business Directory and Buyers Guide

© Mergent Inc. 1-800-342-5647

1187

Mpo Videotronics Inc (PA)...D...... 805 499-8513
5069 Maureen Ln Moorpark (93021) *(P-10876)*

Mpower Holding Corporation (HQ).................................D...... 866 699-8242
515 S Flower St Fl 36 Los Angeles (90071) *(P-11894)*

Mpp Fullerton Div 6061, Fullerton Also Called: Orora Packaging Solutions (P-13020)

Mpp San Diego Div 6064, San Marcos Also Called: Orora Packaging Solutions (P-13015)

Mpressions, Anaheim Also Called: Dean Hesketh Company Inc (P-3752)

MPS Anzon LLC..C...... 626 471-3553
11911 Clark St Arcadia (91006) *(P-10685)*

MPS Medical Inc..E...... 714 672-1090
785 Challenger St Brea (92821) *(P-10571)*

Mq Power, Cypress Also Called: Multiquip Inc (P-12608)

Mr Bug, Anaheim Also Called: Reels Inc (P-12258)

Mr Clean Maintenance Systems, Bloomington Also Called: Chiro Inc (P-12889)

Mr Dj Inc..E...... 213 744-0044
1800 E Washington Blvd Los Angeles (90021) *(P-8425)*

Mr Lock, Corona Also Called: Lock America Inc (P-5928)

MR Mold & Engineering Corp..E...... 714 996-5511
1150 Beacon St Brea (92821) *(P-7083)*

Mr Tortilla Inc...E...... 818 233-8932
1112 Arroyo St San Fernando (91340) *(P-1951)*

MRC Media LLC (PA)..F...... 212 493-4100
100 N Crescent Dr Ste 100 Beverly Hills (90210) *(P-3466)*

Mro Maryruth LLC..C...... 424 343-6650
1171 S Robertson Blvd Ste 148 Los Angeles (90035) *(P-4004)*

Mrs Appletree's Bakery, Baldwin Park Also Called: Distinct Indulgence Inc (P-1462)

MRS Foods Incorporated (PA)...E...... 714 554-2791
4406 W 5th St Santa Ana (92703) *(P-1952)*

Mrs Redds Pie Co Inc..E...... 909 825-4800
150 S La Cadena Dr Colton (92324) *(P-1484)*

Mrv, Chatsworth Also Called: Mrv Communications Inc (P-8848)

Mrv Communications Inc...B...... 818 773-0900
20520 Nordhoff St Chatsworth (91311) *(P-8848)*

Mrv Crane, Delano Also Called: Mrv Service Air Inc (P-17065)

Mrv Service Air Inc...F...... 661 725-3400
937 High St Delano (93215) *(P-17065)*

Mrv Systems LLC...E...... 800 645-7114
6370 Lusk Blvd Ste F100 San Diego (92121) *(P-10217)*

MS Aerospace Inc..B...... 818 833-9095
13928 Balboa Blvd Rancho Cascades (91342) *(P-6449)*

Ms Bellows, Huntington Beach Also Called: Mechanized Science Seals Inc (P-10381)

MS Industrial Shtmtl Inc...C...... 951 272-6610
1731 Pomona Rd Corona (92878) *(P-6276)*

Msblous LLC...D...... 909 929-9689
11671 Dayton Dr Rancho Cucamonga (91730) *(P-11600)*

MSC Metalworking, City Of Industry Also Called: Rutland Tool & Supply Co (P-12876)

MSC-La, City Of Industry Also Called: Material Sciences Corporation (P-5689)

Mscsoftware Corporation (HQ)...C...... 714 540-8900
5161 California Ave Ste 200 Irvine (92617) *(P-16314)*

MSE Enterprises Inc (PA)..D...... 818 223-3500
23622 Calabasas Rd Ste 200 Calabasas (91302) *(P-14834)*

MSI Computer Corp (HQ)...D...... 626 913-0828
901 Canada Ct City Of Industry (91748) *(P-12428)*

MSI Hvac, Fontana Also Called: AC Pro Inc (P-12750)

MSI Orange Showroom & Dist Ctr, Orange Also Called: M S International Inc (P-12356)

MSI Production Services, Vista Also Called: Meeting Services Inc (P-15785)

Msla Management LLC...A...... 626 824-6020
1294 E Colorado Blvd Pasadena (91106) *(P-20363)*

MSM Industries Inc..E...... 951 735-0834
12660 Magnolia Ave Riverside (92503) *(P-19651)*

MSP Group Inc...E...... 310 660-0022
206 W 140th St Los Angeles (90061) *(P-2029)*

Msr Desert Resort LP...A...... 760 564-5730
49499 Eisenhower Dr La Quinta (92253) *(P-14027)*

Msr Hotels & Resorts Inc...C...... 661 325-9700
5101 California Ave Ste 204 Bakersfield (93309) *(P-15039)*

Msr Hotels & Resorts Inc...C...... 310 543-4566
3701 Torrance Blvd Torrance (90503) *(P-15257)*

Msr Resort Lodging Tenant LLC...A...... 760 564-4111
49499 Eisenhower Dr La Quinta (92253) *(P-15258)*

MSRS INC..C...... 310 952-9000
945 E Church St Riverside (92507) *(P-12308)*

Mt Miquel Covenant Village...C...... 619 479-4790
325 Kempton St Spring Valley (91977) *(P-18017)*

Mt Rubidoux Convalescent Hosp, San Bernardino Also Called: Waterman Convalescent
Hosp Inc (P-18073)

Mt Rubidouxidence Opco LLC...C...... 951 681-2200
6401 33rd St Riverside (92509) *(P-18018)*

Mt Sinai Mem Pk & Mortuary, Los Angeles Also Called: Sinai Temple (P-15490)

Mt Sinai Mem Pk & Mortuary, Los Angeles Also Called: Sinai Temple (P-19506)

MTA, San Diego Also Called: MTA Moving Tech In Amer Inc (P-7497)

MTA Moving Tech In Amer Inc...E...... 619 651-7208
10065 Via De La Amistad Ste A1 San Diego (92154) *(P-7497)*

Mtc Financial Inc..D...... 949 252-8300
17100 Gillette Ave Irvine (92614) *(P-20064)*

Mtc Transportation, Twentynine Palms Also Called: Mark Clemons (P-11497)

Mtc Worldwide Corp..D...... 626 839-6800
17837 Rowland St City Of Industry (91748) *(P-12429)*

Mtd Kitchen Inc..D...... 818 764-2254
13213 Sherman Way North Hollywood (91605) *(P-2619)*

MTI De Baja Inc..E...... 951 654-2333
915 Industrial Way San Jacinto (92582) *(P-10004)*

MTI Laboratory Inc..E...... 310 955-3700
201 Continental Blvd Ste 300 El Segundo (90245) *(P-8551)*

Mtil, El Segundo Also Called: MTI Laboratory Inc (P-8551)

Mtn Satellite Communications, Los Angeles Also Called: Maritime Telecom Netwrk Inc
(P-8542)

Mtroiz International...E...... 661 998-8013
150 S Kenmore Ave Los Angeles (90004) *(P-12686)*

MTS Solutions LLC..E...... 661 589-5804
7131 Charity Ave Bakersfield (93308) *(P-364)*

Mufg Americas Leasing Corp (DH).......................................D...... 213 488-3700
445 S Figueroa St Ste 2700 Los Angeles (90071) *(P-15788)*

Mufg Union Bank Foundation...A...... 213 236-5000
445 S Figueroa St Los Angeles (90071) *(P-14171)*

Muhlhauser Enterprises Inc (PA)...F...... 909 877-2792
25825 Adams Ave Murrieta (92562) *(P-6057)*

Muhlhauser Steel, Murrieta Also Called: Muhlhauser Enterprises Inc (P-6057)

Muhlhauser Steel Inc..E...... 909 877-2792
25825 Adams Ave Murrieta (92562) *(P-6058)*

Muir Elementary School, Long Beach Also Called: Long Beach Unified School Dst (P-18973)

Muir-Chase Plumbing Co Inc...D...... 818 500-1940
4530 Brazil St Ste 1 Los Angeles (90039) *(P-795)*

Mulechain Inc..D...... 888 456-8881
2901 W Coast Hwy Ste 200 Newport Beach (92663) *(P-11462)*

Mulgrew Arcft Components Inc..D...... 626 256-1375
1810 S Shamrock Ave Monrovia (91016) *(P-9754)*

Mulholland Brothers...E...... 510 280-5485
11840 Dorothy St Apt 301 Los Angeles (90049) *(P-11601)*

Mulholland SEC & Patrol Inc...B...... 818 755-0202
11454 San Vicente Blvd Los Angeles (90049) *(P-16659)*

Mullen Auto Sales, Brea Also Called: Mullen Technologies Inc (P-9301)

Mullen Technologies Inc (PA)..E...... 714 613-1900
1405 Pioneer St Brea (92821) *(P-9301)*

Mullenlowe US Inc...C...... 424 738-6500
2121 Park Pl Ste 150 El Segundo (90245) *(P-15562)*

Mullenlowe US Inc...C...... 424 738-6600
12130 Millennium Los Angeles (90094) *(P-15563)*

Mullin TBG Insur Agcy Svcs LLC (DH)...................................C
3333 Michelson Dr Ste 820 Irvine (92612) *(P-14615)*

Mullintbg, Irvine Also Called: Mullin TBG Insur Agcy Svcs LLC (P-14615)

Mulroses Usa Inc...D...... 213 489-1761
741 S San Pedro St Los Angeles (90014) *(P-61)*

Multi Plastics, Santa Fe Springs Also Called: Multi-Plastics Inc (P-3955)

Multi-Fineline Electronix Inc (HQ).......................................A...... 949 453-6800
101 Academy Ste 250 Irvine (92617) *(P-8705)*

Multi-Link International Corp...E...... 562 941-5380
933 Montecito Dr San Gabriel (91776) *(P-4894)*

Multi-Plastics Inc..E...... 562 692-1202
11625 Los Nietos Rd Santa Fe Springs (90670) *(P-3955)*

Mergent email: customerrelations@mergent.com
1188

2024 Southern California
Business Directory and Buyers Guide

(P-0000) Products & Services Section entry number
(PA)=Parent Co (HQ)=Headquarters (DH)=Div Headquarters

Multichrome Company Inc (PA)................................E....... 310 216-1086
1013 W Hillcrest Blvd Inglewood (90301) *(P-6641)*

Multicultural Rdo Brdcstg Inc ....D....... 626 844-8882
747 E Green St Pasadena (91101) *(P-11931)*

Multilayer Prototypes Inc ....F....... 805 498-9390
2320 Terra Bella Ln Camarillo (93012) *(P-8706)*

Multiquip Inc (DH)...B...... 310 537-3700
6141 Katella Ave Ste 200 Cypress (90630) *(P-12608)*

Multitaskr ....E....... 619 391-3371
2576 Catamaran Way Chula Vista (91914) *(P-2669)*

Multivest, San Dimas *Also Called: Webmetro (P-16418)*

Mum Industries Inc ....D....... 800 729-1314
2320 Meyers Ave Escondido (92029) *(P-3956)*

Munchkin Inc ....E....... 818 893-5000
27334 San Bernardino Ave Redlands (92374) *(P-4859)*

Munchkin Inc (PA)...C...... 800 344-2229
7835 Gloria Ave Van Nuys (91406) *(P-4860)*

Munekata America Inc ....B...... 619 661-8080
2320 Paseo De Las Americas Ste 112 San Diego (92154) *(P-9087)*

Munger Tolles & Olson LLP ....B...... 213 683-9100
350 S Grand Ave Fl 50 Los Angeles (90071) *(P-18913)*

Munger Bros LLC ....A...... 661 721-0390
786 Road 188 Delano (93215) *(P-49)*

Munger Farm, Delano *Also Called: Munger Bros LLC (P-49)*

Munger Farms, Delano *Also Called: Monarch Nut Company LLC (P-109)*

Munger Tolles Olson Foundation (PA)........................B...... 213 683-9100
350 S Grand Ave Fl 50 Los Angeles (90071) *(P-18914)*

Murad, Los Angeles *Also Called: Murad LLC (P-4171)*

Murad LLC ....D....... 310 906-3100
8207 W 3rd St Los Angeles (90048) *(P-4171)*

Murad LLC (HQ)...C...... 310 726-0600
2121 Park Pl Fl 1 El Segundo (90245) *(P-4172)*

Murad LLC ....C...... 310 726-3300
1340 Storm Pkwy Torrance (90501) *(P-13056)*

Murad LLC ....C...... 310 726-0470
2141 Rosecrans Ave Ste 1151 El Segundo (90245) *(P-15482)*

Murad Spa, El Segundo *Also Called: Murad LLC (P-15482)*

Muranaka Farm ....C...... 805 529-0201
11018 W Los Angeles Ave Moorpark (93021) *(P-84)*

Murcal, Palmdale *Also Called: Murcal Inc (P-12609)*

Murcal Inc ....E....... 661 272-4700
41343 12th St W Palmdale (93551) *(P-12609)*

Murchison & Cumming LLP (PA)..............................D....... 213 623-7400
801 S Grand Ave Ste 900 Los Angeles (90017) *(P-18915)*

Murcor Inc ....C...... 909 623-4001
740 Corporate Center Dr Ste 100 Pomona (91768) *(P-14835)*

Muriel Siebert & Co Inc ....D....... 800 993-2015
9378 Wilshire Blvd Ste 300 Beverly Hills (90212) *(P-14399)*

Murphy Murphy & Murphy Inc ....D....... 562 594-6678
6261 Katella Ave Cypress (90630) *(P-19796)*

Murray Company, E Rncho Dmngz *Also Called: Murray Plumbing and Htg Corp (P-796)*

Murray Plumbing and Htg Corp (PA)..........................B...... 310 637-1500
18414 S Santa Fe Ave E Rncho Dmngz (90221) *(P-796)*

Murrays Iron Works Inc (PA)....................................C...... 323 521-1100
7355 E Slauson Ave Commerce (90040) *(P-2834)*

Murrieta Development Company Inc ....C...... 951 719-1680
42540 Rio Nedo Temecula (92590) *(P-682)*

Murrietta Circuits ....C...... 714 970-2430
5000 E Landon Dr Anaheim (92807) *(P-8707)*

Musclebound Inc ....B...... 818 349-0123
19835 Nordhoff St Northridge (91324) *(P-17408)*

Museum Associates ....B...... 323 857-6172
5905 Wilshire Blvd Los Angeles (90036) *(P-19356)*

Museum of Contemporary Art (PA)...........................C...... 213 626-6222
250 S Grand Ave Los Angeles (90012) *(P-19357)*

Music & Arts ....E....... 951 735-5924
650 E Parkridge Ave Ste 115 Corona (92879) *(P-19012)*

Music Center, Los Angeles *Also Called: Performing Arts Ctr Los Angles (P-17323)*

Music Express Inc (PA)..C...... 818 845-1502
2601 W Empire Ave Burbank (91504) *(P-11399)*

Music Intllgnce Neuro Dev Inst, Irvine *Also Called: Mind Research Institute (P-19935)*

Musick Peeler & Garrett LLP (PA)...........................C...... 213 629-7600
624 S Grand Ave Ste 2000 Los Angeles (90023) *(P-18916)*

Musicmatch Inc ....C...... 858 485-4300
16935 W Bernardo Dr Ste 270 San Diego (92127) *(P-16315)*

Mutesix Group Inc ....C...... 800 935-6856
5800 Bristol Pkwy Ste 500 Culver City (90230) *(P-15564)*

Mutesix, An Iprospect Company, Culver City *Also Called: Mutesix Group Inc (P-15564)*

Muth Development Co Inc ....E....... 714 527-2239
11100 Beach Blvd Stanton (90680) *(P-5389)*

Muth Machine Works (HQ)..E...... 714 527-2239
8042 Katella Ave Stanton (90680) *(P-7949)*

Muth Machine Works ....D....... 951 685-1521
4510 Rutile St Riverside (92509) *(P-20204)*

Mutual Liquid Gas & Eqp Co Inc (PA)........................E...... 310 515-0553
17117 S Broadway Gardena (90248) *(P-12801)*

Mutual Propane, Gardena *Also Called: Mutual Liquid Gas & Eqp Co Inc (P-12801)*

Mutual Trading Co Inc (DH)......................................C...... 213 626-9458
4200 Shirley Ave El Monte (91731) *(P-13382)*

Mv Transportation, Newbury Park *Also Called: Mv Transportation Inc (P-11350)*

Mv Transportation Inc ....C...... 323 666-0856
13690 Vaughn St San Fernando (91340) *(P-11340)*

Mv Transportation Inc ....C...... 818 409-3387
1242 Los Angeles St Glendale (91204) *(P-11341)*

Mv Transportation Inc ....C...... 562 943-6776
15677 Phoebe Ave La Mirada (90638) *(P-11342)*

Mv Transportation Inc ....B...... 323 936-9783
5420 W Jefferson Blvd Los Angeles (90016) *(P-11343)*

Mv Transportation Inc ....B...... 310 638-0556
14011 S Central Ave Los Angeles (90059) *(P-11344)*

Mv Transportation Inc ....C...... 818 374-9145
16738 Stagg St Van Nuys (91406) *(P-11345)*

Mv Transportation Inc ....C...... 760 255-3330
1612 State St Barstow (92311) *(P-11346)*

Mv Transportation Inc ....C...... 760 400-0300
303 Via Del Norte Oceanside (92058) *(P-11347)*

Mv Transportation Inc ....C...... 760 520-0118
755 Norlak Ave Escondido (92025) *(P-11348)*

Mv Transportation Inc ....C...... 805 557-7372
265 S Rancho Rd Thousand Oaks (91361) *(P-11349)*

Mv Transportation Inc ....C...... 805 375-5467
670 Lawrence Dr Newbury Park (91320) *(P-11350)*

Mventix, Woodland Hills *Also Called: Mventix Inc (P-16882)*

Mventix Inc (PA)...D...... 818 337-3747
21600 Oxnard St Ste 1700 Woodland Hills (91367) *(P-16882)*

Mvp Rv Inc ....F....... 951 848-4288
40 E Verdugo Ave Burbank (91502) *(P-9926)*

Mw Compnnts - Anheim Ideal Fas, Anaheim *Also Called: Matthew Warren Inc (P-11072)*

Mw Components - Corona, Corona *Also Called: Ameriflex Inc (P-6837)*

Mw Partners, Irvine *Also Called: Morris & Willner Partners (P-20203)*

Mwd, Los Angeles *Also Called: The Metropolitan Water District of Southern California (P-12150)*

Mws Precision Wire Inds Inc ....D...... 818 991-8553
3000 Camino Del Sol Oxnard (93030) *(P-12560)*

Mws Wire Industries, Oxnard *Also Called: Mws Precision Wire Inds Inc (P-12560)*

Mwss, Irvine *Also Called: In Montrose Wtr Sstnblity Svcs (P-20350)*

MXF Designs Inc ....D...... 323 266-1451
5327 Valley Blvd Los Angeles (90032) *(P-2258)*

MY DAY COUNTS, Anaheim *Also Called: Orange Cnty Adult Achvment Ctr (P-19120)*

My Eye Media LLC ....D...... 818 559-7200
2211 N Hollywood Way Burbank (91505) *(P-16316)*

My Kids Dentist ....B...... 951 600-1062
24635 Madison Ave Ste E Murrieta (92562) *(P-17842)*

My Michelle, La Puente *Also Called: Mymichelle Company LLC (P-2259)*

My Tech USA, Corona *Also Called: Hardy Frames Inc (P-5590)*

Mycase, San Diego *Also Called: Appfolio Inc (P-16171)*

Mydyer.com, Irvine *Also Called: Providence Industries LLC (P-2184)*

Mye Technologies Inc ....E....... 661 964-0217
25060 Avenue Stanford Valencia (91355) *(P-9230)*

Myers & Sons Construction LP ....C...... 424 227-3285
5777 W Century Blvd Ste 600 Los Angeles (90045) *(P-636)*

A L P H A B E T I C

Employee Codes: A=Over 500 employees, B=251-500
C=101-250, D=51-100, E=20-50, F=10-19, G=1-9

2024 Southern California
Business Directory and Buyers Guide

© Mergent Inc. 1-800-342-5647

1189

Myers & Sons Hi-Way Safety Inc (PA)..........................D...... 909 591-1781
13310 5th St Chino (91710) *(P-11139)*

Myers FSI, Ontario Also Called: Myers Power Products Inc *(P-8126)*

Myers Mixers LLC..........................E...... 323 560-4723
8376 Salt Lake Ave Cudahy (90201) *(P-7400)*

Myers Power Products Inc (PA)..........................C...... 909 923-1800
2950 E Philadelphia St Ontario (91761) *(P-8126)*

Myevaluationscom Inc..........................E...... 646 422-0554
11111 W Olympic Blvd Ste 401 Los Angeles (90064) *(P-16078)*

Mygrant Glass Company Inc..........................E...... 858 455-8022
10220 Camino Santa Fe San Diego (92121) *(P-9429)*

Myhhbs Inc..........................D...... 888 969-4427
237 N Central Ave Ste A Glendale (91203) *(P-19114)*

Mymichelle Company LLC (HQ)..........................B...... 626 934-4166
13077 Temple Ave La Puente (91746) *(P-2259)*

Myogenix Incorporated..........................F...... 800 950-0348
4725 Allene Way San Luis Obispo (93401) *(P-4173)*

Myotek Industries Incorporated (DH)..........................D...... 949 502-3776
1278 Glenneyre St Ste 431 Laguna Beach (92651) *(P-9171)*

Myricom, Pasadena Also Called: Myricom Inc *(P-7442)*

Myricom Inc..........................E...... 626 821-5555
3871 E Colorado Blvd Ste 101 Pasadena (91107) *(P-7442)*

Myron L Company..........................D...... 760 438-2021
2450 Impala Dr Carlsbad (92010) *(P-10147)*

Mysmile Oral Care Inc..........................E...... 909 908-4615
8238 Mayten Ave Rancho Cucamonga (91730) *(P-4363)*

Myst Therapeutics Inc..........................D...... 415 516-8450
570 Westwood Plz Bldg 114 Los Angeles (90095) *(P-19862)*

Mytee Products Inc..........................E...... 858 679-1191
13655 Stowe Dr Poway (92064) *(P-7675)*

Mywi Fabricators Inc..........................F...... 626 279-6994
2115 Edwards Ave 2119 South El Monte (91733) *(P-6059)*

N A T C O, Glendale Also Called: North American Textile Co LLC *(P-2536)*

N G I, Brea Also Called: Nevell Group Inc *(P-569)*

N G K Spark Plugs USA Inc..........................E...... 949 855-8278
6 Whatney Irvine (92618) *(P-9430)*

N H A, San Diego Also Called: Neighborhood House Association *(P-19115)*

N H Research LLC..........................D...... 949 474-3900
16601 Hale Ave Irvine (92606) *(P-10218)*

N K Cabinets Inc..........................E...... 818 897-7909
11015 Glenoaks Blvd Ste 22 Pacoima (91331) *(P-2670)*

N P A, Los Angeles Also Called: National Promotions & Advg Inc *(P-15565)*

N Philanthropy LLC..........................F...... 213 278-0754
1132 E 12th St Los Angeles (90021) *(P-16883)*

N Qiagen Amercn Holdings Inc (HQ)..........................C...... 800 426-8157
27220 Turnberry Ln Ste 200 Valencia (91355) *(P-13057)*

N S C Channel Islands Inc..........................B...... 805 485-1908
2300 Wankel Way Oxnard (93030) *(P-17721)*

N Stitches Prints Inc..........................E...... 310 366-7537
16009 S Broadway Gardena (90248) *(P-2521)*

N T S, Woodland Hills Also Called: Network Telephone Services Inc *(P-16884)*

N Trans/Sub Regional Office, Valencia Also Called: Southern California Edison Co *(P-12071)*

N-U Enterprise, Irvine Also Called: Ancca Corporation *(P-967)*

N/S Corporation (PA)..........................D...... 310 412-7074
235 W Florence Ave Inglewood (90301) *(P-7676)*

N2 Acquisition Company Inc..........................D...... 714 942-3563
14440 Myford Rd Irvine (92606) *(P-14936)*

N2 Imaging Systems, Irvine Also Called: N2 Acquisition Company Inc *(P-14936)*

Nabisco, Ontario Also Called: Mondelez Global LLC *(P-13380)*

Nabors Well Services Co..........................D...... 310 639-7074
19431 S Santa Fe Ave Compton (90221) *(P-365)*

Nabors Well Services Co..........................D...... 805 648-2731
2567 N Ventura Ave # C Ventura (93001) *(P-366)*

Nabors Well Services Co..........................C...... 661 588-6140
1025 Earthmover Ct Bakersfield (93314) *(P-367)*

Nabors Well Services Co..........................C...... 661 589-3970
7515 Rosedale Hwy Bakersfield (93308) *(P-368)*

Nabors Well Services Co..........................C...... 661 392-7668
1954 James Rd Bakersfield (93308) *(P-369)*

Nada Appraisal Guide, Costa Mesa Also Called: National Appraisal Guides Inc *(P-3467)*

Nadolife Inc..........................E...... 619 522-0077
1025 Orange Ave Coronado (92118) *(P-5869)*

Naf, Tustin Also Called: New American Funding LLC *(P-14275)*

Nafees Memon..........................D...... 818 997-1666
6819 Sepulveda Blvd Ste 312 Van Nuys (91405) *(P-16660)*

Nafees Mmon Cmmand Intl SEC Sv, Van Nuys Also Called: Nafees Memon *(P-16660)*

Nafhc, Santa Maria Also Called: North American Fire Hose Corp *(P-4710)*

Naftex Westside Partners Limit..........................E...... 310 277-9004
1900 Avenue Of The Stars Los Angeles (90067) *(P-263)*

Nagles Veal Inc..........................D...... 909 383-7075
1411 E Base Line St San Bernardino (92410) *(P-1200)*

Nai, Carlsbad Also Called: Natural Alternatives Intl Inc *(P-4005)*

Nail Alliance - North Amer Inc..........................D...... 714 449-1568
4100 Bonita Pl Fullerton (92835) *(P-15483)*

Nailpro, Encino Also Called: Creative Age Publications Inc *(P-3352)*

Nakamura-Beeman Inc..........................E...... 562 696-1400
8520 Wellsford Pl Santa Fe Springs (90670) *(P-2889)*

Nakase Brothers Whl Nurs LP (PA)..........................D...... 949 855-4388
9441 Krepp Dr Huntington Beach (92646) *(P-13514)*

Nakase Brothers Wholesale Nurs..........................C...... 949 855-4388
20621 Lake Forest Dr Lake Forest (92630) *(P-13515)*

NAKASE BROTHERS WHOLESALE NURSERY, Lake Forest Also Called: Nakase Brothers Wholesale Nurs *(P-13515)*

Naked Juice Co Glendora Inc..........................B...... 626 873-2600
1333 S Mayflower Ave # 100 Monrovia (91016) *(P-13731)*

Nalco Champion, Bakersfield Also Called: Championx LLC *(P-3889)*

Nalco Water, Placentia Also Called: Nalco Wtr Prtrtment Sltons LLC *(P-7677)*

Nalco Wtr Prtrtment Sltons LLC..........................E...... 714 792-0708
1961 Petra Ln Placentia (92870) *(P-7677)*

Nally & Millie, Los Angeles Also Called: MXF Designs Inc *(P-2258)*

Nalu Medical Inc..........................C...... 760 603-8466
2320 Faraday Ave Ste 100 Carlsbad (92008) *(P-18783)*

Namar Company, Paramount Also Called: Namar Foods *(P-1357)*

Namar Foods..........................E...... 562 531-2744
6830 Walthall Way Paramount (90723) *(P-1357)*

Namvars Inc..........................D...... 858 792-5461
11815 Sorrento Valley Rd Ste A San Diego (92121) *(P-207)*

Nan McKay and Associates Inc..........................D...... 619 258-1855
1810 Gillespie Way Ste 202 El Cajon (92020) *(P-20205)*

Nannette Keller, Tehachapi Also Called: Keller Classics Inc *(P-2293)*

Nano Filter Inc..........................D...... 949 316-8866
22310 Bonita St Carson (90745) *(P-11253)*

Nanocellect Biomedical Inc..........................E...... 877 745-7678
6865 Flanders Dr San Diego (92121) *(P-4174)*

Nanocomposix LLC..........................D...... 858 565-4227
4878 Ronson Ct Ste J San Diego (92111) *(P-19937)*

Nanofilm, Westlake Village Also Called: Interntional Photo Plates Corp *(P-6630)*

Nanoprecision Products Inc..........................E...... 310 597-4991
802 Calle Plano Camarillo (93012) *(P-6539)*

Nanovea Inc (PA)..........................E...... 949 461-9292
6 Morgan Ste 156 Irvine (92618) *(P-10277)*

Nantcell Inc..........................B...... 562 397-3639
9920 Jefferson Blvd Culver City (90232) *(P-19863)*

Nantcell Inc..........................C...... 310 883-1300
2040 E Mariposa Ave El Segundo (90245) *(P-19938)*

Nantenergy LLC..........................D...... 310 905-4866
2040 E Mariposa Ave El Segundo (90245) *(P-8152)*

Napca Foundation..........................A...... 800 799-4640
2600 W Olive Ave Ste 500 Burbank (91505) *(P-19013)*

Napd, Bakersfield Also Called: New Advnces For Pple With Dsbl *(P-19336)*

Napoleon Perdis Cosmetics Inc..........................D...... 323 817-3611
16825 Saticoy St Van Nuys (91406) *(P-14140)*

Narayan Corporation..........................E...... 310 719-7330
13432 Estrella Ave Gardena (90248) *(P-4861)*

Narcotics Annymous Wrld Svcs I (PA)..........................E...... 818 773-9999
19737 Nordhoff Pl Chatsworth (91311) *(P-3411)*

Nasco Aircraft Brake Inc..........................D...... 310 532-4430
13300 Estrella Ave Gardena (90248) *(P-9755)*

Nasco Gourmet Foods Inc..........................D...... 714 279-2100
22720 Savi Ranch Pkwy Yorba Linda (92887) *(P-1342)*

Mergent email: customerrelations@mergent.com
1190

2024 Southern California
Business Directory and Buyers Guide

(P-0000) Products & Services Section entry number
(PA)=Parent Co (HQ)=Headquarters (DH)=Div Headquarters

Nashville Wire Pdts Mfg Co LLC .... F...... 714 736-0081
10727 Commerce Way Ste C Fontana (92337) *(P-6821)*

Nasmyth Tmf Inc .... D...... 818 954-9504
29102 Hancock Pkwy Valencia (91355) *(P-6642)*

Naso Industries Corporation .... E...... 805 650-1231
3007 Bunsen Ave Ste Q Ventura (93003) *(P-8708)*

Naso Technologies, Ventura *Also Called: Naso Industries Corporation (P-8708)*

Nassco, San Diego *Also Called: International Mfg Tech Inc (P-5591)*

Nastec International Inc .... D...... 818 222-0355
23875 Ventura Blvd Ste 204 Calabasas (91302) *(P-16661)*

Nasty Gal Inc (HQ) .... E...... 213 542-3436
2049 Century Park E Ste 3400 Los Angeles (90067) *(P-13915)*

Natals Inc .... C...... 323 475-6033
3576 Eastham Dr Culver City (90232) *(P-4175)*

Natel Engineering, Chatsworth *Also Called: Epic Technologies LLC (P-8471)*

Natel Engineering Co Inc .... E...... 760 448-1500
6350 Palomar Oaks Ct Carlsbad (92011) *(P-8849)*

Natel Engineering Company LLC (PA) .... C...... 818 495-8617
9340 Owensmouth Ave Chatsworth (91311) *(P-9088)*

Natel Engineering Holdings Inc .... F...... 818 734-6500
9340 Owensmouth Ave Chatsworth (91311) *(P-8709)*

Nathan Anthony Furniture, Vernon *Also Called: Yen-Nhai Inc (P-2823)*

National Advanced Endoscopy De .... E...... 818 227-2720
22134 Sherman Way Canoga Park (91303) *(P-14141)*

National Air Inc .... C...... 619 299-2500
2053 Kurtz St San Diego (92110) *(P-797)*

National Air and Energy, San Diego *Also Called: National Air Inc (P-797)*

National Appraisal Guides Inc .... E...... 714 556-8511
3186 Airway Ave Ste K Costa Mesa (92626) *(P-3467)*

National Assn For Hispanic, Los Angeles *Also Called: La Asccion Ncnal Pro Prsnas My (P-19107)*

National Attny Collection Svcs .... B...... 818 547-9760
700 N Brand Blvd Fl 2 Glendale (91203) *(P-18917)*

National Band Saw Company .... F...... 661 294-9552
1055 W Avenue L12 Lancaster (93534) *(P-7210)*

National Cement Co Cal Inc (DH) .... E...... 818 728-5200
15821 Ventura Blvd Ste 475 Encino (91436) *(P-5487)*

National Cement Company Inc (HQ) .... E...... 818 728-5200
15821 Ventura Blvd Ste 475 Encino (91436) *(P-5369)*

National Cement Company Inc .... F...... 323 923-4466
2626 E 26th St Vernon (90058) *(P-5488)*

National Cement Ready Mix, Encino *Also Called: National Ready Mixed Con Co (P-5490)*

National Cmnty Renaissance Cal (PA) .... D...... 909 483-2444
9692 Haven Ave Ste 100 Rancho Cucamonga (91730) *(P-14906)*

National Cmnty Renaissance Cal .... C...... 619 223-9222
8265 Aspen St Ste 100 Rancho Cucamonga (91730) *(P-14907)*

National Cnstr Rentals Inc (HQ) .... D...... 818 221-6000
15319 Chatsworth St Mission Hills (91345) *(P-15789)*

National Coatings Corporation .... E...... 805 388-7112
1201 Calle Suerte Camarillo (93012) *(P-4674)*

National Community Renaissance .... C...... 909 948-7579
8590 Malven Ave Rancho Cucamonga (91730) *(P-14728)*

National Copy Cartridge, Tustin *Also Called: US Print & Toner Inc (P-11063)*

National Corset Supply House (PA) .... D...... 323 261-0265
3240 E 26th St Vernon (90058) *(P-2392)*

National Diversified Sales Inc (HQ) .... C...... 559 562-9888
21300 Victory Blvd Ste 215 Woodland Hills (91367) *(P-5110)*

National Emblem Inc (PA) .... E...... 310 515-5055
3925 E Vernon St Long Beach (90815) *(P-2522)*

National Ewp Inc .... F...... 909 931-4014
5566 Arrow Hwy Montclair (91763) *(P-236)*

National Explrtion Wells Pumps, Montclair *Also Called: National Ewp Inc (P-236)*

National Financial Svcs LLC .... A...... 949 476-0157
19200 Von Karman Ave Ste 400 Irvine (92612) *(P-14400)*

National Fitness Testing, Los Angeles *Also Called: Young MNS Chrstn Assn Mtro Los (P-19494)*

National Funding Inc (PA) .... C...... 888 733-2383
9530 Towne Centre Dr Ste 120 San Diego (92121) *(P-14285)*

National Genetics Institute .... C...... 310 996-6610
2440 S Sepulveda Blvd Ste 235 Los Angeles (90064) *(P-19978)*

National Graphics LLC .... E...... 805 644-9212
200 N Elevar St Oxnard (93030) *(P-3642)*

National Hot Rod Association (PA) .... C...... 626 914-4761
140 Via Verde Ste 100 San Dimas (91773) *(P-17387)*

National Hrdwood Flrg Moulding, Van Nuys *Also Called: Katzirs Floor & HM Design Inc (P-12305)*

National Insurance Crime Bur .... D...... 818 895-2867
15545 Devonshire St Ste 309 Mission Hills (91345) *(P-14616)*

National Logistics Team LLC .... E...... 951 369-5841
21496 Main St Grand Terrace (92313) *(P-11535)*

National Manufacturing Co .... A...... 800 346-9445
19701 Da Vinci Lake Forest (92610) *(P-5936)*

National Media Inc (HQ) .... E...... 310 377-6877
609 Deep Valley Dr Ste 200 Rllng Hls Est (90274) *(P-3308)*

National Medical Products Inc .... E...... 949 768-1147
57 Parker Irvine (92618) *(P-5111)*

National Mentor Holdings Inc .... B...... 951 677-1453
30033 Technology Dr Murrieta (92563) *(P-19289)*

National Metal Stampings Inc .... D...... 661 945-1157
42110 8th St E Lancaster (93535) *(P-6540)*

National Monitoring Center, Lake Forest *Also Called: Advanced Protection Inds LLC (P-16721)*

National Notary Association .... C...... 800 876-6827
9350 De Soto Ave Chatsworth (91311) *(P-19398)*

National O Rings, Downey *Also Called: Hutchinson Seal Corporation (P-4733)*

National Packaging Products, Commerce *Also Called: Yavar Manufacturing Co Inc (P-3147)*

National Pen Co LLC (DH) .... C...... 866 900-7367
12121 Scripps Summit Dr Ste 200 San Diego (92131) *(P-11047)*

National Pen Company, San Diego *Also Called: National Pen Co LLC (P-11047)*

National Planning Corporation .... C...... 800 881-7174
100 N Pacific Coast Hwy Ste 1800 El Segundo (90245) *(P-14274)*

National Promotions & Advg Inc .... E...... 310 558-8555
3434 Overland Ave Los Angeles (90034) *(P-15565)*

National Ready Mix .... F...... 818 728-5200
15821 Ventura Blvd Ste 475 Encino (91436) *(P-5489)*

National Ready Mixed Con Co (DH) .... E...... 818 728-5200
15821 Ventura Blvd Ste 475 Encino (91436) *(P-5490)*

National Rent A Fence Co., Mission Hills *Also Called: National Cnstr Rentals Inc (P-15789)*

National Research Group, Los Angeles *Also Called: National Research Group Inc (P-19907)*

National Research Group Inc .... B...... 323 406-6200
12101 Bluff Creek Dr Los Angeles (90094) *(P-19907)*

National Resilience Inc (PA) .... E...... 888 737-2460
3115 Merryfield Row Ste 200 San Diego (92121) *(P-4176)*

National Retail Trnsp Inc .... D...... 951 243-6110
400 Harley Knox Blvd Perris (92571) *(P-11499)*

National School District .... C...... 619 336-7770
1400 N Ave National City (91950) *(P-18976)*

National Security Tech LLC .... B...... 805 681-2432
5520 Ekwill St Ste B Goleta (93111) *(P-19652)*

National Sign & Marketing Corp .... D...... 909 591-4742
13580 5th St Chino (91710) *(P-11140)*

National Signal Inc .... E...... 714 441-7707
2440 Artesia Ave Fullerton (92833) *(P-9935)*

National Stl & Shipbuilding Co (HQ) .... B...... 619 544-3400
2798 Harbor Dr San Diego (92113) *(P-9842)*

National Teleconsultants Inc .... C...... 818 265-4400
550 N Brand Blvd Fl 17 Glendale (91203) *(P-19653)*

National Therapeutic Svcs Inc (PA) .... D...... 866 311-0003
3822 Campus Dr Ste 100 Newport Beach (92660) *(P-18703)*

National Tour Intgrted Rsrces .... E...... 949 215-6330
23141 Arroyo Vis Ste 100 Rcho Sta Marg (92688) *(P-20206)*

National Trench Safety LLC .... C...... 562 602-1642
13217 Laureldale Ave Downey (90242) *(P-15790)*

National Tube & Steel, Mission Hills *Also Called: The National Bus Group Inc (P-15766)*

National Wire and Cable, Los Angeles *Also Called: National Wire and Cable Corporation (P-5621)*

National Wire and Cable Corporation .... C...... 323 225-5611
136 N San Fernando Rd Los Angeles (90031) *(P-5621)*

Nationbuilder, Los Angeles *Also Called: 3dna Corp (P-15950)*

Nationsbenefits LLC .... D...... 877 439-2665
1540 Scenic Ave Costa Mesa (92626) *(P-20207)*

Nationwide, Santa Ana *Also Called: Turnkey Foundation Inc (P-14353)*

Nationwide, Glendale *Also Called: Arthur J Gallagher Risk Mgmt (P-14560)*

Employee Codes: A=Over 500 employees, B=251-500
C=101-250, D=51-100, E=20-50, F=10-19, G=1-9

2024 Southern California
Business Directory and Buyers Guide

© Mergent Inc. 1-800-342-5647

1191

A
L
P
H
A
B
E
T
I
C

Nationwide, San Diego *Also Called: Atlas General Insur Svcs LLC (P-14561)*

Nationwide, Cerritos *Also Called: Auto Insurance Specialists LLC (P-14562)*

Nationwide, Pasadena *Also Called: B&C Liquidating Corp (P-14566)*

Nationwide, Newport Beach *Also Called: Edgewood Partners Insur Ctr (P-14585)*

Nationwide, Riverside *Also Called: Insurance Inc Southern Cal (P-14603)*

Nationwide, San Luis Obispo *Also Called: Morris Grritano Insur Agcy Inc (P-14614)*

Nationwide, Cypress *Also Called: Pacific Pioneer Insur Group (P-14621)*

Nationwide, Cerritos *Also Called: Poliseek Ais Insur Sltions Inc (P-14622)*

Nationwide, Tustin *Also Called: Wood Gutmann Bogart Insur Brkg (P-14646)*

Nationwide, Irvine *Also Called: Sullivncrtsmnroe Insur Svcs LL (P-20250)*

Nationwide, Irvine *Also Called: Alliant Insurance Services Inc (P-20313)*

Nationwide and International, Oceanside *Also Called: Amflex Plastics Incorporated (P-4709)*

Nationwide Guard Services Inc .... B...... 909 608-1112
9327 Fairway View Pl Ste 200 Rancho Cucamonga (91730) *(P-16662)*

Nationwide Technologies Inc .... E...... 909 340-2770
3684 W Uva Ln San Bernardino (92407) *(P-16317)*

Nationwide Theatres Corp ....A...... 562 421-8448
2500 Carson St Lakewood (90712) *(P-17360)*

Nationwide Trans Inc (PA)......................................**D...... 909 355-3211**
11727 Eastend Ave Chino (91710) *(P-11786)*

Natren Inc ....D...... 805 371-4737
3105 Willow Ln Thousand Oaks (91361) *(P-1953)*

Natrol Inc ....C...... 818 739-6000
21411 Prairie St Chatsworth (91311) *(P-4177)*

Natrol LLC (PA)..**C...... 818 739-6000**
21411 Prairie St Chatsworth (91311) *(P-4178)*

Natural Alternatives Intl Inc (PA)...........................**C...... 760 736-7700**
1535 Faraday Ave Carlsbad (92008) *(P-4005)*

Natural Balance Pet Foods LLC (PA).....................**D...... 800 829-4493**
2358 University Ave Ste 2280 San Diego (92104) *(P-1446)*

Natural Balance Pet Foods Inc ....D...... 800 829-4493
1224 Montague Unit 1 Pacoima (91331) *(P-1447)*

NATURAL BALANCE PET FOODS, INC., Pacoima *Also Called: Natural Balance Pet Foods Inc (P-1447)*

Natural Elements, Vernon *Also Called: L A S A M Inc (P-2409)*

Natural Envmtl Protection Co ....E...... 909 620-8028
750 S Reservoir St Pomona (91766) *(P-3957)*

Natural Food Mill, Corona *Also Called: Food For Life Baking Co Inc (P-1469)*

Natural Thoughts Incorporated ....E...... 619 582-0027
4757 Old Cliffs Rd San Diego (92120) *(P-4436)*

Naturalife Eco Vite Labs ....D...... 310 370-1563
20433 Earl St Torrance (90503) *(P-1278)*

Nature-Cide, Canoga Park *Also Called: Pacific Shore Holdings Inc (P-4194)*

Nature's Flavors, Orange *Also Called: Newport Flavors & Fragrances (P-1781)*

Naturelab North America Inc (HQ)..........................**C...... 424 901-0707**
8149 Santa Monica Blvd Ste 361 West Hollywood (90046) *(P-4179)*

Naturemaker Inc ....E...... 760 438-4244
6225 El Camino Real Carlsbad (92009) *(P-11254)*

Natures Best ....B...... 714 255-4600
6 Pointe Dr Ste 300 Brea (92821) *(P-13383)*

Natures Flavors ....E...... 714 744-3700
833 N Elm St Orange (92867) *(P-1954)*

Natures Image Inc ....D...... 949 680-4400
20361 Hermana Cir Lake Forest (92630) *(P-170)*

Natures Produce ....C...... 323 235-4343
3305 Bandini Blvd Vernon (90058) *(P-13334)*

Natureware Inc ....D...... 714 251-4510
6590 Darin Way Cypress (90630) *(P-13058)*

Naturvet, Temecula *Also Called: Garmon Corporation (P-1440)*

Natus Inc ....D...... 626 355-3746
4522 Katella Ave Ste 200 Los Alamitos (90720) *(P-5291)*

Natus Medical Incorporated ....D...... 858 260-2590
5955 Pacific Center Blvd San Diego (92121) *(P-10816)*

Natvar, City Of Industry *Also Called: Tekni-Plex Inc (P-3249)*

Naumann/Hobbs Mtl Hdlg Corp II ....C...... 866 266-2244
86998 Avenue 52 Coachella (92236) *(P-12775)*

Nautilus Seafood, Wilmington *Also Called: J Deluca Fish Company Inc (P-1808)*

Navajo Investments Inc (PA)...................................**D...... 949 863-9200**
17962 Cowan Irvine (92614) *(P-11681)*

Naval Coating Inc ....C...... 619 234-8366
2080 Cambridge Ave Cardiff By The Sea (92007) *(P-1171)*

Naval Facilities Engineer Comm ....D...... 619 532-1158
1220 Pacific Hwy San Diego (92132) *(P-19654)*

Naval Hosp Twntynine Plms Gfeb, Twentynine Palms *Also Called: NAVY UNITED STATES DEPARTMENT (P-18784)*

Naval Medical Center, San Diego *Also Called: NAVY UNITED STATES DEPARTMENT (P-18350)*

Naval Station Child Dev Ctr, San Diego *Also Called: Navy Exchange Service Command (P-19222)*

Navco Security Systems, Fullerton *Also Called: North American Video Corp (P-12688)*

Navcom Technology Inc (HQ).............................**D...... 310 381-2000**
20780 Madrona Ave Torrance (90503) *(P-8552)*

Navigage Foundation (PA)....................................**D...... 818 790-2522**
849 Foothill Blvd Ste 8 La Canada (91011) *(P-18019)*

Navigate Biopharma Svcs Inc ....C...... 866 992-4939
1890 Rutherford Rd Carlsbad (92008) *(P-19864)*

Navigational Services ....F...... 619 477-1564
34 E 17th St Ste C National City (91950) *(P-9843)*

Navigator Yachts, Perris *Also Called: Navigator Yachts and Pdts Inc (P-9864)*

Navigator Yachts and Pdts Inc ....E...... 951 657-2117
364 Malbert St Perris (92570) *(P-9864)*

Navigators Management Co Inc ....C...... 949 255-4860
19100 Von Karman Ave Irvine (92612) *(P-20065)*

Navitas Semiconductor Corp (PA).......................**C...... 901 685-2865**
3520 Challenger St Torrance (90503) *(P-15040)*

Navtrak LLC ....D...... 410 548-2337
20 Enterprise Ste 100 Aliso Viejo (92656) *(P-16748)*

Navy Exchange Service Command ....D...... 619 556-7466
2375 Recreation Way San Diego (92136) *(P-19222)*

NAVY UNITED STATES DEPARTMENT ....A...... 619 556-6033
32nd St Naval Sta San Diego (92136) *(P-9844)*

NAVY UNITED STATES DEPARTMENT ....C...... 805 989-1328
311 Navy Base Ventura County Port Hueneme (93042) *(P-17140)*

NAVY UNITED STATES DEPARTMENT ....B...... 858 577-9849
19871 Mitscher Way San Diego (92145) *(P-17722)*

NAVY UNITED STATES DEPARTMENT ....A...... 619 532-6400
34800 Bob Wilson Dr San Diego (92134) *(P-18350)*

NAVY UNITED STATES DEPARTMENT ....D...... 760 830-2124
1145 Sturgis Rd Twentynine Palms (92278) *(P-18784)*

Nazca Solutions Inc ....E...... 612 279-6100
4 First American Way Santa Ana (92707) *(P-16318)*

NBC, Universal City *Also Called: NBC Subsidiary (knbc-Tv) LLC (P-11959)*

NBC, Universal City *Also Called: NBC Studios Inc (P-17321)*

NBC Consulting Inc ....D...... 310 798-5000
2110 Artesia Blvd Ste 323 Redondo Beach (90278) *(P-20208)*

NBC Studios Inc ....A...... 818 777-1000
100 Universal City Plz Fl 3 Universal City (91608) *(P-17321)*

NBC Subsidiary (knbc-Tv) LLC ....C...... 818 684-5746
100 Universal City Plz Bldg 2120 Universal City (91608) *(P-11959)*

NBC Universal Inc ....A
100 Universal City Plz Universal City (91608) *(P-17202)*

Nbcuniversal Media LLC ....A...... 818 777-1000
100 Universal City Plz Bldg 2160 Universal City (91608) *(P-11932)*

Nbcuniversal Television Dist, Universal City *Also Called: Universal Cy Stdios Prdctons L (P-17230)*

Nbp, Claremont *Also Called: New Bedford Panoramex Corp (P-8376)*

Nbs Systems Inc (PA)..**E...... 217 999-3472**
2477 E Orangethorpe Ave Fullerton (92831) *(P-3831)*

Nbty Manufacturing LLC ....C...... 714 765-8323
5115 E La Palma Ave Anaheim (92807) *(P-4180)*

NC America LLC ....E...... 949 447-6287
400 Spectrum Center Dr Fl 18 Irvine (92618) *(P-16079)*

NC Dynamics, Long Beach *Also Called: NC Dynamics LLC (P-7951)*

NC Dynamics Incorporated ....C...... 562 634-7392
6925 Downey Ave Long Beach (90805) *(P-7950)*

NC Dynamics LLC ....C...... 562 634-7392
3401 E 69th St Long Beach (90805) *(P-7951)*

NC Interactive LLC ....D...... 512 623-8700
660 Newport Center Dr Ste 800 Newport Beach (92660) *(P-16581)*

Nc4 Soltra LLC ....D...... 408 489-5579
21515 Hawthorne Blvd # 52 Torrance (90503) *(P-16319)*

Ncdi, Long Beach *Also Called: NC Dynamics Incorporated (P-7950)*

Nci Group Inc .... E 909 987-4681
9123 Center Ave Rancho Cucamonga (91730) *(P-6387)*

Ncla Inc .... F 562 926-6252
1388 W Foothill Blvd Azusa (91702) *(P-3239)*

Ncn Management LLC .... C 800 275-3243
5838 Edison Pl Ste 100 Carlsbad (92008) *(P-20066)*

Ncompass International, Hawthorne *Also Called: Ncompass International LLC (P-20209)*

Ncompass International LLC .... C 323 785-1700
12101 Crenshaw Blvd Ste 800 Hawthorne (90250) *(P-20209)*

Ncsoft, Newport Beach *Also Called: NC Interactive LLC (P-16581)*

Ncstar Inc .... F 866 627-8278
18031 Cortney Ct City Of Industry (91748) *(P-10329)*

NDC Technologies Inc .... E 626 960-3300
5314 Irwindale Ave Irwindale (91706) *(P-10278)*

Ndga, Irvine *Also Called: Bandai Namco Entrmt Amer Inc (P-12935)*

Nds, Woodland Hills *Also Called: National Diversified Sales Inc (P-5110)*

Nds Americas Inc (DH) .... D 714 434-2100
3500 Hyland Ave Costa Mesa (92626) *(P-11997)*

NDT Systems Inc .... E 714 893-2438
5542 Buckingham Dr Ste A Huntington Beach (92649) *(P-10385)*

Ne-Mos .... F 800 325-2692
416 N Hale Ave Escondido (92029) *(P-1485)*

Nea Electronics Inc .... E 805 292-4010
14370 White Sage Rd Moorpark (93021) *(P-8979)*

Neal Feay Company .... D 805 967-4521
133 S La Patera Ln Goleta (93117) *(P-5704)*

Near Intelligence Inc .... B 628 889-7680
100 W Walnut St Ste A-4 Pasadena (91124) *(P-16508)*

Nearfield Systems Inc .... D 310 525-7000
19730 Magellan Dr Torrance (90502) *(P-10219)*

Neb Cal Printing, San Diego *Also Called: Kovin Corporation Inc (P-3614)*

Neft Vodka USA Inc .... E 415 846-0359
144 Penn St El Segundo (90245) *(P-3789)*

Neighborhood Healthcare .... C 760 737-2000
460 N Elm St Escondido (92025) *(P-17723)*

Neighborhood Healthcare .... D 760 737-6903
401 E Valley Pkwy Escondido (92025) *(P-18785)*

Neighborhood House Association (PA) .... B 858 715-2642
5660 Copley Dr San Diego (92111) *(P-19115)*

Neighborhood Steel LLC (HQ) .... E 714 236-8700
5555 Garden Grove Blvd Ste 250 Westminster (92683) *(P-12561)*

Neighbrhood Bus Advrtsment Ltd .... E 442 300-1803
14752 Crenshaw Blvd Gardena (90249) *(P-11255)*

Neil A Kjos Music Company (PA) .... E 858 270-9800
4382 Jutland Dr San Diego (92117) *(P-3468)*

Neill Aircraft Co .... B 562 432-7981
1260 W 15th St Long Beach (90813) *(P-9756)*

Neiman & Company, Van Nuys *Also Called: Neiman/Hoeller Inc (P-11141)*

Neiman/Hoeller Inc .... D 818 781-8600
6842 Valjean Ave Van Nuys (91406) *(P-11141)*

Nelco Products Inc .... C 714 879-4293
1100 E Kimberly Ave Anaheim (92801) *(P-4837)*

Nelgo Industries Inc .... E 760 433-6434
598 Airport Rd Oceanside (92058) *(P-7952)*

Nelgo Manufacturing, Oceanside *Also Called: Nelgo Industries Inc (P-7952)*

Nellix Inc .... E 650 213-8700
2 Musick Irvine (92618) *(P-10572)*

Nellson Nutraceutical Inc .... B 844 635-5766
5115 E La Palma Ave Anaheim (92807) *(P-1547)*

Nellxo LLC .... E 909 320-8501
5990 Bald Eagle Dr Fontana (92336) *(P-6541)*

Nelson Adams Naco Corporation .... E 909 256-8938
420 S E St San Bernardino (92401) *(P-2782)*

Nelson Aero Space Inc .... E 310 323-6200
14800 S Figueroa St Gardena (90248) *(P-6793)*

Nelson Bros Property MGT Inc .... C 949 916-7300
16b Journey Ste 200 Aliso Viejo (92656) *(P-20067)*

Nelson Brothers Property MGT, Aliso Viejo *Also Called: Nelson Bros Property MGT Inc (P-20067)*

Nelson Case, Placentia *Also Called: Nelson Case Corporation (P-2712)*

Nelson Case Corporation .... E 714 528-2215
650 S Jefferson St Ste A Placentia (92870) *(P-2712)*

Nelson Engineering Llc .... F 714 893-7999
11600 Monarch St Garden Grove (92841) *(P-7953)*

Nelson Honda, El Monte *Also Called: El Monte Automotive Group LLC (P-13761)*

Nelson Name Plate Company (PA) .... D 323 663-3971
708 Nogales St City Of Industry (91748) *(P-6719)*

Nelson Sports Inc .... E 562 944-8081
12810 Florence Ave Santa Fe Springs (90670) *(P-5280)*

Nelson Stud Welding Inc .... C 256 353-1931
630 E Lambert Rd Brea (92821) *(P-12867)*

Nelson-Miller, City Of Industry *Also Called: Nelson Name Plate Company (P-6719)*

Nemos Bakery Inc (HQ) .... D 760 741-5725
416 N Hale Ave Escondido (92029) *(P-1527)*

Neo Tech, Carlsbad *Also Called: Natel Engineering Co Inc (P-8849)*

Neo Tech, Chatsworth *Also Called: Natel Engineering Company LLC (P-9088)*

Neo Tech, Chatsworth *Also Called: Oncore Manufacturing LLC (P-19658)*

Neo Tech Natel Epic Oncore, Chatsworth *Also Called: Oncore Manufacturing Svcs Inc (P-8713)*

Neogov, El Segundo *Also Called: Governmentjobscom (P-16258)*

Neology, Carlsbad *Also Called: Neology Inc (P-10220)*

Neology Inc (PA) .... D 858 391-0260
1917 Palomar Oaks Way Ste 110 Carlsbad (92008) *(P-10220)*

Neomend Inc .... D 949 783-3300
60 Technology Dr Irvine (92618) *(P-10573)*

Neon Rose Inc .... E 619 218-6103
5158 Bristol Rd San Diego (92116) *(P-3871)*

Neonroots LLC .... C 310 907-9210
8560 W Sunset Blvd Ste 500 West Hollywood (90069) *(P-16080)*

Neopacific Holdings Inc .... E 818 786-2900
14940 Calvert St Van Nuys (91411) *(P-5112)*

Neovia Logistics Dist LP .... D 909 657-4900
5750 E Francis St Ontario (91761) *(P-11602)*

Nep Bexel Inc (HQ) .... D 818 565-4399
7850 Ruffner Ave Ste B Van Nuys (91406) *(P-17257)*

Nepco, Pomona *Also Called: Natural Envmtl Protection Co (P-3957)*

Nephrology, Los Angeles *Also Called: Cedars-Sinai Medical Center (P-18197)*

Neptune Foods, Vernon *Also Called: Fishermans Pride Prcessors Inc (P-1806)*

Nerdist Channel LLC .... E 818 333-2705
2900 W Alameda Ave Unit 1500 Burbank (91505) *(P-8553)*

Nerdist Industries, Burbank *Also Called: Nerdist Channel LLC (P-8553)*

Nerys Logistics Inc .... C 619 616-2124
9925 Airway Rd San Diego (92154) *(P-11837)*

Nest Parent Inc .... A 310 551-0101
2125 E Katella Ave Ste 250 Anaheim (92806) *(P-19655)*

Nestle Dist Ctr & Logistics, Jurupa Valley *Also Called: Nestle Usa Inc (P-1396)*

Nestle Ice Cream Company .... A 661 398-3500
7301 District Blvd Bakersfield (93313) *(P-13257)*

Nestle Purina Factory, Maricopa *Also Called: Nestle Purina Petcare Company (P-1436)*

Nestle Purina Petcare Company .... E 314 982-1000
800 N Brand Blvd Fl 5 Glendale (91203) *(P-1435)*

Nestle Purina Petcare Company .... C 661 769-8261
1710 Golden Cat Rd Maricopa (93252) *(P-1436)*

Nestle Usa Inc .... D 877 463-7853
3285 De Forest Cir Jurupa Valley (91752) *(P-1279)*

Nestle Usa Inc .... E 818 549-6000
800 N Brand Blvd Glendale (91203) *(P-1280)*

Nestle Usa Inc .... B 661 398-3536
7301 District Blvd Bakersfield (93313) *(P-1281)*

Nestle Usa Inc .... B 951 360-7200
3450 Dulles Dr Jurupa Valley (91752) *(P-1396)*

Net Shapes Inc (PA) .... D 909 947-3231
1336 E Francis St Ste B Ontario (91761) *(P-5659)*

Netaphor Software Inc .... E 949 470-7955
15510 Rockfield Blvd Ste C100 Irvine (92618) *(P-16320)*

Netapp Inc .... C 818 227-5025
6320 Canoga Ave Ste 1500 Woodland Hills (91367) *(P-16462)*

Netfortris Acquisition Co Inc .... D 877 366-2548
11954 S La Cienega Blvd Hawthorne (90250) *(P-20364)*

Netfortris Acquisition Co Inc .... D 310 861-4300
200 Corporate Pointe Ste 300 Culver City (90230) *(P-20365)*

Netlist, Irvine *Also Called: Netlist Inc (P-8850)*

Netlist Inc (PA)..D...... 949 435-0025
   111 Academy Ste 100 Irvine (92617) *(P-8850)*

Netmarble Us Inc..D...... 213 222-7712
   600 Wilshire Blvd Ste 1100 Los Angeles (90005) *(P-3469)*

Netsol, Encino *Also Called: Netsol Technologies Inc (P-16321)*

Netsol Technologies Inc (PA)............................D...... 818 222-9197
   16000 Ventura Blvd Ste 770 Encino (91436) *(P-16321)*

Network Automation Inc.....................................E...... 213 738-1700
   3530 Wilshire Blvd Ste 1800 Los Angeles (90010) *(P-16322)*

Network Capital, Irvine *Also Called: Network Capital Funding Corp (P-14344)*

Network Capital Funding Corp (PA).....................B...... 949 442-0060
   7700 Irvine Center Dr Fl 3 Irvine (92618) *(P-14344)*

Network Intgrtion Partners Inc............................D...... 909 919-2800
   11981 Jack Benny Dr Ste 103 Rancho Cucamonga (91739) *(P-16463)*

Network Management Group Inc (PA)....................C...... 323 263-2632
   1100 S Flower St Ste 3110 Los Angeles (90015) *(P-20068)*

Network Medical Management Inc.........................C...... 626 282-0288
   1668 S Garfield Ave Ste 100 Alhambra (91801) *(P-20069)*

Network Sltons Prvider USA Inc............................E...... 213 985-2173
   1240 Rosecrans Ave Manhattan Beach (90266) *(P-20366)*

Network Telephone Services Inc (PA)....................D...... 800 742-5687
   21135 Erwin St Woodland Hills (91367) *(P-16884)*

Networkfleet..E...... 904 233-6844
   4510 Executive Dr Ste 315 San Diego (92121) *(P-16323)*

Networks Electronic Co LLC................................E...... 818 341-0440
   9750 De Soto Ave Chatsworth (91311) *(P-6750)*

Netwrix Corporation..E...... 888 638-9749
   300 Spectrum Center Dr Ste 200 Irvine (92618) *(P-16324)*

Neudesic LLC (HQ)...C...... 949 754-4500
   200 Spectrum Center Dr Ste 2000 Irvine (92618) *(P-16081)*

Neuintel LLC (PA)...D...... 949 625-6117
   20 Pacifica Ste 1000 Irvine (92618) *(P-16082)*

Neurasignal Inc..E...... 877 638-7251
   1109 Westwood Blvd Los Angeles (90024) *(P-10817)*

Neurelis Inc (PA)..E...... 858 251-2111
   3430 Carmel Mountain Rd Ste 300 San Diego (92121) *(P-4181)*

Neuro Drinks, Sherman Oaks *Also Called: Neurobrands LLC (P-13384)*

Neurobrands LLC...C...... 310 393-6444
   15303 Ventura Blvd Ste 675 Sherman Oaks (91403) *(P-13384)*

Neurocrine, San Diego *Also Called: Neurocrine Biosciences Inc (P-4325)*

Neurocrine Biosciences Inc (PA)..........................A...... 858 617-7600
   12780 El Camino Real Ste 100 San Diego (92130) *(P-4325)*

Neurocrine Continental Inc.................................E...... 858 617-7941
   12790 El Camino Real San Diego (92130) *(P-4326)*

Neuroptics Inc..E...... 949 250-9792
   9223 Research Dr Irvine (92618) *(P-10574)*

Neuroscience Gamma Knife Ctr, Thousand Oaks *Also Called: Los Robles Regional Med Ctr (P-17710)*

Neurovasc Technologies Inc................................F...... 949 258-9946
   3 Jenner Ste 100 Irvine (92618) *(P-10575)*

Neutraderm Inc...E...... 818 534-3190
   20660 Nordhoff St Chatsworth (91311) *(P-4437)*

Neutrogena, Los Angeles *Also Called: Johnson & Johnson Consumer Inc (P-4424)*

Neutron Plating Inc...F...... 714 632-9241
   2993 E Blue Star St Anaheim (92806) *(P-6643)*

Neutronic Stamping & Plating, Corona *Also Called: Ravlich Enterprises LLC (P-6654)*

Nevell Group Inc (PA)..C...... 714 579-7501
   3001 Enterprise St Ste 200 Brea (92821) *(P-569)*

Nevell Group Inc...B...... 760 598-3501
   3284 Grey Hawk Ct Carlsbad (92010) *(P-570)*

Nevell Group Inc San Diego, Carlsbad *Also Called: Nevell Group Inc (P-570)*

Neversoft Entertainment, Woodland Hills *Also Called: Neversoft Entertainment Inc (P-16083)*

Neversoft Entertainment Inc................................E...... 818 610-4100
   21255 Burbank Blvd Ste 600 Woodland Hills (91367) *(P-16083)*

Nevins Adams Properties, Santa Barbara *Also Called: Nevins/Adams Properties Inc (P-14675)*

Nevins/Adams Properties Inc (PA)........................C...... 805 963-2884
   920 Garden St Ste A Santa Barbara (93101) *(P-14675)*

Nevwest Inc...F...... 619 420-8100
   1225 Exposition Way Ste 140 San Diego (92154) *(P-10005)*

New Advnces For Pple With Dsbl.........................C...... 661 322-9735
   4032 Jewett Ave Bakersfield (93301) *(P-19336)*

New Age Electronics Inc.....................................C...... 310 549-0000
   21950 Arnold Center Rd Carson (90810) *(P-12387)*

New Age Enclosures, Santa Maria *Also Called: Alltec Integrated Mfg Inc (P-4934)*

New Alternatives Incorporated.............................A...... 619 863-5855
   8755 Aero Dr Ste 230 San Diego (92123) *(P-19116)*

New American Funding LLC (PA)..........................A...... 949 430-7029
   14511 Myford Rd Ste 100 Tustin (92780) *(P-14275)*

New Aster Enterprises Inc...................................C...... 213 747-7566
   2901 S Flower St Los Angeles (90007) *(P-15259)*

New Bedford Panoramex Corp..............................E...... 909 982-9806
   1480 N Claremont Blvd Claremont (91711) *(P-8376)*

New Bi US Gaming LLC......................................D...... 858 592-2472
   10920 Via Frontera Ste 420 San Diego (92127) *(P-16325)*

New Brunswick Industries Inc...............................E...... 619 448-4900
   1850 Gillespie Way El Cajon (92020) *(P-8710)*

New Century Industries Inc..................................E...... 562 634-9551
   7231 Rosecrans Ave Paramount (90723) *(P-9431)*

New Century Mortgage, Irvine *Also Called: New Century Mortgage Corp (P-14345)*

New Century Mortgage Corp................................A...... 949 440-7030
   18400 Von Karman Ave Ste 1000 Irvine (92612) *(P-14345)*

New Century Snacks, Commerce *Also Called: Snak Club LLC (P-1562)*

New Century Snacks LLC....................................E...... 323 278-9578
   5560 E Slauson Ave Commerce (90040) *(P-1560)*

New Chef Fashion Inc..D...... 323 581-0300
   3223 E 46th St Vernon (90058) *(P-2152)*

New Childrens Museum.......................................D...... 619 233-8792
   200 W Island Ave San Diego (92101) *(P-19358)*

New Cingular Wireless Svcs Inc............................D...... 619 238-3638
   252 Broadway San Diego (92101) *(P-11851)*

New Classic Furniture, Fontana *Also Called: New Classic HM Furnishing Inc (P-12309)*

New Classic HM Furnishing Inc (PA)......................E...... 909 484-7676
   7351 Mcguire Ave Fontana (92336) *(P-12309)*

New Cntury Mtals Southeast Inc...........................B...... 562 356-6804
   15723 Shoemaker Ave Norwalk (90650) *(P-5725)*

New Crew Production Corp..................................C...... 323 234-8880
   1100 W 135th St Gardena (90247) *(P-16885)*

New Dimension One Spas Inc (DH)........................C...... 800 345-7727
   1819 Aston Ave Ste 105 Carlsbad (92008) *(P-11256)*

New Directions Inc (PA).....................................D...... 310 914-4045
   11303 Wilshire Blvd Bldg 116 Los Angeles (90025) *(P-19117)*

NEW DIRECTIONS FOR VETERANS, Los Angeles *Also Called: New Directions Inc (P-19117)*

New Fashion Products Inc...................................C...... 310 354-0090
   3600 E Olympic Blvd Los Angeles (90023) *(P-2354)*

New First Fincl Resources LLC.............................C...... 949 223-2160
   100 Spectrum Center Dr Ste 400 Irvine (92618) *(P-14438)*

New Flyer of America Inc....................................C...... 909 456-3566
   2880 Jurupa St Ontario (91761) *(P-9302)*

New Generation Engrg Cnstr Inc..........................E...... 424 329-3950
   22815 Frampton Ave Torrance (90501) *(P-12358)*

New Generation Wellness Inc (PA)........................C...... 949 863-0340
   46 Corporate Park Ste 200 Irvine (92606) *(P-4182)*

New Glaspro Inc...E...... 800 776-2368
   9401 Ann St Santa Fe Springs (90670) *(P-5349)*

New Gordon Industries, Santa Fe Springs *Also Called: New Gordon Industries LLC (P-6542)*

New Gordon Industries LLC.................................E...... 562 483-7378
   13750 Rosecrans Ave Santa Fe Springs (90670) *(P-6542)*

New Green Day LLC..E...... 323 566-7603
   1710 E 111th St Los Angeles (90059) *(P-3037)*

New Haven Companies Inc..................................D...... 818 686-7020
   13571 Vaughn St Unit E San Fernando (91340) *(P-2142)*

NEW HORIZONS CENTER & WORKSHOP, North Hills *Also Called: New Hrzns Srving Indvdals With (P-19001)*

New Hrzns Srving Indvdals With (PA).....................D...... 818 894-9301
   15725 Parthenia St North Hills (91343) *(P-19001)*

New Image Commercial Flrg Inc...........................E...... 909 796-3400
   10444 Corporate Dr Ste B Redlands (92374) *(P-13952)*

New Image Flooring, Redlands *Also Called: New Image Commercial Flrg Inc (P-13952)*

New Leaf Biofuel LLC...E...... 619 236-8500
   2285 Newton Ave San Diego (92113) *(P-4646)*

New Legend Inc .... C...... 855 210-2300
8613 Etiwanda Ave Rancho Cucamonga (91739) *(P-11500)*

New Maverick Desk Inc .... C...... 310 217-1554
15100 S Figueroa St Gardena (90248) *(P-2890)*

New Milani Group LLC .... D...... 323 582-9404
10000 Washington Blvd Ste 210 Culver City (90232) *(P-13059)*

New Power Inc .... D...... 800 980-9825
887 Marlborough Ave Riverside (92507) *(P-798)*

New Pride Corporation .... D...... 323 584-6608
5101 Pacific Blvd Vernon (90058) *(P-13138)*

New Pride Tire LLC .... E...... 310 631-7000
1511 E Orangethorpe Ave Ste D Fullerton (92831) *(P-17023)*

New Printing, Van Nuys *Also Called: Digital Room Holdings Inc (P-3753)*

New Spirit Naturals Inc (PA)............................ **E...... 909 592-4445**
615 W Allen Ave San Dimas (91773) *(P-17724)*

New Talco Enterprises LLC .... D...... 310 280-0755
2300 W Empire Ave Burbank (91504) *(P-19797)*

New Tangram LLC .... C...... 562 365-5000
9200 Sorensen Ave Santa Fe Springs (90670) *(P-12287)*

New Technology Plastics Inc .... E...... 562 941-6034
7110 Fenwick Ln Westminster (92683) *(P-3958)*

New Times Media Group, San Luis Obispo *Also Called: Slo New Times Inc (P-3325)*

New Vista Behavioral Hlth LLC .... D...... 949 284-0095
3 Park Plz Ste 550 Irvine (92614) *(P-18091)*

New Vista Health Services .... C...... 310 477-5501
1516 Sawtelle Blvd Los Angeles (90025) *(P-18146)*

New Vista Health Services .... C...... 818 352-1421
8647 Fenwick St Sunland (91040) *(P-18147)*

New Vsta Nrsing Rhbltation Ctr, Sunland *Also Called: New Vista Health Services (P-18147)*

New Vsta Post Acute Care Ctr W, Los Angeles *Also Called: New Vista Health Services (P-18146)*

New Wave Entertainment, Burbank *Also Called: NW Entertainment Inc (P-17203)*

New Way Landscape & Tree Svcs .... C...... 858 505-8300
7485 Ronson Rd San Diego (92111) *(P-208)*

New West Products Inc .... E...... 619 671-9022
7520 Airway Rd Ste 1 San Diego (92154) *(P-5113)*

New World Medical Incorporated .... F...... 909 466-4304
10763 Edison Ct Rancho Cucamonga (91730) *(P-10576)*

New-Indy Containerboard, Ontario *Also Called: New-Indy Ontario LLC (P-3056)*

New-Indy Containerboard, Oxnard *Also Called: New-Indy Oxnard LLC (P-3057)*

New-Indy Containerboard LLC (DH)................... **D...... 909 296-3400**
3500 Porsche Way Ste 150 Ontario (91764) *(P-3055)*

New-Indy Ontario LLC .... C...... 909 390-1055
5100 Jurupa St Ontario (91761) *(P-3056)*

New-Indy Oxnard LLC .... C...... 805 986-3881
5936 Perkins Rd Oxnard (93033) *(P-3057)*

Newbasis LLC .... C...... 951 787-0600
2626 Kansas Ave Riverside (92507) *(P-5427)*

Newbasis West LLC .... C...... 951 787-0600
2626 Kansas Ave Riverside (92507) *(P-5428)*

Newberry Technical Services, Bakersfield *Also Called: Nts Inc (P-683)*

Newby Rubber Inc .... E...... 661 327-5137
320 Industrial St Bakersfield (93307) *(P-4780)*

Newco Auto Leasing, West Hollywood *Also Called: Executive Car Leasing Company (P-16985)*

Newco International Inc .... E...... 818 834-7100
13600 Vaughn St San Fernando (91340) *(P-2783)*

Newcomb Spring Corp .... E...... 714 995-5341
8380 Cerritos Ave Stanton (90680) *(P-6805)*

Newcomb Spring of California, Stanton *Also Called: Newcomb Spring Corp (P-6805)*

Newell Brands Inc .... E...... 760 246-2700
17182 Nevada St Victorville (92394) *(P-5114)*

Newhall Signal, Santa Clarita *Also Called: Signal (P-3323)*

Newlife2 (PA)...**E...... 805 549-8093**
4855 Morabito Pl San Luis Obispo (93401) *(P-7401)*

Newlight Technologies Inc .... E...... 714 556-4500
14382 Astronautics Ln Huntington Beach (92647) *(P-5115)*

Newman and Sons Inc (PA)............................**E...... 805 522-1646**
2655 1st St Ste 210 Simi Valley (93065) *(P-5429)*

Newman Bros California Inc (PA)....................**F...... 951 782-0102**
1901 Massachusetts Ave Riverside (92507) *(P-2620)*

Newmar Power LLC .... C...... 800 854-3906
1580 Sunflower Ave Costa Mesa (92626) *(P-8930)*

Newmeyer & Dillion LLP (PA)............................**C...... 949 854-7000**
895 Dove St Ste 500 Newport Beach (92660) *(P-18918)*

Newport, Irvine *Also Called: Newport Corporation (P-10096)*

Newport Beach Country Club, Newport Beach *Also Called: Newport Beach Country Club Inc (P-17504)*

Newport Beach Country Club Inc .... D...... 949 644-9550
1 Clubhouse Dr Newport Beach (92660) *(P-17504)*

Newport Beach Surgery Ctr LLC .... C...... 949 631-0988
361 Hospital Rd Ste 124 Newport Beach (92663) *(P-17725)*

Newport Brass, Santa Ana *Also Called: Brasstech Inc (P-5963)*

Newport Corporation (HQ).................................**A...... 949 863-3144**
1791 Deere Ave Irvine (92606) *(P-10096)*

Newport Diversified Inc .... C...... 562 921-4359
13963 Alondra Blvd Santa Fe Springs (90670) *(P-16886)*

Newport Diversified Inc .... C...... 619 448-4111
1286 Fletcher Pkwy El Cajon (92020) *(P-16887)*

Newport Electronics Inc .... D...... 714 540-4914
2229 S Yale St Santa Ana (92704) *(P-7252)*

Newport Energy .... E...... 408 230-7545
19200 Von Karman Ave Ste 400 Irvine (92612) *(P-313)*

Newport Fab LLC .... D...... 949 435-8000
4321 Jamboree Rd Newport Beach (92660) *(P-8851)*

Newport Flavors & Fragrances .... E...... 714 771-2200
833 N Elm St Orange (92867) *(P-1781)*

Newport Glassworks, Stanton *Also Called: Newport Optcal Inds Hldngs Ltd (P-10330)*

Newport Hospitality Group Inc .... D...... 661 323-1900
801 Truxtun Ave Bakersfield (93301) *(P-15260)*

Newport Industrial Glass Inc .... E...... 714 484-7500
8610 Central Ave Stanton (90680) *(P-5350)*

Newport Laminates Inc .... E...... 714 545-8335
3121 W Central Ave Santa Ana (92704) *(P-5116)*

Newport Meat Company, Irvine *Also Called: Newport Meat Southern Cal Inc (P-13302)*

Newport Meat Southern Cal Inc .... C...... 949 399-4200
16691 Hale Ave Irvine (92606) *(P-13302)*

Newport Medical Instrs Inc .... D...... 949 642-3910
1620 Sunflower Ave Costa Mesa (92626) *(P-10577)*

Newport Optcal Inds Hldngs Ltd (PA)................**E...... 714 484-8100**
10564 Fern Ave Stanton (90680) *(P-10330)*

NEWPORT SPECIALTY HOSPITAL, Tustin *Also Called: Foothill Regional Medical Ctr (P-18260)*

Newport Specialty Hospital, Los Angeles *Also Called: Tustin Hospital and Medical Center (P-18481)*

Newport Television LLC .... A...... 661 283-1700
2120 L St Bakersfield (93301) *(P-11960)*

News Corp - Fox, Los Angeles *Also Called: Twentieth Cntury Fox Japan Inc (P-15677)*

News Group, The, Orange *Also Called: Great Atlantic News LLC (P-13495)*

Newshire Investment, Los Angeles *Also Called: Otts Asia Moorer Devon (P-15045)*

Newton Heat Treating Co Inc .... D...... 626 964-6528
19235 E Walnut Dr N City Of Industry (91748) *(P-5846)*

Newvac LLC .... C...... 310 990-0401
9330 De Soto Ave Chatsworth (91311) *(P-8635)*

Newvac LLC .... D...... 747 202-7333
9330 De Soto Ave Chatsworth (91311) *(P-8636)*

Newvac LLC .... E...... 747 202-7333
9330 De Soto Ave Chatsworth (91311) *(P-9089)*

Newvac Division, Chatsworth *Also Called: Newvac LLC (P-8635)*

Nexem Staffing, Santa Barbara *Also Called: Partners Prsnnel - MGT Svcs LL (P-15876)*

Nexgen AC & Htg LLC .... D...... 760 616-5870
700 N Valley St Ste K Anaheim (92801) *(P-799)*

Nexgen Air Conditioning & Plbg, Anaheim *Also Called: Nexgen AC & Htg LLC (P-799)*

Nexgen Air Heating and Plbg, Northridge *Also Called: Nexgen Air Los Angeles (P-800)*

Nexgen Air Los Angeles .... C...... 818 900-2525
19205 Parthenia St Northridge (91324) *(P-800)*

Nexgen Pharma, Irvine *Also Called: New Generation Wellness Inc (P-4182)*

Nexgenix Inc (PA)..**B...... 714 665-6240**
2 Peters Canyon Rd # 200 Irvine (92606) *(P-16084)*

Nexgrill Industries, Chino *Also Called: Nexgrill Industries Inc (P-12310)*

Nexgrill Industries Inc (PA).............................**D...... 909 598-8799**
14050 Laurelwood Pl Chino (91710) *(P-12310)*

Employee Codes: A=Over 500 employees, B=251-500
C=101-250, D=51-100, E=20-50, F=10-19, G=1-9
                    2024 Southern California
                    Business Directory and Buyers Guide
© Mergent Inc. 1-800-342-5647
1195

Nexon America, El Segundo *Also Called: M Nexon Inc (P-16297)*

Nexstar Digital LLC ....D...... 310 971-9300
12777 W Jefferson Blvd Ste B100 Los Angeles (90066) *(P-15566)*

Nexstar Pharmaceutical, San Dimas *Also Called: Gilead Sciences Inc (P-4120)*

Next Auto Tech Center ....E...... 323 483-6767
6821 Crenshaw Blvd Los Angeles (90043) *(P-2042)*

Next Day Frame Inc ....D...... 310 886-0851
11560 Wright Rd Lynwood (90262) *(P-2872)*

Next Generation, Commerce *Also Called: J & F Design Inc (P-2331)*

Next Intent, San Luis Obispo *Also Called: Next Intent Inc (P-7954)*

Next Intent Inc ....E...... 805 781-6755
865 Via Esteban San Luis Obispo (93401) *(P-7954)*

Next Level Apparel, Torrance *Also Called: Ys Garments LLC (P-2271)*

Next Point Bearing Group LLC ....E...... 818 988-1880
28364 Avenue Crocker Valencia (91355) *(P-7301)*

Next Semiconductor Tech Inc ....E...... 858 707-7060
4115 Sorrento Valley Blvd San Diego (92121) *(P-8852)*

Next Trucking Inc ....C...... 213 444-2250
301 E Ocean Blvd Ste 1950 Long Beach (90802) *(P-11787)*

Nextel, Irvine *Also Called: Nextel Communications Inc (P-11852)*

Nextel Communications Inc ....C...... 714 368-4509
330 Commerce Irvine (92602) *(P-11852)*

Nextex International, South Gate *Also Called: Nextrade Inc (P-2143)*

Nextgen Healthcare Inc (PA)...B...... 949 255-2600
18111 Von Karman Ave Ste 600 Irvine (92612) *(P-16326)*

Nextivity Inc (PA)..E...... 858 485-9442
16550 W Bernardo Dr Ste 550 San Diego (92127) *(P-8554)*

Nextpoint Inc (PA)..D...... 310 360-5904
8750 Wilshire Blvd Ste 200 Beverly Hills (90211) *(P-11895)*

Nextrade Inc (PA)..E...... 562 944-9950
12411 Industrial Ave South Gate (90280) *(P-2143)*

Nexus Capital Management LP ....A...... 424 330-8820
11100 Santa Monica Blvd Los Angeles (90025) *(P-15041)*

Nexus Dx Inc ....E...... 858 410-4600
6759 Mesa Ridge Rd San Diego (92121) *(P-10578)*

Nexus Is Inc ....B...... 704 969-2200
27202 Turnberry Ln Ste 100 Valencia (91355) *(P-12010)*

Nexxen Apparel Inc (PA)...F...... 323 267-9900
1555 Los Palos St Los Angeles (90023) *(P-2355)*

Neyenesch Printers Inc ....D...... 619 297-2281
2750 Kettner Blvd San Diego (92101) *(P-3643)*

Nfl Network, Culver City *Also Called: Nfl Properties LLC (P-17378)*

Nfl Properties LLC ....D...... 310 840-4635
10950 Washington Blvd Ste 100 Culver City (90232) *(P-17378)*

Nga 911 LLC ....C...... 877 899-8337
8383 Wilshire Blvd Ste 800 Beverly Hills (90211) *(P-16085)*

Ngd Systems Inc ....E...... 949 870-9148
3019 Wilshire Blvd Santa Monica (90403) *(P-7478)*

Ngp Motors Inc ....C...... 818 980-9800
5500 Lankershim Blvd North Hollywood (91601) *(P-13802)*

Nguoi Viet Newspaper, Westminster *Also Called: Nguoi Viet Vtnamese People Inc (P-3309)*

Nguoi Viet Vtnamese People Inc (PA)...........................E...... 714 892-9414
14771 Moran St Westminster (92683) *(P-3309)*

Nhca Inc ....C...... 310 519-8200
2330 Grand Ave Long Beach (90815) *(P-15261)*

Nhk Laboratories Inc (PA)...E...... 562 903-5835
12230 Florence Ave Santa Fe Springs (90670) *(P-4183)*

Nhk Laboratories Inc ....D...... 562 204-5002
10603 Norwalk Blvd Santa Fe Springs (90670) *(P-4184)*

Nhn Global Inc (HQ)..C...... 424 672-1177
2250 Maple Ave Los Angeles (90011) *(P-13139)*

Nhra, San Dimas *Also Called: National Hot Rod Association (P-17387)*

Nhs Western Division Inc ....D...... 909 947-9931
115 S Palm Ave Ontario (91762) *(P-448)*

Ni Industries Inc ....D...... 309 283-3355
7300 E Slauson Ave Commerce (90040) *(P-6402)*

Nibr, San Diego *Also Called: Novartis Inst For Fnctnal Gnmi (P-19866)*

Nic Partners, Rancho Cucamonga *Also Called: Network Intgrtion Partners Inc (P-16463)*

Nice North America LLC (DH)..C...... 760 438-7000
5919 Sea Otter Pl Ste 100 Carlsbad (92010) *(P-14142)*

Nichols Inst Reference Labs (DH)..................................A...... 949 728-4000
33608 Ortega Hwy San Juan Capistrano (92675) *(P-18557)*

Nichols Lumber, Baldwin Park *Also Called: Survey Stake and Marker Inc (P-2763)*

Nichols Lumber & Hardware Co ....D...... 626 960-4802
13470 Dalewood St Baldwin Park (91706) *(P-12337)*

Nick Alexander Imports ....C...... 800 800-6425
6333 S Alameda St Los Angeles (90001) *(P-13803)*

Nico Nat Mfg Corp ....E...... 323 721-1900
2624 Yates Ave Commerce (90040) *(P-2961)*

Niconat Manufacturing, Commerce *Also Called: Nico Nat Mfg Corp (P-2961)*

Niedwick Corporation ....E...... 714 771-9999
967 N Eckhoff St Orange (92867) *(P-7955)*

Niedwick Machine Co, Orange *Also Called: Niedwick Corporation (P-7955)*

Nieves Landscape Inc ....C...... 714 835-7332
1629 E Edinger Ave Santa Ana (92705) *(P-171)*

Nifty Package Co Inc ....E...... 714 863-6058
175 S Cambridge St Orange (92866) *(P-13551)*

Nihon Kohden America LLC (HQ)..................................C...... 949 580-1555
15353 Barranca Pkwy Irvine (92618) *(P-12501)*

Nihon Kohden America, Inc., Irvine *Also Called: Nihon Kohden America LLC (P-12501)*

Niitakaya Usa Inc (PA)..E...... 323 720-5050
1801 Aeros Way Montebello (90640) *(P-13385)*

Nike Inc ....F...... 949 616-4042
20001 Ellipse Foothill Ranch (92610) *(P-2402)*

Nike Usa Inc ....A...... 310 670-6770
222 E Redondo Beach Blvd Ste C Gardena (90248) *(P-17379)*

Nikkel Iron Works Corporation ....F...... 661 746-4904
17045 S Central Valley Hwy Shafter (93263) *(P-6909)*

Nikken Global Inc (HQ)..C...... 949 789-2000
18301 Von Karman Ave Ste 120 Irvine (92612) *(P-12894)*

Nikkiso Acd, Santa Ana *Also Called: Acd LLC (P-6130)*

Nikkiso Cosmodyne, Seal Beach *Also Called: Cosmodyne LLC (P-7229)*

Nikkiso Cryoquip, Escondido *Also Called: Integrted Crygnic Slutions LLC (P-7243)*

Nikko Enterprise Corporation ....E...... 562 941-6080
13168 Sandoval St Santa Fe Springs (90670) *(P-1809)*

Niknejad Inc ....E...... 310 477-0407
6855 Hayvenhurst Ave Van Nuys (91406) *(P-3644)*

Nile Ai Inc ....E...... 818 689-9107
15260 Ventura Blvd Ste 1410 Sherman Oaks (91403) *(P-16327)*

Nina Mia Inc ....D...... 714 773-5588
826 Enterprise Way Fullerton (92831) *(P-1955)*

Ninas Mexican Foods Inc ....E...... 909 468-5888
20631 Valley Blvd Ste A Walnut (91789) *(P-1956)*

Nine Eight Nine LLC ....E...... 310 469-1013
1624 240th St Harbor City (90710) *(P-5263)*

Niner Wine Estates LLC ....E...... 805 239-2233
2400 W Highway 46 Paso Robles (93446) *(P-1648)*

Ninja Jump Inc ....D...... 323 255-5418
3221 N San Fernando Rd Los Angeles (90065) *(P-10963)*

Ninth Avenue Foods, City Of Industry *Also Called: Heritage Distributing Company (P-1273)*

Ninyo More Gtchncal Envmtl Scn (PA)...........................D...... 858 576-1000
5710 Ruffin Rd San Diego (92123) *(P-20367)*

Nippon Cargo Airlines Co Ltd ....D...... 310 417-0801
6501 W Imperial Hwy Hngr 8 Los Angeles (90045) *(P-11667)*

Nippon Express ....C...... 310 782-3000
21250 Hawthorne Blvd Fl 2 Torrance (90503) *(P-11788)*

Nippon Steel Trdg Americas Inc ....E...... 714 367-3910
3100 Bristol St Ste 525 Costa Mesa (92626) *(P-5594)*

Nippon Travel Agency PCF Inc (DH)..............................D...... 310 768-0017
1411 W 190th St Ste 650 Gardena (90248) *(P-11720)*

Nipro Optics Inc ....E...... 949 215-1151
7 Marconi Irvine (92618) *(P-10331)*

Niron Inc ....F...... 909 598-1526
20541 Earlgate St Walnut (91789) *(P-7084)*

Nis America Inc ....E...... 714 540-1199
4 Hutton Centre Dr Ste 650 Santa Ana (92707) *(P-16328)*

Niscayah Inc ....D...... 626 683-8167
751 N Todd Ave Azusa (91702) *(P-12687)*

Nishiba Industries Corporation ....D...... 619 661-8866
2360 Marconi Ct San Diego (92154) *(P-5117)*

Nissan North America Inc ....C...... 714 433-3700
1683 Sunflower Ave Costa Mesa (92626) *(P-12228)*

Mergent email: customerrelations@mergent.com
1196

2024 Southern California
Business Directory and Buyers Guide

(P-0000) Products & Services Section entry number
(PA)=Parent Co (HQ)=Headquarters (DH)=Div Headquarters

Nissan of Tustin .... C..... 714 669-8282
30 Auto Center Dr Tustin (92782) *(P-13804)*

Nissho of California Inc .... B..... 760 727-9719
89055 64th Ave Thermal (92274) *(P-46)*

Nissho of California Inc (PA).............................. C..... 760 727-9719
1902 S Santa Fe Ave Vista (92083) *(P-172)*

Nissin Foods USA Company Inc (DH)................. C..... 310 327-8478
2001 W Rosecrans Ave Gardena (90249) *(P-1842)*

Nite-Lite Signs Inc .... E..... 818 341-0987
25583 Avenue Stanford Valencia (91355) *(P-1172)*

Niterder Tchncal Ltg Vdeo Syst .... E..... 858 268-9316
12255 Crosthwaite Cir Ste A Poway (92064) *(P-8377)*

Niterider, Poway Also Called: Niterder Tchncal Ltg Vdeo Syst *(P-8377)*

Nitto .... E..... 858 750-2012
10614 Science Center Dr San Diego (92121) *(P-4185)*

Nitto, Oceanside Also Called: Nitto Denko Technical Corp *(P-19908)*

Nitto Avecia Pharma Svcs Inc (DH)................... F..... 949 951-4425
10 Vanderbilt Irvine (92618) *(P-4186)*

Nitto Denko Technical Corp .... D..... 760 435-7011
501 Via Del Monte Oceanside (92058) *(P-19908)*

Nivek Industries Inc .... E..... 714 545-8855
230 E Dyer Rd Ste K Santa Ana (92707) *(P-8272)*

Nix Healthcare System, Los Angeles Also Called: Nix Hospitals System LLC *(P-18351)*

Nix Hospitals System LLC (HQ).......................... C..... 210 271-1800
3415 S Sepulveda Blvd Ste 900 Los Angeles (90034) *(P-18351)*

Nixon Inc (PA)... C..... 888 455-9200
2810 Whiptail Loop Ste 1 Carlsbad (92010) *(P-12966)*

Nixon Watches, Carlsbad Also Called: Nixon Inc *(P-12966)*

Nksfb LLC .... C..... 310 277-4657
10960 Wilshire Blvd Fl 5 Los Angeles (90024) *(P-16086)*

NL&a Collections Inc .... E..... 323 277-6266
6323 Maywood Ave Huntington Park (90255) *(P-8296)*

Nliven, San Diego Also Called: Defenseweb Technologies Inc *(P-16563)*

Nlp Furniture Industries Inc .... E..... 619 661-5170
1425 Corporate Center Dr Ste 200 San Diego (92154) *(P-3029)*

Nlyte Software Americas Ltd .... D..... 866 386-5983
1380 El Cajon Blvd Ste 220 El Cajon (92020) *(P-16087)*

NM Holdco Inc .... C..... 323 663-3971
2800 Casitas Ave Los Angeles (90039) *(P-6720)*

NMB (usa) Inc (HQ)... E..... 818 709-1770
9730 Independence Ave Chatsworth (91311) *(P-7302)*

NMB Tech, Chatsworth Also Called: NMB (usa) Inc *(P-7302)*

Nmc Group Inc .... E..... 714 223-3525
300 E Cypress St Brea (92821) *(P-12868)*

Nms Properties Inc .... D..... 310 656-2700
10960 Wilshire Blvd Los Angeles (90024) *(P-14836)*

Nmsp Inc (DH)... D..... 310 484-2322
2205 W 126th St Ste A Hawthorne (90250) *(P-9432)*

Nmsp Inc .... E..... 951 734-2453
1451 E 6th St Corona (92879) *(P-9433)*

NN Jaeschke Inc .... E..... 858 550-7900
9610 Waples St San Diego (92121) *(P-173)*

Nna Insurance Services, Chatsworth Also Called: National Notary Association *(P-19398)*

Nna Insurance Services LLC .... C..... 818 739-4071
9350 De Soto Ave Chatsworth (91311) *(P-14617)*

Nnn Realty Investors LLC .... B..... 714 667-8252
19700 Fairchild Ste 300 Irvine (92612) *(P-15042)*

No Boundaries Inc .... D..... 619 266-2349
789 Gateway Center Way San Diego (92102) *(P-3645)*

No Ordinary Moments Inc .... D..... 714 848-3800
16742 Gothard St Ste 115 Huntington Beach (92647) *(P-18630)*

No Pressure Landscape Services, Murrieta Also Called: No Prssure Prssure Wshg Svcs L *(P-4364)*

No Prssure Prssure Wshg Svcs L .... E..... 951 477-1988
41880 Kalmia St Ste 165 Murrieta (92562) *(P-4364)*

No Second Thoughts Inc .... D..... 619 428-5992
1333 30th St Ste D San Diego (92154) *(P-2153)*

Noah's New York Bagels, Westminster Also Called: Einstein Noah Rest Group Inc *(P-1253)*

Noarus Investments Inc .... D..... 310 649-2440
5850 W Centinela Ave Los Angeles (90045) *(P-13805)*

Noarus Tgg .... D..... 714 895-5595
9444 Trask Ave Garden Grove (92844) *(P-13806)*

Noatum Logistics Usa LLC .... C..... 310 527-2104
1100 W Walnut St Compton (90220) *(P-11789)*

Nobbe Orthopedics .... D..... 805 687-7508
3010 State St Santa Barbara (93105) *(P-10686)*

Nobel Biocare Usa LLC .... B..... 714 282-4800
22715 Savi Ranch Pkwy Yorba Linda (92887) *(P-18572)*

Noble Energy, Seal Beach Also Called: Samedan Oil Corporation *(P-317)*

Noble Investment Group LLC .... C..... 562 436-3000
333 E Ocean Blvd Long Beach (90802) *(P-15262)*

Noble Metals, San Diego Also Called: Johnson Matthey Inc *(P-5682)*

Noble/Utah Long Beach LLC .... C..... 562 436-3000
333 E Ocean Blvd Long Beach (90802) *(P-15263)*

Nobles Medical Tech Inc .... E..... 714 427-0398
17080 Newhope St Fountain Valley (92708) *(P-10579)*

Noblesse Oblige Inc .... C..... 760 353-3336
2015 Silsbee Rd El Centro (92243) *(P-97)*

Nogales Investors LLC .... B..... 310 276-7439
9229 W Sunset Blvd Ste 900 Los Angeles (90069) *(P-15043)*

Nohl Ranch Inn, Anaheim Also Called: Leisure Care LLC *(P-19281)*

Nokia of America Corporation .... E..... 818 880-3500
2000 Corporate Center Dr Newbury Park (91320) *(P-8481)*

Nolte, George S & Associates, San Diego Also Called: Nv5 Inc *(P-19656)*

Nomoflo Enterprises Inc .... D..... 818 767-6528
2840 N Hollywood Way Burbank (91505) *(P-8323)*

Non-Stop Label Corp .... F..... 562 949-2885
16221 Arthur St Cerritos (90703) *(P-3240)*

Nongshim, Rancho Cucamonga Also Called: Nongshim America Inc *(P-13188)*

Nongshim America Inc (HQ)............................... C..... 909 481-3698
12155 6th St Rancho Cucamonga (91730) *(P-13188)*

Noozhawk .... F..... 805 456-7267
1327a State St Santa Barbara (93101) *(P-3310)*

Nor-Cal Beverage Co Inc .... D..... 714 526-8600
1226 N Olive St Anaheim (92801) *(P-16888)*

Nora Lighting Inc .... C..... 323 767-2600
6505 Gayhart St Commerce (90040) *(P-12610)*

Norac Pharma, Azusa Also Called: S&B Pharma Inc *(P-4015)*

Noranco Corona Division, Corona Also Called: Noranco Manufacturing (usa) Acquisition Corp *(P-7122)*

Noranco Manufacturing (usa) Acquisition Corp .... C..... 951 721-8400
345 Cessna Cir Ste 102 Corona (92880) *(P-7122)*

Norberg Crushing Inc .... F..... 619 390-4200
592 Tyrone St El Cajon (92020) *(P-401)*

Norberts Athletic Products Inc .... F..... 310 830-6672
354 W Gardena Blvd Gardena (90248) *(P-11016)*

Norcal Inc .... C..... 714 224-3949
1400 Moonstone Brea (92821) *(P-1020)*

Norcal Beverage Co, Anaheim Also Called: Nor-Cal Beverage Co Inc *(P-16888)*

Norcal Pottery Products Inc .... C..... 909 390-3745
5700 E Airport Dr Ontario (91761) *(P-12311)*

Norcal Waste Services Inc .... D..... 626 357-8666
3514 Emery St Los Angeles (90023) *(P-12175)*

Norchem Corporation (PA).................................. E..... 323 221-0221
5649 Alhambra Ave Los Angeles (90032) *(P-7253)*

Norco Alarms, Riverside Also Called: Home Security Stores Inc *(P-12667)*

Norco Industries Inc (PA)................................... C..... 310 639-4000
365 W Victoria St Compton (90220) *(P-7402)*

Norco Injection Molding Inc .... D..... 909 393-4000
14325 Monte Vista Ave Chino (91710) *(P-5118)*

Norco Plastics, Chino Also Called: Norco Injection Molding Inc *(P-5118)*

Norco Plastics Inc .... D..... 909 393-4000
14325 Monte Vista Ave Chino (91710) *(P-5119)*

Nordhavn Yachts, Dana Point Also Called: Pacific Asian Enterprises Inc *(P-16897)*

Nordon Yestech, Carlsbad Also Called: Nordson Corporation *(P-7311)*

Nordson, Carlsbad Also Called: Nordson Dage Inc *(P-10784)*

Nordson Asymtek, Carlsbad Also Called: Nordson Corporation *(P-7312)*

Nordson Asymtek, Carlsbad Also Called: Nordson California Inc *(P-9182)*

Nordson Asymtek, Carlsbad Also Called: Nordson Asymtek Inc *(P-10148)*

Nordson Asymtek Inc .... C..... 760 431-1919
2747 Loker Ave W Carlsbad (92010) *(P-10148)*

Nordson California Inc .... D..... 760 918-8490
2747 Loker Ave W Carlsbad (92010) *(P-9182)*

ALPHABETIC

Employee Codes: A=Over 500 employees, B=251-500
C=101-250, D=51-100, E=20-50, F=10-19, G=1-9

2024 Southern California
Business Directory and Buyers Guide

© Mergent Inc. 1-800-342-5647
1197

Nordson Corporation	E	760 431-1919
2765 Loker Ave W Carlsbad (92010) *(P-7311)*		
Nordson Corporation	C	760 431-1919
2747 Loker Ave W Carlsbad (92010) *(P-7312)*		
Nordson Dage Inc	E	440 985-4496
2747 Loker Ave W Carlsbad (92010) *(P-10784)*		
Nordson March Inc	D	925 827-1240
2762 Loker Ave W Carlsbad (92010) *(P-7313)*		
Nordson Medical (ca) LLC	D	657 215-4200
7612 Woodwind Dr Huntington Beach (92647) *(P-10580)*		
Nordson Test Insptn Amrcas Inc	E	760 918-8471
2765 Loker Ave W Carlsbad (92010) *(P-7314)*		
Nordstrom, Ontario *Also Called: Nordstrom Inc (P-11603)*		
Nordstrom Inc	B	909 390-1040
1600 S Milliken Ave Ontario (91761) *(P-11603)*		
Norfox, City Of Industry *Also Called: Norman Fox & Co (P-13437)*		
Noritsu-America Corporation (HQ)	**C**	**714 521-9040**
6900 Noritsu Ave Buena Park (90620) *(P-12379)*		
Norlaine Inc	C	626 961-2471
1449 W Industrial Park St Covina (91722) *(P-11257)*		
Norman Fox & Co	E	323 973-4900
5511 S Boyle Ave Vernon (90058) *(P-13436)*		
Norman Fox & Co (PA)	**E**	**800 632-1777**
14970 Don Julian Rd City Of Industry (91746) *(P-13437)*		
Norman Industrial Mtls Inc	D	949 250-3343
2481 Alton Pkwy Irvine (92606) *(P-12562)*		
Norman Industrial Mtls Inc (PA)	**C**	**818 729-3333**
8300 San Fernando Rd Sun Valley (91352) *(P-12563)*		
Norman International, Vernon *Also Called: Norman Paper and Foam Co Inc (P-3188)*		
Norman Paper and Foam Co Inc	E	323 582-7132
4501 S Santa Fe Ave Vernon (90058) *(P-3188)*		
Norman's Nursery, Carpinteria *Also Called: Normans Nursery Inc (P-62)*		
Norman's Nursery, Baldwin Park *Also Called: Normans Nursery Inc (P-13517)*		
Normans Nursery Inc	C	805 684-1411
5770 Casitas Pass Rd Carpinteria (93013) *(P-62)*		
Normans Nursery Inc	C	805 684-5442
5800 Via Real Carpinteria (93013) *(P-13516)*		
Normans Nursery Inc	C	626 285-9795
20500 Ramona Blvd Baldwin Park (91706) *(P-13517)*		
Norotos Inc	C	714 662-3113
201 E Alton Ave Santa Ana (92707) *(P-7956)*		
Norstar Office Products Inc (PA)	**E**	**323 262-1919**
5353 Jillson St Commerce (90040) *(P-2891)*		
North American Acceptance Corp	C	714 868-3195
3191 Red Hill Ave Ste 100 Costa Mesa (92626) *(P-14276)*		
North American Client Svcs Inc (PA)	**C**	**949 240-2423**
25910 Acero Ste 350 Mission Viejo (92691) *(P-20070)*		
North American Composites Co	F	909 605-8977
4990 Vanderbilt St Ontario (91761) *(P-3959)*		
North American Fire Hose Corp	D	805 922-7076
910 Noble Way Santa Maria (93454) *(P-4710)*		
North American Pet Products, Corona *Also Called: Pet Partners Inc (P-11266)*		
North American Textile Co LLC (PA)	**E**	**818 409-0019**
346 W Cerritos Ave Glendale (91204) *(P-2536)*		
North American Video Corp (PA)	**E**	**714 779-7499**
1335 S Acacia Ave Fullerton (92831) *(P-12688)*		
North Amrcn Foam Ppr Cnverters	E	818 255-3383
11835 Wicks St Sun Valley (91352) *(P-4895)*		
North Amrcn SEC Investigations	D	323 634-1911
550 E Carson Plaza Dr Ste 222 Carson (90746) *(P-16663)*		
North Anaheim Surgery Center, Anaheim *Also Called: Vanguard Health Systems Inc (P-17822)*		
North Coast Home Care Inc	D	760 260-8700
5927 Balfour Ct Ste 111 Carlsbad (92008) *(P-18631)*		
North County GMC, Vista *Also Called: County Ford North Inc (P-13749)*		
North County Health Prj Inc	C	760 736-6767
1130 2nd St Encinitas (92024) *(P-17726)*		
North County Health Prj Inc (PA)	**C**	**760 736-6755**
150 Valpreda Rd Frnt San Marcos (92069) *(P-17727)*		
North County Sand and Grav Inc	F	951 928-2881
26227 Sherman Rd Sun City (92585) *(P-407)*		

NORTH COUNTY SERVICES, San Marcos *Also Called: North County Health Prj Inc (P-17727)*		
North County Times (DH)	**C**	**800 533-8830**
350 Camino De La Reina San Diego (92108) *(P-3311)*		
North County Times	E	951 676-4315
28441 Rancho California Rd Ste 103 Temecula (92590) *(P-3312)*		
North Island Credit Union, San Diego *Also Called: North Island Financial Credit Union (P-14250)*		
North Island Financial Credit Union	B	619 656-6525
5898 Copley Dr Ste 100 San Diego (92111) *(P-14250)*		
North Kern S Tulare Hosp Dst	C	661 720-2126
1509 Tokay St Delano (93215) *(P-18352)*		
North La County Regional Ctr (PA)	**B**	**818 778-1900**
9200 Oakdale Ave Ste 100 Chatsworth (91311) *(P-20368)*		
North Orange County Svc Ctr, Fullerton *Also Called: Southern California Edison Co (P-12073)*		
North Ornge Cnty Cmnty Cllege	B	714 992-7008
330 E Chapman Ave Fullerton (92832) *(P-14068)*		
North Park Beer Co., San Diego *Also Called: K A McNair Brewing Co LLC (P-1594)*		
North Ranch Country Club	C	818 889-3531
4761 Valley Spring Dr Westlake Village (91362) *(P-17505)*		
North Ranch Management Corp	D	800 410-2153
9754 Deering Ave Chatsworth (91311) *(P-13964)*		
North Star Acquisition Inc	D	310 515-2200
14912 S Broadway Gardena (90248) *(P-6403)*		
North Star Company, Gardena *Also Called: North Star Acquisition Inc (P-6403)*		
North West Pharmanaturals, Brea *Also Called: Beacon Manufacturing Inc (P-3992)*		
North West Pharmanaturals Inc	E	714 529-0980
1000 Beacon St Brea (92821) *(P-4006)*		
Northbound Treatment Services, Newport Beach *Also Called: National Therapeutic Svcs Inc (P-18703)*		
Northeast Newspapers Inc	E	213 727-1117
621 W Beverly Blvd Montebello (90640) *(P-3313)*		
Northern Reg. Sub Base, Bakersfield *Also Called: Southern California Gas Co (P-12093)*		
Northern Trust, Pasadena *Also Called: Northern Trust of California (inc) (P-14172)*		
Northern Trust of California (inc)	B	
201 S Lake Ave Ste 600 Pasadena (91101) *(P-14172)*		
Northgate Gonzalez Inc	B	323 262-0595
425 S Soto St Los Angeles (90033) *(P-20210)*		
NORTHPOINT DAY TREATMENT SCH, Northridge *Also Called: Child and Family Guidance Ctr (P-18679)*		
Northridge Hospital Med Ctr, Northridge *Also Called: Dignity Health (P-18244)*		
Northrop Grmman Arospc Systems, Palmdale *Also Called: Northrop Grumman Corporation (P-10008)*		
Northrop Grmman Def Mssion Sys, San Diego *Also Called: Northrop Grumman Systems Corp (P-10028)*		
Northrop Grmman Elctrnic Syste, Azusa *Also Called: Northrop Grumman Systems Corp (P-10019)*		
Northrop Grmman Innvtion Syste	B	858 621-5700
9617 Distribution Ave San Diego (92121) *(P-10006)*		
Northrop Grmman Innvtion Syste	D	818 887-8100
9401 Corbin Ave Northridge (91324) *(P-10007)*		
Northrop Grmmn Spce & Mssn Sys	B	310 812-4321
2501 Santa Fe Ave Redondo Beach (90278) *(P-9434)*		
Northrop Grmmn Spce & Mssn Sys	C	909 382-6800
862 E Hospitality Ln San Bernardino (92408) *(P-19865)*		
Northrop Grumman CMS, Woodland Hills *Also Called: Northrop Grumman Systems Corp (P-10027)*		
Northrop Grumman Corporation	E	661 272-7334
3520 E Avenue M Palmdale (93550) *(P-10008)*		
Northrop Grumman Corporation	A	858 967-1221
18701 Caminito Pasadero San Diego (92128) *(P-10009)*		
Northrop Grumman Corporation	E	310 864-7342
198 Willow Grove Pl Escondido (92027) *(P-10010)*		
Northrop Grumman Corporation	C	310 332-1000
1 Hornet Way El Segundo (90245) *(P-10011)*		
Northrop Grumman Corporation	C	949 260-9800
19782 Macarthur Blvd Irvine (92612) *(P-10012)*		
Northrop Grumman Intl Trdg Inc	E	818 715-3607
21240 Burbank Blvd Woodland Hills (91367) *(P-10013)*		
Northrop Grumman Space, San Diego *Also Called: Northrop Grumman Systems Corp (P-10034)*		
Northrop Grumman Systems Corp	C	310 812-5149
1 Space Park Blvd Redondo Beach (90278) *(P-8555)*		

Mergent email: customerrelations@mergent.com
1198

2024 Southern California
Business Directory and Buyers Guide

(P-0000) Products & Services Section entry number
(PA)=Parent Co (HQ)=Headquarters (DH)=Div Headquarters

Northrop Grumman Systems Corp ....B....... 310 812-4321
1 Space Park Blvd # D1 1024 Redondo Beach (90278) *(P-9545)*

Northrop Grumman Systems Corp ....B....... 310 812-1089
1 Space Park Blvd Redondo Beach (90278) *(P-9546)*

Northrop Grumman Systems Corp ....B....... 661 272-7000
3520 E Avenue M Palmdale (93550) *(P-9547)*

Northrop Grumman Systems Corp ....C....... 818 715-2597
21200 Burbank Blvd Woodland Hills (91367) *(P-10014)*

Northrop Grumman Systems Corp ....B....... 818 887-8110
9401 Corbin Ave Northridge (91324) *(P-10015)*

Northrop Grumman Systems Corp ....C....... 714 240-6521
6033 Bandini Blvd Commerce (90040) *(P-10016)*

Northrop Grumman Systems Corp ....D....... 480 355-7716
400 Continental Blvd El Segundo (90245) *(P-10017)*

Northrop Grumman Systems Corp ....D....... 818 249-5252
2550 Honolulu Ave Montrose (91020) *(P-10018)*

Northrop Grumman Systems Corp ....A....... 626 812-1000
1100 W Hollyvale St Azusa (91702) *(P-10019)*

Northrop Grumman Systems Corp ....D....... 661 540-0446
3520 E Avenue M Palmdale (93550) *(P-10020)*

Northrop Grumman Systems Corp ....C....... 855 737-8364
1 Space Park Blvd Redondo Beach (90278) *(P-10021)*

Northrop Grumman Systems Corp ....D....... 310 812-4321
2477 Manhattan Beach Blvd Redondo Beach (90278) *(P-10022)*

Northrop Grumman Systems Corp ....A....... 626 812-1464
1111 W 3rd St Azusa (91702) *(P-10023)*

Northrop Grumman Systems Corp ....B....... 310 332-1000
1 Hornet Way El Segundo (90245) *(P-10024)*

Northrop Grumman Systems Corp ....B....... 310 556-4911
6411 W Imperial Hwy Los Angeles (90045) *(P-10025)*

Northrop Grumman Systems Corp ....A....... 818 715-4040
21240 Burbank Blvd Ms 29 Woodland Hills (91367) *(P-10026)*

Northrop Grumman Systems Corp ....B....... 818 715-4854
21240 Burbank Blvd Woodland Hills (91367) *(P-10027)*

Northrop Grumman Systems Corp ....A....... 410 765-5589
9326 Spectrum Center Blvd San Diego (92123) *(P-10028)*

Northrop Grumman Systems Corp ....B....... 858 592-4518
15120 Innovation Dr San Diego (92128) *(P-10029)*

Northrop Grumman Systems Corp ....C....... 858 618-4349
17066 Goldentop Rd San Diego (92127) *(P-10030)*

Northrop Grumman Systems Corp ....D....... 858 514-9020
9112 Spectrum Center Blvd San Diego (92123) *(P-10031)*

Northrop Grumman Systems Corp ....F....... 858 592-2535
16707 Via Del Campo Ct San Diego (92127) *(P-10032)*

Northrop Grumman Systems Corp ....D....... 858 621-7395
7130 Miramar Rd Ste 100b San Diego (92121) *(P-10033)*

Northrop Grumman Systems Corp ....D....... 858 514-9000
9326 Spectrum Center Blvd San Diego (92123) *(P-10034)*

Northrop Grumman Systems Corp ....D....... 805 278-2074
2700 Camino Del Sol Oxnard (93030) *(P-10035)*

Northrop Grumman Systems Corp ....C....... 805 987-8831
760 Paseo Camarillo Ste 200 Camarillo (93010) *(P-10036)*

Northrop Grumman Systems Corp ....E....... 805 987-9739
5161 Verdugo Way Camarillo (93012) *(P-10037)*

Northrop Grumman Systems Corp ....C....... 805 684-6641
2601 Camino Del Sol Oxnard (93030) *(P-10038)*

Northrop Grumman Systems Corp ....D....... 760 380-4268
Building 806 Fort Irwin (92310) *(P-10039)*

Northrop Grumman Systems Corp ....E....... 703 713-4096
862 E Hospitality Ln San Bernardino (92408) *(P-10040)*

Northrop Grumman Systems Corp ....D....... 714 240-6521
600 Pine Ave Goleta (93117) *(P-10041)*

Northrop Grumman Systems Corp ....D....... 805 315-5728
1467 Fairway Dr Santa Maria (93455) *(P-10042)*

Northstar Dem & Remediation LP (DH).............**C**.... **714 672-3500**
404 N Berry St Brea (92821) *(P-1136)*

Northstar Engineering, Rancho Cucamonga *Also Called: James Magna Ltd (P-17043)*

Northstar Memorial Group LLC ....C....... 800 323-1342
2562 State St Carlsbad (92008) *(P-15488)*

Northwest Circuits Corp ....D....... 619 661-1701
8660 Avenida Costa Blanca San Diego (92154) *(P-8711)*

Northwest Hotel Corporation (PA)........................**C**.... **714 776-6120**
1380 S Harbor Blvd Anaheim (92802) *(P-15264)*

Northwest Pipe Company ....D....... 760 246-3191
12351 Rancho Rd Adelanto (92301) *(P-5638)*

Northwest Recycler Core, Riverside *Also Called: Recycler Core Company Inc (P-12183)*

Northwestern Converting Co ....D....... 800 959-3402
2395 Railroad St Corona (92878) *(P-2479)*

Northwestern Inc ....E....... 818 786-1581
10153 1/2 Riverside Dr # 250 Toluca Lake (91602) *(P-2621)*

Northwestern Mutl Fincl Netwrk (PA).................**D**.... **619 234-3111**
4225 Executive Sq Ste 1250 La Jolla (92037) *(P-14439)*

Northwestern Mutl Inv MGT LLC ....C....... 949 759-5555
610 Newport Center Dr Ste 850 Newport Beach (92660) *(P-14618)*

Northwestern Mutual Investment, Newport Beach *Also Called: Northwestern Mutl Inv MGT LLC (P-14618)*

Norton Packaging Inc ....E....... 323 588-6167
5800 S Boyle Ave Vernon (90058) *(P-5120)*

Norton Smon Mseum Art At Psden ....D....... 626 449-6840
411 W Colorado Blvd Pasadena (91105) *(P-19359)*

Norwalk Unified School Dst, Norwalk *Also Called: Assoction Mxcan Amrcn Edcators (P-19389)*

Not Your Daughters Jeans, Vernon *Also Called: Nydj Apparel LLC (P-13140)*

Nothing To Wear Inc ....F....... 310 328-0408
630 Maple Ave Torrance (90503) *(P-2260)*

Nothing To Wear Inc (PA)................................**E**.... **310 328-0408**
630 Maple Ave Torrance (90503) *(P-2261)*

Notthoff Engineering L A Inc ....D....... 714 894-9802
5416 Argosy Ave Huntington Beach (92649) *(P-9757)*

Noushig Inc ....E....... 805 983-2903
451 Lombard St Oxnard (93030) *(P-1486)*

Nov Inc ....D....... 714 978-1900
759 N Eckhoff St Orange (92868) *(P-6962)*

Nova, Huntington Park *Also Called: NL&a Collections Inc (P-8296)*

Nova Development, Calabasas *Also Called: Avanquest North America LLC (P-15974)*

Nova Lifestyle Inc (PA)................................**E**.... **323 888-9999**
6565 E Washington Blvd Commerce (90040) *(P-2784)*

Nova Skilled Home Health Inc ....C....... 323 658-6232
3300 N San Fernando Blvd Ste 201 Burbank (91504) *(P-18786)*

Nova Steel Company, Corona *Also Called: Ckkm Inc (P-12540)*

Nova Transportation Services, Compton *Also Called: H Rauvel Inc (P-11489)*

Novacap LLC ....B....... 661 295-5920
25111 Anza Dr Valencia (91355) *(P-12689)*

Novalogic Inc (PA)................................**D**.... **818 880-1997**
27489 Agoura Rd Ste 300 Agoura Hills (91301) *(P-16088)*

Novartis Inst For Fnctnal Gnmi ....A....... 858 812-1500
10675 John J Hopkins Dr San Diego (92121) *(P-19866)*

Novasignal, Los Angeles *Also Called: Neurasignal Inc (P-10817)*

Novastor Corporation (PA)...........................**E**.... **805 579-6700**
29209 Canwood St Ste 200 Agoura Hills (91301) *(P-16329)*

Novo Brasil Brewing Co., Chula Vista *Also Called: Otay Lakes Brewery LLC (P-1601)*

Novo Manufacturing LLC ....E....... 949 609-0544
25956 Commercentre Dr Lake Forest (92630) *(P-2622)*

Novolex Holdings LLC ....D....... 626 961-6766
515 Turnbull Canyon Rd City Of Industry (91745) *(P-3189)*

Now Casting Inc ....C....... 818 588-3732
211 N Victory Blvd Burbank (91502) *(P-17347)*

Nowcom LLC ....C....... 323 746-6888
4751 Wilshire Blvd Ste 205 Los Angeles (90010) *(P-16582)*

Nowdocs, Brea *Also Called: Nowdocs International Inc (P-3790)*

Nowdocs International Inc ....E....... 714 986-1559
3230 E Imperial Hwy # 302 Brea (92821) *(P-3790)*

Noymed Corp ....C....... 800 224-2090
1101 N Pacific Ave Ste 303 Glendale (91202) *(P-19867)*

NP Mechanical Inc ....B....... 951 667-4220
9129 Stellar Ct Corona (92883) *(P-801)*

Npg Inc (PA)................................**D**.... **951 940-0200**
1354 Jet Way Perris (92571) *(P-4662)*

Npms Natural Products Mil Svcs, Gardena *Also Called: Sabater Usa Inc (P-1981)*

NRC Research Institute, Los Angeles *Also Called: Orange Cnty Nrpsychtric RES CT (P-19909)*

Employee Codes: A=Over 500 employees, B=251-500
C=101-250, D=51-100, E=20-50, F=10-19, G=1-9

2024 Southern California
Business Directory and Buyers Guide

© Mergent Inc. 1-800-342-5647
1199

Nrea-TRC 711 LLC .... C...... 213 488-3500
711 S Hope St Los Angeles (90017) *(P-15265)*

NRG California South LP .... C...... 909 899-7241
8996 Etiwanda Ave Rancho Cucamonga (91739) *(P-12029)*

NRG California South LP .... C...... 760 254-5241
37000 E Santa Fe St Daggett (92327) *(P-12030)*

NRG California South LP .... C...... 805 984-5241
393 Harbor Blvd Oxnard (93035) *(P-12031)*

NRG Motorsports Inc .... D...... 714 541-1173
861 E Lambert Rd La Habra (90631) *(P-9435)*

NRG Solar LLC .... C...... 760 710-2140
5790 Fleet St Carlsbad (92008) *(P-12032)*

Nri Distribution, Los Angeles *Also Called: Nri Usa LLC (P-11790)*

Nri Usa LLC (PA) .... D...... 323 345-6456
13200 S Broadway Los Angeles (90061) *(P-11790)*

NRLL LLC .... B...... 949 768-7777
1 Mauchly Irvine (92618) *(P-15044)*

Nrp Holding Co Inc (PA) .... C...... 949 583-1000
1 Mauchly Irvine (92618) *(P-14937)*

NS Wash Systems, Inglewood *Also Called: N/S Corporation (P-7676)*

Nsa Holdings Inc .... E...... 951 686-1400
888 Marlborough Ave Riverside (92507) *(P-5121)*

Nsbn, Los Angeles *Also Called: Cliftonlarsonallen LLP (P-19761)*

Nsi - Natural Sourcing Intl, Encino *Also Called: Nsi Group LLC (P-16889)*

Nsi Group LLC (PA) .... F...... 818 639-8335
17031 Ventura Blvd Encino (91316) *(P-16889)*

NSK Prcsion Amer Snta Fe Sprng, Cerritos *Also Called: NSK Precision America Inc (P-12869)*

NSK Precision America Inc .... D...... 562 968-1000
13921 Bettencourt St Cerritos (90703) *(P-12869)*

Nst, San Diego *Also Called: No Second Thoughts Inc (P-2153)*

Nsta Foods, Costa Mesa *Also Called: Nippon Steel Trdg Americas Inc (P-5594)*

Nsv International Corp .... D...... 562 438-3836
1250 E 29th St Signal Hill (90755) *(P-12250)*

Nta Pacific, Gardena *Also Called: Nippon Travel Agency PCF Inc (P-11720)*

NTD Architects .... D...... 858 565-4440
9665 Chesapeake Dr # 365 San Diego (92123) *(P-19739)*

NTD Architecture, San Diego *Also Called: NTD Architects (P-19739)*

Ntrust Infotech Inc .... D...... 562 207-1600
230 Commerce Ste 180 Irvine (92602) *(P-16330)*

Nts Inc .... B...... 661 588-8514
8200 Stockdale Hwy Ste M10306 Bakersfield (93311) *(P-683)*

Nu Health Products, Walnut *Also Called: Nu-Health Products Co (P-4007)*

Nu Venture Diving Co .... E...... 805 815-4044
1600 Beacon Pl Oxnard (93033) *(P-7315)*

Nu-Health Products Co .... E...... 909 869-0666
20875 Currier Rd Walnut (91789) *(P-4007)*

Nu-Hope Laboratories Inc .... E...... 818 899-7711
12640 Branford St Pacoima (91331) *(P-10581)*

Nubs Plastics Inc .... E...... 760 598-2525
991 Park Center Dr Vista (92081) *(P-5122)*

Nucast Industries Inc .... E...... 951 277-8888
23220 Park Canyon Dr Corona (92883) *(P-5430)*

Nucleus Enterprises LLC .... E...... 619 517-8747
888 Prospect St Ste 200 La Jolla (92037) *(P-5123)*

Nucleushealth LLC .... D...... 858 251-3400
13280 Evening Creek Dr S Ste 110 San Diego (92128) *(P-16089)*

Nuconic Packaging LLC .... E...... 323 588-9033
4889 Loma Vista Ave Vernon (90058) *(P-5124)*

Nucor Warehouse Systems Inc (HQ) .... C...... 323 588-4261
3851 S Santa Fe Ave Vernon (90058) *(P-5639)*

Nuface, Vista *Also Called: Carol Cole Company (P-10476)*

Nugier Hydraulics, Gardena *Also Called: Nugier Press Company Inc (P-7035)*

Nugier Press Company Inc .... F...... 310 515-6025
18031 La Salle Ave Gardena (90248) *(P-7035)*

Numatech West (kmp) LLC .... D...... 909 706-3627
1201 E Lexington Ave Pomona (91766) *(P-3119)*

Numatic Engineering Inc .... E...... 818 768-1200
7915 Ajay Dr Sun Valley (91352) *(P-10149)*

Number Holdings Inc (PA) .... C...... 323 980-8145
4000 Union Pacific Ave Commerce (90023) *(P-13687)*

Numecent Inc .... E...... 949 833-2800
530 Technology Dr Ste 375 Irvine (92618) *(P-16331)*

Numerade Labs Inc .... D...... 213 536-1489
1155 Rexford Ave Pasadena (91107) *(P-19979)*

Numotion, Cypress *Also Called: Atg - Designing Mobility Inc (P-12472)*

Nuphoton Technologies Inc .... E...... 951 696-8366
41610 Corning Pl Murrieta (92562) *(P-9231)*

Nura USA LLC .... E...... 949 946-5700
2652 White Rd Irvine (92614) *(P-4187)*

Nursechoice .... D...... 866 557-6050
12400 High Bluff Dr San Diego (92130) *(P-15869)*

Nursecore Management Svcs LLC .... A...... 805 938-7660
1010 S Broadway Ste A Santa Maria (93454) *(P-19290)*

Nursefinders, Los Angeles *Also Called: Nursefinders Inc (P-15870)*

Nursefinders, San Bernardino *Also Called: Nursefinders LLC (P-15871)*

Nursefinders, San Diego *Also Called: Nursefinders LLC (P-15872)*

Nursefinders Inc .... D...... 925 660-1153
5120 W Goldleaf Cir Ste 100 Los Angeles (90056) *(P-15870)*

Nursefinders LLC .... C...... 909 890-2286
1832 Commercenter Cir B San Bernardino (92408) *(P-15871)*

Nursefinders LLC (HQ) .... C...... 858 314-7427
12400 High Bluff Dr San Diego (92130) *(P-15872)*

Nuset Inc .... E...... 626 246-1668
2432 Peck Rd City Of Industry (90601) *(P-5937)*

Nusil, Carpinteria *Also Called: Nusil Technology LLC (P-4781)*

Nusil Technology LLC (DH) .... B...... 805 684-8780
1050 Cindy Ln Carpinteria (93013) *(P-4781)*

Nuspace Inc (HQ) .... E...... 562 497-3200
4401 E Donald Douglas Dr Long Beach (90808) *(P-7957)*

Nutrawise, Irvine *Also Called: Nutrawise Health & Beauty Corp (P-4188)*

Nutrawise Health & Beauty Corp .... D...... 949 900-2400
9600 Toledo Way Irvine (92618) *(P-4188)*

Nutri Granulations, La Mirada *Also Called: JM Huber Micropowders Inc (P-3895)*

Nutrilite, Buena Park *Also Called: Access Business Group LLC (P-13422)*

Nutrition Services, San Bernardino *Also Called: San Brnrdino Cy Unfied Schl Ds (P-18801)*

Nutrition Services, Hemet *Also Called: Hemet Unified School District (P-18969)*

Nuvair, Oxnard *Also Called: Nu Venture Diving Co (P-7315)*

Nuvasive Inc .... F...... 858 909-1800
4223 Ponderosa Ave Ste C San Diego (92123) *(P-10582)*

Nuvasive Inc (HQ) .... D...... 858 909-1800
7475 Lusk Blvd San Diego (92121) *(P-10583)*

Nuvasive Manufacturing LLC (DH) .... E...... 858 909-1800
7475 Lusk Blvd San Diego (92121) *(P-10818)*

Nuvasive Spclzed Orthpdics Inc .... D...... 949 837-3600
101 Enterprise Ste 100 Aliso Viejo (92656) *(P-10584)*

Nuvet Labs, Westlake Village *Also Called: Vitavet Labs Inc (P-11304)*

Nuvision Fincl Federal Cr Un (PA) .... C...... 714 375-8000
7812 Edinger Ave Ste 100 Huntington Beach (92647) *(P-14234)*

Nuvo, Chatsworth *Also Called: Medical Illumination International Inc (P-8322)*

Nuvve Holding Corp (PA) .... E...... 619 456-5161
2488 Historic Decatur Rd Ste 200 San Diego (92106) *(P-8102)*

Nuzuna Corporation .... D...... 949 335-7790
1451 Quail St Ste 104 Newport Beach (92660) *(P-17409)*

Nuzuna Fitness, Newport Beach *Also Called: Nuzuna Corporation (P-17409)*

Nv5 Inc .... C...... 858 385-0500
15092 Avenue Of Science # 200 San Diego (92128) *(P-19656)*

NVE Inc .... D...... 323 512-8400
912 N La Cienega Blvd 2nd Fl Los Angeles (90069) *(P-20211)*

NW Entertainment Inc (PA) .... C...... 818 295-5000
2660 W Olive Ave Burbank (91505) *(P-17203)*

NW Packaging, Pomona *Also Called: NW Packaging LLC (P-13552)*

NW Packaging LLC (PA) .... D...... 909 706-3627
1201 E Lexington Ave Pomona (91766) *(P-13552)*

Nwp Services Corporation (DH) .... C...... 949 253-2500
535 Anton Blvd Ste 1100 Costa Mesa (92626) *(P-16332)*

Nxgn Management LLC .... E...... 949 255-2600
18111 Von Karman Ave Ste 600 Irvine (92612) *(P-16333)*

Nydj Apparel LLC .... C...... 323 581-9040
5401 S Soto St Vernon (90058) *(P-13140)*

Nylok LLC .... E...... 714 635-3993
313 N Euclid Way Anaheim (92801) *(P-6450)*

Mergent email: customerrelations@mergent.com
1200

2024 Southern California
Business Directory and Buyers Guide

(P-0000) Products & Services Section entry number
(PA)=Parent Co (HQ)=Headquarters (DH)=Div Headquarters

Nylok Western Fastener, Anaheim *Also Called: Nylok LLC (P-6450)*

Nylon Molding, Brea *Also Called: Nmc Group Inc (P-12868)*

Nypro Healthcare Baja, Chula Vista *Also Called: Nypro Inc (P-5125)*

Nypro Inc ....D...... 619 498-9250
505 Main St Rm 107 Chula Vista (91911) *(P-5125)*

Nypro San Diego Inc ....D...... 619 482-7033
505 Main St Chula Vista (91911) *(P-5126)*

Nyx Cosmetics, Torrance *Also Called: Nyx Los Angeles Inc (P-4438)*

Nyx Los Angeles Inc ....C...... 323 869-9420
588 Crenshaw Blvd Torrance (90503) *(P-4438)*

Nzxt Inc (PA) ....**B...... 800 228-9395**
15736 E Valley Blvd City Of Industry (91744) *(P-16583)*

O & K Inc (PA) ....**C...... 323 846-5700**
2121 E 37th St Vernon (90058) *(P-13141)*

O & S California Inc ....B...... 619 661-1800
9731 Siempre Viva Rd Ste E San Diego (92154) *(P-9232)*

O & S Precision Inc ....E...... 818 718-8876
20630 Nordhoff St Chatsworth (91311) *(P-7958)*

O C M, Los Angeles *Also Called: Old Country Millwork Inc (P-7152)*

O D I, Riverside *Also Called: Edge Plastics Inc (P-5020)*

O H I, Irvine *Also Called: European Ht Invstors I I A Cal (P-15150)*

O M Y A, Lucerne Valley *Also Called: Omya California Inc (P-3901)*

O P F, Oxnard *Also Called: Oxnard Prcsion Fabrication Inc (P-6280)*

O P I Products Inc (HQ) ....**B...... 818 759-8688**
13034 Saticoy St North Hollywood (91605) *(P-4439)*

O.C. Metro Magazine, Newport Beach *Also Called: Churm Publishing Inc (P-3265)*

O'Connell Landscape Maint, Carson *Also Called: OConnell Landscape Maint Inc (P-209)*

O'Neal U S A, Camarillo *Also Called: Jim ONeal Distributing Inc (P-13900)*

Oak Design Corporation ....F...... 909 628-9597
13272 6th St Chino (91710) *(P-2892)*

Oak Grove Center, Murrieta *Also Called: Oak Grove Inst Foundation Inc (P-17728)*

Oak Grove Inst Foundation Inc (PA) ....**C...... 951 677-5599**
24275 Jefferson Ave Murrieta (92562) *(P-17728)*

Oak Grove Inst Foundation Inc ....C...... 951 238-6022
1251 N A St Perris (92570) *(P-19118)*

OAK HILL RESIDENTIAL CARE, Escondido *Also Called: Life Care Residences Inc (P-17993)*

Oak Paper Products Co Inc (PA) ....**C...... 323 268-0507**
3686 E Olympic Blvd Los Angeles (90023) *(P-13011)*

Oak Springs Nursery Inc ....D...... 818 367-5832
13761 Eldridge Ave Sylmar (91342) *(P-12214)*

Oak Tree Furniture Inc ....F...... 562 944-0754
13681 Newport Ave Ste 8 Tustin (92780) *(P-2785)*

Oak Valley Hotel LLC ....D...... 619 297-1101
2270 Hotel Cir N San Diego (92108) *(P-15266)*

Oak-It Inc ....E...... 310 719-3999
845 Sandhill Ave Carson (90746) *(P-2962)*

Oakcroft Associates Inc (PA) ....**E...... 323 261-5122**
750 Monterey Pass Rd Monterey Park (91754) *(P-12776)*

Oakhurst Industries Inc (PA) ....**C...... 323 724-3000**
2050 S Tubeway Ave Commerce (90040) *(P-1487)*

Oakley Inc (DH) ....**A...... 949 951-0991**
1 Icon Foothill Ranch (92610) *(P-10845)*

Oakley Sales Corp ....C...... 949 672-6925
1 Icon Foothill Ranch (92610) *(P-10846)*

Oakmont Country Club ....C...... 818 542-4260
3100 Country Club Dr Glendale (91208) *(P-17506)*

Oaktree Capital Management LP (DH) ....**C...... 213 830-6300**
333 S Grand Ave Fl 28 Los Angeles (90071) *(P-14424)*

Oaktree Holdings Inc ....A...... 213 830-6300
333 S Grand Ave Fl 28 Los Angeles (90071) *(P-14966)*

Oaktree Real Estate Opprtnties ....A...... 213 830-6300
333 S Grand Ave Fl 28 Los Angeles (90071) *(P-14967)*

Oaktree Strategic Income LLC ....A...... 213 830-6300
333 S Grand Ave Fl 28 Los Angeles (90071) *(P-14968)*

Oakwood Corporate Housing Inc ....C...... 909 922-8272
7922 Day Creek Blvd Rancho Cucamonga (91739) *(P-15431)*

Oakwood Interiors, Ontario *Also Called: Lanpar Inc (P-2777)*

Oakwood Temporary Housing, Long Beach *Also Called: Worldwide Corporate Housing LP (P-15432)*

Oasis Date Garden Inc ....E...... 760 399-5665
59111 Grapefruit Blvd Thermal (92274) *(P-1957)*

Oasis Materials, Poway *Also Called: Oasis Materials Company LLC (P-9090)*

Oasis Materials Company LLC (DH) ....E...... 858 486-8846
12131 Community Rd Poway (92064) *(P-9090)*

Oasis Medical Inc (PA) ....**D...... 909 305-5400**
510 S Vermont Ave 528 Glendora (91741) *(P-10847)*

Oasis Systems LLC ....C...... 805 644-2191
4125 Market St Ste 12 Ventura (93003) *(P-19657)*

Oasis West Realty LLC ....A...... 310 274-8066
1800 Century Park E Ste 500 Los Angeles (90067) *(P-14980)*

Oasis West Realty LLC ....A...... 310 860-6666
9850 Wilshire Blvd Beverly Hills (90210) *(P-15267)*

Oberman Tivoli & Pickert Inc ....C...... 310 440-9600
500 S Sepulveda Blvd Ste 500 Los Angeles (90049) *(P-16464)*

OBryant Electric Inc (PA) ....**C...... 818 407-1986**
9314 Eton Ave Chatsworth (91311) *(P-921)*

OBryant Electric Inc ....C...... 949 341-0025
3 Banting Irvine (92618) *(P-9233)*

Observatories of The Carnegie, Pasadena *Also Called: Carnegie Institution Wash (P-19922)*

Observatory, The, Beverly Hills *Also Called: Live Nation Worldwide Inc (P-17343)*

Oc Direct Shower Door, Orange *Also Called: Dennis DiGiorgio (P-5339)*

OC FOOD BANK, Garden Grove *Also Called: Community Action Prtnr Ornge C (P-19047)*

Oc Metals, Santa Ana *Also Called: Oc Metals Inc (P-6277)*

Oc Metals Inc ....E...... 714 668-0783
2720 S Main St Ste B Santa Ana (92707) *(P-6277)*

Occidental Petroleum Corporation of California ....A
10889 Wilshire Blvd Fl 10 Los Angeles (90024) *(P-264)*

Occidental Petroleum Investment Co Inc ....A...... 310 208-8800
10889 Wilshire Blvd Fl 10 Los Angeles (90024) *(P-314)*

Occupational Therapy Training, Torrance *Also Called: Special Service For Groups Inc (P-19344)*

Ocdm, Tustin *Also Called: Orange County Direct Mail Inc (P-15634)*

Ocean Avenue LLC ....B...... 310 576-7777
101 Wilshire Blvd Santa Monica (90401) *(P-15268)*

Ocean Direct LLC (HQ) ....**C...... 424 266-9300**
13771 Gramercy Pl Gardena (90249) *(P-1810)*

Ocean Park Community Center ....C...... 310 828-6717
1447 16th St Santa Monica (90404) *(P-20369)*

Ocean Protecta Incorporated ....E...... 714 891-2628
14708 Biola Ave La Mirada (90638) *(P-9865)*

Ocean Service, San Diego *Also Called: Overseas Service Corporation (P-20398)*

Ocean Technology Systems, Santa Ana *Also Called: Undersea Systems Intl Inc (P-9265)*

Ocean View Convelesent Hosp, Santa Monica *Also Called: Golden State Health Ctrs Inc (P-18130)*

Ocean's Eleven, Oceanside *Also Called: Oceans Eleven Casino (P-15269)*

Oceania Inc ....E...... 562 926-8886
14209 Gannet St La Mirada (90638) *(P-4816)*

Oceania International LLC ....E...... 949 372-8385
23661 Birtcher Dr Lake Forest (92630) *(P-5726)*

Oceans Eleven Casino ....B...... 760 439-6988
121 Brooks St Oceanside (92054) *(P-15269)*

Oceanscience, Poway *Also Called: Tern Design Ltd (P-10165)*

Oceanside Auto Country Inc (PA) ....**C...... 760 438-2000**
6030 Avenida Encinas Ste 200 Carlsbad (92011) *(P-13807)*

Oceanside Glasstile Company (PA) ....**B...... 760 929-4000**
5858 Edison Pl Carlsbad (92008) *(P-5373)*

Oceanside Harbor Holdings LLC ....C...... 760 331-3177
645 S Beach Blvd Anaheim (92804) *(P-18020)*

Oceanwide Repairs, Long Beach *Also Called: APR Engineering Inc (P-9833)*

Oceanx LLC (PA) ....**D...... 310 774-4088**
100 N Pacific Coast Hwy Ste 1500 El Segundo (90245) *(P-16890)*

Ocelot Engineering Inc ....C...... 800 841-2960
555 S H St San Bernardino (92410) *(P-13902)*

Oci, Santa Fe Springs *Also Called: Office Chairs Inc (P-2893)*

Ocip, Anaheim *Also Called: Orange County Indus Plas Inc (P-13415)*

Ocm Pe Holdings LP ....A...... 213 830-6213
333 S Grand Ave Fl 28 Los Angeles (90071) *(P-9091)*

Ocm Real Estate Opprtnties Fun ....B...... 213 830-6300
333 S Grand Ave Fl 28 Los Angeles (90071) *(P-14969)*

Ocmban, Irvine *Also Called: Ocmbc Inc (P-14346)*

Ocmbc Inc ....B...... 949 679-7400
19000 Macarthur Blvd Ste 200 Irvine (92612) *(P-14346)*

Employee Codes: A=Over 500 employees, B=251-500
C=101-250, D=51-100, E=20-50, F=10-19, G=1-9

2024 Southern California
Business Directory and Buyers Guide

© Mergent Inc. 1-800-342-5647
1201

OConnell Landscape Maint Inc .... A...... 800 339-1106
860 E Watson Center Rd Carson (90745) *(P-209)*

OCP Group Inc .... E...... 858 279-7400
7130 Engineer Rd San Diego (92111) *(P-7498)*

Ocpc Inc .... D...... 949 475-1900
2485 Da Vinci Irvine (92614) *(P-3646)*

Ocs America Inc (DH) .... **E...... 310 417-0650**
22912 Lockness Ave Torrance (90501) *(P-16891)*

Ocs Bookstore, Torrance *Also Called: Ocs America Inc (P-16891)*

Octa, Orange *Also Called: Orange Cnty Trnsp Auth Schlrsh (P-11354)*

Octagon Inc .... C...... 310 967-2473
1840 Century Park E Ste 200 Los Angeles (90067) *(P-20212)*

Odcombe Press (nashville) .... E...... 615 793-5414
2801 Townsgate Rd Westlake Village (91361) *(P-3647)*

Odeh Engineers, Irvine *Also Called: Wsp USA Inc (P-19720)*

Odme Solutions LLC .... D...... 619 227-0059
1963 Christy Ln Del Mar (92014) *(P-20213)*

ODonnell Manufacturing Inc .... E...... 562 944-9671
14811 Via Defrancesco Ave Riverside (92508) *(P-7959)*

Odyssey Innovative Designs, San Gabriel *Also Called: Hsiao & Montano Inc (P-5289)*

OEM, Orange *Also Called: Premier Filters Inc (P-7408)*

Oem LLC .... E...... 714 449-7500
311 S Highland Ave Fullerton (92832) *(P-7960)*

OEM Materials, Santa Ana *Also Called: OEM Materials & Supplies Inc (P-3058)*

OEM Materials & Supplies Inc .... E...... 714 564-9600
1500 Ritchey St Santa Ana (92705) *(P-3058)*

Oeoe Corp .... C...... 213 387-0933
927 S Grand View St # 10 Los Angeles (90006) *(P-16892)*

Off Broadway, La Verne *Also Called: Fortress Inc (P-2883)*

Off Duty Officers Inc .... A...... 888 408-5900
2365 La Mirada Dr Vista (92081) *(P-16664)*

Office Chairs Inc .... D...... 562 802-0464
14815 Radburn Ave Santa Fe Springs (90670) *(P-2893)*

Office Master Inc .... D...... 909 392-5678
1110 Mildred St Ontario (91761) *(P-12288)*

Office of Inspector General, Los Angeles *Also Called: Los Angles Cnty Mtro Trnsp Aut (P-11338)*

Office Star Products, Ontario *Also Called: Blumenthal Distributing Inc (P-12278)*

OfficeMax, Downey *Also Called: OfficeMax North America Inc (P-15650)*

OfficeMax North America Inc .... C...... 562 927-6444
7075 Firestone Blvd Downey (90241) *(P-15650)*

Officeworks Inc .... D...... 951 784-2534
11801 Pierce St Fl 2 Riverside (92505) *(P-15873)*

Officia Imaging Inc (PA) .... **E...... 858 348-0831**
5636 Ruffin Rd San Diego (92123) *(P-14143)*

Offline Inc (PA) .... **E...... 213 742-9001**
2931 S Alameda St Vernon (90058) *(P-2182)*

Ofs Brands Holdings Inc .... A...... 714 903-2257
5559 Mcfadden Ave Huntington Beach (92649) *(P-2894)*

Oggi Corp, Anaheim *Also Called: Asdak International (P-5382)*

Oggis Pizza & Brewing Company .... E...... 760 944-8170
305 Encinitas Blvd Encinitas (92024) *(P-14028)*

Ogio, Carlsbad *Also Called: Ogio International Inc (P-5292)*

Ogio International Inc (HQ) .... **E...... 801 619-4100**
2180 Rutherford Rd Carlsbad (92008) *(P-5292)*

Ogio International Inc .... D...... 800 326-6325
508 Constitution Ave Camarillo (93012) *(P-5293)*

Ogio Powersports, Camarillo *Also Called: Ogio International Inc (P-5293)*

Ogleby Sisters Soap .... E...... 212 518-1172
1804 Garnet Ave San Diego (92109) *(P-15484)*

OH So Original Inc .... B...... 818 841-4770
150 E Angeleno Ave Burbank (91502) *(P-15270)*

Oheck LLC .... F...... 323 923-2700
5830 Bickett St Huntington Park (90255) *(P-2432)*

Ohi Resort Hotels LLC .... D...... 714 867-5555
12021 Harbor Blvd Garden Grove (92840) *(P-15271)*

Ohline Corporation .... E...... 310 327-4630
1930 W 139th St Gardena (90249) *(P-2623)*

Ohmega Solenoid Co Inc .... E...... 562 944-7948
10912 Painter Ave Santa Fe Springs (90670) *(P-8103)*

Oil Field Services, Santa Maria *Also Called: Pacific Petroleum California Inc (P-375)*

Oil Well Service, Santa Paula *Also Called: Oil Well Service Company (P-370)*

Oil Well Service Company .... D...... 805 525-2103
1015 Mission Rock Rd Santa Paula (93060) *(P-370)*

Oil Well Service Company .... D...... 661 746-4809
10255 Enos Ln Shafter (93263) *(P-371)*

Oil Well Service Company (PA) .... **C...... 562 612-0600**
1241 E Burnett St Signal Hill (90755) *(P-372)*

Oil-Dri Corporation America .... D...... 661 765-7194
950 Petroleum Club Rd Taft (93268) *(P-4365)*

Oj Insulation LP (PA) .... **C...... 800 707-9278**
600 S Vincent Ave Azusa (91702) *(P-985)*

Ojai Health & Rehabilitation, Ojai *Also Called: Ojai Healthidence Opco LLC (P-18092)*

Ojai Healthidence Opco LLC .... C...... 805 646-8124
601 N Montgomery St Ojai (93023) *(P-18092)*

Ojai Valley Community Hospital, Ojai *Also Called: Community Memorial Health Sys (P-18227)*

Ojai Valley Inn & Spa, Ojai *Also Called: Ovis LLC (P-15282)*

Ojai Valley School Inc .... **D...... 805 646-1423**
723 El Paseo Rd Ojai (93023) *(P-18977)*

OK International Inc (DH) .... **C...... 714 799-9910**
10800 Valley View St Cypress (90630) *(P-7160)*

Oka & Oka Hawaii LLC .... C...... 808 329-1393
1756 Ruhland Ave Manhattan Beach (90266) *(P-15272)*

Okonite Company Inc .... C...... 805 922-6682
2900 Skyway Dr Santa Maria (93455) *(P-5745)*

Ola Nation LLC .... E...... 310 256-0638
915 W Barbara Ave West Covina (91790) *(P-2286)*

Old Bbh Inc .... A...... 858 715-4000
280 10th Ave San Diego (92101) *(P-1227)*

Old Country Millwork Inc (PA) .... **E...... 323 234-2940**
5855 Hooper Ave Los Angeles (90001) *(P-7152)*

Old English Mil & Woodworks, Santa Clarita *Also Called: Old English Mil Woodworks Inc (P-2624)*

Old English Mil Woodworks Inc (PA) .... **E...... 661 294-9171**
27772 Avenue Scott Santa Clarita (91355) *(P-2624)*

OLD GLOBE, San Diego *Also Called: Old Globe Theatre (P-17322)*

Old Globe Theatre .... B...... 619 234-5623
1363 Old Globe Way San Diego (92101) *(P-17322)*

Old Guys Rule, Ventura *Also Called: Streamline Dsign Slkscreen Inc (P-2223)*

Old Republic, Pasadena *Also Called: Bitco Cnstr Insur Agcy Inc (P-14568)*

Old Spc Inc .... E...... 310 533-0748
202 W 140th St Los Angeles (90061) *(P-6644)*

Old Town Fmly Hospitality Corp .... C...... 619 246-8010
2754 Calhoun St San Diego (92110) *(P-15273)*

Oldcast Precast (DH) .... **E...... 951 788-9720**
2434 Rubidoux Blvd Riverside (92509) *(P-5431)*

Oldcastle Buildingenvelope Inc .... D...... 323 722-2007
5631 Ferguson Dr Commerce (90022) *(P-5351)*

Oldcastle Infrastructure Inc .... E...... 909 428-3700
10650 Hemlock Ave Fontana (92337) *(P-5432)*

Oldcastle Infrastructure Inc .... E...... 951 683-8200
2512 Harmony Grove Rd Escondido (92029) *(P-5433)*

Oldcastle Infrastructure Inc .... E...... 951 928-8713
19940 Hansen Ave Nuevo (92567) *(P-5434)*

Oldcastle Prcast Enclsure Slto, Riverside *Also Called: Carson Industries LLC (P-4985)*

Olde Thompson LLC (DH) .... **E...... 805 983-0388**
3250 Camino Del Sol Oxnard (93030) *(P-4624)*

Olde Thompson LLC .... E...... 805 983-0388
2300 Celsius Ave Oxnard (93030) *(P-13386)*

Olea Kiosks Inc .... D...... 562 924-2644
13845 Artesia Blvd Cerritos (90703) *(P-7556)*

Olen Commercial Realty Corp .... B...... 949 644-6536
7 Corporate Plaza Dr Newport Beach (92660) *(P-14676)*

Olen Residential Realty, Newport Beach *Also Called: Olen Commercial Realty Corp (P-14676)*

Oleumtech Corporation .... D...... 949 305-9009
19762 Pauling Foothill Ranch (92610) *(P-10150)*

Olin Chlor Alkali Logistics .... C...... 562 692-0510
11600 Pike St Santa Fe Springs (90670) *(P-3859)*

OLinn Security Incorporated .... C...... 760 320-5303
1027 S Palm Canyon Dr Palm Springs (92264) *(P-16665)*

Olive Avenue Productions LLC ....B...... 770 214-7052
4000 Warner Blvd Burbank (91522) *(P-17258)*

Olive Crest (PA)..B...... 714 543-5437
2130 E 4th St Ste 200 Santa Ana (92705) *(P-19291)*

Olive Crest, Santa Ana *Also Called: Olive Crest (P-19291)*

Olive Hill Greenhouses Inc ....D...... 760 728-4596
3508 Olive Hill Rd Fallbrook (92028) *(P-63)*

Olive Refinish ....E...... 805 273-5072
9990 Glenoaks Blvd Sun Valley (91352) *(P-4496)*

Olive View-Ucla Medical Center (PA).............................D...... 818 364-1555
14445 Olive View Dr Sylmar (91342) *(P-17729)*

Oliver Healthcare Packaging Co ....D...... 714 864-3500
1145 N Ocean Cir Anaheim (92806) *(P-12802)*

Olivet International Inc (PA)...D...... 951 681-8888
11015 Hopkins St Jurupa Valley (91752) *(P-12981)*

Olli Salumeria Americana LLC ....D
1301 Rocky Point Dr Oceanside (92056) *(P-1201)*

Olloclip, Huntington Beach *Also Called: Premier Systems Usa Inc (P-12432)*

Ols Hotels & Resorts LLC ....A...... 626 962-6000
14635 Baldwin Park Towne Ctr Baldwin Park (91706) *(P-15274)*

Ols Hotels & Resorts LLC ....A...... 310 855-1115
733 N West Knoll Dr West Hollywood (90069) *(P-15275)*

Olson Company LLC (PA)..D...... 562 596-4770
3010 Old Ranch Pkwy Ste 100 Seal Beach (90740) *(P-14908)*

Olson Homes, Seal Beach *Also Called: Olson Company LLC (P-14908)*

Olson Industrial Systems, Santee *Also Called: Olson Irrigation Systems (P-6910)*

Olson Irrigation Systems ....E...... 619 562-3100
10910 Wheatlands Ave Ste A Santee (92071) *(P-6910)*

Oltmans Construction Co ....B...... 805 495-9553
270 Conejo Ridge Ave Ste 210 Thousand Oaks (91361) *(P-513)*

Oltmans Construction Co (PA)..D...... 562 948-4242
10005 Mission Mill Rd Whittier (90601) *(P-514)*

Olympia Convalescent Hospital ....C...... 213 487-3000
1100 S Alvarado St Los Angeles (90006) *(P-18148)*

Olympia Health Care LLC ....A...... 323 938-3161
5900 W Olympic Blvd Los Angeles (90036) *(P-18353)*

Olympia Medical Center, Los Angeles *Also Called: Olympia Health Care LLC (P-18353)*

Olympix Fitness LLC ....D...... 562 366-4600
4101 E Olympic Plz Long Beach (90803) *(P-17410)*

Olympus Building Services Inc ....A...... 760 750-4629
441 La Moree Rd San Marcos (92078) *(P-20297)*

OLYMPUS BUILDING SERVICES INC, San Marcos *Also Called: Olympus Building Services Inc (P-20297)*

Olympus Property ....B...... 661 393-1700
3411 State Rd Bakersfield (93308) *(P-14739)*

Olympus Water Holdings IV LP ....A...... 310 739-6325
360 N Crescent Dr Bldg S Beverly Hills (90210) *(P-4366)*

Om Smart Seating, Ontario *Also Called: Office Master Inc (P-12288)*

Om Tactical, Van Nuys *Also Called: Rizzo Inc (P-10696)*

Omc-Thc Liquidating Inc ....E...... 858 486-8846
12131 Community Rd Poway (92064) *(P-5982)*

OMD Remanufacturing Inc ....E...... 213 220-3851
4395 E Olympic Blvd Los Angeles (90023) *(P-11258)*

Omega, Bell *Also Called: Omega Moulding West LLC (P-12312)*

Omega Accounting Solutions Inc ....D...... 949 348-2433
15101 Alton Pkwy Ste 450 Irvine (92618) *(P-19798)*

Omega Ii Inc ....E...... 619 920-6650
3525 Main St Chula Vista (91911) *(P-6146)*

Omega Industrial Marine, Chula Vista *Also Called: Omega Ii Inc (P-6146)*

Omega Leads Inc ....E...... 310 394-6786
1509 Colorado Ave Santa Monica (90404) *(P-9092)*

Omega Moulding West LLC ....C...... 323 261-3510
5500 Lindbergh Ln Bell (90201) *(P-12312)*

Omega Precision ....E...... 562 946-2491
13040 Telegraph Rd Santa Fe Springs (90670) *(P-7961)*

Omega Products Corp ....E...... 714 935-0900
282 S Anita Dr 3rd Fl Orange (92868) *(P-5571)*

Omega Steel Inc ....E...... 323 726-7669
7140 Bandini Blvd Commerce (90040) *(P-5630)*

Omega/Cinema Props Inc ....D...... 323 466-8201
1515 E 15th St Los Angeles (90021) *(P-17259)*

OMelveny & Myers LLP (PA)..A...... 213 430-6000
400 S Hope St 18th Fl Los Angeles (90071) *(P-18919)*

Omics Group Inc ....B...... 650 268-9744
5716 Corsa Ave Ste 110 Westlake Village (91362) *(P-3373)*

Omni Connection Intl Inc ....B...... 951 898-6232
126 Via Trevizio Corona (92879) *(P-9093)*

Omni Enclosures Inc ....E...... 619 579-6664
505 Raleigh Ave El Cajon (92020) *(P-2963)*

Omni Family Health (PA)...D...... 661 459-1900
4900 California Ave Ste 400b Bakersfield (93309) *(P-17730)*

Omni Hotels, Rancho Mirage *Also Called: Omni Hotels Corporation (P-15276)*

Omni Hotels Corporation ....B...... 760 568-2727
41000 Bob Hope Dr Rancho Mirage (92270) *(P-15276)*

Omni La Costa Resort & Spa LLC (DH).........................C...... 760 438-9111
2100 Costa Del Mar Rd Carlsbad (92009) *(P-15277)*

Omni Metal Finishing Inc (PA).......................................D...... 714 979-9414
11665 Coley River Cir Fountain Valley (92708) *(P-6645)*

Omni Optical Products Inc (PA)......................................E...... 714 634-5700
17282 Eastman Irvine (92614) *(P-10386)*

Omni Optical Products Inc ....E...... 714 692-1400
22605 La Palma Ave Ste 505 Yorba Linda (92887) *(P-17141)*

Omni Pacific, El Cajon *Also Called: Omni Enclosures Inc (P-2963)*

Omni Resource Recovery Inc ....C...... 909 327-2900
1495 N 8th St Ste 150 Colton (92324) *(P-5127)*

Omni Seals, Rancho Cucamonga *Also Called: Smith International Inc (P-6963)*

Omni Seals Inc ....D...... 909 946-0181
11031 Jersey Blvd Ste A Rancho Cucamonga (91730) *(P-4751)*

Omni-Pak Industries, Anaheim *Also Called: Nbty Manufacturing LLC (P-4180)*

Omnia Italian Design LLC ....C...... 909 393-4400
4900 Edison Ave Chino (91710) *(P-12289)*

Omnia Leather Motion Inc ....C...... 909 393-4400
4950 Edison Ave Chino (91710) *(P-2480)*

Omniduct, Buena Park *Also Called: ECB Corp (P-765)*

Omniprint Inc ....E...... 949 833-0080
1923 E Deere Ave Santa Ana (92705) *(P-7557)*

Omnisil ....E...... 805 644-2514
5401 Everglades St Ventura (93003) *(P-8853)*

Omniteam Inc ....C...... 562 923-9660
4380 Ayers Ave Vernon (90058) *(P-12763)*

Omnitracs Midco LLC ....E...... 858 651-5812
9276 Scranton Rd Ste 200 San Diego (92121) *(P-16334)*

Omnitrans ....C...... 909 379-7100
4748 Arrow Hwy Montclair (91763) *(P-11351)*

Omnitrans (PA)..C...... 909 379-7100
1700 W 5th St San Bernardino (92411) *(P-11352)*

Omnitrans ....C...... 909 383-1680
234 S I St San Bernardino (92410) *(P-19292)*

Omnitrans Access, San Bernardino *Also Called: Omnitrans (P-19292)*

Omron Delta Tau, Chatsworth *Also Called: Delta Tau Data Systems Inc Cal (P-7389)*

Omya California Inc ....D...... 760 248-7306
7299 Crystal Creek Rd Lucerne Valley (92356) *(P-3901)*

Omya Inc ....D...... 760 248-5200
7299 Crystal Creek Rd Lucerne Valley (92356) *(P-3902)*

On Central Realty Inc ....B...... 323 543-8500
1648 Colorado Blvd Los Angeles (90041) *(P-14837)*

On-Line Power Incorporated (PA)....................................E...... 323 721-5017
14000 S Broadway Los Angeles (90061) *(P-8104)*

Oncehub Inc ....E...... 650 206-5585
340 S Lemon Ave Ste 5585 Walnut (91789) *(P-16335)*

Oncocyte Corporation (PA)...F...... 949 409-7600
15 Cushing Irvine (92618) *(P-4284)*

Oncor Corp ....F...... 562 944-0230
13115 Barton Rd Ste G-H Whittier (90605) *(P-13060)*

ONCOR CORP, Whittier *Also Called: Oncor Corp (P-13060)*

Oncore Manufacturing LLC ....C...... 760 737-6777
237 Via Vera Cruz San Marcos (92078) *(P-8712)*

Oncore Manufacturing LLC (HQ).....................................A...... 818 734-6500
9340 Owensmouth Ave Chatsworth (91311) *(P-19658)*

Oncore Manufacturing Svcs Inc ....C...... 510 360-2222
9340 Owensmouth Ave Chatsworth (91311) *(P-8713)*

Oncore Velocity, San Marcos *Also Called: Oncore Manufacturing LLC (P-8712)*

ALPHABETIC

One & All Inc (HQ)...C
2 N Lake Ave Ste 600 Pasadena (91101) *(P-15567)*

One California Plaza, Los Angeles *Also Called: Hill Farrer & Burrill (P-18869)*

One Call Plumber Goleta ....D....... 805 284-0441
140 Nectarine Ave Apt 4 Goleta (93117) *(P-15518)*

One Call Plumber Santa Barbara ....D....... 805 364-6337
1016 Cliff Dr Apt 309 Santa Barbara (93109) *(P-802)*

One Clothing, Vernon *Also Called: O & K Inc (P-13141)*

One Events Inc ....D....... 310 498-5471
8581 Santa Monica Blvd West Hollywood (90069) *(P-15519)*

One H.E.A.R.T., San Diego *Also Called: One Heart Worldwide (P-20214)*

One Heart Worldwide ....D....... 415 379-4762
8141 El Extenso Ct San Diego (92119) *(P-20214)*

One Lambda Inc (HQ).......................................D....... **747 494-1000**
22801 Roscoe Blvd West Hills (91304) *(P-19868)*

One Silver Serve LLC ....D....... 818 995-6444
16601 Ventura Blvd Fl 4 Encino (91436) *(P-15730)*

One Step Gps LLC ....E....... 818 659-2031
675 Glenoaks Blvd Unit C San Fernando (91340) *(P-10043)*

One Stop Label Corporation ....E....... 909 230-9380
1641 S Baker Ave Ontario (91761) *(P-3791)*

One Stop Systems Inc ....E....... 858 530-2511
2235 Enterprise St Ste 110 Escondido (92029) *(P-7558)*

One Stop Systems Inc (PA).............................E....... **760 745-9883**
2235 Enterprise St Ste 110 Escondido (92029) *(P-7559)*

One Structural Inc ....E....... 626 252-0778
19326 Ventura Blvd Ste 200 Tarzana (91356) *(P-373)*

One Sun Power Inc ....A....... 844 360-9600
3451 Via Montebello Ste 511 Carlsbad (92009) *(P-19659)*

One Up Manufacturing LLC ....E....... 310 749-8347
550 E Airline Way Gardena (90248) *(P-3069)*

One-Way Manufacturing Inc ....E....... 714 630-8833
1195 N Osprey Cir Anaheim (92807) *(P-6850)*

Onecharge Biz, Garden Grove *Also Called: Onecharge Inc (P-9152)*

Onecharge Inc ....E....... 833 895-8624
12472 Industry St Garden Grove (92841) *(P-9152)*

Onehealth Solutions Inc ....C....... 858 947-6333
420 Stevens Ave Ste 200 Solana Beach (92075) *(P-16584)*

ONeil Capital Management Inc ....C....... 310 448-6400
12655 Beatrice St Los Angeles (90066) *(P-3721)*

ONeil Data Systems LLC ....C....... 310 448-6400
12655 Beatrice St Los Angeles (90066) *(P-12803)*

ONeil Digital Solutions LLC ....C....... 310 448-6407
12655 Beatrice St Los Angeles (90066) *(P-16893)*

ONeill Beverages Co LLC ....E....... 805 239-1616
2975 Mitchell Ranch Way Paso Robles (93446) *(P-1649)*

Oneroof Energy Inc ....C....... 858 458-0533
4445 Eastgate Mall Ste 240 San Diego (92121) *(P-8854)*

Onesource Distributors LLC (DH).....................E....... **760 966-4500**
3951 Oceanic Dr Oceanside (92056) *(P-9234)*

Onewest Bank Group LLC ....A....... 626 535-4870
888 E Walnut St Pasadena (91101) *(P-14216)*

Onex Rf Inc ....F....... 626 358-6639
1824 Flower Ave Duarte (91010) *(P-7161)*

Online Capital, Newport Beach *Also Called: RMR Financial LLC (P-14363)*

Online Marketing Group LLC ....C....... 888 737-9635
530 Technology Dr Ste 100 Irvine (92618) *(P-20215)*

Onni Properties LLC ....C....... 213 568-0278
888 S Olive St Los Angeles (90014) *(P-20071)*

Onshore Technologies Inc ....E....... 310 533-4888
2771 Plaza Del Amo Ste 802-803 Torrance (90503) *(P-9094)*

Ontario Automotive LLC ....C....... 909 974-3800
1401 Auto Center Dr Ontario (91761) *(P-13808)*

Ontario Convention Center Corp ....B....... 909 937-3000
2000 E Convention Center Way Ontario (91764) *(P-16894)*

Ontario Foam Products, Ontario *Also Called: Androp Packaging Inc (P-3079)*

Ontario Mills Shopping Center, Ontario *Also Called: Mills Corporation (P-14673)*

Ontario Vineyard Medical Offs, Ontario *Also Called: Kaiser Foundation Hospitals (P-17675)*

Ontario/Montclair YMCA, Ontario *Also Called: West End Yung MNS Christn Assn (P-19471)*

Ontarioidence Opco LLC ....B....... 909 984-8629
800 E 5th St Ontario (91764) *(P-18093)*

Ontic Engineering and Mfg Inc (PA)..................D....... **818 678-6555**
20400 Plummer St Chatsworth (91311) *(P-12913)*

Ontrac Logistics Inc ....D....... 818 504-9043
11085 Olinda St Sun Valley (91352) *(P-11536)*

Ontraport Inc ....C....... 805 568-1424
2040 Alameda Padre Serra Ste 220 Santa Barbara (93103) *(P-20072)*

Onyx Industries Inc (PA)..................................D....... **310 539-8830**
1227 254th St Harbor City (90710) *(P-6416)*

Onyx Industries Inc ....D....... 310 851-6161
521 W Rosecrans Ave Gardena (90248) *(P-6417)*

Onyx Pharmaceuticals Inc ....A....... 650 266-0000
1 Amgen Center Dr Newbury Park (91320) *(P-4189)*

Onyx Power Inc ....C....... 714 513-1500
4011 W Carriage Dr Santa Ana (92704) *(P-8105)*

Onyx Shutters, Walnut *Also Called: Tje Company (P-6126)*

Op Bancorp (PA)...C....... **213 892-9999**
1000 Wilshire Blvd Ste 500 Los Angeles (90017) *(P-14201)*

Op Games, The, Carlsbad *Also Called: USAopoly Inc (P-10968)*

Opal Service Inc (PA).......................................E....... **714 935-0900**
282 S Anita Dr Orange (92868) *(P-5572)*

OPEN America Inc ....C....... 562 428-9210
4300 Long Beach Blvd Ste 450 Long Beach (90807) *(P-15731)*

Open Systems Inc ....E....... 317 566-6662
5250 Lankershim Blvd Ste 620 North Hollywood (91601) *(P-16336)*

Openworks, Long Beach *Also Called: OPEN America Inc (P-15731)*

Opera Patisserie ....D....... 858 536-5800
8480 Redwood Creek Ln San Diego (92126) *(P-1528)*

Opera Patisserie, San Diego *Also Called: Opera Patisserie (P-1528)*

Operam Inc ....D....... 855 673-7261
1041 N Formosa Ave 500 West Hollywood (90046) *(P-20216)*

Operating Engineers Funds Inc (PA).................C....... **866 400-5200**
100 Corson St Pasadena (91103) *(P-14999)*

Operation Samahan Inc ....C....... 619 477-4451
10737 Camino Ruiz Ste 235138 San Diego (92126) *(P-17731)*

Operation Technology Inc ....D....... 949 462-0100
17 Goodyear Ste 100 Irvine (92618) *(P-16090)*

Ophir Rf, Los Angeles *Also Called: Ophir Rf Inc (P-8556)*

Ophir Rf Inc ....E....... 310 306-5556
5300 Beethoven St Fl 3 Los Angeles (90066) *(P-8556)*

Ophthonix Inc ....E....... 760 842-5600
900 Glenneyre St Laguna Beach (92651) *(P-10848)*

Opolo Vineyards Inc ....E....... 805 238-9593
2801 Townsgate Rd Ste 123 Westlake Village (91361) *(P-1650)*

Oprah Winfrey Network, Burbank *Also Called: Own LLC (P-11998)*

Opsec Specialized Protection ....D....... 661 942-3999
44262 Division St Ste A Lancaster (93535) *(P-16666)*

Optec Displays Inc ....D....... 866 924-5200
1700 S De Soto Pl Ste A Ontario.(91761) *(P-11142)*

Optec Laser Systems LLC ....E....... 858 220-1070
11622 El Camino Real Ste 100 San Diego (92130) *(P-3792)*

Optex Incorporated ....E....... 800 966-7839
10741 Walker St Cypress (90630) *(P-8618)*

Opti-Forms Inc ....E....... 951 296-1300
42310 Winchester Rd Temecula (92590) *(P-6646)*

Optic Arts Holdings Inc ....E....... 213 250-6069
716 Monterey Pass Rd Monterey Park (91754) *(P-8324)*

Optical Corporation (DH)..................................E....... **818 725-9750**
9731 Topanga Canyon Pl Chatsworth (91311) *(P-10332)*

Optical Zonu Corporation ....F....... 818 780-9701
7510 Hazeltine Ave Van Nuys (91405) *(P-8482)*

Optima Family Services Inc ....C....... 323 300-6066
253 N San Gabriel Blvd Pasadena (91107) *(P-19119)*

Optima Office Inc ....D....... 858 361-0481
5120 Shoreham Pl Ste 285 San Diego (92122) *(P-19799)*

Optima Protection Plan, Santa Ana *Also Called: Optima Tax Relief LLC (P-15496)*

Optima Tax Relief LLC ....C....... 714 361-4636
3100 S Harbor Blvd Ste 250 Santa Ana (92704) *(P-15496)*

Optima Technology Corporation ....B....... 949 253-5768
17062 Murphy Ave Irvine (92614) *(P-7560)*

Optimiscorp ....E....... 310 230-2780
200 Mantua Rd Pacific Palisades (90272) *(P-16337)*

Options For All Inc .... B....... 858 565-9870
5050 Murphy Canyon Rd Ste 220 San Diego (92123) *(P-19189)*

Optivus Proton Therapy Inc .... D....... 909 799-8300
1475 Victoria Ct San Bernardino (92408) *(P-10387)*

Opto 22 .... C....... 951 695-3000
43044 Business Park Dr Temecula (92590) *(P-9095)*

Opto Diode Corporation .... E....... 805 499-0335
750 Mitchell Rd Newbury Park (91320) *(P-8855)*

Opto Diode Corporation .... E....... 805 465-8700
1260 Calle Suerte Camarillo (93012) *(P-8856)*

Opto-Knowledge Systems Inc ....E....... 310 756-0520
19805 Hamilton Ave Torrance (90502) *(P-19869)*

Optodyne Incorporation .... E....... 310 635-7481
21345 Hawthorne Blvd Unit 203 Torrance (90503) *(P-8557)*

Optoknowledge, Torrance *Also Called: Opto-Knowledge Systems Inc (P-19869)*

OPTOMETRIC CENTER OF LOS ANGEL, Fullerton *Also Called: Marshall B Ketchum University (P-18991)*

Optosigma Corporation .... E....... 949 851-5881
3210 S Croddy Way Santa Ana (92704) *(P-10333)*

Optotest Corp., Camarillo *Also Called: Santec California Corporation (P-10337)*

Optron Scientific Company Inc ....E....... 818 883-6103
7051 Eton Ave Canoga Park (91303) *(P-10388)*

Optronics, Goleta *Also Called: Karl Storz Imaging Inc (P-10378)*

Optumcare Management LLC (HQ)............................. A....... 310 354-4200
2175 Park Pl El Segundo (90245) *(P-17732)*

Optumcare Management LLC .... C....... 562 988-7000
2600 Redondo Ave Ste 405 Long Beach (90806) *(P-17733)*

Optumcare Medical Group .... D....... 949 364-9112
800 Corporate Dr Ste 100 Ladera Ranch (92694) *(P-18787)*

Optumrx Inc (DH) .... B....... 714 825-3600
2300 Main St Irvine (92614) *(P-14489)*

Optumrx Inc .... B....... 760 804-2399
2858 Loker Ave E Ste 100 Carlsbad (92010) *(P-14490)*

Optumrx PBM Administrator Cal, Irvine *Also Called: Optumrx Inc (P-14489)*

Opus Bank .... A....... 949 250-9800
19900 Macarthur Blvd Ste 1200 Irvine (92612) *(P-14213)*

Oracle, Mission Viejo *Also Called: Oracle Corporation (P-16338)*

Oracle America Inc .... E....... 650 506-7000
17901 Von Karman Ave Ste 800 Irvine (92614) *(P-7443)*

Oracle Corporation .... B....... 626 315-7513
1 Bolero Mission Viejo (92692) *(P-16338)*

Orange Bakery Inc (HQ)... F....... 949 863-1377
17751 Cowan Irvine (92614) *(P-1488)*

Orange Bakery Inc .... C....... 949 454-1247
75 Parker Irvine (92618) *(P-14677)*

Orange Bang Inc .... E....... 818 833-1000
13115 Telfair Ave Sylmar (91342) *(P-1707)*

Orange Circle Studio Corp (PA).................................. E....... 949 727-0800
2 Technology Dr Irvine (92618) *(P-3793)*

Orange Cnty Adult Achvment Ctr .... C....... 714 744-5301
225 W Carl Karcher Way Anaheim (92801) *(P-19120)*

Orange Cnty George M Raymond N, Orange *Also Called: Raymond Group (P-20087)*

Orange Cnty Globl Med Ctr Aux (DH)........................... C....... 714 835-3555
1301 N Tustin Ave Santa Ana (92705) *(P-18354)*

Orange Cnty Hlth Auth A Pub AG .... B....... 714 246-8500
505 City Pkwy W Orange (92868) *(P-19399)*

Orange Cnty Name Plate Co Inc .... D....... 714 522-7693
13201 Arctic Cir Santa Fe Springs (90670) *(P-11143)*

Orange Cnty Nrpsychtric RES CT .... D....... 213 992-9216
1400 S Grand Ave Ste 611 Los Angeles (90015) *(P-19909)*

Orange Cnty Ryale Cnvlscent Ho (PA)......................... B....... 714 546-6450
1030 W Warner Ave Santa Ana (92707) *(P-18149)*

Orange Cnty Trnsp Auth Schlrsh .... D....... 714 560-6282
11790 Cardinal Cir Garden Grove (92843) *(P-11353)*

Orange Cnty Trnsp Auth Schlrsh .... A....... 714 999-1726
600 S Main St Ste 910 Orange (92868) *(P-11354)*

Orange Cnty Trnsp Auth Schlrsh (PA)......................... B....... 714 636-7433
550 S Main St Orange (92868) *(P-11355)*

Orange Coast Magazine, Los Angeles *Also Called: Orange Coast Magazine LLC (P-3374)*

Orange Coast Magazine LLC .... C....... 949 862-1133
5900 Wilshire Blvd # 10 Los Angeles (90036) *(P-3374)*

Orange Coast Memorial Med Ctr (HQ)....................................A....... 714 378-7000
9920 Talbert Ave Fountain Valley (92708) *(P-18355)*

Orange Coast Reprographics Inc .... E....... 949 548-5571
659 W 19th St Costa Mesa (92627) *(P-3648)*

Orange Coast Service Center, Westminster *Also Called: Southern California Edison Co (P-12077)*

Orange Coast Title Company (PA)... D....... 714 558-2836
1551 N Tustin Ave Ste 300 Santa Ana (92705) *(P-16895)*

Orange Coast Wns Med Group Inc ....D....... 949 829-5522
1031 Avenida Pico Ste 204 San Clemente (92673) *(P-17734)*

Orange County Business Journal, Irvine *Also Called: Cbj LP (P-3349)*

Orange County Direct Mail Inc ....E....... 714 444-4412
2672 Dow Ave Tustin (92780) *(P-15634)*

Orange County Erectors Inc ....E....... 714 502-8455
517 E La Palma Ave Anaheim (92801) *(P-6388)*

Orange County Health Authority, Orange *Also Called: Orange Cnty Hlth Auth A Pub AG (P-19399)*

Orange County Health Care Agcy ....D....... 714 568-5683
405 W 5th St Ste 700 Santa Ana (92701) *(P-19400)*

Orange County Indus Plas Inc (PA).. E....... 714 632-9450
4811 E La Palma Ave Anaheim (92807) *(P-13415)*

Orange County Plst Co Inc ....C....... 714 957-1971
3191 Airport Loop Dr Ste B1 Costa Mesa (92626) *(P-986)*

Orange County Printing, Irvine *Also Called: Kelmscott Communications LLC (P-3611)*

Orange County Produce LLC ....D....... 949 451-0880
210 W Walnut Ave Fullerton (92832) *(P-19)*

Orange County Sanitation (PA)... B....... 714 962-2411
10844 Ellis Ave Fountain Valley (92708) *(P-12176)*

Orange County Screw Pdts Inc ....E....... 714 630-7433
2993 E La Palma Ave Anaheim (92806) *(P-7962)*

Orange County Service Center, San Clemente *Also Called: San Diego Gas & Electric Co (P-12107)*

Orange County Services Inc ....D....... 714 541-9753
3022 N Hesperian St Santa Ana (92706) *(P-803)*

Orange County Thermal Inds Inc ....D....... 714 279-9416
1350 N Hundley St Anaheim (92806) *(P-987)*

Orange County Trnsp Auth, Orange *Also Called: Orange Cnty Trnsp Auth Schlrsh (P-11355)*

Orange County-Irvine Med Ctr, Irvine *Also Called: Kaiser Foundation Hospitals (P-14993)*

Orange Countys Credit Union (PA)...C....... 714 755-5900
1721 E Saint Andrew Pl Santa Ana (92705) *(P-14235)*

Orange Courier Inc ....B....... 714 384-3600
15300 Desman Rd La Mirada (90638) *(P-16896)*

Orange Hlthcare Wllness Cntre ....C....... 714 633-3568
920 W La Veta Ave Orange (92868) *(P-18021)*

Orange Logic LLC ....E....... 914 361-9175
29 Cezanne Irvine (92603) *(P-7444)*

Orange Mtal Spnning Stmping In ....F....... 714 754-0770
2601 Orange Ave Santa Ana (92707) *(P-6543)*

Orange Treeidence Opco LLC ....B....... 951 785-6060
4000 Harrison St Riverside (92503) *(P-18094)*

Orange Woodworks Inc ....E....... 714 997-2600
1215 N Parker St Orange (92867) *(P-2625)*

Orangewood Foundation ....D....... 714 619-0200
1575 E 17th St Santa Ana (92705) *(P-19121)*

Orangewood LLC ....C....... 714 750-3000
2085 S Harbor Blvd Anaheim (92802) *(P-15278)*

Orangtree Cnvalescent Hosp Inc ....C....... 951 785-6060
4000 Harrison St Riverside (92503) *(P-18356)*

Orbit Industries Inc ....D....... 213 745-8884
7533 Garfield Ave Bell Gardens (90201) *(P-12611)*

Orbit Intl Inc ....E....... 909 468-5160
4965 Firenza Dr Cypress (90630) *(P-9096)*

Orbital Sciences LLC ....B....... 805 734-5400
Talo Rd Bldg 1555 Lompoc (93437) *(P-10044)*

Orbital Sciences LLC ....C....... 858 618-1847
16707 Via Del Campo Ct San Diego (92127) *(P-10045)*

Orbital Sciences LLC ....C....... 703 406-5000
2401 E El Segundo Blvd Ste 200 El Segundo (90245) *(P-10046)*

Orbital Sciences LLC ....C....... 818 887-8345
1151 W Reeves Ave Ridgecrest (93555) *(P-10047)*

Orbits Lightwave Inc ....E....... 626 513-7400
41 S Chester Ave Pasadena (91106) *(P-5327)*

Orbo Corporation (PA)..D....... 562 806-6171
1000 S Euclid St La Habra (90631) *(P-2934)*

Orbo Manufacturing Inc...E....... 562 222-4535
12740 Lakeland Rd Santa Fe Springs (90670) *(P-2537)*

Orca Arms, San Diego Also Called: Orca Arms LLC *(P-11017)*

Orca Arms LLC...D....... 858 586-0503
9825 Carroll Centre Rd Ste 100 San Diego (92126) *(P-11017)*

Orca Systems Inc...F....... 858 679-9175
3990 Old Town Ave Ste C307 San Diego (92110) *(P-8857)*

Orchard - Post Acute Care Ctr...............................C....... 562 693-7701
12385 Washington Blvd Whittier (90606) *(P-18022)*

Orchem Division, Temecula Also Called: Oreq Corporation *(P-20073)*

Orchid MPS..D....... 714 549-9203
3233 W Harvard St Santa Ana (92704) *(P-10585)*

Orchid Orthopedis, Arcadia Also Called: MPS Anzon LLC *(P-10685)*

Orco Block, Stanton Also Called: Muth Development Co Inc *(P-5389)*

Orco Block & Hardscape (PA)................................D....... **714 527-2239**
11100 Beach Blvd Stanton (90680) *(P-5390)*

Orco Block & Hardscape...F....... 951 685-1521
4510 Rutile St Riverside (92509) *(P-5391)*

Ordermark Inc...C....... 833 673-3762
12045 Waterfront Dr Ste 400 # 3 Playa Vista (90094) *(P-16509)*

Oreco Duct Systems Inc..C....... 626 337-8832
5119 Azusa Canyon Rd Baldwin Park (91706) *(P-6278)*

Oregon PCF Bldg Pdts Maple Inc............................C....... 909 627-4043
2401 E Philadelphia St Ontario (91761) *(P-12338)*

Orepac Millwork Products, Ontario Also Called: Oregon PCF Bldg Pdts Maple Inc *(P-12338)*

Oreq Corporation...D....... 951 296-5076
42306 Remington Ave Temecula (92590) *(P-20073)*

Orexigen, La Jolla Also Called: Orexigen Therapeutics Inc *(P-4190)*

Orexigen Therapeutics Inc.......................................D....... 858 875-8600
3344 N Torrey Pines Ct Ste 200 La Jolla (92037) *(P-4190)*

Orfila Vineyards & Winery, Escondido Also Called: Orfila Vineyards Inc *(P-1651)*

Orfila Vineyards Inc (PA)...F....... **760 738-6500**
13455 San Pasqual Rd Escondido (92025) *(P-1651)*

Orgain LLC...E....... 888 881-4246
16851 Hale Ave Irvine (92606) *(P-4008)*

Organic, Rancho Dominguez Also Called: Organic By Nature Inc *(P-4009)*

Organic By Nature Inc (PA)..E....... **562 901-0177**
2610 Homestead Pl Rancho Dominguez (90220) *(P-4009)*

Organic Gemini LLC..E....... 347 662-2900
325 N Maple Dr Ste 5088 Beverly Hills (90210) *(P-1414)*

Organic Milling Inc (PA)...D....... **800 638-8686**
505 W Allen Ave San Dimas (91773) *(P-1423)*

Organic Milling Corporation.....................................E....... 909 305-0185
305 S Acacia St Ste A San Dimas (91773) *(P-1958)*

Organic Milling Corporation (PA).............................C....... **909 599-0961**
505 W Allen Ave San Dimas (91773) *(P-1959)*

Orgatech Omegalux, Riverside Also Called: Western Lighting Inds Inc *(P-12627)*

Origin LLC..E....... 818 848-1648
119 E Graham Pl Burbank (91502) *(P-11259)*

Original Mowbrays Tree Svc Inc (PA).......................C....... **909 383-7009**
686 E Mill St San Bernardino (92408) *(P-223)*

Original Parts Group Inc (PA)..................................D....... **562 594-1000**
1770 Saturn Way Seal Beach (90740) *(P-13866)*

Original Pennysaver, The, Brea Also Called: Pennysaver USA Publishing LLC *(P-3473)*

Orion Chandelier Inc..F....... 714 668-9668
2202 S Wright St Santa Ana (92705) *(P-8325)*

Orion Construction Corporation...............................D....... 760 597-9660
2185 La Mirada Dr Vista (92081) *(P-684)*

Orion Indemnity Company...D....... 213 742-8700
714 W Olympic Blvd Ste 800 Los Angeles (90015) *(P-14522)*

Orion Ornamental Iron Inc..E....... 818 752-0688
6918 Tujunga Ave North Hollywood (91605) *(P-5938)*

Orion Pictures Corporation.......................................A....... 310 449-3000
245 N Beverly Dr Beverly Hills (90210) *(P-17204)*

Orion Plastics Corporation.......................................D....... 310 223-0370
700 W Carob St Compton (90220) *(P-3960)*

Orion Tech, City Of Industry Also Called: Compucase Corporation *(P-7468)*

Orlandini Entps Pcf Die Cast...................................C....... 323 725-1332
6155 S Eastern Ave Commerce (90040) *(P-5816)*

Orlando Spring Corp..E....... 562 594-8411
5341 Argosy Ave Huntington Beach (92649) *(P-6806)*

Orlando Wilshire Investments..................................D....... 323 658-6600
8384 W 3rd St Los Angeles (90048) *(P-15279)*

Orlando, The, Los Angeles Also Called: Orlando Wilshire Investments *(P-15279)*

Orly International Inc (PA)..D....... **818 994-1001**
7710 Haskell Ave Van Nuys (91406) *(P-4440)*

Ormco Corporation..E....... 909 962-5705
200 S Kraemer Blvd Brea (92821) *(P-10755)*

Ormco Corporation (HQ)..D....... **714 516-7400**
1717 W Collins Ave Orange (92867) *(P-10756)*

Ormet Circuits Inc...E....... 858 831-0010
6555 Nancy Ridge Dr Ste 200 San Diego (92121) *(P-9097)*

Ormond Beach LP...D....... 805 496-4948
1259 E Thousand Oaks Blvd Thousand Oaks (91362) *(P-14678)*

Orora North America, Buena Park Also Called: Orora Packaging Solutions *(P-13013)*

Orora Packaging Solutions.......................................C....... 714 562-6002
6200 Caballero Blvd Buena Park (90620) *(P-13012)*

Orora Packaging Solutions (HQ)...............................D....... **714 562-6000**
6600 Valley View St Buena Park (90620) *(P-13013)*

Orora Packaging Solutions.......................................E....... 909 770-5400
13397 Marlay Ave Ste A Fontana (92337) *(P-13014)*

Orora Packaging Solutions.......................................E....... 760 510-7170
664 N Twin Oaks Valley Rd San Marcos (92069) *(P-13015)*

Orora Packaging Solutions.......................................E....... 805 278-5040
2146 Eastman Ave Oxnard (93030) *(P-13016)*

Orora Packaging Solutions.......................................C....... 323 832-2000
1640 S Greenwood Ave Montebello (90640) *(P-13017)*

Orora Packaging Solutions.......................................E....... 626 284-9524
3201 W Mission Rd Alhambra (91803) *(P-13018)*

Orora Packaging Solutions.......................................E....... 714 525-4900
7001 Village Dr Ste 155 Buena Park (90621) *(P-13019)*

Orora Packaging Solutions.......................................E....... 714 278-6000
1901 E Rosslynn Ave Fullerton (92831) *(P-13020)*

Orora Visual LLC..D....... 714 879-2400
1600 E Valencia Dr Fullerton (92831) *(P-3794)*

Orthalliance Inc...A....... 310 792-1300
21535 Hawthorne Blvd Ste 200 Torrance (90503) *(P-19337)*

Orthalliances, Torrance Also Called: Orthalliance Inc *(P-19337)*

Ortho Engineering Inc (PA).......................................E....... **310 559-5996**
17402 Chatsworth St Ste 200 Granada Hills (91344) *(P-10687)*

Ortho Organizers Inc...C....... 760 448-8600
1822 Aston Ave Carlsbad (92008) *(P-10757)*

Ortho-Clinical Diagnostics Inc................................E....... 714 639-2323
612 W Katella, Ste-B Orange (92867) *(P-4285)*

Orthodental International Inc...................................D....... 760 357-8070
280 Campillo St Ste J Calexico (92231) *(P-10758)*

Orthodyne Electronics Corporation (HQ)...............C....... **949 660-0440**
16700 Red Hill Ave Irvine (92606) *(P-9235)*

Orthopaedic Hospital (PA)...C....... **213 742-1000**
403 W Adams Blvd Los Angeles (90007) *(P-18357)*

Orthopaedic Inst For Children, Los Angeles Also Called: Orthopaedic Hospital *(P-18357)*

Orthopedics Department, Los Angeles Also Called: Southern Cal Prmnnte Med Group *(P-17784)*

Orthotic Holdings Inc...E....... 858 368-8873
8665 Miralani Dr Ste 300 San Diego (92126) *(P-10688)*

Orthowest, Laguna Hills Also Called: South Cnty Orthpd Spclsts A ME *(P-17769)*

Ortronics Inc..C....... 714 776-5420
1443 S Sunkist St Anaheim (92806) *(P-6279)*

Os4labor LLC..C....... 626 838-6745
120 N Fairway Ln Ste A West Covina (91791) *(P-15874)*

Osata Enterprises Inc...D....... 888 445-6237
18105 Bishop Ave Carson (90746) *(P-13163)*

Osca-Arcosa, San Diego Also Called: O & S California Inc *(P-9232)*

OSI Digital Inc (PA)..E....... **818 992-2700**
26745 Malibu Hills Rd Agoura Hills (91301) *(P-16585)*

OSI Electronics Inc (HQ)..D....... **310 978-0516**
12533 Chadron Ave Hawthorne (90250) *(P-8714)*

OSI Industries LLC...B....... 951 684-4500
1155 Mt Vernon Ave Riverside (92507) *(P-1960)*

OSI Laserscan Inc..E....... 310 978-0516
12525 Chadron Ave Hawthorne (90250) *(P-9236)*

Mergent email: customerrelations@mergent.com
1206

2024 Southern California
Business Directory and Buyers Guide

(P-0000) Products & Services Section entry number
(PA)=Parent Co (HQ)=Headquarters (DH)=Div Headquarters

OSI Optoelectronics Inc ....E...... 805 987-0146
1240 Avenida Acaso Camarillo (93012) *(P-8858)*

OSI Optoelectronics Inc (HQ)...........C...... 310 978-0516
12525 Chadron Ave Hawthorne (90250) *(P-8859)*

OSI Staffing Inc ....D...... 562 261-5753
10913 La Reina Ave Ste B Downey (90241) *(P-15875)*

OSI Subsidiary Inc ....D...... 310 978-0516
12525 Chadron Ave Hawthorne (90250) *(P-9237)*

OSI Systems Inc (PA) ....B...... 310 978-0516
12525 Chadron Ave Hawthorne (90250) *(P-8860)*

Osmosis Technology Inc ....E...... 714 670-9303
6900 Hermosa Cir Buena Park (90620) *(P-7678)*

Osmotik, Buena Park *Also Called: Osmosis Technology Inc (P-7678)*

Osr Enterprises Inc ....E...... 805 925-1831
1910 E Stowell Rd Santa Maria (93454) *(P-16339)*

Osram Sylvania Inc ....D...... 858 748-5077
13350 Gregg St Ste 101 Poway (92064) *(P-8251)*

Osram Sylvania Inc ....D...... 909 923-3003
1651 S Archibald Ave Ontario (91761) *(P-11604)*

Oss, Escondido *Also Called: One Stop Systems Inc (P-7559)*

Ossur Americas Inc (HQ)............E...... 800 233-6263
200 Spectrum Center Dr Irvine (92618) *(P-10689)*

Ossur Americas Inc ....E...... 949 382-3883
19762 Pauling Foothill Ranch (92610) *(P-10690)*

Otafuku Foods Inc ....E...... 562 404-4700
13117 Molette St Santa Fe Springs (90670) *(P-1961)*

OTasty Foods Inc ....D...... 626 330-1229
160 S Hacienda Blvd City Of Industry (91745) *(P-13189)*

Otay Hospitality Inc ....D...... 619 422-2600
4450 Main St Chula Vista (91911) *(P-15280)*

Otay Lakes Brewery LLC ....E...... 619 768-0172
901 Lane Ave Ste 100 Chula Vista (91914) *(P-1601)*

Otay River Constructors LLC ....C...... 619 397-7500
860 Harold Pl Chula Vista (91914) *(P-637)*

Otay Water District ....C...... 619 670-2222
2554 Sweetwater Springs Blvd Spring Valley (91978) *(P-12136)*

Otb Acquisition LLC ....C...... 520 458-0540
770 S Brea Blvd Ste 227 Brea (92821) *(P-15281)*

Otis Elevator Company ....C...... 818 241-2828
512 Paula Ave Ste A Glendale (91201) *(P-12804)*

Otis Elevator Company ....C...... 714 758-9593
711 E Ball Rd Ste 200 Anaheim (92805) *(P-12805)*

Otis Elevator Company ....C...... 858 560-5881
3949 Viewridge Ave San Diego (92123) *(P-12806)*

OTONOMY, San Diego *Also Called: Otonomy Inc (P-4191)*

Otonomy Inc ....D...... 619 323-2200
4796 Executive Dr San Diego (92121) *(P-4191)*

Ott Textile Inc ....E...... 626 217-5132
21708 Lasso Ln Walnut (91789) *(P-2144)*

Ott Textile, Inc., Walnut *Also Called: Ott Textile Inc (P-2144)*

Otto Instrument Service Inc (PA).........E...... 909 930-5800
1441 Valencia Pl Ontario (91761) *(P-9758)*

Otts Asia Moorer Devon ....C...... 323 603-6959
10015 Baring Cross St Los Angeles (90044) *(P-15045)*

Our Alchemy LLC ....D...... 310 893-6289
5900 Wilshire Blvd Fl 18 Los Angeles (90036) *(P-17287)*

OUR HOUSE, Victorville *Also Called: Family Assistance Program (P-19079)*

Out of Shell LLC ....C...... 626 401-1923
9658 Remer St South El Monte (91733) *(P-1962)*

Outdoor Dimensions LLC ....C...... 714 578-9555
5325 E Hunter Ave Anaheim (92807) *(P-2757)*

Outdoor Products, View Park *Also Called: Outdoor Rcrtion Group Hldngs L (P-2496)*

Outdoor Rcrtion Group Hldngs L (PA)........E...... 323 226-0830
3450 Mount Vernon Dr View Park (90008) *(P-2496)*

Outdoor Sports Gear Inc ....E
2320 Cousteau Ct Ste 100 Vista (92081) *(P-11018)*

Outer Rebel Inc ....F...... 949 548-3630
760 W 16th St Ste A2 Costa Mesa (92627) *(P-2457)*

Outfront Media LLC ....E...... 323 222-7171
1731 Workman St Los Angeles (90031) *(P-15586)*

Outlook Amusements Inc ....C...... 818 433-3800
3746 Foothill Blvd La Crescenta (91214) *(P-16586)*

Outlook Resources Inc ....D...... 562 623-9328
14930 Alondra Blvd La Mirada (90638) *(P-2523)*

Output Inc ....F...... 888 803-3175
3014 Worthen Ave Los Angeles (90039) *(P-16340)*

Outsource Manufacturing Inc ....D...... 760 795-1295
2460 Ash St Vista (92081) *(P-8861)*

Outsource Utility Contr Corp ....C...... 714 238-9263
17115 Alburtis Ave Artesia (90701) *(P-12033)*

Ovation Fertility, Encino *Also Called: Fpg Services LLC (P-20173)*

Ovation Home Loans, Irvine *Also Called: Carnegie Mortgage LLC (P-14355)*

Ovation R&G LLC (PA)..............F...... 310 430-7575
2850 Ocean Park Blvd Ste 225 Santa Monica (90405) *(P-8558)*

Ovation Tech Inc ....C...... 949 271-0054
17551 Von Karman Ave Irvine (92614) *(P-16587)*

Over & Over Ready Mix Inc ....E...... 818 983-1588
8216 Tujunga Ave Sun Valley (91352) *(P-5435)*

Overair Inc ....E...... 949 503-7503
3001 S Susan St Santa Ana (92704) *(P-9548)*

Overhill Farms Inc (DH)..............C...... 323 582-9977
2727 E Vernon Ave Vernon (90058) *(P-1963)*

Overland Vehicle Systems LLC ....E...... 833 226-4863
9830 Norwalk Blvd Ste 130 Santa Fe Springs (90670) *(P-9436)*

Overseas Service Corporation ....C...... 858 408-0751
8221 Arjons Dr Ste B2 San Diego (92126) *(P-20398)*

Ovis LLC ....A...... 805 646-5511
905 Country Club Rd Ojai (93023) *(P-15282)*

OVS, Ojai *Also Called: Ojai Valley School (P-18977)*

Owb Packers LLC ....E...... 760 351-2700
57 Shank Rd Brawley (92227) *(P-1202)*

Owen Trailers Inc ....E...... 951 361-4557
9020 Jurupa Rd Riverside (92509) *(P-9494)*

Owens & Minor Distribution Inc ....A...... 805 524-0243
452 Sespe Ave Fillmore (93015) *(P-12502)*

Owens Corning, Compton *Also Called: Owens Corning Sales LLC (P-4675)*

Owens Corning Sales LLC ....C...... 310 631-1062
1501 N Tamarind Ave Compton (90222) *(P-4675)*

Owl Education and Training Inc ....B...... 949 797-2000
2465 Campus Dr Irvine (92612) *(P-19190)*

Own LLC ....C...... 323 602-5500
4000 Warner Blvd Burbank (91522) *(P-11998)*

Ownzones Media Network Inc ....E...... 855 466-9696
315 S Beverly Dr Ste 315 Beverly Hills (90212) *(P-7561)*

Oxerra Americas LLC ....D...... 323 269-7311
3700 E Olympic Blvd Los Angeles (90023) *(P-3875)*

Oxford Instrs Asylum RES Inc (HQ)........D...... 805 696-6466
7416 Hollister Ave Santa Barbara (93117) *(P-10279)*

Oxford Nanoimaging Inc ....D...... 650 690-2708
11045 Roselle St Ste 3 San Diego (92121) *(P-10280)*

Oxford Palace Hotel LLC ....D...... 213 382-7756
745 S Oxford Ave Los Angeles (90005) *(P-15283)*

Oxnard 2 Warehouse, Oxnard *Also Called: Sunrise Growers Inc (P-1993)*

Oxnard City Hall, Oxnard *Also Called: City of Oxnard (P-20151)*

Oxnard Lemon Company ....E...... 805 483-1173
2001 Sunkist Cir Oxnard (93033) *(P-1377)*

Oxnard Pallet Company, Oxnard *Also Called: E Vasquez Distributors Inc (P-2717)*

Oxnard Police Department ....B...... 805 385-8300
251 S C St Oxnard (93030) *(P-19457)*

Oxnard Prcsion Fabrication Inc ....E...... 805 985-0447
2200 Teal Club Rd Oxnard (93030) *(P-6280)*

OXY, Los Angeles *Also Called: Occidental Petroleum Corporation of California (P-264)*

OXY Inc ....C...... 310 824-1315
10889 Wilshire Blvd Los Angeles (90024) *(P-11721)*

OXY-World Travel, Los Angeles *Also Called: OXY Inc (P-11721)*

Oxyheal Health Group Inc ....C...... 619 336-2022
3224 Hoover Ave National City (91950) *(P-17142)*

Oxystrap International Inc ....E...... 800 699-6901
8705 Complex Dr San Diego (92123) *(P-4782)*

Oyewan Inc ....E...... 909 869-6200
20501 Earlgate St Walnut (91789) *(P-4441)*

Oz North Coast Y M C A, Oceanside *Also Called: YMCA of San Diego County (P-19490)*

Employee Codes: A=Over 500 employees, B=251-500
C=101-250, D=51-100, E=20-50, F=10-19, G=1-9

2024 Southern California
Business Directory and Buyers Guide

© Mergent Inc. 1-800-342-5647
1207

Ozeri, Ventura *Also Called: Commonpath LLC (P-5337)*

P & L Development LLC ....C....... 323 567-2482
11865 Alameda St Lynwood (90262) *(P-4192)*

P & R Paper Supply Co Inc ....C....... 619 671-2400
1350 Piper Ranch Rd San Diego (92154) *(P-3241)*

P & R Paper Supply Co Inc (HQ) ....D....... 909 389-1807
1898 E Colton Ave Redlands (92374) *(P-13021)*

P A C E, Los Angeles *Also Called: Pacific Asian Cnsrtium In Empl (P-19191)*

P A Motorcars LLC ....A....... 877 433-3517
2016 E Garvey Ave S West Covina (91791) *(P-13809)*

P A P, Anaheim *Also Called: Precision Anodizing & Pltg Inc (P-6650)*

P A S U Inc ....E....... 619 421-1151
1891 Nirvana Ave Chula Vista (91911) *(P-6281)*

P A X Industries, Costa Mesa *Also Called: Tk Pax Inc (P-4715)*

P C A Electronics Inc ....E....... 818 892-0761
16799 Schoenborn St North Hills (91343) *(P-12690)*

P C M, Banning *Also Called: Professional Cmnty MGT Cal Inc (P-14847)*

P C S C, Torrance *Also Called: Proprietary Controls Systems (P-10390)*

P H S, Northridge *Also Called: Progressive Health Care System (P-17740)*

P J J Enterprises Inc ....C....... 619 232-6136
1250 Delevan Dr San Diego (92102) *(P-15791)*

P L C Lighting, Chatsworth *Also Called: PLC Imports Inc (P-12613)*

P L M, Los Angeles *Also Called: Prudential Lighting Corp (P-8328)*

P M C, Cypress *Also Called: Plastic Molded Components Inc (P-5145)*

P M D Holding Corp ....B....... 949 595-4777
26672 Towne Centre Dr Ste 310 El Toro (92610) *(P-12503)*

P M I, San Diego *Also Called: Pacific Maritime Inds Corp (P-6061)*

P P I, Corona *Also Called: Preproduction Plastics Inc (P-5160)*

P P Mfg Co Inc ....F....... 562 921-3640
13130 Arctic Cir Santa Fe Springs (90670) *(P-6544)*

P R L, City Of Industry *Also Called: Prl Glass Systems Inc (P-5354)*

P R P Multisource Inc ....E....... 951 681-6100
3836 Wacker Dr Jurupa Valley (91752) *(P-7353)*

P S E Boilers, Santa Fe Springs *Also Called: Pacific Steam Equipment Inc (P-6147)*

P S I, Beaumont *Also Called: Precision Stampings Inc (P-8274)*

P T I, Torrance *Also Called: Plasma Technology Incorporated (P-6727)*

P T I, Santa Ana *Also Called: Parpro Technologies Inc (P-8715)*

P T Industries Inc ....F....... 562 961-3431
3220 Industry Dr Signal Hill (90755) *(P-6282)*

P T P, Carson *Also Called: Pacific Toll Processing Inc (P-5595)*

P V T Supply, Paramount *Also Called: Wagner Plate Works West Inc (P-6168)*

P-Tabun, El Cajon *Also Called: Pf Bakeries Llc (P-13389)*

P.S. Services, Anaheim *Also Called: 3s Sign Services Inc (P-11093)*

P&O Stg-Carson 4150, Carson *Also Called: US Foods Inc (P-13405)*

P&Y T-Shrts Silk Screening Inc ....E....... 323 585-4604
2126 E 52nd St Vernon (90058) *(P-7178)*

P2s Inc ....C....... 562 497-2999
4660 La Jolla Village Dr San Diego (92122) *(P-19660)*

P5 Graphics and Displays Inc ....E....... 714 808-1645
625 Fee Ana St Placentia (92870) *(P-15671)*

Paamco, Newport Beach *Also Called: Pacific Altrntive Asset MGT LL (P-14425)*

Pabco Building Products LLC ....C....... 323 581-6113
4460 Pacific Blvd Vernon (90058) *(P-5520)*

Pabco Paper, Vernon *Also Called: Pabco Building Products LLC (P-5520)*

Pac Fill Inc ....E....... 818 409-0117
5471 W San Fernando Rd Los Angeles (90039) *(P-1314)*

Pac Foundries Inc ....D....... 805 986-1308
705 Industrial Way Port Hueneme (93041) *(P-5806)*

Pac West Land Care Inc ....C....... 760 630-0231
408 Olive Ave Vista (92083) *(P-174)*

Pac-Dent Inc ....E....... 909 839-0888
670 Endeavor Cir Brea (92821) *(P-10759)*

Pac-Rancho Inc (HQ) ....C....... 909 987-4721
11000 Jersey Blvd Rancho Cucamonga (91730) *(P-5660)*

Pace Lithographers Inc ....E....... 626 913-2108
18030 Cortney Ct City Of Industry (91748) *(P-20399)*

Pace Marketing Communications, City Of Industry *Also Called: Pace Lithographers Inc (P-20399)*

Pace Punches Inc ....D....... 949 428-2750
297 Goddard Irvine (92618) *(P-7085)*

Pace Transducer Co, Canoga Park *Also Called: C J Instruments Incorporated (P-10356)*

Pacer, Commerce *Also Called: Xpo Cartage Inc (P-11470)*

Pacer Print ....E....... 888 305-3144
9207 Eton Ave Chatsworth (91311) *(P-3649)*

Pacer Technology (HQ) ....C....... 909 987-0550
3281 E Guasti Rd Ste 260 Ontario (91761) *(P-4574)*

Pacesetter Inc (DH) ....A....... 818 362-6822
15900 Valley View Ct Sylmar (91342) *(P-10819)*

Pacesetter Inc ....B....... 818 493-2715
13150 Telfair Ave Sylmar (91342) *(P-10820)*

Pacesetter Inc ....B....... 323 773-0591
4946 Florence Ave Bell (90201) *(P-10821)*

Pacesetter Fabrics LLC (HQ) ....F....... 213 741-9999
11450 Sheldon St Sun Valley (91352) *(P-2145)*

Pachulski Stang Zehl Jones LLP (PA) ....D....... 310 277-6910
10100 Santa Monica Blvd Ste 1100 Los Angeles (90067) *(P-18920)*

Pacifcare Hlth Plan Admnstrtor (DH) ....B....... 714 825-5200
3120 W Lake Center Dr Santa Ana (92704) *(P-14491)*

Pacific Aerospace Machine Inc ....E....... 714 534-1444
3002 S Rosewood Ave Santa Ana (92707) *(P-7963)*

Pacific Aggregates Inc ....D....... 951 245-2460
28251 Lake St Lake Elsinore (92530) *(P-5491)*

Pacific Airframe & Engineering, Oxnard *Also Called: American Airframe Inc (P-9622)*

Pacific Alloy Casting Company Inc ....C....... 562 928-1387
5900 Firestone Blvd Fl 1 South Gate (90280) *(P-5647)*

Pacific Altrntive Asset MGT LL (HQ) ....D....... 949 261-4900
660 Newport Center Dr Ste 930 Newport Beach (92660) *(P-14425)*

Pacific American Fish Co Inc (PA) ....C....... 323 319-1551
5525 S Santa Fe Ave Vernon (90058) *(P-1795)*

Pacific Archtectural Mllwk Inc ....D....... 714 525-2059
101 E Commwl Ave Ste A Fullerton (92832) *(P-2626)*

Pacific Archtectural Mllwk Inc ....E....... 562 905-9282
1435 Pioneer St Brea (92821) *(P-2627)*

Pacific Archtectural Mllwk Inc ....D....... 562 905-3200
1031 S Leslie St La Habra (90631) *(P-2628)*

Pacific Artglass Corporation ....E....... 310 516-7828
125 W 157th St Gardena (90248) *(P-5352)*

Pacific Asian Cnsrtium In Empl (PA) ....C....... 213 353-3982
1055 Wilshire Blvd Ste 1475 Los Angeles (90017) *(P-19191)*

Pacific Asian Enterprises Inc (PA) ....E....... 949 496-4848
25001 Dana Dr Dana Point (92629) *(P-16897)*

Pacific Asset Holding LLC ....C....... 949 219-3011
700 Newport Center Dr Newport Beach (92660) *(P-14440)*

Pacific Athletic Wear Inc ....D....... 714 751-8006
7340 Lampson Ave Garden Grove (92841) *(P-2356)*

Pacific Ave Cpitl Partners LLC (PA) ....B....... 424 254-9774
2447 Pacific Coast Hwy Ste 101 Hermosa Beach (90254) *(P-14981)*

Pacific Aviation Corporation (PA) ....C....... 310 646-4015
201 Continental Blvd Ste 220 El Segundo (90245) *(P-11702)*

Pacific Award Metals Inc (HQ) ....D....... 626 814-4410
1450 Virginia Ave Baldwin Park (91706) *(P-6283)*

Pacific Award Metals Inc ....E....... 360 694-9530
10302 Birtcher Dr Jurupa Valley (91752) *(P-6284)*

Pacific Award Metals Inc ....D....... 909 390-9880
10302 Birtcher Dr Jurupa Valley (91752) *(P-12368)*

Pacific Barcode Inc ....E....... 951 587-8717
27531 Enterprise Cir W Ste 201c Temecula (92590) *(P-7188)*

Pacific Bay Lending Group ....D....... 714 367-5125
15020 La Mirada Blvd La Mirada (90638) *(P-14361)*

Pacific Bell Telephone Company ....A....... 310 515-2898
3847 Cardiff Ave Culver City (90232) *(P-11853)*

Pacific Biotech Inc ....E....... 858 552-1100
10165 Mckellar Ct San Diego (92121) *(P-4286)*

Pacific Boat Trailers, Corona *Also Called: Pacific Boat Trailers Inc (P-13907)*

Pacific Boat Trailers Inc (PA) ....F....... 909 902-0094
2855 Sampson Ave Corona (92879) *(P-13907)*

Pacific Broach & Engrg Assoc ....F....... 714 632-5678
1513 N Kraemer Blvd Anaheim (92806) *(P-7964)*

Pacific Building Care Inc (HQ) ....C....... 949 261-1234
3001 Red Hill Ave Bldg 6 Costa Mesa (92626) *(P-15732)*

Mergent email: customerrelations@mergent.com
1208

2024 Southern California
Business Directory and Buyers Guide

(P-0000) Products & Services Section entry number
(PA)=Parent Co (HQ)=Headquarters (DH)=Div Headquarters

Pacific Building Group (PA) .... D...... 858 552-0600
  9752 Aspen Creek Ct Ste 100 San Diego (92126) *(P-571)*

Pacific Building Group .... D...... 858 552-0600
  13541 Stoney Creek Rd San Diego (92129) *(P-988)*

Pacific Cambria Inc .... D...... 805 927-6114
  2905 Burton Dr Cambria (93428) *(P-15284)*

Pacific Cast Cnstr Wtrproofing .... E...... 760 298-3170
  390 Oak Ave Ste A Carlsbad (92008) *(P-449)*

Pacific Cast Fther Cushion LLC (HQ) ....C...... 562 801-9995
  7600 Industry Ave Pico Rivera (90660) *(P-2481)*

Pacific Cast Products, Ontario *Also Called: Alumistar Inc (P-5781)*

Pacific Catalina Hotel Inc .... B...... 310 510-9255
  888 Country Club Dr Avalon (90704) *(P-15285)*

Pacific Chemical, Buena Park *Also Called: Pacific Chemical Dist Corp (P-11634)*

Pacific Chemical Dist Corp (HQ) ....D...... 714 521-7161
  6250 Caballero Blvd Buena Park (90620) *(P-11634)*

Pacific Child and Family Assoc, Glendale *Also Called: Verdugo Hlls Psychthrapy Ctr A (P-17827)*

Pacific City Hotel LLC .... B...... 714 698-6100
  21080 Pacific Coast Hwy Huntington Beach (92648) *(P-15286)*

Pacific Clay Products Inc .... C...... 661 857-1401
  14741 Lake St Lake Elsinore (92530) *(P-12359)*

Pacific Clinics Head Start .... C...... 626 254-5000
  171 N Altadena Dr Pasadena (91107) *(P-19223)*

Pacific Clnics Psdena Calworks .... C...... 626 419-3228
  2550 E Foothill Blvd Pasadena (91107) *(P-18704)*

Pacific Coachworks Inc .... C...... 951 686-7294
  3411 N Perris Blvd Bldg 1 Perris (92571) *(P-9927)*

Pacific Coast Bach Label Inc .... E...... 213 612-0314
  3015 S Grand Ave Los Angeles (90007) *(P-2104)*

Pacific Coast Bolt, Santa Fe Springs *Also Called: Birmingham Fastener & Sup Inc (P-5907)*

Pacific Coast Bus Times Inc .... E...... 805 560-6950
  14 E Carrillo St Ste A Santa Barbara (93101) *(P-3314)*

Pacific Coast Cabling Inc (PA) ....E...... 818 407-1911
  20717 Prairie St Chatsworth (91311) *(P-922)*

Pacific Coast Elevator Corp .... D...... 323 345-2550
  3041 Roswell St Los Angeles (90065) *(P-17143)*

Pacific Coast Feather Cushion, Pico Rivera *Also Called: Pacific Cast Fther Cushion LLC (P-2481)*

Pacific Coast Foam, San Diego *Also Called: PCF Group LLC (P-13553)*

Pacific Coast Home Furn Inc (PA) ....F...... 323 838-7808
  2424 Saybrook Ave Commerce (90040) *(P-2482)*

Pacific Coast Ironworks Inc .... E...... 323 585-1320
  8831 Miner St Los Angeles (90002) *(P-6060)*

Pacific Coast Lacquer, Los Angeles *Also Called: Berg Lacquer Co (P-13523)*

Pacific Coast Laminating, San Diego *Also Called: Higgins Hardwood Inc (P-5047)*

Pacific Coast Lighting, Ventura *Also Called: Lamps Plus Inc (P-8318)*

Pacific Coast Lighting Inc (HQ) ....F...... 800 709-9004
  20238 Plummer St Chatsworth (91311) *(P-8378)*

Pacific Coast Lighting Group, Chatsworth *Also Called: Pacific Coast Lighting Inc (P-8378)*

Pacific Coast Mfg Inc .... D...... 909 627-7040
  5270 Edison Ave Chino (91710) *(P-8220)*

Pacific Coast Sightseeing Tour .... C...... 714 507-1157
  2001 S Manchester Ave Anaheim (92802) *(P-11728)*

Pacific Coast Tree Experts .... C...... 805 506-1211
  21525 Strathern St Canoga Park (91304) *(P-224)*

Pacific Communications, Irvine *Also Called: Allergan Usa Inc (P-4041)*

Pacific Compensation Insur Co ....C...... 818 575-8500
  3011 Townsgate Rd Ste 120 Westlake Village (91361) *(P-14619)*

Pacific Concept Laundry, Los Angeles *Also Called: E & C Fashion Inc (P-16820)*

Pacific Consolidated Inds LLC .... D...... 951 479-0860
  12201 Magnolia Ave Riverside (92503) *(P-7403)*

Pacific Contntl Textiles Inc .... D...... 310 639-1500
  2880 E Ana St Compton (90221) *(P-2105)*

Pacific Contours Corporation .... D...... 714 693-1260
  5340 E Hunter Ave Anaheim (92807) *(P-9759)*

Pacific Couriers, South El Monte *Also Called: Integrated Parcel Network (P-11530)*

Pacific Culinary Group Inc .... E...... 626 284-1328
  566 Monterey Pass Rd Monterey Park (91754) *(P-1964)*

Pacific Defense, El Segundo *Also Called: Pacific Defense Strategies Inc (P-10048)*

Pacific Defense Strategies Inc (PA) ....E...... 310 722-6050
  400 Continental Blvd Ste 100 El Segundo (90245) *(P-10048)*

Pacific Dental Services LLC (PA) ....B...... 714 845-8500
  17000 Red Hill Ave Irvine (92614) *(P-17843)*

Pacific Die Casting, Commerce *Also Called: Orlandini Entps Pcf Die Cast (P-5816)*

Pacific Die Casting Corp .... C...... 323 725-1308
  6155 S Eastern Ave Commerce (90040) *(P-5764)*

Pacific Diversified Capital Co .... C...... 619 696-2000
  101 Ash St San Diego (92101) *(P-10389)*

Pacific Dntl Svcs Holdg Co Inc .... C...... 714 845-8500
  17000 Red Hill Ave Irvine (92614) *(P-17844)*

Pacific Drayage Services LLC .... C...... 833 334-4622
  550 W Artesia Blvd Compton (90220) *(P-11501)*

Pacific Duct Inc .... E...... 909 635-1335
  5499 Brooks St Montclair (91763) *(P-6285)*

Pacific Echo Inc .... D...... 310 539-1822
  23540 Telo Ave Torrance (90505) *(P-12870)*

Pacific Erth Rsrces Ltd A Cal .... D...... 209 892-3000
  315 Hueneme Rd Camarillo (93012) *(P-64)*

Pacific Erth Rsrces Ltd A Cal (PA) ....D...... 805 986-8277
  305 Hueneme Rd Camarillo (93012) *(P-65)*

Pacific Event Productions Inc (PA) ....C...... 858 458-9908
  6989 Corte Santa Fe San Diego (92121) *(P-15520)*

Pacific Fire Safety, Pomona *Also Called: Ferguson Fire Fabrication Inc (P-12740)*

Pacific Foam, Ontario *Also Called: Induspac California Inc (P-3945)*

Pacific Forge Inc .... D...... 909 390-0701
  10641 Etiwanda Ave Fontana (92337) *(P-6467)*

Pacific Gardens Med Ctr LLC .... C...... 562 860-0401
  21530 Pioneer Blvd Hawaiian Gardens (90716) *(P-20074)*

Pacific Gas and Electric Co .... C...... 805 545-4562
  4340 Old Santa Fe Rd San Luis Obispo (93401) *(P-12034)*

Pacific Gas and Electric Co .... A...... 805 506-5280
  9 Mi Nw Of Avila Bch Avila Beach (93424) *(P-12035)*

Pacific Gas and Electric Co .... C...... 805 546-5267
  800 Price Canyon Rd Pismo Beach (93449) *(P-12036)*

Pacific Gas and Electric Co .... D...... 805 434-4418
  160 Cow Meadow Pl Templeton (93465) *(P-12037)*

Pacific Gas and Electric Co .... C...... 760 253-2925
  35863 Fairview Rd Hinkley (92347) *(P-12038)*

Pacific Gas and Electric Co .... C...... 760 326-2615
  145453 National Trails Hway Needles (92363) *(P-12039)*

Pacific Gas and Electric Co .... C...... 661 398-5918
  4201 Arrow St Bakersfield (93308) *(P-12040)*

Pacific Glass, Gardena *Also Called: Pacific Artglass Corporation (P-5352)*

Pacific Green Landscape Inc (PA) ....C...... 619 390-1546
  8834 Winter Gardens Blvd Lakeside (92040) *(P-175)*

Pacific Handy Cutter Inc (DH) ....E...... 714 662-1033
  170 Technology Dr Irvine (92618) *(P-5887)*

Pacific Hardware Sales, Anaheim *Also Called: A J Fasteners Inc (P-6430)*

Pacific Haven Convalescent HM .... D...... 714 534-1942
  12072 Trask Ave Garden Grove (92843) *(P-18150)*

Pacific Health and Welness, Redondo Beach *Also Called: NBC Consulting Inc (P-20208)*

Pacific Health Corporation .... A...... 714 838-9600
  14642 Newport Ave Tustin (92780) *(P-18358)*

Pacific Heritg HM Fashion Inc .... E...... 909 598-5200
  901 Lawson St City Of Industry (91748) *(P-12313)*

Pacific Hospitality Design Inc .... E...... 323 278-7998
  2620 S Malt Ave Commerce (90040) *(P-2935)*

Pacific Hotel Management Inc .... C...... 949 608-1091
  4545 Macarthur Blvd Newport Beach (92660) *(P-15287)*

Pacific Huntington Hotel Corp .... A...... 626 568-3900
  1401 S Oak Knoll Ave Pasadena (91106) *(P-15288)*

Pacific Hydrotech Corporation .... C...... 951 943-8803
  314 E 3rd St Perris (92570) *(P-19661)*

Pacific Indemnity Company .... B...... 213 622-2334
  555 S Flower St Ste 300 Los Angeles (90071) *(P-14620)*

Pacific Insulation, Commerce *Also Called: Farwest Insulation Contracting (P-977)*

Pacific Integrated Mfg Inc .... C...... 619 921-3464
  4364 Bonita Rd Ste 454 Bonita (91902) *(P-10586)*

Pacific Investment MGT Co LLC (DH) ....C...... 949 720-6000
  650 Newport Center Dr Newport Beach (92660) *(P-14970)*

ALPHABETIC

Pacific Kiln, Moreno Valley *Also Called: Pacific Kiln Insulations Inc (P-7370)*

Pacific Kiln Insulations Inc ....E....... 951 697-4422
14370 Veterans Way Moreno Valley (92553) *(P-7370)*

Pacific Lasertec, San Marcos *Also Called: Pacific Lasertec LLC (P-9238)*

Pacific Lasertec LLC (PA)..E....... **760 539-7169**
215 Bingham Dr Ste 110 San Marcos (92069) *(P-9238)*

Pacific Life & Annuity Company ....A....... 949 219-3011
700 Newport Center Dr Newport Beach (92660) *(P-14441)*

Pacific Life Fund Advisors LLC ....B....... 949 260-9000
700 Newport Center Dr Newport Beach (92660) *(P-20075)*

Pacific Lock Company (PA)..E....... **661 294-3707**
25605 Hercules St Valencia (91355) *(P-5939)*

Pacific Lodge Boy's Home, Woodland Hills *Also Called: Pacific Lodge Youth Svcs Inc (P-19293)*

Pacific Lodge Youth Svcs Inc ....C....... 818 347-1577
4900 Serrania Ave Woodland Hills (91364) *(P-19293)*

Pacific Logistics Corp (PA)..C....... **562 478-4700**
7255 Rosemead Blvd Pico Rivera (90660) *(P-11791)*

Pacific Ltg & Standards Co ....E....... 310 603-9344
2815 Los Flores Blvd Lynwood (90262) *(P-8326)*

Pacific Manufacturing MGT Inc ....D....... 323 263-9000
3110 E 12th St Los Angeles (90023) *(P-2985)*

Pacific Marine Sheet Metal Corporation ....C....... 858 869-8900
2650 Jamacha Rd Ste 147 Pmb El Cajon (92019) *(P-6286)*

Pacific Maritime Freight Inc ....D....... 562 590-8188
1512 Pier C St Long Beach (90813) *(P-11651)*

PACIFIC MARITIME FREIGHT, INC., Long Beach *Also Called: Pacific Maritime Freight Inc (P-11651)*

Pacific Maritime Inds Corp ....C....... 619 575-8141
1790 Dornoch Ct San Diego (92154) *(P-6061)*

Pacific Medical Group Inc ....D....... 949 493-1030
212 Avenida Fabricante San Clemente (92672) *(P-12504)*

Pacific Metal Products, Los Angeles *Also Called: Basic Industries Intl Inc (P-6134)*

Pacific Metal Stampings Inc ....E....... 661 257-7656
28415 Witherspoon Pkwy Valencia (91355) *(P-6545)*

Pacific Mfg Inc San Diego ....E....... 619 423-0316
1520 Corporate Center Dr San Diego (92154) *(P-7965)*

Pacific Miniatures, Fullerton *Also Called: Pacmin Incorporated (P-11261)*

Pacific Monarch Resorts Inc (PA)..................................D....... **949 609-2400**
4000 Macarthur Blvd Ste 600 Newport Beach (92660) *(P-14838)*

Pacific Monarch Resorts Inc ....D....... 949 248-2944
34630 Pacific Coast Hwy Capistrano Beach (92624) *(P-15289)*

Pacific National Security Inc ....C....... 310 842-7073
3719 Robertson Blvd Culver City (90232) *(P-16667)*

Pacific Natural Spices, Commerce *Also Called: Pacific Spice Company Inc (P-1965)*

Pacific Naturals, Pacoima *Also Called: Gscm Ventures Inc (P-4417)*

Pacific Oil Cooler Service Inc ....E....... 909 593-8400
1677 Curtiss Ct La Verne (91750) *(P-11703)*

Pacific Outdoor Living, Sun Valley *Also Called: Pacific Pavingstone Inc (P-1080)*

Pacific Packaging McHy LLC ....E....... 951 393-2200
200 River Rd Corona (92878) *(P-7211)*

Pacific Palms Healthcare LLC ....D....... 562 433-6791
1020 Termino Ave Long Beach (90804) *(P-18023)*

Pacific Panel Products, Irwindale *Also Called: Pacific Panel Products Corp (P-2758)*

Pacific Panel Products Corp ....E....... 626 851-0444
15601 Arrow Hwy Irwindale (91706) *(P-2758)*

Pacific Park, Santa Monica *Also Called: Santa Monica Amusements LLC (P-17453)*

Pacific Pavingstone Inc ....C....... 818 244-4000
8309 Tujunga Ave Unit 201 Sun Valley (91352) *(P-1080)*

Pacific Perforating Inc ....E....... 661 768-9224
25090 Highway 33 Fellows (93224) *(P-374)*

Pacific Petroleum California Inc ....B....... 805 925-1947
1615 E Betteravia Rd Ste A Santa Maria (93454) *(P-375)*

Pacific Pharma Inc ....A....... 714 246-4600
18600 Von Karman Ave Irvine (92612) *(P-4193)*

Pacific Pioneer Insur Group (PA)..................................D....... **714 228-7888**
6363 Katella Ave Cypress (90630) *(P-14621)*

Pacific Piston Ring Co Inc ....D....... 310 836-3322
3620 Eastham Dr Culver City (90232) *(P-7701)*

Pacific Plas Injection Molding, Vista *Also Called: Diversified Plastics Inc (P-5013)*

Pacific Plastics Inc ....D....... 714 990-9050
111 S Berry St Brea (92821) *(P-4852)*

Pacific Plating, Sun Valley *Also Called: Kvr Investment Group Inc (P-7246)*

Pacific Plms Conference Resort, City Of Industry *Also Called: Majestic Industry Hills LLC (P-15236)*

Pacific Plstcs-Njction Molding, Vista *Also Called: J A English II Inc (P-5065)*

Pacific Power Systems Integration Inc ....E....... 562 281-0500
14729 Spring Ave Santa Fe Springs (90670) *(P-12612)*

Pacific Precision Inc ....E....... 909 392-5610
1318 Palomares St La Verne (91750) *(P-6418)*

Pacific Precision Metals Inc ....C....... 951 226-1500
1100 E Orangethorpe Ave Ste 253 Anaheim (92801) *(P-6546)*

Pacific Precision Products, Irvine *Also Called: Pacific Precision Products Mfg Inc (P-9760)*

Pacific Precision Products Mfg Inc ....E....... 949 727-3844
9671 Irvine Ctr Dr Koll Ctr Ii Bldg 6 Irvine (92618) *(P-9760)*

Pacific Premier Bancorp Inc ....D....... 951 274-2400
3403 10th St Ste 100 Riverside (92501) *(P-14202)*

Pacific Premier Bancorp Inc ....C....... **949 864-8000**
17901 Von Karman Ave Ste 1200 Irvine (92614) *(P-14203)*

Pacific Press, Anaheim *Also Called: Wasser Filtration Inc (P-7412)*

Pacific Process Systems Inc (PA)..................................D....... **661 321-9681**
7401 Rosedale Hwy Bakersfield (93308) *(P-376)*

Pacific Pulp Molding Inc ....E....... 619 977-5617
11285 Forestview Ln San Diego (92131) *(P-3242)*

Pacific Quality Packaging Corp ....D....... 714 257-1234
660 Neptune Ave Brea (92821) *(P-3120)*

Pacific Rim Mech Contrs Inc ....C....... 714 285-2600
1701 E Edinger Ave Ste F2 Santa Ana (92705) *(P-804)*

Pacific Rim Mech Contrs Inc (PA)..................................B....... **858 974-6500**
9125 Rehco Rd San Diego (92121) *(P-805)*

Pacific Scientific Company (DH)....................................E....... **805 526-5700**
1785 Voyager Ave Simi Valley (93063) *(P-10049)*

Pacific Sd/Pcfic Arbor Nrsries, Camarillo *Also Called: Pacific Erth Rsrces Ltd A Cal (P-65)*

Pacific Seismic Products Inc ....E....... 661 942-4499
233 E Avenue H8 Lancaster (93535) *(P-6768)*

Pacific Select Distrs Inc ....D....... 949 219-3001
700 Newport Center Dr Fl 4 Newport Beach (92660) *(P-14401)*

Pacific Sewer Maintenance Corp ....F....... 800 292-9927
4008 Via Rio Ave Oceanside (92057) *(P-5648)*

Pacific Ship Repr Fbrction Inc (PA)..............................B....... **619 232-3200**
1625 Rigel St San Diego (92113) *(P-9845)*

Pacific Shore Holdings Inc ....E....... 818 998-0996
8236 Remmet Ave Canoga Park (91304) *(P-4194)*

Pacific Sky Supply Inc ....D....... 818 768-3700
8230 San Fernando Rd Sun Valley (91352) *(P-9761)*

Pacific Sod, Camarillo *Also Called: Pacific Erth Rsrces Ltd A Cal (P-64)*

Pacific Spice Company Inc ....C....... 323 726-9190
6430 E Slauson Ave Commerce (90040) *(P-1965)*

Pacific Steam Equipment Inc ....E....... 562 906-9292
11748 Slauson Ave Santa Fe Springs (90670) *(P-6147)*

Pacific Steel, Chula Vista *Also Called: Simec USA Corporation (P-5602)*

Pacific Steel Group (PA)..C....... **858 251-1100**
4805 Murphy Canyon Rd San Diego (92123) *(P-6404)*

Pacific Steel Group ....B....... 858 449-7219
2755 S Willow Ave Bloomington (92316) *(P-12564)*

Pacific Sthwest Structures Inc ....C....... 619 469-2323
7845 Lemon Grove Way Ste A Lemon Grove (91945) *(P-1081)*

Pacific Stone Design Inc ....E....... 714 836-5757
1201 E Wakeham Ave Santa Ana (92705) *(P-5436)*

Pacific Strucframe LLC ....D....... 951 405-8536
1600 Chicago Ave Ste R11 Riverside (92507) *(P-1049)*

Pacific Structures, Venice *Also Called: Pacific Structures Sc Inc (P-1082)*

Pacific Structures Sc Inc (PA)..C....... **415 970-5434**
1212 Abbot Kinney Blvd Apt A Venice (90291) *(P-1082)*

Pacific Suites Hotel, Santa Monica *Also Called: Windsor Capital Group Inc (P-15424)*

Pacific Supply, Orange *Also Called: Beacon Pacific Inc (P-12366)*

Pacific Systems Interiors Inc ....C....... 310 436-6820
190 E Arrow Hwy Ste D San Dimas (91773) *(P-989)*

Pacific Tank & Cnstr Inc ....E....... 805 237-2929
17995 E Highway 46 Shandon (93461) *(P-6148)*

Mergent email: customerrelations@mergent.com
1210

2024 Southern California
Business Directory and Buyers Guide

(P-0000) Products & Services Section entry number
(PA)=Parent Co (HQ)=Headquarters (DH)=Div Headquarters

Pacific Tech Solutions LLC .... C..... 949 830-1623
15530 Rockfield Blvd Ste B4 Irvine (92618) *(P-16091)*

Pacific Toll Processing Inc .... E..... 310 952-4992
24724 Wilmington Ave Carson (90745) *(P-5595)*

Pacific Transformer Corp .... D..... 714 779-0450
5399 E Hunter Ave Anaheim (92807) *(P-8106)*

Pacific Trellis Fruit LLC (PA)................................. **C..... 323 859-9600**
2301 E 7th St Ste C200 Los Angeles (90023) *(P-13335)*

Pacific Trust Bank .... C..... 949 236-5211
18500 Von Karman Ave Ste 1100 Irvine (92612) *(P-14217)*

Pacific Urethanes, Ontario *Also Called: Pacific Urethanes LLC (P-2483)*

Pacific Urethanes LLC .... C..... 909 390-8400
1671 Champagne Ave Ste A Ontario (91761) *(P-2483)*

Pacific Utility Products Inc .... E..... 951 493-8394
2430 Railroad St Corona (92880) *(P-9239)*

Pacific Ventures Ltd .... C..... 626 576-0737
2200 W Valley Blvd Alhambra (91803) *(P-20076)*

Pacific Vial Mfg Inc .... E..... 323 721-7004
2738 Supply Ave Commerce (90040) *(P-5321)*

Pacific Wave Systems Inc .... D..... 714 893-0152
2525 W 190th St Torrance (90504) *(P-8559)*

Pacific West, Anaheim *Also Called: Pacific West Litho Inc (P-3650)*

Pacific West Litho Inc .... D..... 714 579-0868
3291 E Miraloma Ave Anaheim (92806) *(P-3650)*

Pacific West Tree Service, Vista *Also Called: Pac West Land Care Inc (P-174)*

Pacific Western Bank .... B..... 858 756-3023
6110 El Tordo Rancho Santa Fe (92067) *(P-14173)*

Pacific Western Container, Santa Ana *Also Called: Blower-Dempsay Corporation (P-3083)*

Pacific Westline Inc .... D..... 714 956-2442
1536 W Embassy St Anaheim (92802) *(P-2964)*

Pacific Wire Products Inc .... E..... 818 755-6400
10725 Vanowen St North Hollywood (91605) *(P-6822)*

Pacific World Corporation (PA)............................. **D..... 949 598-2400**
100 Technology Dr Ste 200 Irvine (92618) *(P-4442)*

Pacific Wtrprfing Rstrtion Inc .... F..... 909 444-3052
2845 Pomona Blvd Pomona (91768) *(P-4625)*

Pacifica Beauty LLC .... D..... 844 332-8440
1090 Eugenia Pl Ste 200 Carpinteria (93013) *(P-11260)*

Pacifica Emergency Med Assoc, Encino *Also Called: Emergent Medical Associates (P-17649)*

Pacifica Foods LLC .... C..... 951 371-3123
1851 N Delilah St Corona (92879) *(P-1363)*

PACIFICA HOSPITAL OF THE VALLE, Sun Valley *Also Called: Pacifica of Valley Corporation (P-18359)*

Pacifica Hosts Inc .... C..... 858 755-1501
710 Camino Del Mar Del Mar (92014) *(P-15290)*

Pacifica Hosts Inc .... D..... 858 792-8200
717 S Highway 101 Solana Beach (92075) *(P-15291)*

Pacifica International, Carpinteria *Also Called: Pacifica Beauty LLC (P-11260)*

Pacifica of Valley Corporation .... A..... 818 767-3310
9449 San Fernando Rd Sun Valley (91352) *(P-18359)*

Pacifica Services Inc .... D..... 626 405-0131
106 S Mentor Ave Ste 200 Pasadena (91106) *(P-19662)*

Pacificare, Santa Ana *Also Called: Pacifcare Hlth Plan Admnstrtor (P-14491)*

Pacificare Health Systems, Cypress *Also Called: Uhc of California (P-14504)*

Pacificare Health Systems, Cypress *Also Called: Pacificare Health Systems LLC (P-18632)*

Pacificare Health Systems LLC (HQ)....................... A..... 714 952-1121
5995 Plaza Dr Cypress (90630) *(P-18632)*

Pacifictech Molded Pdts Inc .... F..... 714 279-9928
22695 Old Canal Rd Yorba Linda (92887) *(P-4783)*

Pacira Pharmaceuticals Inc (HQ)......................... **E..... 858 625-2424**
10410 Science Center Dr San Diego (92121) *(P-4195)*

Pacira Pharmaceuticals Inc .... D..... 858 625-2424
10578 Science Center Dr San Diego (92121) *(P-4196)*

Paciugo .... E..... 714 536-5388
122 Main St Ste 122 Huntington Beach (92648) *(P-5870)*

Pack West Machinery, Corona *Also Called: Pacific Packaging McHy LLC (P-7211)*

Pack West Machinery Co, Corona *Also Called: W J Ellison Co Inc (P-7356)*

Packaging Corporation America 562 927-7741
9700 E Frontage Rd Ste 20 South Gate (90280) *(P-3121)*

Packaging Corporation America .... C..... 323 263-7581
4240 Bandini Blvd Vernon (90058) *(P-3122)*

Packaging Corporation America .... E..... 909 595-0401
19570 San Jose Ave City Of Industry (91748) *(P-3123)*

Packaging Corporation America ......*........................ E..... 909 888-7008
879 E Rialto Ave San Bernardino (92408) *(P-3124)*

Packaging Manufacturing Inc .... C..... 619 498-9199
2285 Michael Faraday Dr Ste 12 San Diego (92154) *(P-3651)*

Packaging Spectrum, Los Angeles *Also Called: Advance Paper Box Company (P-3078)*

Packaging Systems Inc .... E..... 661 253-5700
26435 Summit Cir Santa Clarita (91350) *(P-4575)*

Packers Bar M, Los Angeles *Also Called: Serv-Rite Meat Company Inc (P-1204)*

Paclights, Chino *Also Called: Paclights LLC (P-8327)*

Paclights LLC (PA)... **F..... 800 980-6386**
15318 El Prado Rd Chino (91710) *(P-8327)*

Paclo, Pico Rivera *Also Called: Pacific Logistics Corp (P-11791)*

Pacmet Aerospace, Corona *Also Called: Pacmet Aerospace LLC (P-6895)*

Pacmet Aerospace LLC .... D..... 909 218-8889
224 Glider Cir Corona (92878) *(P-6895)*

Pacmin Incorporated (PA)................................. **D..... 714 447-4478**
2021 Raymer Ave Fullerton (92833) *(P-11261)*

Pacobond Inc .... E..... 818 768-5002
9344 Glenoaks Blvd Sun Valley (91352) *(P-3200)*

Pacon Inc .... C..... 626 814-4654
4249 Puente Ave Baldwin Park (91706) *(P-3059)*

Pactiv LLC .... C..... 661 392-4000
2024 Norris Rd Bakersfield (93308) *(P-5128)*

Pacwest Air Filter LLC .... E..... 951 698-2228
26550 Adams Ave Murrieta (92562) *(P-7328)*

Pacwest Bancorp (PA)...................................... **C..... 310 887-8500**
9701 Wilshire Blvd Ste 700 Beverly Hills (90212) *(P-14174)*

Pacwest Security Services .... C..... 213 413-3500
1545 Wilshire Blvd Ste 302 Los Angeles (90017) *(P-16668)*

Pacwest Security Services .... C..... 909 948-0279
2990 Inland Empire Blvd Ontario (91764) *(P-16669)*

PACWEST SECURITY SERVICES, Los Angeles *Also Called: Pacwest Security Services (P-16668)*

PACWEST SECURITY SERVICES, Ontario *Also Called: Pacwest Security Services (P-16669)*

Padi, Rcho Sta Marg *Also Called: Padi Americas Inc (P-19401)*

Padi Americas Inc .... C..... 949 858-7234
30151 Tomas Rcho Sta Marg (92688) *(P-19401)*

Padilla Construction Company .... C..... 714 685-8500
1620 N Brian St Orange (92867) *(P-990)*

Padres LP .... A..... 619 795-5000
100 Park Blvd Petco Park San Diego (92101) *(P-17380)*

Pafco, Vernon *Also Called: Pacific American Fish Co Inc (P-1795)*

Page Private School .... D..... 323 272-3429
419 S Robertson Blvd Beverly Hills (90211) *(P-18978)*

Paige LLC (HQ)... **C..... 310 733-2100**
10119 Jefferson Blvd Culver City (90232) *(P-2262)*

Paige Floor Cvg Specialists, National City *Also Called: Paige Sitta & Associates Inc (P-9846)*

Paige Premium Denim, Culver City *Also Called: Paige LLC (P-2262)*

Paige Sitta & Associates Inc (PA)........................ **E..... 619 233-5912**
2050 Wilson Ave Ste B National City (91950) *(P-9846)*

Paiho North America Corp .... E..... 661 257-6611
16051 El Prado Rd Chino (91708) *(P-11074)*

Paint Specialists Inc .... F..... 818 771-0552
8629 Bradley Ave Sun Valley (91352) *(P-6721)*

Painted Rhino Inc (PA)..................................... **E..... 951 656-5524**
14310 Veterans Way Moreno Valley (92553) *(P-4920)*

Paisano Publications LLC (PA)........................... **D..... 818 889-8740**
28210 Dorothy Dr Agoura Hills (91301) *(P-3375)*

Paisano Publications Inc .... D..... 818 889-8740
28210 Dorothy Dr Agoura Hills (91301) *(P-3376)*

Paisleyriversoapco, Paso Robles *Also Called: Melissa Trinidad (P-4434)*

Pak Group LLC .... E..... 626 316-6555
236 N Chester Ave Ste 200 Pasadena (91106) *(P-1522)*

Pak West Paper & Packaging, Santa Ana *Also Called: Blower-Dempsay Corporation (P-3084)*

Pakedge Device & Software Inc .... C..... 714 880-4511
17011 Beach Blvd Ste 600 Huntington Beach (92647) *(P-16341)*

Paklab, Chino *Also Called: Universal Packg Systems Inc (P-4464)*

Paklab, Chino *Also Called: Universal Packg Systems Inc (P-11627)*

Employee Codes: A=Over 500 employees, B=251-500
C=101-250, D=51-100, E=20-50, F=10-19, G=1-9

2024 Southern California
Business Directory and Buyers Guide

© Mergent Inc. 1-800-342-5647

1211

Pala Casino, Pala *Also Called: Pala Casino Spa & Resort (P-15292)*

Pala Casino Spa & Resort .... A....... 760 510-5100
11154 Highway 76 Pala (92059) *(P-15292)*

Pala Mesa Limited Partnership .... C....... 760 728-5881
2001 Old Highway 395 Fallbrook (92028) *(P-15293)*

Pala Mesa Resort, Fallbrook *Also Called: Pala Mesa Limited Partnership (P-15293)*

Paladar Mfg Inc .... D....... 760 775-4222
53973 Polk St Coachella (92236) *(P-10928)*

Palanging International Inc .... D....... 619 948-2459
861 Anchorage Pl Chula Vista (91914) *(P-14839)*

Palermo Family LP .... E....... 213 542-3300
140 W Providencia Ave Burbank (91502) *(P-1966)*

Palette Life Sciences Inc .... D....... 805 869-7020
27 E Cota St Ste 402 Santa Barbara (93101) *(P-4010)*

Pali Adventures, Running Springs *Also Called: Pali Camp (P-15438)*

Pali Camp .... C....... 909 867-5743
30778 Hwy 18 Running Springs (92382) *(P-15438)*

Palisades Beach Club, Los Angeles *Also Called: Fortune Swimwear LLC (P-2070)*

Palisades Group LLC .... C....... 424 280-7560
11755 Wilshire Blvd Ste 1700 Los Angeles (90025) *(P-14402)*

Palisades Ranch Inc .... B....... 323 581-6161
5925 Alcoa Ave Vernon (90058) *(P-13190)*

Pall Corporation .... C....... 858 455-7264
4116 Sorrento Valley Blvd San Diego (92121) *(P-7404)*

Pallet Masters Inc .... D....... 323 758-1713
655 E Florence Ave Los Angeles (90001) *(P-2721)*

Palm Canyon Resort & Spa, Palm Springs *Also Called: Diamond Resorts LLC (P-15129)*

Palm Desert Community Assn, Palm Desert *Also Called: Sun City Palm Dsert Cmnty Assn (P-19465)*

Palm Desert Hospitality LLC .... B....... 760 568-1600
36999 Cook St Palm Desert (92211) *(P-15294)*

PALM GROVE HEALTHCARE, Beaumont *Also Called: David-Kleis II LLC (P-18757)*

Palm Realty Boutique Inc .... D....... 310 545-2490
401 Manhattan Beach Blvd Ste B Manhattan Beach (90266) *(P-14840)*

Palm Springs Art Museum Inc .... D....... 760 322-4800
101 N Museum Dr Palm Springs (92262) *(P-19360)*

Palm Springs Convention Center, Palm Springs *Also Called: Smg Holdings LLC (P-20241)*

Palm Springs Disposal Services .... D....... 760 327-1351
4690 E Mesquite Ave Palm Springs (92264) *(P-12177)*

Palm Springs Health Care Ctr, Palm Springs *Also Called: Mariner Health Care Inc (P-20058)*

Palm Springs Life .... D....... 760 325-2333
303 N Indian Canyon Dr Palm Springs (92262) *(P-3377)*

Palm Springs Motors Inc .... C....... 760 699-6695
69-200a Highway 111 Cathedral City (92234) *(P-13810)*

Palm Sprng Ford Lncoln Mercury, Cathedral City *Also Called: Palm Springs Motors Inc (P-13810)*

Palm Ter Hlthcare Rhbittion Ct, Laguna Hills *Also Called: Gate Three Healthcare LLC (P-17960)*

Palmcrest Grand Care Ctr Inc .... D....... 562 595-4551
3501 Cedar Ave Long Beach (90807) *(P-18024)*

Palmcrest Medallion Convalesc .... D....... 562 595-4336
3355 Pacific Pl Long Beach (90806) *(P-18025)*

Palmdale Water District .... D....... 661 947-4111
2029 E Avenue Q Palmdale (93550) *(P-12137)*

Palmer Tank & Construction Inc .... E....... 661 834-1110
2464 S Union Ave Bakersfield (93307) *(P-377)*

Palmieri Tyler Wner Wlhelm Wld .... D....... 949 851-9400
1900 Main St Ste 700 Irvine (92614) *(P-18921)*

Palo Verde Health Care Dst .... C....... 760 922-4115
250 N 1st St Blythe (92225) *(P-18360)*

Palo Verde Hospital, Blythe *Also Called: Palo Verde Health Care Dst (P-18360)*

Palo Verde Hospital Assn .... C....... 760 922-4115
250 N 1st St Blythe (92225) *(P-18361)*

Palo Verde Irrigation District .... D....... 760 922-3144
180 W 14th Ave Blythe (92225) *(P-12215)*

Palomar Health .... B....... 858 675-5218
152255 Innovation Dr San Diego (92128) *(P-18362)*

Palomar Health .... A....... 760 739-3000
15615 Pomerado Rd Poway (92064) *(P-18363)*

Palomar Health .... C....... 858 613-4000
15615 Pomerado Rd Poway (92064) *(P-18364)*

Palomar Health (PA) .... C....... 442 281-5000
2125 Citracado Pkwy Ste 300 Escondido (92029) *(P-18365)*

Palomar Health .... C....... 760 740-6311
800 W Valley Pkwy Ste 201 Escondido (92025) *(P-18531)*

Palomar Health Medical Group (HQ) .... C....... 858 675-3100
15611 Pomerado Rd Ste 575 Poway (92064) *(P-18366)*

Palomar Health Technology Inc .... C....... 442 281-5000
2140 Enterprise St Escondido (92029) *(P-18367)*

Palomar Medical Center .... B....... 858 613-4000
15615 Pomerado Rd Poway (92064) *(P-18368)*

Palomar Medical Center, Poway *Also Called: Palomar Health (P-18363)*

Palomar Medical Center, Escondido *Also Called: Palomar Health (P-18365)*

Palomar Products Inc .... D....... 949 766-5300
23042 Arroyo Vis Rcho Sta Marg (92688) *(P-8619)*

Palomar Tech Companies (PA) .... E....... 760 931-3600
6305 El Camino Real Carlsbad (92009) *(P-9240)*

Palomar Technologies Inc (PA) .... E....... 760 931-3600
6305 El Camino Real Carlsbad (92009) *(P-7254)*

Palos Verdes Building Corp (PA) .... C....... 951 371-8090
1675 Sampson Ave Corona (92879) *(P-9153)*

Palos Verdes Golf & Cntry CLB, Palos Verdes Estates *Also Called: Palos Verdes Golf Club (P-14051)*

Palos Verdes Golf Club .... D....... 310 375-2759
3301 Via Campesina Palos Verdes Estates (90274) *(P-14051)*

Palp Inc .... C....... 562 599-5841
2230 Lemon Ave Long Beach (90806) *(P-638)*

Palyon Medical Corporation .... E
28432 Constellation Rd Valencia (91355) *(P-10822)*

Pam's Delivery Svc & Nat Msgnr, Compton *Also Called: Madden Corporation (P-11533)*

Pamc Ltd (PA) .... A....... 213 624-8411
531 W College St Los Angeles (90012) *(P-18369)*

Pamc Health Foundation, Los Angeles *Also Called: Pamc Ltd (P-18369)*

Pamco, Sun Valley *Also Called: Precision Arcft Machining Inc (P-7977)*

Pamco Machine Works Inc .... E....... 909 941-7260
9359 Feron Blvd Rancho Cucamonga (91730) *(P-7966)*

Pampa Regional Medical Center, Ontario *Also Called: Prime Hlthcare Svcs - Pmpa LLC (P-18392)*

Pampanga Food Company Inc .... E....... 714 773-0537
1835 N Orangethorpe Park Ste A Anaheim (92801) *(P-1228)*

Pan American Bank Fsb .... B....... 949 224-1917
18191 Von Karman Ave Ste 300 Irvine (92612) *(P-14218)*

Pan Pacific Petroleum Co Inc (PA) .... D....... 562 928-0100
9302 Garfield Ave South Gate (90280) *(P-11502)*

Pan Pacific San Diego, San Diego *Also Called: Pan Pcfic Htels Rsrts Amer Inc (P-15295)*

Pan Pcfic Htels Rsrts Amer Inc .... C....... 619 239-4500
400 W Broadway San Diego (92101) *(P-15295)*

Pan-Pacific Mechanical, Fountain Valley *Also Called: Pan-Pacific Mechanical LLC (P-807)*

Pan-Pacific Mechanical LLC .... B....... 858 764-2464
11622 El Camino Real Ste 100 San Diego (92130) *(P-806)*

Pan-Pacific Mechanical LLC (PA) .... C....... 949 474-9170
18250 Euclid St Fountain Valley (92708) *(P-807)*

Pan-Pacific Plumbing & Mech, San Diego *Also Called: Pan-Pacific Mechanical LLC (P-806)*

Panadent Corporation .... E....... 909 783-1841
580 S Rancho Ave Colton (92324) *(P-10760)*

Panaroma Gardens, Panorama City *Also Called: Ensign Group Inc (P-17940)*

Panasnic Appls Rfrgn Systems C, San Diego *Also Called: Hussmann Tech Corp Amer (P-7616)*

Panasonic Avionics Corporation (DH) .... B....... 949 672-2000
3347 Michelson Dr Ste 100 Irvine (92612) *(P-19663)*

Panasonic Disc Manufacturing Corporation of America ... C....... 310 783-4800
20000 Mariner Ave Ste 200 Torrance (90503) *(P-8462)*

Panattoni Development Co Inc (PA) .... D....... 916 381-1561
2442 Dupont Dr Irvine (92612) *(P-14909)*

Panavision Group, Woodland Hills *Also Called: Panavision Inc (P-15792)*

Panavision Hollywood, Los Angeles *Also Called: Panavision Inc (P-10877)*

Panavision Inc .... E....... 323 464-3800
6735 Selma Ave Los Angeles (90028) *(P-10877)*

Panavision Inc (PA) .... A....... 818 316-1000
6101 Variel Ave Woodland Hills (91367) *(P-15792)*

Panavision International LP (HQ) .... B....... 818 316-1080
6101 Variel Ave Woodland Hills (91367) *(P-10878)*

Panda Express, South Pasadena *Also Called: Citadel Panda Express Inc (P-13997)*

Panda Express, Rosemead *Also Called: Panda Systems Inc (P-14029)*

Panda Systems Inc .... C...... 626 799-9898
2800 Palisades Dr Corona (92878) *(P-8127)*
1683 Walnut Grove Ave Rosemead (91770) *(P-14029)*

Pandemic Studios LLC .... B...... 310 450-5199
5510 Lincoln Blvd Los Angeles (90094) *(P-16092)*

Pandora Media LLC .... C...... 424 653-6803
3000 Ocean Park Blvd Ste 3050 Santa Monica (90405) *(P-11933)*

Panel Products, Long Beach *Also Called: Simulator PDT Solutions LLC (P-10071)*

Panel Shop Inc .... E...... 951 739-7000
2800 Palisades Dr Corona (92878) *(P-8127)*

Panel Works, Tustin *Also Called: JC Hanscom Inc (P-2689)*

Pankl Aerospace Systems .... D...... 562 207-6300
16615 Edwards Rd Cerritos (90703) *(P-5817)*

Pankl Engine Systems Inc .... E...... 949 428-8788
1902 Mcgaw Ave Irvine (92614) *(P-9437)*

Panoramic Doors LLC .... C...... 760 722-1300
3265 Production Ave Ste A Oceanside (92058) *(P-12339)*

Panoramic Software Corporation .... F...... 877 558-8526
9650 Research Dr Irvine (92618) *(P-16342)*

Panosoft, Irvine *Also Called: Panoramic Software Corporation (P-16342)*

Panrosa Enterprises Inc .... D...... 951 339-5888
550 Monica Cir Corona (92878) *(P-4340)*

Papa Cantella's Sausage Plant, Vernon *Also Called: Papa Cantellas Incorporated (P-1229)*

Papa Cantellas Incorporated .... D...... 323 584-7272
3341 E 50th St Vernon (90058) *(P-1229)*

Papaya .... E...... 310 740-6774
14140 Ventura Blvd Ste 209 Sherman Oaks (91423) *(P-16343)*

Pape Material Handling Inc .... D...... 562 692-9311
2600 Peck Rd City Of Industry (90601) *(P-6995)*

Pape Material Handling Inc .... C...... 562 463-8000
2615 Pellissier Pl City Of Industry (90601) *(P-12807)*

Paper Company, The, Irvine *Also Called: Imperial Bag & Paper Co LLC (P-13010)*

Paper Mart Indus & Ret Packg, Orange *Also Called: Frick Paper Company LLC (P-13007)*

Paper Surce Converting Mfg Inc .... E...... 323 583-3800
2015 E 48th St Vernon (90058) *(P-3060)*

Papercon Packaging Division, City Of Industry *Also Called: Bagcraftpapercon I LLC (P-3197)*

Papercutters Inc .... E...... 323 888-1330
6900 Washington Blvd Montebello (90640) *(P-3154)*

Papi Inc., Glendale *Also Called: Glenair Inc (P-8266)*

Pappalecco .... E...... 619 906-5566
3650 5th Ave Ste 104 San Diego (92103) *(P-6870)*

Paq Inc .... D...... 805 227-1660
1465 Creston Rd Paso Robles (93446) *(P-13893)*

Par Services, Los Angeles *Also Called: Exceptional Chld Foundation (P-19183)*

PAR SERVICES, Culver City *Also Called: Exceptional Chld Foundation (P-19184)*

Par Western Line Contrs LLC .... A...... 760 737-0925
11276 5th St Ste 100 Rancho Cucamonga (91730) *(P-16898)*

Para Plate, Cerritos *Also Called: Para-Plate & Plastics Co Inc (P-7189)*

Para Tech Coating, Laguna Hills *Also Called: Metal Improvement Company LLC (P-5841)*

Para-Plate & Plastics Co Inc .... E...... 562 404-3434
15910 Shoemaker Ave Cerritos (90703) *(P-7189)*

Parachute Home Inc .... C...... 310 903-0353
3525 Eastham Dr Culver City (90232) *(P-2484)*

Paraclsus Los Angles Cmnty Hos 323 267-0477
4081 E Olympic Blvd Los Angeles (90023) *(P-18370)*

Paradigm Industries Inc .... D...... 310 965-1900
2522 E 37th St Vernon (90058) *(P-16899)*

Paradigm Packaging East LLC .... E...... 909 985-2750
9595 Utica Ave Rancho Cucamonga (91730) *(P-5129)*

Paradigm Packaging West, Rancho Cucamonga *Also Called: Paradigm Packaging East LLC (P-5129)*

Paradise Electric Inc .... B...... 619 449-4141
697 Greenfield Dr El Cajon (92021) *(P-923)*

Paradise Lessee Inc .... B...... 858 274-4630
1404 Vacation Rd San Diego (92109) *(P-15296)*

Paradise Manufacturing Co Inc .... E...... 909 477-3460
13364 Aerospace Dr # 100 Victorville (92394) *(P-2507)*

Paradise Point Resort, San Diego *Also Called: Westgroup San Diego Associates (P-15415)*

Paradise Point Resort & Spa, San Diego *Also Called: Paradise Lessee Inc (P-15296)*

Paradise Printing Inc .... E...... 714 228-9628
13474 Pumice St Norwalk (90650) *(P-3652)*

Paradise Valley Hospital .... B...... 619 472-7474
180 Otay Lakes Rd Ste 100 Bonita (91902) *(P-18371)*

Paradise Valley Hospital (PA) .... A...... 619 470-4100
2400 E 4th St National City (91950) *(P-18372)*

Paradise Valley Manor, National City *Also Called: Sterling Care Inc (P-18058)*

Paragon Building Products Inc (PA) .... E...... 951 549-1155
2191 5th St Ste 111 Norco (92860) *(P-5437)*

Paragon Industries Inc .... E...... 818 833-0550
16450 Foothill Blvd Ste 100 Sylmar (91342) *(P-1006)*

Paragon Industries Inc .... D...... 714 778-1800
1515 E Winston Rd Anaheim (92805) *(P-13668)*

Paragon Laboratories, Torrance *Also Called: Naturalife Eco Vite Labs (P-1278)*

Paragon Plastics Co Div, Chino *Also Called: Consolidated Plastics Corp (P-13412)*

Paragon Precision, Valencia *Also Called: Princeton Tool Inc (P-9578)*

Paragon Services Engineering, San Diego *Also Called: San Diego Services LLC (P-19685)*

Parallel 6 Inc (PA) .... E...... 619 452-1750
1455 Frazee Rd Ste 900 San Diego (92108) *(P-16093)*

Paramont Metal & Supply Co, Paramount *Also Called: George Jue Mfg Co Inc (P-7145)*

Paramount Asphalt, Paramount *Also Called: Paramount Petroleum Corp (P-4647)*

Paramount Citrus, Delano *Also Called: Wonderful Company LLC (P-45)*

Paramount Citrus Packing Co, Delano *Also Called: Wonderful Citrus Packing LLC (P-118)*

Paramount Dairy Inc .... C...... 562 361-1800
15255 Texaco Ave Paramount (90723) *(P-1315)*

Paramount Fabricators, Rancho Cucamonga *Also Called: Paramunt Plstic Fbricators Inc (P-5131)*

Paramount Farms, Los Angeles *Also Called: Wonderful Pstchios Almonds LLC (P-1563)*

Paramount Forge Inc .... E...... 323 775-6803
1721 E Colon St Wilmington (90744) *(P-6468)*

Paramount Machine Co Inc .... E...... 909 484-3600
10824 Edison Ct Rancho Cucamonga (91730) *(P-7967)*

Paramount Metal & Supply Inc .... E...... 562 634-8180
8140 Rosecrans Ave Paramount (90723) *(P-6365)*

Paramount Panels Inc (PA) .... E...... 909 947-8008
1531 E Cedar St Ontario (91761) *(P-5130)*

Paramount Petroleum Corp (DH) .... C...... 562 531-2060
14700 Downey Ave Paramount (90723) *(P-4647)*

Paramount Pictures Corporation (HQ) .... A...... 323 956-5000
5555 Melrose Ave Los Angeles (90038) *(P-17205)*

Paramount Studios, Los Angeles *Also Called: Paramount Pictures Corporation (P-17205)*

Paramount Swap Meet, Paramount *Also Called: Modern Dev Co A Ltd Partnr (P-16880)*

Paramount Window & Doors, San Bernardino *Also Called: Paramount Windows & Doors (P-2629)*

Paramount Windows & Doors .... F...... 909 888-4688
723 W Mill St San Bernardino (92410) *(P-2629)*

Paramout Farms, Lost Hills *Also Called: Roll Properties Intl Inc (P-15049)*

Paramunt Ovrseas Prdctions Inc .... A...... 323 956-5225
5515 Melrose Ave Los Angeles (90038) *(P-17206)*

Paramunt Plstic Fbricators Inc .... F...... 909 987-4757
11251 Jersey Blvd Rancho Cucamonga (91730) *(P-5131)*

Parcell Steel, Corona *Also Called: Parcell Steel Corp (P-6062)*

Parcell Steel Corp .... C...... 951 471-3200
26365 Earthmover Cir Corona (92883) *(P-6062)*

Parco LLC (DH) .... C...... 909 947-2200
1801 S Archibald Ave Ontario (91761) *(P-4739)*

Parentsquare Inc .... D...... 888 496-3168
6144 Calle Real Ste 200a Goleta (93117) *(P-16344)*

Parex Usa Inc (DH) .... E...... 714 778-2266
2150 Eastridge Ave Riverside (92507) *(P-5573)*

Parex Usa Inc .... F...... 951 653-3549
2150 Eastridge Ave Riverside (92507) *(P-13669)*

Parexel International Corp .... C...... 818 254-7076
1560 E Chevy Chase Dr Ste 140 Glendale (91206) *(P-19870)*

PAREXEL INTERNATIONAL CORPORATION, Glendale *Also Called: Parexel International Corp (P-19870)*

Paris Precision LLC .... C...... 805 239-2500
1650 Ramada Dr Paso Robles (93446) *(P-6287)*

Parisa Lingerie & Swim Wear, Calabasas *Also Called: Afr Apparel International Inc (P-2386)*

Park Engineering and Mfg Co .... E...... 714 521-4660
6430 Roland St Buena Park (90621) *(P-7968)*

Park Hotels & Resorts Inc .... C...... 310 415-3340
9876 Wilshire Blvd Beverly Hills (90210) *(P-15297)*

Park Landscape Maint 1-2-3-4, Rcho Sta Marg *Also Called: Park West Landscape Maint Inc*
(P-211)

Park Management Group LLC .... A...... 404 350-9990
1825 Gillespie Wy Ste 101 North Hollywood (91601) *(P-15298)*

Park Marino Convalescent Ctr .... C...... 626 463-4105
2585 E Washington Blvd Pasadena (91107) *(P-18151)*

Park Place Ford LLC .... D...... 909 946-5555
555 W Foothill Blvd Upland (91786) *(P-13811)*

Park Steel Co Inc .... F...... 310 638-6101
515 E Pine St Compton (90222) *(P-6063)*

Park West Enterprises Inc .... F...... 909 383-8341
2586 Shenandoah Way San Bernardino (92407) *(P-1569)*

Park West Landscape Inc .... D...... 310 363-4100
13105 Crenshaw Blvd Hawthorne (90250) *(P-210)*

Park West Landscape Maint Inc (PA) .... B...... 949 546-8300
22421 Gilberto Ste A Rcho Sta Marg (92688) *(P-211)*

Parkco Building Company .... D...... 714 444-1441
24795 State Highway 74 Perris (92570) *(P-572)*

Parker Aerospace, Irvine *Also Called: Parker-Hannifin Corporation (P-9762)*

Parker Boiler Co, Commerce *Also Called: Sid E Parker Boiler Mfg Co Inc (P-6156)*

Parker Palm Springs LLC .... D...... 760 770-5000
4200 E Palm Canyon Dr Palm Springs (92264) *(P-15299)*

Parker Service Center, Buena Park *Also Called: Parker-Hannifin Corporation (P-4711)*

Parker Station, Calabasas *Also Called: Guarachi Wine Partners Inc (P-13477)*

Parker-Hannifin Corporation .... D...... 714 522-8840
8460 Kass Dr Buena Park (90621) *(P-4711)*

Parker-Hannifin Corporation .... E...... 562 404-1938
14087 Borate St Santa Fe Springs (90670) *(P-6149)*

Parker-Hannifin Corporation .... D...... 951 280-3800
221 Helicopter Cir Corona (92878) *(P-7713)*

Parker-Hannifin Corporation .... C...... 619 661-7000
7664 Panasonic Way San Diego (92154) *(P-7714)*

Parker-Hannifin Corporation .... C...... 310 608-5600
19610 S Rancho Way Rancho Dominguez (90220) *(P-8949)*

Parker-Hannifin Corporation .... C...... 949 833-3000
16666 Von Karman Ave Irvine (92606) *(P-9577)*

Parker-Hannifin Corporation .... C...... 949 833-3000
14300 Alton Pkwy Irvine (92618) *(P-9762)*

Parker-Hannifin Corporation .... D...... 805 484-8533
3800 Calle Tecate Camarillo (93012) *(P-9763)*

Parker-Hannifin Corporation .... C...... 949 465-4519
14300 Alton Pkwy Irvine (92618) *(P-12808)*

Parkhouse Tire, San Diego *Also Called: Parkhouse Tire Service Inc (P-13867)*

Parkhouse Tire, Bell Gardens *Also Called: Parkhouse Tire Service Inc (P-13868)*

Parkhouse Tire Service Inc .... E...... 858 565-8473
4660 Ruffner St San Diego (92111) *(P-13867)*

Parkhouse Tire Service Inc (PA) .... D...... 562 928-0421
6006 Shull St Bell Gardens (90201) *(P-13868)*

Parking Company of America .... D...... 562 862-2118
3165 Garfield Ave Commerce (90040) *(P-16997)*

Parking Concepts Inc .... D...... 626 577-8963
33 E Green St Pasadena (91105) *(P-16998)*

Parking Concepts Inc .... D...... 310 322-5008
12001 Vista Del Mar Playa Del Rey (90293) *(P-16999)*

Parking Concepts Inc .... D...... 310 208-1611
1036 Broxton Ave Los Angeles (90024) *(P-17000)*

Parking Concepts Inc .... C...... 213 746-5764
1801 Georgia St Los Angeles (90015) *(P-17001)*

Parking Concepts Inc .... D...... 310 821-1081
14110 Palawan Way Venice (90292) *(P-17002)*

Parking Concepts Inc .... D...... 213 623-2661
800 Wilshire Blvd Los Angeles (90017) *(P-17003)*

Parking Concepts Inc .... D...... 714 543-5725
1020 W Civic Center Dr Santa Ana (92703) *(P-17004)*

Parking Network Inc .... C...... 213 613-1500
1625 W Olympic Blvd Los Angeles (90015) *(P-1173)*

Parkinson Enterprises Inc .... D...... 714 626-0275
135 S State College Blvd Ste 625 Brea (92821) *(P-2895)*

Parks and Recreation Dept, Pomona *Also Called: County of Los Angeles (P-17422)*

Parkside Health & Wellness Ctr, El Cajon *Also Called: Parkside Healthcare Inc (P-18095)*

Parkside Healthcare Inc .... D...... 619 442-7744
444 W Lexington Ave El Cajon (92020) *(P-18095)*

Parkview Cmnty Hosp Med Ctr .... A...... 951 354-7404
3865 Jackson St Riverside (92503) *(P-18373)*

Parkview Jlian Cnvlescent Hosp .... C...... 661 831-9150
1801 Julian Ave Bakersfield (93304) *(P-18026)*

Parkview Julian LLC .... C...... 661 831-9150
1801 Julian Ave Bakersfield (93304) *(P-18027)*

Parkview Julian Healthcare Ctr, Bakersfield *Also Called: Parkview Julian LLC (P-18027)*

Parkway Bowl, El Cajon *Also Called: Newport Diversified Inc (P-16887)*

Parkwood Landscape Maint Inc .... D...... 818 988-9677
16443 Hart St Van Nuys (91406) *(P-212)*

Parmela Creamery, Moreno Valley *Also Called: Life Is Life LLC (P-1256)*

Parpro Technologies Inc .... C...... 714 545-8886
2700 S Fairview St Santa Ana (92704) *(P-8715)*

Parquet By Dian .... D...... 310 527-3779
16601 S Main St Gardena (90248) *(P-2578)*

Parrot Communications Intl Inc .... E...... 818 567-4700
25461 Rye Canyon Rd Valencia (91355) *(P-3470)*

Parrot Media Network, Valencia *Also Called: Parrot Communications Intl Inc (P-3470)*

Pars Industries Inc .... E...... 619 671-9663
8594 Siempre Viva Rd # C San Diego (92154) *(P-1021)*

Pars Publishing Corp 818 280-0540
6029 Fairview Pl Agoura Hills (91301) *(P-3653)*

PARSONS, Pasadena *Also Called: Parsons Constructors Inc (P-20077)*

Parsons Constructors Inc .... A...... 626 440-2000
100 W Walnut St Pasadena (91103) *(P-20077)*

Parsons Engrg Science Inc (DH) .... B...... 626 440-2000
100 W Walnut St Pasadena (91103) *(P-19664)*

Parsons Government Svcs Inc .... B...... 619 685-0085
525 B St Ste 1600 San Diego (92101) *(P-19665)*

Parsons Intl Cayman Islands .... A...... 626 440-6000
100 W Walnut St Pasadena (91124) *(P-19666)*

Parsons Service Corporation .... A...... 626 440-2000
100 W Walnut St Pasadena (91124) *(P-19667)*

Parsons Wtr Infrastructure Inc .... D...... 626 440-7000
100 W Walnut St Pasadena (91124) *(P-19668)*

Parter Medical Products Inc .... C...... 310 327-4417
17015 Kingsview Ave Carson (90746) *(P-12505)*

Partner Concepts Inc .... D...... 805 745-7199
811 Camino Viejo Santa Barbara (93108) *(P-3378)*

Partner Printing, Glendale *Also Called: Colour Concepts Inc (P-3537)*

Partners Capital Group, Santa Ana *Also Called: Partners Capital Group Inc (P-16900)*

Partners Capital Group Inc (PA) .... D...... 949 916-3900
201 Sandpointe Ave Ste 500 Santa Ana (92707) *(P-16900)*

Partners Information Tech (HQ) .... D...... 714 736-4487
888 S Disneyland Dr Ste 500 Anaheim (92802) *(P-16588)*

Partners Prsnnel - MGT Svcs LL .... A...... 805 689-8191
3820 State St Ste B Santa Barbara (93105) *(P-15876)*

Partnership Staffing Solutions, Santa Clarita *Also Called: Partnership Staffing Svcs Inc*
(P-15877)

Partnership Staffing Svcs Inc .... A...... 661 542-7074
19431 Soledad Canyon Rd A3 Santa Clarita (91351) *(P-15877)*

Partnrship Prmnt Ptro Chnse En, Long Beach *Also Called: Tidelands Oil Production Inc*
(P-268)

Parts Authority LLC .... C...... 805 676-3410
4277 Transport St Ventura (93003) *(P-12251)*

Parts Expediting and Dist Co .... F...... 562 944-3199
10805 Artesia Blvd Ste 112 Cerritos (90703) *(P-9438)*

Parylene Coating Services Inc .... E...... 281 391-7665
35 Argonaut Aliso Viejo (92656) *(P-6722)*

Pasadena Center Operating Co .... C...... 626 795-9311
300 E Green St Pasadena (91101) *(P-16901)*

Pasadena Convention Center, Pasadena *Also Called: Pasadena Center Operating Co*
(P-16901)

Pasadena Hospital Assn Ltd .... B...... 626 397-3322
716 S Fair Oaks Ave Pasadena (91105) *(P-18028)*

Pasadena Hospital Assn Ltd (PA) .... A...... 626 397-5000
100 W California Blvd Pasadena (91105) *(P-18374)*

Pasadena Hotel Dev Ventr LP .... D...... 626 449-4000
303 Cordova St Pasadena (91101) *(P-15300)*

Pasadena Madows Nursing Ctr LP .... D...... 626 796-1103
150 Bellefontaine St Pasadena (91105) *(P-18029)*

Pasadena Newspapers Inc (PA).....................C...... **626 578-6300**
605 E Huntington Dr Ste 100 Monrovia (91016) *(P-3315)*

Pasadena Star-News, Monrovia *Also Called: Pasadena Newspapers Inc (P-3315)*

Pascal Patisserie ....F...... 818 712-9375
21040 Victory Blvd Woodland Hills (91367) *(P-1489)*

Pasco, Buena Park *Also Called: Yeager Enterprises Corp (P-5547)*

Pasco Corporation of America ....E...... 503 289-6500
19191 S Vermont Ave Ste 420 Torrance (90502) *(P-1397)*

Pasea Hotel & Spa, Huntington Beach *Also Called: Pacific City Hotel LLC (P-15286)*

Paso Robles Tank Inc (HQ)........................... D...... **805 227-1641**
825 26th St Paso Robles (93446) *(P-5596)*

Pass, Orange *Also Called: Prototype & Short-Run Svcs Inc (P-6550)*

Passages, Malibu *Also Called: Grasshopper House Partners LLC (P-19085)*

Passages Malibu .... D...... 888 777-8525
6428 Meadows Ct Malibu (90265) *(P-18705)*

Passages Mlibu DRG Rhab Alchol, Malibu *Also Called: Passages Malibu (P-18705)*

Passion Planner LLC .... E...... 619 777-3451
1608 Grayson Ct Chula Vista (91913) *(P-3471)*

Passport Food Group LLC .... C...... 909 627-7312
2539 E Philadelphia St Ontario (91761) *(P-1967)*

Passport Foods (svc) LLC ....C...... 909 627-7312
2539 E Philadelphia St Ontario (91761) *(P-1968)*

Passport Technology Usa Inc .... E...... 818 957-5471
400 N Brand Blvd Ste 800 Glendale (91203) *(P-17144)*

Password Enterprise Inc .... E...... 562 988-8889
3200 E 29th St Long Beach (90806) *(P-14097)*

Passy-Muir Inc (PA)...................................E...... **949 833-8255**
17992 Mitchell S Ste 200 Irvine (92614) *(P-10691)*

Pasta Mia, Fullerton *Also Called: Nina Mia Inc (P-1955)*

Pasta Piccinini Inc .... E...... 626 798-0841
950 N Fair Oaks Ave Pasadena (91103) *(P-13387)*

Patagonia Inc (HQ).....................................B...... **805 643-8616**
259 W Santa Clara St Ventura (93001) *(P-2217)*

Patagonia Works (PA).................................B...... **805 643-8616**
259 W Santa Clara St Ventura (93001) *(P-13935)*

Path .... A...... 323 644-2216
340 N Madison Ave Los Angeles (90004) *(P-19122)*

Pathnostics, Irvine *Also Called: Cap Diagnostics LLC (P-18541)*

Pathology Inc .... B...... 310 769-0561
19951 Mariner Ave Ste 150 Torrance (90503) *(P-20217)*

Pathstone Family Office LLC .... D...... 888 750-7284
1900 Avenue Of The Stars Ste 970 Los Angeles (90067) *(P-14841)*

Pathstone Federal Street, Los Angeles *Also Called: Pathstone Family Office LLC (P-14841)*

Patient Business Services, San Diego *Also Called: Palomar Health (P-18362)*

Patient Safety Technologies Inc .... E...... 949 387-2277
15440 Laguna Canyon Rd Ste 150 Irvine (92618) *(P-10692)*

Patientpop Inc .... D...... 844 487-8399
214 Wilshire Blvd Santa Monica (90401) *(P-16345)*

Patina V, Covina *Also Called: Norlaine Inc (P-11257)*

Patio Guys, Santa Ana *Also Called: Guys Patio Inc (P-17077)*

Patric Communications Inc (PA).....................D...... **619 579-2898**
15215 Alton Pkwy Ste 200 Irvine (92618) *(P-924)*

Patricia Edwards, Commerce *Also Called: Superb Chair Corporation (P-2821)*

Patrick Industries Inc .... E...... 909 350-4440
13414 Slover Ave Fontana (92337) *(P-12360)*

Patriot Brokerage Inc .... D...... 910 227-4142
7840 Foothill Blvd Ste H Sunland (91040) *(P-11792)*

Patriot Logistics Services LLC .... D...... 443 994-9660
1520 Independence Way Vista (92084) *(P-11838)*

Patriot Products, Irwindale *Also Called: Pertronix Inc (P-9172)*

Patriot Wastewater LLC .... C...... 714 921-4545
314 W Freedom Ave Orange (92865) *(P-20370)*

Patrol and Security Services, Los Angeles *Also Called: Guardian Intl Solutions (P-16649)*

Patron Solutions LLC .... C...... 949 823-1700
5171 California Ave Ste 200 Irvine (92617) *(P-16346)*

Pattern Knitting Mills Inc .... E...... 310 801-1126
7963 Paramount Blvd Pico Rivera (90660) *(P-2075)*

Patterns Behavioral Services I .... F...... 657 444-9002
3230 E Imperial Hwy Ste 203 Brea (92821) *(P-7044)*

Patterson Kincaid LLC .... E...... 323 584-3559
5175 S Soto St Vernon (90058) *(P-2357)*

Patton State Hospital, Patton *Also Called: Califrnia Dept State Hospitals (P-18507)*

Paul Ferrante Inc .... E...... 310 854-4412
8464 Melrose Pl West Hollywood (90069) *(P-11262)*

Paul Hastings LLP (PA)...............................A...... **213 683-6000**
515 S Flower St Fl 25 Los Angeles (90071) *(P-18922)*

Paul Hastings LLP .... D...... 858 458-3000
4747 Executive Dr Ste 1200 San Diego (92121) *(P-18923)*

Paul Hubbs Construction Co Inc (PA).............F...... **951 360-3990**
542 W C St Colton (92324) *(P-402)*

Paul Mitchell, Santa Clarita *Also Called: Paul Mitchell John Systems (P-13061)*

Paul Mitchell John Systems (PA)...................D...... **800 793-8790**
20705 Centre Pointe Pkwy Santa Clarita (91350) *(P-13061)*

Paul R Briles Inc .... A...... 310 323-6222
1700 W 132nd St Gardena (90249) *(P-6451)*

Paul-Munroe Entertech Division, Brea *Also Called: Curtiss-Wright Flow Ctrl Corp (P-6789)*

Paulson Manufacturing Corp (PA)..................D...... **951 676-2451**
46752 Rainbow Canyon Rd Temecula (92592) *(P-10693)*

Pauma Band of Mission Indians .... B...... 760 742-2177
777 Pauma Reservation Rd Pauma Valley (92061) *(P-15301)*

Pavement Coatings Co .... C...... 805 647-0693
736 Mission Rock Rd Santa Paula (93060) *(P-12178)*

Pavement Coatings Co, Santa Paula *Also Called: Pavement Coatings Co (P-12178)*

Pavement Recycling Systems Inc .... D...... 661 948-5599
48028 90th St W Lancaster (93536) *(P-4663)*

Pavement Recycling Systems Inc (PA)............C...... **951 682-1091**
10240 San Sevaine Way Jurupa Valley (91752) *(P-12956)*

Paver Decor Masonry Inc .... E...... 909 795-8474
987 Calimesa Blvd Calimesa (92320) *(P-639)*

Pavilion At Ocean Point, The, San Diego *Also Called: Point Loma Rhblitation Ctr LLC (P-18032)*

Pavletich Elc Cmmnications Inc (PA)..............D...... **661 589-9473**
6308 Seven Seas Ave Bakersfield (93308) *(P-925)*

Pavletich Electric, Bakersfield *Also Called: Pavletich Elc Cmmnications Inc (P-925)*

Paw, Chatsworth *Also Called: Performance Automotive Whl Inc (P-14099)*

Pax Tag & Label Inc ....E...... 626 579-2000
9528 Rush St Ste C El Monte (91733) *(P-3795)*

Paychex Benefit Tech Inc .... C...... 800 322-7292
2385 Northside Dr Ste 100 San Diego (92108) *(P-11896)*

Paydarfar Industries Inc .... D...... 949 481-3267
26054 Acero Mission Viejo (92691) *(P-12430)*

Payden & Rygel Inc ....C...... **213 625-1900**
333 S Grand Ave Ste 4000 Los Angeles (90071) *(P-14426)*

Payment Cloud LLC .... D...... 800 988-2215
16501 Ventura Blvd Ste 300 Encino (91436) *(P-16510)*

Paymentcloud, Encino *Also Called: Payment Cloud LLC (P-16510)*

Payne Magnetics Corporation .... D...... 626 332-6207
854 W Front St Covina (91722) *(P-8950)*

Payoff, Torrance *Also Called: Happy Money Inc (P-14261)*

Payoff Inc .... E...... 949 430-0630
3200 Park Center Dr Ste 800 Costa Mesa (92626) *(P-14277)*

Pb Fasteners, Gardena *Also Called: Paul R Briles Inc (P-6451)*

Pb Fasteners, Gardena *Also Called: SPS Technologies LLC (P-12883)*

Pbb Inc .... E...... 909 923-6250
1311 E Philadelphia St Ontario (91761) *(P-12728)*

Pbc Companies, Anaheim *Also Called: Peterson Brothers Cnstr Inc (P-1084)*

Pbc Pavers Inc ....D...... 714 278-0488
2929 E White Star Ave Anaheim (92806) *(P-852)*

Pbf & E LLC .... E...... 213 427-0340
3014 W Olympic Blvd Los Angeles (90006) *(P-14030)*

Pbf Energy Western Region LLC (DH)............. E...... **973 455-7500**
3760 Kilroy Airport Way Ste 640 Long Beach (90806) *(P-4648)*

Pbi, Calabasas *Also Called: Picore Bristain Initiative Inc (P-16670)*

Pbk International LLC .... E...... 866 727-7195
717 E Compton Blvd Rancho Dominguez (90220) *(P-13946)*

PC Cleaner, Pasadena *Also Called: Realdefense LLC (P-16750)*

PC Mechanical Inc .... E...... 805 925-2888
2803 Industrial Pkwy Santa Maria (93455) *(P-378)*

Employee Codes: A=Over 500 employees, B=251-500
C=101-250, D=51-100, E=20-50, F=10-19, G=1-9

2024 Southern California
Business Directory and Buyers Guide

© Mergent Inc. 1-800-342-5647

1215

PC Recycle, Newbury Park *Also Called: Fc Management Services (P-7235)*

PC Specialists Inc (DH)...C....... **858 566-1900**
10620 Treena St Ste 300 San Diego (92131) *(P-12431)*

PC Vaughan Mfg Corp ....D....... 805 278-2555
1278 Mercantile St Oxnard (93030) *(P-5132)*

PC Woo Inc (PA)...D....... 323 887-8138
6443 E Slauson Ave Commerce (90040) *(P-12942)*

PCA Aerospace Inc ....E....... 714 901-5209
15282 Newsboy Cir Huntington Beach (92649) *(P-9549)*

PCA Aerospace Inc (PA)...D....... **714 841-1750**
17800 Gothard St Huntington Beach (92647) *(P-9764)*

PCA/Los Angeles 349, Vernon *Also Called: Packaging Corporation America (P-3122)*

PCA/South Gate 378, South Gate *Also Called: Packaging Corporation America (P-3121)*

Pcam LLC ....D....... 562 862-2118
3165 Garfield Ave Commerce (90040) *(P-17005)*

Pcamp, Commerce *Also Called: Parking Company of America (P-16997)*

Pcb Bancorp (PA)..C....... **213 210-2000**
3701 Wilshire Blvd Ste 100 Los Angeles (90010) *(P-14204)*

PCB BANK (HQ)...C....... **213 210-2000**
3701 Wilshire Blvd Ste 900 Los Angeles (90010) *(P-14205)*

Pcb Fabrication Facility, San Marcos *Also Called: Hughes Circuits Inc (P-8686)*

Pcbc Holdco Inc ....E....... 562 944-9549
12748 Florence Ave Santa Fe Springs (90670) *(P-12871)*

PCC Aerostructures, North Hollywood *Also Called: Klune Industries Inc (P-9732)*

PCC Network Solutions, Chatsworth *Also Called: Pacific Coast Cabling Inc (P-922)*

PCC Rollmet Inc ....D....... 949 221-5333
1822 Deere Ave Irvine (92606) *(P-5675)*

PCF Group LLC ....E....... 858 455-1274
8585 Miramar Pl San Diego (92121) *(P-13553)*

Pcfs 2000, San Diego *Also Called: Pcfs Solutions (P-13974)*

Pcfs Solutions ....E....... 714 674-0009
6353 El Cajon Blvd Ste 124 San Diego (92115) *(P-13974)*

Pch Sheet Metal & AC Inc ....F....... 949 361-9905
118 Calle De Los Molinos San Clemente (92672) *(P-6288)*

PCI, Riverside *Also Called: Pacific Consolidated Inds LLC (P-7403)*

PCI, San Diego *Also Called: Project Concern International (P-19128)*

PCI Holding Company Inc (PA)....................................E....... **951 479-0860**
12201 Magnolia Ave Riverside (92503) *(P-7405)*

PCI Industries Inc ....E....... 323 728-0004
6501 Potello St Commerce (90040) *(P-6289)*

PCI Industries Inc ....E....... 323 889-6770
700 S Vail Ave Montebello (90640) *(P-6290)*

PCI Industries Inc ....E....... 323 889-6770
700 S Vail Ave Montebello (90640) *(P-11263)*

PCI Industries Inc ....E....... 323 728-0004
6490 Fleet St Commerce (90040) *(P-11264)*

PCL Construction Services Inc ....C....... 858 657-3400
4690 Executive Dr Ste 100 San Diego (92121) *(P-573)*

PCL Construction Services Inc ....C....... 818 246-3481
655 N Central Ave Ste 1600 Glendale (91203) *(P-574)*

PCL Construction Services Inc ....D....... 818 509-7816
100 Universal City Plz North Hollywood (91608) *(P-575)*

PCL Industrial Services Inc ....B....... 661 832-3995
1500 S Union Ave Bakersfield (93307) *(P-576)*

Pcm, Laguna Woods *Also Called: Professional Cmnty MGT Cal Inc (P-14848)*

Pcm, Aliso Viejo *Also Called: Professional Community MGT Cal (P-20083)*

Pcm Inc (HQ)..A....... **310 354-5600**
200 N Pacific Coast Hwy Ste 1050 El Segundo (90245) *(P-14098)*

Pcs Link Inc ....B....... 949 655-5000
12424 Wilshire Blvd Ste 1030 Los Angeles (90025) *(P-20371)*

Pcs Mobile Solutions LLC ....D....... 323 567-2490
3534 Tweedy Blvd South Gate (90280) *(P-11897)*

Pcs Property Managment LLC ....E....... 310 231-1000
11859 Wilshire Blvd Ste 600 Los Angeles (90025) *(P-14842)*

Pct, Compton *Also Called: Pacific Contntl Textiles Inc (P-2105)*

Pct-Gw Carbide Tools Usa Inc ....F....... 562 921-7898
13701 Excelsior Dr Santa Fe Springs (90670) *(P-3903)*

Pcv Murcor Real Estate Svcs, Pomona *Also Called: Murcor Inc (P-14835)*

Pcx Aerosystems - Santa Ana, Santa Ana *Also Called: Integral Aerospace LLC (P-9721)*

Pd Group ....E....... 760 674-3028
41945 Boardwalk Ste L Palm Desert (92211) *(P-11144)*

Pdc LLC ....E....... 626 334-5000
4675 Vinita Ct Chino (91710) *(P-7086)*

PDC A Bowman Company, San Diego *Also Called: Project Design Consultants LLC (P-20372)*

Pdc-Identicard, Valencia *Also Called: Precision Dynamics Corporation (P-3173)*

Pdf Print Communications Inc (PA)..............................D....... **562 426-6978**
2630 E 28th St Long Beach (90755) *(P-3654)*

PDM Solutions Inc ....E....... 858 348-1000
8451 Miralani Dr Ste J San Diego (92126) *(P-8716)*

Pdma Ventures Inc ....E....... 714 777-8770
22951 La Palma Ave Yorba Linda (92887) *(P-10761)*

PDQ Engineering Inc ....E....... 805 482-1334
1199 Avenida Acaso Ste F Camarillo (93012) *(P-7969)*

Pds, Compton *Also Called: Pacific Drayage Services LLC (P-11501)*

Pds, Irvine *Also Called: Pacific Dental Services LLC (P-17843)*

Pds Defense Inc ....C....... 214 647-9600
3100 S Harbor Blvd Ste 135 Santa Ana (92704) *(P-15878)*

Pdu Lad Corporation (PA)...E....... **626 442-7711**
11165 Valley Spring Ln North Hollywood (91602) *(P-6723)*

Pe Facility Solutions LLC (PA).....................................D....... **858 467-0202**
4217 Ponderosa Ave Ste A San Diego (92123) *(P-15733)*

Pea Soup Andersen's Restaurant, Buellton *Also Called: Carpenters Southwest ADM Corp (P-13991)*

Peabody Engineering, Corona *Also Called: Peabody Engineering & Sup Inc (P-7255)*

Peabody Engineering & Sup Inc ....E....... 951 734-7711
13435 Estelle St Corona (92879) *(P-7255)*

Peach Inc ....C....... 323 654-2333
1311 N Highland Ave Los Angeles (90028) *(P-11537)*

Peaches, Chatsworth *Also Called: Med Couture Inc (P-2180)*

Peak Seasons, Riverside *Also Called: Tom Leonard Investment Co Inc (P-11296)*

Pearl Management Group Inc ....E....... 818 217-0218
14950 Delano St Van Nuys (91411) *(P-4197)*

Pearpoint Inc ....E....... 760 343-7350
39740 Garand Ln Ste B Palm Desert (92211) *(P-8560)*

Pearson Dental Supplies Inc (PA)................................C....... **818 362-2600**
13161 Telfair Ave Sylmar (91342) *(P-12506)*

Pearson Ford Co (PA)...C....... **877 743-0421**
5900 Sycamore Canyon Blvd Riverside (92507) *(P-13812)*

Pearson Surgical Supply Co, Sylmar *Also Called: Pearson Dental Supplies Inc (P-12506)*

PEC, Torrance *Also Called: Products Engineering Corp (P-5889)*

PEC Tool, Torrance *Also Called: Fun Properties Inc (P-5880)*

Pecc, San Diego *Also Called: Precision Engine Controls Corp (P-6884)*

Pechanga Development Corp ....A....... 951 695-4655
45000 Pechanga Pkwy Temecula (92592) *(P-15302)*

Pechanga Resort & Casino, Temecula *Also Called: Pechanga Development Corp (P-15302)*

Pecific Grinding, Fullerton *Also Called: Kryler Corp (P-6634)*

Peck Jones Construction, Santa Monica *Also Called: Jones Brothers Cnstr Corp (P-561)*

Pecs, Rancho Cucamonga *Also Called: Professnal Elec Cnstr Svcs Inc (P-929)*

Pedavena Mould and Die Co Inc ....E....... 310 327-2814
12464 Mccann Dr Santa Fe Springs (90670) *(P-7970)*

Pedco, Cerritos *Also Called: Parts Expediting and Dist Co (P-9438)*

Pedego LLC (PA)..E....... **800 646-8604**
11310 Slater Ave Fountain Valley (92708) *(P-14064)*

Pedego Electric Bikes, Fountain Valley *Also Called: Pedego LLC (P-14064)*

Pedi, San Diego *Also Called: Providien Injction Molding Inc (P-5169)*

Pedi Center, Bakersfield *Also Called: Dignity Health (P-18242)*

Pediatric & Family Medical Ctr ....C....... 213 342-3325
1530 S Olive St Los Angeles (90015) *(P-17735)*

Pediatric Cancer Research, Orange *Also Called: Childrens Healthcare Cal (P-17617)*

Pediatric Nrology Therapeutics ....D....... 858 304-6440
7090 Miratech Dr San Diego (92121) *(P-17736)*

Pediatric Therapy Network ....C....... 310 328-0276
1815 W 213th St Ste 100 Torrance (90501) *(P-18706)*

Peei, Los Angeles *Also Called: Playboy Enterprises Intl Inc (P-3475)*

Peerigon Medical Distribution, El Toro *Also Called: P M D Holding Corp (P-12503)*

Peerless Building Maint Co, Chatsworth *Also Called: Tuttle Family Enterprises Inc (P-15751)*

Peerless Injection Molding LLC ....E....... 714 689-1920
14321 Corp Dr Garden Grove (92843) *(P-5133)*

Peerless Maintenance Svc Inc ....B....... 714 871-3380
1100 S Euclid St La Habra (90631) *(P-15734)*

Mergent email: customerrelations@mergent.com
1216

2024 Southern California
Business Directory and Buyers Guide

(P-0000) Products & Services Section entry number
(PA)=Parent Co (HQ)=Headquarters (DH)=Div Headquarters

Peerless Materials Company ....E...... 323 266-0313
4442 E 26th St Vernon (90058) *(P-4367)*

Pegasus Building Svcs Co Inc ....B...... 858 444-2290
7966 Arjons Dr Ste A San Diego (92126) *(P-15735)*

Pegasus Elite Aviation Inc ....C...... 818 742-6666
7943 Woodley Ave Van Nuys (91406) *(P-11682)*

Pegasus Foods, Los Angeles *Also Called: Astrochef LLC (P-1384)*

Pegasus HM Hlth Care A Cal Cor ....D...... 818 551-1932
505 N Brand Blvd Ste 1000 Glendale (91203) *(P-18633)*

Pegasus Home Health Services, Glendale *Also Called: Pegasus HM Hlth Care A Cal Cor (P-18633)*

Pegasus Interprint Inc ....E...... 800 926-9873
7111 Hayvenhurst Ave Van Nuys (91406) *(P-3655)*

Pegasus One, Fullerton *Also Called: Aspirez Inc (P-15969)*

Pegasus Squire Inc ....D...... 866 208-6837
12021 Wilshire Blvd Ste 770 Los Angeles (90025) *(P-16589)*

Peggs Company Inc (PA)...**D...... 253 584-9548**
4851 Felspar St Riverside (92509) *(P-17145)*

Peking Noodle Co Inc ....E...... 323 223-0897
1514 N San Fernando Rd Los Angeles (90065) *(P-1843)*

Pelco By Schneider Electric, Chino *Also Called: Schneider Electric Usa Inc (P-11611)*

Pelican, Torrance *Also Called: Pelican Products Inc (P-8379)*

Pelican Biopharma LLC ....F...... 310 326-4700
23215 Early Ave Torrance (90505) *(P-4198)*

Pelican Products Inc (PA)...**C...... 310 326-4700**
23215 Early Ave Torrance (90505) *(P-8379)*

Pelomar Family YMCA, Encinitas *Also Called: YMCA of San Diego County (P-19479)*

Peltek Holdings Inc ....E...... 949 855-8010
35 Argonaut Ste A1 Laguna Hills (92656) *(P-6724)*

Pem, Buena Park *Also Called: Park Engineering and Mfg Co (P-7968)*

Pemko Manufacturing Co ....C...... 800 283-9988
4226 Transport St Ventura (93003) *(P-6115)*

Pencil Grip Inc (PA)..**F...... 310 315-3545**
21200 Superior St Ste A Chatsworth (91311) *(P-3222)*

Pendarvis Manufacturing Inc ....E...... 714 992-0950
1808 N American St Anaheim (92801) *(P-7971)*

Pendry San Diego, San Diego *Also Called: Rgc Gaslamp LLC (P-15325)*

Pendry, The, Irvine *Also Called: Kt Hotels LLC (P-15214)*

Penfield & Smith, Santa Barbara *Also Called: Penfield & Smith Engineers Inc (P-19669)*

Penfield & Smith Engineers Inc ....D...... 805 963-9532
111 E Victoria St Santa Barbara (93101) *(P-19669)*

Pengcheng Aluminum Enterprise Inc USA ....E...... 909 598-7933
19605 E Walnut Dr N Walnut (91789) *(P-5705)*

Penguin Natural Foods Inc ....E...... 323 488-6000
5659 Mansfield Way Bell (90201) *(P-1969)*

Penguin Natural Foods Inc (PA)...................................**E...... 323 727-7980**
4400 Alcoa Ave Vernon (90058) *(P-1970)*

Penguin Pumps Incorporated ....E...... 818 504-2391
7932 Ajay Dr Sun Valley (91352) *(P-7285)*

Penhall Holding Company ....C...... 714 772-6450
1801 W Penhall Way Anaheim (92801) *(P-1083)*

Peninsula Beverly Hill's, Beverly Hills *Also Called: Belvedere Hotel Partnership (P-15090)*

Peninsula Beverly Hills, The, Beverly Hills *Also Called: Belvedere Partnership (P-15091)*

Peninsula Family YMCA Sunshine, San Diego *Also Called: YMCA of San Diego County (P-19484)*

Peninsula Publishing Inc ....F...... 949 631-1307
1602 Monrovia Ave Newport Beach (92663) *(P-3472)*

Penn Elcom Inc (HQ)...**E...... 714 230-6200**
7465 Lampson Ave Garden Grove (92841) *(P-12729)*

Penn Elcom Hardware, Garden Grove *Also Called: Penn Elcom Inc (P-12729)*

Penn Engineering Components ....E...... 818 503-1511
29045 Avenue Penn Valencia (91355) *(P-12730)*

Pennant Group Inc ....B...... 714 978-2534
1800 W Culver Ave Orange (92868) *(P-18030)*

Penney Lawn Service Inc ....D...... 661 587-4788
4000 Allen Rd Bakersfield (93314) *(P-213)*

Penney Opco LLC ....C...... 626 445-6454
400 S Baldwin Ave Lowr Arcadia (91007) *(P-13681)*

Penney Opco LLC ....C...... 626 960-3711
1203 Plaza Dr West Covina (91790) *(P-13682)*

Penney Opco LLC ....C...... 805 497-6811
280 W Hillcrest Dr Thousand Oaks (91360) *(P-13683)*

Pennoyer-Dodge Co ....E...... 818 547-2100
6650 San Fernando Rd Glendale (91201) *(P-7123)*

Penny & Giles Drive Technology, Brea *Also Called: Curtiss-Wrght Cntrls Intgrted (P-10642)*

Penny Lane Centers (PA)...**B...... 818 892-3423**
15305 Rayen St North Hills (91343) *(P-19338)*

Penny Lawn Service, Bakersfield *Also Called: Penney Lawn Service Inc (P-213)*

Pennymac, Agoura Hills *Also Called: Private Nat Mrtg Accptance LLC (P-14347)*

Pennymac Corp ....B...... 818 878-8416
27001 Agoura Rd Agoura Hills (91301) *(P-14362)*

Pennysaver USA Publishing LLC ....A...... 866 640-3900
2830 Orbiter St Brea (92821) *(P-3473)*

Pensinmark Rtirement Group LLC ....C...... 805 456-6260
24 E Cota St Ste 200 Santa Barbara (93101) *(P-20218)*

Penske, West Covina *Also Called: Penske Motor Group LLC (P-16971)*

Penske Business Media LLC ....E...... 310 321-5000
11175 Santa Monica Blvd Los Angeles (90025) *(P-3379)*

Penske Corporation ....C...... 805 983-3788
6551 Ventura Blvd Ventura (93003) *(P-16970)*

Penske Ford Chula Vista, Chula Vista *Also Called: Rp Automotive II Inc (P-16974)*

Penske Honda Ontario, Ontario *Also Called: Ontario Automotive LLC (P-13808)*

Penske Motor Group LLC ....B...... 626 859-1200
2010 E Garvey Ave S West Covina (91791) *(P-16971)*

Penske Motorcars, West Covina *Also Called: P A Motorcars LLC (P-13809)*

Penske Transportation MGT LLC ....D...... 844 847-9518
2280 Wardlow Cir Corona (92878) *(P-16972)*

Pentacon Inc ....B...... 818 727-8000
21123 Nordhoff St Chatsworth (91311) *(P-12872)*

Pentair Equipment Protection, San Diego *Also Called: Schroff Inc (P-17072)*

Pentair Water Treatment, Costa Mesa *Also Called: Shurflo LLC (P-7290)*

Pentel of America Ltd (HQ)..**C...... 310 320-3831**
2715 Columbia St Torrance (90503) *(P-12996)*

Penton Overseas Inc ....F...... 760 809-6030
2310 Camino Vida Roble Ste 105 Carlsbad (92011) *(P-13497)*

Pentrate Metal Processing ....E...... 323 269-2121
3517 E Olympic Blvd Los Angeles (90023) *(P-6647)*

Penwal Industries Inc ....D...... 909 466-1555
10611 Acacia St Rancho Cucamonga (91730) *(P-577)*

People Pets and Vets LLC ....D...... 909 453-4213
10986 Sierra Ave Ste 400 Fontana (92337) *(P-124)*

People Pets and Vets LLC ....C...... 909 329-2860
16055 Sierra Lakes Pkwy Ste 100 Fontana (92336) *(P-125)*

People Concern ....C...... 310 883-1222
1751 Cloverfield Blvd Santa Monica (90404) *(P-19123)*

People Concern ....C...... 310 450-0650
1751 Cloverfield Blvd Santa Monica (90404) *(P-19124)*

People Connect, San Diego *Also Called: Control Group Media Co LLC (P-15533)*

People Creating Success Inc ....D...... 805 644-9480
380 Arneill Rd Camarillo (93010) *(P-17737)*

People Creating Success Inc ....D...... 661 225-9700
1607 E Palmdale Blvd Ste H Palmdale (93550) *(P-19125)*

People Creating Success Inc ....D...... 805 692-5290
5350 Hollister Ave Ste I Santa Barbara (93111) *(P-19126)*

PEOPLE'S CARE INC., Victorville *Also Called: Peoples Care Inc (P-18634)*

PEOPLE'S CARE INC., Santa Fe Springs *Also Called: Peoples Care Inc (P-19224)*

Peoples Care Inc ....C...... 760 962-1900
13901 Amargosa Rd Ste 101 Victorville (92392) *(P-18634)*

Peoples Care Inc ....C...... 562 320-0174
12215 Telegraph Rd Ste 208 Santa Fe Springs (90670) *(P-19224)*

Pep Creations, San Diego *Also Called: Pacific Event Productions Inc (P-15520)*

Pep West, Inc., San Diego *Also Called: Schroff Inc (P-7289)*

Pepitastore, El Segundo *Also Called: Scalefast Inc (P-11901)*

Peppermint Ridge (PA)...**D...... 951 273-7320**
825 Magnolia Ave Corona (92879) *(P-19294)*

Pepsi-Cola, Bakersfield *Also Called: Pepsi-Cola Btlg Co Bakersfield (P-1709)*

Pepsi-Cola, Mojave *Also Called: Pepsi-Cola Metro Btlg Co Inc (P-1710)*

Pepsi-Cola, San Fernando *Also Called: Pepsi-Cola Metro Btlg Co Inc (P-1711)*

Pepsi-Cola, Carson *Also Called: Pepsi-Cola Metro Btlg Co Inc (P-1714)*

Employee Codes: A=Over 500 employees, B=251-500
C=101-250, D=51-100, E=20-50, F=10-19, G=1-9

2024 Southern California
Business Directory and Buyers Guide

© Mergent Inc. 1-800-342-5647

1217

Pepsi-Cola, Buena Park *Also Called: Pepsi-Cola Metro Btlg Co Inc (P-1716)*

Pepsi-Cola, Riverside *Also Called: Pepsi-Cola Metro Btlg Co Inc (P-12764)*

Pepsi-Cola Bottling Group .... D....... 661 635-1100
  215 E 21st St Bakersfield (93305) *(P-1708)*

Pepsi-Cola Btlg Co Bakersfield ....E...... 661 327-9992
  215 E 21st St Bakersfield (93305) *(P-1709)*

Pepsi-Cola Metro Btlg Co Inc ....E...... 661 824-2051
  2471 Nadeau St Mojave (93501) *(P-1710)*

Pepsi-Cola Metro Btlg Co Inc ....D...... 818 898-3829
  1200 Arroyo St San Fernando (91340) *(P-1711)*

Pepsi-Cola Metro Btlg Co Inc ....E...... 805 739-2160
  2345 Thompson Way Santa Maria (93455) *(P-1712)*

Pepsi-Cola Metro Btlg Co Inc ....C...... 858 560-6735
  10057 Marathon Pkwy Lakeside (92040) *(P-1713)*

Pepsi-Cola Metro Btlg Co Inc ....C...... 310 327-4222
  19700 Figueroa St Carson (90745) *(P-1714)*

Pepsi-Cola Metro Btlg Co Inc ....D...... 949 643-5700
  27717 Aliso Creek Rd Aliso Viejo (92656) *(P-1715)*

Pepsi-Cola Metro Btlg Co Inc ....C...... 714 522-9635
  6261 Caballero Blvd Buena Park (90620) *(P-1716)*

Pepsi-Cola Metro Btlg Co Inc ....E...... 951 697-3200
  6659 Sycamore Canyon Blvd Riverside (92507) *(P-12764)*

Pepsico ....E...... 562 818-9429
  1650 E Central Ave San Bernardino (92408) *(P-1717)*

Pepsico, Riverside *Also Called: Bottling Group LLC (P-1688)*

Pepsico, Bakersfield *Also Called: Pepsi-Cola Bottling Group (P-1708)*

Pepsico, Santa Maria *Also Called: Pepsi-Cola Metro Btlg Co Inc (P-1712)*

Pepsico, Lakeside *Also Called: Pepsi-Cola Metro Btlg Co Inc (P-1713)*

Pepsico, Aliso Viejo *Also Called: Pepsi-Cola Metro Btlg Co Inc (P-1715)*

Pepsico, San Bernardino *Also Called: Pepsico (P-1717)*

Pepsico, Beverly Hills *Also Called: Pepsico Inc (P-1718)*

Pepsico, Baldwin Park *Also Called: Pepsico Inc (P-1719)*

Pepsico, Walnut *Also Called: Pepsico Inc (P-1720)*

Pepsico Inc ....F...... 323 785-2820
  8530 Wilshire Blvd Ste 300 Beverly Hills (90211) *(P-1718)*

Pepsico Inc ....E...... 626 338-5531
  4416 Azusa Canyon Rd Baldwin Park (91706) *(P-1719)*

Pepsico Inc ....E...... 909 718-8229
  20445 Business Pkwy Walnut (91789) *(P-1720)*

Peraton Technology Svcs Inc ....F...... 571 313-6000
  2750 Womble Rd Ste 202 San Diego (92106) *(P-19939)*

Perera Cnstr & Design Inc ....E...... 909 484-6350
  2890 Inland Empire Blvd Ste 102 Ontario (91764) *(P-237)*

Perfect Banner, The, Aliso Viejo *Also Called: Perfect Impression Inc (P-16902)*

Perfect Bar LLC ....C...... 866 628-8548
  3931 Sorrento Valley Blvd Ste 100 San Diego (92121) *(P-13388)*

Perfect Choice Mfrs Inc ....E...... 714 792-0322
  17819 Gillette Ave Irvine (92614) *(P-11265)*

Perfect Impression Inc ....E...... 949 305-0797
  27111 Aliso Creek Rd Ste 145 Aliso Viejo (92656) *(P-16902)*

Perfect Snacks, San Diego *Also Called: Perfect Bar LLC (P-13388)*

Performance Aluminum, Ontario *Also Called: Performance Aluminum Products (P-5765)*

Performance Aluminum Products ....E...... 909 391-4131
  520 S Palmetto Ave Ontario (91762) *(P-5765)*

Performance Automotive Whl Inc (PA)..D....... 805 499-8973
  20235 Nordhoff St Chatsworth (91311) *(P-14099)*

Performance Building Services ....C...... 949 364-4364
  22642 Lambert St Ste 409 Lake Forest (92630) *(P-15736)*

Performance Cleanroom Services, Lake Forest *Also Called: Performance Building Services (P-15736)*

Performance Composites Inc ....C...... 310 328-6661
  1418 S Alameda St Compton (90221) *(P-5328)*

Performance Contracting Inc ....D...... 913 310-7120
  4955 E Landon Dr Anaheim (92807) *(P-1138)*

Performance Forge Inc ....E...... 323 722-3460
  7401 Telegraph Rd Montebello (90640) *(P-6469)*

Performance Health Med Group ....D...... 714 740-1778
  13252 Garden Grove Blvd Ste 112 Garden Grove (92843) *(P-18788)*

Performance Machine, La Palma *Also Called: Performance Machine Inc (P-9880)*

Performance Machine Inc ....C...... 714 523-3000
  6892 Marlin Cir La Palma (90623) *(P-9880)*

Performance Machine Tech Inc ....E...... 661 294-8617
  25141 Avenue Stanford Valencia (91355) *(P-7972)*

Performance Materials Corp (HQ)...D....... 805 482-1722
  1150 Calle Suerte Camarillo (93012) *(P-3961)*

Performance Motorsports Inc ....B...... 714 898-9763
  5100 Campus Dr Ste 100 Newport Beach (92660) *(P-7702)*

Performance Nissan, Duarte *Also Called: Gpi Ca-Niii Inc (P-13773)*

Performance Plastics Inc ....D...... 714 343-3928
  7919 Saint Andrews Ave San Diego (92154) *(P-9765)*

Performance Powder Inc ....E...... 714 632-0600
  2940 E La Jolla St Ste A Anaheim (92806) *(P-6725)*

Performance Sheets LLC ....C...... 626 333-0195
  440 Baldwin Park Blvd City Of Industry (91746) *(P-1050)*

Performance Team, El Segundo *Also Called: Maersk Whsng Dist Svcs USA LLC (P-11780)*

Performance Water Products Inc ....F...... 714 736-0137
  6902 Aragon Cir Buena Park (90620) *(P-14111)*

Performing Arts Ctr Los Angles ....C...... 213 972-7512
  135 N Grand Ave Ste 314 Los Angeles (90012) *(P-17323)*

Performnce Engineered Pdts Inc ....E...... 909 594-7487
  3270 Pomona Blvd Pomona (91768) *(P-5134)*

Perimeter Solutions LP ....E...... 909 983-0772
  10667 Jersey Blvd Rancho Cucamonga (91730) *(P-3904)*

Perm Light, Tustin *Also Called: Permlight Products Inc (P-8862)*

Permanente Medical Group Inc ....A...... 310 325-5111
  25825 Vermont Ave Harbor City (90710) *(P-17738)*

Permaswage USA, Gardena *Also Called: Designed Metal Connections Inc (P-9673)*

Permlight Products Inc ....E...... 714 508-0729
  420 W 6th St Tustin (92780) *(P-8862)*

Perricone Juices, Beaumont *Also Called: Beaumont Juice Inc (P-1336)*

Perrin Bernard Supowitz LLC (HQ)...C....... 323 981-2800
  5496 Lindbergh Ln Bell (90201) *(P-13022)*

Perrin Craft, San Marcos *Also Called: Dispensing Dynamics Intl Inc (P-5010)*

Perris Valley Cmnty Hosp LLC ....C...... 909 581-6400
  10841 White Oak Ave Rancho Cucamonga (91730) *(P-18375)*

Perry Coast Construction Inc ....C...... 951 774-0677
  3811 Wacker Dr Jurupa Valley (91752) *(P-578)*

Perry Ford, Poway *Also Called: Perry Ford of Poway LLC (P-13813)*

Perry Ford of Poway LLC ....D...... 858 748-1400
  12740 Poway Rd Poway (92064) *(P-13813)*

Perry Industries, Corona *Also Called: M & O Perry Industries Inc (P-7352)*

Perseption, Vernon *Also Called: W & W Concept Inc (P-2383)*

Persian Bks Englsh-Prsian Bks, Pacoima *Also Called: Ketab Corporation (P-14067)*

Person & Covey Inc ....E...... 818 937-5000
  616 Allen Ave Glendale (91201) *(P-4443)*

Personnel Concepts, Ontario *Also Called: Aio Acquisition Inc (P-3425)*

Personnel Plus Inc ....C...... 562 712-5490
  12052 Imperial Hwy Ste 200 Norwalk (90650) *(P-15934)*

Perspire Sauna Studio, Newport Beach *Also Called: Heatwave LLC (P-17400)*

Pertronix Inc ....E...... 909 599-5955
  15601 Cypress Ave Unit B Irwindale (91706) *(P-9172)*

Pet Partners Inc (PA)...C....... 951 279-9888
  450 N Sheridan St Corona (92878) *(P-11266)*

Petco, San Diego *Also Called: Petco Animal Supplies Inc (P-11823)*

Petco Animal Supplies Inc (DH)..B....... 858 453-7845
  10850 Via Frontera San Diego (92127) *(P-11823)*

Petco Health & Wellness Co Inc 858 453-7845
  10850 Via Frontera San Diego (92127) *(P-14144)*

Petco Park, San Diego *Also Called: City of San Diego (P-17367)*

Petdesk ....D...... 202 431-3045
  2044 1st Ave Ste 200 San Diego (92101) *(P-16094)*

Peter Brasseler Holdings LLC ....D...... 805 658-2643
  4837 Mcgrath St Ventura (93003) *(P-10587)*

Peter Brasseler Holdings LLC ....D...... 805 650-5209
  4837 Mcgrath St Ste J Ventura (93003) *(P-12507)*

Peter Cohen Companies, Los Angeles *Also Called: Piet Retief Inc (P-2359)*

Peter Grimm Ltd ....E...... 800 664-4287
  550 Rancheros Dr San Marcos (92069) *(P-2403)*

Peter Pepper Products Inc (PA)..D....... 310 639-0390
  17929 S Susana Rd Compton (90221) *(P-8620)*

Peter Rabbit Farms, Coachella *Also Called: Amazing Coachella Inc (P-6)*

Mergent email: customerrelations@mergent.com
1218

2024 Southern California
Business Directory and Buyers Guide

(P-0000) Products & Services Section entry number
(PA)=Parent Co (HQ)=Headquarters (DH)=Div Headquarters

Peter Wylan DDS .... D...... 562 925-3765
  10318 Rosecrans Ave Bellflower (90706) *(P-17845)*

Peterson Bros Construction, Anaheim *Also Called: Pbc Pavers Inc (P-852)*

Peterson Brothers Cnstr Inc .... A...... 714 278-0488
  2929 E White Star Ave Anaheim (92806) *(P-1084)*

Peterson's Spices, Pico Rivera *Also Called: GPde Slva Spces Incrporation (P-1908)*

Petes Road Service Inc (PA).. D...... 714 446-1207
  2230 E Orangethorpe Ave Fullerton (92831) *(P-12272)*

Petit Ermitage, West Hollywood *Also Called: Valadon Hotel LLC (P-15402)*

Petro-Lud Inc .... E...... 661 747-4779
  12625 Jomani Dr Ste 104 Bakersfield (93312) *(P-287)*

Petrochem, Long Beach *Also Called: Petrochem Insulation Inc (P-991)*

Petrochem Insulation Inc .... C...... 310 638-6663
  3117 E South St Long Beach (90805) *(P-991)*

Petrochem Manufacturing Inc .... D...... 760 603-0961
  6168 Innovation Way Carlsbad (92009) *(P-4664)*

Petrosian Esthetic Entps LLC .... C...... 818 391-8231
  2919 W Burbank Blvd Burbank (91505) *(P-15485)*

Pexco Aerospace Inc .... E...... 714 894-9922
  5451 Argosy Ave Huntington Beach (92649) *(P-3962)*

Pezeme, Los Angeles *Also Called: Choon Inc (P-2280)*

Pf Bakeries Llc .... E...... 858 263-4863
  1375 Fayette St El Cajon (92020) *(P-13389)*

PF Candle Co .... E...... 323 284-8431
  2213 W Sunset Blvd Los Angeles (90026) *(P-11267)*

Pf Candle Co, Commerce *Also Called: Pommes Frites Candle Co (P-11271)*

Pfenex, San Diego *Also Called: Pfenex Inc (P-4199)*

Pfenex Inc .... D...... 858 352-4400
  10790 Roselle St San Diego (92121) *(P-4199)*

Pff Bancorp Inc (PA).. A...... 213 683-6393
  2058 N Mills Ave Ste 139 Claremont (91711) *(P-14219)*

Pfitech, Huntington Beach *Also Called: Precise Fit Limited One LLC (P-15880)*

Pfizer, San Diego *Also Called: Pfizer Inc (P-4200)*

Pfizer, San Diego *Also Called: Pfizer Inc (P-4201)*

Pfizer Inc .... D...... 858 622-3000
  10777 Science Center Dr San Diego (92121) *(P-4200)*

Pfizer Inc .... E...... 858 622-3001
  10646 Science Center Dr San Diego (92121) *(P-4201)*

Pfp, Chula Vista *Also Called: Precision Fiber Products Inc (P-5747)*

Pfs, Sylmar *Also Called: Professnal Fnshg Systems Sups (P-6548)*

Pg Usa LLC .... D...... 310 954-1040
  5150 W Goldleaf Cir Los Angeles (90056) *(P-13688)*

PG&e, San Luis Obispo *Also Called: Pacific Gas and Electric Co (P-12034)*

PG&e, Avila Beach *Also Called: Pacific Gas and Electric Co (P-12035)*

PG&e, Pismo Beach *Also Called: Pacific Gas and Electric Co (P-12036)*

PG&e, Templeton *Also Called: Pacific Gas and Electric Co (P-12037)*

PG&e, Hinkley *Also Called: Pacific Gas and Electric Co (P-12038)*

PG&e, Needles *Also Called: Pacific Gas and Electric Co (P-12039)*

PG&e, Bakersfield *Also Called: Pacific Gas and Electric Co (P-12040)*

Pga West By Wldorf Astoria MGT, La Quinta *Also Called: Msr Resort Lodging Tenant LLC (P-15258)*

Pgac Corp (PA).. D...... 858 560-8213
  9630 Ridgehaven Ct Ste B San Diego (92123) *(P-3155)*

Pgc Construction Inc .... E...... 760 549-4121
  41731 Corporate Center Ct Murrieta (92562) *(P-450)*

Pgc Scientiifics, San Diego *Also Called: Molecular Bioproducts Svc Corp (P-12530)*

Pgi, San Diego *Also Called: Pgac Corp (P-3155)*

Pgi, City Of Industry *Also Called: Pgi Pacific Graphics Intl (P-3656)*

Pgi Pacific Graphics Intl .... E...... 626 336-7707
  14938 Nelson Ave City Of Industry (91744) *(P-3656)*

PH Design, Commerce *Also Called: Pacific Hospitality Design Inc (P-2935)*

Phamatech Incorporated .... C...... 888 635-5840
  15175 Innovation Dr San Diego (92128) *(P-19980)*

Phaostron Instr Electronic Co .... D...... 626 969-6801
  717 N Coney Ave Azusa (91702) *(P-8128)*

Phaostron Instr Electronic Co, Azusa *Also Called: Phaostron Instr Electronic Co (P-8128)*

Pharma Pac, Grover Beach *Also Called: H J Harkins Company Inc (P-4128)*

Pharmaceutic Litho Label Inc .... D...... 805 285-5162
  3990 Royal Ave Simi Valley (93063) *(P-4202)*

Pharmachem Laboratories LLC .... E...... 714 630-6000
  2929 E White Star Ave Anaheim (92806) *(P-1282)*

PHARMACHEM LABORATORIES, LLC, Anaheim *Also Called: Pharmachem Laboratories LLC (P-1282)*

Pharmaco-Kinesis Corporation .... E...... 310 641-2700
  10604 S La Cienega Blvd Inglewood (90304) *(P-10588)*

Pharmaron Inc .... A...... 949 788-0586
  6 Venture Ste 250 Irvine (92618) *(P-19871)*

Pharmaskincare, Sun Valley *Also Called: Spa De Soleil Inc (P-13070)*

Pharmatek, San Diego *Also Called: Catalent Pharma Solutions Inc (P-4086)*

Pharmavite LLC (DH) .... B...... 818 221-6200
  8531 Fallbrook Ave West Hills (91304) *(P-4011)*

Pharmion Corporation .... E...... 858 335-5744
  12481 High Bluff Dr Ste 200 San Diego (92130) *(P-4203)*

Phase Four Inc .... F...... 310 648-8454
  12605 S Van Ness Ave Hawthorne (90250) *(P-9911)*

Phase II, San Diego *Also Called: Phase II Products Inc (P-3011)*

Phase II Products Inc (PA).. F...... 619 236-9699
  501 W Broadway Ste 2090 San Diego (92101) *(P-3011)*

Phase Ten Strategic Corp .... D...... 619 298-1445
  2445 5th Ave Ste 450 San Diego (92101) *(P-14843)*

Phatboykustomz, Rancho Dominguez *Also Called: Pbk International LLC (P-13946)*

PHC, Irvine *Also Called: Pacific Handy Cutter Inc (P-5887)*

PHC, Irvine *Also Called: PHC Merger Inc (P-5888)*

PHC Merger Inc .... E...... 714 662-1033
  17819 Gillette Ave Irvine (92614) *(P-5888)*

Phenix Enterprises Inc (PA).. E...... 909 469-0411
  1785 Mount Vernon Ave Pomona (91768) *(P-9332)*

Phenix Gourmet LLC .... C...... 562 404-5028
  4225 N Palm St Fullerton (92835) *(P-1523)*

Phenix Technology, Riverside *Also Called: Phenix Technology Corporation (P-7406)*

Phenix Technology Corporation (PA)................................ E...... 951 272-4938
  3453 Durahart St Riverside (92507) *(P-7406)*

Phenix Truck Bodies and Eqp, Pomona *Also Called: Phenix Enterprises Inc (P-9332)*

Phenomenex Inc (HQ).. C...... 310 212-0555
  411 Madrid Ave Torrance (90501) *(P-10281)*

PHF II Burbank LLC .... C...... 818 843-6000
  2500 N Hollywood Way Burbank (91505) *(P-15303)*

Phg Engineering Services LLC .... D...... 714 283-8288
  27481 Ganso Mission Viejo (92691) *(P-19670)*

PHH, Hemet *Also Called: Kpc Global Medical Centers Inc (P-18317)*

PHI (PA).. F...... 626 968-9680
  14955 Salt Lake Ave City Of Industry (91746) *(P-7036)*

PHI Hydraulics, City Of Industry *Also Called: PHI (P-7036)*

Phiaro Incorporated .... E...... 949 727-1261
  9016 Research Dr Irvine (92618) *(P-11268)*

Phibro Animal Health Corp .... D...... 562 698-8036
  8851 Dice Rd Santa Fe Springs (90670) *(P-4626)*

Phibro-Tech Inc .... E...... 562 698-8036
  8851 Dice Rd Santa Fe Springs (90670) *(P-3905)*

Philadelphia Gear, Santa Fe Springs *Also Called: Timken Gears & Services Inc (P-6473)*

Philatron International .... E...... 562 802-2570
  15645 Clanton Cir Santa Fe Springs (90670) *(P-5746)*

Philatron International (PA).. D...... 562 802-0452
  15315 Cornet St Santa Fe Springs (90670) *(P-9241)*

Philip B, West Hollywood *Also Called: Philip B Inc (P-4012)*

Philip B Inc .... E...... 888 376-8236
  9053 Nemo St West Hollywood (90069) *(P-4012)*

Philippe Charriol USA, San Diego *Also Called: Alor International Ltd (P-10895)*

Philips .... E...... 916 337-8008
  3721 Valley Centre Dr Ste 500 San Diego (92130) *(P-8426)*

Philips Image Gded Thrapy Corp (DH)............................. B...... 800 228-4728
  3721 Valley Centre Dr Ste 500 San Diego (92130) *(P-10823)*

Philips North America LLC .... C...... 909 574-1800
  11201 Iberia St Ste A Jurupa Valley (91752) *(P-8297)*

Philips North America LLC .... E...... 858 677-6390
  3721 Valley Centre Dr San Diego (92130) *(P-12635)*

Phillips 66 Co Carbon Group .... E...... 805 489-4050
  2555 Willow Rd Arroyo Grande (93420) *(P-7256)*

Phillips Industries, Santa Fe Springs *Also Called: R A Phillips Industries Inc (P-9445)*

Employee Codes: A=Over 500 employees, B=251-500
C=101-250, D=51-100, E=20-50, F=10-19, G=1-9

2024 Southern California
Business Directory and Buyers Guide

© Mergent Inc. 1-800-342-5647

1219

Phillips Tool & Die Inc ....E....... 909 947-8712
1620 S Marigold Ave Ontario (91761) **(P-7087)**

Phillps-Mdisize Costa Mesa LLC ....C....... 949 477-9495
3545 Harbor Blvd Costa Mesa (92626) **(P-10589)**

Philmont Management Inc ....D....... 213 380-0159
3450 Wilshire Blvd Ste 850 Los Angeles (90010) **(P-579)**

Phoenix Cars LLC ....E....... 909 987-0815
1500 Lakeview Loop Anaheim (92807) **(P-9303)**

Phoenix Cpitl Group Hldngs LLC ....E....... 303 749-0074
18575 Jamboree Rd Ste 830 Irvine (92612) **(P-315)**

Phoenix Custom Packaging, Santa Fe Springs *Also Called: Camper Packaging LLC* **(P-1265)**

Phoenix Engineering, Orange *Also Called: His Industries Inc* **(P-7349)**

Phoenix Engineering Co Inc ....D....... 310 532-1134
2480 Armacost Ave Los Angeles (90064) **(P-15935)**

Phoenix Footwear Group Inc (PA)...............................F....... 760 602-9688
2236 Rutherford Rd Ste 113 Carlsbad (92008) **(P-5273)**

PHOENIX HOUSE, Lake View Terrace *Also Called: Phoenix Houses Los Angeles Inc* **(P-19295)**

Phoenix Houses Los Angeles Inc ....D....... 818 686-3000
11600 Eldridge Ave Lake View Terrace (91342) **(P-19295)**

Phoenix Marketing Services Inc ....C....... 909 399-4000
651 Wharton Dr Claremont (91711) **(P-3657)**

Phoenix Motor Inc (DH)...E....... 909 987-0815
1500 Lakeview Loop Anaheim (92807) **(P-9439)**

Phoenix Motorcars, Anaheim *Also Called: Phoenix Cars LLC* **(P-9303)**

Phoenix Motorcars, Anaheim *Also Called: Phoenix Motor Inc* **(P-9439)**

Phoenix Personnel, Los Angeles *Also Called: Phoenix Engineering Co Inc* **(P-15935)**

Phoenix Technologies Ltd (HQ)...................................E....... 408 570-1000
150 S Los Robles Ave Ste 500 Pasadena (91101) **(P-16347)**

Phoenix Textile Inc (PA)...D....... 310 715-7090
14600 S Broadway Gardena (90248) **(P-13088)**

Phoenix Wheel Company Inc ....E....... 760 598-1960
2611 Commerce Way Ste D Vista (92081) **(P-12252)**

Phone Check Solutions LLC ....B....... 310 365-1855
16027 Ventura Blvd Ste 605 Encino (91436) **(P-16095)**

Phone Ware Inc ....B....... 858 530-8550
8902 Activity Rd Ste A San Diego (92126) **(P-16903)**

Phonecom Inc ....D....... 973 577-6380
14288 Danielson St Poway (92064) **(P-11898)**

Phonesuit Inc ....E....... 310 774-0282
1431 7th St Ste 201 Santa Monica (90401) **(P-8561)**

Photo Fabricators Inc ....D....... 818 781-1010
7648 Burnet Ave Van Nuys (91405) **(P-8717)**

Photo Printing Pros, Goleta *Also Called: Surf To Summit Inc* **(P-11032)**

Photo Research, Chatsworth *Also Called: Photo Research Inc* **(P-10334)**

Photo Research Inc ....E....... 818 341-5151
9731 Topanga Canyon Pl Chatsworth (91311) **(P-10334)**

Photo Sciences Incorporated (PA) ....E....... 310 634-1500
301 9th St Ste 406 Redlands (92374) **(P-7562)**

Photo-Sonics Inc (PA)...E....... 818 842-2141
9131 Independence Ave Chatsworth (91311) **(P-10879)**

Photon Research Associates Inc ....C....... 858 455-9741
9985 Pacific Heights Blvd Ste 200 San Diego (92121) **(P-19671)**

Photonics Division, Carlsbad *Also Called: L3 Technologies Inc* **(P-9985)**

Photronics California, Burbank *Also Called: Photronics Inc* **(P-10881)**

Photronics Inc ....C....... 760 294-1896
1760 Arroyo Gln Escondido (92026) **(P-10880)**

Photronics Inc (DH)..B....... 203 740-5653
2428 N Ontario St Burbank (91504) **(P-10881)**

Phs / Mwa ....C....... 951 695-1008
42374 Avenida Alvarado # A Temecula (92590) **(P-11704)**

Phs Staffing, Seal Beach *Also Called: Premier Healthcare Svcs LLC* **(P-18635)**

Phs/Mwa Aviation Services, Temecula *Also Called: Phs / Mwa* **(P-11704)**

Physician Office Support Svcs, Torrance *Also Called: Torrance Health Assn Inc* **(P-18475)**

Physician Sales & Service, Fullerton *Also Called: McKesson Mdcl-Srgcal Top Hldng* **(P-12498)**

Physician Support Systems Inc (DH)..........................B....... 717 653-5340
1131 W 6th St Ste 300 Ontario (91762) **(P-19800)**

Physicians Choice LLC ....D....... 818 340-9988
21860 Burbank Blvd Ste 120 Woodland Hills (91367) **(P-19801)**

Physicians Datatrust Inc ....C....... 562 860-8771
17215 Studebaker Rd Ste 220 Cerritos (90703) **(P-20219)**

Physicians Formula Inc (DH)......................................D....... 626 334-3395
22067 Ferrero City Of Industry (91789) **(P-4444)**

Physicians Formula Cosmt Inc ....D....... 626 334-3395
22067 Ferrero City Of Industry (91789) **(P-4445)**

Physicians Referral Service, Lancaster *Also Called: Lancaster Crdlgy Med Group Inc* **(P-17705)**

Physpeed Corporation ....D....... 805 259-3101
4055 Mission Oaks Blvd Camarillo (93012) **(P-8863)**

PI Variables, Tustin *Also Called: PI Variables Inc* **(P-8621)**

PI Variables Inc ....E....... 949 415-9411
3002 Dow Ave Ste 138 Tustin (92780) **(P-8621)**

Pic Manufacturing Inc ....F....... 805 238-5451
410 Sherwood Rd Paso Robles (93446) **(P-7190)**

Picnic At Ascot Inc ....E....... 310 674-3098
3237 W 131st St Hawthorne (90250) **(P-2733)**

Picnic Time Inc ....D....... 805 529-7400
5131 Maureen Ln Moorpark (93021) **(P-11269)**

Pico Cleaners Inc (PA)...D....... 310 274-2431
9150 W Pico Blvd Los Angeles (90035) **(P-15464)**

Pico Metal Products Inc ....E....... 562 944-0626
10640 Springdale Ave Santa Fe Springs (90670) **(P-6291)**

Pico Metal Products Since 1919, Santa Fe Springs *Also Called: Pico Metal Products Inc* **(P-6291)**

Pico Pica Foods, Wilmington *Also Called: Juanitas Foods* **(P-1327)**

Picore Bristain Initiative Inc ....D....... 818 888-3659
23679 Calabasas Rd # 215 Calabasas (91302) **(P-16670)**

Picosys Incorporated ....D....... 805 962-3333
320 N Nopal St Santa Barbara (93103) **(P-7124)**

Pictsweet Company ....B....... 805 928-4414
732 Hanson Way Santa Maria (93458) **(P-1398)**

Pie Rise Ltd ....E....... 310 832-4559
29051 S Western Ave Rancho Palos Verdes (90275) **(P-14031)**

Pie Town Productions Inc ....C....... 818 255-9300
5433 Laurel Canyon Blvd North Hollywood (91607) **(P-17207)**

Piecemaker's Country Store, Costa Mesa *Also Called: Piecemakers LLC* **(P-14087)**

Piecemakers LLC ....E....... 714 641-3112
1720 Adams Ave Costa Mesa (92626) **(P-14087)**

Piedmont Airlines Inc ....C....... 562 421-1806
4100 E Donald Douglas Dr Long Beach (90808) **(P-11668)**

Piedmont Plastics, La Mirada *Also Called: Regal-Piedmont Plastics LLC* **(P-13417)**

Piedras Machine Corporation ....F....... 562 602-1500
15154 Downey Ave Ste B Paramount (90723) **(P-7973)**

Piege Co (PA)...D....... 818 727-9100
20120 Plummer St Chatsworth (91311) **(P-13142)**

Piercan Usa Inc ....D....... 760 599-4543
160 Bosstick Blvd San Marcos (92069) **(P-2085)**

Pierce Brothers (DH)..D....... 818 763-9121
10621 Victory Blvd North Hollywood (91606) **(P-15489)**

Pierco, Eastvale *Also Called: Pierco Incorporated* **(P-5135)**

Pierco Incorporated ....D....... 951 361-6400
3900 Hamner Ave Eastvale (91752) **(P-5135)**

Pierre Landscape Inc ....C....... 626 587-2121
5455 2nd St Irwindale (91706) **(P-176)**

Pierre Mitri (PA)..F....... 213 747-1838
1138 Wall St Los Angeles (90015) **(P-2358)**

Piet Retief Inc ....E....... 323 732-8312
1914 6th Ave Los Angeles (90018) **(P-2359)**

Piezo-Metrics Inc (PA)..E....... 805 522-4676
4584 Runway St Simi Valley (93063) **(P-8864)**

Pigeon and Poodle, City Of Industry *Also Called: Ardmore Home Design Inc* **(P-2795)**

Pih Health Inc (PA)...A....... 562 698-0811
12401 Washington Blvd Whittier (90602) **(P-18376)**

Pih Health Downey Hospital (HQ)...............................B....... 562 698-0811
11500 Brookshire Ave Downey (90241) **(P-18377)**

Pih Health Good Samaritan Hosp (HQ)........................A....... 213 977-2121
1225 Wilshire Blvd Los Angeles (90017) **(P-18378)**

Pih Health Hospital - Whitti ....A....... 562 904-5482
11500 Brookshire Ave Downey (90241) **(P-18379)**

Pih Health Whittier Hospital (HQ)................................A....... 562 698-0811
12401 Washington Blvd Whittier (90602) **(P-18380)**

Pilatus Unmanned, Huntington Beach *Also Called: Measure Uas Inc* **(P-10379)**

Pilgrim Operations LLC .... B...... 818 478-4500
  12020 Chandler Blvd Ste 200 North Hollywood (91607) *(P-12380)*

Pilgrim Place In Claremont (PA).. C..... 909 399-5500
  625 Mayflower Rd Claremont (91711) *(P-18152)*

Pilgrim Studios Inc .... D..... 818 728-8800
  12020 Chandler Blvd Ste 200 North Hollywood (91607) *(P-17208)*

Piller Power Systems Inc .... E..... 408 204-9578
  5450 Kiowa Dr Unit 39 La Mesa (91942) *(P-9242)*

Pillsbury, Glendale *Also Called: Pillsbury Company LLC (P-1415)*

Pillsbury, Los Angeles *Also Called: Pillsbury Wnthrop Shaw Pttman (P-18924)*

Pillsbury Company LLC .... E..... 818 522-3952
  220 S Kenwood St Ste 202 Glendale (91205) *(P-1415)*

Pillsbury Wnthrop Shaw Pttman .... C..... 213 488-7100
  725 S Figueroa St Ste 2800 Los Angeles (90017) *(P-18924)*

Pilot Freight Services, San Diego *Also Called: Miramar Transportation Inc (P-11784)*

Pimco, Newport Beach *Also Called: Pacific Investment MGT Co LLC (P-14970)*

Pimco Cyman Trst Pmco Cyman GL .... C..... 949 720-6000
  650 Newport Center Dr Newport Beach (92660) *(P-14971)*

Pin Concepts, Sun Valley *Also Called: Pincraft Inc (P-11067)*

Pincraft Inc .... E..... 818 248-0077
  7933 Ajay Dr Sun Valley (91352) *(P-11067)*

Pindler, Moorpark *Also Called: Pindler & Pindler Inc (P-13089)*

Pindler & Pindler Inc (PA).. D..... 805 531-9090
  11910 Poindexter Ave Moorpark (93021) *(P-13089)*

Pine Grove Hospital Inc .... C..... 818 348-0500
  9449 San Fernando Rd Sun Valley (91352) *(P-18517)*

Pine Grove Industries Inc .... E..... 805 485-3700
  2001 Cabot Pl Oxnard (93030) *(P-3658)*

Pinky Los Angeles, Burbank *Also Called: Vesture Group Incorporated (P-2421)*

PINNACLE COMMUNICATION SERVICE, Glendale *Also Called: Pinnacle Networking Svcs Inc (P-926)*

Pinnacle Escrow Company, Northridge *Also Called: Pinnacle Estate Properties (P-14844)*

Pinnacle Estate Properties (PA)...C..... 818 993-4707
  9137 Reseda Blvd Northridge (91324) *(P-14844)*

Pinnacle Hotels Usa Inc .... D..... 858 974-8201
  8369 Vickers St Ste 101 San Diego (92111) *(P-15304)*

Pinnacle Industrial Supply Inc .... E..... 619 710-4255
  1612 Pacific Rim Ct San Diego (92154) *(P-12873)*

Pinnacle Networking Svcs Inc .... C..... 818 241-6009
  730 Fairmont Ave Glendale (91203) *(P-926)*

Pinnacle Plastic Containers, Oxnard *Also Called: Leading Industry Inc (P-5083)*

Pinnacle Precision Shtmtl Corp (PA)................................... D..... 714 777-3129
  5410 E La Palma Ave Anaheim (92807) *(P-6292)*

Pinnacle Precision Shtmtl Corp .... D..... 714 777-3129
  5410 E La Palma Ave Anaheim (92807) *(P-6293)*

Pinnacle Rvrside Hspitality LP .... C..... 951 784-8000
  3400 Market St Riverside (92501) *(P-15305)*

Pinnacle Travel Services LLC .... C..... 310 414-1787
  390 N Pacific Coast Hwy El Segundo (90245) *(P-11722)*

Pinnpack Capital Holdings LLC .... C..... 805 385-4100
  1151 Pacific Ave Oxnard (93033) *(P-5136)*

Pioneer Broach Company (PA).. E..... 323 728-1263
  6434 Telegraph Rd Commerce (90040) *(P-7125)*

Pioneer Circuits Inc .... B..... 714 641-3132
  3021 S Shannon St Santa Ana (92704) *(P-8718)*

Pioneer Custom Elec Pdts Corp .... D..... 562 944-0626
  10640 Springdale Ave Santa Fe Springs (90670) *(P-8107)*

Pioneer Diecasters Inc .... F..... 323 245-6561
  4209 Chevy Chase Dr Los Angeles (90039) *(P-5766)*

Pioneer Healthcare Svcs LLC .... B..... 800 683-1209
  6255 Ferris Sq # F San Diego (92121) *(P-15879)*

Pioneer Magnetics Inc .... C..... 310 829-6751
  1745 Berkeley St Santa Monica (90404) *(P-9098)*

Pioneer North America Inc (DH)... F..... 310 952-2000
  970 W 190th St Ste 360 Torrance (90502) *(P-12636)*

Pioneer Packing Inc (PA).. E..... 714 540-9751
  2430 S Grand Ave Santa Ana (92705) *(P-13023)*

Pioneer Photo Albums Inc (PA)... C..... 818 882-2161
  9801 Deering Ave Chatsworth (91311) *(P-3839)*

Pioneer Sands LLC .... E..... 949 728-0171
  31302 Ortega Hwy San Juan Capistrano (92675) *(P-409)*

Pioneer Sands LLC .... E..... 661 746-5789
  9952 Enos Lane Bakersfield (93314) *(P-410)*

Pioneer Speakers Inc .... A..... 310 952-2000
  2050 W 190th St Ste 100 Torrance (90504) *(P-8427)*

Pioneer Theatres Inc .... C..... 310 532-8183
  2500 Redondo Beach Blvd Torrance (90504) *(P-16904)*

Pioneers Mem Healthcare Dst (PA)...................................... A..... 760 351-3333
  207 W Legion Rd Brawley (92227) *(P-18381)*

PIONEERS MEMORIAL HOSPITAL, Brawley *Also Called: Pioneers Mem Healthcare Dst (P-18381)*

PIP Printing, Mission Viejo *Also Called: Postal Instant Press Inc (P-3660)*

Pipeline, Rllng Hls Est *Also Called: Graphic Prints Inc (P-2531)*

Pipeline Group LLC .... C..... 949 296-8375
  2850 Redhill Ave Ste 110 Santa Ana (92705) *(P-20078)*

Pipeline Health LLC (PA).. D..... 310 379-2134
  898 N Pacific Coast Hwy Ste 700 El Segundo (90245) *(P-18382)*

Pipeline Products Inc .... F..... 760 744-8907
  1650 Linda Vista Dr Ste 110 San Marcos (92078) *(P-7407)*

Pipeliner Crm .... E..... 424 280-6445
  15243 La Cruz Dr Unit 492 Pacific Palisades (90272) *(P-16348)*

Pipline, Oxnard *Also Called: West Coast Wldg & Piping Inc (P-17099)*

Pipsticks, San Luis Obispo *Also Called: Pipsticks Inc (P-3223)*

Pipsticks Inc .... E..... 805 439-1692
  872 Higuera St San Luis Obispo (93401) *(P-3223)*

Pircher Nichols & Meeks (PA)... D..... 310 201-0132
  1925 Century Park E Ste 1700 Los Angeles (90067) *(P-18925)*

Pitbull Gym Incorporated .... E..... 909 980-7960
  10782 Edison Ct Rancho Cucamonga (91730) *(P-5137)*

Piveg Inc .... C..... 858 436-3070
  3525 Del Mar Heights Rd Ste 1069 San Diego (92130) *(P-13191)*

Pivot Interiors Inc .... E..... 949 988-5400
  3200 Park Center Dr Ste 100 Costa Mesa (92626) *(P-927)*

Pixar .... C..... 510 922-4075
  500 N Buena Vista St Burbank (91505) *(P-16905)*

Pixel Labs LLC .... D..... 512 560-5961
  500 Technology Dr Ste 450 Irvine (92618) *(P-19981)*

Pixomondo LLC .... A..... 310 394-0555
  2055 S Barrington Ave Los Angeles (90025) *(P-17260)*

Pj Printers, Anaheim *Also Called: Jeff Lane (P-3607)*

Pjy LLC .... E..... 323 583-7737
  3251 Leonis Blvd Vernon (90058) *(P-2030)*

Pkl Services Inc .... C..... 858 679-1755
  14265 Danielson St Poway (92064) *(P-17146)*

Pl Development, Lynwood *Also Called: P & L Development LLC (P-4192)*

Pl Machine Corporation .... E..... 714 892-1100
  10716 Reagan St Los Alamitos (90720) *(P-7974)*

Placentia Linda Hospital, Placentia *Also Called: Tenet Healthsystem Medical Inc (P-18537)*

Plainfield Companies, Brea *Also Called: Plainfield Molding Inc (P-5138)*

Plainfield Molding Inc .... D..... 815 436-7806
  135 S State College Blvd # 200 Brea (92821) *(P-5138)*

Plainfield Stamping-Illinois, Brea *Also Called: Plainfield Tool and Engineering Inc (P-5139)*

Plainfield Tool and Engineering Inc .... B..... 815 436-5671
  135 S College Blvd St Brea (92821) *(P-5139)*

Plan Member Financial Corp .... D..... 800 874-6910
  6187 Carpinteria Ave Carpinteria (93013) *(P-14427)*

Planet DDS, Newport Beach *Also Called: Planet DDS Inc (P-16349)*

Planet DDS Inc (PA)... E..... 800 861-5098
  3990 Westerly Pl Ste 200 Newport Beach (92660) *(P-16349)*

Planet Green, Chatsworth *Also Called: Planet Green Cartridges Inc (P-11060)*

Planet Green Cartridges Inc .... D..... 818 725-2596
  20724 Lassen St Chatsworth (91311) *(P-11060)*

Planet Innovation Inc .... E..... 847 943-7270
  2720 Loker Ave W Ste P Carlsbad (92010) *(P-10590)*

Planetizen, Los Angeles *Also Called: Planetizen Inc (P-3474)*

Planetizen Inc .... E..... 877 260-7526
  3530 Wilshire Blvd Ste 1285 Los Angeles (90010) *(P-3474)*

Planmember Services, Carpinteria *Also Called: Plan Member Financial Corp (P-14427)*

Planned Parenthood Los Angeles (PA).................................. D..... 213 284-3200
  400 W 30th St Los Angeles (90007) *(P-18707)*

Planned Prnthood of PCF Sthwes (PA).................................. D..... 619 881-4500
  1075 Camino Del Rio S Ste 100 San Diego (92108) *(P-18708)*

Employee Codes: A=Over 500 employees, B=251-500
C=101-250, D=51-100, E=20-50, F=10-19, G=1-9

2024 Southern California
Business Directory and Buyers Guide

© Mergent Inc. 1-800-342-5647

1221

Planned Prnthood of PCF Sthwes ....D...... 619 881-4500
1964 Via Ctr Vista (92081) *(P-18709)*

Planned Prnthood of PCF Sthwes ....D...... 619 881-4652
4501 Mission Bay Dr Ste 1c San Diego (92109) *(P-18710)*

Plansee USA LLC ....D...... 760 438-9090
1491 Poinsettia Ave Ste 138 Vista (92081) *(P-8865)*

Plant Ranch LLC ....F...... 818 384-9727
242 N Avenue 25 Ste 114 Los Angeles (90031) *(P-1971)*

Plantel Nurseries Inc ....B...... 805 934-4300
3990 Foxen Canyon Rd Santa Maria (93454) *(P-66)*

Plantel Nurseries Inc (PA) ....**E...... 805 349-8952**
2775 E Clark Ave Santa Maria (93455) *(P-67)*

Plantel Tranplanting Services, Santa Maria *Also Called: Plantel Nurseries Inc (P-67)*

Plas-Tal Manufacturing Co, Santa Fe Springs *Also Called: Brunton Enterprises Inc (P-6001)*

Plascor Inc ....C...... 951 328-1010
972 Columbia Ave Riverside (92507) *(P-4862)*

Plasidyne Engineering & Mfg ....E...... 562 531-0510
3230 E 59th St Long Beach (90805) *(P-5140)*

Plaskolite West LLC ....E...... 310 637-2103
2225 E Del Amo Blvd Compton (90220) *(P-3963)*

Plasma Coating Corporation ....E...... 310 532-1951
1900 W Walnut St Compton (90220) *(P-6726)*

Plasma Division, Corona *Also Called: PVA Tepla America Inc (P-7985)*

Plasma Rggedized Solutions Inc ....E...... 714 893-6063
5452 Business Dr Huntington Beach (92649) *(P-6648)*

Plasma Technology Incorporated (PA) ....**D...... 310 320-3373**
1754 Crenshaw Blvd Torrance (90501) *(P-6727)*

Plasthec Molding Inc ....E...... 909 947-4267
1945 S Grove Ave Ontario (91761) *(P-5141)*

Plastic and Metal Center Inc ....E...... 949 770-0610
23162 La Cadena Dr Laguna Hills (92653) *(P-5142)*

Plastic Dress-Up, North Hollywood *Also Called: Pdu Lad Corporation (P-6723)*

Plastic Dress-Up Company ....D...... 626 442-7711
11077 Rush St South El Monte (91733) *(P-5143)*

Plastic Fabrication Tech LLC ....F...... 773 509-1700
2320 E Cherry Indus Cir Long Beach (90805) *(P-5144)*

Plastic Molded Components Inc ....E...... 714 229-0133
5920 Lakeshore Dr Cypress (90630) *(P-5145)*

Plastic Processing Co, Gardena *Also Called: Narayan Corporation (P-4861)*

Plastic Sales, Long Beach *Also Called: Plastic Sales Southern Inc (P-13416)*

Plastic Sales Southern Inc ....E...... 714 375-7900
425 Havana Ave Long Beach (90814) *(P-13416)*

Plastic Services and Products ....A...... 818 896-1101
12243 Branford St Sun Valley (91352) *(P-4896)*

Plastic Specialties & Tech Inc ....C...... 909 869-8069
19555 Arenth Ave City Of Industry (91748) *(P-5146)*

Plastic Technologies Inc ....E...... 951 360-6055
4720 Felspar St Riverside (92509) *(P-5147)*

Plasticolor, Fullerton *Also Called: Plasticolor Molded Pdts Inc (P-13869)*

Plasticolor Molded Pdts Inc (PA) ....**C...... 714 525-3880**
801 S Acacia Ave Fullerton (92831) *(P-13869)*

Plastics Development Corp ....E...... 949 492-0217
960 Calle Negocio San Clemente (92673) *(P-5148)*

Plastics Plus Technology Inc ....E...... 909 747-0555
1495 Research Dr Redlands (92374) *(P-5149)*

Plastics Research Corporation ....D...... 909 391-9050
1400 S Campus Ave Ontario (91761) *(P-4838)*

Plastifab Inc ....E...... 909 596-1927
1425 Palomares St La Verne (91750) *(P-4839)*

Plastifab San Diego ....F...... 858 679-6600
12145 Paine St Poway (92064) *(P-4840)*

Plastifab/Leed Plastics, La Verne *Also Called: Plastifab Inc (P-4839)*

Plastique Unique Inc ....F...... 310 839-3968
3383 Livonia Ave Los Angeles (90034) *(P-5150)*

Plasto Tech International Inc ....E...... 949 458-1880
4 Autry Irvine (92618) *(P-5151)*

Plastopan, Los Angeles *Also Called: Plastopan Industries Inc (P-3137)*

Plastopan Industries Inc (PA) ....E...... 323 231-2225
812 E 59th St Los Angeles (90001) *(P-3137)*

Plastpro 2000 Inc (PA) ....C...... 310 693-8600
5200 W Century Blvd Los Angeles (90045) *(P-5152)*

Plastpro Doors, Los Angeles *Also Called: Plastpro 2000 Inc (P-5152)*

Plateronics Processing, Chatsworth *Also Called: Plateronics Processing Inc (P-6649)*

Plateronics Processing Inc ....E...... 818 341-2191
9164 Independence Ave Chatsworth (91311) *(P-6649)*

Platform Science Inc ....C...... 844 475-8724
9560 Towne Centre Dr # 200 San Diego (92121) *(P-16096)*

Plating, Chatsworth *Also Called: Electro Adapter Inc (P-8262)*

Platinum, Fullerton *Also Called: Ultra Wheel Company (P-9479)*

Platinum Clg Indianapolis LLC ....B...... 310 584-8000
1522 2nd St Santa Monica (90401) *(P-15737)*

Platinum Construction Inc ....D...... 714 527-0700
865 S East St Anaheim (92805) *(P-580)*

Platinum Disc LLC ....D...... 608 784-6620
10203 Santa Monica Blvd Fl 5 Los Angeles (90067) *(P-12982)*

Platinum Distribution, Yorba Linda *Also Called: Nasco Gourmet Foods Inc (P-1342)*

Platinum Empire Group Inc ....C...... 310 821-5888
2430 Amsler St Ste B Torrance (90505) *(P-15936)*

Platinum Group Companies Inc (PA) ....**C...... 818 721-3800**
22560 La Quilla Dr Chatsworth (91311) *(P-14938)*

Platinum Healthcare Staffing, Torrance *Also Called: Platinum Empire Group Inc (P-15936)*

Platinum Landscape Inc ....C...... 760 200-3673
42575 Melanie Pl Ste C Palm Desert (92211) *(P-177)*

Platinum Performance Inc (HQ) ....**E...... 800 553-2400**
90 Thomas Rd Buellton (93427) *(P-13062)*

Platinum Performance Inc ....D...... 800 553-2400
760 Mcmurray Rd Buellton (93427) *(P-17014)*

Platinum Roofing Inc ....D...... 408 280-5028
11500 W Olympic Blvd Ste 530 Los Angeles (90064) *(P-1051)*

Platinum Visual Systems, Corona *Also Called: ABC School Equipment Inc (P-12525)*

Plaxicon Co, Rancho Cucamonga *Also Called: Plaxicon Holding Corporation (P-4863)*

Plaxicon Holding Corporation ....A...... 909 944-6868
10660 Acacia St Rancho Cucamohga (91730) *(P-4863)*

Play Versus Inc ....D...... 949 636-4193
2236 S Barrington Ave Ste A Los Angeles (90064) *(P-19533)*

Playa Proper Jv LLC ....D...... 310 645-0400
8639 Lincoln Blvd Los Angeles (90045) *(P-15306)*

Playboy Enterprises Inc ....D...... 310 424-1800
10960 Wilshire Blvd Fl 22 Los Angeles (90024) *(P-3380)*

Playboy Enterprises Intl Inc ....D...... 310 424-1800
10960 Wilshire Blvd Ste 2200 Los Angeles (90024) *(P-3475)*

Playboy Entrmt Group Inc (DH) ....**C...... 323 276-4000**
2300 W Empire Ave Burbank (91504) *(P-17209)*

Playboy Japan Inc ....E...... 310 424-1800
9346 Civic Center Dr # 200 Beverly Hills (90210) *(P-3381)*

Players West Amusements Inc (PA) ....**E...... 805 983-1400**
2360 Sturgis Rd Ste A Oxnard (93030) *(P-17445)*

Playhaven LLC ....C...... 310 308-9668
1447 2nd St Ste 200 Santa Monica (90401) *(P-16097)*

Playhut Inc ....E...... 909 869-8083
18560 San Jose Ave City Of Industry (91748) *(P-10964)*

Playmax Surfacing Inc ....F...... 951 250-6039
1950 Compton Ave Ste 111 Corona (92881) *(P-4784)*

Playvs, Los Angeles *Also Called: Play Versus Inc (P-19533)*

Plaza Home Mortgage Inc ....C...... 858 346-1208
9808 Scranton Rd San Diego (92121) *(P-14403)*

Plaza Tower 1, Costa Mesa *Also Called: Regus Business Centre LLC (P-16914)*

PLC Imports Inc ....E...... 818 349-1600
9667 Owensmouth Ave Ste 201 Chatsworth (91311) *(P-12613)*

Pleasant Hawaiian Holiday, Westlake Village *Also Called: Pleasant Holidays LLC (P-11723)*

Pleasant Holidays LLC (HQ) ....**B...... 818 991-3390**
2404 Townsgate Rd Westlake Village (91361) *(P-11723)*

Plenums Plus LLC ....D...... 619 422-5515
67 Brisbane St Chula Vista (91910) *(P-6294)*

Plethora ....E...... 323 851-1633
2142 Beachwood Ter Los Angeles (90068) *(P-7975)*

Plg Law Group, Encino *Also Called: Price Law Group A Prof Corp (P-18926)*

Plh Products Inc ....B...... 714 739-6622
10541 Calle Lee Ste 119 Los Alamitos (90720) *(P-2744)*

Plott Family Care Centers, Riverside *Also Called: Orangtree Cnvalescent Hosp Inc (P-18356)*

Pls Diabetic Shoe Company Inc ....E...... 818 734-7080
21500 Osborne St Canoga Park (91304) *(P-4705)*

Plt Enterprises Inc ....D...... 805 389-5335
809 Calle Plano Camarillo (93012) *(P-8273)*

Pluckys Dump Rental LLC ....E...... 323 540-3510
10136 Bowman Ave South Gate (90280) *(P-6150)*

Plug Connection Inc ....D...... 760 631-0992
2627 Ramona Dr Vista (92084) *(P-68)*

Plug Connection LLC ....C...... 760 631-0992
3742 Blue Bird Canyon Rd Vista (92084) *(P-20220)*

Plugg ME LNc ....E...... 949 705-4472
18100 Von Karman Ave # 850 Irvine (92612) *(P-16350)*

Plum Healthcare Group LLC ....C...... 760 471-0388
100 E San Marcos Blvd Ste 200 San Marcos (92069) *(P-18031)*

Plumbing Master, Riverside Also Called: Lozano Plumbing Services Inc *(P-787)*

Plumbing Piping & Cnstr Inc ....D...... 714 821-0490
5950 Lakeshore Dr Cypress (90630) *(P-808)*

Plural Publishing Inc ....E...... 858 492-1555
9177 Aero Dr San Diego (92123) *(P-3412)*

Plus Cbd LLC ....E...... 855 758-7223
591 Camino De La Reina Ste 1200 San Diego (92108) *(P-11270)*

Plus Products, Adelanto Also Called: Carberry LLC *(P-11204)*

Plycraft Industries Inc ....C...... 323 587-8101
2100 E Slauson Ave Huntington Park (90255) *(P-2690)*

Plymouth Village, Redlands Also Called: Humangood Norcal *(P-18134)*

Plz Corp ....E...... 805 498-4531
840 Tourmaline Dr Newbury Park (91320) *(P-3872)*

Plz Corp ....D...... 951 683-2912
2321 3rd St Riverside (92507) *(P-4446)*

Plz Corp ....C...... 951 683-2912
2375 3rd St Riverside (92507) *(P-4447)*

Plz Corp ....D...... 909 393-9475
14425 Yorba Ave Chino (91710) *(P-4448)*

PM Corporate Group Inc (PA)..........................E...... 619 498-9199
2285 Michael Faraday Dr Ste 12 San Diego (92154) *(P-3659)*

PM Packaging, San Diego Also Called: PM Corporate Group Inc *(P-3659)*

PM Realty Group LP ....D...... 949 390-5500
3 Park Plz Ste 450 Irvine (92614) *(P-14679)*

Pmb Group, Poway Also Called: Pmb Group Inc *(P-12508)*

Pmb Group Inc ....F...... 619 690-7300
12778 Brookprinter Pl Poway (92064) *(P-12508)*

Pmb Motorcars LLC ....A...... 626 384-3600
1829 E Garvey Ave N West Covina (91791) *(P-13814)*

Pmc Inc (HQ)..D...... 818 896-1101
12243 Branford St Sun Valley (91352) *(P-9766)*

PMC Capital Partners LLC ....A...... 818 896-1101
12243 Branford St Sun Valley (91352) *(P-15046)*

PMC Global Inc (PA)..D...... 818 896-1101
12243 Branford St Sun Valley (91352) *(P-4897)*

PMC Leaders In Chemicals Inc (HQ)...................C...... 818 896-1101
12243 Branford St Sun Valley (91352) *(P-4898)*

PMC Southwest LLC, Jurupa Valley Also Called: Arcticom Group Rfrgn LLC *(P-17061)*

Pmcs Group Inc ....D...... 562 498-0808
2600 E Pacific Coast Hwy Ste 160 Long Beach (90804) *(P-20221)*

Pmd Inc ....F...... 925 765-0629
12464 Mccann Dr Santa Fe Springs (90670) *(P-9767)*

PMI, Carlsbad Also Called: Petrochem Manufacturing Inc *(P-4664)*

Pml Inc ....E...... 310 671-4345
201 W Beach Ave Inglewood (90302) *(P-16906)*

Pmp Forge, El Cajon Also Called: Jmmca Inc *(P-6463)*

Pmr Precision Mfg & Rbr Co Inc ....E...... 909 605-7525
1330 Etiwanda Ave Ontario (91761) *(P-4785)*

Pmt Crdit Risk Trnsf Tr 2015-1 ....D...... 818 224-7028
3043 Townsgate Rd Westlake Village (91361) *(P-15000)*

Pmt Crdit Risk Trnsf Tr 2015-2 ....C...... 818 224-7442
3043 Townsgate Rd Westlake Village (91361) *(P-15001)*

Pmt Crdit Risk Trnsf Tr 2019-2 ....D...... 818 224-7028
3043 Townsgate Rd Westlake Village (91361) *(P-15002)*

Pmt Crdit Risk Trnsf Tr 2020-1 ....C...... 818 224-7028
3043 Townsgate Rd Westlake Village (91361) *(P-15003)*

PNa Construction Tech Inc ....E...... 661 326-1700
301 Espee St Ste E Bakersfield (93301) *(P-6295)*

PNC Proactive Nthrn Cont LLC ....E...... 909 390-5624
602 S Rockefeller Ave A Ontario (91761) *(P-3125)*

Pneudraulics Inc ....B...... 909 980-5366
8575 Helms Ave Rancho Cucamonga (91730) *(P-10050)*

Pneumatic Conveying Inc ....E...... 909 923-4481
960 E Grevillea Ct Ontario (91761) *(P-6976)*

Pnk Enterprises Inc ....E...... 818 765-3770
12901 Saticoy St North Hollywood (91605) *(P-14145)*

Pnmac Gmsr Issuer Trust ....A...... 818 746-2271
3043 Townsgate Rd Westlake Village (91361) *(P-15004)*

Pocino Foods Company ....D...... 626 968-8000
14250 Lomitas Ave City Of Industry (91746) *(P-1230)*

Point Conception Inc ....E...... 949 589-6890
23121 Arroyo Vis Ste A Rcho Sta Marg (92688) *(P-2360)*

Point Loma Rhblitation Ctr LLC ....C...... 619 308-3200
3202 Duke St San Diego (92110) *(P-18032)*

Point360 ....D...... 818 556-5700
1133 N Hollywood Way Burbank (91505) *(P-17210)*

Point360 (PA)...D...... 818 565-1400
2701 Media Center Dr Los Angeles (90065) *(P-17261)*

Pointdirect Transport Inc ....D...... 909 371-0837
19083 Mermack Ave Lake Elsinore (92532) *(P-11503)*

Pointe At Lantern Crest, The, Santee Also Called: Santee Senior Retirement Com *(P-19136)*

Pokeworks, Irvine Also Called: Beyond Franchise Group Inc *(P-13984)*

Polagram, Los Angeles Also Called: Wellmade Inc *(P-20272)*

Polar Air Cargo LP ....B...... 310 568-4551
100 Oceangate Fl 15 Long Beach (90802) *(P-11669)*

Polar Power, Gardena Also Called: Polar Power Inc *(P-9173)*

Polar Power Inc ....C...... 310 830-9153
249 E Gardena Blvd Gardena (90248) *(P-9173)*

Polar Tankers Inc ....C...... 310 519-8260
60 Berth San Pedro (90731) *(P-11636)*

Polaris E-Commerce Inc ....E...... 714 907-0582
1941 E Occidental St Santa Ana (92705) *(P-7286)*

Polaris Music, Los Angeles Also Called: Eti Systems *(P-10131)*

Polaris Pharmaceuticals Inc (PA)......................E...... 858 452-6688
10675 Sorrento Valley Rd Ste 200 San Diego (92121) *(P-4204)*

Poliseek Ais Insur Sltions Inc ....D...... 866 480-7335
17785 Center Court Dr N Ste 250 Cerritos (90703) *(P-14622)*

Pollstar LLC ....D...... 559 271-7900
1100 Glendon Ave Ste 2100 Los Angeles (90024) *(P-3476)*

Pollstar.com, Los Angeles Also Called: Pollstar LLC *(P-3476)*

Poly Pak America Inc ....D...... 323 264-2400
2939 E Washington Blvd Los Angeles (90023) *(P-4817)*

Poly-Fiber Inc (PA)..F...... 951 684-4280
4343 Fort Dr Riverside (92509) *(P-4497)*

Poly-Tainer Inc (PA)..C...... 805 526-3424
450 W Los Angeles Ave Simi Valley (93065) *(P-4864)*

Polyalloys Injected Metals Inc ....D...... 310 715-9800
14000 Avalon Blvd Los Angeles (90061) *(P-6949)*

Polycell Packaging Corporation ....E...... 562 483-6000
12851 Midway Pl Cerritos (90703) *(P-13554)*

Polycraft Inc ....E...... 951 296-0860
42075 Avenida Alvarado Temecula (92590) *(P-3796)*

Polycycle Solutions LLC ....D...... 626 856-2100
4516 Azusa Canyon Rd Irwindale (91706) *(P-4865)*

Polyfet Rf Devices Inc ....E...... 805 484-9582
1110 Avenida Acaso Camarillo (93012) *(P-8866)*

Polymer Coating Services, Aliso Viejo Also Called: Parylene Coating Services Inc *(P-6722)*

Polymer Logistics Inc ....D...... 951 567-2900
1725 Sierra Ridge Dr Riverside (92507) *(P-5153)*

Polymond Dk Inc ....E...... 213 327-0771
777 E 10th St Ste 110 Los Angeles (90021) *(P-2361)*

Polypeptide Laboratories Inc (HQ)....................D...... 310 782-3569
365 Maple Ave Torrance (90503) *(P-18558)*

Polypeptide Labs San Diego LLC ....D...... 858 408-0808
9395 Cabot Dr San Diego (92126) *(P-4205)*

Polypure, Los Angeles Also Called: Snf Holding Company *(P-4632)*

Polytechnic School ....B...... 626 792-2147
1030 E California Blvd Pasadena (91106) *(P-18979)*

Pom Medical LLC ....D...... 805 306-2105
5456 Endeavour Ct Moorpark (93021) *(P-12509)*

Poma Holding Company Inc ....C...... 909 877-2441
571 W Slover Ave Bloomington (92316) *(P-13453)*

Employee Codes: A=Over 500 employees, B=251-500
C=101-250, D=51-100, E=20-50, F=10-19, G=1-9

2024 Southern California
Business Directory and Buyers Guide

© Mergent Inc. 1-800-342-5647
1223

Pomerado Hospital, Poway *Also Called: Palomar Health (P-18364)*

Pomerado Hospital, Poway *Also Called: Palomar Medical Center (P-18368)*

Pomerado Operations LLC ....D...... 858 487-6242
12696 Monte Vista Rd Poway (92064) *(P-18033)*

Pommes Frites Candle Co ....E...... 213 488-2016
7300 E Slauson Ave Commerce (90040) *(P-11271)*

Pomona Box Co, La Habra *Also Called: Votaw Wood Products Inc (P-2728)*

Pomona Quality Foam LLC ....D...... 909 628-7844
1279 Philadelphia St Pomona (91766) *(P-4899)*

Pomona Service Center, Pomona *Also Called: Altec Industries Inc (P-17028)*

Pomona Valley Hospital Med Ctr (PA)............................**A...... 909 865-9500**
1798 N Garey Ave Pomona (91767) *(P-18383)*

Ponder Environmental Svcs Inc ....E...... 661 589-7771
19484 Broken Ct Shafter (93263) *(P-20298)*

Ponte Winery ....E...... 951 694-8855
35053 Rancho California Rd Temecula (92591) *(P-1652)*

Ponton Industries, Yorba Linda *Also Called: Tom Ponton Industries Inc (P-20262)*

Pontrelli & Larricchia Ltd ....E...... 323 583-6690
6080 Malburg Way Vernon (90058) *(P-13303)*

Pontrlli-Laricchia Sausage Mfg, Vernon *Also Called: Pontrelli & Larricchia Ltd (P-13303)*

Poor Richard's Press, San Luis Obispo *Also Called: Prpco (P-3672)*

Poor Richards Press, San Luis Obispo *Also Called: Ws Packaging-Blake Printery (P-3715)*

Pop Chips, E Rncho Dmngz *Also Called: Sonora Mills Foods Inc (P-1987)*

Popla International Inc ....E...... 909 923-6899
1740 S Sacramento Ave Ontario (91761) *(P-1425)*

Popsalot Gourmet Popcorn, Paramount *Also Called: Popsalot LLC (P-1830)*

Popsalot LLC ....E...... 213 761-0156
7723 Somerset Blvd Paramount (90723) *(P-1830)*

Populus Financial Group Inc ....C...... 951 509-3506
6302 Van Buren Blvd Riverside (92503) *(P-14262)*

Port Brewing ....F...... 760 720-7012
571 Carlsbad Village Dr Carlsbad (92008) *(P-14052)*

Port Logistics Group Inc ....B...... 310 669-2551
19801 S Santa Fe Ave Compton (90221) *(P-11793)*

Port of Long Beach ....B...... 562 283-7000
415 W Ocean Blvd Long Beach (90802) *(P-11644)*

Port of Los Angeles ....B...... 310 732-3508
425 S Palos Verdes St San Pedro (90731) *(P-11645)*

PORT OF SAN DIEGO, San Diego *Also Called: San Diego Unified Port Dst (P-11647)*

Portable Clers Sls Rentals Inc ....F...... 760 747-9591
1250 Pacific Oaks Pl Ste 101 Escondido (92029) *(P-13969)*

Porteous Enterprises Inc (DH)..**C...... 310 549-9180**
1040 E Watson Center Rd Carson (90745) *(P-12731)*

Porter Boiler Service Inc ....E...... 562 426-2528
1166 E 23rd St Signal Hill (90755) *(P-17147)*

Porter Hire Ltd ....E...... 951 674-9999
13013 Temescal Canyon Rd Corona (92883) *(P-15793)*

Porter Valley Catering, Northridge *Also Called: Porter Valley Country Club Inc (P-17507)*

Porter Valley Country Club Inc ....C...... 818 360-1071
19216 Singing Hills Dr Northridge (91326) *(P-17507)*

Portermatt Electric Inc ....D...... 714 596-8788
5431 Production Dr Huntington Beach (92649) *(P-928)*

Porto Vista Hotel, San Diego *Also Called: 1835 Columbia Street LP (P-15063)*

Portofino Hotel Partners LP ....C...... 310 379-8481
260 Portofino Way Redondo Beach (90277) *(P-15307)*

Portofino Inn & Suites Anaheim ....B...... 714 782-7600
1831 S Harbor Blvd Anaheim (92802) *(P-15308)*

Portos Bakery & Cafe, Burbank *Also Called: Portos Bakery Burbank Inc (P-13722)*

Portos Bakery Burbank Inc ....E...... 818 846-9100
3614 W Magnolia Blvd Burbank (91505) *(P-13722)*

Posca Brothers Dental Lab Inc ....D...... 562 427-1811
641 W Willow St Long Beach (90806) *(P-18573)*

Poseida, San Diego *Also Called: Poseida Therapeutics Inc (P-4327)*

Poseida Therapeutics Inc (PA)..**B...... 858 779-3100**
9390 Towne Centre Dr Ste 200 San Diego (92121) *(P-4327)*

Posh'n Bae, Woodland Hills *Also Called: Conquistador International LLC (P-13034)*

Positive Concepts Inc (PA)...**E...... 714 685-5800**
2021 N Glassell St Orange (92865) *(P-3243)*

Post Alarm Systems (PA)..**D...... 626 446-7159**
47 E Saint Joseph St Arcadia (91006) *(P-16749)*

Post Alarm Systems Patrol Svcs, Arcadia *Also Called: Post Alarm Systems (P-16749)*

Post Group Inc (PA)..**C...... 323 462-2300**
1415 N Cahuenga Blvd Los Angeles (90028) *(P-17262)*

Postaer Rubin and Associates ....C...... 312 644-3636
2525 Colorado Ave Ste 100 Santa Monica (90404) *(P-15568)*

Postal Instant Press Inc (HQ)..**E...... 949 348-5000**
26722 Plaza Mission Viejo (92691) *(P-3660)*

Postalio Inc ....D...... 408 616-9284
75 Higuera St Ste 240 San Luis Obispo (93401) *(P-20222)*

Postvision Inc ....F...... 818 840-0777
2605 E Foothill Blvd Ste 103 Glendora (91740) *(P-7479)*

Potential Industries Inc (PA)..**C...... 310 549-5901**
720 East E St Wilmington (90744) *(P-12179)*

Potter Roemer LLC (HQ)...**D...... 626 855-4890**
17451 Hurley St City Of Industry (91744) *(P-12340)*

Poundex Associates Corporation ....D...... 909 444-5878
21490 Baker Pkwy City Of Industry (91789) *(P-12290)*

Pouring With Heart LLC ....D...... 213 817-5321
515 W 7th St Los Angeles (90014) *(P-1653)*

Poway Homecare, San Diego *Also Called: Maxim Healthcare Services Inc (P-18627)*

Poway Toyota, Poway *Also Called: Poway Toyota Scion Inc (P-13815)*

Poway Toyota Scion Inc ....C...... 858 486-2900
13631 Poway Rd Poway (92064) *(P-13815)*

Powder Coating, South El Monte *Also Called: Island Powder Coating (P-6712)*

Powder Painting By Sundial, Sun Valley *Also Called: Sundial Industries Inc (P-6740)*

Powdercoat Services LLC ....E...... 714 533-2251
1747 W Lincoln Ave Ste K Anaheim (92801) *(P-6728)*

Powell Electric ....E...... 310 394-6498
1314 7th St Santa Monica (90401) *(P-9243)*

Powell Works, La Puente *Also Called: Powell Works Inc (P-12809)*

Powell Works Inc ....B...... 909 861-6699
17807 Maclaren St Ste B La Puente (91744) *(P-12809)*

Power Brands Consulting LLC ....E...... 818 989-9646
5805 Sepulveda Blvd Ste 501 Van Nuys (91411) *(P-1602)*

Power Circuits Inc ....D...... 714 327-3000
2630 S Harbor Blvd Santa Ana (92704) *(P-8719)*

Power Digital Marketing Inc (PA)...**B...... 619 501-1211**
2251 San Diego Ave Ste A250 San Diego (92110) *(P-20223)*

Power Fasteners Inc ....E...... 323 232-4362
650 E 60th St Los Angeles (90001) *(P-6452)*

Power Generation Entps Inc ....C...... 818 484-8550
26764 Oak Ave Canyon Country (91351) *(P-12810)*

Power Plus, Corona *Also Called: SRbray LLC (P-939)*

Power Pt Inc (PA)..**E...... 951 490-4149**
1500 Crafton Ave Bldg 100 Mentone (92359) *(P-6996)*

Power Pt Inc ....E...... 714 826-7407
9292 Nancy St Cypress (90630) *(P-6997)*

Power Services, Los Angeles *Also Called: On-Line Power Incorporated (P-8104)*

Power Studios Inc ....C...... 310 314-2800
300 Rose Ave Venice (90291) *(P-17211)*

Power-Right Industries LLC ....F...... 909 628-4397
4722 W Mission Blvd Ontario (91762) *(P-9440)*

Powercords, San Ysidro *Also Called: Volex Inc (P-5244)*

Powered By Fulfillment Inc ....D...... 626 825-9841
20880 Krameria Ave Riverside (92518) *(P-11554)*

Powerflex Systems LLC ....E...... 650 469-3392
15445 Innovation Dr San Diego (92128) *(P-8153)*

Powers Park Healthcare Inc ....D...... 805 687-6651
3880 Via Lucero Santa Barbara (93110) *(P-18034)*

Powersource Talent LLC ....C...... 424 835-0878
12655 W Jefferson Blvd Ste 400 Los Angeles (90066) *(P-20224)*

Ppc Enterprises Inc ....C...... 951 354-5402
5920 Rickenbacker Ave Riverside (92504) *(P-809)*

Ppd Holding LLC (PA)...**D...... 310 733-2100**
10119 Jefferson Blvd Culver City (90232) *(P-2183)*

Ppf, Garden Grove *Also Called: Pure Process Filtration Inc (P-12758)*

PPG Aerospace, Mojave *Also Called: PRC - Desoto International Inc (P-4576)*

PPG Aerospace, Valencia *Also Called: PRC - Desoto International Inc (P-4577)*

PPG Aerospace, Sylmar *Also Called: Sierracin/Sylmar Corporation (P-5204)*

PPG Industries Inc ....E...... 714 894-5252
15541 Commerce Ln Huntington Beach (92649) *(P-4498)*

PPG Industries Inc .... F....... 562 692-4010
  10060 Mission Mill Rd City Of Industry (90601) *(P-4499)*

PPG Industries Inc .... E....... 661 824-4532
  11601 United St Mojave (93501) *(P-4500)*

PPG Paints .... F....... 818 362-6711
  12780 San Fernando Rd Sylmar (91342) *(P-4501)*

Pphm Inc .... D....... 714 508-6100
  14282 Franklin Ave Tustin (92780) *(P-13063)*

Ppmc, Corona *Also Called: Primary Provider MGT Co Inc (P-20081)*

Pponext West Inc .... B....... 888 446-6098
  1501 Hughes Way Ste 400 Long Beach (90810) *(P-18789)*

Ppp LLC .... F....... 323 832-9627
  601 W Olympic Blvd Montebello (90640) *(P-5154)*

Pps Parking Inc .... A....... 949 223-8707
  1800 E Garry Ave Ste 107 Santa Ana (92705) *(P-15521)*

Ppst Inc (PA).. **E....... 800 421-1921**
  17692 Fitch Irvine (92614) *(P-9099)*

PQ LLC .... C....... 323 326-1100
  8401 Quartz Ave South Gate (90280) *(P-3906)*

Prager University Foundation .... D....... 833 772-4378
  15021 Ventura Blvd Ste 552 Sherman Oaks (91403) *(P-17212)*

Pramira Inc .... C....... 800 678-1169
  404 N Berry St Brea (92821) *(P-16590)*

Prana, Carlsbad *Also Called: Prana Living LLC (P-13108)*

Prana Living LLC (HQ).. **D....... 866 915-6457**
  3209 Lionshead Ave Carlsbad (92010) *(P-13108)*

Prata Inc .... E....... 512 823-1002
  202 Bicknell Ave Santa Monica (90405) *(P-16351)*

Praxair, Santa Ana *Also Called: Praxair Distribution Inc (P-3873)*

Praxair Distribution Inc .... E....... 714 564-7311
  1555 E Edinger Ave Santa Ana (92705) *(P-3873)*

PRC, Ontario *Also Called: Plastics Research Corporation (P-4838)*

PRC - Desoto International Inc .... C....... 661 824-4532
  11601 United St Mojave (93501) *(P-4576)*

PRC - Desoto International Inc (HQ)................................ **B....... 661 678-4209**
  24811 Avenue Rockefeller Valencia (91355) *(P-4577)*

PRC Composites LLC (PA).. **D....... 909 391-2006**
  1400 S Campus Ave Ontario (91761) *(P-5155)*

PRC Composites LLC .... E....... 909 464-1520
  13477 12th St Chino (91710) *(P-5156)*

Prdctions N Fremantle Amer Inc (DH)............................. **D....... 818 748-1100**
  2900 W Alameda Ave Unit 800 Burbank (91505) *(P-17324)*

Pre-Con Products .... D....... 805 527-0841
  240 W Los Angeles Ave Simi Valley (93065) *(P-5438)*

Precast Innovations Inc .... E....... 714 921-4060
  1670 N Main St Orange (92867) *(P-5439)*

Precept Advisory Group LLC (DH)................................... **D....... 949 955-1430**
  130 Theory Ste 200 Irvine (92617) *(P-14623)*

Precept Group The, Irvine *Also Called: Precept Advisory Group LLC (P-14623)*

Precise Aerospace Mfg Inc .... C....... 951 898-0500
  22951 La Palma Ave Yorba Linda (92887) *(P-5157)*

Precise Air Systems Inc .... D....... 818 646-9757
  5467 W San Fernando Rd Los Angeles (90039) *(P-810)*

Precise Die and Finishing .... E....... 818 773-9337
  9400 Oso Ave Chatsworth (91311) *(P-7088)*

Precise Engineering Inc .... E....... 858 345-7243
  11280 Turtleback Ct San Diego (92127) *(P-7976)*

Precise Fit Limited One LLC .... B....... 310 824-1800
  17011 Beach Blvd Ste 900 Huntington Beach (92647) *(P-15880)*

Precise Industries Inc .... C....... 714 482-2333
  610 Neptune Ave Brea (92821) *(P-6296)*

Precise Iron Doors Inc .... E....... 818 338-6269
  12331 Foothill Blvd Sylmar (91342) *(P-6116)*

Precise Media Services Inc .... E....... 909 481-3305
  888 Vintage Ave Ontario (91764) *(P-8463)*

Precise Plastic Products, Yorba Linda *Also Called: Precise Aerospace Mfg Inc (P-5157)*

Precise-Full Service Media, Ontario *Also Called: Precise Media Services Inc (P-8463)*

Preciseq Inc .... D....... 310 709-6094
  11601 Wilshire Blvd Ste 500 Los Angeles (90025) *(P-16591)*

Precision Aerospace Corp .... D....... 909 945-9604
  11155 Jersey Blvd Ste A Rancho Cucamonga (91730) *(P-9768)*

Precision Anodizing & Pltg Inc .... D....... 714 996-1601
  1601 N Miller St Anaheim (92806) *(P-6650)*

Precision Arcft Machining Inc .... E....... 818 768-5900
  10640 Elkwood St Sun Valley (91352) *(P-7977)*

Precision Coil Spring Company .... C....... 626 444-0561
  10107 Rose Ave El Monte (91731) *(P-6807)*

Precision Contracting, Irvine *Also Called: Danny Ryan Precision Contg Inc (P-1131)*

Precision Cutting Tools Inc .... E....... 562 921-7898
  5572 Fresca Dr La Palma (90623) *(P-7126)*

Precision Cutting Tools LLC .... E....... 562 921-7898
  5572 Fresca Dr La Palma (90623) *(P-7127)*

Precision Deburring Services .... E....... 562 944-4497
  4440 Manning Rd Pico Rivera (90660) *(P-7017)*

Precision Diecut, Chino *Also Called: Pdc LLC (P-7086)*

Precision Dynamics Corporation (HQ)............................. **C....... 818 897-1111**
  25124 Springfield Ct Ste 200 Valencia (91355) *(P-3173)*

Precision Engine Controls Corp (DH).............................. **C....... 858 792-3217**
  11661 Sorrento Valley Rd San Diego (92121) *(P-6884)*

Precision Fastener Tooling Inc .... E....... 714 898-8558
  11530 Western Ave Stanton (90680) *(P-7037)*

Precision Fiber Products Inc .... E....... 408 946-4040
  642 Palomar St Chula Vista (91911) *(P-5747)*

Precision Forging Dies Inc .... E....... 562 861-1878
  10710 Sessler St South Gate (90280) *(P-7089)*

Precision Frrites Ceramics Inc .... D....... 714 901-7622
  5432 Production Dr Huntington Beach (92649) *(P-7978)*

Precision Glass & Optics, Santa Ana *Also Called: Buk Optics Inc (P-10309)*

Precision Hermetic, Redlands *Also Called: Precision Hermetic Tech Inc (P-9100)*

Precision Hermetic Tech Inc .... D....... 909 381-6011
  1940 W Park Ave Redlands (92373) *(P-9100)*

Precision Information LLC .... F....... 888 345-1285
  501 W Broadway Ste A158 San Diego (92101) *(P-16352)*

Precision Label LLC .... E....... 760 757-7533
  659 Benet Rd Oceanside (92058) *(P-3156)*

Precision Litho Inc .... E....... 760 727-9400
  1185 Joshua Way Vista (92081) *(P-3661)*

Precision Machining & Fab, Anaheim *Also Called: Precision Waterjet Inc (P-7979)*

Precision Measurement Labs, Inglewood *Also Called: Pml Inc (P-16906)*

Precision Metal Crafts Inc .... E....... 562 468-7080
  11965 Rivera Rd Santa Fe Springs (90670) *(P-6064)*

Precision Molded Products Inc .... E....... 951 354-0779
  12660 Magnolia Ave Riverside (92503) *(P-5158)*

Precision Offset Inc .... D....... 949 752-1714
  15201 Woodlawn Ave Tustin (92780) *(P-3662)*

Precision One Medical Inc .... D....... 760 945-7966
  3923 Oceanic Dr Ste 200 Oceanside (92056) *(P-10762)*

Precision Optical, Costa Mesa *Also Called: Sellers Optical Inc (P-10339)*

Precision Pipeline LLC .... B....... 909 229-6858
  10400 Trademark St Rancho Cucamonga (91730) *(P-685)*

Precision Plastics Packaging, Anaheim *Also Called: Interlink Inc (P-3604)*

Precision Pwdred Met Parts Inc .... E....... 909 595-5656
  145 Atlantic St Pomona (91768) *(P-5856)*

Precision Resource Inc .... C....... 714 891-4439
  5803 Engineer Dr Huntington Beach (92649) *(P-6547)*

Precision Resource Cal Div, Huntington Beach *Also Called: Precision Resource Inc (P-6547)*

Precision Services Group, Tustin *Also Called: Precision Offset Inc (P-3662)*

Precision Sheet Metal, Gardena *Also Called: Artistic Welding (P-6193)*

Precision Silicones, Chino *Also Called: Wacker Chemical Corporation (P-4537)*

Precision Stampings Inc (PA)... **E....... 951 845-1174**
  500 Egan Ave Beaumont (92223) *(P-8274)*

Precision Steel Products Inc .... E....... 310 523-2002
  13124 Avalon Blvd Los Angeles (90061) *(P-6297)*

Precision Technology and Mfg .... F....... 951 788-0252
  3147 Durahart St Riverside (92507) *(P-6419)*

Precision Tube Bending .... D....... 562 921-6723
  13626 Talc St Santa Fe Springs (90670) *(P-9769)*

Precision Waterjet, Anaheim *Also Called: Jbb Inc (P-9221)*

Precision Waterjet Inc .... E....... 888 538-9287
  4900 E Hunter Ave Anaheim (92807) *(P-7979)*

Precision Welding Inc .... E....... 661 729-3436
  241 Enterprise Pkwy Lancaster (93534) *(P-6065)*

ALPHABETIC

Employee Codes: A=Over 500 employees, B=251-500
C=101-250, D=51-100, E=20-50, F=10-19, G=1-9

2024 Southern California
Business Directory and Buyers Guide

© Mergent Inc. 1-800-342-5647

1225

Precision Wire Products Inc (PA) .... C...... 323 890-9100
6150 Sheila St Commerce (90040) *(P-6823)*

Precision Woodworks .... F...... 949 215-1185
10 Hammond Ste 300 Irvine (92618) *(P-2671)*

Preco Aircraft Motors Inc .... E...... 626 799-3549
1133 Mission St South Pasadena (91030) *(P-9174)*

Precon Inc .... E...... 714 630-7632
3131 E La Palma Ave Anaheim (92806) *(P-7018)*

Precon Gage, Anaheim *Also Called: Precon Inc (P-7018)*

Pred, San Diego *Also Called: Pred Technologies Usa Inc (P-9101)*

Pred Technologies Usa Inc .... D...... 858 999-2114
4901 Morena Blvd San Diego (92117) *(P-9101)*

Preferred Carrier California, Chino *Also Called: Advanced Multimodal Dist Inc (P-11826)*

Preferred Employers Insur Co .... D...... 619 688-3900
9797 Aero Dr Ste 200 San Diego (92123) *(P-14624)*

Preferred Frzr Svcs - Lbf LLC .... D...... 323 263-8811
4901 Bandini Blvd Vernon (90058) *(P-11555)*

Preferred Hlthcare Rgistry Inc .... C...... 800 787-6787
4909 Murphy Canyon Rd Ste 310 San Diego (92123) *(P-15881)*

Preferred Printing & Packaging Inc .... E...... 909 923-2053
1493 E Philadelphia St Ontario (91761) *(P-3070)*

Pregel America Inc .... C...... 909 598-8980
116 S Brent Cir Walnut (91789) *(P-19225)*

Premier Ambulance, Brea *Also Called: Premier Medical Transport Inc (P-11400)*

Premier Amer Wealth MGT Group, Chatsworth *Also Called: Premier America Credit Union (P-14251)*

Premier America Credit Union (PA) .... C...... 818 772-4000
19867 Prairie St Lbby Chatsworth (91311) *(P-14251)*

Premier Cold Storage & Pkg LLC .... C...... 949 444-8859
1071 E 233rd St Carson (90745) *(P-11556)*

Premier Dealer Services Inc .... D...... 858 810-1700
9449 Balboa Ave Ste 300 San Diego (92123) *(P-14625)*

Premier Dental Holdings Inc (PA) .... B...... 714 480-3000
530 S Main St Ste 600 Orange (92868) *(P-17846)*

Premier Disability Svcs LLC .... D...... 310 280-4000
909 N Pacific Coast Hwy Fl 11 El Segundo (90245) *(P-19339)*

Premier Filters Inc .... E...... 657 226-0091
952 N Elm St Orange (92867) *(P-7408)*

Premier Food Services Inc .... A...... 760 843-8000
14359 Amargosa Rd Ste F Victorville (92392) *(P-13192)*

Premier Fuel Delivery Service, Riverside *Also Called: Premier Fuel Distributors Inc (P-13454)*

Premier Fuel Distributors Inc .... C...... 760 423-3610
156 E La Cadena Dr Riverside (92507) *(P-13454)*

Premier Gear & Machining Inc .... E...... 951 278-5505
2360 Pomona Rd Corona (92878) *(P-6470)*

Premier Healthcare Svcs LLC (DH) .... C...... 626 204-7930
3030 Old Ranch Pkwy Ste 100 Seal Beach (90740) *(P-18635)*

Premier Hlthcare Solutions Inc .... C...... 858 569-8629
12225 El Camino Real San Diego (92130) *(P-20079)*

Premier IMS Insurance Services, San Diego *Also Called: Premier Hlthcare Solutions Inc (P-20079)*

Premier Infsion Hlthcare Svcs .... D...... 310 328-3897
19500 Normandie Ave Torrance (90502) *(P-18636)*

Premier Infusion Care, Torrance *Also Called: Premier Infsion Hlthcare Svcs (P-18636)*

Premier Magnetics Inc .... E...... 949 452-0511
20381 Barents Sea Cir Lake Forest (92630) *(P-8951)*

Premier Meat Company, Vernon *Also Called: Wayne Provision Co Inc (P-13310)*

Premier Medical Transport Inc .... C...... 805 340-5191
260 N Palm St # 200 Brea (92821) *(P-11400)*

Premier Mop & Broom, Corona *Also Called: Northwestern Converting Co (P-2479)*

Premier Otptent Srgery Ctr Inc .... C...... 909 370-2190
900 E Washington St Ste 155 Colton (92324) *(P-17739)*

Premier Packaging LLC .... E...... 909 749-5123
10700 Business Dr Ste 100 Fontana (92337) *(P-4900)*

Premier Pharmacy Service, Baldwin Park *Also Called: Good Health Inc (P-18765)*

Premier Plumbing Company, Riverside *Also Called: Ppc Enterprises Inc (P-809)*

Premier Steel Structures Inc .... E...... 951 356-6655
13345 Estelle St Corona (92879) *(P-6066)*

Premier Systems Usa Inc (PA) .... F...... 657 204-9861
16291 Gothard St Huntington Beach (92647) *(P-12432)*

Premiere Customs Brokers Inc .... A...... 310 410-6825
5951 Skylab Rd Huntington Beach (92647) *(P-11794)*

Premiere Radio Network Inc (DH) .... C...... 818 377-5300
15260 Ventura Blvd Ste 400 Sherman Oaks (91403) *(P-17325)*

Premio Inc (PA) .... C...... 626 839-3100
918 Radecki Ct City Of Industry (91748) *(P-7445)*

Premium Outlet Partners LP .... D...... 951 849-6641
48400 Seminole Dr Cabazon (92230) *(P-14680)*

Premium Outlet Partners LP .... D...... 805 445-8520
740 Ventura Blvd Camarillo (93010) *(P-14681)*

Premium Outlet Partners LP .... D...... 760 804-9045
5620 Paseo Del Norte Ste 100 Carlsbad (92008) *(P-14682)*

Premium Pet Foods, Irwindale *Also Called: J&R Taylor Brothers Assoc Inc (P-1430)*

Premium Plastics Machine Inc .... F...... 562 633-7723
15956 Downey Ave Paramount (90723) *(P-5159)*

Premium Windows, Corona *Also Called: Mediland Corporation (P-5317)*

Preproduction Plastics Inc .... E...... 951 340-9680
210 Teller St Corona (92879) *(P-5160)*

Pres-Tek Plastics Inc (PA) .... E...... 909 360-1600
10700 7th St Rancho Cucamonga (91730) *(P-5161)*

Presbia, Aliso Viejo *Also Called: Presbibio LLC (P-10849)*

Presbibio LLC .... E...... 949 502-7010
36 Plateau Aliso Viejo (92656) *(P-10849)*

Presbyterian Inter Cmnty Hosp, Whittier *Also Called: Interhealth Services Inc (P-18618)*

Prescient Holdings Group LLC .... E...... 858 790-7004
10181 Scripps Gateway Ct San Diego (92131) *(P-4206)*

Prescription Solutions, Carlsbad *Also Called: Optumrx Inc (P-14490)*

Presentation Folder Inc .... E...... 714 289-7000
1130 N Main St Orange (92867) *(P-3204)*

Preserved Treescapes International Inc .... D...... 760 631-6789
180 Vallecitos De Oro San Marcos (92069) *(P-11272)*

Preserved Treescapes Intl, San Marcos *Also Called: Preserved Treescapes International Inc (P-11272)*

President Enterprise LLC .... E...... 714 671-9577
655 Tamarack Ave Brea (92821) *(P-3797)*

Presidio Components Inc .... C...... 858 578-9390
7169 Construction Ct San Diego (92121) *(P-12691)*

Press Colorcom, Santa Fe Springs *Also Called: Ace Commercial Inc (P-3505)*

Press Forge Company .... D...... 562 531-4962
7700 Jackson St Paramount (90723) *(P-6471)*

Press-Enterprise Company (PA) .... A...... 951 684-1200
3450 14th St Riverside (92501) *(P-3316)*

Pressure Profile Systems Inc .... F...... 310 641-8100
5757 W Century Blvd Ste 600 Los Angeles (90045) *(P-10151)*

Prestige Animal Hospital North, Fontana *Also Called: People Pets and Vets LLC (P-125)*

Prestige Animal Hospital South, Fontana *Also Called: People Pets and Vets LLC (P-124)*

Prestige Flag, San Diego *Also Called: Prestige Flag & Banner Co Inc (P-2555)*

Prestige Flag & Banner Co Inc .... D...... 619 497-2220
591 Camino De La Reina Ste 917 San Diego (92108) *(P-2555)*

Prestige Graphics Inc .... E...... 858 560-8213
9630 Ridgehaven Ct Ste B San Diego (92123) *(P-12997)*

Prestige Mold Incorporated .... D...... 909 980-6600
11040 Tacoma Dr Rancho Cucamonga (91730) *(P-7090)*

Prestige Stations Inc (DH) .... C...... 714 670-5145
4 Centerpointe Dr La Palma (90623) *(P-13702)*

Prestone Products Corporation .... E...... 424 271-4836
19500 Mariner Ave Torrance (90503) *(P-4627)*

Pretium Packaging, Chino *Also Called: Pretium Packaging LLC (P-5162)*

Pretium Packaging LLC .... C...... 714 777-9580
13980 Mountain Ave Chino (91710) *(P-5162)*

Prevost Car (us) Inc .... D...... 951 360-2550
3384 De Forest Cir Mira Loma (91752) *(P-12253)*

Price Industries Inc .... D...... 858 673-4451
10883 Thornmint Rd San Diego (92127) *(P-5597)*

Price Law Group A Prof Corp (PA) .... C...... 818 995-4540
15760 Ventura Blvd Ste 800 Encino (91436) *(P-18926)*

Price Manufacturing Co Inc .... E...... 951 371-5660
372 N Smith Ave Corona (92878) *(P-6420)*

Price Pfister Inc (HQ) .... A...... 949 672-4000
19701 Da Vinci Lake Forest (92610) *(P-5972)*

Price Pfister Brass Mfg, Lake Forest *Also Called: Price Pfister Inc (P-5972)*

Price Products Incorporated .... E...... 760 745-5602
106 State Pl Escondido (92029) *(P-7980)*

Pricegrabber.com, Los Angeles *Also Called: Pg Usa LLC (P-13688)*

Pricespider, Irvine *Also Called: Neuintel LLC (P-16082)*

Pricewaterhousecoopers LLP .... C...... 213 356-6000
601 S Figueroa St Ste 900 Los Angeles (90017) *(P-19802)*

Pride Metal Polishing LLC .... F...... 626 350-1326
10822 Saint Louis Dr El Monte (91731) *(P-6651)*

Prima Royale, Pasadena *Also Called: Prima Royale Enterprises Ltd (P-13164)*

Prima Royale Enterprises Ltd .... E...... 626 960-8388
150 S Los Robles Ave Ste 100 Pasadena (91101) *(P-13164)*

Primal Elements, Huntington Beach *Also Called: Primal Elements Inc (P-13064)*

Primal Elements Inc .... D...... 714 899-0757
18062 Redondo Cir Huntington Beach (92648) *(P-13064)*

Primapharma Inc .... E...... 858 259-0969
3443 Tripp Ct San Diego (92121) *(P-4207)*

Primary Care Assod Med Group I .... C...... 760 724-1033
3998 Vista Way Ste B Oceanside (92056) *(P-20080)*

Primary Color Systems Corp .... D...... 818 643-5944
3500 W Burbank Blvd Burbank (91505) *(P-3663)*

Primary Color Systems Corp (PA) .... B...... 949 660-7080
11130 Holder St Ste 210 Cypress (90630) *(P-3798)*

Primary Color Systems Corp .... D...... 310 841-0250
401 Coral Cir El Segundo (90245) *(P-3799)*

Primary Provider MGT Co Inc (HQ) .... D...... 951 280-7700
2115 Compton Ave Ste 301 Corona (92881) *(P-20081)*

Prime Administration LLC .... A...... 323 549-7155
357 S Curson Ave Los Angeles (90036) *(P-15016)*

Prime Converting Corporation .... E...... 909 476-9500
9121 Pittsburgh Ave Ste 100 Rancho Cucamonga (91730) *(P-3244)*

Prime Focus World, Culver City *Also Called: Dneg North America Inc (P-17249)*

Prime Forming & Cnstr Sups Inc .... E...... 714 547-6710
1500a E Chestnut Ave Santa Ana (92701) *(P-5440)*

Prime Group, Los Angeles *Also Called: Prime Administration LLC (P-15016)*

Prime Halthcare Foundation Inc (PA) .... C...... 909 235-4400
3480 E Guasti Rd Ontario (91761) *(P-18384)*

Prime Health Care .... C...... 909 394-2727
1350 W Covina Blvd San Dimas (91773) *(P-19226)*

Prime Healthcare Anaheim LLC .... A...... 714 827-3000
3033 W Orange Ave Anaheim (92804) *(P-18385)*

Prime Healthcare Centinela LLC .... A...... 310 673-4660
555 E Hardy St Inglewood (90301) *(P-18386)*

Prime Healthcare Services, Ontario *Also Called: Bio-Med Services Inc (P-18192)*

Prime Healthcare Services-Mont .... A...... 909 625-5411
5000 San Bernardino St Montclair (91763) *(P-18387)*

Prime Heat Incorporated .... F...... 619 449-6623
1844 Friendship Dr Ste A El Cajon (92020) *(P-7371)*

Prime Hlthcare Hntngton Bch LL .... B...... 714 843-5000
17772 Beach Blvd Huntington Beach (92647) *(P-18388)*

Prime Hlthcare Srvcs-Mntclair (DH) .... C...... 909 625-5411
5000 San Bernardino St Montclair (91763) *(P-18389)*

Prime Hlthcare Srvcs-Mntclair .... C...... 909 625-5411
5000 San Bernardino St Montclair (91763) *(P-18390)*

Prime Hlthcare Svcs - Encino H .... B...... 818 995-5000
16237 Ventura Blvd Encino (91436) *(P-18391)*

Prime Hlthcare Svcs - Pmpa LLC (DH) .... C...... 909 235-4400
3300 E Guasti Rd Ste 300 Ontario (91761) *(P-18392)*

Prime Hlthcare Svcs - San Dmas .... B...... 909 599-6811
1350 W Covina Blvd San Dimas (91773) *(P-18393)*

Prime Hlthcare Svcs - Shrman O .... B...... 818 981-7111
4929 Van Nuys Blvd Sherman Oaks (91403) *(P-18394)*

Prime Hlthcare Svcs - St John (DH) .... D...... 913 680-6000
3500 S 4th St Ontario (91761) *(P-18395)*

Prime Hospitality LLC .... D...... 909 975-5000
2200 E Holt Blvd Ontario (91761) *(P-15309)*

Prime One Inc .... C...... 310 378-1944
22410 Hawthorne Blvd Ste 4 Torrance (90505) *(P-15882)*

Prime Plastic Products Inc .... F...... 760 734-3900
1351 Distribution Way Ste 8 Vista (92081) *(P-5163)*

Prime Plating, Sun Valley *Also Called: Schmidt Industries Inc (P-6661)*

Prime Solutions Inc .... E...... 702 354-7129
7235 Enclave Dr Eastvale (92880) *(P-8867)*

Prime Tech Cabinets Inc .... C...... 949 757-4900
2215 S Standard Ave Santa Ana (92707) *(P-1022)*

Prime Wheel Corporation .... E...... 310 819-4123
17680 S Figueroa St Gardena (90248) *(P-9441)*

Prime Wheel Corporation .... B...... 310 326-5080
23920 Vermont Ave Harbor City (90710) *(P-9442)*

Prime Wheel Corporation (PA) .... A...... 310 516-9126
17705 S Main St Gardena (90248) *(P-9443)*

Prime Wheel of Figueroa, Gardena *Also Called: Prime Wheel Corporation (P-9441)*

Prime Wire & Cable Inc .... C...... 323 266-2010
11701 6th St Rancho Cucamonga (91730) *(P-5748)*

Primeco .... D...... 760 967-8278
220 Oceanside Blvd Oceanside (92054) *(P-853)*

Primetime International Inc .... D...... 760 399-4166
47110 Washington St Ste 103 La Quinta (92253) *(P-13336)*

Primex Clinical Labs Inc (PA) .... D
16742 Stagg St Ste 120 Van Nuys (91406) *(P-18559)*

Primex Farms LLC (PA) .... E...... 661 758-7790
16070 Wildwood Rd Wasco (93280) *(P-1561)*

Primordial Diagnostics Inc .... E...... 800 462-1926
3233 Mission Oaks Blvd Ste P Camarillo (93012) *(P-10152)*

Primoris Services Corporation .... C...... 949 598-9242
26000 Commercentre Dr Lake Forest (92630) *(P-686)*

Primus Inc .... D...... 714 527-2261
17901 Jamestown Ln Huntington Beach (92647) *(P-11145)*

Primus Pipe and Tube Inc (DH) .... D...... 562 808-8000
5855 Obispo Ave Long Beach (90805) *(P-5640)*

Prince Lionheart Inc (PA) .... E...... 805 922-2250
2421 Westgate Rd Santa Maria (93455) *(P-5164)*

Princess Cruise Lines Ltd (HQ) .... A...... 661 753-0000
24305 Town Center Dr Santa Clarita (91355) *(P-11637)*

Princess Cruise Lines Ltd .... A...... 661 753-2197
24833 Anza Dr Santa Clarita (91355) *(P-11724)*

Princess Cruise Lines Ltd .... A...... 661 753-0000
24200 Magic Mountain Pkwy Santa Clarita (91355) *(P-11729)*

Princess Cruise Lines Ltd .... C...... 213 745-0314
1242 E 25th St Los Angeles (90011) *(P-13143)*

Princess Cruises, Santa Clarita *Also Called: Princess Cruise Lines Ltd (P-11637)*

Princess Cruises, Santa Clarita *Also Called: Princess Cruise Lines Ltd (P-11724)*

Princess Paper Inc .... E...... 323 588-4777
4455 Fruitland Ave Vernon (90058) *(P-3206)*

Princess Paradise, Walnut *Also Called: Diana Did-It Designs Inc (P-2449)*

Princeton Case-West Inc .... E...... 805 928-8840
1444 W Mccoy Ln Santa Maria (93455) *(P-5165)*

Princeton Technology Inc .... E...... 949 851-7776
1691 Browning Irvine (92606) *(P-7563)*

Princeton Tool Inc .... F...... 661 257-1380
25620 Rye Canyon Rd Ste A Valencia (91355) *(P-9578)*

Principle Plastics .... E...... 310 532-3411
1136 W 135th St Gardena (90247) *(P-4706)*

Prindle Decker & Amaro LLP (PA) .... D...... 562 436-3946
310 Golden Shore Fl 4 Long Beach (90802) *(P-18927)*

Pringle's Draperies, Garden Grove *Also Called: L C Pringle Sales Inc (P-3010)*

Print Plus, Santa Ana *Also Called: Print Plus Manufacturing Inc (P-2097)*

Print Plus Manufacturing Inc .... E
1939 S Susan St Santa Ana (92704) *(P-2097)*

Print Printing, Placentia *Also Called: Crescent Inc (P-3551)*

Print Shop, San Bernardino *Also Called: San Brnrdino Cmnty College Dst (P-3810)*

Printec Ht Electronics LLC .... E...... 714 484-7597
501 Sally Pl Fullerton (92831) *(P-8868)*

Printech, Placentia *Also Called: High Five Inc (P-3586)*

Printegra Corp .... D...... 714 692-2221
23101 La Palma Ave Yorba Linda (92887) *(P-3832)*

Printing 4him, Ontario *Also Called: Ultimate Print Source Inc (P-3701)*

Printing Impressions, Goleta *Also Called: JD Business Solutions Inc (P-3606)*

Printing Management Associates .... E...... 562 407-9977
17128 Edwards Rd Cerritos (90703) *(P-3664)*

Printing Palace Inc (PA) .... F...... 310 451-5151
2300 Lincoln Blvd Santa Monica (90405) *(P-3665)*

Employee Codes: A=Over 500 employees, B=251-500
C=101-250, D=51-100, E=20-50, F=10-19, G=1-9

2024 Southern California
Business Directory and Buyers Guide

© Mergent Inc. 1-800-342-5647
1227

ALPHABETIC

Printing Solutions, Redlands *Also Called: California Prtg Solutions Inc (P-3526)*

Printivity, San Diego *Also Called: Printivity LLC (P-3666)*

Printivity LLC ....E...... 877 649-5463
8840 Kenamar Dr Ste 405 San Diego (92121) *(P-3666)*

Printronix LLC (PA)...**D...... 714 368-2300**
7700 Irvine Center Dr Ste 700 Irvine (92618) *(P-7564)*

Printrunner LLC ....E...... 888 296-5760
8000 Haskell Ave Van Nuys (91406) *(P-3667)*

Prints 4 Life ....E...... 661 942-2233
43145 Business Ctr Pkwy Lancaster (93535) *(P-3668)*

Printsafe Inc ....E...... 858 748-8600
11895 Community Rd Ste B Poway (92064) *(P-12433)*

Priority Building Services LLC ....B...... 858 695-1326
7313 Carroll Rd Ste G San Diego (92121) *(P-15738)*

Priority Ctr Ending The Gnrtna ....D...... 714 543-4333
1940 E Deere Ave Ste 100 Santa Ana (92705) *(P-19127)*

Priority Lighting Inc ....F...... 800 709-1119
77551 El Duna Ct Ste H Palm Desert (92211) *(P-13965)*

Priority Pallet Inc ....F...... 951 769-9399
1060 E Third St Beaumont (92223) *(P-2722)*

Prism Aerospace ....E...... 951 582-2850
3087 12th St Riverside (92507) *(P-6298)*

Prism Aerospace dba Jet Manufacturing, Corona *Also Called: Jet Manufacturing Inc*
(P-6257)

Prism Software Corporation ....E...... 949 855-3100
184 Technology Dr Ste 201 Irvine (92618) *(P-16353)*

Prismatik Dentalcraft Inc ....D...... 949 399-1930
4141 Macarthur Blvd Newport Beach (92660) *(P-18574)*

Prison Ride Share Network ....E...... 314 703-5245
25310 Stephvon Way Hemet (92544) *(P-3477)*

Prison Rideshare Network, Hemet *Also Called: Prison Ride Share Network (P-3477)*

Private Brand Mdsg Corp ....E...... 213 749-0191
214 W Olympic Blvd Los Angeles (90015) *(P-2287)*

Private Label, City Of Industry *Also Called: Private Label Pc LLC (P-12434)*

Private Label Pc LLC ....C...... 626 965-8686
748 Epperson Dr City Of Industry (91748) *(P-12434)*

Private Medical-Care Inc ....A...... 562 924-8311
12898 Towne Center Dr Cerritos (90703) *(P-14492)*

Private Nat Mrtg Accptance LLC (DH).................**A...... 818 224-7401**
6101 Condor Dr Agoura Hills (91301) *(P-14347)*

Private Suite Lax LLC ....C...... 310 907-9950
6871 W Imperial Hwy Los Angeles (90045) *(P-11356)*

Prl Aluminum Inc ....D...... 626 968-7507
14760 Don Julian Rd City Of Industry (91746) *(P-5706)*

Prl Glass Systems Inc ....D...... 877 775-2586
14760 Don Julian Rd City Of Industry (91746) *(P-5353)*

Prl Glass Systems Inc (PA).................................**C...... 626 961-5890**
13644 Nelson Ave City Of Industry (91746) *(P-5354)*

Prn Ambulance LLC ....B...... 818 810-3600
8928 Sepulveda Blvd North Hills (91343) *(P-11401)*

Prn Radio Networks, Sherman Oaks *Also Called: Premiere Radio Network Inc (P-17325)*

Pro America Premium Tools, Baldwin Park *Also Called: American Kal Enterprises Inc*
(P-12713)

Pro American Premium Tools, Baldwin Park *Also Called: Kal-Cameron Manufacturing Corp*
(P-5883)

Pro Building Maintenance Inc (PA).....................**C...... 951 279-3386**
149 N Maple St Ste H Corona (92878) *(P-15739)*

Pro Cal, South Gate *Also Called: Productivity California Inc (P-5167)*

Pro Circuit Products Inc (PA).............................**E...... 951 738-8050**
2771 Wardlow Rd Corona (92882) *(P-13903)*

Pro Circuit Products & Racing, Corona *Also Called: Pro Circuit Products Inc (P-13903)*

Pro Circuits Manufacturing Inc ....E...... 858 899-4747
16464 Via Esprillo San Diego (92127) *(P-17070)*

Pro Comp, Chula Vista *Also Called: Tap Manufacturing LLC (P-9467)*

Pro Design Group Inc ....E...... 310 767-1032
438 E Alondra Blvd Gardena (90248) *(P-5166)*

Pro Detention Inc ....D...... 714 881-3680
2238 N Glassell St Ste E Orange (92865) *(P-5622)*

Pro Document Solutions Inc (PA)........................**E...... 805 238-6680**
1760 Commerce Way Paso Robles (93446) *(P-3669)*

Pro Energy Services Group LLC ....B...... 760 789-7149
2060 Aldergrove Ave Escondido (92029) *(P-20299)*

Pro Group, Irvine *Also Called: Professnl Rprgraphic Svcs Inc (P-3800)*

Pro Group Inc ....C...... 951 271-3000
4160 Temescal Canyon Rd Ste 500 Corona (92883) *(P-14845)*

Pro Installations Inc (HQ)..................................**E**
13250 Gregg St Ste F Poway (92064) *(P-1034)*

Pro Loaders Inc ....C...... 909 355-5531
14032 Santa Ana Ave Fontana (92337) *(P-11795)*

Pro Safety Inc ....C...... 562 364-7450
20503 Belshaw Ave Carson (90746) *(P-12811)*

Pro Spot International Inc ....F...... 760 407-1414
5932 Sea Otter Pl Carlsbad (92010) *(P-9244)*

Pro Spray Equipment, San Bernardino *Also Called: Wcs Distributing Inc (P-12836)*

Pro Tech Thermal Services ....E...... 951 272-5808
1954 Tandem Norco (92860) *(P-5847)*

Pro Tool Services Inc ....E...... 661 393-9222
1704 Sunnyside Ct Bakersfield (93308) *(P-7128)*

Pro Tour Memorabilia LLC ....E...... 424 303-7200
700 N San Vicente Blvd Ste G696 West Hollywood (90069) *(P-2759)*

Pro Traffic Services Inc ....D...... 760 906-6961
321 Hunter St Ramona (92065) *(P-811)*

Pro Vote Solutions, Paso Robles *Also Called: Pro Document Solutions Inc (P-3669)*

Pro-Action Products, Van Nuys *Also Called: Neopacific Holdings Inc (P-5112)*

Pro-Cast Products Inc (PA)..................................**E...... 909 793-7602**
27417 3rd St Highland (92346) *(P-5441)*

Pro-Craft Construction Inc ....C...... 909 790-5222
500 Iowa St Ste 100 Redlands (92373) *(P-812)*

Pro-Dex, Irvine *Also Called: Pro-Dex Inc (P-10591)*

Pro-Dex Inc (PA)...**C...... 949 769-3200**
2361 Mcgaw Ave Irvine (92614) *(P-10591)*

Pro-Line Paint Company ....F...... 619 232-8968
2646 Main St San Diego (92113) *(P-4502)*

Pro-Lite Inc ....F...... 714 668-9988
3505 Cadillac Ave Ste D Costa Mesa (92626) *(P-11146)*

Pro-Mart Industries Inc ....E...... 949 428-7700
17421 Von Karman Ave Irvine (92614) *(P-2485)*

Pro-Tek Consulting (PA).......................................**C...... 805 807-5571**
21300 Victory Blvd Ste 240 Woodland Hills (91367) *(P-16592)*

Proactive Northern Container, Ontario *Also Called: PNC Proactive Nthrn Cont LLC (P-3125)*

Proactive Risk Management Inc ....D...... 213 840-8856
22617 Hawthorne Blvd Torrance (90505) *(P-20082)*

Probation Department, Lancaster *Also Called: County of Los Angeles (P-19055)*

Probation Department, Los Angeles *Also Called: County of Los Angeles (P-19060)*

Probation Department, Downey *Also Called: County of Los Angeles (P-19061)*

Probation Dept, Los Angeles *Also Called: County of Los Angeles (P-19058)*

Probation Dept, Van Nuys *Also Called: County of Los Angeles (P-19062)*

Probation Dept, Los Angeles *Also Called: County of Los Angeles (P-19063)*

Probation Dept, San Diego *Also Called: County of San Diego (P-19067)*

Probe Racing Components Inc ....E...... 310 784-2977
5022 Onyx St Torrance (90503) *(P-7703)*

Procede Software LP ....E...... 858 450-4800
6815 Flanders Dr Ste 200 San Diego (92121) *(P-16354)*

Procelebrity, Arcadia *Also Called: Tee Top of California Inc (P-13114)*

Process Fab Inc ....C...... 562 921-1979
13153 Lakeland Rd Santa Fe Springs (90670) *(P-7981)*

Processes By Martin Inc ....E...... 310 637-1855
12150 Alameda St Lynwood (90262) *(P-6729)*

Processes Unlimited, Bakersfield *Also Called: Processes Unlimited International Inc (P-19672)*

Processes Unlimited International Inc ....B...... 661 396-3770
5500 Ming Ave Ste 400 Bakersfield (93309) *(P-19672)*

Processors Mailing Inc ....E...... 626 358-5600
761 N Dodsworth Ave Covina (91724) *(P-3670)*

Processors The, Covina *Also Called: Processors Mailing Inc (P-3670)*

Procisedx Inc ....E...... 858 382-4598
9449 Carroll Park Dr San Diego (92121) *(P-10097)*

Procopio Cory Hargreaves & Savitch LLP (PA).....**C...... 619 238-1900**
530 B St Ste 2200 San Diego (92101) *(P-18928)*

Procore Technologies Inc (PA)...........................**A...... 866 477-6267**
6309 Carpinteria Ave Carpinteria (93013) *(P-16098)*

Procter & Gamble, Oxnard *Also Called: Procter & Gamble Paper Pdts Co (P-3207)*

Mergent email: customerrelations@mergent.com
1228

2024 Southern California
Business Directory and Buyers Guide

(P-0000) Products & Services Section entry number
(PA)=Parent Co (HQ)=Headquarters (DH)=Div Headquarters

Procter & Gamble Paper Pdts Co .... A 805 485-8871
800 N Rice Ave Oxnard (93030) *(P-3207)*

Prodata Research, San Diego *Also Called: Soleil Communications LLC (P-19912)*

Producers Meat and Prov Inc .... E 619 232-7593
7651 Saint Andrews Ave San Diego (92154) *(P-13304)*

Product Slingshot Inc (DH) .... E 760 929-9380
2221 Rutherford Rd Carlsbad (92008) *(P-7091)*

Product Solutions Inc .... E 714 545-9757
1182 N Knollwood Cir Anaheim (92801) *(P-7679)*

Production Data Inc .... E 661 327-4776
1210 33rd St Bakersfield (93301) *(P-379)*

Production Engineering & Mch .... E 909 721-2455
14955 Hilton Dr Fontana (92336) *(P-18560)*

Productive Playhouse Inc (PA) .... B 323 250-3445
25231 Paseo De Alicia Ste 205 Laguna Hills (92653) *(P-16907)*

Productivity California Inc .... D 562 923-3100
10533 Sessler St South Gate (90280) *(P-5167)*

Productos Chata, Chula Vista *Also Called: Culinary Hispanic Foods Inc (P-13365)*

Productos Oropeza, Santa Ana *Also Called: La Copa De Oro (P-1927)*

Productplan LLC .... E 805 618-2975
10 E Yanonali St Ste 2a Santa Barbara (93101) *(P-16355)*

Products Engineering Corp .... E 310 787-4500
2645 Maricopa St Torrance (90503) *(P-5889)*

Professional Cabinet Solutions .... C 909 614-2900
2111 Eastridge Ave Riverside (92507) *(P-2672)*

Professional Cabinet Solutions (DH) .... C 909 614-2900
2111 Eastridge Ave Riverside (92507) *(P-2673)*

Professional Cmnty MGT Cal Inc .... D 951 359-2840
11860 Pierce St Ste 100 Riverside (92505) *(P-14846)*

Professional Cmnty MGT Cal Inc .... B 951 845-2191
850 Country Club Dr Banning (92220) *(P-14847)*

Professional Cmnty MGT Cal Inc .... C 949 206-0580
24351 El Toro Rd Laguna Woods (92637) *(P-14848)*

Professional Cmnty MGT Cal Inc .... C 949 597-4200
23522 Paseo De Valencia Laguna Hills (92653) *(P-14849)*

Professional Cmnty MGT Cal Inc .... D 760 918-8040
906 Sycamore Ave Ste 210 Vista (92081) *(P-14850)*

Professional Community MGT, Vista *Also Called: Professional Cmnty MGT Cal Inc (P-14850)*

Professional Community MGT Cal 949 380-0725
23081 Via Campo Verde Aliso Viejo (92656) *(P-20083)*

Professional Cr Reporting Inc .... C 714 556-1570
3560 Hyland Ave Costa Mesa (92626) *(P-14278)*

Professional Maint Systems, San Diego *Also Called: Professional Maint Systems Inc (P-15740)*

Professional Maint Systems Inc .... A 619 276-1150
4912 Naples St San Diego (92110) *(P-15740)*

Professional Parking .... C 949 723-4027
309 Palm St Newport Beach (92661) *(P-17006)*

Professional Plastics Inc (PA) .... E 714 446-6500
1810 E Valencia Dr Fullerton (92831) *(P-3964)*

Professional Produce .... D 323 277-1550
2570 E 25th St Los Angeles (90058) *(P-13337)*

Professional Security Cons (PA) .... D 310 207-7729
11454 San Vicente Blvd 2nd Fl Los Angeles (90049) *(P-16671)*

Professional Security Cons, Los Angeles *Also Called: Professional Security Cons (P-16671)*

Professional Svcs Med Group, Huntington Park *Also Called: All Care Medical Group Inc (P-17584)*

Professnal Elec Cnstr Svcs Inc .... C 909 373-4100
9112 Santa Anita Ave Rancho Cucamonga (91730) *(P-929)*

Professnal Fnshg Systems Sups .... F 818 365-8888
12341 Gladstone Ave Sylmar (91342) *(P-6548)*

Professnal Rprgraphic Svcs Inc .... E 949 748-5400
17622 Armstrong Ave Irvine (92614) *(P-3800)*

Professonal Tele Answering Svc, Chatsworth *Also Called: Seven One Inc (P-16925)*

Profile Planing Mill, Santa Ana *Also Called: Strata Forest Products Inc (P-2567)*

Proform Inc .... D 707 752-9010
1140 S Rockefeller Ave Ontario (91761) *(P-18561)*

Proform Finishing Products LLC .... E 562 435-4465
1850 Pier B St Long Beach (90813) *(P-5521)*

Proform Labs, Ontario *Also Called: Proform Inc (P-18561)*

Proformance Manufacturing Inc .... E 951 279-1230
1922 Elise Cir Corona (92879) *(P-6549)*

Prographics Inc .... E 626 287-0417
9200 Lower Azusa Rd Rosemead (91770) *(P-3671)*

Prographics Screenprinting Inc .... E 760 744-4555
1975 Diamond St San Marcos (92078) *(P-3801)*

Progression Drywall, Lancaster *Also Called: Excel Contractors Inc (P-432)*

Progressive Converting Inc .... F 909 392-2201
280 W Bonita Ave Pomona (91767) *(P-3245)*

Progressive Health Care System .... D 818 707-9603
8510 Balboa Blvd Ste 150 Northridge (91325) *(P-17740)*

Progressive Label Inc .... E 323 415-9770
2545 Yates Ave Commerce (90040) *(P-3246)*

Progressive Management Systems, West Covina *Also Called: RM Galicia Inc (P-15615)*

Progressive Manufacturing, Fullerton *Also Called: Progrssive Intgrated Solutions (P-3802)*

Progressive Marketing, Yorba Linda *Also Called: Progressive Marketing Pdts Inc (P-6389)*

Progressive Marketing Pdts Inc .... D 714 888-1700
4571 Avenida Del Este Yorba Linda (92886) *(P-6389)*

Progrssive Intgrated Solutions .... D 714 237-0980
377 S Acacia Ave Fullerton (92831) *(P-3802)*

Project Concern International (PA) .... C 858 279-9690
5151 Murphy Canyon Rd Ste 320 San Diego (92123) *(P-19128)*

Project Design Consultants LLC .... E 619 235-6471
701 B St Ste 800 San Diego (92101) *(P-20372)*

Project Management, Rcho Sta Marg *Also Called: M-Industrial Enterprises LLC (P-7912)*

Project Skyline Intermediate H .... A 310 712-1850
360 N Crescent Dr Bldg S Beverly Hills (90210) *(P-14939)*

Project Social T LLC .... E 323 266-4500
615 S Clarence St Los Angeles (90023) *(P-2263)*

Prolabs Factory Inc .... E 818 646-3677
15001 Oxnard St Van Nuys (91411) *(P-4449)*

Prolacta Bioscience Inc .... B 626 599-9260
1800 Highland Ave Duarte (91010) *(P-1283)*

Prolacta Bioscience Inc (PA) .... C 626 599-9260
757 Baldwin Park Blvd City Of Industry (91746) *(P-4328)*

Proland Property Managment LLC (PA) .... D 213 738-8175
2510 W 7th St 2nd Fl Los Angeles (90057) *(P-14851)*

Prolifics Testing Inc .... E 925 485-9535
24025 Park Sorrento Ste 405 Calabasas (91302) *(P-16099)*

Proline Concrete Tools Inc .... E 760 758-7240
4645 North Ave Ste 102 Oceanside (92056) *(P-7257)*

Prologic Rdmption Slutions Inc (PA) .... A 310 322-7774
2121 Rosecrans Ave El Segundo (90245) *(P-16908)*

Proma Inc .... E 310 327-0035
730 Kingshill Pl Carson (90746) *(P-10763)*

Promach Filling Systems LLC .... E 951 393-2200
200 River Rd Corona (92878) *(P-10153)*

Promart Dazz, Irvine *Also Called: Pro-Mart Industries Inc (P-2485)*

Promega Biosciences LLC .... D 805 544-8524
277 Granada Dr San Luis Obispo (93401) *(P-4013)*

Promenade Software Inc .... E 949 333-4634
16 Technology Dr Ste 100 Irvine (92618) *(P-16356)*

Prometheus Biosciences Inc .... D 858 422-4300
3050 Science Park Rd San Diego (92121) *(P-4208)*

Prometheus Laboratories Inc .... E 858 583-0131
5739 Pacific Center Blvd San Diego (92121) *(P-4209)*

Prometheus Laboratories Inc .... B 858 824-0895
9410 Carroll Park Dr San Diego (92121) *(P-4210)*

Prometheus Rxdx Inc .... E 858 824-0895
9410 Carroll Park Dr San Diego (92121) *(P-4211)*

Prometheus Therapeutics &Dlagn .... F 858 824-0895
9410 Carroll Park Dr San Diego (92121) *(P-4212)*

Promise Wine LLC .... D 707 260-9094
14909 La Cumbre Dr Pacific Palisades (90272) *(P-1654)*

Promises Promises Inc .... E 213 749-7725
3121 S Grand Ave Los Angeles (90007) *(P-2288)*

Promotonal Design Concepts Inc .... D 626 579-4454
9872 Rush St South El Monte (91733) *(P-4786)*

Promoveo Health LLC .... A 760 931-4794
701 Palomar Airport Rd Carlsbad (92011) *(P-15569)*

Prompt Delivery Inc .... D 858 549-8000
5757 Wilshire Blvd Ph 3 Los Angeles (90036) *(P-16909)*

Pronto Janitorial Svcs Inc .... D 562 273-5997
12561 Persing Dr Whittier (90606) *(P-15741)*

ALPHABETIC

Pronto Products Co (PA)...E....... **619 661-6995**
9850 Siempre Viva Rd San Diego (92154) *(P-7680)*

Pronto Products Co..E....... **800 377-6680**
1801 W Olympic Blvd Pasadena (91199) *(P-7982)*

Proper Hospitality LLC..C...... 310 277-5221
73 Market St Venice (90291) *(P-15310)*

Property Care Building Svc LLC....................................E...... 626 623-6420
126 La Porte St Ste F Arcadia (91006) *(P-15742)*

Property I D, Los Angeles *Also Called: I D Property Corporation (P-14813)*

Property Insight LLC..A...... 877 747-2537
2510 Redhill Ave Santa Ana (92705) *(P-14894)*

Property Management Assoc Inc (PA)............................C...... **323 295-2000**
6011 Bristol Pkwy Culver City (90230) *(P-14852)*

Proplas Technologies, Garden Grove *Also Called: Peerless Injection Molding LLC (P-5133)*

Proponent, Brea *Also Called: Proponent Inc (P-12914)*

Proponent Inc (PA)...C...... **714 223-5400**
3120 Enterprise St Brea (92821) *(P-12914)*

Proprietary Controls Systems.....................................E...... 310 303-3600
3830 Del Amo Blvd # 102 Torrance (90503) *(P-10390)*

Propstream, Lake Forest *Also Called: Equimine (P-16239)*

Pros Incorporated...D...... 661 589-5400
3400 Patton Way Bakersfield (93308) *(P-380)*

Proscape Landscape, Signal Hill *Also Called: Fenderscape Incorporated (P-191)*

Prosciento Inc (PA)..C...... **619 427-1300**
855 Third Ave Ste 3340 Chula Vista (91911) *(P-19872)*

Prosearch Strategies LLC...C...... 877 447-7291
3250 Wilshire Blvd Ste 301 Los Angeles (90010) *(P-19910)*

Proshot Golf, Newport Beach *Also Called: Proshot Investors LLC (P-8562)*

Proshot Investors LLC..F...... 949 586-9500
14 Corporate Plaza Dr Ste 120 Newport Beach (92660) *(P-8562)*

Prosites Inc...C...... 888 932-3644
38977 Sky Canyon Dr Ste 200 Murrieta (92563) *(P-16593)*

Prosoft Technology Inc (HQ).......................................C...... **661 716-5100**
9201 Camino Media Ste 200 Bakersfield (93311) *(P-12011)*

Prospect Enterprises Inc (PA)....................................C...... **213 599-5700**
625 Kohler St Los Angeles (90021) *(P-13283)*

Prospect Medical Group Inc (HQ)................................B...... **714 796-5900**
1920 E 17th St Ste 200 Santa Ana (92705) *(P-20084)*

Prospect Medical Holdings Inc (PA).............................C...... **310 943-4500**
3415 S Sepulveda Blvd Fl 9 Los Angeles (90034) *(P-17741)*

Prospect Medical Systems Inc (HQ).............................C...... **714 667-8156**
600 City Pkwy W Ste 800 Orange (92868) *(P-20085)*

Prospect Mortgage LLC..A
Sherman Oaks (91403) *(P-14940)*

Prospectra Contract Flooring, Poway *Also Called: Pro Installations Inc (P-1034)*

Prost LLC...E...... 619 954-4189
8179 Center St La Mesa (91942) *(P-1603)*

Protab Laboratories..C...... 949 635-1930
25902 Towne Centre Dr Foothill Ranch (92610) *(P-4213)*

Protec Arisawa America Inc...E...... 760 599-4800
2455 Ash St Vista (92081) *(P-6151)*

Protec Association Services (PA)................................C...... **858 569-1080**
10180 Willow Creek Rd San Diego (92131) *(P-15743)*

Protec Building Services, San Diego *Also Called: Protec Association Services (P-15743)*

Protech Design & Manufacturing, San Diego *Also Called: PDM Solutions Inc (P-8716)*

Protect-US..C...... 714 721-8127
3505 Cadillac Ave Costa Mesa (92626) *(P-16672)*

Protection One, Riverside *Also Called: ADT LLC (P-16715)*

Protein Kitchen...E...... 888 899-2956
13448 Manhasset Rd Ste 3 Apple Valley (92308) *(P-13966)*

Proterra Operating Company Inc.................................B...... 864 438-0000
393 Cheryl Ln City Of Industry (91789) *(P-9304)*

Proto Homes LLC...E...... 310 271-7544
11301 W Olympic Blvd Los Angeles (90064) *(P-9928)*

Proto Space Engineering Inc.......................................E...... 626 442-8273
2214 Loma Ave South El Monte (91733) *(P-7983)*

Protocast, Chatsworth *Also Called: John List Corporation (P-7151)*

Protoform, Banning *Also Called: DT Mattson Enterprises Inc (P-10950)*

Protool Co, Tustin *Also Called: Bernhardt and Bernhardt Inc (P-7005)*

Prototype & Short-Run Svcs Inc..................................E...... 714 449-9661
1310 W Collins Ave Orange (92867) *(P-6550)*

Prototype Engineering and Manufacturing Inc...............E...... 310 532-6305
140 E 162nd St Gardena (90248) *(P-19673)*

Prototype Industries Inc (PA).....................................E...... **949 680-4890**
26035 Acero Ste 100 Mission Viejo (92691) *(P-3478)*

Prototypes, Los Angeles *Also Called: Prototypes Centers For Innov (P-19129)*

Prototypes Centers For Innov.....................................C...... 213 542-3838
1000 N Alameda St Ste 390 Los Angeles (90012) *(P-19129)*

Protravel International LLC..D...... 310 271-9566
345 N Maple Dr Beverly Hills (90210) *(P-11725)*

Proulx Manufacturing Inc..E...... 909 980-0662
11433 6th St Rancho Cucamonga (91730) *(P-5168)*

Provena Foods Inc (HQ)...D...... **909 627-1082**
5010 Eucalyptus Ave Chino (91710) *(P-1231)*

Providence, Mission Hills *Also Called: Providence Holy Cross Medical (P-18398)*

Providence Health & Svcs - Ore..................................A...... 818 365-8051
15031 Rinaldi St Mission Hills (91345) *(P-18396)*

Providence Health System..A...... 818 843-5111
501 S Buena Vista St Burbank (91505) *(P-18397)*

Providence Holy Cross Med Ctr, Mission Hills *Also Called: Providence Health & Svcs - Ore (P-18396)*

Providence Holy Cross Medical (PA)...........................B...... **818 365-8051**
15031 Rinaldi St Mission Hills (91345) *(P-18398)*

PROVIDENCE HOME HEALTH ORANGE, Anaheim *Also Called: Providence Medical Foundation (P-18399)*

Providence Industries LLC..D...... 562 420-9091
18191 Von Karman Ave Ste 100 Irvine (92612) *(P-2184)*

Providence Medical Foundation (DH)...........................C...... **714 712-3308**
200 W Center Street Promenade Ste 800 Anaheim (92805) *(P-18399)*

Providence Rest Partners LLC....................................D...... 323 460-4170
5955 Melrose Ave Los Angeles (90038) *(P-15047)*

Providence St Johns Hlth Ctr......................................B...... 971 268-7643
2121 Santa Monica Blvd Santa Monica (90404) *(P-18400)*

Providence Tarzana Medical Ctr..................................A...... 818 881-0800
18321 Clark St Tarzana (91356) *(P-18401)*

Provident Financial Management.................................D...... 310 282-0477
3130 Wilshire Blvd Ste 600 Santa Monica (90403) *(P-20086)*

Providien Injction Molding Inc....................................D...... 760 931-1844
6740 Nancy Ridge Dr San Diego (92121) *(P-5169)*

Providien Machining & Metals Corporation....................D...... 818 367-3161
12840 Bradley Ave Sylmar (91342) *(P-10592)*

Providien Thermoforming Inc......................................E...... 858 850-1591
6740 Nancy Ridge Dr San Diego (92121) *(P-4818)*

Providnce Facey Med Foundation (PA)........................C...... **818 365-9531**
15451 San Fernando Mission Blvd Mission Hills (91345) *(P-17742)*

Providnce Facey Med Foundation...............................D...... 661 513-2100
27924 Seco Canyon Rd Santa Clarita (91350) *(P-17743)*

Providnce Facey Med Foundation...............................D...... 818 365-9531
11165 Sepulveda Blvd Mission Hills (91345) *(P-17744)*

Providnce Facey Med Foundation...............................D...... 805 206-2000
2655 1st St Simi Valley (93065) *(P-17851)*

Providnce Facey Med Foundation...............................D...... 818 861-7831
191 S Buena Vista St Burbank (91505) *(P-17852)*

Providnce Facey Med Foundation...............................C...... 818 837-5677
11211 Sepulveda Blvd Mission Hills (91345) *(P-18790)*

Providnce Facey Med Foundation...............................C...... 661 250-5225
17909 Soledad Canyon Rd Santa Clarita (91387) *(P-18791)*

Providnce Hlth Svcs Fndtn/San..................................A...... 818 843-5111
501 S Buena Vista St Burbank (91505) *(P-18402)*

Providnce Holy Cross Fundation, Burbank *Also Called: Providnce Hlth Svcs Fndtn/San (P-18402)*

Provisio Medical Inc...F...... 508 740-9940
10815 Rancho Bernardo Rd Ste 110 San Diego (92127) *(P-18792)*

Provivi Inc (PA)...E...... **310 828-2307**
1701 Colorado Ave Santa Monica (90404) *(P-4526)*

Prowall Lath and Plaster...D...... 760 480-9001
360 S Spruce St Escondido (92025) *(P-992)*

Prowave Manufacturing, San Marcos *Also Called: Action Electronic Assembly Inc (P-8641)*

Prp Seats, Temecula *Also Called: Kamm Industries Inc (P-2534)*

Prpco..E...... 805 543-6844
2226 Beebee St San Luis Obispo (93401) *(P-3672)*

Prs Industries, Ontario *Also Called: Inland Powder Coating Corp (P-6710)*

Prsi, Jurupa Valley *Also Called: Pavement Recycling Systems Inc (P-12956)*

Prudential, Thousand Oaks *Also Called: Gemmm Corporation (P-14803)*

Prudential, Irvine *Also Called: Hsf Affiliates LLC (P-14812)*

Prudential, Irvine *Also Called: Brer Affiliates LLC (P-15008)*

Prudential Cleanroom Services, Irvine *Also Called: Prudential Overall Supply (P-15470)*

Prudential Lighting Corp (PA)...................................C...... 213 477-1694
1774 E 21st St Los Angeles (90058) *(P-8328)*

Prudential Overall Supply (PA)................................D...... 949 250-4855
1661 Alton Pkwy Irvine (92606) *(P-15470)*

Prutel Joint Venture ....A...... 949 240-5064
1 Ritz Carlton Dr Dana Point (92629) *(P-15311)*

Pryor Products ....E...... 760 724-8244
1819 Peacock Blvd Oceanside (92056) *(P-10593)*

PS, Los Angeles *Also Called: Private Suite Lax LLC (P-11356)*

Psav Holdings LLC (PA)...C...... 562 366-0138
111 W Ocean Blvd Ste 1110 Long Beach (90802) *(P-15794)*

PSC Industrial Outsourcing LP ....D...... 661 833-9991
200 Old Yard Dr Bakersfield (93307) *(P-381)*

Pscmb Repairs Inc ....E...... 626 448-7778
12145 Slauson Ave Santa Fe Springs (90670) *(P-7984)*

Pse Holding LLC (DH)...B...... 248 377-0165
360 N Crescent Dr Beverly Hills (90210) *(P-17381)*

Psemi Corporation (DH)..D...... 858 731-9400
9369 Carroll Park Dr San Diego (92121) *(P-8869)*

Psg, San Diego *Also Called: Pacific Steel Group (P-6404)*

Psg California LLC (HQ)..B...... 909 422-1700
22069 Van Buren St Grand Terrace (92313) *(P-7287)*

PSG Fencing Corporation ....D...... 951 275-9252
330 Main St Riverside (92501) *(P-1174)*

PSI, Glendale *Also Called: PSI Services LLC (P-20373)*

PSI Services LLC (PA)..D...... 818 847-6180
611 N Brand Blvd Ste 10 Glendale (91203) *(P-20373)*

Psitech Inc ....F...... 714 964-7818
18368 Bandilier Cir Fountain Valley (92708) *(P-7446)*

PSM, Oceanside *Also Called: Pacific Sewer Maintenance Corp (P-5648)*

PSM Industries Inc (PA)...D...... 888 663-8256
14000 Avalon Blvd Los Angeles (90061) *(P-6871)*

Psomas ....D...... 714 751-7373
5 Hutton Centre Dr Ste 300 Santa Ana (92707) *(P-19749)*

Psomas (PA)..C...... 213 223-1400
865 S Figueroa St Los Angeles (90017) *(P-19750)*

Psychic Eye Book Shops Inc (PA)...........................D...... 818 906-8263
13435 Ventura Blvd Sherman Oaks (91423) *(P-14069)*

Psyonic Inc ....E...... 888 779-6642
9999 Businesspark Ave Ste B San Diego (92131) *(P-10694)*

Psyonix LLC ....D...... 619 622-8772
401 W A St Ste 2400 San Diego (92101) *(P-16100)*

Pszyjw, Los Angeles *Also Called: Pachulski Stang Zehl Jones LLP (P-18920)*

Pt Gaming LLC ....A...... 323 260-5060
235 Oregon St El Segundo (90245) *(P-15312)*

Ptb, Azusa *Also Called: Ptb Sales Inc (P-9102)*

Ptb Sales Inc (PA)...E...... 626 334-0500
1361 Mountain View Cir Azusa (91702) *(P-9102)*

PTi Sand & Gravel Inc ....E...... 951 272-0140
14925 River Rd Eastvale (92880) *(P-408)*

Pti Technologies Inc (DH)......................................C...... 805 604-3700
501 Del Norte Blvd Oxnard (93030) *(P-9770)*

Ptm & W Industries Inc ....E...... 562 946-4511
10640 Painter Ave Santa Fe Springs (90670) *(P-4841)*

Ptm Images, West Hollywood *Also Called: Pro Tour Memorabilia LLC (P-2759)*

Pts, Tustin *Also Called: Pts Advance (P-15883)*

Pts Advance ....C...... 949 268-4000
1775 Flight Way Ste 100 Tustin (92782) *(P-15883)*

Ptsi Managed Services Inc ....D...... 626 440-3118
100 W Walnut St Pasadena (91124) *(P-19674)*

Public Authority ....D...... 619 731-3705
401 Mile Of Cars Way Ste 200 National City (91950) *(P-12138)*

Public Communications Svcs Inc ....C...... 310 231-1000
11859 Wilshire Blvd Ste 600 Los Angeles (90025) *(P-11899)*

Public Counsel ....D...... 213 385-2977
610 S Ardmore Ave Los Angeles (90005) *(P-18929)*

Public Defender- Main Office, Riverside *Also Called: County of Riverside (P-18841)*

Public Fclities Resources Dept, Santa Ana *Also Called: County of Orange (P-20409)*

Public Hlth Fndation Entps Inc ....C...... 310 518-2835
125 E Anaheim St Wilmington (90744) *(P-18793)*

Public Hlth Fndation Entps Inc ....C...... 626 856-6618
12781 Shama Rd El Monte (91732) *(P-18794)*

Public Hlth Fndation Entps Inc ....C...... 323 261-6388
3648 E Olympic Blvd Los Angeles (90023) *(P-18795)*

Public Hlth Fndation Entps Inc ....C...... 562 801-2323
8666 Whittier Blvd Pico Rivera (90660) *(P-18796)*

Public Hlth Fndation Entps Inc ....C...... 323 733-9381
1649 W Washington Blvd Los Angeles (90007) *(P-18797)*

Public Hlth Fndation Entps Inc ....C...... 626 856-6600
13181 Crossroads Pkwy N City Of Industry (91746) *(P-19130)*

Public Hlth Fndation Entps Inc (PA).......................C...... 800 201-7320
13300 Crossroads Pkwy N Ste 450 City Of Industry (91746) *(P-19458)*

Public Hlth Fndation Entps Inc ....C...... 323 263-0262
277 S Atlantic Blvd Los Angeles (90022) *(P-19459)*

Public Hlth Fndation Entps Inc ....C...... 310 320-5215
1640 W Carson St Ste G Torrance (90501) *(P-19460)*

Public Mdia Group Southern Cal (PA)....................D...... 714 241-4100
2900 W Alameda Ave Unit 600 Burbank (91505) *(P-11961)*

Public Services, Coronado *Also Called: City of Coronado (P-12104)*

Public Social Services, Moreno Valley *Also Called: County of Riverside (P-17636)*

Public Storage (PA)...B...... 818 244-8080
701 Western Ave Glendale (91201) *(P-15017)*

Public Utilites Emts, San Diego *Also Called: City of San Diego (P-10249)*

Public Works, San Diego *Also Called: County of San Diego (P-16808)*

Public Works, Dept of, La Puente *Also Called: County of Los Angeles (P-6929)*

Public Works, Dept of, Malibu *Also Called: County of Los Angeles (P-6930)*

Public Works, Dept of, Los Angeles *Also Called: County of Los Angeles (P-11569)*

Publishers Development Corp ....E...... 858 605-0200
225 W Valley Pkwy Ste 100 Escondido (92025) *(P-3382)*

Puente Ready Mix Services Inc (PA).......................E...... 626 968-0711
209 N California Ave City Of Industry 91744) *(P-5492)*

Puff Candy,, San Diego *Also Called: Puff Global Inc (P-16910)*

Puff Global Inc ....D...... 619 520-3499
402 W Broadway Ste 400 San Diego (92101) *(P-16910)*

Pull-N-Pac, Huntington Park *Also Called: Crown Poly Inc (P-3181)*

Pulltarps Manufacturing, El Cajon *Also Called: Roll-Rite LLC (P-2508)*

Pulltarps Manufacturing, El Cajon *Also Called: Transportation Equipment Inc (P-2511)*

Pulp Story, Orange *Also Called: Quality Produced LLC (P-1378)*

Pulp Studio Incorporated ....D...... 310 815-4999
2100 W 139th St Gardena (90249) *(P-15672)*

Pulse A Yageo Company, San Diego *Also Called: Pulse Electronics Corporation (P-9103)*

Pulse Electronics Inc (HQ)....................................B...... 858 674-8100
15255 Innovation Dr Ste 100 San Diego (92128) *(P-8108)*

Pulse Electronics Corporation (HQ).......................E...... 858 674-8100
15255 Innovation Dr Ste 100 San Diego (92128) *(P-9103)*

Pulse Instruments ....E...... 310 515-5330
22301 S Western Ave Ste 107 Torrance (90501) *(P-10221)*

Pulse Instruments, Camarillo *Also Called: Primordial Diagnostics Inc (P-10152)*

Pulse Sciences, San Diego *Also Called: L3 Applied Technologies Inc (P-8530)*

Puma Biotechnology Inc (PA)................................B...... 424 248-6500
10880 Wilshire Blvd Ste 2150 Los Angeles (90024) *(P-4214)*

Pump-A-Head, San Diego *Also Called: Keco Inc (P-12796)*

Punch Press Products Inc ....D...... 323 581-7151
2035 E 51st St Vernon (90058) *(P-7092)*

Punch Studio LLC (PA)..C...... 310 390-9900
6025 W Slauson Ave Culver City (90230) *(P-12998)*

Pupil Transportation, Whittier *Also Called: County of Los Angeles (P-11420)*

Pura Naturals Inc ....E...... 949 273-8100
3401 Space Center Ct Ste 811a Jurupa Valley (91752) *(P-2857)*

Purchasing Department, Ventura *Also Called: Community Mem Hosp San Bnvntur (P-18226)*

Pure Flo Water, Escondido *Also Called: Pure-Flo Water Co (P-1721)*

Pure Process Filtration Inc ....F...... 714 891-6527
7429 Lampson Ave Garden Grove (92841) *(P-12758)*

Pure Project LLC ....D...... 760 552-7873
1305 Hot Springs Way Vista (92081) *(P-1604)*

A
L
P
H
A
B
E
T
I
C

Employee Codes: A=Over 500 employees, B=251-500
C=101-250, D=51-100, E=20-50, F=10-19, G=1-9

2024 Southern California
Business Directory and Buyers Guide

© Mergent Inc. 1-800-342-5647

1231

Pure-Flo Water Co (PA) .... D...... 619 596-4130
2169 Orange Ave Escondido (92029) *(P-1721)*

Pureformance Cables, Torrance *Also Called: Lynn Products Inc (P-7545)*

Puregear, Irwindale *Also Called: Superior Communications Inc (P-12699)*

Puretek Corporation (PA) .... E...... 818 361-3316
1145 Arroyo St Ste D San Fernando (91340) *(P-4215)*

Puretek Corporation .... C...... 818 361-3949
7900 Nelson Rd Unit A Panorama City (91402) *(P-4216)*

Puri Tech Inc .... E...... 951 360-8380
3167 Progress Cir Jurupa Valley (91752) *(P-7681)*

Puroflux Corporation .... F...... 805 579-0216
2121 Union Pl Simi Valley (93065) *(P-8952)*

Purus International Inc .... F...... 760 775-4500
82860 Avenue 45 Indio (92201) *(P-4787)*

Pusan Pipe America Inc .... B...... 949 655-8000
2100 Main St Ste 100 Irvine (92614) *(P-12565)*

Putnam Accessory Group Inc .... E...... 323 306-1330
4455 Fruitland Ave Vernon (90058) *(P-2362)*

PVA Tepla America Inc (HQ) .... E...... 951 371-2500
251 Corporate Terrace St Corona (92879) *(P-7985)*

Pvd Coatings LLC .... F...... 714 899-4892
5271 Argosy Ave Huntington Beach (92649) *(P-6730)*

Pvhmc, Pomona *Also Called: Pomona Valley Hospital Med Ctr (P-18383)*

Pvp Advanced Eo Systems Inc (DH) .... E...... 714 508-2740
14312 Franklin Ave Ste 100 Tustin (92780) *(P-10335)*

Pw Eagle Inc .... A...... 800 621-4404
5200 W Century Blvd Los Angeles (90045) *(P-4853)*

PW Gillibrand Co Inc (PA) .... E...... 805 526-2195
4537 Ish Dr Simi Valley (93063) *(P-411)*

PWC STRategy& (us) LLC .... C...... 213 356-6000
601 S Figueroa St Ste 900 Los Angeles (90017) *(P-20225)*

Pxise Energy Solutions LLC .... E...... 619 696-2944
1455 Frazee Rd Ste 150 San Diego (92108) *(P-9245)*

Pyr, San Diego *Also Called: Pyr Preservation Services (P-9847)*

Pyr Preservation Services .... E...... 619 338-8395
2393 Newton Ave Ste B San Diego (92113) *(P-9847)*

Pyramid Flowers Inc .... C...... 805 382-8070
3813 Doris Ave Oxnard (93030) *(P-13518)*

Pyramid Mold & Tool .... D...... 909 476-2555
10155 Sharon Cir Rancho Cucamonga (91730) *(P-7093)*

Pyramid Precision Machine Inc .... D...... 858 642-0713
6721 Cobra Way San Diego (92121) *(P-7986)*

Pyrenees French Bakery Inc .... E...... 661 322-7159
717 E 21st St Bakersfield (93305) *(P-1490)*

Pyro, Irvine *Also Called: Pyro-Comm Systems Inc (P-930)*

Pyro-Comm Systems Inc (PA) .... C...... 714 902-8000
15215 Alton Pkwy Irvine (92618) *(P-930)*

Q & B Foods Inc (DH) .... D...... 626 334-8090
15547 1st St Irwindale (91706) *(P-1364)*

Q C M Inc .... E...... 714 414-1173
285 Gemini Ave Brea (92821) *(P-8211)*

Q C Poultry, Montebello *Also Called: Ingenue Inc (P-1245)*

Q Cells, Irvine *Also Called: Hanwha Q Cells America Inc (P-8802)*

Q M C, Fountain Valley *Also Called: Quik Mfg Co (P-6940)*

Q Microwave Inc .... D...... 619 258-7322
1591 Pioneer Way El Cajon (92020) *(P-9104)*

Q Team .... E...... 714 228-4465
6400 Dale St Buena Park (90621) *(P-3673)*

Q Tech Corporation .... C...... 310 836-7900
6161 Chip Ave Cypress (90630) *(P-12692)*

Q-Flex Inc .... F...... 714 664-0101
1301 E Hunter Ave Santa Ana (92705) *(P-8720)*

Q-See, Anaheim *Also Called: Digital Periph Solutions Inc (P-8405)*

Q&A Clothing, Los Angeles *Also Called: Q&A7 LLC (P-2363)*

Q&A7 LLC .... F...... 323 364-4250
2155 E 7th St Ste 150 Los Angeles (90023) *(P-2363)*

Q1 Test Inc .... E...... 909 390-9718
1100 S Grove Ave Ste B2 Ontario (91761) *(P-9771)*

Qad, Santa Barbara *Also Called: Qad Inc (P-16358)*

Qad Inc .... F...... 805 684-6614
6450 Via Real Carpinteria (93013) *(P-16357)*

Qad Inc (HQ) .... C...... 805 566-6000
101 Innovation Pl Santa Barbara (93108) *(P-16358)*

Qantas Vctons Nwmans Vacations, Los Angeles *Also Called: Helloworld Travel Svcs USA Inc (P-11715)*

Qc Manufacturing Inc .... D...... 951 325-6340
26040 Ynez Rd Temecula (92591) *(P-7329)*

Qdoba Mexican Grill, San Diego *Also Called: Qdoba Restaurant Corporation (P-14032)*

Qdoba Restaurant Corporation (HQ) .... C...... 858 766-4900
350 Camino De La Reina Fl 4 San Diego (92108) *(P-14032)*

Qdos Inc .... E...... 949 362-8888
200 Spectrum Center Dr Ste 300 Irvine (92618) *(P-16359)*

QED Software LLC .... E...... 310 214-3118
211 E Ocean Blvd Long Beach (90802) *(P-16360)*

Qf Liquidation Inc (PA) .... C...... 949 930-3400
25242 Arctic Ocean Dr Lake Forest (92630) *(P-9444)*

Qfi Prv Aerospace, Torrance *Also Called: Quality Forming LLC (P-9773)*

Qg Printing Corp .... E...... 951 571-2500
6688 Box Springs Blvd Riverside (92507) *(P-3383)*

Qg Printing IL LLC .... C...... 951 571-2500
6688 Box Springs Blvd Riverside (92507) *(P-3674)*

Qlogic LLC (DH) .... C...... 949 389-6000
15485 Sand Canyon Ave Irvine (92618) *(P-8870)*

Qmerit Electrification LLC (PA) .... C...... 888 272-0090
2 Venture Ste 550 Irvine (92618) *(P-20374)*

Qmp Inc .... E...... 661 294-6860
25070 Avenue Tibbitts Valencia (91355) *(P-7682)*

Qology Direct LLC .... C...... 310 341-4420
12130 Millennium Ste 600 Los Angeles (90094) *(P-16911)*

Qorvo California Inc .... E...... 805 480-5050
950 Lawrence Dr Newbury Park (91320) *(P-9105)*

Qorvo US, Newbury Park *Also Called: Qorvo California Inc (P-9105)*

Qpc Fiber Optic LLC .... E...... 949 361-8855
27612 El Lazo Laguna Niguel (92677) *(P-5749)*

Qpc Laser, Rancho Cascades *Also Called: Laser Operations LLC (P-8827)*

Qpe Inc .... F...... 949 263-0381
1372 Mcgaw Ave Irvine (92614) *(P-3722)*

Qpi Holdings Inc (DH) .... E...... 310 539-2855
22906 Frampton Ave Torrance (90501) *(P-9772)*

Qre Operating LLC .... D...... 213 225-5900
707 Wilshire Blvd Ste 4600 Los Angeles (90017) *(P-316)*

Qsc LLC (PA) .... C...... 800 854-4079
1675 Macarthur Blvd Costa Mesa (92626) *(P-8428)*

Qsc Audio, Costa Mesa *Also Called: Qsc LLC (P-8428)*

Qspac Industries Inc (PA) .... D...... 562 407-3868
15020 Marquardt Ave Santa Fe Springs (90670) *(P-4578)*

Qtc Management Inc (DH) .... D...... 800 682-9701
924 Overland Ct San Dimas (91773) *(P-18798)*

Qtc Mdcal Group Inc A Med Corp .... A...... 800 260-1515
924 Overland Ct San Dimas (91773) *(P-18799)*

Qtc Medical Group, San Dimas *Also Called: Qtc Mdcal Group Inc A Med Corp (P-18799)*

Quad Graphics, Riverside *Also Called: Qg Printing IL LLC (P-3674)*

Quad R Tech, Harbor City *Also Called: Onyx Industries Inc (P-6416)*

Quad-C Jh Holdings Inc .... C...... 800 966-6662
4593 Ish Dr Ste 320 Simi Valley (93063) *(P-12510)*

Quad-C Jh Holdings Inc .... C...... 502 741-0421
1055 E Discovery Ln Anaheim (92801) *(P-12511)*

Quad/Graphics Inc .... E...... 951 689-1122
6688 Box Springs Blvd Riverside (92507) *(P-3675)*

QUAD/GRAPHICS INC., Riverside *Also Called: Quad/Graphics Inc (P-3675)*

Quadriga Americas LLC .... E...... 424 634-4900
17800 S Main St Ste 113 Gardena (90248) *(P-3479)*

Quadrotech Solutions Inc (PA) .... E...... 949 754-8000
20 Enterprise Aliso Viejo (92656) *(P-16361)*

Quadrtech Corporation .... E...... 310 523-1697
521 W Rosecrans Ave Gardena (90248) *(P-10919)*

Quake City Caps, Los Angeles *Also Called: Quake City Casuals Inc (P-13109)*

Quake City Casuals Inc .... C...... 213 746-0540
1800 S Flower St Los Angeles (90015) *(P-13109)*

Quaker, Whittier *Also Called: AC Products Inc (P-4555)*

Quaker City Plating .... C...... 562 945-3721
11729 Washington Blvd Whittier (90606) *(P-6652)*

Mergent email: customerrelations@mergent.com
1232

2024 Southern California
Business Directory and Buyers Guide

(P-0000) Products & Services Section entry number
(PA)=Parent Co (HQ)=Headquarters (DH)=Div Headquarters

Quaker City Plating & Silvrsm, Whittier *Also Called: Quaker City Plating (P-6652)*

QUAKER GARDENS, Stanton *Also Called: California Friends Homes (P-19244)*

Qual-Pro Corporation (HQ)...C....... 310 329-7535
18510 S Figueroa St Gardena (90248) *(P-8721)*

Qualcomm, San Diego *Also Called: Qualcomm Incorporated (P-8563)*

Qualcomm, San Diego *Also Called: Qualcomm Incorporated (P-8564)*

Qualcomm, Carlsbad *Also Called: Qualcomm Incorporated (P-8872)*

Qualcomm, San Diego *Also Called: Qualcomm Incorporated (P-8873)*

Qualcomm, San Diego *Also Called: Qualcomm Incorporated (P-8874)*

Qualcomm, San Diego *Also Called: Qualcomm Incorporated (P-8875)*

Qualcomm, San Diego *Also Called: Qualcomm Limited Partner Inc (P-8876)*

Qualcomm, San Diego *Also Called: Qualcomm International Inc (P-15009)*

Qualcomm Datacenter Tech Inc (HQ) ....E....... 858 567-1121
5775 Morehouse Dr San Diego (92121) *(P-8871)*

Qualcomm Incorporated (PA).....................................A....... 858 587-1121
5775 Morehouse Dr San Diego (92121) *(P-8563)*

Qualcomm Incorporated ....E....... 858 587-1121
4243 Campus Point Ct San Diego (92121) *(P-8564)*

Qualcomm Incorporated ....F..... 858 651-8481
2016 Palomar Airport Rd Ste 100 Carlsbad (92011) *(P-8872)*

Qualcomm Incorporated ....E....... 858 909-0316
5751 Pacific Center Blvd San Diego (92121) *(P-8873)*

Qualcomm Incorporated ....E....... 858 587-1121
9393 Waples St Ste 150 San Diego (92121) *(P-8874)*

Qualcomm Incorporated ....D...... 858 587-1121
10555 Sorrento Valley Rd San Diego (92121) *(P-8875)*

Qualcomm International Inc (HQ) ....A....... 858 587-1121
5775 Morehouse Dr San Diego (92121) *(P-15009)*

Qualcomm Limited Partner Inc ....D...... 858 587-1121
5775 Morehouse Dr San Diego (92121) *(P-8876)*

Qualcomm Mems Technologies Inc ....D...... 858 587-1121
5775 Morehouse Dr San Diego (92121) *(P-8622)*

Qualcomm Technologies Inc (HQ) ....B....... 858 587-1121
5775 Morehouse Dr San Diego (92121) *(P-8877)*

Qualer Inc ....E....... 858 224-9516
10360 Sorrento Valley Rd San Diego (92121) *(P-16362)*

Quali-Tech Manufacturing, Calexico *Also Called: Lakim Industries Incorporated (P-11091)*

Qualigen Inc (HQ)...E....... 760 918-9165
2042 Corte Del Nogal Ste B Carlsbad (92011) *(P-10098)*

Qualis Automotive LLC ....D...... 859 689-7772
21046 Figueroa St Carson (90745) *(P-17036)*

Qualitask Inc ....E....... 714 237-0900
2840 E Gretta Ln Anaheim (92806) *(P-7987)*

Quality Aluminum Forge LLC ....C....... 714 639-8191
793 N Cypress St Orange (92867) *(P-6481)*

Quality Aluminum Forge Div, Orange *Also Called: Gei Industries Inc (P-6478)*

Quality Cabinet and Fixture Co (HQ) ....E....... 619 266-1011
7955 Saint Andrews Ave San Diego (92154) *(P-2674)*

Quality Car Care Products Inc ....E....... 626 359-9174
2734 Huntington Dr Duarte (91010) *(P-3907)*

Quality Control Plating Inc ....E....... 909 605-0206
4425 E Airport Dr Ste 113 Ontario (91761) *(P-6653)*

Quality Control Solutions Inc ....E....... 951 676-1616
43339 Business Park Dr Ste 101 Temecula (92590) *(P-10391)*

Quality Controlled Mfg Inc ....D...... 619 443-3997
9429 Abraham Way Santee (92071) *(P-7988)*

Quality Distributor, El Cajon *Also Called: Benny Enterprises Inc (P-13461)*

Quality Fabrication Inc (PA).....................................D...... 818 407-5015
9631 Irondale Ave Chatsworth (91311) *(P-6299)*

Quality First Woodworks Inc ....C....... 714 632-0480
1264 N Lakeview Ave Anaheim (92807) *(P-2760)*

Quality Foam Packaging, Lake Elsinore *Also Called: Aerofoam Industries Inc (P-2920)*

Quality Foam Packaging Inc ....E....... 951 245-4429
31855 Corydon St Lake Elsinore (92530) *(P-4901)*

Quality Forming LLC ....D...... 310 539-2855
22906 Frampton Ave Torrance (90501) *(P-9773)*

Quality Heat Treating Inc ....E....... 818 840-8212
3305 Burton Ave Burbank (91504) *(P-5848)*

Quality Industry Repair, Santa Fe Springs *Also Called: Pscmb Repairs Inc (P-7984)*

Quality Loan Service Corp ....B....... 619 645-7711
2763 Camino Del Rio S San Diego (92108) *(P-15005)*

Quality Magnetics Corporation ....E....... 310 632-1941
18025 Adria Maru Ln Carson (90746) *(P-6872)*

Quality Marble & Granite, Ontario *Also Called: Regards Enterprises Inc (P-2749)*

Quality Naturally Foods Inc (PA).............................E....... 626 854-6363
18830 San Jose Ave City Of Industry (91748) *(P-13390)*

Quality Packaging and Engrg, Irvine *Also Called: Qpe Inc (P-3722)*

Quality Powder Coating, Bakersfield *Also Called: Elyte Inc (P-6702)*

Quality Produced LLC ....E....... 310 592-8834
987 N Enterprise St Orange (92867) *(P-1378)*

Quality Production Svcs Inc ....D...... 310 406-3350
18711 S Broadwick St Compton (90220) *(P-993)*

Quality Reinforcing Inc ....D...... 858 748-8400
13275 Gregg St Poway (92064) *(P-1111)*

Quality Resources Dist LLC ....E....... 510 378-6861
16254 Beaver Rd Adelanto (92301) *(P-11273)*

Quality Service Pac Industry, Santa Fe Springs *Also Called: Qspac Industries Inc (P-4578)*

Quality Shutters Inc ....E....... 951 683-4939
3359 Chicago Ave Ste A Riverside (92507) *(P-2630)*

Quality Steel Fabricators Inc ....E....... 858 748-8400
13275 Gregg St Poway (92064) *(P-6405)*

Quality Systems, San Diego *Also Called: Quality Systems Intgrated Corp (P-8723)*

Quality Systems Intgrated Corp ....C....... 858 536-3128
7098 Miratech Dr Ste 170 San Diego (92121) *(P-8722)*

Quality Systems Intgrated Corp (PA).....................C..... 858 587-9797
6740 Top Gun St San Diego (92121) *(P-8723)*

Quality Tech Mfg Inc ....E....... 909 465-9565
170 W Mindanao St Bloomington (92316) *(P-9550)*

Qualitylogic Inc ....C....... 208 424-1905
2245 1st St Ste 103 Simi Valley (93065) *(P-7565)*

Quallion LLC ....C....... 818 833-2000
12744 San Fernando Rd Ste 100 Sylmar (91342) *(P-9159)*

Qualls Stud Welding Pdts Inc ....F..... 562 923-7883
9459 Washburn Rd Downey (90242) *(P-12812)*

Qualontime Corporation ....F...... 714 523-4751
19 Senisa Irvine (92612) *(P-7989)*

Qualstaff Resources, San Diego *Also Called: June Group LLC (P-15925)*

Qualy Pak Specialty Foods Inc ....D...... 310 541-3023
2208 Signal Pl San Pedro (90731) *(P-13284)*

Quanex Screens LLC ....E....... 909 349-0600
13611 Santa Ana Ave Fontana (92337) *(P-6117)*

Quanticel Pharmacueticals Inc ....E....... 858 956-3747
9393 Towne Centre Dr Ste 110 San Diego (92121) *(P-4217)*

Quantimetrix ....D...... 310 536-0006
2005 Manhattan Beach Blvd Redondo Beach (90278) *(P-4287)*

Quantos Payroll, Los Angeles *Also Called: Film Payroll Services Inc (P-19776)*

Quantum ....E....... 323 709-8880
220 S Glasgow Ave Inglewood (90301) *(P-7480)*

Quantum Alliance Inc ....F..... 818 415-2085
511 E Mountain St Glendale (91207) *(P-7481)*

Quantum Automation (PA)...E....... 714 854-0800
4400 E La Palma Ave Anaheim (92807) *(P-12614)*

Quantum Corporation ....E....... 949 856-7800
141 Innovation Dr Ste 100 Irvine (92617) *(P-7482)*

Quantum Corporation, Irvine *Also Called: Certance LLC (P-7466)*

Quantum Design Inc (PA)...C....... 858 481-4400
10307 Pacific Center Ct San Diego (92121) *(P-10282)*

Quantum Design International, San Diego *Also Called: Quantum Design Inc (P-10282)*

Quantum Group Inc ....E....... 858 566-9959
6827 Nancy Ridge Dr San Diego (92121) *(P-10392)*

Quantum Magnetics LLC ....A....... 714 258-4400
1251 E Dyer Rd Ste 140 Santa Ana (92705) *(P-10283)*

Quantum Networks LLC ....E....... 212 993-5899
3412 Garfield Ave Commerce (90040) *(P-14100)*

Quantum Technologies, Lake Forest *Also Called: Qf Liquidation Inc (P-9444)*

Quantum World Technologies Inc ....B....... 805 834-0532
4281 Katella Ave Ste 102 Los Alamitos (90720) *(P-15884)*

Quantumsphere Inc ....F...... 714 545-6266
28981 Modjeska Peak Ln Trabuco Canyon (92679) *(P-5857)*

Quartic Solutions LLC ....E....... 858 377-8470
1427 Chalcedony St San Diego (92109) *(P-12435)*

Employee Codes: A=Over 500 employees, B=251-500
C=101-250, D=51-100, E=20-50, F=10-19, G=1-9

2024 Southern California
Business Directory and Buyers Guide

© Mergent Inc. 1-800-342-5647
1233

ALPHABETIC

Quartics Inc ....E....... 949 679-2672
  15241 Laguna Canyon Rd Ste 200 Irvine (92618) *(P-8878)*

Quartus Engineering Inc (PA).................................C....... 858 875-6000
  9689 Towne Centre Dr San Diego (92121) *(P-19675)*

Quatro Composites, Poway *Also Called: Quatro Composites LLC (P-9774)*

Quatro Composites LLC ....C....... 712 707-9200
  13250 Gregg St Ste A1 Poway (92064) *(P-9774)*

Quechan Gaming Commission, Winterhaven *Also Called: Quechan Indian Tribe (P-17561)*

Quechan Indian Tribe ....C....... 760 572-2413
  450 Quechan Rd Winterhaven (92283) *(P-17561)*

Queen Beach Printers Inc ....E....... 562 436-8201
  937 Pine Ave Long Beach (90813) *(P-3676)*

Queen Mary Hotel, Long Beach *Also Called: RMS Foundation Inc (P-15331)*

Queen Mary, The, Long Beach *Also Called: Urban Commons Queensway LLC (P-15398)*

Queen of The Valley Campus, West Covina *Also Called: Citrus Vly Hlth Partners Inc (P-18221)*

Queen of The Valley Hospital, West Covina *Also Called: Emanate Health Medical Center (P-18255)*

Queensbay Hotel LLC ....D....... 562 481-3910
  700 Queensway Dr Long Beach (90802) *(P-15313)*

Queenscare Fmly Clnics - Estsi, Los Angeles *Also Called: Queenscare Health Centers (P-17746)*

Queenscare Health Centers ....D....... 323 644-6180
  4618 Fountain Ave Los Angeles (90029) *(P-17745)*

Queenscare Health Centers ....D....... 323 780-4510
  4816 E 3rd St Los Angeles (90022) *(P-17746)*

Quemetco West LLC ....E....... 626 330-2294
  720 S 7th Ave City Of Industry (91746) *(P-5683)*

Quest, Aliso Viejo *Also Called: Quadrotech Solutions Inc (P-16361)*

Quest Dgnstics Nchols Inst Vln, Valencia *Also Called: Specialty Laboratories Inc (P-18565)*

Quest Diagnostics, San Juan Capistrano *Also Called: Quest Diagnostics Nichols Inst (P-10284)*

Quest Diagnostics, West Hills *Also Called: Unilab Corporation (P-18567)*

Quest Diagnostics Nichols Inst (HQ).......................A....... 949 728-4000
  33608 Ortega Hwy San Juan Capistrano (92675) *(P-10284)*

Quest International, Irvine *Also Called: Quest Intl Monitor Svc Inc (P-16543)*

Quest Intl Monitor Svc Inc (PA)...........................D....... 949 581-9900
  60 Parker 65 Irvine (92618) *(P-16543)*

Quest Software Inc ....D....... 949 754-8000
  20 Enterprise Aliso Viejo (92656) *(P-16363)*

Quest Software Inc (PA)..................................A....... 949 754-8000
  20 Enterprise Ste 100 Aliso Viejo (92656) *(P-16465)*

Quest Solution, Garden Grove *Also Called: Bar Code Specialties Inc (P-7508)*

Quick Box LLC ....C....... 310 436-6444
  13838 S Figueroa St Los Angeles (90061) *(P-11605)*

Quick Crete Products Corp ....C....... 951 737-6240
  731 Parkridge Ave Norco (92860) *(P-5442)*

Quick Draw and Machining Inc ....F....... 805 644-7882
  4869 Mcgrath St Ste 130 Ventura (93003) *(P-6551)*

Quick Lane, San Diego *Also Called: Mossy Ford Inc (P-13799)*

Quick Lane, Riverside *Also Called: Raceway Ford Inc (P-13817)*

Quick Lane, Hawthorne *Also Called: South Bay Ford Inc (P-13826)*

Quick Lane, Fontana *Also Called: Sunrise Ford (P-13833)*

Quickrete, Corona *Also Called: Quikrete California LLC (P-5443)*

Quidel Corporation ....D....... 858 552-1100
  10165 Mckellar Ct San Diego (92121) *(P-4288)*

Quidel Corporation (HQ).................................D....... 858 552-1100
  9975 Summers Ridge Rd San Diego (92121) *(P-4289)*

Quidelortho Corporation (PA)..............................E....... 858 552-1100
  9975 Summers Ridge Rd San Diego (92121) *(P-4290)*

Quiel Bros Elc Sign Svc Co Inc ....E....... 909 885-4476
  272 S I St San Bernardino (92410) *(P-11147)*

Quigley-Simpson & Hepplewhite, Los Angeles *Also Called: Quigly-Simpson Heppelwhite Inc (P-15570)*

Quigly-Simpson Heppelwhite Inc ....C....... 310 996-5800
  11601 Wilshire Blvd Ste 710 Los Angeles (90025) *(P-15570)*

Quik Mfg Co ....E....... 714 754-0337
  18071 Mount Washington St Fountain Valley (92708) *(P-6940)*

Quik Pick Express LLC ....C....... 310 763-3000
  23610 Banning Blvd Carson (90745) *(P-11796)*

Quik-Shor, Downey *Also Called: Westar Manufacturing Inc (P-1185)*

Quikrete California LLC (DH)..............................E....... 951 277-3155
  3940 Temescal Canyon Rd Corona (92883) *(P-5443)*

Quikrete Companies LLC ....E....... 323 875-1367
  11145 Tuxford St Sun Valley (91352) *(P-5444)*

Quiksilver/Dc Shoes, Mira Loma *Also Called: DC Shoes Inc (P-13122)*

Quikstor, Encino *Also Called: Calstar Systems Group Inc (P-9197)*

Quill Distribution Center, Ontario *Also Called: Quill LLC (P-11606)*

Quill LLC ....C....... 909 390-0600
  1500 S Dupont Ave Ontario (91761) *(P-11606)*

Quilt In A Day Inc ....E....... 760 591-0929
  1955 Diamond St San Marcos (92078) *(P-14101)*

Quilter Laboratories LLC ....F....... 714 519-6114
  1791 Reynolds Ave Irvine (92614) *(P-10929)*

Quinn Company ....D....... 661 393-5800
  2200 Pegasus Dr Bakersfield (93308) *(P-12777)*

Quinn Emmanuel Trial Lawyers, Los Angeles *Also Called: Quinn Emnuel Urqhart Sllvan LL (P-18930)*

Quinn Emnuel Urqhart Sllvan LL (PA)......................B....... 213 443-3000
  865 S Figueroa St Fl 10 Los Angeles (90017) *(P-18930)*

Quinn Shepherd Machinery ....B....... 562 463-6000
  10006 Rose Hills Rd City Of Industry (90601) *(P-12778)*

Quinstar Technology Inc ....D....... 310 320-1111
  24085 Garnier St Torrance (90505) *(P-12693)*

Quintiles Pacific Incorporated ....B....... 858 552-3400
  10201 Wateridge Cir Ste 300 San Diego (92121) *(P-19911)*

Quintron, Santa Maria *Also Called: Quintron Systems Inc (P-8483)*

Quintron Systems Inc (PA)................................E....... 805 928-4343
  1290 W Mccoy Ln Santa Maria (93455) *(P-8483)*

Quoc Viet Foods ....D....... 714 283-3663
  12221 Monarch St Garden Grove (92841) *(P-1972)*

Quorex Pharm Inc (PA)....................................E....... 760 602-1910
  2232 Rutherford Rd Carlsbad (92008) *(P-4218)*

Quotit Corporation ....D....... 714 564-5000
  721 S Parker St Ste 330 Orange (92868) *(P-16466)*

Qwest, Burbank *Also Called: Qwest Cybersolutions LLC (P-11900)*

Qwest Cybersolutions LLC ....C....... 818 729-2100
  3015 Winona Ave Burbank (91504) *(P-11900)*

Qycell Corporation ....E....... 909 390-6644
  600 Etiwanda Ave Ontario (91761) *(P-3965)*

Qyk Brands LLC ....C....... 949 312-7119
  12821 Western Ave Garden Grove (92841) *(P-13065)*

R & B Reinforcing Steel Corp ....D....... 909 591-1726
  13581 5th St Chino (91710) *(P-1112)*

R & B Wire Products Inc ....E....... 714 549-3355
  2902 W Garry Ave Santa Ana (92704) *(P-6824)*

R & D Fasteners, Rancho Cucamonga *Also Called: Doubleco Incorporated (P-6438)*

R & D Metal Fabricators Inc ....E....... 714 891-4878
  5250 Rancho Rd Huntington Beach (92647) *(P-6300)*

R & D Partners, San Diego *Also Called: R&D Consulting Group Inc (P-15885)*

R & D Steel Inc ....E....... 310 631-6183
  1136 S Santa Fe Ave Compton (90221) *(P-6067)*

R & I, Ontario *Also Called: R & I Industries Inc (P-6068)*

R & I Industries Inc ....E....... 909 923-7747
  1876 S Taylor Ave Ontario (91761) *(P-6068)*

R & J Fabricators Inc ....E....... 951 817-0300
  1121 Railroad St Ste 102 Corona (92882) *(P-3030)*

R & J Material Handling Inc ....F....... 951 735-0000
  345 Adams Cir Corona (92882) *(P-12813)*

R & R Ductwork, Santa Fe Springs *Also Called: R & R Ductwork LLC (P-6301)*

R & R Ductwork LLC ....F....... 562 944-9660
  12820 Lakeland Rd Santa Fe Springs (90670) *(P-6301)*

R & R Industries, San Clemente *Also Called: Rosen & Rosen Industries Inc (P-11020)*

R & R Industries Inc ....E....... 800 234-5611
  204 Avenida Fabricante San Clemente (92672) *(P-2458)*

R & R Mechanical Contractors Inc ....D....... 619 449-9900
  1400 N Johnson Ave # 114 El Cajon (92020) *(P-813)*

R & R Rubber Molding Inc ....E....... 626 575-8105
  2444 Loma Ave South El Monte (91733) *(P-4788)*

R & R Services Corporation ....E....... 818 889-2562
  3595 Old Conejo Rd Newbury Park (91320) *(P-4789)*

Mergent email: customerrelations@mergent.com
1234

2024 Southern California
Business Directory and Buyers Guide

(P-0000) Products & Services Section entry number
(PA)=Parent Co (HQ)=Headquarters (DH)=Div Headquarters

R & S Automation Inc .... E...... 800 962-3111
283 W Bonita Ave Pomona (91767) *(P-6118)*

R & S Manufacturing & Sup Inc .... F...... 909 622-5881
16616 Garfield Ave Paramount (90723) *(P-4503)*

R & S Ovrhd Doors So-Cal Inc .... E...... 714 680-0600
1617 N Orangethorpe Way Anaheim (92801) *(P-6119)*

R & S Processing Co Inc .... D...... 562 531-0738
15712 Illinois Ave Paramount (90723) *(P-4790)*

R A Phillips Industries Inc (PA).......................... **E...... 562 781-2121**
12012 Burke St Santa Fe Springs (90670) *(P-9445)*

R A Reed Electric Company (PA)......................... **E...... 323 587-2284**
5503 S Boyle Ave Vernon (90058) *(P-17107)*

R and I Holdings Inc .... E...... 562 483-0577
2145 Dashwood St Lakewood (90712) *(P-14941)*

R and L Lopez Associates Inc (PA)..................... **D...... 626 330-5296**
3649 Tyler Ave El Monte (91731) *(P-19676)*

R B III Associates Inc .... C...... 760 471-5370
2386 Faraday Ave Ste 125 Carlsbad (92008) *(P-2295)*

R B R Meat Company Inc .... D...... 323 973-4868
5151 Alcoa Ave Vernon (90058) *(P-1203)*

R C Furniture Inc .... D...... 626 964-4100
1111 Jellick Ave City Of Industry (91748) *(P-2813)*

R C Products Corp .... E...... 949 858-8820
22322 Gilberto Rcho Sta Marg (92688) *(P-5940)*

R D Abbott Co Inc .... D...... 562 944-5354
11958 Monarch St Garden Grove (92841) *(P-13438)*

R D Mathis Company .... E...... 562 426-7049
2840 Gundry Ave Signal Hill (90755) *(P-5609)*

R D Rubber Technology Corp .... E...... 562 941-4800
12870 Florence Ave Santa Fe Springs (90670) *(P-4752)*

R E Barber-Ford .... C...... 805 656-4259
3440 E Main St Ventura (93003) *(P-13816)*

R G Canning Enterprises Inc .... C...... 323 560-7469
4515 E 59th Pl Maywood (90270) *(P-16912)*

R H Strasbaugh (PA).. **D...... 805 541-6424**
825 Buckley Rd San Luis Obispo (93401) *(P-7019)*

R J Lanthier Company Inc .... D...... 760 738-9798
485 Corporate Dr Escondido (92029) *(P-581)*

R J Reynolds Tobacco Company .... D...... 858 625-8453
8380 Miramar Mall Ste 117 San Diego (92121) *(P-2006)*

R K Fabrication Inc .... F...... 714 630-9654
1283 N Grove St Anaheim (92806) *(P-3966)*

R K Properties, Long Beach *Also Called: Rance King Properties Inc (P-14729)*

R Kern Engineering & Mfg Corp .... D...... 909 664-2440
13912 Mountain Ave Chino (91710) *(P-8980)*

R L Jones-San Diego Inc (PA)............................. **D...... 760 357-3177**
1778 Zinetta Rd Ste A Calexico (92231) *(P-11797)*

R M I, Gardena *Also Called: Rotational Molding Inc (P-5186)*

R Mc Closkey Insurance Agency .... C...... 949 223-8100
4001 Macarthur Blvd Ste 300 Newport Beach (92660) *(P-14626)*

R N D Enterprises, Lancaster *Also Called: BDR Industries Inc (P-11969)*

R O S, San Diego *Also Called: Remote Ocean Systems Inc (P-8380)*

R P Direct, Santa Monica *Also Called: Rubin Postaer and Associates (P-15573)*

R P S Resort Corp .... B...... 760 327-8311
1600 N Indian Canyon Dr Palm Springs (92262) *(P-15314)*

R Planet Earth LLC .... C...... 213 320-0601
3200 Fruitland Ave Vernon (90058) *(P-12180)*

R Q Construction Inc .... C...... 760 631-7707
1620 Faraday Ave Carlsbad (92008) *(P-582)*

R R Donnelley, San Diego *Also Called: R R Donnelley & Sons Company (P-3804)*

R R Donnelley & Sons Company .... D...... 310 516-3100
19681 Pacific Gateway Dr Torrance (90502) *(P-3803)*

R R Donnelley & Sons Company .... D...... 619 527-4600
955 Gateway Center Way San Diego (92102) *(P-3804)*

R R Donnelley & Sons Company .... D...... 951 296-2890
40610 County Center Dr Ste 100 Temecula (92591) *(P-12999)*

R Ranch Market .... C...... 714 573-1182
1112 Walnut Ave Tustin (92780) *(P-94)*

R T A, Riverside *Also Called: Riverside Transit Agency (P-11357)*

R T C Group .... F...... 949 226-2000
905 Calle Amanecer Ste 250 San Clemente (92673) *(P-3384)*

R V Best Inc .... E...... 619 448-7300
9335 Stevens Rd Santee (92071) *(P-5170)*

R W Swarens Associates Inc .... E...... 626 579-0943
10768 Lower Azusa Rd El Monte (91731) *(P-8329)*

R Zamora Inc .... E...... 760 597-1130
4645 North Ave Ste 102 Oceanside (92056) *(P-6552)*

R-Cold Inc .... D...... 951 436-5476
1221 S G St Perris (92570) *(P-7620)*

R&C Motor Corporation .... C...... 909 625-1500
601 Auto Center Dr Claremont (91711) *(P-17037)*

R&D Consulting Group Inc .... C...... 415 697-2585
8910 University Center Ln Ste 400 San Diego (92122) *(P-15885)*

R&D Metal, Huntington Beach *Also Called: R & D Metal Fabricators Inc (P-6300)*

R&M Deese Inc .... E...... 951 734-7342
1875 Sampson Ave Corona (92879) *(P-11148)*

R&M Supply Inc .... D...... 951 552-9860
420 Harley Knox Blvd Perris (92571) *(P-6920)*

R1 Concepts Inc (PA)... **E...... 714 777-2323**
13140 Midway Pl Cerritos (90703) *(P-12254)*

RA Industries LLC .... E...... 714 557-2322
900 Glenneyre St Laguna Beach (92651) *(P-7990)*

RA Snyder Properties Inc (PA)............................ **C...... 619 297-0274**
2399 Camino Del Rio S Ste 200 San Diego (92108) *(P-14853)*

Raceline Wheels, Garden Grove *Also Called: Allied Wheel Components Inc (P-13854)*

Racepak LLC .... E...... 949 709-5555
30402 Esperanza Rcho Sta Marg (92688) *(P-9446)*

Raceway Ford Inc .... C...... 951 571-9300
5900 Sycamore Canyon Blvd Riverside (92507) *(P-13817)*

Racing Power Company .... E...... 909 468-3690
815 Tucker Ln Walnut (91789) *(P-9447)*

Rack Installation Services Inc .... E...... 909 261-2243
1256 Brooks St Ste E Ontario (91762) *(P-2986)*

Rackmountpro.com, La Puente *Also Called: Yang-Ming International Corp (P-16479)*

RAD Diversified Reit Inc .... D...... 813 723-7348
3110 E Guasti Rd Ste 300 Ontario (91761) *(P-14854)*

Radcal Corporation .... E...... 626 357-7921
426 W Duarte Rd Monrovia (91016) *(P-10393)*

Radford Cabinets Inc .... D...... 661 729-8931
216 E Avenue K8 Lancaster (93535) *(P-2786)*

Radford Studio Center LLC .... B...... 818 655-5000
4024 Radford Ave Studio City (91604) *(P-17326)*

Radial, Rialto *Also Called: Radial South LP (P-11607)*

Radial South LP .... B...... 610 491-7000
2225 Alder Ave Rialto (92377) *(P-11607)*

Radian Audio Engineering Inc .... E...... 714 288-8900
2720 Kimball Ave Pomona (91767) *(P-8565)*

Radian Memory Systems Inc .... E...... 818 222-4080
5010 N Pkwy Ste 205 Calabasas (91302) *(P-7483)*

Radiance Beauty & Wellness Inc .... E...... 818 812-9740
9016 Fullbright Ave Chatsworth (91311) *(P-4450)*

Radiant Services Corp (PA)................................. **C...... 310 327-6300**
651 W Knox St Gardena (90248) *(P-15445)*

Radiation Onclogy - Cdrs-Snai, Los Angeles *Also Called: Cedars-Sinai Medical Center (P-17613)*

Radio Disney Group LLC 818 569-5000
3800 W Alameda Ave Ste 1150 Burbank (91505) *(P-11934)*

Radiologic Health Branch, San Diego *Also Called: Department of Public Health (P-17641)*

Radiology Partners Inc (HQ)................................ **B...... 424 290-8004**
2101 E El Segundo Blvd Ste 401 El Segundo (90245) *(P-17747)*

Radiology Prtners Holdings LLC (PA)................. **C...... 424 290-8004**
2330 Utah Ave Ste 200 El Segundo (90245) *(P-17748)*

Radiology Support Devices Inc .... E...... 310 518-0527
1904 E Dominguez St Long Beach (90810) *(P-10594)*

Radison Hotel Newport Beach, Newport Beach *Also Called: Pacific Hotel Management Inc (P-15287)*

Radisson Inn, Ontario *Also Called: Prime Hospitality LLC (P-15309)*

Radisson Inn, Los Angeles *Also Called: Radlax Gateway Hotel LLC (P-15315)*

Radix, Los Angeles *Also Called: Radix Textile Inc (P-13090)*

Radix Textile Inc .... D...... 323 234-1667
600 E Washington Blvd Ste C2 Los Angeles (90015) *(P-13090)* ·

Radlax Gateway Hotel LLC .... A...... 310 670-9000
6225 W Century Blvd Los Angeles (90045) *(P-15315)*

Employee Codes: A=Over 500 employees, B=251-500
C=101-250, D=51-100, E=20-50, F=10-19, G=1-9

2024 Southern California
Business Directory and Buyers Guide

© Mergent Inc. 1-800-342-5647

1235

Radnet Inc (PA)..A...... 310 478-7808
1510 Cotner Ave Los Angeles (90025) *(P-18562)*

Rady Childrens Hosp & Hlth Ctr (PA)..................A...... 858 576-1700
3020 Childrens Way San Diego (92123) *(P-18403)*

Rady Chld Hospital-San Diego (HQ).....................A...... 858 576-1700
3020 Childrens Way San Diego (92123) *(P-18404)*

Rael Inc..E...... 800 573-1516
6940 Beach Blvd Unit D301 Buena Park (90621) *(P-3208)*

Raemica Inc..E...... 909 864-1990
7759 Victoria Ave Highland (92346) *(P-1232)*

Rafco Products Brickform, Rancho Cucamonga *Also Called: Rafco-Brickform LLC (P-7129)*

Rafco-Brickform LLC (PA).................................D...... 909 484-3399
11061 Jersey Blvd Rancho Cucamonga (91730) *(P-7129)*

Raffles Lrmitage Beverly Hills............................C...... 310 278-3344
9291 Burton Way Beverly Hills (90210) *(P-15316)*

Rafu Shimpo...E...... 213 629-2231
701 E 3rd St Ste 130 Los Angeles (90013) *(P-3317)*

Raging Waters, San Dimas *Also Called: Raging Waters Group Inc (P-17451)*

Raging Waters Group Inc..................................A...... 909 802-2200
111 Raging Waters Dr San Dimas (91773) *(P-17451)*

RAH Industries Inc (PA)...................................C...... 661 295-5190
24800 Avenue Rockefeller Valencia (91355) *(P-6302)*

Rahn Industries, Whittier *Also Called: Rahn Industries Incorporated (P-7621)*

Rahn Industries Incorporated (PA)......................E...... 562 908-0680
2630 Pacific Park Dr Whittier (90601) *(P-7621)*

Rai Care Centers Colton LLC.............................C...... 909 430-0930
1275 W C St Colton (92324) *(P-18660)*

Rai Care Centers Lynwood LLC.........................D...... 562 401-0155
7700 Imperial Hwy Ste R Downey (90242) *(P-18661)*

Rai Care Ctrs Sthern Cal II LL...........................C...... 310 673-6865
1416 Centinela Ave Inglewood (90302) *(P-18662)*

Rai Care Ctrs Sthern Cal II LL...........................C...... 619 442-4122
858 Fletcher Pkwy El Cajon (92020) *(P-18663)*

Rai Care Ctrs Sthern Cal II LL...........................C...... 619 229-1070
7007 Mission Gorge Rd 1st Fl San Diego (92120) *(P-18664)*

Rai Care Ctrs Sthern Cal II LL...........................C...... 760 346-7588
41501 Corporate Way Palm Desert (92260) *(P-18665)*

Rai Centinela Inglewood, Inglewood *Also Called: Rai Care Ctrs Sthern Cal II LL (P-18662)*

Rai Corporate Way Palm Desert, Palm Desert *Also Called: Rai Care Ctrs Sthern Cal II LL (P-18665)*

Rai West C Colton, Colton *Also Called: Rai Care Centers Colton LLC (P-18660)*

Rai-Fletcher Parkway-El Cajon, El Cajon *Also Called: Rai Care Ctrs Sthern Cal II LL (P-18663)*

Railstech Inc...E...... 267 315-2998
730 Arizona Ave Santa Monica (90401) *(P-16364)*

Rain Bird, Azusa *Also Called: Rain Bird Corporation (P-6794)*

Rain Bird Corporation......................................E...... 626 812-3400
970 W Sierra Madre Ave Azusa (91702) *(P-5973)*

Rain Bird Corporation (PA)...............................C...... 626 812-3400
970 W Sierra Madre Ave Azusa (91702) *(P-6794)*

Rain Bird Corporation......................................E...... 619 674-4068
9491 Ridgehaven Ct San Diego (92123) *(P-6911)*

Rain Bird Distribution Corp...............................E...... 626 963-9311
1000 W Sierra Madre Ave Azusa (91702) *(P-714)*

Rain Bird Golf Division, Azusa *Also Called: Rain Bird Corporation (P-5973)*

Rain For Rent, Bakersfield *Also Called: Western Oilfields Supply Co (P-15806)*

Rain Mstr Irrgtion Systems Inc..........................E...... 805 527-4498
5825 Jasmine St Riverside (92504) *(P-10154)*

Rainbo Record Mfg Corp (PA)...........................E...... 818 280-1100
8960 Eton Ave Canoga Park (91304) *(P-8464)*

Rainbo Records & Cassettes, Canoga Park *Also Called: Rainbo Record Mfg Corp (P-8464)*

Rainbow Disposal Co Inc (HQ)...........................C...... 714 847-3581
17121 Nichols Ln Huntington Beach (92647) *(P-12181)*

Rainbow Refuse Recycling, Huntington Beach *Also Called: Rainbow Disposal Co Inc (P-12181)*

Rainbow Vending & Distributing, San Diego *Also Called: Canteen Vending - San Diego (P-13265)*

Raintree Systems Inc.......................................C...... 951 252-9400
30650 Rancho California Rd Ste 406 Temecula (92591) *(P-16101)*

Raise 3d Technologies Inc.................................E...... 949 482-2040
43 Tesla Irvine (92618) *(P-7566)*

Raj Manufacturing LLC.....................................E...... 714 838-3110
2712 Dow Ave Tustin (92780) *(P-2364)*

Raj Manufacturing Inc (PA)...............................F...... 714 838-3110
2712 Dow Ave Tustin (92780) *(P-2365)*

Rajswim, Tustin *Also Called: Raj Manufacturing LLC (P-2364)*

Rajysan Incorporated (PA).................................E...... 661 775-4920
4175 Guardian St Simi Valley (93063) *(P-12814)*

Rakar Incorporated..E...... 805 487-2721
1680 Universe Cir Oxnard (93033) *(P-5171)*

Rakworx Inc..C...... 949 215-1362
1 Mason Irvine (92618) *(P-16544)*

Ralco Holdings Inc (DH)...................................C...... 949 440-5094
13861 Rosecrans Ave Santa Fe Springs (90670) *(P-12255)*

Raleigh Enterprises Inc (PA)..............................C...... 310 899-8900
5300 Melrose Ave Los Angeles (90038) *(P-15317)*

Raleigh Holdings, Los Angeles *Also Called: Raleigh Enterprises Inc (P-15317)*

Ralis, Orange *Also Called: Ralis Services Corp (P-20226)*

Ralis Services Corp...C...... 844 347-2547
1 City Blvd W Ste 600 Orange (92868) *(P-20226)*

Rally Holdings LLC..A...... 817 919-6833
17771 Mitchell N Irvine (92614) *(P-12256)*

Ralph Brennan Rest Group LLC..........................C...... 714 776-5200
1590 S Disneyland Dr Anaheim (92802) *(P-20227)*

Ralph E Ames Machine Works............................E...... 310 328-8523
2301 Dominguez Way Torrance (90501) *(P-7991)*

Ralph Wilson Plastics, Santa Fe Springs *Also Called: Wilsonart LLC (P-11630)*

Ralphs Logistics - Compton DC, Compton *Also Called: Kroger Co (P-11593)*

Ram Board Inc...E...... 818 848-0400
27460 Avenue Scott Unit A Valencia (91355) *(P-11184)*

Ram Off Road Accessories Inc............................E...... 323 266-3850
3901 Medford St Los Angeles (90063) *(P-9448)*

Ram Plumbing...D...... 800 487-5812
14745 Addison St Sherman Oaks (91403) *(P-814)*

Rama Corporation..E...... 951 654-7351
600 W Esplanade Ave San Jacinto (92583) *(P-7372)*

Rama Food Manufacture Corp (PA)......................F...... 909 923-5305
1486 E Cedar St Ontario (91761) *(P-1973)*

Ramada By Wyndham, Irvine *Also Called: Western National Securities (P-14884)*

Ramada Inn, El Monte *Also Called: Amenities Development Co (P-15071)*

Ramada Inn, Hawthorne *Also Called: Calhot Illinios LLC (P-15106)*

Ramada Inn, Costa Mesa *Also Called: Trigild International Inc (P-15394)*

Ramada Inn, El Cajon *Also Called: W Lodging Inc (P-15406)*

RAMCAR Batteries Inc......................................E...... 323 726-1212
2700 Carrier Ave Commerce (90040) *(P-12257)*

Ramcast Ornamental Sup Co Inc.........................E...... 909 469-4767
1450 E Mission Blvd Pomona (91766) *(P-12566)*

Ramcast Steel, Pomona *Also Called: Ramcast Ornamental Sup Co Inc (P-12566)*

Ramco, Simi Valley *Also Called: Recycled Aggregate Mtls Co Inc (P-4665)*

Ramco Employment Services, Oxnard *Also Called: Ramco Enterprises LP (P-110)*

Ramco Enterprises LP.......................................B...... 805 486-9328
520 E 3rd St Ste B Oxnard (93030) *(P-110)*

Ramco Enterprises LP.......................................B...... 805 922-9888
325 Plaza Dr Ste 1 Santa Maria (93454) *(P-15886)*

Ramda Metal Specialties, Gardena *Also Called: Ramda Metal Specialties Inc (P-6303)*

Ramda Metal Specialties Inc..............................E...... 310 538-2136
13012 Crenshaw Blvd Gardena (90249) *(P-6303)*

Rami Designs Inc...F...... 949 588-8288
24 Hammond Ste E Irvine (92618) *(P-6366)*

Ramirez Pallets Inc..E...... 909 822-2066
8431 Sultana Ave Fontana (92335) *(P-2723)*

Ramko Injection Inc...D...... 951 929-0360
3551 Tanya Ave Hemet (92545) *(P-5172)*

Ramko Mfg Inc..D...... 951 652-3510
3500 Tanya Ave Hemet (92545) *(P-7992)*

Ramona Care Inc...C...... 626 442-5721
11900 Ramona Blvd El Monte (91732) *(P-18035)*

Ramona Community Services Corp (HQ)................C...... 951 658-9288
890 W Stetson Ave Ste A Hemet (92543) *(P-18637)*

Ramona Nrsing Rhbilitation Ctr, El Monte *Also Called: Ramona Care Inc (P-18035)*

Ramona Research Inc..F...... 858 679-0717
13741 Danielson St Ste J Poway (92064) *(P-8566)*

Ramona Rhbittion Post Acute CA .... C....... 951 652-0011
485 W Johnston Ave Hemet (92543) *(P-18405)*

Ramona Rhbittion Post Acute Ca, Hemet *Also Called: Ramona Rhbittion Post Acute CA*
(P-18405)

Ramona Vna & Hospice, Hemet *Also Called: Ramona Community Services Corp (P-18637)*

Ramp Engineering Inc .... E..... 562 531-8030
6850 Walthall Way Paramount (90723) *(P-7993)*

Rampone Industries LLC .... E..... 714 265-0200
168 E Liberty Ave Anaheim (92801) *(P-6825)*

Ramtec Associates Inc .... E..... 714 996-7477
3200 E Birch St Ste B Brea (92821) *(P-5173)*

Rance King Properties Inc (PA) .... C...... 562 240-1000
3737 E Broadway Long Beach (90803) *(P-14729)*

Rancho, Temecula *Also Called: Rancho Ford Inc (P-13818)*

Rancho Bernardo Inn, San Diego *Also Called: JC Resorts LLC (P-20044)*

Rancho California Water Dst (PA) .... C...... 951 296-6900
42135 Winchester Rd Temecula (92590) *(P-12139)*

Rancho Foods Inc .... D..... 323 585-0503
2528 E 37th St Vernon (90058) *(P-13305)*

Rancho Ford Inc .... C..... 951 699-1302
26895 Ynez Rd Temecula (92591) *(P-13818)*

Rancho Laguna Farms LLC .... D..... 805 925-7805
2410 W Main St Santa Maria (93458) *(P-85)*

Rancho Las Palmas Resort & Spa, Rancho Mirage *Also Called: Ksl Rancho Mirage*
Operating Co Inc (P-15212)

Rancho Lomita Food Inds Inc .... E..... 619 464-2800
912 Cardiff St San Diego (92114) *(P-1974)*

Rancho Monterey Apartments, Tustin *Also Called: Irvine APT Communities LP (P-14719)*

Rancho Physical Therapy, San Marcos *Also Called: Rancho Physical Therapy Inc (P-17870)*

Rancho Physical Therapy Inc .... C...... 760 752-1011
277 Rancheros Dr San Marcos (92069) *(P-17870)*

Rancho Pino Verdi, Lucerne Valley *Also Called: Casa Clina Hosp Ctrs For Hlthc (P-19032)*

Rancho Ready Mix .... E..... 951 674-0488
28251 Lake St Lake Elsinore (92530) *(P-5493)*

Rancho Research Institute .... C..... 562 401-8111
7601 Imperial Hwy Downey (90242) *(P-19940)*

Rancho San Antonio Boys HM Inc (PA) .... D...... 818 882-6400
21000 Plummer St Chatsworth (91311) *(P-19296)*

Rancho San Diego Cinema 16, El Cajon *Also Called: Edwards Theatres Circuit Inc (P-17294)*

Rancho Santa Fe, Rancho Santa Fe *Also Called: Pacific Western Bank (P-14173)*

Rancho Santa Fe Association .... C...... 858 756-1182
5827 Viadelacumere Rancho Santa Fe (92067) *(P-17508)*

Rancho Sante Fe Golf Club, Rancho Santa Fe *Also Called: Rancho Santa Fe Association*
(P-17508)

Rancho Sisquoc Winery, Santa Maria *Also Called: Flood Ranch Company (P-1629)*

Rancho Springs Medical Center, Murrieta *Also Called: Southwest Healthcare Sys Aux*
(P-18457)

Rancho Vista, Vista *Also Called: Rancho Vista Health Center (P-18096)*

Rancho Vista Health Center .... C...... 760 941-1480
200 Grapevine Rd Apt 15 Vista (92083) *(P-18096)*

Rancho VIncia Rsort Prtners LL .... B...... 858 756-1123
5921 Valencia Cir Rancho Santa Fe (92067) *(P-15318)*

Rand, Santa Monica *Also Called: The Rand Corporation (P-19948)*

Randall Farms, Vernon *Also Called: Sydney & Anne Bloom Farms Inc (P-13308)*

Rangefinder Publishing Co Inc .... E..... 310 846-4770
11835 W Olympic Blvd Ste 550e Los Angeles (90064) *(P-3385)*

Ranger Patrol, Thousand Oaks *Also Called: Swag Corporation (P-9260)*

Rangers Die Casting Co .... E..... 310 764-1800
10828 Alameda St Lynwood (90262) *(P-5767)*

Ranir LLC .... E..... 866 373-7374
6 Centerpointe Dr Ste 640 La Palma (90623) *(P-10764)*

Ranroy Company .... E..... 858 571-8800
9265 Activity Rd Ste 112 San Diego (92126) *(P-3677)*

Ranroy Printing Company, San Diego *Also Called: Ranroy Company (P-3677)*

Rantec Microwave Systems Inc .... E..... 760 744-1544
2066 Wineridge Pl Escondido (92029) *(P-8567)*

Rantec Microwave Systems Inc (PA) .... D...... 818 223-5000
31186 La Baya Dr Westlake Village (91362) *(P-10051)*

Rantec Power Systems Inc (HQ) .... D...... 805 596-6000
1173 Los Olivos Ave Los Osos (93402) *(P-12694)*

RAP Security Inc .... D...... 323 560-3493
4630 Cecilia St Cudahy (90201) *(P-2987)*

Raphaels Inc .... F
4460 Braeburn Rd San Diego (92116) *(P-2761)*

Raphaels Party Rentals Inc (PA) .... C....... 858 444-1692
8606 Miramar Rd San Diego (92126) *(P-15795)*

Rapid Conn Inc .... E..... 949 951-3722
6 Goddard Irvine (92618) *(P-12567)*

Rapid Manufacturing, Anaheim *Also Called: Rapid Mfg A Cal Ltd Partnr (P-6826)*

Rapid Mfg A Cal Ltd Partnr (PA) .... C....... 714 974-2432
8080 E Crystal Dr Anaheim (92807) *(P-6826)*

Rapid Product Solutions Inc .... E..... 805 485-7234
2240 Celsius Ave Ste D Oxnard (93030) *(P-7994)*

Rapid Rack Holdings Inc .... A
1370 Valley Vista Dr Ste 100 Diamond Bar (91765) *(P-2988)*

Rapid Rack Industries Inc .... D
1370 Valley Vista Dr # 100 Diamond Bar (91765) *(P-2989)*

Rapiscan Systems Inc (HQ) .... C....... 310 978-1457
2805 Columbia St Torrance (90503) *(P-10785)*

Rapp, Los Angeles *Also Called: Rapp Worldwide Inc (P-15571)*

Rapp Worldwide Inc .... C...... 310 563-7200
12777 W Jefferson Blvd Bldg C Los Angeles (90066) *(P-15571)*

Rasmussen Iron Works Inc .... E..... 562 696-8718
12028 Philadelphia St Whittier (90601) *(P-5983)*

Raspadoxpress .... D..... 818 892-6969
8610 Van Nuys Blvd Panorama City (91402) *(P-3480)*

Rastaclat LLC .... E..... 424 287-0902
100 W Broadway Ste 3000 Long Beach (90802) *(P-10909)*

Ratpac Dimmers, Van Nuys *Also Called: Data Lights Rigging LLC (P-8120)*

Raveon Technologies Corp .... E..... 760 444-5995
2320 Cousteau Ct Vista (92081) *(P-8568)*

Ravi Patel MD Inc .... C..... 661 862-7113
6501 Truxtun Ave Bakersfield (93309) *(P-17749)*

Ravine Waterpark LLC .... C...... 805 237-8500
2301 Airport Rd Paso Robles (93446) *(P-17452)*

Ravine Waterpark, The, Paso Robles *Also Called: Ravine Waterpark LLC (P-17452)*

Ravlich Enterprises LLC (PA) .... E..... 714 964-8900
100 Business Center Dr Corona (92878) *(P-6654)*

Ravlich Enterprises LLC .... E..... 310 533-0748
202 W 140th St Los Angeles (90061) *(P-6655)*

Ray Chinn Construction Inc .... E..... 661 327-2731
424 24th St Bakersfield (93301) *(P-7038)*

Ray Products Company Inc .... E..... 888 776-9014
1700 Chablis Ave Ontario (91761) *(P-5174)*

Rayco Electronic Mfg Inc .... E..... 310 329-2660
1220 W 130th St Gardena (90247) *(P-8953)*

Raymond Group (PA) .... D..... 714 771-7670
520 W Walnut Ave Orange (92868) *(P-20087)*

Raymond Handling Solutions Inc (DH) .... C....... 562 944-8067
9939 Norwalk Blvd Santa Fe Springs (90670) *(P-12815)*

Rayotek Scientific, San Diego *Also Called: Rayotek Scientific Inc (P-5355)*

Rayotek Scientific Inc .... E..... 858 558-3671
8845 Rehco Rd San Diego (92121) *(P-5355)*

Raypak Inc (DH) .... B...... 805 278-5300
2151 Eastman Ave Oxnard (93030) *(P-5984)*

Raytheon, San Diego *Also Called: Raytheon Company (P-10052)*

Raytheon, Goleta *Also Called: Raytheon Company (P-10053)*

Raytheon, El Segundo *Also Called: Raytheon Company (P-10055)*

Raytheon, El Segundo *Also Called: Raytheon Company (P-10056)*

Raytheon, El Segundo *Also Called: Raytheon Company (P-10057)*

Raytheon, El Segundo *Also Called: Raytheon Company (P-10058)*

Raytheon, El Segundo *Also Called: Raytheon Secure Information Systems LLC (P-19677)*

Raytheon Applied Sgnal Tech In .... D..... 310 436-7000
2000 E El Segundo Blvd El Segundo (90245) *(P-8569)*

Raytheon Applied Sgnal Tech In .... D....... 714 917-0255
160 N Riverview Dr Ste 300 Anaheim (92808) *(P-8623)*

Raytheon Cmmand Ctrl Sltons LL (DH) .... A....... 714 446-3118
1801 Hughes Dr Fullerton (92833) *(P-12695)*

Raytheon Company .... C....... 805 967-5511
6380 Hollister Ave Goleta (93117) *(P-9246)*

Employee Codes: A=Over 500 employees, B=251-500
C=101-250, D=51-100, E=20-50, F=10-19, G=1-9

2024 Southern California
Business Directory and Buyers Guide

© Mergent Inc. 1-800-342-5647
1237

A
L
P
H
A
B
E
T
I
C

Raytheon Company ....E...... 858 571-6598
8650 Balboa Ave San Diego (92123) *(P-10052)*

Raytheon Company ....D...... 805 562-4611
75 Coromar Dr Goleta (93117) *(P-10053)*

Raytheon Company ....E...... 714 732-0119
1801 Hughes Dr Fullerton (92833) *(P-10054)*

Raytheon Company ....D...... 310 647-1000
1921 E Mariposa Ave El Segundo (90245) *(P-10055)*

Raytheon Company ....E...... 310 647-9438
2000 E El Segundo Blvd El Segundo (90245) *(P-10056)*

Raytheon Company ....A...... 310 647-9438
2000 E El Segundo Blvd El Segundo (90245) *(P-10057)*

Raytheon Company ....B...... 310 647-1000
2000 E El Segundo Blvd El Segundo (90245) *(P-10058)*

Raytheon Dgital Force Tech LLC (DH)............**E...... 858 546-1244**
6779 Mesa Ridge Rd Ste 150 San Diego (92121) *(P-10059)*

Raytheon Lgstics Spport Trning ....B...... 310 647-9438
2000 E El Segundo Blvd El Segundo (90245) *(P-12915)*

Raytheon Secure Information Systems LLC ....C...... 310 647-9438
2000 E El Segundo Blvd El Segundo (90245) *(P-19677)*

Rayzebio Inc ....D...... 619 937-2754
5505 Morehouse Dr Ste 300 San Diego (92121) *(P-4219)*

Rayzist Photomask Inc (PA)..............................**D...... 760 727-8561**
955 Park Center Dr Vista (92081) *(P-11061)*

Razor, Cerritos Also Called: Razor USA LLC *(P-9881)*

Razor USA LLC (PA)..**D...... 562 345-6000**
12723 166th St Cerritos (90703) *(P-9881)*

Rba Builders Inc ....D...... 714 895-9000
16490 Harbor Blvd Ste A Fountain Valley (92708) *(P-583)*

Rbc Lubron Bearing Systems Inc (HQ) ....**E...... 714 841-3007**
13141 Molette St Santa Fe Springs (90670) *(P-5676)*

Rbc Transport Dynamics Corp ....C...... 203 267-7001
3131 W Segerstrom Ave Santa Ana (92704) *(P-12874)*

Rbf Group International ....F...... 626 333-5700
1441 W 2nd St Pomona (91766) *(P-2896)*

Rbf Lifestyle Holdings, Pomona Also Called: Rbf Group International *(P-2896)*

Rbf Lifestyle Holdings LLC ....E...... 626 333-5700
1441 W 2nd St Pomona (91766) *(P-2897)*

Rbm Conveyor Systems Inc ....E...... 909 620-1333
1570 W Mission Blvd Pomona (91766) *(P-7212)*

Rbw Industries Inc ....D...... 909 591-5359
5788 Schaefer Ave Chino (91710) *(P-9449)*

Rbz LLP ....C...... 310 478-4148
11766 Wilshire Blvd Fl 9 Los Angeles (90025) *(P-19803)*

Rbz Vineyards LLC ....E...... 805 542-0133
2324 W Highway 46 Paso Robles (93446) *(P-1655)*

RC Construction Services, Redlands Also Called: Robert Clapper Cnstr Svcs Inc *(P-585)*

RC Maintenance Holdings Inc ....C...... 951 903-6303
569 Bateman Cir Corona (92878) *(P-815)*

RC Wendt Painting Inc ....C...... 714 960-2700
21612 Surveyor Cir Huntington Beach (92646) *(P-854)*

RCP Block & Brick Inc (PA)..............................**D...... 619 460-9101**
8240 Broadway Lemon Grove (91945) *(P-5392)*

RCP Block & Brick Inc ....E...... 619 448-2240
8755 N Magnolia Ave Santee (92071) *(P-5393)*

RCP Block & Brick Inc ....E...... 619 474-1516
75 N 4th Ave Chula Vista (91910) *(P-5394)*

RCP Block & Brick Inc ....E...... 760 753-1164
577 N Vulcan Ave Encinitas (92024) *(P-5395)*

Rcrv Inc (PA)...**E...... 323 235-7300**
4715 S Alameda St Vernon (90058) *(P-13144)*

RCWD, Temecula Also Called: Rancho California Water Dst *(P-12139)*

RD Olson Construction Inc ....C...... 949 474-2001
400 Spectrum Center Dr Ste 1200 Irvine (92618) *(P-584)*

RDfabricators Inc ....F...... 714 634-2078
11880 Western Ave Stanton (90680) *(P-6304)*

RDM Industries ....E...... 714 690-0380
14310 Gannet St La Mirada (90638) *(P-12816)*

Rdmm Legacy Inc ....E...... 323 232-2147
724 E 60th St Los Angeles (90001) *(P-13091)*

Re/Max, Los Alamitos Also Called: College Park Realty Inc *(P-14770)*

Re/Max, Upland Also Called: Diamond Ridge Corporation *(P-14788)*

Re/Max, Santa Clarita Also Called: RE/Max of Valencia Inc *(P-14855)*

Re/Max, Torrance Also Called: Remax Exec King Harbor *(P-14857)*

Re/Max, Northridge Also Called: Remax Olson & Associates Inc *(P-14858)*

Re/Max, Camarillo Also Called: Rgc Services Inc *(P-14860)*

Re/Max, Ventura Also Called: Rgc Services Inc *(P-14861)*

RE/Max of Valencia Inc (PA)..............................**C...... 661 255-2650**
25101 The Old Rd Santa Clarita (91381) *(P-14855)*

Reachlocal, Woodland Hills Also Called: Reachlocal Inc *(P-15572)*

Reachlocal Inc (DH)...**C...... 818 274-0260**
21700 Oxnard St Ste 1600 Woodland Hills (91367) *(P-15572)*

Ready Pac Foods, Irwindale Also Called: Ready Pac Produce Inc *(P-13338)*

Ready Pac Foods Inc (HQ)................................**A...... 626 856-8686**
4401 Foxdale St Irwindale (91706) *(P-1975)*

Ready Pac Produce Inc (DH).............................**C...... 800 800-4088**
4401 Foxdale St Irwindale (91706) *(P-13338)*

Readylink Inc ....D...... 760 343-7000
72030 Metroplex Dr Thousand Palms (92276) *(P-15887)*

Readylink Healthcare ....D...... 760 343-7000
72030 Metroplex Dr Thousand Palms (92276) *(P-15888)*

Readymix -Redlands Rm Dual, Highland Also Called: Cemex Cnstr Mtls PCF LLC *(P-5471)*

Reagent Chemical & RES Inc ....D...... 909 796-4059
1454 S Sunnyside Ave San Bernardino (92408) *(P-3908)*

Real Estate Image Inc (PA)...............................**C...... 714 502-3900**
1415 S Acacia Ave Fullerton (92831) *(P-15635)*

Real Estate Trainers Inc ....E...... 800 282-2352
212 Twne Cntre Pl Ste 100 Anaheim (92806) *(P-19004)*

Real Marketing ....E...... 858 847-0335
8470 Redwood Creek Ln Ste 200 San Diego (92126) *(P-3481)*

Real Mex Foods Inc ....D...... 714 523-0031
5660 Katella Ave Ste 200 Cypress (90630) *(P-13193)*

Real Plating Inc ....E...... 909 623-2304
1245 W 2nd St Pomona (91766) *(P-6656)*

Real Seal, Escondido Also Called: REAL Seal Co Inc *(P-4740)*

REAL Seal Co Inc ....E...... 760 743-7263
1971 Don Lee Pl Escondido (92029) *(P-4740)*

Real Software Systems LLC (PA)......................**E...... 818 313-8000**
21255 Burbank Blvd Ste 220 Woodland Hills (91367) *(P-16365)*

Real Vision Foods, Irvine Also Called: Real Vision Foods LLC *(P-1399)*

Real Vision Foods LLC ....E...... 253 228-5050
72 Knollglen Irvine (92614) *(P-1399)*

Realdefense LLC (PA)...**E...... 801 895-7907**
150 S Los Robles Ave Ste 400 Pasadena (91101) *(P-16750)*

Realselect Inc ....C...... 661 803-5188
3063 W Chapman Ave Apt 6207 Orange (92868) *(P-14856)*

Reapplications Inc ....C...... 619 230-0209
8910 University Center Ln Ste 300 San Diego (92122) *(P-16102)*

Reaps Company LLC ....E...... 212 256-1186
1950 S Santa Fe Ave Los Angeles (90021) *(P-11274)*

Reason Foundation ....E...... 310 391-2245
5737 Mesmer Ave Los Angeles (90230) *(P-16913)*

Rebar Engineering Inc ....C...... 562 946-2461
10706 Painter Ave Santa Fe Springs (90670) *(P-1113)*

Rebas Inc ....C...... 562 941-4155
12907 Imperial Hwy Santa Fe Springs (90670) *(P-12817)*

Rebco Communities Inc ....B...... 714 557-5511
3090 Pullman St Costa Mesa (92626) *(P-472)*

Rebecca International Inc ....E...... 323 973-2602
4587 E 48th St Vernon (90058) *(P-2524)*

Rebel Jeans, Los Angeles Also Called: Be Bop Clothing *(P-2306)*

Reborn Bath Solutions, Anaheim Also Called: Reborn Cabinets LLC *(P-2675)*

Reborn Cabinets LLC (PA).................................**B...... 714 630-2220**
5515 E La Palma Ave Ste 250 Anaheim (92807) *(P-2675)*

Rebound Therapeutics Corp ....E...... 949 305-8111
13900 Alton Pkwy Ste 120 Irvine (92618) *(P-10595)*

Rec Solar, San Luis Obispo Also Called: Mainstream Energy Corporation *(P-791)*

Rec Solar, San Luis Obispo Also Called: Rec Solar Commercial Corp *(P-816)*

Rec Solar Commercial Corp ....C...... 844 732-7652
3450 Broad St Ste 105 San Luis Obispo (93401) *(P-816)*

Rec Van, San Diego Also Called: La Mesa R V Center Inc *(P-13897)*

Mergent email: customerrelations@mergent.com
1238

2024 Southern California
Business Directory and Buyers Guide

(P-0000) Products & Services Section entry number
(PA)=Parent Co (HQ)=Headquarters (DH)=Div Headquarters

Receptos Inc ....E....... 858 652-5700
3033 Science Park Rd Ste 300 San Diego (92121) *(P-4220)*

RECHE CANYON REGIONAL REHAB CE, Colton *Also Called: Cambridge Sierra Holdings LLC (P-17897)*

Recold, Brea *Also Called: SPX Cooling Tech LLC (P-6158)*

Recology, Sun Valley *Also Called: Recology Los Angeles (P-12182)*

Recology Los Angeles ....B....... 818 767-0675
9189 De Garmo Ave Sun Valley (91352) *(P-12182)*

Recom Group ....E....... 909 599-1370
449 Borrego Ct San Dimas (91773) *(P-12696)*

Recon, San Diego *Also Called: Recon Environmental Inc (P-20375)*

Recon Environmental Inc (PA)..............................D....... 619 308-9333
3111 Camino Del Rio N Ste 600 San Diego (92108) *(P-20375)*

Reconserve Inc (HQ)......................................E....... 310 458-1574
2811 Wilshire Blvd Ste 410 Santa Monica (90403) *(P-1448)*

Reconserve of Maryland, Santa Monica *Also Called: Dext Company of Maryland (P-1439)*

Record Technology Inc (PA)...............................E....... 805 484-2747
486 Dawson Dr Ste 4s Camarillo (93012) *(P-8465)*

Recovery Solutions Santa Ana, Santa Ana *Also Called: CRC Health Corporate (P-18685)*

Recruit 360 ....C....... 949 250-4420
457 Ogle St Costa Mesa (92627) *(P-15889)*

Recycled Aggregate Mtls Co Inc (HQ)..............F....... 805 522-1646
2655 1st St Ste 210 Simi Valley (93065) *(P-4665)*

Recycled Paper Products, Santa Fe Springs *Also Called: Gabriel Container (P-3102)*

Recycler Classified, Sherman Oaks *Also Called: E Z Buy & E Z Sell Recycl Corp (P-3274)*

Recycler Core Company Inc ....D....... 951 276-1687
2727 Kansas Ave Riverside (92507) *(P-12183)*

Red Blossom Farms Inc ....D....... 805 686-4747
1389 W Main St Santa Maria (93458) *(P-20)*

Red Blossom Sales Inc ....A....... 805 349-9404
865 Black Rd Santa Maria (93458) *(P-21)*

Red Brick Corporation ....F....... 323 549-9444
5364 Venice Blvd Los Angeles (90019) *(P-3678)*

Red Bull Media Hse N Amer Inc ....D....... 310 393-4647
1630 Stewart St Ste A Santa Monica (90404) *(P-1722)*

Red Bull North America Inc (HQ).........................D....... 310 460-5356
1630 Stewart St Santa Monica (90404) *(P-17348)*

Red Bull TV, Santa Monica *Also Called: Red Bull North America Inc (P-17348)*

Red Chamber Co (PA)...B....... 323 234-9000
1912 E Vernon Ave Vernon (90058) *(P-13285)*

Red Cross, Los Angeles *Also Called: American National Red Cross (P-19020)*

Red Digital Cinema Camera Co, Foothill Ranch *Also Called: Redcom LLC (P-10883)*

Red Earth Casino ....C....... 760 395-1200
3089 Norm Niver Rd Thermal (92274) *(P-15319)*

Red Fish Grill, Anaheim *Also Called: Ralph Brennan Rest Group LLC (P-20227)*

Red Gate Software Inc ....E....... 626 993-3949
144 W Colorado Blvd Ste 200 Pasadena (91105) *(P-16366)*

Red Hill Country Club ....D....... 909 982-1358
8358 Red Hill Country Club Dr Rancho Cucamonga (91730) *(P-17509)*

Red Peak Group LLC ....D....... 818 222-7762
23975 Park Sorrento # 410 Calabasas (91302) *(P-20228)*

Red Pointe Roofing LP (PA)................................D....... 714 685-0010
1814 N Neville St Orange (92865) *(P-1052)*

Red Rock Pallet Company ....E....... 530 852-7744
81153 Red Rock Rd La Quinta (92253) *(P-11798)*

Redbarn Pet Products Inc (PA)............................C....... 562 495-7315
3229 E Spring St Ste 310 Long Beach (90806) *(P-13555)*

Redbarn Premium Pet Products, Long Beach *Also Called: Redbarn Pet Products Inc (P-13555)*

Redcom Inc ....F....... 949 206-7900
94 Icon Foothill Ranch (92610) *(P-10882)*

Redcom LLC ....B....... 949 404-4084
94 Icon Foothill Ranch (92610) *(P-10883)*

Redlands Community Hospital (PA)......................D....... 909 335-5500
350 Terracina Blvd Redlands (92373) *(P-18406)*

REDLANDS COMMUNITY HOSPITAL, Redlands *Also Called: RHS Corp (P-20090)*

Redlands Country Club ....D....... 909 793-2661
1749 Garden St Redlands (92373) *(P-17510)*

Redlands Daily Facts, Redlands *Also Called: Califrnia Nwspapers Ltd Partnr (P-3264)*

Redlands Employment Services ....B....... 951 688-0083
4295 Jurupa St Ste 110 Ontario (91761) *(P-15890)*

Redlands Ford Inc ....D....... 909 793-3211
1121 W Colton Ave Redlands (92374) *(P-17015)*

Redlands Healthcare Center, Redlands *Also Called: Ash Holdings LLC (P-17882)*

Redlands Staffing Services, Ontario *Also Called: Redlands Employment Services (P-15890)*

Redline Detection LLC (PA)................................E....... 714 579-6961
828 W Taft Ave Orange (92865) *(P-10394)*

Redman Equipment & Mfg Co ....E....... 310 329-1134
19800 Normandie Ave Torrance (90502) *(P-17148)*

Redondo Beach Brewing Co Inc ....E....... 310 316-8477
1814 S Catalina Ave Redondo Beach (90277) *(P-14033)*

Redtrac, Bakersfield *Also Called: Water Associates LLC (P-8598)*

Redwood, Culver City *Also Called: Wovexx Holdings Inc (P-12015)*

Redwood Elderlink & Homelink, Escondido *Also Called: Redwood Elderlink Scph (P-19297)*

Redwood Elderlink Scph ....B....... 760 480-1030
710 W 13th Ave Escondido (92025) *(P-19297)*

Redwood Family Care Netwrk Inc ....A....... 909 942-0218
13920 City Center Dr Chino Hills (91709) *(P-17750)*

Redwood Scientific Tech Inc ....E....... 310 693-5401
245 E Main St Ste 115 Alhambra (91801) *(P-4221)*

Redwood Senior Homes & Svcs, Escondido *Also Called: Humangood Socal (P-19275)*

Redwood Wellness LLC ....E....... 323 843-2676
1950 W Corporate Way Anaheim (92801) *(P-2146)*

Reed LLC ....E....... 909 287-2100
13822 Oaks Ave Chino (91710) *(P-7288)*

Reed Electric & Field Service, Vernon *Also Called: R A Reed Electric Company (P-17107)*

Reed Manufacturing, Chino *Also Called: Reed LLC (P-7288)*

Reed Smith LLP ....C....... 213 457-8000
355 S Grand Ave Ste 2900 Los Angeles (90071) *(P-18931)*

Reed Thomas Company Inc ....D....... 714 558-7691
1025 Santiago St Santa Ana (92701) *(P-1125)*

Reedex Inc ....E....... 714 894-0311
15526 Commerce Ln Huntington Beach (92649) *(P-9106)*

Reef, Carlsbad *Also Called: South Cone Inc (P-13166)*

Reel Axis Inc ....F....... 760 826-9246
1902 Wright Pl Ste 200 Carlsbad (92008) *(P-20229)*

Reel Efx Inc ....E....... 818 762-1710
5539 Riverton Ave North Hollywood (91601) *(P-11275)*

Reel Picture Productions LLC ....E....... 858 587-0301
5330 Eastgate Mall San Diego (92121) *(P-9183)*

Reel Security California Inc ....D....... 818 928-4737
15303 Ventura Blvd Ste 1080 Sherman Oaks (91403) *(P-16673)*

Reels Inc ....D....... 714 446-9606
301 E Orangethorpe Ave Anaheim (92801) *(P-12258)*

Reeve Store Equipment Company (PA)...................D....... 562 949-2535
9131 Bermudez St Pico Rivera (90660) *(P-2990)*

Reeves Extruded Products Inc ....E....... 661 854-5970
1032 Stockton Ave Arvin (93203) *(P-5175)*

Refinery, The, Sherman Oaks *Also Called: Waldberg Inc (P-15599)*

Reflex Corporation ....E....... 760 931-9009
1825 Aston Ave Ste A Carlsbad (92008) *(P-2556)*

Reformation, The, Los Angeles *Also Called: Lymi Inc (P-13133)*

Refresco Beverages US Inc ....C....... 951 685-0481
11751 Pacific Ave Fontana (92337) *(P-1343)*

Refresco Beverages US Inc ....E....... 909 915-1400
631 S Waterman Ave San Bernardino (92408) *(P-1723)*

Refresco Beverages US Inc ....E....... 909 915-1430
499 E Mill St San Bernardino (92408) *(P-1724)*

Refriderator Manufacters LLC ....E....... 562 229-0500
17018 Edwards Rd Cerritos (90703) *(P-8227)*

Refrigeration Hdwr Sup Corp ....D....... 800 537-8300
9255 Deering Ave Chatsworth (91311) *(P-12765)*

Refrigerator Manufacters LLC ....E....... 562 926-2006
17018 Edwards Rd Cerritos (90703) *(P-8228)*

Refrigerator Manufacturers LLC ....E....... 562 926-2006
17018 Edwards Rd Cerritos (90703) *(P-7622)*

Refrigrated Trck Solutions LLC ....E....... 323 594-4500
1115 E Dominguez St Carson (90746) *(P-9495)*

Regal Medical Group Inc (PA).............................C....... 818 654-3400
8510 Balboa Blvd Ste 275 Northridge (91325) *(P-19402)*

Regal-Piedmont Plastics LLC ....E....... 562 404-4014
17000 Valley View Ave La Mirada (90638) *(P-13417)*

Regards Enterprises Inc ....F...... 909 983-0655
731 S Taylor Ave Ontario (91761) *(P-2749)*

Regency Enterprises Inc (PA).............B...... 818 901-0255
9261 Jordan Ave Chatsworth (91311) *(P-12615)*

Regency Group, Pasadena Also Called: One & All Inc *(P-15567)*

REGENCY HEALTH SERVICES, Covina Also Called: Covina Rehabilitation Center *(P-17922)*

Regency Inn, Costa Mesa Also Called: US Hotel and Resort MGT Inc *(P-15400)*

Regency Supply, Chatsworth Also Called: Regency Enterprises Inc *(P-12615)*

Regent, Valencia Also Called: Regent Aerospace Corporation *(P-12916)*

Regent LP (PA)...............................D...... 310 299-4100
9720 Wilshire Blvd Fl 6 Beverly Hills (90212) *(P-15048)*

Regent Aerospace Corporation (PA)......C...... 661 257-3000
28110 Harrison Pkwy Valencia (91355) *(P-12916)*

Regents of The University Cal ....D...... 310 267-9308
1250 16th St Santa Monica (90404) *(P-18800)*

Regents Point, Irvine Also Called: Humangood Socal *(P-14715)*

Regional Ctr Orange Cnty Inc (PA).........B...... 714 796-5100
1525 N Tustin Ave Santa Ana (92705) *(P-20415)*

Regional Office, Redlands Also Called: Southern California Gas Co *(P-12098)*

Regional Transportation Comm, San Diego Also Called: San Diego Assn Governments *(P-19384)*

Regis Contractors LP ....B...... 949 253-0455
18825 Bardeen Ave Irvine (92612) *(P-473)*

Regus Business Centre LLC ....C...... 714 371-4000
600 Anton Blvd Ste 1100 Costa Mesa (92626) *(P-16914)*

Reh Company ....C...... 619 238-1818
1055 2nd Ave San Diego (92101) *(P-15320)*

Rehab Alliance ....D...... 949 707-5555
22995 Mill Creek Dr Ste A Laguna Hills (92653) *(P-18711)*

Rehababilities Inc ....C...... 310 473-4448
11835 W Olympic Blvd Ste 1090e Los Angeles (90064) *(P-15891)*

Rehabilitation Ctr Bakersfield, Bakersfield Also Called: Bakersfield Hlthcare Wllness CN *(P-17886)*

REHABILITATION INSTITUTE OF OR, Santa Ana Also Called: Reimagine Network *(P-18712)*

Rehabltion Cntre of Bvrly Hlls ....C...... 323 782-1500
580 S San Vicente Blvd Los Angeles (90048) *(P-18036)*

Rehabltion Ctr of Ornge Cnty ....C...... 714 826-2330
9021 Knott Ave Buena Park (90620) *(P-18037)*

Rehabltion Inst Sthern Cal Ri, Santa Ana Also Called: Rio *(P-18713)*

REHABWORKS AT FREEDOM VILLAGE, Lake Forest Also Called: Freedom Village Healthcare Ctr *(P-17953)*

Rehau Construction LLC ....D...... 951 549-9017
1250 Corona Pointe Ct Ste 301 Corona (92879) *(P-5176)*

Rehrig Pacific Company (HQ).................C...... 323 262-5145
4010 E 26th St Vernon (90058) *(P-5177)*

Rehrig Pacific Holdings Inc (PA).............D...... 323 262-5145
4010 E 26th St Vernon (90058) *(P-5178)*

Reid Metal Finishing, Santa Ana Also Called: Electrode Technologies Inc *(P-6614)*

Reid Plastics Customer Svcs, City Of Industry Also Called: Altium Packaging LLC *(P-4937)*

Reid Products, Apple Valley Also Called: Reid Products Inc *(P-7995)*

Reid Products Inc ....E...... 760 240-1355
21430 Waalew Rd Apple Valley (92307) *(P-7995)*

Reimagine Network (PA)......................C...... 714 633-7400
1601 E Saint Andrew Pl Santa Ana (92705) *(P-18712)*

Reinhold Industries Inc (DH).................C...... 562 944-3281
12827 Imperial Hwy Santa Fe Springs (90670) *(P-5179)*

Reisner Enterprises Inc ....F...... 951 786-9478
1403 W Linden St Riverside (92507) *(P-7996)*

Reiter Affl Companies LLC ....C...... 805 925-8577
124 Carmen Ln Ste A Santa Maria (93458) *(P-22)*

Relational Center ....E...... 323 935-1807
2717 S Robertson Blvd Apt 1 Los Angeles (90034) *(P-16367)*

Relationedge LLC ....C...... 858 451-4665
10120 Pacific Heights Blvd Ste 110 San Diego (92121) *(P-16533)*

Relativity Space Inc (PA).....................B...... 424 393-4309
3500 E Burnett St Long Beach (90815) *(P-9912)*

Reldom Corporation ....E...... 562 498-3346
3241 Industry Dr Signal Hill (90755) *(P-9247)*

Releasepoint, Claremont Also Called: Western Feld Invstigations Inc *(P-16537)*

Reliable Building Products, Downey Also Called: Reliable Building Products Inc *(P-6069)*

Reliable Building Products Inc ....E...... 323 566-5000
9314 Gaymont Ave Downey (90240) *(P-6069)*

Reliable Container Corporation ....B...... 562 861-6226
9206 Santa Fe Springs Rd Santa Fe Springs (90670) *(P-3126)*

Reliable Energy Management Inc ....D...... 562 984-5511
6829 Walthall Way Paramount (90723) *(P-817)*

Reliable Packaging Systems Inc ....F...... 714 572-1094
1300 N Jefferson St Anaheim (92807) *(P-4579)*

Reliable Service Company, Riverside Also Called: Rsvc Company *(P-643)*

Reliable Sheet Metal Works, Fullerton Also Called: Gard Inc *(P-6244)*

Reliable Tape Products, Vernon Also Called: Chua & Sons Co Inc *(P-2054)*

Reliable Wholesale Lumber Inc (PA).........D...... 714 848-8222
7600 Redondo Cir Huntington Beach (92648) *(P-12341)*

Reliance Carpet Cushion, Huntington Park Also Called: Reliance Upholstery Sup Co Inc *(P-2486)*

Reliance Company, Los Angeles Also Called: Zastrow Construction Inc *(P-481)*

Reliance Steel & Aluminum Co ....D...... 562 944-3322
12034 Greenstone Ave Santa Fe Springs (90670) *(P-12568)*

Reliance Steel & Aluminum Co ....C...... 323 583-6111
2537 E 27th St Vernon (90058) *(P-12569)*

Reliance Steel & Aluminum Co ....C...... 714 736-4800
15090 Northam St La Mirada (90638) *(P-12570)*

Reliance Steel Company, Vernon Also Called: Reliance Steel & Aluminum Co *(P-12569)*

Reliance Upholstery Sup Co Inc ....D...... 323 321-2300
4920 S Boyle Ave Huntington Park (90255) *(P-2486)*

Reliance Worldwide Corporation ....F...... 770 863-4005
2750 E Mission Blvd Ontario (91761) *(P-6769)*

Reliant Foodservice, Temecula Also Called: Canadas Finest Foods Inc *(P-1366)*

Reliant Funding Group, San Diego Also Called: Reliant Services Group LLC *(P-14286)*

Reliant Services Group LLC ....C...... 877 850-0998
9540 Towne Centre Dr Ste 100 San Diego (92121) *(P-14286)*

Relief-Mart Inc ....E...... 805 379-4300
28505 Canwood St Ste C Agoura Hills (91301) *(P-14146)*

Relocity Inc ....C...... 323 207-9160
10250 Constellation Blvd Ste 100 Los Angeles (90067) *(P-20088)*

Relton Corporation ....D...... 800 423-1505
317 Rolyn Pl Arcadia (91007) *(P-4628)*

REM Eye Wear, Sun Valley Also Called: REM Optical Company Inc *(P-12531)*

REM Optical Company Inc ....C...... 818 504-3950
10941 La Tuna Canyon Rd Sun Valley (91352) *(P-12531)*

Remax Exec King Harbor ....D...... 310 378-9889
23740 Hawthorne Blvd Torrance (90505) *(P-14857)*

Remax Olson & Associates Inc ....C...... 818 366-3300
11141 Tampa Ave Northridge (91326) *(P-14858)*

Remco Mch & Fabrication Inc ....F...... 909 877-3530
1966 S Date Ave Bloomington (92316) *(P-7997)*

Remec Brdband Wrless Ntwrks LL ....C...... 858 312-6900
17034 Camino San Bernardo San Diego (92127) *(P-8570)*

Remec Broadband Wireless LLC ....C...... 858 312-6900
17034 Camino San Bernardo San Diego (92127) *(P-8571)*

Remec Defense & Space Inc ....A...... 858 560-1301
9404 Chesapeake Dr San Diego (92123) *(P-10060)*

Remedy Intelligent Staffing, Aliso Viejo Also Called: Remedytemp Inc *(P-15937)*

Remedytemp Inc (DH).........................C...... 949 425-7600
101 Enterprise Ste 100 Aliso Viejo (92656) *(P-15937)*

Remington Club I & II, San Diego Also Called: Five Star Senior Living Inc *(P-17952)*

Remington Roll Forming Inc ....E...... 626 350-5196
2445 Chico Ave El Monte (91733) *(P-5631)*

Remn Inc ....D...... 951 697-8135
3400 Central Ave Ste 330 Riverside (92506) *(P-14859)*

Remo Inc (PA).................................B...... 661 294-5600
28101 Industry Dr Valencia (91355) *(P-10930)*

Remote Ocean Systems Inc (PA).............E...... 858 565-8500
9581 Ridgehaven Ct San Diego (92123) *(P-8380)*

Rempex Pharmaceuticals Inc ....E...... 858 875-2840
3013 Science Park Rd 1st Fl San Diego (92121) *(P-4222)*

Remstek Corp, Temecula Also Called: Inners Tasks LLC *(P-7431)*

Renaissance, Indian Wells Also Called: Renaissnce Esmralda Resort Spa *(P-15323)*

Renaissance Doors & Windows, Rcho Sta Marg Also Called: Renaissnce Frnch Dors Sash Inc *(P-2631)*

Mergent email: customerrelations@mergent.com
1240

2024 Southern California
Business Directory and Buyers Guide

(P-0000) Products & Services Section entry number
(PA)=Parent Co (HQ)=Headquarters (DH)=Div Headquarters

Renaissance Hollywood Ht & Spa, Los Angeles Also Called: Cim/H & H Hotel LP (P-15116)

Renaissance Hotel Clubsport, Aliso Viejo Also Called: L & O Aliso Viejo LLC (P-15215)

Renaissance Hotel Operating Co .... B...... 310 337-2800
9620 Airport Blvd Los Angeles (90045) (P-15321)

Renaissance Hotel Operating Co .... A...... 760 773-4444
44400 Indian Wells Ln Indian Wells (92210) (P-15322)

Renaissance Indian Wells, Indian Wells Also Called: Renaissance Hotel Operating Co (P-15322)

Renaissnce Esmralda Resort Spa .... D...... 760 773-4444
44400 Indian Wells Ln Indian Wells (92210) (P-15323)

Renaissnce Frnch Dors Sash Inc (PA)............................... C...... 714 578-0090
38 Segada Rcho Sta Marg (92688) (P-2631)

Renal Center, Orange Also Called: St Joseph Hospital of Orange (P-18464)

Renau Corporation .... E...... 818 341-1994
9309 Deering Ave Chatsworth (91311) (P-10155)

Renau Electronic Laboratories, Chatsworth Also Called: Renau Corporation (P-10155)

Renee Claire Inc, Los Angeles Also Called: Camp Smidgemore Inc (P-2310)

Renew Medical Group Inc .... D...... 310 929-9790
1125 S Beverly Dr Ste 720 Los Angeles (90035) (P-17751)

Renkus-Heinz Inc (PA)... D...... 949 588-9997
19201 Cook St Foothill Ranch (92610) (P-8429)

Reno Tenco, Boron Also Called: Rio Tinto Minerals Inc (P-242)

Renovo Solutions LLC (PA).. B...... 714 599-7969
4 Executive Cir Ste 185 Irvine (92614) (P-20089)

Rent What, Compton Also Called: Sew What Inc (P-2463)

Rentacenter .... D...... 805 769-9030
183 Niblick Rd Paso Robles (93446) (P-15796)

Rentech Inc (PA)... D...... 310 571-9800
10880 Wilshire Blvd Ste 1101 Los Angeles (90024) (P-4691)

Rentech Ntrgn Pasadena Spa LLC .... E...... 310 571-9805
10877 Wilshire Blvd Ste 710 Los Angeles (90024) (P-4541)

Rentokil North America Inc .... D...... 562 802-2238
15415 Marquardt Ave Santa Fe Springs (90670) (P-15687)

Reny & Co Inc .... F...... 626 962-3078
4505 Littlejohn St Baldwin Park (91706) (P-5180)

Renymed, Baldwin Park Also Called: Reny & Co Inc (P-5180)

Renzoni Vineyards Inc .... E...... 951 302-8466
37350 De Portola Rd Temecula (92592) (P-35)

Reotemp Instrument Corporation (PA)............................. D...... 858 784-0710
10656 Roselle St San Diego (92121) (P-10156)

Rep-Kote Products Inc .... F...... 909 355-1288
10938 Beech Ave Fontana (92337) (P-4676)

Repair Tech International, Van Nuys Also Called: Repairtech International Inc (P-11705)

Repairtech International Inc .... E...... 818 989-2681
7850 Gloria Ave Van Nuys (91406) (P-11705)

Repet Inc .... C...... 909 594-5333
14207 Monte Vista Ave Chino (91710) (P-4842)

Replacement Parts Inds Inc .... E...... 818 882-8611
625 Cochran St Simi Valley (93065) (P-10765)

Replanet LLC .... A...... 951 520-1700
800 N Haven Ave Ste 120 Ontario (91764) (P-12818)

Repligen Corporation .... F...... 775 235-5200
2685 Park Center Dr Ste C Simi Valley (93065) (P-4329)

Reprints Desk Inc .... D...... 310 477-0354
15821 Ventura Blvd Ste 165 Encino (91436) (P-16534)

Republic Bag Inc (PA)... D...... 951 734-9740
580 E Harrison St Corona (92879) (P-3190)

Republic Fence Co Inc .... E...... 818 341-5323
11309 Danube Ave Granada Hills (91344) (P-1175)

Republic Floor, Montebello Also Called: Reu Distribution LLC (P-12314)

Republic Flooring, Montebello Also Called: Hardwood Flrg Liquidators Inc (P-2572)

Republic Furniture Mfg Inc .... F...... 323 235-2144
2241 E 49th St Vernon (90058) (P-2814)

Republic Indemnity Co Amer (DH)................................... C...... 818 990-9860
4500 Park Granada Ste 300 Calabasas (91302) (P-14523)

Republic Indemnity Company Cal .... C...... 818 990-9860
15821 Ventura Blvd Ste 370 Encino (91436) (P-14524)

Republic Machinery Co Inc (PA)..................................... E...... 310 518-1100
800 Sprucelake Dr Harbor City (90710) (P-7020)

Republic Nat Distrg Co LLC (PA).................................... C...... 714 368-4615
14402 Franklin Ave Tustin (92780) (P-13480)

Rerubber LLC .... F...... 909 786-2811
115 N Del Rosa Dr Ste C San Bernardino (92408) (P-12184)

RES-Care Inc .... D...... 951 653-1311
22635 Alessandro Blvd Moreno Valley (92553) (P-18097)

RES-Care Inc .... D...... 909 596-5360
2120 Foothill Blvd Ste 205 La Verne (91750) (P-18098)

Res.net, Foothill Ranch Also Called: US Real Estate Services Inc (P-14882)

Reschedge, Walnut Also Called: Oncehub Inc (P-16335)

Research Affiliates, Newport Beach Also Called: Research Affiliates Capital LP (P-14428)

Research Affiliates, Newport Beach Also Called: Research Affiliates MGT LLC (P-14429)

Research Affiliates Capital LP .... D...... 949 325-8700
620 Newport Center Dr Ste 900 Newport Beach (92660) (P-14428)

Research Affiliates MGT LLC .... D...... 949 325-8700
620 Newport Center Dr Ste 900 Newport Beach (92660) (P-14429)

Research Metal Industries Inc .... E...... 310 352-3200
1970 W 139th St Gardena (90249) (P-7998)

Research Tool & Die Works LLC .... D...... 310 639-5722
17124 Keegan Ave Carson (90746) (P-6553)

Reserve Club .... D...... 760 674-2222
49400 Desert Butte Trl Indian Wells (92210) (P-17511)

Reshape Weightloss Inc (HQ)... E...... 949 429-6680
1001 Calle Amanecer San Clemente (92673) (P-10824)

Residence Inn By Marriott, Los Angeles Also Called: 901 West Olympic Blvd Ltd Prtn (P-15068)

Residence Inn By Marriott, Palm Desert Also Called: Ashford Trs Seven LLC (P-15079)

Residence Inn By Marriott, Torrance Also Called: Msr Hotels & Resorts Inc (P-15257)

Residence Inn By Marriott, Los Angeles Also Called: Sunstone Hotel Properties Inc (P-15379)

Residence Inn By Marriott, Manhattan Beach Also Called: Sunstone Hotel Properties Inc (P-15380)

Residence Inn By Marriott, Aliso Viejo Also Called: Sunstone Hotel Properties Inc (P-15381)

Resident Group Services Inc (PA)................................... C...... 714 630-5300
1156 N Grove St Anaheim (92806) (P-214)

Residential Design Services, Irvine Also Called: LARK Industries Inc (P-16860)

Residential Framer, Riverside Also Called: Silverado Framing & Cnstr (P-459)

Resilience, San Diego Also Called: National Resilience Inc (P-4176)

Resilience Us Inc (HQ).. E...... 984 202-0854
3115 Merryfield Row Ste 200 San Diego (92121) (P-4223)

Resinart Corporation .... E...... 949 642-3665
1621 Placentia Ave Costa Mesa (92627) (P-5181)

Resinart Plastics, Costa Mesa Also Called: Resinart Corporation (P-5181)

Resmed, Chatsworth Also Called: Resmed Motor Technologies Inc (P-8154)

Resmed, San Diego Also Called: Resmed Inc (P-10597)

Resmed Corp .... E...... 858 746-2400
14040 Danielson St Poway (92064) (P-10596)

Resmed Inc (PA)... A...... 858 836-5000
9001 Spectrum Center Blvd San Diego (92123) (P-10597)

Resmed Motor Technologies Inc .... C...... 818 428-6400
9540 De Soto Ave Chatsworth (91311) (P-8154)

Resort At Pelican Hill LLC .... B...... 949 467-6800
22701 Pelican Hill Rd S Newport Coast (92657) (P-15324)

Resort Campground Intl, Lytle Creek Also Called: Burlingame Industries Inc (P-15440)

Resort Parking Services Inc .... C...... 760 328-4041
39755 Berkey Dr # B Palm Desert (92211) (P-17007)

Resortime.com, Carlsbad Also Called: Grand Pacific Resorts Inc (P-15160)

Resource Collection Inc .... E...... 310 219-3272
3771 W 242nd St Ste 205 Torrance (90505) (P-15744)

Resource Label Group LLC .... F...... 562 926-1432
13260 Moore St Cerritos (90703) (P-3579)

Resource Label Group LLC .... E...... 310 603-8910
1360 W Walnut Pkwy Compton (90220) (P-3723)

Resource Label Group LLC .... D...... 714 619-7100
1511 E Edinger Ave Santa Ana (92705) (P-3805)

Resources Connection Inc (PA)...................................... C...... 714 430-6400
17101 Armstrong Ave Ste 100 Irvine (92614) (P-20230)

Resources Global Professionals, Irvine Also Called: Resources Connection Inc (P-20230)

Respawn Entertainment LLC .... C...... 818 960-4400
20131 Prairie St Chatsworth (91311) (P-17213)

Response Envelope Inc (PA)... C...... 909 923-5855
1340 S Baker Ave Ontario (91761) (P-3806)

Employee Codes: A=Over 500 employees, B=251-500
C=101-250, D=51-100, E=20-50, F=10-19, G=1-9

2024 Southern California
Business Directory and Buyers Guide

© Mergent Inc. 1-800-342-5647
1241

Response Genetics Inc .... C 323 224-3900
1640 Marengo St Ste 7 Los Angeles (90033) **(P-4291)**

Restaurant Depot, San Diego Also Called: Jetro Cash and Carry Entps LLC **(P-13299)**

Restaurant Investment, Los Angeles Also Called: Providence Rest Partners LLC **(P-15047)**

Restaurants Bars & Food Svcs, Los Angeles Also Called: Fish House Partners One LLC **(P-14008)**

Restorixhealth, Irvine Also Called: Gordian Medical Inc **(P-12489)**

Result Group Inc .... D 480 777-7130
2603 Main St Ste 710 Irvine (92614) **(P-16467)**

Retail Print Media Inc .... E 424 488-6950
2355 Crenshaw Blvd Ste 135 Torrance (90501) **(P-3807)**

Rethink Label Systems, Anaheim Also Called: Labeltronix LLC **(P-3779)**

Rettig Machine Inc .... E 909 793-7811
301 Kansas St Redlands (92373) **(P-17094)**

Reu Distribution LLC .... A 323 201-4200
7227 Telegraph Rd Montebello (90640) **(P-12314)**

Reuben H Fleet Science Center .... C 619 238-1233
1875 El Prado San Diego (92101) **(P-19361)**

Reuland Electric Co (PA) .... **C 626 964-6411**
17969 Railroad St City Of Industry (91748) **(P-8155)**

Reuters Television La, North Hollywood Also Called: Thomson Reuters Corporation **(P-8589)**

Rev Co Spring Mfanufacturing .... F 562 949-1958
9915 Alburtis Ave Santa Fe Springs (90670) **(P-6808)**

Reva Medical Inc (PA) .... **E 858 966-3000**
5751 Copley Dr Ste B San Diego (92111) **(P-10695)**

Revasum Inc .... C 805 541-6424
825 Buckley Rd San Luis Obispo (93401) **(P-8879)**

Revco Industries Inc (PA) .... **E 562 777-1588**
10747 Norwalk Blvd Santa Fe Springs (90670) **(P-12875)**

Revco Products .... D 714 891-6688
7221 Acacia Ave Garden Grove (92841) **(P-16368)**

Reveal Biosciences Inc .... E 858 274-3663
6760 Top Gun St Ste 110 San Diego (92121) **(P-19873)**

Reveal Imaging, Vista Also Called: Leidos Inc **(P-19854)**

Reveal Imaging Tech Inc .... D 571 526-6000
10260 Campus Point Dr Ste 6130 San Diego (92121) **(P-10061)**

Reveal Imaging Tech Inc (DH) .... **E 571 526-6000**
10260 Campus Point Dr Rm 6130 San Diego (92121) **(P-10062)**

Reveal Windows & Doors, La Habra Also Called: Pacific Archtectural Mllwk Inc **(P-2628)**

Reverse Medical, Irvine Also Called: Reverse Medical Corporation **(P-10598)**

Reverse Medical Corporation .... E 949 215-0660
13700 Alton Pkwy Ste 167 Irvine (92618) **(P-10598)**

Revlon Inc .... D 619 372-1379
1125 Joshua Way Ste 12 Vista (92081) **(P-4451)**

Revolt, Los Angeles Also Called: Revolt Media and Tv LLC **(P-11962)**

Revolt Media and Tv LLC .... C 323 645-3000
9200 W Sunset Blvd Fl 3 Los Angeles (90069) **(P-11962)**

Revoltion Cnsmr Sltions CA LLC (DH) .... **C 323 980-0918**
3840 E 26th St Vernon (90058) **(P-13556)**

Rex Creamery, Commerce Also Called: Heritage Distributing Company **(P-1313)**

Rexhall Industries Inc .... E 661 726-5470
26857 Tannahill Ave Canyon Country (91387) **(P-9502)**

Rexnord Industries LLC .... E 805 583-5514
2175 Union Pl Simi Valley (93065) **(P-7213)**

Rey-Crest Roofg Waterproofing .... D 323 257-9329
3065 Verdugo Rd Los Angeles (90065) **(P-1176)**

Rey-Crest Roofg Waterproofing, Los Angeles Also Called: Rey-Crest Roofg Waterproofing **(P-1176)**

Reyes Coca-Cola Bottling LLC .... E 760 241-2653
15346 Anacapa Rd Victorville (92392) **(P-1725)**

Reyes Coca-Cola Bottling LLC .... E 805 644-2211
5335 Walker St Ventura (93003) **(P-1726)**

Reyes Coca-Cola Bottling LLC .... E 805 925-2629
120 E Jones St Santa Maria (93454) **(P-1727)**

Reyes Coca-Cola Bottling LLC .... E 805 614-3702
1000 Fairway Dr Santa Maria (93455) **(P-1728)**

Reyes Coca-Cola Bottling LLC .... E 760 352-1561
126 S 3rd St El Centro (92243) **(P-1729)**

Reyes Coca-Cola Bottling LLC .... D 661 324-6531
4320 Ride St Bakersfield (93313) **(P-1730)**

Reyes Coca-Cola Bottling LLC .... B 909 980-3121
10670 6th St Rancho Cucamonga (91730) **(P-1731)**

Reyes Coca-Cola Bottling LLC .... B 619 266-6300
5255 Federal Blvd San Diego (92105) **(P-1732)**

Reyes Coca-Cola Bottling LLC .... C 323 278-2600
666 Union St Montebello (90640) **(P-1733)**

Reyes Coca-Cola Bottling LLC .... E 213 744-8659
1338 E 14th St Los Angeles (90021) **(P-1734)**

Reyes Coca-Cola Bottling LLC .... D 714 974-1901
700 W Grove Ave Orange (92865) **(P-1735)**

Reyes Coca-Cola Bottling LLC (PA) .... **B 213 744-8616**
3 Park Plz Ste 600 Irvine (92614) **(P-1736)**

Reyes Coca-Cola Bottling LLC .... D 760 396-4500
86375 Industrial Way Coachella (92236) **(P-1737)**

Reyes Coca-Cola Bottling LLC .... D 562 803-8100
8729 Cleta St Downey (90241) **(P-1738)**

Reyes Coca-Cola Bottling LLC .... D 818 362-4307
12925 Bradley Ave Sylmar (91342) **(P-13391)**

Reynaldos Mexican Food Co LLC (PA) .... **C 562 803-3188**
3301 E Vernon Ave Vernon (90058) **(P-1976)**

Reynard Corporation .... E 949 366-8866
1020 Calle Sombra San Clemente (92673) **(P-10336)**

Reyrich Plastics Inc .... E 909 484-8444
1704 S Vineyard Ave Ontario (91761) **(P-5182)**

Rezek Equipment .... F 909 885-6221
970 Reece St San Bernardino (92411) **(P-19678)**

Rezex Corporation .... E 213 622-2015
1930 E 51st St Vernon (90058) **(P-2106)**

Rf Digital Corporation .... C 949 610-0008
1601 Pacific Coast Hwy Ste 290 Hermosa Beach (90254) **(P-8880)**

Rf Industries Ltd (PA) .... **D 858 549-6340**
16868 Via Del Campo Ct Ste 200 San Diego (92127) **(P-8981)**

Rf Surgical Systems LLC .... D 855 522-7027
5927 Landau Ct Carlsbad (92008) **(P-10599)**

Rfc Wire Forms, Ontario Also Called: Rfc Wire Forms Inc **(P-6827)**

Rfc Wire Forms Inc .... D 909 467-0559
525 Brooks St Ontario (91762) **(P-6827)**

RG Costumes & Accessories Inc .... E 626 858-9559
726 Arrow Grand Cir Covina (91722) **(P-2459)**

Rgb Systems Inc (PA) .... **C 714 491-1500**
1025 E Ball Rd Ste 100 Anaheim (92805) **(P-7567)**

Rgbx Inc .... D 714 524-1350
16971 Imperial Hwy Yorba Linda (92886) **(P-19227)**

Rgc Gaslamp LLC .... C 619 738-7000
550 J St San Diego (92101) **(P-15325)**

Rgc Services Inc .... D 805 484-1600
601 E Daily Dr Ste 102 Camarillo (93010) **(P-14860)**

Rgc Services Inc (PA) .... **C 805 644-1242**
5720 Ralston St Ste 100 Ventura (93003) **(P-14861)**

RGF Enterprises Inc .... E 951 734-6922
220 Citation Cir Corona (92878) **(P-6731)**

Rggd Inc (PA) .... **D 323 581-6617**
4950 S Santa Fe Ave Vernon (90058) **(P-12983)**

Rgis LLC .... C 714 938-0663
1937 W Chapman Ave Orange (92868) **(P-16915)**

Rgis LLC .... C 760 736-9241
365 S Rancho Santa Fe Rd Ste 103 San Marcos (92078) **(P-16916)**

Rgis, Llc, Orange Also Called: Rgis LLC **(P-16915)**

Rgis, Llc, San Marcos Also Called: Rgis LLC **(P-16916)**

Rgn-San Diego I LLC .... C 619 344-2500
350 10th Ave Ste 1000 San Diego (92101) **(P-16917)**

Rgs Services, Anaheim Also Called: Resident Group Services Inc **(P-214)**

RH Peterson Co (PA) .... **C 626 369-5085**
14724 Proctor Ave City Of Industry (91746) **(P-8221)**

Rhapsody Clothing Inc .... D 213 614-8887
810 E Pico Blvd Ste 24 Los Angeles (90021) **(P-2366)**

Rhi Inc (PA) .... **D 818 508-3800**
5841 Lankershim Blvd North Hollywood (91601) **(P-13819)**

Rhino Building Services Inc .... C 858 455-1440
6650 Flanders Dr Ste K San Diego (92121) **(P-15745)**

Rhino Linings Corporation (PA) .... **D 858 450-0441**
9747 Businesspark Ave San Diego (92131) **(P-4504)**

RHS Corp ....A....... 909 335-5500
350 Terracina Blvd Redlands (92373) *(P-20090)*

Rhythm & Hues Studios, El Segundo *Also Called: Rhythm and Hues Inc (P-17214)*

Rhythm and Hues Inc (PA)..C....... 310 448-7500
2100 E Grand Ave Ste A El Segundo (90245) *(P-17214)*

Ria Financial Service, Buena Park *Also Called: Continental Exch Solutions Inc (P-14257)*

Rialto Bioenergy Facility LLC ....C....... 760 436-8870
5780 Fleet St Ste 310 Carlsbad (92008) *(P-19679)*

Rialto Concrete Products, Rialto *Also Called: Kti Incorporated (P-5423)*

Ric, Santa Ana *Also Called: Rickenbacker International Corporation (P-10931)*

Rica, Calabasas *Also Called: Republic Indemnity Co Amer (P-14523)*

Ricardo Defense Inc (DH)..E....... 805 882-1884
175 Cremona Dr Ste 140 Goleta (93117) *(P-9450)*

Ricaurte Precision Inc ....E....... 714 667-0632
1550 E Mcfadden Ave Santa Ana (92705) *(P-7999)*

Rice Field Corporation ....C....... 626 968-6917
14500 Valley Blvd City Of Industry (91746) *(P-1233)*

Rich Chicks LLC ....E....... 209 879-4104
13771 Gramercy Pl Gardena (90249) *(P-1248)*

Rich Limited, Oceanside *Also Called: Britcan Inc (P-2974)*

Rich Products Corporation ....E....... 714 338-1145
3401 W Segerstrom Ave Santa Ana (92704) *(P-1529)*

Rich Products Corporation ....D....... 562 946-6396
12805 Busch Pl Santa Fe Springs (90670) *(P-1977)*

Richard Tyler, Alhambra *Also Called: Tyler Trafficante Inc (P-2155)*

Richard Wilson Wellington ....D....... 626 812-7881
1025 N Todd Ave Azusa (91702) *(P-69)*

Richards Neon Shop Inc ....E....... 951 279-6767
4375 Prado Rd Ste 102 Corona (92878) *(P-11149)*

Richards Wtson Grshon A Prof C (PA)..............C....... 213 626-8484
355 S Grand Ave 40th Fl Los Angeles (90071) *(P-18932)*

Richardson Steel Inc ....E....... 619 697-5892
9102 Harness St Ste A Spring Valley (91977) *(P-6070)*

Richfield Engineering Inc ....E....... 714 524-3741
1135 Fee Ana St Placentia (92870) *(P-6152)*

Richman Management Corporation ....B....... 760 832-8520
35400 Bob Hope Dr Ste 107 Rancho Mirage (92270) *(P-16674)*

Richman Management Corporation ....B....... 909 296-6189
41743 Entp Cir N Ste 209 Temecula (92590) *(P-16675)*

Richmond Engineering Co Inc ....C....... 800 589-7058
15472 Markar Rd Poway (92064) *(P-215)*

Richwell Steel Co Inc ....E....... 310 324-4455
134 W 168th St Gardena (90248) *(P-1114)*

Rick Engineering Company, San Diego *Also Called: Glenn A Rick Engrg & Dev Co (P-19600)*

Rick Hamm Construction Inc ....D....... 714 532-0815
201 W Carleton Ave Orange (92867) *(P-640)*

Rick's Hitches & Welding, El Cajon *Also Called: CLP Inc (P-17081)*

Rickenbacker International Corporation ....D....... 714 545-5574
3895 S Main St Santa Ana (92707) *(P-10931)*

Rico Corporation (HQ)..C....... 818 394-2700
8484 San Fernando Rd Sun Valley (91352) *(P-10932)*

Rico Products, Sun Valley *Also Called: Rico Corporation (P-10932)*

Ricoh Electronics Inc ....C....... 714 259-1220
17482 Pullman St Irvine (92614) *(P-7587)*

Ricoh Electronics Inc ....C....... 714 566-6079
2310 Redhill Ave Santa Ana (92705) *(P-10884)*

Ricoh Electronics Inc ....D....... 714 566-2500
1920 W Base Line Rd Rialto (92376) *(P-12388)*

Ricoh Prtg Systems Amer Inc (HQ).......................B....... 805 578-4000
2390 Ward Ave Ste A Simi Valley (93065) *(P-7568)*

Ricon Corp ....C....... 818 267-3000
1135 Aviation Pl San Fernando (91340) *(P-11276)*

Ride On Transportation, San Luis Obispo *Also Called: United Crbral Plsy Assn San Lu (P-19151)*

Ridge, Corona *Also Called: Peppermint Ridge (P-19294)*

Ridge Wallet LLC ....F....... 818 636-2832
2448 Main St Santa Monica (90405) *(P-5304)*

Ridge Wallet, The, Santa Monica *Also Called: Ridge Wallet LLC (P-5304)*

Ridgecrest Healthcare Inc ....D....... 760 446-3591
5808 Monterey Rd Los Angeles (90042) *(P-18038)*

Ridgecrest Regional Hospital (PA)...........................B....... 760 446-3551
1081 N China Lake Blvd Ridgecrest (93555) *(P-18407)*

Ridgecrest Service Center, Ridgecrest *Also Called: Southern California Edison Co (P-12066)*

Ridout Plastics Company (PA)..................................D....... 858 560-1551
5535 Ruffin Rd San Diego (92123) *(P-4819)*

Riedon Inc (PA)..C
300 Cypress Ave Alhambra (91801) *(P-8931)*

Rief Enterprises Inc (PA)...E....... 714 934-3400
15662 Producer Ln Huntington Beach (92649) *(P-12732)*

Right Angle Solutions Inc ....E....... 951 934-3081
6315 Pedley Rd Jurupa Valley (92509) *(P-818)*

Right Hand Manufacturing Inc ....C....... 619 819-5056
180 Otay Lakes Rd Ste 205 Bonita (91902) *(P-8188)*

Right Manufacturing LLC ....E....... 858 566-7002
7949 Stromesa Ct Ste G San Diego (92126) *(P-6851)*

Rightpaq, Santa Ana *Also Called: McDonald Packaging Inc (P-3118)*

Rightway, Vernon *Also Called: R B R Meat Company Inc (P-1203)*

Rigos Equipment Mfg LLC ....E....... 626 813-6621
14501 Joanbridge St Baldwin Park (91706) *(P-6305)*

Rigos Sheet Metal, Baldwin Park *Also Called: Rigos Equipment Mfg LLC (P-6305)*

Rika Corporation ....D....... 949 830-9050
332 W Brenna Ln Orange (92867) *(P-1115)*

Rima Enterprises Inc ....D....... 714 893-4534
16417 Ladona Cir Huntington Beach (92649) *(P-7191)*

Rima-System, Huntington Beach *Also Called: Rima Enterprises Inc (P-7191)*

Rincon Consultants Inc ....C....... 805 547-0900
1530 Monterey St Ste D San Luis Obispo (93401) *(P-20376)*

Rincon Engineering Corporation ....E....... 805 684-0935
6325 Carpinteria Ave Carpinteria (93013) *(P-8000)*

Rincon Engineering Tech ....E....... 805 684-4144
6325 Carpinteria Ave Carpinteria (93013) *(P-8001)*

Rincon Pacific LLC ....B....... 805 986-8806
1312 Del Norte Rd Camarillo (93010) *(P-23)*

Ring Container Tech LLC ....D....... 909 350-8416
8275 Almeria Ave Fontana (92335) *(P-4866)*

Ring LLC (HQ)..B....... 310 929-7085
12515 Cerise Ave Hawthorne (90250) *(P-8109)*

Ring of Fire, Van Nuys *Also Called: Rof LLC (P-2185)*

Rio ....C....... 714 633-7400
1601 E Saint Andrew Pl Santa Ana (92705) *(P-18713)*

Rio Tinto Minerals Inc ....C....... 760 762-7121
14486 Borax Rd Boron (93516) *(P-242)*

Rio Vista Development Co Inc (PA)..........................C....... 818 980-8000
4222 Vineland Ave North Hollywood (91602) *(P-15326)*

Riolo Transportation Inc ....B....... 760 729-4405
2725 Jefferson St Ste 2d Carlsbad (92008) *(P-11839)*

Riot Creative Imaging ....D....... 213 516-3160
934 Venice Blvd Los Angeles (90015) *(P-15651)*

Riot Games, Los Angeles *Also Called: Riot Games Inc (P-16369)*

Riot Games Inc (DH)..E....... 310 207-1444
12333 W Olympic Blvd Los Angeles (90064) *(P-16369)*

Riot Glass Inc ....C....... 800 580-2303
17941 Brookshire Ln Huntington Beach (92647) *(P-9248)*

Rip Curl Inc (DH)...D....... 714 422-3600
3030 Airway Ave Costa Mesa (92626) *(P-11019)*

Rip Curl USA, Costa Mesa *Also Called: Rip Curl Inc (P-11019)*

Risa Tech Inc ....E....... 949 951-5815
27442 Portola Pkwy Ste 200 Foothill Ranch (92610) *(P-16103)*

Risco Inc ....E....... 951 769-2899
390 Risco Cir Beaumont (92223) *(P-6453)*

Risvolds Inc ....D....... 323 770-2674
1234 W El Segundo Blvd Gardena (90247) *(P-1978)*

Rite Engineering & Manufacturing Corporation ......E....... 562 862-2135
5832 Garfield Ave Commerce (90040) *(P-6153)*

Rite Screen, Rancho Cucamonga *Also Called: J T Walker Industries Inc (P-6108)*

Ritec, Simi Valley *Also Called: Rugged Info Tech Eqp Corp (P-7569)*

Ritual, Culver City *Also Called: Natals Inc (P-4175)*

Ritz Carlton Rancho Mirage, Rancho Mirage *Also Called: Ritz-Carlton Hotel Company LLC (P-15327)*

Ritz-Carlton, Dana Point *Also Called: Ritz-Carlton Hotel Company LLC (P-15328)*

Employee Codes: A=Over 500 employees, B=251-500
C=101-250, D=51-100, E=20-50, F=10-19, G=1-9

2024 Southern California
Business Directory and Buyers Guide

© Mergent Inc. 1-800-342-5647
1243

Ritz-Carlton, Santa Barbara *Also Called: Ritz-Carlton Hotel Company LLC (P-15329)*

Ritz-Carlton Hotel Company LLC .... B...... 760 321-8282
68900 Frank Sinatra Dr Rancho Mirage (92270) *(P-15327)*

Ritz-Carlton Hotel Company LLC .... B...... 949 240-5020
1 Ritz Carlton Dr Dana Point (92629) *(P-15328)*

Ritz-Carlton Hotel Company LLC .... A...... 805 968-0100
8301 Hollister Ave Santa Barbara (93117) *(P-15329)*

Ritz-Carlton Laguna Niguel, Dana Point *Also Called: Prutel Joint Venture (P-15311)*

River Ridge Farms Inc .... D...... 805 647-6880
3135 Los Angeles Ave Oxnard (93036) *(P-70)*

River Valley Precast Inc .... E...... 928 764-3839
14796 Washington Dr Fontana (92335) *(P-5445)*

Rivera Sanatarium Inc .... D...... 562 949-2591
7246 Rosemead Blvd Pico Rivera (90660) *(P-18039)*

Riverbench LLC .... E...... 805 324-4100
137 Anacapa St Santa Barbara (93101) *(P-1656)*

Riversd-San Brnrdino Cnty Indi .... C...... 951 654-0803
607 Donna Way San Jacinto (92583) *(P-17752)*

Riversd-San Brnrdino Cnty Indi (PA) .... C...... 909 864-1097
11980 Mount Vernon Ave Grand Terrace (92313) *(P-17753)*

Riverside Auto Auction, Anaheim *Also Called: Califrnia Auto Dalers Exch LLC (P-12223)*

Riverside Blltin Jrupa This We, Riverside *Also Called: Metropolitan News Company (P-3307)*

Riverside Care Inc .... C...... 951 683-7111
4301 Caroline Ct Riverside (92506) *(P-18040)*

Riverside Cement Holdings Company .... B...... 951 774-2500
1500 Rubidoux Blvd Riverside (92509) *(P-5370)*

Riverside Cmnty Hlth Systems (DH) .... A...... 951 788-3000
4445 Magnolia Ave 6th Fl Riverside (92501) *(P-18408)*

Riverside Cnty Flood Ctrl Wtr .... C...... 951 955-1200
1995 Market St Riverside (92501) *(P-20400)*

Riverside Cnty Rgional Med Ctr, Riverside *Also Called: Riverside Univ Hlth Sys Fndtio (P-18409)*

Riverside Community Hospital, Riverside *Also Called: Riverside Cmnty Hlth Systems (P-18408)*

Riverside Companion Services, San Bernardino *Also Called: Maxim Healthcare Services Inc (P-15931)*

Riverside Construction Company Inc .... C...... 951 682-8308
4225 Garner Rd Riverside (92501) *(P-641)*

Riverside Crona Rsrce Cnsrvtio, Riverside *Also Called: County of Riverside (P-19440)*

Riverside District Office, Riverside *Also Called: State Compensation Insur Fund (P-14530)*

Riverside Equities LLC .... B...... 951 688-2222
8487 Magnolia Ave Riverside (92504) *(P-18041)*

Riverside Foundary, Riverside *Also Called: Oldcast Precast (P-5431)*

Riverside Marriott, Riverside *Also Called: Pinnacle Rvrside Hspitality LP (P-15305)*

Riverside Med Clnic Ptient Ctr, Riverside *Also Called: Riverside Medical Clinic Inc (P-17754)*

Riverside Medical Center, Riverside *Also Called: Kaiser Foundation Hospitals (P-17681)*

Riverside Medical Clinic Inc (PA) .... D...... 951 683-6370
3660 Arlington Ave Riverside (92506) *(P-17754)*

Riverside Transit Agency (PA) .... B...... 951 565-5000
1825 3rd St Riverside (92507) *(P-11357)*

Riverside Univ Hlth Sys Fndtio (PA) .... B...... 951 358-5000
4065 County Circle Dr Riverside (92503) *(P-18409)*

Riverside University Health .... B...... 951 486-4000
26520 Cactus Ave Moreno Valley (92555) *(P-18410)*

Riverside-San Bernardino .... C...... 951 849-4761
11555 1/2 Potrero Rd Banning (92220) *(P-18714)*

Riverton Steel Construction .... F...... 323 564-1881
10130 Adella Ave South Gate (90280) *(P-1116)*

Riverwalk Post Acute, Riverside *Also Called: Orange Treeidence Opco LLC (P-18094)*

Riverwalk PST-Cute Rhblitation, Mission Viejo *Also Called: Rock Canyon Healthcare Inc (P-18638)*

Rivian, Irvine *Also Called: Rivian Automotive Inc (P-9305)*

Rivian Automotive Inc (PA) .... B...... 888 748-4261
14600 Myford Rd Irvine (92606) *(P-9305)*

Rivian Automotive LLC .... C...... 309 249-8777
1648 Ashley Way Colton (92324) *(P-9306)*

Riviera Country Club Inc .... C...... 310 454-6591
1250 Capri Dr Pacific Palisades (90272) *(P-17562)*

Riviera Finance of Texas Inc .... D...... 562 777-1300
10430 Pioneer Blvd Ste 1 Santa Fe Springs (90670) *(P-14287)*

Riviera Health Care Center, Pico Rivera *Also Called: Riviera Nursing & Conva (P-18042)*

Riviera Nursing & Conva .... C...... 562 806-2576
8203 Telegraph Rd Pico Rivera (90660) *(P-18042)*

Riviera Palm Sprng A Trbute PR .... C...... 760 327-8311
1600 N Indian Canyon Dr Palm Springs (92262) *(P-15330)*

Riviera Shores, Capistrano Beach *Also Called: Pacific Monarch Resorts Inc (P-15289)*

Rivulis Irrigation Inc (HQ) .... E...... 858 578-1860
7545 Carroll Rd San Diego (92121) *(P-6912)*

Riye Group LLC .... E...... 820 203-9215
2110 W 103rd St Los Angeles (90047) *(P-3482)*

Rizzo Inc .... E...... 818 781-6891
7720 Airport Business Pkwy Van Nuys (91406) *(P-10696)*

RJ Acquisition Corp (PA) .... C...... 323 318-1107
3260 E 26th St Vernon (90058) *(P-3808)*

RJ Noble Company (PA) .... C...... 714 637-1550
15505 E Lincoln Ave Orange (92865) *(P-642)*

RJ Singer International Inc .... F...... 323 735-1717
3737 Ross St Vernon (90058) *(P-5294)*

RJA Industries Inc .... E...... 818 998-5124
9640 Topanga Canyon Pl Ste J Chatsworth (91311) *(P-9107)*

Rjn Investigations Inc .... D...... 951 686-7638
360 E 1st St Ste 696 Tustin (92780) *(P-16676)*

Rks Inc (HQ) .... F...... 858 571-4444
1955 Cordell Ct Ste 104 El Cajon (92020) *(P-9249)*

Rlh Industries Inc .... E...... 714 532-1672
936 N Main St Orange (92867) *(P-8484)*

Rlv Tuned Exhaust Products Inc .... E...... 805 925-5461
2351 Thompson Way Bldg A Santa Maria (93455) *(P-9451)*

RM Galicia Inc .... C...... 626 813-6200
1521 W Cameron Ave Ste 100 West Covina (91790) *(P-15615)*

Rm Partners Inc .... E...... 714 765-5725
1439 S State College Blvd Anaheim (92806) *(P-13953)*

Rmd Group Inc .... B...... 562 866-9288
2311 E South St Long Beach (90805) *(P-20231)*

Rmjv LP (HQ) .... D...... 503 526-5752
3285 Corporate Vw Vista (92081) *(P-7214)*

RMR Financial LLC (DH) .... D...... 408 355-2000
610 Newport Center Dr Newport Beach (92660) *(P-14363)*

RMR Products Inc (PA) .... E...... 818 890-0896
11011 Glenoaks Blvd Ste 1 Pacoima (91331) *(P-5446)*

RMS Foundation Inc .... A...... 562 435-3511
1126 Queens Hwy Long Beach (90802) *(P-15331)*

Rms/Endlgix Sdways Merger Corp .... D...... 949 595-7200
2 Musick Irvine (92618) *(P-10600)*

RNA Ann Arbor Incorporated .... C...... 877 762-7511
508 S Smith Ave Ste A202 Corona (92882) *(P-15746)*

Rnbs Corporation .... E...... 714 998-1828
725 S Paseo Prado Anaheim (92807) *(P-14102)*

Rnd Contractors Inc .... E...... 909 429-8500
14796 Jurupa Ave Ste A Fontana (92337) *(P-6071)*

Rnd Enterprises, Chatsworth *Also Called: BDR Industries Inc (P-7509)*

Rndc, Tustin *Also Called: Republic Nat Distrg Co LLC (P-13480)*

Rnl Design, Los Angeles *Also Called: Stantec Architecture Inc (P-16934)*

RNS Channel Letters, Corona *Also Called: Richards Neon Shop Inc (P-11149)*

Ro Gar Mfg, El Centro *Also Called: Rogar Manufacturing Inc (P-9109)*

Road Champs Inc .... C...... 310 456-7799
22619 Pacific Coast Hwy Ste 250 Malibu (90265) *(P-10965)*

Road Runner Sports Inc (PA) .... D...... 858 974-4200
5549 Copley Dr San Diego (92111) *(P-14103)*

Road Vista, San Diego *Also Called: Gamma Scientific Inc (P-10367)*

Roadex America Inc .... D...... 310 878-9800
2132 E Dominguez St Ste B Long Beach (90810) *(P-11608)*

Roadium Open Air Market, Torrance *Also Called: Pioneer Theatres Inc (P-16904)*

Roadrunner Shuttle, Camarillo *Also Called: Airport Connection Inc (P-11315)*

Roadrunner Sports, San Diego *Also Called: Road Runner Sports Inc (P-14103)*

Roadwire Distinctive Inds, Santa Fe Springs *Also Called: Distinctive Inds Texas Inc (P-2428)*

Roambi, Cardiff By The Sea *Also Called: Mellmo Inc (P-16074)*

Rob Inc .... D...... 562 806-5589
6760 Foster Bridge Blvd Bell Gardens (90201) *(P-2171)*

Robar Enterprises Inc (PA) .... C...... 760 244-5456
17671 Bear Valley Rd Hesperia (92345) *(P-5494)*

Robb Curtco Media LLC .... E....... 310 589-7700
22741 Pacific Coast Hwy Ste 401 Malibu (90265) *(P-3386)*

Robb Report Collection .... E....... 310 589-7700
29160 Heathercliff Rd Ste 200 Malibu (90265) *(P-3387)*

Robbins Geller Rudman Dowd LLP (PA) .... B....... 619 231-1058
655 W Broadway Ste 1900 San Diego (92101) *(P-18933)*

Robbins Precast, Corona *Also Called: Nucast Industries Inc (P-5430)*

Roberson Construction .... E....... 626 578-1936
22 Central Ct Pasadena (91105) *(P-3012)*

Robert B Diemer Trtmnt Plant, Yorba Linda *Also Called: Metropltan Wtr Dst of Sthern C* *(P-12134)*

Robert Ballard Rehab Hospital (HQ) .... D....... 909 473-1200
1760 W 16th St San Bernardino (92411) *(P-17871)*

Robert Clapper Cnstr Svcs Inc .... D....... 909 829-3688
700 New York St Redlands (92374) *(P-585)*

Robert F Chapman Inc .... D....... 661 940-9482
43100 Exchange Pl Lancaster (93535) *(P-6306)*

Robert H Oliva Inc .... E....... 818 700-1035
19863 Nordhoff St Northridge (91324) *(P-8002)*

Robert H Peterson Company, City Of Industry *Also Called: RH Peterson Co (P-8221)*

Robert Heely Construction, Bakersfield *Also Called: Robert Heely Construction LP (P-382)*

Robert Heely Construction LP (PA) .... E....... 661 617-1400
5401 Woodmere Dr Bakersfield (93313) *(P-382)*

Robert Kaufman Co Inc (PA) .... C....... 310 538-3482
129 W 132nd St Los Angeles (90061) *(P-14089)*

Robert Kaufman Fabrics, Los Angeles *Also Called: Robert Kaufman Co Inc (P-14089)*

Robert M Hadley Company Inc .... D....... 805 658-7286
4054 Transport St Ste B Ventura (93003) *(P-8954)*

Robert Michael Ltd .... B....... 562 758-6789
10035 Geary Ave Santa Fe Springs (90670) *(P-2815)*

Robert Moreno Insurance Svcs .... C....... 714 578-3318
3110 E Guasti Rd Ste 500 Ontario (91761) *(P-14627)*

Robert Pool .... E....... 714 556-5277
14751 Franklin Ave Ste B Tustin (92780) *(P-16594)*

Robert Rnzoni Vineyards Winery, Temecula *Also Called: Renzoni Vineyards Inc (P-35)*

Robert's Engineering, Anaheim *Also Called: Roberts Precision Engrg Inc (P-8003)*

Robert's Lumber, Bloomington *Also Called: Roberts Lumber Sales Inc (P-12342)*

Roberts Container Corporation .... E....... 818 727-1700
9131 Oakdale Ave Ste 110 Chatsworth (91311) *(P-16918)*

Roberts Cosmetics and Cntrs, Chatsworth *Also Called: Roberts Container Corporation* *(P-16918)*

Roberts Lumber Sales Inc .... D....... 909 350-9164
2661 S Lilac Ave Bloomington (92316) *(P-12342)*

Roberts Precision Engrg Inc .... E....... 714 635-4485
1345 S Allec St Anaheim (92805) *(P-8003)*

Robertshaw Controls Company .... E....... 951 893-6233
1751 3rd St # 102 Norco (92860) *(P-10106)*

Robertson Honda, North Hollywood *Also Called: Rhi Inc (P-13819)*

Robertson's, Corona *Also Called: Robertsons Rdymx Ltd A Cal Ltd (P-5495)*

Robertsons Rdymx Ltd A Cal Ltd (HQ) .... D....... 951 493-6500
200 S Main St Ste 200 Corona (92882) *(P-5495)*

Robertsons Rdymx Ltd A Cal Ltd .... C....... 909 425-2930
27401 3rd St Highland (92346) *(P-5496)*

Robertsons Ready Mix Ltd .... D....... 760 244-7239
9635 C Ave Hesperia (92345) *(P-5497)*

Robertsons Ready Mix Ltd .... D....... 800 834-7557
5692 Eastgate Dr San Diego (92121) *(P-5498)*

Robertsons Ready Mix Ltd .... D....... 951 685-4600
1310 Simpson Way Escondido (92029) *(P-5499)*

Robertsons Ready Mix Ltd .... D....... 760 373-4815
7900 Moss Ave California City (93505) *(P-5500)*

Robertsons Ready Mix Ltd .... D....... 702 798-0568
16952 S D St Victorville (92395) *(P-12361)*

Robin's Jeans, Bell Gardens *Also Called: Rob Inc (P-2171)*

Robinson Engineering Corp .... F....... 951 361-8000
3575 Grapevine St Jurupa Valley (91752) *(P-7153)*

Robinson Helicopter Co Inc .... A....... 310 539-0508
2901 Airport Dr Torrance (90505) *(P-9775)*

Robinson Pharma Inc .... C....... 714 241-0235
3701 W Warner Ave Santa Ana (92704) *(P-4224)*

Robinson Pharma Inc (PA) .... B....... 714 241-0235
3330 S Harbor Blvd Santa Ana (92704) *(P-4225)*

Robinson Pharma Inc .... C....... 714 241-0235
3300 W Segerstrom Ave Santa Ana (92704) *(P-4226)*

Robinson Printing, Temecula *Also Called: Robinson Printing Inc (P-3809)*

Robinson Printing Inc .... E....... 951 296-0300
42685 Rio Nedo Temecula (92590) *(P-3809)*

Robo 3d Inc .... E....... 844 476-2233
5070 Santa Fe St Ste C San Diego (92109) *(P-3680)*

Robo 3d Printer, San Diego *Also Called: Robo 3d Inc (P-3680)*

Robot-Gxg Inc .... E....... 660 324-0030
8960 Toronto Ave Rancho Cucamonga (91730) *(P-8430)*

ROC-Aire Corp .... E....... 909 784-3385
2198 Pomona Blvd Pomona (91768) *(P-8004)*

Rock Canyon Healthcare Inc .... C....... 719 404-1000
27101 Puerta Real Ste 450 Mission Viejo (92691) *(P-18638)*

Rock Revival, Vernon *Also Called: Rcrv Inc (P-13144)*

Rock Structures-Rip Rap .... E....... 951 371-1112
11126 Silverton Ct Corona (92881) *(P-5557)*

Rock West Composites Inc (PA) .... D....... 858 537-6260
7625 Panasonic Way San Diego (92154) *(P-3967)*

Rock West Composites Inc .... E....... 858 537-6260
7625 Panasonic Way San Diego (92154) *(P-19680)*

Rock-It Cargo USA LLC .... C....... 310 410-0935
5343 W Imperial Hwy Ste 900 Los Angeles (90045) *(P-11799)*

Rock-Ola Manufacturing Corp .... D....... 310 328-1306
1445 Sepulveda Blvd Torrance (90501) *(P-8431)*

Rocker Industries, Huntington Beach *Also Called: Rocker Solenoid Company (P-9108)*

Rocker Solenoid Company .... D....... 310 534-5660
5492 Bolsa Ave Huntington Beach (92649) *(P-9108)*

Rocket Lab Usa Inc (PA) .... D....... 714 465-5737
3881 Mcgowen St Long Beach (90808) *(P-9897)*

Rocket League, San Diego *Also Called: Psyonix LLC (P-16100)*

Rockin Jump Holdings LLC .... B....... 661 233-9907
1301 W Rancho Vista Blvd Ste B Palmdale (93551) *(P-17563)*

Rockin' Jump Trampoline, Palmdale *Also Called: Rockin Jump Holdings LLC (P-17563)*

Rockjock, Corona *Also Called: John Currie Performance Group (P-7245)*

Rockley Photonics Inc (HQ) .... C....... 626 304-9960
234 E Colorado Blvd Ste 600 Pasadena (91101) *(P-8881)*

Rockstar San Diego Inc .... D....... 760 929-0700
2200 Faraday Ave Ste 200 Carlsbad (92008) *(P-16511)*

Rockview Dairies Inc (PA) .... C....... 562 927-5511
7011 Stewart And Gray Rd Downey (90241) *(P-13392)*

Rockwell Collins Inc .... D....... 714 929-3000
1733 Alton Pkwy Irvine (92606) *(P-9776)*

Rockwell Collins Inc .... E....... 714 929-3000
1733 Alton Pkwy Irvine (92606) *(P-10063)*

Rockwell Collins Inc .... E....... 760 768-4732
1757 Carr Rd Ste 100 Calexico (92231) *(P-9777)*

Rockwell Enterprises Inc .... E....... 626 796-1511
20327 Regina Ave Torrance (90503) *(P-13557)*

Rocky Point Investments LLC (HQ) .... C....... 310 482-6500
6601 Center Dr W Ste 400 Los Angeles (90045) *(P-20232)*

Rocky Point RTD, Oceanside *Also Called: Belching Beaver Brewery (P-14046)*

Rode Microphones LLC .... C....... 310 328-7456
2745 Raymond Ave Signal Hill (90755) *(P-8432)*

Roettele Industries .... F....... 909 606-8252
15485 Dupont Ave Chino (91710) *(P-4741)*

Rof LLC .... E....... 818 933-4000
7800 Airport Business Pkwy Van Nuys (91406) *(P-2185)*

Rogar Manufacturing Inc .... C....... 760 335-3700
866 E Ross Ave El Centro (92243) *(P-9109)*

Roger R Caruso Enterprises Inc .... E....... 714 778-6006
2911 Norton Ave Lynwood (90262) *(P-2724)*

Rogers Corporation .... D....... 562 404-8942
13937 Rosecrans Ave Santa Fe Springs (90670) *(P-4791)*

Rogers Holding Company Inc .... E....... 714 257-4850
1130 Columbia St Brea (92821) *(P-9778)*

Rogers Poultry Co (PA) .... D....... 323 585-0802
5050 S Santa Fe Ave Vernon (90058) *(P-13260)*

Rogers Poultry Co .... D....... 800 585-0802
2020 E 67th St Los Angeles (90001) *(P-13261)*

ALPHABETIC

Employee Codes: A=Over 500 employees, B=251-500
C=101-250, D=51-100, E=20-50, F=10-19, G=1-9

2024 Southern California
Business Directory and Buyers Guide

© Mergent Inc. 1-800-342-5647
1245

Rogerson Aircraft Corporation (PA)................................D...... 949 660-0666
16940 Von Karman Ave Irvine (92606) *(P-10064)*

Rogerson Kratos ....C...... 626 449-3090
403 S Raymond Ave Pasadena (91105) *(P-10065)*

Rogue Games, Sherman Oaks Also Called: Rogue Games Inc *(P-16104)*

Rogue Games Inc ....E...... 650 483-8008
4056 Ventura Canyon Ave Sherman Oaks (91423) *(P-16104)*

Rohde & Schwarz Usa Inc ....E...... 818 846-3600
2255 N Ontario St Ste 150 Burbank (91504) *(P-10222)*

Rohr Inc (HQ)...A...... 619 691-4111
850 Lagoon Dr Chula Vista (91910) *(P-9779)*

Rohrback Cosasco Systems Inc (DH)..........................D...... 562 949-0123
11841 Smith Ave Santa Fe Springs (90670) *(P-10157)*

Rojo's, Cypress Also Called: Simply Fresh LLC *(P-1812)*

Rokit Drinks LLC ....E...... 323 654-2740
17383 W Sunset Blvd Ste 300 Pacific Palisades (90272) *(P-1674)*

Roland Corporation US (HQ).....................................C...... 323 890-3700
5100 S Eastern Ave Los Angeles (90040) *(P-12984)*

Rolenn Manufacturing Inc (PA) ....E...... 951 682-1185
2065 Roberta St Riverside (92507) *(P-5183)*

Roll Along Vans Inc ....E...... 714 528-9600
1350 E Yorba Linda Blvd Placentia (92870) *(P-9452)*

Roll Properties Intl Inc ....C...... 661 797-6500
13646 Highway 33 Lost Hills (93249) *(P-15049)*

Roll-A-Shade Inc (PA)...E...... 951 245-5077
12101 Madera Way Riverside (92503) *(P-3013)*

Roll-Rite LLC ....E...... 619 449-8860
1404 N Marshall Ave El Cajon (92020) *(P-2508)*

Roller Bones, Goleta Also Called: Skate One Corp *(P-11027)*

Rolling Hills Country Club ....D...... 424 903-0000
1 Chandler Ranch Rd Palos Verdes Estates (90274) *(P-17512)*

Rolling Hills Vineyard Inc ....E...... 310 541-5098
4213 Pascal Pl Pls Vrds Pnsl (90274) *(P-1657)*

Rolling Hlls Cntry CLB Golf Sp, Palos Verdes Estates Also Called: Rolling Hills Country Club *(P-17512)*

Rolling Sals Whlchair Lacrosse ....E...... 619 677-1431
5333 Mission Center Rd Ste 115 San Diego (92108) *(P-10697)*

Rollins Leasing LLC ....D...... 626 913-7186
18305 Arenth Ave City Of Industry (91748) *(P-16973)*

Rollins Truck Rental-Leasing, City Of Industry Also Called: Rollins Leasing LLC *(P-16973)*

Rolls-Royce High Temperature Composites Inc ....E...... 714 375-4085
5730 Katella Ave Cypress (90630) *(P-5574)*

Rolls-Royce Htc, Cypress Also Called: Rolls-Royce High Temperature Composites Inc *(P-5574)*

Roma Moulding Inc ....E...... 626 334-2539
6230 N Irwindale Ave Irwindale (91702) *(P-2762)*

Romac, Yorba Linda Also Called: Romac Supply Co Inc *(P-8129)*

Romac Supply Co Inc ....D...... 323 721-5810
17722 Neff Ranch Rd Yorba Linda (92886) *(P-8129)*

Romakk Engineering, Northridge Also Called: Robert H Oliva Inc *(P-8002)*

Romakk Engineering, Northridge Also Called: Vision Aerospace LLC *(P-9825)*

Roman Cthlic Bshp of San Diego ....C...... 619 264-3127
4470 Hilltop Dr San Diego (92102) *(P-14862)*

Roman Cthlic Diocese of Orange ....C...... 714 532-6551
7845 E Santiago Canyon Rd Orange (92869) *(P-14917)*

Roman Cthlic Diocese of Orange ....C...... 714 528-1794
801 N Bradford Ave Placentia (92870) *(P-18980)*

Roman Cthlic Diocese of Orange ....C...... 714 544-1533
1311 Sycamore Ave Tustin (92780) *(P-18981)*

Roman Cthlic Diocese of Orange ....C...... 949 766-6000
22062 Antonio Pkwy Rcho Sta Marg (92688) *(P-18982)*

Romar Innovations, Temecula Also Called: Romar Innovations Inc *(P-10099)*

Romar Innovations Inc ....D...... 951 296-3480
42371 Avenida Alvarado Temecula (92590) *(P-10099)*

Romeo Power, Solana Beach Also Called: Romeo Power Inc *(P-9453)*

Romeo Power (HQ)...C...... 833 467-2237
514 Via De La Valle Solana Beach (92075) *(P-9453)*

Romeo Power Technology, Solana Beach Also Called: Romeo Systems Inc *(P-9250)*

Romeo Systems Inc ....C...... 323 675-2180
514 Via De La Valle Solana Beach (92075) *(P-9250)*

Romero General Cnstr Corp ....C...... 760 715-0154
8320 Nelson Way Escondido (92026) *(P-451)*

Romeros Engineering Inc ....E...... 909 481-1170
9175 Milliken Ave Rancho Cucamonga (91730) *(P-8005)*

Romeros Food Products Inc (PA)..............................D...... 562 802-1858
15155 Valley View Ave Santa Fe Springs (90670) *(P-1979)*

Romex Textiles Inc (PA)...E...... 213 749-9090
1430 Griffith Ave Los Angeles (90021) *(P-13092)*

Romla Co ....E...... 619 946-1224
9668 Heinrich Hertz Dr Ste D San Diego (92154) *(P-6307)*

Romla Ventilator Co, San Diego Also Called: Romla Co *(P-6307)*

Ron Rick Holdings Montana LLC ....D...... 406 493-5606
80795 Vista Bonita Trl La Quinta (92253) *(P-14942)*

Ron Teeguarden Enterprises Inc (PA).........................E...... 323 556-8188
10940 Wilshire Blvd Los Angeles (90024) *(P-4014)*

Ronald Reagan Ucla Medical Ctr, Los Angeles Also Called: University Cal Los Angeles *(P-18483)*

Ronan Engineering Company (PA).............................D...... 661 702-1344
28209 Avenue Stanford Valencia (91355) *(P-10158)*

Ronan Engnrng/Rnan Msrment Div, Valencia Also Called: Ronan Engineering Company *(P-10158)*

Roncelli Plastics Inc ....C...... 800 250-6516
330 W Duarte Rd Monrovia (91016) *(P-8006)*

Ronco Plastics, Tustin Also Called: Ronco Plastics Inc *(P-5184)*

Ronco Plastics Inc ....E...... 714 259-1385
15022 Parkway Loop Ste B Tustin (92780) *(P-5184)*

Ronford Products Inc ....E...... 909 622-7446
1116 E 2nd St Pomona (91766) *(P-5185)*

Ronlo Engineering Ltd ....E...... 805 388-3227
955 Flynn Rd Camarillo (93012) *(P-8007)*

Roosevelt Hotel LLC ....C...... 323 466-7000
7000 Hollywood Blvd Los Angeles (90028) *(P-15332)*

Rootstrap Inc ....C...... 310 907-9210
8306 Wilshire Blvd Ste 249 Beverly Hills (90211) *(P-16105)*

Ropers Majeski A Prof Corp ....E...... 213 312-2000
445 S Figueroa St Ste 3000 Los Angeles (90071) *(P-18934)*

Ros Electrical Sup Eqp Co LLC ....E...... 562 695-9000
9529 Slauson Ave Pico Rivera (90660) *(P-12616)*

Rosanna Inc ....C...... 714 751-5100
3350 Avenue Of The Arts Costa Mesa (92626) *(P-15333)*

Roscoe Moss Company, Los Angeles Also Called: Roscoe Moss Manufacturing Co *(P-5641)*

Roscoe Moss Manufacturing Co (PA)..........................D...... 323 261-4185
4360 Worth St Los Angeles (90063) *(P-5641)*

Rose & Shore Inc ....B...... 323 826-2144
5151 Alcoa Ave Vernon (90058) *(P-16919)*

Rose Art Industries, El Segundo Also Called: Mega Brands America Inc *(P-10961)*

Rose Bowl Aquatics Center ....D...... 626 564-0330
360 N Arroyo Blvd Pasadena (91103) *(P-17513)*

Rose Hills Company (DH)...A...... 562 699-0921
3888 Workman Mill Rd Whittier (90601) *(P-14918)*

Rose Hills Holdings Corp (HQ)..................................B...... 562 699-0921
3888 Workman Mill Rd Whittier (90601) *(P-14919)*

Rose Hills Mem Pk & Mortuary, Whittier Also Called: Rose Hills Company *(P-14918)*

Rose Hills Mem Pk & Mortuary, Whittier Also Called: Rose Hills Holdings Corp *(P-14919)*

Rose Lilla Inc ....E...... 888 519-8889
1050 S Cypress St La Habra (90631) *(P-11075)*

Rose Manufacturing Group Inc ....E...... 760 407-0232
2525 Jason Ct Ste 102 Oceanside (92056) *(P-6657)*

Rose Tarlow-Melrose House, West Hollywood Also Called: Rtmh Inc *(P-2817)*

Rose Villa Healthcare Center, Bellflower Also Called: Bell Villa Care Associates LLC *(P-17891)*

Rosecrans Care Center, Gardena Also Called: Healthcare Investments Inc *(P-17971)*

Rosecrans Villa, Hawthorne Also Called: Longwood Management Corp *(P-19282)*

Roselm Industries Inc ....E...... 626 442-6840
2510 Seaman Ave South El Monte (91733) *(P-8572)*

Rosemary Childrens Services Inc ....C...... 626 844-3033
36 S Kinneloa Ave # 200 Pasadena (91107) *(P-19298)*

Rosemead Electrical Supply ....E...... 562 298-4190
9150 Dice Rd Santa Fe Springs (90670) *(P-9251)*

Rosemount Analytical Inc ....A...... 713 396-8880
2400 Barranca Pkwy Irvine (92606) *(P-8189)*

Mergent email: customerrelations@mergent.com
1246

2024 Southern California
Business Directory and Buyers Guide

(P-0000) Products & Services Section entry number
(PA)=Parent Co (HQ)=Headquarters (DH)=Div Headquarters

Rosen & Rosen Industries Inc .... D...... 949 361-9238
204 Avenida Fabricante San Clemente (92672) *(P-11020)*

Rosen Electronics, Ontario *Also Called: Rosen Electronics LLC (P-12985)*

Rosen Electronics LLC .... D...... 951 898-9808
2500 E Francis St Ontario (91761) *(P-12985)*

Rosendin Electric Inc .... A...... 714 739-1334
1730 S Anaheim Way Anaheim (92805) *(P-931)*

Rosewill Inc .... A...... 800 575-9885
17560 Rowland St City Of Industry (91748) *(P-7447)*

Rosewood Court, Fullerton *Also Called: Emeritus Corporation (P-17934)*

Rosewood Miramar Bch Montecito, Santa Barbara *Also Called: Miramar Acquisition Co LLC (P-15038)*

Rosewood Retirement Community, Bakersfield *Also Called: Humangood Norcal (P-18133)*

Roshan Trading Inc .... E...... 213 622-9904
3631 Union Pacific Ave Los Angeles (90023) *(P-2051)*

Ross Bindery Inc .... C...... 562 623-4565
15310 Spring Ave Santa Fe Springs (90670) *(P-3848)*

Ross Name Plate Company .... E...... 323 725-6812
2 Red Plum Cir Monterey Park (91755) *(P-11150)*

Ross Racing Pistons .... D...... 310 536-0100
625 S Douglas St El Segundo (90245) *(P-7704)*

Rossin Steel Inc .... C...... 619 656-9200
9102 Birch St Spring Valley (91977) *(P-12571)*

Rossmoor Pastries MGT Inc .... D...... 562 498-2253
2325 Redondo Ave Signal Hill (90755) *(P-1491)*

Rostar Filters, Oxnard *Also Called: PC Vaughan Mfg Corp (P-5132)*

Rotary and Miission Systems, Fort Irwin *Also Called: Lockheed Martin Corporation (P-11594)*

Rotating Prcsion McHanisms Inc .... E...... 818 349-9774
8750 Shirley Ave Northridge (91324) *(P-8573)*

Rotational Molding Inc .... D...... 310 327-5401
17038 S Figueroa St Gardena (90248) *(P-5186)*

Rotax Incorporated .... E...... 323 589-5999
2940 Leonis Blvd Vernon (90058) *(P-2367)*

Rotech Engineering, Placentia *Also Called: Rotech Engineering Inc (P-9110)*

Rotech Engineering Inc .... E...... 714 632-0532
1020 S Melrose St Ste A Placentia (92870) *(P-9110)*

Roth Capital Partners LLC (PA)............... D...... **800 678-9147**
888 San Clemente Dr Newport Beach (92660) *(P-14404)*

Roth Mkm, Newport Beach *Also Called: Roth Capital Partners LLC (P-14404)*

Roth Staffing Companies LP (PA)............. D...... **714 939-8600**
450 N State College Blvd Orange (92868) *(P-15938)*

Roto Dynamics Inc .... E...... 714 685-0183
1925 N Lime St Orange (92865) *(P-5187)*

Roto Lite Inc .... E...... 909 923-4353
84701 Avenue 48 Coachella (92236) *(P-5188)*

Roto-Die Company Inc .... E...... 714 991-8701
712 N Valley St Ste B Anaheim (92801) *(P-7094)*

Roto-Rooter, Valencia *Also Called: Russell-Warner Inc (P-17149)*

Rotoform Plastics, Santa Paula *Also Called: Westlake Engrg Roto Form (P-5251)*

Rotolo Chevrolet Inc .... C...... 866 756-9776
16666 S Highland Ave Fontana (92336) *(P-13820)*

Rotometrics, Anaheim *Also Called: Roto-Die Company Inc (P-7094)*

Rotron Incorporated .... C...... 619 593-7400
474 Raleigh Ave El Cajon (92020) *(P-7330)*

Roundabout Entertainment Inc .... D...... 818 842-9300
217 S Lake St Burbank (91502) *(P-17215)*

Rove Engineering Inc .... D...... 760 425-0001
398 E Aurora Dr El Centro (92243) *(P-19681)*

Row House, Irvine *Also Called: Row House Franchise LLC (P-17411)*

Row House Franchise LLC .... C...... 949 341-5585
17877 Von Karman Ave Ste 100 Irvine (92614) *(P-17411)*

Row Management Ltd Inc .... B...... 310 887-3671
499 N Canon Dr Beverly Hills (90210) *(P-14863)*

Rowland Convalescent Hosp Inc .... D...... 626 967-2741
330 W Rowland St Covina (91723) *(P-18043)*

ROWLAND, THE, Covina *Also Called: Rowland Convalescent Hosp Inc (P-18043)*

Rox Medical (PA).............................. F...... **949 276-8968**
150 Calle Iglesia Ste A San Clemente (92672) *(P-10601)*

Roy & Val Tool Grinding Inc .... E...... 818 341-2434
10131 Canoga Ave Chatsworth (91311) *(P-8008)*

Roy E Hanson Jr Mfg (PA)...................... D...... 213 747-7514
1600 E Washington Blvd Los Angeles (90021) *(P-6154)*

Roy Miller Freight Lines LLC (PA)............. D...... **714 632-5511**
3165 E Coronado St Anaheim (92806) *(P-11463)*

Royal Adhesives & Sealants LLC .... E...... 310 830-9904
800 E Anaheim St Wilmington (90744) *(P-4629)*

Royal Apparel Inc .... E...... 626 579-5168
4331 Baldwin Ave El Monte (91731) *(P-2368)*

Royal Blue Inc .... E...... 310 888-0156
9025 Wilshire Blvd Ste 301 Beverly Hills (90211) *(P-2487)*

Royal Cabinets, Pomona *Also Called: Royal Cabinets Inc (P-2676)*

Royal Cabinets, Pomona *Also Called: Royal Industries Inc (P-2677)*

Royal Cabinets Inc .... A...... 909 629-8565
1299 E Phillips Blvd Pomona (91766) *(P-2676)*

Royal Coatings, Simi Valley *Also Called: Mabel Baas Inc (P-6717)*

Royal Crown Enterprises Inc .... C...... 626 854-8080
780 Epperson Dr City Of Industry (91748) *(P-13393)*

Royal Custom Designs LLC .... C...... 909 591-8990
13951 Monte Vista Ave Chino (91710) *(P-2816)*

Royal Flex Circuits Inc .... E...... 562 404-0626
15505 Cornet St Santa Fe Springs (90670) *(P-8724)*

Royal Industries, Eastvale *Also Called: Royal Range California Inc (P-8222)*

Royal Industries Inc .... C...... 909 629-8565
1299 E Phillips Blvd Pomona (91766) *(P-2677)*

Royal Interpack North Amer Inc .... E...... 951 787-6925
475 Palmyrita Ave Riverside (92507) *(P-5189)*

Royal Oaks, Duarte *Also Called: Humangood Socal (P-14714)*

Royal Pallets Inc .... F...... 323 580-4364
849 E 29th St Los Angeles (90011) *(P-2725)*

Royal Paper Box Co California (PA)............ C...... **323 728-7041**
1105 S Maple Ave Montebello (90640) *(P-13558)*

Royal Plasticware, Gardena *Also Called: La Palm Furnitures & ACC Inc (P-2516)*

Royal Poultry, Vernon *Also Called: Golden West Trading Inc (P-13246)*

Royal Range California Inc .... D...... 951 360-1600
3245 Corridor Dr Eastvale (91752) *(P-8222)*

Royal Specialty Undwrt Inc .... C...... 818 922-6700
15303 Ventura Blvd Ste 500 Sherman Oaks (91403) *(P-14525)*

Royal Welding & Fabricating, Fullerton *Also Called: Cook and Cook Incorporated (P-6140)*

Royal West Drywall Inc .... D...... 951 271-4600
2008 2nd St Norco (92860) *(P-994)*

Royal Westlake Roofing LLC .... C...... 760 967-0827
3093 Industry St Ste A Oceanside (92054) *(P-1053)*

Royal Westlake Roofing LLC .... F...... 909 822-4407
3511 N Riverside Ave Rialto (92377) *(P-5447)*

Royal Wine Corporation .... E...... 805 983-1560
3201 Camino Del Sol Oxnard (93030) *(P-1658)*

Royal-Pedic Mattress Mfg LLC (PA)............ E...... **310 278-9594**
341 N Robertson Blvd Beverly Hills (90211) *(P-13947)*

Royale Convalescent Hospital, Santa Ana *Also Called: Orange Cnty Ryale Cnvlscent Ho (P-18149)*

Royalty, Irvine *Also Called: Royalty Carpet Mills Inc (P-2119)*

Royalty Carpet Mills Inc .... A...... 949 474-4000
17111 Red Hill Ave Irvine (92614) *(P-2119)*

Roze Room Hospice, Culver City *Also Called: L & A Care Corporation (P-18088)*

Rp Automotive II Inc .... D...... 619 656-2500
560 Auto Park Dr Chula Vista (91911) *(P-16974)*

Rpc Inc .... F...... 619 334-6244
1100 N Magnolia Ave Ste H El Cajon (92020) *(P-383)*

RPC Legacy Inc .... E...... 818 787-9000
14600 Arminta St Van Nuys (91402) *(P-5941)*

Rpd Hotels 18 LLC (PA).......................... A...... 213 746-1531
1801 S La Cienega Blvd Ste 301 Los Angeles (90035) *(P-15334)*

RPI, Simi Valley *Also Called: Replacement Parts Inds Inc (P-10765)*

Rplanet Erth Los Angles Hldngs .... D...... 833 775-2638
5300 S Boyle Ave Vernon (90058) *(P-5190)*

RPM, Northridge *Also Called: Rotating Prcsion McHanisms Inc (P-8573)*

RPM Consolidated Services Inc (HQ)........... D...... **714 388-3500**
1901 Raymer Ave Fullerton (92833) *(P-11609)*

RPM Plastic Molding Inc .... E...... 714 630-9300
2821 E Miraloma Ave Anaheim (92806) *(P-5191)*

Employee Codes: A=Over 500 employees, B=251-500
C=101-250, D=51-100, E=20-50, F=10-19, G=1-9

2024 Southern California
Business Directory and Buyers Guide

© Mergent Inc. 1-800-342-5647

1247

ALPHABETIC

RPM Products Inc (PA)..E....... 949 888-8543
　23201 Antonio Pkwy Rcho Sta Marg (92688) *(P-4742)*

RPM Transportation Inc (DH).............................C....... 714 388-3500
　11660 Arroyo Ave Santa Ana (92705) *(P-11504)*

RPS Inc..E....... 818 350-8088
　20331 Corisco St Chatsworth (91311) *(P-6828)*

Rpsz Construction LLC...E....... 314 677-5831
　1201 W 5th St Ste T340 Los Angeles (90017) *(P-11021)*

Rq Construction LLC..C....... 760 631-7707
　1620 Faraday Ave Carlsbad (92008) *(P-515)*

Rrd Pckaging Solutions - Vista, Vista *Also Called: Precision Litho Inc (P-3661)*

RRI, Downey *Also Called: Rancho Research Institute (P-19940)*

Rri Energy Coolwater Inc......................................D....... 760 254-5290
　37000 E Santa Fe St Daggett (92327) *(P-12041)*

Rrm Design Group (PA)..D....... 805 439-0442
　3765 S Higuera St Ste 102 San Luis Obispo (93401) *(P-19740)*

Rrt Enterprises LP..C....... 323 653-1521
　855 N Fairfax Ave Los Angeles (90046) *(P-18044)*

Rrt Enterprises LP (PA)..C....... 310 397-2372
　3966 Marcasel Ave Los Angeles (90066) *(P-18045)*

RRT ENTERPRISES LP, Los Angeles *Also Called: Rrt Enterprises LP (P-18044)*

Rsa Engineered Products LLC..............................D....... 805 584-4150
　110 W Cochran St Ste A Simi Valley (93065) *(P-9780)*

Rsg Group North America LP.................................C....... 714 609-0572
　7007 Romaine St Ste 101 West Hollywood (90038) *(P-17412)*

Rsg Group USA Inc...A....... 214 574-4653
　7007 Romaine St Ste 101 West Hollywood (90038) *(P-14943)*

Rsg/Aames Security Inc...E....... 562 529-5100
　3300 E 59th St Long Beach (90805) *(P-8624)*

RSI, Anaheim *Also Called: RSI Home Products LLC (P-2836)*

RSI Home Products, Anaheim *Also Called: American Woodmark Corporation (P-2645)*

RSI Home Products Inc..D....... 949 720-1116
　620 Newport Center Dr Ste 1030 Newport Beach (92660) *(P-2835)*

RSI Home Products LLC (HQ)................................A....... 714 449-2200
　400 E Orangethorpe Ave Anaheim (92801) *(P-2836)*

RSI Leasing LLC...D....... 626 966-6129
　1314 E Puente Ave West Covina (91790) *(P-15797)*

Rsk Tool Incorporated...E....... 310 537-3302
　410 W Carob St Compton (90220) *(P-5192)*

RSR Steel Fabrication Inc.....................................E....... 760 244-2210
　11040 I Ave Hesperia (92345) *(P-5598)*

Rsui Group, Sherman Oaks *Also Called: Royal Specialty Undwrt Inc (P-14525)*

Rsvc Company...C....... 951 684-6578
　3051 Myers St Ste B Riverside (92503) *(P-643)*

RT&d, Carson *Also Called: Research Tool & Die Works LLC (P-6553)*

RTC Aerospace, Chatsworth *Also Called: Logistical Support LLC (P-9575)*

RTC Aerospace, Chatsworth *Also Called: Cliffdale Manufacturing LLC (P-9915)*

RTC Arspace - Chtswrth Div Inc (PA)....................C....... 818 341-3344
　20409 Prairie St Chatsworth (91311) *(P-7709)*

Rte Enterprises Inc...D....... 818 999-5300
　21530 Roscoe Blvd Canoga Park (91304) *(P-855)*

Rte Welding, Fontana *Also Called: Tikos Tanks Inc (P-17097)*

Rti Los Angeles, Norwalk *Also Called: New Cntury Mtals Southeast Inc (P-5725)*

Rtie Holdings LLC..F....... 714 765-8200
　1800 E Via Burton Anaheim (92806) *(P-9111)*

Rtm Products Inc...E....... 562 926-2400
　13120 Arctic Cir Santa Fe Springs (90670) *(P-5599)*

Rtmex Inc...C....... 619 391-9913
　1202 Piper Ranch Rd San Diego (92154) *(P-2579)*

Rtmh Inc (PA)...F....... 323 651-2202
　425 N Robertson Blvd West Hollywood (90048) *(P-2817)*

Rtr Industries LLC (PA)..E....... 714 996-0050
　4430 E Miraloma Ave Ste B Anaheim (92807) *(P-7705)*

RTS Powder Coating Inc (PA)...............................E....... 909 393-5404
　15121 Sierra Bonita Ln Chino (91710) *(P-6732)*

Rubber Plastic & Metal Pdts, Rcho Sta Marg *Also Called: RPM Products Inc (P-4742)*

Rubber Teck Division, Long Beach *Also Called: Rubbercraft Corp Cal Ltd (P-4753)*

Rubber-Trim Products Inc.....................................E....... 714 562-0500
　6855 Hermosa Cir Buena Park (90620) *(P-4792)*

Rubbercraft Corp Cal Ltd (HQ)..............................C....... 562 354-2800
　3701 E Conant St Long Beach (90808) *(P-4753)*

Ruben & Leon Inc..E....... 323 937-4445
　5002 Venice Blvd Los Angeles (90019) *(P-17071)*

Ruben and Sharam, Vernon *Also Called: RJ Singer International Inc (P-5294)*

Rubicon Gear, Corona *Also Called: Rubicon Gear Inc (P-6472)*

Rubicon Gear Inc...D....... 951 356-3800
　225 Citation Cir Corona (92878) *(P-6472)*

Rubidoux Family Care Center, Riverside *Also Called: County of Riverside (P-17635)*

Rubin Postaer and Associates (PA).......................C....... 310 394-4000
　2525 Colorado Ave Ste 100 Santa Monica (90404) *(P-15573)*

Rubio Arts Corporation...C....... 407 849-1643
　1313 S Harbor Blvd Anaheim (92802) *(P-20401)*

Ruby Ribbon Inc...E....... 650 449-4470
　4607 Lakeview Canyon Rd Pmb 405 Westlake Village (91361) *(P-13145)*

Ruby Rox, Los Angeles *Also Called: Misyd Corp (P-2411)*

Rucci Inc...E....... 323 778-9000
　6700 11th Ave Los Angeles (90043) *(P-11277)*

Rudolph and Sletten Inc.......................................C....... 949 252-1919
　2855 Michelle Ste 350 Irvine (92606) *(P-586)*

Ruffin Hotel Corp of Cal..B....... 562 425-5210
　4700 Airport Plaza Dr Long Beach (90815) *(P-15335)*

Rugby Laboratories Inc (DH).................................D....... 951 270-1400
　311 Bonnie Cir Corona (92878) *(P-13066)*

Ruggable LLC...B....... 310 295-0098
　17809 S Broadway Gardena (90248) *(P-14104)*

Rugged Info Tech Eqp Corp (PA)...........................E....... 805 577-9710
　25 E Easy St Simi Valley (93065) *(P-7569)*

Rugged Notebooks, Anaheim *Also Called: Rnbs Corporation (P-14102)*

Rugged Systems Inc...C....... 858 391-1006
　13000 Danielson St Ste Q Poway (92064) *(P-7448)*

Ruggeri Marble and Granite Inc............................D....... 310 513-2155
　25028 Vermont Ave Harbor City (90710) *(P-5532)*

Ruhs-Emergency Department, Moreno Valley *Also Called: Riverside University Health (P-18410)*

Ruiteng Internet Technology Co.............................C....... 302 597-7438
　1344 W Foothill Blvd D Azusa (91702) *(P-16512)*

Ruiz Flour Tortillas, Riverside *Also Called: Ruiz Mexican Foods Inc (P-1980)*

Ruiz Mexican Foods Inc (PA)................................C....... 909 947-7811
　1200 Marlborough Ave Ste A Riverside (92507) *(P-1980)*

Runway, Los Angeles *Also Called: Runway Beauty Inc (P-3318)*

Runway Inc...D....... 310 636-2000
　1330 Vine St Los Angeles (90028) *(P-17263)*

Runway Beauty Inc..F....... 844 240-2250
　6075 Rodgerton Dr Los Angeles (90068) *(P-3318)*

Runway Liquidation LLC (HQ)...............................E....... 323 589-2224
　2761 Fruitland Ave Vernon (90058) *(P-13146)*

Rupe's Hydraulics Sales & Svc, San Marcos *Also Called: Hydralic Systems Cmponents Inc (P-17133)*

Rush Business Forms Inc.....................................E....... 714 630-5661
　3860 E Eagle Dr Ste A Anaheim (92807) *(P-14071)*

Rush Press Inc...E....... 619 296-7874
　955 Gateway Center Way San Diego (92102) *(P-3681)*

Rushmore Crrspndent Lnding Svc, Irvine *Also Called: Rushmore Loan MGT Svcs LLC (P-14348)*

Rushmore Loan MGT Svcs LLC (PA)......................A....... 949 727-4798
　15480 Laguna Canyon Rd Ste 100 Irvine (92618) *(P-14348)*

Russ August & Kabat LLP.....................................D....... 310 826-7474
　12424 Wilshire Blvd Ste 1200 Los Angeles (90025) *(P-18935)*

Russ Bassett Corp..C....... 562 945-2445
　8189 Byron Rd Whittier (90606) *(P-2787)*

Russ International Inc..E....... 310 329-7121
　1658 W 132nd St Gardena (90249) *(P-6308)*

Russell Fabrication Corp.......................................E....... 661 861-8495
　4940 Gilmore Ave Bakersfield (93308) *(P-6852)*

Russell-Stanley...E....... 909 980-7114
　9449 Santa Anita Ave Rancho Cucamonga (91730) *(P-5193)*

Russell-Stanley West, Rancho Cucamonga *Also Called: Russell-Stanley (P-5193)*

Russell-Warner Inc..C....... 661 257-9200
　24971 Avenue Stanford Valencia (91355) *(P-17149)*

Rutan & Tucker LLP (PA)..B....... 714 641-5100
　18575 Jamboree Rd Ste 900 Irvine (92612) *(P-18936)*

Rutherford Co Inc (PA)...D....... 323 666-5284
　2107 Crystal St Los Angeles (90039) *(P-995)*

Rutland Tool & Supply Co (HQ)............................C.......562 566-5000
2225 Workman Mill Rd City Of Industry (90601) **(P-12876)**

Rvl Packaging Inc ....C.......818 735-5000
31330 Oak Crest Dr Westlake Village (91361) **(P-16920)**

RW Zant LLC (DH)..D.......323 980-5457
1470 E 4th St Los Angeles (90033) **(P-13306)**

RW&g, Los Angeles Also Called: Richards Wtson Grshon A Prof C **(P-18932)**

Rwh Inc ....E.......818 782-2350
15115 Oxnard St Van Nuys (91411) **(P-5501)**

Rwnm Inc ....E
1240 Simpson Way Escondido (92029) **(P-8110)**

Rx Pro Health LLC ....A.......858 369-4050
12400 High Bluff Dr Ste 100 San Diego (92130) **(P-15939)**

Rxsafe, Vista Also Called: Rxsafe LLC **(P-7258)**

Rxsafe LLC ....D.......760 593-7161
2453 Cades Way Bldg A Vista (92081) **(P-7258)**

Rxsight, Aliso Viejo Also Called: Rxsight Inc **(P-10850)**

Rxsight Inc (PA)...D.......949 521-7830
100 Columbia Ste 120 Aliso Viejo (92656) **(P-10850)**

Ryan Press, Buena Park Also Called: Q Team **(P-3673)**

Ryan's Express, Torrance Also Called: Ryans Express Trnsp Svcs Inc **(P-11402)**

Ryans Express Trnsp Svcs Inc (PA)..................D.......310 219-2960
19500 Mariner Ave Torrance (90503) **(P-11402)**

Rydell Chevrolet-Northridge, Northridge Also Called: San Fernando Valley Auto LLC **(P-13822)**

RYL Inc ....D.......213 503-7968
2738 Supply Ave Commerce (90040) **(P-13559)**

Rynoclad Technologies Inc ....C.......951 264-3441
780 E Francis St Ste M Ontario (91761) **(P-1119)**

Rytan Inc ....F.......310 328-6553
1648 W 134th St Gardena (90249) **(P-7021)**

Ryvec Inc ....E.......714 520-5592
251 E Palais Rd Anaheim (92805) **(P-3876)**

Ryvid Inc (PA) ....E.......650 515-6118
12090 Carson St Ste H504 Hawaiian Gardens (90716) **(P-9454)**

S & C Precision Inc ....E.......626 338-7149
5045 Calmview Ave Baldwin Park (91706) **(P-9112)**

S & H Cabinets and Mfg Inc ....E.......909 357-0551
10860 Mulberry Ave Fontana (92337) **(P-2898)**

S & H Machine Inc ....E.......626 448-5062
9928 Hayward Way South El Monte (91733) **(P-6779)**

S & H Rubber Co ....E.......714 525-0277
1141 E Elm Ave Fullerton (92831) **(P-4793)**

S & M Moving Systems, Santa Fe Springs Also Called: Van Torrance & Storage Company **(P-11523)**

S & R Architectural Metals Inc ....E.......714 226-0108
2609 W Woodland Dr Anaheim (92801) **(P-6072)**

S & S Bakery, Vista Also Called: Baked In The Sun **(P-1452)**

S & S Bindery Inc ....E.......909 596-2213
2366 1st St La Verne (91750) **(P-3849)**

S & S Carbide Tool Inc ....E.......619 670-5214
2830 Via Orange Way Ste D Spring Valley (91978) **(P-7095)**

S & S Construction Co, Beverly Hills Also Called: Shapell Industries LLC **(P-14910)**

S & S Foods LLC, Azusa Also Called: CTI Foods Azusa LLC **(P-1216)**

S & S Numerical Control Inc ....E.......818 341-4141
19841 Nordhoff St Northridge (91324) **(P-8009)**

S & S Paving Inc ....E.......818 591-0668
23875 Ventura Blvd Ste 202 Calabasas (91302) **(P-644)**

S & S Precision Sheetmetal, Canoga Park Also Called: B S K T Inc **(P-7771)**

S & W Plastic Stores Inc (PA)...........................E.......909 390-0090
14270 Albers Way Chino (91710) **(P-13418)**

S & W Plastics Supply, Chino Also Called: S & W Plastic Stores Inc **(P-13418)**

S 2 K, Simi Valley Also Called: S2k Graphics Inc **(P-11151)**

S A Top-U Corporation ....E.......951 916-4025
1794 Illinois Ave Perris (92571) **(P-14080)**

S B H Hotel Corporation ....A.......909 889-0133
285 E Hospitality Ln San Bernardino (92408) **(P-15336)**

S Bravo Systems Inc ....E.......323 888-4133
2929 Vail Ave Commerce (90040) **(P-6155)**

S C A, Victorville Also Called: Comav Technical Services LLC **(P-11693)**

S C A G, Los Angeles Also Called: Cal Southern Assn Governments **(P-20323)**

S C Coatings Corporation ....E.......951 461-9777
41775 Elm St Ste 302 Murrieta (92562) **(P-6733)**

S C Hydraulic Engineering, Brea Also Called: Southern Cal Hydrlic Engrg Cor **(P-12822)**

S C I Industries Inc ....E
1433 Adelia Ave El Monte (91733) **(P-9455)**

S C I R E, Long Beach Also Called: Southern Cal Inst For RES Edca **(P-19945)**

S C P M G, San Dimas Also Called: Southern Cal Prmnnte Med Group **(P-14500)**

S C P M G, Harbor City Also Called: Permanente Medical Group Inc **(P-17738)**

S C P M G, Culver City Also Called: Southern Cal Prmnnte Med Group **(P-17773)**

S C P M G, Inglewood Also Called: Southern Cal Prmnnte Med Group **(P-17774)**

S C P M G, Cudahy Also Called: Southern Cal Prmnnte Med Group **(P-17775)**

S C P M G, Woodland Hills Also Called: Southern Cal Prmnnte Med Group **(P-17776)**

S C P M G, Santa Clarita Also Called: Southern Cal Prmnnte Med Group **(P-17777)**

S C P M G, El Cajon Also Called: Southern Cal Prmnnte Med Group **(P-17786)**

S C P M G, San Diego Also Called: Southern Cal Prmnnte Med Group **(P-17787)**

S C P M G, Escondido Also Called: Southern Cal Prmnnte Med Group **(P-17788)**

S C P M G, Colton Also Called: Southern Cal Prmnnte Med Group **(P-17789)**

S C P M G, Anaheim Also Called: Southern Cal Prmnnte Med Group **(P-17792)**

S C P M G, San Juan Capistrano Also Called: Southern Cal Prmnnte Med Group **(P-17793)**

S C P M G, Santa Ana Also Called: Southern Cal Prmnnte Med Group **(P-17794)**

S C P M G, Fontana Also Called: Southern Cal Prmnnte Med Group **(P-18452)**

S C Village, Bellflower Also Called: S J S Enterprise Inc **(P-17564)**

S D I, Lakeside Also Called: Standard Drywall Inc **(P-998)**

S D I, Camarillo Also Called: Structural Diagnostics Inc **(P-10399)**

S D M, Chino Also Called: Syntech Development & Mfg Inc **(P-5220)**

S D S, Ontario Also Called: Specialized Dairy Service Inc **(P-6914)**

S E - G I Products Inc ....C.......949 297-8530
20521 Teresita Way Lake Forest (92630) **(P-6120)**

S E O P Inc ....C.......949 682-7906
1621 Alton Pkwy Ste 150 Irvine (92606) **(P-16513)**

S E Pipe Line Construction Co ....D.......562 868-9771
11832 Bloomfield Ave Santa Fe Springs (90670) **(P-687)**

S F Technology, Cerritos Also Called: UFO Designs **(P-9478)**

S Fuel LLC ....E.......818 914-4849
4860 Llano Dr Woodland Hills (91364) **(P-4527)**

S G S, Baldwin Park Also Called: Superior Grounding Systems Inc **(P-8277)**

S G S Produce, Los Angeles Also Called: Shapiro-Gilman-Shandler Co **(P-13340)**

S J S Enterprise Inc ....C.......949 489-9000
9030 Somerset Blvd Bellflower (90706) **(P-17564)**

S K Laboratories Inc ....D.......714 695-9800
5420 E La Palma Ave Anaheim (92807) **(P-4227)**

S K Labs, Anaheim Also Called: S K Laboratories Inc **(P-4227)**

S L Fusco Inc (PA)...E.......310 868-1010
1966 E Via Arado Rancho Dominguez (90220) **(P-7022)**

S R C Devices Inccustomer ....B.......866 772-8668
6295 Ferris Sq Ste D San Diego (92121) **(P-8190)**

S R Machining, Norco Also Called: S R Machining-Properties LLC **(P-8011)**

S R Machining Inc ....E.......951 520-9486
640 Parkridge Ave Norco (92860) **(P-8010)**

S R Machining-Properties LLC ....C.......951 520-9486
640 Parkridge Ave Norco (92860) **(P-8011)**

S S, South Gate Also Called: Shultz Steel Company **(P-6482)**

S S I, Long Beach Also Called: Seal Science Inc **(P-4743)**

S S W Mechanical Cnstr Inc ....C.......760 327-1481
670 S Oleander Rd Palm Springs (92264) **(P-819)**

S W K Properties LLC ....C.......714 481-6300
2726 S Grand Ave Lbby Santa Ana (92705) **(P-15337)**

S&B Development Group LLC ....E.......213 446-2818
1901 Avenue Of The Stars 235 Los Angeles (90067) **(P-2043)**

S&B Filters Inc ....D.......909 947-0015
15461 Slover Ave Ste A Fontana (92337) **(P-9456)**

S&B Industry Inc ....E.......909 569-4155
105 S Puente St Brea (92821) **(P-5194)**

S&B Pharma Inc ....D.......626 334-2908
405 S Motor Ave Azusa (91702) **(P-4015)**

S&E Gourmet Cuts Inc ....C.......909 370-0155
1055 E Cooley Ave San Bernardino (92408) **(P-13274)**

Employee Codes: A=Over 500 employees, B=251-500
C=101-250, D=51-100, E=20-50, F=10-19, G=1-9

2024 Southern California
Business Directory and Buyers Guide

© Mergent Inc. 1-800-342-5647

1249

S&S Flavours, Brea *Also Called: Scisorek & Son Flavors Inc (P-1782)*

S&S Precision Mfg Inc .... E....... 714 754-6664
2101 S Yale St Santa Ana (92704) *(P-8012)*

S2k Graphics Inc .... E....... 818 885-3900
4686 Industrial St Simi Valley (93063) *(P-11151)*

SA & G Autotec, Tustin *Also Called: Sunny Amer Globl Autotec Corp (P-9464)*

SA Camp Pump and Drilling Co, Bakersfield *Also Called: SA Camp Pump Company (P-17150)*

SA Camp Pump Company .... D....... 661 399-2976
17876 Zerker Rd Bakersfield (93308) *(P-17150)*

SA Recycling, Orange *Also Called: SA Recycling LLC (P-12185)*

SA Recycling LLC (PA).. C....... **714 632-2000**
2411 N Glassell St Orange (92865) *(P-12185)*

SA Serving Lines Inc .... E....... 714 848-7529
226 W Carleton Ave Orange (92867) *(P-6309)*

Sa-Tech, Oxnard *Also Called: Systems Application & Tech Inc (P-19697)*

Saab Enterprises Inc .... E....... 909 823-2228
1433 Miller Dr Colton (92324) *(P-1234)*

Saalex Corp .... A....... 951 543-9259
27525 Enterprise Cir W Ste 101a Temecula (92590) *(P-16106)*

Saalex Corp (PA).. C....... **805 482-1070**
811 Camarillo Springs Rd Ste A Camarillo (93012) *(P-19682)*

Saalex Solutions, Camarillo *Also Called: Saalex Corp (P-19682)*

Saatchi & Saatchi N Amer LLC .... C....... 310 437-2500
3501 Sepulveda Blvd Torrance (90505) *(P-15574)*

Sabal Capital Partners LLC .... C....... 949 255-1007
680 E Colorado Blvd Ste 350 Pasadena (91101) *(P-15050)*

Saban Brands LLC (HQ).. D....... **310 557-5230**
10100 Santa Monica Blvd Ste 500 Los Angeles (90067) *(P-20233)*

Saban Research Institute, The, Los Angeles *Also Called: Childrens Hospital Los Angeles (P-18216)*

Sabater Usa Inc (PA)... E....... **310 518-2227**
14824 S Main St Gardena (90248) *(P-1981)*

Sabel, Vista *Also Called: Surgistar Inc (P-10610)*

Sabia, San Diego *Also Called: Sabia Incorporated (P-10159)*

Sabia Incorporated (PA)... E....... **858 217-2200**
10919 Technology Pl Ste A San Diego (92127) *(P-10159)*

Sabina Motors & Controls, Anaheim *Also Called: Motors & Controls Whse Inc (P-12685)*

Sabot Publishing Inc (PA).. E....... **310 356-4100**
300 Continental Blvd Ste 650 El Segundo (90245) *(P-3388)*

Sabre Sciences Inc .... F....... 760 448-2750
2233 Faraday Ave Ste K Carlsbad (92008) *(P-4016)*

Sabre Systems Inc .... D....... 619 528-2226
3111 Camino Del Rio N Ste 400 San Diego (92108) *(P-19683)*

Sabred International Packg Inc .... E....... 714 996-2800
3740 Prospect Ave Yorba Linda (92886) *(P-4902)*

Sabrin Corporation .... F....... 626 792-3813
2836 E Walnut St Pasadena (91107) *(P-9781)*

Sabritec .... B....... 714 371-1100
1550 Scenic Ave Ste 150 Costa Mesa (92626) *(P-8982)*

Sac-TEC Labs Inc (PA)... E....... **310 375-5295**
24311 Wilmington Ave Carson (90745) *(P-8882)*

Sacahn JV .... D....... 858 924-1110
15916 Bernardo Center Dr San Diego (92127) *(P-4649)*

Sada, North Hollywood *Also Called: Sada Systems Inc (P-16595)*

Sada Systems Inc (PA)... C....... 818 766-2400
5250 Lankershim Blvd Ste 720 North Hollywood (91601) *(P-16595)*

Saddle Back Valley YMCA, Mission Viejo *Also Called: Young MNS Chrstn Assn Ornge CN (P-19496)*

Saddleback Educational Inc .... F....... 714 640-5200
151 Kalmus Dr Ste J1 Costa Mesa (92626) *(P-3413)*

Saddleback Educational Pubg, Costa Mesa *Also Called: Saddleback Educational Inc (P-3413)*

Saddleback Memorial Med Ctr (HQ).......................... A....... **949 837-4500**
24451 Health Center Dr Fl 1 Laguna Hills (92653) *(P-18411)*

Saddleback Valley Service Ctr, Irvine *Also Called: Southern California Edison Co (P-12076)*

Saddleback Vly .... D....... 949 586-1234
25631 Peter A Hartman Way Mission Viejo (92691) *(P-17514)*

Saddlemen, Compton *Also Called: Saddlemen Corporation (P-12259)*

Saddlemen Corporation .... C....... 310 638-1222
17801 S Susana Rd Compton (90221) *(P-12259)*

Saehan Electronics America Inc (PA)........................ D....... 858 496-1500
7880 Airway Rd Ste B5g San Diego (92154) *(P-8725)*

Saeilo Manufacturing Inds, Santa Fe Springs *Also Called: SMI Ca Inc (P-8029)*

Saf-T-Co Supply .... E....... 714 547-9975
1300 E Normandy Pl Santa Ana (92705) *(P-8283)*

Safariland LLC .... B....... 909 923-7300
4700 E Airport Dr Ontario (91761) *(P-10698)*

Safc Pharma, Carlsbad *Also Called: Sigma-Aldrich Corporation (P-4630)*

Safe Haven, San Fernando *Also Called: Valeda Company LLC (P-10719)*

Safe Plating Inc .... D....... 626 810-1872
18001 Railroad St City Of Industry (91748) *(P-6658)*

Safe Refuge .... D....... 562 987-5722
1041 Redondo Ave Long Beach (90804) *(P-18715)*

Safeco Insurance Company Amer .... C....... 818 956-4250
330 N Brand Blvd Ste 680 Glendale (91203) *(P-14628)*

Safeguard Envirogroup Inc .... E....... 626 512-7585
153 Lowell Ave Glendora (91741) *(P-10285)*

Safeguard Health Entps Inc (HQ)............................. B....... **800 880-1800**
95 Enterprise Ste 100 Aliso Viejo (92656) *(P-14493)*

Safeguard On Demand Inc .... C....... 800 640-2327
11037 Warner Ave # 297 Fountain Valley (92708) *(P-16677)*

Safer Sports Inc .... E....... 760 444-0082
5670 El Camino Real Ste B Carlsbad (92008) *(P-11022)*

Safesmart Access Inc .... E....... 310 410-1525
13238 Florence Ave Santa Fe Springs (90670) *(P-16751)*

Safety Products Holdings LLC .... E....... 714 662-1033
170 Technology Dr Irvine (92618) *(P-7023)*

Safety Systems Hawaii .... F....... 808 847-4017
Irvine (92616) *(P-11152)*

Safeway Inc .... A....... 714 990-8357
200 N Puente St Brea (92821) *(P-14114)*

Safeway Sign Company .... E....... 760 246-7070
9875 Yucca Rd Adelanto (92301) *(P-11153)*

Saffola Quality Foods, Ontario *Also Called: Ventura Foods LLC (P-1250)*

Safran, Anaheim *Also Called: Morphotrak LLC (P-16461)*

Safran Cabin Galleys Us Inc (HQ)............................ A....... **714 861-7300**
17311 Nichols Ln Huntington Beach (92647) *(P-9782)*

Safran Cabin Inc (HQ).. B....... **714 934-0000**
5701 Bolsa Ave Huntington Beach (92647) *(P-9783)*

Safran Cabin Inc .... C....... 562 344-4780
11240 Warland Dr Cypress (90630) *(P-9784)*

Safran Cabin Inc .... C....... 714 891-1906
7330 Lincoln Way Garden Grove (92841) *(P-9785)*

Safran Cabin Inc .... C....... 714 901-2672
12472 Industry St Garden Grove (92841) *(P-9786)*

Safran Cabin Inc .... C....... 714 934-0000
1500 Glenn Curtiss St Carson (90746) *(P-9787)*

Safran Cabin Inc .... C....... 805 922-3013
2850 Skyway Dr Santa Maria (93455) *(P-9788)*

Safran Cabin Inc .... C....... 909 652-9700
8595 Milliken Ave Ste 101 Rancho Cucamonga (91730) *(P-9789)*

Safran Cabin Inc .... C....... 619 661-6292
2695 Customhouse Ct Ste 111 San Diego (92154) *(P-9790)*

Safran Cabin Inc .... C....... 619 671-0430
6754 Calle De Linea Ste 111 San Diego (92154) *(P-9791)*

Safran Cabin Materials LLC .... E....... 909 947-4115
5701 Bolsa Ave Huntington Beach (92647) *(P-9792)*

Safran Cabin Tijuana S.a De Cv, San Diego *Also Called: Safran Cabin Inc (P-9790)*

Safran Power Units, San Diego *Also Called: Safran Pwr Units San Diego LLC (P-9579)*

Safran Pwr Units San Diego LLC .... D....... 858 223-2228
4255 Ruffin Rd Ste 100 San Diego (92123) *(P-9579)*

Safran Seats Santa Maria LLC .... A....... 805 922-5995
2641 Airpark Dr Santa Maria (93455) *(P-9793)*

Sage, Los Angeles *Also Called: Sage Machado Inc (P-10911)*

Sage Goddess Inc .... E....... 650 733-6639
21010 Figueroa St Carson (90745) *(P-10910)*

Sage Hospitality Resources LLC .... C....... 626 357-5211
700 W Huntington Dr Monrovia (91016) *(P-15338)*

Sage Machado Inc .... E....... 323 931-0595
133 N Gramercy Pl Los Angeles (90004) *(P-10911)*

Sage Publications Inc (PA)....................................... C....... **805 499-0721**
2455 Teller Rd Thousand Oaks (91320) *(P-3414)*

Mergent email: customerrelations@mergent.com
1250

2024 Southern California
Business Directory and Buyers Guide

(P-0000) Products & Services Section entry number
(PA)=Parent Co (HQ)=Headquarters (DH)=Div Headquarters

Sage Software Inc .... E...... 949 753-1222
7595 Irvine Center Dr Ste 200 Irvine (92618) *(P-16535)*

Sage Software Holdings Inc (HQ).......................... B...... 866 530-7243
6561 Irvine Center Dr Irvine (92618) *(P-16370)*

Sage Staffing, Valencia *Also Called: Sage Staffing Consultants Inc (P-15940)*

Sage Staffing Consultants Inc (PA)........................ C...... 661 254-4026
27441 Tourney Rd Ste 150 Valencia (91355) *(P-15940)*

SAI Industries .... E...... 818 842-6144
631 Allen Ave Glendale (91201) *(P-6748)*

SAI Management Co Inc .... D...... 714 772-5050
1600 S Harbor Blvd Anaheim (92802) *(P-15339)*

Saic, San Diego *Also Called: Science Applications Intl Corp (P-16468)*

Saic, San Diego *Also Called: Leidos Inc (P-19852)*

Saic, San Diego *Also Called: Leidos Inc (P-19855)*

Saic Government Solutions, San Diego *Also Called: Science Applications Intl Corp (P-16596)*

Sailing Innovation (us) Inc .... A...... 626 965-6665
17870 Castleton St # 220 City Of Industry (91748) *(P-14081)*

Sails Washington Inc .... B...... 425 333-4114
13920 City Center Dr Ste 290 Chino Hills (91709) *(P-18639)*

Saint Cecilia School, Tustin *Also Called: Roman Cthlic Diocese of Orange (P-18981)*

Saint Jhns Hlth Ctr Foundation .... C...... 310 315-6111
2200 Santa Monica Blvd Santa Monica (90404) *(P-17755)*

Saint John's Health Center, Santa Monica *Also Called: Saint Johns Health Center Foundation (P-18412)*

Saint John's Hospital X Ray, Long Beach *Also Called: Dignity Health (P-18243)*

Saint Johns Health Center Foundation (DH).............. A...... 310 829-5511
2121 Santa Monica Blvd Santa Monica (90404) *(P-18412)*

SAINT JOSEPH CENTER VOLUNTEER, Venice *Also Called: St Joseph Center (P-19143)*

Saint Joseph Hlth Sys Hospice, Anaheim *Also Called: St Joseph Hospice (P-19144)*

Saint Jseph Communications Inc (PA)..................... E...... 626 331-3549
1243 E Shamwood St West Covina (91790) *(P-17216)*

Saint Mary Medical Center, Long Beach *Also Called: Dignity Health (P-18245)*

Saint Nine America Inc .... E...... 562 921-5300
10700 Norwalk Blvd Santa Fe Springs (90670) *(P-11023)*

Saint-Gobain Ceramics Plas Inc .... B...... 714 701-3900
4905 E Hunter Ave Anaheim (92807) *(P-4528)*

Saint-Gobain Performance Plas, San Diego *Also Called: Saint-Gobain Solar Gard LLC (P-4820)*

Saint-Gobain Prfmce Plas Corp .... C...... 714 893-0470
7301 Orangewood Ave Garden Grove (92841) *(P-3968)*

Saint-Gobain Prfmce Plas Corp .... D...... 714 630-5818
7301 Orangewood Ave Garden Grove (92841) *(P-3969)*

Saint-Gobain Solar Gard LLC (DH)......................... D...... 866 300-2674
4540 Viewridge Ave San Diego (92123) *(P-4820)*

Sajahtera Inc .... A...... 310 276-2251
9641 Sunset Blvd Beverly Hills (90210) *(P-15340)*

Sakura Finetek USA Inc (HQ)................................ C...... 310 972-7800
1750 W 214th St Torrance (90501) *(P-12512)*

Salad Time Farms, Baldwin Park *Also Called: Tanimura Antle Fresh Foods Inc (P-115)*

Saladish Inc .... D...... 626 304-3100
12 W Colorado Blvd Pasadena (91105) *(P-1982)*

Saleen Automotive Inc (PA)................................. E...... 800 888-8945
2735 Wardlow Rd Corona (92882) *(P-6487)*

Saleen Incorporated (PA).................................... C...... 714 400-2121
2735 Wardlow Rd Corona (92882) *(P-9307)*

Salem Music Network Inc .... F...... 805 987-0400
4880 Santa Rosa Rd Ste 300 Camarillo (93012) *(P-8574)*

Sales Advantage Group, Corona *Also Called: Temps Plus Inc (P-15899)*

Salescatcher, Orange *Also Called: Salescatcher LLC (P-16371)*

Salescatcher LLC .... E...... 714 376-6700
1570 N Batavia St Orange (92867) *(P-16371)*

SALESFORCE.COM, INC., Santa Monica *Also Called: Salesforcecom Inc (P-16372)*

Salesforcecom Inc .... E...... 310 752-7000
1442 2nd St Santa Monica (90401) *(P-16372)*

Salico Farms Inc .... C...... 760 344-5375
4231 Us Highway 86 Ste 4 Brawley (92227) *(P-1330)*

Salis International Inc .... E...... 303 384-3588
3921 Oceanic Dr Ste 802 Oceanside (92056) *(P-11050)*

SALK INSTITUTE, THE, La Jolla *Also Called: The Salk Institute For Biological Studies San Diego California (P-19882)*

Salman, Brea *Also Called: Parkinson Enterprises Inc (P-2895)*

Salsbury Industries, Carson *Also Called: Salsbury Industries Inc (P-2991)*

Salsbury Industries Inc (PA)................................ B...... 800 624-5269
18300 Central Ave Carson (90746) *(P-2991)*

Salson Logistics Inc .... C...... 973 986-0200
1331 Torrance Blvd Torrance (90501) *(P-11800)*

Salvation Army (HQ).. C...... 562 264-3600
30840 Hawthorne Blvd Rancho Palos Verdes (90275) *(P-19131)*

Salvation Army, San Diego *Also Called: Salvation Army Ray & Joan (P-17413)*

Salvation Army Ray & Joan .... B...... 619 287-5762
6845 University Ave San Diego (92115) *(P-17413)*

Salvation Army Western Ttry, Rancho Palos Verdes *Also Called: Salvation Army (P-19131)*

Sam Schaffer Inc .... E...... 323 263-7524
3015 E Echo Hill Way Orange (92867) *(P-17151)*

Sam Sung Fixtures, Los Angeles *Also Called: Trust 1 Sales Inc (P-12465)*

Samaritan Imaging Center .... A...... 213 977-2140
1245 Wilshire Blvd Ste 205 Los Angeles (90017) *(P-18563)*

Same Swim LLC .... D...... 323 582-2588
2333 E 49th St Vernon (90058) *(P-13147)*

Samedan Oil Corporation .... B...... 661 319-5038
1360 Landing Ave Seal Beach (90740) *(P-317)*

Sameday Health, Venice *Also Called: Sameday Technologies Inc (P-16107)*

Sameday Technologies Inc .... C...... 310 697-8126
523 Victoria Ave Venice (90291) *(P-16107)*

Samick Music Corp .... D...... 800 946-6001
10541 Calle Lee Ste 119los Los Alamitos (90720) *(P-12986)*

Sample Tile and Stone Inc .... E...... 951 776-8562
1410 Richardson St San Bernardino (92408) *(P-5533)*

Samson Pharmaceuticals Inc .... E...... 323 722-3066
5635 Smithway St Commerce (90040) *(P-4228)*

Samson Products Inc .... E...... 323 726-9070
6285 Randolph St Commerce (90040) *(P-2992)*

Samsung Electronics Amer Inc .... C...... 323 374-6300
5601 E Slauson Ave Ste 200 Commerce (90040) *(P-12637)*

Samsung International Inc (DH)............................. E...... 619 671-6001
333 H St Ste 6000 Chula Vista (91910) *(P-12697)*

Samsung Research America Inc .... B...... 949 468-1143
18500 Von Karman Ave Ste 700 Irvine (92612) *(P-12436)*

Samtech Automotive Usa Inc .... E...... 310 638-9955
1130 E Dominguez St Carson (90746) *(P-7039)*

Samtech International, Carson *Also Called: Samtech Automotive Usa Inc (P-7039)*

Samuel Son & Co (usa) Inc .... E...... 951 781-7800
2345 Fleetwood Dr Riverside (92509) *(P-5707)*

Samuel Raoof .... E...... 818 534-3180
20660 Nordhoff St Chatsworth (91311) *(P-4452)*

Samy's Digital Imaging, Los Angeles *Also Called: Samys Camera Inc (P-14084)*

Samys Camera Inc (PA)...................................... C...... 310 591-2100
12636 Beatrice St Los Angeles (90066) *(P-14084)*

San Antonio Gift Shop, Los Angeles *Also Called: San Antonio Winery Inc (P-1659)*

San Antonio Regional Hospital (PA)....................... A...... 909 985-2811
999 San Bernardino Rd Upland (91786) *(P-18413)*

San Antonio Winery Inc (PA)................................ C...... 323 223-1401
737 Lamar St Los Angeles (90031) *(P-1659)*

San Bernardino Canning Co., San Bernardino *Also Called: Refresco Beverages US Inc (P-1724)*

San Bernardino Care Company .... C...... 909 884-4781
467 E Gilbert St San Bernardino (92404) *(P-18153)*

San Bernardino Cnty Trnsp Auth .... C...... 909 884-8276
1170 W 3rd St Fl 2 San Bernardino (92410) *(P-11358)*

San Bernardino County Sun, The, San Bernardino *Also Called: Sun Cmpany of San Brnrdino Cal (P-3326)*

San Bernardino Family YMCA, San Bernardino *Also Called: YMCA of East Valley (P-19475)*

San Bernardino Fics, San Bernardino *Also Called: Victor Cmnty Support Svcs Inc (P-18733)*

San Bernardino Hilton (HQ)................................. C...... 909 889-0133
285 E Hospitality Ln San Bernardino (92408) *(P-15341)*

San Bernardino Sheet Plant, San Bernardino *Also Called: Packaging Corporation America (P-3124)*

San Brnrdino Cmnty College Dst .... D...... 909 888-6511
701 S Mount Vernon Ave San Bernardino (92410) *(P-3810)*

San Brnrdino Cmnty College Dst .... C...... 909 384-4444
701 S Mount Vernon Ave San Bernardino (92410) *(P-11935)*

Employee Codes: A=Over 500 employees, B=251-500
C=101-250, D=51-100, E=20-50, F=10-19, G=1-9

2024 Southern California
Business Directory and Buyers Guide

© Mergent Inc. 1-800-342-5647

1251

San Brnrdino Cnty Prbtion Offc .... B...... 909 887-2544
4370 Hallmark Pkwy Ste 105 San Bernardino (92407) *(P-19132)*

San Brnrdino Cnty Rgonal Parks .... D...... 909 387-2583
777 E Rialto Ave San Bernardino (92415) *(P-17565)*

San Brnrdino Cy Unified Schl Ds .... D...... 909 881-8000
1257 Northpark Blvd San Bernardino (92407) *(P-18801)*

San Dego Cnty Rgnal Arprt Auth (PA).......................... C...... 619 400-2400
3225 N Harbor Dr Fl 3 San Diego (92101) *(P-11706)*

San Dego Cnvntion Ctr Corp Inc (PA)............................ B...... 619 782-4388
111 W Harbor Dr San Diego (92101) *(P-16921)*

San Dego Ctr For Chldren Fndti (PA)............................. D...... 858 277-9550
3002 Armstrong St San Diego (92111) *(P-18154)*

San Dego HM Grdn Lfestyles Mag, San Diego *Also Called: McKinnon Enterprises (P-3370)*

San Dego Nghborhood Newspapers, Cypress *Also Called: Community Media Corporation (P-3267)*

San Dego Prcsion Machining Inc .... E...... 858 499-0379
9375 Ruffin Ct San Diego (92123) *(P-5600)*

San Dego Pthlgsts Med Group In .... C...... 619 297-4012
7592 Metropolitan Dr Ste 406 San Diego (92108) *(P-17756)*

San Dego Repertory Theatre Inc .... D...... 619 231-3586
79 Horton Plz San Diego (92101) *(P-17327)*

San Dego Second Chance Program .... E...... 619 266-2506
6145 Imperial Ave San Diego (92114) *(P-19133)*

San Dego Symphony Orchstra Ass .... C...... 619 235-0800
1245 7th Ave San Diego (92101) *(P-17349)*

San Dg-Mprial Cnties Dvlpmntal (PA)........................... B...... 858 576-2996
4355 Ruffin Rd Ste 220 San Diego (92123) *(P-19134)*

San Diego Ace Inc .... C...... 619 206-7339
5363 Sweetwater Trl San Diego (92130) *(P-5195)*

San Diego Arcft Interiors Inc .... E...... 619 474-1997
2381 Boswell Rd Chula Vista (91914) *(P-2788)*

San Diego Assn Governments (PA)................................. C...... 619 699-1900
401 B St Ste 800 San Diego (92101) *(P-19384)*

San Diego Blood Bank (PA)... C...... 619 400-8132
3636 Gateway Center Ave Ste 100 San Diego (92102) *(P-18802)*

San Diego Blood Bnk Foundation, San Diego *Also Called: San Diego Blood Bank (P-18802)*

San Diego Business Journal, San Diego *Also Called: Cbj LP (P-3350)*

San Diego City College, San Diego *Also Called: San Diego Cmnty College Dst (P-18996)*

San Diego Cmnty College Dst .... C...... 619 388-4850
1960 National Ave San Diego (92113) *(P-18983)*

San Diego Cmnty College Dst ....D...... 619 388-3453
1313 Twelfth Ave San Diego (92101) *(P-18996)*

San Diego Cmnty College Dst .... A...... 619 388-2600
7250 Mesa College Dr San Diego (92111) *(P-18997)*

San Diego Composites Inc ....D...... 858 751-0450
9220 Activity Rd Ste 100 San Diego (92126) *(P-19684)*

San Diego Country Club Inc .... C...... 619 422-8895
88 L St Chula Vista (91911) *(P-17515)*

San Diego Country Estates Assn .... C...... 760 789-3788
24157 San Vicente Rd Ramona (92065) *(P-19461)*

San Diego County Credit Union (PA).............................. C...... 877 732-2848
6545 Sequence Dr San Diego (92121) *(P-14236)*

San Diego County Water Auth .... C...... 760 480-1991
610 W 5th Ave Escondido (92025) *(P-12140)*

San Diego County Water Auth (PA)................................D...... 858 522-6600
4677 Overland Ave San Diego (92123) *(P-12141)*

San Diego Crating & Pkg Inc .... F...... 858 748-0100
12678 Brookprinter Pl Poway (92064) *(P-3127)*

San Diego Daily Transcript ....D...... 619 232-4381
34 Emerald Gln Laguna Niguel (92677) *(P-3061)*

San Diego Data Processing Corporation Inc .... A...... 858 581-9600
202 C St 3rd Fl San Diego (92101) *(P-16514)*

San Diego Die Cutting Inc .... E...... 619 297-4453
3112 Moore St San Diego (92110) *(P-13024)*

San Diego District Office, San Diego *Also Called: State Compensation Insur Fund (P-14531)*

San Diego Electric Sign Inc .... F...... 619 258-1775
1890 Cordell Ct Ste 105 El Cajon (92020) *(P-11154)*

San Diego Family, San Diego *Also Called: San Diego Family Magazine LLC (P-3389)*

San Diego Family Care (PA)...D...... 858 279-0925
6973 Linda Vista Rd San Diego (92111) *(P-17757)*

San Diego Family Magazine LLC .... E...... 619 685-6970
1475 6th Ave Ste 500 San Diego (92101) *(P-3389)*

San Diego Farms LLC .... C...... 760 736-4072
570 Quarry Rd San Marcos (92069) *(P-86)*

San Diego Gas & Electric Co .... C...... 858 547-2086
6875c Consolidated Way San Diego (92121) *(P-11610)*

San Diego Gas & Electric Co .... B...... 619 441-3834
104 N Johnson Ave El Cajon (92020) *(P-12042)*

San Diego Gas & Electric Co .... C...... 858 541-5920
5488 Overland Ave San Diego (92123) *(P-12043)*

San Diego Gas & Electric Co .... C...... 619 699-1018
701 33rd St San Diego (92102) *(P-12044)*

San Diego Gas & Electric Co .... B...... 760 432-2508
2300 Harveson Pl Escondido (92029) *(P-12045)*

San Diego Gas & Electric Co .... B...... 858 654-6377
5488 Overland Ave San Diego (92123) *(P-12046)*

San Diego Gas & Electric Co .... C...... 858 613-3216
10975 Technology Pl San Diego (92127) *(P-12047)*

San Diego Gas & Electric Co ....D...... 858 654-1289
8306 Century Park Ct # Cp42c San Diego (92123) *(P-12048)*

San Diego Gas & Electric Co .... C...... 619 696-2000
1801 S Atlantic Blvd Monterey Park (91754) *(P-12049)*

San Diego Gas & Electric Co .... C...... 951 243-2241
14601 Virginia St Moreno Valley (92555) *(P-12082)*

San Diego Gas & Electric Co .... C...... 866 616-5565
8315 Century Park Ct Ste Cp-21d San Diego (92123) *(P-12105)*

San Diego Gas & Electric Co (DH)................................. B...... 619 696-2000
8330 Century Park Ct San Diego (92123) *(P-12106)*

San Diego Gas & Electric Co .... C...... 949 361-8090
662 Camino De Los Mares San Clemente (92673) *(P-12107)*

San Diego Gas & Electric Co .... C...... 760 438-6200
5016 Carlsbad Blvd Carlsbad (92008) *(P-12112)*

San Diego Gas & Electric Co .... C...... 858 654-1135
436 H St Chula Vista (91910) *(P-12113)*

San Diego Hebrew Homes (PA)..................................... C...... 760 942-2695
211 Saxony Rd Encinitas (92024) *(P-18046)*

San Diego Hospice & Palliative, San Diego *Also Called: San Diego Hospice & Palliative Care Corporation (P-18640)*

San Diego Hospice & Palliative Care Corporation .... A...... 619 688-1600
4311 3rd Ave San Diego (92103) *(P-18640)*

San Diego Hotel Company LLC .... C...... 619 696-0234
660 K St San Diego (92101) *(P-15342)*

San Diego Leather Inc .... F...... 619 477-2900
340 National City Blvd National City (91950) *(P-13936)*

San Diego Lessee LLC ....D...... 619 297-5466
7450 Hazard Center Dr San Diego (92108) *(P-15343)*

San Diego Magazine, San Diego *Also Called: San Diego Magazine Pubg Co (P-3390)*

San Diego Magazine Pubg Co .... E...... 619 230-9292
1230 Columbia St Ste 800 San Diego (92101) *(P-3390)*

San Diego Marriott Mission Vly, San Diego *Also Called: Ws Mmv Hotel LLC (P-15427)*

San Diego Mesa College, San Diego *Also Called: San Diego Cmnty College Dst (P-18997)*

San Diego Metro Trnst Sys .... A...... 619 231-1466
1255 Imperial Ave Ste 1000 San Diego (92101) *(P-11359)*

SAN DIEGO METROPOLITAN TRANSIT, San Diego *Also Called: San Diego Transit Corporation (P-11360)*

San Diego Mirror and Window, Vista *Also Called: J & B Manufacturing Corp (P-5344)*

San Diego Mission Bay Resorts ....D...... 619 677-1161
1775 E Mission Bay Dr San Diego (92109) *(P-15344)*

San Diego Museum of Art ....D...... 619 696-1909
1450 El Prado San Diego (92101) *(P-19362)*

San Diego Opera Association .... C...... 619 232-5911
3074 Commercial St San Diego (92113) *(P-17328)*

San Diego Opera Association .... C...... 619 232-5911
3064 Commercial St San Diego (92113) *(P-17329)*

San Diego Padres, San Diego *Also Called: California Sportservice Inc (P-17366)*

San Diego Padres, San Diego *Also Called: Padres LP (P-17380)*

San Diego Pcb Design LLC .... F...... 858 271-5722
461 Whitby Gln Escondido (92027) *(P-8726)*

San Diego Powder Coating, El Cajon *Also Called: BJS&t Enterprises Inc (P-6695)*

San Diego Precast Concrete Inc (DH)............................ E...... 619 240-8000
2735 Cactus Rd San Diego (92154) *(P-5448)*

San Diego Printers, San Diego *Also Called: Three Man Corporation (P-3821)*

San Diego Printing Group Inc .... F...... 858 541-1500
5560 Ruffin Rd Ste 2 San Diego (92123) *(P-3682)*

Mergent email: customerrelations@mergent.com
1252

2024 Southern California
Business Directory and Buyers Guide

(P-0000) Products & Services Section entry number
(PA)=Parent Co (HQ)=Headquarters (DH)=Div Headquarters

San Diego Ready Mix, San Diego *Also Called: Superior Ready Mix Concrete LP (P-13671)*

San Diego Rescue Mission Inc (PA)...................................D...... 619 819-1880
299 17th St San Diego (92101) *(P-19340)*

San Diego Saturn Retailers Inc ....D...... 858 373-3001
9985 Huennekens St San Diego (92121) *(P-17016)*

San Diego Services LLC ....C...... 858 654-0102
5415 Oberlin Dr San Diego (92121) *(P-19685)*

San Diego Sheraton Corporation ....C...... 619 291-6400
1590 Harbor Island Dr San Diego (92101) *(P-15345)*

San Diego Sign Company Inc ....E...... 888 748-7446
5960 Pascal Ct Carlsbad (92008) *(P-12877)*

San Diego State Aztecs, San Diego *Also Called: San Diego State University (P-17516)*

San Diego State University ....C...... 619 594-4263
5302 55th St San Diego (92182) *(P-17516)*

San Diego State University ....D...... 619 594-1515
5200 Campanile Dr San Diego (92182) *(P-18992)*

San Diego Supercomputer Center, La Jolla *Also Called: University Cal San Diego (P-16520)*

San Diego Symphony Foundation ....C...... 619 235-0800
1245 7th Ave San Diego (92101) *(P-17350)*

San Diego Theatres Inc ....C...... 619 615-4007
233 A St Ste 900 San Diego (92101) *(P-14683)*

San Diego Transit Corporation (PA)......................................A...... 619 238-0100
100 16th St San Diego (92101) *(P-11360)*

San Diego Trolley Inc ....B...... 619 595-4933
1341 Commercial St San Diego (92113) *(P-11361)*

SAN DIEGO TROLLEY INC, San Diego *Also Called: San Diego Trolley Inc (P-11361)*

San Diego Unified Hbr Police, San Diego *Also Called: San Diego Unified Port Dst (P-20411)*

San Diego Unified Port Dst ....C...... 619 686-6200
1400 Tidelands Ave National City (91950) *(P-11646)*

San Diego Unified Port Dst (PA)...C...... 619 686-6200
3165 Pacific Hwy San Diego (92101) *(P-11647)*

San Diego Unified Port Dst ....C...... 619 686-6585
3380 N Harbor Dr San Diego (92101) *(P-20411)*

San Diego Unified School Dst ....E...... 619 600-5321
3426 School St San Diego (92116) *(P-2936)*

San Diego Union Tribune, The, San Diego *Also Called: San Diego Union-Tribune LLC (P-3320)*

San Diego Union-Tribune LLC ....E...... 619 299-3131
600 B St San Diego (92101) *(P-3319)*

San Diego Union-Tribune LLC (PA)..A...... 619 299-3131
600 B St Ste 1201 San Diego (92101) *(P-3320)*

San Diego V Inc (PA)..D...... 888 308-2260
5350 Kearny Mesa Rd San Diego (92111) *(P-13821)*

San Diego Volvo, San Diego *Also Called: San Diego V Inc (P-13821)*

San Diego Wild Animal Park, Escondido *Also Called: Zoological Society San Diego (P-19370)*

San Diego Zoo, San Diego *Also Called: Zoological Society San Diego (P-19371)*

San Diego Zoo, San Diego *Also Called: Zoological Society San Diego (P-19372)*

San Diego Zoo Wildlife Aliance, San Diego *Also Called: Zoological Society San Diego (P-19369)*

San Dieguito Printers, San Marcos *Also Called: San Dieguito Publishers Inc (P-3683)*

San Dieguito Publishers Inc ....D...... 760 593-5139
1880 Diamond St San Marcos (92078) *(P-3683)*

San Dimas Community Hospital, San Dimas *Also Called: Prime Hlthcare Svcs - San Dmas (P-18393)*

San Dimas Community Hospital, San Dimas *Also Called: Prime Health Care (P-19226)*

San Fernando City of Inc ....D...... 818 832-2400
10605 Balboa Blvd Ste 100 Granada Hills (91344) *(P-18716)*

San Fernando Valley Auto LLC ....C...... 818 832-1600
18600 Devonshire St Northridge (91324) *(P-13822)*

San Fernando Valley Bus Jurnl, Los Angeles *Also Called: Cbj LP (P-3347)*

San Gabriel Convalescent Ctr, Rosemead *Also Called: Longwood Management Corp (P-18000)*

San Gabriel Country Club ....D...... 626 287-9671
350 E Hermosa Dr San Gabriel (91775) *(P-17517)*

San Gabriel Transit Inc (PA)...C...... 626 258-1310
3650 Rockwell Ave El Monte (91731) *(P-11362)*

San Gabriel Valley Cab Co, El Monte *Also Called: San Gabriel Transit Inc (P-11362)*

San Gabriel Valley Medical Ctr ....A...... 626 289-5454
438 W Las Tunas Dr San Gabriel (91776) *(P-18414)*

San Gabriel Valley Water Assn ....D...... 626 815-1305
725 N Azusa Ave Azusa (91702) *(P-12142)*

San Gabriel Valley Water Co ....C...... 909 822-2201
8440 Nuevo Ave Fontana (92335) *(P-12143)*

San Gabriel Valley Water Co (PA)...C...... 626 448-6183
11142 Garvey Ave El Monte (91733) *(P-12144)*

SAN GABRIEL/POMONA REGIONAL CE, Pomona *Also Called: San Gbrl/Pmona Vlleys Dvlpmnta (P-19135)*

San Gbriel Ambltory Srgery Ctr ....C...... 626 300-5300
207 S Santa Anita St Ste G16 San Gabriel (91776) *(P-17758)*

San Gbrl/Pmona Vlleys Dvlpmnta ....B...... 909 620-7722
75 Rancho Camino Dr Pomona (91766) *(P-19135)*

San Gorgonio Memorial Hospital ....A...... 951 845-1121
600 N Highland Springs Ave Banning (92220) *(P-18415)*

San Grgnio Mem Hosp Foundation (PA)................................C...... 951 845-1121
600 N Highland Springs Ave Banning (92220) *(P-18416)*

San Jacinto Healthcare, Hemet *Also Called: Miramonte Enterprises LLC (P-18014)*

San Joaquin Community Hospital (PA)...................................A...... 661 395-3000
2615 Chester Ave Bakersfield (93301) *(P-18417)*

San Joaquin Refining Co Inc ....C...... 661 327-4257
3500 Shell St Bakersfield (93308) *(P-4650)*

San Joaquin Window Inc ....C...... 909 946-3697
1455 Columbia Ave Riverside (92507) *(P-6121)*

San Jquin Nrsing Rhblttion Ctr, Bakersfield *Also Called: Kern Valleyidence Opco LLC (P-18087)*

San Luis Ambulance Service Inc ....C...... 805 543-2626
3546 S Higuera St San Luis Obispo (93401) *(P-11403)*

San Luis Obispo Golf Cntry CLB ....C...... 805 543-3400
255 Country Club Dr San Luis Obispo (93401) *(P-17518)*

San Luis Obspo Cocmmnty Clgdst ....F...... 805 591-6200
2800 Buena Vista Dr Paso Robles (93446) *(P-3321)*

San Luis Obspo Rgnal Trnst Aut ....D...... 805 781-4465
253 Elks Ln San Luis Obispo (93401) *(P-11363)*

San Manuel Entertainment Auth (PA)....................................A...... 909 864-5050
777 San Manuel Blvd Highland (92346) *(P-17566)*

San Manuel Fire Dept, Highland *Also Called: San Mnuel Band Mission Indians (P-16922)*

San Marcos Mechanical, Vista *Also Called: Industrial Coml Systems Inc (P-778)*

San Marcos Trading Company, San Marcos *Also Called: GK Foods Inc (P-1410)*

San Miguel Produce Inc ....B...... 805 488-0981
600 E Hueneme Rd Oxnard (93033) *(P-11)*

San Mnuel Band Mission Indians ....C...... 909 425-4682
101 Pure Water Ln Highland (92346) *(P-14263)*

San Mnuel Band Mission Indians ....C...... 909 864-6928
26540 Indian Service Rd Highland (92346) *(P-16922)*

San Onofre Child Care Center, Camp Pendleton *Also Called: Marine Corps Community Svcs (P-19217)*

San Pedro Convalescent HM Inc ....D...... 310 832-6431
1430 W 6th St San Pedro (90732) *(P-18047)*

San Pedro Peninsula Hospital ....A...... 310 832-3311
1300 W 7th St San Pedro (90732) *(P-18418)*

San Psqual Band Mssion Indians ....C...... 760 291-5500
16300 Nyemii Pass Rd Valley Center (92082) *(P-15346)*

San Psqual Band Mssion Indians (PA)...................................D...... 760 749-3200
16400 Kumeyaay Way Valley Center (92082) *(P-20407)*

San Val Alarm System, Thousand Palms *Also Called: San Val Corp (P-178)*

San Val Corp (PA)..B...... 760 346-3999
72203 Adelaid St Thousand Palms (92276) *(P-178)*

SAN VICENTE INN & GOLF CLUB, Ramona *Also Called: San Diego Country Estates Assn (P-19461)*

San Ysidro Bb Property LLC ....C...... 805 368-6788
900 San Ysidro Ln Santa Barbara (93108) *(P-15347)*

San Ysidro Health, San Diego *Also Called: Centro De Salud De La Comuni (P-18678)*

San-Mar Construction Co Inc ....C...... 714 693-5400
4875 E La Palma Ave Ste 602 Anaheim (92807) *(P-587)*

SANBAG, San Bernardino *Also Called: San Bernardino Cnty Trnsp Auth (P-11358)*

Sanci Marriott Hotels ....D...... 619 435-3000
2000 2nd St Coronado (92118) *(P-15348)*

Sanctuary Clothing, Burbank *Also Called: Sanctuary Clothing LLC (P-13916)*

Sanctuary Clothing LLC (PA)...E...... 818 505-0018
3611 N San Fernando Blvd Burbank (91505) *(P-13916)*

Sanctuary Spa, San Diego *Also Called: Bay Clubs Company LLC (P-17464)*

Sand Canyon Corporation (HQ)..D...... 949 727-9425
7595 Irvine Center Dr Ste 120 Irvine (92618) *(P-14364)*

Employee Codes: A=Over 500 employees, B=251-500
C=101-250, D=51-100, E=20-50, F=10-19, G=1-9

2024 Southern California
Business Directory and Buyers Guide

© Mergent Inc. 1-800-342-5647

1253

ALPHABETIC

Sandberg Furniture, Vernon *Also Called: Sandberg Furniture Mfg Co Inc (P-2789)*

Sandberg Furniture Mfg Co Inc (PA)...............................C....... 323 582-0711
5705 Alcoa Ave Vernon (90058) *(P-2789)*

Sandberg Industries Inc (PA)................................D...... 949 660-9473
2921 Daimler St Santa Ana (92705) *(P-9113)*

Sandee Plastic Extrusions ....E....... 323 979-4020
14932 Gwenchris Ct Paramount (90723) *(P-5196)*

Sandel, Vista *Also Called: Sandel Avionics Inc (P-10066)*

Sandel Avionics, Vista *Also Called: Sandel Avionics Inc (P-10067)*

Sandel Avionics Inc (PA) ....E....... 760 727-4900
1370 Decision St Ste D Vista (92081) *(P-10066)*

Sandel Avionics Inc ....C....... 760 727-4900
2405 Dogwood Way Vista (92081) *(P-10067)*

Sander Langston LP ....C....... 949 863-9200
17962 Cowan Irvine (92614) *(P-588)*

Sanders & Wohrman Corporation ....C....... 714 919-0446
709 N Poplar St Orange (92868) *(P-856)*

Sanders Candy Factory Inc ....E....... 626 814-2038
5051 Calmview Ave Baldwin Park (91706) *(P-1548)*

Sanders Composites Inc (HQ)...............................E....... 562 354-2800
3701 E Conant St Long Beach (90808) *(P-9794)*

Sanders Composites Industries, Long Beach *Also Called: Sanders Composites Inc (P-9794)*

Sandia Plastics Inc ....E....... 714 901-8400
15571 Container Ln Huntington Beach (92649) *(P-5197)*

Sandm San Dego Mrriott Del Mar ....A....... 858 523-1700
11966 El Camino Real San Diego (92130) *(P-15349)*

Sandpiper of California Inc ....D....... 619 424-2222
687 Anita St Ste A Chula Vista (91911) *(P-5295)*

Sandusky Lee LLC ....E....... 661 854-5551
16125 Widmere Rd Arvin (93203) *(P-2837)*

Sanford Brnham Prbys Med Dscve (PA)...............................A....... 858 795-5000
10901 N Torrey Pines Rd La Jolla (92037) *(P-19941)*

Sangera Buick Inc ....D....... 661 833-5200
5600 Gasoline Alley Dr Bakersfield (93313) *(P-17038)*

Sani-Tech West Inc (HQ)...............................D....... 805 389-0400
1020 Flynn Rd Camarillo (93012) *(P-4712)*

Sanie Manufacturing Company ....F....... 714 751-7700
320 E Alton Ave Santa Ana (92707) *(P-6367)*

Sanisure, Camarillo *Also Called: Sani-Tech West Inc (P-4712)*

Sanittion Dstrcts Los Angles C ....A....... 562 908-4288
1955 Workman Mill Rd Whittier (90601) *(P-12186)*

Sanko Electronics America Inc (HQ)...............................F....... 310 618-1677
2587 Otay Center Dr San Diego (92154) *(P-9457)*

Sanluisina, Chino Hills *Also Called: Andrew LLC (P-1406)*

Sanmina Corporation ....E....... 714 371-2800
2945 Airway Ave Costa Mesa (92626) *(P-8727)*

Sanmina Corporation ....C....... 714 913-2200
2950 Red Hill Ave Costa Mesa (92626) *(P-8728)*

Sansum Clinic ....D....... 805 681-7500
215 Pesetas Ln Santa Barbara (93110) *(P-14056)*

Santa Ana Country Club ....D....... 714 556-3000
20382 Newport Blvd Santa Ana (92707) *(P-17519)*

Santa Ana Creek Development Company ....D....... 714 685-3462
2288 N Batavia St Orange (92865) *(P-1085)*

Santa Ana District Office, Santa Ana *Also Called: State Compensation Insur Fund (P-14529)*

Santa Ana Job Training Program, Santa Ana *Also Called: City of Santa Ana (P-19181)*

Santa Ana Plating (PA)...............................D...... 310 923-8305
1726 E Rosslynn Ave Fullerton (92831) *(P-6659)*

Santa Anita Cnvlscent Hosp Rtr ....C....... 626 579-0310
5522 Gracewood Ave Temple City (91780) *(P-18048)*

Santa Anita Park, Arcadia *Also Called: Los Angeles Turf Club Inc (P-17386)*

Santa Barbara Cnty Social Svcs, Santa Maria *Also Called: Santa Brbara Cttage Hosp Fndti (P-18421)*

Santa Barbara Coffee & Tea Inc ....E....... 805 898-3700
321 Motor Way Santa Barbara (93101) *(P-14034)*

Santa Barbara Control Systems ....F....... 805 683-8833
5375 Overpass Rd Santa Barbara (93111) *(P-10160)*

Santa Barbara Cottage Hospital ....B....... 805 569-7367
400 W Pueblo St Santa Barbara (93105) *(P-18419)*

Santa Barbara Design Studio (PA)...............................D...... 805 966-3883
1600 Pacific Ave Oxnard (93033) *(P-5386)*

Santa Barbara Family YMCA, Santa Barbara *Also Called: Channel Islnds Yung MNS Chrstn (P-19435)*

Santa Barbara Farms LLC ....C....... 805 736-5608
1105 Union Sugar Ave Lompoc (93436) *(P-12)*

Santa Barbara Group, Santa Barbara *Also Called: Tecolote Research Inc (P-20257)*

Santa Barbara Independent Inc ....E....... 805 965-5205
1715 State St Santa Barbara (93101) *(P-3322)*

Santa Barbara Indus Finshg, Goleta *Also Called: Sbif Inc (P-6734)*

Santa Barbara Infrared Inc (DH)...............................D...... 805 965-3669
30 S Calle Cesar Chavez Ste D Santa Barbara (93103) *(P-10068)*

Santa Barbara Instrument GP Inc ....E....... 925 463-3410
150 Castilian Dr Goleta (93117) *(P-10885)*

Santa Barbara Metro Trnst Dst (PA)...............................D...... 805 963-3364
550 Olive St Santa Barbara (93101) *(P-11364)*

Santa Barbara Trnsp Corp ....D....... 661 259-7285
26501 Ruether Ave Santa Clarita (91350) *(P-11413)*

Santa Barbara Trnsp Corp ....C....... 661 510-0566
42138 7th St W Lancaster (93534) *(P-11431)*

Santa Barbara Trnsp Corp ....C....... 805 928-0402
6500 Hollister Ave Ste 100 Goleta (93117) *(P-11432)*

Santa Barbara Trnsp Corp ....C....... 760 746-0850
520 Gannon Pl Escondido (92025) *(P-11433)*

SANTA BARBARA ZOO, Santa Barbara *Also Called: Santa Brbara Zlgcal Foundation (P-19368)*

Santa Barbarba Roasting, Santa Barbara *Also Called: Santa Barbara Coffee & Tea Inc (P-14034)*

Santa Brbara Artfl Kdney Ctr L ....D....... 805 682-9942
1704 State St Santa Barbara (93101) *(P-18666)*

Santa Brbara Cmnty College Dst ....B....... 805 683-4191
525 Anacapa St Santa Barbara (93101) *(P-18998)*

Santa Brbara Cttage Hosp Fndti ....B....... 805 569-7224
400 W Pueblo St Santa Barbara (93105) *(P-18420)*

Santa Brbara Cttage Hosp Fndti ....B....... 805 346-7135
2125 Centerpointe Pkwy Santa Maria (93455) *(P-18421)*

Santa Brbara Cttage Hosp Fndti (HQ)...............................C....... 805 682-7111
400 W Pueblo St Santa Barbara (93105) *(P-18422)*

Santa Brbara Med Frndtion Clnic, Santa Barbara *Also Called: Sansum Clinic (P-14056)*

Santa Brbara Mseum Ntral Hstor ....D....... 805 682-4711
2559 Puesta Del Sol Santa Barbara (93105) *(P-19363)*

Santa Brbara San Luis Obspo RG ....C....... 800 421-2560
4050 Calle Real Santa Barbara (93110) *(P-14455)*

Santa Brbara Zlgcal Foundation ....C....... 805 962-1673
500 Ninos Dr Santa Barbara (93103) *(P-19368)*

Santa Catalina Island Company (PA)...............................C....... 310 510-2000
4 Park Plz Ste 420 Irvine (92614) *(P-11730)*

Santa Clarita Signs ....E....... 661 291-1188
26330 Diamond Pl Santa Clarita (91350) *(P-11155)*

Santa Clarita Valley Wtr Agcy ....C....... 661 259-2737
26521 Summit Cir Santa Clarita (91350) *(P-12145)*

Santa Clarita Water Division, Santa Clarita *Also Called: Santa Clarita Valley Wtr Agcy (P-12145)*

Santa Clrita Plstic Mlding Cor ....E....... 661 294-2257
24735 Avenue Rockefeller Valencia (91355) *(P-5198)*

Santa Clrita Vly Wtr Agcy Fing ....C....... 661 259-2737
27234 Bouquet Canyon Rd Santa Clarita (91350) *(P-12146)*

Santa Fe Enterprises Inc ....E....... 562 692-7596
11654 Pike St Santa Fe Springs (90670) *(P-7096)*

Santa Fe Extruders Inc ....E....... 562 921-8991
15315 Marquardt Ave Santa Fe Springs (90670) *(P-5199)*

Santa Fe Machine Works Inc ....E....... 909 350-6877
14578 Rancho Vista Dr Fontana (92335) *(P-8013)*

Santa Fe Middle School, Hemet *Also Called: Hemet Unified School District (P-18970)*

Santa Fe Rubber Products Inc ....E....... 562 693-2776
12306 Washington Blvd Whittier (90606) *(P-4794)*

Santa Fe Supply Company, Santa Fe Springs *Also Called: Philatron International (P-9241)*

Santa Margarita Water District ....C....... 949 459-6400
26101 Antonio Pkwy Rcho Sta Marg (92688) *(P-12147)*

Santa Maria Enrgy Holdings LLC ....E....... 805 938-3320
2811 Airpark Dr Santa Maria (93455) *(P-318)*

Santa Maria Tire Inc (PA)...............................D...... 805 347-4793
2170 Hutton Rd Bldg A Nipomo (93444) *(P-13870)*

Mergent email: customerrelations@mergent.com
1254

2024 Southern California
Business Directory and Buyers Guide

(P-0000) Products & Services Section entry number
(PA)=Parent Co (HQ)=Headquarters (DH)=Div Headquarters

Santa Monica City of .... B....... 310 458-1975
1685 Main St Santa Monica (90401) *(P-11414)*

Santa Monica Amusements LLC .... B....... 310 451-9641
380 Santa Monica Pier Santa Monica (90401) *(P-17453)*

Santa Monica Bay Physicians He (PA).................. D....... 310 417-5900
5767 W Century Blvd Los Angeles (90045) *(P-17759)*

Santa Monica Hotel Owner LLC .... C....... 310 395-3332
1707 4th St Santa Monica (90401) *(P-15350)*

Santa Monica Millworks .... E....... 805 643-0010
2568 Channel Dr Ventura (93003) *(P-2678)*

Santa Monica Proper Hotel, Santa Monica *Also Called: Santa Monica Proper Jv LLC*
(P-15351)

Santa Monica Proper Jv LLC .... C....... 310 620-9990
700 Wilshire Blvd Santa Monica (90401) *(P-15351)*

Santa Monica Seafood, Rancho Dominguez *Also Called: Santa Monica Seafood Company*
(P-1811)

Santa Monica Seafood Company (PA).................. D....... 310 886-7900
18531 S Broadwick St Rancho Dominguez (90220) *(P-1811)*

Santa Monica Ucla Medical Ctr, Santa Monica *Also Called: Regents of The University Cal*
(P-18800)

Santa Mrgrita Cthlic High Schl, Rcho Sta Marg *Also Called: Roman Cthlic Diocese of Orange*
(P-18982)

Santa Paula Hospital, Santa Paula *Also Called: Ventura County Medical Center (P-17825)*

Santa Rosa Berry Farms LLC .... B....... 805 981-3060
3500 Camino Ave Ste 250 Oxnard (93030) *(P-24)*

Santa Teresita Inc (PA).. B....... 626 359-3243
819 Buena Vista St Duarte (91010) *(P-18423)*

Santa Ynez Valley Marriott, Buellton *Also Called: Kang Family Partners LLC (P-15206)*

Santaluz Club Inc .... C....... 858 759-3120
8170 Caminito Santaluz E San Diego (92127) *(P-17520)*

Santarus Inc .... E....... 858 314-5700
3611 Valley Centre Dr Ste 400 San Diego (92130) *(P-4229)*

Santec Inc .... E....... 310 542-0063
3501 Challenger St Fl 2 Torrance (90503) *(P-5974)*

Santec California Corporation .... E....... 805 987-1700
4750 Calle Quetzal Camarillo (93012) *(P-10337)*

Santee Senior Retirement Com .... C....... 619 955-0901
400 Lantern Crest Way Santee (92071) *(P-19136)*

Santex Group, Carlsbad *Also Called: A R Santex LLC (P-15952)*

Santier Inc .... D....... 858 271-1993
10103 Carroll Canyon Rd San Diego (92131) *(P-8883)*

Santos Precision Inc .... D....... 714 957-0299
2220 S Anne St Santa Ana (92704) *(P-8014)*

Santoshi Corporation .... E....... 626 444-7118
2439 Seaman Ave El Monte (91733) *(P-6660)*

Santourian Manufacturing Inc .... E....... 760 754-3811
2603 Industry St Oceanside (92054) *(P-6310)*

Sanyo Fisher Company, San Diego *Also Called: Sanyo North America Corp (P-20377)*

Sanyo Foods Corp America (DH)............................ E....... 714 891-3671
11955 Monarch St Garden Grove (92841) *(P-1844)*

Sanyo Manufacturing Corporation .... D....... 619 661-1134
2055 Sanyo Ave San Diego (92154) *(P-8433)*

Sanyo North America Corp .... B....... 619 661-1134
2055 Sanyo Ave San Diego (92154) *(P-20377)*

Sapphire Chandelier LLC .... D....... 714 879-3660
505 Porter Way Placentia (92870) *(P-8330)*

Sapphire Clean Rooms LLC .... C....... 714 316-5036
2810 E Coronado St Anaheim (92806) *(P-12532)*

Sapphire Energy Inc .... D....... 858 768-4700
10996 Torreyana Rd Ste 280 San Diego (92121) *(P-4017)*

Sapphire Manufacturing Inc .... E....... 714 401-3117
505 Porter Way Placentia (92870) *(P-6368)*

Sappi North America Inc .... E....... 714 456-0600
21700 Copley Dr Ste 165 Diamond Bar (91765) *(P-3062)*

Saputo Cheese USA Inc .... A....... 562 862-7686
5611 Imperial Hwy South Gate (90280) *(P-1257)*

Sara, Cypress *Also Called: Scientfc Applctons RES Assoc (P-8212)*

Saratech, Mission Viejo *Also Called: Paydarfar Industries Inc (P-12430)*

Sardo Bus & Coach Upholstery, Gardena *Also Called: Louis Sardo Upholstery Inc (P-2932)*

SARR Industries Inc .... E....... 818 998-7735
8975 Fullbright Ave Chatsworth (91311) *(P-8015)*

Sarris Interiors, Paramount *Also Called: Sibyl Shepard Inc (P-2488)*

Sas Manufacturing Inc .... E....... 951 734-1808
405 N Smith Ave Corona (92878) *(P-9114)*

Sas Safety, Long Beach *Also Called: Sas Safety Corporation (P-10699)*

Sas Safety Corporation .... D....... 562 427-2775
3031 Gardenia Ave Long Beach (90807) *(P-10699)*

Sas Textiles Inc .... D....... 323 277-5555
3100 E 44th St Vernon (90058) *(P-2086)*

Satco, El Segundo *Also Called: Satco Inc (P-2726)*

Satco Inc (PA).. C....... 310 322-4719
1601 E El Segundo Blvd El Segundo (90245) *(P-2726)*

Satellite Management Co (PA)................................ C....... 714 558-2411
1010 E Chestnut Ave Santa Ana (92701) *(P-14864)*

Satellite Security Corporation .... E....... 877 437-4199
6779 Mesa Ridge Rd Ste 100 San Diego (92121) *(P-8575)*

Saticoy Country Club .... D....... 805 647-1153
4450 Clubhouse Dr Somis (93066) *(P-17521)*

Saticoy Foods Corporation .... E....... 805 647-5266
554 Todd Rd Santa Paula (93060) *(P-1344)*

Saticoy Fruit Exchange, Ventura *Also Called: Saticoy Lemon Association (P-44)*

Saticoy Fruit Exchange, Santa Paula *Also Called: Saticoy Lemon Association (P-111)*

Saticoy Lemon Association .... D....... 805 654-6500
7560 Bristol Rd Ventura (93003) *(P-44)*

Saticoy Lemon Association (PA)............................ D....... 805 654-6500
103 N Peck Rd Santa Paula (93060) *(P-111)*

Saticoy Lemon Association .... D....... 805 654-6543
600 E 3rd St Oxnard (93030) *(P-19385)*

Satterfield Aerospace, Northridge *Also Called: S & S Numerical Control Inc (P-8009)*

Saturn Fasteners Inc .... C....... 818 973-1807
425 S Varney St Burbank (91502) *(P-5942)*

Sauer Brands Inc .... D....... 805 597-8900
184 Suburban Rd San Luis Obispo (93401) *(P-1983)*

Sauer Brands, Inc, San Luis Obispo *Also Called: Sauer Brands Inc (P-1983)*

Saul Ewing Arnstein & Lehr LLP .... D....... 310 398-6100
1888 Century Park E Fl 19 Los Angeles (90067) *(P-18937)*

Saul Ewing Arnstein & Lehr LLP, Los Angeles *Also Called: Saul Ewing Arnstein & Lehr LLP*
(P-18937)

Sauvage Inc (PA).. F....... 858 408-0100
7717 Formula Pl San Diego (92121) *(P-2218)*

Savage Machining Inc .... E....... 805 584-8047
2235 1st St Ste 116 Simi Valley (93065) *(P-8016)*

Savage Services Corporation .... D....... 562 400-2044
8636 Sorensen Ave Santa Fe Springs (90670) *(P-11464)*

Savedaily Inc .... F....... 562 795-7500
1503 S Coast Dr Ste 330 Costa Mesa (92626) *(P-16373)*

Savi Customs, San Diego *Also Called: Crazy Industries (P-10985)*

Savice Inc .... D....... 949 888-2444
30052 Tomas Rcho Sta Marg (92688) *(P-19462)*

Savitsky Stin Bcon Bcci A Cal, Los Angeles *Also Called: Ground Control Business MGT*
(P-2040)

Saviynt Inc (PA).. C....... 310 641-1664
1301 E El Segundo Blvd Ste D El Segundo (90245) *(P-16374)*

Saw Daily Service Inc .... E....... 323 564-1791
4481 Firestone Blvd South Gate (90280) *(P-12878)*

Say It With A Sock LLC .... F....... 800 208-0879
11111 Santa Monica Blvd Ste 1100 Los Angeles (90025) *(P-2060)*

Sayari Shahrzad .... E....... 310 903-6368
4822 Aqueduct Ave Encino (91436) *(P-13110)*

Sazerac Company Inc .... D....... 310 604-8717
2202 E Del Amo Blvd Carson (90749) *(P-1675)*

Sb Waterman Holdings Inc (PA)............................ C....... 909 883-8611
1700 N Waterman Ave San Bernardino (92404) *(P-17760)*

Sbb Roofing Inc (PA).. C....... 323 254-2888
3310 Verdugo Rd Los Angeles (90065) *(P-1054)*

SBC, Los Angeles *Also Called: AT&T Services Inc (P-11870)*

SBC, Escondido *Also Called: AT&T Services Inc (P-11871)*

Sbcs Corporation .... C....... 619 420-3620
430 F St Chula Vista (91910) *(P-19137)*

SBE, Los Angeles *Also Called: Stockbridge/Sbe Holdings LLC (P-15374)*

SBE Electrical Contracting Inc .... C....... 714 544-5066
2817 Mcgaw Ave Irvine (92614) *(P-932)*

Employee Codes: A=Over 500 employees, B=251-500
C=101-250, D=51-100, E=20-50, F=10-19, G=1-9

2024 Southern California
Business Directory and Buyers Guide

© Mergent Inc. 1-800-342-5647

1255

Sbhis .... D....... 619 427-2689
740 Bay Blvd Chula Vista (91910) *(P-474)*

Sbif Inc .... F..... 805 683-1711
873 S Kellogg Ave Goleta (93117) *(P-6734)*

Sbig Astronomical Instruments, Goleta *Also Called: Santa Barbara Instrument GP Inc*
(P-10885)

Sbir, Santa Barbara *Also Called: Santa Barbara Infrared Inc (P-10068)*

Sbm Dairies Inc .... B....... 626 923-3000
17851 Railroad St City Of Industry (91748) *(P-1739)*

Sbnw LLC (PA) .... C...... 213 234-5122
5600 W Adams Blvd Los Angeles (90016) *(P-5299)*

SBP, La Jolla *Also Called: Sanford Brnham Prbys Med Dscve (P-19941)*

Sbsbtc, National City *Also Called: South Bay Sand Blstg Tank Clg (P-17153)*

SC Bluwood Inc .... F..... 909 519-5470
2604b El Camino Real Ste 356 Carlsbad (92008) *(P-2747)*

SC Fuels, Orange *Also Called: Southern Counties Oil Co (P-13445)*

SC Liquidation Company LLC .... C...... 714 482-1006
566 Vanguard Way Brea (92821) *(P-3174)*

SC Wright Construction Inc .... B....... 619 698-6909
3838 Camino Del Rio N Ste 370 San Diego (92108) *(P-19686)*

Scaled Composites LLC .... B....... 661 824-4541
1624 Flight Line Mojave (93501) *(P-9551)*

Scalefast Inc (PA) .... C...... 310 595-4040
2100 E Grand Ave El Segundo (90245) *(P-11901)*

Scales, Covina *Also Called: American Scale Co Inc (P-12396)*

Scan Group (PA) .... B....... 562 308-2733
3800 Kilroy Airport Way Ste 100 Long Beach (90806) *(P-14494)*

Scan Health Plan, Long Beach *Also Called: Senior Care (P-14495)*

Scanline Vfx Inc .... A..... 310 827-1555
6087 W Sunset Blvd Los Angeles (90028) *(P-17217)*

Scanlinevfx La LLC .... C..... 310 827-1555
6087 W Sunset Blvd Los Angeles (90028) *(P-17218)*

Scantibodies Laboratory Inc (PA) .... C..... 619 258-9300
9336 Abraham Way Santee (92071) *(P-19982)*

Scarborough Farms Inc .... C..... 805 483-9113
731 Pacific Ave Oxnard (93030) *(P-87)*

Scarrott Metallurgical Co, Los Angeles *Also Called: Interntonal Metallurgical Svcs (P-5838)*

Scat Enterprises Inc .... D....... 310 370-5501
1400 Kingsdale Ave Redondo Beach (90278) *(P-12260)*

Scattergood Generation Plant, Playa Del Rey *Also Called: Los Angeles Dept Wtr & Pwr*
(P-12111)

Scb Division, Bell Gardens *Also Called: Cal Southern Braiding Inc (P-9011)*

SCE, Rosemead *Also Called: Southern California Edison Co (P-12072)*

SCE FCU, Baldwin Park *Also Called: SCE Federal Credit Union (P-14237)*

SCE Federal Credit Union (PA) .... D...... 626 960-6888
12701 Schabarum Ave Baldwin Park (91706) *(P-14237)*

Scenario Cockram USA Inc .... C...... 407 613-2949
16340 Roscoe Blvd Van Nuys (91406) *(P-452)*

Scenic Express Inc .... E...... 323 254-4351
9380 San Fernando Rd Sun Valley (91352) *(P-1177)*

Scenic Studio, San Diego *Also Called: San Diego Opera Association (P-17329)*

Sceptre Inc .... E...... 626 369-3698
16800 Gale Ave City Of Industry (91745) *(P-9115)*

Schaefer Ambulance Service Inc .... B....... 323 468-1642
4627 Beverly Blvd Los Angeles (90004) *(P-11404)*

Schaeffler Group USA Inc .... E...... 949 234-9799
34700 Pacific Coast Hwy Ste 203 Capistrano Beach (92624) *(P-7303)*

Schaffer Marine Services Inc .... F...... 562 480-8085
3154 Petaluma Ave Long Beach (90808) *(P-5200)*

SCHAFFER MARINE SERVICES INC, Long Beach *Also Called: Schaffer Marine Services Inc*
(P-5200)

Schaumbond Group Inc (PA) .... B....... 626 215-4998
225 S Lake Ave Ste 300 Pasadena (91101) *(P-14982)*

Schea Holdings Inc .... E...... 818 998-3636
9812 Independence Ave Chatsworth (91311) *(P-11156)*

Schecter Guitar Research Inc .... E...... 818 767-1029
10953 Pendleton St Sun Valley (91352) *(P-10933)*

Schellinger Spring Inc .... E...... 909 373-0799
8477 Utica Ave Rancho Cucamonga (91730) *(P-6784)*

Scher Tire Inc (PA) .... E...... 951 343-3100
3863 Tyler St Riverside (92503) *(P-17024)*

Schick Moving & Storage Co (PA) .... D....... 714 731-5500
2721 Michelle Dr Tustin (92780) *(P-11522)*

Schilling Paradise Corp .... C...... 619 449-4141
697 Greenfield Dr El Cajon (92021) *(P-688)*

Schindler Elevator Corporation .... C...... 818 336-3000
16450 Foothill Blvd Ste 200 Sylmar (91342) *(P-17152)*

Schlumberger Technology Corp .... D....... 661 864-4721
6120 Snow Rd Bakersfield (93308) *(P-384)*

Schmidt Industries Inc .... D....... 818 768-9100
11321 Goss St Sun Valley (91352) *(P-6661)*

Schmitt House, El Monte *Also Called: Hope Hse For Mltple Hndcpped I (P-19272)*

Schneider Elc Buildings LLC .... C...... 310 900-2385
100 W Victoria St Long Beach (90805) *(P-9252)*

Schneider Electric .... E...... 949 713-9200
1660 Scenic Ave Costa Mesa (92626) *(P-9253)*

Schneider Electric Usa Inc .... D....... 909 438-2295
14725 Monte Vista Ave Chino (91710) *(P-11611)*

Schneiders Manufacturing Inc .... E...... 818 771-0082
11122 Penrose St Sun Valley (91352) *(P-8017)*

Scholastic Sports Inc .... D....... 858 496-9221
4878 Ronson Ct Ste Kl San Diego (92111) *(P-3684)*

School-Link Technologies Inc .... D....... 310 434-2700
1437 6th St Santa Monica (90401) *(P-16108)*

Schoolsfirst Federal Credit Un (PA) .... B....... 714 258-4000
2115 N Broadway Santa Ana (92706) *(P-14238)*

Schrey & Sons Mold Co Inc .... E...... 661 294-2260
24735 Avenue Rockefeller Valencia (91355) *(P-7097)*

Schroeder Iron Corporation .... E...... 909 428-6471
8417 Beech Ave Fontana (92335) *(P-6073)*

Schroff Inc .... A...... 800 525-4682
7328 Trade St San Diego (92121) *(P-7289)*

Schroff Inc .... A...... 858 740-2400
7328 Trade St San Diego (92121) *(P-13560)*

Schroff Inc .... E...... 858 740-2400
7328 Trade St San Diego (92121) *(P-17072)*

Schubert Music Publishing Inc .... E...... 310 409-7326
18233 Rayen St Northridge (91325) *(P-3483)*

Schulz Engineering, Sylmar *Also Called: Dg Engineering Corp (P-9970)*

Schurman Fine Papers .... E...... 714 549-0212
3333 Bristol St Costa Mesa (92626) *(P-12819)*

Schweitzers Metal Fabricators, Azusa *Also Called: Todd Street Inc (P-6166)*

Schwing America Inc .... E...... 909 681-6430
3351 Grapevine St Bldg A Jurupa Valley (91752) *(P-6941)*

SCI, Pomona *Also Called: Structural Composites Inds LLC (P-6160)*

SCI, El Monte *Also Called: S C I Industries Inc (P-9455)*

SCI, North Hollywood *Also Called: Pierce Brothers (P-15489)*

SCI-Pharm, Pomona *Also Called: Scientific Pharmaceuticals Inc (P-10766)*

SCI-Tech Glassblowing Inc .... E...... 805 523-9790
5555 Tech Cir Moorpark (93021) *(P-5329)*

Scico, Irvine *Also Called: Santa Catalina Island Company (P-11730)*

Scicon Technologies Corp (PA) .... E...... 661 295-8630
27525 Newhall Ranch Rd Ste 2 Valencia (91355) *(P-19687)*

Science Applications Intl Corp .... A...... 858 826-3061
4015 Hancock St San Diego (92110) *(P-16468)*

Science Applications Intl Corp .... D....... 703 676-4300
4065 Hancock St San Diego (92110) *(P-16596)*

Science of Skincare LLC .... D....... 818 254-7961
3333 N San Fernando Blvd Burbank (91504) *(P-13067)*

Sciencell Research Labs Inc .... E...... 760 602-8549
1610 Faraday Ave Carlsbad (92008) *(P-19942)*

Scientfic Applctons RES Assoc (PA) .... D....... 714 224-4410
6300 Gateway Dr Cypress (90630) *(P-8212)*

Scientific Cutting Tools Inc .... E...... 805 584-9495
220 W Los Angeles Ave Simi Valley (93065) *(P-7130)*

Scientific Drilling Intl Inc .... E...... 661 831-0636
31101 Coberly Rd Shafter (93263) *(P-288)*

Scientific Pharmaceuticals Inc .... E...... 909 595-9922
3221 Producer Way Pomona (91768) *(P-10766)*

Scientific-Atlanta LLC .... E...... 619 679-6000
13112 Evening Creek Dr S San Diego (92128) *(P-10069)*

Sciforma Corporation .... E...... 408 899-0398
600 B St Ste 300 San Diego (92101) *(P-16109)*

Scilex Pharmaceuticals Inc (HQ).................................F...... 949 441-2270
4955 Directors Pl Ste 100 San Diego (92121) *(P-16923)*

Scion Lending, Santa Ana *Also Called: Home Mrtg Aliance Corp Hmac (P-14327)*

Scisorek & Son Flavors Inc ....E...... 714 524-0550
2951 Enterprise St Brea (92821) *(P-1782)*

SCLARC, Los Angeles *Also Called: South Cntl Los Angles Rgnal CT (P-19342)*

SCMG, San Diego *Also Called: Sharp Community Medical Group (P-19403)*

Scmh, Whittier *Also Called: Southern California Material Handling Inc (P-12823)*

Scope, San Diego *Also Called: Scope Orthtics Prosthetics Inc (P-14147)*

Scope City (PA)...E...... 805 522-6646
2978 Topaz Ave Simi Valley (93063) *(P-10338)*

Scope Orthtics Prosthetics Inc (DH)........................ E...... 858 292-7448
7720 Cardinal Ct San Diego (92123) *(P-14147)*

Scope Packaging Inc ....D...... 714 998-4411
13400 Nelson Ave City Of Industry (91746) *(P-3128)*

Scopely Inc (DH)...C...... 323 400-6618
3530 Hayden Ave Ste A Culver City (90232) *(P-16375)*

Score Sports, Wilmington *Also Called: American Soccer Company Inc (P-13929)*

Scorelate Inc ....E...... 818 602-9176
91301 Fairview Pl Ste 2 Agoura Hills (91301) *(P-16376)*

Scorpion Design LLC (PA).......................................A...... 661 702-0100
27750 Entertainment Dr Valencia (91355) *(P-20234)*

Scosche Industries Inc ....C...... 805 486-4450
1550 Pacific Ave Oxnard (93033) *(P-8434)*

Scott A Humphreys Inc (PA).....................................E...... 805 581-2971
4600 Industrial St Simi Valley (93063) *(P-6311)*

Scott Craft Co, Cudahy *Also Called: Merry An Cejka (P-7928)*

Scott Engineering Inc ....D...... 909 594-9637
5051 Edison Ave Chino (91710) *(P-8213)*

Scott Manufacturing Solutions, Chino *Also Called: Scott Engineering Inc (P-8213)*

Scott Turbon Mixer Inc ....E...... 760 246-3430
9351 Industrial Way Adelanto (92301) *(P-7215)*

Scottel Voice & Data Inc ....C...... 310 737-7300
6100 Center Dr Ste 720 Los Angeles (90045) *(P-17073)*

Scottex Inc ....E...... 310 516-1411
12828 S Broadway Los Angeles (90061) *(P-2557)*

Scotts Company LLC ....E...... 661 387-9555
742 Industrial Way Shafter (93263) *(P-4542)*

Scotts Temecula Operations LLC (DH)...................... E...... 951 719-1700
42375 Remington Ave Temecula (92590) *(P-6921)*

Scotts- Hyponex, Jurupa Valley *Also Called: Hyponex Corporation (P-4540)*

SCR Molding Inc ....F...... 951 736-5490
2340 Pomona Rd Corona (92878) *(P-5201)*

Scrape Certified Welding Inc ....E...... 760 728-1308
2525 Old Highway 395 Fallbrook (92028) *(P-6074)*

Screamline Investment Corp ....C...... 323 201-0114
2130 S Tubeway Ave Commerce (90040) *(P-11731)*

Screen Actors Guild - American ....D...... 818 954-9400
3601 W Olive Ave Fl 2 Burbank (91505) *(P-14550)*

Screen Actors Guild-Producers, Burbank *Also Called: Screen Actors Guild - American (P-14550)*

Screening Systems Inc (PA)....................................E...... 949 855-1751
36 Blackbird Ln Aliso Viejo (92656) *(P-10286)*

Screenworks LLC ....A..... 951 279-8877
1900 Compton Ave Ste 101 Corona (92881) *(P-15673)*

Screenworks Nep, Corona *Also Called: Screenworks LLC (P-15673)*

Screwmatic Inc ....D...... 626 334-7831
925 W 1st St Azusa (91702) *(P-8018)*

Scribeamerica LLC ....B...... 877 819-5900
840 Apollo St Ste 231 El Segundo (90245) *(P-18803)*

Scribemd LLC ....D...... 714 543-8911
1310 W Stewart Dr Ste 212 Orange (92868) *(P-17761)*

Scripps Clinic ....C...... 858 794-1250
12395 El Camino Real Ste 112 San Diego (92130) *(P-18424)*

Scripps Clinic Med Group Inc ....C...... 858 554-9000
12395 El Camino Real Ste 112 San Diego (92130) *(P-20091)*

Scripps Green Hospital, La Jolla *Also Called: Scripps Health (P-18430)*

Scripps Health (PA)..A...... 800 727-4777
10140 Campus Point Dr San Diego (92121) *(P-18425)*

Scripps Health ....C...... 619 294-8111
4077 5th Ave San Diego (92103) *(P-18426)*

Scripps Health ....C...... 858 271-9770
15004 Innovation Dr San Diego (92128) *(P-18427)*

Scripps Health ....C...... 760 753-6501
354 Santa Fe Dr Encinitas (92024) *(P-18428)*

Scripps Health ....D...... 619 691-7000
435 H St Chula Vista (91910) *(P-18429)*

Scripps Health ....B...... 858 455-9100
10666 N Torrey Pines Rd La Jolla (92037) *(P-18430)*

Scripps Health ....D...... 619 294-8111
4077 5th Ave San Diego (92103) *(P-18431)*

Scripps Health ....B...... 858 626-6150
9888 Genesee Ave La Jolla (92037) *(P-18432)*

Scripps Health, La Jolla *Also Called: Scripps Mmral-Ximed Med Ctr LP (P-18434)*

Scripps Laboratories ....E...... 858 546-5800
6838 Flanders Dr San Diego (92121) *(P-4330)*

Scripps Mem Hosp - Encinatas, Encinitas *Also Called: Scripps Health (P-18428)*

Scripps Mem Hospital-La Jolla, La Jolla *Also Called: Scripps Health (P-18432)*

Scripps Mercy Hospital ....D...... 619 294-8111
4077 5th Ave # Mer35 San Diego (92103) *(P-18433)*

Scripps Mercy Hospital, San Diego *Also Called: Scripps Health (P-18426)*

Scripps Mercy Hospital, San Diego *Also Called: Scripps Health (P-18431)*

Scripps Mercy Hospitals, Chula Vista *Also Called: Scripps Health (P-18429)*

Scripps Mmral-Ximed Med Ctr LP ....D...... 858 882-8350
9850 Genesee Ave Ste 900 La Jolla (92037) *(P-18434)*

Scripps Rancho Bernardo, San Diego *Also Called: Scripps Health (P-18427)*

Scripps Research Institute (PA)...............................D...... 858 784-1000
10550 N Torrey Pines Rd La Jolla (92037) *(P-19943)*

Scripps Research Institute ....D...... 858 242-1000
11119 N Torrey Pines Rd Ste 100 La Jolla (92037) *(P-19944)*

Scripto-Tokai Corporation (HQ).................................D...... 909 930-5000
2055 S Haven Ave Ontario (91761) *(P-11278)*

Scs Engineers, Long Beach *Also Called: Stearns Conrad and Schmidt Consulting Engineers Inc (P-19696)*

Scully Leather Wear, Oxnard *Also Called: Scully Sportswear Inc (P-2433)*

Scully Sportswear Inc (PA).....................................D...... 805 483-6339
1701 Pacific Ave Oxnard (93033) *(P-2433)*

Scw Contracting Corporation ....D...... 760 728-1308
2525 Old Highway 395 Fallbrook (92028) *(P-689)*

SD Electric Sign, El Cajon *Also Called: San Diego Electric Sign Inc (P-11154)*

SD&a Teleservices Inc (HQ).....................................B
5757 W Century Blvd Ste 300 Los Angeles (90045) *(P-16924)*

SDC Technologies Inc (HQ).......................................E...... 714 939-8300
45 Parker Ste 100 Irvine (92618) *(P-6735)*

SDCCU, San Diego *Also Called: San Diego County Credit Union (P-14236)*

Sdcda ....C...... 619 459-9632
2125 Park Blvd San Diego (92101) *(P-18938)*

Sdcraa, San Diego *Also Called: San Dego Cnty Rgnal Arprt Auth (P-11706)*

Sdg Enterprises ....D...... 805 777-7978
822 Hampshire Rd Ste H Westlake Village (91361) *(P-820)*

SDG&e, Escondido *Also Called: San Diego Gas & Electric Co (P-12045)*

SDG&e, San Diego *Also Called: San Diego Gas & Electric Co (P-12046)*

SDG&e, San Diego *Also Called: San Diego Gas & Electric Co (P-12047)*

SDG&e, San Diego *Also Called: San Diego Gas & Electric Co (P-12048)*

SDG&e, Monterey Park *Also Called: San Diego Gas & Electric Co (P-12049)*

SDG&e, Moreno Valley *Also Called: San Diego Gas & Electric Co (P-12082)*

SDG&E, San Diego *Also Called: San Diego Gas & Electric Co (P-12106)*

SDG&e, Chula Vista *Also Called: San Diego Gas & Electric Co (P-12113)*

SDG&ec, San Diego *Also Called: San Diego Gas & Electric Co (P-12043)*

Sdi, Simi Valley *Also Called: Special Devices Incorporated (P-9461)*

Sdi LLC ....E...... 949 351-1866
21 Morgan Ste 150 Irvine (92618) *(P-8019)*

Sdi Industries Inc (DH)..C...... 818 890-6002
24307 Magic Mountain Pkwy # 443 Valencia (91355) *(P-6977)*

SDI Media USA Inc (HQ)..D...... 310 388-8800
6060 Center Dr Ste 100 Los Angeles (90045) *(P-17219)*

SDS Industries Inc ....C...... 818 492-3500
10241 Norris Ave Pacoima (91331) *(P-6122)*

SE Scher Corporation ....A...... 858 546-8300
2525 Camino Del Rio S Ste 200 San Diego (92108) *(P-15892)*

Employee Codes: A=Over 500 employees, B=251-500
C=101-250, D=51-100, E=20-50, F=10-19, G=1-9

2024 Southern California
Business Directory and Buyers Guide

© Mergent Inc. 1-800-342-5647

1257

Sea Breeze Financial Svcs Inc ....C....... 949 223-9700
  18191 Von Karman Ave Ste 150 Irvine (92612) *(P-14349)*

Sea Breeze Health Care Inc ....C....... 714 847-9671
  7781 Garfield Ave Huntington Beach (92648) *(P-18049)*

Sea Breeze Mortgage Services, Irvine *Also Called: Sea Breeze Financial Svcs Inc (P-14349)*

Sea Electric LLC ....E....... 424 376-3660
  436 Alaska Ave Torrance (90503) *(P-8156)*

Sea Magazine, Fountain Valley *Also Called: Duncan McIntosh Company Inc (P-3357)*

Sea Recovery Corporation ....E....... 310 608-5600
  19610 S Rancho Way Compton (90220) *(P-8020)*

Sea Shield Marine Products ....E....... 909 594-2507
  20832 Currier Rd Walnut (91789) *(P-5768)*

Seabiscuit Motorsports Inc ....E....... 714 898-9763
  10800 Valley View St Cypress (90630) *(P-7706)*

Seaboard Envelope Co Inc ....E....... 626 960-4559
  15601 Cypress Ave Irwindale (91706) *(P-3213)*

Seaborn Canvas ....E....... 310 519-1208
  435 N Harbor Blvd Ste B1 San Pedro (90731) *(P-2558)*

Seacatch Seafoods, El Monte *Also Called: Atlantis Seafood LLC (P-1799)*

Seachrome, Long Beach *Also Called: Seachrome Corporation (P-5960)*

Seachrome Corporation ....C....... 310 427-8010
  1906 E Dominguez St Long Beach (90810) *(P-5960)*

Seaco Technologies Inc ....E....... 661 326-1522
  280 El Cerrito Dr Bakersfield (93305) *(P-7683)*

Seacoast Cmmerce Banc Holdings ....C....... 858 432-7000
  11939 Rancho Bernardo Rd San Diego (92128) *(P-14206)*

Seacomp Inc (PA) ....C....... 760 918-6722
  1525 Faraday Ave Carlsbad (92008) *(P-8214)*

Seafood Family Partners LP ....C....... 310 761-1500
  1123 Cory Ave West Hollywood (90069) *(P-13286)*

Seah Steel America, Irvine *Also Called: Pusan Pipe America Inc (P-12565)*

Seal & Packing Supply, Bakersfield *Also Called: Shar-Craft Inc (P-12879)*

Seal Electric Inc ....C....... 619 449-7323
  1162 Greenfield Dr El Cajon (92021) *(P-933)*

Seal For Life Industries LLC (PA) ....E....... 619 671-0932
  2290 Enrico Fermi Dr Ste 22 San Diego (92154) *(P-4580)*

Seal Methods Inc (PA) ....D....... 562 944-0291
  11915 Shoemaker Ave Santa Fe Springs (90670) *(P-3175)*

Seal Science Inc (HQ) ....D....... 949 253-3130
  3701 E Conant St Long Beach (90808) *(P-4743)*

Sealed Air Corporation ....E....... 619 421-9003
  2311 Boswell Rd Ste 8 Chula Vista (91914) *(P-4903)*

Sealed Air Corporation ....C....... 909 594-1791
  19440 Arenth Ave City Of Industry (91748) *(P-4904)*

Sealing Corporation ....E....... 818 765-7327
  7353 Greenbush Ave # B North Hollywood (91605) *(P-4744)*

Searing Industries, Rancho Cucamonga *Also Called: Searing Industries Inc (P-5601)*

Searing Industries Inc ....C....... 909 948-3030
  8901 Arrow Rte Rancho Cucamonga (91730) *(P-5601)*

Sears, West Covina *Also Called: Sears Home Imprv Pdts Inc (P-453)*

Sears, Long Beach *Also Called: Sears Home Imprv Pdts Inc (P-454)*

Sears, Temple City *Also Called: Sears Home Imprv Pdts Inc (P-455)*

Sears, Ontario *Also Called: Innovel Solutions Inc (P-11773)*

Sears, San Diego *Also Called: Innovel Solutions Inc (P-11774)*

Sears Home Imprv Pdts Inc ....C....... 626 671-1892
  730 S Orange Ave West Covina (91790) *(P-453)*

Sears Home Imprv Pdts Inc ....C....... 562 485-4904
  2900 N Bellflower Blvd Long Beach (90815) *(P-454)*

Sears Home Imprv Pdts Inc ....C....... 626 988-9134
  5665 Rosemead Blvd Temple City (91780) *(P-455)*

Season Produce Co Inc ....B....... 213 689-0008
  1601 E Olympic Blvd Ste 315 Los Angeles (90021) *(P-13339)*

Seaspace Corporation ....E....... 858 746-1100
  9155 Brown Deer Rd San Diego (92121) *(P-8576)*

Seaspine Inc ....D....... 760 727-8399
  5770 Armada Dr Carlsbad (92008) *(P-10700)*

Seaspine Orthopedics Corp (HQ) ....E....... 866 942-8698
  5770 Armada Dr Carlsbad (92008) *(P-10701)*

Seating Component Mfg Inc ....E....... 714 693-3376
  3951 E Miraloma Ave Anaheim (92806) *(P-2873)*

Seating Concepts LLC ....E....... 619 491-3159
  4229 Ponderosa Ave Ste B San Diego (92123) *(P-2937)*

Seating Resource, Azusa *Also Called: Holguin & Holguin Inc (P-2927)*

Seattle Arprt Hospitality LLC ....D....... 310 476-6411
  170 N Church Ln Los Angeles (90049) *(P-15352)*

Seattle Tnnel Prtners A Jint V ....B....... 206 971-8701
  555 Anton Blvd Ste 1000 Costa Mesa (92626) *(P-456)*

Seaward Products Corp ....D....... 562 699-7997
  3721 Capitol Ave City Of Industry (90601) *(P-7623)*

Seaworld Global Logistics ....B....... 310 579-9164
  9350 Wilshire Blvd Ste 203 Beverly Hills (90212) *(P-11801)*

Seaworld Parks & Entrmt LLC ....D....... 619 226-3910
  1660 S Shores Rd San Diego (92109) *(P-17454)*

Seb, Chino *Also Called: Specilty Enzymes Btechnologies (P-4530)*

Sechrist Industries Inc ....A....... 714 579-8400
  4225 E La Palma Ave Anaheim (92807) *(P-10602)*

Seco Industries, Commerce *Also Called: Specialty Enterprises Co (P-4906)*

Secom, Gardena *Also Called: Secom International (P-16469)*

Secom International (PA) ....D....... 310 641-1290
  15905 S Broadway Gardena (90248) *(P-16469)*

Second Generation Inc ....D
  21650 Oxnard St Ste 500 Woodland Hills (91367) *(P-2369)*

Second Hrvest Fd Bnk Ornge CNT ....D....... 949 653-2900
  8014 Marine Way Irvine (92618) *(P-19138)*

Second Image National LLC (PA) ....C....... 800 229-7477
  170 E Arrow Hwy San Dimas (91773) *(P-15652)*

Second Spectrum Inc ....C....... 213 995-6860
  312 E 1st St Los Angeles (90012) *(P-16110)*

Second Street Corporation ....C....... 310 394-5454
  1111 2nd St Santa Monica (90403) *(P-15353)*

Sector9, San Diego *Also Called: Bravo Sports (P-10980)*

Sectran Armored Truck Service, Pico Rivera *Also Called: Sectran Security Incorporated (P-16678)*

Sectran Security Incorporated (PA) ....C....... 562 948-1446
  7633 Industry Ave Pico Rivera (90660) *(P-16678)*

Secura Key, Chatsworth *Also Called: Soundcraft Inc (P-9256)*

Secure Comm Systems Inc (HQ) ....C....... 714 547-1174
  1740 E Wilshire Ave Santa Ana (92705) *(P-8577)*

Secure Net Alliance ....D....... 818 848-4900
  601 S Glenoaks Blvd Ste 409 Burbank (91502) *(P-16679)*

Secure One Data Solutions LLC ....D....... 562 924-7056
  11090 Artesia Blvd Ste D Cerritos (90703) *(P-16515)*

Secure Technology Company ....E....... 714 991-6500
  2000 W Corporate Way Anaheim (92801) *(P-8729)*

Secure-Dmz, Irvine *Also Called: Eighteenth Meridian Inc (P-16021)*

Secureauth Corporation (PA) ....C....... 949 777-6959
  49 Discovery Irvine (92618) *(P-16111)*

Secured Funding Corporation ....A....... 714 689-6749
  2955 Red Hill Ave Costa Mesa (92626) *(P-14365)*

Securitas SEC Svcs USA Inc ....B....... 818 706-6800
  4330 Park Terrace Dr Westlake Village (91361) *(P-16680)*

Securitas Technology Corp ....D....... 858 812-7349
  7002 Convoy Ct San Diego (92111) *(P-16752)*

Securitech Security Svcs Inc ....C....... 213 387-5050
  2733 N San Fernando Rd Los Angeles (90065) *(P-16681)*

Security and Patrol Services, Fountain Valley *Also Called: Safeguard On Demand Inc (P-16677)*

Security Company, Burbank *Also Called: Secure Net Alliance (P-16679)*

Security Front Desk, Mc Kittrick *Also Called: Aera Energy Services Company (P-275)*

Security Indust Spcialists Inc ....A....... 323 924-9147
  477 N Oak St Inglewood (90302) *(P-16682)*

Security Indust Spcialists Inc (PA) ....C....... 310 215-5100
  6071 Bristol Pkwy Culver City (90230) *(P-16683)*

Security Metal Products Corp (DH) ....D....... 310 641-6690
  5678 Concours Ontario (91764) *(P-6123)*

Security Paving Company Inc (PA) ....D....... 818 362-9200
  3075 Townsgate Rd Ste 210 # 200 Westlake Village (91361) *(P-645)*

Security Services, Commerce *Also Called: American Security Force Inc (P-16723)*

Security Textile Corporation ....E....... 213 747-2673
  1457 E Washington Blvd Los Angeles (90021) *(P-2538)*

Securus Inc .... E
14284 Danielson St Poway (92064) *(P-6369)*

Secuto Music, Burbank *Also Called: Roundabout Entertainment Inc (P-17215)*

Sedenquist-Fraser Entps Inc .... E...... 562 924-5763
16730 Gridley Rd Cerritos (90703) *(P-9458)*

Sedgwick, Ontario *Also Called: Sedgwick CMS Holdings Inc (P-14629)*

Sedgwick CMS Holdings Inc .... C...... 909 477-5500
3633 Inland Empire Blvd Ontario (91764) *(P-14629)*

Seeds of Change Inc .... C...... 310 764-7700
31 Mountain Laurel Trabuco Canyon (92679) *(P-13490)*

Seektech, San Diego *Also Called: Seescan Inc (P-7147)*

Seeley Brothers, Brea *Also Called: Norcal Inc (P-1020)*

Seescan Inc (PA) .... C...... 858 244-3300
3855 Ruffin Rd San Diego (92123) *(P-7147)*

Sega Entertainment USA Inc .... A...... 310 217-9500
600 N Brand Blvd 5th Fl Glendale (91203) *(P-17446)*

Sega Holdings USA Inc .... A...... 415 701-6000
9737 Lurline Ave Chatsworth (91311) *(P-11279)*

Sega of America Inc .... B...... 747 477-3708
250 E Olive Ave Ste 200 Burbank (91502) *(P-12943)*

Sega of America Inc (DH) .... E...... 949 788-0455
140 Progress Ste 100 Irvine (92618) *(P-12944)*

Segway Inc .... C...... 603 222-6000
405 E Santa Clara St Ste 100 Arcadia (91006) *(P-9882)*

Sehanson Inc .... E...... 714 778-1900
2121 E Via Burton Anaheim (92806) *(P-9795)*

Seidner-Miller Inc .... C...... 909 305-2000
1949 Auto Centre Dr Glendora (91740) *(P-13823)*

Seiko Epson, Los Alamitos *Also Called: Epson America Inc (P-7527)*

Seirus Innovation, Poway *Also Called: Seirus Innovative ACC Inc (P-11024)*

Seirus Innovative ACC Inc .... D...... 858 513-1212
13975 Danielson St Poway (92064) *(P-11024)*

Seismic Software Inc (HQ) .... D...... 714 404-7069
12390 El Camino Real Ste 300 San Diego (92130) *(P-16377)*

Seiu Local 721 .... C...... 213 368-8660
1545 Wilshire Blvd Ste 100 Los Angeles (90017) *(P-19412)*

Sekai Electronics Inc (PA) .... E...... 949 783-5740
38 Waterworks Way Irvine (92618) *(P-8578)*

Sekisui America Corporation .... D...... 858 452-3198
6659 Top Gun St San Diego (92121) *(P-4292)*

Sela Healthcare Inc .... B...... 818 341-9800
20554 Roscoe Blvd Canoga Park (91306) *(P-18050)*

Sela Healthcare Inc (PA) .... C...... 909 985-1981
867 E 11th St Upland (91786) *(P-18051)*

Selane Products Inc (PA) .... D...... 818 998-7460
9129 Lurline Ave Chatsworth (91311) *(P-10767)*

Select Aircargo Services Inc .... D...... 310 851-8500
12801 S Figueroa St Los Angeles (90061) *(P-11802)*

Select Data, Anaheim *Also Called: Select Data Inc (P-16112)*

Select Data Inc .... C...... 714 577-1000
4175 E La Palma Ave Ste 205 Anaheim (92807) *(P-16112)*

Select Graphics .... E...... 714 537-5250
11931 Euclid St Garden Grove (92840) *(P-3685)*

Select Home Care .... D...... 805 777-3855
2393 Townsgate Rd Ste 100 Westlake Village (91361) *(P-18641)*

Select Home Warranty Ca Inc .... B...... 732 835-0110
222 W 6th St Ste 400 San Pedro (90731) *(P-14537)*

Select Personnel Services, Santa Barbara *Also Called: Select Temporaries LLC (P-15893)*

Select Staffing, Santa Barbara *Also Called: Eastern Staffing LLC (P-15840)*

Select Temporaries LLC (DH) .... D...... 805 882-2200
3820 State St Santa Barbara (93105) *(P-15893)*

Selectabed, Agoura Hills *Also Called: Relief-Mart Inc (P-14146)*

Selectforce, Irvine *Also Called: Accurate Background LLC (P-16524)*

Selectra Industries Corp .... D...... 323 581-8500
5166 Alcoa Ave Vernon (90058) *(P-2393)*

Self Esteem, Montebello *Also Called: All Access Apparel Inc (P-2273)*

Self Realization Fellowship, Los Angeles *Also Called: Self-Realization Fellowship Ch (P-19505)*

Self Serve Auto Dismantlers (PA) .... C...... 714 630-8901
3200 E Frontera St Anaheim (92806) *(P-12957)*

Self-Realization Fellowship Ch (PA) .... E...... 323 225-2471
3880 San Rafael Ave Los Angeles (90065) *(P-19505)*

Sellers Optical Inc .... D...... 949 631-6800
320 Kalmus Dr Costa Mesa (92626) *(P-10339)*

Selman Chevrolet Company .... C...... 714 633-3521
1800 E Chapman Ave Orange (92867) *(P-13824)*

Seloah Gourmet Food, Tustin *Also Called: Country House (P-1536)*

Seltzer Cplan McMhon Vtek A La (PA) .... C...... 619 685-3003
750 B St Ste 2100 San Diego (92101) *(P-18939)*

Sema Construction Inc .... D...... 949 470-0500
320 Goddard Ste 150 Irvine (92618) *(P-646)*

Semco .... E...... 909 799-9666
1495 S Gage St San Bernardino (92408) *(P-10395)*

Semco, Vista *Also Called: Systems Engineering & MGT Co (P-19698)*

Semicoa, Costa Mesa *Also Called: Falkor Partners LLC (P-8796)*

Semicoa Corporation .... D...... 714 979-1900
333 Mccormick Ave Costa Mesa (92626) *(P-8884)*

Semiconductor Process Eqp LLC .... E...... 661 257-0934
27963 Franklin Pkwy Valencia (91355) *(P-8885)*

Semiconductorstore.com, El Segundo *Also Called: Symmetry Electronics LLC (P-8903)*

Semihandmade LLC .... E...... 818 561-4350
3017 W Burbank Blvd Burbank (91505) *(P-2632)*

Seminis, Oxnard *Also Called: Seminis Vegetable Seeds Inc (P-13491)*

Seminis Inc (DH) .... B...... 805 485-7317
2700 Camino Del Sol Oxnard (93030) *(P-19874)*

Seminis Vegetable Seeds Inc (DH) .... A...... 855 733-3834
2700 Camino Del Sol Oxnard (93030) *(P-13491)*

Sempra (PA) .... A...... 619 696-2000
488 8th Ave San Diego (92101) *(P-12108)*

Sempra Energy 619 696-2000
9305 Lightwave Ave San Diego (92123) *(P-12050)*

Sempra Energy, San Diego *Also Called: Sempra Energy (P-12050)*

Sempra Energy Global Entps 619 696-2000
101 Ash St San Diego (92101) *(P-12051)*

Sempra Energy International .... A...... 619 696-2000
101 Ash St San Diego (92101) *(P-12052)*

Sempra Energy Utilities, San Diego *Also Called: Sempra Energy International (P-12052)*

Sempra Global (HQ) .... D...... 619 696-2000
488 8th Ave San Diego (92101) *(P-8111)*

Sempra LNG International LLC .... D...... 661 399-2077
488 8th Ave San Diego (92101) *(P-690)*

Semtech, Camarillo *Also Called: Semtech Corporation (P-8886)*

Semtech Corporation (PA) .... C...... 805 498-2111
200 Flynn Rd Camarillo (93012) *(P-8886)*

Semtech San Diego Corporation .... D...... 858 695-1808
10021 Willow Creek Rd San Diego (92131) *(P-8887)*

Semtek Innvtive Solutions Corp .... E...... 858 436-2270
12777 High Bluff Dr Ste 225 San Diego (92130) *(P-7570)*

Sendx Medical Inc .... C...... 760 930-6300
1945 Palomar Oaks Way Ste 100 Carlsbad (92011) *(P-10603)*

Seneca Family of Agencies .... C...... 714 881-8600
1801 Park Court Pl Bldg H Santa Ana (92701) *(P-14630)*

Seneca Family of Agencies .... C...... 805 278-0355
2130 N Ventura Rd Oxnard (93036) *(P-19139)*

Senegence International, Foothill Ranch *Also Called: Sgii Inc (P-13068)*

Senga Engineering Inc .... E...... 714 549-8011
1525 E Warner Ave Santa Ana (92705) *(P-8021)*

Senior Aerospace Jet Pdts Corp .... D...... 858 278-8400
9150 Balboa Ave San Diego (92123) *(P-8022)*

Senior Aerospace Jet Products, San Diego *Also Called: Senior Operations LLC (P-9580)*

Senior Care (PA) .... A...... 562 989-5100
3800 Kilroy Airport Way Long Beach (90806) *(P-14495)*

Senior Health and Activity Ctr, Los Angeles *Also Called: Altamed Health Services Corp (P-17590)*

Senior Nutrition Program, Los Angeles *Also Called: Jewish Family Svc Los Angeles (P-19101)*

Senior Operations LLC (HQ) .... C...... 858 278-8400
9106 Balboa Ave San Diego (92123) *(P-9580)*

Senior Operations LLC .... D...... 909 627-2723
790 Greenfield Dr El Cajon (92021) *(P-8023)*

Employee Codes: A=Over 500 employees, B=251-500
C=101-250, D=51-100, E=20-50, F=10-19, G=1-9

2024 Southern California
Business Directory and Buyers Guide

© Mergent Inc. 1-800-342-5647
1259

ALPHABETIC

Senior Operations LLC .... D 858 278-8400
  9106 Balboa Ave San Diego (92123) *(P-8024)*

Senior Operations LLC .... B 818 260-2900
  2980 N San Fernando Blvd Burbank (91504) *(P-9796)*

Senior Resource Group LLC .... C 858 519-0890
  850 Del Mar Downs Rd Apt 338 Solana Beach (92075) *(P-14730)*

Senju Usa Inc .... E 818 719-7190
  21515 Hawthorne Blvd Torrance (90503) *(P-4230)*

Sensata Technologies Inc .... D 805 716-0322
  1461 Lawrence Dr Thousand Oaks (91320) *(P-16597)*

Sensei Wellness Holdings Inc .... D 602 499-9862
  1119 Colorado Ave Ste 18 Santa Monica (90401) *(P-18804)*

Sensemetrics Inc .... E 619 738-8300
  750 B St Ste 1630 San Diego (92101) *(P-8888)*

Sensor Systems Inc .... B 818 341-5366
  8929 Fullbright Ave Chatsworth (91311) *(P-10070)*

Sensorex Corporation .... D 714 895-4344
  11751 Markon Dr Garden Grove (92841) *(P-10161)*

Sensoscientific LLC .... E 800 279-3101
  685 Cochran St Ste 200 Simi Valley (93065) *(P-10162)*

Sente Inc .... E 800 205-6774
  2310 Camino Vida Roble Ste 101 Carlsbad (92011) *(P-17762)*

Sentek Consulting Inc .... C 619 543-9550
  2811 Nimitz Blvd Ste G San Diego (92106) *(P-16598)*

Sentek Global, San Diego *Also Called: Sentek Consulting Inc (P-16598)*

Sentinel Monitoring Corp (HQ) .... **D 949 453-1550**
  220 Technology Dr Ste 200 Irvine (92618) *(P-16753)*

Sentinel Offender Services LLC (PA) .... **D 949 453-1550**
  1290 N Hancock St Ste 103 Anaheim (92807) *(P-16754)*

Sentinel Peak Rsources Cal LLC .... D 323 298-2200
  5640 S Fairfax Ave Los Angeles (90056) *(P-319)*

Sentinel Peak Rsources Cal LLC .... D 661 395-5214
  1200 Discovery Dr Ste 100 Bakersfield (93309) *(P-320)*

Sentry Life Insurance Company .... C 661 274-4018
  4720 Aliso Way Oceanside (92057) *(P-14631)*

Sentynl Therapeutics Inc .... E 888 227-8725
  420 Stevens Ave Ste 200 Solana Beach (92075) *(P-4231)*

Sep Group Inc .... E 858 876-4621
  11374 Turtleback Ln San Diego (92127) *(P-19688)*

Separation Engineering Inc .... E 760 489-0101
  931 S Andreasen Dr Ste A Escondido (92029) *(P-7409)*

Sepe Inc .... E 714 241-7373
  245 Fischer Ave Ste C4 Costa Mesa (92626) *(P-7449)*

Sephora Co LLC (PA) .... **E 760 798-7654**
  6103 Obispo Ave Long Beach (90805) *(P-4453)*

Sequenom Inc (HQ) .... **D 858 202-9000**
  3595 John Hopkins Ct San Diego (92121) *(P-19875)*

Sequenom Ctr For Mlclar Mdcine .... B 858 202-9051
  3595 John Hopkins Ct San Diego (92121) *(P-18564)*

Sequenom Laboratories, San Diego *Also Called: Sequenom Ctr For Mlclar Mdcine (P-18564)*

Sequent Medical Inc .... D 949 830-9600
  35 Enterprise Aliso Viejo (92656) *(P-10604)*

Sequoia Exploration Inc .... E 661 303-0564
  5913 Sundale Ave Bakersfield (93309) *(P-265)*

Serampore Inds Private Ltd Inc .... F 877 921-6111
  8333 Almeria Ave Fontana (92335) *(P-8025)*

Serco Inc .... C 858 569-8979
  9350 Waxie Way Ste 400 San Diego (92123) *(P-19689)*

Serco Mold Inc (PA) .... **E 626 331-0517**
  2009 Wright Ave La Verne (91750) *(P-5202)*

Sercomp LLC (PA) .... **D 805 299-0020**
  5401 Tech Cir Ste 200 Moorpark (93021) *(P-11062)*

Serfin Funds Transfer (PA) .... **D 626 457-3070**
  1000 S Fremont Ave Bldg A-O Alhambra (91803) *(P-14264)*

Serpac Electronic Enclosures, La Verne *Also Called: Serco Mold Inc (P-5202)*

Serra Community Med Clinic Inc .... C 818 768-3000
  9375 San Fernando Rd Sun Valley (91352) *(P-17763)*

Serra Community Medical Clinic, Sun Valley *Also Called: Serra Community Med Clinic Inc (P-17763)*

Serra Laser and Waterjet Inc .... E 714 680-6211
  1740 N Orangethorpe Park Anaheim (92801) *(P-9254)*

Serra Manufacturing Corp (PA) .... **D 310 537-4560**
  3039 E Las Hermanas St Compton (90221) *(P-6554)*

Serrano Industries Inc .... E 562 777-8180
  9922 Tabor Pl Santa Fe Springs (90670) *(P-8026)*

Serta Simmons Bedding LLC .... E 951 807-8467
  23700 Cactus Ave Moreno Valley (92553) *(P-2858)*

Serv-Rite Meat Company Inc .... D 323 227-1911
  2515 N San Fernando Rd Los Angeles (90065) *(P-1204)*

Servers Direct LLC .... C 800 576-7931
  20480 Business Pkwy Walnut (91789) *(P-12437)*

Servexo .... B 323 527-9994
  1411 W 190th St Ste 475 Gardena (90248) *(P-16684)*

Servexo Protective Service, Gardena *Also Called: Servexo (P-16684)*

Servi-Tek Inc .... B 858 638-7735
  8765 Sparren Way San Diego (92129) *(P-15747)*

Servi-Tek Janitorial Services, San Diego *Also Called: Servi-Tek Inc (P-15747)*

Service Chemicals, Carson *Also Called: East West Enterprises (P-5614)*

Service Genius Los Angeles Inc .... D 818 200-3379
  8925 Fullbright Ave Chatsworth (91311) *(P-821)*

Service Master By ARS, Gardena *Also Called: Disaster Rstrtion Prfssnals In (P-429)*

ServiceMaster By Best Pros Inc .... D 951 515-9051
  6474 Western Ave Riverside (92505) *(P-15748)*

Servicon Systems Inc .... A 310 970-0700
  3329 Jack Northrop Ave Hawthorne (90250) *(P-1086)*

Servitek Electric Inc .... E 626 227-1650
  618 Brea Canyon Rd Ste J City Of Industry (91789) *(P-12053)*

Servitek Electric Hawaii, City Of Industry *Also Called: Servitek Electric Inc (P-12053)*

SERVPRO Encino/Sherman Oaks, Encino *Also Called: One Silver Serve LLC (P-15730)*

SERVPRO Jeffries Global, Beverly Hills *Also Called: Jeffries Global Inc (P-1164)*

SERVPRO of Beverly Hills, Beverly Hills *Also Called: D&A Endeavors Inc (P-1151)*

Sesa Inc (PA) .... **E 714 779-9700**
  20391 Via Guadalupe Yorba Linda (92887) *(P-15674)*

Sessa Manufacturing & Welding .... E 805 644-2284
  2932 Golf Course Dr Ventura (93003) *(P-6555)*

Setarehshenas Dental Corp .... C 805 583-5700
  1197 E Los Angeles Ave Ste E Simi Valley (93065) *(P-17847)*

Setco LLC .... C: 812 424-2904
  4875 E Hunter Ave Anaheim (92807) *(P-5203)*

Sethi Management Inc .... C 760 692-5288
  6156 Innovation Way Carlsbad (92009) *(P-20092)*

Setschedule LLC .... C 888 222-0011
  100 Spectrum Center Dr Fl 9 Irvine (92618) *(P-16113)*

Settlers Jerky Inc .... E 909 444-3999
  307 Paseo Sonrisa Walnut (91789) *(P-1235)*

Sev Lasers, Burbank *Also Called: Petrosian Esthetic Entps LLC (P-15485)*

Seven California Med Diagnstc, Glendale *Also Called: Advanced Prof Imging Med Group (P-17582)*

Seven Licensing Company LLC .... C 323 780-8250
  801 S Figueroa St Ste 2500 Los Angeles (90017) *(P-13148)*

Seven Oaks Country Club .... C 661 664-6404
  2000 Grand Lakes Ave Bakersfield (93311) *(P-17522)*

Seven One Inc (PA) .... **D 818 904-3435**
  21540 Prairie St Ste E Chatsworth (91311) *(P-16925)*

Seven Sisters of New Orleans, Whittier *Also Called: Indio Products Inc (P-12527)*

Seven7 Brands, Los Angeles *Also Called: Seven Licensing Company LLC (P-13148)*

Severson Group LLC .... C 760 550-9976
  950 Boardwalk Ste 202 San Marcos (92078) *(P-14035)*

Severson Group, The, San Marcos *Also Called: Severson Group LLC (P-14035)*

Seville Classics Inc (PA) .... **C 310 533-3800**
  19401 Harborgate Way Torrance (90501) *(P-12733)*

Sew What Inc .... E 310 639-6000
  1978 E Gladwick St Compton (90220) *(P-2463)*

Sewer Rodding Equipment Co (PA) .... **E 310 301-9009**
  3217 Carter Ave Marina Del Rey (90292) *(P-7684)*

Sewing Collection Inc .... D 323 264-2223
  3113 E 26th St Vernon (90058) *(P-4745)*

Sextant Wines, Paso Robles *Also Called: Rbz Vineyards LLC (P-1655)*

Sexual Recovery Institute Inc .... B 310 360-0130
  1964 Westwood Blvd Ste 400 Los Angeles (90025) *(P-19140)*

Sexy Hair Concepts LLC .... E 818 435-0800
  21551 Prairie St Chatsworth (91311) *(P-14148)*

Mergent email: customerrelations@mergent.com
1260

2024 Southern California
Business Directory and Buyers Guide

(P-0000) Products & Services Section entry number
(PA)=Parent Co (HQ)=Headquarters (DH)=Div Headquarters

Seyfarth Shaw LLP .... C...... 310 277-7200
2029 Century Park E Ste 3300 Los Angeles (90002) *(P-18940)*

Seymour Duncan, Santa Barbara *Also Called: Duncan Carter Corporation (P-10922)*

Seymour Levinger & Co .... E...... 909 673-9800
1455 Citrus St Riverside (92507) *(P-9459)*

SF Broadcasting Wisconsin Inc .... C...... 310 586-2410
2425 Olympic Blvd Santa Monica (90404) *(P-11963)*

Sfadia Inc .... D...... 323 622-1930
8485 Artesia Blvd Ste A Buena Park (90621) *(P-934)*

Sfc, Perris *Also Called: Stretch Forming Corporation (P-6326)*

SFE, Santa Fe Springs *Also Called: Santa Fe Enterprises Inc (P-7096)*

SFMC, Lynwood *Also Called: St Francis Medical Center (P-18460)*

Sfn Group Inc .... A...... 949 727-8500
114 Pacifica Ste 210 Irvine (92618) *(P-15941)*

Sfn Group Inc .... A...... 858 458-9200
4660 La Jolla Village Dr Ste 910 San Diego (92122) *(P-15942)*

Sfpp LP (DH) .... C...... **714 560-4400**
1100 W Town And Country Rd Ste 600 Orange (92868) *(P-11710)*

Sfs, Brea *Also Called: Kirkhill Inc (P-9731)*

SGB Better Baking Co LLC .... D...... 818 787-9992
14528 Blythe St Van Nuys (91402) *(P-1492)*

SGB Bubbles Baking Co LLC .... D...... 818 786-1700
15215 Keswick St Van Nuys (91405) *(P-1493)*

SGB Enterprises Inc .... E...... 661 294-8306
24844 Anza Dr Ste A Valencia (91355) *(P-7499)*

Sggh LLC .... A...... 805 435-1255
15301 Ventura Blvd Ste 400 Sherman Oaks (91403) *(P-12617)*

Sgii Inc (PA) .... C...... 949 521-6161
19651 Alter Foothill Ranch (92610) *(P-13068)*

Sgl Composites Inc (DH) .... D...... **424 329-5250**
1551 W 139th St Gardena (90249) *(P-3138)*

Sgl Technic LLC (DH) .... E...... 661 257-0500
28176 Avenue Stanford Valencia (91355) *(P-5551)*

Sgps Inc .... D...... 310 538-4175
15823 S Main St Gardena (90248) *(P-11280)*

Sgt Dresser-Rand, Chula Vista *Also Called: Curtiss-Wright Corporation (P-17122)*

Shade Structures, Orange *Also Called: Shade Structures Inc (P-6390)*

Shade Structures Inc .... D...... 714 427-6980
115 E 2nd St Ste 101 Tustin (92780) *(P-6312)*

Shade Structures Inc .... E...... 714 427-6980
1085 N Main St Ste C Orange (92867) *(P-6390)*

Shademaster Products, Santee *Also Called: R V Best Inc (P-5170)*

Shadow Holdings LLC .... C...... 661 252-3807
26421 Ruether Ave Santa Clarita (91350) *(P-4454)*

Shadow Holdings LLC (HQ) .... B...... 661 252-3807
26455 Ruether Ave Santa Clarita (91350) *(P-4455)*

Shadow Mtn Rsort Rcquet CLB Tn, Palm Desert *Also Called: Destination Residences LLC (P-15128)*

Shady Canyon Golf Club Inc .... C...... 949 856-7000
100 Shady Canyon Dr Irvine (92603) *(P-17523)*

Shaka Wear, Los Angeles *Also Called: Gino Corporation (P-2158)*

Shamir, San Diego *Also Called: Shamir Insight Inc (P-5330)*

Shamir Insight Inc .... D...... 858 514-8330
9938 Via Pasar San Diego (92126) *(P-5330)*

Shamrock Capital Advisors LLC .... B...... 310 974-6600
1100 Glendon Ave Ste 1600 Los Angeles (90024) *(P-14972)*

Shamrock Companies, The, Anaheim *Also Called: Shamrock Supply Company Inc (P-12734)*

Shamrock Foods Company .... A...... 951 685-6314
12400 Riverside Dr Eastvale (91752) *(P-13394)*

Shamrock Supply Company Inc (PA) .... D...... **714 575-1800**
3366 E La Palma Ave Anaheim (92806) *(P-12734)*

Shanghai Anc Electronic Tech, Moorpark *Also Called: Anc Technology Inc (P-8647)*

Shani Darden Skincare Inc .... E...... 310 745-3150
1800 Century Park E Ste 400 Los Angeles (90067) *(P-4456)*

Shapell Industries .... E...... 323 655-7330
1990 S Bundy Dr Ste 500 Los Angeles (90025) *(P-11281)*

Shapell Industries LLC (HQ) .... D...... **323 655-7330**
8383 Wilshire Blvd Ste 700 Beverly Hills (90211) *(P-14910)*

Shapiro-Gilman-Shandler Co .... C...... 213 593-1200
739 Decatur St Los Angeles (90021) *(P-13340)*

Shapp International Trdg Inc .... C...... 818 348-3000
6000 Reseda Blvd Tarzana (91356) *(P-12343)*

Shapp Internatioonal, Tarzana *Also Called: Shapp International Trdg Inc (P-12343)*

Shar-Craft Inc (PA) .... E...... **661 324-4985**
1103 33rd St Bakersfield (93301) *(P-12879)*

Shara-Tex Inc .... E...... 323 587-7200
3338 E Slauson Ave Vernon (90058) *(P-2079)*

Sharon Care Center LLC .... D...... 323 655-2023
8167 W 3rd St Los Angeles (90048) *(P-18052)*

Sharon Havriluk .... E...... 714 630-1313
1164 N Kraemer Pl Anaheim (92806) *(P-3840)*

Sharp, Torrance *Also Called: Sharp Industries Inc (P-12820)*

Sharp Chula Vista Medical Ctr .... A...... 619 502-5800
751 Medical Center Ct Chula Vista (91911) *(P-18435)*

Sharp Chula Vista Medical Ctr .... D...... 858 499-5150
8695 Spectrum Center Blvd San Diego (92123) *(P-18436)*

Sharp Chula Vista Medical Ctr, Chula Vista *Also Called: Sharp Chula Vista Medical Ctr (P-18435)*

Sharp Community Medical Group .... C...... 858 499-4525
8695 Spectrum Center Blvd San Diego (92123) *(P-19403)*

Sharp Coronado Hospital & Healthcare Center .... A...... 619 522-3600
250 Prospect Pl Coronado (92118) *(P-18437)*

Sharp Fabric, Los Angeles *Also Called: Elijah Textiles Inc (P-12299)*

Sharp Grssmont Hosp Emrgncy Ca, La Mesa *Also Called: Team Health Holdings Inc (P-18470)*

Sharp Health Care, San Diego *Also Called: Sharp Healthcare Aco LLC (P-18442)*

Sharp Health Plan .... D...... 858 499-8300
8520 Tech Way Ste 200 San Diego (92123) *(P-14496)*

Sharp Healthcare (PA) .... A...... **858 499-4000**
8695 Spectrum Center Blvd San Diego (92123) *(P-14057)*

Sharp Healthcare .... D...... 619 460-6200
8860 Center Dr Ste 450 La Mesa (91942) *(P-17764)*

Sharp Healthcare .... C...... 858 499-2000
751 Medical Center Ct Chula Vista (91911) *(P-18438)*

Sharp Healthcare .... C...... 858 939-5434
8008 Frost St Ste 106 San Diego (92123) *(P-18439)*

Sharp Healthcare Aco LLC .... C...... 619 398-2988
7910 Frost St Ste 280 San Diego (92123) *(P-18440)*

Sharp Healthcare Aco LLC .... C...... 619 446-1575
300 Fir St San Diego (92101) *(P-18441)*

Sharp Healthcare Aco LLC .... A...... 858 627-5152
3554 Ruffin Rd Ste Soca San Diego (92123) *(P-18442)*

SHARP HEALTHCARE ACO, LLC, San Diego *Also Called: Sharp Healthcare Aco LLC (P-18440)*

Sharp Healthcare Foundation .... C...... 858 499-4800
8695 Spectrum Center Blvd San Diego (92123) *(P-19341)*

Sharp Industries Inc (PA) .... E...... **310 370-5990**
3501 Challenger St Fl 2 Torrance (90503) *(P-12820)*

Sharp McDonald Center .... A...... 858 637-6920
7989 Linda Vista Rd San Diego (92111) *(P-18532)*

Sharp Memorial Hospital (HQ) .... A...... **858 939-3636**
7901 Frost St San Diego (92123) *(P-18443)*

Sharp Memorial Hospital .... C...... 858 278-4110
7850 Vista Hill Ave San Diego (92123) *(P-18518)*

Sharp Mesa Vista Hospital, San Diego *Also Called: Sharp Memorial Hospital (P-18518)*

Sharp Rees-Stealy, San Diego *Also Called: Sharp Healthcare (P-18439)*

Sharp Rees-Stealy Div, San Diego *Also Called: Sharp Healthcare Aco LLC (P-18441)*

Sharp RES-Stealy Med Group Inc .... C...... 619 644-6405
7862 El Cajon Blvd Ste C La Mesa (91942) *(P-17765)*

Sharp RES-Stealy Med Group Inc .... C...... 619 221-9547
3555 Kenyon St Ste 200 San Diego (92110) *(P-17766)*

Sharpcast, Los Angeles *Also Called: Sugarsync Inc (P-16394)*

Shasta Beverages Inc .... D...... 714 523-2280
14405 Artesia Blvd La Mirada (90638) *(P-1740)*

Shattuck Group, The, Oxnard *Also Called: Steelworks Etc Inc (P-6125)*

Shaver Specialty Co Inc .... E...... 310 370-6941
20608 Earl St Torrance (90503) *(P-7216)*

Shaw Industries Group Inc .... E...... 562 430-4445
11411 Valley View St Cypress (90630) *(P-2120)*

Shawmut Design and Cnstr, Los Angeles *Also Called: Shawmut Woodworking & Sup Inc (P-589)*

**A
L
P
H
A
B
E
T
I
C**

Employee Codes: A=Over 500 employees, B=251-500
C=101-250, D=51-100, E=20-50, F=10-19, G=1-9

2024 Southern California
Business Directory and Buyers Guide

© Mergent Inc. 1-800-342-5647

1261

Shawmut Woodworking & Sup Inc ....C...... 323 602-1000
11390 W Olympic Blvd Fl 2 Los Angeles (90064) *(P-589)*

Shaxon Industries Inc ....D...... 714 779-1140
337 W Freedom Ave Orange (92865) *(P-7484)*

Shea Convalescent Hospital, Whittier *Also Called: Longwood Management Corp (P-18337)*

Shea Homes, Walnut *Also Called: Shea Homes Vantis LLC (P-475)*

Shea Homes At Montage LLC ....C...... 909 594-9500
655 Brea Canyon Rd Walnut (91789) *(P-457)*

Shea Homes For Active Adults, Walnut *Also Called: JF Shea Construction Inc (P-437)*

Shea Homes Ltd Prtnershp, Walnut *Also Called: Vistancia Marketing LLC (P-20269)*

Shea Homes Vantis LLC ....D...... 909 594-9500
655 Brea Canyon Rd Walnut (91789) *(P-475)*

Shea Properties, Aliso Viejo *Also Called: Shea Properties MGT Co Inc (P-14684)*

Shea Properties MGT Co Inc ....B...... 949 389-7000
130 Vantis Dr Ste 200 Aliso Viejo (92656) *(P-14684)*

Shed Media US Inc ....C...... 323 904-4680
3800 Barham Blvd Ste 410 Los Angeles (90068) *(P-15597)*

Sheet Metal Engineering ....E...... 805 306-0390
1780 Voyager Ave Simi Valley (93063) *(P-6313)*

Sheet Metal Prototype Inc ....E...... 818 772-2715
19420 Londelius St Northridge (91324) *(P-6314)*

Sheet Metal Service ....F...... 714 446-0196
2310 E Orangethorpe Ave Anaheim (92806) *(P-6315)*

Sheet Metal Specialists LLC ....F...... 951 351-6828
11698 Warm Springs Rd Riverside (92505) *(P-6316)*

Sheffield Construction, Bakersfield *Also Called: Mark Sheffield Cnstr Inc (P-360)*

Sheffield Manufacturing Inc ....D...... 310 320-1473
9131 Glenoaks Blvd Sun Valley (91352) *(P-8027)*

Sheffield Platers Inc ....D...... 858 546-8484
9850 Waples St San Diego (92121) *(P-6662)*

Sheila Street Properties Inc (PA) ....D...... 323 838-9208
5900 Sheila St Commerce (90040) *(P-6663)*

Shein Technology LLC (PA) ....B...... 213 628-4008
777 S Alameda St Fl 2 Los Angeles (90021) *(P-20235)*

Shelby Carroll Intl Inc (PA) ....E...... 310 538-2914
19021 S Figueroa St Gardena (90248) *(P-9308)*

Shelcore Inc (PA) ....E...... 818 883-2400
7811 Lemona Ave Van Nuys (91405) *(P-10966)*

Shelcore Toys, Van Nuys *Also Called: Shelcore Inc (P-10966)*

Sheldon Mechanical Corporation ....D...... 661 286-1361
26015 Avenue Hall Santa Clarita (91355) *(P-822)*

Shell, Anaheim *Also Called: Shell Oil Company (P-20236)*

Shell Oil Company ....C...... 714 991-9200
511 N Brookhurst St Anaheim (92801) *(P-20236)*

Shelter Island Boatyard, San Diego *Also Called: Shelter Island Ychtways Ltd A (P-9866)*

Shelter Island Ychtways Ltd A ....E...... 619 222-0481
2330 Shelter Island Dr Ste 1 San Diego (92106) *(P-9866)*

Shelter Pointe Hotel & Marina, San Diego *Also Called: Shelter Pointe LLC (P-11652)*

Shelter Pointe LLC ....C...... 619 221-8000
1551 Shelter Island Dr San Diego (92106) *(P-11652)*

Shen Zhen New World II LLC ....D...... 818 980-1212
333 Universal Hollywood Dr Universal City (91608) *(P-15354)*

Shepard Bros Inc (PA) ....C...... 562 697-1366
503 S Cypress St La Habra (90631) *(P-7685)*

Shepard-Thomason Company ....D...... 714 773-5539
901 S Leslie St La Habra (90631) *(P-9460)*

Sheppard Mllin Rchter Hmpton L ....D...... 619 338-6500
501 W Broadway Fl 19 San Diego (92101) *(P-18941)*

Sheppard Mllin Rchter Hmpton L ....D...... 858 720-8900
12275 El Camino Real Ste 100 San Diego (92130) *(P-18942)*

Sheppard Mllin Rchter Hmpton L (PA) ....B...... 213 620-1780
333 S Hope St Fl 43 Los Angeles (90071) *(P-18943)*

Sheppard Mllin Rchter Hmpton L ....D...... 714 513-5100
650 Town Center Dr Fl 10 Costa Mesa (92626) *(P-18944)*

Sheppard Mullin, Los Angeles *Also Called: Sheppard Mllin Rchter Hmpton L (P-18943)*

Sheraton, San Diego *Also Called: 8110 Aero Holding LLC (P-15067)*

Sheraton, Anaheim *Also Called: Anaheim - 1855 S Hbr Blvd Owne (P-15074)*

Sheraton, Los Angeles *Also Called: Hazens Investment LLC (P-15173)*

Sheraton, Universal City *Also Called: Lh Universal Operating LLC (P-15224)*

Sheraton, Los Angeles *Also Called: Nrea-TRC 711 LLC (P-15265)*

Sheraton, Universal City *Also Called: Shen Zhen New World II LLC (P-15354)*

Sheraton, Pomona *Also Called: Starwood Htels Rsrts Wrldwide (P-15372)*

Sheraton Carlsbad Resort & Spa, Carlsbad *Also Called: Grand Pacific Carlsbad Ht LP (P-15159)*

Sheraton Ht San Dego Mssion VI ....D...... 619 321-4602
1433 Camino Del Rio S San Diego (92108) *(P-15355)*

Sheraton Inn Bakersfield, Bakersfield *Also Called: Msr Hotels & Resorts Inc (P-15039)*

Sheraton Pasadena, Pasadena *Also Called: Pasadena Hotel Dev Ventr LP (P-15300)*

Sheraton Pk Ht At Anheim Rsort, Anaheim *Also Called: 1855 S Hbr Blvd Drv Hldngs LLC (P-15064)*

Sheraton San Diego Mission Vly, San Diego *Also Called: Sheraton Ht San Dego Mssion VI (P-15355)*

Shercon LLC ....D
18704 S Ferris Pl Rancho Dominguez (90220) *(P-4795)*

Shercon, Inc., Rancho Dominguez *Also Called: Shercon LLC (P-4795)*

Sherline Products, Vista *Also Called: Sherline Products Incorporated (P-7024)*

Sherline Products Incorporated ....E...... 760 727-5181
3235 Executive Rdg Vista (92081) *(P-7024)*

Sherman Oaks Hospital, Sherman Oaks *Also Called: Prime Hlthcare Svcs - Shrman O (P-18394)*

Sherman Village Hlth Care Ctr, North Hollywood *Also Called: Coldwater Care Center LLC (P-17903)*

Sherman Village Hlth Care Ctr, North Hollywood *Also Called: Hillsdale Group LP (P-18131)*

Sherpa Clinical Packaging LLC ....E...... 858 282-0928
6920 Carroll Rd San Diego (92121) *(P-3157)*

Sherry Kline, Commerce *Also Called: Pacific Coast Home Furn Inc (P-2482)*

Sherwin-Williams, Commerce *Also Called: Sherwin-Williams Company (P-2127)*

Sherwin-Williams Company ....E...... 323 726-7272
5501 E Slauson Ave Commerce (90040) *(P-2127)*

Sherwood Country Club ....C...... 805 496-3036
320 W Stafford Rd Thousand Oaks (91361) *(P-17524)*

Sherwood Guest Home, Lynwood *Also Called: Marlinda Management Inc (P-18144)*

Sherwood Mechanical Inc ....D...... 858 679-3000
6630 Top Gun St San Diego (92121) *(P-823)*

Sherwood Oaks Post Acute, Thousand Oaks *Also Called: Westlake Oaks Healthcare LLC (P-18816)*

Sheryl Lowe Designs LLC ....E...... 805 969-1742
1187 Coast Village Rd Ste 156 Santa Barbara (93108) *(P-16926)*

Sheward & Son & Sons (PA) ....E...... 866 432-8400
3000 Airway Ave Frnt Costa Mesa (92626) *(P-3014)*

Shield AI Inc (PA) ....A...... 619 719-5740
600 W Broadway Ste 250 San Diego (92101) *(P-9552)*

Shield Healthcare, Valencia *Also Called: Shield-Denver Health Care Ctr (P-12513)*

Shield Security Inc ....C...... 818 239-5800
21110 Vanowen St Canoga Park (91303) *(P-16685)*

Shield Security Inc ....B...... 562 283-1100
150 E Wardlow Rd Long Beach (90807) *(P-16686)*

Shield Security Inc (DH) ....B...... 714 210-1501
1551 N Tustin Ave Ste 650 Santa Ana (92705) *(P-16687)*

Shield Security Inc ....B...... 909 920-1173
265 N Euclid Ave Upland (91786) *(P-16688)*

Shield-Denver Health Care Ctr (HQ) ....C...... 661 294-4200
27911 Franklin Pkwy Valencia (91355) *(P-12513)*

SHIELDS, Los Angeles *Also Called: Shields For Families (P-18533)*

Shields For Families (PA) ....D...... 323 242-5000
11601 S Western Ave Los Angeles (90047) *(P-18533)*

Shimada Enterprises Inc ....E...... 562 802-8811
14009 Dinard Ave Santa Fe Springs (90670) *(P-8381)*

Shimadzu Precision Instrs Inc ....D...... 310 217-8855
20101 S Vermont Ave Torrance (90502) *(P-12514)*

Shimano North Amer Holdg Inc (HQ) ....C...... 949 951-5003
1 Holland Irvine (92618) *(P-12931)*

Shimano North America Bicycle, Irvine *Also Called: Shimano North Amer Holdg Inc (P-12931)*

Shimmick Construction Co Inc ....C...... 510 777-5000
16481 Scientific Bldg 2 Irvine (92618) *(P-458)*

Shimmick Construction Co Inc (HQ) ....C...... 949 591-5922
530 Technology Dr Ste 300 Irvine (92618) *(P-715)*

Shimmick Corporation ....A...... 510 777-5000
530 Technology Dr Ste 300 Irvine (92618) *(P-716)*

Shims Bargain Inc ....C...... 323 726-8800
7030 E Slauson Ave Commerce (90040) *(P-516)*

Mergent email: customerrelations@mergent.com
1262
2024 Southern California
Business Directory and Buyers Guide
(P-0000) Products & Services Section entry number
(PA)=Parent Co (HQ)=Headquarters (DH)=Div Headquarters

Shims Bargain Inc (PA)..D...... 323 881-0099
2600 S Soto St Vernon (90058) *(P-13561)*

Shine Food Inc (PA)..E...... 310 329-3829
19216 Normandie Ave Torrance (90502) *(P-1331)*

Shine Food Inc ....D...... 310 533-6010
21100 S Western Ave Torrance (90501) *(P-1400)*

Shining Ocean Inc ....C...... 253 826-3700
10888 7th St Rancho Cucamonga (91730) *(P-13287)*

Shinwoo P&C Usa Inc (HQ).....................................B...... 619 407-7164
2177 Britannia Blvd Ste 203 San Diego (92154) *(P-16927)*

Ship & Shore Environmental Inc ....E...... 562 997-0233
2474 N Palm Dr Signal Hill (90755) *(P-12821)*

Ship Services, San Pedro *Also Called: So Cal Ship Services (P-11640)*

Shiperp, Long Beach *Also Called: Erp Integrated Solutions LLC (P-16028)*

Shipping and Receiving, San Diego *Also Called: General Atomics (P-19841)*

Shire ....D...... 805 372-3000
1445 Lawrence Dr Newbury Park (91320) *(P-4232)*

Shire Rgenerative Medicine Inc ....E...... 858 754-5396
11095 Torreyana Rd San Diego (92121) *(P-4233)*

Shiva-Shakthi, San Diego *Also Called: Marika Group Inc (P-13135)*

Shivay Hospitality Inc ....D...... 323 702-7103
1738 N Las Palmas Ave Los Angeles (90028) *(P-15356)*

Shmaze Custom Coatings, Lake Forest *Also Called: Shmaze Industries Inc (P-6736)*

Shmaze Industries Inc ....E...... 949 583-1448
20792 Canada Rd Lake Forest (92630) *(P-6736)*

Shock Doctor Inc (PA)..D...... 800 233-6956
11488 Slater Ave Fountain Valley (92708) *(P-11025)*

Shock Doctor Inc ....E...... 657 383-4400
11488 Slater Ave Fountain Valley (92708) *(P-11026)*

Shock Doctor Sports, Fountain Valley *Also Called: Shock Doctor Inc (P-11025)*

Shockhound, City Of Industry *Also Called: Hot Topic Inc (P-13934)*

Shoffeitt Pipeline Inc ....D...... 949 581-1600
15801 Rockfield Blvd Ste L Irvine (92618) *(P-691)*

Shogun Labs Inc (PA)...C...... 317 676-2719
340 S Lemon Ave # 1085 Walnut (91789) *(P-19983)*

Shook Hardy & Bacon LLP ....C...... 949 475-1500
5 Park Plz Ste 1600 Irvine (92614) *(P-18945)*

Shop Buru, Los Angeles *Also Called: Bu Ru LLC (P-14092)*

Shop4techcom ....E...... 909 248-2725
13745 Seminole Dr Chino (91710) *(P-7485)*

Shopper Inc ....B...... 805 527-6700
2655 Park Center Dr Ste B Simi Valley (93065) *(P-12463)*

Shopzilla.com, Santa Monica *Also Called: Connexity Inc (P-11876)*

Shore Front LLC ....E...... 714 612-3751
3973 Trolley Ct Brea (92823) *(P-1984)*

Shore Western Manufacturing ....E...... 626 357-3251
19888 Quiroz Ct Walnut (91789) *(P-10287)*

Shores Restaurant, La Jolla *Also Called: La Jolla Bch & Tennis CLB Inc (P-15217)*

Shorett Printing Inc (PA)......................................E...... 714 545-4689
250 W Rialto Ave San Bernardino (92408) *(P-3811)*

Short Load Concrete Inc ....E...... 714 524-7013
605 E Commercial St Anaheim (92801) *(P-5502)*

Short Sale Agent Finder, San Diego *Also Called: Verseio Inc (P-16147)*

Shortcuts Software Inc ....E...... 714 622-6600
7711 Center Ave Ste 550 Huntington Beach (92647) *(P-16378)*

Show Group Production Services, Gardena *Also Called: Sgps Inc (P-11280)*

Show Off Time, Ventura *Also Called: Fnc Medical Corporation (P-4410)*

Showdogs Inc ....E...... 760 603-3269
168 S Pacific St San Marcos (92078) *(P-3015)*

Showerdoordirect LLC ....F...... 310 327-8060
20100 Normandie Ave Torrance (90502) *(P-6317)*

Showershapes, Ventura *Also Called: G W Surfaces (P-1159)*

Showroom Interiors LLC ....C...... 323 348-1551
8905 Rex Rd Pico Rivera (90660) *(P-15798)*

Showtime Custom Coach Inc ....F...... 909 867-7025
2461 Deep Creek Dr Running Springs (92382) *(P-17017)*

Shred Labs LLC ....E...... 781 285-8622
8033 W Sunset Blvd # 1112 Los Angeles (90046) *(P-16379)*

Shrin LLC ....D...... 714 850-0303
900 E Arlee Pl Anaheim (92805) *(P-12261)*

Shriner's Hospital, Pasadena *Also Called: Shriners Hspitals For Children (P-18534)*

Shriners Hspitals For Children ....B...... 626 389-9300
909 S Fair Oaks Ave Pasadena (91103) *(P-18534)*

Shriners Hspitals For Children ....B...... 213 368-3302
3160 Genieva St Montrose (91020) *(F-18535)*

Shriners Hspitals For Children, Pasadena *Also Called: Shriners International (P-19463)*

Shriners International ....C...... 626 389-9300
909 S Fair Oaks Ave Pasadena (91105) *(P-19463)*

Shryne Group Inc ....A...... 323 614-4558
728 E Commercial St Los Angeles (90012) *(P-14944)*

Shultz Steel Company ....B...... 323 357-3200
5321 Firestone Blvd South Gate (90280) *(P-6482)*

Shurflo LLC ....B...... 714 371-1550
3545 Harbor Gtwy S Ste 103 Costa Mesa (92626) *(P-7290)*

Shutters On The Beach, Santa Monica *Also Called: By The Blue Sea LLC (P-15102)*

Shutters On The Beach, Santa Monica *Also Called: Edward Thomas Hospitality Corp (P-15141)*

Shuttle Smart Inc ....C...... 310 338-9466
6150 W 96th St Los Angeles (90045) *(P-11365)*

Shye West Inc (PA)..E...... 949 486-4598
43 Corporate Park Ste 102 Irvine (92606) *(P-11157)*

Shyft Group Inc ....D...... 323 276-1933
1130 S Vail Ave Montebello (90640) *(P-9309)*

Si, Fontana *Also Called: California Steel Inds Inc (P-5583)*

Si Manufacturing Inc ....E...... 714 956-7110
1440 S Allec St Anaheim (92805) *(P-8955)*

Sia Engineering (usa) Inc ....C...... 310 957-2928
7001 W Imperial Hwy Los Angeles (90045) *(P-19690)*

Sibyl Shepard Inc ....E...... 562 531-8612
8225 Alondra Blvd Paramount (90723) *(P-2488)*

Sicor Inc (HQ)...A...... 949 455-4700
19 Hughes Irvine (92618) *(P-4234)*

Sid E Parker Boiler Mfg Co Inc ....D...... 323 727-9800
5930 Bandini Blvd Commerce (90040) *(P-6156)*

Sidakk Distributors ....E...... 619 391-0950
2109 Newton Ave San Diego (92113) *(P-3201)*

Sids Carpet Barn (PA)..E...... 619 477-7000
132 W 8th St National City (91950) *(P-12315)*

Sidus Solutions LLC ....F...... 619 275-5533
7352 Trade St San Diego (92121) *(P-8579)*

Siege Media LLC ....D...... 858 751-4439
624 Broadway Ste 301 San Diego (92101) *(P-12012)*

Siegfried Irvine, Irvine *Also Called: Alliance Medical Products Inc (P-10424)*

Siegfried Irvine, Irvine *Also Called: Alliance Medical Products Inc (P-10425)*

Siemens Energy Inc ....E...... 949 448-0600
6 Journey Ste 200 Aliso Viejo (92656) *(P-3484)*

Siemens Energy Inc ....E...... 310 223-0660
18502 S Dominguez Hills Dr Rancho Dominguez (90220) *(P-7316)*

Siemens Hlthcare Dgnostics Inc ....D...... 310 645-8200
5210 Pacific Concourse Dr Los Angeles (90045) *(P-10605)*

Siemens Industry Inc ....D...... 714 761-2200
6141 Katella Ave Cypress (90630) *(P-12618)*

Siemens Medical Solutions, Los Angeles *Also Called: Siemens Hlthcare Dgnostics Inc (P-10605)*

Siemens Mobility Inc ....E...... 714 284-0206
1026 E Lacy Ave Anaheim (92805) *(P-8485)*

Siemens Rail Automation Corp ....D...... 909 532-5405
9568 Archibald Ave Rancho Cucamonga (91730) *(P-8625)*

Sientra, Irvine *Also Called: Sientra Inc (P-10702)*

Sientra Inc (PA)..D...... 805 562-3500
3333 Michelson Dr Ste 650 Irvine (92612) *(P-10702)*

Sierra, Compton *Also Called: Sierra Cheese Manufacturing Company Inc (P-1258)*

Sierra Alloys Company, Irwindale *Also Called: STS Metals (P-6483)*

Sierra Aluminum, Riverside *Also Called: Samuel Son & Co (usa) Inc (P-5707)*

Sierra Aluminum Company ....E...... 951 781-7800
2345 Fleetwood Dr Riverside (92509) *(P-5708)*

Sierra Automated Sys/Eng Corp ....E...... 818 840-6749
2821 Burton Ave Burbank (91504) *(P-8580)*

Sierra Automated Systems, Burbank *Also Called: Sierra Automated Sys/Eng Corp (P-8580)*

Sierra Canyon Inc ....D...... 818 882-8121
11052 Independence Ave Chatsworth (91311) *(P-18984)*

Employee Codes: A=Over 500 employees, B=251-500
C=101-250, D=51-100, E=20-50, F=10-19, G=1-9

2024 Southern California
Business Directory and Buyers Guide

© Mergent Inc. 1-800-342-5647

1263

Sierra Canyon Day Camp, Chatsworth *Also Called: Sierra Canyon Inc (P-18984)*

Sierra Cheese Manufacturing Company Inc ....E...... 310 635-1216
916 S Santa Fe Ave Compton (90221) *(P-1258)*

Sierra Group Inc ....F..... 760 377-1000
1129 N Calvert Blvd China Lake Ridgecrest (93555) *(P-11707)*

Sierra Lathing Company Inc ....C...... 909 421-0211
1189 Leiske Dr Rialto (92376) *(P-996)*

Sierra Monolithics Inc (HQ)...**E...... 310 698-1000**
103 W Torrance Blvd Redondo Beach (90277) *(P-20378)*

Sierra Pacific Constrs Inc ....D...... 747 888-5000
22212 Ventura Blvd Ste 300 Woodland Hills (91364) *(P-590)*

Sierra Pacific Constructors, Woodland Hills *Also Called: Sierra Pacific Constrs Inc (P-590)*

Sierra Pacific Engrg & Pdts, Long Beach *Also Called: SPEP Acquisition Corp (P-5944)*

Sierra Precision, Anaheim *Also Called: 3d Instruments LLC (P-10112)*

Sierra Springs Apartments, San Bernardino *Also Called: Woodman Realty Inc (P-14886)*

Sierra Vista Extended Stay, Brea *Also Called: Otb Acquisition LLC (P-15281)*

Sierra Vista Hospital Inc (HQ)...**A...... 805 546-7600**
1010 Murray Ave San Luis Obispo (93405) *(P-18444)*

Sierra Vista Regional Med Ctr, San Luis Obispo *Also Called: Sierra Vista Hospital Inc (P-18444)*

Sierracin Corporation (HQ)..**A...... 818 741-1656**
12780 San Fernando Rd Sylmar (91342) *(P-4505)*

Sierracin/Sylmar Corporation ....A...... 818 362-6711
12780 San Fernando Rd Sylmar (91342) *(P-5204)*

Sigma Extruding Corp ....E...... 951 781-8807
1565 Eastwood Ct Riverside (92507) *(P-4821)*

Sigma Stretch Film, Riverside *Also Called: Sigma Extruding Corp (P-4821)*

Sigma Supply & Dist Inc ....F..... 818 246-4624
701 W Harvard St Glendale (91204) *(P-12515)*

Sigma-Aldrich Corporation ....E...... 760 710-6213
6211 El Camino Real Carlsbad (92009) *(P-4630)*

Sign Image Inc ....E...... 818 772-1393
20440 Corisco St Chatsworth (91311) *(P-11158)*

Sign Industries Inc ....E...... 909 930-0303
2101 Carrillo Privado Ontario (91761) *(P-11159)*

Sign Mart, Orange *Also Called: Metal Art of California Inc (P-11137)*

Sign Post Byway Inc ....F..... 949 566-3016
901 Cossa Ct Santa Maria (93454) *(P-11160)*

Sign Specialists Corporation ....E...... 714 641-0064
111 W Dyer Rd Ste F Santa Ana (92707) *(P-11161)*

Sign-A-Rama, Palm Desert *Also Called: Pd Group (P-11144)*

Signage Solutions Corporation ....E...... 714 491-0299
2231 S Dupont Dr Anaheim (92806) *(P-11162)*

Signal ....D...... 661 259-1234
26330 Diamond Pl Ste 100 Santa Clarita (91350) *(P-3323)*

Signal 88, Ontario *Also Called: Signal 88 LLC (P-16689)*

Signal 88 LLC ....A...... 714 713-5306
821 S Rockefeller Ave Ontario (91761) *(P-16689)*

Signal Hill Petroleum Inc ....E...... 562 595-6440
2633 Cherry Ave Signal Hill (90755) *(P-321)*

Signal Pharmaceuticals LLC ....C...... 858 795-4700
10300 Campus Point Dr Ste 100 San Diego (92121) *(P-4235)*

Signal Products Inc (PA)..**D...... 213 748-0990**
5600 W Adams Blvd Ste 200 Los Angeles (90016) *(P-13149)*

Signal Products/Guess Handbags, Los Angeles *Also Called: Signal Products Inc (P-13149)*

Signature Analytics LLC ....D...... 888 284-3842
10120 Pacific Heights Blvd Ste 110 San Diego (92121) *(P-19804)*

Signature Control Systems ....D...... 949 580-3640
16485 Laguna Canyon Rd Ste 130 Irvine (92618) *(P-6913)*

Signature Flexible Packg LLC (PA)..**E...... 909 598-7844**
19310 San Jose Ave City Of Industry (91748) *(P-4581)*

Signature Fresh, City Of Industry *Also Called: Ssre Holdings LLC (P-1205)*

Signature Parking LLC ....D...... 805 969-7275
924 Chapala St Ste B Santa Barbara (93101) *(P-15522)*

Signature Select Personnel LLC ....B...... 626 940-3351
138 W Bonita Ave Ste 207 San Dimas (91773) *(P-15894)*

Signco, Yorba Linda *Also Called: Sesa Inc (P-15674)*

Signet Armorlite Inc (DH)..**B...... 760 744-4000**
5803 Newton Dr Ste A Carlsbad (92008) *(P-10851)*

Signgroup/Karman, Chatsworth *Also Called: Schea Holdings Inc (P-11156)*

Signify North America Corp ....C...... 732 563-3000
3350 Enterprise Dr Bloomington (92316) *(P-8331)*

Signresource LLC (DH)..**C...... 323 771-2098**
6135 District Blvd Maywood (90270) *(P-11163)*

Signs and Services Company ....E...... 714 761-8200
10980 Boatman Ave Stanton (90680) *(P-11164)*

Signtech, San Diego *Also Called: Signtech Electrical Advg Inc (P-11165)*

Signtech Electrical Advg Inc ....C...... 619 527-6100
4444 Federal Blvd San Diego (92102) *(P-11165)*

Signtronix Inc ....D...... 310 534-7500
1445 Sepulveda Blvd Torrance (90501) *(P-11166)*

Sigtronics Corporation ....E...... 909 305-9399
178 E Arrow Hwy San Dimas (91773) *(P-8626)*

Sigue, Sylmar *Also Called: Sigue Corporation (P-16928)*

Sigue Corporation (PA)..**D...... 818 837-5939**
13190 Telfair Ave Sylmar (91342) *(P-16928)*

Sika Corporation ....F..... 562 941-0231
12767 Imperial Hwy Santa Fe Springs (90670) *(P-4631)*

Silao Tortilleria, Rowland Heights *Also Called: Silao Tortilleria Inc (P-1985)*

Silao Tortilleria Inc ....E...... 626 961-0761
18316 Senteno St Rowland Heights (91748) *(P-1985)*

Silc Technologies Inc ....E...... 626 375-1231
181 W Huntington Dr Ste 200 Monrovia (91016) *(P-8889)*

Silgan, Woodland Hills *Also Called: Silgan Can Company (P-5862)*

Silgan, Woodland Hills *Also Called: Silgan Containers Corporation (P-5863)*

Silgan, Woodland Hills *Also Called: Silgan Containers Mfg Corp (P-5865)*

Silgan Can Company ....C...... 818 348-3700
21600 Oxnard St Ste 1600 Woodland Hills (91367) *(P-5862)*

Silgan Containers Corporation (DH)...**D...... 818 710-3700**
21600 Oxnard St Ste 1600 Woodland Hills (91367) *(P-5863)*

Silgan Containers LLC (HQ)..**818 710-3700**
21600 Oxnard St Ste 1600 Woodland Hills (91367) *(P-5864)*

Silgan Containers Mfg Corp (DH)..**C...... 818 710-3700**
21600 Oxnard St Ste 1600 Woodland Hills (91367) *(P-5865)*

Silgan White Cap Corporation ....E...... 818 710-3700
21600 Oxnard St Ste 1600 Woodland Hills (91367) *(P-5205)*

Silica Gel Dessicant Pdts Co ....E...... 800 426-1529
1144 E Hyde Park Blvd Inglewood (90302) *(P-3129)*

Silicon Tech Inc ....B...... 949 476-1130
3009 Daimler St Santa Ana (92705) *(P-7486)*

Silicontech, Santa Ana *Also Called: Silicon Tech Inc (P-7486)*

Silk Screen Shirts Inc ....E...... 760 233-3900
6185 El Camino Real Carlsbad (92009) *(P-2091)*

Silla Automotive LLC ....C...... 800 624-1499
1217 W Artesia Blvd Compton (90220) *(P-12262)*

Silla Cooling Systems, Compton *Also Called: Silla Automotive LLC (P-12262)*

Silmar Division, Hawthorne *Also Called: Ip Corporation (P-3948)*

Silo City Inc ....E
1401 S Union Ave Bakersfield (93307) *(P-6942)*

Silver Creek Industries LLC ....C...... 951 943-5393
2830 Barrett Ave Perris (92571) *(P-591)*

Silver Hawk Freight Inc ....D...... 562 404-0226
16410 Bloomfield Ave Cerritos (90703) *(P-11803)*

Silver Lakes Association ....D...... 760 245-1606
15273 Orchard Hill Ln Helendale (92342) *(P-19464)*

Silver Rock Resort Golf Club ....D...... 760 777-8884
79179 Ahmanson Ln La Quinta (92253) *(P-17441)*

Silver Saddle Ranch & Club Inc ....D...... 818 768-8808
7635 N San Fernando Rd Burbank (91505) *(P-14911)*

Silver Star Distribution, Irvine *Also Called: Str Worldwide Inc (P-13112)*

Silverado Framing & Cnstr ....D...... 951 352-1100
3091 E La Cadena Dr Riverside (92507) *(P-459)*

Silverado Senior Living Inc ....D...... 626 872-3941
1118 N Stoneman Ave Alhambra (91801) *(P-18053)*

Silverado Snior Lving Hldngs ....A...... 949 240-7200
6400 Oak Cyn Ste 200 Irvine (92618) *(P-19299)*

Silvergate San Marcos, San Marcos *Also Called: Americare Hlth Retirement Inc (P-14652)*

Silverlake Motel, Los Angeles *Also Called: New Aster Enterprises Inc (P-15259)*

Silverrest, Fullerton *Also Called: Brentwood Home LLC (P-2845)*

Silverton Business Center, San Diego *Also Called: HG Fenton Property Company (P-14737)*

Mergent email: customerrelations@mergent.com
1264

2024 Southern California
Business Directory and Buyers Guide

(P-0000) Products & Services Section entry number
(PA)=Parent Co (HQ)=Headquarters (DH)=Div Headquarters

Silvester California, Los Angeles *Also Called: Silvestri Studio Inc (P-11282)*

Silvestri Studio Inc (PA)..D....... 323 277-4420
8125 Beach St Los Angeles (90001) *(P-11282)*

Silvus Technologies Inc (PA)...D....... 310 479-3333
10990 Wilshire Blvd Ste 1500 Los Angeles (90024) *(P-8581)*

Sim Ideation, Irvine *Also Called: Specialty Interior Mfg Inc (P-12263)*

Simec USA Corporation ....E....... 619 474-7081
333 H St Ste 5000 Chula Vista (91910) *(P-5602)*

Simex-Iwerks, Valencia *Also Called: Iwerks Entertainment Inc (P-9219)*

Simi Vly Care & Rehabilitation, Simi Valley *Also Called: Chase Group Llc (P-19890)*

Simi Vly Hosp & Hlth Care Svcs ....A....... 805 955-6000
2750 Sycamore Dr Simi Valley (93065) *(P-18445)*

Simi Vly Hosp & Hlth Care Svcs (HQ).............................C....... 805 955-6000
2975 Sycamore Dr Simi Valley (93065) *(P-18446)*

Simi Vly Hosp & Hlth Care Svcs, Simi Valley *Also Called: Simi Vly Hosp & Hlth Care Svcs (P-18446)*

Simi West Inc ....C....... 760 346-5502
999 Enchanted Way Simi Valley (93065) *(P-15357)*

Simmons Family Corporation ....D....... 951 278-4563
350 W Rincon St Corona (92880) *(P-4843)*

Simon G Jewelry Inc ....E....... 818 500-8595
528 State St Glendale (91203) *(P-12967)*

Simon Golub & Sons Inc (DH)..D
514 Via De La Valle Ste 210 Solana Beach (92075) *(P-12968)*

Simons Brick Corporation ....E....... 951 279-1000
4301 Firestone Blvd South Gate (90280) *(P-5561)*

Simonz Machine ....F....... 858 692-5129
4905 Morena Blvd Ste 1309 San Diego (92117) *(P-8028)*

Simple Green, Huntington Beach *Also Called: Sunshine Makers Inc (P-4369)*

Simple Science Inc ....E....... 949 335-1099
1626 Ohms Way Costa Mesa (92627) *(P-16929)*

Simplexgrinnell, San Diego *Also Called: Johnson Cntrls Fire Prtction L (P-8616)*

Simpliphi Power Inc ....E....... 805 640-6700
3100 Camino Del Sol Oxnard (93030) *(P-9154)*

Simply Fresh LLC ....C....... 714 562-5000
11215 Knott Ave Ste A Cypress (90630) *(P-1812)*

Simpson Automotive Inc ....D....... 714 690-6200
6600 Auto Center Dr Buena Park (90621) *(P-13825)*

Simpson Buick Pontiac GMC, Buena Park *Also Called: Simpson Automotive Inc (P-13825)*

Simpson Industries Inc ....E....... 310 605-1224
1093 E Bedmar St Carson (90746) *(P-4236)*

Simpson Strong-Tie Company Inc ....C....... 714 871-8373
12246 Holly St Riverside (92509) *(P-2702)*

Simpsonsimpson Industries, Carson *Also Called: Simpson Industries Inc (P-4236)*

Sims Software, Carlsbad *Also Called: Stratcom Systems Inc (P-16125)*

Simso Tex, Compton *Also Called: Simso Tex Sublimation (P-2539)*

Simso Tex Sublimation (PA)...E....... 310 885-9717
3028 E Las Hermanas St Compton (90221) *(P-2539)*

Simulator PDT Solutions LLC ....E....... 310 830-3331
21818 S Wilmington Ave Ste 411 Long Beach (90810) *(P-10071)*

Simulstat Incorporated ....D....... 858 546-4337
440 Stevens Ave Ste 200 Solana Beach (92075) *(P-16599)*

Sinai Temple ....C....... 323 469-6000
5950 Forest Lawn Dr Los Angeles (90068) *(P-15490)*

Sinai Temple (PA)..B....... 310 474-1518
10400 Wilshire Blvd Los Angeles (90024) *(P-19506)*

Sincere Orient Commercial Corp ....D....... 626 333-8882
15222 Valley Blvd City Of Industry (91746) *(P-1986)*

Sincere Orient Food Company, City Of Industry *Also Called: Sincere Orient Commercial Corp (P-1986)*

Sinecera Inc ....D....... 626 962-1087
5397 3rd St Irwindale (91706) *(P-16930)*

Sing Kung Corp ....E....... 626 358-5838
12061 Clark St Arcadia (91006) *(P-1416)*

Sing Tao Newspapers Ltd ....D....... 626 956-8200
17059 Green Dr City Of Industry (91745) *(P-3324)*

Sing Tao Nwspapers Los Angeles, City Of Industry *Also Called: Sing Tao Newspapers Ltd (P-3324)*

Singapore Airlines Limited ....C....... 310 647-1922
222 N Pacific Coast Hwy Ste 1600 El Segundo (90245) *(P-11670)*

Singer Vehicle Design LLC (PA).......................................C....... 213 592-2728
19500 S Vermont Ave Torrance (90502) *(P-17059)*

Singerlewak, Los Angeles *Also Called: Singerlewak LLP (P-19805)*

Singerlewak LLP (PA)...C....... 310 477-3924
10960 Wilshire Blvd Fl 7 Los Angeles (90024) *(P-19805)*

Singod Investors Vi LLC ....D....... 714 326-7800
1600 S Clementine St Anaheim (92802) *(P-3909)*

SINGULAR GENOMICS, San Diego *Also Called: Singular Genomics Systems Inc (P-10288)*

Singular Genomics Systems Inc ....C....... 858 333-7830
3010 Science Park Rd San Diego (92121) *(P-10288)*

Sir Speedy, Whittier *Also Called: George Coriaty (P-3578)*

Sir Speedy, Mission Viejo *Also Called: Sir Speedy Inc (P-3686)*

Sir Speedy Inc (HQ)...E....... 949 348-5000
26722 Plaza Mission Viejo (92691) *(P-3686)*

Sirius XM Radio Inc ....C....... 323 802-1100
953 N Sycamore Ave Los Angeles (90038) *(P-11936)*

SIS, Culver City *Also Called: Security Indust Spcialists Inc (P-16683)*

Sissell Bros ....E....... 323 261-0106
4322 E 3rd St Los Angeles (90022) *(P-5449)*

Sisters of Nzareth Los Angeles ....D....... 310 839-2361
3333 Manning Ave Los Angeles (90064) *(P-19300)*

Sisters of St Joseph Orange ....A....... 562 430-4638
240 Ocean Ave Seal Beach (90740) *(P-19507)*

Sit On It, Buena Park *Also Called: Exemplis LLC (P-2911)*

Site Crew Inc ....B....... 714 668-0100
3185 Airway Ave Ste G Costa Mesa (92626) *(P-15749)*

Site Helpers LLC ....D....... 877 217-5395
25232 Steinbeck Ave Stevenson Ranch (91381) *(P-20237)*

Site Sltions Cnstr Integration, Riverside *Also Called: Sitesol (P-19691)*

Sitesol ....D....... 562 746-5884
7372 Sycamore Canyon Blvd Riverside (92508) *(P-19691)*

Sitonit, Cypress *Also Called: Exemplis LLC (P-2912)*

Sitonit Seating Inc ....D....... 714 995-4800
6415 Katella Ave Cypress (90630) *(P-12291)*

Sittin Pretty Natural Dog Bky, Ontario *Also Called: JE Rich Company (P-1431)*

Six Continents Hotels Inc ....C....... 661 343-3316
612 Wainwight Ct Lebec (93243) *(P-15358)*

Six Eleven Limited Inc ....F....... 818 764-5810
11921 Sherman Way North Hollywood (91605) *(P-5534)*

Six Flags Magic Mountain, Valencia *Also Called: Magic Mountain LLC (P-17319)*

Six Flags Magic Mountain Inc ....D....... 661 255-4100
26101 Magic Mountain Pkwy Valencia (91355) *(P-17455)*

Sizzix, Lake Forest *Also Called: Ellison Educational Eqp Inc (P-7180)*

SJ&I Bias Binding & Tex Co Inc ....E....... 213 747-5271
1950 E 20th St Vernon (90058) *(P-2540)*

Sjm Facility, Irvine *Also Called: St Jude Medical LLC (P-4240)*

Sk Chemicals America Inc ....E....... 949 336-8088
3 Park Plz Ste 430 Irvine (92614) *(P-3970)*

SK&a, Irvine *Also Called: Iqvia Inc (P-19903)*

Skadden Arps Slate Meagher & F ....C....... 213 687-5000
300 S Grand Ave Ste 3400 Los Angeles (90071) *(P-18946)*

Skanska USA Cvil W Cal Dst Inc (DH)...............................A....... 951 684-5360
1995 Agua Mansa Rd Riverside (92509) *(P-647)*

Skat-Trak ....E....... 909 795-2505
654 Avenue K Calimesa (92320) *(P-4699)*

Skate One Corp ....D....... 805 964-1330
6860 Cortona Dr Ste B Goleta (93117) *(P-11027)*

Skaug Truck Body Works ....F....... 818 365-9123
1404 1st St San Fernando (91340) *(P-9333)*

SKB Corporation (PA)...B....... 714 637-1252
434 W Levers Pl Orange (92867) *(P-5206)*

Skdy of San Diego Inc ....E....... 858 552-9033
6455 Weathers Pl San Diego (92121) *(P-16931)*

SKECHERS, Manhattan Beach *Also Called: Skechers Collection LLC (P-4707)*

SKECHERS, Manhattan Beach *Also Called: Skechers USA Inc (P-5281)*

Skechers Collection LLC ....D....... 310 318-3100
228 Manhattan Beach Blvd Manhattan Beach (90266) *(P-4707)*

Skechers Factory Outlet 335, Moreno Valley *Also Called: Skechers USA Inc (P-13165)*

Skechers USA Inc (PA)...D....... 310 318-3100
228 Manhattan Beach Blvd Ste 200 Manhattan Beach (90266) *(P-5281)*

Employee Codes: A=Over 500 employees, B=251-500
C=101-250, D=51-100, E=20-50, F=10-19, G=1-9

2024 Southern California
Business Directory and Buyers Guide

© Mergent Inc. 1-800-342-5647

1265

ALPHABETIC

Skechers USA Inc ....E...... 951 242-4307
29800 Eucalyptus Ave Moreno Valley (92555) *(P-13165)*

Skechers USA Inc II ....A...... 800 746-3411
228 Manhattan Beach Blvd Ste 200 Manhattan Beach (90266) *(P-13925)*

Skeffington Enterprises Inc ....D...... 714 540-1700
2200 S Yale St Santa Ana (92704) *(P-14945)*

SKF Aptitude Exchange, San Diego Also Called: SKF Condition Monitoring Inc *(P-10396)*

SKF Condition Monitoring Inc (DH) ....C...... 858 496-3400
9444 Balboa Ave Ste 150 San Diego (92123) *(P-10396)*

Skid Row Housing Trust, Los Angeles Also Called: Srht Property Holding LLC *(P-14868)*

Skilled Healthcare LLC (DH) ....C...... 949 282-5800
27442 Portola Pkwy Ste 200 Foothill Ranch (92610) *(P-18054)*

Skin Laundry Holdings Inc ....B...... 424 220-8826
130 Lomita St El Segundo (90245) *(P-20238)*

Skinmedica Inc ....B...... 760 929-2600
18655 Teller Ave Irvine (92612) *(P-4237)*

Skinny Minnie, Maywood Also Called: Ev R Inc *(P-2322)*

Skirball Cultural Center ....C...... 310 440-4500
2701 N Sepulveda Blvd Los Angeles (90049) *(P-19364)*

SKIRBALL CULTURAL CENTER, Los Angeles Also Called: Skirball Cultural Center *(P-19364)*

Skurka Aerospace Inc (DH) ....E...... 805 484-8884
4600 Calle Bolero Camarillo (93012) *(P-8157)*

Sky Court USA Inc ....C...... 805 497-9991
880 S Westlake Blvd Westlake Village (91361) *(P-15359)*

Sky One Inc ....F...... 909 622-3333
1793 W 2nd St Pomona (91766) *(P-5379)*

Sky Rider Equipment Co Inc ....E...... 714 632-6890
1180 N Blue Gum St Anaheim (92806) *(P-2859)*

Skyco Shading Systems Inc ....E...... 714 708-3038
3411 W Fordham Ave Santa Ana (92704) *(P-13967)*

Skylar Creations Inc ....F...... 760 814-8260
5661 Palmer Way Ste C Carlsbad (92010) *(P-14036)*

Skyline Cabinet & Millworks, Bakersfield Also Called: Spalinger Enterprises Inc *(P-2965)*

Skyline Displays of San Diego, San Diego Also Called: Skdy of San Diego Inc *(P-16931)*

SKYLINE HEALTHCARE CENTER, Los Angeles Also Called: Skyline Hlthcare Wllness Ctr L *(P-18055)*

Skyline Hlthcare Wllness Ctr L ....D....: 323 665-1185
3032 Rowena Ave Los Angeles (90039) *(P-18055)*

Skyline Homes Inc ....C...... 951 654-9321
499 W Esplanade Ave San Jacinto (92583) *(P-2742)*

Skylink Travel Inc ....C...... 212 380-2438
18000 Studebaker Rd Ste 330 Cerritos (90703) *(P-11726)*

Skylock Industries ....E...... 201 637-9505
1290 W Optical Dr Azusa (91702) *(P-9797)*

Skylock Industries LLC ....D...... 626 334-2391
1290 W Optical Dr Azusa (91702) *(P-9798)*

Skylon, Perris Also Called: Eci Water Ski Products Inc *(P-14063)*

Skypark At Santa's Village, Skyforest Also Called: Spsv Entertainment LLC *(P-17352)*

Skypower Holdings LLC ....C...... 323 860-4900
4700 Wilshire Blvd Los Angeles (90010) *(P-824)*

Skytech Gaming, Ontario Also Called: Brainstorm Corporation *(P-12400)*

Skyview Capital LLC ....D...... 310 273-6000
2000 Avenue Of The Stars Ste 810 Los Angeles (90067) *(P-14288)*

SKYWORKS, Irvine Also Called: Skyworks Solutions Inc *(P-8892)*

Skyworks Solutions Inc ....F...... 301 874-6408
1767 Carr Rd Ste 105 Calexico (92231) *(P-8215)*

Skyworks Solutions Inc ....E...... 805 480-4400
2427 W Hillcrest Dr Newbury Park (91320) *(P-8890)*

Skyworks Solutions Inc ....E...... 805 480-4227
730 Lawrence Dr Newbury Park (91320) *(P-8891)*

Skyworks Solutions Inc (PA) ....A...... 949 231-3000
5260 California Ave Irvine (92617) *(P-8892)*

SL Blue Garden Corp ....C...... 626 633-2672
3790 Keri Way Fallbrook (92028) *(P-20239)*

Slabs Inc ....E...... 424 289-0275
12555 W Jefferson Blvd Los Angeles (90066) *(P-16380)*

Slalom LLC ....C...... 949 450-1100
300 Spectrum Center Dr Ste 1500 Irvine (92618) *(P-20379)*

SLALOM, LLC, Irvine Also Called: Slalom LLC *(P-20379)*

Slater Inc ....D...... 909 822-6800
11045 Rose Ave Fontana (92337) *(P-717)*

Slauson Plaza Med Group, Pico Rivera Also Called: Altamed Health Services Corp *(P-18740)*

Sld Laser, Goleta Also Called: Kyocera Sld Laser Inc *(P-9225)*

Sleep Data Services LLC ....D...... 619 299-6299
5471 Kearny Villa Rd Ste 200 San Diego (92123) *(P-17767)*

Sleepcomp West LLC ....E...... 562 946-3222
10006 Santa Fe Springs Rd Santa Fe Springs (90670) *(P-4905)*

Slimsuit, Bell Also Called: Carol Wior Inc *(P-2312)*

Slo New Times Inc ....E...... 805 546-8208
1010 Marsh St San Luis Obispo (93401) *(P-3325)*

Sloan Electric Corporation ....E...... 619 239-5174
3520 Main St San Diego (92113) *(P-12619)*

Slogcc, San Luis Obispo Also Called: San Luis Obispo Golf Cntry CLB *(P-17518)*

Slorta, San Luis Obispo Also Called: San Luis Obspo Rgnal Trnst Aut *(P-11363)*

Slr International Corporation ....A...... 949 553-8417
20 Corporate Park Ste 200 Irvine (92606) *(P-20380)*

Sls Hotel At Beverly Hills ....C...... 310 247-0400
465 S La Cienega Blvd Los Angeles (90048) *(P-15360)*

SM Tire, Nipomo Also Called: Santa Maria Tire Inc *(P-13870)*

Smac, Carlsbad Also Called: Systems Mchs Atmtn Cmpnnts Cor *(P-8193)*

Smart LLC ....E...... 866 822-3670
3501 Sepulveda Blvd Torrance (90505) *(P-5207)*

Smart & Final, Los Angeles Also Called: Smart & Final Stores LLC *(P-13222)*

Smart & Final, Los Angeles Also Called: Smart & Final Stores LLC *(P-13223)*

Smart & Final, Los Angeles Also Called: Smart & Final Stores LLC *(P-13225)*

Smart & Final, Los Angeles Also Called: Smart & Final Stores LLC *(P-13226)*

Smart & Final, Commerce Also Called: Smart & Final Stores LLC *(P-13228)*

Smart & Final, Commerce Also Called: Smart Stores Operations LLC *(P-13229)*

Smart & Final, Norwalk Also Called: Smart & Final Stores LLC *(P-13691)*

Smart & Final 341, Los Angeles Also Called: Smart & Final Stores LLC *(P-13224)*

Smart & Final Stores Inc ....B...... 714 549-2362
1308 W Edinger Ave Santa Ana (92704) *(P-13194)*

Smart & Final Stores Inc ....B...... 949 581-1212
26911 Trabuco Rd Mission Viejo (92691) *(P-13195)*

Smart & Final Stores Inc ....C...... 909 773-1813
13346 Limonite Ave Eastvale (92880) *(P-13196)*

Smart & Final Stores Inc ....B...... 805 237-0323
2121 Spring St Paso Robles (93446) *(P-13197)*

Smart & Final Stores Inc ....B...... 805 566-2174
850 Linden Ave Carpinteria (93013) *(P-13198)*

Smart & Final Stores Inc ....B...... 619 449-2396
9870 N Magnolia Ave Santee (92071) *(P-13199)*

Smart & Final Stores Inc ....C...... 619 522-2014
150 B Ave Coronado (92118) *(P-13200)*

Smart & Final Stores Inc ....D...... 619 390-1738
13439 Camino Canada El Cajon (92021) *(P-13201)*

Smart & Final Stores Inc ....B...... 760 732-1480
1845 W Vista Way Vista (92083) *(P-13202)*

Smart & Final Stores Inc ....C...... 760 434-2449
955 Carlsbad Village Dr Carlsbad (92008) *(P-13203)*

Smart & Final Stores Inc ....B...... 619 668-9039
933 Sweetwater Rd Spring Valley (91977) *(P-13204)*

Smart & Final Stores Inc ....B...... 619 291-1842
2235 University Ave San Diego (92104) *(P-13205)*

Smart & Final Stores Inc ....B...... 619 589-7000
2800 Fletcher Pkwy El Cajon (92020) *(P-13206)*

Smart & Final Stores Inc ....B...... 858 578-7343
10740 Westview Pkwy San Diego (92126) *(P-13207)*

Smart & Final Stores Inc ....C...... 818 889-8253
5770 Lindero Canyon Rd Westlake Village (91362) *(P-13208)*

Smart & Final Stores Inc ....B...... 805 647-4276
7800 Telegraph Rd Ventura (93004) *(P-13209)*

Smart & Final Stores Inc ....C...... 805 520-6035
5135 E Los Angeles Ave Simi Valley (93063) *(P-13210)*

Smart & Final Stores Inc ....C...... 323 549-9586
4550 W Pico Blvd Los Angeles (90019) *(P-13211)*

Smart & Final Stores Inc ....B...... 909 592-2190
1005 W Arrow Hwy San Dimas (91773) *(P-13212)*

Smart & Final Stores Inc ....B...... 626 330-2495
15427 Amar Rd La Puente (91744) *(P-13213)*

Smart & Final Stores Inc ....B...... 818 368-6409
18555 Devonshire St Northridge (91324) *(P-13214)*

Mergent email: customerrelations@mergent.com
1266

2024 Southern California
Business Directory and Buyers Guide

(P-0000) Products & Services Section entry number
(PA)=Parent Co (HQ)=Headquarters (DH)=Div Headquarters

Smart & Final Stores Inc .... C 562 438-0450
644 Redondo Ave Long Beach (90814) *(P-13215)*

Smart & Final Stores Inc .... B 323 497-8528
615 N Pacific Coast Hwy Redondo Beach (90277) *(P-13216)*

Smart & Final Stores Inc .... C 323 855-8434
240 S Diamond Bar Blvd Diamond Bar (91765) *(P-13217)*

Smart & Final Stores Inc .... C 818 954-8631
3830 W Verdugo Ave Burbank (91505) *(P-13218)*

Smart & Final Stores Inc .... B 661 722-6210
5038 W Avenue N Palmdale (93551) *(P-13219)*

Smart & Final Stores Inc .... B 562 907-7037
13003 Whittier Blvd Whittier (90602) *(P-13220)*

Smart & Final Stores Inc .... C 626 334-5189
303 E Foothill Blvd Azusa (91702) *(P-13221)*

Smart & Final Stores LLC .... C 323 725-0791
5500 Sheila St Commerce (90040) *(P-11612)*

Smart & Final Stores LLC .... C 310 559-1722
10113 Venice Blvd Los Angeles (90034) *(P-13222)*

Smart & Final Stores LLC .... D 323 466-9289
939 N Western Ave Los Angeles (90029) *(P-13223)*

Smart & Final Stores LLC .... D 323 569-7148
1125 E El Segundo Blvd Los Angeles (90059) *(P-13224)*

Smart & Final Stores LLC .... C 310 207-8688
12210 Santa Monica Blvd Los Angeles (90025) *(P-13225)*

Smart & Final Stores LLC .... C 323 268-9179
2308 E 4th St Los Angeles (90033) *(P-13226)*

Smart & Final Stores LLC .... D 213 747-6697
1216 Compton Ave Los Angeles (90021) *(P-13227)*

Smart & Final Stores LLC (DH) .... D 323 869-7500
600 Citadel Dr Commerce (90040) *(P-13228)*

Smart & Final Stores LLC .... D 562 868-0794
10935 Firestone Blvd Norwalk (90650) *(P-13691)*

SMART & FINAL STORES, INC., Santa Ana *Also Called: Smart & Final Stores Inc (P-13194)*

SMART & FINAL STORES, INC., Mission Viejo *Also Called: Smart & Final Stores Inc (P-13195)*

SMART & FINAL STORES, INC., Eastvale *Also Called: Smart & Final Stores Inc (P-13196)*

SMART & FINAL STORES, INC., Paso Robles *Also Called: Smart & Final Stores Inc (P-13197)*

SMART & FINAL STORES, INC., Carpinteria *Also Called: Smart & Final Stores Inc (P-13198)*

SMART & FINAL STORES, INC., Santee *Also Called: Smart & Final Stores Inc (P-13199)*

SMART & FINAL STORES, INC., Coronado *Also Called: Smart & Final Stores Inc (P-13200)*

SMART & FINAL STORES, INC., El Cajon *Also Called: Smart & Final Stores Inc (P-13201)*

SMART & FINAL STORES, INC., Vista *Also Called: Smart & Final Stores Inc (P-13202)*

SMART & FINAL STORES, INC., Carlsbad *Also Called: Smart & Final Stores Inc (P-13203)*

SMART & FINAL STORES, INC., Spring Valley *Also Called: Smart & Final Stores Inc (P-13204)*

SMART & FINAL STORES, INC., San Diego *Also Called: Smart & Final Stores Inc (P-13205)*

SMART & FINAL STORES, INC., El Cajon *Also Called: Smart & Final Stores Inc (P-13206)*

SMART & FINAL STORES, INC., San Diego *Also Called: Smart & Final Stores Inc (P-13207)*

SMART & FINAL STORES, INC., Westlake Village *Also Called: Smart & Final Stores Inc (P-13208)*

SMART & FINAL STORES, INC., Ventura *Also Called: Smart & Final Stores Inc (P-13209)*

SMART & FINAL STORES, INC., Simi Valley *Also Called: Smart & Final Stores Inc (P-13210)*

SMART & FINAL STORES, INC., Los Angeles *Also Called: Smart & Final Stores Inc (P-13211)*

SMART & FINAL STORES, INC., San Dimas *Also Called: Smart & Final Stores Inc (P-13212)*

SMART & FINAL STORES, INC., La Puente *Also Called: Smart & Final Stores Inc (P-13213)*

SMART & FINAL STORES, INC., Northridge *Also Called: Smart & Final Stores Inc (P-13214)*

SMART & FINAL STORES, INC., Long Beach *Also Called: Smart & Final Stores Inc (P-13215)*

SMART & FINAL STORES, INC., Redondo Beach *Also Called: Smart & Final Stores Inc (P-13216)*

SMART & FINAL STORES, INC., Diamond Bar *Also Called: Smart & Final Stores Inc (P-13217)*

SMART & FINAL STORES, INC., Burbank *Also Called: Smart & Final Stores Inc (P-13218)*

SMART & FINAL STORES, INC., Palmdale *Also Called: Smart & Final Stores Inc (P-13219)*

SMART & FINAL STORES, INC., Whittier *Also Called: Smart & Final Stores Inc (P-13220)*

SMART & FINAL STORES, INC., Azusa *Also Called: Smart & Final Stores Inc (P-13221)*

Smart Action Company LLC .... E 310 776-9200
300 Continental Blvd Ste 350 El Segundo (90245) *(P-16381)*

Smart Circle International LLC (PA) .... D 949 587-9207
4490 Von Karman Ave Newport Beach (92660) *(P-20240)*

Smart Circle, The, Newport Beach *Also Called: Smart Circle International LLC (P-20240)*

Smart Elec & Assembly Inc .... C 714 772-2651
2000 W Corporate Way Anaheim (92801) *(P-8730)*

Smart Electronics, Anaheim *Also Called: Smart Elec & Assembly Inc (P-8730)*

Smart Energy Solar Inc .... C 800 405-1978
1641 Comm St Corona (92880) *(P-825)*

Smart Energy Systems Inc .... C 909 703-9609
Michelson Dr Ste 3370 Irvine (92612) *(P-16114)*

Smart Energy USA, Corona *Also Called: Smart Energy Solar Inc (P-825)*

Smart Energy Water, Irvine *Also Called: Smart Utility Systems Inc (P-16115)*

Smart Foods LLC .... E 800 284-2250
3398 Leonis Blvd Vernon (90058) *(P-1565)*

Smart Stores Operations LLC (DH) .... B 323 869-7500
600 Citadel Dr Commerce (90040) *(P-13229)*

Smart Stores Operations LLC .... C 858 748-0101
12339 Poway Rd Poway (92064) *(P-13230)*

Smart Utility Systems Inc .... D 909 217-3344
19900 Macarthur Blvd Ste 370 Irvine (92612) *(P-16115)*

Smart Wax, Torrance *Also Called: Smart LLC (P-5207)*

Smart-Tek Services Inc (HQ) .... **F 858 798-1644**
11838 Bernardo Plaza Ct Ste 250 San Diego (92128) *(P-16382)*

Smartcover Systems, Escondido *Also Called: Hadronex Inc (P-12152)*

Smartdrive Systems Inc (PA) .... **D 858 225-5550**
9515 Towne Centre Dr San Diego (92121) *(P-16116)*

Smarthomepro, Irvine *Also Called: Smartlabs Inc (P-14149)*

Smartlabs Inc .... D 800 762-7846
1621 Alton Pkwy Ste 100 Irvine (92606) *(P-14149)*

Smartstop Self Storage, Ladera Ranch *Also Called: Sst IV 8020 Las Vgas Blvd S LL (P-11614)*

Smbc Manubank (DH) .... C 213 489-6200
515 S Figueroa St 4th Fl Los Angeles (90071) *(P-14207)*

SMC Grease Specialist Inc .... E 951 788-6042
1600 W Pellisier Rd Colton (92324) *(P-12187)*

SMC Networks Inc (HQ) .... **D 949 679-8029**
20 Mason Irvine (92618) *(P-12438)*

SMC Products Inc .... D 949 753-1099
22651 Lambert St Ste 105 Lake Forest (92630) *(P-12945)*

Smci, Costa Mesa *Also Called: Software Management Cons LLC (P-16119)*

Smci, Glendale *Also Called: Software Management Cons LLC (P-16601)*

Smg, Torrance *Also Called: Storm Manufacturing Group Inc (P-6770)*

Smg Holdings LLC .... D 760 325-6611
277 N Avenida Caballeros Palm Springs (92262) *(P-20241)*

Smg Management Facility, Ontario *Also Called: Ontario Convention Center Corp (P-16894)*

SMI Architectural Millwork Inc .... E 714 567-0112
2116 W Chestnut Ave Santa Ana (92703) *(P-13670)*

SMI Ca Inc .... E 562 926-9407
14340 Iseli Rd Santa Fe Springs (90670) *(P-8029)*

SMI Holdings Inc .... E 800 232-2612
28420 Witherspoon Pkwy Valencia (91355) *(P-8158)*

SMI Millwork, Santa Ana *Also Called: SMI Architectural Millwork Inc (P-13670)*

Smile Brands Group Inc (PA) .... **D 714 668-1300**
100 Spectrum Center Dr Ste 1500 Irvine (92618) *(P-20093)*

Smile Wide Dental, Irvine *Also Called: Universal Care Inc (P-18729)*

Smith Broadcasting Group Inc (PA) .... **C 805 965-0400**
2315 Red Rose Way Santa Barbara (93109) *(P-20094)*

Smith Broadcasting Group Inc .... B 805 882-3933
730 Miramonte Dr Santa Barbara (93109) *(P-11964)*

Smith Brothers, San Diego *Also Called: Smith Brothers Mfg Corp (P-8030)*

Smith Brothers Mfg Corp .... F 619 296-3171
5304 Banks St San Diego (92110) *(P-8030)*

Smith Electric Service, Santa Maria *Also Called: Smith McHncl-Lctrical-Plumbing (P-517)*

Smith International Inc .... C 909 906-7900
11031 Jersey Blvd Ste A Rancho Cucamonga (91730) *(P-6963)*

Smith Ironworks, Hesperia *Also Called: Endura Steel Inc (P-12550)*

Smith McHncl-Lctrical-Plumbing 805 621-5000
1340 W Betteravia Rd Santa Maria (93455) *(P-517)*

Smith Packing Inc .... C 805 348-1817
680 S Simas Rd Santa Maria (93455) *(P-13562)*

Smith-Emery International Inc (PA) .... **C 213 741-8500**
791 E Washington Blvd Fl 3 Los Angeles (90021) *(P-20242)*

Employee Codes: A=Over 500 employees, B=251-500
C=101-250, D=51-100, E=20-50, F=10-19, G=1-9

2024 Southern California
Business Directory and Buyers Guide

© Mergent Inc. 1-800-342-5647

1267

ALPHABETIC

Smithfield Foods, Vernon *Also Called: Clougherty Packing LLC (P-1193)*

Smiths Interconnect Inc .... D....... 805 267-0100
375 Conejo Ridge Ave Thousand Oaks (91361) *(P-9116)*

Smiths Intrcnnect Americas Inc .... B....... 714 371-1100
1231 E Dyer Rd Ste 235 Santa Ana (92705) *(P-9117)*

Smiths Shade & Linoleum Co Inc .... E....... 619 299-2228
6588 Federal Blvd Lemon Grove (91945) *(P-13954)*

SMK, Chula Vista *Also Called: SMK Manufacturing Inc (P-7500)*

SMK Manufacturing Inc .... E....... 619 216-6400
1055 Tierra Del Rey Ste F Chula Vista (91910) *(P-7500)*

Sml Space Maintainers Labs, Chatsworth *Also Called: Selane Products Inc (P-10767)*

Smoke Tree Inc .... D....... 760 327-1221
1850 Smoke Tree Ln Palm Springs (92264) *(P-15361)*

Smoke Tree Ranch, Palm Springs *Also Called: Smoke Tree Inc (P-15361)*

Smooth-Bor Plastics, Laguna Hills *Also Called: Steward Plastics Inc (P-4713)*

Smoothreads Inc .... E....... 800 536-5959
13750 Stowe Dr Ste A Poway (92064) *(P-2541)*

SMS Fabrications Inc .... E....... 951 351-6828
11698 Warm Springs Rd Riverside (92505) *(P-6318)*

SMS Transportation Inc .... D....... 310 527-9200
18516 S Broadway Gardena (90248) *(P-18947)*

SMS Transportation Svcs Inc ....C....... 213 489-5367
865 S Figueroa St Ste 2750 Los Angeles (90017) *(P-11366)*

Smt Electronics Mfg Inc .... E....... 714 751-8894
2630 S Shannon St Santa Ana (92704) *(P-8893)*

Snack It Forward LLC .... E....... 310 242-5517
6080 Center Dr Ste 600 Los Angeles (90045) *(P-1831)*

Snak Club LLC .... D....... 323 278-9578
5560 E Slauson Ave Commerce (90040) *(P-1562)*

Snak-King LLC (PA)... B....... 626 336-7711
16150 Stephens St City Of Industry (91745) *(P-1832)*

Snap Inc (PA)... A....... 310 399-3339
3000 31st St Ste C Santa Monica (90405) *(P-16117)*

Snapchat, Santa Monica *Also Called: Snap Inc (P-16117)*

Snapcomms Inc .... D....... 805 715-0300
155 N Lake Ave Fl 9 Pasadena (91101) *(P-16118)*

Snapnrack Inc .... E....... 877 732-2860
775 Fiero Ln Ste 200 San Luis Obispo (93401) *(P-5943)*

Snapware Corporation ....C....... 951 361-3100
2325 Cottonwood Ave Riverside (92508) *(P-5208)*

Snell & Wilmer, Costa Mesa *Also Called: Snell & Wilmer LLP (P-18948)*

Snell & Wilmer LLP .... D....... 714 427-7000
600 Anton Blvd Ste 1400 Costa Mesa (92626) *(P-18948)*

Snf Holding Company .... F....... 323 266-4435
4690 Worth St Los Angeles (90063) *(P-4632)*

Snf Management .... D....... 310 385-1090
1901 Avenue Of The Stars Los Angeles (90067) *(P-20095)*

Snow Summit, Big Bear Lake *Also Called: Snow Summit Ski Corporation (P-15362)*

Snow Summit Ski Corporation (PA)...............................C....... 909 866-5766
880 Summit Blvd Big Bear Lake (92315) *(P-15362)*

Snow Valley Mountain Sports Pk, Running Springs *Also Called: Snow Valley Mtn Resort LLC (P-15439)*

Snow Valley Mtn Resort LLC .... D....... 909 867-2751
Hwy 18 Running Springs (92382) *(P-15439)*

Snowmass Apparel Inc (PA)..................................... E....... 949 788-0617
15225 Alton Pkwy Irvine (92618) *(P-13150)*

Snowpure LLC .... E....... 949 240-2188
130 Calle Iglesia Ste A San Clemente (92672) *(P-7686)*

Snowpure Water Technologies, San Clemente *Also Called: Snowpure LLC (P-7686)*

Snowsound USA, Santa Fe Springs *Also Called: Atlantic Representations Inc (P-2825)*

Snyder Langston, Irvine *Also Called: Sander Langston LP (P-588)*

So Cal Graphics, San Diego *Also Called: Bretkeri Corporation (P-3739)*

So Cal Sandbags Inc .... D....... 951 277-3404
12620 Bosley Ln Corona (92883) *(P-12880)*

So Cal Ship Services .... D....... 310 519-8411
971 S Seaside Ave San Pedro (90731) *(P-11640)*

So Cal Soft-Pak Incorporated .... E....... 619 283-2338
8525 Gibbs Dr Ste 300 San Diego (92123) *(P-16383)*

SO Tech/Spcl Op Tech Inc (PA)................................. E....... 310 202-9007
206 Star Of India Ln Carson (90746) *(P-13093)*

So-Cal Strl Stl Fbrication Inc .... E....... 909 877-1299
130 S Spruce Ave Rialto (92376) *(P-6075)*

So-Cal Value Added, Camarillo *Also Called: Plt Enterprises Inc (P-8273)*

So-Cal Value Added LLC .... E....... 805 389-5335
809 Calle Plano Camarillo (93012) *(P-9118)*

Soaptronic LLC .... E....... 949 465-8955
20562 Crescent Bay Dr Lake Forest (92630) *(P-4368)*

Soaring America Corporation .... E....... 909 270-2628
8354 Kimball Ave # F360 Chino (91708) *(P-9553)*

Soboba Band Luiseno Indians .... A....... 951 665-1000
22777 Soboba Rd San Jacinto (92583) *(P-16932)*

Soboba Casino, San Jacinto *Also Called: Soboba Band Luiseno Indians (P-16932)*

Soboba Indian Health Clinic, San Jacinto *Also Called: Riversd-San Brnrdino Cnty Indi (P-17752)*

SOBRIETY HOUSE, Long Beach *Also Called: Safe Refuge (P-18715)*

Socal Auto Supply Inc .... E....... 302 360-8373
21418 Osborne St Canoga Park (91304) *(P-15459)*

Socal Cleaning & Insulation, Santa Ana *Also Called: TMC Fluid Systems Inc (P-7335)*

Socal Garment Works LLC .... E....... 323 300-5717
4700 S Boyle Ave Ste C Vernon (90058) *(P-2031)*

Socal Sportsnet LLC .... A....... 619 795-5000
100 Park Blvd San Diego (92101) *(P-17382)*

Socal Technologies LLC .... E....... 619 635-1128
1305 Oakdale Ave El Cajon (92021) *(P-16600)*

Socalgas, Northridge *Also Called: Southern California Gas Co (P-12094)*

Socco Plastic Coating Company .... E....... 909 987-4753
11251 Jersey Blvd Rancho Cucamonga (91730) *(P-6737)*

Social Advctes For Yuth San De ....C....... 619 283-9624
4275 El Cajon Blvd Ste 101 San Diego (92105) *(P-19141)*

Social Gaming Network, Culver City *Also Called: Jam City Inc (P-13973)*

Social Junky Inc .... E....... 213 999-1275
7874 Palmetto Ave Fontana (92336) *(P-16933)*

Social Science Service Center ....D....... 909 421-7120
18612 Santa Ana Ave Bloomington (92316) *(P-18536)*

Social Sciences, Irvine *Also Called: University California Irvine (P-18994)*

Social Service Professionals, Los Angeles *Also Called: Rehababilities Inc (P-15891)*

Societal CDMO San Diego LLC ....D....... 858 623-1520
6828 Nancy Ridge Dr Ste 100 San Diego (92121) *(P-4238)*

Soderberg Manufacturing Co Inc .... D....... 909 595-1291
20821 Currier Rd Walnut (91789) *(P-8349)*

Sodexo Management Inc .... A....... 310 646-3738
450 World Way Los Angeles (90045) *(P-20243)*

Sofa U Love LLC (PA)... E....... 323 464-3397
1207 N Western Ave Los Angeles (90029) *(P-2818)*

Soffa Electric Inc .... E....... 323 728-0230
5901 Corvette St Commerce (90040) *(P-10163)*

Sofitel Los Angeles, Los Angeles *Also Called: Accor Corp (P-13979)*

Soft Gel Technologies Inc (HQ).................................. E....... 323 726-0700
6982 Bandini Blvd Commerce (90040) *(P-4239)*

Soft Pak, San Diego *Also Called: So Cal Soft-Pak Incorporated (P-16383)*

Soft-Touch Tissue, Vernon *Also Called: Paper Surce Converting Mfg Inc (P-3060)*

Softline Home Fashions Inc .... E....... 310 630-4848
13130 S Normandie Ave Gardena (90249) *(P-13094)*

Softscript Inc .... A....... 310 451-2110
2215 Campus Dr El Segundo (90245) *(P-15681)*

Softub Inc (PA)... D....... 858 602-1920
24700 Avenue Rockefeller Valencia (91355) *(P-11283)*

Software, Encino *Also Called: Phone Check Solutions LLC (P-16095)*

Software Management Cons LLC ....C....... 714 662-1841
959 S Coast Dr Ste 415 Costa Mesa (92626) *(P-16119)*

Software Management Cons LLC (HQ)............................ B....... 818 240-3177
500 N Brand Blvd Glendale (91203) *(P-16601)*

Soilmoisture Equipment Corp .... E....... 805 964-3525
801 S Kellogg Ave Goleta (93117) *(P-10397)*

Sol Nova Electric LLC ....C....... 833 765-6682
330 Rancheros Dr Ste 116 San Marcos (92069) *(P-935)*

Sol-Pak Thermoforming Inc .... E....... 323 582-3333
3388 Fruitland Ave Vernon (90058) *(P-5209)*

Solag Disposal Co, San Juan Capistrano *Also Called: Solag Incorporated (P-12188)*

Solag Incorporated .... A....... 949 728-1206
31641 Ortege Hwy San Juan Capistrano (92675) *(P-12188)*

Solar Art, Laguna Hills *Also Called: Budget Enterprises Llc (P-5311)*

Solar Atmospheres Inc ....E....... 909 217-7400
8606 Live Oak Ave Fontana (92335) *(P-5849)*

Solar Electronics Company, North Hollywood *Also Called: A T Parker Inc (P-9189)*

Solar Link International Inc ....C....... 909 605-7789
4652 E Brickell St Ste A Ontario (91761) *(P-12881)*

Solar Shading Systems, Costa Mesa *Also Called: Sheward & Son & Sons (P-3014)*

Solar Spectrum LLC ....B....... 844 777-6527
27368 Via Industria Ste 101 Temecula (92590) *(P-826)*

Solar Turbines Incorporated (HQ)............A....... 619 544-5352
2200 Pacific Hwy San Diego (92101) *(P-6885)*

Solar Turbines Incorporated ....E....... 619 544-5321
2660 Sarnen St San Diego (92154) *(P-6886)*

Solar Turbines Incorporated ....C....... 858 694-6110
9330 Sky Park Ct San Diego (92123) *(P-6887)*

Solar Turbines Incorporated ....D....... 858 715-2060
9250 Sky Park Ct A San Diego (92123) *(P-6888)*

Solar Turbines Intl Co (DH)....................E....... 619 544-5000
2200 Pacific Hwy San Diego (92101) *(P-6889)*

Solara Engineering, Sun Valley *Also Called: Excelity (P-5812)*

Solarflare Communications Inc (DH)........D....... 949 581-6830
7505 Irvine Center Dr Ste 100 Irvine (92618) *(P-7450)*

Solari Enterprises Inc ....C....... 714 282-2520
1507 W Yale Ave Orange (92867) *(P-14685)*

Solariant Capital LLC ....C....... 626 544-0279
301 N Lake Ave Ste 950 Pasadena (91101) *(P-14946)*

Solaris Paper Inc ....C....... 714 687-6657
505 N Euclid St Ste 630 Anaheim (92801) *(P-7588)*

Solarreserve Inc ....D....... 310 315-2200
520 Broadway Fl 6 Santa Monica (90401) *(P-12054)*

Solarreserve LLC (PA)...........................F....... 310 315-2200
520 Broadway 6th Fl Santa Monica (90401) *(P-5985)*

Solartis, Manhattan Beach *Also Called: Solartis LLC (P-16120)*

Solartis LLC ....E....... 310 251-4861
1601 N Sepulveda Blvd Ste 606 Manhattan Beach (90266) *(P-16120)*

Solatube, Vista *Also Called: Solatube International Inc (P-6124)*

Solatube International Inc (DH)...............D....... 888 765-2882
2210 Oak Ridge Way Vista (92081) *(P-6124)*

Solcius LLC ....C....... 951 772-0030
12155 Magnolia Ave Ste 12b/C Riverside (92503) *(P-827)*

SOLCIUS LLC, Riverside *Also Called: Solcius LLC (P-827)*

SOLE Designs Inc ....F....... 626 452-8642
11685 Mcbean Dr El Monte (91732) *(P-2819)*

Sole Society Group Inc ....C....... 310 220-0808
11248 Playa Ct # B Culver City (90230) *(P-5261)*

Sole Technology Inc (PA).......................C....... 949 460-2020
26921 Fuerte Dr Lake Forest (92630) *(P-5282)*

Solecta Inc (PA)..................................E....... 760 630-9643
4113 Avenida De La Plata Oceanside (92056) *(P-2128)*

Solectek Corporation ....E....... 858 450-1220
8375 Camino Santa Fe Ste A San Diego (92121) *(P-8582)*

Soleil Communications LLC ....C....... 619 624-2888
2655 Camino Del Rio N Ste 110 San Diego (92108) *(P-19912)*

Soleo Health, Inglewood *Also Called: Biomed California Inc (P-4073)*

Soleus International, Walnut *Also Called: Mjc America Ltd (P-8238)*

Solex Contracting Inc ....C....... 951 308-1706
42146 Remington Ave Temecula (92590) *(P-692)*

Solheim Lutheran Home ....C....... 323 257-7518
2236 Merton Ave Los Angeles (90041) *(P-19301)*

Solid Oak Software Inc (PA)...................E....... 805 568-5415
319 W Mission St Santa Barbara (93101) *(P-12439)*

Solid State Devices Inc ....C....... 562 404-4474
14701 Firestone Blvd La Mirada (90638) *(P-8894)*

Soligen 2006, Northridge *Also Called: DC Partners Inc (P-5789)*

Solis Capital Partners LLC ....D....... 760 309-9436
3371 Calle Tres Vistas Ste 100 Encinitas (92024) *(P-15051)*

Solo Enterprise Corp ....E....... 626 961-3591
220 N California Ave City Of Industry (91744) *(P-8031)*

Solo Golf, City Of Industry *Also Called: Solo Enterprise Corp (P-8031)*

Solomon Colors Inc ....E....... 909 873-9444
1371 Laurel Ave Rialto (92376) *(P-3877)*

Solow ....E....... 323 664-7772
2907 Glenview Ave Los Angeles (90039) *(P-2370)*

Solpac Inc ....C....... 619 296-6247
2424 Congress St San Diego (92110) *(P-592)*

Solpac Construction Inc ....C....... 619 296-6247
2424 Congress St San Diego (92110) *(P-20096)*

Soltek Pacific, San Diego *Also Called: Solpac Inc (P-592)*

Soltek Pacific Construction Co, San Diego *Also Called: Solpac Construction Inc (P-20096)*

Solugenix, Brea *Also Called: Solugenix Corporation (P-16470)*

Solugenix Corporation (PA)....................C....... 866 749-7658
601 Valencia Ave Ste 260 Brea (92823) *(P-16470)*

Solutions Unlimited, Fullerton *Also Called: Wilsons Art Studio Inc (P-3827)*

Solutionz Inc ....C....... 888 815-0322
1029 Swarthmore Ave Pacific Palisades (90272) *(P-20244)*

Solv Energy LLC (HQ)...........................C....... 858 251-4888
16680 W Bernardo Dr San Diego (92127) *(P-12055)*

Solv Energy LLC ....B....... 858 622-4040
16798 W Bernardo Dr San Diego (92128) *(P-16384)*

Solvang Lutheran Home Inc ....C....... 805 688-3263
636 Atterdag Rd Solvang (93463) *(P-18056)*

Solvay America Inc ....C....... 714 688-4403
1440 N Kraemer Blvd Anaheim (92806) *(P-3910)*

Solvay America Inc ....D....... 225 361-3376
645 N Cypress St Orange (92867) *(P-3911)*

Solvay America Inc ....C....... 562 906-3300
12801 Ann St Santa Fe Springs (90670) *(P-3912)*

SOLVAY AMERICA, INC., Anaheim *Also Called: Solvay America Inc (P-3910)*

SOLVAY AMERICA, INC., Orange *Also Called: Solvay America Inc (P-3911)*

SOLVAY AMERICA, INC., Santa Fe Springs *Also Called: Solvay America Inc (P-3912)*

Solvay Chemicals Inc ....E....... 714 744-5610
645 N Cypress St Orange (92867) *(P-3913)*

Solvay Composite Materials, Anaheim *Also Called: Cytec Engineered Materials Inc (P-5788)*

Solvay Draka Inc (DH)...........................C....... 323 725-7010
6900 Elm St Commerce (90040) *(P-4822)*

Solvay USA Inc ....B....... 310 669-5300
20851 S Santa Fe Ave Long Beach (90810) *(P-3914)*

Solvay USA Inc ....E....... 805 591-3314
7305 Morro Rd Ste 200 Atascadero (93422) *(P-4529)*

Solve All Facility Services, Oceanside *Also Called: Bergensons Property Svcs Inc (P-15695)*

Somacis Inc ....C....... 858 513-2200
13500 Danielson St Poway (92064) *(P-8731)*

Some Crust Bakery, Claremont *Also Called: Feemster Co Inc (P-1465)*

Someone's In The Kitchen, Tarzana *Also Called: JMJ Enterprises Inc (P-14017)*

Son of A Barista Usa LLC (PA)................E....... 323 780-8250
5401 S Soto St Vernon (90058) *(P-1822)*

Sonance ....E....... 949 492-7777
212 Avenida Fabricante San Clemente (92672) *(P-8435)*

Sonance, San Clemente *Also Called: Dana Innovations (P-8404)*

Sonar Entertainment Inc (PA).................D....... 424 230-7140
2834 Colorado Ave Ste 300 Santa Monica (90404) *(P-17279)*

Sondors Inc ....E....... 323 372-3000
2710 Yates Ave Commerce (90040) *(P-9883)*

Sonendo Inc (PA)................................C....... 949 766-3636
26061 Merit Cir Ste 102 Laguna Hills (92653) *(P-10768)*

Sonfarrel ....E....... 714 630-7280
3000 E La Jolla St Anaheim (92806) *(P-5210)*

Sonfarrel Aerospace LLC ....D....... 714 630-7280
3010 E La Jolla St Anaheim (92806) *(P-5798)*

Sonic Industries Inc ....C....... 310 532-8382
20030 Normandie Ave Torrance (90502) *(P-19692)*

Sonic Plating Company, Gardena *Also Called: Granath & Granath Inc (P-6624)*

Sonic Vr, San Diego *Also Called: Sonic Vr LLC (P-16385)*

Sonic Vr LLC ....F....... 206 227-8585
225 Broadway Ste 650 San Diego (92101) *(P-16385)*

Sonix, Torrance *Also Called: Lenntek Corporation (P-8538)*

Sonnet Technologies Inc ....E....... 949 587-3500
8 Autry Irvine (92618) *(P-9255)*

Sonoco Industrial Products Div, City Of Industry *Also Called: Sonoco Products Company (P-3071)*

Sonoco Products Company ....C....... 626 369-6611
166 Baldwin Park Blvd City Of Industry (91746) *(P-3071)*

Employee Codes: A=Over 500 employees, B=251-500
C=101-250, D=51-100, E=20-50, F=10-19, G=1-9

2024 Southern California
Business Directory and Buyers Guide

© Mergent Inc. 1-800-342-5647

1269

Sonoco Products Company .... D...... 562 921-0881
12851 Leyva St Norwalk (90650) *(P-3072)*

Sonora Bakery Inc .... E...... 323 269-2253
4484 Whittier Blvd Los Angeles (90022) *(P-13723)*

Sonora Face Co .... E...... 323 560-8188
5233 Randolph St Maywood (90270) *(P-2691)*

Sonora Mills Foods Inc (PA) .... C...... 310 639-5333
3064 E Maria St E Rncho Dmngz (90221) *(P-1987)*

Sonos, Santa Barbara *Also Called: Sonos Inc (P-8436)*

Sonos Inc (PA) .... D...... 805 965-3001
614 Chapala St Santa Barbara (93101) *(P-8436)*

Sonrava, Orange *Also Called: Premier Dental Holdings Inc (P-17846)*

Sonsray Inc .... D...... 323 585-1271
23935 Madison St Torrance (90505) *(P-8032)*

Sony Electronics Inc .... B...... 858 942-2400
16530 Via Esprillo San Diego (92127) *(P-8437)*

Sony Electronics Inc (DH) .... A...... 858 942-2400
16535 Via Esprillo 1 San Diego (92127) *(P-8438)*

Sony Media Cloud Services LLC .... E...... 877 683-9124
10202 Washington Blvd Culver City (90232) *(P-17220)*

Sony Pctres Wrldwide Acqstons .... C...... 310 244-4000
10202 Washington Blvd Culver City (90232) *(P-17221)*

Sony Pictures Entrmt Inc (DH) .... A...... 310 244-4000
10202 Washington Blvd Culver City (90232) *(P-17222)*

Sony Pictures Imageworks Inc .... A...... 310 840-8000
9050 Washington Blvd Culver City (90232) *(P-16516)*

Sony Pictures Studios, Culver City *Also Called: Sony Pictures Entrmt Inc (P-17222)*

Sony Pictures Studios Inc .... C...... 310 244-4000
10202 Washington Blvd Culver City (90232) *(P-17223)*

Sony Pictures Television (DH) .... B...... 310 244-7625
10202 Washington Blvd Culver City (90232) *(P-17224)*

Sony Style, San Diego *Also Called: Sony Electronics Inc (P-8437)*

Soprano, Los Angeles *Also Called: SSC Apparel Inc (P-2372)*

Sorenson Engineering Inc (PA) .... C...... 909 795-2434
32032 Dunlap Blvd Yucaipa (92399) *(P-6421)*

Sorrento Therapeutics Inc (PA) .... D...... 858 203-4100
4955 Directors Pl San Diego (92121) *(P-4331)*

SOS Beauty Inc .... E...... 424 285-1405
9100 Wilshire Blvd Beverly Hills (90212) *(P-13069)*

SOS Security Incorporated .... C...... 310 392-9600
3000 S Robertson Blvd Ste 100 Los Angeles (90034) *(P-16690)*

Sotec USA LLC .... F...... 909 525-5861
3076 S Edenglen Ave Ontario (91761) *(P-6950)*

Sotera Wireless Inc .... C...... 858 427-4620
5841 Edison Pl Ste 140 Carlsbad (92008) *(P-10825)*

Souldriver Lessee Inc .... D...... 619 819-9500
435 6th Ave San Diego (92101) *(P-15363)*

Sound Image, Escondido *Also Called: Cal Southern Sound Image Inc (P-12651)*

Sound River Corporation .... D...... 661 705-3700
28238 Avenue Crocker Valencia (91355) *(P-936)*

Sound Seal Inc .... E...... 760 806-6400
4675 North Ave Oceanside (92056) *(P-5558)*

Sound United, Carlsbad *Also Called: Dei Headquarters Inc (P-8607)*

Soundcast, Costa Mesa *Also Called: Griswold Industries (P-6777)*

Soundcoat Company Inc .... D...... 631 242-2200
16901 Armstrong Ave Irvine (92606) *(P-8191)*

Soundcraft Inc .... E...... 818 882-0020
20301 Nordhoff St Chatsworth (91311) *(P-9256)*

Soup Bases Loaded Inc .... E...... 909 230-6890
2355 E Francis St Ontario (91761) *(P-1988)*

Source 44 LLC .... C...... 877 916-6337
4660 La Jolla Village Dr Ste 100 San Diego (92122) *(P-20381)*

Source Code LLC .... E...... 562 903-1500
9808 Alburtis Ave Santa Fe Springs (90670) *(P-7451)*

Source Intelligence, San Diego *Also Called: Source 44 LLC (P-20381)*

Source It USA Inc .... E...... 714 318-4428
1150 S Olive St Los Angeles (90015) *(P-16471)*

Source of Health Inc .... E...... 619 409-9500
1055 Bay Blvd Ste A Chula Vista (91911) *(P-1284)*

Source One Staffing LLC .... A...... 626 337-0560
5312 Irwindale Ave Ste 1h Baldwin Park (91706) *(P-15895)*

Source Photonics Usa Inc (PA) .... C...... 818 773-9044
8521 Fallbrook Ave Ste 200 West Hills (91304) *(P-8895)*

Source Photonics Usa Inc .... F...... 818 407-5007
8917 Fullbright Ave Chatsworth (91311) *(P-8896)*

Source Scientific LLC .... E...... 949 231-5096
2144 Michelson Dr Irvine (92612) *(P-10606)*

Souriau Usa Inc (DH) .... E...... 805 238-2840
1740 Commerce Way Paso Robles (93446) *(P-8275)*

South Bay Abrams Mfg & Dist, Huntington Beach *Also Called: Rief Enterprises Inc (P-12732)*

SOUTH BAY CENTER FOR COMMUNITY, Wilmington *Also Called: South Bay Ctr For Counseling (P-19142)*

South Bay Cstm Plstic Extrders .... E...... 619 544-0808
2554 Commercial St San Diego (92113) *(P-5211)*

South Bay Ctr For Counseling .... D...... 310 414-2090
540 N Marine Ave Wilmington (90744) *(P-19142)*

South Bay Ford Inc (PA) .... C...... 310 644-0211
5100 W Rosecrans Ave Hawthorne (90250) *(P-13826)*

South Bay Foundry Inc (HQ) .... E...... 909 383-1823
895 Inland Center Dr San Bernardino (92408) *(P-6076)*

South Bay International Inc .... E...... 909 718-5000
8570 Hickory Ave Rancho Cucamonga (91739) *(P-2860)*

South Bay Post Acute Care, Chula Vista *Also Called: Bayside Healthcare Inc (P-17889)*

South Bay Salt Works, Chula Vista *Also Called: Ggtw LLC (P-4607)*

South Bay Sand Blstg Tank Clg .... D...... 619 238-8338
326 W 30th St National City (91950) *(P-17153)*

South Bay Toyota .... C...... 310 323-7800
18416 S Western Ave Gardena (90248) *(P-13827)*

South Bay Welding, El Cajon *Also Called: M W Reid Welding Inc (P-6042)*

South Bay Wire & Cable Co LLC .... D...... 951 659-2183
54125 Maranatha Dr M-S 67 Idyllwild (92549) *(P-5623)*

South Baylo Acupuncture Clinic, Los Angeles *Also Called: South Baylo University (P-18717)*

South Baylo University .... C...... 213 999-0297
2727 W 6th St Los Angeles (90057) *(P-18717)*

South Cast A Qlty MGT Dst Bldg (PA) .... A...... 909 396-2000
21865 Copley Dr Diamond Bar (91765) *(P-20382)*

South Central Family Hlth Ctr .... D...... 323 908-4200
4425 S Central Ave Los Angeles (90011) *(P-17768)*

South China Sheet Metal Inc .... E...... 323 225-1522
1740 Albion St Los Angeles (90031) *(P-828)*

South Cntl Hlth Rhbltion Prgr .... D...... 310 667-4070
2620 Industry Way Lynwood (90262) *(P-18718)*

South Cntl Los Angles Rgnal CT (PA) .... C...... 213 744-7000
2500 S Western Ave Los Angeles (90018) *(P-19342)*

South Cntl Los Angles Rgnal CT 231 744-8484
650 W Adams Blvd Los Angeles (90007) *(P-19343)*

South Cnty Lxus At Mssion Vejo .... C...... 949 347-3400
28242 Marguerite Pkwy Mission Viejo (92692) *(P-13828)*

South Cnty Orthpd Spclsts A ME .... D...... 949 586-3200
24331 El Toro Rd Ste 200 Laguna Hills (92637) *(P-17769)*

South Coast Auto Insurance, Huntington Beach *Also Called: Freeway Insurance (P-14596)*

South Coast Baking LLC (PA) .... D...... 949 851-9654
1711 Kettering Irvine (92614) *(P-1524)*

South Coast Baking Co., Irvine *Also Called: South Coast Baking LLC (P-1524)*

South Coast Childrens Soc Inc .... C...... 909 478-3377
24950 Redlands Blvd Loma Linda (92354) *(P-18719)*

South Coast Circuits Inc .... D...... 714 966-2108
3506 W Lake Center Dr Ste A Santa Ana (92704) *(P-8732)*

South Coast Global Med Ctr Inc .... D...... 714 754-5454
2701 S Bristol St Santa Ana (92704) *(P-18447)*

South Coast Iron, Placentia *Also Called: Ironwood Fabrication Inc (P-6461)*

South Coast Materials Co, San Diego *Also Called: Forterra Pipe & Precast LLC (P-5415)*

South Coast Plaza LLC .... C...... 714 435-2000
3333 Bristol St Ofc Costa Mesa (92626) *(P-14686)*

South Coast Plaza Mall, Costa Mesa *Also Called: South Coast Plaza LLC (P-14686)*

South Coast Plaza Security .... C...... 714 435-2180
695 Town Center Dr Ste 50 Costa Mesa (92626) *(P-20097)*

South Coast Stairs Inc .... E...... 949 858-1685
30251 Tomas Rcho Sta Marg (92688) *(P-2633)*

South Coast Westin Hotel Co .... D...... 714 540-2500
686 Anton Blvd Costa Mesa (92626) *(P-15364)*

Mergent email: customerrelations@mergent.com
1270

2024 Southern California
Business Directory and Buyers Guide

(P-0000) Products & Services Section entry number
(PA)=Parent Co (HQ)=Headquarters (DH)=Div Headquarters

South Coast Winery Inc .... E 951 587-9463
34843 Rancho California Rd Temecula (92591) *(P-1660)*

South Coast Winery Resort Spa, Temecula *Also Called: South Coast Winery Inc (P-1660)*

South Cone Inc .... C 760 431-2300
5935 Darwin Ct Carlsbad (92008) *(P-13166)*

South Gate Engineering LLC .... C 909 628-2779
13477 Yorba Ave Chino (91710) *(P-6157)*

South Seas Imports, Compton *Also Called: M M Fab Inc (P-13084)*

South Valley Almond Co LLC .... C 661 391-9000
15443 Beech Ave Wasco (93280) *(P-13409)*

South Valley Farms, Wasco *Also Called: South Valley Almond Co LLC (P-13409)*

South West Lubricants Inc .... D 619 449-5000
9266 Abraham Way Santee (92071) *(P-4688)*

Southbay BMW, Torrance *Also Called: Southbay European Inc (P-13829)*

Southbay European Inc .... D 310 939-7300
18800 Hawthorne Blvd Torrance (90504) *(P-13829)*

Southcoast Cabinet Inc (PA) .... E 909 594-3089
755 Pinefalls Ave Walnut (91789) *(P-2679)*

Southcoast Welding & Mfg LLC .... B 619 429-1337
2591 Faivre St Ste 1 Chula Vista (91911) *(P-17095)*

Southeastern Westminster, Westminster *Also Called: Southern California Edison Co (P-12075)*

Souther Cast Stone Inc .... E 760 754-9697
235 Via Del Monte Oceanside (92058) *(P-5450)*

Southern CA Gastroenterology .... D 818 425-9761
50 Alessandro Pl Ste A30 Pasadena (91105) *(P-17770)*

Southern CA Hlth & Rhbltn Prg .... C 310 631-8004
2610 Industry Way Ste A Lynwood (90262) *(P-17771)*

Southern Cal Disc Tire Co Inc .... D 805 639-0166
4640 Telephone Rd Ventura (93003) *(P-13871)*

Southern Cal Disc Tire Co Inc .... C 760 741-9805
550 N Broadway Escondido (92025) *(P-13872)*

Southern Cal Disc Tire Co Inc .... D 760 744-3526
780 Grand Ave San Marcos (92078) *(P-13873)*

Southern Cal Disc Tire Co Inc .... C 760 741-3801
209 S Escondido Blvd Escondido (92025) *(P-13874)*

Southern Cal Disc Tire Co Inc .... C 858 481-6387
685 San Rodolfo Dr Solana Beach (92075) *(P-13875)*

Southern Cal Disc Tire Co Inc .... C 858 486-3600
12651 Poway Rd Poway (92064) *(P-13876)*

Southern Cal Disc Tire Co Inc .... C 760 439-8539
1037 S Coast Hwy Oceanside (92054) *(P-13877)*

Southern Cal Disc Tire Co Inc .... C 760 634-2202
107 N El Camino Real Encinitas (92024) *(P-13878)*

Southern Cal Disc Tire Co Inc .... C 858 278-0661
3935 Convoy St San Diego (92111) *(P-13879)*

Southern Cal Disc Tire Co Inc .... C 310 324-2569
20741 Avalon Blvd Carson (90746) *(P-13880)*

Southern Cal Disc Tire Co Inc .... D 626 335-2883
705 S Grand Ave Glendora (91740) *(P-13881)*

Southern Cal Disc Tire Co Inc .... C 951 929-2130
600 W Florida Ave Hemet (92543) *(P-13882)*

Southern Cal Disc Tire Co Inc .... C 714 901-8226
15672 Springdale St Huntington Beach (92649) *(P-13883)*

Southern Cal Edson - Prvate Ch, Rosemead *Also Called: Southern California Edison Co (P-12064)*

Southern Cal Fd Allergy Inst, Long Beach *Also Called: Transltnl Plmnary Immnlogy RE (P-17806)*

Southern Cal Halthcare Sys Inc (HQ) .... C 310 943-4500
3415 S Sepulveda Blvd 9th Fl Los Angeles (90034) *(P-18448)*

Southern Cal Halthcare Sys Inc .... B 310 836-7000
3828 Delmas Ter Culver City (90232) *(P-18449)*

Southern Cal Hosp At Culver Cy, Culver City *Also Called: Brotman Medical Center Inc (P-18193)*

Southern Cal Hosp At Culver Cy, Culver City *Also Called: Southern Cal Halthcare Sys Inc (P-18449)*

Southern Cal Hydrlic Engrg Cor .... E 714 257-4800
1130 Columbia St Brea (92821) *(P-12822)*

Southern Cal Ibw-Neca Hlth Tr .... D 323 221-5861
100 Corson St Ste 200 Pasadena (91103) *(P-19413)*

Southern Cal Inst For RES Edca .... D 562 826-8139
5901 E 7th St 151 Long Beach (90822) *(P-19945)*

Southern Cal Orthpd Inst LP (PA) .... C 818 901-6600
6815 Noble Ave Van Nuys (91405) *(P-17772)*

Southern Cal Pebblestone, Hawthorne *Also Called: Marleon Inc (P-17093)*

Southern Cal Pipe Trades ADM .... D 619 224-3125
1936 Quivira Way Bldg G San Diego (92109) *(P-14865)*

Southern Cal Prmnnte Med Group .... B 858 974-1000
5855 Copley Dr Ste 250 San Diego (92111) *(P-14497)*

Southern Cal Prmnnte Med Group .... C 619 528-5000
6860 Avenida Encinas Carlsbad (92011) *(P-14498)*

Southern Cal Prmnnte Med Group .... B 800 272-3500
13652 Cantara St Panorama City (91402) *(P-14499)*

Southern Cal Prmnnte Med Group .... C 909 394-2505
1255 W Arrow Hwy San Dimas (91773) *(P-14500)*

Southern Cal Prmnnte Med Group .... B 626 960-4844
1511 W Garvey Ave N West Covina (91790) *(P-14501)*

Southern Cal Prmnnte Med Group .... C 866 984-7483
10800 Magnolia Ave Riverside (92505) *(P-14502)*

Southern Cal Prmnnte Med Group .... C 714 734-4500
17542 17th St Ste 300 Tustin (92780) *(P-14503)*

Southern Cal Prmnnte Med Group .... C 310 737-4900
5620 Mesmer Ave Culver City (90230) *(P-17773)*

Southern Cal Prmnnte Med Group .... C 310 419-3306
110 N La Brea Ave Inglewood (90301) *(P-17774)*

Southern Cal Prmnnte Med Group .... C 323 562-6459
7825 Atlantic Ave Cudahy (90201) *(P-17775)*

Southern Cal Prmnnte Med Group .... C 818 592-3038
21263 Erwin St Woodland Hills (91367) *(P-17776)*

Southern Cal Prmnnte Med Group .... C 661 222-2150
27107 Tourney Rd Santa Clarita (91355) *(P-17777)*

Southern Cal Prmnnte Med Group .... C 661 398-5085
3501 Stockdale Hwy Bakersfield (93309) *(P-17778)*

Southern Cal Prmnnte Med Group .... C 661 334-2020
5055 California Ave Bakersfield (93309) *(P-17779)*

Southern Cal Prmnnte Med Group .... C 310 604-5700
3830 Martin Luther King Jr Blvd Lynwood (90262) *(P-17780)*

Southern Cal Prmnnte Med Group .... C 323 857-2000
6041 Cadillac Ave Los Angeles (90034) *(P-17781)*

Southern Cal Prmnnte Med Group .... C 800 780-1230
25825 Vermont Ave Harbor City (90710) *(P-17782)*

Southern Cal Prmnnte Med Group .... C 323 783-5455
4841 Hollywood Blvd Los Angeles (90027) *(P-17783)*

Southern Cal Prmnnte Med Group .... C 323 783-4893
4760 W Sunset Blvd Los Angeles (90027) *(P-17784)*

Southern Cal Prmnnte Med Group .... B 619 528-5000
4647 Zion Ave San Diego (92120) *(P-17785)*

Southern Cal Prmnnte Med Group .... C 619 528-5000
1630 E Main St El Cajon (92021) *(P-17786)*

Southern Cal Prmnnte Med Group .... C 619 516-6000
4405 Vandever Ave San Diego (92120) *(P-17787)*

Southern Cal Prmnnte Med Group .... C 760 839-7200
732 N Broadway Escondido (92025) *(P-17788)*

Southern Cal Prmnnte Med Group .... C 909 370-2501
789 E Cooley Dr Colton (92324) *(P-17789)*

Southern Cal Prmnnte Med Group .... C 949 262-5780
6 Willard Irvine (92604) *(P-17790)*

Southern Cal Prmnnte Med Group .... C 714 841-7293
18081 Beach Blvd Huntington Beach (92648) *(P-17791)*

Southern Cal Prmnnte Med Group .... C 714 279-4675
411 N Lakeview Ave Anaheim (92807) *(P-17792)*

Southern Cal Prmnnte Med Group .... C 949 234-2139
30400 Camino Capistrano San Juan Capistrano (92675) *(P-17793)*

Southern Cal Prmnnte Med Group .... C 714 967-4760
1900 E 4th St Santa Ana (92705) *(P-17794)*

Southern Cal Prmnnte Med Group .... B 661 290-3100
26415 Carl Boyer Dr Santa Clarita (91350) *(P-18450)*

Southern Cal Prmnnte Med Group .... B 562 657-2200
9353 Imperial Hwy Garden Medical Bldg Flr 3 Downey (90242) *(P-18451)*

Southern Cal Prmnnte Med Group .... B 909 427-5000
9961 Sierra Ave Fontana (92335) *(P-18452)*

Southern Cal Prmnnte Med Group .... C 949 376-8619
23781 Maquina Mission Viejo (92691) *(P-18805)*

ALPHABETIC

Employee Codes: A=Over 500 employees, B=251-500
C=101-250, D=51-100, E=20-50, F=10-19, G=1-9

2024 Southern California
Business Directory and Buyers Guide

© Mergent Inc. 1-800-342-5647

1271

Southern Cal Prmnnte Med Group ....C...... 323 564-7911
1465 E 103rd St Los Angeles (90002) *(P-19014)*

Southern Cal Rgional Rail Auth ....C...... 213 808-7043
2704 N Garey Ave Pomona (91767) *(P-11367)*

Southern Cal Rgional Rail Auth (PA).............**C...... 213 452-0200**
900 Wilshire Blvd Ste 1500 Los Angeles (90017) *(P-11368)*

Southern Cal Spcialty Care Inc......................C...... 626 339-5451
845 N Lark Ellen Ave West Covina (91791) *(P-18453)*

Southern Cal Spcialty Care Inc......................C...... 714 564-7800
1901 College Ave Santa Ana (92706) *(P-18454)*

Southern Cal Spcialty Care Inc, La Mirada *Also Called: Southern Cal Spcialty Care LLC*
(P-18455)

Southern Cal Spcialty Care LLC (DH)............. **D...... 562 944-1900**
14900 Imperial Hwy La Mirada (90638) *(P-18455)*

Southern Cal Tchnical Arts Inc ....E...... 714 524-2626
370 E Crowther Ave Placentia (92870) *(P-8033)*

Southern California Edison Co ....D...... 818 999-1880
3589 Foothill Dr Thousand Oaks (91361) *(P-12056)*

Southern California Edison Co ....D...... 562 529-7301
6900 Orange Ave Long Beach (90805) *(P-12057)*

Southern California Edison Co ....B...... 626 814-4212
13025 Los Angeles St Irwindale (91706) *(P-12058)*

Southern California Edison Co ....C...... 909 592-3757
800 W Cienega Ave San Dimas (91773) *(P-12059)*

Southern California Edison Co ....B...... 562 903-3191
9901 Geary Ave Santa Fe Springs (90670) *(P-12060)*

Southern California Edison Co ....B...... 562 491-3803
125 Elm Ave Long Beach (90802) *(P-12061)*

Southern California Edison Co ....C...... 626 812-7380
6090 N Irwindale Ave Irwindale (91702) *(P-12062)*

Southern California Edison Co ....A...... 626 308-6193
501 S Marengo Ave Alhambra (91803) *(P-12063)*

Southern California Edison Co ....B...... 626 302-1212
2131 Walnut Grove Ave Rosemead (91770) *(P-12064)*

Southern California Edison Co ....B...... 909 274-1925
2 Innovation Way Fl 1 Pomona (91768) *(P-12065)*

Southern California Edison Co ....C...... 760 375-1821
510 S China Lake Blvd Ridgecrest (93555) *(P-12066)*

Southern California Edison Co ....C...... 626 303-8480
1440 S California Ave Monrovia (91016) *(P-12067)*

Southern California Edison Co ....D...... 626 815-7296
6000 N Irwindale Ave Ste A Irwindale (91702) *(P-12068)*

Southern California Edison Co ....A...... 909 469-0251
265 Ne End Ave Pomona (91767) *(P-12069)*

Southern California Edison Co ....B...... 310 608-5029
1924 E Cashdan St Compton (90220) *(P-12070)*

Southern California Edison Co ....C...... 661 607-0207
28250 Gateway Village Dr Valencia (91355) *(P-12071)*

Southern California Edison Co (HQ).............**A...... 626 302-1212**
2244 Walnut Grove Ave Rosemead (91770) *(P-12072)*

Southern California Edison Co ....B...... 714 870-3225
1851 W Valencia Dr Fullerton (92833) *(P-12073)*

Southern California Edison Co ....D...... 800 336-2822
26125 Menifee Rd Romoland (92585) *(P-12074)*

Southern California Edison Co ....A...... 714 895-0420
7300 Fenwick Ln Westminster (92683) *(P-12075)*

Southern California Edison Co ....C...... 949 587-5416
14155 Bake Pkwy Irvine (92618) *(P-12076)*

Southern California Edison Co ....D...... 714 895-0163
7333 Bolsa Ave Westminster (92683) *(P-12077)*

Southern California Gas Co ....B...... 818 701-2592
9400 Oakdale Ave Chatsworth (91311) *(P-12080)*

Southern California Gas Co ....D...... 213 244-1200
25200 Trumble Rd Romoland (92585) *(P-12083)*

Southern California Gas Co (HQ)....................**A..... 213 244-1200**
555 W 5th St Ste 14h1 Los Angeles (90013) *(P-12084)*

Southern California Gas Co ....D...... 714 634-7221
1 Liberty Aliso Viejo (92656) *(P-12085)*

Southern California Gas Co ....C...... 213 244-1200
3050 E La Jolla St Anaheim (92806) *(P-12086)*

Southern California Gas Co ....C...... 800 427-2200
23130 Valencia Blvd Valencia (91355) *(P-12087)*

Southern California Gas Co ....D...... 323 881-3587
333 E Main St Ste J Alhambra (91801) *(P-12088)*

Southern California Gas Co ....D...... 562 803-3341
6738 Bright Ave Whittier (90601) *(P-12089)*

Southern California Gas Co ....B...... 310 823-7945
8141 Gulana Ave Venice (90293) *(P-12090)*

Southern California Gas Co ....C...... 213 244-1200
1600 Corporate Center Dr Monterey Park (91754) *(P-12091)*

Southern California Gas Co ....C...... 909 305-8297
1050 Overland Ct San Dimas (91773) *(P-12092)*

Southern California Gas Co ....C...... 661 399-4431
1510 N Chester Ave Bakersfield (93308) *(P-12093)*

Southern California Gas Co ....B...... 818 363-8542
12801 Tampa Ave Northridge (91326) *(P-12094)*

Southern California Gas Co ....A...... 562 803-7500
9240 Firestone Blvd Downey (90241) *(P-12095)*

Southern California Gas Co ....A...... 213 244-1200
1801 S Atlantic Blvd Monterey Park (91754) *(P-12096)*

Southern California Gas Co ....C...... 213 244-1200
920 S Stimson Ave City Of Industry (91745) *(P-12097)*

Southern California Gas Co ....B...... 909 335-7802
1981 W Lugonia Ave Redlands (92374) *(P-12098)*

Southern California Gas Co ....C...... 909 335-7941
155 S G St San Bernardino (92410) *(P-12099)*

Southern California Gas Tower ....A...... 213 244-1200
555 W 5th St Los Angeles (90013) *(P-12100)*

Southern California Material Handling Inc ....C....... 562 949-1006
12393 Slauson Ave Whittier (90606) *(P-12823)*

Southern California Messenger, Los Angeles *Also Called: Prompt Delivery Inc (P-16909)*

Southern California Mtl Hdlg, Whittier *Also Called: Equipment Depot Inc (P-12790)*

SOUTHERN CALIFORNIA PERMANENTE MEDICAL GROUP, Carlsbad *Also Called:*
Southern Cal Prmnnte Med Group (P-14498)

Southern California Permanente Medical Group, Riverside *Also Called: Southern Cal*
Prmnnte Med Group (P-14502)

SOUTHERN CALIFORNIA PERMANENTE MEDICAL GROUP, Mission Viejo *Also Called:*
Southern Cal Prmnnte Med Group (P-18805)

Southern California Plas Inc ....D...... 714 751-7084
3122 Maple St Santa Ana (92707) *(P-3971)*

Southern California Plating Co ....E...... 619 231-1481
3261 National Ave San Diego (92113) *(P-6664)*

Southern California Regional, Indio *Also Called: Granite Construction Company (P-618)*

Southern California Trane, Brea *Also Called: Trane US Inc (P-7628)*

Southern Contracting Company ....C...... 760 744-0760
559 N Twin Oaks Valley Rd San Marcos (92069) *(P-937)*

Southern Counties Oil Co (DH)......................**D...... 714 744-7140**
1800 W Katella Ave Ste 210 Orange (92867) *(P-13445)*

Southern Counties Terminals ....D...... 310 642-0462
5341 W 104th St Los Angeles (90045) *(P-11465)*

Southern Electronics, Pomona *Also Called: Electrocube Inc (P-9039)*

Southern Glzers Wine Sprits Ca, Cerritos *Also Called: Southern Glzers Wine Sprits LL*
(P-13481)

Southern Glzers Wine Sprits LL ....B...... 562 926-2000
17101 Valley View Ave Cerritos (90703) *(P-13481)*

Southern Home Care Svcs Inc ....D...... 714 979-7413
2900 Bristol St Ste D107 Costa Mesa (92626) *(P-15943)*

Southern Implants Inc ....C...... 949 273-8505
5 Holland Ste 209 Irvine (92618) *(P-20098)*

Southern Indian Health Council (PA)..............**D...... 619 445-1188**
4058 Willows Rd Alpine (91901) *(P-18720)*

Southern International Packg, Rancho Palos Verdes *Also Called: Western Summit Mfg Corp*
(P-4826)

Southern Management Corp ....D...... 213 312-2268
808 S Olive St Los Angeles (90014) *(P-15750)*

Southern Sierra Medical Clinic, Ridgecrest *Also Called: Ridgecrest Regional Hospital*
(P-18407)

Southland Box Company ....C...... 323 583-2231
4201 Fruitland Ave Vernon (90058) *(P-3130)*

Southland Care, San Juan Capistrano *Also Called: Ensign Southland LLC (P-17946)*

Southland Container Corp ....C...... 909 937-9781
1600 Champagne Ave Ontario (91761) *(P-3131)*

Southland Enterprises, Escondido *Also Called: Southland Manufacturing Inc (P-7131)*

Southland Envelope Company Inc ....C...... 619 449-3553
10111 Riverford Rd Lakeside (92040) *(P-3214)*

Southland Manufacturing Inc ....E...... 760 745-7913
1311 Daisy St Escondido (92027) *(P-7131)*

Southland Paving Inc ....D...... 760 747-6895
361 N Hale Ave Escondido (92029) *(P-1087)*

Southland Polymers Inc ....E...... 562 921-0444
14030 Gannet St Santa Fe Springs (90670) *(P-3972)*

Southland Ready Mix Concrete, Escondido *Also Called: Superior Ready Mix Concrete LP*
(P-5510)

Southland Technology Inc ....D...... 858 694-0932
8053 Vickers St San Diego (92111) *(P-12440)*

Southwest Administrators Inc ....B
466 Foothill Blvd La Canada Flintridge (91011) *(P-14551)*

Southwest Airlines, Santa Ana *Also Called: Southwest Airlines Co (P-11671)*

Southwest Airlines Co ....D...... 949 252-5200
18601 Airport Way Ste 237 Santa Ana (92707) *(P-11671)*

Southwest Boulder & Stone Inc (PA).................**E...... 760 451-3333**
5002 2nd St Fallbrook (92028) *(P-14150)*

Southwest Concrete Products ....C...... 909 983-9789
519 S Benson Ave Ontario (91762) *(P-5451)*

Southwest Contractors (PA)...............................**E...... 661 588-0484**
136 Allen Rd # 100 Bakersfield (93314) *(P-693)*

Southwest Crpnters Trning Fund ....D...... 213 386-8590
533 S Fremont Ave Ste 700 Los Angeles (90071) *(P-19414)*

Southwest Data Products, San Bernardino *Also Called: Innovative Metal Inds Inc (P-6399)*

Southwest Greene Intl Inc ....D...... 760 639-4960
4055b Calle Platino Oceanside (92056) *(P-6556)*

Southwest Healthcare Sys Aux ....A...... 800 404-6627
38977 Sky Canyon Dr Ste 200 Murrieta (92563) *(P-18456)*

Southwest Healthcare Sys Aux (HQ)..................**B...... 951 696-6000**
25500 Medical Center Dr Murrieta (92562) *(P-18457)*

Southwest Landscape Inc ....D...... 714 545-1084
2205 S Standard Ave Santa Ana (92707) *(P-179)*

Southwest Machine & Plastic Co ....E...... 626 963-6919
620 W Foothill Blvd Glendora (91741) *(P-9799)*

Southwest Manufacturing Svcs, El Cajon *Also Called: Pacific Marine Sheet Metal Corporation*
(P-6286)

Southwest Material Hdlg Inc (PA).......................**C...... 951 727-0477**
3725 Nobel Ct Jurupa Valley (91752) *(P-13830)*

Southwest Offset Prtg Co Inc (PA).....................**B...... 310 965-9154**
13650 Gramercy Pl Gardena (90249) *(P-3687)*

Southwest Patrol Inc ....D...... 909 861-1884
1800 E Lambert Rd Ste 155 Brea (92821) *(P-16691)*

Southwest Plastics Co, Glendora *Also Called: Southwest Machine & Plastic Co (P-9799)*

Southwest Products LLC ....C...... 619 263-8000
8411 Siempre Viva Rd San Diego (92154) *(P-1989)*

Southwest Protective Svcs Inc ....C...... 760 996-1285
404 W Heil Ave El Centro (92243) *(P-16692)*

Southwest Rgnal Cncil Crpnters ....D...... 714 571-0449
7111 Firestone Blvd Buena Park (90621) *(P-19415)*

Southwest Security, El Centro *Also Called: Southwest Protective Svcs Inc (P-16692)*

Southwest Sign Company, Corona *Also Called: Fovell Enterprises Inc (P-11121)*

Southwest Toyota Lift, Jurupa Valley *Also Called: Southwest Material Hdlg Inc (P-13830)*

Southwest Traders Incorporated (PA)................**C...... 951 699-7800**
27565 Diaz Rd Temecula (92590) *(P-13231)*

Southwestern Industries Inc (PA).......................**D...... 310 608-4422**
2615 Homestead Pl Rancho Dominguez (90220) *(P-7025)*

Southwind Foods LLC (PA).................................**C...... 323 262-8222**
20644 S Fordyce Ave Carson (90810) *(P-1796)*

Southwire Company LLC ....D...... 909 989-2888
9199 Cleveland Ave Ste 100 Rancho Cucamonga (91730) *(P-5690)*

Southwire Inc ....B...... 310 886-8300
20250 S Alameda St Compton (90221) *(P-5691)*

Sovereign Flavors Inc ....E...... 760 455-0446
4030 W Chandler Ave Santa Ana (92704) *(P-1783)*

Sovereign Health, Rancho Mirage *Also Called: Dual Diagnosis Trtmnt Ctr Inc (P-18760)*

Sovereign Health of California, San Clemente *Also Called: Dual Diagnosis Trtmnt Ctr Inc*
(P-18691)

Soxnet Inc ....F...... 626 934-9400
235 S 6th Ave La Puente (91746) *(P-2061)*

Soyfoods of America ....E...... 626 358-3836
1091 Hamilton Rd Duarte (91010) *(P-1990)*

Sp, City Of Industry *Also Called: Scope Packaging Inc (P-3128)*

Sp Craftech I LLC ....E...... 714 630-8117
2941 E La Jolla St Anaheim (92806) *(P-5212)*

Sp Crankshaft, Irvine *Also Called: Pankl Engine Systems Inc (P-9437)*

Spa De Soleil Inc ....E...... 818 504-3200
10443 Arminta St Sun Valley (91352) *(P-13070)*

Spa Havens LP ....C...... 760 945-2055
29402 Spa Haven Way Vista (92084) *(P-17414)*

Spa Resort Casino ....A...... 760 883-1034
100 N Indian Canyon Dr Palm Springs (92262) *(P-15365)*

Spa Resort Casino, Palm Springs *Also Called: Agua Clnte Band Chilla Indians (P-15070)*

Space Components, Commerce *Also Called: Atk Space Systems LLC (P-9954)*

Space Components Division, San Diego *Also Called: Atk Space Systems LLC (P-9952)*

Space Exploration Tech Corp ....E...... 310 848-4410
731 Kelp Rd Slc-4 Vandenberg Afb (93437) *(P-9554)*

Space Exploration Tech Corp (PA).....................**A...... 310 363-6000**
1 Rocket Rd Hawthorne (90250) *(P-9898)*

Space Exploration Tech Corp ....E...... 714 330-8668
2700 Miner St San Pedro (90731) *(P-9899)*

Space Exploration Tech Corp ....E...... 323 754-1285
12520 Wilkie Ave Gardena (90249) *(F-9900)*

Space Exploration Tech Corp ....E...... 310 889-4968
3976 Jack Northrop Ave Hawthorne (90250) *(P-9901)*

Space Micro Inc ....C...... 858 332-0700
15378 Avenue Of Science Ste 200 San Diego (92128) *(P-8583)*

Space Systems Division, El Segundo *Also Called: Orbital Sciences LLC (P-10046)*

Space Vector Corporation ....E...... 818 734-2600
20520 Nordhoff St Chatsworth (91311) *(P-10072)*

Space-Lok Inc ....C...... 310 527-6150
13306 Halldale Ave Gardena (90249) *(P-9800)*

Spacemaker, Santa Ana *Also Called: Watts Spacemaker Inc (P-6170)*

Spaceship Company, The, Mojave *Also Called: Galactic Co LLC (P-9893)*

Spacestor Inc ....E...... 310 410-0220
16411 Carmenita Rd Cerritos (90703) *(P-2899)*

Spacesystems Holdings LLC ....E...... 714 226-1400
4398 Corporate Center Dr Los Alamitos (90720) *(P-8165)*

Spacex, Hawthorne *Also Called: Space Exploration Tech Corp (P-9898)*

Spacex, San Pedro *Also Called: Space Exploration Tech Corp (P-9899)*

Spacex, Hawthorne *Also Called: Space Exploration Tech Corp (P-9901)*

Spacex LLC ....A...... 310 970-5845
12533 Crenshaw Blvd Hawthorne (90250) *(P-9902)*

Spacex Wilkie, Gardena *Also Called: Space Exploration Tech Corp (P-9900)*

Spalinger Enterprises Inc ....E...... 661 834-4550
800 S Mount Vernon Ave Bakersfield (93307) *(P-2965)*

Span-O-Matic Inc ....E...... 714 256-4700
825 Columbia St Brea (92821) *(P-6319)*

Spangler Industries Inc ....C...... 951 735-5000
1711 N Delilah St Corona (92879) *(P-4796)*

Spanish Hills Club LLC ....E...... 805 388-5000
999 Crestview Ave Camarillo (93010) *(P-17525)*

Spanish Hills Country Club (PA).........................**C...... 805 389-1644**
999 Crestview Ave Camarillo (93010) *(P-17526)*

Sparitual, Van Nuys *Also Called: Orly International Inc (P-4440)*

Spark Compass, Los Angeles *Also Called: Total Cmmnicator Solutions Inc (P-16409)*

Sparks Exhbits Envrnments Corp ....D...... 562 941-0101
3143 S La Cienega Blvd Los Angeles (90016) *(P-11284)*

Sparks Los Angeles, Los Angeles *Also Called: Sparks Exhbits Envrnments Corp (P-11284)*

Sparling Instruments LLC ....E...... 626 444-0571
4097 Temple City Blvd El Monte (91731) *(P-10178)*

Spartan Inc ....D...... 661 327-1205
3030 M St Bakersfield (93301) *(P-6077)*

Spartan Manufacturing Co ....E...... 714 894-1955
7081 Patterson Dr Garden Grove (92841) *(P-6422)*

Spartan Truck Company Inc ....E...... 818 899-1111
12266 Branford St Sun Valley (91352) *(P-9334)*

Spartech Plastics, La Mirada *Also Called: Alchem Plastics Inc (P-4831)*

Spates Fabricators, Thermal *Also Called: Spates Fabricators Inc (P-2703)*

ALPHABETIC

Employee Codes: A=Over 500 employees, B=251-500
C=101-250, D=51-100, E=20-50, F=10-19, G=1-9

2024 Southern California
Business Directory and Buyers Guide

© Mergent Inc. 1-800-342-5647

1273

Spates Fabricators Inc .... D....... 760 397-4122
85435 Middleton St Thermal (92274) *(P-2703)*

Spatz Corporation .... C....... 805 487-2122
1600 Westar Dr Oxnard (93033) *(P-4457)*

Spatz Laboratories, Oxnard *Also Called: Spatz Corporation (P-4457)*

Spaulding Crusher Parts, Perris *Also Called: Spaulding Equipment Company (P-6951)*

Spaulding Equipment Company (PA)............................ E....... 951 943-4531
75 Paseo Adelanto Perris (92570) *(P-6951)*

Spc Building Services, Riverside *Also Called: J M V B Inc (P-849)*

SPD Manufacturing Inc .... F....... 985 302-1902
1101 E Truslow Ave Fullerton (92831) *(P-2044)*

Speakercraft LLC .... D....... 951 685-1759
12471 Riverside Dr Eastvale (91752) *(P-8439)*

Spearman Aerospace Inc .... E....... 714 523-4751
9215 Greenleaf Ave Santa Fe Springs (90670) *(P-19693)*

Spearmint Rhino Cmpnies Wrldwi .... D....... 951 371-3788
1875 Tandem Norco (92860) *(P-20099)*

Spearmint Rhino Gentlemens CLB, Torrance *Also Called: Midnight Sun Enterprises Inc (P-20362)*

Spears Manufacturing Co .... D....... 818 364-1611
15860 Olden St Rancho Cascades (91342) *(P-4854)*

Spears Manufacturing Co (PA) .... C....... 818 364-1611
15853 St Rancho Cascades (91342) *(P-12782)*

Spec, Valencia *Also Called: Semiconductor Process Eqp LLC (P-8885)*

Spec Engineering Company Inc .... E....... 818 780-3045
13754 Saticoy St Panorama City (91402) *(P-8034)*

Spec Formliners Inc .... E....... 714 429-9500
1038 E 4th St Santa Ana (92701) *(P-5452)*

Spec Services Inc .... B....... 714 963-8077
10540 Talbert Ave Ste 100e Fountain Valley (92708) *(P-19694)*

Spec Tool Company .... C....... 323 723-9533
11805 Wakeman St Santa Fe Springs (90670) *(P-9801)*

Spec-Built Systems Inc .... D....... 619 661-8100
2150 Michael Faraday Dr San Diego (92154) *(P-6320)*

Special Devices Incorporated .... A....... 805 387-1000
2655 1st St Ste 125 Simi Valley (93065) *(P-9461)*

Special Event Audio Svcs Inc .... E....... 800 518-9144
35889 Shetland Hls E Fallbrook (92028) *(P-17351)*

Special Operations Tech, Carson *Also Called: SO Tech/Spcl Op Tech Inc (P-13093)*

Special Products Group, Chula Vista *Also Called: Sealed Air Corporation (P-4903)*

Special Service For Groups Inc (PA) .... D....... 213 368-1888
905 E 8th St Los Angeles (90021) *(P-19192)*

Special Service For Groups Inc .... C....... 310 323-6887
19401 S Vermont Ave Ste A200 Torrance (90502) *(P-19344)*

Special Service For Groups Inc .... C....... 213 553-1800
520 S La Fayette Park Pl # 30 Los Angeles (90057) *(P-19345)*

Special Service For Groups Ssg, Los Angeles *Also Called: Special Service For Groups Inc (P-19192)*

Special-T, North Hollywood *Also Called: Specialty Coatings & Chem Inc (P-4507)*

Specialist Media Group, Carlsbad *Also Called: L & L Printers Carlsbad LLC (P-3615)*

Specialists In Cstm Sftwr Inc .... E....... 310 315-9660
2574 Wellesley Ave Los Angeles (90064) *(P-16386)*

Speciality Labs, Fullerton *Also Called: Magtech & Power Conversion Inc (P-8945)*

Specialized Dairy Service Inc .... E....... 909 923-3420
1710 E Philadelphia St Ontario (91761) *(P-6914)*

Specialized Milling Corp .... D....... 909 357-7890
10330 Elm Ave Fontana (92337) *(P-4506)*

Specialized Screen Prtg Inc .... F....... 714 964-1230
18435 Bandilier Cir Fountain Valley (92708) *(P-3812)*

Specialteam Medical Svc Inc .... F....... 714 694-0348
22445 La Palma Ave Ste F Yorba Linda (92887) *(P-10607)*

Specialty Brands Incorporated .... A....... 909 477-4851
4200 Concours Ste 100 Ontario (91764) *(P-1401)*

Specialty Coating Systems Inc .... D....... 909 390-8818
4435 E Airport Dr Ste 100 Ontario (91761) *(P-6738)*

Specialty Coatings & Chem Inc .... E....... 818 983-0055
7360 Varna Ave North Hollywood (91605) *(P-4507)*

Specialty Construction Inc .... D....... 805 543-1706
645 Clarion Ct San Luis Obispo (93401) *(P-938)*

Specialty Division, Santa Fe Springs *Also Called: Distinctive Industries (P-2529)*

Specialty Enterprises Co .... D....... 323 726-9721
6858 E Acco St Commerce (90040) *(P-4906)*

Specialty Fabrications Inc .... E....... 805 579-9730
2674 Westhills Ct Simi Valley (93065) *(P-6321)*

Specialty Finishes, Fontana *Also Called: Specialized Milling Corp (P-4506)*

Specialty Interior Mfg Inc .... E....... 714 296-8618
16751 Millikan Ave Irvine (92606) *(P-12263)*

Specialty International Inc .... E....... 818 768-8810
11144 Penrose St Ste 11 Sun Valley (91352) *(P-6557)*

Specialty Laboratories Inc (DH) .... A....... 661 799-6543
27027 Tourney Rd Valencia (91355) *(P-18565)*

Specialty Minerals Inc .... C....... 760 248-5300
6565 Meridian Rd Lucerne Valley (92356) *(P-3915)*

Specialty Motions Inc .... E....... 951 735-8722
5480 Smokey Mountain Way Yorba Linda (92887) *(P-7304)*

Specialty Motors, Valencia *Also Called: SMI Holdings Inc (P-8158)*

Specialty Paper Mills Inc .... C....... 562 692-8737
8844 Millergrove Dr Santa Fe Springs (90670) *(P-3063)*

Specialty Restaurants Corp .... C....... 818 843-5013
1250 E Harvard Rd Burbank (91501) *(P-14037)*

Specialty Sugical Ctr Encino, Encino *Also Called: Symbion Inc (P-17800)*

Specialty Surgical of Westlake, Westlake Village *Also Called: Symbion Inc (P-17799)*

Specialty Team Plastering Inc .... C....... 805 966-3858
4652 Vintage Ranch Ln Santa Barbara (93110) *(P-997)*

Specialty Textile Services LLC .... C....... 619 476-8750
1333 30th St Ste A San Diego (92154) *(P-13095)*

Specilty Enzymes Btechnologies .... F....... 909 613-1660
13591 Yorba Ave Chino (91710) *(P-4530)*

Specilty Enzymes Btechnologies, Chino *Also Called: Cal-India Foods International (P-4517)*

Specimen Contracting, Sunland *Also Called: Brightview Tree Company (P-228)*

Spectra Color Inc .... E....... 951 277-0200
9116 Stellar Ct Corona (92883) *(P-3878)*

Spectra Company .... C....... 909 599-0760
2510 Supply St Pomona (91767) *(P-962)*

Spectra USA, Chino *Also Called: Isiqalo LLC (P-2072)*

Spectral Labs, San Diego *Also Called: Spectral Labs Incorporated (P-10398)*

Spectral Labs Incorporated .... E....... 858 451-0540
15920 Bernardo Center Dr San Diego (92127) *(P-10398)*

Spectrolab Inc .... B....... 818 365-4611
12500 Gladstone Ave Sylmar (91342) *(P-9119)*

Spectrum Accessory Distrs Inc .... F....... 858 653-6470
9770 Carroll Centre Rd San Diego (92126) *(P-9462)*

Spectrum Assembly Inc .... C....... 760 930-4000
6300 Yarrow Dr Ste 100 Carlsbad (92011) *(P-8733)*

Spectrum Bags, Cerritos *Also Called: Ips Industries Inc (P-5063)*

Spectrum Brands Inc .... A....... 949 672-4003
19701 Da Vinci Lake Forest (92610) *(P-9160)*

Spectrum Brands Hdwr HM Imprv, Foothill Ranch *Also Called: Kwikset Corporation (P-5926)*

Spectrum Brands Hhi, Lake Forest *Also Called: Spectrum Brands Inc (P-9160)*

Spectrum Club, Los Angeles *Also Called: Bay Clubs Company LLC (P-17395)*

Spectrum Club Thousand Oaks, Chatsworth *Also Called: Bay Clubs Company LLC (P-17394)*

Spectrum Clubs Inc .... A....... 310 727-9300
840 Apollo St Ste 100 El Segundo (90245) *(P-17415)*

Spectrum Cnstr Group Inc .... D....... 949 299-1400
514 Via De La Valle Ste 210 Solana Beach (92075) *(P-518)*

Spectrum Electronics, Carlsbad *Also Called: Spectrum Assembly Inc (P-8733)*

Spectrum Equipment LLC .... D....... 760 599-8849
2505 Commerce Way Vista (92081) *(P-13519)*

Spectrum Floral Service, Vista *Also Called: Spectrum Equipment LLC (P-13519)*

Spectrum Hotel Group LLC .... D....... 949 471-8888
90 Pacifica Irvine (92618) *(P-15366)*

Spectrum Inc .... C....... 310 885-4600
18617 S Broadwick St Rancho Dominguez (90220) *(P-10608)*

Spectrum Intl Holdings .... A....... 626 333-7225
14421 Bonelli St City Of Industry (91746) *(P-2993)*

Spectrum Lab & Phrm Pdts, Gardena *Also Called: Spectrum Laboratory Pdts Inc (P-13439)*

Spectrum Laboratories, Rancho Dominguez *Also Called: Spectrum Inc (P-10608)*

Spectrum Laboratory Pdts Inc .... E....... 520 292-3103
14422 S San Pedro St Gardena (90248) *(P-13439)*

Mergent email: customerrelations@mergent.com
1274

2024 Southern California
Business Directory and Buyers Guide

(P-0000) Products & Services Section entry number
(PA)=Parent Co (HQ)=Headquarters (DH)=Div Headquarters

Spectrum Lighting, Santa Fe Springs *Also Called: Dab Inc (P-8291)*

Spectrum MGT Holdg Co LLC ....D...... 323 657-0899
3550 Wilshire Blvd Los Angeles (90010) *(P-11999)*

Spectrum MGT Holdg Co LLC ....D...... 619 684-6106
5865 Friars Rd San Diego (92110) *(P-12000)*

Spectrum Plating Company, Los Angeles *Also Called: Ravlich Enterprises LLC (P-6655)*

Spectrum Scientific Inc ....E...... 949 260-9900
16692 Hale Ave Ste A Irvine (92606) *(P-10340)*

Spectrum Security Services Inc (PA).................................**C...... 619 669-6660**
13967 Campo Rd Ste 101 Jamul (91935) *(P-16693)*

Speed-O-Pin International ....F...... 562 433-4911
1401 Freeman Ave Long Beach (90804) *(P-3016)*

Speedo USA, Cypress *Also Called: Speedo USA Inc (P-2219)*

Speedo USA Inc ....B...... 657 465-3800
6251 Katella Ave Cypress (90630) *(P-2219)*

Speedpress Sign Supply, Carlsbad *Also Called: Coplan & Coplan Inc (P-7111)*

Speedwear.com, Huntington Beach *Also Called: Gachupin Enterprises LLC (P-3761)*

Speedy Circuits, Huntington Beach *Also Called: Coast To Coast Circuits Inc (P-8664)*

Speedy Express LLC ....D...... 818 300-7785
4401 W Slauson Ave Ste A Los Angeles (90043) *(P-11538)*

Spencer Forrest Inc ....E
11777 San Vicente Blvd Ste 650 Los Angeles (90049) *(P-14105)*

Spenuzza Inc ....E...... 626 358-8063
913 Oak Ave Duarte (91010) *(P-7687)*

Spenuzza Inc (HQ)...**D...... 951 281-1830**
1128 Sherborn St Corona (92879) *(P-7688)*

SPEP Acquisition Corp (PA)...**D...... 310 608-0693**
4041 Via Oro Ave Long Beach (90810) *(P-5944)*

Sperber Ldscp Companies LLC (PA)....................................**C...... 818 437-1029**
30700 Russell Ranch Rd Ste 120 Westlake Village (91362) *(P-180)*

Spf Capital Real Estate LLC ....D...... 310 519-8200
601 S Palos Verdes St San Pedro (90731) *(P-15367)*

Sphere Alliance Inc ....E...... 951 352-2400
3087 12th St Riverside (92507) *(P-3973)*

Spherion Prof Recruiting Group, San Diego *Also Called: Sfn Group Inc (P-15942)*

Spice Products Company, Anaheim *Also Called: Harris Spice Company Inc (P-13727)*

Spidell Publishing Inc ....E...... 714 776-7850
1134 N Gilbert St Anaheim (92801) *(P-3485)*

Spill Magic Inc ....E...... 714 557-2001
630 Young St Santa Ana (92705) *(P-3064)*

Spilo Worldwide, Santa Monica *Also Called: Spilo Worldwide Inc (P-12895)*

Spilo Worldwide Inc ....D...... 213 687-8600
100 Wilshire Blvd Ste 700 Santa Monica (90401) *(P-12895)*

Spin Products Inc ....E...... 909 590-7000
13878 Yorba Ave Chino (91710) *(P-5213)*

Spinal Elements, Carlsbad *Also Called: Spinal Elements Holdings Inc (P-10609)*

Spinal Elements Holdings Inc ....C...... 877 774-6255
3115 Melrose Dr Ste 200 Carlsbad (92010) *(P-10609)*

Spinergy Inc ....D...... 760 496-2121
1709 La Costa Meadows Dr San Marcos (92078) *(P-9884)*

Spiniello Companies ....C...... 909 629-1000
2650 Pomona Blvd Pomona (91768) *(P-694)*

Spinlaunch Inc ....D...... 650 516-7746
4350 E Conant St Long Beach (90808) *(P-9913)*

Spira Manufacturing Corp ....E...... 818 764-8222
650 Jessie St San Fernando (91340) *(P-4746)*

Spiral Ppr Tube & Core Co Inc ....E...... 562 801-9705
5200 Industry Ave Pico Rivera (90660) *(P-3139)*

Spirent Calabasas, Calabasas *Also Called: Spirent Communications Inc (P-12441)*

Spirent Communications Inc (HQ).......................................**B...... 818 676-2300**
27349 Agoura Rd Calabasas (91301) *(P-12441)*

Spireon Inc (PA)..**C...... 800 557-1449**
18881 Von Karman Ave Ste 1500 Irvine (92612) *(P-16121)*

Spirit Active Wear, Vernon *Also Called: Spirit Clothing Company (P-2371)*

Spirit Clothing Company ....C...... 213 784-0251
2211 E 37th St Vernon (90058) *(P-2371)*

Spitzlift, San Diego *Also Called: Hirok Inc (P-6936)*

Spm, Anaheim *Also Called: Bace Manufacturing Inc (P-4953)*

Spokeo Inc ....C...... 877 913-3088
556 S Fair Oaks Ave Ste 1 Pasadena (91105) *(P-11902)*

Spooners Woodworks, Poway *Also Called: Spooners Woodworks Inc (P-2966)*

Spooners Woodworks Inc ....C...... 858 679-9086
12460 Kirkham Ct Poway (92064) *(P-2966)*

Sport Card Co LLC ....B...... 800 873-7332
5830 El Camino Real Carlsbad (92008) *(P-3688)*

Sport Clips, San Diego *Also Called: Sport Clips Inc (P-15486)*

Sport Clips Inc ....A...... 858 273-9993
4839 Clairemont Dr Ste E San Diego (92117) *(P-15486)*

Sport Kites Inc ....F...... 714 998-6359
500 W Blueridge Ave Orange (92865) *(P-9555)*

Sport Tek, Commerce *Also Called: Sportek International Inc (P-13111)*

Sportek International Inc ....F...... 213 239-6700
2425 S Eastern Ave Commerce (90040) *(P-13111)*

Sportifeye Optics Inc ....E...... 877 742-5000
1854 Business Center Dr Duarte (91010) *(P-10852)*

Sports Venue Padding, Cerritos *Also Called: Artistic Coverings Inc (P-4873)*

Sportsman Steel Gun Safe, Long Beach *Also Called: Sportsmen Steel Safe Fabg Co (P-6873)*

Sportsmen Steel Safe Fabg Co (PA)....................................**E...... 562 984-0244**
6311 N Paramount Blvd Long Beach (90805) *(P-6873)*

Sportsmens Lodge Hotel LLC ....D...... 818 769-4700
12825 Ventura Blvd Studio City (91604) *(P-15368)*

Sportsrobe Inc ....E...... 310 559-3999
8654 Hayden Pl Culver City (90232) *(P-2220)*

Spotify USA Inc ....B...... 213 505-3040
555 Mateo St Los Angeles (90013) *(P-20245)*

Spotlight 29 Casino, Coachella *Also Called: 29 Palms Enterprises Corp (P-17538)*

Spotlite America Corporation (PA)..**E...... 310 829-0200**
9937 Jefferson Blvd Ste 110 Culver City (90232) *(P-5331)*

Spotlite Power Corporation ....E...... 310 838-2367
9937 Jefferson Blvd Ste 110 Culver City (90232) *(P-8332)*

Spoutable LLC ....C...... 609 743-7491
4150 Mission Blvd Ste 220 San Diego (92109) *(P-16517)*

Spragues Ready Mix, Irwindale *Also Called: Spragues Rock and Sand Company (P-5503)*

Spragues Rock and Sand Company (PA)..............................**E...... 626 445-2125**
230 Longden Ave Irwindale (91706) *(P-5503)*

Spray Enclosure Tech Inc ....E...... 909 419-7011
1427 N Linden Ave Rialto (92376) *(P-6322)*

Spray Systems Inc ....E...... 909 397-7511
1363 E Grand Ave Pomona (91766) *(P-8035)*

Spray Tech, Rialto *Also Called: Spray Enclosure Tech Inc (P-6322)*

Spreadco Inc ....E...... 760 351-0747
803 Us Highway 78 Brawley (92227) *(P-2098)*

Spreckels Sugar Company Inc ....B...... 760 344-3110
395 W Keystone Rd Brawley (92227) *(P-1531)*

Spring Industries, Ventura *Also Called: Juengermann Inc (P-6782)*

Spring R&D & Stamp Inc ....F...... 909 465-5166
5757 Chino Ave Chino (91710) *(P-6558)*

Spring Senior Assisted Living, Torrance *Also Called: Genesis Healthcare LLC (P-17962)*

Spring Technologies Corp ....E...... 310 230-4000
10170 Culver Blvd Culver City (90232) *(P-16387)*

Spring Valley Post Acute LLC ....C...... 760 245-6477
14973 Hesperia Rd Victorville (92395) *(P-18057)*

Springcoin Inc ....D...... 847 322-6349
4551 Glencoe Ave Ste 100 Marina Del Rey (90292) *(P-16388)*

Sprint, Temecula *Also Called: Sprint Communications Co LP (P-11859)*

Sprint, Los Angeles *Also Called: Sprint Corporation (P-11862)*

Sprint, South Gate *Also Called: Sprint Corporation (P-11863)*

Sprint, Garden Grove *Also Called: Sprint Communications Co LP (P-11905)*

Sprint Communications Co LP ....C...... 562 943-8907
15582 Whittwood Ln Whittier (90603) *(P-11854)*

Sprint Communications Co LP ....C...... 310 216-9093
5381 W Centinela Ave Los Angeles (90045) *(P-11855)*

Sprint Communications Co LP ....C...... 661 951-8927
44416 Valley Central Way Lancaster (93536) *(P-11856)*

Sprint Communications Co LP ....C...... 310 515-0293
1270 W Redondo Beach Blvd Gardena (90247) *(P-11857)*

Sprint Communications Co LP ....C...... 760 941-4535
4225 Oceanside Blvd Oceanside (92056) *(P-11858)*

Sprint Communications Co LP ....C...... 951 303-8501
31754 Temecula Pkwy Ste A Temecula (92592) *(P-11859)*

**A
L
P
H
A
B
E
T
I
C**

Employee Codes: A=Over 500 employees, B=251-500
C=101-250, D=51-100, E=20-50, F=10-19, G=1-9

2024 Southern California
Business Directory and Buyers Guide

© Mergent Inc. 1-800-342-5647
1275

Sprint Communications Co LP .... C...... 951 461-9786
23865 Clinton Keith Rd Wildomar (92595) *(P-11860)*

Sprint Communications Co LP .... C...... 951 340-1924
3580 Grand Oaks Corona (92881) *(P-11861)*

Sprint Communications Co LP .... C...... 626 339-0430
1316 N Azusa Ave Covina (91722) *(P-11903)*

Sprint Communications Co LP .... C...... 818 755-7100
111 Universal Hollywood Dr Universal City (91608) *(P-11904)*

Sprint Communications Co LP .... C...... 714 534-2107
12913 Harbor Blvd Ste Q4 Garden Grove (92840) *(P-11905)*

Sprint Communications Co LP .... C...... 909 382-6030
1505 E Enterprise Dr San Bernardino (92408) *(P-11906)*

Sprint Corporation .... C...... 213 613-4200
432 S Broadway Los Angeles (90013) *(P-11862)*

Sprint Corporation .... C...... 323 357-0797
4707 Firestone Blvd South Gate (90280) *(P-11863)*

Sprintray Inc (PA) .... **C...... 800 914-8004**
2705 Media Center Dr # 2 Los Angeles (90065) *(P-10769)*

Sprite Industries Incorporated .... E...... 951 735-1015
1791 Railroad St Corona (92878) *(P-10289)*

Sprite Showers, Corona Also Called: Sprite Industries Incorporated *(P-10289)*

Sproutime, Sun Valley Also Called: Foodology LLC *(P-1895)*

Sprouts Farmers Market Inc .... C...... 888 577-7688
280 De Berry St Colton (92324) *(P-11613)*

SPS Holdings Inc .... D...... 310 532-7550
1702 W 134th St Gardena (90249) *(P-15460)*

SPS Technologies LLC .... E...... 714 892-5571
12570 Knott St Garden Grove (92841) *(P-9802)*

SPS Technologies LLC .... B...... 714 545-9311
1224 E Warner Ave Santa Ana (92705) *(P-11076)*

SPS Technologies LLC .... B...... 714 371-1925
1224 E Warner Ave Santa Ana (92705) *(P-11077)*

SPS Technologies LLC .... B...... 949 474-6000
2541 White Rd Irvine (92614) *(P-12882)*

SPS Technologies LLC .... B...... 310 323-6222
1700 W 132nd St Gardena (90249) *(P-12883)*

Spsv Entertainment LLC .... D...... 909 744-9373
28950 State Highway 18 Skyforest (92385) *(P-17352)*

Spus7 125 Cambridgepark LP .... C...... 213 683-4200
515 S Flower St Ste 3100 Los Angeles (90071) *(P-14866)*

Spus7 150 Cambridgepark LP .... C...... 213 683-4200
515 S Flower St Ste 3100 Los Angeles (90071) *(P-14867)*

SPX Cooling Tech LLC .... F...... 714 529-6080
550 Mercury Ln Brea (92821) *(P-6158)*

SPX Flow Us LLC .... E...... 949 455-8150
26561 Rancho Pkwy S Lake Forest (92630) *(P-6159)*

Spy Inc (PA) .... **D...... 760 804-8420**
1896 Rutherford Rd Carlsbad (92008) *(P-10853)*

Sqa Services, Palos Verdes Estates Also Called: Sqa Services Inc *(P-20246)*

Sqa Services Inc .... B...... 800 333-6180
425 Via Corta Ste 203 Palos Verdes Estates (90274) *(P-20246)*

Square Enix Inc .... C...... 310 846-0400
999 N Pacific Coast Hwy Fl 3 El Segundo (90245) *(P-12442)*

Square H Brands Inc .... D...... 323 267-4600
3615 E Vernon Ave Vernon (90058) *(P-519)*

Sr Plastics Company LLC .... D...... 951 479-5394
692 Parkridge Ave Norco (92860) *(P-5214)*

Srax Inc (PA) .... **D...... 323 205-6109**
1014 S Westlake Blvd # 14-299 Westlake Village (91361) *(P-16389)*

SRbray LLC .... D...... 951 898-3850
229 N Sherman Ave Corona (92882) *(P-939)*

Sream Inc .... E...... 951 245-6999
12869 Temescal Canyon Rd Ste A Corona (92883) *(P-5356)*

Srg Holdings LLC (HQ) .... **B...... 858 792-9300**
500 Stevens Ave Ste 100 Solana Beach (92075) *(P-15799)*

Srht Property Holding LLC .... C...... 213 683-0522
1317 E 7th St Los Angeles (90021) *(P-14868)*

Srm Contracting & Paving, San Diego Also Called: Superior Ready Mix Concrete LP *(P-5511)*

SS Heritage Inn Ontario LLC .... D...... 909 937-5000
3595 E Guasti Rd Ontario (91761) *(P-15369)*

SSC Apparel Inc .... F...... 213 748-5511
2025 Long Beach Ave Los Angeles (90058) *(P-2372)*

SSC Construction Inc .... D...... 951 278-1177
4195 Chino Hills Pkwy Chino Hills (91709) *(P-19695)*

Ssco Manufacturing Inc .... E...... 619 628-1022
8155 Mercury Ct Ste 100 San Diego (92111) *(P-7162)*

Ssdi, La Mirada Also Called: Solid State Devices Inc *(P-8894)*

Ssi, Valley Center Also Called: Survival Systems Intl Inc *(P-17156)*

Ssre Holdings LLC .... D...... 800 314-2098
18901 Railroad St City Of Industry (91748) *(P-1205)*

SSS, Carlsbad Also Called: Silk Screen Shirts Inc *(P-2091)*

Sst IV 8020 Las Vgas Blvd S LL .... C...... 949 429-6600
10 Terrace Rd Ladera Ranch (92694) *(P-11614)*

Sst Technologies .... E...... 562 803-3361
9801 Everest St Downey (90242) *(P-8897)*

Sst Vacuum Reflow Systems, Downey Also Called: Sst Technologies *(P-8897)*

Ssw, Palm Springs Also Called: S S W Mechanical Cnstr Inc *(P-819)*

St Annes Family Services .... C...... 213 381-2931
155 N Occidental Blvd Los Angeles (90026) *(P-19302)*

St Bernardine Med Ctr Aux Inc .... C...... 909 881-4320
2101 N Waterman Ave San Bernardino (92404) *(P-18458)*

St Bernardine Medical Center .... C...... 909 883-8711
2101 N Waterman Ave San Bernardino (92404) *(P-18459)*

St Clair Plastics Inc .... E...... 562 946-3115
10031 Freeman Ave Santa Fe Springs (90670) *(P-3974)*

St Francis Medical Center (DH) .... **C...... 310 900-8900**
3630 E Imperial Hwy Lynwood (90262) *(P-18460)*

St George Auto Center Inc .... D...... 657 212-5042
13861 Harbor Blvd Garden Grove (92843) *(P-17044)*

St Jhns Lthran Ch Bakersfield .... C...... 661 665-7815
4500 Buena Vista Rd Bakersfield (93311) *(P-19508)*

St John Knits, Irvine Also Called: St John Knits Inc *(P-2373)*

St John Knits, Irvine Also Called: St John Knits Intl Inc *(P-2374)*

St John Knits Inc (DH) .... **C...... 949 863-1171**
17522 Armstrong Ave Irvine (92614) *(P-2373)*

St John Knits Intl Inc (HQ) .... **C...... 949 863-1171**
17522 Armstrong Ave Irvine (92614) *(P-2374)*

St Johns Lthran Schl Chldren C, Bakersfield Also Called: St Jhns Lthran Ch Bakersfield *(P-19508)*

St Johns Regional Medical Ctr, Oxnard Also Called: Dignity Health *(P-18240)*

St Joseph Center .... D...... 310 396-6468
204 Hampton Dr Venice (90291) *(P-19143)*

St Joseph Health Per Care Svcs .... D...... 800 365-1110
1315 Corona Pointe Ct Ste 201 Corona (92879) *(P-18642)*

St Joseph Hospice .... C...... 714 712-7100
200 W Center Street Promenade Anaheim (92805) *(P-19144)*

St Joseph Hospital of Orange .... C...... 714 771-8222
1310 W Stewart Dr Ste 203 Orange (92868) *(P-18461)*

St Joseph Hospital of Orange .... C...... 714 771-8006
363 S Main St Ste 211 Orange (92868) *(P-18462)*

St Joseph Hospital of Orange .... C...... 714 568-5500
3345 Michelson Dr Ste 100 Irvine (92612) *(P-18463)*

St Joseph Hospital of Orange .... D...... 714 771-8037
1100 W Stewart Dr Orange (92868) *(P-18464)*

St Joseph Hospital of Orange (DH) .... **A...... 714 633-9111**
1100 W Stewart Dr Orange (92868) *(P-18465)*

St Josephs Physical Rehab Svcs, Orange Also Called: St Joseph Hospital of Orange *(P-18461)*

St Josephs School, Placentia Also Called: Roman Cthlic Diocese of Orange *(P-18980)*

St Jseph Heritg Med Group LLC (PA) .... **C...... 714 633-1011**
2212 E 4th St Ste 201 Santa Ana (92705) *(P-17795)*

St Jseph Hlth Sys HM Care Svc .... A...... 714 712-9500
200 W Center Street Promenade Anaheim (92805) *(P-18643)*

St Jude Hospital (DH) .... **A...... 714 871-3280**
101 E Valencia Mesa Dr Fullerton (92835) *(P-18466)*

St Jude Medical LLC .... E...... 949 769-5000
2375 Morse Ave Irvine (92614) *(P-4240)*

St Jude Medical LLC .... E...... 714 992-3000
101 E Valencia Mesa Dr Fullerton (92835) *(P-10703)*

St Jude Medical Center, Fullerton Also Called: St Jude Hospital *(P-18466)*

ST LOUIS RAMS, Agoura Hills Also Called: Los Angeles Rams LLC *(P-17377)*

St Mary Medical Center (DH) .... **A...... 562 491-9000**
1050 Linden Ave Long Beach (90813) *(P-18467)*

St Mary Medical Center LLC (PA)......................A...... 760 242-2311
18300 Us Highway 18 Apple Valley (92307) *(P-18468)*

St Mary Medical Center LLC...................................A...... 760 946-8767
16000 Kasota Rd Apple Valley (92307) *(P-18469)*

ST MARY'S MEDICAL CENTER, Long Beach *Also Called: St Marys Medical Center (P-20247)*

St Mary's School of Nursing, Long Beach *Also Called: St Mary Medical Center (P-18467)*

St Marys Medical Center ....A...... 562 491-9230
1050 Linden Ave Long Beach (90813) *(P-20247)*

St Paul Brands Inc ....E...... 714 903-1000
11842 Monarch St Garden Grove (92841) *(P-3987)*

St Worth Container LLC ....D...... 909 390-4550
727 S Wanamaker Ave Ontario (91761) *(P-3132)*

St. John's Health Center, Santa Monica *Also Called: Providence St Johns Hlth Ctr (P-18400)*

St. Johns Pleasant Valley Hosp, Camarillo *Also Called: Dignity Health (P-18239)*

STA, Thousand Palms *Also Called: Sunline Transit Agency (P-11369)*

STA Pharmaceutical US LLC ....E...... 609 606-6499
6114 Nancy Ridge Dr San Diego (92121) *(P-4241)*

Staar, Lake Forest *Also Called: Staar Surgical Company (P-10854)*

Staar Surgical Company (PA).......................A...... 626 303-7902
25651 Atlantic Ocean Dr Ste A1 Lake Forest (92630) *(P-10854)*

Stabile Plating Company Inc ....E...... 626 339-9091
1150 E Edna Pl Covina (91724) *(P-6665)*

Staco Switch, Irvine *Also Called: Staco Systems Inc (P-8130)*

Staco Systems Inc (HQ)...D...... 949 297-8700
7 Morgan Irvine (92618) *(P-8130)*

Stadco (HQ)...E...... 323 227-8888
107 S Avenue 20 Los Angeles (90031) *(P-7132)*

Staff Assistance, Thousand Oaks *Also Called: Staff Assistance Inc (P-18644)*

Staff Assistance Inc (PA).........................B...... 818 894-7879
72 Moody Ct Ste 100 Thousand Oaks (91360) *(P-18644)*

Staff Assistance Inc ....B...... 805 371-9980
72 Moody Ct Ste 100 Thousand Oaks (91360) *(P-15896)*

Staff Pro Inc ....A...... 619 544-1774
675 Convention Way San Diego (92101) *(P-16694)*

Staff Pro Inc (PA)..A...... 714 230-7200
5455 Garden Grove Blvd Westminster (92683) *(P-16755)*

Staffing Solutions, Montebello *Also Called: L&T Staffing Inc (P-15864)*

Stainless Fixtures Inc ....E...... 909 622-1615
1250 E Franklin Ave Pomona (91766) *(P-3031)*

Stainless Industrial Companies ....E...... 310 575-9400
11111 Santa Monica Blvd Ste 1120 Los Angeles (90025) *(P-7098)*

Stainless Micro-Polish Inc ....F...... 714 632-8903
1286 N Grove St Anaheim (92806) *(P-6666)*

Stainless Stl Fabricators Inc ....D...... 714 739-9904
15120 Desman Rd La Mirada (90638) *(P-12824)*

Stake Fastener, Chino *Also Called: Dupree Inc (P-6440)*

Stamps.com, El Segundo *Also Called: Stampscom Inc (P-15636)*

Stampscom Inc (PA)....................................C...... 310 482-5800
1990 E Grand Ave El Segundo (90245) *(P-15636)*

Stance, San Clemente *Also Called: Stance Inc (P-13151)*

Stance Inc (PA)...C...... 949 391-9030
197 Avenida La Pata San Clemente (92673) *(P-13151)*

Stand 8 Technology Services, Seal Beach *Also Called: Talent & Acquisition LLC (P-16130)*

Standard Armament, Glendale *Also Called: SAI Industries (P-6748)*

Standard Chartered Bank ....D...... 626 639-8000
601 S Figueroa St Ste 2775 Los Angeles (90017) *(P-14208)*

Standard Concrete Products Inc (HQ)............................E...... 310 829-4537
13550 Live Oak Ln Baldwin Park (91706) *(P-5504)*

Standard Drywall Inc (HQ)..........................B...... 619 443-7034
9831 Channel Rd Lakeside (92040) *(P-998)*

Standard Filter Corporation (PA).................E...... 866 443-3615
3801 Ocean Ranch Blvd Ste 107 Oceanside (92056) *(P-7331)*

Standard Industries Inc ....D...... 661 387-1110
6505 Zerker Rd Shafter (93263) *(P-12369)*

Standard Lumber Company Inc (HQ)..........................E...... 559 651-2037
27770 Entertainment Dr Valencia (91355) *(P-2727)*

Standard Metal Products Inc ....E...... 310 532-9861
1541 W 132nd St Gardena (90249) *(P-6667)*

Standard Sales Llc (PA).............................E...... 323 269-0510
2801 E 12th St Los Angeles (90023) *(P-11028)*

Standard Tool & Die Co, Los Angeles *Also Called: Stadco (P-7132)*

Standard Wire & Cable Co (PA).................E...... 310 609-1811
2050 E Vista Bella Way Rancho Dominguez (90220) *(P-5750)*

Standard-Southern Corporation ....D...... 213 624-1831
400 S Central Ave Los Angeles (90013) *(P-11557)*

Standard-Southern Corporation ....C...... 213 624-1831
440 S Central Ave Los Angeles (90013) *(P-11558)*

Standard-Southern Corporation ....C...... 213 624-1831
715 E 4th St Los Angeles (90013) *(P-11559)*

Standardvision LLC ....E...... 323 222-3630
3370 N San Fernando Rd Ste 206 Los Angeles (90065) *(P-11167)*

Standdesk Inc ....E...... 213 634-0665
5042 Wilshire Blvd # 44689 Los Angeles (90036) *(P-2874)*

Standish Precision Products, Fallbrook *Also Called: Fallbrook Industries Inc (P-6516)*

Standridge Granite Corporation ....E...... 562 946-6334
9437 Santa Fe Springs Rd Santa Fe Springs (90670) *(P-5535)*

Staness Jonekos Entps Inc ....E...... 818 606-2710
4000 W Magnolia Blvd D Burbank (91505) *(P-1991)*

Stanford Advanced Materials, Lake Forest *Also Called: Oceania International LLC (P-5726)*

Stanford Mu Corporation ....E...... 310 605-2888
20725 Annalee Ave Carson (90746) *(P-9921)*

Stanford Sign & Awning Inc (PA)................E...... 619 423-6200
2556 Faivre St Chula Vista (91911) *(P-11168)*

Stang Industrial Products, Chino *Also Called: Stang Industries Inc (P-11285)*

Stang Industries Inc ....F...... 914 479-9810
8778 Kimball Ave Chino (91708) *(P-11285)*

Stanley Black & Decker Inc ....F...... 909 491-6322
15750 Jurupa Ave Fontana (92337) *(P-7148)*

Stanley G Alexander Inc (PA).....................C...... 714 731-1658
2942 Dow Ave Tustin (92780) *(P-11505)*

Stanley National Hardware, Lake Forest *Also Called: National Manufacturing Co (P-5936)*

Stanley Steemer Carpet Cleaner, San Diego *Also Called: Colt Services Inc (P-15467)*

Stansport, Los Angeles *Also Called: Standard Sales Llc (P-11028)*

Stantec Architecture Inc ....B...... 213 955-9775
801 S Figueroa St Ste 300 Los Angeles (90017) *(P-16934)*

Stantec Architecture Inc ....B...... 949 923-6000
38 Technology Dr Ste 200 Irvine (92618) *(P-19741)*

Stantec Architecture Inc ....D...... 626 796-9141
300 N Lake Ave Ste 400 Pasadena (91101) *(P-19742)*

Stantec Consulting Svcs Inc ....C...... 949 923-6000
38 Technology Dr Ste 100 Irvine (92618) *(P-19743)*

Stantec Holdings Del III Inc ....B...... 661 396-3770
5500 Ming Ave Ste 300 Bakersfield (93309) *(P-14947)*

Stantec Oil and Gas, Bakersfield *Also Called: Stantec Holdings Del III Inc (P-14947)*

Stanton Carpet Corp ....E...... 562 945-8711
2209 Pine Ave Manhattan Beach (90266) *(P-2121)*

Stantru Reinforcing Steel, Fontana *Also Called: Stantru Resources Inc (P-520)*

Stantru Resources Inc ....D...... 909 587-1441
11175 Redwood Ave Fontana (92337) *(P-520)*

Stanzino Inc (PA)..E...... 213 746-8822
16325 S Avalon Blvd Gardena (90248) *(P-2032)*

Stanzino Inc ....C...... 818 602-5171
17937 Santa Rita St Encino (91316) *(P-2033)*

Star Die Casting Inc ....D...... 562 698-0627
12209 Slauson Ave Santa Fe Springs (90670) *(P-5945)*

Star Food 316 Inc ....E...... 213 858-2512
2370 E 48th St Vernon (90058) *(P-1402)*

Star Food Snacks, Colton *Also Called: Star Food Snacks Intl Inc (P-1236)*

Star Food Snacks Intl Inc ....D...... 909 825-8882
125 E Laurel St Colton (92324) *(P-1236)*

Star Ford Lincoln Mercury, Glendale *Also Called: Los Feliz Ford Inc (P-13791)*

Star Laundry Services Inc ....D...... 619 572-1009
3410 Main St San Diego (92113) *(P-15465)*

Star Lion, Los Angeles *Also Called: Starlion Inc (P-2162)*

Star Milling Co ....C...... 951 657-3143
23901 Water St Perris (92570) *(P-1449)*

Star Nail International, Valencia *Also Called: Star Nail Products Inc (P-13071)*

Star Nail Products Inc ....D...... 661 257-3376
29120 Avenue Paine Valencia (91355) *(P-13071)*

Star of Ca LLC ....D...... 805 379-1401
501 Marin St Thousand Oaks (91360) *(P-18806)*

A
L
P
H
A
B
E
T
I
C

Employee Codes: A=Over 500 employees, B=251-500
C=101-250, D=51-100, E=20-50, F=10-19, G=1-9

2024 Southern California
Business Directory and Buyers Guide

© Mergent Inc. 1-800-342-5647
1277

Star of Ca LLC (HQ)...C...... 805 644-7827
4880 Market St Ventura (93003) *(P-18807)*

Star of Ca LLC ....D...... 818 986-7827
15260 Ventura Blvd Sherman Oaks (91403) *(P-18808)*

Star of California ....D...... 805 466-1638
8834 Morro Rd Atascadero (93422) *(P-18809)*

STAR OF CALIFORNIA, A PROFESSIONAL PSYCHOLOGICAL CORPORATION, Atascadero
Also Called: Star of California (P-18809)

Star Plastic Design ....D...... 310 530-7119
25914 President Ave Harbor City (90710) *(P-5215)*

Star Pro Security Patrol Inc ....C...... 714 617-5056
3303 Harbor Blvd Ste B3 Costa Mesa (92626) *(P-16695)*

Star Services, San Diego *Also Called: Star Laundry Services Inc (P-15465)*

Star Shield Solutions LLC ....D...... 866 662-4477
4315 Santa Ana St Ontario (91761) *(P-5216)*

Star Trac, Irvine *Also Called: Star Trac Health & Fitness Inc (P-11029)*

Star Trac, Irvine *Also Called: Unisen Inc (P-11039)*

Star Trac Fitness, Irvine *Also Called: Star Trac Strength Inc (P-11030)*

Star Trac Health & Fitness Inc ....E...... 714 669-1660
14410 Myford Rd Irvine (92606) *(P-11029)*

Star Trac Strength Inc ....B...... 714 669-1660
14410 Myford Rd Irvine (92606) *(P-11030)*

Star Waggons LLC ....D...... 818 367-5946
13334 Ralston Ave Sylmar (91342) *(P-17264)*

Starco Enterprises Inc (PA)...................................**D...... 323 266-7111**
3137 E 26th St Vernon (90058) *(P-7259)*

Stardust Diamond Corp ....E...... 213 239-9999
550 S Hill St Ste 1420 Los Angeles (90013) *(P-10920)*

Stardust Studios Inc ....D...... 310 399-6047
1823 Colorado Ave Santa Monica (90404) *(P-20248)*

Stark Awning & Canvas, Chula Vista *Also Called: Stark Mfg Co (P-2509)*

Stark Mfg Co ....E...... 619 425-5880
76 Broadway Chula Vista (91910) *(P-2509)*

Starlineoem Inc ....E...... 949 342-8889
3183f Airway Ave Ste 112 Costa Mesa (92626) *(P-8112)*

Starlion Inc ....E...... 323 233-8823
706 E 32nd St Los Angeles (90011) *(P-2162)*

Starpint 1031 Property MGT LLC ....C...... 310 247-0550
450 N Roxbury Dr Ste 1050 Beverly Hills (90210) *(P-14869)*

Starrett Kinemetric Engrg Inc ....E...... 949 348-1213
26052 Merit Cir Ste 103 Laguna Hills (92653) *(P-7133)*

Starscroll, Los Angeles *Also Called: Twelve Signs Inc (P-3392)*

Startel Corporation (PA)...**D...... 949 863-8700**
16 Goodyear B-125 Irvine (92618) *(P-16122)*

Starwood Inc ....C...... 888 559-1749
402 W Broadway Ste 400 San Diego (92101) *(P-15370)*

Starwood Hotel ....C...... 310 641-7740
5990 Green Valley Cir Culver City (90230) *(P-15371)*

Starwood Hotels & Resorts, San Diego *Also Called: San Diego Sheraton Corporation (P-15345)*

Starwood Hotels & Resorts, Costa Mesa *Also Called: South Coast Westin Hotel Co (P-15364)*

Starwood Hotels & Resorts, Culver City *Also Called: Starwood Hotel (P-15371)*

Starwood Hotels & Resorts, San Diego *Also Called: Starwood Htels Rsrts Wrldwide (P-15373)*

Starwood Htels Rsrts Wrldwide ....C...... 909 622-2220
601 W Mckinley Ave Pomona (91768) *(P-15372)*

Starwood Htels Rsrts Wrldwide ....C...... 619 239-2200
910 Broadway Cir San Diego (92101) *(P-15373)*

Starz Inc ....F...... 877 595-6789
23016 Lake Forest Dr Ste D303 Laguna Hills (92653) *(P-12516)*

Starz Tipz, Laguna Hills *Also Called: Starz Inc (P-12516)*

Statco, Huntington Beach *Also Called: DSI Process Systems LLC (P-12789)*

Statco Engrg & Fabricators LLC (PA)....................**E...... 714 375-6300**
7595 Reynolds Cir Huntington Beach (92647) *(P-12825)*

State Bar of California ....D...... 805 544-7551
755 Santa Rosa St Ste 310 San Luis Obispo (93401) *(P-19404)*

State Bar of California ....D...... 213 765-1520
845 S Figueroa St Los Angeles (90017) *(P-19405)*

State Compensation Insur Fund ....C...... 888 782-8338
2901 N Ventura Rd Ste 100 Oxnard (93036) *(P-14456)*

State Compensation Insur Fund ....A...... 818 888-4750
21300 Victory Blvd Ste 600 Woodland Hills (91367) *(P-14526)*

State Compensation Insur Fund ....C...... 323 266-5000
900 Corporate Center Dr Monterey Park (91754) *(P-14527)*

State Compensation Insur Fund ....D...... 661 664-4000
9801 Camino Media Ste 101 Bakersfield (93311) *(P-14528)*

State Compensation Insur Fund ....C...... 714 565-5000
1750 E 4th St Fl 3 Santa Ana (92705) *(P-14529)*

State Compensation Insur Fund ....C...... 888 782-8338
6301 Day St Riverside (92507) *(P-14530)*

State Compensation Insur Fund ....C...... 888 782-8338
10105 Pacific Heights Blvd Ste 120 San Diego (92121) *(P-14531)*

State Farm General Insur Co ....D...... 619 227-5777
945 Otay Lakes Rd Ste K Chula Vista (91913) *(P-14632)*

State Farm Insurance, Chula Vista *Also Called: State Farm General Insur Co (P-14632)*

State Fish Co Inc ....C...... 310 547-9530
624 W 9th St Ste 100 San Pedro (90731) *(P-1813)*

State Pipe & Supply Inc ....E...... 909 356-5670
2180 N Locust Ave Rialto (92377) *(P-5603)*

State Ready Mix Inc ....F...... 805 647-2817
3127 Los Angeles Ave Oxnard (93036) *(P-5505)*

State Ready Mix Inc (PA)..**E...... 805 647-2817**
1011 Azahar St Ste 1 Ventura (93004) *(P-5506)*

Statek, Orange *Also Called: Statek Corporation (P-9121)*

Statek Corporation ....E...... 714 639-7810
1449 W Orange Grove Ave Orange (92868) *(P-9120)*

Statek Corporation (HQ)...**C...... 714 639-7810**
512 N Main St Orange (92868) *(P-9121)*

Stater Bros Markets ....E...... 714 963-0949
10114 Adams Ave Huntington Beach (92646) *(P-13703)*

Stater Bros Markets ....E...... 714 991-5310
1131 N State College Blvd Anaheim (92806) *(P-13704)*

States Logistics Services Inc (PA)........................**C...... 714 521-6520**
5650 Dolly Ave Buena Park (90621) *(P-11804)*

Statewide Distributors, Ontario *Also Called: USA Sales Inc (P-2007)*

Statewide Trffic Sfety Sgns In (HQ).......................**E...... 949 553-8272**
2722 S Fairview St Fl 2 Santa Ana (92704) *(P-8627)*

Statewide Trffic Sfety Sgns In ....E...... 714 468-1919
2722 S Fairview St Santa Ana (92704) *(P-11169)*

Statewide Trffic Sfety Sgns In ....E...... 949 553-8272
1100 Main St Ste 100 Irvine (92614) *(P-11170)*

Statrad - Radconnect, San Diego *Also Called: Nucleushealth LLC (P-16089)*

Staub Metals LLC ....D...... 562 602-2200
7747 Rosecrans Ave Paramount (90723) *(P-12572)*

Stauber, Fullerton *Also Called: Stauber Prfmce Ingredients Inc (P-4019)*

Stauber California Inc ....D...... 714 441-3900
4120 N Palm St Fullerton (92835) *(P-4018)*

Stauber Prfmce Ingredients Inc (HQ)....................**D...... 714 441-3900**
4120 N Palm St Fullerton (92835) *(P-4019)*

Stauber USA, Fullerton *Also Called: Stauber California Inc (P-4018)*

Stavatti Industries Ltd ....E...... 651 238-5369
3670 El Camino Dr San Bernardino (92404) *(P-235)*

Stavros Enterprises Inc ....E...... 888 463-2293
681 Arrow Grand Cir Covina (91722) *(P-17154)*

Stci, Rancho Cucamonga *Also Called: Superior Tank Co Inc (P-6161)*

Steadfast Companies, Irvine *Also Called: Steadfast Management Co Inc (P-14870)*

Steadfast Management Co Inc (PA).........................**D...... 949 748-3000**
18100 Von Karman Ave Ste 500 Irvine (92612) *(P-14870)*

Steady Clothing Inc ....F...... 714 444-2058
2851 E White Star Ave Ste A Anaheim (92806) *(P-2221)*

Stearns Conrad and Schmidt Consulting Engineers Inc (PA)...............**D...... 562 426-9544**
3900 Kilroy Airport Way Ste 100 Long Beach (90806) *(P-19696)*

Stearns Corporation ....E...... 805 582-2710
2280 Ward Ave Ste 100 Simi Valley (93065) *(P-4458)*

Stearns Product Dev Corp (PA)...............................**D...... 951 657-0379**
20281 Harvill Ave Perris (92570) *(P-7410)*

Stec (HQ)...**B...... 415 222-9996**
3355 Michelson Dr Ste 100 Irvine (92612) *(P-7487)*

Stec International Holding Inc ....C...... 949 476-1180
3001 Daimler St Santa Ana (92705) *(P-7488)*

Steel Products International, Los Angeles *Also Called: Precision Steel Products Inc (P-6297)*

Steel Works Etc, Oxnard *Also Called: Millworks Etc Inc (P-6113)*

Mergent email: customerrelations@mergent.com
1278

2024 Southern California
Business Directory and Buyers Guide

(P-0000) Products & Services Section entry number
(PA)=Parent Co (HQ)=Headquarters (DH)=Div Headquarters

Steel-Tech Industrial Corp ....E...... 951 270-0144
1268 Sherborn St Corona (92879) *(P-6078)*

Steelcase Authorized Dealer, Camarillo Also Called: BKM Office Environments Inc *(P-13939)*

Steelco USA, Chino Also Called: Wcs Equipment Holdings LLC *(P-5666)*

Steelco USA, Chino Also Called: Wcs Equipment Holdings LLC *(P-6343)*

Steeldeck Inc ....E...... 323 290-2100
13147 S Western Ave Gardena (90249) *(P-11286)*

Steeldyne Industries ....E...... 714 630-6200
2871 E La Cresta Ave Anaheim (92806) *(P-6323)*

Steelhead, Los Angeles Also Called: Deutsch La Inc *(P-15537)*

Steelscape LLC ....F...... 909 987-4711
11200 Arrow Rte Rancho Cucamonga (91730) *(P-6739)*

Steelwave LLC ....A...... 310 821-1111
4553 Glencoe Ave Ste 300 Marina Del Rey (90292) *(P-14912)*

Steelworks Etc Inc ....E...... 805 487-3000
2230 Statham Blvd Ste 100 Oxnard (93033) *(P-6125)*

Steico, Oceanside Also Called: Steico Industries Inc *(P-6559)*

Steico Industries Inc ....C...... 760 438-8015
1814 Ord Way Oceanside (92056) *(P-6559)*

Stein Industries Inc (PA)...**E...... 714 522-4560**
4005 Artesia Ave Fullerton (92833) *(P-6324)*

Stein Sam & Rose Education Ctr, San Diego Also Called: Vista Hill Foundation *(P-19015)*

Steiny & Company, Corona Also Called: Computer Service Company *(P-8605)*

Steiny and Company Inc ....B...... 213 382-2331
221 N Ardmore Ave Los Angeles (90004) *(P-940)*

Stell Industries Inc ....E...... 951 369-8777
1951 S Parco Ave Ste B Ontario (91761) *(P-6391)*

Stellant Systems Inc (DH)...**A...... 310 517-6000**
3100 Lomita Blvd Torrance (90505) *(P-10073)*

Stellar Engineering, Anaheim Also Called: APT Manufacturing LLC *(P-7004)*

Stellar Exploration Inc ....E...... 805 459-1425
835 Airport Dr San Luis Obispo (93401) *(P-9903)*

Stellar Microelectronics Inc ....C...... 661 775-3500
9340 Owensmouth Ave Chatsworth (91311) *(P-8898)*

Stemconnector LLC ....D...... 424 543-4074
1500 Rosecrans Ave Ste 500 Manhattan Beach (90266) *(P-16602)*

STEMCONNECTOR LLC, Manhattan Beach Also Called: Stemconnector LLC *(P-16602)*

Stepan Company ....B...... 714 776-9870
1208 N Patt St Anaheim (92801) *(P-3975)*

Stepstone Inc ....E...... 310 327-7474
13238 S Figueroa St Los Angeles (90061) *(P-5453)*

Stepstone Inc (PA)...**E...... 310 327-7474**
17025 S Main St Gardena (90248) *(P-5454)*

Steren Electronic Solutions, San Diego Also Called: Steren Electronics Intl LLC *(P-12698)*

Steren Electronics Intl LLC (PA)...............................**D...... 800 266-3333**
8445 Camino Santa Fe San Diego (92121) *(P-12698)*

Stereo D LLC ....D...... 818 861-3100
3355 W Empire Ave 1st Fl Burbank (91504) *(P-17265)*

Stereod, Burbank Also Called: Stereo D LLC *(P-17265)*

Steril-Aire Inc ....E...... 818 565-1128
25060 Avenue Stanford Ste 160 Valencia (91355) *(P-8382)*

Steris, San Diego Also Called: Steris Corporation *(P-10704)*

Steris Corporation ....C...... 858 586-1166
9020 Activity Rd Ste D San Diego (92126) *(P-10704)*

Steris Isomedix, Temecula Also Called: Isomedix Operations Inc *(P-10674)*

Sterisyn Inc ....E...... 805 991-9694
11969 Challenger Ct Moorpark (93021) *(P-4242)*

Sterisyn Scientific, Moorpark Also Called: Sterisyn Inc *(P-4242)*

Sterling BMW, Newport Beach Also Called: Sterling Motors Ltd *(P-13831)*

Sterling Care Inc ....C...... 619 470-6700
2575 E 8th St National City (91950) *(P-18058)*

Sterling Carpets & Flooring, Anaheim Also Called: Rm Partners Inc *(P-13953)*

Sterling Motors Ltd ....D...... 949 645-5900
3000 W Coast Hwy Newport Beach (92663) *(P-13831)*

Sterling Pacific Meat Co., Commerce Also Called: Interstate Meat Co Inc *(P-7202)*

Sterling Plumbing Inc ....D...... 714 641-5480
3111 W Central Ave Santa Ana (92704) *(P-829)*

Sterling Sleep Systems, Westminster Also Called: American Pacific Plastic Fabricators Inc *(P-3922)*

Steve P Rados Inc ....C...... 619 328-1360
1638 Pioneer Way El Cajon (92020) *(P-655)*

Steven Global Freight Services, Redondo Beach Also Called: Stevens Global Logistics Inc *(P-11805)*

Steven Handelman Studios Inc (PA)..........................**E...... 805 884-9070**
716 N Milpas St Santa Barbara (93103) *(P-5650)*

Steven Label Corporation (PA)...................................**C...... 562 698-9971**
11926 Burke St Santa Fe Springs (90670) *(P-13096)*

Stevens Global Logistics Inc (PA)..............................**D...... 800 229-7284**
3700 Redondo Beach Ave Redondo Beach (90278) *(P-11805)*

Stevens Transportation Inc ....C...... 661 366-3286
7100 E Brundage Ln Bakersfield (93307) *(P-11506)*

Stevens Trucking, Bakersfield Also Called: Stevens Transportation Inc *(P-11506)*

Steves Plating Corporation ....C...... 818 842-2184
3111 N San Fernando Blvd Burbank (91504) *(P-2994)*

Steward Plastics Inc ....C...... 949 581-9530
23322 Del Lago Dr Laguna Hills (92653) *(P-4713)*

Stewart Filmscreen Corp (PA)....................................**C...... 310 784-5300**
1161 Sepulveda Blvd Torrance (90502) *(P-10886)*

Stewart Title California Inc (DH).................................**C...... 619 692-1600**
7676 Hazard Center Dr Ste 1400 San Diego (92108) *(P-14545)*

Stewart Title California Inc ....C...... 818 502-2700
525 N Brand Blvd Ste 200 Glendale (91203) *(P-14895)*

Stg Auto Group, Garden Grove Also Called: St George Auto Center Inc *(P-17044)*

Stic-Adhesive Products Co Inc ....C...... 323 268-2956
3950 Medford St Los Angeles (90063) *(P-4582)*

Stickypos, Santa Ana Also Called: Documotion Research Inc *(P-3564)*

Stigtec Manufacturing, San Marcos Also Called: Ed Stiglic *(P-7823)*

Stillhouse LLC ....E...... 323 498-1111
8201 Beverly Blvd Ste 300 Los Angeles (90048) *(P-1676)*

Stines Machine Inc ....E...... 760 599-9955
2481 Coral St Vista (92081) *(P-8036)*

Stir Foods, Corona Also Called: Pacifica Foods LLC *(P-1363)*

Stir Foods LLC ....E...... 714 871-9231
1851 N Delilah St Corona (92879) *(P-1403)*

Stitch Industries Inc ....E...... 888 282-0842
767 S Alameda St Ste 360 Los Angeles (90021) *(P-2820)*

Stjohn God Rtirement Care Ctr ....C...... 323 731-0641
2468 S St Andrews Pl Los Angeles (90018) *(P-18059)*

Stm Networks Inc ....E...... 949 273-6800
2 Faraday Irvine (92618) *(P-8584)*

Stm Wireless, Irvine Also Called: Stm Networks Inc *(P-8584)*

Stn Digital LLC ....D...... 619 292-8683
3033 Bunker Hill St San Diego (92109) *(P-15575)*

Stockbridge/Sbe Holdings LLC ....A...... 323 655-8000
5900 Wilshire Blvd Ste 3100 Los Angeles (90036) *(P-15374)*

Stockdale Christian School, Bakersfield Also Called: First Assmbly of God Bkrsfld *(P-18966)*

Stockdale Country Club ....D...... 661 832-0310
7001 Stockdale Hwy Bakersfield (93309) *(P-17527)*

Stockdale Medical Offices, Bakersfield Also Called: Kaiser Foundation Hospitals *(P-17697)*

Stockmar Industrial, Long Beach Also Called: Elite Craftsman *(P-15710)*

Stoll Metalcraft Inc ....C...... 661 295-0401
24808 Anza Dr Valencia (91355) *(P-6325)*

Stolo Cabinets Inc (PA)...**E...... 714 529-7303**
860 Challenger St Brea (92821) *(P-2900)*

Stolo Custom Cabinets, Brea Also Called: Stolo Cabinets Inc *(P-2900)*

Stone Brewing Co LLC ....A...... 760 471-4999
1999 Citracado Pkwy Escondido (92029) *(P-14053)*

Stone Brewing Co., Escondido Also Called: Stone Brewing Co LLC *(P-14053)*

Stone Canyon Inds Holdings LLC (PA).......................**D...... 424 316-2061**
1875 Century Park E Ste 320 Los Angeles (90067) *(P-20249)*

Stone Canyon Industries LLC ....A...... 310 570-4869
1875 Century Park E Ste 320 Los Angeles (90067) *(P-5217)*

Stone Entertainment, Costa Mesa Also Called: Volcom LLC *(P-16959)*

Stone Harbor Inc ....F...... 323 277-2777
5015 District Blvd Vernon (90058) *(P-2147)*

Stone Manufacturing Company, Gardena Also Called: Tomorrows Heirlooms Inc *(P-5946)*

Stone Yard Inc ....F...... 858 586-1580
6056 Corte Del Cedro Carlsbad (92011) *(P-2875)*

Stonebridge Rlty Advisors Inc ....A...... 949 597-8700
27102 Towne Centre Dr Foothill Ranch (92610) *(P-15375)*

Employee Codes: A=Over 500 employees, B=251-500
C=101-250, D=51-100, E=20-50, F=10-19, G=1-9

2024 Southern California
Business Directory and Buyers Guide

© Mergent Inc. 1-800-342-5647
1279

ALPHABETIC

Stonecalibre LLC (PA) ....D....... 310 774-0014
2049 Century Park E Ste 2550 Los Angeles (90067) *(P-15052)*

Stonehouse Restaurant, Santa Barbara *Also Called: San Ysidro Bb Property LLC (P-15347)*

Stoneriver Inc ....D....... 714 705-8227
770 The City Dr S Ste 5000 Orange (92868) *(P-16123)*

Stoneybrook Publishing Inc ....E....... 858 674-4600
10815 Rancho Bernardo Rd Ste 300 San Diego (92127) *(P-3415)*

Stony Apparel Corp (PA)..C....... 323 981-9080
1201 S Grand Ave Los Angeles (90015) *(P-2264)*

Stop Hop Center, Carson *Also Called: Anschutz Sthern Cal Spt Cmplex (P-17540)*

Storage West, Marina Del Rey *Also Called: Laaco Ltd (P-14738)*

Store 3, El Cajon *Also Called: Wetzels Pretzels LLC (P-13724)*

Stories International Inc ....E....... 310 242-8409
400 Corporate Pointe Culver City (90230) *(P-3486)*

Storm, Torrance *Also Called: Storm Industries Inc (P-6915)*

Storm Industries Inc (PA) ....D....... 310 534-5232
23223 Normandie Ave Torrance (90501) *(P-6915)*

Storm Manufacturing, Torrance *Also Called: FCkingston Co (P-6764)*

Storm Manufacturing Group Inc ....D....... 310 326-8287
23201 Normandie Ave Torrance (90501) *(P-6770)*

Storyland Studios, Lake Elsinore *Also Called: Harrington & Sons Inc (P-5568)*

Stoughton Printing Co ....E....... 626 961-3678
130 N Sunset Ave City Of Industry (91744) *(P-3689)*

Str Worldwide Inc ....A....... 949 276-5990
17462 Von Karman Ave Irvine (92614) *(P-13112)*

Stracon Inc ....F....... 949 851-2288
1672 Kaiser Ave Ste 1 Irvine (92614) *(P-9257)*

Stradling Ycca Crlson Ruth A P (PA) ....C....... 949 725-4000
660 Newport Center Dr Ste 1600 Newport Beach (92660) *(P-18949)*

Straight Down Clothing Company, San Luis Obispo *Also Called: Straight Down Enterprises (P-2222)*

Straight Down Enterprises (PA)....................................E....... 805 543-3086
625 Clarion Ct San Luis Obispo (93401) *(P-2222)*

Straight Forwarding Inc ....D....... 909 594-3400
20275 Business Pkwy Walnut (91789) *(P-11806)*

Straight Smile LLC (HQ) ....F....... 424 389-4551
3435 Ocean Park Blvd Ste 107-252 Santa Monica (90405) *(P-10770)*

Straight Talk Counseling Ctr, La Mirada *Also Called: Straight Talk Inc (P-19145)*

Straight Talk Inc ....D....... 562 943-0195
13710 La Mirada Blvd La Mirada (90638) *(P-19145)*

Strand Art Company Inc ....E....... 714 777-0444
4700 E Hunter Ave Anaheim (92807) *(P-5218)*

Strand Products Inc (PA) ....E....... 800 343-7985
2233 Knoll Dr Ventura (93003) *(P-10826)*

Strasbaugh, San Luis Obispo *Also Called: R H Strasbaugh (P-7019)*

Strat Edge, Santee *Also Called: Stratedge Corporation (P-8899)*

Strata Forest Products Inc (PA) ....E....... 714 751-0800
2600 S Susan St Santa Ana (92704) *(P-2567)*

Strata Information Group Inc ....D....... 619 296-0170
3935 Harney St Ste 203 San Diego (92110) *(P-16603)*

Strata USA Llc ....E....... 888 878-7282
333 City Blvd W Fl 17 Orange (92868) *(P-14112)*

Stratacare, Irvine *Also Called: Stratacare Llc (P-16124)*

Stratacare Llc ....C....... 949 743-1200
17838 Gillette Ave Ste D Irvine (92614) *(P-16124)*

Stratcom Systems Inc ....E....... 858 481-9292
2701 Loker Ave W Ste 130 Carlsbad (92010) *(P-16125)*

Stratedge Corporation ....E....... 866 424-4962
9424 Abraham Way Ste A Santee (92071) *(P-8899)*

Strategic Asset Services LLC ....D....... 949 713-0053
27422 Portola Pkwy Ste 150 Foothill Ranch (92610) *(P-14687)*

Strategic Distribution L P ....E....... 818 671-2100
9800 De Soto Ave Chatsworth (91311) *(P-2186)*

Strategic Operations Inc ....C....... 858 244-0559
4705 Ruffin Rd San Diego (92123) *(P-16935)*

Strategy Companion Corp ....D....... 714 460-8398
100 Pacifica Ste 220 Irvine (92618) *(P-16390)*

Stratgic Hlthcare Programs LLC ....D....... 805 963-9446
6500 Hollister Ave Ste 210 Goleta (93117) *(P-16126)*

Stratoflex Product Division, Camarillo *Also Called: Parker-Hannifin Corporation (P-9763)*

Stratos Renewables Corporation ....E....... 310 402-5901
9440 Santa Monica Blvd Ste 401 Beverly Hills (90210) *(P-4531)*

Stratus Group Duo LLC ....E....... 323 581-3663
4401 S Downey Rd Vernon (90058) *(P-1741)*

Stratus Real Estate Inc ....D....... 626 441-5549
435 Garfield Ave South Pasadena (91030) *(P-14366)*

Stratus Real Estate Inc ....D....... 310 549-7028
1100 N Banning Blvd Apt 111 Wilmington (90744) *(P-14367)*

Stratus Realestate, South Pasadena *Also Called: Stratus Real Estate Inc (P-14366)*

Straub Distributing Co Ltd (PA) ....C....... 714 779-4000
4633 E La Palma Ave Anaheim (92807) *(P-13472)*

Streamelements Inc ....D....... 323 928-7848
11400 W Olympic Blvd Los Angeles (90064) *(P-19913)*

Streamland Media LLC ....C....... 416 909-2103
1117 W Isabel St Burbank (91506) *(P-20100)*

Streamline Avionics Inc ....E....... 949 861-8151
17672 Armstrong Ave Irvine (92614) *(P-8113)*

Streamline Dsign Slkscreen Inc (PA) ....D....... 805 884-1025
1299 S Wells Rd Ventura (93004) *(P-2223)*

Streamline Finishes Inc ....D....... 949 600-8964
26429 Rancho Pkwy S Ste 140 Lake Forest (92630) *(P-593)*

Strech Plastics Incorporated ....E....... 951 922-2224
900 John St Ste J Banning (92220) *(P-12917)*

Street Smart 247, El Segundo *Also Called: Street Smart LLC (P-16391)*

Street Smart LLC ....E....... 866 924-4644
100 N Pacific Coast Hwy El Segundo (90245) *(P-16391)*

Streets Ahead Inc ....E....... 323 277-0860
5510 S Soto St Unit B Vernon (90058) *(P-2435)*

Stremicks Heritage Foods LLC (HQ) ....B....... 714 775-5000
4002 Westminster Ave Santa Ana (92703) *(P-1316)*

Stress-O-Pedic, Ontario *Also Called: Stress-O-Pedic Mattress Co Inc (P-2861)*

Stress-O-Pedic Mattress Co Inc ....D....... 909 605-2010
2060 S Wineville Ave Ste A Ontario (91761) *(P-2861)*

Stretch Forming Corporation ....D....... 951 443-0911
804 S Redlands Ave Perris (92570) *(P-6326)*

Streuter Fastel Timtel, San Clemente *Also Called: Streuter Technologies (P-12573)*

Streuter Technologies ....F....... 949 369-7676
208 Avenida Fabricante Ste 200 San Clemente (92672) *(P-12573)*

Strike Technology Inc ....E....... 562 437-3428
24311 Wilmington Ave Carson (90745) *(P-9122)*

Stringking Inc (PA)..E....... 310 503-8901
19100 S Vermont Ave Gardena (90248) *(P-2154)*

Stromasys Inc ....D....... 919 239-8450
871 Marlborough Ave Riverside (92507) *(P-16392)*

Stroock & Stroock & Lavan, Los Angeles *Also Called: Stroock & Stroock & Lavan LLP (P-18950)*

Stroock & Stroock & Lavan LLP ....C....... 310 556-5800
2029 Century Park E Ste 1800 Los Angeles (90002) *(P-18950)*

Strottman, Irvine *Also Called: Strottman International Inc (P-10943)*

Strottman International Inc (PA)....................................E....... 949 623-7900
36 Executive Park Ste 200 Irvine (92614) *(P-10943)*

Strouk Group LLC ....C....... 323 939-7792
6333 W 3rd St Ste 150 Los Angeles (90036) *(P-13307)*

Structral Prsrvtion Systems LL ....B....... 714 891-9080
11800 Monarch St Garden Grove (92841) *(P-1088)*

Structural Composites Inds LLC (DH) ....E....... 909 594-7777
336 Enterprise Pl Pomona (91768) *(P-6160)*

Structural Diagnostics Inc ....E....... 805 987-7755
650 Via Alondra Camarillo (93012) *(P-10399)*

Structural Stl Fabricators Inc ....E....... 714 761-1695
10641 Sycamore Ave Stanton (90680) *(P-6079)*

Structurecast, Bakersfield *Also Called: Golden Empire Con Pdts Inc (P-5417)*

STS Instruments Inc ....E....... 580 223-4773
2802 Kelvin Ave Ste 100 Irvine (92614) *(P-10223)*

STS Metals ....D....... 626 969-6711
5467 Ayon Ave Irwindale (91706) *(P-6483)*

Stuart C. Gildred Family YMCA, Santa Ynez *Also Called: Channel Islnds Yung MNS Chrstn (P-19437)*

Stuart F Cooper Co ....C....... 213 747-7141
1565 E 23rd St Los Angeles (90011) *(P-3724)*

Stuart-Dean Co Inc ....E....... 714 544-4460
14731 Franklin Ave Ste L Tustin (92780) *(P-6668)*

Mergent email: customerrelations@mergent.com
1280

2024 Southern California
Business Directory and Buyers Guide

(P-0000) Products & Services Section entry number
(PA)=Parent Co (HQ)=Headquarters (DH)=Div Headquarters

Stud Welding Products, Downey *Also Called: Qualls Stud Welding Pdts Inc (P-12812)*

Student Transportation America, Santa Clarita *Also Called: Santa Barbara Trnsp Corp (P-11413)*

Student Transportation America, Goleta *Also Called: Santa Barbara Trnsp Corp (P-11432)*

Student Transportation America, Escondido *Also Called: Santa Barbara Trnsp Corp (P-11433)*

Studex, Gardena *Also Called: Quadrtech Corporation (P-10919)*

Studio 71 LP .... C...... 323 370-1500
8383 Wilshire Blvd Ste 1050 Beverly Hills (90211) *(P-15598)*

Studio City .... D...... 818 557-7777
5161 Lankershim Blvd # 200 North Hollywood (91601) *(P-17225)*

Studio Depot, Pacoima *Also Called: Mole-Richardson Co Ltd (P-8375)*

Studio Distribution Svcs LLC .... C...... 818 954-6000
4000 Warner Blvd Burbank (91522) *(P-17226)*

Studio OH, Irvine *Also Called: Orange Circle Studio Corp (P-3793)*

Studio Systems Inc (PA) .... **E...... 323 634-3400**
5700 Wilshire Blvd Ste 600 Los Angeles (90036) *(P-3487)*

Studio9d8 Inc .... E...... 626 350-0832
9743 Alesia St South El Monte (91733) *(P-2076)*

Stull Industries Inc .... F...... 951 248-9789
1315 W Flint St Lake Elsinore (92530) *(P-9463)*

Sturgeon Services Intl Inc .... B...... 661 322-4408
3511 Gilmore Ave Bakersfield (93308) *(P-6943)*

Sturgeon Son Grading & Pav Inc (PA) .... **C...... 661 322-4408**
3511 Gilmore Ave Bakersfield (93308) *(P-1126)*

Stussy, Irvine *Also Called: Stussy Inc (P-13113)*

Stussy Inc .... D...... 949 474-9255
17426 Daimler St Irvine (92614) *(P-13113)*

Stutz Packing LLC .... E...... 760 342-1666
82689 Avenue 45 Indio (92201) *(P-1358)*

Stutz Packing Company, Indio *Also Called: Stutz Packing LLC (P-1358)*

Stv Architects Inc .... C...... 213 482-9444
1055 W 7th St Ste 3150 Los Angeles (90017) *(P-19744)*

Stx Entertainment, Burbank *Also Called: Stx Financing LLC (P-17227)*

Stx Financing LLC .... C...... 310 742-2300
3900 W Alameda Ave Fl 32 Burbank (91505) *(P-17227)*

Style Network, Los Angeles *Also Called: E Entertainment Television Inc (P-11992)*

Styrotek Inc .... C...... 661 725-4957
345 Road 176 Delano (93215) *(P-4907)*

Subject Technologies Inc .... E...... 310 243-6484
345 N Maple Dr Beverly Hills (90210) *(P-16393)*

Sublitex Inc .... E...... 323 582-9596
1515 E 15th St Los Angeles (90021) *(P-2289)*

Sublitex Sublimation Tech, Los Angeles *Also Called: Sublitex Inc (P-2289)*

Subsidy of Be Aerospace, Fullerton *Also Called: ADB Industries (P-5822)*

Substance Abuse Program .... E...... 951 791-3350
1370 S State St Ste A Hemet (92543) *(P-8900)*

Subtle Luxury, Torrance *Also Called: Nothing To Wear Inc (P-2260)*

Subway, Brea *Also Called: Shore Front LLC (P-1984)*

Success Healthcare 1 LLC .... A.... 626 288-1160
7500 Hellman Ave Rosemead (91770) *(P-17796)*

Successor Agcy To Nrco Cmnty R, Norco *Also Called: City of Norco (P-20329)*

Suderman Contg Stevedores Inc (PA) .... **D...... 409 762-8131**
3806 Worsham Ave Long Beach (90808) *(P-11648)*

Suez Water Indiana LLC .... D...... 310 414-0183
1935 S Hughes Way El Segundo (90245) *(P-10164)*

Sugar Foods, Westlake Village *Also Called: Sugar Foods LLC (P-4532)*

Sugar Foods LLC .... D...... 323 727-8290
6190 E Slauson Ave Commerce (90040) *(P-1494)*

Sugar Foods LLC (PA) .... **E...... 805 396-5000**
3059 Townsgate Rd Ste 101 Westlake Village (91361) *(P-4532)*

Sugar Foods LLC .... C...... 818 768-7900
9500 El Dorado Ave Sun Valley (91352) *(P-16936)*

Sugarfina Inc .... E...... 818 302-0765
779 Americana Way Glendale (91210) *(P-1549)*

Sugarfina Inc .... E...... 949 301-9482
4353 La Jolla Village Dr San Diego (92122) *(P-1550)*

Sugarfina Inc .... E...... 424 290-0777
840 S Pacific Coast Hwy El Segundo (90245) *(P-1551)*

Sugarfina Inc .... E...... 424 284-8518
20 Hugus Aly Pasadena (91103) *(P-1552)*

Sugarfina Inc .... E...... 855 784-2734
9495 Santa Monica Blvd Beverly Hills (90210) *(P-1553)*

Sugarsync Inc .... E...... 650 571-5105
6922 Hollywood Blvd Ste 500 Los Angeles (90028) *(P-16394)*

Suheung-America Corporation .... E...... 714 671-9095
540 W Lambert Rd Brea (92821) *(P-4243)*

Suissa Miller Advertising LLC .... D...... 310 392-9666
8687 Melrose Ave West Hollywood (90069) *(P-15576)*

Suitecentric Lcc .... F...... 760 520-1611
5857 Owens Ave Ste 300 Carlsbad (92008) *(P-8466)*

Sukarne, City Of Industry *Also Called: Viz Cattle Corporation (P-1208)*

Sukut Construction LLC .... D...... 714 540-5351
4010 W Chandler Ave Santa Ana (92704) *(P-695)*

Sukut Construction Inc .... C...... 714 540-5351
4010 W Chandler Ave Santa Ana (92704) *(P-1127)*

Sullins Connector Solutions, San Marcos *Also Called: Sullins Electronics Corp (P-8276)*

Sullins Electronics Corp .... C...... 760 744-0125
801 E Mission Rd # B San Marcos (92069) *(P-8276)*

Sullivan, San Diego *Also Called: Sullivan International Group Inc (P-12211)*

Sullivan International Group Inc .... C...... 619 260-1432
2750 Womble Rd Ste 100 San Diego (92106) *(P-12211)*

Sullivans Stone Factory Inc .... E...... 760 347-5535
83778 Avenue 45 Indio (92201) *(P-5536)*

Sullivncrtsmnroe Insur Svcs LL (PA) .... **C...... 800 427-3253**
1920 Main St Ste 600 Irvine (92614) *(P-20250)*

Sully Miller Contracting, Brea *Also Called: United Rock Products Corp (P-651)*

Sully-Miller Holding Corp .... C...... 714 578-9600
135 S State College Blvd Ste 400 Brea (92821) *(P-648)*

Sulpizio Cardiovascular Center .... C...... 858 657-7000
9434 Medical Center Dr La Jolla (92037) *(P-17797)*

Sulzer Bingham Pumps, Santa Fe Springs *Also Called: Sulzer Pump Services (us) Inc (P-7291)*

Sulzer Elctr-Mchncal Svcs US I .... E...... 909 825-7971
620 S Rancho Ave Colton (92324) *(P-17108)*

Sulzer Pump Services (us) Inc .... E...... 562 903-1000
9856 Jordan Cir Santa Fe Springs (90670) *(P-7291)*

Sumitomo Elc Semicdtr Mtls Inc .... D...... 503 693-3100
915 Armorlite Dr San Marcos (92069) *(P-8901)*

Sumitomo Mitsui Banking Corp .... C...... 213 452-7800
601 S Figueroa St Ste 1800 Los Angeles (90017) *(P-14214)*

Sumitomo Rubber North Amer Inc (HQ) .... **C...... 909 466-1116**
8656 Haven Ave Rancho Cucamonga (91730) *(P-12273)*

Sumitronics USA Inc .... E...... 619 661-0450
9335 Airway Rd Ste 212 San Diego (92154) *(P-8734)*

Summer Fridays LLC .... E...... 612 804-0868
9180 Wilshire Blvd Beverly Hills (90212) *(P-4459)*

Summer Systems Inc .... D...... 661 257-4419
28942 Hancock Pkwy Valencia (91355) *(P-594)*

Summerland Wine Brands, Buellton *Also Called: Terravant Wine Company LLC (P-1663)*

Summerwood Winery & Inn Inc .... E...... 805 227-1365
2175 Arbor Rd Paso Robles (93446) *(P-15376)*

Summit Electric & Data Inc .... F...... 661 775-9901
27913 Smyth Dr Valencia (91355) *(P-9258)*

Summit Enterprises Inc .... E...... 858 679-2100
2471 Montecito Rd Ste A Ramona (92065) *(P-3247)*

Summit Erosion Control, Ramona *Also Called: Summit Enterprises Inc (P-3247)*

Summit Interconnect Inc (HQ) .... **C...... 714 239-2433**
223 N Crescent Way Anaheim (92801) *(P-8735)*

Summit Interconnect - Anaheim, Anaheim *Also Called: Kca Electronics Inc (P-8695)*

Summit Interconnect Orange, Orange *Also Called: Fabricated Components Corp (P-8676)*

Summit Machine LLC .... C...... 909 923-2744
2880 E Philadelphia St Ontario (91761) *(P-9803)*

SUN & SAIL CLUB, Lake Forest *Also Called: Lake Frest No II Mstr Hmwners (P-19453)*

Sun & Sun Industries Inc ....D...... 714 210-5141
2101 S Yale St Santa Ana (92704) *(P-8333)*

Sun Air Jets LLC .... C...... 805 389-9301
855 Aviation Dr Ste 200 Camarillo (93010) *(P-11683)*

Sun Badge Co .... E...... 909 930-1444
2248 S Baker Ave Ontario (91761) *(P-11287)*

Sun Chemical Corporation .... E...... 562 946-2327
12963 Park St Santa Fe Springs (90670) *(P-4591)*

Sun City Palm Dsert Cmnty Assn (PA)..............................D.......760 200-2100
  38180 Del Webb Blvd Palm Desert (92211) *(P-19465)*

Sun Cmpany of San Brnrdino Cal (HQ)......................B.......909 889-9666
  4030 Georgia Blvd San Bernardino (92407) *(P-3326)*

Sun Coast Merchandise Corp ....C.......323 720-9700
  6405 Randolph St Commerce (90040) *(P-12987)*

Sun Dairy Co, Los Angeles *Also Called: Pac Fill Inc (P-1314)*

Sun Diego Charter, National City *Also Called: Sureride Charter Inc (P-11418)*

Sun Electric LP ....D.......714 210-3744
  2101 S Yale St Ste B Santa Ana (92704) *(P-941)*

Sun Glo Foods, Fullerton *Also Called: Khyber Foods Incorporated (P-1922)*

Sun Healthcare Group Inc (DH) ....B
  27442 Portola Pkwy Ste 200 Foothill Ranch (92610) *(P-17798)*

Sun Hill Properties Inc ....B.......818 506-2500
  555 Universal Hollywood Dr Universal City (91608) *(P-15377)*

Sun Ice USA, Riverside *Also Called: Mackie International Inc (P-1299)*

Sun Industries, Torrance *Also Called: Sun Industries Corporation (P-7332)*

Sun Industries, Santa Ana *Also Called: Sun & Sun Industries Inc (P-8333)*

Sun Industries Corporation ....E.......310 782-1188
  370 Amapola Ave Ste 101 Torrance (90501) *(P-7332)*

SUN MAR HEALTH CARE, Riverside *Also Called: Riverside Equities LLC (P-18041)*

Sun Microsystems, Irvine *Also Called: Oracle America Inc (P-7443)*

Sun Pacific Cold Storage, Bakersfield *Also Called: Exeter Packers Inc (P-11551)*

Sun Pacific Farming, Bakersfield *Also Called: 7th Standard Ranch Company (P-26)*

Sun Pacific Farming, Bakersfield *Also Called: Sun Pacific Marketing Coop Inc (P-13341)*

Sun Pacific Farming Coop Inc ....D.......661 399-0376
  33374 Lerdo Hwy Bakersfield (93308) *(P-138)*

Sun Pacific Farms, Bakersfield *Also Called: Sun Pacific Farming Coop Inc (P-138)*

Sun Pacific Marketing Coop Inc ....B.......661 847-1015
  31452 Old River Rd Bakersfield (93311) *(P-13341)*

Sun Pacific Marketing Coop Inc ....B.......213 612-9957
  33502 Lerdo Hwy Bakersfield (93308) *(P-20251)*

Sun Pacific Shippers, Pasadena *Also Called: Exeter Packers Inc (P-42)*

Sun Plastics Inc ....E.......323 888-6999
  7140 E Slauson Ave Commerce (90040) *(P-3191)*

Sun Precision Machining Inc ....F.......951 817-0056
  1651 Market St Ste A Corona (92880) *(P-8037)*

Sun Rich Foods Intl Corp ....F.......714 632-7577
  1240 N Barsten Way Anaheim (92806) *(P-1992)*

Sun Stone Sales, Temecula *Also Called: Sunstone Components Group Inc (P-6560)*

Sun Ten Labs Liquidation Co ....F.......949 587-0509
  9250 Jeronimo Rd Irvine (92618) *(P-13395)*

Sun Valley Extrusion, Los Angeles *Also Called: Sun Valley Products Inc (P-5710)*

Sun Valley Ltg Standards Inc ....E.......661 233-2000
  660 W Avenue O Palmdale (93551) *(P-8334)*

Sun Valley Products Inc (HQ)..E.......818 247-8350
  4626 Sperry St Los Angeles (90039) *(P-5709)*

Sun Valley Products Inc ....E.......818 247-8350
  4640 Sperry St Los Angeles (90039) *(P-5710)*

Sun West Mortgage Company Inc (PA).........................C.......562 326-5732
  18303 Gridley Rd Cerritos (90703) *(P-14350)*

Sun World Inc ....A.......805 833-6460
  5544 California Ave Ste 280 Bakersfield (93309) *(P-112)*

Sun World International Inc (PA)...................................A.......661 392-5000
  16351 Driver Rd Bakersfield (93308) *(P-113)*

Sun-Gro Commodities Inc (PA)......................................E.......661 393-2612
  34575 Famoso Rd Bakersfield (93308) *(P-1450)*

SunAmerica, Los Angeles *Also Called: SunAmerica Inc (P-14254)*

SunAmerica, Los Angeles *Also Called: SunAmerica Life Insurance Company (P-14442)*

SunAmerica, Los Angeles *Also Called: SunAmerica Investments Inc (P-20101)*

SunAmerica Inc (HQ)..A.......310 772-6000
  1 Sun America Ctr Fl 38 Los Angeles (90067) *(P-14254)*

SunAmerica Investments Inc (DH)................................D.......310 772-6000
  1 Sun America Ctr Fl 37 Los Angeles (90067) *(P-20101)*

SunAmerica Life Insurance Company ....C.......310 772-6000
  1 Sun America Ctr Fl 36 Los Angeles (90067) *(P-14442)*

Sunbeam, Fontana *Also Called: Sunbeam Products Inc (P-8223)*

Sunbeam Products Inc ....F.......951 727-3901
  13052 Jurupa Ave Fontana (92337) *(P-8223)*

Sunbritetv LLC (DH)..F.......805 214-7250
  2630 Townsgate Rd Ste F Westlake Village (91361) *(P-8585)*

Sunco Lighting Inc ....E.......844 334-9938
  27811 Hancock Pkwy Ste A Valencia (91355) *(P-12620)*

Suncoast Post, Ontario *Also Called: Suncoast Post-Tension Ltd (P-12735)*

Suncoast Post-Tension Ltd ....F.......909 673-0490
  1528 E Cedar St Ontario (91761) *(P-12735)*

Suncore Inc ....E.......949 450-0054
  15 Hubble Ste 200 Irvine (92618) *(P-8902)*

Sundance Custom Golf Carts, El Cajon *Also Called: Sundance Custom Golf Carts Inc (P-12918)*

Sundance Custom Golf Carts Inc ....F.......619 449-0822
  1240 Vernon Way El Cajon (92020) *(P-12918)*

Sundance Spas, Chino *Also Called: Jacuzzi Brands LLC (P-11233)*

Sundance Spas, Irvine *Also Called: Sundance Spas Inc (P-11288)*

Sundance Spas Inc (DH)...E.......909 606-7733
  17872 Gillette Ave Ste 300 Irvine (92614) *(P-11288)*

Sunderstorm LLC ....E.......818 605-6682
  1146 N Central Ave Glendale (91202) *(P-11289)*

Sundial Industries Inc ....E.......818 767-4477
  8421 Telfair Ave Sun Valley (91352) *(P-6740)*

Sundial Powder Coatings Inc ....E.......818 767-4477
  8421 Telfair Ave Sun Valley (91352) *(P-6741)*

Sundown Foods, Fontana *Also Called: Sundown Foods USA Inc (P-1345)*

Sundown Foods USA Inc ....E.......909 606-6797
  10891 Business Dr Fontana (92337) *(P-1345)*

Sundown Liquidating Corp (PA).....................................D.......714 540-8950
  401 Goetz Ave Santa Ana (92707) *(P-5318)*

Suneva Medical Inc (PA)...E.......858 550-9999
  5870 Pacific Center Blvd San Diego (92121) *(P-4460)*

Sunfood Corporation ....D.......619 596-7979
  1830 Gillespie Way Ste 101 El Cajon (92020) *(P-13396)*

Sunfood Superfoods, El Cajon *Also Called: Sunfood Corporation (P-13396)*

Sunfusion Energy Systems Inc ....E.......800 544-0282
  9020 Kenamar Dr Ste 204 San Diego (92121) *(P-9155)*

Sungard, Calabasas *Also Called: Sungard Treasury Systems Inc (P-16395)*

Sungard Treasury Systems Inc ....C.......818 223-2300
  23975 Park Sorrento Ste 100 Calabasas (91302) *(P-16395)*

Sungear Inc ....E.......858 549-3166
  8535 Arjons Dr Ste G San Diego (92126) *(P-9804)*

Sungevity, Temecula *Also Called: Solar Spectrum LLC (P-826)*

Sunkist Growers Inc (PA)...C.......661 290-8900
  27770 Entertainment Dr Valencia (91355) *(P-13342)*

Sunland Aerospace Fasteners ....E.......818 485-8929
  12920 Pierce St Pacoima (91331) *(P-6454)*

Sunland Ford Inc ....D.......760 241-7751
  15330 Palmdale Rd Victorville (92392) *(P-13832)*

Sunland Ford-Lincoln-Mercury, Victorville *Also Called: Sunland Ford Inc (P-13832)*

Sunland Shutters, Long Beach *Also Called: Ta Chen International Inc (P-12574)*

Sunline Transit Agency (PA)..C.......760 343-3456
  32505 Harry Oliver Trl Thousand Palms (92276) *(P-11369)*

Sunline Transit Agency ....C.......760 972-4059
  790 Vine Ave Coachella (92236) *(P-11405)*

Sunn America Inc ....E.......909 944-5756
  10280 Indiana Ct Rancho Cucamonga (91730) *(P-15800)*

Sunnova Energy Corporation ....A.......877 757-7697
  6531 Irvine Center Dr Ste 200 Irvine (92618) *(P-12078)*

Sunny Amer Globl Autotec Corp ....E.......714 544-0400
  2681 Dow Ave Ste A Tustin (92780) *(P-9464)*

Sunny View Care Center, Los Angeles *Also Called: Longwood Management Corp (P-18137)*

Sunnygem, Wasco *Also Called: Sunnygem LLC (P-1346)*

Sunnygem LLC (PA)...B.......661 758-0491
  500 N F St Wasco (93280) *(P-1346)*

Sunon Inc (PA)...E.......714 255-0208
  1075 W Lambert Rd Ste A Brea (92821) *(P-7333)*

Sunopta Fruit Group Inc ....D.......323 774-6000
  12128 Center St South Gate (90280) *(P-1784)*

Sunopta Grains and Foods Inc ....D.......323 774-6000
  12128 Center St South Gate (90280) *(P-1417)*

Sunpower By Green Convergence, Valencia *Also Called: Green Convergence (P-12742)*

Sunrise Ford .... C...... 909 822-4401
16005 Valley Blvd Fontana (92335) *(P-13833)*

Sunrise Ford, North Hollywood *Also Called: Ngp Motors Inc (P-13802)*

Sunrise Growers Inc .... A...... 612 619-9545
2640 Sturgis Rd Oxnard (93030) *(P-1993)*

Sunrise Growers Inc .... C...... 714 706-6090
701 W Kimberly Ave # 210 Placentia (92870) *(P-13343)*

Sunrise Jewelry Mfg Corp .... F...... 619 270-5624
4425 Convoy St Ste 226 San Diego (92111) *(P-10912)*

Sunrise Med HM Hlth Care Group, Chula Vista *Also Called: Vcp Mobility Holdings Inc (P-10720)*

Sunrise Medical Inc .... E...... 619 930-1500
2382 Faraday Ave Ste 200 Carlsbad (92008) *(P-10705)*

Sunrise Respiratory Care Inc .... C...... 949 398-6555
1881 Langley Ave Irvine (92614) *(P-12517)*

Sunrise Senior Living MGT Inc .... C...... 760 720-9898
3140 El Camino Real Carlsbad (92008) *(P-18060)*

Sunrise Senior Living MGT Inc .... C...... 909 447-5259
120 W San Jose Ave Claremont (91711) *(P-19303)*

Sunroad Asset Management Inc .... C...... 858 362-8500
4445 Eastgate Mall Ste 400 San Diego (92121) *(P-20102)*

Sunsation Inc .... E...... 909 542-0280
100 S Cambridge Ave Claremont (91711) *(P-1379)*

Sunset Landscape Maintenance .... D...... 949 455-4636
27201 Burbank El Toro (92610) *(P-216)*

Sunset Manor Convalescent Hosp, El Monte *Also Called: Gibraltar Cnvalescent Hosp Inc (P-18128)*

Sunset Property Services, Irvine *Also Called: Jonset LLC (P-12209)*

Sunset Signs and Printing Inc .... E...... 714 255-9104
2906 E Coronado St Anaheim (92806) *(P-11171)*

Sunsets Inc .... E...... 310 784-3600
24511 Frampton Ave Harbor City (90710) *(P-2077)*

Sunsets Separates, Harbor City *Also Called: Sunsets Inc (P-2077)*

Sunshine, Montebello *Also Called: Sunshine Fpc Inc (P-3192)*

Sunshine Communications SE Inc .... C...... 619 448-7600
350 Cypress Ln Ste D El Cajon (92020) *(P-942)*

Sunshine Enterprises, Monterey Park *Also Called: DHm International Corp (P-2319)*

Sunshine Fpc Inc .... D...... 323 721-8168
1600 Gage Rd Montebello (90640) *(P-3192)*

Sunshine Makers Inc (PA) .... D...... 562 795-6000
15922 Pacific Coast Hwy Huntington Beach (92649) *(P-4369)*

Sunshine Metal Clad Inc .... D...... 661 366-0575
7201 Edison Hwy Bakersfield (93307) *(P-999)*

Sunsports LP .... E...... 949 273-6202
7 Holland Irvine (92618) *(P-5262)*

Sunstar Spa Covers Inc (HQ) .... E...... 858 602-1950
26074 Avenue Hall Ste 13 Valencia (91355) *(P-11290)*

Sunstone Components Group Inc (HQ) .... E...... 951 296-5010
42136 Avenida Alvarado Temecula (92590) *(P-6560)*

Sunstone Durante LLC .... C...... 858 792-5200
15575 Jimmy Durante Blvd Del Mar (92014) *(P-15378)*

Sunstone Hotel Properties Inc .... C...... 310 228-4100
1177 S Beverly Dr Los Angeles (90035) *(P-15379)*

Sunstone Hotel Properties Inc .... C...... 310 546-7627
1700 N Sepulveda Blvd Manhattan Beach (90266) *(P-15380)*

Sunstone Hotel Properties Inc (DH) .... C...... 949 330-4000
120 Vantis Dr Ste 350 Aliso Viejo (92656) *(P-15381)*

Sunstone Top Gun Lessee Inc .... C...... 949 330-4000
4550 La Jolla Village Dr San Diego (92122) *(P-15382)*

Suntsu, Irvine *Also Called: Suntsu Electronics Inc (P-9123)*

Suntsu Electronics Inc .... E...... 949 783-7300
142 Technology Dr Ste 150 Irvine (92618) *(P-9123)*

Sunvair, Valencia *Also Called: Sunvair Inc (P-9805)*

Sunvair Inc (HQ) .... E...... 661 294-3777
29145 The Old Rd Valencia (91355) *(P-9805)*

Sunvair Aerospace Group Inc (PA) .... D...... 661 294-3777
29145 The Old Rd Valencia (91355) *(P-17155)*

Sunvair Overhaul Inc .... E...... 661 257-6123
29145 The Old Rd Valencia (91355) *(P-9806)*

Sunwest Electric Inc .... C...... 714 630-8700
3064 E Mariloma Anaheim (92806) *(P-943)*

Supacolor Usa Inc .... D...... 844 973-2862
16198 Gramercy Pl Ste B Gardena (90247) *(P-3813)*

Super 8 Motel, Bakersfield *Also Called: Tiburon Hospitality LLC (P-15390)*

Super Center Concepts Inc .... C...... 323 562-8980
7300 Atlantic Ave Cudahy (90201) *(P-13705)*

Super Center Concepts Inc .... D...... 323 241-6789
10211 Avalon Blvd Los Angeles (90003) *(P-13706)*

Super Center Concepts Inc .... C...... 323 223-3878
133 W Avenue 45 Los Angeles (90065) *(P-16937)*

Super Color Digital, Irvine *Also Called: Super Color Digital LLC (P-3814)*

Super Color Digital LLC (PA) .... E...... 949 622-0010
16761 Hale Ave Irvine (92606) *(P-3814)*

Super D Phantom Distribution, Irvine *Also Called: C D Listening Bar Inc (P-12970)*

Super Dyeing and Finishing, Santa Fe Springs *Also Called: Super Dyeing LLC (P-2092)*

Super Dyeing LLC .... D...... 562 692-9500
8825 Millergrove Dr Santa Fe Springs (90670) *(P-2092)*

Super Glue, Ontario *Also Called: Pacer Technology (P-4574)*

Super Services, Anaheim *Also Called: E Z Services (P-14259)*

Super Struct Bldg Systems Inc .... E...... 760 322-2522
1251 Montalvo Way Ste F Palm Springs (92263) *(P-2917)*

Super Welding Southern Cal Inc .... E...... 619 239-8003
1668 Newton Ave San Diego (92113) *(P-7163)*

Super73 Inc (PA) .... E...... 949 649-4607
16591 Noyes Ave Irvine (92606) *(P-9885)*

Superb Chair Corporation .... E...... 562 776-1771
6861 Watcher St Commerce (90040) *(P-2821)*

Superbam Inc .... E...... 310 845-5784
214 Main St El Segundo (90245) *(P-3488)*

Supercolor, Irvine *Also Called: Digital Supercolor Inc (P-3562)*

Superior Awning Inc .... E...... 818 780-7200
14555 Titus St Panorama City (91402) *(P-2510)*

Superior Bias Trims, Vernon *Also Called: SJ&I Bias Binding & Tex Co Inc (P-2540)*

Superior Communications Inc (PA) .... C...... 877 522-4727
5027 Irwindale Ave Ste 900 Irwindale (91706) *(P-12699)*

Superior Connector Plating Inc .... E...... 714 774-1174
1901 E Cerritos Ave Anaheim (92805) *(P-6669)*

Superior Construction Inc .... D...... 951 808-8780
265 N Joy St Corona (92879) *(P-460)*

Superior Duct Fabrication Inc .... C...... 909 620-8565
1683 Mount Vernon Ave Pomona (91768) *(P-6327)*

Superior Elec Mech & Plbg Inc .... B...... 909 357-9400
8613 Helms Ave Rancho Cucamonga (91730) *(P-944)*

Superior Electric Mtr Svc Inc .... F...... 323 583-1040
4622 Alcoa Ave Vernon (90058) *(P-17109)*

Superior Electrical Advg Inc (PA) .... D...... 562 495-3808
1700 W Anaheim St Long Beach (90813) *(P-11172)*

Superior Equipment Solutions .... D...... 323 722-7900
1085 Bixby Dr Hacienda Heights (91745) *(P-8224)*

Superior Essex Inc .... C...... 909 481-4804
5250 Ontario Mills Pkwy Ste 300 Ontario (91764) *(P-5751)*

Superior Food Machinery Inc .... E...... 562 949-0396
8311 Sorensen Ave Santa Fe Springs (90670) *(P-7217)*

Superior Fruit LLC .... C...... 805 485-2519
4324 E Vineyard Ave Oxnard (93036) *(P-25)*

Superior Grocers, Los Angeles *Also Called: Super Center Concepts Inc (P-16937)*

Superior Grounding Systems Inc .... E...... 626 814-1981
16021 Arrow Hwy Ste A Baldwin Park (91706) *(P-8277)*

Superior Gunite (HQ) .... C...... 818 896-9199
12306 Van Nuys Blvd Sylmar (91342) *(P-1089)*

Superior Honey Company, San Bernardino *Also Called: Millers American Honey Inc (P-1945)*

Superior Inds Intl Hldings LLC (HQ) .... D...... 818 781-4973
7800 Woodley Ave Van Nuys (91406) *(P-9465)*

Superior Jig Inc .... E...... 714 525-4777
1540 N Orangethorpe Way Anaheim (92801) *(P-7099)*

Superior Lithographics Inc .... D...... 323 263-8400
3055 Bandini Blvd Vernon (90058) *(P-3690)*

Superior Machining Mfg Co Inc .... F...... 714 529-6000
322 Oak Pl Brea (92821) *(P-8038)*

Superior Metal Fabricators Inc .... E...... 951 360-2474
4768 Felspar St Riverside (92509) *(P-6328)*

Employee Codes: A=Over 500 employees, B=251-500
C=101-250, D=51-100, E=20-50, F=10-19, G=1-9
2024 Southern California
Business Directory and Buyers Guide
© Mergent Inc. 1-800-342-5647
1283

Superior Metal Shapes Inc .... E...... 909 947-3455
4730 Eucalyptus Ave Chino (91710) *(P-5711)*

Superior Mold Co .... E...... 909 947-7028
1927 E Francis St Ontario (91761) *(P-5219)*

Superior Nut Co Inc .... F...... 323 223-2431
5200 Valley Blvd Los Angeles (90032) *(P-13275)*

Superior Paving Company Inc .... D...... 951 739-9200
1880 N Delilah St Corona (92879) *(P-649)*

Superior Plating, Anaheim *Also Called: Superior Connector Plating Inc (P-6669)*

Superior Press, Santa Fe Springs *Also Called: Superior Printing Inc (P-3815)*

Superior Printing Inc .... D...... 888 590-7998
9440 Norwalk Blvd Santa Fe Springs (90670) *(P-3815)*

Superior Quality Foods Inc .... D...... 909 923-4733
2355 E Francis St Ontario (91761) *(P-1332)*

Superior Ready Mix Concrete, Corona *Also Called: Superior Ready Mix Concrete LP (P-5507)*

Superior Ready Mix Concrete, Thousand Palms *Also Called: Superior Ready Mix Concrete LP (P-5509)*

Superior Ready Mix Concrete LP .... D...... 951 277-3553
24635 Temescal Canyon Rd Corona (92883) *(P-5507)*

Superior Ready Mix Concrete LP .... D...... 951 658-9225
1130 N State St Hemet (92543) *(P-5508)*

Superior Ready Mix Concrete LP .... D...... 760 343-3418
72270 Varner Rd Thousand Palms (92276) *(P-5509)*

Superior Ready Mix Concrete LP (PA) ....**E...... 760 745-0556**
1564 Mission Rd Escondido (92029) *(P-5510)*

Superior Ready Mix Concrete LP .... D...... 619 265-0955
7192 Mission Gorge Rd San Diego (92120) *(P-5511)*

Superior Ready Mix Concrete LP .... D...... 619 265-0296
7500 Mission Gorge Rd San Diego (92120) *(P-5512)*

Superior Ready Mix Concrete LP .... D...... 760 728-1128
1564 Mission Rd Escondido (92029) *(P-5513)*

Superior Ready Mix Concrete LP .... D...... 619 443-7510
12494 Highway 67 Lakeside (92040) *(P-5514)*

Superior Ready Mix Concrete LP .... D...... 760 352-4341
802 E Main St El Centro (92243) *(P-5515)*

Superior Ready Mix Concrete LP .... D...... 858 695-0666
9245 Camino Santa Fe San Diego (92121) *(P-13671)*

Superior Sod I LP .... C...... 909 923-5068
17821 17th St Ste 165 Tustin (92780) *(P-71)*

Superior Spring Company .... E...... 714 490-0881
1260 S Talt Ave Anaheim (92806) *(P-6809)*

Superior Super Warehouse, Cudahy *Also Called: Super Center Concepts Inc (P-13705)*

Superior Tank Co Inc (PA) ....**E...... 909 912-0580**
9500 Lucas Ranch Rd Rancho Cucamonga (91730) *(P-6161)*

Superior Thread Rolling Co .... D...... 818 504-3626
12801 Wentworth St Arleta (91331) *(P-8039)*

Superior Touch, Ontario *Also Called: Superior Quality Foods Inc (P-1332)*

Superior Trailer Works .... E...... 909 350-0185
13700 Slover Ave Fontana (92337) *(P-6998)*

Superior Wall Systems Inc .... B...... 714 278-0000
1232 E Orangethorpe Ave Fullerton (92831) *(P-1000)*

Superior Warehouse, Los Angeles *Also Called: Super Center Concepts Inc (P-13706)*

Superior Window Coverings Inc .... E...... 818 762-6685
7683 N San Fernando Rd Burbank (91505) *(P-2464)*

Superior-Studio Spc Inc .... E...... 323 278-0100
2239 Yates Ave Commerce (90040) *(P-11291)*

Supermedia LLC .... D...... 562 594-5101
3131 Katella Ave Los Alamitos (90720) *(P-3489)*

Supernal LLC .... C...... 202 422-3275
15555 Laguna Canyon Rd Irvine (92618) *(P-5799)*

Superpak, Tustin *Also Called: Durabag Company Inc (P-3182)*

Supersprings International Inc .... E...... 805 745-5553
5251 6th St Carpinteria (93013) *(P-6785)*

Supervision of Shipbuilding, San Diego *Also Called: NAVY UNITED STATES DEPARTMENT (P-9844)*

Supplier Diversity, San Diego *Also Called: San Diego Gas & Electric Co (P-12105)*

Supplier Diversity Program, Carlsbad *Also Called: Life Technologies Corporation (P-10271)*

Support Equipment, Escondido *Also Called: C & H Machine Inc (P-7708)*

SUPPORT, TREATMENT, & EDUCATIO, Irvine *Also Called: In Stepps Inc (P-17860)*

Supra National Express Inc .... C...... 310 549-7105
1421 Charles Willard St Carson (90746) *(P-11807)*

Supreme Abrasives .... E...... 949 250-8644
1021 Fuller St Santa Ana (92701) *(P-5544)*

Supreme Almonds California Inc .... D...... 661 746-6475
16897 Highway 43 Wasco (93280) *(P-38)*

Supreme Enterprise, Santa Fe Springs *Also Called: Kingsolver Inc (P-11090)*

Supreme Graphics Inc .... F...... 310 531-8300
1201 N Miller St Anaheim (92806) *(P-3691)*

Supreme Machine Products Inc .... F...... 909 974-0349
302 Sequoia Ave Ontario (91761) *(P-8040)*

Sure Grip International .... D...... 562 923-0724
5519 Rawlings Ave South Gate (90280) *(P-11031)*

Sure Power Inc .... E...... 619 661-6292
9255 Customhouse Plz San Diego (92154) *(P-8159)*

Sure Power Inc .... E...... 310 542-8561
1111 Knox St Torrance (90502) *(P-9124)*

Surecraft Supply Inc C
2875 Executive Pl Escondido (92029) *(P-1023)*

Surefire LLC .... E...... 714 545-9444
17680 Newhope St Ste B Fountain Valley (92708) *(P-10706)*

Surefire LLC .... E...... 714 545-9444
17760 Newhope St Ste A Fountain Valley (92708) *(P-10707)*

Surefire LLC .... E...... 714 641-0483
2110 S Anne St Santa Ana (92704) *(P-10708)*

Surefire LLC .... E...... 714 545-9444
18300 Mount Baldy Cir Fountain Valley (92708) *(P-10709)*

Surefire LLC .... E...... 714 545-9444
2121 S Yale St Santa Ana (92704) *(P-10710)*

Surefire LLC .... E...... 714 641-0483
2300 S Yale St Santa Ana (92704) *(P-10711)*

Surefire LLC (PA) ....**C...... 714 545-9444**
18300 Mount Baldy Cir Fountain Valley (92708) *(P-8383)*

Sureride Charter Inc .... C...... 619 336-9200
522 W 8th St National City (91950) *(P-11418)*

Surf Sand Hotel, Laguna Beach *Also Called: JC Resorts LLC (P-20042)*

Surf To Summit Inc .... F...... 805 964-1896
7234 Hollister Ave Goleta (93117) *(P-11032)*

Surface Optics Corporation .... E...... 858 675-7404
11555 Rancho Bernardo Rd San Diego (92127) *(P-10224)*

Surface Pumps Inc (PA) ....**D...... 661 393-1545**
3301 Unicorn Rd Bakersfield (93308) *(P-12826)*

Surface Technologies Corp .... E...... 619 564-8320
3170 Commercial St San Diego (92113) *(P-8192)*

Surface-Tech LLC .... F...... 619 880-0265
888 Prospect St Ste 200 La Jolla (92037) *(P-4666)*

SURFSIDE RACE PLACE AT DEL MAR, Del Mar *Also Called: Del Mar Thoroughbred Club (P-17385)*

Surge Globl Bkries Hldings LLC (PA) ....**D...... 818 896-0525**
13336 Paxton St Pacoima (91331) *(P-13397)*

Surgeon Worldwide Inc .... E...... 707 501-7962
3855 S Hill St Los Angeles (90037) *(P-5279)*

Surgistar Inc (PA) ....**E...... 760 598-2480**
2310 La Mirada Dr Vista (92081) *(P-10610)*

Surrounding Elements LLC .... E...... 949 582-9000
33051 Calle Aviador Ste A San Juan Capistrano (92675) *(P-2838)*

Survey Stake and Marker Inc .... E...... 626 960-4802
13470 Dalewood St Baldwin Park (91706) *(P-2763)*

Surveysavvy.com, San Diego *Also Called: Luth Research Inc (P-19905)*

Survios Inc .... E...... 310 736-1503
4501 Glencoe Ave Marina Del Rey (90292) *(P-16472)*

Survival Systems Intl Inc (PA) ....**D...... 760 749-6800**
34140 Valley Center Rd Valley Center (92082) *(P-17156)*

Susan J Harris Inc .... C...... 619 498-8450
344 F St Ste 100 Chula Vista (91910) *(P-19304)*

Suss McRtec Phtnic Systems Inc .... D...... 951 817-3700
2520 Palisades Dr Corona (92882) *(P-9259)*

Suss Microtec Inc (HQ) ....**C...... 408 940-0300**
2520 Palisades Dr Corona (92882) *(P-7260)*

Sustainable Agriculture, Trabuco Canyon *Also Called: Seeds of Change Inc (P-13490)*

Sutter Securities Inc .... D...... 415 352-6300
6 Venture Ste 395 Irvine (92618) *(P-14405)*

Suzhou South .... B...... 626 322-0101
18351 Colima Rd Ste 82 Rowland Heights (91748) *(P-7585)*

Suzuki Motor of America Inc (HQ)............................C....... 714 996-7040
3251 E Imperial Hwy Brea (92821) *(P-13834)*

Suzuki USA, Brea *Also Called: Suzuki Motor of America Inc (P-13834)*

Svf Flow Controls Inc ....E....... 562 802-2255
5595 Fresca Dr La Palma (90623) *(P-12827)*

Svf Flow Controls LLC ....E....... 562 802-2255
5595 Fresca Dr La Palma (90623) *(P-7707)*

Svo Enterprise LLC ....E....... 626 406-4770
9854 Baldwin Pl El Monte (91731) *(P-2423)*

SW Fixtures Inc ....F....... 909 595-2506
3940 Valley Blvd Ste C Walnut (91789) *(P-2967)*

Swabplus Inc ....E....... 909 987-7898
9669 Hermosa Ave Rancho Cucamonga (91730) *(P-4747)*

Swag Corporation ....E....... 805 499-6555
1534 N Moorpark Rd Pmb 353 Thousand Oaks (91360) *(P-9260)*

Swan Fence Incorporated ....E....... 310 669-8000
600 W Manville St Compton (90220) *(P-13672)*

Swaner Hardwood Co Inc (PA)...............................D....... 818 953-5350
5 W Magnolia Blvd Burbank (91502) *(P-2692)*

Swarco McCain Inc (DH)..C....... 760 727-8100
2365 Oak Ridge Way Vista (92081) *(P-12828)*

Swartz Glass Co Inc (PA).......................................F....... 310 392-0001
821 Lincoln Blvd Venice (90291) *(P-13674)*

Swatfame Inc (PA)..B....... 626 961-7928
16425 Gale Ave City Of Industry (91745) *(P-13152)*

Sway-A-Way Inc ....E....... 818 700-9712
9530 Cozycroft Ave Chatsworth (91311) *(P-9466)*

Swds, Irvine *Also Called: Swds Holdings Inc (P-14948)*

Swds Holdings Inc ....B....... 800 395-5277
8659 Research Dr Irvine (92618) *(P-14948)*

Sweda, City Of Industry *Also Called: Sweda Company LLC (P-12969)*

Sweda Company LLC ....B....... 626 357-9999
17411 E Valley Blvd City Of Industry (91744) *(P-12969)*

Sweden & Martina Inc ....E....... 844 862-7846
600 Anton Blvd Ste 1134 Costa Mesa (92626) *(P-10611)*

Sweetener Products, Vernon *Also Called: Edna H Pagel Inc (P-501)*

Sweetener Products Inc (PA)..................................E....... 323 234-2200
2050 E 38th St Vernon (90058) *(P-13398)*

Sweetener Products Company, Vernon *Also Called: Sweetener Products Inc (P-13398)*

Sweetwter Auth Employees Cmmtte (PA)..................C....... 619 420-1413
505 Garrett Ave Chula Vista (91910) *(P-12148)*

Sweis Inc (PA)..D....... 310 375-0558
20000 Mariner Ave Torrance (90503) *(P-12896)*

Swell Cafe, The, San Diego *Also Called: Swell Coffee Roasting Co LP (P-13399)*

Swell Coffee Roasting Co LP ....E....... 619 504-9244
501 W Broadway Ste 290 San Diego (92101) *(P-13399)*

Swift Beef Company ....C....... 951 571-2237
15555 Meridian Pkwy Riverside (92518) *(P-1237)*

Swift Engineering, San Clemente *Also Called: Swift Engineering Inc (P-9807)*

Swift Engineering Inc ....D....... 949 492-6608
1141a Via Callejon San Clemente (92673) *(P-9807)*

Swift Fab, Gardena *Also Called: Carla Senter (P-6210)*

Swift Leasing Co LLC ....B....... 909 347-0500
14392 Valley Blvd Fontana (92335) *(P-11507)*

Swift Tactical Systems Inc ....E....... 800 547-9438
1141 A Via Callejon San Clemente (92673) *(P-9556)*

Swift-Cor Precision Inc ....E....... 310 354-1207
344 W 157th St Gardena (90248) *(P-6329)*

Swinerton Builders, San Diego *Also Called: Solv Energy LLC (P-16384)*

Swinerton Renewable Energy ....C....... 858 622-4040
16680 W Bernardo Dr San Diego (92127) *(P-20252)*

Swiss Dairy, City Of Industry *Also Called: Dean Socal LLC (P-1309)*

Swiss Port Corp ....B....... 310 417-0258
11001 Aviation Blvd Los Angeles (90045) *(P-20300)*

Swiss-Micron Inc ....D....... 949 589-0430
22361 Gilberto Ste A Rcho Sta Marg (92688) *(P-6423)*

Swissport, Los Angeles *Also Called: Swiss Port Corp (P-20300)*

Swissport Cargo Services LP ....C....... 310 910-9541
11001 Aviation Blvd Los Angeles (90045) *(P-11708)*

Swisstex California Inc (PA)...................................C....... 310 516-6800
13660 S Figueroa St Los Angeles (90061) *(P-16938)*

Switching Systems, Anaheim *Also Called: Xp Power Inc (P-9141)*

Swm, El Cajon *Also Called: Delstar Technologies Inc (P-4810)*

Sws, Fullerton *Also Called: Superior Wall Systems Inc (P-1000)*

Swt Stockton, Temecula *Also Called: Southwest Traders Incorporated (P-13231)*

Swvp Del Mar Hotel LLC ....D....... 858 481-5900
11915 El Camino Real San Diego (92130) *(P-15383)*

Swvp Westlake LLC ....C....... 805 557-1234
880 S Westlake Blvd Westlake Village (91361) *(P-15384)*

Swwc Utilities Inc (DH)..C
1325 N Grand Ave Ste 100 Covina (91724) *(P-12149)*

Sybron Dental Specialties Inc ....E....... 909 596-0276
1332 S Lone Hill Ave Glendora (91740) *(P-10771)*

Sybron Dental Specialties Inc (PA)..........................C....... 714 516-7400
1717 W Collins Ave Orange (92867) *(P-10772)*

Sybron Endo, Orange *Also Called: Ormco Corporation (P-10756)*

Sycuan Casino ....A....... 619 445-6002
5469 Casino Way El Cajon (92019) *(P-15385)*

Sycuan Casino (PA)..C....... 619 445-6002
5459 Casino Way El Cajon (92019) *(P-17567)*

Sycuan Resort, El Cajon *Also Called: Sycuan Tribal Development (P-14038)*

Sycuan Resort and Casino, El Cajon *Also Called: Sycuan Casino (P-17567)*

Sycuan Tribal Development ....C....... 619 442-3425
1530 Hilton Head Rd Ste 210 El Cajon (92019) *(P-14038)*

Sydata Inc ....C....... 760 444-4368
6494 Weathers Pl Ste 100 San Diego (92121) *(P-11907)*

Sydell Hotels LLC ....C....... 213 381-7411
3515 Wilshire Blvd Los Angeles (90010) *(P-15386)*

Sydney & Anne Bloom Farms Inc ....A....... 323 261-6565
2900 Ayers Ave Vernon (90058) *(P-13308)*

Sygma, Santa Fe Springs *Also Called: Sygma Inc (P-7134)*

Sygma, Lancaster *Also Called: Sygma Network Inc (P-13232)*

Sygma Inc ....F....... 562 906-8880
13168 Flores St Santa Fe Springs (90670) *(P-7134)*

Sygma Network Inc ....C....... 661 723-0405
46905 47th St W Lancaster (93536) *(P-13232)*

Sygma Network, The, Sun Valley *Also Called: Sugar Foods LLC (P-16936)*

Sylmark Group, Van Nuys *Also Called: Sylmark Inc (P-20103)*

Sylmark Inc (PA)..D....... 818 217-2000
7821 Orion Ave Ste 200 Van Nuys (91406) *(P-20103)*

Symantec ....D....... 213 489-3262
1200 W 7th St Los Angeles (90017) *(P-16396)*

Symantec, Los Angeles *Also Called: Symantec (P-16396)*

Symbion Inc ....C....... 805 413-7920
696 Hampshire Rd Ste 100 Westlake Village (91361) *(P-17799)*

Symbion Inc ....C....... 818 501-1080
16501 Ventura Blvd Ste 103 Encino (91436) *(P-17800)*

Symbolic Displays Inc ....D....... 714 258-2811
1917 E Saint Andrew Pl Santa Ana (92705) *(P-9808)*

Symcoat Metal Processing Inc ....C....... 858 451-3313
7887 Dunbrook Rd Ste C San Diego (92126) *(P-6670)*

Symitar Systems Inc ....C....... 619 542-6700
8985 Balboa Ave San Diego (92123) *(P-16127)*

Symmetry Electronics LLC (DH)..............................E....... 310 536-6190
222 Pacific Coast Hwy El Segundo (90245) *(P-8903)*

Symons Fire Protection Inc ....C....... 619 588-6364
9475 Chesapeake Dr Ste A San Diego (92123) *(P-16756)*

Synaptics Inc ....E....... 949 483-5594
1929 Main St Ste 105 Irvine (92614) *(P-7571)*

Synbiotics LLC ....E....... 858 451-3771
16420 Via Esprillo San Diego (92127) *(P-4293)*

Sync Brokerage Inc ....D....... 818 770-3663
22020 Clarendon St Ste 200 Woodland Hills (91367) *(P-16939)*

Synear Foods, Chatsworth *Also Called: Synear Foods Usa LLC (P-521)*

Synear Foods Usa LLC ....E....... 818 341-3588
9601 Canoga Ave Chatsworth (91311) *(P-521)*

Synergetic Tech Group Inc ....E....... 909 305-4711
1712 Earhart La Verne (91750) *(P-9809)*

Synergeyes, Carlsbad *Also Called: Synergeyes Inc (P-10341)*

Synergeyes Inc (PA)...D....... 760 476-9410
2236 Rutherford Rd Ste 115 Carlsbad (92008) *(P-10341)*

Employee Codes: A=Over 500 employees, B=251-500
C=101-250, D=51-100, E=20-50, F=10-19, G=1-9

2024 Southern California
Business Directory and Buyers Guide

© Mergent Inc. 1-800-342-5647

1285

Synergy Beverages, Vernon *Also Called: Gts Living Foods LLC (P-1697)*

Synergy Direct Response, Santa Ana *Also Called: Cowboy Direct Response (P-11106)*

Synergy Health Ast LLC (DH)...............E...... 858 586-1166
9020 Activity Rd Ste D San Diego (92126) *(P-10612)*

Synergy Microsystems Inc (DH)...............D...... 858 452-0020
28965 Avenue Penn Valencia (91355) *(P-7452)*

Synergy One Lending Inc...............D...... 385 273-5250
3131 Camino Del Rio N Ste 150 San Diego (92108) *(P-14351)*

Synergy Orthpd Specialists Inc...............D...... 858 450-7118
4445 Eastgate Mall Ste 103 San Diego (92121) *(P-18810)*

Syneron Inc (DH)...............D...... 866 259-6661
3 Goodyear Ste A Irvine (92618) *(P-10827)*

Syneron Candela, Irvine *Also Called: Syneron Inc (P-10827)*

Synertech PM Inc...............F...... 714 898-9151
11711 Monarch St Garden Grove (92841) *(P-5818)*

Syng Inc (PA)...............D...... 770 354-0915
120 Mildred Ave Venice (90291) *(P-8440)*

Synsus Prvate Lbel Prtners LLC...............C...... 713 714-0225
980 Rancheros Dr San Marcos (92069) *(P-4370)*

Syntech Development & Mfg Inc (PA)...............E...... 909 465-5554
13948 Mountain Ave Chino (91710) *(P-5220)*

Synthorx, La Jolla *Also Called: Synthorx Inc (P-4244)*

Synthorx Inc...............E...... 858 352-5100
11099 N Torrey Pines Rd Ste 190 La Jolla (92037) *(P-4244)*

Syntiant Corp (PA)...............E...... 949 774-4887
7555 Irvine Center Dr Ste 200 Irvine (92618) *(P-8904)*

Syntron Bioresearch Inc...............B...... 760 930-2200
2774 Loker Ave W Carlsbad (92010) *(P-4294)*

Sypris Data Systems Inc (HQ)...............E...... 909 962-9400
160 Via Verde San Dimas (91773) *(P-7489)*

Sysco, Walnut *Also Called: Sysco Los Angeles Inc (P-13233)*

Sysco, Poway *Also Called: Sysco San Diego Inc (P-13235)*

Sysco, Oxnard *Also Called: Sysco Ventura Inc (P-13236)*

Sysco Los Angeles Inc...............A...... 909 595-9595
20701 Currier Rd Walnut (91789) *(P-13233)*

Sysco Riverside Inc...............B...... 951 601-5300
15750 Meridian Pkwy Riverside (92518) *(P-13234)*

Sysco San Diego Inc...............B...... 858 513-7300
12180 Kirkham Rd Poway (92064) *(P-13235)*

Sysco Ventura Inc...............B...... 805 205-7000
3100 Sturgis Rd Oxnard (93030) *(P-13236)*

Syspro, Tustin *Also Called: Syspro Impact Software Inc (P-12443)*

Syspro Impact Software Inc...............C...... 714 437-1000
1775 Flight Way Ste 150 Tustin (92782) *(P-12443)*

Systech, Escondido *Also Called: Systech Corporation (P-8628)*

Systech Corporation...............E...... 858 674-6500
118 State Pl Ste 101 Escondido (92029) *(P-8628)*

Systech Solutions Inc (PA)...............D...... 818 550-9690
500 N Brand Blvd Ste 1900 Glendale (91203) *(P-16128)*

Systechs, Orange *Also Called: Cruz Modular Inc (P-11518)*

System Pavers, Santa Ana *Also Called: System Pavers LLC (P-650)*

System Pavers LLC...............C...... 949 243-2072
1570 Brookhollow Dr Santa Ana (92705) *(P-650)*

System Supply Stationery Corp...............F...... 310 223-0880
1251 E Walnut St Carson (90746) *(P-13000)*

System1 Inc (PA)...............B...... 310 924-6037
4235 Redwood Ave Los Angeles (90066) *(P-16397)*

Systems Application & Tech Inc...............D...... 805 487-7373
1000 Town Center Dr Ste 110 Oxnard (93036) *(P-19697)*

Systems Engineering & MGT Co (PA)...............E...... 760 727-7800
1430 Vantage Ct Vista (92081) *(P-19698)*

Systems Integrated LLC...............F...... 714 998-0900
2200 N Glassell St Orange (92865) *(P-10400)*

Systems Mchs Atmtn Cmpnnts Cor (PA)...............C...... 760 929-7575
5807 Van Allen Way Carlsbad (92008) *(P-8193)*

Systems Technology Inc...............D...... 909 799-9950
1350 Riverview Dr San Bernardino (92408) *(P-7354)*

Syston Cable Technology Corp...............E...... 888 679-7866
15278 El Prado Rd Chino (91710) *(P-9261)*

T - Y Nursery Inc...............C...... 760 742-2151
15335 Highway 76 Pauma Valley (92061) *(P-13520)*

T & F Sheet Mtls Fab McHning I...............E...... 310 516-8548
15607 New Century Dr Gardena (90248) *(P-6330)*

T & H Store Fixtures, Commerce *Also Called: Teichman Enterprises Inc (P-2995)*

T & J Sausage Kitchen, Anaheim *Also Called: T&J Sausage Kitchen Inc (P-1238)*

T & M Machining...............E...... 805 983-6716
331 Irving Dr Oxnard (93030) *(P-8041)*

T & T Box Company Inc...............E...... 909 465-0848
1353 Philadelphia St Ste 101 Pomona (91766) *(P-3146)*

T & T Enterprises, Corona *Also Called: Thalasinos Enterprises Inc (P-12884)*

T & T Foods Inc...............E...... 323 588-2158
3080 E 50th St Vernon (90058) *(P-1333)*

T Allance One - Palm Sprng LLC...............D...... 760 322-7000
67967 Vista Chino Cathedral City (92234) *(P-17568)*

T and B Boots Inc...............D...... 805 434-9904
72 S Main St B Templeton (93465) *(P-13926)*

T B Penick & Sons Inc...............C...... 858 558-1800
15435 Innovation Dr Ste 200 San Diego (92128) *(P-522)*

T C Construction Company Inc...............C...... 619 448-4560
10540 Prospect Ave Santee (92071) *(P-696)*

T E M P, Gardena *Also Called: Thermlly Engnred Mnfctred Pdts (P-6164)*

T G T Enterprises Inc...............C...... 858 413-0300
12650 Danielson Ct Poway (92064) *(P-20253)*

T Hasegawa USA Inc...............E...... 949 461-3344
25882 Wright Foothill Ranch (92610) *(P-1785)*

T Hasegawa USA Inc (HQ)...............E...... 714 522-1900
14017 183rd St Cerritos (90703) *(P-1786)*

T Hasegawa USA Inc...............E...... 714 522-1900
8720 Rochester Ave Rancho Cucamonga (91730) *(P-1787)*

T Hasegawa USA Inc...............E...... 951 264-1121
2026 Cecilia Cir Corona (92881) *(P-1994)*

T I B Inc...............F...... 619 562-3071
9525 Pathway St Santee (92071) *(P-8042)*

T L Fabrications LP...............D...... 562 802-3980
2921 E Coronado St Anaheim (92806) *(P-17096)*

T L Timmerman Cnstr Inc...............E...... 760 244-2532
9845 Santa Fe Ave E Hesperia (92345) *(P-2704)*

T M B, San Fernando *Also Called: Jme Inc (P-12599)*

T M Cobb Company (PA)...............E...... 951 248-2400
500 Palmyrita Ave Riverside (92507) *(P-2634)*

T M I, Gardena *Also Called: Timbucktoo Manufacturing Inc (P-7689)*

T M I, San Diego *Also Called: Toward Maximum Independence (P-19146)*

T M P Services Inc (PA)...............E...... 951 213-3900
2929 Kansas Ave Riverside (92507) *(P-6392)*

t McGee Electric Inc...............D...... 909 591-6461
2390 S Reservoir St Pomona (91766) *(P-945)*

T McGee Electric Inc...............F...... 909 591-6461
12375 Mills Ave Ste 2 Chino (91710) *(P-8278)*

T R I, Yucaipa *Also Called: Technical Resource Industries (P-8279)*

T R L, Rancho Cucamonga *Also Called: TRL Systems Incorporated (P-948)*

T S I, Valencia *Also Called: Tape Specialty Inc (P-12702)*

T S M, Los Angeles *Also Called: Tubular Specialties Mfg Inc (P-5378)*

T Y R, Seal Beach *Also Called: Tyr Sport Inc (P-13155)*

T-12 Three LLC...............B...... 619 702-3000
207 5th Ave San Diego (92101) *(P-15387)*

T-Force, Newport Beach *Also Called: T-Force Inc (P-20383)*

T-Force Inc (PA)...............D...... 949 208-1527
4695 Macarthur Ct Newport Beach (92660) *(P-20383)*

T-Rex Grilles, Corona *Also Called: T-Rex Truck Products Inc (P-6488)*

T-Rex Truck Products Inc...............D...... 800 287-5900
2365 Railroad St Corona (92878) *(P-6488)*

T.B.S. Irrigation, Santee *Also Called: TBs Irrigation Products Inc (P-5975)*

T.com Ontario Fc T-9479, Ontario *Also Called: Target Corporation (P-11617)*

T/O Printing, Westlake Village *Also Called: Thousand Oaks Prtg & Spc Inc (P-16943)*

T/Q Systems Inc...............E...... 949 455-0478
25131 Arctic Ocean Dr Lake Forest (92630) *(P-8043)*

T&J Sausage Kitchen Inc...............E...... 714 632-8350
2831 E Miraloma Ave Anaheim (92806) *(P-1238)*

T2c Inc...............F...... 213 741-5232
1348 S Flower St Los Angeles (90015) *(P-2265)*

Mergent email: customerrelations@mergent.com
1286

2024 Southern California
Business Directory and Buyers Guide

(P-0000) Products & Services Section entry number
(PA)=Parent Co (HQ)=Headquarters (DH)=Div Headquarters

T3 Micro Inc (PA)..F...... 310 452-2888
880 Apollo St Ste 200 El Segundo (90245) *(P-8239)*

Ta Aerospace Co ....C...... 661 702-0448
28065 Franklin Pkwy Valencia (91355) *(P-3976)*

Ta Aerospace Co (DH)..C...... 661 775-1100
28065 Franklin Pkwy Valencia (91355) *(P-4797)*

Ta Chen International Inc (HQ)............................C...... 562 808-8000
5855 Obispo Ave Long Beach (90805) *(P-12574)*

Ta Division, Valencia *Also Called: Ta Aerospace Co (P-3976)*

TA Industries Inc (HQ)..E...... 562 466-1000
11130 Bloomfield Ave Santa Fe Springs (90670) *(P-12748)*

Tabc Inc (DH)..B...... 562 984-3305
6375 N Paramount Blvd Long Beach (90805) *(P-9335)*

Taber Company Inc ....D...... 714 543-7100
121 Waterworks Way Ste 100 Irvine (92618) *(P-2635)*

Tablas Creek Vineyard LLC ....F...... 805 237-1231
9339 Adelaida Rd Paso Robles (93446) *(P-1661)*

Tabor Communications Inc ....E...... 858 625-0070
8445 Camino Santa Fe Ste 101 San Diego (92121) *(P-3490)*

Tacer, Van Nuys *Also Called: Town & Cntry Event Rentals Inc (P-15802)*

Tachyon Networks Incorporated ....E...... 858 882-8100
9339 Carroll Park Dr Ste 150 San Diego (92121) *(P-8586)*

Tacna International Corp ....F...... 619 661-1261
9255 Customhouse Plz Ste G San Diego (92154) *(P-20254)*

Taco Bell, Irvine *Also Called: Taco Bell Corp (P-14039)*

Taco Bell Corp (HQ)..A...... 949 863-4500
1 Glen Bell Way Irvine (92618) *(P-14039)*

Taco Works Inc ....E...... 805 541-1556
3424 Sacramento Dr San Luis Obispo (93401) *(P-1833)*

Tactical Command Inds Inc (DH)........................E...... 925 219-1097
4700 E Airport Dr Ontario (91761) *(P-8629)*

Tactical Communications Corp ....E...... 805 987-4100
473 Post St Camarillo (93010) *(P-8630)*

Tactical Engrg & Analis Inc (PA)........................D...... 858 573-9869
6050 Santo Rd Ste 250 San Diego (92124) *(P-16604)*

Tactical Micro Inc (DH)..F...... 714 547-1174
1740 E Wilshire Ave Santa Ana (92705) *(P-9262)*

Tacticombat Inc ....F...... 626 315-4433
11640 Mcbean Dr El Monte (91732) *(P-11033)*

Tactsquad, Corona *Also Called: Amwear USA Inc (P-2148)*

Tacupeto Chips & Salsa Inc ....F...... 760 597-9400
1330 Distribution Way Ste A Vista (92081) *(P-1834)*

Tad Group LLC ....C...... 949 476-3601
5000 Birch St Ste 3000 Newport Beach (92660) *(P-16757)*

Tad Pgs Inc ....A...... 800 261-3779
12062 Valley View St Ste 108 Garden Grove (92845) *(P-15944)*

Tad Pgs Inc ....A...... 571 451-2428
10805 Holder St Ste 250 Cypress (90630) *(P-15945)*

Tadin Herb & Tea Co., Vernon *Also Called: Tadin Inc (P-13400)*

Tadin Inc ....D...... 213 406-8880
3345 E Slauson Ave Vernon (90058) *(P-13400)*

Tadpole Cartesia Inc ....F...... 760 929-8345
2237 Faraday Ave Ste 120 Carlsbad (92008) *(P-16129)*

Tae Technologies, Foothill Ranch *Also Called: Tae Technologies Inc (P-19876)*

Tae Technologies Inc (PA)..................................C...... 949 830-2117
19631 Pauling Foothill Ranch (92610) *(P-19876)*

Taft Electric Company (PA)..................................C...... 805 642-0121
1694 Eastman Ave Ventura (93003) *(P-946)*

Taft Production Company ....D...... 661 765-7194
950 Petroleum Club Rd Taft (93268) *(P-243)*

Tag Rag, Los Angeles *Also Called: Fetish Group Inc (P-2204)*

Tag Toys Inc ....D...... 310 639-4566
1810 S Acacia Ave Compton (90220) *(P-11292)*

Tag-It Pacific Inc ....E...... 818 444-4100
21900 Burbank Blvd Ste 270 Woodland Hills (91367) *(P-2107)*

Tagtime Usa Inc ....B...... 323 587-1555
4601 District Blvd Vernon (90058) *(P-3248)*

Taheem Johnson Inc ....D...... 818 835-3785
1237 S Victoria Ave Oxnard (93035) *(P-16605)*

Tahiti Cabinets Inc ....D...... 714 693-0618
5419 E La Palma Ave Anaheim (92807) *(P-3032)*

Tahiti Trading Company, Riverside *Also Called: Tropical Functional Labs LLC (P-1287)*

Tahoe Stag, Brea *Also Called: Griffith Company (P-622)*

Tailbroom Media Grop, North Hollywood *Also Called: Pilgrim Operations LLC (P-12380)*

Tailgate Printing Inc ....D...... 714 966-3035
2930 S Fairview St Santa Ana (92704) *(P-3692)*

Taisei Construction Corporation ....C...... 714 886-1530
970 W 190th St 920 Torrance (90502) *(P-523)*

Tait & Associates Inc ....D...... 714 560-8222
2131 S Dupont Dr Anaheim (92806) *(P-6162)*

Tajen Graphics Inc ....E...... 714 527-3122
2100 W Lincoln Ave Ste B Anaheim (92801) *(P-3693)*

Tajima /Crl, Vernon *Also Called: Tajima USA Dissolving Corp (P-6370)*

Tajima Usa Inc ....E...... 310 604-8200
19925 S Susana Rd Compton (90221) *(P-7179)*

Tajima USA Dissolving Corp ....E...... 323 588-1281
2503 E Vernon Ave Vernon (90058) *(P-6370)*

Takane USA Inc ....C...... 909 923-5511
2055 S Haven Ave Ontario (91761) *(P-11615)*

Take A Break Paper ....E...... 323 333-7773
263 W Olive Ave # 307 Burbank (91502) *(P-3327)*

Takeda Dev Ctr Americas Inc (HQ)....................C...... 858 622-8528
9625 Towne Centre Dr San Diego (92121) *(P-19946)*

Takken's Comfort Shoes, Templeton *Also Called: T and B Boots Inc (P-13926)*

Takyo Tyco, Los Angeles *Also Called: Ruben & Leon Inc (P-17071)*

Tala, Santa Monica *Also Called: Inventure Capital Corporation (P-15033)*

Talbert Archtctral Panl Door I ....D...... 714 671-9700
711 S Stimson Ave City Of Industry (91745) *(P-2636)*

Talco Plastics Inc ....D...... 562 630-1224
3270 E 70th St Long Beach (90805) *(P-5221)*

Talco Plastics Inc (PA)..D...... 951 531-2000
1000 W Rincon St Corona (92878) *(P-12189)*

Talega Golf Club, San Clemente *Also Called: Heritage Golf Group LLC (P-17431)*

Talent & Acquisition LLC ....C...... 888 970-9575
3020 Old Ranch Pkwy Ste 300 Seal Beach (90740) *(P-16130)*

Talimar Systems Inc ....E...... 714 557-4884
3105 W Alpine St Santa Ana (92704) *(P-2938)*

Talis Lending, San Diego *Also Called: Lendsure Mortgage Corp (P-14332)*

Talladium Inc (PA)..E...... 661 295-0900
27360 Muirfield Ln Valencia (91355) *(P-10773)*

Talley & Associates, Santa Fe Springs *Also Called: Talley Inc (P-12700)*

Talley Farms ....C...... 805 489-2508
2900 Lopez Dr Arroyo Grande (93420) *(P-114)*

Talley Inc (PA)..C...... 562 906-8000
12976 Sandoval St Santa Fe Springs (90670) *(P-12700)*

Talley Metal Fabrication, San Jacinto *Also Called: J Talley Corporation (P-6359)*

Tallgrass Pictures LLC ....E...... 619 227-2701
710 13th St Ste 300 San Diego (92101) *(P-1495)*

Talmo & Chinn Inc ....E...... 626 443-1741
9537 Telstar Ave Ste 131 El Monte (91731) *(P-8905)*

Talon International Inc (PA)................................D...... 818 444-4100
21900 Burbank Blvd Ste 101 Woodland Hills (91367) *(P-13097)*

Talon Therapeutics Inc ....D...... 949 788-6700
18200 Von Karman Ave Ste 700 Irvine (92612) *(P-19877)*

Talsco, Garden Grove *Also Called: Jvr Sheetmetal Fabrication Inc (P-9542)*

Talsco Inc ....E...... 714 841-2464
7101 Patterson Dr Garden Grove (92841) *(P-9810)*

Tam O'Shanter Inn, Los Angeles *Also Called: Lawrys Restaurants II Inc (P-14022)*

Tam Printing Inc ....F...... 714 224-4488
2961 E White Star Ave Anaheim (92806) *(P-3694)*

Tamco (HQ)..E...... 909 899-0660
5425 Industrial Pkwy San Bernardino (92407) *(P-5604)*

Tamco ....B...... 949 552-9714
1000 Quail St Ste 260 Newport Beach (92660) *(P-6406)*

Tammy Taylor Nails Inc ....E...... 949 250-9287
2001 E Deere Ave Santa Ana (92705) *(P-3977)*

Tampico Spice Co Incorporated ....E...... 323 235-3154
5901 S Central Ave # 5941 Los Angeles (90001) *(P-1995)*

Tampico Spice Company, Los Angeles *Also Called: Tampico Spice Co Incorporated (P-1995)*

Tamshell, Corona *Also Called: Tamshell Corp (P-5222)*

Tamshell Corp ....D...... 951 272-9395
237 Glider Cir Corona (92878) *(P-5222)*

A L P H A B E T I C

Employee Codes: A=Over 500 employees, B=251-500
C=101-250, D=51-100, E=20-50, F=10-19, G=1-9

2024 Southern California
Business Directory and Buyers Guide

© Mergent Inc. 1-800-342-5647
1287

Tamura Corporation of America (HQ)......................E....... 800 472-6624
277 Rancheros Dr Ste 190 San Marcos (92069) *(P-12701)*

Tandem Design Inc ....E....... 714 978-7272
1846 W Sequoia Ave Orange (92868) *(P-11293)*

Tandem Diabetes Care, San Diego Also Called: Tandem Diabetes Care Inc *(P-10613)*

Tandem Diabetes Care Inc (PA) ....A....... 877 801-6901
12400 High Bluff Dr San Diego (92130) *(P-10613)*

Tandem Exhibit, Orange Also Called: Tandem Design Inc *(P-11293)*

Tandem Medical Inc ....E....... 858 673-3900
535 Encinitas Blvd Ste 109 Encinitas (92024) *(P-10614)*

Tandex Test Labs Inc ....E....... 626 962-7166
15849 Business Center Dr Irwindale (91706) *(P-19984)*

Tangerine Express Inc ....E....... 702 260-6650
4870 Adohr Ln A Camarillo (93012) *(P-14151)*

Tangerine Office Systems, Camarillo Also Called: Tangerine Express Inc *(P-14151)*

Tangoe-PI Inc C
9920 Pacific Heights Blvd Ste 200 San Diego (92121) *(P-20384)*

Tanimura Antle Fresh Foods Inc ....C....... 831 424-6100
4401 Foxdale St Baldwin Park (91706) *(P-115)*

Tanimura Antle Fresh Foods Inc ....C....... 805 483-2358
761 Commercial Ave Oxnard (93030) *(P-11616)*

Tank Holding Corp ....B....... 952 446-1945
13878 Yorba Ave Chino (91710) *(P-5223)*

Tanner Research Inc ....E....... 626 471-9700
1851 Huntington Dr Duarte (91010) *(P-19878)*

Tanvex Biopharma Usa Inc (PA) ....C....... 858 210-4100
10394 Pacific Center Ct San Diego (92121) *(P-19879)*

Tao of Wllness Snta Mnica A PR ....D....... 626 397-1000
171 S Los Robles Ave Pasadena (91101) *(P-17872)*

Taotao Manufacturer Inc ....F....... 626 688-9880
9073 Arcadia Ave San Gabriel (91775) *(P-11294)*

Tap Manufacturing LLC ....F....... 619 216-1444
2390 Boswell Rd Chula Vista (91914) *(P-9467)*

Tape and Label Converters Inc ....E....... 562 945-3486
8231 Allport Ave Santa Fe Springs (90670) *(P-3176)*

Tape Specialty Inc ....E....... 661 702-9030
24831 Avenue Tibbitts Valencia (91355) *(P-12702)*

Tapestry Solutions Inc (HQ) ....C....... 858 503-1990
6910 Carroll Rd San Diego (92121) *(P-16131)*

Tapetech Tool Company ....A....... 858 268-0656
7360 Convoy Ct San Diego (92111) *(P-15053)*

Tapetech Tool Company, San Diego Also Called: Tapetech Tool Company *(P-15053)*

Tapia Brothers Co, Maywood Also Called: Tapia Enterprises Inc *(P-13237)*

Tapia Enterprises Inc (PA) ....D....... 323 560-7415
6067 District Blvd Maywood (90270) *(P-13237)*

Taproom Beer Co ....E....... 619 539-7738
2000 El Cajon Blvd San Diego (92104) *(P-1605)*

Taral Plastics, Corona Also Called: Martin Chancey Corporation *(P-5091)*

Tarantino Wholesale Fd Distrs, San Diego Also Called: Producers Meat and Prov Inc *(P-13304)*

Tarbell Financial Corporation (PA) ....D....... 714 972-0988
1403 N Tustin Ave Ste 380 Santa Ana (92705) *(P-14368)*

Tarbell Realtors, Santa Ana Also Called: F M Tarbell Co *(P-14793)*

Target, Fontana Also Called: Target Corporation *(P-11618)*

Target Corporation ....C....... 909 937-5500
1505 S Haven Ave Ontario (91761) *(P-11617)*

Target Corporation ....C....... 909 355-6000
14750 Miller Ave Fontana (92336) *(P-11618)*

Target Mdia Prtners Intractive, North Hollywood Also Called: Target Mdia Prtners Intrctive *(P-3816)*

Target Mdia Prtners Intrctive (HQ) ....E....... 323 930-3123
5200 Lankershim Blvd Ste 350 North Hollywood (91601) *(P-3816)*

Target Specialty Products, Santa Fe Springs Also Called: Rentokil North America Inc *(P-15687)*

Target Specialty Products Inc ....D....... 562 865-9541
15415 Marquardt Ave Santa Fe Springs (90670) *(P-13492)*

Target Technology Company LLC ....E....... 949 788-0909
3420 Bristol St Costa Mesa (92626) *(P-9184)*

Targeted Medical Pharma Inc ....F....... 310 474-9809
2980 N Beverly Glen Cir Ste 100 Los Angeles (90077) *(P-18811)*

Targus, Anaheim Also Called: Targus International LLC *(P-13563)*

Targus International LLC (PA) ....C....... 714 765-5555
1211 N Miller St Anaheim (92806) *(P-13563)*

Targus US LLC ....E....... 714 765-5555
1211 N Miller St Anaheim (92806) *(P-5296)*

Tarpin Corporation ....E....... 714 891-6944
5361 Business Dr Huntington Beach (92649) *(P-7100)*

Tarrant Apparel Group ....D....... 323 780-8250
5401 S Soto St Vernon (90058) *(P-13153)*

Tarrant Apparel Group, Los Angeles Also Called: C M G Inc *(P-2309)*

Tarsadia Hotels, Newport Beach Also Called: Uka LLC *(P-15396)*

Tarsco Holdings LLC ....C....... 562 869-0200
11905 Regentview Ave Downey (90241) *(P-17157)*

Tartan Fashion Inc ....E....... 626 575-2828
4357 Rowland Ave El Monte (91731) *(P-2224)*

Tarzana Treatment Centers Inc (PA) ....C....... 818 996-1051
18646 Oxnard St Tarzana (91356) *(P-18721)*

Tarzana Treatment Centers Inc ....C....... 562 218-1868
2101 Magnolia Ave Long Beach (90806) *(P-18722)*

Tarzana Treatment Centers Inc ....C....... 661 726-2630
44447 10th St W Lancaster (93534) *(P-18723)*

Tarzana Treatment Centers Inc ....D....... 562 428-4111
5190 Atlantic Ave Lakewood (90805) *(P-18724)*

Tarzana Treatment Ctr, Lancaster Also Called: Tarzana Treatment Centers Inc *(P-18723)*

Tarzana Trtmnt Ctrs LNG Bch O, Lakewood Also Called: Tarzana Treatment Centers Inc *(P-18724)*

Taseon Inc ....F....... 408 240-7800
515 S Flower St Fl 25 Los Angeles (90071) *(P-10225)*

Tasteful Selections LLC ....C....... 661 854-3998
13003 Di Giorgio Rd Arvin (93203) *(P-3)*

Tastepoint By Iff, Corona Also Called: Tastepoint Inc *(P-4533)*

Tastepoint Inc ....C....... 951 734-6620
790 E Harrison St Corona (92879) *(P-4533)*

Tatung Company America Inc (HQ) ....D....... 310 637-2105
2157 Mount Shasta Dr San Pedro (90732) *(P-8587)*

Tavistock Restaurants LLC ....C....... 714 939-8686
20 City Blvd W Ste R1 Orange (92868) *(P-14054)*

Tawa Supermarket Inc ....D....... 714 521-8899
6363 Regio Ave Buena Park (90620) *(P-524)*

Tawa Supermarket Inc (PA) ....D....... 714 521-8899
6281 Regio Ave Buena Park (90620) *(P-1404)*

Tax and Financial Group, Newport Beach Also Called: R Mc Closkey Insurance Agency *(P-14626)*

Tax Credit Co, The, Los Angeles Also Called: The Tax Credit Company *(P-15624)*

Tay Ho, Santa Ana Also Called: West Lake Food Corporation *(P-1209)*

Tayco Engineering Inc ....C....... 714 952-2240
10874 Hope St Cypress (90630) *(P-9904)*

Taylor Graphics Inc ....E....... 949 752-5200
1582 Browning Irvine (92606) *(P-3817)*

Taylor Guitars, El Cajon Also Called: Taylor-Listug Inc *(P-12988)*

Taylor Technology Services Inc ....D....... 714 986-1559
3230 E Imperial Hwy Ste 302 Brea (92821) *(P-3818)*

Taylor-Dunn Manufacturing LLC (HQ) ....D....... 714 956-4040
2114 W Ball Rd Anaheim (92804) *(P-6999)*

Taylor-Listug Inc (PA) ....C....... 619 258-1207
1980 Gillespie Way El Cajon (92020) *(P-12988)*

Taylored Fmi LLC ....C....... 909 510-4800
1495 E Locust St Ontario (91761) *(P-11619)*

Taylored Services, Ontario Also Called: Taylored Services LLC *(P-11620)*

Taylored Services, Ontario Also Called: Taylored Services Holdings LLC *(P-11621)*

Taylored Services LLC (DH) ....D....... 909 510-4800
1495 E Locust St Ontario (91761) *(P-11620)*

Taylored Services Holdings LLC (DH) ....D....... 909 510-4800
1495 E Locust St Ontario (91761) *(P-11621)*

Taylored Svcs Parent Co Inc (PA) ....D....... 909 510-4800
1495 E Locust St Ontario (91761) *(P-11808)*

Taylored Transload LLC ....C....... 909 510-4800
1495 E Locust St Ontario (91761) *(P-11840)*

Tbp Indoor Facilities Inc ....D....... 877 778-9587
3905 State St Santa Barbara (93105) *(P-4245)*

Tbs, Costa Mesa Also Called: Transprttion Brkg Spclists Inc *(P-11466)*

Mergent email: customerrelations@mergent.com
1288

2024 Southern California
Business Directory and Buyers Guide

(P-0000) Products & Services Section entry number
(PA)=Parent Co (HQ)=Headquarters (DH)=Div Headquarters

TBs Irrigation Products Inc .... E 619 579-0520
8787 Olive Ln Bldg 3 Santee (92071) *(P-5975)*

Tbwa Chiat/Day Inc .... B 310 305-5000
5353 Grosvenor Blvd Los Angeles (90066) *(P-16940)*

Tc Construction Company, Santee *Also Called: T C Construction Company Inc (P-696)*

Tc Cosmotronic Inc .... C 949 660-0740
4663 E Guasti Rd Ste A Ontario (91761) *(P-8736)*

Tc Technology, Carlsbad *Also Called: Tadpole Cartesia Inc (P-16129)*

Tcal, San Diego *Also Called: Takeda Dev Ctr Americas Inc (P-19946)*

Tcg Capital Management LP .... C 310 633-2900
12180 Millennium Ste 500 Playa Vista (90094) *(P-15054)*

Tcg Software Services Inc .... B 714 665-6200
320 Commerce Ste 200 Irvine (92602) *(P-16132)*

TCI Engineering Inc .... D 909 984-1773
1416 Brooks St Ontario (91762) *(P-9310)*

TCI Texarkana Inc (DH) .... **E 562 808-8000**
5855 Obispo Ave Long Beach (90805) *(P-5692)*

TCI Transportation Services .... C 909 355-8545
14561 Merrill Ave Bldg B Fontana (92335) *(P-11508)*

Tcj Manufacturing LLC .... E 213 488-8400
2744 E 11th St Los Angeles (90023) *(P-2375)*

Tcl Electronics, Irvine *Also Called: Tte Technology Inc (P-12638)*

TCS, Chatsworth *Also Called: Telemtry Cmmnctons Systems Inc (P-8588)*

TCS Space & Component Tech, Torrance *Also Called: Trident Space & Defense LLC (P-8913)*

Tct Mobile Inc .... D 949 892-2990
189 Technology Dr Irvine (92618) *(P-20104)*

Tcw Group Inc (PA) .... **B 213 244-0000**
865 S Figueroa St Ste 1800 Los Angeles (90017) *(P-14430)*

Tcw Trends Inc .... E 310 533-5177
2886 Columbia St Torrance (90503) *(P-2376)*

Tcwglobal, San Diego *Also Called: Wmbe Payrolling Inc (P-15904)*

Tdg Aerospace Inc .... F 760 466-1040
2180 Chablis Ct Ste 106 Escondido (92029) *(P-9811)*

Tdi Signs .... E 562 436-5188
13158 Arctic Cir Santa Fe Springs (90670) *(P-11173)*

Tdi2 Custom Packaging Inc .... F 714 751-6782
17391 Mount Cliffwood Cir Fountain Valley (92708) *(P-3193)*

Tdk-Lambda Americas Inc .... C 619 575-4400
401 Mile Of Cars Way Ste 325 National City (91950) *(P-12703)*

Tdmi, Gardena *Also Called: Twin Dragon Marketing Inc (P-2034)*

Tdo Software Inc .... E 858 558-3696
6235 Lusk Blvd San Diego (92121) *(P-16398)*

Te Connectivity Corporation .... E 805 684-4560
550 Linden Ave Carpinteria (93013) *(P-8194)*

Te Connectivity Corporation .... D 760 757-7500
3390 Alex Rd Oceanside (92058) *(P-8983)*

Te Connectivity MOG, El Cajon *Also Called: Brantner and Associates Inc (P-8961)*

Tea Financial Services .... E 951 301-8884
32100 Menifee Rd Menifee (92584) *(P-12932)*

Tea Tree Essentials, Rcho Sta Marg *Also Called: Forespar Products Corp (P-5917)*

Teac, Santa Fe Springs *Also Called: Teac America Inc (P-12444)*

Teac America Inc (HQ) .... **F 323 726-0303**
10410 Pioneer Blvd Ste 1 Santa Fe Springs (90670) *(P-12444)*

Teacher Created Materials Inc .... C 714 891-2273
5301 Oceanus Dr Huntington Beach (92649) *(P-3491)*

Teacher Created Resources Inc .... C 714 230-7060
12621 Western Ave Garden Grove (92841) *(P-3416)*

Teague Custom Marine Inc .... F 661 295-7000
28115 Avenue Stanford Valencia (91355) *(P-17158)*

Teal Electronics Corporation (PA) .... D 858 558-9000
10350 Sorrento Valley Rd San Diego (92121) *(P-8195)*

Tealium Inc (PA) .... A 858 779-1344
11095 Torreyana Rd Fl 2 San Diego (92121) *(P-16518)*

Tealove Inc .... E 714 408-8245
9810 Sierra Ave Ste A Fontana (92335) *(P-13732)*

Team Inc .... E 310 514-2312
1515 240th St Harbor City (90710) *(P-5850)*

Team Air Inc (PA) .... **E 909 823-1957**
12771 Brown Ave Riverside (92509) *(P-7624)*

Team Air Conditioning Eqp, Riverside *Also Called: Team Air Inc (P-7624)*

Team Beachbody Canada LLC .... E 310 883-9000
400 Continental Blvd Ste 400 El Segundo (90245) *(P-1285)*

Team Brda RE Svcs - Cldwell Bn .... D 858 621-5284
16787 Bernardo Center Dr Ste 6 San Diego (92128) *(P-14871)*

Team Companies LLC (PA) .... **D 818 558-3261**
2300 W Empire Ave Ste 500 Burbank (91504) *(P-19806)*

Team Finish Inc .... D 714 671-9190
155 Arovista Cir Ste A Brea (92821) *(P-1090)*

Team Health Holdings Inc .... B 619 740-4401
5555 Grossmont Center Dr La Mesa (91942) *(P-18470)*

Team Industrial Services, Harbor City *Also Called: Team Inc (P-5850)*

Team Manufacturing Inc .... E 310 639-0251
2625 Homestead Pl Rancho Dominguez (90220) *(P-6561)*

Team Post-Op, Irvine *Also Called: Team Post-Op Inc (P-12518)*

Team Post-Op Inc .... C 949 253-5500
17256 Red Hill Ave Irvine (92614) *(P-12518)*

Team Risk MGT Strategies LLC .... A 877 767-8728
3131 Camino Del Rio N Ste 650 San Diego (92108) *(P-20385)*

Team Services, Burbank *Also Called: Team Companies LLC (P-19806)*

Team So-Cal Inc .... B 805 650-9946
1811 Knoll Dr Ste A Ventura (93003) *(P-17528)*

Team West Contracting Corp .... D 951 340-3426
2733 S Vista Ave Bloomington (92316) *(P-1178)*

Team-One Staffing Services Inc .... A 951 616-3515
16030 Ventura Blvd Ste 430 Encino (91436) *(P-15897)*

Teamone Employment, Encino *Also Called: Team-One Staffing Services Inc (P-15897)*

Teamwork Athletic Apparel, Carlsbad *Also Called: R B III Associates Inc (P-2295)*

Tebra Technologies Inc (PA) .... C 888 775-2736
1111 Bayside Dr Ste 150 Corona Del Mar (92625) *(P-16133)*

TEC, Compton *Also Called: Thermal Equipment Corporation (P-6163)*

TEC Color Craft (PA) .... **E 909 392-9000**
1860 Wright Ave La Verne (91750) *(P-3819)*

TEC Color Craft Products, La Verne *Also Called: TEC Color Craft (P-3819)*

Tecan Sp Inc .... D 626 962-0010
14180 Live Oak Ave Baldwin Park (91706) *(P-12533)*

Tech Knowledge Associates LLC .... D 714 735-3810
1 Centerpointe Dr Ste 200 La Palma (90623) *(P-17159)*

Tech Plate, Orange *Also Called: Dunham Metal Processing Inc (P-6612)*

Tech Systems Inc .... C 714 523-5404
7372 Walnut Ave Ste J Buena Park (90620) *(P-12704)*

Techflow Inc (PA) .... **C 858 412-8000**
9889 Willow Creek Rd Ste 100 San Diego (92131) *(P-20301)*

Techflow Scntfc A Div Tchflow, San Diego *Also Called: Techflow Inc (P-20301)*

Techmer Pm Inc .... B 310 632-9211
18420 S Laurel Park Rd Compton (90220) *(P-3978)*

Technclor Crative Svcs USA Inc .... B 818 260-1214
8921 Lindblade St Culver City (90232) *(P-17266)*

Technclor Vdocassette Mich Inc (DH) .... **B 805 445-1122**
3601 Calle Tecate Ste 120 Camarillo (93012) *(P-17267)*

Techni-Cast Corp .... D 562 923-4585
11220 Garfield Ave South Gate (90280) *(P-5819)*

Techni-Tools, Moorpark *Also Called: Testequity LLC (P-17075)*

Technic Inc .... E 714 632-0200
1170 N Hawk Cir Anaheim (92807) *(P-6671)*

Technical Arts, Placentia *Also Called: Southern Cal Tchnical Arts Inc (P-8033)*

Technical Associates, Canoga Park *Also Called: Optron Scientific Company Inc (P-10388)*

Technical Cable Concepts Inc .... E 714 835-1081
350 Lear Ave Costa Mesa (92626) *(P-9125)*

Technical Devices, Torrance *Also Called: Winther Technologies Inc (P-7165)*

Technical Devices Company .... E 310 618-8437
560 Alaska Ave Torrance (90503) *(P-7164)*

Technical Heaters Inc .... F 818 361-7185
10959 Tuxford St Sun Valley (91352) *(P-4714)*

Technical Manufacturing W LLC .... E 661 295-7226
24820 Avenue Tibbitts Valencia (91355) *(P-11295)*

Technical Micro Cons Inc (PA) .... **E 310 559-3982**
807 N Park View Dr Ste 150 El Segundo (90245) *(P-20255)*

Technical Resource Industries (PA) .... **E 909 446-1109**
12854 Daisy Ct Yucaipa (92399) *(P-8279)*

Technical Services, San Bernardino *Also Called: Northrop Grumman Systems Corp (P-10040)*

ALPHABETIC

Employee Codes: A=Over 500 employees, B=251-500
C=101-250, D=51-100, E=20-50, F=10-19, G=1-9

2024 Southern California
Business Directory and Buyers Guide

© Mergent Inc. 1-800-342-5647

1289

Technicolor, Hollywood *Also Called: Technicolor Usa Inc (P-8442)*

Technicolor Inc .... B...... 818 260-4577
2255 N Ontario St Ste 180 Burbank (91504) *(P-16762)*

Technicolor Connected USA, Lebec *Also Called: Technicolor Usa Inc (P-8441)*

Technicolor Creative Studios, Culver City *Also Called: Technclor Crative Svcs USA Inc (P-17266)*

Technicolor Disc Services Corp (HQ) .... C...... 805 445-1122
3601 Calle Tecate Ste 120 Camarillo (93012) *(P-9185)*

Technicolor Entertainment Svcs, Burbank *Also Called: Technicolor Thomson Group Inc (P-17268)*

Technicolor Lab, Burbank *Also Called: Technicolor Inc (P-16762)*

Technicolor Thomson Group Inc (HQ) .... B
2233 N Ontario St Ste 300 Burbank (91504) *(P-17268)*

Technicolor Usa Inc .... B...... 661 496-1309
4049 Industrial Parkway Dr Lebec (93243) *(P-8441)*

Technicolor Usa Inc (HQ) .... A...... 317 587-4287
6040 W Sunset Blvd Hollywood (90028) *(P-8442)*

Technicolor Video Service, Camarillo *Also Called: Technclor Vdocassette Mich Inc (P-17267)*

Technicolor Video Services, Camarillo *Also Called: Vantiva Sup Chain Slutions Inc (P-17271)*

Technicon Design Corporation .... C...... 949 218-1300
30011 Ivy Glenn Dr Ste 115 Laguna Niguel (92677) *(P-16941)*

Technicote Inc .... E...... 951 372-0627
1587 E Bentley Dr Corona (92879) *(P-4583)*

Technifex Products LLC .... E...... 661 294-3800
25261 Rye Canyon Rd Valencia (91355) *(P-5545)*

Techniform International Corp .... C...... 909 877-6886
375 S Cactus Ave Rialto (92376) *(P-8044)*

Technip Usa Inc .... B...... 909 447-3600
555 W Arrow Hwy Claremont (91711) *(P-19699)*

Technipfmc Usa Inc .... E...... 949 238-4150
6400 Oak Cyn Ste 100 Irvine (92618) *(P-6964)*

Techno Coatings Inc (PA) .... C...... 714 635-1130
1391 S Allec St Anaheim (92805) *(P-595)*

Techno West, Anaheim *Also Called: Techno Coatings Inc (P-595)*

Technocel, Simi Valley *Also Called: Foreign Trade Corporation (P-12660)*

Technology Integration Group, San Diego *Also Called: PC Specialists Inc (P-12431)*

Technology Management Concepts, El Segundo *Also Called: Technical Micro Cons Inc (P-20255)*

Technology Training Corp .... D...... 310 644-7777
3238 W 131st St Hawthorne (90250) *(P-3695)*

Technosylva Inc .... F...... 858 729-3648
2261 Caminito Preciosa Norte La Jolla (92037) *(P-12445)*

Technotronix Inc .... E...... 714 630-9200
1381 N Hundley St Anaheim (92806) *(P-8737)*

Technovative Applications .... D...... 714 996-0104
3160 Enterprise St Ste A Brea (92821) *(P-10074)*

Techture Inc .... E...... 323 347-6209
1010 Wilshire Blvd Apt 1206 Los Angeles (90017) *(P-3492)*

Tecma Group LLC .... A...... 619 918-7371
6020 Progressive Ave San Diego (92154) *(P-16942)*

Tecnadyne, San Diego *Also Called: Tecnova Advanced Systems Inc (P-10075)*

Tecno Industrial Engrg Inc .... E...... 562 623-4517
13528 Pumice St Norwalk (90650) *(P-8045)*

Tecnova Advanced Systems Inc .... E...... 858 586-9660
9770 Carroll Centre Rd Ste A San Diego (92126) *(P-10075)*

Teco Diagnostics .... D...... 714 693-7788
1268 N Lakeview Ave Anaheim (92807) *(P-4295)*

Tecolote Research Inc .... C...... 310 640-4700
2120 E Grand Ave Ste 200 El Segundo (90245) *(P-20256)*

Tecolote Research Inc .... C...... 805 964-6963
5266 Hollister Ave Ste 301 Santa Barbara (93111) *(P-20257)*

Tecom Industries Incorporated .... C...... 805 267-0100
375 Conejo Ridge Ave Thousand Oaks (91361) *(P-12705)*

Tecomet, Azusa *Also Called: Tecomet Inc (P-10615)*

Tecomet Inc .... A...... 626 334-1519
503 S Vincent Ave Azusa (91702) *(P-10615)*

Tecon Pacific, Ontario *Also Called: Clark - Pacific Corporation (P-5404)*

Tecxel, Oceanside *Also Called: R Zamora Inc (P-6552)*

Ted Ford Jones Inc .... C...... 760 438-9171
5555 Paseo Del Norte Carlsbad (92008) *(P-13835)*

Ted Ford Jones Inc (PA) .... C...... 714 521-3110
6211 Beach Blvd Buena Park (90621) *(P-17039)*

Ted Levine Drum Co (PA) .... D...... 626 579-1084
1817 Chico Ave South El Monte (91733) *(P-17160)*

Tee -N -Jay Manufacturing Inc .... E...... 818 504-2961
9145 Glenoaks Blvd Sun Valley (91352) *(P-6331)*

Tee Styled Inc .... E...... 323 983-9988
5383 Alcoa Ave Vernon (90058) *(P-3820)*

Tee Top of California Inc (PA) .... E...... 626 303-1868
11801 Goldring Rd Arcadia (91006) *(P-13114)*

Teefor2 Inc .... F...... 909 613-0055
5460 Vine St Chino (91710) *(P-3696)*

Teg Staffing Inc .... A...... 800 918-1678
2385 Northside Dr Ste 250 San Diego (92108) *(P-15898)*

Tegra118 Wealth Solutions Inc (HQ) .... C...... 888 800-0188
700 N San Vicente Blvd Ste G605 West Hollywood (90069) *(P-16519)*

Tei Struthers Wells, Santa Fe Springs *Also Called: Wells Struthers Corporation (P-6171)*

Teichert Enrgy Utlties Group I .... D...... 916 484-3011
3780 Kilroy Airport Way Long Beach (90806) *(P-20105)*

Teichman Enterprises Inc .... E...... 323 278-9000
6100 Bandini Blvd Commerce (90040) *(P-2995)*

Tek84 Inc (PA) .... D...... 858 676-5382
13495 Gregg St Poway (92064) *(P-10828)*

Tekia Inc .... E...... 949 699-1300
17 Hammond Ste 414 Irvine (92618) *(P-10855)*

Teklam, Corona *Also Called: Simmons Family Corporation (P-4843)*

Tekni-Plex Inc .... D...... 909 589-4366
19555 Arenth Ave City Of Industry (91748) *(P-3249)*

Teknor Apex, City Of Industry *Also Called: Teknor Color Company (P-3980)*

Teknor Apex Company .... C...... 626 968-4656
420 S 6th Ave City Of Industry (91746) *(P-3979)*

Teknor Color Company .... E...... 626 336-7709
420 S 6th Ave City Of Industry (91746) *(P-3980)*

Teksun Inc .... E...... 310 479-0794
1549 N Poinsettia Pl Apt 1 Los Angeles (90046) *(P-5224)*

Tektest Inc .... E...... 626 446-6175
5108 Azusa Canyon Rd Baldwin Park (91706) *(P-8984)*

Telair International, Anaheim *Also Called: AAR Manufacturing Inc (P-6129)*

Telecare Corporation .... C...... 562 630-8672
6060 N Paramount Blvd Long Beach (90805) *(P-18725)*

Telecommunication, Beverly Hills *Also Called: Nga 911 LLC (P-16085)*

Teledyne, San Diego *Also Called: Teledyne Instruments Inc (P-8907)*

Teledyne, Los Angeles *Also Called: Teledyne Technologies Inc (P-9127)*

Teledyne Analytical Instrs, City Of Industry *Also Called: Teledyne Instruments Inc (P-10403)*

Teledyne API, San Diego *Also Called: Teledyne Instruments Inc (P-10401)*

Teledyne Battery Products, Redlands *Also Called: Teledyne Technologies Inc (P-9156)*

Teledyne Controls, El Segundo *Also Called: Teledyne Technologies Inc (P-9126)*

Teledyne Controls LLC .... A...... 310 765-3600
501 Continental Blvd El Segundo (90245) *(P-10076)*

Teledyne Defense Elec LLC .... C...... 310 823-5491
1001 Knox St Torrance (90502) *(P-8906)*

Teledyne Flir LLC .... D...... 805 964-9797
6769 Hollister Ave Goleta (93117) *(P-10077)*

Teledyne Flir Coml Systems Inc (DH) .... B...... 805 964-9797
6769 Hollister Ave Goleta (93117) *(P-10290)*

Teledyne Hanson Research Inc .... E...... 818 882-7266
9810 Variel Ave Chatsworth (91311) *(P-10291)*

Teledyne Impulse, San Diego *Also Called: Teledyne Instruments Inc (P-8280)*

Teledyne Instruments Inc .... D...... 858 842-3100
9855 Carroll Canyon Rd San Diego (92131) *(P-8280)*

Teledyne Instruments Inc .... E...... 858 842-3127
9855 Carroll Canyon Rd San Diego (92131) *(P-8907)*

Teledyne Instruments Inc .... C...... 858 842-2600
14020 Stowe Dr Poway (92064) *(P-10078)*

Teledyne Instruments Inc .... E...... 818 882-7266
9810 Variel Ave Chatsworth (91311) *(P-10292)*

Teledyne Instruments Inc .... D...... 619 239-5959
9970 Carroll Canyon Rd Ste A San Diego (92131) *(P-10401)*

Teledyne Instruments Inc .... D...... 858 657-9800
9970 Carroll Canyon Rd San Diego (92131) *(P-10402)*

Teledyne Instruments Inc ....C...... 626 934-1500
 16830 Chestnut St City Of Industry (91748) *(P-10403)*

Teledyne Judson Technologies, Camarillo *Also Called: Teledyne Scentific Imaging LLC*
(P-19880)

Teledyne Lecroy Inc ....F...... 434 984-4500
 1049 Camino Dos Rios Thousand Oaks (91360) *(P-10226)*

Teledyne Optmum Optcal Systems, Camarillo *Also Called: Teledyne Scentific Imaging LLC*
(P-10342)

Teledyne Rd Instruments, Poway *Also Called: Teledyne Instruments Inc (P-10078)*

Teledyne Rd Instruments Inc ....C...... 858 842-2600
 14020 Stowe Dr Poway (92064) *(P-10079)*

Teledyne Redlake Masd LLC (DH) .... E...... 805 373-4545
 1049 Camino Dos Rios Thousand Oaks (91360) *(P-10293)*

Teledyne Reson Inc .... E...... 805 964-6260
 5212 Verdugo Way Camarillo (93012) *(P-12919)*

Teledyne Reynolds, Torrance *Also Called: Teledyne Defense Elec LLC (P-8906)*

Teledyne Reynolds Inc ....C...... 310 823-5491
 1001 Knox St Torrance (90502) *(P-4584)*

Teledyne Risi Inc (HQ).. E...... 818 718-6640
 19735 Dearborn St Chatsworth (91311) *(P-4585)*

Teledyne Scentific Imaging LLC .... E
 4153 Calle Tesoro Camarillo (93012) *(P-10342)*

Teledyne Scentific Imaging LLC .... D...... 805 373-4979
 5212 Verdugo Way Camarillo (93012) *(P-19880)*

Teledyne Scentific Imaging LLC (HQ)............................C...... 805 373-4545
 1049 Camino Dos Rios Thousand Oaks (91360) *(P-19881)*

Teledyne Scientific Company, Thousand Oaks *Also Called: Teledyne Scentific Imaging LLC*
(P-19881)

Teledyne Seabotix Inc ....D...... 619 239-5959
 2877 Historic Decatur Rd # 100 San Diego (92106) *(P-7172)*

TELEDYNE TECHNOLOGIES, Thousand Oaks *Also Called: Teledyne Technologies Inc*
(P-9128)

Teledyne Technologies Inc ....B...... 310 765-3600
 501 Continental Blvd El Segundo (90245) *(P-9126)*

Teledyne Technologies Inc ....B...... 310 822-8229
 12964 Panama St Los Angeles (90066) *(P-9127)*

Teledyne Technologies Inc (PA)..C...... 805 373-4545
 1049 Camino Dos Rios Thousand Oaks (91360) *(P-9128)*

Teledyne Technologies Inc ....D...... 909 793-3131
 840 W Brockton Ave Redlands (92374) *(P-9156)*

Teleflora, Los Angeles *Also Called: The Wonderful Company LLC (P-116)*

Telemtry Cmmnctons Systems Inc .... E...... 818 718-6248
 10020 Remmet Ave Chatsworth (91311) *(P-8588)*

Telenet, El Segundo *Also Called: Telenet Voip Inc (P-17074)*

Telenet Voip Inc ....D...... 310 253-9000
 850 N Park View Dr El Segundo (90245) *(P-17074)*

Teleperformance, Pasadena *Also Called: Tpusa - Fhcs Inc (P-16540)*

Telescape, Los Angeles *Also Called: Truconnect Communications Inc (P-11910)*

Telesector Resources Group Inc ....B...... 626 813-4538
 5010 Azusa Canyon Rd Baldwin Park (91706) *(P-20258)*

Telesign Holdings Inc (DH) .... E...... 310 740-9700
 13274 Fiji Way Ste 600 Marina Del Rey (90292) *(P-16399)*

Telesis Bio Inc ....C...... 858 526-3080
 10431 Wateridge Cir Ste 150 San Diego (92121) *(P-10294)*

Telesis Community Credit Union (PA)............................D...... 818 885-1226
 9301 Winnetka Ave Chatsworth (91311) *(P-14239)*

Telestar International Corp .... E...... 818 582-3018
 5536 Balboa Blvd Encino (91316) *(P-20259)*

Telestar Material, Encino *Also Called: Telestar International Corp (P-20259)*

Teletrac Inc (PA)..C...... 714 897-0877
 310 Commerce Ste 100 Irvine (92602) *(P-12013)*

Teletrac Navman US Ltd (HQ)... E...... 866 527-9896
 310 Commerce Ste 100 Irvine (92602) *(P-10080)*

Teletronics Technology Corp .... E...... 661 273-7033
 190 Sierra Ct Ste A3 Palmdale (93550) *(P-10081)*

Telisimo International Corp ....B...... 619 325-1593
 2330 Shelter Island Dr Ste 210a San Diego (92106) *(P-11908)*

Telit Wireless Solutions Inc ....C...... 949 461-7150
 7700 Irvine Center Dr Irvine (92618) *(P-12706)*

Tellabs Access LLC (HQ)... E...... 630 798-8671
 338 Pier Ave Hermosa Beach (90254) *(P-8631)*

Tellkamp Systems Inc (PA)... E...... 562 802-1621
 15523 Carmenita Rd Santa Fe Springs (90670) *(P-10107)*

Temblor Brewing LLC .... E...... 661 489-4855
 3200 Buck Owens Blvd Bakersfield (93308) *(P-1606)*

Temco, Pomona *Also Called: C & B Delivery Service (P-11566)*

Temco Logistics, Lake Forest *Also Called: Home Express Delivery Svc LLC (P-11770)*

Temecula Hhg Hotel Dev LP ....D...... 951 331-3622
 28400 Rancho California Rd Temecula (92590) *(P-15388)*

Temecula Homecare, Temecula *Also Called: Maxim Healthcare Services Inc (P-15932)*

Temecula Quality Plating Inc .... E...... 951 296-9875
 42147 Roick Dr Temecula (92590) *(P-6672)*

Temecula Stadium Cinemas 15, Temecula *Also Called: Edwards Theatres Circuit Inc*
(P-17298)

Temecula Valley Winery MGT LLC ....D...... 951 699-8896
 27495 Diaz Rd Temecula (92590) *(P-1662)*

Temeka Advertising Inc ....D...... 951 277-2525
 9073 Pulsar Ct Corona (92883) *(P-2968)*

Temeka Group, Corona *Also Called: Temeka Advertising Inc (P-2968)*

Temeka Incorporated .... E...... 951 296-3570
 150 W Walnut Ave Perris (92571) *(P-11174)*

Temeku Hills, Temecula *Also Called: McMillin Communities Inc (P-17437)*

Temple Community Hospital, Los Angeles *Also Called: Temple Hospital Corporation*
(P-18471)

Temple Custom Jewelers LLC .... E...... 800 988-3844
 1640 Camino Del Rio N Ste 220 San Diego (92108) *(P-10913)*

Temple Hospital Corporation ....B...... 213 355-3200
 242 N Hoover St Los Angeles (90004) *(P-18471)*

Temple Israel of Hollywood (PA)....................................D...... 323 876-8330
 7300 Hollywood Blvd Los Angeles (90046) *(P-15491)*

Tempo Communications Inc (PA)....................................D...... 800 642-2155
 1390 Aspen Way Vista (92081) *(P-11909)*

Tempo Industries, Irvine *Also Called: Wpmg Inc (P-8342)*

Tempo Industries Inc ....C...... 415 552-8074
 2137 E 55th St Vernon (90058) *(P-2862)*

Temporary Staffing Union .... A...... 714 728-5186
 19800 Macarthur Blvd Ste 300 Irvine (92612) *(P-19416)*

Temps Plus Inc ....C...... 951 549-8309
 268 N Lincoln Ave Ste 12 Corona (92882) *(P-15899)*

Tempted Apparel Corp ....D...... 323 859-2480
 4516 Loma Vista Ave Vernon (90058) *(P-2377)*

Temptron Engineering Inc .... E...... 818 346-4900
 7823 Deering Ave Canoga Park (91304) *(P-10404)*

Ten Publishing Media LLC (PA)......................................C...... 310 531-9900
 831 S Douglas St El Segundo (90245) *(P-17269)*

Ten Stone Wbster Prcess Tech ....B...... 909 447-3600
 555 W Arrow Hwy Claremont (91711) *(P-19700)*

Ten-X, Irvine *Also Called: Ten-X Finance Inc (P-14872)*

Ten-X Finance Inc ....C...... 949 465-8523
 15295 Alton Pkwy Irvine (92618) *(P-14872)*

Tencate Performance Composite, Camarillo *Also Called: Performance Materials Corp*
(P-3961)

Tenenblatt Corporation ....C...... 323 232-2061
 3750 Broadway Pl Los Angeles (90007) *(P-2080)*

Tenet, Palm Springs *Also Called: Desert Regional Med Ctr Inc (P-18237)*

Tenet Health Systems Norris ....B...... 323 865-3000
 1441 Eastlake Ave Los Angeles (90089) *(P-18472)*

Tenet Healthsystem Medical Inc ....B...... 562 531-2550
 3700 South St Lakewood (90712) *(P-17801)*

Tenet Healthsystem Medical Inc ....B...... 805 546-7698
 3751 Katella Ave Los Alamitos (90720) *(P-17802)*

Tenet Healthsystem Medical Inc ....C...... 562 493-9581
 1661 Golden Rain Rd Seal Beach (90740) *(P-17803)*

Tenet Healthsystem Medical Inc ....C...... 714 428-6800
 1400 S Douglass Rd Ste 250 Anaheim (92806) *(P-18473)*

Tenet Healthsystem Medical Inc ....B...... 714 993-2000
 1301 N Rose Dr Placentia (92870) *(P-18537)*

Tenex Health Inc ....D...... 949 454-7500
 26902 Vista Ter Lake Forest (92630) *(P-10616)*

Tenma America Corporation ....C...... 619 754-2250
 333 H St Ste 5000 Chula Vista (91910) *(P-5225)*

Tensorcom Inc .... E...... 760 496-3264
 3530 John Hopkins Ct San Diego (92121) *(P-8908)*

ALPHABETIC

Tensoriot Inc .... D..... 909 342-2459
625 The City Dr S Ste 485 Orange (92868) *(P-16606)*

Tensys Medical Inc .... E..... 858 552-1941
12625 High Bluff Dr Ste 213 San Diego (92130) *(P-10829)*

Teradata, San Diego *Also Called: Teradata Corporation (P-16400)*

Teradata Corporation (PA) .... A..... 866 548-8348
17095 Via Del Campo San Diego (92127) *(P-16400)*

Teradata Operations Inc (HQ) .... D..... 937 242-4030
17095 Via Del Campo San Diego (92127) *(P-7453)*

Teradyne Inc .... D..... 818 991-2900
30701 Agoura Rd Agoura Hills (91301) *(P-9129)*

TERI COMMON GROUNDS CAFE & COF, Oceanside *Also Called: E R I T Inc (P-19260)*

Teridian Semiconductor Corp (DH) .... D..... 714 508-8800
6440 Oak Cyn Ste 100 Irvine (92618) *(P-8909)*

Teris - San Diego LLC .... E..... 619 231-3282
600 W Broadway Ste 340 San Diego (92101) *(P-3328)*

Terminal Freezers, Oxnard *Also Called: Fresh Innovations LLC (P-1836)*

Termo Company .... E..... 562 595-7401
3275 Cherry Ave Long Beach (90807) *(P-322)*

Tern Design Ltd .... E..... 760 754-2400
14020 Stowe Dr Poway (92064) *(P-10165)*

Terra Bella Nursery, San Diego *Also Called: Bella Terra Nursery Inc (P-13503)*

Terra Furniture Inc .... E
1950 Salto Dr Hacienda Heights (91745) *(P-2822)*

Terra Nova Technologies Inc .... D..... 619 596-7400
10770 Rockville St Ste A Santee (92071) *(P-6978)*

Terra Pacific Landscape (HQ) .... D..... 714 567-0177
12891 Nelson St Garden Grove (92840) *(P-181)*

Terra Universal Inc .... C..... 714 526-0100
800 S Raymond Ave Fullerton (92831) *(P-7334)*

Terra Vista Management, San Diego *Also Called: Terra Vista Management Inc (P-14873)*

Terra Vista Management Inc .... B..... 858 581-4200
2211 Pacific Beach Dr San Diego (92109) *(P-14873)*

Terrace, The, Grand Terrace *Also Called: Emeritus Corporation (P-17931)*

Terraces At Squaw Peak, Duarte *Also Called: Humangood (P-18132)*

Terranea Resort, Rancho Palos Verdes *Also Called: Long Point Development LLC (P-15231)*

Terravant Wine, Buellton *Also Called: Terravant Wine Company LLC (P-1664)*

Terravant Wine Company LLC .... D..... 805 686-9400
35 Industrial Way Buellton (93427) *(P-1663)*

Terravant Wine Company LLC (PA) .... E..... 805 688-4245
70 Industrial Way Buellton (93427) *(P-1664)*

Terravino, Pasadena *Also Called: Eurobizusa Inc (P-1625)*

Terry Hines & Assoc, Burbank *Also Called: GL Nemirow Inc (P-15540)*

Terry Hinge & Hardware, Van Nuys *Also Called: RPC Legacy Inc (P-5941)*

Terry Town Corporation .... D..... 619 421-5354
8851 Kerns St Ste 100 San Diego (92154) *(P-2424)*

Terumo Americas Holding Inc .... F..... 714 258-8001
1311 Valencia Ave Tustin (92780) *(P-10295)*

Tesancia La Jlla Ht Spa Resort, La Jolla *Also Called: Destination Residences LLC (P-15506)*

Tesco Controls Inc .... E..... 916 395-8800
42015 Remington Ave Ste 102 Temecula (92590) *(P-10227)*

TESCO CONTROLS, INC., Temecula *Also Called: Tesco Controls Inc (P-10227)*

Tesco Products .... E..... 661 257-0153
25601 Avenue Stanford Santa Clarita (91355) *(P-7026)*

Teserra (PA) .... B..... 760 340-9000
86100 Avenue 54 Coachella (92236) *(P-1179)*

Tesoro Refining & Mktg Co LLC .... D..... 562 728-2215
5905 N Paramount Blvd Long Beach (90805) *(P-4651)*

Tesoro Refining & Mktg Co LLC .... C..... 877 837-6762
2101 E Pacific Coast Hwy Wilmington (90744) *(P-13455)*

Tessa Mia Corp .... E..... 877 740-5757
9565 Vassar Ave Chatsworth (91311) *(P-2680)*

Tessitura Network Inc .... C..... 888 643-5778
2295 Fletcher Pkwy Ste 101 El Cajon (92020) *(P-16401)*

Test-Rite Products Corp (DH) .... D..... 909 605-9899
1900 Burgundy Pl Ontario (91761) *(P-12316)*

Testequity, Moorpark *Also Called: Testequity Inc (P-12829)*

Testequity Inc .... D..... 805 498-9933
6100 Condor Dr Moorpark (93021) *(P-12829)*

Testequity LLC (PA) .... C..... 805 498-9933
6100 Condor Dr Moorpark (93021) *(P-17075)*

Testronic Inc .... C..... 818 845-3223
111 N First St Ste 204 Burbank (91502) *(P-17270)*

Testronic Labs, Burbank *Also Called: Testronic Inc (P-17270)*

Tetra Tech, Pasadena *Also Called: Tetra Tech Inc (P-19701)*

Tetra Tech Inc (PA) .... C..... 626 351-4664
3475 E Foothill Blvd Pasadena (91107) *(P-19701)*

Tetra Tech Inc .... D..... 949 263-0846
17885 Von Karman Ave Ste 500 Irvine (92614) *(P-19702)*

Tetra Tech Ec Inc .... E..... 949 809-5000
17885 Von Karman Ave # 500 Irvine (92614) *(P-10296)*

Tetra Tech Executive Svcs Inc .... C..... 626 470-2400
3475 E Foothill Blvd Pasadena (91107) *(P-15900)*

Tetra Tech Nus Inc .... C..... 412 921-7090
3475 E Foothill Blvd Pasadena (91107) *(P-19703)*

Teva Foods Inc .... E..... 323 267-8110
4401 S Downey Rd Vernon (90058) *(P-1996)*

Teva Parenteral Medicines Inc .... A..... 949 455-4700
19 Hughes Irvine (92618) *(P-4246)*

Texas Home Health America LP (PA) .... D..... 972 201-3800
1455 Auto Center Dr Ste 200 Ontario (91761) *(P-18645)*

Texas Home Health of America, Ontario *Also Called: Texas Home Health America LP (P-18645)*

Texas Tst Inc .... E..... 951 685-2155
13428 Benson Ave Chino (91710) *(P-5684)*

Texican Inc .... E..... 310 384-7000
21031 Ventura Blvd Ste 1000 Woodland Hills (91364) *(P-16402)*

Texolini Inc .... C..... 310 537-3400
2575 E El Presidio St Long Beach (90810) *(P-2129)*

Textile Unlimited Corporation (PA) .... D..... 310 263-7400
20917 Higgins Ct Torrance (90501) *(P-2163)*

Texture Design, Anaheim *Also Called: Textured Design Furniture Inc (P-2790)*

Textured Design Furniture Inc .... E..... 714 502-9121
1303 S Claudina St Anaheim (92805) *(P-2790)*

TFC Manufacturing Inc .... D..... 562 426-9559
4001 Watson Plaza Dr Lakewood (90712) *(P-6332)*

Tfd Incorporated .... E..... 714 630-7127
1180 N Tustin Ave Anaheim (92807) *(P-10343)*

Tfi of California Inc .... C..... 844 362-3222
9955 6th St Rancho Cucamonga (91730) *(P-1239)*

Tfi of California Inc (DH) .... E..... 844 362-3222
10646 Fulton Ct Rancho Cucamonga (91730) *(P-1240)*

Tfn Architectural Signage Inc (PA) .... E..... 714 556-0990
527 Fee Ana St Placentia (92870) *(P-11175)*

Tga Franchise Spt Holdings LLC .... D..... 310 333-0622
1960 E Grand Ave Ste 811 El Segundo (90245) *(P-17529)*

Tga Premier Sports, El Segundo *Also Called: Tga Franchise Spt Holdings LLC (P-17529)*

Tgg Accounting .... D..... 760 697-1033
10188 Telesis Ct Ste 130 San Diego (92121) *(P-19807)*

Thaihot Investment Co US Ltd .... A..... 949 242-5300
18201 Von Karman Ave Ste 600 Irvine (92612) *(P-18566)*

Thalasinos Enterprises Inc .... E..... 951 340-0911
1220 Railroad St Corona (92882) *(P-12884)*

Thales Avionics Inc .... E..... 949 381-3033
48 Discovery Irvine (92618) *(P-9812)*

Thales Avionics Inc .... E..... 949 790-2500
51 Discovery Ste 100 Irvine (92618) *(P-9813)*

Thales Avionics Inc .... E..... 949 829-5808
9975 Toledo Way Irvine (92618) *(P-9814)*

The Aerospace Corporation (PA) .... A..... 310 336-5000
2310 E El Segundo Blvd El Segundo (90245) *(P-19947)*

The Alternative Copy Shop Inc .... D..... 805 569-2116
3887 State St Ste 12 Santa Barbara (93105) *(P-15653)*

The Bobrick Corporation (PA) .... D..... 818 764-1000
6901 Tujunga Ave North Hollywood (91605) *(P-2996)*

The China Press, San Gabriel *Also Called: Asia-Pacific California Inc (P-3257)*

The Clear Group Inc, Los Angeles *Also Called: Clear Group Inc (P-15119)*

The Coding Source LLC .... C..... 866 235-7553
3415 S Sepulveda Blvd Ste 900 Los Angeles (90034) *(P-19005)*

The Copley Press Inc .... A..... 858 454-0411
7776 Ivanhoe Ave La Jolla (92037) *(P-16759)*

The Eberly Company, Beverly Hills *Also Called: Charles & Cynthia Eberly Inc (P-14705)*

Mergent email: customerrelations@mergent.com
1292

2024 Southern California
Business Directory and Buyers Guide

(P-0000) Products & Services Section entry number
(PA)=Parent Co (HQ)=Headquarters (DH)=Div Headquarters

The Enkeboll Co .... E....... 310 532-1400
16506 Avalon Blvd Carson (90746) *(P-2637)*

The Full Void 2 Inc .... B....... 818 891-5999
16320 Roscoe Blvd Ste 100 Van Nuys (91406) *(P-3417)*

The Gersh Agency LLC (PA) .... D....... 310 274-6611
9465 Wilshire Blvd Fl 6 Beverly Hills (90212) *(P-17330)*

The Goodwin Company, Garden Grove *Also Called: Goodwin Ammonia Company LLC*
(P-4337)

The Heat Factory Inc .... E....... 760 893-8300
2793 Loker Ave W Carlsbad (92010) *(P-3194)*

The Hunter Spice Inc .... D....... 805 597-8900
184 Suburban Rd San Luis Obispo (93401) *(P-1997)*

The J Paul Getty Trust (PA) .... A....... 310 440-7300
1200 Getty Center Dr Ste 500 Los Angeles (90049) *(P-19365)*

The Korea Times Los Angeles Inc (PA) .... C....... 323 692-2000
3731 Wilshire Blvd Ste 1000 Los Angeles (90010) *(P-3329)*

The Ligature Inc (HQ) .... E....... 323 585-6000
4909 Alcoa Ave Vernon (90058) *(P-3697)*

The Lodge At Torrey Pines Partnership L P .... B
998 W Mission Bay Dr San Diego (92109) *(P-15389)*

The Lubrizol Corporation .... F....... 949 212-1863
30211 Avenida De Las Bandera Rancho Santa Margari (92688) *(P-4633)*

The Lunada Bay Corporation (PA) .... D....... 714 490-1313
2000 E Winston Rd Anaheim (92806) *(P-2418)*

The Macsmith Corporation .... E....... 323 321-8881
1563 W 130th St Gardena (90249) *(P-6562)*

The Metropolitan Water District of Southern California (PA) ...... A....... 213 217-6000
700 N Alameda St Los Angeles (90012) *(P-12150)*

The National Bus Group Inc (PA) .... D....... 818 221-6000
15319 Chatsworth St Mission Hills (91345) *(P-15766)*

The Orange County Printing Co, Irvine *Also Called: Ocpc Inc (P-3646)*

The Original Cult Inc .... D....... 323 260-7308
40 E Verdugo Ave Burbank (91502) *(P-2378)*

The Orthopedic Institute of .... A....... 213 977-2010
616 Witmer St Los Angeles (90017) *(P-17804)*

The Ortiz Corporation .... D....... 619 434-7925
2000 Mckinley Ave National City (91950) *(P-697)*

The Palace of Auburn Hills, Beverly Hills *Also Called: Pse Holding LLC (P-17381)*

The Pines Ltd .... C....... 619 447-1880
1423 E Washington Ave El Cajon (92019) *(P-14731)*

The Rand Corporation (PA) .... A....... 310 393-0411
1776 Main St Santa Monica (90401) *(P-19948)*

The Rule Group, Newport Beach *Also Called: Trg Insurance Services (P-14636)*

The Rutter Group, North Hollywood *Also Called: West Publishing Corporation (P-3420)*

The Ryland Group Inc .... A....... 805 367-3800
3011 Townsgate Rd Ste 200 Westlake Village (91361) *(P-487)*

The Salk Institute For Biological Studies San Diego California ...... A....... 858 453-4100
10010 N Torrey Pines Rd La Jolla (92037) *(P-19882)*

The San Diego Yacht Club .... C....... 619 221-8400
1011 Anchorage Ln San Diego (92106) *(P-17530)*

The Strand Energy Company .... B....... 213 225-5900
515 S Flower St Ste 4800 Los Angeles (90071) *(P-266)*

The Sweet Life Enterprises Inc .... C....... 949 261-7400
2350 Pullman St Santa Ana (92705) *(P-1418)*

The Tax Credit Company .... D....... 323 927-0750
6464 W Sunset Blvd # 1150 Los Angeles (90028) *(P-15624)*

The Timing Inc .... E....... 323 589-5577
2807 S Santa Fe Ave Vernon (90058) *(P-13154)*

The Tristaff Group, San Diego *Also Called: Garich Inc (P-15847)*

The Wave, Manhattan Beach *Also Called: Wave Community Newspapers Inc (P-3336)*

The White Sheet, Palm Desert *Also Called: Associated Desert Shoppers Inc (P-3428)*

The Wonderful Company LLC (PA) .... C....... 310 966-5700
11444 W Olympic Blvd Ste 210 Los Angeles (90064) *(P-116)*

Theater Arts Fndtion San Dego .... C....... 858 623-3366
2910 La Jolla Village Dr La Jolla (92093) *(P-19466)*

Thebouqs.com, Marina Del Rey *Also Called: Bouqs Company (P-13504)*

Theodore, Los Angeles *Also Called: Country Club Fashions Inc (P-13912)*

Theorem LLC, Woodland Hills *Also Called: Citrusbyte LLC (P-15994)*

Therapy Specialist, Chula Vista *Also Called: Susan J Harris Inc (P-19304)*

Therm Core Products, San Bernardino *Also Called: Caldesso LLC (P-14124)*

Therm Pacific, Commerce *Also Called: Hkf Inc (P-12756)*

Therm-O-Namel Inc .... E....... 310 631-7866
2780 Martin Luther King Jr Blvd Lynwood (90262) *(P-6742)*

Thermal Dynamics, Ontario *Also Called: Thmx Holdings LLC (P-9469)*

Thermal Energy Solutions Inc .... E....... 661 489-4100
100 Quantico Ave Bakersfield (93307) *(P-698)*

Thermal Engineering, Cerritos *Also Called: Thermal Engrg Intl USA Inc (P-19704)*

Thermal Engrg Intl USA Inc (HQ) .... D....... 323 726-0641
18000 Studebaker Rd Ste 400 Cerritos (90703) *(P-19704)*

Thermal Equipment Corporation .... E....... 310 328-6600
2146 E Gladwick St Compton (90220) *(P-6163)*

Thermal Rite, Commerce *Also Called: Crowntonka California Inc (P-7606)*

Thermal Solutions Mfg Inc .... E....... 909 796-0754
1390 S Tippecanoe Ave Ste B San Bernardino (92408) *(P-9468)*

Thermal Structures Inc (DH) .... B....... 951 736-9911
2362 Railroad St Corona (92878) *(P-9581)*

Thermal Structures Inc .... E....... 951 256-8051
2380 Railroad St Corona (92878) *(P-9582)*

Thermal-Vac Technology Inc .... E....... 714 997-2601
1221 W Struck Ave Orange (92867) *(P-5851)*

Thermalflex, San Diego *Also Called: Tacna International Corp (P-20254)*

Thermalrite, Rancho Cucamonga *Also Called: Everidge Inc (P-7613)*

Thermaprint Corporation .... E....... 949 583-0800
11 Autry Ste B Irvine (92618) *(P-10887)*

Thermasol Steam Bath, Simi Valley *Also Called: DMA Enterprises Inc (P-11212)*

Thermech Corporation .... E....... 714 533-3183
1773 W Lincoln Ave Ste I Anaheim (92801) *(P-3158)*

Thermech Engineering, Anaheim *Also Called: Thermech Corporation (P-3158)*

Thermlly Engnred Mnfctred Pdts .... E....... 310 523-9934
543 W 135th St Gardena (90248) *(P-6164)*

Thermo Fisher Scientific, Carlsbad *Also Called: Thermo Fisher Scientific Inc (P-10300)*

Thermo Fisher Scientific Inc .... E....... 781 622-1000
5823 Newton Dr Carlsbad (92008) *(P-10297)*

Thermo Fisher Scientific Inc .... D....... 858 453-7551
9389 Waples St San Diego (92121) *(P-10298)*

Thermo Fisher Scientific Inc .... E....... 760 603-7200
5791 Van Allen Way Carlsbad (92008) *(P-10299)*

Thermo Fisher Scientific Inc .... E....... 760 268-8641
5781 Van Allen Way Carlsbad (92008) *(P-10300)*

Thermo Fsher Scntific Psg Corp (HQ) .... C....... 760 603-7200
5791 Van Allen Way Carlsbad (92008) *(P-10301)*

Thermo Power Industries .... E....... 562 799-0087
10570 Humbolt St Los Alamitos (90720) *(P-1001)*

Thermo Power Industries, Los Alamitos *Also Called: Thermo Power Industries (P-1001)*

Thermo Trilogy, Wasco *Also Called: Certis USA LLC (P-4547)*

Thermobile, Santa Ana *Also Called: Hood Manufacturing Inc (P-5051)*

Thermocraft .... D....... 619 813-2985
2554 Commercial St San Diego (92113) *(P-7625)*

Thermodyne International Ltd .... C....... 909 923-9945
1841 S Business Pkwy Ontario (91761) *(P-5226)*

Thermolab, Sun Valley *Also Called: Technical Heaters Inc (P-4714)*

Thermometrics Corporation (PA) .... F....... 818 886-3755
18714 Parthenia St Northridge (91324) *(P-10166)*

Thermomix, Thousand Oaks *Also Called: Vorwerk LLC (P-6567)*

Thermtronix Corporation (PA) .... E....... 760 246-4500
17129 Muskrat Ave Adelanto (92301) *(P-7373)*

Theta Oilfield Services Inc .... E....... 661 633-2792
5201 California Ave Ste 370 Bakersfield (93309) *(P-385)*

Thetradedesk, Ventura *Also Called: Trade Desk Inc (P-16137)*

Thewrap .... D....... 424 273-4787
2260 S Centinela Ave Ste 150 Los Angeles (90064) *(P-3330)*

Thg Brands Inc .... E....... 844 694-8327
1810 Abalone Ave Torrance (90501) *(P-1998)*

Thi Inc .... D....... 714 444-4643
1525 E Edinger Ave Santa Ana (92705) *(P-10617)*

Thi Holdings (delaware) Inc .... B....... 661 266-7423
2140 E Palmdale Blvd Ste O Palmdale (93550) *(P-14633)*

Thienes Apparel Inc .... E....... 626 575-2818
1811 Floradale Ave South El Monte (91733) *(P-2078)*

Thiessen Products Inc .... C....... 805 482-6913
555 Dawson Dr Ste A Camarillo (93012) *(P-8046)*

Thin Film Devices, Anaheim *Also Called: Tfd Incorporated (P-10343)*

Thin-Lite Corporation ....E....... 805 987-5021
530 Constitution Ave Camarillo (93012) *(P-8384)*

Thingap, Camarillo *Also Called: Thingap Inc (P-8160)*

Thingap Inc ....E....... 805 477-9741
4035 Via Pescador Camarillo (93012) *(P-8160)*

Think Together ....B....... 562 236-3835
12016 Telegraph Rd Santa Fe Springs (90670) *(P-17416)*

Think Together ....B....... 951 571-9944
22620 Goldencrest Dr Ste 104 Moreno Valley (92553) *(P-19228)*

Think Together ....B....... 909 723-1400
202 E Airport Dr Ste 200 San Bernardino (92408) *(P-19229)*

Think Together ....B....... 626 373-2311
800 S Barranca Ave Ste 120 Covina (91723) *(P-19230)*

Think Together ....B....... 760 269-1230
17270 Bear Valley Rd Ste 103 Victorville (92395) *(P-19534)*

Thinkbasic Inc ....C....... 858 755-6922
350 10th Ave San Diego (92101) *(P-15675)*

Thinkcp Technologies, Irvine *Also Called: H Co Computer Products (P-7473)*

Thinkom Solutions Inc ....C....... 310 371-5486
4881 W 145th St Hawthorne (90250) *(P-12014)*

Third Floor North Company, Placentia *Also Called: Tfn Architectural Signage Inc (P-11175)*

Thirty Three Threads Inc (PA).............................. E....... **877 486-3769**
1330 Park Center Dr Vista (92081) *(P-2225)*

This Is Rocknroll LLC ....F....... 323 384-3966
3950 Los Feliz Blvd Apt 208 Los Angeles (90027) *(P-7454)*

Thistle Roller Co Inc ....E....... 323 685-5322
209 Van Norman Rd Montebello (90640) *(P-7192)*

Thmx Holdings LLC ....C....... 909 390-3944
4850 E Airport Dr Ontario (91761) *(P-9469)*

Thomas Container & Packaging, Pomona *Also Called: T & T Box Company Inc (P-3146)*

Thomas James Capital Inc ....C....... 949 481-7026
26940 Aliso Viejo Pkwy Ste 100 Aliso Viejo (92656) *(P-14431)*

Thomas James Homes Inc ....C....... 949 424-2356
26880 Aliso Viejo Pkwy Ste 100 Aliso Viejo (92656) *(P-14874)*

Thomas Properties Group Inc ....C....... 213 613-1900
515 S Flower St Fl 6 Los Angeles (90071) *(P-14875)*

Thomas St John Inc ....D....... 424 273-1172
10877 Wilshire Blvd Ste 1550 Los Angeles (90024) *(P-20260)*

Thompco Inc ....E....... 805 933-8048
899 Mission Rock Rd Santa Paula (93060) *(P-12779)*

Thompson ADB Industries, Westminster *Also Called: Thompson Industries Ltd (P-9815)*

Thompson Building Materials, Fontana *Also Called: Valori Sand & Gravel Company (P-12363)*

Thompson Gundrilling Inc ....E....... 323 873-4045
13840 Saticoy St Van Nuys (91402) *(P-5649)*

Thompson Industries Ltd ....D....... 310 679-9193
7155 Fenwick Ln Westminster (92683) *(P-9815)*

Thompson Magnetics Inc ....E....... 951 676-0243
42255 Baldaray Cir Ste C Temecula (92590) *(P-9130)*

Thompson Pipe Group Inc (PA).............................. E....... **909 822-0200**
3011 N Laurel Ave Rialto (92377) *(P-3250)*

Thompson Tank Inc ....F....... 562 869-7711
8029 Phlox St Downey (90241) *(P-6165)*

Thomson Reuters Corporation ....E....... 310 287-2360
3280 Motor Ave Ste 200 Los Angeles (90034) *(P-3493)*

Thomson Reuters Corporation ....F....... 949 400-7782
163 Albert Pl Costa Mesa (92627) *(P-3494)*

Thomson Reuters Corporation ....E....... 877 518-2761
5161 Lankershim Blvd # 250 North Hollywood (91601) *(P-8589)*

Thorn Street Brewing Company, San Diego *Also Called: Tsb2 Llc (P-1608)*

Thornton Steel & Ir Works Inc ....F....... 714 491-8800
1323 S State College Pkwy Anaheim (92806) *(P-6371)*

Thornton Technologies, Oceanside *Also Called: Thornton Technology Corp (P-12920)*

Thornton Technology Corp ....E....... 760 471-9969
2608 Temple Heights Dr Oceanside (92056) *(P-12920)*

Thornton Winery ....D....... 951 699-0099
32575 Rancho California Rd Temecula (92591) *(P-1665)*

Thoro--Packaging (DH)... C....... **951 278-2100**
1467 Davril Cir Corona (92878) *(P-13564)*

Thorpe Technologies Inc (DH) ....E....... 562 903-8230
449 W Allen Ave Ste 119 San Dimas (91773) *(P-19705)*

Thorwear Inc ....F....... 760 224-3393
5674 El Camino Real Carlsbad (92008) *(P-12519)*

Thousand Oaks Prtg & Spc Inc ....C....... 818 706-8330
5334 Sterling Center Dr Westlake Village (91361) *(P-16943)*

Thousand Oaks Service Center, Thousand Oaks *Also Called: Southern California Edison Co (P-12056)*

Thousand Oaks Surgical Hosp LP ....D....... 805 777-7750
401 Rolling Oaks Dr Thousand Oaks (91361) *(P-18474)*

Thq Inc ....A....... 818 591-1310
21900 Burbank Blvd Woodland Hills (91367) *(P-16403)*

Thq San Diego, Woodland Hills *Also Called: Thq Inc (P-16403)*

Three Man Corporation ....E....... 858 684-5200
10025 Huennekens St San Diego (92121) *(P-3821)*

Three Sons Inc ....D....... 562 801-4100
5201 Industry Ave Pico Rivera (90660) *(P-13309)*

Three Star Rfrgn Engrg Inc ....E....... 310 327-9090
21720 S Wilmington Ave Ste 309 Long Beach (90810) *(P-7626)*

Three Wise Men Inc ....E....... 909 477-6698
11818 San Marino St Ste B Rancho Cucamonga (91730) *(P-12317)*

Three-D Plastics Inc (PA)....................................... E....... **323 849-1316**
430 N Varney St Burbank (91502) *(P-5227)*

Three-D Traffics Works, Burbank *Also Called: Three-D Plastics Inc (P-5227)*

Three-Way Chevrolet Co (PA)................................. C....... **661 847-6400**
4501 Wible Rd Bakersfield (93313) *(P-13836)*

Threesixty Group, Irvine *Also Called: Merchsource LLC (P-12940)*

Thrifty Oil Co (PA)... F....... **562 921-3581**
13116 Imperial Hwy Santa Fe Springs (90670) *(P-14688)*

Thrifty Payless Inc ....A....... 626 571-0122
9200 Telstar Ave El Monte (91731) *(P-1300)*

Thrio Inc ....E....... 858 299-7191
5230 Las Virgenes Rd Ste 210 Calabasas (91302) *(P-16404)*

Thrive Mortgage LLC ....D....... 909 527-3736
9587 Foothill Blvd Rancho Cucamonga (91730) *(P-14352)*

Thums Long Beach Company ....C....... 562 624-3400
111 W Ocean Blvd Ste 800 Long Beach (90802) *(P-267)*

Thunderbird Industries Inc ....F....... 909 394-1633
695 W Terrace Dr San Dimas (91773) *(P-7101)*

Thunderbolt Manufacturing Inc ....E....... 714 632-0397
641 S State College Blvd Fullerton (92831) *(P-8047)*

Thursby Software Systems LLC ....E....... 817 478-5070
1900 Carnegie Ave Santa Ana (92705) *(P-16405)*

Thyde Inc (PA)... C....... **951 817-2300**
300 El Sobrante Rd Corona (92879) *(P-16944)*

Thyssenkrupp Bilstein Amer Inc ....E....... 858 386-5900
13225 Danielson St # 100 Poway (92064) *(P-9470)*

TI Limited LLC (PA)... D....... **323 877-5991**
20335 Ventura Blvd Ste 231-239 Woodland Hills (91364) *(P-16406)*

TI Wire, Walnut *Also Called: Tree Island Wire (USA) Inc (P-5626)*

Tianello Inc ....C....... 323 231-0599
138 W 38th St Los Angeles (90037) *(P-2266)*

Tianello By Steve Barraza, Los Angeles *Also Called: Tianello Inc (P-2266)*

Tiburon Hospitality LLC ....C....... 661 322-1012
901 Real Rd Bakersfield (93309) *(P-15390)*

Ticketmaster, Los Angeles *Also Called: Ticketmaster Corporation (P-17569)*

Ticketmaster, Los Angeles *Also Called: Ticketmaster Group Inc (P-17571)*

Ticketmaster, Beverly Hills *Also Called: Ticketmster New Vntres Hldngs (P-17572)*

Ticketmaster Corporation ....A....... 323 769-4600
7060 Hollywood Blvd Ste 2 Los Angeles (90028) *(P-17569)*

Ticketmaster Entertainment LLC ....A....... 800 653-8000
8800 W Sunset Blvd West Hollywood (90069) *(P-17570)*

Ticketmaster Group Inc ....A....... 800 745-3000
3701 Wilshire Blvd Fl 9 Los Angeles (90010) *(P-17571)*

Ticketmster New Vntres Hldngs (HQ)..................... C....... **800 653-8000**
325 N Maple Dr Beverly Hills (90210) *(P-17572)*

Tickets.com, Inc., Costa Mesa *Also Called: Ticketscom LLC (P-17331)*

Ticketscom LLC (DH)... E....... **714 327-5400**
535 Anton Blvd Ste 250 Costa Mesa (92626) *(P-17331)*

Ticketsocket Inc ....E....... 888 633-7105
6150 Lusk Blvd Ste 201 San Diego (92121) *(P-16407)*

Tidelands Oil Production Inc ....E....... 562 436-9918
301 E Ocean Blvd St 300 Long Beach (90802) *(P-268)*

Mergent email: customerrelations@mergent.com
1294

2024 Southern California
Business Directory and Buyers Guide

(P-0000) Products & Services Section entry number
(PA)=Parent Co (HQ)=Headquarters (DH)=Div Headquarters

Tidings .... E 213 637-7360
3424 Wilshire Blvd Los Angeles (90010) *(P-3331)*

Tidwell Excav Acquisition Inc .... D 805 647-4707
1691 Los Angeles Ave Ventura (93004) *(P-1128)*

Tidwell Excavating, Ventura *Also Called: Tidwell Excav Acquisition Inc (P-1128)*

Tierra Del Sol Foundation .... D 909 626-8301
250 W 1st St Ste 120 Claremont (91711) *(P-17573)*

Tierra Del Sol Foundation (PA) .... D 818 352-1419
9919 Sunland Blvd Sunland (91040) *(P-19305)*

Tierra Del Soul, Claremont *Also Called: Tierra Del Sol Foundation (P-17573)*

Tiffany Coach Builders, Perris *Also Called: Warlock Industries (P-9313)*

Tiffany Coachworks, Corona *Also Called: Tiffany Coachworks Inc (P-9311)*

Tiffany Coachworks, Perris *Also Called: Limos By Tiffany Inc (P-9330)*

Tiffany Coachworks Inc .... F 951 657-2680
420 N Mckinley St # 111-465 Corona (92879) *(P-9311)*

Tiffany Dale Inc (PA) .... D 714 739-2700
14765 Firestone Blvd La Mirada (90638) *(P-12318)*

Tiffany Homecare Inc (PA) .... B 818 886-1602
9700 Reseda Blvd Ste 105 Northridge (91324) *(P-18646)*

Tig/M LLC .... E 818 709-8500
9160 Jordan Ave Chatsworth (91311) *(P-6979)*

Tiger Business Holdings Inc .... F 714 763-4180
32052 Sea Island Dr Dana Point (92629) *(P-8738)*

Tiger Case Hole Services, Signal Hill *Also Called: Tiger Cased Hole Services Inc (P-386)*

Tiger Cased Hole Services Inc .... E 562 426-4044
2828 Junipero Ave Signal Hill (90755) *(P-386)*

Tiger Tanks Inc .... E 661 363-8335
3397 Edison Hwy Bakersfield (93307) *(P-9931)*

Tiger Woods Learning Center .... D 714 765-8040
1 Tiger Woods Way Anaheim (92801) *(P-19231)*

Tigerconnect Inc (PA) .... D 310 401-1820
2054 Broadway Santa Monica (90404) *(P-16607)*

Tikos Tanks Inc .... E 951 757-8014
14561 Hawthorne Ave Fontana (92335) *(P-17097)*

Tikun Olam Adelanto LLC .... E 833 468-4586
541 S Spring St Unit 213 Los Angeles (90013) *(P-4020)*

Tile & Marble Design Co Inc .... E 714 847-6472
7421 Vincent Cir Huntington Beach (92648) *(P-1007)*

Tiling and Stone Counter Tops, Ontario *Also Called: Calvillo Construction Corp (P-424)*

Tilton Engineering Inc .... E 805 688-2353
25 Easy St Buellton (93427) *(P-9471)*

Timbucktoo Manufacturing Inc .... E 310 323-1134
1633 W 134th St Gardena (90249) *(P-7689)*

Timco, Hesperia *Also Called: T L Timmerman Cnstr Inc (P-2704)*

Timco/Cal Rf Inc .... E 805 582-1777
3910 Royal Ave Ste A Simi Valley (93063) *(P-8985)*

Time Masters, Glendale *Also Called: AMG Employee Management Inc (P-10891)*

Time Warner, Los Angeles *Also Called: Spectrum MGT Holdg Co LLC (P-11999)*

Time Warner, San Diego *Also Called: Spectrum MGT Holdg Co LLC (P-12000)*

Time Warner, Santa Monica *Also Called: Time Warner Companies Inc (P-12001)*

Time Warner Companies Inc .... A 310 315-4437
2939 Nebraska Ave Santa Monica (90404) *(P-12001)*

Timec, E Rncho Dmngz *Also Called: Timec Companies Inc (P-718)*

Timec Companies Inc .... C 310 885-4710
2997 E Maria St E Rncho Dmngz (90221) *(P-718)*

Timec Companies Inc .... E 661 322-8177
6861 Charity Ave Bakersfield (93308) *(P-7261)*

Timec Southern California, Bakersfield *Also Called: Timec Companies Inc (P-7261)*

Timely Prefinished Steel, Pacoima *Also Called: SDS Industries Inc (P-6122)*

Timemed Labeling Systems Inc (DH) .... D 818 897-1111
27770 Entertainment Dr Ste 200 Valencia (91355) *(P-4798)*

Timevalue Software .... E 949 727-1800
22 Mauchly Irvine (92618) *(P-16408)*

Timing Fashion, Vernon *Also Called: The Timing Inc (P-13154)*

Timken Gears & Services Inc .... E 310 605-2600
12935 Imperial Hwy Santa Fe Springs (90670) *(P-6473)*

Timmons Wood Products Inc .... E 951 940-4700
4675 Wade Ave Perris (92571) *(P-2764)*

Tinco Sheet Metal Inc .... C 323 263-0511
958 N Eastern Ave Los Angeles (90063) *(P-1055)*

Tinker & Rasor .... E 909 890-0700
791 S Waterman Ave San Bernardino (92408) *(P-10082)*

Tiodize Co Inc (PA) .... F 714 898-4377
5858 Engineer Dr Huntington Beach (92649) *(P-6743)*

Tiodize Co Inc .... E 714 898-4377
15701 Industry Ln Huntington Beach (92649) *(P-13456)*

Tireco Inc (PA) .... C 310 767-7990
500 W 190th St Ste 600 Gardena (90248) *(P-12274)*

Tires Warehouse LLC .... B 714 432-8851
18203 Mount Baldy Cir Fountain Valley (92708) *(P-13884)*

Tissue-Grown Corporation .... D 805 525-1975
15245 W Telegraph Rd Santa Paula (93060) *(P-19883)*

Titan, Camarillo *Also Called: Titan Metal Fabricators Inc (P-6080)*

Titan Led .... D 805 523-7500
11959 Discovery Ct Moorpark (93021) *(P-14689)*

Titan Metal Fabricators Inc (PA) .... D 805 487-5050
352 Balboa Cir Camarillo (93012) *(P-6080)*

Titan Oilfield Services, Bakersfield *Also Called: Titan Oilfield Services Inc (P-387)*

Titan Oilfield Services Inc .... D 661 861-1630
21535 Kratzmeyer Rd Bakersfield (93314) *(P-387)*

Titan Solar, Woodland Hills *Also Called: Memeged Tevuot Shemesh (P-793)*

Titan Wolrdwide, Cerritos *Also Called: Silver Hawk Freight Inc (P-11803)*

Titanum Health Care .... D 213 765-8123
1414 S Grand Ave Los Angeles (90015) *(P-20261)*

Title Resource Group LLC .... D 818 291-4400
801 N Brand Blvd Glendale (91203) *(P-14896)*

TITLE RESOURCE GROUP LLC, Glendale *Also Called: Title Resource Group LLC (P-14896)*

Titleist, Carlsbad *Also Called: Acushnet Company (P-10970)*

Tivoli LLC .... E 714 957-6101
17110 Armstrong Ave Irvine (92614) *(P-8252)*

Tivoli Industries Inc .... E 714 957-6101
1550 E Saint Gertrude Pl Santa Ana (92705) *(P-8385)*

Tj Aerospace, Garden Grove *Also Called: Tj Aerospace Inc (P-9816)*

Tj Aerospace Inc .... E 714 891-3564
12601 Monarch St Garden Grove (92841) *(P-9816)*

Tje Company .... F 909 869-7777
20805 Currier Rd Walnut (91789) *(P-6126)*

Tjs Metal Manufacturing Inc .... E 310 604-1545
10847 Drury Ln Lynwood (90262) *(P-6372)*

Tk Elevator Corporation .... C 619 596-7220
1965 Gillespie Way Ste 101 El Cajon (92020) *(P-12830)*

Tk Pax Inc .... E 714 850-1330
1545 Macarthur Blvd Costa Mesa (92626) *(P-4715)*

Tka, La Palma *Also Called: Tech Knowledge Associates LLC (P-17159)*

Tl Enterprises LLC .... E 805 981-8393
2750 Park View Ct Ste 240 Oxnard (93036) *(P-3391)*

Tl Fab LP .... C 562 802-3980
2921 E Coronado St Anaheim (92806) *(P-6081)*

Tl Machine Inc .... D 714 554-4154
14272 Commerce Dr Garden Grove (92843) *(P-6424)*

TL Montgomery & Associates Inc .... C 323 583-1645
2833 Leonis Blvd Ste 205 Vernon (90058) *(P-13401)*

TL Shield & Associates Inc .... E 818 509-8228
1030 Arroyo St San Fernando (91340) *(P-6967)*

Tld Acquisition Co LLC C
505 S 7th Ave City Of Industry (91746) *(P-13402)*

Tld Distribution Co, City Of Industry *Also Called: Tld Acquisition Co LLC (P-13402)*

Tlm Publishing Inc .... E 213 627-3737
110 E 9th St Ste A777 Los Angeles (90079) *(P-3495)*

Tlmf Inc .... D 212 764-2334
1515 E 15th St Los Angeles (90021) *(P-2290)*

Tm Claims Service Inc .... D 626 568-7800
800 E Colorado Blvd Pasadena (91101) *(P-14634)*

Tm Highland Insurance Services, South Pasadena *Also Called: Tokio Marine Highland Insurance Services Inc (P-14635)*

TMC Aero, Los Angeles *Also Called: TMC Ice Protection Systems LLC (P-10083)*

TMC Aero, Murrieta *Also Called: TMC Ice Protection Systems LLC (P-10084)*

TMC Fluid Systems Inc .... F 714 553-0944
1228 Village Way Ste H Santa Ana (92705) *(P-7335)*

TMC Ice Protection Systems LLC (PA) .... E 951 677-6934
10850 Wilshire Blvd Ste 1250 Los Angeles (90024) *(P-10083)*

Employee Codes: A=Over 500 employees, B=251-500
C=101-250, D=51-100, E=20-50, F=10-19, G=1-9

2024 Southern California
Business Directory and Buyers Guide

© Mergent Inc. 1-800-342-5647
1295

ALPHABETIC

TMC Ice Protection Systems LLC ....E....... 951 677-6934
25775 Jefferson Ave Murrieta (92562) *(P-10084)*

TMI Products Inc ....C....... 951 272-1996
1493 E Bentley Dr Ste 102 Corona (92879) *(P-9472)*

TMI Visualogic, Corona *Also Called: TMI Products Inc (P-9472)*

TMJ Concepts, Ventura *Also Called: TMJ Solutions LLC (P-10618)*

TMJ Solutions LLC ....D....... 805 650-3391
6059 King Dr Ventura (93003) *(P-10618)*

Tmt Intrntonal Observatory LLC ....D....... 626 395-1651
100 W Walnut St Ste 300 Pasadena (91124) *(P-19949)*

TMW Corporation (PA) ....**C....... 818 362-5665**
15148 Bledsoe St Sylmar (91342) *(P-9817)*

Tmx Aerospace ....C....... 562 215-4410
12821 Carmenita Rd Unit F Santa Fe Springs (90670) *(P-12575)*

Tmx Engineering and Mfg Corp ....D....... 714 641-5884
2141 S Standard Ave Santa Ana (92707) *(P-8048)*

TN Sheet Metal Inc ....F....... 714 593-0100
18385 Bandilier Cir Fountain Valley (92708) *(P-6333)*

Tnk Therapeutics Inc (HQ) ....**C....... 858 210-3700**
9380 Judicial Dr San Diego (92121) *(P-19884)*

TNT Plastic Molding Inc (PA) ....**D....... 951 808-9700**
725 E Harrison St Corona (92879) *(P-5228)*

TO HELP EVERYONE HEALTH AND WE, Los Angeles *Also Called: Clinic Inc (P-17623)*

Toad & Co, Santa Barbara *Also Called: Toad & Co International Inc (P-2379)*

Toad & Co International Inc (PA) ....**E....... 800 865-8623**
2020 Alameda Padre Serra Ste 125 Santa Barbara (93103) *(P-2379)*

Toan D Nguyen DDS Inc ....D....... 909 599-3398
213 N San Dimas Ave San Dimas (91773) *(P-17848)*

TOAN D NGUYEN DDS INC, San Dimas *Also Called: Toan D Nguyen DDS Inc (P-17848)*

Tobin Lucks, West Hills *Also Called: Tobin Lucks A Prof Corp (P-18951)*

Tobin Lucks A Prof Corp (PA) ....**D....... 818 226-3400**
8511 Fallbrook Ave Ste 400 West Hills (91304) *(P-18951)*

Tobin Steel Company Inc ....D....... 714 541-2268
817 E Santa Ana Blvd Santa Ana (92701) *(P-6082)*

Tocanw Wholesaler ....E....... 619 376-2860
2801 Cmino Del Rio S Mssi San Diego (92108) *(P-8114)*

Todays IV ....A....... 213 835-4016
404 S Figueroa St Ste 516 Los Angeles (90071) *(P-15391)*

Todd Street Inc ....E....... 626 815-1175
770 N Todd Ave Azusa (91702) *(P-6166)*

Toesox, Vista *Also Called: Thirty Three Threads Inc (P-2225)*

Tognazzini Beverage Service ....E....... 805 928-1144
241 Roemer Way Santa Maria (93454) *(P-1742)*

Tokio Marine Highland Insurance Services Inc (DH) ....D....... 626 463-6486
899 El Centro St South Pasadena (91030) *(P-14635)*

Tokio Marine Michido, Pasadena *Also Called: Tm Claims Service Inc (P-14634)*

Tokyopop Inc (PA) ....D....... 323 920-5967
4136 Del Rey Ave Marina Del Rey (90292) *(P-3418)*

Tolar Manufacturing Co Inc ....E....... 951 808-0081
258 Mariah Cir Corona (92879) *(P-6083)*

Toleeto Fastener International ....E....... 619 662-1355
1580 Jayken Way Chula Vista (91911) *(P-11078)*

Tolemar Inc ....E....... 714 362-8166
5221 Oceanus Dr Huntington Beach (92649) *(P-9886)*

Tolemar Manufacturing, Huntington Beach *Also Called: Tolemar Inc (P-9886)*

TOLL GLOBAL FORWARDING SCS (USA) INC., Jurupa Valley *Also Called: Toll Global Fwdg Scs USA Inc (P-11810)*

Toll Global Fwdg Scs USA Inc ....D....... 732 750-9000
400 Westmont Dr 450 San Pedro (90731) *(P-11809)*

Toll Global Fwdg Scs USA Inc ....D....... 951 360-8310
3355 Dulles Dr Jurupa Valley (91752) *(P-11810)*

Toller Enterprises Inc (PA) ....**E....... 805 374-9455**
2251 Townsgate Rd Westlake Village (91361) *(P-13894)*

Tolosa Winery, San Luis Obispo *Also Called: Courtside Cellars LLC (P-1619)*

Tom Anderson Guitarworks ....F....... 805 498-1747
845 Rancho Conejo Blvd Newbury Park (91320) *(P-10934)*

Tom Bell Chevrolet, Redlands *Also Called: Dick Dewese Chevrolet Inc (P-13757)*

Tom Leonard Investment Co Inc ....E....... 951 351-7778
7240 Sycamore Canyon Blvd Riverside (92508) *(P-11296)*

Tom Ponton Industries Inc ....F....... 714 998-9073
22901 Savi Ranch Pkwy Ste B Yorba Linda (92887) *(P-20262)*

Tom York Enterprises Inc ....E....... 323 581-6194
2050 E 48th St Vernon (90058) *(P-5229)*

Tomi Engineering Inc ....D....... 714 556-1474
414 E Alton Ave Santa Ana (92707) *(P-8049)*

Tomitribe Corporation ....E....... 310 526-7676
1519 6th St Apt 503 Santa Monica (90401) *(P-16134)*

Tomorrows Heirlooms Inc ....E....... 310 323-6720
1636 W 135th St Gardena (90249) *(P-5946)*

Tomorrows Look Inc ....D....... 949 596-8400
17462 Von Karman Ave Irvine (92614) *(P-2093)*

Toms Truck Center Inc ....C....... 714 835-1978
1008 E 4th St Santa Ana (92701) *(P-13837)*

Tonbo Biosciences, San Diego *Also Called: Tonbo Biotechnologies Corp (P-3916)*

Tonbo Biotechnologies Corp ....E....... 858 888-7300
10840 Thornmint Rd San Diego (92127) *(P-3916)*

Tone It Up Inc ....E....... 310 376-7645
1110 Manhattan Ave Manhattan Beach (90266) *(P-13733)*

Toneonel Lavash, Los Angeles *Also Called: Lavash Corporation of America (P-1480)*

Tonnage Industrial LLC ....E....... 800 893-9681
2130 W Cowles St Long Beach (90813) *(P-12885)*

Tonys Express Inc (PA) ....**C....... 909 427-8700**
10613 Jasmine St Fontana (92337) *(P-11622)*

Tool Components Inc (PA) ....**E....... 310 323-5613**
240 E Rosecrans Ave Gardena (90248) *(P-12576)*

Tool Specialty Co, Los Angeles *Also Called: Tosco - Tool Specialty Company (P-7135)*

Toolbox Medical Innovations, Carlsbad *Also Called: Foundry Med Innovations Inc (P-10510)*

Top Finance Company, Chatsworth *Also Called: Platinum Group Companies Inc (P-14938)*

Top Heavy Clothing Company Inc (PA) ....**D....... 951 442-8839**
28381 Vincent Moraga Dr Temecula (92590) *(P-2164)*

Top Line Mfg Inc ....E....... 562 633-0605
7032 Alondra Blvd Paramount (90723) *(P-5947)*

Top Notch Mfg Inc ....F....... 619 588-2033
1488 Pioneer Way Ste 17 El Cajon (92020) *(P-6563)*

Top Source, The, Anaheim *Also Called: Block Tops Inc (P-2944)*

Top-Shelf Fixtures LLC ....D....... 909 627-7423
5263 Schaefer Ave Chino (91710) *(P-6829)*

Topa Property Group Inc (HQ) ....**C....... 310 203-9199**
1800 Avenue Of The Stars Ste 1400 Los Angeles (90067) *(P-14690)*

Topaz Lighting Company LLC ....E....... 818 838-3123
225 Parkside Dr San Fernando (91340) *(P-8335)*

Topaz Systems Inc (PA) ....**E....... 805 520-8282**
875 Patriot Dr Ste A Moorpark (93021) *(P-7572)*

Topco Sales, Simi Valley *Also Called: Wsm Investments LLC (P-15011)*

Topgolf Callaway Brands Corp (PA) ....**B....... 760 931-1771**
2180 Rutherford Rd Carlsbad (92008) *(P-11034)*

Topline Manufacturing Inc ....F....... 562 633-0605
7032 Alondra Blvd Paramount (90723) *(P-11297)*

Toppik, Los Angeles *Also Called: Spencer Forrest Inc (P-14105)*

Topson Downs, Culver City *Also Called: Topson Downs California Inc (P-13917)*

Topson Downs California Inc ....C....... 310 558-0300
3545 Motor Ave Los Angeles (90034) *(P-2296)*

Topson Downs California Inc (PA) ....**C....... 310 558-0300**
3840 Watseka Ave Culver City (90232) *(P-13917)*

Toray Membrane Usa Inc (DH) ....**D....... 858 218-2360**
13435 Danielson St Poway (92064) *(P-4634)*

Toray PMC, Camarillo *Also Called: Toray Prfmce Mtls Corp USA (P-8166)*

Toray Prfmce Mtls Corp USA ....E....... 805 402-6664
1150 Calle Suerte Camarillo (93012) *(P-8166)*

Toro Company ....C....... 619 562-2950
1588 N Marshall Ave El Cajon (92020) *(P-6916)*

Toro Company ....D....... 951 688-9221
5825 Jasmine St Riverside (92504) *(P-6917)*

Torrance Care Center West Inc ....C....... 310 370-4561
4333 Torrance Blvd Torrance (90503) *(P-18061)*

Torrance Health Assn Inc (PA) ....**A....... 310 325-9110**
3330 Lomita Blvd Torrance (90505) *(P-18475)*

Torrance Memorial Breast Diagn, Manhattan Beach *Also Called: Torrance Memorial Medical Ctr (P-18477)*

Torrance Memorial Medical Ctr (HQ) ....**A....... 310 325-9110**
3330 Lomita Blvd Torrance (90505) *(P-18476)*

Mergent email: customerrelations@mergent.com
1296

2024 Southern California
Business Directory and Buyers Guide

(P-0000) Products & Services Section entry number
(PA)=Parent Co (HQ)=Headquarters (DH)=Div Headquarters

Torrance Memorial Medical Ctr .... B....... 310 939-7847
855 Manhattan Beach Blvd Ste 208 Manhattan Beach (90266) *(P-18477)*

Torrance Memorial Medical Ctr .... B....... 310 784-6316
3333 Skypark Dr Ste 200 Torrance (90505) *(P-18478)*

Torrance Memorial Medical Ctr .... B....... 310 784-3740
22411 Hawthorne Blvd Torrance (90505) *(P-18479)*

Torrance Refining Company LLC .... A....... 310 212-2800
3700 W 190th St Torrance (90504) *(P-4652)*

Torrance Steel Window Co Inc .... E....... 310 328-9181
1819 Abalone Ave Torrance (90501) *(P-6127)*

Torrence Aluminum Window, Redlands *Also Called: Window Enterprises Inc (P-6128)*

Torrey Suites LP .... D....... 858 720-9500
3939 Ocean Bluff Ave San Diego (92130) *(P-15392)*

Torrid Merchandising Inc .... B....... 626 667-1002
18501 San Jose Ave City Of Industry (91748) *(P-20263)*

Tortoise Industries Inc .... E....... 323 258-7776
3052 Treadwell St Los Angeles (90065) *(P-6744)*

Tortoise Tube, Los Angeles *Also Called: Tortoise Industries Inc (P-6744)*

Toscana Country Club Inc .... C....... 760 404-1444
76009 Via Club Villa Indian Wells (92210) *(P-17531)*

Tosco - Tool Specialty Company .... E....... 323 232-3561
1011 E Slauson Ave Los Angeles (90011) *(P-7135)*

Toshiba, Irvine *Also Called: Toshiba Amer Elctrnc Cmpnnts (P-8443)*

Toshiba, Lake Forest *Also Called: Toshiba Amer Bus Solutions Inc (P-12389)*

Toshiba Amer Bus Solutions Inc (DH) .... B....... 949 462-6000
25530 Commercentre Dr Lake Forest (92630) *(P-12389)*

Toshiba Amer Elctrnc Cmpnnts (DH) .... B....... 949 462-7700
5231 California Ave Irvine (92617) *(P-8443)*

Toshiba Amer Info Systems Inc .... C....... 949 583-3000
9740 Irvine Blvd Fl 1 Irvine (92618) *(P-7455)*

Toshiba America Inc .... A....... 212 596-0600
5241 California Ave Ste 200 Irvine (92617) *(P-8444)*

Total Cmmnicator Solutions Inc .... D....... 619 277-1488
11150 Sta Monica Ste 600 Los Angeles (90025) *(P-16409)*

Total Cost Involved, Ontario *Also Called: TCI Engineering Inc (P-9310)*

Total Debt Management, Irvine *Also Called: Egs Financial Care Inc (P-15611)*

Total Garments, Westlake Village *Also Called: Hec Inc (P-12663)*

Total Gym Commercial LLC .... F....... 858 586-6080
100 Chesterfield Dr # G Cardiff By The Sea (92007) *(P-11035)*

Total Health Environment LLC .... E....... 714 637-1010
743 W Taft Ave Orange (92865) *(P-12520)*

Total Intermodal Services Inc (PA) .... E....... 562 427-6300
7101 Jackson St Paramount (90723) *(P-11649)*

Total Mont LLC .... E....... 562 983-1374
790 W 12th St Long Beach (90813) *(P-5357)*

Total Process Solutions LLC .... E....... 661 829-7910
1400 Norris Rd Bakersfield (93308) *(P-7292)*

Total Recon Solutions Inc .... D....... 949 584-8417
27 Oakbrook Trabuco Canyon (92679) *(P-20264)*

Total Resources Intl Inc (PA) .... E....... 909 594-1220
420 S Lemon Ave Walnut (91789) *(P-10712)*

Total Structures, Ventura *Also Called: Total Structures Inc (P-8386)*

Total Structures Inc .... E....... 805 676-3322
1696 Walter St Ventura (93003) *(P-8386)*

Total Vision LLC .... C....... 949 652-7242
27271 Las Ramblas Ste 200a Mission Viejo (92691) *(P-17856)*

Total Warehouse Inc .... C....... 480 582-3954
2895 E Miraloma Ave Anaheim (92806) *(P-11623)*

Total-Western Inc (HQ) .... E....... 562 220-1450
8049 Somerset Blvd Paramount (90723) *(P-388)*

Totally Bamboo, San Marcos *Also Called: Hollywood Chairs (P-2775)*

Totally Kids Rhbilitation Hosp, Loma Linda *Also Called: Mountain View Child Care Inc (P-18348)*

Totally Kids Spcalty Hlth Care, Sun Valley *Also Called: Mountain View Child Care Inc (P-19221)*

Totally Radical Associates Inc .... E....... 714 630-0653
1025 Ortega Way Ste A Placentia (92870) *(P-5230)*

Totex Manufacturing Inc .... D....... 310 326-2028
3050 Lomita Blvd Torrance (90505) *(P-5231)*

Totten Tubes Inc (PA) .... D....... 626 812-0220
500 W Danlee St Azusa (91702) *(P-12577)*

Touch International Display Enhancements Corp .... E....... 512 646-0310
11231 Jola Ln Garden Grove (92843) *(P-10344)*

Touchdown Technologies Inc .... E....... 626 472-6732
5188 Commerce Dr Baldwin Park (91706) *(P-8910)*

Touchtone Corporation .... E....... 714 755-2810
3151 Airway Ave Ste I3 Costa Mesa (92626) *(P-16135)*

TOUGHBUILT, Irvine *Also Called: Toughbuilt Industries Inc (P-5890)*

Toughbuilt Industries Inc (PA) .... B....... 949 528-3100
8669 Research Dr Irvine (92618) *(P-5890)*

Tour Master, Calabasas Hills *Also Called: Helmet House LLC (P-13104)*

Tourcoach Transportation, Commerce *Also Called: Screamline Investment Corp (P-11731)*

Tow Industries, West Covina *Also Called: Baatz Enterprises Inc (P-9280)*

Toward Maximum Independence (PA) .... C....... 858 467-0600
4740 Murphy Canyon Rd Ste 300 San Diego (92123) *(P-19146)*

Tower Glass Inc .... D....... 619 596-6199
9570 Pathway St Ste A Santee (92071) *(P-1120)*

Tower Hmtlogy Onclogy Med Grou .... E....... 310 888-8680
9090 Wilshire Blvd Ste 200 Beverly Hills (90211) *(P-17805)*

Tower Industries Inc .... C....... 909 947-2723
1720 S Bon View Ave Ontario (91761) *(P-8050)*

Tower Mechanical Products Inc .... C....... 714 947-2723
1720 S Bon View Ave Ontario (91761) *(P-10085)*

Tower Semicdtr Newport Bch Inc (DH) .... A....... 949 435-8000
4321 Jamboree Rd Newport Beach (92660) *(P-8911)*

Towerjazz, Newport Beach *Also Called: Tower Semicdtr Newport Bch Inc (P-8911)*

Towmaster Tire & Wheel, Anaheim *Also Called: Greenball Corp (P-12269)*

Town & Cntry Event Rentals Inc .... B....... 805 770-5729
1 N Calle Cesar Chavez Santa Barbara (93103) *(P-15801)*

Town & Cntry Event Rentals Inc (PA) .... B....... 818 908-4211
7725 Airport Business Pkwy Van Nuys (91406) *(P-15802)*

Town and Country, San Diego *Also Called: Atlas Hotels Inc (P-15080)*

Town and Country Hotel, San Diego *Also Called: Hotel Circle Property LLC (P-15186)*

Town Cntry Mnor of Chrstn Mssn .... C....... 714 547-7581
555 E Memory Ln Side Santa Ana (92706) *(P-18062)*

Towne Allpoints, Santa Ana *Also Called: Towne Inc (P-15637)*

Towne Inc .... C....... 714 540-3095
3441 W Macarthur Blvd Santa Ana (92704) *(P-15637)*

Towne Park Brew Inc .... E....... 714 844-2492
1566 W Lincoln Ave Anaheim (92801) *(P-1607)*

TownePlace Suites El Centro, El Centro *Also Called: El Centro Hospitality 2 LLC (P-15143)*

Townsend Design, Bakersfield *Also Called: Townsend Industries Inc (P-10715)*

Townsend Industries Inc .... D....... 661 837-1795
4401 Stine Rd Bakersfield (93313) *(P-10713)*

Townsend Industries Inc .... D....... 661 837-1795
4833 N Hills Dr Bakersfield (93308) *(P-10714)*

Townsend Industries Inc (DH) .... C....... 661 837-1795
4615 Shepard St Bakersfield (93313) *(P-10715)*

Townsteel Inc .... D....... 626 965-8917
17901 Railroad St City Of Industry (91748) *(P-5948)*

Toy Barn, Oxnard *Also Called: Players West Amusements Inc (P-17445)*

Toye Corporation .... E....... 818 882-4000
9230 Deering Ave Chatsworth (91311) *(P-7573)*

Toymax International Inc (HQ) .... D....... 310 456-7799
22619 Pacific Coast Hwy Malibu (90265) *(P-10967)*

Toyo Tire Hldings Americas Inc (HQ) .... E....... 714 229-6100
3565 Harbor Blvd Costa Mesa (92626) *(P-4700)*

Toyon Research Corporation (PA) .... C....... 805 968-6787
6800 Cortona Dr Goleta (93117) *(P-19706)*

Toyota Arena .... D....... 909 244-5500
4000 E Ontario Center Pkwy Ontario (91764) *(P-17574)*

Toyota Carlsbad, Carlsbad *Also Called: Oceanside Auto Country Inc (P-13807)*

Toyota Downtown La .... C....... 213 342-3646
714 W Olympic Blvd Ste 1131 Los Angeles (90015) *(P-13885)*

Toyota Logistics Services Inc (DH) .... C....... 310 468-4000
19001 S Western Ave Torrance (90501) *(P-13838)*

Toyota Material Hdlg Solutions, Santa Fe Springs *Also Called: Rebas Inc (P-12817)*

Toyota of Downtown L.A., Los Angeles *Also Called: Toyota Downtown La (P-13885)*

Toyota of El Cajon, El Cajon *Also Called: K Motors Inc (P-13851)*

Toyota of Glendora, Glendora *Also Called: Seidner-Miller Inc (P-13823)*

Employee Codes: A=Over 500 employees, B=251-500
C=101-250, D=51-100, E=20-50, F=10-19, G=1-9

2024 Southern California
Business Directory and Buyers Guide

© Mergent Inc. 1-800-342-5647

1297

Toyota of Orange Inc .... C....... 714 639-6750
   1400 N Tustin St Orange (92867) *(P-13839)*

Toyota of Oxnard, Oxnard *Also Called: DCH California Motors Inc (P-13755)*

Toyota of Riverside Inc ....C....... 951 687-1622
   7870 Indiana Ave Riverside (92504) *(P-13840)*

Toyota Scion Place, Garden Grove *Also Called: Noarus Tgg (P-13806)*

TP Products, San Fernando *Also Called: Triumph Precision Products (P-6425)*

TP USA, Claremont *Also Called: Technip Usa Inc (P-19699)*

Tp-Link USA Corporation ....D....... 562 528-7700
   3760 Kilroy Airport Way Ste 600 Long Beach (90806) *(P-12446)*

Tpl Communications, Panorama City *Also Called: D X Communications Inc (P-8507)*

Tpusa - Fhcs Inc (DH) .... C....... 213 873-5100
   215 N Marengo Ave Ste 160 Pasadena (91101) *(P-16540)*

Tpx Communications, Los Angeles *Also Called: Mpower Holding Corporation (P-11894)*

Tra Medical, Placentia *Also Called: Totally Radical Associates Inc (P-5230)*

Trace3, Irvine *Also Called: Trace3 LLC (P-16473)*

Trace3 LLC (HQ) ....C....... 949 333-2300
   7505 Irvine Center Dr Ste 100 Irvine (92618) *(P-16473)*

Trackr Inc ....D....... 855 981-1690
   7410 Hollister Ave Santa Barbara (93117) *(P-16136)*

Tracy Industries Inc ....C....... 562 692-9034
   3200 E Guasti Rd Ste 100 Ontario (91761) *(P-6896)*

Trade Desk Inc (PA) ....B....... 805 585-3434
   42 N Chestnut St Ventura (93001) *(P-16137)*

Trade Leasing Inc ....E....... 714 538-4614
   1818 E Rosslynn Ave Fullerton (92831) *(P-9336)*

Tradebeyond, San Diego *Also Called: Cbx Software Inc (P-16195)*

Trademark Construction Co Inc (PA) ....D....... 760 489-5647
   15916 Bernardo Center Dr San Diego (92127) *(P-9175)*

Trademark Cosmetics Inc ....E....... 951 683-2631
   545 Columbia Ave Riverside (92507) *(P-4461)*

Trademark Plastics Inc ....C....... 909 941-8810
   807 Palmyrita Ave Riverside (92507) *(P-7262)*

Tradenet Enterprise Inc ....D....... 888 595-3956
   1580 Magnolia Ave Corona (92879) *(P-11176)*

Tradition Golf Club, La Quinta *Also Called: Chapman Golf Development LLC (P-17421)*

Traffic Control & Safety Corp ....F....... 858 679-7292
   13755 Blaisdell Pl Poway (92064) *(P-11177)*

Traffic Control Service Inc C
   4695 Macarthur Ct Ste 1100 Newport Beach (92660) *(P-15803)*

Traffic Management Inc ....C....... 562 595-4278
   4900 Airport Plaza Dr Ste 300 Long Beach (90815) *(P-16945)*

Traffic Management Pdts Inc ....A....... 800 763-3999
   4900 Airport Plaza Dr Ste 300 Long Beach (90815) *(P-16410)*

Traffic Works Inc ....E....... 323 582-0616
   5720 Soto St Huntington Park (90255) *(P-4823)*

Trailer Park Inc (PA) ....D....... 310 845-3000
   6922 Hollywood Blvd Fl 12 Los Angeles (90028) *(P-15577)*

Train Reaction, Huntington Beach *Also Called: West Coast Trends Inc (P-11041)*

Trak Machine Tools, Rancho Dominguez *Also Called: Southwestern Industries Inc (P-7025)*

Trane, San Diego *Also Called: Trane US Inc (P-7627)*

Trane, Walnut *Also Called: Trane US Inc (P-7629)*

Trane Technologies Company LLC ....F....... 323 583-4771
   2845 Pellissier Pl City Of Industry (90601) *(P-7293)*

Trane US Inc ....D....... 858 292-0833
   3565 Corporate Ct Fl 1 San Diego (92123) *(P-7627)*

Trane US Inc ....D....... 626 913-7123
   3253 E Imperial Hwy Brea (92821) *(P-7628)*

Trane US Inc ....E....... 626 913-7913
   20450 E Walnut Dr N Walnut (91789) *(P-7629)*

Trans-Dapt California Inc ....E....... 562 921-0404
   12438 Putnam St Whittier (90602) *(P-9473)*

Trans-Pak Incorporated ....C....... 310 618-6937
   2601 S Garnsey St Santa Ana (92707) *(P-16946)*

Trans-West Services Inc ....B....... 661 381-2900
   8503 Crippen St Bakersfield (93311) *(P-16696)*

Transamerica Occidental Life Insurance Company ....A....... 213 742-2111
   1150 S Olive St Fl 23 Los Angeles (90015) *(P-14443)*

Transamerican, Escondido *Also Called: Transamerican Direct Inc (P-15638)*

Transamerican Direct Inc ....D....... 760 745-5343
   355 State Pl Escondido (92029) *(P-15638)*

Transamerican Dissolution LLC (HQ) ....C....... 310 900-5500
   400 W Artesia Blvd Compton (90220) *(P-13886)*

Transcendia Inc ....E....... 909 944-9981
   9000 9th St Ste 140 Rancho Cucamonga (91730) *(P-13419)*

Transcentra Inc ....B....... 310 603-0105
   20500 Belshaw Ave Carson (90746) *(P-16474)*

Transco, El Monte *Also Called: Transgo LLC (P-9474)*

Transcom Telecommunication Inc ....F....... 562 424-9616
   1390 E Burnett St Ste C Signal Hill (90755) *(P-8590)*

Transcontinental Ontario Inc ....E....... 909 390-8866
   5601 Santa Ana St Ontario (91761) *(P-3159)*

Transcontinental US LLC ....E....... 909 390-8866
   5601 Santa Ana St Ontario (91761) *(P-3195)*

Transcosmos Omniconnect LLC ....D....... 310 630-0072
   879 W 190th St Ste 1050 Gardena (90248) *(P-20106)*

Transdev Services Inc ....A....... 626 357-7912
   5640 Peck Rd Arcadia (91006) *(P-11406)*

Transdev Services Inc ....C....... 619 401-4503
   544 Vernon Way El Cajon (92020) *(P-11407)*

Transdigm Inc ....D....... 323 269-9181
   5000 Triggs St Commerce (90022) *(P-9818)*

Transducer Techniques LLC ....E....... 951 719-3965
   42480 Rio Nedo Temecula (92590) *(P-10405)*

Transglobal Holding Company ....D....... 626 447-7888
   1045 W Huntington Dr Ste 200 Arcadia (91007) *(P-14369)*

Transgo LLC ....E....... 626 443-7456
   2621 Merced Ave El Monte (91733) *(P-9474)*

Transico Inc ....E....... 714 835-6000
   1240 Pioneer St Ste A Brea (92821) *(P-9131)*

Transilwrap Company, Rancho Cucamonga *Also Called: Transcendia Inc (P-13419)*

Transit Air Cargo Inc ....D....... 714 571-0393
   2204 E 4th St Santa Ana (92705) *(P-11811)*

Transline Technology Inc ....E....... 714 533-8300
   1106 S Technology Cir Anaheim (92805) *(P-8739)*

Translogic Incorporated ....E....... 714 890-0058
   5641 Engineer Dr Huntington Beach (92649) *(P-10167)*

Transltnal Plmnary Immnlogy RE ....D....... 562 490-9900
   701 E 28th St Ste 419 Long Beach (90806) *(P-17806)*

Transnational Computer Tech, El Segundo *Also Called: Mesfin Enterprises (P-16457)*

Transom Capital Group LLC (PA) ....D....... 424 293-2818
   10990 Wilshire Blvd Ste 440 Los Angeles (90024) *(P-15055)*

Transom Post Midco LLC ....C....... 312 254-3300
   100 N Pacific Coast Hwy # 17 El Segundo (90245) *(P-14949)*

Transonic Combustion Inc ....E....... 805 465-5145
   461 Calle San Pablo Camarillo (93012) *(P-6897)*

Transpak Los Angeles, Santa Ana *Also Called: Trans-Pak Incorporated (P-16946)*

Transparent Devices Inc ....E....... 805 499-5000
   853 Lawrence Dr Newbury Park (91320) *(P-7574)*

Transparent Products Inc ....E....... 661 294-9787
   28064 Avenue Stanford Unit E Valencia (91355) *(P-7501)*

Transphorm Inc (PA) ....D....... 805 456-1300
   75 Castilian Dr Ste 200 Goleta (93117) *(P-8912)*

Transportation Department, Long Beach *Also Called: Long Beach Unified School Dst (P-11430)*

Transportation Department, Culver City *Also Called: City of Culver City (P-20404)*

Transportation Equipment Inc ....E....... 619 449-8860
   1404 N Marshall Ave El Cajon (92020) *(P-2511)*

Transportation Power LLC ....E....... 858 248-4255
   2057 Aldergrove Ave Escondido (92029) *(P-9475)*

Transpower, Escondido *Also Called: Transportation Power LLC (P-9475)*

Transprttion Brkg Spclists Inc ....B....... 714 754-4236
   3151 Airway Ave Ste F208 Costa Mesa (92626) *(P-11466)*

Transprttion Oprtion MGT Slton ....C....... 858 391-0260
   1917 Palomar Oaks Way Ste 110 Carlsbad (92008) *(P-16947)*

Transprttion Oprtons MGT Slton, Irvine *Also Called: Shimmick Construction Co Inc (P-715)*

Transtar Metals Corp ....B....... 562 630-1400
   14001 Orange Ave Paramount (90723) *(P-12578)*

Transtech Engineers Inc (PA) ....D....... 909 595-8599
   13367 Benson Ave Chino (91710) *(P-19707)*

Transwestern Publishing, San Diego *Also Called: Transwestern Publishing Company LLC (P-3496)*

Mergent email: customerrelations@mergent.com
1298

2024 Southern California
Business Directory and Buyers Guide

(P-0000) Products & Services Section entry number
(PA)=Parent Co (HQ)=Headquarters (DH)=Div Headquarters

Transwestern Publishing Company LLC .... A 858 467-2800
8344 Clairemont Mesa Blvd San Diego (92111) *(P-3496)*

Trantronics Inc .... E 949 553-1234
1822 Langley Ave Irvine (92614) *(P-8740)*

Travelerhelpdesk.com, San Diego *Also Called: Lbf Travel Inc (P-11719)*

Travelers Choice Travelware .... D 909 529-7688
2805 S Reservoir St Pomona (91766) *(P-5297)*

Travelodge, Santa Ana *Also Called: Chen & Huang Partners LP (P-15114)*

Travelodge Hotels Inc .... C 800 257-2297
3327 Del Mar Ave Rosemead (91770) *(P-15393)*

TRAVERE, San Diego *Also Called: Travere Therapeutics Inc (P-4247)*

Travere Therapeutics Inc (PA) .... C 888 969-7879
3611 Valley Centre Dr Ste 300 San Diego (92130) *(P-4247)*

Travis Industries, Sun Valley *Also Called: Travis-American Group LLC (P-2638)*

Travis Snyder .... E 909 338-6302
27248 Hwy 189 Ste Ab-06 Blue Jay (92317) *(P-6944)*

Travis-American Group LLC .... E 714 258-1200
11450 Sheldon St Sun Valley (91352) *(P-2638)*

TravisMathew LLC (HQ) .... E 562 799-6900
15202 Graham St Huntington Beach (92649) *(P-2226)*

Traxero North America LLC .... D 423 497-1164
1730 E Holly Ave Ste 740 El Segundo (90245) *(P-16411)*

Traxx Corporation .... D 909 623-8032
1201 E Lexington Ave Pomona (91766) *(P-11298)*

TRC Solutions Inc (HQ) .... C 949 753-0101
9685 Research Dr Ste 100 Irvine (92618) *(P-20386)*

Tre Milano LLC .... E 310 260-8888
2730 Monterey St Ste 101 Torrance (90503) *(P-11299)*

Treana Winery LLC .... E 805 237-2932
4280 Second Wind Way Paso Robles (93446) *(P-1666)*

Treasure Garden Inc (PA) .... E 626 814-0168
13401 Brooks Dr Baldwin Park (91706) *(P-13680)*

Treasury Wine Estates Americas .... E 805 237-6000
7000 E Highway 46 Paso Robles (93446) *(P-36)*

Tree House Pad & Paper Inc .... D 800 213-4184
2341 Pomona Rd Ste 108 Corona (92878) *(P-3224)*

Tree Island Wire (usa) Inc .... C 909 594-7511
13470 Philadelphia Ave Fontana (92337) *(P-5624)*

Tree Island Wire (usa) Inc .... C 909 595-6617
3880 W Valley Blvd Pomona (91769) *(P-5625)*

Tree Island Wire (usa) Inc .... C 909 899-1673
5080 Hallmark Pkwy San Bernardino (92407) *(P-6830)*

Tree Island Wire (USA) Inc (DH) .... C 909 594-7511
3880 Valley Blvd Walnut (91789) *(P-5626)*

Tree Island Wire USA, San Bernardino *Also Called: Tree Island Wire (usa) Inc (P-6830)*

Treebeard Landscape Inc .... D 619 697-8302
9917 Campo Rd Spring Valley (91977) *(P-182)*

Treesap Farms LLC .... C 760 990-7770
2500 Rainbow Valley Blvd Fallbrook (92028) *(P-88)*

Treivush Industries Inc .... D 213 745-7774
940 W Washington Blvd Los Angeles (90015) *(P-2380)*

Trellborg Sling Sltions US Inc .... E 805 239-4284
3077 Rollie Gates Dr Paso Robles (93446) *(P-5232)*

Trellborg Sling Sltions US Inc (DH) .... C 714 415-0280
2761 Walnut Ave Tustin (92780) *(P-10619)*

Trelleborg Sealing Solutions .... D 805 239-4284
3034 Propeller Dr Paso Robles (93446) *(P-10620)*

TRELLEBORG SEALING SOLUTIONS TUSTIN, INC., Paso Robles *Also Called: Trelleborg Sealing Solutions (P-10620)*

Trellisware Technologies Inc (HQ) .... C 858 753-1600
10641 Scripps Summit Ct Ste 100 San Diego (92131) *(P-11864)*

Trench Plate Rental, Downey *Also Called: National Trench Safety LLC (P-15790)*

Trend Design Inc .... F 805 498-0457
1200 Lawrence Dr Ste 465 Newbury Park (91320) *(P-15676)*

Trend Graphics Screenprinting, Newbury Park *Also Called: Trend Design Inc (P-15676)*

Trend Manor Furn Mfg Co Inc .... E 626 964-6493
17047 Gale Ave City Of Industry (91745) *(P-2791)*

Trend Offset Printing, Los Alamitos *Also Called: Trend Offset Printing Services Inc (P-3698)*

Trend Offset Printing Services Inc (HQ) .... E 562 598-2446
3701 Catalina St Los Alamitos (90720) *(P-3698)*

TREND OFFSET PRINTING SERVICES INCORPORATED, Los Alamitos *Also Called: Trend Offset Printing Svcs Inc (P-3699)*

Trend Offset Printing Svcs Inc .... B 562 598-2446
3791 Catalina St Los Alamitos (90720) *(P-3699)*

Trend Technologies, Chino *Also Called: Trend Technologies LLC (P-6334)*

Trend Technologies LLC (DH) .... C 909 597-7861
4626 Eucalyptus Ave Chino (91710) *(P-6334)*

Trepanning Specialities Inc .... E 562 633-8110
16201 Illinois Ave Paramount (90723) *(P-8051)*

Trepanning Specialties, Paramount *Also Called: Trepanning Specialities Inc (P-8051)*

Treston IAC LLC .... E 714 990-8997
8175 E Brookdale Ln Anaheim (92807) *(P-3033)*

Trey Arch LLC .... B 310 581-4700
3420 Ocean Park Blvd Ste 2000 Santa Monica (90405) *(P-12447)*

Trg Inc .... D 310 396-6750
1350 Abbot Kinney Blvd # 101 Venice (90291) *(P-14876)*

Trg Insurance Services .... C 949 474-1550
4675 Macarthur Ct Newport Beach (92660) *(P-14636)*

Tri City Mental Health Center, Pomona *Also Called: Tri-City Mental Health Auth (P-18726)*

Tri Models Inc .... D 714 896-0823
5191 Oceanus Dr Huntington Beach (92649) *(P-9557)*

Tri Pointe, Irvine *Also Called: Tri Pointe Homes Inc (P-476)*

Tri Pointe Homes Inc (HQ) .... D 949 438-1400
3161 Michelson Dr Ste 1500 Irvine (92612) *(P-476)*

Tri Pointe Homes Inc .... C 714 389-5933
57 Furlong Irvine (92602) *(P-477)*

Tri Pointe Homes Inc .... C 949 478-8600
5 Peters Canyon Rd Ste 100 Irvine (92606) *(P-488)*

Tri Precision Sheetmetal Inc .... E 714 632-8838
845 N Elm St Orange (92867) *(P-6335)*

Tri Star Engineering Inc .... D 619 710-8038
6774 Calle De Linea Ste 106 San Diego (92154) *(P-19708)*

Tri State Truss Corporation .... E 760 326-3868
600 River Rd Needles (92363) *(P-2705)*

Tri-Ad .... C 760 743-7555
221 W Crest St Ste 300 Escondido (92025) *(P-14637)*

Tri-Ad, Escondido *Also Called: Tri-Ad Actuaries Inc (P-20265)*

Tri-Ad Actuaries Inc .... C 760 743-7555
221 W Crest St Ste 300 Escondido (92025) *(P-20265)*

Tri-City Hospital District .... B 760 931-3171
6250 El Camino Real Carlsbad (92009) *(P-17417)*

Tri-City Hospital District (PA) .... A 760 724-8411
4002 Vista Way Oceanside (92056) *(P-18480)*

Tri-City Medical Center, Oceanside *Also Called: Tri-City Hospital District (P-18480)*

Tri-City Mental Health Auth (PA) .... D 909 623-6131
2008 N Garey Ave Pomona (91767) *(P-18726)*

Tri-City Wellness Center, Carlsbad *Also Called: Tri-City Hospital District (P-17417)*

Tri-Cnties Assn For Dvlpmntlly .... C 805 543-2833
1146 Farmhouse Ln San Luis Obispo (93401) *(P-19147)*

Tri-Co Building Supply Inc .... E 805 343-2555
695 Obispo St Guadalupe (93434) *(P-2706)*

Tri-Counties Regional Center, San Luis Obispo *Also Called: Tri-Cnties Assn For Dvlpmntlly (P-19147)*

Tri-Dim Filter Corporation .... E 626 826-5893
15271 Fairfield Ranch Rd Ste 150 Chino Hills (91709) *(P-7336)*

Tri-J Metal Heat Treating Co (PA) .... F 909 622-9999
327 E Commercial St Pomona (91767) *(P-5852)*

Tri-Modal Dist Svcs Inc .... D 310 522-1844
22560 Lucerne St Carson (90745) *(P-11624)*

Tri-Mountain, Irwindale *Also Called: Mountain Gear Corporation (P-13107)*

Tri-Net Inc .... E 909 483-3555
14721 Hilton Dr Fontana (92336) *(P-10228)*

Tri-Net Technology Inc .... C 909 598-8818
21709 Ferrero Walnut (91789) *(P-7575)*

Tri-Pack Enterprises Inc .... C 760 737-7995
946 S Andreasen Dr Escondido (92029) *(P-3160)*

Tri-Signal Integration Inc (PA) .... D 818 566-8558
28110 Avenue Stanford Unit D Santa Clarita (91355) *(P-947)*

Tri-Star Dyeing & Finshg Inc .... D 562 483-0123
15125 Marquardt Ave Santa Fe Springs (90670) *(P-2052)*

Tri-Star Laminates Inc .... E 949 587-3200
20322 Windrow Dr Ste 100 Lake Forest (92630) *(P-8741)*

Tri-Tech Logistics LLC .... C 855 373-7049
1370 Brea Blvd Ste 200 Fullerton (92835) *(P-11812)*

ALPHABETIC

Tri-Tech Metals Inc ....F...... 909 948-1401
9039 Charles Smith Ave Rancho Cucamonga (91730) *(P-12579)*

Tri-Tech Precision Inc ....F...... 714 970-1363
1863 N Case St Orange (92865) *(P-9819)*

Tri-Tech Systems Inc (PA) ....B...... 818 222-6811
23801 Calabasas Rd Ste 2022 Calabasas (91302) *(P-16138)*

Tri-Tek Electronics, Valencia Also Called: Interconnect Solutions Co LLC *(P-9062)*

Tri-Union Seafoods LLC (DH) ....D...... 424 397-8556
2150 E Grand Ave El Segundo (90245) *(P-13288)*

Tri-Valley Corporation ....E...... 661 864-0500
4927 Calloway Dr Ste 101 Bakersfield (93312) *(P-269)*

Tri-West Ltd (PA) ....C...... 562 692-9166
12005 Pike St Santa Fe Springs (90670) *(P-12319)*

Triad Bellows, Anaheim Also Called: Triad Bellows Design & Mfg Inc *(P-6084)*

Triad Bellows Design & Mfg Inc ....E...... 714 204-4444
2897 E La Cresta Ave Anaheim (92806) *(P-6084)*

Triad Components Group Inc (PA) ....F...... 619 993-3800
1675 Pioneer Way Ste C El Cajon (92020) *(P-9132)*

Triad Systems International, Calabasas Also Called: Tri-Tech Systems Inc *(P-16138)*

Triangle Distributing Co ....B...... 562 699-3424
12065 Pike St Santa Fe Springs (90670) *(P-13473)*

Triangle Rock Products LLC ....B...... 818 553-8820
500 N Brand Blvd Ste 500 Glendale (91203) *(P-403)*

Triangle West, Santa Fe Springs Also Called: Gale/Triangle Inc *(P-11453)*

Tribe Mdia Corp A Cal Nnprfit ....E...... 213 368-1661
3250 Wilshire Blvd Los Angeles (90010) *(P-3332)*

Tribridge Holdings LLC ....A...... 813 287-8887
523 W 6th St Ste 830 Los Angeles (90014) *(P-16139)*

Tribute Portfolio Hotels, Palm Springs Also Called: Riviera Palm Sprng A Trbute PR *(P-15330)*

Trical Inc ....E...... 951 737-6960
1029 Railroad St Corona (92882) *(P-4553)*

Trical Inc ....E...... 661 824-2494
1667 Purdy Rd Mojave (93501) *(P-4554)*

Trico Leasing Company LLC ....D...... 877 259-9997
30154 Rhone Dr Rancho Palos Verdes (90275) *(P-12886)*

Tricom Management Inc ....C...... 714 630-2029
4025 E La Palma Ave Ste 101 Anaheim (92807) *(P-20107)*

Tricom Research Inc ....D...... 949 250-6024
17791 Sky Park Cir Ste J Irvine (92614) *(P-8591)*

Tricom Research Inc ....D...... 949 250-6024
17791 Sky Park Cir Ste J Irvine (92614) *(P-8592)*

Tricon American Homes LLC ....C...... 844 874-2661
15771 Red Hill Ave Tustin (92780) *(P-461)*

Tricor Refining LLC ....E...... 661 393-7110
1134 Manor St Bakersfield (93308) *(P-4653)*

Trident Dental Labratories, Hawthorne Also Called: Trident Labs LLC *(P-18575)*

Trident Labs LLC ....C...... 310 915-9121
12000 Aviation Blvd Hawthorne (90250) *(P-18575)*

Trident Maritime Systems Inc ....E...... 619 346-3800
651 Drucker Ln San Diego (92154) *(P-9848)*

Trident Plating Inc ....E...... 562 906-2556
10046 Romandel Ave Santa Fe Springs (90670) *(P-6673)*

Trident Space & Defense LLC ....E...... 310 214-5500
19951 Mariner Ave Torrance (90503) *(P-8913)*

Trident Technologies, San Diego Also Called: Chemtreat Inc *(P-4600)*

Trigild International Inc ....C...... 949 645-2221
1680 Superior Ave Costa Mesa (92627) *(P-15394)*

Trigon Electronics Inc ....F...... 714 633-7442
22865 Savi Ranch Pkwy Ste A Yorba Linda (92887) *(P-9263)*

Trilar Management Group ....C...... 951 925-2021
1025 S Gilbert St Hemet (92543) *(P-20108)*

Trilink Biotechnologies LLC ....C...... 800 863-6801
10770 Wateridge Cir Ste 200 San Diego (92121) *(P-19885)*

Trilogy Golf At La Quinta ....B...... 760 771-0707
60151 Trilogy Pkwy La Quinta (92253) *(P-17442)*

Trilogy Plumbing Inc ....C...... 714 441-2952
1525 S Sinclair St Anaheim (92806) *(P-830)*

Trim Quick, Corona Also Called: Vinylvisions Company LLC *(P-4508)*

Trim-Lok, Buena Park Also Called: Rubber-Trim Products Inc *(P-4792)*

Trim-Lok Inc (PA) ....C...... 714 562-0500
6855 Hermosa Cir Buena Park (90620) *(P-5233)*

Trimark Orange County, Irvine Also Called: Trimark Raygal LLC *(P-12464)*

Trimark Raygal LLC ....C...... 949 474-1000
210 Commerce Dr Irvine (92602) *(P-12464)*

Trimas Aerospace, Simi Valley Also Called: Rsa Engineered Products LLC *(P-9780)*

Trimatic, Pasadena Also Called: C & D Precision Components Inc *(P-7792)*

Trimco Finish Inc ....C...... 714 708-0300
3130 W Harvard St Santa Ana (92704) *(P-1024)*

Trinamix Inc (PA) ....B...... 408 507-3583
35 Amoret Dr Irvine (92602) *(P-20266)*

Trinity Brdcstg Netwrk Inc ....C...... 714 665-3619
2442 Michelle Dr Tustin (92780) *(P-11965)*

Trinity Christn Ctr Santa Ana, Tustin Also Called: Trinity Brdcstg Netwrk Inc *(P-11965)*

Trinity Health Systems (PA) ....D...... 626 960-1971
14318 Ohio St Baldwin Park (91706) *(P-18063)*

Trinity International Inds LLC ....E...... 800 985-5506
930 E 233rd St Carson (90745) *(P-5234)*

Trinity Lighweight, Frazier Park Also Called: Trnlwb LLC *(P-11300)*

Trinity Process Solutions Inc ....E...... 714 701-1112
4740 E Bryson St Anaheim (92807) *(P-6853)*

Trinity Robotics Automtn LLC ....F...... 562 690-4525
4582 Brickell Privado St Ontario (91761) *(P-7173)*

Trinity Sports Inc ....B...... 323 277-9288
2067 E 55th St Vernon (90058) *(P-2291)*

Trinity Woodworks Inc ....E...... 760 639-5351
2620 Temple Heights Dr Oceanside (92056) *(P-2639)*

Trinium Technologies, Long Beach Also Called: QED Software LLC *(P-16360)*

Trinus Corporation ....C...... 818 246-1143
35 N Lake Ave Ste 710 Pasadena (91101) *(P-16140)*

Trio, Azusa Also Called: Trio Engineered Products Inc *(P-6945)*

Trio Engineered Products Inc (HQ) ....E...... 626 851-3966
505 W Foothill Blvd Azusa (91702) *(P-6945)*

Trio Manufacturing Inc ....C...... 310 640-6123
601 Lairport St El Segundo (90245) *(P-9820)*

Trio Metal Stamping, City Of Industry Also Called: Trio Metal Stamping Inc *(P-6336)*

Trio Metal Stamping Inc ....D...... 626 336-1228
15318 Proctor Ave City Of Industry (91745) *(P-6336)*

Tripalink Corp ....C...... 323 717-9139
600 Wilshire Blvd Ste 1540 Los Angeles (90005) *(P-20109)*

Triple A Containers Inc ....D...... 562 404-7433
16069 Shoemaker Ave Cerritos (90703) *(P-3133)*

Triple D and DS ....E
4040 Calle Platino Ste 105 Oceanside (92056) *(P-3251)*

Triple DOT Corp ....E...... 714 241-0888
3302 S Susan St Santa Ana (92704) *(P-4867)*

Triple Five Nutrition LLC ....E...... 310 502-2277
17120 S Figueroa St Gardena (90248) *(P-1286)*

Triple H Food Processors LLC ....D...... 951 352-5700
5821 Wilderness Ave Riverside (92504) *(P-1999)*

Triple R Transportation Inc ....D...... 661 725-6494
978 Rd 192 Delano (93215) *(P-11408)*

Tristaff Group, Fallbrook Also Called: Garich Inc *(P-15848)*

Tristar Insurance Group Inc (PA) ....A...... 562 495-6600
100 Oceangate Ste 700 Long Beach (90802) *(P-14532)*

Tristar Risk Management, Long Beach Also Called: Tristar Insurance Group Inc *(P-14532)*

Tristar Service Company Inc (HQ) ....B...... 562 495-6600
100 Oceangate Ste 700 Long Beach (90802) *(P-14638)*

Triton, Newport Beach Also Called: Triton Chandelier Inc *(P-8336)*

Triton Chandelier Inc ....F...... 714 957-9600
1301 Dove St Ste 900 Newport Beach (92660) *(P-8336)*

Triton Structural Concrete Inc ....C...... 858 866-2450
15435 Innovation Dr Ste 225 San Diego (92128) *(P-596)*

Triumph Acttion Systems - Vlnc ....C...... 661 702-7537
28150 Harrison Pkwy Valencia (91355) *(P-9821)*

Triumph Group, Valencia Also Called: Triumph Acttion Systems - Vlnc *(P-9821)*

Triumph Group, Calexico Also Called: Triumph Insulation Systems LLC *(P-9822)*

Triumph Insulation Systems LLC ....A...... 760 618-7543
1754 Carr Rd Ste 103 Calexico (92231) *(P-9822)*

Triumph Precision Products ....F...... 818 897-4700
13636 Vaughn St Ste A San Fernando (91340) *(P-6425)*

Triumph Proc - Embee Div Inc ....B...... 714 546-9842
2158 S Hathaway St Santa Ana (92705) *(P-6674)*

Mergent email: customerrelations@mergent.com
1300

2024 Southern California
Business Directory and Buyers Guide

(P-0000) Products & Services Section entry number
(PA)=Parent Co (HQ)=Headquarters (DH)=Div Headquarters

Triumph Processing Inc .... C 323 563-1338
2605 Industry Way Lynwood (90262) *(P-6675)*

Triumph Structures, City Of Industry *Also Called: Triumph Structures - Everett Inc (P-9823)*

Triumph Structures - Brea, Chatsworth *Also Called: Alatus Aerosystems (P-9617)*

Triumph Structures - Everett Inc .... C 425 348-4100
17055 Gale Ave City Of Industry (91745) *(P-9823)*

Triune Enterprises Inc .... E 310 719-1600
13711 S Normandie Ave Gardena (90249) *(P-3161)*

Triune Enterprises Mfg, Gardena *Also Called: Triune Enterprises Inc (P-3161)*

Trius Therapeutics Inc .... C 858 452-0370
4747 Executive Dr Ste 1100 San Diego (92121) *(P-4248)*

Trivascular Inc (DH) .... E 707 543-8800
2 Musick Irvine (92618) *(P-10621)*

Trivascular Technologies Inc (HQ) .... C 707 543-8800
2 Musick Irvine (92618) *(P-10622)*

Triview, La Habra *Also Called: Triview Glass Industries LLC (P-5358)*

Triview Glass Industries LLC .... D 626 363-7980
279 Shawnan Ln La Habra (90631) *(P-5358)*

Trixxi Clothing Company Inc (PA) .... E 323 585-4200
6817 E Acco St Commerce (90040) *(P-2292)*

Triyar Sv LLC (PA) .... B 310 234-2888
10850 Wilshire Blvd Ste 1050 Los Angeles (90024) *(P-14877)*

TRL Systems Incorporated .... D 909 390-8392
9531 Milliken Ave Rancho Cucamonga (91730) *(P-948)*

Trlg Corporate Holdings LLC (PA) .... D 323 266-3072
1888 Rosecrans Ave Manhattan Beach (90266) *(P-2419)*

Trlggc Services LLC .... B 323 266-3072
1888 Rosecrans Ave Manhattan Beach (90266) *(P-13115)*

TRM Manufacturing Inc .... C 951 256-8550
375 Trm Cir Corona (92879) *(P-4824)*

Trnlwb LLC .... A 661 245-3736
17410 Lockwood Valley Rd Frazier Park (93225) *(P-11300)*

Troesh Readymix Inc .... E 805 928-3764
2280 Hutton Rd Nipomo (93444) *(P-5516)*

Trojan Battery Company LLC (DH) .... C 562 236-3000
12380 Clark St Santa Fe Springs (90670) *(P-9161)*

Trojan Battery Holdings LLC .... E 800 423-6569
12380 Clark St Santa Fe Springs (90670) *(P-9157)*

Trojan Professional Svcs Inc .... D 714 816-7169
11075 Knott Ave Ste A Cypress (90630) *(P-16536)*

Trona Railway Company .... A 760 372-2312
13068 Main St Trona (93562) *(P-11312)*

Troon Golf LLC .... C 760 346-4653
44500 Indian Wells Ln Indian Wells (92210) *(P-20110)*

Troop Real Estate Inc .... C 805 402-3028
4165 E Thousand Oaks Blvd Ste 100 Westlake Village (91362) *(P-14878)*

Troop Real Estate Inc .... C 805 921-0030
586 W Main St Santa Paula (93060) *(P-14879)*

Troop Real Estate Inc .... C 805 640-1440
236 W Ojai Ave Ste 100 Ojai (93023) *(P-14880)*

Troop Real Estate Inc (PA) .... D 805 581-3200
1308 Madera Rd Ste 8 Simi Valley (93065) *(P-14881)*

Tropi-Con Foods Inc .... E 949 472-2200
3691 Noakes St Los Angeles (90023) *(P-6874)*

Tropical Functional Labs LLC .... E 951 688-2619
7111 Arlington Ave Ste F Riverside (92503) *(P-1287)*

Tropical Plaza Nursery Inc .... D 714 998-4100
9642 Santiago Blvd Villa Park (92867) *(P-217)*

Tropical Preserving Co Inc .... E 213 748-5108
5 Lewiston Ct Ladera Ranch (92694) *(P-1347)*

Tropicale Foods LLC (PA) .... D 909 635-1000
1237 W State St Ontario (91762) *(P-1301)*

Tropicana, City Of Industry *Also Called: Tropicana Products Inc (P-1348)*

Tropicana Products Inc .... E 626 968-1299
240 N Orange Ave City Of Industry (91744) *(P-1348)*

Tropitone Furniture Co Inc (DH) .... B 949 595-2010
5 Marconi Irvine (92618) *(P-2839)*

Trouble At The Mill, Huntington Park *Also Called: Cotton Generation Inc (P-2406)*

Troutman Ppper Hmlton Snders L .... D 949 622-2700
5 Park Plz Ste 1400 Irvine (92614) *(P-18952)*

Troutman Sanders, Irvine *Also Called: Troutman Ppper Hmlton Snders L (P-18952)*

Trovata, Solana Beach *Also Called: Trovata Inc (P-16141)*

Trovata Inc (PA) .... D 312 914-8106
312 S Cedros Ave Ste 312 Solana Beach (92075) *(P-16141)*

Troy Metal Products, Goleta *Also Called: Neal Feay Company (P-5704)*

Troy Products, Montebello *Also Called: Troy Sheet Metal Works Inc (P-6489)*

Troy Sheet Metal Works Inc (PA) .... D 323 720-4100
1024 S Vail Ave Montebello (90640) *(P-6489)*

Troy-Csl Lighting Inc .... C 626 336-4511
14508 Nelson Ave City Of Industry (91744) *(P-8298)*

Troygould PC .... D 310 553-4441
1801 Century Park E Ste 1600 Los Angeles (90067) *(P-18953)*

Trs Rentelco, Jurupa Valley *Also Called: Mobile Modular Management Corp (P-6385)*

Trs Staffing Solutions, Aliso Viejo *Also Called: Fluor Corporation (P-19590)*

Tru Form Industries, Santa Fe Springs *Also Called: Tru-Form Industries Inc (P-6564)*

Tru-Cut Inc .... E 310 630-0422
141 E 157th St Gardena (90248) *(P-6922)*

Tru-Duct Inc .... E 619 660-3858
2515 Industry St Oceanside (92054) *(P-6337)*

Tru-Form Industries Inc (PA) .... D 562 802-2041
14511 Anson Ave Santa Fe Springs (90670) *(P-6564)*

Tru-Form Plastics Inc .... E 310 327-9444
14600 Hoover St Westminster (92683) *(P-5235)*

Tru-Wood Products, Azusa *Also Called: McMurtrie & Mcmurtrie Inc (P-2576)*

Truabutment Inc .... D 714 956-1488
17666 Fitch Irvine (92614) *(P-10774)*

Truaire, Santa Fe Springs *Also Called: TA Industries Inc (P-12748)*

Truck Underwriters Association .... A 323 932-3200
6303 Owensmouth Ave Fl 1 Woodland Hills (91367) *(P-14444)*

Truck Underwriters Association (DH) .... A 323 932-3200
4680 Wilshire Blvd Los Angeles (90010) *(P-19406)*

Truconnect Communications Inc (PA) .... C 512 919-2641
1149 S Hill St Ste 400 Los Angeles (90015) *(P-11910)*

True Air Mechanical Inc .... C 888 316-0642
1801 California Ave Corona (92881) *(P-831)*

True Cast Concrete Products, Sun Valley *Also Called: Quikrete Companies LLC (P-5444)*

True Cast Concrete Products, Sun Valley *Also Called: Gibbel Bros Inc (P-5478)*

True Classic Tees LLC .... E 323 419-1092
26635 Agoura Rd Ste 105 Calabasas (91302) *(P-2165)*

True Digital Surgery, Goleta *Also Called: Digital Surgery Systems Inc (P-10494)*

True Fresh Hpp LLC .... E 949 922-8801
6535 Caballero Blvd Unit B Buena Park (90620) *(P-10108)*

True Home Heating and AC, Corona *Also Called: True Air Mechanical Inc (P-831)*

True Investments LLC (PA) .... E 949 258-9720
2260 University Dr Newport Beach (92660) *(P-15056)*

True Investments LLC .... E 949 258-9720
6535 Caballero Blvd Unit B Buena Park (90620) *(P-15057)*

True Investments LLC, Buena Park *Also Called: True Investments LLC (P-15057)*

True Position Technologies LLC .... D 661 294-0030
24900 Avenue Stanford Valencia (91355) *(P-8052)*

True Precision Machining Inc .... E 805 964-4545
175 Industrial Way Buellton (93427) *(P-8053)*

True Religion Apparel, Gardena *Also Called: Guru Denim LLC (P-13908)*

True Religion Apparel Inc (HQ) .... B 323 266-3072
500 W 190th St Ste 300 Gardena (90248) *(P-2172)*

True Religion Brand Jeans, Gardena *Also Called: True Religion Apparel Inc (P-2172)*

True Warrior LLC .... E 661 237-6588
21226 Lone Star Way Santa Clarita (91390) *(P-2460)*

Truecare .... C 760 736-6767
150 Valpreda Rd San Marcos (92069) *(P-17807)*

Trueclass, Foothill Ranch *Also Called: Twila True Collaborations LLC (P-4463)*

Truevision 3d Surgical, Goleta *Also Called: Truevision Systems Inc (P-10623)*

Truevision Systems Inc .... E 805 963-9700
315 Bollay Dr Ste 101 Goleta (93117) *(P-10623)*

Trugreen, San Diego *Also Called: Landcare USA LLC (P-198)*

Trugreen, Santa Ana *Also Called: Landcare USA LLC (P-199)*

Truitt Oilfield Maint Corp .... B 661 871-4099
1051 James Rd Bakersfield (93308) *(P-389)*

Trulite GL Alum Solutions LLC .... D 800 877-8439
19430 San Jose Ave City Of Industry (91748) *(P-5712)*

Employee Codes: A=Over 500 employees, B=251-500
C=101-250, D=51-100, E=20-50, F=10-19, G=1-9

2024 Southern California
Business Directory and Buyers Guide

© Mergent Inc. 1-800-342-5647

1301

ALPHABETIC

Truly Green Solutions LLC ....E...... 818 206-4404
9601 Variel Ave Chatsworth (91311) *(P-8387)*

Trumed Systems Incorporated ....E...... 844 878-6331
4370 La Jolla Village Dr Ste 200 San Diego (92122) *(P-7630)*

Trump Nat Golf CLB Los Angeles, Rancho Palos Verdes *Also Called: Estates At Trump Nat Golf CLB (P-17427)*

Truspro, Guadalupe *Also Called: Tri-Co Building Supply Inc (P-2706)*

Trussworks International Inc ....D...... 714 630-2772
1275 E Franklin Ave Pomona (91766) *(P-6085)*

Trust 1 Sales Inc ....D...... 323 732-3300
1737 S Vermont Ave Los Angeles (90006) *(P-12465)*

Trust Automation Inc ....D...... 805 544-0761
125 Venture Dr Ste 110 San Luis Obispo (93401) *(P-19709)*

Trust Company of West ....A...... 213 244-0000
865 S Figueroa St Ste 1800 Los Angeles (90017) *(P-14406)*

Trust Employee ADM & MGT, San Diego *Also Called: Team Risk MGT Strategies LLC (P-20385)*

Trustee Corps, Irvine *Also Called: Mtc Financial Inc (P-20064)*

Truxtun Radiology Med Group LP ....C...... 661 822-6619
20960 Sage Ln Ste B Tehachapi (93561) *(P-17808)*

Truxtun Radiology Med Group LP ....C...... 661 325-6200
3940 San Dimas St Bakersfield (93301) *(P-17809)*

Truxtun Radiology Med Group LP ....C...... 661 616-1201
1917 Truxtun Ave Bakersfield (93301) *(P-17810)*

Truxtun Radiology Med Group LP ....C...... 661 205-6567
11622 Harrington St Bakersfield (93311) *(P-17811)*

Tryad Service Corporation ....D...... 661 391-1524
5900 E Lerdo Hwy Shafter (93263) *(P-390)*

TS Enterprises Inc ....E...... 760 360-5991
78250 Highway 111 La Quinta (92253) *(P-14040)*

Tsb2 Llc ....D...... 619 255-9679
1745 National Ave San Diego (92113) *(P-1608)*

TSC Auto ID Technology America (HQ).....................**C...... 909 468-0100**
3040 Saturn St Ste 200 Brea (92821) *(P-12887)*

Tst Inc (PA)..**B...... 951 685-2155**
13428 Benson Ave Chino (91710) *(P-5685)*

Tst Inc ....E...... 310 835-0115
2132 E Dominguez St Long Beach (90810) *(P-12958)*

TST Molding LLC ....E...... 951 296-6200
42322 Avenida Alvarado Temecula (92590) *(P-5236)*

Tst/Impreso Inc ....E...... 909 357-7190
10589 Business Dr Fontana (92337) *(P-3833)*

TT Elctrnics Pwr Sltons US Inc ....C...... 626 967-6021
1330 E Cypress St Covina (91724) *(P-9133)*

TT Electronics, Brea *Also Called: Bi Technologies Corporation (P-9005)*

Tte Technology Inc ....C...... 877 300-8837
189 Technology Dr Irvine (92618) *(P-12638)*

Ttg Engineers ....B...... 626 463-2800
300 N Lake Ave Fl 14 Pasadena (91101) *(P-19710)*

TTI Floor Care North Amer Inc ....D...... 440 996-2802
13055 Valley Blvd Fontana (92335) *(P-4716)*

TTI Performance Exhaust, Corona *Also Called: Tube Technologies Inc (P-9476)*

Ttm, Santa Ana *Also Called: Ttm Technologies Inc (P-8743)*

Ttm Printed Circuit Group Inc (HQ).........................**C...... 714 327-3000**
2630 S Harbor Blvd Santa Ana (92704) *(P-8742)*

Ttm Technologies Inc (PA).......................................**B...... 714 327-3000**
200 Sandpointe Ave Ste 400 Santa Ana (92707) *(P-8743)*

Ttm Technologies Inc ....B...... 714 241-0303
2630 S Harbor Blvd Santa Ana (92704) *(P-8744)*

Ttm Technologies Inc ....B...... 714 688-7200
3140 E Coronado St Anaheim (92806) *(P-8745)*

Ttm Technologies Inc ....C...... 858 874-2701
5037 Ruffner St San Diego (92111) *(P-8746)*

TTT Concrete, Lakeside *Also Called: Superior Ready Mix Concrete LP (P-5514)*

TTT Innovations, Chatsworth *Also Called: TTT Innovations LLC (P-11301)*

TTT Innovations LLC ....E...... 818 201-8828
20850 Plummer St Chatsworth (91311) *(P-11301)*

Tu Madre Romana Inc ....C...... 323 321-6041
13633 S Western Ave Gardena (90249) *(P-2000)*

Tu-K Industries Inc ....E...... 562 927-3365
5702 Firestone Pl South Gate (90280) *(P-4462)*

Tube Lighting Products, El Cajon *Also Called: Tujayar Enterprises Inc (P-8337)*

Tube Technologies Inc ....E...... 951 371-4878
1555 Consumer Cir Corona (92878) *(P-9476)*

Tube-Line Technologies ....F...... 951 834-3123
340 Via El Centro Oceanside (92058) *(P-5605)*

Tube-Tainer Inc ....E...... 562 945-3711
8174 Byron Rd Whittier (90606) *(P-3140)*

Tubing Seal Cap Co, Anaheim *Also Called: Pacific Precision Metals Inc (P-6546)*

Tuboscope, Bakersfield *Also Called: Tuboscope Pipeline Svcs Inc (P-391)*

Tuboscope Pipeline Svcs Inc ....F...... 661 328-5500
3003 Fairhaven Dr Ste B Bakersfield (93308) *(P-391)*

Tubular Specialties Mfg Inc ....D...... 310 515-4801
13011 S Spring St Los Angeles (90061) *(P-5378)*

Tuffer Manufacturing Co Inc ....E...... 714 526-3077
163 E Liberty Ave Anaheim (92801) *(P-10086)*

Tuffstuff Fitness Intl Inc ....D...... 909 629-1600
155 N Riverview Dr Anaheim (92808) *(P-11036)*

Tujayar Enterprises Inc ....E...... 619 442-0577
1346 Pioneer Way El Cajon (92020) *(P-8337)*

Tumbleweed Day Camp, Los Angeles *Also Called: Tumbleweed Eductl Entps Inc (P-17575)*

Tumbleweed Eductl Entps Inc ....C...... 310 444-3232
1024 Hanley Ave Los Angeles (90049) *(P-17575)*

Tur-Bo Jet Products Co Inc ....D...... 626 285-1294
5025 Earle Ave Rosemead (91770) *(P-8956)*

Turbine Repair Services LLC (PA)..............................**E...... 909 947-2256**
1838 E Cedar St Ontario (91761) *(P-6890)*

Turbo Coil Inc ....E...... 626 644-6254
1532 Sinaloa Ave Pasadena (91104) *(P-7631)*

Turbo Coil Manufacturing Inc ....E...... 626 599-7777
1740 Evergreen St Duarte (91010) *(P-8957)*

Turbotax, San Diego *Also Called: Intuit Inc (P-16273)*

Turn Around Communications Inc ....C...... 626 443-2400
100 N Barranca St Ste 260 West Covina (91791) *(P-699)*

Turn Key Scaffold LLC ....C...... 619 642-0880
410 W 30th St National City (91950) *(P-1180)*

Turner Construction Company ....B...... 714 940-9000
1900 S State College Blvd Ste 200 Anaheim (92806) *(P-597)*

Turner Fiberfill Inc ....E...... 323 724-7957
1600 Date St Montebello (90640) *(P-3988)*

Turner Precision, Gardena *Also Called: Aldo Fragale (P-7750)*

TURNING POINT COUNSELING, Fullerton *Also Called: Turning Point Ministries (P-19149)*

Turning Point For God ....D...... 619 258-3600
San Diego (92163) *(P-19148)*

Turning Point Ministries ....D...... 800 998-6329
1370 Brea Blvd Ste 245 Fullerton (92835) *(P-19149)*

Turning Point Therapeutics Inc ....D...... 858 926-5251
10300 Campus Point Dr San Diego (92121) *(P-19886)*

Turnkey Foundation Inc ....D...... 949 557-6203
1805 E Garry Ave Ste 130 Santa Ana (92705) *(P-14353)*

Turret Lathe Specialists Inc ....F...... 714 520-0058
875 S Rose Pl Anaheim (92805) *(P-8054)*

Turtle Beach, San Diego *Also Called: Voyetra Turtle Beach Inc (P-7579)*

Turtle Rock Cdc, Irvine *Also Called: Child Development Incorporated (P-19205)*

Turtle Storage Ltd ....E...... 805 933-3688
401 S Beckwith Rd Santa Paula (93060) *(P-2997)*

Turtleback Case, Sylmar *Also Called: Leather Pro Inc (P-5302)*

Tusimple, San Diego *Also Called: Tusimple Holdings Inc (P-16475)*

Tusimple Holdings Inc (PA).......................................**B...... 619 916-3144**
9191 Towne Centre Dr Ste 600 San Diego (92122) *(P-16475)*

Tustin Executive Center, Tustin *Also Called: Southern Cal Prmnnte Med Group (P-14503)*

Tustin Hospital, Tustin *Also Called: Pacific Health Corporation (P-18358)*

Tustin Hospital and Medical Center ....B...... 714 619-7700
3699 Wilshire Blvd # 540 Los Angeles (90010) *(P-18481)*

Tustin Ranch Golf Club, Tustin *Also Called: Crown Golf Properties LP (P-20160)*

Tustin Saab, Tustin *Also Called: Nissan of Tustin (P-13804)*

Tustin Unified School District ....C...... 714 542-4271
16791 E Main St Tustin (92780) *(P-18985)*

TUTOR PERINI, Rancho Cascades *Also Called: Tutor Perini Corporation (P-598)*

Tutor Perini Corporation (PA)...................................**C...... 818 362-8391**
15901 Olden St Rancho Cascades (91342) *(P-598)*

Tutor Time Learning Ctrs LLC ....C...... 714 484-1000
5805 Corporate Ave Cypress (90630) *(P-19232)*

Tutor Time Learning Ctrs LLC ....C...... 818 710-1677
5855 De Soto Ave Woodland Hills (91367) *(P-19233)*

Tutor-Saliba Corporation (HQ).....................................**D...... 818 362-8391**
15901 Olden St Rancho Cascades (91342) *(P-599)*

Tutor-Saliba Perini ....A...... 818 362-8391
15901 Olden St Sylmar (91342) *(P-600)*

Tuttle Click Ford, Irvine *Also Called: Tuttle-Click Ford Inc (P-13841)*

Tuttle Family Enterprises Inc ....B...... 818 534-2566
9510 Topanga Canyon Blvd Chatsworth (91311) *(P-15751)*

Tuttle-Click Ford Inc ....C...... 949 855-1704
43 Auto Center Dr Irvine (92618) *(P-13841)*

TV Ears Inc ....E...... 619 797-1600
2701 Via Orange Way Ste 1 Spring Valley (91978) *(P-12707)*

TV Guide Entrmt Group LLC ....D...... 310 360-1441
2700 Colorado Ave Ste 200 Santa Monica (90404) *(P-12639)*

TW Holdings Inc ....A...... 858 217-8750
10805 Rancho Bernardo Rd Ste 120 San Diego (92127) *(P-17418)*

TW Security Corp (DH)..**C...... 949 932-1000**
5 Park Plz Ste 400 Irvine (92614) *(P-12448)*

TW Services Inc ....B...... 714 441-2400
1801 W Romneya Dr Ste 601 Anaheim (92801) *(P-11841)*

Twdc Enterprises 18 Corp (HQ)....................................**A...... 818 560-1000**
500 S Buena Vista St Burbank (91521) *(P-11966)*

Twed-Dells Inc ....E...... 714 754-6900
1900 S Susan St Santa Ana (92704) *(P-5359)*

Twelve Signs Inc ....F...... 310 553-8000
3369 S Robertson Blvd Los Angeles (90034) *(P-3392)*

Twenteth Cntury Fox HM Entrmt (PA)...........................A...... 310 369-1000
10201 W Pico Blvd Los Angeles (90064) *(P-17228)*

Twentieth Cntury Fox Intl TV In ....A...... 310 369-1000
10201 W Pico Blvd Los Angeles (90064) *(P-11967)*

Twentieth Cntury Fox Intl Corp (HQ)............................**C...... 310 369-1000**
10201 W Pico Blvd Bldg 1 Los Angeles (90064) *(P-17280)*

Twentieth Cntury Fox Japan Inc ....A...... 310 369-4636
10201 W Pico Blvd Los Angeles (90064) *(P-15677)*

Twenty Mile Productions LLC ....C...... 412 251-0767
11833 Mississippi Ave Ste 101 Los Angeles (90025) *(P-17353)*

Twenty4seven Hotels Corp ....B...... 949 734-6400
520 Newport Center Dr Ste 520 Newport Beach (92660) *(P-20111)*

Twila True Collaborations LLC ....E...... 949 258-9720
27156 Burbank Foothill Ranch (92610) *(P-4463)*

Twin Cities Community Hosp Inc ....B...... 805 434-3500
1100 Las Tablas Rd Templeton (93465) *(P-17812)*

Twin Dragon Marketing Inc (PA)....................................**E...... 310 715-7070**
14600 S Broadway Gardena (90248) *(P-2034)*

Twin Eagles Inc ....C...... 562 802-3488
13259 166th St Cerritos (90703) *(P-8225)*

Twin Med Inc ....B
5900 Wilshire Blvd Ste 2600 Los Angeles (90036) *(P-12521)*

Twin Oaks Growers Intl, San Marcos *Also Called: Twin Oaks Growers Intl Inc (P-72)*

Twin Oaks Growers Intl Inc ....E...... 760 744-5581
1969 Marilyn Ln San Marcos (92069) *(P-72)*

Twin Oaks Power LP (HQ)...**D...... 619 696-2034**
101 Ash St Hq10b San Diego (92101) *(P-12079)*

Twin Peak Industries Inc ....E...... 800 259-5906
12420 Montague St Ste E Pacoima (91331) *(P-11037)*

Twin Power Indus Solutions, Murrieta *Also Called: Twin Power Usa LLC (P-949)*

Twin Power Usa LLC ....E...... 714 609-6014
40424 Jacob Way Murrieta (92563) *(P-949)*

Twining Inc (PA)..**D...... 562 426-3355**
2883 E Spring St Ste 300 Long Beach (90806) *(P-19985)*

Twining Laboratories, Long Beach *Also Called: Twining Inc (P-19985)*

Twist Tite Mfg Inc ....E...... 562 229-0990
13344 Cambridge St Santa Fe Springs (90670) *(P-6455)*

Two Bit Circus, Los Angeles *Also Called: Two Bit Circus Dtla LLC (P-17354)*

Two Bit Circus Dtla LLC ....D...... 323 438-9808
634 Mateo St Los Angeles (90021) *(P-17354)*

Two Brothers Racing Inc ....F...... 714 550-6070
3474 Niki Way Riverside (92507) *(P-9887)*

Two Lads Inc (PA)..**E...... 323 584-0064**
5001 Hampton St Vernon (90058) *(P-11079)*

Two Palms Nursing Center Inc ....C...... 626 796-1103
150 Bellefontaine St Pasadena (91105) *(P-18155)*

Twomagnets Inc ....A...... 408 837-0116
440 N Barranca Ave Ste 5028 Covina (91723) *(P-15901)*

TWR Enterprises Inc ....C...... 951 279-2000
1661 Railroad St Corona (92878) *(P-1025)*

Txi Riverside Cement, Riverside *Also Called: Riverside Cement Holdings Company (P-5370)*

Tydg Enterprises Inc ....D...... 562 903-9030
10232 Palm Dr Santa Fe Springs (90670) *(P-14950)*

Tyler Trafficante Inc (PA)..**E...... 323 869-9299**
700 S Palm Ave Alhambra (91803) *(P-2155)*

Typecraft Inc ....E...... 626 795-8093
2040 E Walnut St Pasadena (91107) *(P-3700)*

Typecraft Wood & Jones, Pasadena *Also Called: Typecraft Inc (P-3700)*

Tyr Sport Inc (HQ)..**F...... 714 897-0799**
1790 Apollo Ct Seal Beach (90740) *(P-13155)*

Tyra Biosciences Inc ....E...... 619 728-4760
2656 State St Carlsbad (92008) *(P-4296)*

Tystar Corporation ....E...... 310 781-9219
7050 Lampson Ave Garden Grove (92841) *(P-7263)*

Tyte Jeans, Commerce *Also Called: 4 What Its Worth Inc (P-2189)*

Tyvak Nn-Satellite Systems Inc (DH)............................**D...... 949 753-1020**
15330 Barranca Pkwy Irvine (92618) *(P-9905)*

U C I Distribution Plus, Pasadena *Also Called: United Couriers Inc (P-11673)*

U C L Incorporated (PA)...**D...... 323 235-0099**
620 S Hacienda Blvd City Of Industry (91745) *(P-11509)*

U C S D Medical Center, San Diego *Also Called: University Cal San Diego (P-18485)*

U C San Diego Foundation ....C...... 858 534-1032
9500 Gilman Dr La Jolla (92093) *(P-19535)*

U F C Pension Trust Fund, Cypress *Also Called: Cal Southern United Food (P-14547)*

U F P, San Marcos *Also Called: Unique Functional Products (P-9496)*

U I G, Lake Forest *Also Called: United Industries Group Inc (P-19712)*

U M C, Costa Mesa *Also Called: Universal Motion Components Co Inc (P-7359)*

U S Architectural Lighting, Palmdale *Also Called: US Pole Company Inc (P-8339)*

U S Battery Mfg Co, Corona *Also Called: Palos Verdes Building Corp (P-9153)*

U S C, Burbank *Also Called: Universal Switching Corp (P-8281)*

U S C, Glendale *Also Called: Usc Vrdugo Hlls Hosp Fundation (P-18494)*

U S Circuit Inc ....D...... 760 489-1413
2071 Wineridge Pl Escondido (92029) *(P-9134)*

U S L, San Luis Obispo *Also Called: Ultra-Stereo Labs Inc (P-9264)*

U S Medical Instruments Inc (PA)..................................**E...... 619 661-5500**
888 Prospect St Ste 100 La Jolla (92037) *(P-10624)*

U S Precision Manufacturing, Riverside *Also Called: US Precision Sheet Metal Inc (P-6338)*

U S Saw & Blades, Santa Ana *Also Called: US Saws Inc (P-6946)*

U S Technical Institute, Placentia *Also Called: US Computers Inc (P-7577)*

U S Trust Company NA ....B...... 213 861-5000
515 S Flower St Ste 2700 Los Angeles (90071) *(P-14432)*

U S Weatherford L P ....C...... 661 589-9483
2815 Fruitvale Ave Bakersfield (93308) *(P-392)*

U S Wheel Corporation ....E...... 714 892-0021
15702 Producer Ln Huntington Beach (92649) *(P-9477)*

U S Xpress Inc ....B...... 760 768-6707
363 Nina Lee Rd Calexico (92231) *(P-11510)*

U W G Southern California Div, Los Angeles *Also Called: Unified Grocers Inc (P-11625)*

U-Blox San Diego Inc ....E...... 858 847-9611
12626 High Bluff Dr Ste 200 San Diego (92130) *(P-8486)*

U-Haul, Corona *Also Called: U-Haul Business Consultants (P-16975)*

U-Haul, Moreno Valley *Also Called: U-Haul Leasing & Sales Co (P-16976)*

U-Haul Business Consultants ....C...... 951 736-7811
314 E 6th St Corona (92879) *(P-16975)*

U-Haul Leasing & Sales Co ....B...... 951 485-2003
23730 Sunnymead Blvd Moreno Valley (92553) *(P-16976)*

U-Nited Printing and Copy Ctr, Van Nuys *Also Called: Printrunner LLC (P-3667)*

U-T Direct ....F...... 619 293-1484
350 Camino De La Reina San Diego (92108) *(P-3333)*

U. S. Grant Hotel, San Diego *Also Called: American Prprty-Mnagement Corp (P-15073)*

U.S. Airconditioning Distrs, City Of Industry *Also Called: US Airconditioning Distributors Inc (P-12759)*

Employee Codes: A=Over 500 employees, B=251-500
C=101-250, D=51-100, E=20-50, F=10-19, G=1-9

2024 Southern California
Business Directory and Buyers Guide

© Mergent Inc. 1-800-342-5647

1303

A
L
P
H
A
B
E
T
I
C

U.S. Continental, Corona *Also Called: US Continental Marketing Inc (P-4371)*

U.S. Horizon Mfg, Valencia *Also Called: US Horizon Manufacturing Inc (P-5319)*

U.S. Specialty Vehicles, Yorba Linda *Also Called: American HX Auto Trade Inc (P-9277)*

UAS, Los Angeles *Also Called: Cal State La Univ Aux Svcs Inc (P-20009)*

Ubiq, San Diego *Also Called: Ubiq Security Inc (P-12449)*

Ubiq Security Inc .... E....... 888 434-6674
4660 La Jolla Village Dr Ste 100 San Diego (92122) *(P-12449)*

Ubm Canon LLC (DH) ....**E....... 310 445-4200**
2901 28th St Ste 100 Santa Monica (90405) *(P-3393)*

UBS Americas Inc .... C....... 619 557-2400
600 W Broadway Ste 2800 San Diego (92101) *(P-14407)*

Ubtech Robotics Corp .... E....... 213 261-7153
767 S Alameda St Los Angeles (90021) *(P-7174)*

Uc Irvine Health .... D....... 714 456-6191
200 S Manchester Ave Ste 400 Orange (92868) *(P-18812)*

Uc Irvine Hlth Rgonal Burn Ctr, Orange *Also Called: University California Irvine (P-17817)*

Uc Irvine Medical Center, Orange *Also Called: University California Irvine (P-18488)*

Uc Riverside RES Economic Dev, Riverside *Also Called: University Cal Riverside (P-19914)*

UC SAN DIEGO, La Jolla *Also Called: U C San Diego Foundation (P-19535)*

Ucan Zippers, Los Angeles *Also Called: Catame Inc (P-11069)*

Uce Holdings Inc .... D....... 213 217-4235
411 Center St Los Angeles (90012) *(P-2001)*

UCI Cancer Center, Orange *Also Called: University California Irvine (P-18487)*

UCI Construction Inc .... D....... 661 587-0192
3900 Fruitvale Ave Bakersfield (93308) *(P-19711)*

UCI Division Plastic Surgery, Orange *Also Called: University California Irvine (P-19809)*

UCI Family Health Center, Santa Ana *Also Called: University California Irvine (P-17818)*

UCI Health Blood Donor Center, Irvine *Also Called: University California Irvine (P-18813)*

UCI Westminster Medical Center, Westminster *Also Called: University California Irvine (P-18490)*

Ucla Dept of Design Media, Los Angeles *Also Called: Associated Students UCLA (P-18989)*

Ucla Foundation .... B....... 310 794-3193
10889 Wilshire Blvd Ste 1100 Los Angeles (90024) *(P-14985)*

Ucla Hbr Dlysis Ctr Med Fndtio, Torrance *Also Called: Harbor-Ucla Med Foundation Inc (P-18659)*

Ucla Health Auxiliary .... A....... 310 267-4327
10920 Wilshire Blvd Ste 400 Los Angeles (90024) *(P-18647)*

Ucla Mdcn SC Phrmclgy, Los Angeles *Also Called: Associated Students UCLA (P-17596)*

Ucp of Orange County, Santa Ana *Also Called: United Crbral Plsy Assn Ornge (P-19150)*

Ucsd, San Diego *Also Called: Kelly Thomas MD Ucsd Hlth Care (P-18774)*

Ucsd Fac & Design, La Jolla *Also Called: University Cal San Diego (P-19745)*

Ucsd Neuroscience Center .... D....... 619 287-7661
6645 Alvarado Rd San Diego (92120) *(P-17813)*

Ucsd Thornton Hospital, La Jolla *Also Called: University Cal San Diego (P-18484)*

UDC, Anaheim *Also Called: Universal Dust Clictr Mfg Sup (P-525)*

Ue Authority Co .... D....... 800 466-4178
225 Broadway Ste 2200 San Diego (92101) *(P-15578)*

UFO Designs .... E....... 562 924-5763
16730 Gridley Rd Cerritos (90703) *(P-9478)*

UFO Inc .... E....... 323 588-5450
2110 Belgrave Ave Huntington Park (90255) *(P-5237)*

Ufp Technologies Inc .... E....... 714 662-0277
20211 S Susana Rd Compton (90221) *(P-4908)*

Ugm Citatah Inc (PA) ....**C....... 562 921-9549**
13220 Cambridge St Santa Fe Springs (90670) *(P-12362)*

Ugmc, Santa Fe Springs *Also Called: Ugm Citatah Inc (P-12362)*

Uhc of California (DH) ....A....... 952 936-6615
5995 Plaza Dr Cypress (90630) *(P-14504)*

Uhg Lax Prop Llc ....C....... 310 322-0999
1985 E Grand Ave El Segundo (90245) *(P-15395)*

Uhp Healthcare, Inglewood *Also Called: Watts Health Foundation Inc (P-18103)*

UHS, Chino *Also Called: Canyon Ridge Hospital Inc (P-18509)*

Uhs-Corona Inc (HQ) ....**A....... 951 737-4343**
800 S Main St Corona (92882) *(P-18482)*

Uhs-Corona Inc .... C....... 951 736-7200
730 Magnolia Ave Corona (92879) *(P-18727)*

Ui Medical LLC .... E....... 562 453-1515
1670 W Park Ave Redlands (92373) *(P-3209)*

UIC, Orange *Also Called: University California Irvine (P-17816)*

Uka LLC .... B....... 949 610-8000
620 Newport Center Dr Ste 1400 Newport Beach (92660) *(P-15396)*

Uke Corporation .... D....... 858 513-9100
13400 Danielson St Poway (92064) *(P-11038)*

Ulmer Industries Inc .... E....... 909 823-7111
15243 Valley Blvd Fontana (92335) *(P-6086)*

Uls Express Inc .... C....... 310 631-0800
2850 E Del Amo Blvd Compton (90221) *(P-11467)*

Ultimate, Long Beach *Also Called: Altamed Health Services Corp (P-17586)*

Ultimate Builders Inc .... D....... 818 481-2627
23679 Calabasas Rd Calabasas (91302) *(P-462)*

ULTIMATE BUILDERS INC, Calabasas *Also Called: Ultimate Builders Inc (P-462)*

Ultimate Demo, Pomona *Also Called: Ultimate Removal Inc (P-463)*

Ultimate Ears Consumer LLC .... A....... 949 502-8340
3 Jenner Ste 180 Irvine (92618) *(P-10716)*

Ultimate Fghting Prdctons Intl 310 285-9000
9601 Wilshire Blvd Beverly Hills (90210) *(P-17383)*

Ultimate Landscaping MGT .... D....... 714 502-9711
700 E Sycamore St Anaheim (92805) *(P-218)*

Ultimate Metal Finishing Corp ....E....... 323 890-9100
6150 Sheila St Commerce (90040) *(P-6745)*

Ultimate Paper Box Company, City Of Industry *Also Called: Boxes R Us Inc (P-3086)*

Ultimate Print Source Inc .... E....... 909 947-5292
2070 S Hellman Ave Ontario (91761) *(P-3701)*

Ultimate Removal Inc .... C....... 909 524-0800
2168 Pomona Blvd Pomona (91768) *(P-463)*

Ultimate Solutions, Huntington Beach *Also Called: Sandia Plastics Inc (P-5197)*

Ultimate Sound Inc .... B....... 909 861-6200
1200 S Diamond Bar Blvd Ste 200 Diamond Bar (91765) *(P-8445)*

Ultimate Staffing Services, Orange *Also Called: Roth Staffing Companies LP (P-15938)*

Ultimatte Corporation .... E....... 818 993-8007
5828 Calvin Ave Tarzana (91356) *(P-8593)*

Ultisat Inc .... A....... 240 243-5107
11839 Sorrento Valley Rd San Diego (92121) *(P-16476)*

Ultra Built Kitchens Inc .... E....... 323 232-3362
1814 E 43rd St Los Angeles (90058) *(P-2681)*

Ultra Communications Inc .... F....... 760 652-0011
990 Park Center Dr Ste H Vista (92081) *(P-11911)*

Ultra Pro Acquisition LLC .... E....... 323 725-1975
6049 E Slauson Ave Commerce (90040) *(P-3841)*

Ultra Pro International LLC .... C....... 323 890-2100
6049 E Slauson Ave Commerce (90040) *(P-12946)*

Ultra Wheel Company .... E....... 714 449-7100
586 N Gilbert St Fullerton (92833) *(P-9479)*

Ultra-Stereo Labs Inc .... E....... 805 549-0161
181 Bonetti Dr San Luis Obispo (93401) *(P-9264)*

Ultracare Services LLC .... D....... 818 266-9668
1117 W Manchester Blvd Ste B Inglewood (90301) *(P-18648)*

Ultraglas Inc .... E....... 818 772-7744
3392 Hampton Ct Thousand Oaks (91362) *(P-12373)*

Ultragraphics Inc .... E....... 818 295-3994
2800 N Naomi St Burbank (91504) *(P-15655)*

Ultramar Inc .... E....... 661 944-2496
9508 E Palmdale Blvd Palmdale (93591) *(P-4654)*

Ultramet .... D....... 818 899-0236
12173 Montague St Pacoima (91331) *(P-6676)*

Ultrasigns Electrical Advg, San Diego *Also Called: Jones Sign Co Inc (P-11127)*

Ultrasigns Electrical Advg, San Diego *Also Called: Jones Signs Co Inc (P-12461)*

Ultron Systems Inc .... F....... 805 529-1485
5105 Maureen Ln Moorpark (93021) *(P-8914)*

Ultura, Long Beach *Also Called: Ultura Inc (P-20302)*

Ultura Inc .... C....... 562 661-4999
3605 Long Beach Blvd Ste 201 Long Beach (90807) *(P-20302)*

Umbrla Inc .... D....... 888 909-5564
3242 Halladay St Ste 202 Santa Ana (92705) *(P-6918)*

Umc Acquisition Corp (PA) ....**E....... 562 940-0300**
9151 Imperial Hwy Downey (90242) *(P-5727)*

Umex, Downey *Also Called: Universal Mlding Extrusion Inc (P-5713)*

Umgd, Santa Monica *Also Called: Universal Mus Group Dist Corp (P-3497)*

Umgee USA Inc .... F...... 323 526-9138
1565 E 23rd St Los Angeles (90011) *(P-2267)*

Umpco Inc .... D..... 714 897-3531
7100 Lampson Ave Garden Grove (92841) *(P-5949)*

Un Deux Trois Inc (PA) .... E...... 323 588-1067
2301 E 7th St Los Angeles (90023) *(P-2420)*

Unbroken Studios LLC .... D..... 310 741-2670
2120 Park Pl Ste 110 El Segundo (90245) *(P-16412)*

Undercar Plus Company, Van Nuys *Also Called: Kalaydjain Shahe Inc (P-9408)*

Undersea Systems Intl Inc .... D..... 714 754-7848
3133 W Harvard St Santa Ana (92704) *(P-9265)*

Underwater Kinetics, Poway *Also Called: Uke Corporation (P-11038)*

Uneekor Inc .... E...... 949 328-7790
15770 Laguna Canyon Rd Ste 100 Irvine (92618) *(P-16413)*

Unger Fabrik LLC (PA) .... C...... 626 469-8080
18525 Railroad St City Of Industry (91748) *(P-2268)*

UNI Filter Inc .... F...... 714 535-6933
1468 Manhattan Ave Fullerton (92831) *(P-9480)*

UNI Hosiery Co Inc (PA) .... C..... 213 228-0100
1911 E Olympic Blvd Los Angeles (90021) *(P-13116)*

UNI-Caps LLC .... E...... 714 529-8400
540 Lambert Rd Brea (92821) *(P-4021)*

UNI-Sport Inc .... E...... 310 217-4587
16933 Gramercy Pl Gardena (90247) *(P-3702)*

Unibal-Rodamco-Westfield Group .... C..... 310 478-4456
2049 Century Park E 41st Fl Los Angeles (90067) *(P-14691)*

Unicare Medical Transportation, Riverside *Also Called: Empire Med Transportations LLC (P-11758)*

Unicel, Chatsworth *Also Called: Meissner Mfg Co Inc (P-7674)*

Unico Incorporated .... F...... 619 209-6124
8880 Rio San Diego Dr Fl 8 San Diego (92108) *(P-238)*

Unicor, Lompoc *Also Called: Federal Prison Industries (P-11120)*

Unified Field Services Corp .... E...... 661 325-8962
6906 Downing Ave Bakersfield (93308) *(P-270)*

Unified Grocers Inc .... D..... 323 232-6124
457 E Martin Luther King Jr Blvd Los Angeles (90011) *(P-11625)*

Unified Nutrimeals .... D..... 323 923-9335
5469 Ferguson Dr Commerce (90022) *(P-14041)*

Unifirst, Ontario *Also Called: Unifirst Corporation (P-15471)*

Unifirst Corporation .... C..... 909 390-8670
700 Etiwanda Ave Ste C Ontario (91761) *(P-15471)*

Unify Fincl Cr Un Prof Corp (PA) .... D..... 877 254-9328
2305b W 190th St Torrance (90504) *(P-14240)*

Unigro, San Bernardino *Also Called: L & L Nursery Supply Inc (P-13488)*

Unilab Corporation (HQ) .... B..... 818 737-6000
8401 Fallbrook Ave West Hills (91304) *(P-18567)*

Unimark, Gardena *Also Called: Matsui International Co Inc (P-4619)*

Union 76, Los Angeles *Also Called: Kim Chong (P-16853)*

Union Building Maintenance, Commerce *Also Called: Uniserve Facilities Svcs Corp (P-15753)*

Union Carbide Corporation .... E...... 310 214-5300
19206 Hawthorne Blvd Torrance (90503) *(P-3073)*

Union Pacific Lines, Long Beach *Also Called: Union Pacific Railroad Company (P-11313)*

Union Pacific Railroad Company .... B..... 562 490-7000
2401 E Sepulveda Blvd Long Beach (90810) *(P-11313)*

Union Sup Comsy Solutions Inc .... B..... 785 357-5005
2301 E Pacifica Pl Rancho Dominguez (90220) *(P-13238)*

Union Technology Corp .... E...... 323 266-6871
718 Monterey Pass Rd Monterey Park (91754) *(P-12708)*

Unique Carpets Ltd .... D..... 951 352-8125
7360 Jurupa Ave Riverside (92504) *(P-12320)*

Unique Functional Products .... C..... 760 744-1610
135 Sunshine Ln San Marcos (92069) *(P-9496)*

Unique Functional Products, San Marcos *Also Called: Dexter Axle Company (P-9493)*

Unique Lighting Systems Inc .... F...... 800 955-4831
5825 Jasmine St Riverside (92504) *(P-8388)*

Unique Protective Services, Santa Clarita *Also Called: Cottrell Paul Enterprises LLC (P-16635)*

Unique Sales, Vernon *Also Called: Zk Enterprises Inc (P-2228)*

Unirex Corp .... E...... 323 589-4000
2288 E 27th St Vernon (90058) *(P-8915)*

Unirex Technologies, Vernon *Also Called: Unirex Corp (P-8915)*

Unis LLC .... D..... 310 747-7388
19914 S Via Baron Rancho Dominguez (90220) *(P-11626)*

Unis LLC (PA) .... C..... 909 839-2600
218 Machlin Ct Ste A Walnut (91789) *(P-11813)*

Unisen Inc .... E...... 714 669-1660
14410 Myford Rd Irvine (92606) *(P-11039)*

Uniserve Facilities Svcs Corp .... B..... 310 440-6747
1200 Getty Center Dr Los Angeles (90049) *(P-15752)*

Uniserve Facilities Svcs Corp (PA) .... B..... 213 533-1000
2363 S Atlantic Blvd Commerce (90040) *(P-15753)*

Unisource Solutions Inc (PA) .... C..... 562 654-3500
8350 Rex Rd Pico Rivera (90660) *(P-12292)*

Unisun Multinational, Chino *Also Called: Ht Multinational Inc (P-9403)*

Unisys Corporation .... C..... 949 380-5000
9701 Jeronimo Rd Ste 100 Irvine (92618) *(P-16142)*

Unite Eurotherapy Inc .... D..... 760 585-1800
2870 Whiptail Loop Ste 100 Carlsbad (92010) *(P-13072)*

Unite Hair .... D..... 760 585-1800
2870 Whiptail Loop Ste 100 Carlsbad (92010) *(P-19417)*

United Aeronautical Corp .... E...... 818 764-2102
7360 Laurel Canyon Blvd North Hollywood (91605) *(P-12921)*

United Airlines Inc .... D..... 310 258-3319
7300 World Way W Rm 144 Los Angeles (90045) *(P-11672)*

United Amrcn Indian Invlvment (PA) .... C..... 213 202-3970
1125 W 6th St Ste 103 Los Angeles (90017) *(P-18728)*

United Artist Releasing, Beverly Hills *Also Called: United Artists Films Company (P-17282)*

United Artists Corporation .... C..... 310 449-3000
10250 Constellation Blvd Fl 19 Los Angeles (90067) *(P-17281)*

United Artists Films Company (DH) .... C..... 310 449-3000
245 N Beverly Dr Beverly Hills (90210) *(P-17282)*

United Artists Productions Inc .... C..... 310 449-3000
10250 Constellation Blvd Fl 19 Los Angeles (90067) *(P-17283)*

United Artists Television Corp .... B..... 310 449-3000
10250 Constellation Blvd Fl 27 Los Angeles (90067) *(P-17284)*

United Audio Video Group Inc .... B..... 818 980-6700
7651 Densmore Ave Van Nuys (91406) *(P-9186)*

United Bakery Equipment Co Inc (PA) .... D..... 310 635-8121
15315 Marquardt Ave Santa Fe Springs (90670) *(P-7355)*

United Biologics Inc .... E...... 949 345-7490
2871 Pullman St Santa Ana (92705) *(P-10717)*

United Brands Company Inc .... E...... 619 461-5220
5930 Cornerstone Ct W Ste 170 San Diego (92121) *(P-1788)*

United Brothers Concrete Inc .... C..... 760 346-1013
41905 Boardwalk Ste K Palm Desert (92211) *(P-1091)*

United Cabinet Company Inc .... E...... 909 796-3015
1510 S Mountain View Ave San Bernardino (92408) *(P-2682)*

United California, Downey *Also Called: United Drill Bushing Corp (P-7136)*

United California Corporation .... E...... 562 803-1521
12200 Woodruff Ave Downey (90241) *(P-7102)*

United Cargo Logistics, City Of Industry *Also Called: U C L Incorporated (P-11509)*

United Carports LLC .... E...... 800 757-6742
7280 Sycamore Canyon Blvd Ste 1 Riverside (92508) *(P-6393)*

United Convalescent Facilities .... D..... 213 748-0491
230 E Adams Blvd Los Angeles (90011) *(P-18156)*

United Couriers Inc (DH) .... C..... 213 383-3611
3280 E Foothill Blvd Pasadena (91107) *(P-11673)*

United Crbral Plsy Assn Ornge .... C..... 949 333-6400
1251 E Dyer Rd Ste 150 Santa Ana (92705) *(P-19150)*

United Crbral Plsy Assn San Lu .... D..... 805 543-2039
3620 Sacramento Dr Ste 201 San Luis Obispo (93401) *(P-19151)*

United Detector Technology, Hawthorne *Also Called: OSI Optoelectronics Inc (P-8859)*

United Drill Bushing Corp .... C..... 562 803-1521
12200 Woodruff Ave Downey (90241) *(P-7136)*

United Facility Solutions Inc .... B..... 310 743-3000
19208 S Vermont Ave Ste 200 Gardena (90248) *(P-16697)*

United Farm Workers America (PA) .... C..... 661 822-5571
29700 Woodford Tehachapi Rd Keene (93531) *(P-19418)*

United Fmly Care Inc A Med Cor .... C..... 909 874-1679
8110 Mango Ave Ste 104 Fontana (92335) *(P-17814)*

United Guard Security Inc .... C..... 714 242-4051
1100 W Town And Country Rd Ste 1250 Orange (92868) *(P-16698)*

ALPHABETIC

United Guard Security Inc ....C....... 909 402-0754
473 E Carnegie Dr Ste 200 San Bernardino (92408) *(P-16699)*

United Imaging, Woodland Hills *Also Called: United Ribbon Company Inc (P-12390)*

United Industries Group Inc ....E....... 949 759-3200
11 Rancho Cir Lake Forest (92630) *(P-19712)*

United International Tech Inc ....E....... 818 772-9400
9207 Deering Ave Ste B Chatsworth (91311) *(P-8747)*

United Lab Services Inc ....D....... 951 444-0467
2479 S Vicentia Ave Corona (92882) *(P-18568)*

United Launch Alliance LLC ....B....... 303 269-5876
1579 Utah Ave, Bldg. 7525 Vandenberg Afb (93437) *(P-9906)*

United Marketing Group Inc ....D....... 323 778-4283
5957 S St Andrews Pl Los Angeles (90047) *(P-1026)*

United Media Services Inc ....C....... 714 693-8168
4955 E Hunter Ave Anaheim (92807) *(P-9187)*

United Medical Devices LLC ....E....... 310 551-4100
16250 Ventura Blvd Encino (91436) *(P-10625)*

United Medical Management Inc ....C....... 909 886-5291
1680 N Waterman Ave San Bernardino (92404) *(P-18157)*

United Memorial Products, Inc., Whittier *Also Called: Mhk Investment Holdings Inc (P-5424)*

United Network Info Svcs, Walnut *Also Called: Unis LLC (P-11813)*

United Orthopedic Corp USA, Irvine *Also Called: Uoc USA Inc (P-10626)*

United Owners Services, Anaheim *Also Called: Tricom Management Inc (P-20107)*

United Pacific Designs, Vernon *Also Called: UPD INC (P-10944)*

United Parcel Service Inc ....C....... 310 217-2646
17115 S Western Ave Gardena (90247) *(P-11539)*

United Parcel Service Inc ....B....... 404 828-6000
16000 Arminta St Van Nuys (91406) *(P-11540)*

United Parcel Service Inc ....B....... 562 404-3236
13233 Moore St Cerritos (90703) *(P-11541)*

United Parcel Service Inc ....B....... 626 814-6216
1100 Baldwin Park Blvd Baldwin Park (91706) *(P-11542)*

United Parcel Service Inc ....A....... 909 974-7212
3140 Jurupa St Ontario (91761) *(P-11543)*

United Parcel Service Inc ....A....... 909 279-5111
7925 Ronson Rd San Diego (92111) *(P-11544)*

United Parcel Service Inc ....C....... 619 482-8119
2300 Boswell Ct Chula Vista (91914) *(P-11545)*

United Parcel Service Inc ....A....... 949 643-6634
22 Brookline Aliso Viejo (92656) *(P-11546)*

United Parcel Service Inc ....C....... 800 742-5877
1457 E Victoria Ave San Bernardino (92408) *(P-11674)*

United Parcel Service Inc ....C....... 909 605-7740
3110 Jurupa St Ontario (91761) *(P-11675)*

United Parcel Service Inc ....C....... 323 260-8957
3333 S Downey Rd Vernon (90058) *(P-11678)*

United Paving Company, Corona *Also Called: Superior Paving Company Inc (P-649)*

United Pharma LLC ....C....... 714 738-8999
2317 Moore Ave Fullerton (92833) *(P-4635)*

United Precision Corp ....E....... 818 576-9540
20810 Plummer St Chatsworth (91311) *(P-8055)*

United Pumping Service Inc ....D....... 626 961-9326
14000 Valley Blvd City Of Industry (91746) *(P-11468)*

United Ribbon Company Inc ....D....... 818 716-1515
21201 Oxnard St Woodland Hills (91367) *(P-12390)*

United Riggers & Erectors Inc (PA)...............................D....... **909 978-0400**
4188 Valley Blvd Walnut (91789) *(P-1139)*

United Rock Products Corp ....C....... 714 578-9600
135 S State College Blvd Ste 400 Brea (92821) *(P-651)*

United Scope LLC (HQ)...............................F....... **714 942-3202**
14370 Myford Rd Ste 150 Irvine (92606) *(P-10345)*

United Security Products Inc ....E....... 800 227-1592
12675 Danielson Ct Ste 405 Poway (92064) *(P-9266)*

United Sports Brands, Fountain Valley *Also Called: Shock Doctor Inc (P-11026)*

United States Bakery ....E....... 323 232-6124
457 E Martin Luther King Jr Blvd Los Angeles (90011) *(P-1496)*

United States Gypsum Company ....D....... 908 232-8900
401 Van Ness Ave Torrance (90501) *(P-5522)*

United States Gypsum Company ....D....... 760 358-3200
3810 Evan Hewes Hwy Imperial (92251) *(P-5523)*

United States Logistics Group ....E....... 562 989-9555
2700 Rose Ave Ste A Signal Hill (90755) *(P-9497)*

United States Marine Corps ....D....... 760 725-3564
Marine Corps Air Stn Bldg 23122 (Camp Pendleton) Oceanside (92049) *(P-12922)*

United States Mineral Pdts Co ....E....... 909 473-3027
4062 Georgia Blvd San Bernardino (92407) *(P-5559)*

United States Technical Svcs ....C....... 714 374-6300
16541 Gothard St Ste 214 Huntington Beach (92647) *(P-16608)*

United States Tile Co ....C....... 951 739-4613
909 Railroad St Corona (92882) *(P-5376)*

United Stationers, City Of Industry *Also Called: Essendant Co (P-12993)*

United Sttes Dept Enrgy Brkley ....C....... 510 486-7089
555 W Imperial Hwy Brea (92821) *(P-19950)*

United Studios Self Def Inc ....D....... 949 293-1391
28251 Marguerite Pkwy Ste J Mission Viejo (92692) *(P-17576)*

United Studios Self Def Inc ....D....... 858 486-8773
13331 Poway Rd Poway (92064) *(P-17577)*

United Sunshine American Industries Corporation ....E
2808 E Marywood Ln Orange (92867) *(P-6831)*

United Support Services Inc ....C....... 858 373-9500
3252 Holiday Ct Ste 110 La Jolla (92037) *(P-16143)*

United Surface Solutions LLC ....E....... 562 693-0202
11901 Burke St Santa Fe Springs (90670) *(P-7264)*

United Svcs Amer Federal Cr Un (PA)...............................D....... **858 831-8100**
9999 Willow Creek Rd San Diego (92131) *(P-14241)*

United Syatt America Corp (PA)...............................C....... **714 568-1938**
920 E 1st St Santa Ana (92701) *(P-13887)*

United Talent Agency LLC ....C....... 310 776-8160
9336 Civic Center Dr Beverly Hills (90210) *(P-16948)*

United Talent Agency, LLC, Beverly Hills *Also Called: United Talent Agency LLC (P-16948)*

United Technologies, Anaheim *Also Called: Otis Elevator Company (P-12805)*

United Tote Company ....D....... 858 279-4250
4205 Ponderosa Ave San Diego (92123) *(P-7576)*

United Vision Financial Inc ....C....... 818 285-0211
16027 Ventura Blvd # 200 Encino (91436) *(P-14370)*

United Way Inc (PA)...............................D....... **213 808-6220**
1150 S Olive St Ste T-500 Los Angeles (90015) *(P-19346)*

United Way Greater Los Angeles, Los Angeles *Also Called: United Way Inc (P-19346)*

United Western Enterprises Inc ....E....... 805 389-1077
850 Flynn Rd Ste 200 Camarillo (93012) *(P-6746)*

United Wholesale Lumber Co, Valencia *Also Called: Standard Lumber Company Inc (P-2727)*

Unity Courier Service Inc (DH)...............................C....... **323 255-9800**
3231 Fletcher Dr Los Angeles (90065) *(P-11547)*

Unity Digital, Costa Mesa *Also Called: Unity Sales International Inc (P-10888)*

Unity Sales International Inc ....F....... 714 800-1700
2950 Airway Ave Ste A12 Costa Mesa (92626) *(P-10888)*

Univar Solutions USA Inc ....C....... 323 727-7005
2600 Garfield Ave Commerce (90040) *(P-13440)*

Universal Card Inc ....B....... 949 861-4000
9012 Research Dr Ste 200 Irvine (92618) *(P-16949)*

Universal Care Inc (HQ)...............................B....... **562 424-6200**
19762 Macarthur Blvd Ste 100 Irvine (92612) *(P-18729)*

Universal Christian Music Pubg, Santa Monica *Also Called: Universal Music Publishing Inc (P-3498)*

Universal City Studios Lllp ....A....... 818 622-8477
100 Universal City Plz Universal City (91608) *(P-17229)*

Universal Cushion Company Inc (PA)...............................E....... **323 887-8000**
1610 Mandeville Canyon Rd Los Angeles (90049) *(P-2489)*

Universal Custom Cabinets, Pacoima *Also Called: N K Cabinets Inc (P-2670)*

Universal Custom Courier, San Fernando *Also Called: Universal Mail Delivery Svc (P-15639)*

Universal Cy Stdios Prdctons L (DH)...............................E....... **818 777-1000**
100 Universal City Plz Universal City (91608) *(P-17230)*

Universal Defense ....E....... 909 626-4178
412 Cucamonga Ave Claremont (91711) *(P-6167)*

Universal Dust Cllctr Mfg Sup (PA)...............................D....... **714 630-8588**
1041 N Kraemer Pl Anaheim (92806) *(P-525)*

Universal Dynamics Inc ....F....... 626 480-0035
5313 3rd St Irwindale (91706) *(P-323)*

Universal Elastic & Garment Supply Inc ....E....... 213 748-2995
2200 S Alameda St Vernon (90058) *(P-2056)*

Universal Framing Products, Santa Clarita *Also Called: Universal Wood Moulding Inc (P-12321)*

Universal Home Care Inc ....C....... 323 653-9222
151 N San Vicente Blvd Ste 200 Beverly Hills (90211) *(P-18649)*

Universal Hosiery Inc ....D...... 661 702-8444
28337 Constellation Rd Valencia (91355) *(P-2062)*

Universal Mail Delivery Svc (PA).................................D...... 818 365-3144
501 S Brand Blvd # 104 San Fernando (91340) *(P-15639)*

Universal Meat Company, Rancho Cucamonga Also Called: Formosa Meat Company Inc
(P-1218)

Universal Metal Plating (PA).....................................F...... 626 969-7931
626 1/2 S Gerhart Ave Los Angeles (90022) *(P-17018)*

Universal Mlding Extrusion Inc (DH).............................E...... 562 401-1015
9151 Imperial Hwy Downey (90242) *(P-5713)*

Universal Molding Company (HQ)...............................C...... 310 886-1750
9151 Imperial Hwy Downey (90242) *(P-5728)*

Universal Molding Company, Downey Also Called: Umc Acquisition Corp *(P-5727)*

Universal Motion Components Co Inc ....E...... 714 437-9600
2920 Airway Ave Costa Mesa (92626) *(P-7359)*

Universal Mus Group Dist Corp (DH)..........................D...... 310 235-4700
2220 Colorado Ave Santa Monica (90404) *(P-3497)*

Universal Mus Group Dist Corp ....D...... 818 508-9550
111 Universal Hollywood Dr Ste 1420 Universal City (91608) *(P-16950)*

Universal Mus Investments Inc (HQ)...........................D...... 888 583-7176
2220 Colorado Ave Santa Monica (90404) *(P-16951)*

Universal Music Group Inc (HQ)................................D...... 310 865-0770
2220 Colorado Ave Santa Monica (90404) *(P-16952)*

Universal Music Publishing Inc ....C...... 310 235-4700
1601 Cloverfield Blvd Santa Monica (90404) *(P-3498)*

Universal Orthodontic Lab Inc ....F...... 562 484-0500
11917 Front St Norwalk (90650) *(P-10775)*

Universal Packaging West Inc (HQ)............................E...... 603 889-8311
43225 Business Park Dr Temecula (92590) *(P-5238)*

Universal Packg Systems Inc (PA)...............................A...... 909 517-2442
14570 Monte Vista Ave Chino (91710) *(P-4464)*

Universal Packg Systems Inc ....C...... 909 517-2442
14570 Monte Vista Ave Chino (91710) *(P-11627)*

Universal Pictures Intl, Universal City Also Called: Nbcuniversal Media LLC *(P-11932)*

Universal Plant Svcs Cal Inc ....D...... 310 618-1600
20545 Belshaw Ave # A Carson (90746) *(P-8056)*

Universal Plastic Mold, Baldwin Park Also Called: Upm Inc *(P-7103)*

Universal Products, Rancho Cucamonga Also Called: Proulx Manufacturing Inc *(P-5168)*

Universal Protection Svc LP (HQ)..............................D...... 866 877-1965
450 Exchange Ste 100 Irvine (92602) *(P-16700)*

Universal Prtction SEC Systems (DH)..........................D...... 714 923-3700
1815 E Wilshire Ave Ste 910 Santa Ana (92705) *(P-16701)*

Universal Prtein Spplmnts Corp ....F...... 732 545-3130
3441 Gato Ct Riverside (92507) *(P-4249)*

Universal Punch Corp ....D...... 714 556-4488
4001 W Macarthur Blvd Santa Ana (92704) *(P-7040)*

Universal Services America LP ....A...... 714 923-3700
1815 E Wilshire Ave Ste 912 Santa Ana (92705) *(P-15754)*

Universal Services America LP ....A...... 760 200-2865
77725 Enfield Ln Palm Desert (92211) *(P-16702)*

Universal Services America LP (HQ)............................D...... 866 877-1965
450 Exchange Irvine (92602) *(P-16703)*

Universal Shopping Plaza A CA ....C...... 714 521-8899
6281 Regio Ave Buena Park (90620) *(P-14692)*

Universal Stdios Licensing LLC ....C...... 818 695-1273
100 Universal City Plz Universal City (91608) *(P-15010)*

Universal Steel Services Inc ....D...... 626 960-1455
5034 Heintz St Baldwin Park (91706) *(P-6087)*

Universal Studios, Universal City Also Called: Creative Park Productions LLC *(P-17179)*

Universal Studios, Universal City Also Called: Universal City Studios Lllp *(P-17229)*

Universal Studios Company LLC (DH)...........................A...... 818 777-1000
100 Universal City Plz North Hollywood (91608) *(P-17231)*

Universal Surveillance Systems, Rancho Cucamonga Also Called: Universal Surveillance
Systems LLC *(P-9267)*

Universal Surveillance Systems LLC ....D...... 909 484-7870
11172 Elm Ave Rancho Cucamonga (91730) *(P-9267)*

Universal Switching Corp ....E...... 818 785-0200
7671 N San Fernando Rd Burbank (91505) *(P-8281)*

Universal Technical Inst Inc ....C...... 909 484-1929
9494 Haven Ave Rancho Cucamonga (91730) *(P-19006)*

Universal Wood Moulding Inc (PA).............................E...... 661 362-6262
21139 Centre Pointe Pkwy Santa Clarita (91350) *(P-12321)*

UNIVERSITY BOOKSTORE, Long Beach Also Called: Forty-Niner Shops Inc *(P-14066)*

University Business Ctr Assoc ....D...... 601 354-3555
5383 Hollister Ave Ste 120 Santa Barbara (93111) *(P-14693)*

University Cal Los Angeles ....A...... 310 825-9111
757 Westwood Plz Los Angeles (90095) *(P-18483)*

University Cal Los Angeles ....C...... 310 825-7852
420 Westwood Plz Rm 7702 Los Angeles (90095) *(P-18993)*

University Cal Riverside ....C...... 951 827-4801
1160 University Ave Riverside (92507) *(P-19914)*

University Cal San Diego ....A...... 858 534-2377
9500 Gilman Dr Dept 908 La Jolla (92093) *(P-15678)*

University Cal San Diego ....B...... 858 534-5000
10100 Hopkins Dr La Jolla (92093) *(P-16520)*

University Cal San Diego ....A...... 858 657-7000
9300 Campus Point Dr La Jolla (92037) *(P-18484)*

University Cal San Diego ....C...... 619 543-6170
402 Dickinson St Ste 380 San Diego (92103) *(P-18485)*

University Cal San Diego ....A...... 619 543-6654
200 W Arbor Dr Frnt San Diego (92103) *(P-18486)*

University Cal San Diego ....D...... 858 534-2377
10280 N Torrey Pines Rd Ste 470 La Jolla (92037) *(P-19745)*

University California Irvine ....C...... 949 824-6483
1001 Health Sciences Rd Irvine (92617) *(P-16953)*

University California Irvine ....C...... 714 456-7890
101 The City Dr S Orange (92868) *(P-17815)*

University California Irvine ....D...... 714 456-6966
101 The City Dr S Ste 313 Orange (92868) *(P-17816)*

University California Irvine ....A...... 714 456-6170
101 The City Dr S Bldg 1a Orange (92868) *(P-17817)*

University California Irvine ....B...... 714 480-2443
800 N Main St Santa Ana (92701) *(P-17818)*

University California Irvine ....B...... 714 456-8000
101 The City Dr S Orange (92868) *(P-18487)*

University California Irvine ....A...... 714 456-6011
101 The City Dr S Orange (92868) *(P-18488)*

University California Irvine ....C...... 714 456-5558
200 S Manchester Ave Ste 400 Orange (92868) *(P-18489)*

University California Irvine ....C...... 714 775-3066
15355 Brookhurst St Ste 102 Westminster (92683) *(P-18490)*

University California Irvine ....D...... 949 824-2662
106 B Student Ctr Irvine (92697) *(P-18813)*

University California Irvine ....D...... 949 939-7106
31865 Circle Dr Laguna Beach (92651) *(P-18814)*

University California Irvine ....C...... 949 824-7725
3151 Social Science Plz Irvine (92697) *(P-18994)*

University California Irvine ....D...... 949 824-6828
120 Theory Ste 200 Irvine (92617) *(P-19808)*

University California Irvine ....D...... 714 456-6655
200 S Manchester Ave Ste 650 Orange (92868) *(P-19809)*

University California Irvine ....A...... 949 824-2819
2220 Engineering Gtwy Irvine (92697) *(P-19887)*

University Credit Union ....C...... 310 477-6628
1500 S Sepulveda Blvd Los Angeles (90025) *(P-14242)*

University Frames Inc ....E...... 714 575-5100
3060 E Miraloma Ave Anaheim (92806) *(P-2765)*

University Marelich Mech Inc ....D...... 714 632-2600
1000 N Kraemer Pl Anaheim (92806) *(P-832)*

University Park Healthcare Ctr, Los Angeles Also Called: United Convalescent Facilities
(P-18156)

University Readers, San Diego Also Called: Cognella Inc *(P-3402)*

University Southern California ....A...... 323 442-8500
1500 San Pablo St Los Angeles (90033) *(P-18491)*

Uniweb, Corona Also Called: Uniweb Inc *(P-2998)*

Uniweb Inc (PA)..D...... 951 279-7999
222 S Promenade Ave Corona (92879) *(P-2998)*

Uniwell Corporation ....C...... 714 522-7000
7000 Beach Blvd Buena Park (90620) *(P-15397)*

Unix Packaging LLC (PA).......................................C...... 213 627-5050
9 Minson Way Montebello (90640) *(P-1743)*

Unix Packaging LLC ....B...... 213 627-5050
5361 Alexander St Commerce (90040) *(P-13565)*

Employee Codes: A=Over 500 employees, B=251-500
C=101-250, D=51-100, E=20-50, F=10-19, G=1-9

2024 Southern California
Business Directory and Buyers Guide

© Mergent Inc. 1-800-342-5647
1307

ALPHABETIC

Unlimited Innovations Inc .... E....... 714 998-0866
180 N Rverview Dr Ste 320 Anaheim (92808) *(P-16414)*

Uns Electric Inc .... E....... 714 690-3660
6565 Valley View St La Palma (90623) *(P-12621)*

Unspoken Language Services Inc .... B....... 626 532-8096
1370 Valley Vista Dr Ste 200 Diamond Bar (91765) *(P-16954)*

Uoc USA Inc .... F....... 949 328-3366
15251 Alton Pkwy Ste 100 Irvine (92618) *(P-10626)*

UPD INC .... D....... 323 588-8811
4507 S Maywood Ave Vernon (90058) *(P-10944)*

UPF Corporation .... F....... 661 323-8227
3747 Standard St Bakersfield (93308) *(P-5560)*

Upland Community Care Inc .... C....... 909 985-1903
1221 E Arrow Hwy Upland (91786) *(P-18064)*

Upland Fab Inc .... E....... 909 986-6565
1445 Brooks St Ste L Ontario (91762) *(P-8057)*

Upland Highlanders High Ptsa .... D....... 909 949-7880
565 W 11th St Upland (91786) *(P-19467)*

Uplift Family Services .... D....... 626 287-2988
9353 Valley Blvd Ste C Rosemead (91770) *(P-17819)*

Uplift Family Services .... A....... 626 254-5000
800 S Santa Anita Ave Arcadia (91006) *(P-19152)*

Upm Inc .... B....... 626 962-4001
13245 Los Angeles St Baldwin Park (91706) *(P-7103)*

Upm Raflatac Inc .... F....... 909 390-4657
1105 Auto Center Dr Ontario (91761) *(P-3177)*

Upper Deck Company (PA) .... E....... 800 873-7332
5830 El Camino Real Carlsbad (92008) *(P-3499)*

UPS, Gardena *Also Called: United Parcel Service Inc (P-11539)*

UPS, Van Nuys *Also Called: United Parcel Service Inc (P-11540)*

UPS, Cerritos *Also Called: United Parcel Service Inc (P-11541)*

UPS, Baldwin Park *Also Called: United Parcel Service Inc (P-11542)*

UPS, Ontario *Also Called: United Parcel Service Inc (P-11543)*

UPS, San Diego *Also Called: United Parcel Service Inc (P-11544)*

UPS, Chula Vista *Also Called: United Parcel Service Inc (P-11545)*

UPS, Aliso Viejo *Also Called: United Parcel Service Inc (P-11546)*

UPS, San Bernardino *Also Called: United Parcel Service Inc (P-11674)*

UPS, Ontario *Also Called: United Parcel Service Inc (P-11675)*

UPS, Vernon *Also Called: United Parcel Service Inc (P-11678)*

UPS Store Inc (HQ) .... B....... 858 455-8800
6060 Cornerstone Ct W San Diego (92121) *(P-16955)*

Upstanding LLC .... C....... 949 788-9900
440 Exchange Ste 100 Irvine (92602) *(P-16415)*

Uptown, Los Angeles *Also Called: Lets Go Apparel Inc (P-2453)*

Upwind Blade Solutions Inc .... B....... 866 927-3142
2869 Historic Decatur Rd Ste 100 San Diego (92106) *(P-17161)*

Uqora Inc .... E....... 888 313-1372
4250 Executive Sq La Jolla (92037) *(P-1288)*

Urban Armor Gear LLC (HQ) .... E....... 949 329-0500
1601 Alton Pkwy Irvine (92606) *(P-5239)*

Urban Commons Queensway LLC .... A....... 562 499-1611
1126 Queens Hwy Long Beach (90802) *(P-15398)*

Urban Concepts, Vernon *Also Called: Anns Trading Company Inc (P-13527)*

Urban Corps San Diego County .... C....... 619 235-6884
3127 Jefferson St San Diego (92110) *(P-19468)*

Urban Decay, Newport Beach *Also Called: Urban Decay Cosmetics LLC (P-13073)*

Urban Decay Cosmetics LLC .... B....... 949 631-4504
833 W 16th St Newport Beach (92663) *(P-13073)*

Urban Expressions Inc .... E....... 310 593-4574
5500 Union Pacific Ave Commerce (90022) *(P-5300)*

Urban Insight Inc .... E....... 213 792-2000
3530 Wilshire Blvd Ste 1285 Los Angeles (90010) *(P-16477)*

Uremet Corporation .... E....... 657 257-4027
7012 Belgrave Ave Garden Grove (92841) *(P-3981)*

Urgent Care Center, Montclair *Also Called: Prime Hlthcare Srvcs-Mntclair (P-18390)*

Uriman Inc (HQ) .... F....... 714 257-2080
650 N Puente St Brea (92821) *(P-9176)*

Urovant Sciences Inc .... E....... 949 226-6029
5281 California Ave Ste 100 Irvine (92617) *(P-4250)*

URS, Long Beach *Also Called: URS Group Inc (P-19713)*

URS Group Inc .... D....... 562 420-2933
3995 Via Oro Ave Long Beach (90810) *(P-19713)*

US Airconditioning Distributors Inc (PA) .... C....... 626 854-4500
16900 Chestnut St City Of Industry (91748) *(P-12759)*

US Architectural Lighting, Palmdale *Also Called: Sun Valley Ltg Standards Inc (P-8334)*

US Armor Corporation .... E....... 562 207-4240
10715 Bloomfield Ave Santa Fe Springs (90670) *(P-10718)*

US Best Repair Service Inc .... C....... 888 750-2378
1652 Edinger Ave Ste E Tustin (92780) *(P-464)*

US Best Repairs, Tustin *Also Called: US Best Repair Service Inc (P-464)*

US Blanks, LLC (PA) .... E....... 310 225-6774
14700 S San Pedro St Gardena (90248) *(P-3982)*

US Borax Inc .... A....... 760 762-7000
14486 Borax Rd Boron (93516) *(P-3917)*

US Carenet Services LLC .... C....... 661 945-7350
42225 10th St W Ste 2b Lancaster (93534) *(P-18650)*

US Computers Inc .... F....... 714 528-0514
181 W Orangethorpe Ave Ste C Placentia (92870) *(P-7577)*

US Concrete Precast, San Diego *Also Called: San Diego Precast Concrete Inc (P-5448)*

US Continental Marketing Inc (PA) .... D....... 951 808-8888
310 Reed Cir Corona (92879) *(P-4371)*

US Critical, Lake Forest *Also Called: US Critical LLC (P-7490)*

US Critical LLC (PA) .... E....... 949 916-9326
6 Orchard Ste 150 Lake Forest (92630) *(P-7490)*

US Critical LLC .... E....... 800 884-8945
25422 Trabuco Rd # 320 Lake Forest (92630) *(P-7491)*

US Data Management LLC (PA) .... D....... 888 231-0816
535 Chapala St Santa Barbara (93101) *(P-16609)*

US Dental Inc .... E....... 562 404-3500
13043 166th St Cerritos (90703) *(P-10776)*

US Dermatology Medical Management Inc .... D....... 817 962-2157
1401 N Batavia St Ste 204 Orange (92867) *(P-17820)*

US Display Group Inc .... E....... 951 444-4567
235 Radio Rd Corona (92879) *(P-3134)*

US Divers Co Inc .... D....... 760 597-5000
2340 Cousteau Ct Vista (92081) *(P-11040)*

US Donuts & Yogurt .... F....... 562 695-8867
11719 Whittier Blvd Whittier (90601) *(P-14042)*

US Duty Gear Inc .... F....... 909 391-8800
1946 S Grove Ave Ontario (91761) *(P-5310)*

US Electrical Services Inc .... E....... 714 982-1534
1501 E Orangethorpe Ave Ste 140 Fullerton (92831) *(P-12622)*

US Energy Technologies Inc .... E....... 714 617-8800
14370 Myford Road Ste 100 Walnut (91789) *(P-8338)*

US Foods Inc .... C....... 714 670-3500
15155 Northam St La Mirada (90638) *(P-13239)*

US Foods Inc .... C....... 562 806-2445
8457 Eastern Ave Bell Gardens (90201) *(P-13403)*

US Foods Inc .... C....... 213 623-4150
636 Stanford Ave Los Angeles (90021) *(P-13404)*

US Foods Inc .... C....... 310 632-6265
1610 E Sepulveda Blvd Carson (90745) *(P-13405)*

US Gold Trading Inc .... F....... 818 558-7766
117 E Providencia Ave Burbank (91502) *(P-10914)*

US Grant Hotel Ventures LLC .... D....... 619 744-2007
326 Broadway San Diego (92101) *(P-15399)*

US Hanger Company LLC .... E....... 310 323-8030
17501 S Denver Ave Gardena (90248) *(P-5627)*

US Horizon Manufacturing Inc .... E....... 661 775-1675
28539 Industry Dr Valencia (91355) *(P-5319)*

US Hotel and Resort MGT Inc .... C....... 949 650-2988
2544 Newport Blvd Costa Mesa (92627) *(P-15400)*

US Hybrid Corporation (HQ) .... E....... 310 212-1200
2660 Columbia St Torrance (90503) *(P-9481)*

US Industrial Tool & Sup Co .... E....... 310 464-8400
14083 S Normandie Ave Gardena (90249) *(P-7041)*

US Joiner LLC .... E....... 619 233-3993
2800 Harbor Dr San Diego (92113) *(P-719)*

US Lighting Tech, Walnut *Also Called: US Energy Technologies Inc (P-8338)*

US Logistics, Signal Hill *Also Called: United States Logistics Group (P-9497)*

US Motor Works LLC (PA) .... E....... 562 404-0488
14722 Anson Ave Santa Fe Springs (90670) *(P-9482)*

Mergent email: customerrelations@mergent.com
1308

2024 Southern California
Business Directory and Buyers Guide

(P-0000) Products & Services Section entry number
(PA)=Parent Co (HQ)=Headquarters (DH)=Div Headquarters

US Pole Company Inc (PA)..C....... 800 877-6537
  660 W Avenue O Palmdale (93551) *(P-8339)*

US Polymers Inc (PA)...D...... 323 728-3023
  1057 S Vail Ave Montebello (90640) *(P-5240)*

US Polymers Inc ....D...... 323 727-6888
  5910 Bandini Blvd Commerce (90040) *(P-5714)*

US Precision Sheet Metal Inc ....D...... 951 276-2611
  4020 Garner Rd Riverside (92501) *(P-6338)*

US Print & Toner Inc ....E....... 619 562-6995
  14751 Franklin Ave Ste B Tustin (92780) *(P-11063)*

US Radiator Corporation (PA) ....E....... 323 826-0965
  4423 District Blvd Vernon (90058) *(P-9483)*

US Real Estate Services Inc ....D...... 949 598-9920
  27442 Portola Pkwy Ste 300 Foothill Ranch (92610) *(P-14882)*

US Rigging Supply Corp ....E....... 714 545-7444
  1600 E Mcfadden Ave Santa Ana (92705) *(P-6832)*

US Rubber Recycling Inc ....E....... 909 825-1200
  1231 Lincoln St Colton (92324) *(P-4799)*

US Rubber Roller Company Inc ....F....... 951 682-2221
  1516 7th St Riverside (92507) *(P-4800)*

US Saws Inc (PA)..F....... 860 668-2402
  3702 W Central Ave Santa Ana (92704) *(P-6946)*

US Security Associates, Burbank *Also Called: US Security Associates Inc (P-16704)*

US Security Associates Inc ....B...... 818 697-1809
  455 N Moss St Burbank (91502) *(P-16704)*

US Security Associates Inc ....B...... 714 352-0773
  2275 W 190th St Ste 100 Torrance (90504) *(P-16705)*

US Sensor Corp ....D...... 714 639-1000
  1832 W Collins Ave Orange (92867) *(P-8916)*

US Skillserve Inc ....A...... 909 621-4751
  9620 Fremont Ave Montclair (91763) *(P-18065)*

US Toyo Fan Corporation ....D...... 626 338-1111
  16025 Arrow Hwy Ste F Irwindale (91706) *(P-7337)*

US Trust, Los Angeles *Also Called: U S Trust Company NA (P-14432)*

US Union Tool Inc (HQ) ....E....... 714 521-6242
  1260 N Fee Ana St Anaheim (92807) *(P-7027)*

US Wheel, Huntington Beach *Also Called: U S Wheel Corporation (P-9477)*

USA Enterprise Inc ....B...... 310 750-4246
  9777 Wilshire Blvd Ste 400 Beverly Hills (90212) *(P-15058)*

USA Federal Credit Union, San Diego *Also Called: United Svcs Amer Federal Cr Un (P-14241)*

USA Industries, Orange *Also Called: United Sunshine American Industries Corporation (P-6831)*

USA Sales Inc ....E....... 909 390-9606
  1560 S Archibald Ave Ontario (91761) *(P-2007)*

USA Travel Services LLC ....A...... 207 899-8803
  714 Washington Blvd Marina Del Rey (90292) *(P-19536)*

USA Vision Systems Inc (HQ) ....E....... 949 583-1519
  9301 Irvine Blvd Irvine (92618) *(P-9268)*

USA Waste of California Inc ....D...... 818 252-3112
  9081 Tujunga Ave Sun Valley (91352) *(P-12190)*

Usamp, Encino *Also Called: Instantly Inc (P-19900)*

USAopoly Inc ....D...... 760 431-5910
  5999 Avenida Encinas Ste 150 Carlsbad (92008) *(P-10968)*

Usc Arcadia Hospital (PA)..A...... 626 898-8000
  300 W Huntington Dr Arcadia (91007) *(P-18492)*

Usc Hsc Purchasing Svc ....F....... 213 740-8165
  3560 Watt Way Mc0656 Los Angeles (90089) *(P-4636)*

Usc Information Sciences Inst ....C...... 310 448-9438
  4676 Admiralty Way Ste 1001 Marina Del Rey (90292) *(P-19951)*

Usc University Hospital, Los Angeles *Also Called: University Southern California (P-18491)*

Usc Verdugo Hills Hospital LLC ....A...... 818 790-7100
  1812 Verdugo Blvd Glendale (91208) *(P-18493)*

Usc Vrdugo Hlls Hosp Fundation (HQ) ....B...... 800 872-2273
  1812 Verdugo Blvd Glendale (91208) *(P-18494)*

Uscb Inc (PA)...C...... 213 985-2111
  355 S Grand Ave Ste 3200 Los Angeles (90071) *(P-15616)*

Uscb America, Los Angeles *Also Called: Uscb Inc (P-15616)*

Usdm Life Science, Santa Barbara *Also Called: US Data Management LLC (P-16609)*

Used Cardboard Boxes Inc ....C...... 323 724-2500
  4032 Wilshire Blvd Ste 402 Los Angeles (90010) *(P-13025)*

Ushio America Inc (HQ) ....D...... 714 236-8600
  5440 Cerritos Ave Cypress (90630) *(P-12623)*

Usit Co, Gardena *Also Called: US Industrial Tool & Sup Co (P-7041)*

Usl Parallel Products Cal ....E....... 909 980-1200
  12281 Arrow Rte Rancho Cucamonga (91739) *(P-4534)*

USP Inc ....D...... 760 842-7700
  1818 Ord Way Oceanside (92056) *(P-4465)*

USS Cal Builders Inc ....C...... 714 828-4882
  8031 Main St Stanton (90680) *(P-601)*

UST, Aliso Viejo *Also Called: UST Global Inc (P-16144)*

UST Global Inc (HQ)..D...... 949 716-8757
  5 Polaris Way Aliso Viejo (92656) *(P-16144)*

Usts, Huntington Beach *Also Called: United States Technical Svcs (P-16608)*

Utak Laboratories Inc ....E....... 661 294-3935
  25020 Avenue Tibbitts Valencia (91355) *(P-4535)*

Utbbb Inc ....D...... 562 594-4411
  10711 Bloomfield St Los Alamitos (90720) *(P-1525)*

Utc, Mas, Costa Mesa *Also Called: Carrier Fire SEC Americas Corp (P-8604)*

Uti, Rancho Cucamonga *Also Called: Universal Technical Inst Inc (P-19006)*

Utility Refrigerator ....E....... 818 764-6200
  12160 Sherman Way North Hollywood (91605) *(P-7632)*

Utility Traffic Services LLC ....B...... 562 264-2355
  2845 E Spring St Long Beach (90806) *(P-19714)*

Utility Trailer Manufacturing (PA)...............................B...... 626 965-1514
  17295 Railroad St Ste A City Of Industry (91748) *(P-9498)*

Utility Trailer Mfg Co ....C...... 909 428-8300
  15567 Valley Blvd Fontana (92335) *(P-9499)*

Utility Trailer Mfg Co ....C...... 909 594-6026
  17295 Railroad St Ste A City Of Industry (91748) *(P-9500)*

Utility Trlr Sls Southern Cal, Fontana *Also Called: Utility Trailer Mfg Co (P-9499)*

Utility Trlr Sls Sthern Cal LL (PA).............................D...... 877 275-4887
  15567 Valley Blvd Fontana (92335) *(P-12229)*

Utility Vault, Fontana *Also Called: Oldcastle Infrastructure Inc (P-5432)*

Utility Vault, Escondido *Also Called: Oldcastle Infrastructure Inc (P-5433)*

Uwe, Camarillo *Also Called: United Western Enterprises Inc (P-6746)*

V & F Fabrication Company Inc ....E....... 714 265-0630
  13902 Seaboard Cir Garden Grove (92843) *(P-6088)*

V & L Produce Inc ....C...... 323 589-3125
  2550 E 25th St Vernon (90058) *(P-13344)*

V & M Company ....F....... 310 532-5633
  14024 Avalon Blvd Los Angeles (90061) *(P-6677)*

V & M Precision Grinding Co., Brea *Also Called: Rogers Holding Company Inc (P-9778)*

V & P Scientific Inc ....F....... 858 455-0643
  9823 Pacific Heights Blvd Ste T San Diego (92121) *(P-10302)*

V & S Engineering Company Ltd ....E....... 714 898-7869
  5766 Research Dr Huntington Beach (92649) *(P-8058)*

V 3, Oxnard *Also Called: V3 Printing Corporation (P-3703)*

V B I, Simi Valley *Also Called: Vanderhorst Brothers Industries Inc (P-8061)*

V C A Central Animal Hospital ....D...... 909 981-2855
  281 N Central Ave Upland (91786) *(P-126)*

V J Provision Inc ....F....... 818 843-3945
  410 S Varney St Burbank (91502) *(P-1206)*

V M S, Glendora *Also Called: Venue Management Systems Inc (P-16706)*

V P H, Van Nuys *Also Called: Valley Presbyterian Hospital (P-18496)*

V Q Orthocare, Vista *Also Called: Vision Quest Industries Inc (P-10721)*

V R Gifts, Brea *Also Called: Vesuki Inc (P-14088)*

V Todays Inc ....C...... 310 781-9100
  19800 S Vermont Ave Torrance (90502) *(P-15401)*

V Twest Inc ....F....... 714 521-2167
  16222 Phoebe Ave La Mirada (90638) *(P-2969)*

V Twin Magazine, Agoura Hills *Also Called: Paisano Publications LLC (P-3375)*

V-T Industries Inc ....E....... 714 521-2008
  9818 Firestone Blvd Downey (90241) *(P-5241)*

V/ Twins, Agoura Hills *Also Called: Paisano Publications Inc (P-3376)*

V&H Performance LLC ....D...... 562 921-7461
  13861 Rosecrans Ave Santa Fe Springs (90670) *(P-9888)*

V3, Oxnard *Also Called: Ventura Printing Inc (P-3705)*

V3 Printing Corporation ....D...... 805 981-2600
  200 N Elevar St Oxnard (93030) *(P-3703)*

Vacation Interval Realty, Newport Beach *Also Called: Pacific Monarch Resorts Inc (P-14838)*

Vacco Industries (DH)..C...... 626 443-7121
  10350 Vacco St South El Monte (91733) *(P-6795)*

Employee Codes: A=Over 500 employees, B=251-500
C=101-250, D=51-100, E=20-50, F=10-19, G=1-9

2024 Southern California
Business Directory and Buyers Guide

© Mergent Inc. 1-800-342-5647

1309

Vadnais Trenchless Svcs Inc .... D....... 858 550-1460
   11858 Bernardo Plaza Ct Ste 100 San Diego (92128) *(P-700)*

Vae Industries Corporation .... E....... 714 842-7500
   5402 Research Dr Huntington Beach (92649) *(P-2512)*

Vagabond Inns, Los Angeles *Also Called: Rpd Hotels 18 LLC (P-15334)*

Vagrant Records Inc .... F....... 323 302-0100
   6351 Wilshire Blvd Ste 101 Los Angeles (90048) *(P-3842)*

Vahe Enterprises Inc .... D....... 323 235-6657
   750 E Slauson Ave Los Angeles (90011) *(P-9337)*

Vahi Toyota Inc (PA) .... **C....... 760 241-6484**
   14612 Valley Center Dr Victorville (92395) *(P-13842)*

Val USA Manufacturer Inc .... E....... 626 839-8069
   1050 W Central Ave Ste A Brea (92821) *(P-11302)*

Val-Pro Inc (PA) .... **C....... 213 627-8736**
   1601 E Olympic Blvd Ste 300 Los Angeles (90021) *(P-13345)*

Valadon Hotel LLC .... D....... 310 854-1114
   8822 Cynthia St West Hollywood (90069) *(P-15402)*

Valco Planer Works Inc .... E....... 323 582-6355
   6131 Maywood Ave Huntington Park (90255) *(P-7104)*

Valco Precision Works, Huntington Park *Also Called: Valco Planer Works Inc (P-7104)*

Valeant Biomedicals Inc (DH) .... D....... 949 461-6000
   1 Enterprise Aliso Viejo (92656) *(P-13441)*

Valeda Company LLC .... E....... 800 421-8700
   13571 Vaughn St Unit E San Fernando (91340) *(P-10719)*

Valence Los Angeles, Gardena *Also Called: Coast Plating Inc (P-6604)*

Valence Lynwood, Lynwood *Also Called: Triumph Processing Inc (P-6675)*

Valence Surface Tech LLC .... F....... 562 531-7666
   7718 Adams St Paramount (90723) *(P-6089)*

Valencia Country Club, Valencia *Also Called: Heritage Golf Group LLC (P-17432)*

Valencia Gardens Health Care Center, Riverside *Also Called: Riverside Care Inc (P-18040)*

Valencia Group LLC .... C....... 949 379-6489
   94 Mayfair Irvine (92620) *(P-15403)*

Valencia Pipe Company .... E....... 661 257-3923
   28305 Livingston Ave Valencia (91355) *(P-4855)*

Valero, Wilmington *Also Called: Valero Ref Company-California (P-4655)*

Valero Ref Company-California .... A....... 562 491-6754
   2401 E Anaheim St Wilmington (90744) *(P-4655)*

Valet Parking Service, Los Angeles *Also Called: Valet Parking Svc A Cal Partnr (P-17008)*

Valet Parking Svc A Cal Partnr (PA) .... A....... 323 465-5873
   6933 Hollywood Blvd Los Angeles (90028) *(P-17008)*

Valet Services, Bell Gardens *Also Called: Anitsa Inc (P-15444)*

Valew Welding & Fabrication, Adelanto *Also Called: Hayes Welding Inc (P-17085)*

Valex Corp (HQ) .... D....... 805 658-0944
   6080 Leland St Ventura (93003) *(P-6678)*

Valiant Technical Services Inc .... D....... 757 628-9500
   1785 Utah Ave Lompoc (93437) *(P-9849)*

Validyne Engineering Corp .... E....... 818 886-8488
   8626 Wilbur Ave Northridge (91324) *(P-10406)*

Valle Vsta Cnvlescent Hosp Inc .... D....... 760 745-1288
   1025 W 2nd Ave Escondido (92025) *(P-18158)*

Vallecitos Water District, San Marcos *Also Called: Vallecitos Water District Financing Corporation (P-12151)*

Vallecitos Water District Financing Corporation (HQ) .... D....... 760 744-0460
   201 Vallecitos De Oro San Marcos (92069) *(P-12151)*

Valley Animal Medical Center .... A....... 760 342-4711
   46920 Jefferson St Indio (92201) *(P-127)*

Valley Base Materials, Westlake Village *Also Called: Security Paving Company Inc (P-645)*

Valley Box Co Inc .... E....... 619 449-2882
   10611 Prospect Ave Santee (92071) *(P-13026)*

Valley Bulk Inc .... D....... 760 843-0574
   17649 Turner Rd Victorville (92394) *(P-11511)*

Valley Business Printers Inc .... D....... 818 362-7771
   6355 Topanga Canyon Blvd Ste 225 Woodland Hills (91367) *(P-3704)*

Valley Cabinet, El Cajon *Also Called: Vcsd Inc (P-2683)*

Valley Care Olive View Med Ctr, Sylmar *Also Called: Olive View-Ucla Medical Center (P-17729)*

Valley Community Healthcare .... B....... 818 763-8836
   6801 Coldwater Canyon Ave Ste 1b North Hollywood (91605) *(P-17821)*

Valley Detriot Diesel, Bakersfield *Also Called: Valley Power Systems Inc (P-12831)*

Valley Enerprises Inc .... F....... 951 789-0843
   18600 Van Buren Blvd Riverside (92508) *(P-11178)*

Valley Engravers, Santa Clarita *Also Called: Valley Precision Metal Product (P-6339)*

Valley Fruit & Produce Co, Los Angeles *Also Called: Val-Pro Inc (P-13345)*

Valley Garbage Rubbish Co Inc .... C....... 805 614-1131
   1850 W Betteravia Rd Santa Maria (93455) *(P-12191)*

Valley Healthcare, San Bernardino *Also Called: United Medical Management Inc (P-18157)*

Valley Hospital Medical Center Foundation .... A....... 818 885-8500
   18300 Roscoe Blvd Northridge (91325) *(P-18495)*

Valley Hunt Club .... D....... 626 793-7134
   520 S Orange Grove Blvd Pasadena (91105) *(P-19469)*

Valley Insurance Service Inc .... A....... 949 707-4080
   23181 Verdugo Dr Ste 100b Laguna Hills (92653) *(P-14639)*

Valley Lght Ctr For Scial Advn .... D....... 626 337-6200
   109 W 6th St Azusa (91702) *(P-19193)*

VALLEY LIGHT INDUSTRIES, Azusa *Also Called: Valley Lght Ctr For Scial Advn (P-19193)*

Valley Manor Convalescent Hosp, North Hollywood *Also Called: Golden Care Inc (P-18129)*

Valley Metal Treating Inc .... E....... 909 623-6316
   355 Se End Ave Pomona (91766) *(P-5853)*

Valley Metals LLC .... E....... 858 513-1300
   13125 Gregg St Poway (92064) *(P-5642)*

Valley News Gardens, Gardena *Also Called: Gardena Valley News Inc (P-3278)*

Valley Oak Cabinets, Santa Ynez *Also Called: Valley Oaks Industries (P-2901)*

Valley Oaks Industries .... F....... 805 688-2754
   3550 E Highway 246 Ste Ae Santa Ynez (93460) *(P-2901)*

Valley of Sun Cosmetics LLC .... C....... 310 327-9062
   535 Patrice Pl Gardena (90248) *(P-13074)*

Valley of The Sun Labs, Gardena *Also Called: Valley of Sun Cosmetics LLC (P-13074)*

Valley Perforating LLC .... D....... 661 324-4964
   3201 Gulf St Bakersfield (93308) *(P-8059)*

Valley Power Services Inc .... E....... 909 969-9345
   425 S Hacienda Blvd City Of Industry (91745) *(P-8161)*

Valley Power Systems Inc .... D....... 661 325-9001
   4000 Rosedale Hwy Bakersfield (93308) *(P-12831)*

Valley Power Systems Inc (PA) .... **D....... 626 333-1243**
   425 S Hacienda Blvd City Of Industry (91745) *(P-12832)*

Valley Precision Metal Product .... E....... 661 607-0100
   27771 Avenue Hopkins Santa Clarita (91355) *(P-6339)*

Valley Presbyterian Hospital .... A....... 818 782-6600
   15107 Vanowen St Van Nuys (91405) *(P-18496)*

Valley Printers, Woodland Hills *Also Called: Valley Business Printers Inc (P-3704)*

Valley Resource Center, Hemet *Also Called: Valley Resource Center Inc (P-19194)*

Valley Resource Center Inc (PA) .... **E....... 951 766-8659**
   1285 N Santa Fe St Hemet (92543) *(P-19194)*

Valley Spuds, Oxnard *Also Called: McK Enterprises Inc (P-1944)*

Valley Substation, Romoland *Also Called: Southern California Edison Co (P-12074)*

Valley Tool and Machine Co Inc .... D....... 909 595-2205
   111 Explorer St Pomona (91768) *(P-8060)*

Valley View Casino, Valley Center *Also Called: San Psqual Band Mssion Indians (P-15346)*

Valley Village .... C....... 818 446-0366
   8727 Fenwick St Sunland (91040) *(P-18099)*

Valley Vsta Nrsing Trnstnal CA .... C....... 818 763-6275
   6120 Vineland Ave North Hollywood (91606) *(P-18066)*

Valley Vsta Nrsing Trnstnal Ca, North Hollywood *Also Called: Valley Vsta Nrsing Trnstnal CA (P-18066)*

Valley-HI Toyota Honda, Victorville *Also Called: Vahi Toyota Inc (P-13842)*

Valley-Todeco Inc (DH) .... **D....... 800 992-4444**
   135 N Unruh Ave City Of Industry (91744) *(P-6456)*

Valleycrest Productions Ltd .... D....... 818 560-5391
   500 S Buena Vista St Burbank (91521) *(P-11968)*

Valori Sand & Gravel Company .... C....... 909 350-3000
   11027 Cherry Ave Fontana (92337) *(P-12363)*

Valterra Products LLC (HQ) .... **E....... 818 898-1671**
   15235 Brand Blvd Ste A101 Mission Hills (91345) *(P-6796)*

Valtron Technologies Inc .... D....... 805 257-0333
   28309 Avenue Crocker Santa Clarita (91355) *(P-16545)*

Valudor Products LLC .... F....... 760 635-8500
   179 Calle Magdalena Ste 100 Encinitas (92024) *(P-13442)*

Value Wholesaler Inc .... F....... 626 263-5933
   1830 Flower Ave Duarte (91010) *(P-2002)*

Valueoptions of California Inc, Cerritos *Also Called: Carelon Bhavioral Hlth Cal Inc (P-14571)*

Valumark, Tustin *Also Called: Logomark Inc (P-13545)*

Valverde Construction Inc ....C..... 562 906-1826
10936 Shoemaker Ave Santa Fe Springs (90670) *(P-701)*

Valvoline Instant Oil Change, Costa Mesa *Also Called: EZ Lube LLC (P-17055)*

Van Can Company ....C..... 858 391-8084
13230 Evening Creek Dr S Ste 212 San Diego (92128) *(P-5866)*

Van Daele Development Corp ....C..... 951 354-6800
2900 Adams St Ste C25 Riverside (92504) *(P-489)*

Van Daele Homes, Riverside *Also Called: Van Daele Development Corp (P-489)*

Van Torrance & Storage Company (PA).............D
12128 Burke St Santa Fe Springs (90670) *(P-11523)*

Van's Gifts, Long Beach *Also Called: Farm Street Designs Inc (P-13476)*

Vance & Hines, Santa Fe Springs *Also Called: V&H Performance LLC (P-9888)*

Vance Executive Protection, Los Angeles *Also Called: Andrews International Inc (P-16621)*

Vanderhorst Brothers Industries Inc ....D..... 805 583-3333
1715 Surveyor Ave Simi Valley (93063) *(P-8061)*

Vanderra Resources LLC ....B..... 817 439-2220
1801 Century Park E Ste 2400 Los Angeles (90067) *(P-393)*

Vanderveer Industrial Plas LLC ....E..... 714 579-7700
515 S Melrose St Placentia (92870) *(P-4844)*

Vanderveer Industrial Plastics, Placentia *Also Called: Vanderveer Industrial Plas LLC (P-4844)*

Vanguard Electronics Company (PA)............E..... 714 842-3330
18292 Enterprise Ln Huntington Beach (92648) *(P-8958)*

Vanguard Health Systems Inc ....B..... 714 635-6272
1154 N Euclid St Anaheim (92801) *(P-17822)*

Vanguard Industries East Inc ....E..... 800 433-1334
2440 Impala Dr Carlsbad (92010) *(P-2559)*

Vanguard Industries West Inc (PA).............C..... 760 438-4437
2440 Impala Dr Carlsbad (92010) *(P-2560)*

Vanguard Lgistics Svcs USA Inc (HQ)..........D..... 310 847-3000
5000 Airport Plaza Dr Ste 200 Long Beach (90815) *(P-11814)*

Vanguard Space Tech Inc ....C..... 858 587-4210
4398 Corporate Center Dr Los Alamitos (90720) *(P-19715)*

Vanguard Tool & Manufacturing, Rancho Cucamonga *Also Called: Vanguard Tool & Mfg Co Inc (P-6565)*

Vanguard Tool & Mfg Co Inc ....E..... 909 980-9392
8388 Utica Ave Rancho Cucamonga (91730) *(P-6565)*

Vanguard Univ Southern Cal ....C..... 714 668-6163
55 Fair Dr Costa Mesa (92626) *(P-18995)*

Vanlaw Food Products Inc (HQ)..................D..... 714 870-9091
2325 Moore Ave Fullerton (92833) *(P-1365)*

Vans Inc (DH)...B..... 714 755-4000
1588 S Coast Dr Costa Mesa (92626) *(P-4708)*

Vans Manufacturing Inc ....F..... 805 522-6267
330 E Easy St Ste C Simi Valley (93065) *(P-8062)*

Vans Shoes, Costa Mesa *Also Called: Vans Inc (P-4708)*

Vantage Apparel, Santa Ana *Also Called: Vantage Custom Classics Inc (P-13117)*

Vantage Associates Inc ....E..... 800 995-8322
12333 Los Nietos Rd Santa Fe Springs (90670) *(P-4921)*

Vantage Associates Inc ....D..... 562 968-1400
12333 Los Nietos Rd Santa Fe Springs (90670) *(P-5242)*

Vantage Associates Inc ....E..... 562 968-1400
12333 Los Nietos Rd Santa Fe Springs (90670) *(P-9824)*

Vantage Associates Inc (PA)......................E..... 619 477-6940
12333 Los Nietos Rd Santa Fe Springs (90670) *(P-9922)*

Vantage Custom Classics Inc ....C..... 714 755-1133
3321 S Susan St Santa Ana (92704) *(P-13117)*

Vantage Led, Corona *Also Called: Tradenet Enterprise Inc (P-11176)*

Vantage Master Machine Company, Santa Fe Springs *Also Called: Vantage Associates Inc (P-9824)*

Vantage Point Products Corp (PA)...............E..... 562 946-1718
9115 Dice Rd Ste 18 Santa Fe Springs (90670) *(P-8446)*

Vantage Vehicle Group, Corona *Also Called: Vantage Vehicle Intl Inc (P-9177)*

Vantage Vehicle Intl Inc ....E..... 951 735-1200
1740 N Delilah St Corona (92879) *(P-9177)*

Vantari Medical LLC ....E..... 949 783-5300
15440 Laguna Canyon Rd # 26 Irvine (92618) *(P-10407)*

Vantiva Sup Chain Slutions Inc (HQ)............B..... 805 445-1122
3601 Calle Tecate Ste 120 Camarillo (93012) *(P-17271)*

Vantiva Sup Chain Slutions Inc ....C..... 909 974-2016
5491 E Philadelphia St Ontario (91761) *(P-17272)*

Vape Craft LLC ....E..... 760 295-7484
2100 Palomar Airport Rd Ste 210 Carlsbad (92011) *(P-14116)*

Vapex-Genex-Precision, Los Angeles *Also Called: Electrical Rebuilders Sls Inc (P-9166)*

Vapor Delux Inc ....E..... 818 370-8308
2148 Glendale Galleria Glendale (91210) *(P-3843)*

Vaquero Energy Inc ....E..... 661 616-0600
4700 Stockdale Hwy Ste 120 Bakersfield (93309) *(P-394)*

Vaquero Energy Incorporated ....E..... 661 363-7240
15545 Hermosa Rd Bakersfield (93307) *(P-271)*

Varco De Mexico Holdings Inc ....E..... 714 978-1900
743 N Eckhoff St Orange (92868) *(P-15804)*

Varco Heat Treating, Garden Grove *Also Called: Diversfied Mtllrgical Svcs Inc (P-5836)*

Varco Systems, Orange *Also Called: Varco De Mexico Holdings Inc (P-15804)*

Varda Space Industries Inc ....D..... 833 707-0020
225 S Aviation Blvd El Segundo (90245) *(P-9907)*

Varner Bros Inc ....C..... 661 399-2944
1808 Roberts Ln Bakersfield (93308) *(P-12192)*

Varner Family Ltd Partnership (PA)..............D..... 661 399-1163
5900 E Lerdo Hwy Shafter (93263) *(P-15006)*

Varsity Contractors Inc ....C..... 949 586-8283
24155 Laguna Hills Mall Laguna Hills (92653) *(P-15755)*

Vas Engineering Inc ....E..... 858 569-1601
4750 Viewridge Ave San Diego (92123) *(P-9135)*

Vascular Therapies, Irvine *Also Called: Covidien LP (P-10487)*

Vastek Inc ....C..... 925 948-5701
1230 Columbia St Ste 1180 San Diego (92101) *(P-16956)*

Vaughans Industrial Repair Inc ....E..... 562 633-2660
16224 Garfield Ave Paramount (90723) *(P-12833)*

Vault Prep Inc ....E..... 310 971-9091
2500 Broadway Ste F125 Santa Monica (90404) *(P-5455)*

Vault Pro ....F..... 800 299-6929
13607 Pumice St Santa Fe Springs (90670) *(P-6875)*

Vaya Workforce Solutions LLC ....C..... 866 687-7390
5930 Cornerstone Ct W Ste 300 San Diego (92121) *(P-15946)*

Vbc Holdings Inc ....E..... 310 322-7357
134 Main St El Segundo (90245) *(P-1497)*

Vbx Labs LLC ....E..... 747 256-0103
9631 Topanga Canyon Pl Chatsworth (91311) *(P-11303)*

VCA, Los Angeles *Also Called: VCA Inc (P-14152)*

VCA Animal Hospitals Inc ....D..... 310 473-2951
1900 S Sepulveda Blvd Los Angeles (90025) *(P-128)*

VCA Inc (DH)..C..... 310 571-6500
12401 W Olympic Blvd Los Angeles (90064) *(P-14152)*

VCA West Los Angles Anmal Hosp, Los Angeles *Also Called: VCA Animal Hospitals Inc (P-128)*

Vcc, Carlsbad *Also Called: Visual Communications Company LLC (P-9137)*

Vci Construction LLC (HQ).........................D..... 909 946-0905
1921 W 11th St Ste A Upland (91786) *(P-702)*

Vci Event Technology Inc ....C..... 714 772-2002
25172 Arctic Ocean Dr Ste 102 Lake Forest (92630) *(P-15805)*

Vclad Laminates Inc ....E..... 626 442-2100
2103 Seaman Ave South El Monte (91733) *(P-4845)*

Vcp Mobility Holdings Inc ....E..... 619 213-6500
745 Design Ct Ste 602 Chula Vista (91911) *(P-10720)*

Vcsd Inc ....E..... 619 579-6886
585 Vernon Way El Cajon (92020) *(P-2683)*

Vdi Motor Sports, Lake Elsinore *Also Called: Vertical Doors Inc (P-3017)*

Vector, Huntington Beach *Also Called: Vector Launch LLC (P-6751)*

Vector Electronics & Tech Inc ....E..... 818 985-8208
11115 Vanowen St North Hollywood (91605) *(P-8748)*

Vector Launch LLC (PA)............................C..... 202 888-3063
15261 Connector Ln Huntington Beach (92649) *(P-6751)*

Vector Resources Inc (PA).........................C..... 310 436-1000
20917 Higgins Ct Torrance (90501) *(P-950)*

Vectorusa, Torrance *Also Called: Vector Resources Inc (P-950)*

Vectron Inc ....F..... 858 621-2400
345 6th Ave San Diego (92101) *(P-7265)*

Veeco Electro Fab Inc ....E..... 714 630-8020
1176 N Osprey Cir Anaheim (92807) *(P-8749)*

Veeco Process Equipment Inc ....D..... 805 967-2700
112 Robin Hill Rd Goleta (93117) *(P-8063)*

Employee Codes: A=Over 500 employees, B=251-500
C=101-250, D=51-100, E=20-50, F=10-19, G=1-9

2024 Southern California
Business Directory and Buyers Guide

© Mergent Inc. 1-800-342-5647

1311

Veeco Process Equipment Inc ....D...... 805 967-1400
112 Robin Hill Rd Goleta (93117) *(P-10303)*

Veezee Inc ....E...... 949 265-0800
121 Waterworks Way Irvine (92618) *(P-2269)*

Vefo Inc ....E...... 909 598-3856
3202 Factory Dr Pomona (91768) *(P-4909)*

Veg Fresh, Corona *Also Called: Veg-Fresh Farms LLC (P-13346)*

Veg Fresh Logistics LLC ....C...... 714 446-8800
1400 W Rincon St Corona (92878) *(P-11815)*

Veg-Fresh Farms LLC (PA) ....**C...... 800 422-5535**
1400 W Rincon St Corona (92878) *(P-13346)*

Vege - Kurl Inc ....D...... 818 956-5582
412 W Cypress St Glendale (91204) *(P-4466)*

Vege-Mist Inc ....D...... 310 353-2300
407 E Redondo Beach Blvd Gardena (90248) *(P-7633)*

Vege-Tech Company, Glendale *Also Called: Vege - Kurl Inc (P-4466)*

Veinviewer, Cypress *Also Called: Christie Medical Holdings Inc (P-10796)*

Velaro Incorporated ....D...... 800 983-5276
1234 N La Brea Ave West Hollywood (90038) *(P-13975)*

Velasco Carwash Supplies Corp ....E...... 310 715-3000
1601 Perrino Pl Los Angeles (90023) *(P-9312)*

Velher LLC ....E...... 619 494-6310
350 10th Ave Ste 1000 San Diego (92101) *(P-10229)*

Vellios Automotive Machine Sp, Lawndale *Also Called: Vellios Machine Shop Inc (P-8064)*

Vellios Machine Shop Inc ....F...... 310 643-8540
4625 29th Manhattan Beach Blvd Lawndale (90260) *(P-8064)*

Velocity Vehicle Group, Whittier *Also Called: Los Angeles Truck Centers LLC (P-17034)*

Velvet Heart, Los Angeles *Also Called: Tcj Manufacturing LLC (P-2375)*

Venco Western Inc ....C...... 805 981-2400
2400 Eastman Ave Oxnard (93030) *(P-219)*

Vendor Direct Solutions LLC (PA) ....**C...... 213 362-5622**
515 S Figueroa St Ste 1900 Los Angeles (90071) *(P-16145)*

Vengroff Williams & Assoc Inc ....C...... 714 889-6200
2099 S State College Blvd Ste 600 Anaheim (92806) *(P-15617)*

Venice Fmly Clinic Foundation (PA) ....**D...... 310 664-7703**
604 Rose Ave Venice (90291) *(P-17823)*

Ventegra Inc A Cal Beneft Corp ....D...... 858 551-8111
450 N Brand Blvd Ste 600 Glendale (91203) *(P-20387)*

Ventritex, Sylmar *Also Called: Pacesetter Inc (P-10819)*

Ventura Cnty Md-Cal Mnged Care ....D...... 888 301-1228
711 E Daily Dr Ste 106 Camarillo (93010) *(P-18815)*

Ventura Cnty Obstet Gynclgic M ....D...... 805 643-8695
2795 Loma Vista Rd Ventura (93003) *(P-17824)*

Ventura Coastal LLC (PA) ....**D...... 805 653-7000**
2325 Vista Del Mar Dr Ventura (93001) *(P-1380)*

Ventura County Credit Union (PA) ....**D...... 805 477-4000**
2575 Vista Del Mar Dr Ste 100 Ventura (93001) *(P-14243)*

Ventura County Lemon Coop ....D...... 805 385-3345
2620 Sakioka Dr Oxnard (93030) *(P-13347)*

Ventura County Medical Center ....C...... 805 933-8600
845 N 10th St Ste 3 Santa Paula (93060) *(P-17825)*

Ventura County Medical Center ....C...... 805 652-6201
3291 Loma Vista Rd Bldg 343 Ventura (93003) *(P-17826)*

Ventura County Medical Center ....C...... 805 652-6729
300 Hillmont Ave Ventura (93003) *(P-17873)*

Ventura County Medical Center ....D...... 805 677-5184
825 N 10th St Santa Paula (93060) *(P-20267)*

Ventura Family YMCA, Ventura *Also Called: Channel Islnds Yung MNS Chrstn (P-19439)*

Ventura Feed and Pet Sups Inc ....E...... 805 648-5035
980 E Front St Ventura (93001) *(P-13918)*

Ventura Foods LLC ....E...... 323 262-9157
2900 Jurupa St Ontario (91761) *(P-1250)*

Ventura Foods LLC ....D...... 714 257-3700
2900 Jurupa St Ontario (91761) *(P-1573)*

Ventura Foods LLC (PA) ....**C...... 714 257-3700**
40 Pointe Dr Brea (92821) *(P-1574)*

Ventura Harbor Boatyard Inc ....E...... 805 654-1433
1415 Spinnaker Dr Ventura (93001) *(P-9867)*

Ventura Hsptality Partners LLC ....C...... 805 648-2100
450 Harbor Blvd Ventura (93001) *(P-15404)*

Ventura Hydrulic Mch Works Inc ....E...... 805 656-1760
1555 Callens Rd Ventura (93003) *(P-8065)*

Ventura Medical Management LLC ....B...... 805 477-6220
2601 E Main St Ventura (93003) *(P-20112)*

Ventura Pacific Co, Oxnard *Also Called: Ventura County Lemon Coop (P-13347)*

Ventura Printing Inc (PA) ....**D...... 805 981-2600**
200 N Elevar St Oxnard (93030) *(P-3705)*

Ventura Technology Group ....E...... 805 581-0800
855 E Easy St Ste 104 Simi Valley (93065) *(P-8917)*

Ventura Yuth Crrctional Fcilty, Camarillo *Also Called: Juvenile Justice Division Cal (P-20046)*

Venturedyne Ltd ....D...... 909 793-2788
1320 W Colton Ave Redlands (92374) *(P-7338)*

Venue Management Systems Inc ....A...... 626 445-6000
2041 E Gladstone St Ste A Glendora (91740) *(P-16706)*

Venus Alloys Inc (PA) ....**E...... 714 635-8800**
1415 S Allec St Anaheim (92805) *(P-5769)*

Venus Bridal Gowns, San Gabriel *Also Called: Lotus Orient Corp (P-2285)*

Venus Foods Inc ....E...... 626 369-5188
770 S Stimson Ave City Of Industry (91745) *(P-1207)*

Venus Group Inc (PA) ....**D...... 949 609-1299**
25861 Wright St Foothill Ranch (92610) *(P-12322)*

Venus Laboratories Inc ....D...... 714 891-3100
11150 Hope St Cypress (90630) *(P-3918)*

Venus Textiles, Foothill Ranch *Also Called: Venus Group Inc (P-12322)*

Veolia Wts Services Usa Inc ....D...... 562 942-2200
7777 Industry Ave Pico Rivera (90660) *(P-7690)*

Veolia Wts Usa Inc ....D...... 805 545-3743
8.5 Miles Nw Avila Beach Avila Beach (93424) *(P-4637)*

Ver Sales Inc (PA) ....**E...... 818 567-3000**
2509 N Naomi St Burbank (91504) *(P-12580)*

Vera Bradley Inc ....E...... 858 320-9020
4525 La Jolla Village Dr San Diego (92122) *(P-13920)*

Veratex, Chatsworth *Also Called: Avitex Inc (P-2011)*

Verdeco Recycling Inc ....E...... 323 537-4617
8685 Bowers Ave South Gate (90280) *(P-12193)*

Verdugo Hills Hospital Inc ....C...... 818 790-7100
1812 Verdugo Blvd Glendale (91208) *(P-18497)*

Verdugo Hlls Psychthrapy Ctr A (PA) ....**C...... 818 241-6780**
410 Arden Ave Ste 201 Glendale (91203) *(P-17827)*

Verdugo Tool & Engrg Co Inc ....F...... 818 998-1101
20600 Superior St Chatsworth (91311) *(P-6566)*

Verdugo Vista Healthcare Ctr, La Crescenta *Also Called: Mariner Health Care Inc (P-18006)*

Verenium Corporation ....C...... 858 431-8500
3550 John Hopkins Ct San Diego (92121) *(P-4536)*

Veridiam Inc (DH) ....**D...... 619 448-1000**
1717 N Cuyamaca St El Cajon (92020) *(P-7137)*

Veris Manufacturing, Brea *Also Called: Q C M Inc (P-8211)*

Veritas Health Services Inc ....A...... 909 464-8600
5451 Walnut Ave Chino (91710) *(P-18498)*

Veritas Technologies LLC ....C...... 310 202-0757
16501 Ventura Blvd Ste 400 Encino (91436) *(P-16146)*

Verizon, Los Alamitos *Also Called: Supermedia LLC (P-3489)*

Verizon, Santa Monica *Also Called: Verizon Services Corp (P-11865)*

Verizon, Goleta *Also Called: Verizon South Inc (P-11866)*

Verizon, San Fernando *Also Called: Frontier California Inc (P-11880)*

Verizon, Westlake Village *Also Called: Frontier California Inc (P-11881)*

Verizon, Santa Maria *Also Called: Frontier California Inc (P-11882)*

Verizon, Huntington Beach *Also Called: Frontier California Inc (P-11883)*

Verizon, Indio *Also Called: Frontier California Inc (P-11884)*

Verizon, Baldwin Park *Also Called: Telesector Resources Group Inc (P-20258)*

Verizon Connect Telo Inc (DH) ....**C...... 844 617-1100**
15505 Sand Canyon Ave Irvine (92618) *(P-16521)*

Verizon Services Corp ....B...... 310 315-1100
2530 Wilshire Blvd Fl 1 Santa Monica (90403) *(P-11865)*

Verizon South Inc ....C...... 805 681-8527
424 S Patterson Ave Goleta (93111) *(P-11866)*

Vermont Care Center, Torrance *Also Called: Geri-Care II Inc (P-18127)*

Vernon Central Warehouse Inc ....C...... 323 234-2200
2050 E 38th St Vernon (90058) *(P-11524)*

Vernon Warehouse Co, Vernon *Also Called: Vernon Central Warehouse Inc (P-11524)*

Versa Products Inc (PA) ....**C...... 310 353-7100**
14105 Avalon Blvd Los Angeles (90061) *(P-2918)*

Versa Stage, Torrance *Also Called: Forrester Eastland Corporation (P-11216)*

Versaclimber, Santa Ana *Also Called: Heart Rate Inc (P-10996)*

Versafab Corp (PA) .... E...... **800 421-1822**
15919 S Broadway Gardena (90248) *(P-6340)*

Versaform Corporation .... D...... 760 599-4477
1377 Specialty Dr Vista (92081) *(P-6341)*

Versatables.com, Los Angeles *Also Called: Versa Products Inc (P-2918)*

Verseio Inc .... D...... 888 373-9942
550 W B St Fl 4 San Diego (92101) *(P-16147)*

Vertechs Enterprises Inc (PA) .... E...... **858 578-3900**
1071 Industrial Pl El Cajon (92020) *(P-5776)*

Vertechs Enterprises Inc .... F...... 858 578-3900
400 Raleigh Ave El Cajon (92020) *(P-9583)*

Vertex China, Pomona *Also Called: Sky One Inc (P-5379)*

Vertex Diamond Tool Co Inc .... F...... 909 599-1129
940 W Cienega Ave San Dimas (91773) *(P-7138)*

Vertex Lcd Inc .... E...... 714 223-7111
600 S Jefferson St Ste K Placentia (92870) *(P-9136)*

Vertex Phrmctcals San Dego LLC (HQ) .... C...... **858 404-6600**
3215 Merryfield Row San Diego (92121) *(P-4251)*

Vertical Doors Inc .... F...... 951 273-1069
542 3rd St Lake Elsinore (92530) *(P-3017)*

Vertical Fiber Technologies, Montebello *Also Called: Vft Inc (P-2490)*

Vertiflex Inc .... E...... 442 325-5900
25155 Rye Canyon Loop Valencia (91355) *(P-10627)*

Vertiv, Escondido *Also Called: Vertiv It Systems Inc (P-7502)*

Vertiv, Irvine *Also Called: Vertiv Corporation (P-10168)*

Vertiv Corporation .... D...... 949 457-3600
35 Parker Irvine (92618) *(P-10168)*

Vertiv It Systems Inc .... D...... 760 504-5451
970 W Valley Pkwy Ste 425 Escondido (92025) *(P-7502)*

Vertos Medical Inc LLC .... D...... 949 349-0008
95 Enterprise Ste 325 Aliso Viejo (92656) *(P-10628)*

Very Special Chocolats Inc .... C...... 626 334-7838
760 N Mckeever Ave Azusa (91702) *(P-1555)*

Verys, Santa Ana *Also Called: Verys LLC (P-16610)*

Verys LLC .... C...... 949 423-3295
1251 E Dyer Rd Ste 210 Santa Ana (92705) *(P-16610)*

Vescio Manufacturing Intl, Santa Fe Springs *Also Called: Vescio Threading Co (P-8066)*

Vescio Threading Co .... D...... 562 802-1868
14002 Anson Ave Santa Fe Springs (90670) *(P-8066)*

Vescom Corporation (PA) .... A...... **207 945-5051**
1125 W 190th St Gardena (90248) *(P-16707)*

Vessels Club Restaurant, Cypress *Also Called: Los Alamitos Race Course (P-14024)*

Vest Inc .... D...... 800 421-6370
6023 Alcoa Ave Vernon (90058) *(P-7154)*

Vesta, Corona *Also Called: Extrumed Inc (P-5027)*

Vesta Foodservice, Santa Fe Springs *Also Called: LA Specialty Produce Co (P-13332)*

Vesta Luxury Home Staging, Pico Rivera *Also Called: Showroom Interiors LLC (P-15798)*

Vestis Services LLC .... A...... 818 973-3700
115 N First St Ste 203 Burbank (91502) *(P-15472)*

Vesture Group Incorporated .... D...... 818 842-0200
3405 W Pacific Ave Burbank (91505) *(P-2421)*

Vesuki Inc .... F...... 562 245-4000
1350 W Lambert Rd Ste A Brea (92821) *(P-14088)*

Vet National Inc .... E...... 805 692-8487
3621 State St Santa Barbara (93105) *(P-12624)*

Vet National Mail, Santa Barbara *Also Called: Vet National Inc (P-12624)*

Veterans EZ Info, San Diego *Also Called: Veterans EZ Info Inc (P-20388)*

Veterans EZ Info Inc .... C...... 866 839-1329
1901 1st Ave Ste 192 San Diego (92101) *(P-20388)*

Veterans Health Administration .... A...... 310 478-3711
11301 Wilshire Blvd Los Angeles (90073) *(P-17828)*

Veterans Health Administration .... A...... 909 825-7084
11201 Benton St Loma Linda (92357) *(P-17829)*

Veterans Med RES Fndtion San D .... C...... 858 642-3080
3350 La Jolla Village Dr Ste 151a San Diego (92161) *(P-19470)*

Veterinary Centers America VCA, Los Angeles *Also Called: Vicar Operating Inc (P-131)*

Veterinary Pet Insurance Services Inc .... B...... 714 989-0555
1800 E Imperial Hwy Ste 145 Brea (92821) *(P-14640)*

Veterinary Pet Services Inc .... C...... 714 989-0555
3060 Saturn St Brea (92821) *(P-14641)*

Veterinary Practice Assoc Inc .... C...... 949 833-9020
10435 Sorrento Valley Rd San Diego (92121) *(P-129)*

Veterinary Specialty Hosp .... C...... 858 875-7500
10435 Sorrento Valley Rd San Diego (92121) *(P-130)*

Veterinary Specialty Hospital, San Diego *Also Called: Veterinary Practice Assoc Inc (P-129)*

Veterinary Specialty Hospital, San Diego *Also Called: Veterinary Specialty Hosp (P-130)*

Vetronix Corporation .... C...... 805 966-2000
2030 Alameda Padre Serra Santa Barbara (93103) *(P-9484)*

Vets Securing America Inc .... A...... 310 645-6200
1125 W 190th St Gardena (90248) *(P-16708)*

Vfs Fire Protection Services, Orange *Also Called: Bernel Inc (P-743)*

Vft Inc .... E...... 323 728-2280
1040 S Vail Ave Montebello (90640) *(P-2490)*

Vgp Holdings LLC .... B...... 562 906-6200
9520 John St Santa Fe Springs (90670) *(P-12264)*

Vi-Star Gear Co Inc .... E...... 323 774-3750
7312 Jefferson St Paramount (90723) *(P-6474)*

Viacyte Inc .... D...... 858 455-3708
5580 Morehouse Dr Ste 100 San Diego (92121) *(P-19952)*

Viade Products Inc .... F...... 805 484-2114
354 Dawson Dr Camarillo (93012) *(P-10777)*

Vianh Company Inc .... E...... 714 590-9808
13841 A Better Way Ste 10c Garden Grove (92843) *(P-8067)*

Viant, Irvine *Also Called: Interactive Media Holdings Inc (P-15550)*

Viasat, Carlsbad *Also Called: Viasat Inc (P-8595)*

Viasat Inc .... E...... 760 476-2129
2426 Town Garden Rd Carlsbad (92009) *(P-8594)*

Viasat Inc (PA) .... A...... **760 476-2200**
6155 El Camino Real Carlsbad (92009) *(P-8595)*

Viasensor, Colton *Also Called: Landtec North America Inc (P-20359)*

Viasys Respiratory Care Inc .... D...... 714 283-2228
22745 Savi Ranch Pkwy Yorba Linda (92887) *(P-10629)*

Vibiana, Los Angeles *Also Called: Vibiana Events LLC (P-15523)*

Vibiana Events LLC .... D...... 213 626-1507
214 S Main St Los Angeles (90012) *(P-15523)*

Vibra Finish Co (PA) .... E...... **805 578-0033**
2220 Shasta Way Simi Valley (93065) *(P-5546)*

Vibra Healthcare LLC .... C...... 619 260-8300
555 Washington St San Diego (92103) *(P-18499)*

Vibra Hospital of San Diego, San Diego *Also Called: Vibra Healthcare LLC (P-18499)*

Vibrahone, Simi Valley *Also Called: Vibra Finish Co (P-5546)*

Vibrex, Valencia *Also Called: M W Sausse & Co Inc (P-8185)*

Vicar Operating Inc (DH) .... D...... 310 571-6500
12401 W Olympic Blvd Los Angeles (90064) *(P-131)*

Vicki Marsha Uniforms, Huntington Beach *Also Called: Marsha Vicki Originals Inc (P-2179)*

Victor Cmnty Support Svcs Inc .... C...... 951 212-1770
1105 E Florida Ave Hemet (92543) *(P-18730)*

Victor Cmnty Support Svcs Inc .... C...... 760 987-8225
15095 Amargosa Rd Ste 201 Victorville (92394) *(P-18731)*

Victor Cmnty Support Svcs Inc .... C...... 760 245-4695
14360 St Andrews Dr Ste 11 Victorville (92395) *(P-18732)*

Victor Cmnty Support Svcs Inc .... C...... 909 890-5930
1908 Business Center Dr Ste 109 San Bernardino (92408) *(P-18733)*

Victor Treatment Centers, San Bernardino *Also Called: Victor Treatment Centers Inc (P-19306)*

Victor Treatment Centers Inc .... D...... 951 436-5200
1053 N D St San Bernardino (92410) *(P-19306)*

Victoria Care Center .... D...... 805 642-1736
5445 Everglades St Ventura (93003) *(P-18067)*

Victoria Care Center, Ventura *Also Called: Victoria Vntura Healthcare LLC (P-18069)*

Victoria Club .... C...... 951 683-5323
2521 Arroyo Dr Riverside (92506) *(P-17532)*

Victoria Vntura Asssted Lving .... D...... 805 642-1736
27101 Puerta Real Ste 450 Mission Viejo (92691) *(P-18068)*

Victoria Vntura Healthcare LLC .... B...... 805 642-1736
5445 Everglades St Ventura (93003) *(P-18069)*

Victorville Homecare, San Bernardino *Also Called: Maxim Healthcare Services Inc (P-18628)*

Victorville Speedwash Inc .... D...... 760 998-2482
13311 Main St Hesperia (92345) *(P-17049)*

Employee Codes: A=Over 500 employees, B=251-500
C=101-250, D=51-100, E=20-50, F=10-19, G=1-9

2024 Southern California
Business Directory and Buyers Guide

© Mergent Inc. 1-800-342-5647
1313

Victorville Speedwash Inc .... D...... 760 388-0112
15200 Palmdale Rd Victorville (92392) *(P-17050)*

Victorville Speedwash Inc .... D...... 760 388-0113
12875 Bear Valley Rd Victorville (92392) *(P-17051)*

Victory Display & Store Fixs, Compton *Also Called: Gemco Display and Str Fixs LLC*
(P-12454)

Victory Foam Inc (PA).. D...... **949 474-0690**
3 Holland Irvine (92618) *(P-13566)*

Victory Intl Group LLC .... C...... 949 407-5888
14748 Pipeline Ave Ste B Chino Hills (91709) *(P-12947)*

Victory Koredrry, Huntington Beach *Also Called: Victory Professional Pdts Inc (P-2381)*

Victory Professional Pdts Inc .... E...... 714 887-0621
5601 Engineer Dr Huntington Beach (92649) *(P-2381)*

Victory Sportswear, Duarte *Also Called: Victory Sportswear Inc (P-13567)*

Victory Sportswear Inc .... E...... 866 308-0798
2381 Buena Vista St Duarte (91010) *(P-13567)*

Victory Studio, Burbank *Also Called: Warner Bros Entertainment Inc (P-17235)*

Vid, Vista *Also Called: Vista Irrigation District (P-12216)*

Vida Lease Corporation .... E...... 626 839-4912
17807 Maclaren St Ste A City Of Industry (91744) *(P-9188)*

VIDA NUEVA, Los Angeles *Also Called: Tidings (P-3331)*

Video Sensing Division, Tustin *Also Called: Canon Medical Systems USA Inc (P-12480)*

Video Vice Data Communications (PA).................. C...... **714 897-6300**
7391 Lincoln Way Garden Grove (92841) *(P-12002)*

Videoamp Inc (PA)... D...... **424 272-7774**
2229 S Carmelina Ave Los Angeles (90064) *(P-16416)*

Videocam, Lake Forest *Also Called: Vci Event Technology Inc (P-15805)*

Videssence LLC (PA)... E...... **626 579-0943**
10768 Lower Azusa Rd El Monte (91731) *(P-8299)*

Vie De France 108, Vernon *Also Called: Vie De France Yamazaki Inc (P-14043)*

Vie De France Yamazaki Inc .... A...... 323 582-1241
3046 E 50th St Vernon (90058) *(P-14043)*

Viele & Sons Inc (PA).. D...... **714 447-3663**
1820 E Valencia Dr Fullerton (92831) *(P-13240)*

Viele & Sons Instnl Groc, Fullerton *Also Called: Viele & Sons Inc (P-13240)*

View Heights Convalescent Hosp, Los Angeles *Also Called: Amada Enterprises Inc*
(P-17879)

View Park Convalescent Center, Los Angeles *Also Called: Burlington Convalescent Hosp*
(P-17894)

View Park Convalescent Center, Los Angeles *Also Called: Burlington Convalescent Hosp*
(P-17895)

Viewsonic, Brea *Also Called: Viewsonic Corporation (P-7578)*

Viewsonic Corporation (PA)..................................... C...... **909 444-8888**
10 Pointe Dr Ste 200 Brea (92821) *(P-7578)*

Vigilant Drone Defense Inc .... E...... 424 275-8282
1055 W 7th St 33rd Fl Los Angeles (90017) *(P-6876)*

Vignolo Farms Inc .... C...... 661 746-2148
33342 Dresser Ave Bakersfield (93308) *(P-2)*

Vigobyte Tape Corporation .... A...... 866 803-8446
2498 Roll Dr Ste 916 San Diego (92154) *(P-7492)*

Vigor Systems Inc .... E...... 866 748-4467
4660 La Jolla Village Dr Ste 500 San Diego (92122) *(P-8596)*

Vijall Inc .... E...... 818 700-0071
21900 Marilla St Chatsworth (91311) *(P-13443)*

Viking Office Products Inc (DH)............................... B...... **562 490-1000**
3366 E Willow St Signal Hill (90755) *(P-13001)*

Viking Products, Orange *Also Called: Pro Detention Inc (P-5622)*

Viking Products Inc .... E...... 949 379-5100
20 Doppler Irvine (92618) *(P-7139)*

Viking Range LLC .... E...... 909 662-3504
14680 Monte Vista Ave Chino (91710) *(P-8226)*

Viking Rubber Products Inc .... F...... 310 868-5200
2600 Homestead Pl Compton (90220) *(P-4801)*

Viking Therapeutics Inc (PA).................................. E...... **858 704-4660**
12340 El Camino Real Ste 250 San Diego (92130) *(P-4252)*

Viktor Benes Bakeries, Westlake Village *Also Called: Mamolos Cntntl Bailey Bakeries*
(P-13721)

Villa Convalescent Hosp Inc .... D...... 951 689-5788
8965 Magnolia Ave Riverside (92503) *(P-18070)*

VILLA CONVALESCENT HOSPITAL, Riverside *Also Called: Villa Convalescent Hosp Inc*
(P-18070)

Villa De La Mar Inc .... C...... 562 494-5001
5001 E Anaheim St Long Beach (90804) *(P-18159)*

Villa Del Rey Retirement Inn, Escondido *Also Called: Emeritus Corporation (P-14706)*

Villa Ford Inc .... C...... 714 637-8222
2550 N Tustin St Orange (92865) *(P-13843)*

Villa Furniture Mfg Co .... C...... 714 535-7272
13760 Midway St Cerritos (90703) *(P-2939)*

Villa International, Cerritos *Also Called: Villa Furniture Mfg Co (P-2939)*

Villa Maria Care Center, Baldwin Park *Also Called: Trinity Health Systems (P-18063)*

Villa Roma Sausage Co, Ontario *Also Called: Heatherfield Foods Inc (P-1197)*

Villa Venetia .... B...... 714 540-1800
2775 Mesa Verde Dr E Costa Mesa (92626) *(P-14371)*

Village At Northridge .... D...... 818 514-4497
9222 Corbin Ave Northridge (91324) *(P-19307)*

Village Center Ultramar, Palmdale *Also Called: Ultramar Inc (P-4654)*

Village Green Foods Inc .... E...... 949 261-0111
1732 Kaiser Ave Irvine (92614) *(P-2003)*

Village Management Svcs Inc .... D...... 949 597-4360
24351 El Toro Rd Laguna Woods (92637) *(P-20113)*

Village Marine Technology, Gardena *Also Called: Aqua Pro Properties Vii LP (P-7222)*

Village News Inc .... E...... 760 451-3488
41740 Enterprise Cir S Temecula (92590) *(P-3334)*

Village Nurseries Whl LLC .... B...... 951 657-3940
20099 Santa Rosa Mine Rd Perris (92570) *(P-13521)*

Village The, San Juan Capistrano *Also Called: Freedom Properties-Hemet LLC (P-14662)*

Village West Health Center, Riverside *Also Called: Air Force Village West Inc (P-17877)*

Villanueva Plastic Company Inc .... E...... 909 581-3870
372 W Tullock St Rialto (92376) *(P-4846)*

Villas De Crlsbad Ltd A Cal Lt .... D...... 760 434-7116
3500 Lake Blvd Oceanside (92056) *(P-19308)*

Vim Tools, La Verne *Also Called: Durston Manufacturing Company (P-5878)*

Vincent Contractors Inc .... B...... 714 660-0165
4501 E La Palma Ave Ste 200 Anaheim (92807) *(P-963)*

Vincent Scaffolding, Anaheim *Also Called: Vincent Contractors Inc (P-963)*

Vinci Brands LLC (PA)... C...... **949 838-5111**
1775 Flight Way Ste 300 Tustin (92782) *(P-7456)*

Vinculums, Irvine *Also Called: Vinculums Services LLC (P-20389)*

Vinculums Services LLC .... C...... 949 783-3552
10 Pasteur Ste 100 Irvine (92618) *(P-20389)*

Vintage Associates Inc .... C...... 760 772-3673
78755 Darby Rd Bermuda Dunes (92203) *(P-220)*

Vintage Club .... D...... 760 340-0500
75001 Vintage Dr W Indian Wells (92210) *(P-17533)*

Vintage Design LLC .... D...... 858 695-9544
8310 Juniper Creek Ln San Diego (92126) *(P-16957)*

Vintage Nursery, Bermuda Dunes *Also Called: Vintage Associates Inc (P-220)*

Vintage Production California, Santa Clarita *Also Called: California Resources Prod Corp*
(P-255)

Vintage Senior Management Inc .... A...... 818 954-9500
2721 W Willow St Burbank (91505) *(P-19153)*

VINTAGE SENIOR MANAGEMENT, INC., Burbank *Also Called: Vintage Senior Management*
Inc (P-19153)

Vintique Inc .... E...... 714 634-1932
1828 W Sequoia Ave Orange (92868) *(P-9485)*

Vinyl Technology Inc (PA).. C...... **626 443-5257**
200 Railroad Ave Monrovia (91016) *(P-3162)*

Vinylvisions Company LLC .... E...... 800 321-8746
1233 Enterprise Ct Corona (92882) *(P-4508)*

VIP Rubber Company Inc (PA)................................. C...... **562 905-3456**
540 S Cypress St La Habra (90631) *(P-4802)*

Virco Inc (HQ)... C...... **310 533-0474**
2027 Harpers Way Torrance (90501) *(P-12293)*

Virco Mfg Corporation (PA)..................................... D...... **310 533-0474**
2027 Harpers Way Torrance (90501) *(P-2940)*

Virgin Fish Inc (PA)... C...... **310 391-6161**
1000 Corporate Pointe Ste 150 Culver City (90230) *(P-11409)*

Virgin Orbit Holdings Inc (HQ)................................ F...... **562 388-4400**
4022 E Conant St Long Beach (90808) *(P-10087)*

Virginia Cntry CLB of Long Bch .... C...... 562 427-0924
4602 N Virginia Rd Long Beach (90807) *(P-17534)*

Mergent email: customerrelations@mergent.com
1314

2024 Southern California
Business Directory and Buyers Guide

(P-0000) Products & Services Section entry number
(PA)=Parent Co (HQ)=Headquarters (DH)=Div Headquarters

Viridos Inc .... D...... 858 754-2900
250 W Schrimpf Rd Calipatria (92233) *(P-19888)*

Virtium, Rcho Sta Marg *Also Called: Virtium Technology Inc (P-8918)*

Virtium LLC .... D...... 949 888-2444
30052 Tomas Rcho Sta Marg (92688) *(P-12450)*

Virtium Technology Inc .... E...... 949 888-2444
30052 Tomas Rcho Sta Marg (92688) *(P-8918)*

Vish Consulting Services Inc .... D...... 916 800-3762
9655 Granite Ridge Dr Ste 200 San Diego (92123) *(P-15902)*

Vishay Spectoral Electronics, Ontario *Also Called: Vishay Thin Film LLC (P-8919)*

Vishay Spectro, Ontario *Also Called: Vishay Techno Components LLC (P-8196)*

Vishay Techno Components LLC .... D...... 909 923-3313
4051 Greystone Dr Ontario (91761) *(P-8196)*

Vishay Thin Film LLC .... E...... 909 923-3313
4051 Greystone Dr Ontario (91761) *(P-8919)*

Vision Aerospace LLC .... E...... 818 700-1035
19863 Nordhoff St Northridge (91324) *(P-9825)*

Vision Engineering, Palmdale *Also Called: Vision Engrg Met Stamping Inc (P-8340)*

Vision Engrg Met Stamping Inc .... D...... 661 575-0933
114 Grand Cypress Ave Palmdale (93551) *(P-8340)*

Vision Envelope & Prtg Co Inc (PA)............................E...... 310 324-7062
13707 S Figueroa St Los Angeles (90061) *(P-3215)*

Vision Imaging Supplies Inc .... E...... 818 885-4515
9540 Cozycroft Ave Chatsworth (91311) *(P-11064)*

Vision Manufacturing Inc .... D...... 760 689-0020
1398 Poinsettia Ave # 101 Vista (92081) *(P-8750)*

Vision Quest Industries Inc .... C...... 949 261-6382
1390 Decision St Ste A Vista (92081) *(P-10721)*

Vision Realty Managements, Beverly Hills *Also Called: Starpint 1031 Property MGT LLC (P-14869)*

Vision Solutions Inc (HQ) .... D...... 949 253-6500
15300 Barranca Pkwy Irvine (92618) *(P-16148)*

Vision Systems Inc .... D...... 619 258-7300
11322 Woodside Ave N Santee (92071) *(P-5715)*

Visionaire Lighting, Rancho Dominguez *Also Called: Visionaire Lighting LLC (P-8341)*

Visionaire Lighting LLC .... D...... 310 512-6480
19645 S Rancho Way Rancho Dominguez (90220) *(P-8341)*

Visionary Contact Lens Inc .... E...... 714 237-1900
2940 E Miraloma Ave Anaheim (92806) *(P-10856)*

Visionary Sleep LLC .... D...... 909 605-2010
2060 S Wineville Ave Ste A Ontario (91761) *(P-2863)*

Visionary Vr Inc .... E...... 323 868-7443
409 N Plymouth Blvd Los Angeles (90004) *(P-16417)*

Visiting Nrse Assn of Inland C (PA)...........................A...... 951 413-1200
600 W Santa Ana Blvd Ste 114 Santa Ana (92701) *(P-18651)*

Visiting Nurse & Hospice .... C...... 805 965-5555
512 E Gutierrez St Santa Barbara (93103) *(P-18652)*

Visiting Nurse & Hospice Care (PA)...........................C...... 805 965-5555
509 E Montecito St Ste 200 Santa Barbara (93103) *(P-18653)*

VISITING NURSE & HOSPICE CARE, Santa Barbara *Also Called: Visiting Nurse & Hospice Care (P-18653)*

Vista Care Group LLC (PA)..D...... 760 295-3900
1863 Devon Pl Vista (92084) *(P-19154)*

Vista Community Clinic (PA)..B...... 760 631-5000
1000 Vale Terrace Dr Vista (92084) *(P-17853)*

Vista Del Mar Child Fmly Svcs (PA)............................B...... 310 836-1223
3200 Motor Ave Los Angeles (90034) *(P-18986)*

Vista Del Mar Child Fmly Svcs .... C...... 310 836-1223
1533 Euclid St Santa Monica (90404) *(P-19309)*

Vista Del Mar Health Centers, Vista *Also Called: Life Care Centers America Inc (P-18136)*

Vista Gardens, Vista *Also Called: Vista Care Group LLC (P-19154)*

Vista Hill Foundation .... D...... 619 281-5511
6145 Decena Dr San Diego (92120) *(P-19015)*

Vista Hill Foundation .... D...... 619 266-0166
4125 Alpha St San Diego (92113) *(P-19155)*

Vista Hospital Riverside, Rancho Cucamonga *Also Called: Perris Valley Cmnty Hosp LLC (P-18375)*

Vista Hospital San Gabriel Vly, Baldwin Park *Also Called: Vista Spclty Hosp Sthern Cal L (P-18500)*

Vista Industrial Products Inc .... C...... 760 599-5050
3210 Executive Rdg Vista (92081) *(P-8068)*

Vista Irrigation District .... D...... 760 597-3100
1391 Engineer St Vista (92081) *(P-12216)*

Vista JV Partners LLC .... B...... 214 738-2771
2035 Corte Del Nogal Ste 200 Carlsbad (92011) *(P-17874)*

Vista Knoll Spclzed Care Fclty, Vista *Also Called: Vista Woods Health Assoc LLC (P-18072)*

Vista Metals Corp (PA)...C...... 909 823-4278
13425 Whittram Ave Fontana (92335) *(P-5716)*

Vista Pacifica Center, Jurupa Valley *Also Called: Vista Pacifica Enterprises Inc (P-18071)*

Vista Pacifica Enterprises Inc (PA)..............................C...... 951 682-4833
3674 Pacific Ave Jurupa Valley (92504) *(P-18071)*

Vista Paint Corporation (PA).......................................C...... 714 680-3800
2020 E Orangethorpe Ave Fullerton (92831) *(P-13675)*

Vista Spclty Hosp Sthern Cal L .... D...... 626 388-2700
14148 Francisquito Ave Baldwin Park (91706) *(P-18500)*

Vista Steel Co Inc .... E...... 805 653-1189
331 W Lewis St Ventura (93001) *(P-720)*

VISTA STEEL CO INC, Ventura *Also Called: Vista Steel Co Inc (P-720)*

Vista Steel Company (PA)..E...... 805 964-4732
6100 Francis Botello Rd Ste C Goleta (93117) *(P-6090)*

Vista Woods Health Assoc LLC .... C...... 760 630-2273
2000 Westwood Rd Vista (92083) *(P-18072)*

Vistage International Inc (PA)......................................D...... 858 523-6800
4840 Eastgate Mall San Diego (92121) *(P-20268)*

Vistancia Marketing LLC .... C...... 909 594-9500
655 Brea Canyon Rd Walnut (91789) *(P-20269)*

Visterra Credit Union .... C...... 951 656-4411
23520 Cactus Ave Moreno Valley (92553) *(P-14252)*

Visual Communications Company LLC .... C...... 800 522-5546
2173 Salk Ave Ste 175 Carlsbad (92008) *(P-9137)*

Visual Information Systems Co, Chino *Also Called: National Sign & Marketing Corp (P-11140)*

Visual Pak San Diego LLC .... C...... 847 689-1000
2320 Paseo De Las Americas Ste 201 San Diego (92154) *(P-16958)*

VIT Products Inc .... E...... 760 480-6702
2063 Wineridge Pl Escondido (92029) *(P-5950)*

Vita Juice Corporation .... D...... 818 899-1195
10725 Sutter Ave Pacoima (91331) *(P-1349)*

Vita-Herb Nutriceuticals Inc .... E...... 714 632-3726
172 E La Jolla St Placentia (92870) *(P-13734)*

Vita-Pakt Citrus Products Co (PA)...............................E...... 626 332-1101
10000 Stockdale Hwy Ste 390 Bakersfield (93311) *(P-1350)*

Vitabri Canopies, Huntington Beach *Also Called: Vae Industries Corporation (P-2512)*

Vitachrome Graphics, Montrose *Also Called: Vitachrome Graphics Group Inc (P-3822)*

Vitachrome Graphics Group Inc .... E...... 818 957-0900
3710 Park Pl Montrose (91020) *(P-3822)*

Vitajoy USA Inc .... E...... 626 965-8830
14165 Ramona Ave Chino (91710) *(P-4022)*

Vitamer Laboratories, Irvine *Also Called: Anabolic Incorporated (P-4050)*

Vitamins Unlimited, Brea *Also Called: North West Pharmanaturals Inc (P-4006)*

Vitas Healthcare Corporation .... D...... 858 805-6254
9106 Pulsar Ct Ste D Corona (92883) *(P-18100)*

Vitas Healthcare Corporation .... D...... 805 437-2100
333 N Lantana St Ste 124 Camarillo (93010) *(P-18101)*

Vitatech Nutritional Sciences Inc .... B...... 714 832-9700
2802 Dow Ave Tustin (92780) *(P-4253)*

Vitavet Labs Inc .... E...... 818 865-2600
5717 Corsa Ave Westlake Village (91362) *(P-11304)*

Vitawest Nutraceuticals Inc .... E...... 888 557-8012
1502 Arrow Hwy La Verne (91750) *(P-1289)*

Vitco Distributors Inc .... C...... 909 355-1300
715 E California St Ontario (91761) *(P-13241)*

Vitco Food Service, Ontario *Also Called: Vitco Distributors Inc (P-13241)*

Vitek Indus Video Pdts Inc .... E...... 661 294-8043
28492 Constellation Rd Valencia (91355) *(P-10889)*

Vitesse Manufacturing & Dev .... C...... 805 388-3700
11861 Western Ave Garden Grove (92841) *(P-8920)*

Vitesse Semiconductor, Garden Grove *Also Called: Vitesse Manufacturing & Dev (P-8920)*

Vitrek LLC (PA)...E...... 858 689-2755
12169 Kirkham Rd Ste C Poway (92064) *(P-10230)*

Vitro, San Diego *Also Called: Vitrorobertson LLC (P-15579)*

Vitrorobertson LLC .... D...... 619 234-0408
225 Broadway San Diego (92101) *(P-15579)*

Employee Codes: A=Over 500 employees, B=251-500
C=101-250, D=51-100, E=20-50, F=10-19, G=1-9

2024 Southern California
Business Directory and Buyers Guide

© Mergent Inc. 1-800-342-5647

1315

ALPHABETIC

Viva Concepts, Vernon Also Called: Viva Holdings LLC (P-3225)

Viva Holdings LLC (PA) .... F...... 818 243-1363
4210 Charter St Vernon (90058) (P-3225)

Viva Life Science Inc .... C...... 949 645-6100
350 Paularino Ave Costa Mesa (92626) (P-13075)

Viva Print LLC (HQ) .... F...... 818 243-1363
1025 N Brand Blvd Ste 300 Glendale (91202) (P-3226)

Vive Organic Inc .... E...... 877 774-9291
2554 Lincoln Blvd Ste 772 Venice (90291) (P-1351)

Vivometrics Inc .... F...... 805 667-2225
16030 Ventura Blvd # 470 Encino (91436) (P-10830)

Viz Cattle Corporation .... E...... 310 884-5260
17890 Castleton St Ste 350 City Of Industry (91748) (P-1208)

Vizio, Irvine Also Called: Vizio Holding Corp (P-8449)

Vizio Inc .... C...... 213 746-7730
2601 S Bdwy Unit B Los Angeles (90007) (P-8447)

Vizio Inc (HQ) .... C...... 855 833-3221
39 Tesla Irvine (92618) (P-8448)

Vizio Holding Corp (PA) .... C...... 949 428-2525
39 Tesla Irvine (92618) (P-8449)

Vizualogic LLC .... C...... 407 509-3421
1493 E Bentley Dr Corona (92879) (P-7266)

Vline Industries, Simi Valley Also Called: Computer Metal Products Corp (P-6217)

Vm International, Riverside Also Called: MSRS INC (P-12308)

Vmc Holdings Group Corp .... E...... 818 993-1466
9667 Owensmouth Ave Ste 202 Chatsworth (91311) (P-7457)

Vna of Greater Los Angeles Inc .... D...... 951 252-5314
17682 Mitchell N Ste 100 Irvine (92614) (P-18654)

VNA PRIVATE DUTY CARE, San Bernardino Also Called: Vnacare (P-18655)

Vnacare (PA) .... D...... 909 624-3574
412 E Vanderbilt Way Ste 100 San Bernardino (92408) (P-18655)

Vnaic, Santa Ana Also Called: Visiting Nrse Assn of Inland C (P-18651)

Voa, Los Angeles Also Called: Volunteers of Amer Los Angeles (P-19164)

Voa Plainview Head Start, Tujunga Also Called: Volunteers of Amer Los Angeles (P-19161)

Vocational Imprv Program Inc (PA) .... D...... 909 483-5924
9210 Rochester Ave Rancho Cucamonga (91730) (P-19195)

Vocational Visions .... C...... 949 837-7280
26041 Pala Mission Viejo (92691) (P-19196)

Voestalpine High Prfmce Mtls, Walnut Also Called: Edro Engineering LLC (P-7067)

Vogue Sign Inc .... E...... 805 487-7222
715 Commercial Ave Oxnard (93030) (P-11179)

Vogue Sign Company, Oxnard Also Called: Vogue Sign Inc (P-11179)

Voice of San Diego .... E...... 619 325-0525
110 W A St Ste 650 San Diego (92101) (P-3335)

Voipment, Tustin Also Called: Xbp Inc (P-16151)

Voit Real Estate Services LLC .... C...... 949 851-5100
2020 Main St Irvine (92614) (P-14913)

Volcano, San Diego Also Called: Philips Image Gded Thrapy Corp (P-10823)

Volcom LLC (HQ) .... C...... 949 646-2175
1740 Monrovia Ave Costa Mesa (92627) (P-16959)

Volex De Mexico, San Ysidro Also Called: Volex Inc (P-5243)

Volex Inc .... E...... 619 205-4900
511 E San Ysidro Blvd 509 San Ysidro (92173) (P-5243)

Volex Inc (HQ) .... E...... 669 444-1740
511 E San Ysidro Blvd Ste 509 San Ysidro (92173) (P-5244)

Volkswagen of Van Nuys Inc .... D...... 323 873-3311
300 Hitchcock Way Santa Barbara (93105) (P-13844)

Volkswagen Santa Monica Inc (PA) .... C...... 310 829-1888
2440 Santa Monica Blvd Santa Monica (90404) (P-13845)

Volt Management Corp .... D...... 858 576-3140
7676 Hazard Center Dr Ste 1000 San Diego (92108) (P-15947)

Volt Management Corp .... B...... 800 654-2624
2411 N Glassell St Orange (92865) (P-15948)

Volt Telecom Group, Corona Also Called: Volt Telecom Group Inc (P-20390)

Volt Telecom Group Inc .... B...... 951 493-8900
218 Helicopter Cir Corona (92878) (P-20390)

Volt Temporary Services, Orange Also Called: Volt Management Corp (P-15948)

Volt Workforce Solutions, San Diego Also Called: Volt Management Corp (P-15947)

Voltege Inc .... E...... 714 369-8068
10571 Los Alamitos Blvd Los Alamitos (90720) (P-16960)

Volume Services Inc .... B...... 619 525-5800
111 W Harbor Dr San Diego (92101) (P-17578)

Volume Services Inc .... B...... 323 644-6038
5333 Zoo Dr Los Angeles (90027) (P-17579)

Volunteers America Head Start, San Fernando Also Called: Child Care Resource Center Inc (P-19204)

Volunteers of Amer Los Angeles .... D...... 714 426-9834
2100 N Broadway Ste 300 Santa Ana (92706) (P-19156)

Volunteers of Amer Los Angeles .... C...... 213 749-0362
1032 W 18th St Los Angeles (90015) (P-19157)

Volunteers of Amer Los Angeles .... C...... 323 780-3770
522 N Dangler Ave Los Angeles (90022) (P-19158)

Volunteers of Amer Los Angeles .... D...... 626 337-9878
1760 W Cameron Ave Ste 104 West Covina (91790) (P-19159)

Volunteers of Amer Los Angeles .... D...... 661 290-2829
25141 Avenida Rondel Valencia (91355) (P-19160)

Volunteers of Amer Los Angeles .... C...... 818 352-5974
10819 Plainview Ave Tujunga (91042) (P-19161)

Volunteers of Amer Los Angeles .... C...... 818 769-3617
6724 Tujunga Ave North Hollywood (91606) (P-19162)

Volunteers of Amer Los Angeles .... C...... 818 506-0597
11243 Kittridge St North Hollywood (91606) (P-19163)

Volunteers of Amer Los Angeles .... C...... 213 627-8002
515 E 6th St Fl 9 Los Angeles (90021) (P-19164)

Volunteers of Amer Los Angeles .... D...... 818 834-8957
12550 Van Nuys Blvd Pacoima (91331) (P-19165)

Volunteers of Amer Los Angeles .... C...... 310 830-3404
334 Figueroa St Wilmington (90744) (P-19166)

Volunteers of America, Santa Ana Also Called: Volunteers of Amer Los Angeles (P-19156)

Volunteers of America, Los Angeles Also Called: Volunteers of Amer Los Angeles (P-19157)

Volunteers of America, Los Angeles Also Called: Volunteers of Amer Los Angeles (P-19158)

Volunteers of America, West Covina Also Called: Volunteers of Amer Los Angeles (P-19159)

Volunteers of America, Valencia Also Called: Volunteers of Amer Los Angeles (P-19160)

Volunteers of America, North Hollywood Also Called: Volunteers of Amer Los Angeles (P-19162)

Volunteers of America, Pacoima Also Called: Volunteers of Amer Los Angeles (P-19165)

Volunteers of America, Wilmington Also Called: Volunteers of Amer Los Angeles (P-19166)

Voluspa, Irvine Also Called: Flame and Wax Inc (P-11215)

Vomar, Canoga Park Also Called: Vomar Products Inc (P-3823)

Vomar Products Inc .... E...... 818 610-5115
7800 Deering Ave Canoga Park (91304) (P-3823)

Vomela, Santa Fe Springs Also Called: Vomela Specialty Company (P-3706)

Vomela Specialty Company .... C...... 562 944-3853
9810 Bell Ranch Dr Santa Fe Springs (90670) (P-3706)

Vons 2030, Stevenson Ranch Also Called: Vons Companies Inc (P-13711)

Vons 2111, Newhall Also Called: Vons Companies Inc (P-13708)

Vons 2124, Tujunga Also Called: Vons Companies Inc (P-13707)

Vons 2381, Corona Also Called: Vons Companies Inc (P-13709)

Vons 2407, Brawley Also Called: Vons Companies Inc (P-13712)

Vons 2560, Grover Beach Also Called: Vons Companies Inc (P-13710)

Vons Companies Inc .... C...... 818 353-4917
7789 Foothill Blvd Tujunga (91042) (P-13707)

Vons Companies Inc .... C...... 661 259-9214
24160 Lyons Ave Newhall (91321) (P-13708)

Vons Companies Inc .... C...... 951 278-8284
535 N Mckinley St Corona (92879) (P-13709)

Vons Companies Inc .... C...... 805 481-2492
1758 W Grand Ave Grover Beach (93433) (P-13710)

Vons Companies Inc .... C...... 661 254-3570
25850 The Old Rd Stevenson Ranch (91381) (P-13711)

Vons Companies Inc .... C...... 760 351-3002
475 W Main St Brawley (92227) (P-13712)

Vortech, Oxnard Also Called: Vortech Engineering Inc (P-7339)

Vortech Engineering Inc .... E...... 805 247-0226
1650 Pacific Ave Oxnard (93033) (P-7339)

Vortex Doors, Irvine Also Called: Vortex Industries Inc (P-1027)

Vortex Industries Inc (PA) .... E...... 714 434-8000
20 Odyssey Irvine (92618) (P-1027)

Vortox Air Technology Inc .... E...... 909 621-3843
121 S Indian Hill Blvd Claremont (91711) (P-7340)

Mergent email: customerrelations@mergent.com
1316

2024 Southern California
Business Directory and Buyers Guide

(P-0000) Products & Services Section entry number
(PA)=Parent Co (HQ)=Headquarters (DH)=Div Headquarters

Vorwerk LLC .... D...... 888 867-9375
3255 E Thousand Oaks Blvd Ste B Thousand Oaks (91362) *(P-6567)*

Votaw, Santa Fe Springs Also Called: Votaw Precision Technologies *(P-10088)*

Votaw Precision Technologies .... C...... 562 944-0661
13153 Lakeland Rd Santa Fe Springs (90670) *(P-10088)*

Votaw Wood Products Inc .... E...... 714 871-0932
301 W Imperial Hwy La Habra (90631) *(P-2728)*

Voyant Beauty, Chatsworth Also Called: Aware Products LLC *(P-4381)*

Voyetra Turtle Beach Inc (DH)... D...... 914 345-2255
11011 Via Frontera Ste A San Diego (92127) *(P-7579)*

Vpb Operating Co LLC 805 773-1011
147 Stimson Ave Pismo Beach (93449) *(P-15405)*

Vpet Usa LLC .... D...... 909 605-1668
12925b Marlay Ave Fontana (92337) *(P-5245)*

Vpm Management Inc .... C...... 949 863-1500
2400 Main St Ste 201 Irvine (92614) *(P-20114)*

Vpt Direct, Santa Fe Springs Also Called: Vantage Point Products Corp *(P-8446)*

Vroom Automotive Finance Corp (HQ)............................ B...... 949 224-1226
1071 Camelback St Ste 100 Newport Beach (92660) *(P-17040)*

Vsmpo-Tirus US Inc .... D...... 909 230-9020
2850 E Cedar St Ontario (91761) *(P-5729)*

VT Milcom Inc .... D...... 619 424-9024
1660 Logan Ave Ste 2 San Diego (92113) *(P-19716)*

Vtc Enterprises (PA)... D...... 805 928-5000
2445 A St Santa Maria (93455) *(P-19197)*

Vti Instruments Corporation (HQ)................................... E...... 949 955-1894
2031 Main St Irvine (92614) *(P-9269)*

Vtl Amplifiers Inc .... E...... 909 627-5944
4774 Murietta St Ste 10 Chino (91710) *(P-8450)*

Vts Sheetmetal Specialist Co .... E...... 714 237-1420
1041 N Grove St Anaheim (92806) *(P-6342)*

Vubiquity, Sherman Oaks Also Called: Vubiquity Holdings Inc *(P-12003)*

Vubiquity Holdings Inc (DH)... C...... 818 526-5000
15301 Ventura Blvd Ste 3000 Sherman Oaks (91403) *(P-12003)*

Vulcan Materials, Glendale Also Called: Calmat Co *(P-4657)*

Vulcan Materials Co .... B...... 760 737-3486
849 W Washington Ave Escondido (92025) *(P-5517)*

Vurger Co (usa) Corp .... E...... 929 318-9546
1800 Century Park E Ste 600 Los Angeles (90067) *(P-1498)*

Vvd Communications, Garden Grove Also Called: Video Vice Data Communications *(P-12002)*

Vxb & Orfwid Inc .... E...... 213 222-0030
5041 S Santa Fe Ave Unit B Vernon (90058) *(P-2382)*

Vxi Global Solutions, Los Angeles Also Called: Vxi Global Solutions LLC *(P-16961)*

Vxi Global Solutions LLC (PA).. A...... 213 739-4720
220 W 1st St Fl 3 Los Angeles (90012) *(P-16961)*

Vyaire Medical Inc .... E...... 714 919-3265
510 Technology Dr Ste 100 Irvine (92618) *(P-10630)*

Vytalogy Wellness LLC .... C...... 818 867-4440
15233 Ventura Blvd Sherman Oaks (91403) *(P-4023)*

W & F Mfg Inc .... E...... 818 394-6060
10635 Keswick St Sun Valley (91352) *(P-5951)*

W & M Textile, Vernon Also Called: Jml Textile Inc *(P-2025)*

W & W Concept Inc .... D...... 323 803-3090
4890 S Alameda St Vernon (90058) *(P-2383)*

W A Benjamin Electric Co .... E...... 213 749-7731
1615 Staunton Ave Los Angeles (90021) *(P-8131)*

W A Rasic Cnstr Co Inc (PA)... C...... 562 928-6111
4150 Long Beach Blvd Long Beach (90807) *(P-703)*

W B Mason Co Inc .... E...... 888 926-2766
5911 E Washington Blvd Commerce (90040) *(P-14072)*

W B Powell Inc .... D...... 951 270-0095
630 Parkridge Ave Norco (92860) *(P-2640)*

W B Walton Enterprises Inc .... E...... 951 683-0930
4185 Hallmark Pkwy San Bernardino (92407) *(P-8597)*

W C I, Oxnard Also Called: West Coast Industries Inc *(P-3035)*

W E O'Neil Construction, Rancho Cucamonga Also Called: WE Oneil Construction Co Cal *(P-602)*

W G A, Irvine Also Called: Western Growers Association *(P-19386)*

W G Holt Inc .... D...... 949 859-8800
101 Columbia Aliso Viejo (92656) *(P-8921)*

W J Ellison Co Inc .... E...... 626 814-4766
200 River Rd Corona (92878) *(P-7356)*

W L Rubottom Co .... D...... 805 648-6943
320 W Lewis St Ventura (93001) *(P-2684)*

W Lodging Inc .... A...... 619 258-6565
1825 Gillespie Way Ste 10 El Cajon (92020) *(P-15406)*

W Los Angeles .... B...... 310 208-8765
930 Hilgard Ave Los Angeles (90024) *(P-15407)*

W M Lyles Co .... C...... 951 296-2354
42142 Roick Dr Temecula (92590) *(P-704)*

W M Lyles Co .... C...... 661 387-1600
2810 Unicorn Rd Bakersfield (93308) *(P-19717)*

W Machine Works Inc .... E...... 818 890-8049
13814 Del Sur St San Fernando (91340) *(P-8069)*

W P Keith Co Inc .... E...... 562 948-3636
8323 Loch Lomond Dr Pico Rivera (90660) *(P-7374)*

W Plastics Inc .... E...... 800 442-9727
41573 Dendy Pkwy Ste 2543 Temecula (92590) *(P-4825)*

W R Grace & Co .... F....... 562 927-8513
7237 E Gage Ave Commerce (90040) *(P-3919)*

W R Grace & Co-Conn .... F....... 760 244-6107
17434 Mojave St Hesperia (92345) *(P-10304)*

W R Grace Construction Pdts, Commerce Also Called: W R Grace & Co *(P-3919)*

W R Meadows Inc .... E...... 909 469-2606
2300 Valley Blvd Pomona (91768) *(P-5456)*

W T E, Ontario Also Called: Wallner Expac Inc *(P-7175)*

W. R. Meadows Southern Cal, Pomona Also Called: W R Meadows Inc *(P-5456)*

W/S Packaging Group Inc .... D...... 714 992-2574
531 Airpark Dr Fullerton (92833) *(P-3252)*

W&J Business Ventures LLC .... D...... 310 645-7700
8620 Airport Blvd Los Angeles (90045) *(P-15408)*

W5 Concepts Inc .... E...... 323 231-2415
2049 E 38th St Vernon (90058) *(P-2270)*

Waag, Van Nuys Also Called: Wsw Corp *(P-9488)*

Wabash National Trlr Ctrs Inc 765 771-5300
16025 Slover Ave Fontana (92337) *(P-12265)*

Wac Lighting, Ontario Also Called: Wangs Alliance Corporation *(P-8300)*

Wacker Biotech US Inc .... E...... 858 875-4700
10390 Pacific Center Ct San Diego (92121) *(P-4254)*

Wacker Chemical Corporation .... D...... 909 590-8822
13910 Oaks Ave Chino (91710) *(P-4537)*

Waco Products, Santa Ana Also Called: Ackley Metal Products Inc *(P-7734)*

Wadco Industries Inc .... E...... 909 874-7800
2625 S Willow Ave Bloomington (92316) *(P-6091)*

Wadco Steel Sales, Bloomington Also Called: Wadco Industries Inc *(P-6091)*

Waddington North America Inc .... C...... 626 913-4022
1135 Samuelson St City Of Industry (91748) *(P-5246)*

Waev Inc (PA)... E...... 714 956-4040
2114 W Ball Rd Anaheim (92804) *(P-7000)*

Wagner Die Supply Inc (PA)... E...... 909 947-3044
2041 Elm Ct Ontario (91761) *(P-7105)*

Wagner Plate Works West Inc (PA)................................... E...... 562 531-6050
14015 Garfield Ave Paramount (90723) *(P-6168)*

Wahlco, Chino Also Called: Wahlco Inc *(P-8070)*

Wahlco Inc .... C...... 714 979-7300
4774 Murrietta St Ste 3 Chino (91710) *(P-8070)*

Wakunaga of America Co Ltd (HQ)................................... D...... 949 855-2776
23501 Madero Mission Viejo (92691) *(P-4255)*

Walashek Industrial & Mar Inc .... E...... 619 498-1711
1428 Mckinley Ave National City (91950) *(P-9850)*

Waldberg Inc .... D...... 818 843-0004
15301 Ventura Blvd Ste 300 Sherman Oaks (91403) *(P-15599)*

Walden House Inc .... C...... 626 258-0300
845 E Arrow Hwy Pomona (91767) *(P-19310)*

Walden Structures Inc .... B...... 909 389-9100
1000 Bristol St N # 126 Newport Beach (92660) *(P-2745)*

Waldorf Astoria Beverly Hills, Beverly Hills Also Called: Oasis West Realty LLC *(P-15267)*

Waldorf Astria Mnrc Bch Rsort, Dana Point Also Called: Cph Monarch Hotel LLC *(P-15123)*

Walin Group Inc .... E...... 714 444-5980
1117 Baker St Ste A Costa Mesa (92626) *(P-7411)*

Employee Codes: A=Over 500 employees, B=251-500
C=101-250, D=51-100, E=20-50, F=10-19, G=1-9

2024 Southern California
Business Directory and Buyers Guide

© Mergent Inc. 1-800-342-5647

1317

Walk Vascular LLC .... E 949 752-9642
17171 Daimler St Irvine (92614) *(P-12522)*

Walker, Ontario *Also Called: Walker Spring & Stamping Corp (P-6569)*

Walker Corporation .... E 909 390-4300
1555 S Vintage Ave Ontario (91761) *(P-6568)*

Walker Design Inc .... E 818 252-7788
9255 San Fernando Rd Sun Valley (91352) *(P-9851)*

Walker Engineering Enterprises, Sun Valley *Also Called: Walker Design Inc (P-9851)*

Walker Foods Inc .... D 323 268-5191
237 N Mission Rd Los Angeles (90033) *(P-1352)*

Walker Products .... E 714 554-5151
14291 Commerce Dr Garden Grove (92843) *(P-9486)*

WALKER PRODUCTS, Garden Grove *Also Called: Walker Products (P-9486)*

Walker Spring & Stamping Corp .... C 909 390-4300
1555 S Vintage Ave Ontario (91761) *(P-6569)*

Walking Company Holdings Inc (PA) .... **C 805 963-8727**
1800 Avenue Of The Stars Ste 300 Los Angeles (90067) *(P-13924)*

Wall Street Alley T-Shirt Co .... E 661 324-6207
4125 E Brundage Ln Bakersfield (93307) *(P-13156)*

Wallace E Miller Inc .... E 818 998-0444
9155 Alabama Ave Ste B Chatsworth (91311) *(P-8071)*

Wallner Expac Inc (PA) .... **D 909 481-8800**
1274 S Slater Cir Ontario (91761) *(P-7175)*

Wally & Pat Enterprises .... E 310 532-2031
13530 S Budlong Ave Gardena (90247) *(P-11305)*

Wally Parking, Los Angeles *Also Called: All Star Parking (P-16988)*

Walmart, Riverside *Also Called: Walmart Inc (P-11628)*

Walmart, Rialto *Also Called: Walmart Inc (P-13684)*

Walmart Inc .... C 951 320-5722
1001 Columbia Ave Riverside (92507) *(P-11628)*

Walmart Inc .... C 909 820-9912
1366 S Riverside Ave Rialto (92376) *(P-13684)*

Walnut Investment Corp .... A 714 238-9240
2940 E White Star Ave Anaheim (92806) *(P-12344)*

Walt Disney Company (PA) .... **A 818 560-1000**
500 S Buena Vista St Burbank (91521) *(P-17456)*

Walt Disney Music Company (DH) .... **C 818 560-1000**
500 S Buena Vista St Burbank (91521) *(P-17232)*

Walt Disney Pictures .... B 818 409-2200
811 Sonora Ave Glendale (91201) *(P-17233)*

Walt Disney Records Direct (DH) .... **A 818 560-1000**
500 S Buena Vista St Burbank (91521) *(P-17234)*

Walt Dsney Imgnring RES Dev In .... E 714 781-3152
1200 N Miller St Unit D Anaheim (92806) *(P-2461)*

Walt Dsney Imgnring RES Dev In (DH) .... **A 818 544-6500**
1401 Flower St Glendale (91201) *(P-17273)*

Walter Anderson Plumbing Inc .... C 619 449-7646
1830 John Towers Ave El Cajon (92020) *(P-833)*

Walter Foster Publishing Inc .... E 949 380-7510
6 Orchard Ste 100 Lake Forest (92630) *(P-3419)*

Walter N Coffman Inc .... D 619 266-2642
5180 Naranja St San Diego (92114) *(P-4910)*

Walters Auto Sales and Svc Inc .... C 888 316-4097
3213 Adams St Riverside (92504) *(P-13846)*

Walters Family Partnership .... C 760 320-6868
400 E Tahquitz Canyon Way Palm Springs (92262) *(P-15409)*

Walters Wholesale Electric Co (HQ) .... **E 562 988-3100**
18626 S Susana Rd Compton (90221) *(P-12625)*

Walton Company Inc .... F 714 847-8800
17900 Sampson Ln Huntington Beach (92647) *(P-2766)*

Walton Construction Inc .... D 909 267-7777
358 E Foothill Blvd Ste 100 San Dimas (91773) *(P-478)*

Walton Construction Services, San Dimas *Also Called: Walton Construction Inc (P-478)*

Walton Electric Corporation .... C 909 981-5051
755 N Central Ave Ste A Upland (91786) *(P-8632)*

Wamc Company Inc .... D 858 454-2753
7420 Clairemont Mesa Blvd San Diego (92111) *(P-14732)*

Wamco Inc (PA) .... **F 714 545-5560**
17752 Fitch Irvine (92614) *(P-12626)*

Wand Topco Inc .... A 323 734-3333
4774 W Adams Blvd Los Angeles (90016) *(P-17019)*

Wangs Alliance Corporation .... E 909 230-9401
1750 S Archibald Ave Ontario (91761) *(P-8300)*

Warco, Orange *Also Called: West American Rubber Co LLC (P-4803)*

Warco, Orange *Also Called: West American Rubber Co LLC (P-4804)*

Wardlow 2 LP (PA) .... **D 562 432-8066**
333 S Grand Ave Ste 4070 Los Angeles (90071) *(P-17162)*

Ware Disposal Inc .... C 714 834-0234
1451 Manhattan Ave Fullerton (92831) *(P-12194)*

Ware Malcomb (PA) .... **C 949 660-9128**
10 Edelman Irvine (92618) *(P-19746)*

Warlock Industries .... E 951 657-2680
23129 Cajalco Rd Ste A Perris (92570) *(P-9313)*

Warmelin Precision Products, Hawthorne *Also Called: DL Horton Enterprises Inc (P-7819)*

Warmington, Costa Mesa *Also Called: Warmington Mr 14 Assoc LLC (P-20115)*

Warmington Homes (PA) .... **C 714 434-4435**
3090 Pullman St Costa Mesa (92626) *(P-490)*

Warmington Homes .... C 949 679-3100
15615 Alton Pkwy Ste 150 Irvine (92618) *(P-491)*

Warmington Homes California, Costa Mesa *Also Called: Rebco Communities Inc (P-472)*

Warmington Mr 14 Assoc LLC .... D 714 557-5511
3090 Pullman St Costa Mesa (92626) *(P-20115)*

Warmington Residential Cal Inc .... C 714 557-5511
3090 Pullman St Costa Mesa (92626) *(P-465)*

Warner Bros, Burbank *Also Called: Warner Bros Transatlantic Inc (P-17285)*

Warner Bros Consumer Pdts Inc (DH) .... **C 818 954-7980**
4001 W Olive Ave Burbank (91505) *(P-20391)*

Warner Bros Distributing Inc .... B 818 954-6000
4000 Warner Blvd Bldg 154 Burbank (91522) *(P-20116)*

Warner Bros Entertainment Inc (DH) .... **C 818 954-6000**
4000 Warner Blvd Burbank (91522) *(P-17235)*

Warner Bros Entertainment Inc .... C 818 954-2209
3500 W Olive Ave Ste 200 Burbank (91505) *(P-17236)*

Warner Bros Home Entrmt Inc (DH) .... **D 818 954-6000**
4000 Warner Blvd Bldg 160 Burbank (91522) *(P-17237)*

Warner Bros Intl TV Dist Inc .... D 818 954-6000
4000 Warner Blvd Burbank (91522) *(P-17238)*

Warner Bros Records Inc (DH) .... **B 818 846-9090**
777 S Santa Fe Ave Los Angeles (90021) *(P-16962)*

Warner Bros Studio Facilities, Burbank *Also Called: Warner Bros Entertainment Inc (P-17236)*

Warner Bros Transatlantic Inc .... B 818 977-6384
3300 W Olive Ave Ste 200 Burbank (91505) *(P-17285)*

Warner Bros Transatlantic Inc .... B 818 954-5990
4001 W Olive Ave Burbank (91505) *(P-17286)*

Warner Chemicals Mfg, Los Angeles *Also Called: Velasco Carwash Supplies Corp (P-9312)*

Warner Food Management Co Inc .... C 818 285-2160
4917 Genesta Ave Encino (91316) *(P-14044)*

Warner Geometric Music, Los Angeles *Also Called: Warner/Chappell Music Inc (P-3500)*

Warner/Chappell Music Inc (DH) .... **C 310 441-8600**
777 S Santa Fe Ave Los Angeles (90021) *(P-3500)*

Warren Collins and Assoc Inc (PA) .... **E 909 548-6708**
5470 Daniels St Chino (91710) *(P-721)*

Warren E & P, Long Beach *Also Called: Warren E&P Inc (P-324)*

Warren E&P Inc .... D 214 393-9688
400 Oceangate Ste 200 Long Beach (90802) *(P-324)*

Wasco Medical Plaza, Wasco *Also Called: Adventist Health Delano (P-14987)*

Wasco Sales and Marketing Inc .... E 805 739-2747
2245 A St Santa Maria (93455) *(P-8282)*

Wasco Switches & Sensors, Santa Maria *Also Called: Wasco Sales and Marketing Inc (P-8282)*

Wash Mltfmily Ldry Systems LLC (PA) .... **C 800 421-6897**
2200 195th St Torrance (90501) *(P-15462)*

Washburn Grove Management Inc .... E 909 322-4690
27781 Fairview Ave Hemet (92544) *(P-2562)*

Washington C3 Center, San Diego *Also Called: Mitre Corporation (P-19936)*

Washington Garment Dyeing (PA) .... **E 213 747-1111**
1341 E Washington Blvd Los Angeles (90021) *(P-2099)*

Washington Grment Dyg Fnshg In .... E 213 747-1111
1332 E 18th St Los Angeles (90021) *(P-2094)*

Washington Inventory Service .... A 858 565-8111
9265 Sky Park Ct Ste 100 San Diego (92123) *(P-16963)*

Mergent email: customerrelations@mergent.com
1318

2024 Southern California
Business Directory and Buyers Guide

(P-0000) Products & Services Section entry number
(PA)=Parent Co (HQ)=Headquarters (DH)=Div Headquarters

Washington Iron Works, Gardena *Also Called: Washington Orna Ir Works Inc (P-1181)*

Washington Orna Ir Works Inc (PA).................................C...... 310 327-8660
17926 S Broadway Gardena (90248) *(P-1181)*

Wassco ....C...... 858 679-0444
12778 Brookprinter Pl Poway (92064) *(P-12834)*

Wassco Sales, Poway *Also Called: Wassco (P-12834)*

Wasser Filtration Inc (PA).................................D...... 714 696-6450
1215 N Fee Ana St Anaheim (92807) *(P-7412)*

Wasserman, Los Angeles *Also Called: Wasserman Media Group LLC (P-20270)*

Wasserman Comden & Casselman (PA).................D...... 323 872-0995
5567 Reseda Blvd Ste 330 Tarzana (91356) *(P-18954)*

Wasserman Media Group LLC (PA).................C...... 310 407-0200
10900 Wilshire Blvd Ste 1200 Los Angeles (90024) *(P-20270)*

Waste Management, Sun Valley *Also Called: Waste Management Recycling (P-11469)*

Waste Management, Corona *Also Called: Waste Management Cal Inc (P-12195)*

Waste Management, Sun Valley *Also Called: Waste Management Cal Inc (P-12196)*

Waste Management, Simi Valley *Also Called: Waste Management Cal Inc (P-12197)*

Waste Management, El Cajon *Also Called: Waste Management Cal Inc (P-12198)*

Waste Management, Oceanside *Also Called: Waste Management Cal Inc (P-12199)*

Waste Management, Palmdale *Also Called: Waste Management Cal Inc (P-12200)*

Waste Management, Gardena *Also Called: Waste MGT Collectn Recycl Inc (P-12201)*

Waste Management, Baldwin Park *Also Called: Waste MGT Collectn Recycl Inc (P-12202)*

Waste Management, Moreno Valley *Also Called: Waste MGT Collectn Recycl Inc (P-12203)*

Waste Management, Irvine *Also Called: Waste MGT Collectn Recycl Inc (P-12204)*

Waste Management Cal Inc ....C...... 951 277-1740
10910 Dawson Canyon Rd Corona (92883) *(P-12195)*

Waste Management Cal Inc (HQ).................C...... 877 836-6526
9081 Tujunga Ave Sun Valley (91352) *(P-12196)*

Waste Management Cal Inc ....C...... 805 522-7023
2801 N Madera Rd Simi Valley (93065) *(P-12197)*

Waste Management Cal Inc ....C...... 619 596-5100
1001 W Bradley Ave El Cajon (92020) *(P-12198)*

Waste Management Cal Inc ....C...... 760 439-2824
2141 Oceanside Blvd Oceanside (92054) *(P-12199)*

Waste Management Cal Inc ....C...... 661 947-7197
1200 W City Ranch Rd Palmdale (93551) *(P-12200)*

Waste Management Recycling ....D...... 818 767-6180
9227 Tujunga Ave Sun Valley (91352) *(P-11469)*

Waste MGT Collectn Recycl Inc ....D...... 310 532-6511
1449 W Rosecrans Ave Gardena (90249) *(P-12201)*

Waste MGT Collectn Recycl Inc ....C...... 626 960-7551
13940 Live Oak Ave Baldwin Park (91706) *(P-12202)*

Waste MGT Collectn Recycl Inc ....C...... 951 242-0421
17700 Indian St Moreno Valley (92551) *(P-12203)*

Waste MGT Collectn Recycl Inc ....C...... 949 451-2600
16122 Construction Cir E Irvine (92606) *(P-12204)*

Wastech Controls & Engrg Inc ....D...... 818 998-3500
20600 Nordhoff St Chatsworth (91311) *(P-12835)*

Watch L.A., Los Angeles *Also Called: Pierre Mitri (P-2358)*

Water & Power Department, Long Beach *Also Called: County of Los Angeles (P-12117)*

Water Associates LLC ....E...... 661 281-6077
5060 California Ave Bakersfield (93309) *(P-8598)*

Water Purification, Rancho Dominguez *Also Called: Parker-Hannifin Corporation (P-8949)*

Water Treatment Plant, Riverside *Also Called: City of Riverside (P-7649)*

Water Works Inc ....E...... 858 499-0119
5490 Complex St Ste 601 San Diego (92123) *(P-7691)*

Wateranywhere, Vista *Also Called: Applied Membranes Inc (P-7639)*

Waterbox LLC ....E...... 323 743-8070
2500 E Imperial Hwy Ste 201 Brea (92821) *(P-3074)*

Watercrest Inc ....C...... 909 390-3944
4850 E Airport Dr Ontario (91761) *(P-6169)*

Waterfi LLC ....F...... 619 438-0058
4379 30th St Ste 2 San Diego (92104) *(P-12709)*

Waterfront Design Group LLC ....E...... 213 746-5800
122 E Washington Blvd Los Angeles (90015) *(P-2227)*

Waterfront Hotel LLC ....B...... 714 845-8000
21100 Pacific Coast Hwy Huntington Beach (92648) *(P-15410)*

Waterman Canyon Post Acute, San Bernardino *Also Called: Watermanidence Opco LLC (P-18102)*

Waterman Convalescent Hosp Inc (PA).................C...... 909 882-1215
1850 N Waterman Ave San Bernardino (92404) *(P-18073)*

Watermanidence Opco LLC ....B...... 909 882-1215
1850 N Waterman Ave San Bernardino (92404) *(P-18102)*

Watermark, Riverside *Also Called: Irrometer Company Inc (P-10375)*

Watermark Rtrment Cmmnties Inc ....D...... 760 346-5420
41505 Carlotta Dr Palm Desert (92211) *(P-18074)*

Watersentinel, Temecula *Also Called: Aquamor LLC (P-7642)*

Waterstone Faucets, Murrieta *Also Called: Waterstone Faucets LLC (P-12749)*

Waterstone Faucets LLC ....C...... 951 304-0520
41180 Raintree Ct Murrieta (92562) *(P-12749)*

Watertite Products Inc 901 853-5001
455 W Victoria St Compton (90220) *(P-5976)*

Waterway Plastics, Oxnard *Also Called: B & S Plastics Inc (P-4951)*

Watg, Irvine *Also Called: Wimberly Allson Tong Goo NA In (P-19747)*

Watkins Manufacturing Corp ....B...... 760 598-6464
1325 Hot Springs Way Vista (92081) *(P-4922)*

Watkins Manufacturing Corp (HQ).................C...... 760 598-6464
1280 Park Center Dr Vista (92081) *(P-11306)*

Watkins Wellness, Vista *Also Called: Watkins Manufacturing Corp (P-11306)*

WATTS HEALTH, Los Angeles *Also Called: Watts Healthcare Corporation (P-17830)*

Watts Health Foundation Inc (HQ).................B...... 310 424-2220
3405 W Imperial Hwy Ste 304 Inglewood (90303) *(P-18103)*

Watts Health Systems Inc (PA).................A...... 310 424-2220
3405 W Imperial Hwy Inglewood (90303) *(P-20271)*

Watts Healthcare Corporation (PA).................C...... 323 564-4331
10300 Compton Ave Los Angeles (90002) *(P-17830)*

Watts Labor Community Action ....C...... 323 563-5639
4142 Palmwood Dr Apt 11 Los Angeles (90008) *(P-19167)*

Watts Spacemaker Inc ....E...... 714 542-4649
1918 W Chestnut Ave Santa Ana (92703) *(P-6170)*

Wave Community Newspapers Inc (PA).................E...... 323 290-3000
1007 N Sepulveda Blvd Manhattan Beach (90266) *(P-3336)*

Wavenet Inc (PA).................F...... 310 885-4200
707 E Sepulveda Blvd Carson (90745) *(P-5752)*

Wavestream Corporation (HQ).................C...... 909 599-9080
545 W Terrace Dr San Dimas (91773) *(P-9138)*

Wax Jean By Ambiance, Los Angeles *Also Called: Ambiance USA Inc (P-2300)*

Waxie Sanitary Supply, San Diego *Also Called: Waxies Enterprises LLC (P-12897)*

Waxie Sanitary Supply, Santa Ana *Also Called: Waxies Enterprises LLC (P-14153)*

Waxies Enterprises LLC ....D...... 714 545-8441
3220 S Fairview St Santa Ana (92704) *(P-14153)*

Waxies Enterprises LLC (DH).................C...... 800 995-4466
9353 Waxie Way San Diego (92123) *(P-12897)*

Way Out West Inc ....E...... 310 769-6937
1440 W 135th St Gardena (90249) *(P-2187)*

Wayne Gossett Ford Inc ....D...... 760 753-6286
1424 Encinitas Blvd Encinitas (92024) *(P-13847)*

Wayne Perry Inc (PA).................C...... 714 826-0352
8281 Commonwealth Ave Buena Park (90621) *(P-1182)*

Wayne Provision Co Inc (PA).................D...... 323 277-5888
5030 Gifford Ave Vernon (90058) *(P-13310)*

Wayne Tool & Die Co ....E...... 818 364-1611
15853 Olden St Sylmar (91342) *(P-5606)*

Wb Music Corp (DH).................C...... 310 441-8600
10585 Santa Monica Blvd Ste 200 Los Angeles (90025) *(P-3501)*

Wbi Inc ....A...... 800 673-4968
8201 Woodley Ave Van Nuys (91406) *(P-10890)*

Wbt Group LLC ....E...... 323 735-1201
1401 S Shamrock Ave Monrovia (91016) *(P-11307)*

Wbt Industries, Monrovia *Also Called: Wbt Group LLC (P-11307)*

Wcbm Company (PA).................E...... 323 262-3274
1812 W 135th St Gardena (90249) *(P-11080)*

Wco Hotels Inc ....A...... 714 635-2300
1600 S Disneyland Dr Anaheim (92802) *(P-15411)*

WCP Inc ....D...... 562 653-9797
17730 Crusader Ave Cerritos (90703) *(P-5247)*

Wcs Distributing ....E...... 909 888-2015
268 W Orange Show Ln San Bernardino (92408) *(P-12836)*

Wcs Equipment Holdings LLC ....D...... 909 993-5700
1350 E Lexington Ave Pomona (91766) *(P-5665)*

Employee Codes: A=Over 500 employees, B=251-500
C=101-250, D=51-100, E=20-50, F=10-19, G=1-9

2024 Southern California
Business Directory and Buyers Guide

© Mergent Inc. 1-800-342-5647
1319

Wcs Equipment Holdings LLC (HQ)......................D...... 909 393-8405
13568 Vintage Pl Chino (91710) *(P-5666)*

Wcs Equipment Holdings LLC......................D...... 909 393-8405
13066 14th St Chino (91710) *(P-6343)*

Wd-40 Company......................C...... 619 275-1400
9715 Businesspark Ave San Diego (92131) *(P-4656)*

WD-40 Company (PA)......................C...... 619 275-1400
9715 Businesspark Ave San Diego (92131) *(P-4689)*

Wdm Group, San Diego Also Called: White Digital Media Inc *(P-13498)*

We Do Graphics Inc......................E...... 714 997-7390
1150 N Main St Orange (92867) *(P-3707)*

We Five-R Corporation......................F...... 323 263-6757
1507 S Sunol Dr Los Angeles (90023) *(P-6679)*

We Imagine Inc......................D...... 818 709-0064
9371 Canoga Ave Chatsworth (91311) *(P-8751)*

WE Oneil Construction Co Cal......................C...... 909 466-5300
9485 Haven Ave Ste 101 Rancho Cucamonga (91730) *(P-602)*

We Pack It All LLC......................C...... 626 301-9214
2745 Huntington Dr Duarte (91010) *(P-16964)*

We See Dragons LLC......................C...... 310 361-5700
1100 Glendon Ave Ste 1700 Los Angeles (90024) *(P-16611)*

We The Pie People LLC......................E...... 818 349-1880
9909 Topanga Canyon Blvd # 159 Chatsworth (91311) *(P-1302)*

Weapon X Security Inc......................D...... 818 818-9950
297 Country Club Dr Simi Valley (93065) *(P-20402)*

Weapons System Division, Northridge Also Called: Northrop Grumman Systems Corp *(P-10015)*

Weartech International Inc......................E...... 714 683-2430
1177 N Grove St Anaheim (92806) *(P-7305)*

Weatherford International LLC......................F...... 805 933-0242
201 Hallock Dr Santa Paula (93060) *(P-395)*

Webasto Charging Systems Inc (DH)......................D...... 626 415-4000
1333 S Mayflower Ave Ste 100 Monrovia (91016) *(P-12266)*

Webb, Riverside Also Called: Albert A Webb Associates *(P-19543)*

Webb Del California Corp (DH)......................B...... 760 772-5300
39755 Berkey Dr Palm Desert (92211) *(P-14914)*

Webcor Builders, San Diego Also Called: Webcor Construction LP *(P-603)*

Webcor Builders, Los Angeles Also Called: Webcor Construction LP *(P-604)*

Webcor Construction LP......................C...... 619 798-3891
2150 W Washington St Ste 308 San Diego (92110) *(P-603)*

Webcor Construction LP......................C...... 213 239-2800
333 S Grand Ave Ste 4400 Los Angeles (90071) *(P-604)*

Weber, Rancho Cucamonga Also Called: American Fruits & Flavors LLC *(P-1755)*

Weber Distribution, Norwalk Also Called: Weber Distribution LLC *(P-11629)*

Weber Distribution LLC......................C...... 562 404-9996
15301 Shoemaker Ave Norwalk (90650) *(P-11629)*

Weber Drilling Co Inc......................E...... 310 670-7708
4028 W 184th St Torrance (90504) *(P-8072)*

Weber Metals Inc (HQ)......................E...... 562 602-0260
16706 Garfield Ave Paramount (90723) *(P-6484)*

Weber Metals Inc......................B...... 562 543-3316
233 E Manville St Compton (90220) *(P-6485)*

Weber Orthopedic LP (PA)......................D...... 800 221-5465
1185 E Main St Santa Paula (93060) *(P-10722)*

Weber Precision Graphics, Santa Ana Also Called: Artisan Nameplate Awards Corp *(P-3735)*

Weber Printing Company Inc......................E...... 310 639-5064
1124 E Del Amo Blvd Long Beach (90807) *(P-3708)*

Webmetro......................D...... 909 599-8885
160 Via Verde Ste 1 San Dimas (91773) *(P-16418)*

Weckerle Cosmetic, Torrance Also Called: Weckerle Cosmetics Usa Inc *(P-13076)*

Weckerle Cosmetics Usa Inc......................E...... 310 328-7000
525 Maple Ave Torrance (90503) *(P-13076)*

Wedbush Securities Inc (HQ)......................B...... 213 688-8000
1000 Wilshire Blvd Ste 900 Los Angeles (90017) *(P-14408)*

Weddingchannelcom Inc......................C...... 213 599-4100
5757 Wilshire Blvd Ste 504 Los Angeles (90036) *(P-3502)*

Wedgewood Inc (PA)......................D...... 310 640-3070
2015 Manhattan Beach Blvd Ste 100 Redondo Beach (90278) *(P-15059)*

WEI-Chuan USA Inc (PA)......................C...... 626 225-7168
13031 Temple Ave City Of Industry (91746) *(P-13249)*

Weider Health and Fitness......................B...... 818 884-6800
21100 Erwin St Woodland Hills (91367) *(P-1789)*

Weingart Center Association......................C...... 213 622-6359
566 S San Pedro St Los Angeles (90013) *(P-19168)*

WEINGART CENTER FOR THE HOMELE, Los Angeles Also Called: Weingart Center Association *(P-19168)*

Weiser Iron Inc......................F...... 909 429-4600
64 Sundance Dr Pomona (91766) *(P-6092)*

Weiser Lock Corporation......................F...... 949 672-4000
19701 Da Vinci Foothill Ranch (92610) *(P-5952)*

Weiss Sheet Metal Company......................E...... 310 354-2700
1715 W 135th St Gardena (90249) *(P-1056)*

Welaco, Bakersfield Also Called: Well Analysis Corporation Inc *(P-2563)*

Welbilt Inc......................E...... 310 339-1555
3835 E Thousand Oaks Blvd Unit 315 Westlake Village (91362) *(P-396)*

WELCOME BABY, Santa Ana Also Called: Priority Ctr Ending The Gnrtna *(P-19127)*

Weld-It Co, Orange Also Called: Sam Schaffer Inc *(P-17151)*

Weld-On Adhesives, Compton Also Called: Ips Corporation *(P-4571)*

Weldex Corporation (PA)......................C...... 714 761-2100
6751 Katella Ave Cypress (90630) *(P-8922)*

Weldlogic Inc......................D...... 805 375-1670
2651 Lavery Ct Newbury Park (91320) *(P-17098)*

Weldlogic Gas & Supply, Newbury Park Also Called: Weldlogic Inc *(P-17098)*

Weldmac Manufacturing Company......................E...... 619 440-2300
1533 N Johnson Ave El Cajon (92020) *(P-8073)*

Weldmac Manufacturing Company......................E...... 619 440-2300
1451 N Johnson Ave El Cajon (92020) *(P-8074)*

Welk Group Inc (PA)......................B...... 760 749-3000
11400 W Olympic Blvd Ste 760 Los Angeles (90064) *(P-15412)*

Welk Group Inc......................B...... 760 749-3000
8860 Lawrence Welk Dr Escondido (92026) *(P-15413)*

Welk Group Inc......................C...... 760 749-3225
8860 Lawrence Welk Dr Escondido (92026) *(P-17443)*

Welk Group Inc......................C...... 760 749-0983
10333 Meadow Glen Way E Escondido (92026) *(P-17535)*

Welk Music Group, Los Angeles Also Called: Welk Group Inc *(P-15412)*

Welk Resort Center, San Marcos Also Called: Whv Resort Group Inc *(P-14885)*

Welk Resort Center, Escondido Also Called: Welk Group Inc *(P-15413)*

Well Analysis Corporation Inc (PA)......................E...... 661 283-9510
5500 Woodmere Dr Bakersfield (93313) *(P-2563)*

Wella Corporation (HQ)......................C...... 800 422-2336
4500 Park Granada # 100 Calabasas (91302) *(P-4467)*

Wella Operations US LLC......................B...... 818 999-5112
4500 Park Granada Ste 100 Calabasas (91302) *(P-13077)*

Wellington Crt Asssted Lving C, Arcadia Also Called: Leisure Care LLC *(P-19280)*

Wellington Foods Inc......................C...... 951 547-7000
1930 California Ave Corona (92881) *(P-1290)*

Wellmade Inc......................D...... 213 221-1123
800 E 12th St Los Angeles (90021) *(P-20272)*

Wellnest......................D...... 323 766-2345
3787 S Vermont Ave Los Angeles (90007) *(P-14694)*

Wellnest Emtonal Hlth Wellness (PA)......................C...... 323 373-2400
3031 S Vermont Ave Los Angeles (90007) *(P-19169)*

Wells Fargo Capital Fin LLC (DH)......................D...... 310 453-7300
2450 Colorado Ave Ste 3000w Santa Monica (90404) *(P-14292)*

Wells Fargo Capital Finance Inc......................C...... 310 453-7300
2450 Colo Ave 3000w 3rd Fl Santa Monica (90404) *(P-16965)*

Wells Fargo Investments LLC......................D...... 619 702-6949
401 B St Ste 101 San Diego (92101) *(P-14175)*

Wells Fargo Investments LLC......................D...... 310 546-4235
603 14th St Manhattan Beach (90266) *(P-14176)*

Wells Fargo Securities LLC......................A...... 310 479-3500
1800 Century Park E Ste 1100 Los Angeles (90067) *(P-14409)*

Wells Frgo Insur Svcs Minn Inc......................C...... 909 481-3802
4141 Inland Empire Blvd Ontario (91764) *(P-14642)*

Wells Media Group Inc (PA)......................F...... 619 584-1100
3570 Camino Del Rio N Ste 100 San Diego (92108) *(P-18955)*

Wells Struthers Corporation......................E...... 814 726-1000
10375 Slusher Dr Santa Fe Springs (90670) *(P-6171)*

Welltower Om Group LLC......................C...... 626 254-0552
301 W Huntington Dr Ste 5 Arcadia (91007) *(P-14695)*

Welovefine, Los Angeles Also Called: Mf Inc *(P-2256)*

Mergent email: customerrelations@mergent.com
1320
2024 Southern California
Business Directory and Buyers Guide
(P-0000) Products & Services Section entry number
(PA)=Parent Co (HQ)=Headquarters (DH)=Div Headquarters

Wems Inc (PA)..D....... 310 644-0251
4650 W Rosecrans Ave Hawthorne (90250) *(P-7341)*

Wems Electronics, Hawthorne *Also Called: Wems Inc (P-7341)*

Wepower LLC ....E...... 866 385-9463
32 Journey Ste 250 Aliso Viejo (92656) *(P-6891)*

Werfen, San Diego *Also Called: Inova Diagnostics Inc (P-19847)*

Wermers, San Diego *Also Called: Wermers Multi-Family Corp (P-479)*

Wermers Multi-Family Corp ....C...... 858 535-1475
5120 Shoreham Pl Ste 150 San Diego (92122) *(P-479)*

Werner Corporation ....E...... 951 277-4586
25050 Maitri Rd Corona (92883) *(P-5518)*

Werner Systems Inc ....E...... 714 838-4444
14321 Myford Rd Tustin (92780) *(P-5722)*

Wes Go Inc ....E...... 818 504-1200
8211 Lankershim Blvd North Hollywood (91605) *(P-3824)*

Wesanco Inc ....E...... 714 739-4989
14870 Desman Rd La Mirada (90638) *(P-9826)*

Wesco Aircraft, Valencia *Also Called: Falcon Aerospace Holdings LLC (P-12907)*

Wesco Aircraft Hardware Corp ....B...... 661 775-7200
27727 Avenue Scott Valencia (91355) *(P-12923)*

Wescom Central Credit Union (PA).................B...... 888 493-7266
123 S Marengo Ave Pasadena (91101) *(P-14253)*

Wesfac Inc (HQ)..F....... 562 861-2160
9300 Hall Rd Downey (90241) *(P-7692)*

Weslar Inc ....D...... 661 702-1362
28310 Constellation Rd Valencia (91355) *(P-1028)*

Weslend Financial, Santa Ana *Also Called: Lenox Financial Mortgage Corp (P-14333)*

Wesley Allen Inc ....C...... 323 231-4275
1001 E 60th St Los Angeles (90001) *(P-2840)*

Wespac, Downey *Also Called: Wesfac Inc (P-7692)*

Wessco International, Los Angeles *Also Called: Wessco Intl Ltd A Cal Ltd Prtn (P-2561)*

Wessco Intl Ltd A Cal Ltd Prtn (PA).............D...... 310 477-4272
11400 W Olympic Blvd Ste 450 Los Angeles (90064) *(P-2561)*

Wessex Industries Inc ....E...... 562 944-5760
8619 Red Oak St Rancho Cucamonga (91730) *(P-6854)*

West American Energy Corp ....F...... 661 747-7732
4949 Buckley Way Ste 207 Bakersfield (93309) *(P-289)*

West American Rubber Co LLC ....C...... 714 532-3355
750 N Main St Orange (92868) *(P-4803)*

West American Rubber Co LLC (PA)...............C...... 714 532-3355
1337 W Braden Ct Orange (92868) *(P-4804)*

West Anaheim Care Center, Anaheim *Also Called: Mark & Fred Enterprises (P-18009)*

West Anaheim Medical Center, Anaheim *Also Called: Prime Healthcare Anaheim LLC (P-18385)*

West Angeles Ch God In Chrst ....C...... 323 731-2567
3010 Crenshaw Blvd Los Angeles (90016) *(P-18987)*

West Angeles Christian Academy, Los Angeles *Also Called: West Angeles Ch God In Chrst (P-18987)*

West Area Opportunity Center, Santa Monica *Also Called: Casa De Hermandad (P-10983)*

West Bay Imports Inc ....E...... 323 720-5777
7245 Oxford Way Commerce (90040) *(P-13568)*

West Bent Bolt Division, Santa Fe Springs *Also Called: Mid-West Fabricating Co (P-9425)*

West Bond Inc (PA).....................................E...... 714 978-1551
1551 S Harris Ct Anaheim (92806) *(P-8075)*

West Bsin Wtr Rclamation Plant, El Segundo *Also Called: Suez Water Indiana LLC (P-10164)*

West Capital Lending Inc ....C...... 818 501-2666
15233 Ventura Blvd Ste 120 Sherman Oaks (91403) *(P-20273)*

West Cast Stl Proc Hldings LLC (PA)..............E...... 909 393-8405
13568 Vintage Pl Chino (91710) *(P-5607)*

West Central Food Service, Norwalk *Also Called: West Central Produce Inc (P-13348)*

West Central Produce Inc ....B...... 213 629-3600
12840 Leyva St Norwalk (90650) *(P-13348)*

West Cntinela Vly Care Ctr Inc ....D...... 310 674-3216
950 S Flower St Inglewood (90301) *(P-18075)*

West Coast AC Co Inc ....C...... 619 561-8000
1155 Pioneer Way Ste 101 El Cajon (92020) *(P-834)*

West Coast Aerospace Inc (PA)......................D...... 310 518-3167
220 W E St Wilmington (90744) *(P-11081)*

West Coast Aerospace Inc ....F...... 310 518-0633
24224 Broad St Carson (90745) *(P-12888)*

West Coast Airlines, Riverside *Also Called: West Coast Unlimited (P-9314)*

West Coast Arborists Inc ....C...... 909 783-6544
21718 Walnut Ave Grand Terrace (92313) *(P-225)*

West Coast Arborists Inc ....C...... 805 671-5092
11405 Nardo St Ventura (93004) *(P-226)*

West Coast Arborists Inc ....C...... 858 566-4204
8163 Commercial St La Mesa (91942) *(P-466)*

West Coast Arborists Inc (PA).......................D...... 714 991-1900
2200 E Via Burton Anaheim (92806) *(P-221)*

West Coast Button Mfg Co, Gardena *Also Called: Wcbm Company (P-11080)*

West Coast Chain Mfg Co ....E...... 909 923-7800
4245 Pacific Privado Ontario (91761) *(P-9270)*

West Coast Construction, Jurupa Valley *Also Called: Perry Coast Construction Inc (P-578)*

West Coast Consulting LLC ....C...... 949 250-4102
9233 Research Dr Ste 200 Irvine (92618) *(P-16419)*

West Coast Corporation ....E...... 909 923-7800
4245 Pacific Privado Ontario (91761) *(P-9271)*

West Coast Countertops Inc ....D...... 951 719-3670
1200 Marlborough Ave Ste B Riverside (92507) *(P-1183)*

West Coast Coupon Inc ....E...... 818 341-2400
9400 Oso Ave Chatsworth (91311) *(P-15604)*

West Coast Custom Sheet Metal ....E...... 818 252-7500
8125 Lankershim Blvd North Hollywood (91605) *(P-6344)*

West Coast Dental Labs LLC ....B...... 855 220-5600
12002 Aviation Blvd Hawthorne (90250) *(P-18576)*

West Coast Distribution Inc ....D...... 323 588-6508
4440 E 26th St Vernon (90058) *(P-526)*

West Coast Drywall & Co Inc ....B...... 951 778-3592
1610 W Linden St Riverside (92507) *(P-1002)*

West Coast Drywall & Paint, Riverside *Also Called: West Coast Drywall & Co Inc (P-1002)*

West Coast Firestopping Inc ....E...... 714 935-1104
1130 W Trenton Ave Orange (92867) *(P-1184)*

West Coast Foundry LLC (HQ).......................E...... 323 583-1421
2450 E 53rd St Huntington Park (90255) *(P-5667)*

West Coast Furn Framers Inc ....E...... 760 669-5275
17402 Eucalyptus St Hesperia (92345) *(P-2580)*

West Coast Gasket Co ....D...... 714 869-0123
300 Ranger Ave Brea (92821) *(P-4748)*

West Coast Industries Inc ....E...... 213 627-1113
707 E 7th St Los Angeles (90021) *(P-3034)*

West Coast Industries Inc (PA)......................E...... 415 621-6656
361 Bernoulli Cir Oxnard (93030) *(P-3035)*

West Coast Interiors Inc ....A...... 951 778-3592
1610 W Linden St Riverside (92507) *(P-857)*

West Coast Iron Inc ....D...... 619 464-8456
9302 Jamacha Rd Spring Valley (91977) *(P-1140)*

West Coast Labels, Placentia *Also Called: Cinton LLC (P-3168)*

West Coast Laboratories Inc ....E...... 310 527-6163
156 E 162nd St Gardena (90248) *(P-4256)*

West Coast Ltg & Enrgy Inc ....D...... 951 296-0680
18550 Minthorn St Lake Elsinore (92530) *(P-951)*

West Coast Manufacturing, Stanton *Also Called: West Coast Manufacturing Inc (P-6570)*

West Coast Manufacturing Inc ....E...... 714 897-4221
11822 Western Ave Stanton (90680) *(P-6570)*

West Coast Metal Stamping, Irvine *Also Called: Perfect Choice Mfrs Inc (P-11265)*

West Coast Metal Stamping Incorporated ....E...... 714 792-0322
550 W Crowther Ave Placentia (92870) *(P-6571)*

West Coast Mfg & Whsng, Ontario *Also Called: Idx Los Angeles LLC (P-2981)*

West Coast Milling, Lancaster *Also Called: Pavement Recycling Systems Inc (P-4663)*

West Coast Motor Sports, Perris *Also Called: West Coast Yamaha Inc (P-7381)*

West Coast Naturals LLC ....E...... 310 467-3007
4591 Firestone Blvd South Gate (90280) *(P-1790)*

West Coast Operations, Chula Vista *Also Called: East Cast Repr Fabrication LLC (P-6022)*

West Coast Painting, Riverside *Also Called: West Coast Interiors Inc (P-857)*

West Coast Physical Therapy, Laguna Niguel *Also Called: Mission Internal Med Group Inc (P-17713)*

West Coast Pvd Inc ....E...... 714 822-6362
3280 Corporate Vw Vista (92081) *(P-6680)*

West Coast Sales Office & Whse, Oxnard *Also Called: Amiad USA Inc (P-7636)*

West Coast Service Center, Ontario *Also Called: Vsmpo-Tirus US Inc (P-5729)*

Employee Codes: A=Over 500 employees, B=251-500
C=101-250, D=51-100, E=20-50, F=10-19, G=1-9

2024 Southern California
Business Directory and Buyers Guide

© Mergent Inc. 1-800-342-5647
1321

West Coast Surfaces Inc .... E...... 951 699-0600
  27620 Commerce Center Dr Ste 107 Temecula (92590) *(P-1035)*

West Coast Switchgear (DH) ....**D**...... **562 802-3441**
  13837 Bettencourt St Cerritos (90703) *(P-8132)*

West Coast Trends Inc .... E...... 714 843-9288
  17811 Jamestown Ln Huntington Beach (92647) *(P-11041)*

West Coast Trimming Corp .... E...... 323 587-0701
  7100 Wilson Ave Los Angeles (90001) *(P-2057)*

West Coast Unlimited .... E...... 951 352-1234
  11161 Pierce St Riverside (92505) *(P-9314)*

West Coast Vinyl Windows, Cerritos *Also Called: WCP Inc (P-5247)*

West Coast Wldg & Piping Inc .... D...... 805 246-5841
  750 W Hueneme Rd Oxnard (93033) *(P-17099)*

West Coast Wood Preserving LLC .... C...... 661 833-0429
  5601 District Blvd Bakersfield (93313) *(P-2748)*

West Coast Yamaha Inc .... E...... 951 943-2061
  1622 Illinois Ave Perris (92571) *(P-7381)*

West Coast-Accudyne Inc .... E...... 562 927-2546
  7180 Scout Ave Bell (90201) *(P-7042)*

West Covina Medical Clinic Inc (PA) ....**C**...... **626 960-8614**
  1500 W West Covina Pkwy Ste 100 West Covina (91790) *(P-17831)*

WEST COVINA PHYSICAL THERAPY, West Covina *Also Called: Doctors Hospital W Covina Inc (P-18246)*

West Dermatology, Newport Beach *Also Called: West Dermatology Med MGT Inc (P-17832)*

West Dermatology Med MGT Inc (PA) .... A...... 909 793-3000
  680 Newport Center Dr Ste 150 Newport Beach (92660) *(P-17832)*

West Edge, Chula Vista *Also Called: West Edge Inc (P-14883)*

West Edge Inc ....D...... 619 475-4095
  1061 Tierra Del Rey Chula Vista (91910) *(P-14883)*

West End Yung MNS Christn Assn .... C...... 909 477-2780
  1257 E D St Ontario (91764) *(P-19471)*

West End Yung MNS Christn Assn .... C...... 909 597-7445
  5665 Edison Ave Chino (91710) *(P-19472)*

West Health Care, Bonita *Also Called: Paradise Valley Hospital (P-18371)*

West Hollywood Edition .... D...... 310 795-7103
  9040 W Sunset Blvd West Hollywood (90069) *(P-15414)*

West Lake Food Corporation (PA) ....**E**...... **714 973-2286**
  301 N Sullivan St Santa Ana (92703) *(P-1209)*

West Los Angeles V A Med Ctr, Los Angeles *Also Called: Veterans Health Administration (P-17828)*

West Newport Oil Company .... E...... 949 631-1100
  5800 W Coast Hwy Newport Beach (92663) *(P-272)*

West Pacific Medical Lab, Santa Fe Springs *Also Called: California Lab Sciences LLC (P-19960)*

West Pacific Services Inc .... C...... 888 401-0188
  4445 Eastgate Mall Ste 200 San Diego (92121) *(P-605)*

West Pak Avocado Inc (PA) ....**C**...... **951 296-5757**
  38655 Sky Canyon Dr Murrieta (92563) *(P-117)*

West Pico Foods Inc .... C...... 323 586-9050
  5201 S Downey Rd Vernon (90058) *(P-13250)*

West Publishing Corporation .... B...... 800 747-3161
  5161 Lankershim Blvd North Hollywood (91601) *(P-3420)*

West Publishing Corporation .... B...... 619 296-7862
  2801 Camino Del Rio S San Diego (92108) *(P-3503)*

West Publishing Corporation .... A...... 424 243-2100
  800 Corporate Pointe Ste 150 Culver City (90230) *(P-16478)*

West Side Rehab Corporation .... C...... 323 231-4174
  1755 E Martin Luther King Jr Blvd Los Angeles (90069) *(P-14696)*

West Valley Occupational Ctr, Woodland Hills *Also Called: Los Angeles Unified School Dst (P-18974)*

West Valley Post Acute, West Hills *Also Called: West Valleyidence Opco LLC (P-18104)*

West Valleyidence Opco LLC .... C...... 818 348-8422
  7057 Shoup Ave West Hills (91307) *(P-18104)*

West Wood Products Inc (PA) ....**F**...... **310 631-8978**
  2943 E Las Hermanas St Compton (90221) *(P-12345)*

West World Productions Inc .... E...... 310 276-9500
  420 N Camden Dr Beverly Hills (90210) *(P-3394)*

West-Bag Inc .... E...... 323 264-0750
  1161 Monterey Pass Rd Monterey Park (91754) *(P-5248)*

Westair Gases & Equipment, Bakersfield *Also Called: Westair Gases & Equipment Inc (P-12837)*

Westair Gases & Equipment Inc .... C...... 661 387-6800
  3901 Buck Owens Blvd Bakersfield (93308) *(P-12837)*

Westamerica Graphics Corporation ....D...... 949 462-3600
  26012 Atlantic Ocean Dr Lake Forest (92630) *(P-3709)*

Westar Manufacturing Inc .... E...... 562 633-0581
  13217 Laureldale Ave Downey (90242) *(P-1185)*

Westar Nutrition Corp (PA) ....**E**...... **949 645-6100**
  350 Paularino Ave Costa Mesa (92626) *(P-4024)*

Westates Inc ....F...... 714 523-7600
  6800 Orangethorpe Ave Ste H Buena Park (90620) *(P-14106)*

Westates Automotive Promotions, Buena Park *Also Called: Westates Inc (P-14106)*

Westco Industries Inc .... E...... 909 874-8700
  2625 S Willow Ave Bloomington (92316) *(P-6093)*

Westcoast Brush Mfg Inc .... E...... 909 627-7170
  1330 Philadelphia St Pomona (91766) *(P-11092)*

Westcoast Iron, Spring Valley *Also Called: West Coast Iron Inc (P-1140)*

Westcoast Rotor Inc .... E...... 310 327-5050
  119 W 154th St Gardena (90248) *(P-12838)*

Westcorp Engineering, Riverside *Also Called: Reisner Enterprises Inc (P-7996)*

Westech Products Inc (PA) ....**E**...... **951 279-4496**
  1242 Enterprise Ct Corona (92882) *(P-11051)*

Westech Wax Products, Corona *Also Called: Westech Products Inc (P-11051)*

Westerlay Orchids, Carpinteria *Also Called: Westerlay Orchids LP (P-73)*

Westerlay Orchids LP .... C...... 805 684-5411
  3504 Via Real Carpinteria (93013) *(P-73)*

Western Allied Corporation .... E...... 562 944-6341
  12046 Florence Ave Santa Fe Springs (90670) *(P-835)*

Western Asset Core Plus Bond P ....C...... 626 844-9400
  385 E Colorado Blvd Pasadena (91101) *(P-14973)*

Western Asset Mrtg Capitl Corp .... A...... 626 844-9400
  385 E Colorado Blvd Pasadena (91101) *(P-15018)*

Western Bagel Baking Corp .... E...... 818 887-5451
  21749 Ventura Blvd Woodland Hills (91364) *(P-1499)*

Western Bagel Baking Corp (PA) ....**C**...... **818 786-5847**
  7814 Sepulveda Blvd Van Nuys (91405) *(P-1500)*

Western Bay Sheet Metal Inc .... E...... 619 233-1753
  1410 Hill St El Cajon (92020) *(P-6094)*

Western Cactus Growers Inc .... E...... 760 726-1710
  1860 Monte Vista Dr Vista (92084) *(P-6923)*

Western Case Incorporated ....D...... 951 214-6380
  231 E Alessandro Blvd Riverside (92508) *(P-5249)*

Western Cnc Inc ....D...... 760 597-7000
  1001 Park Center Dr Vista (92081) *(P-8076)*

Western Converting Spc Inc .... E...... 909 392-4578
  2886 Metropolitan Pl Pomona (91767) *(P-3825)*

Western Corrugated Design Inc .... E...... 562 695-9295
  8741 Pioneer Blvd Santa Fe Springs (90670) *(P-3135)*

Western Costume Co (HQ) ....**E**...... **818 760-0900**
  11041 Vanowen St North Hollywood (91605) *(P-15524)*

Western Dental & Orthodontics, Orange *Also Called: Western Dental Services Inc (P-17849)*

Western Dental Services Inc (HQ) ....**B**...... **714 480-3000**
  530 S Main St Ste 600 Orange (92868) *(P-17849)*

Western Design, Irvine *Also Called: Meggitt Western Design Inc (P-10105)*

Western Digital .... E...... 510 557-7553
  19600 S Western Ave Torrance (90501) *(P-9139)*

Western Digital Corporation ....C...... 949 672-7000
  3337 Michelson Dr Irvine (92612) *(P-7493)*

Western Division Regional Off, Long Beach *Also Called: Southern California Edison Co (P-12061)*

Western Drug Medical Supply, San Bernardino *Also Called: H and H Drug Stores Inc (P-12491)*

Western Energy Services Corp ....C...... 403 984-5916
  3430 Getty St Bakersfield (93308) *(P-15767)*

Western Environmental Inc .... E...... 760 396-0222
  62150 Gene Welmas Dr Mecca (92254) *(P-10109)*

Western Equipment Mfg, Corona *Also Called: Western Equipment Mfg Inc (P-6947)*

Western Equipment Mfg Inc .... E...... 951 284-2000
  1160 Olympic Dr Corona (92881) *(P-6947)*

Western Feld Invstigations Inc (PA) ....**D**...... **800 999-9589**
  405 W Foothill Blvd Ste 204 Claremont (91711) *(P-16537)*

Western Filter A Division of Donaldson Company Inc ....D...... 661 295-0800
  26235 Technology Dr Valencia (91355) *(P-7413)*

2024 Southern California
Business Directory and Buyers Guide

Western Fire Protection Inc (PA) .... D...... 858 513-4949
13630 Danielson St Poway (92064) *(P-836)*

Western Forge Die, Huntington Beach Also Called: Tarpin Corporation *(P-7100)*

Western Gage Corporation .... E...... 805 445-1410
3316 Maya Linda Ste A Camarillo (93012) *(P-7140)*

Western General Insurance Co .... C...... 818 880-9070
5230 Las Virgenes Rd Ste 100 Calabasas (91302) *(P-14643)*

Western Golf Car Mfg Inc .... D...... 760 671-6691
69391 Dillon Rd Desert Hot Springs (92241) *(P-11042)*

Western Golf Car Sales Co, Desert Hot Springs Also Called: Western Golf Car Mfg Inc *(P-11042)*

Western Growers Association (PA) .... C...... 949 863-1000
6501 Irvine Center Dr Irvine (92618) *(P-19386)*

Western Hardware Company .... F...... 909 595-6201
161 Commerce Way Walnut (91789) *(P-5953)*

Western Hardware Company, Walnut Also Called: Hardware Imports Inc *(P-9328)*

Western Highway Products, Huntington Beach Also Called: Primus Inc *(P-11145)*

Western Hose & Gasket, National City Also Called: Westflex Inc *(P-4717)*

Western Hydrostatics Inc (PA) .... E...... 951 784-2133
1956 Keats Dr Riverside (92501) *(P-7715)*

Western Integrated Mtls Inc (PA) .... E...... 562 634-2823
3310 E 59th St Long Beach (90805) *(P-2641)*

Western Lighting Inds Inc .... E...... 626 969-6820
12203 Magnolia Ave Ste 1 Riverside (92503) *(P-12627)*

Western Medical Center Aux, Santa Ana Also Called: Orange Cnty Globl Med Ctr Aux *(P-18354)*

Western Mesquite Mines Inc .... E...... 928 341-4653
6502 E Us Highway 78 Brawley (92227) *(P-5677)*

Western Methods, Santa Ana Also Called: Western Methods Machinery Corporation *(P-9827)*

Western Methods Machinery Corporation .... C...... 949 252-6600
2344 Pullman St Santa Ana (92705) *(P-9827)*

Western Mfg & Distrg LLC .... E...... 805 988-1010
835 Flynn Rd Camarillo (93012) *(P-9889)*

Western Mill Fabricators Inc .... E...... 714 993-3667
670 S Jefferson St Ste B Placentia (92870) *(P-3036)*

Western National Contractors .... D...... 949 862-6200
8 Executive Cir Irvine (92614) *(P-20117)*

Western National Prpts LLC (PA) .... C...... 949 862-6200
8 Executive Cir Irvine (92614) *(P-480)*

Western National Securities (PA) .... C...... 949 862-6200
8 Executive Cir Irvine (92614) *(P-14884)*

Western Oilfields Supply Co (PA) .... C...... 661 399-9124
3404 State Rd Bakersfield (93308) *(P-15806)*

Western Operations, Rancho Cucamonga Also Called: Gentex Corporation *(P-19844)*

Western Operations Center, Westlake Village Also Called: Securitas SEC Svcs USA Inc *(P-16680)*

Western Outdoor News, San Clemente Also Called: Western Outdoors Publications *(P-3337)*

Western Outdoors Publications (PA) .... E...... 949 366-0030
901 Calle Amanecer Ste 115 San Clemente (92673) *(P-3337)*

Western Pacific Distrg LLC .... C...... 714 974-6837
341 W Meats Ave Orange (92865) *(P-12364)*

Western Pacific Pulp and Paper (HQ) .... D...... 562 803-4401
9400 Hall Rd Downey (90241) *(P-3038)*

Western Pacific Roofing Corp .... C...... 661 273-1336
3462 E La Campana Way Palm Springs (92262) *(P-1057)*

Western PCF Stor Solutions Inc (PA) .... D...... 909 451-0303
300 E Arrow Hwy San Dimas (91773) *(P-2999)*

Western Penn AAA Insur Agcy .... B...... 805 682-5811
3712 State St Santa Barbara (93105) *(P-14644)*

Western Plastics Temecula, Temecula Also Called: W Plastics Inc *(P-4825)*

Western Precision Aero LLC .... E...... 714 893-7999
11600 Monarch St Garden Grove (92841) *(P-8077)*

Western Printing and Label, Orange Also Called: Western Prtg & Graphics LLC *(P-3710)*

Western Prtg & Graphics LLC (PA) .... E...... 714 532-3946
675 N Main St Orange (92868) *(P-3710)*

Western Psychological Services, Torrance Also Called: Manson Western LLC *(P-3409)*

Western Pump Inc (PA) .... D...... 619 239-9988
3235 F St San Diego (92102) *(P-17163)*

Western Refining Inc .... E...... 714 708-2200
1201 Baker St Costa Mesa (92626) *(P-12839)*

Western Refining Inc .... E...... 310 834-1297
22232 Wilmington Ave Carson (90745) *(P-12840)*

Western Refining Inc .... E...... 323 264-8500
4357 E Cesar E Chavez Ave Los Angeles (90022) *(P-12841)*

Western Rim Pipeline, Lakeside Also Called: A M Ortega Construction Inc *(P-859)*

Western Saw, Oxnard Also Called: Western Saw Manufacturers Inc *(P-5893)*

Western Saw Manufacturers Inc .... E...... 805 981-0999
3200 Camino Del Sol Oxnard (93030) *(P-5893)*

Western Screw Products Inc .... E...... 562 698-5793
11770 Slauson Ave Santa Fe Springs (90670) *(P-6426)*

Western Sheet Metals Inc .... F...... 951 272-3600
280 E Harrison St Corona (92879) *(P-6345)*

Western Sign Systems, San Marcos Also Called: Western Sign Systems Inc *(P-11180)*

Western Sign Systems Inc .... E...... 760 736-6070
261 S Pacific St San Marcos (92078) *(P-11180)*

Western States Envelope Corp .... D...... 714 449-0909
2301 Raymer Ave Fullerton (92833) *(P-3826)*

Western States Glass, Long Beach Also Called: Total Mont LLC *(P-5357)*

Western States Packaging Inc .... E...... 818 686-6045
13276 Paxton St Pacoima (91331) *(P-3196)*

Western States Wholesale Inc (PA) .... D...... 909 947-0028
1420 S Bon View Ave Ontario (91761) *(P-5396)*

Western Summit Mfg Corp .... E...... 626 333-3333
30200 Cartier Dr Rancho Palos Verdes (90275) *(P-4826)*

Western Supreme Inc .... E...... 213 627-3861
846 Produce Ct Los Angeles (90021) *(P-1249)*

Western Telematic Inc .... E...... 949 586-9950
5 Sterling Irvine (92618) *(P-7580)*

Western Tube & Conduit Corp (HQ) .... D...... 310 537-6300
2001 E Dominguez St Long Beach (90810) *(P-8284)*

Western Valve, Bakersfield Also Called: Western Valve Inc *(P-6771)*

Western Valve Inc .... E...... 661 327-7660
201 Industrial St Bakersfield (93307) *(P-6771)*

Westfall Technik, Walnut Also Called: 10 Day Parts Inc *(P-4923)*

Westfall Technik Inc .... B...... 951 734-5600
1100 Citrus St Riverside (92507) *(P-5250)*

Westfield LLC (DH) .... B...... 310 478-4456
2049 Century Park E 41st Fl Los Angeles (90067) *(P-14697)*

Westfield America Inc (HQ) .... C...... 310 478-4456
2049 Century Park E 41st Fl Los Angeles (90067) *(P-14698)*

Westfield America Ltd Partnr .... B...... 310 277-3898
2049 Century Park E Ste 4100 Los Angeles (90067) *(P-14699)*

Westflex Inc (PA) .... E...... 619 474-7400
325 W 30th St National City (91950) *(P-4717)*

Westgate Hotel, San Diego Also Called: Reh Company *(P-15320)*

Westgate Manufacturing, Vernon Also Called: Westgate Mfg Inc *(P-9272)*

Westgate Mfg Inc .... D...... 323 826-9490
2462 E 28th St Vernon (90058) *(P-9272)*

Westgroup Kona Kai LLC .... D...... 619 221-8000
1551 Shelter Island Dr San Diego (92106) *(P-17536)*

Westgroup San Diego Associates .... E...... 858 274-4630
1404 Vacation Rd San Diego (92109) *(P-15415)*

Westin, San Dimas Also Called: Westin Automotive Products Inc *(P-2542)*

Westin Automotive Products Inc (PA) .... E...... 626 960-6762
320 W Covina Blvd San Dimas (91773) *(P-2542)*

Westin Bonaventure Ht & Suites, Los Angeles Also Called: Todays IV *(P-15391)*

Westin Long Beach Hotel, The, Long Beach Also Called: Noble Investment Group LLC *(P-15262)*

Westin Long Beach Hotel, The, Long Beach Also Called: Noble/Utah Long Beach LLC *(P-15263)*

Westin Rncho Mrage Golf Rsort, Rancho Mirage Also Called: Hst Lessee Mission Hills LP *(P-15188)*

Westin San Diego, San Diego Also Called: Diamondrock San Dego Tnant LLC *(P-15130)*

Westlake Engrg Roto Form .... E...... 805 525-8800
1041 E Santa Barbara St Santa Paula (93060) *(P-5251)*

Westlake Financial Services, Los Angeles Also Called: Westlake Services LLC *(P-14293)*

Westlake Health Care Center .... B...... 805 494-1233
1101 Crenshaw Blvd Los Angeles (90019) *(P-18076)*

Westlake Oaks Healthcare LLC .... C...... 805 494-1233
250 Fairview Rd Thousand Oaks (91361) *(P-18816)*

Employee Codes: A=Over 500 employees, B=251-500
C=101-250, D=51-100, E=20-50, F=10-19, G=1-9

2024 Southern California
Business Directory and Buyers Guide

© Mergent Inc. 1-800-342-5647

1323

Westlake Properties Inc .... C...... 818 889-0230
31943 Agoura Rd Westlake Village (91361) *(P-15416)*

Westlake Royal Stone LLC .... D...... 800 255-1727
3817 Ocean Ranch Blvd Oceanside (92056) *(P-5537)*

Westlake Services LLC (HQ) .... **C...... 323 692-8800**
4751 Wilshire Blvd Ste 100 Los Angeles (90010) *(P-14293)*

Westlake Village Inn, Westlake Village *Also Called: Westlake Properties Inc (P-15416)*

Westmed Ambulance Inc .... C...... 310 456-3830
3872 Las Flores Canyon Rd Malibu (90265) *(P-11410)*

Westmed Ambulance Inc .... C...... 310 219-1779
2537 Old San Pasqual Rd Escondido (92027) *(P-11411)*

WESTMED AMBULANCE, INC, Malibu *Also Called: Westmed Ambulance Inc (P-11410)*

WESTMED AMBULANCE, INC, Escondido *Also Called: Westmed Ambulance Inc (P-11411)*

Westminster Press Inc .... E...... 714 210-2881
4906 W 1st St Santa Ana (92703) *(P-3711)*

Westpac Labs Inc .... B...... 562 906-5227
10200 Pioneer Blvd # 500 Santa Fe Springs (90670) *(P-19986)*

Westpac Materials, Orange *Also Called: Western Pacific Distrg LLC (P-12364)*

Westprint, Orange *Also Called: Comprehensive Print Group LLC (P-3538)*

Westrec Properties Inc .... B...... 818 907-0400
16633 Ventura Blvd Fl 6 Encino (91436) *(P-20118)*

Westridge Laboratories Inc .... E...... 714 259-9400
1671 E Saint Andrew Pl Santa Ana (92705) *(P-4468)*

Westrock Cp LLC .... D...... 951 273-7900
2577 Research Dr Corona (92882) *(P-3712)*

Westside Accessories Inc (PA) .... **F...... 626 858-5452**
8920 Vernon Ave Ste 128 Montclair (91763) *(P-2436)*

Westside Bldg San Diego LLC .... E...... 858 566-4343
11620 Sorrento Valley Rd San Diego (92121) *(P-12346)*

Westside Building Materials, San Diego *Also Called: Westside Bldg San Diego LLC (P-12346)*

Westside Crdvsclar Med Group I .... C...... 310 289-9955
99 N La Cienega Blvd Ste 203 Beverly Hills (90211) *(P-17833)*

Westside Jewish Cmnty Ctr Inc (PA) .... **C...... 323 938-2531**
5870 W Olympic Blvd Los Angeles (90036) *(P-19347)*

Westside Resources Inc .... E...... 800 944-3939
8850 Research Dr Irvine (92618) *(P-10778)*

Westside Security Patrol, Bakersfield *Also Called: M & S Security Services Inc (P-16658)*

Weststar Cinemas Inc .... C...... 805 379-8966
180 Promenade Way Ste R Westlake Village (91362) *(P-17304)*

Weststar Cinemas Inc .... C...... 661 723-9392
742 W Lancaster Blvd Lancaster (93534) *(P-17332)*

Westview Services Inc .... D...... 714 635-2444
1655 S Euclid St Ste A Anaheim (92802) *(P-19198)*

Westview Services Inc .... D...... 626 962-0956
1515 W Cameron Ave Ste 310 West Covina (91790) *(P-19199)*

Westview Vocational Services, Anaheim *Also Called: Westview Services Inc (P-19198)*

Westwind Engineering Inc .... C...... 310 831-3454
625 Esplanade Unit 70 Redondo Beach (90277) *(P-19718)*

Westwind Equity Investors, Newport Beach *Also Called: Windjmmer Cpitl Invstors III L (P-15060)*

Westwood Building Materials Co .... E...... 310 643-9158
15708 Inglewood Ave Lawndale (90260) *(P-5519)*

Westwood Healthcare Center LP .... D...... 310 826-0821
12121 Santa Monica Blvd Los Angeles (90025) *(P-18077)*

Westwood Insurance Agency LLC (HQ) .... **D...... 818 990-9715**
6320 Canoga Ave Woodland Hills (91367) *(P-14645)*

Westwood Laboratories LLC (PA) .... **E...... 626 969-3305**
710 S Ayon Ave Azusa (91702) *(P-4469)*

Westwood Marquis Hotel & Grdns, Los Angeles *Also Called: W Los Angeles (P-15407)*

Wet (PA) .... **C...... 818 769-6200**
10847 Sherman Way Sun Valley (91352) *(P-16966)*

Wet Design, Sun Valley *Also Called: Wet (P-16966)*

Wetmore Cutting Tools, Chino *Also Called: Wetmore Tool and Engrg Co (P-7141)*

Wetmore Tool and Engrg Co .... D...... 909 364-1000
5091 G St Chino (91710) *(P-7141)*

Wetzels Pretzels LLC .... E...... 619 588-1074
525 Parkway Plz Unit 525 El Cajon (92020) *(P-13724)*

Wexler Corporation .... A...... 818 846-9381
1111 S Victory Blvd Burbank (91502) *(P-12710)*

Wexler Video, Burbank *Also Called: Wexler Corporation (P-12710)*

Wfb Archives Inc .... D
13500 Danielson St Poway (92064) *(P-8752)*

Wfcf Technology E2040-030, Santa Monica *Also Called: Wells Fargo Capital Finance Inc (P-16965)*

WG Best Weinkellerei Inc .... F...... 858 627-1747
888 W E St San Diego (92101) *(P-1667)*

Whalen Furniture Manufacturing, San Diego *Also Called: Whalen LLC (P-2792)*

Whalen LLC (DH) .... **E...... 619 423-9948**
1578 Air Wing Rd San Diego (92154) *(P-2792)*

Whaley, Kevin Enterprises, Santee *Also Called: Kevin Whaley (P-6819)*

Whaling Bar & Grill, La Jolla *Also Called: Lav Hotel Corp (P-15220)*

Whaling Packaging Co .... E...... 310 518-6021
21020 S Wilmington Ave Carson (90810) *(P-11824)*

Wham-O Inc .... D...... 818 963-4200
6301 Owensmouth Ave Ste 700 Woodland Hills (91367) *(P-12948)*

Wharf, The, Ventura *Also Called: Ventura Feed and Pet Sups Inc (P-13918)*

Whb Corporation .... A...... 213 624-1011
506 S Grand Ave Los Angeles (90071) *(P-15417)*

Wheat Group Inc .... E...... 858 673-2070
9950 Summers Ridge Rd Ste 160 San Diego (92121) *(P-16967)*

Wheel and Tire Club Inc .... E...... 714 422-3505
1301 Burton St Fullerton (92831) *(P-5608)*

Whelan Security Co .... C...... 310 343-8628
400 Continental Blvd El Segundo (90245) *(P-16709)*

Whi Solutions Inc .... C...... 661 257-2120
28470 Avenue Stanford Ste 200 Valencia (91355) *(P-12451)*

Whip Media Group, Santa Monica *Also Called: Mediamorph Inc (P-16304)*

Whiskey Girl .... C...... 619 236-1616
702 5th Ave San Diego (92101) *(P-20119)*

White & Case LLP .... C...... 213 620-7724
555 S Flower St Ste 2700 Los Angeles (90071) *(P-18956)*

White Bottle Inc .... E...... 949 788-1998
10579 Dale Ave Stanton (90680) *(P-5252)*

White Cap 301, Santa Clarita *Also Called: White Cap Supply Group Inc (P-12374)*

White Cap Supply Group Inc .... A...... 661 294-7737
28255 Kelly Johnson Pkwy Santa Clarita (91355) *(P-12374)*

White Digital Media Inc .... E...... 760 827-7800
3394 Carmel Mountain Rd Ste 250 San Diego (92121) *(P-13498)*

White Fire Tagets, San Bernardino *Also Called: Reagent Chemical & RES Inc (P-3908)*

White Memorial Medical Center .... A...... 323 260-5739
1720 E Cesar E Chavez Ave Los Angeles (90033) *(P-17834)*

White Memorial Medical Center (HQ) .... **A...... 323 268-5000**
1720 E Cesar E Chavez Ave Los Angeles (90033) *(P-18501)*

White Rabbit Partners Inc .... C...... 310 975-1450
9000 W Sunset Blvd Ste 1500 West Hollywood (90069) *(P-19311)*

White Sands of La Jolla Clinic, La Jolla *Also Called: Humangood Socal (P-19274)*

White Wave Foods, City Of Industry *Also Called: Wwf Operating Company LLC (P-1318)*

Whitefox Defense Tech Inc .... E...... 805 225-4506
854 Monterey St San Luis Obispo (93401) *(P-5777)*

Whites Steel Inc (PA) .... **F...... 760 347-3401**
45524 Towne St Indio (92201) *(P-1117)*

Whitewater Rock & Sup Co Inc .... E...... 760 325-2747
58645 Old Highway 60 Whitewater (92282) *(P-12365)*

Whiting Door Mfg Corp .... D...... 909 877-0120
301 S Milliken Ave Ontario (91761) *(P-17164)*

Whiting-Turner Contracting Co .... B...... 949 863-0800
250 Commerce Ste 150 Irvine (92602) *(P-606)*

Whitlock Industries Inc .... F...... 760 231-9262
609 Mission Ave Oceanside (92054) *(P-11308)*

Whitlock Surfboards, Oceanside *Also Called: Whitlock Industries Inc (P-11308)*

Whitmor Plstic Wire Cable Corp .... E...... 661 257-2400
28420 Avenue Stanford Valencia (91355) *(P-6833)*

Whitmor Plstic Wire Cable Corp (PA) .... **E...... 661 257-2400**
27737 Avenue Hopkins Santa Clarita (91355) *(P-6834)*

Whitmor Wire and Cable, Santa Clarita *Also Called: Whitmor Plstic Wire Cable Corp (P-6834)*

Whitmor Wirenetics, Valencia *Also Called: Whitmor Plstic Wire Cable Corp (P-6833)*

Whittaker Corporation .... E...... 805 526-5700
1955 Surveyor Ave Fl 2 Simi Valley (93063) *(P-9828)*

Whittier Fertilizer Company .... D...... 562 699-3461
9441 Kruse Rd Pico Rivera (90660) *(P-4543)*

Whittier Filtration Inc (DH).......... E...... 714 986-5300
120 S State College Blvd Ste 175 Brea (92821) *(P-7693)*

Whittier Hills Health Care Ctr, Whittier Also Called: Ensign Group Inc *(P-17941)*

Whittier Hospital Med Ctr Inc .... C...... 562 945-3561
9080 Colima Rd Whittier (90605) *(P-18502)*

Whittier Inst For Diabetes ....D...... 877 944-8843
10140 Campus Point Dr San Diego (92121) *(P-19953)*

Whittier Mailing Products Inc (PA) .... F...... 562 464-3000
13019 Park St Santa Fe Springs (90670) *(P-7589)*

Whittier Service Center, Santa Fe Springs Also Called: Southern California Edison Co *(P-12060)*

Whittier Union High Schl Dist .... C...... 562 693-8826
7200 Greenleaf Ave Ste 170 Whittier (90602) *(P-18988)*

Who What Wear, West Hollywood Also Called: Clique Brands Inc *(P-3351)*

Wholesale 46, Irvine Also Called: Disco Print Whl 46 A Ltd Lblty *(P-16440)*

Wholesale Displays, Carlsbad Also Called: San Diego Sign Company Inc *(P-12877)*

Wholesale Shade, San Marcos Also Called: Showdogs Inc *(P-3015)*

Whv Resort Group Inc (HQ) .... C...... 760 652-4913
300 Rancheros Dr Ste 310 San Marcos (92069) *(P-14885)*

Whv Resort Group Inc .... A...... 760 770-9755
34567 Cathedral Canyon Dr Cathedral City (92234) *(P-15418)*

Wic, El Monte Also Called: Public Hlth Fndation Entps Inc *(P-18794)*

Wic, Torrance Also Called: Public Hlth Fndation Entps Inc *(P-19460)*

Wick Communications Co .... E...... 760 379-3667
6404 Lake Isabella Blvd Lake Isabella (93240) *(P-3338)*

Widly Inc .... C...... 951 279-0900
785 E Harrison St Ste 100 Corona (92879) *(P-2864)*

Wiedenbach-Brown, Fullerton Also Called: US Electrical Services Inc *(P-12622)*

Wiens Cellars LLC .... E...... 951 694-9892
35055 Via Del Ponte Temecula (92592) *(P-1668)*

Wilbur Curtis Co Inc .... B...... 800 421-6150
6913 W Acco St Montebello (90640) *(P-14951)*

Wilcompute .... E...... 818 674-0506
38713 Tierra Subida Ave Ste 200 Palmdale (93551) *(P-10231)*

Wilcox Machine Co .... D...... 562 927-5353
7180 Scout Ave Bell Gardens (90201) *(P-8078)*

Wild Lizard, Los Angeles Also Called: Bb Co Inc *(P-2305)*

Wildcat Discovery Tech Inc .... D...... 858 550-1980
6255 Ferris Sq Ste A San Diego (92121) *(P-19889)*

Wilden Pump, Grand Terrace Also Called: Psg California LLC *(P-7287)*

Wildomar Medical Offices, Wildomar Also Called: Kaiser Foundation Hospitals *(P-18304)*

Will-Mann Inc .... E...... 714 870-0350
225 E Santa Fe Ave Fullerton (92832) *(P-6346)*

Willard Marine Inc .... D...... 714 666-2150
4602 North Ave Oceanside (92056) *(P-9868)*

Willdan Group Inc (PA) .... C...... 800 424-9144
2401 E Katella Ave Ste 300 Anaheim (92806) *(P-19719)*

William Bounds Ltd .... F...... 310 375-0505
23625 Madison St Torrance (90505) *(P-7218)*

William Morris Consulting, Beverly Hills Also Called: William Mrris Endvor Entrmt LL *(P-17334)*

William Mrris Endvor Entrmt FN (DH) .... C...... 310 285-9000
9601 Wilshire Blvd Fl 3 Beverly Hills (90210) *(P-17333)*

William Mrris Endvor Entrmt LL (DH) .... C...... 212 586-5100
9601 Wilshire Blvd Beverly Hills (90210) *(P-15903)*

William Mrris Endvor Entrmt LL .... B...... 310 285-9000
9601 Wilshire Blvd Fl 3 Beverly Hills (90210) *(P-17334)*

William Warren Properties Inc .... D...... 310 454-1500
201 Wilshire Blvd Ste 102 Santa Monica (90401) *(P-14733)*

Williams Aerospace & Mfg Inc (HQ) .... E...... 805 586-8699
999 Avenida Acaso Camarillo (93012) *(P-12924)*

Williams Comfort Products, Colton Also Called: Williams Furnace Co *(P-7634)*

Williams East Heating A & Plbg .... D...... 818 678-9699
2290 Agate Ct Ste A Simi Valley (93065) *(P-837)*

Williams Furnace Co (DH) .... C...... 562 450-3602
250 W Laurel St Colton (92324) *(P-7634)*

Williams Scotsman Inc .... C...... 619 710-8468
14015 Kirkham Way Poway (92064) *(P-15605)*

Willis Electric Inc .... E...... 661 324-2781
4465 Buck Owens Blvd Bakersfield (93308) *(P-17076)*

Willis Electric Company, Bakersfield Also Called: Willis Electric Inc *(P-17076)*

Willis Insurance Services Cal, Irvine Also Called: Willis North America Inc *(P-20274)*

Willis Machine Inc .... E...... 805 604-4500
11000 Alto Dr Oak View (93022) *(P-8079)*

Willis North America Inc .... C...... 909 476-3300
18101 Von Karman Ave Ste 600 Irvine (92612) *(P-20274)*

Willow, Vernon Also Called: Complete Clothing Company *(P-2281)*

Wills Wing, Orange Also Called: Sport Kites Inc *(P-9555)*

Wilmar, Vernon Also Called: Jobbers Meat Packing Co LLC *(P-1198)*

Wilmington Ironworks, Wilmington Also Called: Wilmington Machine Inc *(P-8080)*

Wilmington Machine Inc .... E...... 310 518-3213
432 W C St Wilmington (90744) *(P-8080)*

Wilorco, Carson Also Called: Strike Technology Inc *(P-9122)*

Wilsey Foods Inc .... A...... 714 257-3700
40 Pointe Dr Brea (92821) *(P-1575)*

Wilshire 2015 Fund .... D...... 310 451-3051
1299 Ocean Ave Ste 700 Santa Monica (90401) *(P-14974)*

Wilshire Advisors LLC (PA) .... C...... 310 451-3051
1299 Ocean Ave Ste 700 Santa Monica (90401) *(P-20275)*

Wilshire Bancorp Inc .... A...... 213 387-3200
3200 Wilshire Blvd Los Angeles (90010) *(P-14209)*

Wilshire Bank .... B...... 213 427-1000
3200 Wilshire Blvd Fl 10 Los Angeles (90010) *(P-14210)*

Wilshire Country Club .... D...... 323 934-6050
301 N Rossmore Ave Los Angeles (90004) *(P-17537)*

Wilshire Kingsley Inc .... D...... 213 382-6677
3575 Wilshire Blvd Los Angeles (90010) *(P-14700)*

Wilshire Precision Pdts Inc .... E...... 818 765-4571
7353 Hinds Ave North Hollywood (91605) *(P-8081)*

Wilshire State Bank, Los Angeles Also Called: Wilshire Bank *(P-14210)*

Wilson Creek Winery, Temecula Also Called: Wilson Creek Wnery Vnyards Inc *(P-1669)*

Wilson Creek Wnery Vnyards Inc .... C...... 951 699-9463
35960 Rancho California Rd Temecula (92591) *(P-1669)*

Wilson Cycles Sports Corp .... E...... 951 894-5545
26145 Jefferson Ave Ste 205 Murrieta (92562) *(P-13848)*

Wilsonart LLC .... E...... 562 921-7426
13911 Gannet St Santa Fe Springs (90670) *(P-11630)*

Wilsons Art Studio Inc .... D...... 714 870-7030
501 S Acacia Ave Fullerton (92831) *(P-3827)*

Wilwood Engineering (PA) .... C...... 805 388-1188
4700 Calle Bolero Camarillo (93012) *(P-9487)*

Wimberly Allson Tong Goo NA In .... D...... 949 574-8500
300 Spectrum Center Dr Ste 500 Irvine (92618) *(P-19747)*

Win Soon Inc .... E...... 323 564-5070
4569 Firestone Blvd South Gate (90280) *(P-1317)*

Win Time Ltd (PA) .... C...... 858 695-2300
9335 Kearny Mesa Rd San Diego (92126) *(P-15419)*

Win-Dor Inc (PA) .... E...... 714 576-2030
450 Delta Ave Brea (92821) *(P-1029)*

Win-Holt Equip, Pomona Also Called: Win-Holt Equipment Corp *(P-7001)*

Win-Holt Equipment Corp .... E...... 909 625-2624
2717 N Towne Ave Pomona (91767) *(P-7001)*

Winc Inc .... C...... 855 282-5829
927 S Santa Fe Ave Los Angeles (90021) *(P-1670)*

Winchester Interconnect EC LLC .... D...... 714 230-6122
12691 Monarch St Garden Grove (92841) *(P-12711)*

Winchster Intrcnnect CM CA Inc .... C...... 800 848-4257
1810 Diamond St San Marcos (92078) *(P-5753)*

Winchster Intrcnnect Micro LLC .... C...... 714 637-7099
1872 N Case St Orange (92865) *(P-8986)*

Wind River Systems Inc .... F...... 858 824-3100
12770 High Bluff Dr Ste 300 San Diego (92130) *(P-16420)*

Windermere RE Coachella Vly, Indian Wells Also Called: Bennion Deville Fine Homes Inc *(P-14749)*

Windes Inc (PA) .... D...... 562 435-1191
3780 Kilroy Airport Way Ste 600 Long Beach (90806) *(P-19810)*

Windjmmer Capitl Investors III, Santa Ana Also Called: Jwc Environmental Inc *(P-12794)*

Windjmmer Cpitl Invstors III L .... A...... 949 706-9989
610 Newport Center Dr Ste 1100 Newport Beach (92660) *(P-15060)*

Windjmmer Cpitl Invstors IV LP .... B...... 919 706-9989
610 Newport Center Dr Ste 1100 Newport Beach (92660) *(P-15061)*

Employee Codes: A=Over 500 employees, B=251-500
C=101-250, D=51-100, E=20-50, F=10-19, G=1-9

2024 Southern California
Business Directory and Buyers Guide

© Mergent Inc. 1-800-342-5647
1325

Window Enterprises Inc ....E....... 951 943-4894
430 Nevada St Redlands (92373) *(P-6128)*

Windsor Anaheim Healthcare (PA).....................................C....... **714 826-8950**
3415 W Ball Rd Anaheim (92804) *(P-18078)*

Windsor Capital Group Inc ....C....... 805 735-8311
1117 N H St Lompoc (93436) *(P-15420)*

Windsor Capital Group Inc ....A....... 951 676-5656
29345 Rancho California Rd Temecula (92591) *(P-15421)*

Windsor Capital Group Inc ....C....... 714 990-6000
900 E Birch St Brea (92821) *(P-15422)*

Windsor Capital Group Inc ....C....... 714 241-3800
1325 E Dyer Rd Santa Ana (92705) *(P-15423)*

Windsor Capital Group Inc ....C....... 310 566-1100
2800 28th St Ste 385 Santa Monica (90405) *(P-15424)*

Windsor Cypress Garden, Riverside *Also Called: Windsor Cypress Grdns Hlthcare (P-18160)*

Windsor Cypress Grdns Hlthcare ....A....... 951 688-3643
9025 Colorado Ave Riverside (92503) *(P-18160)*

Windsor Foods, Ontario *Also Called: Ajinomoto Foods North Amer Inc (P-1382)*

Windsor Foods, Ontario *Also Called: Windsor Quality Food Company Ltd (P-1405)*

Windsor Grdns Cnvlescent Ctr A, Anaheim *Also Called: Windsor Anaheim Healthcare (P-18078)*

Windsor Manor, Glendale *Also Called: Humangood Socal (P-14713)*

Windsor Palms Care Ctr Artesia, Artesia *Also Called: Windsor Twin Plms Hlthcare Ctr (P-18079)*

Windsor Quality Food Company Ltd ....A....... 713 843-5200
4200 Concours Ste 100 Ontario (91764) *(P-1405)*

Windsor Twin Plms Hlthcare Ctr ....C....... 562 865-0271
11900 Artesia Blvd Artesia (90701) *(P-18079)*

Windward Life Care, San Diego *Also Called: Buena Vista MGT Svcs LLC (P-18599)*

Wine Country Party & Events, Torrance *Also Called: Bright Event Rentals LLC (P-15772)*

Wine Dept, Los Angeles *Also Called: Youngs Market Company LLC (P-13484)*

Winfield Locks Inc ....A....... 949 722-5400
1721 Whittier Ave Costa Mesa (92627) *(P-5954)*

Wing Hing, Los Angeles *Also Called: Wing Hing Foods LLC (P-1334)*

Wing Hing Foods LLC ....D....... 323 232-8899
1659 E 23rd St Los Angeles (90011) *(P-1334)*

Wing Hing Noodle Company, Ontario *Also Called: Passport Food Group LLC (P-1967)*

Wingert Grbing Brbker Jstkie L ....D....... 619 232-8151
1230 Columbia St Ste 400 San Diego (92101) *(P-18957)*

Winit America Inc ....E....... 626 606-0308
381 Brea Canyon Rd Walnut (91789) *(P-7581)*

Winners Only Inc ....C....... 760 599-0300
1365 Park Center Dr Vista (92081) *(P-12294)*

Winonics Inc ....C....... 714 626-3755
1257 S State College Blvd Fullerton (92831) *(P-8753)*

Winstar Textile Inc ....F....... 626 357-1133
16815 E Johnson Dr City Of Industry (91745) *(P-2412)*

Wintergreen Apts, San Diego *Also Called: Hanken Cono Assad & Co Inc (P-14810)*

Winther Technologies Inc (PA).......................................E....... **310 618-8437**
560 Alaska Ave Torrance (90503) *(P-7165)*

Wintriss Engineering Corp ....E....... 858 550-7300
9010 Kenamar Dr Ste 101 San Diego (92121) *(P-10346)*

Wira Co, El Monte *Also Called: Jans Enterprises Corporation (P-13371)*

Wire Cut Company Inc ....E....... 714 994-1170
6750 Caballero Blvd Buena Park (90620) *(P-8082)*

Wire Harness & Cable Assembly, Santa Monica *Also Called: Omega Leads Inc (P-9092)*

Wire Technology Corporation ....E....... 310 635-6935
9527 Laurel St Los Angeles (90002) *(P-5754)*

Wireless Technology Inc ....E....... 805 339-9696
2064 Eastman Ave Ste 113 Ventura (93003) *(P-8451)*

Wirenetics Co, Valencia *Also Called: Circle W Enterprises Inc (P-6815)*

Wiretech Inc (PA)...D....... **323 722-4933**
6440 Canning St Commerce (90040) *(P-5628)*

Wirtz Quality Installations ....D....... 858 569-3816
7932 Armour St San Diego (92111) *(P-964)*

Wirz & Co ....F....... 909 825-6970
444 Colton Ave Colton (92324) *(P-3713)*

Wis, San Diego *Also Called: Washington Inventory Service (P-16963)*

Wiser Foods Inc ....D....... 310 895-0888
5405 E Village Rd Unit 8219 Long Beach (90808) *(P-1744)*

Wismettac Asian Foods Inc (HQ)...................................C....... **562 802-1900**
13409 Orden Dr Santa Fe Springs (90670) *(P-13242)*

Wismettac Fresh Fish, Santa Fe Springs *Also Called: Wismettac Asian Foods Inc (P-13242)*

With Inc ....E....... 714 617-1991
7 Studebaker 1 Irvine (92618) *(P-16149)*

Withers Bergman, San Diego *Also Called: Withers Bergman LLP (P-18958)*

Withers Bergman LLP ....B....... 203 974-0412
12830 El Camino Real Ste 350 San Diego (92130) *(P-18958)*

Wj Newport LLC ....C....... 949 476-2001
4500 Macarthur Blvd Newport Beach (92660) *(P-15425)*

WJB Bearings Inc ....E....... 909 598-6238
535 Brea Canyon Rd City Of Industry (91789) *(P-6486)*

WKS Restaurant Corporation (PA)..................................C....... **562 425-1402**
5856 Corporate Ave Ste 200 Cypress (90630) *(P-14045)*

Wlcac, Los Angeles *Also Called: Watts Labor Community Action (P-19167)*

Wm Bolthouse Farms Inc (HQ)......................................A....... **661 366-7209**
7200 E Brundage Ln Bakersfield (93307) *(P-1381)*

Wm Technology, Irvine *Also Called: Wm Technology Inc (P-16421)*

Wm Technology Inc ....B....... 844 933-3627
41 Discovery Irvine (92618) *(P-16421)*

Wmbe Payrolling Inc ....C....... 858 810-3000
3545 Aero Ct San Diego (92123) *(P-15904)*

WMc Prcsion McHning Grnding ....F....... 714 773-0059
1234 E Ash Ave Ste A Fullerton (92831) *(P-8083)*

Wme, Beverly Hills *Also Called: William Mrris Endvor Entrmt LL (P-15903)*

Wme Bi LLC ....D....... 877 592-2472
17075 Camino San Diego (92127) *(P-16422)*

Wme Img LLC (DH)..C....... **212 586-5100**
9601 Wilshire Blvd Beverly Hills (90210) *(P-17384)*

Wna City of Industry, City Of Industry *Also Called: Waddington North America Inc (P-5246)*

Wna City of Industry, City Of Industry *Also Called: Wna Comet West Inc (P-5253)*

Wna Comet West Inc ....C....... 626 913-0724
927 S Azusa Ave City Of Industry (91748) *(P-5253)*

Wolf & Raven LLC ....D....... 800 431-6471
206 W 4th St Ste 439 Santa Ana (92701) *(P-20120)*

Wolfe Industries, Santa Fe Springs *Also Called: C Wolfe Industries Inc (P-6502)*

Wolfpack Inc ....E....... 760 736-4500
2440 Grand Ave Ste B Vista (92081) *(P-11181)*

Wolfpack Sign Group, Vista *Also Called: Wolfpack Inc (P-11181)*

Womanhaven ....D....... 760 353-6922
510 W Main St Ste 106 El Centro (92243) *(P-19170)*

Womble Bond Dickinson (us) LLP ....C....... 310 207-3800
400 Spectrum Center Dr Irvine (92618) *(P-18959)*

Wonderful Agency ....A....... 310 966-8600
11444 W Olympic Blvd Ste 210 Los Angeles (90064) *(P-15580)*

Wonderful Citrus Cooperative ....A....... 661 720-2400
5001 California Ave Ste 230 Bakersfield (93309) *(P-19387)*

Wonderful Citrus Packing LLC (HQ).................................B....... **661 720-2400**
1901 S Lexington St Delano (93215) *(P-118)*

Wonderful Citrus Packing LLC ....F....... 661 720-2400
1701 S Lexington St Delano (93215) *(P-1353)*

Wonderful Company LLC ....B....... 661 720-2400
1901 S Lexington St Delano (93215) *(P-45)*

Wonderful Company LLC ....A....... 559 781-7438
5001 California Ave Bakersfield (93309) *(P-119)*

Wonderful Company LLC ....A....... 661 399-4456
6801 E Lerdo Hwy Shafter (93263) *(P-120)*

Wonderful Company LLC ....B....... 661 720-2609
11444 W Olympic Blvd Ste 210 Los Angeles (90064) *(P-121)*

Wonderful Orchards LLC ....B....... 661 797-6400
13646 Highway 33 Lost Hills (93249) *(P-39)*

Wonderful Orchards LLC ....D....... 661 797-2509
21707 Lerdo Hwy Mc Kittrick (93251) *(P-40)*

Wonderful Orchards LLC (HQ)..C....... **661 399-4456**
6801 E Lerdo Hwy Shafter (93263) *(P-41)*

Wonderful Pstchios Almonds LLC (HQ)..............................E....... **310 966-4650**
11444 W Olympic Blvd Ste 310 Los Angeles (90064) *(P-1563)*

Wonderfulpistachiosandalmonds, Lost Hills *Also Called: Wonderful Orchards LLC (P-39)*

Wonderware, Lake Forest *Also Called: Aveva Software LLC (P-16430)*

Wonderware Corporation (DH)..B....... **949 727-3200**
26561 Rancho Pkwy S Lake Forest (92630) *(P-16423)*

Mergent email: customerrelations@mergent.com
1326

2024 Southern California
Business Directory and Buyers Guide

(P-0000) Products & Services Section entry number
(PA)=Parent Co (HQ)=Headquarters (DH)=Div Headquarters

Wondros, Los Angeles *Also Called: Hungry Heart Media Inc (P-17196)*

Wood Candle Wick Tech Inc ....E...... 310 488-5885
9750 Irvine Blvd Ste 106 Irvine (92618) *(P-11309)*

Wood Craft Company, The, San Diego *Also Called: Pars Industries Inc (P-1021)*

Wood Gutmann Bogart Insur Brkg ....D...... 714 505-7000
15901 Red Hill Ave Ste 100 Tustin (92780) *(P-14646)*

Wood Gutmann Bogart Insur Brks ....C..... 714 505-7000
15901 Red Hill Ave Ste 100 Tustin (92780) *(P-14647)*

Wood Space Industries Inc ....F...... 714 996-4552
429 W Levers Pl Orange (92867) *(P-11635)*

Woodbridge Glass, Tustin *Also Called: Werner Systems Inc (P-5722)*

Woodbridge Glass Inc ....C..... 714 838-4444
14321 Myford Rd Tustin (92780) *(P-1121)*

Woodman Realty Inc ....C..... 909 425-5324
26030 Base Line St Apt 97 San Bernardino (92410) *(P-14886)*

Woodpecker Cabinets Inc ....E...... 310 404-4805
21512 Nordhoff St Chatsworth (91311) *(P-2685)*

Woodridge Press Inc ....E...... 949 475-1900
2485 Da Vinci Irvine (92614) *(P-3714)*

Woodruff Convalescent Center, Duarte *Also Called: Estrella Inc (P-17949)*

Woodruff Corporation ....E...... 310 378-1611
109 Calle Mayor Redondo Beach (90277) *(P-8084)*

Woods Maintenance Services Inc ....C..... 818 764-2515
7250 Coldwater Canyon Ave North Hollywood (91605) *(P-1186)*

Woodward Duarte, Duarte *Also Called: Woodward Hrt Inc (P-9829)*

Woodward Hrt Inc (HQ)...**A...... 661 294-6000**
25200 Rye Canyon Rd Santa Clarita (91355) *(P-8197)*

Woodward Hrt Inc ....C..... 626 359-9211
1700 Business Center Dr Duarte (91010) *(P-9829)*

Woodwork Pioneers Corp ....E...... 714 991-1017
1757 S Claudina Way Anaheim (92805) *(P-2642)*

Woongjin Coway USA Inc., Los Angeles *Also Called: Coway Usa Inc (P-14129)*

Word & Brown Insurance Administrators Inc (PA)....................**B...... 714 835-5006**
721 S Parker St Ste 300 Orange (92868) *(P-14648)*

Word For Today ....E...... 714 825-9673
3232 W Macarthur Blvd # A Santa Ana (92704) *(P-14107)*

Wordsmart Corporation ....D
10025 Mesa Rim Rd San Diego (92121) *(P-16424)*

Work Force Services Inc ....C..... 661 327-5019
1811 Oak St Bakersfield (93301) *(P-15949)*

Work Force Staffing, Bakersfield *Also Called: Work Force Services Inc (P-15949)*

Work Inc ....D...... 805 739-0451
3070 Skyway Dr Ste 104 Santa Maria (93455) *(P-19171)*

Workcare Inc ....C..... 714 978-7488
300 S Harbor Blvd Ste 600 Anaheim (92805) *(P-20303)*

Working With Autism Inc ....D...... 818 501-4240
14724 Ventura Blvd Ste 1110 Sherman Oaks (91403) *(P-18734)*

Workrite Uniform Company Inc (DH)....................................**B...... 805 483-0175**
1701 Lombard St Ste 200 Oxnard (93030) *(P-15473)*

Workway Inc ....C..... 619 278-0012
3111 Camino Del Rio N Ste 400 San Diego (92108) *(P-15905)*

Workway Inc ....C..... 949 553-8700
19742 Macarthur Blvd Ste 235 Irvine (92612) *(P-15906)*

World Class Cheerleading Inc ....E...... 877 923-2645
20212 Hart St Winnetka (91306) *(P-11043)*

World Gym Fitness Centers, Los Angeles *Also Called: World Gym International LLC (P-17419)*

World Gym International LLC ....C..... 310 557-8804
1901 Avenue Of The Stars Ste 1100 Los Angeles (90067) *(P-17419)*

World Journal La LLC (HQ)...**C..... 323 268-4982**
1588 Corporate Center Dr Monterey Park (91754) *(P-3339)*

World Mvie Awrds Orgnztion Wma ....D...... 833 375-5857
9171 Wilshire Blvd # 500a Beverly Hills (90210) *(P-19473)*

World Oil Corp ....C..... 562 928-0100
9302 Garfield Ave South Gate (90280) *(P-273)*

World Oil Marketing Company (PA)....................................**E...... 562 928-0100**
9302 Garfield Ave South Gate (90280) *(P-13713)*

World Peas Brand, Los Angeles *Also Called: Snack It Forward LLC (P-1831)*

World Private Security Inc ....C..... 818 894-1800
16921 Parthenia St Ste 201 Northridge (91343) *(P-16710)*

WORLD SERVICE OFFICE, Chatsworth *Also Called: Narcotics Annymous Wrld Svcs I (P-3411)*

World Svc Wst/La Inflght Svc L ....C..... 310 538-7000
1812 W 135th St Gardena (90249) *(P-11709)*

World Trade Ctr Ht Assoc Ltd ....D...... 562 983-3400
701 W Ocean Blvd Long Beach (90831) *(P-15426)*

World Trade Printing Company, Garden Grove *Also Called: Wtpc Inc (P-3716)*

World Variety Produce Inc ....B...... 800 588-0151
5325 S Soto St Vernon (90058) *(P-13349)*

World Vision International (PA)..**C..... 626 303-8811**
800 W Chestnut Ave Monrovia (91016) *(P-19537)*

World Water Inc ....E...... 562 940-1964
9848 Everest St Downey (90242) *(P-10169)*

World Wind & Solar, Tehachapi *Also Called: World Wind Electrical Svcs Inc (P-952)*

World Wind & Solar, Paso Robles *Also Called: Worldwind Services LLC (P-953)*

World Wind Electrical Svcs Inc ....B...... 661 822-4877
228 W Tehachapi Blvd Tehachapi (93561) *(P-952)*

Worldbridge Partners ....C..... 661 775-9999
25000 Avenue Stanford Ste 250 Valencia (91355) *(P-15907)*

Worldwide, Monrovia *Also Called: Worldwide Energy and Mfg USA (P-8923)*

Worldwide Aeros Corp ....D...... 818 344-3999
3971 Fredonia Dr Los Angeles (90068) *(P-9558)*

Worldwide Corporate Housing LP ....B...... 972 392-4747
1 World Trade Ctr Ste 2400 Long Beach (90831) *(P-15432)*

Worldwide Energy and Mfg USA (PA)..................................**A...... 650 692-7788**
1800 S Myrtle Ave Monrovia (91016) *(P-8923)*

Worldwide Envmtl Pdts Inc (PA)...**D...... 714 990-2700**
1100 Beacon St Brea (92821) *(P-10170)*

Worldwide Holdings Inc (PA)..**D...... 213 236-4500**
725 S Figueroa St Ste 1900 Los Angeles (90017) *(P-14649)*

Worldwide Produce, Los Angeles *Also Called: Green Farms Inc (P-13327)*

Worldwide Security Assoc Inc (HQ)....................................**B...... 310 743-3000**
10311 S La Cienega Blvd Los Angeles (90045) *(P-16711)*

Worldwide Specialties Inc ....C..... 323 587-2200
2420 Modoc St Los Angeles (90021) *(P-2004)*

Worldwind Services LLC ....A...... 661 822-4877
1222 Vine St Ste 301 Paso Robles (93446) *(P-953)*

Worthington Cylinder Corp ....E...... 909 594-7777
336 Enterprise Pl Pomona (91768) *(P-6172)*

Wovexx Holdings Inc (DH)...**D...... 310 424-2080**
10381 Jefferson Blvd Culver City (90232) *(P-12015)*

Wpmg Inc ....E...... 949 442-1601
1961 Mcgaw Ave Irvine (92614) *(P-8342)*

Wpromote LLC (PA)...**D...... 310 421-4844**
101 Continental Blvd El Segundo (90245) *(P-20276)*

Wright Business Graphics Calif, Chino *Also Called: Wright Business Graphics LLC (P-3834)*

Wright Business Graphics LLC ....E...... 909 614-6700
13602 12th St Ste A Chino (91710) *(P-3834)*

Wright Ford Young & Co ....D...... 949 910-2727
16140 Sand Canyon Ave Irvine (92618) *(P-19811)*

Wrights Supply Inc ....D...... 661 254-8400
25838 Springbrook Ave Santa Clarita (91350) *(P-17110)*

Writers Guild America West Inc ....C..... 323 951-4000
7000 W 3rd St Los Angeles (90048) *(P-19419)*

Ws Mmv Hotel LLC ....D...... 619 692-3800
8757 Rio San Diego Dr San Diego (92108) *(P-15427)*

Ws Packaging-Blake Printery ....E...... 805 543-6844
2224 Beebee St San Luis Obispo (93401) *(P-3715)*

Wsa Group Inc ....A...... 310 743-3000
19208 S Vermont Ave # 200 Gardena (90248) *(P-16712)*

Wsm Investments LLC ....C..... 818 332-4600
3990b Heritage Oak Ct Simi Valley (93063) *(P-15011)*

Wsp USA Inc ....D...... 714 973-4880
15231 Laguna Canyon Rd Irvine (92618) *(P-19720)*

Wsw Corp (PA)...**E...... 818 989-5008**
16000 Strathern St Van Nuys (91406) *(P-9488)*

Wti, Ventura *Also Called: Wireless Technology Inc (P-8451)*

Wtpc Inc ....E...... 714 903-2500
12082 Western Ave Garden Grove (92841) *(P-3716)*

Wun, Goleta *Also Called: Yardi Kube Inc (P-16426)*

Wurms Janitorial Service Inc ....D...... 951 582-0003
601 S Milliken Ave Ontario (91761) *(P-15756)*

Wurth Louis and Company (DH)...**D...... 714 529-1771**
895 Columbia St Brea (92821) *(P-12736)*

Employee Codes: A=Over 500 employees, B=251-500
C=101-250, D=51-100, E=20-50, F=10-19, G=1-9

2024 Southern California
Business Directory and Buyers Guide

© Mergent Inc. 1-800-342-5647
1327

WV Communications Inc .... E....... 805 376-1820
1125 Business Center Cir Ste A Newbury Park (91320) *(P-8599)*

Ww San Diego Harbor Island LLC .... C....... 619 291-6700
1960 Harbor Island Dr San Diego (92101) *(P-15428)*

Ww Woodworks .... E....... 760 887-4708
9771 Cedar St Oak Hills (92344) *(P-2643)*

Wwf Operating Company LLC .... D....... 626 810-1775
18275 Arenth Ave Bldg 1 City Of Industry (91748) *(P-1318)*

Wyatt Precision Machine Inc .... E....... 562 634-0524
3301 E 59th St Long Beach (90805) *(P-6427)*

Wyatt Technology, Goleta *Also Called: Wyatt Technology LLC (P-10305)*

Wyatt Technology LLC (HQ) .... C....... 805 681-9009
6330 Hollister Ave Goleta (93117) *(P-10305)*

Wymore Inc .... E....... 760 352-2045
697 S Dogwood Rd El Centro (92243) *(P-17100)*

Wyndcrest Dd Florida, Los Angeles *Also Called: Digital Domain Media Group Inc (P-15664)*

Wyndham Anaheim Garden Grove, Garden Grove *Also Called: Ohi Resort Hotels LLC (P-15271)*

Wyndham Collection LLC .... E....... 888 522-8476
1175 Aviation Pl San Fernando (91340) *(P-2686)*

Wyndham Hotels & Resorts, Fullerton *Also Called: Anaheim Park Hotel (P-15075)*

Wyndham Residence, Arroyo Grande *Also Called: Compass Health Inc (P-19251)*

Wyndham San Diego Bayside, San Diego *Also Called: Bhr Operations LLC (P-15095)*

Wyrefab Inc .... E....... 310 523-2147
15711 S Broadway Gardena (90248) *(P-6835)*

Wyvern Technologies .... E....... 714 966-0710
1205 E Warner Ave Santa Ana (92705) *(P-9140)*

X-Chair LLC .... E....... 844 492-4247
6415 Katella Ave Cypress (90630) *(P-2919)*

X1 Discovery Inc .... E....... 877 999-1347
617 W 7th St Ste 604 Los Angeles (90017) *(P-16150)*

X3 Management Services Inc .... D....... 760 597-9336
700 La Terraza Blvd Ste 110 Escondido (92025) *(P-954)*

Xbiz .... F....... 310 820-0228
4929 Wilshire Blvd Ste 960 Los Angeles (90010) *(P-3395)*

Xbp Inc .... D....... 888 895-7116
333 El Camino Real Ste 201 Tustin (92780) *(P-16151)*

XCEL Mechanical Systems Inc .... E....... 310 660-0090
1710 W 130th St Gardena (90249) *(P-838)*

Xcor, Mojave *Also Called: Xcor Aerospace Inc (P-9908)*

Xcor Aerospace Inc .... D....... 661 824-4714
1314 Flight Line Mojave (93501) *(P-9908)*

Xcvi LLC (PA) .... D....... 213 749-2661
15236 Burbank Blvd Sherman Oaks (91411) *(P-2035)*

Xdbs Corporation .... C....... 844 932-7356
3501 Jack Northrop Ave Hawthorne (90250) *(P-19915)*

Xdbsb2b, Hawthorne *Also Called: Xdbs Corporation (P-19915)*

Xdr Radiology, Los Angeles *Also Called: Cyber Medical Imaging Inc (P-10734)*

XEL Group, Laguna Hills *Also Called: XEL USA Inc (P-8924)*

XEL USA Inc .... E....... 949 425-8686
23501 Ridge Route Dr Ste F Laguna Hills (92653) *(P-8924)*

Xencor, Pasadena *Also Called: Xencor Inc (P-4257)*

Xencor Inc .... C....... 626 305-5900
465 N Halstead St Ste 200 Pasadena (91107) *(P-4257)*

Xerox Education Services LLC (DH) .... D....... 310 830-9847
2277 E 220th St Long Beach (90810) *(P-12391)*

Xerxes Corporation .... C....... 714 630-0012
1210 N Tustin Ave Anaheim (92807) *(P-3983)*

Xgrass Turf Direct, Anaheim *Also Called: Leonards Carpet Service Inc (P-2960)*

Xiamen Hongfa Electroacoustic, Lake Forest *Also Called: Hongfa America Inc (P-8182)*

Xirgo Technologies LLC .... D....... 805 319-4079
188 Camino Ruiz Fl 2 Camarillo (93012) *(P-9273)*

Xirrus Inc .... E....... 805 262-1600
2545 W Hillcrest Dr Ste 220 Newbury Park (91320) *(P-10171)*

Xitron Technologies, Poway *Also Called: Vitrek LLC (P-10230)*

Xl Staffing Inc .... C....... 619 579-0442
826 Jackman St El Cajon (92020) *(P-15908)*

Xlr8 Ems, San Clemente *Also Called: Xlr8 Services Inc (P-19721)*

Xlr8 Services Inc .... E....... 949 498-9578
1020 Calle Negocio Ste A San Clemente (92673) *(P-19721)*

Xmultiple Technologies (PA) .... E....... 805 579-1100
1919 Williams St Ste 325 Simi Valley (93065) *(P-7458)*

Xmultiple/Xrjax, Simi Valley *Also Called: Xmultiple Technologies (P-7458)*

Xos, Los Angeles *Also Called: Xos Inc (P-9178)*

Xos Inc (PA) .... E....... 818 316-1890
3550 Tyburn St Ste 100 Los Angeles (90065) *(P-9178)*

Xos Fleet Inc .... E....... 855 909-4407
3550 Tyburn St Ste 100 Los Angeles (90065) *(P-9315)*

Xos Trucks, Los Angeles *Also Called: Xos Fleet Inc (P-9315)*

Xp Power Inc .... D....... 714 712-2642
1590 S Sinclair St Anaheim (92806) *(P-9141)*

Xpdel Inc .... D....... 805 267-1214
2625 Townsgate Rd Ste 330 Westlake Village (91361) *(P-16425)*

Xplain Corporation .... E....... 805 494-9797
705 Lakefield Rd Ste I Westlake Village (91361) *(P-3396)*

Xpo, Torrance *Also Called: Lomita Logistics LLC (P-15633)*

Xpo Cartage Inc .... D....... 800 837-7584
5800 Sheila St Commerce (90040) *(P-11470)*

Xpo Logistics Freight Inc .... D....... 951 685-1244
13364 Marlay Ave Fontana (92337) *(P-11512)*

Xpo Logistics Freight Inc .... C....... 213 744-0664
1955 E Washington Blvd Los Angeles (90021) *(P-11513)*

Xpo Logistics Freight Inc .... D....... 562 946-8331
12903 Lakeland Rd Santa Fe Springs (90670) *(P-11514)*

Xpo Logistics Freight Inc .... D....... 714 282-7717
2102 N Batavia St Orange (92865) *(P-11515)*

Xpo Logistics Supply Chain Inc .... C....... 909 390-9799
5200b E Airport Dr Ontario (91761) *(P-11816)*

Xponential Fitness Inc (PA) .... B....... 949 346-3000
17877 Von Karman Ave Ste 100 Irvine (92614) *(P-17420)*

Xport Forwarding LLC .... D....... 949 354-0609
620 Newport Center Dr Ste 1100 Newport Beach (92660) *(P-11817)*

Xpower Manufacture Inc .... E....... 626 285-3301
668 S 6th Ave City Of Industry (91746) *(P-10110)*

Xr LLC .... E....... 714 847-9292
15251 Pipeline Ln Huntington Beach (92649) *(P-10723)*

Xr Studios LLC .... F....... 513 446-5621
6700 Santa Monica Blvd Los Angeles (90038) *(P-8467)*

Xrp Inc (PA) .... F....... 562 861-4765
5630 Imperial Hwy South Gate (90280) *(P-13888)*

Xs Scuba Inc (PA) .... E....... 714 424-0434
4040 W Chandler Ave Santa Ana (92704) *(P-11044)*

Xse Group Inc .... C....... 888 272-8340
92 Argonaut Ste 235 Aliso Viejo (92656) *(P-13002)*

Xsolla, Sherman Oaks *Also Called: Xsolla (usa) Inc (P-11912)*

Xsolla (usa) Inc (PA) .... A....... 818 435-6613
15260 Ventura Blvd Ste 2230 Sherman Oaks (91403) *(P-11912)*

Xylem Water Solutions USA Inc .... E....... 949 474-1679
17942 Cowan Irvine (92614) *(P-7294)*

Xylem Water Systems (california) Inc .... E....... 619 575-7466
830 Bay Blvd Ste 101 Chula Vista (91911) *(P-7295)*

Y I C, Carson *Also Called: Yun Industrial Co Ltd (P-8754)*

Y K K U S A, Anaheim *Also Called: YKK (usa) Inc (P-11082)*

Y, The, San Diego *Also Called: YMCA of San Diego County (P-19491)*

Y&R-Wcj Spectrum, Irvine *Also Called: Young & Rubicam LLC (P-15582)*

Yaamava Rsort Csino At San Mnu, Highland *Also Called: San Manuel Entertainment Auth (P-17566)*

Yaesu Usa Inc .... E....... 714 827-7600
6125 Phyllis Dr Cypress (90630) *(P-8600)*

Yahoo Cv LLC .... C....... 408 349-3300
11985 Bluff Creek Dr Playa Vista (90094) *(P-16522)*

Yale/Chase Equipment and Services Inc .... C....... 562 463-8000
2615 Pellissier Pl City Of Industry (90601) *(P-12842)*

Yamagata America Inc .... C....... 858 751-1010
3760 Convoy St Ste 219 San Diego (92111) *(P-3504)*

Yamaha Corporation of America (HQ) .... B....... 714 522-9011
6600 Orangethorpe Ave Buena Park (90620) *(P-12989)*

Yamaha Guitar Group Inc (HQ) .... C....... 818 575-3600
26580 Agoura Rd Calabasas (91302) *(P-10935)*

Yamaha Guitar Group Inc .... E....... 818 575-3900
26664 Agoura Rd Calabasas (91302) *(P-10936)*

Mergent email: customerrelations@mergent.com
1328

2024 Southern California
Business Directory and Buyers Guide

(P-0000) Products & Services Section entry number
(PA)=Parent Co (HQ)=Headquarters (DH)=Div Headquarters

Yamaha Motor Corporation USA (HQ)......................B...... **714 761-7300**
6555 Katella Ave Cypress (90630) *(P-13904)*

Yamaha Music Corporation U S A, Buena Park *Also Called: Yamaha Corporation of America (P-12989)*

Yamamoto of Orient Inc (HQ).............................C...... **909 594-7356**
122 Voyager St Pomona (91768) *(P-14701)*

Yamamotoyama of America, Pomona *Also Called: Yamamoto of Orient Inc (P-14701)*

Yamasa Enterprises .... E...... 213 626-2211
515 Stanford Ave Los Angeles (90013) *(P-1797)*

Yamasa Fish Cake, Los Angeles *Also Called: Yamasa Enterprises (P-1797)*

Yamazaki California Inc .... E...... 213 624-2773
123 Japanese Village Plaza Mall Los Angeles (90012) *(P-13725)*

Yanchewski & Wardell Entps Inc .... D...... 760 754-1960
2241 La Mirada Dr Vista (92081) *(P-7694)*

Yang-Ming International Corp .... E...... 626 956-0100
595 Yorbita Rd La Puente (91744) *(P-16479)*

Yankon Industries Inc (PA).............................**E...... 909 591-2345**
13445 12th St Chino (91710) *(P-8343)*

Yardi Kube Inc .... D...... 805 699-2040
430 S Fairview Ave Goleta (93117) *(P-16426)*

Yardi Systems Inc (PA)..................................**B...... 805 699-2040**
430 S Fairview Ave Santa Barbara (93117) *(P-16152)*

Yardney Water MGT Systems, Riverside *Also Called: Yardney Water MGT Systems Inc (P-7695)*

Yardney Water MGT Systems Inc (PA)..........**E...... 951 656-6716**
6666 Box Springs Blvd Riverside (92507) *(P-7695)*

Yavar Manufacturing Co Inc .... E...... 323 722-2040
1900 S Tubeway Ave Commerce (90040) *(P-3147)*

Yawitz Inc .... E...... 909 865-5599
1379 Ridgeway St Pomona (91768) *(P-8301)*

Ybcc Inc ....E...... 626 213-3945
17800 Castleton St Ste 386 City Of Industry (91748) *(P-1291)*

Yeager Enterprises Corp .... D...... 714 994-2040
7100 Village Dr Buena Park (90621) *(P-5547)*

Yebo Group LLC .... C...... 949 502-3317
2652 Dow Ave Tustin (92780) *(P-14073)*

Yebo Printing, Tustin *Also Called: Yebo Group LLC (P-14073)*

Yee Yuen Laundry and Clrs Inc ....D...... 323 734-7205
2575 S Normandie Ave Los Angeles (90007) *(P-15461)*

Yee Yuen Linen Service, Los Angeles *Also Called: Yee Yuen Laundry and Clrs Inc (P-15461)*

Yellow Jacket Drlg Svcs LLC .... C...... 909 989-8563
9460 Lucas Ranch Rd Rancho Cucamonga (91730) *(P-1096)*

Yellow Luxury, Calabasas *Also Called: Abbyson Living Corp (P-12276)*

Yellowpagescom LLC (DH).............................B...... **818 937-5500**
611 N Brand Blvd Ste 500 Glendale (91203) *(P-16968)*

Yen-Nhai Inc .... E...... 323 584-1315
4940 District Blvd Vernon (90058) *(P-2823)*

Yesco, Jurupa Valley *Also Called: Young Electric Sign Company (P-11182)*

Yesterdays Sportswear, Paso Robles *Also Called: Lakeshirts LLC (P-2517)*

Yf Art Holdings Gp LLC .... A...... 678 441-1400
9130 W Sunset Blvd Los Angeles (90069) *(P-14952)*

Yg Laboratories Inc .... E...... 714 474-2800
11520 Warner Ave Fountain Valley (92708) *(P-4470)*

Yhb Long Beach LLC .... D...... 562 597-4401
2640 N Lakewood Blvd Long Beach (90815) *(P-15429)*

YKK (usa) Inc .... E...... 714 701-1200
5001 E La Palma Ave Anaheim (92807) *(P-11082)*

Ylopo LLC .... C...... 818 915-9150
4712 Admiralty Way 548 Marina Del Rey (90292) *(P-14887)*

YMCA, Newport Beach *Also Called: Young MNS Chrstn Assn Ornge CN (P-19495)*

YMCA Camp Edwards, Angelus Oaks *Also Called: YMCA of East Valley (P-19474)*

YMCA Child Care Resource Svcs, San Diego *Also Called: YMCA of San Diego County (P-19486)*

YMCA Crescenta-Canada, La Canada *Also Called: Crescenta-Canada YMCA (P-19441)*

YMCA of East Valley .... C...... 909 794-1702
42842 Jenks Lake Rd E Angelus Oaks (92305) *(P-19474)*

YMCA of East Valley .... C...... 909 881-9622
808 E 21st St San Bernardino (92404) *(P-19475)*

YMCA of East Valley (PA)..............................C...... **909 798-9622**
500 E Citrus Ave Redlands (92373) *(P-19476)*

YMCA of San Diego County .... B...... 858 453-3483
8355 Cliffridge Ave La Jolla (92037) *(P-19477)*

YMCA of San Diego County .... C...... 619 428-1168
3085 Beyer Blvd Ste 105 San Diego (92154) *(P-19478)*

YMCA of San Diego County .... C...... 760 745-7490
200 Saxony Rd Encinitas (92024) *(P-19479)*

YMCA of San Diego County .... C...... 619 464-1323
8881 Dallas St La Mesa (91942) *(P-19480)*

YMCA of San Diego County .... B...... 619 280-9622
5505 Friars Rd San Diego (92110) *(P-19481)*

YMCA of San Diego County .... B...... 858 292-4034
200 Saxony Rd Encinitas (92024) *(P-19482)*

YMCA of San Diego County .... C...... 619 281-8313
2927 Meade Ave San Diego (92116) *(P-19483)*

YMCA of San Diego County .... B...... 619 226-8888
2150 Beryl St Ste 18 San Diego (92109) *(P-19484)*

YMCA of San Diego County .... C...... 619 264-0144
5505 Friars Rd San Diego (92110) *(P-19485)*

YMCA of San Diego County .... C...... 619 521-3055
3333 Camino Del Rio S Ste 400 San Diego (92108) *(P-19486)*

YMCA of San Diego County .... C...... 760 765-0642
4761 Pine Hills Rd Julian (92036) *(P-19487)*

YMCA of San Diego County .... C...... 619 298-3576
5505 Friars Rd San Diego (92110) *(P-19488)*

YMCA of San Diego County .... C...... 760 758-0808
200 Saxony Rd Encinitas (92024) *(P-19489)*

YMCA of San Diego County .... C...... 760 721-8930
215 Barnes St Oceanside (92054) *(P-19490)*

YMCA of San Diego County (PA).....................C...... **858 292-9622**
3708 Ruffin Rd San Diego (92123) *(P-19491)*

YMCA Overnight Camp, Julian *Also Called: YMCA of San Diego County (P-19487)*

YMCA Youth & Family Services, San Diego *Also Called: YMCA of San Diego County (P-19483)*

YMi Jeanswear Inc .... D...... 213 746-6681
1015 Wall St Ste 115 Los Angeles (90015) *(P-2384)*

Yobs, Los Angeles *Also Called: Yobs Technologies Inc (P-17239)*

Yobs Technologies Inc .... E...... 213 713-3825
615 Childs Way Tro 370 Los Angeles (90089) *(P-17239)*

Yoga Box LLC .... E...... 619 994-1915
909 Grand Ave San Diego (92109) *(P-17580)*

Yokohama Corp North America (HQ)................C...... **540 389-5426**
1 Macarthur Pl Santa Ana (92707) *(P-4701)*

Yokohama Tire, Santa Ana *Also Called: Yokohama Corp North America (P-4701)*

Yokohama Tire Corporation (DH).....................C...... **714 870-3800**
1 Macarthur Pl Ste 800 Santa Ana (92707) *(P-12275)*

Yokohama Tire USA, Santa Ana *Also Called: Yokohama Tire Corporation (P-12275)*

Yonekyu USA Inc .... D...... 323 581-4194
611 N 20th St Montebello (90640) *(P-1241)*

Yorba Linda Country Club, Garden Grove *Also Called: Sanyo Foods Corp America (P-1844)*

Yorba Park Medical Group, Santa Ana *Also Called: St Jseph Heritg Med Group LLC (P-17795)*

York Enterprises South Inc .... D...... 714 842-6611
18255 Beach Blvd Huntington Beach (92648) *(P-13849)*

Yoshimasa, Pomona *Also Called: Yoshimasa Display Case Inc (P-2970)*

Yoshimasa Display Case Inc .... E...... 213 637-9999
108 Pico St Pomona (91766) *(P-2970)*

Yoshimura RES & Dev Amer Inc .... D...... 909 628-4722
5420 Daniels St Ste A Chino (91710) *(P-12267)*

You ME and Sciences Inc .... D...... 310 406-7350
202 W Manchester Ave Playa Del Rey (90293) *(P-17355)*

You Should Have It, San Diego *Also Called: Highlander Home Inc (P-13578)*

Youbar Inc (PA)..D...... **626 537-1851**
445 Wilson Way City Of Industry (91744) *(P-13276)*

Youbetcom Inc (HQ).....................................C...... **818 668-2100**
2600 W Olive Ave Fl 5 Burbank (91505) *(P-17388)*

Youcare Pharma (usa) Inc .... D...... 951 258-3114
132 Business Center Dr Corona (92878) *(P-4258)*

Young & Rubicam LLC .... C...... 213 930-5000
4751 Wilshire Blvd Ste 201 Los Angeles (90010) *(P-15581)*

Young & Rubicam LLC .... B...... 949 754-2000
7535 Irvine Center Dr Irvine (92618) *(P-15582)*

Young & Rubicam LLC .... C...... 949 754-2100
7535 Irvine Center Dr Irvine (92618) *(P-15583)*

ALPHABETIC

Young & Rubicam LLC .... B....... 949 224-6300
1735 Irvine Center Dr Irvine (92618) *(P-20277)*

Young Dental, Cerritos *Also Called: US Dental Inc (P-10776)*

Young Electric Sign Company .... C....... 909 923-7668
10235 Bellegrave Ave Jurupa Valley (91752) *(P-11182)*

Young Engineering & Mfg Inc (PA) .... E....... 909 394-3225
560 W Terrace Dr San Dimas (91773) *(P-10172)*

Young Engineers Inc .... D....... 949 581-9411
25841 Commercentre Dr Lake Forest (92630) *(P-5955)*

Young Machine Inc .... F....... 909 464-0405
12282 Colony Ave Chino (91710) *(P-8085)*

Young Mens Christn Assocation, La Mesa *Also Called: YMCA of San Diego County (P-19480)*

Young MNS Chrstn Assn Brbank C (PA) .... D....... 818 845-8551
321 E Magnolia Blvd Burbank (91502) *(P-19492)*

Young MNS Chrstn Assn Glndale .... D....... 818 484-8256
140 N Louise St Glendale (91206) *(P-19493)*

Young MNS Chrstn Assn Mtro Los .... C....... 323 467-4161
1553 Schrader Blvd Los Angeles (90028) *(P-19494)*

Young MNS Chrstn Assn Ornge CN .... D....... 949 642-9990
2300 University Dr Newport Beach (92660) *(P-19495)*

Young MNS Chrstn Assn Ornge CN .... D....... 949 859-9622
27341 Trabuco Cir Mission Viejo (92692) *(P-19496)*

Young Wns Chrstn Assn Grter Lo .... C....... 323 295-4288
2519 W Vernon Ave Los Angeles (90008) *(P-19497)*

Young Wns Chrstn Assn Grter Lo .... C....... 323 295-4280
2501 W Vernon Ave Los Angeles (90008) *(P-19498)*

Youngdale Manufacturing Corp .... E....... 760 727-0644
1216 Liberty Way Ste B Vista (92081) *(P-5956)*

Younger Mfg Co (PA) .... B....... 310 783-1533
2925 California St Torrance (90503) *(P-10857)*

Younger Optics, Torrance *Also Called: Younger Mfg Co (P-10857)*

Youngs Holdings Inc (PA) .... D....... 714 368-4615
15 Enterprise Ste 100 Aliso Viejo (92656) *(P-13482)*

Youngs Market Company LLC (HQ) .... B....... 800 317-6150
14402 Franklin Ave Tustin (92780) *(P-13483)*

Youngs Market Company LLC .... B....... 213 629-3929
500 S Central Ave Los Angeles (90013) *(P-13484)*

Youngvity Essntial Lf Sciences, Chula Vista *Also Called: Al Global Corporation (P-14091)*

Your Practice Online LLC (PA) .... C....... 877 388-8569
4590 Macarthur Blvd Ste 500 Newport Beach (92660) *(P-20278)*

Your Way Fumigation Inc .... D....... 951 699-9116
1660 Chicago Ave Ste N9 Riverside (92507) *(P-15688)*

Youth To People Inc .... D....... 309 648-5500
888 N Douglas St El Segundo (90245) *(P-4471)*

Youthglow, Fountain Valley *Also Called: Yg Laboratonies Inc (P-4470)*

Ys Garments LLC (HQ) .... E....... 310 631-4955
588 Crenshaw Blvd Torrance (90503) *(P-2271)*

Ytel Inc .... D....... 800 382-4913
26632 Towne Centre Dr Ste 300 Lake Forest (92610) *(P-11913)*

Yucaipa Companies LLC (PA) .... C....... 310 789-7200
9130 W Sunset Blvd Los Angeles (90069) *(P-20392)*

Yucaipa Disposal Inc .... D....... 909 429-4200
9890 Cherry Ave Fontana (92335) *(P-12205)*

Yuciapa & Calimesa News Mirror, Yucaipa *Also Called: Hi-Desert Publishing Company (P-3281)*

Yum Yum Donut Shop, City Of Industry *Also Called: Quality Naturally Foods Inc (P-13390)*

Yuma Lakes Resort, Earp *Also Called: Colorado River Adventures Inc (P-15442)*

Yumi, Los Angeles *Also Called: Caer Inc (P-1320)*

Yun Industrial Co Ltd .... E....... 310 715-1898
161 Selandia Ln Carson (90746) *(P-8754)*

Yusen Logistics Americas Inc .... C....... 310 518-3008
2417 E Carson St Ste 100 Carson (90810) *(P-11818)*

YWCA, Los Angeles *Also Called: Young Wns Chrstn Assn Grter Lo (P-19498)*

Yyk Enterprises Operations LLC (PA) .... C....... 619 474-6229
3475 E St San Diego (92102) *(P-1187)*

Z C & R Coating For Optics Inc .... E....... 310 381-3060
1401 Abalone Ave Torrance (90501) *(P-10347)*

Z Industries, Los Angeles *Also Called: Active Window Products (P-6097)*

Z Microsystems, San Diego *Also Called: Zmicro Inc (P-16480)*

Z P M Inc .... E....... 805 681-3511
5770 Thornwood Dr Ste C Goleta (93117) *(P-7696)*

Z Willing J A Henckels, Commerce *Also Called: Zwilling JA Henckels LLC (P-12323)*

Z-Best Concrete Inc .... D....... 951 774-1870
2575 Main St Riverside (92501) *(P-1092)*

Z-Tronix Inc .... E....... 562 808-0800
6327 Alondra Blvd Paramount (90723) *(P-9142)*

Z57 Inc .... C....... 858 623-5577
2443 Impala Dr Ste B Carlsbad (92010) *(P-16523)*

Za Management .... D....... 310 271-2200
101 N Robertson Blvd Beverly Hills (90211) *(P-20121)*

Zaca Mesa Winery, Los Olivos *Also Called: Cushman Winery Corporation (P-13475)*

Zadara Storage Inc .... D....... 949 251-0360
6 Venture Ste 140 Irvine (92618) *(P-7494)*

Zadro Inc .... E....... 714 892-9200
14462 Astronautics Ln Ste 101 Huntington Beach (92647) *(P-5360)*

Zadro Products Inc .... E....... 714 892-9200
14462 Astronautics Ln Ste 101 Huntington Beach (92647) *(P-5361)*

Zamboni, Paramount *Also Called: Zamboni Company Usa Inc (P-7267)*

Zamboni Company Usa Inc .... E....... 562 633-0751
15714 Colorado Ave Paramount (90723) *(P-7267)*

Zapp Packaging Inc .... D....... 909 930-1500
1921 S Business Pkwy Ontario (91761) *(P-3075)*

Zastrow Construction Inc .... D....... 323 478-1956
3267 Verdugo Rd Los Angeles (90065) *(P-481)*

Zbe Inc .... E....... 805 576-1600
1035 Cindy Ln Carpinteria (93013) *(P-8198)*

Zbs Law LLP .... D....... 714 848-7920
30 Corporate Park Ste 450 Irvine (92606) *(P-18960)*

Zebra Technologies Corporation .... D....... 805 579-1800
30601 Agoura Rd Agoura Hills (91301) *(P-7582)*

Zeco Systems Inc .... C....... 888 751-8560
767 S Alameda St Ste 200 Los Angeles (90021) *(P-13446)*

Zefr Inc .... B....... 310 392-3555
4101 Redwood Ave Los Angeles (90066) *(P-19916)*

Zeghani, Glendale *Also Called: Simon G Jewelry Inc (P-12967)*

Zenith A Fairfax Company, The, Woodland Hills *Also Called: Zenith Insurance Company (P-14533)*

Zenith Insurance Company (DH) .... B....... 818 713-1000
21255 Califa St Woodland Hills (91367) *(P-14533)*

Zenith Manufacturing Inc .... E....... 818 767-2106
3087 12th St Riverside (92507) *(P-9830)*

Zenith Screw Products Inc .... E....... 562 941-0281
10910 Painter Ave Santa Fe Springs (90670) *(P-6428)*

Zenlayer Inc .... B....... 909 718-3558
21680 Gateway Center Dr Ste 350 Diamond Bar (91765) *(P-11914)*

Zenleads Inc .... B....... 415 640-9303
440 N Barranca Ave # 4750 Covina (91723) *(P-20279)*

Zenner Usa Inc .... E....... 951 849-8822
1910 E Westward Ave Banning (92220) *(P-10179)*

Zeons Inc .... B....... 323 302-8299
291 S La Cienega Blvd Ste 102 Beverly Hills (90211) *(P-5332)*

Zep Inc .... C....... 877 428-9937
1000 Railroad St Corona (92882) *(P-13444)*

Zephyr Manufacturing Co Inc .... D....... 310 410-4907
201 Hindry Ave Inglewood (90301) *(P-7149)*

Zephyr Tool Group, Inglewood *Also Called: Zephyr Manufacturing Co Inc (P-7149)*

Zerep Management Corporation (PA) .... C....... 626 855-5522
17445 Railroad St City Of Industry (91748) *(P-12206)*

Zero Energy Contracting Inc .... C....... 626 701-3180
13850 Cerritos Corporate Dr Ste D Cerritos (90703) *(P-839)*

Zero Energy Contracting LLC .... D....... 626 701-3180
13850 Cerritos Corporate Dr Ste D Cerritos (90703) *(P-840)*

Zero Gravity Consulting LLC .... A....... 310 989-7989
458 N Doheny Dr West Hollywood (90069) *(P-20393)*

Zero Gravity Management .... D....... 310 656-9440
11110 Ohio Ave Ste 100 Los Angeles (90025) *(P-20122)*

Zest Anchors LLC .... D....... 760 743-7744
2230 Enterprise St Escondido (92029) *(P-12523)*

Zest Dental Solutions, Escondido *Also Called: Zest Anchors LLC (P-12523)*

Zest.ai, Burbank *Also Called: Zestfinance Inc (P-16153)*

Zestfinance Inc .... D....... 323 450-3000
3900 W Alameda Ave Ste 1600 Burbank (91505) *(P-16153)*

Mergent email: customerrelations@mergent.com
1330

2024 Southern California
Business Directory and Buyers Guide

(P-0000) Products & Services Section entry number
(PA)=Parent Co (HQ)=Headquarters (DH)=Div Headquarters

Zet-Tek Precision Machining, Yorba Linda *Also Called: Pdma Ventures Inc (P-10761)*
Zettler Components Inc (PA)............................C...... 949 831-5000
  75 Columbia Orange (92868) *(P-8633)*

Zettler Magnetics Inc ....C...... 949 831-5000
  2410 Birch St Vista (92081) *(P-8115)*

Zevia LLC ....D...... 310 202-7000
  15821 Ventura Blvd Ste 145 Encino (91436) *(P-1745)*

Zevia Pbc (PA) ....E...... 855 469-3842
  15821 Ventura Blvd Ste 145 Encino (91436) *(P-1746)*

Zhong W Ang Group, Walnut *Also Called: Pengcheng Aluminum Enterprise Inc USA (P-5705)*
Zia Aamir ....E...... 714 337-7861
  2043 Imperial St Los Angeles (90021) *(P-6095)*

Zico, El Segundo *Also Called: Zico Beverages LLC (P-1747)*
Zico Beverages LLC (HQ)..............................E...... 866 729-9426
  2101 E El Segundo Blvd Ste 403 El Segundo (90245) *(P-1747)*

Ziegenfelder Company ....D...... 909 509-0493
  12262 Colony Ave Chino (91710) *(P-1303)*

Ziegenfelder Company ....D...... 909 590-0493
  12290 Colony Ave Chino (91710) *(P-1304)*

Ziehm Instrumentarium ....E...... 407 615-8560
  4181 Latham St Riverside (92501) *(P-10786)*

Ziffren B B F G-L S&C Fnd ....C...... 310 552-3388
  1801 Century Park W Fl 7 Los Angeles (90067) *(P-18961)*

Zim Industries Inc ....C...... 661 393-9661
  7212 Fruitvale Ave Bakersfield (93308) *(P-1097)*

Zimmer Dental Inc ....B...... 800 854-7019
  1900 Aston Ave Carlsbad (92008) *(P-10724)*

Zimmer Gnsul Frsca Archtcts LL ....C...... 213 617-1901
  515 S Flower St Ste 3700 Los Angeles (90071) *(P-19748)*

Zimmer Gnsul Frsca Partnr Amer, Los Angeles *Also Called: Zimmer Gnsul Frsca Archtcts LL (P-19748)*
Zimmer Melia & Associates Inc (PA)..............E...... 615 377-0118
  6832 Presidio Dr Huntington Beach (92648) *(P-10725)*

Zion Automotive Group, Cerritos *Also Called: R1 Concepts Inc (P-12254)*
Zions Bancorporation ....A...... 424 290-5123
  200 N Pacific Coast Hwy Ste 1850 El Segundo (90245) *(P-15909)*

Zions Bank, El Segundo *Also Called: Zions Bancorporation (P-15909)*
Zipco, Riverside *Also Called: Zenith Manufacturing Inc (P-9830)*
ZIPRECRUITER, Santa Monica *Also Called: Ziprecruiter Inc (P-20280)*
Ziprecruiter Inc ....A...... 877 252-1062
  604 Arizona Ave Santa Monica (90401) *(P-20280)*

Zk Enterprises Inc ....E...... 213 622-7012
  4368 District Blvd Vernon (90058) *(P-2228)*

Zmicro Inc (PA) ....D...... 858 831-7000
  9820 Summers Ridge Rd San Diego (92121) *(P-16480)*

Zo Skin Health Inc (DH) ....D...... 949 988-7524
  9685 Research Dr Irvine (92618) *(P-4472)*

Zo Skin Health Inc ....F...... 949 988-3153
  15375 Barranca Pkwy Irvine (92618) *(P-4473)*

Zodiac Aerospace ....F...... 909 652-9700
  11340 Jersey Blvd Rancho Cucamonga (91730) *(P-9831)*

Zodiac Pool Solutions LLC (PA) ....E...... 760 599-9600
  2882 Whiptail Loop Ste 100 Carlsbad (92010) *(P-7697)*

Zodiac Pool Systems LLC (HQ) ....C...... 760 599-9600
  2882 Whiptail Loop Ste 100 Carlsbad (92010) *(P-7698)*

Zodiac Wtr Waste Aero Systems ....D...... 310 884-7000
  1500 Glenn Curtiss St Carson (90746) *(P-9832)*

Zoek, Irvine *Also Called: Online Marketing Group LLC (P-20215)*
Zoetis Inc ....F...... 858 312-7082
  16420 Via Esprillo San Diego (92127) *(P-4259)*

Zoic Inc ....C...... 310 838-0770
  3582 Eastham Dr Culver City (90232) *(P-17240)*

Zoic Studios, Culver City *Also Called: Zoic Inc (P-17240)*
Zonda Intelligence, Newport Beach *Also Called: Metrostudy Inc (P-20198)*
Zonda Media, Newport Beach *Also Called: Hanley Wood Media Inc (P-3455)*
Zonex Systems, Huntington Beach *Also Called: California Economizer (P-8172)*
Zonson Company Inc ....E...... 760 597-0338
  3197 Lionshead Ave Carlsbad (92010) *(P-11045)*

Zonu, Van Nuys *Also Called: Optical Zonu Corporation (P-8482)*
Zoo, El Segundo *Also Called: Zoo Digital Production LLC (P-17241)*
Zoo Digital Production LLC ....C...... 310 220-3939
  2201 Park Pl Ste 100 El Segundo (90245) *(P-17241)*

Zoo Med Laboratories Inc ....C...... 805 542-9988
  3650 Sacramento Dr San Luis Obispo (93401) *(P-11310)*

Zoo Printing Inc (PA) ....E...... 310 253-7751
  1225 Los Angeles St Glendale (91204) *(P-3717)*

Zoo Printing Trade Printer, Glendale *Also Called: Zoo Printing Inc (P-3717)*
Zooey Apparel Inc ....E...... 310 315-2880
  1526 Cloverfield Blvd C Santa Monica (90404) *(P-2385)*

Zoological Society San Diego (PA) ....A...... 619 231-1515
  2920 Zoo Dr San Diego (92101) *(P-19369)*

Zoological Society San Diego ....C...... 760 747-8702
  15500 San Pasqual Valley Rd Escondido (92027) *(P-19370)*

Zoological Society San Diego ....C...... 619 744-3325
  2920 Zoo Dr San Diego (92101) *(P-19371)*

Zoological Society San Diego ....C...... 619 231-1515
  10946 Willow Ct Ste 200 San Diego (92127) *(P-19372)*

Zoominfo Technologies LLC ....A...... 360 783-6924
  Dept La 24789 Pasadena (91185) *(P-16538)*

Zosano, Los Angeles *Also Called: Zp Opco Inc (P-4260)*
Zp Opco Inc ....A...... 510 745-1200
  355 S Grand Ave Ste 1450 Los Angeles (90071) *(P-4260)*

Zpower LLC ....C...... 805 445-7789
  5171 Clareton Dr Agoura Hills (91301) *(P-8216)*

Zuffa Mexico LLC ....C...... 310 285-9000
  9601 Wilshire Blvd Fl 3 Beverly Hills (90210) *(P-17581)*

Zuza LLC ....D...... 760 494-9000
  2304 Faraday Ave Carlsbad (92008) *(P-3718)*

Zwift Inc (PA) ....B...... 855 469-9438
  111 W Ocean Blvd Ste 1800 Long Beach (90802) *(P-16427)*

Zwilling JA Henckels LLC ....C...... 323 597-1421
  100 Citadel Dr Ste 575 Commerce (90040) *(P-12323)*

Zygo Corporation ....E...... 714 918-7433
  2031 Main St Irvine (92614) *(P-10348)*

Zygo Optical Systems, Irvine *Also Called: Zygo Corporation (P-10348)*
Zyris Inc ....E...... 805 560-9888
  6868 Cortona Dr Ste A Santa Barbara (93117) *(P-10779)*

Zyxel, Anaheim *Also Called: Zyxel Communications Inc (P-11915)*
Zyxel Communications Inc ....D...... 714 632-0882
  1130 N Miller St Anaheim (92806) *(P-11915)*

ALPHABETIC

Employee Codes: A=Over 500 employees, B=251-500
C=101-250, D=51-100, E=20-50, F=10-19, G=1-9

2024 Southern California
Business Directory and Buyers Guide

© Mergent Inc. 1-800-342-5647
1331

COUNTY/CITY CROSS-REFERENCE INDEX

ENTRY #	ENTRY #	ENTRY #	ENTRY #	ENTRY #
Julian	Santa Ysabel	Morro Bay	Guadalupe	Newbury Park
La Jolla	Santee	Nipomo	Lompoc	Oak Park
La Mesa	Solana Beach	Paso Robles	Los Olivos	Oak View
Lakeside	Spring Valley	Pismo Beach	New Cuyama	Ojai
Lemon Grove	Tecate	San Luis Obispo	Orcutt	Oxnard
National City	Valley Center	San Miguel	Santa Barbara	Piru
Oceanside	Vista	San Simeon	Santa Maria	Port Hueneme
Pala		Shandon	Santa Ynez	Santa Paula
Pauma Valley	**San Luis Obispo**	Shell Beach	Solvang	Santa Rosa Valley
Poway		Templeton	Vandenberg Afb	Simi Valley
Ramona	Arroyo Grande			Somis
Rancho Santa Fe	Atascadero	**Santa Barbara**	**Ventura**	Thousand Oaks
San Diego	Avila Beach			Ventura
San Marcos	Cambria	Buellton	Camarillo	Westlake Village
San Ysidro	Grover Beach	Carpinteria	Fillmore	
	Los Osos	Goleta	Moorpark	

GEOGRAPHIC SECTION

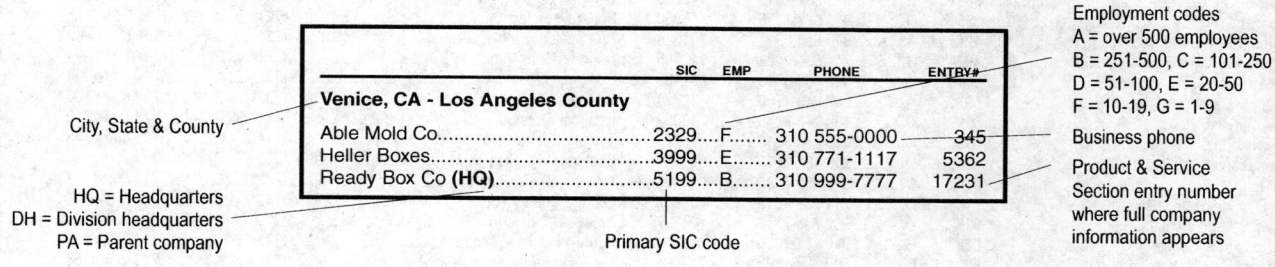

		SIC	EMP	PHONE	ENTRY#
Venice, CA - Los Angeles County					
Able Mold Co		2329	F	310 555-0000	345
Heller Boxes		3999	E	310 771-1117	5362
Ready Box Co **(HQ)**		5199	B	310 999-7777	17231

City, State & County

HQ = Headquarters
DH = Division headquarters
PA = Parent company

Primary SIC code

Employment codes
A = over 500 employees
B = 251-500, C = 101-250
D = 51-100, E = 20-50
F = 10-19, G = 1-9

Business phone

Product & Service
Section entry number
where full company
information appears

- Listings in this section are sorted alphabetically by city.
- Listings within each city are sorted alphabetically by company name.

	SIC	EMP	PHONE	ENTRY#
ACTON, CA - Los Angeles County				
County of Los Angeles	8069	C	661 223-8700	18527
ADELANTO, CA - San Bernardino County				
Commercial Wood Products Company	1751	C	760 246-4530	1009
Flavor House Inc	2087	E	760 246-9131	1769
Adelanto Elementary School Dst	2099	E	760 530-7680	1846
Furniture Technologies Inc	2426	E	760 246-9180	2570
California Silica Products LLC	2819	D	909 947-0028	3883
Dar-Ken Inc	3053	E	760 246-4010	4726
Fiber Care Baths Inc	3088	B	760 246-0019	4915
Hee Environmental Engineering LLC	3089	E	760 530-1409	5045
Inca Plastics Molding Co Inc	3089	F	760 246-8087	5059
Molded Fiber GL Companies - W	3089	D	760 246-4042	5105
Clark - Pacific Corporation	3272	E	626 962-8755	5403
Mk Magnetics Inc	3315	D	760 246-6373	5620
Northwest Pipe Company	3317	E	760 246-3191	5638
McElroy Metal Mill Inc	3448	E	760 246-5545	6383
Cageco Inc	3523	E	800 605-4859	6902
Hayward Gordon Us Inc	3556	B	760 246-3430	7201
Scott Turbon Mixer Inc	3556	E	760 246-3430	7215
Thermtronix Corporation **(PA)**	3567	E	760 246-4500	7373
Andersen Industries Inc	3715	E	760 246-8766	9489
General Atomic Aeron	3721	C	760 388-8208	9534
Ducommun Aerostructures Inc	3728	D	760 246-4191	9676
Safeway Sign Company	3993	E	760 246-7070	11153
Carberry LLC **(HQ)**	3999	E	800 564-0842	11204
Quality Resources Dist LLC	3999	E	510 378-6861	11273
Apex Bulk Commodities Inc **(PA)**	4212	C	760 246-6077	11442
Hayes Welding Inc **(PA)**	7692	D	760 246-4878	17085
AGOURA, CA - Los Angeles County				
Joni and Friends Foundation **(PA)**	8322	D	818 707-5664	19103
AGOURA HILLS, CA - Los Angeles County				
James H Cowan & Associates Inc	0782	D	310 457-2574	196
1st Century Builders Inc	1521	F	818 254-7183	418
Ess LLC	1711	D	888 303-6424	768
Acorn Newspaper Inc	2711	E	818 706-0266	3254
Paisano Publications LLC **(PA)**	2721	E	818 889-8740	3375
Paisano Publications Inc	2721	E	818 889-8740	3376
Pars Publishing Corp	2752	E	818 280-0540	3653
Bendpak Inc **(PA)**	3559	C	805 933-9970	7227
Edge Solutions Consulting Inc **(PA)**	3571	E	818 591-3500	7424
Internet Machines Corporation **(PA)**	3577	D	818 575-2100	7538
Zebra Technologies Corporation	3577	D	805 579-1800	7582
Zpower LLC	3629	C	805 445-7789	8216
Teradyne Inc	3679	D	818 991-2900	9129
Relief-Mart Inc	5999	E	805 379-4300	14146
Athas Capital Group Inc	6162	C	877 877-1477	14301
Private Nat Mrtg Accptance LLC **(DH)**	6162	A	818 224-7401	14347
Pennymac Corp	6163	B	818 878-8416	14362
Davidson Hotel Partners Lp	7011	A	818 707-1220	15127
Novalogic Inc **(PA)**	7371	D	818 880-1997	16088
Novastor Corporation **(PA)**	7372	E	805 579-6700	16329
Scorelate Inc	7372	E	818 602-9176	16376
OSI Digital Inc **(PA)**	7379	E	818 992-2700	16585
Los Angeles Rams LLC **(PA)**	7941	D	314 982-7267	17377

	SIC	EMP	PHONE	ENTRY#
AGUA DULCE, CA - Los Angeles County				
Agua Dulce Vineyards LLC	2084	E	661 268-7402	1610
ALHAMBRA, CA - Los Angeles County				
Tyler Trafficante Inc **(PA)**	2311	E	323 869-9299	2155
Gracing Brand Management Inc	2369	B	626 297-2472	2416
Copy Solutions Inc	2752	E	323 307-0900	3545
Comprhnsive Crdvsclar Spclsts **(PA)**	2834	F	626 281-8663	4091
Redwood Scientific Tech Inc	2834	E	310 693-5401	4221
Alhambra Foundry Company Ltd	3321	E	626 289-4294	5643
Coast To Coast Met Finshg Corp	3471	E	626 282-2122	6605
Crown Pavers Inc	3531	E	323 636-3365	6931
Emcore Corporation	3674	C	626 293-3400	8791
Emcore Corporation **(PA)**	3674	C	626 293-3400	8792
Riedon Inc **(PA)**	3676	C		8931
Be Services Company Inc	3679	B	626 284-9901	9004
Ecoflow Technology Inc	4911	E	407 247-6023	12020
Southern California Edison Co	4911	A	626 308-6193	12063
Southern California Gas Co	4924	D	323 881-3587	12088
County of Los Angeles	4941	B	626 458-4000	12118
Orora Packaging Solutions	5113	E	626 284-9524	13018
Alhambra Motors Inc	5511	C	626 576-1114	13737
Lola Belle Brands LLC	5621	F	855 226-3526	13914
FB Corporation	6022	B	626 300-0880	14196
Serfin Funds Transfer **(PA)**	6099	D	626 457-3070	14264
County of Los Angeles	6324	D	626 299-5300	14467
Holmes Body Shop-Alhambra	7532	C	626 282-6173	17010
Atherton Baptist Homes	8051	C	626 863-1710	17884
Silverado Senior Living Inc	8051	D	626 872-3941	18053
Alhambra Hospital Med Ctr LP	8062	C	626 570-1606	18172
Eastern Los Angles Rgnal Ctr F **(PA)**	8322	C	626 299-4700	19074
Binoptics LLC	8711	D	607 257-3200	19553
Network Medical Management Inc	8741	C	626 282-0288	20069
Pacific Ventures Ltd	8741	C	626 576-0737	20076
ALISO VIEJO, CA - Orange County				
LMC Hollywood Highland	1542	B	949 448-1600	565
Fluor Daniel Construction Co **(DH)**	1622	B	949 349-2000	653
Pepsi-Cola Metro Btlg Co Inc	2086	D	949 643-5700	1715
Siemens Energy Inc	2741	E	949 448-0600	3484
Avanir Pharmaceuticals Inc **(DH)**	2834	D	949 389-6700	4061
Biovail Technologies Ltd	2834	D	703 995-2400	4075
Epicuren Discovery	2835	E	949 588-5807	4273
Custom Iron Corporation	3441	E	949 939-4379	6016
Parylene Coating Services Inc	3479	E	281 391-7665	6722
Wepower LLC	3511	E	866 385-9463	6891
Centon Electronics Inc **(PA)**	3572	C	949 855-9111	7465
Ace Tube Bending	3599	E	949 362-2220	7733
Astronic	3672	C	949 454-1180	8650
Agile Technologies Inc	3674	E	949 454-8030	8762
CNT Acquisition Corp **(DH)**	3674	E	949 380-6100	8780
Indie Semiconductor Inc **(PA)**	3674	E	949 608-0854	8806
Ixys Intgrted Crcits Div AV In	3674	A	949 831-4622	8820
W G Holt Inc	3674	D	949 859-8800	8921
Screening Systems Inc **(PA)**	3826	E	949 855-1751	10286
Glaukos Corporation **(PA)**	3841	C	949 367-9600	10517
Merit Medical Systems Inc	3841	E	801 208-4793	10564
Microvention Inc **(DH)**	3841	C	714 258-8800	10567
Nuvasive Spclzed Orthpdics Inc	3841	D	949 837-3600	10584
Sequent Medical Inc	3841	D	949 830-9600	10604

Employee Codes: A=Over 500 employees, B=251-500
C=101-250, D=51-100, E=20-50, F=10-19, G=1-9

2024 Southern California
Business Directory and Buyers Guide

© Mergent Inc. 1-800-342-5647
1335

GEOGRAPHIC

	SIC	EMP	PHONE	ENTRY#
Vertos Medical Inc LLC	3841	D	949 349-0008	10628
Presbibio LLC	3851	E	949 502-7010	10849
Rxsight Inc **(PA)**	3851	D	949 521-7830	10850
United Parcel Service Inc	4215	A	949 643-6634	11546
Southern California Gas Co	4924	D	714 634-7221	12085
Datallegro Inc	5045	C	949 680-3000	12406
Hd Supply Distribution Services LLC	5072	A	949 643-4700	12724
Xse Group Inc	5112	C	888 272-8340	13002
Metagenics LLC **(PA)**	5122	C	949 366-0818	13055
Valeant Biomedicals Inc **(DH)**	5169	D	949 461-6000	13441
Efuel LLC	5172	D	949 330-7145	13450
Youngs Holdings Inc **(PA)**	5182	D	714 368-4615	13482
Clearedge Lending	6162	D	562 708-7706	14307
Thomas James Capital Inc	6282	C	949 481-7026	14431
Safeguard Health Entps Inc **(HQ)**	6324	B	800 880-1800	14493
Shea Properties MGT Co Inc	6512	E	949 389-7000	14684
First Team RE - Orange Cnty	6531	C	949 389-0004	14799
Thomas James Homes Inc	6531	C	949 424-2356	14874
L & O Aliso Viejo LLC	7011	D	949 643-6700	15215
Sunstone Hotel Properties Inc **(DH)**	7011	C	949 330-4000	15381
Cloudstaff LLC	7299	B	888 551-5339	15502
Adecco Employment Services	7361	C	949 586-2342	15810
Remedytemp Inc **(DH)**	7363	C	949 425-7600	15937
Itrex Group USA Corporation	7371	D	213 436-7785	16060
UST Global Inc **(HQ)**	7371	D	949 716-8757	16144
Gaikai Inc	7372	D		16253
Global Wave Group	7372	F	949 916-9800	16257
Quadrotech Solutions Inc **(PA)**	7372	E	949 754-8000	16361
Quest Software Inc	7372	D	949 754-8000	16363
Information MGT Resources Inc **(PA)**	7373	C	949 215-8889	16449
Quest Software Inc **(PA)**	7373	A	949 754-8000	16465
Navtrak LLC	7382	D	410 548-2337	16748
Perfect Impression Inc	7389	E	949 305-0797	16902
Covenant Care LLC **(PA)**	8051	B	949 349-1200	17919
Hcr Manorcare Med Svcs Fla LLC	8051	C	949 587-9000	17969
American Assn Crtcal Care Nrse	8299	C	949 362-2000	19007
Lauras House	8322	D	949 361-3775	19108
Midi Manufacturers Assn Inc	8611	D	714 227-0068	19383
Fluor Corporation	8711	D	949 349-2000	19590
Fluor Daniel Eurasia Inc **(DH)**	8711	E	949 349-2000	19591
Fluor Plant Services Intl Inc	8711	D	949 349-2000	19592
Clarient Diagnostic Svcs Inc	8734	D	888 443-3310	19963
Nelson Bros Property MGT Inc	8741	C	949 916-7300	20067
Professional Community MGT Cal	8741	C	949 380-0725	20083
Basketball Marketing Co Inc	8742	C	610 249-2255	20139
Channelwave Software Inc	8748	D	949 448-4500	20328
Indie LLC	8748	C	949 608-0854	20351

ALPINE, CA - San Diego County

	SIC	EMP	PHONE	ENTRY#
Abhe & Svoboda Inc	1542	D	619 659-1320	527
Mountain Materials Inc	3273	E	619 445-4150	5486
Caster Civil Inc	3562	E	626 201-1300	7297
Alpine Convalescent Center Inc	8093	D	619 659-3120	18667
Southern Indian Health Council **(PA)**	8093	D	619 445-1188	18720

ALTADENA, CA - Los Angeles County

	SIC	EMP	PHONE	ENTRY#
Honeybee Robotics LLC	3569	E	303 774-7613	7393
Anre Technologies Inc	7371	C	818 627-5433	15964
Maimone Liquidating Corp **(PA)**	7532	D	626 286-5691	17012
Altadena Town and Country Club	7997	D	626 345-9088	17459
Five Acres - The Bys Grls Aid	8361	B	626 798-6793	19262

ANAHEIM, CA - Orange County

	SIC	EMP	PHONE	ENTRY#
Harvest Landscape Entps Inc **(PA)**	0781	C	714 693-8100	164
Marina Maintenance Group Inc	0781	B	714 939-6600	166
Resident Group Services Inc **(PA)**	0782	C	714 630-5300	214
Ultimate Landscaping MGT	0782	D	714 502-9711	218
West Coast Arborists Inc **(PA)**	0782	E	714 991-1900	221
Capsule Manufacturing Inc	1389	D	949 245-4151	335
Brownco Construction Co Inc	1521	D	714 935-9600	423
Gray Construction Inc	1521	D	714 491-1315	434
Katerra	1521	D	720 449-3909	439
Katerra Construction LLC	1521	A	720 449-3909	440
Gray West Construction Inc	1541	D	714 491-1317	504
Universal Dust Cllctr Mfg Sup **(PA)**	1541	D	714 630-8588	525
Platinum Construction Inc	1542	D	714 527-0700	580
San-Mar Construction Co Inc	1542	C	714 693-5400	587
Techno Coatings Inc **(PA)**	1542	C	714 635-1130	595
Turner Construction Company	1542	B	714 940-9000	597
Control Air Conditioning Corporation	1711	B	714 777-8600	755
Ken Starr Inc	1711	C	714 632-8789	783
Nexgen AC & Htg LLC	1711	D	760 616-5870	799
Trilogy Plumbing Inc	1711	C	714 441-2952	830

	SIC	EMP	PHONE	ENTRY#
University Marelich Mech Inc	1711	D	714 632-2600	832
Borbon Incorporated	1721	C	714 994-0170	843
Pbc Pavers Inc	1721	D	714 278-0488	852
C G Systems Inc	1731	E	714 632-8882	875
Donco & Sons Inc	1731	E	714 779-0099	891
Rosendin Electric Inc	1731	A	714 739-1334	931
Sunwest Electric Inc	1731	C	714 630-8700	943
Hba Incorporated	1741	D	714 635-8602	958
Vincent Contractors Inc	1741	B	714 660-0165	963
Best Interiors Inc **(PA)**	1742	C	714 490-7999	969
Mowery Thomason Inc	1742	C	714 666-1717	984
Orange County Thermal Inds Inc	1742	D	714 279-9416	987
Arciero Brothers Inc	1771	C	714 238-6600	1058
Penhall Holding Company	1771	C	714 772-6450	1083
Peterson Brothers Cnstr Inc	1771	A	714 278-0488	1084
Performance Contracting Inc	1796	E	913 310-7120	1138
A-1 Enterprises Inc	1799	E	714 630-3390	1141
ATI Restoration LLC **(PA)**	1799	D	714 283-9990	1143
Bravo Sign & Design Inc	1799	F	714 284-0500	1145
Bloomfield Food Inc	2011	E	714 779-7273	1189
Pampanga Food Company Inc	2013	E	714 773-0537	1228
T&J Sausage Kitchen Inc	2013	E	714 632-8350	1238
Pharmachem Laboratories LLC	2023	E	714 630-6000	1282
180 Snacks Inc	2064	E	714 238-1192	1532
Nellson Nutraceutical Inc	2064	B	844 635-5766	1547
Towne Park Brew Inc	2082	E	714 844-2492	1607
Sun Rich Foods Intl Corp	2099	F	714 632-7577	1992
Fantasia Distribution Inc	2131	E	714 817-8300	2008
Alstyle Apparel LLC	2211	A	714 765-0400	2009
Harrys Dye and Wash Inc	2261	E	714 446-0300	2089
Expo Dyeing & Finishing Inc	2269	C	714 220-9583	2100
Redwood Wellness LLC	2299	E	323 843-2676	2146
Joe Wells Enterprises Inc	2329	E		2209
Steady Clothing Inc	2329	F	714 444-2058	2221
The Lunada Bay Corporation **(PA)**	2369	D	714 490-1313	2418
Walt Dsney Imgnring RES Dev In	2389	E	714 781-3152	2461
Display Fabrication Group Inc	2399	E	714 373-2100	2548
Highland Lumber Sales Inc	2431	E	714 778-2293	2605
Millcraft Inc	2431	D	714 632-9621	2615
Woodwork Pioneers Corp	2431	E	714 991-1017	2642
American Woodmark Corporation	2434	B	714 449-2200	2645
Cabinets R US	2434	E	562 483-6886	2652
Reborn Cabinets LLC **(PA)**	2434	B	714 630-2220	2675
D-Mac LLC	2451	E	714 808-3918	2736
Outdoor Dimensions LLC	2499	C	714 578-9555	2757
Quality First Woodworks	2499	E	714 632-0480	2760
University Frames Inc	2499	E	714 575-5100	2765
Textured Design Furniture Inc	2511	E	714 502-9121	2790
M&J Design Inc	2512	E	714 687-9918	2807
RSI Home Products LLC **(HQ)**	2514	A	714 449-2200	2836
Sky Rider Equipment Co Inc	2515	E	714 632-6890	2859
Seating Component Mfg Inc	2519	E	714 693-3376	2873
Commercial Furniture	2521	F	714 350-7045	2880
Furniture Solutions Inc	2521	E	714 666-0424	2884
Block Tops Inc **(PA)**	2541	E	714 978-5080	2944
Leonards Carpet Service Inc **(PA)**	2541	D	714 630-1930	2960
Pacific Westline Inc	2541	D	714 956-2442	2964
Tahiti Cabinets Inc	2599	D	714 693-0618	3032
Treston IAC LLC	2599	E	714 990-8997	3033
Global Paper Solutions Inc	2621	E	714 687-6102	3046
International Paper Company	2621	D	714 776-6060	3048
Mozaik LLC	2652	E	562 207-1900	3076
Jellco Container Inc	2653	D	714 666-2728	3112
Absolute Packaging Inc	2657	E	714 630-3020	3145
Thermec Corporation	2671	E	714 533-3183	3158
Felix Schoeller North Amer Inc	2672	E	315 298-8425	3171
Apple Paper Converting Inc	2679	E	714 632-3195	3229
Digital Label Solutions LLC	2679	E	714 982-5000	3235
Affluent Target Marketing Inc	2721	E	714 446-6280	3343
Spidell Publishing Inc	2741	E	714 776-7850	3485
Anchored Prints	2752	E	714 929-9317	3511
Creative Press LLC **(PA)**	2752	E	714 774-5060	3549
Creative Press LLC	2752	E	714 774-5060	3550
Inland Litho LLC	2752	D	714 993-6000	3599
Interlink Inc	2752	D	714 905-7700	3604
Jeff Lane	2752	E	714 779-8484	3607
Lester Lithograph Inc	2752	E	714 491-3981	3622
Man-Grove Industries Inc	2752	D	714 630-3020	3629
Pacific West Litho Inc	2752	D	714 579-0868	3650
Supreme Graphics Inc	2752	F	310 531-8300	3691
Tajen Graphics Inc	2752	E	714 527-3122	3693
Tam Printing Inc	2752	F	714 224-4488	3694
Adcraft Products Co Inc	2759	E	714 776-1230	3729

Company	SIC	EMP	PHONE	ENTRY#
Brook & Whittle Limited	2759	E	714 634-3466	3741
C T L Printing Inds Inc	2759	E	714 635-2980	3742
Dean Hesketh Company Inc	2759	E	714 236-2138	3752
Diversified Images Inc	2759	F	661 702-0003	3754
Labeltronix LLC (HQ)	2759	D	800 429-4321	3779
Sharon Havriluk	2782	E	714 630-1313	3840
Ryvec Inc	2816	E	714 520-5592	3876
Cytec Solvay Group	2819	E	714 630-9400	3890
Singod Investors Vi LLC	2819	D	714 326-7800	3909
Solvay America Inc	2819	C	714 688-4403	3910
Cytec Engineered Materials Inc	2821	E	714 632-8444	3935
Mer-Kote Products Inc	2821	E	714 778-2266	3954
R K Fabrication Inc	2821	E	714 630-9654	3966
Stepan Company	2821	B	714 776-9870	3975
Xerxes Corporation	2821	C	714 630-0012	3983
B & C Nutritional Products Inc	2833	D	714 238-7225	3991
Excelsior Nutrition Inc	2833	D	657 999-5188	4001
Gmp Laboratories America Inc (PA)	2834	E	714 630-2467	4122
Nbty Manufacturing LLC	2834	C	714 765-8323	4180
S K Laboratories Inc	2834	E	714 695-9800	4227
Teco Diagnostics	2835	D	714 693-7788	4295
Botanx LLC	2844	E	714 854-1601	4385
Buds Cotton Inc	2844	E	714 223-7800	4386
Firmenich	2869	E	714 535-2871	4520
Firmenich Incorporated	2869	D	714 535-2871	4521
Innovative Organics Inc	2869	F	714 701-3900	4522
Saint-Gobain Ceramics Plas Inc	2869	B	714 701-3900	4528
Reliable Packaging Systems Inc	2891	F	714 572-1094	4579
Haddads Fine Arts Inc	2893	E	714 996-2100	4589
Graffiti Shield Inc	3081	E	714 575-1100	4812
Custom Laminators Inc	3083	E	714 778-0895	4832
Nelco Products Inc	3083	C	714 879-4293	4837
Clean Cut Technologies LLC	3086	D	714 864-3500	4878
Foam Concepts Inc	3086	E	714 693-1037	4882
Aquatic Co	3088	E	714 993-1220	4912
Aquatic Industries Inc	3088	E	800 877-2005	4913
Anaheim Custom Extruders Inc	3089	E	714 693-8508	4941
Bace Manufacturing Inc (HQ)	3089	A	714 630-6002	4953
Beemak Plastics LLC	3089	D	800 421-4393	4958
Berry Global Inc	3089	D	714 777-5200	4962
Charmaine Plastics Inc	3089	D	714 630-8117	4989
Demoldco Plastics Inc	3089	E	714 577-9391	5005
Edco Plastics Inc	3089	E	714 772-1986	5019
GT Styling Corp	3089	E	714 644-9214	5044
RPM Plastic Molding Inc	3089	E	714 630-9300	5191
Setco LLC	3089	C	812 424-2904	5203
Sonfarrel	3089	E	714 630-7280	5210
Sp Craftech I LLC	3089	E	714 630-8117	5212
Strand Art Company Inc	3089	E	714 777-0444	5218
Targus US LLC	3161	E	714 765-5555	5296
Custom Industries Inc	3231	E	714 779-9101	5338
Elysium Tiles Inc	3253	F	714 991-7885	5372
Asdak International	3269	E	714 449-0733	5382
Short Load Concrete Inc	3273	E	714 524-7013	5502
Maverick Abrasives Corporation	3291	D	714 854-9531	5543
Anaheim Extrusion Co Inc	3354	D	714 630-3111	5693
Coast 2 Coast Cables LLC	3357	E	714 666-1062	5740
Venus Alloys Inc (PA)	3363	E	714 635-8800	5769
Cytec Engineered Materials Inc	3365	C	714 632-1174	5788
Sonfarrel Aerospace LLC	3365	D	714 630-7280	5798
Craftsman Cutting Dies Inc (PA)	3423	E	714 776-8995	5876
Craftsman Unity LLC	3423	C	714 776-8995	5877
B & B Specialties Inc (PA)	3429	E	714 985-3000	5903
Mid-West Wholesale Hardware Co	3429	E	714 630-4751	5932
Aerofab Industries	3441	F	714 635-0902	5989
Hitech Metal Fabrication Corp	3441	E	714 635-3505	6029
S & R Architectural Metals Inc	3441	E	714 226-0108	6072
TI Fab LP	3441	E	562 802-3980	6081
Triad Bellows Design & Mfg Inc	3441	E	714 204-4444	6084
R & S Ovrhd Doors So-Cal Inc	3442	E	714 680-0600	6119
AAR Manufacturing Inc	3443	C	714 634-8807	6129
Tait & Associates Inc	3443	D	714 560-8222	6162
AMF Anaheim LLC	3444	C	714 363-9206	6188
California Chassis Inc	3444	C	714 666-8511	6209
International West Inc	3444	E	714 632-9190	6254
Metal-Fab Services Indust Inc	3444	E	714 630-7771	6272
Ortronics Inc	3444	C	714 776-5420	6279
Pinnacle Precision Shtmtl Corp (PA)	3444	E	714 777-3129	6292
Pinnacle Precision Shtmtl Corp	3444	D	714 777-3129	6293
Sheet Metal Service	3444	F	714 446-0196	6315
Steeldyne Industries	3444	E	714 630-6200	6323
Vts Sheetmetal Specialist Co	3444	E	714 237-1420	6342
K & J Wire Products Corp	3446	E	714 816-0360	6362
Thornton Steel & Ir Works Inc	3446	F	714 491-8800	6371
Orange County Erectors Inc	3448	E	714 502-8455	6388
A J Fasteners Inc	3452	E	714 630-1556	6430
Butler Inc	3452	F	310 323-3114	6435
CBS Fasteners Inc	3452	E	714 779-6368	6436
Dgl Holdings Inc	3452	E	714 630-7840	6437
Nylok LLC	3452	E	714 635-3993	6450
Ascent Manufacturing LLC	3469	E	714 540-6414	6496
Pacific Precision Metals Inc	3469	C	951 226-1500	6546
Advance-Tech Plating Inc	3471	E	714 630-7093	6575
Artistic Pltg & Met Finshg Inc	3471	E	619 661-1691	6586
Black Oxide Industries Inc	3471	E	714 870-9610	6591
Neutron Plating Inc	3471	F	714 632-9241	6643
Precision Anodizing & Pltg Inc	3471	D	714 996-1601	6650
Stainless Micro-Polish Inc	3471	E	714 632-8903	6666
Superior Connector Plating Inc	3471	E	714 774-1174	6669
Technic Inc	3471	E	714 632-0200	6671
A-1 Engraving Co Inc	3479	E	562 861-2216	6681
Crest Coating Inc	3479	D	714 635-7090	6698
Performance Powder Inc	3479	E	714 632-0600	6725
Powdercoat Services LLC	3479	E	714 533-2251	6728
Superior Spring Company	3495	E	714 490-0881	6809
Anaheim Wire Products Inc	3496	E	714 563-8300	6811
Rampone Industries LLC	3496	E	714 265-0200	6825
Rapid Mfg A Cal Ltd Partnr (PA)	3496	C	714 974-2432	6826
Bassani Manufacturing	3498	E	714 630-1821	6839
One-Way Manufacturing Inc	3498	E	714 630-8833	6850
Trinity Process Solutions Inc	3498	E	714 701-1112	6853
J&S Goodwin Inc (HQ)	3537	D	714 956-4040	6994
Taylor-Dunn Manufacturing LLC (HQ)	3537	D	714 956-4040	6999
Waev Inc (PA)	3537	E	714 956-4040	7000
APT Manufacturing LLC	3541	F	714 632-0040	7004
Precon Inc	3541	E	714 630-7632	7018
US Union Tool Inc (HQ)	3541	E	714 521-6242	7027
Computed Tool & Engrg Inc	3544	E	714 630-3911	7062
Gemini Mfg & Engrg Inc	3544	E	714 999-0010	7073
Roto-Die Company Inc	3544	E	714 991-8701	7094
Superior Jig Inc	3544	E	714 525-4777	7099
Kempton Machine Works Inc	3545	E	714 990-0596	7118
Weartech International Inc	3562	E	714 683-2430	7305
Adwest Technologies Inc (HQ)	3564	E	714 632-8595	7317
Hepa Corporation	3564	D	714 630-5700	7323
Wasser Filtration Inc (PA)	3569	D	714 696-6450	7412
Foreseeson Custom Displays Inc (PA)	3577	E	714 300-0540	7529
Rgb Systems Inc (PA)	3577	C	714 491-1500	7567
Solaris Paper Inc	3579	E	714 687-6657	7588
Manitwoc Fdsrvice Cmpanies LLC	3585	B	323 245-3761	7618
J L Wingert Company	3589	E	714 379-5519	7664
Product Solutions Inc	3589	E	714 545-9757	7679
Rtr Industries LLC (PA)	3592	E	714 996-0050	7705
3d Machine Co Inc	3599	E	714 777-8985	7718
A & D Precision Mfg Inc	3599	E	714 779-2714	7723
Brek Manufacturing Co	3599	C	310 329-7638	7788
Cheek Machine Corp	3599	E	714 279-9486	7798
Cresco Manufacturing Inc	3599	E	714 525-2326	7810
Jaco Engineering	3599	E	714 991-1680	7885
Kerleylegacy63 Inc	3599	D	714 630-7286	7897
Moseys Production Machinists Inc (PA)	3599	E	714 693-4840	7947
Orange County Screw Pdts Inc	3599	E	714 630-7433	7962
Pacific Broach & Engrg Assoc	3599	F	714 632-5678	7964
Pendarvis Manufacturing Inc	3599	E	714 992-0950	7971
Precision Waterjet Inc	3599	E	888 538-9287	7979
Qualitask Inc	3599	E	714 237-0900	7987
Roberts Precision Engrg Inc	3599	E	714 635-4485	8003
Turret Lathe Specialists Inc	3599	F	714 520-0058	8054
West Bond Inc (PA)	3599	E	714 978-1551	8075
Pacific Transformer Corp	3612	D	714 779-0450	8106
Anaheim Automation Inc	3625	D	714 992-6990	8168
Hestan Commercial Corporation	3639	C	714 869-2280	8243
Intense Lighting LLC	3646	D	714 630-9877	8317
Birchwood Lighting Inc	3648	E	714 550-7118	8355
Emazing Lights LLC	3648	E	626 628-6482	8365
Anacom General Corporation	3651	E	714 774-8484	8393
Digital Periph Solutions Inc	3651	E	714 998-3440	8405
Siemens Mobility Inc	3661	E	714 284-0206	8485
L3 Technologies Inc	3663	C	714 758-4222	8536
L3harris Interstate Elec Corp	3663	E	714 758-3395	8537
Econolite Control Products Inc (PA)	3669	C	714 630-3700	8609
Raytheon Applied Sgnal Tech In	3669	D	714 917-0255	8623
American Circuit Tech Inc (PA)	3672	E	714 777-2480	8646
APT Electronics Inc	3672	E	714 687-6760	8648
Chad Industries Incorporated	3672	E	714 938-0080	8659
Copper Clad Mltilayer Pdts Inc	3672	E	714 237-1388	8666

Employee Codes: A=Over 500 employees, B=251-500
C=101-250, D=51-100, E=20-50, F=10-19, G=1-9

2024 Southern California
Business Directory and Buyers Guide

© Mergent Inc. 1-800-342-5647

1337

GEOGRAPHIC

	SIC	EMP	PHONE	ENTRY#
Excello Circuits Inc	3672	D	714 993-0560	8674
Jabil Inc	3672	E	714 938-0080	8692
Kca Electronics Inc	3672	C	714 239-2433	8695
Murrietta Circuits Inc	3672	C	714 970-2430	8707
Secure Technology Company	3672	E	714 991-6500	8729
Smart Elec & Assembly Inc	3672	C	714 772-2651	8730
Summit Interconnect Inc (HQ)	3672	C	714 239-2433	8735
Technotronix Inc	3672	E	714 630-9200	8737
Transline Technology Inc	3672	E	714 533-8300	8739
Ttm Technologies Inc	3672	B	714 688-7200	8745
Veeco Electro Fab Inc	3672	E	714 630-8020	8749
Advanced Thermal Sciences Corp (DH)	3674	E	714 688-4200	8759
Si Manufacturing Inc	3677	E	714 956-7110	8955
Cristek Interconnects LLC (DH)	3678	C	714 696-5200	8968
C & S Assembly Inc	3679	E	866 779-8939	9009
General Power Systems Inc	3679	E	714 956-9321	9048
Ges US (new England) Inc	3679	C	978 459-4434	9049
Interlog Corporation	3679	E	714 529-7808	9065
Jasper Electronics	3679	E	714 917-0749	9069
Magnetic Sensors Corporation	3679	E	714 630-8380	9080
Micrometals Inc (PA)	3679	C	714 970-9400	9085
Rtie Holdings LLC	3679	F	714 765-8200	9111
Xp Power Inc	3679	D	714 712-2642	9141
United Media Services Inc	3695	C	714 693-8168	9187
Jbb Inc	3699	E	888 538-9287	9221
Serra Laser and Waterjet Inc	3699	E	714 680-6211	9254
Phoenix Cars LLC	3711	E	909 987-0815	9303
American Fabrication Corp (PA)	3714	D	714 632-1709	9351
McLeod Racing LLC	3714	E	714 630-2764	9421
Phoenix Motor Inc (DH)	3714	E	909 987-0815	9439
Aerospace Parts Holdings Inc	3728	A	949 877-3630	9607
Arden Engineering Inc (DH)	3728	E	949 877-3642	9629
Astro Spar Inc	3728	E	626 839-7858	9634
Astro-Tek Industries LLC	3728	D	714 238-0022	9635
B/E Aerospace Macrolink	3728	E	714 777-8800	9642
Cadence Aerospace LLC (HQ)	3728	C	949 877-3630	9648
Cadence Aerospace LLC	3728	F	425 353-0405	9649
Cal Tech Precision Inc	3728	D	714 992-4130	9650
Canyon Composites Incorporated	3728	E	714 991-8181	9653
D & D Gear Incorporated	3728	C	714 692-6570	9670
Ferra Aerospace Inc	3728	E	918 787-2220	9687
Gear Manufacturing Inc	3728	E	714 792-2895	9698
Giddens Industries Inc (DH)	3728	E	425 353-0405	9700
Gledhill/Lyons Inc	3728	E	714 502-0274	9701
Goodrich Corporation	3728	C	714 984-1461	9704
Pacific Contours Corporation	3728	D	714 693-1260	9759
Sehanson Inc	3728	E	714 778-1900	9795
DG Performance Spc Inc	3799	D	714 961-8850	9933
Apex Technology Holdings Inc	3812	A	321 270-3630	9944
Cummins Aerospace LLC (PA)	3812	E	714 879-2800	9967
Employer Defense Group	3812	F	949 200-0137	9974
L3 Technologies Inc	3812	E	714 956-9200	9987
Tuffer Manufacturing Co Inc	3812	E	714 526-3077	10086
3d Instruments LLC	3823	D	714 399-9200	10112
L3harris Interstate Elec Corp	3825	E	714 758-0500	10210
L3harris Interstate Elec Corp	3825	E	714 758-0500	10211
L3harris Interstate Elec Corp (DH)	3825	B	714 758-0500	10212
Endress & Hauser Conducta Inc	3826	E	800 835-5474	10256
Mako Industries SC Inc	3826	E	714 632-1400	10272
Tfd Incorporated	3827	E	714 630-7127	10343
Mettler Electronics Corp	3841	E	714 533-2221	10565
Sechrist Industries Inc	3841	A	714 579-8400	10602
Hanger Prsthtics Orthtics W In (HQ)	3842	E	714 961-2112	10667
Danville Materials LLC	3843	E	714 399-0334	10736
Diamodent Inc	3843	E	888 281-8850	10741
Visionary Contact Lens Inc	3851	E	714 237-1900	10856
Golf Supply House Usa Inc	3949	D	714 983-0050	10995
Tuffstuff Fitness Intl Inc	3949	D	909 629-1600	11036
Matthew Warren Inc	3965	E	714 630-7840	11072
YKK (usa) Inc	3965	E	714 701-1200	11082
3s Sign Services Inc	3993	E	714 683-1120	11093
Coast Sign Incorporated	3993	C	714 520-9144	11104
Signage Solutions Corporation	3993	E	714 491-0299	11162
Sunset Signs and Printing Inc	3993	E	714 255-9104	11171
Halonus Inc	3999	B	714 345-0822	11225
Jorge Ulloa	3999	F	714 630-0499	11235
LA Spas Inc	3999	C	714 630-1150	11240
Falck Mobile Health Corp	4119	B	714 828-7750	11386
Filyn Corporation	4119	C	714 632-0225	11387
Roy Miller Freight Lines LLC (PA)	4212	D	714 632-5511	11463
All Counties Courier Inc	4215	C	714 599-9300	11525
Di Overnite LLC	4215	D	877 997-7447	11528
Total Warehouse Inc	4225	C	480 582-3954	11623
Aircraft Repair & Overhaul Svc (PA)	4581	E	714 630-9494	11686
Pacific Coast Sightseeing Tour	4725	C	714 507-1157	11728
DSV Solutions LLC	4731	D	714 630-0110	11757
L&L Foods Holdings LLC	4783	C	714 254-1430	11821
TW Services Inc	4789	B	714 441-2400	11841
AT&T Corp	4812	C	714 284-2878	11843
Zyxel Communications Inc	4813	D	714 632-0882	11915
Southern California Gas Co	4924	C	213 244-1200	12086
City of Anaheim	4971	D	714 254-0125	12212
Califrnia Auto Dalers Exch LLC	5012	B	714 996-2400	12223
Cal-State Auto Parts Inc (PA)	5013	C	714 630-5950	12236
Empi Inc	5013	D	714 446-9606	12240
Reels Inc	5013	D	714 446-9606	12258
Shrin LLC	5013	D	714 850-0303	12261
Greenball Corp (PA)	5014	E	714 782-3060	12269
Atrium Door & Win Co Ariz Inc	5031	C	714 693-0601	12324
Walnut Investment Corp	5031	A	714 238-9240	12344
Best Cheer Stone Inc (PA)	5032	C	714 399-1588	12348
Kretus Group Inc (PA)	5032	E	714 738-6640	12355
General Procurement Inc (PA)	5045	D	949 679-7960	12415
Genesis Computer Systems Inc	5045	E	714 632-3648	12416
Quad-C Jh Holdings Inc	5047	C	502 741-0421	12511
Sapphire Clean Rooms LLC	5049	C	714 316-5036	12532
Quantum Automation (PA)	5063	E	714 854-0800	12614
Etekcity Corporation	5064	C	855 686-3835	12631
Bisco Inc	5065	C	714 693-2901	12647
Bisco Industries Inc (HQ)	5065	D	800 323-1232	12648
L3harris Interstate Elec Corp	5065	C	714 758-0500	12676
Motors & Controls Whse Inc	5065	E	714 956-0480	12685
B & B Specialties Inc	5072	D	714 985-3075	12716
Chuaolson Enterprises Inc	5072	E	714 630-4751	12717
Macpherson Wstn TI Sup Co LLC	5072	F	714 666-4100	12726
Shamrock Supply Company Inc (PA)	5072	E	714 575-1800	12734
Dust Collector Services Inc	5075	E	714 237-1690	12751
George T Hall Co Inc (PA)	5075	E	909 825-9751	12754
Oliver Healthcare Packaging Co	5084	D	714 864-3500	12802
Otis Elevator Company	5084	C	714 758-9593	12805
Midland Industries	5085	D	800 821-5725	12865
Self Serve Auto Dismantlers (PA)	5093	C	714 630-8901	12957
Ft 2 Inc	5099	C	714 765-5555	12975
Bunzl Distribution Cal LLC (DH)	5113	D	714 688-1900	13004
Alstyle AP & Activewear MGT Co (HQ)	5137	A	714 765-0400	13118
Advantage-Crown Sls & Mktg LLC (DH)	5141	A	714 780-3000	13168
Bridgford Marketing Company (DH)	5147	D	714 526-5533	13291
Family Tree Produce Inc	5148	C	714 693-5688	13321
Legacy Farms LLC	5148	D	714 736-1800	13333
Harris Freeman & Co Inc (PA)	5149	B	714 765-7525	13370
Orange County Indus Plas Inc (PA)	5162	E	714 632-9450	13415
Straub Distributing Co Ltd (PA)	5181	C	714 779-4000	13472
Hippo Corporation	5199	F	714 229-9152	13541
Targus International LLC (PA)	5199	C	714 765-5555	13563
Home Depot USA Inc	5211	D	714 921-1215	13586
Lowes Home Centers LLC	5211	C	714 447-6140	13656
Paragon Industries Inc	5211	D	714 778-1800	13668
Stater Bros Markets	5411	E	714 991-5310	13704
Harris Spice Company Inc (HQ)	5499	E	714 507-1919	13727
Emergency Vehicle Group Inc	5511	E	714 238-0110	13762
Isuzu North America Corp (HQ)	5511	E	714 935-9300	13781
Kendon Industries LLC	5561	F	714 630-7144	13896
Cintas Corporation	5699	D	714 646-2550	13931
Rm Partners Inc	5713	E	714 765-5725	13953
Rush Business Forms Inc	5943	E	714 630-5661	14071
Melton Intl Tackle Inc	5961	E	714 978-9192	14095
Rnbs Corporation	5961	E	714 998-1828	14102
E Z Services	6099	D	714 635-7599	14259
Carrington Mrtg Holdings LLC	6162	C	888 267-0584	14305
Caballero & Sons Inc	6221	E	562 368-1644	14410
First Team RE - Orange Cnty	6531	C	714 974-9191	14798
House Seven Gables RE Inc	6531	D	714 282-0306	14811
Fortress Holding Group LLC	6719	D	714 202-8710	14929
1855 S Hbr Blvd Drv Hldngs LLC	7011	D	714 750-1811	15064
American Koyu Corporation	7011	C	626 793-0669	15072
Anaheim - 1855 S Hbr Blvd Owne	7011	D	714 750-1811	15074
Anaheim Plaza Hotel Inc	7011	D	714 772-5900	15076
Best Western Stovalls Inn (PA)	7011	D	714 956-4430	15092
Cinderella Motel	7011	D	559 432-0118	15117
Comfort California Inc	7011	C	714 750-3131	15121
Disney Enterprises Inc	7011	A	714 778-6600	15131
Disneyland International	7011	A	714 956-6746	15132
Edward Thomas Companies	7011	C	714 782-7500	15140
Fairfeld Inn By Mrrott Ltd Prt	7011	C	714 772-6777	15151
Fjs Inc	7011	D	714 905-1050	15153
Ken Real Estate Lease Ltd	7011	D	714 778-1700	15208

2024 Southern California
Business Directory and Buyers Guide

(P-0000) Products & Services Section entry number
(PA)=Parent Co (HQ)=Headquarters (DH)=Div Headquarters

	SIC	EMP	PHONE	ENTRY#
Makar Anaheim LLC	7011	A	714 740-4431	15237
Northwest Hotel Corporation **(PA)**	7011	C	714 776-6120	15264
Orangewood LLC	7011	B	714 750-3000	15278
Portofino Inn & Suites Anaheim	7011	B	714 782-7600	15308
SAI Management Co Inc	7011	A	714 772-5050	15339
Wco Hotels Inc	7011	A	714 635-2300	15411
GBS Linens Inc **(PA)**	7213	D	714 778-6448	15451
Fci Lender Services Inc	7322	C	800 931-2424	15612
Vengroff Williams & Assoc Inc	7322	C	714 889-6200	15617
Advantage Mailing LLC **(PA)**	7331	C	714 538-3881	15627
AST Sportswear Inc	7331	B	714 223-2030	15628
Consolidated Design West Inc	7336	E	714 999-1476	15659
Infosend Inc **(PA)**	7338	E	714 993-2690	15680
Coastal Building Services Inc	7349	B	714 775-2855	15700
DMS Facility Services Inc	7349	A	949 975-1366	15709
Hunter Easterday Corporation	7349	C	714 238-3400	15713
Go-Staff Inc	7361	A	657 242-9350	15850
Anamex Corporation **(PA)**	7371	E	714 779-7055	15963
Select Data Inc	7371	C	714 577-1000	16112
Bpoms Inc **(HQ)**	7372	D	714 974-2670	16188
Unlimited Innovations Inc	7372	E	714 998-0866	16414
Morphotrak LLC **(DH)**	7373	C	714 238-2000	16461
Cyber-Pro Systems Inc	7374	C	562 256-3800	16489
Bcp Systems Inc	7378	D	714 202-3900	16541
Etherwan Systems Inc	7379	C	714 779-3800	16566
Partners Information Tech **(HQ)**	7379	C	714 736-4487	16588
Califrnia Suthland Private SEC	7381	C	714 367-4005	16628
ADT LLC	7382	C	714 450-6461	16716
ADT LLC	7382	C	626 593-1020	16717
G4s Justice Services LLC	7382	D	800 589-6003	16737
Kesa Incorporated	7382	E	714 956-2827	16744
Sentinel Offender Services LLC **(PA)**	7382	C	949 453-1550	16754
Cppg Inc	7389	F	714 572-3662	16809
Freeman Expositions LLC	7389	C	714 254-3400	16829
MB Coatings Inc	7389	C	714 625-2118	16869
Nor-Cal Beverage Co Inc	7389	C	714 526-8600	16888
Alamo Rental (us) Inc	7514	D	714 748-7368	16978
T L Fabrications LP	7692	D	562 802-3980	17096
Disney Enterprises Inc	7812	D	407 397-6000	17182
Disney Enterprises Inc	7812	C	714 781-1651	17183
Hob Entertainment LLC	7929	C	714 520-2310	17337
Anaheim Arena Management LLC	7941	A	714 704-2400	17361
Anaheim Ducks Hockey Club LLC **(PA)**	7941	D	714 940-2900	17362
Angels Baseball LP **(PA)**	7941	A	714 940-2000	17363
Disneyland International **(DH)**	7996	C	714 781-4565	17448
Adventure City Inc	7999	C	714 821-3311	17539
Agile Occupational Medicine PC	8011	D	949 464-4036	17583
Kaiser Foundation Hospitals	8011	C	714 279-4675	17683
Southern Cal Prmnnte Med Group	8011	C	714 279-4675	17792
Vanguard Health Systems Inc	8011	B	714 635-6272	17822
Coventry Court Health Center	8051	C	714 636-2800	17921
Mark & Fred Enterprises	8051	C	714 821-1993	18009
Oceanside Harbor Holdings LLC	8051	C	760 331-3177	18020
Windsor Anaheim Healthcare **(PA)**	8051	C	714 826-8950	18078
Ahmc Anheim Rgional Med Ctr LP	8062	A	714 774-1450	18166
Ahmc Anheim Rgional Med Ctr LP **(PA)**	8062	A	714 774-1450	18167
Anaheim Global Medical Center	8062	A	714 533-6220	18179
Anaheim Regional Medical Ctr	8062	C	714 774-1450	18180
Anaheim Regional Medical Ctr	8062	C	714 999-3847	18181
Kaiser Foundation Hospitals	8062	A	714 644-2000	18307
Prime Healthcare Anaheim LLC	8062	A	714 827-3000	18385
Providence Medical Foundation **(DH)**	8062	C	714 712-3308	18399
Tenet Healthsystem Medical Inc	8062	C	714 428-6800	18473
Korean Community Services Inc	8069	C	714 527-6561	18529
St Jseph Hlth Sys HM Care Svc	8082	A	714 712-9500	18643
Behavioral Health Works Inc	8093	D	800 249-1266	18670
Real Estate Trainers Inc	8249	E	800 282-2352	19004
Orange Cnty Adult Achvment Ctr	8322	C	714 744-5301	19120
St Joseph Hospice	8322	C	714 712-7100	19144
Westview Services Inc	8331	D	714 635-2444	19198
Tiger Woods Learning Center	8351	D	714 765-8040	19231
Leisure Care LLC	8361	C	714 974-1616	19281
Automobile Club Southern Cal	8699	D	714 774-2392	19519
Development Resource Cons Inc **(PA)**	8711	D	714 685-6860	19571
DMS Facility Services LLC	8711	A	949 975-1366	19575
Fortel Traffic Inc	8711	F	714 701-9800	19593
Nest Parent LLC	8711	A	310 551-0101	19655
Willdan Group Inc **(PA)**	8711	A	800 424-9144	19719
Country Villa Service Corp **(PA)**	8741	D	310 574-3733	20021
Tricom Management Inc	8741	C	714 630-2029	20107
Branded Group Inc	8742	C	323 940-1444	20144
Concrete West Construction Inc	8742	F	949 448-9940	20155
Consumer Resource Network LLC	8742	B	800 291-4794	20156

	SIC	EMP	PHONE	ENTRY#
Ralph Brennan Rest Group LLC	8742	C	714 776-5200	20227
Shell Oil Company	8742	C	714 991-9200	20236
Workcare Inc	8744	C	714 978-7488	20303
Aliantel Inc	8748	D	714 829-1650	20312
C M E Corp	8748	C	714 632-6939	20322
Edge Mortgage Advisory Co LLC	8748	D	714 564-5800	20332
Rubio Arts Corporation	8999	C	407 849-1643	20401

ANGELUS OAKS, CA - San Bernardino County

	SIC	EMP	PHONE	ENTRY#
YMCA of East Valley	8641	C	909 794-1702	19474

ANZA, CA - Riverside County

	SIC	EMP	PHONE	ENTRY#
Cahuilla Creek Rest & Casino	7999	C	951 763-1200	17543

APPLE VALLEY, CA - San Bernardino County

	SIC	EMP	PHONE	ENTRY#
Brightview Tree Company	0781	D	760 955-2560	155
American Integrity Corp	3089	E	760 247-1082	4939
Cemex Cement Inc	3273	C	760 381-7616	5470
Dicken Enterprises Inc	3567	E	760 246-7333	7364
Reid Products Inc	3599	E	760 240-1355	7995
Cco Holdings LLC	4841	C	760 810-4076	11980
Lowes Home Centers LLC	5211	C	760 961-3000	13642
Protein Kitchen	5719	E	888 899-2956	13966
Inland Valley Hospice Co	8052	D	760 243-2501	18086
St Mary Medical Center LLC **(PA)**	8062	A	760 242-2311	18468
St Mary Medical Center LLC	8062	A	760 946-8767	18469
BEST Opportunities Inc	8331	C	760 628-0111	19177
High Dsert Prtnr In Acdmic Exc	8732	B	760 946-5414	19896

ARCADIA, CA - Los Angeles County

	SIC	EMP	PHONE	ENTRY#
Sing Kung Corp	2041	E	626 358-5838	1416
Dear John Denim Inc	2211	F	626 350-5100	2018
Harvest Pack Inc	2656	F	888 727-7225	3143
Relton Corporation	2899	D	800 423-1505	4628
Danco Anodizing Inc **(PA)**	3471	E	626 445-3303	6610
Bendick Precision Inc	3599	E	626 445-0217	7780
Enas Media Inc	3652	F	626 962-1115	8457
Segway Inc	3751	C	603 222-6000	9882
MPS Anzon LLC	3842	C	626 471-3553	10685
Transdev Services Inc	4119	A	626 357-7912	11406
Coach Usa Inc	4142	C	626 357-7912	11416
365 Delivery Inc	4212	D	818 815-5005	11436
Gar Enterprises **(PA)**	5045	C	626 574-1175	12413
Tee Top of California Inc **(PA)**	5136	C	626 303-1868	13114
Penney Opco LLC	5311	C	626 445-6454	13681
Burlington Coat Fctry Whse of	5651	C	626 447-8784	13921
Ikrusher Inc	5993	D	626 256-3449	14115
Transglobal Holding Company	6163	D	626 447-7888	14369
Welltower Om Group LLC	6512	C	626 254-0552	14695
Coldwell Banker Residential RE	6531	C	626 445-5500	14767
Property Care Building Svc LLC	7349	E	626 623-6420	15742
Post Alarm Systems **(PA)**	7382	C	626 446-7159	16749
Los Angeles Turf Club Inc **(DH)**	7948	C	626 574-6330	17386
Country Villa Service Corp	8051	C	626 445-2421	17916
Arcadia Gardens MGT Corp	8052	C	626 574-8571	18080
Arcadia Convalescent Hosp Inc **(PA)**	8059	C	626 445-2170	18110
Usc Arcadia Hospital **(PA)**	8062	A	626 898-8000	18492
Uplift Family Services	8322	A	626 254-5000	19152
Leisure Care LLC	8361	C	626 447-0106	19280

ARLETA, CA - Los Angeles County

	SIC	EMP	PHONE	ENTRY#
Superior Thread Rolling Co	3599	D	818 504-3626	8039

ARROYO GRANDE, CA - San Luis Obispo County

	SIC	EMP	PHONE	ENTRY#
Greenheart Farms Inc	0191	B	805 481-2234	82
Talley Farms	0723	C	805 489-2508	114
Anderson Burton Cnstr Inc **(PA)**	1542	C	805 481-5096	529
Corbett Vineyards LLC	2084	E	805 782-9463	1617
Laetitia Vineyard & Winery Inc	2084	D	805 481-1772	1642
Crosno Construction Inc	3441	C	805 343-7437	6015
Phillips 66 Co Carbon Group	3559	E	805 489-4050	7256
Cco Holdings LLC	4841	C	805 904-1047	11977
Ameri-Kleen	7349	C	805 546-0706	15592
Compass Health Inc	8051	C	805 489-8137	17909
Arroyo Grande Community Hospital	8062	B	805 473-7626	18187
Mhm Services Inc	8093	C	805 904-6678	18702
Compass Health Inc	8361	C	805 474-7260	19251

ARTESIA, CA - Los Angeles County

	SIC	EMP	PHONE	ENTRY#
California Dairies Inc	2026	D	562 809-2595	1307
Cal Plate Inc	3555	D	562 403-3000	7183
Outsource Utility Contr Corp	4911	C	714 238-9263	12033
Kukdong Apparel America Inc	7389	E	562 403-0044	16857

Employee Codes: A=Over 500 employees, B=251-500
C=101-250, D=51-100, E=20-50, F=10-19, G=1-9

2024 Southern California
Business Directory and Buyers Guide

© Mergent Inc. 1-800-342-5647

1339

GEOGRAPHIC

	SIC	EMP	PHONE	ENTRY#
Windsor Twin Plms Hlthcare Ctr.	8051	C	562 865-0271	18079
Artesia Christian Home Inc.	8059	C	562 865-5218	18111

ARVIN, CA - Kern County

	SIC	EMP	PHONE	ENTRY#
Tasteful Selections LLC	0134	C	661 854-3998	3
Grimmway Enterprises Inc.	0723	B	661 854-6250	104
Grimmway Enterprises Inc.	0723	A	661 854-6200	105
Kern Ridge Growers LLC	0723	B	661 854-3141	107
Grimmway Enterprises Inc.	1541	C	661 854-6240	505
Moore Farms Inc.	2099	E	661 854-5588	1949
Sandusky Lee LLC	2514	E	661 854-5551	2837
Reeves Extruded Products Inc.	3089	D	661 854-5970	5175
Grimmway Enterprises Inc.	4212	D	307 302-0090	11458
Blue Beacon USA LP	7542	C	661 858-2090	17045
Evergreen Health Care LLC	8051	A	661 854-4475	17951
Grimmway Enterprises Inc.	8741	D	661 854-6200	20036

ATASCADERO, CA - San Luis Obispo County

	SIC	EMP	PHONE	ENTRY#
Chemlogics Group LLC	2869	E	805 591-3314	4518
Solvay USA Inc.	2869	E	805 591-3314	4529
Central Coast Seafoods	5146	C	805 462-3474	13278
Compass Health Inc.	8051	C	805 466-9254	17910
Califrnia Dept State Hospitals	8063	A	805 468-2000	18508
Star of California	8099	D	805 466-1638	18809

AVALON, CA - Los Angeles County

	SIC	EMP	PHONE	ENTRY#
Pacific Catalina Hotel Inc.	7011	B	310 510-9255	15285
Intervrsity Chrstn Fllwshp/Usa	7032	A	310 510-0015	15436

AVILA BEACH, CA - San Luis Obispo County

	SIC	EMP	PHONE	ENTRY#
Veolia Wts Usa Inc.	2899	D	805 545-3743	4637
Pacific Gas and Electric Co.	4911	A	805 506-5280	12035

AZUSA, CA - Los Angeles County

	SIC	EMP	PHONE	ENTRY#
Monrovia Nursery Company (PA)	0181	A	626 334-9321	60
Richard Wilson Wellington	0181	D	626 812-7881	69
Rain Bird Distribution Corp.	1629	E	626 963-9311	714
Berger Bros Inc.	1742	B	626 334-2699	968
Oj Insulation LP (PA)	1742	C	800 707-9278	985
CTI Foods Azusa LLC	2013	C	626 633-1609	1216
McKeever Danlee Confectionary	2064	D	626 334-8964	1546
Very Special Chocolats Inc.	2066	E	626 334-7838	1555
Mat Cactus Mfg Co.	2273	E	626 969-0444	2117
Bojer Inc.	2392	E	626 334-1711	2467
McMurtrie & Mcmurtrie Inc.	2426	E	626 815-0177	2576
Carters Metal Fabricators Inc.	2522	E	626 815-4225	2906
Holguin & Holguin Inc.	2531	E	626 815-0168	2927
Mortech Manufacturing	2531	D	626 334-1471	2933
Ncla Inc.	2679	F	562 926-6252	3239
Artisan Screen Printing Inc.	2759	C	626 815-2700	3736
S&B Pharma Inc.	2833	D	626 334-2908	4015
Bbeautiful LLC	2844	E	626 610-2332	4382
Westwood Laboratories LLC (PA)	2844	E	626 969-3305	4469
D W Mack Co Inc.	3053	E	626 969-1817	4724
California Amforge Corporation	3312	C	626 334-4931	5581
Inwesco Incorporated (PA)	3315	D	626 334-7115	5618
Inovativ Inc.	3334	E	626 969-5300	5671
Magparts (HQ)	3365	C	626 334-7897	5797
Rain Bird Corporation	3432	E	626 812-3400	5973
Melco Steel Inc.	3443	E	626 334-7875	6145
Todd Street Inc.	3443	E	626 815-1175	6166
Lindsey Manufacturing Co.	3463	C	626 969-3471	6479
Mc William & Son Inc.	3469	F	626 969-1821	6535
Rain Bird Corporation (PA)	3494	C	626 812-3400	6794
Gale Banks Engineering	3519	C	626 969-9600	6894
Trio Engineered Products Inc (HQ)	3531	E	626 851-3966	6945
Ancra International LLC	3537	C	626 765-4818	6984
Ancra International LLC (HQ)	3537	C	626 765-4800	6985
Marples Gears Inc.	3566	E	626 570-1744	7357
Acme Portable Machines Inc.	3571	E	626 610-1888	7414
A & B Aerospace	3599	E	626 334-2976	7722
Kemac Technology Inc.	3599	E	626 334-1519	7896
Screwmatic Inc.	3599	D	626 334-7831	8018
Phaostron Instr Electronic Co.	3613	D	626 969-6801	8128
Ptb Sales Inc (PA)	3679	E	626 334-0500	9102
Skylock Industries	3728	E	201 637-9505	9797
Skylock Industries Inc.	3728	E	626 334-2391	9798
Northrop Grumman Systems Corp.	3812	A	626 812-1000	10019
Northrop Grumman Systems Corp.	3812	A	626 812-1464	10023
Tecomet Inc.	3841	A	626 334-1519	10615
BK Signs Inc.	3993	F	626 334-5600	11099
Dhb Delivery LLC.	4215	D	626 588-7562	11527
Cco Holdings LLC	4841	C	626 513-0204	11974

	SIC	EMP	PHONE	ENTRY#
San Gabriel Valley Water Assn.	4941	D	626 815-1305	12142
Hanson Distributing Company (PA)	5013	C	626 224-9800	12241
Cemex Cement Inc.	5032	E	626 969-1747	12349
Totten Tubes Inc (PA)	5051	D	626 812-0220	12577
Niscayah Inc.	5065	D	626 683-8167	12687
Smart & Final Stores Inc.	5141	C	626 334-5189	13221
Buena Vista Food Products Inc (DH)	5149	C	626 815-8859	13356
Arrietta Incorporated	5411	E	626 334-0302	13694
Mc-40 (PA)	7349	C	323 225-4111	15723
Ruiteng Internet Technology Co.	7374	C	302 597-7438	16512
I2k LLC.	7911	E	626 969-7780	17308
Casa Clina Hosp Ctrs For Hlthc.	8049	C	626 334-8735	17858
Valley Lght Ctr For Scial Advn.	8331	D	626 337-6200	19193

BAKERSFIELD, CA - Kern County

	SIC	EMP	PHONE	ENTRY#
J G Boswell Company	0131	B	661 327-7721	1
Vignolo Farms Inc.	0131	C	661 746-2148	2
Bolthouse Farms.	0161	A	661 366-7205	7
Generis Holdings LP (PA)	0161	C	661 366-7209	10
7th Standard Ranch Company.	0172	B	661 399-0416	26
Giumarra Vineyards Corporation	0172	C	661 395-7071	30
Crystal Organic Farms LLC	0191	A	661 845-5200	79
Dv Custom Farming LLC	0191	D	661 858-2888	80
AC Irrigation Holdco LLC.	0711	C	661 368-3550	95
Grimmway Enterprises Inc.	0723	C	661 845-5200	106
Sun World Inc.	0723	A	805 833-6460	112
Sun World International Inc (PA)	0723	A	661 392-5000	113
Wonderful Company LLC.	0723	A	559 781-7438	119
Ag-Wise Enterprises Inc (PA)	0762	C	661 325-1567	134
Illume Agriculture LLC.	0762	C	661 587-5198	136
Sun Pacific Farming Coop Inc.	0762	D	661 399-0376	138
Penney Lawn Service Inc.	0782	E	661 587-4788	213
Aera Energy LLC.	1311	A	661 665-5000	245
Berry Petroleum Company LLC (HQ)	1311	E	661 616-3900	247
Hathaway LLC.	1311	E	661 393-2004	261
Sequoia Exploration Inc.	1311	E	661 303-0564	265
Tri-Valley Corporation	1311	E	661 864-0500	269
Unified Field Services Corp.	1311	E	661 325-8962	270
Vaquero Energy Incorporated.	1311	E	661 363-7240	271
Aera Energy Services Company (HQ)	1381	A	661 665-5000	277
Elysium Jennings LLC.	1381	C	661 679-1700	280
Excalibur Well Services Corp.	1381	C	661 589-5338	281
Geo Guidance Drilling Svcs Inc (PA)	1381	E	661 833-9999	282
Golden State Drilling Inc.	1381	D	661 589-0730	283
Petro-Lud Inc.	1381	E	661 747-4779	287
West American Energy Corp.	1381	F	661 747-7732	289
California Resources Corp.	1382	A	661 395-8000	293
E & B Ntral Resources Mgt Corp (PA)	1382	D	661 679-1714	300
Freeport-Mcmoran Oil & Gas LLC.	1382	E	661 322-7600	306
Linnco LLC.	1382	A	661 616-3900	310
Macpherson Oil Company LLC.	1382	E	661 556-6096	311
Sentinel Peak Rsources Cal LLC.	1382	D	661 395-5214	320
Ally Enterprises.	1389	E	661 412-9933	326
Anatesco Inc.	1389	F	661 399-6990	327
Basic Energy Services Inc.	1389	E	661 588-3800	329
C & H Testing Service Inc (PA)	1389	E	661 589-4030	331
C&J Well Services LLC.	1389	A	661 589-5222	332
Calpi Inc.	1389	E	661 589-5648	334
Casing Specialties Inc.	1389	E	661 399-5522	336
Central California Cnstr Inc.	1389	E	661 978-8230	337
CJ Berry Well Services MGT LLC.	1389	A	661 589-5220	338
CL Knox Inc.	1389	D	661 837-0477	340
Engineered Well Svc Intl Inc.	1389	F	866 913-6283	345
First Energy Services Inc.	1389	E	661 387-1972	347
Grayson Service Inc.	1389	F	661 589-5444	348
Halliburton Company.	1389	D	661 393-8111	350
Hills Wldg & Engrg Contr Inc.	1389	D	661 746-5400	352
John M Phillips LLC.	1389	E	661 327-3118	357
Mark Sheffield Cnstr Inc.	1389	F	661 589-5826	360
Mmi Services Inc.	1389	C	661 589-9366	363
MTS Solutions LLC.	1389	E	661 589-5804	364
Nabors Well Services Co.	1389	C	661 588-6140	367
Nabors Well Services Co.	1389	C	661 589-3970	368
Nabors Well Services Co.	1389	C	661 392-7668	369
Pacific Process Systems Inc (PA)	1389	D	661 321-9681	376
Palmer Tank & Construction Inc.	1389	E	661 834-1110	377
Production Data Inc.	1389	E	661 327-4776	379
Pros Incorporated.	1389	E	661 589-5400	380
PSC Industrial Outsourcing LP	1389	D	661 833-9991	381
Robert Heely Construction LP (PA)	1389	E	661 617-1400	382
Schlumberger Technology Corp.	1389	E	661 864-4721	384
Theta Oilfield Services Inc.	1389	C	661 633-2792	385
Titan Oilfield Services Inc.	1389	D	661 861-1630	387

(P-0000) Products & Services Section entry number
(PA)=Parent Co (HQ)=Headquarters (DH)=Div Headquarters

	SIC	EMP	PHONE	ENTRY#
Truitt Oilfield Maint Corp	1389	B	661 871-4099	389
Tuboscope Pipeline Svcs Inc	1389	F	661 328-5500	391
U S Weatherford L P	1389	C	661 589-9483	392
Vaquero Energy Inc	1389	E	661 616-0600	394
Pioneer Sands LLC	1446	E	661 746-5789	410
PCL Industrial Services Inc	1542	B	661 832-3995	576
Griffith Company	1611	B	661 392-6640	621
Construction Specialty Svc Inc	1623	D	661 864-7573	667
Diversified Utility Svcs Inc	1623	B	661 325-3212	668
K S Fabrication & Machine Inc	1623	C	661 617-1700	678
KS Industries LP (PA)	1623	A	661 617-1700	680
Nts Inc	1623	B	661 588-8514	683
Southwest Contractors (PA)	1623	E	661 588-0484	693
Thermal Energy Solutions Inc	1623	E	661 489-4100	698
Frontier Mechanical Inc	1711	D	661 589-6203	772
Hps Mechanical Inc (PA)	1711	C	661 397-2121	777
Contra Costa Electric Inc	1731	C	661 322-4036	885
Electrical & Instrumentation Unlimi	1731	C		893
Energy Watch	1731	D	661 324-0930	896
Ensign US Drlg Cal Inc	1731	E	661 387-8400	898
Pavletich Elc Cmmnications Inc (PA)	1731	D	661 589-9473	925
Sunshine Metal Clad Inc	1742	D	661 366-0575	999
Grant Construction Inc	1751	C	661 588-4586	1012
Baymarr Constructors Inc	1771	C	661 395-1676	1059
Kenai Drilling Limited	1781	C	661 587-0117	1095
Zim Industries Inc	1781	D	661 393-9661	1097
Sturgeon Son Grading & Pav Inc (PA)	1794	C	661 322-4408	1126
Davidson Enterprises Inc	1799	E	661 325-2145	1152
Nestle Usa Inc	2023	B	661 398-3536	1281
Vita-Pakt Citrus Products Co (PA)	2033	E	626 332-1101	1350
Laumiere Gourmet Fruits Co LLC	2034	F	661 218-9768	1356
Wm Bolthouse Farms Inc (HQ)	2037	A	661 366-7209	1381
Sun-Gro Commodities Inc (PA)	2048	E	661 393-2612	1450
Pyrenees French Bakery Inc	2051	E	661 322-7159	1490
Temblor Brewing LLC	2082	E	661 489-4855	1606
Giumarra Vineyards Corporation	2084	D	661 395-7000	1633
American Bottling Company	2086	D	661 323-7921	1681
Crystal Geyser Water Company	2086	E	661 323-6296	1692
Crystal Geyser Water Company	2086	E	661 321-0896	1693
Pepsi-Cola Bottling Group	2086	D	661 635-1100	1708
Pepsi-Cola Btlg Co Bakersfield	2086	E	661 327-9992	1709
Reyes Coca-Cola Bottling LLC	2086	E	661 324-6531	1730
Alfred Louie Incorporated	2099	F	661 831-2520	1849
American Yeast Corporation	2099	E	661 834-1050	1851
Well Analysis Corporation Inc (PA)	2411	E	661 283-9510	2563
Hoover Treated Wood Pdts Inc	2491	E	661 833-0429	2746
West Coast Wood Preserving LLC	2491	C	661 833-0429	2748
Spalinger Enterprises Inc	2541	E	661 834-4550	2965
Harrell Holdings (PA)	2711	C	661 322-5627	3280
Amber Chemical Inc	2819	E	661 325-2072	3880
Championx LLC	2819	E	661 834-0454	3889
Aqseptence Group Inc	2821	C	661 323-1506	3925
Glam and Glits Nail Design Inc	2844	D	661 393-4800	4414
Kern Oil & Refining Co (HQ)	2911	C	661 845-0761	4642
San Joaquin Refining Co Inc	2911	C	661 327-4257	4650
Tricor Refining LLC	2911	D	661 393-7110	4653
Delta Trading LP	2951	E	661 834-5560	4658
Asphalt Dr Inc	2952	E	661 437-5995	4667
Newby Rubber Inc	3069	E	661 327-5137	4780
Georg Fischer Harvel LLC	3084	E	661 396-0653	4848
Hancor Inc	3084	E	661 366-1520	4849
Domino Plastics Mfg Inc	3089	E	661 396-3744	5014
Pactiv LLC	3089	C	661 392-4000	5128
Carlos Shower Doors Inc	3231	F	661 204-6689	5335
Golden Empire Con Pdts Inc	3272	D	661 833-4490	5417
Lux LLC	3281	E	661 479-2926	5531
Consolidated Fibrgls Pdts Co	3296	D	661 323-6026	5553
UPF Corporation	3296	F	661 323-8227	5560
Kern Steel Fabrication Inc (PA)	3441	D	661 327-9588	6037
Metal Tek Company	3441	E	661 832-6011	6052
Spartan Inc	3441	E	661 327-1205	6077
Bryant Fuel Systems LLC	3443	F	661 334-5462	6135
PNa Construction Tech Inc	3444	E	661 326-1700	6295
Jts Modular Inc	3448	E	661 835-9270	6381
Elyte Inc	3479	F	661 832-1000	6702
Bvi International Inc	3491	E	661 834-1775	6755
Western Valve Inc	3491	E	661 327-7660	6771
Russell Fabrication Corp	3498	E	661 861-8495	6852
Material Control Inc	3499	D	661 617-6033	6869
Marie Edward Vineyards Inc	3523	E	661 363-5038	6908
Altec Inc	3531	E	661 679-4177	6924
Silo City Inc	3531	E		6942
Sturgeon Services Intl Inc	3531	B	661 322-4408	6943
Chancellor Oil Tools Inc	3533	E	661 324-2213	6954
Downhole Stabilization Inc	3533	E	661 631-1044	6957
Global Elastomeric Pdts Inc	3533	D	661 831-5380	6958
Hydril Company	3533	D	661 588-9332	6959
JB Rogers Consulting Inc	3533	F	661 397-4987	6960
Kba Engineering LLC	3533	D	661 323-0487	6961
Mobile Equipment Company	3536	E	661 327-8476	6983
Ensign US Drlg Cal Inc (HQ)	3541	E	661 589-0111	7012
Ray Chinn Construction Inc	3542	E	661 327-2731	7038
Pro Tool Services Inc	3545	E	661 393-9222	7128
Timec Companies Inc	3559	E	661 322-8177	7261
Total Process Solutions LLC	3561	E	661 829-7910	7292
Acco Engineered Systems Inc	3585	E	661 631-1975	7593
M D Manufacturing Inc	3589	F	661 283-7550	7669
Mazzei Injector Company LLC	3589	E	661 363-6500	7672
Seaco Technologies Inc	3589	E	661 326-1522	7683
B & B Pipe and Tool Co	3599	E	661 323-8208	7770
Bakersfield Machine Co Inc	3599	D	661 709-1992	7773
Energy Link Indus Svcs Inc	3599	E	661 765-4444	7827
Valley Perforating LLC	3599	E	661 324-4964	8059
Water Associates Inc	3663	E	661 281-6077	8598
Custom Truck One Source LP	3713	E	316 627-2608	9320
Douglass Truck Bodies Inc	3713	E	661 327-0258	9322
Tiger Tanks Inc	3795	E	661 363-8335	9931
Computational Systems Inc	3823	D	661 832-5306	10124
Townsend Industries Inc	3842	E	661 837-1795	10713
Townsend Industries Inc	3842	D	661 837-1795	10714
Townsend Industries Inc (DH)	3842	C	661 837-1795	10715
Dunbar Electric Sign Company	3993	E	661 323-2600	11110
Golden Empire Transit District (PA)	4111	C	661 869-2438	11321
Gazelle Transportation LLC	4212	C	661 322-8868	11455
Esparza Enterprises Inc	4213	A	661 631-0347	11484
Stevens Transportation Inc	4213	C	661 366-3286	11506
Exeter Packers Inc	4222	C	661 399-0416	11551
AGM California Inc	4832	C	661 328-0118	11919
Buck Owens Production Co Inc (PA)	4832	C	661 326-1011	11920
Newport Television LLC	4833	A	661 283-1700	11960
Prosoft Technology Inc (HQ)	4899	C	661 716-5100	12011
Pacific Gas and Electric Co	4911	C	661 398-5918	12040
Southern California Gas Co	4924	C	661 399-4431	12093
MP Environmental Svcs Inc (PA)	4953	C	800 458-3036	12174
Varner Bros Inc	4953	C	661 399-2944	12192
Bakersfield Shingles Wholesale Inc	5039	D	661 327-3727	12370
Jims Supply Co Inc (PA)	5051	E	661 616-6977	12556
Cameron West Coast Inc	5082	D		12766
Gottstein Corporation	5082	C	661 322-8934	12769
Quinn Company	5082	C	661 393-5800	12777
Ace Hydraulic Sales & Svc Inc	5084	F	661 327-0571	12783
Industrial Data Communications	5084	E	661 589-4477	12791
Measurment Instrmnttion Cntrls	5084	E	661 401-0070	12799
Surface Pumps Inc (PA)	5084	D	661 393-1545	12826
Valley Power Systems Inc	5084	D	661 325-9001	12831
Westair Gases & Equipment Inc	5084	C	661 387-6800	12837
Custom Building Products LLC	5085	D	661 393-0422	12850
Dhv Industries Inc	5085	D	661 392-8948	12852
Shar-Craft Inc (PA)	5085	E	661 324-4985	12879
Wall Street Alley T-Shirt Co	5137	E	661 324-6207	13156
Nestle Ice Cream Company	5143	A	661 398-3500	13257
Frito-Lay North America Inc	5145	C	661 328-6034	13269
Sun Pacific Marketing Coop Inc	5148	B	661 847-1015	13341
Aspire Bakeries LLC	5149	C	661 832-0409	13352
Core-Mark International Inc	5149	C	661 366-2673	13363
Geo Drilling Fluids Inc (PA)	5169	E	661 325-5919	13434
Advance Beverage Co Inc	5181	D	661 833-3783	13457
Emser Tile LLC	5211	E	661 837-4400	13574
Lowes Home Centers LLC	5211	C	661 889-9000	13626
Haberfelde Ford (PA)	5511	C	661 328-3600	13776
Motor City Sales & Service (PA)	5511	C	661 836-9000	13801
Three-Way Chevrolet Co (PA)	5511	C	661 847-6400	13836
Mexicali Inc	5812	C	661 327-3861	14026
Kern Federal Credit Union	6061	D	661 327-9461	14228
Golden Empire Mortgage Inc (PA)	6162	D	661 328-1600	14320
Golden Empire Mortgage Inc (PA)	6162	D	661 328-1600	14321
Health Net LLC	6324	C	661 321-3904	14468
State Compensation Insur Fund	6331	D	661 664-4000	14528
Olympus Property	6519	B	661 393-1700	14739
Bakersfield Westwind Corp	6531	C	661 327-2121	14748
Stantec Holdings Del III Inc	6719	B	661 396-3770	14947
Msr Hotels & Resorts Inc	6799	C	661 325-9700	15039
Bakersfield Hospitality LLC	7011	D	661 393-1277	15084
Cni Thl Propco Fe LLC	7011	D	661 325-9700	15120
Golden West Partners Inc	7011	C	661 324-6936	15157
Newport Hospitality Group Inc	7011	D	661 323-1900	15260

GEOGRAPHIC

	SIC	EMP	PHONE	ENTRY#
Tiburon Hospitality LLC	7011	C	661 322-1012	15390
Banks Pest Control	7342	B	661 323-7858	15682
Western Energy Services Corp	7353	C	403 984-5916	15767
Western Oilfields Supply Co (PA)	7359	C	661 399-9124	15806
Century Hlth Staffing Svcs Inc	7361	C	661 322-0606	15832
Esparza Enterprises Inc	7361	A	661 631-0347	15845
Maxim Healthcare Services Inc	7363	D	661 322-3039	15928
Work Force Services Inc	7363	C	661 327-5019	15949
Lightspeed Software Inc	7372	E	661 716-7600	16294
M & S Security Services Inc	7381	D	661 397-9616	16658
Trans-West Services Inc	7381	B	661 381-2900	16696
Sangera Buick Inc	7538	D	661 833-5200	17038
Car Wash Partners Inc	7542	C	661 377-1020	17046
Willis Electric Inc	7629	E	661 324-2781	17076
Bakersfield Elc Mtr Repr Inc	7694	E	661 327-3583	17101
Electric Motor Works Inc	7694	E	661 327-4271	17104
SA Camp Pump Company	7699	D	661 399-2976	17150
Seven Oaks Country Club	7997	E	661 664-6404	17522
Stockdale Country Club	7997	D	661 832-0310	17527
Bakersfield Family Medical Group Inc (PA)	8011	D	661 327-4411	17597
Central Cardiology Med Clinic	8011	C	661 395-0000	17614
Clinica Sierra Vista (PA)	8011	D	661 635-3050	17625
Cns Inc	8011	D	661 872-3408	17626
Kaiser Foundation Hospitals	8011	C	661 398-5011	17697
Kaiser Foundation Hospitals	8011	D	661 334-2020	17698
Kern Health Systems Inc	8011	C	661 664-5000	17701
Mohawk Medical Group Inc	8011	C	661 324-4747	17715
Omni Family Health (PA)	8011	D	661 459-1900	17730
Ravi Patel MD Inc	8011	C	661 862-7113	17749
Southern Cal Prmnnte Med Group	8011	C	661 398-5085	17778
Southern Cal Prmnnte Med Group	8011	D	661 334-2020	17779
Truxtun Radiology Med Group LP	8011	C	661 325-6200	17809
Truxtun Radiology Med Group LP	8011	C	661 616-1201	17810
Truxtun Radiology Med Group LP	8011	C	661 205-6567	17811
Bakersfeld Hlthcare Wllness CN	8051	D	661 872-2121	17886
Bakersfieldidence Opco LLC	8051	C	661 399-2472	17887
Evergreen At Lakeport LLC	8051	C	661 871-3133	17950
Parkview Jlian Cnvlescent Hosp	8051	C	661 831-9150	18026
Parkview Julian LLC	8051	C	661 831-9150	18027
Kern Valleyidence Opco LLC	8052	C	661 323-2894	18087
Crestwood Behavioral Hlth Inc	8059	C	661 363-8127	18120
Humangood Norcal	8059	C	661 834-0620	18133
Adventist Hlth Systm/West Corp	8062	B	661 316-6000	18164
Bakersfield Memorial Hospital	8062	A	661 327-1792	18189
County of Kern	8062	A	661 326-2054	18230
Dignity Health	8062	B	661 663-6000	18242
Good Smrtan Hosp A Cal Ltd Prt	8062	B	661 903-9555	18271
Kaiser Foundation Hospitals	8062	C	661 412-6777	18301
Kern County Hospital Authority (PA)	8062	B	661 326-2102	18315
San Joaquin Community Hospital (PA)	8062	A	661 395-3000	18417
Bakersfeld Bhvral Hlthcare Hos	8063	C	661 398-1800	18505
Centre For Neuro Skills (PA)	8093	C	661 872-3408	18677
Kern County Hospital Authority	8093	A	661 843-7980	18700
First Assmbly of God Bkrsfield	8211	C	661 327-2227	18966
City of Bakersfield	8322	E	661 852-7300	19045
Dean L Davis MD	8322	E	661 632-5000	19070
Bakersfeld Assn For Rtrded Ctz	8331	D	661 834-2272	19176
Alliance Childrens Services	8361	C	661 863-0350	19236
Community Action Partnr Kern	8399	D	661 835-5405	19320
Kern Regional Center (PA)	8399	C	661 327-8531	19331
New Advnces For Pple With Dsbl	8399	C	661 322-9735	19336
Wonderful Citrus Cooperative	8611	C	661 720-2400	19387
Boys Girls Clubs of Kern Cnty	8641	B	661 325-3730	19427
St Jhns Lthran Ch Bakersfield	8661	C	661 665-7815	19508
Diversified Prj Svcs Intl Inc (PA)	8711	D	661 371-2800	19574
Innovative Engrg Systems Inc (PA)	8711	B	661 381-7800	19614
Processes Unlimited International Inc	8711	B	661 396-3770	19672
UCI Construction Inc	8711	C	661 587-0192	19711
W M Lyles Co	8711	C	661 387-1600	19717
Analytical Pace Services LLC	8734	C	800 878-4911	19958
Healthcare Finance Direct LLC	8742	D	661 616-4400	20180
Sun Pacific Marketing Coop Inc	8742	B	213 612-9957	20251
County of Kern	9441	C	661 336-6871	20416

BALDWIN PARK, CA - Los Angeles County

	SIC	EMP	PHONE	ENTRY#
Tanimura Antle Fresh Foods Inc	0723	C	831 424-6100	115
Crosstown Elec & Data Inc	1731	D	626 813-6693	887
Distinct Indulgence Inc	2051	E	818 546-1700	1462
Sanders Candy Factory Inc	2064	E	626 814-2038	1548
Pepsico Inc	2086	E	626 338-5531	1719
Survey Stake and Marker Inc	2499	E	626 960-4802	2763
Pacon Inc	2621	C	626 814-4654	3059
Checkworks Inc	2782	D	626 333-1444	3835

	SIC	EMP	PHONE	ENTRY#
Mission Kleensweep Prod Inc	2841	D	323 223-1405	4339
Hemosure Inc	2899	E	888 436-6787	4608
Anura Plastic Engineerign	3089	E	626 814-9684	4942
Hillcor Distribution Inc	3089	F	626.960-8789	5049
Reny & Co Inc	3089	F	626 962-3078	5180
Standard Concrete Products Inc (HQ)	3273	E	310 829-4537	5504
Kal-Cameron Manufacturing Corp (HQ)	3423	D	626 338-7308	5883
Universal Steel Services Inc	3441	D	626 960-1455	6087
Lawrence Roll Up Doors Inc (PA)	3442	E	626 962-4163	6111
Fabtronics Inc	3444	E	626 962-3293	6239
Oreco Duct Systems Inc	3444	C	626 337-8832	6278
Pacific Award Metals Inc (HQ)	3444	D	626 814-4410	6283
Rigos Equipment Mfg LLC	3444	E	626 813-6621	6305
Upm Inc	3544	B	626 962-4001	7103
G & I Islas Industries Inc (PA)	3556	E	626 960-5020	7199
Meritek Electronics Corp (PA)	3559	D	626 373-1728	7249
Global Silicon Electronics Inc	3572	E	626 336-1888	7470
George Fischer Inc (HQ)	3599	C	626 571-2770	7847
Superior Grounding Systems Inc	3643	E	626 814-1981	8277
Touchdown Technologies Inc	3674	E	626 472-6732	8910
Tektest Inc	3678	E	626 446-6175	8984
S & C Precision Inc	3679	E	626 338-7149	9112
Front Edge Technology Inc	3691	E	626 856-8979	9149
Cera Inc	3821	E	626 814-2688	10089
Ametek Ameron LLC (HQ)	3823	D	626 856-0101	10116
Georg Fischer Signet LLC	3823	D	626 571-2770	10135
Freudenberg Medical LLC	3841	C	626 814-9684	10511
Denovo Dental Inc	3843	E	626 480-0182	10738
Condor Outdoor Products Inc (PA)	3949	C	626 358-3270	10984
United Parcel Service Inc	4215	B	626 814-6216	11542
Cedarwood-Young Company (PA)	4953	C	626 962-4047	12165
Waste MGT Collectn Recycl Inc	4953	C	626 960-7551	12202
Nichols Lumber & Hardware Co	5031	D	626 960-4802	12337
Tecan Sp Inc	5049	D	626 962-0010	12533
Lighting Technologies Intl LLC	5063	C	626 480-0755	12601
American Kal Enterprises Inc (PA)	5072	D	626 338-7308	12713
Cedarwood-Young Company	5093	C	626 962-4047	12952
Normans Nursery Inc	5193	C	626 285-9795	13517
Home Depot USA Inc	5211	C	626 813-7131	13609
Treasure Garden Inc (PA)	5261	E	626 814-0168	13680
SCE Federal Credit Union (PA)	6061	D	626 960-6888	14237
Kaiser Foundation Hospitals	6324	A	626 851-1011	14474
Baldwin Hospitality LLC	7011	D	626 446-2988	15085
Ols Hotels & Resorts LLC	7011	A	626 962-6000	15274
Haynes Building Service LLC	7349	C	626 359-6100	15712
Source One Staffing LLC	7361	A	626 337-0560	15895
Alphatech General Inc	7699	D	626 337-4640	17114
Golden State Habilitation Conv (PA)	8051	E	626 962-3274	17965
Trinity Health Systems (PA)	8051	D	626 960-1971	18063
Vista Spclty Hosp Sthern Cal L	8062	D	626 388-2700	18500
Good Health Inc	8099	E	714 961-7930	18765
Eben-Ezer Chld Day Care Ctr	8351	D	626 960-7100	19209
American Mzhou Dngpo Group Inc	8741	D	626 820-9239	19997
Telesector Resources Group Inc	8742	B	626 813-4538	20258

BANNING, CA - Riverside County

	SIC	EMP	PHONE	ENTRY#
Zenner Usa Inc	3824	E	951 849-8822	10179
DT Mattson Enterprises Inc	3944	E	951 849-9781	10950
Strech Plastics Incorporated	5088	E	951 922-2224	12917
Green Thumb Produce Inc	5148	C	951 849-4711	13328
Professional Cmnty MGT Cal Inc	6531	B	951 845-2191	14847
San Gorgonio Memorial Hospital	8062	A	951 845-1121	18415
San Grgnio Mem Hosp Foundation (PA)	8062	C	951 845-1121	18416
Riverside-San Bernardino	8093	C	951 849-4761	18714

BARSTOW, CA - San Bernardino County

	SIC	EMP	PHONE	ENTRY#
Kar Ice Service Inc (PA)	2097	F	760 256-2648	1837
Five Star Food Containers Inc	3086	D	626 437-6219	4881
Mv Transportation Inc	4111	C	760 255-3330	11346
Life Care Centers America Inc	8051	C	760 252-2515	17986
Hospital of Barstow Inc (DH)	8062	D	760 256-1761	18288

BEAUMONT, CA - Riverside County

	SIC	EMP	PHONE	ENTRY#
Beaumont Juice Inc	2033	D	951 769-7171	1336
Priority Pallet Inc	2448	F	951 769-9399	2722
Dpp 2020 Inc (DH)	3089	E	951 845-3161	5017
Anderson Chrnesky Strl Stl Inc	3441	D	951 769-5700	5992
Risco Inc	3452	E	951 769-2899	6453
Precision Stampings Inc (PA)	3643	E	951 845-1174	8274
CJ Foods Mfg Beaumont Corp	3999	E	951 916-9300	11208
David-Kleis II LLC	8099	E	951 845-3125	18757
Beaumont Unfied Schl Dst Pub F	8211	B	951 845-6580	18963
Childhelp Inc	8361	C	951 845-6737	19248

Mergent email: customerrelations@mergent.com
1342

2024 Southern California
Business Directory and Buyers Guide

(P-0000) Products & Services Section entry number
(PA)=Parent Co (HQ)=Headquarters (DH)=Div Headquarters

	SIC	EMP	PHONE	ENTRY#

BELL, CA - Los Angeles County

Company	SIC	EMP	PHONE	ENTRY#
Penguin Natural Foods Inc	2099	E	323 488-6000	1969
Fam LLC **(PA)**	2231	D	323 888-7755	2049
Carol Wior Inc	2339	D	562 927-0052	2312
Marika LLC	2339	D	323 888-7755	2350
Hain Celestial Group Inc	2844	C	323 859-0553	4418
Custom Building Products LLC	2891	C	323 582-0846	4562
West Coast-Accudyne Inc	3542	E	562 927-2546	7042
Pacesetter Inc	3845	B	323 773-0591	10821
De Well Container Shipping Inc	4731	D	310 735-8600	11750
Omega Moulding West LLC	5023	C	323 261-3510	12312
Fam Ppe LLC	5099	C	323 888-7755	12974
Perrin Bernard Supowitz LLC **(HQ)**	5113	A	323 981-2800	13022
Lovin Enterprises Inc	5137	D	323 268-0220	13132
H & T Seafood Inc	5146	E	323 526-0888	13281
El Aviso Magazine	5192	D	323 586-9199	13494
Fedex Services	7389	D	323 881-3400	16824
Leonid M Glsman DDS A Dntl Cor	8021	C	323 560-4514	17839
Jwch Institute Inc	8733	C	323 562-5813	19931

BELL GARDENS, CA - Los Angeles County

Company	SIC	EMP	PHONE	ENTRY#
C T and F Inc	1731	D	562 927-2339	876
Rob Inc	2325	D	562 806-5589	2171
Carnevale & Lohr Inc	3281	E	562 927-8311	5526
Eurocraft Archtectural Met Inc	3446	E	323 771-1323	6357
Metal Surfaces Intl LLC	3471	E	562 927-1331	6639
McLane Manufacturing Inc	3524	D	562 633-8158	6919
Barber Welding and Mfg Co	3599	E	562 928-2570	7775
Wilcox Machine Co	3599	D	562 927-5353	8078
Cal Southern Braiding Inc	3679	D	562 927-5531	9011
Flexco Inc	3728	E	562 927-2525	9689
Orbit Industries Inc	5063	D	213 745-8884	12611
US Foods Inc	5149	C	562 806-2445	13403
Parkhouse Tire Service Inc **(PA)**	5531	D	562 928-0421	13868
Anitsa Inc	7211	C	213 237-0533	15444
Bell Gardens Bicycle Club Inc	7999	A	562 806-4646	17541
Del Rio Sanitarium Inc	8051	D	562 927-6586	17924

BELLFLOWER, CA - Los Angeles County

Company	SIC	EMP	PHONE	ENTRY#
KI Decorator Sales	2431	E	562 920-0268	2610
Cutting Edge Creative LLC	2542	D	562 907-7007	2978
Bryant Rubber Corp	3053	C	310 530-2530	4720
Danco Valve Company	3491	E	562 925-2588	6763
Empire Transportation Inc	4141	B	562 529-2676	11415
George Chevrolet	5511	C	562 925-2500	13772
Hollywood Sports Park LLC	7389	D	562 867-9600	16841
S J S Enterprise Inc	7999	C	949 489-9000	17564
Peter Wylan DDS	8021	C	562 925-3765	17845
Bell Villa Care Associates LLC	8051	C	562 925-4252	17891
Life Care Centers America Inc	8051	C	562 867-1761	17991
Jwch Institute Inc	8099	C	562 867-7999	18772
Harbor Health Care Inc	8361	C	562 866-7054	19266

BERMUDA DUNES, CA - Riverside County

Company	SIC	EMP	PHONE	ENTRY#
Vintage Associates Inc	0782	C	760 772-3673	220

BEVERLY HILLS, CA - Los Angeles County

Company	SIC	EMP	PHONE	ENTRY#
Atlas Lithium Corporation	1499	E	213 590-2500	415
D&A Endeavors Inc	1799	D	310 390-7540	1151
Jeffries Global Inc	1799	D	888 255-3488	1164
Organic Gemini LLC	2041	E	347 662-2900	1414
Sugarfina Inc	2064	E	855 784-2734	1553
Pepsico Inc	2086	F	323 785-2820	1718
Lorber Industries California	2261	F	310 275-1568	2090
Alanic International Corp	2299	E	855 525-2642	2133
Lisa Factory Inc	2321	D	213 536-5326	2161
Etro USA Incorporated	2331	F	310 248-2855	2238
Instant Tuck Inc	2392	D	310 955-8824	2472
Royal Blue Inc	2392	E	310 888-0156	2487
Hollywood Reporter	2711	E	323 525-2150	3286
Hollywood Reporter LLC	2711	E	323 525-2000	3287
L F P Inc **(PA)**	2721	D	323 651-3525	3364
Playboy Japan Inc	2721	D	310 424-1800	3381
West World Productions Inc	2721	E	310 276-9500	3394
Activision	2741	E	424 320-9000	3423
MRC Media LLC **(PA)**	2741	F	212 493-4100	3466
Kate Somerville Skincare LLC **(HQ)**	2834	D	323 655-7546	4150
Olympus Water Holdings IV LP	2842	A	310 739-6325	4366
Summer Fridays LLC	2844	D	612 804-0868	4459
Stratos Renewables Corporation	2869	E	310 402-5901	4531
Zeons Inc	3229	B	323 302-8299	5332
Altmans Products LLC	3431	E	310 274-5896	5957
American Solar LLC	3433	E	323 250-1307	5977

Company	SIC	EMP	PHONE	ENTRY#
King Holding Corporation	3452	A	586 254-3900	6448
B-Reel Films Inc	3571	E	917 388-3836	7419
Ownzones Media Network Inc	3577	E	855 466-9696	7561
Dasol Inc	3641	C	310 327-6700	8245
Lorser Industries Inc	3672	E	619 917-4298	8699
Protravel International LLC	4724	D	310 271-9566	11725
Seaworld Global Logistics	4731	B	310 579-9164	11801
Nextpoint Inc **(PA)**	4813	D	310 360-5904	11895
Maurice Kraiem & Company	5094	E	213 629-0038	12964
SOS Beauty LLC	5122	E	424 285-1405	13069
Fashion World Incorporated	5136	C	310 273-6544	13102
Royal-Pedic Mattress Mfg LLC **(PA)**	5712	C	310 278-9594	13947
BW Hotel LLC	5812	A	310 275-5200	13987
Fat Brands Inc **(PA)**	5812	B	310 319-1850	14006
City National Securities Inc	6021	C	310 888-6393	14165
Pacwest Bancorp **(PA)**	6021	C	310 887-8500	14174
Gores Group LLC **(PA)**	6211	D	310 209-3010	14380
M L Stern & Co LLC **(DH)**	6211	C	323 658-4400	14387
Muriel Siebert & Co Inc	6211	D	800 993-2015	14399
Charles & Cynthia Eberly Inc	6513	C	323 937-6468	14705
Keller Wllams Rlty Bvrly Hills	6531	D	310 432-6400	14819
Kennedy-Wilson Inc **(PA)**	6531	D	310 887-6400	14820
Row Management Ltd Inc	6531	B	310 887-3671	14863
Starpint 1031 Property MGT LLC	6531	C	310 247-0550	14869
Century Pacific Realty Corp	6552	C	310 729-9922	14898
Shapell Industries LLC **(HQ)**	6552	D	323 655-7330	14910
Project Skyline Intermediate H	6719	A	310 712-1850	14939
Regent LP **(PA)**	6799	D	310 299-4100	15048
USA Enterprise Inc	6799	B	310 750-4246	15058
Belvedere Hotel Partnership	7011	C	310 551-2888	15090
Belvedere Partnership	7011	B	310 551-2888	15091
Honeymoon Real Estate LP	7011	D	310 277-5221	15184
Oasis West Realty LLC	7011	C	310 860-6666	15267
Park Hotels & Resorts Inc	7011	D	310 415-3340	15297
Raffles Lrmitage Beverly Hills	7011	C	310 278-3344	15316
Sajahtera Inc	7011	A	310 276-2251	15340
Mob Scene LLC **(PA)**	7311	C	323 648-7200	15560
Studio 71 LP	7313	C	323 370-1500	15598
William Mrris Endvor Entrmt LL **(DH)**	7361	C	212 586-5100	15903
Anderson Assoc Staffing Corp **(PA)**	7363	C	323 930-3170	15913
Nga 911 LLC	7371	C	877 899-8337	16085
Rootstrap Inc	7371	C	310 907-9210	16105
1on1 LLC	7371	E	310 998-7473	16154
Ateliere Creative Tech Inc	7372	E	800 921-4252	16179
Klooma Holdings Inc	7372	E	305 747-3315	16286
Subject Technologies Inc	7372	E	310 243-6484	16393
Mission Cloud Services Inc **(PA)**	7379	C	855 647-7466	16580
American Health Connection	7389	A	424 226-0420	16776
Heritage Auctions Inc	7389	D	310 300-8390	16839
Live Nation Entertainment Inc **(PA)**	7389	C	310 867-7000	16863
United Talent Agency LLC	7389	C	310 776-8160	16948
Modern Parking Inc	7521	C	310 271-1125	16993
Brillstein Entrmt Partners LLC **(HQ)**	7812	D	310 205-5100	17172
Metro-Goldwyn-Mayer Inc **(DH)**	7812	B	310 449-3000	17201
Orion Pictures Corporation	7812	A	310 449-3000	17204
Condor Productions LLC	7819	C	310 449-3000	17246
United Artists Films Company **(DH)**	7822	C	310 449-3000	17282
Agency For Performing Arts Inc **(PA)**	7922	D	310 557-9049	17311
Management 360	7922	D	310 272-7000	17320
The Gersh Agency LLC **(PA)**	7922	D	310 274-6611	17330
William Mrris Endvor Entrmt FN **(DH)**	7922	C	310 285-9000	17333
William Mrris Endvor Entrmt LL	7922	B	310 285-9000	17334
Live Nation Worldwide Inc **(HQ)**	7929	A	310 867-7000	17343
Endeavor Group Holdings Inc **(PA)**	7941	C	310 285-9000	17368
Gemini Basketball LLC	7941	D	213 929-1300	17371
Live Nation Worldwide Inc	7941	C	310 867-7000	17376
Pse Holding LLC **(DH)**	7941	B	248 377-0165	17381
Ultimate Fghting Prdctons Intl	7941	C	310 285-9000	17383
Wme Img LLC **(DH)**	7941	C	212 586-5100	17384
Ba Sports Nutrition LLC	7991	D	718 357-7402	17392
Ticketmster New Vntres Hldngs **(HQ)**	7999	C	800 653-8000	17572
Zuffa Mexico LLC	7999	C	310 285-9000	17581
Tower Hmtlogy Onclogy Med Grou	8011	D	310 888-8680	17805
Westside Crdvsclar Med Group I	8011	C	310 289-9955	17833
GPh Medical & Legal Services **(PA)**	8051	C	213 207-2700	17966
Cedars-Sinai Medical Center	8062	C	310 967-1884	18206
Cedars-Sinai Medical Center	8062	A	310 385-3400	18210
Universal Home Care Inc	8082	C	323 653-9222	18649
BD&j PC	8111	D	855 906-3699	18828
Page Private School	8211	D	323 272-3429	18978
Academy Mpic Arts & Sciences **(PA)**	8621	C	310 247-3000	19388
World Mvie Awrds Orgnztion Wma	8641	D	833 375-5857	19473
Collective MGT Group LLC	8741	C	323 655-8585	20015

Employee Codes: A=Over 500 employees, B=251-500
C=101-250, D=51-100, E=20-50, F=10-19, G=1-9

2024 Southern California
Business Directory and Buyers Guide

© Mergent Inc. 1-800-342-5647

1343

GEOGRAPHIC

	SIC	EMP	PHONE	ENTRY#
Ghp Management Corporation	8741	C	310 432-1441	20034
Za Management	8741	D	310 271-2200	20121
Magic Workforce Solutions LLC	8743	A	310 246-6153	20285
MGM and Ua Services Company	8999	A	310 449-3000	20397

BIG BEAR LAKE, CA - San Bernardino County

	SIC	EMP	PHONE	ENTRY#
Big Bear Bowling Barn Inc	1799	E	909 878-2695	1144
Hi-Desert Publishing Company	5994	E	909 866-3456	14117
Snow Summit Ski Corporation (PA)	7011	C	909 866-5766	15362
Bear Vly Cmnty Healthcare Dst (PA)	8062	C	909 866-6501	18190

BLOOMINGTON, CA - San Bernardino County

	SIC	EMP	PHONE	ENTRY#
Team West Contracting Corp	1799	D	951 340-3426	1178
Aspire Bakeries LLC	2052	E	714 478-4656	1507
Frito-Lay North America Inc	2096	E	909 877-0902	1825
Dura Technologies Inc	2851	C	909 877-8477	4486
Hogan Co Inc	3315	E	909 421-0245	5617
Wadco Industries Inc	3441	E	909 874-7800	6091
Westco Industries Inc	3441	E	909 874-8700	6093
Hydraulic Shop Inc	3537	E	909 875-9336	6992
Heater Designs Inc	3567	E	909 421-0971	7367
Mitco Industries Inc (PA)	3599	E	909 877-0800	7941
Remco Mch & Fabrication Inc	3599	F	909 877-3530	7997
Signify North America Corp	3646	C	732 563-3000	8331
Cooper Lighting LLC	3648	A	909 605-6615	8359
Cooper Crouse-Hinds LLC	3699	E	951 241-8766	9201
Quality Tech Mfg Inc	3721	E	909 465-9565	9550
Ftdi West Inc	4225	D	909 473-1111	11580
Gxo Logistics Supply Chain Inc	4225	A	336 309-6201	11583
Roberts Lumber Sales Inc	5031	D	909 350-9164	12342
Pacific Steel Group	5051	B	858 449-7219	12564
Chiro Inc (PA)	5087	C	909 879-1160	12889
Atlas Pacific Corporation (PA)	5093	E	909 421-1200	12950
Empire Oil Co	5172	C	909 877-0226	13451
Poma Holding Company Inc	5172	C	909 877-2441	13453
Social Science Service Center	8069	D	909 421-7120	18536

BLUE JAY, CA - San Bernardino County

	SIC	EMP	PHONE	ENTRY#
Travis Snyder	3531	E	909 338-6302	6944

BLYTHE, CA - Riverside County

	SIC	EMP	PHONE	ENTRY#
Fisher Ranch LLC	0723	D	760 922-4151	102
Crawford Associates	1771	E	760 922-6804	1068
Palo Verde Irrigation District	4971	D	760 922-3144	12215
Palo Verde Health Care Dst	8062	C	760 922-4115	18360
Palo Verde Hospital Assn	8062	C	760 922-4115	18361

BONITA, CA - San Diego County

	SIC	EMP	PHONE	ENTRY#
International Plating Svc LLC (PA)	3471	E	619 454-2135	6629
Right Hand Manufacturing Inc	3625	E	619 819-5056	8188
Pacific Integrated Mfg Inc	3841	E	619 921-3464	10586
John Collins Co Inc	6513	D	818 227-2190	14724
Crockett & Coinc (PA)	7992	E	619 267-6410	17423
Crockett & Coinc	7992	E	619 267-1103	17424
Paradise Valley Hospital	8062	C	619 472-7474	18371

BONSALL, CA - San Diego County

	SIC	EMP	PHONE	ENTRY#
Euroamerican Propagators LLC	0181	B	760 731-6029	53

BORON, CA - Kern County

	SIC	EMP	PHONE	ENTRY#
Rio Tinto Minerals Inc	1241	C	760 762-7121	242
US Borax Inc	2819	A	760 762-7000	3917

BORREGO SPRINGS, CA - San Diego County

	SIC	EMP	PHONE	ENTRY#
Borrego Cmnty Hlth Foundation (PA)	8011	C	855 436-1234	17605

BRAWLEY, CA - Imperial County

	SIC	EMP	PHONE	ENTRY#
Esparza Enterprises Inc	0762	A	760 344-2031	135
Owb Packers LLC	2011	E	760 351-2700	1202
Salico Farms Inc	2032	C	760 344-5375	1330
Crown Citrus Company Inc	2037	E	760 344-1930	1368
Fiesta Mexican Foods Inc	2051	E	760 344-3580	1466
Spreckels Sugar Company Inc	2063	B	760 344-3110	1531
Spreadco Inc	2262	E	760 351-0747	2098
Western Mesquite Mines Inc	3339	E	928 341-4653	5677
Broma Applicators LLC	5191	E	760 351-0101	13487
Vons Companies Inc	5411	C	760 351-3002	13712
Pioneers Mem Healthcare Dst (PA)	8062	A	760 351-3333	18381
Brawley Union High School Dist (PA)	8211	D	760 312-6068	18964

BREA, CA - Orange County

	SIC	EMP	PHONE	ENTRY#
Linn Energy LLC	1382	E	714 257-1600	309
Beazer Mortgage Corporation	1531	D	714 480-1635	482

	SIC	EMP	PHONE	ENTRY#
Bergman Kprs LLC (PA)	1542	C	714 924-7000	535
Kprs Construction Services Inc (PA)	1542	D	714 672-0800	564
Nevell Group Inc (PA)	1542	C	714 579-7501	569
Griffith Company (PA)	1611	C	714 984-5500	622
Sully-Miller Holding Corp	1611	C	714 578-9600	648
United Rock Products Corp	1611	C	714 578-9600	651
Coolsys Coml Indus Sltions Inc (DH)	1711	C	714 510-9609	756
Norcal Inc	1751	C	714 224-3949	1020
Win-Dor Inc (PA)	1751	C	714 576-2030	1029
Team Finish Inc	1771	D	714 671-9190	1090
Northstar Dem & Remediation LP (DH)	1795	C	714 672-3500	1136
Fresh Start Bakeries Inc	2051	A	714 256-8900	1470
Ventura Foods LLC (PA)	2079	C	714 257-3700	1574
Wilsey Foods Inc	2079	A	714 257-3700	1575
La Paz Products Inc	2087	F	714 990-0982	1780
Scisorek & Son Flavors Inc	2087	E	714 524-0550	1782
Benevolence Food Products LLC	2099	E	888 832-3738	1856
Shore Front LLC	2099	E	714 612-3751	1984
BOa Inc	2329	E	714 256-8960	2197
AST Sportswear Inc (PA)	2361	D	714 223-2030	2405
Absolute Screenprint Inc	2396	C	714 529-2120	2525
Pacific Archtectural Mllwk Inc	2431	E	562 905-9282	2627
Parkinson Enterprises Inc	2521	D	714 626-0275	2895
Stolo Cabinets Inc (PA)	2521	E	714 529-7303	2900
Waterbox LLC	2631	E	323 743-8070	3074
Pacific Quality Packaging Corp	2653	D	714 257-1234	3120
Avery Dennison Corporation	2672	B	714 674-8500	3164
SC Liquidation Company LLC	2672	C	714 482-1006	3174
Avery Dennison Office Products Co Inc	2678	A		3216
Avery Products Corporation (DH)	2678	C	714 674-8500	3218
Educational Ideas Incorporated	2741	E	714 990-4332	3443
Pennysaver USA Publishing LLC	2741	A	866 640-3900	3473
Coyle Reproductions Inc (PA)	2752	C	866 269-5373	3548
Nowdocs International Inc	2759	E	714 986-1559	3790
President Enterprise LLC	2759	E	714 671-9577	3797
Taylor Technology Services Inc	2759	D	714 986-1559	3818
Moravek Biochemicals Inc (PA)	2819	E	714 990-2018	3900
Beacon Manufacturing Inc	2833	E	714 529-0980	3992
North West Pharmanaturals Inc	2833	E	714 529-0980	4006
UNI-Caps LLC	2833	E	714 529-8400	4021
Lifebloom Corporation	2834	E	562 944-6800	4159
Suheung-America Corporation	2834	E	714 671-9095	4243
Kirkhill Inc	3053	A	714 529-4901	4737
West Coast Gasket Co	3053	D	714 869-0123	4748
Pacific Plastics Inc	3084	D	714 990-9050	4852
Plainfield Molding Inc	3089	D	815 436-7806	5138
Plainfield Tool and Engineering Inc	3089	B	815 436-5671	5139
Ramtec Associates Inc	3089	E	714 996-7477	5173
S&B Industry Inc	3089	E	909 569-4155	5194
Metals USA Building Pdts LP (DH)	3355	A	713 946-9000	5720
Consolidated Aerospace Mfg LLC	3429	D	714 989-2802	5912
Moeller Mfg & Sup LLC	3429	E	714 999-5551	5933
SPX Cooling Tech LLC	3443	F	714 529-6080	6158
Precise Industries Inc	3444	C	714 482-2333	6296
Span-O-Matic Inc	3444	E	714 256-4700	6319
3-V Fastener Co Inc	3452	D	949 888-7700	6429
Bristol Industries LLC	3452	C	714 990-4121	6434
Caran Precision Engineering & Manuf (PA)	3469	D	714 447-5400	6506
Imperial Cal Products Inc	3469	E	714 990-9100	6523
Electronic Precision Spc Inc	3471	E	714 256-8950	6619
Amada America Inc	3479	D	714 739-2111	6688
Curtiss-Wright Flow Ctrl Corp	3491	E	949 271-7500	6761
Curtiss-Wright Flow Ctrl Corp	3491	D	714 528-2301	6762
Curtiss-Wright Flow Ctrl Corp (DH)	3494	D	714 528-1365	6789
Patterns Behavioral Services I	3543	F	657 444-9002	7044
Kingson Mold & Machine Inc	3544	E	714 871-0221	7078
MR Mold & Engineering Corp	3544	E	714 996-5511	7083
Sunon Inc (PA)	3564	E	714 255-0208	7333
Baker Furnace Inc	3567	F	714 223-7262	7361
Moxa Americas Inc	3577	E	714 528-6777	7554
Viewsonic Corporation (PA)	3577	C	909 444-8888	7578
Trane US Inc	3585	D	626 913-7123	7628
Media Blast & Abrasive Inc	3589	F	714 257-0484	7673
Whittier Filtration Inc (DH)	3589	E	714 986-5300	7693
Superior Machining Mfg Co Inc	3599	E	714 529-6000	8038
Energy Cnvrsion Applctions Inc	3612	F	714 256-2166	8095
Q C M Inc	3629	E	714 414-1173	8211
Jade Range LLC	3631	C	714 961-2400	8218
Foxlink International Inc (HQ)	3643	E	714 256-1777	8265
Ledconn Corp	3648	E	714 256-2111	8371
Kworld (usa) Computer Inc	3663	E	626 581-0867	8528
Fine Line Circuits & Tech Inc	3672	E	714 529-2942	8677
Aeroflite Enterprises Inc	3678	D	714 773-4251	8959

Mergent email: customerrelations@mergent.com
1344

2024 Southern California
Business Directory and Buyers Guide

(P-0000) Products & Services Section entry number
(PA)=Parent Co (HQ)=Headquarters (DH)=Div Headquarters

	SIC	EMP	PHONE	ENTRY#
Bi Technologies Corporation **(HQ)**	3679	B	714 447-2300	9005
Cks Solution Incorporated	3679	E	714 292-6307	9018
Instrment Dsign Engrg Assoc In	3679	E	714 525-3302	9060
Transico Inc	3679	E	714 835-6000	9131
Uriman Inc	3694	F	714 257-2080	9176
Mullen Technologies Inc **(PA)**	3711	C	714 613-1900	9301
Harbor Truck Bodies Inc	3713	D	714 996-0411	9327
Lund Motion Products Inc	3714	E	888 983-2204	9417
Aerospace Engineering LLC **(PA)**	3728	D	714 996-8178	9604
Applied Cmpsite Structures Inc **(HQ)**	3728	E	714 990-6300	9627
Dynamic Fabrication Inc	3728	E	714 662-2440	9681
Kirkhill Inc **(HQ)**	3728	C	714 529-4901	9731
Rogers Holding Company Inc	3728	E	714 257-4850	9778
Belt Drives Ltd	3751	E	714 693-1313	9874
Garmin International Inc	3812	B	909 444-5000	9977
Technovative Applications	3812	E	714 996-0104	10074
Worldwide Envmtl Pdts Inc **(PA)**	3823	E	714 990-2700	10170
Beckman Coulter Inc **(HQ)**	3826	A	714 993-5321	10238
Beckman Coulter Inc	3841	C	818 970-2161	10451
Carolina Lquid Chmistries Corp	3841	E	336 722-8910	10477
Life Science Outsourcing Inc	3841	E	714 672-1090	10546
MPS Medical Inc	3841	E	714 672-1090	10571
Curtiss-Wrght Cntrls Intgrted	3842	E	714 982-1860	10642
Dcii North America LLC **(PA)**	3843	E	714 817-7000	10737
DH Dental Business Svcs LLC **(HQ)**	3843	E	714 817-7000	10740
Envista Holdings Corporation **(PA)**	3843	E	714 817-7000	10743
Ormco Corporation	3843	E	909 962-5705	10755
Pac-Dent Inc	3843	E	909 839-0888	10759
Val USA Manufacturer Inc	3999	E	626 839-8069	11302
Emergency Ambulance Svc Inc	4119	D	714 990-1331	11382
Premier Medical Transport Inc	4119	C	805 340-5191	11400
Hot Dogger Tours Inc	4142	C	714 988-4088	11417
Kelly-Wright Hardwoods Inc	5031	F	714 632-9930	12336
Wurth Louis and Company **(DH)**	5072	D	714 529-1771	12736
Southern Cal Hydrlic Engrg Cor	5084	E	714 257-4800	12822
Nelson Stud Welding Inc	5085	E	256 353-1931	12867
Nmc Group Inc	5085	E	714 223-3525	12868
TSC Auto ID Technology America **(HQ)**	5085	C	909 468-0100	12887
Proponent Inc **(PA)**	5088	C	714 223-5400	12914
Acosta Inc	5141	C	714 988-1500	13167
Natures Best	5149	B	714 255-4600	13383
Hill Brothers Chemical Company **(PA)**	5169	C	714 998-8800	13435
Jewelscent Inc	5199	D	800 550-1762	13542
American Suzuki Motor Corporation	5511	B	714 996-7040	13738
Suzuki Motor of America Inc **(HQ)**	5511	C	714 996-7040	13834
Levity of Brea LLC	5813	D	714 482-0700	14049
Beverages & More Inc	5921	C	714 990-2060	14059
Jewelers Touch	5944	E	714 579-1616	14076
Vesuki Inc	5947	F	562 245-4000	14088
Safeway Inc	5992	A	714 990-8357	14114
Capitalsource Bank	6022	C	714 989-4600	14184
American First Credit Union **(PA)**	6061	D	562 691-1112	14222
Adelfi Credit Union	6062	C	714 671-5700	14244
Amwest Funding Corp	6153	C	714 831-3333	14279
American Financial Network Inc **(PA)**	6162	C	714 831-4000	14294
Emet Lending Group Inc	6162	E	714 933-9800	14312
Morgan Stnley Smith Barney LLC	6211	C	714 674-4100	14397
Mercury Casualty Company **(HQ)**	6331	A	323 937-1060	14512
Mercury Insurance Company	6331	C	714 671-6700	14515
Mercury Insurance Company	6331	A	714 255-5000	14516
Veterinary Pet Insurance Services Inc	6411	B	714 989-0555	14640
Veterinary Pet Services Inc	6411	C	714 989-0555	14641
Otb Acquisition LLC	7011	C	520 458-0540	15281
Windsor Capital Group Inc	7011	C	714 990-6000	15422
Glen Ivy Hot Springs	7299	C	714 990-2090	15508
Cmre Financial Services Inc	7322	B	714 528-3200	15609
Contract Services Group Inc	7349	C	714 582-1800	15702
Crossroads Software Inc	7372	F	714 990-6433	16216
Maxxess Systems Inc **(PA)**	7372	F	714 772-1000	16301
Solugenix Corporation **(PA)**	7373	C	866 749-7658	16470
Pramira Inc	7379	C	800 678-1169	16590
Southwest Patrol Inc	7381	C	909 861-1884	16691
Aer Technologies Inc	7699	B	714 871-7357	17112
Burns & McDonnell Inc	8711	D	714 256-1595	19558
Lance Soll & Lunghard LLP	8721	C	714 672-0022	19787
American Regent Inc	8733	C	714 989-5058	19917
United Sttes Dept Enrgy Brkley	8733	C	510 486-7089	19950
Acepex Management Corporation	8744	C	909 625-6900	20286

BUELLTON, CA - Santa Barbara County

	SIC	EMP	PHONE	ENTRY#
Central Coast Agriculture Inc **(PA)**	0191	E	805 694-8594	78
Firestone Walker Inc	2082	D	805 254-4205	1590
Foley Fmly Wines Holdings Inc	2084	D	805 450-7225	1630

	SIC	EMP	PHONE	ENTRY#
Terravant Wine Company LLC	2084	D	805 686-9400	1663
Terravant Wine Company LLC **(PA)**	2084	D	805 688-4245	1664
Aero Industries LLC	3599	B	805 688-6734	7741
True Precision Machining Inc	3599	E	805 964-4545	8053
Infraredvision Technology Corp	3674	D	805 686-8848	8810
Materion Prcsion Optics Thin F	3674	D	805 688-4949	8835
Tilton Engineering Inc	3714	E	805 688-2353	9471
Platinum Performance Inc **(HQ)**	5122	E	800 553-2400	13062
Carpenters Southwest ADM Corp	5812	C	805 688-5581	13991
Kang Family Partners LLC	7011	C	805 688-1000	15206
Platinum Performance Inc	7532	D	800 553-2400	17014

BUENA PARK, CA - Orange County

	SIC	EMP	PHONE	ENTRY#
Tawa Supermarket Inc	1541	D	714 521-8899	524
ECB Corp **(PA)**	1711	D	714 385-8900	765
Sfadia Inc	1731	D	323 622-1930	934
Gresean Industries Inc	1751	E		1013
Wayne Perry Inc **(PA)**	1799	C	714 826-0352	1182
Mondelez Global LLC	2013	F	714 690-7428	1226
Cleughs Frozen Foods Inc	2037	E		1367
La Mexicana LLC	2038	E	323 277-3660	1393
Tawa Supermarket Inc **(PA)**	2038	E	714 521-8899	1404
Island Snacks Inc	2064	E	714 994-1228	1544
Ameripec Inc	2086	E	714 690-9191	1683
Pepsi-Cola Metro Btlg Co Inc	2086	C	714 522-9635	1716
Bridport-Air Carrier Inc **(HQ)**	2394	D	253 872-7205	2499
Manhattan Stitching Co Inc	2395	E	714 521-9479	2518
Haley Bros Inc **(HQ)**	2431	D	714 670-2112	2604
Exemplis LLC	2522	E	714 995-4800	2911
Elwin Inc	2591	E	714 752-6962	3005
Mashindustries Inc	2599	E	714 736-9600	3028
Blue Ribbon Cont & Display Inc	2653	E	562 944-1217	3085
Express Container Inc	2653	E	909 798-3857	3099
Rael Inc	2676	E	800 573-1516	3208
Cyu Lithographics Inc	2752	E	888 878-9898	3554
Q Team	2752	E	714 228-4465	3673
Interntional Color Posters Inc	2759	E	949 768-1005	3771
Awesome Products Inc **(PA)**	2842	C	714 562-8873	4343
BASF Corporation	2869	E	714 521-6085	4515
Parker-Hannifin Corporation	3052	D	714 522-8840	4711
Rubber-Trim Products Inc	3069	F	714 562-0500	4792
Creative Impressions Inc	3081	F	714 521-4441	4808
Abad Foam Inc	3086	E	714 994-2223	4868
Trim-Lok Inc **(PA)**	3089	C	714 562-0500	5233
Yeager Enterprises Corp	3291	D	714 994-2040	5547
Alloy Die Casting Co	3363	C	714 521-9800	5756
Metals USA Building Pdts LP	3441	C	714 522-7852	6053
Jaz Distribution Inc	3462	F	714 521-3888	6462
AW Die Engraving Inc	3544	E	714 521-7910	7053
Mar Cor Purification Inc	3589	E	800 633-3080	7671
Osmosis Technology Inc	3589	E	714 670-9303	7678
CJ Advisors Inc	3599	E	714 956-3388	7799
Hi-Tech Labels Incorporated	3599	E	714 670-2150	7861
Park Engineering and Mfg Co	3599	E	714 521-4660	7968
Wire Cut Company Inc	3599	E	714 994-1170	8082
Erika Records Inc	3652	E	714 228-5420	8458
Amcor Industries Inc	3714	E	323 585-2862	9350
Leach International Corp **(DH)**	3728	B	714 736-7537	9735
True Fresh Hpp LLC	3822	E	949 922-8801	10108
Pacific Chemical Dist Corp **(HQ)**	4226	D	714 521-7161	11634
States Logistics Services Inc **(PA)**	4731	C	714 521-6520	11804
Communications Supply Corp	4899	C	714 670-7711	12004
Cambium Business Group Inc **(PA)**	5021	C	714 670-1171	12279
Atlas Construction Supply Inc	5032	E	714 441-9500	12347
Noritsu-America Corporation **(HQ)**	5043	C	714 521-9040	12379
Hochiki America Corporation **(HQ)**	5063	D	714 522-2246	12598
Tech Systems Inc	5065	E	714 523-5404	12704
AM Machining Inc	5088	F	714 367-0830	12901
Yamaha Corporation of America **(HQ)**	5099	B	714 522-9011	12989
Orora Packaging Solutions	5113	C	714 562-6002	13012
Orora Packaging Solutions **(HQ)**	5113	C	714 562-6000	13013
Orora Packaging Solutions	5113	E	714 525-4900	13019
Derm Cosmetic Labs Inc **(PA)**	5122	E	714 562-8873	13038
Matesta Corporation	5137	C	949 874-6052	13136
Access Business Group LLC	5169	B	714 562-6200	13421
Access Business Group LLC	5169	E	714 562-7914	13422
G & G Door Products Inc	5211	E	714 228-2008	13575
Simpson Automotive Inc	5511	C	714 690-6200	13825
Westates Inc	5961	F	714 523-7600	14106
Performance Water Products Inc	5963	E	714 736-0137	14111
Continental Exch Solutions Inc **(HQ)**	6099	C	714 522-7044	14257
Universal Shopping Plaza A CA	6512	C	714 521-8899	14692
True Investments LLC	6799	E	949 258-9720	15057

Employee Codes: A=Over 500 employees, B=251-500
C=101-250, D=51-100, E=20-50, F=10-19, G=1-9

2024 Southern California
Business Directory and Buyers Guide

© Mergent Inc. 1-800-342-5647

1345

GEOGRAPHIC

	SIC	EMP	PHONE	ENTRY#
Knotts Berry Farm LLC	7011	D	714 995-1111	15211
Uniwell Corporation	7011	C	714 522-7000	15397
Medieval Times Entrmt Inc (HQ)	7041	A	714 523-1100	15443
Healthcare Resource Group	7363	C	562 945-7224	15922
A J Parent Company Inc (PA)	7389	D	714 521-1100	16763
Ted Ford Jones Inc (PA)	7538	C	714 521-3110	17039
Bridport Erie Aviation Inc	7699	E	714 634-8801	17117
Krikorian Premiere Theatre LLC	7832	D	714 826-7469	17303
Knotts Berry Farm LLC (HQ)	7996	B	714 827-1776	17449
Rehablttion Ctr of Ornge Cnty	8051	C	714 826-2330	18037
Southwest Rgnal Cncil Crpnters	8631	D	714 571-0449	19415

BURBANK, CA - Los Angeles County

	SIC	EMP	PHONE	ENTRY#
Honey Isabells Inc	0279	E	800 708-8485	92
V J Provision Inc	2011	F	818 843-3945	1206
Aries Beef LLC	2013	E	818 526-4855	1211
Excelline Food Products LLC	2038	E	818 701-7710	1390
Divine Pasta Company	2099	E	818 559-7440	1885
Palermo Family LP	2099	E	213 542-3300	1966
Staness Jonekos Entps Inc	2099	E	818 606-2710	1991
Mortex Corporation	2329	C		2216
Eastwest Clothing Inc (PA)	2331	F	323 980-1177	2237
The Original Cult Inc	2339	D	323 260-7308	2378
Vesture Group Incorporated	2369	D	818 842-0200	2421
Superior Window Coverings Inc	2391	E	818 762-6685	2464
Semihandmade LLC	2431	E	818 561-4350	2632
Swaner Hardwood Co Inc (PA)	2435	D	818 953-5350	2692
Arte De Mexico Inc (PA)	2522	D	818 753-4559	2904
Steves Plating Corporation	2542	C	818 842-2184	2994
Take A Break Paper	2711	E	323 333-7773	3327
Alternative Press Magazine Inc	2721	E	216 631-1510	3344
Disney Publishing Worldwide (DH)	2721	A	212 633-4400	3356
Disney Book Group LLC (DH)	2731	E	818 560-1000	3406
Advanced Publishing Tech Inc	2741	F	818 557-3035	3424
Color West Inc	2752	C	818 840-8881	3533
G Printing Inc	2752	F	818 246-1156	3577
Imagic	2752	E	818 333-1670	3591
Midnight Oil Agency LLC	2752	B	818 295-6100	3637
Primary Color Systems Corp	2752	E	818 643-5944	3663
Effective Graphics NC Inc	2796	C	310 323-2223	3852
Hutchinson Arospc & Indust Inc	3069	C	818 843-1000	4767
Matz Rubber Company Inc	3069	E	323 849-5170	4776
Three-D Plastics Inc (PA)	3089	E	323 849-1316	5227
Cydwoq Inc	3131	E	818 848-8307	5260
California Insulated Wire &	3357	D	818 569-4930	5736
Burbank Steel Treating Inc	3398	E	818 842-0975	5831
Quality Heat Treating Inc	3398	E	818 840-8212	5848
Saturn Fasteners Inc	3429	C	818 973-1807	5942
ESM Aerospace Inc	3444	E	818 841-3653	6233
Connell Processing Inc	3471	E	818 845-7661	6607
Haskel International LLC (HQ)	3561	C	818 843-4000	7281
Key Code Media Inc (PA)	3571	E	818 303-3900	7435
Comco Inc	3589	E	818 333-8500	7651
Centerpoint Mfg Co Inc	3599	D	818 842-2147	7795
Fortner Eng & Mfg Inc	3599	E	818 240-7740	7833
Hydra-Electric Company (PA)	3613	C	818 843-6211	8123
Litegear Inc	3641	E	818 358-8542	8249
Universal Switching Corp	3643	E	818 785-0200	8281
Nomoflo Enterprises Inc	3646	D	818 767-6528	8323
Dolby Laboratories Inc	3651	E	818 562-1101	8406
Doremi Labs Inc	3651	E	818 562-1101	8407
Magnasync/Moviola Corporation	3651	E	818 845-8066	8421
Hollywood Records Inc	3652	E	818 560-5670	8461
24/7 Studio Equipment Inc	3663	D	818 840-8247	8487
Astra Communications Inc	3663	F	818 859-7305	8497
Draco Broadcast Inc	3663	E	818 736-5788	8510
Nerdist Channel LLC	3663	E	818 333-2705	8553
Sierra Automated Sys/Eng Corp	3663	E	818 840-6749	8580
Graphic Research Inc	3672	E	818 886-7340	8683
Accratronics Seals Corporation	3679	D	818 843-1500	8990
Acsco Products Inc	3714	E	818 953-2240	9341
Gerhardt Gear Co Inc	3714	E	818 842-6700	9396
Bandy Manufacturing LLC	3728	D	818 846-9020	9643
Cardona Manufacturing Corp	3728	E	818 841-8358	9656
Crane Aerospace Inc	3728	D	818 526-2600	9667
Hutchinson Arospc & Indust Inc	3728	C	818 843-1000	9707
Hydro-Aire Inc (HQ)	3728	B	818 526-2600	9712
Hydro-Aire Aerospace Corp	3728	C	818 526-2600	9713
Senior Operations LLC	3728	B	818 260-2900	9796
Mvp Rv Inc	3792	F	951 848-4288	9926
Rohde & Schwarz Usa Inc	3825	E	818 846-3600	10222
Eckert Zegler Isotope Pdts Inc	3829	E	661 309-1010	10362
Avid Technology Inc	3861	E	818 557-2520	10859

	SIC	EMP	PHONE	ENTRY#
Photronics Inc (DH)	3861	B	203 740-5653	10881
US Gold Trading Inc	3911	F	818 558-7766	10914
Insomniac Games Inc (PA)	3944	D	818 729-2400	10955
Aramark Uniform Mfg Co	3999	E	800 999-8989	11190
Origin LLC	3999	E	818 848-1648	11259
Music Express Inc (PA)	4119	C	818 845-1502	11399
Ardwin Inc	4213	C	818 767-7777	11471
Ameriflight LLC	4512	C	818 847-0000	11659
Avjet Corporation	4522	D	818 841-6190	11680
Gat - Arln Ground Support Inc	4581	C	818 847-9127	11698
Mis Sciences Corp	4813	C	818 847-0213	11892
Qwest Cybersolutions LLC	4813	C	818 729-2100	11900
Deluxe Encore Inc	4822	C	323 466-7663	11916
ABC Cable Networks Group (HQ)	4832	B	818 460-7477	11918
Disney Enterprises Inc (DH)	4832	A	818 560-1000	11922
Krca License LLC	4832	C	818 840-1400	11927
Liberman Broadcasting Inc (PA)	4832	D	818 729-5300	11929
Radio Disney Group LLC	4832	E	818 569-5000	11934
ABC Signature Studios Inc	4833	D	818 560-1000	11937
Cw Network LLC (HQ)	4833	C	818 977-2500	11943
Public Mdia Group Southern Cal (PA)	4833	C	714 241-4100	11961
Twdc Enterprises 18 Corp (HQ)	4833	A	818 560-1000	11966
Valleycrest Productions Ltd	4833	D	818 560-5391	11968
International Fmly Entrmt Inc (DH)	4841	C	818 560-1000	11996
Own LLC	4841	C	323 602-5500	11998
City of Burbank	4931	B	818 238-3550	12103
Ver Sales Inc (PA)	5051	E	818 567-3000	12580
Wexler Corporation	5065	A	818 846-9381	12710
Sega of America Inc	5092	B	747 477-3708	12943
Mel Bernie and Company Inc (PA)	5094	C	818 841-1928	12965
Science of Skincare LLC	5122	D	818 254-7961	13067
Smart & Final Stores Inc	5141	C	818 954-8631	13218
Mader News Inc	5192	D	818 551-5000	13496
Lowes Home Centers LLC	5211	C	818 557-2300	13629
Portos Bakery Burbank Inc	5461	E	818 846-9100	13722
Sanctuary Clothing LLC (PA)	5621	E	818 505-0018	13916
Specialty Restaurants Corp	5812	C	818 843-5013	14037
Filmtools Inc (PA)	5946	E	323 467-1116	14082
Logix Federal Credit Union (PA)	6061	C	888 718-5328	14230
Allianz Globl Risks US Insur (DH)	6331	C		14505
Screen Actors Guild - American	6371	D	818 954-9400	14550
Silver Saddle Ranch & Club Inc	6552	D	818 768-8808	14911
OH So Original Inc	7011	B	818 841-4770	15270
PHF II Burbank LLC	7011	C	818 843-6000	15303
Vestis Services LLC	7218	A	818 973-3700	15472
Petrosian Esthetic Entps LLC	7231	C	818 391-8231	15485
GL Nemirow Inc	7311	D	818 562-9433	15540
Legendary Pictures Films LLC	7311	D	818 688-7003	15553
Dvs Media Services (PA)	7334	E	818 841-6750	15647
Ultragraphics Inc	7335	A	818 295-3994	15655
Come Land Maint Svc Co Inc	7349	A	818 567-2455	15701
M-N-Z Janitorial Services Inc	7349	C	323 851-4115	15722
J L Fisher Inc	7359	D	818 846-8366	15782
Blu Digital Group Inc (PA)	7371	C	818 527-2763	15985
Cheque Guard Inc	7371	D	818 563-9335	15991
Disney Interactive Studios Inc	7371	B	818 553-5000	16015
Global Service Resources Inc	7371	D	800 679-7658	16040
Zestfinance Inc	7371	D	323 450-3000	16153
Annex Pro Inc	7372	E	800 682-6639	16167
Jam City Inc	7372	D	804 920-8760	16280
My Eye Media LLC	7372	D	818 569-7200	16316
Integrated Media Tech Inc (PA)	7379	D	818 761-9770	16571
Andrews International Inc (DH)	7381	A	818 487-4060	16620
Secure Net Alliance	7381	E	818 848-4900	16679
US Security Associates Inc	7381	B	818 697-1809	16704
Buena Vista Television (DH)	7383	C	818 560-1878	16758
Coloredge	7384	E	818 842-1121	16760
Jake Hey Incorporated	7384	C	323 856-5280	16761
Technicolor Inc	7384	B	818 260-4577	16762
Pixar	7389	D	510 922-4075	16905
ABC Family Worldwide Inc (HQ)	7812	B	818 560-1000	17165
Barnstorm Vfx Inc	7812	D	818 792-1899	17170
Buena Vista International Inc	7812	C	818 295-5200	17173
Disney Incorporated (DH)	7812	C	818 560-1000	17185
NW Entertainment Inc (PA)	7812	B	818 295-5000	17203
Playboy Entrmt Group Inc (DH)	7812	C	323 276-4000	17209
Point360	7812	D	818 556-5700	17210
Roundabout Entertainment Inc	7812	B	818 842-9300	17215
Studio Distribution Svcs LLC	7812	B	818 954-6000	17226
Stx Financing LLC	7812	C	310 742-2300	17227
Walt Disney Music Company (DH)	7812	C	818 560-1000	17232
Walt Disney Records Direct (DH)	7812	A	818 560-1000	17234
Warner Bros Entertainment Inc (DH)	7812	C	818 954-6000	17235

	SIC	EMP	PHONE	ENTRY#
Warner Bros Entertainment Inc	7812	C	818 954-2209	17236
Warner Bros Home Entrmt Inc **(DH)**	7812	D	818 954-6000	17237
Warner Bros Intl TV Dist Inc	7812	C	818 954-6000	17238
Foto-Kem Industries Inc **(PA)**	7819	C	818 846-3102	17253
Olive Avenue Productions LLC	7819	B	770 214-7052	17258
Stereo D LLC	7819	D	818 861-3100	17265
Technicolor Thomson Group Inc **(HQ)**	7819	B		17268
Testronic Inc	7819	C	818 845-3223	17270
Warner Bros Transatlantic Inc	7822	B	818 977-6384	17285
Warner Bros Transatlantic Inc	7822	B	818 954-5990	17286
Eros Stx Global Corporation	7841	A	818 524-7000	17307
Prdctions N Fremantle Amer Inc **(DH)**	7922	D	818 748-1100	17324
Esl Gaming America Inc	7929	D	818 861-7315	17336
Now Casting Inc	7929	D	818 588-3732	17347
Youbetcom Inc **(HQ)**	7948	C	818 668-2100	17388
Lakeside Golf Club	7992	D	818 984-0601	17434
Walt Disney Company **(PA)**	7996	A	818 560-1000	17456
Disney Regional Entrmt Inc **(DH)**	7999	D	818 560-1000	17545
Providnce Facey Med Foundation	8031	D	818 861-7831	17852
Providence Health System	8062	A	818 843-5111	18397
Providnce Hlth Svcs Fndtn/San.	8062	A	818 843-5111	18402
Kan-Di-Ki LLC **(HQ)**	8071	D	818 549-1880	18554
Burbank Dental Laboratory Inc	8072	C	818 841-2256	18569
Nova Skilled Home Health Inc	8099	C	323 658-6232	18786
Napca Foundation	8299	A	800 799-4640	19013
Vintage Senior Management Inc	8322	A	818 954-9500	19153
American Fdrtion Mscans Lcal 4	8631	D	323 462-2161	19407
Boys Grls CLB Brbank Grter E V	8641	D	818 842-9333	19428
Young MNS Chrstn Assn Brbank C **(PA)**	8641	D	818 845-8551	19492
Cast & Crew LLC **(PA)**	8721	C	818 570-6180	19760
Entertainment Partners Inc **(PA)**	8721	B	818 955-6000	19772
New Talco Enterprises LLC	8721	D	310 280-0755	19797
Team Companies LLC **(PA)**	8721	D	818 558-3261	19806
Certified Laboratories LLC	8734	A	818 845-0070	19962
Dcl Maritime LLC	8741	C	818 560-1000	20026
IKEA Purchasing Svcs US Inc	8741	D	818 841-3500	20040
Streamland Media LLC	8741	C	416 909-2103	20100
Warner Bros Distributing Inc	8741	B	818 954-6000	20116
Enbio Corp.	8742	D	818 953-9976	20168
Modern Hr Inc	8742	D	877 842-4988	20202
Warner Bros Consumer Pdts Inc **(DH)**	8748	C	818 954-7980	20391

BUTTONWILLOW, CA - Kern County

	SIC	EMP	PHONE	ENTRY#
J G Boswell Company	0173	B	661 764-9000	37
B W Implement Co	3523	E	661 764-5254	6900

CABAZON, CA - Riverside County

	SIC	EMP	PHONE	ENTRY#
Hadley Fruit Orchards Inc **(PA)**	5961	E	951 849-5255	14094
Premium Outlet Partners LP	6512	D	951 849-6641	14680
Morongo Band Mission Indians	7999	C	951 849-3080	17559

CALABASAS, CA - Los Angeles County

	SIC	EMP	PHONE	ENTRY#
Ultimate Builders Inc	1521	D	818 481-2627	462
S & S Paving Inc	1611	E	818 591-0668	644
Blk International LLC **(PA)**	2086	E	424 282-3443	1686
True Classic Tees LLC	2321	E	323 419-1092	2165
Afr Apparel International Inc	2341	D	818 773-5000	2386
Electric Solidus LLC	2741	E	917 692-7764	3444
Wella Corporation **(HQ)**	2844	C	800 422-2336	4467
Radian Memory Systems Inc	3572	E	818 222-4080	7483
Fulcrum Microsystems Inc	3674	D	818 871-8100	8798
Apex Precision Technologies Inc	3714	E	317 821-1000	9353
Ixia	3825	E	818 871-1800	10207
Ixia **(HQ)**	3825	E	818 871-1800	10208
Yamaha Guitar Group Inc **(HQ)**	3931	E	818 575-3600	10935
Yamaha Guitar Group Inc	3931	E	818 575-3900	10936
Durham School Services L P	4151	C	818 880-4257	11423
Amawaterways LLC **(PA)**	4724	C	800 626-0126	11713
Las Virgenes Municipal Wtr Dst	4941	C	818 251-2100	12127
Abbyson Living Corp.	5021	C	805 465-5500	12276
Spirent Communications Inc **(HQ)**	5045	B	818 676-2300	12441
Central Purchasing LLC **(HQ)**	5085	B	800 444-3353	12847
Goldco Direct LLC	5094	D	818 343-0186	12962
Wella Operations US LLC	5122	B	818 999-5112	13077
Guarachi Wine Partners Inc	5182	D	818 225-5100	13477
Arcs Commercial Mortgage Co LP **(DH)**	6162	C	818 676-3274	14300
Republic Indemnity Co Amer **(DH)**	6331	C	818 990-9860	14523
Far West Bond Services Cal Inc **(PA)**	6351	B	818 704-1111	14536
Cartel Marketing Inc	6411	C	818 483-1130	14572
Western General Insurance Co.	6411	C	818 880-9070	14643
Alliant Asset MGT Co LLC **(HQ)**	6531	D	818 668-2805	14743
Dg Real Estate Inc	6531	D	818 591-8800	14787
Marcus & Millichap Inc **(PA)**	6531	C	818 212-2250	14829

	SIC	EMP	PHONE	ENTRY#
MSE Enterprises Inc **(PA)**	6531	D	818 223-3500	14834
Grant & Weber **(PA)**	7322	D	818 878-7700	15613
Avanquest North America LLC **(HQ)**	7371	D	818 591-9600	15974
Ellie Mae Inc	7371	B	818 223-2000	16024
Fattail Inc **(PA)**	7371	E	818 615-0380	16031
Prolifics Testing Inc	7371	E	925 485-9535	16099
Tri-Tech Systems Inc **(PA)**	7371	D	818 222-6811	16138
Catapult Communications Corp **(DH)**	7372	D	818 871-1800	16194
Estify Inc	7372	E	801 341-1911	16240
Sungard Treasury Systems Inc	7372	C	818 223-2300	16395
Thrio Inc.	7372	E	858 299-7191	16404
David Shield Security Inc	7381	D	310 849-4950	16637
Nastec International Inc	7381	D	818 222-0355	16661
Picore Bristain Initiative Inc	7381	D	818 888-3659	16670
Able Cable Inc **(PA)**	7629	C	818 223-3600	17067
Dts Inc **(DH)**	7819	C	818 436-1000	17250
Insomniac Inc	7929	C	323 874-7020	17342
Help Children World Foundation	8322	B	818 706-9848	19088
Davis Research LLC	8732	D	818 591-2408	19891
Informa Research Services Inc **(HQ)**	8732	D	818 880-8877	19899
Red Peak Group LLC	8742	D	818 222-7762	20228

CALABASAS HILLS, CA - Los Angeles County

	SIC	EMP	PHONE	ENTRY#
Helmet House LLC **(PA)**	5136	D	800 421-7247	13104
Ccf China Operating Corp.	5812	E	818 871-3000	13993
Cheesecake Factory Bakery Inc	5812	B	818 871-3000	13994
Cheesecake Factory Inc **(PA)**	5812	B	818 871-3000	13995
Houston Cheesecake Fctry Corp.	5812	B	818 871-3000	14013

CALEXICO, CA - Imperial County

	SIC	EMP	PHONE	ENTRY#
Cooper Lighting LLC	1731	C	760 357-4760	886
Imperial Valley Foods Inc.	2037	B	760 203-1896	1371
Bradford Soap Mexico Inc.	2841	C	760 768-4539	4334
4I Technologies Inc.	3555	C	817 538-0974	7181
Skyworks Solutions Inc.	3629	F	301 874-6408	8215
Celestica LLC.	3643	F	760 357-4880	8256
Creation Tech Calexico Inc **(HQ)**	3672	E		8667
Lorenz Inc.	3699	E	760 427-1815	9227
Garrett Motion Inc.	3714	C	973 867-7016	9393
Chromalloy Gas Turbine LLC	3724	C	760 768-3723	9565
Garrett Motion Inc.	3724	E	760 357-3297	9568
Honeywell International Inc.	3724	F	760 312-5300	9571
Rockwell Collins Inc.	3728	E	760 768-4732	9777
Triumph Insulation Systems LLC	3728	A	760 618-7543	9822
Orthodental International Inc.	3843	D	760 357-8070	10758
Clover Envmtl Solutions LLC	3861	E	760 357-9277	10863
Lakim Industries Incorporated **(PA)**	3991	E	310 637-8900	11091
U S Xpress Inc.	4213	B	760 768-6707	11510
R L Jones-San Diego Inc **(PA)**	4731	D	760 357-3177	11797
ARC - Imperial Valley	8093	E	760 768-1944	18669

CALIFORNIA CITY, CA - Kern County

	SIC	EMP	PHONE	ENTRY#
Creative Accents	2273	E	760 373-1222	2112
Robertsons Ready Mix Ltd	3273	D	760 373-4815	5500

CALIMESA, CA - Riverside County

	SIC	EMP	PHONE	ENTRY#
Paver Decor Masonry Inc.	1611	E	909 795-8474	639
Skat-Trak.	3011	E	909 795-2505	4699

CALIPATRIA, CA - Imperial County

	SIC	EMP	PHONE	ENTRY#
Calenergy LLC.	1731	B	402 231-1527	877
Earthrise Nutritionals LLC	2099	E	760 348-5027	1886
Viridos Inc.	8731	D	858 754-2900	19888

CAMARILLO, CA - Ventura County

	SIC	EMP	PHONE	ENTRY#
Boskovich Farms Inc	0161	C	805 987-1443	8
Rincon Pacific LLC.	0171	D	805 986-8806	23
Pacific Erth Rsrces Ltd A Cal.	0181	D	209 892-3000	64
Pacific Erth Rsrces Ltd A Cal **(PA)**	0181	D	805 986-8277	65
Houwelings Camarillo Inc.	0182	B	805 250-1600	75
Hi-Temp Insulation Inc.	1742	B	805 484-2774	979
Califrnia Dsgners Chice Cstm C	2434	E	805 987-5820	2654
Americon.	2521	F	805 987-0412	2877
Galtech Computer Corporation	2521	E	805 376-1060	2885
Crockett Graphics Inc **(PA)**	2653	C	805 987-8577	3095
Lundberg Survey Incorporated	2721	E	805 383-2400	3368
Bestforms Inc.	2761	E	805 388-0503	3829
Performance Materials Corp **(HQ)**	2821	D	805 482-1722	3961
Gsms Inc **(PA)**	2834	D	805 477-9866	4125
National Coatings Corporation	2952	E	805 388-7112	4674
Sani-Tech West Inc **(HQ)**	3052	D	805 389-0400	4712
Ogio International Inc.	3161	E	800 326-6325	5293
Koltov Inc **(PA)**	3172	E	805 764-0280	5301

Employee Codes: A=Over 500 employees, B=251-500
C=101-250, D=51-100, E=20-50, F=10-19, G=1-9

2024 Southern California
Business Directory and Buyers Guide

© Mergent Inc. 1-800-342-5647

1347

GEOGRAPHIC

	SIC	EMP	PHONE	ENTRY#
Engense Inc	3312	F	805 484-8317	5589
Gc International Inc **(PA)**	3365	E	805 389-4631	5794
Gms Landscapes Inc	3432	D	805 402-3925	5971
Titan Metal Fabricators Inc **(PA)**	3441	D	805 487-5050	6080
Abel Automatics LLC	3451	E	805 388-3721	6407
Nanoprecision Products Inc	3469	E	310 597-4991	6539
United Western Enterprises Inc	3479	E	805 389-1077	6746
Transonic Combustion Inc	3519	E	805 465-5145	6897
Western Gage Corporation	3545	C	805 445-1410	7140
Hales Engineering Coinc	3599	E		7856
Hte Acquisition LLC	3599	E	805 987-5449	7868
PDQ Engineering Inc	3599	E	805 482-1334	7969
Ronlo Engineering Ltd	3599	E	805 388-3227	8007
Thiessen Products Inc	3599	C	805 482-6913	8046
Arnold Magnetics Corporation	3612	D	805 484-4221	8087
Califrnia State Univ Chnnel Is	3612	E	805 437-2670	8089
Barta - Schoenewald Inc **(PA)**	3621	C	805 389-1935	8135
Magicall Inc	3621	E	805 484-4300	8150
Skurka Aerospace Inc **(DH)**	3621	E	805 484-8884	8157
Thingap Inc	3621	E	805 477-9741	8160
Toray Prfmce Mtls Corp USA	3624	E	805 402-6664	8166
Plt Enterprises Inc	3643	D	805 389-5335	8273
Thin-Lite Corporation	3648	E	805 987-5021	8384
Mediapointe Inc	3651	E	805 480-3700	8423
Gc International Inc	3652	E	805 389-4631	8460
Record Technology Inc **(PA)**	3652	E	805 484-2747	8465
Salem Music Network Inc	3663	E	805 987-0400	8574
Tactical Communications Corp	3669	E	805 987-4100	8630
Multilayer Prototypes Inc	3672	F	805 498-9390	8706
Former Luna Subsidiary Inc **(HQ)**	3674	D		8797
Interconnect Systems Intl LLC **(DH)**	3674	E	805 482-2870	8814
Microsemi Communications Inc **(DH)**	3674	D	805 388-3700	8840
Opto Diode Corporation	3674	E	805 465-8700	8856
OSI Optoelectronics Inc	3674	E	805 987-0146	8858
Physpeed Corporation	3674	D	805 259-3101	8863
Polyfet Rf Devices Inc	3674	E	805 484-9582	8866
Semtech Corporation **(PA)**	3674	C	805 498-2111	8886
Johanson Technology Inc	3675	C	805 575-0124	8929
Meissner Filtration Pdts Inc **(PA)**	3677	E	805 388-9911	8946
Cooper Interconnect Inc **(DH)**	3678	F	805 484-0543	8966
Ciao Wireless Inc	3679	D	805 389-3224	9016
Gtran Inc **(PA)**	3679	E	805 445-4500	9051
Lucix Corporation **(HQ)**	3679	D	805 987-6645	9079
Mercury LLC - Rf Integrated Solutions	3679	C	805 388-1345	9083
So-Cal Value Added LLC	3679	E	805 389-5335	9118
Battery-Biz Inc	3694	C	800 848-6782	9164
Technicolor Disc Services Corp **(HQ)**	3695	C	805 445-1122	9185
Xirgo Technologies LLC	3699	D	805 319-4079	9273
Artisan Vehicle Systems Inc	3711	D	805 402-6856	9278
Wilwood Engineering **(PA)**	3714	C	805 388-1188	9487
Airborne Technologies Inc	3728	E	805 389-3700	9611
Camar Aircraft Parts Co	3728	E	805 389-8944	9652
Parker-Hannifin Corporation	3728	D	805 484-8533	9763
Western Mfg & Distrg LLC	3751	E	805 988-1010	9889
Northrop Grumman Systems Corp	3812	C	805 987-8831	10036
Northrop Grumman Systems Corp	3812	E	805 987-9739	10037
Hanson Lab Solutions Inc	3821	E	805 498-3121	10094
CK Technologies Inc **(PA)**	3823	E	805 987-4801	10123
Innovative Integration Inc	3823	E	805 520-3300	10140
Primordial Diagnostics Inc	3823	E	800 462-1926	10152
Merex Inc	3825	C	805 446-2700	10216
Bruker Corporation	3826	F	805 388-3326	10247
Interglobal Waste MGT Inc	3826	D	805 388-1588	10266
Santec California Corporation	3827	E	805 987-1700	10337
Teledyne Scentific Imaging LLC	3827	E		10342
Structural Diagnostics Inc	3829	E	805 987-7755	10399
Infab LLC	3842	D	805 987-5255	10671
Kinamed Inc	3842	E	805 384-2748	10678
Medical Packaging Corporation	3842	E	805 388-2383	10680
Belport Company Inc **(PA)**	3843	F	805 484-1051	10730
Viade Products Inc	3843	F	805 484-2114	10777
Cal Simba Inc **(PA)**	3914	E	805 240-1177	10915
Airport Connection Inc	4111	C	805 389-8196	11315
Sun Air Jets LLC	4522	C	805 389-9301	11683
California Internet LP **(PA)**	4813	C	805 225-4638	11875
Directv Group Holdings LLC	4841	C	805 207-6675	11989
Data Exchange Corporation **(PA)**	5045	B	805 388-1711	12405
Golden State Medical Sup Inc	5047	C	805 477-9866	12488
Teledyne Reson Inc	5088	E	805 964-6260	12919
Williams Aerospace & Mfg Inc **(HQ)**	5088	E	805 586-8699	12924
Golden State Medical Supply	5099	D	805 477-8966	12977
Home Depot USA Inc	5211	B	805 389-9918	13600
Jim ONeal Distributing Inc	5571	E	805 426-3300	13900
BKM Office Environments Inc **(PA)**	5712	F	805 339-6388	13939
Tangerine Express Inc	5999	E	702 260-6650	14151
Al Hewitt Inc	6282	C	661 945-7050	14413
Premium Outlet Partners LP	6512	D	805 445-8520	14681
Cushman & Wakefield Cal Inc	6531	B	805 322-7244	14781
Rgc Services Inc	6531	D	805 484-1600	14860
Barrett Business Services Inc	7361	A	805 987-0331	15821
Applied Engineering MGT Corp	7371	C	805 484-1909	15965
Market Scan Info Systems Inc	7371	D	800 658-7226	16071
Modern Campus USA Inc **(PA)**	7371	D	805 484-9400	16077
Electronic Clearing House Inc **(HQ)**	7372	D	805 419-8700	16236
Gbl Systems Corporation	7373	E	805 987-4345	16443
Dial Security Inc **(PA)**	7382	C	805 389-6700	16729
Technclor Vdocassette Mich Inc **(DH)**	7819	B	805 445-1122	17267
Vantiva Sup Chain Slutions Inc **(HQ)**	7819	B	805 445-1122	17271
La Workout Inc	7991	C	805 482-8884	17404
Las Posas Country Club	7997	C	805 482-4518	17498
Spanish Hills Club LLC	7997	C	805 388-5000	17525
Spanish Hills Country Club **(PA)**	7997	D	805 389-1644	17526
People Creating Success Inc	8011	D	805 644-9480	17737
Institute For Applied Bhvior A	8049	D	805 987-5886	17864
Vitas Healthcare Corporation	8052	D	805 437-2100	18101
Dignity Health	8062	C	805 389-5800	18239
Ventura Cnty Md-Cal Mnged Care	8099	D	888 301-1228	18815
Casa Pcfica Ctrs For Chldren F **(PA)**	8322	C	805 482-3260	19034
Interface Community **(PA)**	8322	D	805 485-6114	19096
Channel Islnds Yung MNS Chrstn	8641	D	805 484-0423	19438
Dex Corporation	8711	D	805 388-1711	19572
Saalex Corp **(PA)**	8711	C	805 482-1070	19682
Amt Datasouth Corp **(PA)**	8731	E	805 388-5799	19819
Teledyne Scentific Imaging LLC	8731	D	805 373-4999	19880
Camarillo Healthcare Center	8741	D	805 482-9805	20010
Juvenile Justice Division Cal	8741	A	805 485-7951	20046

CAMBRIA, CA - San Luis Obispo County

	SIC	EMP	PHONE	ENTRY#
Linns Fruit Bin Inc **(PA)**	5431	E	805 927-1499	13714
Moonstone Management Corp **(PA)**	6531	C	805 927-4200	14832
Moonstone Bch Innvstors A Cal	7011	C	805 927-8661	15254
Pacific Cambria Inc	7011	D	805 927-6114	15284

CAMP PENDLETON, CA - San Diego County

	SIC	EMP	PHONE	ENTRY#
Marine Corps Community Svcs	7999	C	760 725-6195	17557
Marine Corps Community Svcs	8351	C	760 725-7311	19217
Lion-Vallen Ltd Partnership	8741	D	760 385-4885	20055

CAMPO, CA - San Diego County

	SIC	EMP	PHONE	ENTRY#
Campo Band Missions Indians	7993	B	619 938-6000	17444

CANOGA PARK, CA - Los Angeles County

	SIC	EMP	PHONE	ENTRY#
American Landscape Inc	0781	C	818 999-2041	139
American Landscape MGT Inc **(PA)**	0781	C	818 999-2041	140
Pacific Coast Tree Experts	0783	C	805 506-1211	224
Rte Enterprises Inc	1721	D	818 999-5300	855
Mark Land Electric Inc	1731	E	818 883-5110	915
Flowers Bkg Co Henderson LLC	2051	D	818 884-8970	1467
Modern Woodworks Inc	2499	E	800 575-3475	2756
Barrys Printing Inc	2752	E	818 998-8600	3517
Vomar Products Inc	2759	E	818 610-5115	3823
Pacific Shore Holdings Inc	2834	E	818 998-0996	4194
Den-Mat Corporation	2844	C	800 445-0345	4401
Aerojet Rocketdyne De Inc **(DH)**	2869	C	818 586-1000	4510
Pls Diabetic Shoe Company Inc	3021	E	818 734-7080	4705
Glastar Corporation	3559	E	818 341-0301	7239
B S K T Inc	3599	F	818 349-1566	7771
Rainbo Record Mfg Corp **(PA)**	3652	E	818 280-1100	8464
Aerojet Rocketdyne De Inc	3724	A	818 586-1000	9562
Micro Steel Inc	3769	E	818 348-8701	9920
C J Instruments Incorporated	3829	E	818 996-4131	10356
Optron Scientific Company Inc	3829	E	818 883-6103	10388
Temptron Engineering Inc	3829	E	818 346-4900	10404
Azimc Investments Inc	5013	C	818 678-1200	12233
H2w	5099	C	800 578-3088	12979
Green Thumb International Inc	5193	D	818 340-6400	13507
Atlantis Enterprises Inc	5199	C	818 712-0572	13528
National Advanced Endoscopy De	5999	E	818 227-2720	14141
Socal Auto Supply Inc	7213	C	302 360-8373	15459
Computrition Inc **(HQ)**	7371	D	818 961-3999	16000
Hvantage Technologies Inc **(PA)**	7371	D	818 661-6301	16048
Shield Security Inc	7381	E	818 239-5800	16685
Decor Interior Design Inc	7389	E	818 962-4800	16815
Sela Healthcare Inc	8051	B	818 341-9800	18050
APn Business Resources Inc	8742	D	818 717-9980	20133

Mergent email: customerrelations@mergent.com
1348

2024 Southern California
Business Directory and Buyers Guide

(P-0000) Products & Services Section entry number
(PA)=Parent Co (HQ)=Headquarters (DH)=Div Headquarters

	SIC	EMP	PHONE	ENTRY#

CANYON COUNTRY, CA - Los Angeles County

	SIC	EMP	PHONE	ENTRY#
Commercial Display Systems LLC	3585	E	818 361-8160	7603
Rexhall Industries Inc	3716	E	661 726-5470	9502
Power Generation Entps Inc	5084	C	818 484-8550	12810

CANYON LAKE, CA - Riverside County

	SIC	EMP	PHONE	ENTRY#
Alexander Dennis Incorporated	5012	A	951 244-9429	12220

CAPISTRANO BEACH, CA - Orange County

	SIC	EMP	PHONE	ENTRY#
Schaeffler Group USA Inc	3562	E	949 234-9799	7303
Pacific Monarch Resorts Inc	7011	D	949 248-2944	15289

CARDIFF BY THE SEA, CA - San Diego County

	SIC	EMP	PHONE	ENTRY#
Naval Coating Inc	1799	C	619 234-8366	1171
Total Gym Commercial LLC	3949	F	858 586-6080	11035
Mellmo Inc	7371	C	858 847-3272	16074
Igrad Inc	7372	E	858 705-2917	16268

CARLSBAD, CA - San Diego County

	SIC	EMP	PHONE	ENTRY#
James Allison Estates & Homes	1521	C	866 463-5780	436
Pacific Cast Cnstr Wrtrproofing	1521	E	760 298-3170	449
Rq Construction LLC	1541	C	760 631-7707	515
Nevell Group Inc	1542	B	760 598-3501	570
R Q Construction Inc	1542	C	760 631-7707	582
Anaergia Services LLC	1629	E	760 436-8870	705
Hellas Construction Inc	1629	B	760 891-8090	710
Bergelectric Corp (PA)	1731	D	760 638-2374	869
Bergelectric Corp	1731	A	760 746-1003	870
Ipitek Inc	1731	C	760 438-1010	909
Mellace Family Brands Inc	2068	E	760 448-1940	1556
Mellace Family Brands Cal Inc	2068	E	760 448-1940	1557
Mfb Liquidation Inc	2068	E	760 448-1940	1558
Bitchin Inc (PA)	2099	E	760 224-7447	1858
Bitchin Sauce LLC	2099	D	737 248-2446	1859
Living Wellness Partners LLC	2099	E	800 642-3754	1936
Silk Screen Shirts Inc	2261	E	760 233-3900	2091
Ashworth Inc	2329	A	760 438-6610	2195
R B III Associates Inc	2337	C	760 471-5370	2295
Eevelle LLC	2399	E	760 434-2231	2550
Reflex Corporation	2399	E	760 931-9009	2556
Vanguard Industries East Inc	2399	E	800 433-1334	2559
Vanguard Industries West Inc (PA)	2399	C	760 438-4437	2560
Finishing Touch Moulding Inc	2434	D	760 444-1019	2659
SC Bluwood Inc	2491	F	909 519-5470	2747
Stone Yard Inc	2519	F	858 586-1580	2875
The Heat Factory Inc	2673	E	760 893-8300	3194
Upper Deck Company (PA)	2741	E	800 873-7332	3499
Gsg Printing Inc (PA)	2752	E	760 752-9500	3582
L & L Printers Carlsbad LLC	2752	E	760 477-0321	3615
Sport Card Co LLC	2752	B	800 873-7332	3688
Zuza LLC	2752	D	760 494-9000	3718
Hudson Printing Inc	2759	D	760 602-1260	3768
Iris Group Inc	2759	C	760 431-1103	3773
Air Products and Chemicals Inc	2813	B	760 931-9555	3861
Natural Alternatives Intl Inc (PA)	2833	C	760 736-7700	4005
Sabre Sciences Inc	2833	F	760 448-2750	4016
Akcea Therapeutics Inc (HQ)	2834	D	617 207-0202	4038
Carlsbad Technology Inc	2834	D	760 431-8284	4084
Carlsbad Technology Inc (DH)	2834	E	760 431-8284	4085
Design Therapeutics Inc	2834	E	858 293-4900	4101
Greenwich Biosciences LLC (DH)	2834	E	760 795-2200	4124
Hikma Pharmaceuticals USA Inc	2834	E	760 683-0901	4131
Imprimisrx LLC	2834	D	844 446-6979	4134
Ionis Pharmaceuticals Inc	2834	E	760 603-3567	4139
Ionis Pharmaceuticals Inc	2834	E	760 931-9200	4140
Ionis Pharmaceuticals Inc (PA)	2834	B	760 931-9200	4141
Quorex Pharm Inc (PA)	2834	E	760 602-1910	4218
Biosource International Inc	2835	E	805 659-5759	4270
Life Technologies Corporation (HQ)	2835	C	760 603-7200	4280
Molecular Probes Inc	2835	E	760 603-7200	4282
Syntron Bioresearch Inc	2835	B	760 930-2200	4294
Tyra Biosciences Inc	2835	E	619 728-4760	4296
Dnatrix Inc	2836	E	832 930-2401	4312
Lineage Cell Therapeutics Inc (PA)	2836	E	510 521-3390	4324
Alastin Skincare Inc	2844	C	844 858-7546	4377
Coola LLC	2844	D	760 940-2125	4392
Eden Beauty Concepts Inc	2844	E	760 330-9941	4408
Sigma-Aldrich Corporation	2899	E	760 710-6213	4630
Petrochem Manufacturing Inc	2951	D	760 603-0961	4664
Modus Advanced Inc	3069	D	925 960-8700	4779
Allbirds Inc	3143	F	442 273-5519	5270
Phoenix Footwear Group Inc (PA)	3143	E	760 602-9688	5273
Ogio International Inc (HQ)	3161	E	801 619-4100	5292

	SIC	EMP	PHONE	ENTRY#
Oceanside Glasstile Company (PA)	3253	B	760 929-4000	5373
Product Slingshot Inc (DH)	3544	E	760 929-9380	7091
Coplan & Coplan Inc	3545	E	760 268-0583	7111
Palomar Technologies Inc (PA)	3559	E	760 931-3600	7254
Nordson Corporation	3563	E	760 431-1919	7311
Nordson Corporation	3563	C	760 431-1919	7312
Nordson March Inc	3563	D	925 827-1240	7313
Nordson Test Insptn Amrcas Inc	3563	E	760 918-8471	7314
Borsos Engineering Inc	3571	F	760 930-0296	7420
Mercury Computer System Inc	3571	E	760 494-9600	7440
Aqua Products Inc (DH)	3589	E	973 857-2700	7640
Fluidra Usa LLC (PA)	3589	E	904 378-0999	7658
Zodiac Pool Solutions LLC (PA)	3589	E	760 599-9600	7697
Zodiac Pool Systems LLC (HQ)	3589	C	760 599-9600	7698
Diligent Solutions Inc	3599	E	760 814-8960	7818
Gtr Enterprises Incorporated	3599	E	760 931-1192	7854
Laurelwood Industries Inc	3599	F	760 705-1649	7907
Machine Craft of San Diego	3599	E	858 642-0509	7913
Aih LLC (DH)	3621	E	760 930-4600	8134
Systems Mchs Atmtn Cmpnnts Cor (PA)	3625	C	760 929-7575	8193
Seacomp Inc (PA)	3629	C	760 918-6722	8214
Mercotac Inc	3643	F	760 431-7723	8270
Anchor Audio Inc	3651	D	760 827-7100	8394
Arlo Technologies Inc (PA)	3651	E	408 890-3900	8396
Ecolink Intelligent Tech Inc	3651	E	855 432-6546	8409
Suitecentric Lcc	3652	F	760 520-1611	8466
Excelsus A Division of Pulse	3661	E	760 476-1511	8472
Aethercomm Inc	3663	C	760 208-6002	8489
Calamp Corp	3663	E	760 444-0952	8503
Denso Wireless Systems America Inc	3663	C	760 734-4600	8508
Global Microwave Systems Inc	3663	E	760 496-0046	8520
Viasat Inc	3663	E	760 476-2129	8594
Viasat Inc (PA)	3663	A	760 476-2200	8595
Dei Headquarters Inc	3669	B	760 598-6200	8607
Dei Holdings Inc (HQ)	3669	E	760 598-6200	8608
H M Electronics Inc	3669	E	858 535-6139	8613
Cal-Comp USA (san Diego) Inc	3672	C	858 587-6900	8655
Crown Circuits Inc	3672	E	949 922-0144	8668
Electro Surface Tech Inc	3672	E	760 431-8306	8671
Spectrum Assembly Inc	3672	E	760 930-4000	8733
Luxtera LLC	3674	C	760 448-3520	8831
Maxlinear Inc (PA)	3674	E	760 692-0711	8836
Maxlinear Technologies LLC (HQ)	3674	C	760 692-0711	8837
Natel Engineering Co Inc	3674	E	760 448-1500	8849
Qualcomm Incorporated	3674	F	858 651-8481	8872
Visual Communications Company LLC	3679	C	800 522-5546	9137
Nordson California Inc	3695	D	760 918-8490	9182
Palomar Tech Companies (PA)	3699	E	760 931-3600	9240
Pro Spot International Inc	3699	F	760 407-1414	9244
American Rim Supply Inc	3714	E	760 431-3666	9352
Machinetek LLC	3728	F	760 438-6644	9740
Matthew Smith Crampton	3732	C	760 840-8404	9862
Aqua-Lung America Inc (DH)	3812	C	760 376-9813	9945
L3 Technologies Inc	3812	C	760 431-6800	9985
Laird R & F Products Inc (DH)	3812	E	760 916-9410	9992
Qualigen Inc (HQ)	3821	C	760 918-9165	10098
Myron L Company	3823	D	760 438-2021	10148
Nordson Asymtek Inc	3823	C	760 431-1919	10148
Neology Inc (PA)	3825	E	858 391-0260	10220
Beckman Coulter Inc	3826	C	760 438-9151	10237
Invitrogen Ip Holdings Inc (DH)	3826	D	760 603-7200	10267
Life Technologies Corporation	3826	C	760 918-0135	10270
Life Technologies Corporation	3826	E	760 918-4259	10271
Means Engineering Inc	3826	D	760 931-9452	10273
Thermo Fisher Scientific Inc	3826	E	781 622-1000	10297
Thermo Fisher Scientific Inc	3826	E	760 603-7200	10299
Thermo Fisher Scientific Inc	3826	E	760 268-8641	10300
Thermo Fsher Scntfic Psg Corp (HQ)	3826	C	760 603-7200	10301
Idex Health & Science LLC	3827	C	760 438-2131	10319
Intevac Photonics Inc	3827	E	760 476-0339	10321
Melles Griot Inc	3827	E	760 438-2131	10327
Melles Griot Inc	3827	D	760 438-2254	10328
Synergeyes Inc	3827	C	760 476-9410	10341
California Sensor Corporation	3829	E	760 438-0525	10358
Aalto Scientific Ltd	3841	E	800 748-6674	10408
Acutus Medical Inc	3841	B	442 232-6080	10416
Alphatec Holdings Inc (PA)	3841	C	760 431-9286	10426
Bolt Medical Inc	3841	E	949 287-3207	10460
Breg Inc (HQ)	3841	C	760 599-3000	10463
Canary Medical USA LLC	3841	E	760 448-5066	10468
Covidien Holding Inc	3841	C	760 603-5020	10485
Eklin Medical Systems Inc	3841	E	760 918-9626	10500
Foundry Med Innovations Inc	3841	F	888 445-2333	10510

Employee Codes: A=Over 500 employees, B=251-500
C=101-250, D=51-100, E=20-50, F=10-19, G=1-9

2024 Southern California
Business Directory and Buyers Guide

© Mergent Inc. 1-800-342-5647
1349

GEOGRAPHIC

Company	SIC	EMP	PHONE	ENTRY#
Genmark Diagnostics Inc (DH)	3841	B	760 448-4300	10516
Impedimed Inc (HQ)	3841	E	760 585-2100	10528
Medtronic Inc	3841	E	760 214-3009	10558
Planet Innovation Inc	3841	E	847 943-7270	10590
Rf Surgical Systems LLC	3841	D	855 522-7027	10599
Sendx Medical Inc	3841	C	760 930-6300	10603
Spinal Elements Holdings Inc	3841	C	877 774-6255	10609
Alphatec Spine Inc (HQ)	3842	C	760 431-9286	10634
Djo LLC	3842	E	800 321-9549	10646
Drs Own Inc (PA)	3842	E	760 804-0751	10649
Seaspine Inc	3842	D	760 727-8399	10700
Seaspine Orthopedics Corp (HQ)	3842	E	866 942-8698	10701
Sunrise Medical Inc	3842	E	619 930-1500	10705
Zimmer Dental Inc	3842	B	800 854-7019	10724
Lancer Orthodontics Inc (PA)	3843	E	760 744-5585	10754
Ortho Organizers Inc	3843	C	760 448-8600	10757
Nordson Dage Inc	3844	C	440 985-4496	10784
Hygeia II Medical Group Inc	3845	E	714 515-7571	10807
Sotera Wireless Inc	3845	C	858 427-4620	10825
Signet Armorlite Inc (DH)	3851	B	760 744-4000	10851
Spy Inc (PA)	3851	D	760 804-8420	10853
USAopoly Inc	3944	D	760 431-5910	10968
Acushnet Company	3949	B	760 804-6500	10970
Aldila Golf Corp (DH)	3949	D	858 513-1801	10973
Fujikura Composite America Inc	3949	E	760 598-6060	10992
Hyperfly Inc	3949	E	760 300-0909	11001
Liquid Force Wakeboards Inc	3949	E	760 943-8364	11009
Lucite Intl Prtnr Holdings Inc	3949	D	760 929-0001	11010
Safer Sports Inc	3949	E	760 444-0082	11022
Topgolf Callaway Brands Corp (PA)	3949	B	760 931-1771	11034
Zonson Company Inc	3949	E	760 597-0338	11045
Naturemaker Inc	3999	E	760 438-4244	11254
New Dimension One Spas Inc (DH)	3999	C	800 345-7727	11256
Riolo Transportation Inc	4789	B	760 729-4405	11839
Adicio Inc	4813	D	760 602-9502	11869
NRG Solar LLC	4911	C	760 710-2140	12032
San Diego Gas & Electric Co.	4939	C	760 438-6200	12112
Diakont Advanced Tech Inc	5043	E	858 551-5551	12377
Carlsbad International Export Inc	5047	E	760 438-5323	12481
Thorwear Inc	5047	F	760 224-3393	12519
Equity International Inc	5065	A	978 664-2712	12658
HM Electronics Inc (PA)	5065	B	858 535-6000	12666
Matrix-Focalspot Inc	5065	E	858 536-5050	12681
San Diego Sign Company Inc	5085	E	888 748-7446	12877
Bikes Online Inc	5091	D	650 272-3378	12926
Full-Swing Golf Inc	5091	E	858 675-1100	12929
Industrial Strength Corp	5094	F	760 795-1068	12963
Nixon Inc (PA)	5094	C	888 455-9200	12966
Golden Eye Media Usa Inc	5113	F	760 688-9962	13009
Colorescience Inc	5122	C	866 426-5673	13033
Unite Eurotherapy Inc	5122	D	760 585-1800	13072
Prana Living LLC (HQ)	5136	D	866 915-6457	13108
South Cone Inc	5139	C	760 431-2300	13166
Smart & Final Stores Inc	5141	C	760 434-2449	13203
Penton Overseas Inc	5192	F	760 809-6030	13497
Kendal Floral Supply LLC (PA)	5193	D	888 828-9875	13511
La Costa Coffee Roasting Co (PA)	5499	E	760 438-8160	13729
Bob Baker Volkswagen	5511	D	760 438-2200	13740
Hoehn Company Inc	5511	C	760 438-1818	13778
Oceanside Auto Country Inc (PA)	5511	C	760 438-2000	13807
Ted Ford Jones Inc	5511	C	760 438-9171	13835
Skylar Creations Inc	5812	F	760 814-8260	14036
Port Brewing	5813	F	760 720-7012	14052
Vape Craft LLC	5993	E	760 295-7484	14116
Gunnar Optiks LLC	5995	E	858 769-2500	14118
Nice North America LLC (DH)	5999	C	760 438-7000	14142
First Community Bancorp	6021	D	858 756-3023	14166
Merrill Lynch Prce Fnner Smith	6211	D	760 930-3100	14389
Morgan Stnley Smith Barney LLC	6211	C	760 438-5100	14395
Optumrx Inc	6324	B	760 804-2399	14490
Southern Cal Prmnnte Med Group	6324	C	619 528-5000	14498
Premium Outlet Partners LP	6512	D	760 804-9045	14682
Front Porch Communities & Svcs	6513	C	760 729-4983	14710
Integral Senior Living LLC	6513	C	760 547-2863	14717
Common Grounds Holdings LLC	6531	D	760 206-7861	14771
Grand Pacific Resorts Inc (PA)	6531	C	760 431-8500	14805
Aviara Fsrc Associates Limited	7011	A	760 603-6800	15081
Grand Pacific Carlsbad Ht LP	7011	B	760 827-2400	15159
Grand Pacific Resorts Inc.	7011	C	760 431-8500	15160
Grand Pacific Resorts Svcs LP	7011	C	760 431-8500	15161
Hilton Garden Inns MGT LLC	7011	C	760 476-0800	15177
Hyatt Corp As Agt Brcp Hef Ht.	7011	D	760 603-6851	15192
Lc Trs Inc.	7011	A	760 438-9111	15221
Omni La Costa Resort & Spa LLC (DH)	7011	C	760 438-9111	15277
Northstar Memorial Group LLC	7261	C	800 323-1342	15488
High Moon Studios LLC	7299	C	760 448-3000	15509
JC Weight Loss Centres Inc (PA)	7299	C	760 696-4000	15514
Jon Renau Collection Inc	7299	D	760 598-0067	15516
Havas Edge LLC (DH)	7311	D	760 929-0041	15542
Promoveo Health LLC	7311	A	760 931-4794	15569
Basepoint Analytics LLC	7323	B	760 602-4971	15619
Continuing Lf Communities LLC (PA)	7361	D	760 704-6400	15833
A R Santex LLC (PA)	7371	E	888 622-7098	15952
Alogent Holdings Inc	7371	D	760 410-9000	15961
Applied Spectral Imaging Inc	7371	F	760 929-2840	15966
Aveva Software LLC	7371	C	760 268-7700	15975
C Squared Social	7371	D	858 386-7400	15990
Chromacode Inc	7371	E	442 244-4369	15992
Happyco Inc (PA)	7371	C	415 230-9832	16044
Stratcom Systems Inc	7371	E	858 481-9292	16125
Tadpole Cartesia Inc	7371	F	760 929-8345	16129
2b Advice LLC	7372	E	858 366-9750	16155
Aira Tech Corp.	7372	D	800 835-1934	16161
Applied Biosystems LLC (DH)	7372	C		16172
Brendan Technologies Inc	7372	E	760 929-7500	16190
Lawinfocom Inc	7372	E	800 397-3743	16289
Microvision Development Inc.	7372	E	760 438-7781	16305
Electronic Online Systems International	7373	D	760 431-8400	16441
Cofa Media Group LLC	7374	D	877 293-2007	16487
Rockstar San Diego Inc.	7374	D	760 929-0700	16511
Z57 Inc.	7374	D	858 623-5577	16523
Alphabold	7379	D	949 637-7148	16551
Boughts Inc.	7379	E	619 895-7246	16557
Exois Inc.	7379	C	408 777-6630	16567
Transprttion Oprtion MGT Slton	7389	C	858 391-0260	16947
El Camino Rental	7513	E	760 438-7368	16969
Legend Films	7819	B	858 793-4420	17256
24 Hour Fitness Usa LLC (HQ)	7991	C	925 543-3100	17389
24 Hour Fitness Worldwide Inc	7991	A	925 543-3100	17390
Jazzercise Inc (PA)	7991	D	760 476-1750	17401
Tri-City Hospital District.	7991	B	760 931-3171	17417
Legoland California LLC	7996	B	760 450-3661	17450
Sente Inc.	8011	E	800 205-6774	17762
Carbon Health Technologies Inc.	8031	C	760 603-3221	17850
Vista JV Partners LLC	8049	B	214 738-2771	17874
Sunrise Senior Living MGT Inc.	8051	C	760 720-9898	18060
North Coast Home Care Inc.	8082	D	760 260-8700	18631
Che Behavioral Health Services.	8099	C	760 300-3664	18753
Monarch Hlthcare A Med Group I.	8099	C	760 730-9448	18782
Nalu Medical Inc.	8099	C	760 603-8466	18783
Gemological Institute Amer Inc (PA)	8249	A	760 603-4000	19003
Buffini & Company (PA)	8331	C	760 827-2100	19178
Unite Hair	8631	D	760 585-1800	19417
Carlsbad Firefighters Assn.	8699	D	760 729-3730	19527
One Sun Power Inc.	8711	A	844 360-9600	19659
Rialto Bioenergy Facility LLC.	8711	C	760 436-8870	19679
Navigate Biopharma Svcs Inc.	8731	C	866 992-4939	19864
Hisamitsu Pharmaceutical Co Inc.	8733	A	760 931-1756	19927
Sciencell Research Labs Inc.	8733	E	760 602-8549	19942
Ncn Management LLC.	8741	C	800 275-3243	20066
Sethi Management Inc.	8741	C	760 692-5288	20092
Corporate Visions Inc.	8742	C	760 458-0914	20157
Human Resource Capitl Cons Inc.	8742	C	760 518-8816	20182
Reel Axis Inc.	8742	F	760 826-9246	20229
Camston Wrather LLC.	8744	C	858 525-9999	20290
3E Company Env Ec n Eng (PA)	8748	C	760 602-8700	20304
By Referral Only Inc.	8748	D	760 707-1300	20321

CARPINTERIA, CA - Santa Barbara County

Company	SIC	EMP	PHONE	ENTRY#
Jimenez Nursery Inc.	0181	D	805 684-7955	58
Normans Nursery Inc.	0181	C	805 684-1411	62
Westerlay Orchids LP	0181	C	805 684-5411	73
Dsy Educational Corporation.	2399	E	805 684-8111	2549
Nusil Technology LLC (DH)	3069	B	805 684-8780	4781
Forms and Surfaces Company LLC	3272	C	805 684-8626	5414
Forms and Surfaces Inc.	3446	E	805 684-8626	6358
Supersprings International Inc.	3493	E	805 745-5553	6785
Clipper Windpower PLC	3511	A	805 690-3275	6879
Dac International Inc.	3541	E	805 684-8307	7009
Rincon Engineering Corporation.	3599	E	805 684-0935	8000
Rincon Engineering Tech.	3599	E	805 684-4144	8001
Te Connectivity Corporation.	3625	E	805 684-4560	8194
Zbe Inc.	3625	E	805 576-1600	8198
Bega North America Inc.	3648	D	805 684-0533	8354
Essex Electronics Inc.	3674	E	805 684-7601	8795
Agilent Technologies Inc.	3825	E	805 566-6655	10180

2024 Southern California
Business Directory and Buyers Guide
(P-0000) Products & Services Section entry number
(PA)=Parent Co (HQ)=Headquarters (DH)=Div Headquarters

	SIC	EMP	PHONE	ENTRY#
Agilent Technologies Inc	3825	D	805 566-1405	10181
Freudenberg Medical LLC **(DH)**	3842	C	805 684-3304	10663
Freudenberg Medical LLC	3842	D	805 576-5308	10664
Freudenberg Medical LLC	3842	E	805 684-3304	10665
Inhealth Technologies	3842	C	800 477-5969	10672
Pacifica Beauty LLC	3999	D	844 332-8440	11260
Dako North America Inc	5122	B	805 566-6655	13036
Smart & Final Stores Inc	5141	B	805 566-2174	13198
Applied Silicone Company LLC	5169	C	805 525-5657	13424
Normans Nursery Inc	5193	C	805 684-5442	13516
Plan Member Financial Corp	6282	D	800 874-6910	14427
AGIA Inc **(PA)**	6411	C	805 566-9191	14554
Procore Technologies Inc **(PA)**	7371	A	866 477-6267	16098
Qad Inc	7372	F	805 684-6614	16357

CARSON, CA - Los Angeles County

	SIC	EMP	PHONE	ENTRY#
Gs Brothers Inc **(PA)**	0782	C	310 833-1369	193
OConnell Landscape Maint Inc	0782	A	800 339-1106	209
Ampam Parks Mechanical Inc	1711	A	310 835-1532	731
Clay Dunn Enterprises Inc	1711	C	310 549-1698	754
General Mills Inc	2026	D	310 605-6108	1311
Giuliano-Pagano Corporation	2051	D	310 537-7700	1473
Anheuser-Busch LLC	2082	E	310 761-4600	1579
Sazerac Company Inc	2085	D	310 604-8717	1675
Pepsi-Cola Metro Btlg Co Inc	2086	E	310 327-4222	1714
American Fruits & Flavors LLC	2087	E	310 522-1844	1751
Southwind Foods LLC **(PA)**	2091	C	323 262-8222	1796
Arctic Glacier USA Inc	2097	C	310 638-0321	1835
Mountain Water Ice Company Inc **(PA)**	2097	C	310 638-0321	1838
Bristol Farms **(HQ)**	2099	D	310 233-4700	1860
Cedarlane Natural Foods Inc **(PA)**	2099	D	310 886-7720	1868
Kts Kitchens Inc	2099	C	310 764-0850	1923
Dynamex Corporation	2298	C	310 329-0399	2131
Js Apparel Inc	2329	E	310 631-6333	2210
Cali-Fame Los Angeles Inc	2353	C	310 747-5263	2399
The Enkeboll Co	2431	E	310 532-1400	2637
Cal-Coast Pkg & Crating Inc	2441	E	310 518-7215	2711
Morettis Design Collection Inc	2511	E	310 638-5555	2781
Arktura LLC **(HQ)**	2519	E	310 532-1050	2868
Oak-It Inc	2541	E	310 719-3999	2962
Salsbury Industries Inc **(PA)**	2542	B	800 624-5269	2991
International Paper Company	2621	E	310 549-5525	3050
Empire Container Corporation	2653	D	310 537-8190	3098
Elite 4 Print Inc	2752	E	310 366-1344	3569
Marchem Technologies LLC	2819	E	310 638-9352	3897
Avient Corporation	2821	E	310 513-7100	3926
Ineos Polypropylene LLC	2821	E	310 847-8523	3947
AOE International Inc	2834	E		4053
Leiner Health Products Inc **(DH)**	2834	C	631 200-2000	4156
Simpson Industries Inc	2834	E	310 605-1224	4236
Cosway Company Inc **(PA)**	2844	E	310 900-4100	4398
Dermalogica LLC **(HQ)**	2844	C	310 900-4000	4402
Dan-Loc Group LLC	3053	D	310 538-2322	4725
Johnson Laminating Coating Inc	3083	D	310 635-4929	4834
Altium Packaging LLC	3085	D	310 952-8736	4856
Caplugs Inc	3089	E	310 900-8323	4983
CCL Tube Inc **(HQ)**	3089	C	310 635-4444	4987
Trinity International Inds LLC	3089	E	800 985-5506	5234
Avalon Glass & Mirror Company	3231	D	323 321-8806	5334
Pacific Toll Processing Inc	3312	E	310 952-4992	5595
East West Enterprises	3315	E	310 632-9933	5614
Howmet Corporation	3324	A	310 847-8152	5654
Belden Inc	3357	A	310 639-9473	5731
Wavenet Inc **(PA)**	3357	F	310 885-4200	5752
Mag Aerospace Industries LLC	3431	B	801 400-7944	5959
Capital Cooking Equipment Inc	3433	D	562 903-1168	5978
Crate Modular Inc	3448	D	310 405-0829	6375
Huck International Inc	3452	D	310 830-8200	6445
Research Tool & Die Works LLC	3469	D	310 639-5722	6553
Calwest Galvanizing Corp	3479	D	310 549-2200	6696
Quality Magnetics Corporation	3499	E	310 632-1941	6872
Samtech Automotive Usa Inc	3542	E	310 638-9955	7039
Mestek Inc	3585	C	310 835-7500	7619
A & R Engineering Co Inc	3599	E	310 603-9060	7726
Universal Plant Svcs Cal Inc	3599	E	310 618-1600	8056
DMC Power Inc **(PA)**	3643	E	310 323-1616	8261
Dmf Inc	3645	D	323 934-7779	8292
Yun Industrial Co Ltd	3672	E	310 715-1898	8754
Sac-TEC Labs Inc **(PA)**	3674	E	310 375-5295	8882
Daico Industries Inc	3679	D	310 507-3242	9027
Strike Technology Inc	3679	E	562 437-3428	9122
Coast Wire & Plastic Tech LLC	3699	A	310 639-9473	9199
Refrigrated Trck Solutions LLC	3715	E	323 594-4500	9495

	SIC	EMP	PHONE	ENTRY#
Boeing Company	3721	C	310 522-2809	9514
Ducommun Aerostructures Inc	3728	C	310 513-7200	9675
Ducommun Labarge Tech Inc **(HQ)**	3728	C	310 513-7200	9680
Hydroform USA Incorporated	3728	C	310 632-6353	9714
Long-Lok LLC	3728	E	424 209-8726	9738
Safran Cabin Inc	3728	C	714 934-0000	9787
Zodiac Wtr Waste Aero Systems	3728	C	310 884-7000	9832
Stanford Mu Corporation	3769	C	310 605-2888	9921
Mp Solutions Inc	3812	E		10003
Megiddo Global LLC	3842	E	844 477-7007	10682
Proma Inc	3843	E	310 327-0035	10763
Sage Goddess Inc	3911	E	650 733-6639	10910
C Preme Limited LLC	3949	E	310 355-0498	10982
Chris Putrimas	3999	E	877 434-1666	11207
Nano Filter Inc	3999	D	949 316-8866	11253
Premier Cold Storage & Pkg LLC	4222	E	949 444-8859	11556
Tri-Modal Dist Svcs Inc	4225	D	310 522-1844	11624
Air Group Leasing Inc	4731	A	310 684-4095	11738
Mainfreight Inc **(HQ)**	4731	D	310 900-1974	11782
Quik Pick Express LLC	4731	C	310 763-3000	11796
Supra National Express Inc	4731	C	310 549-7105	11807
Yusen Logistics Americas Inc	4731	C	310 518-3008	11818
Whaling Packaging Co	4783	E	310 518-6021	11824
Apw Knox-Seeman Warehouse Inc **(HQ)**	5013	D	310 604-4373	12231
New Age Electronics Inc	5044	C	310 549-0000	12387
JB Dental Supply Co Inc **(PA)**	5047	C	310 202-8855	12495
Parter Medical Products Inc	5047	C	310 327-4417	12505
Long-Lok Fasteners Corporation	5072	F	424 213-4570	12725
Porteous Enterprises Inc **(DH)**	5072	C	310 549-9180	12731
Industrial Parts Depot LLC **(HQ)**	5084	D	310 530-1900	12792
Pro Safety Inc	5084	E	562 364-7450	12811
Western Refining Inc	5084	E	310 834-1297	12840
West Coast Aerospace Inc	5085	F	310 518-0633	12888
System Supply Stationery Corp	5112	F	310 223-0880	13000
H D Smith LLC	5122	D	641 681-1885	13044
SO Tech/Spcl Op Tech Inc **(PA)**	5131	E	310 202-9007	13093
Osata Enterprises Inc	5139	D	888 445-6237	13163
US Foods Inc	5149	C	310 632-6265	13405
Cirrus Enterprises LLC	5162	D	310 204-6159	13410
Coastal Doors	5211	E	562 665-5585	13570
Home Depot USA Inc	5211	C	310 835-7547	13610
Dianas Mexican Food Pdts Inc	5411	E	310 834-4886	13696
Southern Cal Disc Tire Co Inc	5531	C	310 324-2569	13880
Carson Operating Company LLC	7011	E	310 830-9200	15108
Transcentra Inc	7373	B	310 603-0105	16474
North Amrcn SEC Investigations	7381	D	323 634-1901	16663
Qualis Automotive LLC	7538	C	859 689-7772	17036
Interface Welding	7699	E	310 323-4944	17135
Anschutz Sthern Cal Spt Cmplex	7999	C	310 630-2000	17540
Kaiser Foundation Hospitals	8093	C	310 513-6707	18699
Forensic Analytical Spc Inc	8734	D	310 763-2374	19972

CASTAIC, CA - Los Angeles County

	SIC	EMP	PHONE	ENTRY#
Castaic Truck Stop Inc	2911	E	661 295-1374	4639
County of Los Angeles	8069	D	661 223-8700	18526

CATHEDRAL CITY, CA - Riverside County

	SIC	EMP	PHONE	ENTRY#
Palm Springs Motors Inc	5511	C	760 699-6695	13810
Whv Resort Group Inc	7011	A	760 770-9755	15418
Big Lgue Dreams Consulting LLC	7032	C	760 324-5600	15434
T Allance One - Palm Sprng LLC	7999	D	760 322-7000	17568
Califrnia Dept Dvlpmental Svcs	8099	B	760 770-6248	18749

CERRITOS, CA - Los Angeles County

	SIC	EMP	PHONE	ENTRY#
Zero Energy Contracting Inc	1711	C	626 701-3180	839
Zero Energy Contracting LLC	1711	D	626 701-3180	840
Helix Electric Inc	1731	A	562 941-7200	906
Captek Holdings LLC	2023	F	562 921-9511	1266
Better Beverages Inc **(PA)**	2087	E	562 924-8321	1757
T Hasegawa USA Inc **(HQ)**	2087	E	714 522-1900	1786
AB Mauri Food Inc	2099	E	562 483-4619	1845
Fleischmanns Vinegar Company Inc **(DH)**	2099	E	562 483-4619	1894
Dool Fna Inc	2221	E	562 483-4100	2037
Insta-Lettering Machine Co **(PA)**	2253	E	562 404-3000	2071
LA Triumph Inc	2326	E	562 404-7657	2178
Caravan Canopy Intl Inc	2394	E	714 367-3000	2502
Eide Industries Inc	2394	E	562 402-8335	2503
Spacestor Inc	2521	E	310 410-0220	2899
Villa Furniture Mfg Co	2531	E	714 535-7272	2939
Award Packaging Spc Corp	2653	E	323 727-1200	3080
Triple A Containers Inc	2653	E	562 404-7433	3133
Non-Stop Label Corp	2679	F	562 949-2885	3240
Molino Company	2752	D	323 726-1000	3640

Employee Codes: A=Over 500 employees, B=251-500
C=101-250, D=51-100, E=20-50, F=10-19, G=1-9

2024 Southern California
Business Directory and Buyers Guide

© Mergent Inc. 1-800-342-5647

1351

GEOGRAPHIC

	SIC	EMP	PHONE	ENTRY#
Printing Management Associates	2752	F	562 407-9977	3664
Resource Label Group LLC	2752	F	562 926-1432	3679
Blc Wc Inc (PA)	2759	C	562 926-1452	3738
Apperson Inc (PA)	2761	D	562 356-3333	3828
Captek Softgel Intl Inc (DH)	2834	B	562 921-9511	4081
International Coatings Co Inc (PA)	2891	E	562 926-1010	4570
Artistic Coverings Inc	3086	E	562 404-9343	4873
Foam Molders and Specialties	3086	E	562 924-7757	4884
Foam Molders and Specialties (PA)	3086	E	562 924-7757	4885
Ips Industries Inc	3089	D	562 623-2555	5063
WCP Inc	3089	D	562 653-9797	5247
Pankl Aerospace Systems	3369	D	562 207-6300	5817
Madison Inc of Oklahoma	3441	D	918 224-6990	6043
Blairs Metal Polsg Pltg Co Inc	3471	F	562 860-7106	6592
Bermingham Cntrls Inc A Cal Co (PA)	3491	E	562 860-0463	6754
Clio Inc	3495	E	562 926-3724	6802
Para-Plate & Plastics Co Inc	3555	E	562 404-3434	7189
Atlas Copco Compressors LLC	3563	E	562 484-6370	7306
Aline Systems Corporation	3565	E	562 229-9727	7344
Mpd Holdings Inc	3577	E	213 210-2591	7555
Olea Kiosks Inc	3577	D	562 924-2644	7556
ARI Industries Inc	3585	D	714 993-3700	7600
Refrigerator Manufacturers LLC	3585	E	562 926-2006	7622
Advanced Uv Inc (PA)	3589	E	562 407-0299	7635
A & H Engineering & Mfg Inc	3599	E	562 623-9717	7724
West Coast Switchgear (DH)	3613	D	562 802-3441	8132
Calnetix Technologies LLC (HQ)	3621	D	562 293-1660	8136
Twin Eagles Inc	3631	C	562 802-3488	8225
Refriderator Manufacturers LLC	3632	E	562 229-0500	8227
Refrigerator Manufacturers Inc (PA)	3632	E	562 926-2006	8228
Big 5 Electronics Inc	3651	E	562 941-4669	8401
IPC Cal Flex Inc	3672	E	714 952-0373	8689
Corelis Inc	3679	E	562 926-6727	9022
Lapco West LLC	3714	E	562 348-4850	9411
Parts Expediting and Dist Co	3714	F	562 944-3199	9438
Sedenquist-Fraser Entps Inc	3714	E	562 924-5763	9458
UFO Designs	3714	E	562 924-5763	9478
Ctcoa LLC	3728	E	562 407-5375	9668
Razor USA LLC (PA)	3751	D	562 345-6000	9881
Alpha Dental of Utah Inc	3843	D	562 467-7759	10728
US Dental Inc	3843	E	562 404-3500	10776
Dji Technology Inc	3861	D	818 235-0789	10864
United Parcel Service Inc	4215	B	562 404-3236	11541
Skylink Travel Inc	4724	C	212 380-2438	11726
Silver Hawk Freight Inc	4731	E	562 404-0226	11803
R1 Concepts Inc (PA)	5013	E	714 777-2323	12254
Microtek Lab Inc (HQ)	5044	C	310 687-5823	12386
Arjo Inc	5047	B	714 412-1170	12471
McNichols Company	5051	F	562 921-3344	12559
Memorex Products Inc	5064	C	562 653-2800	12634
NSK Precision America Inc	5085	D	562 968-1000	12869
Southern Glzers Wine Sprits LL	5182	B	562 926-2000	13481
Midway International Inc	5199	D	800 826-2383	13548
Polycell Packaging Corporation	5199	E	562 483-6000	13554
Bargain Rent-A-Car	5511	C	562 865-7447	13739
Docusource Inc	5999	D	562 447-2600	14131
Enterprise Bank & Trust	6022	C	562 345-9092	14194
Sun West Mortgage Company Inc (PA)	6162	C	562 326-5732	14350
Caremore Health Plan (HQ)	6321	C	562 622-2950	14451
Private Medical-Care Inc	6324	A	562 924-8311	14492
Allstate Floral Inc	6411	C	562 926-2989	14557
Auto Insurance Specialists LLC (DH)	6411	C	562 345-6247	14562
Carelon Bhavioral Hlth Cal Inc	6411	A	800 228-1286	14571
Poliseek Ais Insur Sltions Inc	6411	D	866 480-7335	14622
Eplica Inc	7361	C	562 977-4300	15842
Lloyd Staffing Inc	7363	F	631 777-7600	15926
Auditboard Inc (PA)	7371	D	877 769-5444	15970
Secure One Data Solutions LLC	7374	D	562 924-7056	16515
Geek Squad Inc	7379	D	562 402-1555	16568
Commercial Protective Svcs Inc	7381	A	310 515-5290	16630
College Hospital Inc (PA)	8063	B	562 924-9581	18511
Axelacare Holdings Inc	8082	C	714 522-8802	18591
Atkinson Andlson Loya Ruud Rom (PA)	8111	C	562 653-3200	18821
Thermal Engrg Intl USA Inc (HQ)	8711	D	323 726-0641	19704
Biospace Inc	8731	D	323 932-6503	19829
Caremore Medical Management Company	8741	A	562 741-4300	20011
Management Trust Assn Inc	8742	C	562 926-3372	20193
Physicians Datatrust Inc	8742	C	562 860-8771	20219
City of Cerritos	9111	C	562 916-8500	20403

CHATSWORTH, CA - Los Angeles County

	SIC	EMP	PHONE	ENTRY#
Synear Foods Usa LLC	1541	E	818 341-3588	521
Service Genius Los Angeles Inc	1711	D	818 200-3379	821

	SIC	EMP	PHONE	ENTRY#
Comet Electric Inc	1731	C	818 340-0965	882
OBryant Electric Inc (PA)	1731	C	818 407-1986	921
Pacific Coast Cabling Inc (PA)	1731	E	818 407-1911	922
Jt Windows Inc	1751	E	818 709-7950	1017
We The Pie People LLC	2024	E	818 349-1880	1302
Avitex Inc (PA)	2211	E	818 994-6487	2011
Med Couture Inc	2326	D	214 231-2500	2180
Strategic Distribution L P	2326	C	818 671-2100	2186
Almack Liners Inc	2335	E	818 718-5878	2274
Apparel Prod Svcs Globl LLC	2339	E	818 700-3700	2303
Academic Ch Choir Gwns Mfg Inc	2389	E	818 886-8697	2437
Califrnia Dluxe Wndows Inds In (PA)	2431	E	818 349-5566	2588
Tessa Mia Corp	2434	E	877 740-5757	2680
Woodpecker Cabinets Inc	2434	E	310 404-4805	2685
Heritage Cabinet Co Inc	2541	F	818 786-4900	2954
Califrnia Trade Converters Inc	2631	E	818 899-1455	3065
Pencil Grip Inc (PA)	2678	F	310 315-3545	3222
Avn Media Network Inc	2731	E	818 718-5788	3398
Narcotics Annymous Wrld Svcs I (PA)	2731	E	818 773-9999	3411
Cal Southern Graphics Corp (HQ)	2752	D	310 559-3600	3524
Impress Communications Inc	2752	D	818 701-8800	3594
Pacer Print	2752	E	888 305-3144	3649
Labeling Hurst Systems LLC	2759	F	818 701-0710	3778
Pioneer Photo Albums Inc (PA)	2782	C	818 882-2161	3839
H2u Technologies Inc	2813	E	626 344-0505	3866
Erbaviva Inc	2833	E	818 998-7112	3998
Bio-Nutraceuticals Inc (PA)	2834	F	818 727-0246	4072
Natrol Inc	2834	C	818 739-6000	4177
Natrol LLC (PA)	2834	C	818 739-6000	4178
Henkel US Operations Corp	2843	E	818 435-0889	4373
Aware Products Inc	2844	F	818 206-6700	4380
Aware Products LLC	2844	C	818 206-6700	4381
Classic Cosmetics Inc (PA)	2844	E	818 773-9042	4388
Clm Group Inc	2844	E	818 349-2549	4389
Formology Lab Inc	2844	E	424 452-0377	4411
Kdc/One Chatsworth Inc (DH)	2844	C	818 709-1345	4427
Kdc/One Chatsworth Inc	2844	C	818 709-1345	4428
Neutraderm Inc	2844	E	818 534-3190	4437
Radiance Beauty & Wellness Inc	2844	E	818 812-9740	4450
Samuel Raoof	2844	E	818 534-3180	4452
Aerojet Rocketdyne De Inc	2869	C	818 586-1000	4512
Teledyne Risi Inc (HQ)	2892	E	818 718-6640	4585
Line One Laboratories Inc USA	3069	F	818 886-2288	4775
3d Cam Inc	3089	E	818 407-0220	4924
A & S Mold and Die Corp	3089	D	818 341-5393	4925
Lehrer Brllnprfktion Werks Inc	3089	D	818 407-1890	5084
Dwa Composite Specialties Inc	3354	F	818 885-8654	5695
Ftg Aerospace Inc (DH)	3364	C	818 407-4024	5775
Dwa Aluminum Composites USA Inc	3365	E	818 998-1504	5791
Metal Improvement Company LLC	3398	D	818 407-6280	5845
Alliance Metal Products Inc	3444	C	818 709-1204	6184
Armorcast Products Company Inc (DH)	3444	C	818 982-3600	6191
Dynamo Aviation Inc	3444	D	818 785-9561	6229
Keith E Archambeau Sr Inc	3444	C	818 718-6110	6260
Quality Fabrication Inc (PA)	3444	D	818 407-5015	6299
Federal Manufacturing Corp	3452	E	818 341-9825	6441
Golden Bolt LLC	3452	E	818 626-8261	6443
Verdugo Tool & Engrg Co Inc	3469	F	818 998-1101	6566
Metal Chem Inc	3471	E	818 727-9951	6638
Plateronics Processing Inc	3471	E	818 341-2191	6649
Networks Electronic Co LLC	3489	E	818 341-0440	6750
Aquasyn LLC	3491	E	818 350-0423	6753
RPS Inc	3496	E	818 350-8088	6828
Bey-Berk International (PA)	3499	E	818 773-7534	6857
Double K Industries Inc	3523	F	818 772-2887	6904
Invelop Inc	3523	E	818 772-2887	6906
Tig/M LLC	3535	E	818 709-8500	6979
Colbrit Manufacturing Co Inc	3544	E	818 709-3608	7061
Precise Die and Finishing	3544	E	818 773-9337	7088
John List Corporation	3547	E	818 882-7848	7151
NMB (usa) Inc (HQ)	3562	E	818 709-1770	7302
Delta Tau Data Systems Inc Cal (HQ)	3569	C	818 998-2095	7389
Aleratec Inc	3571	E	818 678-6900	7415
Vmc Holdings Group Corp	3571	E	818 993-1466	7457
Globalvision Systems Inc	3572	E	888 227-7967	7471
BDR Industries Inc	3577	E	818 341-2112	7509
Best Data Products Inc	3577	D	818 534-1414	7511
Ciphertex LLC	3577	E	818 773-8989	7515
Logicube Inc (PA)	3577	C	888 494-8832	7543
Toye Corporation	3577	E	818 882-4000	7573
Meissner Mfg Co Inc (PA)	3589	E	818 678-0400	7674
RTC Arspace - Chtswrth Div Inc (PA)	3593	C	818 341-3344	7709
3dcam International Corp	3599	F	818 773-8777	7719

Mergent email: customerrelations@mergent.com
1352

2024 Southern California
Business Directory and Buyers Guide

(P-0000) Products & Services Section entry number
(PA)=Parent Co (HQ)=Headquarters (DH)=Div Headquarters

Company	SIC	EMP	PHONE	ENTRY#
Aben Machine Products Inc	3599	F	818 960-4502	7728
Aero Mechanism Precision Inc	3599	E	818 886-1855	7742
Aram Precision Tool & Die Inc	3599	E	818 998-1000	7758
Delta Fabrication Inc	3599	D	818 407-4000	7815
Delta Hi-Tech	3599	C	818 407-4000	7816
Expand Machinery LLC	3599	F	818 349-9166	7828
Houston Ontic Inc	3599	F	818 678-6555	7867
International Precision Inc	3599	F	818 882-3933	7874
Molnar Engineering Inc	3599	E	818 993-3495	7944
Mono Engineering Corp	3599	E	818 772-4998	7946
O & S Precision Inc	3599	E	818 718-8876	7958
Roy & Val Tool Grinding Inc	3599	E	818 341-2434	8008
SARR Industries Inc	3599	E	818 998-7735	8015
United Precision Corp	3599	E	818 576-9540	8055
Wallace E Miller Inc	3599	E	818 998-0444	8071
Jackson Engineering Co Inc	3612	E	818 886-9567	8099
Custom Control Sensors LLC (PA)	3613	C	818 341-4610	8119
Resmed Motor Technologies Inc	3621	C	818 428-6400	8154
Custom Control Sensors Inc	3625	E	818 341-4610	8176
Litepanels Inc	3641	E	818 752-7009	8250
Electro Adapter Inc	3643	D	818 998-1198	8262
Micro Plastics Inc	3643	F	818 882-0244	8271
Lf Illumination LLC	3646	D	818 885-1335	8319
Medical Illumination International Inc (PA)	3646	E	818 838-3025	8322
Lighting Control & Design Inc	3648	E	323 226-0000	8373
Pacific Coast Lighting Inc (HQ)	3648	F	800 709-9004	8378
Truly Green Solutions LLC	3648	E	818 206-4404	8387
Epic Technologies LLC	3661	A	908 707-4085	8471
Dynamic Sciences Intl Inc	3663	E	818 226-6262	8511
Telemtry Cmmnctons Systems Inc	3663	E	818 718-6248	8588
Canoga Perkins Corporation (HQ)	3669	D	818 718-6300	8603
Newvac LLC	3671	C	310 990-0401	8635
Newvac LLC	3671	E	747 202-7333	8636
Circuit Services Llc	3672	E	818 701-5391	8662
Ftg Circuits Inc (DH)	3672	E	818 407-4024	8679
Natel Engineering Holdings Inc	3672	F	818 734-6500	8709
Oncore Manufacturing Svcs Inc	3672	C	510 360-2222	8713
United International Tech Inc	3672	E	818 772-9400	8747
We Imagine Inc	3672	D	818 709-0064	8751
Iog Products LLC	3674	E	818 350-5077	8817
Mrv Communications Inc	3674	B	818 773-0900	8848
Source Photonics Usa Inc	3674	B	818 407-5007	8896
Stellar Microelectronics Inc	3674	C	661 775-3500	8898
Mercury Magnetics Inc	3677	E	818 998-7791	8947
Celesco Transducer Products	3679	E	818 701-2701	9015
Dytran Instruments Inc	3679	E	818 700-7818	9033
Natel Engineering Company LLC (PA)	3679	C	818 495-8617	9088
Newvac LLC	3679	E	747 202-7333	9089
RJA Industries Inc	3679	E	818 998-5124	9107
Aitech Defense Systems Inc	3699	D	818 700-2000	9193
Aitech Rugged Group Inc (PA)	3699	E	818 700-2000	9194
Soundcraft Inc	3699	E	818 882-0020	9256
Automoco LLC	3714	E	707 544-4761	9357
Sway-A-Way Inc	3714	E	818 700-9712	9466
Logistical Support LLC	3724	C	818 341-3344	9575
Alatus Aerosystems	3728	D	626 498-7376	9615
Alatus Aerosystems (PA)	3728	D	610 965-1630	9616
Alatus Aerosystems	3728	D	714 732-0559	9617
Align Aerospace LLC (PA)	3728	B	818 727-7800	9618
Hydraulics International Inc (PA)	3728	B	818 998-1231	9709
Hydraulics International Inc	3728	E	818 998-1236	9710
Hydraulics International Inc	3728	E	818 998-1231	9711
Cliffdale Manufacturing LLC	3769	C	818 341-3344	9915
Hydromach Inc	3769	E	818 341-0915	9918
Aeroantenna Technology Inc	3812	E	818 993-3842	9937
Firan Tech Group USA Corp (HQ)	3812	D	818 407-4024	9976
Moog Inc	3812	D	818 341-5156	10001
Sensor Systems Inc	3812	B	818 341-5366	10070
Space Vector Corporation	3812	E	818 734-2600	10072
Renau Corporation	3823	E	818 341-1994	10155
Intelligent Cmpt Solutions Inc (PA)	3825	E	818 998-5805	10205
Teledyne Hanson Research Inc	3826	E	818 882-7266	10291
Teledyne Instruments Inc	3826	E	818 882-7266	10292
Optical Corporation (DH)	3827	E	818 725-9750	10332
Photo Research Inc	3827	E	818 341-5151	10334
California Dynamics Corp (PA)	3829	E	323 223-3882	10357
Measurement Specialties Inc	3829	D	818 701-2750	10380
Ansell Sndel Med Solutions LLC	3842	E	818 534-2500	10637
Boyd Chatsworth Inc	3842	D	818 998-1477	10640
Selane Products Inc (PA)	3843	E	818 998-7460	10767
Photo-Sonics Inc (PA)	3861	E	818 842-2141	10879
General Ribbon Corp	3955	B	818 709-1234	11057
Planet Green Cartridges Inc	3955	D	818 725-2596	11060
Vision Imaging Supplies Inc	3955	E	818 885-4515	11064
Maxwell Alarm Screen Mfg Inc	3993	E	818 773-5533	11134
Schea Holdings Inc	3993	E	818 998-3636	11156
Sign Image Inc	3993	E	818 772-1393	11158
Advanced Cosmetic RES Labs Inc	3999	E	818 709-9945	11187
Sega Holdings USA Inc	3999	A	415 701-6000	11279
TTT Innovations LLC	3999	E	818 201-8828	11301
Vbx Labs LLC	3999	E	747 256-0103	11303
Los Angles Cnty Mtro Trnsp Aut	4111	A	213 922-6308	11327
Southern California Gas Co	4922	B	818 701-2592	12080
Allstate Imaging Inc (PA)	5044	D	818 678-4550	12381
Levlad LLC	5047	C	818 882-2951	12497
Cooner Sales Company LLC (PA)	5051	F	818 882-8311	12544
PLC Imports Inc	5063	E	818 349-1600	12613
Regency Enterprises Inc (PA)	5063	B	818 901-0255	12615
Air Electro Inc (PA)	5065	C	818 407-5400	12642
Cbol Corporation	5065	C	818 704-8200	12653
Refrigeration Hdwr Sup Corp	5078	D	800 537-8300	12765
Maloof Naman Builders	5082	D	818 775-0040	12774
Wastech Controls & Engrg Inc	5084	D	818 998-3500	12835
Clover Envmtl Solutions LLC	5085	A	815 431-8100	12848
Pentacon Inc	5085	B	818 727-8000	12872
Logistical Support LLC	5088	C	818 341-3344	12912
Ontic Engineering and Mfg Inc (PA)	5088	D	818 678-6555	12913
MGA Entertainment Inc	5092	A	800 222-4685	12941
Medical Research Institute	5122	C	818 739-6000	13054
Piege Co (PA)	5137	D	818 727-9100	13142
Chemsil Silicones Inc	5169	E	818 700-0302	13429
Vijall Inc	5169	E	818 700-0071	13443
North Ranch Management Corp	5719	D	800 410-2153	13964
Gameworks Entertainment LLC (PA)	5812	A	206 521-0952	14010
Performance Automotive Whl Inc (PA)	5961	D	805 499-8973	14099
Cosmetic Laboratories of America LLC	5999	B	818 717-6140	14127
Sexy Hair Concepts LLC	5999	E	818 435-0800	14148
Telesis Community Credit Union (PA)	6061	D	818 885-1226	14239
Premier America Credit Union (PA)	6062	C	818 772-4000	14251
Nna Insurance Services LLC	6411	C	818 739-4071	14617
Platinum Group Companies Inc (PA)	6719	C	818 721-3800	14938
Bellami Hair LLC	7231	D	844 235-5264	15479
West Coast Coupon Inc	7319	E	818 341-2400	15604
Aaron Thomas & Associates Inc	7331	E	818 727-9040	15625
Tuttle Family Enterprises Inc	7349	B	818 534-2566	15751
Datadirect Networks Inc (PA)	7371	C	818 700-7600	16009
ADT LLC	7382	C	818 464-5001	16718
Guardian Integrated SEC Inc (PA)	7382	C	800 400-3167	16739
American Copak Corporation	7389	C	818 576-1000	16775
Roberts Container Corporation	7389	E	818 727-1700	16918
Seven One Inc (PA)	7389	D	818 904-3435	16925
Ironman Inc	7692	E	818 341-0980	17087
Cali Framing Supplies LLC	7699	E	818 899-7777	17118
Duclos Lenses Inc	7699	F	818 773-0600	17124
Genesis Tech Partners LLC	7699	C	800 950-2647	17130
Respawn Entertainment LLC	7812	C	818 960-4400	17213
Bay Clubs Company LLC	7991	B	805 778-0888	17394
Cpcc Inc	8059	D	818 882-3200	18119
Sierra Canyon Inc	8211	D	818 882-8121	18984
Child Care Resource Center Inc (PA)	8322	C	818 717-1000	19038
Rancho San Antonio Boys HM Inc (PA)	8361	D	818 882-6400	19296
Health Advocates LLC	8399	B	818 995-9500	19328
National Notary Association	8621	C	800 876-6827	19398
Accunex Inc	8711	E	818 882-5858	19540
Oncore Manufacturing LLC (HQ)	8711	A	818 734-6500	19658
Color Design Laboratory Inc (PA)	8734	D	818 341-5100	19964
North La County Regional Ctr (PA)	8748	B	818 778-1900	20368

CHINO, CA - San Bernardino County

Company	SIC	EMP	PHONE	ENTRY#
American Beef Packers Inc	0751	C	909 628-4888	132
DL Long Landscaping Inc	0781	D	909 628-5531	159
Generation Construction Inc	1521	C	909 923-2077	433
Flatiron West Inc	1622	C	909 597-8413	652
Warren Collins and Assoc Inc (PA)	1629	E	909 548-6708	721
Interior Experts Gen Bldrs Inc	1742	D	909 203-4922	980
Duke Pacific Inc	1761	D	909 591-0191	1043
Diversified Coatings Linings	1771	E	909 591-6366	1069
R & B Reinforcing Steel Corp	1791	E	909 591-1726	1112
Provena Foods Inc (HQ)	2013	D	909 627-1082	1231
Fenchem Inc (HQ)	2023	E	909 597-8880	1270
Ziegenfelder Company	2024	D	909 509-0493	1303
Ziegenfelder Company	2024	D	909 590-0493	1304
Hira Paris Inc	2064	C	909 634-3900	1542
Gluten Free Foods Mfg LLC (PA)	2099	E	909 823-8230	1903
Isiqalo LLC	2253	B	714 683-2820	2072
Omnia Leather Motion Inc	2392	C	909 393-4400	2480

Employee Codes: A=Over 500 employees, B=251-500
C=101-250, D=51-100, E=20-50, F=10-19, G=1-9

2024 Southern California
Business Directory and Buyers Guide

© Mergent Inc. 1-800-342-5647

1353

GEOGRAPHIC

	SIC	EMP	PHONE	ENTRY#
El & El Wood Products Corp **(DH)**	2431	D	909 591-0339	2599
Corona Millworks Company **(PA)**	2434	D	909 606-3288	2655
Hanson Truss Inc	2439	B	909 591-9256	2699
Alaco Ladder Company	2499	E	909 591-7561	2750
B E & P Enterprises LLC **(PA)**	2499	E	909 591-7561	2751
Mikhail Darafeev Inc	2511	D	909 613-1818	2780
Royal Custom Designs LLC	2512	C	909 591-8990	2816
Oak Design Corporation	2521	F	909 628-9597	2892
Eastwest Container Group Inc	2631	E	626 523-1523	3067
Contixo Inc	2678	E	909 465-5668	3221
GLS US Freight Inc	2741	E	909 627-2538	3450
Impact Printing & Graphics	2752	E	909 614-1678	3592
Teefor2 Inc	2752	F	909 613-0055	3696
Wright Business Graphics LLC	2761	E	909 614-6700	3834
Ferco Color Inc **(PA)**	2821	E	909 930-0773	3940
Vitajoy USA Inc	2833	E	626 965-8830	4022
Amphastar Pharmaceuticals Inc	2834	E	909 590-1828	4048
Genlabs **(PA)**	2842	C	909 591-8451	4350
Diamond Wipes Intl Inc	2844	E	909 230-9888	4405
Diamond Wipes Intl Inc **(PA)**	2844	D	909 230-9888	4406
Plz Corp	2844	D	909 393-9475	4448
Universal Packg Systems Inc **(PA)**	2844	A	909 517-2442	4464
Avient Colorants USA LLC	2869	E	909 606-1325	4513
Cal-India Foods International	2869	E	909 613-1660	4517
Specilty Enzymes Btechnologies	2869	F	909 613-1660	4530
Wacker Chemical Corporation	2869	D	909 590-8822	4537
Gro-Power Inc	2873	E	909 393-3744	4539
Roettele Industries	3053	E	909 606-8252	4741
Berry Global Films LLC	3081	C	909 517-2872	4807
Flexcon Company Inc	3081	C	909 465-0408	4811
Repet Inc	3083	C	909 594-5333	4842
Inter-Packing Inc	3086	F	909 465-5555	4891
Jacuzzi Products Co	3088	B	909 548-7732	4917
Acorn-Gencon Plastics LLC	3089	D	909 591-8461	4927
Altium Packaging LP	3089	E	909 590-7334	4938
Berry Global Inc	3089	C	909 465-9055	4961
C G Motor Sports Inc	3089	F	909 628-1440	4973
Dacha Enterprises Inc **(HQ)**	3089	E	951 273-7777	5000
Envision Plastics Industries LLC	3089	E	909 590-7334	5025
Karat Packaging Inc **(PA)**	3089	E	626 965-8882	5075
Liner Technologies Inc	3089	E	909 594-6610	5085
Norco Injection Molding Inc	3089	D	909 393-4000	5118
Norco Plastics Inc	3089	D	909 393-4000	5119
PRC Composites LLC	3089	E	909 464-1520	5156
Pretium Packaging LLC	3089	C	714 777-9580	5162
Spin Products Inc	3089	E	909 590-7000	5213
Syntech Development & Mfg Inc **(PA)**	3089	E	909 465-5554	5220
Tank Holding Corp	3089	B	952 446-1945	5223
West Cast Stl Proc Hldings LLC **(PA)**	3312	E	909 393-8405	5607
Wcs Equipment Holdings LLC **(HQ)**	3325	D	909 393-8405	5666
Texas Tst Inc	3341	E	951 685-2155	5684
Tst Inc **(PA)**	3341	B	951 685-2155	5685
Superior Metal Shapes Inc	3354	E	909 947-3455	5711
Kemper Enterprises Inc	3423	E	909 627-6191	5884
Larin Corp	3423	E	909 464-0605	5885
Acornvac Inc	3432	E	909 902-1141	5961
Kumar Industries	3441	E	909 591-0722	6038
South Gate Engineering LLC	3443	C	909 628-2779	6157
Great Pacific Elbow LLC	3444	E	909 606-6551	6248
Trend Technologies LLC **(DH)**	3444	C	909 597-7861	6334
Wcs Equipment Holdings LLC	3444	D	909 393-8405	6343
Dupree Inc	3452	E	909 597-4889	6440
Spring R&D & Stamp Inc	3469	F	909 465-5166	6558
RTS Powder Coating Inc **(PA)**	3479	E	909 393-5404	6732
C & M Spring Engrg Co Inc	3495	C	909 597-2030	6801
Top-Shelf Fixtures LLC	3496	D	909 627-7423	6829
Albers Mfg Co Inc **(PA)**	3523	E	909 597-5537	6898
Pdc LLC	3544	E	626 334-5000	7086
Wetmore Tool and Engrg Co	3545	D	909 364-1000	7141
Churchill Aerospace LLC	3546	E	909 266-3116	7144
Imperial Rubber Products Inc	3555	E	909 393-0528	7186
Morehouse-Cowles LLC	3559	E	909 627-7222	7250
Reed LLC	3561	E	909 287-2100	7288
Dick Farrell Industries Inc	3567	F	909 613-9424	7363
Shop4techcom	3572	E	909 248-2725	7485
Hussmann Corporation	3585	B	909 590-4910	7615
Aranda Tooling Inc	3599	D	714 379-6565	7759
Arnold-Gonsalves Engrg Inc	3599	E	909 465-1579	7761
Bti Aerospace & Electronics	3599	E	909 465-1569	7789
Fortune Manufacturing Inc	3599	E	909 591-1547	7834
Wahlco Inc	3599	C	714 979-7300	8070
Young Machine Inc	3599	F	909 464-0405	8085
Custom Magnetics Cal Inc	3612	E	909 620-3877	8091

	SIC	EMP	PHONE	ENTRY#
Desco Industries Inc **(PA)**	3629	D	909 627-8178	8204
Scott Engineering Inc	3629	D	909 594-9637	8213
Pacific Coast Mfg Inc	3631	D	909 627-7040	8220
Viking Range LLC	3631	E	909 662-3504	8226
T McGee Electric Inc	3643	F	909 591-6461	8278
Anthony California Inc **(PA)**	3645	E	909 627-0351	8287
Artiva USA Inc **(PA)**	3645	E	909 628-1388	8288
Base Lite Corporation	3645	E	909 444-2776	8290
Lights of America Inc **(PA)**	3645	B	909 594-7883	8294
Hi-Lite Manufacturing Co Inc	3646	D	909 465-1999	8316
Paclights LLC **(PA)**	3646	F	800 980-6386	8327
Yankon Industries Inc **(PA)**	3646	E	909 591-2345	8343
Delta Tech Industries LLC	3647	E	909 673-1900	8345
Vtl Amplifiers Inc	3651	E	909 627-5944	8450
Balaji Trading Inc	3661	D	909 444-7999	8468
General Photonics Corp	3661	D	909 590-5473	8474
Manley Laboratories Inc	3663	E	909 627-4256	8541
Asrock America Inc	3672	E	909 590-8308	8649
American Solar Advantage Inc	3674	E	877 765-2388	8764
R Kern Engineering & Mfg Corp	3678	D	909 664-2440	8980
Eaglerise E&E Inc	3679	E	215 675-5953	9034
Enersys	3691	E	909 464-8251	9145
Syston Cable Technology Corp	3699	E	888 679-7866	9261
Esslinger Engineering Inc	3714	E	909 539-0544	9389
Ht Multinational Inc	3714	E	909 325-8582	9403
McO Inc	3714	E	909 627-3574	9422
Rbw Industries Inc	3714	E	909 591-5359	9449
Soaring America Corporation	3721	E	909 270-2628	9553
Alvarado Manufacturing Co Inc	3829	C	909 591-8431	10351
Paiho North America Corp	3965	E	661 257-6611	11074
Myers & Sons Hi-Way Safety Inc **(PA)**	3993	D	909 591-1781	11139
National Sign & Marketing Corp	3993	D	909 591-4742	11140
Jacuzzi Brands LLC	3999	E	909 606-1416	11233
Macro Industries Inc	3999	F	909 606-2218	11246
Stang Industries Inc	3999	F	914 479-9810	11285
CRST Expedited Inc	4213	C	909 563-5606	11478
Schneider Electric Usa Inc	4225	D	909 438-2295	11611
Universal Packg Systems Inc	4225	C	909 517-2442	11627
Aviation Maintenance Group Inc	4581	D	714 469-0515	11690
Nationwide Trans Inc **(PA)**	4731	D	909 355-3211	11786
Advanced Multimodal Dist Inc	4789	C	800 838-3058	11826
Inland Empire Utlties Agcy A M **(PA)**	4941	D	909 993-1600	12123
Yoshimura RES & Dev Amer Inc	5013	D	909 628-4722	12267
Omnia Italian Design LLC	5021	C	909 393-4400	12289
Nexgrill Industries Inc **(PA)**	5023	D	909 598-8799	12310
A Plus International Inc **(PA)**	5047	E	909 591-5168	12466
Harrington Industrial Plas LLC **(PA)**	5074	D	909 597-8641	12744
Hill Phoenix Inc	5078	D	909 592-8830	12762
Consolidated Plastics Corp **(PA)**	5162	E	909 393-8222	13412
S & W Plastic Stores LLC **(PA)**	5162	D	909 390-0090	13418
General Electric Company	5169	F	909 517-2560	13433
Home Depot USA Inc	5211	C	909 393-5205	13604
M K Smith Chevrolet	5511	C	909 628-8961	13792
Kaiser Foundation Hospitals	6324	C	888 750-0036	14480
Mission Linen Supply	7213	C	909 393-6857	15453
Baronhr LLC	7361	D	909 517-3800	15818
Contract Labeling Service Inc	7389	E	909 937-0344	16805
Math Holdings Inc **(PA)**	7389	C	909 517-2200	16868
El Prado Golf Course LP	7992	D	909 597-1751	17426
Chino Medical Group Inc	8011	D	909 591-6446	17620
James M Lally Do	8011	D	909 464-8600	17673
Veritas Health Services Inc	8062	A	909 464-8600	18498
Canyon Ridge Hospital Inc	8063	B	909 590-3700	18509
West End Yung MNS Christn Assn	8641	C	909 597-7445	19472
Automobile Club Southern Cal	8699	C	909 591-9451	19516
Transtech Engineers Inc **(PA)**	8711	D	909 595-8599	19707
Hyundai Amer Technical Ctr Inc	8734	C	909 627-3525	19974
Lollicup Franchising LLC	8742	C	626 965-8882	20190

CHINO HILLS, CA - San Bernardino County

	SIC	EMP	PHONE	ENTRY#
Andrew LLC	2041	F	909 270-9356	1406
Jacuzzi Products Co **(DH)**	3088	C	909 606-1416	4916
Dur-Red Products	3444	E	323 771-9000	6228
Advanced Mold Technology Inc	3544	F		7047
Tri-Dim Filter Corporation	3564	E	626 826-5893	7336
Dynamic Enterprises Inc	3599	E	562 944-0271	7822
Victory Intl Group LLC	5092	C	949 407-5888	12947
Lowes Home Centers LLC	5211	C	909 438-9000	13644
Crmls LLC	6512	C	909 859-2040	14657
Gateway Fresh LLC	6719	C	951 378-5439	14930
Harkins Theatres Inc	7832	D	909 627-8010	17299
Los Serranos Golf Club	7992	C	909 597-1769	17435
Redwood Family Care Netwrk Inc	8011	A	909 942-0218	17750

Mergent email: customerrelations@mergent.com
1354

2024 Southern California
Business Directory and Buyers Guide

(P-0000) Products & Services Section entry number
(PA)=Parent Co (HQ)=Headquarters (DH)=Div Headquarters

	SIC	EMP	PHONE	ENTRY#
Sails Washington Inc	8082	B	425 333-4114	18639
Boys Republic **(PA)**	8361	C	909 902-6690	19241
SSC Construction Inc	8711	D	951 278-1177	19695

CHULA VISTA, CA - San Diego County

	SIC	EMP	PHONE	ENTRY#
Merchants Landscape Services	0782	D	619 778-6239	205
Sbhis	1522	D	619 427-2689	474
FJ Willert Contracting Co	1542	C	619 421-1980	551
Otay River Constructors LLC	1611	C	619 397-7500	637
Foshay Electric Co Inc	1731	D	858 277-7676	903
Home Carpet Investment Inc **(PA)**	1752	D	619 262-8040	1030
Legacy Reinforcing Steel LLC	1791	D	619 646-0205	1107
Source of Health Inc	2023	E	619 409-9500	1284
Otay Lakes Brewery LLC	2082	E	619 768-0172	1601
Boochery Inc	2085	D	619 207-0530	1672
Canvas Concepts Inc	2394	E	619 424-3428	2500
Stark Mfg Co	2394	E	619 425-5880	2509
Multitaskr	2434	E	619 391-3371	2669
San Diego Arcft Interiors Inc	2511	E	619 474-1997	2788
Califrnia Furn Collections Inc	2519	C	619 621-2455	2869
Latina & Associates Inc **(PA)**	2711	E	619 426-1491	3296
Passion Planner LLC	2741	E	619 777-3451	3471
Lamb Fuels Inc	2869	E	619 777-9135	4524
Ggtw LLC	2899	C	619 423-3388	4607
Sealed Air Corporation	3086	E	619 421-9003	4903
Nypro Inc	3089	D	619 498-9250	5125
Nypro San Diego Inc	3089	D	619 482-7033	5126
Tenma America Corporation	3089	E	619 754-2250	5225
Sandpiper of California Inc	3161	D	619 424-2222	5295
Aker International Inc	3199	E	619 423-5182	5305
RCP Block & Brick Inc	3271	E	619 474-1516	5394
Simec USA Corporation	3312	E	619 474-7081	5602
Precision Fiber Products Inc	3357	E	408 946-4040	5747
McMahon Steel Company Inc	3429	C	619 671-9700	5931
East Cast Repr Fabrication LLC	3441	E	619 591-9577	6022
Omega Ii Inc	3443	E	619 920-6650	6146
P A S U Inc	3444	E	619 421-1151	6281
Plenums Plus LLC	3444	D	619 422-5515	6294
Curtiss-Wright Corporation	3491	D	619 482-3405	6759
Flexible Metal Inc	3498	C	734 516-3017	6846
Lyon Technologies Inc	3523	E		6907
Harcon Precision Metals Inc	3531	E	619 423-5544	6935
Circor Naval Solutions LLC **(DH)**	3561	D	413 436-7711	7272
Xylem Water Systems (california) Inc	3561	E	619 575-7466	7295
Integrated Energy Technologies Inc	3562	C	619 421-1151	7300
American Metal Filter Company	3564	F	619 628-1917	7318
Hyspan Precision Products Inc **(PA)**	3568	D	619 421-1355	7378
SMK Manufacturing Inc	3575	E	619 216-6400	7500
Ace Industries Inc	3599	E	619 482-2700	7731
Advanced McHning Solutions Inc	3599	E	619 671-3055	7738
Miller Machine Works LLC	3599	F	619 501-9866	7938
Ichia USA Inc	3674	D	619 482-2222	8804
Kev-Ton Inc	3679	E	619 482-2600	9076
Tap Manufacturing LLC	3714	F	619 216-1444	9467
Astor Manufacturing	3728	E	661 645-5585	9633
Goodrich Corporation	3728	C	619 691-4111	9705
Rohr Inc **(HQ)**	3728	A	619 691-4111	9779
Colonnas Shipyard West LLC	3731	E	757 545-2414	9835
Integrated Marine Services Inc	3731	D	619 429-0300	9839
Adept Process Services Inc	3732	E	619 434-3194	9852
Bae Systems Land Armaments LP	3812	E	619 455-0213	9957
Vcp Mobility Holdings LLC	3842	C	619 213-6500	10720
Toleeto Fastener International	3965	E	619 662-1355	11078
Stanford Sign & Awning Inc **(PA)**	3993	C	619 423-6200	11168
Estes Express Lines	4213	A	619 425-4040	11488
United Parcel Service Inc	4215	C	619 482-8119	11545
San Diego Gas & Electric Co	4939	C	858 654-1135	12113
Sweetwter Auth Emplyees Cmmtte **(PA)**	4941	C	619 420-1413	12148
Samsung International Inc **(DH)**	5065	E	619 671-6001	12697
Heartland Meat Company Inc	5147	D	619 407-3668	13296
California Baking Company	5149	B	619 591-8289	13358
Culinary Hispanic Foods Inc	5149	A	619 955-6101	13365
Home Depot USA Inc	5211	C	619 421-0639	13597
Lowes Home Centers LLC	5211	C	619 739-9060	13648
Al Global Corporation **(HQ)**	5961	E	619 934-3980	14091
Amnet Esop Corporation	6162	C	877 354-1110	14297
Loandepot Inc	6162	B	619 245-0115	14336
State Farm General Insur Co	6411	D	619 227-5777	14632
Palanging International Inc	6531	D	619 948-2459	14839
West Edge Inc	6531	E	619 475-4095	14883
Otay Hospitality Inc	7011	E	619 422-2600	15280
Kineticom Inc **(PA)**	7361	C	619 330-3100	15861
Ado Staffing Inc	7363	C	619 691-3659	15911

	SIC	EMP	PHONE	ENTRY#
Rp Automotive II Inc	7513	D	619 656-2500	16974
Southcoast Welding & Mfg LLC	7692	B	619 429-1337	17095
Curtiss-Wright Corporation	7699	E	619 656-4740	17122
Marine Group Boat Works LLC	7699	D	619 427-6767	17137
San Diego Country Club Inc	7997	C	619 422-8895	17515
Community Health Group	8011	C	800 224-7766	17628
Bayside Healthcare Inc	8051	C	619 426-8611	17889
Front Porch Communities & Svcs	8051	C	619 427-2777	17955
Healthcare Management Systems Inc	8051	C	619 521-9641	17972
Scripps Health	8062	D	619 691-7000	18429
Sharp Chula Vista Medical Ctr	8062	A	619 502-5800	18435
Sharp Healthcare	8062	A	858 499-2000	18438
Sbcs Corporation	8322	C	619 420-3620	19137
Metroplitan Area Advsory Cmmtte **(PA)**	8331	D	619 426-3595	19188
Susan J Harris Inc	8361	C	619 498-8450	19304
CHG Foundation	8699	B	619 422-0422	19528
Gryphon Marine LLC	8711	D	619 407-4010	19602
Lockheed Martin Services LLC	8711	B	619 271-9831	19640
Estudysite	8731	C	619 955-5246	19837
Prosciento Inc **(PA)**	8731	C	619 427-1300	19872

CITY OF INDUSTRY, CA - Los Angeles County

	SIC	EMP	PHONE	ENTRY#
Alta-Dena Certified Dairy LLC **(DH)**	0241	B	626 964-6401	89
Frize Corporation	1541	D	800 834-2127	502
Morrow-Meadows Corporation **(PA)**	1731	A	858 974-3650	920
Closet World	1751	A	626 855-0846	1008
Home Organizers Inc	1751	A	562 699-9945	1015
Performance Sheets LLC	1761	C	626 333-0195	1050
Ssre Holdings LLC	2011	D	800 314-2098	1205
Venus Foods Inc	2011	E	626 369-5188	1207
Viz Cattle Corporation	2011	E	310 884-5260	1208
Derek and Constance Lee Corp **(PA)**	2013	D	909 595-8831	1217
Gaytan Foods LLC	2013	D	626 330-4553	1219
Pocino Foods Company	2013	D	626 968-8000	1230
Rice Field Corporation	2013	C	626 968-6917	1233
Heritage Distributing Company	2023	E	626 333-9526	1273
Ybcc Inc	2023	E	626 213-3945	1291
Berkeley Farms LLC	2026	B	510 265-8600	1306
Dean Socal LLC	2026	C	951 734-3950	1309
Wwf Operating Company LLC	2026	E	626 810-1775	1318
Tropicana Products Inc	2033	E	626 968-1299	1348
Gff Inc	2035	D	323 232-6255	1360
Lee Kum Kee (usa) Foods Inc **(PA)**	2035	C	626 709-1888	1361
Morehouse Foods Inc	2035	E	626 854-1655	1362
Langers Juice Company Inc	2037	B	626 336-3100	1375
Golden State Foods Corp	2038	B	626 465-7500	1391
Harbor Green Grain LP	2048	C	310 991-8089	1441
Cfp Chocolate Holdings LLC	2066	C	661 257-3700	1554
Sbm Dairies Inc	2086	B	626 923-3000	1739
Blue Pacific Flavors Inc **(PA)**	2087	E	626 934-0099	1759
Snak-King LLC **(PA)**	2096	B	626 336-7711	1832
Best Formulations LLC **(HQ)**	2099	E	626 912-9998	1857
Cali-Nat Products Inc	2099	E	626 581-5555	1864
Cosmos Food Co Inc	2099	E	323 221-9142	1873
Delori-Nutifood Products Inc	2099	E	626 965-3006	1882
Sincere Orient Commercial Corp	2099	D	626 333-8882	1986
Bentley Mills Inc **(PA)**	2273	C	626 333-4585	2110
American Foam Fiber & Sups Inc **(PA)**	2299	E	626 969-7268	2135
Unger Fabrik LLC **(PA)**	2331	C	626 469-8080	2268
Winstar Textile Inc	2361	F	626 357-1133	2412
Continental Marketing Svc Inc	2393	F	626 626-8888	2492
Exxel Outdoors Inc	2399	C	626 369-7278	2551
Hitex Dyeing & Finishing Inc	2399	E	626 363-0160	2554
Talbert Archtctral Panl Door I	2431	D	714 671-9700	2636
McConnell Cabinets Inc	2434	A	626 937-2200	2667
Commercial Lbr & Pallet Co Inc	2448	C	626 968-0631	2715
Fremarc Industries Inc **(PA)**	2511	C	626 965-0802	2773
Trend Manor Furn Mfg Co Inc	2511	E	626 964-6493	2791
Ardmore Home Design Inc **(PA)**	2512	C	626 803-7769	2795
Burton James Inc	2512	D	626 961-7221	2796
E J Lauren LLC	2512	C	562 803-1113	2800
R C Furniture Inc	2512	D	626 964-4100	2813
Miracle Bedding Corporation	2515	E	562 908-2370	2856
Closets By Design Inc	2541	C	562 699-9945	2948
Spectrum Intl Holdings	2542	A	626 333-7225	2993
Harvard Label LLC	2621	C	626 333-8881	3047
Sonoco Products Company	2631	C	626 369-6611	3071
Boxes R Us Inc	2653	D	626 820-5410	3086
Fleetwood Fibre LLC	2653	C	626 968-8503	3100
Golden West Packg Group LLC **(PA)**	2653	B	888 501-5893	3105
Goldencorr Sheets LLC	2653	C	626 369-6446	3106
Hoover Containers Inc	2653	D	909 444-9454	3109
Packaging Corporation America	2653	E	909 595-0401	3123

Employee Codes: A=Over 500 employees, B=251-500
C=101-250, D=51-100, E=20-50, F=10-19, G=1-9

2024 Southern California
Business Directory and Buyers Guide

© Mergent Inc. 1-800-342-5647

1355

	SIC	EMP	PHONE	ENTRY#
Scope Packaging Inc	2653	D	714 998-4411	3128
Mercury Plastics Inc (HQ)	2673	B	626 961-0165	3186
Novolex Holdings LLC	2673	D	626 961-6766	3189
Bagcraftpapercon I LLC	2674	D	626 961-6766	3197
Tekni-Plex Inc	2679	D	909 589-4366	3249
Sing Tao Newspapers Ltd	2711	D	626 956-8200	3324
Ideal Printing Company	2752	E	626 964-2019	3588
K-1 Packaging Group LLC (PA)	2752	D	626 964-9384	3609
Marrs Printing Inc	2752	D	909 594-9459	3631
Pgi Pacific Graphics Intl	2752	E	626 336-7707	3656
Stoughton Printing Co	2752	E	626 961-3678	3689
Hill Brothers Chemical Company	2812	F	626 333-2251	3857
Teknor Apex Company	2821	C	626 964-4656	3979
Teknor Color Company	2821	E	626 336-7709	3980
Accolade Pharma USA	2834	E	626 279-9699	4032
Best Formulations Inc	2834	C	626 912-9998	4069
Prolacta Bioscience Inc (PA)	2836	C	626 599-9260	4328
Maintex Inc (PA)	2842	C	800 446-1888	4359
Physicians Formula Inc (DH)	2844	D	626 334-3395	4444
Physicians Formula Cosmt Inc	2844	D	626 334-3395	4445
Cardinal Paint and Powder Inc	2851	C	626 937-6767	4484
PPG Industries Inc	2851	F	562 692-4010	4499
General Sealants	2891	C	626 961-0211	4566
Henkel US Operations Corp	2891	D	626 968-6511	4569
Signature Flexible Packg LLC (PA)	2891	E	909 598-7844	4581
Acorn Engineering Company (PA)	2899	A	800 488-8999	4593
Coi Rubber Products Inc	3069	B	626 965-9966	4759
Sealed Air Corporation	3086	C	909 594-1791	4904
Altium Packaging LLC	3089	D	888 425-7343	4937
Engineering Model Assoc Inc (PA)	3089	E	626 912-7011	5024
J & L Cstm Plstic Extrsons Inc	3089	E	626 442-0711	5064
Plastic Specialties & Tech Inc	3089	C	909 869-8069	5146
Waddington North America Inc	3089	C	626 913-4022	5246
Wna Comet West Inc	3089	C	626 913-0724	5253
Prl Glass Systems Inc	3231	D	877 775-2586	5353
Prl Glass Systems Inc (PA)	3231	C	626 961-5890	5354
Puente Ready Mix Services Inc (PA)	3273	E	626 968-0711	5492
Jon Brooks Inc (PA)	3295	D	626 330-0631	5550
Cast Parts Inc	3324	C	626 937-3444	5651
Quemetco West LLC	3341	C	626 330-2294	5683
Alum-A-Fold Pacific Inc	3353	E	562 699-4550	5686
Material Sciences Corporation	3353	C	562 699-4550	5689
Hydro Extrusion Usa LLC	3354	B	626 964-3411	5699
Prl Aluminum Inc	3354	D	626 968-7507	5706
Trulite GL Alum Solutions LLC	3354	D	800 877-8439	5712
Aremac Heat Treating Inc	3398	E	626 333-3898	5824
Newton Heat Treating Co Inc	3398	D	626 964-6528	5846
Monadnock Company	3429	C	626 964-6581	5934
Nuset Inc	3429	E	626 246-1668	5937
Townsteel Inc	3429	C	626 965-8917	5948
Integral Engrg Fabrication Inc	3441	E	626 369-0958	6033
Adams-Campbell Company Ltd (PA)	3444	D	626 330-3425	6177
Cemco LLC (DH)	3444	C	800 775-2362	6213
Trio Metal Stamping Inc	3444	C	626 336-1228	6336
Dennison Inc	3446	C	626 965-8917	6356
Valley-Todeco Inc (DH)	3452	D	800 992-4444	6456
WJB Bearings Inc	3463	E	909 594-6238	6486
Safe Plating Inc	3471	D	626 810-1872	6658
Nelson Name Plate Company (PA)	3479	D	323 663-3971	6719
Evans Industries Inc	3499	D	626 912-1688	6862
Pape Material Handling Inc	3537	D	562 692-9311	6995
PHI (PA)	3542	F	626 968-9680	7036
Trane Technologies Company LLC	3561	F	323 583-4771	7293
Clayton Manufacturing Company (PA)	3569	C	626 443-9381	7386
Clayton Manufacturing Inc (HQ)	3569	C	626 443-9381	7387
Premio Inc (PA)	3571	C	626 839-3100	7445
Rosewill Inc	3571	A	800 575-9885	7447
Compucase Corporation	3572	A	626 336-6588	7468
Seaward Products Corp	3585	D	562 699-7997	7623
Metal Cutting Service	3599	F	626 968-4764	7929
Solo Enterprise Corp	3599	E	626 961-3591	8031
Reuland Electric Co (PA)	3621	C	626 964-6411	8155
Valley Power Services Inc	3621	E	909 969-9345	8161
ITT LLC	3625	D	562 908-4144	8184
RH Peterson Co (PA)	3631	C	626 369-5085	8221
Maxim Lighting Intl Inc	3645	E	626 956-4200	8295
Troy-Csl Lighting Inc	3645	C	626 336-4511	8298
Kim Lighting Inc	3648	A	626 968-5666	8370
D-Tech Optoelectronics Inc	3669	E	626 956-1100	8606
Adtech Photonics Inc	3674	C	626 956-1000	8757
Invenlux Corporation	3674	E	626 277-4163	8815
Cooper Interconnect Inc	3679	D	617 389-7080	9021
Sceptre Inc	3679	E	626 369-3698	9115
Battery Technology Inc (PA)	3691	D	626 336-6878	9143
Vida Lease Corporation	3695	E	626 839-4912	9188
Proterra Operating Company Inc	3711	B	864 438-0000	9304
Blackseries Campers Inc	3715	E	833 822-6737	9490
Utility Trailer Manufacturing (PA)	3715	E	626 965-1514	9498
Utility Trailer Mfg Co	3715	C	909 594-6026	9500
Acromil LLC (HQ)	3728	C	626 964-2522	9589
Acromil Corporation (PA)	3728	C	626 964-2522	9590
Maverick Aerospace Inc	3728	D	714 578-1700	9745
Triumph Structures - Everett Inc	3728	C	425 348-4100	9823
Chronomite Laboratories Inc	3822	E	310 534-2300	10101
Xpower Manufacture Inc	3822	E	626 285-3301	10110
Ncstar Inc	3827	F	866 627-8278	10329
Teledyne Instruments Inc	3829	C	626 934-1500	10403
Johnson Wilshire Inc	3842	E	562 777-0088	10677
Astrophysics Inc (PA)	3844	C	909 598-5488	10781
Jada Group Inc (DH)	3944	E	626 810-8382	10956
Playhut Inc	3944	E	909 869-8083	10964
Easy Reach Supply LLC	3991	E	601 582-7866	11087
Gordon Brush Mfg Co (PA)	3991	C	323 724-7777	11089
Abis Signs Inc	3993	F	626 818-4329	11094
Cambro Manufacturing Company	3999	C	909 354-8962	11201
H & H Specialties Inc	3999	E	626 575-0776	11224
United Pumping Service Inc	4212	D	626 961-9326	11468
Estes Express Lines	4213	D	626 333-9090	11486
U C L Incorporated (PA)	4213	D	323 235-0099	11509
Cryomax USA Inc (HQ)	4225	F	626 330-3388	11570
Servitek Electric Inc	4911	E	626 227-1650	12053
Southern California Gas Co	4924	C	213 244-1200	12097
Arakelian Enterprises Inc	4953	B	626 336-3636	12155
Arakelian Enterprises Inc (PA)	4953	B	626 336-3636	12156
Zerep Management Corporation (PA)	4953	C	626 855-5522	12206
Furniture America Cal Inc (PA)	5021	C	866 923-8500	12281
Furniture America Cal Inc	5021	E	909 718-7276	12282
Poundex Associates Corporation	5021	D	909 444-5878	12290
Pacific Heritg HM Fashion Inc	5023	E	909 598-5200	12313
Potter Roemer LLC (HQ)	5031	D	626 855-4890	12340
American Future Tech Corp	5045	C	888 462-3899	12395
Avatar Technology Inc	5045	E	909 598-7696	12398
GBT Inc	5045	E	626 854-9338	12414
Magnell Associate Inc (DH)	5045	C	800 685-3471	12425
Micro-Technology Concepts Inc	5045	D	626 839-6800	12427
MSI Computer Corp (HQ)	5045	C	626 913-0828	12428
Mtc Worldwide Corp	5045	D	626 839-6800	12429
Private Label Pc LLC	5045	C	626 965-8686	12434
Durasafe Inc	5047	F	626 965-1588	12484
Grifols Usa LLC	5047	A	626 435-2600	12490
California Steel and Tube	5051	C	626 968-5511	12537
Maxim Lighting Intl Inc (PA)	5063	C	626 956-4200	12606
Databyte Technology Inc (PA)	5064	E	626 305-0500	12628
Assa Abloy Rsdential Group Inc	5072	A	626 369-4718	12714
Elmco Sales Inc (PA)	5074	C	626 855-4831	12738
US Airconditioning Distributors Inc (PA)	5075	C	626 854-4500	12759
Quinn Shepherd Machinery	5082	B	562 463-6000	12778
Airgas Safety Inc	5084	E	562 699-5239	12784
Pape Material Handling Inc	5084	C	562 463-8000	12807
Valley Power Systems Inc (PA)	5084	D	626 333-1243	12832
Yale/Chase Equipment and Services Inc	5084	C	562 463-8000	12842
Bridgestone Hosepower LLC	5085	E	562 699-9500	12845
Rutland Tool & Supply Co (HQ)	5085	C	562 566-5000	12876
Delta Creative Inc	5092	C	800 423-4135	12937
Design International Group Inc	5092	E	626 369-2289	12938
Sweda Company LLC	5094	B	626 357-9999	12969
Cenveo Worldwide Limited	5112	B	626 369-4921	12992
Essendant Co	5112	C	626 961-0011	12993
Markwins Beauty Brands Inc (PA)	5122	C	909 595-8898	13052
Foria International Inc	5136	E	626 912-8836	13103
Swatfame Inc (PA)	5137	B	626 961-7928	13152
Fortune Dynamic Inc	5139	D	909 979-8318	13162
Marquez Brothers Entps Inc	5141	C	626 330-3310	13185
Mercado Latino Inc (PA)	5141	D	626 333-6862	13187
OTasty Foods Inc	5141	D	626 330-1229	13189
WEI-Chuan USA Inc (PA)	5142	C	626 225-7168	13249
Clemson Distribution Inc (PA)	5143	E	909 595-2770	13253
Dfa Dairy Brands Fluid LLC	5143	B	800 395-7004	13254
Los Altos Food Products LLC	5143	C	626 330-6555	13255
Youbar Inc (PA)	5145	D	626 537-1851	13276
D&D Wholesale Distributors LLC	5148	D	626 333-2111	13318
Freshpoint Inc	5148	C	626 855-1400	13324
Freshpoint Southern Cal Inc	5148	C	626 855-1400	13325
Lee Kum Kee (usa) Inc (DH)	5149	E	626 709-1888	13376
Quality Naturally Foods Inc (PA)	5149	C	626 854-6363	13390
Royal Crown Enterprises Inc	5149	C	626 854-8080	13393

	SIC	EMP	PHONE	ENTRY#
Tld Acquisition Co LLC	5149	C		13402
Norman Fox & Co **(PA)**	5169	E	800 632-1777	13437
Classic Bev Southern Cal LLC	5181	B	626 934-3700	13463
American Paper & Plastics LLC	5199	C	626 444-0000	13526
Consolidated Devices Inc **(HQ)**	5251	E	626 965-0668	13676
Langer Juice Company Inc	5499	B	626 336-3100	13730
Dna Motor Inc	5531	E	626 965-8898	13858
Hot Topic Inc **(DH)**	5699	A	626 839-4681	13934
Dacor **(DH)**	5719	D	626 799-1000	13959
Labels-R-Us Inc	5932	C	626 333-4001	14062
Sailing Innovation (us) Inc	5945	A	626 965-6665	14081
Citifinancial Credit Company	6141	D	626 712-8780	14270
Cubeworkcom LLC	6531	C	909 991-6669	14774
Majestic Realty Co **(PA)**	6531	C	562 692-9581	14828
Bethar Corporation	6719	C		14924
Benefits Prgram Adminstration	6733	D	562 463-5000	14988
Majestic Industry Hills LLC	7011	A	626 810-4455	15236
Major Gloves & Safety Inc	7218	E	626 330-8022	15469
Boiling Point Rest S CA Inc	7361	B	626 551-5181	15822
Management Applied Prgrm Inc **(PA)**	7374	D	562 463-5000	16503
Nzxt Inc **(PA)**	7379	C	800 228-9395	16583
Easterncctv (usa) LLC	7382	C	626 961-8999	16731
Ezviz Inc	7382	E	855 693-9849	16736
Hikvision USA Inc **(HQ)**	7382	C	909 895-0400	16741
Rollins Leasing LLC	7513	D	626 913-7186	16973
Allied Entertainment Group Inc **(PA)**	7812	B	626 330-0600	17168
Public Hlth Fndation Entps Inc	8322	C	626 856-6600	19130
Public Hlth Fndation Entps Inc **(PA)**	8641	C	800 201-7320	19458
Torrid Merchandising Inc	8742	B	626 667-1002	20263
Pace Lithographers Inc	8999	E	626 913-2108	20399

CLAREMONT, CA - Los Angeles County

	SIC	EMP	PHONE	ENTRY#
Sunsation Inc	2037	E	909 542-0280	1379
Feemster Co Inc	2051	F	909 621-9772	1465
Green Spot Packaging Inc	2086	E	909 625-8771	1695
Phoenix Marketing Services Inc	2752	D	909 399-4000	3657
Universal Defense	3443	E	909 626-4178	6167
Micro Matrix Systems **(PA)**	3469	E	909 626-8544	6538
Vortox Air Technology Inc	3564	C	909 621-3843	7340
Baumann Engineering	3599	D	909 621-4181	7776
HI Rel Connectors Inc	3643	B	909 626-1820	8267
New Bedford Panoramex Corp	3648	C	909 982-9806	8376
Pff Bancorp Inc **(PA)**	6035	A	213 683-6393	14219
Western Feld Invstigations Inc **(PA)**	7375	D	800 999-9589	16537
R&C Motor Corporation	7538	C	909 625-1500	17037
Claremont Tennis Club	7997	C	909 625-9515	17478
Tierra Del Sol Foundation	7999	D	909 626-8301	17573
Pilgrim Place In Claremont **(PA)**	8059	A	909 399-5500	18152
Sunrise Senior Living MGT Inc	8361	C	909 447-5259	19303
Technip Usa Inc	8711	B	909 447-3600	19699
Ten Stone Wbster Prcess Tech	8711	B	909 447-3600	19700
Bon Appetit Management Co	8741	C	909 607-2788	20006

COACHELLA, CA - Riverside County

	SIC	EMP	PHONE	ENTRY#
Amazing Coachella Inc	0161	D	760 398-0151	6
Anthony Vineyards Inc	0172	D	760 391-5488	27
Teserra **(PA)**	1799	B	760 340-9000	1179
Reyes Coca-Cola Bottling LLC	2086	A	760 396-4500	1737
Roto Lite Inc	3089	E	909 923-4353	5188
Armtec Defense Products Co **(DH)**	3489	B	760 398-0143	6749
Armtec Countermeasures Co **(DH)**	3812	N	760 398-0143	9948
Paladar Mfg Inc	3931	D	760 775-4222	10928
Sunline Transit Agency	4119	C	760 972-4059	11405
Naumann/Hobbs Mtl Hdlg Corp II	5082	D	866 266-2244	12775
Desert Valley Date LLC	5149	C	760 340-0999	13366
Imperial Western Products Inc A Cal **(HQ)**	5159	E	760 398-0815	13408
Esparza Enterprises Inc	7361	A	760 398-0349	15844
Augustine Gaming MGT Corp	7371	D	760 391-9500	15971
29 Palms Enterprises Corp	7999	A	760 775-5566	17538

COLTON, CA - San Bernardino County

	SIC	EMP	PHONE	ENTRY#
Paul Hubbs Construction Co Inc **(PA)**	1429	F	951 360-3990	402
Lozano Caseworks Inc	1751	D	909 783-7530	1019
Boyd Specialties LLC	2013	D	909 219-5120	1214
Hawa Corporation **(PA)**	2013	F	909 825-8882	1220
Saab Enterprises Inc	2013	B	909 823-2228	1234
Star Food Snacks Intl Inc	2013	F	909 825-8882	1236
Ardent Mills LLC	2041	E	951 201-1170	1407
Brill Inc	2051	C	909 825-7343	1456
California Churros Corporation	2051	B	909 370-4777	1458
Mrs Redds Pie Co Inc	2051	E	909 825-4800	1484
Masterbrand Cabinets LLC	2434	E	951 682-1535	2666
Frank Kams & Associates Inc	2449	E	909 382-0047	2731

	SIC	EMP	PHONE	ENTRY#
Banner Mattress Inc	2515	D	909 835-4200	2844
Clariant Corporation	2672	E	909 825-1793	3169
Wirz & Co	2752	F	909 825-6970	3713
US Rubber Recycling Inc	3069	D	909 825-1200	4799
Microdyne Plastics Inc	3089	D	909 503-4010	5099
Omni Resource Recovery Inc	3089	C	909 327-2900	5127
Cemex Materials LLC	3273	D	909 825-1500	5472
Als Garden Art Inc **(PA)**	3299	B	909 424-0221	5564
Darnell-Rose Inc	3429	E	626 912-1688	5915
Elizabeth Shutters Inc	3442	C	909 825-1531	6104
Black Diamond Blade Company **(PA)**	3531	E	800 949-9014	6926
Williams Furnace Co **(DH)**	3585	C	562 450-3602	7634
A-Z Emissions Solutions Inc	3699	E	951 781-1856	9190
Rivian Automotive LLC	3711	D	309 249-8777	9306
Erf Enterprises Inc	3713	F	909 825-4080	9325
McNeilus Truck and Mfg Inc	3713	E	909 370-2100	9331
Panadent Corporation	3843	E	909 783-1841	10760
Cummings Resources LLC	3993	E	951 248-1130	11108
Gxo Logistics Supply Chain Inc	4225	D	951 512-1201	11584
Sprouts Farmers Market Inc	4225	A	888 577-7688	11613
Entercom Media Corp	4832	D	909 825-9525	11924
Ecology Recycling Services LLC	4953	D	909 370-1318	12168
SMC Grease Specialist Inc	4953	E	951 788-6042	12187
A-Z Bus Sales Inc **(PA)**	5012	C	951 781-7444	12217
Brithinee Electric	5063	D	909 825-7971	12588
Greenpath Recovery West Inc	5093	D	909 954-0686	12955
Jon-Lin Frozen Foods **(PA)**	5142	D	909 825-8542	13247
Sulzer Elctr-Mchncal Svcs US I	7694	C	909 825-7971	17108
Premier Otptent Srgery Ctr Inc	8011	C	909 370-2190	17739
Southern Cal Prmnnte Med Group	8011	C	909 370-2501	17789
Cambridge Sierra Holdings LLC	8051	B	909 370-4411	17897
Charter Hospice Colton LLC	8052	C	909 825-2969	18082
Arrowhead Regional Medical Ctr	8062	A	909 580-1000	18186
Rai Care Centers Colton LLC	8092	C	909 430-0930	18660
Landtec North America Inc	8748	E	909 783-3636	20359

COMMERCE, CA - Los Angeles County

	SIC	EMP	PHONE	ENTRY#
Shims Bargain Inc	1541	C	323 726-8800	516
Freedom Forever LLC	1711	A	714 955-8735	769
Farwest Insulation Contracting	1742	D	310 634-2800	977
Heritage Distributing Company **(PA)**	2026	E	323 838-1225	1313
Oakhurst Industries Inc **(PA)**	2051	E	323 724-3000	1487
Sugar Foods LLC	2051	D	323 727-8290	1494
New Century Snacks LLC	2068	D	323 278-9578	1560
Snak Club LLC	2068	E	323 278-9578	1562
Chameleon Beverage Company Inc **(PA)**	2086	E	323 724-8223	1690
Carmi Flvr & Fragrance Co Inc **(PA)**	2087	E	323 888-9240	1762
Key Essentials Inc	2087	D		1779
Caffe DAmore Inc	2095	C		1816
Gruma Corporation	2096	B	323 803-1400	1827
Fungs Village Inc	2098	E	323 881-1600	1839
Arevalo Tortilleria Inc	2099	E	323 888-1711	1852
Gold Coast Ingredients Inc	2099	D	323 724-8935	1904
Interntional Tea Importers Inc **(PA)**	2099	E	562 801-9600	1916
Mojave Foods Corporation **(HQ)**	2099	C	323 890-8900	1948
Pacific Spice Company Inc	2099	C	323 726-9190	1965
Artcraft Bedspreads Mfg Inc	2211	E		2010
Bonded Fiberloft Inc	2211	B	323 726-7820	2013
Hidden Jeans Inc	2211	E	213 746-4223	2024
J Michelle of California	2269	F	323 585-8500	2102
American & Efird LLC	2284	F	323 724-6884	2123
Sherwin-Williams Company	2295	C	323 726-7272	2127
4 What Its Worth Inc **(PA)**	2329	D	323 728-4503	2189
Alliance Apparel Inc	2331	E	323 888-8900	2229
Bluprint Clothing Corp	2331	D	323 780-4347	2232
Trixxi Clothing Company Inc **(PA)**	2335	E	323 585-4200	2292
AB&r Inc	2339	E	323 727-0007	2298
DNam Apparel Industries LLC	2339	E	323 859-0114	2321
J & F Design Inc	2339	D	323 526-4444	2331
Evy of California Inc	2361	E	213 746-4647	2407
Ajg Inc	2386	E	323 346-0171	2425
Pacific Coast Home Furn Inc **(PA)**	2392	F	323 838-7808	2482
Canvas Specialty Inc	2394	E		2501
Hospitality Wood Products Inc	2431	E	562 806-5564	2607
Apex Drum Company Inc	2449	F	323 721-8994	2730
Greif Inc	2449	E	323 724-7500	2732
Furniture Technics Inc	2511	E	562 802-0261	2774
JP Products LLC	2511	E	310 237-6237	2776
Nova Lifestyle Inc **(PA)**	2511	E	323 888-9999	2784
Commercial Intr Resources Inc	2512	D	562 692-5885	2798
Superb Chair Corporation	2512	C	562 776-1771	2821
Murrays Iron Works Inc **(PA)**	2514	E	323 521-1100	2834
Kingdom Mattress Co Inc	2515	E	562 630-5531	2853

Employee Codes: A=Over 500 employees, B=251-500
C=101-250, D=51-100, E=20-50, F=10-19, G=1-9
2024 Southern California
Business Directory and Buyers Guide
© Mergent Inc. 1-800-342-5647
1357
GEOGRAPHIC

	SIC	EMP	PHONE	ENTRY#
Deskmakers Inc.	2521	E	323 264-2260	2882
Norstar Office Products Inc (PA)	2521	E	323 262-1919	2891
Ergocraft Contract Solutions	2522	E		2909
Pacific Hospitality Design Inc	2531	E	323 278-7998	2935
Nico Nat Mfg Corp	2541	E	323 721-1900	2961
Samson Products Inc	2542	E	323 726-9070	2992
Teichman Enterprises Inc	2542	E	323 278-9000	2995
American Graphic Board Inc	2621	D	323 721-0585	3041
Yavar Manufacturing Co Inc	2657	E	323 722-2040	3147
Amcor Flexibles LLC	2671	A	323 721-6777	3148
Liberty Packg & Extruding Inc	2673	E	323 722-5124	3184
Sun Plastics Inc	2673	E	323 888-6999	3191
Progressive Label Inc	2679	E	323 415-9770	3246
Bridge Publications Inc (PA)	2731	E	323 888-6200	3400
La Xpress Air & Heating Svcs	2741	D	310 856-9678	3461
Colorcom Inc	2752	E	323 246-4640	3534
Hanover Accessories Corp	2782	C		3838
Ultra Pro Acquisition LLC	2782	E	323 725-1975	3841
W R Grace & Co	2819	F	562 927-8513	3919
Ineos Composites Us LLC	2821	D	323 767-1300	3946
Biorx Pharmaceuticals Inc	2834	E	323 723-3100	4074
Samson Pharmaceuticals Inc	2834	E	323 722-3066	4228
Soft Gel Technologies Inc (HQ)	2834	E	323 726-0700	4239
American Intl Inds Inc	2844	A	323 728-2999	4378
Ink Systems Inc (PA)	2893	D	323 720-4000	4590
Indio Products Inc	2899	E	323 720-9117	4611
Lion Tank Line Inc	2911	F	323 726-1966	4643
Solvay Draka Inc (DH)	3081	C	323 767-7010	4822
Huhtamaki Inc	3086	C	323 269-0151	4890
Specialty Enterprises Co	3086	D	323 726-9721	4906
API Kirk Containers	3089	E	323 278-5400	4943
Arthurmade Plastics Inc	3089	E	323 721-7325	4949
Bottlemate Inc (PA)	3089	E	323 887-9009	4969
Urban Expressions Inc	3171	E	310 593-4574	5300
Mascorro Leather Inc	3199	D	323 724-6759	5309
Pacific Vial Mfg Inc	3221	E	323 721-7004	5321
Oldcastle Buildingenvelope Inc	3231	D	323 722-2007	5351
Wiretech Inc (PA)	3315	D	323 722-4933	5628
Omega Steel Inc	3316	E	323 726-7669	5630
Globe Iron Foundry Inc	3321	D	323 723-8983	5645
Kaiser Aluminum Corporation	3354	B	323 726-8011	5700
Kaiser Aluminum Fab Pdts LLC	3354	F	323 722-7151	5701
US Polymers Inc	3354	D	323 727-6888	5714
Century Wire & Cable Inc	3357	D	800 999-5566	5739
Gehr Industries Inc (HQ)	3357	C	323 728-5558	5742
Pacific Die Casting Corp	3363	C	323 725-1308	5764
Alcast Mfg Inc (PA)	3365	E	310 542-3581	5780
Orlandini Entps Pcf Die Cast.	3369	E	323 725-1332	5816
Alarin Aircraft Hinge Inc	3429	E	323 725-1666	5896
Asco Sintering Co	3429	E	323 725-3550	5897
Hollywood Bed Spring Mfg Inc (PA)	3429	D	323 887-9500	5922
Monogram Aerospace Fas Inc	3429	C	323 722-4760	5935
American Brass & Alum Fndry Co	3432	E	800 545-9988	5962
Capitol Steel Fabricators Inc	3441	E	323 721-5460	6006
Air Louvers Inc	3442	E	800 554-6077	6099
Rite Engineering & Manufacturing Corporation	3443	E	562 862-2135	6153
S Bravo Systems Inc	3443	E	323 888-4133	6155
Sid E Parker Boiler Mfg Co Inc	3443	D	323 727-9800	6156
A-1 Metal Products Inc	3444	E	323 721-3334	6175
PCI Industries Inc	3444	E	323 728-0004	6289
Architectural Enterprises Inc	3446	E	323 268-4000	6351
Ni Industries Inc	3449	D	309 283-3355	6402
Sheila Street Properties Inc (PA)	3471	D	323 838-9208	6663
Haley Indus Ctings Linings Inc	3479	E	323 588-8086	6708
Ultimate Metal Finishing Corp	3479	E	323 890-9100	6745
Advanced Process Services Inc.	3491	E	323 278-6530	6752
Matthew Warren Inc	3495	D	800 237-5225	6804
Precision Wire Products Inc (PA)	3496	C	323 890-9100	6823
Deamco Corporation	3535	E	323 890-1190	6972
Ctd Machines Inc	3541	F	213 689-4455	7008
Pioneer Broach Company (PA)	3545	E	323 728-1263	7125
Interstate Meat Co Inc	3556	D	323 838-9400	7202
Martin Sprocket & Gear Inc	3566	C	323 728-8117	7358
Crowntonka California Inc	3585	E	909 230-6720	7606
MGM Transformer Co	3612	D	323 726-0888	8101
Image Micro Spare Parts Inc	3621	F	562 776-9808	8145
Iworks Us Inc	3641	D	323 278-8363	8247
Acclaim Lighting LLC	3646	E	323 213-4626	8303
Deco Enterprises Inc	3646	D	323 726-2575	8307
Edison Price Lighting Inc (PA)	3646	C	718 685-0700	8310
Hallmark Lighting LLC	3646	E	818 885-5010	8315
Elation Lighting Inc	3648	E	323 582-3322	8363
Elite Lighting	3648	C	323 888-1973	8364

	SIC	EMP	PHONE	ENTRY#
Eti Sound Systems Inc	3651	E	323 835-6660	8410
B & B Battery (usa) Inc (PA)	3692	F	323 278-1900	9158
Dynaflex Products (PA)	3713	D	323 724-1555	9323
Fastener Dist Holdings LLC	3721	E	213 620-9950	9522
Transdigm Inc	3728	D	323 269-9181	9818
Sondors Inc	3751	E	323 372-3000	9883
Atk Space Systems LLC (DH)	3812	E	323 722-0222	9954
Northrop Grumman Systems Corp	3812	C	714 240-6521	10016
Soffa Electric Inc	3823	E	323 728-0230	10163
PCI Industries Inc	3999	E	323 728-0004	11264
Pommes Frites Candle Co	3999	E	213 488-2016	11271
Superior-Studio Spc Inc	3999	E	323 278-0100	11291
Eastwestproto Inc	4119	B	888 535-5728	11381
Xpo Cartage Inc	4212	D	800 837-7584	11470
Dart International A Corp (HQ)	4225	C	323 264-8746	11572
Dart Warehouse Corporation (HQ)	4225	B	323 264-1011	11573
Smart & Final Stores LLC	4225	C	323 725-0791	11612
Screamline Investment Corp.	4725	C	323 201-0114	11731
RAMCAR Batteries Inc	5013	E	323 726-1212	12257
ITD Arizona Inc	5014	C	323 722-8542	12270
Gibson Overseas Inc (PA)	5023	B	323 832-8900	12303
Zwilling JA Henckels LLC	5023	C	323 597-1421	12323
Insul-Therm International Inc (PA)	5033	E	323 728-0558	12367
Interstate Electric Co Inc.	5046	D	800 225-5432	12458
Justman Packaging & Display (PA)	5046	D	323-728-8888	12462
Adj Products LLC (PA)	5063	E	323 582-2650	12582
Kobert & Company Inc	5063	D	323 725-1000	12600
Nora Lighting Inc	5063	C	323 767-2600	12610
Samsung Electronics Amer Inc	5064	C	323 374-6300	12637
Hkf Inc (PA)	5075	D	323 225-1318	12756
Fastener Dist Holdings LLC (HQ)	5085	E	213 620-9950	12854
PC Woo Inc (PA)	5092	D	323 887-8138	12942
Ultra Pro International LLC	5092	C	323 890-2100	12946
D J American Supply Inc.	5099	C	323 582-2650	12972
Sun Coast Merchandise Corp.	5099	C	323 720-9700	12987
Glamour Industries Co (PA)	5122	B	323 728-2999	13042
Charming Trim & Packaging	5131	A	415 302-7021	13081
Matrix International Tex Inc.	5131	E	323 582-9100	13085
Sportek International Inc.	5136	F	213 239-6700	13111
BP Clothing LLC	5137	C		13119
Smart & Final Stores LLC (DH)	5141	D	323 869-7500	13228
Smart Stores Operations LLC (DH)	5141	B	323 869-7500	13229
Balance Foods Inc	5145	E	323 838-5555	13264
Century Snacks LLC	5145	C	323 278-9578	13266
4 Earth Farms LLC (PA)	5148	B	323 201-5800	13311
Buy Fresh Produce Inc	5148	D	323 796-0127	13315
El Guapo Spices Inc (PA)	5149	D	213 312-1300	13367
Jfc International Inc (HQ)	5149	C	323 721-6100	13372
Jfc International Inc.	5149	C	323 721-6900	13373
Elkay Plastics Co Inc (PA)	5162	D	323 722-7073	13413
Univar Solutions USA Inc.	5169	C	323 727-7005	13440
Breakthru Beverage Cal LLC (HQ)	5182	B	800 331-2829	13474
99 Cents Only Stores LLC (HQ)	5199	B	323 980-8145	13524
Bio Hazard Inc	5199	E	213 625-2116	13529
Blisterpak Inc	5199	E	323 728-5555	13530
Ernest Packaging (PA)	5199	C	800 233-7788	13535
Misa Imports Inc.	5199	D	562 281-6773	13549
RYL Inc	5199	D	213 503-7968	13559
Unix Packaging LLC	5199	B	213 627-5050	13565
West Bay Imports Inc	5199	E	323 720-5777	13568
Home Depot USA Inc	5211	C	323 727-9600	13613
Dunn-Edwards Corporation (DH)	5231	C	888 337-2468	13673
Number Holdings Inc (PA)	5331	C	323 980-8145	13687
Unified Nutrimeals.	5812	D	323 923-9335	14041
W B Mason Co Inc	5943	E	888 926-2766	14072
Quantum Networks LLC	5961	C	212 993-5899	14100
California Commerce Club Inc.	7011	A	323 721-2100	15107
Uniserve Facilities Svcs Corp (PA)	7349	B	213 533-1000	15753
American Security Force Inc.	7382	D	323 722-8585	16723
Ceramic Decorating Company Inc.	7389	E	323 268-5135	16800
Parking Company of America	7521	D	562 862-2118	16997
Pcam LLC	7521	D	562 862-2118	17005
Altamed Health Services Corp (PA)	8011	C	323 725-8751	17591
County of Los Angeles	8322	B	323 889-3405	19056
Mexican Amrcn Oprtnty Fndation	8322	D	323 890-1555	19113
Maravilla Foundation (PA)	8641	C	323 721-4162	19455
Ivy Enterprises Inc.	8748	B	323 887-8661	20354

COMPTON, CA - Los Angeles County

	SIC	EMP	PHONE	ENTRY#
Demenno Kerdoon	1382	E	310 537-7100	298
Nabors Well Services Co	1389	D	310 639-7074	365
Alameda Construction Svcs Inc.	1442	E	310 635-3277	404
Quality Production Svcs Inc	1742	D	310 406-3350	993

	SIC	EMP	PHONE	ENTRY#
Foster Poultry Farms	2015	A	310 223-1499	1243
Sierra Cheese Manufacturing Company Inc	2022	E	310 635-1216	1258
Lekos Dye & Finishing Inc **(PA)**	2231	D	310 763-0900	2050
Pacific Contntl Textiles Inc	2269	D	310 639-1500	2105
American Dawn Inc **(PA)**	2299	D	800 821-2221	2134
Edmund Kim International Inc **(PA)**	2329	E	310 604-1100	2202
Magic Apparel Group Inc	2353	E	310 223-4000	2401
Sew What Inc	2391	E	310 639-6000	2463
Simso Tex Sublimation **(PA)**	2396	E	310 885-9717	2539
Elliotts Designs Inc	2514	E	310 631-4931	2830
Jbi LLC	2514	E	310 537-2910	2832
Cri Sub 1 **(DH)**	2521	E	310 537-1657	2881
International Paper Company	2621	E	310 639-2310	3051
Great Eastern Entertainment Co **(PA)**	2741	E	310 638-5058	3454
Kmr Label LLC	2754	E	310 603-8910	3719
Resource Label Group LLC	2754	E	310 603-8910	3723
Carbon Activated Corporation **(PA)**	2819	E	310 885-4555	3887
Crossfield Products Corp **(PA)**	2821	E	310 886-9100	3934
Orion Plastics Corporation	2821	D	310 223-0370	3960
Plaskolite West LLC	2821	E	310 637-2103	3963
Techmer Pm Inc	2821	B	310 632-9211	3978
Flo-Kem Inc	2842	E	310 632-7124	4349
LMC Enterprises	2842	E	310 632-7124	4358
Henkel US Operations Corp	2843	C	562 297-6840	4374
Ips Corporation **(HQ)**	2891	E	310 898-3300	4571
De Menno-Kerdoon Trading Co **(HQ)**	2911	C	310 537-7100	4640
Owens Corning Sales LLC	2952	C	310 631-1062	4675
Viking Rubber Products Inc	3069	F	310 868-5200	4801
Foam Factory Inc	3086	E	310 603-9808	4883
Ufp Technologies Inc	3086	E	714 662-0277	4908
Advanced Materials Inc **(HQ)**	3089	E	310 537-5444	4930
Idemia America Corp	3089	C	310 884-7900	5057
Rsk Tool Incorporated	3089	E	310 537-3302	5192
Andrew Alexander Inc	3111	D	323 752-0066	5254
Performance Composites Inc	3229	C	310 328-6661	5328
Southwire Inc	3353	B	310 886-8300	5691
Magnesium Alloy Pdts Co Inc	3363	E	310 605-1440	5762
Magnesium Alloy Products Co LP	3363	E	323 636-2276	5763
Fleetwood Continental Inc	3366	D	310 609-1477	5802
Fs - Precision Tech Co LLC	3369	E	310 638-0595	5814
Watertite Products Inc	3432	D	901 853-5001	5976
Park Steel Co Inc	3441	F	310 638-6101	6063
R & D Steel Inc	3441	E	714 631-6183	6067
Mnm Manufacturing Inc	3442	D	310 898-1099	6114
Thermal Equipment Corporation	3443	E	310 328-6600	6163
Anoroc Precision Shtmtl Inc	3444	E	310 515-6015	6189
Fastener Innovation Tech Inc	3451	D	310 538-1111	6414
Continental Forge Company LLC	3463	D	310 603-1014	6477
Weber Metals Inc	3463	B	562 543-3316	6485
Innovative Stamping Inc	3469	E	310 537-6996	6524
Serra Manufacturing Corp **(PA)**	3469	D	310 537-4560	6554
AAA Plating & Inspection Inc	3471	D	323 979-8930	6573
BHC Industries Inc	3471	E	310 632-2000	6590
Bowman Plating Co Inc	3471	C	310 639-4343	6594
E M E Inc	3471	E	310 639-1621	6613
Morrells Electro Plating Inc	3471	E	310 639-1024	6640
Kens Spray Equipment Inc	3479	E	310 635-9995	6715
Plasma Coating Corporation	3479	E	310 532-1951	6726
Ilco Industries Inc	3498	E	310 631-8655	6847
Ace Clearwater Enterprises Inc	3544	E	310 538-5380	7045
Concrete Mold Corporation	3544	E	310 537-5171	7063
Tajima Usa Inc	3552	E	310 604-8200	7179
Barkens Hardchrome Inc	3559	E	310 632-2000	7226
Flowserve Corporation	3561	D	310 667-4220	7278
Circle Industrial Mfg Corp **(PA)**	3567	E	310 638-5101	7362
Norco Industries Inc **(PA)**	3569	C	310 639-4000	7402
Classic Tents	3585	E	310 328-5060	7602
Sea Recovery Corporation	3599	E	310 608-5600	8020
Allan Kidd	3643	E	310 762-1600	8254
Jimway Inc	3648	D	310 886-3718	8369
Peter Pepper Products Inc **(PA)**	3669	D	310 639-0390	8620
ESP Corp	3679	E	310 639-2535	9042
Martins Quality Truck Body Inc	3711	E	310 632-5978	9297
Complete Truck Body Repair Inc	3713	E	323 445-2675	9318
AITA Clutch Inc	3714	E	323 585-4140	9349
Fmf Racing	3751	E	310 631-4363	9876
Essilor Laboratories Amer Inc	3851	E	310 604-8668	10839
Hf Group Inc **(PA)**	3861	E	310 605-0755	10868
Artboxx Framing Inc	3999	E	310 604-6933	11191
Mercado Latino Inc	3999	E	310 537-1062	11251
Tag Toys Inc	3999	D	310 639-4566	11292
Durham School Services L P	4151	C	310 767-5820	11421
Ajr Trucking Inc	4212	D	310 707-1120	11440

	SIC	EMP	PHONE	ENTRY#
Uls Express Inc	4212	C	310 631-0800	11467
H Rauvel Inc	4213	C	562 989-3333	11489
Pacific Drayage Services LLC	4213	C	833 334-4622	11501
Fox Transportation Inc	4214	C	310 971-0867	11520
Madden Corporation	4215	D	714 922-1670	11533
F R T International Inc **(PA)**	4225	D	310 604-8208	11576
Foamex LP	4225	C	323 774-5600	11579
Kroger Co	4225	B	859 630-6959	11593
Apex Logistics Intl Inc **(PA)**	4731	C	310 665-0288	11740
Dhx-Dependable Hawaiian Ex Inc **(PA)**	4731	C	310 537-2000	11753
Global Mail Inc	4731	C	310 735-0800	11763
M-7 Consolidation Inc	4731	C	310 898-3456	11779
Noatum Logistics Usa LLC	4731	C	310 527-2104	11789
Port Logistics Group Inc	4731	B	310 669-2551	11793
Southern California Edison Co	4911	A	310 608-5029	12070
4 Wheel Parts Wholesalers LLC	5013	B	310 900-7725	12230
Dna Specialty Inc	5013	D	310 767-4070	12238
Saddlemen Corporation	5013	E	310 638-1222	12259
Silla Automotive LLC	5013	F	800 624-1499	12262
West Wood Products Inc **(PA)**	5031	F	310 631-8978	12345
Concrete Tie Industries Inc	5032	D	310 628-2328	12352
Gemco Display and Str Fixs LLC **(PA)**	5046	E	800 262-1126	12454
Jack Rubin & Sons Inc **(PA)**	5051	E	310 635-5407	12554
Cordelia Lighting Inc	5063	C	310 886-3490	12591
Walters Wholesale Electric Co **(HQ)**	5063	E	562 988-3100	12625
Florence Filter Corporation	5075	D	310 637-1137	12753
JOHN TILLMAN COMPANY **(DH)**	5084	D	310 764-0110	12793
Industrial Valco Inc **(PA)**	5085	E	310 635-0711	12860
M M Fab Inc	5131	D	310 763-3800	13084
Colosseum Athletics Corp	5136	D	310 667-8341	13100
Gourmet Foods Inc **(PA)**	5141	D	310 632-3300	13182
Interstate Foods Inc	5144	C	310 635-2442	13259
General Petroleum LLC **(HQ)**	5172	C	562 983-7300	13452
Beauchamp Distributing Company	5181	C	310 639-5320	13460
Swan Fence Incorporated	5211	E	310 669-8000	13672
Kraco Enterprises LLC	5531	C	310 639-0666	13864
Transamerican Dissolution LLC **(HQ)**	5531	C	310 900-5500	13886
Diamond Mattress Company Inc **(PA)**	5712	E	310 638-0363	13941
Celebrity Casinos Inc	7011	B	310 631-3838	15110
Color Ad Inc	7311	E	310 632-5500	15532
Hydroprocessing Associates LLC	7389	D	310 667-6456	16842
Evans Hydro Inc	7699	E	310 608-5801	17126
Brinderson LLC **(DH)**	8711	C	714 466-7100	19557
Dxterity Diagnostics Inc **(PA)**	8733	C	310 537-7857	19925
Element Mtrls Tech HB Inc	8734	D	310 632-8500	19969
Beyondsoft Consulting Inc	8748	C	310 532-2822	20318

CORONA, CA - Riverside County

	SIC	EMP	PHONE	ENTRY#
Excel Landscape Inc	0782	C	951 735-9650	190
Landscape Development Inc	0782	C	951 371-9370	201
Chandler Aggregates Inc **(PA)**	1411	E	951 277-1341	397
Gail Materials Inc	1442	E	951 667-6106	406
Champion Home Builders Inc	1521	D	951 256-4617	425
Superior Construction Inc	1521	D	951 808-8780	460
Clay Corona Company **(PA)**	1542	E	951 277-2667	543
All American Asphalt	1611	C	951 736-7617	608
Ebs General Engineering Inc	1611	D	951 279-6869	616
Kec Engineering	1611	C	951 734-3010	627
Superior Paving Company Inc	1611	D	951 739-9200	649
Arizona Pipeline Company	1623	C	951 270-3100	659
Boudreau Pipeline Corporation	1623	B	951 493-6780	663
HP Communications Inc **(PA)**	1623	D	951 572-1200	674
Couts Heating & Cooling Inc	1711	C	951 278-5560	758
Infinity Plumbing Designs Inc	1711	B	951 737-4436	779
LDI Mechanical Inc **(PA)**	1711	C	951 340-9685	785
NP Mechanical Inc	1711	B	951 667-4220	801
RC Maintenance Holdings Inc	1711	C	951 903-6303	815
Smart Energy Solar Inc	1711	C	800 405-1978	825
True Air Mechanical Inc	1711	C	888 316-0642	831
SRbray LLC	1731	D	951 898-3850	939
Laurence-Hovenier Inc	1751	C	951 736-2990	1018
TWR Enterprises Inc	1751	C	951 279-2000	1025
A Class Precision Inc	1761	F	951 549-9706	1036
Cornerstone Concrete Inc	1771	D	951 279-2221	1067
Empire Demolition Inc	1795	D	909 393-8300	1132
Wellington Foods Inc	2023	C	951 547-7000	1290
Pacifica Foods LLC	2035	C	951 371-3123	1363
Stir Foods LLC	2038	E	714 871-9231	1403
Food For Life Baking Co Inc **(PA)**	2051	D	951 273-3031	1469
Monster Beverage 1990 Corporation	2086	A	951 739-6200	1704
Monster Beverage Company	2086	A	866 322-4466	1705
Monster Beverage Corporation **(PA)**	2086	A	951 739-6200	1706
Frutarom	2087	E	951 734-6620	1774

Employee Codes: A=Over 500 employees, B=251-500
C=101-250, D=51-100, E=20-50, F=10-19, G=1-9

2024 Southern California
Business Directory and Buyers Guide

© Mergent Inc. 1-800-342-5647

1359

	SIC	EMP	PHONE	ENTRY#
Cadence Gourmet LLC (PA)	2099	F	951 444-9269	1862
T Hasegawa USA Inc	2099	E	951 264-1121	1994
Amrapur Overseas Incorporated (PA)	2299	E	714 893-8808	2137
Amwear USA Inc	2311	E	800 858-6755	2148
Lejon of California Inc	2387	E	951 736-1229	2434
Anatomic Global Inc	2392	C	800 874-7237	2465
Northwestern Converting Co	2392	D	800 959-3402	2479
CTA Manufacturing Inc	2393	E	951 280-2400	2493
Best- In- West	2395	E	909 947-6507	2514
Leepers Wood Turning Co Inc (PA)	2431	E	562 422-6525	2613
Excel Cabinets Inc	2434	E	951 279-4545	2658
Fleetwood Homes of Kentucky (DH)	2451	E	800 688-1745	2741
American National Mfg Inc	2515	D	951 273-7888	2842
AMF Support Surfaces Inc (DH)	2515	C	951 549-6800	2843
Della Robbia Inc	2515	E	951 372-9199	2847
Widly Inc	2515	C	951 279-0900	2864
Ergononmic Comfort Design Inc	2522	F	951 277-1558	2910
Temeka Advertising Inc	2541	D	951 277-2525	2968
Uniweb Inc (PA)	2542	D	951 279-7999	2998
Century Blinds Inc	2591	D	951 734-3762	3003
R & J Fabricators Inc	2599	E	951 817-0300	3030
General Container	2653	D	714 562-8700	3103
US Display Group Inc	2653	E	951 444-4567	3134
Republic Bag Inc	2673	E	951 734-9740	3190
Tree House Pad & Paper Inc	2678	D	800 213-4184	3224
Dietzgen Corporation	2679	E	951 278-3259	3234
Big Horn Wealth Management Inc	2752	D	951 273-7900	3519
Handbill Printers LP	2752	E	951 547-5910	3584
Westrock Cp LLC	2752	E	951 273-7900	3712
Spectra Color Inc	2816	E	951 277-0200	3878
Cgpc America Corporation	2821	E	951 332-4100	3930
Actavis LLC	2834	E	951 493-5582	4033
Actavis LLC	2834	D	909 270-1400	4034
Youcare Pharma (usa) Inc	2834	E	951 258-3114	4258
Panrosa Enterprises Inc	2841	D	951 339-5888	4340
US Continental Marketing Inc (PA)	2842	D	951 808-8888	4371
Adonis Inc	2844	E	951 432-3960	4376
Vinylvisions Company LLC	2851	E	800 321-8746	4508
Tastepoint Inc	2869	C	951 734-6620	4533
Trical Inc	2879	E	951 737-6960	4553
Technicote Inc	2891	E	951 372-0627	4583
Playmax Surfacing Inc	3069	F	951 250-6039	4784
Spangler Industries Inc	3069	C	951 735-5000	4796
Arvinyl Laminates LP	3081	E	951 371-7800	4806
TRM Manufacturing Inc	3081	C	951 256-8550	4824
Simmons Family Corporation	3083	D	951 278-4563	4843
Dart Container Corp California (PA)	3086	B	951 735-8115	4879
Aquatic Co	3088	B	714 993-1220	4911
Le Elegant Bath Inc	3088	C	951 734-0238	4919
Carr Management Inc	3089	D	951 277-4800	4984
Dacha Enterprises Inc	3089	D	951 273-7777	5001
Extrumed Inc (DH)	3089	E	951 547-7400	5027
Fischer Mold Incorporated	3089	D	951 279-1140	5028
Hoosier Inc	3089	D	951 272-3070	5052
Martin Chancey Corporation	3089	E	510 972-6300	5091
Merrick Engineering Inc (PA)	3089	C	951 737-6040	5097
Preproduction Plastics Inc	3089	E	951 340-9680	5160
Rehau Construction LLC	3089	D	951 549-9017	5176
SCR Molding Inc	3089	F	951 736-5490	5201
Tamshell Corp	3089	D	951 272-9395	5222
TNT Plastic Molding Inc (PA)	3089	D	951 808-9700	5228
Mediland Corporation	3211	D	562 630-9696	5317
Sream Inc	3231	E	951 245-6999	5356
Maruhachi Ceramics America Inc	3259	E	800 736-6221	5375
United States Tile Co	3259	C	951 739-4613	5376
Acker Stone Industries Inc (DH)	3272	E	951 674-0047	5397
Nucast Industries Inc	3272	E	951 277-8888	5430
Quikrete California LLC (DH)	3272	E	951 277-3155	5443
Robertsons Rdymx Ltd A Cal Ltd (HQ)	3273	D	951 493-6500	5495
Superior Ready Mix Concrete LP	3273	E	951 277-3553	5507
Werner Corporation	3273	E	951 277-4586	5518
3M Company	3295	D	951 737-3441	5548
Rock Structures-Rip Rap	3296	E	951 371-1112	5557
Carter Holt Harvey Holdings	3312	E	951 272-8180	5585
Hardy Frames Inc	3312	D	951 245-9525	5590
Lexani Wheel Corporation	3312	E	951 808-4220	5592
Merit Aluminum Inc (PA)	3354	C	951 735-1770	5703
Actron Manufacturing Inc	3429	D	951 371-0885	5895
Lock America Inc	3429	F	951 277-5180	5928
Columbia Aluminum Products LLC	3441	E	323 728-7361	6008
Johasee Rebar Inc	3441	E	661 589-0972	6036
Parcell Steel Corp	3441	C	951 471-3200	6062
Premier Steel Structures Inc	3441	E	951 356-6655	6066
Steel-Tech Industrial Corp	3441	E	951 270-0144	6078
Tolar Manufacturing Co Inc	3441	E	951 808-0081	6083
Computrus Inc	3443	E	951 245-9103	6138
Decra Roofing Systems Inc (DH)	3444	D	951 272-8180	6226
Fletcher Bldg Holdings USA Inc (DH)	3444	D	951 272-8180	6241
Four Seasons Rest Eqp Inc	3444	E	951 278-9100	6242
Jet Manufacturing Inc	3444	E	951 736-9316	6257
MS Industrial Shtmtl Inc	3444	C	951 272-6610	6276
Western Sheet Metals Inc	3444	F	951 272-3600	6345
LMS Reinforcing Steel Usa LP (HQ)	3449	E	604 598-9930	6401
Price Manufacturing Co Inc	3451	E	951 371-5660	6420
Premier Gear & Machining Inc	3462	E	951 278-5505	6470
Rubicon Gear Inc	3462	D	951 356-3800	6472
Saleen Automotive Inc (PA)	3465	E	800 888-8945	6487
T-Rex Truck Products Inc	3465	D	800 287-5900	6488
David Engineering & Mfg Inc	3469	E	951 735-5200	6509
Proformance Manufacturing Inc	3469	E	951 279-1230	6549
Ravlich Enterprises LLC (PA)	3471	E	714 964-8900	6654
RGF Enterprises Inc	3479	E	951 734-6922	6731
Circor Aerospace Inc (DH)	3491	C	951 270-6200	6757
Circor Instrmentation Tech Inc	3492	D	951 270-6200	6773
Eibach Inc	3493	E	951 256-8300	6781
Brasscraft Manufacturing Co	3494	D	951 735-4375	6788
Mission Rubber Company LLC	3494	C	951 736-1313	6792
California Wire Products Corp	3496	E	951 371-7730	6814
Ameriflex Inc	3498	D	951 737-5557	6837
Laminated Shim Company Inc	3499	E	951 273-3900	6867
Pacmet Aerospace LLC	3519	E	909 218-8889	6895
Western Equipment Mfg Inc	3531	E	951 284-2000	6947
Cremach Tech Inc	3541	D	951 735-3194	7006
Cremach Tech Inc (PA)	3541	E	951 735-3194	7007
David Engineering & Manufacturing Inc	3544	E	951 735-5200	7066
Noranco Manufacturing (usa) Acquisition Corp	3545	C	951 721-8400	7122
Pacific Packaging McHy LLC	3556	E	951 393-2200	7211
John Currie Performance Group	3559	E	714 367-1580	7245
Peabody Engineering & Sup Inc	3559	E	951 734-7711	7260
Suss Microtec Inc (HQ)	3559	C	408 940-0300	7260
Vizualogic LLC	3559	C	407 509-3421	7266
Kobelco Compressors Amer Inc	3563	D	951 739-3030	7309
Kobelco Compressors Amer Inc (DH)	3563	B	951 739-3030	7310
M & O Perry Industries Inc	3565	E	951 734-9838	7352
W J Ellison Co Inc	3565	E	626 814-4766	7356
Jhawar Industries LLC	3567	E	951 340-4646	7368
Anaco Inc	3568	C	951 372-2732	7375
Avt Inc	3581	E	951 737-1057	7590
Ace Heaters LLC	3585	E	951 738-2230	7594
Aqueous Technologies Corp	3589	E	909 944-7771	7643
Blue Desert International Inc	3589	D	951 273-7575	7646
Engineered Food Systems	3589	E	714 921-9913	7656
Spenuzza Inc (HQ)	3589	E	951 281-1830	7688
Parker-Hannifin Corporation	3594	D	951 280-3800	7713
Btl Machine	3599	E	951 808-9929	7790
F & L Tools Corporation	3599	F	951 277-1555	7830
MD Engineering Inc	3599	E	951 736-5390	7924
Millworx Prcsion Machining Inc	3599	E	951 371-2683	7940
PVA Tepla America Inc (HQ)	3599	E	951 371-2500	7985
Sun Precision Machining Inc	3599	F	951 817-0056	8037
Panel Shop Inc	3613	E	951 739-7000	8127
Motor Technology Inc	3621	D	951 270-6200	8151
Absolute Graphic Tech USA Inc	3625	E	909 597-1133	8167
Esl Power Systems Inc	3643	D	800 922-4188	8264
Computer Service Company	3669	E	951 738-1444	8605
Corona Magnetics Inc	3677	C	951 735-7558	8939
Jayco Interface Technology Inc	3679	E	951 738-2000	9071
Jayco/Mmi Inc	3679	E	951 738-2000	9072
Omni Connéction Intl Inc	3679	B	951 898-6232	9093
Sas Manufacturing Inc	3679	E	951 734-1808	9114
Palos Verdes Building Corp (PA)	3691	C	951 371-8090	9153
Vantage Vehicle Intl Inc	3694	E	951 735-1200	9177
Pacific Utility Products Inc	3699	E	951 493-8394	9239
Suss McRtec Phtnic Systems Inc	3699	D	951 817-3700	9259
Saleen Incorporated (PA)	3711	E	714 400-2121	9307
Tiffany Coachworks Inc	3711	F	951 657-2680	9311
Advanced Flow Engineering Inc (PA)	3714	E	951 493-7155	9345
Advanced Flow Engineering Inc	3714	E	951 493-7100	9346
Currie Enterprises	3714	D	714 528-6957	9377
Gibson Performance Corporation	3714	D	951 372-1220	9397
Nmsp Inc	3714	E	951 734-2453	9433
TMI Products Inc	3714	C	951 272-1996	9472
Tube Technologies Inc	3714	E	951 371-4878	9476
Accurate Grinding and Mfg Corp	3724	E	951 479-0909	9560
International Wind Inc (PA)	3724	E	562 240-3963	9573
Thermal Structures Inc (DH)	3724	B	951 736-9911	9581

2024 Southern California
Business Directory and Buyers Guide

(P-0000) Products & Services Section entry number
(PA)=Parent Co (HQ)=Headquarters (DH)=Div Headquarters

	SIC	EMP	PHONE	ENTRY#
Thermal Structures Inc	3724	E	951 256-8051	9582
Acromil LLC	3728	D	951 808-9929	9588
Aero-Craft Hydraulics Inc	3728	E	951 736-4690	9599
Approved Aeronautics LLC	3728	E	951 200-3730	9628
Asturies Manufacturing Co Inc	3728	E	951 270-1766	9636
Irwin Aviation Inc	3728	E	951 372-9555	9725
Johnson Caldraul Inc	3728	E	951 340-1067	9729
Electrasem Corp	3822	C	951 371-6140	10103
Promach Filling Systems LLC	3823	E	951 393-2200	10153
Sprite Industries Incorporated	3826	E	951 735-1015	10289
Kap Medical	3829	E	951 340-4360	10377
All Manufacturers Inc	3841	C	951 280-4200	10423
Biolase Inc	3843	D	949 361-1200	10732
Dansereau Health Products	3843	E	951 549-1400	10735
Fender Musical Instrs Corp	3931	A	480 596-9690	10924
Westech Products Inc (PA)	3952	E	951 279-4496	11051
Architectural Design Signs Inc (PA)	3993	E	951 278-0680	11097
Fovell Enterprises Inc	3993	E	951 734-6275	11121
R&M Deese Inc	3993	E	951 734-7342	11148
Richards Neon Shop Inc	3993	E	951 279-6767	11149
Tradenet Enterprise Inc	3993	D	888 595-3956	11176
Developlus Inc	3999	C	951 738-8595	11211
Interstate Cabinet Inc	3999	C	951 736-0777	11232
Kurz Transfer Products LP	3999	D	951 738-9521	11238
Pet Partners Inc (PA)	3999	C	951 279-9888	11266
Mission Ambulance Inc	4119	D	951 272-2300	11398
Veg Fresh Logistics LLC	4731	C	714 446-8800	11815
Sprint Communications Co LP	4812	C	951 340-1924	11861
Combustion Associates Inc	4911	E	951 272-6999	12018
Agile Sourcing Partners Inc	4939	C	951 279-4154	12109
Talco Plastics Inc (PA)	4953	C	951 531-2000	12189
Waste Management Cal Inc	4953	C	951 277-1740	12195
Fleetwood Aluminum Products Inc	5031	C	800 736-7363	12329
ABC School Equipment Inc	5049	E	951 817-2200	12525
Ckkm Inc (PA)	5051	E	951 371-8484	12540
Joor Bros Welding Inc	5051	E	951 737-3950	12557
Corona Clipper Inc	5072	D	951 737-6515	12719
R & J Material Handling Inc	5084	F	951 735-0000	12813
So Cal Sandbags Inc	5085	D	951 277-3404	12880
Thalasinos Enterprises Inc	5085	E	951 340-0911	12884
Aqua Performance Inc	5091	E	951 340-2056	12925
Amerisourcebergen Drug Corp	5122	C	951 371-2000	13028
Rugby Laboratories Inc (DH)	5122	D	951 270-1400	13066
Marie Cllender Wholesalers Inc	5142	A	951 737-6760	13248
Index Fresh Inc (PA)	5148	D	909 877-0999	13330
Veg-Fresh Farms LLC (PA)	5148	C	800 422-5535	13346
Monster Energy Company (HQ)	5149	B	866 322-4466	13381
Zep Inc	5169	C	877 428-9937	13444
Thoro--Packaging (DH)	5199	C	951 278-2100	13564
Ganahl Lumber Company	5211	D	951 278-4000	13576
Home Depot USA Inc	5211	C	951 808-0327	13583
Lowes Home Centers LLC	5211	C	951 256-9004	13666
Vons Companies Inc	5411	C	951 278-8284	13709
Freedom Prfmce Exhaust Inc	5531	E	951 898-4733	13861
Pro Circuit Products Inc (PA)	5571	E	951 738-8050	13903
Irwin International Inc (PA)	5599	D	951 372-9555	13906
Pacific Boat Trailers Inc (PA)	5599	F	909 902-0094	13907
Hub Distributing Inc (HQ)	5611	B	951 340-3149	13909
Aurelio Felix Barreto III	5699	C	951 354-9528	13930
Ames Construction Inc	5712	B	951 356-1275	13938
Kaiser Fndtion Hlth Plan GA In	6324		951 270-1200	14472
Pro Group Inc	6531	C	951 271-3000	14845
Bellota US Corp	6722	C	951 737-6515	14959
JJ Mac Intyre Co Inc (PA)	7322	C	951 898-4300	15614
Screenworks LLC	7336	A	951 279-8877	15673
Pro Building Maintenance Inc (PA)	7349	C	951 279-3386	15739
RNA Ann Arbor Incorporated	7349	C	877 762-7511	15746
Porter Hire Ltd	7359	E	951 674-9999	15793
Temps Plus Inc	7361	C	951 549-8309	15899
Eknowledge Group Inc	7372	E	951 256-4076	16235
American Power SEC Svc Inc	7381	D	866 974-9994	16617
Aztecs Telecom Inc	7389	D	714 373-1560	16785
General Water Systems	7389	F	951 278-8992	16832
Thyde Inc (PA)	7389	C	951 817-2300	16944
Penske Transportation MGT LLC	7513	D	844 847-9518	16972
U-Haul Business Consultants	7513	C	951 736-7811	16975
Metro Truck Body Inc	7532	E	310 532-5570	17013
Ironman Renewal LLC	7538	D	951 735-3710	17032
Moyes Custom Furniture Inc	7641	E	714 729-0234	17078
General Conveyor Inc	7699	E	951 734-3460	17129
Green River Golf Corporation	7992	D	714 970-8411	17430
Corona Regional Med Ctr LLC	8011	C	951 737-4343	17632
Vitas Healthcare Corporation	8052	D	858 805-6254	18100

	SIC	EMP	PHONE	ENTRY#
Uhs-Corona Inc (HQ)	8062	A	951 737-4343	18482
United Lab Services Inc	8071	D	951 444-0467	18568
St Joseph Health Per Care Svcs	8082	D	800 365-1110	18642
Uhs-Corona Inc	8093	C	951 736-7200	18727
Crossrads Chrstn Schols Corona	8299	C	951 278-3199	19009
Music & Arts	8299	E	951 735-5924	19012
Ability Counts Inc (PA)	8331	D	951 734-6595	19172
Peppermint Ridge (PA)	8361	D	951 273-7320	19294
K&B Electric LLC	8711	C	951 808-9501	19628
K&B Engineering	8711	C	951 808-9501	19629
Primary Provider MGT Co Inc (HQ)	8741	C	951 280-7700	20081
Kpc Group Inc (PA)	8742	C	951 782-8812	20189
Volt Telecom Group Inc	8748	B	951 493-8900	20390

CORONA DEL MAR, CA - Orange County

	SIC	EMP	PHONE	ENTRY#
Cpaperless LLC	3652	D	949 510-3365	8454
Tebra Technologies Inc (PA)	7371	C	888 775-2736	16133

CORONADO, CA - San Diego County

	SIC	EMP	PHONE	ENTRY#
Industrial Metal Cleaning Co.	3398	F	314 621-4209	5837
Nadolife Inc	3421	E	619 522-0077	5869
Lockheed Martin Corporation	3812	D	619 437-7230	9994
City of Coronado	4931	C	619 522-7380	12104
Smart & Final Stores Inc	5141	C	619 522-2014	13200
Coronado Brewing Company Inc (PA)	5813	E	619 437-4452	14047
51st St & 8th Ave Corp	7011	C	619 424-4000	15065
Ksl Resorts Hotel Del Coronado	7011	C	619 435-6611	15213
Sanci Marriott Hotels	7011	D	619 435-3000	15348
Mariner Systems Inc (PA)	7389	C	305 266-7255	16867
Sharp Coronado Hospital & Healthcare Center	8062	A	619 522-3600	18437

COSTA MESA, CA - Orange County

	SIC	EMP	PHONE	ENTRY#
Hexagon Agility Inc	1321	D	949 236-5520	274
Mdm Solutions LLC	1389	B	800 669-6361	361
Brookfeld Sthland Holdings LLC	1521	C	714 427-6868	422
Seattle Tnnel Prtners A Jint V	1521	B	206 971-8701	456
Warmington Residential Cal Inc	1521	C	714 557-5511	465
Rebco Communities Inc	1522	B	714 557-5511	472
Warmington Homes (PA)	1531	C	714 434-4435	490
Andrew L Youngquist Cnstr Inc	1542	C	949 862-5611	530
Adopt-A-Highway Maintenance	1611	C	800 200-0003	607
Beador Construction Co Inc	1611	D	951 674-7352	610
Dragados Usa Inc	1611	D	657 229-7800	615
Lombardy Holdings Inc (PA)	1623	C	951 808-4550	681
Pivot Interiors Inc	1731	D	949 988-5400	927
Orange County Plst Co Inc	1742	C	714 957-1971	986
El Metate Inc	2051	C	949 646-9362	1463
Associated Microbreweries Inc	2082	D	714 546-2739	1584
3 Point Distribution LLC	2329	E	949 266-2700	2188
Hurley International LLC (PA)	2329	C	949 548-9375	2207
Outer Rebel Inc	2389	F	949 548-3630	2457
I D Brand LLC	2396	E	949 422-7057	2532
Fxc Corporation	2399	D	714 557-8032	2553
Fineline Woodworking Inc	2431	D	714 540-5468	2600
L & L Custom Shutters Inc	2431	F	714 996-9539	2612
Sheward & Son & Sons (PA)	2591	E	866 432-8400	3014
Locale Lifestyle Magazine LLC	2721	E	949 436-8910	3366
Saddleback Educational Inc	2731	F	714 640-5200	3413
National Appraisal Guides Inc	2741	E	714 556-8511	3467
Thomson Reuters Corporation	2741	F	949 400-7782	3494
Orange Coast Reprographics Inc	2752	E	949 548-5571	3648
ID Supply	2759	E	714 728-6478	3769
Westar Nutrition Corp (PA)	2833	E	949 645-6100	4024
Moleculum	2911	F	714 619-5139	4645
Toyo Tire Hldings Americas Inc (HQ)	3011	E	714 229-6100	4700
Vans Inc (DH)	3021	B	714 755-4000	4708
Tk Pax Inc	3052	E	714 850-1330	4715
CCI Industries Inc (PA)	3089	E	714 662-3879	4986
Husky Injection Mlding Systems	3089	D	714 545-8200	5056
JG Plastics Group LLC	3089	E	714 751-4266	5073
Resinart Corporation	3089	E	949 642-3665	5181
Cevians LLC (PA)	3211	D	714 619-5135	5313
Ceradyne Esk LLC	3299	C	714 549-0421	5566
Nippon Steel Trdg Americas Inc	3312	D	714 367-3910	5594
Contech Engnered Solutions Inc	3317	A	714 281-7883	5633
Griswold Industries (PA)	3365	B	949 722-4800	5795
Baier Marine Company Inc	3429	E	800 455-3917	5904
Fxc Corporation (PA)	3429	E	714 556-7400	5919
Winfield Locks Inc	3429	A	949 722-5400	5954
Coast Sheet Metal Inc	3444	E	949 645-2224	6215
Flare Group	3471	E	714 549-0202	6621
Inveco Inc	3471	E	949 378-3850	6631
Griswold Industries	3492	F	949 722-4831	6777

Employee Codes: A=Over 500 employees, B=251-500
C=101-250, D=51-100, E=20-50, F=10-19, G=1-9

2024 Southern California
Business Directory and Buyers Guide

© Mergent Inc. 1-800-342-5647

1361

GEOGRAPHIC

	SIC	EMP	PHONE	ENTRY#
Kyocera Tycom Corporation	3541	B	714 428-3600	7015
Criterion Machine Works	3545	E		7113
Shurflo LLC	3561	B	714 371-1550	7290
Universal Motion Components Co Inc	3566	E	714 437-9600	7359
Walin Group Inc	3569	E	714 444-5980	7411
International Bus Mchs Corp	3571	E	714 472-2237	7432
Sepe Inc	3571	E	714 241-7373	7449
Delphi Display Systems Inc	3577	D	714 825-3400	7522
Dynamic Cooking Systems Inc	3589	A	714 372-7000	7654
GSP Precision Inc	3599	E	818 845-2212	7853
Starlineoem Inc	3612	E	949 342-8889	8112
Balboa Water Group LLC (HQ)	3625	D	714 384-0384	8170
Fisher & Paykel Appliances Inc (DH)	3639	E	949 790-8900	8242
Candle Lamp Holdings LLC	3641	B	951 682-9600	8244
Flexfire Leds Inc	3646	E	925 273-9080	8312
Qsc LLC (PA)	3651	C	800 854-4079	8428
Impac Technologies Inc	3663	E	714 427-2000	8524
Bdfco Inc	3669	D	714 228-2900	8601
Carrier Fire SEC Americas Corp	3669	C	949 737-7800	8604
Sanmina Corporation	3672	E	714 371-2800	8727
Sanmina Corporation	3672	E	714 913-2200	8728
Falkor Partners LLC	3674	E	714 721-8772	8796
Irvine Sensors Corporation	3674	E	714 444-8700	8819
Semicoa Corporation	3674	D	714 979-1900	8884
Newmar Power LLC	3675	C	800 854-3906	8930
I O Interconnect Ltd (PA)	3678	E	714 564-1111	8973
Sabritec	3678	B	714 371-1100	8982
Technical Cable Concepts Inc	3679	E	714 835-1081	9125
Target Technology Company LLC	3695	E	949 788-0909	9184
Isc8 Inc	3699	E	714 549-8211	9218
Schneider Electric	3699	E	949 713-9200	9253
Fisker Automotive Inc	3711	D		9285
Flare Group	3728	E	714 850-2080	9688
Macgregor Yacht Corporation	3732	E	310 621-2206	9861
Maurer Marine Inc	3732	F	949 645-7673	9863
Anduril Industries Inc (PA)	3812	E	949 891-1607	9943
Lambda Research Optics Inc	3826	D	714 327-0600	10268
Sellers Optical Inc	3827	D	949 631-6800	10339
Advanced Micro Instruments Inc	3829	E	714 848-5533	10349
Newport Medical Instrs Inc	3841	D	949 642-3910	10577
Phillps-Mdisize Costa Mesa LLC	3841	C	949 477-9495	10589
Sweden & Martina Inc	3841	E	844 862-7846	10611
Unity Sales International Inc	3861	F	714 800-1700	10888
Rip Curl Inc (DH)	3949	C	714 422-3600	11019
Hartley Company	3951	E	949 646-9643	11046
Pro-Lite Inc	3993	F	714 668-9988	11146
Transprttion Brkg Spclists Inc	4212	B	714 754-4236	11466
Flowspace Inc	4225	D	323 741-1325	11578
County of Orange	4581	C	949 252-5006	11694
Nds Americas Inc (DH)	4841	D	714 434-2100	11997
Flat White Economy Inv USA LLC	4953	C	949 344-5013	12170
ABC Bus Inc	5012	D	714 444-5888	12218
Nissan North America Inc	5012	C	714 433-3700	12228
Altametrics Hosting LLC	5045	C	800 676-1281	12393
Schurman Fine Papers	5084	E	714 549-0212	12819
Western Refining Inc	5084	E	714 708-2200	12839
Viva Life Science Inc	5122	C	949 645-6100	13075
Food Sales West Inc	5141	C	714 966-2900	13180
Home Depot USA Inc	5211	C	949 646-4220	13590
Grand Prix Road Trends Inc (PA)	5531	F	323 962-8600	13863
511 Inc (DH)	5699	E	949 800-1511	13927
Annas Linens Inc	5719	A	714 850-0504	13956
El Pollo Loco Holdings Inc (PA)	5812	C	714 599-5000	14004
Fgr 1 LLC	5812	E	800 653-3517	14007
Piecemakers LLC	5947	E	714 641-3112	14087
North American Acceptance Corp	6141	E	714 868-3195	14276
Payoff Inc	6141	D	949 430-0630	14277
Professional Cr Reporting Inc	6141	C	714 556-1570	14278
Balboa Capital Corporation (DH)	6153	C	949 756-0800	14280
Metropolitan Home Mortgage Inc	6162	D	949 428-0161	14340
Secured Funding Corporation	6163	A	714 689-6749	14365
Villa Venetia	6163	B	714 540-1800	14371
Merrill Lynch Prce Fnner Smith	6211	A	714 429-2800	14388
Auto Club Enterprises (PA)	6321	A	714 850-5111	14447
Automobile Club Southern Cal	6411	C	714 885-1343	14563
Medical Eye Services Inc	6411	D	714 619-4660	14612
Donahue Schriber Rlty Group LP (PA)	6512	D	714 545-1400	14659
South Coast Plaza LLC	6512	C	714 435-2000	14686
Donahue Schrber Rlty Group Inc (PA)	6531	D	714 545-1400	14789
Hanford Hotels Inc	7011	C	714 557-3000	15169
Rosanna Inc	7011	C	714 751-5100	15333
South Coast Westin Hotel Co	7011	D	714 540-2500	15364
Trigild International Inc	7011	C	949 645-2221	15394

	SIC	EMP	PHONE	ENTRY#
US Hotel and Resort MGT Inc	7011	C	949 650-2988	15400
Klientboost LLC	7311	C	657 203-7866	15552
Marshall Advertising and Design Inc	7311	E	714 545-5757	15556
Experian Info Solutions Inc (DH)	7323	A	714 830-7000	15622
Experian Mktg Solutions LLC	7323	A	714 830-7000	15623
All-Rite Leasing Company Inc	7349	B	714 957-1822	15691
Pacific Building Care Inc (HQ)	7349	C	949 261-1234	15732
Site Crew Inc	7349	B	714 668-0100	15749
Career Strategies Tmpry Inc	7361	C	714 824-6840	15827
Recruit 360	7361	C	949 250-4420	15889
Southern Home Care Svcs Inc	7363	D	714 979-7413	15943
Marigold Usa Inc	7371	C	617 385-6786	16070
Software Management Cons LLC	7371	C	714 662-1841	16119
Touchtone Corporation	7371	E	714 755-2810	16135
Mirth Corporation	7372	D	714 389-1200	16308
Nwp Services Corporation (DH)	7372	C	949 253-2500	16332
Savedaily Inc	7372	F	562 795-7500	16373
Filenet Corporation	7373	C	800 345-3638	16442
Protect-US	7381	C	714 721-8127	16672
Star Pro Security Patrol Inc	7381	C	714 617-5056	16695
Benrich Service Company Inc	7389	E	714 241-0284	16792
Carecredit LLC	7389	C	800 300-3046	16798
Creative Design Consultants (PA)	7389	D	714 641-4868	16810
Regus Business Centre LLC	7389	C	714 371-4000	16914
Simple Science Inc	7389	E	949 335-1099	16929
Volcom LLC (HQ)	7389	C	949 646-2175	16959
EZ Lube LLC	7549	C	714 966-1647	17055
Metropro Road Services Inc	7549	D	714 556-7600	17058
Kone Inc	7699	E	714 890-7080	17136
Edwards Theatres Circuit Inc	7832	C	714 428-0962	17296
Ticketscom LLC (DH)	7922	E	714 327-5400	17331
Aspyr Holdings LLC	7991	B	714 651-1840	17391
Mesa Verde Partners	7992	C	714 540-7500	17438
Mesa Verde Country Club	7997	C	714 549-0377	17500
Beaver Dam Health Care Center	8051	D	949 642-0387	17890
Mesa Vrde Cnvalescent Hosp Inc	8051	C	949 548-5584	18013
College Hospital Costa Mesa Mso Inc (HQ)	8062	C	949 642-2734	18223
Hoag Family Cancer Institute	8062	C	949 764-7777	18282
Califrnia Dept State Hospitals	8063	A	714 957-5000	18506
Accredited Nursing Services	8082	C	714 973-1234	18584
Baker & Hostetler LLP	8111	C	714 754-6600	18824
Cooksey Tlen Gage Dffy Woog A (PA)	8111	D	714 431-1100	18839
Latham & Watkins LLP	8111	B	714 540-1235	18890
Lewis Brsbois Bsgard Smith LLP	8111	C	714 545-9200	18895
Sheppard Mllin Rchter Hmpton L	8111	D	714 513-5100	18944
Snell & Wilmer LLP	8111	D	714 427-7000	18948
Vanguard Univ Southern Cal	8221	C	714 668-6163	18995
Califrnia Dept Dvlpmental Svcs	8331	A	714 957-5151	19179
Ds Lakeshore LP	8641	D	916 286-5231	19444
Deloitte & Touche LLP	8721	C	714 436-7419	19768
Marcum LLP	8721	D	949 236-5600	19794
South Coast Plaza Security	8741	C	714 435-2180	20097
Warmington Mr 14 Assoc LLC	8741	D	714 557-5511	20115
Nationsbenefits LLC	8742	D	877 439-2665	20207
Innovative Cnstr Solutions	8744	C	714 893-6366	20294

COVINA, CA - Los Angeles County

	SIC	EMP	PHONE	ENTRY#
Brutoco Engineering & Construction Inc	1611	C		612
RG Costumes & Accessories Inc	2389	E	626 858-9559	2459
Processors Mailing Inc	2752	E	626 358-5600	3670
Ink Fx Corporation	2759	E	909 673-1950	3770
Matrix Document Imaging Inc	2759	F	626 966-9959	3786
Composites Horizons LLC (DH)	2821	C	626 331-0861	3932
Chemeor Inc (PA)	2843	E	626 966-3808	4372
Anvil Cases Inc	3161	C	626 968-4100	5284
Stabile Plating Company Inc	3471	E	626 339-9091	6665
Caco-Pacific Corporation (PA)	3544	C	626 331-3361	7055
Dauntless Industries Inc	3544	C	626 966-4494	7065
Payne Magnetics Corporation	3677	D	626 332-6207	8950
TT Elctrnics Pwr Sltons US Inc	3679	C	626 967-6021	9133
Cozzia USA LLC (HQ)	3699	F	626 667-2272	9202
Azusa Engineering Inc	3714	F	626 966-4071	9358
Cdc International Inc	3714	E	626 347-7705	9370
Composites Horizons LLC	3728	C	626 331-0861	9662
Apricot Designs Inc	3841	D	626 966-3299	10438
Haemonetics Manufacturing Inc (HQ)	3841	E	626 339-7388	10519
Moores Ideal Products LLC	3944	C	626 339-9007	10962
Bright Glow Candle Company Inc (PA)	3999	E	909 469-4733	11198
Norlaine Inc	3999	C	626 961-2471	11257
Sprint Communications Co LP	4813	C	626 339-0430	11903
Swwc Utilities Inc (DH)	4941	C		12149
American Scale Co Inc	5045	E	800 773-7225	12396
Twomagnets Inc	7361	A	408 837-0116	15901

Mergent email: customerrelations@mergent.com
1362

2024 Southern California
Business Directory and Buyers Guide

(P-0000) Products & Services Section entry number
(PA)=Parent Co (HQ)=Headquarters (DH)=Div Headquarters

	SIC	EMP	PHONE	ENTRY#
Stavros Enterprises Inc	7699	E	888 463-2293	17154
Davita Magan Management Inc **(DH)**	8011	C	626 331-6411	17640
Covina Rehabilitation Center	8051	C	626 967-3874	17922
Rowland Convalescent Hosp Inc	8051	D	626 967-2741	18043
Emanate Health Medical Center	8062	B	626 858-8515	18254
Emanate Health Medical Center	8062	A	626 331-7331	18256
Emanate Health Medical Group **(PA)**	8062	A	626 331-7331	18258
Charter Bhvral Hlth Sys S C/Ch	8063	C	626 966-1632	18510
Citrus Vly Hlth Partners Inc	8099	B	626 732-3100	18754
Eggleston Youth Centers Inc **(PA)**	8322	D	626 480-8107	19075
Think Together	8351	B	626 373-2311	19230
Los Angeles Engineering Inc	8711	C	626 869-1400	19641
Zenleads Inc	8742	B	415 640-9303	20279

CUDAHY, CA - Los Angeles County

	SIC	EMP	PHONE	ENTRY#
RAP Security Inc	2542	D	323 560-3493	2987
Day-Glo Color Corp	2816	F	323 560-2000	3874
Consolidated Foundries Inc	3365	C	323 773-2363	5787
Myers Mixers LLC	3569	E	323 560-4723	7400
Merry An Cejka	3599	E	323 560-3949	7928
HF Cox Inc	4212	B	323 587-2359	11460
Super Center Concepts Inc	5411	C	323 562-8980	13705
Southern Cal Prmnnte Med Group	8011	C	323 562-6459	17775
Kaiser Foundation Hospitals	8062	C	323 562-6400	18297

CULVER CITY, CA - Los Angeles County

	SIC	EMP	PHONE	ENTRY#
Advanced Crtcal Care Emrgncy S	0742	C	310 558-6111	122
Farchitecture Bb LLC	2024	E	917 701-2777	1297
Ppd Holding LLC **(PA)**	2326	D	310 733-2100	2183
Sportsrobe Inc	2329	E	310 559-3999	2220
Fortune Casuals LLC **(PA)**	2331	D	310 733-2100	2240
Paige LLC **(HQ)**	2331	D	310 733-2100	2262
Carbon 38 Inc	2339	D	888 723-5838	2311
Metric Products Inc **(PA)**	2342	E	310 815-9000	2396
Parachute Home Inc	2392	C	310 903-0353	2484
Stories International Inc	2741	E	310 242-8409	3486
Natals Inc	2834	C	323 475-6033	4175
Cambridge Equities LP	2836	E	858 350-2300	4307
Henkel US Operations Corp	2844	E	626 321-4100	4419
Joico Laboratories Inc	2844	E	626 321-4100	4425
Sole Society Group Inc	3131	C	310 220-0808	5261
Spotlite America Corporation **(PA)**	3229	E	310 829-0200	5331
Magnet Sales & Mfg Co Inc **(HQ)**	3264	D	310 391-7213	5381
Integrated Tech Group Inc **(PA)**	3499	C	310 391-7213	6864
Borin Manufacturing Inc	3561	E	310 822-1000	7270
Pacific Piston Ring Co Inc	3592	D	310 836-3322	7701
Chargie LLC	3621	E	310 621-0024	8137
CMI Integrated Tech Inc	3621	E		8138
Integrated Magnetics Inc	3621	E	310 391-7213	8146
Spotlite Power Corporation	3646	E	310 838-2367	8332
Beats Electronics LLC	3651	B	424 326-4679	8399
Apic Corporation	3674	D	310 642-7975	8767
Loaded Boards Inc	3751	F	310 839-1800	9878
Moldex-Metric Inc	3842	B	310 837-6500	10684
Given Imaging Los Angeles LLC	3845	C	310 641-8492	10804
Virgin Fish Inc **(PA)**	4119	C	310 391-6161	11409
Makespace Labs Inc	4225	C	800 920-9440	11596
Pacific Bell Telephone Company	4812	A	310 515-2898	11853
Globecast America Incorporated	4841	C	310 845-3900	11995
Wovexx Holdings **(DH)**	4899	D	310 424-2080	12015
Punch Studio LLC **(PA)**	5112	C	310 390-9900	12998
New Milani Group LLC	5122	D	323 582-9404	13059
M M S Trading Inc	5199	E	323 587-1082	13546
Topson Downs California Inc **(PA)**	5621	C	310 558-0300	13917
Jam City Inc **(PA)**	5734	E	310 205-4800	13973
GK Management Co Inc **(PA)**	6531	C	310 204-2050	14804
Property Management Assoc Inc **(PA)**	6531	C	323 295-2000	14852
Goldrich & Kest Industries LLC	6552	A	310 204-2050	14899
Goldrich Kest Hirsch Stern LLC **(PA)**	6552	C	310 204-2050	14900
Hirsch3667 Corp	6719	C	310 641-6690	14933
Starwood Hotel	7011	C	310 641-7740	15371
Clutter Inc	7299	C	800 805-4023	15503
Mutesix Group Inc	7311	C	800 935-6856	15564
Carat N Amer Dntsu Aegis Ntwrk	7319	C	310 255-1000	15600
Amazon Studios LLC	7371	C	818 804-0884	15962
Docupace Technologies LLC **(PA)**	7371	C	310 445-7722	16018
Genex **(DH)**	7371	C	424 672-9500	16039
Liveoffice LLC	7372	D	877 253-2793	16295
Scopely Inc **(DH)**	7372	C	323 400-6618	16375
Spring Technologies Corp	7372	E	310 230-4000	16387
West Publishing Corporation	7373	A	424 243-2100	16478
Sony Pictures Imageworks Inc	7374	A	310 840-8000	16516
Aegis SEC & Investigations Inc	7381	C	310 838-2787	16613

	SIC	EMP	PHONE	ENTRY#
Pacific National Security Inc	7381	C	310 842-7073	16667
Security Indust Spcialists Inc **(PA)**	7381	C	310 215-5100	16683
Event Intelligence Group	7382	D	310 237-5375	16735
Innovation Specialties	7389	C	888 827-2387	16847
Mktg Inc	7389	B	310 972-7900	16879
Columbia Pictures Inds Inc **(DH)**	7812	C	310 244-4000	17177
Crunchyroll LLC **(DH)**	7812	D	972 355-7300	17180
Sony Media Cloud Services LLC	7812	E	877 683-9124	17220
Sony Pctres Wrldwide Acqstons	7812	C	310 244-4000	17221
Sony Pictures Entrmt Inc **(DH)**	7812	A	310 244-4000	17222
Sony Pictures Studios Inc	7812	A	310 244-4000	17223
Sony Pictures Television Inc **(DH)**	7812	B	310 244-7625	17224
Zoic Inc	7812	C	310 838-0770	17240
Dneg North America Inc **(PA)**	7819	D	323 461-7887	17249
Technclor Crative Svcs USA Inc	7819	B	818 260-1214	17266
Maker Studios **(DH)**	7929	C	310 606-2182	17346
Nfl Properties LLC	7941	D	310 840-4635	17378
Southern Cal Prmnnte Med Group	8011	C	310 737-4900	17773
Institute For Applied Bhvior A **(PA)**	8049	C	310 649-0499	17862
L & A Care Corporation	8052	C	310 202-7693	18088
Marycrest Manor	8059	D	310 838-2778	18145
Brotman Medical Center Inc	8062	B	310 836-7000	18193
Southern Cal Halthcare Sys Inc	8062	B	310 836-7000	18449
Didi Hirsch Psychiatric Svc **(PA)**	8322	C	310 390-6612	19072
Exceptional Chld Foundation **(PA)**	8331	C	310 204-3300	19184
Allies For Every Child Inc	8351	C	310 846-4100	19200
Exceptional Chld Foundation	8641	C	310 915-6606	19446
Hawkins Brown USA Inc	8712	B	310 600-2695	19730
Lamar Jhnson Collaborative Inc	8712	C	424 361-3960	19734
Kpmg LLP	8721	D	703 286-8175	19784
Nantcell Inc	8731	B	562 397-3639	19863
HI LLC **(PA)**	8732	E	757 655-4113	19895
Ipsos Otx Corporation **(HQ)**	8732	C	310 736-3400	19902
Altruist Corp	8742	C	949 370-5096	20128
Netfortris Acquisition Co Inc	8748	D	310 861-4300	20365
City of Culver City	9111	D	310 253-6525	20404

CYPRESS, CA - Orange County

	SIC	EMP	PHONE	ENTRY#
Plumbing Piping & Cnstr Inc	1711	D	714 821-0490	808
Lt Foods Americas Inc **(HQ)**	2041	F	562 340-4040	1413
Simply Fresh LLC	2092	C	714 562-5000	1812
Shaw Industries Group Inc	2273	C	562 430-4445	2120
Speedo USA Inc	2329	B	657 465-3800	2219
Awake Inc	2335	E	818 365-9361	2277
Manhattan Beachwear LLC **(PA)**	2369	D	657 384-2110	2417
Exemplis LLC **(PA)**	2522	E	714 995-4800	2912
X-Chair LLC	2522	E	844 492-4247	2919
Johnson Controls Inc	2531	C	562 594-3200	2930
Community Media Corporation **(PA)**	2711	E	714 220-0292	3267
Creative Teaching Press Inc **(PA)**	2731	D	714 799-2100	3404
Primary Color Systems Corp **(PA)**	2759	B	949 660-7080	3798
Venus Laboratories Inc	2819	D	714 891-3100	3918
Diasorin Molecular LLC	2835	C	562 240-6500	4272
Merger Sub Gotham 2 LLC	3089	C	714 462-4603	5096
Plastic Molded Components Inc	3089	E	714 229-0133	5145
Rolls-Royce High Temperature Composites Inc	3299	E	714 375-4085	5574
Dameron Alloy Foundries **(PA)**	3325	D	310 631-5165	5662
Hyatt Die Cast and Engineering Corp **(PA)**	3363	D	714 826-7550	5759
Hilti US Manufacturing Inc	3425	E	714 230-7410	5892
Cavotec Inet US Inc	3531	D	714 947-0005	6928
Cavotec US Holdings Inc **(HQ)**	3532	F	714 545-7900	6948
Power Pt Inc	3537	D	714 826-7407	6997
OK International Inc **(DH)**	3548	C	714 799-9910	7160
Seabiscuit Motorsports Inc	3592	E	714 898-9763	7706
J & F Machine Inc	3599	E	714 527-3499	7878
Magna Tool Inc	3599	E	714 826-2500	7915
Hitachi Automotive Systems	3621	D	310 212-0200	8144
Scientfc Applctons RES Assoc **(PA)**	3629	C	714 224-4410	8212
Luma Comfort Inc	3634	C	855 963-9247	8237
Mission Microwave Tech LLC	3663	D	951 893-4925	8547
Yaesu Usa Inc	3663	E	714 827-7600	8600
Optex Incorporated	3669	C	800 966-7839	8618
Drs Ntwork Imaging Systems LLC	3674	D	714 220-3800	8789
Weldex Corporation **(PA)**	3674	C	714 761-2100	8922
Mitsubshi Elc Vsual Sltons AME	3679	C	800 553-7278	9086
Orbit Inni Inc	3679	C	909 468-5160	9096
Cavotec Dabico US Inc	3728	E	714 947-0005	9657
Inet Airport Systems Inc	3728	C	714 888-2700	9718
Safran Cabin Inc	3728	C	562 344-4780	9784
Tayco Engineering Inc	3761	C	714 952-2240	9904
Focus Technologies Holding Co	3826	E	800 838-4548	10260
Dentis USA Corporation	3843	F	323 677-4363	10739
Christie Medical Holdings Inc	3845	E	714 236-8610	10796

Employee Codes: A=Over 500 employees, B=251-500
C=101-250, D=51-100, E=20-50, F=10-19, G=1-9

2024 Southern California
Business Directory and Buyers Guide

© Mergent Inc. 1-800-342-5647

1363

GEOGRAPHIC

	SIC	EMP	PHONE	ENTRY#
Christie Digital Systems Inc (HQ)	3861	D	714 236-8610	10862
Sitonit Seating Inc	5021	D	714 995-4800	12291
Atg - Designing Mobility Inc (DH)	5047	E	562 921-0258	12472
Multiquip Inc (DH)	5063	B	310 537-3700	12608
Siemens Industry Inc	5063	D	714 761-2200	12618
Ushio America Inc (HQ)	5063	D	714 236-8600	12623
Interntional Tech Systems Corp	5065	E	714 761-8886	12671
Mitsubishi Electric Us Inc (DH)	5065	C	714 220-2500	12683
Q Tech Corporation	5065	C	310 836-7900	12692
Beverages & More Inc	5078	C	714 891-1242	12760
ME & My Big Ideas LLC	5092	C	240 348-5240	12939
Natureware Inc	5122	D	714 251-4510	13058
Hybrid Promotions LLC (PA)	5136	C	714 952-3866	13105
Real Mex Foods Inc	5141	D	714 523-0031	13193
Yamaha Motor Corporation USA (HQ)	5571	B	714 761-7300	13904
Los Alamitos Race Course	5812	C	714 820-2800	14024
WKS Restaurant Corporation (PA)	5812	C	562 425-1402	14045
Eno Brands Inc	5944	E	714 220-1318	14075
Mitsubishi Motors Cr Amer Inc (DH)	6141	B	714 799-4730	14272
Uhc of California (DH)	6324	A	952 936-6615	14504
Cal Southern United Food	6371	C	714 220-2297	14547
Healthsmart Management Service	6411	D	714 947-8600	14601
Pacific Pioneer Insur Group (PA)	6411	D	714 228-7888	14621
DAndrea Graphic Corportion	7336	D	310 642-0260	15662
B2b Staffing Services Inc	7363	B	714 243-4104	15915
Tad Pgs Inc	7363	A	571 451-2428	15945
Mercury Defense Systems Inc	7374	C	714 898-8200	16504
Mercury Systems Inc	7374	C	714 898-8200	16505
Trojan Professional Svcs Inc	7375	C	714 816-7169	16536
Consoldted Med Bo-Analysis Inc (PA)	8071	C	714 657-7369	18543
Focus Diagnostics Inc	8071	A	714 220-1900	18550
Pacificare Health Systems LLC (HQ)	8082	A	714 952-1121	18632
Tutor Time Learning Ctrs LLC	8351	C	714 484-1000	19232
Murphy Murphy & Murphy Inc	8721	C	562 594-6678	19796
Applied Research Assoc Inc	8731	D	505 881-8074	19821

DAGGETT, CA - San Bernardino County

	SIC	EMP	PHONE	ENTRY#
NRG California South LP	4911	C	760 254-5241	12030
Rri Energy Coolwater Inc	4911	D	760 254-5290	12041

DANA POINT, CA - Orange County

	SIC	EMP	PHONE	ENTRY#
Tiger Business Holdings Inc	3672	F	714 763-4180	8738
Kanstul Musical Instrs Inc	3931	E	714 563-1000	10926
Cph Monarch Hotel LLC	7011	A	949 234-3200	15123
Prutel Joint Venture	7011	A	949 240-5064	15311
Ritz-Carlton Hotel Company LLC	7011	B	949 240-5020	15328
Ciri - Stroup Inc	7299	C	949 488-3104	15501
Pacific Asian Enterprises Inc (PA)	7389	E	949 496-4848	16897
Monarch Beach Golf Links (HQ)	7992	C	949 240-8247	17440
Gfk Etilize Inc	8732	D	888 608-1212	19893
Alter Management LLC	8741	C	949 629-0214	19993

DEL MAR, CA - San Diego County

	SIC	EMP	PHONE	ENTRY#
Crest Beverage Company Inc	5181	C	858 452-2300	13465
Liquid Investments Inc (PA)	5181	C	858 509-8510	13471
Dayton Dmh Inc	6514	C	858 350-4400	14735
Lhoberge Lessee Inc	7011	E	858 259-1515	15226
Pacifica Hosts Inc	7011	C	858 755-1501	15290
Sunstone Durante LLC	7011	C	858 792-5200	15378
Del Mar Fairgrounds	7299	D	858 792-4288	15505
Del Mar Blue Print Co Inc	7334	E	858 755-5134	15646
Culver Personnel Agencies Inc	7361	C	888 600-5733	15835
Del Mar Thoroughbred Club	7948	B	858 755-1141	17385
LLC Bates White	8111	C	858 523-2150	18899
Humetrix Holdings Inc	8742	E	858 259-8987	20183
Odme Solutions LLC	8742	D	619 227-0059	20213
California Dept Fd Agriculture	9641	A	858 755-1161	20419

DELANO, CA - Kern County

	SIC	EMP	PHONE	ENTRY#
M Caratan Disc Inc	0172	C	661 725-2566	34
Hronis Inc A California Corp (PA)	0174	C	661 725-2503	43
Wonderful Company LLC	0174	B	661 720-2400	45
Munger Bros LLC	0179	A	661 721-0390	49
Cal Treehouse Almonds LLC	0723	C	661 725-6334	100
Monarch Nut Company LLC	0723	C	661 725-6458	109
Wonderful Citrus Packing LLC (HQ)	0723	B	661 720-2400	118
Ayo Foods LLC	2026	E	661 345-5457	1305
Wonderful Citrus Packing LLC	2033	F	661 720-2400	1353
Delano Growers Grape Products	2087	D	661 725-3255	1765
Agri-Cel Inc	3086	C	661 792-2107	4870
Styrotek Inc	3086	C	661 725-4957	4907
Anthony Welded Products Inc (PA)	3537	E	661 721-7211	6986
City of Delano	3589	E	661 721-3352	7648

	SIC	EMP	PHONE	ENTRY#
Triple R Transportation Inc	4119	D	661 725-6494	11408
Mrv Service Air Inc	7623	F	661 725-3400	17065
Delano Dst Sklled Nrsing Fclty	8051	C	661 720-2100	17926
Adventist Health Delano	8062	C	661 721-5337	18161
Adventist Health Delano (HQ)	8062	A	661 725-4800	18162
North Kern S Tulare Hosp Dst	8062	C	661 720-2126	18352
Crowne Cold Storage LLC	8742	E	661 725-6458	20161

DESERT HOT SPRINGS, CA - Riverside County

	SIC	EMP	PHONE	ENTRY#
Western Golf Car Mfg Inc	3949	D	760 671-6691	11042
Desert Hot Sprng Real Prpts In	6512	D	760 329-6000	14658
Forest Lawn Mortuary	7261	B	760 329-8737	15487
Borrego Cmnty Hlth Foundation	8011	C	760 251-0044	17603

DIAMOND BAR, CA - Los Angeles County

	SIC	EMP	PHONE	ENTRY#
Genius Products Nt Inc	2086	C	510 671-0219	1694
Rapid Rack Holdings Inc	2542	A		2988
Rapid Rack Industries Inc	2542	D		2989
Sappi North America Inc	2621	E	714 456-0600	3062
K2 Label & Printing Inc	2752	E	626 922-8108	3610
Gohz Inc	3621	E	800 603-1219	8142
Ultimate Sound Inc	3651	B	909 861-6200	8445
Ecmm Services Inc	3955	C	714 988-9388	11056
Call-The-Car	4119	D	855 282-6968	11378
Zenlayer Inc	4813	C	909 718-3558	11914
Graybar Electric Company Inc	5063	C	909 451-4300	12596
Smart & Final Stores Inc	5141	C	323 855-8434	13217
24-Hour Med Staffing Svcs LLC	7361	C	909 895-8960	15807
Liferay Inc (PA)	7373	A	877 543-3729	16454
Unspoken Language Services Inc	7389	B	626 532-8096	16954
Central Health Plan Cal Inc	8082	C	626 938-7120	18601
Motech Americas LLC	8731	B	302 451-7500	19861
South Cast A Qlty MGT Dst Bldg (PA)	8748	A	909 396-2000	20382

DOWNEY, CA - Los Angeles County

	SIC	EMP	PHONE	ENTRY#
Meruelo Enterprises Inc (PA)	1542	A	562 745-2300	568
Westar Manufacturing Inc	1799	E	562 633-0581	1185
Reyes Coca-Cola Bottling LLC	2086	D	562 803-8100	1738
Western Pacific Pulp and Paper (HQ)	2611	D	562 803-4401	3038
Loudlabs News LLC	2711	F	310 877-8374	3300
Instant Web LLC	2752	C	562 658-2020	3601
Hutchinson Seal Corporation (DH)	3053	C	248 375-4190	4733
Bradley Manufacturing Co Inc	3089	E	562 923-5556	4970
V-T Industries Inc	3089	E	714 521-2008	5241
Universal Mlding Extrusion Inc (DH)	3354	E	562 401-1015	5713
Umc Acquisition Corp (PA)	3356	C	562 940-0300	5727
Universal Molding Company (HQ)	3356	C	310 886-1750	5728
Reliable Building Products Inc	3441	E	323 566-5000	6069
Thompson Tank Inc	3443	F	562 869-7711	6165
Cal Pipe Manufacturing Inc (PA)	3498	E	562 803-4388	6840
MD Stainless Services	3498	E	562 904-7022	6849
Detroit Diesel Corporation	3519	D	562 929-7016	6893
Downey Grinding Inc	3541	E	562 803-5556	7011
United California Corporation	3544	D	562 803-1521	7102
United Drill Bushing Corp	3545	C	562 803-1521	7136
Can Lines Engineering Inc (PA)	3565	D	562 861-2996	7346
Wesfac Inc (HQ)	3589	F	562 861-2160	7692
Sst Technologies	3674	E	562 803-3361	8897
Commercial Truck Eqp Co LLC	3713	C	562 803-4466	9317
Ebus Inc	3713	E	562 904-3474	9324
World Water Inc	3823	E	562 940-1964	10169
California Ribbon Carbn Co Inc	3955	D		11054
Advanced Building Systems Inc	3999	E	818 652-4252	11186
Liberty Ambulance LLC	4119	C	562 741-6230	11393
Mike Campbell & Associates Ltd	4222	A	626 369-3981	11552
Southern California Gas Co	4924	A	562 803-7500	12095
Keyline Sales Inc	5074	C	562 904-3910	12745
Qualls Stud Welding Pdts Inc	5084	F	562 923-7883	12812
Rockview Dairies Inc (PA)	5149	C	562 927-5511	13392
Leach Grain & Milling Co Inc	5191	E	562 869-4451	13489
Home Depot USA Inc	5211	A	562 776-2200	13619
Florence Meat Packing Co Inc	5812	E	562 401-0760	14009
Kaiser Foundation Hospitals	6324	B	562 657-9000	14475
Kaiser Foundation Hospitals	6324	A	562 622-4190	14478
OfficeMax North America Inc	7334	C	562 927-6444	15650
National Trench Safety LLC	7359	C	562 602-1642	15790
OSI Staffing Inc	7361	D	562 261-5753	15875
Biu Inc	7389	C	909 556-1311	16794
Kpwr Radio LLC	7389	C	562 745-2300	16856
Lakewood Park Health Ctr Inc (PA)	7389	B	562 869-0978	16859
Jobsite Stud Welding	7692	C	855 885-7883	17090
Tarsco Holdings LLC	7699	E	562 869-0200	17157
City of Downey	7922	C	562 861-8211	17313

	SIC	EMP	PHONE	ENTRY#
Downey Community Health Center	8051	C	562 862-6506	17928
Ensign Group Inc	8051	C	562 923-9301	17942
Healthcare Ctr of Downey LLC	8051	C	562 869-0978	17970
Los Angeles Cnty Rncho Los Amgo	8052	A	562 385-7111	18090
Pih Health Downey Hospital (HQ)	8062	B	562 698-0811	18377
Pih Health Hospital - Whitti	8062	A	562 904-5482	18379
Southern Cal Prmnnte Med Group	8062	B	562 657-2200	18451
Rai Care Centers Lynwood LLC	8092	D	562 401-0155	18661
County of Los Angeles	8093	C	562 401-7088	18683
Jwch Institute Inc	8099	C	562 862-1000	18773
County of Los Angeles	8322	D	562 940-6856	19061
Automobile Club Southern Cal	8699	C	562 904-5970	19524
Rancho Research Institute	8733	C	562 401-8111	19940
County of Los Angeles	8741	C	562 940-2907	20022

DUARTE, CA - Los Angeles County

	SIC	EMP	PHONE	ENTRY#
Prolacta Bioscience Inc	2023	B	626 599-9260	1283
Soyfoods of America	2099	E	626 358-3836	1990
Value Wholesaler Inc	2099	F	626 263-5933	2002
Cosmo Fiber Corporation (PA)	2759	F	626 256-6098	3750
Quality Car Care Products Inc	2819	E	626 359-9174	3907
Baxco Pharmaceutical Inc	2834	F	626 610-7088	4067
Justice Bros Dist Co Inc	2843	E	626 359-9174	4375
Onex Rf Inc	3548	F	626 358-6639	7161
Spenuzza Inc	3589	E	626 358-8063	7687
Assembly Automation Industries	3599	E	626 303-2777	7764
Delafield Corporation (PA)	3599	C	626 303-0740	7814
Accu-Sembly Inc	3672	D	626 357-3447	8638
Turbo Coil Manufacturing Inc	3677	E	626 599-7777	8957
Woodward Hrt Inc	3728	C	626 359-9211	9829
Sportifeye Optics Inc	3851	E	877 742-5000	10852
A & B Brush Mfg Corp	3991	F	626 303-8856	11083
Victory Sportswear Inc	5199	E	866 308-0798	13567
Advantage Ford Lincoln Mercury	5511	D	626 305-9188	13735
Gpi Ca-Niii Inc	5511	D	626 305-3000	13773
Bay Vista Senior Housing	6513	B	925 924-7100	14704
Humangood Socal	6513	E	626 357-1632	14714
We Pack It All LLC	7389	C	626 301-9214	16964
Beckman RES Inst of The Cy Hop	8011	C	626 359-8111	17601
Estrella Inc	8051	C	562 925-6418	17949
Humangood (PA)	8059	C	602 906-4024	18132
City Hope National Medical Ctr (HQ)	8062	A	626 256-4673	18222
Santa Teresita Inc (PA)	8062	B	626 359-3243	18423
Maryvale Day Care Center	8351	C	626 357-1514	19218
Humangood Socal	8361	C	626 359-8141	19273
City of Hope	8399	B	213 202-5735	19319
Tanner Research Inc	8731	E	626 471-9700	19878
City of Hope (PA)	8741	B	626 256-4673	20013

E RNCHO DMNGZ, CA - Los Angeles County

	SIC	EMP	PHONE	ENTRY#
Timec Companies Inc	1629	C	310 885-4710	718
Murray Plumbing and Htg Corp (PA)	1711	B	310 637-1500	796
Sonora Mills Foods Inc (PA)	2099	C	310 639-5333	1987
Audio Video Color Corporation (PA)	2671	E	424 213-7500	3149
Modern Concepts Inc	3089	C	310 637-0013	5103
Coy Industries Inc	3444	D	310 603-2970	6220
Industrial Tctnics Brings Corp (DH)	3562	C	310 537-3750	7299
Dependable Global Express Inc (PA)	4731	C	310 537-2000	11751

EARP, CA - San Bernardino County

	SIC	EMP	PHONE	ENTRY#
Colorado River Adventures Inc (PA)	7033	C	760 663-3737	15442

EASTVALE, CA - Riverside County

	SIC	EMP	PHONE	ENTRY#
PTi Sand & Gravel Inc	1442	E	951 272-0140	408
Pierco Incorporated	3089	D	951 361-6400	5135
Jose Perez	3535	E	920 318-6527	6975
Royal Range California Inc	3631	D	951 360-1600	8222
Speakercraft LLC	3651	D	951 685-1759	8439
Prime Solutions Inc	3674	E	702 354-7129	8867
Edwards Lifesciences	3842	E	951 749-3316	10651
CJ Logistics America LLC	4212	C	909 605-7233	11450
Keystone Automotive Warehouse	5013	D	951 277-5237	12245
Smart & Final Stores Inc	5141	C	909 773-1813	13196
Shamrock Foods Company	5149	A	951 685-6314	13394
Home Depot USA Inc	5211	D	951 727-0324	13580

EDISON, CA - Kern County

	SIC	EMP	PHONE	ENTRY#
Giumarra Vineyards Corporation (PA)	0172	B	661 395-7000	31
Kirschenman Enterprises Sls LP	7389	C	661 366-5736	16854

EDWARDS, CA - Kern County

	SIC	EMP	PHONE	ENTRY#
Jt3 LLC	8711	A	661 277-4900	19627

EL CAJON, CA - San Diego County

	SIC	EMP	PHONE	ENTRY#
Hess Contracting Inc	1382	E	619 442-6333	308
Rpc Inc	1389	F	619 334-6244	383
Azusa Rock LLC	1422	E	619 440-2363	398
Norberg Crushing Inc	1429	F	619 390-4200	401
California Shtmtl Works Inc	1541	D	619 562-7010	497
Steve P Rados Inc	1622	E	619 328-1360	655
Cass Construction Inc (PA)	1623	B	619 590-0929	666
Schilling Paradise Corp	1623	C	619 449-4141	688
J Cloud Incorporated	1629	E	619 593-9020	713
Astro Mechanical Contractors Inc	1711	D	619 442-9686	737
Cascade Thermal Solutions LLC (PA)	1711	E	619 562-8852	750
Countywide Mech Systems LLC	1711	C	619 449-9900	757
Helix Mechanical Inc	1711	C	619 440-1518	776
R & R Mechanical Contractors Inc	1711	C	619 449-9900	813
Walter Anderson Plumbing Inc	1711	C	619 449-7646	833
West Coast AC Co Inc	1711	C	619 561-8000	834
City-Wide Electronic Systems Inc	1731	D	619 444-0219	880
Dynalectric Company	1731	B	619 328-4007	892
Paradise Electric Inc	1731	B	619 449-4141	923
Seal Electric Inc	1731	C	619 449-7323	933
Sunshine Communications SE Inc	1731	C	619 448-7600	942
Artimex Iron Inc	1791	C	619 444-3155	1100
Flight Suits	2386	D	619 440-2700	2430
Roll-Rite LLC	2394	E	619 449-8860	2508
Transportation Equipment Inc	2394	E	619 449-8860	2511
Flexsystems Usa Inc	2399	F	619 401-1858	2552
Lexar Incorporated	2426	F	619 252-8265	2575
Hollands Custom Cabinets Inc	2434	E	619 443-6081	2660
Vcsd Inc	2434	E	619 579-6886	2683
Omni Enclosures Inc	2541	E	619 579-6664	2963
First Class Packaging Inc	2631	E	619 579-7166	3068
Doctors Signature Sales (PA)	2833	E	800 531-4877	3997
Delstar Technologies Inc	3081	E	619 258-1503	4810
Damar Plastics Inc	3089	E	619 283-2300	5002
JP Gunite Inc	3273	E	619 938-0228	5484
Vertechs Enterprises Inc (PA)	3364	F	858 578-3900	5776
Decco Castings Inc	3369	C	619 444-9437	5810
Certified Metal Craft Inc	3398	E	619 593-3636	5832
M W Reid Welding Inc	3441	D	619 401-5880	6042
Western Bay Sheet Metal Inc	3441	E	619 233-1753	6094
Asm Construction Inc	3444	E	619 449-1966	6194
Bay Sheet Metal Inc	3444	E	619 401-9270	6200
Dave Whipple Sheet Metal Inc	3444	E	619 562-6962	6224
Pacific Marine Sheet Metal Corporation	3444	C	858 869-8900	6286
Access Professional Inc	3446	F	858 571-4444	6347
Jmmca Inc (PA)	3462	D	619 448-2711	6463
Top Notch Mfg Inc	3469	F	619 588-2033	6563
BJS&t Enterprises Inc	3479	E	619 448-7795	6695
Alturdyne Power Systems Inc	3511	E	619 343-3204	6877
Toro Company	3523	C	619 562-2950	6916
Veridiam Inc (DH)	3545	C	619 448-1000	7137
Rotron Incorporated	3564	C	619 593-7400	7330
Prime Heat Incorporated	3567	F	619 449-6623	7371
Campbell Membrane Tech Inc	3569	E	619 938-2481	7384
Hi-Tech Welding & Forming Inc	3599	E	619 562-5929	7862
High Prcsion Grnding McHning I	3599	E	619 440-0303	7863
Senior Operations LLC	3599	D	909 247-7000	8023
Weldmac Manufacturing Company	3599	E	619 440-2300	8073
Weldmac Manufacturing Company	3599	E	619 440-2300	8074
Tujayar Enterprises Inc	3646	E	619 442-0577	8337
Micro-Mode Products Inc	3663	E	619 449-3844	8544
New Brunswick Industries Inc	3672	E	619 448-4900	8710
Brantner and Associates Inc (DH)	3678	C	619 562-7070	8961
Q Microwave Inc	3679	D	619 258-7322	9104
Triad Components Group Inc (PA)	3679	F	619 993-3800	9132
Rks Inc (HQ)	3699	F	858 571-4444	9249
Gear Vendors Inc	3714	E	619 562-0060	9395
GKN Aerospace Chem-Tronics Inc (DH)	3724	A	619 258-5500	9570
Vertechs Enterprises Inc	3724	F	858 578-3900	9583
Jet Air Fbo LLC	3728	C	619 448-5991	9728
Dn Tanks Inc	3795	C	619 440-8181	9929
Dyk Incorporated (HQ)	3795	C	619 440-8181	9930
Get Engineering Corp	3823	F	619 443-8295	10136
Calbiotech Export Inc	3841	E	619 660-6162	10465
Johnson Outdoors Inc	3949	C	619 402-1023	11007
California Neon Products	3993	D	619 283-2191	11101
Integrated Sign Associates	3993	E	619 579-2229	11125
San Diego Electric Sign Inc	3993	F	619 258-1775	11154
Cal AM Manufacturing Co Inc	3999	E	800 992-0499	11199
Transdev Services Inc	4119	C	619 401-0543	11407
San Diego Gas & Electric Co	4911	B	619 441-3834	12042
Waste Management Cal Inc	4953	C	619 596-5100	12198

Employee Codes: A=Over 500 employees, B=251-500
C=101-250, D=51-100, E=20-50, F=10-19, G=1-9

2024 Southern California
Business Directory and Buyers Guide

© Mergent Inc. 1-800-342-5647

1365

	SIC	EMP	PHONE	ENTRY#
Denardi Machinery Inc	5082	C	619 749-0039	12767
Tk Elevator Corporation	5084	C	619 596-7220	12830
Sundance Custom Golf Carts Inc	5088	F	619 449-0822	12918
Taylor-Listug Inc (PA)	5099	C	619 258-1207	12988
Graphic Business Solutions Inc	5112	E	619 258-4081	12994
Smart & Final Stores Inc	5141	B	619 390-1738	13201
Smart & Final Stores Inc	5141	B	619 589-7000	13206
Pf Bakeries Llc	5149	E	858 263-4863	13389
Sunfood Corporation	5149	E	619 596-7979	13396
Benny Enterprises Inc	5181	E	619 592-4455	13461
Home Depot USA Inc	5211	D	619 401-6610	13598
Wetzels Pretzels LLC	5461	E	619 588-1074	13724
K Motors Inc	5521	C	619 270-3000	13851
Sycuan Tribal Development	5812	C	619 442-3425	14038
EC Closing Corp	6162	D	800 546-1531	14311
The Pines Ltd	6513	C	619 447-1880	14731
Sycuan Casino	7011	A	619 445-6002	15385
W Lodging Inc	7011	B	619 258-6565	15406
Beauty Boutique Inc	7231	C	619 442-3407	15478
Cartwright Trmt Pest Ctrl Inc	7342	E	619 442-9613	15684
XI Staffing Inc	7361	C	619 579-0442	15908
Nlyte Software Americas Ltd	7371	D	866 386-5983	16087
Tessitura Network Inc	7372	C	888 643-5778	16401
Socal Technologies LLC	7379	E	619 635-1128	16600
Newport Diversified Inc	7389	C	619 448-4111	16887
El Cajon Motors (PA)	7515	D	619 579-8888	16984
CLP Inc (PA)	7692	E	619 444-3105	17081
Edwards Theatres Circuit Inc	7832	C	619 660-3460	17294
Sycuan Casino (PA)	7999	C	619 445-6002	17567
Kaiser Foundation Hospitals	8011	D	619 528-5000	17678
Southern Cal Prmnnte Med Group	8011	C	619 528-5000	17786
Country Hills Health Care Inc	8051	C	619 441-8745	17912
Eldorado Care Center LP	8051	B	619 440-1211	17930
Parkside Healthcare Inc	8052	C	619 442-7744	18095
Kaiser Foundation Hospitals	8062	C	619 528-5000	18310
Apheresis Care Group Inc	8092	D	619 440-4612	18656
Rai Care Ctrs Sthern Cal II LL	8092	C	619 442-4122	18663
Home Guiding Hands Corporation (PA)	8361	B	619 938-2850	19271
ARC of San Diego	8399	B	619 448-2415	19312
Nan McKay and Associates Inc	8742	D	619 258-1855	20205

EL CENTRO, CA - Imperial County

	SIC	EMP	PHONE	ENTRY#
Braga Fresh Family Farms Inc	0191	C	760 353-1155	77
Joe Heger Farms LLC	0191	C	760 353-5111	83
Noblesse Oblige Inc	0722	C	760 353-3336	97
Reyes Coca-Cola Bottling LLC	2086	E	760 352-1561	1729
Labrucherie Produce LLC	2099	C	760 352-2170	1932
Associated Desert Newspaper (DH)	2711	E	760 337-3400	3258
Coyne Companies LLC	2741	F	760 353-1016	3438
Imperial Printers (PA)	2752	F	760 352-4374	3593
Superior Ready Mix Concrete LP	3273	D	760 352-4341	5515
Complete Metal Fabrication Inc	3441	F	760 353-0260	6011
Ew Corprtion Indus Fabricators (PA)	3441	D	760 337-0020	6023
Rogar Manufacturing Inc	3679	C	760 335-3700	9109
Lowes Home Centers LLC	5211	D	760 337-6700	13625
El Centro Motors	5511	D	760 336-2100	13759
El Centro Hospitality Inc	7011	C	760 353-2600	15142
El Centro Hospitality 2 LLC	7011	C	760 370-3800	15143
I N C Builders Inc	7363	B	760 352-4200	15924
Southwest Protective Svcs Inc	7381	C	760 996-1285	16692
Wymore Inc	7692	E	760 352-2045	17100
El Centro Rgnal Med Ctr Fndtio (PA)	8062	A	760 339-7100	18252
Accentcare HM Hlth El Cntro In	8082	B	760 352-4022	18580
Womanhaven	8322	D	760 353-6922	19170
Rove Engineering Inc	8711	D	760 425-0001	19681

EL MONTE, CA - Los Angeles County

	SIC	EMP	PHONE	ENTRY#
Envirogenics Systems Company	1629	D	818 573-9220	708
LA Web Inc	1721	F	626 453-8800	850
Thrifty Payless Inc	2024	A	626 571-0122	1300
Atlantis Seafood LLC	2092	D	626 626-4900	1799
Dianas Mexican Food Pdts Inc	2099	D	626 444-0555	1883
El Gallito Market Inc	2099	E	626 442-1190	1887
La Chapalita Inc (PA)	2099	E	626 443-8556	1925
Andari Fashion Inc	2329	C	626 575-2759	2192
Tartan Fashion Inc	2329	E	626 575-2828	2224
Royal Apparel Inc	2339	E	626 579-5168	2368
Svo Enterprise LLC	2381	E	626 406-4770	2423
SOLE Designs Inc	2512	F	626 452-8642	2819
Hunter Douglas Inc	2591	A	858 679-7500	3007
LAweb Offset Printing Inc	2759	F	626 454-2469	3780
Pax Tag & Label Inc	2759	E	626 579-2000	3795
Gill Corporation (PA)	3089	C	626 443-6094	5040

	SIC	EMP	PHONE	ENTRY#
Remington Roll Forming Inc	3316	E	626 350-5196	5631
Industrial Machine & Mfg Co	3441	E	626 444-0181	6032
Fanboys Window Factory Inc (PA)	3442	E	626 280-8787	6106
Castle Industries Inc of California	3444	E	909 390-0899	6212
Jansen Ornamental Supply Co	3446	E	626 442-0271	6360
BIG Enterprises	3448	E	626 448-1449	6374
All New Stamping Co	3469	C	626 443-8813	6494
Pride Metal Polishing LLC	3471	F	626 350-1326	6651
Santoshi Corporation	3471	E	626 444-7118	6660
Applied Coatings & Linings	3479	E	626 280-6354	6690
Precision Coil Spring Company	3495	C	626 444-0561	6807
Craneveyor Corp (PA)	3536	D	626 442-1524	6980
Mercury Broach Co Inc	3545	F	626 443-5904	7119
Lith-O-Roll Corporation	3555	C	626 579-0340	7187
Lawrence Equipment Leasing Inc (PA)	3556	C	626 442-2894	7206
Justin Inc	3612	E	626 444-4516	8100
Videssence LLC (PA)	3645	E	626 579-0943	8299
R W Swarens Associates Inc	3646	E	626 579-0943	8329
Talmo & Chinn Inc	3674	E	626 443-1741	8905
S C I Industries Inc	3714	E		9455
Transgo LLC	3714	E	626 443-7456	9474
Sparling Instruments LLC	3824	E	626 444-0571	10178
Tacticombat Inc	3949	F	626 315-4433	11033
Access Services	4111	D	213 270-6000	11314
First Student Inc	4111	C	626 448-9446	11316
San Gabriel Transit Inc (PA)	4111	C	626 258-1310	11362
San Gabriel Valley Water Co (PA)	4941	C	626 448-6183	12144
Los Angeles Ltg Mfg Co Inc	5063	D	626 454-8300	12602
Burke Engineering Co	5074	E	626 579-6763	12737
Jans Enterprises Corporation	5149	E	626 575-2000	13371
Mutual Trading Co Inc (DH)	5149	C	213 626-9458	13382
D Longo Inc	5511	B	626 580-6000	13752
El Monte Automotive Group Inc	5511	D	626 580-6200	13760
El Monte Automotive Group LLC	5511	D	626 444-0321	13761
Cathay Capital Trust II	6022	D	213 625-4700	14186
Amenities Development Co	7011	E	626 350-9588	15071
Herald Christian Health Center (PA)	8011	D	626 286-8700	17664
Georgia Atkison Snf LLC	8051	D	626 444-2535	17963
Ramona Care Inc	8051	C	626 442-5721	18035
Gibraltar Cnvalescent Hosp Inc	8059	D	626 443-9425	18128
Ahm Gemch Inc	8062	E	626 579-7777	18165
Fulgent Genetics Inc (PA)	8071	A	626 350-0537	18551
Altamed Health Services Corp	8099	C	626 453-8466	18741
Public Hlth Fndation Entps Inc	8099	C	626 856-6618	18794
Foothill Family Service	8322	E	626 246-1240	19082
Hope Hse For Mltple Hndcpped I (PA)	8361	D	626 443-1313	19272
R and L Lopez Associates Inc (PA)	8711	D	626 330-5296	19676

EL SEGUNDO, CA - Los Angeles County

	SIC	EMP	PHONE	ENTRY#
Irwin Industries Inc	1629	A	704 457-5117	712
Beyond Meat Inc	2013	C	866 756-4112	1213
Team Beachbody Canada LLC	2023	E	310 883-9000	1285
Beyond Meat Inc (PA)	2038	E	866 756-4112	1385
El Segundo Bread Bar LLC	2051	E	310 615-9898	1464
Vbc Holdings Inc	2051	E	310 322-7357	1497
Sugarfina Inc	2064	E	424 290-0777	1551
Zico Beverages LLC (HQ)	2086	E	866 729-9426	1747
Berri Pro Inc	2087	F	781 929-8288	1756
Lambs & Ivy Inc	2392	E	310 322-3800	2475
Satco Inc (PA)	2448	C	310 322-4719	2726
Artissimo Designs LLC (HQ)	2679	D	310 906-3700	3230
Los Angles Tmes Cmmnctions LLC (PA)	2711	A	213 237-5000	3299
Sabot Publishing Inc (PA)	2721	C	310 356-4100	3388
Browntrout Publishers Inc (PA)	2741	E	424 290-6122	3433
Golden State Company LLC	2741	E	310 376-7800	3451
Superbam Inc	2741	E	310 845-5784	3488
Continental Graphics Corp	2752	E	310 662-2307	3543
Neft Vodka USA Inc	2759	E	415 846-0359	3789
Primary Color Systems Corp	2759	D	310 841-0250	3799
Murad LLC (HQ)	2834	C	310 726-0600	4172
Youth To People Inc	2844	D	309 648-5500	4471
Hco Holding II Corporation	2952	A	310 955-9200	4669
Henry Company LLC (HQ)	2952	D	310 955-9200	4670
Hnc Parent Inc (PA)	2952	D	310 955-9200	4671
Allbirds Inc	3143	F	424 502-2383	5265
Craig Tools Inc	3545	D	310 322-0614	7112
Flight Microwave Corporation	3559	D	310 607-9819	7237
Belkin International Inc (DH)	3577	A	310 751-5100	7510
Ross Racing Pistons	3592	E	310 536-0100	7704
Metalore Inc	3599	E	310 643-0360	7930
Glentek Inc	3621	D	310 322-3026	8141
Nantenergy LLC	3621	D	310 905-4866	8152
T3 Micro Inc (PA)	3634	F	310 452-2888	8239

	SIC	EMP	PHONE	ENTRY#
Belkin Inc.	3651	A	800 223-5546	8400
Boeing Satellite Systems Inc (HQ)	3663	E	310 791-7450	8500
Millennium Space Systems Inc (HQ)	3663	E	310 683-5840	8546
MTI Laboratory Inc.	3663	E	310 955-3700	8551
Raytheon Applied Sgnal Tech In	3663	D	310 436-7000	8569
Display Products Inc.	3674	E	310 640-0442	8787
Efficient Pwr Conversion Corp (PA)	3674	D	310 615-0279	8790
Infineon Tech Americas Corp (HQ)	3674	A	310 726-8200	8807
Infineon Tech Americas Corp.	3674	C	310 252-7116	8808
Infineon Tech Americas Corp.	3674	E	310 726-8000	8809
Integra Technologies Inc.	3674	E	310 606-0855	8813
Symmetry Electronics (DH)	3679	E	310 536-6190	8903
J L Cooper Electronics Inc.	3679	E	310 322-9990	9067
Teledyne Technologies Inc.	3679	B	310 765-3600	9126
Loop Inc.	3694	E	888 385-6674	9167
Allclear Inc.	3721	E	424 316-1596	9508
Boeing Coml Satellite Svcs Inc (HQ)	3721	F	310 335-6682	9512
Boeing Satellite Systems Inc.	3721	A	310 568-2735	9518
Aerospace Engrg Support Corp.	3728	E	310 297-4050	9606
Trio Manufacturing Inc.	3728	C	310 640-6123	9820
Kinkisharyo (usa) Inc.	3743	E	424 276-1803	9869
Kinkisharyo Int LLC (HQ)	3743	F	424 276-1803	9870
Abl Space Systems Company.	3761	D	424 321-5049	9890
Varda Space Industries Inc.	3761	E	833 707-0020	9907
Morpheus Space Inc (PA)	3764	F	562 766-8470	9910
Aerojet Rcketdyne Holdings Inc (HQ)	3812	D	310 252-8100	9938
Atk Space Systems LLC.	3812	C	310 343-3799	9955
Northrop Grumman Corporation.	3812	C	310 332-1000	10011
Northrop Grumman Systems Corp.	3812	D	480 355-7716	10017
Northrop Grumman Systems Corp.	3812	B	310 332-1000	10024
Orbital Sciences LLC.	3812	E	703 406-5000	10046
Pacific Defense Strategies Inc (PA)	3812	E	310 722-6050	10048
Raytheon Company.	3812	D	310 647-1000	10055
Raytheon Company.	3812	E	310 647-9438	10056
Raytheon Company.	3812	A	310 647-9438	10057
Raytheon Company.	3812	D	310 647-1000	10058
Teledyne Controls LLC.	3812	A	310 765-3600	10076
Suez Water Indiana LLC.	3823	D	310 414-0183	10164
Karl Storz Endscpy-America Inc (HQ)	3841	B	424 218-8100	10542
Mod-Electronics Inc.	3873	E	310 322-2136	10893
Far Out Toys Inc.	3942	E	310 480-7554	10938
Mattel Inc (PA)	3942	A	310 252-2000	10940
Mattel Investment Inc.	3942	E	310 252-2000	10941
Moose Toys LLC.	3942	D	310 341-4642	10942
Mattel Direct Import Inc (HQ)	3944	E	310 252-2000	10959
Mattel Operations Inc.	3944	E	310 252-2000	10960
Mega Brands America Inc (DH)	3944	D	949 727-9009	10961
Beach House Group LLC.	3999	D	310 356-6180	11194
Cls Trnsprttion Los Angles LLC (HQ)	4119	C	310 414-8189	11380
Air New Zealand Limited.	4512	C	310 648-7000	11657
Singapore Airlines Limited.	4512	C	310 647-1922	11670
F & E Arcft Mint Los Angles LL.	4581	B	310 338-0063	11697
Pacific Aviation Corporation (PA)	4581	C	310 646-4015	11702
Pinnacle Travel Services LLC.	4724	C	310 414-1787	11722
Dfds International Corporation.	4731	D	310 414-1516	11752
L E Coppersmith Inc (PA)	4731	D	310 607-8000	11777
Maersk Whsng Dist Svcs USA LLC (HQ)	4731	C	562 345-2200	11780
AT&T Corp.	4812	D	303 596-8431	11844
Directv Group Holdings LLC (HQ)	4812	C	310 964-5000	11847
Infonet Services Corporation (DH)	4813	A	310 335-2600	11889
Scalefast (PA)	4813	C	310 595-4040	11901
Directv Inc.	4841	B	888 388-4249	11985
Directv Enterprises LLC.	4841	A	310 535-5000	11986
Directv Group Inc (DH)	4841	C	310 964-5000	11990
Directv International Inc (DH)	4841	C	310 964-6460	11991
En Pointe Technologies Sls LLC.	5045	C	310 337-6151	12408
Jal Avionet USA (HQ)	5045	E	310 606-1000	12422
Square Enix Inc.	5045	C	310 846-0400	12442
Boeing Stllite Systems Intl In (HQ)	5088	C	310 364-4000	12903
Com Dev Usa LLC.	5088	D	424 456-8000	12904
Itochu Aviation Inc (DH)	5088	E	310 640-2770	12909
Raytheon Lgstics Spport Trning.	5088	B	310 647-9438	12915
A-Mark Precious Metals Inc (PA)	5094	C	310 587-1477	12959
Jlo Beauty & Lifestyle LLC.	5122	E	888 853-3169	13049
Tri-Union Seafoods LLC (DH)	5146	D	424 397-8556	13288
Chevron Corporation.	5541	C	310 615-5000	13890
Cookingcom Inc.	5719	C	310 664-1283	13958
Gurucul Solutions LLC.	5734	E	213 291-6888	13972
Merqbiz LLC.	5961	E	855 637-7249	14096
Pcm Inc (PA)	5961	A	310 354-5600	14098
Cosmetix West (PA)	5999	C	310 726-3080	14128
Intelligent Beauty LLC.	5999	A	310 683-0940	14137
Manhattan Bancorp.	6021	C	310 606-8000	14169
Bank of Manhattan.	6029	C	310 606-8000	14211
National Planning Corporation.	6141	C	800 881-7174	14274
Charger Investment Partners LP.	6211	D	310 372-5525	14375
Computershare Inc.	6289	B	800 522-6645	14434
Associated Third Party Administrators Inc.	6371			14546
Lyon Stahl Investment RE Inc.	6531	D	310 425-9838	14826
American Academic Hlth Sys LLC.	6719	A	310 414-7200	14922
Asp Henry Holdings Inc.	6719	A	310 955-9200	14923
Hco Holding I Corporation (HQ)	6719	D	323 583-5000	14932
Transom Post Midco LLC.	6719	C	312 254-3300	14949
Century Pk Capitl Partners LLC (PA)	6726	C	310 867-2210	14977
Ld Acquisition Company 16 LLC.	6799	C	310 294-8160	15034
Djont Operations LLC.	7011	C	310 640-3600	15133
Pt Gaming LLC.	7011	A	323 260-5060	15312
Uhg Lax Prop Llc.	7011	C	310 322-0999	15395
Esaloncom LLC.	7231	C	866 550-2424	15480
Murad LLC.	7231	C	310 726-0470	15482
David & Goliath LLC.	7311	C	310 445-5200	15535
Ignited LLC (PA)	7311	C	310 773-3100	15548
Liquid Advertising Inc.	7311	D	310 450-2653	15554
Mh Sub I LLC (PA)	7311	C	310 280-4000	15558
Mullenlowe US Inc.	7311	C	424 738-6500	15562
Beachbody LLC (HQ)	7313	C	310 883-9000	15588
Stampscom Inc (PA)	7331	C	310 482-5800	15636
Softscript Inc.	7338	A	310 451-2110	15681
Ibftech Inc.	7361	D	424 217-8010	15853
Zions Bancorporation.	7361	A	424 290-5123	15909
Altech Services Inc.	7363	B	888 725-8324	15912
Agent Image Inc.	7371	B	310 577-9222	15958
Artic Sentinel Inc.	7371	E	310 227-8230	15967
Crescentone Inc (HQ)	7371	C	310 563-7000	16004
Irise (PA)	7371	D	800 556-0399	16058
Liminex Inc (PA)	7371	C	888 310-0410	16065
BMC.	7372	E	310 321-5555	16187
Governmentjobscom Inc.	7372	C	310 426-6304	16258
Hr Cloud Inc.	7372	E	510 909-1993	16266
M Nexon Inc.	7372	E	213 858-5930	16297
Saviynt Inc (PA)	7372	C	310 641-1664	16374
Smart Action Company LLC.	7372	E	310 776-9200	16381
Street Smart LLC.	7372	C	866 924-4644	16391
Traxero North America LLC.	7372	D	423 497-1164	16411
Unbroken Studios LLC.	7372	C	310 741-2670	16412
Mesfin Enterprises.	7373	B	310 615-0881	16457
Design People Inc.	7374	C	800 969-5799	16490
Crowdstrike Inc.	7379	C	888 512-8906	16560
Ispace Inc.	7379	C	310 563-3800	16573
Cornerstone Protective Svcs.	7381	C	888 848-4791	16634
Whelan Security Co.	7381	C	310 343-8628	16709
Da Vinci Schools Fund.	7389	C	310 725-5800	16813
Oceanx LLC (PA)	7389	D	310 774-4088	16890
Prologic Rdmption Slutions Inc (PA)	7389	A	310 322-7774	16908
Telenet Voip Inc.	7629	D	310 253-9000	17074
Crafty Apes LLC (PA)	7812	A	310 837-3900	17178
Rhythm and Hues Inc (PA)	7812	C	310 448-7500	17214
Zoo Digital Production LLC.	7812	C	310 220-3939	17241
Ten Publishing Media LLC (PA)	7819	C	310 531-9900	17269
Spectrum Clubs Inc.	7991	A	310 727-9300	17415
American Golf Corporation (HQ)	7997	A	310 664-4000	17460
Tga Franchise Spt Holdings LLC.	7997	D	310 333-0622	17529
Optumcare Management LLC (HQ)	8011	A	310 354-4200	17732
Radiology Partners Inc.	8011	B	424 290-8004	17747
Radiology Prtners Holdings LLC (PA)	8011	C	424 290-8004	17748
Pipeline Health LLC (PA)	8062	D	310 379-2134	18382
Scribeamerica LLC.	8099	B	877 819-5900	18803
BMC Group LLC.	8111	D	310 321-5555	18830
Carson Kurtzman Consultants (DH)	8111	C	310 823-9000	18834
Michael Sullivan & Assoc LLP.	8111	C	310 337-4480	18906
Premier Disability Svcs LLC.	8399	D	310 280-4000	19339
Raytheon Secure Information Systems LLC.	8711	C	310 647-9438	19677
Infineon Tech Americas Corp.	8721	A	310 726-8000	19781
Nantcell Inc.	8733	C	310 883-1300	19938
The Aerospace Corporation (PA)	8733	A	310 336-5000	19947
Anthos Group Inc.	8742	E	888 778-2986	20132
Avasant LLC (PA)	8742	D	310 643-3030	20136
Skin Laundry Holdings Inc.	8742	D	424 220-8826	20238
Technical Micro Cons Inc (PA)	8742	D	310 559-3982	20255
Tecolote Research Inc.	8742	C	310 640-4700	20256
Wpromote LLC (PA)	8742	D	310 421-4844	20276

EL TORO, CA - Orange County

	SIC	EMP	PHONE	ENTRY#
Sunset Landscape Maintenance.	0782	D	949 455-4636	216
Black & Decker Corporation.	3546	E	949 672-4000	7142
P M D Holding Corp.	5047	B	949 595-4777	12503

Employee Codes: A=Over 500 employees, B=251-500
C=101-250, D=51-100, E=20-50, F=10-19, G=1-9

2024 Southern California
Business Directory and Buyers Guide

© Mergent Inc. 1-800-342-5647

GEOGRAPHIC

	SIC	EMP	PHONE	ENTRY#

ENCINITAS, CA - San Diego County

	SIC	EMP	PHONE	ENTRY#
Dramm and Echter Inc.	0181	D	760 436-0188	52
Baked Bear LLC	2024	F	760 704-8140	1292
Coast News Inc	2711	E	760 436-9737	3266
RCP Block & Brick Inc.	3271	E	760 753-1164	5395
Cratex Manufacturing Co Inc	3291	D	760 942-2877	5540
Access Scientific Inc.	3841	F	858 354-8761	10412
Tandem Medical Inc.	3841	E	858 673-3900	10614
Black Box Distribution LLC	3949	D	760 268-1174	10978
Flock Freight Inc.	4731	C	855 744-7585	11761
Black Box Inc.	5136	D	760 804-3300	13098
Valudor Products LLC	5169	F	760 635-8500	13442
El Nopalito Inc (PA)	5411	D	760 436-5775	13697
Wayne Gossett Ford Inc.	5511	D	760 753-6286	13847
Southern Cal Disc Tire Co Inc	5531	C	760 634-2202	13878
Lofty Coffee Inc.	5812	D	760 230-6747	14023
Oggis Pizza & Brewing Company	5812	E	760 944-8170	14028
Solis Capital Partners LLC.	6799	D	760 309-9436	15051
North County Health Prj Inc.	8011	C	760 736-6767	17726
San Diego Hebrew Homes (PA)	8051	C	760 942-2695	18046
Scripps Health.	8062	E	760 753-6501	18428
YMCA of San Diego County.	8641	C	760 745-7490	19479
YMCA of San Diego County.	8641	B	858 292-4034	19482
YMCA of San Diego County.	8641	C	760 758-0808	19489
Dudek Inc (PA)	8711	D	760 942-5147	19577

ENCINO, CA - Los Angeles County

	SIC	EMP	PHONE	ENTRY#
Zevia LLC.	2086	D	310 202-7000	1745
Zevia Pbc (PA)	2086	E	855 469-3842	1746
Stanzino Inc.	2211	C	818 602-5171	2033
Etrade 24 Inc.	2299	E	818 712-0574	2140
Aquarius Rags LLC (PA)	2335	D	213 895-4400	2275
ABS By Allen Schwartz LLC (HQ)	2339	E	213 895-4400	2299
Creative Age Publications Inc.	2721	E	818 782-7328	3352
Ect News Network Inc.	2741	E	818 461-9700	3442
California Respiratory Care.	2899	D	818 379-9999	4598
National Cement Company Inc (HQ)	3241	E	818 728-5200	5369
Concrete Holding Co Cal Inc.	3273	A	818 788-4228	5473
National Cement Co Cal Inc (DH)	3273	E	818 728-5200	5487
National Ready Mix.	3273	F	818 728-5200	5489
National Ready Mixed Con Co (DH)	3273	E	818 728-5200	5490
Columbia Fabricating Co Inc.	3446	E	818 247-4220	6354
Capna Fabrication.	3556	E	888 416-6777	7193
Calstar Systems Group Inc.	3699	E	818 922-2000	9197
United Medical Devices LLC.	3841	E	310 551-4100	10625
Vivometrics Inc.	3845	F	805 667-2225	10830
Sayari Shahrzad.	5136	E	310 903-6368	13110
Benihana Inc.	5812	D	818 788-7121	13983
Warner Food Management Co Inc.	5812	C	818 285-2160	14044
United Vision Financial Inc.	6163	C	818 285-0211	14370
Republic Indemnity Company Cal.	6331	C	818 990-9860	14524
Lowe Enterprises Rlty Svcs Inc.	6531	A	818 990-9555	14824
One Silver Serve LLC.	7349	D	818 995-6444	15730
Team-One Staffing Services Inc.	7361	A	951 616-3515	15897
Phone Check Solutions LLC.	7371	B	310 365-1855	16095
Veritas Technologies LLC.	7371	C	310 202-0757	16146
Artkive.	7372	E	310 975-9809	16175
Culture AMP Inc (HQ)	7372	F	415 326-8453	16217
D3publisher of America Inc.	7372	D	310 268-0820	16219
Ipr Software Inc.	7372	E	310 499-0544	16276
Netsol Technologies Inc (PA)	7372	D	818 222-9197	16321
Payment Cloud LLC.	7374	C	800 988-2215	16510
Reprints Desk Inc.	7375	C	310 477-0354	16534
Life Alert Emrgncy Rsponse Inc (PA)	7382	C	800 247-0000	16746
Answer Financial Inc (HQ)	7389	C	818 644-4000	16781
Metropolitan Imports LLC.	7389	C	646 980-5343	16878
Nsi Group LLC (PA)	7389	F	818 639-8335	16889
Encino Living LLC.	7991	C	818 907-1343	17396
Emergent Medical Associates.	8011	D	818 995-5350	17649
Exer Holding Company LLC.	8011	C	818 287-0894	17651
Symbion Inc.	8011	C	818 501-1080	17800
Prime Hlthcare Svcs - Encino H.	8062	B	818 995-5000	18391
Elizabeth Glaser Pedia.	8099	B	310 231-0400	18762
Price Law Group A Prof Corp (PA)	8111	C	818 995-4540	18926
Baker Tilly Us LLP.	8721	B	818 981-2600	19752
F6s Network Limited.	8731	D	619 818-4363	19838
Instantly Inc.	8732	C	866 872-4006	19900
Westrec Properties Inc.	8741	B	818 907-0400	20118
Fpg Services LLC.	8742	D	818 858-1080	20173
Telestar International Corp.	8742	E	818 582-3018	20259

ESCONDIDO, CA - San Diego County

	SIC	EMP	PHONE	ENTRY#
Eleven Western Builders Inc (PA)	1521	D	760 796-6346	431
Innovative Communities Inc (PA)	1521	D	760 690-5225	435
Romero General Cnstr Corp.	1521	C	760 715-0154	451
Erickson-Hall Construction Co (PA)	1542	E	760 796-7700	550
R J Lanthier Company Inc.	1542	D	760 738-9798	581
Marathon General Inc.	1611	D	760 738-9714	633
JR Filanc Cnstr Co Inc (PA)	1623	E	760 941-7130	677
Associate Mech Contrs Inc.	1711	C	760 294-3517	736
Baker Electric & Renewables LLC.	1731	A	760 745-2001	868
Bergelectric Corp.	1731	D	760 291-8100	871
Hmt Electric Inc.	1731	D	858 458-9771	908
Laser Electric Inc.	1731	C	760 658-6626	912
X3 Management Services Inc.	1731	D	760 597-9336	954
Prowall Lath and Plaster.	1742	D	760 480-9001	992
Surecraft Supply Inc.	1751	C		1023
Southland Paving Inc.	1771	D	760 747-6895	1087
Ne-Mos.	2051	F	800 325-2692	1485
Nemos Bakery Inc (HQ)	2053	D	760 741-5725	1527
Orfila Vineyards Inc (PA)	2084	F	760 738-6500	1651
Pure-Flo Water Co (PA)	2086	D	619 596-4130	1721
Esperanzas Tortilleria.	2099	E	760 743-5908	1888
Tri-Pack Enterprises Inc.	2671	C	760 737-7995	3160
Publishers Development Corp.	2721	E	858 605-0200	3382
Mum Industries Inc.	2821	D	800 729-1314	3956
REAL Seal Co Inc.	3053	E	760 743-7263	4740
Dcc General Engrg Contrs Inc.	3272	D	760 480-7400	5408
Oldcastle Infrastructure Inc.	3272	E	951 683-8200	5433
Robertsons Ready Mix Ltd.	3273	D	951 685-4600	5499
Superior Ready Mix Concrete LP (PA)	3273	D	760 745-0556	5510
Superior Ready Mix Concrete LP.	3273	D	760 728-1128	5513
Vulcan Materials Co.	3273	B	760 737-3486	5517
VIT Products Inc.	3429	E	760 480-6702	5950
Freeberg Indus Fbrication Corp.	3441	E	760 737-7614	6027
A & D Plating Inc.	3471	F	760 480-4580	6572
Southland Manufacturing Inc.	3545	E	760 745-7913	7131
Count Numbering Machine Inc.	3555	E	760 739-9357	7184
Integrted Crygnic Slutions LLC.	3559	E	951 234-0899	7243
Capstone Fire Management Inc (PA)	3569	E	760 839-2290	7385
Separation Engineering Inc.	3569	E	760 489-0101	7409
Vertiv It Systems Inc.	3575	D	760 504-5451	7502
One Stop Systems Inc.	3577	E	858 530-2511	7558
One Stop Systems Inc (PA)	3577	E	760 745-9883	7559
C & H Machine Inc.	3593	D	760 746-6459	7708
Frans Manufacturing Inc.	3599	E	760 741-9135	7837
H & M Four-Slide Inc.	3599	E	951 461-8244	7855
J Flying Machine Inc.	3599	F	760 504-0323	7883
Meziere Enterprises Inc.	3599	E	800 208-1755	7932
Price Products Incorporated.	3599	E	760 745-5602	7980
Rwnm Inc.	3612	E		8110
Bliss Holdings LLC.	3648	E	626 506-8696	8357
Rantec Microwave Systems Inc.	3663	E	760 744-1544	8567
Systech Corporation.	3669	D	858 674-6500	8628
San Diego Pcb Design LLC.	3672	F	858 271-5722	8726
Avr Global Technologies Inc (PA)	3679	C	949 391-1180	8999
Csr Technology Inc.	3679	E	619 823-7919	9024
U S Circuit Inc.	3679	D	760 489-1413	9134
Heatshield Products Inc.	3714	E	760 751-0441	9400
Mgp Exhausts Usa Inc.	3714	E	760 445-1235	9424
Transportation Power LLC.	3714	E	858 248-4255	9475
Tdg Aerospace Inc.	3728	F	760 466-1040	9811
Northrop Grumman Corporation.	3812	E	310 864-7342	10010
Arch Med Sltons - Escndido LLC.	3841	C	760 432-9785	10439
Photronics Inc.	3861	C	760 294-1896	10880
Brainstormproducts LLC.	3944	E	760 871-1135	10948
Adti Media LLC.	3993	E	951 795-4446	11095
Cbdsd Inc.	3999	E	760 738-4200	11205
Mv Transportation Inc.	4111	C	760 520-0118	11348
Westmed Ambulance Inc.	4119	C	310 219-1779	11411
Santa Barbara Trnsp Corp.	4151	C	760 746-0850	11433
AT&T Services Inc.	4813	C	760 489-3187	11871
San Diego Gas & Electric Co.	4911	B	760 432-2508	12045
San Diego County Water Auth.	4941	C	760 480-1991	12140
Hadronex Inc.	4952	E	760 291-1980	12152
Zest Anchors LLC.	5047	D	760 743-7744	12523
Cal Southern Sound Image Inc (PA)	5065	D	760 737-3900	12651
Klein Electronics Inc.	5065	E	760 781-3220	12675
Giumarra Agricom Intl LLC.	5148	A	760 480-8502	13326
Home Depot USA Inc.	5211	C	760 233-1285	13596
Lowes Home Centers LLC.	5211	D	760 484-5113	13650
Brecht Enterprises Inc.	5511	D	760 745-3000	13743
Escondido Motors LLC.	5511	C	760 745-5000	13763
Jack Pwell Chrysler - Ddge Inc.	5511	D	760 745-2880	13783
Southern Cal Disc Tire Co Inc.	5531	C	760 741-9805	13872
Southern Cal Disc Tire Co Inc.	5531	C	760 741-3801	13874

	SIC	EMP	PHONE	ENTRY#
Portable Clers Sls Rentals Inc	5722	F	760 747-9591	13969
Stone Brewing Co LLC	5813	A	760 471-4999	14053
Tri-Ad	6411	C	760 743-7555	14637
Emeritus Corporation	6513	C	760 741-3055	14706
Welk Group Inc	7011	B	760 749-3000	15413
ARS National Services Inc (PA)	7322	C	800 456-5053	15607
Transamerican Direct Inc	7331	D	760 745-5343	15638
Dish For All Inc	7622	E	760 690-3869	17060
Welk Group Inc	7992	C	760 749-3225	17443
Welk Group Inc	7997	C	760 749-0983	17535
Borrego Cmnty Hlth Foundation	8011	C	760 466-1080	17604
Graybill Medical Group Inc (PA)	8011	C	866 228-2236	17661
Kaiser Foundation Hospitals	8011	C	619 528-5000	17679
Neighborhood Healthcare	8011	C	760 737-2000	17723
Southern Cal Prmnnte Med Group	8011	C	760 839-7200	17788
Life Care Centers America Inc	8051	C	760 741-6109	17987
Life Care Residences Inc	8051	E	760 743-8843	17993
Mek Escondido LLC	8051	C	760 747-0430	18012
Valle Vsta Cnvlescent Hosp Inc	8059	D	760 745-1288	18158
Palomar Health (PA)	8062	C	442 281-5000	18365
Palomar Health Technology Inc	8062	C	442 281-5000	18367
Palomar Health	8069	C	760 740-6311	18531
Cox Enterprises LLC	8082	D	858 822-8587	18606
Elizabeth Hospice Inc (PA)	8082	C	760 737-2050	18612
Neighborhood Healthcare	8099	C	760 737-6903	18785
Interfaith Community Svcs Inc	8322	D	760 489-6380	19097
Atria Management Company LLC	8361	B	760 480-8155	19239
Humangood Socal	8361	C	760 747-4306	19275
Las Villas Del Norte	8361	C	760 741-1047	19279
Meadowbrook Vlg Chrstn Rtrment	8361	C	760 746-2500	19286
Redwood Edrlink Scph	8361	B	760 480-1030	19297
Califrnia Ctr For Arts Escndid	8412	C	760 839-4138	19351
Zoological Society San Diego	8422	C	760 747-8702	19370
Automobile Club Southern Cal	8699	C	760 745-2124	19515
Blanchard Training and Dev Inc (PA)	8742	C	760 489-5005	20141
Tri-Ad Actuaries Inc	8742	C	760 743-7555	20265
Pro Energy Services Group LLC	8744	B	760 789-7149	20299

FALLBROOK, CA - San Diego County

	SIC	EMP	PHONE	ENTRY#
Olive Hill Greenhouses Inc	0181	D	760 728-4596	63
Treesap Farms LLC	0191	C	760 990-7770	88
Executive Landscape Inc	0781	C	760 731-9036	160
Scw Contracting Corporation	1623	D	760 728-1308	689
Scrape Certified Welding Inc	3441	E	760 728-1308	6074
Fallbrook Industries Inc	3469	E	760 728-7229	6516
Axelgaard Manufacturing Co (PA)	3845	D	760 723-7554	10790
Axelgaard Manufacturing Co	3845	C	760 723-7554	10791
Med-Fit Systems Inc	3949	F	760 723-3618	11013
Altman Specialty Plants LLC	5193	B	800 348-4881	13499
Major Market Inc	5411	C	760 723-0857	13701
Southwest Boulder & Stone Inc (PA)	5999	E	760 451-3333	14150
Pala Mesa Limited Partnership	7011	C	760 728-5881	15293
Garich Inc	7361	B	951 302-4750	15848
Special Event Audio Svcs Inc	7929	C	800 518-9144	17351
Crestwood Behavioral Hlth Inc	8059	C	760 451-4165	18122
Edsi	8711	D	760 731-3501	19578
SL Blue Garden Corp	8742	C	626 633-2672	20239

FELLOWS, CA - Kern County

	SIC	EMP	PHONE	ENTRY#
Dwaynes Engineering & Cnstr	1389	E	661 762-7261	343
Pacific Perforating Inc	1389	E	661 768-9224	374

FILLMORE, CA - Ventura County

	SIC	EMP	PHONE	ENTRY#
Brightview Tree Company	0811	D	714 546-7975	227
Honey Bennetts Farm	2099	E	805 521-1375	1912
Ameron International Corp	3272	C	425 258-2616	5398
Ameron International Corp	3272	D	805 524-0223	5399
Owens & Minor Distribution Inc	5047	A	805 524-0243	12502

FONTANA, CA - San Bernardino County

	SIC	EMP	PHONE	ENTRY#
People Pets and Vets LLC	0742	C	909 453-4213	124
People Pets and Vets LLC	0742	C	909 329-2860	125
Brightview Landscape Svcs Inc	0781	C	909 946-3196	149
Stantru Resources Inc	1541	D	909 587-1441	520
Engel Holdings Inc	1542	C	866 950-9862	548
Foundation Pile Inc	1629	D	909 350-1584	709
Slater Inc	1629	D	909 822-6800	717
B&B Industrial Services Inc (PA)	1741	B	909 428-3167	955
Gonsalves & Santucci Inc	1771	B	909 350-0474	1072
Refresco Beverages US Inc	2033	C	951 685-0481	1343
Sundown Foods USA Inc	2033	E	909 606-6797	1345
Mohawk Industries Inc	2273	E	909 357-1064	2118
A&R Tarpaulins Inc	2394	E	909 829-4444	2497

	SIC	EMP	PHONE	ENTRY#
Ramirez Pallets Inc	2448	E	909 822-2066	2723
S & H Cabinets and Mfg Inc	2521	E	909 357-0551	2898
Allied West Paper Corp	2621	D	909 349-0710	3040
Tst/Impreso Inc	2761	E	909 357-7190	3833
Kemira Water Solutions Inc	2819	E	909 350-5678	3896
Indorama Vntres Sstnble Sltion	2821	D	951 727-8318	3944
J-M Manufacturing Company Inc	2821	D	909 822-3009	3949
Bluefield Associates Inc	2844	E	909 476-6027	4384
Specialized Milling Corp	2851	D	909 357-7990	4506
Kemira Water Solutions Inc	2899	E	909 350-5678	4613
Fontana Paper Mills Inc	2952	D	909 823-4100	4668
Rep-Kote Products Inc	2952	F	909 355-1288	4676
TTI Floor Care North Amer Inc	3052	D	440 596-9000	4716
Cannon Gasket Inc	3053	E	909 355-1547	4721
Ring Container Tech LLC	3085	D	909 350-8416	4866
Premier Packaging LLC	3086	E	909 749-5123	4900
Dorel Juvenile Group Inc	3089	C	909 428-0295	5015
Mission Custom Extrusion Inc	3089	E	909 822-1581	5101
Vpet Usa LLC	3089	D	909 605-1668	5245
Avilas Garden Art (PA)	3272	D	909 350-4546	5401
Hanson Roof Tile LLC	3272	B	888 509-4787	5418
Jensen Enterprises Inc	3272	B	909 357-7264	5422
Oldcastle Infrastructure Inc	3272	E	909 428-3700	5432
River Valley Precast Inc	3272	E	928 764-3839	5445
California Steel Inds Inc	3312	B	909 350-6300	5582
California Steel Inds Inc (HQ)	3312	B	909 350-6300	5583
Tree Island Wire (usa) Inc	3315	C	909 594-7511	5624
Vista Metals Corp (PA)	3354	C	909 823-4298	5716
American Die Casting Inc	3364	E	909 356-7768	5771
Fontana Foundry Corporation	3365	F	909 822-6128	5793
Solar Atmospheres Inc	3398	E	909 217-7400	5849
Greif Inc	3412	D	909 350-2112	5867
Allegion Access Tech LLC	3423	E	909 628-9272	5873
Corbell Products Inc (PA)	3441	F	909 574-9139	6013
Fabco Steel Fabrication Inc	3441	E	909 350-1535	6024
Rnd Contractors Inc	3441	E	909 429-8500	6071
Schroeder Iron Corporation	3441	E	909 428-6471	6073
Ulmer Industries Inc	3441	E	909 823-7111	6086
Door Components Inc	3442	C	909 770-5700	6103
Quanex Screens LLC	3442	E	909 349-0600	6117
LLC Walker West	3444	D	951 685-9660	6262
Lynam Industries Inc (PA)	3444	D	951 360-1919	6263
Alabama Metal Industries Corp	3446	C	909 350-9280	6350
Morin Corporation	3448	E	909 428-3747	6386
Fab Services West Inc	3449	D	909 350-7500	6397
Forged Metals Inc	3462	C	909 350-9260	6459
Pacific Forge Inc	3462	D	909 390-0701	6467
Nellxo LLC	3469	E	909 320-8501	6541
Betts Company	3495	E	909 427-9988	6800
Nashville Wire Pdts Mfg Co LLC	3496	F	714 736-0001	6821
American Security Products Co	3499	C	951 685-9680	6855
Superior Trailer Works	3537	E	909 350-0185	6998
Stanley Black & Decker Inc	3546	F	909 491-6322	7148
Cvc Technologies Inc	3565	E	909 355-0311	7347
Santa Fe Machine Works Inc	3599	E	909 350-6877	8013
Serampore Inds Private Ltd Inc	3599	F	877 921-6111	8025
Crown Technical Systems (PA)	3613	C	951 332-4170	8118
Eaton Electrical Inc	3625	C	951 685-5788	8179
Sunbeam Products Inc	3631	F	951 727-3901	8223
Harman Professional Inc	3651	C	844 776-4899	8414
Becker Specialty Corporation	3677	D	909 356-1095	8935
DSM&t Co Inc	3694	C	909 357-7960	9165
Kovatch Mobile Equipment Corp	3711	E	951 685-1224	9295
Bab Steering Hydraulics (PA)	3714	E	208 573-4502	9360
Carlstar Group LLC	3714	E	909 829-1703	9369
S&B Filters Inc	3714	C	909 947-0015	9456
Utility Trailer Mfg Co	3715	D	909 428-8300	9499
Tri-Net Inc	3825	E	909 483-3555	10228
Cargo Solution Brokerage Inc	4212	C	909 350-1644	11447
Hub Group Trucking Inc	4212	B	909 770-8950	11461
Cargo Solution Express Inc (PA)	4213	C	909 350-1644	11473
Estes Express Lines	4213	C	909 427-9850	11487
Heartland Express Inc Iowa	4213	A	319 626-3600	11490
Swift Leasing Co LLC	4213	B	909 347-0500	11507
TCI Transportation Services	4213	C	909 355-8545	11508
Xpo Logistics Freight Inc	4213	D	951 685-1244	11512
Advanced Strlztion Pdts Svcs I	4225	B	909 350-6987	11561
Dalton Trucking Inc (PA)	4225	C	909 823-0663	11571
Target Corporation	4225	C	909 355-6000	11618
Tonys Seeds Inc (PA)	4225	C	909 427-8700	11622
DSV Solutions LLC	4226	C	909 829-5804	11632
Blackrock Logistics Inc	4731	C	909 259-5357	11742
DSV Solutions LLC	4731	C	909 349-6100	11755

GEOGRAPHIC

Employee Codes: A=Over 500 employees, B=251-500
C=101-250, D=51-100, E=20-50, F=10-19, G=1-9

2024 Southern California
Business Directory and Buyers Guide

© Mergent Inc. 1-800-342-5647

1369

	SIC	EMP	PHONE	ENTRY#
Pro Loaders Inc.	4731	C	909 355-5531	11795
San Gabriel Valley Water Co.	4941	C	909 822-2201	12143
Burrtec Waste Industries Inc **(HQ)**	4953	C	909 429-4200	12160
Yucaipa Disposal Inc.	4953	D	909 429-4200	12205
Inland Kenworth Inc **(HQ)**	5012	C	909 823-9955	12225
Los Angeles Truck Centers LLC	5012	C	909 510-4000	12226
Utility Trlr Sls Sthern Cal LL **(PA)**	5012	D	877 275-4887	12229
Maxzone Vehicle Lighting Corp **(HQ)**	5013	E	909 822-3288	12246
Wabash National Trlr Ctrs Inc	5013	E	765 771-5300	12265
New Classic HM Furnishing Inc **(PA)**	5023	E	909 484-7676	12309
James Hardie Building Pdts Inc.	5031	C	909 355-6500	12333
Patrick Industries Inc.	5032	E	909 350-4440	12360
Valori Sand & Gravel Company	5032	C	909 350-3000	12363
Daniel Gerard Worldwide Inc.	5051	D	951 361-1111	12546
AC Pro Inc **(PA)**	5075	C	951 360-7849	12750
Orora Packaging Solutions.	5113	E	909 770-5400	13014
Lowes Home Centers LLC	5211	C	909 350-7900	13640
Tealove Inc.	5499	E	714 408-8245	13732
Rotolo Chevrolet Inc.	5511	C	866 756-9776	13820
Sunrise Ford.	5511	C	909 822-4401	13833
Boyd Flotation Inc.	5712	E	314 997-5222	13940
Castle Importing Inc.	5812	E	909 428-9200	13992
Kaiser Foundation Hospitals.	6324	B	909 427-3910	14481
Kaiser Permanente.	6324	C	909 427-3910	14483
Guzman Grading and Paving Corp.	7359	D	909 428-5960	15780
Integrated Intermodal Svcs Inc.	7379	D	909 355-4100	16570
Social Junky Inc.	7389	C	213 999-1275	16933
Bridgestone Americas.	7534	E	909 770-8523	17020
Eight Point Trailer Corp.	7539	F	909 357-9227	17042
Amerit Fleet Solutions Inc.	7549	A	909 357-0100	17052
Jeti Inc.	7692	F	909 357-2966	17089
Tikos Tanks Inc.	7692	E	951 757-8014	17097
Kaiser Foundation Hospitals.	8011	A	909 427-5000	17676
United Fmly Care Inc A Med Cor.	8011	C	909 874-1679	17814
Southern Cal Prmnnte Med Group.	8062	B	909 427-5000	18452
Production Engineering & Mch.	8071	C	909 721-2455	18560
Fontana Resources At Work.	8331	E	909 428-3833	19185
Lamer Street Kreations Corp.	8711	E	909 305-4824	19637

FOOTHILL RANCH, CA - Orange County

	SIC	EMP	PHONE	ENTRY#
T Hasegawa USA Inc.	2087	E	949 461-3344	1785
Nike Inc.	2353	F	949 616-4042	2402
Avion Graphics Inc.	2752	C	949 472-0438	3514
Protab Laboratories.	2834	C	949 635-1930	4213
Twila True Collaborations LLC	2844	E	949 258-9720	4463
Kaiser Aluminum Fab Pdts LLC **(HQ)**	3353	A	949 614-1740	5688
Kwikset Corporation	3429	A	949 672-4000	5926
Weiser Lock Corporation	3429	F	949 672-4000	5952
A & J Manufacturing Company.	3469	E	714 544-9570	6490
Bal Seal Engineering LLC **(DH)**	3495	C	949 460-2100	6799
Azure Microdynamics Inc.	3599	D	949 699-3344	7769
Renkus-Heinz Inc **(PA)**	3651	D	949 588-9997	8429
Allied Components Intl.	3677	E	949 356-1780	8933
Carttronics LLC **(HQ)**	3699	C	888 696-2278	9198
Gatekeeper Systems Inc **(PA)**	3699	D	888 808-9433	9212
Oleumtech Corporation.	3823	D	949 305-9009	10150
Chroma Systems Solutions Inc **(HQ)**	3825	E	949 297-4848	10190
Ossur Americas Inc.	3842	E	949 382-3883	10690
Oakley Inc **(DH)**	3851	A	949 951-0991	10845
Oakley Sales Corp.	3851	C	949 672-6925	10846
Redcom Inc.	3861	F	949 206-7900	10882
Redcom LLC.	3861	B	949 404-4084	10883
Belshire Trnsp Svcs Inc.	4212	C	949 460-5200	11444
Venus Group Inc **(PA)**	5023	D	949 609-1299	12322
Hampton Products Intl Corp **(PA)**	5072	D	949 472-4256	12723
Sgii Inc **(PA)**	5122	C	949 521-6161	13068
Kawasaki Motors Corp USA **(HQ)**	5571	B	949 837-4683	13901
Debisys Inc **(PA)**	6099	D	949 699-1401	14258
Loandepotcom LLC **(DH)**	6162	A	888 337-6888	14339
Strategic Asset Services LLC	6512	C	949 713-0053	14687
US Real Estate Services Inc.	6531	D	949 598-9920	14882
Stonebridge Rlty Advisors Inc.	7011	A	949 597-8700	15375
Image Options **(PA)**	7319	D	949 586-7665	15603
Risa Tech Inc.	7371	E	949 951-5815	16103
Sun Healthcare Group Inc **(DH)**	8011	B		17798
Skilled Healthcare LLC **(DH)**	8051	C	949 282-5800	18054
Healthcare Talent.	8099	C	714 341-1197	18769
Tae Technologies Inc **(PA)**	8731	C	949 830-2117	19876

FOREST FALLS, CA - San Bernardino County

	SIC	EMP	PHONE	ENTRY#
Forest Home Inc.	7032	C	909 389-2300	15435

FORT IRWIN, CA - San Bernardino County

	SIC	EMP	PHONE	ENTRY#
Northrop Grumman Systems Corp.	3812	D	760 380-4268	10039
Lockheed Martin Corporation.	4225	C	760 386-2572	11594

FOUNTAIN VALLEY, CA - Orange County

	SIC	EMP	PHONE	ENTRY#
Brightview Companies LLC.	0782	C	714 437-1586	184
Rba Builders Inc.	1542	D	714 895-9000	583
Pan-Pacific Mechanical LLC **(PA)**	1711	C	949 474-9170	807
ML Kishigo Mfg Co LLC.	2389	D	949 852-1963	2456
Action Bag & Cover Inc.	2393	D	714 965-7777	2491
Tdi2 Custom Packaging Inc.	2673	F	714 751-6782	3193
Duncan McIntosh Company Inc **(PA)**	2721	E	949 660-6150	3357
Microscale Industries Inc.	2752	F	714 593-1422	3636
Moreland Manufacturing Inc.	2759	F	714 426-1411	3788
Specialized Screen Prtg Inc.	2759	F	714 964-1230	3812
Yg Laboratories Inc.	2844	E	714 474-2800	4470
Epe Industries Usa Inc **(HQ)**	3086	F	800 315-0336	4880
Gaffoglio Fmly Mtlcrafters Inc **(PA)**	3231	C	714 444-2000	5340
KB Sheetmetal Fabrication Inc.	3444	E	714 979-1780	6259
TN Sheet Metal Inc.	3444	F	714 593-0100	6333
Omni Metal Finishing Inc **(PA)**	3471	D	714 979-9414	6645
Quik Mfg Co.	3531	E	714 754-0337	6940
Meyco Machine and Tool Inc.	3545	E	714 435-1546	7120
Psitech Inc.	3571	F	714 964-7818	7446
Kingston Digital Inc **(HQ)**	3577	E	714 435-2600	7539
Kingston Technology Corp **(PA)**	3577	B	714 435-2600	7540
Avatar Machine LLC.	3599	E	714 434-2737	7767
Infocus Cnc Machining Inc.	3599	E	714 979-1253	7872
Advanced Charging Tech Inc.	3629	E	877 228-5922	8199
Interconnect Solutions Co LLC **(PA)**	3629	D	909 545-6140	8209
Surefire LLC **(PA)**	3648	C	714 545-9444	8383
Ktc-Tu Corporation.	3674	E	714 435-2600	8822
Mobis Parts America LLC.	3714	E	949 450-0014	9427
Nobles Medical Tech Inc.	3841	E	714 427-0398	10579
Surefire LLC.	3842	E	714 545-9444	10706
Surefire LLC.	3842	E	714 545-9444	10707
Surefire LLC.	3842	E	714 545-9444	10709
Moving Image Technologies LLC.	3861	E	714 751-7998	10875
Shock Doctor Inc **(PA)**	3949	D	800 233-6956	11025
Shock Doctor Inc.	3949	E	657 383-4400	11026
Joy Products California Inc.	3953	E	714 437-7250	11052
Orange County Sanitation **(PA)**	4953	B	714 962-2411	12176
Hyundai Motor America **(HQ)**	5012	B	714 965-3000	12224
Mobis Parts America LLC **(HQ)**	5013	D	786 515-1101	12249
Kingston Technology Company Inc **(PA)**	5045	A	714 435-2600	12424
Motive Energy Inc **(PA)**	5063	D	714 888-2525	12607
Tires Warehouse LLC.	5531	B	714 432-8851	13884
Pedego LLC **(PA)**	5941	C	800 646-8604	14064
Ceridian Tax Service Inc.	7291	B	714 963-1311	15494
Freightgate Inc.	7372	C	714 799-2833	16252
Hyundai Autoever America LLC.	7378	C	714 965-3000	16542
Safeguard On Demand Inc.	7381	C	800 640-2327	16677
Mile Square Golf Course.	7992	C	714 962-5541	17439
Fountain Vly Rgnal Hosp Med CT.	8062	A	714 966-7200	18261
Memorial Health Services **(PA)**	8062	B	714 377-2900	18342
Orange Coast Memorial Med Ctr **(HQ)**	8062	A	714 378-7000	18355
Boys Grls Clubs Huntington Vly **(PA)**	8641	D	714 531-2582	19430
Spec Services Inc.	8711	B	714 963-8077	19694
Memorial Healthtec Labratories.	8731	A	714 962-4677	19859

FRAZIER PARK, CA - Kern County

	SIC	EMP	PHONE	ENTRY#
Trnlwb LLC.	3999	A	661 245-3736	11300

FULLERTON, CA - Orange County

	SIC	EMP	PHONE	ENTRY#
Orange County Produce LLC.	0171	D	949 451-0880	19
AMS American Mech Svcs MD Inc.	1711	C	714 888-6820	732
C & L Refrigeration Corp.	1711	C	800 901-4822	749
AJ Kirkwood & Associates Inc.	1731	B	714 505-1977	862
Superior Wall Systems Inc.	1742	H	714 278-0000	1000
Gaylords HRI Meats.	2011	F	714 526-2278	1195
Kraft Heinz Foods Company.	2033	D	714 870-8235	1340
Vanlaw Food Products Inc **(HQ)**	2035	D	714 870-9091	1365
Charlies Specialties Inc.	2052	E	724 346-2350	1512
Phenix Gourmet LLC.	2052	E	562 404-5028	1523
Byrnes & Kiefer Co.	2087	D	714 554-4000	1760
Common Collabs LLC **(PA)**	2087	E	714 519-3245	1763
Dr Smoothie Brands Inc.	2087	E	714 449-9787	1766
Dr Smoothie Enterprises.	2087	E	714 449-9787	1767
Chefmaster.	2099	E	714 554-4000	1870
Khyber Foods Incorporated.	2099	F	714 879-0900	1922
Nina Mia Inc.	2099	D	714 773-5588	1955
Dae Shin Usa Inc.	2221	D	714 578-8900	2036
Fabtex Inc.	2221	C	714 538-0877	2039

Mergent email: customerrelations@mergent.com
1370

2024 Southern California
Business Directory and Buyers Guide

(P-0000) Products & Services Section entry number
(PA)=Parent Co (HQ)=Headquarters (DH)=Div Headquarters

	SIC	EMP	PHONE	ENTRY#
SPD Manufacturing Inc.	2221	F	985 302-1902	2044
Delta Pacific Activewear Inc.	2253	D	714 871-9281	2066
Anderco Inc.	2431	E	714 446-9508	2583
Pacific Archtectural Mllwk Inc.	2431	D	714 525-2059	2626
Accurate Laminated Pdts Inc.	2434	E	714 632-2773	2644
Brentwood Home LLC (PA)	2515	C	562 949-3759	2845
Michael Nicholas Designs Inc.	2519	C	714 562-8101	2871
Amtrend Corporation	2541	E	714 630-2070	2942
Advanced Equipment Corporation (PA)	2542	E	714 635-5350	2972
Corru-Kraft IV	2653	F	714 773-0124	3093
W/S Packaging Group Inc.	2679	D	714 992-2574	3252
Lava Products Inc.	2752	E	949 951-7191	3619
Mail Handling Group Inc.	2752	D	952 975-5000	3628
Graphics 2000 LLC	2759	D	714 879-1188	3764
Orora Visual LLC	2759	D	714 879-2400	3794
Progrssive Intgrated Solutions	2759	D	714 237-0980	3802
Western States Envelope Corp.	2759	E	714 449-0909	3826
Wilsons Art Studio Inc.	2759	E	714 870-7030	3827
Nbs Systems Inc (PA)	2761	E	217 999-3472	3831
Professional Plastics Inc (PA)	2821	E	714 446-6500	3964
Cargill Incorporated	2833	D	714 449-6708	3994
Stauber California Inc.	2833	E	714 441-3900	4018
Stauber Prfmce Ingredients Inc (HQ)	2833	D	714 441-3900	4019
McKenna Labs Inc (PA)	2834	E	714 687-6888	4165
United Pharma LLC.	2899	C	714 738-8999	4635
S & H Rubber Co.	3069	E	714 525-0277	4793
Foam-Craft Inc.	3086	C	714 459-9971	4886
Future Foam Inc.	3086	E	714 459-9971	4888
Future Foam Inc.	3086	E	714 871-2344	4889
Chubby Gorilla Inc (PA)	3089	E	844 365-5218	4990
Wheel and Tire Club Inc.	3312	E	714 422-3505	5608
Kip Steel Inc.	3316	E	714 461-1051	5629
Howmet Globl Fstning Systems I.	3324	D	714 871-1550	5655
Cablesys LLC.	3357	E	562 356-3222	5734
ADB Industries.	3398	B	310 679-9193	5822
Cook and Cook Incorporated	3443	E	714 680-6669	6140
Gard Inc.	3444	E	714 738-5891	6244
Stein Industries Inc (PA)	3444	E	714 522-4560	6324
Will-Mann Inc.	3444	E	714 870-0350	6346
Kims Welding and Iron Works.	3462	F	714 680-7700	6464
Kryler Corp.	3471	E	714 871-9611	6634
Santa Ana Plating (PA)	3471	E	310 923-8305	6659
Aerofit LLC.	3498	C	714 521-5060	6836
Golden Pacific Seafoods Inc.	3556	E	714 589-8888	7200
Terra Universal Inc.	3564	C	714 526-0100	7334
Label-Aire Inc (PA)	3565	D	714 449-5155	7351
Greenbridge Technology Inc.	3567	E	714 991-0200	7366
HP It Services Incorporated.	3577	E	714 844-7737	7531
Jonel Engineering.	3596	E	714 879-2360	7716
Ejays Machine Co Inc.	3599	E	714 879-0558	7824
Ellingson Inc.	3599	E	714 773-1923	7825
Lange Precision Inc.	3599	F	714 870-5420	7903
Laser Industries Inc.	3599	E	714 532-3271	7905
Oem LLC.	3599	E	714 449-7500	7960
Thunderbolt Manufacturing Inc.	3599	E	714 632-0397	8047
WMc Prcsion McHning Grnding.	3599	F	714 773-0059	8083
Direct Drive Systems Inc.	3621	D	714 872-5500	8140
Custom Autosound Mfg Inc.	3651	F	714 535-1091	8403
Interntnal Cnnctors Cable Corp.	3661	C	888 275-4422	8475
Golden West Technology.	3672	D	714 738-3775	8682
Winonics Inc.	3672	E	714 626-3755	8753
Printec Ht Electronics LLC.	3674	E	714 484-7597	8868
General Linear Systems Inc.	3677	F	714 994-4822	8944
Magtech & Power Conversion Inc.	3677	E	714 451-0106	8945
Gigatera Communications.	3679	E	714 515-1100	9050
Delta Stag Manufacturing.	3713	E	562 904-6444	9321
Trade Leasing Inc.	3713	E	714 538-4614	9336
Ultra Wheel Company.	3714	E	714 449-7100	9479
UNI Filter Inc.	3714	F	714 535-6933	9480
Marton Precision Mfg LLC.	3724	E	714 808-6523	9576
Adams Rite Aerospace Inc (DH)	3728	D	714 278-6500	9592
Hydraflow.	3728	B	714 773-2600	9708
National Signal Inc.	3799	E	714 441-7707	9935
Consolidated Aerospace Mfg LLC (HQ)	3812	E	714 989-2797	9965
Raytheon Company.	3812	A	714 732-0119	10054
Beckman Instruments Inc.	3826	E	714 871-4848	10239
St Jude Medical LLC.	3842	E	714 992-3000	10703
Aurident Incorporated.	3843	E	714 870-1851	10729
Bbe Sound Inc (PA)	3931	E	714 897-6766	10921
Bushnell Ribbon Corporation.	3955	E	562 948-1410	11053
Pacmin Incorporated (PA)	3999	D	714 447-4478	11261
RPM Consolidated Services Inc (HQ)	4225	D	714 388-3500	11609
Hub Group Los Angeles LLC.	4731	D	714 449-6300	11771

	SIC	EMP	PHONE	ENTRY#
Tri-Tech Logistics LLC.	4731	C	855 373-7049	11812
Southern California Edison Co.	4911	B	714 870-3225	12073
Ware Disposal Inc.	4953	C	714 834-0234	12194
Petes Road Service Inc (PA)	5014	D	714 446-1207	12272
McKesson Mdcl-Srgcal Top Hldng.	5047	B	800 300-4350	12498
US Electrical Services Inc.	5063	E	714 982-1534	12622
North American Video Corp (PA)	5065	E	714 779-7499	12688
Raytheon Cmmand Cntrl Sltons LL (DH)	5065	A	714 446-3118	12695
Orora Packaging Solutions.	5113	E	714 278-6000	13020
Viele & Sons Inc (PA)	5141	D	714 447-3663	13240
Hidden Villa Ranch Produce Inc (HQ)	5144	B	714 680-3447	13258
Bakery Ex Southern Cal LLC.	5149	D	714 446-9470	13354
Home Depot USA Inc.	5211	C	714 459-4909	13585
Vista Paint Corporation (PA)	5231	C	714 680-3800	13675
Kaylas Cake Corporation.	5461	E	714 869-1522	13718
Plasticolor Molded Pdts Inc (PA)	5531	E	714 525-3880	13869
North Ornge Cnty Cmnty Cllege.	5942	B	714 992-7008	14068
Altura Holdings LLC.	6722	B	714 948-8400	14955
Anaheim Park Hotel.	7011	C	714 992-1700	15075
Huoyen International Inc.	7011	D	714 635-9000	15191
Merritt Hospitality LLC.	7011	C	714 738-7800	15248
American Window Covering Inc.	7216	F	714 879-3880	15463
Nail Alliance - North Amer Inc.	7231	C	714 449-1568	15483
Advanced Image Direct LLC.	7331	E	714 502-3900	15626
Real Estate Image Inc (PA)	7331	C	714 502-3900	15635
Aspirez Inc.	7371	E	714 485-8104	15969
New Pride Tire LLC.	7534	E	310 631-7000	17023
Emeritus Corporation.	8051	C	714 441-0644	17934
Fullerton Hlthcare Wllness CNT.	8051	C	714 992-5701	17956
St Jude Hospital (DH)	8062	A	714 871-3280	18466
Marshall B Ketchum University (PA)	8221	C	714 463-7567	18991
Autism Spctrum Intrvntions Inc.	8322	C	562 972-4846	19024
Turning Point Ministries.	8322	C	800 998-6329	19149
Corecare I I I.	8361	E	714 256-8000	19252
Florence Crttnton Svcs Ornge C.	8361	B	714 680-9000	19263
Independent Options Inc.	8361	D	714 738-4991	19277
Bon Suisse Inc.	8748	E	714 578-0001	20319

GARDEN GROVE, CA - Orange County

	SIC	EMP	PHONE	ENTRY#
Terra Pacific Landscape (HQ)	0781	D	714 567-0177	181
Envise (HQ)	1711	C	800 613-6240	767
Structral Prsrvtion Systems LL.	1771	B	714 891-9080	1088
Cali Food Company Inc.	2032	E	714 821-8630	1321
Sanyo Foods Corp America (DH)	2098	E	714 891-3671	1844
House Foods America Corp (HQ)	2099	E	714 901-4350	1913
Quoc Viet Foods.	2099	D	714 283-3663	1972
Pacific Athletic Wear Inc.	2339	C	714 751-8006	2356
Bodywaves Inc (PA)	2369	E	714 898-9900	2414
L C Pringle Sales Inc (PA)	2591	E	714 892-1524	3010
Commercial Cstm Sting Uphl Inc.	2599	D	714 850-0520	3021
Teacher Created Resources Inc.	2731	C	714 230-7060	3416
Select Graphics.	2752	C	714 537-5250	3685
Wtpc Inc.	2752	E	714 903-2500	3716
Elasco Inc.	2821	E	714 373-4767	3938
Elasco Urethane Inc.	2821	E	714 895-7031	3939
Saint-Gobain Prfmce Plas Corp.	2821	D	714 893-0470	3968
Saint-Gobain Prfmce Plas Corp.	2821	D	714 630-5818	3969
Uremet Corporation.	2821	E	657 257-4027	3981
St Paul Brands Inc.	2824	C	714 903-1000	3987
A Q Pharmaceuticals Inc.	2834	C	714 903-1000	4026
Beauty & Health International.	2834	E	714 903-9730	4068
Leiner Health Products Inc.	2834	E	714 898-9936	4157
Goodwin Ammonia Company LLC.	2841	E	714 894-0531	4337
Cali Chem Inc.	2844	E	714 265-3740	4387
Advanced Chemistry & Technology Inc.	2891	D	714 373-8118	4556
GKN Arspace Trnsprncy Systems.	3089	B	714 893-7531	5041
Jason Tool and Engineering Inc.	3089	E	714 895-5067	5067
Monco Products Inc.	3089	E	714 891-2788	5108
Peerless Injection Molding LLC.	3089	E	714 891-7669	5133
Customfab Inc.	3111	E	714 891-9119	5256
Cham-Cal Engineering Co.	3231	D	714 898-9721	5336
CTS Cement Manufacturing Corp (PA)	3241	E	714 379-8260	5365
Hyatt Die Cast Engrg Corp - S.	3363	E	714 622-2131	5760
Synertech PM Inc.	3369	F	714 898-9151	5818
Diversfied Mtllrgical Svcs Inc.	3398	E	714 895-7777	5836
Kittyhawk Products CA LLC.	3398	E	714 895-5024	5839
Kpi Services Inc.	3398	E	714 895-5024	5840
Container Supply Company Incorporated.	3411	C	714 892-8321	5858
Baton Lock and Hardware Co Inc.	3429	E	714 265-3636	5906
Umpco Inc.	3429	E	714 897-3531	5949
V & F Fabrication Company Inc.	3441	E	714 265-0630	6088
F T B & Son Inc.	3444	E	714 891-8003	6237
Spartan Manufacturing Co.	3451	E	714 894-1955	6422

GEOGRAPHIC

	SIC	EMP	PHONE	ENTRY#
TI Machine Inc	3451	D	714 554-4154	6424
Houston Bazz Co	3469	D	714 898-2666	6522
Coastline Metal Finishing Corp	3471	E	714 895-9099	6606
Electron Plating III Inc	3471	E	714 554-2210	6617
Associated Components Technology Inc	3496	E	714 265-4800	6812
Intra Storage Systems Inc	3499	E	714 373-2346	6865
Tystar Corporation	3559	E	310 781-9219	7263
American Metal Bearing Company	3562	E	714 892-5527	7296
Bar Code Specialties Inc	3577	E	877 411-2633	7508
Advanced Aerospace	3585	E	714 265-6200	7595
Chemical Methods Assoc LLC (DH)	3589	E	714 898-8781	7647
Aero Dynamic Machining Inc	3599	D	714 379-1073	7740
I Copy Inc	3599	E	562 921-0202	7870
Infinite Engineering Inc	3599	F	714 534-4688	7871
Kimberly Machine Inc	3599	E	714 539-0151	7899
Nelson Engineering Llc	3599	F	714 893-7999	7953
Vianh Company Inc	3599	E	714 590-9808	8067
Western Precision Aero LLC	3599	E	714 893-7999	8077
Microsemi Corp-Power MGT Group	3625	C	714 994-6500	8186
Fei-Zyfer Inc (HQ)	3663	E	714 933-4000	8517
Exigent Sensors LLC	3669	E	949 439-1321	8611
Microsemi Corp - Anlog Mxed Sg (DH)	3674	D	714 898-8121	8841
Microsemi Corp - High Prfmce T (DH)	3674	D	949 380-6100	8842
Microsemi Corporation (HQ)	3674	E	949 380-6100	8843
Microsemi Corporation	3674	C	714 898-7112	8844
Vitesse Manufacturing & Dev	3674	E	805 388-3700	8920
Basic Electronics Inc	3679	E	714 530-2400	9002
Onecharge Inc	3691	E	833 895-8624	9152
Driveshaftpro	3714	E	714 893-4585	9384
King Shock Technology Inc	3714	D	719 394-3754	9410
Walker Products	3714	E	714 554-5151	9486
GKN Aerospace	3721	E	714 653-7531	9536
Jvr Sheetmetal Fabrication Inc	3721	E	714 841-2464	9542
Align Precision - Anaheim Inc (DH)	3728	D	714 961-9200	9619
B & E Manufacturing Co Inc	3728	E	714 898-2269	9640
C&D Zodiac Aerospace	3728	E	714 801-0683	9646
Safran Cabin Inc	3728	C	714 891-1906	9785
Safran Cabin Inc	3728	C	714 901-2672	9786
SPS Technologies LLC	3728	E	714 892-5571	9802
Talsco Inc	3728	E	714 841-2464	9810
Tj Aerospace Inc	3728	E	714 891-3564	9816
King Instrument Company Inc	3823	E	714 891-0008	10143
Sensorex Corporation	3823	D	714 895-4344	10161
Touch International Display Enhance	3827	C	512 646-0310	10344
Hycor Biomedical LLC	3841	C	714 933-3000	10522
Elite Screens Inc	3861	E	877 511-1211	10865
Iron Grip Barbell Company Inc	3949	C	714 850-6900	11005
Evans Manufacturing Inc (HQ)	3993	E	714 379-6100	11116
Expo-3 International Inc	3993	E	714 379-8383	11117
Innovative Casework Mfg Inc	3999	E	714 890-9100	11230
Orange Cnty Trnsp Auth Schlrsh	4111	D	714 560-6282	11353
Modivcare Solutions LLC	4731	C	714 503-6871	11785
Sprint Communications Co LP	4813	C	714 534-2107	11905
Video Vice Data Communications (PA)	4841	C	714 897-6300	12002
Battery Systems Inc	5013	C	714 667-9320	12234
Innovative Metal Designs Inc	5013	E	714 799-6700	12244
Winchester Interconnect EC LLC	5065	D	714 230-6122	12711
Penn Elcom Inc (HQ)	5072	E	714 230-6200	12729
Pure Process Filtration Inc	5075	F	714 891-6527	12758
Advanced Phrm Svcs Inc	5122	F	714 903-1006	13027
Kush Supply Co LLC	5122	D	714 243-4023	13050
Qyk Brands LLC	5122	E	949 312-7119	13065
R D Abbott Co Inc	5169	D	562 944-5354	13438
Home Depot USA Inc	5211	C	714 539-0319	13593
Noarus Tgg	5511	D	714 895-5595	13806
Allied Wheel Components Inc	5531	E	714 893-4160	13854
Irvine APT Communities LP	6513	C	714 537-8500	14718
Cushman & Wakefield Cal Inc	6531	B	714 591-0451	14777
Embassy Suites & Hotel	7011	C	714 539-3300	15145
Ohi Resort Hotels LLC	7011	D	714 867-5555	15271
Mastroianni Family Entps Ltd	7299	B	310 952-1700	15517
Compass Group Usa Inc	7359	C	714 899-2520	15777
Tad Pgs Inc	7363	A	800 261-3779	15944
Revco Products	7372	C	714 891-6688	16368
Brinks Incorporated	7381	C	714 903-9272	16627
Lao-Hmong Security Agency Inc	7381	D	714 533-6776	16656
Aaron Thomas Company Inc (PA)	7389	C	714 894-4468	16765
St George Auto Center Inc	7539	D	657 212-5042	17044
Kaiser Foundation Hospitals	8011	C	714 741-3448	17684
Garden Grove Medical Investors (HQ)	8051	D	714 534-1041	17958
Pacific Haven Convalescent HM	8059	D	714 534-1942	18150
Childrens Hospital Orange Cnty	8062	B	714 638-5990	18220
Kenneth Corp	8062	A	714 537-5160	18314
Performance Health Med Group	8099	D	714 740-1778	18788
Garden Grove Unified Schl Dst	8211	E	714 663-6101	18967
Boys Grls Clubs Grdn Grove Inc (PA)	8299	C	714 530-0430	19008
Community Action Prtnr Ornge C	8322	C	714 897-6670	19047
Garden Grove Unified Schl Dst	8351	D	714 663-6437	19211
Crystal Cathedral Ministries (PA)	8661	C	714 622-2900	19500
Buffalo Spot MGT Group LLC	8741	C	949 354-0884	20007

GARDENA, CA - Los Angeles County

	SIC	EMP	PHONE	ENTRY#
Brightview Landscape Svcs Inc	0781	C	310 327-8700	153
K C Restoration Co Inc	1389	E	310 280-0597	358
Disaster Rstrtion Prfssnals In	1521	D	310 301-8030	429
XCEL Mechanical Systems Inc	1711	C	310 660-0090	838
Arena Painting Contractors Inc	1721	E	310 316-2446	842
Martin Bros/Marcowall Inc (PA)	1742	C	310 532-5335	982
Best Contracting Services Inc (PA)	1761	B	310 328-9176	1037
Weiss Sheet Metal Company	1761	E	310 354-2700	1056
Anvil Steel Corporation	1791	D	310 329-5811	1099
Richwell Steel Co Inc	1791	E	310 324-4455	1114
Washington Orna Ir Works Inc (PA)	1799	C	310 327-8660	1181
Rich Chicks LLC	2015	E	209 879-4104	1248
Better Nutritionals LLC	2023	C	310 356-9019	1263
Triple Five Nutrition LLC	2023	E	310 502-2277	1286
La Mousse Desserts Inc	2038	E	310 478-6051	1394
Hannahmax Baking Inc	2051	C	310 380-6778	1477
Little Brothers Bakery LLC	2051	D	310 225-3790	1481
Ocean Direct LLC (HQ)	2092	C	424 266-9300	1810
Nissin Foods USA Company Inc (DH)	2098	C	310 327-8478	1842
Bcd Food Inc	2099	F	310 323-1200	1855
Lets Do Lunch	2099	B	310 523-3664	1934
Risvolds Inc	2099	D	323 770-2674	1978
Sabater Usa Inc (PA)	2099	E	310 518-2227	1981
Tu Madre Romana Inc	2099	E	323 321-6041	2000
Stanzino Inc (PA)	2211	E	213 746-8822	2032
Twin Dragon Marketing Inc (PA)	2211	E	310 715-7070	2034
Caitac Garment Processing Inc	2261	B	310 217-9888	2087
Barco Uniforms Inc	2311	B	310 323-7315	2149
Stringking Inc (PA)	2311	E	310 503-8901	2154
True Religion Apparel Inc (HQ)	2325	B	323 266-3072	2172
Knk Apparel Inc	2326	F	310 768-3333	2177
Way Out West Inc	2326	E	310 769-6937	2187
Global Casuals Inc	2329	D	310 817-2828	2206
Gloria Lance Inc (PA)	2331	E	310 767-4400	2241
La Palm Furnitures & ACC Inc (PA)	2395	E	310 217-2700	2516
N Stitches Prints Inc	2395	E	310 366-7537	2521
D and J Marketing Inc	2396	E	310 538-1583	2528
Baxstra Inc	2426	E	323 770-4171	2568
Parquet By Dian	2426	D	310 527-3779	2578
American Cabinet Works Inc	2431	E	310 715-6815	2582
Ohline Corporation	2431	E	310 327-4630	2623
Hammer Collection Inc	2512	F	310 515-0276	2804
Martin/Brattrud Inc	2512	E	323 770-4171	2810
A M Cabinets Inc (PA)	2521	D	310 532-1919	2876
New Maverick Desk Inc	2521	C	310 217-1554	2890
Louis Sardo Upholstery Inc (PA)	2531	D	310 327-0532	2932
Custom Displays Inc	2541	E	323 770-8074	2951
One Up Manufacturing LLC	2631	E	310 749-8347	3069
Sgl Composites Inc (DH)	2655	D	424 329-5250	3138
Triune Enterprises Inc	2671	E	310 719-1600	3161
Gardena Valley News Inc	2711	D	310 329-6351	3278
Bremik International Inc	2741	D	310 715-6622	3432
Quadriga Americas LLC	2741	E	424 634-4900	3479
Americhip Inc (PA)	2752	E	310 323-3697	3510
Matsuda House Printing Inc	2752	E	310 532-1533	3632
Southwest Offset Prtg Co Inc (PA)	2752	B	310 965-9154	3687
UNI-Sport Inc	2752	E	310 217-4587	3702
Supacolor Usa Inc	2759	D	844 973-2862	3813
Continental Bdr Specialty Corp (PA)	2782	C	310 324-8227	3836
US Blanks LLC (PA)	2821	E	310 225-6774	3982
CH Laboratories Inc (PA)	2834	E	310 516-8273	4090
West Coast Laboratories Inc	2834	E	310 527-6163	4256
Cilajet LLC	2842	E	310 320-8000	4347
Grow More Inc	2879	D	310 515-1700	4551
Matsui International Co Inc (HQ)	2899	C	310 767-7812	4619
Evergreen Oil Inc (HQ)	2992	E	949 757-7770	4684
Principle Plastics	3021	E	310 532-3411	4706
Lite Extrusions Mfg Inc	3085	E	323 770-4298	4836
Narayan Corporation	3085	D	310 719-7330	4861
Advanced Foam Inc	3086	F	310 515-0728	4869
Amfoam Inc (PA)	3086	E	310 327-4003	4872
Barnes Plastics Inc	3089	E	310 329-6301	4957
Geiger Plastics Inc	3089	E	310 327-9926	5035
Getpart La Inc	3089	E	424 331-9599	5038

Mergent email: customerrelations@mergent.com
1372

2024 Southern California
Business Directory and Buyers Guide

(P-0000) Products & Services Section entry number
(PA)=Parent Co (HQ)=Headquarters (DH)=Div Headquarters

	SIC	EMP	PHONE	ENTRY#
Pro Design Group Inc	3089	E	310 767-1032	5166
Rotational Molding Inc	3089	D	310 327-5401	5186
Pacific Artglass Corporation	3231	E	310 516-7828	5352
Arto Brick / California Pavers	3251	E	310 768-8500	5371
Stepstone Inc (PA)	3272	E	310 327-7474	5454
US Hanger Company LLC	3315	E	310 323-8030	5627
Del Mar Industries (PA)	3364	D	323 321-0600	5773
Cast-Rite International Inc (PA)	3369	D	310 532-2080	5809
International Die Casting Inc	3369	E	310 324-2278	5815
Abrasive Finishing Co	3398	F	310 323-7175	5820
Melling Tool Rush Metals LLC	3399	E	580 725-3295	5854
Tomorrows Heirlooms Inc	3429	E	310 323-6720	5946
A and M Welding Inc	3441	E	310 329-2700	5986
Maya Steel Fabrications Inc	3441	D	310 532-8830	6045
Columbia Holding Corp	3442	B	310 327-4107	6102
Thermlly Engnred Mnfctred Pdts	3443	E	310 523-9934	6164
Aero ARC	3444	E	310 324-3400	6179
All-Ways Metal Inc	3444	E	310 217-1177	6183
American Aircraft Products Inc	3444	D	310 532-7434	6186
Artistic Welding	3444	E	310 515-4922	6193
Bay Cities Tin Shop Inc	3444	C	310 660-0351	6199
Carla Senter	3444	F	310 366-7295	6210
Hi-Craft Metal Products	3444	E	310 323-6949	6252
Meadows Sheet Metal and AC Inc	3444	E	310 615-1125	6269
Ramda Metal Specialties Inc	3444	E	310 538-2136	6303
Russ International Inc	3444	E	310 329-7121	6308
Swift-Cor Precision Inc	3444	E	310 354-1207	6329
T & F Sheet Mtls Fab McHning I	3444	E	310 516-8548	6330
Versafab Corp (PA)	3444	E	800 421-1822	6340
Lni Custom Manufacturing Inc	3446	E	310 978-2000	6364
North Star Acquisition Inc	3449	E	310 515-2200	6403
GT Precision Inc	3451	C	310 323-4374	6415
Onyx Industries Inc	3451	D	310 851-6161	6417
Briles Aerospace LLC	3452	E	424 320-3817	6433
Paul R Briles Inc	3452	A	310 323-6222	6451
Binder Metal Products Inc	3469	E	800 233-0896	6499
Metco Manufacturing Inc	3469	E	310 516-6547	6537
The Macsmith Corporation	3469	E	323 321-8881	6562
Coast Plating Inc (PA)	3471	E	323 770-0240	6604
Granath & Granath Inc	3471	F	310 327-5740	6624
Gsp Metal Finishing Inc	3471	E	818 744-1328	6625
Standard Metal Products Inc	3471	E	310 532-9861	6667
Faber Enterprises Inc	3492	C	310 323-6200	6776
Nelson Aero Space Inc	3494	E	310 323-6200	6793
Wyrefab Inc	3496	E	310 523-2147	6835
Mark IV Metal Products Inc	3498	E	310 217-9700	6848
Tru-Cut Inc	3524	E	310 630-0422	6922
Rytan Inc	3541	F	310 328-6553	7021
Nugier Press Company Inc	3542	F	310 515-6025	7035
US Industrial Tool & Sup Co	3542	E	310 464-8400	7041
Cast-Rite Corporation	3544	D	310 532-2080	7056
Aqua Pro Properties Vii LP	3559	B	310 516-9911	7222
Custom Metal Finishing Inc	3559	D	310 532-5075	7233
Mars Air Systems LLC	3564	D	310 532-1555	7327
American Condenser & Coil LLC	3585	D	310 327-8600	7598
Vege-Mist Inc	3585	D	310 353-2300	7633
Timbucktoo Manufacturing Inc	3589	E	310 323-1134	7689
A & A Machine & Dev Co Inc	3599	F	310 532-7706	7721
Aldo Fragale	3599	E	310 324-0050	7750
Brek Manufacturing Co (HQ)	3599	E	310 329-7638	7787
Century Precision Engrg Inc	3599	E	310 538-0015	7796
German Machined Products Inc	3599	E	310 532-4480	7848
J & S Inc	3599	E	310 719-7144	7880
Research Metal Industries Inc	3599	E	310 352-3200	7998
California Pak Intl Inc	3612	E	310 223-2500	8088
Kc Hilites Inc	3647	E	928 635-2607	8348
Mj Best Videographer LLC	3651	C	209 208-8432	8424
Centron Industries Inc	3663	E	310 324-6443	8504
Qual-Pro Corporation (HQ)	3672	C	310 329-7535	8721
Inca One Corporation	3675	E	310 808-0001	8928
Rayco Electronic Mfg Inc	3677	E	310 329-2660	8953
Polar Power Inc	3694	E	310 830-9153	9173
Harbinger Motors Inc	3711	E	914 299-3998	9293
Shelby Carroll Intl Inc (PA)	3711	E	310 538-2914	9308
Prime Wheel Corporation	3714	E	310 819-4123	9441
Prime Wheel Corporation (PA)	3714	B	310 516-9126	9443
Ducommun Aerostructures Inc (HQ)	3724	D	310 380-5390	9566
Ace Air Manufacturing	3728	F	310 323-7246	9586
Ahf-Ducommun Incorporated (HQ)	3728	C	310 380-5390	9608
Avcorp Cmpsite Fabrication Inc	3728	B	310 970-5658	9638
Designed Metal Connections Inc (DH)	3728	C	310 323-6200	9673
Impresa Aerospace LLC	3728	C	310 354-1200	9717
Nasco Aircraft Brake Inc	3728	D	310 532-4430	9755
Space-Lok Inc	3728	C	310 527-6150	9800
Space Exploration Tech Corp	3761	E	323 754-1285	9900
Quadrtech Corporation	3915	E	310 523-1697	10919
Cloud B Inc	3942	E	310 781-3833	10937
I & I Sports Supply Company (PA)	3949	E	310 715-6800	11002
Norberts Athletic Products Inc	3949	F	310 830-6672	11016
Wcbm Company (PA)	3965	E	323 262-3274	11080
Clegg Industries Inc	3993	C	310 225-3800	11103
Elro Manufacturing Company (PA)	3993	E	310 380-7444	11112
Maneri Sign Co Inc	3993	E	310 327-6261	11133
Neighbrhood Bus Advrtsment Ltd	3999	E	442 300-1803	11255
Sgps Inc	3999	D	310 538-4175	11280
Steeldeck Inc	3999	E	323 290-2100	11286
Wally & Pat Enterprises	3999	E	310 532-2031	11305
First Transit Inc	4111	D	323 222-0010	11317
Global Paratransit Inc	4119	B	310 715-7550	11390
Administrative Svcs Coop Inc	4121	C	310 715-1968	11412
First Student Inc	4151	A	310 769-2400	11429
United Parcel Service Inc	4215	C	310 217-2646	11539
World Svc Wst/La Inflght Svc L	4581	C	310 538-7000	11709
Nippon Travel Agency PCF Inc (DH)	4724	D	310 768-0017	11720
Hanjin Transportation Co Ltd	4731	C	310 522-5030	11767
Comprehensive Dist Svcs Inc	4789	D	310 523-1546	11830
Sprint Communications Co LP	4812	C	310 515-0293	11857
California Waste Services LLC	4953	C	310 538-5998	12163
Waste MGT Collectn Recycl Inc	4953	D	310 532-6511	12201
Cleanstreet LLC	4959	C	800 225-7316	12208
Tireco Inc (PA)	5014	C	310 767-7990	12274
Mariak Industries Inc	5023	B	310 661-4400	12307
Jk Imaging Ltd	5043	D	310 755-6848	12378
Canon Business Solutions-West Inc	5044	B	310 217-3000	12382
Tool Components Inc (PA)	5051	E	310 323-5613	12576
Magnetika Inc (PA)	5063	C	310 527-8100	12603
Mutual Liquid Gas & Eqp Co Inc (PA)	5084	E	310 515-0553	12801
Westcoast Rotor Inc	5084	C	310 327-5050	12838
A Royal Wolf Portable Stor Inc	5085	E	310 719-1048	12843
SPS Technologies LLC	5085	B	310 323-6222	12883
Valley of Sun Cosmetics LLC	5122	C	310 327-9062	13074
Phoenix Textile Inc (PA)	5131	D	310 715-7090	13088
Softline Home Fashions Inc	5131	E	310 630-4848	13094
La Dye & Print Inc	5137	E	310 327-3200	13130
Lily Bleu Inc	5137	E	310 225-2522	13131
Field Fresh Foods Incorporated	5148	A	310 719-8422	13323
Spectrum Laboratory Pdts Inc	5169	E	520 292-3103	13439
Harbor Distributing LLC	5181	D	310 538-5483	13469
DCH Gardena Honda	5511	C	310 515-5700	13756
South Bay Toyota	5511	C	310 323-7800	13827
Carson Trailer Inc (PA)	5599	D	310 835-0876	13905
Guru Denim LLC (DH)	5611	C	323 266-3072	13908
J & M Sales Inc	5651	A	310 324-9962	13922
B & W Tile Co Inc (PA)	5713	E	310 538-9579	13948
Air Fayre USA Inc	5812	C	310 808-1061	13980
Kings Hawaiian Bakery W Inc (HQ)	5812	C	310 533-3250	14019
Ruggable LLC	5961	B	310 295-0098	14104
Episource LLC	6411	E	714 452-1961	14586
Monark LP	6513	D	310 769-6669	14727
El Dorado Enterprises Inc	7011	A	310 719-9800	15144
Radiant Services Corp (PA)	7211	C	310 327-6300	15445
SPS Holdings Inc	7213	C	310 532-7550	15460
CM Laundry LLC	7219	D	310 436-6170	15474
Pulp Studio Incorporated	7336	D	310 815-4999	15672
Los Angeles Unified School Dst	7349	D	310 808-1500	15721
Maxim Healthcare Services Inc	7363	C	310 329-9115	15927
Secom International (PA)	7373	D	310 641-1290	16469
American Guard Services Inc (PA)	7381	B	310 645-6200	16616
Construction Protective Services Inc (PA)	7381	A	800 257-5512	16632
Eagle Security Services Inc	7381	A	310 642-0656	16639
Servexo	7381	B	323 527-9994	16684
United Facility Solutions Inc	7381	A	310 743-3000	16697
Vescom Corporation (PA)	7381	A	207 945-5051	16707
Vets Securing America Inc	7381	A	310 645-6200	16708
Wsa Group Inc	7381	A	310 743-3000	16885
New Crew Production Corp	7389	C	323 234-8880	16885
Hansens Welding Inc	7692	E	310 329-6888	17084
Nike Usa Inc	7941	A	310 670-6770	17379
Gardena Retirement Center Inc	8051	C	310 327-4091	17959
Healthcare Investments Inc (PA)	8051	C	310 323-3194	17971
Clear View Sanitarium Inc	8059	C	310 538-2323	18117
Gardena Hospital LP	8062	A	310 532-4200	18263
Kaiser Foundation Hospitals	8062	C	310 517-2956	18298
SMS Transportation Inc	8111	D	310 527-9200	18947
Counseling and Research Assoc (PA)	8361	C	310 715-2020	19253
Elite Engineering Contrs Inc	8711	E	310 465-8333	19580

Employee Codes: A=Over 500 employees, B=251-500
C=101-250, D=51-100, E=20-50, F=10-19, G=1-9

2024 Southern California
Business Directory and Buyers Guide

© Mergent Inc. 1-800-342-5647
1373

Company	SIC	EMP	PHONE	ENTRY#
Prototype Engineering and Manufacturing Inc.	8711	E	310 532-6305	19673
Transcosmos Omniconnect LLC	8741	D	310 630-0072	20106

GLENDALE, CA - Los Angeles County

Company	SIC	EMP	PHONE	ENTRY#
Triangle Rock Products LLC	1429	B	818 553-8820	403
Kennard Development Group	1522	D	818 241-0800	471
PCL Construction Services Inc.	1542	C	818 246-3481	574
H L Moe Co Inc (PA)	1711	C	818 572-2100	775
Pinnacle Networking Svcs Inc	1731	C	818 241-6009	926
Nestle Usa Inc	2023	C	818 549-6000	1280
Pillsbury Company LLC	2041	E	818 522-3952	1415
Nestle Purina Petcare Company	2047	E	314 982-1000	1435
Sugarfina Inc.	2064	E	818 302-0765	1549
Custom Characters Inc.	2389	F	818 507-5940	2446
North American Textile Co LLC (PA)	2396	C	818 409-0019	2536
Avery Dennison Foundation	2672	D	626 304-2000	3166
Avery Dnnson Ret Info Svcs LLC (HQ)	2678	D	626 304-2000	3217
Viva Print LLC (HQ)	2678	F	818 243-1363	3226
California Community News LLC	2711	D	818 843-8700	3260
Axiomprint Inc.	2752	F	747 888-7777	3515
Chromatic Inc Lithographers	2752	E	818 242-5785	3529
Color Inc.	2752	E	818 240-1350	3532
Colour Concepts Inc.	2752	C		3537
Zoo Printing Inc (PA)	2752	E	310 253-7751	3717
4 Over LLC (HQ)	2759	E	818 246-1170	3725
Legion Creative Group	2759	E	323 498-1100	3782
Vapor Delux Inc.	2782	E	818 370-8308	3843
Person & Covey Inc.	2844	E	818 937-5000	4443
Vege - Kurl Inc.	2844	D	818 956-5582	4466
Calmat Co (DH)	2951	C	818 553-8821	4657
Hintex	3272	F	320 400-0009	5420
JP Weaver & Company	3299	E	818 500-1740	5569
Cygnet Stampng & Fabrictng Inc (PA)	3469	E	818 240-7574	6508
Automation Plating Corporation	3471	E	323 245-4951	6588
SAI Industries	3484	C	818 842-6144	6748
Ambrit Industries Inc.	3542	E	818 243-1224	7029
Pennoyer-Dodge Co.	3545	C	818 547-2100	7123
Cryst Mark Inc A Swan Techno C	3559	F	818 240-7520	7232
International Bus Mchs Corp.	3571	A	818 553-8100	7433
Quantum Alliance Inc.	3572	F	818 415-2085	7481
All 4-Pcb North America Inc.	3599	F	866 734-9403	7751
HI Temp Forming Co.	3599	E	714 529-6556	7860
McCoppin Enterprises.	3599	E	818 240-4840	7923
Modern Engine Inc.	3599	E	818 409-9494	7943
Arecont Vision LLC	3629	C	818 937-0700	8200
Glenair Inc (PA)	3643	A	818 247-6000	8266
Bittree Incorporated.	3663	E	818 500-8142	8499
Coda Energy Holdings LLC.	3699	F	626 775-3900	9200
Kalap Inc.	3861	F	818 332-6916	10871
AMG Employee Management Inc.	3873	E	323 254-7448	10891
LDI Operations LLC.	3999	C	818 240-7500	11241
Sunderstorm LLC.	3999	F	818 605-6682	11289
Mv Transportation Inc.	4111	C	818 409-3387	11341
Ambiance Transportation LLC.	4789	D	818 955-5757	11827
American Transportation Co LLC.	4789	C	818 660-2343	11828
Sigma Supply & Dist Inc.	5047	F	818 246-4624	12515
Global Plumbing & Fire Supply.	5074	C	818 550-8444	12741
Otis Elevator Company.	5084	C	818 241-2828	12804
Simon G Jewelry Inc.	5094	E	818 500-8595	12967
Alexander Henry Fabrics Inc.	5131	E	818 562-8200	13079
Los Feliz Ford Inc (PA)	5511	D	818 502-1901	13791
Chop Stop Inc.	5812	D	818 369-7350	13996
Forest Lawn Memorial-Park Assn (PA)	5992	B	323 254-3131	14113
Los Angeles Federal Credit Un (PA)	6061	D	818 242-8640	14231
California Credit Union (PA)	6062	C	818 291-6700	14245
Countrywide Home Loans Inc.	6162	A	818 550-8700	14309
Carelon Med Benefits MGT Inc.	6321	A	847 310-0366	14450
Cigna Behavioral Health of Cal.	6324	B	800 753-0540	14465
Cigna Healthcare Cal Inc (DH)	6324	B	818 500-6262	14466
Arthur J Gallagher Risk Mgmt.	6411	E	818 539-2300	14560
Califrnia Insur Guarantee Assn.	6411	C	818 844-4300	14570
Dedicted Dfned Beneft Svcs LLC.	6411	C	415 931-1990	14583
Safeco Insurance Company Amer.	6411	C	818 956-1263	14628
Glendale Associates Ltd.	6512	D	818 246-6737	14663
Humangood Socal.	6513	C	818 244-7219	14713
Equity Title Company (DH)	6541	D	818 291-4400	14888
Stewart Title California Inc.	6541	C	818 502-2700	14895
Title Resource Group LLC.	6541	D	818 291-4400	14896
Forest Lawn Co.	6553	C	818 241-4151	14915
Public Storage (PA)	6798	B	818 244-8080	15017
Asab Inc (DH)	7338	C	818 551-7300	15679
AppleOne Inc.	7361	C	818 240-8688	15813
AppleOne Inc (HQ)	7361	C	818 240-8688	15814
E Z Staffing Inc (PA)	7361	B	818 845-2500	15839
Hrn Services Inc.	7361	D	323 951-1450	15851
Akkodis Inc.	7371	C	818 546-2848	15959
Disney Cnsmr Pdts Intrctive MD.	7371	D	818 263-1374	16014
Disney Interactive Studios Inc.	7371	B	818 560-1000	16016
Systech Solutions Inc (PA)	7371	C	818 550-9690	16128
Btrade LLC.	7372	E	818 334-4433	16191
Informtion Intgrtion Group Inc.	7372	E	818 956-3744	16271
Legalzoomcom Inc (PA)	7374	B	323 962-8600	16502
Assign Corporation.	7379	C	818 247-7100	16552
General Networks Corporation.	7379	D	818 249-1962	16569
Software Management Cons LLC (HQ)	7379	B	818 240-3177	16601
Grandall Distributing Co Inc.	7389	C	818 242-6640	16837
Isovac Engineering Inc.	7389	E	818 552-6200	16851
Yellowpagescom LLC (DH)	7389	B	818 937-5500	16968
Passport Technology Usa Inc.	7699	E	818 957-5471	17144
Bunim-Murray Productions.	7812	C	818 756-5100	17174
Disney Enterprises Inc.	7812	D	818 553-4103	17184
Dreamworks Animation Pubg LLC.	7812	A	818 695-5000	17186
Dwa Holdings LLC (DH)	7812	A	818 695-5000	17187
Walt Disney Pictures.	7812	B	818 409-2200	17233
Walt Dsney Imgnring RES Dev In (DH)	7819	A	818 544-6500	17273
Sega Entertainment USA Inc.	7993	A	310 217-9500	17446
Oakmont Country Club.	7997	C	818 542-4260	17506
Advanced Prof Imging Med Group.	8011	C	818 244-4646	17582
Insite Digestive Health Care.	8011	E	626 817-2900	17671
Kaiser Foundation Hospitals.	8011	C	818 552-3000	17693
Verdugo Hlls Psychthrapy Ctr A (PA)	8011	C	818 241-6780	17827
Country Villa Service Corp.	8051	C	818 246-5516	17914
Emeritus Corporation.	8051	C	818 246-7457	17937
Mariner Health Care Inc.	8051	D	818 246-5677	18004
Buena Ventura Care Center Inc.	8059	D	818 247-4476	18115
Front Prch Cmmnties Oprting Gr.	8059	A	800 233-3709	18125
Longwood Management Corp.	8059	D	818 246-7174	18138
American Hlthcare Systems Corp (PA)	8062	B	818 646-9933	18177
Glendale Adventist Medical Ctr (HQ)	8062	A	818 409-8000	18265
Glendale Mem Hlth Foundation.	8062	C	818 502-2375	18266
Glendale Memorial Health Corp.	8062	A	818 502-2323	18267
Glendale Memorial Health Corporation.	8062	A	818 502-1900	18268
Glenoaks Convalescent Hospital.	8062	D	818 240-4300	18269
Usc Verdugo Hills Hospital LLC.	8062	A	818 790-7100	18493
Usc Vrdugo Hlls Hosp Fundation (HQ)	8062	B	800 872-2273	18494
Verdugo Hills Hospital Inc.	8062	C	818 790-7100	18497
Pegasus HM Hlth Care A Cal Cor.	8082	D	818 551-1932	18633
Interstate Rhbltation Svcs LLC.	8093	C	818 244-5656	18698
Health Services Advisory Group.	8099	C	818 409-9220	18768
Christie Parker & Hale LLP (PA)	8111	C	626 795-9900	18836
La Folltte Jhnson De Haas Fsle (PA)	8111	C	213 426-3600	18888
National Attny Collection Svcs.	8111	B	818 547-9760	18917
Myhhbs Inc.	8322	D	888 969-4427	19114
Young MNS Chrstn Assn Glndale.	8641	D	818 484-8256	19493
City of Glendale.	8711	C	818 548-3945	19563
National Teleconsultants Inc.	8711	C	818 265-4400	19653
Avery Corp.	8731	C	626 304-2000	19823
Disney Research Pittsburgh.	8731	C	412 623-1800	19833
Noymed Corp.	8731	C	800 224-2090	19867
Parexel International Corp.	8731	C	818 254-7076	19870
Allzone Management Svcs Inc.	8741	B	213 291-8879	19992
Amco Foods Inc.	8742	C	818 247-4716	20130
Gavin De Becker & Assoc GP LLC.	8742	C	818 505-0177	20175
PSI Services LLC (PA)	8748	D	818 847-6180	20373
Ventegra Inc A Cal Beneft Corp.	8748	D	858 551-8111	20387

GLENDORA, CA - Los Angeles County

Company	SIC	EMP	PHONE	ENTRY#
CJd Construction Svcs Inc.	1389	E	626 335-1116	339
BR Building Resources Co.	1542	C	626 963-4880	537
Building Elctronic Contrls Inc (PA)	1731	E	909 305-1600	874
Deccofelt Corporation.	2299	E	626 963-8511	2139
G R Leonard & Co Inc.	2741	E	847 797-8101	3448
Calportland Company (DH)	3241	D	626 852-6200	5362
Calportland.	3273	E	760 343-3403	5466
CPC Services Inc.	3273	E	626 852-6200	5475
Hallmark Metals Inc.	3444	C	626 335-1263	6250
Action Stamping Inc.	3469	C	626 914-7466	6493
HP Core Co Inc.	3543	F	323 582-1688	7043
Postvision Inc.	3572	F	818 840-0777	7479
Millipart Inc (PA)	3599	F	626 963-4101	7939
Mackenzie Laboratories Inc.	3674	C	909 394-9007	8832
Electro-Tech Products Inc.	3679	E	909 592-1434	9038
Southwest Machine & Plastic Co.	3728	C	626 963-6919	9799
Safeguard Envirogroup Inc.	3826	C	626 512-7585	10285
Sybron Dental Specialties Inc.	3843	C	909 596-0276	10771
Oasis Medical Inc (PA)	3851	D	909 305-5400	10847

	SIC	EMP	PHONE	ENTRY#
Seidner-Miller Inc.	5511	C	909 305-2000	13823
Southern Cal Disc Tire Co Inc.	5531	D	626 335-2883	13881
Venue Management Systems Inc.	7381	A	626 445-6000	16706
Jans Towing Inc.	7549	C	909 596-9060	17057
Glendora Country Club.	7997	D	626 335-4051	17486
Harbor Glen Care Center.	8051	C	626 963-7531	17968
Ensign San Dimas LLC.	8059	C	626 963-7531	18123
East Valley Glendora Hosp LLC.	8062	B	626 852-5000	18248
Emanate Health.	8062	B	626 857-3477	18253
Emanate Hlth Fthill Prsbt Hosp (PA).	8062	D	626 857-3145	18259
Care Unlimited Health Svcs Inc.	8082	C	626 332-3767	18600
Berkshire Hathaway Home Servic.	8322	C	626 335-6001	19028
Inland Empire Chptr-Ssction Cr.	8699	D	512 478-9000	19530

GOLETA, CA - Santa Barbara County

	SIC	EMP	PHONE	ENTRY#
Apeel Technology Inc (PA).	0723	B	805 203-0146	98
Kitson Landscape MGT Inc.	0782	B	805 681-9460	197
Arguello Inc.	1382	E	805 567-1632	290
Alexs Tile Works Inc.	1743	E	805 967-5308	1003
Deckers Outdoor Corporation (PA).	2389	A	805 967-7611	2447
Boone Printing & Graphics Inc.	2752	E	805 683-2349	3520
JD Business Solutions Inc.	2752	E	805 962-8193	3606
Neal Feay Company.	3354	D	805 967-4521	5704
AEC - Able Engineering Company Inc.	3441	C	805 685-2262	5988
Vista Steel Company (PA).	3441	C	805 964-4732	6090
Ipt Holding Inc (PA).	3469	F	805 683-3414	6525
Sbif Inc.	3479	F	805 683-1711	6734
Flir Motion Ctrl Systems Inc.	3559	C	650 692-3900	7238
Mann+hmmel Wtr Fluid Sltons In (DH).	3589	D	805 964-8003	7670
Z P M Inc.	3589	E	805 681-3511	7696
Cnc Machining Inc.	3599	E	805 681-8855	7802
Intri-Plex Technologies Inc (HQ).	3599	C	805 683-3414	7876
Veeco Process Equipment Inc.	3599	E	805 967-2700	8063
Calient Technologies Inc (PA).	3661	E	805 695-4800	8469
L3 Technologies Inc.	3663	D	805 683-3881	8534
Moseley Associates Inc (HQ).	3663	E	805 968-9621	8550
Atomica Corp.	3674	C	805 681-2807	8771
Transphorm Inc (PA).	3674	D	805 456-1300	8912
Kyocera Sld Laser Inc (HQ).	3699	E	805 696-6999	9225
Raytheon Company.	3699	C	805 967-5511	9246
Ricardo Defense Inc (DH).	3714	E	805 882-1884	9450
Launchpint Elc Prplsion Sltons.	3728	E	805 683-9659	9734
Atk Space Systems LLC.	3812	E	805 685-2262	9953
Lockheed Martin Corporation.	3812	E	805 571-2346	9995
Mission Research Corporation (DH).	3812	E	805 690-2447	9999
Moog Inc.	3812	D	805 618-3900	10000
Northrop Grumman Systems Corp.	3812	D	714 240-6521	10041
Raytheon Company.	3812	D	805 562-4611	10053
Teledyne Flir LLC.	3812	D	805 964-9797	10077
Biopac Systems Inc.	3826	E	805 685-0066	10244
Teledyne Flir Coml Systems Inc (DH).	3826	B	805 964-9797	10290
Veeco Process Equipment Inc.	3826	D	805 967-1400	10303
Wyatt Technology LLC (HQ).	3826	C	805 681-9009	10305
Far West Technology Inc.	3829	F	805 964-3615	10364
Karl Storz Imaging Inc (HQ).	3829	B	805 968-5563	10378
Soilmoisture Equipment Corp.	3829	E	805 964-3525	10397
Digital Surgery Systems Inc.	3841	E	805 978-5400	10494
Inogen Inc (PA).	3841	D	805 562-0500	10531
Karl Storz Endscpy-America Inc.	3841	E	800 964-5563	10541
Karl Storz Imaging Inc.	3841	E	805 968-5563	10543
Truevision Systems Inc.	3841	E	805 963-9700	10623
Advanced Vision Science Inc.	3851	E	805 683-3851	10831
Santa Barbara Instrument GP Inc.	3861	E	925 463-3410	10885
Skate One Corp.	3949	D	805 964-1330	11027
Surf To Summit Inc.	3949	E	805 964-1896	11032
Santa Barbara Trnsp Corp.	4151	C	805 928-0402	11432
Hanson Aggrgtes Md-Pacific Inc.	4212	F	805 967-2371	11459
Verizon South Inc.	4812	C	805 681-8527	11866
Marborg Recovery LP.	4953	C	805 963-1852	12173
Enerpro Inc.	5065	E	805 683-2114	12657
Integrated Procurement Tech (PA).	5088	D	805 682-0842	12908
Moss Motors Ltd (PA).	5531	C	805 967-4546	13865
Exxon Mobil Corporation.	5541	C	805 961-4093	13892
CMC Rescue Inc.	5999	C	805 562-9120	14126
Mesa Insurance Solutions Inc.	6411	C	805 308-6308	14613
6500 Hllister Ave Partners LLC.	6512	D	805 722-1362	14650
One Call Plumber Goleta.	7299	D	805 284-0441	15518
Citrix Online LLC.	7371	B	805 690-6400	15993
Image-X Enterprises Inc.	7371	F	805 964-3535	16050
Stratgic Hlthcare Programs LLC.	7371	D	805 963-9446	16126
Connectpoint Inc.	7372	F	805 682-8900	16211
Parentsquare Inc.	7372	D	888 496-3168	16344
Yardi Kube Inc.	7372	D	805 699-2040	16426

	SIC	EMP	PHONE	ENTRY#
Glen Annie Golf Club.	7992	D	805 968-6400	17428
Bay Clubs Company LLC.	7997	B	805 964-0556	17465
Devereux Foundation.	8093	B	805 968-2525	18689
Intouch Technologies Inc (HQ).	8399	C	805 562-8686	19330
L3 Maripro Inc.	8711	D	805 683-3881	19636
National Security Tech LLC.	8711	E	805 681-2432	19652
Toyon Research Corporation (PA).	8711	C	805 968-6787	19706

GRANADA HILLS, CA - Los Angeles County

	SIC	EMP	PHONE	ENTRY#
Republic Fence Co Inc (PA).	1799	E	818 341-5323	1175
Instrumentation Tech Systems.	3577	F	818 886-2034	7537
Ortho Engineering Inc (PA).	3842	C	310 559-5996	10687
Financial Info Netwrk Inc.	7371	F	818 782-0331	16033
Longwood Management Corp.	8051	D	818 360-1864	17998
Aegis Senior Communities LLC.	8082	E	818 363-3373	18586
San Fernando City of Inc.	8093	D	818 832-2400	18716

GRAND TERRACE, CA - San Bernardino County

	SIC	EMP	PHONE	ENTRY#
West Coast Arborists Inc.	0783	C	909 783-6544	225
Duncan Bros Inc.	3441	E	909 877-1904	6021
Griswold Pump Company.	3561	E	909 422-1700	7279
Psg California LLC (HQ).	3561	B	909 422-1700	7287
National Logistics Team LLC.	4215	E	951 369-5841	11535
Riversd-San Brnrdino Cnty Indi (PA).	8011	C	909 864-1097	17753
Emeritus Corporation.	8051	D	909 420-0153	17931
Keystone NPS LLC (DH).	8399	D	909 633-6354	19333

GROVER BEACH, CA - San Luis Obispo County

	SIC	EMP	PHONE	ENTRY#
Hotlix (PA).	2064	E	805 473-0596	1543
H J Harkins Company Inc.	2834	E	805 929-1333	4128
California Fine Wire Co (PA).	3357	E	805 489-5144	5735
Vons Companies Inc.	5411	C	805 481-2492	13710

GUADALUPE, CA - Santa Barbara County

	SIC	EMP	PHONE	ENTRY#
Tri-Co Building Supply Inc.	2439	E	805 343-2555	2706
Guadalupe Union School Dst (PA).	8211	C	805 343-2114	18968

HACIENDA HEIGHTS, CA - Los Angeles County

	SIC	EMP	PHONE	ENTRY#
Terra Furniture Inc.	2512	E		2822
Superior Equipment Solutions.	3631	D	323 722-7900	8224
Lg-Led Solutions Limited.	3648	E	626 587-8506	8372
Brio Water Technology Inc.	5078	E	800 781-1680	12761

HARBOR CITY, CA - Los Angeles County

	SIC	EMP	PHONE	ENTRY#
Bennett Entps A Cal Ldscp Cntg.	0781	D	310 534-3543	143
Brea Canon Oil Co Inc.	1311	F	310 326-4002	251
La Espanola Meats Inc.	2013	E	310 539-0455	1225
Corn Maiden Foods Inc.	2032	E	310 784-0400	1322
Sunsets Inc.	2253	E	310 784-3600	2077
Miller Woodworking Inc.	2431	E	310 257-6806	2616
A & J Industries Inc.	2441	E	310 216-2170	2707
Cal Partitions Inc.	2542	E	310 539-1911	2975
Star Plastic Design.	3089	D	310 530-7119	5215
Nine Eight Nine LLC.	3142	E	310 469-1013	5263
Ruggeri Marble and Granite Inc.	3281	D	310 513-2155	5532
Team Inc.	3398	E	310 514-2312	5850
Joanka Inc.	3442	F	310 326-8940	6109
Basmat Inc (PA).	3444	D	310 325-2063	6198
Onyx Industries Inc (PA).	3451	D	310 539-8830	6416
Decco Graphics Inc.	3469	F	310 534-2861	6511
Republic Machinery Co Inc (PA).	3541	D	310 518-1100	7020
Hansen Engineering Co.	3599	D	310 534-3870	7857
Judco Manufacturing Inc (PA).	3643	C	310 534-0959	8268
Prime Wheel Corporation.	3714	B	310 326-5080	9442
Allied Protection Services Inc.	7381	C	310 330-8314	16614
Kaiser Foundation Hospitals.	8011	A	310 325-5111	17691
Permanente Medical Group Inc.	8011	A	310 325-5111	17738
Southern Cal Prmnnte Med Group.	8011	C	800 780-1230	17782

HAWAIIAN GARDENS, CA - Los Angeles County

	SIC	EMP	PHONE	ENTRY#
Consolidated Color Corporation.	2851	E	562 420-7714	4485
Ryvid Inc (PA).	3714	E	650 515-6118	9454
Hawaiian Gardens Casino.	7011	A	562 860-5887	15171
Hawaiian Gardens Casino.	7999	A	562 860-5887	17554
Gardens Regional Hospital and Medic.	8062	B	877 877-1104	18264
Pacific Gardens Med Ctr LLC.	8741	C	562 860-0401	20074

HAWTHORNE, CA - Los Angeles County

	SIC	EMP	PHONE	ENTRY#
Park West Landscape Inc.	0782	D	310 363-4100	210
Servicon Systems Inc.	1771	A	310 970-0700	1086
Firstclass Foods - Trojan Inc.	2011	E	310 676-2500	1194
Picnic At Ascot Inc.	2449	E	310 674-3098	2733
Huntington Industries Inc.	2512	C	323 772-5575	2806

Employee Codes: A=Over 500 employees, B=251-500
C=101-250, D=51-100, E=20-50, F=10-19, G=1-9

2024 Southern California
Business Directory and Buyers Guide

© Mergent Inc. 1-800-342-5647

1375

GEOGRAPHIC

	SIC	EMP	PHONE	ENTRY#
Lithographix Inc (PA)	2752	B	323 770-1000	3624
Marina Graphic Center Inc	2752	C	310 970-1777	3630
Technology Training Corp	2752	D	310 644-7777	3695
Marco Fine Arts Galleries Inc	2759	E	310 615-1818	3784
Ip Corporation	2821	E	323 757-1801	3948
Moleaer Inc	3561	D	424 558-3567	7284
Wems Inc (PA)	3564	D	310 644-0251	7341
Amag Technology Inc (DH)	3577	E	310 518-2380	7505
DL Horton Enterprises Inc	3599	D	323 777-1700	7819
Fulham Co Inc	3612	E	323 779-2980	8096
Ring LLC (HQ)	3612	B	310 929-7085	8109
Calpak Usa Inc	3672	E	310 937-7335	8656
OSI Electronics Inc (HQ)	3672	D	310 978-0516	8714
OSI Optoelectronics Inc (HQ)	3674	C	310 978-0516	8859
OSI Systems Inc (PA)	3674	B	310 978-0516	8860
Glen - Mac Swiss Co	3678	E	310 978-4555	8971
OSI Laserscan Inc	3699	E	310 978-0516	9236
OSI Subsidiary Inc	3699	D	310 978-0516	9237
Nmsp Inc (DH)	3714	D	310 484-2322	9432
Space Exploration Tech Corp (PA)	3761	A	310 363-6000	9898
Space Exploration Tech Corp	3761	E	310 889-4968	9901
Spacex LLC	3761	A	310 970-5845	9902
Phase Four Inc	3764	F	310 648-8454	9911
Medical Tactile Inc	3841	E	310 641-8228	10555
Dolphin Medical Inc (HQ)	3845	D	800 448-6506	10800
Local Neon Company Inc	3993	E	310 978-2000	11130
Advanced Air LLC	4522	C	310 644-3344	11679
Expeditors Intl Wash Inc	4731	C	310 343-6200	11760
Thinkom Solutions Inc	4899	C	310 371-5486	12014
Home Depot USA Inc	5211	C	310 644-9600	13612
Lowes Home Centers LLC	5211	C	323 327-4000	13630
South Bay Ford Inc (PA)	5511	C	310 644-0211	13826
Arch Motorcycle Company Inc	5571	E	970 443-1380	13898
EC Design LLC	5943	E	310 220-2362	14070
Ayres Group	7011	D	310 220-6447	15083
Calhot Illinios LLC	7011	E	310 536-9800	15106
Inspectorate America Corp	7389	C	800 424-0099	16848
Marleon Inc	7692	F	310 679-1242	17093
Eastbiz Corporation	7999	C	310 212-7134	17548
Longwood Management Corp	8051	C	310 679-1461	17997
Trident Labs LLC	8072	C	310 915-9121	18575
West Coast Dental Labs LLC	8072	B	855 220-5600	18576
Longwood Management Corp	8361	D	310 675-9163	19282
Interntonal Strl Engineers Inc	8711	E	310 643-7310	19616
Xdbs Corporation	8732	C	844 932-7356	19915
Analysts Inc	8734	C	800 424-0099	19957
Ncompass International LLC	8742	C	323 785-1700	20209
Netfortris Acquisition Co Inc	8748	D	877 366-2548	20364

HEBER, CA - Imperial County

	SIC	EMP	PHONE	ENTRY#
Gibson & Schaefer Inc (PA)	3273	E	619 352-3535	5479

HELENDALE, CA - San Bernardino County

	SIC	EMP	PHONE	ENTRY#
Lockheed Martin Corporation	3812	D	760 952-4200	9993
Silver Lakes Association	8641	D	760 245-1606	19464

HEMET, CA - Riverside County

	SIC	EMP	PHONE	ENTRY#
Lpsh Holdings Inc	1711	B	951 926-1176	788
Lpsh Holdings Inc (PA)	1711	D	855 647-5061	789
Washburn Grove Management Inc	2411	E	909 322-4690	2562
Prison Ride Share Network	2741	E	314 703-5245	3477
EZ Lube LLC	2992	D	951 766-1996	4685
Ramko Injection Inc	3089	D	951 929-0360	5172
Superior Ready Mix Concrete LP	3273	D	951 658-9225	5508
Brazeau Thoroughbred Farms LP	3523	E	951 201-2278	6901
Ramko Mfg Inc	3599	D	951 652-3510	7992
Substance Abuse Program	3674	E	951 791-3350	8900
McCrometer Inc (HQ)	3823	C	951 652-6811	10145
Jack Gosch Ford Inc	5511	D	951 652-3181	13782
Southern Cal Disc Tire Co Inc	5531	C	951 929-2130	13882
Emeritus Corporation	8051	C	951 744-9861	17935
Miramonte Enterprises LLC	8051	C	951 658-9441	18014
Hemet Valley Medical Center-Education	8062	A	951 652-2811	18278
Kpc Global Medical Centers Inc (DH)	8062	C	714 953-3500	18317
Ramona Rhblttion Post Acute CA	8062	C	951 652-0011	18405
Ramona Community Services Corp (HQ)	8082	C	951 658-9288	18637
Victor Cmnty Support Svcs Inc	8093	C	951 212-1770	18730
Hemet Unified School District	8211	D	951 765-5100	18969
Hemet Unified School District	8211	D	951 765-6287	18970
Valley Resource Center Inc (PA)	8331	E	951 766-8659	19194
Casa-Pacifica Inc	8361	D	951 658-3369	19246
Casa-Pacifica Inc	8361	B	951 766-5116	19247
Trilar Management Group	8741	C	951 925-2021	20108

HERMOSA BEACH, CA - Los Angeles County

	SIC	EMP	PHONE	ENTRY#
Easy Reader Inc	2711	E	310 372-4611	3275
Hammitt Inc	3161	D	310 292-5200	5288
Tellabs Access LLC (HQ)	3669	C	630 798-8671	8631
Rf Digital Corporation	3674	C	949 610-0008	8880
Marlin Equity Partners LLC (PA)	6282	D	310 364-0100	14423
Pacific Ave Cpitl Partners LLC (PA)	6726	B	424 254-9774	14981

HESPERIA, CA - San Bernardino County

	SIC	EMP	PHONE	ENTRY#
Arizona Pipeline Company (PA)	1623	B	760 244-8212	660
Hesperia Unified School Dst	2099	D	760 948-1051	1910
West Coast Furn Framers Inc	2426	E	760 669-5275	2580
Brown Hnycutt Truss Systems In	2439	F	760 244-8887	2693
Hesperia Holding Inc	2439	D	760 244-8787	2700
T L Timmerman Cnstr Inc	2439	E	760 244-2532	2704
Brent-Wood Products Inc	2499	E	800 400-7335	2752
C & M Wood Industries	2591	E	760 949-3292	3002
Robar Enterprises Inc (PA)	3273	C	760 244-5456	5494
Robertsons Ready Mix Ltd	3273	D	760 244-7239	5497
RSR Steel Fabrication Inc	3312	E	760 244-2210	5598
Maurice & Maurice Engrg Inc	3334	E	760 949-5151	5672
CAr Enterprises Inc	3578	F	760 947-6411	7584
Dial Precision Inc	3599	E	760 947-3557	7817
Geeriraj Inc	3672	E	760 244-6149	8681
W R Grace & Co-Conn	3826	F	760 244-6107	10304
El Dorado Broadcasters LLC	4832	C	760 241-1313	11923
Best Way Disposal Co Inc	4953	C	760 244-9773	12159
Endura Steel Inc (HQ)	5051	F	760 244-9325	12550
Global Customer Services Inc	7389	D	760 995-7949	16833
Victorville Speedwash Inc	7542	D	760 998-2482	17049
Davita Inc	8092	C	310 536-2406	18657

HIGHLAND, CA - San Bernardino County

	SIC	EMP	PHONE	ENTRY#
Kcb Towers Inc	1791	D	909 862-0322	1106
Raemica Inc	2013	E	909 864-1990	1232
Pro-Cast Products Inc (PA)	3272	E	909 793-7602	5441
Cemex Cnstr Mtls PCF LLC	3273	F	909 335-3105	5471
Robertsons Rdymx Ltd A Cal Ltd	3273	D	909 425-2930	5496
Innovative Product Brands Inc	3841	E	909 864-7477	10530
Cco Holdings LLC	4841	C	909 742-8273	11981
Lowes Home Centers LLC	5211	D	909 557-9010	13645
San Mnuel Band Mission Indians	6099	C	909 425-4682	14263
San Mnuel Band Mission Indians	7389	C	909 864-6928	16922
San Manuel Entertainment Auth (PA)	7999	A	909 864-5050	17566
Beaver Medical Group LP (HQ)	8011	C	909 425-3321	17600
Cedar Holdings LLC	8051	D	909 862-0611	17898

HINKLEY, CA - San Bernardino County

	SIC	EMP	PHONE	ENTRY#
Pacific Gas and Electric Co	4911	C	760 253-2925	12038

HOLLYWOOD, CA - Los Angeles County

	SIC	EMP	PHONE	ENTRY#
Body Glove International LLC	2329	E	310 374-3441	2199
Technicolor Usa Inc (HQ)	3651	A	317 587-4287	8442
Loews Hollywood Hotel LLC	7011	B	323 450-2235	15229

HUNTINGTON BEACH, CA - Orange County

	SIC	EMP	PHONE	ENTRY#
Coastline Cnstr & Awng Co Inc	1521	D	714 891-9798	426
Galkos Construction Inc	1542	D	714 373-8545	552
Grani Installation Inc (PA)	1542	D	714 898-0441	554
Aire-Rite AC & Rfrgn LLC	1711	E	714 895-2338	728
Critchfeld Mech Inc Sthern Cal	1711	D	949 390-2900	759
RC Wendt Painting Inc	1721	C	714 960-2700	854
Portermatt Electric Inc	1731	D	714 596-8788	928
Tile & Marble Design Co Inc	1743	E	714 847-6472	1007
California Closet Company Inc	1799	C	714 899-4905	1146
Armor Dermalogics LLC	2023	E	714 202-6424	1259
Creative Costuming Designs Inc	2211	E	714 895-0982	2017
Gearment Inc (PA)	2269	C	866 236-5476	2101
Marsha Vicki Originals Inc	2326	F	714 895-6371	2179
Boardriders Inc (HQ)	2329	A	714 889-5404	2198
DC Shoes Inc (DH)	2329	E	714 889-4206	2200
TravisMathew LLC (HQ)	2329	E	562 799-6900	2226
Bare Nothings Inc (PA)	2339	E	714 848-8532	2304
Jolyn Clothing Company LLC	2339	E	714 794-2149	2336
Victory Professional Pdts Inc	2339	E	714 887-0621	2381
Vae Industries Corporation	2394	E	714 842-7500	2512
Kastle Stair Inc (PA)	2431	E	714 596-2600	2609
Walton Company Inc	2499	F	714 847-8800	2766
Ofs Brands Holdings Inc	2521	A	714 903-2257	2894
Highmark Smart Reliable Seating Inc	2522	C	714 903-2257	2913
JCM Industries Inc (PA)	2542	E	714 902-9000	2982
K-Jack Engineering Co Inc	2542	D	310 327-8389	2983
Lifoam Industries LLC	2653	E	714 891-5035	3116

Mergent email: customerrelations@mergent.com
1376

2024 Southern California
Business Directory and Buyers Guide

(P-0000) Products & Services Section entry number
(PA)=Parent Co (HQ)=Headquarters (DH)=Div Headquarters

	SIC	EMP	PHONE	ENTRY#
Harris Industries Inc **(PA)**	2672	E	714 898-8048	3172
Maxwell Petersen Associates	2721	E	714 230-3150	3369
Teacher Created Materials Inc	2741	C	714 891-2273	3491
Inkwright LLC	2752	E	714 892-3300	3598
Gachupin Enterprises LLC	2759	F	714 375-4111	3761
HB Products LLC	2759	E	714 799-6967	3766
Pexco Aerospace Inc	2821	E	714 894-9922	3962
Sunshine Makers Inc **(PA)**	2842	D	562 795-6000	4369
Laird Coatings Corporation	2851	D	714 894-5252	4492
PPG Industries Inc	2851	E	714 894-5252	4498
Custom Building Products LLC **(DH)**	2891	D	800 272-8786	4561
Home & Body Company **(PA)**	2899	B	714 842-8000	4609
All West Plastics Inc	3082	E	714 894-9922	4827
Innovative Plastics Inc	3083	E	714 891-8800	4833
Marko Foam Products Inc **(PA)**	3086	E	949 417-3307	4893
Advanced Cmpsite Pdts Tech Inc	3089	E	714 895-5544	4928
Bent Manufacturing Co Inc	3089	E	714 842-0600	4959
Cambro Manufacturing Company	3089	D	714 848-1555	4977
Cambro Manufacturing Company **(PA)**	3089	B	714 848-1555	4978
Cambro Manufacturing Company	3089	C	714 848-1555	4979
Delfin Design & Mfg Inc	3089	E	949 888-4644	5004
Newlight Technologies Inc	3089	E	714 556-4500	5115
Sandia Plastics Inc	3089	E	714 901-8400	5197
Donoco Industries Inc	3229	E	714 893-7889	5324
Zadro Inc	3231	E	714 892-9200	5360
Zadro Products Inc	3231	E	714 892-9200	5361
Fox Hills Industries	3321	E	714 893-1940	5644
Dynamet Incorporated	3356	E	714 375-3150	5723
Paciugo	3421	E	714 536-5388	5870
Advanced Cutting Tools Inc	3423	E	714 842-9376	5871
Crenshaw Manufacturing Inc	3429	E	949 475-5505	5914
California Faucets Inc	3432	E	657 400-1639	5965
California Faucets Inc **(PA)**	3432	E	800 822-8855	5966
Evans Alloys	3444	E	714 373-2515	6235
R & D Metal Fabricators Inc	3444	E	714 841-4878	6300
Precision Resource Inc	3469	C	714 891-4439	6547
Cal-Aurum Industries	3471	E	714 898-0996	6598
Plasma Rggedized Solutions Inc	3471	E	714 893-6063	6648
Pvd Coatings LLC	3479	F	714 899-4892	6730
Tiodize Co Inc **(PA)**	3479	E	714 898-4377	6743
Vector Launch LLC **(PA)**	3489	C	202 888-3063	6751
Iconn Engineering LLC	3495	E	714 696-8826	6803
Orlando Spring Corp	3495	E	562 594-8411	6806
American Precision Hydraulics	3542	E	714 903-8610	7030
Mjc Engineering and Tech Inc	3542	F	714 890-0618	7034
Crenshaw Die and Mfg Corp	3544	D	949 475-5505	7064
M I T Inc	3544	E	714 899-6066	7079
Tarpin Corporation	3544	E	714 891-6944	7100
Guhring Inc	3545	E	714 841-3582	7116
Lytle Screen Printing Inc	3552	F	714 969-2424	7177
Rima Enterprises Inc	3555	D	714 893-4534	7191
Fotis and Son Imports Inc **(PA)**	3556	E	714 894-9022	7196
JGM Automotive Tooling Inc	3559	F	714 895-7001	7244
Curlin Medical Inc **(HQ)**	3561	C	714 897-9301	7275
Lynde-Ordway Company Inc	3579	F	714 957-1311	7586
Aerodynamic Engineering Inc	3599	E	714 891-2651	7744
Aerodyne Prcsion Machining Inc	3599	E	714 841-1311	7745
Fibreform Electronics Inc	3599	E	714 898-9641	7831
Hytron Mfg Co Inc	3599	E	714 903-6701	7869
Johnson Manufacturing Inc	3599	E	714 903-0393	7889
Milco Wire Edm Inc	3599	F	714 373-0098	7937
Momeni Engineering LLC	3599	E	714 897-9301	7945
Precision Frrites Ceramics Inc	3599	D	714 901-7622	7978
V & S Engineering Company Ltd	3599	E	714 898-7869	8058
California Economizer	3625	E	714 898-9963	8172
Coast To Coast Circuits Inc **(PA)**	3672	E	714 891-9441	8664
Vanguard Electronics Company **(PA)**	3677	E	714 842-3330	8958
Reedex Inc	3679	E	714 894-0311	9106
Rocker Solenoid Company	3679	D	310 534-5660	9108
Riot Glass Inc	3699	E	800 580-2303	9248
Dynatrac Products LLC	3714	E	714 596-4461	9385
U S Wheel Corporation	3714	E	714 892-0021	9477
Boeing Intllctual Prprty Lcnsi	3721	B	562 797-2020	9517
PCA Aerospace Inc	3721	E	714 901-5209	9549
Tri Models Inc	3721	D	714 896-0823	9557
Irish International	3724	C	949 559-0930	9574
Airtech International Inc **(PA)**	3728	C	714 899-8100	9613
AMG Torrance LLC **(DH)**	3728	E	310 515-2584	9623
Boeing Encore Interiors LLC	3728	E	949 559-0930	9645
Encore Seats Inc	3728	E	949 559-0930	9683
Forming Specialties Inc	3728	E	310 639-1122	9693
Irish Interiors Inc	3728	C	562 344-1700	9722
Irish Interiors Inc **(HQ)**	3728	C	949 559-0930	9723
Mission Crtical Composites LLC	3728	E	714 831-2100	9753
Notthoff Engineering L A Inc	3728	D	714 894-9802	9757
PCA Aerospace Inc **(PA)**	3728	D	714 841-1750	9764
Safran Cabin Galleys Us Inc **(HQ)**	3728	A	714 861-7300	9782
Safran Cabin Inc **(HQ)**	3728	B	714 934-0000	9783
Safran Cabin Materials LLC	3728	E	909 947-4115	9792
Tolemar Inc	3751	E	714 362-8166	9886
Boeing Company	3761	B	714 896-3311	9892
American Automated Engrg Inc	3769	D	714 898-9951	9914
Leda Corporation	3769	E	714 841-7821	9919
Translogic Incorporated	3823	E	714 890-0058	10167
Blue-White Industries Ltd **(PA)**	3824	D	714 893-8529	10173
Enhanced Vision Systems Inc **(HQ)**	3827	D	800 440-9476	10314
Measure Uas Inc	3829	E	714 916-6166	10379
Mechanized Science Seals Inc	3829	E	714 898-5602	10381
NDT Systems Inc	3829	E	714 893-2438	10385
Electronic Waveform Lab Inc	3841	E	714 843-0463	10501
Nordson Medical (ca) LLC	3841	D	657 215-4200	10580
Xr LLC	3842	E	714 847-9292	10723
Zimmer Melia & Associates Inc **(PA)**	3842	E	615 377-0118	10725
Kettenbach LP	3843	E	877 532-2123	10750
West Coast Trends Inc	3949	E	714 843-9288	11041
Primus Inc	3993	D	714 527-2261	11145
Leoben Company	3999	E	951 284-9653	11243
C & C Boats Inc	4499	F	714 969-0900	11654
Premiere Customs Brokers Inc	4731	A	310 410-6825	11794
Frontier California Inc	4813	B	714 375-6713	11883
Rainbow Disposal Co Inc **(HQ)**	4953	C	714 847-3581	12181
Reliable Wholesale Lumber Inc	5031	D	714 848-8222	12341
Premier Systems Usa Inc **(PA)**	5045	F	657 204-9861	12432
Bartco Lighting Inc	5063	D	714 230-3200	12585
Rief Enterprises Inc **(PA)**	5072	E	714 934-3400	12732
DSI Process Systems LLC	5084	E	314 382-1525	12789
Statco Engrg & Fabricators LLC **(PA)**	5084	E	714 375-6300	12825
Primal Elements Inc	5122	D	714 899-0757	13064
Kings Seafood Company LLC	5146	A	714 793-1177	13282
Astra Oil Company Inc	5172	C	714 969-6569	13447
Tiodize Co Inc	5172	E	714 898-4377	13456
Harbor Distributing LLc **(HQ)**	5181	C	714 933-2400	13468
Nakase Brothers Whl Nurs LP **(PA)**	5193	D	949 855-4388	13514
Stater Bros Markets	5411	E	714 963-0949	13703
York Enterprises South Inc	5511	D	714 842-6611	13849
Classic Camaro Inc	5531	C	714 847-6888	13857
Southern Cal Disc Tire Co Inc	5531	C	714 901-8226	13883
Boiling Crab Operations LLC	5812	B	714 636-4885	13985
Nuvision Fincl Federal Cr Un **(PA)**	6061	C	714 375-8000	14234
GFS Capital Holdings	6162	B	714 720-3918	14317
Managed Health Network	6324	C	714 934-5519	14488
Confie Holding II Co **(PA)**	6411	C	714 252-2500	14579
Freeway Insurance **(PA)**	6411	C	714 252-2500	14596
Huntington Bch Senior Hsing LP	6513	C	714 842-4006	14716
Burleigh Point LLC	6531	C	949 428-3200	14754
Child Development Incorporated	6531	B	714 842-4064	14764
Lincoln Prprty No 2087 Ltd Prt	6552	C	214 740-3300	14903
Pacific City Hotel LLC	7011	B	714 698-6100	15286
Waterfront Hotel LLC	7011	B	714 845-8000	15410
Grupo Gallegos	7311	D	562 256-3600	15541
Innocean Wrldwide Americas LLC **(HQ)**	7311	C	714 861-5200	15549
Graphic Ink Corp	7336	E	714 901-2805	15666
Direct Chassislink Inc	7359	A	657 216-5846	15779
Huntington Beach Union High	7361	C	714 478-7684	15852
Precise Fit Limited One LLC	7361	B	310 824-1800	15880
Infomagnus LLC	7371	D	714 810-3430	16053
Pakedge Device & Software Inc	7372	C	714 880-4511	16341
Shortcuts Software Inc	7372	E	714 622-6600	16378
United States Technical Svcs	7379	C	714 374-6300	16608
Horsemen Inc	7381	D	714 847-4243	16652
Global Exprnce Specialists Inc	7389	C	619 498-6300	16834
Century Theatres Inc	7832	C	714 373-4573	17289
Covid Clinic Inc	8011	B	877 219-8378	17638
Southern Cal Prmnnte Med Group	8011	C	714 841-7293	17791
Douglas Fir Holdings LLC	8051	C	714 842-5551	17927
Sea Breeze Health Care Inc	8051	C	714 847-9671	18049
Prime Hlthcare Hntngton Bch LL	8062	B	714 843-5000	18388
Landmark Health LLC	8082	B	657 237-2450	18623
No Ordinary Moments Inc	8082	B	714 848-3800	18630
Goodwill Inds Orange Cnty Cal	8331	C	714 881-3986	19186
Element Materials **(DH)**	8734	C	714 892-1961	19968
BJs Restaurant Operations Co	8741	B	714 500-2440	20003
Michaelson Connor & Boul **(PA)**	8742	D	714 230-3600	20200
Innovative Vhcl Solutions LLC	8748	C	714 896-8267	20352

Employee Codes: A=Over 500 employees, B=251-500
C=101-250, D=51-100, E=20-50, F=10-19, G=1-9

2024 Southern California
Business Directory and Buyers Guide

© Mergent Inc. 1-800-342-5647

1377

	SIC	EMP	PHONE	ENTRY#

HUNTINGTON PARK, CA - Los Angeles County

	SIC	EMP	PHONE	ENTRY#
Kuk Rim USA Inc.	2281	C	323 277-9256	2122
Citizens of Humanity LLC (PA)	2339	C	323 923-1240	2313
Cotton Generation Inc.	2361	F	323 581-8555	2406
Oheck LLC	2386	F	323 923-2700	2432
Reliance Upholstery Sup Co Inc.	2392	D	323 321-2300	2486
G - L Veneer Co Inc (PA)	2435	D	323 582-5203	2687
Plycraft Industries Inc.	2435	C	323 587-8101	2690
Crown Poly Inc.	2673	C	323 585-5522	3181
Cal-Pac Chemical Co Inc.	2819	F	323 585-2178	3881
Traffic Works Inc.	3081	E	323 582-0616	4823
UFO Inc.	3089	E	323 588-5450	5237
West Coast Foundry LLC (HQ)	3325	E	323 583-1421	5667
Acme Castings Inc.	3366	E	323 583-3129	5800
Montclair Bronze Inc (PA)	3366	E	909 986-2664	5805
Canterbury Designs Inc.	3446	E	323 936-7111	6352
Bodycote Thermal Proc Inc.	3471	D	323 583-1231	6593
Los Angeles Galvanizing Co.	3479	D	323 583-2263	6716
Valco Planer Works Inc.	3544	E	323 582-6355	7104
Los Angles Pump Valve Pdts Inc.	3561	E	323 277-7788	7282
NL&a Collections Inc.	3645	E	323 277-6266	8296
Home Depot USA Inc.	5211	C	323 587-5520	13621
Fred M Boerner Motor Co (PA)	5531	D	323 560-3882	13860
Bancolmbia PR Intrnacional Inc.	7389	D	323 582-2255	16787
All Care Medical Group Inc.	8011	D	408 278-3550	17584
Altamed Health Services Corp.	8011	A	323 277-7678	17585
Aircraft Xray Laboratories Inc.	8734	D	323 587-4141	19955

IDYLLWILD, CA - Riverside County

	SIC	EMP	PHONE	ENTRY#
South Bay Wire & Cable Co LLC.	3315	D	951 659-2183	5623

IMPERIAL, CA - Imperial County

	SIC	EMP	PHONE	ENTRY#
United States Gypsum Company	3275	D	760 358-3200	5523
Empire Southwest LLC.	3531	E	760 545-6200	6932
Imperial Irrigation District (PA)	4911	A	800 303-7756	12027

IMPERIAL BEACH, CA - San Diego County

	SIC	EMP	PHONE	ENTRY#
Boys & Girls Clubs South Cnty.	8641	D	619 424-2266	19426

INDIAN WELLS, CA - Riverside County

	SIC	EMP	PHONE	ENTRY#
Bennion Deville Fine Homes Inc.	6531	B	760 674-3452	14749
Hyatt Corporation	7011	A	760 341-1000	15201
Lh Indian Wells Operating LLC.	7011	C	760 341-2200	15223
Renaissance Hotel Operating LLC	7011	A	760 773-4444	15322
Renaissnce Esmralda Resort Spa.	7011	A	760 773-4444	15323
Dhccnp.	7997	D	760 340-4646	17481
Eldorado Country Club.	7997	C	760 346-8081	17483
Reserve Club.	7997	C	760 674-2222	17511
Toscana Country Club Inc.	7997	C	760 404-1444	17531
Vintage Club.	7997	D	760 340-0500	17533
Bjz LLC.	8082	C	760 851-0740	18594
Troon Golf LLC.	8741	C	760 346-4653	20110

INDIO, CA - Riverside County

	SIC	EMP	PHONE	ENTRY#
Valley Animal Medical Center.	0742	A	760 342-4711	127
Granite Construction Company.	1611	B	760 775-7500	618
All Wall Inc.	1742	D	760 600-5108	966
Whites Steel Inc (PA)	1791	F	760 347-3401	1117
Stutz Packing LLC.	2034	E	760 342-1666	1358
Cabinets By Prcision Works Inc.	2434	E	760 342-1133	2651
Purus International Inc.	3069	F	760 775-4500	4787
Lindsey Doors Inc.	3083	E	760 775-1959	4835
Coronet Concrete Products Inc (PA)	3273	E	760 398-2441	5474
Cortima Co.	3281	F	760 347-5535	5528
Sullivans Stone Factory Inc.	3281	E	760 347-5535	5536
Frontier California Inc.	4813	A	760 342-0500	11884
Fiesta Ford Inc.	5511	C	760 775-7777	13767
Cabazon Band Mission Indians.	7011	A	760 342-5000	15105
East Valley Tourist Dev Auth.	7999	A	760 342-5000	17547
JFK Memorial Hospital Inc.	8062	C	760 347-6191	18291
John F Kennedy Mem Hosp Aux.	8062	A	760 347-6191	18292

INGLEWOOD, CA - Los Angeles County

	SIC	EMP	PHONE	ENTRY#
Flowers Bkg Co Henderson LLC.	2051	D	310 695-9846	1468
Goodman Food Products Inc (PA)	2099	C	310 674-3180	1907
K B Socks Inc (DH)	2252	D	310 670-3235	2059
Silica Gel Dessicant Pdts Co.	2653	E	800 426-1529	3129
Biomed California Inc.	2834	D	310 665-1121	4073
Everbrands Inc.	2844	E	855 595-2999	4409
Centinela Consulting Group Inc.	3272	F	310 674-2115	5402
Heidelberg Mtls Sthwest Agg LL.	3273	D	310 419-1520	5480
Multichrome Company Inc.	3471	E	310 216-1086	6641
Zephyr Manufacturing Co Inc.	3546	D	310 410-4907	7149

	SIC	EMP	PHONE	ENTRY#
Quantum.	3572	E	323 709-8880	7480
N/S Corporation (PA)	3589	D	310 412-7074	7676
Engineered Magnetics Inc.	3629	E	310 649-9000	8205
Empower Rf Systems Inc (PA)	3663	D	310 412-8100	8514
Doorking Inc (PA)	3699	C	310 645-0023	9207
Marvin Land Systems Inc.	3711	E	310 674-5030	9298
Farrar Grinding Company.	3728	E	323 678-4879	9686
Autonomous Medical Devices Inc.	3826	E	310 641-2700	10235
Minus K Technology Inc.	3829	C	310 348-9656	10384
Pharmaco-Kinesis Corporation.	3841	E	310 641-2700	10588
First Transit Inc.	4111	D	310 216-9584	11318
Iron Mountain Info MGT LLC.	4731	C	818 649-9766	11775
Mittal Ram.	5074	D	310 769-6669	12747
Home Depot USA Inc.	5211	C	310 677-1944	13622
L and W Developers LLC.	6552	E	310 654-8428	14902
Inglewood Park Cemetery (PA)	6553	C	310 412-6500	14916
Century Gaming Management Inc.	7011	A	310 330-2800	15111
Hollywood Park Casino Co Inc.	7011	C	310 330-2800	15183
After-Party2 Inc (DH)	7359	C	310 202-0011	15769
After-Party6 Inc.	7359	C	310 966-4900	15770
Classic Party Rentals Inc.	7359	A	310 966-4900	15775
Leads360 LLC.	7372	E	888 843-1777	16292
American Egle Prtctive Svcs In.	7381	D	310 412-0019	16615
Hayes Protective Services Inc.	7381	C	323 755-2282	16651
Security Indust Spcialists Inc.	7381	C	323 924-9147	16682
Aero Port Services Inc (PA)	7382	C	310 623-8230	16722
Pml Inc.	7389	E	310 671-4345	16906
Alamo Rental (us) Inc.	7514	C	310 649-2242	16980
Kaiser Foundation Hospitals.	8011	A	310 419-3303	17696
Southern Cal Prmnnte Med Group.	8011	A	310 419-3306	17774
Centinela Sklled Nrsing Wllnes.	8051	D	310 674-3216	17900
West Cntinela Vly Care Ctr Inc.	8051	D	310 674-3216	18075
Watts Health Foundation Inc (HQ)	8052	B	310 424-2220	18103
Cfhs Holdings Inc.	8062	A	310 673-4660	18212
Prime Healthcare Centinela LLC.	8062	A	310 673-4660	18386
Ultracare Services LLC.	8082	D	818 266-9668	18648
Rai Care Ctrs Sthern Cal II LL.	8092	C	310 673-6865	18662
Girl Scuts Greater Los Angeles (PA)	8641	C	626 677-2265	19447
Marvin Engineering Co Inc (PA)	8711	A	310 674-5030	19643
Watts Health Systems Inc (PA)	8742	A	310 424-2220	20271

INYOKERN, CA - Kern County

	SIC	EMP	PHONE	ENTRY#
Herbert Rizzardini.	5251	F	760 377-4571	13678

IRVINE, CA - Orange County

	SIC	EMP	PHONE	ENTRY#
Medterra Cbd LLC.	0139	D	800 971-1288	5
Hines Horticulture Inc (PA)	0181	B	949 559-4444	57
Earthrise Nutritionals LLC (HQ)	0191	E	949 623-0980	81
Mission Ldscp Companies Inc.	0781	D	800 545-9963	169
Newport Energy.	1382	E	408 230-7545	313
Phoenix Cpitl Group Hldngs LLC.	1382	E	303 749-0074	315
De Vries International Inc (PA)	1389	D	949 252-1212	342
A Clark/Mccarthy Joint Venture.	1521	A	714 429-9779	419
Shimmick Construction Co Inc.	1521	C	510 777-5000	458
Regis Contractors LP.	1522	D	949 253-0455	473
Tri Pointe Homes Inc (HQ)	1522	D	949 438-1400	476
Tri Pointe Homes Inc.	1522	C	714 389-5933	477
Western National Prpts LLC (PA)	1522	C	949 862-6200	480
Fieldstone Communities Inc (PA)	1531	C	949 790-5400	483
Lennar Corporation.	1531	D	949 349-8000	485
Tri Pointe Homes Inc.	1531	C	949 478-8600	488
Warmington Homes.	1531	E	949 679-3100	491
Clark Cnstr Group - Cal Inc.	1541	B	714 754-0764	498
Clark Cnstr Group - Cal LP.	1542	B	714 429-9779	542
Interior Lgic Group Hldngs IV (PA)	1542	D	800 959-8333	559
RD Olson Construction Inc.	1542	C	949 474-2001	584
Rudolph and Sletten Inc.	1542	D	949 252-1919	586
Sander Langston LP.	1542	B	949 863-9200	588
Whiting-Turner Contracting Co.	1542	B	949 863-0800	606
Atkinson Construction Inc.	1611	B	303 410-2540	609
Sema Construction Inc.	1611	D	949 470-0500	646
A & H Communications Inc.	1623	C	949 250-4555	656
Shoffeitt Pipeline Inc.	1623	D	949 581-1600	691
Shimmick Construction Co Inc (HQ)	1629	C	949 591-5922	715
Shimmick Corporation.	1629	C	510 777-5000	716
Baywa RE Operation Svcs LLC.	1711	E	949 398-3915	741
Brightview Landscape Dev Inc.	1711	C	714 546-7975	747
Bromic Heating Pty Limited.	1711	D	855 552-7432	748
Cfp Fire Protection Inc.	1711	C	949 727-3277	751
Mesa Energy Systems Inc (HQ)	1711	C	949 460-0460	794
Empcc Inc.	1721	B	888 278-8200	844
Leading Edge Aviation Svcs Inc.	1721	A	714 556-0576	851
Anderson & Howard Electric Inc.	1731	C	949 250-4555	867

	SIC	EMP	PHONE	ENTRY#
Kite Electric Incorporated	1731	C	949 380-7471	911
Patric Communications Inc **(PA)**	1731	D	619 579-2898	924
Pyro-Comm Systems Inc **(PA)**	1731	C	714 902-8000	930
SBE Electrical Contracting Inc	1731	C	714 544-5066	932
Ancca Corporation	1742	D	949 553-0084	967
Vortex Industries Inc **(PA)**	1751	E	714 434-8000	1027
Interior Specialists Inc	1752	B	800 959-8333	1032
Dri Commercial Corporation	1761	C	949 266-1900	1041
Dri Companies	1761	B	949 266-1900	1042
Ekedal Concrete Inc	1771	C	949 729-8082	1070
Danny Ryan Precision Contg Inc	1795	D	949 642-6664	1131
Antis Roofg Waterproofing LLC	1799	D	949 461-9222	1142
Courtney Inc **(PA)**	1799	D	949 222-2050	1149
Hormel Foods Corp Svcs LLC	2013	E	949 753-5350	1221
Bio-Nutritional RES Group Inc	2023	C	714 427-6990	1264
Danone Us LLC	2024	E	949 474-9670	1296
Good Culture LLC	2026	E	949 545-9945	1312
Kraft Heinz Foods Company	2032	E	949 250-4080	1328
Real Vision Foods LLC	2038	E	253 228-5050	1399
Justfoodfordogs LLC **(PA)**	2047	E	866 726-9509	1432
Orange Bakery Inc **(HQ)**	2051	F	949 863-1377	1488
South Coast Baking LLC **(PA)**	2052	D	949 851-9654	1524
Ezaki Glico USA Corporation	2064	F	949 251-0144	1538
Fertile Soil LLC	2084	E	949 981-9026	1627
Reyes Coca-Cola Bottling LLC **(PA)**	2086	B	213 744-8616	1736
Golden State Foods Corp **(PA)**	2087	E	949 247-8000	1775
Maruchan Inc	2098	C	949 789-2300	1840
Maruchan Inc **(HQ)**	2099	B	949 789-2300	1939
Marukome USA Inc	2099	F	949 863-0110	1942
Village Green Foods Inc	2099	E	949 261-0111	2003
Tomorrows Look Inc	2261	D	949 596-8400	2093
INX Prints Inc	2262	E	949 660-9190	2096
Royalty Carpet Mills Inc	2273	A	949 474-4000	2119
Lee	2325	E	213 200-1000	2170
Providence Industries LLC	2326	C	562 420-9091	2184
Birdwell Enterprises Inc	2329	E	714 557-7040	2196
Lost International LLC	2329	D	949 600-6950	2215
Lspace America LLC	2331	D	949 750-2292	2255
Veezee Inc	2331	E	949 265-0800	2269
Boardriders Wholesale LLC	2339	E	949 916-3060	2307
St John Knits Inc **(DH)**	2339	C	949 863-1171	2373
St John Knits Intl Inc **(HQ)**	2339	C	949 863-1171	2374
Pro-Mart Industries Inc	2392	E	949 428-7700	2485
Taber Company Inc	2431	D	714 543-7100	2635
Precision Woodworks	2434	F	949 215-1185	2671
Dellarobbia Inc **(PA)**	2512	E	949 251-9532	2799
Marlin Designs LLC	2512	C	949 637-7257	2809
Tropitone Furniture Co Inc **(DH)**	2514	B	949 595-2010	2839
Craftwood Industries Inc	2522	E	616 796-1209	2907
Krueger International Inc	2531	E	949 748-7000	2931
CK Manufacturing & Trading Inc	2541	E	949 529-3400	2947
Cycle News Inc **(PA)**	2711	E	949 863-7082	3268
Advanstar Communications Inc	2721	D	714 513-8400	3341
Cbj LP	2721	E	949 833-8373	3349
Entrepreneur Media Inc **(PA)**	2721	D	949 261-2325	3358
Haymarket Worldwide Inc	2721	E	949 417-6700	3361
Kelley Blue Book Co Inc **(DH)**	2721	C	949 770-7704	3363
Informa Business Media Inc	2741	E	949 252-1146	3457
Advanced Vsual Image Dsign LLC	2752	E	951 279-2138	3507
Digital Supercolor Inc	2752	D	949 622-0010	3562
DOT Printer Inc **(PA)**	2752	E	949 474-1100	3566
Kelmscott Communications LLC	2752	B	949 475-1900	3611
L T Litho & Printing Co	2752	E	949 466-8584	3616
Ocpc Inc	2752	D	949 475-1900	3646
Woodridge Press Inc	2752	E	949 475-1900	3714
Qpe Inc	2754	F	949 263-0381	3722
ABC Imaging of Washington	2759	F	949 419-3728	3726
Lps Agency Sales & Posting Inc	2759	E	714 247-7500	3783
Orange Circle Studio Corp **(PA)**	2759	E	949 727-0800	3793
Professnal Rprgraphic Svcs Inc	2759	E	949 748-5400	3800
Super Color Digital LLC **(PA)**	2759	E	949 622-0010	3814
Taylor Graphics Inc	2759	E	949 752-5200	3817
Sk Chemicals America Inc	2821	E	949 336-8088	3970
Bio-RAD Laboratories Inc	2833	D	949 598-1200	3993
Orgain LLC	2833	E	888 881-4246	4008
Allergan Sales LLC **(DH)**	2834	A	862 261-7000	4039
Allergan Spclty Thrpeutics Inc	2834	A	714 246-4500	4040
Allergan Usa Inc	2834	A	714 427-1900	4041
Anabolic Incorporated	2834	E	949 863-0340	4050
Anchen Pharmaceuticals Inc	2834	C	949 639-8100	4052
Cg Oncology Inc	2834	E	949 409-3700	4089
Edwards Lifesciences LLC **(HQ)**	2834	A	949 250-2500	4103
Endo Pharmaceuticals Inc	2834	E	949 767-9420	4105
Formex LLC	2834	E	858 529-6600	4112
International Vitamin Corp	2834	C	951 361-1120	4137
Ista Pharmaceuticals Inc	2834	B	949 788-6000	4142
New Generation Wellness Inc **(PA)**	2834	C	949 863-0340	4182
Nitto Avecia Pharma Svcs Inc **(DH)**	2834	F	949 951-4425	4186
Nura USA LLC	2834	E	949 946-5700	4187
Nutrawise Health & Beauty Corp	2834	D	949 900-2400	4188
Pacific Pharma Inc	2834	A	714 246-4600	4193
Sicor Inc **(PA)**	2834	A	949 455-4700	4234
Skinmedica Inc	2834	B	760 929-2600	4237
St Jude Medical LLC	2834	B	949 769-5000	4240
Teva Parenteral Medicines Inc	2834	A	949 455-4700	4246
Urovant Sciences Inc	2834	E	949 226-6029	4250
Biomerica Inc **(PA)**	2835	F	949 645-2111	4268
Oncocyte Corporation **(PA)**	2835	F	949 409-7600	4284
California Scents LLC	2842	E		4346
Meguiars Inc **(HQ)**	2842	E	949 752-8000	4360
Pacific World Corporation **(PA)**	2844	D	949 598-2400	4442
Zo Skin Health Inc **(DH)**	2844	D	949 988-7524	4472
Zo Skin Health Inc	2844	F	949 988-3153	4473
FSI Coating Technologies Inc	2851	E	949 540-1140	4491
Desmond Ventures Inc	2891	C	949 474-0400	4563
Henkel Chemical Management LLC	2891	C	888 943-6535	4567
Henkel Corporation	2891	C	714 368-8000	4568
Mitsubishi Chemical Crbn Fbr	2891	C	800 929-5471	4573
Evergreen Holdings Inc **(PA)**	2992	C	949 757-7770	4683
Jsn Packaging Products Inc	3082	D	949 458-0050	4830
Jsn Industries Inc	3089	D	949 458-0050	5074
National Medical Products Inc	3089	E	949 768-1147	5111
Plasto Tech International Inc	3089	E	949 458-1880	5151
Urban Armor Gear LLC **(HQ)**	3089	E	949 329-0500	5239
Sunsports LP	3131	E	949 273-6202	5262
Bloom Designs Corp	3161	F	949 250-4929	5285
Gary Bale Redi-Mix Con Inc	3273	D	949 786-9441	5477
3M Technical Ceramics Inc **(HQ)**	3299	D	949 862-9600	5562
3M Technical Ceramics Inc	3299	E	949 756-0642	5563
Cwi Steel Technologies Corporation	3325	E	949 476-7600	5661
PCC Rollmet Inc	3339	D	949 221-5333	5675
Supernal LLC	3365	C	202 422-3275	5799
Joseph Company Intl Inc	3411	E	949 474-2200	5859
Pacific Handy Cutter Inc **(DH)**	3423	E	714 662-1033	5887
PHC Merger Inc	3423	E	714 662-1033	5888
Toughbuilt Industries Inc **(PA)**	3423	B	949 528-3100	5890
Jonathan Engrned Slutions Corp **(HQ)**	3429	E	714 665-4400	5925
M A G Engineering Mfg Co	3429	E		5930
Columbia Sanitary Products Inc	3432	E	949 474-0777	5969
Atlas Sheet Metal Inc	3444	F	949 600-8787	6195
Cartel Industries LLC	3444	E	949 474-3200	6211
Rami Designs Inc	3446	F	949 588-8288	6366
Global Pcci (gpc) **(PA)**	3469	C	757 637-9000	6519
Electrolurgy	3471	D	949 250-4494	6616
Global Metal Solutions Inc	3471	E	949 872-2995	6623
M P C Industrial Products Inc	3471	E	949 863-0106	6636
SDC Technologies Inc **(HQ)**	3479	C	714 939-9600	6735
Interntnal Plymr Solutions Inc	3491	E	949 458-3731	6766
Griswold Controls LLC **(PA)**	3494	D	949 559-6000	6791
Cummins Pacific LLC **(HQ)**	3519	C	949 253-6000	6892
Signature Control Systems	3523	D	949 580-3640	6913
Control Systems Intl Inc	3533	E	949 238-4150	6955
Technipfmc Usa Inc	3533	E	949 238-4150	6964
Safety Products Holdings LLC	3541	E	714 662-1033	7023
Barrot Corporation	3544	E	949 852-1640	7054
Pace Punches Inc	3544	D	949 428-2750	7085
Viking Products Inc	3545	E	949 379-5100	7139
M K Products Inc	3548	D	949 798-1234	7159
Aquatec International Inc	3561	D	949 225-2200	7269
Xylem Water Solutions USA Inc	3561	E	949 474-1679	7294
Jeremywell International Inc	3569	F	949 588-6888	7396
Knight LLC **(PA)**	3569	D	949 595-4800	7398
Lubrication Scientifics LLC	3569	E	714 557-0664	7399
Cybernet Manufacturing Inc	3571	A	949 600-8000	7422
Dynabook Americas Inc **(HQ)**	3571	B	949 583-3000	7423
Gateway Inc **(DH)**	3571	C	949 471-7000	7427
Gateway US Retail Inc	3571	C	949 471-7000	7428
I/O Magic Corporation	3571	E	949 707-4800	7430
Mediatek USA Inc	3571	C	408 526-1899	7439
Oracle America Inc	3571	E	650 506-7000	7443
Orange Logic LLC	3571	E	914 361-9175	7444
Solarflare Communications Inc **(DH)**	3571	D	949 581-6830	7450
Toshiba Amer Info Systems Inc	3571	C	949 583-3000	7455
Certance LLC **(HQ)**	3572	E	949 856-7800	7466
H Co Computer Products **(PA)**	3572	E	949 833-3222	7473
Memory Experts Intl USA Inc **(HQ)**	3572	E	714 258-3000	7477

Employee Codes: A=Over 500 employees, B=251-500
C=101-250, D=51-100, E=20-50, F=10-19, G=1-9

2024 Southern California
Business Directory and Buyers Guide

© Mergent Inc. 1-800-342-5647

1379

GEOGRAPHIC

	SIC	EMP	PHONE	ENTRY#
Quantum Corporation	3572	E	949 856-7800	7482
Stec Inc (HQ)	3572	B	415 222-9996	7487
Western Digital Corporation	3572	E	949 672-7000	7493
Zadara Storage Inc	3572	D	949 251-0360	7494
Gateway Manufacturing LLC	3575	D	949 471-7000	7495
Cs Systems Inc	3577	E	949 475-9100	7519
Emulex Corporation (DH)	3577	C		7525
Encrypted Access Corporation	3577	C	714 371-4125	7526
Finis LLC	3577	D	949 250-4929	7528
Goodix Technology Inc	3577	E	858 554-0352	7530
Incipio Technologies Inc (PA)	3577	E	888 893-1638	7532
Innovative Tech & Engrg Inc	3577	E	949 955-2501	7535
Lasergraphics Inc	3577	E	949 753-8282	7541
Livescribe Inc	3577	E		7542
Logitech Inc	3577	A	510 795-8500	7544
Optima Technology Corporation	3577	B	949 253-5768	7560
Princeton Technology Inc	3577	E	949 851-7776	7563
Printronix LLC (PA)	3577	D	714 368-2300	7564
Raise 3d Technologies Inc	3577	E	949 482-2040	7566
Synaptics Inc	3577	E	949 483-5594	7571
Western Telematic Inc	3577	E	949 586-9950	7580
Ricoh Electronics Inc	3579	C	714 259-1220	7587
Filtronics Inc	3589	F	714 630-5040	7657
Jacuzzi Inc (DH)	3589	C	909 606-7733	7665
Cp-Carrillo Inc (DH)	3592	E	949 567-9000	7699
Cp-Carrillo Inc	3592	E	949 567-9000	7700
Coast Composites LLC	3599	E	949 455-0665	7804
Computer Assisted Mfg Tech LLC	3599	E	949 263-8911	7806
Qualontime Corporation	3599	F	714 523-4751	7989
Sdi LLC	3599	E	949 351-1866	8019
Streamline Avionics Inc	3612	E	949 861-8151	8113
Iconn Inc	3613	D	800 286-6742	8124
Staco Systems Inc (HQ)	3613	D	949 297-8700	8130
ITT Cannon LLC	3625	C	714 557-4700	8183
Rosemount Analytical Inc	3625	A	713 396-8880	8189
Soundcoat Company Inc	3625	E	631 242-2200	8191
Tivoli LLC	3641	E	714 957-6101	8252
Connectec Company Inc (PA)	3643	D	949 252-1077	8257
Ctc Global Corporation (PA)	3643	C	949 428-8500	8258
Wpmg Inc	3646	E	949 442-1601	8342
Acti Corporation Inc	3651	E	949 753-0352	8390
Henrys Adio Vsual Slutions Inc	3651	E	714 258-7238	8417
Toshiba Amer Elctrnic Cmpnnts (DH)	3651	B	949 462-7700	8443
Toshiba America Inc	3651	A	212 596-0600	8444
Vizio Inc (HQ)	3651	C	855 833-3221	8448
Vizio Holding Corp (PA)	3651	C	949 428-2525	8449
Lg-Ericsson USA Inc	3661	E	877 828-2673	8477
Anydata Corporation	3663	D	949 900-6040	8496
Fleet Management Solutions Inc	3663	E	800 500-6009	8518
Microwave Dynamics LLC	3663	E	949 679-7788	8545
Mophie Inc (DH)	3663	F	888 866-7443	8549
Sekai Electronics Inc (PA)	3663	E	949 783-5740	8578
Stm Networks Inc	3663	E	949 273-6800	8584
Tricom Research Inc	3663	D	949 250-6024	8591
Tricom Research Inc	3663	D	949 250-6024	8592
General Monitors Inc (DH)	3669	C	949 581-4464	8612
Choose Manufacturing Co LLC	3672	E	714 327-1698	8660
Concept Development Llc	3672	E	949 623-8000	8665
Irvine Electronics LLC	3672	D	949 250-0315	8690
Lifetime Memory Products Inc	3672	E	949 794-9000	8698
Mflex Delaware Inc	3672	A	949 453-6800	8704
Multi-Fineline Electronix Inc (HQ)	3672	A	949 453-6800	8705
Trantronics Inc	3672	E	949 553-1234	8740
Aeroflex Incorporated	3674	E	800 843-1553	8761
American Arium	3674	E	949 623-7090	8763
Baywa RE Epc LLC	3674	E	949 398-3915	8773
Baywa RE Solar Projects LLC (DH)	3674	C	949 398-3915	8774
Broadcom Corporation	3674	D	949 926-5000	8775
Broadcom Corporation	3674	E	714 376-5029	8776
Clariphy Communications Inc (DH)	3674	D	949 861-3074	8779
Conexant Systems LLC (HQ)	3674	E	949 483-4600	8782
Cooper Microelectronics Inc	3674	E	949 553-8352	8783
Data Circle Inc	3674	E	949 260-6569	8784
Global Locate Inc	3674	E	949 926-5000	8800
Hanwha Q Cells America Inc (DH)	3674	F	949 748-5996	8802
Marvell Semiconductor Inc	3674	A	949 614-7700	8833
Masimo Semiconductor Inc	3674	E	603 595-8900	8834
Morse Micro Inc	3674	D	949 501-7080	8847
Netlist Inc (PA)	3674	D	949 435-0025	8850
Qlogic LLC (DH)	3674	C	949 389-6000	8870
Quartics Inc	3674	E	949 679-2672	8878
Skyworks Solutions Inc (PA)	3674	A	949 231-3000	8892
Suncore Inc	3674	E	949 450-0054	8902
Syntiant Corp (PA)	3674	E	949 774-4887	8904
Teridian Semiconductor Corp (DH)	3674	D	714 508-8800	8909
Astron Corporation	3677	E	949 458-7277	8934
Circuit Assembly Corp (PA)	3678	F	949 855-7887	8962
Corsair Elec Connectors Inc	3678	C	949 833-0273	8967
Infinite Electronics Intl Inc (DH)	3678	D	949 261-1920	8974
Min-E-Con LLC	3678	D	949 250-0087	8978
3y Power Technology Inc	3679	F	949 450-0152	8987
American Audio Component Inc	3679	E	909 596-3788	8995
Bi-Search International Inc	3679	D	714 258-4500	9006
Bivar Inc	3679	E	949 951-8808	9007
Dynalloy Inc	3679	E	714 436-1206	9032
EMI Solutions Inc	3679	F	949 206-9960	9040
Fema Electronics Corporation	3679	E	714 825-0140	9045
Infinite Electronics Inc (HQ)	3679	E	949 261-1920	9059
Interctive Dsplay Slutions Inc	3679	E	949 727-1959	9063
Interlink Electronics Inc	3679	E	805 484-8855	9064
Ppst Inc (PA)	3679	E	800 421-1921	9099
Suntsu Electronics Inc	3679	E	949 783-7300	9123
Enevate Corporation	3691	D	949 243-0399	9146
Farstone Technology Inc	3695	C	949 336-4321	9181
Agents West Inc	3699	E	949 614-0293	9192
Femto Blanc Inc	3699	D	408 409-2900	9210
OBryant Electric Inc	3699	E	949 341-0025	9233
Orthodyne Electronics Corporation (HQ)	3699	C	949 660-0440	9235
Sonnet Technologies Inc	3699	E	949 587-3500	9255
Stracon Inc	3699	F	949 851-2288	9257
USA Vision Systems Inc (HQ)	3699	E	949 583-1519	9268
Vti Instruments Corporation (HQ)	3699	E	949 955-1894	9269
Karma Automotive LLC	3711	A	855 565-2762	9294
Mazda Motor of America Inc (HQ)	3711	B	949 727-1990	9299
Rivian Automotive Inc (PA)	3711	B	888 748-4261	9305
Coda Automotive Inc	3714	D	949 830-7000	9372
Innova Electronics Corporation	3714	E	714 241-6800	9406
N G K Spark Plugs USA Inc	3714	E	949 855-8278	9430
Pankl Engine Systems Inc	3714	E	949 428-8788	9437
American Scence Tech As T Corp	3721	D	310 773-1978	9509
Boeing	3721	E	949 623-2222	9511
Parker-Hannifin Corporation	3724	C	949 833-3000	9577
A-Info Inc	3728	E	949 346-7326	9585
Coast Composites LLC (PA)	3728	D	949 455-0665	9659
Eaton Corporation	3728	F	714 272-4700	9682
Fmh Aerospace Corp	3728	D	714 751-1000	9692
Meggitt Defense Systems Inc	3728	B	949 465-7700	9747
Pacific Precision Products Mfg Inc	3728	E	949 727-3844	9760
Parker-Hannifin Corporation	3728	C	949 833-3000	9762
Rockwell Collins Inc	3728	D	714 929-3000	9776
Thales Avionics Inc	3728	E	949 381-3033	9812
Thales Avionics Inc	3728	E	949 790-2500	9813
Thales Avionics Inc	3728	E	949 929-5808	9814
American Eagle Mfg Co	3751	E	949 251-0722	9872
Super73 Inc (PA)	3751	E	949 649-4607	9885
Tyvak Nn-Satellite Systems Inc (DH)	3761	D	949 753-1020	9905
Eaton Aerospace LLC	3812	E	949 452-9500	9971
Northrop Grumman Corporation	3812	E	949 260-9800	10012
Rockwell Collins Inc	3812	E	714 929-3000	10063
Rogerson Aircraft Corporation (PA)	3812	D	949 660-0666	10064
Teletrac Navman US Ltd (HQ)	3812	E	866 527-9896	10080
Newport Corporation (HQ)	3821	A	949 863-3144	10096
Meggitt Western Design Inc	3822	C	949 465-7700	10105
3d Infotech (PA)	3823	E	949 980-0200	10111
Biodot Inc (HQ)	3823	D	949 440-3685	10119
Futek Advanced Sensor Tech Inc	3823	C	949 465-0900	10134
Graphtec America Inc (DH)	3823	E	949 770-6010	10137
Vertiv Corporation	3823	D	949 457-3600	10168
Emcor Facilities Services Inc	3824	C	949 475-6020	10175
Astronics Test Systems Inc (HQ)	3825	C	800 722-2528	10185
Equus Products Inc	3825	E	714 424-6779	10197
Hid Global Corporation	3825	E	949 732-2000	10204
Marvin Test Solutions Inc	3825	D	949 263-2222	10215
N.H Research LLC	3825	D	949 474-3900	10218
STS Instruments Inc	3825	E	580 223-4773	10223
Biorad Inc	3826	E	949 598-1200	10245
Broadley-James Corporation	3826	D	949 829-5555	10246
Capillary Biomedical Inc	3826	E	949 317-1701	10248
Combimatrix Corporation (HQ)	3826	E	949 753-0624	10250
Horiba Americas Holding Inc (HQ)	3826	A	949 250-4811	10262
Horiba Instruments Inc (DH)	3826	C	949 250-4811	10263
Mp Biomedicals LLC (HQ)	3826	E	949 833-2500	10276
Nanovea Inc (PA)	3826	E	949 461-9292	10277
Tetra Tech Ec Inc	3826	E	949 809-5000	10296
Nipro Optics Inc	3827	E	949 215-1151	10331
Spectrum Scientific Inc	3827	E	949 260-9900	10340

2024 Southern California
Business Directory and Buyers Guide

(P-0000) Products & Services Section entry number
(PA)=Parent Co (HQ)=Headquarters (DH)=Div Headquarters

	SIC	EMP	PHONE	ENTRY#
United Scope LLC (HQ)	3827	F	714 942-3202	10345
Zygo Corporation	3827	E	714 918-7433	10348
Horiba International Corp	3829	A	949 250-4811	10371
International Sensor Tech	3829	E	949 452-9000	10374
Meggitt (orange County) Inc (DH)	3829	B	949 493-8181	10382
Omni Optical Products Inc (PA)	3829	E	714 634-5700	10386
Vantari Medical LLC	3829	E	949 783-5300	10407
Acclarent Inc	3841	B	650 687-5888	10413
Advanced Sterlization (HQ)	3841	C	800 595-0200	10417
Alcon Lensx Inc (DH)	3841	D	949 753-1393	10419
Alcon Research Ltd	3841	D	949 387-2142	10420
Alcon Vision LLC	3841	A	949 753-6488	10422
Alliance Medical Products Inc	3841	E	949 664-9616	10424
Alliance Medical Products Inc (DH)	3841	E	949 768-4690	10425
Applied Cardiac Systems Inc	3841	E	949 855-9366	10431
Aspen Medical Products LLC	3841	E	949 681-0200	10441
B Braun Medical Inc	3841	A	610 691-5400	10444
B Braun Medical Inc	3841	E	949 660-3151	10445
B Braun Medical Inc	3841	E	949 660-2581	10446
Baxter Healthcare Corporation	3841	C	949 474-6301	10449
Bio-Medical Devices Inc	3841	E	949 752-9642	10453
Bio-Medical Devices Intl Inc	3841	E	949 752-9642	10454
Cas Medical Systems Inc (HQ)	3841	E	203 488-6056	10478
Chen-Tech Industries Inc (DH)	3841	E	949 855-6716	10480
Covidien LP	3841	C	949 837-3700	10487
Devax Inc	3841	E	949 461-0450	10490
Diality Inc	3841	D	949 916-5851	10493
Easydial Inc	3841	E	949 916-5851	10497
Edwards Lfsciences Cardiaq LLC	3841	D	949 387-2615	10499
Endologix Inc (PA)	3841	D	949 595-7200	10503
Endologix Canada Inc	3841	D	949 595-7200	10504
Envveno Medical Corporation	3841	F	949 261-2900	10505
Fluxergy Inc	3841	F	949 305-4201	10508
Fluxergy Inc	3841	F	949 305-4201	10509
Hoya Surgical Optics Inc	3841	E	909 680-3900	10521
I-Flow LLC	3841	A	800 448-3569	10524
Inari Medical Inc (PA)	3841	D	877 927-4747	10529
Irvine Biomedical Inc	3841	C	949 851-3053	10537
Links Medical Products Inc (PA)	3841	E	949 753-0001	10547
Masimo Americas Inc	3841	D	949 297-7000	10551
Medtronic Inc	3841	C	949 837-3700	10559
Medtronic PS Medical Inc (DH)	3841	C	805 571-3769	10563
Micro Therapeutics Inc (HQ)	3841	E	949 837-3700	10566
Nellix Inc	3841	E	650 213-8700	10572
Neomend Inc	3841	D	949 783-3300	10573
Neuroptics Inc	3841	E	949 250-9792	10574
Neurovasc Technologies Inc	3841	F	949 258-9946	10575
Pro-Dex Inc (PA)	3841	C	949 769-3200	10591
Rebound Therapeutics Corp	3841	E	949 305-8111	10595
Reverse Medical Corporation	3841	E	949 215-0660	10598
Rms/Endlgix Sdways Merger Corp	3841	D	949 595-7200	10600
Source Scientific LLC	3841	E	949 231-5096	10606
Trivascular (DH)	3841	E	707 543-8800	10621
Trivascular Technologies Inc (HQ)	3841	C	707 543-8800	10622
Uoc USA Inc	3841	F	949 328-3366	10626
Vyaire Medical Inc	3841	E	714 919-3265	10630
Biomet Inc	3842	E	949 453-3200	10638
Breathe Technologies Inc	3842	E	949 988-7700	10641
Edwards Lifesciences Corp	3842	F	949 250-3522	10652
Edwards Lifesciences Corp (PA)	3842	A	949 250-2500	10653
Edwards Lifesciences Corp	3842	C	949 250-2500	10654
Edwards Lifesciences Corp PR	3842	C	949 250-2500	10655
Ethicon Inc	3842	B	949 581-5799	10658
Interpore Cross Intl Inc (DH)	3842	D	949 453-3200	10673
Mentor Worldwide LLC (DH)	3842	C	800 636-8678	10683
Ossur Americas Inc (HQ)	3842	C	800 233-6263	10689
Passy-Muir Inc (PA)	3842	E	949 833-8255	10691
Patient Safety Technologies Inc	3842	E	949 387-2277	10692
Sientra Inc (PA)	3842	D	805 562-3500	10702
Ultimate Ears Consumer LLC	3842	A	949 502-8340	10716
3M Company	3843	B	949 863-1360	10726
Bien Air Usa Inc	3843	D	949 477-6050	10731
Evolve Dental Technologies Inc	3843	E	949 713-0909	10744
Keystone Dental Inc	3843	E	781 328-3324	10751
Keystone Dental Inc	3843	E	781 328-3382	10752
Truabutment Inc	3843	D	714 956-1488	10774
Westside Resources Inc	3843	E	800 944-3939	10778
Immport Therapeutics Inc	3844	F	949 679-4068	10783
Ampronix LLC	3845	D	949 273-8000	10789
Beta Bionics Inc	3845	D	949 297-6635	10792
Biosense Webster Inc (HQ)	3845	C	909 839-8500	10794
Edwards Lifesciences US Inc (HQ)	3845	D	949 250-2500	10801
Flexicare Incorporated	3845	E	949 450-9999	10802
Johnson Jhnson Srgcal Vsion In (HQ)	3845	B	949 581-5799	10809
Masimo Corporation (PA)	3845	B	949 297-7000	10811
Masimo Corporation	3845	E	949 297-7000	10812
Masimo Corporation	3845	E	949 297-7000	10813
Masimo Corporation	3845	F	949 297-7000	10814
Syneron Inc (DH)	3845	D	866 259-6661	10827
Barton Perreira LLC	3851	E	949 305-5360	10832
Bausch & Lomb Incorporated	3851	C	949 788-6000	10833
Eyeonics Inc	3851	E	949 788-6000	10840
Medennium Inc (PA)	3851	E	949 789-9000	10844
Tekia Inc	3851	E	949 699-1300	10855
Thermaprint Corporation	3861	E	949 583-0800	10887
Quilter Laboratories LLC	3931	F	714 559-6114	10929
Strottman International Inc (PA)	3942	E	949 623-7900	10943
Bandai Nmco Toys Cllctbles AME (DH)	3944	D	949 271-6000	10947
Hyper Ice Inc (PA)	3949	E	949 565-4994	11000
Melin LLC	3949	E	323 489-3274	11014
Mission Hockey Company (PA)	3949	F	949 585-9390	11015
Star Trac Health & Fitness Inc	3949	E	714 669-1660	11029
Star Trac Strength Inc	3949	B	714 669-1660	11030
Unisen Inc	3949	E	714 669-1660	11039
Lasercare Technologies Inc (PA)	3955	E	310 202-4200	11059
Foampro Mfg Inc	3991	D	949 252-0112	11088
Media Nation Enterprises LLC (PA)	3993	E	888 502-8222	11136
Safety Systems Hawaii	3993	F	808 847-4017	11152
Shye West Inc (PA)	3993	E	949 486-4598	11157
Statewide Trffic Sfety Sgns In	3993	E	949 553-8272	11170
Above & Beyond Balloons Inc	3999	E	949 586-8470	11185
Edwards Lifesciences Fing LLC	3999	E	949 250-3480	11214
Flame and Wax Inc	3999	C	949 752-4000	11215
Fringe Studio LLC	3999	E	310 390-9900	11218
Perfect Choice Mfrs Inc	3999	E	714 792-0322	11265
Phiaro Incorporated	3999	E	949 727-1261	11268
Sundance Spas Inc (DH)	3999	E	909 606-7733	11288
Wood Candle Wick Tech Inc	3999	E	310 488-5885	11309
Albertsons LLC	4225	D	949 855-2465	11563
Navajo Investments Inc (PA)	4522	D	949 863-9200	11681
Santa Catalina Island Company (PA)	4725	C	310 510-2000	11730
Agility Holdings Inc (DH)	4731	D	714 617-6300	11735
Agility Logistics Corp (DH)	4731	C	714 617-6300	11736
Glovis America Inc (HQ)	4731	C	714 427-0944	11764
Cofiroute Usa LLC	4785	C	949 754-0198	11825
Nextel Communications Inc	4812	C	714 368-4509	11852
3h Communication Systems Inc	4813	E	949 529-1583	11867
Boldyn Networks US Services LL	4813	B	877 999-7070	11872
Boldyn Ntwrks US Oprations LLC	4813	E	949 515-1500	11873
Incomnet Communications Corp	4813	D	949 251-8000	11888
Jynormus LLC	4813	F	949 436-2112	11890
Horizon Communication Tech Inc	4899	D	714 982-3900	12007
Teletrac Inc (PA)	4899	C	714 897-0877	12013
Chestnut Ridge Energy Company	4911	C		12017
Edison Capital	4911	C	909 594-3789	12022
Hanwha Q Cells USA Corp	4911	D	949 748-5996	12026
Southern California Edison Co	4911	C	949 587-5416	12076
Sunnova Energy Corporation	4911	A	877 757-7697	12078
Irvine Ranch Water District	4941	C	949 453-5300	12124
Irvine Ranch Water District (PA)	4941	C	949 453-5300	12125
Waste MGT Collectn Recycl Inc	4953	C	949 451-2600	12204
Ampco Contracting Inc	4959	C	949 955-2255	12207
Jonset LLC	4959	D	949 551-5151	12209
Asian European Products Inc	5013	C	949 553-3900	12232
Rally Holdings LLC	5013	A	817 919-6833	12256
Specialty Interior Mfg Inc	5013	E	714 296-8618	12263
Ledra Brands Inc	5023	C	714 259-9959	12306
Decwood Inc	5031	F	949 588-9663	12327
Canon USA Inc	5043	B	949 753-4000	12376
Integrus LLC	5044	D	949 538-9211	12384
Kyocera Dcment Solutions W LLC	5044	C	800 996-9591	12385
Aluratek Inc	5045	E	866 580-1978	12394
Aten Technology Inc	5045	D	949 453-8782	12397
D-Link Systems Incorporated	5045	C	714 885-6000	12403
Dane Elec Corp USA (HQ)	5045	E	949 450-2900	12404
Eworkplace Manufacturing Inc	5045	C	949 583-1646	12412
Getac Inc	5045	D	949 681-2900	12418
Hitachi Solutions America Ltd (DH)	5045	E	949 242-1300	12419
Ingram Micro Inc (HQ)	5045	A	714 566-1000	12420
Ingram Micro Services LLC	5045	C	714 566-1000	12421
Samsung Research America Inc	5045	B	949 468-1143	12436
SMC Networks Inc (HQ)	5045	D	949 679-8029	12438
TW Security Corp (DH)	5045	C	949 932-1000	12448
Trimark Raygal LLC	5046	C	949 474-1000	12464
Alphaeon Corporation	5047	C	949 284-4555	12467
American Medical Tech Inc	5047	D	949 553-0359	12469

GEOGRAPHIC

Employee Codes: A=Over 500 employees, B=251-500
C=101-250, D=51-100, E=20-50, F=10-19, G=1-9

2024 Southern California
Business Directory and Buyers Guide

© Mergent Inc. 1-800-342-5647

1381

	SIC	EMP	PHONE	ENTRY#
Balt Usa LLC	5047	D	949 788-1443	12475
Fisher & Paykel Healthcare Inc	5047	C	949 453-4000	12487
Gordian Medical Inc	5047	B	714 556-0200	12489
Horibaabx Inc	5047	C	949 453-0500	12493
Nihon Kohden America LLC **(HQ)**	5047	C	949 580-1555	12501
Sunrise Respiratory Care Inc	5047	C	949 398-6555	12517
Team Post-Op Inc	5047	C	949 253-5500	12518
Walk Vascular LLC	5047	E	949 752-9642	12522
Norman Industrial Mtls Inc	5051	D	949 250-3343	12562
Pusan Pipe America Inc	5051	B	949 655-8000	12565
Rapid Conn Inc	5051	E	949 951-3722	12567
Wamco Inc **(PA)**	5063	F	714 545-5560	12626
Tte Technology Inc	5064	C	877 300-8837	12638
Jae Electronics Inc **(HQ)**	5065	E	949 753-2600	12672
Linksys LLC	5065	C	408 526-4000	12678
Linksys LLC	5065	C	310 751-5100	12679
Linksys Usa Inc	5065	D	949 270-8500	12680
Telit Wireless Solutions Inc	5065	C	949 461-7150	12706
Parker-Hannifin Corporation	5084	C	949 465-4519	12808
General Tool Inc	5085	D	949 261-2322	12856
SPS Technologies LLC	5085	B	949 474-6000	12882
Nikken Global Inc **(HQ)**	5087	C	949 789-2000	12894
Shimano North Amer Holdg Inc **(HQ)**	5091	C	949 951-5003	12931
Bandai Namco Entrmt Amer Inc	5092	C	408 235-2000	12935
Merchsource LLC **(DH)**	5092	C	800 374-2744	12940
Sega of America Inc **(DH)**	5092	E	949 788-0455	12944
C D Listening Bar Inc	5099	A	949 225-1170	12970
Blue Sky The Clor Imgntion LLC	5112	D	714 389-7700	12991
Imperial Bag & Paper Co LLC	5113	D	800 834-6248	13010
Momentum Textiles LLC **(PA)**	5131	E	949 833-8886	13086
Str Worldwide Inc	5136	A	949 276-5990	13112
Stussy Inc	5136	D	949 474-9255	13113
Delta Galil USA Inc	5137	C	949 296-0380	13123
Fox Head Inc **(HQ)**	5137	B	949 757-9500	13127
Snowmass Apparel Inc **(PA)**	5137	E	949 788-0617	13150
Asics America Corporation **(HQ)**	5139	C	949 453-8888	13158
Newport Meat Southern Cal Inc	5147	C	949 399-4200	13302
Kids Healthy Foods LLC	5149	E	949 260-4950	13374
Mhh Holdings Inc	5149	C	949 651-9903	13378
Sun Ten Labs Liquidation Co	5149	F	949 587-0509	13395
Graphic Packaging Intl LLC	5199	D	949 250-0900	13540
Victory Foam Inc **(PA)**	5199	D	949 474-0690	13566
Tuttle-Click Ford Inc	5511	C	949 855-1704	13841
Impressions Vanity Company **(PA)**	5719	E	844 881-0790	13961
Beyond Franchise Group Inc	5812	C	949 398-7338	13984
Taco Bell Corp **(HQ)**	5812	A	949 863-4500	14039
Arbonne International LLC **(DH)**	5999	E	949 770-2610	14121
Arbonne International Dist Inc	5999	D	800 272-6663	14122
Smartlabs Inc	5999	D	800 762-7846	14149
California Republic Bank	6022	B	949 270-9700	14183
First Foundation Inc **(PA)**	6022	C	949 202-4160	14197
Pacific Premier Bancorp Inc **(PA)**	6022	C	949 864-8000	14203
Opus Bank	6029	A	949 250-9800	14213
Pacific Trust Bank	6035	C	949 236-5211	14217
Pan American Bank Fsb	6035	B	949 224-1917	14218
Cig Financial LLC	6141	C	877 244-4442	14269
Hyundai Protection Plan Inc	6141	C	949 468-4000	14271
Change Lending LLC	6162	D	949 769-3526	14306
Decision Ready Solutions Inc	6162	E	949 400-1126	14310
Goodleap LLC	6162	D	916 290-9999	14322
Guaranteed Rate Inc	6162	C	424 354-5344	14323
Impac Mortgage Corp	6162	B	949 475-3600	14328
Lenders Investment Corp	6162	D	714 540-4747	14331
Loandepot Inc **(PA)**	6162	B	888 337-6888	14334
Mission Hills Mortgage Corp **(HQ)**	6162	C	714 972-3832	14341
Mission Loans LLC	6162	C	855 959-4500	14342
Network Capital Funding Corp **(PA)**	6162	B	949 442-0060	14344
New Century Mortgage Corp	6162	A	949 440-7030	14345
Ocmbc Inc	6162	B	949 679-7400	14346
Rushmore Loan MGT Svcs LLC **(PA)**	6162	A	949 727-4798	14348
Sea Breeze Financial Svcs Inc	6162	C	949 223-9700	14349
5 Arches LLC	6163	D	949 387-8092	14354
Carnegie Mortgage LLC	6163	C	949 379-7000	14355
Clearpath Lending	6163	C	949 502-3577	14357
Sand Canyon Corporation **(HQ)**	6163	D	949 727-9425	14364
Hyundai ABS Funding LLC	6211	C	949 732-2697	14381
National Financial Svcs LLC	6211	A	949 476-0157	14400
Sutter Securities Inc	6211	C	415 352-6300	14405
American Funds Service Company **(DH)**	6289	B	949 975-5000	14433
New First Fincl Resources LLC	6311	C	949 223-2160	14438
Liberty Dental Plan Cal Inc	6324	C	949 223-0007	14484
Liberty Dental Plan Corp **(PA)**	6324	D	888 703-6999	14485
Optumrx Inc **(DH)**	6324	B	714 825-3600	14489
Lawyers Title Insurance Corp	6361	C	949 223-5575	14543
Automobile Club Southern Cal	6411	C	714 973-1211	14565
Lexisnexis Risk Assets Inc	6411	C	949 222-0028	14607
Mullin TBG Insur Agcy Svcs LLC **(DH)**	6411	C		14615
Precept Advisory Group LLC **(DH)**	6411	D	949 955-1430	14623
Ford Motor Land Dev Corp	6512	C	949 242-6606	14661
Orange Bakery Inc	6512	C	949 454-1247	14677
PM Realty Group LP	6512	D	949 390-5500	14679
Humangood Socal	6513	C	949 854-9500	14715
Irvine APT Communities LP	6513	C	949 854-4942	14721
Irvine APT Communities LP **(HQ)**	6513	C	949 720-5600	14722
Action Property Management Inc **(PA)**	6514	D	949 450-0202	14734
Atlas Hospitality Group	6531	D	949 622-3400	14745
Auctioncom Inc	6531	C	800 499-6199	14746
Auctioncom LLC **(PA)**	6531	C	949 859-2777	14747
Cushman & Wakefield Cal Inc	6531	A	949 474-4004	14778
First Amercn Prof RE Svcs Inc **(HQ)**	6531	C	714 250-1400	14794
First Team RE - Orange Cnty **(PA)**	6531	C	949 988-3000	14800
Firstsrvice Rsidential Cal LLC **(HQ)**	6531	C	949 448-6000	14802
Hsf Affiliates LLC	6531	D	949 794-7900	14812
J & M Realty Company **(PA)**	6531	C	949 261-2727	14816
Steadfast Management Co Inc **(PA)**	6531	D	949 748-3000	14870
Ten-X Finance Inc	6531	C	949 465-8523	14872
Western National Securities **(PA)**	6531	C	949 862-6200	14884
Guardian Title Company	6541	D	949 495-9306	14893
Panattoni Development Co Inc **(PA)**	6552	D	916 381-1561	14909
Voit Real Estate Services LLC	6552	C	949 851-5100	14913
N2 Acquisition Company Inc	6719	D	714 942-3563	14936
Nrp Holding Co Inc **(PA)**	6719	C	949 583-1000	14937
Swds Holdings Inc	6719	B	800 395-5277	14948
Acorns Grow Incorporated **(PA)**	6726	B	949 251-0095	14975
Impac Secured Assets Corp	6733	D	949 475-3600	14992
Kaiser Foundation Hospitals	6733	D	949 932-5000	14993
Brer Affiliates LLC **(DH)**	6794	C	949 794-7900	15008
Centerline Mortgage Capitl Inc	6799	B	949 221-6685	15024
Nnn Realty Investors LLC	6799	B	714 667-8252	15042
NRLL LLC	6799	B	949 768-7777	15044
Dkn Hotel LLC **(PA)**	7011	B	714 427-4320	15135
European Ht Invstors I I A Cal	7011	D	949 474-7368	15150
Golden Hotels Ltd Partnership	7011	C	949 833-2770	15156
Greens Group Inc	7011	C	949 829-4902	15162
Hyatt Corporation	7011	D	949 975-1234	15199
Kt Hotels LLC	7011	C	949 715-5000	15214
Marriott International Inc	7011	B	949 724-3606	15242
Montage Hotels & Resorts LLC **(PA)**	7011	A	949 715-5002	15253
Spectrum Hotel Group LLC	7011	D	949 471-8888	15366
Valencia Group LLC	7011	C	949 379-6489	15403
Prudential Overall Supply **(PA)**	7218	D	949 250-4855	15470
Americor Funding Inc	7299	C	866 333-8686	15498
Alcone Marketing Group Inc **(HQ)**	7311	D	949 595-5322	15529
Ignite Health LLC **(PA)**	7311	D	949 861-3200	15547
Interactive Media Holdings Inc	7311	C	949 861-8888	15550
Local Corporation **(PA)**	7311	D	949 784-0800	15555
Young & Rubicam LLC	7311	B	949 754-2000	15582
Young & Rubicam LLC	7311	C	949 754-2100	15583
Ghost Management Group LLC	7313	C	949 870-1400	15593
Egs Financial Care Inc **(DH)**	7322	B	877 217-4433	15611
Corelogic Credco LLC **(DH)**	7323	C	800 255-0792	15621
Bzya Corporation	7349	D	949 656-3220	15696
Calico Building Services Inc	7349	C	949 380-8707	15698
Certified Wtr Dmage Rstrtion E	7349	E	800 447-1776	15699
Creative Maintenance Systems	7349	D	949 852-2871	15703
Innovative Cleaning Svcs LLC	7349	B	949 251-9188	15716
Celtic Leasing Corp	7359	C	949 263-3880	15773
Cybercoders Inc	7361	C	949 885-5151	15836
Jwilliams Staffing Inc	7361	C	949 250-1923	15857
Kore1 LLC	7361	C	949 706-6990	15862
Loan Administration Netwrk Inc	7361	D	949 752-5246	15865
Workway Inc	7361	C	949 553-8700	15906
Sfn Group Inc	7363	A	949 727-8500	15941
Avamar Technologies Inc	7371	D	949 743-5100	15973
Axon Networks Inc **(PA)**	7371	D	949 310-4429	15976
Big Cart Corporation	7371	F	949 250-7064	15980
Buddy Group Inc	7371	D	949 468-0042	15989
Codazen Inc	7371	D	949 916-6266	15996
Eighteenth Meridian Inc	7371	B	714 706-3643	16021
Einfochips Inc	7371	D	949 527-6459	16022
Frontech N Fujitsu Amer Inc **(DH)**	7371	C	877 766-7545	16035
Gan Limited	7371	B	702 964-5777	16037
Home Junction Inc	7371	D	858 777-9533	16046
Kofax Inc **(PA)**	7371	B	949 783-1000	16062
NC America LLC	7371	E	949 447-6287	16079
Neudesic LLC **(HQ)**	7371	C	949 754-4500	16081

Company	SIC	EMP	PHONE	ENTRY#
Neuintel LLC (PA)	7371	D	949 625-6117	16082
Nexgenix Inc (PA)	7371	B	714 665-6240	16084
Operation Technology Inc	7371	D	949 462-0100	16090
Pacific Tech Solutions LLC	7371	C	949 830-1623	16091
Secureauth Corporation (PA)	7371	C	949 777-6959	16111
Setschedule LLC	7371	C	888 222-0011	16113
Smart Energy Systems Inc	7371	C	909 703-9609	16114
Smart Utility Systems Inc	7371	D	909 217-3344	16115
Spireon Inc (PA)	7371	C	800 557-1449	16121
Startel Corporation (PA)	7371	D	949 863-8700	16122
Stratacare Llc	7371	C	949 743-1200	16124
Tcg Software Services Inc	7371	B	714 665-6200	16132
Unisys Corporation	7371	C	949 380-5000	16142
Vision Solutions Inc (HQ)	7371	D	949 253-6500	16148
With Inc	7371	E	714 617-1991	16149
Activision Blizzard Inc	7372	D	949 955-1380	16156
Advisys Inc	7372	E	949 250-0794	16159
Alphastar Tech Solutions LLC	7372	F	562 961-7827	16162
Astea International Inc	7372	E	949 784-5000	16178
Blind Squirrel Games Inc	7372	D	714 460-0860	16184
Blizzard Entertainment Inc (DH)	7372	D	949 955-1380	16186
Calamp Corp (PA)	7372	D	949 600-5600	16192
Cloudcover Iot Inc	7372	E	888 511-2022	16205
Cloudvirga Inc	7372	D	949 799-2643	16206
Club Speed LLC (PA)	7372	E	951 817-7073	16207
Commerce Velocity LLC	7372	E	949 756-8950	16208
Compugroup Medical Inc	7372	E	949 789-0500	16209
Dacenso Inc	7372	E	888 513-9367	16220
Dorado Network Systems Corp	7372	C	650 227-7300	16228
Eagle Topco LP	7372	A	949 585-4329	16231
Egl Holdco Inc	7372	A	800 678-7423	16234
Eturns Inc	7372	E	949 265-2626	16241
Foundation Inc	7372	E	310 294-8955	16250
Global Cash Card Inc	7372	C	949 751-0360	16256
Illumnate Educatn Holdings Inc (PA)	7372	E	949 656-3133	16269
Justenough Software Corp Inc (HQ)	7372	E	949 706-5400	16282
Kofax Limited (PA)	7372	E	949 783-1000	16287
Magic Software Enterprises Inc (PA)	7372	D	714 918-1310	16298
Medata Inc (PA)	7372	C	714 540-8900	16302
Mscsoftware Corporation (HQ)	7372	E	949 470-7955	16314
Netaphor Software Inc	7372	E	888 638-9749	16320
Netwrix Corporation	7372	B	949 255-2600	16324
Nextgen Healthcare Inc (PA)	7372	D	562 207-1600	16326
Ntrust Infotech Inc	7372	E	949 833-2800	16330
Numecent Inc	7372	E	949 255-2600	16331
Nxgn Management LLC	7372	F	877 558-8526	16333
Panoramic Software Corporation	7372	C	949 823-1700	16342
Patron Solutions LLC	7372	E	949 705-4472	16346
Plugg ME LNc	7372	E	949 855-3100	16350
Prism Software Corporation	7372	E	949 333-4634	16353
Promenade Software Inc	7372	E	949 362-8888	16356
Qdos Inc	7372	B	866 530-7243	16359
Sage Software Holdings Inc (HQ)	7372	D	714 460-8398	16370
Strategy Companion Corp	7372	E	949 727-1800	16390
Timevalue Software	7372	E	949 328-7790	16408
Uneekor Inc	7372	C	949 788-9900	16413
Upstanding LLC	7372	C	949 250-4102	16415
West Coast Consulting LLC	7372	B	844 933-3627	16419
Wm Technology Inc	7372	E	888 836-4274	16421
Alteryx Inc (PA)	7373	E	714 665-6507	16428
Computer Tech Resources Inc	7373	E	949 261-8457	16436
Disco Print Whl 46 A Ltd Lblty	7373	E	714 694-0536	16440
Genea Energy Partners Inc	7373	E	714 805-9283	16445
Greenwave Reality Inc	7373	D	877 425-8725	16446
Icl Systems Inc	7373	F	949 509-6589	16448
Leadingway Corporation (PA)	7373	D	480 777-7130	16453
Result Group Inc	7373	C	949 333-2300	16467
Trace3 LLC (HQ)	7373	C	949 751-0360	16473
Automatic Data Processing Inc	7374	C	949 214-1000	16482
Celestial-Saturn Parent Inc (PA)	7374	B	949 797-7160	16486
Enclarity Inc	7374	C	949 682-7906	16493
S E O P Inc	7374	C	844 617-1100	16513
Verizon Connect Telo Inc (DH)	7374	B	800 784-3911	16521
Accurate Background LLC (PA)	7375	E	949 753-1222	16524
Sage Software Inc	7375	D	949 581-9900	16535
Quest Intl Monitor Svc Inc (PA)	7378	C	949 215-1362	16543
Rakworx Inc	7378	E	949 583-9500	16544
Blytheco Inc (PA)	7379	C	800 215-9124	16556
Caylent Inc	7379	C	888 512-8906	16558
Crowdstrike Inc	7379	C	888 512-8906	16561
Crowdstrike Inc	7379	C	949 271-6700	16562
Dyntek Inc (PA)	7379	C	844 563-3552	16565
Kodella LLC	7379	C	949 706-6990	16576
Kore1 Inc	7379	D	949 706-6990	16577
McLaren Strategic Solutions	7379	D	310 564-6754	16579
Ovation Tech Inc	7379	C	949 271-0054	16587
ABM Onsite Services Inc	7381	A	949 863-9100	16612
Landmark Event Staffing	7381	A	714 293-4248	16654
Universal Protection Svc LP (HQ)	7381	D	866 877-1965	16700
Universal Services America LP (HQ)	7381	D	866 877-1965	16703
Sentinel Monitoring Corp (HQ)	7382	D	949 453-1550	16753
Alorica Customer Care Inc	7389	C	941 906-9000	16772
Alorica Inc (PA)	7389	D	866 256-7422	16773
Andrew Lauren Company Inc	7389	C	949 861-4222	16778
Baxalta US Inc	7389	C	949 474-6301	16790
Boost Mobile LLC	7389	A	949 451-1563	16795
Consoldted Fire Protection LLC (HQ)	7389	A	949 727-3277	16804
Data Council LLC	7389	C	904 512-3200	16814
Edison Energy LLC	7389	C	949 491-1633	16822
Flagship Credit Acceptance LLC	7389	C	949 748-7172	16826
Global Language Solutions LLC	7389	D	949 798-1400	16835
La Jolla Group Inc (PA)	7389	B	949 428-2800	16858
LARK Industries Inc (DH)	7389	D	714 701-4200	16860
Universal Card Inc	7389	B	949 861-4000	16949
University California Irvine	7389	C	949 824-6483	16953
Ameripark LLC	7521	B	949 279-7525	16989
Dynamic Auto Images Inc	7542	B	714 771-3400	17047
Bsh Home Appliances Corp (DH)	7629	C	949 440-7100	17069
Melan Inc	7699	D	818 489-1745	17139
Edwards Theatres Circuit Inc	7832	C	949 854-8811	17297
Equinox-76th Street Inc	7991	D	949 296-1700	17399
Row House Franchise LLC	7991	C	949 341-5585	17411
Xponential Fitness Inc (PA)	7991	B	949 346-3000	17420
Shady Canyon Golf Club Inc	7997	C	949 856-7000	17523
Cor Medica Technology (PA)	8011	E	949 353-4554	17631
Monarch Healthcare A Medical (HQ)	8011	D	949 923-3200	17720
Southern Cal Prmnnte Med Group	8011	C	949 262-5780	17790
Pacific Dental Services LLC (PA)	8021	B	714 845-8500	17843
Pacific Dntl Svcs Holdg Co Inc	8021	C	714 845-8500	17844
In Stepps Inc	8049	D	949 474-1493	17860
Home Street Operations LLC	8052	D	949 449-2500	18085
New Vista Behavioral Hlth LLC	8052	D	949 284-0095	18091
Childrens Hospital Orange Cnty	8062	C	949 387-2586	18218
Hoag Hospital Irvine	8062	C	949 764-4624	18283
Kaiser Foundation Hospitals	8062	C	949 262-5780	18305
St Joseph Hospital of Orange	8062	C	714 568-5500	18463
Alliance Healthcare Svcs Inc (DH)	8071	C	800 544-3215	18538
Cap Diagnostics LLC	8071	C	714 966-1221	18541
Healthquest Clinical Lab Inc	8071	D	909 445-9727	18552
Thaihot Investment Co US Ltd	8071	A	949 242-5300	18566
Keating Dental Arts Inc	8072	C	949 955-2100	18571
Vna of Greater Los Angeles Inc	8082	D	951 252-5314	18654
Davita Inc	8092	B	949 930-4400	18658
Discovery Practice MGT Inc	8093	C	714 828-1800	18690
Universal Care Inc (HQ)	8093	B	562 424-6200	18729
University California Irvine	8099	D	949 824-2662	18813
Crowell & Moring LLP	8111	C	949 263-8400	18845
Fisher & Phillips LLP	8111	C	949 851-2424	18855
Gibson Dunn & Crutcher LLP	8111	D	949 451-3800	18860
Greenberg Traurig LLP	8111	D	949 732-6500	18866
Knobbe Martens Olson Bear LLP (PA)	8111	B	949 760-0404	18886
Law Offces Les Zeve A Prof Cor	8111	C	714 848-7920	18893
Malcolm & Cisneros A Law Corp	8111	C	949 252-9400	18902
Palmieri Tyler Wner Wlhelm Wld	8111	D	949 851-9400	18921
Rutan & Tucker LLP (PA)	8111	B	714 641-5100	18936
Shook Hardy & Bacon LLP	8111	C	949 475-1500	18945
Troutman Ppper Hmlton Snders L	8111	D	949 622-2700	18952
Womble Bond Dickinson (us) LLP	8111	C	310 207-3800	18959
Zbs Law LLC	8111	D	714 848-7920	18960
University California Irvine	8221	C	949 824-7725	18994
It Division Inc	8243	C	678 648-2709	19000
Learning Ovations Inc	8299	E	734 904-1459	19011
Council On Aging - Sthern Cal	8322	D	714 479-0107	19052
Second Hrvest Fd Bnk Ornge CNT	8322	C	949 653-2900	19138
Owl Education and Training Inc	8331	B	949 797-2000	19190
Child Development Incorporated	8351	B	949 854-5060	19205
Leport Educational Inst Inc	8351	D	914 374-8860	19214
Leport Schools	8351	D	714 377-6035	19215
Silverado Snior Lving Hldngs	8361	A	949 240-7200	19299
Western Growers Association (PA)	8611	C	949 863-1000	19386
Temporary Staffing Union	8631	A	714 728-5186	19416
ABM Facility Services LLC	8711	A	949 330-1555	19538
ABS Consulting Inc	8711	D	714 734-4242	19539
ACS Engineering Inc	8711	E	949 297-3777	19541
Es Engineering Services LLC	8711	D	949 988-3500	19587
Fuscoe Engineering Inc (PA)	8711	D	949 474-1960	19597

GEOGRAPHIC

Employee Codes: A=Over 500 employees, B=251-500
C=101-250, D=51-100, E=20-50, F=10-19, G=1-9

2024 Southern California
Business Directory and Buyers Guide

© Mergent Inc. 1-800-342-5647

1383

	SIC	EMP	PHONE	ENTRY#
Gradient Engineers Inc.	8711	C	949 477-0555	19601
Hunsaker & Assoc Irvine Inc **(PA)**	8711	D	949 583-1010	19611
Hyundai Amer Technical Ctr Inc.	8711	C	734 337-2500	19612
Jacobs Engineering Group Inc.	8711	D	949 224-7500	19620
Jacobs Government Services Co.	8711	C	949 224-7500	19623
Jacobs Project Management Co.	8711	C	949 224-7695	19625
Kpff Inc.	8711	D	949 252-1022	19634
Mgc Systems Corp.	8711	E	714 442-2064	19645
Mobilenet Services Inc **(PA)**	8711	C	949 951-4444	19649
Modelo Group Inc.	8711	E	562 446-5091	19650
Panasonic Avionics Corporation **(DH)**	8711	B	949 672-2000	19663
Tetra Tech Inc.	8711	D	949 263-0846	19702
Wsp USA Inc.	8711	D	714 973-4880	19720
Gkk Corporation **(PA)**	8712	D	949 250-1500	19729
LPA Inc **(PA)**	8712	C	949 261-1001	19735
Stantec Architecture Inc.	8712	B	949 923-6000	19741
Stantec Consulting Svcs Inc.	8712	C	949 923-6000	19743
Ware Malcomb **(PA)**	8712	C	949 660-9128	19746
Wimberly Allson Tong Goo NA In.	8712	D	949 574-8500	19747
Baker Tilly Us LLP.	8721	A	949 222-2999	19754
Ernst & Young LLP.	8721	B	949 794-2300	19773
Kpmg LLP.	8721	C	949 885-5400	19785
LLP Moss Adams.	8721	C	949 221-4000	19788
Omega Accounting Solutions Inc.	8721	D	949 348-2433	19798
University California Irvine.	8721	C	949 824-6828	19808
Wright Ford Young & Co.	8721	C	949 910-2727	19811
Agendia Inc.	8731	C	949 540-6300	19814
Bioduro LLC.	8731	B	858 529-6600	19824
Fluxergy Inc **(PA)**	8731	E	949 305-4201	19839
Invasix Inc.	8731	D	855 418-5306	19848
Isotis Orthobiologics Inc.	8731	C	949 595-8710	19850
Pharmaron Inc.	8731	A	949 788-0586	19871
Talon Therapeutics Inc.	8731	D	949 788-6700	19877
University California Irvine.	8731	C	949 824-2819	19887
Henkel US Operations Corp.	8732	C	714 368-8000	19894
Iqvia Inc **(DH)**	8732	D	866 267-4479	19903
Mind Research Institute.	8733	C	949 345-8700	19935
Aptim Corp.	8734	A	949 261-6441	19959
Pixel Labs LLC.	8734	D	512 560-5961	19981
Legacy Prtners Residential Inc.	8741	C	949 930-6600	20051
Mtc Financial Inc.	8741	D	949 252-8300	20064
Navigators Management Co Inc.	8741	C	949 255-4860	20065
Renovo Solutions LLC **(PA)**	8741	B	714 599-7969	20089
Smile Brands Group Inc **(PA)**	8741	C	714 668-1300	20093
Southern Implants Inc.	8741	C	949 273-8505	20098
Tct Mobile Inc.	8741	C	949 892-2990	20104
Vpm Management Inc.	8741	C	949 863-1500	20114
Western National Contractors.	8741	C	949 862-6200	20117
Advantage Sales & Mktg Inc **(DH)**	8742	C	949 797-2900	20125
Advantage Sales & Mktg LLC **(DH)**	8742	C	949 797-2900	20126
Beacon Resources LLC.	8742	C	949 955-1773	20140
Bridgwter Consulting Group Inc.	8742	C	949 535-1755	20145
City of Irvine.	8742	C	949 724-7600	20150
Denken Solutions Inc.	8742	C	949 630-5263	20162
Exult Inc.	8742	A	949 856-8800	20169
Morris & Willner Partners.	8742	D	949 705-0682	20203
Online Marketing Group LLC.	8742	C	888 737-9635	20215
Resources Connection Inc.	8742	C	714 430-6400	20230
Sullivncrtsmnroe Insur Svcs LL **(PA)**	8742	C	800 427-3253	20250
Trinamix Inc **(PA)**	8742	B	408 507-3583	20266
Willis North America Inc.	8742	C	909 476-3300	20274
Young & Rubicam LLC.	8742	B	949 224-6300	20277
Alliant Insurance Services Inc **(PA)**	8748	C	949 756-0271	20313
Datatrace Title.	8748	D	800 221-2056	20330
Fryman Management Inc.	8748	D	949 481-5211	20336
Ies Commercial Inc.	8748	D	949 222-0320	20349
In Montrose Wtr Sstnblity Svcs.	8748	D	949 988-3500	20350
Lsa Associates Inc **(PA)**	8748	C	949 553-0666	20360
Qmerit Electrification LLC **(PA)**	8748	C	888 272-0090	20374
Slalom LLC.	8748	C	949 450-1100	20379
Slr International Corporation.	8748	A	949 553-8417	20380
TRC Solutions Inc **(HQ)**	8748	C	949 753-0101	20386
Vinculums Services LLC.	8748	C	949 783-3552	20389

IRWINDALE, CA - Los Angeles County

	SIC	EMP	PHONE	ENTRY#
Pierre Landscape Inc.	0781	C	626 587-2121	176
Mariposa Landscapes Inc **(PA)**	0782	C	626 960-0196	204
Universal Dynamics Inc.	1382	F	626 480-0035	323
Church & Larsen Inc.	1742	C	626 303-8741	976
Kifuki USA Co Inc **(HQ)**	2015	C	626 334-8090	1246
Huy Fong Foods Inc.	2033	E	626 286-8328	1337
Q & B Foods Inc **(DH)**	2035	D	626 334-8090	1364
J&R Taylor Brothers Assoc Inc.	2047	D	626 334-9301	1430

	SIC	EMP	PHONE	ENTRY#
Miller Brewing Co.	2082	E	626 353-1604	1600
Califrnia Cstm Frits Flvors In **(PA)**	2087	E	626 736-4130	1761
Ready Pac Foods Inc **(HQ)**	2099	A	626 856-8686	1975
Decore-Ative Spc NC LLC.	2431	C	626 960-7731	2595
Pacific Panel Products Corp.	2499	E	626 851-0444	2758
Roma Moulding Inc.	2499	E	626 334-2539	2762
Seaboard Envelope Co Inc.	2677	E	626 960-4559	3213
Alpha Printing & Graphics Inc.	2752	E	626 851-9800	3508
Km Printing Production Inc.	2752	F	626 821-0008	3613
Million Corporation.	2759	D	626 969-1888	3787
Matheson Tri-Gas Inc.	2813	E	626 334-2905	3868
Esmond Natural Inc.	2833	E	626 337-1588	3999
Bimeda Inc.	2834	C	626 815-1680	4071
Chem Arrow Corp.	2992	E	626 358-2255	4679
Polycycle Solutions LLC.	3085	D	626 856-2100	4865
Altium Packaging.	3089	C	626 856-2100	4936
Clark - Pacific Corporation.	3272	E	626 962-8751	5405
Spragues Rock and Sand Company **(PA)**	3273	E	626 445-2125	5503
Davis Wire Corporation **(HQ)**	3315	C	626 969-7651	5612
STS Metals.	3463	D	626 969-6711	6483
US Toyo Fan Corporation.	3564	C	626 338-1111	7337
A & M Engineering Inc.	3599	D	626 813-2020	7725
Arrow Engineering.	3599	E	626 960-2806	7762
Cni Mfg Inc.	3599	F	626 962-6646	7803
Fine Ptch Elctrnic Assmbly LLC.	3672	E	626 337-2800	8678
Halcyon Microelectronics Inc.	3674	F	626 814-4688	8801
American Capacitor Corporation.	3675	E	626 814-4444	8925
Pertronix Inc.	3694	E	909 599-5955	9172
Bsst LLC.	3714	E	626 593-4500	9361
NDC Technologies Inc.	3826	E	626 960-3300	10278
Johnson & Johnson.	3842	B	909 839-8650	10676
Best Overnite Express Inc **(PA)**	4213	D	626 256-6340	11472
Southern California Edison Co.	4911	C	626 814-4212	12058
Southern California Edison Co.	4911	C	626 812-7380	12062
Southern California Edison Co.	4911	D	626 815-7296	12068
Ihealth Manufacturing Inc.	5047	C	216 785-0107	12494
Essilor Laboratories Amer Inc.	5048	E	626 969-6181	12524
Superior Communications Inc **(PA)**	5065	C	877 522-4727	12699
Assa Abloy Rsdential Group Inc **(HQ)**	5072	C	626 961-0413	12715
Blue Ridge Home Fashions Inc.	5131	E	626 960-6069	13080
Mountain Gear Corporation.	5136	E	626 851-2488	13107
Ready Pac Produce Inc **(DH)**	5148	C	800 800-4088	13338
Sinecera Inc.	7389	D	626 962-1087	16930
Tandex Test Labs Inc.	8734	E	626 962-7166	19984
Calibre International LLC **(PA)**	8743	C	626 969-4660	20283

JAMUL, CA - San Diego County

	SIC	EMP	PHONE	ENTRY#
Mikes Metal Works Inc.	3441	F	619 440-8804	6054
Spectrum Security Services Inc **(PA)**	7381	C	619 669-6660	16693

JOSHUA TREE, CA - San Bernardino County

	SIC	EMP	PHONE	ENTRY#
Hdmc Holdings LLC.	8062	C	760 366-3711	18274

JULIAN, CA - San Diego County

	SIC	EMP	PHONE	ENTRY#
YMCA of San Diego County.	8641	C	760 765-0642	19487

JURUPA VALLEY, CA - Riverside County

	SIC	EMP	PHONE	ENTRY#
Perry Coast Construction Inc.	1542	C	951 774-0677	578
Christian Brothers Mechanical Services Inc.	1711	C	951 361-2247	752
Right Angle Solutions Inc.	1711	E	951 934-3081	818
Hartmark Cab Design & Mfg Inc.	1799	E	909 391-9153	1160
Nestle Usa Inc.	2023	D	877 463-7853	1279
Del Real LLC **(PA)**	2038	D	951 681-0395	1388
Nestle Usa Inc.	2038	B	951 360-7200	1396
Langlois Company.	2045	E	951 360-3900	1424
Levecke LLC.	2084	E	951 681-8600	1644
A and G Inc **(HQ)**	2329	A	714 765-0400	2190
Activeapparel Inc **(PA)**	2329	F	951 361-0060	2191
Charles Komar & Sons Inc.	2341	B	951 934-1377	2387
Blue and Butter LLC.	2389	F	951 763-8808	2442
Advanced Innvtive Rcvery Tech.	2515	E	949 273-8100	2841
Pura Naturals Inc.	2515	E	949 273-8100	2857
Calpaco Papers Inc **(PA)**	2679	C	323 767-2800	3232
Adam Nutrition Inc.	2834	E	951 361-1120	4035
Hyponex Corporation.	2873	B	909 597-2811	4540
Highland Plastics Inc.	3089	C	951 360-9587	5048
Aluminum Die Casting Co Inc.	3363	D	951 681-3900	5757
Metal Container Corporation.	3411	C	951 360-4500	5861
Pacific Award Metals Inc.	3444	E	360 694-9530	6284
Mobile Modular Management Corp.	3448	D	800 819-1084	6385
Cryoworks Inc.	3498	D	951 360-0920	6842
Schwing America Inc.	3531	E	909 681-6430	6941
Brothers Machine & Tool Inc.	3542	E	951 361-9454	7032

(P-0000) Products & Services Section entry number
(PA)=Parent Co (HQ)=Headquarters (DH)=Div Headquarters

	SIC	EMP	PHONE	ENTRY#
Cte California Tl & Engrg Inc	3545	E		7114
Robinson Engineering Corp	3547	F	951 361-8000	7153
P R P Multisource Inc	3565	E	951 681-6100	7353
Puri Tech Inc	3589	E	951 360-8380	7681
Philips North America LLC	3645	C	909 574-1800	8297
Genbody America LLC	3841	E	949 561-0664	10515
Enhance America Inc	3993	E	951 361-3000	11115
Young Electric Sign Company	3993	C	909 923-7668	11182
March Products Inc	3999	D	909 622-4800	11249
Landjet (PA)	4119	C	909 873-4636	11391
Act Fulfillment Inc (PA)	4225	C	909 930-9083	11560
Costco Wholesale Corporation	4225	A	951 361-3606	11568
Home Depot USA Inc	4225	C	951 361-1235	11586
Toll Global Fwdg Scs USA Inc	4731	D	951 360-8310	11810
Highline Aftermarket LLC	5013	D	951 361-0331	12242
Hino Motors Mfg USA Inc	5013	D	951 727-0286	12243
Pacific Award Metals Inc	5033	D	909 390-9880	12368
Pavement Recycling Systems Inc (PA)	5093	C	951 682-1091	12956
Olivet International Inc (PA)	5099	D	951 681-8888	12981
Galassos Bakery (PA)	5149	C	951 360-1211	13368
Southwest Material Hdlg Inc (PA)	5511	C	951 727-0477	13830
Express Contractors Inc	7217	D	951 360-6500	15468
Arcticom Group Rfrgn LLC	7623	B	916 484-3190	17061
Vista Pacifica Enterprises Inc (PA)	8051	C	951 682-4833	18071

KEENE, CA - Kern County

	SIC	EMP	PHONE	ENTRY#
United Farm Workers America (PA)	8631	C	661 822-5571	19418

LA CANADA, CA - Los Angeles County

	SIC	EMP	PHONE	ENTRY#
La Canada Flintridge Cntry CLB	7997	D	818 790-0611	17492
Navigage Foundation (PA)	8051	D	818 790-2522	18019
Crescenta-Canada YMCA (PA)	8641	C	818 790-0123	19441

LA CANADA FLINTRIDGE, CA - Los Angeles County

	SIC	EMP	PHONE	ENTRY#
Southwest Administrators Inc	6371	B		14551
Bis Computer Solutions Inc (PA)	7371	E	818 248-4282	15984

LA CRESCENTA, CA - Los Angeles County

	SIC	EMP	PHONE	ENTRY#
Hamo Constraction	1389	E	818 415-3334	351
Modular Communications Systems	3663	E	818 764-1333	8548
EAM Enterprises Inc (PA)	6531	D	818 248-9100	14791
Outlook Amusements Inc	7379	C	818 433-3800	16586
Mariner Health Care Inc	8051	C	818 957-0850	18006

LA HABRA, CA - Orange County

	SIC	EMP	PHONE	ENTRY#
Albd Electric and Cable	1731	D	949 440-1216	863
Pacific Archtectural Mllwk Inc	2431	D	562 905-3200	2628
Votaw Wood Products Inc	2448	E	714 871-0932	2728
Eurotec Seating Incorporated	2531	E	562 806-6171	2926
Orbo Corporation (PA)	2531	E	562 806-6171	2934
VIP Rubber Company Inc (PA)	3069	C	562 905-3456	4802
Triview Glass Industries LLC	3231	D	626 363-7980	5358
Mmp Sheet Metal Inc	3444	E	562 691-1055	6273
Ckd Industries Inc	3469	F	714 871-5600	6507
Jcr Aircraft Deburring LLC	3471	C	714 870-4427	6632
J C Ford Company (HQ)	3556	C	714 871-7361	7203
B&W Custom Restaurant Eqp Inc	3589	C	714 578-0352	7645
Shepard Bros Inc (PA)	3589	C	562 697-1366	7685
NRG Motorsports Inc	3714	D	714 541-1173	9435
Shepard-Thomason Company	3714	D	714 773-5539	9460
Rose Lilla Inc	3965	D	888 519-8889	11075
Home Depot USA Inc	5211	D	562 690-6006	13587
Lowes Home Centers LLC	5211	C	562 690-5122	13657
Peerless Maintenance Svc Inc	7349	B	714 871-3380	15734
Life Care Centers America Inc	8051	C	562 690-0852	17992

LA HABRA HEIGHTS, CA - Orange County

	SIC	EMP	PHONE	ENTRY#
Hacienda Golf Club	7997	D	562 694-1081	17487

LA JOLLA, CA - San Diego County

	SIC	EMP	PHONE	ENTRY#
Kitchen Expo	1799	F		1166
Uqora	2023	E	888 313-1372	1288
Berenice 2 AM Corp	2024	E	858 255-8693	1293
Champion Home Builders Inc	2451	D	858 456-3507	2735
Jumper Media LLC	2741	D	831 333-6202	3458
Dm Luxury LLC	2759	C	858 366-9721	3755
Ambrx Inc (PA)	2834	E	858 875-2400	4043
Auspex Pharmaceuticals Inc	2834	E	858 558-2400	4060
Calporta Therapeutics Inc	2834	E	858 750-4700	4078
Equillium Inc (PA)	2834	F	858 412-5302	4107
Kyowa Kirin Phrm RES Inc (DH)	2834	E	858 952-7000	4154
Longboard Pharmaceuticals Inc	2834	E	619 592-9775	4160
Manna Health LLC	2834	E	877 576-2662	4162

	SIC	EMP	PHONE	ENTRY#
Metabasis Therapeutics Inc	2834	E	858 550-7500	4168
Orexigen Therapeutics Inc	2834	D	858 875-8600	4190
Synthorx Inc	2834	E	858 352-5100	4244
Inhibrx Inc (PA)	2836	E	858 795-4220	4323
Surface-Tech LLC	2951	F	619 880-0265	4666
Nucleus Enterprises LLC	3089	D	619 517-8747	5123
Imperial Valley Steel Company	3441	E	858 900-2011	6031
Ensemble Communications Inc	3663	C	858 458-1400	8515
Agilent Technologies Inc	3825	D	858 373-6300	10182
U S Medical Instruments Inc (PA)	3841	E	619 661-5500	10624
Technosylva Inc	5045	F	858 729-3648	12445
Morgan Stnley Smith Barney LLC	6211	C	212 761-4000	14396
Northwestern Mutl Fincl Netwrk (PA)	6311	D	619 234-3111	14439
Front Porch Communities & Svcs	6513	C	858 454-2151	14709
Malk Partners	6722	D	858 914-1125	14965
Estancia Hotel LLC	7011	C	949 474-7368	15148
La Jolla Bch & Tennis CLB Inc	7011	B	858 459-8271	15217
Lav Hotel Corp	7011	C	858 454-0771	15220
Marriott International Inc	7011	C	858 587-1414	15244
Destination Residences LLC	7299	C	858 550-1000	15506
University Cal San Diego	7336	A	858 534-2377	15678
Host Healthcare Inc	7363	C	858 999-3579	15923
Abacus Data Systems Inc	7371	D	858 529-0020	15954
Education Systems Inc	7371	E	858 454-9765	16020
United Support Services Inc	7371	C	858 373-9500	16143
Edgewave Inc	7372	D	800 782-3762	16233
Eventscom Inc	7372	E	858 257-2300	16242
University Cal San Diego	7374	B	858 534-5000	16520
The Copley Press Inc	7383	A	858 454-0411	16759
Life Time Inc	7991	D	858 459-0281	17405
La Jolla Bch & Tennis CLB Inc (PA)	7997	C	858 454-7126	17494
La Jolla Country Club Inc	7997	D	858 454-9601	17495
Balboa Nphrology Med Group Inc	8011	D	858 810-8000	17598
La Jolla Orthpdic Srgery Ctr L	8011	B	858 657-0055	17702
Sulpizio Cardiovascular Center	8011	C	858 657-7000	17797
Covenant Care La Jolla LLC	8051	C	858 453-5810	17918
Scripps Health	8062	B	858 455-9100	18430
Scripps Health	8062	B	858 626-6150	18432
Scripps Mmral-Ximed Med Ctr LP	8062	D	858 882-8350	18434
University Cal San Diego	8062	A	858 657-7000	18484
Discovery Health Services	8099	B	858 459-0785	18758
Humangood Socal	8361	C	858 454-4201	19274
Lawrence Fmly Jwish Cmnty Ctrs (PA)	8399	C	858 362-1144	19334
Theater Arts Fndtion San Dego	8641	C	858 623-3366	19466
YMCA of San Diego County	8641	B	858 453-3483	19477
U C San Diego Foundation	8699	C	858 534-1032	19535
University Cal San Diego	8712	D	858 534-2177	19745
Agouron Pharmaceuticals Inc	8731	B	858 622-3000	19816
Coi Pharmaceuticals Inc	8731	E	858 750-4700	19831
The Salk Institute For Biological S	8731	A	858 453-4100	19882
California Institute For Biomedical Research	8733	C	858 242-1000	19920
J Craig Venter Institute Inc (PA)	8733	B	301 795-7000	19930
La Jolla Inst For Immunology	8733	B	858 752-6500	19933
Sanford Brnham Prbys Med Dscve (PA)	8733	A	858 795-5000	19941
Scripps Research Institute (PA)	8733	D	858 784-1000	19943
Scripps Research Institute	8733	D	858 242-1000	19944

LA MESA, CA - San Diego County

	SIC	EMP	PHONE	ENTRY#
West Coast Arborists Inc	1521	C	858 566-4204	466
Crew Builders Inc	1542	C	619 587-2033	544
Brady Company/San Diego Inc	1742	B	619 462-2600	971
Brady Socal Incorporated	1742	C	619 462-2600	972
Prost LLC	2082	E	619 954-4189	1603
California Countertop Inc (PA)	2542	F	619 460-0205	2976
Piller Power Systems Inc	3699	E	408 204-9578	9242
Magnebit Holding Corp	3825	E	858 573-0727	10214
Bob Stall Chevrolet	5511	C	619 460-1311	13741
Drew Ford	5511	C	619 464-7777	13758
Kaiser Foundation Hospitals	6324	C	619 528-5000	14482
Fancy Life Enterprises LLC (PA)	7812	C	619 560-9890	17190
Sharp Healthcare	8011	D	619 460-6200	17764
Sharp RES-Stealy Med Group Inc	8011	C	619 644-6405	17765
Community Care Center	8051	C	619 465-0702	17904
Grossmont Hospital Corporation (HQ)	8062	A	619 740-6000	18272
Grossmont Hospital Corporation	8062	B	619 667-1900	18273
Team Health Holdings Inc	8062	B	619 740-4401	18470
Bh-SD Opco LLC (PA)	8093	D	619 465-4411	18673
Helix Healthcare Inc	8093	D	619 465-4411	18694
YMCA of San Diego County	8641	C	619 464-1323	19480

LA MIRADA, CA - Los Angeles County

	SIC	EMP	PHONE	ENTRY#
Gemsa Enterprises LLC	2079	E	714 521-1736	1571
Shasta Beverages Inc	2086	D	714 523-2280	1740

Employee Codes: A=Over 500 employees, B=251-500
C=101-250, D=51-100, E=20-50, F=10-19, G=1-9

2024 Southern California
Business Directory and Buyers Guide

© Mergent Inc. 1-800-342-5647

1385

GEOGRAPHIC

	SIC	EMP	PHONE	ENTRY#
Outlook Resources Inc	2395	D	562 623-9328	2523
Harbor Furniture Mfg Inc **(PA)**	2512	E	323 636-1201	2805
V Twest Inc	2541	F	714 521-2167	2969
Golden Kraft Inc	2679	B	562 926-8888	3238
JM Huber Micropowders Inc	2819	E	714 994-7855	3895
Captek Softgel Intl Inc	2834	E	657 325-0412	4082
Imcd Us LLC	2834	D	714 562-7660	4133
Oceania Inc	3081	E	562 926-8886	4816
Alchem Plastics Inc	3083	C	714 523-2260	4831
Headwaters Construction Inc	3241	E	714 523-1530	5366
Jdh Pacific Inc **(PA)**	3321	E	818 269-6274	5646
Lindblade Metalworks Inc	3441	E	714 670-7172	6041
Fooma America Inc	3549	E	310 921-0717	7169
MEMC Liquidating Corporation	3556	C	818 637-7200	7209
MEI Rigging & Crating LLC	3559	D	714 712-5888	7248
Iqair North America Inc	3564	E	877 715-4247	7324
Jmg Machine Inc	3599	E	714 522-6221	7888
American Power Solutions Inc	3648	E	714 626-0300	8352
Gallagher Rental Inc	3648	E	714 690-1559	8367
Solid State Devices Inc	3674	C	562 404-4474	8894
Wesanco Inc	3728	E	714 739-4989	9826
Ocean Protecta Incorporated	3732	E	714 891-2628	9865
Mv Transportation Inc	4111	C	562 943-6776	11342
Estes Express Lines	4213	C	714 994-3770	11485
Home Depot USA Inc	4225	D	714 522-8651	11589
Mejico Express Inc **(PA)**	4513	C	714 690-8300	11677
Tiffany Dale Inc **(PA)**	5023	D	714 739-2700	12318
Reliance Steel & Aluminum Co	5051	C	714 736-4800	12570
Makita USA Inc **(HQ)**	5072	C	714 522-8088	12727
RDM Industries	5084	E	714 690-0380	12816
Stainless Stl Fabricators Inc	5084	D	714 739-9904	12824
US Foods Inc	5141	C	714 670-3500	13239
Regal-Piedmont Plastics LLC	5162	E	562 404-4014	13417
Calwax LLC **(DH)**	5169	E	626 969-4334	13426
Living Spaces Furniture LLC **(PA)**	5712	C	877 266-7300	13944
IL Fornaio (america) LLC	5812	E	714 752-7052	14015
Georgia-Pacific LLC	5999	E	562 926-8888	14133
Pacific Bay Lending Group	6163	D	714 367-5125	14361
Cha La Mirada LLC	7011	C	714 739-8500	15112
Diversified Mailing Incorporated	7331	C	714 994-6245	15630
Bigge Group	7353	C	714 523-4092	15758
Orange Courier Inc	7389	B	714 384-3600	16896
Crothall Services Group	7699	A	714 562-9275	17121
Life Care Centers America Inc	8051	C	562 947-8691	17988
Life Care Centers America Inc	8051	C	562 943-7156	17990
Southern Cal Spcialty Care LLC **(DH)**	8062	D	562 944-1900	18455
Straight Talk Inc	8322	C	562 943-0195	19145

LA PALMA, CA - Orange County

	SIC	EMP	PHONE	ENTRY#
Isec Incorporated	1751	C	714 761-5151	1016
CJ Foods Inc **(HQ)**	2099	D	714 367-7200	1871
Precision Cutting Tools Inc	3545	E	562 921-7898	7126
Precision Cutting Tools LLC	3545	E	562 921-7898	7127
Svf Flow Controls LLC	3592	C	562 802-2255	7707
Performance Machine Inc	3751	E	714 523-3000	9880
Ranir LLC	3843	E	866 373-7374	10764
Uns Electric Inc	5063	E	714 690-3660	12621
Svf Flow Controls LLC	5084	E	562 802-2255	12827
Prestige Stations Inc **(DH)**	5411	C	714 670-5145	13702
Atlantic Richfield Company **(DH)**	5541	A	800 333-3991	13889
Commercial Crrers Insur Agcy I	6411	D	562 404-4900	14577
Tech Knowledge Associates LLC	7699	C	714 735-3810	17159
Kaiser Foundation Hospitals	8011	C	714 562-3420	17685
La Palma Hospital Medical Center	8062	B	714 670-7400	18319
Applecare Medical MGT LLC	8741	C	714 443-4507	19998

LA PUENTE, CA - Los Angeles County

	SIC	EMP	PHONE	ENTRY#
AZ Construction Inc **(PA)**	1521	C	626 333-0727	421
Ley Grand Foods Corporation	2099	E	626 336-2244	1935
Soxnet Inc	2252	F	626 934-9400	2061
Mymichelle Company LLC **(HQ)**	2331	B	626 934-4166	2259
Cortez Pallets Service Inc **(PA)**	2448	F	626 961-9891	2716
Genesis Tc Inc	2512	E	626 968-4455	2802
Bomark Inc	2893	E	626 968-1666	4586
Cad Works Inc	3441	E	626 336-5491	6003
Cott Technologies Inc	3498	F	626 961-3399	6841
County of Los Angeles	3531	E	626 968-3312	6929
Athens Disposal Company Inc **(PA)**	4953	B	626 336-3636	12158
Powell Works Inc	5084	B	909 861-6699	12809
Smart & Final Stores Inc	5141	B	626 330-2495	13213
Cacique Distributors US	5143	C	626 961-3399	13251
Cacique Foods LLC	5143	C	626 961-3399	13252
Living Doll LLC	5621	F	213 222-1010	13913

	SIC	EMP	PHONE	ENTRY#
Aperto Property Management Inc	6513	B	626 965-1961	14703
Yang-Ming International Corp	7373	E	626 956-0100	16479
Enki Health and RES Systems	8011	D	626 961-8971	17650

LA QUINTA, CA - Riverside County

	SIC	EMP	PHONE	ENTRY#
Red Rock Pallet Company	4731	E	530 852-7744	11798
Imperial Irrigation District	4939	C	760 398-5811	12110
Primetime International Inc	5148	D	760 399-4166	13336
Lowes Home Centers LLC	5211	C	760 771-5566	13661
Hideaway	5812	C	760 777-7400	14012
Msr Desert Resort LP	5812	A	760 564-5730	14027
TS Enterprises Inc	5812	E	760 360-5991	14040
Ron Rick Holdings Montana LLC	6719	D	406 493-5606	14942
HP Lq Investment LP	7011	C	760 564-4111	15187
Lqr Property LLC	7011	C	760 564-4111	15233
Msr Resort Lodging Tenant LLC	7011	A	760 564-4111	15258
Career Strategies Tmpry Inc	7361	C	760 564-5959	15828
Chapman Golf Development LLC	7992	D	760 564-8723	17421
Golf Management Operating LLC	7992	A	760 777-4839	17429
Ksl Recreation Management Operations LLC	7992	A	760 564-8000	17433
Madison Club Owners Assn	7992	C	760 777-9320	17436
Silver Rock Resort Golf Club	7992	D	760 777-8884	17441
Trilogy Golf At La Quinta	7992	B	760 771-0707	17442
Hideaway Club	7997	B	760 777-7400	17488
Eisenhower Medical Center	8062	C	760 610-7200	18249

LA VERNE, CA - Los Angeles County

	SIC	EMP	PHONE	ENTRY#
Andersen Commercial Plbg Inc	1711	C	909 599-5950	733
Vitawest Nutraceuticals Inc	2023	E	888 557-8012	1289
G & M Mattress and Foam Corporation	2515	D	909 593-1000	2849
Fortress Inc	2521	E	909 593-8600	2883
Mohawk Western Plastics Inc	2673	E	909 593-7547	3187
Layton Printing & Mailing	2752	F	909 592-4419	3620
TEC Color Craft **(PA)**	2759	E	909 392-9000	3819
S & S Bindery Inc	2789	E	909 596-2213	3849
Gilead Sciences Inc	2834	D	650 522-2771	4121
Plastifab Inc	3083	E	909 596-1927	4839
Serco Mold Inc **(PA)**	3089	E	626 331-0517	5202
Gainey Ceramics Inc	3269	E	909 596-4464	5384
Durston Manufacturing Company	3423	F	909 593-1506	5878
Pacific Precision Inc	3451	E	909 392-5610	6418
Mesa Industries Inc	3531	E	626 712-1708	6938
Crown Equipment Corporation	3537	E	626 968-0556	6989
Marman Industries Inc	3544	D	909 392-2136	7082
Juicy Whip Inc	3556	E	909 392-7500	7205
Boom Industrial Inc	3559	D	909 945-3555	7228
Beonca Machine Inc	3599	F	909 392-9991	7781
Inseat Solutions LLC	3634	E	562 447-1780	8236
Micro Analog Inc	3674	C	909 392-8277	8838
DPI Labs Inc	3728	E	909 392-5777	9674
Synergetic Tech Group Inc	3728	E	909 305-4711	9809
Jet Delivery Inc **(PA)**	4215	D	800 716-7177	11531
Pacific Oil Cooler Service Inc	4581	E	909 593-8400	11703
Metropltan Wtr Dst of Sthern C	4941	B	909 593-7474	12133
Edwards Theatres Inc	7832	E	844 462-7342	17293
RES-Care Inc	8052	D	909 596-5360	18098
Brethren Hillcrest Homes	8361	C	909 593-4917	19242
David and Margaret Home Inc	8361	C	909 596-5921	19259
Haynes Family Programs Inc	8361	C	909 593-2581	19268

LADERA RANCH, CA - Orange County

	SIC	EMP	PHONE	ENTRY#
Tropical Preserving Co Inc	2033	E	213 748-5108	1347
Bau Furniture Mfg Inc	2511	D	949 643-2729	2767
Enchannel Medical Ltd	3841	E	949 694-6802	10502
Sst IV 8020 Las Vgas Blvd S LL	4225	D	949 429-6600	11614
Optumcare Medical Group	8099	C	949 364-9112	18787

LAGUNA BEACH, CA - Orange County

	SIC	EMP	PHONE	ENTRY#
Langlois Fancy Frozen Foods Inc	2038	E	949 497-1741	1395
Flavor Infusion LLC	2087	E	949 715-4369	1770
Cantare Foods Inc	2099	E		1866
Firebrand Media LLC	2752	F	949 715-4100	3573
RA Industries LLC	3599	E	714 557-2322	7990
Myotek Industries Incorporated **(DH)**	3694	D	949 502-3776	9171
Ophthonix Inc	3851	E	760 842-5600	10848
K31 Road Engineering LLC	3999	E	305 928-1968	11236
Durham School Services L P	4151	C	949 376-0376	11427
Cabo Foods Inc **(PA)**	5149	C	949 463-2373	13357
Data Processing Design Inc	7371	E	714 695-1000	16008
Atlantis Computing Inc	7372	C	650 917-9471	16180
Laguna Playhouse **(PA)**	7922	C	949 497-2787	17317
University California Irvine	8099	D	949 939-7106	18814
JC Resorts LLC	8741	A	949 376-2779	20042

	SIC	EMP	PHONE	ENTRY#
Montage Hotels & Resorts LLC	8741	A	949 715-6000	20063

LAGUNA HILLS, CA - Orange County

	SIC	EMP	PHONE	ENTRY#
Five Star Plastering Inc	1742	D	949 683-5091	978
Bingo Publishers Incorporated	2741	E	949 581-5410	3430
Steward Plastics Inc	3052	D	949 581-9530	4713
Chavers Gasket Corporation	3053	E	949 472-8118	4722
Eurotech Showers Inc	3088	E	949 716-4099	4914
Plastic and Metal Center Inc	3089	E	949 770-0610	5142
Budget Enterprises Llc	3211	E	949 697-9544	5311
Associated Cnstr & Engrg Inc (PA)	3272	E	949 455-2682	5400
Metal Improvement Company LLC	3398	E	949 855-8010	5841
Peltek Holdings Inc	3479	E	949 855-8010	6724
Starrett Kinemetric Engrg Inc	3545	E	949 348-1213	7133
Garrett Precision Inc	3599	F	949 855-9710	7843
Djh Enterprises	3663	E	714 424-6500	8509
XEL USA Inc	3674	E	949 425-8686	8924
Adco Products Inc	3679	D	937 339-6267	8991
Advanced Waveguide Tech	3679	E	949 297-3564	8992
Ecliptek Inc	3679	E	714 433-1200	9035
Fox Enterprises LLC (HQ)	3679	E	239 693-0099	9046
Sonendo Inc (PA)	3843	C	949 766-3636	10768
Moulton Nguel Wtr Dst Pub Fclt	4941	D	949 831-2500	12135
Starz Inc	5047	F	877 595-6789	12516
Cynergy Prof Systems LLC	5065	E	800 776-7978	12655
Valley Insurance Service Inc	6411	A	949 707-4080	14639
Jamboree Realty Corp (PA)	6531	C	949 380-0300	14817
Professional Cmnty MGT Cal Inc	6531	C	949 597-4200	14849
Varsity Contractors Inc	7349	C	949 586-8283	15755
Groundwork Open Source Inc	7375	D	415 992-4500	16529
Productive Playhouse Inc (PA)	7389	B	323 250-3445	16907
Cirrus Health II LP	8011	D	949 855-0562	17621
South Cnty Orthpd Spclsts A ME	8011	E	949 586-3200	17769
Gate Three Healthcare LLC	8051	E	949 587-9000	17960
Saddleback Memorial Med Ctr (HQ)	8062	A	949 837-4500	18411
Laguna Home Health Svcs LLC	8082	C	949 707-5023	18622
Rehab Alliance	8093	D	949 707-5555	18711

LAGUNA NIGUEL, CA - Orange County

	SIC	EMP	PHONE	ENTRY#
Beverages & More Inc	2086	C	949 643-3020	1685
San Diego Daily Transcript	2621	E	619 232-4381	3061
Qpc Fiber Optic LLC	3357	E	949 361-8855	5749
Alcon Vision LLC	3841	B	949 753-6218	10421
Interface Associates Inc	3841	C	949 448-7056	10535
Home Depot USA Inc	5211	C	949 831-3698	13584
First Team RE - Orange Cnty	6531	B	949 240-7979	14796
Technicon Design Corporation	7389	C	949 218-1300	16941
Mission Internal Med Group Inc	8011	D	949 364-3605	17713
Life Time Fitness Inc	8099	C	949 238-2700	18776
Aegis Senior Communities LLC	8361	C	949 496-8080	19235

LAGUNA WOODS, CA - Orange County

	SIC	EMP	PHONE	ENTRY#
Laguna Woods Village	6531	A	949 597-4267	14822
Professional Cmnty MGT Cal Inc	6531	C	949 206-0580	14848
Village Management Svcs Inc	8741	D	949 597-4360	20113

LAKE ARROWHEAD, CA - San Bernardino County

	SIC	EMP	PHONE	ENTRY#
Gildan USA Inc	2252	F	909 485-1475	2058
Hi-Desert Publishing Company	2711	E	909 336-3555	3282
Lake Arrwhead Rsort Oprtor Inc (HQ)	7011	C	909 336-1511	15218
Mountains Community Hosp Fndtn	8062	C	909 336-3651	18349

LAKE ELSINORE, CA - Riverside County

	SIC	EMP	PHONE	ENTRY#
West Coast Ltg & Enrgy Inc	1731	D	951 296-0680	951
Gbc Concrete Masnry Cnstr Inc	1741	E	951 245-2355	957
Hakes Sash & Door Inc	1751	C	951 674-2414	1014
Edje-Enterprises	1761	E	951 245-7070	1045
Aerofoam Industries Inc	2531	C	951 245-4429	2920
Vertical Doors Inc	2591	F	951 273-1069	3017
Quality Foam Packaging Inc	3086	E	951 245-4429	4901
Pacific Aggregates Inc	3273	D	951 245-2460	5491
Rancho Ready Mix	3273	C	951 674-0488	5493
Harrington & Sons Inc	3299	E	951 674-0998	5568
Boozak Inc	3444	C	951 245-6045	6203
American Compaction Eqp Inc	3531	E	949 661-2921	6925
Stull Industries Inc	3714	F	951 248-9789	9463
Pointdirect Transport Inc	4213	D	909 371-0837	11503
Pacific Clay Products Inc	5032	C	661 857-1401	12359
Lowes Home Centers LLC	5211	C	951 253-6000	13667
Albertsons LLC	5411	C	951 245-4461	13693
Lake Chevrolet	5511	C	951 674-3116	13790
Champion Motosports Inc (PA)	5531	C	951 245-9464	13856
AWI Management Corporation	8741	C	951 674-8200	20000

LAKE FOREST, CA - Orange County

	SIC	EMP	PHONE	ENTRY#
Natures Image Inc	0781	D	949 680-4400	170
Juniper Rock Corporation	1423	F	949 500-1797	400
Streamline Finishes Inc	1542	D	949 600-8964	593
Hardy & Harper Inc	1611	E	714 444-1851	623
Arb Inc (HQ)	1623	C	949 598-9242	658
Primoris Services Corporation	1623	C	949 598-9242	686
Cbr Electric Inc	1731	C	949 455-0331	879
Mission Pools of Escondido	1799	C	949 588-0100	1169
Big Train Inc	2024	D	949 340-8800	1294
Crumbl Cookies	2052	D	949 519-0791	1513
ABC Custom Wood Shutters Inc	2431	E	949 595-0300	2581
Novo Manufacturing LLC	2431	E	949 609-0544	2622
Cod USA Inc	2531	E	949 381-7367	2924
Walter Foster Publishing Inc	2731	D	949 380-7510	3419
Westamerica Graphics Corporation	2752	D	949 462-3600	3709
Soaptronic LLC	2842	E	949 465-8955	4368
JB Brananne Inc	3089	E	949 215-7704	5068
Sole Technology Inc (PA)	3149	C	949 460-2020	5282
Oceania International LLC	3356	E	949 372-8385	5726
Dynacast LLC	3364	C	949 707-1211	5774
Baldwin Hardware Corporation (HQ)	3429	A	949 672-4000	5905
National Manufacturing Co	3429	A	800 346-9445	5936
Young Engineers Inc	3429	D	949 581-9411	5955
Price Pfister Inc (HQ)	3432	A	949 672-4000	5972
S E - G I Products Inc	3442	C	949 297-8530	6120
SPX Flow Us LLC	3443	E	949 455-8150	6159
Berry-Perussi Inc	3469	E	949 461-7000	6498
Camisasca Automotive Mfg Inc (PA)	3469	E	949 452-0195	6504
Camisasca Automotive Mfg Inc	3469	E	949 452-0195	6505
Shmaze Industries Inc	3479	E	949 583-1448	6736
Campbell Engineering Inc	3545	E	949 859-3965	7109
Ellison Educational Eqp Inc (PA)	3554	E	949 598-8822	7180
Cameo Technologies Inc	3572	E	949 672-7000	7464
I/Omagic Corporation (PA)	3572	E	949 707-4800	7474
US Critical LLC (PA)	3572	E	949 916-9326	7490
US Critical LLC	3572	E	800 884-8945	7491
IMC Networks Corp (PA)	3575	E	949 465-3000	7496
Innovative Control Systems Inc	3589	C	800 246-3469	7662
American Deburring Inc	3599	E	949 457-9790	7757
T/Q Systems Inc	3599	E	949 455-0478	8043
Leoch Battery Corporation (DH)	3621	D	949 588-5853	8148
Hongfa America Inc	3625	E	714 669-2888	8182
Focus Industries Inc	3646	D	949 830-1350	8314
Greenshine New Energy LLC	3648	D	949 609-9636	8368
Laminating Company of America	3672	E	949 587-3300	8696
Tri-Star Laminates Inc	3672	E	949 587-3200	8741
Advantest Test Solutions Inc	3674	D	949 523-6900	8760
Premier Magnetics Inc	3677	E	949 452-0511	8951
Cac Inc	3679	E	949 587-3328	9010
Spectrum Brands Inc	3692	A	949 672-4003	9160
Qf Liquidation Inc (PA)	3714	C	949 930-3400	9444
AC&a Enterprises LLC (HQ)	3724	E	949 716-3511	9559
Karem Aircraft Inc	3728	C	949 859-4444	9730
Monobind Sales Inc (PA)	3841	E	949 951-2665	10570
Tenex Health Inc	3841	D	949 454-7500	10616
Staar Surgical Company (PA)	3851	A	626 303-7902	10854
Aminco International USA Inc	3911	D	949 457-3261	10897
Associated Electrics Inc (HQ)	3944	F	949 544-7500	10946
Media Nation Enterprises LLC	3993	E	714 371-9494	11135
Home Express Delivery Svc LLC	4731	A	949 715-9844	11770
Ytel Inc	4813	D	800 382-4913	11913
Toshiba Amer Bus Solutions Inc (DH) *	5044	B	949 462-6000	12389
SMC Products Inc	5092	D	949 753-1099	12945
Nakase Brothers Wholesale Nurs	5193	C	949 855-4388	13515
Cloudradiant Corp (PA)	5199	C	408 256-1527	13534
Home Depot USA Inc	5211	D	949 609-0221	13591
Del Taco Restaurants Inc (PA)	5812	C	949 462-9300	14000
Loandepot Inc	6162	B	949 470-6263	14335
Performance Building Services	7349	C	949 364-4364	15736
Vci Event Technology Inc	7359	C	714 772-2002	15805
Equimine	7372	E	877 204-9040	16239
Wonderware Corporation (DH)	7372	B	949 727-3200	16423
Aveva Software LLC (DH)	7373	B	949 727-3200	16430
Avidex Industries LLC	7379	D	949 428-6333	16553
Itek Services Inc	7379	D	949 770-4835	16574
Advanced Protection Inds LLC	7382	D	800 662-1711	16721
Freedom Village Healthcare Ctr	8051	C	949 472-4733	17953
Lake Frest No II Mstr Hmwners	8641	D	949 586-0860	19453
United Industries Group Inc	8711	E	949 759-3200	19712
Alcon Vision LLC	8734	B	949 505-6890	19956
Beech Street Corporation (HQ)	8741	E	949 672-1000	20002
Caelus Corporation	8741	E	949 877-7170	20008

Employee Codes: A=Over 500 employees, B=251-500
C=101-250, D=51-100, E=20-50, F=10-19, G=1-9

2024 Southern California
Business Directory and Buyers Guide

© Mergent Inc. 1-800-342-5647

1387

GEOGRAPHIC

	SIC	EMP	PHONE	ENTRY#
Mike Rovner Construction Inc	8741	C	949 458-1562	20062
Environmental Resolutions Inc	8748	B	949 457-8950	20334
Higher Ground Education Inc (PA)	8748	B	949 836-9401	20343
Ibaset Inc (PA)	8748	E	949 598-5200	20347

LAKE ISABELLA, CA - Kern County

	SIC	EMP	PHONE	ENTRY#
Wick Communications Co	2711	E	760 379-3667	3338
Kern Valley Hosp Foundation (PA)	5912	B	760 379-2681	14055

LAKE VIEW TERRACE, CA - Los Angeles County

	SIC	EMP	PHONE	ENTRY#
Phoenix Houses Los Angeles Inc	8361	D	818 686-3000	19295

LAKESIDE, CA - San Diego County

	SIC	EMP	PHONE	ENTRY#
Pacific Green Landscape Inc (PA)	0781	C	619 390-1546	175
Enniss Inc	1442	E	619 561-1101	405
Minshew Brothers Stl Cnstr Inc	1541	C		511
Lb3 Enterprises Inc	1611	D	619 579-6161	630
Hazard Construction Company	1622	B	858 587-3600	654
A M Ortega Construction Inc (PA)	1731	C	619 390-1988	859
Standard Drywall Inc (HQ)	1742	B	619 443-7034	998
Clauss Construction	1795	C	619 390-4940	1130
Layfield USA Corporation (DH)	1799	C	619 562-1200	1167
Pepsi-Cola Metro Btlg Co Inc	2086	E	858 560-6735	1713
Southland Envelope Company Inc	2677	C	619 449-3553	3214
Superior Ready Mix Concrete LP	3273	A	619 443-7510	5514
Blue Star Steel Inc	3441	E	619 448-5520	5998
Clark Steel Fabricators Inc	3446	E	619 390-1502	6353
Christian Bros Flrg Intrors In	5713	D	619 443-9500	13950
Barona Resort & Casino	7011	A	619 443-2300	15086

LAKEWOOD, CA - Los Angeles County

	SIC	EMP	PHONE	ENTRY#
Cusa Properties Inc	2092	E	562 432-7300	1802
TFC Manufacturing Inc	3444	D	562 426-9559	6332
Magma Products LLC	3631	D	562 627-0500	8219
Eve Hair Inc (PA)	5199	E	562 377-1020	13537
Berkshire Hathaway Home Servic	6331	D	562 809-1331	14507
R and I Holdings	6719	C	562 483-0577	14941
Nationwide Theatres Corp	7933	A	562 421-8448	17360
Tenet Healthsystem Medical Inc	8011	B	562 531-2550	17801
Butterfly Imprints LLC	8049	C	657 464-5188	17857
Lakewood Regional Med Ctr Inc	8062	A	562 531-2550	18322
Center For Dscovery Adolescent	8093	D	562 425-6404	18676
Tarzana Treatment Centers Inc	8093	D	562 428-4111	18724
County of Los Angeles	8322	D	562 497-3500	19057

LAMONT, CA - Kern County

	SIC	EMP	PHONE	ENTRY#
Grimmway Enterprises Inc	5148	B	661 845-3758	13329
Clinica Sierra Vista	8011	D	661 845-3717	17624

LANCASTER, CA - Los Angeles County

	SIC	EMP	PHONE	ENTRY#
Desert Haven Enterprises	0782	A	661 948-8402	187
Excel Contractors Inc	1521	D	661 942-6944	432
Granite Construction Inc	1611	D	805 667-8210	620
Harvest Farms Inc	2038	D	661 945-3636	1392
Radford Cabinets Inc	2511	D	661 729-8931	2786
Antelope Valley Newspapers Inc	2711	E	661 940-1000	3255
Aerotech News and Review Inc (PA)	2721	E	661 945-5634	3342
Prints 4 Life	2752	E	661 942-2233	3668
Pavement Recycling Systems Inc	2951	E	661 948-5599	4663
Griff Industries Inc	3089	F	661 728-0111	5043
Arrow Transit Mix	3273	E	661 945-7600	5460
McWhirter Steel Inc	3441	D	661 951-8998	6048
Precision Welding Inc	3441	E	661 729-3436	6065
Robert F Chapman Inc	3444	D	661 940-9482	6306
Mobile Mini Inc	3448	F	909 356-1690	6384
National Metal Stampings Inc	3469	D	661 945-1157	6540
Pacific Seismic Products Inc	3491	E	661 942-4499	6768
National Band Saw Company	3556	F	661 294-9552	7210
J & R Machine Works	3599	E	661 945-8826	7879
A V Poles and Lighting Inc	3646	E	661 945-2731	8302
Advanced Clutch Technology Inc	3714	E	661 940-7555	9344
Morton Grinding Inc	3965	C	661 298-0895	11073
Keolis Transit America Inc	4111	D	661 341-3910	11323
Antelope Vly Schl Trnsp Agcy	4151	C	661 952-3106	11419
Santa Barbara Trnsp Corp	4151	C	661 510-0566	11431
Sprint Communications Co LP	4812	C	661 951-8927	11856
BDR Industries Inc (PA)	4841	D	661 940-8554	11969
Directv Group Holdings LLC	4841	C	661 632-6562	11987
Sygma Network Inc	5141	C	661 723-0405	13232
H W Hunter Inc (PA)	5511	D	661 948-8411	13775
Johnson Ford (PA)	5511	C	888 483-0454	13785
Loandepotcom LLC	6162	A	661 202-1700	14337
Mission Linen Supply	7213	D	661 948-5052	15452

	SIC	EMP	PHONE	ENTRY#
Opsec Specialized Protection	7381	D	661 942-3999	16666
Lancaster Cmnty Svcs Fndtion I	7538	C	661 723-6230	17033
Weststar Cinemas Inc	7922	C	661 723-9392	17332
City of Lancaster	7996	C	661 723-6071	17447
Antelope Valley Hospital Inc	8011	B	661 726-6180	17594
High Dsert Med Corp A Med Grou (PA)	8011	C	661 945-5984	17665
Lancaster Crdlgy Med Group Inc (PA)	8011	C	661 726-3058	17705
Antelope Vly Retirement HM Inc	8051	C	661 949-5584	17881
Antelope Vly Retirement HM Inc	8059	C	661 949-5524	18106
Antelope Vly Retirement HM Inc	8059	C	661 948-7501	18107
Antelope Valley Health Care Di (PA)	8062	A	661 949-5000	18182
Antelope Valley Hospital Inc	8062	C	661 949-5000	18183
Antelope Valley Hospital Inc	8062	C	661 726-6050	18184
Antelope Valley Hospital Inc	8062	C	661 949-5936	18185
Kaiser Foundation Hospitals	8062	A	661 726-2500	18303
US Carenet Services LLC	8082	C	661 945-7350	18650
Tarzana Treatment Centers Inc	8093	C	661 726-2630	18723
County of Los Angeles	8322	D	661 940-4181	19055
County of Los Angeles	8711	C	661 723-6088	19567
County of Los Angeles	9222	D	661 974-7700	20412

LAWNDALE, CA - Los Angeles County

	SIC	EMP	PHONE	ENTRY#
Westwood Building Materials Co	3273	E	310 643-9158	5519
Curry Company LLC	3545	E	310 643-8400	7115
Vellios Machine Shop Inc	3599	F	310 643-8540	8064
Los Angles Cnty Mtro Trnsp Aut	4111	B	310 643-3804	11335

LEBEC, CA - Kern County

	SIC	EMP	PHONE	ENTRY#
Technicolor Usa Inc	3651	B	661 496-1309	8441
Six Continents Hotels Inc	7011	C	661 343-3316	15358

LEMON GROVE, CA - San Diego County

	SIC	EMP	PHONE	ENTRY#
Aztec Landscaping Inc (PA)	0782	C	619 464-3303	183
Condon-Johnson & Assoc Inc	1522	D	858 530-9165	469
Pacific Sthwest Structures Inc	1771	C	619 469-2323	1081
RCP Block & Brick Inc (PA)	3271	D	619 460-9101	5392
Jci Metal Products (PA)	3441	D	619 229-8206	6035
Micro Tool & Manufacturing Inc	3545	E	619 582-2884	7121
Home Depot USA Inc	5211	C	619 589-2999	13599
Smiths Shade & Linoleum Co Inc	5714	E	619 299-2228	13954
Lemon Grove Health Assoc LLC	8051	B	619 463-0294	17985
Family Hlth Ctrs San Diego Inc	8099	B	619 515-2550	18764

LITTLEROCK, CA - Los Angeles County

	SIC	EMP	PHONE	ENTRY#
Hi-Grade Materials Co	3273	D	661 533-3100	5481

LOMA LINDA, CA - San Bernardino County

	SIC	EMP	PHONE	ENTRY#
Bakell LLC	1541	D	800 292-2137	494
Dvele Inc	2451	E	909 796-2561	2737
Dvele Omega Corporation	2451	E	909 796-2561	2738
Loma Linda Univ Chld Hosp	6733	C	909 558-8000	14997
ABI Document Support Svcs LLC	7389	D	909 793-0613	16766
Linda Loma Univ Hlth Care (PA)	8011	A	909 558-4729	17706
Loma Lnda Univ Fmly Med Group	8011	D	909 558-6600	17707
Veterans Health Administration	8011	A	909 825-7084	17829
Heritage Health Care Inc	8051	C	909 796-0216	17973
Linda Loma Univ Hlth Care (HQ)	8062	A	909 558-2806	18323
Loma Linda University Med Ctr (DH)	8062	A	909 558-4000	18326
Loma Linda University Med Ctr	8062	C	909 558-4385	18329
Loma Lnda - Inland Empire Cnsr	8062	C	909 558-4000	18330
Mountain View Child Care Inc (PA)	8062	C	909 796-6915	18348
South Coast Childrens Soc Inc	8093	C	909 478-3377	18719

LOMPOC, CA - Santa Barbara County

	SIC	EMP	PHONE	ENTRY#
Santa Barbara Farms LLC	0161	C	805 736-5608	12
Babcock Enterprises Inc	0172	E	805 736-1455	28
Horizon Well Logging Inc	1389	E	805 733-0972	354
Imerys Minerals California Inc (HQ)	1499	D	805 736-1221	417
Kustom Kanopies Inc	1541	E	801 399-3400	509
Dierberg Starlane Vineyard	2084	F	805 736-0757	1623
Hilliard Bruce Vineyards LLC (PA)	2084	F	805 736-5366	1637
Kugler Wines LLC	2084	E	630 306-4634	1641
Valiant Technical Services Inc	3731	C	757 628-9500	9849
Orbital Sciences LLC	3812	B	805 734-5400	10044
Federal Prison Industries	3993	F	805 735-2771	11120
Windsor Capital Group Inc	7011	D	805 735-8311	15420
Lompoc Valley Medical Center	8062	C	805 735-9229	18331
Lompoc Valley Medical Center (PA)	8062	B	805 737-3300	18332
Crestwood Behavioral Hlth Inc	8361	D	805 308-8720	19258
Channel Islnds Yung MNS Chrstn	8641	D	805 736-3483	19434

LONG BEACH, CA - Los Angeles County

	SIC	EMP	PHONE	ENTRY#
Beta Operating Company LLC	1311	D	562 628-1526	250

Mergent email: customerrelations@mergent.com
1388

2024 Southern California
Business Directory and Buyers Guide

(P-0000) Products & Services Section entry number
(PA)=Parent Co (HQ)=Headquarters (DH)=Div Headquarters

	SIC	EMP	PHONE	ENTRY#
California Resources Corp **(PA)**	1311	D	888 848-4754	254
Thums Long Beach Company	1311	C	562 624-3400	267
Tidelands Oil Production Inc	1311	E	562 436-9918	268
Dick Howells Hole Drlg Svc Inc	1381	F	562 633-9898	279
Kuster Co Oil Well Services	1381	E	562 595-0661	284
Termo Company	1382	E	562 595-7401	322
Warren E&P Inc	1382	D	214 393-9688	324
B & B Pipe and Tool Co **(PA)**	1389	E	562 424-0704	328
Sears Home Imprv Pdts Inc	1521	C	562 485-4904	454
Palp Inc	1611	C	562 599-5841	638
W A Rasic Cnstr Co Inc **(PA)**	1623	C	562 928-6111	703
Curtin Maritime Corp	1629	B	562 983-7257	707
Herzog Contracting Corp	1629	D	562 595-7414	711
Lite Solar Corp	1711	C	562 256-1249	786
Petrochem Insulation Inc	1742	C	310 638-6663	991
Wiser Foods Inc	2086	D	310 895-0888	1744
Everson Spice Company Inc	2099	E	562 595-4785	1889
Texollini Inc	2297	C	310 537-3400	2129
L A Cstm AP & Promotions Inc **(PA)**	2329	E	562 595-1770	2212
Brentwood Originals Inc **(PA)**	2392	D	310 637-6804	2468
National Emblem Inc **(PA)**	2395	C	310 515-5055	2522
Western Integrated Mtls Inc **(PA)**	2431	E	562 634-2823	2641
Harding Containers Intl Inc	2448	E	310 549-7272	2719
F-J-E Inc	2541	E	562 437-7466	2953
Speed-O-Pin International	2591	F	562 433-4911	3016
Jbi LLC **(PA)**	2599	C	310 886-8034	3027
Ld Products Inc	2621	C	888 321-2552	3054
Medianews Group Inc	2711	E	562 435-1161	3303
Continental Graphics Corp	2752	E	714 827-1752	3541
Continental Graphics Corp	2752	E	714 503-4200	3542
Crestec Usa Inc	2752	C	310 327-9000	3552
Pdf Print Communications Inc **(PA)**	2752	D	562 426-6978	3654
Queen Beach Printers Inc	2752	E	562 436-8201	3676
Weber Printing Company Inc	2752	E	310 639-5064	3708
Air Source Industries Inc	2813	F	562 426-4017	3862
Airgas Inc	2813	E	510 429-4216	3863
California Carbon Company Inc	2819	E	562 436-1962	3882
Eco Services Operations Corp	2819	E	310 885-6719	3891
Solvay USA Inc	2819	B	310 669-5300	3914
Evolife Scientific Llc	2833	E	888 750-0310	4000
FP Nutraceuticals LLC	2834	D	562 944-7821	4113
Sephora Co LLC **(PA)**	2844	E	760 798-7654	4453
Morton Salt Inc	2899	C	562 437-0071	4623
Pbf Energy Western Region LLC **(DH)**	2911	E	973 455-7500	4648
Tesoro Refining & Mktg Co LLC	2911	E	562 728-2215	4651
Lubeco Inc	2992	E	562 602-1791	4686
Bryant Rubber Corp **(PA)**	3053	E	310 530-2530	4719
Seal Science Inc **(HQ)**	3053	D	949 253-3130	4743
Mikron Products Inc	3061	E	909 545-8600	4750
Rubbercraft Corp Cal Ltd **(HQ)**	3061	C	562 354-2800	4753
Kirkhill Rubber Company	3069	D	562 803-1117	4772
G B Remanufacturing Inc	3089	D	562 272-7333	5033
Jacobson Plastics Inc	3089	D	562 433-4911	5066
Medway Plastics Corporation	3089	C	562 630-1175	5095
Plasidyne Engineering & Mfg	3089	E	562 531-0510	5140
Plastic Fabrication Tech LLC	3089	F	773 509-1700	5144
Schaffer Marine Services Inc	3089	F	562 480-8085	5200
Talco Plastics Inc	3089	D	562 630-1224	5221
Total Mont LLC	3231	E	562 983-1374	5357
Mitsubishi Cement Corporation	3241	B	562 495-0600	5367
Proform Finishing Products LLC	3275	E	562 435-4465	5521
American Plant Services Inc **(PA)**	3312	E	562 630-1773	5576
Primus Pipe and Tube Inc **(DH)**	3317	D	562 808-8000	5640
Certified Alloy Products Inc	3341	C	562 595-6621	5678
TCI Texarkana Inc **(DH)**	3353	C	562 808-8000	5692
SPEP Acquisition Corp **(PA)**	3429	D	310 608-0693	5944
Seachrome Corporation	3431	C	310 427-8010	5960
Cw Industries	3441	E	562 432-5421	6018
Foss Maritime Company	3441	F	562 437-6098	6026
Cowelco	3444	E	562 432-5766	6219
H Roberts Construction	3448	D	562 590-4825	6379
Wyatt Precision Machine Inc	3451	E	562 634-0524	6427
Crane Co	3492	C	562 426-2531	6774
Cunico Corporation	3498	E	562 733-4600	6843
Sportsmen Steel Safe Fabg Co **(PA)**	3499	E	562 984-0244	6873
Crown Equipment Corporation	3537	D	310 952-6600	6990
Ferguson Co	3585	F	562 428-3300	7614
Three Star Rfrgn Engrg Inc	3585	E	310 327-9090	7626
Berns Bros Inc	3599	F	562 437-0471	7783
Cavanaugh Machine Works Inc	3599	E	562 437-1126	7794
Frontier Engrg & Mfg Tech Inc	3599	E	562 606-2655	7838
NC Dynamics Incorporated	3599	C	562 634-7392	7950
NC Dynamics LLC	3599	C	562 634-7392	7951
Nuspace Inc **(HQ)**	3599	E	562 497-3200	7957
Kbr Inc	3624	E	562 436-9281	8164
Control Switches Intl Inc	3625	E	562 498-7331	8173
Western Tube & Conduit Corp **(HQ)**	3644	D	310 537-6300	8284
Rsg/Aames Security Inc	3669	E	562 529-5100	8624
Ixys Long Beach Inc **(DH)**	3674	E	562 296-6584	8821
Mercury Security Products LLC	3699	F	562 986-9105	9229
Schneider Elc Buildings LLC	3699	C	310 900-2385	9252
Tabc Inc **(DH)**	3713	B	562 984-3305	9335
Acme Headlining Co	3714	D	562 432-0281	9340
Arias Industries Inc	3714	E	310 532-9737	9354
Metra Electronics Corporation	3714	E	562 470-6601	9423
Aibot US Operation Inc	3721	E	562 283-3286	9507
Boeing Company	3721	A	562 496-1000	9513
Boeing Company	3721	A	562 593-5511	9515
Gulf Streams	3721	E	562 420-1818	9537
Gulfstream Aerospace Corp GA	3721	A	562 420-1818	9538
Jetzero Inc	3721	E	949 474-8222	9541
A Cdg Boeing Company	3728	C	562 608-2000	9584
Neill Aircraft Co	3728	B	562 432-7981	9756
Sanders Composites Inc **(PA)**	3728	E	562 354-2800	9794
APR Engineering Inc	3731	E	562 983-3800	9833
Indel Engineering Inc	3732	E	562 594-0995	9860
Rocket Lab Usa Inc **(PA)**	3761	D	714 465-5737	9897
Relativity Space Inc **(PA)**	3764	B	424 393-4309	9912
Spinlaunch Inc	3764	C	650 516-7746	9913
Custom Fibreglass Mfg Co	3792	C	562 432-5454	9923
Simulator PDT Solutions LLC	3812	E	310 830-3331	10071
Virgin Orbit Holdings Inc **(HQ)**	3812	F	562 388-4400	10087
Fundamental Tech Intl Inc	3823	E	562 595-0661	10133
Beauty Health Company **(PA)**	3841	B	800 603-4996	10450
Hydrafacial LLC **(HQ)**	3841	D	800 603-4996	10523
Radiology Support Devices Inc	3841	E	310 518-0527	10594
Ferraco Inc **(HQ)**	3842	E	562 988-2414	10659
Sas Safety Corporation	3842	D	562 427-2775	10699
Rastaclat LLC	3911	E	424 287-0902	10909
Superior Electrical Advg Inc **(PA)**	3993	D	562 495-3808	11172
Carberry LLC	3999	E	562 264-5078	11203
Guzzler Manufacturing Inc	3999	E	562 436-0250	11223
Macs Lift Gate Inc **(PA)**	3999	E	562 529-3465	11247
Union Pacific Railroad Company	4011	B	562 490-7000	11313
Long Beach Public Trnsp Co	4111	D	562 591-2301	11324
Long Beach Public Trnsp Co **(PA)**	4111	A	562 599-8571	11325
Atlantic Express Trnsp	4119	C	562 997-6868	11375
Long Beach Unified School Dst	4151	C	562 426-6176	11430
Hydrafacial LLC	4225	E	562 391-2052	11590
Kair Harbor Express LLC **(PA)**	4225	D	562 432-6800	11591
Roadex America Inc	4225	D	310 878-9800	11608
International Trnsp Svc LLC **(PA)**	4491	C	562 435-7781	11641
Lbct LLC	4491	C	562 951-6000	11642
Port of Long Beach	4491	B	562 283-7000	11644
Suderman Contg Stevedores Inc **(PA)**	4491	D	409 762-8131	11648
Pacific Maritime Freight Inc	4492	D	562 590-8188	11651
Hanjin Shipping Co Ltd	4499	A	201 291-4600	11655
Jetblue Airways Inc	4512	D	562 394-4397	11662
Piedmont Airlines Inc	4512	C	562 421-1806	11668
Polar Air Cargo LP	4512	B	310 568-4551	11669
Cargomatic Inc **(PA)**	4731	C	866 513-2343	11743
Hapag-Lloyd (america) LLC	4731	C	562 435-0771	11768
Next Trucking Inc	4731	C	213 444-2250	11787
Vanguard Lgistics Svcs USA Inc **(HQ)**	4731	C	310 847-3000	11814
Free Conferencing Corporation	4813	C	562 437-1411	11879
California Broadcast Ctr LLC	4841	D	310 233-2425	11970
Cco Holdings LLC	4841	C	562 228-1262	11975
Intelsat US LLC	4899	C	310 525-5500	12008
AES Alamitos LLC	4911	D	562 493-7891	12016
Southern California Edison Co	4911	D	562 529-7301	12057
Southern California Edison Co	4911	B	562 491-3803	12061
County of Los Angeles	4941	D	213 367-3196	12117
Covanta Long Bch Rnwble Enrgy	4953	C	562 436-0636	12166
Denso Pdts & Svcs Americas Inc **(DH)**	5013	B	310 834-6352	12237
Intex Recreation Corp	5021	D	310 549-5400	12285
Xerox Education Services LLC **(DH)**	5044	D	310 830-9847	12391
Tp-Link USA Corporation	5045	D	562 528-7700	12446
Jfe Shoji America Holdings Inc **(DH)**	5051	D	562 637-3500	12555
Ta Chen International Inc **(HQ)**	5051	C	562 808-8000	12574
Jvckenwood USA Corporation **(HQ)**	5065	C	310 639-9000	12674
Clarendon Specialty Fas Inc	5072	D	714 842-2603	12718
Airgas Usa LLC	5084	A	562 497-1991	12785
Tonnage Industrial LLC	5085	E	800 869-9463	12885
Aircraft Hardware West	5088	E	562 961-9324	12899
Intex Properties S Bay Corp **(PA)**	5091	D	310 549-5400	12930
Tst Inc	5093	E	310 835-0115	12958

Employee Codes: A=Over 500 employees, B=251-500
C=101-250, D=51-100, E=20-50, F=10-19, G=1-9

2024 Southern California
Business Directory and Buyers Guide

© Mergent Inc. 1-800-342-5647

1389

	SIC	EMP	PHONE	ENTRY#
A W Chang Corporation (PA)	5131	E	310 764-2000	13078
Smart & Final Stores Inc	5141	C	562 438-0450	13215
Plastic Sales Southern Inc	5162	E	714 375-7900	13416
Casey Company (PA)	5172	C	562 436-9685	13448
Farm Street Designs Inc	5182	C	562 985-0026	13476
Redbarn Pet Products Inc (PA)	5199	C	562 495-7315	13555
Home Depot USA Inc	5211	D	562 595-9200	13617
Cabe Brothers	5511	D	562 595-7411	13744
Belmont Brewing Company Inc	5812	E	562 433-3891	13982
Forty-Niner Shops Inc	5942	A	562 985-5093	14066
Password Enterprise Inc	5961	E	562 988-8889	14097
Innovative Dialysis Partners Inc	5999	B	562 495-8075	14136
Citibank FSB	6021	C	562 999-3453	14161
Farmers Merchants Bnk Long Bch (HQ)	6022	C	562 437-0011	14195
Molina Hlthcare Cal Prtner Pla	6321	B	562 435-3666	14454
California Physicians Service	6324	D	310 744-2668	14463
Scan Group (PA)	6324	B	562 308-2733	14494
Senior Care (PA)	6324	A	562 989-5100	14495
Tristar Insurance Group Inc (PA)	6331	A	562 495-6600	14532
Tristar Service Company Inc (HQ)	6411	D	562 495-6600	14638
Intex Recreation Corp	6512	C	310 549-5400	14667
Rance King Properties Inc (PA)	6513	C	562 240-1000	14729
American Development Corp (PA)	6531	D	562 989-3730	14744
Coastal Alliance Holdings Inc	6531	C	562 370-1000	14766
Cushman & Wakefield Cal Inc	6531	B	562 276-1400	14776
Gh Group Inc	6719	C	562 264-5078	14931
HEI Long Beach LLC	7011	C	562 983-3400	15176
Hyatt Corporation	7011	B	562 432-0161	15198
Merritt Hospitality LLC	7011	C	562 983-3400	15247
Nhca Inc	7011	C	310 519-8200	15261
Noble Investment Group LLC	7011	C	562 436-3000	15262
Noble/Utah Long Beach LLC	7011	C	562 436-3000	15263
Queensbay Hotel LLC	7011	D	562 481-3910	15313
RMS Foundation Inc	7011	A	562 435-3511	15331
Ruffin Hotel Corp of Cal	7011	C	562 425-5210	15335
Urban Commons Queensway LLC	7011	A	562 499-1611	15398
World Trade Ctr Ht Assoc Ltd	7011	C	562 983-3400	15426
Yhb Long Beach LLC	7011	D	562 597-4401	15429
Worldwide Corporate Housing LP	7021	B	972 392-4747	15432
Choura Venue Services	7299	D	562 426-0555	15500
Continental Graphics Corp (HQ)	7336	C	714 503-4200	15660
Designory Inc (HQ)	7336	C	562 624-0200	15663
Motion Theory Inc	7336	C	310 396-9433	15669
Elite Craftsman (PA)	7349	C	562 989-3511	15710
Mida Industries Inc	7349	C	562 616-1020	15728
OPEN America Inc	7349	C	562 428-9210	15731
Bragg Investment Company Inc (PA)	7353	B	562 984-2400	15759
Psav Holdings LLC (PA)	7359	C	562 366-0138	15794
Compulink Management Ctr Inc (PA)	7371	C	562 988-1688	15998
Design Science Inc	7371	E	562 442-4779	16012
Erp Integrated Solutions LLC	7371	D	562 425-7800	16028
QED Software LLC	7372	E	310 214-3118	16360
Traffic Management Pdts Inc	7372	A	800 763-3999	16410
Zwift Inc (PA)	7372	C	855 469-9438	16427
Shield Security Inc	7381	D	562 283-1100	16686
Goodwill Srving The Pple Sther (PA)	7389	D	562 435-3411	16836
Macro-Pro Inc (PA)	7389	C	562 595-0900	16866
Traffic Management Inc (PA)	7389	C	562 595-4278	16945
Cw Industries Inc (PA)	7692	E	562 432-5421	17082
DK Valve & Supply Inc	7699	E	562 529-8400	17123
Olympix Fitness LLC	7991	D	562 366-4600	17410
Virginia Cntry CLB of Long Bch	7997	D	562 427-0924	17534
Altamed Health Services Corp	8011	C	562 923-9414	17586
CB Tang MD Incorporated	8011	D	562 437-0831	17611
Childrens Clnic Srving Chldren	8011	C	562 264-4638	17616
Healthsmart Pacific Inc	8011	B	562 595-1911	17663
Molina Healthcare Inc (PA)	8011	A	562 435-3666	17716
Molina Healthcare California	8011	C	800 526-8196	17717
Molina Pathways LLC	8011	C	562 491-5773	17718
Optumcare Management LLC	8011	C	562 988-7000	17733
Transltnal Plmnary Immnlogy RE	8011	D	562 490-9900	17806
Alamitos-Belmont Rehab Inc	8051	C	562 434-8421	17878
Intercommunity Care Ctrs Inc	8051	D	562 427-8915	17978
Long Beach Care Center Inc	8051	C	562 426-6141	17996
Marlora Investments LLC	8051	C	562 494-3311	18010
Pacific Palms Healthcare LLC	8051	D	562 433-6791	18023
Palmcrest Grand Care Ctr Inc	8051	D	562 595-4551	18024
Palmcrest Medallion Convalesc	8051	D	562 595-4336	18025
Blyth/Wndsor Cntry Pk Hlthcare	8052	D	310 385-1090	18081
Lexington Group International	8059	C	562 428-4681	18135
Longwood Management Corp	8059	C	562 432-5751	18142
Villa De La Mar Inc	8059	C	562 494-5001	18159
Catholic Hlthcare W Sthern Cal (HQ)	8062	C	562 491-9000	18196
Community Hospital Long Beach	8062	A	562 494-0600	18225
Dignity Health	8062	B	805 988-2868	18243
Dignity Health	8062	C	562 491-9000	18245
Healthsmart Pacific Inc (PA)	8062	A	562 595-1911	18277
Long Beach Medical Center	8062	C	562 933-0085	18333
Long Beach Medical Center	8062	C	562 933-7701	18334
Long Beach Medical Center (HQ)	8062	A	562 933-2000	18335
Long Beach Memorial Med Ctr	8062	C	562 933-0432	18336
Memorial Hlth Svcs - Univ Cal (PA)	8062	A	562 933-2000	18343
St Mary Medical Center (DH)	8062	A	562 491-9000	18467
Posca Brothers Dental Lab Inc	8072	D	562 427-1811	18573
Coastal Cmnty Senior Care LLC	8082	C	562 596-4884	18603
Safe Refuge	8093	D	562 987-5722	18715
Tarzana Treatment Centers Inc	8093	C	562 218-1868	18722
Telecare Corporation	8093	C	562 630-8672	18725
Easy Care Mso LLC	8099	C	562 676-9600	18761
Industrial Medical Support Inc	8099	A	877 878-9185	18771
Los Angles Cnty Dept Mntal HLT	8099	D	213 738-4431	18777
Medasend Biomedical Inc (PA)	8099	C	800 200-3581	18780
Molina Healthcare Inc	8099	C	562 435-3666	18781
Pponext West Inc	8099	B	888 446-6098	18789
Fulwider and Patton LLP	8111	D	310 824-5555	18856
Keesal Young Logan A Prof Corp (PA)	8111	D	562 436-2000	18881
Prindle Decker & Amaro LLP (PA)	8111	D	562 436-3946	18927
Long Beach Unified School Dst	8211	D	562 426-5571	18973
Childnet Youth & Fmly Svcs Inc (PA)	8322	C	562 498-5500	19041
Interval House	8322	D	562 594-4555	19099
Jewish Community Ctr Long Bch	8322	C	562 426-7601	19100
Life Steps Foundation Inc	8322	D	562 436-0751	19109
Advocacy For Rspect Chice - Lo (PA)	8331	D	562 597-7716	19173
Conservation Corps Long Beach	8331	C	562 986-1249	19182
McKinley Child Development Ctr	8351	D	562 531-6182	19219
Brittany House LLC	8361	C	562 421-4717	19243
Aquarium of Pacific (PA)	8422	C	562 590-3100	19366
Assocted Stdnts Cal State Univ	8641	C	562 985-4994	19424
Automobile Club Southern Cal	8699	D	562 425-8350	19521
Memorial Medical Center Foundation	8699	A	562 933-2273	19532
Capital Engineering LLC	8711	D	562 612-1302	19561
Jacobs Civil Inc	8711	C	310 847-2500	19618
Mangan Inc (PA)	8711	D	310 835-8080	19642
Stearns Conrad and Schmidt Consulti (PA)	8711	D	562 426-9544	19696
URS Group Inc	8711	D	562 420-2933	19713
Utility Traffic Services LLC	8711	B	562 264-2355	19714
California State Univ Long Bch	8721	C	562 985-1764	19759
Windes Inc (PA)	8721	C	562 435-1191	19810
Southern Cal Inst For RES Edca	8733	D	562 826-8139	19945
Twining Inc	8734	D	562 426-3355	19985
Avsc Intllctual Prprty MGT Inc	8741	B	562 366-1924	19999
Country Villa Service Corp	8741	C	562 597-8817	20018
Teichert Enrgy Utlties Group I	8741	D	916 484-3011	20105
Aunt Rubys LLC	8742	E	562 326-6783	20135
Pmcs Group Inc	8742	D	562 498-0808	20221
Rmd Group Inc	8742	B	562 866-9288	20231
St Marys Medical Center	8742	A	562 491-9230	20247
Argus Management Company LLC	8744	B	562 299-5200	20289
Ultura Inc	8744	C	562 661-4999	20302
Envent Corporation Inc	8748	C	562 997-9465	20333
Healthcare Services Group Inc	8999	A	562 494-7939	20396
City of Long Beach	9431	C	562 570-4000	20413

LOS ALAMITOS, CA - Orange County

	SIC	EMP	PHONE	ENTRY#
Carol Electric Company Inc	1731	D	562 431-1870	878
Kdc Inc (HQ)	1731	C	714 828-7000	910
Thermo Power Industries	1742	E	562 799-0087	1001
Bloomfield Bakers	2052	A	626 610-2253	1511
Utbbb Inc	2052	D	562 594-4411	1525
Blue Sphere Inc	2311	D	714 953-7555	2150
Kids Line LLC	2392	C	310 660-0110	2474
Plh Products Inc	2452	B	714 739-6622	2744
Supermedia LLC	2741	D	562 594-5101	3489
Mittera Group Inc	2752	E	562 598-2446	3638
Trend Offset Printing Services Inc (HQ)	2752	E	562 598-2446	3698
Trend Offset Printing Svcs Inc	2752	B	562 598-2446	3699
Lab Clean Inc	2842	C	714 689-0063	4356
Natus Inc	3161	D	626 355-3746	5291
International Consulting Unltd	3317	C	657 256-1761	5635
Grating Pacific Inc (PA)	3441	E	562 684-4314	6028
Epson America Inc (DH)	3577	A	800 463-7766	7527
PI Machine Corporation	3599	E	714 892-1100	7974
Alliance Spacesystems LLC	3624	C	714 226-1400	8162
Spacesystems Holdings LLC	3624	C	714 226-1400	8165
Dwi Enterprises	3651	E	714 842-2236	8408
Epson Electronics America Inc (DH)	3674	E	408 922-0200	8793

Mergent email: customerrelations@mergent.com
1390

2024 Southern California
Business Directory and Buyers Guide

(P-0000) Products & Services Section entry number
(PA)=Parent Co (HQ)=Headquarters (DH)=Div Headquarters

	SIC	EMP	PHONE	ENTRY#
Arrowhead Products Corporation	3728	A	714 822-2513	9632
Flowline Inc.	3829	E	562 598-3015	10366
Samick Music Corp.	5099	D	800 946-6001	12986
College Park Realty Inc (PA)	6531	D	562 594-6753	14770
Quantum World Technologies Inc.	7361	B	805 834-0532	15884
Voltege Inc.	7389	E	714 369-8068	16960
Tenet Healthsystem Medical Inc.	8011	B	805 546-7698	17802
Katella Properties.	8051	D	562 596-5561	17981
Los Alamitos Medical Ctr Inc (HQ)	8062	A	714 826-6400	18338
Institute of Elec Elec Engnrs.	8611	D	714 821-8380	19379
Vanguard Space Tech Inc.	8711	C	858 587-4210	19715
Military California Department.	8744	B	562 795-2065	20296

LOS ANGELES, CA - Los Angeles County

	SIC	EMP	PHONE	ENTRY#
Eclipse Berry Farms LLC.	0171	D	310 207-7879	14
Mulroses Usa Inc.	0181	D	213 489-1761	61
Hokto Kinoko Company.	0182	D	323 526-1155	74
The Wonderful Company LLC (PA)	0723	C	310 966-5700	116
Wonderful Company LLC.	0723	B	661 720-2609	121
Mercy For Animals Inc.	0742	C	347 839-6464	123
VCA Animal Hospitals Inc.	0742	D	310 473-2951	128
Vicar Operating Inc (DH)	0742	D	310 571-6500	131
Camp Bow Wow Franchising Inc.	0752	C	310 571-6500	133
Greenscreen.	0781	E	310 837-0526	163
Breitburn Energy Partners LP.	1311	A	213 225-5900	252
Breitburn GP LLC.	1311	E	213 225-5900	253
Naftex Westside Partners Limit.	1311	E	310 277-9004	263
Occidental Petroleum Corporation of California.	1311	A		264
The Strand Energy Company.	1311	B	213 225-5900	266
Breitburn Energy Holdings LLC.	1382	F	213 225-5900	292
Freeport-Mcmoran Oil & Gas LLC.	1382	E	323 298-2200	305
Occidental Petroleum Investment Co Inc.	1382	A	310 208-8800	314
Qre Operating LLC.	1382	D	213 225-5900	316
Sentinel Peak Rsources Cal LLC.	1382	C	323 298-2200	319
Hirsh Inc.	1389	E	213 622-9441	353
Vanderra Resources LLC.	1389	B	817 439-2220	393
KB Home Grater Los Angeles Inc (HQ)	1521	D	310 231-4000	441
Zastrow Construction Inc.	1522	C	323 478-1956	481
KB Home (PA)	1531	D	310 231-4000	484
Austin Commercial LP.	1542	C	310 421-0269	532
Hitt Contracting Inc.	1542	B	424 326-1042	557
Philmont Management Inc.	1542	D	213 380-0159	579
Shawmut Woodworking & Sup Inc.	1542	C	323 602-1000	589
Webcor Construction LP.	1542	C	213 239-2800	604
Myers & Sons Construction LP.	1611	C	424 227-3285	636
Arrowhead Brass & Plumbing LLC.	1711	D	800 332-4267	734
Muir-Chase Plumbing Co Inc.	1711	C	818 500-1940	795
Precise Air Systems Inc.	1711	D	818 646-9757	810
Skypower Holdings LLC.	1711	C	323 860-4900	824
South China Sheet Metal Inc.	1711	E	323 225-1522	828
American Solar Direct Inc.	1731	C	424 214-6700	866
First Fire Systems Inc (PA)	1731	D	310 559-0900	900
Steiny and Company Inc.	1731	B	213 382-2331	940
Capital Drywall LP.	1742	C	909 599-6818	974
Rutherford Co Inc (PA)	1742	C	323 666-5284	995
United Marketing Group Inc.	1751	D	323 778-4283	1026
Platinum Roofing Inc.	1761	D	408 280-5028	1051
Sbb Roofing Inc (PA)	1761	C	323 254-2888	1054
Tinco Sheet Metal Inc.	1761	C	323 263-0511	1055
Giroux Glass Inc (PA)	1793	D	213 747-7406	1118
Closet Factory Inc (PA)	1799	C	310 516-7000	1148
Parking Network Inc.	1799	C	213 613-1500	1173
Rey-Crest Roofg Waterproofing.	1799	D	323 257-9329	1176
Serv-Rite Meat Company Inc.	2011	C	323 227-1911	1204
Commodity Sales Co.	2015	D	323 980-5463	1242
Los Angeles Poultry Co Inc.	2015	C	323 232-1619	1247
Western Supreme Inc.	2015	C	213 627-3861	1249
Pac Fill Inc.	2026	E	818 409-0117	1314
Caer Inc.	2032	E	415 879-9864	1320
Dolores Canning Co Inc.	2032	E	323 263-9155	1323
Wing Hing Foods LLC.	2032	D	323 232-8899	1334
Jackson Manufacturing LLC.	2033	F	213 399-9300	1339
Walker Foods Inc.	2033	D	323 268-5191	1352
J Hellman Frozen Foods Inc (PA)	2037	E	213 243-9105	1372
La Aloe LLC.	2037	E	888 968-2563	1374
Astrochef LLC.	2038	D	213 627-9860	1384
Grain Craft Inc.	2041	D	323 585-0131	1411
East West Tea Company LLC.	2043	C	310 275-9891	1420
Arthur Dogswell LLC (PA)	2047	E	888 559-8833	1427
Bakers Kneaded LLC.	2051	E	310 819-8700	1453
Frisco Baking Company Inc.	2051	C	323 225-6111	1471
Global Impact Inv Partners LLC.	2051	E	310 592-2000	1474
Lavash Corporation of America.	2051	E	323 663-5249	1480
Lupitas Bakery Inc (PA)	2051	F	323 752-2391	1482
United States Bakery.	2051	F	323 232-6124	1496
Vurger Co (usa) Corp.	2051	E	929 318-9546	1498
Amays Bakery & Noodle Co Inc (PA)	2052	D	213 626-2713	1502
Aspire Bakeries Holdco LLC (HQ)	2052	D	844 992-7747	1503
Aspire Bakeries Holdings LLC (DH)	2052	E	844 992-7747	1504
Aspire Bakeries LLC (DH)	2052	C	844 992-7747	1505
Aspire Bakeries Midco LLC (DH)	2052	F	844 992-7747	1508
Grandville Llc.	2052	E	213 382-3878	1518
Wonderful Pstchios Almonds LLC (HQ)	2068	E	310 966-4650	1563
Darling Ingredients Inc.	2077	E	323 583-6311	1568
Angel City Public Hse & Brewry.	2082	E	562 983-6880	1576
Pouring With Heart LLC.	2084	D	213 817-5321	1653
San Antonio Winery Inc (PA)	2084	C	323 223-1401	1659
Winc Inc.	2084	C	855 282-5829	1670
Stillhouse LLC.	2085	E	323 498-1111	1676
Aquahydrate Inc.	2086	E	310 559-5058	1684
Reyes Coca-Cola Bottling LLC.	2086	E	213 744-8659	1734
American Fruits & Flavors LLC.	2087	E	818 899-9574	1748
American Fruits & Flavors LLC.	2087	E	818 899-9574	1749
American Fruits & Flavors LLC.	2087	D	213 624-1831	1750
Felbro Food Products Inc.	2087	E	323 936-5266	1768
Herbalife Manufacturing LLC (DH)	2087	E	866 866-4744	1776
Yamasa Enterprises.	2091	E	213 626-2211	1797
Gourmet Coffee Warehouse Inc (PA)	2095	E	323 871-8930	1820
Snack It Forward LLC.	2096	E	310 242-5517	1831
Peking Noodle Co Inc.	2098	E	323 223-0897	1843
Albany Farms Inc (PA)	2099	E	877 832-8269	1847
C & F Foods Inc.	2099	B	626 723-1000	1861
Crave Foods Inc.	2099	E	562 900-7272	1874
Everytable Pbc.	2099	E	323 296-0311	1890
Jsl Foods Inc (PA)	2099	D	323 223-2484	1919
La Barca Tortilleria Inc.	2099	E	323 268-1744	1924
La Fortaleza Inc.	2099	E	323 261-1211	1928
La Gloria Foods Corp.	2099	E	323 263-6755	1929
La Gloria Foods Corp (PA)	2099	E	323 262-0410	1930
La Princesita Tortilleria Inc (PA)	2099	F	323 267-0673	1931
Plant Ranch LLC.	2099	F	818 384-9727	1971
Tampico Spice Co Incorporated.	2099	E	323 235-3154	1995
Uce Holdings Inc.	2099	D	213 217-4235	2001
Worldwide Specialties Inc.	2099	C	323 587-2200	2004
BTS Trading Inc.	2211	E	213 800-6655	2014
Colormax Industries Inc (PA)	2211	E	213 748-6600	2016
East Shore Garment Company LLC.	2211	E	323 923-4454	2019
Factory One Studio Inc.	2211	E	323 752-1670	2020
G Kagan and Sons Inc (PA)	2211	E	323 583-1400	2022
Knit Generation Group Inc.	2211	E	213 221-5081	2026
MSP Group Inc.	2211	E	310 660-0022	2029
Ground Control Business MGT (DH)	2221	F	310 315-6200	2040
Juicy Couture Inc.	2221	C	888 824-8826	2041
Next Auto Tech Center.	2221	E	323 483-6767	2042
S&B Development Group LLC.	2221	E	213 446-2818	2043
American AP Dyg & Finshg Inc.	2231	E	310 644-4001	2045
Cmk Manufacturing LLC.	2231	E		2047
Roshan Trading Inc.	2231	E	213 622-9904	2051
Ax II Inc.	2241	E	310 292-6523	2053
West Coast Trimming Corp.	2241	E	323 587-0701	2057
Say It With A Sock LLC.	2252	F	800 208-0879	2060
Byer California.	2253	C	323 780-7615	2064
Crew Knitwear LLC.	2253	D	323 526-3888	2065
Design Knit Inc.	2253	E	213 742-1234	2067
Fortune Swimwear LLC (HQ)	2253	E	310 733-2130	2070
Tenenblatt Corporation.	2257	C	323 232-2061	2080
Azitex Trading Corp.	2259	E	213 745-7072	2083
Midthrust Imports Inc.	2259	E	213 749-6651	2084
Washington Grment Dyg Fnshg In.	2261	E	213 747-1111	2094
Washington Garment Dyeing (PA)	2262	E	213 747-1111	2099
Matchmaster Dyg & Finshg Inc (PA)	2269	E	323 232-2061	2103
Pacific Coast Bach Label Inc.	2269	E	213 612-0314	2104
Durkan Patterned Carpets Inc.	2273	C	310 838-2898	2113
Interfaceflor LLC.	2273	D	213 741-2139	2115
AMpm Maintenance Corporation.	2299	E	424 230-1300	2136
Gino Corporation.	2321	E	323 234-7979	2158
Starlion Inc.	2321	E	323 233-8823	2162
Fashiongo.	2323	F	213 745-2667	2166
J&C Apparel.	2323	E	323 490-6600	2168
Aries 33 LLC.	2329	E	310 355-8330	2194
Doh Quest LLC.	2329	E	213 651-3441	2201
Fear of God LLC.	2329	E	310 466-9751	2203
Fetish Group Inc (PA)	2329	E	323 587-7873	2204
Jh Design Group.	2329	D	213 747-5700	2208
Waterfront Design Group LLC.	2329	E	213 746-5800	2227
Boulevard Style Inc.	2331	E	213 749-1551	2233

Employee Codes: A=Over 500 employees, B=251-500
C=101-250, D=51-100, E=20-50, F=10-19, G=1-9

2024 Southern California
Business Directory and Buyers Guide

© Mergent Inc. 1-800-342-5647
1391

GEOGRAPHIC

	SIC	EMP	PHONE	ENTRY#
C-Quest Inc	2331	E	323 980-1400	2234
Colon Manufacturing Inc (PA)	2331	F	213 749-6149	2235
Guru Knits Inc	2331	D	323 235-9424	2242
Harari Inc (PA)	2331	E	323 734-5302	2243
Harkham Industries Inc (PA)	2331	E	323 586-4600	2244
J Heyri Inc	2331	E	323 588-1234	2245
Judy Ann of California Inc	2331	C	213 623-9233	2246
Juntee of California Inc	2331	E	213 742-0246	2247
K Too	2331	E	213 747-7766	2248
La Mamba LLC	2331	E	323 526-3526	2251
Leebe Apparel Inc	2331	E	323 897-5585	2252
Mf Inc	2331	C	213 627-2498	2256
Monrow Inc	2331	E	213 741-6007	2257
MXF Designs Inc	2331	D	323 266-1451	2258
Project Social T LLC	2331	E	323 266-4500	2263
Stony Apparel Corp (PA)	2331	C	323 981-9080	2264
T2c Inc	2331	F	213 741-5232	2265
Tianello Inc	2331	C	323 231-0599	2266
Umgee USA Inc	2331	F	323 526-9138	2267
Avalon Apparel LLC (PA)	2335	C	323 581-3511	2276
California Blue Apparel Inc	2335	E	213 745-5400	2278
Choon Inc (PA)	2335	E	213 225-2500	2280
J C Trimming Company Inc	2335	D	323 235-4458	2282
Jodi Kristopher LLC (PA)	2335	D	323 890-8000	2283
Jwc Studio Inc (PA)	2335	E	323 231-8222	2284
Private Brand Mdsg Corp	2335	E	213 749-0191	2287
Promises Promises Inc	2335	E	213 749-7725	2288
Sublitex Inc	2335	E	323 582-9596	2289
Tlmf Inc	2335	D	212 764-2334	2290
Komarov Enterprises Inc	2337	D	213 244-7000	2294
Topson Downs California Inc	2337	C	310 558-0300	2296
Ambiance USA Inc	2339	E	213 765-9600	2300
Ambiance USA Inc	2339	E	323 587-0007	2301
Ambiance USA Inc (PA)	2339	E	323 587-0007	2302
Bb Co Inc	2339	E	213 550-1158	2305
Be Bop Clothing	2339	B	323 846-0121	2306
Burning Torch Inc	2339	E	323 733-7700	2308
C M G Inc (PA)	2339	E	323 780-8250	2309
Camp Smidgemore Inc (DH)	2339	E	323 634-0333	2310
Clothing Illustrated Inc (PA)	2339	E	213 403-9950	2314
Crew Knitwear LLC (PA)	2339	D	323 526-3888	2315
Dda Holdings Inc	2339	E	213 624-5200	2317
Dmbm LLC	2339	E	714 321-6032	2320
Good American LLC (PA)	2339	E	213 357-5100	2325
Gypsy 05 Inc	2339	E	323 265-2700	2326
Jd/Cmc Inc	2339	E	818 767-2260	2334
JT Design Studio Inc (PA)	2339	E	213 891-1500	2338
Klk Forte Industry Inc (PA)	2339	E	323 415-9181	2342
L Y A Group Inc	2339	E	213 683-1123	2344
L&L Manufacturing Co Inc	2339	B		2345
Lee Thomas Inc (PA)	2339	E	310 532-7560	2347
Lefty Production Co LLC	2339	E	323 515-9266	2348
MGT Industries Inc (PA)	2339	D	310 516-5900	2352
Monterey Canyon LLC (PA)	2339	D	213 741-0209	2353
New Fashion Products Inc	2339	C	310 354-0090	2354
Nexxen Apparel Inc (PA)	2339	F	323 267-9900	2355
Pierre Mitri (PA)	2339	E	213 747-1838	2358
Piet Retief Inc	2339	E	323 732-8312	2359
Polymond Dk Inc	2339	E	213 327-0771	2361
Q&A7 LLC	2339	F	323 364-4250	2363
Rhapsody Clothing Inc	2339	D	213 614-8887	2366
Solow	2339	E	323 664-7772	2370
SSC Apparel Inc	2339	F	213 748-5511	2372
Tcj Manufacturing LLC	2339	E	213 488-8400	2375
Treivush Industries Inc	2339	D	213 745-7774	2380
YMi Jeanswear Inc	2339	E	213 746-6681	2384
Delta Galil USA Inc	2341	B	213 488-4859	2388
Guess Inc	2341	A	213 765-3100	2389
Harper Wilde Inc	2341	E	213 510-1608	2390
Honest Company Inc (PA)	2341	C	310 917-9199	2391
Foh Group Inc (PA)	2342	E		2395
Agron Inc	2353	D	310 473-7223	2397
Kwdz Manufacturing LLC (PA)	2361	D	323 526-3526	2408
Misyd Corp (PA)	2361	D	213 742-1800	2411
Baby Guess Inc	2369	E	213 765-3100	2413
Un Deux Trois Inc (PA)	2369	E	323 588-1067	2420
Chrome Hearts LLC (PA)	2386	E	323 957-7544	2426
Euro Bello USA	2386	E	213 446-2818	2429
American Apparel (usa) LLC	2389	E	213 488-0226	2439
App Winddown LLC (HQ)	2389	C		2441
Califrnia Cstume Cllctions Inc (PA)	2389	E	323 262-8383	2443
Conquer Nation Inc	2389	C	310 651-5555	2445
Gilli Inc	2389	F	213 744-9808	2451
Havuni LLC	2389	E	917 428-1183	2452
Lets Go Apparel Inc (PA)	2389	E	213 863-1767	2453
Los Angeles Apparel Inc (PA)	2389	B	213 275-3120	2454
Mdc Interior Solutions LLC	2389	E	800 621-4006	2455
Amtex California Inc	2391	E	323 859-2200	2462
Big League Pillows LLC	2392	F	949 422-8443	2466
Matteo LLC	2392	E	213 617-2813	2477
Universal Cushion Company Inc (PA)	2392	E	323 887-8000	2489
Gma Cover Corp	2394	C		2505
American Quilting Company Inc	2395	E	323 233-2500	2513
Amoseastern Apparel Inc	2396	E	323 909-1010	2526
Atelier Luxury Group LLC	2396	E	310 751-2444	2527
Security Textile Corporation	2396	E	213 747-2673	2538
Scottex Inc	2399	E	310 516-1411	2557
Wessco Intl Ltd A Cal Ltd Prtn (PA)	2399	D	310 477-4272	2561
Bromack Company	2434	E	323 227-5000	2649
Mikada Cabinets LLC	2434	D	713 681-6116	2668
Ultra Built Kitchens Inc	2434	E	323 232-3362	2681
Arnies Supply Service Ltd (PA)	2448	E	323 263-1696	2714
Pallet Masters Inc	2448	D	323 758-1713	2721
Royal Pallets Inc	2448	F	323 580-4364	2725
Marge Carson Inc (PA)	2512	D	626 571-1111	2808
Minson Corporation	2512	B	323 513-1041	2811
Sofa U Love LLC (PA)	2512	E	323 464-3397	2818
Stitch Industries Inc	2512	E	888 282-0842	2820
A A Cater Truck Mfg Co Inc	2514	E	323 233-2343	2824
Wesley Allen Inc	2514	C	323 231-4275	2840
Cristal Materials Inc	2515	E	323 855-1688	2846
Don Alderson Associates Inc	2519	E	310 837-5141	2870
Standdesk Inc	2519	E	213 634-0665	2874
American Furniture Systems Inc	2522	E	626 457-9900	2902
Angell & Giroux Inc	2522	D	323 269-8596	2903
Versa Products Inc (PA)	2522	C	310 353-7100	2918
LA Cabinet & Millwork Inc	2541	E	323 227-5000	2959
Felbro Inc	2542	C	323 263-8686	2979
Pacific Manufacturing MGT Inc	2542	D	323 263-9000	2985
Hd Window Fashions Inc (DH)	2591	B	213 749-6333	3006
6th Street Partners LLC	2599	F	213 377-5277	3019
David Haid	2599	E	323 752-8096	3022
West Coast Industries Inc	2599	E	213 627-1113	3034
New Green Day LLC	2611	E	323 566-7603	3037
Boise Cascade Company	2621	F	310 815-2200	3042
Advance Paper Box Company	2653	C	323 750-2550	3078
Plastopan Industries Inc (PA)	2655	E	323 231-2225	3137
Vision Envelope & Prtg Co Inc (PA)	2677	E	310 324-7062	3215
Argonaut	2711	E	310 822-1629	3256
Associated Students UCLA	2711	C	310 825-2787	3259
California Community News LLC (DH)	2711	B	626 388-1017	3261
Daily Journal Corporation (PA)	2711	D	213 229-5300	3270
Grace Communications Inc (PA)	2711	E	213 628-4384	3279
Hollywood Reporter	2711	C	323 525-2000	3285
Investors Business Daily Inc (HQ)	2711	C	800 831-2525	3289
Joongangilbo Usa Inc (DH)	2711	C	213 368-2512	3291
La Opinion LP	2711	B	213 896-2222	3293
La Opinion LP (HQ)	2711	D	213 891-9191	3294
La Times	2711	E	213 237-2279	3295
Los Angeles Sentinel Inc	2711	D	323 299-3800	3298
Met News	2711	E	310 346-0033	3306
Rafu Shimpo	2711	E	213 629-2231	3317
Runway Beauty Inc	2711	F	844 240-2250	3318
The Korea Times Los Angeles Inc (PA)	2711	C	323 692-2000	3329
Thewrap	2711	D	424 273-4787	3330
Tidings	2711	E	213 637-7360	3331
Tribe Mdia Corp A Cal Nnprfit	2711	E	213 368-1661	3332
Cbj LP	2721	D	818 676-1750	3347
Cbj LP	2721	E	323 549-5225	3348
Flaunt Magazine	2721	F	323 836-1044	3359
Los Angeles Bus Jurnl Assoc	2721	E	323 549-5225	3367
Mnm Corporation	2721	E	213 627-3737	3372
Orange Coast Magazine LLC	2721	C	949 862-1133	3374
Penske Business Media LLC	2721	E	310 321-5000	3379
Playboy Enterprises Inc	2721	D	310 424-1800	3380
Rangefinder Publishing Co Inc	2721	E	310 846-4770	3385
Twelve Signs Inc	2721	F	310 553-8000	3392
Xbiz	2721	F	310 820-0228	3395
Judy O Productions Inc	2731	E	323 938-8513	3408
Microfilm Company of Cal Inc	2731	F	310 354-2610	3410
418 Media LLC	2741	E	614 350-3960	3421
Acceptedcom LLC	2741	E	310 815-9553	3422
American Soc Cmpsers Athors Pb	2741	D	323 883-1000	3427
Audience Inc	2741	E	323 413-2370	3429
Blavity Inc	2741	C	818 669-9162	3431
Brud Inc	2741	F	310 806-2283	3434

Company	SIC	EMP	PHONE	ENTRY#
Den Editorial LLC	2741	E	949 292-6475	3440
Good Worldwide LLC	2741	E	323 206-6495	3452
Netmarble Us Inc	2741	D	213 222-7712	3469
Planetizen Inc	2741	E	877 260-7526	3474
Playboy Enterprises Intl Inc	2741	E	310 424-1800	3475
Pollstar LLC	2741	D	559 271-7900	3476
Riye Group LLC	2741	E	820 203-9215	3482
Studio Systems Inc (PA)	2741	E	323 634-3400	3487
Techture Inc	2741	E	323 347-6209	3492
Thomson Reuters Corporation	2741	E	310 287-2360	3493
Tlm Publishing Inc	2741	E	213 627-3737	3495
Warner/Chappell Music Inc (DH)	2741	C	310 441-8600	3500
Wb Music Corp (DH)	2741	C	310 441-8600	3501
Weddingchannelcom Inc	2741	C	213 599-4100	3502
Anderson La Inc	2752	D	323 460-4115	3512
Apple Graphics Inc	2752	E	626 301-4287	3513
Boss Litho Inc	2752	E	626 912-7088	3521
Cdr Graphics Inc (PA)	2752	E	310 474-7600	3527
Digital Printing Systems Inc (PA)	2752	D	626 815-1888	3561
Ikonick LLC	2752	E	516 680-7765	3589
Ink & Color Inc	2752	E	310 280-6060	3595
LA Printing & Graphics Inc	2752	E	310 527-4526	3617
Madisn/Grham Clor Graphics Inc	2752	B	323 261-7171	3627
Red Brick Corporation	2752	F	323 549-9444	3678
ONeil Capital Management Inc	2754	C	310 448-6400	3721
Stuart F Cooper Co	2754	C	213 747-7141	3724
American Zabin Intl Inc	2759	E	213 746-3770	3733
Consolidated Graphics Inc	2759	D	323 460-4115	3748
CR & A Custom Apparel Inc	2759	E	213 749-4440	3751
Fabfad LLC	2759	F	213 488-0456	3759
Vagrant Records Inc	2782	E	323 302-0100	3842
Automation Printing Co (PA)	2791	E	213 488-1230	3850
Gemini GEL Llc	2796	E	323 651-0513	3854
Oxerra Americas LLC	2816	D	323 269-7311	3875
Merelex Corporation	2819	E	310 208-0551	3899
Huntsman Advanced Materials AM	2821	C	818 265-7221	3943
Chromadex Corporation (PA)	2833	E	310 388-6706	3995
Mro Maryruth LLC	2833	C	424 343-6650	4004
Ron Teeguarden Enterprises Inc (PA)	2833	E	323 556-8188	4014
Tikun Olam Adelanto LLC	2833	E	833 468-4586	4020
Abraxis Bioscience LLC (DH)	2834	C	800 564-0216	4030
Baxalta US Inc	2834	A	818 240-5600	4066
Cougar Biotechnology Inc	2834	D	310 943-8040	4094
Dnib Unwind Inc	2834	C	213 617-2717	4102
Hylands Consumer Health Inc (PA)	2834	B	310 768-0700	4132
Murad LLC	2834	D	310 906-3100	4171
Puma Biotechnology Inc (PA)	2834	B	424 248-6500	4214
Zp Opco Inc	2834	E	510 745-1200	4260
Response Genetics Inc	2835	C	323 224-3900	4291
Grifols Biologicals LLC (DH)	2836	D	323 225-2221	4319
Ecolab	2841	D	323 292-7752	4336
Global Sales Inc	2844	E	310 474-7700	4415
Johnson & Johnson Consumer Inc	2844	D	310 642-1150	4424
Merle Norman Cosmetics Inc (PA)	2844	B	310 641-3000	4435
Shani Darden Skincare Inc	2844	E	310 745-3150	4456
America Wood Finishes Inc	2851	E	323 232-8256	4474
Ennis Traffic Safety Solutions	2851	E	323 758-1147	4488
Cvr Nitrogen LP (HQ)	2873	E	310 571-9800	4538
Rentech Ntrgn Pasadena Spa LLC	2873	E	310 571-9805	4541
CTS Cement Manufacturing Corp	2891	E	310 472-4004	4560
Stic-Adhesive Products Co Inc	2891	C	323 268-2956	4582
Gans Ink and Supply Co Inc (PA)	2893	E	323 264-2200	4588
American Consumer Products LLC	2899	D	323 289-6610	4595
Everspring Chemical Inc	2899	E	310 707-1600	4604
Snf Holding Company	2899	F	323 266-4435	4632
Usc Hsc Purchasing Svc	2899	F	213 740-8165	4636
Rentech Inc (PA)	2999	D	310 571-9800	4691
K-Swiss Inc (DH)	3021	E	323 675-2700	4703
K-Swiss Sales Corp	3021	E	323 675-2700	4704
Ames Rubber Mfg Co Inc	3069	E	818 240-9313	4756
Exrox Inc	3069	E	213 536-5290	4761
Falcon Waterfree Tech LLC (HQ)	3069	E	310 209-7250	4762
Mercury Plastics Inc	3081	D	323 264-2400	4814
Poly Pak America Inc	3081	E	323 264-2400	4817
J-M Manufacturing Company Inc (PA)	3084	C	310 693-8200	4850
Pw Eagle Inc	3084	A	800 621-4404	4853
Dial Industries Inc	3089	D	323 263-6878	5008
Dial Industries Inc (PA)	3089	D	323 263-6878	5009
Housewares International Inc	3089	E	323 581-3000	5054
Jet Plastics (PA)	3089	E	323 268-6706	5072
Plastique Unique Inc	3089	F	310 839-3968	5150
Plastpro 2000 Inc (PA)	3089	C	310 693-8600	5152
Stone Canyon Industries LLC	3089	A	310 570-4869	5217
Teksun Inc	3089	E	310 479-0794	5224
Bella K	3111	E	213 559-7916	5255
La La Land Production & Design	3111	E	323 406-9223	5258
Allbirds Inc	3143	F	213 374-2354	5267
Millennial Brands LLC	3144	E	925 230-0617	5278
Surgeon Worldwide LLC	3144	E	707 501-7962	5279
Jan-Al Innerprizes Inc	3161	E	323 260-7212	5290
Sbnw LLC (PA)	3171	C	213 234-5122	5299
Malibu Leather Inc	3172	C	310 985-0707	5303
Aputure Imaging Industries	3229	E	626 295-6133	5322
Judson Studios Inc	3231	E	323 255-0131	5345
Tubular Specialties Mfg Inc	3261	D	310 515-4801	5378
Sissell Bros	3272	E	323 261-0106	5449
Stepstone Inc	3272	E	310 327-7474	5453
American Marble & Onyx Coinc	3281	F	323 776-0900	5524
Best-Way Marble & Tile Co Inc	3281	E	323 266-6794	5525
National Wire and Cable Corporation	3315	C	323 225-5611	5621
Roscoe Moss Manufacturing Co (PA)	3317	D	323 261-4185	5641
David H Fell & Co Inc (PA)	3341	E	323 722-9992	5679
Sun Valley Products Inc (HQ)	3354	E	818 247-8350	5709
Sun Valley Products Inc	3354	E	818 247-8350	5710
Interstate Steel Center Co Inc	3355	E	323 583-0855	5719
Wire Technology Corporation	3357	E	310 635-6935	5754
Pioneer Diecasters Inc	3363	F	323 245-6561	5766
Cast Partner Inc	3369	E	323 876-9000	5808
Interntonal Metallurgical Svcs	3398	F	310 645-7300	5838
Micro Surface Engr Inc (PA)	3399	E	323 582-7348	5855
Augerscope Inc	3423	E		5874
Doval Industries Inc	3429	D	323 226-0335	5916
Champion-Arrowhead LLC	3432	D	323 221-9137	5967
Commercial Shtmtl Works Inc	3441	E	213 748-7321	6010
Medsco Fabrication & Dist Inc	3441	D	323 263-0511	6049
Pacific Coast Ironworks Inc	3441	E	323 585-1320	6060
Zia Aamir	3441	E	714 337-7861	6095
Active Window Products	3442	D	323 245-5185	6097
Hehr International Inc	3442	C	323 663-1261	6107
Basic Industries Intl Inc (PA)	3443	E	951 226-1500	6134
Roy E Hanson Jr Mfg (PA)	3443	D	213 747-7514	6154
A & A Feros Non Feros Met LLC	3444	E	213 622-9995	6173
A & M Sculptured Metals LLC	3444	F	323 263-2221	6174
Able Sheet Metal Inc (PA)	3444	E	323 269-2181	6176
Aero Precision Engineering	3444	E	310 642-9747	6181
Precision Steel Products Inc	3444	E	310 523-2002	6297
King Wire Partitions Inc	3449	E	323 256-4848	6400
Power Fasteners Inc	3452	E	323 232-4362	6452
Bandel Mfg Inc	3469	E	818 246-7493	6497
Larry Spun Products Inc	3469	E	323 881-6300	6532
Accurate Plating Company	3471	E	323 268-8567	6574
Alco Plating Corp (PA)	3471	E	213 749-7561	6576
Alpha Polishing Corporation (PA)	3471	D	323 263-7593	6581
Anodizing Industries Inc	3471	E	323 227-4916	6584
Barry Avenue Plating Co Inc	3471	D	310 478-0078	6589
Brite Plating Co Inc	3471	E	323 263-7593	6596
Bronze-Way Plating Corporation (PA)	3471	E	323 266-6933	6597
Cemcoat Inc	3471	E	323 733-0125	6600
Chromal Plating Company	3471	E	323 222-0119	6602
CP Auto Products Inc	3471	E	323 266-3850	6609
Electrolizing Inc	3471	E	213 749-7876	6615
Genes Plating Works Inc (PA)	3471	E	323 269-8748	6622
Old Spc Inc	3471	E	310 533-0748	6644
Pentrate Metal Processing	3471	E	323 269-2121	6647
Ravlich Enterprises LLC	3471	E	310 533-0748	6655
V & M Company	3471	F	310 532-5633	6677
We Five-R Corporation	3471	F	323 263-6757	6679
Adfa Incorporated	3479	E	213 627-8004	6688
Certified Enameling Inc (PA)	3479	D	323 264-4403	6697
NM Holdco Inc	3479	C	323 663-3971	6720
Tortoise Industries Inc	3479	E	323 258-7776	6744
Atlas Spring Mfgcorp	3495	E	310 532-6200	6798
Edmund A Gray Co (PA)	3498	D	213 625-0376	6845
PSM Industries Inc (PA)	3499	D	888 663-8256	6871
Tropi-Con Foods Inc	3499	E	949 472-2200	6874
Vigilant Drone Defense Inc	3499	E	424 275-8282	6876
Mixmor Inc	3531	F	323 664-1941	6939
Polyalloys Injected Metals Inc	3532	D	310 715-9800	6949
Elevator Research & Mfg Co	3534	E	213 746-1914	6965
Gleason Industrial Pdts Inc	3537	C	574 532-1141	6991
Avis Roto Die Co	3544	E	323 255-7070	7052
Idea Tooling and Engrg Inc	3544	D	310 608-7488	7077
Stainless Industrial Companies	3544	E	310 575-9400	7098
Stadco (HQ)	3545	E	323 227-8888	7132
Tosco - Tool Specialty Company	3545	E	323 232-3561	7135
Old Country Millwork Inc (PA)	3547	E	323 234-2940	7152

Employee Codes: A=Over 500 employees, B=251-500
C=101-250, D=51-100, E=20-50, F=10-19, G=1-9

2024 Southern California
Business Directory and Buyers Guide

© Mergent Inc. 1-800-342-5647

1393

GEOGRAPHIC

Company	SIC	EMP	PHONE	ENTRY#
Ubtech Robotics Corp	3549	E	213 261-7153	7174
Machine Building Spc Inc	3556	E	323 666-8289	7207
Meat Packers Butchers Sup Inc	3556	F	323 268-8514	7208
Avanzato Technology Corp	3559	E	312 509-0506	7225
Industrial Tools Inc	3559	E	805 483-1111	7242
Norchem Corporation (PA)	3559	E	323 221-0221	7253
Mjw Inc	3561	D	323 778-8900	7283
Allhealth	3571	E	213 538-0762	7416
This Is Rocknroll LLC	3571	F	323 384-3966	7454
Efaxcom (DH)	3577	D	323 817-3207	7523
Denim-Tech LLC	3582	D	323 277-8998	7592
City of Santa Monica	3589	C	310 826-6712	7650
Plethora	3599	E	323 851-1633	7975
On-Line Power Incorporated (PA)	3612	E	323 721-5017	8104
W A Benjamin Electric Co	3613	E	213 749-7731	8131
Concurrent Holdings LLC	3629	A	310 473-3065	8203
IaMplus LLC	3629	D	323 210-3852	8207
Capital Brands Distribution L (PA)	3634	D	800 523-5993	8231
Alger-Triton Inc	3645	E	310 229-9500	8285
Alcon Lighting Inc	3646	E	310 733-1248	8304
Prudential Lighting Corp (PA)	3646	C	213 477-1694	8328
Eema Industries Inc	3648	E	323 904-0200	8362
Absolute Usa Inc	3651	E	213 744-0044	8389
Mr Dj Inc	3651	E	213 744-0044	8425
Vizio Inc	3651	C	213 746-7730	8447
Capitol-Emi Music Inc	3652	A	323 462-6252	8452
CMH Records Inc	3652	F	323 663-8098	8453
Xr Studios LLC	3652	F	513 446-5621	8467
Hbc Solutions Holdings LLC	3663	E	321 727-9100	8522
Katz Millennium Sls & Mktg Inc	3663	C	323 966-5066	8527
Lifesinnovations Inc	3663	E	866 603-8456	8539
Maritime Telecom Netwrk Inc (DH)	3663	C		8542
Ophir Rf Inc	3663	E	310 306-5556	8556
Silvus Technologies Inc (PA)	3663	D	310 479-3333	8581
Bitmax LLC (PA)	3669	F	323 978-7878	8602
ABB Enterprise Software Inc	3674	D	213 743-4819	8755
Esi Inc	3674	E	310 670-4974	8794
Micross Holdings Inc	3674	D	215 997-3200	8845
A M I/Coast Magnetics Inc	3677	E	323 936-6188	8932
Crucial Power Products	3679	F	323 721-5017	9023
Dcx-Chol Enterprises Inc (PA)	3679	D	310 516-1692	9028
Ocm Pe Holdings LP	3679	A	213 830-6213	9091
Teledyne Technologies Inc	3679	B	310 822-8229	9127
Electrical Rebuilders Sls Inc (PA)	3694	D	323 249-7545	9166
Xos Inc (PA)	3694	E	818 316-1890	9178
Gores Radio Holdings LLC	3699	D	310 209-3010	9213
Flyer Defense LLC	3711	D	310 324-5650	9288
Velasco Carwash Supplies Corp	3711	E	310 715-3000	9312
Xos Fleet Inc	3711	E	855 909-4407	9315
Ctbla Inc	3713	D	323 276-1933	9319
Vahe Enterprises Inc	3713	D	323 235-6657	9337
Coda Automotive Inc	3714	D	310 820-3611	9373
Grover Products Co	3714	D	323 263-9981	9399
Leet Technology Inc	3714	F	877 238-4492	9412
Ram Off Road Accessories Inc	3714	E	323 266-3850	9448
Worldwide Aeros Corp	3721	D	818 344-3999	9558
Chol Enterprises Inc	3728	D	310 516-1328	9658
Coating Specialties Inc	3728	F	310 639-6900	9660
Gali Corporation	3728	E	310 477-1224	9696
Helicopter Tech Co Ltd Partnr	3728	E	310 523-2750	9706
Gambol Industries Inc	3732	E	562 901-2470	9858
Proto Homes LLC	3792	E	310 271-7544	9928
L3harris Technologies Inc	3812	E	310 481-6000	9990
Northrop Grumman Systems Corp	3812	B	310 556-4911	10025
TMC Ice Protection Systems LLC (PA)	3812	E	951 677-6934	10083
Eti Systems	3823	D	310 684-3664	10131
ITI Electro-Optic Corporation	3823	E	310 312-4526	10141
ITI Electro-Optic Corporation (PA)	3823	E	310 445-8900	10142
Pressure Profile Systems Inc	3823	F	310 641-8100	10151
First Legal Network	3825	E	213 250-1111	10200
Taseon Inc	3825	F	408 240-7800	10225
Bruin Biometrics LLC	3841	F	310 268-9494	10464
Siemens Hlthcare Dgnostics Inc	3841	D	310 645-8200	10605
Dynamics Orthtics Prsthtics In	3842	E	213 383-9212	10650
Hanger Prsthtics Orthtics W In	3842	D	213 250-7850	10666
Cyber Medical Imaging Inc	3843	E	888 937-9729	10734
Sprintray Inc (PA)	3843	C	800 914-8004	10769
Neurasignal Inc	3845	E	877 638-7251	10817
March Vision Care Inc	3851	E	310 665-0975	10843
Anschutz Film Group LLC (HQ)	3861	E	310 887-1000	10858
Carolense Entrmt Group LLC	3861	D	405 493-1120	10860
Cds California LLC	3861	F	818 766-5000	10861
Fpc Inc	3861	E	323 468-5778	10867
Panavision Inc	3861	E	323 464-3800	10877
Americas Gold Inc	3911	E	213 688-4904	10896
Giving Keys Inc	3911	E	213 935-8791	10902
Kesmor Associates	3911	E	213 629-2300	10903
LA Gem and Jewelry Design (PA)	3911	E	213 488-1290	10906
Sage Machado Inc	3911	E	323 931-0595	10911
Stardust Diamond Corp	3915	E	213 239-9999	10920
Exploding Kittens LLC	3944	E	310 788-8699	10952
Ninja Jump Inc	3944	D	323 255-5418	10963
Addaday Inc	3949	E	424 259-3368	10971
Martin Sports Inc (PA)	3949	E	509 529-2554	11012
Rpsz Construction LLC	3949	E	314 677-5831	11021
Standard Sales Llc (PA)	3949	E	323 269-0510	11028
Catame Inc (PA)	3965	F	213 749-2610	11069
Brush Research Mfg Co Inc	3991	C	323 261-2193	11085
La6721 LLC	3993	F	323 484-4070	11129
Standardvision LLC	3993	E	323 222-3630	11167
Beauty Tent Inc	3999	E	323 717-7131	11195
L A Hq Inc	3999	E	310 880-7433	11239
OMD Remanufacturing Inc	3999	E	213 220-3851	11258
PF Candle Co	3999	E	323 284-8431	11267
Reaps Company LLC	3999	E	212 256-1186	11274
Rucci Inc	3999	E	323 778-9000	11277
Shapell Industries	3999	E	323 655-7330	11281
Silvestri Studio Inc (PA)	3999	D	323 277-4420	11282
Sparks Exhbits Envrnments Corp	3999	D	562 941-0101	11284
Forrest Group LLC (PA)	4111	D	619 808-9798	11320
Los Angles Cnty Mtro Trnsp Aut (PA)	4111	A	323 466-3876	11326
Los Angles Cnty Mtro Trnsp Aut	4111	A	213 922-5887	11328
Los Angles Cnty Mtro Trnsp Aut	4111	B	213 922-6301	11329
Los Angles Cnty Mtro Trnsp Aut	4111	B	213 922-6203	11330
Los Angles Cnty Mtro Trnsp Aut	4111	A	213 922-6202	11331
Los Angles Cnty Mtro Trnsp Aut	4111	A	213 922-6207	11332
Los Angles Cnty Mtro Trnsp Aut	4111	B	213 533-1506	11334
Los Angles Cnty Mtro Trnsp Aut	4111	A	213 922-5012	11336
Los Angles Cnty Mtro Trnsp Aut	4111	A	213 244-6783	11338
Los Angles Cnty Mtro Trnsp Aut	4111	A	213 626-4455	11339
Mv Transportation Inc	4111	B	323 936-9783	11343
Mv Transportation Inc	4111	B	310 638-0556	11344
Private Suite Lax LLC	4111	C	310 907-9950	11356
Shuttle Smart Inc	4111	C	310 338-9466	11365
SMS Transportation Svcs Inc	4111	C	213 489-5367	11366
Southern Cal Rgional Rail Auth (PA)	4111	C	213 452-0200	11368
Bls Lmsine Svc Los Angeles Inc	4119	B	323 644-7166	11376
Falck Mobile Health Corp	4119	B	323 720-1578	11385
Flixbus Inc	4119	C	925 577-4164	11388
Schaefer Ambulance Service Inc	4119	B	323 468-1642	11404
Greyhound Lines Inc	4173	D	213 629-8400	11435
Dlf Logistics LLC	4212	D	626 387-3797	11452
Gateway Logistics Tech LLC	4212	C	732 750-9000	11454
Southern Counties Terminals	4212	D	310 642-0462	11465
Dependable Companies	4213	C	800 548-8608	11481
Dependable Highway Express Inc (PA)	4213	B	323 526-2200	11482
Xpo Logistics Freight Inc	4213	C	213 744-0664	11513
Kxp Carrier Services LLC	4215	C	424 320-5300	11532
Peach Inc	4215	C	323 654-2333	11537
Speedy Express LLC	4215	D	818 500-7785	11538
Unity Courier Service Inc (DH)	4215	C	323 255-9800	11547
Standard-Southern Corporation	4222	D	213 624-1831	11557
Standard-Southern Corporation	4222	C	213 624-1831	11558
Standard-Southern Corporation	4222	C	213 624-1831	11559
County of Los Angeles	4225	D	626 458-1707	11569
Edmund A Gray Co	4225	E	213 625-2725	11575
Mulholland Brothers	4225	E	510 280-5485	11601
Quick Box LLC	4225	C	310 436-6444	11605
Unified Grocers Inc	4225	C	323 232-6124	11625
Aerotransporte De Carge Union	4512	B	310 649-0069	11656
American Airlines Inc	4512	B	310 646-4553	11658
China Airlines Ltd	4512	C	310 484-1818	11660
China Airlines Ltd	4512	C	310 646-4293	11661
Korean Air Lines Co Ltd	4512	C	310 646-4866	11663
Korean Airlines Co Ltd	4512	C	310 410-2000	11664
Korean Airlines Co Ltd	4512	D	213 484-1900	11665
L A Air Inc	4512	C	310 215-8245	11666
Nippon Cargo Airlines Co Ltd	4512	D	310 417-0801	11667
United Airlines Inc	4512	D	310 258-3319	11672
Federal Express Corporation	4513	D	800 463-3339	11676
Airport Terminal MGT Inc	4581	B	310 988-1492	11687
Alliance Ground Intl LLC	4581	A	310 646-2446	11688
Department of Arprts of The Cy	4581	A	855 463-5252	11695
Los Angeles World Airports	4581	C	424 646-9118	11699
Los Angeles World Airports	4581	B	424 646-5900	11700
Los Angeles World Airports (PA)	4581	C	855 463-5252	11701

	SIC	EMP	PHONE	ENTRY#
Swissport Cargo Services LP	4581	C	310 910-9541	11708
Altour International Inc	4724	B	310 571-6000	11711
Altour International Inc **(PA)**	4724	D	310 571-6000	11712
Americantours Intl LLC **(HQ)**	4724	C	310 641-9953	11714
Helloworld Travel Svcs USA Inc	4724	C	310 535-1005	11715
OXY Inc	4724	C	310 824-1315	11721
Antenna Audio Inc **(PA)**	4725	A	203 523-0320	11727
Korean Airlines Co Ltd	4729	B	213 484-5700	11732
Matrix Aviation Services Inc	4729	C	310 337-3037	11733
Able Freight Services LLC **(PA)**	4731	D	310 568-8883	11734
Nri Usa LLC **(PA)**	4731	D	323 345-6456	11790
Rock-It Cargo USA LLC	4731	D	310 410-0935	11799
Select Aircargo Services Inc	4731	D	310 851-8500	11802
Fluor Fltron Blfour Btty Drgdo	4789	D	949 420-5000	11831
Hyperloop Technologies Inc	4789	C	213 800-3270	11834
Ea Mobile Inc	4812	C	310 754-7125	11848
Sprint Communications Co LP	4812	C	310 216-9093	11855
Sprint Corporation	4812	C	213 613-4200	11862
AT&T Services Inc	4813	E	213 975-4089	11870
Fox Interactive Media Inc	4813	C	310 969-7000	11878
Hulu LLC	4813	A	888 631-4858	11886
Media Temple Inc	4813	C	877 578-4000	11891
Mpower Holding Corporation **(HQ)**	4813	D	866 699-8242	11894
Public Communications Svcs Inc	4813	C	310 231-1000	11899
Truconnect Communications Inc **(PA)**	4813	C	512 919-2641	11910
J2 Cloud Services LLC **(HQ)**	4822	D	323 860-9200	11917
Dash Radio Inc	4832	C	310 456-9993	11921
Entercom Media Corp	4832	C	323 930-7317	11925
Sirius XM Radio Inc	4832	C	323 802-1100	11936
Cnn America Inc	4833	C	323 993-5000	11942
Disney Networks Group LLC **(DH)**	4833	D	310 369-1000	11944
Entravsion Communications Corp	4833	D	323 900-6100	11946
Fox Inc **(DH)**	4833	A	310 369-1000	11948
Fox Broadcasting Company LLC **(HQ)**	4833	C	310 369-1000	11949
Fox Sports Inc **(DH)**	4833	C	310 369-1000	11950
Fox Television Stations Inc **(HQ)**	4833	B	310 584-2000	11951
King World Productions Inc	4833	C	310 264-3549	11955
Lifetime Entrmt Svcs LLC	4833	B	310 556-7500	11957
Revolt Media and Tv LLC	4833	C	323 645-3000	11962
Twenteth Cntury Fox Intl TV In	4833	A	310 369-1000	11967
Directv	4841	D	323 810-2032	11984
E Entertainment Television Inc	4841	A	323 954-2400	11992
Fx Networks LLC	4841	C	310 369-1000	11993
Spectrum MGT Holdg Co LLC	4841	D	323 657-0899	11999
Discovery Communications Inc **(PA)**	4899	B	310 975-5906	12006
Southern California Gas Co **(HQ)**	4924	A	213 244-1200	12084
Southern California Gas Tower	4924	A	213 244-1200	12100
Los Angeles Dept Wtr & Pwr **(HQ)**	4941	A	213 367-1320	12128
Los Angeles Dept Wtr & Pwr	4941	A	213 367-5706	12129
Los Angeles Dept Wtr & Pwr	4941	A	323 256-8079	12130
Los Angeles Dept Wtr & Pwr	4941	A	213 367-4211	12132
The Metropolitan Water District of **(PA)**	4941	A	213 217-6000	12150
Norcal Waste Services Inc	4953	D	626 357-8666	12175
EC Group Inc **(PA)**	5021	D	310 815-2700	12280
Elijah Textiles Inc	5023	D	310 666-3443	12299
GA Gertmenian and Sons LLC **(PA)**	5023	C	213 250-7777	12301
Emser Tile LLC **(PA)**	5032	B	323 650-2000	12354
Hannam Chain USA Inc **(PA)**	5046	C	213 382-2922	12455
Jetro Holdings LLC	5046	B	213 516-0301	12459
Trust 1 Sales Inc	5046	D	323 732-3300	12465
Twin Med Inc	5047	B		12521
Lexicon Marketing (usa) Inc **(PA)**	5049	D	323 782-8282	12528
Earle M Jorgensen Company	5051	D	323 567-1122	12548
Gvs Italy	5051	D	424 382-4343	12552
AAA Electric Motor Sales & Svc **(PA)**	5063	F	213 749-2367	12581
Eaton Aerospace LLC	5063	B	818 409-0200	12592
Ecosense Lighting Inc **(PA)**	5063	D	855 632-6736	12593
Homeland Housewares LLC	5064	D	310 996-7200	12633
Bear Communications Inc	5065	D	310 854-2327	12645
Calrad Electronics Inc	5065	E	323 465-2131	12652
Mtroiz International	5065	E	661 998-8013	12686
ONeil Data Systems LLC	5084	C	310 448-6400	12803
Western Refining Inc	5084	E	323 264-8500	12841
Duhig and Co Inc	5085	E		12853
75s Corp	5093	E	323 234-7708	12949
C&C Jewelry Mfg Inc	5094	D	213 623-6800	12960
Mizari Enterprises Inc **(PA)**	5099	E	323 549-9400	12980
Platinum Disc LLC	5099	D	608 784-6620	12982
Roland Corporation US **(HQ)**	5099	E	323 890-3700	12984
Image Source Inc **(PA)**	5112	C	310 477-0700	12995
E & S Paper Co	5113	D	310 538-8700	13006
Oak Paper Products Co Inc **(PA)**	5113	C	323 268-0507	13011
Used Cardboard Boxes Inc	5113	C	323 724-2500	13025
Dhouse Brands Inc // Comune	5122	E	213 291-7576	13039
Hatchbeauty Products LLC **(PA)**	5122	D	310 396-7070	13046
Radix Textile Inc	5131	D	323 234-1667	13090
Rdmm Legacy Inc	5131	E	323 232-2147	13091
Romex Textiles Inc **(PA)**	5131	E	213 749-9090	13092
Quake City Casuals Inc	5136	C	213 746-0540	13109
UNI Hosiery Co Inc **(PA)**	5136	C	213 228-0100	13116
California Rain Company Inc	5137	D	213 623-6061	13120
Damo Textile Inc	5137	E	213 741-1323	13121
Edgemine Inc	5137	E	323 267-8222	13124
Fiesta Fashion Co Inc **(PA)**	5137	E	213 748-5775	13125
Flirt Inc	5137	E	213 748-4442	13126
Lymi Inc **(PA)**	5137	D	855 756-0560	13133
Nhn Global Inc **(HQ)**	5137	C	424 672-1177	13139
Princess Cruise Lines Ltd	5137	C	213 745-0314	13143
Seven Licensing Company LLC	5137	C	323 780-8250	13148
Signal Products Inc **(PA)**	5137	E	213 748-0990	13149
Aci International **(PA)**	5139	D	310 889-3400	13157
Afc Trading & Wholesale Inc	5141	E	323 223-7738	13170
Buffalo Market Inc	5141	C	650 337-0078	13174
Canton Food Co Inc	5141	C	213 688-7707	13175
Smart & Final Stores Inc	5141	C	323 549-9586	13211
Smart & Final Stores LLC	5141	C	310 559-1722	13222
Smart & Final Stores LLC	5141	D	323 466-9289	13223
Smart & Final Stores LLC	5141	D	323 569-7148	13224
Smart & Final Stores LLC	5141	D	310 207-8688	13225
Smart & Final Stores LLC	5141	C	323 268-9179	13226
Smart & Final Stores LLC	5141	D	213 747-6697	13227
Rogers Poultry Co	5144	D	800 585-0802	13261
Consolidated Svc Distrs Inc	5145	D	908 687-5800	13267
Superior Nut Co Inc	5145	F	323 223-2431	13275
Prospect Enterprises Inc **(PA)**	5146	C	213 599-5700	13283
Al Foods Corporation **(PA)**	5147	E	323 222-0827	13289
L & T Meat Co	5147	D	323 262-2815	13300
RW Zant **(DH)**	5147	D	323 980-5457	13306
Strouk Group LLC	5147	C	323 939-7792	13307
Borg Produce Sales LLC	5148	C	213 624-2674	13313
Coast Produce Company **(PA)**	5148	C	213 955-4900	13317
Davalan Sales Inc	5148	C	213 623-2500	13319
Green Farms Inc	5148	D	858 831-7701	13327
Pacific Trellis Fruit LLC **(PA)**	5148	C	323 859-9600	13335
Professional Produce	5148	D	323 277-1550	13337
Season Produce Co Inc	5148	B	213 689-0008	13339
Shapiro-Gilman-Shandler Co	5148	C	213 593-1200	13340
Val-Pro Inc **(PA)**	5148	C	213 627-8736	13345
App Wholesale LLC	5149	B	323 980-8315	13350
CJ America Inc **(HQ)**	5149	C	213 338-2700	13360
US Foods Inc	5149	C	213 623-4150	13404
ESE INC	5169	E	213 614-0102	13432
Zeco Systems Inc	5171	D	888 751-8560	13446
Youngs Market Company LLC	5182	B	213 629-3929	13484
Delta Floral Distributors Inc	5193	C	323 751-8116	13506
Berg Lacquer Co **(PA)**	5198	D	323 261-8114	13523
Gaju Market Corporation	5199	C	213 382-9444	13539
Home Depot USA Inc	5211	C	323 292-1397	13606
Home Depot USA Inc	5211	C	323 342-9495	13607
Home Depot USA Inc	5211	C	310 822-3330	13614
Goodwill Inds Southern Cal **(PA)**	5331	A	323 223-1211	13686
Pg Usa LLC	5331	D	310 954-1040	13688
Super Center Concepts Inc	5411	D	323 241-6789	13706
Sonora Bakery Inc	5461	E	323 269-2253	13723
Yamazaki California Inc	5461	E	213 624-2773	13725
Al Asher & Sons Inc	5511	E	800 896-2480	13736
FAA Beverly Hills Inc	5511	D	323 801-1430	13765
Felix Chevrolet LP **(PA)**	5511	C	213 748-6141	13766
Fox Hills Auto Inc **(PA)**	5511	C	310 649-3673	13769
Nick Alexander Imports	5511	C	800 800-6425	13803
Noarus Investments Inc	5511	D	310 649-2440	13805
Toyota Downtown La	5531	C	213 342-3646	13885
Evgo Services LLC	5541	B	310 954-2900	13891
Meundies Inc	5611	B	888 552-6775	13910
American Rag Compagnie	5621	D	323 935-3154	13911
Country Club Fashions Inc	5621	E	323 965-2707	13912
Nasty Gal Inc **(HQ)**	5621	E	213 542-3436	13915
Walking Company Holdings Inc **(PA)**	5651	C	805 963-8727	13924
ABC Home Furnishings Inc	5712	A	212 473-3000	13937
Aero Shade Co Inc **(PA)**	5719	E	323 938-2314	13955
Bebe Studio Inc	5719	E	213 362-2323	13957
La Linen Inc	5719	E	213 745-4004	13962
Linen Salvage Et Cie LLC	5719	E	323 904-3100	13963
Accor Corp	5812	C	310 278-5444	13979
Bonaventure Brewing Co Inc	5812	E	213 236-0802	13986
Calimex Deli	5812	E	323 261-7271	13990

Employee Codes: A=Over 500 employees, B=251-500
C=101-250, D=51-100, E=20-50, F=10-19, G=1-9

2024 Southern California
Business Directory and Buyers Guide

© Mergent Inc. 1-800-342-5647

1395

Company	SIC	EMP	PHONE	ENTRY#
Fish House Partners One LLC	5812	D	323 460-4170	14008
Lawrys Restaurants II Inc	5812	C	323 664-0228	14022
Magic Castles Inc	5812	D	323 851-3313	14025
Pbf & E LLC	5812	E	213 427-0340	14030
L & L Diamond Co	5944	F	213 622-5752	14077
Samys Camera Inc (PA)	5946	C	310 591-2100	14084
Robert Kaufman Co Inc (PA)	5949	C	310 538-3482	14089
Bu Ru LLC	5961	F	424 316-2878	14092
Spencer Forrest Inc	5961	E		14105
Avery Group Inc	5963	B	310 217-1070	14108
AAA Flag & Banner Mfg Co Inc (PA)	5999	C	310 836-3200	14119
Coway Usa Inc	5999	E	213 486-1600	14129
Evoqua Water Technologies LLC	5999	E	213 748-8511	14132
VCA Inc (DH)	5999	C	310 571-6500	14152
Federal Rsrve Bnk San Frncisco	6011	A	213 683-2300	14154
Bank of Hope (HQ)	6021	C	213 639-1700	14158
Bbcn Bank	6021	A	213 251-2222	14159
Bny Mellon National Assn	6021	A	310 551-7600	14160
City National Bank	6021	C	310 888-6500	14162
City National Bank (DH)	6021	B	310 888-6000	14163
City National Corporation	6021	A		14164
Hope Bancorp Inc (PA)	6021	D	213 639-1700	14168
Mufg Union Bank Foundation	6021	A	213 236-5000	14171
Busa Servicing Inc (PA)	6022	C	310 203-3400	14181
Cathay Bank (HQ)	6022	C	626 279-3698	14185
Cathay General Bancorp (PA)	6022	C	213 625-4700	14187
Op Bancorp (PA)	6022	C	213 892-9999	14201
Pcb Bancorp (PA)	6022	C	213 210-2000	14204
PCB BANK (HQ)	6022	C	213 210-2000	14205
Smbc Manubank (DH)	6022	C	213 489-6200	14207
Standard Chartered Bank	6022	D	626 639-8000	14208
Wilshire Bancorp Inc	6022	A	213 387-3200	14209
Wilshire Bank	6022	B	213 427-1000	14210
Sumitomo Mitsui Banking Corp	6029	C	213 452-7800	14214
Greenbox Loans Inc	6035	D	800 919-1086	14215
Mizuho Bank Ltd	6036	C	213 243-4500	14220
First Entertainment Credit Un (PA)	6061	D	323 851-3673	14225
University Credit Union	6061	C	310 477-6628	14242
SunAmerica Inc (HQ)	6091	A	310 772-6000	14254
Fcti Inc (PA)	6099	C	310 405-0022	14260
Deutsche Bank National Tr Co	6111	C	310 788-6200	14265
Hana Commercial Finance LLC	6153	D	213 240-1234	14282
Skyview Capital LLC	6153	C	310 273-6000	14288
Capitalsource Inc	6159	A	213 443-7700	14289
Capnet Financial Services Inc (PA)	6159	D	877 980-0558	14290
Westlake Services LLC (HQ)	6159	C	323 692-8800	14293
Federal Home Loan Mrtg Corp	6162	A	213 337-4200	14314
Gold Parent LP	6211	A	310 954-0444	14378
Goldman Sachs & Co LLC	6211	C	310 407-5700	14379
Imperial Capital LLC (PA)	6211	D	310 246-3700	14382
Leonard Green & Partners LP (PA)	6211	D	310 954-0444	14384
Morgan Stnley Smith Barney LLC	6211	C	213 891-3200	14392
Palisades Group LLC	6211	C	424 280-7560	14402
Trust Company of West	6211	A	213 244-0000	14406
Wedbush Securities Inc (HQ)	6211	B	213 688-8000	14408
Wells Fargo Securities LLC	6211	A	310 479-3500	14409
Adviceperiod	6282	A	424 281-3600	14412
Anderson Kayne Capital	6282	B	800 231-7414	14415
Atlas Capital Group LLC	6282	D	213 988-8890	14416
Capital Group Companies Inc (PA)	6282	A	213 486-9200	14420
Capital Research and MGT Co (HQ)	6282	B	213 486-9200	14421
Houlihan Lokey Inc (PA)	6282	B	310 788-5200	14422
Oaktree Capital Management LP (DH)	6282	C	213 830-6300	14424
Payden & Rygel (PA)	6282	C	213 625-1900	14426
Tcw Group Inc (PA)	6282	B	213 244-0000	14430
U S Trust Company NA	6282	B	213 861-5000	14432
Golden State Mutl Lf Insur Co (PA)	6311	D	713 526-4361	14435
SunAmerica Life Insurance Company	6311	C	310 772-6000	14442
Transamerica Occidental Life Insura	6311	A	213 742-2111	14443
Kaiser Fndtion Hosp Gift Shppe	6324	C	323 857-3290	14473
Local Inttive Hlth Auth For Lo (PA)	6324	A	213 694-1250	14486
Mercury General Corporation (PA)	6331	C	323 937-1060	14513
Mercury Insurance Company (HQ)	6331	C	323 937-1060	14514
Mercury Insurance Services LLC	6331	C	323 937-1060	14520
Orion Indemnity Company	6331	D	213 742-8700	14522
American Contrs Indemnity Co (DH)	6351	C	213 330-1309	14534
Cap-Mpt (PA)	6351	C	213 473-8600	14535
Allstate Financial Svcs LLC	6411	D	323 981-8520	14556
Automobile Club Southern Cal (PA)	6411	C	213 741-3686	14564
California Fair Plan Assn	6411	C	213 487-0111	14569
Gnet Agency	6411	D	323 951-9399	14598
John Hancock Life Insur Co USA (DH)	6411	A	213 689-0813	14604
Lockton Cmpnies LLC - PCF Srie (HQ)	6411	B	213 689-0500	14608
Marsh Risk & Insurance Svcs	6411	A	213 624-5555	14611
Pacific Indemnity Company	6411	B	213 622-2334	14620
Worldwide Holdings Inc (PA)	6411	D	213 236-4500	14649
Arden Realty Inc	6512	B	310 966-2600	14653
CB Richard Ellis Strgc Prtners	6512	D	213 683-4200	14655
Cdcf III PCF Lndmark Scrmnto L	6512	D	310 552-7211	14656
Insignia/Esg Ht Partners Inc (DH)	6512	B	310 765-2600	14666
La County	6512	D	310 417-5184	14669
Los Angeles Conven and Exh	6512	B	213 741-1151	14671
Topa Property Group Inc (HQ)	6512	C	310 203-9199	14690
Unibal-Rodamco-Westfield Group	6512	C	310 478-4456	14691
Wellnest	6512	D	323 766-2345	14694
West Side Rehab Corporation	6512	C	323 231-4174	14696
Westfield LLC (DH)	6512	B	310 478-4456	14697
Westfield America Inc (HQ)	6512	C	310 478-4456	14698
Westfield America Ltd Partnr	6512	B	310 277-3898	14699
Wilshire Kingsley Inc	6512	C	213 382-6677	14700
Abode Communities LLC	6531	C	213 629-2702	14741
Caruso MGT Ltd A Cal Ltd Prtnr (PA)	6531	D	323 900-8100	14758
Cbre Globl Value Investors LLC (DH)	6531	C	213 683-4200	14760
Charles Dunn RE Svcs Inc (PA)	6531	D	213 270-6200	14763
Cushman & Wakefield Cal Inc	6531	B	310 556-1805	14775
Cushman Realty Corporation	6531	C	213 627-4700	14784
Evoq Properties Inc	6531	D	213 988-8890	14792
I D Property Corporation	6531	C	213 625-0100	14813
Keller Williams	6531	D	323 300-1700	14818
Kor Realty Group LLC (PA)	6531	D	323 930-3700	14821
M & S Acquisition Corporation (PA)	6531	C	213 385-1515	14827
Memco Holdings Inc	6531	D	310 277-0057	14831
Nms Properties Inc	6531	D	310 656-2700	14836
On Central Realty Inc	6531	B	323 543-8600	14837
Pathstone Family Office LLC	6531	D	888 750-7284	14841
Pcs Property Managmnt LLC	6531	D	310 231-1000	14842
Proland Property Managmnt LLC (PA)	6531	D	213 738-8175	14851
Spus7 125 Cambridgepark LP	6531	C	213 683-4200	14866
Spus7 150 Cambridgepark LP	6531	C	213 683-4200	14867
Srht Property Holding LLC	6531	C	213 683-0522	14868
Thomas Properties Group Inc	6531	C	213 613-1900	14875
Triyar Sv LLC (PA)	6531	B	310 234-2888	14877
Lowe Enterprises RE Group	6552	C	310 820-6661	14904
LPC Commercial Services Inc	6552	C	213 362-9080	14905
Banamex USA Bancorp (DH)	6712	C	310 203-3440	14920
Shryne Group Inc	6719	A	323 614-4558	14944
Yf Art Holdings Gp LLC	6719	A	678 441-1400	14952
Alliancebernstein LP	6722	C	310 286-6000	14954
American Funds Distrs Inc (DH)	6722	C	213 486-9200	14956
American Mutual Fund	6722	C	213 486-9200	14957
Ares Management Corporation (PA)	6722	C	310 201-4100	14958
Causeway Capital MGT LLC	6722	C	310 231-6100	14961
Los Angeles Capital MGT LLC (PA)	6722	D	310 479-9998	14964
Oaktree Holdings Inc	6722	A	213 830-6300	14966
Oaktree Real Estate Opprtnties	6722	A	213 830-6300	14967
Oaktree Strategic Income LLC	6722	A	213 830-6300	14968
Ocm Real Estate Opprtnties Fun	6722	B	213 830-6300	14969
Shamrock Capital Advisors LLC	6722	C	310 974-6600	14972
Kingswood Capital MGT LP	6726	C	424 744-8238	14979
Oasis West Realty LLC	6726	A	310 274-8066	14980
Empower Our Youth	6732	D	323 203-5436	14983
Greater Los Angles Vtrans RES	6732	C	310 312-1554	14984
Ucla Foundation	6732	B	310 794-3193	14985
Capital Guardian Trust Company (HQ)	6733	D	213 486-9200	14989
Epidaurus	6733	A	213 743-9075	14990
Kaiser Foundation Hospitals	6733	D	323 881-5516	14996
Moelis & Company LLC	6733	C	310 443-2300	14998
Coresite LLC	6798	B	213 327-1231	15013
Prime Administration LLC	6798	A	323 549-7155	15016
Broadreach Capitl Partners LLC	6799	A	310 691-5760	15022
Call To Action Partners Llc (PA)	6799	D	310 996-7200	15023
Clearview Capital LLC	6799	A	310 806-9555	15025
Corridor Capital LLC (PA)	6799	C	310 442-7000	15026
Emp III Inc	6799	D	323 231-4174	15028
Golden International	6799	D	213 628-1388	15029
Intrepid Inv Bankers LLC	6799	A	310 478-9000	15032
Nexus Capital Management LP	6799	A	424 330-8820	15041
Nogales Investors LLC	6799	B	310 276-7439	15043
Otts Asia Moorer Devon	6799	C	323 660-6959	15045
Providence Rest Partners LLC	6799	A	323 460-4170	15047
Stonecalibre LLC (PA)	6799	C	310 774-0014	15052
Transom Capital Group LLC (PA)	6799	C	424 293-2818	15055
6417 Selma Hotel LLC	7011	C	323 844-6417	15066
901 West Olympic Blvd Ltd Prtn	7011	C	347 992-5707	15068
Andaz West Hollywood	7011	D	323 656-1234	15077
Ascot Hotel LP	7011	C	310 476-6411	15078

2024 Southern California
Business Directory and Buyers Guide

(P-0000) Products & Services Section entry number
(PA)=Parent Co (HQ)=Headquarters (DH)=Div Headquarters

	SIC	EMP	PHONE	ENTRY#
Behringer Harvard Wilshire Blv	7011	D	310 475-8711	15089
Beverly Hills Luxury Hotel LLC	7011	B	310 274-9999	15093
Brisam Lax (de) LLC	7011	D	310 649-5151	15097
Burton Way Hotels LLC	7011	D	310 273-2222	15099
Burton-Way House Ltd A CA	7011	D	310 273-2222	15101
Cim Group LP (PA)	7011	C	323 860-4900	15115
Cim/H & H Hotel LP	7011	B	323 856-1200	15116
Clear Group Inc	7011	C	603 325-5600	15119
Crestline Hotels & Resorts Inc (HQ)	7011	C	213 629-1200	15124
Custom Hotel LLC	7011	B	310 645-0400	15126
Donald T Sterling Corporation	7011	D	310 275-5575	15137
Emerik Hotel Corp	7011	D	213 748-1291	15146
Fortuna Enterprises LP	7011	B	310 410-4000	15154
Hazens Investment LLC	7011	B	310 642-1111	15173
Hotel Bel-Air	7011	B	310 472-1211	15185
Humnit Hotel At Lax LLC	7011	D	424 702-1234	15189
Hyatt Corporation	7011	B	312 750-1234	15196
Hyatt Corporation	7011	C	323 656-1234	15197
Hyatt Regency Century Plaza	7011	A	310 228-1234	15202
Ihg Management (maryland) LLC	7011	D	310 642-7500	15203
Ihg Management (maryland) LLC	7011	D	213 688-7777	15204
Irp Lax Hotel LLC	7011	C	310 645-4600	15205
Kava Holdings Inc (DH)	7011	C	310 472-1211	15207
Kimpton Hotel & Rest Group LLC	7011	C	323 852-6000	15209
L-O Bedford Operating LLC	7011	C	781 275-5500	15216
Lightstone Dt La LLC	7011	B	310 669-9252	15228
Lowe Enterprises Inc (PA)	7011	C	310 820-6661	15232
Marriott International Inc	7011	A	310 641-5700	15243
Metropolis Hotel MGT LLC	7011	D	213 683-4855	15249
Morgans Hotel Group MGT LLC	7011	C	323 650-8999	15256
New Aster Enterprises Inc	7011	C	213 747-7566	15259
Nrea-TRC 711 LLC	7011	D	213 488-3500	15265
Orlando Wilshire Investments	7011	D	323 658-6600	15279
Oxford Palace Hotel LLC	7011	D	213 382-7756	15283
Playa Proper Jv LLC	7011	D	310 645-0400	15306
Radlax Gateway Hotel LLC	7011	A	310 670-9000	15315
Raleigh Enterprises Inc (PA)	7011	C	310 899-8900	15317
Renaissance Hotel Operating Co	7011	C	310 337-2800	15321
Roosevelt Hotel LLC	7011	C	323 466-7000	15332
Rpd Hotels 18 LLC (PA)	7011	A	213 746-1531	15334
Seattle Arprt Hospitality LLC	7011	C	310 476-6411	15352
Shivay Hospitality Inc	7011	D	323 702-7103	15356
Sls Hotel At Beverly Hills	7011	C	310 247-0400	15360
Stockbridge/Sbe Holdings LLC	7011	A	323 655-8000	15374
Sunstone Hotel Properties Inc	7011	C	310 228-4100	15379
Sydell Hotels LLC	7011	C	213 381-7411	15386
Todays IV	7011	A	213 835-4016	15391
W Los Angeles	7011	B	310 208-8765	15407
W&J Business Ventures LLC	7011	D	310 645-7700	15408
Welk Group Inc (PA)	7011	B	760 749-3000	15412
Whb Corporation	7011	A	213 624-1011	15417
M-Aurora Worldwide (us) LP (PA)	7021	C	800 888-0808	15430
American Textile Maint Co	7213	D	213 749-4433	15446
American Textile Maint Co	7213	C	323 735-1661	15447
Morgan Services Inc	7213	D	213 485-9666	15458
Yee Yuen Laundry and Clrs Inc	7213	D	323 734-7205	15461
Pico Cleaners Inc (PA)	7216	D	310 274-2431	15464
Corbis Images LLC (PA)	7221	F	323 602-5700	15476
Miniluxe Inc	7231	D	424 442-1630	15481
Sinai Temple	7261	B	323 469-6000	15490
Temple Israel of Hollywood (PA)	7261	D	323 876-8330	15491
Andersen Tax LLC	7291	C	213 593-2300	15493
Eharmony Inc (HQ)	7299	C	424 258-1199	15507
Jet Fleet International Corp	7299	E	310 440-3820	15515
Vibiana Events LLC	7299	D	213 626-1507	15523
180la LLC	7311	D	310 382-1400	15525
Campbell-Ewald Company	7311	C	310 358-4800	15530
Cimarron Partner Associates LLC	7311	C	323 337-0300	15531
Daviselen Advertising Inc (PA)	7311	C	213 688-7000	15536
Deutsch La Inc	7311	D	310 862-3000	15537
Dg2 Worldwide Group LLC	7311	E	310 809-0899	15538
Digitas Inc	7311	E	617 867-1000	15539
Horizon Media Inc	7311	B	310 282-0909	15545
Mediabrands Worldwide Inc	7311	B	323 370-8000	15557
Mullenlowe US Inc	7311	C	424 738-6600	15563
National Promotions & Advg Inc	7311	E	310 508-8555	15565
Nexstar Digital LLC	7311	D	310 971-9300	15566
Quigly-Simpson Heppelwhite Inc	7311	C	310 996-5800	15570
Rapp Worldwide Inc	7311	C	310 563-7200	15571
Trailer Park Inc (PA)	7311	D	310 845-3000	15577
Wonderful Agency	7311	A	310 966-8600	15580
Young & Rubicam LLC	7311	C	213 930-5000	15581
Bamko Inc	7312	C	310 470-5859	15584
Outfront Media LLC	7312	E	323 222-7171	15586
Attn Inc	7313	C	323 413-2878	15587
BLT Cmmnctions LLC A Ltd Lblty	7313	C	323 860-4000	15590
Mediaalpha Inc (PA)	7313	D	213 316-6256	15596
Shed Media US Inc	7313	C	323 904-4680	15597
Gils Distributing Service	7319	D	213 627-0539	15602
Uscb Inc (PA)	7322	C	213 985-2111	15616
The Tax Credit Company	7323	D	323 927-0750	15624
Concord Document Services Inc (PA)	7334	E	213 745-3175	15643
CP Document Technologies LLC	7334	C	310 575-6640	15644
Cybercopy Inc (PA)	7334	F	310 736-1001	15645
Lasr Inc	7334	C	877 591-9979	15649
Riot Creative Imaging	7334	D	213 516-3160	15651
BLT & Associates Inc	7336	C	323 860-4000	15657
Cinnabar	7336	C	818 842-8190	15658
County of Los Angeles	7336	C	213 922-6210	15661
Digital Domain Media Group Inc	7336	A		15664
Twentieth Cntury Fox Japan Inc	7336	A	310 369-4636	15677
Aramark Facility Services LLC	7349	C	213 740-8968	15693
Crown Energy Services Inc	7349	A	213 765-7800	15706
Southern Management Corp	7349	D	213 312-2268	15750
Uniserve Facilities Svcs Corp	7349	B	310 440-6747	15752
Aercap Global Aviation Trust (HQ)	7359	C	310 788-1999	15768
Air Lease Corporation (PA)	7359	D	310 553-0555	15771
Hana Financial Inc (PA)	7359	D	213 240-1234	15781
Mufg Americas Leasing Corp (DH)	7359	D	213 488-3700	15788
Attorney Network Services Inc	7361	D	213 430-0440	15816
Career Group Inc (PA)	7361	A	310 277-8188	15826
Creative Solutions Svcs LLC	7361	C	646 495-1558	15834
Kimco Staffing Services Inc	7361	A	310 622-1616	15860
Korn Ferry (PA)	7361	C	310 552-1834	15863
Nursefinders Inc	7361	D	925 660-1153	15870
Rehababilities Inc	7361	C	310 473-4448	15891
Phoenix Engineering Co Inc	7363	D	310 532-1134	15935
3dna Corp (PA)	7371	C	213 992-4809	15950
Adcolony Inc	7371	C	650 625-1262	15956
Automotus Inc	7371	D	805 504-5750	15972
Bahare	7371	C	516 472-1457	15977
Bellrock Media Inc (PA)	7371	E	310 315-2727	15978
Boulevard Labs Inc	7371	D	323 310-2093	15987
Coalition Technologies LLC	7371	E	310 905-8268	15995
County of Los Angeles	7371	A	562 940-4343	16003
Cyberdefender Corporation	7371	F	323 449-0774	16007
Daz Systems LLC	7371	B	310 640-1300	16011
Deviation Games LLC	7371	D	310 873-5225	16013
Equator LLC (HQ)	7371	C	310 469-9500	16027
Gehry Technologies Inc	7371	C	310 862-1200	16038
Honey Science LLC	7371	C	949 795-1695	16047
Ktb Software LLC	7371	D	213 935-0902	16064
Myevaluationscom Inc	7371	C	646 422-0554	16078
Nksfb LLC	7371	C	310 277-4657	16086
Pandemic Studios LLC	7371	B	310 450-5199	16092
Second Spectrum Inc	7371	C	213 995-6860	16110
Tribridge Holdings LLC	7371	A	813 287-8887	16139
Vendor Direct Solutions LLC (PA)	7371	C	213 362-5622	16145
X1 Discovery Inc	7371	E	877 999-1347	16150
Adexa Inc	7372	E	310 642-2100	16158
Agencycom LLC	7372	B	415 817-3800	16160
AMS	7372	E	714 376-2464	16165
App LLC	7372	E	213 703-7294	16169
Bitmax	7372	E	323 978-7878	16182
Chrome River Technologies Inc	7372	C	888 781-0088	16201
Cloud Sftwr Group Holdings Inc	7372	F	800 424-8749	16204
Consensus Cloud Solutions Inc (PA)	7372	D	323 860-9200	16212
Dave Inc	7372	D	844 857-3283	16222
Evocative Inc	7372	D	888 365-2656	16244
Flash Code Solutions LLC	7372	F	800 633-7467	16247
Hoylu Inc	7372	F	213 440-2993	16265
IaMplus Electronics Inc (PA)	7372	E	323 210-3852	16267
Invisble Prtection Systems Inc	7372	E	213 254-0463	16275
Jurny Inc	7372	E	888 875-8769	16281
Luna Imaging Inc	7372	E	323 908-1400	16296
Mangomint Inc	7372	E	310 496-8677	16300
Media Gobbler Inc	7372	F	323 203-3222	16303
Mindshow	7372	E	213 531-0277	16306
Mitratech Holdings Inc	7372	C	323 964-0000	16309
Mod2 Inc	7372	E	213 747-8424	16311
Network Automation Inc	7372	E	213 738-1700	16322
Output Inc	7372	F	888 803-3175	16340
Relational Center	7372	E	323 935-1807	16367
Riot Games Inc (DH)	7372	E	310 207-1444	16369
Shred Labs LLC	7372	E	781 285-8622	16379
Slabs Inc	7372	E	424 289-0275	16380

Employee Codes: A=Over 500 employees, B=251-500
C=101-250, D=51-100, E=20-50, F=10-19, G=1-9

2024 Southern California
Business Directory and Buyers Guide

© Mergent Inc. 1-800-342-5647
1397

	SIC	EMP	PHONE	ENTRY#
Specialists In Cstm Sftwr Inc	7372	E	310 315-9660	16386
Sugarsync Inc	7372	E	650 571-5105	16394
Symantec Inc	7372	D	213 489-3262	16396
System1 Inc (PA)	7372	B	310 924-6037	16397
Total Cmmnicator Solutions Inc	7372	D	619 277-1488	16409
Videoamp Inc (PA)	7372	D	424 272-7774	16416
Visionary Vr Inc	7372	E	323 868-7443	16417
Cordoba Corporation	7373	D	213 895-0224	16437
Internet Corp For Assgned Nmes (PA)	7373	C	310 823-9358	16450
Oberman Tivoli & Pickert Inc	7373	C	310 440-9600	16464
Source It USA Inc	7373	E	714 318-4428	16471
Urban Insight Inc	7373	E	213 792-2000	16477
Enervee Corporation	7374	C	844 363-7833	16494
Honk Technologies Inc	7374	C	800 979-3162	16499
Mocean LLC	7374	C	310 481-0808	16507
County of Los Angeles	7375	C	213 974-0515	16525
E-Times Corporation (PA)	7375	B	213 452-6720	16526
Elavon Inc	7375	B	865 403-7000	16528
Adams Comm & Engrg Tech Inc	7379	C	301 861-5000	16547
Aiminsight Solutions Inc	7379	F	310 313-0047	16549
Bitscopic Inc	7379	E	650 503-3120	16555
Nowcom LLC	7379	C	323 746-6888	16582
Pegasus Squire Inc	7379	D	866 208-6837	16589
Preciseq Inc	7379	D	310 709-6094	16591
We See Dragons LLC	7379	C	310 361-5700	16611
Andrews International Inc	7381	B	310 575-4844	16621
Garda CL West Inc (HQ)	7381	B	213 383-3611	16643
Guardian Intl Solutions	7381	B	323 528-6555	16649
Mulholland SEC & Patrol Inc	7381	B	818 755-0202	16659
Pacwest Security Services	7381	C	213 413-3500	16668
Professional Security Cons (PA)	7381	D	310 207-7729	16671
Securitech Security Svcs Inc	7381	C	213 387-5050	16681
SOS Security Incorporated	7381	C	310 392-9600	16690
Worldwide Security Assoc Inc (HQ)	7381	B	310 743-3000	16711
Dtiq Holdings Inc	7382	C	323 576-1400	16730
Elite Intractive Solutions Inc	7382	E	310 740-5426	16733
Assocted Ldscp Dsplay Group In	7389	D	714 558-6100	16783
B Riley Securities Inc	7389	C	310 966-1444	16786
County of Los Angeles	7389	C	323 267-2771	16807
Diba Fashions Inc	7389	D	323 232-3775	16818
E & C Fashion Inc	7389	B	323 262-0099	16820
Facter Direct Ltd	7389	C	323 634-1999	16823
Forever 21 Logistics LLC	7389	B	888 494-3837	16828
Gelfand Rennert & Feldman LLP (PA)	7389	C	310 553-1707	16831
High Times Productions Inc	7389	C	844 933-3287	16840
Ingenuity Studios Intl Inc	7389	C	323 460-6096	16846
Ipayment Inc	7389	B	213 387-1353	16850
Kim Chong	7389	E	323 581-4700	16853
Laundry Design LLC	7389	C	323 933-2800	16861
Lindsey & Sons	7389	D	657 306-5369	16862
Medholdings of Newnan LLC	7389	A	213 462-6252	16870
N Philanthropy LLC	7389	F	213 278-0754	16883
Oeoe Corp	7389	C	213 387-0933	16892
ONeil Digital Solutions LLC	7389	C	310 448-6407	16893
Prompt Delivery Inc	7389	C	858 549-8000	16909
Qology Direct LLC	7389	C	310 341-4420	16911
Reason Foundation	7389	C	310 391-2245	16913
SD&a Teleservices Inc (HQ)	7389	B		16924
Stantec Architecture Inc	7389	B	213 955-9775	16934
Super Center Concepts Inc	7389	C	323 223-3878	16937
Swisstex California Inc (PA)	7389	C	310 516-6800	16938
Tbwa Chiat/Day Inc	7389	B	310 305-5000	16940
Vxi Global Solutions LLC (PA)	7389	A	213 739-4720	16961
Warner Bros Records Inc (DH)	7389	B	818 846-9090	16962
Fox Rent A Car Inc	7514	C	310 342-5155	16982
ABM Parking Services Inc	7521	A	213 284-7600	16987
All Star Parking	7521	C	310 337-1944	16988
Everpark Inc	7521	C	310 987-6922	16990
L and R Auto Parks Inc	7521	C	213 784-3018	16991
Laz Karp Associates LLC	7521	C	323 464-4190	16992
Parking Concepts Inc	7521	D	310 208-1611	17000
Parking Concepts Inc	7521	C	213 746-5764	17001
Parking Concepts Inc	7521	D	213 623-2661	17003
Valet Parking Svc A Cal Partnr (PA)	7521	A	323 465-5873	17008
Universal Metal Plating (PA)	7532	F	626 969-7931	17018
Wand Topco Inc	7532	A	323 734-3333	17019
Mission Service Inc	7538	A	323 266-2593	17035
Authorized Cellular Service	7629	D	310 466-4144	17068
Ruben & Leon Inc	7629	E	323 937-4445	17071
Scottel Voice & Data Inc	7629	C	310 737-7300	17073
Excel Picture Frames Inc	7699	E	323 231-0244	17127
Pacific Coast Elevator Corp	7699	D	323 345-2550	17143
Wardlow 2 LP (PA)	7699	D	562 432-8066	17162
Advanced Digital Services Inc (PA)	7812	D	323 962-8585	17166
Digital Domain 30 Inc (PA)	7812	B	213 797-3100	17181
Efilm LLC	7812	C	323 463-7041	17188
Fonco Creative Services	7812	F	415 254-5460	17193
Fox Net Inc	7812	A	310 369-1000	17194
Hungry Heart Media Inc	7812	C	323 951-0010	17196
Ignition Creative LLC	7812	D	310 315-6300	17197
Merlot Film Productions Inc	7812	D	323 575-2906	17200
Paramount Pictures Corporation (HQ)	7812	A	323 956-5000	17205
Paramunt Ovrseas Prdctions Inc	7812	A	323 956-5225	17206
Scanline Vfx Inc	7812	A	310 827-1555	17217
Scanlinevfx La LLC	7812	C	310 827-1555	17218
SDI Media USA Inc (HQ)	7812	D	310 388-8800	17219
Twenteth Cntury Fox HM Entrmt (PA)	7812	A	310 369-1000	17228
Yobs Technologies Inc	7812	E	213 713-3825	17239
A Filml Inc	7819	D	213 977-8600	17242
Alan Gordon Enterprises Inc	7819	E	323 466-3561	17243
Directors Guild America Inc (PA)	7819	C	310 289-2000	17248
For Cali Productions LLC	7819	B	323 956-9500	17252
Hollywood Rntals Prod Svcs LLC (PA)	7819	C	818 407-7800	17255
Omega/Cinema Props Inc	7819	C	323 466-8201	17259
Pixomondo LLC	7819	A	310 394-0555	17260
Point360 (PA)	7819	D	818 565-1400	17261
Post Group Inc (PA)	7819	C	323 462-2300	17262
Runway Inc	7819	A	310 636-2000	17263
Brat Inc	7822	D	619 410-3403	17274
Twentieth Cntury Fox Intl Corp (HQ)	7822	C	310 369-1000	17280
United Artists Corporation	7822	A	310 449-3000	17281
United Artists Productions Inc	7822	A	310 449-3000	17283
United Artists Television Corp	7822	B	310 449-3000	17284
Our Alchemy LLC	7829	D	310 893-6289	17287
Decurion Corporation (PA)	7832	D	310 659-9432	17290
AEG Presents LLC (DH)	7922	C	323 930-5700	17310
Center Thtre Group Los Angeles (PA)	7922	C	213 972-7344	17312
Creative Artsts Agcy Hldngs LL (PA)	7922	A	424 288-2000	17314
J C Entertainment Ltg Svcs Inc	7922	C	818 252-7481	17316
Los Angeles Opera Company	7922	B	213 972-7219	17318
Performing Arts Ctr Los Angles	7922	C	213 972-7512	17323
Anschutz Entrmt Group Inc (HQ)	7929	C	213 763-7700	17335
Hob Entertainment LLC (DH)	7929	C	323 769-4600	17338
House of Blues Concerts Inc (DH)	7929	C	323 769-4977	17339
Los Angeles Philharmonic Assn (PA)	7929	C	213 972-7300	17344
Los Angeles Philharmonic Assn	7929	A	323 850-2060	17345
Twenty Mile Productions LLC	7929	C	412 251-0767	17353
Two Bit Circus Dtla LLC	7929	D	323 438-9808	17354
Lucky Strike Entertainment Inc	7933	B	213 542-4880	17357
Fox Baseball Holdings Inc	7941	C	323 224-1500	17369
Fox BSB Holdco Inc (HQ)	7941	B	323 224-1500	17370
Immortals LLC	7941	D	310 554-8267	17372
La Clippers LLC	7941	C	213 742-7500	17374
LA Sports Properties Inc	7941	C	213 742-7500	17375
Bay Clubs Company LLC	7991	B	310 216-3060	17395
Equinox-76th Street Inc	7991	C	310 479-5200	17397
Equinox-76th Street Inc	7991	C	310 552-0420	17398
Los Angeles Athletic Club Inc	7991	C	213 625-2211	17407
World Gym International LLC	7991	C	310 557-8804	17419
Bel-Air Country Club	7997	C	310 472-9563	17472
Brentwood Country Club Los Angeles	7997	C	310 451-8011	17477
Hillcrest Country Club	7997	C	310 553-8911	17489
Lafc Partners Lllp	7997	B	213 334-4239	17496
Los Angeles Country Club	7997	C	310 276-6104	17499
Wilshire Country Club	7997	C	323 934-6050	17537
Faze Clan Inc	7999	B	818 688-6373	17550
Faze Holdings Inc (PA)	7999	B	818 688-6373	17551
Fortiss LLC	7999	D	323 415-4900	17553
Ticketmaster Corporation	7999	A	323 769-4600	17569
Ticketmaster Group Inc	7999	A	800 745-3000	17571
Tumbleweed Eductl Entps Inc	7999	C	310 444-3232	17575
Volume Services Inc	7999	B	323 644-6038	17579
Altamed Health Services Corp	8011	C	323 980-4466	17588
Altamed Health Services Corp	8011	C	323 269-0421	17589
Altamed Health Services Corp	8011	C	323 728-0411	17590
Arroyo Vsta Fmly Hlth Fndation	8011	D	323 224-2188	17595
Associated Students UCLA	8011	D	310 825-9451	17596
Cedars-Sinai Medical Center	8011	B	310 423-3849	17612
Cedars-Sinai Medical Center	8011	A	310 423-4208	17613
Cha Health Systems Inc (PA)	8011	A	213 487-3211	17615
Clinic Inc	8011	C	323 730-1920	17623
County of Los Angeles	8011	C	323 226-7131	17633
County of Los Angeles	8011	C	213 744-3919	17634
Garden Grove Advanced Imaging	8011	C	310 445-2800	17658
Good Samaritan Hospital Aux	8011	B	213 977-2121	17660
House Ear Clinic Inc (PA)	8011	D	213 483-9930	17666

Mergent email: customerrelations@mergent.com
1398

2024 Southern California
Business Directory and Buyers Guide

(P-0000) Products & Services Section entry number
(PA)=Parent Co (HQ)=Headquarters (DH)=Div Headquarters

	SIC	EMP	PHONE	ENTRY#
Kaiser Foundation Hospitals	8011	C	323 857-2000	17688
Kaiser Foundation Hospitals	8011	A	323 857-2000	17689
Kaiser Foundation Hospitals	8011	D	323 783-7955	17692
Kaiser Foundation Hospitals	8011	C	323 783-8306	17695
Keck Medical Center of Usc	8011	D	323 371-9535	17700
Lac & Usc Medical Center	8011	C	323 409-2345	17704
Los Angeles Free Clinic	8011	C	323 653-1990	17708
Pediatric & Family Medical Ctr	8011	C	213 342-3325	17735
Prospect Medical Holdings Inc (PA)	8011	C	310 943-4500	17741
Queenscare Health Centers	8011	D	323 644-6180	17745
Queenscare Health Centers	8011	D	323 780-4510	17746
Renew Medical Group Inc	8011	C	310 929-9790	17751
Santa Monica Bay Physicians He (PA)	8011	D	310 417-5900	17759
South Central Family Hlth Ctr	8011	C	323 908-4200	17768
Southern Cal Prmnnte Med Group	8011	C	323 857-2000	17781
Southern Cal Prmnnte Med Group	8011	C	323 783-5455	17783
Southern Cal Prmnnte Med Group	8011	C	323 783-4893	17784
The Orthopedic Institute of	8011	A	213 977-2010	17804
Veterans Health Administration	8011	A	310 478-3711	17828
Watts Healthcare Corporation (PA)	8011	C	323 564-4331	17830
White Memorial Medical Center	8011	A	323 260-5739	17834
Che Snior Psychlogical Svcs PC	8049	C	888 307-0893	17859
Intercare Therapy Inc	8049	C	323 866-1880	17865
Amada Enterprises Inc	8051	C	323 757-1881	17879
Beverly West Health Care Inc	8051	D	323 938-2451	17892
Burlington Convalescent Hosp (PA)	8051	D	213 381-5585	17894
Burlington Convalescent Hosp	8051	C	323 295-7737	17895
Cha Hollywood Medical Ctr LP	8051	A	213 413-3000	17901
Country Villa Nursing Ctr Inc	8051	C	213 484-9730	17913
Culver West Health Center LLC	8051	D	310 390-9506	17923
Front Porch Communities & Svcs	8051	C	323 661-1128	17954
Garden Crest Cnvlscent Hosp In	8051	C	323 663-8281	17957
Hyde Pk Rehabilitation Ctr LLC	8051	C	323 753-1354	17975
J P H Consulting Inc	8051	C	323 934-5660	17979
Lighthouse Healthcare Ctr LLC	8051	C	323 564-4461	17994
Longwood Management Corp	8051	C	323 933-1560	18001
Rehabltion Cntre of Bvrly Hlls	8051	C	323 782-1500	18036
Ridgecrest Healthcare Inc	8051	D	760 446-3591	18038
Rrt Enterprises LP	8051	C	323 653-1521	18044
Rrt Enterprises LP (PA)	8051	C	310 397-2372	18045
Sharon Care Center LLC	8051	D	323 655-2023	18052
Skyline Hlthcare Wllness Ctr L	8051	C	323 665-1185	18055
Stjohn God Rtirement Care Ctr	8051	C	323 731-0641	18059
Westlake Health Care Center	8051	B	805 494-1233	18076
Westwood Healthcare Center LP	8051	C	310 826-0821	18077
Amberwood Convalescent Hosp	8059	C	323 254-3407	18105
Ararat Home Los Angeles Inc	8059	C	323 256-8012	18108
Genesis Healthcare LLC	8059	A	323 461-9961	18126
Longwood Management Corp	8059	D	323 735-5146	18137
Longwood Management Corp	8059	C	213 382-8461	18139
New Vista Health Services	8059	C	310 477-5501	18146
Olympia Convalescent Hospital	8059	C	213 487-3000	18148
United Convalescent Facilities	8059	D	213 748-0491	18156
Alta Healthcare System LLC (HQ)	8062	C	323 267-0477	18173
Califrnia Hosp Med Ctr Fndtion	8062	A	213 742-5867	18194
Cedars-Sinai Medical Center	8062	B	310 824-3664	18197
Cedars-Sinai Medical Center	8062	C	310 423-6451	18200
Cedars-Sinai Medical Center	8062	C	310 423-2587	18201
Cedars-Sinai Medical Center	8062	B	310 423-8965	18202
Cedars-Sinai Medical Center	8062	C	310 423-3277	18207
Cedars-Sinai Medical Center	8062	C	310 423-9520	18208
Childrens Hospital Los Angeles	8062	A	323 361-2751	18216
County of Los Angeles	8062	B	310 668-4545	18232
County of Los Angeles	8062	C	323 226-6021	18233
County of Los Angeles	8062	C	213 473-6100	18234
East Los Angles Dctors Hosp In	8062	B		18247
Hollywood Cmnty Hosp Med Ctr I	8062	C	323 462-2271	18286
Hollywood Medical Center LP	8062	A	213 413-3000	18287
Jupiter Bellflower Doctors Hospital	8062	B		18293
Kaiser Foundation Hospitals	8062	C	323 783-4011	18295
Kaiser Permanente Watts C	8062	D	323 564-7911	18311
Keck Hospital of Usc	8062	A	800 872-2273	18312
Keck School	8062	D	323 442-1179	18313
LA Metropolitan Medical Center	8062	A	323 730-7300	18318
Lac Usc County Hospital	8062	D	323 226-2622	18320
Lac Usc Medical Center	8062	C		18321
Memorial Hospital of Gardena	8062	B	323 268-5514	18344
Nix Hospitals System LLC (HQ)	8062	C	210 271-1800	18351
Olympia Health Care LLC	8062	A	323 938-3161	18353
Orthopaedic Hospital (PA)	8062	C	213 742-1000	18357
Pamc Ltd (PA)	8062	A	213 624-8411	18369
Paraclsus Los Angles Cmnty Hos	8062	C	323 267-0477	18370
Pih Health Good Samaritan Hosp (HQ)	8062	A	213 977-2121	18378
Southern Cal Halthcare Sys Inc (HQ)	8062	C	310 943-4500	18448
Temple Hospital Corporation	8062	B	213 355-3200	18471
Tenet Health Systems Norris	8062	C	323 865-3000	18472
Tustin Hospital and Medical Center	8062	B	714 619-7700	18481
University Cal Los Angeles	8062	A	310 825-9111	18483
University Southern California	8062	A	323 442-8500	18491
White Memorial Medical Center (HQ)	8062	A	323 268-5000	18501
Gateways Hosp Mental Hlth Ctr (PA)	8063	C	323 644-2000	18513
Kaiser Foundation Hospitals	8063	C	213 580-7200	18514
Kedren Community Hlth Ctr Inc (PA)	8063	B	323 233-0425	18515
Barlow Group (PA)	8069	C	213 250-4200	18520
Barlow Respiratory Hospital (PA)	8069	C	213 250-4200	18522
Childrens Hospital Los Angeles (PA)	8069	A	323 660-2450	18524
County of Los Angeles	8069	C	323 226-3468	18525
Shields For Families (PA)	8069	D	323 242-5000	18533
Radnet Inc (PA)	8071	A	310 478-7808	18562
Samaritan Imaging Center	8071	A	213 977-2140	18563
Clinics On Demand Inc	8082	C	310 709-7355	18602
Livhome Inc (PA)	8082	A	800 807-5854	18625
Maxim Healthcare Services Inc	8082	B	866 465-5678	18626
Ucla Health Auxiliary	8082	A	310 267-4327	18647
Amanecer Cmnty Cnsling Svc A N	8093	D	213 481-7464	18668
Behavioral Learning Netwrk LLC	8093	D	310 871-6800	18671
Brand Therapy LLC	8093	D	415 336-6411	18674
Comprehensive Cancer Centers Inc	8093	C	323 966-3400	18682
County of Los Angeles	8093	B	323 897-6187	18684
Evolve Treatment Centers	8093	D	310 622-1420	18692
Planned Parenthood Los Angeles (PA)	8093	D	213 284-3200	18707
South Baylo University	8093	C	213 999-0297	18717
United Amrcn Indian Invlvment (PA)	8093	D	213 202-3970	18728
Altamed Health Services Corp	8099	C	323 307-0400	18739
Camden Center Inc	8099	D	310 526-3807	18751
Drip Hydration	8099	D	323 333-9634	18759
Los Angles Cnty Dvlpmntal Svcs	8099	C	213 383-1300	18778
Martin Lther King Jr-Los Angle	8099	B	424 338-8000	18779
Public Hlth Fndation Entps Inc	8099	C	323 261-6388	18795
Public Hlth Fndation Entps Inc	8099	C	323 733-9381	18797
Targeted Medical Pharma Inc	8099	F	310 474-9809	18811
A Buchalter Professional Corp (PA)	8111	C	213 891-0700	18817
Allen Mtkins Leck Gmble Mllory (PA)	8111	C	213 622-5555	18819
Arnold Porter Kaye Scholer LLP	8111	D	213 243-4000	18820
Austin Sidley CA LLP	8111	C	213 896-6000	18822
Baker & Hostetler LLP	8111	D	310 820-8800	18823
Baker & McKenzie LLP	8111	C	310 201-4728	18825
Barnes & Thornburg LLP	8111	C	310 284-3880	18826
Barnes Firm LC	8111	D	800 800-0000	18827
Blakely Sokoloff Taylor & Zafman LLP	8111	C	310 207-3800	18829
Bonne Brdges Mller Okefe Nchol (PA)	8111	D	213 480-1900	18831
Burke Williams & Sorensen LLP (PA)	8111	D	213 236-0600	18832
County of Los Angeles	8111	C	213 974-3512	18840
Covington & Burling LLP	8111	C	424 332-4800	18843
Cox Castle & Nicholson LLP (PA)	8111	C	310 284-2200	18844
Crowell & Moring LLP	8111	C	213 622-4750	18846
Davis Wright Tremaine LLP	8111	C	213 633-6800	18847
Dentons US LLP	8111	C	213 623-9300	18848
Dla Piper LLP (us)	8111	C	310 595-3000	18849
Dominguez Law Group PC	8111	D	213 388-7788	18850
Elkins Kalt Wntraub Rben Grtsi	8111	D	310 746-4431	18851
Ellis Grge Cpllone Obrien Anng	8111	D	310 274-7100	18852
Epstein Becker & Green PC	8111	C	310 556-8861	18853
Gibson Dunn & Crutcher Inc	8111	C	213 229-7000	18857
Gibson Dunn & Crutcher LLP (PA)	8111	B	213 229-7000	18858
Gibson Dunn & Crutcher LLP	8111	C	310 552-8500	18859
Girardi Keese (PA)	8111	D	213 977-0211	18861
Glaser Weil Fink Jacobs (PA)	8111	C	310 553-3000	18862
Gordon Rees Scully Mansukhani	8111	C	213 576-5000	18863
Greenberg Glsker Flds Clman Mc	8111	C	310 553-3610	18865
Haight Brown & Bonesteel LLP (PA)	8111	D	213 542-8000	18867
Hill Farrer & Burrill	8111	D	213 620-0460	18869
Holland & Knight LLP	8111	C	213 896-2400	18870
Hueston Hennigan LLP	8111	D	213 788-4340	18871
Imhoff & Associates PC	8111	D	310 691-2200	18872
Immigrant Defenders Law Center	8111	D	213 634-0999	18873
Irell & Manella LLP (PA)	8111	C	310 277-1010	18875
Jackoway Tyrman Wrthmer Asten	8111	C	310 553-0305	18876
Jacoby & Meyers Attys LLP	8111	C	310 312-3300	18877
Jeffer Mngels Btlr Mtchell LLP (PA)	8111	C	310 203-8080	18878
Jones Day Limited Partnership	8111	C	213 489-3939	18879
K&L Gates LLP	8111	D	310 552-5000	18880
Kirkland & Ellis LLP	8111	C	310 552-4200	18882
Kirkland & Ellis LLP	8111	D	213 680-8400	18883
Kirkland & Ellis LLP	8111	B	213 680-8400	18884
Knight Law Group LLP	8111	D	424 355-1155	18885

	SIC	EMP	PHONE	ENTRY#
La Folette Johnson Dehass Sesl	8111	D	213 426-3600	18887
Latham & Watkins LLP	8111	B	213 891-7108	18889
Latham & Watkins LLP **(PA)**	8111	A	213 485-1234	18891
Lewis Brsbois Bsgard Smith LLP **(PA)**	8111	A	213 250-1800	18896
Liner LLP	8111	C	310 500-3500	18898
LLP Mayer Brown	8111	B	213 229-9500	18900
Loeb & Loeb LLP **(PA)**	8111	C	310 282-2000	18901
Manatt Phelps & Phillips LLP **(PA)**	8111	B	310 312-4000	18903
Manning Kass Ellrod Rmrez Trst **(PA)**	8111	C	213 624-6900	18904
Milbank Tweed Hdley McCloy LLP	8111	C	424 386-4000	18907
Mitchell Silberberg Knupp LLP **(PA)**	8111	C	310 312-2000	18909
Morris Polich & Purdy LLP **(PA)**	8111	D	213 891-9100	18910
Morrison & Foerster LLP	8111	C	213 892-5200	18911
Munger Tolles & Olson LLP	8111	B	213 683-9100	18913
Munger Tolles Olson Foundation **(PA)**	8111	B	213 683-9100	18914
Murchison & Cumming LLP **(PA)**	8111	D	213 623-7400	18915
Musick Peeler & Garrett LLP **(PA)**	8111	C	213 629-7600	18916
OMelveny & Myers LLP **(PA)**	8111	A	213 430-6000	18919
Pachulski Stang Zehl Jones LLP **(PA)**	8111	D	310 277-6910	18920
Paul Hastings LLP **(PA)**	8111	A	213 683-6000	18922
Pillsbury Wnthrop Shaw Pttman	8111	C	213 488-7100	18924
Pircher Nichols & Meeks LLP	8111	D	310 201-0132	18925
Public Counsel	8111	D	213 385-2977	18929
Quinn Emnuel Urqhart Sllvan LL **(PA)**	8111	B	213 443-3000	18930
Reed Smith LLP	8111	C	213 457-8000	18931
Richards Wtson Grshon A Prof C **(PA)**	8111	C	213 626-8484	18932
Ropers Majeski A Prof Corp.	8111	C	213 312-2000	18934
Russ August & Kabat LLP	8111	D	310 826-7474	18935
Saul Ewing Arnstein & Lehr LLP	8111	D	310 398-6100	18937
Seyfarth Shaw LLP	8111	C	310 277-7200	18940
Sheppard Mllin Rchter Hmpton L **(PA)**	8111	B	213 620-1780	18943
Skadden Arps Slate Meagher & F	8111	C	213 687-5000	18946
Stroock & Stroock & Lavan LLP	8111	C	310 556-5800	18950
Troygould PC	8111	D	310 553-4441	18953
White & Case LLP	8111	C	213 620-7724	18956
Ziffren B B F G-L S&C Fnd.	8111	C	310 552-3388	18961
Vista Del Mar Child Fmly Svcs **(PA)**	8211	B	310 836-1223	18986
West Angeles Ch God In Chrst.	8211	C	323 731-2567	18987
Associated Students UCLA	8221	C	310 206-8282	18989
Los Angeles Unified School Dst.	8221	D	213 763-2900	18990
University Cal Los Angeles.	8221	D	310 825-7852	18993
The Coding Source LLC.	8249	C	866 235-7553	19005
Greenwood Hall Inc	8299	C	310 905-8300	19010
Southern Cal Prmnnte Med Group.	8299	C	323 564-7911	19014
Aids Project Los Angeles **(PA)**	8322	C	213 201-1600	19017
American National Red Cross	8322	C	310 445-9900	19020
American Red Cross Los Angles **(PA)**	8322	C	310 445-9900	19021
Aviva Family & Childrens Svcs **(PA)**	8322	D	323 876-0550	19025
Blc Residential Care Inc	8322	D	310 722-7541	19029
Braille Institute America Inc **(PA)**	8322	C	323 663-1111	19030
Childrens Bureau Southern Cal	8322	C	213 342-0100	19042
Childrens Inst Los Angeles.	8322	A	213 383-2765	19043
Childrens Institute Inc **(PA)**	8322	C	213 385-5100	19044
Core Cmnty Orgnzed Rlief Effor.	8322	B	323 934-4400	19051
County of Los Angeles.	8322	D	213 974-9331	19058
County of Los Angeles.	8322	D	323 226-8511	19060
County of Los Angeles.	8322	C	323 780-2185	19063
County of Los Angeles.	8322	C	213 351-7257	19064
Crystal Stairs Inc **(PA)**	8322	B	323 299-8998	19069
East Los Angles Rmrkble Ctzens.	8322	D	323 223-3079	19073
First 5 La.	8322	C	213 482-5920	19081
Homeboy Industries **(PA)**	8322	B	323 526-1254	19090
International Medical Corps **(PA)**	8322	A	310 826-7800	19098
Jewish Family Svc Los Angeles.	8322	C	323 937-5900	19101
Jvs Socal.	8322	C	323 761-8879	19104
Kedren Community Hlth Ctr Inc.	8322	C	323 524-0634	19106
La Asccion Ncnal Pro Prsnas My.	8322	A	213 202-5900	19107
Los Angeles Homeless Svcs Auth.	8322	A	213 683-3333	19110
New Directions Inc **(PA)**	8322	D	310 914-4045	19117
Path.	8322	A	323 644-2216	19122
Prototypes Centers For Innov.	8322	C	213 542-3838	19129
Sexual Recovery Institute Inc.	8322	B	310 360-0130	19140
Volunteers of Amer Los Angeles.	8322	C	213 749-0362	19157
Volunteers of Amer Los Angeles.	8322	C	323 780-3770	19158
Volunteers of Amer Los Angeles.	8322	C	213 627-8002	19164
Watts Labor Community Action.	8322	C	323 563-5639	19167
Weingart Center Association.	8322	C	213 622-6359	19168
Wellnest Emtonal Hlth Wellness **(PA)**	8322	C	323 373-2400	19169
Asian Rehabilitation Svc Inc.	8331	C	213 680-3790	19175
Chinatown Service Center **(PA)**	8331	D	213 808-1701	19180
Exceptional Chld Foundation.	8331	C	213 748-3556	19183
Pacific Asian Cnsrtium In Empl **(PA)**	8331	C	213 353-3982	19191
Special Service For Groups Inc **(PA)**	8331	D	213 368-1888	19192
California Childrens Academy	8351	C	323 263-3846	19201
Carousel Child Care Corp.	8351	C	310 216-6641	19203
County of Los Angeles	8361	D	323 226-8611	19254
Covenant House California	8361	C	323 461-3131	19255
Hamburger Home **(PA)**	8361	D	323 876-0550	19265
Hathaway-Sycmres Child Fmly Svc.	8361	D	323 257-9600	19267
Lamp Inc.	8361	C	213 488-9559	19278
Sisters of Nzareth Los Angeles	8361	D	310 839-2361	19300
Solheim Lutheran Home.	8361	C	323 257-7518	19301
St Annes Family Services.	8361	C	213 381-2931	19302
Associated Students UCLA **(PA)**	8399	B	310 794-8836	19315
Associated Students UCLA.	8399	C	310 794-0242	19316
California Endowment **(PA)**	8399	C	213 928-8800	19318
Community Partners **(PA)**	8399	D	213 346-3200	19323
Essential Access Health **(PA)**	8399	D	213 386-5614	19325
Greater Los Angeles Zoo Assn.	8399	C	323 644-4200	19326
Interntnal Fndtion For Krea Un.	8399	B	213 550-2182	19329
Los Angeles Lgbt Center **(PA)**	8399	C	323 993-7618	19335
South Cntl Los Angles Rgnal CT **(PA)**	8399	C	213 744-7000	19342
South Cntl Los Angles Rgnal CT.	8399	C	231 744-8484	19343
Special Service For Groups Inc **(PA)**	8399	C	213 553-1800	19345
United Way Inc **(PA)**	8399	D	213 808-6220	19346
Westside Jewish Cmnty Ctr Inc **(PA)**	8399	C	323 938-2531	19347
Academy Museum Motion Pictures.	8412	C	310 247-3000	19348
Armand Hmmer Mseum of Art Cltr.	8412	C	310 443-7000	19349
Autry Museum of American West.	8412	C	323 667-2000	19350
Califrnia Scnce Ctr Foundation	8412	B	213 744-2545	19352
Los Angeles Cnty Mseum of Art.	8412	B	323 857-6000	19355
Museum Associates	8412	C	323 857-6172	19356
Museum of Contemporary Art **(PA)**	8412	C	213 626-6222	19357
Skirball Cultural Center.	8412	C	310 440-4500	19364
The J Paul Getty Trust **(PA)**	8412	A	310 440-7300	19365
California Assn Realtors Inc **(PA)**	8611	C	213 739-8200	19374
California RE Assn Inc.	8611	D	213 739-8200	19375
Los Angles Area Chmber Cmmerce.	8611	D	213 580-7500	19380
Attainment Holdco LLC.	8621	C	310 954-1578	19390
Cooprtive Amrcn Physcians Inc **(PA)**	8621	C	213 473-8600	19393
County of Los Angeles.	8621	C	213 240-8412	19394
Los Angeles County Bar Assn **(PA)**	8621	C	213 627-2727	19396
State Bar of California.	8621	C	213 765-1520	19405
Truck Underwriters Association **(DH)**	8621	A	323 932-3200	19406
Seiu Local 721	8631	C	213 368-8660	19412
Southwest Crpnters Trning Fund.	8631	D	213 386-8590	19414
Writers Guild America West Inc.	8631	C	323 951-4000	19419
California Club.	8641	C	213 622-1391	19431
Catholic Education Founda.	8641	D	213 637-7475	19432
Greater Los Angles Area Cncil **(PA)**	8641	D	213 413-4400	19449
Jewish Cmnty Fndtion Los Angle **(PA)**	8641	C	323 761-8700	19450
Jonathan Club **(PA)**	8641	C	213 624-0881	19451
La County Sheriff PDC No.	8641	C	661 294-6312	19452
Public Hlth Fndation Entps Inc.	8641	C	323 263-0262	19459
Young MNS Chrstn Assn Mtro Los.	8641	C	323 467-4161	19494
Young Wns Chrstn Assn Grter Lo.	8641	C	323 295-4288	19497
Young Wns Chrstn Assn Grter Lo.	8641	C	323 295-4280	19498
Crenshaw Chrstn Ctr Ch Los Ang **(PA)**	8661	B	323 758-3777	19499
Hospitller Order of St John Go.	8661	B	323 731-0641	19501
Interntnal Ch of Frsqare Gospl **(PA)**	8661	D	714 701-1818	19502
Self-Realization Fellowship Ch **(PA)**	8661	E	323 225-2471	19505
Sinai Temple **(PA)**	8661	B	310 474-1518	19506
Best Friends Animal Society.	8699	C	818 643-3989	19526
Los Angeles Mem Coliseum Comm.	8699	B	213 747-7111	19531
Play Versus Inc.	8699	D	949 636-4193	19533
Arup North America Limited.	8711	C	310 578-4182	19549
Fire Protection Group Amer Inc.	8711	E	323 732-4200	19588
Flint Energy Services Inc.	8711	C	213 593-8000	19589
Fti Consulting Inc.	8711	D	213 689-1200	19596
Linquest Corporation **(PA)**	8711	C	323 924-1600	19639
Sia Engineering (usa) Inc.	8711	C	310 957-2928	19690
Aecom Services Inc **(HQ)**	8712	C	213 593-8000	19722
Dlr Group Inc **(HQ)**	8712	C	213 800-9400	19727
Gehry Partners LLP.	8712	C	310 482-3000	19728
Hellmuth Obata & Kassabaum Inc.	8712	D	310 838-9555	19731
Johnson Fain Inc.	8712	D	323 224-6000	19733
M Arthur Gensler Jr Assoc Inc.	8712	C	213 927-3600	19737
Martin AC Partners Inc.	8712	C	213 683-1900	19738
Stv Architects Inc.	8712	C	213 482-9444	19744
Zimmer Gnsul Frsca Archtcts LL.	8712	C	213 617-1901	19748
Psomas.	8713	C	213 223-1400	19750
Armanino LLP.	8721	B	310 478-4148	19751
Baker Tilly Us LLP.	8721	A	310 826-4474	19753
Cliftonlarsonallen LLP.	8721	D	310 273-2501	19761
County of Los Angeles.	8721	A	323 267-2136	19764
Deloitte & Touche LLP.	8721	A	213 688-0800	19767

Mergent email: customerrelations@mergent.com
1400

2024 Southern California
Business Directory and Buyers Guide

(P-0000) Products & Services Section entry number
(PA)=Parent Co (HQ)=Headquarters (DH)=Div Headquarters

	SIC	EMP	PHONE	ENTRY#
Deloitte Tax LLP	8721	C	404 885-6754	19769
Ernst & Young LLP	8721	A	213 977-3200	19774
Film Payroll Services Inc (PA)	8721	D	310 440-9600	19776
Green Hasson & Janks LLP	8721	C	310 873-1600	19777
Gursey Schneider & Co LLC (PA)	8721	C	310 552-0960	19778
Holthouse Carlin Van Trigt LLP (PA)	8721	C	310 566-1900	19780
Macias Gini & OConnell LLP	8721	C	213 408-8700	19791
Macias Gini & OConnell LLP	8721	C	323 653-8300	19792
Macias Gini & OConnell LLP	8721	C	916 928-4600	19793
Pricewaterhousecoopers LLP	8721	C	213 356-6000	19802
Rbz LLP	8721	C	310 478-4148	19803
Singerlewak LLP (PA)	8721	C	310 477-3924	19805
Aerospace Corporation	8731	D	310 336-7270	19813
Environmental Science Assoc	8731	C	213 599-4300	19836
Myst Therapeutics Inc	8731	D	415 516-8450	19862
Material Holdings LLC (PA)	8732	C	310 553-0550	19906
National Research Group Inc	8732	B	323 406-6200	19907
Orange Cnty Nrpsychtric RES CT	8732	D	213 992-9216	19909
Prosearch Strategies LLC	8732	C	877 447-7291	19910
Streamelements Inc	8732	C	323 928-7848	19913
Zefr Inc	8732	B	310 392-3555	19916
Brentwood Bmdical RES Inst Inc	8733	C	310 312-1554	19919
Childrens Inst Los Angeles (PA)	8733	C	213 385-5100	19923
House Research Institute	8733	C	213 353-7012	19928
County of Los Angeles	8734	C	323 267-6167	19966
Ellison Institute LLC (PA)	8734	C	310 228-6400	19970
National Genetics Institute	8734	C	310 996-6610	19978
AEG Management Lacc LLC	8741	C	213 741-1151	19989
Ajit Healthcare Inc	8741	D	213 484-0510	19990
Bon Appetit Management Co	8741	C	310 440-6209	20004
Bon Appetit Management Co	8741	C	310 440-6052	20005
Cal State La Univ Aux Svcs Inc	8741	A	323 343-2531	20009
Chan Family Partnership LP	8741	D	626 322-7132	20012
Country Villa Service Corp	8741	C	323 734-9122	20016
Country Villa Service Corp	8741	C	323 666-1544	20017
Country Villa Service Corp	8741	C	323 734-1101	20020
Far East National Bank	8741	B	213 687-1300	20030
Firstsrvice Rsidential Cal LLC	8741	C	213 213-0886	20032
Hotchkis Wiley Capitl MGT LLC (PA)	8741	C	213 430-1000	20038
Keiro Services	8741	B	213 873-5700	20048
La 1000 Santa Fe LLC	8741	C	213 205-1000	20049
Los Angeles Rams LLC	8741	C	310 277-4700	20057
Network Management Group Inc (PA)	8741	C	323 263-2632	20068
Onni Properties LLC	8741	C	213 568-0278	20071
Relocity Inc	8741	C	323 207-9160	20088
Snf Management	8741	D	310 385-1090	20095
SunAmerica Investments Inc (DH)	8741	C	310 772-6000	20101
Tripalink Corp	8741	C	323 717-9139	20109
Zero Gravity Management	8741	D	310 656-9440	20122
Alvarez Mrsal Bus Cnslting LLC	8742	D	310 975-2600	20129
Bain & Company Inc	8742	C	310 229-3000	20138
Cashmere Agency Inc	8742	C	323 928-5080	20147
Catalyst Speech LLC	8742	B	213 346-9945	20148
Diagnostic Health Corporation	8742	C	310 665-7180	20163
Egon Zehnder International	8742	C	213 337-1500	20167
Hatchbeauty Agency LLC (PA)	8742	E	310 396-7070	20179
Heidelberg Investment Group In	8742	C	213 884-7747	20181
Korn Ferry (us) (HQ)	8742	C	310 552-1834	20188
Northgate Gonzalez Inc	8742	B	323 262-0595	20210
NVE Inc	8742	D	323 512-8400	20211
Octagon Inc	8742	C	310 967-2473	20212
Powersource Talent LLC	8742	C	424 835-0878	20224
PWC STRategy& (us) LLC	8742	C	213 356-6000	20225
Rocky Point Investments LLC (HQ)	8742	C	310 482-6500	20232
Saban Brands LLC (HQ)	8742	D	310 557-5230	20233
Shein Technology LLC (PA)	8742	B	213 628-4008	20235
Smith-Emery International Inc (PA)	8742	C	213 741-8500	20242
Sodexo Management Inc	8742	A	310 646-3738	20243
Spotify USA Inc	8742	C	213 505-3040	20245
Stone Canyon Inds Holdings LLC (PA)	8742	D	424 316-2061	20249
Thomas St John Inc	8742	D	424 273-1172	20260
Titanum Health Care	8742	D	213 765-8123	20261
Wasserman Media Group LLC (PA)	8742	C	310 407-0200	20270
Wellmade Inc	8742	C	213 221-1123	20272
Swiss Port Corp	8744	B	310 417-0258	20300
Aecom Technical Services Inc (HQ)	8748	D	213 593-8100	20307
Aecom Usa Inc	8748	D	213 593-8000	20309
Aecom Usa Inc	8748	D	213 330-7200	20310
Ankura Consulting Group LLC	8748	C	213 223-2109	20314
Broadband Telecom Inc	8748	C	818 450-5714	20320
Cal Southern Assn Governments (PA)	8748	C	213 236-1800	20323
Cdsnet LLC	8748	B	310 981-9500	20325
Deloitte Consulting LLP	8748	B	212 489-1600	20331

	SIC	EMP	PHONE	ENTRY#
Lusive Decor	8748	D	323 227-9207	20361
Pcs Link Inc	8748	B	949 655-5000	20371
Yucaipa Companies LLC (PA)	8748	C	310 789-7200	20392
Essense	8999	A	323 202-4650	20395
Los Angles Cnty Mseum Ntral Hs (PA)	9111	C	213 763-3466	20406
County of Los Angeles	9431	C	213 738-4601	20414

LOS OLIVOS, CA - Santa Barbara County

	SIC	EMP	PHONE	ENTRY#
Beckmen Vineyards	0172	E	805 688-8664	29
Firestone Vineyard LP	2084	D	805 688-3940	1628
Cushman Winery Corporation	5182	E	805 688-9339	13475

LOS OSOS, CA - San Luis Obispo County

	SIC	EMP	PHONE	ENTRY#
Rantec Power Systems Inc (HQ)	5065	D	805 596-6000	12694

LOST HILLS, CA - Kern County

	SIC	EMP	PHONE	ENTRY#
Wonderful Orchards LLC	0173	B	661 797-6400	39
Roll Properties Intl Inc	6799	C	661 797-6500	15049

LUCERNE VALLEY, CA - San Bernardino County

	SIC	EMP	PHONE	ENTRY#
Omya California Inc	2819	D	760 248-7306	3901
Omya Inc	2819	D	760 248-5200	3902
Specialty Minerals Inc	2819	C	760 248-5300	3915
Mitsubishi Cement Corporation	3241	C	760 248-7373	5368
Casa Clina Hosp Ctrs For Hlthc	8322	C	760 248-6245	19032

LYNWOOD, CA - Los Angeles County

	SIC	EMP	PHONE	ENTRY#
Hgc Holdings Inc	2064	E	323 567-2226	1541
First Finish Inc	2211	E	310 631-6717	2021
Aaron Corporation	2339	C	323 235-5959	2297
Kayo of California (PA)	2339	E	323 233-6107	2340
Roger R Caruso Enterprises Inc	2448	E	714 778-6006	2724
Amerasia Furn Cmpnnts Mfg Impr	2512	E	310 638-0570	2794
Gomen Furniture Mfg Inc	2512	E	310 635-4894	2803
Golden Mattress Co Inc	2515	D	323 887-1888	2851
Next Day Frame Inc	2519	E	310 886-0851	2872
P & L Development LLC	2834	C	323 567-2482	4192
Rangers Die Casting Co	3363	E	310 764-1800	5767
Metal Improvement Company LLC	3398	D	323 585-2168	5843
Bleeker Brothers Inc1	3444	E	310 639-4367	6202
Tjs Metal Manufacturing Inc	3446	E	310 604-1545	6372
Bowman-Field Inc	3471	D	310 638-8519	6595
Triumph Processing Inc	3471	C	323 563-1338	6675
Processes By Martin Inc	3479	C	310 637-1855	6729
Therm-O-Namel Inc	3479	E	310 631-7866	6742
Ace Machine Shop Inc	3599	D	310 608-2277	7732
Pacific Ltg & Standards Co	3646	E	310 603-9344	8326
Midas Express Los Angeles Inc	4225	C	310 609-0366	11598
Earle M Jorgensen Company (HQ)	5051	C	323 567-1122	12549
Altamed Health Services Corp	8011	C	310 632-0415	17587
Southern CA Hlth & Rhbltn Prg	8011	D	310 631-8004	17771
Southern Cal Prmnnte Med Group	8011	C	810 604-5700	17780
Country Villa Service Corp	8051	C	310 537-2500	17915
Marlinda Management Inc (PA)	8059	C	310 631-6122	18144
St Francis Medical Center (DH)	8062	C	310 900-8900	18460
South Cntl Hlth Rhbltition Prgr	8093	D	310 667-4070	18718
Baymark Health Services La Inc	8099	C	310 761-4762	18744
Lynwood Unified School Dst	8211	D	310 631-7308	18975
Jwch Institute Inc	8322	C	310 223-1035	19105

LYTLE CREEK, CA - San Bernardino County

	SIC	EMP	PHONE	ENTRY#
Inland Pacific Coatings Inc	3479	E	909 822-0594	6709
Burlingame Industries Inc	7033	C	909 887-7038	15440

MALIBU, CA - Los Angeles County

	SIC	EMP	PHONE	ENTRY#
Kor Shots Inc	2037	E	805 351-0700	1373
Malibu Times Inc	2711	F	310 456-5507	3301
Curtco Robb Media LLC (PA)	2721	E	310 589-7700	3353
Robb Curtco Media LLC	2721	E	310 589-7700	3386
Robb Report Collection	2721	E	310 589-7700	3387
County of Los Angeles	3531	E	310 456-8014	6930
Road Champs Inc	3944	C	310 456-7799	10965
Toymax International Inc (HQ)	3944	D	310 456-7799	10967
Westmed Ambulance Inc	4119	C	310 456-3830	11410
Cco Holdings LLC	4841	C	310 589-3008	11972
Malibu Conference Center Inc	6512	B	818 889-6440	14672
Credibility Corp	7389	A	310 456-8271	16811
Passages Malibu	8093	A	888 777-8525	18705
Grasshopper House Partners LLC	8322	C	310 589-2880	19085
Hrl Laboratories LLC	8732	A	310 317-5000	19898

MANHATTAN BEACH, CA - Los Angeles County

	SIC	EMP	PHONE	ENTRY#
Ebc Inc (PA)	1521	D	310 753-6407	430

Employee Codes: A=Over 500 employees, B=251-500
C=101-250, D=51-100, E=20-50, F=10-19, G=1-9

2024 Southern California
Business Directory and Buyers Guide

© Mergent Inc. 1-800-342-5647

1401

GEOGRAPHIC

	SIC	EMP	PHONE	ENTRY#
Stanton Carpet Corp.	2273	E	562 945-8711	2121
Trlg Corporate Holdings LLC **(PA)**	2369	D	323 266-3072	2419
Wave Community Newspapers Inc **(PA)**	2711	E	323 290-3000	3336
Skechers Collection LLC	3021	E	310 318-3100	4707
Skechers USA Inc **(PA)**	3149	C	310 318-3100	5281
De Nora Water Technologies LLC	3589	F	310 618-9700	7653
Fisker Group Inc **(HQ)**	3711	E	833 434-7537	9286
Fisker Inc **(PA)**	3711	E	833 434-7537	9287
Enersponse Inc	3825	C	949 829-3901	10196
Fox US Productions 27 Inc	4833	C	310 727-2550	11952
I Brands LLC	5083	C	424 336-5216	12781
Trlggc Services LLC	5136	B	323 266-3072	13115
Tone It Up Inc	5499	E	310 376-7645	13733
Skechers USA Inc II	5661	A	800 746-3411	13925
Wells Fargo Investments LLC	6021	D	310 546-4235	14176
Kinecta Federal Credit Union **(PA)**	6061	C	310 643-5400	14229
Coverance Insur Solutions Inc	6411	C	310 856-9925	14580
Palm Realty Boutique Inc	6531	D	310 545-2490	14840
Oka & Oka Hawaii LLC	7011	E	808 329-1393	15272
Sunstone Hotel Properties Inc	7011	C	310 546-7627	15380
Distillery Tech Inc	7371	C	310 776-6234	16017
Solartis LLC	7371	E	310 251-4861	16120
Stemconnector LLC	7379	E	424 543-4074	16602
1334 Partners LP	7997	C	310 546-5656	17457
Kaiser Foundation Hospitals	8062	C	310 937-4311	18294
Torrance Memorial Medical Ctr	8062	B	310 939-7847	18477
Automobile Club Southern Cal	8699	C	310 376-0521	19525
M & E Technical Services L L C	8744	D	256 964-6486	20295
Jag Professional Services Inc	8748	C	310 945-5648	20355
Network Sltons Prvider USA Inc	8748	E	213 985-2173	20366

MARICOPA, CA - Kern County

	SIC	EMP	PHONE	ENTRY#
Aera Energy Services Company	1381	C	661 665-3200	276
Calmat Co	1422	C	661 858-2673	399
Nestle Purina Petcare Company	2047	C	661 769-8261	1436

MARINA DEL REY, CA - Los Angeles County

	SIC	EMP	PHONE	ENTRY#
Lf Sportswear Inc **(PA)**	2331	E	310 437-4100	2253
Tokyopop Inc **(PA)**	2731	D	323 920-5967	3418
Armata Pharmaceuticals Inc **(PA)**	2836	C	310 665-2928	4300
Dr Squatch LLC	2844	C	631 229-7068	4407
Ace Iron Inc	3446	E	510 324-3300	6348
Dollar Shave Club Inc **(HQ)**	3541	C	310 975-8528	7010
Sewer Rodding Equipment Co **(PA)**	3589	C	310 301-9009	7684
Eti Partners IV LLC	3672	E	949 273-4990	8673
Executive Network Entps Inc **(PA)**	4119	D	310 447-2759	11383
Bouqs Company	5193	D	888 320-2687	13504
Gelsons Markets	5411	D	310 306-3192	13699
Marina City Club LP A Cali	6513	C	310 822-0611	14726
Laaco Ltd **(HQ)**	6519	C	213 622-1254	14738
Ylopo LLC	6531	C	818 915-9150	14887
Steelwave LLC	6552	A	310 821-1111	14912
Apotheka Systems Inc	7372	E	844 777-4455	16168
Springcoin Inc	7372	D	847 322-6349	16388
Telesign Holdings Inc **(DH)**	7372	E	310 740-9700	16399
Survios Inc	7373	E	310 736-1503	16472
Modern Parking Inc	7521	C	310 821-1081	16994
EZ Lube LLC	7549	C	310 821-2517	17056
Deluxe Nms Inc	7822	C	310 760-8500	17276
Diagnstic Intrvntnal Srgcal CT	8011	D	310 574-0400	17645
Cfhs Holdings Inc	8062	A	310 823-8911	18213
Cfhs Holdings Inc	8062	A	310 448-7800	18214
USA Travel Services LLC	8699	A	207 899-8803	19536
Usc Information Sciences Inst	8733	C	310 448-9438	19951

MAYWOOD, CA - Los Angeles County

	SIC	EMP	PHONE	ENTRY#
Kitchen Cuts LLC	2013	D	323 560-7415	1222
KSM Garment Inc	2331	E	323 585-8811	2250
Ev R Inc	2339	E	323 312-5400	2322
Sonora Face Co	2435	E	323 560-8188	2691
Gemini Film & Bag Inc **(PA)**	3089	E	323 582-0901	5036
Heritage Leather Company Inc	3111	E	323 983-0420	5257
Cook Induction Heating Co Inc	3398	C	323 560-1327	5834
Signresource LLC **(DH)**	3993	C	323 771-2098	11163
Tapia Enterprises Inc **(PA)**	5141	D	323 560-7415	13237
R G Canning Enterprises Inc	7389	C	323 560-7469	16912

MC FARLAND, CA - Kern County

	SIC	EMP	PHONE	ENTRY#
Jakov Dulcich and Sons LLC	0172	C	661 792-6360	33
Aptco **(PA)**	2821	D	661 792-2107	3924
Amaretto Orchards LLC	3999	E	661 399-9697	11188
A G Hacienda Incorporated	4212	B	661 792-2418	11437

MC KITTRICK, CA - Kern County

	SIC	EMP	PHONE	ENTRY#
Wonderful Orchards LLC	0173	D	661 797-2509	40
Aera Energy LLC	1311	D	661 334-3100	244
California Resources Prod Corp	1311	E	661 869-8000	256
Aera Energy Services Company	1381	C	661 665-4400	275

MECCA, CA - Riverside County

	SIC	EMP	PHONE	ENTRY#
Kerry Inc	2023	D	760 396-2116	1274
Califrnia Nutritional Pdts Inc	2043	D	760 485-3000	1419
Western Environmental Inc	3822	E	760 396-0222	10109

MENIFEE, CA - Riverside County

	SIC	EMP	PHONE	ENTRY#
Davids Natural Toothpaste Inc	2844	E	949 933-1185	4399
Big Brand Tire & Service	3011	D	951 679-6266	4693
Datatronics Romoland Inc	3612	D	951 928-7700	8093
Grove Lumber & Bldg Sups Inc **(PA)**	5031	C	909 947-0277	12331
Tea Financial Services	5091	E	951 301-8884	12932
Lowes Home Centers LLC	5211	D	951 723-1930	13659
City of Menifee	8741	D	951 672-6777	20014

MENTONE, CA - San Bernardino County

	SIC	EMP	PHONE	ENTRY#
International Paving Svcs Inc	1611	D	909 794-2101	626
Bausman and Company Inc **(PA)**	2521	C	909 947-0139	2878
Bristol Omega Inc	2541	E	909 794-6862	2945
Power Pt Inc **(PA)**	3537	C	951 490-4149	6996
Marwell Corporation	3613	F	909 794-4192	8125

MIRA LOMA, CA - Riverside County

	SIC	EMP	PHONE	ENTRY#
Prevost Car (us) Inc	5013	C	951 360-2550	12253
DC Shoes Inc	5137	E	951 361-7712	13122

MISSION HILLS, CA - Los Angeles County

	SIC	EMP	PHONE	ENTRY#
Valterra Products LLC **(HQ)**	3494	E	818 898-1671	6796
Electric Gate Store Inc	3699	C	818 361-6872	9209
National Insurance Crime Bur	6411	D	818 895-2867	14616
The National Bus Group Inc **(PA)**	7353	D	818 221-6000	15766
National Cnstr Rentals Inc **(HQ)**	7359	C	818 221-6000	15789
Providnce Facey Med Foundation **(PA)**	8011	C	818 365-9531	17742
Providnce Facey Med Foundation	8011	C	818 365-9531	17744
Ararat Home Los Angeles	8059	C	818 837-1800	18109
Providence Health & Svcs - Ore	8062	A	818 365-8051	18396
Providence Holy Cross Medical **(PA)**	8062	B	818 365-8051	18398
Providnce Facey Med Foundation	8099	C	818 837-5677	18790
El Nido Family Centers **(PA)**	8322	C	818 830-3646	19076

MISSION VIEJO, CA - Orange County

	SIC	EMP	PHONE	ENTRY#
Gregg Hammork Enterprises Inc	1311	E	949 586-7902	260
Prototype Industries Inc **(PA)**	2741	E	949 680-4890	3478
Franchise Services Inc **(PA)**	2752	E	949 348-5400	3576
Postal Instant Press Inc **(HQ)**	2752	E	949 348-5000	3660
Sir Speedy Inc **(HQ)**	2752	E	949 348-5000	3686
Wakunaga of America Co Ltd **(HQ)**	2834	D	949 855-2776	4255
James Hardie Trading Co Inc	2952	C	949 582-2378	4672
Elixir Industries	3469	D	949 860-5000	6514
Ironwood Electric Inc	3699	E	714 630-2350	9217
Medix Ambulance Service Inc **(PA)**	4119	C	949 470-8915	11395
Black Dot Wireless LLC	4812	D	949 502-3800	11845
Paydarfar Industries Inc	5045	D	949 481-3267	12430
Advanced Mp Technology LLC **(DH)**	5065	C	800 492-3113	12641
Smart & Final Stores Inc	5141	B	949 581-1212	13195
Home Depot USA Inc	5211	A	949 364-1900	13592
South Cnty Lxus At Mssion Vejo	5511	C	949 347-3400	13828
Camden Development Inc	6531	C	949 427-4674	14756
Coldwell Bnkr Rsdntial Rfrral **(DH)**	6531	C	949 367-1800	14768
Dimar Enterprises Inc	7349	C	949 492-1100	15708
Foundstone Inc	7372	E	949 297-5600	16251
Oracle Corporation	7372	B	626 315-7513	16338
Edwards Theatres Inc	7832	C	949 582-4078	17291
Mission Viejo Country Club	7997	C	949 582-1550	17502
Saddleback Vly	7997	D	949 586-1234	17514
United Studios Self Def Inc	7999	C	949 293-1391	17576
Hutchins Healthcare Inc	8011	C	949 487-9500	17668
Mission Internal Med Group Inc	8011	D	949 364-3570	17714
Total Vision LLC	8042	C	949 652-7242	17856
Bridgestone Living LLC	8051	D	949 487-9500	17893
Jewish HM For The Aging Ornge	8051	C	949 364-9685	17980
Victoria Vntura Asssted Lving	8051	D	805 642-1736	18068
Auxilary of Mssion Hosp Mssion	8062	A	949 364-1400	18188
Mission Hosp Regional Med Ctr **(PA)**	8062	A	949 364-1400	18345
Brightstar Care Lake Forest	8082	B	949 837-7000	18598
Rock Canyon Healthcare Inc	8082	C	719 404-1000	18638
Southern Cal Prmnnte Med Group	8099	C	949 376-8619	18805
Vocational Visions	8331	C	949 837-7280	19196

Mergent email: customerrelations@mergent.com
1402
2024 Southern California
Business Directory and Buyers Guide
(P-0000) Products & Services Section entry number
(PA)=Parent Co (HQ)=Headquarters (DH)=Div Headquarters

	SIC	EMP	PHONE	ENTRY#
Atria Assisted Living Group	8361	C	949 427-8191	19237
Morningstar Senior MGT LLC	8361	C	949 298-3675	19288
Lake Mission Viejo Association	8641	D	949 770-1313	19454
Young MNS Chrstn Assn Ornge CN	8641	D	949 859-9622	19496
Phg Engineering Services LLC	8711	D	714 283-8288	19670
North American Client Svcs Inc (PA)	8741	C	949 240-2423	20070

MOJAVE, CA - Kern County

	SIC	EMP	PHONE	ENTRY#
Golden Queen Mining Co LLC	1041	C	661 824-4300	233
Pepsi-Cola Metro Btlg Co Inc	2086	E	661 824-2051	1710
PPG Industries Inc	2851	E	661 824-4532	4500
Trical Inc	2879	E	661 824-2494	4554
PRC - Desoto International Inc	2891	E	661 824-4532	4576
Calportland Company	3241	C	661 824-2401	5364
Commodity Resource Envmtl Inc	3339	E	661 824-2416	5674
Innovative Coatings Technology Corporation	3479	C	661 824-8101	6711
Scaled Composites LLC	3721	B	661 824-4541	9551
Astrobotic Technology Inc	3761	D	888 488-8455	9891
Galactic Co LLC (DH)	3761	F	661 824-6600	9893
Masten Space Systems Inc	3761	E	888 488-8455	9896
Xcor Aerospace Inc	3761	D	661 824-4714	9908
Bae Systems Tech Sol Srvc Inc	3812	A	661 816-3474	9959

MONROVIA, CA - Los Angeles County

	SIC	EMP	PHONE	ENTRY#
Cell-Crete Corporation (PA)	1771	D	626 357-3500	1063
Burnett & Son Meat Co Inc	2011	D	626 357-2165	1190
Kruse and Son Inc	2013	E	626 358-4536	1224
Decore-Ative Spc NC LLC (PA)	2431	A	626 254-9191	2594
Vinyl Technology Inc (PA)	2671	C	626 443-5257	3162
Califrnia Nwspapers Ltd Partnr (DH)	2711	B	626 962-8811	3262
Medianews Group Inc	2711	C	818 713-3000	3304
Pasadena Newspapers Inc (PA)	2711	E	626 578-6300	3315
Global Compliance Inc	2741	E	626 303-6855	3449
Genzyme Corporation	2834	D	626 471-9922	4117
Decco US Post-Harvest Inc (HQ)	2879	F	800 221-0925	4549
Mask-Off Company Inc	2891	E	626 359-3261	4572
3M Company	3069	E	626 358-0136	4754
Duracold Refrigeration Mfg LLC	3448	E	626 358-1710	6376
Jan-Kens Enameling Company Inc	3479	E	626 358-1849	6713
Amada Weld Tech Inc (DH)	3548	E	626 303-5676	7155
Belco Packaging Systems Inc	3565	E	626 357-9566	7345
Micro/Sys Inc	3571	E	818 244-4600	7441
Aremac Associates Inc	3599	E	626 303-8795	7760
Roncelli Plastics Inc	3599	C	800 250-6516	8006
Silc Technologies Inc	3674	E	626 375-1231	8889
Worldwide Energy and Mfg USA (PA)	3674	A	650 692-7788	8923
Clary Corporation	3679	E	626 359-4486	9019
Foote Axle & Forge LLC	3714	E	323 268-4151	9391
Aerovironment Inc	3721	E	626 357-9983	9503
Aerovironment Inc	3721	E	626 357-9983	9505
Aerovironment Inc	3721	E	626 357-9983	9506
Ducommun Aerostructures Inc	3728	E	626 358-3211	9677
Ducommun Incorporated	3728	E	626 358-3211	9678
Mulgrew Arcft Components Inc	3728	D	626 256-1375	9754
L3harris Technologies Inc	3812	E	626 305-6230	9991
Hoya Holdings Inc	3827	D	626 739-5200	10317
Radcal Corporation	3829	E	626 357-7921	10393
Amada Weld Tech Inc	3841	E	626 303-5676	10427
Chromologic LLC	3841	E	626 381-9974	10481
Konigsberg Instruments Inc	3841	E	626 775-6500	10544
3M Unitek Corporation	3843	E	626 445-7960	10727
Wbt Group LLC	3999	E	323 735-1201	11307
Southern California Edison Co	4911	C	626 303-8480	12067
Webasto Charging Systems Inc (DH)	5013	D	626 415-4000	12266
Home Depot USA Inc	5211	E	626 256-0580	13623
Naked Juice Co Glendora Inc	5499	B	626 873-2600	13731
Doubltree By Hlton Ht Monrovia	7011	C	626 357-1900	15138
Sage Hospitality Resources LLC	7011	E	626 357-5211	15338
Executive Auto Reconditioning	7542	E	626 416-3322	17048
Ctour Holiday LLC	7999	B	323 261-8811	17544
Childrens Oncology Group	8011	C	626 241-1500	17618
Alakor Healthcare LLC	8062	E	626 408-9800	18171
Curative-Korva LLC	8071	D	424 645-7575	18544
California Cancer Specialists Medical Group Inc.	8621	B	626 775-3200	19391
World Vision International (PA)	8699	C	626 303-8811	19537
California Business Bureau Inc	8721	C	626 303-1515	19758
Eurofins Eaton Analytical LLC (DH)	8734	C	626 386-1100	19971
Country Villa Service Corp	8741	C	626 358-4547	20019
Curative Inc	8741	A	650 713-8928	20023
Financial Tech Sltons Intl Inc	8742	C	818 241-9571	20171

MONTCLAIR, CA - San Bernardino County

	SIC	EMP	PHONE	ENTRY#
Cls Landscape Management Inc	0783	B	909 628-3005	222

	SIC	EMP	PHONE	ENTRY#
National Ewp Inc	1081	F	909 931-4014	236
Elements Food Group Inc	2052	D	909 983-2011	1516
Ingredients By Nature LLC	2099	E	909 230-6200	1915
Westside Accessories Inc (PA)	2387	F	626 858-5452	2436
Arcadia Cabinetry LLC	2434	F	909 550-0074	2646
California Offset Printers Inc (PA)	2752	D	818 291-1100	3525
Cpd Industries	3089	E	909 465-5596	4997
Falcon Abrasive Mfg Inc	3291	F	909 598-3078	5541
Empire Products Inc	3433	D	909 399-3355	5979
Amazing Steel Company	3441	E	909 590-0393	5991
Mitchell Fabrication	3441	E	909 590-0393	6056
Pacific Duct Inc	3444	E	909 635-1335	6285
John L Conley Inc	3448	D	909 627-0981	6380
Ampac Usa Inc	3589	E	435 291-0961	7638
Cosmo Products LLC	3634	F	626 416-5411	8232
American Nail Plate Ltg Inc	3645	D	909 982-1807	8286
Dm Technology & Energy Inc	3646	E	909 627-1600	8308
Copp Industrial Mfg Inc	3728	E	909 593-7448	9665
Omnitrans	4111	C	909 379-7100	11351
Expo Power Systems Inc	5063	E	800 506-9884	12595
Industrial Wood Products Inc	5211	F	909 625-1247	13624
Giant Inland Empire Rv Ctr Inc (PA)	5561	C	909 981-0444	13895
US Skillserve Inc	8051	A	909 621-4751	18065
Prime Healthcare Services-Mont	8062	A	909 625-5411	18387
Prime Hlthcare Srvcs-Mntclair (DH)	8062	C	909 625-5411	18389
Prime Hlthcare Srvcs-Mntclair	8062	C	909 625-5411	18390
Hampton Tdder Tchncal Svcs Inc	8734	F	909 628-1256	19973

MONTEBELLO, CA - Los Angeles County

	SIC	EMP	PHONE	ENTRY#
Holiday Tree Farms Inc	0811	C	323 276-1900	229
Yonekyu USA Inc	2013	D	323 581-4194	1241
Ingenue Inc	2015	E	323 726-8084	1245
Bimbo Bakeries Usa Inc	2051	F	323 720-6099	1455
J & R Bottling and Distributing Inc	2086	E	323 724-4076	1698
La Bottleworks Inc	2086	E	323 724-4076	1702
Reyes Coca-Cola Bottling LLC	2086	E	323 278-2600	1733
Unix Packaging LLC (PA)	2086	C	213 627-5050	1743
Arevalo Tortilleria Inc (PA)	2099	D	323 888-1711	1853
Bltee LLC	2331	E	213 802-1736	2231
All Access Apparel Inc (PA)	2335	C	323 889-4300	2273
Vft Inc	2392	E	323 728-2280	2490
J & M Richman Corporation	2395	E	800 422-9646	2515
Hardwood Flrg Liquidators Inc (PA)	2426	D	323 201-4200	2572
Big Tree Furniture & Inds Inc (PA)	2511	E	310 894-7500	2768
Atlas Survival Shelters LLC	2514	E	323 727-7084	2826
Gateway Mattress Co Inc	2515	D	323 725-1923	2850
Papercutters Inc	2671	E	323 888-1330	3154
Sunshine Fpc Inc	2673	D	323 721-8168	3192
LA Envelope Incorporated	2677	E	323 838-9300	3212
Northeast Newspapers Inc	2711	E	213 727-1117	3313
Monarch Litho Inc (PA)	2752	E	323 727-0300	3641
Turner Fiberfill Inc	2824	E	323 724-7957	3988
Cobe Chemical Co Inc	2844	D	877 691-3590	4390
Desser Tire & Rubber Co LLC (DH)	3011	E	323 721-4900	4695
Montebello Plastics LLC	3081	E	323 728-6814	4815
Delamo Manufacturing Inc	3089	D	323 936-3566	5003
Ppp Inc	3089	F	323 832-9627	5154
US Polymers Inc (PA)	3089	E	323 728-3023	5240
Beacon Concrete Inc	3273	F	323 889-7775	5463
Howmet Aerospace Inc	3353	C	323 728-3901	5687
PCI Industries Inc	3444	E	323 889-6770	6290
Performance Forge Inc	3462	E	323 722-3460	6469
Troy Sheet Metal Works Inc (PA)	3465	E	323 720-4100	6489
H & L Tooth Company (PA)	3531	D	323 721-5146	6934
Ingalls Conveyors Inc	3535	E	323 887-9900	6974
Thistle Roller Co Inc	3555	E	323 685-5322	7192
General Industrial Repair	3599	E	323 278-0873	7845
Dow-Elco Inc	3612	E	323 723-1288	8094
Amplifier Technologies Inc (HQ)	3663	E	323 278-0001	8494
Shyft Group Inc	3711	D	323 276-1933	9309
Craig Manufacturing Company (PA)	3714	E	323 726-7355	9375
Commerce On Demand LLC	3999	D	562 360-4819	11210
PCI Industries Inc	3999	E	323 889-6770	11263
Reu Distribution LLC	5023	A	323 201-4200	12314
Desser Tire & Rubber Co LLC	5088	E	323 837-1497	12906
Orora Packaging Solutions	5113	C	323 832-2000	13017
Niitakaya Usa Inc (PA)	5149	E	323 720-5050	13385
Katzkin Leather Inc (PA)	5199	D	323 725-1243	13543
Royal Paper Box Co California (PA)	5199	E	323 728-7041	13558
Costco Wholesale Corporation	5399	C	323 890-1904	13689
Johnstone Supply Inc	5722	D	323 722-2859	13968
Btg Textiles Inc	5963	E	323 586-9488	14109
Desser Holding Company LLC (HQ)	6719	E	323 721-4900	14927

Employee Codes: A=Over 500 employees, B=251-500
C=101-250, D=51-100, E=20-50, F=10-19, G=1-9

2024 Southern California
Business Directory and Buyers Guide

© Mergent Inc. 1-800-342-5647

1403

GEOGRAPHIC

	SIC	EMP	PHONE	ENTRY#
Wilbur Curtis Co Inc	6719	B	800 421-6150	14951
Montebello Unified School Dst	7349	D	323 887-2140	15729
L&T Staffing Inc	7361	B	323 727-9056	15864
Leidos Government Services Inc	7379	C	323 721-6979	16578
Code Red Fire Inc	7382	E	323 726-0982	16725
Montebello Unified School Dst	7389	D	323 440-2899	16881
Beverly Community Hosp Assn (PA)	8062	A	323 726-1222	18191
Mexican Amrcn Oprtnty Fndation (PA)	8322	D	323 890-9600	19112
Altura Management Services LLC	8741	B	323 768-2898	19994

MONTEREY PARK, CA - Los Angeles County

	SIC	EMP	PHONE	ENTRY#
Alltech Industries Inc	1731	E	323 450-2168	865
Asia Food Inc	2011	E	626 284-1328	1188
La Colonial Tortilla Pdts Inc	2099	C	626 289-3647	1926
Pacific Culinary Group Inc	2099	E	626 284-1328	1964
DHm International Corp	2339	F	323 263-3888	2319
Architectural Woodworking Co	2541	D	626 570-4125	2943
International Daily News Inc (PA)	2711	E	323 265-1317	3288
World Journal La LLC (HQ)	2711	C	323 268-4982	3339
Graphic Color Systems Inc	2752	D	323 283-3000	3580
Inertech Supply Inc	3053	E	626 282-2000	4735
West-Bag Inc	3089	E	323 264-0750	5248
Aero Powder Coating Inc	3479	E	323 264-6405	6685
L C Miller Company	3567	E	323 268-3611	7369
Optic Arts Holdings Inc	3646	E	213 250-6069	8324
Ross Name Plate Company	3993	E	323 725-6812	11150
Carmichael International Svc (DH)	4731	D	213 353-0800	11744
Logisteed America Inc	4731	E	323 263-8100	11778
San Diego Gas & Electric Co	4911	C	619 696-2000	12049
Southern California Gas Co	4924	C	213 244-1200	12091
Southern California Gas Co	4924	A	213 244-1200	12096
Union Technology Corp	5065	E	323 266-6871	12708
Oakcroft Associates Inc (PA)	5082	C	323 261-5122	12776
El Primo Foods Inc	5142	C	626 289-5054	13245
Care 1st Health Plan (PA)	6321	C	323 889-6638	14449
State Compensation Insur Fund	6331	C	323 266-5000	14527
Farmers Insurance	6411	C	626 288-0870	14589
Innovations Building Svcs LLC	7349	D	323 787-6068	15715
Merchants Building Maint Co	7349	E	323 881-8902	15725
Guard-Systems Inc	7381	A	323 881-6715	16648
Garfield Imaging Center Inc	8011	C	626 572-0912	17659
Ahmc Garfield Medical Ctr LP	8051	C	626 573-2222	17876
Monterey Park Hospital	8062	H	626 570-9000	18346
Childrens Law Center Cal (PA)	8111	D	323 980-8700	18835

MONTROSE, CA - Los Angeles County

	SIC	EMP	PHONE	ENTRY#
Vitachrome Graphics Group Inc	2759	E	818 957-0900	3822
Northrop Grumman Systems Corp	3812	D	818 249-5252	10018
Gloves In A Bottle Inc	5122	E	818 248-9980	13043
Shriners Hspitals For Children	8069	B	213 368-3302	18535

MOORPARK, CA - Ventura County

	SIC	EMP	PHONE	ENTRY#
Muranaka Farm	0191	C	805 529-0201	84
Corporate Graphics & Printing	2752	F	805 529-5333	3546
Sterisyn Inc	2834	D	805 991-9694	4242
Insparation Inc	2844	D	805 553-0820	4423
Kamsut Incorporated	2844	E	805 495-7479	4426
Husky Injection Mlding Systems	3089	D	805 523-9593	5055
SCI-Tech Glassblowing Inc	3229	E	805 523-9790	5329
G T Water Products Inc	3432	F	805 529-2900	5970
Topaz Systems Inc (PA)	3577	E	805 520-8282	7572
Glendee Corp	3599	E	805 523-2422	7849
Glendee Corp (PA)	3599	E	805 523-2422	7850
Mac M Mc Cully Corporation	3621	E	805 529-0661	8149
Anc Technology Inc	3672	D	805 530-3958	8647
Benchmark Elec Mfg Sltons Mrpa	3672	A	805 532-2800	8653
Laritech Inc	3672	C	805 529-5000	8697
Ultron Systems Inc	3674	F	805 529-1485	8914
Nea Electronics Inc	3678	E	805 292-4010	8979
Ensign-Bickford Arospc Def Co	3812	C	805 292-4000	9975
Gooch and Housego Cal LLC	3827	D	805 529-3324	10316
Koros USA Inc	3841	E	805 529-0825	10545
Mpo Videotronics Inc (PA)	3861	D	805 499-8513	10876
Conversion Technology Co Inc (PA)	3952	D	805 378-0033	11049
Sercomp LLC (PA)	3955	D	805 299-0020	11062
Global Uxe Inc	3999	D	805 583-4600	11220
Globaluxe Inc	3999	D	805 583-4600	11221
Picnic Time Inc	3999	D	805 529-7400	11269
Pom Medical LLC	5047	D	805 306-2105	12509
Testequity Inc	5084	D	805 498-9933	12829
Lifetech Resources LLC	5122	D	805 944-1199	13051
Pindler & Pindler Inc (PA)	5131	D	805 531-9090	13089
Kretek International Inc (DH)	5194	D	805 531-8888	13522

	SIC	EMP	PHONE	ENTRY#
Titan Led	6512	D	805 523-7500	14689
Citrus North Venture LLC	7011	D	256 428-2000	15118
Cardservice International Inc (DH)	7389	B		16797
Testequity LLC (PA)	7629	C	805 498-9933	17075

MORENO VALLEY, CA - Riverside County

	SIC	EMP	PHONE	ENTRY#
Life Is Life LLC	2022	E	310 584-7541	1256
Masonite Entry Door Corp	2431	F	951 243-2261	2614
Serta Simmons Bedding LLC	2515	E	951 807-8467	2858
Bms Investments LLC	2834	E	714 376-2535	4077
Hsb Holdings Inc	3011	E	951 214-6590	4697
Painted Rhino Inc (PA)	3088	E	951 656-5524	4920
Cardinal Glass Industries Inc	3211	C	951 485-9007	5312
Modular Metal Fabricators Inc	3444	C	951 242-3154	6275
Pacific Kiln Insulations Inc	3567	E	951 697-4422	7370
Harman Professional Inc	3651	C	951 242-2927	8415
Accuturn Corporation	3812	E	951 656-6621	9936
Bcd Industries Corp	3999	F	760 927-8988	11193
Access Info Holdings LLC	4226	A	909 459-1417	11631
Capstone Logistics LLC	4789	C	770 414-1929	11829
San Diego Gas & Electric Co	4924	C	951 243-2241	12082
Waste MGT Collectn Recycl Inc	4953	C	951 242-0421	12203
Skechers USA Inc	5139	E	951 242-4307	13165
Home Depot USA Inc	5211	D	951 485-5400	13581
Lowes Home Centers LLC	5211	D	951 656-1859	13664
Akh Company Inc	5531	C	951 924-5356	13853
Certified Tire & Svc Ctrs Inc	5531	E	951 656-6466	13855
Visterra Credit Union	6062	C	951 656-4411	14252
Kaiser Foundation Hospitals	6733	N	951 601-6174	14994
Butler America Holdings Inc	7361	B	951 563-0020	15823
U-Haul Leasing & Sales Co	7513	B	951 485-2003	16976
Community Health Systems Inc	8011	C	951 571-2300	17629
County of Riverside	8011	A	951 486-4000	17636
County of Riverside	8011	B	951 486-4000	17637
Kaiser Foundation Hospitals	8011	A	951 243-0811	17682
RES-Care Inc	8052	D	951 653-1311	18097
Riverside University Health	8062	B	951 486-4000	18410
Think Together	8351	B	951 571-9944	19228

MORRO BAY, CA - San Luis Obispo County

	SIC	EMP	PHONE	ENTRY#
Compass Health Inc	8051	C	805 772-7372	17908

MOUNTAIN PASS, CA - San Bernardino County

	SIC	EMP	PHONE	ENTRY#
Mp Materials Corp	1099	E	702 844-6111	239
Chevron Mining Inc	1221	C	760 856-7625	240
Mp Mine Operations LLC	1481	C	702 277-0848	414

MURRIETA, CA - Riverside County

	SIC	EMP	PHONE	ENTRY#
West Pak Avocado Inc (PA)	0723	C	951 296-5757	117
Pgc Construction Inc	1521	E	760 549-4121	450
Twin Power Usa LLC	1731	E	714 609-6014	949
Global Link Sourcing Inc	2671	D	951 698-1977	3152
Gold Prospectors Assn Amer LLC	2721	D	951 699-4749	3360
Kingman Industries Inc	2841	E	951 698-1812	4338
No Prssure Prssure Wshg Svcs L	2842	E	951 477-1988	4364
Medical Extrusion Tech Inc (PA)	3089	E	951 698-4346	5094
Muhlhauser Enterprises Inc (PA)	3441	E	909 877-2792	6057
Muhlhauser Steel Inc	3441	E	909 877-2792	6058
Inland Metal Trading Inc	3444	F	833 396-0740	6253
S C Coatings Corporation	3479	E	951 461-9777	6733
Apex Conveyor Corp	3535	E	951 304-7808	6970
Chip-Makers Tooling Supply Inc	3544	F	562 698-5840	7058
Hexco International	3559	C	951 677-2081	7240
Pacwest Air Filter LLC	3564	C	951 698-2228	7328
Fireblast Global Inc	3569	E	951 277-8319	7392
Bigfogg Inc (PA)	3585	F	951 587-2460	7601
Cryogenic Industries Inc	3634	C	951 677-2060	8233
CMS Circuit Solutions Inc	3672	E	951 698-4452	8663
American Industrial Manufacturing Services Inc	3694	C	951 698-3379	9162
Nuphoton Technologies Inc	3699	E	951 696-8366	9231
Denso Pdts & Svcs Americas Inc	3714	D	951 698-3379	9381
Ikhana Group LLC	3728	C	951 600-0009	9716
Coherent Aerospace & Defense Inc (HQ)	3812	C	951 926-2994	9963
TMC Ice Protection Systems LLC	3812	E	951 677-6934	10084
Abbott Vascular Inc	3841	A	408 845-3186	10410
Lobue Laser & Eye Medical Ctrs	3845	E	951 696-1135	10810
Avenue Medical Equipment Inc	5047	E	949 680-7444	12473
Battery Systems Inc	5065	D	951 894-2960	12643
Waterstone Faucets LLC	5074	C	951 304-0520	12749
Copan Diagnostics Inc (DH)	5122	F	951 696-6957	13035
Home Depot USA Inc	5211	D	951 698-1555	13582
Lowes Home Centers LLC	5211	C	951 461-8916	13663
Wilson Cycles Sports Corp	5511	E	951 894-5545	13848

	SIC	EMP	PHONE	ENTRY#
Carmax Inc.	5521	C	951 387-3887	13850
ARC Document Solutions LLC	7334	A	951 445-4480	15642
Busy Bee LLC	7342	D	951 404-9900	15683
Mintle Enterprises Inc	7372	F	951 506-4005	16307
Prosites Inc	7379	C	888 932-3644	16593
Elite Enfrcment SEC Sltons Inc	7381	C	866 354-8308	16640
Glare Technology Usa Inc	7382	C	909 437-6999	16738
Complete Coach Works	7549	C	800 300-3751	17054
Oak Grove Inst Foundation Inc (PA)	8011	C	951 677-5599	17728
My Kids Dentist	8021	B	951 600-1062	17842
Michael G Frtnsce Physcl Thrap	8049	C	626 446-7027	17869
Southwest Healthcare Sys Aux	8062	A	800 404-6627	18456
Southwest Healthcare Sys Aux (HQ)	8062	B	951 696-6000	18457
National Mentor Holdings Inc	8361	B	951 677-1453	19289

NATIONAL CITY, CA - San Diego County

	SIC	EMP	PHONE	ENTRY#
Brightview Landscape Svcs Inc	0781	D	619 474-4478	148
The Ortiz Corporation	1623	D	619 434-7925	697
Ehmcke Sheet Metal Corp	1761	D	619 477-6484	1046
Turn Key Scaffold LLC	1799	C	619 642-0880	1180
Family Loompya Corporation	2099	E	619 477-2125	1892
Gmi Inc	2393	E	619 429-4479	2494
Westflex Inc (PA)	3052	E	619 474-7400	4717
B and P Plastics	3089	E	619 477-1893	4952
Gary Manufacturing Inc	3089	E	619 429-4479	5034
Bay City Marine Inc (PA)	3441	E	619 477-3991	5994
Carroll Metal Works Inc	3441	E	619 477-9125	6007
Fabrication Tech Inds Inc	3441	E	619 477-4141	6025
G V Industries Inc	3599	E	619 474-3013	7841
Craft Labor & Support Svcs LLC	3731	C	619 336-9977	9837
Navigational Services	3731	F	619 477-1564	9843
Paige Sitta & Associates Inc (PA)	3731	E	619 233-5912	9846
Walashek Industrial & Mar Inc	3731	E	619 498-1711	9850
Hyperbaric Technologies Inc	3845	D	619 336-2022	10808
Costco Wholesale Corporation	3851	C	619 336-3412	10835
Sureride Charter Inc	4142	C	619 336-9200	11418
San Diego Unified Port Dst	4491	C	619 686-6200	11646
Public Authority	4941	D	619 731-3705	12138
Sids Carpet Barn (PA)	5023	E	619 477-7000	12315
Dragon Trade Intl Corp	5064	C	619 816-6062	12629
Tdk-Lambda Americas Inc	5065	C	619 575-4400	12703
Centerline Industrial Inc	5084	E	858 505-0838	12788
Del Mar Holding LLC	5147	A	313 659-7300	13292
Harvest Meat Company Inc	5147	D	619 477-0185	13294
Harvest Meat Company Inc (HQ)	5147	D	619 477-0185	13295
Fornaca Inc (PA)	5531	C	866 308-9461	13859
San Diego Leather Inc	5699	F	619 477-2900	13936
Adventist Health System/West	6513	D	619 475-5040	14702
Motivational Systems Inc (PA)	7336	D	619 474-8246	15670
HI Welding Inc	7692	C	619 336-9231	17086
Oxyheal Health Group Inc	7699	C	619 336-2022	17142
South Bay Sand Blstg Tank Clg	7699	D	619 238-8338	17153
Imaginative Horizons Inc	8051	D	619 477-1176	17976
Sterling Care Inc	8051	C	619 470-6700	18058
Paradise Valley Hospital (PA)	8062	A	619 470-4100	18372
National School District	8211	C	619 336-7770	18976
Episcopal Community Services	8322	C	619 470-0720	19077
Epsilon Systems Solutions Inc	8611	C	619 474-3252	19378
Hii Fleet Support Group LLC	8711	C	619 474-8820	19604

NEEDLES, CA - San Bernardino County

	SIC	EMP	PHONE	ENTRY#
Tri State Truss Corporation	2439	E	760 326-3868	2705
Pacific Gas and Electric Co	4911	C	760 326-2615	12039
Community Hlthcare Partner Inc	8011	D	760 326-4531	17630

NEW CUYAMA, CA - Santa Barbara County

	SIC	EMP	PHONE	ENTRY#
E & B Ntral Resources MGT Corp	1382	E	661 766-2501	301

NEWBERRY SPRINGS, CA - San Bernardino County

	SIC	EMP	PHONE	ENTRY#
5e Boron Americas LLC	1474	E	442 292-2120	413
Elementis Specialties Inc	2819	D	760 257-9112	3892

NEWBURY PARK, CA - Ventura County

	SIC	EMP	PHONE	ENTRY#
Bnk Petroleum (us) Inc	1382	E	805 484-3613	291
Kota Construction LLC	1521	D	855 800-5682	443
Coast Index Co Inc	2678	D	805 499-6844	3220
Juniper Publishers	2741	E	909 563-8215	3460
Plz Corp	2813	E	805 498-4531	3872
Amgen Inc	2834	C	805 447-1000	4045
Onyx Pharmaceuticals Inc	2834	A	650 266-0000	4189
Shire	2834	D	805 372-3000	4232
Cosmetic Technologies LLC	2844	D	805 376-9960	4395
R & R Services Corporation	3069	E	818 889-2562	4789

	SIC	EMP	PHONE	ENTRY#
JBW Precision Inc	3444	E	805 499-1973	6255
Diamond Ground Products Inc	3548	E	805 498-3837	7158
Fc Management Services	3559	E	805 499-0050	7235
Transparent Devices Inc	3577	E	805 499-5000	7574
CHE Precision Inc	3599	E	805 499-8885	7797
Nokia of America Corporation	3661	E	818 880-3500	8481
CPI Malibu Division	3663	D	805 383-1829	8505
WV Communications Inc	3663	E	805 376-1820	8599
Opto Diode Corporation	3674	E	805 499-0335	8855
Skyworks Solutions Inc	3674	E	805 480-4400	8890
Skyworks Solutions Inc	3674	E	805 480-4227	8891
Qorvo California Inc	3679	E	805 480-5050	9105
Condor Pacific Industries Inc (PA)	3812	E	818 889-2150	9964
Xirrus Inc	3823	E	805 262-1600	10171
Eca Medical Instruments (DH)	3841	E	805 376-2509	10498
Tom Anderson Guitarworks	3931	F	805 498-1747	10934
Amgen Manufacturing Limited	3999	E	787 656-2000	11189
Mv Transportation Inc	4111	C	805 375-5467	11350
McBain Systems A Cal Ltd Prtnr	5049	E	805 581-6800	12529
Carefree Communities Inc	6515	C	805 498-2612	14736
Hawaiian Hotels & Resorts Inc	7011	C	805 480-0052	15172
Trend Design Inc	7336	F	805 498-0457	15676
Compulink Business Systems Inc (PA)	7372	C	805 446-2050	16210
Isolutecom Inc	7372	E	805 498-6259	16278
Weldlogic Inc	7692	D	805 375-1670	17098
Mary Hlth of Sick Cnvlscent Nr	8051	A	805 498-3644	18011

NEWHALL, CA - Los Angeles County

	SIC	EMP	PHONE	ENTRY#
Berry Petroleum Company LLC	1311	D	661 255-6066	248
Green Thumb International Inc	5261	D	661 259-1071	13679
Vons Companies Inc	5411	C	661 259-9214	13708
Hollenbeck Palms	8361	C	323 263-6195	19270

NEWPORT BEACH, CA - Orange County

	SIC	EMP	PHONE	ENTRY#
West Newport Oil Company	1311	E	949 631-1100	272
Houalla Enterprises Ltd	1542	D	949 515-4350	558
Koll Construction LP	1542	D	949 833-3030	563
McCarthy Bldg Companies Inc	1542	B	949 851-8383	566
A Shoc Beverage LLC	2048	F	949 490-1612	1437
Crossport Mocean	2311	F	949 646-1701	2151
Hmr Building Systems LLC	2421	E	951 749-4700	2566
Walden Structures Inc	2452	B	909 389-9100	2745
RSI Home Products Inc	2514	D	949 720-1116	2835
Churm Publishing Inc (PA)	2711	E	714 796-7000	3265
Hanley Wood Media Inc (HQ)	2741	F	202 736-3300	3455
Peninsula Publishing Inc	2741	F	949 631-1307	3472
Evolus Inc (PA)	2834	D	949 284-4555	4111
American Vanguard Corporation (PA)	2879	D	949 260-1200	4545
Amvac Chemical Corporation (HQ)	2879	E	323 264-3910	4546
Lewis Barricade Inc	2951	E	661 363-0912	4661
Crm Co LLC (PA)	3061	E	949 263-9100	4749
Allbirds Inc	3143	F	949 942-1233	5264
A & A Ready Mixed Concrete Inc (PA)	3273	E	949 253-2800	5457
Associated Ready Mixed Con Inc (PA)	3273	E	949 253-2800	5462
Lebata Inc	3273	E	949 253-2800	5485
Tamco	3449	B	949 552-9714	6406
Hixson Metal Finishing	3471	C	800 900-9798	6627
Jacksam Corporation	3565	E	800 605-3580	7350
Gst Inc	3572	E	949 510-1142	7472
Performance Motorsports Inc	3592	B	714 898-9763	7702
Triton Chandelier Inc	3646	F	714 957-9600	8336
Adaptive Digital Systems Inc	3663	E	949 955-3116	8488
Proshot Investors LLC	3663	F	949 586-9500	8562
Conexant Holdings Inc	3674	A	415 983-2706	8781
Mindspeed Technologies LLC (HQ)	3674	D	949 579-3000	8846
Newport Fab LLC	3674	E	949 435-8000	8851
Tower Semicdtr Newport Bch Inc (DH)	3674	A	949 435-8000	8911
Kelly Pneumatics Inc	3699	E	800 704-7552	9223
Center Line Wheel Corporation	3714	E	562 921-9670	9371
Comac America Corporation	3721	E	760 616-9614	9520
C&H Hydraulics Inc	3728	E	949 646-6230	9647
Anacapa Marine Services (PA)	3732	F	805 985-1818	9854
Basin Marine Inc	3732	E	949 673-0360	9855
Imagegrid Inc	3829	E	949 852-1000	10372
Mmxviii Holdings Inc	3993	E	800 672-3974	11138
CDM Company Inc	3999	E	949 644-2820	11206
Mulechain Inc	4212	D	888 456-8881	11462
Hornblower Yachts LLC	4724	E	949 650-2412	11716
Xport Forwarding LLC	4731	D	949 354-0609	11817
Mbit Wireless Inc (PA)	4812	C	949 205-4559	11850
Clean Energy	4924	A	949 437-1000	12081
Bitcentral Inc	5065	E	949 253-9000	12649
Hard Candy LLC	5122	E	949 515-3923	13045

Employee Codes: A=Over 500 employees, B=251-500
C=101-250, D=51-100, E=20-50, F=10-19, G=1-9

2024 Southern California
Business Directory and Buyers Guide

© Mergent Inc. 1-800-342-5647

1405

GEOGRAPHIC

	SIC	EMP	PHONE	ENTRY#
Urban Decay Cosmetics LLC	5122	B	949 631-4504	13073
Sterling Motors Ltd	5511	D	949 645-5900	13831
Monex Deposit A Cal Ltd Partnr	5944	D	800 444-8317	14079
American Security Bank	6022	D	949 440-5200	14179
Bny Mellon National Assn	6022	A	877 420-6377	14180
Electronic Commerce LLC	6159	D	800 770-5520	14291
RMR Financial LLC (DH)	6163	D	408 355-2000	14363
Pacific Select Distrs Inc	6211	D	949 219-3011	14401
Roth Capital Partners LLC (PA)	6211	D	800 678-9147	14404
Allianz Global Investors of America LP	6282	A	949 219-2200	14414
Pacific Altrntive Asset MGT LL (HQ)	6282	D	949 261-4900	14425
Research Affiliates Capital LP	6282	D	949 325-8700	14428
Research Affiliates MGT LLC	6282	D	949 325-8700	14429
John Hancock Life Insur Co USA	6311	D	949 254-1440	14437
Pacific Asset Holding LLC	6311	C	949 219-3011	14440
Pacific Life & Annuity Company	6311	A	949 219-3011	14441
Lawyers Title Insurance Corp	6361	C	949 223-5575	14542
Edgewood Partners Insur Ctr	6411	C	949 263-0606	14585
Northwestern Mutl Inv MGT LLC	6411	C	949 759-5555	14618
R Mc Closkey Insurance Agency	6411	C	949 223-8100	14626
Trg Insurance Services	6411	C	949 474-1550	14636
Entrepreneurial Capital Corp	6512	C	949 809-3900	14660
Olen Commercial Realty Corp	6512	B	949 644-6536	14676
BKM Diablo 227 LLC	6531	D	602 688-6409	14752
Buchanan Street Partners LP	6531	C	949 721-1414	14753
C B Coast Newport Properties	6531	A	949 644-1600	14755
Cbre Globl Value Investors LLC	6531	C	949 725-8500	14761
Citivest Inc	6531	C	949 705-0420	14765
Coldwell Bnkr Rsdntial Rfrral	6531	A	949 673-8700	14769
Core Realty Holdings MGT Inc	6531	D	949 863-1031	14773
Greystar Management Svcs LP	6531	C	949 705-0010	14806
Marshall Reddick Realty Inc	6531	C	949 885-8180	14830
Pacific Monarch Resorts Inc (PA)	6531	D	949 609-2400	14838
Absolute Return Portfolio	6722	A	800 800-7646	14953
Pacific Investment MGT Co LLC (DH)	6722	C	949 720-6000	14970
Pimco Cyman Trst Pmco Cyman GL	6722	C	949 720-6000	14971
Irvine Eastgate Office II LLC	6798	A	949 720-2000	15014
True Investments LLC (PA)	6799	E	949 258-9720	15056
Windjmmer Cpitl Invstors III L	6799	A	949 706-9989	15060
Windjmmer Cpitl Invstors IV LP	6799	B	919 706-9989	15061
Hyatt Corporation	7011	B	949 729-1234	15200
Pacific Hotel Management Inc	7011	C	949 608-1091	15287
Uka LLC	7011	B	949 610-8000	15396
Wj Newport LLC	7011	C	949 476-2001	15425
Beauty Barrage LLC	7231	C	949 771-3399	15477
Traffic Control Service Inc	7359	C		15803
Heat Waves LLC	7371	C	719 651-4942	16045
Conversionpoint Holdings Inc	7372	D	888 706-6764	16214
Planet DDS Inc (PA)	7372	E	800 861-5098	16349
Elevated Resources Inc (PA)	7374	C	949 419-6632	16491
Lifescript Inc	7375	C	949 454-0422	16530
Ajilon LLC	7379	C	949 955-0100	16550
NC Interactive LLC	7379	D	512 623-8700	16581
Tad Group LLC	7382	C	949 476-3601	16757
Professional Parking	7521	C	949 723-4027	17006
Vroom Automotive Finance Corp (HQ)	7538	B	949 224-1226	17040
Edwards Theatres Inc (DH)	7832	C	949 640-4600	17292
Heatwave LLC	7991	D	949 717-7588	17400
Nuzuna Corporation	7991	D	949 335-7790	17409
Balboa Bay Club Inc (HQ)	7997	B	949 645-5000	17463
Big Canyon Country Club	7997	C	949 645-5404	17474
International Bay Clubs LLC (PA)	7997	B	949 645-5000	17490
Newport Beach Country Club Inc	7997	C	949 644-9550	17504
Micha-Rettenmaier Partnership	8011	D	714 280-1645	17712
Newport Beach Surgery Ctr LLC	8011	C	949 631-0988	17725
West Dermatology Med MGT Inc (PA)	8011	A	909 793-3000	17832
Hoag Clinic	8062	B	949 764-1888	18281
Hoag Memorial Hospital Presbt (PA)	8062	A	949 764-4624	18284
Hoag Orthopedic Institute LLC	8062	B	949 515-0708	18285
Akua Behavioral Health Inc (PA)	8069	C	949 777-2283	18519
James R Gldwell Dntl Crmics In (PA)	8072	A	949 440-2600	18570
Prismatik Dentalcraft Inc	8072	D	949 399-1930	18574
National Therapeutic Svcs Inc (PA)	8093	D	866 311-0003	18703
Harbor Health Systems LLC	8099	C	949 273-7020	18767
Irell & Manella LLP	8111	B	949 760-0991	18874
Newmeyer & Dillion LLP (PA)	8111	C	949 854-7000	18918
Stradling Ycca Crlson Ruth A P (PA)	8111	C	949 725-4000	18949
Childrens Hospital Orange Cnty	8351	C	949 631-2062	19206
Young MNS Chrstn Assn Ornge CN	8641	D	949 642-9990	19495
Bkf Engineers/Ags.	8711	D	949 526-8400	19555
Concept Technology Inc (PA)	8711	D	949 854-7047	19565
M Arthur Gensler Jr Assoc Inc	8712	C	949 863-9434	19736
Hagen Streiff Newton & Oshiro Accountants PC.	8721	D	949 390-7647	19779
JS Held LLC	8721	D	949 390-7647	19782
LFC Corporate Services Inc	8741	D	949 640-4950	20054
Mig Management Services LLC	8741	D	949 474-5800	20061
Pacific Life Fund Advisors LLC	8741	B	949 260-9000	20075
Twenty4seven Hotels Corp	8741	B	949 734-6400	20111
Greenhouse Agency Inc	8742	C	949 752-7542	20178
Metrostudy Inc	8742	C	714 619-7800	20198
Smart Circle International LLC (PA)	8742	C	949 587-9207	20240
Your Practice Online LLC (PA)	8742	C	877 388-8569	20278
T-Force Inc (PA)	8748	D	949 208-1527	20383

NEWPORT COAST, CA - Orange County

	SIC	EMP	PHONE	ENTRY#
Krystal Ventures LLC	3911	E	213 507-2215	10904
Resort At Pelican Hill LLC	7011	B	949 467-6800	15324

NIPOMO, CA - San Luis Obispo County

	SIC	EMP	PHONE	ENTRY#
Troesh Readymix Inc	3273	E	805 928-3764	5516
Condition Monitoring Svcs Inc	3826	E	888 359-3277	10251
LR Baggs Corporation	3931	E	805 929-3545	10927
Santa Maria Tire Inc (PA)	5531	D	805 347-4793	13870

NORCO, CA - Riverside County

	SIC	EMP	PHONE	ENTRY#
Cal-West Nurseries Inc	0782	C	951 270-0667	185
Royal West Drywall Inc	1742	D	951 271-4600	994
Guy Yocom Construction Inc (PA)	1771	C	951 284-3456	1073
Better Nutritionals LLC	2023	D	310 356-9019	1261
Better Nutritionals LLC	2023	D	310 356-9019	1262
International E-Z Up Inc (PA)	2394	D	800 457-4233	2506
W B Powell Inc	2431	C	951 270-0095	2640
Legal Vision Group LLC	2752	E	310 945-5550	3621
Sr Plastics Company LLC	3089	C	951 479-5394	5214
Paragon Building Products Inc (PA)	3272	E	951 549-1155	5437
Quick Crete Products Corp.	3272	C	951 737-6240	5442
Pro Tech Thermal Services	3398	E	951 272-5808	5847
S R Machining Inc.	3599	C	951 520-9486	8010
S R Machining-Properties LLC.	3599	C	951 520-9486	8011
Avid Idntification Systems Inc (PA)	3674	C	951 371-7505	8772
Robertshaw Controls Company	3822	E	951 893-6233	10106
Clima-Tech Inc.	7623	D	909 613-5513	17062
Spearmint Rhino Cmpnies Wrldwi	8741	C	951 371-3788	20099
City of Norco	8748	D	951 270-5617	20329

NORTH HILLS, CA - Los Angeles County

	SIC	EMP	PHONE	ENTRY#
Morris Enterprises Inc	3089	F	818 894-9103	5109
Alpha Aviation Components Inc (PA)	3599	E	818 894-8801	7754
Learjet Inc	3721	E	818 894-8241	9543
Moore Industries-International Inc (PA)	3823	C	818 894-7111	10146
Imperial Toy LLC (PA)	3944	C	818 536-6500	10954
Prn Ambulance LLC.	4119	B	818 810-3600	11401
Battery Systems Inc.	5063	D	818 474-1500	12586
P C A Electronics Inc.	5065	E	818 892-0761	12690
Galpin Motors Inc (PA)	5511	B	818 787-3800	13770
New Hrzns Srving Indvdals With (PA)	8243	D	818 894-9301	19001
Penny Lane Centers (PA)	8399	C	818 892-3423	19338

NORTH HOLLYWOOD, CA - Los Angeles County

	SIC	EMP	PHONE	ENTRY#
PCL Construction Services Inc.	1542	D	818 509-7816	575
Circulating Air Inc (PA)	1711	D	818 764-0530	753
M Gaw Inc.	1799	D	818 503-7997	1168
Woods Maintenance Services Inc.	1799	C	818 764-2515	1186
Alpena Sausage Inc.	2013	E	818 505-9482	1210
Mave Enterprises Inc.	2064	E	818 767-4533	1545
Groundwork Coffee Roasters LLC	2095	C	818 506-6020	1821
Ahs Trinity Group Inc (PA)	2389	E	818 508-2105	2438
Mtd Kitchen Inc.	2431	D	818 764-2254	2619
Artcrafters Cabinets	2434	E	818 752-8960	2647
Kobis Windows & Doors Mfg Inc.	2434	E	818 764-6400	2664
Armored Group Inc.	2441	E	818 767-3030	2708
Basaw Manufacturing Inc.	2441	E	818 765-6650	2709
Basaw Manufacturing Inc (PA)	2441	E	818 765-6650	2710
A & S Case Company Inc.	2449	E	800 394-6181	2729
Bobrick Washroom Equipment Inc (HQ)	2542	D	818 764-1000	2973
The Bobrick Corporation (PA)	2542	D	818 764-1000	2996
West Publishing Corporation.	2731	B	800 747-3161	3420
Jungotv LLC	2741	D	650 207-6227	3459
Dennis Bolton Enterprises Inc.	2752	E	818 982-1800	3558
Graphic Visions Inc.	2752	E	818 845-8393	3581
Harman Press Inc.	2752	E	818 432-0570	3585
Corporate Impressions La Inc.	2759	E	818 761-9295	3749
G-2 Graphic Service Inc.	2759	C	818 623-3100	3760
Target Mdia Prtners Intrctive (HQ)	2759	E	323 930-3123	3816
Wes Go Inc.	2759	E	818 504-1200	3824
O P I Products Inc (HQ)	2844	B	818 759-8688	4439

	SIC	EMP	PHONE	ENTRY#
Specialty Coatings & Chem Inc	2851	E	818 983-0055	4507
Sealing Corporation	3053	E	818 765-7327	4744
Capco/Psa	3089	F	818 762-4276	4981
Hope Plastics Co Inc	3089	E	818 769-5560	5053
Meco-Nag Corporation	3144	F	818 764-2020	5277
Encore Cases Inc	3161	E	818 768-8803	5286
Six Eleven Limited Inc	3281	F	818 764-5810	5534
Dowell Aluminum Foundry Inc	3365	E	323 877-9645	5790
Metal Improvement Company LLC	3398	D	818 983-1952	5844
Cal-June Inc (PA)	3429	E	323 877-4164	5909
Orion Ornamental Iron Inc	3429	E	818 752-0688	5938
Lexington Acquisition Inc	3441	C	818 768-5768	6039
Davis California Industries Ltd	3444	E	818 980-6178	6225
Modern-Aire Ventilating Inc	3444	E	818 765-9870	6274
West Coast Custom Sheet Metal	3444	E	818 252-7500	6344
Astro Chrome and Polsg Corp	3479	E	818 781-1463	6693
Pdu Lad Corporation (PA)	3479	E	626 442-7711	6723
Allan Aircraft Supply Co LLC	3494	E	818 765-4992	6786
Pacific Wire Products Inc	3496	E	818 755-6400	6822
Artisan House Inc	3499	E	818 767-7476	6856
Enviro-Intercept Inc	3585	E	818 982-6063	7612
Utility Refrigerator	3585	E	818 764-6200	7632
Mar Engineering Company	3599	E	818 765-4805	7918
Wilshire Precision Pdts Inc	3599	E	818 765-4571	8081
Arte De Mexico Inc	3646	D	818 753-4510	8305
Thomson Reuters Corporation	3663	E	877 518-2761	8589
Vector Electronics & Tech Inc	3672	E	818 985-8208	8748
A T Parker Inc (PA)	3699	E	818 755-1700	9189
Anmar Precision Components Inc	3728	E	818 764-0901	9625
Avibank Mfg Inc (DH)	3728	C	818 392-2100	9639
Curtiss-Wright Controls Inc	3728	E	818 503-0998	9669
Klune Industries Inc (DH)	3728	B	818 503-8100	9732
Meggitt North Hollywood Inc (DH)	3728	E	818 765-8160	9748
Americh Corporation (PA)	3842	C	818 982-1711	10636
General Wax Co Inc (PA)	3999	D	818 765-5800	11219
Reel Efx Inc	3999	E	818 762-1710	11275
Ambulnz Health LLC	4119	B	877 311-5555	11370
Messenger Express (PA)	4215	C	213 614-0475	11534
Buster and Punch Inc	5023	E	818 392-3827	12297
Pilgrim Operations LLC	5043	B	818 478-4500	12380
Electronic Hardware Limited (PA)	5065	E	818 982-6100	12656
E B Bradley Co	5072	F	800 533-3030	12722
Fastener Technology Corp	5085	C	818 764-6467	12855
United Aeronautical Corp	5088	E	818 764-2102	12921
Fluids Manufacturing Inc	5159	C	818 264-4657	13407
Century West LLC	5511	D	818 432-5800	13747
Ngp Motors Inc	5511	E	818 980-9800	13802
Rhi Inc (PA)	5511	E	818 508-3800	13819
King Express Inc	5812	F	818 503-2772	14018
Pnk Enterprises Inc	5999	E	818 765-3770	14145
Kaiser Foundation Hospitals	6324	C	818 503-7082	14479
Financial Group Inc	6411	C	818 308-8527	14593
Marcus Hotels Inc	7011	E	818 980-8000	15239
Park Management Group LLC	7011	A	404 350-9990	15298
Rio Vista Development Co Inc (PA)	7011	E	818 980-8000	15326
Pierce Brothers (DH)	7261	D	818 763-9121	15489
Western Costume Co (HQ)	7299	E	818 760-0900	15524
Cats USA Inc	7342	D	818 506-1000	15685
Diamond Contract Services Inc	7349	B	818 565-3554	15707
Open Systems Inc	7372	E	317 566-6662	16336
Core Bts Inc	7373	C	818 766-2400	16438
Sada Systems Inc (PA)	7379	C	818 766-2400	16595
Babylon Security Services Inc	7381	D	818 766-8122	16623
Airdraulics Inc	7539	E	818 982-1400	17041
Bento Box Entertainment LLC	7812	B	818 333-7700	17171
Endemol Shine North America	7812	D	747 529-8000	17189
Pie Town Productions Inc	7812	C	818 255-9300	17207
Pilgrim Studios Inc	7812	D	818 728-8800	17208
Studio City	7812	D	818 557-7777	17225
Universal Studios Company LLC (DH)	7812	A	818 777-1000	17231
Chapmn/Lnard Stdio Eqp Cnada I (PA)	7819	C	323 877-5309	17245
Century Theatres Inc	7833	B	818 508-1943	17306
IPC Healthcare Inc (DH)	8011	C	888 447-2362	17672
Valley Community Healthcare	8011	B	818 763-8836	17821
Coldwater Care Center LLC	8051	C	818 766-6105	17903
Valley Vsta Nrsing Trnstnal CA	8051	C	818 763-6275	18066
Golden Care Inc	8059	D	818 763-6275	18129
Hillsdale Group LP	8059	E	818 623-2170	18131
Dubnoff Ctr For Child Dev Edct (PA)	8211	D	818 755-4950	18965
Concorde Career Colleges Inc	8249	B	818 239-6151	19002
Volunteers of Amer Los Angeles	8322	C	818 769-3617	19162
Volunteers of Amer Los Angeles	8322	C	818 506-0597	19163
Iatse Affl Prprty Crftsprson L	8631	C	818 769-2500	19409
Miller Kaplan Arase LLP (PA)	8721	C	818 769-2010	19795

NORTHRIDGE, CA - Los Angeles County

	SIC	EMP	PHONE	ENTRY#
Nexgen Air Los Angeles	1711	C	818 900-2525	800
Kitchen Pro Cabinetry Inc	2434	E	877 210-6361	2663
Artistry In Motion Inc	2679	E	818 994-7388	3231
Schubert Music Publishing Inc	2741	E	310 409-7326	3483
Kindeva Drug Delivery LP	2834	B	818 341-1300	4152
Monocent Inc	2835	F	424 310-0777	4283
Burns Environmental Svcs Inc	2842	E	800 577-4009	4345
DC Partners Inc (PA)	3365	E	714 558-9444	5789
Sheet Metal Prototype Inc	3444	E	818 772-2715	6314
Instrument Bearing Factory USA	3452	E	818 989-5052	6446
Maroney Company	3599	F	818 882-2722	7919
Robert H Oliva Inc	3599	E	818 700-1035	8002
S & S Numerical Control Inc	3599	E	818 341-4141	8009
Harman Professional Inc	3651	B	818 893-8411	8416
Rotating Prcsion McHanisms Inc	3663	E	818 349-9774	8573
Dxray Inc	3679	E	818 280-0177	9031
Lloyd Design Corporation	3714	D	818 768-6001	9414
Infinity Aerospace Inc (PA)	3728	E	818 998-9811	9719
Vision Aerospace LLC	3728	E	818 700-1035	9825
Alliant Tchsystems Oprtons LLC	3812	B	818 887-8195	9939
Alliant Tchsystems Oprtons LLC	3812	B	818 887-8195	9941
Arete Associates (PA)	3812	C	818 885-2200	9946
Northrop Grmman Innvtion Syste	3812	B	818 887-8100	10007
Northrop Grumman Systems Corp	3812	B	818 887-8110	10015
Chemat Technology Inc	3821	E	818 727-9786	10090
Thermometrics Corporation (PA)	3823	F	818 886-3755	10166
Validyne Engineering Corp	3829	E	818 886-8488	10406
Medtronic Minimed Inc (DH)	3841	A	800 646-4633	10562
Southern California Gas Co	4924	B	818 363-8542	12094
Harman-Kardon Incorporated	5064	E	818 841-4600	12632
Harman International Inds Inc	5065	A	818 893-8411	12662
Smart & Final Stores Inc	5141	C	818 368-6409	13214
Lowes Home Centers LLC	5211	C	818 477-9022	13634
San Fernando Valley Auto LLC	5511	C	818 832-1600	13822
Pinnacle Estate Properties (PA)	6531	C	818 993-4707	14844
Remax Olson & Associates Inc	6531	C	818 366-3300	14858
Assisted Home Recovery Inc (PA)	7361	C	818 894-8117	15815
Ikano Communications Inc (PA)	7374	D	801 924-0900	16500
Contemporary Services Corp (PA)	7381	A	818 885-5150	16633
World Private Security Inc	7381	C	818 894-1800	16710
Musclebound Inc	7991	E	818 349-0123	17408
Porter Valley Country Club Inc	7997	C	818 360-1071	17507
Progressive Health Care System	8011	D	818 707-9603	17740
Institute For Applied Bhvior A	8049	D	818 341-1933	17863
Dignity Health	8062	A	818 885-8500	18244
Valley Hospital Medical Center Foundation	8062	A	818 885-8500	18495
Tiffany Homecare Inc	8082	B	818 886-1602	18646
Child and Family Guidance Ctr (PA)	8093	C	818 739-5140	18679
Charles Rver Labs Cell Sltons (HQ)	8099	D	877 310-0717	18752
Village At Northridge	8361	D	818 514-4497	19307
Regal Medical Group Inc (PA)	8621	C	818 654-3400	19402
Lakeside Systems Inc	8741	A	866 654-3471	20050

NORWALK, CA - Los Angeles County

	SIC	EMP	PHONE	ENTRY#
Doty Bros Equipment Co (HQ)	1623	D	562 864-6566	669
Cargill Meat Solutions Corp	2011	E	562 345-5240	1191
Dianas Mexican Food Pdts Inc (PA)	2099	E	562 926-5802	1884
Golden Specialty Foods LLC	2099	E	562 802-2537	1906
Cabinets 2000 LLC	2434	C	562 868-0909	2650
McDowell Craig Off Systems Inc	2522	D	562 921-4441	2915
Sonoco Products Company	2631	D	562 921-0881	3072
El Clasificado (PA)	2711	E	323 837-4095	3276
Paradise Printing Inc	2752	E	714 228-9628	3652
Jason Markk Inc (PA)	2842	E	213 687-7060	4354
Eriks North America Inc	3053	D	562 802-7782	4727
ARC Plastics Inc	3089	E	562 802-2929	4945
New Cntury Mtals Southeast Inc	3356	B	562 356-6804	5725
Aerotec Alloys Inc	3363	E	562 809-1378	5755
Argo Spring Mfg Co Inc	3493	D	800 252-2740	6780
Aerospace Tool & Grinding Inc	3541	E	562 802-3339	7002
Tecno Industrial Engrg Inc	3599	E	562 623-4517	8045
AG Global Products LLC	3634	F	323 334-2900	8229
Icarcover Inc	3714	E	714 469-7759	9404
Master Research & Mfg Inc	3728	E	562 483-8789	9744
Universal Orthodontic Lab Inc	3843	F	562 484-0500	10775
Weber Distribution LLC	4225	C	562 404-9996	11629
Cco Holdings LLC	4841	C	562 239-2761	11973
Aquirecorps Norwalk Auto Auctn	5012	C	562 864-7464	12222
West Central Produce Inc	5148	B	213 629-3600	13348
Lowes Home Centers LLC	5211	D	562 926-0826	13635

	SIC	EMP	PHONE	ENTRY#
Smart & Final Stores LLC	5399	D	562 868-0794	13691
Keystone Ford Inc (PA)	5511	C	562 868-0825	13789
Personnel Plus Inc	7363	C	562 712-5490	15934
Bally Total Fitness Corporation	7991	A	562 484-2000	17393
Life Care Centers America Inc	8051	D	562 921-6624	17989
Assoction Mxcan Amrcn Edcators	8621	D	562 868-0431	19389
Jwch Institute Inc	8733	C	562 281-0306	19932

NUEVO, CA - Riverside County

	SIC	EMP	PHONE	ENTRY#
Oldcastle Infrastructure Inc	3272	E	951 928-8713	5434

OAK HILLS, CA - San Bernardino County

	SIC	EMP	PHONE	ENTRY#
Ww Woodworks	2431	E	760 887-4708	2643
Double Eagle Trnsp Corp	4213	C	760 956-3770	11483

OAK PARK, CA - Ventura County

	SIC	EMP	PHONE	ENTRY#
Foldimate Inc	3634	E	805 876-4418	8235

OAK VIEW, CA - Ventura County

	SIC	EMP	PHONE	ENTRY#
Willis Machine Inc	3599	E	805 604-4500	8079

OCEANSIDE, CA - San Diego County

	SIC	EMP	PHONE	ENTRY#
Primeco	1721	D	760 967-8278	853
Royal Westlake Roofing LLC	1761	C	760 967-0827	1053
Fencecorp Inc	1799	C	760 721-2101	1156
Olli Salumeria Americana LLC	2011	D		1201
American Food Ingredients Inc	2034	E	760 967-6287	1354
Julians Foods LLC	2043	E	760 583-9358	1422
Dibella Baking Company Inc	2052	D	951 797-4144	1515
Hammond Inc Which Will Do Bus	2085	E	925 381-5392	1673
Linksoul LLC	2211	E	760 231-7069	2027
Solecta Inc (PA)	2295	E	760 630-9643	2128
Kapan - Kent Company Inc	2396	E	760 631-1716	2535
Custom Win & Door Design Inc	2431	E	760 439-6213	2591
Trinity Woodworks Inc	2431	E	760 639-5351	2639
Britcan Inc	2542	E	760 722-2300	2974
Precision Label LLC	2671	E	760 757-7533	3156
Triple D and DS	2679	E		3251
Car Sound Exhaust System Inc	2819	D	949 888-1625	3885
Envirnmental Catalyst Tech LLC	2819	E	949 459-3870	3893
Genentech Inc	2834	A	760 231-2440	4114
Gilead Palo Alto Inc	2834	C	760 945-7701	4119
Guckenheimer Enterprises Inc	2834	D	760 414-3659	4126
USP Inc	2844	D	760 842-7700	4465
Hydranautics (DH)	2899	B	760 901-2500	4610
Amflex Plastics Incorporated	3052	E	760 643-1756	4709
Advanced Thrmlforming Entp Inc	3089	E	760 722-4400	4931
Cal-Mil Plastic Products Inc (PA)	3089	E	800 321-9069	4975
Eldorado Stone LLC (DH)	3272	E	800 925-1491	5410
Souther Cast Stone Inc	3272	E	760 754-9697	5450
Westlake Royal Stone LLC	3281	D	800 255-1727	5537
Kainalu Blue Inc	3296	E	760 806-6400	5555
Sound Seal Inc	3296	E	760 806-6400	5558
Tube-Line Technologies	3312	F	951 834-3123	5605
Pacific Sewer Maintenance Corp	3321	F	800 292-9927	5648
Campbell Certified Inc	3441	E	760 722-9353	6004
Santourian Manufacturing Inc	3444	E	760 754-3811	6310
Tru-Duct Inc	3444	E	619 660-3858	6337
Balda HK Plastics Inc	3451	E	760 757-1100	6412
Balda Precision Inc (DH)	3451	D	760 757-1100	6413
R Zamora Inc	3469	E	760 597-1130	6552
Southwest Greene Intl Inc	3469	D	760 639-4960	6556
Steico Industries Inc	3469	C	760 438-8015	6559
Rose Manufacturing Group Inc	3471	E	760 407-0232	6657
Proline Concrete Tools Inc	3559	E	760 758-7240	7257
Standard Filter Corporation (PA)	3564	E	866 443-3615	7331
Kellermyer Bergensons Svcs LLC (PA)	3589	E	760 631-5111	7667
BMw Precision Machining Inc	3599	E	760 439-6813	7785
Landmark Mfg Inc	3599	E	760 941-6626	7902
Nelgo Industries Inc	3599	E	760 433-6434	7952
Amerillum LLC	3648	D	760 727-7675	8353
Foxfury LLC	3648	E	760 945-4231	8366
HI Tech Electronic Mfg Corp	3672	D	858 657-0908	8685
Te Connectivity Corporation	3678	D	760 757-7500	8983
Blisslights Inc	3699	E	888 868-4603	9196
Onesource Distributors LLC (DH)	3699	E	760 966-4500	9234
Car Sound Exhaust System Inc (PA)	3714	D	949 858-5900	9368
Horstman Manufacturing Co Inc	3714	F	760 598-2100	9402
Hobie Cat Company (PA)	3732	C	760 758-9100	9859
Willard Marine Inc	3732	D	714 666-2150	9868
Hexagon Mfg Intelligence Inc	3825	D	760 994-1401	10203
Dupaco Inc	3841	E	760 758-4550	10495
Pryor Products	3841	E	760 724-8244	10593

	SIC	EMP	PHONE	ENTRY#
Precision One Medical Inc	3843	D	760 945-7966	10762
Absolute Board Co Inc	3949	F	760 295-2201	10969
Hobie Cat Company II LLC	3949	E	760 758-9100	10997
JBL Enterprises Inc	3949	E	760 754-2727	11006
Salis International Inc	3952	E	303 384-3588	11050
Federal Heath Sign Company LLC	3993	C	760 941-0715	11119
Whitlock Industries Inc	3999	F	760 231-9262	11308
Mv Transportation Inc	4111	C	760 400-0300	11347
Mountain Water Ice Company	4222	E	760 722-7611	11553
Sprint Communications Co LP	4812	C	760 941-4535	11858
Agri Service Inc	4953	E	760 295-6255	12153
Waste Management Cal Inc	4953	C	760 439-2824	12199
Panoramic Doors Inc	5031	C	760 722-1300	12339
Thornton Technology Corp	5088	E	760 471-9969	12920
United States Marine Corps	5088	D	760 725-3564	12922
Chemi-Source Inc	5122	E	760 477-8177	13032
Mellano & Co	5193	C	760 433-9550	13513
Lowes Home Centers LLC	5211	C	760 966-7140	13646
Julian Bakery Inc	5461	E	760 721-5200	13717
Southern Cal Disc Tire Co Inc	5531	C	760 439-8539	13877
Belching Beaver Brewery	5813	C	760 599-5832	14046
Frontwave Credit Union (PA)	6061	C	760 430-7511	14227
Monterey Financial Svcs Inc (PA)	6141	C	760 639-3500	14273
Sentry Life Insurance Company	6411	C	661 274-4018	14631
Oceans Eleven Casino	7011	B	760 439-6988	15269
Mission Linen Supply	7213	C	760 757-9099	15454
Bus-Let Inc	7331	E	323 728-6245	15629
Bergensons Property Svcs Inc	7349	A	760 631-5111	15695
Go-Staff Inc	7361	A	760 730-8520	15809
McKenna Boiler Works Inc	7699	E	323 221-1171	17138
Marine Corps Community Svcs	8021	C	760 725-5187	17841
Tri-City Hospital District (PA)	8062	A	760 724-8411	18480
Marine Corps United States	8069	A	760 725-1304	18530
Marine Corps Community Svcs	8351	C	760 725-2817	19216
Aegis Asssted Living Prpts LLC	8361	C	760 806-3600	19234
E R I T Inc (PA)	8361	D	760 433-6024	19260
Villas De Crlsbad Ltd A Cal Lt	8361	D	760 434-7116	19308
YMCA of San Diego County	8641	C	760 721-8930	19490
Goodwill Inds San Diego Cnty	8699	D	760 806-7670	19529
Hetherington Engineering (PA)	8711	C	760 931-1917	19603
Nitto Denko Technical Corp	8732	D	760 435-7011	19908
Primary Care Assod Med Group I	8741	C	760 724-1033	20080

OJAI, CA - Ventura County

	SIC	EMP	PHONE	ENTRY#
Casa Barranca Inc	2084	E	805 640-1255	1615
Troop Real Estate Inc	6531	C	805 640-1440	14880
Ovis LLC	7011	A	805 646-5511	15282
Ojai Healthidence Opco LLC	8052	C	805 646-8124	18092
Community Memorial Health Sys	8062	C	805 646-1401	18227
Help Unlmted Personnel Svc Inc	8082	A	805 962-4646	18616
Ojai Valley School (PA)	8211	D	805 646-1423	18977
Financial Group Inc	8741	C	805 646-7974	20031

ONTARIO, CA - San Bernardino County

	SIC	EMP	PHONE	ENTRY#
C C Graber Co	0179	F	909 983-1761	47
Perera Cnstr & Design Inc	1081	E	909 484-6350	237
Calvillo Construction Corp	1521	E	310 985-3911	424
Nhs Western Division Inc	1521	D	909 947-9931	448
Fullmer Construction	1541	C	909 947-9467	503
Bomel Construction Co Inc	1542	D	909 923-3319	536
CA Station Management Inc	1623	C	909 245-6251	664
Integrated Energy Group LLC	1711	C	605 381-7859	780
Communication Tech Svcs LLC	1731	C	508 382-2700	884
Gregg Electric Inc	1731	C	909 983-1794	905
Martinez Steel Corporation	1791	C	909 946-0686	1109
Rynoclad Technologies Inc	1793	C	951 264-3441	1119
Heatherfield Foods Inc	2011	E	877 460-3060	1197
Ventura Foods LLC	2021	E	323 262-9157	1250
Tropicale Foods LLC (PA)	2024	D	909 635-1000	1301
Adesa International LLC (PA)	2032	E	909 321-8240	1319
Superior Quality Foods Inc	2032	D	909 923-4733	1332
Ajinomoto Foods North Amer Inc	2038	C	909 477-4700	1382
Ajinomoto Foods North Amer Inc (DH)	2038	D	909 477-4700	1383
Cardenas Markets LLC	2038	B	909 923-7426	1386
Specialty Brands Incorporated	2038	A	909 477-4851	1401
Windsor Quality Food Company Ltd	2038	A	713 843-5200	1405
Popla International Inc	2045	E	909 923-6899	1425
JE Rich Company	2047	E	909 464-1872	1431
Ventura Foods LLC	2079	D	714 257-3700	1573
Coca-Cola Company	2086	D	909 975-5200	1691
Five Star Gourmet Foods Inc (PA)	2099	C	909 390-0032	1893
Fuji Natural Foods Inc (HQ)	2099	D	909 947-1008	1902
Gold Star Foods Inc (HQ)	2099	D	909 843-9600	1905

Mergent email: customerrelations@mergent.com
1408

2024 Southern California
Business Directory and Buyers Guide

(P-0000) Products & Services Section entry number
(PA)=Parent Co (HQ)=Headquarters (DH)=Div Headquarters

Company	SIC	EMP	PHONE	ENTRY#
Haliburton International Foods Inc	2099	B	909 428-8520	1909
Minsley Inc	2099	E	909 458-1100	1946
Passport Food Group LLC	2099	C	909 627-7312	1967
Passport Foods (svc) LLC	2099	C	909 627-7312	1968
Rama Food Manufacture Corp (PA)	2099	F	909 923-5305	1973
Soup Bases Loaded Inc	2099	E	909 230-6890	1988
USA Sales Inc	2111	E	909 390-9606	2007
Jomar Table Linens Inc	2392	D	909 390-1444	2473
Pacific Urethanes LLC	2392	E	909 390-8400	2483
Gold Crest Industries Inc	2393	E	909 930-9069	2495
Melmarc Products Inc	2395	C	714 549-2170	2519
A Lot To Say Inc	2399	E	877 366-8448	2543
Action Embroidery Corp (PA)	2399	C	909 983-1359	2544
Artesia Sawdust Products Inc	2421	E	909 947-5983	2564
Hallmark Home Interiors Inc (PA)	2426	F	909 947-7736	2571
Kls Doors LLC	2431	D	909 605-6468	2611
Moldings Plus Inc	2431	E	909 947-3310	2618
K & Z Cabinet Co Inc	2434	D	909 947-3567	2662
Regards Enterprises Inc	2493	F	909 983-0655	2749
Dorel Home Furnishings Inc	2511	D	909 390-5705	2771
Lanpar Inc	2511	E	541 484-1962	2777
Leggett & Platt Incorporated	2515	D	909 937-1010	2854
Stress-O-Pedic Mattress Co Inc	2515	E	909 605-2010	2861
Visionary Sleep LLC	2515	E	909 605-2010	2863
Kushwood Chair Inc	2521	E	909 930-2100	2887
Korden Inc	2522	E	909 988-8979	2914
Compatico Inc	2541	E	616 940-1772	2950
Ivars Display (PA)	2541	E	909 923-2761	2956
CTA Fixtures Inc	2542	D	909 390-6744	2977
Idx Los Angeles LLC	2542	C	909 212-8333	2981
LLC Walker West	2542	E	800 767-9378	2984
Rack Installation Services Inc	2542	E	909 261-2243	2986
Forbes Industries Div	2599	C	909 923-4559	3025
Crown Paper Converting Inc	2621	E	909 923-5226	3043
New-Indy Containerboard LLC (DH)	2621	D	909 296-3400	3055
New-Indy Ontario LLC	2621	D	909 390-1055	3056
Caraustar Industries Inc	2631	E	951 685-5544	3066
Preferred Printing & Packaging Inc	2631	E	909 923-2053	3070
Zapp Packaging Inc	2631	D	909 930-1500	3075
Androp Packaging Inc	2653	E	909 605-8842	3079
Commander Packaging West Inc	2653	E	714 921-9350	3092
Ecko Products Group LLC	2653	E	909 628-5678	3097
PNC Proactive Nthrn Cont LLC	2653	E	909 390-5624	3125
Southland Container Corp	2653	C	909 937-9781	3131
St Worth Container LLC	2653	D	909 390-4550	3132
Greif Bros Corp	2655	E	909 941-4570	3136
Fineline Settings LLC	2656	E	845 369-6100	3142
Transcontinental Ontario Inc	2671	E	909 390-8866	3159
Upm Raflatac Inc	2672	F	909 390-4657	3177
Transcontinental US LLC	2673	E	909 390-8866	3195
Encorr Sheets LLC	2679	E	626 523-4661	3236
Califrnia Nwspapers Ltd Partnr	2711	E	909 987-6397	3263
Aio Acquisition Inc (HQ)	2741	D	800 333-3795	3425
Advanced Color Graphics	2752	E	909 930-1500	3506
Bert-Co Industries Inc	2752	E	323 669-5700	3518
Eclipse Prtg & Graphics LLC	2752	E	909 390-2452	3568
Fgs-Wi LLC	2752	E	909 467-8300	3572
GW Reed Printing Inc	2752	E	909 947-0599	3583
Ultimate Print Source Inc	2752	E	909 947-5292	3701
L A Supply Co	2759	E	949 470-9900	3775
One Stop Label Corporation	2759	E	909 230-9380	3791
Response Envelope Inc (PA)	2759	C	909 923-5855	3806
Linde Inc	2813	E	909 390-0283	3867
Induspac California Inc	2821	E	909 390-4422	3945
North American Composites LLC	2821	F	909 605-8977	3959
Qycell Corporation	2821	E	909 390-6644	3965
Genvivo Incorporated	2834	D	626 441-6695	4116
Amrep Inc	2842	B	770 422-2071	4342
Diamond Wipes Intl Inc	2844	C	909 230-9888	4404
Pacer Technology (HQ)	2891	C	909 987-0550	4574
Kik Pool Additives Inc	2899	C	909 390-9912	4614
Able Industrial Products Inc (PA)	3053	E	909 930-1585	4718
Parco LLC (DH)	3053	C	909 947-2200	4739
Abba Roller LLC (DH)	3069	F	909 947-1244	4755
Kirkhill Inc	3069	D	562 803-1117	4771
KMC Acquisition LLC (PA)	3069	D	562 396-0121	4773
Pmr Precision Mfg & Rbr Co Inc	3069	E	909 605-7525	4785
Plastics Research Corporation	3083	D	909 391-9050	4838
Classic Containers Inc	3085	B	909 930-3610	4857
Liqui-Box Corporation	3085	E	909 390-4400	4858
Akra Plastic Products Inc	3089	E	909 930-1999	4932
Armorcast Products Company Inc	3089	E	909 390-1365	4948
Axium Packaging LLC	3089	A	909 969-0766	4950
Balda C Brewer Inc (DH)	3089	D	714 630-6810	4954
Bandlock Corporation	3089	D	909 947-7500	4955
Bericap LLC	3089	D	905 634-2248	4960
Bomatic Inc	3089	D	909 947-3900	4968
California Quality Plas Inc	3089	E	909 930-5667	4976
Dorel Juvenile Group LLC	3089	C	909 390-5705	5016
Inca Plastics Molding Co Inc	3089	F	909 923-3235	5060
Inline Plastics Inc	3089	E	909 923-1033	5061
LLC Walker West	3089	C	909 390-4300	5086
Medegen LLC (DH)	3089	C	909 390-9080	5092
Medegen Inc	3089	C	909 390-9080	5093
Mission Plastics Inc	3089	E	909 947-7287	5102
Paramount Panels Inc (PA)	3089	E	909 947-8008	5130
Plasthec Molding Inc	3089	E	909 947-4267	5141
PRC Composites LLC (PA)	3089	D	909 391-2006	5155
Ray Products Company Inc	3089	E	888 776-9014	5174
Reyrich Plastics Inc	3089	E	909 484-8444	5182
Star Shield Solutions LLC	3089	E	866 662-4477	5216
Superior Mold Co	3089	E	909 947-7028	5219
Thermodyne International Ltd	3089	C	909 923-9945	5226
US Duty Gear Inc	3199	F	909 391-8800	5310
Larry Mthvin Installations Inc (HQ)	3231	C	909 563-1700	5346
Western States Wholesale Inc (PA)	3271	D	909 947-0028	5396
Clark - Pacific Corporation	3272	E	909 823-1453	5404
Southwest Concrete Products	3272	C	909 983-9789	5451
Foundry Service & Supplies Inc	3299	E	909 284-5000	5567
Halsteel Inc (DH)	3315	E	909 937-1001	5615
Net Shapes Inc (PA)	3324	D	909 947-3231	5659
Century American Aluminum Inc	3354	F	909 390-2384	5694
Metals USA Building Pdts LP	3355	D	800 325-1305	5721
Vsmpo-Tirus US Inc	3356	D	909 230-9000	5729
Bee Wire & Cable Inc	3357	E	909 923-5800	5730
Superior Essex Inc	3357	C	909 481-4804	5751
Performance Aluminum Products	3363	E	909 391-4131	5765
California Die Casting Inc	3364	C	909 947-9947	5772
Alumistar Inc	3365	E	562 633-6673	5781
Calidad Inc	3365	E	909 947-3937	5784
Employee Owned PCF Cast Pdts I	3365	E	562 633-6673	5792
Lynwood Pattern Service Inc	3365	E	310 631-2225	5796
Everest Group USA Inc	3423	E	909 923-1818	5879
Garden Pals Inc	3423	E	909 605-0200	5881
Halex Corporation (DH)	3423	E	909 629-6219	5882
J L M C Inc	3441	E	909 947-2980	6034
Lightcap Industries Inc	3441	E	909 930-3772	6040
Maximum Quality Metal Pdts Inc	3441	E	909 902-5018	6044
R & I Industries Inc	3441	E	909 923-7747	6068
Security Metal Products Corp (DH)	3442	D	310 641-6690	6123
Watercrest Inc	3443	E	909 390-3944	6169
AMD International Tech LLC	3444	E	909 985-8300	6185
Barzillai Manufacturing Co Inc	3444	F	909 947-4200	6197
Compumeric Engineering Inc	3444	E	909 605-7666	6216
Empire Sheet Metal Inc	3444	E	909 923-2927	6231
Eugenios Sheet Metal Inc	3444	E	909 923-2002	6234
Metal Engineering Inc	3444	E	626 334-1819	6270
Stell Industries Inc	3448	E	951 369-8777	6391
DB Building Fasteners Inc (PA)	3449	F	909 581-6740	6396
Alger Precision Machining LLC	3451	C	909 986-4591	6408
Athanor Group Inc	3451	E	909 467-1205	6411
Duncan Bolt Co	3452	F	909 581-6740	6439
Alum-Alloy Co Inc	3463	E	909 986-0410	6475
Kitchen Equipment Mfg Co Inc	3469	E	909 923-3153	6529
Walker Corporation	3469	E	909 390-4300	6568
Walker Spring & Stamping Corp	3469	C	909 390-4300	6569
Danco Anodizing Inc	3471	C	909 923-0562	6611
Quality Control Plating Inc	3471	E	909 605-0206	6653
Inland Powder Coating Corp	3479	E	909 947-1122	6710
Specialty Coating Systems Inc	3479	D	909 390-8818	6738
James Jones Company	3491	A	909 418-2558	6767
Reliance Worldwide Corporation	3491	F	770 863-4005	6769
C M C Steel Fabricators Inc	3496	F	909 899-9993	6813
Lexco Imports Inc	3496	E	800 883-1454	6820
Rfc Wire Forms Inc	3496	D	909 467-0559	6827
Turbine Repair Services LLC (PA)	3511	E	909 947-2256	6890
Tracy Industries Inc	3519	C	562 692-9034	6896
Specialized Dairy Service Inc	3523	E	909 923-3420	6914
Sotec USA LLC	3523	F	909 525-5891	6950
Pneumatic Conveying Inc	3535	E	909 923-4481	6976
Konecranes Inc	3536	E	909 930-0108	6982
Crown Equipment Corporation	3537	E	909 923-8357	6988
Phillips Tool & Die Inc	3544	E	909 947-8712	7087
Wagner Die Supply Inc (PA)	3544	E	909 947-3044	7105
Broco Inc	3548	E	909 483-3222	7156
Bmci Inc	3549	E	951 361-8000	7167

Employee Codes: A=Over 500 employees, B=251-500
C=101-250, D=51-100, E=20-50, F=10-19, G=1-9

2024 Southern California
Business Directory and Buyers Guide

© Mergent Inc. 1-800-342-5647

1409

GEOGRAPHIC

	SIC	EMP	PHONE	ENTRY#		SIC	EMP	PHONE	ENTRY#
Eubanks Engineering Co **(PA)**	3549	E	909 483-2456	7168	Xpo Logistics Supply Chain Inc	4731	C	909 390-9799	11816
Trinity Robotics Automtn LLC	3549	F	562 690-4525	7173	Taylored Transload LLC	4789	C	909 510-4800	11840
Wallner Expac Inc **(PA)**	3549	D	909 481-8800	7175	Comcast Corporation	4841	D	909 890-0886	11982
Amrep Manufacturing Co LLC	3559	B	877 468-9278	7221	Blumenthal Distributing Inc **(PA)**	5021	C	909 930-2000	12278
C M Automotive Systems Inc **(PA)**	3563	E	909 869-7912	7307	Office Master Inc	5021	D	909 392-5678	12288
Future Commodities Intl Inc	3565	E	888 588-2378	7348	Norcal Pottery Products Inc	5023	C	909 390-3745	12311
Apple Tree International Corp	3571	F	626 679-7025	7418	Test-Rite Products Corp **(DH)**	5023	D	909 605-9899	12316
Chenbro Micom (usa) Inc	3572	E	909 937-0100	7467	Oregon PCF Bldg Pdts Maple Inc	5031	C	909 627-4043	12338
Am-Tek Engineering Inc	3599	E	909 673-1633	7756	Cemex Construction Mtls Inc **(DH)**	5032	C	909 974-5500	12350
Gamma Aerospace LLC	3599	E	310 532-4480	7842	Brainstorm Corporation	5045	C	888 370-8882	12400
Hera Technologies LLC	3599	E	951 751-6191	7859	Bionime USA Corporation	5047	E	909 781-6969	12477
Supreme Machine Products Inc	3599	F	909 974-0349	8040	Discus Dental LLC **(PA)**	5047	C	310 845-8600	12483
Tower Industries Inc	3599	C	909 947-2723	8050	Maury Microwave Inc **(PA)**	5065	C	909 987-4715	12682
Upland Fab Inc	3599	D	909 986-6565	8057	DH Caster International Inc	5072	F	909 930-6400	12720
Myers Power Products Inc **(PA)**	3613	C	909 923-1800	8126	Pbb Inc	5072	E	909 923-6250	12728
HI Perfrmnce Elc Vhcl Systems	3621	E	909 923-1973	8143	Suncoast Post-Tension Ltd	5072	F	909 673-0490	12735
Vishay Techno Components LLC	3625	D	909 923-3313	8196	Heat Transfer Pdts Group LLC	5075	C	909 786-3669	12755
Ledvance LLC	3641	E	909 923-3003	8248	Replanet LLC	5084	A	951 520-1700	12818
Wangs Alliance Corporation	3645	E	909 230-9401	8300	Index Fasteners Inc **(PA)**	5085	F	909 923-5002	12859
Mag Instrument Inc **(PA)**	3648	A	909 947-1006	8374	Solar Link International Inc	5085	C	909 605-7789	12881
Discopylabs	3652	E	909 390-3800	8456	Jcm Engineering Corp	5088	D	909 923-3730	12910
Precise Media Services Inc	3652	E	909 481-3305	8463	Dennis Foland Inc **(PA)**	5099	E	909 930-9900	12973
Tactical Command Inds Inc **(DH)**	3669	E	925 219-1097	8629	Rosen Electronics LLC	5099	D	951 898-9808	12985
Celestica Aerospace Tech Corp	3672	C	512 310-7540	8658	Beauty 21 Cosmetics Inc	5122	C	909 945-2220	13030
Tc Cosmotronic Inc	3672	E	949 660-0740	8736	Concord Foods Inc **(HQ)**	5141	D	909 975-2000	13176
Vishay Thin Film LLC	3674	E	909 923-3313	8919	Dpi Specialty Foods West Inc **(DH)**	5141	C	909 975-1019	13178
Aamp of America	3699	E	805 338-6800	9191	Dpi Specialty Foods West Inc	5141	C	909 975-1019	13179
Kanex	3699	E	714 332-1681	9222	Vitco Distributors Inc	5141	C	909 355-1300	13241
West Coast Chain Mfg Co	3699	E	909 923-7800	9270	Aspire Bakeries LLC	5149	C	909 472-3500	13351
West Coast Corporation	3699	E	909 923-7800	9271	Mondelez Global LLC	5149	D	909 605-0140	13380
New Flyer of America Inc	3711	C	909 456-3566	9302	Coast Plastics Inc **(PA)**	5162	F	626 812-9174	13411
TCI Engineering Inc	3711	D	909 984-1773	9310	Lowes Home Centers LLC	5211	C	909 969-9053	13643
Arrow Truck Bodies & Eqp Inc	3713	E	909 947-3991	9316	Eggs West	5399	F	909 947-6207	13690
Egr Incorporated **(DH)**	3714	E	909 923-7075	9387	Citrus Motors Ontario Inc **(PA)**	5511	C	909 390-0930	13748
Lenco Racing Transmissions Inc	3714	F	909 673-9000	9413	Jeep Chrysler of Ontario	5511	D	909 390-9898	13784
Power-Right Industries LLC	3714	F	909 628-4397	9440	Mark Christopher Chevrolet Inc **(PA)**	5511	C	909 321-5860	13794
Thmx Holdings LLC	3714	C	909 390-3944	9469	Ontario Automotive LLC	5511	C	909 974-3800	13808
Maney Aircraft Inc	3728	E	909 390-2500	9741	American Business Bank	6022	D	909 919-2040	14178
Otto Instrument Service Inc **(PA)**	3728	E	909 930-5800	9758	Citizens Business Bank **(HQ)**	6022	C	909 980-4030	14188
Q1 Test Inc	3728	C	909 390-9718	9771	Cvb Financial Corp **(PA)**	6022	C	909 980-4030	14190
Summit Machine LLC	3728	C	909 923-2744	9803	First Mortgage Corporation	6162	B	909 595-1996	14316
Tower Mechanical Products Inc	3812	C	714 947-2723	10085	Invapharm Inc	6221	E	909 757-1818	14411
Aaren Scientific Inc **(DH)**	3827	D	909 937-1033	10306	Adminsure Inc	6411	D	909 718-1200	14553
Carl Zeiss Meditec Prod LLC	3827	D	877 644-4657	10310	Robert Moreno Insurance Svcs	6411	C	714 578-3318	14627
F & D Flores Enterprises Inc	3829	E	909 975-4853	10363	Sedgwick CMS Holdings Inc	6411	C	909 477-5500	14629
B Braun Medical Inc	3841	C	909 906-7575	10447	Wells Frgo Insur Svcs Minn Inc	6411	C	909 481-3802	14642
Marlee Manufacturing Inc	3841	E	909 390-3222	10550	Mills Corporation	6512	D	909 484-8300	14673
Isomedix Operations Inc	3842	E	909 390-9942	10675	Cushman & Wakefield Cal Inc	6531	B	909 483-0077	14782
Safariland LLC	3842	B	909 923-7300	10698	Cushman & Wakefield Cal Inc	6531	B	909 980-3781	14783
Ashtel Studios Inc	3844	E	909 434-0911	10780	RAD Diversified Reit Inc	6531	D	813 723-7348	14854
Aliquantum International Inc	3944	E	909 773-0880	10945	Prime Hospitality LLC	7011	D	909 975-5000	15309
Horizon Hobby LLC	3944	D	909 390-9595	10953	SS Heritage Inn Ontario LLC	7011	C	909 937-5000	15369
American Fleet & Ret Graphics	3993	E	909 937-7570	11096	Unifirst Corporation	7218	C	909 390-8670	15471
Astro Display Company Inc	3993	E	909 605-2875	11098	Wurms Janitorial Service Inc	7349	D	951 582-0003	15756
Edelmann Usa Inc **(DH)**	3993	F	323 669-5700	11111	Diversity Bus Solutions Inc	7361	C	909 395-0243	15838
Encore Image Inc	3993	E	909 986-4632	11113	Kimco Staffing Services Inc	7361	A	909 390-9881	15859
Optec Displays Inc	3993	D	866 924-5239	11142	Redlands Employment Services	7361	B	951 688-0083	15890
Sign Industries Inc	3993	E	909 930-0303	11159	Care Stffing Professionals Inc	7363	D	909 906-2060	15919
California Exotic Novlt LLC	3999	D	909 606-1950	11200	CU Direct Corporation **(PA)**	7371	C	833 908-0121	16005
Scripto-Tokai Corporation **(HQ)**	3999	D	909 930-5000	11278	Guard-Systems Inc	7381	A	909 947-5400	16647
Sun Badge Co	3999	D	909 930-1444	11287	Pacwest Security Services	7381	A	909 948-0279	16669
C P S Express	4212	C	951 685-1041	11446	Signal 88 LLC	7381	A	714 713-5306	16689
CRST Expedited Inc	4213	B	909 563-5606	11479	Arvato USA LLC	7389	C	502 356-8063	16782
Jack Jones Trucking Inc	4213	D	909 456-2500	11492	Merchant of Tennis Inc	7389	A	909 923-3388	16873
Las Vegas / LA Express Inc **(PA)**	4213	C	909 972-3100	11494	Ontario Convention Center Corp	7389	B	909 937-3000	16894
Ltl Pros Inc	4213	D	909 350-1600	11496	Alamo Rental (us) Inc	7514	D	888 826-6893	16979
United Parcel Service Inc	4215	A	909 974-7212	11543	Fox Rent A Car Inc	7514	D	909 635-6390	16983
Americold Logistics LLC	4222	C	909 937-2200	11549	Automotive Tstg & Dev Svcs Inc **(PA)**	7549	C	909 390-1100	17053
Americold Logistics LLC	4222	D	909 390-4950	11550	Whiting Door Mfg Corp	7699	D	909 877-0120	17164
Coastal Pacific Fd Distrs Inc	4225	D	909 947-2066	11567	Vantiva Sup Chain Slutions Inc	7819	C	909 974-2016	17272
Neovia Logistics Dist LP	4225	D	909 657-4900	11602	Toyota Arena	7999	D	909 244-5500	17574
Nordstrom Inc	4225	B	909 390-1040	11603	Kaiser Foundation Hospitals	8011	C	909 605-7000	17675
Osram Sylvania Inc	4225	C	909 923-3003	11604	Inland Chrstn HM Fundation Inc	8051	C	909 395-9322	17977
Quill LLC	4225	C	909 390-0600	11606	Ontarioidence Opco LLC	8052	B	909 984-8629	18093
Takane USA Inc	4225	C	909 923-5511	11615	Bio-Med Services Inc	8062	D	909 235-4400	18192
Target Corporation	4225	C	909 937-5500	11617	Prime Healthcare Foundation Inc **(PA)**	8062	D	909 235-4400	18384
Taylored Fmi LLC	4225	C	909 510-4800	11619	Prime Hlthcare Svcs - Pmpa LLC **(DH)**	8062	C	909 235-4400	18392
Taylored Services LLC **(DH)**	4225	D	909 510-4800	11620	Prime Hlthcare Svcs - St John **(DH)**	8062	C	913 680-6000	18395
Taylored Services Holdings LLC **(DH)**	4225	D	909 510-4800	11621	Proform Inc	8071	D	707 752-9010	18561
United Parcel Service Inc	4512	C	909 605-7740	11675	Accentcare Home Hlth Yuma Inc	8082	A	909 605-7000	18581
DSV Solutions Inc	4731	C	909 390-4563	11756	Texas Home Health America LP **(PA)**	8082	D	972 201-3800	18645
Innovel Solutions Inc	4731	A	909 605-1446	11773	In-Roads Creative Programs	8322	B	909 947-9142	19093
Taylored Svcs Parent Co Inc **(PA)**	4731	D	909 510-4800	11808	West End Yung MNS Christn Assn	8641	C	909 477-2780	19471

Mergent email: customerrelations@mergent.com
1410

2024 Southern California
Business Directory and Buyers Guide

(P-0000) Products & Services Section entry number
(PA)=Parent Co (HQ)=Headquarters (DH)=Div Headquarters

Name	SIC	EMP	PHONE	ENTRY#
Hntb Corporation	8711	D	909 727-5600	19606
HMC Group (HQ)	8712	C	909 989-9979	19732
Physician Support Systems Inc (DH)	8721	B	717 653-5340	19800
Aveta Health Solution Inc	8742	B	909 605-8000	20137

ORANGE, CA - Orange County

Name	SIC	EMP	PHONE	ENTRY#
Marina Landscape Inc	0782	B	714 939-6600	203
Ggg Demolition Inc (PA)	1542	D	714 699-9350	553
McCarthy Bldg Companies Inc	1542	D	949 851-8383	567
Rick Hamm Construction Inc	1611	C	714 532-0815	640
RJ Noble Company (PA)	1611	C	714 637-1550	642
Bernel Inc	1711	C	714 778-6070	743
General Underground	1711	C	714 632-8646	773
K & S Air Conditioning Inc	1711	C	714 685-0077	782
General Coatings Corporation	1721	D	858 587-1277	845
Sanders & Wohrman Corporation	1721	C	714 919-0446	856
Calderon Drywall Contrs Inc	1742	C	714 696-2977	973
John Jory Corporation (PA)	1742	B	714 279-7901	981
Martin Integrated Systems	1742	E	714 998-9100	983
Padilla Construction Company	1742	C	714 685-8500	990
Cmf Inc	1761	D	714 637-2409	1039
Danny Letner Inc	1761	C	714 633-0030	1040
Red Pointe Roofing LP (PA)	1761	C	714 685-0010	1052
Beach Paving Inc	1771	E	714 978-2414	1060
Jezowski & Markel Contrs Inc	1771	C	714 978-2222	1076
Santa Ana Creek Development Company	1771	D	714 685-3462	1085
Bapko Metal Inc	1791	D	714 639-9380	1101
Rika Corporation	1791	D	949 830-9050	1115
Miller Environmental Inc	1795	C	714 385-0099	1135
West Coast Firestopping Inc	1799	D	714 935-1104	1184
Quality Produced LLC	2037	E	310 592-8834	1378
Don Miguel Mexican Foods Inc (HQ)	2038	C	714 385-4500	1389
American Bottling Company	2086	C	714 974-8560	1680
Reyes Coca-Cola Bottling LLC	2086	C	714 974-1901	1735
Newport Flavors & Fragrances	2087	C	714 771-2200	1781
Natures Flavors	2099	E	714 744-3700	1954
Orange Woodworks Inc	2431	E	714 997-2600	2625
Amscan Inc	2656	E	714 972-2626	3141
J J Foil Company Inc	2675	E	714 998-9920	3202
K & D Graphics	2675	E	714 639-8900	3203
Presentation Folder Inc	2675	E	714 289-7000	3204
Positive Concepts Inc (PA)	2679	E	714 685-5800	3243
American PCF Prtrs College Inc	2752	E	949 250-3212	3509
Comprehensive Print Group LLC	2752	E	949 255-4067	3538
Fisher Printing Inc (PA)	2752	C	714 998-9200	3574
We Do Graphics Inc	2752	E	714 997-7390	3707
Western Prtg & Graphics LLC (PA)	2752	E	714 532-3946	3710
Label Impressions Inc	2759	E	714 634-3466	3776
Solvay America Inc	2819	D	225 361-3376	3911
Solvay Chemicals Inc	2819	E	714 744-5610	3913
Coastal Enterprises	2821	E	714 771-4969	3931
Ameripharma Specialty Phrm Div	2834	F	877 778-3773	4044
Harpers Pharmacy Inc	2834	C	877 778-3773	4129
Ortho-Clinical Diagnostics Inc	2835	E	714 639-2323	4285
BASF Corporation	2869	C	714 921-1430	4514
Cytec Engineered Materials Inc	2899	D	714 630-9400	4603
California Gasket and Rbr Corp (PA)	3069	E	310 323-4250	4758
West American Rubber Co LLC	3069	C	714 532-3355	4803
West American Rubber Co LLC (PA)	3069	C	714 532-3355	4804
Allen Mold Inc	3089	F	714 538-6517	4933
King Plastics Inc	3089	D	714 997-7540	5080
Roto Dynamics Inc	3089	E	714 685-0183	5187
SKB Corporation (PA)	3089	B	714 637-1252	5206
Dennis DiGiorgio	3231	E	714 408-7527	5339
Precast Innovations Inc	3272	E	714 921-4060	5439
Merlex Stucco Inc	3299	E	877 547-8822	5570
Omega Products Corp	3299	E	714 935-0900	5571
Opal Service Inc (PA)	3299	E	714 935-0900	5572
Pro Detention Inc	3315	D	714 881-3680	5622
Thermal-Vac Technology Inc	3398	E	714 997-2601	5851
Commercial Metal Forming Inc	3443	E	714 532-6321	6137
Facility Makers Inc	3444	D	714 544-1702	6240
SA Serving Lines Inc	3444	E	714 848-7529	6309
Tri Precision Sheetmetal Inc	3444	E	714 632-8838	6335
Allied Mdular Bldg Systems Inc (PA)	3448	E	714 516-1188	6373
Shade Structures Inc	3448	E	714 427-6980	6390
Anillo Industries Inc (PA)	3452	E	714 637-7000	6431
Independent Forge Company	3462	E	714 997-7337	6460
Gel Industries Inc	3463	C	714 639-8191	6478
Quality Aluminum Forge LLC	3463	C	714 639-8191	6481
Prototype & Short-Run Svcs Inc	3469	E	714 449-9661	6550
Continuous Coating Corp (PA)	3471	D	714 637-4642	6608
Dunham Metal Processing Inc	3471	E	714 532-5551	6612
Hightower Plating & Mfg Co	3471	E	714 637-9110	6626
Fletcher Coating Co	3479	E	714 637-4763	6705
United Sunshine American Industries	3496	E		6831
Nov Inc	3533	D	714 978-1900	6962
Air Tube Transfer Systems Inc	3535	E	714 363-0700	6968
Dematic Corp	3535	E	714 388-8803	6973
Hightower Metal Products	3544	D	714 637-7000	7075
His Industries Inc	3565	E	949 383-4308	7349
Premier Filters Inc	3569	E	657 226-0091	7408
Shaxon Industries Inc	3572	E	714 779-1140	7484
Data Aire Inc (HQ)	3585	D	800 347-2473	7608
G A Systems Inc	3589	F	714 848-7529	7659
Hyperion Motors LLC	3594	E	714 363-5858	7712
All Diameter Grinding Inc	3599	E	714 744-1200	7752
D Mills Grnding Machining Inc	3599	C	951 697-6847	7812
ISI Detention Contg Group Inc	3599	D	714 288-1770	7877
Niedwick Corporation	3599	E	714 771-9999	7955
Rlh Industries Inc	3661	E	714 532-1672	8484
Jtb Supply Company Inc	3669	F	714 639-9558	8617
Zettler Magnetics Inc (PA)	3669	C	949 831-5000	8633
Avantec Manufacturing Inc	3672	E	714 532-6197	8652
Fabricated Components Corp	3672	C	714 974-8590	8676
US Sensor Corp	3674	D	714 639-1000	8916
Winchster Intrcnnect Micro LLC	3678	C	714 637-7099	8986
Coastal Component Inds Inc	3679	E	714 685-6677	9020
Statek Corporation	3679	C	714 639-7810	9120
Statek Corporation (HQ)	3679	C	714 639-7810	9121
Vintique Inc	3714	E	714 634-1932	9485
APM Manufacturing	3721	C	714 453-0100	9510
Sport Kites Inc	3721	F	714 998-6359	9555
Ducommun Aerostructures Inc	3724	C	714 637-4401	9567
Air Cabin Engineering Inc	3728	E	714 637-4111	9609
APM Manufacturing (HQ)	3728	C	714 453-0100	9626
Arden Engineering Inc	3728	E	714 998-6410	9630
Arden Engineering Holdings Inc (DH)	3728	E	714 998-6410	9631
Tri-Tech Precision Inc	3728	F	714 970-1363	9819
Cleatech LLC	3821	E	714 754-6668	10091
Califrnia Anlytical Instrs Inc	3823	D	714 974-5560	10121
Fieldpiece Instruments Inc (PA)	3825	D	714 634-1844	10199
Redline Detection LLC (PA)	3829	E	714 579-6961	10394
Systems Integrated LLC	3829	F	714 998-0900	10400
Fusion Biotec Inc	3841	E	949 264-3437	10512
Dux Industries Inc	3843	D	805 488-1122	10742
Handpiece Parts & Products Inc	3843	E	714 997-4331	10745
Jeneric/Pentron Incorporated (HQ)	3843	C	203 265-7397	10748
Kerr Corporation (HQ)	3843	C	714 516-7400	10749
Ormco Corporation (HQ)	3843	C	714 516-7400	10756
Sybron Dental Specialties Inc (PA)	3843	C	714 516-7400	10772
John Bishop Design Inc	3993	E	714 744-2300	11126
Metal Art of California Inc (PA)	3993	D	714 532-7100	11137
Do It Right Products LLC	3999	E	714 998-8152	11213
Tandem Design Inc	3999	E	714 978-7272	11293
Orange Cnty Trnsp Auth Schlrsh	4111	A	714 999-1726	11354
Orange Cnty Trnsp Auth Schlrsh (PA)	4111	B	714 636-7433	11355
Xpo Logistics Freight Inc	4213	D	714 282-7717	11515
Cruz Modular Inc (PA)	4214	D	714 283-2890	11518
Wood Space Industries Inc	4226	F	714 996-4552	11635
Sfpp LP (DH)	4613	C	714 560-4400	11710
Cco Holdings LLC	4841	C	714 509-5861	11976
SA Recycling LLC (PA)	4953	C	714 632-2000	12185
M S International Inc (PA)	5032	B	714 685-7500	12356
Western Pacific Distrg LLC	5032	C	714 974-6837	12364
Beacon Pacific Inc	5033	C	714 288-1974	12366
Total Health Environment LLC	5047	C	714 637-1010	12520
Everfocus Electronics Corp (HQ)	5065	E	626 844-8888	12659
Intellipower Inc	5065	C	714 921-1580	12670
Lonestar Sierra LLC	5085	C	866 575-5680	12862
Frick Paper Company LLC	5113	C	714 787-4900	13007
Cencora Inc	5122	C	610 727-7000	13031
Bluetriton Brands Inc	5149	C	714 532-6220	13355
Southern Counties Oil Co (DH)	5171	D	714 744-7140	13445
Great Atlantic News LLC	5192	C	770 863-9000	13495
Nifty Package Co Inc	5199	E	714 863-6058	13551
Home Depot USA Inc	5211	C	714 538-9600	13589
Selman Chevrolet Company	5511	C	714 633-3521	13824
Toyota of Orange Inc	5511	C	714 639-6750	13839
Villa Ford Inc	5511	C	714 637-8222	13843
Aquarian Accessories Corp	5736	F	714 632-0230	13976
Fahetas LLC (PA)	5812	D	949 280-1983	14005
Tavistock Restaurants LLC	5813	C	714 939-8686	14054
Beverages & More Inc	5921	C	714 279-8131	14058
Strata USA Llc	5963	E	888 878-7282	14112
Cashcall Inc	6141	A	949 752-4600	14268

Employee Codes: A=Over 500 employees, B=251-500
C=101-250, D=51-100, E=20-50, F=10-19, G=1-9

2024 Southern California
Business Directory and Buyers Guide

© Mergent Inc. 1-800-342-5647

GEOGRAPHIC

1411

	SIC	EMP	PHONE	ENTRY#
Alignment Health Plan	6324	D	323 728-7232	14458
Alignment Healthcare Inc **(PA)**	6324	D	844 310-2247	14459
Choic Admini Insur Servi	6411	B	714 542-4200	14576
Conexis Bnfits Admnstrators LP **(HQ)**	6411	C	714 835-5006	14578
Word & Brown Insurance Administrato **(PA)**	6411	B	714 835-5006	14648
Solari Enterprises Inc	6512	C	714 282-2520	14685
Irvine APT Communities LP	6513	C	714 937-8900	14720
Kisco Senior Living LLC	6513	C	714 997-5355	14725
Absolutely Zero Corporation	6531	B	949 269-3300	14742
Lres Corporation **(PA)**	6531	C	714 520-5737	14825
Realselect Inc	6531	C	661 803-5188	14856
Roman Cthlic Diocese of Orange	6553	C	714 532-6551	14917
Varco De Mexico Holdings Inc	7359	E	714 978-1900	15804
Emergncy Mdcine Spclist Ornge	7363	D	714 543-8911	15920
Roth Staffing Companies LP **(PA)**	7363	D	714 939-8600	15938
Volt Management Corp	7363	B	800 654-2624	15948
Ashunya Inc	7371	C	714 385-1900	15968
Infinite Technologies LLC	7371	C	786 408-7995	16052
Maintech Incorporated	7371	C	714 921-8000	16068
Stoneriver Inc	7371	D	714 705-8227	16123
Lcptracker Inc	7372	E	714 669-0052	16290
Salescatcher LLC	7372	E	714 376-6700	16371
Quotit Corporation	7373	C	714 564-5000	16466
Invision Networking LLC	7379	C	949 309-3441	16572
Tensoriot Inc	7379	C	909 342-2459	16606
United Guard Security Inc	7381	C	714 242-4051	16698
Cirtech Inc	7389	E	714 921-0860	16802
Merical LLC	7389	C	714 685-0977	16875
Merical LLC	7389	B	714 283-9551	16876
Merical LLC	7389	C	714 238-7225	16877
Rgis LLC	7389	C	714 938-0663	16915
Enterprise Rnt--car Los Angles **(DH)**	7514	D	657 221-4400	16981
Sam Schaffer Inc	7699	E	323 263-7524	17151
Lucky Strike Entertainment LLC	7933	D	248 374-3420	17359
Childrens Healthcare Cal	8011	B	714 997-3000	17617
Scribemd LLC	8011	C	714 543-8911	17761
University California Irvine	8011	C	714 456-7890	17815
University California Irvine	8011	C	714 456-6966	17816
University California Irvine	8011	A	714 456-6170	17817
US Dermatology Medical Management Inc	8011	D	817 962-2157	17820
Premier Dental Holdings Inc **(PA)**	8021	B	714 480-3000	17846
Western Dental Services Inc **(HQ)**	8021	B	714 480-3000	17849
Emeritus Corporation	8051	C	714 639-3590	17933
Orange Hlthcare Wllness Cntre	8051	C	714 633-3568	18021
Pennant Group Inc	8051	B	714 978-2534	18030
Chapman Global Medical Ctr Inc	8062	B	714 633-0011	18215
Childrens Hospital Orange Cnty	8062	B	949 365-2416	18217
Childrens Hospital Orange Cnty **(PA)**	8062	A	714 509-8300	18219
St Joseph Hospital of Orange	8062	C	714 771-8222	18461
St Joseph Hospital of Orange	8062	C	714 771-8006	18462
St Joseph Hospital of Orange	8062	D	714 771-8037	18464
St Joseph Hospital of Orange **(DH)**	8062	A	714 633-9111	18465
University California Irvine	8062	B	714 456-8000	18487
University California Irvine	8062	A	714 456-6011	18488
University California Irvine	8062	C	714 456-5558	18489
Childrens Healthcare Cal **(PA)**	8069	A	714 997-3000	18523
Arbormed Inc **(PA)**	8099	C	714 689-1500	18742
Uc Irvine Health	8099	D	714 456-6191	18812
City Orange Police Assn Inc	8611	C	714 457-5340	19376
Orange Cnty Hlth Auth A Pub AG	8621	B	714 246-8500	19399
Aclu Fndation Southern Cal LLC	8641	D	213 977-9500	19421
Boyle Engineering Corporation	8711	C	949 476-3300	19556
Eichleay Inc	8711	C	562 256-8600	19579
Holmes & Narver Inc **(HQ)**	8711	C	714 567-2400	19609
Architects Orange Inc	8712	C	714 639-9860	19723
University California Irvine	8721	D	714 456-6655	19809
Micro Prcision Calibration Inc	8734	C	714 901-5659	19976
American Intgrted Rsources Inc	8741	C	714 921-4100	19995
Prospect Medical Systems Inc **(HQ)**	8741	C	714 667-8156	20085
Raymond Group **(PA)**	8741	D	714 771-7670	20087
Medical Spc Managers Inc	8742	C	714 571-5000	20197
Ralis Services Corp	8742	C	844 347-2547	20226
Aecom Usa Inc	8748	C	714 567-2501	20308
Goldman Data LLC	8748	D	714 283-5889	20341
Patriot Wastewater LLC	8748	C	714 921-4545	20370
California Dept of Pub Hlth	9199	C	714 567-2906	20408

ORCUTT, CA - Santa Barbara County

	SIC	EMP	PHONE	ENTRY#
Den-Mat Corporation **(DH)**	2844	B	805 922-8491	4400

ORO GRANDE, CA - San Bernardino County

	SIC	EMP	PHONE	ENTRY#
Calportland Company	3241	E	760 245-5321	5363

OXNARD, CA - Ventura County

	SIC	EMP	PHONE	ENTRY#
Fresh Venture Farms LLC	0161	D	805 754-4449	9
San Miguel Produce Inc	0161	B	805 488-0981	11
Etchandy Farms LLC	0171	D	805 983-4700	15
Las Posas Berry Farms LLC	0171	D	805 483-1000	18
Santa Rosa Berry Farms LLC	0171	B	805 981-3060	24
Superior Fruit LLC	0171	C	805 485-2519	25
Marathon Land Inc	0181	C	805 488-3585	59
River Ridge Farms Inc	0181	D	805 647-6880	70
Scarborough Farms Inc	0191	C	805 483-9113	87
Boskovich Farms Inc **(PA)**	0723	C	805 487-2299	99
Mission Produce Inc **(PA)**	0723	C	805 981-3650	108
Ramco Enterprises LP	0723	B	805 486-9328	110
Venco Western Inc	0782	C	805 981-2400	219
Dcor LLC **(PA)**	1382	C	805 535-2000	297
Eagle Dominion Energy Corp	1382	E	805 272-9557	302
Freeport-Mcmoran Oil & Gas LLC	1382	F	805 567-1601	304
Blois Construction Inc	1623	C	805 485-0011	662
Kaiser Air Conditioning and Sheet Metal Inc	1761	E	805 988-1800	1047
J M Smucker Company	2033	D	805 487-5483	1338
Oxnard Lemon Company	2037	C	805 483-1173	1377
Noushig Inc	2051	E	805 983-2903	1486
Royal Wine Corporation	2084	C	805 983-1560	1658
Kevita Inc **(HQ)**	2086	D	805 200-2250	1701
Fresh Innovations LLC	2097	E	805 483-2265	1836
McK Enterprises Inc	2099	D	805 483-5292	1944
Sunrise Growers Inc	2099	A	612 619-9545	1993
Scully Sportswear Inc **(PA)**	2386	D	805 483-6339	2433
California Woodworking Inc	2434	E	805 982-9090	2653
E Vasquez Distributors Inc	2448	E	805 487-8458	2717
Casualway Usa LLC	2514	D	805 660-7408	2827
Ergonom Corporation	2599	D	805 981-9978	3023
Ergonom Corporation **(PA)**	2599	D	805 981-9978	3024
West Coast Industries Inc **(PA)**	2599	E	415 621-6656	3035
New-Indy Oxnard LLC	2621	C	805 986-3881	3057
Procter & Gamble Paper Pdts Co	2676	A	805 485-8871	3207
TI Enterprises LLC	2721	C	805 981-8393	3391
National Graphics LLC	2752	E	805 644-9212	3642
Pine Grove Industries Inc	2752	C	805 485-3700	3658
V3 Printing Corporation	2752	D	805 981-2600	3703
Ventura Printing Inc **(PA)**	2752	D	805 981-2600	3705
Complyright Dist Svcs Inc	2761	C	805 981-0992	3830
Cdti Advanced Materials Inc **(PA)**	2819	C	805 639-9458	3888
Kim Laube & Company Inc	2844	E	805 240-1300	4429
Spatz Corporation	2844	C	805 487-2122	4457
Monsanto Company	2879	E	805 827-2341	4552
Olde Thompson LLC **(DH)**	2899	C	805 983-0388	4624
B & S Plastics Inc	3089	C	805 981-0262	4951
Cool-Pak LLC	3089	D	805 981-2434	4995
Leading Industry Inc	3089	E	805 385-4100	5083
PC Vaughan Mfg Corp	3089	D	805 278-2555	5132
Pinnpack Capital Holdings LLC	3089	C	805 385-4100	5136
Rakar Incorporated	3089	E	805 487-2721	5171
Masters In Metal Inc	3263	E	805 988-1992	5380
Santa Barbara Design Studio **(PA)**	3269	E	805 966-3883	5386
Diversified Minerals Inc	3273	E	805 247-1069	5476
State Ready Mix Inc	3273	F	805 647-2817	5505
Western Saw Manufacturers Inc	3425	E	805 981-0999	5893
Raypak Inc **(DH)**	3433	B	805 278-5300	5984
Millworks Etc Inc	3442	E	805 499-3400	6113
Steelworks Etc Inc	3442	E	805 487-3000	6125
Oxnard Prcsion Fabrication Inc	3444	E	805 985-0447	6280
Advanced Structural Tech Inc	3462	C	805 204-9133	6457
Elite Metal Finishing LLC **(PA)**	3471	C	805 983-4320	6620
Applied Powdercoat Inc	3479	E	805 981-1991	6691
Ets Express LLC **(DH)**	3479	E	805 278-7771	6703
Haas Automation Inc **(PA)**	3541	A	805 278-1800	7013
Acme Cryogenics Inc	3559	E	805 981-4500	7219
Cryogenic Experts Inc	3559	E	805 981-4500	7231
Nu Venture Diving Co	3563	E	805 815-4044	7315
Vortech Engineering Inc	3564	E	805 247-0226	7339
Amiad USA Inc	3589	E	805 988-3323	7636
Amiad USA Inc	3589	E	805 988-3323	7637
Aerotek Inc	3599	A	805 604-3000	7747
Rapid Product Solutions Inc	3599	E	805 485-7234	7994
T & M Machining	3599	E	805 983-6716	8041
Birns Oceanographics Inc	3648	F	805 487-5393	8356
Boss International LLC **(PA)**	3651	E	805 988-0192	8402
Scosche Industries Inc	3651	C	805 486-4450	8434
Calamp Corp	3663	D	949 600-5600	8502
Esco Technologies Inc	3669	E	805 604-3875	8610
Mercury Systems Inc	3672	C	805 388-1345	8702
Mercury Systems Inc	3672	C	805 751-1100	8703

Mergent email: customerrelations@mergent.com
1412

2024 Southern California
Business Directory and Buyers Guide

(P-0000) Products & Services Section entry number
(PA)=Parent Co (HQ)=Headquarters (DH)=Div Headquarters

	SIC	EMP	PHONE	ENTRY#
Alpha Products Inc	3678	E	805 981-8666	8960
Component Equipment Coinc	3678	E	805 988-8004	8964
Delta Microwave LLC	3679	D	805 751-1100	9030
Harwil Precision Products	3679	E	805 988-6800	9055
Simpliphi Power Inc	3691	E	805 640-6700	9154
Becker Automotive Designs Inc	3711	E	805 487-5227	9281
Granatelli Motor Sports Inc	3714	E	805 486-6644	9398
American Airframe Inc	3728	E	805 240-1608	9622
Pti Technologies Inc (DH)	3728	E	805 604-3700	9770
Northrop Grumman Systems Corp	3812	D	805 278-2074	10035
Northrop Grumman Systems Corp	3812	C	805 684-6641	10038
Catalytic Solutions Inc (HQ)	3822	E	805 486-4649	10100
Frank Stubbs Co Inc	3842	E	805 278-4300	10661
Golf Sales West Inc	3949	E	805 988-3363	10994
Illah Sports Inc	3949	E	805 240-7790	11004
Vogue Sign Inc	3993	E	805 487-7222	11179
Mgr Design International Inc	3999	C	805 981-6400	11252
Durham School Services L P	4151	C	805 483-6076	11426
Tanimura Antle Fresh Foods Inc	4225	C	805 483-2358	11616
NRG California South LP	4911	C	805 984-5241	12031
Bragg Investment Company Inc	5013	D	805 485-2106	12235
American Tooth Industries	5047	D	805 487-9868	12470
Aluminum Precision Pdts Inc	5051	A	805 488-4401	12534
Mws Precision Wire Inds Inc	5051	A	818 991-8553	12560
Orora Packaging Solutions	5113	D	805 278-5040	13016
Sysco Ventura Inc	5141	B	805 205-7000	13236
McConnells Fine Ice Creams LLC	5143	E	805 963-8813	13256
Boskovich Fresh Cut LLC	5148	C	805 487-2299	13314
Ventura County Lemon Coop	5148	C	805 385-3345	13347
Olde Thompson LLC	5149	E	805 983-0388	13386
AG Rx (PA)	5191	D	805 487-0696	13486
Seminis Vegetable Seeds Inc (DH)	5191	A	855 733-3834	13491
Grolink Plant Company Inc (PA)	5193	C	805 984-7958	13509
Pyramid Flowers Inc	5193	C	805 382-8070	13518
Home Depot USA Inc	5211	C	805 983-0653	13601
DCH California Motors Inc	5511	C	805 988-7900	13755
State Compensation Insur Fund	6321	D	888 782-8338	14456
Lawyers Title Insurance Corp	6361	A	805 484-2701	14544
Milwood Healthcare Inc	6512	D	626 274-4345	14674
Courtyard Oxnard	7011	D	805 988-3600	15122
Djont/Jpm Hsptlity Lsg Spe LLC	7011	D	805 984-2500	15134
Mission Linen Supply	7213	D	805 485-6794	15455
Workrite Uniform Company Inc (DH)	7218	B	805 483-0175	15473
H G Group Inc	7291	B	805 486-6463	15495
Taheem Johnson Inc	7379	D	818 835-3785	16605
Boyd and Associates	7381	C	805 988-8298	16625
West Coast Wldg & Piping Inc	7692	D	805 246-5841	17099
Players West Amusements Inc (PA)	7993	E	805 983-1400	17445
Comedy Club Oxnard LLC	7997	D	805 535-5400	17479
Cabrillo Crdolgy Med Group Inc	8011	D	805 983-0922	17607
N S C Channel Islands Inc	8011	B	805 485-1908	17721
Dignity Health	8062	A	805 988-2500	18240
Inclusive Edcatn Cmnty Prtnr I	8211	B	805 985-4808	18971
Amigo Baby Inc	8322	E	805 901-1237	19023
Child Dev Rsrces of Vntura CNT (PA)	8322	C	805 485-7878	19039
Seneca Family of Agencies	8322	E	805 278-0355	19139
Saticoy Lemon Association	8611	C	805 654-6543	19385
Oxnard Police Department	8641	B	805 385-8300	19457
Jsl Technologies Inc	8711	B	805 985-7700	19626
Systems Application & Tech Inc	8711	B	805 487-7373	19697
Seminis Inc (DH)	8731	E	805 485-7317	19874
City of Oxnard (PA)	8742	C	805 385-7803	20151
Behavioral Science Technology Inc (PA)	8748	D	805 646-0166	20317

PACIFIC PALISADES, CA - Los Angeles County

	SIC	EMP	PHONE	ENTRY#
Promise Wine LLC	2084	D	707 260-9094	1654
Rokit Drinks LLC	2085	E	323 654-2740	1674
Aadi Bioscience Inc (PA)	2834	E	424 744-8055	4027
Fuego Living LLC	3631	E	415 558-7151	8217
Chilicon Power LLC (PA)	3825	D	310 800-1396	10189
Optimiscorp	7372	E	310 230-2780	16337
Pipeliner Crm	7372	E	424 280-6445	16348
Bel-Air Bay Club Ltd	7997	C	310 230-4700	17471
Riviera Country Club Inc	7999	C	310 454-6591	17562
Solutionz Inc	8742	C	888 815-0322	20244

PACOIMA, CA - Los Angeles County

	SIC	EMP	PHONE	ENTRY#
Vita Juice Corporation	2033	D	818 899-1195	1349
Hrk Pet Food Products Inc	2048	F	818 897-2521	1442
Natural Balance Pet Foods Inc	2048	D	800 829-4493	1447
American Fruits & Flavors LLC (HQ)	2087	E	818 899-9574	1754
Creative Fire Kiln and Kit LLC	2099	E	818 486-3899	1875
LA Hardwood Flooring Inc (PA)	2426	F	818 361-0099	2574

	SIC	EMP	PHONE	ENTRY#
N K Cabinets Inc	2434	E	818 897-7909	2670
Western States Packaging Inc	2673	E	818 686-6045	3196
Cosmetic Enterprises Ltd	2844	F	818 896-5355	4393
Cosmetic Group Usa Inc	2844	C	818 767-2889	4394
Gscm Ventures Inc	2844	E	818 303-2600	4417
Flamemaster Corporation	2891	E	818 890-1401	4565
Moc Products Company Inc (PA)	2899	D	818 794-3500	4622
Molding Corporation America	3089	E	818 890-7877	5106
RMR Products Inc (PA)	3281	E	818 890-0896	5446
D & M Steel Inc	3441	E	818 896-2070	6019
SDS Industries Inc	3442	C	818 492-3500	6122
American Range Corporation	3444	C	818 897-0808	6187
Mayoni Enterprises	3444	D	818 896-0026	6268
Anwright Corporation	3451	E	818 896-2465	6410
Sunland Aerospace Fasteners	3452	C	818 485-8929	6454
APT Metal Fabricators Inc	3469	E	818 896-7478	6495
Cabrac Inc	3469	C	818 834-0177	6503
Hanmar LLC (PA)	3469	D	818 890-2802	6520
Metalite Manufacturing Company	3469	E	818 890-2802	6536
M & R Plating Corporation	3471	F	818 896-2700	6635
Ultramet	3471	D	818 899-0236	6676
American Etching & Mfg	3479	E	323 875-3910	6689
Kitch Engineering Inc	3599	E	818 897-7133	7900
JKL Components Corporation	3647	E	818 896-0019	8347
Mole-Richardson Co Ltd (PA)	3648	D	323 851-0111	8375
Dw and Bb Consulting Inc	3769	D	818 896-9899	9917
Nu-Hope Laboratories Inc	3841	E	818 899-7711	10581
Twin Peak Industries Inc	3949	E	800 259-5906	11037
California Signs Inc	3993	E	818 899-1888	11102
Energy Club Inc	5145	D		13268
Surge Globl Bkries Hldings LLC (PA)	5149	D	818 896-0525	13397
Lowes Home Centers LLC	5211	C	818 686-4300	13627
Ketab Corporation	5942	D	310 477-7477	14067
Golden West Security	7381	C	818 897-5965	16644
Florence Wstn Med Clinic Inc	8011	C	818 896-2999	17657
Hillview Mental Health Ctr Inc	8093	D	818 896-1161	18696
Hathaway-Sycmres Child Fmly Svc	8322	C	626 395-7100	19086
Volunteers of Amer Los Angeles	8322	D	818 834-8957	19165

PALA, CA - San Diego County

	SIC	EMP	PHONE	ENTRY#
Pala Casino Spa & Resort	7011	A	760 510-5100	15292

PALM DESERT, CA - Riverside County

	SIC	EMP	PHONE	ENTRY#
Platinum Landscape Inc	0781	C	760 200-3673	177
Breeze Air Conditioning LLC	1711	D	760 346-0855	746
Dave Williams Plbg & Elec Inc	1711	D	760 296-1397	761
United Brothers Concrete Inc	1771	C	760 346-1013	1091
La Quinta Brewing Company LLC	2082	D	760 200-2597	1598
Clarios LLC	2531	E	760 200-5225	2923
Associated Desert Shoppers Inc (DH)	2741	D	760 346-1729	3428
Daniels Inc (PA)	2741	E	801 621-3355	3439
Farley Paving Stone Co Inc	3272	D	760 773-3960	5412
Jordahl USA Inc	3444	E	866 332-6687	6258
Pearpoint Inc	3663	E	760 343-7350	8560
Pd Group	3993	D	760 674-3028	11144
Gary Cardiff Enterprises Inc	4119	D	760 568-1403	11389
Coachlla Vly Wtr Dst Pub Fclti	4941	C	760 398-2651	12115
Coachlla Vly Wtr Dst Pub Fclti (PA)	4941	C	760 398-2651	12116
Priority Lighting Inc	5719	F	800 709-1119	13965
Morgan Stnley Smith Barney LLC	6022	C	760 568-3500	14200
Webb Del California Corp (DH)	6552	B	760 772-5300	14914
Ashford Trs Seven LLC	7011	D	760 776-0050	15079
Destination Residences LLC	7011	B	760 346-4647	15128
Palm Desert Hospitality LLC	7011	B	760 568-1600	15294
Universal Services America LP	7381	A	760 200-2865	16702
Califrnia Clnic Plstic Surgery	7389	C	760 346-0611	16796
Resort Parking Services Inc	7521	C	760 328-4041	17007
Friends of Cultural Center Inc	7922	D	760 346-6505	17315
Desert Willow Golf Resort Inc	7992	C	760 346-0015	17425
Bighorn Golf Club Charities	7997	C	760 773-2468	17475
Lakes Country Club Assn Inc (PA)	7997	C	760 568-4321	17497
Mountain Vista Golf Course At	7999	D	760 200-2200	17560
Eisenhower Medical Center	8011	A	760 836-0232	17647
Mariner Health Care Inc	8051	C	760 776-7700	18008
Watermark Rtrment Cmmnties Inc	8051	D	760 346-5420	18074
Rai Care Ctrs Sthern Cal II LL	8092	C	760 346-7588	18665
Able Health Group LLC	8099	C	760 610-2093	18735
Desert ARC	8322	B	760 346-1611	19071
Living Desert	8422	C	760 346-5694	19367
Leighton Group Inc	8621	C	760 776-4192	19395
Sun City Palm Dsert Cmnty Assn (PA)	8641	D	760 200-2100	19465

GEOGRAPHIC

Employee Codes: A=Over 500 employees, B=251-500
C=101-250, D=51-100, E=20-50, F=10-19, G=1-9

2024 Southern California
Business Directory and Buyers Guide

© Mergent Inc. 1-800-342-5647

1413

	SIC	EMP	PHONE	ENTRY#

PALM SPRINGS, CA - Riverside County

	SIC	EMP	PHONE	ENTRY#
S S W Mechanical Cnstr Inc	1711	C	760 327-1481	819
Western Pacific Roofing Corp	1761	C	661 273-1336	1057
BMW of Palm Springs	2426	E	760 324-7071	2569
Super Struct Bldg Systems Inc	2522	E	760 322-2522	2917
Desert Sun Publishing Co **(DH)**	2711	C	760 322-8889	3273
Adams Trade Press LP **(PA)**	2721	E	760 318-7000	3340
Desert Publications Inc **(PA)**	2721	E	760 325-2333	3355
Palm Springs Life	2721	D	760 325-2333	3377
Matches Inc	2824	B	760 899-1919	3986
Iqd Frequency Products Inc	3679	E	408 250-1435	9066
Carefusion 207 Inc	3841	B	760 778-7200	10470
Carefusion Corporation	3841	D	760 778-7200	10473
Joe Blasco Enterprises Inc	3999	E	323 467-4949	11234
American Medical Response Inc	4119	C	760 883-5000	11372
First Student Inc	4151	B	760 320-4659	11428
Desert Water Agency Fing Corp	4941	D	760 323-4971	12120
Palm Springs Disposal Services	4953	D	760 327-1351	12177
Lowes Home Centers LLC	5211	C	760 866-1901	13662
Loandepotcom LLC	6162	A	760 797-6000	14338
Agua Clnte Band Chilla Indians	7011	B	800 854-1279	15070
Diamond Resorts LLC	7011	D	760 866-1800	15129
Margartvlle Rsort Orlndo Rsort	7011	C	760 327-8311	15240
Parker Palm Springs LLC	7011	D	760 770-5000	15299
R P S Resort Corp	7011	B	760 327-8311	15314
Riviera Palm Sprng A Trbute PR	7011	C	760 327-8311	15330
Smoke Tree Inc	7011	D	760 327-1221	15361
Spa Resort Casino	7011	A	760 883-1034	15365
Walters Family Partnership	7011	C	760 320-6868	15409
OLinn Security Incorporated	7381	C	760 320-5303	16665
Best Signs Inc **(PA)**	7389	E	760 320-3042	16793
Alamo Rental (us) Inc	7514	D	760 778-6271	16977
Desert Medical Group Inc **(PA)**	8011	C	760 320-8814	17643
Ensign Palm I LLC	8051	C	760 323-2638	17944
Desert Regional Med Ctr Inc **(HQ)**	8062	A	760 323-6511	18237
Eisenhower Medical Center	8062	C	760 325-6621	18250
Palm Springs Art Museum Inc	8412	D	760 322-4800	19360
Agua Clnte Band Chilla Indians **(PA)**	8699	A	760 699-6800	19510
Mariner Health Care Inc	8741	D	760 327-8541	20058
Kings Garden LLC	8742	C	760 275-4969	20187
Smg Holdings LLC	8742	D	760 325-6611	20241

PALMDALE, CA - Los Angeles County

	SIC	EMP	PHONE	ENTRY#
Dac Heating and AC	1711	F	661 441-2787	760
Csi Electrical Contractors Inc	1731	B	661 723-0869	888
D & J Printing Inc	2752	D	661 265-1995	3555
Ultramar Inc	2911	E	661 944-2496	4654
Aero Bending Company	3444	D	661 948-2363	6180
Lusk Quality Machine Products	3599	E	661 272-0630	7910
Sun Valley Ltg Standards Inc	3646	E	661 233-2000	8334
US Pole Company Inc **(PA)**	3646	C	800 877-6537	8339
Vision Engrg Met Stamping Inc	3646	D	661 575-0933	8340
Kennedy Engineered Pdts Inc	3714	F	661 272-1147	9409
Northrop Grumman Systems Corp	3721	B	661 272-7000	9547
Lockheed Martin Corporation	3812	A	661 572-7428	9996
Northrop Grumman Corporation	3812	E	661 272-7334	10008
Northrop Grumman Systems Corp	3812	D	661 540-0446	10020
Teletronics Technology Corp	3812	E	661 273-7033	10081
Wilcompute	3825	D	818 674-0506	10231
Battle-Tested Strategies LLC	4215	D	661 802-6509	11526
Palmdale Water District	4941	D	661 947-4111	12137
Waste Management Cal Inc	4953	C	661 947-7197	12200
Murcal Inc	5063	C	661 272-4700	12609
Smart & Final Stores Inc	5141	B	661 722-6210	13219
Lowes Home Centers LLC	5211	D	661 267-9888	13632
Golden Empire Mortgage Inc	6162	B	661 949-3388	14319
Thi Holdings (delaware) Inc	6411	C	661 266-7423	14633
Delta Scientific Corporation **(PA)**	7382	C	661 575-1100	16728
Africajun LLC	7812	E	310 403-1673	17167
Antelope Vly Cntry CLB Imprv	7997	C	661 947-3142	17462
Rockin Jump Holdings LLC	7999	B	661 233-9907	17563
Child Care Resource Center Inc	8322	C	661 723-3246	19037
People Creating Success Inc	8322	D	661 225-9700	19125
Kinkisharyo International	8748	C	661 265-1647	20357

PALOS VERDES ESTATES, CA - Los Angeles County

	SIC	EMP	PHONE	ENTRY#
Douglas Furniture of California LLC	2514	A	310 749-0003	2828
Palos Verdes Golf Club	5813	D	310 375-2759	14051
Grosvenor Inv MGT US Inc	6411	D	310 265-0297	14599
Rolling Hills Country Club	7997	D	424 903-0000	17512
Sqa Services Inc	8742	B	800 333-6180	20246

PALOS VERDES PENINSU, CA - Los Angeles County

	SIC	EMP	PHONE	ENTRY#
County of Los Angeles	8062	C	310 222-2401	18231

PANORAMA CITY, CA - Los Angeles County

	SIC	EMP	PHONE	ENTRY#
Crestview Landscape Inc	0781	D	818 962-7771	158
Superior Awning Inc	2394	E	818 780-7200	2510
Raspadoxpress	2741	D	818 892-6969	3480
Puretek Corporation	2834	C	818 361-3949	4216
Spec Engineering Company Inc	3599	E	818 780-3045	8034
D X Communications Inc	3663	E	323 256-3000	8507
Southern Cal Prmnnte Med Group	6324	B	800 272-3500	14499
American Protection Group Inc **(PA)**	7381	C	818 279-2433	16618
Kaiser Foundation Hospitals	8011	C	818 375-4023	17687
Kaiser Foundation Hospitals	8011	A	818 375-2000	17690
Ensign Group Inc	8051	C	818 893-6385	17940
Deanco Healthcare LLC	8062	A	818 787-2222	18236

PARAMOUNT, CA - Los Angeles County

	SIC	EMP	PHONE	ENTRY#
Drillmec Inc	1382	D	281 885-0777	299
Total-Western Inc **(HQ)**	1389	E	562 220-1450	388
Reliable Energy Management Inc	1711	D	562 984-5511	817
Advanced Industrial Svcs Inc	1721	D	562 940-8305	841
MB Herzog Electric Inc	1731	C	562 531-2002	916
Ariza Cheese Co Inc	2022	E	562 630-4144	1251
Ariza Global Foods Inc	2022	E	562 630-4144	1252
Paramount Dairy Inc	2026	C	562 361-1800	1315
Namar Foods	2034	E	562 531-2744	1357
Popsalot LLC	2096	E	213 761-0156	1830
Jayone Foods Inc	2099	E	562 633-7400	1917
Jimenes Food Inc	2099	E	562 602-2505	1918
Marukan Vinegar U S A Inc **(HQ)**	2099	E	562 630-6060	1940
Marukan Vinegar U S A Inc	2099	E	562 630-6060	1941
Cosmo Textiles Inc	2258	D	562 220-1177	2081
Sibyl Shepard Inc	2392	E	562 531-8612	2488
Drees Wood Products Inc	2431	E	562 633-7337	2597
Drees Wood Products Inc **(PA)**	2434	E	562 633-7337	2656
Graphic Trends Incorporated	2759	E	562 531-2339	3763
Hoffman Plastic Compounds Inc	2821	D	323 636-3346	3942
LMC Enterprises **(PA)**	2842	E	562 602-2116	4357
Kum Kang Trading USA Inc	2844	E	562 531-6111	4430
R & S Manufacturing & Sup Inc	2851	F	909 622-5881	4503
Paramount Petroleum Corp **(DH)**	2911	C	562 531-2060	4647
R & S Processing Co Inc	3069	D	562 531-0738	4790
Premium Plastics Machine Inc	3089	F	562 633-7723	5159
Sandee Plastic Extrusions	3089	E	323 979-4020	5196
Ener-Tech Metals Inc	3325	D	562 529-5034	5663
Fenico Precision Castings Inc	3369	D	562 634-5000	5813
Aerocraft Heat Treating Co Inc	3398	D	562 674-2400	5823
Avantus Aerospace Inc	3429	E	562 633-6626	5901
California Screw Products Corp	3429	E	562 633-6626	5910
Top Line Mfg Inc	3429	E	562 633-0605	5947
Valence Surface Tech LLC	3441	F	562 531-7666	6089
Wagner Plate Works West Inc **(PA)**	3443	F	562 531-6050	6168
C & J Metal Products Inc	3444	E	562 634-3101	6206
Jeffrey Fabrication LLC	3444	E	562 634-3101	6256
Paramount Metal & Supply Inc	3446	E	562 634-8180	6365
Mattco Forge Inc	3462	E	562 634-8635	6465
Mattco Forge Inc **(HQ)**	3462	F	562 634-8635	6466
Press Forge Company	3462	D	562 531-4962	6471
Vi-Star Gear Co Inc	3462	E	323 774-3750	6474
Carlton Forge Works	3463	B	562 633-1131	6476
Weber Metals Inc **(HQ)**	3463	E	562 602-0260	6484
Anaplex Corporation	3471	E	714 522-4481	6583
Denmac Industries Inc	3479	E	562 634-2714	6699
George Jue Mfg Co Inc	3546	D	562 634-8181	7145
Golden State Engineering Inc	3549	C	562 634-3125	7170
Excellon Acquisition LLC **(HQ)**	3559	E	310 668-7700	7234
Zamboni Company Usa Inc	3559	E	562 633-0751	7267
Extrude Hone Deburring Svc Inc	3599	E	562 531-2976	7829
J and K Manufacturing Inc	3599	E	562 630-8417	7881
Piedras Machine Corporation	3599	F	562 602-1500	7973
Ramp Engineering Inc	3599	E	562 531-8030	7993
Trepanning Specialities Inc	3599	E	562 633-8110	8051
Amsco US Inc	3679	C	562 630-0333	8996
Z-Tronix Inc	3679	D	562 808-0800	9142
Amrex-Zetron Inc	3699	F	310 527-6868	9195
New Century Industries Inc	3714	E	562 634-9551	9431
Topline Manufacturing Inc	3999	F	562 633-0605	11297
Durham School Services L P	4151	C	562 408-1206	11422
Cnet Express	4212	C	949 357-5475	11451
Contractors Cargo Company **(PA)**	4213	D	310 609-1957	11476
Total Intermodal Services Inc **(PA)**	4491	C	562 427-6300	11649
Calmet Inc **(PA)**	4953	C	323 721-8120	12164

Mergent email: customerrelations@mergent.com
1414

2024 Southern California
Business Directory and Buyers Guide

(P-0000) Products & Services Section entry number
(PA)=Parent Co (HQ)=Headquarters (DH)=Div Headquarters

	SIC	EMP	PHONE	ENTRY#
Staub Metals LLC	5051	D	562 602-2200	12572
Transtar Metals Corp	5051	B	562 630-1400	12578
Vaughans Industrial Repair Inc	5084	E	562 633-2660	12833
Aylesva Inc	5139	C	562 688-0592	13159
Home Depot USA Inc	5211	D	562 272-8055	13608
Blue Ribbon Draperies Inc	5713	E	562 425-4637	13949
CCC Property Holdings LLC	6719	C	310 609-1957	14926
Braun Linen Service (PA)	7213	C	909 623-2678	15449
Modern Dev Co A Ltd Partnr	7389	D	949 646-6400	16880

PASADENA, CA - Los Angeles County

	SIC	EMP	PHONE	ENTRY#
Exeter Packers Inc	0174	C	626 993-6245	42
Boswell Properties Inc	0722	B	626 583-3000	96
Dpr Construction A Gen Partnr	1542	D	626 463-1265	547
Acco Engineered Systems Inc (PA)	1711	A	818 244-6571	726
Pak Group LLC	2052	E	626 316-6555	1522
Sugarfina Inc	2064	E	424 284-8518	1552
Eurobizusa Inc	2084	F	626 793-0032	1625
Saladish Inc	2099	D	626 304-3100	1982
AGS Usa LLC	2335	C	323 588-2200	2272
Max Leon Inc (PA)	2339	C	626 797-6886	2351
Cisco Bros Corp (PA)	2512	C	323 778-8612	2797
Roberson Construction	2591	E	626 578-1936	3012
Avery Dennison Corporation	2672	C	626 304-2000	3165
House of Printing Inc	2752	E	626 793-7034	3587
Licher Direct Mail Inc	2752	E	626 795-3333	3623
Typecraft Inc	2752	E	626 795-8093	3700
Grant Dahlstrom Inc	2791	F	626 798-0858	3851
Materia Inc (DH)	2819	C	626 584-8400	3898
Xencor Inc	2834	C	626 305-5900	4257
Allbirds Inc	3143	F	626 344-2622	5266
Evolution Design Lab Inc	3144	E	626 960-8388	5275
Orbits Lightwave Inc	3229	E	626 513-7400	5327
Hamilton Metalcraft Inc	3444	E	626 795-4811	6251
Fvo Solutions Inc	3479	D	626 449-0218	6706
Honeybee Robotics LLC	3569	E	510 207-4555	7394
American Reliance Inc	3571	E	626 443-6818	7417
Myricom Inc	3571	E	626 821-5555	7442
Cire Group Inc	3577	C	626 321-8822	7516
Turbo Coil Inc	3585	E	626 644-6254	7631
Lifesource Water Systems Inc (PA)	3589	E	626 792-9996	7668
C & D Precision Components Inc	3599	E	626 799-7109	7792
Pronto Products Co	3599	E	800 377-6680	7982
Caelux Corporation	3674	E	626 502-7033	8778
Rockley Photonics Inc (HQ)	3674	C	626 304-9960	8881
Byd Motors LLC (HQ)	3714	E	213 748-3980	9363
Advanced Mtls Joining Corp (PA)	3728	E	626 449-2696	9596
Sabrin Corporation	3728	F	626 792-3813	9781
Atk Space Systems LLC	3812	D	626 351-0205	9956
Rogerson Kratos	3812	E	626 449-3090	10065
Gmto Corporation	3827	D	626 204-0500	10315
Hemodialysis Inc	3841	D	626 792-0548	10520
Arts Elegance Inc	3911	E	626 793-4794	10898
L A Steel Craft Products (PA)	3949	E	626 798-7401	11008
United Couriers Inc (DH)	4512	C	213 383-3611	11673
Spokeo Inc	4813	D	877 913-3088	11902
Multicultural Rdo Brdcstg Inc	4832	D	626 844-8882	11931
American Multimedia TV USA	4833	D	626 466-1038	11938
Blue Chip Stamps Inc	5051	A	626 585-6700	12536
Curiosity Ink Media LLC	5085	C	561 287-5776	12849
Prima Royale Enterprises Ltd	5139	C	626 960-8388	13164
Deliverr Inc	5141	B	213 534-8686	13177
Mhh Holdings Inc	5149	C	626 744-9370	13379
Pasta Piccinini Inc	5149	C	626 798-0841	13387
George L Throop Co	5211	C	626 796-0285	13577
Idealab (HQ)	5511	D	626 356-3654	13780
Dine Brands Global Inc (PA)	5812	B	818 240-6055	14002
Northern Trust of California (inc)	6021	B		14172
Community Bank	6022	B	626 577-1700	14189
East West Bancorp Inc (PA)	6022	B	626 768-6000	14191
East West Bank (HQ)	6022	B	626 768-6000	14192
First Foundation Inc	6029	C	626 993-1300	14212
Onewest Bank Group LLC	6035	A	626 535-4870	14216
Firefighters First Credit Un (PA)	6061	C	323 254-1700	14224
First Financial Federal Cr Un	6061	C	800 537-8491	14226
Wescom Central Credit Union (PA)	6062	B	888 493-7266	14253
Law School Financial	6111	C	626 243-1800	14266
Merrill Lynch Prce Fnner Smith	6211	C	800 637-7455	14390
Los Angles Cnty Employees Rtrme (PA)	6371	C	626 564-6000	14548
B&C Liquidating Corp (PA)	6411	C	626 799-7000	14566
Bitco Cnstr Insur Agcy Inc	6411	D	626 683-5200	14568
Tm Claims Service Inc	6411	D	626 568-7800	14634
Invitation Homes Inc	6531	D	805 372-2900	14815

	SIC	EMP	PHONE	ENTRY#
Solariant Capital LLC	6719	C	626 544-0279	14946
Western Asset Core Plus Bond P	6722	C	626 844-9400	14973
Schaumbond Group Inc (PA)	6726	B	626 215-4998	14982
Operating Engineers Funds Inc (PA)	6733	C	866 400-5200	14999
Western Asset Mrtg Capitl Corp	6798	A	626 844-9400	15018
Are/Cal-Sd Region No 62 LLC	6799	D	626 578-0777	15020
Idealab Holdings LLC (PA)	6799	A	626 585-6900	15031
Sabal Capital Partners LLC	6799	C	949 255-1007	15050
Langham Hotels Pacific Corp	7011	C	617 451-1900	15219
Pacific Huntington Hotel Corp	7011	A	626 568-3900	15288
Pasadena Hotel Dev Ventr LP	7011	D	626 449-4000	15300
One & All Inc (HQ)	7311	C		15567
Tetra Tech Executive Svcs Inc	7361	C	626 470-2400	15900
Bluebeam Inc (PA)	7371	C	626 788-4100	15986
Foremay Inc (PA)	7371	E	408 228-3468	16034
Snapcomms Inc	7371	D	805 715-0300	16118
Trinus Corporation	7371	C	818 246-1143	16140
Everbridge Inc (PA)	7372	C	818 230-9700	16243
Evolution Robotics Inc	7372	C	626 993-3300	16245
Floor Covering Soft	7372	E	626 583-8188	16248
Guidance Software Inc (HQ)	7372	C	626 229-9191	16261
Phoenix Technologies Ltd (HQ)	7372	E	408 570-1000	16347
Red Gate Software Inc	7372	E	626 993-3949	16366
Gemalto Cogent Inc (HQ)	7373	D	626 325-9600	16444
I3dnet LLC	7373	A	800 482-6910	16447
Greensoft Technology Inc	7374	C	323 254-5961	16498
Near Intelligence Inc	7374	B	628 889-7680	16508
Zoominfo Technologies LLC	7375	A	360 783-6924	16538
Tpusa - Fhcs Inc (DH)	7376	C	213 873-5100	16540
Inter-Con Security Systems Inc (PA)	7381	A	626 535-2200	16653
Realdefense LLC (PA)	7382	E	801 895-7907	16750
Pasadena Center Operating Co	7389	C	626 795-9311	16901
Parking Concepts Inc	7521	C	626 577-8963	16998
Fremont & Purdon Inc	7534	E	626 795-6282	17021
Annandale Golf Club	7997	C	626 796-6125	17461
Rose Bowl Aquatics Center	7997	D	626 564-0330	17513
Huntington Medical Foundation	8011	D	626 795-4210	17667
Kaiser Foundation Hospitals	8011	C	626 440-5639	17694
Kaiser Prmnnte Schl Anesthesia	8011	C	626 564-3016	17699
Southern CA Gastroenterology	8011	C	818 425-9761	17770
Tao of Wllness Snta Mnica A PR	8049	D	626 397-1000	17872
Accredited Nursing Services	8051	C	626 573-1234	17875
Highland Hlthcare Cmllia Grdns	8051	C	626 798-6777	17974
Pasadena Hospital Assn Ltd	8051	B	626 397-3322	18028
Pasadena Madows Nursing Ctr LP	8051	D	626 796-1103	18029
Brighton Convalescent Center	8059	D	626 798-9873	18114
Park Marino Convalescent Ctr	8059	C	626 463-4105	18151
Two Palms Nursing Center Inc	8059	C	626 796-1103	18155
Huntington Medical Foundation	8062	C	626 792-3141	18289
Kaiser Foundation Hospitals	8062	B	626 440-5659	18300
Pasadena Hospital Assn Ltd (PA)	8062	A	626 397-5000	18374
Aurora Las Encinas LLC	8063	C	626 795-9901	18504
Gooden Center	8069	D	626 356-0078	18528
Shriners Hspitals For Children	8069	B	626 389-9300	18534
Lotus Clinical Research LLC	8071	B	626 381-9830	18556
Confido LLC	8082	A	310 361-8558	18604
Grandcare Health Services LLC (PA)	8082	C	866 554-2447	18615
Huntington Care LLC	8082	C	877 405-6990	18617
Pacific Clnics Psdena Calworks	8093	C	626 419-3228	18704
Legacy Healthcare Center LLC	8099	D	626 798-0558	18775
Polytechnic School	8211	B	626 792-2147	18979
Foothill Family Service	8322	C	626 795-6907	19083
Hillsides	8322	B	323 254-2274	19089
Optima Family Services Inc	8322	C	323 300-6066	19119
Pacific Clinics Head Start	8351	C	626 254-5000	19223
Monte Vista Grove Homes	8361	D	626 796-6135	19287
Rosemary Childrens Services (PA)	8361	C	626 844-3033	19298
DVeal Corporation	8399	C	626 296-8900	19324
Kidspce A Prticipatory Museum	8412	D	626 449-9144	19354
Norton Smon Mseum Art At Psden	8412	C	626 449-6840	19359
Southern Cal Ibw-Neca Hlth Tr	8631	D	323 221-5861	19413
Shriners International	8641	C	626 389-9300	19463
Valley Hunt Club	8641	C	626 793-7134	19469
Jacobs Atcs Fema A Joint Ventr	8711	D	571 218-1115	19617
Jacobs Engineering Company	8711	A	626 449-2171	19619
Jacobs Engineering Group Inc	8711	A	626 578-3500	19621
Jacobs Engineering Inc (DH)	8711	C	626 578-3500	19622
Jacobs International Ltd Inc	8711	B	626 578-3500	19624
Kinemetrics Inc (DH)	8711	D	626 795-2220	19630
Pacifica Services Inc	8711	C	626 405-0131	19647
Parsons Engrg Science Inc (DH)	8711	B	626 440-2000	19664
Parsons Intl Cayman Islands	8711	A	626 440-6000	19666
Parsons Service Corporation	8711	A	626 440-2000	19667

Employee Codes: A=Over 500 employees, B=251-500
C=101-250, D=51-100, E=20-50, F=10-19, G=1-9

2024 Southern California
Business Directory and Buyers Guide

© Mergent Inc. 1-800-342-5647

1415

GEOGRAPHIC

	SIC	EMP	PHONE	ENTRY#
Parsons Wtr Infrastructure Inc.	8711	D	626 440-7000	19668
Ptsi Managed Services Inc.	8711	D	626 440-3118	19674
Tetra Tech Inc **(PA)**	8711	C	626 351-4664	19701
Tetra Tech Nus Inc.	8711	C	412 921-7090	19703
Ttg Engineers.	8711	B	626 463-2800	19710
Stantec Architecture Inc.	8712	D	626 796-9141	19742
Cachet Financial Services.	8721	E	626 578-9400	19757
Kbkg Inc.	8721	C	626 449-4225	19783
Krost **(PA)**	8721	C	626 449-4225	19786
California Institute Tech.	8733	A	818 354-9154	19921
Carnegie Institution Wash.	8733	E	626 577-1122	19922
Doheny Eye Institute **(PA)**	8733	D	323 342-7120	19924
Tmt Intrntonal Observatory LLC.	8733	D	626 395-1651	19949
Numerade Labs LLC.	8734	D	213 536-1489	19979
Parsons Constructors Inc.	8741	A	626 440-2000	20077
Dowling Advisory Group.	8742	D	626 319-1369	20164
Msla Management LLC.	8748	A	626 824-6020	20363

PASO ROBLES, CA - San Luis Obispo County

	SIC	EMP	PHONE	ENTRY#
J & L Vineyards.	0172	D	559 268-1627	32
Treasury Wine Estates Americas.	0172	E	805 237-6000	36
All Risk Shield Inc.	1389	E	866 991-7190	325
City of Paso Robles.	1611	D	805 237-3999	613
Boneso Brothers Cnstr Inc.	1711	D	805 227-4450	745
Worldwind Services LLC.	1731	A	661 822-4877	953
Mge Underground Inc.	1794	B	805 238-3510	1124
Firestone Walker Inc.	2082	D	805 226-8514	1588
Firestone Walker Inc **(PA)**	2082	C	805 225-5911	1589
Daou Family Estates LLC.	2084	D	805 226-5460	1622
Eos Estate Winery.	2084	E	805 239-2562	1624
Halter Properties LLC.	2084	E	805 226-9455	1634
Halter Winery LLC **(PA)**	2084	E	805 226-9455	1635
Hearst Ranch Winery.	2084	F	805 467-2241	1636
J Lohr Winery Corporation.	2084	D	805 239-8900	1638
James Tobin Cellars Inc.	2084	E	805 239-2204	1640
Niner Wine Estates LLC.	2084	E	805 239-2233	1648
ONeill Beverages Co LLC.	2084	E	805 239-1616	1649
Rbz Vineyards LLC.	2084	E	805 542-0133	1655
Tablas Creek Vineyard LLC.	2084	F	805 237-1231	1661
Treana Winery LLC.	2084	E	805 237-2932	1666
Lakeshirts LLC.	2395	E	805 239-1290	2517
Hogue Bros Inc.	2426	E	805 239-1440	2573
Lindamar Industries Inc.	2673	D	805 237-1910	3185
San Luis Obspo Cocmmnty Clgdst.	2711	F	805 591-6200	3321
Pro Document Solutions Inc **(PA)**	2752	E	805 238-6680	3669
Melissa Trinidad.	2844	E	805 536-0954	4434
Lubrizol Global Management Inc.	2899	E	805 239-1550	4617
Cornucopia Tool & Plastics Inc.	3089	E	805 238-7660	4996
Trellborg Sling Sltions US Inc.	3089	E	805 239-4284	5232
Acme Vial & Glass Co.	3221	E	805 239-2666	5320
Paso Robles Tank Inc **(HQ)**	3312	D	805 227-1641	5596
Paris Precision LLC.	3444	C	805 239-2500	6287
AMC Machining Inc.	3449	E	805 238-5452	6394
Pic Manufacturing Inc.	3555	F	805 238-5451	7190
Souriau Usa Inc **(DH)**	3643	E	805 238-2840	8275
Joslyn Sunbank Company LLC.	3678	B	805 238-2840	8976
Advance Adapters Inc.	3714	E	805 238-7000	9342
Advance Adapters LLC.	3714	E	805 238-7000	9343
Esterline Technologies Corp.	3728	E	805 238-2840	9685
Flight Environments Inc.	3728	E		9690
Arbiter Systems Incorporated **(PA)**	3825	E	805 237-3831	10184
Applied Technologies Assoc Inc **(HQ)**	3829	C	805 239-9100	10352
JIT Manufacturing Inc.	3841	E	805 238-5000	10540
Trelleborg Sealing Solutions.	3841	D	805 239-4284	10620
Cco Holdings LLC.	4841	E	805 400-1002	11978
Ctek Inc.	4899	E	310 241-2973	12005
Smart & Final Stores Inc.	5141	B	805 237-0323	13197
Lowes Home Centers LLC.	5211	D	805 602-9051	13653
Paq Inc.	5541	D	805 227-1660	13893
Heritage Oaks Bancorp.	6022	B	805 369-5200	14198
Heritage Oaks Bank.	6022	C	805 239-5200	14199
Emeritus Corporation.	6513	C	805 239-1313	14707
Ayres - Paso Robles LP.	7011	E	714 850-0409	15082
Summerwood Winery & Inn Inc.	7011	E	805 227-1365	15376
Kings Oil Tools Inc **(PA)**	7353	E	805 238-9311	15765
Rentacenter.	7359	D	805 769-9030	15796
Iqms LLC **(PA)**	7372	E	805 227-1122	16277
Eagle Med Pckg Strlization Inc.	7389	E	805 238-7401	16821
Ravine Waterpark LLC.	7996	E	805 237-8500	17452
Carbon Health Technologies Inc.	8011	C	805 226-4222	17608

PATTON, CA - San Bernardino County

	SIC	EMP	PHONE	ENTRY#
Califrnia Dept State Hospitals.	8063	A	909 425-7000	18507

PAUMA VALLEY, CA - San Diego County

	SIC	EMP	PHONE	ENTRY#
T - Y Nursery Inc.	5193	C	760 742-2151	13520
Pauma Band of Mission Indians.	7011	B	760 742-2177	15301

PERRIS, CA - Riverside County

	SIC	EMP	PHONE	ENTRY#
Parkco Building Company.	1542	D	714 444-1441	572
Silver Creek Industries LLC.	1542	C	951 943-5393	591
Mamco Inc **(PA)**	1611	C	951 776-9300	632
HB Parkco Construction Inc **(PA)**	1771	B	714 567-4752	1074
Integrity Rebar Placers.	1791	C	951 696-6843	1105
Jimenez Mexican Foods Inc.	2032	E	951 351-0102	1326
Star Milling Co.	2048	E	951 657-3143	1449
Aoc LLC.	2295	D	951 657-5161	2124
Avalon Shutters Inc.	2431	C	909 937-4900	2586
California Trusframe LLC **(HQ)**	2439	D	951 350-4880	2694
California Trusframe LLC.	2439	C	951 657-7491	2695
California Truss Company **(PA)**	2439	C	951 657-7491	2696
Inland Truss Inc **(PA)**	2439	D	951 300-1758	2701
AAA Pallet Recycling & Mfg Inc.	2448	E	951 681-7748	2713
Timmons Wood Products Inc.	2499	E	951 940-4700	2764
Alpha Corporation of Tennessee.	2821	C	951 657-5161	3921
J-M Manufacturing Company Inc.	2821	E	951 657-7400	3950
Accu-Blend Corporation.	2911	F	626 334-7744	4638
Goldstar Asphalt Products Inc.	2951	E	951 940-1610	4660
Npg Inc **(PA)**	2951	D	951 940-0200	4662
Coreslab Structures La Inc.	3272	C	951 943-9119	5406
J & R Concrete Products Inc.	3272	E	951 943-5855	5421
Canyon Steel Fabricators Inc.	3441	E	951 683-2352	6005
Craftech Metal Forming Inc.	3441	E	951 940-6444	6014
Stretch Forming Corporation.	3444	C	951 443-0911	6326
R&M Supply Inc.	3524	D	951 552-9860	6920
Spaulding Equipment Company **(PA)**	3532	E	951 943-4531	6951
West Coast Yamaha Inc.	3568	E	951 943-2061	7381
Stearns Product Dev Corp **(PA)**	3569	C	951 657-0379	7410
R-Cold Inc.	3585	D	951 436-5476	7620
Axxis Corporation.	3599	E	951 436-9921	7768
Warlock Industries Inc.	3711	E	951 657-2680	9313
Limos By Tiffany Inc.	3713	E	951 657-2680	9330
Navigator Yachts and Pdts Inc.	3732	E	951 657-2117	9864
Pacific Coachworks Inc.	3792	C	951 686-7294	9927
Temeka Incorporated.	3993	E	951 296-3570	11174
Claybourne Industries Inc.	3999	E	951 675-4508	11209
National Retail Trnsp Inc.	4213	D	951 243-6110	11499
Lowes Home Centers LLC.	4225	B	951 443-2500	11595
Eastern Municipal Water Dst.	4941	C	951 657-7469	12121
Eastern Municipal Water Dst **(PA)**	4941	B	951 928-3777	12122
Eldorado Stone LLC.	5032	A	951 601-3838	12353
Herca Telecomm Services Inc.	5082	D	951 940-5941	12770
Jpl Global LLC.	5082	E	888 274-7744	12773
Griswold Industries.	5085	F	951 657-1718	12857
Global Plastics Inc.	5093	C	951 657-5466	12954
Village Nurseries Whl LLC.	5193	B	951 657-3940	13521
Iherb LLC **(PA)**	5499	A	951 616-3600	13728
Eci Water Ski Products Inc.	5941	E	951 940-9999	14063
S A Top-U Corporation.	5944	E	951 916-4025	14080
Big Lgue Dreams Consulting LLC.	7941	C	619 846-8855	17364
Dropzone Waterpark.	7999	E	951 210-1600	17546
Oak Grove Inst Foundation Inc.	8322	C	951 238-6022	19118
Pacific Hydrotech Corporation.	8711	B	951 943-8803	19661

PICO RIVERA, CA - Los Angeles County

	SIC	EMP	PHONE	ENTRY#
Genesis Foods Corporation.	2064	D	323 890-5890	1540
Mixed Nuts Inc.	2068	E	323 587-6887	1559
GPde Slva Spces Incrporation **(PA)**	2099	D	562 407-2643	1908
Pattern Knitting Mills Inc.	2253	E	310 801-1126	2075
Coop Home Goods LLC.	2392	E	888 316-1886	2470
Pacific Cast Fther Cushion LLC **(HQ)**	2392	C	562 801-9995	2481
Reeve Store Equipment Company **(PA)**	2542	D	562 949-2535	2990
Bay Cities Container Corp **(PA)**	2653	D	562 948-3751	3082
CD Container Inc.	2653	D	562 948-1910	3089
Coastal Container Inc.	2653	E	562 801-4595	3091
Jkv Inc.	2653	D	562 948-3000	3113
Spiral Ppr Tube & Core Co Inc.	2655	E	562 801-9705	3139
Endpak Packaging Inc.	2674	D	562 801-0281	3199
Lombard Enterprises Inc.	2752	E	562 692-7070	3626
Coastwide Tag & Label Co Inc.	2759	E	323 721-1501	3746
Kater-Crafts Incorporated.	2789	E	562 692-0665	3847
Whittier Fertilizer Company.	2873	D	562 699-3461	4543
Aoclsc Inc.	2992	E	813 248-1988	4677
Lubricating Specialties Company.	2992	C	562 776-4000	4687
Metal Tite Products **(PA)**	3442	D	562 695-0645	6112
C&O Manufacturing Company Inc.	3444	E	562 692-7525	6207
Arnaco Industrial Coatings.	3479	E	562 222-1022	6692

Mergent email: customerrelations@mergent.com
1416

2024 Southern California
Business Directory and Buyers Guide

(P-0000) Products & Services Section entry number
(PA)=Parent Co (HQ)=Headquarters (DH)=Div Headquarters

	SIC	EMP	PHONE	ENTRY#
Precision Deburring Services	3541	E	562 944-4497	7017
W P Keith Co Inc	3567	E	562 948-3636	7374
Veolia Wts Services Usa Inc	3589	D	562 942-2200	7690
Feit Electric Company Inc (PA)	3645	C	562 463-2852	8293
Pacific Logistics Corp (PA)	4731	C	562 478-4700	11791
Unisource Solutions Inc (PA)	5021	C	562 654-3500	12292
Ros Electrical Sup Eqp Co LLC	5063	E	562 695-9000	12616
Aurora World Inc	5092	C	562 205-1222	12934
Three Sons Inc	5147	D	562 801-4100	13309
Bakemark USA LLC (PA)	5149	C	562 949-1054	13353
Lowes Home Centers LLC	5211	C	562 942-9909	13631
Showroom Interiors LLC	7359	C	323 348-1551	15798
Sectran Security Incorporated (PA)	7381	C	562 948-1446	16678
Los Angeles Unified School Dst	7389	C	562 654-9007	16864
Krikorian Premiere Theatre LLC	7832	D	562 205-3456	17302
Mariner Health Care Inc	8051	D	562 942-7019	18005
Rivera Sanatarium Inc	8051	E	562 949-2591	18039
Riviera Nursing & Conva	8051	E	562 806-2576	18042
Altamed Health Services Corp	8099	C	562 949-8717	18740
Bms Healthcare Inc	8099	C	562 942-7019	18748
Public Hlth Fndation Entps Inc	8099	C	562 801-2323	18796

PIRU, CA - Ventura County

	SIC	EMP	PHONE	ENTRY#
La Verne Nursery Inc	5193	D	805 521-0111	13512

PISMO BEACH, CA - San Luis Obispo County

	SIC	EMP	PHONE	ENTRY#
Alliance Ready Mix Inc	3273	D	805 556-3015	5458
Pacific Gas and Electric Co	4911	C	805 546-5267	12036
Brooks Restaurant Group Inc (PA)	5141	E	559 485-8520	13173
Vpb Operating Co LLC	7011	D	805 773-1011	15405

PLACENTIA, CA - Orange County

	SIC	EMP	PHONE	ENTRY#
Mddr Inc	1711	C	714 792-1993	792
GD Heil Inc	1795	C	714 687-9100	1133
Nelson Case Corporation	2441	C	714 528-2215	2712
Western Mill Fabricators Inc	2599	E	714 993-3667	3036
Cinton LLC	2672	E	714 961-8808	3168
CF&b Manufacturing Inc	2673	E	714 744-8361	3180
Crescent Inc	2752	E	714 992-6030	3551
High Five Inc	2752	E	714 847-2200	3586
Eclectic Printing & Design LLC	2759	F	714 528-8040	3756
Label Specialties Inc	2759	E	714 861-8074	3777
General Rewinding Inc	2789	E	714 776-5561	3845
Cardinal Health 414 LLC	2834	E	714 572-9900	4083
Arlon Graphics LLC (HQ)	3081	C	714 985-6300	4805
Vanderveer Industrial Plas LLC	3083	E	714 579-7700	4844
Excalibur Extrusion Inc	3084	E	714 528-8834	4847
Fruth Custom Plastics Inc	3089	D	714 993-9955	5032
Totally Radical Associates Inc	3089	E	714 630-0653	5230
Eisel Enterprises Inc	3272	E	714 993-1706	5409
Crd Mfg Inc	3429	E	714 871-3300	5913
Hartwell Corporation (DH)	3429	C	714 993-4200	5920
Richfield Engineering Inc	3443	C	714 524-3741	6152
Gerard Roof Products LLC (DH)	3444	C	714 529-0407	6245
Sapphire Manufacturing Inc	3446	E	714 401-3117	6368
Ironwood Fabrication Inc	3462	F	714 576-7320	6461
West Coast Metal Stamping Incorporated	3469	E	714 792-0322	6571
Industrial Metal Finishing Inc	3471	E	714 628-8808	6628
Coast Aerospace Mfg Inc	3544	E	714 893-8066	7060
US Computers Inc	3577	F	714 528-0514	7577
Nalco Wtr Prtrtment Sltons LLC	3589	E	714 792-0708	7677
Auger Industries Inc	3599	F	714 577-9350	7765
J B Tool Inc	3599	F	714 993-7173	7882
Mike Kenney Tool Inc	3599	E	714 577-9262	7935
Mkt Innovations	3599	D	714 524-7668	7942
Southern Cal Tchnical Arts Inc	3599	E	714 524-2626	8033
Sapphire Chandelier LLC	3646	D	714 879-3660	8330
Altinex Inc	3663	E	714 990-0877	8493
Cartel Electronics LLC	3672	C	714 993-0270	8657
Microplex Inc	3674	F	714 630-8220	8839
L & M Machining Corporation	3678	D	714 414-0923	8977
Rotech Engineering Inc	3679	E	714 632-0532	9110
Vertex Lcd Inc	3679	E	714 223-7111	9136
Roll Along Vans Inc	3714	E	714 528-9600	9452
Alva Manufacturing Inc	3728	E	714 237-0925	9621
Bioplate Inc	3841	E	310 815-2100	10458
Bioseal	3841	E	714 528-4695	10459
Tfn Architectural Signage Inc (PA)	3993	E	714 556-0990	11175
Hardy Window Company (PA)	5031	C	714 996-1807	12332
Sunrise Growers Inc	5148	C	714 706-6090	13343
Vita-Herb Nutriceuticals Inc	5499	E	714 632-3726	13734
P5 Graphics and Displays Inc	7336	E	714 808-1645	15671
Interface Rehab Inc	8049	A	714 646-8300	17866

	SIC	EMP	PHONE	ENTRY#
Tenet Healthsystem Medical Inc	8069	B	714 993-2000	18537
Roman Cthlic Diocese of Orange	8211	C	714 528-1794	18980

PLAYA DEL REY, CA - Los Angeles County

	SIC	EMP	PHONE	ENTRY#
Chipton-Ross Inc	3721	D	310 414-7800	9519
Los Angeles Dept Wtr & Pwr	4939	A	310 524-8500	12111
Parking Concepts Inc	7521	D	310 322-5008	16999
You ME and Sciences Inc	7929	D	310 406-7350	17355

PLAYA VISTA, CA - Los Angeles County

	SIC	EMP	PHONE	ENTRY#
Cpl Holdings LLC	5331	C	310 348-6800	13685
Lmb Opco LLC	6163	B	310 348-6800	14360
Tcg Capital Management LP	6799	C	310 633-2900	15054
Canvas Worldwide LLC	7313	C	424 303-4300	15591
Commercial RE Exch Inc	7371	C	888 273-0423	15997
Chownow Inc	7372	D	888 707-2469	16200
Ordermark Inc	7374	C	833 673-3762	16509
Yahoo Cv LLC	7374	C	408 349-3300	16522
Lowermybills Inc	7375	C	310 348-6800	16532

PLS VRDS PNSL, CA - Los Angeles County

	SIC	EMP	PHONE	ENTRY#
Rolling Hills Vineyard Inc	2084	E	310 541-5098	1657
Episcopal Communities & Servic	8051	D	310 544-2204	17948

POMONA, CA - Los Angeles County

	SIC	EMP	PHONE	ENTRY#
Centrescapes Inc	0781	D	909 392-3303	157
Ultimate Removal Inc	1521	C	909 524-0800	463
Henkels & McCoy Inc	1623	B	909 517-3011	672
Spiniello Companies	1623	C	909 629-1000	694
t McGee Electric Inc	1731	E	909 591-6461	945
Frank S Smith Masonry Inc	1741	E	909 468-0525	956
Spectra Company	1741	C	909 599-0760	962
Anheuser-Busch LLC	2082	A	951 782-3935	1577
Los Pericos Food Products LLC	2099	E	909 623-5625	1937
Lift-It Manufacturing Co Inc	2298	E	909 469-2251	2132
Bragel International Inc	2342	E	909 598-8808	2394
Elite Stone & Cabinet Inc	2434	E	909 629-6988	2657
Royal Cabinets Inc	2434	A	909 629-8565	2676
Royal Industries Inc	2434	C	909 629-8565	2677
Rbf Group International	2521	F	626 333-5700	2896
Rbf Lifestyle Holdings LLC	2521	E	626 333-5700	2897
Yoshimasa Display Case Inc	2541	E	213 637-9999	2970
Kittrich Corporation (PA)	2591	C	714 736-1000	3009
Stainless Fixtures Inc	2599	E	909 622-1615	3031
Numatech West (kmp) LLC	2653	D	909 706-3627	3119
T & T Box Company Inc	2657	E	909 465-0848	3146
Federated Diversified Sls Inc	2671	E	909 591-1733	3151
California Plastix Inc	2673	E	909 629-8288	3179
Inland Envelope Company	2677	D	909 622-2016	3211
FDS Manufacturing Company (PA)	2679	D	909 591-1733	3237
Progressive Converting Inc	2679	F	909 392-2201	3245
K-1 Packaging Group	2752	C	626 964-9384	3608
Western Converting Spc Inc	2759	E	909 392-4578	3825
Natural Envmtl Protection Co	2821	E	909 620-8028	3957
Essential Pharmaceutical Corp	2834	E	909 623-4565	4109
K-Max Health Products Corp	2834	F	909 455-0158	4149
Kc Pharmaceuticals Inc (PA)	2834	D	909 598-9499	4151
Med-Pharmex Inc	2834	C	909 593-7875	4166
Alere San Diego Inc	2835	A	909 482-0840	4265
Ecosmart Technologies Inc	2879	E	770 667-0006	4550
Pacific Wtrprfing Rstrtion Inc	2899	F	909 444-3052	4625
Mitchell Processing LLC	3069	E	909 519-5759	4777
Pomona Quality Foam LLC	3086	D	909 628-7844	4899
Vefo Inc	3086	E	909 598-3856	4909
L & H Mold & Engineering Inc (PA)	3089	E	909 930-1547	5081
Performnce Engineered Pdts Inc	3089	E	909 594-7487	5134
Ronford Products Inc	3089	E	909 622-7446	5185
Travelers Choice Travelware	3161	D	909 529-7688	5297
El Jinete Leather & Western	3199	F	951 264-8396	5307
Lippert Components Mfg Inc	3231	E	909 628-5557	5347
Sky One Inc	3262	F	909 622-3333	5379
Headwaters Incorporated	3272	E	909 627-9066	5419
W R Meadows Inc	3272	E	909 469-2606	5456
Desicare Inc	3295	E	909 444-8272	5549
Tree Island Wire (usa) Inc	3315	C	909 595-6617	5625
CFI Holdings Corp	3324	E	909 595-2252	5653
Wcs Equipment Holdings LLC	3325	D	909 993-5700	5665
Gemini Aluminum Corporation	3354	C	909 595-7403	5697
Consolted Precision Pdts Corp	3365	C	909 595-2252	5786
Tri-J Metal Heat Treating Co (PA)	3398	F	909 622-9999	5852
Valley Metal Treating Inc	3398	E	909 623-6316	5853
Precision Pwdred Met Parts Inc	3399	C	909 595-5656	5856
Able Iron Works	3441	E	909 397-5300	5987

	SIC	EMP	PHONE	ENTRY#
Trussworks International Inc	3441	D	714 630-2772	6085
Weiser Iron Inc	3441	F	909 429-4600	6092
R & S Automation Inc	3442	E	800 962-3111	6118
Structural Composites Inds LLC **(DH)**	3443	E	909 594-7777	6160
Worthington Cylinder Corp	3443	E	909 594-7777	6172
Equipment Design & Mfg Inc	3444	D	909 594-2229	6232
Superior Duct Fabrication Inc	3444	C	909 620-8565	6327
Galleher Acquisition Corp	3452	E	909 623-5888	6442
Real Plating Inc	3471	C	909 623-2304	6656
DOT Blue Safes Corporation	3499	E	909 445-8888	6860
Camlever Inc	3531	F	909 629-9669	6927
Industrial Design Products Inc	3537	E	909 468-0693	6993
Win-Holt Equipment Corp	3537	E	909 625-2624	7001
Casa Herrera Inc **(PA)**	3556	D	909 392-3930	7194
Rbm Conveyor Systems Inc	3556	E	909 620-1333	7212
Central Blower Co	3564	E	626 330-3182	7321
Cooltec Refrigeration Corp	3585	E	909 865-2229	7605
Dow Hydraulic Systems Inc	3599	D	909 596-6602	7820
Holland & Herring Mfg Inc	3599	E	909 469-4700	7866
ROC-Aire Corp	3599	E	909 784-3385	8004
Spray Systems Inc	3599	E	909 397-7511	8035
Valley Tool and Machine Co Inc	3599	D	909 595-2205	8060
Yawitz Inc	3645	E	909 865-5599	8301
Radian Audio Engineering Inc	3663	E	714 288-8900	8565
Mil-Spec Magnetics Inc	3677	E	909 598-8116	8948
Electrocube Inc **(PA)**	3679	E	909 595-1821	9039
Phenix Enterprises Inc **(PA)**	3713	E	909 469-0411	9332
American Mtal Mfg Resource Inc	3724	E	909 620-4500	9563
Analytical Industries Inc	3823	E	909 392-6900	10117
Gould & Bass Company Inc	3825	E	909 623-6793	10202
Diagnostixx of California Corp	3841	E	909 482-0840	10492
Scientific Pharmaceuticals Inc	3843	E	909 595-9922	10766
American Rotary Broom Co Inc	3991	E	909 629-9117	11084
Westcoast Brush Mfg Inc	3991	E	909 627-7170	11092
Traxx Corporation	3999	D	909 623-8032	11298
Southern Cal Rgional Rail Auth	4111	C	213 808-7043	11367
Covenant Transport Inc	4213	A	909 469-0130	11477
C & B Delivery Service	4225	D	909 623-4708	11566
Kkw Trucking Inc **(PA)**	4225	A	909 869-1200	11592
Southern California Edison Co	4911	B	909 274-1925	12065
Southern California Edison Co	4911	A	909 469-0251	12069
Ramcast Ornamental Sup Co Inc	5051	E	909 469-4767	12566
Ferguson Fire Fabrication Inc **(DH)**	5074	D	909 517-3085	12740
Especial T Hvac Shtmtl Fttngs	5075	E	909 869-9150	12752
Injen Technology Company Ltd	5075	E	909 839-0706	12757
Als Group Inc	5084	E	909 622-7555	12786
Cape Robbin Inc	5139	C	626 810-8080	13160
NW Packaging LLC **(PA)**	5199	D	909 706-3627	13552
Lereta LLC **(PA)**	6211	B	626 543-1765	14385
Yamamoto of Orient Inc **(HQ)**	6512	E	909 594-7356	14701
Murcor Inc	6531	C	909 623-4001	14835
Starwood Htels Rsrts Wrldwide	7011	C	909 622-2220	15372
Merchants Building Maint Co	7349	A	909 622-8260	15724
Global Rental Co Inc	7353	C	909 469-5160	15761
Maxim Healthcare Services Inc	7363	D	626 962-6453	15930
Altec Industries Inc	7538	C	909 444-0444	17028
County of Los Angeles	7992	C	909 231-0549	17422
Fairplex Enterprises Inc	7999	C	909 623-3111	17549
Los Angeles County Fair Assn **(PA)**	7999	D	909 623-3111	17556
Inland Valley Partners LLC	8049	C	909 623-7100	17861
Casa Clina Hosp Ctrs For Hlthc **(HQ)**	8062	B	909 596-7733	18195
Pomona Valley Hospital Med Ctr **(PA)**	8062	A	909 865-9500	18383
Landmark Medical Services Inc	8063	D	909 593-2585	18516
Immunalysis Corporation	8071	D	909 482-0840	18553
Latara Enterprise Inc **(PA)**	8071	C	909 623-9301	18555
Tri-City Mental Health Auth **(PA)**	8093	C	909 623-6131	18726
American National Red Cross	8322	C	909 859-7006	19019
Casa Colina Inc **(PA)**	8322	A	909 596-7733	19033
San Gbrl/Pmona Vlleys Dvlpmnta	8322	B	909 620-7722	19135
Walden House Inc	8361	C	626 258-0300	19310

PORT HUENEME, CA - Ventura County

	SIC	EMP	PHONE	ENTRY#
Consoldted Precision Pdts Corp	3365	D	805 488-6451	5785
Pac Foundries Inc	3366	D	805 986-1308	5806
Brusco Tug & Barge Inc	4492	C	805 986-1600	11650
NAVY UNITED STATES DEPARTMENT	7699	C	805 989-1328	17140

PORTER RANCH, CA - Los Angeles County

	SIC	EMP	PHONE	ENTRY#
Design Todays Inc **(PA)**	2339	E	213 745-3091	2318
JNJ Apparel Inc	2339	E	323 584-9700	2335
Cyberpolicy Inc	6411	C	877 626-9991	14582
Kaiser Foundation Hospitals	8062	D	833 574-2273	18299

POWAY, CA - San Diego County

	SIC	EMP	PHONE	ENTRY#
Benchmark Landscape Svcs Inc	0781	C	858 513-7190	142
Richmond Engineering Co Inc	0782	C	800 589-7058	215
Kiewit Corporation	1542	D	858 208-4285	562
Harper Federal Cnstr LLC	1611	D	619 543-1296	624
BCM Customer Service	1711	D	858 679-5757	742
Western Fire Protection Inc **(PA)**	1711	D	858 513-4949	836
Electronic Control Systems LLC	1731	C	858 513-1911	894
Gould Electric Inc	1731	C	858 486-1727	904
Morrow-Meadows Corporation	1731	B	858 974-3650	919
Pro Installations Inc **(HQ)**	1752	E		1034
Quality Reinforcing Inc	1791	D	858 748-8400	1111
Creative Foods LLC	2099	E	858 748-0070	1876
Disguise Inc **(HQ)**	2389	E	858 391-3600	2450
Smoothreads Inc	2396	E	800 536-5959	2541
B Young Enterprises Inc	2434	D	858 748-0935	2648
Spooners Woodworks Inc	2541	C	858 679-9086	2966
Hpi Liquidations Inc	2653	C	858 391-7302	3110
Liberty Diversified Intl Inc	2653	C	858 391-7302	3115
San Diego Crating & Pkg Inc	2653	F	858 748-0100	3127
Digital One Color	2752	F	858 576-3600	3560
Digitalpro Inc	2752	D	858 874-7750	3563
Alfa Scientific Designs Inc	2835	D	858 513-3888	4266
Granite Gold Inc	2842	D	858 499-8933	4352
Henkel US Operations Corp	2844	E	203 655-8911	4420
Diversfied Nano Solutions Corp	2893	E	858 924-1013	4587
Aldila Materials Tech Corp **(DH)**	2895	E	858 486-6970	4592
Toray Membrane Usa Inc **(DH)**	2899	D	858 218-2360	4634
Plastifab San Diego	3083	F	858 679-6600	4840
Eagle Mold Technologies Inc	3089	E	858 530-0888	5018
K-Tube Corporation	3317	D	858 513-9229	5636
Valley Metals LLC	3317	E	858 513-1300	5642
Omc-Thc Liquidating Inc	3433	E	858 486-8846	5982
Gaines Manufacturing Inc	3444	E	858 486-7100	6243
L & T Precision LLC	3444	C	858 513-7874	6261
Securus Inc	3446	E		6369
Quality Steel Fabricators Inc	3449	E	858 748-8400	6405
Aztec Manufacturing Inc **(PA)**	3452	E	858 513-4350	6432
Advanced Machining Tooling Inc	3544	E	858 486-9050	7046
Masterbilt Atmtn Solutions Inc	3549	E	858 748-6700	7171
Delta Design Inc **(HQ)**	3569	B	858 848-8000	7388
Gateway Inc	3571	E	858 451-9933	7426
Rugged Systems Inc	3571	C	858 391-1006	7448
Apricorn LLC	3577	E	858 513-2000	7507
Delkin Devices Inc **(PA)**	3577	D	858 391-1234	7521
Mytee Products Inc	3589	E	858 679-1191	7675
Advanced Engineering & EDM Inc	3599	F	858 679-6800	7735
Advanced Enginering and EDM	3599	E	858 679-6800	7736
Darmark Corporation	3599	D	858 679-3970	7813
Franklins Inds San Diego Inc	3599	E	858 486-9399	7836
EPC Power Corp **(PA)**	3629	C	858 748-5590	8206
Osram Sylvania Inc	3641	D	858 748-5077	8251
Niterder Tchncal Ltg Vdeo Syst	3648	C	858 268-9316	8377
Littlefeet Inc	3661	E	858 375-6400	8478
Broadcast Microwave Svcs LLC **(PA)**	3663	C	858 391-3050	8501
Ramona Research Inc	3663	F	858 679-0717	8566
Somacis Inc	3672	C	858 513-2200	8731
Wfb Archives Inc	3672	D		8752
Data Device Corporation	3674	E	858 503-3300	8785
Oasis Materials Company LLC **(DH)**	3679	E	858 486-8846	9090
United Security Products Inc	3699	E	800 227-1592	9266
Thyssenkrupp Bilstein Amer Inc	3714	E	858 386-5900	9470
General Atmics Arntcal Systems **(DH)**	3721	B	858 312-2810	9523
General Atmics Arntcal Systems	3721	E	858 455-3358	9524
General Atmics Arntcal Systems	3721	E	858 312-4247	9526
General Atmics Arntcal Systems	3721	C	858 455-3000	9527
General Atmics Arntcal Systems	3721	E	858 762-6700	9530
General Atomic Aeron	3721	E	858 455-4560	9531
General Atomic Aeron	3721	E	858 312-3428	9532
General Atomic Aeron	3721	E	858 312-2543	9533
Quatro Composites LLC	3728	C	712 707-9200	9774
Teledyne Instruments Inc	3812	E	858 842-2600	10078
Teledyne Rd Instruments Inc	3812	E	858 842-2600	10079
Tern Design Ltd	3823	E	760 754-2400	10165
Cohu Inc **(PA)**	3825	E	858 848-8100	10191
Cohu Interface Solutions LLC **(HQ)**	3825	D	858 848-8000	10192
Delta Design (littleton) Inc	3825	A	858 848-8100	10194
Vitrek LLC **(PA)**	3825	E	858 689-2755	10230
Resmed Corp	3841	E	858 746-2400	10596
Decision Sciences Med Co LLC	3845	E	858 602-1600	10799
Tek84 Inc **(PA)**	3845	C	858 676-5382	10828
Aldila Golf Corp	3949	C	858 513-1801	10972
Hoist Fitness Systems Inc	3949	D	858 578-7676	10998

	SIC	EMP	PHONE	ENTRY#
Seirus Innovative ACC Inc	3949	D	858 513-1212	11024
Uke Corporation	3949	D	858 513-9100	11038
Traffic Control & Safety Corp	3993	F	858 679-7292	11177
Corovan Corporation (PA)	4214	C	858 762-8100	11516
Corovan Moving & Storage Co (HQ)	4214	D	858 748-1100	11517
Home Depot USA Inc	4225	C	858 859-4143	11588
Phonecom Inc	4813	D	973 577-6380	11898
IMS Electronics Recycling Inc	4953	C	858 679-1555	12171
Printsafe Inc	5045	E	858 748-8600	12433
Pmb Group Inc	5047	F	619 690-7300	12508
Bay City Equipment Inds Inc	5063	D	619 938-8200	12587
Wassco	5084	C	858 679-0444	12834
Motion Industries Inc	5085	E	858 602-1500	12866
Chef Works Inc (PA)	5136	C	858 643-5600	13099
Smart Stores Operations LLC	5141	C	858 748-0101	13230
Sysco San Diego Inc	5141	B	858 513-7300	13235
Perry Ford of Poway LLC	5511	D	858 748-1400	13813
Poway Toyota Scion Inc	5511	D	858 486-2900	13815
Southern Cal Disc Tire Co Inc	5531	C	858 486-3600	13876
Geico General Insurance Co	6411	A	858 848-8200	14597
Champion Investment Corp	7011	D	917 712-7807	15113
Williams Scotsman Inc	7319	C	619 710-8468	15605
Digirad Imaging Solutions Inc	7352	C	800 947-6134	15757
Dynovas Inc	7389	E	508 717-7494	16819
Bay City Electric Works Inc	7694	F	858 486-1054	17102
Pkl Services Inc	7699	E	858 679-1755	17146
United Studios Self Def Inc	7999	D	858 486-8773	17577
Pomerado Operations LLC	8051	C	858 487-6242	18033
Palomar Health	8062	A	760 739-3000	18363
Palomar Health	8062	C	858 613-4000	18364
Palomar Health Medical Group (HQ)	8062	C	858 675-3100	18366
Palomar Medical Center	8062	B	858 613-4000	18368
Liberty Residential Svcs Inc	8082	D	858 500-0852	18624
Community Food Connection	8322	N	858 751-4613	19048
Community Dev Inst Head Start	8351	B	858 668-2985	19208
ISE Corporation	8731	C	858 413-1720	19849
T G T Enterprises Inc	8742	C	858 413-0300	20253

RAMONA, CA - San Diego County

	SIC	EMP	PHONE	ENTRY#
Demler Brothers LLC	0252	D	760 789-2457	91
Pro Traffic Services Inc	1711	D	760 906-6961	811
In-Line Fence & Railing Co Inc	1799	E	760 789-0282	1162
Summit Enterprises Inc	2679	E	858 679-2100	3247
Micron Machine Company	3599	E	858 486-5900	7933
EMD Millipore Corporation	3826	E	760 788-9692	10255
San Diego Country Estates Assn	8641	C	760 789-3788	19461

RANCHO CASCADES, CA - Los Angeles County

	SIC	EMP	PHONE	ENTRY#
Tutor Perini Corporation (PA)	1542	C	818 362-8391	598
Tutor-Saliba Corporation (HQ)	1542	C	818 362-8391	599
Desert Mechanical Inc	1711	A	702 873-7333	763
Fisk Electric Company	1731	C	818 884-1166	902
A A Gonzalez Inc	1742	D	818 367-2242	965
Spears Manufacturing Co	3084	B	818 364-1611	4854
MS Aerospace Inc	3452	B	818 833-9095	6449
Laser Operations LLC	3674	E	818 986-0000	8827
Janco Corporation	3679	C	818 361-3366	9068
Mason Electric Co	3728	B	818 361-3366	9743
Spears Manufacturing Co (PA)	5083	C	818 364-1611	12782

RANCHO CUCAMONGA, CA - San Bernardino County

	SIC	EMP	PHONE	ENTRY#
Merchants Landscape Services	0781	D	909 981-1022	167
American De Rosa Lamparts LLC	1541	D	800 777-4440	493
David L Manwarren Corp	1542	E	909 989-5883	545
Penwal Industries Inc	1542	D	909 466-1555	577
WE Oneil Construction Co Cal	1542	E	909 466-5300	602
Precision Pipeline LLC	1623	B	909 229-6858	685
General Coatings Corporation	1721	D	909 204-4150	847
Professnal Elec Cnstr Svcs Inc	1731	C	909 373-4100	929
Superior Elec Mech & Plbg Inc	1731	B	909 357-9400	944
TRL Systems Incorporated	1731	D	909 390-8392	948
Yellow Jacket Drlg Svcs LLC	1781	C	909 989-8563	1096
Cargill Meat Solutions Corp	2011	D	909 476-3120	1192
Formosa Meat Company Inc	2013	E	909 987-0470	1218
Tfi of California Inc	2013	C	844 362-3222	1239
Tfi of California Inc (DH)	2013	E	844 362-3222	1240
Honeyville Grain Inc	2041	E	909 243-1050	1412
Reyes Coca-Cola Bottling LLC	2086	B	909 980-3121	1731
American Fruits & Flavors LLC	2087	E	909 291-2620	1755
Frozen Bean Inc	2087	E	855 837-6936	1773
T Hasegawa USA Inc	2087	E	714 522-1900	1787
Aquamar Inc	2091	C	909 481-4700	1791
Gruma Corporation	2096	C	909 980-3566	1826

	SIC	EMP	PHONE	ENTRY#
Mizkan America Inc	2099	C	909 484-8743	1947
Hollywood Ribbon Industries Inc	2241	B	323 266-0670	2055
Ecmd Inc	2431	D	909 980-1775	2598
Ifco Systems Us LLC	2448	D	909 484-4332	2720
Brownwood Furniture Inc	2511	C	909 945-5613	2769
ES Kluft & Company Inc (DH)	2515	C	909 373-4211	2848
South Bay International Inc	2515	E	909 718-5000	2860
Modular Office Solutions Inc	2522	E	909 476-4200	2916
Ironwood Packaging LLC	2671	E	909 581-0077	3153
Avery Dennison Corporation	2672	D	909 987-4631	3163
Prime Converting Corporation	2679	E	909 476-9500	3244
Chick Publications Inc	2731	E	909 987-0771	3401
Continental Graphics Corp	2752	E	909 758-9800	3539
Kindred Litho Incorporated	2752	E	909 944-4015	3612
Heartland Label Printers LLC	2759	A	909 243-7151	3767
Perimeter Solutions LP	2819	E	909 983-0772	3904
Dow Company Foundation	2821	C	909 476-4127	3936
Criticalpoint Capital LLC	2822	E	909 987-9533	3985
Amphastar Pharmaceuticals Inc (PA)	2834	C	909 980-9484	4047
Mysmile Oral Care Inc	2842	E	909 908-4615	4363
Usl Parallel Products Cal	2869	E	909 980-1200	4534
Advantage Adhesives Inc	2891	E	909 204-4990	4557
Master Builders LLC	2899	A	909 987-1758	4618
Swabplus Inc	3053	E	909 987-7898	4747
Omni Seals Inc	3061	D	909 946-0181	4751
Good-West Rubber Corp (PA)	3069	C	909 987-1774	4764
Goodwest Rubber Linings Inc	3069	E	888 499-0085	4765
Plaxicon Holding Corporation	3085	A	909 944-6868	4863
Creu LLC	3089	E	909 483-4888	4998
Diverse Optics Inc	3089	E	909 593-9330	5012
Paradigm Packaging East LLC	3089	E	909 985-2519	5129
Paramunt Plstic Fbricators Inc	3089	F	909 987-4757	5131
Pitbull Gym Incorporated	3089	E	909 980-7960	5137
Pres-Tek Plastics Inc (PA)	3089	E	909 360-1600	5161
Proulx Manufacturing Inc	3089	E	909 980-0662	5168
Russell-Stanley	3089	E	909 980-7114	5193
American Traveler Inc	3161	E	909 466-4000	5283
Searing Industries Inc	3312	C	909 948-3030	5601
Pac-Rancho Inc (HQ)	3324	C	909 987-4721	5660
Southwire Company LLC	3353	C	909 989-2888	5690
Prime Wire & Cable Inc	3357	C	323 266-2010	5748
J T Walker Industries Inc	3442	A	909 481-1909	6108
Superior Tank Co Inc (PA)	3443	E	909 912-0580	6161
M-5 Steel Mfg Inc (PA)	3444	E	323 263-9383	6264
Gcn Supply LLC	3448	E	909 643-4603	6378
Nci Group Inc	3448	E	909 987-4681	6387
Doubleco Incorporated	3452	D	909 481-0799	6438
Vanguard Tool & Mfg Co Inc	3469	D	909 980-9392	6565
Metal Coaters California Inc	3479	D	909 987-4681	6718
Socco Plastic Coating Company	3479	E	909 987-4753	6737
Steelscape LLC	3479	F	909 987-4711	6739
Schellinger Spring Inc	3493	E	909 373-0799	6784
Wessex Industries Inc	3498	E	562 944-5760	6854
Executive Safe and SEC Corp	3499	E	909 947-7020	6863
Smith International Inc	3533	C	909 906-7900	6963
Prestige Mold Incorporated	3544	D	909 980-6600	7090
Pyramid Mold & Tool	3544	D	909 947-2555	7093
Rafco-Brickform LLC (PA)	3545	D	909 484-3399	7129
Everidge Inc	3585	E	909 605-6419	7613
Bernell Hydraulics Inc (PA)	3594	E	909 899-1751	7710
All Star Precision	3599	E	909 944-8373	7753
Intra Aerospace LLC	3599	E	909 476-0343	7875
JCPM Inc	3599	E	909 484-9040	7886
Jet Cutting Solutions Inc	3599	E	909 948-2424	7887
Pamco Machine Works Inc	3599	E	909 941-7260	7966
Paramount Machine Co Inc	3599	E	909 484-3600	7967
Romeros Engineering Inc	3599	E	909 481-1170	8005
Electro Switch Corp	3613	D	909 581-0855	8121
Fluorescent Supply Co Inc	3646	E	909 948-8878	8313
Robot-Gxg Inc	3651	E	660 324-0030	8430
Digital Flex Media Inc	3652	D	909 484-8440	8455
Siemens Rail Automation Corp	3669	D	909 532-5405	8625
B & G Electronic Assembly Inc	3679	E	909 608-2077	9001
Electro Switch Corp	3679	E	909 581-0855	9036
Hunt Electronic Usa Inc	3699	F	909 987-6999	9215
Universal Surveillance Systems LLC	3699	D	909 484-7870	9267
Greenpower Motor Company Inc	3711	D	909 308-0960	9291
Air Components Inc	3728	E	909 980-8224	9610
Lanic Engineering Inc (PA)	3728	E	877 763-0411	9733
Marino Enterprises Inc	3728	E	909 476-0343	9742
Precision Aerospace Corp	3728	D	909 945-9604	9768
Safran Cabin Inc	3728	C	909 652-9700	9789
Zodiac Aerospace	3728	F	909 652-9700	9831

Employee Codes: A=Over 500 employees, B=251-500
C=101-250, D=51-100, E=20-50, F=10-19, G=1-9

2024 Southern California
Business Directory and Buyers Guide

© Mergent Inc. 1-800-342-5647

1419

GEOGRAPHIC

	SIC	EMP	PHONE	ENTRY#
Pneudraulics Inc.	3812	B	909 980-5366	10050
Mindrum Precision Inc.	3824	E	909 989-1728	10177
Endress+hser Optcal Analis Inc.	3826	E	909 477-2329	10257
Davidson Optronics Inc.	3829	E	626 962-5181	10360
Eagle Labs LLC.	3841	D	909 481-0011	10496
New World Medical Incorporated.	3841	F	909 466-4304	10576
Alcoa Fastening Systems.	3965	C	909 483-2333	11068
Butler Home Products LLC.	3991	C	909 476-3884	11086
Fan Fave Inc.	3993	E	909 975-4999	11118
Durham School Services L P.	4151	C	909 899-1809	11425
New Legend Inc.	4213	C	855 210-2300	11500
Honeyville Inc.	4221	D	909 980-9500	11548
Distribution Alternatives Inc.	4225	D	909 746-5600	11574
Home Depot USA Inc.	4225	D	909 483-8115	11587
Msblous LLC.	4225	D	909 929-9689	11600
NRG California South LP.	4911	C	909 899-7241	12029
Cucamonga Valley Water Dst.	4941	D	909 987-2591	12119
Falken Tire Holdings Inc.	5014	C	800 723-2553	12268
Sumitomo Rubber North Amer Inc (HQ).	5014	C	909 466-1116	12273
Bradshaw International Inc (PA).	5023	B	909 476-3884	12296
Three Wise Men Inc.	5023	E	909 477-6698	12317
Innovative Displayworks Inc.	5046	C	909 447-8254	12457
Tri-Tech Metals Inc.	5051	F	909 948-1401	12579
California Box II.	5113	D	909 944-9202	13005
L & R Distributors Inc.	5131	C	909 980-3807	13083
Nongshim America Inc (HQ).	5141	C	909 481-3698	13188
Frito-Lay North America Inc.	5145	B	909 941-6214	13271
Frito-Lay North America Inc.	5145	C	909 941-6218	13272
Shining Ocean Inc.	5146	C	253 826-3700	13287
Evolution Fresh Inc.	5148	C	800 794-9986	13320
Transcendia Inc.	5162	E	909 944-9981	13419
Home Depot USA Inc.	5211	D	909 948-9200	13605
Lowes Home Centers LLC.	5211	C	909 476-9697	13637
Handels Homemade Ice Cream.	5812	E	909 989-7065	14011
Klatch Coffee Inc (PA).	5812	E	909 481-4031	14020
M & G Jewelers Inc.	5944	D	909 989-2929	14078
Arrowhead Central Credit Union (PA).	6061	B	866 212-4333	14223
CU Cooperative Systems Inc (PA).	6062	B	909 948-2500	14247
Thrive Mortgage LLC.	6162	D	909 527-3736	14352
Carrington Mortgage Svcs LLC.	6211	C	909 226-7963	14373
Agent Franchise LLC.	6321	C	949 930-5025	14446
Inland Empire Health Plan (PA).	6321	A	909 890-2000	14452
Lereta LLC.	6512	C	626 332-1942	14670
National Community Renaissance.	6513	C	909 948-7579	14728
National Cmnty Renaissance Cal (PA).	6552	C	909 483-2444	14906
National Cmnty Renaissance Cal.	6552	C	619 223-9222	14907
Oakwood Corporate Housing Inc.	7021	C	909 922-8272	15431
Collection Technology Inc.	7322	D	800 743-4284	15610
Sunn America Inc.	7359	E	909 944-5756	15800
Butler America Holdings Inc.	7361	B	909 417-3660	15824
Career Strategies Tmpry Inc.	7361	C	909 230-4504	15830
Network Intgrtion Partners Inc.	7373	D	909 919-2800	16463
Diplomatic Security Svcs LLC.	7381	D	909 463-8409	16638
Nationwide Guard Services Inc.	7381	B	909 608-1112	16662
Harrison Iyke.	7382	D	909 463-8409	16740
Par Western Line Contrs LLC.	7389	A	760 737-0925	16898
H & A Transmissions Inc.	7537	E	909 941-9020	17025
James Magna Ltd.	7539	F	909 391-2025	17043
Kathleen Brugger.	7692	E	909 226-1372	17092
Red Hill Country Club.	7997	D	909 982-1358	17509
Grove Diagnstc Imaging Ctr Inc.	8011	B	909 982-8638	17662
Knd Development 55 LLC.	8062	C	909 581-6400	18316
Perris Valley Cmnty Hosp LLC.	8062	C	909 581-6400	18375
Branlyn Prominence Inc (PA).	8082	D	909 476-9030	18596
Universal Technical Inst Inc.	8249	C	909 484-1929	19006
Horrigan Enterprises Inc.	8322	C	909 481-9663	19091
In-Roads Creative Programs.	8322	B	909 989-9944	19092
Vocational Imprv Program Inc (PA).	8331	D	909 483-5924	19195
Monte Vista Child Care Ctr Inc.	8351	D	909 476-6780	19220
AMP Display Inc (PA).	8711	E	909 980-1310	19547
Bas Engineering Inc.	8711	F	909 484-2575	19552
CDM Constructors Inc.	8711	C	909 579-3500	19562
Meeder Equipment Company.	8711	F	909 463-0600	19644
Eide Bailly LLP.	8721	B	909 466-4410	19771
Gentex Corporation.	8731	D	909 481-7667	19844

RANCHO DOMINGUEZ, CA - Los Angeles County

	SIC	EMP	PHONE	ENTRY#
Global Agri-Trade (PA).	2076	E	562 320-8550	1564
Bi Nutraceuticals Inc.	2087	C	310 669-2100	1758
Ethos Seafood Group LLC.	2092	D	312 858-3474	1803
Santa Monica Seafood Company (PA).	2092	D	310 886-7900	1811
Mars Food Us LLC (HQ).	2099	B	310 933-0670	1938
Carol Anderson Inc (PA).	2335	E	310 638-3333	2279

	SIC	EMP	PHONE	ENTRY#
Organic By Nature Inc (PA).	2833	E	562 901-0177	4009
Biocell Laboratories Inc.	2835	E	310 537-3300	4267
Giovanni Cosmetics Inc.	2844	D	310 952-9960	4413
Shercon LLC.	3069	D		4795
Caplugs Inc.	3089	D	310 537-2300	4982
Expanded Rubber & Plastics Corp.	3089	E	310 324-6692	5026
Buff and Shine Mfg Inc.	3291	E	310 886-5111	5538
Standard Wire & Cable Co (PA).	3357	C	310 609-1811	5750
Aerol Co Inc.	3365	E	310 762-2660	5779
Bodycote Thermal Proc Inc.	3398	E	310 604-8000	5828
Adf Incorporated.	3446	E	310 669-9700	6349
Team Manufacturing Inc.	3469	E	310 639-0251	6561
S L Fusco Inc (PA).	3541	E	310 868-1010	7022
Southwestern Industries Inc (PA).	3541	D	310 608-4422	7025
Dresser-Rand Company.	3563	C	310 223-0600	7308
Siemens Energy Inc.	3563	C	310 223-0660	7316
Enlink Geoenergy Services Inc.	3585	E	424 242-1200	7611
Grand General Accessories LLC.	3612	C	310 631-2589	8097
DSA Phototech LLC.	3646	E	866 868-1602	8309
Visionaire Lighting LLC.	3646	D	310 512-6480	8341
Parker-Hannifin Corporation.	3677	C	310 608-5600	8949
Spectrum Inc.	3841	E	310 885-4600	10608
Laclede Inc.	3843	E	310 605-4280	10753
Fairway Import-Export Inc.	3949	E	262 788-7313	10989
Unis LLC.	4225	D	310 747-7388	11626
CDS Moving Equipment Inc (PA).	5084	D	310 631-1100	12787
Afc Distribution Inc.	5141	C	310 604-3630	13169
Union Sup Comsy Solutions Inc.	5141	B	785 357-5005	13238
Pbk International LLC.	5712	C	866 727-7195	13946
Advanced Fresh Concepts Corp (PA).	6794	E	310 604-3630	15007
Bioquip Products Inc.	8731	E	310 667-8800	19828

RANCHO MIRAGE, CA - Riverside County

	SIC	EMP	PHONE	ENTRY#
Agua Clnte Band Chilla Indians.	7011	A	760 321-2000	15069
Hst Lessee Mission Hills LP.	7011	D	760 328-5955	15188
Ksl Rancho Mirage Operating Co Inc.	7011	B	760 568-2727	15212
Omni Hotels Corporation.	7011	B	760 568-2727	15276
Ritz-Carlton Hotel Company LLC.	7011	A	760 321-8282	15327
Richman Management Corporation.	7381	D	760 832-8520	16674
Country Villa Service Corp.	7389	C	760 340-0053	16806
Df One Operator LLC.	7389	D	310 961-9739	16817
Mission Hills Country Club Inc.	7997	D	760 324-9400	17501
Desert Crdlgy Cons Med Group I.	8011	C	760 346-0642	17642
Eisenhower Medical Center (PA).	8062	A	760 340-3911	18251
Eisenhower Medical Center.	8071	E	760 773-1364	18547
Eisenhower Medical Center.	8082	C	760 773-1888	18611
Betty Ford Center (HQ).	8093	C	760 773-4100	18672
Dual Diagnosis Trtmnt Ctr Inc.	8099	C	949 324-4531	18760
Country Vlla Rncho Mrage Hlthc.	8322	C	760 340-0053	19054
Ameritac Inc (PA).	8744	D	925 989-2942	20288

RANCHO PALOS VERDES, CA - Los Angeles County

	SIC	EMP	PHONE	ENTRY#
Ki-P C USA Jeans Inc.	2325	C	310 234-8185	2169
Western Summit Mfg Corp.	3081	E	626 333-3333	4826
Trico Leasing Company LLC.	5085	E	877 259-9997	12886
Pie Rise Ltd.	5812	E	310 832-4559	14031
Long Point Development LLC.	7011	A	310 265-2800	15231
CAW Cowie Inc (PA).	7389	E	212 396-9007	16799
Estates At Trump Nat Golf CLB.	7992	C	310 265-5000	17427
Bay Clubs Company LLC.	7997	B	310 541-2582	17469
Salvation Army (HQ).	8322	E	562 264-3600	19131

RANCHO SANTA FE, CA - San Diego County

	SIC	EMP	PHONE	ENTRY#
First National Bank.	6021	B	858 756-3023	14167
Pacific Western Bank.	6021	B	858 756-3023	14173
Archipelago Development Inc.	6552	D	858 699-6272	14897
Groves Capital Inc.	6799	C	619 519-4453	15030
Huntington Hotel Company.	7011	B	858 756-1131	15190
Rancho Vlncia Rsort Prtners LL.	7011	B	858 756-1123	15318
Del Mar Country Club Inc.	7997	B	858 759-5500	17480
Fairbanks Ranch Cntry CLB Inc.	7997	C	858 259-8811	17484
Rancho Santa Fe Association.	7997	D	858 756-1182	17508

RANCHO SANTA MARGARI, CA - Orange County

	SIC	EMP	PHONE	ENTRY#
The Lubrizol Corporation.	2899	F	949 212-1863	4633
Glas Werk Inc.	3229	E	949 766-1296	5325
Allstar Microelectronics Inc.	3572	F	949 546-0888	7462
Foundation 9 Entertainment Inc (PA).	7372	C	949 698-1500	16249
Jipc Management Inc.	8741	A	949 916-2000	20045

RCHO STA MARG, CA - Orange County

	SIC	EMP	PHONE	ENTRY#
Park West Landscape Maint Inc (PA).	0782	B	949 546-8300	211
Barr Engineering Inc.	1711	D	562 944-1722	740

	SIC	EMP	PHONE	ENTRY#
Point Conception Inc.	2339	E	949 589-6890	2360
Renaissnce Frnch Dors Sash Inc (PA)	2431	C	714 578-0090	2631
South Coast Stairs Inc.	2431	E	949 858-1685	2633
Environmental Catalyst Tech.	2819	E	949 888-1625	3894
At Apollo Technologies LLC	2899	E	949 888-0573	4596
Mc Products Inc.	2899	E	949 888-7100	4620
RPM Products Inc (PA)	3053	E	949 888-8543	4742
Forespar Products Corp (PA)	3429	E	949 858-8820	5917
Light Composite Corporation.	3429	E	949 858-8820	5927
R C Products Corp.	3429	E	949 858-8820	5940
Swiss-Micron Inc.	3451	D	949 589-0430	6423
C C I	3491	E	910 616-7426	6756
IMI Critical Engineering LLC (DH)	3491	B	949 858-1877	6765
Ats Tool Inc.	3544	E	949 888-1744	7051
Ats Workholding Llc (PA)	3545	E	800 321-1833	7107
Ep Holdings Inc.	3572	E	949 713-4600	7469
Form Grind Corporation.	3599	E	949 858-7000	7832
M-Industrial Enterprises LLC	3599	E	949 413-7513	7912
Palomar Products Inc.	3669	D	949 766-5300	8619
Virtium Technology Inc.	3674	E	949 888-2444	8918
Abracon.	3679	E	949 546-8000	8989
Impact LLC.	3679	E	714 546-6000	9058
Laser Spectrum Inc.	3699	E	949 726-2978	9226
Car Sound Exhaust System Inc.	3714	C	949 858-5900	9366
Car Sound Exhaust System Inc.	3714	E	949 858-5900	9367
Racepak LLC.	3714	E	949 709-5555	9446
Applied Manufacturing LLC.	3841	A	949 713-8000	10432
Applied Medical Corporation (PA)	3841	C	949 713-8000	10433
Applied Medical Corporation.	3841	E	949 713-2174	10434
Applied Medical Dist Corp.	3841	A	949 713-8000	10435
Applied Medical Resources.	3841	E	949 459-1042	10436
Applied Medical Resources Corp (HQ)	3841	D	949 713-8000	10437
Santa Margarita Water District.	4941	C	949 459-6400	12147
Virtium LLC.	5045	D	949 888-2444	12450
Grandma Lucys LLC.	5999	F	949 206-8547	14134
Melissa Data Corporation (PA)	7371	E	949 858-3000	16073
Roman Cthlic Diocese of Orange.	8211	C	949 766-6000	18982
Capital Invstmnts Vntures Corp (PA)	8621	C	949 858-0647	19392
Padi Americas Inc.	8621	E	949 858-7234	19401
Savice Inc.	8641	D	949 888-2444	19462
National Tour Intgrted Rsrces.	8742	E	949 215-6330	20206

REDLANDS, CA - San Bernardino County

	SIC	EMP	PHONE	ENTRY#
Larry Jacinto Farming Inc.	0762	D	909 794-2276	137
Bradco Industrial Corporation.	0851	F	888 272-3261	230
Robert Clapper Cnstr Svcs Inc.	1542	D	909 829-3688	585
Larry Jacinto Construction Inc.	1611	D	909 794-2151	629
Ach Mechanical Contractors Inc.	1711	D	909 307-2850	727
Pro-Craft Construction Inc.	1711	C	909 790-5222	812
Enerpath Services Inc.	1731	D	909 335-1699	897
Faith Electric LLC.	1731	C	909 767-2682	899
Mobiz It Inc.	1731	D	909 453-6700	918
Keurig Green Mountain Inc.	2086	E	909 557-6513	1700
Caseworx Inc (PA)	2521	E	909 799-8550	2879
Ui Medical LLC.	2676	E	562 453-1515	3209
Continental Datalabel Inc.	2679	F	909 307-3600	3233
Califrnia Nwspapers Ltd Partnr.	2711	E	909 793-3221	3264
California Prtg Solutions Inc.	2752	F	909 307-2032	3526
Clorox Manufacturing Company.	2842	D	909 307-2756	4348
Munchkin Inc.	3085	E	818 893-5000	4859
Plastics Plus Technology Inc.	3089	E	909 747-0555	5149
Window Enterprises Inc.	3442	E	951 943-4894	6128
Venturedyne Ltd.	3564	D	909 793-2788	7338
Garner Holt Productions Inc.	3571	E	909 799-3030	7425
Photo Sciences Incorporated (PA)	3577	E	310 634-1500	7562
Precision Hermetic Tech Inc.	3679	D	909 381-6011	9100
Teledyne Technologies Inc.	3691	D	909 793-3131	9156
Low Cost Interlock Inc.	3694	E	844 387-0326	9168
C C I Redlands Inc.	3751	E	909 307-6500	9875
Becton Dickinson and Company.	3826	D	909 748-7300	10241
Kyocera Medical Tech Inc.	3842	E	909 557-2360	10679
Ifit Inc.	3949	A	909 335-2888	11003
Advanced Chemical Trnspt Inc.	4212	E	951 790-7989	11439
CJ Logistics America LLC.	4213	D	909 363-4354	11475
Ashley Furniture Inds LLC.	4225	B	909 825-4900	11565
Maersk Whsng Dist Svcs USA LLC.	4731	C	801 301-1732	11781
Southern California Gas Co.	4924	D	909 335-7802	12098
Environmental Systems Research Inst (PA)	5045	A	909 793-2853	12409
Esri International LLC.	5045	E	909 793-2853	12411
Hulsey Contracting Inc.	5082	E	951 549-3665	12771
Hydro Tek Systems Inc.	5087	D	909 799-9222	12892
P & R Paper Supply Co Inc (HQ)	5113	D	909 389-1807	13021
Haralambos Beverage Co.	5181	B	562 347-4300	13467

	SIC	EMP	PHONE	ENTRY#
Home Depot USA Inc.	5211	C	909 748-0505	13602
Lowes Home Centers LLC.	5211	D	909 307-8883	13641
Dick Dewese Chevrolet Inc.	5511	E	909 793-2681	13757
Ken Grody Redlands LLC.	5511	D	909 793-3211	13786
Akh Company Inc.	5531	D	909 748-5016	13852
New Image Commercial Flrg Inc.	5713	E	909 796-3400	13952
Mountain West Financial Inc (PA)	6162	B	909 793-1500	14343
Lois Lauer Realty (PA)	6531	E	909 748-7000	14823
ABI Attorneys Service Inc (PA)	7334	D	909 793-0613	15640
Envirnmntal Systems RES Inst I.	7372	E	909 793-2853	16237
Redlands Ford Inc.	7532	D	909 793-3211	17015
Advanced Innovative Tech Corp.	7538	D	417 831-9444	17026
Rettig Machine Inc.	7692	E	909 793-7811	17094
Chp.	7822	D	909 213-3788	17275
Harkins Theatres Inc.	7832	E	909 793-7993	17300
Redlands Country Club.	7997	D	909 793-2661	17510
Beaver Medical Clinic Inc (PA)	8011	C	909 793-3311	17599
Kaiser Foundation Hospitals.	8011	C	888 750-0036	17674
Ash Holdings LLC.	8051	C	909 793-2609	17882
Humangood Norcal.	8059	C	909 793-1233	18134
Loma Linda University Med Ctr.	8062	D	909 558-4000	18327
Loma Linda University Med Ctr.	8062	D	909 558-9275	18328
Redlands Community Hospital (PA)	8062	C	909 335-5500	18406
Interntional Un Oper Engineers.	8631	A	909 307-8700	19410
YMCA of East Valley (PA)	8641	C	909 798-9622	19476
Epic Management LP (PA)	8741	C	909 799-1818	20029
RHS Corp.	8741	A	909 335-5500	20090
Bon Appetit Management Co.	8742	C	909 748-8970	20143

REDONDO BEACH, CA - Los Angeles County

	SIC	EMP	PHONE	ENTRY#
Gms Molds.	2431	E	310 403-9870	2602
Quantimetrix.	2835	D	310 536-0006	4287
Alcast Mfg Inc.	3364	E	310 542-3581	5770
Woodruff Corporation.	3599	E	310 378-1611	8084
Northrop Grumman Systems Corp.	3663	C	310 812-5149	8555
Northrop Grmmn Spce & Mssn Sys.	3714	B	310 812-4321	9434
Northrop Grumman Systems Corp.	3721	C	310 812-4321	9545
Northrop Grumman Systems Corp.	3721	E	310 812-1089	9546
Impulse Space Inc.	3761	E	949 315-5540	9894
Jariet Technologies Inc.	3812	E	310 698-1001	9984
Northrop Grumman Systems Corp.	3812	C	855 737-8364	10021
Northrop Grumman Systems Corp.	3812	C	310 812-4321	10022
Advanced Arm Dynamics (PA)	3842	C	310 372-3050	10631
Dsd Trucking Inc.	4581	C	310 338-3395	11696
Mapcargo Global Logistics (PA)	4731	E	310 297-8300	11783
Stevens Global Logistics Inc (PA)	4731	C	800 229-7284	11805
Scat Enterprises Inc.	5013	C	310 370-5501	12260
Brownstone Companies Inc.	5065	A	310 297-3600	12650
Smart & Final Stores Inc.	5141	B	323 497-8528	13216
Bicara Inc.	5147	B	310 316-6222	13290
Redondo Beach Brewing Co Inc.	5812	E	310 316-8477	14033
HMC Assets LLC.	6331	D	310 535-9293	14509
Greenhedge Escrow.	6541	D	310 640-3040	14892
Wedgewood Inc (PA)	6799	D	310 640-3070	15059
Portofino Hotel Partners LP.	7011	D	310 379-8481	15307
K & P Janitorial Services.	7349	D	310 540-8878	15717
Cputer Inc.	7379	D	844 394-1538	16559
Gsg Protective Services CA Inc.	7381	C	310 371-5300	16645
Gable House Inc.	7933	D	310 378-2265	17356
Beach Cities Health District.	8399	C	310 374-3426	19317
Westwind Engineering Inc.	8711	C	310 831-3454	19718
NBC Consulting Inc.	8742	D	310 798-5000	20208
Sierra Monolithics Inc (HQ)	8748	E	310 698-1000	20378

RESEDA, CA - Los Angeles County

	SIC	EMP	PHONE	ENTRY#
Eisenberg Vlg of The Los Angle.	8051	D	818 774-3372	17929
Los Angles Jewish HM For Aging.	8051	B	818 774-3000	18002
Los Angles Jewish HM For Aging (PA)	8051	B	818 774-3000	18003
Child Development Institute.	8322	D	818 888-4559	19040
Chase Group Llc.	8742	B	818 708-3533	20149

RIALTO, CA - San Bernardino County

	SIC	EMP	PHONE	ENTRY#
Sierra Lathing Company Inc.	1742	C	909 421-0211	996
Arnett Construction Inc.	1794	E	909 421-7960	1122
Biscomerica Corp.	2052	E	909 877-5997	1510
Thompson Pipe Group Inc (PA)	2679	C	909 822-0200	3250
ABF Prints Inc.	2759	F	909 875-7163	3728
Solomon Colors Inc.	2816	C	909 873-9444	3877
B & B Plastics Inc.	2821	E	909 581-3870	3927
Villanueva Plastic Company Inc.	3083	E	909 829-3606	4846
Eagle Roofing Products Fla LLC.	3259	C	909 822-6000	5374
Creative Stone Mfg Inc (PA)	3272	C	909 357-8295	5407
Kti Incorporated.	3272	D	909 434-1888	5423

Employee Codes: A=Over 500 employees, B=251-500
C=101-250, D=51-100, E=20-50, F=10-19, G=1-9

2024 Southern California
Business Directory and Buyers Guide

© Mergent Inc. 1-800-342-5647

1421

GEOGRAPHIC

	SIC	EMP	PHONE	ENTRY#
Royal Westlake Roofing LLC	3272	F	909 822-4407	5447
Burlingame Industries Inc	3299	C	909 355-7000	5565
State Pipe & Supply Inc	3312	E	909 356-5670	5603
Columbia Steel Inc	3441	D	909 874-8840	6009
So-Cal Strl Stl Fbrication Inc	3441	E	909 877-1299	6075
Spray Enclosure Tech Inc	3444	E	909 419-7011	6322
H Wayne Lewis Inc	3449	E	909 874-2213	6398
Martinez and Turek Inc	3599	C	909 820-6800	7920
Mike Dyell Machine Shop Inc (PA)	3599	F	909 350-4101	7934
Techniform International Corp	3599	C	909 877-6886	8044
Lippert Components Inc	3711	E	909 873-0061	9296
Medical Depot Inc	3841	E	877 224-0946	10554
Radial South LP	4225	B	610 491-7000	11607
Jeld-Wen Inc	5031	C	909 879-8700	12334
Ricoh Electronics Inc	5044	D	714 566-2500	12388
B & B Plastics Recyclers Inc (PA)	5093	E	909 829-3606	12951
Distribution Alternatives Inc	5122	D	909 770-8900	13040
Walmart Inc	5311	C	909 820-9912	13684
Burlingame Industries Inc (PA)	7033	D	909 355-7000	15441
Mercy Air Tri-County LLC	7623	C	909 829-1051	17064

RIDGECREST, CA - Kern County

	SIC	EMP	PHONE	ENTRY#
Mpb Furniture Corporation	2512	E	760 375-4800	2812
Orbital Sciences LLC	3812	C	818 887-8345	10047
Sierra Group Inc	4581	F	760 377-1000	11707
Directv Group Holdings LLC	4841	C	760 375-8300	11988
Southern California Edison Co	4911	C	760 375-1821	12066
Home Depot USA Inc	5211	C	760 375-4614	13618
Desert Area Resources Training (PA)	5932	D	760 375-9787	14060
Altaone Federal Credit Union (PA)	6061	C	760 371-7000	14221
Ridgecrest Regional Hospital (PA)	8062	B	760 446-3551	18407
Community Action Partnr Kern	8399	D	760 371-1469	19321

RIVERSIDE, CA - Riverside County

	SIC	EMP	PHONE	ENTRY#
Corona - Cllege Hts Ornge Lmon	0723	B	951 359-6451	101
Azteca Landscape	0781	D	951 369-9210	141
Brightview Tree Care Svcs Inc	0781	E	951 684-2730	154
Liberty Landscaping Inc (PA)	0782	C	951 683-2999	202
County of Riverside	1521	C	951 955-4800	427
MGB Construction Inc	1521	C	951 342-0303	447
Silverado Framing & Cnstr	1521	C	951 352-1100	459
Van Daele Development Corp	1531	C	951 354-6800	489
Hal Hays Construction Inc (PA)	1541	C	951 788-0703	506
Bens Asphalt & Maint Co Inc	1611	D	951 248-1103	611
Riverside Construction Company Inc	1611	C	951 682-8308	641
Rsvc Company	1611	C	951 684-6578	643
Skanska USA Cvil W Cal Dst Inc (DH)	1611	A	951 684-5360	647
Hci LLC (HQ)	1623	B	951 520-4200	671
Herman Weissker Inc (HQ)	1623	C	951 826-8800	673
Kana Pipeline Inc	1623	D	714 986-1400	679
20/20 Plumbing & Heating Inc (PA)	1711	C	951 396-2020	722
Dynamic Plumbing Systems Inc	1711	B	951 343-1200	764
Lozano Plumbing Services Inc	1711	C	951 683-4840	787
M & M Plumbing Inc	1711	C	951 354-5388	790
New Power Inc	1711	D	800 980-9825	798
Ppc Enterprises Inc	1711	C	951 354-5402	809
Solcius LLC	1711	C	951 772-0030	827
J M V B Inc	1721	D	714 288-9797	849
West Coast Interiors Inc	1721	A	951 778-3592	857
Elite Electric	1731	D	951 681-5811	895
J Ginger Masonry LP (PA)	1741	B	951 688-5050	959
Masonry Group Nevada Inc	1741	D	951 509-5300	961
West Coast Drywall & Co Inc	1742	E	951 778-3592	1002
Craftsman Lath and Plaster Inc	1751	B	951 685-9922	1010
Hy-Tech Tile Inc	1752	C	951 788-0550	1031
Pacific Strucframe LLC	1761	C	951 405-8536	1049
Century West Concrete Inc	1771	B	951 712-4065	1065
Inland Cc Inc	1771	C	909 355-1318	1075
Z-Best Concrete Inc	1771	D	951 774-1870	1092
Allied Steel Co Inc	1791	D	951 241-7000	1098
Fencecorp Inc (HQ)	1799	C	951 686-3170	1157
Fenceworks Inc (PA)	1799	C	951 788-5620	1158
PSG Fencing Corporation	1799	D	951 275-9252	1174
West Coast Countertops Inc	1799	C	951 719-3670	1183
Swift Beef Company	2013	C	951 571-2237	1237
Better Bar Manufacturing LLC	2023	E	951 525-3111	1260
Tropical Functional Labs LLC	2023	E	951 688-2619	1287
Mackie International Inc (PA)	2024	E	951 346-0530	1299
Ludfords Inc	2033	E	909 948-0797	1341
Inland Empire Foods Inc (PA)	2034	E	951 682-8222	1355
Canine Caviar Pet Foods De Inc	2047	F	714 223-1800	1428
Canine Caviar Pet Foods Inc	2048	E	714 223-1800	1438
American Bottling Company	2086	D	951 341-7500	1678

	SIC	EMP	PHONE	ENTRY#
Bottling Group LLC	2086	E	951 697-3200	1688
Inland Cold Storage	2092	E	951 369-0230	1807
OSI Industries LLC	2099	B	951 684-4500	1960
Ruiz Mexican Foods Inc (PA)	2099	C	909 947-7811	1980
Triple H Food Processors LLC	2099	D	951 352-5700	1999
Newman Bros California Inc (PA)	2431	F	951 782-0102	2620
Quality Shutters Inc	2431	E	951 683-4939	2630
T M Cobb Company (PA)	2431	E	951 248-2400	2634
Professional Cabinet Solutions	2434	C	909 614-2900	2672
Professional Cabinet Solutions (DH)	2434	C	909 614-2900	2673
Simpson Strong-Tie Company Inc	2439	C	714 871-8373	2702
G C Pallets Inc	2448	E	909 357-8515	2718
Cavco Industries Inc	2451	E	951 688-5353	2734
Fleetwood Homes California Inc (DH)	2451	C	951 351-2494	2739
Fleetwood Homes of Florida (DH)	2451	C	909 261-4274	2740
Autonomous Inc	2522	E	844 949-3879	2905
Ideal Products Inc	2541	E	951 727-8600	2955
Roll-A-Shade Inc (PA)	2591	E	951 245-5077	3013
Heritage Container Inc	2653	D	951 360-1900	3107
Highlander Newspaper	2711	E	951 827-3457	3284
Metropolitan News Company	2711	E	951 369-5890	3307
Press-Enterprise Company (PA)	2711	A	951 684-1200	3316
Qg Printing Corp	2721	E	951 571-2500	3383
Qg Printing II LLC	2752	C	951 571-2500	3674
Quad/Graphics Inc	2752	E	951 689-1122	3675
Sphere Alliance Inc	2821	E	951 352-2400	3973
Cosmedx Science Inc	2834	E	951 371-0509	4093
Universal Prtein Spplmnts Corp	2834	F	732 545-3130	4249
Gar Laboratories Inc	2844	C	951 788-0700	4412
Plz Corp	2844	D	951 683-2912	4446
Plz Corp	2844	E	951 683-2912	4447
Trademark Cosmetics Inc	2844	E	951 683-2631	4461
Poly-Fiber Inc (PA)	2851	F	951 684-4280	4497
Mitchell Rubber Products LLC (PA)	3069	C	951 681-5655	4778
US Rubber Roller Company Inc	3069	F	951 682-2221	4800
Sigma Extruding Corp	3081	E	951 781-8807	4821
Plascor Inc	3085	C	951 328-1010	4862
Carpenter Co	3086	D	951 354-7550	4877
Advanced Engrg Mlding Tech Inc	3089	E	888 264-0392	4929
Altium Holdings LLC	3089	A	951 340-9390	4935
Blow Molded Products Inc	3089	E	951 360-6055	4964
Bm Extrusion Inc	3089	E	951 782-9020	4965
Carson Industries LLC	3089	A	951 788-9720	4985
Edge Plastics Inc (PA)	3089	E	951 786-4750	5020
Hi-Rel Plastics & Molding Corp	3089	E	951 354-0258	5046
Nsa Holdings Inc	3089	E	951 686-1400	5121
Plastic Technologies Inc	3089	E	951 360-6055	5147
Polymer Logistics Inc	3089	D	951 567-2900	5153
Precision Molded Products Inc	3089	E	951 354-0779	5158
Rolenn Manufacturing Inc (PA)	3089	E	951 682-1185	5183
Royal Interpack North Amer Inc	3089	E	951 787-6925	5189
Snapware Corporation	3089	C	951 361-3100	5208
Western Case Incorporated	3089	D	951 214-6380	5249
Westfall Technik Inc	3089	B	951 734-5600	5250
Riverside Cement Holdings Company	3241	B	951 774-2500	5370
Orco Block & Hardscape	3271	F	951 685-1521	5391
Newbasis LLC	3272	C	951 787-0600	5427
Newbasis West LLC	3272	C	951 787-0600	5428
Oldcast Precast (DH)	3272	C	951 788-9720	5431
Alpha Materials Inc	3273	E	951 788-5150	5459
Parex Usa Inc (DH)	3299	E	714 778-2266	5573
Borrmann Metal Center	3312	E	951 367-1510	5578
Barrette Outdoor Living Inc	3315	F	800 336-2383	5610
Dayton Superior Corporation	3315	E	951 782-9517	5613
Merchants Metals LLC	3315	D	951 686-1888	5619
Imperial Pipe Services LLC	3317	E	951 682-3307	5634
Luxfer Inc	3354	E	951 684-5110	5702
Samuel Son & Co (usa) Inc	3354	E	951 781-7800	5707
Sierra Aluminum Company	3354	E	951 781-7800	5708
Metal Container Corporation	3411	C	951 354-0444	5860
Bell Bros Steel Inc	3441	E	951 784-0903	5995
Blazing Industrial Steel Inc	3441	D	951 360-8340	5997
Millers Fab & Weld Corp	3441	E	951 359-3100	6055
Kawneer Company Inc	3442	D	951 410-4779	6110
San Joaquin Window Inc	3442	C	909 946-3697	6121
Atco Rubber Products Inc	3443	F	951 788-4345	6132
Ba Holdings Inc (DH)	3443	E	951 684-5110	6133
Clarkwestern Dietrich Building	3444	E	951 360-3500	6214
Prism Aerospace	3444	E	951 582-2850	6298
Sheet Metal Specialists LLC	3444	F	951 351-6828	6316
SMS Fabrications Inc	3444	E	951 351-6828	6318
Superior Metal Fabricators Inc	3444	E	951 360-2474	6328
US Precision Sheet Metal Inc	3444	D	951 276-2611	6338

Company	SIC	EMP	PHONE	ENTRY#
T M P Services Inc (PA)	3448	E	951 213-3900	6392
United Carports LLC	3448	E	800 757-6742	6393
Precision Technology and Mfg	3451	F	951 788-0252	6419
Luxfer Inc	3463	E	951 351-4100	6480
Main Steel LLC	3471	D	951 231-4949	6637
Dura Coat Products Inc (PA)	3479	E	951 341-6500	6700
Ejay Filtration Inc	3496	E	951 683-0805	6817
Toro Company	3523	D	951 688-9221	6917
Jlg Industries Inc	3531	D	951 358-1915	6937
American Quality Tools Inc	3545	E	951 280-4700	7106
Karbide Inc	3545	E	951 354-0900	7117
John Bean Technologies Corp	3556	D	951 222-2300	7204
Mega Machinery Inc	3559	E	951 300-9300	7247
Trademark Plastics Inc	3559	C	909 941-8810	7262
Codysales Inc	3561	F	951 786-3650	7273
Pacific Consolidated Inds LLC	3569	D	951 479-0860	7403
PCI Holding Company Inc (PA)	3569	D	951 479-0860	7405
Phenix Technology Corporation (PA)	3569	E	951 272-4938	7406
Team Air Inc (PA)	3585	E	909 823-1957	7624
City of Riverside	3589	C	951 351-6140	7649
Yardney Water MGT Systems Inc (PA)	3589	E	951 656-6716	7695
Western Hydrostatics Inc (PA)	3594	E	951 784-2133	7715
Cody Cylinder Service LLC	3599	E	951 786-3650	7805
Future Tech Metals Inc	3599	E	951 781-4801	7839
Metric Machining (PA)	3599	E	909 947-9222	7931
ODonnell Manufacturing Inc	3599	E	562 944-9671	7959
Reisner Enterprises Inc	3599	F	951 786-9478	7996
Unique Lighting Systems Inc	3648	E	800 955-4831	8388
Bourns Inc (PA)	3677	C	951 781-5500	8936
Astro Seal Inc	3679	E	951 787-6670	8998
Be Services Company Inc (HQ)	3679	E	626 284-9901	9003
Aleph Group Inc	3711	E	951 213-4815	9275
Coachworks Holdings Inc	3711	F	951 684-9585	9282
Eldorado National Cal Inc (HQ)	3711	B	951 727-9300	9284
West Coast Unlimited	3711	E	951 352-1234	9314
Krystal Infinity LLC	3713	B		9329
Automax Styling Inc	3714	E	951 530-1876	9356
Dee Engineering Inc	3714	E	909 947-5616	9379
Evans Walker Enterprises	3714	E	951 784-7223	9390
LSI Products Inc	3714	F	951 343-9270	9416
Seymour Levinger & Co	3714	E	909 673-9800	9459
Owen Trailers Inc	3715	E	951 361-4557	9494
Fleetwood Motor Homes-Califinc (DH)	3716	C	951 354-3000	9501
Luxfer Inc (DH)	3728	D	951 684-5110	9739
Zenith Manufacturing Inc	3728	E	818 767-2106	9830
K & N Engineering Inc (PA)	3751	A	951 826-4000	9877
Two Brothers Racing Inc	3751	E	714 550-6070	9887
Fleetwood Travel Trlrs Ind Inc (DH)	3792	C	951 354-3000	9924
Fleetwood Travel Trlrs of MD (DH)	3792	E	951 351-3500	9925
Club Car LLC	3799	C	951 735-4675	9932
Rain Mstr Irrgtion Systems Inc	3823	E	805 527-4498	10154
DOE & Ingalls Cal Oper LLC	3826	E	951 801-7175	10253
Brenner-Fiedler & Assoc Inc (PA)	3829	E	562 404-2721	10355
Irrometer Company Inc	3829	F	951 682-9505	10375
Ziehm Instrumentarium	3844	E	407 615-8560	10786
AM Castenada Inc	3915	E	951 686-3966	10916
Cummings Resources LLC	3993	E	951 248-1130	11107
Fusion Sign & Design Inc (PA)	3993	F	877 477-8777	11122
Luxury Signs Inc	3993	E	951 446-9303	11132
Valley Enerprises Inc	3993	F	951 789-0843	11178
Tom Leonard Investment Co Inc	3999	E	951 351-7778	11296
Riverside Transit Agency (PA)	4111	B	951 565-5000	11357
American Med Rspnse Inland Emp (HQ)	4119	D	951 782-5200	11371
Powered By Fulfillment Inc	4222	D	626 825-9841	11554
Walmart Inc	4225	C	951 320-5722	11628
Empire Med Transportations LLC	4731	D	877 473-6029	11758
20/20 Mobile Corp	4812	D	909 587-2973	11842
Jurupa Community Services Dst	4941	D	951 685-7073	12126
Arakelian Enterprises Inc	4953	C	951 342-3300	12157
Recycler Core Company Inc	4953	C	951 276-1687	12183
Gtt International Inc	5023	E	951 788-8729	12304
MSRS INC	5023	C	310 952-9000	12308
Unique Carpets Ltd	5023	E	951 352-8125	12320
Crystal PCF Win & Door Sys LLC	5031	E	951 779-9300	12326
Crest Steel Corporation	5051	D	951 727-2600	12545
Harbor Pipe and Steel Inc	5051	E	951 369-3990	12553
Western Lighting Inds Inc	5063	E	626 969-6820	12627
Home Security Stores Inc	5065	E	951 782-8494	12667
Pepsi-Cola Metro Btlg Co Inc	5078	C	951 697-3200	12764
Johnson Machinery Co (PA)	5082	C	951 686-4560	12772
McLane Foodservice Inc	5141	C	951 867-3727	13186
Sysco Riverside Inc	5141	B	951 601-5300	13234
Cibaria International Inc	5149	E	951 823-8490	13359
Premier Fuel Distributors Inc	5172	C	760 423-3610	13454
B & B Nurseries Inc	5193	C	951 352-8383	13501
Boise Cascade Company	5211	D	951 343-3000	13569
Dixieline Lumber Company LLC	5211	A	951 224-8491	13571
Home Depot USA Inc	5211	C	951 358-1370	13579
Lowes Home Centers LLC	5211	C	951 509-5500	13660
Parex Usa Inc	5211	F	951 653-3549	13669
Albertsons LLC	5411	D	951 656-6603	13692
David A Campbell Corporation	5511	C	951 785-4444	13753
Pearson Ford Co (PA)	5511	C	877 743-0421	13812
Raceway Ford Inc	5511	C	951 571-9300	13817
Toyota of Riverside Inc	5511	C	951 687-1622	13840
Walters Auto Sales and Svc Inc	5511	C	888 316-4097	13846
Fairprice Enterprises Inc	5713	D	951 684-8578	13951
Alin Party Supply Co	5947	E	951 682-7441	14085
Pacific Premier Bancorp Inc	6022	C	951 274-2400	14202
Populus Financial Group Inc	6099	C	951 509-3506	14262
Morgan Stnley Smith Barney LLC	6211	C	951 682-1181	14398
Southern Cal Prmnnte Med Group	6324	C	866 984-7483	14502
State Compensation Insur Fund	6331	C	888 782-8338	14530
Farmers Insurance	6411	C	951 681-1068	14588
Insurance Inc Southern Cal	6411	D	951 300-9333	14603
Professional Cmnty MGT Cal Inc	6531	D	951 359-2840	14846
Remn Inc	6531	D	951 697-8135	14859
Historic Mission Inn Corp	7011	B	951 784-0300	15180
Pinnacle Rvrside Hspitality LP	7011	C	951 784-8000	15305
Brimad Enterprises Inc	7312	E	951 354-8187	15585
A-Check America LLC (HQ)	7323	C	951 750-1501	15618
Your Way Fumigation Inc	7342	C	951 699-9116	15688
ServiceMaster By Best Pros Inc	7349	D	951 515-9051	15748
Kimco Staffing Services Inc	7361	A	951 686-3800	15858
Officeworks Inc	7361	D	951 784-2534	15873
Stromasys Inc	7372	D	919 239-8450	16392
Interntnal Communications Corp	7373	E	951 934-0531	16451
Allied Digital Services Inc	7376	C	310 431-2361	16539
Barrys Security Services Inc (PA)	7381	C	951 789-7575	16624
313 Acquisition LLC	7382	A	801 234-6374	16713
ADT LLC	7382	C	951 782-6900	16715
Corporate Alnce Strategies Inc	7382	C	877 777-7487	16727
Scher Tire Inc (PA)	7534	E	951 343-3100	17024
Grech Motors LLC (PA)	7694	E	951 688-8347	17106
Fleetwood Motor Homes-Califinc	7699	C	951 274-2000	17128
Innovative Emergency Equipment	7699	E	951 222-2270	17134
Peggs Company Inc (PA)	7699	D	253 584-9548	17145
Adventist Media Center Inc (PA)	7922	C	805 955-7777	17309
Victoria Club	7997	C	951 683-5323	17532
County of Riverside	8011	C	951 955-0840	17635
Kaiser Foundation Hospitals	8011	D	951 353-3790	17680
Kaiser Foundation Hospitals	8011	A	951 353-2000	17681
Riverside Medical Clinic Inc (PA)	8011	D	951 683-6370	17754
Air Force Village West Inc	8051	B	951 697-2000	17877
Community Care On Palm Rvrside	8051	D	951 686-9001	17905
Mt Rubidouxidence Opco LLC	8051	C	951 681-2200	18018
Riverside Care Inc	8051	C	951 683-7111	18040
Riverside Equities LLC	8051	B	951 688-2222	18041
Villa Convalescent Hosp Inc	8051	D	951 689-5788	18070
Orange Treeidence Opco LLC	8052	D	951 785-6060	18094
Magnolia Rhblttion Nursing Ctr	8059	C	951 688-4321	18143
Windsor Cypress Grdns Hlthcare	8059	D	951 688-3643	18160
Orangtree Cnvalescent Hosp Inc	8062	C	951 785-6060	18356
Parkview Cmnty Hosp Med Ctr	8062	A	951 354-7404	18373
Riverside Cmnty Hlth Systems (DH)	8062	A	951 788-3000	18408
Riverside Univ Hlth Sys Fndtio (PA)	8062	B	951 358-5000	18409
Interim Healthcare Inc	8082	C	951 684-6111	18619
CRC Health Group Inc	8093	C	951 784-8010	18686
County of Riverside	8111	C	951 955-6000	18841
Carolyn E Wylie Ctr For Chldre	8322	D	951 683-5193	19031
County of Riverside	8322	D	951 955-4900	19066
FSA Arlanza Child Dev Ctr	8351	D	951 353-0129	19210
Keystone NPS LLC	8399	C	951 785-0504	19332
County of Riverside	8641	C	951 683-7691	19440
Automobile Club Southern Cal	8699	D	951 684-4250	19518
Albert A Webb Associates (PA)	8711	D	951 686-1070	19543
Construction Tstg & Engrg Inc	8711	B	951 571-4081	19566
Current Renewables Engrg Inc	8711	F	951 405-1733	19568
Hunsaker & Assoc Irvine Inc	8711	B	951 352-7200	19616
MSM Industries Inc	8711	E	951 735-0834	19651
Sitesol	8711	E	562 746-5884	19691
University Cal Riverside	8732	C	951 827-4801	19914
Inland Cnties Regional Ctr Inc	8741	C	951 826-2600	20041
Muth Machine Works	8742	C	951 685-1521	20204
Riverside Cnty Flood Ctrl Wtr	8999	C	951 955-1200	20400
County of Riverside	9441	C	951 358-5000	20417

Employee Codes: A=Over 500 employees, B=251-500
C=101-250, D=51-100, E=20-50, F=10-19, G=1-9

2024 Southern California
Business Directory and Buyers Guide

© Mergent Inc. 1-800-342-5647

1423

GEOGRAPHIC

	SIC	EMP	PHONE	ENTRY#

RLLNG HLS EST, CA - Los Angeles County

	SIC	EMP	PHONE	ENTRY#
Graphic Prints Inc.	2396	E	310 870-1239	2531
National Media Inc (HQ)	2711	E	310 377-6877	3308
Malmberg Engineering Inc	3599	E	925 606-6500	7916
Dincloud Inc.	7372	D	310 929-1101	16226

ROLLING HILLS, CA - Los Angeles County

	SIC	EMP	PHONE	ENTRY#
California Digital Inc (PA)	3577	D	310 217-0500	7514

ROMOLAND, CA - Riverside County

	SIC	EMP	PHONE	ENTRY#
Datatronic Distribution Inc.	3612	F		8092
Southern California Edison Co.	4911	D	800 336-2822	12074
Southern California Gas Co.	4924	D	213 244-1200	12083

ROSEMEAD, CA - Los Angeles County

	SIC	EMP	PHONE	ENTRY#
Irish Communication Company (DH)	1623	D	626 288-6170	675
Irish Construction (HQ)	1623	C	626 288-8530	676
Lonix Pharmaceutical Inc.	2023	F	626 287-4700	1276
Chinese Overseas Mktg Svc Corp (PA)	2741	E	626 280-8588	3436
Prographics Inc.	2752	E	626 287-0417	3671
M Argeso & Co Inc.	2911	E	626 573-3000	4644
Tur-Bo Jet Products Co Inc.	3677	C	626 285-1294	8956
Hermetic Seal Corporation (DH)	3679	C	626 443-8931	9056
Beckman Instruments Inc.	3826	D	626 309-0110	10240
Durham School Services L P	4151	A	626 573-3769	11424
Cco Holdings LLC.	4841	C	626 500-1214	11971
Edison International (PA)	4911	A	626 302-2222	12023
Edison Mission Energy (PA)	4911	C	626 302-5778	12024
Edison Mission Midwest Holdings	4911	A	626 302-2222	12025
Southern California Edison Co.	4911	B	626 302-1212	12064
Southern California Edison Co (HQ)	4911	A	626 302-1212	12072
Panda Systems Inc.	5812	C	626 799-9898	14029
Travelodge Hotels Inc.	7011	A	800 257-2297	15393
Success Healthcare 1 LLC	8011	C	626 288-1160	17796
Uplift Family Services	8011	D	626 287-2988	17819
Ensign Group Inc.	8051	D	626 607-2400	17943
Longwood Management Corp.	8051	C	626 280-2293	17999
Longwood Management Corp.	8051	E	626 280-4820	18000
Bhc Alhambra Hospital Inc.	8099	B	626 286-1191	18745
Maryvale	8361	C	626 280-6510	19284

ROWLAND HEIGHTS, CA - Los Angeles County

	SIC	EMP	PHONE	ENTRY#
Silao Tortilleria Inc.	2099	E	626 961-0761	1985
Diack 1 Inc.	3355	E	626 961-2491	5718
Suzhou South	3578	B	626 322-0101	7585
Emanate Health	8011	C	626 912-5282	17648

RUNNING SPRINGS, CA - San Bernardino County

	SIC	EMP	PHONE	ENTRY#
Pali Camp	7032	C	909 867-5743	15438
Snow Valley Mtn Resort LLC	7032	D	909 867-2751	15439
Showtime Custom Coach Inc.	7532	F	909 867-7025	17017

SAN BERNARDINO, CA - San Bernardino County

	SIC	EMP	PHONE	ENTRY#
Original Mowbrays Tree Svc Inc (PA)	0783	C	909 383-7009	223
Stavatti Industries Ltd.	1041	E	651 238-5369	235
Legend Pump & Well Service Inc.	1381	E	909 384-1000	285
Matich Corporation (PA)	1611	D	909 382-7400	634
Davidsons AC & Htg Inc.	1711	D	909 885-2703	762
Caston Inc.	1742	D	909 381-1619	975
Nagles Veal Inc.	2011	E	909 383-7075	1200
Kmb Foods Inc (PA)	2013	E	626 447-0545	1223
Farmdale Creamery Inc.	2026	D	909 888-4938	1310
Live Fresh Corporation	2037	E	909 478-0895	1376
Ardent Mills LLC.	2041	E	909 887-3407	1408
Mars Petcare Us Inc.	2047	E	909 887-8131	1433
Adams and Brooks Inc.	2064	C	909 880-2305	1533
Park West Enterprises Inc.	2077	F	909 383-8341	1569
Pepsico.	2086	E	562 818-9429	1717
Refresco Beverages US Inc.	2086	E	909 915-1400	1723
Refresco Beverages US Inc.	2086	E	909 915-1430	1724
Anitas Mexican Foods Corp	2096	E	909 884-8706	1823
Anitas Mexican Foods Corp (PA)	2096	D	909 884-8706	1824
Dean Distributors Inc.	2099	E	323 587-8147	1881
Millers American Honey Inc.	2099	F	909 825-1722	1945
Haley Bros Inc.	2431	C	800 854-5951	2603
Paramount Windows & Doors.	2431	F	909 888-4688	2629
United Cabinet Company Inc.	2434	E	909 796-3015	2682
Nelson Adams Naco Corporation.	2511	E	909 256-8938	2782
Packaging Corporation America.	2653	E	909 888-7008	3124
Sun Cmpany of San Brnrdino Cal (HQ)	2711	B	909 889-9666	3326
San Brnrdino Cmnty College Dst.	2759	D	909 888-6511	3810
Shorett Printing Inc (PA)	2759	E	714 545-4689	3811
Reagent Chemical & RES Inc.	2819	D	909 796-4059	3908

	SIC	EMP	PHONE	ENTRY#
Mapei Corporation	2821	E	909 475-4100	3953
Innocor West LLC	3069	B	909 307-3737	4768
Back Support Systems Inc	3086	F	760 329-1472	4876
Foamex LP	3086	E	909 824-8981	4887
C-Pak Industries Inc.	3089	E	909 880-6017	4974
Container Options	3089	F	909 478-0045	4994
Fiore Stone Inc.	3272	E	909 424-0221	5413
Holliday Rock Trucking Inc.	3273	D	888 273-2200	5482
Sample Tile and Stone Inc.	3281	E	951 776-8562	5533
United States Mineral Pdts Co.	3296	E	909 473-3027	5559
Tamco (HQ)	3312	E	909 899-0660	5604
Caesar Hardware Intl Ltd.	3429	E	800 306-3829	5908
South Bay Foundry Inc (HQ)	3441	E	909 383-1823	6076
Hayden Products LLC	3443	D	951 736-2600	6143
Brydenscot Metal Products Inc.	3444	F	909 799-0088	6205
CMC Steel Us LLC.	3449	E	909 646-7827	6395
Innovative Metal Inds Inc.	3449	D	909 796-6200	6399
Anco International Inc.	3494	E	909 887-2521	6787
American Wire Inc.	3496	F	909 884-9990	6810
Tree Island Wire (usa) Inc.	3496	C	909 899-1673	6830
Ground Hog Inc.	3531	E	909 478-5700	6933
Macroair Technologies Inc (PA)	3564	E	909 890-2270	7326
Systems Technology Inc.	3565	D	909 799-9950	7354
W B Walton Enterprises Inc.	3663	E	951 683-0930	8597
DSPM Inc.	3677	E	714 970-2304	8941
Allianz Sweeper Company.	3711	C		9276
Global Environmental Pdts Inc.	3711	E	909 713-1600	9289
Thermal Solutions Mfg Inc.	3714	D	909 796-0754	9468
Northrop Grumman Systems Corp.	3812	E	703 713-4096	10040
Tinker & Rasor.	3812	E	909 890-0700	10082
Optivus Proton Therapy Inc.	3829	D	909 799-8300	10387
Semco.	3829	E	909 799-9666	10395
Quiel Bros Elc Sign Svc Co Inc.	3993	E	909 885-4476	11147
Omnitrans (PA)	4111	C	909 379-7100	11352
San Bernardino Cnty Trnsp Auth.	4111	C	909 884-8276	11358
Amazoncom Inc.	4225	D	626 260-6954	11564
United Parcel Service Inc.	4512	C	800 742-5877	11674
Aviation & Defense Inc.	4581	C	909 382-3487	11689
CJ Logistics America LLC.	4731	C	540 377-2302	11747
Gxo Logistics Supply Chain Inc.	4731	D	909 838-5631	11766
Gunderson Rail Services LLC.	4789	C	909 478-0541	11833
Meridian Rail Acquisition.	4789	C	909 478-0541	11836
Sprint Communications Co LP.	4813	C	909 382-6030	11906
San Brnrdino Cmnty College Dst.	4832	C	909 384-4444	11935
Southern California Gas Co.	4924	C	909 335-7941	12099
Burrtec Waste Industries Inc.	4953	C	909 889-1969	12161
Rerubber LLC.	4953	F	909 786-2811	12184
Metropolitan Automotive Warehouse.	5013	A	909 885-2886	12248
H and H Drug Stores Inc.	5047	D	909 890-9700	12491
California Steel Services Inc.	5051	E	909 796-2222	12538
CMC Rebar West.	5051	C	909 713-1130	12541
Wcs Distributing Inc.	5084	E	909 888-2015	12836
Laymon Candy Co Inc.	5145	E	909 825-4408	13273
S&E Gourmet Cuts Inc.	5145	C	909 370-0155	13274
Gate City Beverage Distrs (PA)	5181	B	909 799-0281	13466
L & L Nursery Supply Inc (HQ)	5191	C	909 591-0461	13488
Harbill Inc.	5511	D	909 883-8833	13777
Ocelot Engineering Inc.	5571	C	800 841-2960	13902
Caldesso LLC.	5999	D	909 888-2882	14124
Inland Empire Health Plan.	6324	A	866 228-4347	14471
Woodman Realty Inc.	6531	C	909 425-5324	14886
S B H Hotel Corporation.	7011	A	909 889-0133	15336
San Bernardino Hilton (HQ)	7011	A	909 889-0133	15341
Job Options Incorporated.	7219	A	909 890-4612	15475
Avalon Building Maint Inc.	7349	B	714 693-2407	15694
Barrett Business Services Inc.	7361	A	909 890-3633	15819
Nursefinders LLC.	7361	C	909 890-2286	15871
Maxim Healthcare Services Inc.	7363	D	951 684-4148	15931
Nationwide Technologies Inc.	7372	E	909 340-2770	16317
United Guard Security Inc.	7381	C	909 402-0754	16699
ADT LLC.	7382	C	951 824-7205	16720
Jenco Productions Inc (PA)	7389	C	909 381-9453	16852
Jon Steel Erectors Inc.	7692	E	909 799-0005	17091
Inland Empire 66ers Bsbal CLB.	7941	C	909 888-9922	17373
San Brnrdino Cnty Rgonal Parks.	7999	D	909 387-2583	17565
Sb Waterman Holdings Inc (PA)	8011	C	909 883-8611	17760
Boyd Dental Corporation.	8021	D	909 880-0421	17835
Robert Ballard Rehab Hospital (HQ)	8049	D	909 473-1200	17871
Del Rosa Villa Inc.	8051	C	909 885-3261	17925
Waterman Convalescent Hosp Inc (PA)	8051	C	909 882-1215	18073
Del Rosa Villaidence Opco LLC.	8052	B	909 885-3261	18083
Watermanidence Opco LLC.	8052	B	909 882-1215	18102
San Bernardino Care Company.	8059	C	909 884-4781	18153

Mergent email: customerrelations@mergent.com
1424

2024 Southern California
Business Directory and Buyers Guide

(P-0000) Products & Services Section entry number
(PA)=Parent Co (HQ)=Headquarters (DH)=Div Headquarters

	SIC	EMP	PHONE	ENTRY#
United Medical Management Inc	8059	C	909 886-5291	18157
Community Hosp San Bernardino **(DH)**	8062	B	909 887-6333	18224
St Bernardine Med Ctr Aux Inc	8062	C	909 881-4320	18458
St Bernardine Medical Center	8062	C	909 883-8711	18459
Maxim Healthcare Services Inc	8082	C	760 243-3377	18628
Vnacare **(PA)**	8082	D	909 624-3574	18655
Institute For Bhvoral Hlth Inc	8093	B	909 289-1041	18697
Victor Cmnty Support Svcs Inc	8093	C	909 890-5930	18733
Bio-Medics Inc	8099	C	909 883-9501	18746
Blood Bnk San Brnrdino Rvrside **(HQ)**	8099	C	909 885-6503	18747
San Brnrdino Cy Unified Schl Ds	8099	D	909 881-8000	18801
California City San Bernardino	8111	B	909 384-7272	18833
Inland Cnties Regional Ctr Inc **(PA)**	8322	C	909 890-3000	19095
San Brnrdino Cnty Prbtion Offc	8322	B	909 887-2544	19132
Think Together	8351	B	909 723-1400	19229
Omnitrans	8361	C	909 383-1680	19292
Victor Treatment Centers Inc	8361	D	951 436-5200	19306
Community Action Prtnr San Brn	8399	C	909 723-1500	19322
YMCA of East Valley	8641	C	909 881-9622	19475
Allen Engineering Contractor Inc	8711	C	909 478-5500	19544
Rezek Equipment	8711	F	909 885-6221	19678
Northrop Grmmn Spce & Mssn Sys	8731	C	909 382-6800	19865
Mentor Mdia USA Sup Chain MGT	8741	D	909 930-0800	20060
Amtex Supply Holdings Inc	8742	C	909 985-8918	20131
Gibson Overseas Inc	8748	C	323 832-8900	20340

SAN CLEMENTE, CA - Orange County

	SIC	EMP	PHONE	ENTRY#
Bemus Landscape Inc	1629	B	714 557-7910	706
Millennium Reinforcing Inc	1791	B	949 361-9730	1110
Custom Ingredients Inc **(PA)**	2087	E	949 276-7995	1764
Fig313 Inc	2092	E	949 218-4406	1804
Freshrealm Inc **(PA)**	2099	C	800 264-1297	1899
Cornerstone Apparel Inc	2299	E	949 498-2664	2138
R & R Industries Inc	2389	C	800 234-5611	2458
Kui Co Inc	2621	E	949 369-7949	3053
Western Outdoors Publications **(PA)**	2711	E	949 366-0030	3337
R T C Group	2721	F	949 226-2000	3384
Four Star Distribution	3021	E	949 369-4420	4702
International Rubber Pdts Inc **(HQ)**	3069	D	909 947-1244	4769
Kelcourt Plastics Inc **(DH)**	3089	E	949 361-0774	5077
Plastics Development Corp	3089	E	949 492-0217	5148
Pch Sheet Metal & AC Inc	3444	F	949 361-9905	6288
Clean Wave Management Inc	3562	C	949 370-0740	7298
Snowpure LLC	3589	E	949 240-2188	7686
Dana Innovations **(PA)**	3651	C	949 492-7777	8404
Sonance	3651	E	949 492-7777	8435
Fleming Metal Fabricators	3713	E	323 723-8203	9326
Bunker Corp **(PA)**	3714	D	949 361-3935	9362
Swift Tactical Systems Inc	3721	E	800 547-9438	9556
Swift Engineering Inc	3728	E	949 492-6608	9807
Reynard Corporation	3827	D	949 366-8866	10336
Capistrano Labs Inc	3841	F	949 492-0390	10469
Composite Manufacturing Inc	3841	E	949 361-7580	10484
Epica Medical Innovations LLC	3841	E	949 238-6323	10506
Icu Medical Inc **(PA)**	3841	D	949 366-2183	10525
Icu Medical Sales Inc **(HQ)**	3841	D	949 366-2183	10526
Rox Medical Inc	3841	E	949 276-8968	10601
Reshape Weightloss Inc **(HQ)**	3845	E	949 429-6680	10824
Dragon Alliance Inc	3851	D	760 931-4900	10836
Electric Visual Evolution LLC **(PA)**	3851	E	949 940-9125	10837
Rosen & Rosen Industries Inc	3949	C	949 361-9238	11020
San Diego Gas & Electric Co	4931	C	949 361-8090	12107
Elotek Systems Inc **(PA)**	5045	E	949 366-4404	12407
Buyefficient LLC	5046	C	949 382-3129	12452
Cameron Ashley Inc	5047	D	949 940-4000	12479
Pacific Medical Group Inc	5047	C	949 493-1030	12504
Streuter Technologies	5051	F	949 369-7676	12573
Liberty Synergistics Inc	5085	D	949 361-1100	12861
Stance Inc **(PA)**	5137	C	949 391-9030	13151
Grain To Green Inc	5153	C	760 845-6107	13406
Lowes Home Centers LLC	5211	D	949 369-4644	13655
Matsushita International Corp **(PA)**	6799	D	949 498-1000	15035
Model Match Inc	7372	F	949 525-9405	16312
Life Time Inc	7991	E	949 492-1515	17406
Heritage Golf Group LLC	7992	D	949 369-6226	17431
Bella Collina San Clemente	7997	D	949 498-6604	17473
Monarch Healthcare A Medical	8011	C	949 489-1960	17719
Orange Coast Wns Med Group Inc	8011	D	949 829-5522	17734
Dual Diagnosis Trtmnt Ctr Inc **(PA)**	8093	C	949 276-5553	18691
Xlr8 Services Inc	8711	E	949 498-9578	19721

SAN DIEGO, CA - San Diego County

	SIC	EMP	PHONE	ENTRY#
Veterinary Practice Assoc Inc	0742	C	949 833-9020	129
Veterinary Specialty Hosp	0742	C	858 875-7500	130
Brightview Landscape Dev Inc	0781	B	858 458-9900	146
Brightview Landscape Svcs Inc	0781	B	858 458-1900	147
NN Jaeschke Inc	0781	E	858 550-7900	173
Heavliand Enterprises Inc	0782	E	858 412-1576	194
Landcare USA LLC	0782	C	858 453-1755	198
Namvars Inc	0782	D	858 792-5461	207
New Way Landscape & Tree Svcs	0782	C	858 505-8300	208
Unico Incorporated	1081	F	619 209-6124	238
Elk Hills Power LLC	1382	E	661 763-2730	303
CP Kelco US Inc	1455	E	619 595-5000	412
Aptim Federal Services LLC	1521	A	619 239-1690	420
Largo Concrete Inc	1521	C	619 356-2142	444
Fairfield Development Inc **(PA)**	1522	C	858 457-2123	470
Wermers Multi-Family Corp	1522	C	858 535-1475	479
Amaya Curiel Corporation	1522	A	619 661-1230	492
Biotix Inc	1541	E	858 875-5479	496
CMC Rebar West	1541	C	858 737-7700	500
Isec Incorporated	1541	C	858 279-9085	507
Kevcon Inc	1541	D	760 432-0307	508
Ledcor CMI Inc	1541	D	602 595-3017	510
T B Penick & Sons Inc	1541	C	858 558-1800	522
Austin Commercial LP	1542	C	619 446-5637	531
Balfour Beatty Cnstr LLC	1542	C	858 635-7400	533
Barnhart Inc	1542	B	858 635-7400	534
Bycor General Contractors Inc	1542	C	858 587-1901	538
C W Driver Incorporated	1542	C	619 696-5100	539
Dpr Construction A Gen Partnr	1542	C	858 646-0757	546
Harvey Inc	1542	C	858 769-4000	556
Pacific Building Group **(PA)**	1542	D	858 552-0600	571
PCL Construction Services Inc	1542	C	858 657-3400	573
Solpac Inc	1542	C	619 296-6247	592
Triton Structural Concrete Inc	1542	C	858 866-2450	596
Webcor Construction LP	1542	C	619 798-3891	603
West Pacific Services Inc	1542	C	888 401-0188	605
City of San Diego	1611	C	619 527-7482	614
Ies Commercial Inc	1611	C	858 210-4900	625
Cameron Intrstate Pipeline LLC	1623	C	619 696-3110	665
Sempra LNG International LLC	1623	D	661 399-2077	690
Vadnais Trenchless Svcs Inc	1623	C	858 550-1460	700
US Joiner LLC	1629	E	619 233-3993	719
A & D Fire Protection Inc	1711	D	619 258-7697	724
A O Reed & Co LLC	1711	B	858 565-4131	725
Alpha Mechanical Inc	1711	C	858 278-3500	729
Alpha Mechanical Heating & Air Cond	1711	C	858 279-1300	730
ASI Hastings Inc	1711	C	619 590-9300	735
Atlas Mechanical Inc **(PA)**	1711	D	858 554-0700	738
Bill Howe Plumbing Inc	1711	D	800 245-5469	744
Greater San Diego AC Co Inc	1711	C	619 469-7818	774
Jackson & Blanc	1711	C	858 831-7900	781
National Air Inc	1711	C	619 299-2500	797
Pacific Rim Mech Contrs Inc **(PA)**	1711	B	858 974-6500	805
Pan-Pacific Mechanical LLC	1711	B	858 764-2464	806
Sherwood Mechanical Inc	1711	D	858 679-3000	823
General Coatings Corporation **(PA)**	1721	C	858 587-1277	846
4liberty Inc	1731	D	619 400-1000	858
Allied Universal	1731	C	619 444-0219	864
Commuction Wirg Spcalists Inc	1731	D	858 278-4545	883
Fishel Company	1731	C	858 658-0830	901
Helix Electric Inc **(PA)**	1731	C	858 535-0505	907
Wirtz Quality Installations	1741	D	858 569-3816	964
Best Interiors Inc	1742	D	858 715-3760	970
Pacific Building Group	1742	C	858 552-0600	988
Pars Industries Inc	1751	E	619 671-9663	1021
J W Floor Covering Inc **(PA)**	1752	C	858 536-8565	1033
Ben F Smith Inc	1771	C	858 271-4320	1061
Cement Cutting Inc	1771	D	619 296-9592	1064
Coffman Specialties Inc **(PA)**	1771	C	858 536-3100	1066
Heavy Metal Steel Company Inc	1791	E	858 433-4800	1104
Dehart Inc	1799	E	858 695-0882	1153
Demor Enterprises Inc	1799	E	858 625-0003	1154
Herzog Contracting Corp	1799	D	619 849-6990	1161
Yyk Enterprises Operations LLC **(PA)**	1799	C	619 474-6229	1187
Old Bbh Inc	2013	A	858 715-4000	1227
El Indio Shops Incorporated	2023	D	619 299-0333	1267
Gerlait Group Inc	2023	E	858 587-0400	1272
Husks Unlimited **(PA)**	2037	E	619 476-8301	1370
Intelligent Blends LP	2043	E	858 888-7937	1421
Honest Kitchen Inc	2047	D	619 544-0018	1429
Natural Balance Pet Foods LLC **(PA)**	2048	D	800 829-4493	1446
Fusion Food Factory	2051	E	858 578-8001	1472
Lauras Orgnal Bston Brwnies In	2051	F	619 855-3258	1479
Tallgrass Pictures LLC	2051	E	619 227-2701	1495

Employee Codes: A=Over 500 employees, B=251-500
C=101-250, D=51-100, E=20-50, F=10-19, G=1-9

2024 Southern California
Business Directory and Buyers Guide

© Mergent Inc. 1-800-342-5647

1425

GEOGRAPHIC

Company	SIC	EMP	PHONE	ENTRY#
Opera Patisserie	2053	D	858 536-5800	1528
Azumex Corp	2061	E	619 710-8855	1530
El Super Leon Pnchin Sncks Inc	2064	E	619 426-2968	1537
Sugarfina Inc	2064	E	949 301-9482	1550
Anheuser-Busch LLC	2082	D	858 581-7000	1580
Associated Microbreweries Inc	2082	D	858 587-2739	1581
Associated Microbreweries Inc	2082	D	619 234-2739	1582
Associated Microbreweries Inc (PA)	2082	D	858 273-2739	1583
Assocted McRbrwries Ltd A Cal	2082	F	858 273-2739	1585
Home Brew Mart Inc	2082	B	858 790-6900	1591
Jdz Inc	2082	D	858 549-9888	1593
K A McNair Brewing Co LLC	2082	E	858 254-3238	1594
Karl Strauss Brewing Company (PA)	2082	E	858 273-2739	1595
Kings & Convicts Bp LLC	2082	C	619 255-7213	1596
Kings & Convicts Bp LLC	2082	E	619 295-2337	1597
Mikkeller Brewing San Diego	2082	E	858 381-3500	1599
Taproom Beer Co	2082	E	619 539-7738	1605
Tsb2 Llc	2082	D	619 255-9679	1608
Cydea Inc	2084	E	800 710-9939	1620
WG Best Weinkellerei Inc	2084	F	858 627-1747	1667
Reyes Coca-Cola Bottling LLC	2086	B	619 266-6300	1732
United Brands Company Inc	2087	E	619 461-5220	1788
Bumble Bee Foods LLC (HQ)	2091	F	800 800-8572	1792
Bumble Bee Seafoods LP	2091	C	858 715-4000	1794
Blue Nalu Inc	2092	E	858 703-8703	1800
Monzu Holdings LLC	2098	D	619 255-5032	1841
Foods On Fly LLC	2099	E	858 404-0642	1896
Fuji Food Products Inc	2099	C	619 268-3118	1901
Juneshine Inc	2099	C	619 501-8311	1920
Rancho Lomita Food Inds Inc	2099	E	619 464-2800	1974
Southwest Products LLC	2099	C	619 263-8000	1989
R J Reynolds Tobacco Company	2111	D	858 625-8453	2006
Masterpiece Artist Canvas LLC	2211	E	619 710-2500	2028
California Industrial Fabrics	2231	E	619 661-7166	2046
Balboa Manufacturing Co LLC (PA)	2253	E	858 715-0060	2063
Mad Engine Global LLC (HQ)	2253	D	858 558-5270	2074
Custom Logos Inc	2261	E	858 277-1886	2088
No Second Thoughts Inc	2311	D	619 428-5992	2153
Creative Design Industries	2321	C	619 710-2525	2157
Sauvage Inc (PA)	2329	F	858 408-0100	2218
Hylete Inc	2339	E	858 225-8998	2329
Legendary Holdings Inc	2353	E	619 872-6100	2400
A Thanks Million Inc	2361	F	858 432-7744	2404
Terry Town Corporation	2384	D	619 421-5354	2424
Krasnes Inc	2386	E	619 232-2066	2431
Lofta	2392	E	858 299-8000	2476
Four Seasons Design Inc (PA)	2396	E	619 761-5151	2530
Autoliv Asp Inc	2399	E	619 662-8018	2546
Autoliv Safety Technology Inc	2399	A	619 662-8000	2547
Prestige Flag & Banner Co Inc	2399	D	619 497-2220	2555
Cabinets Glore Orange Cnty Inc	2421	E	858 586-0555	2565
Rtmex Inc	2426	C	619 391-9913	2579
Canyon Graphics Inc	2431	D	858 646-0444	2589
Design Synthesis Inc	2431	E	858 271-8480	2596
Jeld-Wen Inc	2431	C	800 468-3667	2608
Quality Cabinet and Fixture Co (HQ)	2434	E	619 266-1011	2674
Cri 2000 LP (PA)	2499	E	619 542-1975	2753
Magic-Flight General Mfg Inc	2499	E	619 288-4638	2755
Raphaels Inc	2499	F		2761
Whalen LLC (DH)	2511	E	619 423-9948	2792
Elite Leather LLC	2512	D	909 548-8600	2801
Ideal Mattress Company Inc	2515	E	619 595-0003	2852
Ana Global LLC (PA)	2517	D	619 482-9990	2865
Gilbert Martin Wdwkg Co Inc (PA)	2517	E	800 268-5669	2866
Interior Wood of San Diego	2521	F	619 295-6469	2886
Montbleau & Associates Inc (PA)	2521	D	619 263-5550	2888
Ecr4kids LP	2531	E	619 323-2005	2925
J L Furnishings LLC	2531	B	310 605-6600	2928
San Diego Unified School Dst	2531	E	619 600-5321	2936
Seating Concepts LLC	2531	E	619 491-3159	2937
Bonded Window Coverings Inc	2591	E	858 576-8400	3001
Custom Brands Group	2591	E	213 749-6333	3004
Phase II Products Inc (PA)	2591	F	619 236-9699	3011
Hire Elegance	2599	F	858 740-7862	3026
Nlp Furniture Industries Inc	2599	E	619 661-5170	3029
Dynamic Resources Inc	2621	D	619 268-3070	3044
Corrugados De Baja California	2653	A	619 662-8672	3094
Global Packaging Solutions Inc	2653	B	619 710-2661	3104
Pgac Corp (PA)	2671	D	858 560-8213	3155
Sherpa Clinical Packaging LLC	2671	E	858 282-0928	3157
Sidakk Distributors	2674	E	619 391-0950	3201
Avery Products Corporation	2678	C	619 671-1022	3219
P & R Paper Supply Co Inc	2679	C	619 671-2400	3241
Pacific Pulp Molding Inc	2679	E	619 977-5617	3242
Joong-Ang Daily News Cal Inc	2711	D	858 573-1111	3290
Kaar Drect Mail Flfillment LLC	2711	E	619 382-3670	3292
North County Times (DH)	2711	C	800 533-8830	3311
San Diego Union-Tribune LLC	2711	E	619 299-3131	3319
San Diego Union-Tribune LLC (PA)	2711	A	619 299-3131	3320
Teris - San Diego LLC	2711	E	619 231-3282	3328
U-T Direct	2711	F	619 293-1484	3333
Voice of San Diego	2711	E	619 325-0525	3335
Cbj LP	2721	E	858 277-6359	3350
McKinnon Enterprises	2721	F	858 571-1818	3370
San Diego Family Magazine LLC	2721	E	619 685-6970	3389
San Diego Magazine Pubg Co	2721	E	619 230-9292	3390
Cognella Inc	2731	D	858 552-1120	3402
Dawn Sign Press Inc	2731	E	858 625-0600	3405
Houghton Mifflin Harcourt Pubg	2731	E	617 351-5000	3407
Plural Publishing Inc	2731	E	858 492-1555	3412
Stoneybrook Publishing Inc	2731	E	858 674-4600	3415
Elsevier Inc	2741	D	619 231-6616	3445
Elsevier Inc	2741	E	619 231-6616	3446
Equity Ford Research	2741	E	858 755-1327	3447
Marcoa Media LLC (PA)	2741	E	858 635-9627	3463
Marcoa Quality Publishing LLC	2741	F	858 695-9600	3464
Mitchell Repair Info Co LLC (HQ)	2741	E	858 391-5000	3465
Neil A Kjos Music Company (PA)	2741	E	858 270-9800	3468
Real Marketing	2741	E	858 847-0335	3481
Tabor Communications Inc	2741	E	858 625-0070	3490
Transwestern Publishing Company LLC	2741	A	858 467-2800	3496
West Publishing Corporation	2741	B	619 296-7862	3503
Yamagata America Inc	2741	C	858 751-1010	3504
Brehm Communications Inc (PA)	2752	E	858 451-6200	3522
Continental Graphics Corp	2752	E	858 552-6520	3540
Diego & Son Printing Inc	2752	E	619 233-5373	3559
Elum Designs Inc	2752	E	858 650-3586	3570
Instant Imprints Franchising	2752	F	858 642-4848	3600
JA Ferrari Print Imaging LLC	2752	F	619 295-8307	3605
Kovin Corporation Inc	2752	E	858 558-0100	3614
Modern Printing & Mailing Inc	2752	E	619 222-0535	3639
Neyenesch Printers Inc	2752	D	619 297-2281	3643
No Boundaries Inc	2752	E	619 266-2349	3645
Packaging Manufacturing Inc	2752	C	619 498-9199	3651
PM Corporate Group Inc (PA)	2752	E	619 498-9199	3659
Printivity LLC	2752	E	877 649-5463	3666
Ranroy Company	2752	E	858 571-8800	3677
Robo 3d Inc	2752	E	844 476-2233	3680
Rush Press Inc	2752	E	619 296-7874	3681
San Diego Printing Group Inc	2752	F	858 541-1500	3682
Scholastic Sports Inc	2752	D	858 496-9221	3684
Bretkeri Corporation	2759	F	858 292-4919	3739
Colmol Inc	2759	E	858 693-7575	3747
Electronic Prtg Solutions LLC	2759	E	858 576-3000	3757
Express Business Systems Inc	2759	E	858 549-9828	3758
Kieran Label Corp	2759	E	619 449-4457	3774
Optec Laser Systems LLC	2759	E	858 220-1070	3792
R R Donnelley & Sons Company	2759	EMP	619 527-4600	3804
Three Man Corporation	2759	E	858 684-5200	3821
Neon Rose Inc	2813	E	619 218-6103	3871
Carbomer Inc	2819	D	858 552-0992	3886
Tonbo Biotechnologies Corp	2819	E	858 888-7300	3916
Lamkin Corporation (PA)	2821	E	619 661-7090	3952
Rock West Composites Inc (PA)	2821	E	858 537-6260	3967
Allermed Laboratories Inc	2833	E	858 292-1060	3989
Sapphire Energy Inc	2833	D	858 768-4700	4017
1859 Inc	2834	D	858 648-2470	4025
Acadia Pharmaceuticals Inc (PA)	2834	A	858 558-2871	4031
Aegis Life Inc	2834	E	650 666-5287	4036
Agouron Pharmaceuticals Inc (HQ)	2834	E	858 622-3000	4037
Ambit Biosciences Corporation	2834	D	858 334-2100	4042
Amylin Ohio LLC	2834	A	858 552-2200	4049
Anaptysbio Inc (PA)	2834	D	858 362-6295	4051
Applied Mlecular Evolution Inc (HQ)	2834	E	858 597-4990	4054
Arcturus Thrptics Holdings Inc (PA)	2834	C	858 900-2660	4055
Arizeke Pharmacueticals Inc	2834	E	858 455-6907	4057
Arrowhead Pharmaceuticals Inc	2834	E	626 304-3400	4058
Atxco Inc	2834	E	650 334-2079	4059
Avidity Biosciences Inc	2834	D	858 401-7900	4064
Bms Finance Inc	2834	E	619 284-9801	4076
Capricor Therapeutics Inc (PA)	2834	F	310 358-3200	4079
Catalent Pharma Solutions Inc	2834	C	858 805-6383	4086
Catalent Pharma Solutions Inc	2834	E	877 587-1835	4087
Celgene Corporation	2834	E	858 795-4961	4088
Crinetics Pharmaceuticals Inc (PA)	2834	D	858 450-6464	4095
Cv Sciences Inc (PA)	2834	E	866 290-2157	4096

Mergent email: customerrelations@mergent.com

1426

2024 Southern California
Business Directory and Buyers Guide

(P-0000) Products & Services Section entry number
(PA)=Parent Co (HQ)=Headquarters (DH)=Div Headquarters

Company	SIC	EMP	PHONE	ENTRY#
Cymbiotika LLC (PA)	2834	E	770 910-4945	4097
Cymbiotika LLC	2834	D	949 652-8177	4098
Defender SD Manufacturing LLC	2834	E	314 697-1330	4099
Elitra Pharmaceuticals	2834	D	858 410-3030	4104
Entos Pharmaceuticals Inc	2834	F	800 727-0884	4106
Erasca Inc	2834	C	858 465-6511	4108
Evofem Biosciences Inc (PA)	2834	E	858 550-1900	4110
Genetronics Inc	2834	E	858 410-3112	4115
Gossamer Bio Inc (PA)	2834	E	858 684-1300	4123
Gyre Therapeutics Inc (PA)	2834	D	650 266-8674	4127
Heron Therapeutics Inc (PA)	2834	C	858 251-4400	4130
Inova Diagnostics Inc	2834	C	858 586-9900	4135
Janssen Research & Dev LLC	2834	C	858 450-2000	4143
Janux Therapeutics Inc	2834	E	858 751-4493	4144
Kura Oncology Inc (PA)	2834	E	858 500-8800	4153
Levena Biopharma Us Inc	2834	E	858 720-1439	4158
Lorem Cytori Usa Inc	2834	E	858 746-8696	4161
Maravai Lfscences Holdings Inc (PA)	2834	E	858 546-0004	4163
MEI Pharma Inc	2834	E	858 369-7100	4167
Metacrine Inc	2834	E	858 369-7800	4169
Mirati Therapeutics Inc (PA)	2834	A	858 332-3410	4170
Nanocellect Biomedical Inc	2834	E	877 745-7678	4174
National Resilience Inc (PA)	2834	E	888 737-2460	4176
Neurelis Inc (PA)	2834	E	858 251-2111	4181
Nitto	2834	E	858 750-2012	4185
Otonomy Inc	2834	D	619 323-2200	4191
Pacira Pharmaceuticals Inc (HQ)	2834	E	858 625-2424	4195
Pacira Pharmaceuticals Inc	2834	D	858 625-2424	4196
Pfenex Inc	2834	D	858 352-4400	4199
Pfizer Inc	2834	D	858 622-3000	4200
Pfizer Inc	2834	E	858 622-3001	4201
Pharmion Corporation	2834	E	858 335-5744	4203
Polaris Pharmaceuticals Inc (PA)	2834	E	858 452-6688	4204
Polypeptide Labs San Diego LLC	2834	E	858 408-0808	4205
Prescient Holdings Group LLC	2834	E	858 790-7004	4206
Primapharma Inc	2834	E	858 259-0969	4207
Prometheus Biosciences Inc	2834	D	858 422-4300	4208
Prometheus Laboratories Inc	2834	E	858 583-0131	4209
Prometheus Laboratories Inc	2834	B	858 824-0895	4210
Prometheus Rxdx Inc	2834	E	858 824-0895	4211
Prometheus Therapeutics &Dlagn	2834	F	858 824-0895	4212
Quanticel Pharmaceuticals Inc	2834	E	858 956-3747	4217
Rayzebio Inc	2834	D	619 937-2754	4219
Receptos Inc	2834	E	858 652-5700	4220
Rempex Pharmaceuticals Inc	2834	E	858 875-2840	4222
Resilience Us Inc (HQ)	2834	E	984 202-0854	4223
Santarus Inc	2834	E	858 314-5700	4229
Shire Rgenerative Medicine Inc	2834	E	858 754-5396	4233
Signal Pharmaceuticals Inc	2834	C	858 795-4700	4235
Societal CDMO San Diego LLC	2834	D	858 623-1520	4238
STA Pharmaceutical US LLC	2834	E	609 606-6499	4241
Travere Therapeutics Inc (PA)	2834	C	888 969-7879	4247
Trius Therapeutics LLC	2834	C	858 452-0370	4248
Vertex Phrmctcals San Dego LLC (HQ)	2834	E	858 404-6600	4251
Viking Therapeutics Inc (PA)	2834	E	858 704-4660	4252
Wacker Biotech US Inc	2834	E	858 875-4700	4254
Zoetis Inc	2834	F	858 312-7082	4259
Acon Laboratories Inc (PA)	2835	E	858 875-8000	4261
Alere Inc	2835	D	858 805-2000	4262
Alere Inc	2835	F	858 805-3810	4263
Alere San Diego Inc (DH)	2835	C	858 455-4808	4264
Bioserv Corporation	2835	E	917 817-1326	4269
Dermtech Inc (PA)	2835	E	866 450-4223	4271
Gateway Genomics LLC	2835	D	858 886-7250	4274
Gen-Probe Incorporated	2835	D	858 410-8000	4275
Innovacon Inc	2835	D	858 805-8900	4277
Inova Diagnostics Inc	2835	C	858 586-9900	4278
Lifeome Biolabs Inc	2835	E	619 302-0129	4281
Pacific Biotech Inc	2835	E	858 552-1100	4286
Quidel Corporation	2835	C	858 552-1100	4288
Quidel Corporation (HQ)	2835	D	858 552-1100	4289
Quidelortho Corporation (PA)	2835	E	858 552-1100	4290
Sekisui America Corporation	2835	D	858 452-3198	4292
Synbiotics LLC	2835	E	858 451-3771	4293
Ark Animal Health Inc	2836	E	858 203-4100	4299
Atyr Pharma Inc (PA)	2836	E	858 731-8389	4302
Bioatla Inc	2836	E	858 558-0708	4306
Cidara Therapeutics Inc (PA)	2836	D	858 752-6170	4309
Excellos Incorporated	2836	E	619 400-8235	4314
Gb007 Inc	2836	E	858 684-1300	4318
Halozyme Therapeutics Inc (PA)	2836	E	858 794-8889	4321
Immunitybio Inc (PA)	2836	D	844 696-5235	4322
Neurocrine Biosciences Inc (PA)	2836	A	858 617-7600	4325
Neurocrine Continental Inc	2836	E	858 617-7941	4326
Poseida Therapeutics Inc (PA)	2836	B	858 779-3100	4327
Scripps Laboratories	2836	E	858 546-5800	4330
Sorrento Therapeutics Inc (PA)	2836	D	858 203-4100	4331
Natural Thoughts Incorporated	2844	E	619 582-0027	4436
Suneva Medical Inc (PA)	2844	E	858 550-9999	4460
Frazee Industries Inc	2851	A	858 626-3600	4490
Mast Technologies LLC	2851	F	858 452-1700	4493
Pro-Line Paint Company	2851	F	619 232-8968	4502
Rhino Linings Corporation (PA)	2851	D	858 450-0441	4504
BASF Enzymes LLC (DH)	2869	D	858 431-8520	4516
Verenium Corporation	2869	C	858 431-8500	4536
Cibus Inc	2879	C	858 450-0008	4548
Seal For Life Industries LLC (PA)	2891	E	619 671-0932	4580
Chemdiv Inc	2899	E	858 794-4860	4599
Chemtreat Inc	2899	C	804 935-2000	4600
Coatinc United States Inc	2899	E	619 638-7261	4601
CP Kelco US Inc	2899	E	619 652-5326	4602
Firmenich Incorporated	2899	E	858 646-8323	4606
New Leaf Biofuel LLC	2911	E	619 236-8500	4646
Sacahn JV	2911	D	858 924-1110	4649
Wd-40 Company	2911	C	619 275-1400	4656
WD-40 Company (PA)	2992	C	619 275-1400	4689
Bridgestone Americas Inc	3011	E	858 874-3109	4694
Morgan Polymer Seals LLC (PA)	3053	E	619 498-9221	4738
Apon Medical Molding and Assembly Inc	3069	D	619 793-4887	4757
Oxystrap International Inc	3069	E	800 609-6901	4782
Laird Plastics Inc	3081	E	858 560-1551	4813
Providien Thermoforming Inc	3081	D	858 850-1591	4818
Ridout Plastics Company (PA)	3081	D	858 560-1551	4819
Saint-Gobain Solar Gard LLC (DH)	3081	D	866 300-2674	4820
Atlas Roofing Corporation	3086	E	626 334-5358	4875
KB Foam Inc	3086	F	619 661-1870	4892
Walter N Coffman Inc	3086	D	619 266-2642	4910
Apon Industries Corp	3089	C		4944
Bh-Tech Inc	3089	A	858 694-0900	4963
Custom Engineering Plastics LP	3089	F	858 452-0961	4999
Grand Fusion Housewares Inc	3089	E	909 292-5776	5042
Higgins Hardwood Inc	3089	F	775 856-1653	5047
Ikegami Mold Corp America	3089	F	619 858-6855	5058
Jem-Hd Co Inc	3089	E	619 710-1443	5071
MI Technologies Inc	3089	A	619 710-2637	5098
New West Products Inc	3089	E	619 671-9022	5113
Nishiba Industries Corporation	3089	D	619 661-8866	5117
Providien Injction Molding Inc	3089	D	760 931-1844	5169
San Diego Ace Inc	3089	C	619 206-7339	5195
South Bay Cstm Plstic Extrders	3089	E	619 544-0808	5211
Allbirds Inc	3143	F	858 987-9533	5271
Eleanor Rigby Leather Co	3199	D	619 356-5590	5308
Shamir Insight Inc	3229	D	858 514-8330	5330
Rayotek Scientific Inc	3231	E	858 558-3671	5355
Forterra Pipe & Precast LLC	3272	E	858 715-5600	5415
San Diego Precast Concrete Inc (DH)	3272	E	619 240-8000	5448
California Commercial Asp LLC	3273	F	858 513-0611	5465
Robertsons Ready Mix Ltd	3273	D	800 834-7557	5498
Superior Ready Mix Concrete LP	3273	D	619 265-0955	5511
Superior Ready Mix Concrete LP	3273	D	619 265-0955	5512
Lamart California Inc	3296	E	973 772-6262	5556
International Mfg Tech Inc (DH)	3312	E	619 544-7741	5591
Price Industries Inc	3312	D	858 673-4451	5597
San Dego Prcsion Machining Inc	3312	E	858 499-0379	5600
Initium Aerospace LLC	3324	F	818 324-3684	5656
Argen Corporation (PA)	3339	C	858 455-7900	5673
Johnson Matthey Inc	3341	C	858 716-2400	5682
Bridgewave Communications Inc	3357	E	408 567-6900	5732
Centurum Information Tech Inc	3357	C	619 224-1100	5738
Van Can Company	3411	C	858 391-8084	5866
Allegion Access Tech LLC	3423	E	858 431-5940	5872
Hodge Products Inc	3429	E	800 778-2217	5921
Lucky Line Products Inc	3429	E	858 549-6699	5929
Pacific Maritime Inds Corp	3441	C	619 575-8141	6061
Hyundai Translead (HQ)	3441	D	619 574-1500	6144
AP Precision Metals Inc	3444	E	619 628-0003	6190
Arrk North America Inc	3444	E	858 552-1587	6192
Concise Fabricators Inc	3444	E	520 746-3226	6218
Marine & Rest Fabricators Inc	3444	E	619 232-7267	6266
Metal Master Inc	3444	E	858 292-8880	6271
Romla Co	3444	E	619 946-1224	6307
Spec-Built Systems Inc	3444	D	619 661-8100	6320
Pacific Steel Group (PA)	3449	E	858 251-1100	6404
HI Tech Honeycomb Inc	3469	C	858 974-1600	6521
Sheffield Platers Inc	3471	D	858 546-8484	6662
Southern California Plating Co	3471	E	619 231-1481	6664

Employee Codes: A=Over 500 employees, B=251-500
C=101-250, D=51-100, E=20-50, F=10-19, G=1-9

2024 Southern California
Business Directory and Buyers Guide

© Mergent Inc. 1-800-342-5647
1427

GEOGRAPHIC

	SIC	EMP	PHONE	ENTRY#
Symcoat Metal Processing Inc	3471	E	858 451-3313	6670
Action Powder Coating LLC	3479	F	858 566-2288	6683
All Source Coatings Inc	3479	E	858 586-0903	6686
Alphacoat Finishing LLC	3479	E	949 748-7796	6687
Flame-Spray Inc	3479	E	619 283-2007	6704
Dha America Inc	3496	D	858 925-3246	6816
Innovive LLC (PA)	3496	E	858 309-6620	6818
Right Manufacturing LLC	3498	E	858 566-7002	6851
Pappalecco	3499	E	619 906-5566	6870
Precision Engine Controls Corp (DH)	3511	C	858 792-3217	6884
Solar Turbines Incorporated (HQ)	3511	A	619 544-5352	6885
Solar Turbines Incorporated	3511	E	619 544-5321	6886
Solar Turbines Incorporated	3511	C	858 694-6110	6887
Solar Turbines Incorporated	3511	D	858 715-2060	6888
Solar Turbines Intl Co (DH)	3511	E	619 544-5000	6889
Aquaneering Inc	3523	E	858 578-2028	6899
DRTS Enterprises Ltd	3523	E	858 270-7244	6905
Rain Bird Corporation	3523	E	619 674-4068	6911
Rivulis Irrigation Inc (HQ)	3523	E	858 578-1860	6912
Hirok Inc	3531	E	619 713-5066	6936
California Air Tools Inc	3546	E	619 407-7905	7143
Seescan Inc (PA)	3546	C	858 244-3300	7147
Ssco Manufacturing Inc	3548	E	619 628-1022	7162
Super Welding Southern Cal Inc	3548	E	619 239-8003	7163
Teledyne Seabotix Inc	3549	D	619 239-5959	7172
Innova Design Inc	3552	F	858 535-9389	7176
Fabric8labs Inc	3555	D	858 215-1142	7185
Asml Us LLC	3559	A	858 385-6500	7224
CP Manufacturing Inc (HQ)	3559	C	619 477-3175	7230
Morgan Polymer Seals LLC	3559	B	619 498-9221	7251
Vectron Inc	3559	F	858 621-2400	7265
Schroff Inc	3561	A	800 525-4682	7289
Industrial Fire Sprnklr Co Inc	3569	E	619 266-6030	7395
Pall Corporation	3569	C	858 455-7264	7404
Continuous Computing Corp	3571	C	858 882-8800	7421
HP Inc	3571	B	858 924-5117	7429
Kontron America Incorporated	3571	D	800 822-7522	7436
Matri Kart	3571	E	858 609-0933	7438
Teradata Operations Inc (HQ)	3571	D	937 242-4030	7453
Advanced Hpc Inc	3572	F	858 716-8262	7460
Vigobyte Tape Corporation	3572	A	866 803-8446	7492
MTA Moving Tech In Amer Inc	3575	E	619 651-7208	7497
OCP Group Inc	3575	E	858 279-7400	7498
Acces I/O Products Inc	3577	F	858 550-9559	7503
C Enterprises Inc	3577	D	760 599-5111	7513
Congatec Inc	3577	E	858 457-2600	7518
Mad Catz Inc	3577	C	858 790-5008	7546
Magma Inc	3577	E	858 530-2511	7547
Mission Technology Group Inc	3577	E	858 530-2511	7551
Mitek Systems Inc	3577	C	619 269-6800	7552
Semtek Innvtive Solutions Corp	3577	E	858 436-2270	7570
United Tote Company	3577	D	858 279-4250	7576
Voyetra Turtle Beach Inc (DH)	3577	D	914 345-2255	7579
Asteres Inc (PA)	3578	E	858 777-8600	7583
Alliance Air Products Llc (DH)	3585	D	619 428-9688	7596
Alliance Air Products Llc	3585	B	619 664-0027	7597
Elco Rfrgn Solutions LLC	3585	A	858 888-9447	7609
Energy Labs Inc (DH)	3585	E	619 671-0100	7610
Hussmann Tech Corp Amer	3585	D	619 661-1134	7616
Thermocraft	3585	D	619 813-2985	7625
Trane US Inc	3585	E	858 292-0833	7627
Trumed Systems Incorporated	3585	E	844 878-6331	7630
Pronto Products Co (PA)	3589	E	619 661-6995	7680
Water Works Inc	3589	E	858 499-0119	7691
Parker-Hannifin Corporation	3594	C	619 661-7000	7714
5th Axis Inc (PA)	3599	E	858 505-0432	7720
Futuristics Machine Inc	3599	E	858 450-0644	7840
Inno Tech Manufacturing Inc	3599	F	858 545-4556	7873
J I Machine Company Inc	3599	E	858 695-1787	7884
Pacific Mfg Inc San Diego	3599	E	619 423-0316	7965
Precise Engineering Inc	3599	E	858 345-7243	7976
Pyramid Precision Machine Inc	3599	D	858 642-0713	7986
Senior Aerospace Jet Pdts Corp	3599	D	858 278-8400	8022
Senior Operations LLC	3599	D	858 278-8400	8024
Simonz Machine	3599	F	858 692-5129	8028
Smith Brothers Mfg Corp	3599	F	619 296-3171	8030
His Company Inc	3612	F	858 513-7748	8098
Nuvve Holding Corp (PA)	3612	E	619 456-5161	8102
Pulse Electronics Inc (HQ)	3612	B	858 674-8100	8108
Sempra Global	3612	D	619 696-2000	8111
Tocanw Wholesaler	3612	E	619 376-2860	8114
Aemi Holdings LLC	3613	D	858 481-0210	8116
Powerflex Systems LLC	3621	E	650 469-3392	8153
Sure Power Inc	3621	E	619 661-6292	8159
Cal-Comp Electronics (usa) Co Ltd	3625	B	858 587-6900	8171
Crydom Inc (DH)	3625	D	619 210-1590	8174
General Dynamics Mission	3625	D	619 671-5400	8181
S R C Devices Inccustomer	3625	E	866 772-8668	8190
Surface Technologies Corp	3625	E	619 564-8320	8192
Teal Electronics Corporation (PA)	3625	D	858 558-9000	8195
Intelligent Technologies LLC	3629	C	858 458-1500	8208
Maxwell Technologies Inc	3629	E	858 503-3493	8210
Autosplice Parent Inc (PA)	3643	C	858 535-0077	8255
Teledyne Instruments Inc	3643	D	858 842-3100	8280
Enertron Technologies Inc	3646	E	800 537-7649	8311
Clear Blue Energy Corp	3648	D	858 451-1549	8358
Deepsea Power & Light Inc	3648	E	858 576-1261	8361
Remote Ocean Systems Inc (PA)	3648	E	858 565-8500	8380
Activeon Inc (PA)	3651	E	858 798-3300	8391
Al Shellco LLC (HQ)	3651	C	570 296-6444	8392
Genasys Inc (PA)	3651	D	858 676-1112	8413
Ksc Industries Inc	3651	E	619 671-0110	8419
Philips	3651	E	916 337-8008	8426
Sanyo Manufacturing Corporation	3651	D	619 661-1134	8433
Sony Electronics Inc	3651	B	858 942-2400	8437
Sony Electronics Inc (DH)	3651	A	858 942-2400	8438
Franklin Wireless Corp	3661	D	858 623-0000	8473
U-Blox San Diego Inc	3661	E	858 847-9611	8486
Air-Trak	3663	E	858 677-9950	8490
Airgain Inc (PA)	3663	E	760 579-0200	8491
Atx Networks (san Diego) Corp (DH)	3663	E	858 546-5050	8498
E-Band Communications LLC	3663	E	858 408-0660	8512
Ectron Corporation	3663	E	858 278-0600	8513
Flo TV Incorporated	3663	E	858 651-1645	8519
Ingenu Inc (PA)	3663	E		8525
Interdigital Inc	3663	E	858 210-4800	8526
Kyocera AVX Cmpnnts San Dego I (DH)	3663	E	858 550-3820	8529
L3 Applied Technologies Inc (DH)	3663	E	858 404-7824	8530
L3 Technologies Inc	3663	B	858 279-0411	8531
L3 Technologies Inc	3663	D	858 552-9716	8532
L3 Technologies Inc	3663	B	858 552-9500	8533
Marketspark Sub Inc	3663	D	844 900-0599	8543
Nextivity Inc (PA)	3663	E	858 485-9442	8554
Qualcomm Incorporated (PA)	3663	A	858 587-1121	8563
Qualcomm Incorporated	3663	E	858 587-1121	8564
Remec Brdband Wrless Ntwrks LL	3663	C	858 312-6900	8570
Remec Broadband Wireless LLC	3663	E	858 312-6900	8571
Satellite Security Corporation	3663	E	877 437-4199	8575
Seaspace Corporation	3663	E	858 746-1100	8576
Sidus Solutions LLC	3663	F	619 275-5533	8579
Solectek Corporation	3663	E	858 450-1220	8582
Space Micro Inc	3663	C	858 332-0700	8583
Tachyon Networks Incorporated	3663	E	858 882-8100	8586
Vigor Systems Inc	3663	E	866 748-4467	8596
Indyme Solutions LLC	3669	E	858 268-0717	8614
Indyme Solutions LLC	3669	D	858 268-0717	8615
Johnson Cntrls Fire Prtction L	3669	E	858 633-9100	8616
Qualcomm Mems Technologies Inc	3669	E	858 587-1121	8622
Ecoatm LLC (DH)	3671	C	858 999-3200	8634
Aurum Assembly Plus Inc	3672	E	858 578-8710	8651
Benchmark Elec Phoenix Inc	3672	B	619 397-2402	8654
Electronic Surfc Mounted Inds	3672	E	858 455-1710	8672
Northwest Circuits Corp	3672	D	619 661-1701	8711
PDM Solutions Inc	3672	E	858 348-1000	8716
Quality Systems Intgrated Corp	3672	C	858 536-3128	8722
Quality Systems Intgrated Corp (PA)	3672	C	858 587-9797	8723
Saehan Electronics America Inc (PA)	3672	D	858 496-1500	8725
Sumitomics USA Inc	3672	E	619 661-0450	8734
Ttm Technologies Inc	3672	C	858 874-2701	8746
Anokiwave Inc (PA)	3674	E	858 792-9910	8766
Arm Inc	3674	A	858 453-1900	8768
Broadcom Corporation	3674	C	858 385-8800	8777
Daylight Solutions Inc (DH)	3674	C	858 432-7500	8786
Hermes-Microvision Inc	3674	E	858 385-6500	8803
Ikanos Communications Inc (DH)	3674	F	858 587-1121	8805
Innophase Inc	3674	D	619 541-8280	8811
Io Semiconductor Incorporated	3674	E	858 362-4074	8816
Iq-Analog Corporation	3674	E	858 200-0388	8818
Kulr Technology Corporation	3674	E	408 675-7002	8823
Kyocera America Inc	3674	E	858 576-2600	8824
Kyocera International Inc (HQ)	3674	D	858 492-1456	8825
Next Semiconductor Tech Inc	3674	E	858 707-7060	8852
Oneroof Energy Inc	3674	C	858 458-0533	8854
Orca Systems Inc	3674	F	858 679-9175	8857
Psemi Corporation (DH)	3674	D	858 731-9400	8869
Qualcomm Datacenter Tech Inc (HQ)	3674	E	858 567-1121	8871

Mergent email: customerrelations@mergent.com
1428
2024 Southern California
Business Directory and Buyers Guide
(P-0000) Products & Services Section entry number
(PA)=Parent Co (HQ)=Headquarters (DH)=Div Headquarters

Company	SIC	EMP	PHONE	ENTRY#
Qualcomm Incorporated	3674	E	858 909-0316	8873
Qualcomm Incorporated	3674	E	858 587-1121	8874
Qualcomm Incorporated	3674	D	858 587-1121	8875
Qualcomm Limited Partner Inc	3674	D	858 587-1121	8876
Qualcomm Technologies Inc (HQ)	3674	B	858 587-1121	8877
Santier Inc	3674	D	858 271-1993	8883
Semtech San Diego Corporation	3674	D	858 695-1808	8887
Sensemetrics Inc	3674	E	619 738-8300	8888
Teledyne Instruments Inc	3674	E	858 842-3127	8907
Tensorcom Inc	3674	E	760 496-3264	8908
General Atomics Electronic Systems Inc	3675	B	858 522-8495	8927
Rf Industries Ltd (PA)	3678	E	858 549-6340	8981
Cali Resources Inc	3679	E	619 661-5741	9012
CCM Assembly & Mfg Inc (PA)	3679	E	760 560-1310	9014
Custom Sensors & Tech Inc	3679	A	805 716-0322	9025
Delta Group Electronics Inc	3679	E	858 569-1681	9029
Enfora Inc	3679	E	972 234-1689	9041
Hannspree North America Inc	3679	D	909 992-5025	9053
Integrated Microwave Corp	3679	D	858 259-2600	9061
Katolec Development Inc	3679	E	619 710-0075	9074
Munekata America Inc	3679	B	619 661-8080	9087
Ormet Circuits Inc	3679	E	858 831-0010	9097
Pred Technologies Usa Inc	3679	D	858 999-2114	9101
Pulse Electronics Corporation (HQ)	3679	E	858 674-8100	9103
Vas Engineering Inc	3679	E	858 569-1601	9135
Ereplacements LLC	3691	E	714 361-2652	9147
Gold Peak Industries (north America) Inc	3691	E	858 674-6099	9150
Sunfusion Energy Systems Inc	3691	E	800 544-0282	9155
Arriver Holdco Inc	3694	A	858 587-1121	9163
Maxwell Technologies Inc (HQ)	3694	D	858 503-3300	9170
Trademark Construction Co Inc (PA)	3694	D	760 489-5647	9175
Elm System Inc	3695	F	408 694-2750	9180
Reel Picture Productions LLC	3695	E	858 587-0301	9183
Cubic Defense Applications Inc (DH)	3699	A	858 776-5664	9203
Cubic Defense Applications Inc	3699	C	858 505-2870	9204
Cymer LLC (HQ)	3699	A	858 385-7300	9205
Hc West LLC	3699	B	858 277-3473	9214
Instruments Incorporated	3699	E	858 571-1111	9216
O & S California Inc	3699	B	619 661-1800	9232
Pxise Energy Solutions LLC	3699	E	619 696-2944	9245
Azaa Investments Inc (PA)	3711	E	858 569-8111	9279
Achates Power Inc	3714	D	858 535-9920	9339
B & I Fender Trims Inc	3714	E	718 326-4323	9359
Coda Automotive Inc	3714	D	619 291-2040	9374
Crower Engrg & Sls Co Inc	3714	D	619 661-6477	9376
Mygrant Glass Company Inc	3714	E	858 455-8022	9429
Sanko Electronics America Inc (HQ)	3714	F	310 618-1677	9457
Spectrum Accessory Distrs Inc	3714	F	858 653-6470	9462
Boeing Company	3721	A	619 545-8382	9516
General Atomics Arntcal Systems	3721	B	858 964-6700	9525
General Atomics Arntcal Systems	3721	A	858 762-6700	9528
General Atomics Arntcal Systems	3721	B	858 455-2810	9529
Shield AI Inc (PA)	3721	A	619 719-5740	9552
Chromalloy Component Svcs Inc	3724	E	858 877-2800	9564
Safran Pwr Units San Diego LLC	3724	D	858 223-2228	9579
Senior Operations LLC (HQ)	3724	C	858 278-8400	9580
Coi Ceramics Inc	3728	E	858 621-5700	9661
Delta Airlines Inc	3728	E	619 491-2886	9672
General Dynamics Ots Cal Inc	3728	C	619 671-5411	9699
Meggitt (san Diego) Inc (HQ)	3728	C	858 824-8976	9746
Performance Plastics Inc	3728	D	714 343-3928	9765
Safran Cabin Inc	3728	C	619 661-6292	9790
Safran Cabin Inc	3728	C	619 671-0430	9791
Sungear Inc	3728	E	858 549-3166	9804
Bae Systems San Dego Ship Repr	3731	A	619 238-1000	9834
Continental Maritime Inds Inc	3731	B	619 234-8851	9836
Hii San Diego Shipyard Inc	3731	B	619 234-8851	9838
Miller Marine	3731	E	619 791-1500	9841
National Stl & Shipbuilding Co (HQ)	3731	B	619 544-3400	9842
NAVY UNITED STATES DEPARTMENT	3731	A	619 556-6033	9844
Pacific Ship Repr Fbrction Inc (PA)	3731	B	619 232-3200	9845
Pyr Preservation Services	3731	E	619 338-8395	9847
Trident Maritime Systems Inc	3731	E	619 346-3800	9848
Driscoll Inc	3732	E	619 226-2500	9857
Shelter Island Ychtways Ltd A	3732	E	619 222-0481	9866
Kratos Def & SEC Solutions Inc (PA)	3761	A	858 812-7300	9895
Composite Optics Incorporated	3769	A	937 490-4145	9916
Argon St Inc	3812	D	703 270-6927	9947
Atk Launch Systems LLC	3812	B	858 592-2509	9950
Atk Space Systems LLC	3812	D	858 487-0970	9951
Atk Space Systems LLC	3812	D	858 621-5700	9952
Bae Systems Tech Sltons Svcs I	3812	E	858 278-3042	9958
Biospherical Instruments Inc	3812	E	619 686-1888	9960
Caes Systems LLC	3812	C	858 560-1301	9961
Cubic Corporation (HQ)	3812	A	858 277-6780	9966
Decatur Electronics Inc (HQ)	3812	D	888 428-4315	9969
Global A Lgistics Training Inc	3812	E	760 688-0365	9979
Lockheed Martin Orincon Corp (HQ)	3812	C	858 455-5530	9997
Lytx Inc (PA)	3812	B	858 430-4000	9998
Nevwest Inc	3812	F	619 420-8100	10005
Northrop Grmman Innvtion Syste	3812	B	858 621-5700	10006
Northrop Grumman Corporation	3812	A	858 967-1221	10009
Northrop Grumman Systems Corp	3812	A	410 765-5589	10028
Northrop Grumman Systems Corp	3812	B	858 592-4518	10029
Northrop Grumman Systems Corp	3812	C	858 618-4349	10030
Northrop Grumman Systems Corp	3812	D	858 514-9020	10031
Northrop Grumman Systems Corp	3812	F	858 592-2535	10032
Northrop Grumman Systems Corp	3812	D	858 621-7395	10033
Northrop Grumman Systems Corp	3812	D	858 514-9000	10034
Orbital Sciences LLC	3812	C	858 618-1847	10045
Raytheon Company	3812	E	858 571-6598	10052
Raytheon Dgital Force Tech LLC (DH)	3812	E	858 546-1244	10059
Remec Defense & Space Inc	3812	A	858 560-1301	10060
Reveal Imaging Tech Inc	3812	E	571 526-6000	10061
Reveal Imaging Tech Inc (DH)	3812	E	571 526-6000	10062
Scientific-Atlanta LLC	3812	E	619 679-6000	10069
Tecnova Advanced Systems Inc	3812	E	858 586-9660	10075
Genetronics Inc	3821	E	858 597-6006	10093
Isec Incorporated	3821	D	858 279-9085	10095
Procisedx Inc	3821	E	858 382-4598	10097
Contrctor Cmpliance Monitoring	3822	E	619 472-9065	10102
Honeywell International Inc	3822	C	619 671-5612	10104
Advanced Electromagnetics Inc	3823	E	619 449-9492	10113
Continental Controls Corp	3823	E	858 453-9880	10125
Digivision Inc	3823	E	858 530-0100	10128
Embedded Designs Inc	3823	E	858 673-6050	10130
Hardy Process Solutions	3823	E	858 278-2900	10139
Reotemp Instrument Corporation (PA)	3823	D	858 784-0710	10156
Sabia Incorporated (PA)	3823	E	858 217-2200	10159
D & K Engineering (PA)	3824	D	858 451-8999	10174
Ametek Programmable Power Inc (HQ)	3825	B	858 450-0085	10183
Bae Systems Info Elctrnic Syst	3825	A	858 592-5000	10187
Bae Systems National Security Solutions Inc	3825	A	858 592-5000	10188
CONCISYS	3825	E	858 292-5888	10193
L3harris Interstate Elec Corp	3825	D	858 552-5600	10209
Litel Instruments Inc	3825	E	858 546-3788	10213
Mrv Systems LLC	3825	E	800 645-7114	10217
Surface Optics Corporation	3825	E	858 675-7404	10224
Velher LLC	3825	E	619 494-6310	10229
Affymetrix Inc	3826	E	858 642-2058	10232
Bionano Genomics Inc (PA)	3826	D	858 888-7600	10243
City of San Diego	3826	C	619 758-2310	10249
Cue Health Inc	3826	A	858 412-8151	10252
Filmetrics Inc (HQ)	3826	E	858 573-9300	10259
Illumina Inc	3826	E	800 809-4566	10264
Illumina Inc (PA)	3826	A	858 202-4500	10265
Molecular Bioproducts Inc (DH)	3826	C	858 453-7551	10274
Oxford Nanoimaging Inc	3826	D	650 690-2708	10280
Quantum Design Inc (PA)	3826	C	858 481-4400	10282
Singular Genomics Systems Inc	3826	C	858 333-7830	10288
Telesis Bio Inc	3826	E	858 526-3080	10294
Thermo Fisher Scientific Inc	3826	D	858 453-7551	10298
V & P Scientific Inc	3826	F	858 455-0643	10302
Wintrliss Engineering Corp	3827	E	858 550-7300	10346
Fitbit Inc	3829	D	415 513-1000	10365
Gamma Scientific Inc	3829	E	858 635-9008	10367
Gantner Instruments Inc	3829	E	888 512-5788	10368
Meps Real-Time Inc	3829	C	760 448-9500	10383
Pacific Diversified Capital Co	3829	C	619 696-2000	10389
Quantum Group Inc	3829	E	858 566-9959	10392
SKF Condition Monitoring Inc (DH)	3829	C	858 496-3400	10396
Spectral Labs Incorporated	3829	E	858 451-0540	10398
Teledyne Instruments Inc	3829	D	619 239-5959	10401
Teledyne Instruments Inc	3829	D	858 657-9800	10402
Abbott Rapid Dx North Amer LLC	3841	E	858 805-3804	10409
Accriva Dgnostics Holdings Inc (DH)	3841	B	858 404-8203	10414
Ajinomoto Althea Inc (HQ)	3841	C	858 882-0123	10418
Ameditech Inc	3841	C	858 535-1968	10428
Apex Medical Technologies Inc	3841	E	858 535-0012	10430
Becton Dickinson and Company	3841	D	888 876-4287	10452
Biogeneral Inc	3841	E	858 453-4451	10456
Bioject Inc	3841	E	503 692-8001	10457
Branan Medical Corporation (PA)	3841	E	949 598-7166	10462
Camino Neurocare	3841	E	858 455-1115	10467
Carefusion 213 LLC (DH)	3841	B	800 523-0502	10471
Carefusion Corporation	3841	D	858 617-4271	10472

GEOGRAPHIC

	SIC	EMP	PHONE	ENTRY#
Carefusion Solutions LLC **(DH)**	3841	A	858 617-2100	10475
Chart Sequal Technologies Inc.	3841	D	858 202-3100	10479
Companion Medical Inc.	3841	C	858 522-0252	10483
Covidien Holding Inc.	3841	C	619 690-8500	10486
Cytori Therapeutics Inc.	3841	E	858 458-0900	10488
Dexcom Inc **(PA)**.	3841	A	858 200-0200	10491
Genalyte Inc **(PA)**	3841	F	858 956-1200	10514
Glysens Incorporated.	3841	E	858 638-7708	10518
Inova Labs Inc.	3841	D	866 647-0691	10532
Integer Holdings Corporation.	3841	C	619 498-9448	10533
Integra Lfscnces Holdings Corp.	3841	E	609 529-9748	10534
International Technidyne Corp **(DH)**	3841	C	858 263-2300	10536
Ivera Medical LLC.	3841	E	888 861-8228	10539
Magnabiosciences LLC.	3841	E	858 481-4400	10549
Mast Biosurgery USA Inc.	3841	E	858 550-8050	10552
Med-Safe Systems Inc.	3841	E	855 236-2772	10553
Medtronic Inc.	3841	E	949 798-3934	10557
Modular Medical Inc.	3841	E	858 800-3500	10569
Nexus Dx Inc.	3841	E	858 410-4600	10578
Nuvasive Inc.	3841	F	858 909-1800	10582
Nuvasive Inc **(HQ)**.	3841	D	858 909-1800	10583
Resmed Inc **(PA)**	3841	A	858 836-5000	10597
Synergy Health Ast LLC **(DH)**	3841	E	858 586-1166	10612
Tandem Diabetes Care Inc **(PA)**	3841	A	877 801-6901	10613
Honeywell Safety Pdts USA Inc.	3842	C	619 661-8383	10668
Howmedica Osteonics Corp.	3842	D	800 621-6104	10669
Orthotic Holdings Inc.	3842	E	858 368-8873	10688
Psyonic Inc.	3842	E	888 779-6642	10694
Reva Medical Inc **(PA)**	3842	E	858 966-3000	10695
Rolling Sals Whlchair Lacrosse.	3842	E	619 677-1431	10697
Steris Corporation.	3842	C	858 586-1166	10704
Alere Connect LLC.	3845	E	888 876-3327	10788
Carefusion Corporation **(HQ)**	3845	B	858 617-2000	10795
Coastline International.	3845	C	888 748-7177	10797
Daylight Defense LLC.	3845	C	858 432-7500	10798
Gen-Probe Sales & Service Inc.	3845	E	858 410-8000	10803
Hologic Inc.	3845	E	858 410-8792	10805
Hologic Inc.	3845	C	858 410-8000	10806
Natus Medical Incorporated.	3845	D	858 260-2590	10816
Nuvasive Manufacturing LLC **(DH)**	3845	E	858 909-1800	10818
Philips Image Gded Thrapy Corp **(DH)**	3845	B	800 228-4728	10823
Tensys Medical Inc.	3845	E	858 552-1941	10829
Blenders Eyewear LLC.	3851	D	858 490-2178	10834
Essilor Laboratories Amer Inc.	3851	E	858 565-0751	10838
Hoya Corporation.	3851	E	858 309-6050	10841
Fastec Imaging Corporation.	3861	E	858 592-2342	10866
Alor International Ltd.	3911	E	858 454-0011	10895
Sunrise Jewelry Mfg Corp.	3911	F	619 270-5624	10912
Temple Custom Jewelers LLC.	3911	E	800 988-3844	10913
Bravo Sports.	3949	E	858 408-0083	10980
Crazy Industries.	3949	E	619 270-9090	10985
Diving Unlimited Intl Inc.	3949	D	619 236-1203	10987
Fitness Warehouse LLC **(PA)**	3949	E	858 578-7676	10991
Orca Arms LLC.	3949	D	858 586-0503	11017
National Pen Co LLC **(DH)**	3951	C	866 900-7367	11047
Jones Sign Inc.	3993	C	858 569-1400	11127
Signtech Electrical Advg Inc.	3993	C	619 527-6100	11165
Holiday Foliage Inc.	3999	E	619 661-9094	11227
Huntington Ingalls Industries.	3999	E	858 522-6000	11228
Lotus and Luna LLC.	3999	E	805 216-4451	11245
Plus Cbd LLC.	3999	E	855 758-7223	11270
San Diego Metro Trnst Sys.	4111	A	619 231-1466	11359
San Diego Transit Corporation **(PA)**	4111	A	619 238-0100	11360
San Diego Trolley Inc.	4111	B	619 595-4933	11361
Americare Ambulance.	4119	C	760 739-9723	11374
Care Medical Trnsp Inc.	4119	C	858 653-4520	11379
United Parcel Service Inc.	4215	A	909 279-5111	11544
MCR Printing and Packg Corp.	4225	C	619 488-3012	11597
San Diego Gas & Electric Co.	4225	C	858 547-2086	11610
Hornblower Yachts LLC.	4489	D	619 686-8700	11639
San Diego Unified Port Dst **(PA)**	4491	C	619 686-6200	11647
Shelter Pointe LLC.	4493	C	619 221-8000	11652
Air 88 LLC.	4581	D	858 277-1453	11685
San Dego Cnty Rgnal Arprt Auth **(PA)**	4581	C	619 400-2400	11706
Lbf Travel Inc.	4724	B	858 429-7599	11719
Golden Hour Data Systems Inc.	4731	C	858 768-2500	11765
Innovel Solutions Inc.	4731	A	619 497-1123	11774
Miramar Transportation Inc.	4731	D	858 693-0071	11784
Chandler Packaging A Transpak Company.	4783	D	858 292-5674	11819
Mek Enterprises Inc.	4783	D	619 527-0957	11822
Petco Animal Supplies Inc **(DH)**	4783	B	858 453-7845	11823
Nerys Logistics Inc.	4789	C	619 616-2124	11837
Cubic Secure Communications I.	4812	B	858 505-2000	11846
New Cingular Wireless Svcs Inc.	4812	D	619 238-3638	11851
Trellisware Technologies Inc **(HQ)**	4812	C	858 753-1600	11864
Fortitude Technology Inc.	4813	D	858 974-5080	11877
Mp3com Inc.	4813	D	858 623-7000	11893
Paychex Benefit Tech Inc.	4813	C	800 322-7292	11896
Sydata Inc.	4813	C	760 444-4368	11907
Telisimo International Corp.	4813	B	619 325-1593	11908
Kifm Smooth Jazz 981 Inc.	4832	C	619 297-3698	11926
Local Media San Diego LLC.	4832	D	858 888-7000	11930
Bay City Television Inc **(PA)**	4833	C	858 279-6666	11939
EW Scripps Company.	4833	C	619 237-1010	11947
Herring Networks Inc.	4833	C	858 270-6900	11954
McKinnon Publishing Company.	4833	A	858 571-5151	11958
Cox Communications Cal LLC.	4841	B	619 262-1122	11983
Spectrum MGT Holdg Co LLC.	4841	D	619 684-6106	12000
Ips Group Inc **(PA)**	4899	E	858 404-0607	12009
Siege Media LLC.	4899	D	858 751-4439	12012
Edf Renewables Inc **(PA)**	4911	C	858 521-3300	12021
San Diego Gas & Electric Co.	4911	C	858 541-5920	12043
San Diego Gas & Electric Co.	4911	C	619 696-1018	12044
San Diego Gas & Electric Co.	4911	B	858 654-6377	12046
San Diego Gas & Electric Co.	4911	B	858 613-3216	12047
San Diego Gas & Electric Co.	4911	D	858 654-1289	12048
Sempra Energy.	4911	A	619 696-2000	12050
Sempra Energy Global Entps.	4911	A	619 696-2000	12051
Sempra Energy International.	4911	A	619 696-2000	12052
Solv Energy LLC **(HQ)**	4911	C	858 251-4888	12055
Twin Oaks Power LP **(PA)**	4911	D	619 696-2034	12079
American Green Lights LLC.	4931	E	858 547-8837	12101
Calpine Energy Solutions LLC **(DH)**	4931	C	877 273-6772	12102
San Diego Gas & Electric Co.	4931	C	866 616-5565	12105
San Diego Gas & Electric Co **(DH)**	4931	B	619 696-2000	12106
Sempra **(PA)**	4932	C	619 696-2000	12108
San Diego County Water Auth **(PA)**	4941	D	858 522-6600	12141
California Marine Cleaning Inc **(PA)**	4953	C	619 231-8788	12162
Sullivan International Group Inc.	4959	C	619 260-1432	12211
Adesa Corporation LLC.	5012	D	619 661-5565	12219
Meridian Rack & Pinion Inc.	5013	C	888 875-0026	12247
Goforth & Marti **(PA)**	5021	D	800 686-6583	12283
Expo Industries Inc.	5031	D	858 566-3110	12328
Westside Bldg San Diego LLC.	5031	E	858 566-4343	12346
Baker & Taylor Holdings LLC.	5045	A	858 457-2500	12399
Broadway Typewriter Co Inc.	5045	D	800 998-9199	12401
Eset LLC **(HQ)**	5045	C	619 876-5400	12410
Mediatek USA Inc.	5045	D	858 731-9200	12426
PC Specialists Inc **(DH)**	5045	C	858 566-1900	12431
Quartic Solutions LLC.	5045	E	858 377-8470	12435
Southland Technology Inc.	5045	D	858 694-0932	12440
Ubiq Security Inc.	5045	E	888 434-6674	12449
Jetro Holdings LLC.	5046	B	858 564-0466	12460
Jones Signs Co Inc.	5046	C	858 569-1400	12461
Better Night LLC.	5047	E	619 299-6299	12476
Biosite Inc.	5047	E	510 683-9063	12478
Mobility Solutions Inc **(PA)**	5047	C	858 278-0591	12500
Molecular Bioproducts Svc Corp **(HQ)**	5049	E	858 875-7696	12530
Century Tubes Inc.	5051	C	858 586-0550	12539
Cableconn Industries Inc.	5063	D	858 517-7111	12589
Graybar Electric Company Inc.	5063	D	858 578-8606	12597
Main Electric Supply Co LLC.	5063	E	858 737-7000	12605
Sloan Electric Corporation.	5063	E	619 239-5174	12619
Philips North America LLC.	5064	D	858 677-6390	12635
Bear Communications Inc.	5065	D	619 263-2159	12644
Impact Components A California Limi.	5065	E	858 634-4800	12669
Lightpointe Communications Inc.	5065	E	858 834-4083	12677
Motorola Mobility LLC.	5065	E	858 455-1500	12684
Presidio Components Inc.	5065	C	858 578-9390	12691
Steren Electronics Intl LLC **(PA)**	5065	D	800 266-3333	12698
Waterfi LLC.	5065	F	619 438-0058	12709
Eurodrip USA Inc.	5083	C	559 674-2670	12780
Keco Inc.	5084	E	619 298-3800	12796
Otis Elevator Company.	5084	E	858 560-5881	12806
Carpenter Group.	5085	E	619 233-5625	12846
Pinnacle Industrial Supply Inc.	5085	E	619 710-4255	12873
Waxies Enterprises LLC **(DH)**	5087	C	800 995-4466	12897
Kettenburg Marine Corporation.	5088	C	619 224-8211	12911
Prestige Graphics Inc.	5112	E	858 560-8213	12997
San Diego Die Cutting Inc.	5113	E	619 297-4453	13024
Irisys Inc.	5122	E	858 623-1520	13047
Specialty Textile Services LLC.	5131	E	619 476-8750	13095
Mad Engine Global LLC.	5137	B	858 558-5270	13134
Marika Group Inc.	5137	E	858 537-5300	13135
Piveg Inc.	5141	C	858 436-3070	13191
Smart & Final Stores Inc.	5141	B	619 291-1842	13205

Mergent email: customerrelations@mergent.com
1430
2024 Southern California
Business Directory and Buyers Guide
(P-0000) Products & Services Section entry number
(PA)=Parent Co (HQ)=Headquarters (DH)=Div Headquarters

	SIC	EMP	PHONE	ENTRY#
Smart & Final Stores Inc.	5141	B	858 578-7343	13207
Canteen Vending - San Diego	5145	A	619 527-1900	13265
Catalina Offshore Products Inc.	5146	D	619 297-9797	13277
Jensen Meat Company Inc.	5147	D	619 754-6400	13298
Jetro Cash and Carry Entps LLC	5147	D	619 233-0200	13299
Mpci Holdings Inc.	5147	C	619 294-2222	13301
Producers Meat and Prov Inc.	5147	E	619 232-7593	13304
Coast Citrus Distributors (PA)	5148	C	619 661-7950	13316
Lenore John & Co (PA)	5149	C	619 232-6136	13377
Perfect Bar LLC	5149	C	866 628-8548	13388
Swell Coffee Roasting Co LP	5149	E	619 504-9244	13399
Chembridge Corporation (PA)	5169	B	858 451-7400	13428
Clipper Oil Inc.	5172	E	619 692-9701	13449
Crest Beverage LLC	5181	B	858 452-2300	13464
Montesquieu Corp.	5182	D	877 705-5669	13479
Baker & Taylor LLC	5192	C	858 457-2500	13493
White Digital Media Inc.	5192	C	760 827-7800	13498
Bella Terra Nursery Inc.	5193	D	619 585-1118	13503
PCF Group LLC	5199	E	858 455-1274	13553
Schroff Inc.	5199	A	858 740-2400	13560
Dixieline Lumber Company LLC (DH)	5211	D	619 224-4120	13572
Highlander Home Inc.	5211	E	858 261-4068	13578
Home Depot USA Inc.	5211	D	619 263-1533	13595
Lowes Home Centers LLC	5211	D	619 584-5500	13654
Superior Ready Mix Concrete LP	5211	D	858 695-0666	13671
El Tigre Inc.	5411	C	619 429-8212	13698
Courtesy Chevrolet Center	5511	D	619 297-4321	13750
Europa Auto Imports Inc.	5511	C	858 569-6900	13764
Mossy Automotive Group Inc (PA)	5511	D	858 581-4000	13798
Mossy Ford Inc.	5511	C	858 273-7500	13799
Mossy Nissan Inc.	5511	C	858 565-6608	13800
San Diego V Inc (PA)	5511	D	888 308-2260	13821
Parkhouse Tire Service Inc.	5531	E	858 565-8473	13867
Southern Cal Disc Tire Co Inc.	5531	C	858 278-0661	13879
La Mesa R V Center Inc (PA)	5561	C	858 874-8000	13897
Vera Bradley Inc.	5632	E	858 320-9020	13920
Madewell Inc.	5651	E	619 491-0549	13923
Adrenaline Lacrosse Inc.	5699	C	888 768-8479	13928
Cintas Corporation No 3	5699	D	619 239-1001	13933
Gosecure Inc (PA)	5734	C	301 442-3432	13971
Pcfs Solutions	5734	E	714 674-0009	13974
Carvin Corp.	5736	C	858 487-1600	13977
Cafe 21 Gaslamp Inc.	5812	E	619 795-0721	13988
California Garlic Company Inc.	5812	E	951 506-8883	13989
Citrus Restaurant LLC	5812	C	858 277-8888	13998
Jack In Box Inc (PA)	5812	A	858 571-2121	14016
Qdoba Restaurant Corporation (HQ)	5812	C	858 766-4900	14032
Harland Brewing Co LLC	5813	E	858 800-4566	14048
Mission Brewery Inc.	5813	E	619 818-7147	14050
Sharp Healthcare (PA)	5912	A	858 499-4000	14057
Road Runner Sports Inc (PA)	5961	D	858 974-4200	14103
Greatcall Inc.	5999	A	800 733-6632	14135
Officia Imaging Inc (PA)	5999	A	858 348-0831	14143
Petco Health & Wellness Co Inc.	5999	A	858 453-7845	14144
Scope Orthtics Prosthetics Inc (DH)	5999	E	858 292-7448	14147
Wells Fargo Investments LLC	6021	D	619 702-6949	14175
California Bank & Trust.	6022	A	801 844-7637	14182
Enterprise Bank & Trust.	6022	C	858 432-7000	14193
Seacoast Cmmerce Banc Holdings	6022	C	858 432-7000	14206
Mission Federal Credit Union	6061	C	858 531-5106	14232
Mission Federal Services LLC	6061	C	858 524-2850	14233
San Diego County Credit Union (PA)	6061	C	877 732-2848	14236
United Svcs Amer Federal Cr Un (PA)	6061	D	858 831-8100	14241
North Island Financial Credit Union.	6062	B	619 656-6525	14250
Encore Capital Group Inc (PA)	6153	A	877 445-4581	14281
Midland Credit Management Inc.	6153	C	877 240-2377	14284
National Funding Inc (PA)	6153	C	888 733-2383	14285
Reliant Services Group LLC	6153	C	877 850-0998	14286
American Internet Mortgage Inc.	6162	C	888 411-4246	14295
Amnet Mortgage LLC	6162	A	858 909-1200	14298
Berkshire Hthway HM Svcs Cal P	6162	C	619 302-8082	14302
Blufi Lending Corporation	6162	C		14303
Goal Financial LLC	6162	C	619 684-7600	14318
Guaranteed Rate Inc.	6162	C	760 310-6008	14324
Guild Holdings Company (PA)	6162	B	858 560-6330	14326
Integrity Mortgage Group	6162	D	858 225-5000	14329
Iserve Residential Lending LLC	6162	C	858 486-4169	14330
Lendsure Mortgage Corp.	6162	C	888 707-7811	14332
Synergy One Lending Inc.	6162	C	385 273-5250	14351
Change Lending LLC	6163	D	858 500-3060	14356
Charles Schwab Corporation.	6211	C	800 435-4000	14376
Lpl Financial Holdings Inc (PA)	6211	B	800 877-7210	14386
Morgan Stnley Smith Barney LLC	6211	C	619 238-1226	14393
Plaza Home Mortgage Inc.	6211	C	858 346-1208	14403
UBS Americas Inc.	6211	C	619 557-2400	14407
Brandes Inv Partners Inc (PA)	6282	C	858 755-0239	14418
C2 Financial Corporation.	6282	C	858 220-2112	14419
American Spclty Hlth Group Inc.	6324	B	858 754-2000	14460
Blue Shield Cal Lf Hlth Insur.	6324	A	619 686-4200	14462
Sharp Health Plan.	6324	D	858 499-8300	14496
Southern Cal Prmnnte Med Group.	6324	B	858 974-1000	14497
Arrowhead Gen Insur Agcy Inc (HQ)	6331	C	619 881-8600	14506
Golden Eagle Insurance Corp (DH)	6331	C	619 744-6000	14508
Icw Group Holdings Inc (PA)	6331	C	858 350-2400	14510
Mercury Insurance Company.	6331	A	858 694-4100	14517
State Compensation Insur Fund.	6331	C	888 782-8338	14531
Stewart Title California Inc (DH)	6361	C	619 692-1600	14545
AIG Direct Insurance Svcs Inc.	6411	B	858 309-3000	14555
American Spclty Insur Agcy Inc.	6411	B	619 297-8100	14558
Anchor General Insur Agcy Inc.	6411	C	858 527-3600	14559
Atlas General Insur Svcs LLC	6411	C	858 529-6700	14561
Barney & Barney Inc.	6411	C	800 321-4696	14567
Cbiz Life Insur Solutions Inc.	6411	C	858 444-3100	14573
Customzed Svcs Admnstrtors Inc.	6411	C	858 810-2004	14581
Insurance Company of West (HQ)	6411	D	858 350-2400	14602
John Hancock Life Insur Co USA.	6411	C	858 292-1667	14605
Marsh & McLennan Agency LLC	6411	C	858 457-3414	14610
Preferred Employers Insur Co.	6411	D	619 688-3900	14624
Premier Dealer Services Inc.	6411	D	858 810-1700	14625
C & D Wax Inc.	6512	C	858 292-5954	14654
Icw Valencia LLC	6512	C	858 350-2600	14665
San Diego Theatres Inc.	6512	C	619 615-4007	14683
Ffrt Residential LLC	6513	C	858 457-2123	14708
HG Fenton Company.	6513	C	619 400-0120	14712
Wamc Company Inc.	6513	D	858 454-2753	14732
HG Fenton Property Company (PA)	6519	C	619 400-0120	14737
Cbre Inc.	6531	C	858 546-4600	14759
Conam Management Corporation (PA)	6531	A	858 614-7200	14772
Cushman & Wakefield Cal Inc.	6531	A	858 452-6500	14779
Daymark Realty Advisors Inc.	6531	B	714 975-2999	14785
Dorothy Sarkozy.	6531	C	858 259-0555	14790
Hanken Cono Assad & Co Inc.	6531	C	619 575-3100	14810
Phase Ten Strategic Corp.	6531	C	619 298-1445	14843
RA Snyder Properties Inc (PA)	6531	C	619 297-0274	14853
Roman Cthlic Bshp of San Diego.	6531	C	619 264-3127	14862
Southern Cal Pipe Trades ADM.	6531	D	619 224-3125	14865
Team Brda RE Svcs - Cldwell Bn.	6531	C	858 621-5284	14871
Terra Vista Management Inc.	6531	B	858 581-4400	14873
Bridge Group Hh Inc.	6719	C	858 455-5000	14925
DMS Ue Acqisition Holdings Inc.	6719	D	800 466-4178	14928
Mlim Holdings LLC	6719	A	619 299-3131	14935
Bridgewest Ventures LLC (PA)	6726	A	858 529-6600	14976
Charles Schwab Corporation.	6726	C	800 435-4000	14978
Guild Mortgage Company LLC (HQ)	6733	C	800 365-4441	14991
Kaiser Foundation Hospitals.	6733	A	619 528-5888	14995
Quality Loan Service Corp.	6733	B	619 645-7711	15005
Qualcomm International Inc (HQ)	6794	A	858 587-1121	15009
Biomed Realty Trust Inc (PA)	6798	B	858 207-2513	15012
7th & C Investments LLC	6799	C	619 233-7327	15019
McMillin Companies LLC (PA)	6799	D	619 477-4117	15036
Medimpact Holdings Inc (PA)	6799	A	858 566-2727	15037
Tapetech Tool Company.	6799	A	858 268-0656	15053
1835 Columbia Street LP	7011	D	619 564-3993	15063
8110 Aero Holding LLC.	7011	C	858 277-8888	15067
American Prprty-Mnagement Corp.	7011	C	619 232-3121	15073
Atlas Hotels Inc.	7011	A	619 291-2232	15080
Bartell Hotels.	7011	D	619 291-6700	15087
Bh Partnership LP (PA)	7011	C	858 539-7635	15094
Bhr Operations LLC.	7011	C	619 232-3861	15095
Braemar Partnership.	7011	B	858 488-1081	15096
C N L Hotel Del Partners LP.	7011	C	619 522-8299	15103
Diamondrock San Dego Tnant LLC.	7011	B	619 239-4500	15130
Grand Del Mar Resort LP.	7011	C	858 314-2000	15158
Gringteam Inc.	7011	C	619 297-5466	15163
Gringteam Inc.	7011	C	858 485-4145	15164
Hampstead Lafayette Hotel LLC.	7011	C	619 296-2101	15167
Handlery Hotels Inc.	7011	C	415 781-4550	15168
Harbor View Hotel Ventures LLC.	7011	D	619 239-6800	15170
Historical Properties Inc (PA)	7011	D	619 230-8417	15181
Hotel Circle Property LLC.	7011	B	619 291-7131	15186
Hyatt Corporation.	7011	C	858 453-0018	15193
Hyatt Corporation.	7011	C	619 232-1234	15194
Hyatt Corporation.	7011	C	619 849-1234	15195
Lfs Development LLC.	7011	C	619 501-5400	15222
Lho Mssion Bay Rsie Lessee Inc.	7011	B	619 276-4010	15225
Libor Management LLC.	7011	C	858 450-7175	15227

Employee Codes: A=Over 500 employees, B=251-500
C=101-250, D=51-100, E=20-50, F=10-19, G=1-9

2024 Southern California
Business Directory and Buyers Guide

© Mergent Inc. 1-800-342-5647
1431

GEOGRAPHIC

	SIC	EMP	PHONE	ENTRY#
M4dev LLC	7011	D	619 696-6300	15235
Manchester Grand Resorts LP	7011	A	619 232-1234	15238
Mbp Land LLC	7011	A	619 291-5720	15245
Mhf Mv Operating VI LLC	7011	D	619 481-5881	15250
Oak Valley Hotel LLC	7011	D	619 297-1101	15266
Old Town Fmly Hospitality Corp	7011	C	619 246-8010	15273
Pan Pcfic Htels Rsrts Amer Inc	7011	C	619 239-4500	15295
Paradise Lessee Inc	7011	B	858 274-4630	15296
Pinnacle Hotels Usa Inc	7011	D	858 974-8201	15304
Reh Company	7011	C	619 238-1818	15320
Rgc Gaslamp LLC	7011	C	619 738-7000	15325
San Diego Hotel Company LLC	7011	C	619 696-0234	15342
San Diego Lessee LLC	7011	D	619 297-5466	15343
San Diego Mission Bay Resorts	7011	C	619 677-1161	15344
San Diego Sheraton Corporation	7011	C	619 291-6400	15345
Sandm San Dego Mrriott Del Mar	7011	A	858 523-1700	15349
Sheraton Ht San Dego Mssion VI	7011	D	619 321-4602	15355
Souldriver Lessee Inc	7011	D	619 819-9500	15363
Starwood Inc	7011	C	888 559-1749	15370
Starwood Htels Rsrts Wrldwide	7011	C	619 239-2200	15373
Sunstone Top Gun Lessee Inc	7011	C	949 330-4000	15382
Swvp Del Mar Hotel LLC	7011	D	858 481-5900	15383
T-12 Three LLC	7011	B	619 702-3000	15387
The Lodge At Torrey Pines Partnership L P	7011	B		15389
Torrey Suites LP	7011	D	858 720-9500	15392
US Grant Hotel Ventures LLC	7011	D	619 744-2007	15399
Westgroup San Diego Associates	7011	C	858 274-4630	15415
Win Time Ltd (PA)	7011	C	858 695-2300	15419
Ws Mmv Hotel LLC	7011	D	619 692-3800	15427
Ww San Diego Harbor Island LLC	7011	C	619 291-6700	15428
Star Laundry Services Inc	7216	D	619 572-1009	15465
Bonded Inc (PA)	7217	D	858 576-8400	15466
Colt Services Inc	7217	D	858 271-9910	15467
Ogleby Sisters Soap	7231	E	212 518-1172	15484
Sport Clips Inc	7231	A	858 273-9993	15486
Beyond Finance LLC	7299	C	800 282-7186	15499
Instant Checkmate LLC	7299	C	800 222-8985	15511
Intelicare Direct Llc	7299	D	858 299-3636	15512
Intelius LLC	7299	C	888 245-1655	15513
Pacific Event Productions Inc (PA)	7299	C	858 458-9908	15520
Control Group Media Co LLC	7311	D	858 242-1350	15533
Hayes Company Inc	7311	E	949 375-3113	15543
Homes Media Solutions LLC	7311	C	888 510-8795	15544
Mindgruve Holdings Inc	7311	C	619 757-1325	15559
Stn Digital LLC	7311	D	619 292-8683	15575
Ue Authority Co	7311	D	800 466-4178	15578
Vitrorobertson LLC	7311	C	619 234-0408	15579
Corelogic Credco LLC	7323	B	619 938-7028	15620
Full/Tech Systems Inc	7331	E	619 297-0454	15632
American Legal Copy - Oc LLC	7334	D	415 777-4449	15641
Knox Attorney Service Inc (PA)	7334	C	619 233-9700	15648
Mirum Inc	7336	C	619 237-5552	15668
Thinkbasic Inc	7336	C	858 755-6922	15675
Crown Building Maintenance Co	7349	B	858 560-5785	15705
GMI Building Services Inc	7349	C	858 279-6262	15711
Kbm Fclity Sltons Holdings LLC	7349	B	858 467-0202	15718
Life Cycle Engineering Inc	7349	C	619 785-5990	15720
Merchants Building Maint Co	7349	B	858 455-0163	15726
Pe Facility Solutions LLC (PA)	7349	D	858 467-0202	15733
Pegasus Building Svcs Co Inc	7349	C	858 444-2290	15735
Priority Building Services LLC	7349	B	858 695-1326	15738
Professional Maint Systems Inc	7349	A	619 276-1150	15740
Protec Association Services (PA)	7349	C	858 569-1080	15743
Rhino Building Services Inc	7349	C	858 455-1440	15745
Servi-Tek Inc	7349	B	858 638-7735	15747
Hawthorne Machinery Co (PA)	7353	C	858 674-7000	15763
Hawthorne Rent-It Service (HQ)	7353	D	858 674-7000	15764
P J J Enterprises Inc	7359	C	619 232-6136	15791
Raphaels Party Rentals Inc (PA)	7359	C	858 444-1692	15795
Access Nurses Inc	7361	D	858 458-4400	15808
Advanced Med Prsonnel Svcs Inc	7361	D	386 756-4395	15811
Amn Healthcare Inc	7361	D	800 282-0300	15812
Barrett Business Services Inc	7361	A	858 314-1100	15820
Carter Aston Inc	7361	C	858 609-2062	15831
Eplica Corporate Services Inc	7361	A	619 282-1400	15843
Garich Inc (PA)	7361	B	858 453-1331	15847
Innovative Placements Inc	7361	C	800 322-9796	15854
Integrated Associates Inc	7361	C	858 412-6189	15855
Merritt Hawkins & Assoc LLC (HQ)	7361	C	858 792-0711	15868
Nursechoice	7361	D	866 567-6050	15869
Nursefinders LLC (HQ)	7361	C	858 314-7427	15872
Pioneer Healthcare Svcs LLC	7361	B	800 683-1209	15879
Preferred Hlthcare Rgistry Inc	7361	C	800 787-6787	15881
R&D Consulting Group Inc	7361	C	415 697-2585	15885
SE Scher Corporation	7361	A	858 546-8300	15892
Teg Staffing Inc	7361	A	800 918-1678	15898
Vish Consulting Services Inc	7361	D	916 800-3762	15902
Wmbe Payrolling Inc	7361	C	858 810-3000	15904
Workway Inc	7361	C	619 278-0012	15905
Aya Healthcare Inc (PA)	7363	B	858 458-4410	15914
Cardinal Point Captains Inc	7363	D	760 438-7361	15918
Eplica Inc (PA)	7363	C	619 260-2000	15921
June Group LLC	7363	D	858 450-4290	15925
Mek Industries Inc	7363	C	858 610-9601	15933
Rx Pro Health LLC	7363	A	858 369-4050	15939
Sfn Group Inc	7363	A	858 458-9200	15942
Vaya Workforce Solutions LLC	7363	C	866 687-7390	15946
Volt Management Corp	7363	D	858 576-3140	15947
Abacus Data Systems Inc (PA)	7371	C	858 452-4280	15953
Adaptamed Inc	7371	C	877 478-7773	15955
Algorithmic Objective Corp	7371	E	858 249-9580	15960
Biosero (PA)	7371	E	858 880-7376	15981
Brain Corporation	7371	C	858 689-7600	15988
Computer Proc Unlimited Inc	7371	C	858 530-0875	15999
Corelation Inc	7371	C	619 876-5074	16001
Cubic Trnsp Systems Inc (DH)	7371	A	858 268-3100	16006
Daybreak Game Company LLC	7371	B	858 239-0500	16010
Einstein Industries Inc	7371	C	858 459-1182	16023
Evernote Corporation (PA)	7371	B	650 216-7700	16029
G2 Software Systems Inc	7371	C	619 222-8025	16036
H & R Accounts Inc	7371	C	619 819-8844	16043
ID Analytics LLC	7371	C	858 312-6200	16049
Innovasystems Intl LLC	7371	C	619 955-5890	16054
Isaac Fair Corporation	7371	C	858 369-8000	16059
Logility Inc	7371	D	858 565-4238	16066
Mango Technologies Inc (PA)	7371	A	888 625-4258	16069
Medimizer Software	7371	E	760 642-2000	16072
Mir3 Inc	7371	D	858 724-1200	16075
Mitchell International Inc (PA)	7371	C	858 368-7000	16076
Nucleushealth LLC	7371	D	858 251-3400	16089
Parallel 6 Inc (PA)	7371	E	619 452-1750	16093
Petdesk	7371	D	202 431-3045	16094
Platform Science Inc	7371	C	844 475-8724	16096
Psyonix LLC	7371	D	619 622-8772	16100
Reapplications Inc	7371	C	619 230-0209	16102
Sciforma Corporation	7371	E	408 899-0398	16109
Smartdrive Systems Inc (PA)	7371	C	858 225-5550	16116
Symitar Systems Inc	7371	C	619 542-6700	16127
Tapestry Solutions Inc (HQ)	7371	C	858 503-1990	16131
Verseio Inc	7371	D	888 373-9942	16147
Altumind Inc	7372	E	858 382-3956	16163
Ancora Software Inc (PA)	7372	E	888 476-4839	16166
Appfolio Inc	7372	E	866 648-1536	16171
Ascender Software Inc	7372	B	877 561-7501	16177
Blitz Rocks Inc	7372	F	310 883-5183	16185
Cbx Software Inc	7372	E	858 264-1133	16195
Chatmeter Inc	7372	D	619 300-1050	16199
Classy Inc	7372	C	619 961-1892	16202
Conservice Mtring Slutions Inc	7372	F	858 356-7534	16213
Curemetrix Inc	7372	E	858 333-5830	16218
Dassault Systemes Biovia Corp (DH)	7372	E	858 799-5000	16221
Dcatalog Inc	7372	E	408 824-5648	16223
Decisionlogic LLC	7372	E	858 586-0202	16224
Digital Arbitrage Dist Inc (PA)	7372	E	888 392-9478	16225
Dreamstart Labs Inc	7372	E	408 914-1234	16230
Edgate Holdings Inc	7372	E	858 712-9341	16232
Galley Solutions Inc	7372	F	818 636-1538	16254
Intuit Inc	7372	C	858 780-2846	16272
Intuit Inc	7372	B	858 215-8000	16273
Kazuhm Inc	7372	E	858 771-3861	16283
Kintera Inc (HQ)	7372	D	858 795-3000	16285
Kyriba Corp (HQ)	7372	E	858 210-3560	16288
Leadcrunch Inc (PA)	7372	E	888 708-6649	16291
Momco App Inc	7372	E	619 450-6340	16313
Musicmatch Inc	7372	E	858 485-4300	16315
Networkfleet Inc	7372	E	904 233-6844	16323
New Bi US Gaming LLC	7372	D	858 592-2472	16325
Omnitracs Midco LLC	7372	E	858 651-5812	16334
Precision Information LLC	7372	F	888 345-1285	16352
Procede Software LP	7372	E	858 450-4800	16354
Qualer Inc	7372	E	858 224-9516	16362
Seismic Software Inc (HQ)	7372	D	714 404-7069	16377
Smart-Tek Services Inc (HQ)	7372	F	858 798-1644	16382
So Cal Soft-Pak Incorporated	7372	E	619 283-2338	16383
Solv Energy LLC	7372	B	858 622-4040	16384
Sonic Vr LLC	7372	F	206 227-8585	16385

(P-0000) Products & Services Section entry number
(PA)=Parent Co (HQ)=Headquarters (DH)=Div Headquarters

Company	SIC	EMP	PHONE	ENTRY#
Tdo Software Inc.	7372	E	858 558-3696	16398
Teradata Corporation (PA)	7372	A	866 548-8348	16400
Ticketsocket Inc.	7372	E	888 633-7105	16407
Wind River Systems Inc.	7372	F	858 824-3100	16420
Wme Bi LLC	7372	D	877 592-2472	16422
Wordsmart Corporation	7372	D		16424
Automation Holdco Inc.	7373	E	858 967-8650	16429
Caci Enterprise Solutions LLC	7373	B	619 881-6000	16431
Captiva Software Corporation (DH)	7373	C	858 320-1000	16432
Clarity Design Inc.	7373	F	858 746-3500	16433
Clinicomp International Inc (PA)	7373	D	858 546-8202	16434
Cubic Corporation	7373	A	858 277-6780	16439
Koam Engineering Systems Inc	7373	C	858 292-0922	16452
Miro Technologies Inc	7373	C	858 677-2100	16458
Miva Inc.	7373	C	858 490-2570	16459
Mobisystems Inc	7373	C	858 350-0315	16460
Science Applications Intl Corp.	7373	A	858 826-3061	16468
Tusimple Holdings Inc (PA)	7373	B	619 916-3144	16475
Ultisat Inc.	7373	A	240 243-5107	16476
Zmicro Inc (PA)	7373	D	858 831-7000	16480
Amazon Processing LLC	7374	C	858 565-1135	16481
Emerald Connect LLC (HQ)	7374	D	800 233-2834	16492
San Diego Data Processing Corporation Inc.	7374	A	858 581-9600	16514
Spoutable LLC	7374	C	609 743-7491	16517
Tealium Inc (PA)	7374	C	858 779-1344	16518
Relationedge LLC	7375	C	858 451-4665	16533
Bernardo Technical Services	7379	F	858 779-9276	16554
Defenseweb Technologies Inc.	7379	D	858 272-8505	16563
Science Applications Intl Corp.	7379	D	703 676-4300	16596
Sentek Consulting Inc.	7379	C	619 543-9550	16598
Strata Information Group Inc.	7379	D	619 296-0170	16603
Tactical Engrg & Analis Inc (PA)	7379	D	858 573-9869	16604
ATI Systems International Inc.	7381	A	858 715-8484	16622
Elite Show Services Inc.	7381	C	619 574-1589	16641
Guard Management Inc.	7381	C	858 279-8282	16646
Locator Services Inc.	7381	C	619 229-6100	16657
Staff Pro Inc.	7381	A	619 544-1774	16694
Accurate Security Pros Inc.	7382	E	858 271-1155	16714
Brightcloud Inc.	7382	B	858 652-4803	16724
Kratos Public Safety & Security Solutions Inc.	7382	D	858 812-7300	16745
Securitas Technology Corp.	7382	D	858 812-7349	16752
Symons Fire Protection Inc.	7382	C	619 588-6364	16756
Affinity Auto Programs Inc.	7389	B	858 643-9324	16769
Alorica Customer Care Inc.	7389	D	619 298-7103	16771
Beaumont Nielsen Marine Inc.	7389	E	619 223-2628	16791
Cetera Financial Group Inc (PA)	7389	B	866 489-3100	16801
County of San Diego.	7389	B	858 694-2960	16808
Interior Specialists Inc.	7389	B	909 983-5386	16849
Mabie Marketing Group Inc.	7389	C	858 279-5585	16865
Phone Ware Inc.	7389	B	858 530-8550	16903
Puff Global Inc.	7389	D	619 520-3499	16910
Rgn-San Diego I LLC	7389	C	619 344-2500	16917
San Dego Cnvntion Ctr Corp Inc (PA)	7389	B	619 782-4388	16921
Scilex Pharmaceuticals Inc (HQ)	7389	F	949 441-2270	16923
Shinwoo P&C Usa Inc (HQ)	7389	B	619 407-7164	16927
Skdy of San Diego Inc.	7389	E	858 552-9033	16931
Strategic Operations Inc.	7389	C	858 244-0559	16935
Tecma Group LLC	7389	A	619 918-7371	16942
UPS Store Inc (HQ)	7389	B	858 455-8800	16955
Vastek Inc.	7389	C	925 948-5701	16956
Vintage Design LLC	7389	D	858 695-9544	16957
Visual Pak San Diego LLC	7389	C	847 689-1000	16958
Washington Inventory Service.	7389	A	858 565-8111	16963
Wheat Group Inc.	7389	E	858 673-2070	16967
Modern Parking Inc.	7521	C	619 233-0412	16996
San Diego Saturn Retailers Inc.	7532	D	858 373-3001	17016
City Chevrolet of San Diego.	7538	C	619 276-6171	17031
Pro Circuits Manufacturing Inc.	7629	E	858 899-4747	17070
Schroff Inc.	7629	C	858 740-2400	17072
Action Cleaning Corporation.	7699	E	619 233-1881	17111
Chromalloy San Diego Corp.	7699	C	858 877-2800	17119
Upwind Blade Solutions Inc.	7699	B	866 927-3142	17161
Western Pump Inc (PA)	7699	D	619 239-9988	17163
Edwards Theatres Circuit Inc.	7832	C	858 635-7716	17295
Old Globe Theatre.	7922	B	619 234-5623	17322
San Diego Repertory Theatre Inc.	7922	D	619 231-3586	17327
San Diego Opera Association.	7922	C	619 232-5911	17328
San Diego Opera Association.	7922	C	619 232-5911	17329
Inmotion Entrmt Group LLC.	7929	C	904 332-0459	17341
San Dego Symphony Orchstra Ass.	7929	C	619 235-0800	17349
San Diego Symphony Foundation.	7929	C	619 235-0800	17350
California Sportservice Inc.	7941	B	619 795-5000	17366
City of San Diego.	7941	B	619 795-5000	17367
Padres LP.	7941	A	619 795-5000	17380
Socal Sportsnet LLC.	7941	A	619 795-5000	17382
Salvation Army Ray & Joan.	7991	B	619 287-5762	17413
TW Holdings Inc.	7991	A	858 217-8750	17418
Seaworld Parks & Entrmt LLC.	7996	D	619 226-3910	17454
Bay Clubs Company LLC.	7997	B	858 509-9933	17464
San Diego State University.	7997	C	619 594-4263	17516
Santaluz Club Inc.	7997	C	858 759-3120	17520
The San Diego Yacht Club.	7997	C	619 221-8400	17530
Westgroup Kona Kai LLC.	7997	D	619 221-8000	17536
Fit Athletic Club.	7999	C	858 592-2440	17552
Marine Corps Community Svcs.	7999	B	858 577-1061	17558
Volume Services Inc.	7999	B	619 525-5800	17578
Yoga Box LLC.	7999	E	619 994-1915	17580
Amn Healthcare Inc (HQ)	8011	B	858 792-0711	17592
Cardionet Inc.	8011	D	619 243-7500	17610
Childrens Spclsts of San Dego (PA)	8011	B	858 576-1700	17619
Curology Inc.	8011	D	617 959-2480	17639
Department of Public Health.	8011	C	619 338-2493	17641
Family Hlth Ctrs San Diego Inc.	8011	B	619 515-2526	17652
Family Hlth Ctrs San Diego Inc.	8011	B	619 515-2435	17653
Family Hlth Ctrs San Diego Inc.	8011	B	619 515-2400	17654
Family Hlth Ctrs San Diego Inc.	8011	B	619 515-2444	17656
Imaging Hlthcare Spcalists LLC.	8011	C	619 229-2299	17669
La Maestra Family Clinic Inc (PA)	8011	C	619 584-1612	17703
MainStay Medical Limited.	8011	D	619 261-9144	17711
NAVY UNITED STATES DEPARTMENT.	8011	B	858 577-9849	17722
Operation Samahan Inc.	8011	C	619 477-4451	17731
Pediatric Nrology Therapeutics.	8011	C	858 304-6440	17736
San Dego Pthlgsts Med Group In.	8011	C	619 297-4012	17756
San Diego Family Care (PA)	8011	D	858 279-0925	17757
Sharp RES-Stealy Med Group Inc.	8011	C	619 221-9547	17766
Sleep Data Services LLC.	8011	C	619 299-6299	17767
Southern Cal Prmnnte Med Group.	8011	B	619 528-5000	17785
Southern Cal Prmnnte Med Group.	8011	C	619 516-6000	17787
Ucsd Neuroscience Center.	8011	C	619 287-7661	17813
Family Hlth Ctrs San Diego Inc.	8021	B	619 515-2300	17837
Lance Rygg Dental Corp.	8021	C	858 492-9300	17838
Chirotech Inc.	8041	C	619 528-0040	17854
James G Meyers & Associates.	8042	E	858 622-2165	17855
Locums Unlimited LLC.	8049	A	619 550-3763	17868
Emeritus Corporation.	8051	C	858 292-8044	17932
Five Star Senior Living Inc.	8051	C	858 673-6300	17952
La Jolla Skilled Inc.	8051	C	858 625-8700	17984
Mission Hills Health Care Inc.	8051	D	619 297-4086	18015
Point Loma Rhblitation Ctr LLC.	8051	C	619 308-3200	18032
Bernardo Hts Healthcare Inc.	8059	C	858 673-0101	18113
Crestwood Behavioral Hlth Inc.	8059	C	619 481-6790	18121
San Dego Ctr For Chldren Fndti (PA)	8059	D	858 277-9550	18154
Alvarado Hospital LLC (DH)	8062	C	619 287-3270	18175
Alvarado Hospital Med Ctr Inc.	8062	A	619 287-3270	18176
Kaiser Foundation Hospitals.	8062	C	619 528-2583	18308
Kaiser Foundation Hospitals.	8062	C	858 573-1504	18309
NAVY UNITED STATES DEPARTMENT.	8062	A	619 532-6400	18350
Palomar Health.	8062	B	858 675-5218	18362
Rady Childrens Hosp & Hlth Ctr (PA)	8062	A	858 576-1700	18403
Rady Chld Hospital-San Diego (HQ)	8062	A	858 576-1700	18404
Scripps Clinic.	8062	C	858 794-1250	18424
Scripps Health (PA)	8062	A	800 727-4777	18425
Scripps Health.	8062	C	619 294-8111	18426
Scripps Health.	8062	C	858 271-9770	18427
Scripps Health.	8062	D	619 294-8111	18431
Scripps Mercy Hospital.	8062	C	619 294-8111	18433
Sharp Chula Vista Medical Ctr.	8062	D	858 499-5150	18436
Sharp Healthcare.	8062	C	858 939-5454	18439
Sharp Healthcare Aco LLC.	8062	C	619 398-2988	18440
Sharp Healthcare Aco LLC.	8062	C	619 446-1575	18441
Sharp Healthcare Aco LLC.	8062	A	858 627-5152	18442
Sharp Memorial Hospital (HQ)	8062	A	858 939-3636	18443
University Cal San Diego.	8062	C	619 543-6170	18485
University Cal San Diego.	8062	A	619 543-6654	18486
Vibra Healthcare LLC.	8062	C	619 260-8300	18499
County of San Diego.	8063	C	619 692-8200	18512
Sharp Memorial Hospital.	8063	B	858 278-4110	18518
Sharp McDonald Center.	8069	A	858 637-6920	18532
Biora Therapeutics Inc (PA)	8071	D	855 293-2639	18539
Biotheranostics Inc (HQ)	8071	E	877 886-6739	18540
Decipher Corp.	8071	D	888 975-4540	18545
DR Systems Inc.	8071	C	858 625-3344	18546
Epic Sciences Inc.	8071	C	858 356-6610	18548
Sequenom Ctr For Mlclar Mdcine.	8071	B	858 202-9051	18564
ABC Home Health Care Llc.	8082	C	858 455-5000	18578
Accentcare Inc.	8082	B	858 576-7410	18579

Employee Codes: A=Over 500 employees, B=251-500
C=101-250, D=51-100, E=20-50, F=10-19, G=1-9

2024 Southern California
Business Directory and Buyers Guide

© Mergent Inc. 1-800-342-5647

1433

GEOGRAPHIC

	SIC	EMP	PHONE	ENTRY#
Accredited Nursing Services	8082	C	818 986-1234	18583
All Valley Home Hlth Care Inc	8082	D	619 276-8001	18588
Bridge Home Health LLC	8082	D	858 277-5200	18597
Buena Vista MGT Svcs LLC	8082	C	619 450-4300	18599
Faith Jones & Associates Inc **(PA)**	8082	C	619 297-9601	18613
Firstat Nursing Services Inc	8082	C	619 220-7600	18614
Interim Hlthcare San Diego LLC	8082	B	858 576-9501	18620
Maxim Healthcare Services Inc	8082	B	619 299-9350	18627
Mission HM Hlth San Diego LLC	8082	D	619 757-2700	18629
San Diego Hospice & Palliative Care	8082	A	619 688-1600	18640
Rai Care Ctrs Sthern Cal II LL	8092	C	619 229-1070	18664
Center For Atism RES Evltion S	8093	C	858 444-8823	18675
Centro De Salud De La Comuni **(PA)**	8093	D	619 428-4463	18678
Planned Prnthood of PCF Sthwes **(PA)**	8093	D	619 881-4500	18708
Planned Prnthood of PCF Sthwes	8093	D	619 881-4652	18710
Aya Locums Services Inc	8099	A	866 687-7390	18743
Cortica Healthcare Inc	8099	B	858 304-6440	18756
Examone World Wide Inc	8099	D	619 299-3926	18763
Kelly Thomas MD Ucsd Hlth Care	8099	C	619 543-2885	18774
Provisio Medical Inc	8099	F	508 740-9940	18792
San Diego Blood Bank **(PA)**	8099	C	619 400-8132	18802
Synergy Orthpd Specialists Inc	8099	D	858 450-7118	18810
Aldridge Pite LLP	8111	B	858 750-7700	18818
County of San Diego	8111	C	619 531-4040	18842
Fish & Richardson PC	8111	C	858 678-5070	18854
Gordon Rees Scully Mansukhani	8111	C	619 696-6700	18864
Higgs Fletcher & Mack Llp	8111	C	619 236-1551	18868
Latham & Watkins LLP	8111	B	858 523-5400	18892
Lewis Brsbois Bsgard Smith LLP	8111	C	619 233-1006	18897
Mintz Levin Cohn Ferris GL	8111	D	858 314-1500	18908
Morrison & Foerster LLP	8111	B	858 720-5100	18912
Paul Hastings LLP	8111	D	858 458-3000	18923
Procopio Cory Hargreaves & Savitch LLP **(PA)**	8111	C	619 238-1900	18928
Robbins Geller Rudman Dowd LLP **(PA)**	8111	B	619 231-1058	18933
Sdcda	8111	C	619 459-9632	18938
Seltzer Cplan McMhon Vtek A La **(PA)**	8111	C	619 685-3003	18939
Sheppard Mllin Rchter Hmpton L	8111	D	619 338-6500	18941
Sheppard Mllin Rchter Hmpton L	8111	D	858 720-8900	18942
Wells Media Group Inc **(PA)**	8111	F	619 584-1100	18955
Wingert Grbing Brbker Jstkie L	8111	D	619 232-8151	18957
Withers Bergman LLP	8111	B	203 974-0412	18958
San Diego Cmnty College Dst	8211	C	619 388-4850	18983
San Diego State University	8221	D	619 594-1515	18992
San Diego Cmnty College Dst	8222	D	619 388-3453	18996
San Diego Cmnty College Dst	8222	A	619 388-2600	18997
Vista Hill Foundation	8299	D	619 281-5511	19015
American Red Cross San Dg-Mpri **(PA)**	8322	D	858 309-1200	19022
Aya Living Inc	8322	C	619 446-6469	19026
Behavral Hlthcare Slutions Inc	8322	C	858 573-2600	19027
County of San Diego	8322	A	619 515-8202	19067
Essence of America	8322	E	312 805-9365	19078
G&L Penasquitos Inc	8322	A	858 538-0802	19084
Jewish Family Svc San Diego **(PA)**	8322	C	858 637-3000	19102
Neighborhood House Association **(PA)**	8322	B	858 715-2642	19115
New Alternatives Incorporated	8322	A	619 863-5855	19116
Project Concern International **(PA)**	8322	C	858 279-9690	19128
San Dego Second Chance Program	8322	E	619 266-2506	19133
San Dg-Mprial Cnties Dvlpmntal **(PA)**	8322	B	858 576-2996	19134
Social Advctes For Yuth San De	8322	C	619 283-9624	19141
Toward Maximum Independence **(PA)**	8322	C	858 467-0600	19146
Turning Point For God	8322	D	619 258-3600	19148
Vista Hill Foundation	8322	D	619 266-0166	19155
Options For All Inc	8331	B	858 565-9870	19189
Harmonium Inc **(PA)**	8351	C	858 684-3080	19212
Kare Klub	8351	C	858 538-5437	19213
Navy Exchange Service Command	8351	D	619 556-7466	19222
Atria Management Company LLC	8361	C	619 326-0190	19238
Casa De Las Campanas Inc **(PA)**	8361	C	858 451-9152	19245
Collwood Ter Stellar Care Inc	8361	D	619 287-2920	19250
Independent Options Inc	8361	D	858 598-5260	19276
ARC of San Diego **(PA)**	8399	C	619 685-1175	19314
San Diego Rescue Mission Inc **(PA)**	8399	D	619 819-1880	19340
Sharp Healthcare Foundation	8399	C	858 499-4800	19341
New Childrens Museum	8412	C	619 233-8792	19358
Reuben H Fleet Science Center	8412	C	619 238-1233	19361
San Diego Museum of Art	8412	D	619 696-1909	19362
Zoological Society San Diego **(PA)**	8422	A	619 231-1515	19369
Zoological Society San Diego	8422	C	619 744-3325	19371
Zoological Society San Diego	8422	C	619 231-1515	19372
Electra Owners Assoc	8611	C	619 234-3310	19377
San Diego Assn Governments **(PA)**	8611	C	619 699-1900	19384
Medimpact Hlthcare Systems Inc **(HQ)**	8621	C	858 566-2727	19397
Sharp Community Medical Group	8621	C	858 499-4525	19403
Interntional Un Oper Engineers	8631	A	619 295-3186	19411
Armed Services YMCA of USA	8641	C	858 751-5755	19423
Girl Scuts San Dg-Mprial Cncil **(PA)**	8641	D	619 610-0751	19448
Urban Corps San Diego County	8641	C	619 235-6884	19468
Veterans Med RES Fndtion San D	8641	C	858 642-3080	19470
YMCA of San Diego County	8641	C	619 428-1168	19478
YMCA of San Diego County	8641	B	619 280-9622	19481
YMCA of San Diego County	8641	C	619 281-8313	19483
YMCA of San Diego County	8641	C	619 226-8888	19484
YMCA of San Diego County	8641	C	619 264-0144	19485
YMCA of San Diego County	8641	C	619 521-3055	19486
YMCA of San Diego County	8641	B	619 298-3576	19488
YMCA of San Diego County **(PA)**	8641	C	858 292-9622	19491
Morris Crullo World Evangelism **(PA)**	8661	D	858 277-2200	19504
Affinity Development Group Inc	8699	C	858 643-9324	19509
Assocted Stdnts San Dego State **(PA)**	8699	A	619 594-0234	19511
Assocted Stdnts San Dego State	8699	C	619 594-5200	19512
Automobile Club Southern Cal	8699	C	858 483-4960	19513
Automobile Club Southern Cal	8699	D	619 233-1000	19514
Ausgar Technologies Inc	8711	C	855 428-7427	19550
Bae Systems Maritime Engineering &	8711	B	619 238-1000	19551
Bit Medtech LLC	8711	D	858 613-1200	19554
DMS Facility Services LLC	8711	A	858 560-4191	19576
Encore Semi Inc	8711	D	858 225-4993	19582
Engineering Partners Inc	8711	D	858 824-1761	19583
Enginring Sftwr Sys Sltons Inc **(PA)**	8711	D	619 338-0380	19584
Epsilon Systems Sltons Mssion	8711	D	619 702-1700	19585
Epsilon Systems Solutions Inc **(PA)**	8711	C	619 702-1700	19586
Forward Slope Incorporated **(PA)**	8711	D	619 299-4400	19594
Geocon Incorporated	8711	D	858 558-6900	19599
Glenn A Rick Engrg & Dev Co **(PA)**	8711	C	619 291-0708	19600
Hntb Corporation	8711	C	619 684-6586	19605
Indus Technology Inc	8711	C	619 299-2555	19613
Kleinfelder Inc **(HQ)**	8711	C	619 831-4600	19631
Kleinfelder Associates	8711	C	619 831-4600	19632
Kleinfelder Group Inc **(PA)**	8711	C	619 831-4600	19633
Kratos Tech Trning Sltions Inc **(HQ)**	8711	D	858 812-7300	19635
Naval Facilities Engineer Comm	8711	D	619 532-1158	19654
Nv5 Inc	8711	C	858 385-0500	19656
P2s Inc	8711	C	562 497-2999	19660
Parsons Government Svcs Inc	8711	B	619 685-0085	19665
Photon Research Associates Inc	8711	C	858 455-9741	19671
Quartus Engineering Inc **(PA)**	8711	C	858 875-6000	19675
Rock West Composites Inc	8711	E	858 537-6260	19680
Sabre Systems Inc	8711	D	619 528-2226	19683
San Diego Composites Inc	8711	C	858 751-0450	19684
San Diego Services LLC	8711	C	858 654-0102	19685
SC Wright Construction Inc	8711	B	619 698-6909	19686
Sep Group Inc	8711	E	858 876-4621	19688
Serco Inc	8711	C	858 569-8979	19689
Tri Star Engineering Inc	8711	D	619 710-8038	19708
VT Milcom Inc	8711	C	619 424-9024	19716
Architectural Mtls USA Inc	8712	C	888 219-2126	19724
Austin Veum Rbbins Prtners Inc **(PA)**	8712	D	619 231-1960	19725
NTD Architects	8712	D	858 565-4440	19739
Baker Tilly Us LLP	8721	B	858 597-4100	19755
Considine Cnsdine An Accntncy	8721	C	619 231-1977	19763
Deloitte & Touche LLP	8721	A	619 232-6500	19766
Ernst & Young LLP	8721	C	858 535-7200	19775
LLP Moss Adams	8721	D	858 627-1400	19790
Optima Office Inc	8721	D	858 361-0481	19799
Signature Analytics LLC	8721	C	888 284-3842	19804
Tgg Accounting	8721	D	760 697-1033	19807
Acea Biosciences Inc	8731	D	858 724-0928	19812
Agouron Pharmaceuticals Inc	8731	C	858 455-3200	19815
Alimentiv US Inc	8731	D	858 356-5665	19817
Allele Bio & Pharmaceuticals	8731	C	858 410-0299	19818
Ansun Biopharma Inc	8731	E	858 452-2631	19820
Arcturus Therapeutics Inc	8731	C	858 900-2660	19822
Bioduro LLC **(PA)**	8731	E	858 529-6600	19825
Biolegend Inc **(HQ)**	8731	C	858 455-9588	19826
Biolegend Cns Inc	8731	E	781 915-5200	19827
Cibus Global Ltd	8731	D	858 450-0008	19830
Dermtech Operations Inc	8731	B	866 450-4223	19832
Ebioscience Inc	8731	C	858 642-2058	19835
General Atomics	8731	D	858 455-4141	19841
General Atomics	8731	D	858 676-7100	19842
General Atomics	8731	D	858 455-4000	19843
Halozyme Inc	8731	C	858 794-8889	19845
Hii Fleet Support Group LLC	8731	B	858 522-6319	19846
Inova Diagnostics Inc **(HQ)**	8731	B	858 586-9900	19847
Leidos Inc	8731	D	858 826-6000	19852
Leidos Inc	8731	C	858 826-9416	19853

Mergent email: customerrelations@mergent.com
1434

2024 Southern California
Business Directory and Buyers Guide

(P-0000) Products & Services Section entry number
(PA)=Parent Co (HQ)=Headquarters (DH)=Div Headquarters

	SIC	EMP	PHONE	ENTRY#
Leidos Inc	8731	C	703 676-4300	19855
Leidos Engrg & Sciences LLC	8731	C	619 542-3130	19856
M&B Sciences Inc	8731	E	858 812-8735	19857
Maravai Lf Scnces Holdings LLC (HQ)	8731	C	650 697-3600	19858
Novartis Inst For Fnctnal Gnmi	8731	E	858 812-1500	19866
Reveal Biosciences	8731	D	858 274-3663	19873
Sequenom Inc (HQ)	8731	D	858 202-9000	19875
Tanvex Biopharma Usa Inc (PA)	8731	C	858 210-4100	19879
Tnk Therapeutics Inc (HQ)	8731	C	858 210-3700	19884
Trilink Biotechnologies LLC	8731	C	800 863-6801	19885
Turning Point Therapeutics Inc	8731	D	858 926-5251	19886
Wildcat Discovery Tech Inc	8731	C	858 550-1980	19889
General Atomics (HQ)	8732	A	858 455-2810	19892
Luth Research Inc (PA)	8732	B	619 234-5884	19905
Quintiles Pacific Incorporated	8732	B	858 552-3400	19911
Soleil Communications LLC	8732	C	619 624-2888	19912
Biosplice Therapeutics Inc	8733	D	858 926-2900	19918
Healthpoint Capital LLC (PA)	8733	C	212 935-7780	19926
Institute For Defense Analyses	8733	C	858 622-5439	19929
Mitre Corporation	8733	D	619 758-7818	19936
Nanocomposix LLC	8733	D	858 565-4227	19937
Peraton Technology Svcs Inc	8733	F	571 313-6000	19939
Takeda Dev Ctr Americas Inc (HQ)	8733	C	858 622-8528	19946
Viacyte Inc	8733	C	858 455-3708	19952
Whittier Inst For Diabetes	8733	C	877 944-8843	19953
Catalent San Diego Inc	8734	C	858 805-6383	19961
Intertek Usa Inc	8734	C	858 558-2599	19975
Millennium Health LLC	8734	B	877 451-3534	19977
Phamatech Incorporated	8734	C	888 635-5840	19980
Activcare Living Inc (PA)	8741	C	858 565-4424	19988
Allegis Residential Svcs Inc	8741	D	858 430-5700	19991
Azul Hospitality Group Inc	8741	C	619 223-4200	20001
Hotel Managers Group Llc	8741	B	858 673-1534	20039
JC Resorts LLC	8741	B	760 944-1936	20043
JC Resorts LLC	8741	C	858 675-8500	20044
Ka Management II Inc	8741	D	858 404-6080	20047
Premier Hlthcare Solutions Inc	8741	C	858 569-8629	20079
Scripps Clinic Med Group Inc	8741	C	858 554-9000	20091
Solpac Construction Inc	8741	C	619 296-6247	20096
Sunroad Asset Management Inc	8741	D	858 362-8500	20102
Whiskey Girl	8741	C	619 236-1616	20119
AA Blocks LLC	8742	C	858 523-8231	20123
Accenture Federal Services LLC	8742	A	619 574-2400	20124
Artemis Consulting LLC	8742	D	619 573-6328	20134
Blue Sky Elearn LLC	8742	E	877 925-8375	20142
Co-Production Intl Inc	8742	A	619 429-4344	20153
Covario Inc	8742	C	858 397-1500	20158
Eastern Goldfields Inc	8742	C	619 497-2555	20165
Ecg Management Consultant	8742	C	206 689-2200	20166
Fairway Technologies LLC (PA)	8742	D	858 454-4471	20170
Gcorp Consulting	8742	C	619 587-3160	20176
Independent Fincl Group LLC	8742	C	858 436-3180	20184
Lotus Workforce LLC	8742	A	480 264-0773	20191
Lpl Holdings Inc (HQ)	8742	D	858 450-9606	20192
Mapp Digital Us LLC	8742	E	619 342-4340	20194
Medical Management Cons Inc	8742	A	858 587-0609	20196
Mindlance Inc	8742	A	858 433-9298	20201
One Heart Worldwide	8742	D	415 379-4762	20214
Power Digital Marketing Inc (PA)	8742	B	619 501-1211	20223
Swinerton Renewable Energy	8742	D	858 622-4040	20252
Tacna International Corp	8742	F	619 661-1261	20254
Vistage International Inc (PA)	8742	D	858 523-6800	20268
Havas Formula LLC	8743	D	619 234-0345	20284
Chugach Government Svcs Inc	8744	B	858 578-0276	20291
Techflow Inc (PA)	8744	C	858 412-8000	20301
Aecom Usa Inc	8748	C	858 947-7144	20311
Aptim Corp	8748	B	619 239-1690	20315
BE Smith Inc	8748	B	913 341-9116	20316
Cask Nx LLC	8748	C	858 232-8900	20324
Center For Sustainable Energy	8748	D	858 244-1177	20326
Environmental Science Assoc	8748	C	858 638-0900	20335
Geocon Consultants Inc (PA)	8748	D	858 558-6900	20338
Humano LLC	8748	D	844 448-6266	20345
Icf Jones & Stokes Inc	8748	D	858 578-8964	20348
Johnson Johnson Innovation LLC	8748	A	858 242-1504	20356
Ninyo More Gtchncal Envmtl Scn (PA)	8748	D	858 576-1000	20367
Project Design Consultants LLC	8748	D	619 235-6471	20372
Recon Environmental Inc (PA)	8748	D	619 308-9333	20375
Sanyo North America Corp	8748	B	619 661-1134	20377
Source 44 LLC	8748	C	877 916-6337	20381
Tangoe-PI Inc	8748	C		20384
Team Risk MGT Strategies LLC	8748	A	877 767-8728	20385
Veterans EZ Info Inc	8748	C	866 839-1329	20388
Overseas Service Corporation	8999	C	858 408-0751	20398
County of San Diego	9199	D	858 505-6100	20410
San Diego Unified Port Dst	9221	C	619 686-6585	20411

SAN DIMAS, CA - Los Angeles County

	SIC	EMP	PHONE	ENTRY#
Walton Construction Inc	1522	D	909 267-7777	478
Pacific Systems Interiors Inc	1742	C	310 436-6820	989
Organic Milling Inc (PA)	2043	D	800 638-8686	1423
Organic Milling Corporation	2099	E	909 305-0185	1958
Organic Milling Corporation (PA)	2099	C	909 599-0961	1959
Westin Automotive Products Inc (PA)	2396	E	626 960-6762	2542
M724 Inc	2514	F	951 314-1333	2833
Western PCF Stor Solutions Inc (PA)	2542	D	909 451-0303	2999
Gilead Palo Alto Inc	2834	C	909 394-4000	4118
Gilead Sciences Inc	2834	E	909 394-4000	4120
Hagen-Renaker Inc (PA)	3269	D	909 599-2341	5385
Aircraft Stamping Company Inc	3444	E	323 283-1239	6182
Danrich Welding Co Inc	3444	E	562 634-4811	6223
Gms Elevator Services Inc	3534	E	909 599-3904	6966
Magor Mold LLC	3544	D	909 592-3663	7081
Thunderbird Industries Inc	3544	E	909 394-1633	7101
Vertex Diamond Tool Co Inc	3545	F	909 599-1129	7138
Bluelab Corporation Usa Inc	3569	E	909 599-1940	7383
Sypris Data Systems Inc (HQ)	3572	E	909 962-9400	7489
Kap Manufacturing Inc	3599	E	909 599-2525	7894
AC Propulsion Inc	3621	E	909 592-5399	8133
Sigtronics Corporation	3669	E	909 305-9399	8626
Landmark Electronics Inc	3679	E	626 967-2857	9077
Wavestream Corporation (HQ)	3679	C	909 599-9080	9138
Young Engineering & Mfg Inc (PA)	3823	E	909 394-3225	10172
Hamilton Sundstrand Corp	3826	C	909 593-5300	10261
Hamilton Sundstrand Spc Systms	3829	D	909 288-5300	10370
Elba Jewelry Inc	3911	F	909 394-5803	10901
Medic-1 Ambulance Service Inc	4119	D	909 592-8840	11394
Southern California Edison Co	4911	C	909 592-3757	12059
Southern California Gas Co	4924	C	909 305-8297	12092
American States Water Company (PA)	4941	A	909 394-3600	12114
Recom Group	5065	E	909 599-1370	12696
Smart & Final Stores Inc	5141	B	909 592-2190	13212
Southern Cal Prmnnte Med Group	6324	C	909 394-2505	14500
Second Image National LLC (PA)	7334	C	800 229-7477	15652
Industrial Janitor Service	7349	D	818 782-5658	15714
Signature Select Personnel LLC	7361	B	626 940-3351	15894
Webmetro	7372	C	909 599-8885	16418
Automatic Data Processing Inc	7374	C	800 225-5237	16483
Financial Ctrs Coop Inc	7389	C	909 751-1213	16825
National Hot Rod Association (PA)	7948	C	626 914-4761	17387
Raging Waters Group Inc	7996	A	909 802-2200	17451
New Spirit Naturals Inc (PA)	8011	E	909 592-4445	17724
Toan D Nguyen DDS Inc	8021	D	909 599-3398	17848
Emeritus Corporation	8051	C	909 394-0304	17936
Kaiser Foundation Hospitals	8062	C	909 394-2530	18296
Prime Hlthcare Svcs - San Dmas	8062	B	909 599-6811	18393
Qtc Management Inc (DH)	8099	C	800 682-9701	18798
Qtc Mdcal Group Inc A Med Corp	8099	A	800 260-1515	18799
Legal Solutions Holdings Inc	8111	C	800 244-3495	18894
Med-Legal LLC	8111	C	626 653-5160	18905
Prime Health Care	8351	C	909 394-2727	19226
McKinley Childrens Center Inc (PA)	8361	C	909 599-1227	19285
Thorpe Technologies Inc (DH)	8711	E	562 903-8230	19705
Brault	8721	C	626 447-0296	19756
Ego Inc	8721	C	626 447-0296	19770

SAN FERNANDO, CA - Los Angeles County

	SIC	EMP	PHONE	ENTRY#
Bernards Builders Inc	1522	B	818 898-1521	467
La Solar Group Inc	1711	D	818 373-0077	784
Karoun Dairies Inc (PA)	2022	E	818 767-7000	1255
American Bottling Company	2086	B	818 898-1471	1677
Bluecan Company LLC	2086	E	818 450-3290	1687
Pepsi-Cola Metro Btlg Co Inc	2086	A	818 898-3829	1711
Fresh & Ready Foods LLC (PA)	2099	D	818 837-7600	1898
Lehman Foods Inc	2099	D	818 837-7600	1933
Mr Tortilla Inc	2099	E	818 233-8932	1951
New Haven Companies Inc	2299	D	818 686-7020	2142
Wyndham Collection LLC	2434	E	888 522-8476	2686
Newco International Inc	2511	E	818 834-7100	2783
Airo Industries Company	2531	E	818 838-1008	2921
Abex Display Systems Inc (PA)	2653	C	800 537-0231	3077
Araca Merchandise LP	2759	D	818 743-5400	3734
Puretek Corporation	2834	E	818 361-3316	4215
Blue Cross Beauty Products Inc	2844	E	818 896-8681	4383
All American Products Group Inc	2899	E	818 361-0059	4594
J Miller Co Inc	3053	E	818 837-0181	4736

Employee Codes: A=Over 500 employees, B=251-500
C=101-250, D=51-100, E=20-50, F=10-19, G=1-9

2024 Southern California
Business Directory and Buyers Guide

© Mergent Inc. 1-800-342-5647

1435

GEOGRAPHIC

	SIC	EMP	PHONE	ENTRY#
Spira Manufacturing Corp	3053	E	818 764-8222	4746
C A Schroeder Inc **(PA)**	3296	E	818 365-9561	5552
American Intrntnl-Steel Cast D	3365	E	818 365-8000	5782
Art Bronze Inc	3366	F	818 897-2222	5801
J & M Products Inc	3429	D	818 837-0205	5924
Bellows Mfg & RES Inc	3441	E	818 838-1333	5996
Haimetal Duct Inc	3444	E	818 768-2315	6249
Triumph Precision Products	3451	F	818 897-4700	6425
TL Shield & Associates Inc	3534	E	818 509-8228	6967
Metromedia Technologies Inc	3577	E	818 552-6500	7550
General Production Services	3599	E	818 365-4211	7846
W Machine Works Inc	3599	E	818 890-8049	8069
Topaz Lighting Company LLC	3646	E	818 838-3123	8335
Skaug Truck Body Works	3713	F	818 365-9123	9333
Frazier Aviation Inc	3728	E	818 898-1998	9695
One Step Gps LLC	3812	E	818 659-2031	10043
J L Shepherd and Assoc Inc	3829	E	818 898-2361	10376
Valeda Company LLC	3842	E	800 421-8700	10719
Laser Technologies & Services LLC	3861	D		10872
Dg-Displays LLC	3993		877 358-5976	11109
Ricon Corp	3999	E	818 267-3000	11276
Mv Transportation Inc	4111	C	323 666-0856	11340
Frontier California Inc	4813	B	818 365-0542	11880
Jme Inc **(PA)**	5063	D	201 896-8600	12599
Ahi Investment Inc **(DH)**	5199	E	818 979-0030	13525
Cousins Foods LLC	5411	E	818 767-3842	13695
Don Whittemore Corp	5812	E	818 994-0111	14003
American Fruits & Flavors LLC	7299	B	818 899-9574	15497
Universal Mail Delivery Svc **(PA)**	7331	C	818 365-3144	15639
A Thread Ahead Inc	7389	E	818 837-1984	16764
Industrial Stitchtech Inc	7389	C	818 361-6319	16845
De La Mare Engineering Inc	7819	C	818 365-9208	17247
Child Care Resource Center Inc	8351	C	818 837-0097	19204
All State Association Inc	8611	C	877 425-2558	19373

SAN GABRIEL, CA - Los Angeles County

	SIC	EMP	PHONE	ENTRY#
Black Drop Coffee Inc	2095	F	323 742-5666	1815
Comfort Industries Inc	2231	E	562 692-8288	2048
Lotus Orient Corp **(PA)**	2335	F	626 285-5796	2285
Asia-Pacific California Inc	2711	E	626 281-8500	3257
BF Suma Pharmaceuticals Inc	2834	E	626 285-8366	4070
Diamond Wipes Intl Inc	2844	D	626 309-0033	4403
Multi-Link International Corp	3086	E	562 941-5380	4894
Hsiao & Montano Inc	3161	E	626 588-2528	5289
Taotao Manufacturer Inc	3999	F	626 688-9880	11294
Inveserve Corporation	6531	D	626 458-3435	14814
Informtion Rfrral Fdrtion of L	7299	D	626 350-1841	15510
San Gabriel Country Club	7997	D	626 287-9671	17517
San Gbriel Ambltory Srgery Ctr	8011	C	626 300-5300	17758
Country Villa Service Corp	8059	C	626 285-2165	18118
Longwood Management Corp	8059	C	626 289-3763	18141
Ahmc Healthcare Inc **(PA)**	8062	C	626 943-7526	18168
San Gabriel Valley Medical Ctr	8062	A	626 289-5454	18414
Ahmc Healthcare Inc	8099	B	626 248-3452	18737

SAN JACINTO, CA - Riverside County

	SIC	EMP	PHONE	ENTRY#
Skyline Homes Inc	2451	C	951 654-9321	2742
Edelbrock Foundry Corp	3363	C	951 654-6677	5758
Matthews International Corp	3366	F	951 537-6615	5804
J Talley Corporation **(PA)**	3446	D	951 654-2123	6359
Rama Corporation	3567	E	951 654-7351	7372
MTI De Baja Inc	3812	C	951 654-2333	10004
Agri-Empire	5148	C	951 654-7311	13312
Soboba Band Luiseno Indians	7389	A	951 665-1000	16932
Borrego Cmnty Hlth Foundation	8011	C	951 487-8506	17602
Riversd-San Brnrdino Cnty Indi	8011	C	951 654-0803	17752

SAN JUAN CAPISTRANO, CA - Orange County

	SIC	EMP	PHONE	ENTRY#
Devil Mountain Whl Nurs LLC	0181	D	949 496-9356	51
Brightview Landscape Svcs Inc	0781	C	714 546-7843	151
Pioneer Sands LLC	1446	E	949 728-0171	409
Surrounding Elements LLC	2514	E	949 582-9000	2838
Fluidmaster Inc **(PA)**	3089	C	949 728-2000	5030
Conax Usa Inc	3728	C	949 690-4880	9664
Quest Diagnostics Nichols Inst **(HQ)**	3826	A	949 728-4000	10284
Solag Incorporated	4953	A	949 728-1206	12188
Mission Volkswagen Inc	5511	D	949 493-4511	13797
Las Glondrinas Mexican Fd Pdts **(PA)**	5812	F	949 240-3440	14021
Freedom Properties-Hemet LLC	6512	C	949 489-0430	14662
Marriott International Inc	7011	D	949 503-5700	15241
Diamond Peo LLC	7361	C	714 728-5186	15837
Medusind Solutions Inc **(PA)**	7389	D	949 240-8895	16871
Southern Cal Prmnnte Med Group	8011	C	949 234-2139	17793

	SIC	EMP	PHONE	ENTRY#
Endura Healthcare Inc	8051	C	949 487-9500	17939
Ensign Services Inc	8051	D	949 487-9500	17945
Ensign Southland LLC	8051	C	949 487-9500	17946
Grand Avenue Hlth Holdings LLC	8051	D	949 487-9500	17967
Clarient Inc	8071	C	949 445-7300	18542
Nichols Inst Reference Labs **(DH)**	8071	A	949 728-4000	18557
Infospan	8742	A	949 260-9990	20186

SAN LUIS OBISPO, CA - San Luis Obispo County

	SIC	EMP	PHONE	ENTRY#
Mainstream Energy Corporation	1711	B	805 528-9705	791
Rec Solar Commercial Corp	1711	C	844 732-7652	816
Specialty Construction Inc	1731	D	805 543-1706	938
Cattaneo Bros Inc	2013	E	805 543-7188	1215
Courtside Cellars LLC **(PA)**	2084	E	805 782-0500	1619
Taco Works Inc	2096	E	805 541-1556	1833
Sauer Brands Inc	2099	D	805 597-8900	1983
The Hunter Spice Inc	2099	D	805 597-8900	1997
Straight Down Enterprises **(PA)**	2329	E	805 543-3086	2222
Pipsticks Inc	2678	E	805 439-1692	3223
Slo New Times Inc	2711	E	805 546-8208	3325
David B Anderson	2752	E	805 489-0661	3556
Prpco	2752	D	805 543-6844	3672
Ws Packaging-Blake Printery	2752	E	805 543-6844	3715
Promega Biosciences LLC	2833	D	805 544-8524	4013
Myogenix Incorporated	2834	F	800 950-0348	4173
ITW Global Tire Repair Inc	3011	D	805 489-0490	4698
Air-Vol Block Inc	3271	E	805 543-1314	5387
Whitefox Defense Tech Inc	3364	E	805 225-4506	5777
Inspired Flight Tech Inc	3429	E	805 776-3640	5923
Snapnrack Inc	3429	E	877 732-2860	5943
R H Strasbaugh **(PA)**	3541	D	805 541-6424	7019
Entegris Gp Inc	3569	E	805 541-9299	7391
Newlife2 **(PA)**	3569	E	805 549-8093	7401
Next Intent Inc	3599	E	805 781-6755	7954
Revasum Inc	3674	C	805 541-6424	8879
Ultra-Stereo Labs Inc	3699	E	805 549-0161	9264
Empirical Systems Arospc Inc **(PA)**	3721	E	805 474-5900	9521
Stellar Exploration Inc	3761	E	805 459-1425	9903
Edge Autonomy Slo LLC	3812	E	805 544-0932	9972
Crystal Engineering Corp	3823	E	805 595-5477	10127
Imdex Technology Usa LLC	3829	E	805 540-2017	10373
Fziomed Inc **(PA)**	3841	E	805 546-0610	10513
L Spark	3911	C	805 626-0511	10905
Ernie Ball Inc **(PA)**	3931	C	805 544-7726	10923
Kairos Manufacturing Inc	3999	F	805 544-2216	11237
Zoo Med Laboratories Inc	3999	C	805 542-9988	11310
First Transit Inc	4111	C	805 544-2730	11319
San Luis Obspo Rgnal Trnst Aut	4111	D	805 781-4465	11363
San Luis Ambulance Service Inc	4119	C	805 543-2626	11403
Eschat	4812	D	805 541-5044	11849
Ksby Communications LLC	4833	C	805 541-6666	11956
Pacific Gas and Electric Co	4911	C	805 545-4562	12034
Amk Foodservices Inc	5141	C	805 544-7600	13171
Madonna Inn Inc	5461	C	805 543-3000	13720
Apple Farm Collections-Slo Inc **(PA)**	5812	B	805 544-2040	13981
Goodwill Central Coast	5932	C	805 544-0542	14061
Mission Community Bancorp	6021	C	805 782-5000	14170
Guaranteed Rate Inc	6162	C	805 550-6933	14325
Morris Grritano Insur Agcy Inc	6411	D	805 543-6887	14614
Harvest Management Sub LLC	6513	A	805 543-0187	14711
King Ventures	6552	C	805 544-4444	14901
3i Infotech Inc	7371	E	805 544-8327	15951
Dozuki	7372	D	805 464-0573	16229
Lockheed Martin Unmanned	7373	D	805 503-4340	16455
Mindbody Inc **(PA)**	7374	C	877 755-4279	16506
San Luis Obispo Golf Cntry CLB	7997	D	805 543-3400	17518
Bayshore Healthcare Inc	8051	C	805 544-5100	17888
Compass Health Inc	8051	D	805 543-0210	17907
County of San Luis Obispo	8062	C	805 781-4753	18235
French Hospital Medical Center **(DH)**	8062	B	805 543-5353	18262
Sierra Vista Hospital Inc **(HQ)**	8062	A	805 546-7600	18444
Community Action Prtnr San Lui	8093	C	805 544-2478	18681
Community Action Partnership	8322	D	805 541-4122	19046
Tri-Cnties Assn For Dvlpmntlly	8322	C	805 543-2833	19147
United Crbral Plsy Assn San Lu	8322	D	805 543-2039	19151
Community Action Prtnr San Lui	8351	C	805 541-2272	19207
State Bar of California	8621	C	805 544-7551	19404
AME Unmanned Air Systems Inc	8711	D	805 541-4448	19545
Trust Automation Inc	8711	D	805 544-0761	19709
Rrm Design Group **(PA)**	8712	D	805 439-0442	19740
Entegris Inc	8741	C	805 541-9299	20028
Postalio Inc	8742	D	408 616-9284	20222
Rincon Consultants Inc	8748	C	805 547-0900	20376

Mergent email: customerrelations@mergent.com
1436

2024 Southern California
Business Directory and Buyers Guide

(P-0000) Products & Services Section entry number
(PA)=Parent Co (HQ)=Headquarters (DH)=Div Headquarters

	SIC	EMP	PHONE	ENTRY#

SAN MARCOS, CA - San Diego County

	SIC	EMP	PHONE	ENTRY#
Twin Oaks Growers Intl Inc.	0181	E	760 744-5581	72
San Diego Farms LLC	0191	C	760 736-4072	86
Hollandia Dairy Inc (PA)	0241	C	760 744-3222	90
Doose Landscape Incorporated	0782	D	760 591-4500	189
Airx Utility Surveyors Inc (PA)	1623	D	760 480-2347	657
20/20 Plumbing & Heating Inc.	1711	C	760 535-3101	723
Csi Electrical Contractors Inc.	1731	B	760 227-0577	889
Sol Nova Electric LLC	1731	C	833 765-6682	935
Southern Contracting Company.	1731	C	760 744-0760	937
M Bar C Construction Inc.	1791	D	760 744-4131	1108
Clear Sign & Design Inc.	1799	F	760 736-8111	1147
GK Foods Inc.	2041	E	760 752-5230	1410
Manchester Feeds Inc (PA)	2048	F	714 637-7062	1445
California Spirits Company LLC	2086	E	619 677-7066	1689
Fish House Foods Inc.	2092	B	760 597-1270	1805
Equal Exchange Inc.	2095	D	619 335-6259	1818
Culinary Specialties Inc.	2099	C	760 744-8220	1878
Piercan Usa Inc.	2259	E	760 599-4543	2085
Leemarc Industries LLC	2329	E	760 598-0505	2213
Peter Grimm Ltd.	2353	E	800 664-4287	2403
Escondido Roof Truss Co Inc.	2439	F	760 744-4040	2697
Hollywood Chairs Inc.	2511	E	760 471-6600	2775
Showdogs Inc.	2591	E	760 603-2600	3015
San Dieguito Publishers Inc.	2752	D	760 593-5139	3683
Prographics Screenprinting Inc.	2759	E	760 744-4555	3801
Cliniqa Corporation	2836	D	760 744-1900	4310
Cliniqa Corporation	2836	D	760 744-1900	4311
Synsus Prvate Lbel Prtners LLC	2842	C	713 714-0225	4370
Innovative Biosciences Corp	2844	E	760 603-0772	4422
Avista Technologies Inc.	2899	F	760 744-0536	4597
Dispensing Dynamics Intl Inc (PA)	3089	D	626 961-3691	5010
L&S Stone LLC (DH)	3281	E	760 736-3232	5530
Columbia Stone Products.	3291	F	760 737-3215	5539
Winchster Intrcnnect CM CA Inc.	3357	C	800 848-4257	5753
Independent Energy Solutions Inc.	3433	E	760 752-9706	5980
Crown Products Inc.	3444	E	760 471-1188	6222
Electro Tech Coatings Inc.	3479	E	760 746-0292	6701
Craneworks Southwest Inc.	3537	C	760 735-9793	6987
Enstrom Mold & Engineering Inc.	3544	F	760 744-1880	7068
Accu-Seal Sencorpwhite Inc.	3565	F	760 591-9800	7342
Pipeline Products Inc.	3569	F	760 744-8907	7407
Accu-Tech Laser Processing Inc.	3599	E	760 744-6692	7729
Duplan Industries	3599	E	760 744-4047	7821
Ed Stiglic.	3599	F	760 744-7239	7823
K-Tech Machine Inc.	3599	C	800 274-9424	7893
Sullins Electronics Corp.	3643	D	760 744-0125	8276
Action Electronic Assembly Inc.	3672	E	760 510-0003	8641
Hughes Circuits Inc.	3672	C	760 744-0300	8686
Hughes Circuits Inc (PA)	3672	C	760 744-0300	8687
Impact Project Management Inc.	3672	E	760 747-6616	8688
Oncore Manufacturing LLC	3672	C	760 737-6777	8712
Sumitomo Elc Semicdtr Mtls Inc.	3674	C	503 693-3100	8901
Bree Engineering Corp.	3679	E	760 510-4950	9008
Pacific Lasertec LLC (PA)	3699	E	760 539-7169	9238
Dexter Axle Company.	3715	E	760 744-1610	9493
Unique Functional Products.	3715	E	760 744-1610	9496
Spinergy Inc.	3751	D	760 496-2121	9884
Fluid Components Intl LLC (PA)	3823	E	760 744-6950	10132
Aci Medical LLC	3841	E	760 744-4400	10415
Western Sign Systems Inc.	3993	E	760 736-6070	11180
Hexoden Holdings Inc.	3999	D	858 201-3412	11226
Preserved Treescapes International Inc.	3999	E	760 631-6789	11272
Vallecitos Water District Financing (HQ)	4941	C	760 744-0460	12151
Hunter Industries Incorporated (PA)	4971	C	760 744-5240	12213
BIP Corporation.	5065	F	760 591-9822	12646
Tamura Corporation of America (HQ)	5065	E	800 472-6624	12701
Orora Packaging Solutions.	5113	E	760 510-7170	13015
La Provence Inc.	5149	D	760 736-3299	13375
Mack Packaging Inc.	5199	C	760 752-3500	13547
La Fe Tortilla Factory Inc (PA)	5461	E	760 752-8350	13719
Southern Cal Disc Tire Co Inc.	5531	D	760 744-3526	13873
Bestop Baja LLC.	5571	C	760 560-2252	13899
Severson Group LLC	5812	C	760 550-9976	14035
Quilt In A Day Inc.	5961	E	760 591-0929	14101
Centurion Group Inc (PA)	6211	C	760 471-8536	14374
Americare Hlth Retirement Inc.	6512	C	760 744-4484	14652
Whv Resort Group Inc (HQ)	6531	C	760 652-4913	14885
Golden Door Properties LLC	7011	C	760 744-5777	15155
Corkys Pest Control Inc.	7342	D	760 432-8801	15686
Diamond Environmental Svcs LP.	7359	C	760 744-7191	15778
Magic Touch Software Intl.	7372	E	800 714-6490	16299
Rgis LLC.	7389	C	760 736-9241	16916

	SIC	EMP	PHONE	ENTRY#
Control Air Enterprises LLC	7623	B	760 744-2727	17063
Hydralic Systems Cmponents Inc.	7699	E	760 744-9350	17133
North County Health Prj Inc (PA)	8011	C	760 736-6755	17727
Truecare.	8011	C	760 736-6767	17807
Rancho Physical Therapy Inc.	8049	C	760 752-1011	17870
Plum Healthcare Group LLC.	8051	C	760 471-0388	18031
ARC of San Diego.	8399	B	760 740-6800	19313
Olympus Building Services Inc.	8744	A	760 750-4629	20297
Kros-Wise.	8748	C	619 607-2899	20358

SAN MARINO, CA - Los Angeles County

	SIC	EMP	PHONE	ENTRY#
Feihe International Inc (PA)	2023	A	626 757-8885	1269
Huntington Lib Art Cllctons BT	8231	B	626 405-2100	18999

SAN MIGUEL, CA - San Luis Obispo County

	SIC	EMP	PHONE	ENTRY#
Courtside Cellars LLC	2084	F	805 467-2882	1618

SAN PEDRO, CA - Los Angeles County

	SIC	EMP	PHONE	ENTRY#
Cleantek Electric Inc.	1731	E	424 400-3315	881
State Fish Co Inc.	2092	C	310 547-9530	1813
Seaborn Canvas.	2399	E	310 519-1208	2558
Flexline Incorporated.	2796	E	562 921-4141	3853
Tatung Company America Inc (HQ)	3663	D	310 637-2105	8587
Larson Al Boat Shop.	3731	E	310 514-4100	9840
Space Exploration Tech Corp.	3761	C	714 330-8668	9899
Polar Tankers Inc.	4424	C	310 519-8260	11636
Catalina Channel Express Inc (HQ)	4489	C	310 519-7971	11638
So Cal Ship Services.	4489	D	310 519-8411	11640
Marine Terminals Corporation.	4491	B	310 519-2300	11643
Port of Los Angeles.	4491	B	310 732-3508	11645
APM Terminals Pacific LLC.	4731	B	310 221-4000	11741
Crowley Marine Services Inc.	4731	E	310 732-6500	11748
Toll Global Fwdg Scs USA Inc.	4731	D	732 750-9000	11809
Contessa Liquidating Co Inc.	5142	C		13243
Qualy Pak Specialty Foods Inc.	5146	D	310 541-3023	13284
Select Home Warranty Ca Inc.	6351	B	732 835-0110	14537
Meristar San Pedro Hilton LLC.	7011	C	310 514-3344	15246
Spf Capital Real Estate LLC.	7011	D	310 519-8200	15367
Advent Resources Inc.	7371	D	241 241-1500	15957
Little Ssters of The Poor Los.	8051	D	310 548-0625	17995
San Pedro Convalescent HM Inc.	8051	D	310 832-6431	18047
San Pedro Peninsula Hospital.	8062	A	310 832-3311	18418
Healthview Inc (PA)	8361	C	310 638-4113	19269
City of Los Angeles.	9621	A	310 732-3734	20418

SAN SIMEON, CA - San Luis Obispo County

	SIC	EMP	PHONE	ENTRY#
Cavalier Inn Inc.	7011	D	805 927-4688	15109

SAN YSIDRO, CA - San Diego County

	SIC	EMP	PHONE	ENTRY#
Volex Inc.	3089	E	619 205-4900	5243
Volex Inc (HQ)	3089	E	669 444-1740	5244

SANTA ANA, CA - Orange County

	SIC	EMP	PHONE	ENTRY#
Bill & Daves Ldscp Maint Inc.	0781	C	714 850-0213	144
Brightview Landscape Svcs Inc.	0781	B	714 546-7843	152
Mission Ldscp Companies Inc.	0781	C	714 545-9962	168
Nieves Landscape Inc.	0781	C	714 835-7332	171
Southwest Landscape Inc.	0781	C	714 545-1084	179
Landcare USA LLC.	0782	D	949 559-7771	199
Mpl Enterprises Inc.	0782	D	714 545-1717	206
John M Frank Construction Inc.	1542	D	714 210-3600	560
Macro-Z-Technology Company (PA)	1611	D	714 564-1130	631
System Pavers LLC.	1611	C	949 243-2072	650
Sukut Construction LLC.	1623	D	714 540-5351	695
Orange County Services Inc.	1711	D	714 541-9753	803
Pacific Rim Mech Contrs Inc.	1711	C	714 285-2600	804
Sterling Plumbing Inc.	1711	C	714 641-5480	829
Gps Painting Wallcovering Inc.	1721	C	714 730-8904	848
Sun Electric LP.	1731	D	714 210-3744	941
Kirby Industries Inc.	1743	F	714 437-0789	1005
Prime Tech Cabinets Inc.	1751	C	949 757-4900	1022
Trimco Finish Inc.	1751	C	714 708-0300	1024
Reed Thomas Company Inc.	1794	D	714 558-7691	1125
Sukut Construction Inc.	1794	D	714 540-5351	1127
West Lake Food Corporation (PA)	2011	E	714 973-2286	1209
Brothers Intl Desserts (PA)	2024	D	949 655-0080	1295
Stremicks Heritage Foods LLC (HQ)	2026	B	714 775-5000	1316
The Sweet Life Enterprises Inc.	2041	E	949 261-7400	1418
Corbin-Hill Inc.	2051	E	714 966-6695	1459
Gold Coast Baking Company Inc.	2051	E	714 545-2253	1476
D F Stauffer Biscuit Co Inc.	2052	E	714 546-6855	1514
Laguna Cookie Company Inc.	2052	E	714 546-6855	1521
Bonerts Incorporated.	2053	E	714 540-3535	1526

Employee Codes: A=Over 500 employees, B=251-500
C=101-250, D=51-100, E=20-50, F=10-19, G=1-9

2024 Southern California
Business Directory and Buyers Guide

© Mergent Inc. 1-800-342-5647

1437

GEOGRAPHIC

	SIC	EMP	PHONE	ENTRY#
Rich Products Corporation	2053	E	714 338-1145	1529
Kerns Beverages LLC **(DH)**	2086	E	888 655-3767	1699
Sovereign Flavors Inc	2087	E	760 455-0446	1783
DAd Investments	2099	E	714 751-8500	1880
La Copa De Oro	2099	E	714 554-9925	1927
MRS Foods Incorporated **(PA)**	2099	E	714 554-2791	1952
Hook It Up	2111	E	714 600-0100	2005
Print Plus Manufacturing Inc	2262	E		2097
Atlas Carpet Mills Inc	2273	C	323 724-7930	2109
Fabrica International Inc	2273	E	949 261-7181	2114
J Miller Canvas LLC	2295	E	714 641-0052	2126
Cotton Links LLC	2321	E	714 444-4700	2156
Image Apparel For Business Inc	2326	E	714 541-5247	2174
Funny-Bunny Inc **(PA)**	2329	D	714 957-1114	2205
Liquid Graphics Inc	2329	C	949 486-3588	2214
Modern Embroidery Inc	2395	E	714 436-9960	2520
Airborne Systems N Amer CA Inc	2399	C	714 662-1400	2545
Strata Forest Products Inc **(PA)**	2421	E	714 751-0800	2567
Talimar Systems Inc	2531	E	714 557-4884	2938
Abtech Incorporated	2542	E	714 550-9961	2971
Acme United Corporation	2621	E	714 557-2001	3039
Envelopments Inc	2621	E	714 569-3300	3045
OEM Materials & Supplies Inc	2621	E	714 564-9600	3058
Spill Magic Inc	2621	E	714 557-2001	3064
Blower-Dempsay Corporation	2653	E	714 547-9266	3083
Blower-Dempsay Corporation **(PA)**	2653	C	714 481-3800	3084
Heritage Paper Co **(HQ)**	2653	E	714 540-9737	3108
McDonald Packaging Inc	2653	C		3118
A Plus Label Inc	2679	E	714 229-9811	3228
2100 Freedom Inc **(HQ)**	2711	D	714 796-7000	3253
Freedom Communications Inc	2711	A	714 796-7000	3277
B and Z Printing Inc	2752	E	714 892-2000	3516
Documotion Research Inc	2752	F	714 662-3800	3564
DOT Corp	2752	E	714 708-5960	3565
Foster Printing Company Inc	2752	E	714 731-2000	3575
Integrated Communications Inc	2752	E	310 851-8066	3603
Laborlawcenter LLC	2752	E	800 745-9970	3618
Mekong Printing Inc	2752	E	714 558-9595	3633
Metro Digital Printing Inc	2752	E	714 545-8400	3635
Tailgate Printing Inc	2752	D	714 966-3035	3692
Westminster Press Inc	2752	E	714 210-2881	3711
Artisan Nameplate Awards Corp	2759	E	714 556-6222	3735
Blackburn Alton Invstments LLC	2759	E	714 731-2000	3737
Brixen & Sons Inc	2759	E	714 566-1444	3740
Resource Label Group LLC	2759	D	714 619-7100	3805
B J Bindery Inc	2789	D	714 835-7342	3844
Praxair Distribution Inc	2813	E	714 564-7311	3873
Acp Noxtat Inc	2821	F	714 547-5477	3920
Southern California Plas Inc	2821	D	714 751-7084	3971
Tammy Taylor Nails Inc	2821	E	949 250-9287	3977
McGuff Otsurcing Solutions Inc	2834	E	800 603-4795	4164
Robinson Pharma Inc	2834	C	714 241-0235	4224
Robinson Pharma Inc **(PA)**	2834	B	714 241-0235	4225
Robinson Pharma Inc	2834	E	714 241-0235	4226
Helica Biosystems Inc	2835	F	714 578-7830	4276
Lehman Millet Incorporated	2835	E	714 850-7900	4279
Fujifilm Irvine Scientific Inc **(DH)**	2836	E	949 261-7800	4317
Gps Associates Inc	2842	E	949 408-3162	4351
Westridge Laboratories Inc	2844	E	714 259-9400	4468
Behr Holdings Corporation **(HQ)**	2851	E	714 545-7101	4475
Behr Process Corporation **(DH)**	2851	A	714 545-7101	4476
Behr Process Corporation	2851	E	714 545-7101	4477
Behr Process Corporation	2851	F	714 545-7101	4478
Behr Process Corporation	2851	E	714 545-7101	4479
Behr Process Corporation	2851	F	714 545-7101	4480
Behr Sales Inc **(HQ)**	2851	C	714 545-7101	4481
Color Science Inc	2865	E	714 434-1033	4509
Axiom Materials Inc	2891	E	949 623-4400	4558
Insultech LLC **(PA)**	2899	E	714 384-0506	4612
Yokohama Corp North America **(HQ)**	3011	C	540 389-5426	4701
Ciasons Industrial Inc	3053	E	714 259-0838	4723
Freudenberg-Nok General Partnr	3053	E	714 834-0602	4728
Hdz Brothers Inc	3053	E	714 953-4010	4732
Hitt Companies	3069	E	714 979-1405	4766
Bird B Gone LLC	3082	D	949 472-3122	4828
Triple DOT Corp	3085	E	714 241-0888	4867
Altium Packaging LP	3086	D	714 241-6640	4871
Arlon LLC	3089	C	714 540-2811	4947
Clear-Ad Inc	3089	E	866 627-9718	4992
Codan US Corporation	3089	E	714 545-2111	4993
Fit-Line Inc	3089	E	714 549-9091	5029
Hood Manufacturing Inc	3089	D	714 979-7681	5051
JB Plastics Inc	3089	E	714 541-8500	5069
Jdr Engineering Cons Inc **(PA)**	3089	D	714 751-7084	5070
Modified Plastics Inc **(PA)**	3089	E	714 546-4667	5104
Newport Laminates Inc	3089	E	714 545-8335	5116
CL Solutions LLC	3211	D	714 597-6499	5314
International Skylights	3211	C	800 325-4355	5316
Sundown Liquidating Corp **(PA)**	3211	D	714 540-8950	5318
Twed-Dells Inc	3231	E	714 754-6900	5359
Lotus Hygiene Systems Inc	3261	E	714 259-8805	5377
Pacific Stone Design Inc	3272	E	714 836-5757	5436
Prime Forming & Cnstr Sups Inc	3272	E	714 547-6710	5440
Spec Formliners Inc	3272	E	714 429-9500	5452
Bender Ready Mix Inc	3273	E	714 560-0744	5464
Supreme Abrasives	3291	E	949 250-8644	5544
Easyflex Inc	3312	E	888 577-8999	5588
Metal Cast Inc	3325	E	714 285-9792	5664
Aluminum Precision Pdts Inc **(PA)**	3334	A	714 546-8125	5669
Gemini Industries Inc	3341	D	949 250-4011	5680
Calmont Engrg & Elec Corp **(PA)**	3357	E	714 549-0336	5737
ADM Works LLC	3365	E	714 245-0536	5778
Curtiss-Wright Surfc Tech LLC	3398	F	714 546-4160	5835
Metal Improvement Company LLC	3398	E	714 546-4160	5842
Brasstech Inc **(HQ)**	3432	C	949 417-5207	5963
Brasstech Inc	3432	C	714 796-9278	5964
Tobin Steel Company Inc	3441	C	714 541-2268	6082
Accent Industries Inc **(PA)**	3442	F	714 708-1389	6096
Acd LLC **(DH)**	3443	D	949 261-7533	6130
Ajax Boiler Inc	3443	D	714 437-9050	6131
Watts Spacemaker Inc	3443	E	714 542-4649	6170
Bend-Tek Inc	3444	D	714 210-8966	6201
Cal Pac Sheet Metal Inc	3444	E	714 979-2733	6208
CPC Fabrication Inc	3444	E	714 554-2426	6221
Fabrication Concepts Corporation	3444	C	714 881-2000	6238
GKN Aerospace Camarillo Inc	3444	F	805 383-6684	6246
Oc Metals Inc	3444	E	714 668-0783	6277
Sanie Manufacturing Company	3446	F	714 751-7700	6367
Madison Industries **(HQ)**	3448	E	323 583-4061	6382
Acrontos Manufacturing Inc	3469	E	714 850-9133	6492
Kaga (usa) Inc	3469	E	714 540-2697	6527
Orange Mtal Spnning Stmping In	3469	F	714 754-0770	6543
Anodyne Inc	3471	E	714 549-3321	6585
Chrome Tech Inc	3471	C	714 543-4092	6603
Electrode Technologies Inc	3471	E	714 549-3771	6614
JD Processing Inc	3471	E	714 972-8161	6633
Triumph Proc - Embee Div Inc	3471	B	714 546-9842	6674
Gemtech Inds Good Earth Mfg	3479	E	714 848-2517	6707
R & B Wire Products Inc	3496	E	714 549-3355	6824
US Rigging Supply Corp	3496	E	714 545-7444	6832
Ecoolthing Corp	3499	E	714 368-4791	6861
Umbrla Inc	3523	D	888 909-5564	6918
US Saws Inc **(PA)**	3531	F	860 668-2402	6946
K-V Engineering Inc	3541	D	714 229-9977	7014
Universal Punch Corp	3542	E	714 556-4488	7040
Ambrit Engineering Corporation	3544	D	714 557-1074	7048
Adapt Automation Inc	3549	E	714 662-4454	7166
Newport Electronics Inc	3559	D	714 540-4914	7252
Polaris E-Commerce Inc	3561	E	714 907-0582	7286
TMC Fluid Systems Inc	3564	F	714 553-0944	7335
Atr Sales Inc	3568	E	714 432-8411	7376
Deschner Corporation	3569	E	714 557-1261	7390
Silicon Tech Inc	3572	B	949 476-1130	7486
Stec International Holding Inc	3572	C	949 476-1180	7488
Marway Power Systems Inc **(PA)**	3577	E	714 917-6200	7549
Omniprint Inc	3577	E	949 833-0080	7557
Jwc Environmental Inc	3589	D	714 662-5829	7666
A-Z Mfg Inc	3599	E	714 444-4446	7727
Accurate Prfmce Machining Inc	3599	E	714 434-7811	7730
Ackley Metal Products Inc	3599	F	714 979-7431	7734
Advanced Joining Technologies Inc	3599	E	949 756-8091	7737
Aero-k	3599	E	626 350-5125	7743
AGA Precision Systems Inc	3599	E	714 540-3163	7748
Alco Engrg & Tooling Corp	3599	E	714 556-6060	7749
Automation West Inc	3599	E	714 556-7381	7766
Connelly Machine Wks	3599	E	714 558-6855	7808
GBF Enterprises Inc	3599	E	714 979-7131	7844
Helfer Enterprises	3599	E	714 557-2733	7858
Johnson Precision Products Inc	3599	F	714 824-6971	7890
K-P Engineering Corp	3599	E	714 545-7045	7892
Kilgore Machine Company Inc	3599	E	714 540-3659	7898
M & W Machine Corporation	3599	E	714 541-2652	7911
Maul Mfg Inc **(PA)**	3599	E	714 641-0727	7922
Motorvac Technologies Inc	3599	E	714 558-4822	7948
Norotos Inc	3599	C	714 662-3113	7956
Pacific Aerospace Machine Inc	3599	E	714 534-1444	7963

2024 Southern California
Business Directory and Buyers Guide

(P-0000) Products & Services Section entry number
(PA)=Parent Co (HQ)=Headquarters (DH)=Div Headquarters

	SIC	EMP	PHONE	ENTRY#
Ricaurte Precision Inc	3599	E	714 667-0632	7999
S&S Precision Mfg Inc	3599	E	714 754-6664	8012
Santos Precision Inc	3599	D	714 957-0299	8014
Senga Engineering Inc	3599	E	714 549-8011	8021
Tmx Engineering and Mfg Corp	3599	D	714 641-5884	8048
Tomi Engineering Inc	3599	E	714 556-1474	8049
Onyx Power Inc	3612	C	714 513-1500	8105
Cole Instrument Corp	3621	D	714 556-3100	8139
Frontera Solutions Inc	3624	E	714 368-1631	8163
AP Parpro Inc	3625	E	619 498-9004	8169
Data Solder Inc	3643	F	714 429-9866	8259
Nivek Industries Inc	3643	E	714 545-8855	8272
Saf-T-Co Supply	3644	E	714 547-9975	8283
Orion Chandelier Inc	3646	F	714 668-9668	8325
Sun & Sun Industries Inc	3646	D	714 210-5141	8333
Dana Creath Designs Ltd	3648	E	714 662-0111	8360
Tivoli Industries Inc	3648	E	714 957-6101	8385
Aurasound Inc	3651	D	949 829-4000	8397
Honav Usa Inc	3651	F	858 634-0617	8418
Leader Electronics (na) Inc	3661	E	714 435-0505	8476
Secure Comm Systems Inc **(HQ)**	3663	C	714 547-1174	8577
Statewide Trffic Sfety Sgns In **(HQ)**	3669	E	949 553-8272	8627
Accurate Circuit Engrg Inc	3672	D	714 546-2162	8639
Allied Electronic Services Inc	3672	E	714 245-2500	8643
Almatron Electronics Inc	3672	E	714 557-6000	8644
Dynasty Electronic Company LLC	3672	D	714 550-1197	8670
K L Electronic Inc	3672	E	714 751-5611	8694
Matrix USA Inc	3672	E	714 825-0404	8700
Maxtrol Corporation	3672	E	714 245-0506	8701
Parpro Technologies Inc	3672	C	714 545-8886	8715
Pioneer Circuits Inc	3672	B	714 641-3132	8718
Power Circuits Inc	3672	E	714 327-3000	8719
Q-Flex Inc	3672	F	714 664-0101	8720
South Coast Circuits Inc	3672	E	714 966-2108	8732
Ttm Printed Circuit Group Inc **(HQ)**	3672	C	714 327-3000	8742
Ttm Technologies Inc **(PA)**	3672	B	714 327-3000	8743
Ttm Technologies Inc	3672	B	714 241-0303	8744
Accelerated Memory Prod Inc	3674	E	714 460-9800	8756
Labarge/Stc Inc	3674	B	281 207-1400	8826
Smt Electronics Mfg Inc	3674	E	714 751-8894	8893
Flexible Manufacturing LLC	3678	D	714 259-7996	8970
Express Manufacturing Inc **(PA)**	3679	B	714 979-2228	9043
IJ Research Inc	3679	E	714 546-8522	9057
Jolo Industries Inc	3679	F	714 554-6840	9073
Mask Technology Inc	3679	F	714 557-3383	9082
Sandberg Industries Inc **(PA)**	3679	E	949 660-9473	9113
Smiths Intrcnnect Americas Inc	3679	B	714 371-1100	9117
Wyvern Technologies	3679	E	714 966-0710	9140
CD Video Manufacturing Inc	3695	D	714 265-0770	9179
Kulicke Sffa Wedge Bonding Inc	3699	C	949 660-0440	9224
Tactical Micro Inc **(DH)**	3699	F	714 547-1174	9262
Undersea Systems Intl Inc	3699	D	714 754-7848	9265
Greenkraft Inc	3711	F	714 545-7777	9290
Agility Fuel Systems LLC **(DH)**	3714	E	949 236-5520	9347
Danchuk Manufacturing Inc	3714	D	714 540-4363	9378
Garrison Manufacturing Inc	3714	E	714 549-4880	9394
Impco Technologies Inc **(HQ)**	3714	C	714 656-1200	9405
Overair Inc	3721	E	949 503-7503	9548
Advanced Digital Mfg LLC	3728	E	714 245-0536	9595
Aerospace Driven Tech Inc	3728	F	949 553-1606	9601
Aerospace Engineering Inc	3728	E	714 641-5884	9605
California Composites MGT Inc	3728	E	714 258-0405	9651
Ducommun Incorporated **(PA)**	3728	C	657 335-3665	9679
Integral Aerospace LLC	3728	C	949 250-3123	9721
Meggitt North Hollywood Inc	3728	E	818 691-6258	9749
Symbolic Displays Inc	3728	D	714 258-2811	9808
Western Methods Machinery Corporation	3728	E	949 252-2600	9827
All American Racers Inc	3751	E	714 540-1771	9871
Markland Industries Inc **(PA)**	3751	D	714 245-2850	9879
Anduril Industries Inc	3812	E	949 891-1607	9942
Ascent Aerospace	3812	D	586 726-0500	9949
Bambeck Systems Inc **(PA)**	3823	F	949 250-3100	10118
E D Q Inc	3823	E	714 546-6010	10129
Autonomous Medical Devices Inc **(PA)**	3826	E	657 660-6800	10236
Quantum Magnetics LLC	3826	A	714 258-4400	10283
Buk Optics Inc	3827	E	714 384-9620	10309
Deltronic Corporation	3827	D	714 545-5800	10312
Infinite Optics Inc	3827	E	714 557-2299	10320
Mark Optics Inc	3827	E	714 545-6684	10326
Optosigma Corporation	3827	E	949 851-5881	10333
AMO Usa Inc	3841	C	714 247-8200	10429
Medtronic Inc	3841	B	949 474-3943	10560
Medtronic Ats Medical Inc	3841	C	949 380-9333	10561
Orchid MPS	3841	D	714 549-9203	10585
Thi Inc	3841	D	714 444-4643	10617
Diamond Gloves	3842	E	714 667-0506	10643
Surefire LLC	3842	E	714 641-0483	10708
Surefire LLC	3842	E	714 545-9444	10710
Surefire LLC	3842	E	714 641-0483	10711
United Biologics Inc	3842	E	949 345-7490	10717
Medtronic 3f Therapeutics Inc	3845	C	949 399-1675	10815
Ricoh Electronics Inc	3861	C	714 566-6079	10884
Leonard Craft Co LLC	3911	D	714 549-0678	11008
Rickenbacker International Corporation	3931	D	714 545-5574	10931
Diamond Baseball Company Inc	3949	E	800 366-2999	10986
Heart Rate Inc	3949	E	714 850-9716	10996
Xs Scuba Inc **(PA)**	3949	E	714 424-0434	11044
Aardvark Clay & Supplies Inc **(PA)**	3952	E	714 541-4157	11048
Bob Siemon Designs Inc	3961	D	714 549-0678	11065
SPS Technologies LLC	3965	B	714 545-9311	11076
SPS Technologies LLC	3965	B	714 371-1925	11077
Cal-Sign Wholesale Inc	3993	F	209 523-7446	11100
Cowboy Direct Response	3993	E	714 824-3780	11106
Sign Specialists Corporation	3993	E	714 641-0064	11161
Statewide Trffic Sfety Sgns In	3993	E	714 468-1919	11169
Durham School Services L P	4173	B	714 542-8989	11434
RPM Transportation Inc **(DH)**	4213	C	714 388-3500	11504
Southwest Airlines Co	4512	D	949 252-5200	11671
Transit Air Cargo Inc	4731	E	714 571-0393	11811
Lbi Media Holdings Inc	4832	B	714 554-5000	11928
Yokohama Tire Corporation **(DH)**	5014	C	714 870-3800	12275
Contractors Flrg Svc Cal Inc	5023	C	714 556-6100	12298
Foundation Building Mtls Inc **(HQ)**	5031	C	714 380-3127	12330
AAA Imaging & Supplies Inc	5043	E	714 431-0570	12375
Advantage Manufacturing Inc	5063	E	714 505-1166	12583
Ace Wireless & Trading Inc	5065	E	949 748-5901	12640
Hirsch Electronics LLC	5065	D	949 250-8888	12665
Jwc Environmental Inc **(DH)**	5084	E	949 833-3888	12794
Rbc Transport Dynamics Corp	5085	C	203 267-7001	12874
Pioneer Packing Inc **(PA)**	5113	E	714 540-9751	13023
Michael Gerald Ltd	5136	E	562 921-9611	13106
Vantage Custom Classics Inc	5136	C	714 755-1133	13117
Smart & Final Stores Inc	5141	B	714 549-2362	13194
Ingardia Bros Produce Inc	5148	C	949 645-1365	13331
Coastal Cocktails Inc **(PA)**	5149	D	949 250-8951	13361
Goglanian Bakeries Inc **(HQ)**	5149	B	714 338-1145	13369
Embee Performance LLC	5169	E	714 540-1354	13431
Jenny Silks Inc	5193	F	714 597-7272	13510
Home Depot USA Inc	5211	C	714 966-8551	13588
Home Depot USA Inc	5211	D	714 259-1030	13594
SMI Architectural Millwork Inc	5211	E	714 567-0112	13670
Crevier Classics LLC	5511	B	714 835-3171	13751
Toms Truck Center Inc	5511	E	714 835-1978	13837
United Syatt America Corp **(PA)**	5531	C	714 568-1938	13887
Skyco Shading Systems Inc	5719	E	714 708-3038	13967
DAd Investments	5812	E	714 751-8500	13999
Word For Today	5961	E	714 825-9657	14107
Alignmed Inc	5999	F	866 987-5433	14120
Waxies Enterprises LLC	5999	E	714 545-8441	14153
Banc California National Assn **(HQ)**	6021	D	877 770-2262	14156
Banc of California Inc	6021	C	855 361-2262	14157
Orange Countys Credit Union **(PA)**	6061	C	714 755-5900	14235
Schoolsfirst Federal Credit Un **(PA)**	6061	B	714 258-4000	14238
Continental Currency Svcs Inc **(PA)**	6099	D	714 667-6699	14256
Home Mrtg Aliance Corp Hmac **(PA)**	6162	B	800 900-7040	14327
Lenox Financial Mortgage Corp	6162	*	949 428-5100	14333
Turnkey Foundation Inc	6162	D	949 557-6203	14353
Tarbell Financial Corporation **(PA)**	6163	C	714 972-0988	14368
Admar Corporation	6324	C	714 953-9600	14457
Pacifcare Hlth Plan Admnstrtor **(DH)**	6324	B	714 825-5200	14491
State Compensation Insur Fund	6331	C	714 565-5000	14529
First American Financial Corp **(PA)**	6361	A	714 250-3000	14539
First American Mortgage Svcs	6361	B	714 250-4210	14540
First American Title Insur Co **(HQ)**	6361	B	800 854-3643	14541
First Amrcn Prprty Insur Cslty	6411	C	949 474-7500	14595
H & H Agency Inc	6411	D	949 260-8840	14600
Seneca Family of Agencies	6411	C	714 881-8600	14630
F M Tarbell Co **(HQ)**	6531	C	714 972-0988	14793
Grubb & Ellis Company	6531	A	714 667-8252	14808
Grubb & Ellis Management Services Inc	6531	A	412 201-8200	14809
Satellite Management Co **(PA)**	6531	C	714 558-2411	14864
First American Title Company	6541	A	714 250-3109	14891
Property Insight LLC	6541	A	877 747-2537	14894
Skeffington Enterprises Inc	6719	C	714 540-1700	14945
2100 Trust LLC **(PA)**	6733	C	877 469-7344	14986
Chen & Huang Partners LP	7011	D	714 557-8700	15114

Employee Codes: A=Over 500 employees, B=251-500
C=101-250, D=51-100, E=20-50, F=10-19, G=1-9

2024 Southern California
Business Directory and Buyers Guide

© Mergent Inc. 1-800-342-5647

1439

GEOGRAPHIC

	SIC	EMP	PHONE	ENTRY#
S W K Properties LLC	7011	C	714 481-6300	15337
Windsor Capital Group Inc	7011	C	714 241-3800	15423
Cintas Sales Corporation	7213	D	714 957-2852	15450
Optima Tax Relief LLC	7291	C	714 361-4636	15496
Pps Parking Inc	7299	A	949 223-8707	15521
Financial Statement Svcs Inc **(PA)**	7331	C	714 436-3326	15631
Towne Inc	7331	C	714 540-3095	15637
Advanced Clnroom McRclean Corp	7349	C	714 751-1152	15690
Merchants Building Maint Co	7349	B	714 973-9272	15727
Universal Services America LP	7349	A	714 923-3700	15754
County of Orange	7353	D	714 647-1552	15760
Executive Personnel Services	7361	B	714 310-9506	15846
Pds Defense Inc	7361	C	214 647-9600	15878
Dm Software Inc	7372	E	714 953-2653	16227
Itc Sftware Slutions Group LLC **(PA)**	7372	E	877 248-2774	16279
Nazca Solutions Inc	7372	E	612 279-6100	16318
Nis America Inc	7372	E	714 540-1199	16328
Thursby Software Systems LLC	7372	E	817 478-5070	16405
Cognizant Trztto Sftwr Group I	7373	C	714 481-0396	16435
Black Knight Infoserv LLC	7374	C	904 854-5100	16484
Compushare Inc	7374	C	714 427-1000	16488
Verys LLC	7379	C	949 423-3295	16610
Community Patrol Inc	7381	D	657 247-4744	16631
Guardsmark LLC **(DH)**	7381	C	714 619-9700	16650
Shield Security Inc **(DH)**	7381	B	714 210-1501	16687
Universal Prtction SEC Systems **(DH)**	7381	A	714 923-3700	16701
Anovia Payments LLC	7389	D	469 621-0166	16780
Dekra-Lite Industries Inc	7389	C	714 436-0705	16816
Fntech	7389	D	714 429-7833	16827
Fresh Grill LLC	7389	C	714 444-2126	16830
Orange Coast Title Company **(PA)**	7389	D	714 558-2836	16895
Partners Capital Group Inc **(PA)**	7389	D	949 916-3900	16900
Trans-Pak Incorporated	7389	C	310 618-6937	16946
Parking Concepts Inc	7521	D	714 543-5725	17004
Brake Depot Systems Inc	7538	B	714 623-9030	17029
Guys Patio Inc	7641	E	844 968-7485	17077
American Cooling Tower Inc **(PA)**	7699	F	714 898-2436	17115
Collectors Universe Inc **(PA)**	7699	C	949 567-1234	17120
La Boxing Franchise Corp	7991	B	714 668-0911	17403
Santa Ana Country Club	7997	C	714 556-3000	17519
Carbon Health Technologies Inc	8011	C	714 710-3030	17609
Kaiser Foundation Hospitals	8011	C	714 967-4700	17686
Southern Cal Prmnnte Med Group	8011	C	714 967-4700	17794
St Jseph Heritg Med Group LLC **(PA)**	8011	C	714 633-1011	17795
University California Irvine	8011	B	714 480-2443	17818
Chromium Dental II LLC	8021	C	949 733-3111	17836
Intergro Rehab Service	8049	D	714 901-4200	17867
Town Cntry Mnor of Chrstn Mssn	8051	C	714 547-7581	18062
Orange Cnty Ryale Cnvlscent Ho **(PA)**	8059	B	714 546-6450	18149
Health Resources Corp	8062	A	714 754-5454	18276
Orange Cnty Globl Med Ctr Aux **(DH)**	8062	C	714 835-3555	18354
South Coast Global Med Ctr Inc	8062	D	714 754-5454	18447
Southern Cal Spcialty Care Inc	8062	C	714 564-7800	18454
Ctsh LLC	8082	C	949 916-6705	18608
Visiting Nrse Assn of Inland C **(PA)**	8082	A	951 413-1200	18651
Child Guidance Center Inc	8093	C	714 953-4455	18680
CRC Health Corporate	8093	A	714 542-3581	18685
Reimagine Network **(PA)**	8093	C	714 633-7400	18712
Rio	8093	C	714 633-7400	18713
Orangewood Foundation	8322	D	714 619-0200	19121
Priority Ctr Ending The Gnrtna	8322	D	714 543-4333	19127
United Crbral Plsy Assn Ornge	8322	B	949 333-6400	19150
Volunteers of Amer Los Angeles	8322	D	714 426-9834	19156
City of Santa Ana	8331	D	714 647-6545	19181
Calvary Church Santa Ana Inc	8351	C	714 973-4800	19202
Olive Crest **(PA)**	8361	B	714 543-5437	19291
Discovery Scnce Ctr Ornge Cnty	8412	C	866 552-2823	19353
Mercy House Living Centers	8611	C	714 836-7188	19382
Orange County Health Care Agcy	8621	D	714 568-5683	19400
Air Liquide Electronics US LP	8711	A	713 624-8000	19542
Concept Technology Inc	8711	B	949 851-6550	19564
Custom Built Machinery Inc	8711	E	714 424-9250	19570
Embee Processing LLC	8711	C	714 540-9842	19581
Hntb Corporation	8711	C	714 460-1600	19607
Hntb Gerwick Water Solutions	8711	C	714 460-1600	19608
Michael Baker International Inc **(DH)**	8711	B	949 472-3505	19646
Psomas	8713	D	714 751-7373	19749
Dhs Consulting LLC	8741	D	714 276-1135	20027
Medical Network Inc	8741	D	949 863-0022	20059
Pipeline Group LLC	8741	C	949 296-8375	20078
Prospect Medical Group Inc **(HQ)**	8741	B	714 796-5900	20084
Wolf & Raven LLC	8741	D	800 431-6471	20120
Alan B Whitson Company Inc	8742	A	949 955-1200	20127
Behr Process Sales Company	8743	E	714 545-7101	20281
Chambers Group Inc **(PA)**	8748	D	949 261-5414	20327
Iaccess Technologies Inc **(PA)**	8748	E	714 922-9158	20346
Irvine Technology Corporation	8748	C	714 445-2624	20353
Data Trace Info Svcs LLC **(HQ)**	8999	D	714 250-6700	20394
County of Orange	9199	E	714 567-7444	20409
Regional Ctr Orange Cnty Inc **(PA)**	9431	B	714 796-5100	20415

SANTA BARBARA, CA - Santa Barbara County

	SIC	EMP	PHONE	ENTRY#
Brightview Golf Maint Inc	0781	D	805 968-6400	145
Dennis Allen Associates **(PA)**	1521	D	805 884-8777	428
Granite Construction Company	1611	C	805 964-9951	619
One Call Plumber Santa Barbara	1711	D	805 364-6337	802
Specialty Team Plastering Inc	1742	C	805 966-3858	997
Esperer Webstores LLC	2023	F	805 880-1900	1268
Jeannines Bkg Co Santa Barbara **(PA)**	2051	F	805 687-8701	1478
Adriennes Gourmet Foods	2052	D	805 964-6848	1501
Riverbench LLC	2084	E	805 324-4100	1656
Honey	2099	B	805 963-8300	1911
Kate Farms Inc	2099	C	805 845-2446	1921
Toad & Co International Inc **(PA)**	2339	E	800 865-8623	2379
Architctral Mllwk Snta Barbara	2431	E	805 965-7011	2584
Daily Nexus	2711	D	805 893-4006	3271
Dailymedia Inc **(PA)**	2711	F	541 821-5207	3272
Noozhawk	2711	F	805 456-7267	3310
Pacific Coast Bus Times Inc	2711	E	805 560-6950	3314
Santa Barbara Independent Inc	2711	E	805 965-5205	3322
Partner Concepts Inc	2721	D	805 745-7199	3378
ABC - Clio Inc **(HQ)**	2731	C	805 968-1911	3397
Graphiq LLC	2741	C	805 335-2433	3453
Palette Life Sciences Inc	2833	D	805 869-7020	4010
Tbp Indoor Facilities Inc	2834	D	877 778-9587	4245
Invenios LLC	3231	D	805 962-3333	5343
Steven Handelman Studios Inc **(PA)**	3322	E	805 884-9070	5650
Helistrand Inc	3357	E	805 963-4518	5743
Aqueos Corporation **(PA)**	3533	E	805 364-0570	6952
Picosys Incorporated	3545	D	805 962-3333	7124
Foodtools Consolidated Inc **(PA)**	3556	C	805 962-8383	7195
Efaxcom	3577	E	805 692-0064	7524
Motion Engineering Inc **(DH)**	3577	D	805 696-1200	7553
Kollmorgen Corporation	3621	D	805 696-1236	8147
Sonos Inc **(PA)**	3651	D	805 965-3001	8436
Clearpathgps LLC	3678	E	805 979-3442	8963
Agile Rf Inc	3679	E	805 968-5159	8993
Freedom Photonics LLC	3699	E	805 967-4900	9211
Vetronix Corporation	3714	C	805 966-2000	9484
Channel Technologies Group LLC	3812	A	805 967-0171	9962
Santa Barbara Infrared Inc **(DH)**	3812	D	805 965-3669	10068
Santa Barbara Control Systems	3823	F	805 683-8833	10160
International Transducer Corp	3825	C	805 683-2575	10206
Oxford Instrs Asylum RES Inc **(HQ)**	3826	D	805 696-6466	10279
Electro-Optical Industries LLC	3827	E	805 964-6701	10313
Ircamera LLC	3827	E	805 965-9650	10322
Arthrex Inc	3841	C	805 964-8104	10440
Nobbe Orthopedics Inc	3842	D	805 687-7508	10686
Zyris Inc	3843	E	805 560-9888	10779
Duncan Carter Corporation **(PA)**	3931	D	805 964-9749	10922
Bloomios Inc	3999	E	805 222-6330	11197
Santa Barbara Metro Trnst Dst **(PA)**	4111	D	805 963-3364	11364
Smith Broadcasting Group Inc	4833	B	805 882-3933	11964
Marborg Industries **(PA)**	4953	C	805 963-1852	12172
Curvature LLC **(DH)**	5045	D	800 230-6638	12402
Solid Oak Software Inc **(PA)**	5045	E	805 568-5415	12439
Mentor Worldwide LLC	5047	D	805 681-6000	12499
Vet National Inc	5063	E	805 692-8487	12624
Jordanos Inc **(PA)**	5181	C	805 964-0611	13470
Volkswagen of Van Nuys Inc	5511	D	323 873-3311	13844
Santa Barbara Coffee & Tea Inc	5812	E	805 898-3700	14034
Sansum Clinic	5912	D	805 681-7500	14056
Morgan Stnley Smith Barney LLC	6211	C	805 963-3381	14394
Santa Brbara San Luis Obspo RG	6321	C	800 421-2560	14455
Chicago Title Insurance Co **(HQ)**	6361	C	805 565-6900	14538
Western Penn AAA Insur Agcy	6411	B	805 682-5811	14644
Nevins/Adams Properties Inc **(PA)**	6512	C	805 963-2884	14675
University Business Ctr Assoc	6512	D	601 354-3555	14693
Miramar Acquisition Co LLC	6799	C	805 900-8338	15038
1260 Bb Property LLC	7011	B	805 969-2261	15062
Bcra Resort Services Inc	7011	C	805 571-3176	15088
Encina Pepper Tree Joint Ventr	7011	B	805 682-7277	15147
Fess Prker-Red Lion Gen Partnr	7011	C	805 564-4333	15152
H D G Associates	7011	C	805 963-0744	15166
Morgans Hotel Group MGT LLC	7011	C	805 969-2203	15255
Ritz-Carlton Hotel Company LLC	7011	A	805 968-0100	15329

Mergent email: customerrelations@mergent.com
1440

2024 Southern California
Business Directory and Buyers Guide

(P-0000) Products & Services Section entry number
(PA)=Parent Co (HQ)=Headquarters (DH)=Div Headquarters

Company	SIC	EMP	PHONE	ENTRY#
San Ysidro Bb Property LLC	7011	C	805 368-6788	15347
Mission Linen Supply	7213	C	805 962-7687	15456
Signature Parking LLC	7299	D	805 969-7275	15522
Fastclick Inc	7319	A	805 689-9839	15601
The Alternative Copy Shop Inc	7334	D	805 569-2116	15653
Town & Cntry Event Rentals Inc	7359	B	805 770-5729	15801
Butler International Inc (PA)	7361	C	805 882-2200	15825
Eastern Staffing LLC	7361	A	805 882-2200	15840
Partners Prsnnel - MGT Svcs LL	7361	A	805 689-8191	15876
Select Temporaries LLC (DH)	7361	D	805 882-2200	15893
Butler Service Group Inc (HQ)	7363	D	201 891-5312	15916
Trackr Inc	7371	D	855 981-1690	16136
Yardi Systems Inc (PA)	7371	B	805 699-2040	16152
Appfolio Inc (PA)	7372	B	805 364-6093	16170
Axia Technologies Inc	7372	E	855 376-2942	16181
Green Hills Software LLC (HQ)	7372	C	805 965-6044	16259
Inform Solution Incorporated	7372	E	805 879-6000	16270
Learning Explorer Inc	7372	F	888 909-9035	16293
Mixmode Inc	7372	E	858 225-2352	16310
Productplan LLC	7372	E	805 618-2975	16355
Qad Inc (HQ)	7372	C	805 566-6000	16358
Logicmonitor Inc (PA)	7375	C	805 394-8632	16531
US Data Management LLC (PA)	7379	D	888 231-0816	16609
Sheryl Lowe Designs LLC	7389	E	805 969-1742	16926
Bay Clubs Company LLC	7997	B	805 965-0999	17466
Bay Clubs Company LLC	7997	B	805 563-8700	17467
La Cumbre Country Club	7997	D	805 687-2421	17493
Montecito Country Club Inc	7997	D	805 969-0800	17503
Anesthsia Med Group Snta Brbar	8011	D	805 682-7751	17593
Compass Health Inc	8051	C	805 687-6651	17911
Covenant Care California LLC	8051	D	805 964-4871	17917
Covenant Rtirement Communities	8051	D	805 687-0701	17920
Montecito Retirement Assn	8051	B	805 969-8011	18016
Powers Park Healthcare Inc	8051	C	805 687-6651	18034
Hillside House	8052	D	805 687-0788	18084
Front Porch Communities & Svcs	8059	D	805 687-0793	18124
Goleta Valley Cottage Hosp Aux	8062	B	805 681-6468	18270
Santa Barbara Cottage Hospital	8062	B	805 569-7367	18419
Santa Brbara Cttage Hosp Fndti	8062	B	805 569-7224	18420
Santa Brbara Cttage Hosp Fndti (HQ)	8062	C	805 682-7111	18422
Visiting Nurse & Hospice	8082	C	805 965-5555	18652
Visiting Nurse & Hospice Care (PA)	8082	C	805 965-5555	18653
Santa Brbara Artfl Kdney Ctr L	8092	D	805 682-9942	18666
Laguna Blanca School (PA)	8211	D	805 687-2461	18972
Santa Brbara Cmnty College Dst	8222	B	805 683-4191	18998
Family Svc Agcy Snta Brbara CN	8322	D	805 965-1001	19080
People Creating Success Inc	8322	D	805 692-5290	19126
Cliff View Terrace Inc	8361	D	805 682-7443	19249
Covenant Living West	8361	C	805 687-0701	19256
Santa Brbara Mseum Ntral Hstor	8412	D	805 682-4711	19363
Santa Brbara Zlgcal Foundation	8422	D	805 962-1673	19368
African Women Rising	8641	C	415 278-1784	19422
Channel Islnds Yung MNS Chrstn	8641	C	805 963-8775	19433
Channel Islnds Yung MNS Chrstn	8641	D	805 687-7727	19435
Channel Islnds Yung MNS Chrstn	8641	D	805 969-3288	19436
Automobile Club Southern Cal	8699	C	805 682-5811	19517
Lash Construction Inc	8711	D	805 963-3553	19638
MNS Engineers Inc (PA)	8711	C	805 692-6921	19648
Penfield & Smith Engineers Inc	8711	D	805 963-9532	19669
Dupont Displays Inc	8731	D	805 562-5400	19834
Ontraport Inc	8741	C	805 568-1424	20072
Smith Broadcasting Group Inc (PA)	8741	D	805 965-0400	20094
Pensinmark Rtirement Group LLC	8742	D	805 456-6260	20218
Tecolote Research Inc	8742	C	805 964-6963	20257

SANTA CLARITA, CA - Los Angeles County

Company	SIC	EMP	PHONE	ENTRY#
Gothic Landscaping Inc (PA)	0782	C	661 678-1400	192
California Resources Prod Corp (HQ)	1311	C	661 869-8000	255
Califrnia Rsrces Elk Hills LLC	1382	B	661 412-0000	294
Califrnia Rsurces Long Bch Inc	1382	D	888 848-4754	295
CRC Services LLC	1382	F	888 848-4754	296
Sheldon Mechanical Corporation	1711	D	661 286-1361	822
Tri-Signal Integration Inc (PA)	1731	D	818 566-8558	947
Blending Lab Inc	2084	E	323 424-4051	1612
True Warrior LLC	2389	E	661 237-6588	2460
Frametent Inc	2394	E	661 290-3375	2504
California Millworks Corp	2431	E	661 294-2345	2587
Old English Mil Woodworks Inc (PA)	2431	E	661 294-9171	2624
Applied Polytech Systems Inc	2452	E	818 504-9261	2743
Signal	2711	D	661 259-1234	3323
Daisy Publishing Company Inc	2721	E	661 295-1910	3354
Living Way Industries Inc	2752	F	661 298-3200	3625
3d/International Inc	2842	C	661 250-2020	4341

Company	SIC	EMP	PHONE	ENTRY#
B&D Investment Partners Inc (PA)	2842	E	661 255-0955	4344
Shadow Holdings LLC	2844	C	661 252-3807	4454
Shadow Holdings LLC (HQ)	2844	B	661 252-3807	4455
Packaging Systems Inc	2891	E	661 253-5700	4575
Certified Thermoplastics Inc	3089	E	661 222-3006	4988
Lamsco West Inc	3089	D	661 295-8620	5082
Magic Plastics Inc (PA)	3089	E	800 369-0303	5089
Valley Precision Metal Product	3444	E	661 607-0100	6339
Curtiss-Wright Corporation	3491	E	661 257-4430	6758
Whitmor Plstic Wire Cable Corp (PA)	3496	E	661 257-2400	6834
Tesco Products	3541	E	661 257-0153	7026
B&B Manufacturing Co (PA)	3599	C	661 257-2161	7772
Lansair Corporation	3599	E	661 294-9503	7904
Curtiss-Wrght Cntrls Elctrnic (DH)	3625	E	661 702-1494	8175
Woodward Hrt Inc (HQ)	3625	A	661 294-6000	8197
Custom Suppression Inc	3677	F	818 718-1040	8940
Madn Aircraft Hinge	3721	E	661 257-3430	9544
Aerospace Dynamics Intl Inc	3728	B	661 310-6986	9603
Aircraft Hinge Inc	3728	E	661 257-3434	9612
Santa Clarita Signs	3993	E	661 291-1188	11155
Santa Barbara Trnsp Corp	4131	D	661 259-7285	11413
Funnelcloudsales	4215	C	661 284-6032	11529
Princess Cruise Lines Ltd (HQ)	4481	A	661 753-0000	11637
Princess Cruise Lines Ltd	4724	A	661 753-2197	11724
Princess Cruise Lines Ltd	4725	A	661 753-0000	11729
CBS Studios Inc	4833	B	661 964-6020	11941
Santa Clarita Valley Wtr Agcy	4941	C	661 259-2737	12145
Santa Clrita Vly Wtr Agcy Fing	4941	C	661 259-2737	12146
Marathon Industries Inc	5012	C	661 286-1520	12227
Universal Wood Moulding Inc (PA)	5023	E	661 362-6262	12321
White Cap Supply Group Inc	5039	A	661 294-7737	12374
Aq Lighting Group Texas Inc	5063	E	818 534-5300	12584
Paul Mitchell John Systems (PA)	5122	D	800 793-8790	13061
Allied Company Holdings Inc	5181	C	661 510-6533	13458
Home Depot USA Inc	5211	D	661 252-7800	13616
Lowes Home Centers LLC	5211	C	661 678-4430	13636
RE/Max of Valencia Inc (PA)	6531	C	661 255-2650	14855
Jt Resources Inc	7361	C	661 367-6827	15856
Partnership Staffing Svcs Inc	7361	A	661 542-7074	15877
Canon Recruiting Group LLC	7363	D	661 252-7400	15917
Execuprint Inc	7374	F	818 993-8184	16496
Valtron Technologies Inc	7378	D	805 257-0333	16545
Cottrell Paul Enterprises LLC (PA)	7381	C	661 212-2357	16635
5 Star Service Inc	7629	E	323 647-7777	17066
Wrights Supply Inc	7694	D	661 254-8400	17110
Providnce Facey Med Foundation	8011	D	661 513-2100	17743
Southern Cal Prmnnte Med Group	8011	C	661 222-2150	17777
Southern Cal Prmnnte Med Group	8062	B	661 290-3100	18450
Providnce Facey Med Foundation	8099	C	661 250-5225	18791
Child & Family Center	8322	C	661 259-9439	19036
Los Angeles Residential Comm F	8361	D	661 296-8636	19283
Applied Companies	8711	E	661 257-0090	19548
Curtiss-Wrght Cntrls Elctrnic	8711	C	661 257-4430	19569

SANTA FE SPRINGS, CA - Los Angeles County

Company	SIC	EMP	PHONE	ENTRY#
Ethosenergy Field Services LLC (DH)	1389	E	310 639-3523	346
CMC Rebar West	1541	D	714 692-7082	499
Kiewit Infrastructure West Co	1611	C	562 946-1816	628
S E Pipe Line Construction Co	1623	C	562 868-9771	687
Valverde Construction Inc	1623	C	562 906-1826	701
Western Allied Corporation	1711	E	562 944-6341	835
Csi Electrical Contractors Inc (HQ)	1731	C	562 946-0700	890
Leed Electric Inc	1731	C	562 270-9500	913
Masonry Concepts Inc	1741	D	562 802-3700	960
Coast Iron & Steel Co	1791	E	562 946-4421	1103
Rebar Engineering Inc	1791	C	562 946-2461	1113
Crown Fence Co	1799	D	562 864-5177	1150
Camper Packaging LLC	2023	F	562 239-6167	1265
Food Technology and Design LLC (PA)	2064	E	562 944-7821	1539
Liberty Vegetable Oil Company	2079	E	562 921-3567	1572
Anheuser-Busch LLC	2082	E	562 699-3424	1578
American Fruits & Flavors LLC	2087	E	562 320-2802	1753
J & J Processing Inc	2087	E	562 926-2333	1777
Bumble Bee Foods LLC	2091	D	562 483-7474	1793
Nikko Enterprise Corporation	2092	E	562 941-6080	1809
Apffels Coffee Inc	2095	D	562 309-0400	1814
Fuji Food Products Inc (PA)	2099	D	562 404-2590	1900
MCI Foods Inc	2099	C	562 977-4000	1943
Otafuku Foods Inc	2099	E	562 404-4700	1961
Rich Products Corporation	2099	C	562 946-6396	1977
Romeros Food Products Inc (PA)	2099	D	562 802-1858	1979
Gda Inc	2211	F	702 260-1949	2023
Tri-Star Dyeing & Finshg Inc	2231	D	562 483-0123	2052

Employee Codes: A=Over 500 employees, B=251-500
C=101-250, D=51-100, E=20-50, F=10-19, G=1-9

2024 Southern California
Business Directory and Buyers Guide

© Mergent Inc. 1-800-342-5647

1441

GEOGRAPHIC

Name	SIC	EMP	PHONE	ENTRY#
Super Dyeing LLC	2261	D	562 692-9500	2092
Final Finish Inc	2262	F	562 777-7774	2095
Catalina Carpet Mills Inc (PA)	2273	E	562 926-5811	2111
Cableco	2298	E	562 942-8076	2130
Distinctive Inds Texas Inc	2386	E	323 889-5766	2427
Distinctive Inds Texas Inc	2386	E	512 491-3500	2428
Distinctive Industries	2396	B	800 421-9777	2529
Orbo Manufacturing Inc	2396	E	562 222-4535	2537
Day Star Industries	2431	F	562 926-8800	2593
Larson-Juhl US LLC	2499	E	562 946-6873	2754
Robert Michael Ltd	2512	B	562 758-6789	2815
Atlantic Representations Inc	2514	E	562 903-9550	2825
Nakamura-Beeman Inc	2521	E	562 696-1400	2889
Office Chairs Inc	2521	D	562 802-0464	2893
Elite Mfg Corp	2522	C	888 354-8356	2908
Alegacy Fdsrvice Pdts Group In	2599	D	562 320-3100	3020
International Paper Company	2621	E	562 692-9465	3049
J R C Industries Inc	2621	E	562 698-0171	3052
Specialty Paper Mills Inc	2621	C	562 692-8737	3063
Bay Cities Container Corp	2653	F	562 302-2552	3081
C B Sheets Inc	2653	E	562 921-1223	3087
California Box Company (PA)	2653	E	562 921-1223	3088
Cflute Corp	2653	C	562 404-6221	3090
Gabriel Container (PA)	2653	C	562 699-1051	3102
International Paper Company	2653	E	323 946-6100	3111
Reliable Container Corporation	2653	B	562 861-6226	3126
Western Corrugated Design Inc	2653	E	562 695-9295	3135
Bay Cities Container Corp	2671	E	562 551-2946	3150
Seal Methods Inc (PA)	2672	D	562 944-0291	3175
Tape and Label Converters Inc	2672	E	562 945-3486	3176
Ace Commercial	2752	E	562 946-6664	3505
Crt Color Printing Inc	2752	F	562 906-1517	3553
Ink Spot Inc	2752	E	626 338-4500	3596
Inkovation Inc	2752	F	800 465-4174	3597
Vomela Specialty Company	2752	C	562 944-3853	3706
ABC Imaging of Washington	2759	F	562 375-7280	3727
All-Star Lettering Inc	2759	E	562 404-5995	3731
Martin E-Z Stick Labels	2759	F	562 906-1577	3785
Superior Printing Inc	2759	D	888 590-7998	3815
Ross Bindery Inc	2789	C	562 623-4565	3848
Olin Chlor Alkali Logistics	2812	C	562 692-0510	3859
Airgas Usa LLC	2813	D	562 945-1383	3864
Airgas Usa LLC	2813	E	562 906-8700	3865
Pct-Gw Carbide Tools Usa Inc	2819	E	562 921-7898	3903
Phibro-Tech Inc	2819	E	562 698-8036	3905
Solvay America Inc	2819	C	562 906-3300	3912
Bdc Epoxy Systems Inc	2821	E	562 944-6177	3928
Ecowise Inc	2821	E	626 759-3997	3937
Multi-Plastics Inc	2821	E	562 692-1202	3955
Southland Polymers Inc	2821	E	562 921-0444	3972
St Clair Plastics Inc	2821	E	562 946-3115	3974
Jarrow Industries LLC (PA)	2834	D	562 906-1919	4145
Jarrow Industries LLC	2834	E	562 631-9330	4146
Jarrow Industries LLC	2834	E	562 631-9330	4147
Jarrow Industries LLC	2834	E	562 631-9330	4148
Nhk Laboratories Inc (PA)	2834	E	562 903-5835	4183
Nhk Laboratories Inc	2834	D	562 204-5002	4184
Kik-Socal Inc	2842	A	562 946-6427	4355
Morgan Gallacher Inc	2842	E	562 695-1232	4361
Master Powder Coating Inc	2851	E	562 863-4135	4494
Qspac Industries Inc (PA)	2891	D	562 407-3868	4578
Sun Chemical Corporation	2893	E	562 946-2327	4591
L M Scofield Company (DH)	2899	E	323 720-3000	4615
Phibro Animal Health Corp	2899	D	562 698-8036	4626
Sika Corporation	2899	F	562 941-0231	4631
Golden West Refining Company	2911	E	562 921-3581	4641
Gasket Manufacturing Co	3053	E	310 217-5600	4731
R D Rubber Technology Corp	3061	E	562 941-4800	4752
Duro-Flex Rubber Products Inc	3069	E	562 946-5533	4760
Rogers Corporation	3069	D	562 404-8942	4791
Ptm & W Industries Inc	3083	E	562 946-4511	4841
Sleepcomp West LLC	3086	E	562 946-3222	4905
Vantage Associates Inc	3088	E	800 995-8322	4921
Barber-Webb Company Inc (PA)	3089	E	541 488-4821	4956
Bolero Inds Inc A Cal Corp	3089	E	562 693-3000	4966
Clack Corporation	3089	D	562 789-1702	4991
Elastpro Silicone Sheeting LLC	3089	F	562 348-2348	5022
Reinhold Industries Inc (DH)	3089	C	562 944-3281	5179
Santa Fe Extruders Inc	3089	E	562 921-8991	5199
Vantage Associates Inc	3089	D	562 968-1400	5242
Nelson Sports Inc	3149	E	562 944-8081	5280
GP Merger Sub Inc	3231	D	562 946-7722	5342
New Glaspro Inc	3231	E	800 776-2368	5349
Standridge Granite Corporation	3281	E	562 946-6334	5535
Brown-Pacific Inc	3312	E	562 921-3471	5579
Rtm Products Inc	3312	E	562 926-2400	5599
Maruichi American Corporation	3317	D	562 903-8600	5637
Corrpro Companies Inc	3331	E	562 944-1636	5668
Rbc Lubron Bearing Systems Inc (HQ)	3339	E	714 841-3007	5676
Heraeus Prcous Mtls N Amer LLC (DH)	3341	C	562 921-7464	5681
Fry Reglet Corporation (PA)	3354	D	800 237-9773	5696
Philatron International	3357	E	562 802-2570	5746
Bodycote Thermal Proc Inc	3398	D	562 946-1717	5827
Bodycote W Cast Anlytcal Svc I	3398	E	562 948-2225	5830
Continental Heat Treating Inc	3398	D	562 944-8808	5833
Accuride International Inc (PA)	3429	E	562 903-0200	5894
Birmingham Fastener & Sup Inc	3429	E	562 944-9549	5907
Calmex Fireplace Eqp Mfg Inc	3429	E	716 645-2901	5911
Star Die Casting Inc	3429	E	562 698-0627	5945
Collicutt Energy Services Inc	3432	E	562 944-4413	5968
Brunton Enterprises Inc	3441	C	562 945-0013	6001
Custom Steel Fabrication Inc	3441	F	562 907-2777	6017
Precision Metal Crafts Inc	3441	E	562 468-7080	6064
Best Roll-Up Door Inc	3442	E	562 802-2233	6101
Cji Process Systems Inc	3443	D	562 777-0614	6136
Pacific Steam Equipment Inc	3443	E	562 906-9292	6147
Parker-Hannifin Corporation	3443	E	562 404-1938	6149
Wells Struthers Corporation	3443	E	814 726-1000	6171
Excel Sheet Metal Inc (PA)	3444	D	562 944-0701	6236
Grayd-A Prcsion Met Fbricators	3444	E	562 944-8951	6247
Pico Metal Products Inc	3444	E	562 944-0626	6291
R & R Ductwork LLC	3444	F	562 944-9660	6301
Western Screw Products Inc	3451	E	562 698-5793	6426
Zenith Screw Products Inc	3451	E	562 941-0281	6428
Twist Tite Mfg Inc	3452	E	562 229-0990	6455
Timken Gears & Services Inc	3462	E	310 605-2600	6473
A-W Engineering Company Inc	3469	E	562 945-1041	6491
C Wolfe Industries Inc	3469	E	626 443-7185	6502
Eagleware Manufacturing Co Inc	3469	E	562 320-3100	6513
Ftr Associates Inc	3469	E	562 945-7504	6518
New Gordon Industries LLC	3469	E	562 483-7378	6542
P P Mfg Co Inc	3469	F	562 921-3640	6544
Tru-Form Industries Inc (PA)	3469	D	562 802-2041	6564
Allblack Co Inc	3471	E	562 946-2955	6580
Associated Plating Company	3471	E	562 946-5525	6587
Cal-Tron Plating Inc	3471	E	562 945-1181	6599
Electronic Chrome Grinding Inc	3471	E	562 946-6671	6618
Trident Plating Inc	3471	E	562 906-2556	6673
Rev Co Spring Mfanufacturing	3495	E	562 949-1958	6808
Vault Pro	3499	F	800 299-6929	6875
Conveyor Service & Electric	3535	E	562 777-1221	6971
Konecranes Inc	3536	E	562 903-1371	6981
Medlin Ramps	3542	E	877 948-3546	7033
Express Die Supply Inc	3544	E	562 903-1700	7069
Santa Fe Enterprises Inc	3544	E	562 692-7596	7096
Sygma Inc	3545	C	562 906-8880	7134
FPec Corporation A Cal Corp (PA)	3556	F	562 802-3727	7197
Superior Food Machinery Inc	3556	E	562 949-0396	7217
United Surface Solutions LLC	3559	E	562 693-0202	7264
Cascade Pump Company	3561	D	562 946-1414	7271
Sulzer Pump Services (us) Inc	3561	E	562 903-1000	7291
United Bakery Equipment Co Inc (PA)	3565	D	310 635-8121	7355
Industrial Sprockets Gears Inc	3568	E	323 233-7221	7380
Source Code LLC	3571	E	562 903-1500	7451
Aferin LLC	3572	E	562 903-1500	7461
Whittier Mailing Products Inc (PA)	3579	F	562 464-3000	7589
Lmw Enterprises LLC	3585	E	562 944-1969	7617
Gorlitz Sewer & Drain Inc	3589	E	562 944-3060	7660
Aero Chip Inc	3599	E	562 404-6300	7739
C & C Die Engraving	3599	E	562 944-3399	7791
Golden West Machine Inc	3599	E	562 903-1111	7852
JR Machine Company Inc	3599	E	562 903-9477	7891
Machine Precision Components	3599	F	562 404-0500	7914
Omega Precision	3599	E	562 946-2491	7961
Pedavena Mould and Die Co Inc	3599	E	310 327-2814	7970
Process Fab Inc	3599	C	562 921-1979	7981
Pscmb Repairs Inc	3599	E	626 448-7778	7984
Serrano Industries Inc	3599	E	562 777-8180	8026
SMI Ca Inc	3599	E	562 926-9407	8029
Vescio Threading Co	3599	D	562 802-1868	8066
Ohmega Solenoid Co Inc	3612	E	562 944-7948	8103
Pioneer Custom Elec Pdts Corp	3612	D	562 944-0626	8107
Age Incorporated	3613	E	562 483-7300	8117
General Switchgear Inc	3613	E		8122
Artiva USA Inc	3645	E	562 298-8968	8289
Dab Inc	3645	D	562 623-4773	8291

2024 Southern California
Business Directory and Buyers Guide

(P-0000) Products & Services Section entry number
(PA)=Parent Co (HQ)=Headquarters (DH)=Div Headquarters

Name	SIC	EMP	PHONE	ENTRY#
Shimada Enterprises Inc	3648	E	562 802-8811	8381
Funai Corporation Inc (HQ)	3651	E	310 787-3000	8411
Vantage Point Products Corp (PA)	3651	E	562 946-1718	8446
Royal Flex Circuits Inc	3672	E	562 404-0626	8724
Detoronics Corp	3678	E	626 579-7130	8969
Trojan Battery Holdings LLC	3691	E	800 423-6569	9157
Trojan Battery Company LLC (DH)	3692	C	562 236-3000	9161
M & H Electric Fabricators Inc	3694	E	562 926-9552	9169
Philatron International (PA)	3699	D	562 802-0452	9241
Rosemead Electrical Supply	3699	E	562 298-4190	9251
Auto Motive Power Inc	3714	C	800 894-7104	9355
Los Angeles Sleeve Co Inc	3714	E	562 945-7578	9415
M E D Inc	3714	D	562 921-0464	9418
Maxon Industries Inc	3714	D	562 464-0099	9420
Mid-West Fabricating Co	3714	E	562 698-9615	9425
Overland Vehicle Systems LLC	3714	E	833 226-4863	9436
R A Phillips Industries Inc (PA)	3714	E	562 781-2121	9445
US Motor Works LLC (PA)	3714	E	562 404-0488	9482
Advanced Grund Systems Engrg L (HQ)	3724	E	562 906-9300	9561
All Power Manufacturing Co	3728	C	562 802-2640	9620
Goodrich Corporation	3728	D	562 944-4441	9703
Lefiell Manufacturing Company	3728	C	562 921-3411	9736
Pmd Inc	3728	F	925 765-0629	9767
Precision Tube Bending	3728	D	562 921-6723	9769
Spec Tool Company	3728	D	323 723-9533	9801
Vantage Associates Inc	3728	E	562 968-1400	9824
V&H Performance Inc	3751	D	562 921-7461	9888
Vantage Associates Inc (PA)	3769	E	619 477-6940	9922
Deca International Corp	3812	E	714 367-5900	9968
Votaw Precision Technologies	3812	C	562 944-0661	10088
Tellkamp Systems Inc (PA)	3822	E	562 802-1621	10107
Cosasco Inc	3823	D	562 949-0123	10126
Rohrback Cosasco Systems Inc (DH)	3823	D	562 949-0123	10157
I-Coat Company LLC	3827	E	562 941-9989	10318
Endotec Inc	3842	E	714 681-6306	10657
US Armor Corporation	3842	E	562 207-4240	10718
Bravo Sports (HQ)	3949	D	562 484-5100	10981
Saint Nine America Inc	3949	E	562 921-5300	11023
Kingsolver Inc	3991	F	562 945-7590	11090
K S Designs Inc	3993	E	562 929-3973	11128
Orange Cnty Name Plate Co Inc	3993	D	714 522-7693	11143
Tdi Signs	3993	E	562 436-5188	11173
Altro Usa Inc	3996	D	562 944-8292	11183
Golden Supreme Inc	3999	E	562 903-1063	11222
Gale/Triangle Inc (PA)	4212	D	562 741-1300	11453
General Lgstics Systems US Inc	4212	C	562 577-6037	11456
Savage Services Corporation	4212	D	562 400-2044	11464
Xpo Logistics Freight Inc	4213	D	562 946-8331	11514
FN Logistics Llc	4214	A	213 625-5900	11519
Great Amrcn Logistics Dist Inc	4214	D	562 229-3601	11521
Van Torrance & Storage Company (PA)	4214	D		11523
Wilsonart LLC	4225	E	562 921-7426	11630
Diversified Logistic Svcs Inc	4783	E	562 941-3600	11820
Southern California Edison Co	4911	B	562 903-3191	12060
Egge Machine Company Inc (PA)	5013	E	562 945-3419	12239
Ralco Holdings Inc (DH)	5013	C	949 440-5094	12255
Vgp Holdings LLC	5013	B	562 906-6200	12264
Lakin Tire West Incorporated (PA)	5014	C	562 802-2752	12271
Janus Et Cie (PA)	5021	C	310 601-2958	12286
New Tangram LLC	5021	C	562 365-5000	12287
Galleher LLC (PA)	5023	C	562 944-8885	12302
Tri-West Ltd (PA)	5023	C	562 692-9166	12319
Ugm Citatah Inc (PA)	5032	C	562 921-9549	12362
Teac America Inc (HQ)	5045	F	323 726-0303	12444
Bergsen Inc	5051	E	562 236-9787	12535
Coast Aluminum Inc (PA)	5051	C	562 946-6061	12542
Conquest Industries Inc	5051	E	562 906-1111	12543
Fry Steel Company	5051	C	562 802-2721	12551
Reliance Steel & Aluminum Co	5051	D	562 944-3322	12568
Tmx Aerospace	5051	C	562 215-4410	12575
Pacific Power Systems Integration Inc	5063	E	562 281-0500	12612
Talley Inc (PA)	5065	E	562 906-8000	12700
Larsen Supply Co (PA)	5074	D	562 698-0731	12746
TA Industries Inc (HQ)	5074	E	562 466-1000	12748
Material Handling Supply Inc (HQ)	5084	D	562 921-7715	12797
Maxon Lift Corp (PA)	5084	C	562 464-0099	12798
Menke Marking Devices Inc	5084	E	562 921-1380	12800
Raymond Handling Solutions Inc (DH)	5084	C	562 944-8067	12815
Rebas Inc	5084	E	562 941-4155	12817
Lord & Sons Inc	5085	D	562 529-2500	12863
McMaster-Carr Supply Company	5085	B	562 692-5911	12864
Pcbc Holdco Inc	5085	E	562 944-9549	12871
Revco Industries Inc (PA)	5085	E	562 777-1588	12875
Kelly Spicers Inc (HQ)	5111	C	562 698-1199	12990
Georgia-Pacific LLC	5113	B	562 861-6226	13008
Danne Montague-King Co (PA)	5122	F	562 944-0230	13037
McKesson Corporation	5122	C	562 463-2100	13053
Steven Label Corporation (PA)	5131	E	562 698-9971	13096
Mias Fashion Mfg Co Inc	5137	B	562 906-1060	13137
Wismettac Asian Foods Inc (HQ)	5141	C	562 802-1900	13242
LA Specialty Produce Co (PA)	5148	B	562 741-2200	13332
Laird Plastics Inc	5162	E	562 464-9929	13414
Access Business Group LLC	5169	B	808 422-9482	13420
Brenntag Pacific Inc (DH)	5169	C	562 903-9626	13425
Triangle Distributing Co	5181	B	562 699-3424	13473
Target Specialty Products Inc	5191	D	562 865-9955	13492
Chus Packaging Supplies Inc	5199	E	562 944-6411	13533
Global Trade Alliance Inc	5531	C	562 944-6422	13862
Freestyle Sales Co Ltd Partnr	5946	D	323 660-3460	14083
Riviera Finance of Texas Inc	6153	D	562 777-1300	14287
Thrifty Oil Co (PA)	6512	F	562 921-3581	14688
Tydg Enterprises Inc	6719	C	562 903-9030	14950
Rentokil North America Inc	7342	D	562 802-2238	15687
Crossing Guard Company	7381	A	310 202-8284	16636
Johnson Controls	7382	C	562 405-3817	16743
Safesmart Access Inc	7382	E	310 410-1525	16751
Newport Diversified Inc	7389	C	562 921-4359	16886
El Monte Rents Inc (HQ)	7519	C	562 404-9300	16986
E & L Electric	7694	F	562 903-9272	17103
Think Together	7991	B	562 236-3835	17416
Crescent Healthcare Inc (DH)	8082	C	714 520-6300	18607
Peoples Care Inc	8351	C	562 320-0174	19224
Spearman Aerospace Inc	8711	E	714 523-4751	19693
California Lab Sciences LLC	8734	B	562 758-6900	19960
Westpac Labs Inc	8734	B	562 906-5227	19986
Fujitec America Inc	8741	C	310 464-8270	20033
Matt Construction Corporation (PA)	8742	C	562 903-2277	20195
Greater Los Angles Cnty Vctor	8748	C	562 944-7976	20342

SANTA MARIA, CA - Santa Barbara County

Name	SIC	EMP	PHONE	ENTRY#
Darensberries LLC	0171	C	805 937-8000	13
Freshway Farms LLC	0171	C	805 349-7170	16
J&G Berry Farms LLC	0171	C	831 750-9408	17
Red Blossom Farms Inc	0171	D	805 686-4747	20
Red Blossom Sales Inc	0171	A	805 349-9404	21
Reiter Affl Companies LLC	0171	C	805 925-8577	22
Glad-A-Way Gardens Inc	0181	C	805 938-0569	55
Plantel Nurseries Inc	0181	B	805 934-4300	66
Plantel Nurseries Inc (PA)	0181	E	805 349-8952	67
Blackjack Frms De La Csta Cntl	0191	C	805 347-1333	76
Rancho Laguna Farms LLC	0191	D	805 925-7805	85
Greka Integrated Inc (PA)	1382	C	805 347-8700	307
Santa Maria Enrgy Holdings LLC	1382	E	805 938-3320	318
Cal Coast Acidizing Co	1389	E	805 934-2411	333
Engel & Gray Inc	1389	E	805 925-2771	344
Pacific Petroleum California Inc	1389	B	805 925-1947	375
PC Mechanical Inc	1389	E	805 925-2888	378
Smith McHncl-Lctrical-Plumbing	1541	E	805 621-5000	517
Pictsweet Company	2038	B	805 928-4414	1398
ARC Vineyards LLC	2084	E	805 937-3901	1611
Central Coast Wine Warehouse (PA)	2084	F	805 928-9210	1616
Flood Ranch Company	2084	E	805 937-3616	1629
Foxen Vineyard Inc	2084	E	805 937-4251	1631
Jackson Family Wines Inc	2084	E	805 938-7300	1639
American Bottling Company	2086	D	805 928-1001	1682
Pepsi-Cola Metro Btlg Co Inc	2086	E	805 739-2160	1712
Reyes Coca-Cola Bottling LLC	2086	E	805 925-2629	1727
Reyes Coca-Cola Bottling LLC	2086	E	805 614-3702	1728
Tognazzini Beverage Service	2086	E	805 928-1144	1742
Curation Foods Inc (HQ)	2099	D	800 454-1355	1879
Amass Brands Inc	2833	E	619 204-2560	3990
North American Fire Hose Corp	3052	D	805 922-7076	4710
Alltec Integrated Mfg Inc	3089	E	805 595-3500	4934
Prince Lionheart Inc (PA)	3089	E	805 922-2250	5164
Princeton Case-West Inc	3089	E	805 928-8840	5165
Impo International Inc	3144	E	805 922-7753	5276
Mid-State Concrete Pdts Inc	3272	E	805 928-2855	5425
Okonite Company Inc	3357	C	805 922-6682	5745
Matthew Warren Inc	3493	E	805 928-3851	6783
Melfred Borzall Inc	3541	E	805 614-4344	7016
Fresh Venture Foods LLC	3556	E	805 928-3374	7198
Atlas Copco Mafi-Trench Co LLC (DH)	3564	C	805 928-5757	7319
Helical Products Company Inc	3568	E	805 928-3851	7377
Arrow Screw Products Inc	3599	E	805 928-2269	7763
Wasco Sales and Marketing Inc	3643	E	805 739-2747	8282
Quintron Systems Inc (PA)	3661	E	805 928-4343	8483

Employee Codes: A=Over 500 employees, B=251-500
C=101-250, D=51-100, E=20-50, F=10-19, G=1-9

2024 Southern California
Business Directory and Buyers Guide

© Mergent Inc. 1-800-342-5647

1443

GEOGRAPHIC

	SIC	EMP	PHONE	ENTRY#
Gavial Engineering & Mfg Inc	3672	E	805 614-0060	8680
Alan Johnson Prfmce Engrg Inc	3711	E	805 922-1202	9274
Rlv Tuned Exhaust Products Inc	3714	E	805 925-5461	9451
Safran Cabin Inc	3728	C	805 922-3013	9788
Safran Seats Santa Maria LLC	3728	A	805 922-5995	9793
Northrop Grumman Systems Corp	3812	D	805 315-5728	10042
Sign Post Byway Inc	3993	F	949 566-3016	11160
Certified Frt Logistics Inc (PA)	4213	C	800 592-5906	11474
Adient Aerospace LLC (PA)	4581	C	949 514-1851	11684
Frontier California Inc	4813	B	805 925-0000	11882
Valley Garbage Rubbish Co Inc	4953	C	805 614-1131	12191
Coast Rock Products Inc	5032	E	805 925-2505	12351
Hardy Diagnostics Inc (PA)	5047	B	805 346-2766	12492
Foothill Packing Inc	5141	D	805 925-7900	13181
Central Coast Distributing LLC	5181	D	805 922-2108	13462
Smith Packing Inc	5199	C	805 348-1817	13562
Coasthills Credit Union (PA)	6062	D	805 733-7600	14246
H & H LLC (PA)	7011	F	805 925-2036	15165
Mission Linen Supply	7213	D	805 922-3579	15457
Ramco Enterprises LP	7361	B	805 922-9888	15886
Osr Enterprises Inc	7372	C	805 925-1831	16339
J and D Stl Fbrication Repr LP	7692	F	805 928-9674	17088
Genesis Healthcare LLC	8051	A	805 922-3558	17961
Dignity Health	8062	E	805 739-3000	18241
Marian Community Clinic	8062	D	805 739-3867	18340
Marian Medical Center	8062	A	805 739-3000	18341
Santa Brbara Cttage Hosp Fndti	8062	B	805 346-7135	18421
Work Inc	8322	D	805 739-0451	19171
Vtc Enterprises (PA)	8331	C	805 928-5000	19197
Ensign Group Inc	8361	C	805 925-8713	19261
Nursecore Management Svcs LLC	8361	A	805 938-7660	19290
Microwave Applications Group	8711	E	805 928-5711	19647
American Management Svcs W LLC	8741	C	805 352-1921	19996

SANTA MONICA, CA - Los Angeles County

	SIC	EMP	PHONE	ENTRY#
Morley Builders Inc (PA)	1541	C	310 399-1600	512
Jones Brothers Cnstr Corp (PA)	1542	D	310 470-1885	561
Morley Construction Company (HQ)	1771	D	310 399-1600	1079
Dext Company of Maryland (DH)	2048	E	310 458-1574	1439
International Processing Corp (DH)	2048	E	310 458-1574	1443
Reconserve Inc (HQ)	2048	E	310 458-1574	1448
Bake R Us Inc	2051	C	310 630-5873	1451
Liquid Death Mountain Water	2086	D	818 521-5500	1703
Red Bull Media Hse N Amer Inc	2086	D	310 393-4647	1722
Figs Inc	2326	B	424 300-8330	2173
Koral LLC	2329	E	323 391-1060	2211
Koral Industries LLC (PA)	2339	E	323 585-5343	2343
Zooey Apparel Inc	2339	E	310 315-2880	2385
Mammoth Media Inc	2711	D	832 315-0833	3302
Ubm Canon LLC (DH)	2721	E	310 445-4200	3393
Alg Inc	2741	B	424 258-8026	3426
C Publishing LLC	2741	E	310 393-3800	3435
Universal Mus Group Dist Corp (DH)	2741	D	310 235-4700	3497
Universal Music Publishing Inc	2741	D	310 235-4700	3498
Printing Palace Inc (PA)	2752	F	310 451-5151	3665
Archipelago Inc	2844	C	213 743-9200	4379
Lanza Research International	2844	E	310 393-5227	4431
Provivi Inc (PA)	2869	E	310 828-2307	4526
Kas Engineering Inc (PA)	3089	E	310 450-8925	5076
Careismatic Brands LLC (PA)	3143	C	818 671-2100	5272
Ridge Wallet LLC	3172	F	818 636-2832	5304
Vault Prep Inc	3272	E	310 971-9091	5455
Coast Flagstone Co	3281	D	310 829-4010	5527
Hamrock Inc	3315	C	562 944-0255	5616
Solarreserve LLC (PA)	3433	F	310 315-2200	5985
Ngd Systems Inc	3572	E	949 870-9148	7478
Apogee Electronics Corporation	3651	E	310 584-9394	8395
Extreme Group Holdings LLC	3652	E	310 899-3200	8459
Ovation R&G LLC (PA)	3663	F	310 430-7575	8558
Phonesuit Inc	3663	E	310 774-0282	8561
Omega Leads Inc	3679	E	310 394-6786	9092
Pioneer Magnetics Inc	3679	C	310 829-6751	9098
Powell Electric	3699	E	310 394-6498	9243
Straight Smile LLC (HQ)	3843	F	424 389-4551	10770
Carr Corporation (PA)	3844	E	310 587-1113	10782
Jakks Pacific Inc (PA)	3944	D	424 268-9444	10957
Bravo Highline LLC	3949	E	562 484-5100	10979
Casa De Hermandad (PA)	3949	E	310 477-8272	10983
Executive Network Entps Inc	4119	A	310 457-8822	11384
Santa Monica City of	4131	B	310 458-1975	11414
Verizon Services Corp	4812	D	310 315-1100	11865
Connexity Inc (DH)	4813	C	310 571-1235	11876
Hulu LLC (HQ)	4813	B	310 571-4700	11887

	SIC	EMP	PHONE	ENTRY#
Pandora Media LLC	4832	C	424 653-6803	11933
Entravsion Communications Corp (PA)	4833	C	310 447-3870	11945
SF Broadcasting Wisconsin Inc	4833	C	310 586-2410	11963
Game Show Network Music LLC (DH)	4841	C	310 255-6800	11994
Time Warner Companies Inc	4841	A	310 315-4437	12001
Cypress Creek Holdings LLC	4911	D	310 581-6299	12019
Inspire Energy Holdings LLC	4911	D	866 403-2620	12028
Solarreserve Inc	4911	D	310 315-2200	12054
K-Micro Inc	5045	D	310 442-3200	12423
Trey Arch LLC	5045	B	310 581-4700	12447
TV Guide Entrmt Group LLC	5064	D	310 360-1441	12639
Glamour Industries Co	5087	D	213 687-8600	12891
Spilo Worldwide Inc	5087	D	213 687-8600	12895
Genius Products Inc	5099	C	310 453-1222	12976
Guthy-Renker LLC	5099	D	310 581-6250	12978
Johnny Was LLC	5137	D	310 656-0600	13128
Converse Inc	5139	D	310 451-0314	13161
Ford of Santa Monica Inc	5511	D	310 451-1588	13768
Volkswagen Santa Monica Inc (PA)	5511	C	310 829-1888	13845
Hallmark Labs LLC	5947	C	424 210-3600	14086
Wells Fargo Capital Fin LLC (DH)	6159	D	310 453-7300	14292
Mercury Insurance Company	6331	B	310 451-4943	14519
Gumbiner Savett Inc	6512	D	310 828-9798	14664
Irvine APT Communities LP	6513	C	310 255-1221	14723
William Warren Properties Inc	6513	C	310 454-1500	14733
Carmel Partners LLC	6722	C	916 479-5286	14960
Clearlake Capital Group LP (PA)	6722	B	310 400-8800	14962
Guggenheim Prtners Inv MGT LLC	6722	D	310 576-1270	14963
Wilshire 2015 Fund	6722	C	310 451-3051	14974
Macerich Company (PA)	6798	D	310 394-6000	15015
Inventure Capital Corporation (PA)	6799	A	213 262-6903	15033
By The Blue Sea LLC	7011	B	310 458-0030	15102
C W Hotels Ltd	7011	D	310 395-9700	15104
Dtrs Santa Monica LLC	7011	B	310 458-6700	15139
Edward Thomas Hospitality Corp	7011	B	310 458-0030	15141
Et Whitehall Seascape LLC	7011	C	310 581-5533	15149
M&C Hotel Interests Inc	7011	B	310 399-9344	15234
Ocean Avenue LLC	7011	B	310 576-7777	15268
Santa Monica Hotel Owner LLC	7011	C	310 395-3332	15350
Santa Monica Proper Jv LLC	7011	C	310 620-9990	15351
Second Street Corporation	7011	C	310 394-5454	15353
Windsor Capital Group Inc	7011	C	310 566-1100	15424
Ad Populum LLC	7311	D	619 818-7644	15526
Adconion Media Inc (PA)	7311	C	310 382-5521	15527
Advertise Purple	7311	D	424 272-7400	15528
Movers and Shakers LLC	7311	D	310 893-7051	15561
Postaer Rubin and Associates	7311	C	312 644-3636	15568
Rubin Postaer and Associates (PA)	7311	C	310 394-4000	15573
Beachbody Company Inc (PA)	7313	C	310 883-9000	15589
Edmundscom Inc (HQ)	7313	A	310 309-6300	15592
Kargo Global Inc	7313	C	212 979-9000	15595
Platinum Clg Indianapolis LLC	7349	B	310 584-8000	15737
Bird Rides Inc	7371	C	866 205-2442	15982
Fair Financial Corp (PA)	7371	C	800 584-5000	16030
Playhaven LLC	7371	C	310 308-9668	16097
School-Link Technologies Inc	7371	D	310 434-2700	16108
Snap Inc (PA)	7371	A	310 399-3339	16117
Tomitribe Corporation	7371	E	310 526-7676	16134
Activision Blizzard Inc (HQ)	7372	B	310 255-2000	16157
Amber Holding Inc	7372	D	603 324-3000	16164
Clearlake Capital Partners	7372	A	310 400-8800	16203
Cornerstone Ondemand Inc (HQ)	7372	B	310 752-0200	16215
Gumgum Inc (PA)	7372	E	310 260-9666	16262
Hooked	7372	E	805 551-4981	16264
Kingcom(us) LLC (DH)	7372	E	424 744-5697	16284
Mediamorph Inc (HQ)	7372	E	212 643-0762	16304
Patientpop Inc	7372	D	844 487-8399	16345
Prata Inc	7372	E	512 823-1002	16351
Railstech Inc	7372	E	267 315-2998	16364
Salesforcecom Inc	7372	E	310 752-7000	16372
Epochcom LLC	7374	C	310 664-5700	16495
Goodrx Holdings Inc (PA)	7374	C	855 268-2822	16497
Leaf Group Ltd (HQ)	7374	C	310 394-6400	16501
Edmunds Holding Company (PA)	7375	A	310 309-6300	16527
Tigerconnect Inc (PA)	7379	D	310 401-1820	16607
Advanstar Communications Inc	7389	E	310 857-7500	16767
Advanstar Communications Inc (DH)	7389	E	310 857-7500	16768
Hct Packaging Inc (PA)	7389	C	310 260-7680	16838
Universal Mus Investments Inc (HQ)	7389	D	888 583-7176	16951
Universal Music Group Inc (HQ)	7389	D	310 865-0770	16952
Wells Fargo Capital Finance Inc	7389	C	310 453-7300	16965
M2 Automotive	7532	A	310 399-3887	17011
Artisan Entertainment Inc	7812	A	310 449-9200	17169

Mergent email: customerrelations@mergent.com
1444

2024 Southern California
Business Directory and Buyers Guide

(P-0000) Products & Services Section entry number
(PA)=Parent Co (HQ)=Headquarters (DH)=Div Headquarters

	SIC	EMP	PHONE	ENTRY#
Focus Features LLC (DH)	7812	D		17192
Lions Gate Films Inc	7812	C	310 449-9200	17198
Luma Pictures Inc	7812	C	310 888-8738	17199
Lionsgate Productions Inc	7822	B	310 255-3937	17278
Sonar Entertainment Inc (PA)	7822	D	424 230-7140	17279
Illumination Entertainment	7929	C	626 298-1879	17340
Red Bull North America Inc (HQ)	7929	D	310 460-5356	17348
Santa Monica Amusements LLC	7996	B	310 451-9641	17453
Bay Clubs Company LLC	7997	B	310 829-4995	17470
Jonathan Club	7997	C	310 393-9245	17491
Saint Jhns Hlth Ctr Foundation	8011	C	310 315-6111	17755
American Retirement Corp	8051	C	310 399-3227	17880
Asmb LLC	8051	D	949 347-7100	17883
Berkeley E Convalescent Hosp	8059	C	310 829-5377	18112
Golden State Health Ctrs Inc	8059	C	310 451-9706	18130
Providence St Johns Hlth Ctr	8062	B	971 268-7643	18400
Saint Johns Health Center Foundation (DH)	8062	A	310 829-5511	18412
Regents of The University Cal	8099	C	310 267-9308	18800
Sensei Wellness Holdings Inc	8099	D	602 499-9862	18804
People Concern	8322	C	310 883-1222	19123
People Concern	8322	C	310 450-0650	19124
Vista Del Mar Child Fmly Svcs	8361	C	310 836-1223	19309
Mens Apparel Guild In Cal Inc	8611	C	310 857-7500	19381
Boys Grls CLB Snta Monica Inc	8641	D	310 361-8500	19429
Elizabeth Glser Pdtric Aids FN	8641	B	310 593-0047	19445
Milken Family Foundation	8641	C	310 570-4800	19456
Los Angeles Intl Ch Chrst	8661	C	213 351-2300	19503
Automobile Club Southern Cal	8699	C	310 453-1909	19520
California Semiconductor Tech	8711	C	310 579-2939	19560
Bjarke Ingels Group Nyc LLC	8712	C	347 549-4141	19726
Kite Pharma Inc (HQ)	8731	D	310 824-9999	19851
The Rand Corporation (PA)	8733	A	310 393-0411	19948
911 Health Inc	8734	D	310 560-8509	19954
Global-Dining Inc California	8741	D	310 576-9922	20035
Provident Financial Management	8741	D	310 282-0477	20086
Cloud9 Esports Inc	8742	D	424 256-8391	20152
Mgid Inc	8742	D	424 322-8059	20199
Stardust Studios Inc	8742	D	310 399-6047	20248
Wilshire Advisors LLC (PA)	8742	C	310 451-3051	20275
Ziprecruiter Inc	8742	A	877 252-1062	20280
Ocean Park Community Center	8748	C	310 828-6717	20369

SANTA PAULA, CA - Ventura County

	SIC	EMP	PHONE	ENTRY#
Saticoy Lemon Association (PA)	0723	D	805 654-6500	111
Carbon California Company LLC	1311	E	805 933-1901	258
Oil Well Service Company	1389	D	805 525-2103	370
Weatherford International LLC	1389	F	805 933-0242	395
Keller North America Inc	1799	D	805 933-1331	1165
Saticoy Foods Corporation	2033	E	805 647-5266	1344
Calavo Growers Inc (PA)	2099	C	805 525-1245	1863
Turtle Storage Ltd	2542	E	805 933-3688	2997
Westlake Engrg Roto Form	3089	E	805 525-8800	5251
Calpipe Industries LLC	3312	C	562 803-4388	5584
Automotive Racing Products Inc	3429	C	805 525-1497	5899
Coastal Cnting Indus Scale Inc	3545	E	805 487-0403	7110
Abrisa Industrial Glass Inc (HQ)	3827	D	805 525-4902	10307
Abrisa Technologies	3827	E	805 525-4902	10308
Weber Orthopedic LP (PA)	3842	D	800 221-5465	10722
Pavement Coatings Co	4953	C	805 647-0693	12178
Thompco Inc	5082	E	805 933-8048	12779
Troop Real Estate Inc	6531	C	805 921-0030	14879
Ventura County Medical Center	8011	A	805 933-8600	17825
Tissue-Grown Corporation	8731	D	805 525-1975	19883
Ventura County Medical Center	8742	D	805 677-5184	20267

SANTA ROSA VALLEY, CA - Ventura County

	SIC	EMP	PHONE	ENTRY#
Hyper-Tech LLC	7389	F	805 988-2000	16843

SANTA YNEZ, CA - Santa Barbara County

	SIC	EMP	PHONE	ENTRY#
Gainey Vineyard	2084	E	805 688-0558	1632
Valley Oaks Industries	2521	F	805 688-2754	2901
Channel Islnds Yung MNS Chrstn	8641	D	805 686-2037	19437

SANTA YSABEL, CA - San Diego County

	SIC	EMP	PHONE	ENTRY#
Dudleys Bakery Inc	5461	E	760 765-0488	13715

SANTEE, CA - San Diego County

	SIC	EMP	PHONE	ENTRY#
Lustros Inc	1021	E	619 449-4800	231
T C Construction Company Inc	1623	C	619 448-4560	696
Challenger Sheet Metal Inc	1761	D	619 596-8040	1038
Tower Glass Inc	1793	D	619 596-6199	1120
Lauren Anthony & Co Inc	2511	E	619 590-1141	2778
CCM Enterprises (PA)	2541	D	619 562-2605	2946

	SIC	EMP	PHONE	ENTRY#
European Wholesale Counter	2541	C	619 562-0565	2952
South West Lubricants Inc	2992	D	619 449-5000	4688
Delstar Holding Corp	3081	E	619 258-1503	4809
C&M Manufacturing Company Inc (PA)	3082	E	619 449-7200	4829
Argee Mfg Co San Diego Inc	3089	D	619 449-5050	4946
R V Best Inc	3089	E	619 448-7300	5170
RCP Block & Brick Inc	3271	E	619 448-2240	5393
Vision Systems Inc	3354	D	619 258-7300	5715
TBs Irrigation Products Inc	3432	E	619 579-0520	5975
Davis Gregg Enterprises Inc	3443	F	619 449-4250	6141
Aymar Engineering	3444	F	619 562-1121	6196
Kevin Whaley	3496	E	619 596-4000	6819
Olson Irrigation Systems	3523	E	619 562-3100	6910
Terra Nova Technologies Inc	3535	D	619 596-7400	6978
Ds Fibertech Corp	3567	E	619 562-7001	7365
Alts Tool & Machine Inc	3599	D	619 562-6653	7755
Computer Intgrted McHining Inc	3599	E	619 596-9246	7807
Cozza Inc	3599	E	619 749-5663	7809
Mathy Machine Inc	3599	E	619 448-0404	7921
Quality Controlled Mfg Inc	3599	D	619 443-3997	7988
T I B Inc	3599	F	619 562-3071	8042
Stratedge Corporation	3674	*	866 424-4962	8899
Lhv Power Corporation (PA)	3679	E	619 258-7700	9078
Compucraft Industries Inc	3728	E	619 448-0787	9663
Air & Gas Tech Inc	3732	E	619 955-5980	9853
Interocean Industries Inc	3812	E	858 292-0808	9982
Interocean Systems LLC	3812	E	858 565-8400	9983
Valley Box Co Inc	5113	E	619 449-2882	13026
Smart & Final Stores Inc	5141	C	619 449-2396	13199
Lowes Home Centers LLC	5211	C	619 212-4100	13649
Santee Senior Retirement Com	8322	E	619 955-0901	19136
Scantibodies Laboratory Inc (PA)	8734	D	619 258-9300	19982

SAUGUS, CA - Los Angeles County

	SIC	EMP	PHONE	ENTRY#
Hasa Inc (PA)	2812	D	661 259-5848	3856

SEAL BEACH, CA - Orange County

	SIC	EMP	PHONE	ENTRY#
Hellman Properties LLC	1311	E	562 431-6022	262
Samedan Oil Corporation	1382	B	661 319-5038	317
Dendreon Pharmaceuticals LLC (HQ)	2834	E	562 252-7500	4100
Modular Wind Energy Inc	3511	D	562 304-6782	6883
Cosmodyne LLC	3559	E	562 795-5990	7229
Magtek Inc (PA)	3577	C	562 546-6400	7548
Amonix Inc	3674	E	562 344-4750	8765
Irish Interiors Holdings Inc	3728	E	949 559-0930	9724
Diversified Tchncal Systems Inc (HQ)	3825	E	562 493-0158	10195
Tyr Sport Inc (HQ)	5137	F	714 897-0799	13155
Original Parts Group Inc (PA)	5531	E	562 594-1000	13866
First Team RE - Orange Cnty	6531	C	562 596-9911	14801
Olson Company LLC (PA)	6552	C	562 596-4770	14908
Talent & Acquisition LLC	7371	C	888 970-9575	16130
Tenet Healthsystem Medical Inc	8011	C	562 493-9581	17803
Action Hlth Care Prsnnel Svcs	8082	C	562 799-5523	18585
Premier Healthcare Svcs LLC (DH)	8082	C	626 204-7930	18635
Country Villa Service Corp	8322	C	562 598-2477	19053
Sisters of St Joseph Orange	8661	A	562 430-4638	19507
Fisheries Resource Vlntr Corps	8742	C	562 596-9261	20172

SHAFTER, CA - Kern County

	SIC	EMP	PHONE	ENTRY#
Garlic Company	0139	C	661 393-4212	4
Wonderful Orchards LLC (HQ)	0173	B	661 399-4456	41
Grimmway Enterprises Inc	0723	B	661 393-3320	103
Wonderful Company LLC	0723	B	661 399-4456	120
Scientific Drilling Intl Inc	1381	E	661 831-0636	288
Cummings Vacuum Service Inc	1389	E	661 746-1786	341
M-I LLC	1389	E	661 321-5400	359
Oil Well Service Company	1389	E	661 746-4809	371
Tryad Service Corporation	1389	E	661 391-1524	390
Scotts Company LLC	2873	E	661 387-9555	4542
Elk Corporation of Texas	3272	D	661 391-3900	5411
McM Fabricators Inc	3441	C	661 589-2774	6047
Nikkel Iron Works Corporation	3523	E	661 746-4904	6909
Frank Russell Inc	3599	F	661 324-5575	7835
Standard Industries Inc	5033	E	661 387-1110	12369
Varner Family Ltd Partnership (PA)	6733	E	661 399-1163	15006
Central California Power	7538	E	661 589-2870	17030
Ponder Environmental Svcs Inc	8744	E	661 589-7771	20298

SHANDON, CA - San Luis Obispo County

	SIC	EMP	PHONE	ENTRY#
Pacific Tank & Cnstr Inc	3443	E	805 237-2929	6148

SHELL BEACH, CA - San Luis Obispo County

	SIC	EMP	PHONE	ENTRY#
Dolphin Bay Ht & Residence Inc	7011	D	805 773-4300	15136

Employee Codes: A=Over 500 employees, B=251-500
C=101-250, D=51-100, E=20-50, F=10-19, G=1-9

2024 Southern California
Business Directory and Buyers Guide

© Mergent Inc. 1-800-342-5647

1445

GEOGRAPHIC

	SIC	EMP	PHONE	ENTRY#
La Bonne Vie Inc	7991	D	805 773-5003	17402

SHERMAN OAKS, CA - Los Angeles County

	SIC	EMP	PHONE	ENTRY#
Ram Plumbing	1711	D	800 487-5812	814
Coastal Tile Inc	1743	D	818 988-6134	1004
Forever Rich International LLC	2023	E	310 867-4723	1271
American Naturals Company LLC	2099	E	323 201-6891	1850
Xcvi LLC (PA)	2211	D	213 749-2661	2035
E Z Buy & E Z Sell Recycl Corp (DH)	2711	C	310 886-7808	3274
Vytalogy Wellness LLC	2833	C	818 867-4440	4023
Envion LLC	3564	E	818 217-2500	7322
American Med O & P Clinic Inc	3842	E	818 281-5747	10635
Lucky Strike Entertainment Inc (PA)	3949	E	818 933-3752	11011
Ameritrans Express Inc	4731	F	818 201-0524	11739
Xsolla (usa) Inc (PA)	4813	A	818 435-6613	11912
Vubiquity Holdings Inc (DH)	4841	C	818 526-5000	12003
Sggh LLC	5063	A	805 435-1255	12617
Jarrow Formulas Inc (PA)	5122	C	310 204-6936	13048
Neurobrands LLC	5149	C	310 393-6444	13384
Center Automotive Inc	5511	D	818 907-9995	13746
Miller Automotive Group Inc (HQ)	5511	B	818 787-8400	13796
Psychic Eye Book Shops Inc (PA)	5942	C	818 906-8263	14069
Homebridge Financial Svcs Inc	6163	A	818 981-0606	14359
Royal Specialty Undwrt Inc	6331	C	818 922-6700	14525
Beverly and Company Inc	6531	C	323 422-3253	14751
Moss Management Services Inc	6531	C	818 990-5999	14833
Prospect Mortgage LLC	6719	A		14940
Burbank Partners LLC	7011	D	818 263-8704	15098
Grabit Interactive Inc	7313	E	844 472-2488	15594
Waldberg Inc	7313	E	818 843-0004	15599
Caine & Weiner Company Inc (PA)	7322	D	818 226-6000	15608
Branded Entrmt Netwrk Inc (PA)	7335	C	310 342-1500	15654
Ben Group Inc	7371	B	310 342-1500	15979
Rogue Games Inc	7371	E	650 483-8008	16104
Nile Ai Inc	7372	E	818 689-9107	16327
Papaya	7372	E	310 740-6774	16343
Reel Security California Inc	7381	D	818 928-4737	16673
Alternative Ira Services LLC	7389	C	877 936-7175	16774
Mega Appraisers Inc	7389	A	818 246-7370	16872
Prager University Foundation	7812	D	833 772-4378	17212
Premiere Radio Network Inc (DH)	7922	E	818 377-5300	17325
Lucky Strike Entertainment LLC	7933	D	248 374-3420	17358
Prime Hlthcare Svcs - Shrman O	8062	B	818 981-7111	18394
Dynamic Home Care Service Inc (PA)	8082	C	818 981-4446	18610
Help Group West (PA)	8093	C	818 781-0360	18695
Working With Autism Inc	8093	D	818 501-4240	18734
Star of Ca LLC	8099	D	818 986-7827	18808
West Capital Lending Inc	8742	C	818 501-2666	20273

SIERRA MADRE, CA - Los Angeles County

	SIC	EMP	PHONE	ENTRY#
Group H Engineering	1389	E	818 999-0999	349
Deasy Penner Podley	6531	C	626 408-1280	14786

SIGNAL HILL, CA - Los Angeles County

	SIC	EMP	PHONE	ENTRY#
Fenderscape Incorporated	0782	C	562 988-2228	191
Signal Hill Petroleum Inc	1382	E	562 595-6440	321
Black Gold Pump & Supply Inc	1389	F	323 298-0077	330
Oil Well Service Company Inc	1389	C	562 612-0600	372
Tiger Cased Hole Services Inc	1389	E	562 426-4044	386
Jmh Engineering and Cnstr	1521	D	562 317-1700	438
Har-Bro LLC (HQ)	1542	D	562 528-8000	555
Gregg Drilling LLC	1781	C	562 427-6899	1094
Lovco Construction Inc	1794	D	562 595-1601	1123
Rossmoor Pastries MGT Inc	2051	D	562 498-2253	1491
Clariant Corporation	2869	F	562 322-6647	4519
R D Mathis Company	3313	E	562 426-7049	5609
P T Industries Inc	3444	F	562 961-3431	6282
Dawson Enterprises (PA)	3533	E	562 424-8564	6956
CJ Precision Industries Inc	3599	E	562 426-3708	7800
Rode Microphones LLC	3651	C	310 328-7456	8432
Transcom Telecommunication Inc	3663	F	562 424-9616	8590
Harper & Two Inc (PA)	3679	F	562 424-3030	9054
Reldom Corporation	3699	E	562 498-3346	9247
United States Logistics Group	3715	E	562 989-9555	9497
Blueridge Technology Inc	3823	E	562 762-5914	10120
Asphalt Fabric and Engrg Inc	3949	D	562 997-4129	10975
Ancon Marine LLC	4212	C	562 326-5900	11441
Edco Disposal Corporation (PA)	4953	C	619 287-7555	12169
Nsv International Corp	5013	D	562 438-3836	12250
Ship & Shore Environmental Inc	5084	E	562 997-0233	12821
Viking Office Products Inc (DH)	5112	B	562 490-1000	13001
Boulevard Automotive Group (PA)	5511	E	562 492-1000	13742
Adaptive Tech Group Inc	5961	E	562 424-1100	14090

	SIC	EMP	PHONE	ENTRY#
First American Team Realty Inc (PA)	6531	C	562 427-7765	14795
Applied Business Software Inc	7372	E	562 426-2188	16173
Porter Boiler Service Inc	7699	E	562 426-2528	17147
Accountbl Hlth Cre IPA A Prof	8099	C	562 435-3333	18736

SIMI VALLEY, CA - Ventura County

	SIC	EMP	PHONE	ENTRY#
PW Gillibrand Co Inc (PA)	1446	E	805 526-2195	411
Williams East Heating A & Plbg	1711	D	818 678-9699	837
Millworks By Design Inc	2431	E	818 597-1326	2617
Clarios LLC	2531	E	805 522-5555	2922
Lca Promotions Inc	2759	E	818 773-9170	3781
Pharmaceutic Litho Label Inc	2834	D	805 285-5162	4202
Repligen Corporation	2836	F	775 235-5200	4329
Stearns Corporation	2844	E	805 582-2710	4458
Microblend Inc	2851	E	330 998-4602	4495
Recycled Aggregate Mtls Co Inc (HQ)	2951	F	805 522-1646	4665
Poly-Tainer Inc (PA)	3085	C	805 526-3424	4864
Milgard Manufacturing LLC	3231	C	805 581-6325	5348
Newman and Sons Inc (PA)	3272	E	805 522-1646	5429
Pre-Con Products	3272	D	805 527-0841	5438
Vibra Finish Co (PA)	3291	E	805 578-0033	5546
Calabasas Tms Center	3312	D	805 261-0824	5580
Cal State Site Services	3315	E	800 499-5757	5611
Fiberoptic Systems Inc	3357	E	805 579-6600	5741
Delt Industries Inc	3369	F	805 579-0213	5811
Advanced Metal Mfg Inc	3444	E	805 322-4161	6178
Computer Metal Products Corp	3444	D	805 520-6966	6217
Scott A Humphreys Inc (PA)	3444	E	805 581-2971	6311
Sheet Metal Engineering	3444	E	805 306-0390	6313
Specialty Fabrications Inc	3444	E	805 579-9730	6321
Mabel Baas Inc	3479	E	805 520-8075	6717
Chatsworth Products Inc (PA)	3499	E	818 735-6100	6858
Custom Iron Design	3499	E	805 581-3763	6859
Scientific Cutting Tools Inc	3545	E	805 584-9495	7130
Rexnord Industries LLC	3556	E	805 583-5514	7213
Xmultiple Technologies (PA)	3571	E	805 579-1100	7458
Datametrics Corporation	3577	E	805 577-9710	7520
Qualitylogic Inc	3577	C	208 424-1905	7565
Ricoh Prtg Systems Amer Inc (HQ)	3577	B	805 578-4000	7568
Rugged Info Tech Eqp Corp (PA)	3577	E	805 577-9710	7569
Savage Machining Inc	3599	E	805 584-8047	8016
Vanderhorst Brothers Industries Inc	3599	D	805 583-3333	8061
Vans Manufacturing Inc	3599	F	805 522-6267	8062
Embedded Systems Inc	3625	E	805 624-6030	8180
Aveox Inc	3629	E	805 915-0200	8201
Lumificient Corporation	3646	E	763 424-3702	8321
Circuit Express Inc	3672	E	805 581-2172	8661
Dpa Labs Inc	3674	E	805 581-9200	8788
Piezo-Metrics Inc (PA)	3674	E	805 522-4676	8864
Ventura Technology Group	3674	E	805 581-0800	8917
Componetics Inc	3677	E	805 498-0939	8938
Frontier Electronics Corp	3677	F	805 522-9998	8943
Puroflux Corporation	3677	F	805 579-0216	8952
Timco/Cal Rf Inc	3678	E	805 582-1777	8985
Jaxx Manufacturing Inc	3679	E	805 526-4979	9070
Meggitt Safety Systems Inc (DH)	3699	C	805 584-4100	9228
Enderle Fuel Injection	3714	E	805 526-3838	9388
Milodon Incorporated	3714	E	805 577-5950	9426
Special Devices Incorporated	3714	A	805 387-1000	9461
Aerovironment Inc	3721	E	805 520-8350	9504
Meggitt Safety Systems Inc	3728	D	805 584-4100	9750
Meggitt Safety Systems Inc	3728	C	805 584-4100	9751
Meggitt-Usa Inc (DH)	3728	B	805 526-5700	9752
Rsa Engineered Products LLC	3728	D	805 584-4150	9780
Whittaker Corporation	3728	E	805 526-5700	9828
Catalina Yachts Inc (PA)	3732	C	818 884-7700	9856
L3 Technologies Inc	3812	D	805 584-1717	9986
Pacific Scientific Company (DH)	3812	E	805 526-5700	10049
Sensoscientific LLC	3823	E	800 279-3101	10162
Interscan Corporation	3824	E	805 823-8301	10176
Bemco Inc (PA)	3826	E	805 583-4970	10242
Entech Instruments Inc	3826	D	805 527-5939	10258
Scope City Inc	3827	E	805 522-6646	10338
Fluid Line Technology Corp	3841	E	818 998-8848	10507
Freedom Designs Inc	3842	C	805 582-0077	10662
Replacement Parts Inds Inc	3843	E	818 882-8611	10765
S2k Graphics Inc	3993	E	818 885-3900	11151
DMA Enterprises Inc (PA)	3999	F	805 520-2468	11212
Waste Management Cal Inc	4953	C	805 522-7023	12197
Shopper Inc	5046	B	805 527-6700	12463
Electromed Inc	5047	D	805 523-7500	12485
Quad-C Jh Holdings Inc	5047	C	800 966-6662	12510
Foreign Trade Corporation	5065	C	805 823-8400	12660

Mergent email: customerrelations@mergent.com
1446

2024 Southern California
Business Directory and Buyers Guide

(P-0000) Products & Services Section entry number
(PA)=Parent Co (HQ)=Headquarters (DH)=Div Headquarters

	SIC	EMP	PHONE	ENTRY#
Rajysan Incorporated **(PA)**	5084	E	661 775-4920	12814
Howmet Globl Fstning Systems I **(HQ)**	5085	C	805 426-2270	12858
Andwin Corporation **(PA)**	5113	D	818 999-2828	13003
Smart & Final Stores Inc	5141	C	805 520-6035	13210
Eurow and OReilly Corp.	5199	E	800 747-7452	13536
Lowes Home Centers LLC	5211	C	805 426-2780	13652
Coast To Coast Cmpt Pdts Inc	5734	C	805 244-9500	13970
Troop Real Estate Inc **(PA)**	6531	D	805 581-3200	14881
Wsm Investments LLC	6794	C	818 332-4600	15011
Holiday Inn Express	7011	C	805 584-6006	15182
Simi West Inc.	7011	C	760 346-5502	15357
Arxis Technology Inc.	7372	E	805 306-7890	16176
CFS Tax Software Inc.	7372	F	805 522-1157	16198
Edgeworth Integration LLC	7382	C	805 915-0211	16732
Jims Tire Center Simi Vly Inc.	7534	F	805 581-1104	17022
American Vision Windows Inc	7699	C	805 582-1833	17116
Setarehshenas Dental Corp.	8021	C	805 583-5700	17847
Providnce Facey Med Foundation.	8031	D	805 206-2000	17851
Simi Vly Hosp & Hlth Care Svcs	8062	A	805 955-6000	18445
Simi Vly Hosp & Hlth Care Svcs **(HQ)**	8062	A	805 955-6000	18446
Good Shepherd Lutheran HM of W.	8361	C	805 526-2482	19264
Computerized Mgt Svcs Inc.	8721	D	805 522-5940	19762
Chase Group Llc	8732	B	805 522-9155	19890
Weapon X Security Inc.	8999	D	818 818-9950	20402

SKYFOREST, CA - San Bernardino County

	SIC	EMP	PHONE	ENTRY#
Spsv Entertainment LLC	7929	D	909 744-9373	17352

SOLANA BEACH, CA - San Diego County

	SIC	EMP	PHONE	ENTRY#
Spectrum Cnstr Group Inc	1541	D	949 299-1400	518
Mc Allister Industries Inc **(PA)**	2754	E	858 755-0683	3720
Sentynl Therapeutics Inc.	2834	C	888 227-8725	4231
Romeo Systems Inc.	3699	C	323 675-2180	9250
Romeo Power Inc **(HQ)**	3714	C	833 467-2237	9453
Clearpoint Neuro Inc **(PA)**	3841	D	949 900-6833	10482
Simon Golub & Sons Inc **(DH)**	5094	D		12968
Southern Cal Disc Tire Co Inc.	5531	C	858 481-6387	13875
Senior Resource Group LLC	6513	C	858 519-0890	14730
Pacifica Hosts Inc.	7011	D	858 792-8200	15291
Srg Holdings LLC **(HQ)**	7359	B	858 792-9300	15799
Lumiradx Inc.	7371	C	951 201-9384	16067
Trovata Inc **(PA)**	7371	D	312 914-8106	16141
Onehealth Solutions Inc.	7379	D	858 947-6333	16584
Simulstat Incorporated	7379	D	858 546-4337	16599

SOLVANG, CA - Santa Barbara County

	SIC	EMP	PHONE	ENTRY#
Lucas & Lewellen Vineyards Inc **(PA)**	5182	E	805 686-9336	13478
Holzheus El Rancho Market Inc.	5411	D	805 688-4300	13700
Alisal Properties **(PA)**	7032	C	805 688-6411	15433
Solvang Lutheran Home Inc.	8051	C	805 688-3263	18056
Cottage Health.	8062	D	805 688-6432	18229

SOMIS, CA - Ventura County

	SIC	EMP	PHONE	ENTRY#
Dudes Brewing Company.	2082	E	424 271-2915	1586
Saticoy Country Club.	7997	D	805 647-1153	17521

SOUTH EL MONTE, CA - Los Angeles County

	SIC	EMP	PHONE	ENTRY#
Bali Construction Inc.	1623	D	626 442-8003	661
American Wrecking Inc.	1795	D	626 350-8303	1129
California Snack Foods Inc.	2064	E	626 444-4508	1534
Out of Shell LLC.	2099	C	626 401-1923	1962
Cala Action Inc.	2211	E	213 272-9759	2015
Studio9d8 Inc.	2253	E	626 350-0832	2076
Thienes Apparel Inc.	2253	E	626 575-2818	2078
Antaeus Fashions Group Inc.	2329	F	626 452-0797	2193
Jowett Garments Factory Inc.	2339	E	626 350-0515	2337
88 Special Sweet Inc.	2657	E	909 525-7055	3144
Asia Plastics Inc.	2673	E	626 448-8100	3178
88 Special Sweet Inc.	2679	C	909 525-7055	3227
Golden Color Printing Inc.	2752	F	626 455-0850	3579
Interntnal Mdction Systems Ltd.	2834	A	626 442-6757	4138
Lee Pharmaceuticals.	2844	D	626 442-3141	4432
Cardinal Industrial Finishes **(PA)**	2851	D	626 444-9274	4482
Cardinal Paint and Powder Inc.	2851	D	626 444-9274	4483
Euhomy LLC.	3011	E	213 265-5081	4696
Promotnal Design Concepts Inc.	3069	D	626 579-4454	4786
R & R Rubber Molding Inc.	3069	E	626 575-8105	4788
Vclad Laminates Inc.	3083	D	626 442-2100	4845
Plastic Dress-Up Company.	3089	D	626 442-7711	5143
Design Shapes In Steel Inc.	3312	E	626 579-2032	5587
Brass Unique Inc.	3441	E	626 444-8977	6000
Mywi Fabricators Inc.	3441	F	626 279-6994	6059
Master Enterprises Inc.	3444	E	626 442-1821	6267

	SIC	EMP	PHONE	ENTRY#
Abacus Powder Coating.	3479	E	626 443-7556	6682
Island Powder Coating.	3479	E	626 279-2460	6712
S & H Machine Inc.	3492	E	626 448-5062	6779
Vacco Industries **(DH)**	3494	C	626 443-7121	6795
Grover Smith Mfg Corp.	3561	E	323 724-3444	7280
Bci Inc.	3599	E	626 579-4234	7778
Hoefner Corporation.	3599	E	626 443-3258	7865
Melkes Machine Inc.	3599	E	626 448-5062	7926
Mikelson Machine Shop Inc.	3599	E	626 448-3920	7936
Proto Space Engineering Inc.	3599	E	626 442-8273	7983
Brands Republic Inc.	3634	E	302 401-1195	8230
C W Cole & Company Inc.	3646	E	626 443-2473	8306
Roselm Industries Inc.	3663	E	626 442-6840	8572
Fabricast **(PA)**	3679	E	626 443-3247	9044
Halcore Group Inc.	3711	E	626 575-0880	9292
Amro Fabricating Corporation **(PA)**	3728	C	626 579-2200	9624
Bestsio LLC.	3911	F	626 841-8543	10899
California Med Response Inc.	4119	D	562 968-1818	11377
Leader Industries Inc.	4119	C	626 575-0880	11392
Integrated Parcel Network.	4215	B	714 278-6100	11530
Gama Contracting Services Inc.	5082	C	626 442-7200	12768
Creative Baby Inc.	5092	E	626 330-2289	12936
Ted Levine Drum Co **(PA)**	7699	C	626 579-1084	17160
Ahmc Healthcare Inc.	8062	D	626 579-7777	18169
Lincoln Trning Ctr Rhblttion W.	8331	D	626 442-0621	19187

SOUTH GATE, CA - Los Angeles County

	SIC	EMP	PHONE	ENTRY#
World Oil Corp.	1311	C	562 928-0100	273
Riverton Steel Construction.	1791	F	323 564-1881	1116
Interior Rmoval Specialist Inc.	1795	C	323 357-6900	1134
Saputo Cheese USA Inc.	2022	A	562 862-7686	1257
Win Soon Inc.	2026	E	323 564-5070	1317
Sunopta Grains and Foods Inc.	2041	D	323 774-6000	1417
Sunopta Fruit Group Inc.	2087	E	323 774-6000	1784
West Coast Naturals LLC	2087	E	310 467-3007	1790
Marquez Marquez Inc.	2096	E	562 408-0960	1829
Nextrade Inc **(PA)**	2299	E	562 944-9950	2143
AG Adriano Goldschmied Inc **(PA)**	2325	E	323 357-1111	2167
Janin.	2339	C	323 564-0995	2332
General Veneer Mfg Co.	2435	E	323 564-2661	2688
Liberty Container Company.	2653	C	323 564-4211	3114
Packaging Corporation America.	2653	C	562 927-7741	3121
PQ LLC.	2819	C	323 326-1100	3906
Arnco.	2822	E	323 249-7500	3984
Granitize Products Inc.	2842	D	562 923-5438	4353
Tu-K Industries Inc.	2844	E	562 927-3365	4462
Lunday-Thagard Company.	2952	B	562 928-6990	4673
Demenno/Kerdoon Holdings **(DH)**	2992	C	562 231-1550	4681
Lunday-Thagard Company **(HQ)**	2999	C	562 928-7000	4690
Productivity California Inc.	3089	D	562 923-3100	5167
Custom Leathercraft Mfg LLC **(DH)**	3199	C	323 752-2221	5306
Gwla Acquisition Corp **(PA)**	3211	F	323 789-7800	5315
Glasswerks La Inc **(HQ)**	3231	B	888 789-7810	5341
Johns Manville Corporation.	3296	D	323 568-2220	5554
Simons Brick Corporation.	3297	C	951 279-1000	5561
Artsons Manufacturing Company.	3312	E	323 773-3469	5577
Pacific Alloy Casting Company Inc.	3321	C	562 928-1387	5647
Buddy Bar Casting LLC.	3365	C	562 861-9664	5783
Techni-Cast Corp.	3369	C	562 923-4585	5819
Accurate Steel Treating Inc.	3398	E	562 927-6528	5821
Astro Aluminum Treating Co.	3398	D	562 923-4344	5825
Frameless Hardware Company LLC.	3429	C	888 295-4531	5918
Metal Supply Inc.	3441	D	562 634-9940	6051
Arcadia Inc.	3442	E	310 665-0490	6100
Pluckys Dump Rental LLC.	3443	E	323 540-3510	6150
Shultz Steel Company.	3463	B	323 357-3200	6482
Anadite Cal Restoration Tr.	3471	C	562 861-2205	6582
Hughes Bros Aircrafters Inc.	3544	E	323 773-4541	7076
Precision Forging Dies Inc.	3544	E	562 861-1878	7089
M D H Burner & Boiler Co Inc.	3564	F	562 630-2875	7325
Mercury Engineering Corp.	3599	E	562 861-7816	7927
Cie Manufacturing LLC.	3715	E	877 711-0725	9491
Cimc Intermodal Equipment LLC **(HQ)**	3715	D	562 904-8600	9492
Bell Foundry Co **(PA)**	3949	D	323 564-5701	10977
Sure Grip International.	3949	E	562 923-0724	11031
Pan Pacific Petroleum Co Inc **(PA)**	4213	D	562 928-0100	11502
Sprint Corporation.	4812	C	323 357-0797	11863
Pcs Mobile Solutions LLC.	4813	C	323 567-2490	11897
Verdeco Recycling Inc.	4953	E	323 537-4617	12193
Saw Daily Service Inc.	5085	E	323 564-1791	12878
Firma Plastic Co Inc.	5093	C	323 567-7767	12953
World Oil Marketing Company **(PA)**	5411	E	562 928-0100	13713
Xrp Inc **(PA)**	5531	F	562 861-4765	13888

	SIC	EMP	PHONE	ENTRY#
Berkshire Hthway HM Svcs CA Rp	6531	D	562 307-5636	14750
Century 21 A Better Svc Rlty	6531	D	562 806-1000	14762
Koos Manufacturing Inc	7389	A	323 249-1000	16855
Meribear Productions Inc	7389	D	310 204-5353	16874
Altamed Health Services Corp	8099	C	323 562-6700	18738
Dickson Testing Co Inc **(DH)**	8734	D	562 862-8378	19967

SOUTH PASADENA, CA - Los Angeles County

	SIC	EMP	PHONE	ENTRY#
Albany Farms Inc	2099	E	213 330-6573	1848
Finesse Apparel Inc	2339	E	213 747-7077	2323
Preco Aircraft Motors Inc	3694	E	626 799-3549	9174
Citadel Panda Express Inc	5812	C	626 799-9898	13997
Equity Smart Home Loans Inc	6162	D	626 864-8774	14313
Stratus Real Estate Inc	6163	E	626 441-5549	14366
Tokio Marine Highland Insurance Ser **(DH)**	6411	D	626 463-6486	14635
Ellens Silk Screening Inc	7336	E	626 441-4415	15665
City of Hope	8011	A	626 396-2900	17622

SPRING VALLEY, CA - San Diego County

	SIC	EMP	PHONE	ENTRY#
Treebeard Landscape Inc	0781	D	619 697-8302	182
Martin Brown Construction Inc	1521	F	619 660-0988	445
Casper Company	1771	C	619 589-6001	1062
West Coast Iron Inc	1796	D	619 464-8456	1140
J&M Keystone Inc	1799	C	619 466-9876	1163
Modern Stairways Inc	3272	E	619 466-1484	5426
Homestead Sheet Metal	3441	E	619 469-4373	6030
Richardson Steel Inc	3441	E	619 697-5892	6070
S & S Carbide Tool Inc	3544	E	619 670-5214	7095
East Penn Manufacturing	3691	E	619 660-0016	9144
Bish Inc	3728	E	619 660-6220	9644
Burns and Sons Trucking Inc	4212	D	619 460-5394	11445
Otay Water District	4941	E	619 670-2222	12136
Marjan Stone Inc	5032	E	619 825-6000	12357
Rossin Steel Inc	5051	E	619 656-9200	12571
TV Ears Inc	5065	E	619 797-1600	12707
Smart & Final Stores Inc	5141	B	619 668-9039	13204
Deering Banjo Company Inc	5736	E	619 464-8252	13978
Kaizen Syndicate LLC	7379	C	858 309-2028	16575
Family Hlth Ctrs San Diego Inc	8011	B	619 515-2555	17655
B-Spring Valley LLC	8051	D	619 797-3991	17885
Mt Miguel Covenant Village	8051	C	619 479-4790	18017
365 Home Care	8082	C	310 908-5179	18577
Covenant Living West	8361	D	619 931-1114	19257
D A V Industries	8641	E	619 337-9244	19443

STANTON, CA - Orange County

	SIC	EMP	PHONE	ENTRY#
USS Cal Builders Inc	1542	C	714 828-4882	601
White Bottle Inc	3089	E	949 788-1998	5252
Newport Industrial Glass Inc	3231	E	714 484-7500	5350
Muth Development Co Inc	3271	E	714 527-2239	5389
Orco Block & Hardscape **(PA)**	3271	D	714 527-2239	5390
Structural Stl Fabricators Inc	3441	E	714 761-1695	6079
Design Form Inc	3443	E	714 952-3700	6142
RDfabricators Inc	3444	F	714 634-2078	6304
West Coast Manufacturing Inc	3469	E	714 897-4221	6570
All Metals Processing of San Diego Inc	3471	C	714 828-8238	6578
All Mtals Proc Orange Cnty LLC	3471	C	714 828-8238	6579
Field Time Target Training LLC	3483	E	714 677-2841	6747
Newcomb Spring Corp	3495	E	714 995-5341	6805
Custom Pipe & Fabrication Inc **(HQ)**	3498	D	800 553-3058	6844
Precision Fastener Tooling Inc	3542	E	714 898-8558	7037
Blaga Precision Inc	3599	E	714 891-9509	7784
Boudraux Prcsion McHining Corp	3599	E	714 894-4523	7786
Manti - Machine Co Inc	3599	E	714 902-1465	7917
Muth Machine Works **(HQ)**	3599	E	714 527-2239	7949
Newport Optcal Inds Hldngs Ltd **(PA)**	3827	E	714 484-8100	10330
Signs and Services Company	3993	E	714 761-8200	11164
Haulaway Storage Cntrs Inc	4225	B	800 826-9040	11585
Cameron Welding Supply **(PA)**	7692	E	714 530-9353	17080
California Friends Homes	8361	B	714 530-9100	19244

STEVENSON RANCH, CA - Los Angeles County

	SIC	EMP	PHONE	ENTRY#
Vons Companies Inc	5411	C	661 254-3570	13711
Site Helpers LLC	8742	D	877 217-5395	20237

STUDIO CITY, CA - Los Angeles County

	SIC	EMP	PHONE	ENTRY#
Allbirds Inc	3143	F	213 374-3533	5268
CBS Broadcasting Inc	4833	C	818 655-8500	11940
Hallmark Media US LLC **(DH)**	4833	D	818 755-2400	11953
Motion Pcture Indust Pnsion HI	6371	C	818 769-0007	14549
Backbone Capital Advisors LLC	6799	D	818 769-8016	15021
Sportsmens Lodge Hotel LLC	7011	D	818 769-4700	15368
CBS Studios Inc	7812	C	818 655-5160	17175

	SIC	EMP	PHONE	ENTRY#
Columbia Pictures Inds Inc	7812	D	818 655-5820	17176
Radford Studio Center LLC	7922	B	818 655-5000	17326
Longwood Management Corp	8059	C	818 980-8200	18140
American Private Duty Inc	8082	D	818 386-6358	18589
Art Drctors Gild Itse Lcal 876	8631	C	818 762-9995	19408

SUN CITY, CA - Riverside County

	SIC	EMP	PHONE	ENTRY#
North County Sand and Grav Inc	1442	F	951 928-2881	407
Forterra Pipe & Precast LLC	3272	E	951 523-7039	5416

SUN VALLEY, CA - Los Angeles County

	SIC	EMP	PHONE	ENTRY#
Ble Inc	1381	E	818 504-9577	278
Leon Krous Drilling Inc	1381	E	818 833-4654	286
Pacific Pavingstone Inc	1771	C	818 244-4000	1080
Scenic Express Inc	1799	E	323 254-4351	1177
Glenoaks Food Inc	2015	E	818 768-9091	1244
High Road Craft Ice Cream Inc **(PA)**	2024	E	678 701-7623	1298
Gedney Foods Company	2035	C	952 448-2612	1359
Aries Prepared Beef Company	2047	F	818 771-0181	1426
Foodology LLC	2099	D	818 252-1888	1895
Four Seasons Hummus Inc	2099	F	305 409-0449	1897
Pacesetter Fabrics LLC **(HQ)**	2299	F	213 741-9999	2145
Travis-American Group LLC	2431	E	714 258-1200	2638
Acrylic Distribution Corp	2519	E	818 767-8448	2867
Columbia Showcase & Cab Co Inc	2541	C	818 765-9710	2949
Marfred Industries	2653	B		3117
E-Z Mix Inc **(PA)**	2674	E	818 768-0568	3198
Pacobond Inc	2674	E	818 768-5002	3200
Colorfx Inc	2752	E	818 767-7671	3536
Insua Graphics Incorporated	2752	E	818 767-7007	3602
Cosrich Group Inc	2844	E	818 686-2500	4397
Olive Refinish	2851	E	805 273-5072	4496
Desert Block Co Inc	2951	E	661 824-2624	4659
Technical Heaters Inc	3052	F	818 361-7185	4714
North Amrcn Foam Ppr Cnverters	3086	E	818 255-3383	4895
Plastic Services and Products	3086	A	818 896-1101	4896
PMC Global Inc **(PA)**	3086	D	818 896-1101	4897
PMC Leaders In Chemicals Inc **(HQ)**	3086	E	818 896-1101	4898
M & A Plastics Inc	3089	E	818 768-0479	5088
Angelus Block Co Inc **(PA)**	3271	E	714 637-8594	5388
Over & Over Ready Mix Inc	3272	E	818 983-1588	5435
Quikrete Companies LLC	3272	E	323 875-1367	5444
Associated Ready Mix Con Inc	3273	D	818 504-3100	5461
Capital Ready Mix Inc	3273	E	818 771-1122	5468
Gibbel Bros Inc	3273	F	323 875-1367	5478
Kenwalt Die Casting Corp	3363	E	818 768-5800	5761
Excelity	3369	D	818 767-1000	5812
W & F Mfg Inc	3429	E	818 394-6060	5951
C A Buchen Corp	3441	E	818 767-5408	6002
Tee -N -Jay Manufacturing Inc	3444	E	818 504-2961	6331
JMI Steel Inc	3446	E	818 768-3955	6361
Kitcor Corporation	3469	E	323 875-2820	6530
Specialty International Inc	3469	E	818 768-8810	6557
Alert Plating Company	3471	E	818 771-9304	6577
Schmidt Industries Inc	3471	D	818 768-9100	6661
Paint Specialists Inc	3479	F	818 771-0552	6721
Sundial Industries Inc	3479	E	818 767-4477	6740
Sundial Powder Coatings Inc	3479	E	818 767-4477	6741
L A Propoint Inc	3499	E	818 767-6800	6866
American Plastic Products Inc	3544	E	818 504-1073	7049
Art Mold Die Casting Inc	3544	E	818 767-6464	7050
Kvr Investment Group Inc	3559	D	818 896-1102	7246
Penguin Pumps Incorporated	3561	E	818 504-2391	7285
AVX Filters Corporation	3569	D	818 767-6770	7382
Impulse Industries Inc	3581	E	818 767-4258	7591
L A Gauge Company Inc	3599	D	818 767-7193	7901
Precision Arcft Machining Inc	3599	E	818 768-5900	7977
Schneiders Manufacturing Inc	3599	E	818 771-0082	8017
Sheffield Manufacturing Inc	3599	D	310 320-1473	8027
Abbott Technologies Inc	3612	E	818 504-0644	8086
American Grip Inc	3648	E	818 768-8922	8351
Accurate Engineering Inc	3672	E	818 768-3919	8640
De Leon Entps Elec Spclist Inc	3672	E	818 252-6690	8669
ASC Group Inc	3674	A	818 896-1101	8769
Industrial Battery Engrg Inc	3691	E	818 767-7067	9151
Jack J Engel Manufacturing Inc	3699	E	818 767-6220	9220
Spartan Truck Company Inc	3713	E	818 899-1111	9334
Forgiato Inc	3714	D	818 771-9779	9392
K & G Latirovian Inc	3714	D	818 319-2862	9407
Coronado Manufacturing LLC	3728	E	818 768-5010	9666
Pacific Sky Supply Inc	3728	D	818 768-3700	9761
Pmc Inc **(HQ)**	3728	E	818 896-1101	9766
Walker Design Inc	3731	E	818 252-7788	9851

2024 Southern California
Business Directory and Buyers Guide

(P-0000) Products & Services Section entry number
(PA)=Parent Co (HQ)=Headquarters (DH)=Div Headquarters

	SIC	EMP	PHONE	ENTRY#
Numatic Engineering Inc.	3823	E	818 768-1200	10149
Emergent Group Inc **(DH)**	3842	D	818 394-2800	10656
Hollywood Film Company	3861	E	818 683-1130	10869
Rico Corporation **(HQ)**	3931	C	818 394-2700	10932
Schecter Guitar Research Inc	3931	E	818 767-1029	10933
Pincraft Inc	3961	E	818 248-0077	11067
Los Angles Cnty Mtro Trnsp Aut	4111	A	213 922-6215	11333
Arakelian Enterprises Inc	4212	C	818 768-2644	11443
Waste Management Recycling	4212	D	818 767-6180	11469
Ontrac Logistics Inc	4215	C	818 504-9043	11536
Los Angeles Dept Wtr & Pwr	4941	A	213 367-1342	12131
Araco Enterprises LLC	4953	B	818 767-0675	12154
Recology Los Angeles	4953	C	818 767-0675	12182
USA Waste of California Inc	4953	D	818 252-3112	12190
Waste Management Cal Inc **(HQ)**	4953	C	877 836-6526	12196
Builders Fence Company Inc **(PA)**	5031	E	818 768-5500	12325
REM Optical Company Inc	5049	C	818 504-3950	12531
Norman Industrial Mtls Inc **(PA)**	5051	C	818 729-3333	12563
Spa De Soleil Inc	5122	E	818 504-3200	13070
PMC Capital Partners LLC	6799	A	818 896-1101	15046
Magic Jump Inc	7359	C	818 847-1313	15784
Sugar Foods LLC	7389	C	818 768-7900	16936
Wet **(PA)**	7389	C	818 769-6200	16966
Dip Braze Inc	7692	E	818 768-1555	17083
Hawker Pacific Aerospace	7699	B	818 765-6201	17131
Serra Community Med Clinic Inc	8011	C	818 768-3000	17763
Pacifica of Valley Corporation	8062	A	818 767-3310	18359
Pine Grove Hospital Corp	8063	C	818 348-0500	18517
Mountain View Child Care Inc	8351	C	818 252-5863	19221

SUNLAND, CA - Los Angeles County

	SIC	EMP	PHONE	ENTRY#
Brightview Tree Company	0811	D	818 951-5500	228
Patriot Brokerage Inc	4731	D	910 227-4142	11792
Valley Village	8052	C	818 446-0366	18099
New Vista Health Services	8059	C	818 352-1421	18147
Tierra Del Sol Foundation **(PA)**	8361	D	818 352-1419	19305

SYLMAR, CA - Los Angeles County

	SIC	EMP	PHONE	ENTRY#
Tutor-Saliba Perini	1542	A	818 362-8391	600
Paragon Industries Inc	1743	E	818 833-0550	1006
Superior Gunite **(HQ)**	1771	C	818 896-9199	1089
Fantasy Cookie Corporation **(PA)**	2052	E	818 361-6901	1517
Orange Bang Inc	2086	E	818 833-1000	1707
Clear Image Printing Inc	2752	E	818 547-4684	3531
Imagemover Inc	2752	F	818 485-8840	3590
Abbott Laboratories	2834	E	818 493-2388	4028
PPG Paints	2851	F	818 362-6711	4501
Sierracin Corporation **(HQ)**	2851	A	818 741-1656	4505
International Academy of Fin **(PA)**	2869	E	818 361-7724	4523
Gasket Associates LP **(PA)**	3053	F	310 217-5630	4730
Atlas Foam Products	3086	F	818 837-3626	4874
C & G Plastics	3089	E	818 837-3773	4971
Gibraltar Plastic Pdts Corp	3089	E	818 365-9318	5039
Sierracin/Sylmar Corporation	3089	A	818 362-6711	5204
Leather Pro Inc	3172	E	818 833-8822	5302
Anthony Inc	3231	E	818 365-9451	5333
Wayne Tool & Die Co	3312	E	818 364-1611	5606
Precise Iron Doors Inc	3442	E	818 338-6269	6116
JW Manufacturing Inc	3452	E	805 498-4594	6447
Professnal Fnshg Systems Sups	3469	F	818 365-8888	6548
Anthony Inc **(DH)**	3585	A	818 365-9451	7599
Kay & James Inc	3599	D	818 998-0357	7895
Eagle Access Ctrl Systems Inc	3625	E	818 837-7900	8178
L3 Technologies Inc	3663	C	818 367-0111	8535
ISU Petasys Corp	3672	D	818 833-5800	8691
Spectrolab Inc	3679	B	818 365-4611	9119
Quallion LLC	3692	C	818 833-2000	9159
Acufast Aircraft Products Inc	3728	E	818 365-7077	9591
Llamas Plastics Inc	3728	C	818 362-0371	9737
TMW Corporation **(PA)**	3728	C	818 362-5665	9817
Dg Engineering Corp **(PA)**	3812	E	818 364-9024	9970
Goldak Inc	3812	E	818 240-2666	9980
Providni Machining & Metals Corporation	3841	D	818 367-3161	10592
Advanced Bionics LLC **(HQ)**	3842	B	661 362-1400	10632
Pacesetter Inc **(DH)**	3845	A	818 362-6822	10819
Pacesetter Inc	3845	E	818 493-2715	10820
Matthews Studio Equipment Inc	3861	E	818 843-6715	10873
Carroll Fulmer Logistics Corp	4731	B	626 435-9940	11745
Oak Springs Nursery Inc	4971	D	818 367-5832	12214
Pearson Dental Supplies Inc **(PA)**	5047	C	818 362-2600	12506
American Nuts LLC **(HQ)**	5145	C	818 364-8855	13262
Reyes Coca-Cola Bottling LLC	5149	D	818 362-4307	13391
Allied Company Holdings Inc **(PA)**	5181	D	818 493-6400	13459

	SIC	EMP	PHONE	ENTRY#
Modern Candle Co Inc	5199	E	323 441-0104	13550
Home Depot USA Inc	5211	C	818 365-7662	13615
Sigue Corporation **(PA)**	7389	D	818 837-5939	16928
Schindler Elevator Corporation	7699	C	818 336-3000	17152
Star Waggons Inc	7819	D	818 367-5946	17264
Olive View-Ucla Medical Center **(PA)**	8011	D	818 364-1555	17729

TAFT, CA - Kern County

	SIC	EMP	PHONE	ENTRY#
Taft Production Company	1241	D	661 765-7194	243
Berry Petroleum Company LLC	1311	D	661 769-8820	249
Jerry Melton & Sons Cnstr Inc	1389	C	661 765-5546	356
General Production Svc Cal Inc	1623	C	661 765-5330	670
Oil-Dri Corporation America	2842	D	661 765-7194	4365
Mashburn Trnsp Svcs Inc	4213	C	661 763-5724	11498

TARZANA, CA - Los Angeles County

	SIC	EMP	PHONE	ENTRY#
One Structural Inc	1389	E	626 252-0778	373
Ultimatte Corporation	3663	E	818 993-8007	8593
Cgm Inc	3915	E	818 609-7088	10917
Shapp International Trdg Inc	5031	C	818 348-3000	12343
Extensions Plus Inc	5087	E	818 881-5611	12890
Airey Enterprises LLC	5088	C	818 530-3362	12900
JMJ Enterprises Inc	5812	C	818 343-5151	14017
Braemar Country Club Inc	7997	C	323 873-6880	17476
El Caballero Country Club	7997	C	818 654-3000	17482
Amisub of California Inc **(DH)**	8062	A	818 881-0800	18178
Providence Tarzana Medical Ctr	8062	A	818 881-0800	18401
Tarzana Treatment Centers Inc **(PA)**	8093	C	818 996-1051	18721
Wasserman Comden & Casselman **(PA)**	8111	C	323 872-0995	18954
Avantgarde Senior Living	8361	C	818 881-0055	19240

TECATE, CA - San Diego County

	SIC	EMP	PHONE	ENTRY#
Formula Plastics Inc	3089	B	866 307-1362	5031
Fusion Product Mfg Inc	3544	D	619 819-5521	7072
Alpha Sensors Inc	3823	E	949 250-6578	10114
Alpha Technics Inc	3823	E	949 250-6578	10115
Benchpro Inc	5021	C	619 478-9400	12277

TEHACHAPI, CA - Kern County

	SIC	EMP	PHONE	ENTRY#
World Wind Electrical Svcs Inc	1731	B	661 822-4877	952
Keller Classics Inc **(PA)**	2337	E	805 524-1322	2293
Chemtool Incorporated	2992	C	661 823-7190	4680
GE Wind Energy LLC	3511	C	661 823-6423	6880
GE Wind Energy LLC **(HQ)**	3511	C	661 822-6835	6881
CMS Products LLC	3577	E	714 424-5520	7517
Adaptive Aerospace Corporation	3728	C	661 300-0616	9593
Henway Inc	3965	F	661 822-6873	11070
LLC Woodward West	7032	C	661 822-7900	15437
Truxtun Radiology Med Group LP	8011	C	661 822-6619	17808
Adventist Health Med Tehachapi **(PA)**	8062	C	661 750-4848	18163
Bear Valley Springs Assn	8641	C	661 821-5537	19425

TEMECULA, CA - Riverside County

	SIC	EMP	PHONE	ENTRY#
Renzoni Vineyards Inc	0172	E	951 302-8466	35
Hines Growers Inc	0181	A	800 554-4065	56
Irriscape Construction Inc	0782	D	951 694-6936	195
Lost Dutchmans Minings Inc **(DH)**	1041	E	951 699-4749	234
Murrieta Development Company Inc	1623	C	951 719-1680	682
Solex Contracting Inc	1623	C	951 308-1706	692
W M Lyles Co	1623	C	951 296-2354	704
Freedom Forever LLC **(PA)**	1711	C	888 557-6431	770
Freedom Solar Services	1711	C	888 557-6431	771
Solar Spectrum LLC	1711	B	844 777-6527	826
Medley Communications Inc **(PA)**	1731	C	951 245-5200	917
West Coast Surfaces Inc	1752	E	951 699-0660	1035
Leonard Roofing Inc	1761	D	951 506-3811	1048
Canadas Finest Foods Inc	2037	D	951 296-1040	1366
Garmon Corporation **(PA)**	2048	D	888 628-8783	1440
Bottaia Wines LP	2084	E	951 252-1799	1613
Callaway Vineyard & Winery	2084	D	951 676-4001	1614
Danza Del Sol Winery Inc	2084	D	951 302-6363	1621
Falkner Winery Inc	2084	D	951 676-6741	1626
Leonesse Cellars LLC	2084	D	951 302-7601	1643
Lorimar Winery	2084	D	951 240-5177	1645
Louidar LLC	2084	D	951 676-5047	1646
Maurice Carrie Winery	2084	F	951 676-1711	1647
Ponte Winery	2084	C	951 694-8855	1652
South Coast Winery Inc	2084	C	951 587-9463	1660
Temecula Valley Winery MGT LLC	2084	D	951 699-8896	1662
Thornton Winery	2084	D	951 699-0099	1665
Wiens Cellars LLC	2084	C	951 694-9892	1668
Wilson Creek Wnery Vnyards Inc	2084	C	951 699-9463	1669
Top Heavy Clothing Company Inc **(PA)**	2321	D	951 442-8839	2164

GEOGRAPHIC

	SIC	EMP	PHONE	ENTRY#
Kamm Industries Inc	2396	E	800 317-6253	2534
North County Times	2711	E	951 676-4315	3312
Village News Inc	2711	E	760 451-3488	3334
Inland Empire Media Group Inc	2721	E	951 682-3026	3362
Polycraft Inc	2759	E	951 296-0860	3796
Robinson Printing Inc	2759	E	951 296-0300	3809
Abbott Vascular Inc	2834	B	951 941-2400	4029
EMD Millipore Corporation	2836	D	951 676-8080	4313
Bostik Inc	2891	E	951 296-6425	4559
W Plastics Inc	3081	E	800 442-9727	4825
Bomatic Inc (DH)	3089	E	909 947-3900	4967
Designer Sash and Door Sys Inc	3089	E	951 657-4179	5007
Milgard Manufacturing LLC	3089	B	480 763-6000	5100
Molding Intl & Engrg Inc	3089	E	951 296-5010	5107
TST Molding LLC	3089	E	951 296-6200	5236
Universal Packaging West Inc (HQ)	3089	E	603 889-8311	5238
MAC Products Inc	3312	E	951 296-3077	5593
Jeb Holdings Corp	3357	E	951 296-9900	5744
Marathon Finishing Systems Inc	3444	E	310 791-5601	6265
Sunstone Components Group Inc (HQ)	3469	E	951 296-5010	6560
Opti-Forms Inc	3471	E	951 296-1300	6646
Temecula Quality Plating Inc	3471	E	951 296-9875	6672
Aard Industries Inc	3495	E	951 296-0844	6797
Scotts Temecula Operations LLC (DH)	3524	E	951 719-1700	6921
Pacific Barcode Inc	3555	E	951 587-8717	7188
Flowserve Corporation	3561	D	951 296-2464	7276
Qc Manufacturing Inc	3564	D	951 325-6340	7329
Inners Tasks LLC	3571	E	951 225-9696	7431
Infineon Tech Americas Corp	3577	A	951 375-6008	7534
Aquamor LLC (PA)	3589	E	951 541-9517	7642
Axeon Water Technologies	3589	D	760 723-5417	7644
3-D Precision Machine Inc	3599	E	951 296-5449	7717
Banner American Products Inc	3599	F	951 296-9780	7774
Long Machine Inc	3599	E	951 296-0194	7908
Motorola Sltons Cnnctivity Inc (HQ)	3661	C	951 719-2100	8480
Electro-Support Systems Corp	3679	E	951 676-2751	9037
Opto 22	3679	C	951 695-3000	9095
Thompson Magnetics Inc	3679	E	951 676-0243	9130
Douglas Technologies Group Inc (PA)	3714	E	760 758-5560	9383
Ice Management Systems Inc	3728	E	951 676-2751	9715
Romar Innovations Inc	3821	D	951 296-3480	10099
Tesco Controls Inc	3825	E	916 395-8800	10227
EMD Millipore Corporation	3826	D	951 676-8080	10254
Quality Control Solutions Inc	3829	E	951 676-1616	10391
Transducer Techniques LLC	3829	E	951 719-3965	10405
Abbott Vascular Inc	3841	A	951 914-2400	10411
Isomedix Operations Inc	3842	D	951 694-9340	10674
Medline Industries LP	3842	E	951 296-2600	10681
Paulson Manufacturing Corp (PA)	3842	D	951 676-2451	10693
Artificial Grass Liquidators	3999	E	951 677-3377	11192
Phs / Mwa	4581	C	951 695-1008	11704
Kaydan Logistics LLC	4789	D	951 961-9000	11835
Sprint Communications Co LP	4812	C	951 303-8501	11859
Rancho California Water Dst (PA)	4941	C	951 296-6900	12139
Genica Corporation	5045	B	855 433-5747	12417
R R Donnelley & Sons Company	5112	D	951 296-2890	12999
FFF Enterprises Inc (PA)	5122	B	951 296-2500	13041
Southwest Traders Incorporated (PA)	5141	C	951 699-7800	13231
Advantage Chemical LLC	5169	E	951 225-4631	13423
Emser Tile LLC	5211	E	951 296-3671	13573
Lowes Home Centers LLC	5211	C	951 296-1618	13665
DCH Acura of Temecula	5511	D	877 847-9532	13754
Rancho Ford Inc	5511	C	951 699-1302	13818
Cal Mutual Inc	6162	D	888 700-4650	14304
Charles Schwab Corporation	6211	C	800 435-4000	14377
Pechanga Development Corp	7011	A	951 695-4655	15302
Temecula Hhg Hotel Dev LP	7011	D	951 331-3622	15388
Windsor Capital Group Inc	7011	A	951 676-5656	15421
Maxim Healthcare Services Inc	7363	C	951 694-0100	15932
Raintree Systems Inc	7371	E	951 252-9400	16101
Saalex Corp	7371	A	951 543-9259	16106
Applied Statistics & MGT Inc	7372	D	951 699-4600	16174
Richman Management Corporation	7381	B	909 296-6189	16675
Identity Intlligence Group LLC	7382	C	626 522-7993	16742
Incircle LLC	7389	A	800 843-7477	16844
Edwards Theatres Circuit Inc	7832	E	951 296-0144	17298
McMillin Communities LLC	7992	A	951 506-3303	17437
James Rebecca Prouty Entps Inc	8082	D	951 292-9777	18621
Ameresco Solar LLC	8711	B	888 967-6527	19546
Oreq Corporation	8741	D	951 296-5076	20073
Hqe Systems Inc	8748	D	800 967-3036	20344

TEMPLE CITY, CA - Los Angeles County

	SIC	EMP	PHONE	ENTRY#
Sears Home Imprv Pdts Inc	1521	C	626 988-9134	455
California Flexrake Corp	3423	E	626 443-4026	5875
D D Wire Co Inc (PA)	3441	E	626 442-0459	6020
Jon Davler Inc	5999	E	626 941-6558	14139
Santa Anita Cnvlscent Hosp Rtr	8051	C	626 579-0310	18048

TEMPLETON, CA - San Luis Obispo County

	SIC	EMP	PHONE	ENTRY#
Pacific Gas and Electric Co	4911	D	805 434-4418	12037
T and B Boots Inc	5661	D	805 434-9904	13926
Twin Cities Community Hosp Inc	8011	B	805 434-3500	17812
Compass Health Inc	8051	C	805 434-3035	17906

THERMAL, CA - Riverside County

	SIC	EMP	PHONE	ENTRY#
Nissho of California Inc	0175	B	760 727-9719	46
Oasis Date Garden Inc	2099	E	760 399-5665	1957
Spates Fabricators Inc	2439	D	760 397-4122	2703
Red Earth Casino	7011	C	760 395-1200	15319

THOUSAND OAKS, CA - Ventura County

	SIC	EMP	PHONE	ENTRY#
Oltmans Construction Co	1541	B	805 495-9553	513
General Pavement Management Inc	1771	D	805 933-0909	1071
Cal-State Steel Corporation	1791	C	310 632-2772	1102
Natren Inc	2099	D	805 371-4737	1953
August Hat Company Inc (PA)	2353	E	805 983-4651	2398
Sage Publications Inc (PA)	2731	C	805 499-0721	3414
Midnight Manufacturing LLC	2833	E	714 833-6130	4003
Amgen USA Inc (HQ)	2834	D	805 447-1000	4046
Instacure Healing Products	2834	E	818 222-9600	4136
Amgen Inc (PA)	2836	A	805 447-1000	4298
Atara Biotherapeutics Inc (PA)	2836	A	650 278-8930	4301
Fujifilm Dsynth Btchnlgies Cal	2836	E	914 789-8100	4315
Fujifilm Dsynth Btchnlgies USA	2836	C	805 669-5579	4316
Vorwerk LLC	3469	D	888 867-9375	6567
Ale USA Inc	3663	A	818 880-3500	8492
Custom Sensors & Tech Inc (HQ)	3679	A	805 716-0322	9026
Kavlico Corporation (DH)	3679	A	805 523-2000	9075
Maple Imaging LLC (HQ)	3679	D	805 373-4545	9081
Smiths Interconnect Inc	3679	D	805 267-0100	9116
Teledyne Technologies Inc (PA)	3679	C	805 373-4545	9128
Swag Corporation	3699	E	805 499-6555	9260
Teledyne Lecroy Inc	3825	F	434 984-4500	10226
Teledyne Redlake Masd LLC (DH)	3826	C	805 373-4545	10293
BEI North America LLC (DH)	3829	C	805 716-0642	10354
Carros Sensors Systems Co LLC (DH)	3829	C	805 968-0782	10359
Baxalta US Inc	3841	B	805 498-8664	10448
Easton Hockey Inc	3949	A	818 782-6445	10988
Mv Transportation Inc	4111	C	805 557-7372	11349
Full Scale Logistics LLC	4789	D	805 279-6799	11832
Southern California Edison Co	4911	D	818 999-1880	12056
Ultraglas Inc	5039	E	818 772-7744	12373
Tecom Industries Incorporated	5065	C	805 267-0100	12705
Easton Baseball / Softball Inc	5091	E	800 632-7866	12927
Easton Diamond Sports LLC	5091	D	800 632-7866	12928
Penney Opco LLC	5311	C	805 497-6811	13683
Countrywide Home Loans Inc (HQ)	6162	A		14308
Ormond Beach LP	6512	D	805 496-4948	14678
Gemmm Corporation (PA)	6531	D	805 496-0555	14803
American Recovery Service Inc (DH)	7322	C	805 379-8500	15606
Staff Assistance Inc	7361	B	805 371-9980	15896
A P R Inc	7363	C	805 379-3400	15910
Sensata Technologies Inc	7379	C	805 716-0322	16597
Carmike Cinemas LLC	7832	C	805 494-4702	17288
Bay Clubs Company LLC	7997	B	310 643-6878	17468
Sherwood Country Club	7997	C	805 496-3036	17524
Los Robles Regional Med Ctr	8011	B	805 494-0880	17710
Los Robles Regional Med Ctr (DH)	8062	A	805 497-2727	18339
Thousand Oaks Surgical Hosp LP	8062	D	805 777-7750	18474
Staff Assistance Inc (PA)	8082	C	818 894-7879	18644
La Ventana Treatment Programs	8093	D	805 644-5745	18701
Star of Ca LLC	8099	D	805 379-1401	18806
Westlake Oaks Healthcare LLC	8099	C	805 494-1233	18816
Teledyne Scientfic Imaging LLC (HQ)	8731	C	805 373-4545	19881
Briotix	8742	C	805 864-2711	20146

THOUSAND PALMS, CA - Riverside County

	SIC	EMP	PHONE	ENTRY#
San Val Corp (PA)	0781	B	760 346-3999	178
Superior Ready Mix Concrete LP	3273	D	760 343-3418	5509
A R Electronics Inc	3679	E	760 343-1200	8988
Sunline Transit Agency (PA)	4111	C	760 343-3456	11369
Readylink Inc	7361	D	760 343-7000	15887
Readylink Healthcare	7361	D	760 343-7000	15888

(P-0000) Products & Services Section entry number
(PA)=Parent Co (HQ)=Headquarters (DH)=Div Headquarters

	SIC	EMP	PHONE	ENTRY#
TOLUCA LAKE, CA - Los Angeles County				
Northwestern Inc	2431	E	818 786-1581	2621
TORRANCE, CA - Los Angeles County				
Finleys Tree & Landcare Inc	0781	C	310 326-9818	161
Magnetron Power Inventions Inc	1382	E	310 462-6970	312
Dicaperl Corporation **(DH)**	1499	D	610 667-6640	416
MC&a Usa LLC	1521	E	504 267-8145	446
Taisei Construction Corporation	1541	C	714 886-1530	523
ACS Communications Inc	1731	C	310 767-2145	861
Vector Resources Inc **(PA)**	1731	C	310 436-1000	950
Excelpro Inc **(PA)**	2022	F	323 415-8544	1254
Naturalife Eco Vite Labs	2023	D	310 370-1563	1278
Shine Food Inc **(PA)**	2032	E	310 329-3829	1331
Pasco Corporation of America	2038	E	503 289-6500	1397
Shine Food Inc	2038	D	310 533-6010	1400
Advanced Fresh Cncpts Frnchise	2092	E	310 604-3200	1798
Asiana Cuisine Enterprises Inc	2099	A	310 327-2223	1854
Morinaga Nutritional Foods Inc **(HQ)**	2099	F	310 787-0200	1950
Thg Brands Inc	2099	E	844 694-8327	1998
Just For Fun Inc	2321	E	310 320-1327	2160
Textile Unlimited Corporation **(PA)**	2321	D	310 263-7400	2163
Image Solutions Apparel Inc	2326	C	310 464-8991	2175
Alpinestars USA	2331	D	310 891-0222	2230
Nothing To Wear Inc	2331	E	310 328-0408	2260
Nothing To Wear Inc **(PA)**	2331	E	310 328-0408	2261
Ys Garments LLC **(HQ)**	2331	E	310 631-4955	2271
Marcea Inc	2339	F	213 746-5191	2349
Tcw Trends Inc	2339	E	310 533-5177	2376
Micronova Manufacturing Inc	2392	E	310 784-6990	2478
A-Aztec Rents & Sells Inc **(PA)**	2394	C	310 347-3010	2498
His Life Woodworks	2431	E	310 756-0170	2606
Doug Mockett & Company Inc	2511	D	310 318-2491	2772
Virco Mfg Corporation **(PA)**	2531	C	310 533-0474	2940
Field Manufacturing Corp **(PA)**	2542	E	310 781-9292	2980
Union Carbide Corporation	2631	E	310 214-5300	3073
Daily Breeze	2711	E	310 540-5622	3269
Medianews Group Inc	2711	E	310 540-5511	3305
Bbm Fairway Inc **(PA)**	2721	C		3345
Bobit Business Media Inc	2721	B	310 533-2400	3346
Minority Success Pubg Group	2721	E	310 736-2462	3371
Manson Western LLC	2731	C	424 201-8800	3409
Classic Litho & Design Inc	2752	E	310 224-5200	3530
R R Donnelley & Sons Company	2759	D	310 516-3100	3803
Retail Print Media Inc	2759	E	424 488-6950	3807
Arkema Inc	2812	D	310 214-5327	3855
Jci Jones Chemicals Inc	2812	F	310 523-1629	3858
Messer LLC	2813	D	310 533-8394	3870
Americas Styrenics LLC	2821	E	424 488-3757	3923
Pelican Biopharma LLC	2834	F	310 326-4700	4198
Senju Usa Inc	2834	E	818 719-7190	4230
Bachem Americas Inc **(DH)**	2836	E	310 784-4440	4303
Bachem Americas Inc	2836	D	310 784-4440	4304
Bachem Bioscience Inc	2836	E	310 784-7322	4305
Colonial Enterprises Inc	2844	E	909 822-8700	4391
Nyx Los Angeles Inc	2844	C	323 869-9420	4438
Mercfuel LLC	2869	F	310 827-5778	4525
Teledyne Reynolds Inc	2892	C	310 823-5491	4584
Lg Nanoh2o LLC	2899	E	424 218-4000	4616
Medical Chemical Corporation	2899	E	310 787-6800	4621
Prestone Products Corporation	2899	E	424 271-4836	4627
Torrance Refining Company LLC	2911	A	310 212-2800	4652
G F Cole Corporation **(PA)**	3053	F	310 320-0601	4729
Industrial Gasket and Sup Co	3053	E	310 530-1771	4734
Kakuichi America Inc	3084	D	310 539-1590	4851
Kepner Plas Fabricators Inc	3089	E	310 325-3162	5078
Smart LLC	3089	E	866 822-3670	5207
Totex Manufacturing Inc	3089	D	310 326-2028	5231
Carley **(PA)**	3229	C	310 325-8474	5323
Catalina Pacific Concrete	3273	E	310 532-4600	5469
United States Gypsum Company	3275	D	908 232-8900	5522
Lisi Aerospace North Amer Inc	3324	A	310 326-8110	5657
Howmet Aerospace Inc	3334	B	212 836-2674	5670
Broadata Communications Inc	3357	D	310 530-1416	5733
Alliedsignal Arospc Svc Corp **(HQ)**	3369	D	310 323-9500	5807
Fun Properties Inc **(PA)**	3423	D	310 787-4500	5880
Products Engineering Corp	3423	E	310 787-4500	5889
Diamond K2	3425	E	310 539-6116	5891
Santec Inc	3432	E	310 542-0063	5974
Torrance Steel Window Co Inc	3442	E	310 328-9181	6127
Showerdoordirect LLC	3444	F	310 327-8060	6317
Hi-Shear Corporation **(DH)**	3452	A	310 326-8110	6444
KB Delta Inc	3469	E	310 530-1539	6528
Kopykake Enterprises Inc **(PA)**	3469	F	310 373-8906	6531
Plasma Technology Incorporated **(PA)**	3479	D	310 320-3373	6727
FCkingston Co	3491	E	310 326-8287	6764
Storm Manufacturing Group Inc	3491	D	310 326-8287	6770
Magnetic Component Engrg LLC **(PA)**	3499	D	310 784-3100	6868
Storm Industries Inc **(PA)**	3523	D	310 534-5232	6915
American Ultraviolet West Inc	3535	E	310 784-2930	6969
Barranca Holdings Ltd	3545	C	310 523-5867	7108
Mk Diamond Products Inc **(PA)**	3546	D	310 539-5221	7146
Creative Pathways Inc	3548	E	310 530-1965	7157
Technical Devices Company	3548	E	310 618-8437	7164
Winther Technologies Inc **(PA)**	3548	E	310 618-8437	7165
Shaver Specialty Co Inc	3556	E	310 370-6941	7216
William Bounds Ltd	3556	F	310 375-0505	7218
Industrial Dynamics Co Ltd **(PA)**	3559	C	310 325-5633	7241
Camfil Farr Inc	3564	D	973 616-7300	7320
Sun Industries Corporation	3564	E	310 782-1188	7332
M2 Marketplace Inc	3571	E		7437
Bnl Technologies Inc	3572	E	310 320-7272	7463
Bixolon America Inc	3577	E	858 764-4580	7512
Lynn Products Inc	3577	A	310 530-5966	7545
Probe Racing Components Inc	3592	E	310 784-2977	7703
Aeroliant Manufacturing Inc	3599	E	310 257-1903	7746
Beranek LLC	3599	E	310 328-9094	7782
Ely Co Inc	3599	E	310 539-5831	7826
Goeppner Industries Inc	3599	E	310 784-2800	7851
Laserod Technologies LLC	3599	E	310 328-5869	7906
Ralph E Ames Machine Works	3599	E	310 328-8523	7991
Sonsray Inc	3599	D	323 585-1271	8032
Weber Drilling Co Inc	3599	E	310 670-7708	8072
Sea Electric LLC	3621	E	424 376-3660	8156
Moog Inc	3625	B	310 533-1178	8187
Breville Usa Inc	3639	E	310 755-3000	8241
Aero-Electric Connector Inc **(PA)**	3643	B	310 618-3737	8253
Emp Connectors Inc	3643	E	310 533-6799	8263
Lyncole Grunding Solutions LLC	3643	E	310 214-4000	8269
All Access Stging Prdctons Inc **(PA)**	3648	E	310 784-2464	8350
Pelican Products Inc **(PA)**	3648	C	310 326-4700	8379
Funai Corporation Inc	3651	D	201 727-4560	8412
Marshall Electronics Inc **(PA)**	3651	D	310 333-0606	8422
Pioneer Speakers Inc	3651	A	310 952-2000	8427
Rock-Ola Manufacturing Corp	3651	D	310 328-1306	8431
Panasonic Disc Manufacturing Corpor	3652	C	310 783-4800	8462
Antcom Corporation	3663	E	310 782-1076	8495
CPI Satcom & Antenna Tech Inc	3663	C	310 539-6704	8506
Escape Communications Inc	3663	F	310 997-1300	8516
Hadrian Automation Inc	3663	D	503 807-4490	8521
Lenntek Corporation	3663	E	310 534-2738	8538
Mainline Equipment Inc	3663	D	800 444-2288	8540
Navcom Technology Inc **(HQ)**	3663	D	310 381-2000	8552
Optodyne Incorporation	3663	E	310 635-7481	8557
Pacific Wave Systems Inc	3663	D	714 893-0152	8559
Global Comm Semiconductors LLC	3674	E	310 530-7274	8799
Ledtronics Inc **(PA)**	3674	E	310 534-1505	8828
Teledyne Defense Elec LLC	3674	C	310 823-5491	8906
Trident Space & Defense LLC	3674	E	310 214-5500	8913
Coast/Dvnced Chip Mgnetics Inc	3677	F	310 370-8188	8937
Conesys Inc	3678	C	310 212-0065	8965
J - T E C H	3678	E	310 533-6700	8975
Onshore Technologies Inc	3679	E	310 533-4888	9094
Sure Power Inc	3679	E	310 542-8561	9124
Western Digital	3679	E	510 557-7553	9139
Czv Inc	3711	D	424 603-1450	9283
Canoo Inc **(PA)**	3714	E	424 271-2144	9365
Edelbrock LLC	3714	E	310 781-2290	9386
Motorcar Parts of America Inc **(PA)**	3714	A	310 212-7910	9428
US Hybrid Corporation **(HQ)**	3714	E	310 212-1200	9481
Garrett Transportation I Inc **(HQ)**	3724	D	973 455-2000	9569
Honeywell International Inc	3724	A	310 323-9500	9572
Ace Clearwater Enterprises Inc **(PA)**	3728	E	310 323-2140	9587
Dasco Engineering Corp	3728	C	310 326-2277	9671
Qpi Holdings Inc **(DH)**	3728	E	310 539-2855	9772
Quality Forming LLC	3728	E	310 539-2855	9773
Robinson Helicopter Co Inc	3728	A	310 539-0508	9775
Microcosm Inc	3764	E	310 219-2700	9909
Hall Associates Racg Pdts Inc	3799	F	310 326-4111	9934
General Forming Corporation	3812	E	310 326-0624	9978
Intellisense Systems Inc	3812	C	310 320-1827	9981
Moog Inc	3812	B	310 533-1178	10002
Stellant Systems Inc **(DH)**	3812	A	310 517-6000	10073
Fischer Cstm Cmmunications Inc **(PA)**	3825	E	310 303-3300	10201
Nearfield Systems Inc	3825	D	310 525-7000	10219
Pulse Instruments	3825	E	310 515-5330	10221

GEOGRAPHIC

Company	SIC	EMP	PHONE	ENTRY#
Phenomenex Inc (HQ)	3826	C	310 212-0555	10281
Luminit LLC (PA)	3827	E	310 320-1066	10324
Z C & R Coating For Optics Inc	3827	E	310 381-3060	10347
AES NDT	3829	E	310 947-6755	10350
Proprietary Controls Systems	3829	E	310 303-3600	10390
Axiom Medical Incorporated	3841	E	818 919-1657	10443
Igenomix Usa LLC	3841	E	818 919-1657	10527
Lisi Aerospace	3841	E	310 326-8110	10548
Medicool Inc	3841	F	310 782-2200	10556
Finest Hour Holdings Inc	3842	E	310 533-9966	10660
Rapiscan Systems Inc (HQ)	3844	C	310 978-1457	10785
Younger Mfg Co (PA)	3851	B	310 783-1533	10857
Stewart Filmscreen Corp (PA)	3861	C	310 784-5300	10886
Crislu Corp	3911	E	310 322-3444	10900
Dreamgear LLC	3944	E	310 222-5522	10949
Ergo Baby Carrier Inc (HQ)	3944	E	213 283-2090	10951
Encore Image Group Inc (PA)	3993	D	310 534-7500	11114
George P Johnson Company	3993	E	310 965-4300	11123
Signtronix Inc	3993	D	310 534-7500	11166
Forrester Eastland Corporation	3999	E	310 784-2464	11216
Learning Resources Inc	3999	E	800 995-4436	11242
Tre Milano LLC	3999	E	310 260-8888	11299
Ryans Express Trnsp Svcs Inc (PA)	4119	D	310 219-2960	11402
Fashion Logistics Inc	4225	D	424 201-4100	11577
Express Imaging Services Inc	4226	C	888 846-8804	11633
Jtb Americas Ltd (HQ)	4724	D	310 406-3121	11718
Air Express Intl USA Inc	4731	D	310 297-4401	11737
Ceva Logistics LLC	4731	B	310 223-6500	11746
Dcw Dcw Inc	4731	C	310 324-3147	11749
Expeditors Intl Wash Inc	4731	B	310 343-6200	11759
Fns Inc (PA)	4731	C	661 615-2300	11762
Hitachi Transport System (america) Ltd	4731	B	310 787-3420	11769
Kuehne + Nagel Inc	4731	C	310 641-5500	11776
Nippon Express	4731	C	310 782-3000	11788
Salson Logistics Inc	4731	C	973 986-0200	11800
American Honda Motor Co Inc (HQ)	5012	A	310 783-2000	12221
Virco Inc (HQ)	5021	C	310 533-0474	12293
New Generation Engrg Cnstr Inc	5032	E	424 329-3950	12358
Convaid Products LLC	5047	E	310 618-0111	12482
Elers Medical Usa Inc	5047	E	858 336-4900	12486
Sakura Finetek USA Inc (HQ)	5047	D	310 972-7800	12512
Shimadzu Precision Instrs Inc	5047	E	310 217-8855	12514
Pioneer North America Inc (DH)	5064	F	310 952-2000	12636
I C Class Components Corp (PA)	5065	D	310 539-5500	12668
Quinstar Technology Inc	5065	D	310 320-1111	12693
Seville Classics Inc (PA)	5072	C	310 533-3800	12733
Sharp Industries Inc (PA)	5084	E	310 370-5990	12820
Pacific Echo Inc	5085	D	310 539-1822	12870
Sweis Inc (PA)	5087	D	310 375-0558	12896
Citizen Watch Company of America Inc (HQ)	5094	C	800 321-1023	12961
Pentel of America Ltd (HQ)	5112	C	310 320-3831	12996
Murad LLC	5122	C	310 726-3300	13056
Weckerle Cosmetics Usa Inc	5122	E	310 328-7000	13076
Frito-Lay North America Inc	5145	C	310 224-5600	13270
Ezcaretech Usa Inc	5199	B	424 558-3191	13538
Rockwell Enterprises Inc	5199	E	626 796-1511	13557
Lowes Home Centers LLC	5211	C	310 787-1469	13633
Jessie Lord Bakery LLC	5461	E	310 533-6010	13716
General Motors LLC	5511	E	313 556-5000	13771
Martin Chevrolet	5511	D	323 772-6494	13795
Southbay European Inc	5511	D	310 939-7300	13829
Toyota Logistics Services Inc (DH)	5511	C	310 468-4000	13838
Enagic Usa Inc (PA)	5963	D	310 542-7700	14110
American Business Bank	6022	D	310 808-1200	14177
Unify Fincl Cr Un Prof Corp (PA)	6061	D	877 254-9328	14240
Happy Money Inc	6099	B	949 430-0630	14261
American Honda Finance Corp (DH)	6141	C	310 972-2239	14267
Keenan & Associates (HQ)	6411	C	310 212-3344	14606
Alpine Village	6512	C	310 327-4384	14651
Remax Exec King Harbor	6531	C	310 378-9889	14857
AME-Gyu Co Ltd	6719	A	310 214-9572	14921
Navitas Semiconductor Corp (PA)	6799	C	901 685-2865	15040
Ctc Group Inc (DH)	7011	C	310 540-0500	15125
Kintetsu Enterprises Co Amer (HQ)	7011	D	310 782-9300	15210
Long Beach Golden Sails Inc	7011	D	562 596-1631	15230
Msr Hotels & Resorts Inc	7011	C	310 543-4566	15257
V Todays Inc	7011	C	310 781-9100	15401
Wash Mltfmily Ldry Systems LLC (PA)	7215	C	800 421-6897	15462
Saatchi & Saatchi N Amer LLC	7311	C	310 437-2500	15574
Lomita Logistics LLC	7331	C	310 784-8485	15633
Resource Collection Inc	7349	E	310 219-3272	15744
Bright Event Rentals LLC (PA)	7359	C	310 202-0011	15772
Choura Events	7359	D	310 320-6200	15774
Classic/Prime Inc	7359	D	310 328-5060	15776
Act 1 Group Inc (PA)	7361	D	310 750-3400	15809
Prime One Inc	7361	C	310 378-1944	15882
Platinum Empire Group Inc	7363	C	310 821-5888	15936
Good Sports Plus Ltd	7371	B	310 671-4400	16041
Indizen Optical Tech Amer LLC	7371	F	310 783-1533	16051
BQE Software Inc	7372	D	310 602-4020	16189
Epirus Inc	7372	E	310 620-8678	16238
Nc4 Soltra LLC	7372	D	408 489-5579	16319
Luxury Presence Inc	7373	C	310 955-1077	16456
CCH Incorporated	7374	A	310 800-9800	16485
Delta Computer Consulting	7379	C	310 541-9440	16564
US Security Associates Inc	7381	B	714 352-0773	16705
Contemporary Services Corp	7382	C	310 320-8418	16726
Bankcard Services (PA)	7389	C	213 365-1122	16788
Credit Card Services Inc (PA)	7389	C	213 365-1122	16812
Ocs America Inc (DH)	7389	E	310 417-0650	16891
Pioneer Theatres Inc	7389	C	310 532-8183	16904
Singer Vehicle Design LLC (PA)	7549	C	213 592-2728	17059
Aeroworx Inc	7699	D	310 891-0300	17113
Redman Equipment & Mfg Co	7699	E	310 329-1134	17148
Louis F Mascola DDS	8021	C	310 986-2930	17840
Genesis Healthcare LLC	8051	C	310 370-3594	17962
Geri-Care Inc	8051	D	310 320-0961	17964
Mariner Health Care Inc	8051	C	310 371-4628	18007
Torrance Care Center West Inc	8051	C	310 370-4561	18061
Geri-Care II Inc	8059	C	310 328-0812	18127
Cedars-Sinai Medical Center	8062	A	310 967-1900	18209
Little Company Mary Hospital	8062	A	310 540-7676	18324
Little Company of Mary Health Services	8062	A	310 540-7676	18325
Torrance Health Assn Inc (PA)	8062	A	310 325-9110	18475
Torrance Memorial Medical Ctr (HQ)	8062	A	310 325-9110	18476
Torrance Memorial Medical Ctr	8062	B	310 784-6316	18478
Torrance Memorial Medical Ctr	8062	B	310 784-3740	18479
Polypeptide Laboratories Inc (HQ)	8071	D	310 782-3569	18558
Premier Infsion Hlthcare Svcs	8082	D	310 328-3897	18636
Harbor-Ucla Med Foundation Inc	8092	B	310 533-0413	18659
Del AMO Hospital Inc	8093	B	310 530-1151	18687
Pediatric Therapy Network	8093	C	310 328-0276	18706
Collinson Law A Prof Corp	8111	C	424 212-7777	18837
Compex Legal Services Inc (PA)	8111	C	310 782-1801	18838
Harbor Dvlpmntal Dsblties Fndt	8399	C	310 540-1711	19327
Orthalliance Inc	8399	A	310 792-1300	19337
Special Service For Groups Inc	8399	C	310 323-6887	19344
21515 Hawthorne Owner LLC	8641	D	310 406-3730	19420
Public Hlth Fndation Entps Inc	8641	C	310 320-5215	19460
Automobile Club Southern Cal	8699	C	310 325-3111	19523
Divergent Technologies Inc	8711	C	424 542-2158	19573
Friction Materials LLC	8711	C	248 362-3600	19595
International Energy Services USA Inc	8711	C	310 257-8222	19615
Sonic Industries Inc	8711	C	310 532-8382	19692
Garrett Motion Inc	8731	C	310 512-5424	19840
Mercury Mission Systems LLC	8731	E	310 320-3088	19860
Opto-Knowledge Systems Inc	8731	E	310 756-0520	19869
Honda R&D Americas LLC	8732	A	310 781-5500	19897
Lundquist Institute For Biomedical	8733	A	877 452-2674	19934
Daicel America Holdings Inc	8741	B	480 798-6737	20025
Harbor-Ucla Med Foundation Inc (PA)	8741	D	310 222-5015	20037
Proactive Risk Management Inc	8741	D	213 840-8856	20082
Pathology Inc	8742	B	310 769-0561	20217
Advanced Corporate Svcs Inc	8748	E	310 937-6848	20306
Midnight Sun Enterprises Inc	8748	C	310 532-2427	20362

TRABUCO CANYON, CA - Orange County

Company	SIC	EMP	PHONE	ENTRY#
Quantumsphere Inc	3399	F	714 545-6266	5857
Seeds of Change Inc	5191	C	310 764-7700	13490
Total Recon Solutions Inc	8742	D	949 584-8417	20264

TRONA, CA - San Bernardino County

Company	SIC	EMP	PHONE	ENTRY#
Dv Natural Resources LLC	1041	F		232
Trona Railway Company	4011	A	760 372-2312	11312

TUJUNGA, CA - Los Angeles County

Company	SIC	EMP	PHONE	ENTRY#
American Foothill Pubg Co Inc	2759	E	818 352-7878	3732
David Kopf Instruments	3841	E	818 352-3274	10489
Vons Companies Inc	5411	C	818 353-4917	13707
F J & J Corporation	7819	F	505 452-1700	17251
Volunteers of Amer Los Angeles	8322	C	818 352-5974	19161
Crescenta-Canada YMCA	8641	C	818 352-3255	19442

TUPMAN, CA - Kern County

Company	SIC	EMP	PHONE	ENTRY#
Midstream Energy Partners USA	1231	E	661 765-4087	241

	SIC	EMP	PHONE	ENTRY#

TUSTIN, CA - Orange County

	SIC	EMP	PHONE	ENTRY#
Superior Sod I LP	0181	C	909 923-5068	71
R Ranch Market	0291	C	714 573-1182	94
Mec-CCC S All N One	1389	E	909 529-0013	362
Tricon American Homes LLC	1521	C	844 874-2661	461
US Best Repair Service Inc	1521	C	888 750-2378	464
Bergelectric Corp	1731	C	949 250-7005	872
Briggs Electric Inc (PA)	1731	D	714 544-2500	873
Woodbridge Glass Inc	1793	C	714 838-4444	1121
Meganutra Inc	2023	E	949 331-2503	1277
Dawn Food Products Inc	2051	C	714 258-1223	1461
Country House	2064	F	714 505-8988	1536
Bar None Inc	2085	F	714 259-8450	1671
JI Design Enterprises Inc	2321	D	714 479-0240	2159
Raj Manufacturing LLC	2339	F	714 838-3110	2364
Raj Manufacturing Inc (PA)	2339	F	714 838-3110	2365
Custom Quilting Inc	2392	E	714 731-7271	2471
GL Woodworking Inc	2431	D	949 515-2192	2601
JC Hanscom Inc	2435	F	562 789-9955	2689
Oak Tree Furniture Inc	2511	F	562 944-0754	2785
Durabag Company Inc	2673	D	714 259-8811	3182
Landscape Communications Inc	2721	E	714 979-5276	3365
Colbi Technologies Inc	2741	E	714 505-9544	3437
Diversified Printers Inc	2741	D	714 994-3400	3441
Meridian Graphics Inc	2752	D	949 833-3500	3634
Precision Offset Inc	2752	D	949 752-1714	3662
Docupak Inc	2782	F	714 670-7944	3837
Bjb Enterprises Inc	2821	E	714 734-8450	3929
Avid Bioservices Inc (PA)	2834	C	714 508-6100	4062
Avid Bioservices Inc	2834	C	714 508-6000	4063
Vitatech Nutritional Sciences Inc	2834	B	714 832-9700	4253
Design West Technologies Inc	3089	D	714 731-0201	5006
Ronco Plastics Inc	3089	C	714 259-1385	5184
Ifiber Optix Inc	3229	E	714 665-9796	5326
Werner Systems Inc	3355	E	714 838-4444	5722
Shade Structures Inc	3444	C	714 427-6980	6312
Braxton Caribbean Mfg Co Inc	3469	C	714 508-3570	6501
Stuart-Dean Co Inc	3471	E	714 544-4460	6668
Bernhardt and Bernhardt Inc	3541	C	714 544-0708	7005
Anajet LLC	3555	E	714 662-3200	7182
Johnston International Corporation	3569	E	714 542-4487	7397
Vinci Brands LLC (PA)	3571	C	949 838-5111	7456
Add-On Cmpt Peripherals LLC	3572	E	949 546-8200	7459
LGarde Inc	3572	C	714 259-0771	7476
Add-On Cmpt Peripherals Inc	3577	C	949 546-8200	7504
Compass Water Solutions Inc (PA)	3589	E	949 222-5777	7652
PI Variables Inc	3669	E	949 415-9411	8621
Expert Assembly Services Inc	3672	E	714 258-8880	8675
Jmp Electronics Inc	3672	E	714 730-2086	8693
Permlight Products Inc	3674	E	714 508-0729	8862
Distribution Electrnics Vlued	3699	E	714 368-1717	9206
Millenworks	3711	D	714 426-5500	9300
89908 Inc	3714	E	949 221-0023	9338
Sunny Amer Globl Autotec Corp	3714	E	714 544-0400	9464
Motionloft Inc	3826	E	415 580-7671	10275
Terumo Americas Holding Inc	3826	F	714 258-8001	10295
Coherent Aerospace & Def Inc	3827	D	714 247-7100	10311
Lightworks Optics Inc	3827	E	714 247-7100	10323
Pvp Advanced Eo Systems Inc (DH)	3827	E	714 508-2740	10335
Issac Medical Inc	3841	B	805 239-4284	10538
Microvention Inc	3841	E	714 258-8001	10568
Trellborg Sling Sltions US Inc (DH)	3841	E	714 415-0280	10619
US Print & Toner Inc	3955	E	619 562-6995	11063
Bio-Reigns Inc	3999	D	949 922-2032	11196
Stanley G Alexander Inc (PA)	4213	C	714 731-1658	11505
Schick Moving & Storage Co (PA)	4214	C	714 731-5500	11522
AB Cellular Holding LLC	4813	A	562 468-6846	11868
Trinity Brdcstg Netwrk Inc	4833	C	714 665-3619	11965
Lsf9 Cypress LP (PA)	5039	C	714 380-3127	12371
Lsf9 Cypress Parent 2 LLC	5039	A	714 380-3127	12372
Syspro Impact Software Inc	5045	C	714 437-1000	12443
Canon Medical Systems USA Inc (DH)	5047	B	714 730-5000	12480
Ecosense Lighting Inc	5063	C	714 823-1014	12594
Pphm Inc	5122	D	714 508-6100	13063
Ansar Gallery Inc	5141	C	949 220-0000	13172
Republic Nat Distrg Co LLC (PA)	5182	C	714 368-4615	13480
Youngs Market Company LLC (HQ)	5182	B	800 317-6150	13483
Logomark Inc	5199	C	714 675-6100	13545
Lowes Home Centers LLC	5211	E	714 913-2663	13658
Nissan of Tustin	5511	E	714 669-8282	13804
Dickeys Barbecue Rest Inc	5812	E	714 602-3874	14001
Yebo Group LLC	5943	C	949 502-3317	14073
Diamond Goldenwest Corporation (PA)	5944	C	714 542-9000	14074

	SIC	EMP	PHONE	ENTRY#
New American Funding LLC (PA)	6141	A	949 430-7029	14275
Southern Cal Prmnnte Med Group	6324	C	714 734-4500	14503
Wood Gutmann Bogart Insur Brkg	6411	D	714 505-7000	14646
Wood Gutmann Bogart Insur Brks	6411	C	714 505-7000	14647
Irvine APT Communities LP	6513	B	714 505-7181	14719
First Team RE - Orange Cnty	6531	B	714 544-5456	14797
Crestmont Capital LLC	6799	C	949 537-3882	15027
Orange County Direct Mail Inc	7331	C	714 444-4412	15634
Crown Building Maintenance Co	7349	B	714 434-9494	15704
B2 Services Llc	7361	D	714 363-3451	15817
Pts Advance	7361	C	949 268-4000	15883
Xbp Inc	7371	D	888 895-7116	16151
A P R Consulting Inc	7379	A	714 544-3696	16546
Robert Pool	7379	E	714 556-5277	16594
Rjn Investigations Inc	7381	D	951 686-7638	16676
Autocrib Inc	7389	C	714 274-0400	16784
Coastal Intl Holdings LLC	7389	B	714 635-1200	16803
Caliber Bodyworks Texas Inc	7532	D	714 665-3905	17009
Allied Lube Inc	7538	D	949 651-8814	17027
Alta Hospitals System LLC	8062	A	714 619-7700	18174
Foothill Regional Medical Ctr	8062	C	310 943-4500	18260
Health Investment Corporation	8062	A	714 669-2085	18275
Kaiser Foundation Hospitals	8062	C	951 353-4000	18306
Pacific Health Corporation	8062	A	714 838-9600	18358
Core Holdings Inc	8082	C	714 969-2342	18605
Roman Cthlic Diocese of Orange	8211	C	714 544-1533	18981
Tustin Unified School District	8211	A	714 542-4271	18985
Crown Golf Properties LP	8742	C	714 730-1611	20160

TWENTYNINE PALMS, CA - San Bernardino County

	SIC	EMP	PHONE	ENTRY#
HI Pro Inc	4213	C	760 367-7734	11491
Mark Clemons	4213	C	760 361-1531	11497
NAVY UNITED STATES DEPARTMENT	8099	D	760 830-2124	18784

UNIVERSAL CITY, CA - Los Angeles County

	SIC	EMP	PHONE	ENTRY#
Sprint Communications Co LP	4813	C	818 755-7100	11904
Nbcuniversal Media LLC	4832	A	818 777-1000	11932
NBC Subsidiary (knbc-Tv) LLC	4833	C	818 684-5746	11959
Universal Stdios Licensing LLC	6794	C	818 695-1273	15010
Hilton Los Angles Universal Cy	7011	C	818 506-2500	15178
Lh Universal Operating LLC	7011	B	818 980-1212	15224
Shen Zhen New World II LLC	7011	D	818 980-1212	15354
Sun Hill Properties Inc	7011	B	818 506-2500	15377
Universal Mus Group Dist Corp	7389	D	818 508-9550	16950
Creative Park Productions LLC	7812	C	818 622-3702	17179
NBC Universal Inc	7812	A		17202
Universal City Studios Lllp	7812	A	818 622-8477	17229
Universal Cy Stdios Prdctons L (DH)	7812	E	818 777-1000	17230
Gramercy Productions LLC	7822	D	818 777-1677	17277
NBC Studios Inc	7922	A	818 777-1000	17321

UPLAND, CA - San Bernardino County

	SIC	EMP	PHONE	ENTRY#
V C A Central Animal Hospital	0742	D	909 981-2855	126
California Skateparks	0781	C	909 949-1601	156
California Ldscp & Design Inc	0782	C	909 949-1601	186
Lewis Companies (PA)	1531	D	909 985-0971	486
Vci Construction LLC (HQ)	1623	D	909 946-0905	702
Largo Concrete Inc	1771	C	909 981-7844	1078
Montclair Wood Corporation	2426	E	909 985-0302	2577
La Bath Vanity Inc (PA)	2434	F	909 303-3323	2665
Judith Von Hopf Inc	2541	E	909 481-1884	2957
CCL Label Inc	2759	D	909 608-2655	3743
CCL Label (delaware) Inc	2759	C	909 608-2260	3744
Holliday Trucking Inc (PA)	3273	D	909 982-1553	5483
Dimic Steel Tech Inc	3444	E	909 946-6767	6227
Lock-Ridge Tool Company Inc	3469	D	909 865-8309	6533
Charles Meisner Inc	3544	E	909 946-8216	7057
Engineered Machinery Group Inc	3547	F	909 579-0088	7150
Walton Electric Corporation	3669	C	909 981-5051	8632
Gar Enterprises	3679	E	909 985-4575	9047
Guided Wave Inc	3823	E	919 264-9651	10138
Analytik Jena US LLC	3826	F	781 376-9899	10233
Applied Instrument Tech Inc	3826	E	909 204-3700	10234
Dependble Break Rm Sltions Inc	5046	D	909 982-5933	12453
Lowes Home Centers LLC	5211	E	909 982-4795	13639
Park Place Ford LLC	5511	D	909 946-5555	13811
Diamond Ridge Corporation	6531	C	909 949-0605	14788
Employnet Inc	7361	A	909 458-0961	15841
Shield Security Inc	7381	B	909 920-1173	16688
Sela Healthcare Inc (PA)	8051	C	909 985-1981	18051
Upland Community Care Inc	8051	C	909 985-1903	18064
San Antonio Regional Hospital (PA)	8062	A	909 985-2811	18413
Upland Highlanders High Ptsa	8641	D	909 949-7880	19467

GEOGRAPHIC

Employee Codes: A=Over 500 employees, B=251-500
C=101-250, D=51-100, E=20-50, F=10-19, G=1-9

2024 Southern California
Business Directory and Buyers Guide

© Mergent Inc. 1-800-342-5647

1453

	SIC	EMP	PHONE	ENTRY#
Garrett J Gentry Gen Engrg Inc	8711	D	909 693-3391	19598
Lewis Management Corp.	8741	C	909 985-0971	20052
Lexxiom Inc	8741	B	909 581-7313	20053
Bni Enterprises Inc	8743	A	909 305-1818	20282

VALENCIA, CA - Los Angeles County

	SIC	EMP	PHONE	ENTRY#
Gothic Landscaping Inc	0781	C	661 257-5085	162
Landscape Development Inc **(PA)**	0782	B	661 295-1970	200
California Strl Concepts Inc	1542	D	661 257-6903	540
Summer Systems Inc	1542	E	661 257-4419	594
Awhap Acquisition Corp	1711	C	888 611-4328	739
AAA Elctrcal Cmmunications Inc **(PA)**	1731	C	800 892-4784	860
Sound River Corporation	1731	D	661 705-3700	936
Weslar Inc	1751	D	661 702-1362	1028
JT Wimsatt Contg Co Inc **(PA)**	1771	B	661 775-8090	1077
Nite-Lite Signs Inc	1799	E	818 341-0987	1172
Lief Organics LLC **(PA)**	2023	E	661 775-2500	1275
Bestway Sandwiches Inc **(PA)**	2051	E	818 361-1800	1454
Chocolates A La Carte Inc	2064	C	661 257-3700	1535
King Henrys Inc	2096	E	818 536-3692	1828
Universal Hosiery Inc	2252	D	661 702-8444	2062
Mechanix Wear LLC **(PA)**	2381	E	800 222-4296	2422
Contractors Wardrobe Inc **(PA)**	2431	C	661 257-1177	2590
Standard Lumber Company Inc **(HQ)**	2448	E	559 651-2037	2727
Legacy Commercial Holdings Inc	2511	E	818 767-6626	2779
Fruit Growers Supply Company **(PA)**	2653	E	888 997-4855	3101
Precision Dynamics Corporation **(HQ)**	2672	C	818 897-1111	3173
Bertelsmann Inc	2731	A	661 702-2700	3399
HI Torque Publicatio	2741	E	661 367-2134	3456
Parrot Communications Intl Inc	2741	E	818 567-4700	3470
Delta Printing Solutions Inc	2752	C	661 257-0584	3557
Cosmic Plastics Inc **(PA)**	2821	E	661 257-3274	3933
Ta Aerospace Co	2821	C	661 702-0448	3976
Creatons Grdn Ntral Fd Mkts In	2833	C	661 877-4280	3996
Ibg Holdings Inc	2844	E	661 702-8680	4421
Mastey De Paris Inc	2844	E	661 257-4814	4433
Utak Laboratories Inc	2869	E	661 294-3935	4535
PRC - Desoto International Inc **(HQ)**	2891	B	661 678-4209	4577
Leonards Molded Products Inc	3069	E	661 253-2227	4774
Ta Aerospace Co **(DH)**	3069	E	661 775-1100	4797
Timemed Labeling Systems Inc **(DH)**	3069	D	818 897-1111	4798
Valencia Pipe Company	3084	E	661 257-3923	4855
King Bros Enterprises LLC	3088	C	661 257-3262	4918
Canyon Plastics LLC	3089	C	800 350-6325	4980
King Bros Industries	3089	C		5079
Santa Clrita Plstic Mlding Cor	3089	E	661 294-2257	5198
US Horizon Manufacturing Inc	3211	E	661 775-1675	5319
Technifex Products LLC	3291	E	661 294-3800	5545
Sgl Technic LLC **(DH)**	3295	E	661 257-0500	5551
Galaxy Die and Engineering Inc	3366	E	661 775-9301	5803
Avibank Mfg Inc	3429	D	661 257-2329	5902
Pacific Lock Company **(PA)**	3429	E	661 294-3707	5939
Hydro Systems Inc **(PA)**	3431	D	661 775-0686	5958
RAH Industries Inc **(PA)**	3444	C	661 295-5190	6302
Stoll Metalcraft Inc	3444	C	661 295-0401	6325
CURRAN ENGINEERING COMPANY I	3446	E	800 643-6353	6355
Lavi Industries **(PA)**	3446	D	877 275-5284	6363
Bloomers Metal Stampings Inc	3469	E	661 257-2955	6500
Pacific Metal Stampings Inc	3469	E	661 257-7656	6545
Nasmyth Tmf Inc	3471	D	818 954-9504	6642
Curtiss-Wright Flow Control	3491	C	626 851-3100	6760
Acousticfab LLC **(DH)**	3492	D	661 257-2242	6772
Electrofilm Mfg Co LLC	3492	E	661 257-2242	6775
Industrial Tube Company LLC	3492	D	661 295-4000	6778
G-G Distribution & Dev Co Inc	3494	C	661 257-5700	6790
Circle W Enterprises Inc.	3496	E	661 257-2400	6815
Whitmor Plstic Wire Cable Corp	3496	E	661 257-2400	6833
LA Turbine **(HQ)**	3511	D	661 294-8290	6882
Sdi Industries Inc **(DH)**	3535	C	818 890-6002	6977
Gruber Systems Inc	3544	E	661 257-0464	7074
Schrey & Sons Mold Co Inc.	3544	E	661 294-2260	7097
Next Point Bearing Group LLC	3562	E	818 988-1880	7301
ASC Process Systems Inc	3567	C	818 833-0088	7360
Indu-Electric North Amer Inc **(PA)**	3568	E	310 578-2144	7379
Western Filter A Division of Donald	3569	D	661 295-0800	7413
Synergy Microsystems Inc **(DH)**	3571	D	858 452-0020	7452
SGB Enterprises Inc	3575	E	661 294-8306	7499
Transparent Products Inc	3575	E	661 294-9787	7501
Input/Output Technology Inc	3577	E	661 257-1000	7536
Aquafine Corporation **(HQ)**	3589	D	661 257-4770	7641
Qmp Inc	3589	E	661 294-6860	7682
Crissair Inc	3594	C	661 367-3300	7711
Bayless Manufacturing LLC	3599	C	661 257-3373	7777
Classic Wire Cut Company Inc	3599	C	661 257-0558	7801
Luran Inc	3599	F	661 257-6303	7909
Performance Machine Tech Inc	3599	E	661 294-8617	7972
True Position Technologies LLC	3599	D	661 294-0030	8052
SMI Holdings Inc	3621	E	800 232-2612	8158
M W Sausse & Co Inc **(PA)**	3625	D	661 257-3311	8185
Capax Technologies Inc	3629	E	661 257-7666	8202
Lightway Industries	3646	E	661 257-0286	8320
Steril-Aire Inc	3648	E	818 565-1128	8382
A & M Electronics Inc	3672	E	661 257-3680	8637
Hamby Corporation	3672	E	661 257-1924	8684
Advanced Semiconductor Inc	3674	D	818 982-1200	8758
Asi Semiconductor Inc	3674	E	818 982-1200	8770
Lockwood Industries LLC **(HQ)**	3674	D	661 702-6999	8829
Semiconductor Process Eqp LLC	3674	E	661 257-0934	8885
Interconnect Solutions Co LLC	3679	D	661 295-0020	9062
Iwerks Entertainment Inc	3699	D	661 678-1800	9219
Mye Technologies Inc	3699	E	661 964-0217	9230
Summit Electric & Data Inc	3699	F	661 775-9901	9258
Air Flow Research Heads Inc	3714	E	661 257-8124	9348
Del West Engineering Inc **(PA)**	3714	C	661 295-5700	9380
Donaldson Company Inc	3714	E	661 295-0800	9382
Princeton Tool Inc	3724	F	661 257-1380	9578
Adept Fasteners Inc **(PA)**	3728	E	661 257-6600	9594
Aero Engineering & Mfg Co LLC	3728	D	661 295-0875	9597
Aerospace Dynamics Intl Inc **(DH)**	3728	C	661 257-3535	9602
Avantus Aerospace Inc **(DH)**	3728	C	661 295-8620	9637
Canyon Engineering Pdts Inc	3728	D	661 294-0084	9654
Flight Line Products Inc	3728	E	661 775-8366	9691
Forrest Machining LLC	3728	C	661 257-0231	9694
Global Aerospace Tech Corp	3728	E	818 407-5600	9702
ITT Aerospace Controls LLC **(HQ)**	3728	D	315 568-7258	9726
ITT Aerospace Controls LLC.	3728	B	661 295-4000	9727
Sunvair Inc **(HQ)**	3728	C	661 294-3777	9805
Sunvair Overhaul Inc	3728	E	661 257-6123	9806
Triumph Acttion Systems - VInc	3728	C	661 702-7537	9821
L3 Technologies Inc	3812	C	818 367-0111	9988
Ronan Engineering Company **(PA)**	3823	D	661 702-1344	10158
Eckert Zegler Isotope Pdts Inc **(HQ)**	3829	E	661 309-1010	10361
H2scan Corporation **(PA)**	3829	E	661 775-9575	10369
Avita Therapeutics Inc	3841	F	661 367-9170	10442
Boston Scientific Corporation	3841	E	800 678-2575	10461
Vertiflex Inc	3841	E	442 325-5900	10627
Advanced Bionics Corporation **(HQ)**	3842	C	661 362-1400	10633
Boston Scntfic Nrmdlation Corp **(HQ)**	3842	B	661 949-4310	10639
Talladium Inc **(PA)**	3843	E	661 295-0900	10773
Advanced Bionics LLC.	3845	C	310 819-4004	10787
Bioness Inc.	3845	C	661 362-4850	10793
Palyon Medical Corporation	3845	E		10822
Vitek Indus Video Pdts Inc	3861	E	661 294-8043	10889
Remo Inc **(PA)**	3931	B	661 294-5600	10930
Fasthouse Inc	3949	E	661 775-5963	10990
Cornerstone Display Group Inc	3993	E	661 705-1700	11105
Ram Board Inc	3996	E	818 848-0400	11184
Medical Brkthrugh Mssage Chirs	3999	E	408 677-7702	11250
Softub Inc **(PA)**	3999	D	858 602-1920	11283
Sunstar Spa Covers Inc **(HQ)**	3999	E	858 602-1950	11290
Technical Manufacturing W LLC	3999	E	661 295-7226	11295
Central States Logistics Inc	4212	C	661 295-7222	11449
D C Shower Doors Inc	4213	C	661 257-1177	11480
Advantage Media Services Inc	4225	C	661 705-7588	11562
Nexus Is Inc	4899	B	704 969-2200	12010
Southern California Edison Co.	4911	C	661 607-0207	12071
Southern California Gas Co.	4924	C	800 427-2200	12087
Whi Solutions Inc	5045	C	661 257-2120	12451
American Med & Hosp Sup Co Inc	5047	E	661 294-1213	12468
Avita Medical Americas LLC	5047	C	661 367-9170	12474
Klm Laboratories Inc	5047	D	661 295-2600	12496
Shield-Denver Health Care Ctr **(HQ)**	5047	C	661 294-4200	12513
Sunco Lighting Inc	5063	E	844 334-9938	12620
Cicoil LLC	5065	C	661 295-1295	12654
Novacap LLC	5065	B	661 295-5920	12689
Tape Specialty Inc	5065	C	661 702-9030	12702
Allied International LLC	5072	E	818 364-2333	12712
Penn Engineering Components	5072	E	818 503-1511	12730
Green Convergence **(PA)**	5074	D	661 294-9495	12742
H2o Innovation USA Holding Inc	5074	D	418 688-0170	12743
Malys of California Inc	5087	B	661 295-8317	12893
Air Frame Mfg & Supply Co Inc	5088	E	661 257-7728	12898
Falcon Aerospace Holdings LLC	5088	A	661 775-7200	12907
Regent Aerospace Corporation **(PA)**	5088	E	661 257-3000	12916
Wesco Aircraft Hardware Corp.	5088	B	661 775-7200	12923
N Qiagen Amercn Holdings Inc **(HQ)**	5122	C	800 426-8157	13057

Mergent email: customerrelations@mergent.com
1454

2024 Southern California
Business Directory and Buyers Guide

(P-0000) Products & Services Section entry number
(PA)=Parent Co (HQ)=Headquarters (DH)=Div Headquarters

	SIC	EMP	PHONE	ENTRY#
Star Nail Products Inc	5122	D	661 257-3376	13071
Sunkist Growers Inc **(PA)**	5148	C	661 290-8900	13342
Bluemark Inc	5199	C	323 230-0770	13531
Magic Acquisition Corp	5511	B	661 382-4700	13793
At Battery Company Inc	5999	E	661 775-2020	14123
Dharma Ventures Group Inc **(PA)**	5999	C	661 294-4200	14130
Mercury Insurance Company	6331	A	661 291-6470	14518
Farmers Insurance	6411	C	661 257-0844	14591
Black Anchor Supply Co LLC	7336	F	661 309-1193	15656
Worldbridge Partners	7361	C	661 775-9999	15907
Maxim Healthcare Services Inc	7363	D	661 964-6350	15929
Sage Staffing Consultants Inc **(PA)**	7363	C	661 254-4026	15940
Krg Technologies Inc **(PA)**	7371	B	661 257-9967	16063
Fpk Security Inc	7381	C	661 702-9091	16642
ADT LLC	7382	C	818 373-6200	16719
Hrd Aero Systems Inc **(PA)**	7699	C	661 295-0670	17132
Russell-Warner Inc	7699	C	661 257-9200	17149
Sunvair Aerospace Group Inc **(PA)**	7699	D	661 294-3777	17155
Teague Custom Marine Inc	7699	F	661 295-7000	17158
Magic Mountain LLC	7922	C	661 255-4100	17319
Heritage Golf Group LLC	7992	C	661 254-4401	17432
Six Flags Magic Mountain Inc	7996	D	661 255-4100	17455
Henry Mayo Newhall Mem Hosp **(PA)**	8062	A	661 253-8000	18279
Henry Mayo Nwhall Mem Hlth Fnd	8062	A	661 253-8000	18280
Specialty Laboratories Inc **(DH)**	8071	C	661 799-6543	18565
Volunteers of Amer Los Angeles	8322	D	661 290-2829	19160
Scicon Technologies Corp **(PA)**	8711	E	661 295-8630	19687
Scorpion Design LLC **(PA)**	8742	A	661 702-0100	20234
Geologics Corporation	8748	B	661 259-5767	20339

VALLEY CENTER, CA - San Diego County

	SIC	EMP	PHONE	ENTRY#
Brax Company Inc	1781	E	760 749-2209	1093
Mercy Medical Trnsp Inc	4119	C	760 739-8026	11397
Hcal LLC	7011	B	760 751-3100	15174
San Psqual Band Mssion Indians	7011	C	760 291-5500	15346
Survival Systems Intl Inc **(PA)**	7699	D	760 749-6800	17156
Caesars Entrtnment Oprtng Inc	7999	A	760 751-3100	17542
Indian Health Council Inc **(PA)**	8011	D	760 749-1410	17670
San Psqual Band Mssion Indians **(PA)**	9131	D	760 749-3200	20407

VALLEY VILLAGE, CA - Los Angeles County

	SIC	EMP	PHONE	ENTRY#
FB Productions Inc	2752	E	818 773-9337	3571
Cannalogic	3999	F	619 458-0775	11202
Douglas Steel Supply Inc **(PA)**	5051	D	323 587-7676	12547
Adat ARI EI	8211	C	818 766-4992	18962

VAN NUYS, CA - Los Angeles County

	SIC	EMP	PHONE	ENTRY#
Parkwood Landscape Maint Inc	0782	D	818 988-9677	212
Scenario Cockram USA Inc	1521	C	407 613-2949	452
Energy Enterprises USA Inc **(PA)**	1711	D	424 339-0005	766
Eberhard	1761	D	818 782-4604	1044
Mp Aero LLC	1799	D	818 901-9828	1170
Bubbles Baking Company	2051	E	818 786-1700	1457
Danish Baking Co Inc	2051	D	818 786-1700	1460
SGB Better Baking Co LLC	2051	E	818 787-9992	1492
SGB Bubbles Baking Co LLC	2051	E	818 786-1700	1493
Western Bagel Baking Corp **(PA)**	2051	C	818 786-5847	1500
Aspire Bakeries LLC	2052	A	818 904-8230	1506
Power Brands Consulting LLC	2082	E	818 989-9646	1602
Chef Merito LLC **(PA)**	2099	E	818 787-0100	1869
Rof LLC	2326	E	818 933-4000	2185
Kandy Kiss of California Inc	2331	D		2249
Leigh Jerry California Inc **(PA)**	2361	B	818 909-6200	2410
Danmer Inc	2431	C	516 670-5125	2592
I and E Cabinets Inc	2434	E	818 933-6480	2661
All American Cabinetry Inc	2541	F	818 376-0500	2941
Cpp/Belwin Inc	2731	B	818 891-5999	3403
The Full Void 2 Inc	2731	E	818 891-5999	3417
C & L Graphics Inc	2752	F	818 785-8310	3523
Challenge Graphics Inc	2752	F	818 892-0123	3528
Niknejad Inc	2752	E	310 477-0407	3644
Pegasus Interprint Inc	2752	E	800 926-9873	3655
Printrunner LLC	2752	E	888 296-5760	3667
Digital Room Holdings Inc **(HQ)**	2759	D	310 575-4440	3753
Great Western Packaging LLC	2759	D	818 464-3800	3765
Investment Enterprises Inc **(PA)**	2759	E	818 464-3800	3772
Pearl Management Group Inc	2834	E	818 217-0218	4197
Mpm Building Services Inc	2842	E	818 708-9676	4362
Orly International Inc **(PA)**	2844	E	818 994-1001	4440
Prolabs Factory Inc	2844	E	818 646-3677	4449
Munchkin Inc **(PA)**	3085	C	800 344-2229	4860
Neopacific Holdings Inc	3089	E	818 786-2900	5112
Linea Pelle Inc **(PA)**	3111	F	310 231-9950	5259
Rwh Inc	3273	E	818 782-2350	5501
Thompson Gundrilling Inc	3321	E	323 873-4045	5649
RPC Legacy Inc	3429	E	818 787-9000	5941
Advance Overhead Door Inc	3442	F	818 781-5590	6098
Consolidated Fabricators Corp **(PA)**	3443	C	800 635-8335	6139
Broadway AC Htg & Shtmtl	3444	E	818 781-1477	6204
Edwards Sheet Metal Supply Inc	3444	E	818 785-8600	6230
Dayton Rogers of California Inc	3469	C	763 784-7714	6510
Enterprises Industries Inc	3469	C	818 989-6103	6515
Capstone Green Energy Corp **(PA)**	3511	C		6878
Industrial Elctrnc Engnrs In	3577	D	818 787-0311	7533
Data Lights Rigging LLC	3613	F	818 786-0536	8120
Optical Zonu Corporation	3661	F	818 780-9701	8482
Advanced Circuits Inc	3672	E	818 345-1993	8642
Ambay Circuits Inc	3672	E	818 786-8241	8645
Photo Fabricators Inc	3672	D	818 781-1010	8717
Alyn Industries Inc	3679	D	818 988-7696	8994
Cicon Engineering Inc **(PA)**	3679	C	818 909-6060	9017
Microfabrica Inc	3679	E	888 964-2763	9084
United Audio Video Group Inc	3695	E	818 980-6700	9186
Kalaydjian Shahe Inc	3714	E	818 988-3700	9408
Superior Inds Intl Hldings LLC **(HQ)**	3714	D	818 781-4973	9465
Wsw Corp **(PA)**	3714	E	818 989-5008	9488
Gulfstream Aerospace Corp GA	3721	B	805 236-5755	9540
Aeroshear Aviation Svcs Inc **(PA)**	3728	E	818 779-1650	9600
Edo Communications and Countermeasu	3812	D	818 464-2475	9973
L3harris Technologies Inc	3812	E	818 901-2523	9989
Rizzo Inc	3842	E	818 781-6891	10696
Kazak-Mars Inc	3851	E	818 375-1033	10842
Modern Studio Equipment Inc	3861	F	818 764-8574	10874
Wbi Inc	3861	A	800 673-4968	10890
Allison-Kaufman Co	3911	E	818 373-5100	10894
Shelcore Inc **(PA)**	3944	E	818 883-2400	10966
E Alko Inc	3955	E	818 587-9700	11055
Neiman/Hoeller Inc	3993	D	818 781-8600	11141
Keolis Transit America Inc	4111	C	818 616-5254	11322
Mv Transportation Inc	4111	C	818 374-9145	11345
American Prof Ambulance Corp	4119	D	818 996-2200	11373
Medresponse **(PA)**	4119	C	818 442-9222	11396
Catered Fit Corp	4212	C	855 400-2348	11448
United Parcel Service Inc	4215	B	404 828-6000	11540
Moulton Logistics Management	4225	C	818 997-1800	11599
Pegasus Elite Aviation Inc	4522	C	818 742-6666	11682
Clay Lacy Aviation Inc **(PA)**	4581	B	818 989-2900	11691
Repairtech International Inc	4581	E	818 989-2681	11705
Broadview Networks Inc	4813	D	818 939-0015	11874
Katzirs Floor & HM Design Inc **(PA)**	5023	E	818 988-9663	12305
E & S International Entps Inc **(PA)**	5064	C	818 887-0700	12630
American Industrial Source Inc	5085	D	800 661-0622	12844
Anatex Enterprises Inc	5092	E	818 908-1888	12933
Home Depot USA Inc	5211	C	818 780-5448	13620
Keyes Motors Inc **(PA)**	5511	D	818 782-0122	13787
Keylex Inc **(PA)**	5511	E	818 379-4000	13788
Cinema Secrets Inc	5999	D	818 846-0579	14125
Napoleon Perdis Cosmetics Inc	5999	E	323 817-3611	14140
Los Angeles Police Credit Un **(PA)**	6062	B	818 787-6520	14249
Century-National Insurance Co **(DH)**	6411	B	818 760-0880	14574
Dewitt Stern Group Inc	6411	D	818 933-2700	14584
1370 Realty Corp	6531	F	818 817-0092	14740
Icon Media Direct Inc **(PA)**	7311	D	818 995-6400	15546
Lees Maintenance Service Inc	7349	B	818 988-6644	15719
L A Party Rents Inc	7359	C	818 989-4300	15783
Microlease Inc **(DH)**	7359	C	866 520-0200	15787
Town & Cntry Event Rentals Inc **(PA)**	7359	B	818 908-4211	15802
Certemy Inc	7372	F	866 907-4088	16176
Hollywood Software Inc	7372	E	818 205-2121	16263
Nafees Memon	7381	D	818 997-1666	16660
Louroe Electronics Inc	7382	E	818 994-6498	16747
Anheuser-Busch LLC	7389	B	805 381-4700	16779
Modern Parking Inc	7521	C	818 783-3143	16995
EDN Aviation Inc	7699	E	818 988-8826	17125
Harpo Productions Inc	7812	C	312 633-1000	17195
Fusefx LLC	7819	E	818 237-5052	17254
Nep Bexel Inc **(HQ)**	7819	D	818 565-4399	17257
Southern Cal Orthpd Inst LP **(PA)**	8011	C	818 901-6600	17772
Valley Presbyterian Hospital	8062	A	818 782-6600	18496
Alta Hllywood Cmnty Hosp Van N	8063	D	818 787-1511	18503
Primex Clinical Labs Inc **(PA)**	8071	E		18559
Americare Home Health Inc	8082	D	818 881-0005	18590
Greater Valley Medical Group	8093	C	818 781-7097	18693
County of Los Angeles	8322	C	818 374-2000	19062
Apprentice Jrnymen Trning Tr F	8331	C	310 604-0892	19174
Interviewing Service Amer LLC **(PA)**	8732	C	818 989-1044	19901

Employee Codes: A=Over 500 employees, B=251-500
C=101-250, D=51-100, E=20-50, F=10-19, G=1-9

2024 Southern California
Business Directory and Buyers Guide

© Mergent Inc. 1-800-342-5647

1455

GEOGRAPHIC

	SIC	EMP	PHONE	ENTRY#
Consumer Safety Analytics LLC	8734	D	818 922-2416	19965
Sylmark Inc (PA)	8741	D	818 217-2000	20103
Cockram Construction Inc	8742	B	818 650-0999	20154
Ganz USA LLC	8742	C	818 901-0077	20174

VANDENBERG AFB, CA - Santa Barbara County

	SIC	EMP	PHONE	ENTRY#
Space Exploration Tech Corp	3721	E	310 848-4410	9554
United Launch Alliance LLC	3761	B	303 269-5876	9906
Henry Call Inc	8744	C	805 734-2762	20292
Indyne Inc	8744	B	805 606-7225	20293

VENICE, CA - Los Angeles County

	SIC	EMP	PHONE	ENTRY#
Pacific Structures Sc Inc (PA)	1771	C	415 970-5434	1082
Vive Organic Inc	2033	E	877 774-9291	1351
Indie Source	2326	E	424 200-2027	2176
Frankies Bikinis LLC	2369	E	323 354-4133	2415
Flex Company (PA)	3069	E	424 209-2711	4763
Allbirds Inc	3143	F	424 295-9968	5269
Alpargatas Usa Inc	3144	E	646 277-7171	5274
Flat Planet Inc	3559	E	888 656-6872	7236
Fellow Industries Inc	3634	E	415 649-0361	8234
Syng Inc (PA)	3651	D	770 354-0915	8440
Los Angles Cnty Mtro Trnsp Aut	4111	A	310 392-8636	11337
Load Delivered Logistics LLC	4213	C	310 822-0215	11495
Southern California Gas Co	4924	A	310 823-7945	12090
Swartz Glass Co Inc (PA)	5231	F	310 392-0001	13674
Trg Inc	6531	D	310 396-6750	14876
Proper Hospitality LLC	7011	C	310 277-5221	15310
Dynasty Marketplace Inc	7371	B	804 837-0119	16019
Sameday Technologies Inc	7371	C	310 697-8126	16107
Gamemine LLC	7372	E	310 310-3105	16255
Parking Concepts Inc	7521	C	310 821-1081	17002
Power Studios Inc	7812	C	310 314-2800	17211
Venice Fmly Clinic Foundation (PA)	8011	C	310 664-7703	17823
St Joseph Center	8322	D	310 396-6468	19143
Gateb Consulting Inc	8748	D	310 526-8323	20337

VENTURA, CA - Ventura County

	SIC	EMP	PHONE	ENTRY#
Saticoy Lemon Association	0174	D	805 654-6500	44
Floral Gift HM Decor Intl Inc	0181	E	818 849-8832	54
Brightview Landscape Svcs Inc	0781	C	805 642-9300	150
West Coast Arborists Inc	0783	C	805 671-5092	226
Bentley-Simonson Inc	1311	E	805 650-2794	246
Calnrg Operating LLC (PA)	1311	E	805 477-9805	257
Instrument Control Services	1389	E	805 642-1999	355
Nabors Well Services Co	1389	D	805 648-2731	366
Ais Construction Company	1542	D	805 928-9467	528
Vista Steel Co Inc	1629	E	805 653-1189	720
Taft Electric Company (PA)	1731	C	805 642-0121	946
Tidwell Excav Acquisition Inc	1794	D	805 647-4707	1128
G W Surfaces (PA)	1799	D	805 642-5004	1159
Dairy Farmers America Inc	2026	D	805 653-0042	1308
Ventura Coastal LLC (PA)	2037	D	805 653-7000	1380
Better Bakery LLC	2052	C	661 294-9882	1509
Fermented Sciences Inc	2082	E	818 427-8442	1587
Reyes Coca-Cola Bottling LLC	2086	E	805 644-2211	1726
Fabricmate Systems Inc	2221	E	805 642-7470	2038
Patagonia Inc (HQ)	2329	B	805 643-8616	2217
Streamline Dsign Slkscreen Inc (PA)	2329	E	805 884-1025	2223
Hearts Delight	2339	E	805 648-7123	2327
Art Glass Etc Inc	2431	E	805 644-4494	2585
Santa Monica Millworks	2434	E	805 643-0010	2678
W L Rubottom Co	2434	D	805 648-6943	2684
Goldenwood Truss Corporation	2439	D	805 659-2520	2698
Edwards Assoc Cmmnications Inc (PA)	2672	C	805 658-2626	3170
Hennis Enterprises Inc	2821	E	805 477-0257	3941
Fnc Medical Corporation	2844	E	805 644-7576	4410
Jh Biotech Inc (PA)	2875	E	805 650-8933	4544
C & R Molds Inc	3089	E	805 658-7098	4972
Commonpath LLC	3231	F	858 922-8116	5337
State Ready Mix Inc (PA)	3273	E	805 647-2817	5506
Chapala Iron & Manufacturing	3312	F	805 654-9803	5586
Assa Abloy ACC Door Cntrls Gro	3429	C	805 642-2600	5898
Automotive Racing Products Inc (PA)	3429	D	805 339-2200	5900
Pemko Manufacturing Co	3442	C	800 283-9988	6115
Quick Draw and Machining Inc	3469	F	805 644-7882	6551
Sessa Manufacturing & Welding	3469	E	805 644-2284	6555
Valex Corp (HQ)	3471	D	805 658-0944	6678
Juengermann Inc	3493	E	805 644-7165	6782
Aqueos Corporation	3533	C	805 676-4330	6953
Aquastar Pool Products Inc	3561	E	877 768-2717	7268
HMcompany	3599	F	805 650-2651	7864
Ventura Hydrulic Mch Works Inc	3599	E	805 656-1760	8065

	SIC	EMP	PHONE	ENTRY#
Dow-Key Microwave Corporation	3625	C	805 650-0260	8177
Lamps Plus Inc	3646	E	805 642-9007	8318
Total Structures Inc	3648	E	805 676-3322	8386
Wireless Technology Inc	3651	E	805 339-9696	8451
Coastal Connections	3661	E	805 644-5051	8470
Naso Industries Corporation	3672	E	805 650-1231	8708
Omnisil	3674	E	805 644-2514	8853
Robert M Hadley Company Inc	3677	D	805 658-7286	8954
Holland Electronics LLC	3678	E	805 339-9060	8972
Magnuson Products LLC	3714	E	805 642-8833	9419
Ventura Harbor Boatyard Inc	3732	E	805 654-1433	9867
Barnett Tool & Engineering	3751	D	805 642-9435	9873
Peter Brasseler Holdings LLC	3841	D	805 658-2643	10587
TMJ Solutions LLC	3841	D	805 650-3391	10618
Implantech Associates Inc	3842	E	805 289-1665	10670
Strand Products Inc (PA)	3845	E	800 343-7985	10826
Blue Ocean Marine LLC	4499	E	805 658-2628	11653
Cco Holdings LLC	4841	C	805 232-5887	11979
E J Harrison & Sons Inc	4953	C	805 647-1414	12167
Parts Authority LLC	5013	C	805 676-3410	12251
Canon Solutions America Inc	5044	E	844 443-4636	12383
Peter Brasseler Holdings LLC	5047	D	805 650-5209	12507
M-H Ironworks Inc	5051	D		12558
High Tech Pet Products	5065	C	805 644-1797	12664
Smart & Final Stores Inc	5141	B	805 647-4276	13209
Del Mar Seafoods Inc	5146	C	805 850-0421	13279
Lowes Home Centers LLC	5211	C	805 675-8800	13651
Gregory Consulting Inc (PA)	5511	C	805 642-0111	13774
R E Barber-Ford	5511	C	805 656-4259	13816
Southern Cal Disc Tire Co Inc	5531	D	805 639-0166	13871
Ventura Feed and Pet Sups Inc	5621	C	805 648-5035	13918
Patagonia Works (PA)	5699	B	805 643-8616	13935
Cold Steel Inc (PA)	5961	F	805 650-8481	14093
Ventura County Credit Union (PA)	6061	D	805 477-4000	14243
Fin-West Group	6162	C	805 658-7435	14315
Rgc Services Inc (PA)	6531	C	805 644-1242	14861
Ventura Hsptality Partners LLC	7011	C	805 648-2100	15404
MCM Harvesters Inc	7361	C	805 659-6833	15866
Trade Desk Inc (PA)	7371	C	805 585-3434	16137
Boyd and Associates (PA)	7381	C	818 752-1888	16626
Penske Corporation	7513	C	805 983-3788	16970
Century Theatres Inc	7833	C	805 641-6555	17305
Agi Holding Corp (PA)	7997	B	805 667-4100	17458
Team So-Cal Inc	7997	E	805 650-9946	17528
Ventura Cnty Obstet Gynclgic M	8011	D	805 643-8695	17824
Ventura County Medical Center	8011	C	805 652-6201	17826
Ventura County Medical Center	8049	C	805 652-6729	17873
Coastal View Halthcare Ctr LLC	8051	D	805 642-4101	17902
Victoria Care Center	8051	D	805 642-1736	18067
Victoria Vntura Healthcare LLC	8051	D	805 642-1736	18069
Community Mem Hosp San Bnvntur	8062	D	805 652-5072	18226
Community Memorial Health Sys (PA)	8062	A	805 652-5011	18228
Aegis Senior Communities LLC	8082	D	805 650-1114	18587
Califrnia Frnsic Med Group Inc	8099	C	805 654-3343	18750
Star of Ca LLC (HQ)	8099	C	805 644-7827	18807
Catholic Chrties Snta Clara CN	8322	D	805 643-4694	19035
County of Ventura	8322	C	805 654-2561	19068
Channel Islnds Yung MNS Chrstn	8641	D	805 484-0423	19439
C D Lyon Construction Inc (PA)	8711	D	805 653-0173	19559
Oasis Systems LLC	8711	C	805 644-2191	19657
County of Ventura	8721	C	805 654-3152	19765
Livingston Mem Vna Hlth Corp	8741	B	805 642-0239	20056
Ventura Medical Management LLC	8741	B	805 477-6220	20112
County of Ventura	9111	D	805 652-6100	20405

VERNON, CA - Los Angeles County

	SIC	EMP	PHONE	ENTRY#
Edna H Pagel Inc	1541	D	323 234-2200	501
Square H Brands Inc	1541	D	323 267-4600	519
West Coast Distribution Inc	1541	D	323 588-6508	526
Littlejohn-Reuland Corporation	1731	E	323 587-5255	914
Clougherty Packing LLC (DH)	2011	B	323 583-4621	1193
Golden West Food Group Inc (PA)	2011	E	888 807-3663	1196
Jobbers Meat Packing Co LLC	2011	C	323 585-6328	1198
K & M Packing Co Inc	2011	E	323 585-5318	1199
R B R Meat Company Inc	2011	D	323 973-4868	1203
Bar-S Foods Co	2013	E	323 589-3600	1212
Papa Cantellas Incorporated	2013	D	323 584-7272	1229
Expro Manufacturing Corporation	2032	E	323 415-8544	1324
Fresh Packing Corporation	2032	F	213 612-0136	1325
Masongate Inc	2032	E	323 415-8544	1329
T & T Foods Inc	2032	E	323 588-2158	1333
Culinary Brands Inc (PA)	2038	E	626 289-3000	1387
Star Food 316 Inc	2038	E	213 858-2512	1402

	SIC	EMP	PHONE	ENTRY#
General Mills Inc.	2041	E	323 584-3433	1409
Mochi Ice Cream Company LLC **(PA)**	2051	E	323 587-5504	1483
Interntnal Desserts Delicacies **(PA)**	2052	F	818 549-0056	1519
J & J Snack Foods Corp Cal **(HQ)**	2052	C	323 581-0171	1520
Smart Foods LLC.	2076	C	800 284-2250	1565
Baker Commodities Inc **(PA)**	2077	C	323 268-2801	1566
D & D Services Inc.	2077	E	323 261-4176	1567
Coast Packing Company.	2079	D	323 277-7700	1570
American Bottling Company.	2086	C	323 268-7779	1679
Gts Living Foods LLC.	2086	E	323 581-7787	1696
Gts Living Foods LLC **(PA)**	2086	A	323 581-7787	1697
Stratus Group Duo LLC.	2086	E	323 581-3663	1741
American Fruits & Flavors LLC.	2087	E	323 881-8321	1752
Pacific American Fish Co Inc **(PA)**	2091	C	323 319-1551	1795
Fishermans Pride Prcessors Inc.	2092	B	323 232-1980	1806
Eberine Enterprises Inc.	2095	E	323 587-1111	1817
F Gavina & Sons Inc.	2095	B	323 582-0671	1819
Son of A Barista Usa LLC **(PA)**	2095	E	323 780-8250	1822
Camino Real Foods Inc **(PA)**	2099	C	323 585-6599	1865
Cargill Meat Solutions Corp.	2099	C	515 735-9800	1867
Clw Foods LLC.	2099	F	323 432-4600	1872
Culinary International LLC **(PA)**	2099	C	626 289-3000	1877
F I O Imports Inc.	2099	C	323 263-5100	1891
Overhill Farms Inc **(DH)**	2099	C	323 582-9977	1963
Penguin Natural Foods Inc **(PA)**	2099	E	323 727-7980	1970
Reynaldos Mexican Food Co LLC **(PA)**	2099	C	562 803-3188	1976
Teva Foods Inc.	2099	E	323 267-8110	1996
Belagio Enterprises Inc.	2211	E	323 731-6934	2012
Jml Textile Inc.	2211	F	323 584-2323	2025
Pjy LLC.	2211	E	323 583-7737	2030
Socal Garment Works LLC.	2211	E	323 300-5717	2031
Chua & Sons Co Inc.	2241	E	323 588-8044	2054
Universal Elastic & Garment Supply Inc.	2241	E	213 748-2995	2056
Fantasy Activewear Inc **(PA)**	2253	E	213 705-4111	2068
Fantasy Dyeing & Finishing Inc.	2253	E	323 983-9988	2069
Latigo Inc.	2253	E	323 583-8000	2073
Shara-Tex Inc.	2257	E	323 587-7200	2079
Sas Textiles Inc.	2259	D	323 277-5555	2086
Rezex Corporation.	2269	E	213 622-2015	2106
American Cover Design 26 Inc.	2273	E	323 582-8666	2108
Marspring Corporation **(PA)**	2273	E	323 589-5637	2116
California Combining Corp.	2295	E	323 589-5727	2125
J H Textiles Inc.	2299	E	323 585-4124	2141
Stone Harbor Inc.	2299	F	323 277-2777	2147
New Chef Fashion Inc.	2311	D	323 581-0300	2152
Mexapparel Inc **(PA)**	2326	E	323 364-8600	2181
Offline Inc **(PA)**	2326	E	213 742-9001	2182
Zk Enterprises Inc.	2329	E	213 622-7012	2228
Crestone LLC.	2331	E	323 588-8857	2236
Final Touch Apparel Inc.	2331	F	323 484-9621	2239
Lovemarks Inc.	2331	D	213 514-5888	2254
W5 Concepts Inc.	2331	E	323 231-2415	2270
Complete Clothing Company **(PA)**	2335	E	323 277-1470	2281
Trinity Sports Inc.	2335	B	323 277-9288	2291
David Grment Cctng Fsing Svc In.	2339	E	323 216-1574	2316
Gaze USA Inc.	2339	E	213 622-0022	2324
Heather By Bordeaux Inc.	2339	E	213 622-0555	2328
It Jeans Inc.	2339	E	323 588-2156	2330
Jaya Apparel Group LLC **(PA)**	2339	D	323 584-3500	2333
Just For Wraps Inc **(PA)**	2339	C	213 239-0503	2339
Kim & Cami Productions Inc.	2339	E	323 584-1300	2341
LAT LLC.	2339	E	323 233-3017	2346
Patterson Kincaid LLC.	2339	E	323 584-3559	2357
Putnam Accessory Group Inc.	2339	E	323 306-1330	2362
Rotax Incorporated.	2339	E	323 589-5999	2367
Spirit Clothing Company.	2339	C	213 784-0251	2371
Tempted Apparel Corp.	2339	D	323 859-2480	2377
Vxb & Orfwid Inc.	2339	E	213 222-0030	2382
W & W Concept Inc.	2339	D	323 803-3090	2383
National Corset Supply House **(PA)**	2341	D	323 261-0265	2392
Selectra Industries Corp.	2341	D	323 581-8500	2393
L A S A M Inc.	2361	F	323 586-8717	2409
Streets Ahead Inc.	2387	E	323 277-0860	2435
Anaya Brothers Cutting LLC.	2389	D	323 582-5758	2440
Classic Slip Covers Inc.	2392	F	323 583-0804	2469
Rebecca International Inc.	2395	E	323 973-2602	2524
J & H Production.	2396	E	323 261-6600	2533
SJ&I Bias Binding & Tex Co Inc.	2396	E	213 747-5271	2540
Sandberg Furniture Mfg Co Inc **(PA)**	2511	C	323 582-0711	2789
A Rudin Inc.	2512	D	323 589-5547	2793
Republic Furniture Mfg Inc.	2512	F	323 235-2144	2814
Yen-Nhai Inc.	2512	E	323 584-1315	2823
Marspring Corporation.	2515	D	310 484-6849	2855
Tempo Industries Inc.	2515	C	415 552-8074	2862
Paper Surce Converting Mfg Inc.	2621	E	323 583-3800	3060
Crown Carton Company Inc.	2653	E	323 582-3053	3096
Packaging Corporation America.	2653	C	323 263-7581	3122
Southland Box Company.	2653	C	323 583-2231	3130
Great American Packaging.	2673	E	323 582-2247	3183
Norman Paper and Foam Co Inc.	2673	E	323 582-7132	3188
Princess Paper Inc.	2676	E	323 588-4777	3206
Viva Holdings LLC **(PA)**	2678	F	818 243-1363	3225
Tagtime Usa Inc.	2679	B	323 587-1555	3248
Colorfast Dye & Print Hse Inc.	2752	E	323 581-1656	3535
Corporate Graphics Intl Inc.	2752	D	323 826-3440	3547
Superior Lithographics Inc.	2752	D	323 263-8400	3690
The Ligature Inc **(HQ)**	2752	E	323 585-6000	3697
RJ Acquisition Corp **(PA)**	2759	C	323 318-1107	3808
Tee Styled Inc.	2759	E	323 983-9988	3820
Advanced Chemical Technology.	2819	E	800 527-9607	3879
Joes Plastics Inc.	2821	E	323 771-8433	3951
Continental Vitamin Co Inc.	2834	D	323 581-0176	4092
Peerless Materials Company.	2842	E	323 266-0313	4367
Engineered Coating Tech Inc.	2851	E	323 588-0260	4487
Evonik Corporation.	2899	C	323 264-0311	4605
Aoclsc Inc.	2992	E	562 776-4000	4678
Demenno/Kerdoon Holdings.	2992	E	323 268-3387	4682
Sewing Collection Inc.	3053	D	323 264-2223	4745
A&A Global Imports LLC **(PA)**	3089	D	888 315-2453	4926
Edris Plastics Mfg Inc.	3089	E	323 581-7000	5021
Geo Plastics.	3089	E	323 277-8106	5037
Home Concepts Products Inc.	3089	E	866 981-0500	5050
Makabi 26 Inc.	3089	F	323 588-7666	5090
Norton Packaging Inc.	3089	E	323 588-6167	5120
Nuconic Packaging LLC.	3089	E	323 588-9033	5124
Rehrig Pacific Company **(HQ)**	3089	C	323 262-5145	5177
Rehrig Pacific Holdings Inc **(PA)**	3089	D	323 262-5145	5178
Rplanet Erth Los Angles Hldngs.	3089	E	833 775-2638	5190
Sol-Pak Thermoforming Inc.	3089	E	323 582-3333	5209
Tom York Enterprises Inc.	3089	E	323 581-6194	5229
G & G Quality Case Co Inc.	3161	D	323 233-2482	5287
RJ Singer International Inc.	3161	F	323 735-1717	5294
Isabelle Handbag Inc.	3171	E	323 277-9888	5298
Berney-Karp Inc.	3269	D	323 260-7122	5383
Calportland Company.	3273	F	800 272-1891	5467
National Cement Company Inc.	3273	E	323 923-4466	5488
Pabco Building Products LLC.	3275	C	323 581-6113	5520
Charman Manufacturing Inc.	3317	F	213 489-7000	5632
Nucor Warehouse Systems Inc **(HQ)**	3317	C	323 588-4601	5639
Global Truss America LLC.	3354	D	323 415-6225	5698
Arcadia Products LLC **(HQ)**	3355	C	323 771-9819	5717
Bodycote Usa Inc.	3398	A	323 264-0111	5829
Kai USA Ltd.	3421	E	323 589-2600	5868
Tajima USA Dissolving Corp.	3446	E	323 588-1281	6370
Ajax Forge Company **(PA)**	3462	F	323 582-6307	6458
Luppen Holdings Inc **(PA)**	3469	E	323 581-8121	6534
Certified Steel Treating Corp.	3471	E	323 583-8711	6601
Atlas Galvanizing LLC.	3479	E	323 587-6247	6694
Kennedy Name Plate Co.	3479	E	323 585-0121	6714
Baker Coupling Company Inc.	3498	E	323 583-3444	6838
Angelus Machine Corp Intl.	3542	D	323 583-2171	7031
Punch Press Products Inc.	3544	D	323 581-7151	7092
Vest Inc.	3547	D	800 421-6370	7154
P&Y T-Shrts Silk Screening Inc.	3552	E	323 585-4604	7178
Starco Enterprises Inc **(PA)**	3559	D	323 266-7111	7259
Flowserve Corporation.	3561	B	323 584-1890	7277
J F Duncan Industries Inc **(PA)**	3589	D	562 862-4269	7663
Bender Ccp Inc **(PA)**	3599	E	707 745-9970	7779
Brentwood Appliances Inc.	3639	E	323 266-4600	8240
Hollywood Lamp & Shade Co.	3641	E	323 585-3999	8246
AMP Plus Inc.	3647	D	323 231-2600	8344
Unirex Corp.	3674	E	323 589-4000	8915
Westgate Mfg Inc.	3699	D	323 826-9490	9272
C R Laurence Co Inc **(HQ)**	3714	B	323 588-1281	9364
US Radiator Corporation **(PA)**	3714	E	323 826-0965	9483
Evergreen Industries Inc **(DH)**	3821	D	323 583-1331	10092
Barksdale Inc **(DH)**	3829	C	323 583-6243	10353
LA Gem and Jwly Design Inc.	3911	D	213 488-1290	10907
Mahar Manufacturing Corp **(PA)**	3942	E	323 581-9988	10939
UPD INC.	3942	E	323 588-8811	10944
Labeltex Mills Inc **(PA)**	3965	C	323 582-0228	11071
Two Lads Inc **(PA)**	3965	E	323 584-0064	11079
Los Angeles Junction Rlwy Co.	4011	C	323 277-2004	11311
Vernon Central Warehouse Inc.	4214	C	323 234-2200	11524
Preferred Frzr Svcs - Lbf LLC.	4222	D	323 263-8811	11555
Generational Properties Inc.	4225	B	323 583-3163	11582

Employee Codes: A=Over 500 employees, B=251-500
C=101-250, D=51-100, E=20-50, F=10-19, G=1-9

2024 Southern California
Business Directory and Buyers Guide

© Mergent Inc. 1-800-342-5647

1457

GEOGRAPHIC

	SIC	EMP	PHONE	ENTRY#
United Parcel Service Inc	4513	C	323 260-8957	11678
R Planet Earth LLC	4953	C	213 320-0601	12180
Reliance Steel & Aluminum Co	5051	C	323 583-6111	12569
E B Bradley Co (PA)	5072	E	323 585-9917	12721
Omniteam Inc	5078	C	562 923-9660	12763
Kafco Sales Company	5084	E	323 588-7141	12795
Rggd Inc (PA)	5099	D	323 581-6617	12983
Morgan Fabrics Corporation (PA)	5131	D	323 583-9981	13087
Karen Kane Inc (PA)	5137	C	323 588-0000	13129
New Pride Corporation	5137	D	323 584-6608	13138
Nydj Apparel LLC	5137	C	323 581-9040	13140
O & K Inc (PA)	5137	C	323 846-5700	13141
Rcrv Inc (PA)	5137	E	323 235-7300	13144
Runway Liquidation LLC (HQ)	5137	E	323 589-2224	13146
Same Swim LLC	5137	D	323 582-2588	13147
Tarrant Apparel Group	5137	D	323 780-8250	13153
The Timing Inc	5137	E	323 589-5577	13154
Palisades Ranch Inc	5141	B	323 581-6161	13190
Contessa Premium Foods Inc	5142	C	310 832-8000	13244
Golden West Trading Inc	5142	C	323 581-3663	13246
West Pico Foods Inc	5142	C	323 586-9050	13250
Rogers Poultry Co (PA)	5144	C	323 585-0802	13260
H & N Foods International Inc (HQ)	5146	C	323 586-9300	13280
Red Chamber Co (PA)	5146	E	323 234-9000	13285
Eastland Corporation	5147	C	323 261-5388	13293
HV Randall Foods LLC	5147	C	323 261-6565	13297
Pontrelli & Larricchia Ltd	5147	C	323 583-6690	13303
Rancho Foods Inc	5147	D	323 585-0503	13305
Sydney & Anne Bloom Farms Inc	5147	A	323 261-6565	13308
Wayne Provision Co Inc (PA)	5147	D	323 277-5888	13310
Farmers Link Inc	5148	D	213 623-5242	13322
Natures Produce	5148	C	323 235-4343	13334
V & L Produce Inc	5148	C	323 589-3125	13344
World Variety Produce Inc	5148	B	800 588-0151	13349
Completely Fresh Foods Inc	5149	C	323 722-9136	13362
Core-Mark International Inc	5149	C	323 583-6531	13364
Sweetener Products Inc (PA)	5149	E	323 234-2200	13398
Tadin Inc	5149	D	213 406-8880	13400
TL Montgomery & Associates Inc	5149	C	323 583-1645	13401
Cherokee Chemical Co Inc (PA)	5169	E	323 265-1112	13430
Norman Fox & Co	5169	E	323 973-4900	13436
Anns Trading Company Inc	5199	E	323 585-4702	13527
BTG S CORP (PA)	5199	D	323 582-4444	13532
Revoltion Cnsmr Sltions CA LLC (DH)	5199	C	323 980-0918	13556
Shims Bargain Inc (PA)	5199	D	323 881-0099	13561
Kaiser Foundation Hospitals	5712	C	323 264-4310	13942
Modernica Inc (PA)	5712	E	323 826-1600	13945
Good Fellas Industries Inc	5719	D	323 924-9495	13960
Huxtables Kitchen Inc	5812	D	323 923-2900	14014
Vie De France Yamazaki Inc	5812	A	323 582-1241	14043
Kelly Toys Holdings LLC	6719	C	323 923-1300	14934
Ameripride Services Inc	7213	C	323 587-3941	15448
Paradigm Industries Inc	7389	D	310 965-1900	16899
Rose & Shore Inc	7389	B	323 826-2144	16919
R A Reed Electric Company (PA)	7694	E	323 587-2284	17107
Superior Electric Mtr Svc Inc	7694	F	323 583-1040	17109
Los Angeles Regional Food Bank	8322	C	323 234-3030	19111
D I F Group Inc	8741	E	323 231-8800	20024

VICTORVILLE, CA - San Bernardino County

	SIC	EMP	PHONE	ENTRY#
Baja Fresh Supermarket	0291	B	760 843-7730	93
Cwp Cabinets Inc	1751	C	760 246-4530	1011
Mars Petcare Us Inc	2047	D	760 261-7900	1434
Reyes Coca-Cola Bottling LLC	2086	E	760 241-2653	1725
Paradise Manufacturing Co Inc	2394	D	909 477-3460	2507
Graco Childrens Products Inc	2514	B	770 418-7200	2831
Church & Dwight Co Inc	2841	E	609 613-1551	4335
Newell Brands Inc	3089	C	760 246-2700	5114
Afakori Inc	3441	E	949 859-4277	5990
Daikin Comfort Tech Mfg LP	3585	D	760 955-7770	7607
General Electric Company	3721	E	760 530-5200	9535
A-Team Delivers LLC	4212	D	858 254-8401	11438
Landforce Corporation	4213	C	760 843-7839	11493
Valley Bulk Inc	4213	D	760 843-0574	11511
Comav LLC	4581	C	760 523-5100	11692
Comav Technical Services LLC	4581	C	760 530-2400	11693
Robertsons Ready Mix Ltd	5032	D	702 798-0568	12361
Excel Scientific LLC	5049	E	760 246-4545	12526
Comav LLC (PA)	5088	D	760 523-5100	12905
Centerline Wood Products	5099	D	760 246-4530	12971
Premier Food Services Inc	5141	A	760 843-8000	13192
Home Depot USA Inc	5211	C	760 955-2999	13603
Lowes Home Centers LLC	5211	D	760 949-9565	13638

	SIC	EMP	PHONE	ENTRY#
Sunland Ford Inc	5511	D	760 241-7751	13832
Vahi Toyota Inc (PA)	5511	C	760 241-6484	13842
American Prtctive Svcs Invstgt	7381	C	626 705-8600	16619
Victorville Speedwash Inc	7542	D	760 388-0112	17050
Victorville Speedwash Inc	7542	D	760 388-0113	17051
Desert Valley Med Group Inc (PA)	8011	B	760 241-8000	17644
Knolls Convalescent Hosp Inc (PA)	8051	C	760 245-5361	17982
Knolls West Enterprise	8051	C	760 245-0107	17983
Spring Valley Post Acute LLC	8051	C	760 245-6477	18057
Desert Valley Hospital Inc (DH)	8062	C	760 241-8000	18238
Branlyn Prominence Inc	8082	C	760 843-5655	18595
Peoples Care Inc	8082	C	760 962-1900	18634
Victor Cmnty Support Svcs Inc	8093	C	760 987-8225	18731
Victor Cmnty Support Svcs Inc	8093	C	760 245-4695	18732
Heritage Medical Group	8099	B	760 956-1286	18770
Family Assistance Program	8322	C	760 843-0701	19079
Think Together	8699	B	760 269-1230	19534

VIEW PARK, CA - Los Angeles County

	SIC	EMP	PHONE	ENTRY#
Outdoor Rcrtion Group Hldngs L (PA)	2393	E	323 226-0830	2496
Hathawy-Sycmres Child Fmly Svc	8322	C	323 733-0322	19087

VILLA PARK, CA - Orange County

	SIC	EMP	PHONE	ENTRY#
Tropical Plaza Nursery Inc	0782	D	714 998-4100	217
Manufactured Solutions LLC	3999	E	714 548-6915	11248

VISTA, CA - San Diego County

	SIC	EMP	PHONE	ENTRY#
Color Spot Holdings Inc (PA)	0181	A	760 695-1430	50
Plug Connection Inc	0181	D	760 631-0992	68
I Pwlc Inc	0781	D	760 630-0231	165
Nissho of California Inc (PA)	0781	C	760 727-9719	172
Pac West Land Care Inc	0781	C	760 630-0231	174
Orion Construction Corporation	1623	D	760 597-9660	684
Industrial Coml Systems Inc	1711	C	760 300-4094	778
Excel Mdular Scaffold Lsg Corp	1799	C	760 598-0050	1155
Baked In The Sun	2051	C	760 591-9045	1452
J&L Eppig Brewing LLC	2082	F	760 295-2009	1592
Pure Project LLC	2082	F	760 552-7873	1604
Great Western Malting Co	2083	D	360 991-0888	1609
Javo Beverage Company Inc	2087	D	760 560-5286	1778
Tacupeto Chips & Salsa Inc	2096	F	760 597-9400	1834
Jif-Pak Manufacturing Inc (PA)	2258	D	760 597-2665	2082
Thirty Three Threads Inc (PA)	2329	C	877 486-3769	2225
Earthlite LLC (DH)	2514	D	760 599-1112	2829
Killion Industries Inc (PA)	2541	D	760 727-5102	2958
Astro Converters Inc (PA)	2677	C	800 752-5003	3210
Continental Litho Inc	2752	E	760 598-0291	3544
Precision Litho Inc	2752	E	760 727-9400	3661
Advanced Web Offset Inc	2759	D	760 727-1700	3730
Golden Rule Bindery Inc	2789	E	760 471-0013	3846
J & D Laboratories Inc	2833	B	760 734-6800	4002
Bachem Americas Inc	2834	D	888 422-2436	4065
Captek Midco Inc	2834	D	760 734-6000	4080
American Peptide Company Inc	2836	D	408 733-7604	4297
Grifols Usa LLC	2836	D	760 931-8444	4320
All One God Faith Inc (PA)	2841	C	844 937-2551	4332
All One God Faith Inc	2841	D	760 549-4010	4333
Revlon Inc	2844	D	619 372-1379	4451
American General Tool Group	3011	E	760 745-7993	4692
Watkins Manufacturing Corp	3088	D	760 598-6464	4922
Distinctive Plastics Inc	3089	D	760 599-9100	5011
Diversified Plastics Inc	3089	D	760 598-5333	5013
J A English II Inc	3089	C	760 598-5333	5065
Nubs Plastics Inc	3089	D	760 598-2525	5122
Prime Plastic Products Inc	3089	F	760 734-3900	5163
J & B Manufacturing Corp	3231	E	760 846-6316	5344
Kammerer Enterprises Inc	3281	D	760 560-0550	5529
Monster Tool LLC	3423	C	760 477-1000	5886
Youngdale Manufacturing Corp	3429	E	760 727-0644	5956
Aztec Technology Corporation (PA)	3441	E	760 727-2300	5993
McCain Manufacturing Inc	3441	D	760 295-9290	6046
Solatube International Inc (DH)	3442	C	888 765-2882	6124
Protec Arisawa America Inc	3443	C	760 599-4800	6151
Versaform Corporation	3444	D	760 599-4477	6341
Diversified Tool & Die	3469	E	760 598-9100	6512
J-Mark Manufacturing Inc	3469	C	760 727-6956	6526
West Coast Pvd Inc	3471	E	714 822-6362	6680
Dig Corporation	3523	E	760 727-0914	6903
Western Cactus Growers Inc	3524	D	760 726-1710	6923
Affinity Lath & Plaster Inc	3541	E	760 207-5311	7003
Sherline Products Incorporated	3541	E	760 727-5181	7024
Addition Manufacturing Technologies CA Inc	3542	E	760 597-5220	7028
Flotron	3544	E	760 727-2700	7071

2024 Southern California
Business Directory and Buyers Guide

(P-0000) Products & Services Section entry number
(PA)=Parent Co (HQ)=Headquarters (DH)=Div Headquarters

	SIC	EMP	PHONE	ENTRY#
Rmjv LP **(HQ)**	3556	D	503 526-5752	7214
Asml Us Inc	3559	B	760 443-6244	7223
Rxsafe LLC	3559	D	760 593-7161	7258
Accutek Packaging Equipment Co **(PA)**	3565	E	760 734-4177	7343
Apem Inc **(HQ)**	3577	E	978 372-1602	7506
Applied Membranes Inc	3589	C	760 727-3711	7639
Enaqua	3589	E	760 599-2644	7655
Yanchewski & Wardell Entps Inc	3589	D	760 754-1960	7694
Stines Machine Inc	3599	E	760 599-9955	8036
Vista Industrial Products Inc	3599	C	760 599-5050	8068
Western Cnc Inc	3599	D	760 597-7000	8076
Zettler Magnetics Inc	3612	C	949 831-5000	8115
Ddh Enterprise Inc **(PA)**	3643	D	760 599-0171	8260
M Klemme Technology Corp	3651	E	760 727-0593	8420
Raveon Technologies Corp	3663	E	760 444-5995	8568
Vision Manufacturing Inc	3672	D	760 689-0020	8750
Outsource Manufacturing Inc	3674	D	760 795-1295	8861
Plansee USA LLC	3674	E	760 438-9090	8865
Csi Technologies Inc	3675	F	760 682-2222	8926
Apem Inc	3679	D	760 598-2518	8997
AZ Displays Inc	3679	E	949 831-5000	9000
Flux Power Holdings Inc **(PA)**	3691	C	877 505-3589	9148
Dutek Incorporated	3699	E	760 566-8888	9208
Carbon By Design LLC	3728	D	760 643-1300	9655
Sandel Avionics Inc **(PA)**	3812	C	760 727-4900	10066
Sandel Avionics Inc	3812	C	760 727-4900	10067
Leica Biosystems Imaging Inc **(HQ)**	3826	D	760 539-1100	10269
Machine Vision Products Inc **(PA)**	3827	E	760 438-1138	10325
Biofilm Inc	3841	D	760 727-9030	10455
Carol Cole Company	3841	C	888 360-9171	10476
Surgistar Inc **(PA)**	3841	E	760 598-2480	10610
Djo LLC	3842	D	760 727-1280	10644
Djo LLC	3842	E	800 321-9549	10645
Djo Consumer LLC	3842	F	760 727-1280	10647
Djo Holdings LLC **(DH)**	3842	C	760 727-1280	10648
Vision Quest Industries Inc	3842	C	949 261-6382	10721
Conamco SA De CV	3843	D	760 586-4356	10733
Amron International Inc **(PA)**	3949	D	760 208-6500	10974
Aza Industries Inc	3949	E	760 560-0440	10976
Outdoor Sports Gear Inc	3949	E		11018
US Divers Co Inc	3949	D	760 597-5000	11040
Rayzist Photomask Inc **(PA)**	3955	D	760 727-8561	11061
Wolfpack Inc	3993	E	760 736-4500	11181
Integrated Mfg Solutions LLC	3999	E	760 599-4300	11231
Watkins Manufacturing Corp **(HQ)**	3999	C	760 598-6464	11306
Directed LLC	4731	C	800 876-0800	11754
Patriot Logistics Services LLC	4789	D	443 994-9660	11838
Tempo Communications Inc **(PA)**	4813	D	800 642-2155	11909
Ultra Communications Inc	4813	F	760 652-0011	11911
Vista Irrigation District	4971	D	760 597-3100	12216
Phoenix Wheel Company Inc	5013	E	760 598-1960	12252
Winners Only Inc	5021	C	760 599-0300	12294
American Faucet Coatings Corp	5023	E	760 598-5895	12295
Jeld-Wen Inc	5031	B	760 597-4201	12335
California Breakers Inc	5063	E	760 598-1528	12590
Swarco McCain Inc **(DH)**	5084	C	760 727-8100	12828
D & D Saw Works Inc	5085	C		12851
Apical Industries Inc	5088	E	760 724-5300	12902
Eliel & Co	5136	E	760 877-8469	13101
Smart & Final Stores Inc	5141	B	760 732-1480	13202
Altman Specialty Plants LLC **(PA)**	5193	A	800 348-4881	13500
Bandy Ranch Floral Corp	5193	E	805 757-9905	13502
Gringo Ventures LLC	5193	B	760 477-7999	13508
Spectrum Equipment LLC	5193	D	760 599-8849	13519
Lee-Mar Aquarium & Pet Sups	5199	D	760 727-1300	13544
Lowes Home Centers LLC	5211	D	760 631-6255	13647
Coromega Company Inc **(PA)**	5499	E	760 599-6088	13726
County Ford North Inc **(PA)**	5511	C	760 945-9900	13749
Living Spaces Furniture LLC	5712	C	760 945-6805	13943
Bni Publications Inc	5942	E	760 734-1113	14065
Professional Cmnty MGT Cal Inc	6531	D	760 918-8040	14850
Meeting Services Inc	7359	D	858 348-0100	15785
Epitec Inc	7371	A	760 650-2515	16026
International Lottery & Totalizator Systems Inc	7371	E	760 598-1655	16056
Interntnal Lttery Ttlztor Syst	7371	E	760 598-1655	16057
Off Duty Officers Inc	7381	A	888 408-5900	16664
All-Pro Bail Bonds Inc	7389	E	760 512-1969	16770
Amkom Design Group Inc	7389	E	760 295-1957	16777
Krikorian Premiere Theatre LLC	7832	E	760 945-7469	17301
Spa Havens LP	7991	E	760 945-2055	17414
Kaiser Foundation Hospitals	8011	D	619 528-5000	17677
Vista Community Clinic **(PA)**	8031	B	760 631-5000	17853
Vista Woods Health Assoc LLC	8051	C	760 630-2273	18072
Rancho Vista Health Center	8052	C	760 941-1480	18096
Care Choice Health Systems Inc	8059	C	760 798-4508	18116
Life Care Centers America Inc	8059	C	760 724-8222	18136
Exagen Inc	8071	C	505 272-7966	18549
Planned Prnthood of PCF Sthwes	8093	C	619 881-4500	18709
Grifols Bio Supplies Inc	8099	C	760 651-4042	18766
Alpha Project For Homeless	8322	C	760 630-9922	19018
Community Interface Services	8322	C	760 729-3866	19049
Vista Care Group LLC **(PA)**	8322	D	760 295-3900	19154
Systems Engineering & MGT Co **(PA)**	8711	C	760 727-7800	19698
Leidos Inc	8731	C	858 826-9090	19854
Plug Connection LLC	8742	C	760 631-0992	20220

WALNUT, CA - Los Angeles County

	SIC	EMP	PHONE	ENTRY#
JF Shea Construction Inc **(HQ)**	1521	C	909 594-9500	437
Shea Homes At Montage LLC	1521	C	909 594-9500	457
Shea Homes Vantis LLC	1522	D	909 594-9500	475
United Riggers & Erectors Inc **(PA)**	1796	C	909 978-0400	1139
Settlers Jerky Inc	2013	E	909 444-3999	1235
Pepsico Inc	2086	B	909 598-8229	1720
Imperfect Foods Inc **(HQ)**	2099	D	510 595-6683	1914
Ninas Mexican Foods Inc	2099	D	909 468-5888	1956
Ott Textile Inc	2299	E	626 217-5132	2144
Charades LLC **(PA)**	2389	E	626 435-0077	2444
Diamond Collection LLC	2389	E	626 435-0077	2448
Diana Did-It Designs Inc	2389	E	970 226-5062	2449
Southcoast Cabinet Inc **(PA)**	2434	E	909 594-3089	2679
SW Fixtures Inc	2541	F	909 595-2506	2967
All Strong Industry (usa) Inc **(PA)**	2591	E	909 598-6494	3000
1perfectchoice	2599	F	909 594-8855	3018
Golden Applexx Co Inc	2759	E	909 594-9788	3762
Nu-Health Products Co	2833	E	909 869-0666	4007
Oyewan Inc	2844	E	909 869-6200	4441
Essentra International LLC	2891	A	708 315-7498	4564
10 Day Parts Inc	3089	E	951 279-4810	4923
AMS Plastics Inc **(HQ)**	3089	D	619 713-2000	4940
2nd Source Wire & Cable Inc	3312	D	714 482-2866	5575
Tree Island Wire (USA) Inc **(DH)**	3315	C	909 594-7511	5626
Cast Parts Inc	3324	C	909 595-2252	5652
Pengcheng Aluminum Enterprise Inc USA	3354	E	909 598-7933	5705
Sea Shield Marine Products	3363	E	909 594-2507	5768
Western Hardware Company	3429	F	909 595-6201	5953
Tje Company	3442	F	909 869-7777	6126
Edro Engineering LLC **(DH)**	3544	E	909 594-5751	7067
Fairway Injection Molds Inc	3544	E	909 595-2201	7070
Niron Inc	3544	E	909 598-1526	7084
Amergence Technology Inc	3559	E	909 859-8400	7220
In Win Development USA Inc	3572	E	909 348-0588	7475
Tri-Net Technology Inc	3577	D	909 598-8818	7575
Winit America Inc	3577	E	626 606-0308	7581
Trane US Inc	3585	E	626 913-7913	7629
Crush Master Grinding Corp	3599	E	909 595-2249	7811
Mjc America Ltd **(PA)**	3634	E	888 876-5387	8238
US Energy Technologies Inc	3646	E	714 617-8800	8338
Excellence Opto Inc **(PA)**	3647	E	909 468-0550	8346
Soderberg Manufacturing Co Inc	3647	D	909 595-1291	8349
Hardware Imports Inc	3713	E	909 595-6201	9328
Racing Power Company	3714	E	909 468-3690	9447
Aero Pacific Corporation	3728	E	714 961-9200	9598
Alatus Aerosystems	3728	E	909 217-9047	9614
Shore Western Manufacturing	3826	E	626 357-3251	10287
Total Resources Intl Inc **(PA)**	3842	E	909 594-1220	10712
Jakks Pacific Inc	3944	C	909 594-7771	10958
Hupa International Inc	3949	E	909 598-9876	10999
Loungefly LLC	3961	E	818 718-5600	11066
Infinity Watch Corporation	3993	E	626 289-9878	11124
General Electric Company	4225	D	909 869-7404	11581
Straight Forwarding Inc	4731	D	909 594-3400	11806
Unis LLC **(PA)**	4731	C	909 839-2600	11813
Adesso Inc	5045	D	909 839-2929	12392
Servers Direct LLC	5045	C	800 576-7931	12437
Sysco Los Angeles Inc	5141	A	909 595-9595	13233
Ahg Inc	7291	B	703 596-0111	15492
Identigraphix Inc	7336	E	909 468-4741	15667
Gremlin Inc	7372	E	408 214-9885	16260
Oncehub Inc	7372	E	650 206-5585	16335
Emeritus Corporation	8051	C	909 595-5030	17938
Pregel America Inc	8351	C	909 598-8980	19225
Shogun Labs Inc **(PA)**	8734	C	317 676-2719	19983
Vistancia Marketing LLC	8742	C	909 594-9500	20269

WASCO, CA - Kern County

	SIC	EMP	PHONE	ENTRY#
Supreme Almonds California Inc	0173	D	661 746-6475	38

Company	SIC	EMP	PHONE	ENTRY#
Bethlehem Construction Inc	1541	D	661 758-1001	495
Sunnygem LLC (PA)	2033	B	661 758-0491	1346
Primex Farms LLC (PA)	2068	E	661 758-7790	1561
Certis USA LLC	2879	E	661 758-8471	4547
Carter Pump & Machine Inc	3599	F	661 393-8620	7793
Hec Asset Management Inc	5046	C	661 587-2250	12456
South Valley Almond Co LLC	5159	C	661 391-9000	13409
Adventist Health Delano	6733	D	661 758-4184	14987
Ag-Weld Inc	7692	F	661 758-3061	17079
Community Support Options Inc	8322	C	661 758-5331	19050

WEST COVINA, CA - Los Angeles County

Company	SIC	EMP	PHONE	ENTRY#
Sears Home Imprv Pdts Inc	1521	C	626 671-1892	453
Turn Around Communications Inc	1623	C	626 443-2400	699
Ola Nation LLC	2335	E	310 256-0638	2286
Interspace Battery Inc (PA)	3356	E	626 813-1234	5724
Macdonald Carbide Co	3544	E	626 960-4034	7080
Baatz Enterprises Inc	3711	E	323 660-4866	9280
Penney Opco LLC	5311	C	626 960-3711	13682
P A Motorcars LLC	5511	A	877 433-3517	13809
Pmb Motorcars LLC	5511	A	626 384-3600	13814
Iheartraves LLC	5632	F	626 628-6482	13919
Kaiser Foundation Hospitals	6324	D	626 856-3045	14477
Southern Cal Prmnnte Med Group	6324	B	626 960-4844	14501
RM Galicia Inc	7322	C	626 813-6200	15615
RSI Leasing LLC	7359	D	626 966-6129	15797
Os4labor LLC	7361	C	626 838-6745	15874
Penske Motor Group LLC	7513	B	626 859-1200	16971
Saint Jseph Communications Inc (PA)	7812	E	626 331-3549	17216
Big Lgue Dreams Consulting LLC	7941	C	626 839-1100	17365
West Covina Medical Clinic Inc (PA)	8011	C	626 960-8614	17831
Citrus Vly Hlth Partners Inc	8062	A	626 962-4011	18221
Doctors Hospital W Covina Inc	8062	C	626 338-8481	18246
Emanate Health Medical Center	8062	B	626 963-8411	18255
Emanate Health Medical Center (PA)	8062	A	626 962-4011	18257
Southern Cal Spcialty Care Inc	8062	C	626 339-5451	18453
Volunteers of Amer Los Angeles	8322	D	626 337-9878	19159
Westview Services Inc	8331	D	626 962-0956	19199

WEST HILLS, CA - Los Angeles County

Company	SIC	EMP	PHONE	ENTRY#
Flavor Producers LLC (PA)	2087	E	661 257-3400	1771
Pharmavite LLC (DH)	2833	B	818 221-6200	4011
Aerojet Rocketdyne De Inc	2869	E	818 586-9629	4511
Jj Acquisitions LLC	3069	E	818 772-0100	4770
Source Photonics Usa Inc (PA)	3674	C	818 773-9044	8895
Lowes Home Centers LLC	5211	D	818 610-1960	13628
First Amercn HM Warranty Corp	6541	E	818 781-5050	14890
911 Restoration Entps Inc	7349	B	832 887-2582	15689
Citiguard Inc	7381	B	800 613-5903	16629
Leisure Care LLC	8052	C	818 713-0900	18089
West Valleyidence Opco LLC	8052	C	818 348-8422	18104
Unilab Corporation (HQ)	8071	B	818 737-6000	18567
Tobin Lucks A Prof Corp (PA)	8111	D	818 226-3400	18951
One Lambda Inc (HQ)	8731	C	747 494-1000	19868

WEST HOLLYWOOD, CA - Los Angeles County

Company	SIC	EMP	PHONE	ENTRY#
Pro Tour Memorabilia LLC	2499	E	424 303-7200	2759
Dedon Inc	2511	E	310 388-4721	2770
Rtmh Inc (PA)	2512	F	323 651-2202	2817
Clique Brands Inc (PA)	2721	E	310 623-6916	3351
Philip B Inc	2833	E	888 376-8236	4012
Naturelab North America Inc (HQ)	2834	C	424 901-0707	4179
Cosmo International Corp	2844	D	310 271-1100	4396
Chase-Durer Ltd (PA)	3873	F	310 550-7280	10892
Fountainhead Industries	3999	E	310 248-2444	11217
Paul Ferrante Inc	3999	E	310 854-4412	11262
Hwood Group	5021	D	310 859-1011	12284
J Robert Scott Inc (PA)	5131	C		13082
Seafood Family Partners LP	5146	C	310 761-1500	13286
Velaro Incorporated	5734	D	800 983-5276	13975
Auto Club Enterprises	6321	B	310 914-8500	14448
Carlyle Group Inc (PA)	6531	D	310 550-8656	14757
Rsg Group USA Inc	6719	A	214 574-4653	14943
Mondrian Holdings LLC	7011	B	323 848-6004	15252
Ols Hotels & Resorts LLC	7011	A	310 855-1115	15275
Valadon Hotel LLC	7011	B	310 854-1114	15402
West Hollywood Edition	7011	B	310 795-7103	15414
One Events Inc	7299	D	310 498-5471	15519
Dailey & Associates	7311	D	323 490-3847	15534
Suissa Miller Advertising LLC	7311	C	310 392-9666	15576
Bird Rides Inc (HQ)	7371	F	866 205-2442	15983
Ficto Holdings LLC	7371	F	424 250-2400	16032
Grindr LLC	7371	C	310 776-6680	16042

Company	SIC	EMP	PHONE	ENTRY#
Neonroots LLC	7371	C	310 907-9210	16080
Tegra118 Wealth Solutions Inc (HQ)	7374	C	888 800-0188	16519
Executive Car Leasing Company (PA)	7515	D	800 800-3932	16985
Annapurna Pictures LLC	7819	D	310 385-7701	17244
Rsg Group North America LP	7991	C	714 609-0572	17412
Kids Empire USA LLC	7999	D	424 527-1039	17555
Ticketmaster Entertainment LLC	7999	A	800 653-8000	17570
Cedars-Sinai Medical Center	8062	B	310 855-7701	18198
Cedars-Sinai Medical Center	8062	D	310 423-5468	18199
Cedars-Sinai Medical Center	8062	C	310 423-5841	18203
Cedars-Sinai Medical Center	8062	C	310 423-5147	18204
Cedars-Sinai Medical Center	8062	C	310 423-9310	18205
Cedars-Sinai Medical Center	8062	C	310 423-8780	18211
White Rabbit Partners Inc	8361	C	310 975-1450	19311
Automobile Club Southern Cal	8699	D	323 525-0018	19522
Cpe Hr Inc	8742	D	310 270-9800	20159
Operam Inc	8742	D	855 673-7261	20216
Zero Gravity Consulting LLC	8748	A	310 989-7989	20393

WESTLAKE VILLAGE, CA - Ventura County

Company	SIC	EMP	PHONE	ENTRY#
Dole Holding Company LLC	0179	A	818 879-6600	48
Sperber Ldscp Companies LLC (PA)	0781	C	818 437-1029	180
Welbilt Inc	1389	E	310 339-1555	396
The Ryland Group Inc	1531	A	805 367-3800	487
Castle & Cooke Investments Inc	1542	C	310 208-3636	541
Security Paving Company Inc (PA)	1611	D	818 362-9200	645
Sdg Enterprises	1711	D	805 777-7978	820
Dole Packaged Foods LLC (HQ)	2037	A	805 601-5500	1369
Opolo Vineyards Inc	2084	D	805 238-9593	1650
Omics Group Inc	2721	B	650 268-9744	3373
Xplain Corporation	2721	E	805 494-7997	3396
Earth Print Inc	2752	F	818 879-6050	3567
Odcombe Press (nashville)	2752	E	615 793-5414	3647
Arcutis Biotherapeutics Inc (PA)	2834	C	805 418-5006	4056
Kythera Biopharmaceuticals Inc	2834	C	818 587-4500	4155
Capsida Biotherapeutics Inc (PA)	2836	C	805 410-2673	4308
Sugar Foods LLC (PA)	2869	C	805 396-5000	4532
Ember Technologies Inc	3089	E	520 400-9337	5023
Interntional Photo Plates Corp	3471	E	805 496-5031	6630
Hydrodex LLC	3589	C	800 218-8813	7661
Baltic Ltvian Unvrsal Elec LLC	3651	E	818 879-5200	8398
Sunbritetv LLC (DH)	3663	F	805 214-7250	8585
Inphi International Pte Ltd.	3674	E	805 719-2300	8812
Carros Americas Inc	3679	C	805 267-7176	9013
Rantec Microwave Systems Inc (PA)	3812	D	818 223-5000	10051
Erp Power LLC (PA)	3825	E	805 517-1300	10198
Caldera Medical Inc	3841	D	818 879-6555	10466
Implant Direct Sybron Intl LLC (HQ)	3843	D	818 444-3000	10746
Implant Direct Sybron Mfg LLC	3843	C	818 444-3300	10747
Gamebreaker Inc (PA)	3949	C	818 224-7424	10993
Vitavet Labs Inc	3999	E	818 865-2600	11304
Pleasant Holidays LLC (HQ)	4724	C	818 991-3390	11723
Frontier California Inc	4813	B	805 372-6000	11881
Hec Inc	5065	B	818 879-7414	12663
Jri Inc	5065	C	818 706-2424	12673
Baxter Healthcare Corporation	5122	D	805 372-3000	13029
Ruby Ribbon Inc	5137	C	650 449-4470	13145
Smart & Final Stores Inc	5141	C	818 889-8253	13208
Country Floral Supply Inc (PA)	5193	C	805 520-8026	13505
Mamolos Cntntl Bailey Bakeries	5461	C	805 496-0045	13721
Cadillac Motor Div Area	5511	C	805 373-9575	13745
Toller Enterprises Inc (PA)	5551	E	805 374-9455	13894
Jafra Cosmetics Intl Inc (DH)	5999	D	805 449-3000	14138
Bana Home Loan Servicing	6021	A	213 345-7975	14155
Amerihome Inc	6162	A	888 469-0810	14296
Anchor Loans LP	6162	C	310 395-0010	14299
Dignified Home Loans LLC	6163	D	818 421-7753	14358
Amerihome Mortgage Company LLC	6211	B	888 469-0810	14372
Kramer-Wilson Company Inc (PA)	6331	C	818 760-0880	14511
Chivaroli & Assoc Inc	6411	C	208 338-6640	14575
Pacific Compensation Insur Co	6411	C	818 575-8500	14619
Cushman & Wakefield Cal Inc	6531	B	805 418-5811	14780
Troop Real Estate Inc	6531	C	805 402-3028	14878
Fidelity Nat Title Insur Co NY	6541	C	805 370-1400	14889
Pmt Crdit Risk Trnsf Tr 2015-1	6733	D	818 224-7028	15000
Pmt Crdit Risk Trnsf Tr 2015-2	6733	C	818 224-7442	15001
Pmt Crdit Risk Trnsf Tr 2019-2	6733	D	818 224-7028	15002
Pmt Crdit Risk Trnsf Tr 2020-1	6733	C	818 224-7028	15003
Pnmac Gmsr Issuer Trust	6733	B	818 746-2271	15004
Burton Way Htels Ltd A Cal Ltd	7011	B	818 575-3000	15100
Sky Court USA Inc	7011	C	805 497-9991	15359
Swwp Westlake LLC	7011	C	805 557-1234	15384
Westlake Properties Inc	7011	C	818 889-0230	15416

	SIC	EMP	PHONE	ENTRY#
C&W Facility Services Inc	7349	A	805 267-7123	15697
Microfinancial Incorporated	7359	C	805 367-8900	15786
Cforia Software LLC	7372	E	818 871-9687	16197
Facefirst LLC	7372	E	805 482-8428	16246
Srax Inc (PA)	7372	D	323 205-6109	16389
Xpdel Inc	7372	E	805 267-1214	16425
Lantz Security Systems Inc	7381	C	805 496-5775	16655
Securitas SEC Svcs USA Inc	7381	B	818 706-6800	16680
Bankcard USA Merchant Srvc	7389	D	818 597-7000	16789
Rvl Packaging Inc	7389	C	818 735-5000	16920
Thousand Oaks Prtg & Spc Inc	7389	C	818 706-8330	16943
Weststar Cinemas Inc	7832	C	805 379-8966	17304
North Ranch Country Club	7997	C	818 889-3531	17505
Coastal Rdtion Onclogy Med Gro	8011	D	805 494-4483	17627
Los Robles Regional Med Ctr	8011	B	805 370-4531	17709
Symbion Inc	8011	C	805 413-7920	17799
Select Home Care	8082	D	805 777-3855	18641
Comprhnsive Indus Dsblity MGT	8099	C	866 301-6568	18755
JD Power and Associates Inc	8732	C	805 418-8000	19904

WESTMINSTER, CA - Orange County

	SIC	EMP	PHONE	ENTRY#
Emerald Acquisition LLC	1611	C	714 891-8752	617
Maintech Resources Inc	1796	E	562 804-0664	1137
Einstein Noah Rest Group Inc	2022	A	714 847-4609	1253
Nguoi Viet Vtnamese People Inc (PA)	2711	E	714 892-9414	3309
American Pacific Plastic Fabricators Inc	2821	E	714 891-3191	3922
New Technology Plastics Inc	2821	E	562 941-6034	3958
Intertrade Industries Ltd	3089	D	714 894-5566	5062
Tru-Form Plastics Inc	3089	E	310 327-9444	5235
Bodycote Thermal Proc Inc	3398	E	714 893-6561	5826
Cgr/Thompson Industries Inc	3612	C	714 678-4200	8090
B/E Aerospace Inc	3728	C	714 896-9001	9641
Thompson Industries Ltd	3728	C	310 679-9193	9815
Lexor Inc	3999	D	714 444-4144	11244
Inlog Inc	4731	D	949 212-3867	11772
Southern California Edison Co	4911	C	714 895-0420	12075
Southern California Edison Co	4911	A	714 895-0163	12077
Neighborhood Steel LLC (HQ)	5051	E	714 236-8700	12561
Honda World Westminster	5511	C	714 890-8900	13779
Lbs Financial Credit Union (PA)	6062	C	562 598-9007	14248
Staff Pro Inc (PA)	7382	A	714 230-7200	16755
University California Irvine	8062	C	714 775-3066	18490
Abrazar Inc	8322	D	714 893-3581	19016
County of Orange	8322	C	714 896-7188	19065
360 Health Plan Inc	8741	C	800 446-8888	19987

WHITEWATER, CA - Riverside County

	SIC	EMP	PHONE	ENTRY#
Whitewater Rock & Sup Co Inc	5032	E	760 325-2747	12365

WHITTIER, CA - Los Angeles County

	SIC	EMP	PHONE	ENTRY#
Oltmans Construction Co (PA)	1541	D	562 948-4242	514
Russ Bassett Corp	2511	C	562 945-2445	2787
Johnson Controls Inc	2531	E	562 698-8301	2929
JC Window Fashions Inc	2591	E	909 364-8888	3008
Tube-Tainer Inc	2655	E	562 945-3711	3140
Georgia Pacific Holdings Inc	2676	A	626 926-1474	3205
George Coriaty	2752	E	562 698-7513	3578
Coastal Tag & Label Inc	2759	D	562 946-4318	3745
Messer LLC	2813	E	562 903-1290	3869
Epmar Corporation	2851	E	562 946-8781	4489
AC Products Inc	2891	E	714 630-7311	4555
Santa Fe Rubber Products Inc	3069	E	562 693-2776	4794
Mhk Investment Holdings Inc	3272	E	562 699-3578	5424
Jason Incorporated	3291	E	562 921-9821	5542
Miller Castings Inc (PA)	3324	B	562 695-0461	5658
Rasmussen Iron Works Inc	3433	C	562 696-8718	5983
Consteel Industrial Inc	3441	E	562 806-4575	6012
Fred R Rippy Inc	3469	C	562 698-9801	6517
Quaker City Plating	3471	C	562 945-3721	6652
Christos Engineering Inc	3544	F	562 907-4463	7059
Cryostar USA LLC	3561	D	562 903-1290	7274
Compu Aire Inc	3585	C	562 945-8971	7604
Rahn Industries Incorporated (PA)	3585	D	562 908-0680	7621
Medlin and Son Engrg Svc Inc	3599	E	562 464-5889	7925
Hedman Manufacturing (PA)	3714	E	562 204-1031	9401
Trans-Dapt California Inc	3714	C	562 921-0404	9473
Gulfstream Aerospace Corp GA	3721	B	562 907-9300	9539
Cameron Technologies Us LLC	3823	E	562 222-8440	10122
Harris Organs Inc	3931	E	562 693-3442	10925
Loren Industries	3993	E	562 699-1122	11131
County of Los Angeles	4151	C	562 945-2581	11420
Sprint Communications Co LP	4812	C	562 943-8907	11854
Southern California Gas Co	4924	D	562 803-3341	12089

	SIC	EMP	PHONE	ENTRY#
Sanittion Dstrcts Los Angles C	4953	A	562 908-4288	12186
Los Angles Cnty Snttion Dstrct (PA)	4959	A	562 699-7411	12210
Indio Products Inc (PA)	5049	C	323 720-1188	12527
Main Electric Supply Co LLC	5063	E	323 753-5131	12604
General Transistor Corporation (PA)	5065	E	310 578-7344	12661
Eps Corporate Holdings Inc	5074	F	562 698-7774	12739
Equipment Depot Inc	5084	C	562 949-1000	12790
Southern California Material Handling Inc	5084	C	562 949-1006	12823
Oncor Corp	5122	F	562 944-0230	13060
Grand Supercenter Inc	5141	D	562 318-3451	13183
Smart & Final Stores Inc	5141	B	562 907-7037	13220
Champion Chemical Co Cal Inc	5169	E	562 945-1456	13427
Home Depot USA Inc	5211	C	562 789-4121	13611
Cintas Corporation No 3	5699	D	562 692-8741	13932
US Donuts & Yogurt	5812	F	562 695-8867	14042
Kaiser Foundation Hospitals	6324	C	866 340-5974	14476
Katella Properties	6512	D	562 704-8695	14668
Rose Hills Company (DH)	6553	A	562 699-0921	14918
Rose Hills Holdings Corp (HQ)	6553	B	562 699-0921	14919
Pronto Janitorial Svcs Inc	7349	D	562 273-5997	15741
Los Angeles Truck Centers LLC (PA)	7538	D	562 447-1200	17034
Eurton Electric Company Inc	7694	E	562 946-4477	17105
Friendly Hlls Cntry CLB Fndtio	7997	C	562 698-0331	17485
Bright Health Physicians (PA)	8011	C	562 947-8478	17606
Ensign Group Inc	8051	C	562 947-7817	17941
Ensign Whittier East LLC	8051	C	562 947-7817	17947
Orchard - Post Acute Care Ctr	8051	C	562 693-7701	18022
Ahmc Whittier Hosp Med Ctr LP	8062	A	562 945-3561	18170
Longwood Management Corp	8062	D	562 693-5240	18337
Pih Health Inc (PA)	8062	A	562 698-0811	18376
Pih Health Whittier Hospital (HQ)	8062	A	562 698-0811	18380
Whittier Hospital Med Ctr Inc	8062	C	562 945-3561	18502
Barlow Respiratory Hospital	8069	A	562 698-0811	18521
Interhealth Services Inc (HQ)	8082	C	562 698-0811	18618
Whittier Union High Schl Dist	8211	C	562 693-8826	18988
County of Los Angeles	8322	D	562 908-3119	19059
Inclusion Services LLC	8322	C	562 945-2000	19094

WILDOMAR, CA - Riverside County

	SIC	EMP	PHONE	ENTRY#
Diverscape Inc	0782	D	951 245-1686	188
KB Home Grater Los Angeles Inc	1521	C	951 691-5300	442
Fcp Inc (PA)	3448	D	951 678-4571	6377
General Lgstics Systems US Inc	4212	C	951 677-3972	11457
Sprint Communications Co LP	4812	C	951 461-9786	11860
Inland Vly Rgional Med Ctr Inc	8062	B	951 677-1111	18290
Kaiser Foundation Hospitals	8062	C	951 353-2000	18304

WILMINGTON, CA - Los Angeles County

	SIC	EMP	PHONE	ENTRY#
Cooper & Brain Inc	1311	E	310 834-4411	259
Juanitas Foods	2032	C	310 834-5339	1327
Cfwf Inc	2092	C	310 221-6280	1801
J Deluca Fish Company Inc	2092	C	310 221-6500	1808
Air Liquide Electronics US LP	2813	A	310 549-7079	3860
California Sulphur Company	2819	E	562 437-0768	3884
Royal Adhesives & Sealants LLC	2899	C	310 830-9904	4629
Valero Ref Company-California	2911	A	562 491-6754	4655
Paramount Forge Inc	3462	E	323 775-6803	6468
Wilmington Machine Inc	3599	E	310 518-3213	8080
West Coast Aerospace Inc (PA)	3965	D	310 518-3167	11081
Potential Industries Inc (PA)	4953	C	310 549-5901	12179
Icpk Corporation	5141	D	310 830-8020	13184
Tesoro Refining & Mktg Co LLC	5172	C	877 837-6762	13455
Acx Intermodal Inc	5191	C	310 241-6229	13485
Coordnted Wire Rope Rgging Inc (HQ)	5251	E	310 834-8535	13677
American Soccer Company Inc (PA)	5699	C	310 830-6161	13929
Stratus Real Estate Inc	6163	D	310 549-7028	14367
Harbor Industrial Svcs Corp	7353	E	310 522-1193	15762
Public Hlth Fndation Entps Inc	8099	C	310 518-2835	18793
South Bay Ctr For Counseling	8322	C	310 414-2090	19142
Volunteers of Amer Los Angeles	8322	C	310 830-3404	19166
Advanced Cleanup Tech Inc	8744	B	310 763-1423	20287

WINNETKA, CA - Los Angeles County

	SIC	EMP	PHONE	ENTRY#
World Class Cheerleading Inc	3949	E	877 923-2645	11043

WINTERHAVEN, CA - Imperial County

	SIC	EMP	PHONE	ENTRY#
Quechan Indian Tribe	7999	C	760 572-2413	17561

WOODLAND HILLS, CA - Los Angeles County

	SIC	EMP	PHONE	ENTRY#
Blh Construction Company	1522	C	818 905-3837	468
Environmental Construction Inc	1542	D	818 449-8920	549
Sierra Pacific Constrs Inc	1542	E	747 888-5000	590
Memeged Tevuot Shemesh (PA)	1711	C	866 575-1211	793

GEOGRAPHIC

Employee Codes: A=Over 500 employees, B=251-500
C=101-250, D=51-100, E=20-50, F=10-19, G=1-9

2024 Southern California
Business Directory and Buyers Guide

© Mergent Inc. 1-800-342-5647

1461

	SIC	EMP	PHONE	ENTRY#
Legacy Epoch LLC	2048	D	844 673-7305	1444
Gold Coast Baking Company LLC (PA)	2051	D	818 575-7280	1475
Pascal Patisserie	2051	F	818 712-9375	1489
Western Bagel Baking Corp	2051	E	818 887-5451	1499
Weider Health and Fitness	2087	B	818 884-6800	1789
Tag-It Pacific Inc	2269	E	818 444-4100	2107
Second Generation Inc	2339	D		2369
Los Angeles Daily News Pubg Co	2711	E	818 713-3883	3297
Leadmmatic Inc	2741	E	310 857-4511	3462
Valley Business Printers Inc	2752	D	818 362-7771	3704
Graham Webb International Inc (HQ)	2844	D	760 918-3600	4416
S Fuel LLC	2869	E	818 914-4849	4527
National Diversified Sales Inc (HQ)	3089	C	559 562-9888	5110
Silgan White Cap Corporation	3089	E	818 710-3700	5205
Silgan Can Company	3411	C	818 348-3700	5862
Silgan Containers Corporation (DH)	3411	D	818 710-3700	5863
Silgan Containers LLC (HQ)	3411	C	818 710-3700	5864
Silgan Containers Mfg Corp (DH)	3411	C	818 710-3700	5865
Lynx Phtnic Ntworks A Del Corp.	3661	F	818 802-0244	8479
Hillside Capital Inc	3663	C	650 367-2011	8523
Lumio Inc	3674	E	586 861-2408	8830
Alliant Tchsystems Oprtons LLC	3812	F	818 887-8185	9940
Northrop Grumman Intl Trdg Inc	3812	E	818 715-3607	10013
Northrop Grumman Systems Corp.	3812	C	818 715-2597	10014
Northrop Grumman Systems Corp.	3812	A	818 715-4040	10026
Northrop Grumman Systems Corp.	3812	B	818 715-4854	10027
King Nutronics LLC	3823	E	818 887-5460	10144
Panavision International LP (HQ)	3861	B	818 316-1080	10878
Lucent Diamonds Inc	3915	C	424 781-7127	10918
Keytonex Inc	3955	E	310 828-2207	11058
ICON Line Inc	3999	F	818 709-4266	11229
IDS Inc.	4724	C	866 297-5757	11717
Ev Ray Inc	5023	C	818 346-5381	12300
United Ribbon Company Inc	5044	C	818 716-1515	12390
Wham-O Inc	5092	C	818 963-4200	12948
Conquistador International LLC	5122	D	424 249-9304	13034
Talon International Inc (PA)	5131	C	818 444-4100	13097
Assocted Fgn Exch Holdings Inc (HQ)	6099	C	818 386-2702	14255
Input 1 LLC	6153	C	818 340-0030	14283
Interlink Securities Corp	6211	C	818 992-6700	14383
Morgan Stnley Smith Barney LLC	6211	C	818 715-1800	14391
Beating Wall Street Inc (PA)	6282	C	818 332-9696	14417
John Alden Life Insurance Co.	6311	C	818 595-7600	14436
Truck Underwriters Association	6311	A	323 932-3200	14444
21st Century Lf & Hlth Co Inc (PA)	6321	C	818 887-4436	14445
Lifecare Assurance Company	6321	C	818 887-4436	14453
Blue Cross of California (HQ)	6324	C	805 557-6050	14461
California Physicians Service	6324	C	818 598-8000	14464
Health Net LLC (HQ)	6324	C	818 676-6000	14469
Health Net Inc.	6324	A	818 676-6000	14470
Managed Dental Care	6324	C	818 598-6599	14487
Mid-Century Insurance Company	6331	C	323 932-7116	14521
State Compensation Insur Fund	6331	A	818 888-4750	14526
Zenith Insurance Company	6331	B	818 713-1000	14533
21st Century Life Insurance Co (DH)	6411	C	877 310-5687	14552
Farmers Group Inc (HQ)	6411	A	323 932-3200	14587
Farmers Insurance.	6411	B	818 876-3400	14590
Farmers Insurance Exchange (DH)	6411	A	888 327-6335	14592
Fire Insurance Exchange (PA)	6411	A	323 932-3200	14594
Markel Corp.	6411	B	818 595-0600	14609
Westwood Insurance Agency LLC (HQ)	6411	C	818 990-9715	14645
Greystar Management Svcs LP	6531	C	818 596-2180	14807
HEI Hospitality LLC.	7011	C	818 887-4800	15175
Hilton Woodland Hills & Towers.	7011	C	818 595-1000	15179
Conduit Lngage Specialists Inc.	7299	D	859 299-3178	15504
Kern Organization Inc.	7311	D	818 703-8775	15551
Reachlocal Inc (DH)	7311	C	818 274-0260	15572
Panavision Inc (PA)	7359	A	818 316-1000	15792
Career Strategies Tmpry Inc.	7361	C	818 883-0440	15829
Mediscan Diagnostic Svcs LLC	7361	C	818 758-4224	15867
Citrusbyte LLC.	7371	E	888 969-2983	15994
Corptax LLC.	7371	C	818 316-2400	16002
Emids Tech Private Ltd Corp.	7371	A	805 304-5986	16025
Intelex Systems Inc.	7371	C	818 992-2969	16055
Javanan Inc.	7371	E	310 741-0011	16061
Neversoft Entertainment Inc.	7371	E	818 610-4100	16083
Blackline Inc (PA)	7372	E	818 223-9008	16183
Intuit Inc.	7372	C	818 436-7800	16274
Real Software Systems LLC (PA)	7372	E	818 313-8000	16365
Texican Inc.	7372	E	310 384-7000	16402
Thq Inc.	7372	A	818 591-1310	16403
TI Limited LLC (PA)	7372	D	323 877-5991	16406
Netapp Inc.	7373	C	818 227-5025	16462
Adcom Interactive Media Inc.	7379	D	800 296-7104	16548
Pro-Tek Consulting (PA)	7379	C	805 807-5571	16592
Mventix Inc (PA)	7389	D	818 337-3747	16882
Network Telephone Services Inc (PA)	7389	D	800 742-5687	16884
Sync Brokerage Inc.	7389	D	818 770-3663	16939
Film Roman Llc.	7812	C	818 748-4000	17191
Southern Cal Prmnnte Med Group	8011	C	818 592-3038	17776
Kaiser Foundation Hospitals.	8062	A	818 719-2000	18302
Motion Picture and TV Fund (PA)	8062	A	818 876-1777	18347
Accredited Fms Inc.	8082	A	818 435-4200	18582
Barry & Taffy Inc.	8082	A	818 986-1234	18592
Berger Inc.	8082	A	818 986-1234	18593
Dunn & Berger Inc.	8082	B	818 986-1234	18609
Destinations For Teens.	8093	D	818 737-2221	18688
Los Angeles Unified School Dst.	8211	C	818 346-3540	18974
Tutor Time Learning Ctrs LLC.	8351	C	818 710-1677	19233
Pacific Lodge Youth Svcs Inc.	8361	C	818 347-1577	19293
LLP Moss Adams.	8721	C	310 477-0450	19789
Physicians Choice Inc.	8721	D	818 340-9988	19801
Goetzman Group Inc.	8742	C	818 595-1112	20177
Information Forecast Inc.	8742	E	818 888-4445	20185
8020 Consulting LLC.	8748	D	818 523-3201	20305

WRIGHTWOOD, CA - San Bernardino County

	SIC	EMP	PHONE	ENTRY#
MHRP Resort Inc.	7011	D	760 249-5808	15251

YORBA LINDA, CA - Orange County

	SIC	EMP	PHONE	ENTRY#
Mesa Contracting Corporation	1611	C		635
Aseptic Technology LLC.	2033	C	714 694-0168	1335
Nasco Gourmet Foods Inc.	2033	D	714 279-2100	1342
Fpg Oc Inc.	2087	E	714 692-2950	1772
Beckers Fabrication Inc.	2672	C	714 692-1600	3167
Printegra Corp.	2761	D	714 692-2221	3832
Pacifictech Molded Pdts Inc.	3069	F	714 279-9928	4783
Sabred International Packg Inc.	3086	E	714 996-2800	4902
Loritz & Associates Inc.	3089	C	714 694-0200	5087
Precise Aerospace Mfg Inc.	3089	E	951 898-0500	5157
Infrared Dynamics Inc.	3433	C	714 572-4050	5981
Boyd Corporation (PA)	3441	E	714 533-2375	5999
Euroline Steel Windows.	3442	E	877 590-2741	6105
Progressive Marketing Pdts Inc.	3448	D	714 888-1700	6389
Alpha Omega Swiss Inc.	3451	E	714 692-8009	6409
Specialty Motions Inc.	3562	C	951 735-8722	7304
Ixi Technology Inc.	3571	C	714 221-5000	7434
Romac Supply Co Inc.	3613	D	323 721-5810	8129
Filter Concepts Incorporated.	3677	C	714 545-7003	8942
Gunjoy Inc.	3679	C	714 289-0055	9052
Trigon Electronics Inc.	3699	F	714 633-7442	9263
American HX Auto Trade Inc.	3711	D	909 484-1010	9277
Engineering Jk Aerospace & Def.	3728	C	714 499-9092	9684
GE Aviation Systems LLC.	3728	C	714 692-0200	9697
Inflight Warning Systems Inc.	3728	F	714 993-9394	9720
B&K Precision Corporation (PA)	3825	F	714 921-9095	10186
Carefusion Corporation.	3841	D	800 231-2466	10474
Specialteam Medical Svc Inc.	3841	F	714 694-0348	10607
Viasys Respiratory Care Inc.	3841	D	714 283-2228	10629
Pdma Ventures Inc.	3843	E	714 777-8770	10761
Jondo Ltd (HQ)	3861	D	714 279-2300	10870
Metropltan Wtr Dst of Sthern C.	4941	D	714 577-5031	12134
Sesa Inc (PA)	7336	D	714 779-9700	15674
Enterprise Security Inc (PA)	7382	D	714 630-9100	16734
Omni Optical Products Inc.	7699	E	714 692-1400	17141
Nobel Biocare Usa LLC.	8072	B	714 282-4800	18572
Rgbx Inc.	8351	D	714 524-1350	19227
Tom Ponton Industries Inc.	8742	E	714 998-9073	20262

YUCAIPA, CA - San Bernardino County

	SIC	EMP	PHONE	ENTRY#
Hi-Desert Publishing Company.	2711	E	909 795-8145	3281
Merrimans Incorporated.	3441	E	909 795-5301	6050
Sorenson Engineering Inc (PA)	3451	C	909 795-2434	6421
Technical Resource Industries (PA)	3643	E	909 446-1109	8279
Google International LLC (DH)	4813	C	650 253-0000	11885
B B G Management Group (PA)	5145	E	909 797-9581	13263
Calimesa Operations LLC.	8051	C	909 795-2421	17896
Cedar Operations LLC.	8051	C	909 790-2273	17899

YUCCA VALLEY, CA - San Bernardino County

	SIC	EMP	PHONE	ENTRY#
Hi-Desert Publishing Company (HQ)	2711	D	760 365-3315	3283
Catalyst Development Corp.	7372	E	760 228-9653	16193
Eisenhower Medical Center.	8011	D	760 228-9900	17646

Mergent email: customerrelations@mergent.com
1462

2024 Southern California
Business Directory and Buyers Guide

(P-0000) Products & Services Section entry number
(PA)=Parent Co (HQ)=Headquarters (DH)=Div Headquarters